Rating system

★★★★★ Excellent
★★★★ Very Good
★★★ Good
★★ Fair
🦃 Turkey

Also by Mick Martin and Marsha Porter
Published by Ballantine Books:

VIDEO MOVIE GUIDE FOR FAMILY VIEWING

VIDEO MOVIE GUIDE 2001

Mick Martin
and Marsha Porter

Contributing Editor:
Derrick Bang

BALLANTINE BOOKS • NEW YORK

A Ballantine Book
Published by The Ballantine Publishing Group
Copyright © 2000 by Mick Martin and Marsha Porter

www.randomhouse.com/BB/

ISSN 1095-6190

ISBN 0-345-44417-5

Cover design by Dreu Pennington-McNeil
Cover photos: *The Sixth Sense* © Spyglass Entertainment Group, LP (courtesy of The Kobal Collection). *Toy Story 2* © Disney/Pixar (courtesy of The Kobal Collection). *The Blair Witch Project* © Artisan Entertainment (courtesy of The Kobal Collection). *American Beauty* © Dreamworks LLC. Photographer: Lorey Sebastian (courtesy of The Kobal Collection).

Manufactured in the United States of America

Revised Edition: October 2000

10 9 8 7 6 5 4 3 2 1

CONTENTS

FOREWORD/INTRODUCTION

You hold in your hands the most comprehensive critical guide to movies on video available. Where other movie-review books contain films that may never be released to video stores, *Video Movie Guide (VMG)* concentrates only on what you can rent at your local shop or purchase through the mail. Even so, that still puts this fifteenth annual edition at more than 19,000 titles.

Video Movie Guide is also a book written by people who love movies *for* people who love movies. We treat this annual publication like some kind of holy quest, searching out obscure titles and oddball distributors in order to pack *VMG* with as many titles as possible. This is why you'll find more B-movies, foreign films, old-time and spaghetti Westerns, TV movies, direct-to-video releases, silent films, and TV series covered here than in any other movie guide.

As in previous years, we have covered all the major movie releases available in stores as well as several months' worth of upcoming titles, which we reviewed while they were in theatrical release. Also, we have gone backward as much as forward, catching up on whatever obscure or previously unreleased titles we may have missed in earlier editions. We honestly believe that you cannot find a more complete critical review of entertainment on video.

In past years, reviews in *VMG* have been broken down into genre categories. Now, by popular demand, we are listing all movies together in alphabetical order. As our readers have pointed out, so many movies today mix genres—horror with comedy, science fiction with mystery, for example—there are no clear-cut categories anymore. So we decided it was time to put an end to the confusion.

To help you find movies reviewed in this book, we have several features: a cast index, a director index, an index of Academy Award winners, and a complete alphabetical listing of alternate titles at the back of the book. Alternate titles have been listed so that a film like *The Christmas Tree,* for example, can be found under its video title, *When Wolves Cry,* in the text, and so on. In addition, a bullet (•) has been placed next to each new review.

A few readers have expressed dismay because we reevaluate films from edition to edition. We feel this is necessary. A good movie might catch us on a bad day or vice versa and lead to a less-than-objective analysis. Some of the better-known film critics balk at being considered consumer guides, but that is exactly what we strive to be. Not everyone is going to like everything. But if a film has merit, even if we don't particularly care for it, we have strived to call attention to its attributes. We want this book to be, given the capriciousness of opinion, the most accurate and useful critical guide to movies.

This is why we rate genre movie against genre movie. For example, dramas are rated against dramas, Westerns against Westerns, and so on. There is no way the John Wayne/Johnny Mack Brown B-plus Western, *Hell Town*, could be compared with *Lawrence of Arabia*, for example, so we try to keep things in perspective.

Our rating system runs from five stars to a turkey. A five-star movie is a must-see; a four-star rating means it's well worth watching. The desirability of a film with a lesser rating depends on how much one likes a particular type of motion picture or a movie star. A turkey by any other name is still a bad movie, which is why we give at least a two-star rating to so-bad-they're-good movies, such as *Plan 9 from Outer Space* and *Robot Monster*. If a film is particularly offensive even though it has a big-name star, we want you to know why. Likewise, if a little-known gem has special attributes, we've done our best to call your attention to them.

When a film has been rated G, PG, PG-13, R, X, or NC-17 by the Motion Picture Association of America (MPAA), we have noted it. Only theatrically released films distributed after November 1967 were considered by the MPAA ratings board, so we have attempted to indicate the potentially objectionable content in films released before then, as well as in unrated made-for-cable and direct-to-video products. These ratings are confusing at times, so, wherever appropriate, we have explained them.

Please see the section entitled TO ORDER VIDEOS for a list of companies that specialize in selling and renting videos.

We welcome comments from our readers, but can only answer those that come with a self-addressed, stamped envelope. Our mailing address is Video Movie Guide, P.O. Box 189674, Sacramento, CA 95818. Or you may e-mail us at bang@dcn.davis.ca.us. Until next year, happy viewing!

TO ORDER VIDEOS

Video Movie Guide (VMG) is meant to function as a viewing guide to what is available in video stores for rent and a buyer's guide to titles available by mail order. As with books, some movies may go "out of print" and become unavailable for purchase. A number of video companies have gone out of business in the last two years. However, many videos that can no longer be purchased still can be found for rent in many stores. So we do not delete any titles.

A number of Disney titles are released for a brief period of time and then placed on moratorium, which means you can find them for viewing purposes at a rental store, but cannot currently buy them—although they will be rereleased eventually. More and more video companies are using this approach. Other titles that were available at one time exist in some kind of never-never land now, as rights have been transferred from one company to another.

Still others, like Richard Lester's *Three* (and *Four*) *Musketeers* and Jules Dassin's *Topkapi*, were pulled by their respective distributors and currently are not available for purchase. But they were available on video at one time, so we include them in our book. After all, *Those Magnificent Men in Their Flying Machines* was rereleased, so anything can happen.

We regret any inconvenience a reader might have in attempting to buy a particular title listed in this book. However, as much as we would like to help, we do not have the time or resources to find movies for readers who want to buy them. But help is available.

Mike Antonaros has graciously agreed to answer letters from *VMG* readers about the availability and price of desired movies. Write to him at Dickens Video, 5325 Elkhorn Boulevard #292, Sacramento, CA 95842, or call toll free at (800) 228-4246.

Readers interested in buying their favorite movies on video cannot order them directly from the distributor, which is why we do not list video companies in the book. Instead, we have found a number of mail-order houses that sell and rent videos.

There are other sources for movies on video, but we have not dealt personally with any of them. We welcome comments from readers on whether we should or should not list them in the book.

Most of the following mail-order companies carry a line of recent video releases in addition to their specialty:

Classic, foreign, silent, and contemporary films for rent and for sale: Facets Multimedia, 1517 Fullerton Avenue, Chicago, IL 60614, (800) 331-6197.

Rental outlets: Home Video Festival, P.O. Box 2032, Scranton, PA 18501-9952, (800) 258-FILM; Video Library, 7157 Germantown Avenue, Philadelphia, PA 19119, (800) 669-7157. Eddie Brandt's Saturday Matinee, 6310 Colfax Avenue, North Hollywood, CA 91606, (818) 506-4242 or (818) 506-7722.

Various: Columbia House Video Club, 1400 North Fruitridge Avenue, Terre Haute, IN 47812-9621, (800) 544-4431; Critics' Choice Video, P.O. Box 549, Elk Grove Village, IL 60009-0549; Value Video International, P.O. Box 22565, Denver, CO 80222; the National Film Board of Canada, (800) 542-2164.

Classic and creaky oldies (many of which are in the public domain): Video Classic, P.O. Box 293, White River Junction, VT 05001-0293, (802) 295-4903; Outre Products, P.O. Box 1900, Evanston, IL 60204, (847) 866-7155; Discount Video, P.O. Box 7122, Burbank, CA 91510; Video Yesteryear, Box C, Sandy Hook, CT 06482; Blackhawk Films, 15959 Triumph Street, Commerce, CA 90040-1688; Hollywood Attic, 138 Fifth Avenue, Pelham, NY 10803; Foothill Video Inc., P.O. Box 547, Tujanga, CA 91043, (818) 353-8591; Grapevine Video, P.O. Box 46161, Phoenix, AZ 85063, (602) 245-0210; Mike LeBell's Video, 75 Fremont Place, Los Angeles, CA 90005, (213) 938-3333.

Cult, foreign, classic, independent, and out-of-print: Kim's Video & Music, 350 Bleecker St., New York, NY 10014, (212) 675-8996.

Canadian and specialty titles: The National Film Board of Canada, (800) 542-2164 (from the United States and elsewhere); or (800) 267-7710 (from Canada).

1950s TV shows: Shokus Video, P.O. Box 3125, Chatsworth, CA 91313.

Horror films: Sinister Cinema, P.O. Box 4369, Medford, OR 97501-0168, (541) 773-6860; Something Weird, P. O. Box 33664, Seattle, WA 98133, (206) 361-3759.

B Westerns: Boyd Magers, Video West, 1312 Stagecoach Road SE, Albuquerque, NM 87123.

Serials: Stokey's Serials, P.O. Box 426, Selden, NY 11784.

For Beta tapes: Absolute Beta Movies, P.O. Box 130, Remington, VA 22734, (540) 439-3259.

The Internet is, of course, becoming an increasingly popular source for video sales. We've tried to be careful with our endorsements here, as many companies spring up and disappear in a matter of months or years, but we do feel comfortable with these three sites: www.reel.com, www.videoexpress.com, and www.kencranes.com.

In Canada: Videomatica, Ltd., 1859 West 4th Avenue, Vancouver, B.C. V6J-1M4, (604) 734-0411 (for rentals), (604) 734-5752 (for sales), (800) 665-1469 (toll free in Canada only).

A number of these companies have 35mm or 16mm copies of old fright flicks or shoot-'em-ups from which they make their copies. Quality can vary greatly depending on the condition of the original print and the integrity of the company itself. We have seen videos that were obviously duplicated from other videos instead of an original print. So let the buyer beware. The list of mail-order houses in *VMG* is purely a service for our readers and does not constitute an endorsement on the part of the authors or the publisher. Good luck!

ACKNOWLEDGMENTS

The authors are grateful to a number of wonderful people without whose help *Video Movie Guide (VMG)* would not be a reality. Health-and-nutrition expert Cary Nosler (a.k.a. Captain Carrot) planted the seed. Our first editor, Marilyn Abraham, helped define the book's form and nurture its growth, and our current editor, Cathy Repetti, is a consistent source of support, sage advice, and inspiration.

Derrick Bang, a founding contributor, is the entertainment editor for *Davis Enterprise* as well as the host/producer/writer of the *Cable Connection* TV series. He continues to play an important role in the yearly creation of *VMG* as consulting editor.

Copy editor Steve Connell is the former features-and-entertainment editor for the now-defunct *Sacramento Union,* so he's still keeping Mick on his toes.

Research editors Derrick Tribble and William Glines serve as our source points. Derrick and Bill keep our staff up on the latest films to hit video. In addition, Bill is our number-one fact checker.

Our chief contributors, a splendid crew of film critics, movie buffs, and historians, have also contributed greatly to this tome. Allow us to introduce them:

M. Faust has written about movies and video over the past twenty years for numerous publications, including *Movies on TV, Video* magazine, the *Motion Picture Guide,* FamilyWonder.com, and the *Buffalo News.* He is also the owner of Mondo Video, the coolest video store in upstate New York.

Rochelle O'Gorman reviews videos for *Pulse!* magazine and is a nationally syndicated audiobook critic whose reviews can be found in the *Los Angeles Times, Boston Globe, New York Post,* and on audiobookscafe.com. She has been writing about film, video, and audiobooks for eighteen years.

Jack Garner is the chief film critic for *Gannett News Service.* Just look at the movie ads, and you'll see his name.

Rich Garrison is a free-lance writer and movie buff.

Ed Grant writes for *TV Guide.*

Mark Halverson and Jim Lane share film-critic duties at the *Sacramento News and Review.* They have been reviewing movies for more than twenty years.

John Larsen has been the film editor of the *Ventura County & Coast Reporter* for twenty years. He reviews for numerous publications and radio stations. His latest Internet Web site, www.lightviews.com, covers video and film. In addition, he is a screenwriter and script doctor working on several projects. He also is responsible for bringing R. Scott Bolton, another main contributor, into the fold.

Richard Leathers is a free-lance writer from Seattle, perhaps the biggest movie town in the country.

Classic-films expert Bob Polunsky is the film critic for San Antonio's KENS-TV, WOAI-AM, and KAJA-FM.

Bob Shaw is the film reviewer for KTVU Channel 2's *10 O'Clock News* in San Francisco and a real witty guy.

Bob Strauss is the film critic for the *Los Angeles Daily News.* His writings also appear in the *Boston Globe* and the *Chicago Sun-Times.*

Motion-picture historian and collector Tom Tolley is another founding contributor whose amazing knowledge of movies has been a key factor in shaping this book.

Lori J. Tribble is an independent video producer, assistant media specialist at a Sacramento, CA, hospital, and a film buff.

Another chief contributor since the beginning, Robert Young Jr., is the author of *Roscoe "Fatty" Arbuckle,* a bio-bibliograpy of the life and career of the silent-comedy star, and last year appeared on A&E's *Biography* special on the great clown. He also wrote *Movie Memo,* a short history of the MGM studios, ghosted the autobiography of Sessue Hayakawa, and was a contributing editor for *American Classic Screen.*

In addition, Terry Hayes, Gayna Lamb-Bang, Jason Damron, Harvey Burgess, Devin Davis, Jean Fournier, Paul Freeman, Bob Holman, Chris Hunter, Scott Hunter, David Linck, Simon Macmillan, Boyd Magers, Bill MacLeod, Craig Modderno, Bill O'Brien, Linda Rajotte, Mike Reynolds, Vicki and Mark Sazaki, Bill Smith, Lisa Smith-Youngs, and John Tibbetts also wrote reviews.

VMG is dedicated to the memory of Bill Creter, a lifelong movie buff whose knowledge of the history of movies, sage advice, and warm heart will be sorely missed.

Thanks also to our familes for their support and patience. Eileen and Chuck Porter, Hada Martin, Matt and Norma Condo, and Diane Martin have pitched in to help on numerous occasions. Even Francesca Martin has done her bit.

We'd also like to thank Mike and Betty Antonaros, Louise Braverman, Norton Buffalo, Keith Burton, Tayen Chen, Henry Chung, Bernard Dauphinais, George Davidson, Jim Dixon, Betsy Flagler, Stan Goman, Caron Harris, Carol Johnson, David Johnson, Bob Kronenberg, Stacey Mendonca, Steve Palmer, Gary Quattrin, Marcia Raphael, Helen Rees, Mark Rifkin, Michael Riesenberg, Russ Solomon, Jon Souza, Roger Sperberg, Jerry and Karen Sterchi, Milos Strehlik, Nicolas Sywak, Steven Taveira, Walter von Hauffe, Tami Walker, and Bob Wilkins.

A COEUR JOIE (HEAD OVER HEELS) 💔 Sixties fluff about a woman torn between two men. Original title in its American release: *Two Weeks in September*. In French with English subtitles. 89m. **DIR:** Serge Bourguignon. **CAST:** Brigitte Bardot, Laurent Terzieff. 1967

A LA MODE ★★★ A French teenager (Ken Hegelin) becomes apprenticed to an eccentric Jewish tailor and dreams of success in the world of fashion design. This lightweight, easygoing, coming-of-age comedy profits from good performances, especially by Jean Yonne as the old tailor, and from its witty, satirical jabs at the flashy world of haute couture. In French with English subtitles. Rated R for sexual scenes and mild profanity. 81m. **DIR:** Remy Duchemin. **CAST:** Ken Hegelin, Jean Yonne, Francois Hautesserre, Florence Darel, Maurice Benichou. 1993

A NOS AMOURS ★★★ This winner of the Cesar (French Oscar) for best film of 1983 examines the life of a working-class girl of 15 (Sandrine Bonnaire) who engages in one sexual relationship after another. In French with English subtitles. Rated R for nudity. 110m. **DIR:** Maurice Pialat. **CAST:** Sandrine Bonnaire, Dominique Besnehard, Maurice Pialat. 1983

A NOUS LA LIBERTE ★★1/2 Louis and Emile are two prisoners who plan an escape. Only Louis gets away and, surprisingly, he becomes a rich, successful businessman. There are some slapstick segments, and many believe that this film was the inspiration for Charlie Chaplin's *Modern Times*. In French with English subtitles. B&W; 87m. **DIR:** René Clair. **CAST:** Raymond Cordy, Henri Marchand. 1931

AARON LOVES ANGELA ★★★ This Harlem love affair features a black youth (Kevin Hooks) falling for a sweet Puerto Rican girl (Irene Cara). Their relative innocence contrasts with the drug-dealing violence around them. Rated R for violence and profanity. 99m. **DIR:** Gordon Parks Jr. **CAST:** Moses Gunn, Kevin Hooks, Irene Cara, Ernestine Jackson, Robert Hooks. 1975

ABBOTT AND COSTELLO GO TO MARS ★★1/2 The comedy team was getting a little tired when they made this movie, which has become a cult favorite. It's set in space, but the plot is the same as a TV sitcom. B&W; 78m. **DIR:** Charles Lamont. **CAST:** Bud Abbott, Lou Costello, Mari Blanchard, Jack Kruschen, Horace McMahon, Martha Hyer, Robert Paige, Anita Ekberg. 1953

ABBOTT AND COSTELLO IN HOLLYWOOD ★★ Lesser Abbott and Costello effort has Bud and Lou trying to make it big as movie stars. Best scenes occur early in the film, with Lou playing a barber. B&W; 83m. **DIR:** S. Sylvan Simon. **CAST:** Bud Abbott, Lou Costello, Frances Rafferty, Robert Stanton. 1945

ABBOTT AND COSTELLO IN THE FOREIGN LEGION ★★★1/2 Costello inadvertently buys a slave girl in the Sahara just because he waved at the girl flirting with him. Watch for some of the team's funniest routines. B&W; 79m. **DIR:** Charles Lamont.

CAST: Bud Abbott, Lou Costello, Walter Slezak, Patricia Medina, Douglass Dumbrille. 1950 DVD

ABBOTT AND COSTELLO MEET CAPTAIN KIDD ★★ One of Abbott and Costello's few color films, this is strictly preschooler fare. The boys get chased around uncharted islands, pirate ships, etc., by the infamous Captain Kidd, as portrayed by Charles Laughton, who makes every effort to retain his dignity. 70m. **DIR:** Charles Lamont. **CAST:** Bud Abbott, Lou Costello, Charles Laughton, Hillary Brooke, Leif Erickson. 1952

ABBOTT AND COSTELLO MEET DR. JEKYLL AND MR. HYDE ★★★1/2 Fun mixture of comedy and horror has the team up against the smooth Dr. Jekyll and the maniacal Mr. Hyde. One of the boys' better films of the 1950s. Boris Karloff is in top form in the dual role, and don't miss the hilarious scene in which Lou is turned into a mouse! B&W; 77m. **DIR:** Charles Lamont. **CAST:** Bud Abbott, Lou Costello, Boris Karloff. 1953

ABBOTT AND COSTELLO MEET FRANKENSTEIN ★★★★ For Bud Abbott and Lou Costello, this film meant a resurgence of popularity after a slow fall from favor as the 1940s box-office champs. Yet it never compromises the characters of Dracula (Bela Lugosi), the Wolfman (Lon Chaney Jr.), or the Frankenstein monster (Glenn Strange). B&W; 83m. **DIR:** Charles Barton. **CAST:** Bud Abbott, Lou Costello, Lon Chaney Jr., Bela Lugosi, Glenn Strange. 1948

ABBOTT AND COSTELLO MEET THE INVISIBLE MAN ★★ Bud and Lou are private eyes hired by a prizefighter to clear him of his manager's murder. The fighter injects himself with a serum that renders him invisible and helps Lou kayo his opponents in the ring before the real murderer is exposed. B&W; 82m. **DIR:** Charles Lamont. **CAST:** Bud Abbott, Lou Costello, Arthur Franz, Nancy Guild, Adele Jergens, Sheldon Leonard, William Frawley. 1951

ABBOTT AND COSTELLO MEET THE KEYSTONE KOPS ★★★1/2 A boon for nostalgia buffs, this film features pie-in-the-face director Mack Sennett and three of the surviving Keystone Kops in a climactic chase scene. B&W; 78m. **DIR:** Charles Lamont. **CAST:** Bud Abbott, Lou Costello, Maxie Rosenbloom, Lynn Bari, Mack Sennett, Harold Goodwin, Heinie Conklin, Hank Mann, Carol Costello. 1955

ABBOTT AND COSTELLO MEET THE KILLER, BORIS KARLOFF ★★★ Second in the duo's *Abbott and Costello Meet ...* series, brought on by the tremendous popularity of their *Frankenstein* send-up the year before. In this enjoyable outing, Bud and Lou match wits with Boris Karloff, in classic form as a sinister swami doing away with his enemies at a posh hotel. B&W; 84m. **DIR:** Charles Barton. **CAST:** Bud Abbott, Lou Costello, Boris Karloff, Lenore Aubert, Gar Moore, James Flavin. 1949

ABBOTT AND COSTELLO MEET THE MUMMY ★★ Final (and overdue) entry in the seven-year cycle of "horror comedies" pitting Abbott and Costello against Universal Pictures' monster stable. Not without amusing moments, but mostly, the same tired vaudeville routines are dragged out as the boys flee two mummies—one real, one fake—in Egypt. B&W;

79m. **DIR:** Charles Lamont. **CAST:** Bud Abbott, Lou Costello, Marie Windsor, Richard Deacon. **1955**

ABBOTT AND COSTELLO SHOW, THE (TV SERIES) ★★★ Set in Hollywood, this comedy series depicts Bud Abbott's and Lou Costello's efforts to improve their financial situation. Though the comics appear somewhat weary and the humor is often forced, enough of the gags work to make the episodes worth a glance. Many of Abbott and Costello's classic routines are incorporated into the shows, boosting the slim plots. 53m. **DIR:** Various. **CAST:** Bud Abbott, Lou Costello, Sidney Fields, Hillary Brooke, Joe Besser. **1952–1954 DVD**

ABDUCTED ★★1/2 This is not as sleazy as the video box art would have you believe. A backwoods jogger (Roberta Weiss) is abducted by a crazed mountain man and taken back to his cabin. Nothing new, but some good chase scenes. Not rated, but has violence, profanity, and adult subject matter. 87m. **DIR:** Boon Collins. **CAST:** Roberta Weiss, Lawrence King Phillip, Dan Haggerty. **1985**

ABDUCTED II ★★1/2 Less a sequel than a remake, this time with three young lovelies terrorized by mountain man Lawrence King. Rated R for violence and nudity. 91m. **DIR:** Boon Collins. **CAST:** Jan-Michael Vincent, Dan Haggerty, Raquel Bianca, Lawrence King. **1994**

ABDUCTION ★★ This film comes across as a cheap exploitation of the Patty Hearst kidnapping. It includes theories that may or may not be true. As in the real incident, Patty is kidnapped from the house she shares with her boyfriend. Rated R for profanity, violence, nudity, and sex. 100m. **DIR:** Joseph Zito. **CAST:** Gregory Rozakis, Leif Erickson, Dorothy Malone, Lawrence Tierney. **1975**

ABDUCTORS, THE 🎬 Sequel to *Ginger* is even nastier. Rated R for nudity, violence, and sexual situations. 88m. **DIR:** Don Schain. **CAST:** Cheri Caffaro, Jennifer Brooks. **1972**

ABE LINCOLN IN ILLINOIS ★★★★ Based on Sherwood Anderson's Broadway play, this is a reverent look at the early career and loves of the sixteenth president. As contrasted with John Ford's *Young Mr. Lincoln*, this is a more somber, historically accurate, and better-acted version. B&W; 110m. **DIR:** John Cromwell. **CAST:** Raymond Massey, Ruth Gordon, Gene Lockhart, Mary Howard. **1934**

ABEL GANCE'S BEETHOVEN ★★★★ Originally titled *Un Grand Amour de Beethoven*, this contains some of Abel Gance's finest work with sound, especially in the scene at the Heiligenstadt Mill when Beethoven first begins to lose his hearing. In French with English subtitles. B&W; 116m. **DIR:** Abel Gance. **CAST:** Harry Baur, Annie Ducaux. **1937**

•**ABERRATION** 🎬 A bunch of rubber lizards attacks a young couple in their cabin in the hills. Dullsville. Rated R for language and gore. 93m. **DIR:** Tim Boxell. **CAST:** Pamela Gidley, Simon Bossell, Valery Nikolaev. **1997**

ABIGAIL'S PARTY ★★★★★ A superb slice of acerbic British social commentary. Beverly is a gin-sodden shrew with middle-class aspirations, who holds a small get-together for the neighbors. This movie is like an English version of *Who's Afraid of Virginia*

Woolf, a group of adults congregate, imbibe vast amounts of alcohol, and squirm-inducing disaster ensues. 105m. **DIR:** Mike Leigh. **CAST:** Alison Steadman. **1977**

ABILENE TOWN ★★★ Cattlemen and homesteaders are at loggerheads in the 1870s in this fast-paced shoot-'em-up. Randolph Scott is the trusty tall man with the star. Edgar Buchanan is sly, as always. B&W; 89m. **DIR:** Edwin L. Marin. **CAST:** Randolph Scott, Ann Dvorak, Rhonda Fleming, Lloyd Bridges, Edgar Buchanan. **1946**

ABOMINABLE DR. PHIBES, THE ★★★1/2 Stylish horror film features Vincent Price in one of his best latter-day roles as a man disfigured in a car wreck taking revenge. Rated PG. 93m. **DIR:** Robert Fuest. **CAST:** Vincent Price, Joseph Cotten, Hugh Griffith, Terry-Thomas. **1971**

ABOMINABLE SNOWMAN OF THE HIMALAYAS, THE ★★★ The writer and director of the British *Quatermass* series worked on what is probably the only intelligent yeti movie. Peter Cushing and Forrest Tucker are a botanist and an exploitative promoter (American, of course) searching for the legendary giant creatures in Nepal. B&W; 85m. **DIR:** Val Guest. **CAST:** Peter Cushing, Forrest Tucker, Maureen Connell. **1957**

ABOUT LAST NIGHT ... ★★★★ A slick adaptation of David Mamet's play, *Sexual Perversity in Chicago*. Demi Moore and Rob Lowe meet for a one-night stand and then realize they *like* each other. Jim Belushi and Elizabeth Perkins turn in solid performances, but the film belongs to Moore. Rated R for nudity and explicit adult situations. 113m. **DIR:** Edward Zwick. **CAST:** Rob Lowe, Demi Moore, James Belushi, Elizabeth Perkins, George DiCenzo. **1986 DVD**

ABOVE AND BEYOND ★★★1/2 Good account of the secret training led by Paul Tibbets (Robert Taylor) to prepare for the first atomic-bomb attack on Hiroshima. Bogs down some when dealing with his home life, but overall a fine biographical drama. Jim Backus has a cameo as General Curtis E. LeMay. B&W; 122m. **DIR:** Melvin Frank. **CAST:** Robert Taylor, Eleanor Parker, James Whitmore, Larry Keating, Jeff Richards, Jim Backus. **1952**

ABOVE SUSPICION (1943) ★★★★ Newlyweds Joan Crawford and Fred MacMurray, while honeymooning on the Continent at the outbreak of World War II, innocently become involved in espionage. Conrad Veidt, who died before the movie was released, steals every scene in which he appears. Not rated, but good family entertainment. B&W; 90m. **DIR:** Richard Thorpe. **CAST:** Joan Crawford, Fred MacMurray, Conrad Veidt, Basil Rathbone, Reginald Owen. **1943**

ABOVE SUSPICION (1994) ★★★1/2 In a positively spooky precursor to the accident that would end his career, Christopher Reeve stars as a dedicated cop who becomes crippled during a bust gone sour. Confined to a wheelchair and clinically depressed, he begins to question the wisdom of staying alive. Ah, but things are not as they seem in this deliciously twisty script from Jerry Lazarus, W. H. Macy, and Steven Schachter. You'll be guessing to the last frame—this one's very clever. Rated R for nudity, violence, profanity, and simulated sex. 92m. DIR: Steven Schachter. CAST: Christopher Reeve, Joe Mantegna, Kim Cattrall, Edward Kerr, Geoffrey Rivas, Finola Hughes, William H. Macy. **1994**

ABOVE THE LAW ★★★1/2 Director Andrew Davis, who gave credibility to Chuck Norris in *Code of Silence*, teams up with karate expert Steven Seagal (who cowrote the story and coproduced with Davis) for this tough, action-filled cop thriller. Seagal is a Chicago cop and Vietnam veteran who takes on the CIA. The result is a strong entry for action buffs. Rated R for lots of violence, profanity, and drug use. 97m. DIR: Andrew Davis. CAST: Steven Seagal, Pam Grier, Sharon Stone, Daniel Faraldo, Henry Silva. **1988 DVD**

ABOVE THE RIM ★★1/2 Two brothers clash as they try to influence a morally struggling young man in this Manhattan melodrama about inner-city crime, broken dreams, and one high-school athlete's attempt to climb out of the dangerous Harlem street scene. The laws and rhythms of the street are brought to life by a magnetic cast, but this bold bite out of the dark side of the Big Apple has a familiar taste to it. Rated R for violence and language. 96m. DIR: Jeff Pollack. CAST: Duane Martin, Leon, Tupac Shakur, Bernie Mac, Marlon Wayans. **1994**

ABRAHAM ★★★1/2 Abraham and Sarah prove their faith by obeying a divine command to undertake a difficult journey to the Promised Land and later to sacrifice son Isaac. Handsome production values and a fine cast. Not rated. 150m. DIR: Joseph Sargent. CAST: Richard Harris, Barbara Hershey, Maximilian Schell, Vittorio Gassman. **1994**

ABRAHAM LINCOLN ★★★★ A milestone in many ways, this episodic film is legendary director Griffith's first "talkie," Hollywood's first sound biography of an American, the first attempt to cover Lincoln's life from cradle to grave, and the first about the martyred president to include the Civil War. Walter Huston's peerless performance in the title role dominates throughout. B&W; 91m. DIR: D. W. Griffith. CAST: Walter Huston, Una Merkel, Kay Hammond, Ian Keith, Hobart Bosworth, Jason Robards Sr., Henry B. Walthall. **1930**

ABRAXAS GUARDIAN OF THE UNIVERSE ★★ A renegade alien peace officer flees to Earth and impregnates a young woman, only to be caught and sent to prison. Five years later he escapes and returns to Earth to engage in countless, violent chase scenes. Not rated; contains violence. 87m. DIR: Damien Lee. CAST: Jesse Ventura, Marjorie Bransfield, Sven-Ole Thorsen. **1992 DVD**

ABSENCE OF MALICE ★★★★ Sally Field is a Miami reporter who writes a story implicating an innocent man (Paul Newman) in the mysterious disappearance—and possible murder—of a union leader in this taut, thoughtful drama about the ethics of journalism. It's sort of *All the President's Men* turned inside out. Rated PG because of minor violence. 116m. DIR: Sydney Pollack. CAST: Paul Newman, Sally Field, Bob Balaban, Melinda Dillon, Wilford Brimley. **1982 DVD**

ABSENT-MINDED PROFESSOR, THE ★★★★ One of Disney's best live-action comedies, this stars Fred MacMurray in the title role of a scientist who discovers "flubber" (flying rubber). Only trouble is, no one will believe him—except Keenan Wynn, who tries to steal his invention. B&W; 104m. DIR: Robert Stevenson. CAST: Fred MacMurray, Nancy Olson, Tommy Kirk, Ed Wynn, Keenan Wynn. **1961**

ABSOLUTE BEGINNERS ★★★★ Based on the cult novel by Colin MacInnes, who chronicled the musical and social scene in London during the pivotal summer of 1958. Occasionally the accents are too thick and the references too obscure for Americans, but the overall effect is an unequivocal high. Rated PG-13 for stylized, but rather intense, violence and some profanity. 107m. DIR: Julien Temple. CAST: Eddie O'Connell, Patsy Kensit, David Bowie, James Fox, Ray Davies, Anita Morris, Sade Adu, Mandy Rice-Davies. **1986**

ABSOLUTE POWER ★★★★ A gripping thriller in the tradition of *Tightrope*, this is Clint Eastwood at his most cynical. He is a professional thief in the middle of plying his trade when a middle-aged man brings a young woman into the bedroom. Hidden in a vault behind a one-way mirror, Eastwood witnesses the woman's rape and murder. He also gets a clear look at the killer: the president of the United States (Gene Hackman). Now the question is what to do about what he's seen, and how to stay alive long enough to do it. Rated R for violence, rape, profanity, and simulated sex. 121m. DIR: Clint Eastwood. CAST: Clint Eastwood, Gene Hackman, Ed Harris, Laura Linney, Judy Davis, Scott Glenn, E. G. Marshall. **1997 DVD**

ABSOLUTELY FABULOUS ★★★★★ This is not your parents' sitcom. Two middle-aged English tarts smoke, swallow, and bed everything in their paranoid paths, and are all the more fun for being unedited and abashedly vulgar. Jennifer Saunders is the queen of excess and Joanna Lumley her promiscuous best friend in this ground-breaking, sidesplitting satire. Available on video are all eighteen 30-minute episodes, a 30-minute special, and a 90-minute made-for-television movie. Not rated; contains profanity and adult themes. 660m. DIR: Bob Spiers. CAST: Jennifer Saunders, Joanna Lumley, Julia Sawalha, Jane Horrocks, June Whitfield. **1993–1996**

ABSOLUTION ★★1/2 Slow-moving but interesting tale of a priest's emotional and physical battle with one of his students at an English school for boys. As the priest, Richard Burton gives his usual compelling performance. Nice plot twist at the end. Not rated; contains violence. 91m. DIR: Anthony Page. CAST: Richard Burton, Dominic Guard, Andrew Keir, Billy Connolly. **1977**

ABYSS, THE ★★★★ After suffering the deep-sea disappointments in *Leviathan* and *Deepstar Six*, viewers are likely to be a little cautious of getting back into the water with this thriller–adventure–fantasy film. They shouldn't be. The third time's the charm with the underwater plot, thanks to the inventiveness of director James Cameron (*The Terminator*, *Aliens*). Rated PG-13. 145m. DIR: James Cameron. CAST: Ed Harris, Mary Elizabeth Mastrantonio, Michael Biehn. **1989 DVD**

ACCATTONE ★★1/2 Director Pier Paolo Pasolini's first feature film adapted from his own novel follows the desperate existence of a pimp living in the slums of southern Italy. Lacks emotional depth and raw power. In Italian with (virtually unreadable) English subtitles. B&W; 116m. **DIR:** Pier Paolo Pasolini. **CAST:** Franco Citti. 1961

ACCEPTABLE RISKS ★★★ Heavy-handed message film about the risks a chemical plant poses to the inhabitants of a new housing development. Unbelievable amount of carelessness by plant workers and blind greed by owners reduce this TV movie to near sci-fi rather than gritty docudrama. 97m. **DIR:** Rick Wallace. **CAST:** Brian Dennehy, Kenneth McMillan, Christine Ebersole, Cicely Tyson. 1986

ACCESS CODE 🍿 Dreadful action film about an Orwellian Big Brother surveillance system that takes over the country's national security complex. Not rated, has profanity. 90m. **DIR:** Mark Sobel. **CAST:** Martin Landau, Michael Ansara, Macdonald Carey. 1984

ACCIDENT ★★★★ Harold Pinter's complicated play retains its subtleties in this sometimes baffling British film. Dirk Bogarde is excellent as a married professor pursuing an attractive student. There are enough twists and turns in the characters' actual desires to maintain your complete attention. 105m. **DIR:** Joseph Losey. **CAST:** Dirk Bogarde, Stanley Baker, Jacqueline Sassard, Michael York. 1967

ACCIDENTAL MEETING ★★ In this made-for-cable movie, two women joke about having each other murder someone they don't like. However, one of the women takes it seriously. For a better version of this plot, rent Hitchcock's *Strangers on a Train*. Not rated; contains violence and sexual situations. 95m. **DIR:** Michael Zinberg. **CAST:** Linda Gray, Linda Purl, Leigh McCloskey, Ernie Lively, David Hayward, Kent McCord. 1993

ACCIDENTAL TOURIST, THE ★★★★ William Hurt and Kathleen Turner team again for this compelling adaptation of Anne Tyler's novel. Hurt's the writer of travel guides who distances himself from everybody—including wife Turner—after the death of their young son; Geena Davis is the earthy, colorful free spirit who tries to break through his wall of self-imposed isolation. Filled with strong emotional highs and lows. Rated PG. 120m. **DIR:** Lawrence Kasdan. **CAST:** William Hurt, Kathleen Turner, Geena Davis, Bill Pullman, Amy Wright, David Ogden Stiers, Ed Begley Jr. 1988

ACCOMPANIST, THE ★★1/2 In Nazi-occupied Paris, a young pianist works for, and later flees to London with, a famous concert singer and her manager/husband. Lovely pastel photography and wonderful music but it's a bit too measured and deliberate. In French with English subtitles. Rated PG. 111m. **DIR:** Claude Miller. **CAST:** Richard Bohringer, Elena Safonova, Romane Bohringer, Samuel Labarthe, Julien Rassam. 1993

ACCUSED, THE ★★★★ Superb, emotionally intense retelling of the precedent-setting New Bedford, Massachusetts, gang-rape case, with Jodie Foster as an innocent but definitely not saintly victim, and Kelly McGillis as a tough DA. An excellent and wrenching film. Rated R for adult themes, language, nudity, and sexual violence. 105m. **DIR:** Jonathan Ka-

plan. **CAST:** Jodie Foster, Kelly McGillis, Bernie Coulson, Steve Antin, Leo Rossi, Woody Brown. 1988

ACE DRUMMOND ★★1/2 An arch villain known as The Dragon has thwarted every effort by an international group attempting to establish a round-the-world airline service. Aviation whiz Ace Drummond jumps from the Sunday funnies to the silver screen. Laughable in many respects, this is still a pretty good serial and the only filming of this character's adventures. B&W; 250m. **DIR:** Ford Beebe, Cliff Smith. **CAST:** John King, Jean Rogers, Noah Beery Jr., Lon Chaney Jr. 1936

ACE HIGH ★★ In this violent spaghetti Western written and directed by Giuseppe Colizzi, a condemned outlaw is offered a chance to save himself from the hangman's noose. Having just completed the entertaining *The Good, The Bad, and The Ugly*, Eli Wallach is wasted. There is some humor, but the dialogue and dubbing are simply terrible. 123m. **DIR:** Giuseppe Colizzi. **CAST:** Eli Wallach, Brock Peters, Terence Hill, Kevin McCarthy, Bud Spencer. 1969

ACE OF ACES ★★★1/2 Aviation drama set in World War I. Richard Dix, as the hero, raises this tough film above literally dozens of flying ace movies made in the early 1930s. B&W; 70m. **DIR:** J. Walter Ruben. **CAST:** Richard Dix, Elizabeth Allan, Ralph Bellamy. 1933

ACE OF HEARTS ★★1/2 Unlikely love triangle between a girl and two ardent anarchists. Lon Chaney Sr. plays the weepy suitor who loses the girl but redeems himself when he saves the loving couple. Chaney plays it low-key throughout the film, but there's a great segment featuring his character and an attentive dog and the finale is one of his finest moments. B&W; 62m. **DIR:** Wallace Worsley. **CAST:** Lon Chaney Sr., Leatrice Joy, John Bowers, Raymond Hatton. 1921

ACE VENTURA: PET DETECTIVE ★★1/2 Gangly Jim Carrey of TV's *In Living Color* proves that comedy doesn't have to be pretty to be a scream. Carrey hams it up as a goofy Florida gumshoe who cracks missing-animal cases. This giddy, crude comedy doesn't really have a personality of its own—it's an extension of Carrey's own hyper-nuttiness. Ace must locate the Miami Dolphins' mascot and star quarterback just before the Super Bowl. Rated PG-13 for violence, profanity, and suggested sex. 85m. **DIR:** Tom Shadyac. **CAST:** Jim Carrey, Sean Young, Courteney Cox, Tone Loc, Dan Marino. 1994 DVD

ACE VENTURA: WHEN NATURE CALLS ★★ Diminishing returns hit this series pretty quickly, with Jim Carrey's patented gross-out humor employed to shore up a thin script. This time out our hero must retrieve a sacred animal abducted from an African tribe, before war is declared. Although only small children are likely to enjoy the infantile slapstick, they're hardly the right audience for some of Carrey's tasteless sexual gags. Rated PG-13 for profanity, violence, and blue sexual material. 91m. **DIR:** Steve Oedekerk. **CAST:** Jim Carrey, Ian McNeice, Simon Callow, Maynard Eziashi, Bob Gunton. 1995 DVD

ACES AND EIGHTS ★★1/2 Although lacking in action, this Tim McCoy Western nevertheless has its moments. McCoy comes to the aid of a young Mexican unfairly accused of murder. B&W; 62m. **DIR:** Sam Newfield. **CAST:** Tim McCoy, Luana Walters. **1936**

ACES GO PLACES (1–3) (MAD MISSION 1–3) ★★★1/2 These high-spirited slapstick spy capers center on a daredevil burglar. Best of the series is number 3, an over-the-top parody of *Mission Impossible* and James Bond. In Cantonese with English subtitles. Not rated; contains some strong violence. 94/100/110m. **DIR:** Eric Tsang, Tsui Hark. **CAST:** Samuel Hui, Sylvia Chang, Karl Maka. **1981–1984**

ACES: IRON EAGLE III ★★★1/2 Surprisingly effective and entertaining reworking of *The Magnificent Seven/Seven Samurai* formula bears no resemblance to the other two films in the *Iron Eagle* series. It features Lou Gossett Jr. as the character of Chappy. This time, he must lead a group of World War II veterans on a mission to save a village from drug dealers. Rated R for violence and profanity. 98m. **DIR:** John Glen. **CAST:** Lou Gossett Jr., Rachel McLish, Paul Freeman, Horst Buchholz, Christopher Cazenove, Sonny Chiba, Fred Dalton Thompson, Mitchell Ryan. **1992**

ACROSS 110TH STREET ★★★1/2 This one is a real sleeper! An action-packed, extremely violent film concerning gang warfare between the Mafia and their black counterparts. Entire cast is very good, as are the action scenes. Rated R for violence and language. 102m. **DIR:** Barry Shear. **CAST:** Anthony Quinn, Yaphet Kotto, Anthony Franciosa, Richard Ward. **1972**

ACROSS THE GREAT DIVIDE ★★ Family entertainment at its most unchallenging. Two kids (Heather Rattray and Mark Hall) meet up with a shifty gambler (Robert Logan), and the three eventually unite for safety on their monotonous trek through valleys, mountains, and rivers. Rated G. 89m. **DIR:** Stewart Raffill. **CAST:** Robert Logan, George "Buck" Flower, Heather Rattray, Mark Edward Hall. **1976**

ACROSS THE MOON ★★★ Personable romantic comedy about two very different women and the circumstances that bring them together: their hoodlum boyfriends botch a robbery and are sent to prison. Elizabeth Peña and Christina Applegate are winning as the sisters-in-arms. Rated R for strong language and adult situations. 88m. **DIR:** Lisa Gottlieb. **CAST:** Christina Applegate, Elizabeth Peña, James Remar, Michael McKean, Tony Fields, Peter Berg, Michael Aniel Mundra. **1993 DVD**

ACROSS THE PACIFIC ★★★★ Prior to going off to war himself, director John Huston reassembled three of the stars from *The Maltese Falcon* for this high-spirited World War II propaganda piece. Humphrey Bogart woos Mary Astor while battling spy Sydney Greenstreet. Hugely enjoyable action film. B&W; 97m. **DIR:** John Huston. **CAST:** Humphrey Bogart, Mary Astor, Sydney Greenstreet, Victor Sen Yung, Keye Luke, Richard Loo. **1942**

ACROSS THE RIO GRANDE ★★★1/2 Jimmy Wakely straightens out a young lawyer involved with border silver-ore smugglers and captures the killer of the lawyer's father. Noteworthy as the first film appearance of Polly Bergen. B&W; 55m. **DIR:** Oliver Drake. **CAST:** Jimmy Wakely, Dub Taylor, Polly Bergen. **1949**

ACROSS THE TRACKS ★★★★ Two brothers compete for a scholarship in a county track championship. The soundtrack is excellent, the acting is convincing, and the screenplay deals with believable, real-life situations. Rated PG. 101m. **DIR:** Sandy Tung. **CAST:** Rick Schroder, Brad Pitt, Carrie Snodgress. **1990**

ACROSS THE WIDE MISSOURI ★★1/2 Scenery is the big and only plus in this plotless pedestrian tale of fortune seekers led by a Kentucky trapper seeking wealth in Indian-held virgin beaver territory. 78m. **DIR:** William Wellman. **CAST:** Clark Gable, Ricardo Montalban, Adolphe Menjou, John Hodiak, J. Carrol Naish, Alan Napier, Jack Holt. **1951**

ACT, THE ★★★ A comedy-drama with a convoluted plot of political chicanery, double cross, and robbery. The overall quality is erratic and yet this ends up being a good effort from a veteran cast. Trivia fans may note John Sebastian's involvement in the musical score. Rated R for sexual situations and language. 90m. **DIR:** Sig Shore. **CAST:** Robert Ginty, Sarah Langenfeld, Jill St. John, Eddie Albert, Pat Hingle. **1982**

ACT OF AGGRESSION ★★1/2 After his wife and daughter are raped and murdered, Jean-Louis Trintignant takes the law into his own hands in this unpleasant Gallic contribution to the *Death Wish* genre. In French with English subtitles. Not rated; contains brief nudity and violence. 94m. **DIR:** Gilbert Pires. **CAST:** Jean-Louis Trintignant, Catherine Deneuve, Claude Brasseur. **1975**

ACT OF PASSION ★★ In this made-for-television movie, Marlo Thomas plays a single woman who picks up a stranger (Kris Kristofferson) at a party. She is subsequently subjected to harassment by the police and the press when the man turns out to be a suspected terrorist. Harsh and blatantly exaggerated. 95m. **DIR:** Simon Langton. **CAST:** Marlo Thomas, Kris Kristofferson, Jon De Vries, David Rasche, Linda Thorson, Edward Winter, George Dzundza. **1984**

ACT OF PIRACY ★★1/2 When modern-day pirate Ray Sharkey and his gang rip off Gary Busey's state-of-the-art yacht, accidentally kidnapping his children at the same time, our hero embarks on a no-holds-barred mission to get his property back. Hohum action movie. Not rated, the film has profanity, violence, nudity, and simulated sex. 101m. **DIR:** John "Bud" Cardos. **CAST:** Gary Busey, Belinda Bauer, Ray Sharkey, Nancy Mulford, Ken Gampu. **1990**

ACT OF VENGEANCE ★★★★ In this first-rate drama, a suprisingly effective Charles Bronson plays Jock Yablonski, an honest man who wants to turn his coal-miners union around. When he runs for union president against the thoroughly corrupt incumbent (played brilliantly by Wilford Brimley), the threatened leader resorts to strong-arm tactics. Not rated; contains violence and profanity. 97m. **DIR:** John Mackenzie. **CAST:** Charles Bronson, Ellen Burstyn, Wilford Brimley, Hoyt Axton, Ellen Barkin. **1985**

ACTING ON IMPULSE ★★ A rather muddled thriller concerning needlessly warped horror-film star Linda Fiorentino, a conservative young salesman (C. Thomas Howell), and the obligatory assassin. The leads are better than the script deserves, and director Sam Irvin elicits stunningly awful performances from a host of cameo players. Rated R for profanity, violence, drug use, and kinky sexuality. 94m. DIR: Sam Irvin. CAST: C. Thomas Howell, Linda Fiorentino, Nancy Allen, Paul Bartel, Isaac Hayes, Adam Ant. 1993

ACTION IN ARABIA ★★1/2 George Sanders fights against time and Nazi agents as he attempts to inform the Allied authorities about German plans for a pact with the Arabs in this wartime romance-adventure. The love of a woman helps to turn the tide for the western powers in this sandy adventure. B&W; 75m. DIR: Leonide Moguy. CAST: George Sanders, Virginia Bruce, Gene Lockhart, Robert Armstrong, Michael Ansara. 1944

ACTION IN THE NORTH ATLANTIC ★★★1/2 Somewhat stodgy, flag-waving morale-booster features a fine cast in World War II-era tribute to the merchant marine. Officers Humphrey Bogart and Raymond Massey must rally their courage and crew when their convoy is attacked by a German U-boat. B&W; 127m. DIR: Lloyd Bacon. CAST: Humphrey Bogart, Raymond Massey, Alan Hale Sr., Julie Bishop, Ruth Gordon, Sam Levene, Dane Clark. 1943

ACTION JACKSON ★★ A maverick cop (Carl Weathers) is on the trail of a corrupt auto tycoon (Craig T. Nelson). Unfortunately, *Action Jackson* is a gabfest punctuated by not-so-hot sex scenes. There are a couple of good stunt scenes, though. Rated R for violence, drug use, simulated sex, nudity, and profanity. 95m. DIR: Craig R. Baxley. CAST: Carl Weathers, Craig T. Nelson, Vanity, Sharon Stone, Thomas F. Wilson, Bill Duke. 1988 DVD

ACTORS AND SIN ★★1/2 Two short films: *Actor's Blood* is a drama starring Edward G. Robinson as the devoted father of a successful Broadway actress (Marsha Hunt). *Woman's Sin* is a comedy starring Eddie Albert as an irrepressible Hollywood agent who finds a winning screenplay but loses its author. B&W; 86m. DIR: Ben Hecht, Lee Garmes. CAST: Edward G. Robinson, Eddie Albert, Marsha Hunt, Alan Reed, Dan O'Herlihy. 1952

•ACTOR'S REVENGE, AN ★★★1/2 Stylized drama set in the 1800s about a female impersonator in a Kabuki theater who seeks revenge on the killers of his parents. There's a little bit of everything in this somewhat confusing but intriguing import. In Japanese with English subtitles. 113m. DIR: Kon Ichikawa. CAST: Kazuo Hasegawa. 1963

ACTS OF BETRAYAL 💓 Movies this bad are usually relegated to cable at 3 A.M. Unfortunately this tale of a woman on the run from the mob is available to rent twenty-four hours a day. Not rated; contains violence. 112m. DIR: Joakim Ersgard. CAST: Maria Conchita Alonso, Matt McColm, Muse Watson, David Groh, Joe Estevez. 1997

A.D. POLICE FILES, VOLS. 1–3 ★★★ Animated spin-off from the *Bubblegum Crisis* series that chronicles the cases of Mega Tokyo's special A.D. Police, who handle ultraviolent crimes. Dark and graphic, this series is not for younger audiences, but animation buffs will enjoy the fine artwork, music, and gritty stories. In Japanese with English subtitles. Not rated; contains violence and nudity. 40m. each DIR: Ikegami Takamasa. 1993

ADAM ★★★★ Daniel J. Travanti and JoBeth Williams deliver fine performances in this chillingly real account of John and Reve Walsh's search for their missing 6-year-old son, Adam. A quite believable picture, detailing the months of uncertainty and anguish that surrounded the child's disappearance from a department store. This ordeal resulted in the formation of the Missing Children's Bureau. Made for television. 97m. DIR: Michael Tuchner. CAST: Daniel J. Travanti, JoBeth Williams, Richard Masur. 1983

ADAM AND EVELYN ★★★ An uneven mixture of comedy and drama that parallels the history of man's passion for woman. A middle-aged gambler adopts a homeless young woman and lavishes her with gifts and fatherly attention. His attitude toward her changes when his own brother starts courting her. The storyline is dated, but the performances are refreshingly personable. B&W; 80m. DIR: Harold French. CAST: Jean Simmons, Stewart Granger, Wilfrid Hyde-White, Helen Cherry, Edwin Styles. 1949

ADAM AT 6 A.M. ★★★ In his second film, Michael Douglas—in a coming-of-age role—leaves his California professorship to find his roots in rural Missouri. There he falls in love with a small-town girl (Lee Purcell) while working as a road laborer. Ending is a gem! Rated PG for violence. 100m. DIR: Robert Scheerer. CAST: Michael Douglas, Lee Purcell, Joe Don Baker, Grayson Hall. 1970

ADAM HAD FOUR SONS ★★★★ This classic has it all: good acting, romance, seduction, betrayal, tears, and laughter. Ingrid Bergman plays the good governess, and Susan Hayward plays the seductive hussy who tries to turn brother against brother. Warner Baxter offers a fine performance as Adam, the father. B&W; 81m. DIR: Gregory Ratoff. CAST: Ingrid Bergman, Warner Baxter, Susan Hayward. 1941

ADAM'S RIB (1949) ★★★★1/2 The screen team of Spencer Tracy and Katharine Hepburn was always watchable, but never more so than in this comedy. As husband-and-wife lawyers on opposing sides of a same case, they remind us of what movie magic is really all about. The supporting performances by Judy Holliday, Tom Ewell, David Wayne, and Jean Hagen greatly add to the fun. B&W; 101m. DIR: George Cukor. CAST: Spencer Tracy, Katharine Hepburn, Judy Holliday, Tom Ewell, David Wayne. 1949 DVD

ADAM'S RIB (1993) ★★★1/2 Four single women representing three generations try to live together in a small flat in a large Russian city. Gentle humor can be found in the forced intimacy and bittersweet relationships of these women as they try to maintain their independence while stepping on top of one another. In Russian with English subtitles. Not rated; contains adult themes and brief nudity. 77m. DIR: Vyacheslav Krishtofovich. CAST: Inna Churikova, Svetlana Ryabova, Maria Golubkina, Elena Bogdanova. 1993

ADDAMS FAMILY, THE ★★★1/2 It's murder and mayhem at the Addams mansion when two sleazy promoters try to force a fake Uncle Fester (Christopher Lloyd) on the unassuming Morticia (Anjelica Huston) and Gomez (Raul Julia). Perfectly cast and filled with touches of macabre humor. This movie actually improves upon the cult television series. Rated PG-13 for brief profanity and goofy violence. 101m. **DIR:** Barry Sonnenfeld. **CAST:** Anjelica Huston, Raul Julia, Christopher Lloyd, Christina Ricci, Jimmy Workman, Judith Malina, Elizabeth Wilson, Dan Hedaya. **1991 DVD**

ADDAMS FAMILY VALUES ★★★★ Fine performances mark this second big-screen romp of the Addams family. The zany plot involves the birth of a new family member and the seduction of Uncle Fester by a femme fatale. Forget sense and enjoy the nonsense. Rated PG-13 for ghoulish goings-on. 88m. **DIR:** Barry Sonnenfeld. **CAST:** Anjelica Huston, Raul Julia, Christopher Lloyd, Joan Cusack, Carol Kane, Peter Graves. **1993 DVD**

ADDAMS FAMILY REUNION ★★★1/2 This third entry in the *Addams Family* franchise is a different but nonetheless engaging beast. Tim Curry and Daryl Hannah are Gomez and Morticia, who pack up the family for a little vacation when they accidentally receive an invitation for another Addams family reunion. Familiar faces, witty humor, and outrageous sight gags work splendidly on this direct-to-video. Rated PG. 90m. **DIR:** David Payne. **CAST:** Tim Curry, Daryl Hannah, Estelle Harris, Ed Begley Jr., Kevin McCarthy, Alice Ghostley. **1998**

ADDAMS FAMILY, THE (TV SERIES) ★★★ Mid-Sixties television viewers never knew quite what to make of the deliciously bent humor in *The Addams Family*, which stretched Charles Addams' *New Yorker* cartoons into offbeat T.V. entertainment. John Astin played Gomez with maniacal intensity, while his lady-love, Morticia, was brought to somber life by Carolyn Jones. Fans of the 1991 big-screen rendition are encouraged to investigate these delightful origins. Each tape contains two half-hour episodes. each 52m. **DIR:** Arthur Hiller, Jerry Hopper, Sidney Lanfield. **CAST:** Carolyn Jones, John Astin, Jackie Coogan, Ted Cassidy. **1964–1966**

ADDICTED TO LOVE ★★★1/2 Robert Gordon's script is a wonderfully wacky ode to love gone sour. Nice guy Matthew Broderick unwisely allows childhood sweetheart Kelly Preston to accept a "temporary" job in New York; when she doesn't return, he follows and finds her in the arms—and bed—of an amorous Frenchman. Our hero sets up housekeeping across the street and watches, hoping to be present when his ex comes to her senses … and then things get truly bent when the Frenchman's ex-fiancée (Meg Ryan) shows up. Although things get a bit nasty toward the end, true love emerges in this mostly delightful, *truly* screwball comedy. Rated R for profanity, nudity, and strong sexual content. 100m. **DIR:** Griffin Dunne. **CAST:** Meg Ryan, Matthew Broderick, Kelly Preston, Tcheky Karyo, Maureen Stapleton. **1997 DVD**

ADDICTED TO MURDER ★★ Low-budget vampire flick attempts to inject some new blood into the tired old formula but never really takes off. Not rated; contains violence, gore, and profanity. 90m. **DIR:** Kevin J. Lindénmuth. **CAST:** Mick McCleery, Sasha Graham. **1995**

ADDICTION, THE ★★★ Director Abel Ferrara once again walks on the dark side with this fatalistic, beautifully photographed tale of the supernatural. Lili Taylor is a naïve New York City philosophy student who learns a painful afterlife lesson from master vampire Christopher Walken. Allegorical and atmospheric, this is intriguing but too internalized and slow moving. Letterboxed. Not rated; contains profanity, violence, and sexual situations. B&W; 82m. **DIR:** Abel Ferrara. **CAST:** Christopher Walken, Annabella Sciorra, Lili Taylor. **1995**

•ADDRESS UNKNOWN ★★★1/2 A teen discovers that his father's accidental death may not have been an accident after all when he uncovers a letter written ten years before. Though intended primarily for younger viewers, this mystery will entertain parents as well. Rated PG. 92m. **DIR:** Shawn Levy. **CAST:** Kyle Howard, Johna Stewart, Corbin Allred, Patrick Renna. **1997**

ADIOS AMIGO ★★★ Writer-director-actor-producer Fred Williamson's whimsical parody of the Hollywood Western is about the misadventures of a cowboy (Williamson) and his sly, con-man partner (hilariously performed by Richard Pryor). Rated PG for profanity, but not much violence. 87m. **DIR:** Fred Williamson. **CAST:** Fred Williamson, Richard Pryor, Thalmus Rasulala, James Brown, Mike Henry. **1975**

ADIOS, HOMBRE ★★ Tiny, a sleazy outlaw, and his gang try to rob a bank but find it empty, so they decide to take the town hostage until the next gold shipment arrives. Enter a falsely accused escaped convict, Will Flagherty, out to prove his innocence and a one-man war is unleashed against the outlaw gang. Good action and an over-the-top performance by Eduardo Fajardo as Tiny. Not rated; contains violence. 90m. **DIR:** Mario Caiano. **CAST:** Craig Hill, Giulia Rubini, Piero Lulli, Eduardo Fajardo, Nazzareno Zemperla, Jacques Herlin, Nello Pazzafini, Roberto Camardiel. **1966**

ADJUSTER, THE ★★ Elias Koteas stars as an insurance adjuster. His wife is obsessed with the pornography and violence she views every day as a film censor. Another couple enter their lives—a wealthy duo who spend all their money and time on elaborate sex games. If you're looking for clarity and plot, abandon faith, all ye who enter here. 102m. **DIR:** Atom Egoyan. **CAST:** Elias Koteas, Arsinée Khanjian, Maury Chaykin, Gabrielle Rose. **1992**

ADMIRABLE CRICHTON, THE ★★★ A super-efficient butler takes command when he and his aristocratic employers are shipwrecked and marooned on a desert island. Love blossoms between the social classes, but all reverts to pre-wreck status following rescue. Love does not conquer all. Somewhat dated, but entertaining anyway. 93m. **DIR:** Lewis Gilbert. **CAST:** Sally Ann Howes, Martita Hunt, Kenneth More, Cecil Parker, Diane Cilento. **1957**

ADMIRAL WAS A LADY, THE ★★1/2 Romantic comedy about a group of ex-GI's asked to watch over a young woman until she can be reunited with her fiancé. Clichéd and somewhat bland, it's not without a certain amount of charm. B&W; 87m. **DIR:** Albert S. Rogell. **CAST:** Edmond O'Brien, Wanda Hendrix, Rudy Vallee, Johnny Sands. **1948**

ADORABLE JULIA ★★1/2 Somerset Maugham tale of a middle-aged stage actress who has an affair with a younger man while her husband waits in the wings. About as original as it sounds, though the cast lends it a bit of charm. Dubbed. Not rated. B&W; 97m. **DIR:** Alfred Weidenmann. **CAST:** Lilli Palmer, Charles Boyer, Jean Sorel. 1962

ADRENALIN: FEAR THE RUSH ★★★ Creepy, effective thriller that's sure to appeal to fans of *The X-Files*. Set in the not-too-distant future, the film stars Christopher Lambert and Natasha Henstridge as police officers trying to capture an elusive killer. What they don't know is that their prey is a government experiment gone awry: a crazed, killing machine carrying a virus that could wipe out the rest of mankind. Director Albert Pyun has created an intense thriller. Rated R for profanity and violence. 76m. **DIR:** Albert Pyun. **CAST:** Christopher Lambert, Natasha Henstridge, Norbert Weisser, Elizabeth Barondes, Nicholas Guest. 1995

ADRIFT ★★ Derivative made-for-TV thriller proves those behind it saw *Dead Calm*. Kate Jackson and Kenneth Welsh are the good couple whose voyage is interrupted when they pick up bad couple Bruce Greenwood and Kelly Rowan. Predictable high-seas terror. Not rated. 92m. **DIR:** Christian Duguay. **CAST:** Kate Jackson, Kenneth Welsh, Bruce Greenwood, Kelly Rowan. 1993

ADULTRESS, THE ★ Abysmal film about an impotent husband who hires a gigolo to service his wife. 85m. **DIR:** Norbert Meisel. **CAST:** Tyne Daly, Eric Braeden, Greg Morton. 1973

ADVENTURE ★★1/2 Flat and slow-moving romantic drama has a rough merchant sailor involved with a staid librarian. Neither Joan Blondell nor Thomas Mitchell (in his patented drunk Irishman role) can save this one. B&W; 125m. **DIR:** Victor Fleming. **CAST:** Clark Gable, Greer Garson, Joan Blondell, Thomas Mitchell, Tom Tully, John Qualen, Lina Romay, Harry Davenport. 1946

ADVENTURE OF SHERLOCK HOLMES' SMARTER BROTHER, THE ★★1/2 Even discounting the effrontery of writer-director-star Gene Wilder's creating a smarter sibling, Sigerson Holmes (Gene Wilder), one is still left with a highly uneven romp. Though the principals—who also include Marty Feldman and Dom DeLuise—try hard, the film's soggy structure (and Wilder's poor research into the canon) plunge the whole thing into mediocrity. Rated PG. 91m. **DIR:** Gene Wilder. **CAST:** Gene Wilder, Madeline Kahn, Marty Feldman, Dom DeLuise. 1975

ADVENTURES BEYOND BELIEF ❤ In this incoherent excuse for madcap comedy, an Elvis Presley fan helps a mobster's daughter escape from an all-girls' school. Not rated. 95m. **DIR:** Marcus Tompson. **CAST:** Skyler Cole, Jill Whitlow, Elke Sommer, Stella Stevens, Edie Adams, John Astin, Larry Storch. 1987

ADVENTURES IN BABYSITTING ★★★1/2 A sort of *After Hours* for the teen crowd, this is a surprisingly entertaining film about what happens when 17-year-old Chris Parker (Elisabeth Shue) accepts a babysitting assignment. There are a number of hilarious moments—our favorite being a sequence in a blues club presided over by superguitarist Albert Collins. Rated PG-13 for profanity and violence. 100m. **DIR:**

Chris Columbus. **CAST:** Elisabeth Shue, Keith Coogan, Anthony Rapp, Maia Brewton, Penelope Ann Miller, Vincent D'Onofrio. 1987 DVD

ADVENTURES IN DINOSAUR CITY ★★ Three teens enter a dimension in which cartoon characters—dinosaurs—become real. Muppet-like creatures are very well done but can't make up for the flimsy plot and silly dialogue. Rated PG for comical violence. 88m. **DIR:** Brett Thompson. **CAST:** Omri Katz, Shawn Hoffman. 1991

ADVENTURES IN SPYING ★★1/2 In this harmless romp, bored Bernie Coulson and Jill Schoelen learn that a recent acquaintance is actually a hired killer presumed dead. Now that he knows that they know his secret, they have to outrun numerous bad guys, ranging from crooked cops to evil chemists. G. Gordon Liddy makes a great villain. Rated PG-13 for violence. 91m. **DIR:** Hil Covington. **CAST:** Bernie Coulson, Jill Schoelen, Seymour Cassel, Michael Emil, G. Gordon Liddy. 1991

ADVENTURES OF A GNOME NAMED GNORM, THE ❤ A buffoonish young cop and a hairy, stubby creature from a mystic underworld team up to nab a jewel thief in this overly violent fantasy-caper. Rated PG for language and violence. 86m. **DIR:** Stan Winston. **CAST:** Anthony Michael Hall, Claudia Christian, Jerry Orbach. 1993

ADVENTURES OF A PRIVATE EYE ★★ Boring British comedy about a detective's assistant who tries his hand at investigating a blackmail case while his boss is on vacation. The film has plenty of nudity and some scenes of rather explicit sex. Not rated. 96m. **DIR:** Stanley Long. **CAST:** Christopher Neil, Suzy Kendall, Harry H. Corbett, Diana Dors, Fred Emney, Liz Fraser, Irene Handl, Ian Lavender, Jon Pertwee, Adrienne Posta. 1987

ADVENTURES OF AN AMERICAN RABBIT, THE ★★★ In this enjoyable-for-kids feature-length cartoon, mild-mannered and sweet-natured Rob Rabbit becomes the heir to the Legacy, which magically transforms him into the star-spangled protector of all animalkind, the American Rabbit. Rated G. 85m. **DIR:** Steward Moskowitz. 1986

ADVENTURES OF BARON MÜNCHAUSEN, THE ★★★★ Terry Gilliam, that inspired madman of the movies, completes the fantasy trilogy—which began with *Time Bandits* and *Brazil*—with this one about the celebrated eighteenth-century liar. In the Age of Reason a small theatrical troupe attempts to put on a play about Münchausen, only to have an old soldier turn up claiming to be the real thing. He goes on to prove his identity with a series of wild tales. Rated PG for violence. 126m. **DIR:** Terry Gilliam. **CAST:** John Neville, Robin Williams, Eric Idle, Oliver Reed, Uma Thurman, Sarah Polley. 1989 DVD

ADVENTURES OF BUCKAROO BANZAI, THE ★★★★ Peter Weller plays Buckaroo Banzai, a skilled neurosurgeon and physicist who becomes bored with his scientific and medical work and embarks on a career as a rock star and two-fisted defender of justice. This offbeat genre film is a silly movie for smart people. Rated PG. 103m. **DIR:** W. D. Richter. **CAST:** Peter Weller, John Lithgow, Ellen Barkin, Jeff Goldblum. 1984

ADVENTURES OF BULLWHIP GRIFFIN, THE ★★ Typical, flyweight Disney comedy fails to offer anything original. Roddy McDowall plays a proper English butler who finds himself smack-dab in the wilds of California during the Gold Rush. Okay for the kids but not much to recommend for a discriminating audience. 110m. **DIR:** James Neilson. **CAST:** Roddy McDowall, Suzanne Pleshette, Karl Malden, Harry Guardino, Richard Haydn, Hermione Baddeley, Cecil Kellaway, Bryan Russell. **1966**

ADVENTURES OF CAPTAIN MARVEL, THE ★★★★ Fawcett Comics' Captain Marvel is splendidly brought to life by Republic Studios in what is generally regarded as the best serial of all time, certainly the best superhero chapterplay ever produced. Sincerely acted by all involved, this serial set the standards for flying stunts for years to come. B&W; 12 chapters. **DIR:** William Witney, John English. **CAST:** Tom Tyler, Frank Coghlan Jr., William Benedict, Louise Currie. **1941**

ADVENTURES OF DON JUAN, THE ★★★★ Despite the obvious use of footage from *The Adventures of Robin Hood* and *The Private Lives of Elizabeth and Essex*, this is a solid swashbuckler. Errol Flynn plays the great lover and swordsman of the title with tongue planted firmly in cheek. The years of drinking were beginning to show on his once boyishly handsome face. Yet this is quite appropriate to his portrayal of the famous libertine. 110m. **DIR:** Vincent Sherman. **CAST:** Errol Flynn, Viveca Lindfors, Robert Douglas, Alan Hale Sr., Romney Brent, Ann Rutherford, Robert Warwick, Jerry Austin, Douglas Kennedy, Una O'Connor. **1949**

•ADVENTURES OF ELMO IN GROUCHLAND, THE ★★★ Little woolly red creature Elmo from TV's *Sesame Street* dives into Oscar the Grouch's garbage can to retrieve his beloved blanket. He gets sucked down a tunnel into a yucky universe where a selfish tyrant takes whatever he wants from his disgruntled subjects. This crisply paced adventure includes messages about sharing and cooperation, and encourages interaction from the audience. Rated G. 73m. **DIR:** Gary Halvorson. **CAST:** Mandy Patinkin, Vanessa Williams. **1999 DVD**

ADVENTURES OF FORD FAIRLANE, THE ★★ Foulmouthed shock comic Andrew Clay stars as rock 'n' roll private dick Ford Fairlane. There's something here to offend everybody, especially women. Rated R for profanity and violence. 101m. **DIR:** Renny Harlin. **CAST:** Andrew Clay, Priscilla Presley, Wayne Newton, Robert Englund, Ed O'Neill. **1990**

ADVENTURES OF GALGAMETH, THE ★★ Mildly diverting effort will please only the most forgiving children. Devin Oatway stars as young Prince Davin, whose fight with the evil knight El El over his father's throne is aided by a goofy, metal-eating creature who can balloon up to the size of a building. Too bad he couldn't inflate the obviously low budget. Rated PG. 99m. **DIR:** Sean McNamara. **CAST:** Devin Oatway, Stephen Macht, Johna Stewart. **1997**

ADVENTURES OF GALLANT BESS ★★ Minor melodrama about a man who seems to be more in love with his horse than he is with the woman in his life. The photography is quite good and the performances are passable, but it is still only fair. 73m. **DIR:** Lew Landers. **CAST:** Cameron Mitchell, Audrey Long, Fuzzy Knight. **1948**

ADVENTURES OF HERCULES, THE ♥ This is the sequel to *Hercules*, the 1983 bomb with Lou "the Hulk" Ferrigno. The first Ferrigno folly was a laughfest. This tiresome piece of junk would only benefit insomniacs. Rated PG for violence (yes, even *that* can be boring). 89m. **DIR:** Lewis Coates. **CAST:** Lou Ferrigno, Milly Carlucci. **1984**

ADVENTURES OF HUCKLEBERRY FINN, THE **(1939)** ★★★★ Fun-filled telling of the misadventures of Mark Twain's "other hero," as he outdoes the evil thieves, "King" and "Duke," becomes smitten over Mary Jane, and develops a conscience concerning the treatment of blacks. Mickey Rooney is fine in a subdued performance, and Rex Ingram is impressive as the slave, Jim. Originally released as *Huckleberry Finn.* B&W; 90m. **DIR:** Richard Thorpe. **CAST:** Mickey Rooney, Walter Connolly, William Frawley, Rex Ingram, Minor Watson, Lynne Carver. **1939**

ADVENTURES OF HUCKLEBERRY FINN, THE **(1960)** ★★★★ A delightful version of the Mark Twain classic produced to commemorate the seventy-fifth anniversary of its publication. A host of colorful players bring the famous characters to life. 107m. **DIR:** Michael Curtiz. **CAST:** Eddie Hodges, Archie Moore, Buster Keaton, Tony Randall, Andy Devine, Patty McCormack, Judy Canova, John Carradine, Mickey Shaughnessy, Sterling Holloway, Neville Brand. **1960**

ADVENTURES OF HUCKLEBERRY FINN, THE **(1978)** ★★ This drawn-out version of Mark Twain's classic has its moments but lacks continuous action. In it, young Huck fakes his own drowning to avoid attendance at a proper eastern school for boys. When his friend, Jim (Brock Peters), is accused of his murder, he must devise a plan to free him. 97m. **DIR:** Jack B. Hively. **CAST:** Forrest Tucker, Larry Storch, Brock Peters. **1978**

ADVENTURES OF HUCK FINN, THE (1993) ★★★★ In this high-gloss family film from Walt Disney Pictures that recalls Hollywood's golden age, adaptor-director Stephen Sommers lovingly captures Mark Twain's witty, wink-of-the-eye style. Elijah Wood is delightful as the barefoot boy who learns some important life lessons while traveling. Rated PG for brief violence. 108m. **DIR:** Stephen Sommers. **CAST:** Elijah Wood, Courtney B. Vance, Robbie Coltrane, Jason Robards Jr., Ron Perlman, Dana Ivey, Anne Heche, James Gammon, Curtis Armstrong. **1993**

ADVENTURES OF MARCO POLO, THE ★★★ Disappointing tale of the travels of the thirteenth-century Italian merchant and his "discovery" in China of spaghetti, coal, and gunpowder for civilized Europe. Should have been a rousing epic. Screenplay by Robert E. Sherwood. Look for Lana Turner as an attendant in the court of Kublai Khan. B&W; 100m. **DIR:** Archie Mayo. **CAST:** Gary Cooper, Sigrid Gurie, Basil Rathbone, George Barbier, Ernest Truex, Binnie Barnes, Alan Hale Sr., H. B. Warner, Lana Turner. **1938**

ADVENTURES OF MARK TWAIN, THE (1944) ★★★1/2 This very episodic tale follows Samuel Clemens (Fredric March) from boyhood and young manhood on his beloved Mississippi River to recognition as a writer and lecturer. A nice bit of license is taken when he is involved in a frog-jump contest with Bret Harte (John Carradine). B&W; 130m. **DIR:** Irving Rapper. **CAST:** Fredric March, Alexis Smith, Donald Crisp, Alan Hale Sr., C. Aubrey Smith, John Carradine, Walter Hampen, Joyce Reynolds, Percy Kilbride. 1944

ADVENTURES OF MARK TWAIN, THE (1985) ★★★★ A superior work of Claymation provides insights into the creative genius of Samuel Clemens. Includes vignettes of Twain's "The Diary of Adam and Eve" and "The Mysterious Stranger" in which the character of Satan spouts an existential perspective on life and death. 86m. **DIR:** Will Vinton. 1985

ADVENTURES OF MILO AND OTIS, THE ★★★★ Japanese director Masanori Hata spent four years making this splendid family film, in which a dog named Otis sets out to rescue his lifelong friend, a kitten named Milo, when the feline is carried away by a rushing river. Adults will enjoy this one as much as their children. Rated G. 76m. **DIR:** Masanori Hata. **CAST:** Dudley Moore. 1989 DVD

ADVENTURES OF MILO IN THE PHANTOM TOLLBOOTH, THE ★★★ An assortment of cartoon talents, including director Chuck Jones and voice greats like Mel Blanc, Hans Conried, Daws Butler, and June Foray, make this unusual but entertaining film coalesce. Live-action footage combines with animation to tell the story of a young boy who enters a booth that takes him into the Land of Wisdom. Rated G. 89m. **DIR:** Chuck Jones, Abe Levitow, Dave Monahan. **CAST:** Butch Patrick. 1969

ADVENTURES OF MOLE, THE ★★★ Engaging animated tale based on Kenneth Grahame's beloved children's stories. This outing, Mole and his friends journey down the river in search of excitement and adventure. They find plenty of both in this tune-filled excursion that features colorful animation and kid-friendly lessons in life. Not rated. 60m. **DIR:** Martin Gates. 1995

ADVENTURES OF NELLIE BLY, THE ★★ In this made-for-television film, Linda Purl shines as a reporter who uncovers serious problems in factories and insane asylums. The script unfortunately is weak and the direction is uninspired. 100m. **DIR:** Henning Schellerup. **CAST:** Linda Purl, Gene Barry, John Randolph, Raymond Buktenica, J. D. Cannon. 1981

ADVENTURES OF OZZIE AND HARRIET, THE (TV SERIES) ★★★★ This prototypical family sitcom, primarily remembered for its all-American wholesomeness, was genuinely funny. That remarkable accomplishment must be largely credited to Ozzie Nelson, who produced, directed, and co-wrote, as well as starred as the earnest father who could create chaos out of the simplest situations. Real-life wife Harriet and sons Ricky and David added warmth and naturalness. B&W; 60m. **DIR:** Ozzie Nelson. **CAST:** Ozzie Nelson, Harriet Nelson, Ricky Nelson, David Nelson, Kris Nelson, June Nelson, Don DeFore, Lyle Talbot. 1952–1966

ADVENTURES OF PICASSO, THE ★★★ Witty, off-the-wall Swedish comedy about the life of Picasso. The rubber-faced Gosta Eckman looks like Buster Keaton playing Picasso, and Bernard Cribbins is a scream in drag as Gertrude Stein. Some truly funny moments make this semislapstick film shine. In overly simplistic Spanish, French, and English, so no subtitles are needed. Not rated; contains some ribald humor. 94m. **DIR:** Tage Danielsson. **CAST:** Gosta Ekman, Hans Alfredson, Margaretha Krook, Bernard Cribbins, Wilfred Brambell. 1988

ADVENTURES OF PINOCCHIO, THE ★★★1/2 Martin Landau is impressive as the lonely puppet maker, Geppetto, whose latest creation takes on a life of its own. Jonathan Taylor Thomas, the voice for the wooden Pinocchio and eventually the real little boy, maintains an irresistible sense of awe and wonderment. This film, based on Carlo Collodi's fable, is a veritable special-effects bonanza combining Jim Henson's Creature Shop wizardry, animatronics, miniatures, and computer-generated images to perfection. Rated G. 88m. **DIR:** Steve Barron. **CAST:** Martin Landau, Jonathan Taylor Thomas, Genevieve Bujold, Udo Kier, Bebe Neuwirth, Rob Schneider. 1996

ADVENTURES OF PRISCILLA, QUEEN OF THE DESERT, THE ★★★★ Those who enjoyed the exuberant energy of *Strictly Ballroom* will be equally delighted by this spirited Australian import that follows three cross-dressing entertainers through small-town stops en route to a big-city gig. Not rated; contains mild profanity and frank sexual situations. 102m. **DIR:** Stephan Elliott. **CAST:** Terence Stamp, Hugo Weaving, Guy Pearce, Bill Hunter, Sarah Chadwick. 1994 DVD

ADVENTURES OF RED RYDER ★★★★1/2 Action-packed serial as Red Ryder thwarts at every turn a banker's attempts to defraud ranchers whose land is wanted for a coming railroad. B&W; 12 chapters. **DIR:** William Witney, John English. **CAST:** Don Barry, Tommy Cook, Noah Beery Sr. 1940

ADVENTURES OF REX AND RINTY ★★★1/2 A trio of unscrupulous Americans steal the God-Horse, Rex, from the island of Sujan and sell it to a greedy United States ranch owner. Rex escapes, meets Rinty, and the animals team up to avoid capture by the thieves. B&W; 12 chapters. **DIR:** Ford Beebe, B. Reeves "Breezy" Eason. **CAST:** Rin Tin Tin Jr., Kane Richmond, Norma Taylor, Smiley Burnette, Harry Woods. 1935

ADVENTURES OF ROBIN HOOD, THE ★★★★★ This classic presents Errol Flynn at his swashbuckling best. He is backed up in this color spectacular by a perfect cast of supporting actors. Lavish sets and a stirring musical score help place *Robin Hood* among the very best adventure films. 106m. **DIR:** Michael Curtiz, William Keighley. **CAST:** Errol Flynn, Basil Rathbone, Ian Hunter, Olivia de Havilland, Claude Rains, Alan Hale Sr., Eugene Pallette. 1938

ADVENTURES OF SADIE ★★ Three men and a very young Joan Collins shipwrecked on a desert island; you can guess the rest. 88m. **DIR:** Noel Langley. **CAST:** George Cole, Kenneth More, Joan Collins, Hattie Jacques, Hermione Gingold. 1953

•**ADVENTURES OF SEBASTIAN COLE, THE** ★★★★ Insightful film about a high-school boy and the eclectic characters who, in some way, influence his life and his future. Well-written, brilliantly acted and directed. Rated R for profanity. 112m. **DIR:** Tod

Williams. **CAST:** Adrian Grenier, Clark Gregg, Aleksa Pallodino, Margaret Colin, John Shea, Rory Cochrane. **1998 DVD**

ADVENTURES OF SHERLOCK HOLMES, THE ★★★★1/2 The best of all the Basil Rathbone–Nigel Bruce Sherlock Holmes movies, this pits the great detective against his arch-nemesis, Dr. Moriarty (played by George Zucco). The period setting, atmospheric photography, and the spirited performances of the cast (which includes a young Ida Lupino as Holmes's client) make this a must-see for mystery fans. B&W; 85m. **DIR:** Alfred Werker. **CAST:** Basil Rathbone, Nigel Bruce, Ida Lupino, George Zucco. **1939**

ADVENTURES OF SHERLOCK HOLMES, THE (TV SERIES) ★★★ Originally created as a television series for the European market, these 36 episodes hold up reasonably well. The original scripts are much lighter than Conan Doyle's stories, resulting in a finished tone that suggests the cast had a good time. Suitable for family viewing. B&W; 52m. **DIR:** Steve Previn, Sheldon Reynolds. **CAST:** Ronald Howard, H. Marion Crawford, Archie Duncan. **1955**

ADVENTURES OF SHERLOCK HOLMES, THE (SERIES) ★★★★★ Jeremy Brett portrays Holmes as twitchy, arrogant, wan, humorless, and often downright rude—in short, everything Conan Doyle's hero was described to be. David Burke brings youthful dash and intelligent charm to Dr. Watson. Each episode is impeccably scripted and superbly acted. Not rated; contains frank discussions of violence and drug abuse. 52m. **DIR:** Paul Annett, John Bruce, David Carson, Ken Grieve, Alan Grint, Derek Marlowe. **CAST:** Jeremy Brett, David Burke. **1986**

ADVENTURES OF SINBAD, THE ★★ Slow retelling of a tale from *The Thousand and One Nights.* Sinbad the sailor sets out to retrieve the proverbial magic lamp when it is stolen by the Old Man of the Sea. 48m. **DIR:** Richard Slapczynski. **1979**

ADVENTURES OF TARTU ★★1/2 Robert Donat steals the show as a British spy entrusted with the crippling of a poison gas factory behind enemy lines. He is joined in this blend of comedy and suspense by lovely Valerie Hobson and perky Glynis Johns. Nothing really special about this one, but it's fun. B&W; 103m. **DIR:** Harold S. Bucquet. **CAST:** Robert Donat, Valerie Hobson, Glynis Johns, Walter Rilla, Phyllis Morris. **1943**

ADVENTURES OF TARZAN, THE ★★1/2 Early action star Elmo Lincoln dons a wig for the third time to portray the Lord of the Jungle in this ambitious chapterplay. Lincoln finds himself fighting unscrupulous Bolsheviks, wild animals, a claimant to his family name, and the hordes of the lost city of Opar. Loosely adapted from two Tarzan novels. Silent. B&W; 15 chapters. **DIR:** Robert Hill. **CAST:** Elmo Lincoln, Louise Lorraine, Percy Pembroke. **1921**

ADVENTURES OF THE GREAT MOUSE DETECTIVE, THE ★★★★ Before going on to even more spectacular success with *The Little Mermaid,* directors John Musker and Ron Clements collaborated on this charming adaptation of Eve Titus's *Basil of Baker Street,* a children's book inspired by the stories of Conan Doyle. Featuring the voice of Vincent Price as the villain, Rattigan, and a delightful, suspenseful story, this film gave the first indication that the Walt Disney animation department had at last awoken from its long slumber. Rated G. 90m. **DIR:** John Musker, Ron Clements, Dave Michener, Bunny Mattison. **1986**

ADVENTURES OF THE KUNG FU RASCALS, THE ★★ Wacky spoof of the kung fu genre is helped by decent special effects and creature makeup. Three Stooges–like heroes—Lao Ze, Reepo, and Chen Chow Mein—fight to free their land from an evil ruler. Toilet humor is unnecessarily offensive. Rated PG-13 for comic-book violence. 90m. **DIR:** Steve Wang. **CAST:** Steve Wang, Troy Fromin, Johnnie Saiko Espiritu, Les Claypool, Ted Smith, Aaron Sims. **1991**

ADVENTURES OF THE WILDERNESS FAMILY ★★★1/2 This is a variation on the Swiss Family Robinson story. A family (oddly enough named Robinson) moves to the Rocky Mountains to escape the frustrations and congestion of life in Los Angeles. They're sick of smog, hassles, and crime. They build a cabin and brave the dangers of the wild. Rated G. 100m. **DIR:** Stewart Raffill. **CAST:** Robert Logan, Susan D. Shaw, Ham Larsen, Heather Rattray, George "Buck" Flower, Hollye Holmes. **1975 DVD**

ADVENTURES OF TOM SAWYER, THE ★★★★ One of the better screen adaptations of Mark Twain's works. Tommy Kelly is a perfect Tom Sawyer, but it's Victor Jory as the villainous Indian Joe who steals the show. Good sets and beautiful cinematography make this one work. Fine family entertainment for young and old. B&W; 93m. **DIR:** Norman Taurog. **CAST:** Tommy Kelly, Jackie Moran, Victor Jory, May Robson, Walter Brennan, Ann Gillis. **1938**

ADVENTURES OF TOPPER, THE ★★★ This television comedy consistently earned chuckles, if not an abundance of belly laughs as this video compilation attests. Leo G. Carroll is delightful as Cosmo Topper, the henpecked bank vice president who is the only one who can see a trio of ghosts—Marion Kirby (Anne Jeffreys), her husband George (Robert Sterling), "that most sporting spirit," and their boozeswilling Saint Bernard, Neil. 93m. **DIR:** Philip Rapp. **CAST:** Anne Jeffreys, Robert Sterling, Leo G. Carroll, Lee Patrick, Thurston Hall, Kathleen Freeman. **1953–1956**

✦ADVENTURES OF YOUNG BRAVE, THE ★★ Fanciful family adventure that will appeal more to kids than adults. Two children are helped by the spirit of an Indian in their quest for gold, and then must help the ghost complete an act of bravery in order to return to the spirit world. A little silly and not very demanding, the film still exudes some charm. Also released as *Waking Up Horton.* Rated PG. 88m. **DIR:** Harry Bromley Davenport. **CAST:** Dirk Benedict, Barbara Carrera, Kenneth Hughes, Billy Maddox. **1998 DVD**

ADVERSARY, THE ★★★ Vivid and disturbing account of a college graduate who has been out of work for months. Satyajit Ray's neorealist sense of tragedy is unforgettably dramatized in this heartfelt film. In Bengali with English subtitles. B&W; 110m. **DIR:** Satyajit Ray. **CAST:** Dhritiman Chatterjee. **1971**

ADVISE AND CONSENT ★★★1/2 An engrossing adaptation of Allen Drury's bestseller about behind-the-scenes Washington. Fine performances abound as the U.S. Senate is called upon to confirm a controversial nominee for Secretary of State (Henry Fonda). Easily the most riveting is Charles Laughton, at his scene-stealing best, as a smiling old crocodile of a southern senator. B&W; 140m. **DIR:** Otto Preminger. **CAST:** Henry Fonda, Don Murray, Charles Laughton, Franchot Tone, Lew Ayres, Walter Pidgeon, Peter Lawford; Paul Ford, Burgess Meredith, Gene Tierney. **1962**

ADVOCATE, THE ★★1/2 In medieval France, a country lawyer defends a pig accused of murder. It may sound like a Monty Python skit, but the film is really a serious examination of social, religious, and legal attitudes during the fifteenth century. It gets high marks for daring and originality, and for its fine cast, but the script is unnecessarily confusing and the pacing is cumbersome. Rated R for nudity and sexual scenes. 101m. **DIR:** Leslie Megahey. **CAST:** Colin Firth, Amina Annabi, Donald Pleasence, Nicol Williamson, Michael Gough. **1993**

AELITA: QUEEN OF MARS ★★★ Deeply esoteric entertainment here. A silent Russian movie concerning a disenchanted man who takes a spaceship to Mars to meet the woman of his dreams. He encounters a proletariat uprising on the planet and realizes daydreams are not all they seem. Silent. B&W; 113m. **DIR:** Yakov Protázanov. **CAST:** Yulia Solntseva. **1924 DVD**

AFFAIR, THE (1973) ★★★ Touching, honest story of a crippled songwriter (Natalie Wood) tentatively entering into her first love affair—with an attorney (Robert Wagner). This is an unusually well-acted, sensitively told TV movie. 74m. **DIR:** Gilbert Cates. **CAST:** Natalie Wood, Robert Wagner, Bruce Davison, Kent Smith, Pat Harrington. **1973 DVD**

AFFAIR, THE (1995) ★★★★ Actual events suggested this compelling WWII drama, which concerns the forbidden romance between an unhappily married British woman and a black American soldier. Although treated decently by their English hosts, black soldiers found the color barrier just as insurmountable. A pall of impending doom hangs over this story from its first moments, but the resolution is no less tragic for its foreshadowing. Rated R for profanity, violence, nudity, and simulated sex. 105m. **DIR:** Paul Seed. **CAST:** Courtney B. Vance, Kerry Fox, Leland Gantt, Bill Nunn, Ned Beatty. **1995**

AFFAIR IN TRINIDAD ★★★ Sultry, enticing café singer Rita Hayworth teams with brother-in-law Glenn Ford to trap her husband's murderer. The two fall in love en route. 98m. **DIR:** Vincent Sherman. **CAST:** Glenn Ford, Rita Hayworth, Alexander Scourby, Torin Thatcher. **1952**

AFFAIR TO REMEMBER, AN ★★★★ Leo McCarey's gorgeous, haunting remake of his Oscar-nominated *Love Affair*. Cary Grant and Deborah Kerr have a shipboard romance, then part for six months. They agree to meet atop the Empire State Building in six months, but an accident prevents it. 115m. **DIR:** Leo McCarey. **CAST:** Cary Grant, Deborah Kerr, Richard Denning, Cathleen Nesbitt, Robert Q. Lewis. **1957 DVD**

AFFAIRS OF ANNABEL, THE ★★★★ The pre–*I Love Lucy* Lucille Ball is very funny in this fast-paced comedy as a none-too-bright movie star whose manager (Jack Oakie) is continually dreaming up outrageous publicity stunts for her. The supporting cast of familiar Thirties faces also provides plenty of laughs, especially Fritz Feld as a supercilious foreign director. 73m. **DIR:** Ben Stoloff. **CAST:** Jack Oakie, Lucille Ball, Ruth Donnelly, Fritz Feld, Thurston Hall. **1937**

AFFAIRS OF DOBIE GILLIS, THE ★★★★ This delightful college comedy that is sexy but not obvious about it focuses on an overamorous undergrad who dates girls in spite of their parents' objections. Good songs and lively dances by solid pros lift this one above the ordinary. B&W; 74m. **DIR:** Don Weis. **CAST:** Debbie Reynolds, Bobby Van, Bob Fosse, Hans Conried, Lurene Tuttle. **1953**

AFFLICTION ★★★1/2 Small-town New Hampshire constable Nick Nolte investigates an accidental shooting that he suspects was murder; meanwhile, his personal life disintegrates as he is haunted by memories of a childhood terrorized by his drunken, abusive father (Oscar-winner James Coburn). Acting is excellent, though the story is bleak, melodramatic, and depressing. Rated R for profanity. 114m. **DIR:** Paul Schrader. **CAST:** Nick Nolte, Sissy Spacek, James Coburn, Willem Dafoe, Jim True, Mary Beth Hurt. **1998 DVD**

AFRAID OF THE DARK ★★ A young boy losing his eyesight seeks out a slasher who targets the blind. Scary in places, but the thrills are few and too far between. Rated R for nudity and violence. 91m. **DIR:** Mark Peploe. **CAST:** James Fox, Fanny Ardant, Paul McGann. **1992**

AFRICA SCREAMS ★★ Bud and Lou are joined by circus great Clyde Beatty and Frank (*Bring 'Em Back Alive*) Buck in this thin but enjoyable comedy, one of their last feature films. Most of the jungle and safari clichés are evident in this fast-paced, oddball film but they work acceptably. Fun for the kids as well as the adults. B&W; 79m. **DIR:** Charles Barton. **CAST:** Bud Abbott, Lou Costello, Hillary Brooke, Shemp Howard, Max Baer, Clyde Beatty, Frank Buck. **1949 DVD**

AFRICA—TEXAS STYLE! ★★ The idea of a movie about cowboys rounding up animals in Africa must have sounded good in theory. But in practice, it's pretty dull going. Even the location photography doesn't help. Give us *Hatari!* any day. 106m. **DIR:** Andrew Marton. **CAST:** Hugh O'Brian, John Mills, Tom Nardini. **1966**

AFRICAN DREAM, AN ★★★★ Powerful film about a British-educated black man (John Kani) who returns to Africa as a teacher. Enter Kitty Aldridge as a joyful young woman who has just become a part of the nearby British colony, circa 1906. Inspirational portrayal of two people who dare to dream of a better world. Rated PG for violence. 94m. **DIR:** John Smallcombe. **CAST:** Kitty Aldridge, John Kani. **1990**

AFRICAN QUEEN, THE ★★★★★ Humphrey Bogart and Katharine Hepburn star in this exciting World War I adventure film. Bogart's a drunkard, and Hepburn's the spinster sister of a murdered missionary. Together they take on the Germans and, in doing so, are surprised to find themselves falling in love. 106m. **DIR:** John Huston. **CAST:** Humphrey Bogart,

Katharine Hepburn, Peter Bull, Robert Morley, Theodore Bikel. **1951**

AFRICAN RAGE ★★★1/2 Anthony Quinn is a nurse in an African hospital where a tribal leader is admitted amid heavy security. Quinn's kidnapping of the leader, played with great dignity and warmth by Simon Sabela, takes some very unusual and interesting turns. A surprisingly moving film. Not rated. 105m. **DIR:** Peter Collinson. **CAST:** Anthony Quinn, John Phillip Law, Marius Weyers, Sandra Prinsloo, Ken Gampu, Simon Sabela. **1985**

AFTER DARK, MY SWEET ★★★1/2 Jason Patric gives a spellbinding performance as a moody, wandering ex-boxer who may or may not be as punch drunk as he seems. He meets a beguiling widow (Rachel Ward) and an ex-detective con man (Bruce Dern) and gets mixed up in a kidnap-ransom scheme that soon turns sour. Style and atmosphere dominate this gritty adaptation of Jim Thompson's hardboiled novel. Rated R for language. 114m. **DIR:** James Foley. **CAST:** Jason Patric, Rachel Ward, Bruce Dern. **1990 DVD**

AFTER DARKNESS 🎬 An odd thriller about twin brothers who share visions of their parents' deaths. 105m. **DIR:** Dominique Othenin-Girard. **CAST:** John Hurt, Julian Sands, Victoria Abril. **1985**

AFTER HOURS ★★★★ The most brutal and bizarre black comedy we are ever likely to see. Griffin Dunne stars as a computer operator who unwillingly spends a night in downtown Manhattan. A trio of strange women mystify, seduce, and horrify our hapless hero, and his life soon becomes a total nightmare. Rated R for profanity, nudity, violence, and general weirdness. 94m. **DIR:** Martin Scorsese. **CAST:** Griffin Dunne, Rosanna Arquette, Teri Garr, John Heard, Linda Fiorentino, Richard "Cheech" Marin, Tommy Chong, Catherine O'Hara, Verna Bloom. **1985**

AFTER JULIUS ★★1/2 Slow-paced British soap about a widow and the effect her husband's death has on her and her daughters. Not rated; contains nudity. 150m. **DIR:** John Glenister. **CAST:** Faith Brook, John Carson, Cyd Hayman. **1978**

•**AFTER LIFE** ★★★★ Every Monday a group of dead people walks into a postmortem screening area where they are asked by staff counselors to pick a single memory to take into eternity. The memory is then reenacted and captured on film at the end of the week. The deceased then segue into the Great Beyond with a celluloid slice of their past and the process begins anew. This delicate, magnetic fable about how and what we remember (and making movies) escorts us into provocative speculation as emotions and relationships evolve between staff and clients. In Japanese with English subtitles. Not rated. 118m. **DIR:** Hirokazu Kore-eda. **CAST:** Arata, Erika Oda, Taketoshi Naito, Susumu Terajima, Takashi Naito. **1999**

AFTER MIDNIGHT ★★ University students taking a course on fear form a study group to tell each other scary stories. The film has a few thrills and chills, but it suffers from its lack of originality. Rated PG-13 for violence and profanity. 98m. **DIR:** Ken Wheat, Jim Wheat. **CAST:** Pamela Segall, Marc McClure, Marg Helgenberger. **1989**

AFTER PILKINGTON ★★★ A strange tale about an Oxford professor who meets up with his childhood sweetheart. He will do anything for her, even bury a dead body. Good acting, but the plot is weird. Not rated; contains violence and nudity. 100m. **DIR:** Christopher Morahan. **CAST:** Bob Peck, Miranda Richardson, Barry Foster, Gary Waldhorn, Mary Miller. **1988**

AFTER THE FALL OF NEW YORK 🎬 Michael Sopkiw as a two-fisted, post-apocalyptic hero. Rated R for violence and profanity. 91m. **DIR:** Martin Dolman. **CAST:** Michael Sopkiw, Valentine Monnier, Anna Kanakis. **1983**

AFTER THE FOX 🎬 Peter Sellers is at his worst, playing an Italian movie director in this flat farce. 103m. **DIR:** Vittorio De Sica. **CAST:** Peter Sellers, Victor Mature, Britt Ekland, Martin Balsam. **1966**

AFTER THE PROMISE ★★ An uneducated laborer (Mark Harmon) loses custody of his sons following the death of his ailing wife. His efforts to get them back lead him down a road of red tape. Shamelessly maudlin and predictable TV movie. 93m. **DIR:** David Greene. **CAST:** Mark Harmon, Diana Scarwid, Donnelly Rhodes. **1987**

AFTER THE REHEARSAL ★★★1/2 This Ingmar Bergman movie made for Swedish television is about a director (Erland Josephson) who is approached by a young actress with a proposition: she wants to have an affair with him. In Swedish with English subtitles. 72m. **DIR:** Ingmar Bergman. **CAST:** Erland Josephson. **1984**

AFTER THE SHOCK ★★ A telemovie depicting the heroics of a group of Bay Area residents after the October 17, 1989 earthquake. Gary Sherman shot the movie with a home-movie, you-are-there feel. 92m. **DIR:** Gary A. Sherman. **CAST:** Scott Valentine, Jack Scalia, Yaphet Kotto. **1990**

AFTER THE THIN MAN ★★★★1/2 Second of the six wonderful *Thin Man* films made with William Powell and Myrna Loy. Powell, Loy, and Asta, the incorrigible terrier, trade quips and drinks in this decent murder mystery. The dialogue is fast-paced and quite droll, and Powell and Loy demonstrate a chemistry that explains the dozen hits they had together. Not to be missed. B&W; 113m. **DIR:** W. S. Van Dyke. **CAST:** William Powell, Myrna Loy, James Stewart, Elissa Landi, Joseph Calleia, Sam Levene. **1936**

AFTERBURN ★★★★★ Made-for-cable drama doesn't get much better than this scathing indictment of government air force contracts, and the lengths to which life-threatening mistakes will be buried beneath red tape. Laura Dern superbly handles her role as fiery Janet Harduvel, who singlehandedly forced General Dynamics to acknowledge that the F-16 fighter plane that killed her husband went down due to faulty design, rather than "pilot error." 103m. **DIR:** Robert Markowitz. **CAST:** Laura Dern, Robert Loggia, Michael Rooker, Vincent Spano. **1992**

AFTERGLOW ★★1/2 Writer-director Alan Rudolph's contrived round-robin of adultery flounders uncertainly from melodrama to farce without developing any conviction, and the arch double entendres of the dialogue become coy and labored. The acting is better than the script deserves—especially by Julie Christie, who seems to grow more radiant and complex with each passing year. Rated R for profanity, nudity, and sexual situations. 113m. DIR: Alan Rudolph. CAST: Julie Christie, Nick Nolte, Lara Flynn Boyle, Jonny Lee Miller. **1997**

AFTERMATH, THE ★★1/2 Two astronauts return to Earth after a nuclear war and battle the crazies who survived. Low-budget sci-fi flick strives to go above the subject matter. Not rated; contains violence. 94m. DIR: Steve Barkett. CAST: Steve Barkett, Lynne Margulies, Sid Haig. **1981**

AGAINST A CROOKED SKY ★★ Nothing new in this familiar tale of a boy searching for his sister, who has been kidnapped by Indians. Another inferior reworking of John Ford's classic Western *The Searchers*. For fans who watch anything with a horse and a saddle. Rated PG for violence. 89m. DIR: Earl Bellamy. CAST: Richard Boone, Clint Ritchie, Henry Wilcoxon, Stewart Peterson. **1975**

AGAINST ALL FLAGS ★★★ Though Errol Flynn's energy and attractiveness had seriously ebbed by this time, he still possessed the panache to make this simple swashbuckler fun to watch. He portrays a dashing British soldier who infiltrates a pirate stronghold, pausing only to romance the fiery Maureen O'Hara. 83m. DIR: George Sherman. CAST: Errol Flynn, Maureen O'Hara, Anthony Quinn, Mildred Natwick. **1952**

AGAINST ALL ODDS (1968) (KISS AND KILL, BLOOD OF FU MANCHU) 🎬 The evil Fu Manchu hatches another dastardly plan for world domination. A complete bore. Rated PG. 93m. DIR: Jess (Jesus) Franco. CAST: Christopher Lee, Richard Greene, Shirley Eaton. **1968**

AGAINST ALL ODDS (1984) ★★★1/2 A respectable remake of *Out of the Past*, a 1947 *film noir* classic, this release stars Jeff Bridges as a man hired by a wealthy gangster (James Woods) to track down his girlfriend (Rachel Ward), who allegedly tried to kill him. Bridges finds her, they fall in love, and that's when the plot's twists really begin. Rated R for nudity, suggested sex, violence, and profanity. 128m. DIR: Taylor Hackford. CAST: Jeff Bridges, Rachel Ward, Alex Karras, James Woods. **1984 DVD**

AGAINST THE WALL ★★★★ This crackling thriller dramatizes the events leading to 1971s Attica Prison riots, which ultimately resulted in fortythree deaths, as seen through the eyes of impressionable new guard Kyle MacLachlan. It's hard to tear your eyes from the screen. Rated R for violence, profanity, and nudity. 111m. DIR: John Frankenheimer. CAST: Kyle MacLachlan, Samuel L. Jackson, Clarence Williams III, Frederic Forrest, Harry Dean Stanton. **1994**

AGATHA ★★1/2 Supposedly based on a true event in the life of mystery author Agatha Christie (during which she disappeared for eleven days in 1926), this is a moderately effective thriller. Vanessa Redgrave is excellent in the title role, but costar Dustin Hoffman is miscast as the American detective on her trail. Rated PG. 98m. DIR: Michael Apted. CAST: Dustin Hoffman, Vanessa Redgrave, Celia Gregory. **1979**

AGE ISN'T EVERYTHING 🎬 Age-reversal comedy with a twist: young Jonathan Silverman has his body taken over by an old man in a comedy that's as old as the hills and just as dusty. Rated R for language. 91m. DIR: Douglas Katz. CAST: Jonathan Silverman, Robert Prosky, Rita Moreno, Paul Sorvino. **1991**

AGE OF GOLD ★★★ Filmmaker Luis Buñuel's surrealist masterpiece is a savage assault on organized religion, the bourgeoisie, and social ethics. Salvador Dalí contributed a few ideas to the production. In French with English subtitles. B&W; 62m. DIR: Luis Buñuel. CAST: Pierre Prevert, Gaston Modot, Lya Lys, Max Ernst. **1930**

AGE OF INNOCENCE, THE ★★★★ Daniel Day-Lewis and Michelle Pfeiffer are star-crossed lovers in this romance that also examines the mores and morals of New York in the 1870s. The film belongs to the luminous Winona Ryder, who plays Lewis's patient and formidable fiancée. Narrated by Joanne Woodward. Rated PG for suggestion of impropriety. 133m. DIR: Martin Scorsese. CAST: Daniel Day-Lewis, Michelle Pfeiffer, Winona Ryder, Geraldine Chaplin, Alec McCowen, Richard E. Grant, Mary Beth Hurt, Stuart Gordon, Robert Sean Leonard, Sian Phillips, Carolyn Farina, Michael Gough, Miriam Margolyes, Alexis Smith, Jonathan Pryce, Norman Lloyd. **1993**

AGE-OLD FRIENDS ★★★★1/2 This poignant study of aging, adapted by Bob Larbey from his Broadway play *A Month of Sundays*, makes a superb vehicle for star Hume Cronyn. While enthusiastically flirting with his kind young nurse or testily enduring his monthly Inspection Day—a visit from his estranged daughter—Cronyn's crusty codger puts his effort and concern into the well-being of best friend Vincent Gardenia. 90m. DIR: Allan Kroeker. CAST: Hume Cronyn, Vincent Gardenia, Tandy Cronyn, Esther Rolle. **1989**

AGENCY ★★ Despite the presence of Robert Mitchum, this Canadian feature about a power struggle in the world of advertising doesn't convince. Rated PG. 94m. DIR: George Kaczender. CAST: Robert Mitchum, Lee Majors, Saul Rubinek, Valerie Perrine. **1981**

•AGENT OF DEATH ★★ This formulaic thriller about a staged kidnapping that turns into the real thing has a twist: The victim is the president of the United States. The payoff is that the only man who can save him is a CIA agent still bitter over the death of his wife and daughter, who were murdered during a presidential-ordered assassination. Rated R for adult situations, language, and violence. 105m. DIR: Sam Firstenberg. CAST: Eric Roberts, Michael Madsen, Ice T, Bryan Genesse. **1999**

AGENT ON ICE ★★★1/2 This exciting action film features Tom Ormeny as John Pope, a former CIA agent who has become a target for both the CIA and the Mafia. Clifford David plays the corrupt CIA official who has been laundering money for Mafia leader Frank Matera (Louis Pastore). Rated R for violence and obscenities. 96m. DIR: Clark Worswick. CAST: Tom Ormeny, Clifford David, Louis Pastore, Matt Craven. **1985**

AGGIE APPLEBY, MAKER OF MEN ★★ The heroine teaches a wimp to act like a tough guy so he can impersonate her tough boyfriend. A mixed bag that's watchable in spite of itself. But only up to a point.

B&W; 73m. **DIR:** Mark Sandrich. **CAST:** Wynne Gibson, William Gargan, Charles Farrell, ZaSu Pitts, Jane Darwell, Betty Furness. **1933**

AGNES OF GOD ★★★ This fascinating drama features tour-de-force performances by Jane Fonda, Anne Bancroft, and Meg Tilly. Tilly's character, the childlike novice of an extremely sheltered convent, is discovered one night with the bloodied body of a baby. Psychiatrist Fonda is sent to determine Tilly's sanity in anticipation of a court hearing; Bancroft, as the Mother Superior, struggles to prevent the young girl's loss of innocence. Rated PG-13 for subject matter. 101m. **DIR:** Norman Jewison. **CAST:** Jane Fonda, Anne Bancroft, Meg Tilly, Anne Pitoniak, Winston Rekert. **1985**

AGONY AND THE ECSTASY, THE ★★★ Handsomely mounted but plodding historical drama based on Irving Stone's bestselling novel about Pope Julius II (Rex Harrison) engaging Michelangelo (Charlton Heston) to paint the ceiling of the Sistine Chapel. Heston overacts and the direction is heavy-handed. 140m. **DIR:** Carol Reed. **CAST:** Charlton Heston, Rex Harrison, Diane Cilento, Harry Andrews. **1965**

AGUIRRE: WRATH OF GOD ★★★★ Klaus Kinski gives one of his finest screen performances as the mad, traitorous Spanish conquistador who leads an expedition through the South American wilds in a quest for the lost city of El Dorado. It's a spectacular adventure story. In German with English subtitles. Not rated, the film has violence. 94m. **DIR:** Werner Herzog. **CAST:** Klaus Kinski, Ruy Guerra, Del Negro, Helena Rojo. **1972**

AH, WILDERNESS ★★★★ An American classic, this story of a family in 1910 mid-America is one of the most tasteful coming-of-age stories ever written. Playwright Eugene O'Neill based his stage play on memories of his youth at the turn of the century. B&W; 101m. **DIR:** Clarence Brown. **CAST:** Wallace Beery, Lionel Barrymore, Aline MacMahon, Cecilia Parker, Mickey Rooney, Eric Linden, Bonita Granville, Frank Albertson. **1935**

AILEEN WUORNOS: SELLING OF A SERIAL KILLER ★★★ Chilling, disturbing, and maddening, this documentary examines the postarrest life of America's first female serial killer and those around her, including her attorney and a born-again Christian—who are either doing everything in their power to help her or attempting to cash in on the tragedy. The audience is left to decide. Not rated; contains harsh language and adult themes. 87m. **DIR:** Nick Broomfield. **CAST:** Aileen Wuornos, Arlene Pralle, Steven Glazer, Tyria Moore. **1992**

AIR AMERICA ★★★★ The cop/buddy formula takes to the air when veteran pilot Mel Gibson teams up with rookie Robert Downey Jr. to fly top-secret U.S. missions behind enemy lines in the early Vietnam War–era jungles of Laos. Plenty of action and comedy bits make this a fun romp for the action crowd. Rated R for profanity and violence. 100m. **DIR:** Roger Spottiswoode. **CAST:** Mel Gibson, Robert Downey Jr. **1990 DVD**

AIR BUD ★★★ In true Disney form, this family film successfully combines laughter with tears. A custody battle erupts over a talented pooch when the dog's abusive clown owner takes him from the lonely boy who really loves him. Beyond this heartwarming angle is the unbelievable transition the dog makes from mascot to basketball team player. The kids will love it, and adults will be moved by the dog's plight. Rated PG for suggested animal and child abuse. 96m. **DIR:** Charles Martin Smith. **CAST:** Michael Jeter, Kevin Zegers, Wendy Makkena, Eric Christmas, Bill Cobbs. **1997 DVD**

AIR BUD: GOLDEN RECEIVER ★★1/2 Corny but cute Disney film features a talented Golden Retriever able to turn a losing football team into champs. Circus villains dognap the lovable pooch right before the big game (of course!). Heartwarming and amusing moments make for good family fun. Rated G. 90m. **DIR:** Richard Martin. **CAST:** Kevin Zegers, Gregory Harrison, Cynthia Stevenson, Nora Dunn. **1999**

AIR FORCE ★★★★ This is essentially wartime propaganda about a flying fortress and its crew taking on the enemy at Pearl Harbor, Manila, and the Coral Sea. However, the direction by Howard Hawks puts the film head and shoulders above similar motion pictures. B&W; 124m. **DIR:** Howard Hawks. **CAST:** John Garfield, John Ridgely, Gig Young, Charles Drake, Harry Carey, Arthur Kennedy, George Tobias. **1943**

AIR FORCE ONE ★★★★ Russian terrorists hijack the United States' most valuable aircraft and promise to kill a hostage every half hour until an imprisoned tyrant is released. But the bad guys don't know that this particular chief of state is Harrison Ford. Wolfgang Petersen's crisp thriller unfolds smoothly and intelligently, and this is far better than most genre entries. Rated R for violence and profanity. 118m. **DIR:** Wolfgang Petersen. **CAST:** Harrison Ford, Gary Oldman, Glenn Close, Wendy Crewson, Paul Guilfoyle, William H. Macy, Liesel Matthews, Dean Stockwell, Xander Berkeley. **1997 DVD**

AIR RAID WARDENS ★★ The title tells all in this lesser effort from Stan Laurel and Oliver Hardy, which has them messing up on the home front until they capture a nest of saboteurs. Dated and disappointing. B&W; 67m. **DIR:** Edward Sedgwick. **CAST:** Stan Laurel, Oliver Hardy, Edgar Kennedy, Stephen McNally, Donald Meek. **1943**

AIR UP THERE, THE ★★ Aggressive college-basketball coach Kevin Bacon tries to recruit a Kenyan tribesman in a predictable, *Rocky*-type comedy-adventure about global sports imperialism. The white, alleged hero—who has a terminal me-first attitude—ends up leading the Winabi tribe in a hoops game against a rival clan for ancestral lands. Shot on location in South Africa and Kenya. Rated PG. 107m. **DIR:** Paul Michael Glaser. **CAST:** Kevin Bacon, Charles Gitonga Maina. **1994**

AIRBORNE ★★★ California-surf teen moves in with nerdy Cincinnati relatives and becomes a target of local toughs in this pubescent comedy. The landlocked hotdogger embraces a Gandhiesque pacifism when confronted by toughs, dates one bully's sister and—when the Midwest frost thaws—struts some amazing stuff on roller blades in a scorching downhill race finale. The rock-charged soundtrack includes original music by former Police drummer Stewart Copeland. Rated PG. 89m. **DIR:** Rob Bowman. **CAST:** Shane McDermott, Seth Green, Brittney Powell, Chris Conrad, Patrick O'Brien. **1993 DVD**

AIRHEADS 🦃 A metal band takes a radio station hostage until it plays a demo tape. Poor performances, gimmicky direction, and shallow characters make this movie a dud. Rated PG-13 for language. 115m. **DIR:** Michael Lehmann. **CAST:** Brendan Fraser, Steve Buscemi, Adam Sandler, Joe Mantegna. **1994**

AIRPLANE! ★★★★ This is a hilarious spoof of the *Airport* series—and movies in general. While the jokes don't always work, there are so many of them that this comedy ends up with enough laughs for three movies. Rated PG. 88m. **DIR:** Jim Abrahams, David Zucker, Jerry Zucker. **CAST:** Robert Hays, Julie Hagerty, Leslie Nielsen, Kareem Abdul-Jabbar, Lloyd Bridges, Peter Graves, Robert Stack. **1980**

AIRPLANE II: THE SEQUEL ★★★1/2 Viewers who laughed uncontrollably through *Airplane!* will find much to like about this sequel. The stars of the original are back, with silly jokes and sight gags galore. However, those who thought the original was more stupid than funny undoubtedly will mutter the same about the sequel. Rated PG for occasional adult content. 85m. **DIR:** Ken Finkleman. **CAST:** Robert Hays, Julie Hagerty, Peter Graves, William Shatner. **1982**

AIRPORT ★★★★ The daddy of them all, this *Grand Hotel* in the air is slick, enjoyable entertainment. Taking place on a fateful winter night, it miraculously rises above some stiff performances and an often hackneyed plot. Rated G. 137m. **DIR:** George Seaton. **CAST:** Burt Lancaster, Dean Martin, Helen Hayes, Jacqueline Bisset, Van Heflin, Jean Seberg, George Kennedy. **1970 DVD**

AIRPORT 1975 🦃 Poor sequel. Rated PG. 106m. **DIR:** Jack Smight. **CAST:** Charlton Heston, George Kennedy, Karen Black, Sid Caesar, Helen Reddy. **1974 DVD**

AIRPORT '77 🦃 If you've seen one *Airport*, you've seen them all. Rated PG for violence. 113m. **DIR:** Jerry Jameson. **CAST:** Jack Lemmon, Lee Grant, George Kennedy, Christopher Lee. **1977 DVD**

AIRPORT '79: THE CONCORDE 🦃 Bring your own airsickness bag. Rated PG. 113m. **DIR:** David Lowell Rich. **CAST:** Alain Delon, Robert Wagner, Susan Blakely, George Kennedy, Eddie Albert, Cicely Tyson. **1979**

AKIRA ★★★★ Based on writer-director Katsuhiro Otomo on his popular comic book, this is a spectacular film set in twenty-first-century post–World War III Japan, where a member of a motorcycle gang becomes an unwilling guinea pig in a scientific experiment that backfires. Not rated, the film has oodles of violence. 124m. **DIR:** Katsuhiro Otomo. **1990**

AKIRA KUROSAWA'S DREAMS ★★★★ Celebrated Japanese director Akira Kurosawa delves into his dreams for this episodic motion picture. Like real dreams, Kurosawa's *Dreams* are snippets of situations and ideas. As such, they are often anti-climactic and even frustrating. Yet the images are breathtakingly beautiful. In Japanese with English subtitles. Rated PG. 120m. **DIR:** Akira Kurosawa. **CAST:** Akira Terao, Martin Scorsese. **1990**

AL CAPONE ★★★1/2 Rod Steiger is mesmerizing as Al Capone in this perceptive portrait of the legendary Chicago gangster. The film covers Capone's life from his first job for $75 a week to his ultimate fate behind prison walls. Filmed in black and white with a documentary-style narrative, which heightens the quality of this film. The supporting cast—Fay Spain in particular—is just right. B&W; 104m. **DIR:** Richard Wilson. **CAST:** Rod Steiger, Fay Spain, James Gregory, Martin Balsam, Nehemiah Persoff. **1959**

ALADDIN (1987) ★★ Update of the Aladdin tale, with Bud Spencer as the genie from the lamp, discovered this time by a boy in a junk shop in a modern city. A little too cute at times, and the humor is forced. Not rated; contains some violence. 95m. **DIR:** Bruno Corbucci. **CAST:** Bud Spencer, Luca Venantini, Janet Agren. **1987**

ALADDIN (1992) ★★★★★ The over-the-edge, manic voice work of an unleashed Robin Williams, as the genie of the lamp, supplies the laughs in this exquisite magic-carpet ride from Walt Disney Pictures. A worthy successor to *The Little Mermaid* and *Beauty and the Beast*, *Aladdin* is a classic feature-length cartoon blessed with excellent songs and a story that will fascinate all ages. The crowning touch is the deft illustration by Disney's animators. Rated G. 83m. **DIR:** John Musker, Ron Clements. **1992**

ALADDIN AND HIS MAGIC LAMP ★★★ Artful animation helps to make this an engrossing version of the classic story. Young Aladdin finds the magic lamp and rescues the genie, but things go amiss when a black-hearted sorcerer puts the genie's power to evil use. 70m. **DIR:** Jean Image. **1985**

ALADDIN & THE KING OF THIEVES ★★★★ Robin Williams returns as the voice of the genie in this lively sequel. While the genie helps prepare for Aladdin and Jasmine's royal wedding, Aladdin discovers that his father is still alive, and is the leader of the infamous Forty Thieves. Clever animation, exciting adventures, and Williams's irrepressible humor make this second sequel much better than the first. Rated G. 80m. **DIR:** Tad Stones. **CAST:** Robin Williams, Gilbert Gottfried, Jerry Orbach, John Rhys-Davies (voices). **1996**

ALAKAZAM THE GREAT ★★1/2 Musical morality play for kids about the evils of pride and the abuse of power. When naïve little Alakazam the monkey is made king of the animals, he quickly develops an abusive personality that can only be set to rights through an arduous pilgrimage. Somewhat muddled, but watchable. 84m. **DIR:** James H. Nicholson, Samuel Z. Arkoff. **1961**

ALAMO, THE ★★★1/2 This Western, directed by and starring John Wayne, may have seemed overlong when originally released. But today it's the answer to a Duke-deprived fan's dream. Of course, there's the expected mushy flag-waving here and there. However, once Davy Crockett (Wayne), Jim Bowie (Richard Widmark), Will Travis (Laurence Harvey), and their respective followers team up to take on Santa Ana's forces, it's a humdinger of a period war movie. 161m. **DIR:** John Wayne. **CAST:** John Wayne, Richard Widmark, Laurence Harvey, Frankie Avalon, Richard Boone, Chill Wills. **1960**

ALAMO, THE: THIRTEEN DAYS TO GLORY 🦃 Jim Bowie, Davy Crockett, Col. William Travis and their men defend the Texas fort to the death, in this made-for-TV movie. The two-part film suffers from inaccuracies, and the significance of the siege is trivialized by focusing on bickering between Travis and Bowie. 168m. **DIR:** Burt Kennedy. **CAST:** James Arness, Brian Keith, Alec Baldwin, David Ogden Stiers, Raul Julia, Lorne Greene. **1987**

ALAMO BAY ★★★★ French director Louis Malle once again looks at the underbelly of the American dream. This time, he takes us to the Gulf Coast of Texas in the late 1970s where Vietnamese refugees arrived, expecting the land of opportunity, and came face-to-face, instead, with the Ku Klux Klan. Rated R for nudity, violence, and profanity. 105m. **DIR:** Louis Malle. **CAST:** Ed Harris, Amy Madigan, Ho Nguyen, Donald Moffat. **1985**

ALAN AND NAOMI ★★ Well-intentioned but muddled story about a high school student in the Forties and his attempts to help a victim of Nazi terrorism. The performances add a level of quality, but they are thwarted by the funereal tone and an inexcusably abrupt conclusion. Rated PG for mature themes. 98m. **DIR:** Sterling Vanwagenen. **CAST:** Lukas Haas, Vanessa Zaoui, Michael Gross, Amy Aquino, Kevin Connolly, Zohra Lampert. **1992**

ALAN SMITHEE FILM, AN—BURN HOLLYWOOD BURN 🎦 Director Alan Smithee steals the negative to his latest movie so producer can't ruin it in editing. Writer Joe Eszterhas vents his spleen on the incompetence of Hollywood in this witless comedy; it's a clear case of the pot calling the kettle black. (The joke is that "Alan Smithee" is the pseudonym used when a director orders his name taken off a film—which, ironically, is exactly what Arthur Hiller wisely did with this one.) Rated R for profanity. 83m. **CAST:** Ryan O'Neal, Coolio, Chuck D, Richard Jeni, Eric Idle, Sylvester Stallone, Whoopi Goldberg, Jackie Chan. **1997**

ALARMIST, THE ★★★ Honest home-security system salesman has an affair with his first client and learns that his reptilian boss and business associate are staging residential break-ins to bolster company sales. Engaging black comedy about greed, office politics, crime, paranoia, and sex is based on Keith Reddin's off-Broadway play, *Life During Wartime.* Rated R for simulated sex, language, and violence. 95m. **DIR:** Evan Dunsky. **CAST:** David Arquette, Stanley Tucci, Kate Capshaw, Mary McCormack, Ryan Reynolds. **1998 DVD**

ALASKA ★★★ Under his son's direction, Charlton Heston has the art of acting ruthless down to a science. While poaching polar bear, he meets a brother and sister on a mission to find their missing dad. Since the kids are being followed by the orphaned cub Heston wants, he keeps track of the kids. Coming-of-age element, physical dangers, and gorgeous panoramic shots of glaciers and forests are all a plus. Rated PG for mild profanity and simulated cruelty to animals. 109m. **DIR:** Fraser Heston. **CAST:** Charlton Heston, Vincent Kartheiser, Thora Birch, Dirk Benedict. **1996**

ALBERTO EXPRESS ★★★1/2 When a young man leaves home, his father demands that he repay the costs of his upbringing before he starts his own family. Fifteen years later, with his wife pregnant, the son

frantically struggles to find the money before she gives birth. Fast-paced comedy will have you laughing out loud. In Italian with English subtitles. 98m. **DIR:** Arthur Joffe. **CAST:** Sergio Castellitto, Nino Manfredi, Jeanne Moreau. **1990**

ALBINO 🎦 African terrorists, led by an albino chief, frighten natives. Not rated. 96m. **DIR:** Jurgen Goslar. **CAST:** Christopher Lee, Trevor Howard, James Faulkner, Sybil Danning. **1976**

ALBINO ALLIGATOR ★★1/2 Three robbers and five hostages are cornered by the police and media in a subterranean New Orleans bar in this familiar hostage drama. This claustrophobic story (written by Christian Forte, son of 1950s pop star Fabian) is about inner struggles between good and evil, and the moral ambiguity that can arise in the name of survival. It's a character study that is imaginatively directed but often feels more like an actors'-workshop exercise than a real movie. Rated R for language and violence. 97m. **DIR:** Kevin Spacey. **CAST:** Matt Dillon, Faye Dunaway, Gary Sinise, William Fichtner, Viggo Mortensen, John Spencer, Skeet Ulrich, M. Emmet Walsh, Joe Mantegna. **1996 DVD**

ALDRICH AMES: TRAITOR WITHIN ★★★1/2 Timothy Hutton plays Ames, a browbeaten husband who just wanted to pad his paycheck a bit. Elizabeth Peña is more convincing as his materialistic wife, a shrew who doesn't care where the money comes from. The film really belongs to Joan Plowright as the resourceful agency investigator who carefully closes the net that eventually traps Ames. Rated PG for profanity and dramatic content. 98m. **DIR:** John Mackenzie. **CAST:** Timothy Hutton, Joan Plowright, Elizabeth Peña, C. David Johnson, Eugene Lipinski. **1998**

ALEX ★★★ Courageous story of a young Australian woman who fought against the odds to compete in the 1960 Rome Olympics. Lauren Jackson is strong as the freestyle swimmer who balanced a full college workload and dealt with the death of her boyfriend while training for the Games. Not rated. 93m. **DIR:** Megan Simpson. **CAST:** Lauren Jackson, Chris Haywood, Josh Picker, Cathy Gobold, Elizabeth Hawthorne. **1993**

ALEX IN WONDERLAND ★★ A self-conscious look at the film world that misses its mark in spite of good performances and some sharp jabs at the greed that controls Hollywood. Donald Sutherland is appropriately humble as a movie director trying to follow his first film with an even better one. Rated R. 110m. **DIR:** Paul Mazursky. **CAST:** Donald Sutherland, Ellen Burstyn, Paul Mazursky, Jeanne Moreau, Federico Fellini. **1970**

ALEXANDER NEVSKY ★★★★ Another classic from the inimitable Russian director Sergei Eisenstein (*Ivan the Terrible; Battleship Potemkin*), this film is a Soviet attempt to prepare Russia for the coming conflict with Hitlerian Germany via portrayal of Alexander Nevsky, a thirteenth-century Russian prince, and his victories over the Teutonic knights of that era. As with all state-commissioned art, the situations can be corny, but the direction is superb. In Russian with English subtitles. B&W; 105m. **DIR:**

Sergei Eisenstein. **CAST:** Nikolai Cherkassov, Dmitri Orlov. **1938 DVD**

ALEXANDER THE GREAT ★★★1/2 The strange, enigmatic, self-possessed Macedonian conqueror of Greece and most of the civilized world of his time rides again. Richard Burton, with his enthralling voice and uniquely hypnotic eyes, dominates an outstanding cast in this lavish epic. 141m. **DIR:** Robert Rossen. **CAST:** Richard Burton, Fredric March, Claire Bloom, Danielle Darrieux. **1956**

ALEXANDER'S RAGTIME BAND ★★★★★ The first all-star epic musical to feature classic Irving Berlin tunes. The story of a Nob Hill elitist who starts a ragtime band on the Barbary Coast is a suitable setting for over two dozen Berlin songs composed between World War I and the early days of World War II. Tyrone Power glamorizes the setting, while the music and the nostalgia element still have the magic to involve an audience emotionally. B&W; 105m. **DIR:** Henry King. **CAST:** Alice Faye, Tyrone Power, Don Ameche, Ethel Merman, Jack Haley, Dixie Dunbar. **1938**

ALEXINA ★★1/2 Confusing erotic tale about a young woman who discovers she's not really a girl, after indulging in a relationship with another woman in this strange concoction of metamorphosis and identity crisis. Pretty baffling. Not rated; contains nudity. In French with English subtitles. 98m. **DIR:** René Feret. **CAST:** Valerie Stroh, Bernard Freyd. **1991**

ALEX'S APARTMENT ♥ When a young woman starts a new life in a coastal town, she's confronted by a maniac who kills women as "gifts" to her. Poor script. Not rated, contains violence. 79m. **DIR:** W. Mel Martins. **CAST:** Miki Welling. **1992**

ALFIE ★★★★ Wild and ribald comedy about a Cockney playboy (Michael Caine) who finds "birds" irresistible. Full of sex and delightful charm, this quick-moving film also tells the poignant tragedy of a man uncertain about his lifestyle. Nominated for five Oscars, including best picture and best actor. 113m. **DIR:** Lewis Gilbert. **CAST:** Michael Caine, Shelley Winters, Millicent Martin, Julia Foster, Shirley Anne Field. **1966**

ALFRED HITCHCOCK PRESENTS (TV SERIES) ★★★★ This classic anthology series features a broad range of mystery and suspense. First-rate casts add to the fun. During breaks, Alfred Hitchcock himself drolly comments on the action. One of the four episodes on the initial video release, "Lamb to the Slaughter," stars Barbara Bel Geddes in a deliciously ironic tale of murder. Black humor and surprise endings are trademarks of the show. Hitchcock directed the episodes featured on Volume 1. 120m. **DIR:** Alfred Hitchcock. **CAST:** Barbara Bel Geddes, Tom Ewell, John Williams. **1962 DVD**

ALFRED HITCHCOCK'S BON VOYAGE AND ADVENTURE MALGACHE ★★★ Alfred Hitchcock made these two intriguing propaganda films for the war effort and, strangely, they were never released to American audiences. *Bon Voyage* follows a downed RAF flyer and a Polish POW as they are passed from hand to hand by the French Resistance. *Aventure Malgache* chronicles the tensions in the French colony of Madagascar after the fall of France. In French with English subtitles. B&W; 57m. **DIR:** Alfred Hitchcock. **CAST:** John Blythe, The Molière Players. **1944 DVD**

ALFREDO ALFREDO ★★ At the height of his popularity in the early 1970s, Dustin Hoffman ventured over to Italy to make this marriage farce for director Pietro Germi (*Divorce—Italian Style*). Hoffman plays a man married to a woman he doesn't love in pursuit of one he does. Complications arise when Alfredo tries to get around Italy's tough divorce laws. Broad at best, this farce doesn't hold up well by today's standards. It's odd to see Hoffman dubbed into Italian by another actor. In Italian with English subtitles. Rated R for adult situations. 97m. **DIR:** Pietro Germi. **CAST:** Dustin Hoffman, Stefania Sandrelli, Carla Gravina. **1972**

ALI BABA AND THE FORTY THIEVES ★★★ Youthful Ali Baba flees from an evil vizier and is protected and raised by forty thieves, the only hope of his downtrodden people. Sit back and enjoy this lighthearted sword-and-turban adventure. Now what are we to do with the forty jars if the thieves are the good guys? 87m. **DIR:** Arthur Lubin. **CAST:** Jon Hall, Maria Montez, Turhan Bey, Andy Devine, Fortunio Bonanova, Crispin Martin, Kurt Katch, Frank Puglia, Scotty Beckett. **1944**

ALI: FEAR EATS THE SOUL ★★★1/2 Outrageous albeit touching story about a love affair between an old German floor washer and an inarticulate young Arab mechanic. Rainer Warner Fassbinder delicately explores this troubled relationship with deeplyfelt humanism and cool irony. Winner of the International Critics' Prize at the Cannes Film Festival. In German with English subtitles. Not rated; contains profanity and nudity. 94m. **DIR:** Rainer Werner Fassbinder. **CAST:** Brigitte Mira, El Hedi Ben Salem, Rainer Werner Fassbinder. **1974**

ALICE (1981) ♥ In this bizarre adaptation of *Alice in Wonderland*, Alice falls for a jogger called Rabbit. Not rated. 80m. **DIR:** Jerzy Gruza, Jacek Bromski. **CAST:** Sophie Barjac, Jean-Pierre Cassel, Susannah York, Paul Nicholas. **1981**

ALICE (1988) ★★★★ Outstanding adaptation of Lewis Carroll's story by Jan Svankmajer, one of the world's leading figures in animation. The film brilliantly captures the surreal world of little Alice with bizarre erotic overtones. Not rated. 85m. **DIR:** Jan Svankmajer. **CAST:** Kristyna Kohoutova. **1988**

ALICE (1990) ★★★1/2 In this takeoff on *Alice in Wonderland*, Mia Farrow plays a wealthy New Yorker whose inner self is no longer fulfilled by an immense shopping habit. So she turns to a Chinese doctor whose magical herbs bring romance, spirituality, and even invisibility into her life. Rated PG-13 for profanity and sexual frankness. 100m. **DIR:** Woody Allen. **CAST:** Mia Farrow, Alec Baldwin, Blythe Danner, Judy Davis, William Hurt, Julie Kavner, Keye Luke, Joe Mantegna, Bernadette Peters, Cybill Shepherd. **1990**

ALICE ADAMS ★★★★ Life and love in a typical mid-American small town when there were still such things as concerts in the park and ice-cream socials. Hepburn is a social-climbing girl wistfully seeking love while trying to overcome the stigma of her father's lack of money and ambition. High point of the film is the dinner scene, at once a comic gem and painful insight into character. B&W; 99m. DIR: George Stevens. CAST: Katharine Hepburn, Fred Mac-Murray, Evelyn Venable, Fred Stone, Frank Albertson, Hattie McDaniel, Charley Grapewin, Hedda Hopper. 1935

ALICE DOESN'T LIVE HERE ANYMORE ★★★1/2 The feature film that spawned the television series *Alice* is a memorable character study about a woman (Ellen Burstyn, who won an Oscar for her performance) attempting to survive after her husband's death has left her penniless and with a young son to support. Rated PG for profanity and violence. 113m. DIR: Martin Scorsese. CAST: Ellen Burstyn, Kris Kristofferson, Harvey Keitel, Billy Green Bush, Alfred Lutter, Jodie Foster, Vic Tayback, Diane Ladd. 1975

ALICE IN THE CITY ★★★ Another road movie from Wim Wenders. While touring the US, a German journalist stumbles upon a precocious 9-year-old girl who has been abandoned by her mother. Excellent eccentric tragicomedy. In German with English subtitles. B&W; 110m. DIR: Wim Wenders. CAST: Rudiger Vogler, Yella Rottlander, Lisa Kreuzer. 1974

ALICE IN WONDERLAND (1951) ★★★1/2 The magic of the Walt Disney Studio animators is applied to Lewis Carroll's classic in this feature-length cartoon with mostly entertaining results. As with the book, the film is episodic and lacking the customary Disney warmth. But a few wonderful sequences—like the Mad Hatter's tea party and the appearances of the Cheshire cat—make it worth seeing. Rated G. 75m. DIR: Clyde Geronimi, Hamilton Luske, Wilfred Jackson. 1951 DVD

ALICE IN WONDERLAND (1985) ★★★1/2 Charming live-action TV adaptation of the Lewis Carroll classic. Adults will enjoy some of their favorite stars as zany characters; Steve Allen wrote the witty original songs. Followed by a continuation, 1985's *Alice through the Looking Glass*. 94m. DIR: Harry Harris. CAST: Natalie Gregory, Sheila Allen, Scott Baio, Red Buttons, Sid Caesar, Imogene Coca, Sammy Davis Jr., Sherman Hemsley, Arte Johnson, Roddy McDowall, Jayne Meadows, Robert Morley, Anthony Newley, Donald O'Connor, Martha Raye, Telly Savalas, Ringo Starr, Shelley Winters. 1985

ALICE IN WONDERLAND (1999) ★★1/2 The fabulous sets and marvelous critters from Jim Henson's Creature Shop notwithstanding, this is little more than an excuse for its stars to parade about in strange costumes. The focus is very odd, with certain familiar scenes extended, shortened, or changed until they no longer make sense or seem relevant, even in this wacky universe. Absent the insightful political commentary that made Carroll's originals so enchanting to readers of *all* ages, this unsatisfying Peter Barnes adaptation merely lurches from one scene to the next. Rated G. 128m. DIR: Nick Willing. CAST: Tina Majorino, Robbie Coltrane, Whoopi Goldberg, Ben Kingsley, Christopher Lloyd, Pete Postlethwaite, Miranda Richardson, Martin Short, Peter Ustinov, George Wendt, Gene Wilder. 1999 DVD

ALICE, SWEET ALICE (COMMUNION, HOLY TERROR) ★★ A 12-year-old girl goes on a chopping spree. Brooke Shields only has a small role in this,

her first film. But after the success of *Pretty Baby*, the distributor changed the title, gave Brooke top billing, and rereleased this uninteresting thriller. Rated R for violence. 96m. DIR: Alfred Sole. CAST: Brooke Shields, Tom Signorelli, Paula E. Sheppard, Lillian Roth. 1977 DVD

ALICE THROUGH THE LOOKING GLASS (1966) ★★★1/2 Another version of Lewis Carroll's immortal classic? Why not? When you've got such a talented cast working with a great story, you've got a winner. In this made-for-TV version, Alice makes an attempt to become the Queen of Wonderland by visiting the Royal Castle. 72m. DIR: Alan Handley. CAST: Ricardo Montalban, Judy Rolin, Nanette Fabray, Robert Coote, Agnes Moorehead, Jack Palance, Jimmy Durante, Tom Smothers, Dick Smothers, Roy Castle, Richard Denning. 1966

ALICE THROUGH THE LOOKING GLASS (1985) ★★★1/2 A continuation of 1985s *Alice in Wonderland* with Natalie Gregory returning to the mystical land in search of her missing parents. The chase scenes with the monster Jabberwocky may be too scary for very young viewers. Made for TV. 93m. DIR: Harry Harris. CAST: Natalie Gregory, Sheila Allen, Steve Allen, Ernest Borgnine, Beau Bridges, Lloyd Bridges, Red Buttons, Carol Channing, Patrick Duffy, George Gobel, Eydie Gorme, Merv Griffin, Ann Jillian, Arte Johnson, Harvey Korman, Steve Lawrence, Karl Malden, Roddy McDowall, Jayne Meadows, Donna Mills, Noriyuki "Pat" Morita, Robert Morley, Anthony Newley, Louis Nye, John Stamos, Sally Struthers, Jack Warden, Jonathan Winters. 1985

ALICE TO NOWHERE ★★★★ A bungled jewel heist sets in motion this fast-paced adventure. A nurse assigned to a job in central Australia is unknowingly carrying the stolen jewels. The action never lets up as she is pursued by the robbers to the outback. Made for Australian television and shown on independent stations in the United States. 210m. DIR: John Power. CAST: John Waters, Steve Jacobs, Rosie Jones, Ruth Cracknell. 1986

ALICE'S ADVENTURES IN WONDERLAND ★★ This British live-action version of Lewis Carroll's classic tale is too long and boring. It is a musical that employs an endless array of silly songs, dances, and riddles. Although it sticks closely to the book, it's not as entertaining as Disney's fast-paced animated version of 1951. Rated G. 97m. DIR: William Sterling. CAST: Fiona Fullerton, Dudley Moore, Peter Sellers, Ralph Richardson, Spike Milligan. 1973

ALICE'S RESTAURANT ★★★1/2 This film was based on Arlo Guthrie's hit record of the same name. Some insights into the 1960s counterculture can be found in the story of Guthrie's attempt to stay out of the draft. Some fine acting by a basically unknown cast. Rated PG for language and some nudity. 111m. DIR: Arthur Penn. CAST: Arlo Guthrie, Pat Quinn, James Broderick, Michael McClanathan, Geoff Outlaw, Tina Chen. 1969

ALIEN ★★★★1/2 A superb cinematic combination of science fiction and horror, this is a heart-pounding, visually astounding shocker. The players are all excellent as the crew of a futuristic cargo ship that picks up an unwanted passenger: an alien that lives on human flesh and continually changes form. Rated R. 116m. DIR: Ridley Scott. CAST: Tom Skerritt, Sigourney Weaver, John Hurt, Ian Holm, Harry Dean Stanton, Yaphet Kotto, Veronica Cartwright. 1979 DVD

ALIENS ★★★1/2 Fifty-seven years have passed during Warrant Officer Ripley's (Sigourney Weaver) deep-space sleep; when she wakes, the planet LV-426—where the crew of the ill-fated *Nostromo* first encountered the nasty extraterrestrial—has been colonized. Then, to everybody's surprise except Ripley's, contact is lost with the colonists. Equal to, although different from, the original. Rated R for considerable violence and profanity. 137m. DIR: James Cameron. CAST: Sigourney Weaver, Carrie Henn, Michael Biehn, Paul Reiser, Lance Henriksen, Jenette Goldstein. 1986 DVD

ALIEN 3 ★★★ Ripley (Sigourney Weaver) crashlands on an all-but-deserted penal colony for madmen and rapists. The acid-spitting, flesh-eating space creature has, unfortunately for them all, hitched a ride with our heroine, and the battle rages once again. More like *Alien* than *Aliens*, this visually stunning atmospheric thriller by first-time filmmaker David Fincher disintegrates into an outer space version of Agatha Christie's *And Then There Were None*. Rated R for profanity and violence. 115m. DIR: David Fincher. CAST: Sigourney Weaver, Charles Dutton, Charles Dance, Paul McGann, Brian Glover. 1992 DVD

ALIEN AGENDA, THE (TV SERIES) ★★ Made for the cost of several *Star Wars* models, this ambitious trilogy attempts to tell the epic story of a war between extraterrestrials for control of Earth. Each director follows a different set of people and how they are affected; as can be expected, the results are highly varied. Titles are *Out of the Darkness*, *Endangered Species*, and *Under the Skin*. Not rated; contains violence, profanity, and gore. 80–102m. DIR: Kevin J. Lindenmuth, Mick McCleery, Tim Ritter, Gabriel Campisi, Ron Ford, Tom Vollman, Michael Legge. CAST: Sasha Graham, Debbie Rochon, Joel Wynkoop, Joseph Zaso. 1996–1997

•ALIEN ARSENAL ★★1/2 Producer Charles Band remakes his earlier films *Laserblast* and *Deadly Weapon* with only so-so results in this sci-fi thriller. Two teen misfits discover a cache of weapons in their high-school basement; can the alien owners be far behind? Good production values, but a weak script hurts the film. Rated PG-13 for violence and profanity. 90m. DIR: Julian Breen. CAST: Josh Hammond, Danielle Hoover. 1999

ALIEN CHASER ★★ After being trapped on Earth for five thousand years, an alien is awakened from hibernation by archaeologists in search of a powerful artifact in his possession. A promising premise is soon abandoned in favor of endless chases in this made-for-video release. Rated R for strong violence and profanity. 95m. DIR: Mark Roper. CAST: Frank Zagarino, Todd Jensen, Jennifer MacDonald. 1996 DVD

ALIEN DEAD ✂ Low-grade, alien-loose-on-Earth drivel. Rated R. 87m. DIR: Fred Olen Ray. CAST: Buster Crabbe, Linda Lewis. 1980

ALIEN FACTOR, THE ★★★ As an amateur film, this is pretty decent. The cast and production crew are one and the same. There are four aliens on the planet Earth. Only one alien is good, and the Earthlings have a hard time figuring out which one is on their side. Rated PG. 82m. DIR: Don Dohler. CAST: Don Leifert, Tom Griffith. 1977

ALIEN FORCE ✂ Alien warrior races to destroy a meteor bearing the souls of a billion monsters in this cheapo clone of *Starman* and *The Hidden*. Not rated; contains sexual situations and violence. 85m. DIR: Ron Ford. CAST: Tyrone Wade, Roxanne Coyne, Burt Ward. 1997

ALIEN FROM L.A. ★★1/2 When a nerdy valley girl goes in search of her archaeologist father, she embarks on the adventure of her life. Although this is a low-budget film, it has enough action and humor to be appropriate for most family members. Rated PG for light violence. 88m. DIR: Albert Pyun. CAST: Kathy Ireland, Linda Kerridge, William R. Moses. 1983

ALIEN INTRUDER ★★1/2 An alien virus disguises itself as a femme fatale to lure space warriors to their doom. This low-budgeter rips off so many sci-fi hits that it sustains interest. Rated R for violence and profanity. 94m. DIR: Ricardo Jacques Gale. CAST: Billy Dee Williams, Maxwell Caulfield, Tracy Scoggins, Jeff Conaway. 1992

ALIEN NATION ★★★ There are some slow moments, but just sit back and enjoy the ride through familiar territory in this cop-buddy movie with a sci-fi slant. James Caan plays a detective in Los Angeles of the future. Mandy Patinkin is the "newcomer," as the aliens are called, who is teamed with Caan to ferret out the perpetrators of a series of mysterious murders among the aliens. Rated R for profanity, violence, and nudity. 96m. DIR: Graham Baker. CAST: James Caan, Mandy Patinkin, Terence Stamp. 1988

ALIEN NATION, DARK HORIZON ★★★1/2 Made-for-TV film that picks up where the canceled series' cliffhanger left off. After five years of assimilation into Los Angeles life, the Tenctonese aliens are targeted for extermination by humans. To add to their woes, the slavers from whom they escaped want them back. Compelling viewing with a parallel message about tolerance. Not rated; contains violence. 93m. DIR: Kenneth Johnson. CAST: Michele Scarabelli, Terri Treas, Scott Patterson, Jeff Marcus, Gary Graham, Eric Pierpoint. 1994

ALIEN P.I. ★★ A new twist to the old private eye theme. This time the private investigator is from the planet Styx. He's just vacationing on our planet when he stumbles onto an intergalactic crime involving an ancient Egyptian disc. Rated R for violence and nudity. 90m. DIR: Viktor. CAST: Nikki Fastinetti, John Alexander. 1987

ALIEN PREDATORS ✂ Three young American adventurers stumble into an alien invasion. Rated R for violence and gore. 92m. DIR: Deran Sarafian. CAST: Dennis Christopher, Martin Hewitt, Lynn-Holly Johnson. 1986

ALIEN PREY ✂ This savage alien is on a protein mission. This film contains sexual and cannibalistic scenes, making it unsuitable for the squeamish. 85m. DIR: Norman J. Warren. CAST: Barry Stokes, Sally Faulkner. 1984

ALIEN RESURRECTION ★★★★ Following the disappointment delivered by *Alien 3*, it seemed likely we'd never see another adventure of the two-fisted alien fighter, Ripley (Sigourney Weaver), who, of course, died at the end of the initial trilogy. But she's back—through the miracle of cloning—some two hundred years later, dealing once again with the stupidity of corporate greed and the mother of all man-eaters. It's an edge-of-your-seat sci-fi knockout. Rated R for violence, profanity, and nudity. 108m. DIR: Jean-Pierre Jeunet. CAST: Sigourney Weaver, Winona Ryder, Ron Pearlman, Dominique Pinon, Michael Wincott, Dan Hedaya, J. E. Freeman, Brad Dourif, Raymond Cruz, Kim Flowers. **1997 DVD**

ALIEN SPACE AVENGER 🎬 Low-budget reworking of *The Hidden*, detailing the plight of four alien convicts being stalked by an alien bounty hunter through the streets of New York. In true sci-fi fashion, they get around by hiding inside poor New Yorkers. All this time we thought they were just rude. Not rated; contains violence. 88m. DIR: Richard W. Haines. CAST: Robert Prichard. **1991**

ALIEN TERMINATOR ★★ Giant, mutant rat goes on a killing rampage in this cheesy effort. Five miles underground, scientists messing with DNA create a killer rat that likes the taste of flesh and stupid scientists who dabble with DNA. Fun on a campy level, with all the prerequisite shock effects and bare ladies. Rated R for nudity, violence, and adult language. 95m. DIR: David Payne. CAST: Maria Ford, Roger Halston, Emile Levisetti, Cassandra Leigh. **1995**

ALIEN WARRIOR 🎬 In this unwatchable film, a father on another planet sends his son to Earth to confront the ultimate evil—a pimp. Rated R for nudity, violence, and profanity. 100m. DIR: Edward Hunt. CAST: Brett Clark, Pamela Saunders. **1985**

ALIEN WITHIN, THE 🎬 Relentlessly stupid, bargain-basement retread of *Alien* from producer Roger Corman, with vapid characters who barely become interesting when they are taken over by the tentacled beastie. Rated R for violence, drug use, and nudity. 79m. DIR: Scott Levy. CAST: Roddy McDowall, Alex Hyde-White, Melanie Shatner, Don Stroud. **1995**

ALIENATOR 🎬 Lame *Terminator* clone. Rated R for violence. 93m. DIR: Fred Olen Ray. CAST: Jan-Michael Vincent, John Phillip Law, P. J. Soles. **1989**

•ALIENS AMONG US 🎬 Much ado about nothing as the family from *Welcome to Planet Earth* takes on the duties of sheriff of a western town. Low-budget mush. Also released as *Alien Avengers II*. Rated R for adult situations, language, nudity, and violence. 89m. DIR: David Payne. CAST: George Wendt, Julie Brown, Anastasia Sakelaris, Christopher M. Brown. **1997**

ALISON'S BIRTHDAY ★★1/2 A slow but interesting Australian horror story. A young girl is told by her father's ghost to leave home before her nineteenth birthday, but as you may guess, she's summoned back days before the big day, and things get nasty. 99m. DIR: Ian Coughlan. CAST: Joanne Samuel, Lou Brown. **1984**

ALIVE ★★★1/2 This gripping adaptation of Piers Paul Read's bestseller benefits from Frank Marshall's crackling direction and a reasonably unflinching script from John Patrick Shanley (*Moonstruck*). After a horrifyingly realistic plane crash in the Andes, the surviving members of a South American rugby team eventually steel themselves to the requirements of staying alive. Rated R for language. 123m. DIR: Frank Marshall. CAST: Ethan Hawke, Vincent Spano, Josh Hamilton, Bruce Ramsay. **1993**

•ALIVE & KICKING ★★★ Engaging tale of a dancer and a therapist who find true love despite the odds. Jason Flemyng and Antony Sher are wonderful as the couple who try to make their relationship work in the new swinging London. Screenwriter Martin Sherman explores a gay relationship without resorting to the usual clichés, while director Nancy Meckler does a splendid job of making all this matter with a tender, human touch. Rated R for adult situations. 100m. DIR: Nancy Meckler. CAST: Jason Flemyng, Antony Sher, Dorothy Tutin, Anthony Higgins. **1996 DVD**

ALL ABOUT EVE ★★★★★ The behind-the-scenes world of the New York theater is the subject of this classic. The picture won several Academy Awards, including best picture, but it is Bette Davis as Margo Channing whom most remember. The dialogue sparkles, and the performances are of high caliber. B&W; 138m. DIR: Joseph L. Mankiewicz. CAST: Bette Davis, Anne Baxter, Marilyn Monroe, George Sanders, Celeste Holm, Gary Merrill. **1950 DVD**

•ALL ABOUT MY MOTHER ★★1/2 A Madrid nurse travels to Barcelona in search of her dead son's father and becomes part of an extended family that includes a pregnant nun, a transsexual whore, a transvestite, and lesbian actresses. This brightly colored, self-conscious, campy tale of sisterhood, motherhood, and stormy relationships is patterned after, and references, Hollywood's melodramas of yesteryear. Rated R for profanity, nudity, sex, and drug use. 105m. DIR: Pedro Almodóvar. CAST: Celia Roth, Eloy Azorín, Marisa Paredes, Penelope Cruz, Candela Peña, Antonia San Juan, Rosa Maria Sardà, Toni Cantó. **1999**

ALL-AMERICAN MURDER ★★★ This murder mystery holds a lot of surprises. Charlie Schlatter is an ex-con who is implicated in the death of a beautiful coed. Christopher Walken is the cop who has a hunch and lets him off to prove his innocence. Unfortunately for Schlatter, dead bodies keep turning up wherever he goes. Rated R for violence, profanity, and nudity. 94m. DIR: Anson Williams. CAST: Christopher Walken, Charlie Schlatter, Josie Bissett, Amy Davis, Richard Kind, Joanna Cassidy. **1991**

ALL CREATURES GREAT AND SMALL ★★★1/2 This feature-length film picks up where the popular British television series left off, with veterinarian James Herriot (Christopher Timothy) returning to his home and practice after having served in World War II. Although he has been away for years, things quickly settle into a comfortable routine. The animal stories are lifted from Dr. Herriot's poignant, bittersweet books, with a few moments likely to require a hanky or two. 94m. DIR: Terence Dudley. CAST: Christopher Timothy, Robert Hardy, Peter Davison. **1986**

ALL DOGS GO TO HEAVEN ★★1/2 Somewhat disappointing feature-length cartoon from Disney defector Don Bluth. The convoluted story, about a con-artist dog who gets a glimpse of the afterlife, is more crude than charming. Burt Reynolds, Dom DeLuise, Loni Anderson, and Vic Tayback are among those who supply the voices. Rated G. 80m. **DIR:** Don Bluth. **1989**

ALL DOGS GO TO HEAVEN 2 ★★ This dreary, animated musical begins in heaven where a nasty bulldog plans to steal Gabriel's horn, which allows entry through heaven's pearly gates. When the horn falls to Earth, hero hound Charlie, who is tired of heaven's sedate environment, and his reluctant pal Itchy, return to Earth to prevent the evil Red from turning Alcatraz into a dank, eternal dog pound. Featuring the voices of Charlie Sheen, Ernest Borgnine, Sheena Easton, and Dom DeLuise. Rated G. 75m. **DIR:** Paul Sabella, Larry Leker. **1996**

ALL FALL DOWN ★★1/2 Sporadically powerful William Inge soap opera about the love affair of a young man (Warren Beatty) and an older woman (Eva Marie Saint), with a subplot about the man's adoring younger brother (Brandon de Wilde). Slightly overlong and handicapped by the puritanical Hollywood production code of the time. B&W; 110m. **DIR:** John Frankenheimer. **CAST:** Warren Beatty, Eva Marie Saint, Karl Malden, Angela Lansbury, Brandon de Wilde. **1962**

ALL GOD'S CHILDREN ★★ Forced busing to achieve educational integration is the crux of this story of two families, one white and one black. The cast is excellent, but a wandering script makes comprehension difficult. Rated PG for violence. 107m. **DIR:** Jerry Thorpe. **CAST:** Richard Widmark, Ned Beatty, Ossie Davis, Ruby Dee. **1980**

ALL I DESIRE ★★1/2 Serious sudser in which aging vaudevillian Barbara Stanwyck returns to her small-town roots and the family she abandoned. Stanwyck is the bright spot in this morality lesson as a tough cookie tired of being so worldly. Not rated. B&W; 80m. **DIR:** Douglas Sirk. **CAST:** Barbara Stanwyck, Richard Carlson, Lyle Bettger, Maureen O'Sullivan, Marcia Henderson, Lori Nelson. **1953**

ALL I WANT FOR CHRISTMAS ★★★ All 7-year-old Thora Birch wants for Christmas is to see her divorced mother and father get back together, so she enlists the aid of a department-store Santa. It's a charming little movie, but be forewarned: children of divorced parents could get the wrong idea and be quite disturbed by the story. Rated G. 89m. **DIR:** Robert Lieberman. **CAST:** Harley Jane Kozak, Jamey Sheridan, Lauren Bacall, Leslie Nielsen, Kevin Nealon; Thora Birch. **1991**

ALL IN A NIGHT'S WORK ★★★ The heir to a publishing empire falls in love with a girl he believes has, at one time, been the mistress of his own uncle. This comedy starts well but lags before the finale. Harmless fun. 94m. **DIR:** Joseph Anthony. **CAST:** Shirley MacLaine, Dean Martin, Charlie Ruggles, Cliff Robertson, Gale Gordon, Jack Weston. **1961**

ALL MINE TO GIVE ★★★ Reaching for the heartstrings, this melodrama follows the lives of a Scottish family in 1850s Wisconsin. The backwoods life is brutal and by the film's midpoint both the mother and father have died and left the oldest child the

task of parceling out his little brothers and sisters to the far-flung neighbors. A fairly decent weeper. 102m. **DIR:** Allen Reisner. **CAST:** Glynis Johns, Cameron Mitchell, Patty McCormack, Hope Emerson. **1957**

ALL MY SONS (1948) ★★★ A man recently returned from combat discovers that his father profited by selling the government inferior material that may have cost lives. Edward G. Robinson as the all-too-human monster lacking a sense of responsibility for his actions is fine, but Arthur Miller's powerful play comes across as heavy-handed and preachy on film. B&W; 94m. **DIR:** Irving Reis. **CAST:** Edward G. Robinson, Burt Lancaster, Mady Christians, Howard Duff, Lloyd Gough, Arlene Francis, Harry Morgan. **1948**

ALL MY SONS (1986) ★★★1/2 An excellent adaptation of the Arthur Miller play. A family must deal with the death of one son in World War II and the father's profit made by selling plane parts during the war. James Whitmore is the guilt-ridden father, Michael Learned his distraught wife. Made for TV. 122m. **DIR:** Jack O'Brien. **CAST:** James Whitmore, Aidan Quinn, Michael Learned, Joan Allen. **1986**

ALL NIGHT LONG ★★★ Praised by some for its offbeat style and story, this comedy, starring the odd couple of Gene Hackman and Barbra Streisand, is only occasionally convincing. Hackman stars as an executive demoted to the position of managing a twenty-four-hour grocery store. There, he meets a daffy housewife (played by a miscast Streisand) and love blooms. 95m. **DIR:** Jean-Claude Tramont. **CAST:** Gene Hackman, Barbra Streisand. **1981**

ALL OF ME ★★★★1/2 Steve Martin finds himself haunted from within by the soul of a recently deceased Lily Tomlin when an attempt to put her spirit in another woman's body backfires. This delightful comedy gives its two stars the best showcase for their talents to date. Rated PG for suggested sex, violence, and profanity. 93m. **DIR:** Carl Reiner. **CAST:** Steve Martin, Lily Tomlin, Victoria Tennant, Richard Libertini. **1984 DVD**

ALL OVER ME ★★★1/2 Urban Manhattan makes a suitably gritty backdrop for this story of two teenage girls whose lifelong friendship may be on the verge of coming apart as their lives change. While Ellen (Tara Subkoff) starts dating a drug dealer, Claude (Alison Folland) reacts to her absence with more warmth than either of them expected. Low-budget film wears its independent attitude on its sleeve, but has some affecting moments along with its heavy-duty attitude. Rated R for sexuality, drug use, and profanity. 90m. **DIR:** Alex Sichel. **CAST:** Alison Folland, Tara Subkoff, Cole Hauser, Wilson Cruz, Leisha Hailey. **1996**

ALL OVER TOWN ★★1/2 Stage favorites of the 1920s and 1930s, Olsen and Johnson display their zany patter and antics as they try to produce a show in a theater on which a hex has been put. Some funny moments, but most of this low-budget comedy is antiquated. B&W; 62m. **DIR:** James W. Horne. **CAST:** Chic Johnson, Ole Olsen, Franklin Pangborn, Mary Howard, James Finlayson. **1937**

ALL QUIET ON THE WESTERN FRONT (1930) ★★★★★ Despite some dated moments and an "old movie" look, this film still stands as a powerful statement against war and man's inhumanity to man. Lew Ayres and Louis Wolheim star in this story, set during World War I, which follows several young men into battle, examining their disillusionment and eventual deaths. B&W; 130m. DIR: Lewis Milestone. CAST: Lew Ayres, Louis Wolheim. **1930 DVD**

ALL QUIET ON THE WESTERN FRONT (1979) ★★1/2 This is a television remake of the 1930 film, which was taken from Erich Maria Remarque's classic antiwar novel. It attempts to recall all the horrors of World War I, but even the great detail issued to this film can't hide its TV mentality and melodramatic characters. Despite this major flaw, the film is watchable for its rich look and compelling story. 126m. DIR: Delbert Mann. CAST: Richard Thomas, Ernest Borgnine, Donald Pleasence, Ian Holm, Patricia Neal, Keith Carradine. **1979 DVD**

ALL SCREWED UP ★★★1/2 Minor but entertaining Lina Wertmuller comedy-drama about farmers confronted with the noise and chaos of life in the big city. Lacks subtlety. Rated PG. Dubbed in English. 105m. DIR: Lina Wertmuller. CAST: Luigi Diberti, Nino Bignamini. **1976**

•**ALL THAT HEAVEN ALLOWS** ★★★1/2 Douglas Sirk was Hollywood's master of the classy soap opera, and this is one of his best. Jane Wyman plays a suburban widow who is scorned by her neighbors when she is courted by a young gardener (Rock Hudson). 89m. DIR: Douglas Sirk. CAST: Jane Wyman, Rock Hudson, Agnes Moorehead, Conrad Nagel. **1955**

ALL THAT JAZZ ★★★★ While it may not be what viewers expect from a musical, this story of a gifted choreographer, Joe Gideon (Roy Scheider, in his finest performance), who relentlessly drives himself to exhaustion is daring, imaginative, shocking, and visually stunning. Rated R. 123m. DIR: Bob Fosse. CAST: Roy Scheider, Ann Reinking, Jessica Lange. **1979**

ALL THE BROTHERS WERE VALIANT ★★★ Whaling captain Robert Taylor proves his brother (Stewart Granger) innocent of desertion but is betrayed by the latter in a quest for pearls. Some good action scenes. The last movie for the gifted Lewis Stone. 96m. DIR: Richard Thorpe. CAST: Robert Taylor, Stewart Granger, Ann Blyth, Betta St. John, Keenan Wynn, James Whitmore, Kurt Kasznar, Lewis Stone. **1953**

ALL THE KIND STRANGERS ★★ This made-for-TV thriller lacks overt terror. A family of orphans lures kind strangers to their isolated home and then forces them to act as their parents. If the strangers don't measure up, they're murdered. Interesting in an eerie way. 74m. DIR: Burt Kennedy. CAST: Stacy Keach, Samantha Eggar, John Savage, Robby Benson, Arlene Farber. **1974**

ALL THE KING'S MEN ★★★★ Broderick Crawford and Mercedes McCambridge won Academy Awards for their work in this adaptation of Robert Penn Warren's Pulitzer Prize–winning novel about a corrupt politician's ascension to power. The film retains its relevance and potency. B&W; 109m. DIR: Robert Rossen. CAST: Broderick Crawford, Joanne Dru, John Ireland, Mercedes McCambridge, John Derek. **1949**

ALL THE MARBLES ♥ Peter Falk stars as the unscrupulous manager of two female wrestlers. Rated

R because of nudity, violence, and profanity. 113m. DIR: Robert Aldrich. CAST: Peter Falk, Vicki Frederick, Laurene Landon, Burt Young, Tracy Reed. **1981**

ALL THE PRESIDENT'S MEN ★★★★ Robert Redford, who also produced, and Dustin Hoffman star in this gripping reenactment of the exposure of the Watergate conspiracy by reporters Bob Woodward and Carl Bernstein. What's so remarkable about this docudrama is, although we know how it eventually comes out, we're on the edge of our seats from beginning to end. That's inspired moviemaking. Rated PG. 136m. DIR: Alan J. Pakula. CAST: Dustin Hoffman, Robert Redford, Jason Robards Jr., Jane Alexander, Jack Warden, Martin Balsam. **1976 DVD**

ALL THE RIGHT MOVES ★★★1/2 Tom Cruise stars in this entertaining coming-of-age picture as a blue-collar high school senior trying to get out of a Pennsylvania mill town by way of a football scholarship. Rated R for profanity, sex, and nudity. 91m. DIR: Michael Chapman. CAST: Tom Cruise, Craig T. Nelson, Christopher Penn, Lea Thompson. **1983**

•**ALL THE VERMEERS IN NEW YORK** ★★1/2 A stockbroker and a young Frenchwoman who meet at an art gallery in front of a Vermeer painting seem to be headed for a relationship. Whether they get there is a subject for speculation. Not rated; contains mild sexual situations. 86m. DIR: Jon Jost. CAST: Emmanuelle Chaulet, Katherine Bean, Grace Phillips. **1990**

ALL THESE WOMEN ★ A comedy by Ingmar Bergman that is a not-so-subtle attack upon the legions of biographers who were pursuing them. The story is about a deceased cellist, Felix, who (we learn in a series of flashbacks) had been hounded by an erstwhile biographer. Bergman's first exercise in color, the movie suffers from a contrived, episodic structure. In Swedish with English subtitles. 80m. DIR: Ingmar Bergman. CAST: Bibi Andersson. **1964**

ALL THIS AND HEAVEN TOO ★★★★ Based on a true murder case, this film, set in Paris in 1840, casts Bette Davis as the governess who wins Charles Boyer's heart. Barbara O'Neil is the uncaring mother and obsessed wife who becomes jealous. When she is found murdered, Davis and Boyer become prime suspects. A classic. B&W; 121m. DIR: Anatole Litvak. CAST: Bette Davis, Charles Boyer, Jeffrey Lynn, Barbara O'Neil, Virginia Weidler, Henry Daniell, Ann Todd, June Lockhart, Harry Davenport. **1940**

ALL THROUGH THE NIGHT ★★★1/2 Humphrey Bogart and his gang take on Nazi spies in this star-studded romp. The plot is typical World War II flag-waving. But the dialogue and the cast—oh, my! This one's worth a look if only to see Jackie Gleason and Phil Silvers clowning it up a full decade before they'd become icons of the small screen. B&W; 107m. DIR: Vincent Sherman. CAST: Humphrey Bogart, Conrad Veidt, Kaaren Verne, Jane Darwell, Frank McHugh, Peter Lorre, Judith Anderson, William Demarest, Jackie Gleason, Phil Silvers, Wallace Ford, Barton MacLane, Edward Brophy, Martin Kosleck. **1942**

ALL TIED UP ★★ Zach Galligan promises to give up his wild bachelor days for Teri Hatcher, but her roommates don't believe him. When he wavers, they kidnap him to teach him a lesson. Bondage has never been so mundane. Rated R for language and adult situations. 90m. **DIR:** John Mark Robinson. **CAST:** Zach Galligan, Teri Hatcher, Lara Harris, Tracy Griffith, Abel Folk. **1992**

ALLAN QUARTERMAIN AND THE LOST CITY OF GOLD ❤ As if they weren't bad enough in the original, Richard Chamberlain and Sharon Stone reprise their roles from the tongue-in-beak turkey, *King Solomon's Mines*. Rated PG. 95m. **DIR:** Gary Nelson. **CAST:** Richard Chamberlain, Sharon Stone, James Earl Jones, Henry Silva, Robert Donner, Cassandra Peterson (Elvira). **1987**

ALLEGHENY UPRISING ★★★ John Wayne and Claire Trevor were reteamed the same year of their costarring triumph in *Stagecoach* for this potboiler set in the pre-Revolutionary American colonies, but the results were hardly as auspicious. Still, it's a decent time passer and features Brian Donlevy in one of his better villain roles. B&W; 81m. **DIR:** William A. Seiter. **CAST:** John Wayne, Claire Trevor, George Sanders, Chill Wills, Brian Donlevy. **1939**

ALLEGRO NON TROPPO ★★★★ An animated spoof of Disney's *Fantasia* by Italian filmmaker Bruno Bozzetto, this release entertainingly weds stylish slapstick with the music of Debussy, Ravel, Vivaldi, Stravinsky, Dvorak, and Sibelius. Rated PG. 75m. **DIR:** Bruno Bozzetto. **1976**

ALLEY CATS, THE ★★★ Director Radley Metzger set the screen on fire in the mid-1960s with this daring tale of a European socialite who becomes bored with her husband and decides to take a lover. Her quest eventually leads her to another woman, who unlocks her lesbian desires. Racy stuff for the period. Not rated; contains adult situations and nudity. B&W; 83m. **DIR:** Radley Metzger. **CAST:** Anna Arthur, Sabrina Koch, Karin Field, Chaz Holman. **1965 DVD**

ALLIGATOR ★★★1/2 The wild imagination of screenwriter John Sayles invests this comedy-horror film with wit and style. It features Robert Forster as a cop tracking down a giant alligator. It's good, unpretentious fun, but you have to be on your toes to catch all the gags (be sure to read the hilarious graffiti). Rated R. 94m. **DIR:** Lewis Teague. **CAST:** Robert Forster, Michael Gazzo, Robin Riker, Perry Lang, Jack Carter, Bart Braverman, Henry Silva, Dean Jagger. **1980**

ALLIGATOR II ★★1/2 An evil land developer prevents cops from stopping the groundbreaking ceremonies of his lakefront project, despite the fact that a mutant alligator is making lunch of anyone near the lake. Doesn't have the bite of the original John Sayles script, but manages to dig its teeth into you nonetheless. Rated R for violence. 94m. **DIR:** Brandon Clark. **CAST:** Joseph Bologna, Dee Wallace, Richard Lynch, Steve Railsback. **1990**

ALLIGATOR EYES ★★ A group of friends pick up a hitchhiking blind woman. Nonthrilling, would-be thriller. Rated R for nudity and violence. 101m. **DIR:** John Feldman. **CAST:** Annabelle Larsen, Roger Kabler, Mary McLain. **1990**

ALLIGATOR PEOPLE, THE ★★ At his laboratory in a Florida swamp, a scientist experiments with using alligator tissue to regenerate human flesh. Standard 1950s science fiction, obviously inspired (to put it

kindly) by *The Fly*. B&W; 74m. **DIR:** Roy Del Ruth. **CAST:** Beverly Garland, George Macready, Lon Chaney Jr., Richard Crane, Bruce Bennett. **1959**

ALLIGATOR SHOES ★★ This is pretty much a home movie by two brothers, Gary and Clay Borris. Although their characters here are grownup, they still live at home. When their mentally disturbed aunt moves in, trouble arises. This drama becomes strained before its fatal conclusion. Not rated. 98m. **DIR:** Clay Borris. **CAST:** Gary Borris, Clay Borris, Ronalda Jones, Rose Mallais-Borris. **1982**

ALLNIGHTER, THE ★ Terminally dumb 1980s beach movie. Rated PG-13. 90m. **DIR:** Tamar Simon Hoffs. **CAST:** Susanna Hoffs, John Terlesky, Joan Cusack, Dedee Pfeiffer, James Anthony Shanta, Janelle Brady. **1987 DVD**

•**ALLONSONFAN** ★★★ Marcello Mastroianni stars as a disillusioned nineteenth-century Italian nobleman in this handsomely filmed but impenetrable political drama. Imprisoned for revolutionary activities, he is released and cooperates in a plot to capture the leader of his group. In Italian with English subtitles. 100m. **DIR:** Paolo Taviani, Vittorio Taviani. **CAST:** Marcello Mastroianni, Lea Massari, Mimsy Farmer. **1974**

ALL'S FAIR ★★ Male corporate executives battle their wives and female coworkers in a weekend war game. Good cast and a promising premise are both wasted in a lot of second-rate slapstick. Rated PG-13 for double entendre humor. 89m. **DIR:** Rocky Lane. **CAST:** George Segal, Sally Kellerman, Robert Carradine, Jennifer Edwards, Jane Kaczmarek, Lou Ferrigno. **1989**

ALMOS' A MAN ★★1/2 You'll have trouble finding firm moral ground in this adaptation of Richard Wright's short story about a boy (LeVar Burton) impatient to achieve adulthood. The conclusion leaves an unpleasant taste. Introduced by Henry Fonda; unrated and suitable for family viewing. 51m. **DIR:** Stan Lathan. **CAST:** LeVar Burton, Madge Sinclair, Robert DoQui, Christopher Brooks, Garry Goodrow. **1976**

... ALMOST ★★★ This Australian comedy is almost—but not quite—hilarious. Uneven timing takes the punch out of many of the sight gags as Rosanna Arquette re-creates her bored wife ready-for-adventure role from *Desperately Seeking Susan.* Rated PG. 87m. **DIR:** Michael Pattinson. **CAST:** Rosanna Arquette, Bruce Spence. **1990**

ALMOST AN ANGEL ★★1/2 Paul Hogan gets his first non-"Crocodile" Dundee role as a professional thief in Los Angeles who becomes a probational angel in heaven. The film falls from there, as Hogan's comedy turns decidedly downbeat. Rated PG for mild profanity. 96m. **DIR:** John Cornell. **CAST:** Paul Hogan, Elias Koteas, Linda Kozlowski. **1990**

ALMOST ANGELS ★★1/2 Schmaltzy film focusing on the Vienna Boys' Choir and the problems one boy encounters when his voice changes and he can no longer sing in the choir. Rated G. 93m. **DIR:** Steve Previn. **CAST:** Peter Weck, Hans Holt, Fritz Eckhardt, Bruni Lobel, Sean Scully. **1962**

ALMOST BLUE ★★1/2 Jazz saxophonist Michael Madsen is overwhelmed with grief after his wife dies. He attempts to soothe his troubled soul by immersing himself in his music and new girlfriend Lynette Walden, but they only remind him of his loss. Moody and atmospheric, the film is rather downbeat, but that's the blues. Rated R for language and adult situations. 98m. **DIR:** Keoni Waxman. **CAST:** Michael Madsen, Lynette Walden. **1992**

ALMOST HEROES 🎭 Alcoholic frontier guide is hired in 1804 by a prissy aristocrat to chart a path to the Pacific Ocean before Lewis and Clark can complete the same task in this loud, crude spoof. Rated PG-13 for language, partial nudity, and violence. 87m. **DIR:** Christopher Guest. **CAST:** Chris Farley, Matthew Perry, Eugene Levy, Kevin Dunn. **1998**

ALMOST HUMAN 🎭 Italian grade-Z auteur Umberto Lenzi ground out this flat, routine kidnap potboiler during a break between his horror and cannibal epics. Rated R. 92m. **DIR:** Umberto Lenzi. **CAST:** Tomas Milian, Henry Silva. **1974**

ALMOST PERFECT AFFAIR, AN ★★★1/2 A very human love triangle evolves amidst the frenzy of film politics that surrounds the Cannes Film Festival. This romantic comedy about a young American filmmaker and the worldly but lovable wife of a powerful Italian film mogul is slow to start, but leaves you with a warm feeling. Rated PG with suggested sex and partial nudity. 92m. **DIR:** Michael Ritchie. **CAST:** Keith Carradine, Monica Vitti, Raf Vallone. **1979**

ALMOST PREGNANT ★★1/2 Bedroom farce features Tanya Roberts as Jeff Conaway's desperate-to-be-pregnant wife. She recruits both a neighbor and an in-law as donors while her husband finds his own diversions. In both an R and an unrated version, each containing nudity and profanity. 93m. **DIR:** Michael DeLuise. **CAST:** Tanya Roberts, Jeff Conaway, Joan Severance, Dom DeLuise. **1991**

ALMOST YOU ★★★★ Brooke Adams and Griffin Dunne give excellent performances as a restless husband and his down-to-earth wife. Dunne perfectly emulates the frustrated over-30 businessman and husband with comic results. Adams plays his wife, who is recovering from a car accident that gives her a new perspective on life. Rated R for language, sex, and nudity. 91m. **DIR:** Adam Brooks. **CAST:** Brooke Adams, Griffin Dunne, Karen Young, Marty Watt. **1985**

ALOHA, BOBBY AND ROSE ★★ B-movie treatment of two kids on the lam for a murder they didn't mean to commit. Paul LeMat's first starring role after *American Graffiti.* He is interesting, but the film is downbeat and uninspired. Rated R. 88m. **DIR:** Floyd Mutrux. **CAST:** Paul LeMat, Dianne Hull, Tim McIntire. **1975 DVD**

ALOHA SUMMER ★★★1/2 Chris Makepeace stars as a middle-class, Italian-American teenager who goes to the Hawaiian islands with his family in 1959. Once there, he learns important lessons about life and love. Instead of being just another empty-headed teen exploitation flick, *Aloha Summer* is blessed with sensitivity and insight. Rated PG for violence. 97m. **DIR:** Tommy Lee Wallace. **CAST:** Chris Makepeace, Don Michael Paul, Tia Carrere. **1988**

ALONE IN THE DARK 🎭 The inmates of a New Jersey mental institution break out to terrorize a doctor and his family. Rated R. 92m. **DIR:** Jack Sholder. **CAST:** Jack Palance, Donald Pleasence, Martin Landau,

Dwight Schultz, Deborah Hedwall, Erland Van Lidth. **1982**

ALONE IN THE NEON JUNGLE ★★★ Suzanne Pleshette is top-notch in this superior made-for-TV crime-drama about a woman police captain, heading up the tough Los Angeles Southeast Precinct, called "the sewer." Excellent writing pits Pleshette and her force against drugs and gangs, and a cop killer still on the loose. 90m. **DIR:** Georg Stanford Brown. **CAST:** Suzanne Pleshette, Danny Aiello, Joe Morton. **1991**

ALONE IN THE WOODS ★★1/2 Preteens will best appreciate this action-comedy about a wayward 10-year-old who accidentally wanders into the wrong van during a pit stop. It isn't until later that young Justin realizes he's in the company of two bumbling crooks who have kidnapped a toy magnate's young daughter. Now it's up to Justin to save the day. Rated PG for violence. 81m. **DIR:** John Putch. **CAST:** Laraine Newman, Chick Vennera, Matthias Hues, Daniel McVicar, Brady Bluhm. **1997**

ALONG CAME JONES ★★★★ Highly watchable comic Western with Gary Cooper as an innocent cowboy who's mistaken for an infamous outlaw. Both lawmen and the real outlaw (Dan Duryea) pursue him. B&W; 90m. **DIR:** Stuart Heisler. **CAST:** Gary Cooper, Loretta Young, Dan Duryea. **1945**

ALONG THE GREAT DIVIDE ★★1/2 With his usual determination and grit, lawman Kirk Douglas fights a sandstorm to capture an escaped criminal. The pace is slow, but the scenery is grand. B&W; 88m. **DIR:** Raoul Walsh. **CAST:** Kirk Douglas, John Agar, Walter Brennan, Virginia Mayo. **1951**

ALONG THE NAVAJO TRAIL ★★★ Deputy Marshal Roy Rogers investigates the disappearance of another government agent on Dale Evans's ranch and discovers land grabbers. Standard fare, exciting climax. B&W; 70m. **DIR:** Frank McDonald. **CAST:** Roy Rogers, George "Gabby" Hayes, Dale Evans, Douglas Fowley, Estelita Rodriguez. **1945**

ALPHA INCIDENT, THE ★★ A deadly organism from Mars, an attempted government cover-up, a radiation leak, panic, and havoc. Okay, if you like this sort of now-tired thing. Rated PG. 84m. **DIR:** Bill Rebane. **CAST:** Ralph Meeker. **1977**

ALPHABET CITY 🎭 Pretentious movie set in Manhattan's Lower East Side. Rated R for profanity, nudity, and violence. 98m. **DIR:** Amos Poe. **CAST:** Vincent Spano, Kate Vernon, Michael Winslow, Zohra Lampert, Raymond Serra. **1984**

ALPHABET MURDERS, THE ★★★ A semicomic Agatha Christie mystery with Tony Randall as Hercule Poirot and Margaret Rutherford in a cameo bit as Miss Marple. Poirot goes after a serial killer who polishes off his victims in alphabetical order. Christie fans might regard the movie as blasphemous, but Randall's fans should love it. B&W; 90m. **DIR:** Frank Tashlin. **CAST:** Tony Randall, Robert Morley, Anita Ekberg, Margaret Rutherford, James Villiers, Guy Rolfe. **1966**

ALPHAVILLE ★★★ Eddie Constantine portrays Lemmy Caution, French private eye extraordinaire, who is sent into the future to rescue a trapped scientist. It's a Dick Tracy–type of story with sci-fi leanings. In French with English subtitles. 98m. **DIR:**

Jean-Luc Godard. **CAST:** Eddie Constantine, Anna Karina, Akim Tamiroff. **1965 DVD**

ALSINO AND THE CONDOR ★★ This is an earnest attempt to dramatize the conflict between the Central American governments and the Sandinista rebels in Nicaragua. The film revolves around the story of one young boy caught in the turmoil. Alan Esquivel is Alsino, the boy who escapes into a fantasy world of flight. 90m. **DIR:** Miguel Littin. **CAST:** Alan Esquivel, Dean Stockwell, Carmen Bunster. **1983**

ALTERED STATES ★★★1/2 At times you can't help but be swept along … and almost overwhelmed. William Hurt, Blair Brown, Bob Balaban, and Charles Haid star in this suspenseful film as scientists involved in the potentially dangerous exploration of the mind. Rated R for nudity, profanity, and violence. 102m. **DIR:** Ken Russell. **CAST:** William Hurt, Blair Brown, Bob Balaban, Charles Haid, Drew Barrymore. **1980 DVD**

ALVAREZ KELLY ★★ Edward Dymtryk unimaginatively directed this plodding Western, starring William Holden as a cattle driver supplying beef to the Yankees. Confederate officer Richard Widmark wants him to steal that much-needed food for the South. Dull. 116m. **DIR:** Edward Dmytryk. **CAST:** William Holden, Richard Widmark, Janice Rule, Patrick O'Neal, Victoria Shaw. **1966 DVD**

ALWAYS (1984) ★★★ Largely autobiographical, *Always* follows Henry Jaglom and Patrice Townsend through their breakup and their reckoning of the relationship. This movie has a bittersweet feeling that is reminiscent of some of Woody Allen's films dealing with romance. Unfortunately, the movie doesn't have the laughs that Allen provides. Rated R for profanity and nudity. 105m. **DIR:** Henry Jaglom. **CAST:** Henry Jaglom, Patrice Townsend, Joanna Frank, Alan Rachins, Melissa Leo. **1984**

ALWAYS (1989) ★★★★ Steven Spielberg's transcendent remake of *A Guy Named Joe* is touching, funny, life-affirming, and lightweight. Richard Dreyfuss is in top form as a daredevil pilot who dies after saving the life of his buddy (John Goodman). Holly Hunter is the girl Dreyfuss leaves behind—until, that is, he comes back as a guardian angel to a fledgling pilot. Rated PG for brief profanity. 106m. **DIR:** Steven Spielberg. **CAST:** Richard Dreyfuss, Holly Hunter, John Goodman, Audrey Hepburn, Brad Johnson. **1989 DVD**

ALWAYS OUTNUMBERED ★★★★★ Sensational adaptation by author Walter Mosley of *Always Outnumbered, Always Outgunned*. Laurence Fishburne tears up the screen as an inner-city ex-con with a violent temper who tries to gain respect in all the wrong places. The film is episodic, reflecting its roots in a series of short stories, but all are superbly integrated. Mostly, though, it's Fishburne's show; you won't be able to take your eyes off him. Rated R for violence, profanity, nudity, and simulated sex. 105m. **DIR:** Michael Apted. **CAST:** Laurence Fishburne, Bill Cobbs, Natalie Cole, Bill Duke, Laurie Metcalf, Bill Nunn, Isaiah Washington, Cicely Tyson. **1998**

AMADEUS ★★★★★ F. Murray Abraham, who won an Oscar for his performance, gives a haunting portrayal of Antonio Salieri, the court composer for Hapsburg Emperor Joseph II. A second-rate musician, Salieri felt jealousy and admiration for the young musical genius Wolfgang Amadeus Mozart (Tom Hulce), who died at the age of thirty-five—perhaps by Salieri's hand. It's a stunning film full of great music, drama, and wit. Rated PG for mild violence. 158m. **DIR:** Milos Forman. **CAST:** Tom Hulce, F. Murray Abraham, Elizabeth Berridge. **1984 DVD**

AMANDA AND THE ALIEN ★★ Science-fiction giant Robert Silverberg's original story is ill-served by this comic spin on *Starman*, which stars Nicole Eggert as an oh-so-hip Valley Girl who rescues a cannibalistic alien being pursued by nasty government agents. The humor is pretty strained, and the one-joke premise quickly wears thin. Rated R for profanity, nudity, violence, and simulated sex. 94m. **DIR:** Jon Kroll. **CAST:** Nicole Eggert, Michael Dorn, Michael Bendetti, Stacy Keach, John Diehl. **1995**

AMARCORD ★★★★★ This landmark film is based on director Federico Fellini's reflections of his youth in a small town in prewar Italy. While celebrating the kinship that exists in the town, Fellini examines the serious shortcomings that would pave the route for fascism. Brilliantly photographed by Giuseppe Rotunno. Italian dubbed in English. 127m. **DIR:** Federico Fellini. **CAST:** Magali Noel, Bruno Zanin, Pupella Maggio. **1974 DVD**

AMATEUR, THE (1982) ★★★1/2 A CIA computer technologist (John Savage) blackmails The Company into helping him avenge the terrorist murder of his girlfriend, only to find himself abandoned—and hunted—by the CIA. Rated R for violence. 111m. **DIR:** Charles Jarrott. **CAST:** John Savage, Christopher Plummer, Marthe Keller, John Marley. **1982**

AMATEUR (1995) ★★★★ An amnesiac teams up with a nymphomaniac/virgin ex-nun to try to discover his true identity. Meanwhile, his porn star ex-wife tries to get away from him and the international crime cartel that's after them both. Great dialogue and eccentric plotting mark this deadpan comic *film noir* that is nowhere near as smutty as it sounds. Rated R for violence, language, and some sexual situations. 105m. **DIR:** Hal Hartley. **CAST:** Isabelle Huppert, Martin Donovan, Elina Lowensohn, Damian Young. **1995**

AMAZING ADVENTURE ★★★ Feeling guilty after inheriting a fortune, Cary Grant sets out to earn his living in this comedy of stout hearts among the poor-but-honest in England during the Depression. B&W; 70m. **DIR:** Alfred Zeisler. **CAST:** Cary Grant, Mary Brian, Peter Gawthorne, Henry Kendall, Leon M. Lion. **1936**

AMAZING COLOSSAL MAN, THE ★★ Exposed to a nuclear blast, an army colonel grows as big as a house … and keeps on growing, as scientists and his understandably worried fiancée search for a cure. Basically a C-budget rip-off of one of Jack Arnold's stylish Universal International chillers of the Fifties. Best scene: the struggle with a king-size syringe. B&W; 80m. **DIR:** Bert I. Gordon. **CAST:** Glenn Langan, Cathy Downs, William Hudson, James Seay, Larry Thor. **1957**

AMAZING DOBERMANS ★★ Third in a series of films about do-gooder dogs pits a treasury agent (James Franciscus) against inept crooks who can't compete with the dogged determination of the Dobermans. Harmless, but hardly inspired. Rated G. 94m. **DIR:** David Chudnow, Byron Chudnow. **CAST:** James Franciscus, Barbara Eden, Fred Astaire, Jack Carter. **1976**

●**AMAZING DR. CLITTERHOUSE, THE** ★★1/2 Psychiatrist attempting to tap into the criminal mind involves himself with a gang and ends up directing their capers. Melodrama with a comic touch has a good cast but its play-bound roots tangle it up and the finished product is lightweight. B&W; 87m. **DIR:** Anatole Litvak. **CAST:** Edward G. Robinson, Claire Trevor, Humphrey Bogart, Gale Page, Donald Crisp, Allen Jenkins, Thurston Hall. **1938**

AMAZING GRACE AND CHUCK ♥ Paranoid fantasy about what happens when a 12-year-old Little Leaguer (Joshua Zuehlke) decides to give up baseball in protest of nuclear arms. Rated PG. 115m. **DIR:** Mike Newell. **CAST:** Jamie Lee Curtis, Alex English, Gregory Peck, William L. Petersen, Dennis Lipscomb, Lee Richardson. **1987**

AMAZING HOWARD HUGHES, THE ★★ Howard Hughes was amazing, but little in this account of his life and career would so indicate. Best portrayal is Ed Flanders as longtime, finally turned-upon associate Noah Dietrich. An ambitious TV production that falls short of the mark. 215m. **DIR:** William A. Graham. **CAST:** Tommy Lee Jones, Ed Flanders, Tovah Feldshuh, Sorrell Booke, Lee Purcell, Arthur Franz. **1977**

AMAZING MR. BLUNDEN, THE ★★★ Neat little ghost story about children from the twentieth century (Lynne Frederick, Garry Miller) helping right a wrong done 100 years previously. Laurence Naismith is the mysterious (and amazing) Mr. Blunden, a nineteenth-century lawyer who is at home in the twentieth century. The children seem a little old, but on the whole the story is delightful. Rated PG. 100m. **DIR:** Lionel Jeffries. **CAST:** Laurence Naismith, Lynne Frederick, Garry Miller, Dorothy Alison, Diana Dors. **1972**

AMAZING MR. X ★★★ This drama about a bogus medium and the woman he plans to hoodwink is leisurely paced but well written and acted by a solid cast. A pleasant surprise. B&W; 78m. **DIR:** Bernard Vorhaus. **CAST:** Turhan Bey, Cathy O'Donnell, Lynn Bari. **1948**

AMAZING PANDA ADVENTURE, THE ★★★ Annoying, self-involved 12-year-old evolves after spending his vacation on a panda reserve and saving a cub that poachers hope to sell to a zoo. Rick Baker of Cinovation Studios creates the animatronic pandas that are used intermittently with actual animals. Chinese highland forestry shots are absolutely breathtaking. Rated PG for violence. 85m. **DIR:** Christopher Cain. **CAST:** Ryan Slater, Ding Yi, Fei Wang, Stephen Lang. **1995**

AMAZING SPIDERMAN, THE ★★ Marvel Comics' popular character makes his live-action debut in this made-for-TV adaptation that involves Spidey's origin. Although fairly well-acted, it's missing many of the wisecracking elements that made the comic-book character popular. The production values and special effects are decent, though, especially the wall-crawling scenes. Not rated, but appropriate for all ages. 93m. **DIR:** E. W. Swackhamer. **CAST:** Nicholas Hammond, David White, Michael Pataki, Hilly Hicks, Lisa Eilbacher. **1977**

AMAZING STORIES (TV SERIES) ★★★1/2 The best of Steven Spielberg's *Amazing Stories* have been paired up for video release. "Book Two" is by far the strongest, highlighted by director Robert Zemeckis's "Go to the Head of the Class," and Tim Burton's manic "Family Dog," an animated short that beat *The Simpsons* by several years. "Book One" includes Spielberg's overlong segment, "The Mission," in which a World War II bomber takes enemy fire and seems doomed, until rescue arrives from a most unlikely source. Danny DeVito rounds out that tape by directing and starring in the occasionally uproarious "The Wedding Ring." 70–71m. **DIR:** Steven Spielberg, Robert Zemeckis, Danny DeVito, Brad Bird. **CAST:** Kevin Costner, Kiefer Sutherland, Christopher Lloyd, Mary Stuart Masterson, Casey Siemaszko, Danny DeVito, Rhea Perlman, Scott Coffey. **1985–1986**

AMAZING TRANSPARENT MAN, THE ★★ This zero-budget thriller from cult director Edgar Ulmer has gotten a bad rap over the years, while the talky sci-fi film shot back-to-back with it, *Beyond the Time Barrier*, has been overpraised. The admittedly lame premise has a refugee scientist blackmailed into turning an escaped convict invisible so he can commit bank robberies—but Ulmer provides some thrills, including an exciting, sadistic climax. B&W; 58m. **DIR:** Edgar G. Ulmer. **CAST:** Douglas Kennedy, Marguerite Chapman, James Griffith. **1960 DVD**

AMAZON ★★1/2 On the lam, Kari Vaananen hightails it into the jungles of the Amazon, where he's befriended by pilot Robert Davi. Politically correct film is only so-so. Rated R for violence and language. 88m. **DIR:** Mika Kaurismaki. **CAST:** Robert Davi, Kari Vaananen, Rae Dawn Chong. **1992**

AMAZON WOMEN ON THE MOON ★★★ This silly scrapbook send-up of Saturday-morning, sci-fi, and sitcom-TV schlock stitches together star-strewn skits, but many of the plots are threadbare. When on the mark the chuckles come easily. More often, it's like the Not Ready for Prime Time Players on a not-so-prime night. Rated R for nudity. 85m. **DIR:** John Landis, Joe Dante, Carl Gottlieb, Peter Horton, Robert K. Weiss. **CAST:** Rosanna Arquette, Ralph Bellamy, Carrie Fisher, Sybil Danning, Steve Allen, Griffin Dunne, Steve Guttenberg, Ed Begley Jr., Arsenio Hall, Howard Hesseman, Russ Meyer, B. B. King, Henny Youngman. **1987 DVD**

AMAZONS ♥ The ridiculousness of the fight scenes in this film rivals that of the worst kung fu flick. This silly film is rated R for nudity, violence, and sex. 76m. **DIR:** Alex Sessa. **CAST:** Windsor Taylor Randolph, Penelope Reed, Joseph Whipp, Danitza Kingsley, Willie Nelson. **1986**

AMBASSADOR, THE ★★★1/2 *The Ambassador* confronts the Arab-Israeli conflict with a clear head and an optimistic viewpoint. Robert Mitchum plays the controversial U.S. ambassador to Israel, who tries to solve the Palestinian question while being criticized by all factions. Rock Hudson (in his last big-screen role) is the security officer who saves the ambassador's life. Rated R for violence, profanity, sex, and nudity. 97m. DIR: J. Lee Thompson. CAST: Robert Mitchum, Rock Hudson, Ellen Burstyn, Fabio Testi, Donald Pleasence. 1984

AMBASSADOR BILL ★★★ This contrived comedy of pompous protocol versus common sense has amiable inexperienced cowpoke Will Rogers appointed ambassador to a revolution-wracked monarchy somewhere in Europe. Funny dialogue and absurd situations give the star plenty of laugh opportunities. B&W; 68m. DIR: Sam Taylor. CAST: Will Rogers, Marguerite Churchill, Gustav von Seyffertitz, Ray Milland. 1931

AMBASSADOR MAGMA ★★ Dull artistry and an average story make this Japanese animated series rather tedious as Ambassador Magma, a giant golden robot, battles the evil would-be ruler of the universe and his army of weird demons. Dubbed in English. Not rated; contains violence. 70m. DIR: Yutaka Maseba. 1993

AMBASSADOR'S DAUGHTER, THE ★★★ A beautiful Olivia de Havilland and a handsome John Forsythe star in this sophisticated romantic comedy about a congressman (Edward Arnold) attempting to curtail the amorous adventures of GIs in Paris. Winningly performed by all. 102m. DIR: Norman Krasna. CAST: Olivia de Havilland, John Forsythe, Myrna Loy, Adolphe Menjou, Tommy Noonan, Edward Arnold. 1956

AMBITION 💔 An unpublished author is so obsessed with a paroled slasher that he befriends the reformed psycho. Rated R for violence, language, and nudity. 100m. DIR: Scott Goldstein. CAST: Lou Diamond Phillips, Clancy Brown, Cecilia Peck, Richard Bradford, Willard E. Pugh, Grace Zabriskie. 1991

AMBULANCE, THE ★★★★ Cartoonist Eric Roberts stumbles onto what may be a weird abduction conspiracy when dream gal Janine Turner is whisked away by a mysterious ambulance and never shows up at any of the local hospitals. Campy, strange, infused with black humor and several exciting chase scenes, this is an intriguing flick. Adding to its oddball patina is James Earl Jones as a cop on the edge. Rated R for profanity and violence. 95m. DIR: Larry Cohen. CAST: Eric Roberts, Janine Turner, James Earl Jones, Eric Braeden. 1993

AMBUSH MURDERS, THE ★★★ Formulaic TV adaptation of a true story. The title refers to the killing of two California policemen in a black neighborhood. A black activist is framed and it's up to hardworking lawyer James Brolin to get him acquitted. Intermittently engrossing. 98m. DIR: Steven H. Stern. CAST: James Brolin, Dorian Harewood, Amy Madigan, Antonio Fargas. 1982

AMBUSHERS, THE 💔 Only hard-core Dean Martin fans will want to bother with this one, the third movie in the Matt Helm secret agent series. 102m. DIR: Henry Levin. CAST: Dean Martin, Senta Berger, Janice Rule, James Gregory, Albert Salmi, Kurt Kasznar, Beverly Adams. 1968

AMELIA EARHART: THE FINAL FLIGHT ★★1/2 Diane Keaton portrays Amelia Earhart as a tantrum-throwing, whining know-it-all in this disappointing Turner Pictures production. Earhart's fabled heroism is strangely lacking in this rendition of her final flight. Only Rutger Hauer, as her drunken navigator, seems to believe in his character. Not rated; contains mild profanity. 93m. DIR: Yves Simoneau. CAST: Diane Keaton, Bruce Dern, Rutger Hauer, Paul Guilfoyle, Denis Arndt. 1994

AMERICA 💔 This mess has a down-and-out cable station trying to get financial support from New York's latest $10 million lottery winner. Rated R. 90m. DIR: Robert Downey. CAST: Zack Norman, Tammy Grimes, Michael J. Pollard, Richard Belzer, Laura Ashton, Liz Torres. 1986 DVD

AMERICAN ANTHEM 💔 Starring 1984 Olympic gold medal gymnast Mitch Gaylord, this film features superb gymnastics. Rated PG. 100m. DIR: Albert Magnoli. CAST: Mitch Gaylord, Janet Jones, Michelle Phillips. 1986

AMERICAN ARISTOCRACY, AN ★★★★ One of those early Douglas Fairbanks gems when he was more interested in strenuous acrobatics and satiric commentary than ponderous costume adventures. This one deflates the pretensions of Rhode Island society. Silent. B&W; 52m. DIR: Lloyd Ingraham. CAST: Douglas Fairbanks Sr., Jewel Carmen. 1916

AMERICAN BLUE NOTE ★★★ Offbeat nostalgic tale about struggling jazz musicians, circa 1960. Peter MacNicol, in an engaging performance, plays the ever-hopeful but constantly thwarted bandleader who desperately tries to keep his quintet together. Rated PG-13 for profanity. 96m. DIR: Ralph Toporoff. CAST: Peter MacNicol, Charlotte d'Amboise, Trini Alvarado. 1989

AMERICAN BOYFRIENDS ★★★1/2 Precocious Canadian Sandy Wilcox, last seen as the gawky 12-year-old of My American Cousin, has matured in this sequel from writer-director Sandy Wilson. This time Sandy attends the wedding of her cousin Butch (John Wildman) in Portland, Oregon. Margaret Langrick, as Sandy, has added drop-dead cuteness to her spunky personality; but Wilson's story has a decidedly bittersweet tone. Rated PG-13 for sexual connotations. 90m. DIR: Sandy Wilson. CAST: Margaret Langrick, John Wildman. 1989

AMERICAN BUFFALO ★★1/2 David Mamet's slight stage play becomes an equally unsatisfying film: a claustrophobic and needlessly talky exercise between two men with nothing much to say. Junk-shop owner Dennis Franz allows himself to be persuaded into sharing a potential burglary with twitchy Dustin Hoffman, but the caper never moves past the planning stage. Hoffman's nervous tics are laughably overplayed and are no substitute for credible characterization. Rated R for profanity and violence. 88m. DIR: Michael Corrente. CAST: Dustin Hoffman, Dennis Franz, Sean Nelson. 1996

AMERICAN CHRISTMAS CAROL, AN ★★ Lackluster made-for-television rendering of Charles Dickens's Christmas favorite, set in 1930s New England. Scrooge is played by Henry Winkler with some panache. 100m. DIR: Eric Till. CAST: Henry Winkler, David Wayne, Dorian Harewood, Chris Wiggins. 1979 DVD

AMERICAN CINEMA ★★★★ Directors Martin Scorsese, Steven Spielberg, Billy Wilder, and Joseph Mankiewicz top the who's who of more than 150 filmmakers sharing their insights in this revealing examination of the $20-billion-per-year American movie industry. All aspects of Hollywood-style creation and production are discussed in detail. B&W/color; 10 hours on five cassettes. **DIR:** Lawrence Pitkethly. **1995**

AMERICAN CLOCK, THE ★★★★ Telling and thought-provoking look at the stock-market crash of 1929 and the great depression that followed. Engrossing story line, vivid characterizations, and wonderful performances make this a winner based on the Arthur Miller stage play. Made for cable television. 95m. **DIR:** Bob Clark. **CAST:** Kelly Preston, John Randolph, David Strathairn, Joanna Miles, Darren McGavin, Mary McDonnell, Estelle Parsons, Yaphet Kotto, Eddie Bracken, Jim Dale, Tony Roberts, Roberts Blossom, Loren Dean. **1993**

AMERICAN COP ★★ Vanity effort from director-actor Wayne Crawford, who plays Elmo LaGrange, a dedicated cop finally taking a vacation—which is cut short when he lands in Moscow and is mistaken by the Russian mob for someone else. The usual complications and encounters come his way. Rated PG-13 for violence. 91m. **DIR:** Wayne Crawford. **CAST:** Daniele Quinn, Wayne Crawford, Ashley Laurence, William Katt. **1994**

AMERICAN CYBORG: STEEL WARRIOR ★★ Futuristic kick-boxing thriller is marred by laughable performances and a derivative storyline stolen from *The Terminator.* Rated R for violence and profanity. 95m. **DIR:** Boaz Davidson. **CAST:** Joe Lara, Nicole Hansen, John P. Ryan. **1994**

AMERICAN DREAM ★★★★ Oscar-winning documentary about the Local P-9 (meat packers) union in Austin, Minnesota, and their struggle to renegotiate wages with the Hormel Corporation. The local union bypasses its international chapter and hires a corporate image consultant. A good mix of interviews between the strikers, Hormel executives, and the international chapter. This documentary lets the viewers decide for themselves which side they should take. Rated PG-13 for profanity. 98m. **DIR:** Barbara Kopple. **1990**

AMERICAN DREAMER ★★★ JoBeth Williams plays Cathy Palmer, a would-be novelist who, in a short story contest, successfully captures the style of adventure stories that feature a superspy named Rebecca Ryan and wins a trip to Paris. But once there, Palmer is hit by a car and wakes up believing she is the fictional character. The picture never quite shines as brightly as one expects. Rated PG for violence. 105m. **DIR:** Rick Rosenthal. **CAST:** JoBeth Williams, Tom Conti, Giancarlo Giannini. **1984**

AMERICAN EAGLE ✦ Rehashed garbage about a CIA hit man who wants out of the game. Rated R for violence and profanity. 92m. **DIR:** Robert J. Smawley. **CAST:** Asher Brauner, Robert F. Lyons. **1989**

AMERICAN EMPIRE ★★★ A formula film featuring the now-standard grand opening, dramatic problemposing center, and slam-bang breathtaking climax, but a good, entertaining Western nonetheless. Richard Dix and Preston Foster team to found a cattle empire in Texas. Villain Leo Carrillo makes most of the trouble the pair encounters. Fans of the genre will love it. B&W; 82m. **DIR:** William McGann. **CAST:**

Richard Dix, Frances Gifford, Preston Foster, Leo Carrillo, Guinn Williams. **1942**

AMERICAN FLATULATORS ✦ This spoof of television's *American Gladiators* stinks to high heaven, and then some. Totally tasteless. Not rated; contains adult situations. 54m. **DIR:** Nolan T. Michaels. **1996**

AMERICAN FLYERS ★★★1/2 Another bicycle-racing tale from writer Steve Tesich (*Breaking Away*), who correctly decided he could milk that theme at least one more time. Kevin Costner and David Marshall Grant star as estranged brothers who get to know and like each other again during a grueling three-day overland race. Rated PG-13 for brief nudity and language. 113m. **DIR:** John Badham. **CAST:** Kevin Costner, David Marshall Grant, Rae Dawn Chong, Alexandra Paul, Janice Rule, John Amos. **1985 DVD**

AMERICAN FRIEND, THE ★★★★1/2 Tense story of an American criminal (Dennis Hopper) in Germany talking a picture framer into murdering a gangster. Extremely well-done, with lots of surprises. Cameo appearances by American film directors Sam Fuller and Nicholas Ray. Rated R for language, violence. 127m. **DIR:** Wim Wenders. **CAST:** Dennis Hopper, Bruno Ganz, Lisa Kreuzer, Gerard Blain. **1977**

AMERICAN FRIENDS ★★★★1/2 Michael Palin is an uptight Oxford instructor who learns to loosen up after meeting two American women while hiking in Switzerland. Co-writer Palin based this leisurely, elegant period piece, set in 1861, on one of his upstart ancestors. Witty and wonderful, it is a true romance in every sense of the word. Rated PG for adult themes. 95m. **DIR:** Tristram Powell. **CAST:** Michael Palin, Trini Alvarado, Connie Booth, Alfred Molina. **1993**

AMERICAN GIGOLO ★★ This story of a male hooker, Julian Kay (Richard Gere), who attends to the physical needs of bored, rich, middle-aged women in Beverly Hills, may be something different. But who needs it? This is sensationalism in the guise of social comment, though it has some incidental humor and impressive performances by Gere and Lauren Hutton. Rated R for explicit depictions of a low lifestyle. 117m. **DIR:** Paul Schrader. **CAST:** Richard Gere, Lauren Hutton, Hector Elizondo, Nina Van Pallandt. **1980 DVD**

AMERICAN GOTHIC ★★★1/2 Inventive, chilling, and atmospheric horror film pits a group of vacationers on a remote island against a grotesque, creepy family headed by Ma and Pa (Rod Steiger and Yvonne De Carlo). The latter's children, middle-aged adults who act and dress like kids, delight in killing off the newcomers one by one. An absence of gore and an emphasis on characterization make this an uncommonly satisfying film for horror buffs. Rated R for violence and profanity. 90m. **DIR:** John Hough. **CAST:** Rod Steiger, Yvonne De Carlo, Michael J. Pollard. **1988**

AMERICAN GRAFFITI ★★★★1/2 *Star Wars* creator George Lucas discovered his talent for creating lighthearted, likable entertainment with this film about the coming-of-age of a group of high school students in northern California. Blessed with a superb rock 'n' roll score and fine performances, it's the best of its kind and inspired the long-running television series *Happy Days.* Rated PG. 110m. **DIR:**

George Lucas. **CAST:** Richard Dreyfuss, Ron Howard, Paul LeMat, Cindy Williams, Candy Clark, Mackenzie Phillips, Harrison Ford, Bo Hopkins, Charles Martin Smith. **1973 DVD**

AMERICAN HEART ★★★1/2 Tough, realistic film follows the volatile relationship of a recently released convict and his 15-year-old son. As the father and son attempt reconciliation, they are drawn into life on the streets. Movie benefits greatly from gritty location filming and memorable performances, especially Jeff Bridges and Edward Furlong. Rated R for violence and language. 117m. **DIR:** Martin Bell. **CAST:** Jeff Bridges, Edward Furlong, Lucinda Jenney, Don Harvey. **1991**

AMERICAN HISTORY X ★★★★ Racism ravages an American middle-class family in this incendiary drama about breaking a daisy chain of hatred. A neo-Nazi skinhead returns from prison to his Venice Beach home. His evolution from young bright jock to thug to enlightened parolee and his relationship with a younger brother who is following in his toxic footsteps are captured in gripping flashbacks. The acting is excellent. Rated R for language, sex, and violence. 118m. **DIR:** Tony Kaye. **CAST:** Edward Norton, Edward Furlong, Fairuza Balk, Beverly D'Angelo, Stacy Keach, Jennifer Lien, Elliott Gould. **1998 DVD**

AMERICAN HOT WAX ★★★1/2 Though facts may be in short supply in this bio-pic of pioneer rock disc jockey Alan Freed, abundant energy and spirit make this movie a winner. Tim McIntire gives a remarkable performance as Freed. Rated PG. 91m. **DIR:** Floyd Mutrux. **CAST:** Tim McIntire, Fran Drescher, Jay Leno, John Lehne, Laraine Newman, Jeff Altman, Chuck Berry, Jerry Lee Lewis. **1978**

AMERICAN IN PARIS, AN ★★★★★ One of Gene Kelly's classic musicals, this Oscar-winning best picture features the hoofer as the free-spirited author of the title. The picture is a heady mixture of light entertainment and the music of George Gershwin. 115m. **DIR:** Vincente Minnelli. **CAST:** Gene Kelly, Leslie Caron, Nina Foch, Oscar Levant. **1951 DVD**

AMERICAN JUSTICE ★★1/2 Small-town cops near the Mexican border become involved in an illegal alien/slavery ring. It's brutal and violent and probably truer than you'd think. A fair attempt by TV's *Simon and Simon* to work together in different roles. Rated R for violence, sex, and language. 79m. **DIR:** Gary Grillo. **CAST:** Gerald McRaney, Jameson Parker, Wilford Brimley. **1986**

AMERICAN KICKBOXER ★★ A former world-champion kick boxer must fight his way back to the top following a jail term for manslaughter. Rated R for profanity. 93m. **DIR:** Frans Nel. **CAST:** John Barrett. **1991**

AMERICAN ME ★★★★★ Brilliant directorial debut by Edward James Olmos has him adopting the storytelling style of his mentor, director Robert M. Young, in depicting thirty years in the life of an East Los Angeles Latino family. Olmos stars as the pivotal character, a hardened criminal who finds his soul too late. A cinema milestone. Rated R for violence, nudity, and profanity. 126m. **DIR:** Edward James Olmos. **CAST:** Edward James Olmos, William Forsythe, Pepe Serna, Danny De La Paz, Evelina Fernandez. **1992**

•**AMERICAN MOVIE** ★★★★ This documentary portrait of amateur Wisconsin filmmaker Mark Borchardt is a deadpan scream. It chronicles his two-year obsession with making a cheesy horror flick that will hopefully help finance another pet project. Borchardt plows through numerous personal, economic, and artistic snags, and his talent is suspect. But he and his relatives and friends (which include a grizzled, octogenarian uncle and permanently stoned musician pal) are certainly a colorful brood. Rated R for language and suggested violence. 104m. **DIR:** Chris Smith. **1999 DVD**

AMERICAN NINJA 🖤 An American soldier (Michael Dudikoff) single-handedly takes on an army of martial arts mercenaries in the Philippines. Rated R for profanity and violence. 95m. **DIR:** Sam Firstenberg. **CAST:** Michael Dudikoff, Guich Koock, Judie Aronson, Steve James. **1985**

AMERICAN NINJA II ★★ Michael Dudikoff continues to set new standards for nonacting in this mindless but enjoyable-for-fans martial arts movie. Dudikoff and Steve James, who is as watchable as ever, play army rangers who come to the aid of the Marines and wipe out a passel of heroin dealers. Rated R. 96m. **DIR:** Sam Firstenberg. **CAST:** Michael Dudikoff, Steve James, Larry Poindexter, Gary Conway. **1987**

AMERICAN NINJA III 🖤 Comic-book movie filled with cartoon characters. Rated R for violence and profanity. 89m. **DIR:** Cedric Sundstrom. **CAST:** Steve James, David Bradley, Marjoe Gortner. **1989**

AMERICAN NINJA IV: THE ANNIHILATION 🖤 This paint-by-numbers action flick has martial arts experts trying to rescue a group of Americans held captive by a mad Arab. Rated R for violence and profanity; 96m. **DIR:** Cedric Sundstrom. **CAST:** Michael Dudikoff, David Bradley, James Booth, Robin Stille, Ken Gampu. **1991**

•**AMERICAN PIE** ★★ Four high-school chums vow to lose their virginity by the time they graduate. Crude, rampantly sexist, amateurish, and cheap-looking, this adolescent sex comedy was nevertheless a big box-office hit; think of it as *Porky's* for the 1990s. Rated R for profanity and sexual scenes. 95m. **DIR:** Paul Weitz. **CAST:** Jason Biggs, Chris Klein, Mena Suvari, Alyson Hannigan, Eugene Levy. **1999 DVD**

AMERICAN PRESIDENT, THE ★★★★★ Ah, if only American politics were blessed with so much nobility! Michael Douglas is just right as a chief of state who enjoys unprecedented popularity until venturing back into the "dating scene." American citizens admire a man who grieves for his wife's untimely death, but they're not so sure what to make of his growing passion for a perky environmental lobbyist (Annette Bening). Aaron Sorkin's script is clearly a populist fantasy, but so what? Rated PG-13 for profanity and adult themes. 120m. **DIR:** Rob Reiner. **CAST:** Michael Douglas, Annette Bening, Martin Sheen, Michael J. Fox, David Paymer, Anna Deavere Smith, Samantha Mathis. **1995 DVD**

•**AMERICAN PSYCHO** ★★★1/2 The notorious Bret Easton Ellis novel about a yuppie serial killer (Christian Bale) makes a comparatively restrained and surprisingly effective film. The script is by Guinevere

Turner and director Mary Harron mercifully avoids most of the stomach-churning excesses of the book, although the last half hour becomes increasingly disconnected and leaves too many loose ends. Still, Harron's wry satire of 1980s materialism and Bale's fine performance in the title role make it worthwhile. Rated R for violence, sex, and profanity. 104m. **DIR:** Mary Harron. **CAST:** Christian Bale, Willem Dafoe, Jared Leto, Reese Witherspoon, Samantha Mathis, Chloe Sevigny. **2000**

AMERICAN ROULETTE ★★ Political thriller about a deposed president (Andy Garcia) of a South American nation living in exile in London. The ex-president's life is constantly in jeopardy from Latin death squads—and the CIA and KGB play a tug of war with his loyalities. Robert Stephens gives a fine performance as a sleazy British agent. Light on action, long on talk, with a sappy ending. Rated R. 102m. **DIR:** Maurice Hatton. **CAST:** Andy Garcia, Kitty Aldridge, Robert Stephens. **1988**

AMERICAN SHAOLIN: KING OF THE KICKBOXERS II ★★1/2 A kick boxer is humiliated during a tournament and decides he will travel to China to become a Shaolin monk. By the end you'll be rooting for him. Rated PG-13 for violence. 103m. **DIR:** Lucas Lowe. **CAST:** Reese Madigan, Daniel Dae Kim, Billy Chang, Cliff Lenderman, Zhang Zhi Yen, Trent Bushey, Kim Chan. **1991**

AMERICAN SOLDIER, THE ★★★ A German-American Vietnam veteran is hired by the Munich police to murder local criminals. Slight but significant early film by Rainer Werner Fassbinder. Is at once an homage to and a critique of American crime-dramas, particularly as seen by German viewers. In German with English subtitles. Not rated. B&W; 80m. **DIR:** Rainer Werner Fassbinder. **CAST:** Karl Scheydt, Elga Sorbas, Margarethe Von Trotta, Rainer Werner Fassbinder. **1970**

AMERICAN STORY, AN ★★★1/2 Powerful *Hallmark Hall of Fame* television special focuses on six WWII vets who return to their hometown only to find that it has been taken over by a corrupt mayor and brutal sheriff. Challenging the diabolical duo in the election, they're forced to arm themselves in order to free their community from its home-grown tyranny. Rated PG for violence and adult themes. 97m. **DIR:** John Gray. **CAST:** Brad Johnson, Kathleen Quinlan, Tom Sizemore, Josef Sommer, David Labiosa. **1992**

AMERICAN STRAYS ★★★1/2 Episodic film featuring various losers on the road in Texas. A surprisingly good showcase for a solid group of actors who seldom fare so well with feature-length scripts. Particularly good is Eric Roberts as a family man whose family is making his life a living hell. Rated R for violence, profanity, and sexual situations. 93m. **DIR:** Michael Covert. **CAST:** Eric Roberts, Jennifer Tilly, John Savage, Carol Kane, Luke Perry, Sam Jones. **1996 DVD**

AMERICAN SUMMER, AN 🎔 A teenage boy is shipped off to live with his aunt, only to become embroiled in sex, drugs, and murder. Rated R for profanity, violence, and nudity. 100m. **DIR:** James Slocum. **CAST:** Michael Landes, Amber Susa, Brian Austin Green, Joanna Kerns. **1991**

AMERICAN TAIL, AN ★★★ An immigrant mouse becomes separated from his family while voyaging to the United States. The execution and lavish animation make up for the trite and predictable story. Film picks up steam with the introduction of Dom DeLuise, as a vegetarian cat. Rated G. 82m. **DIR:** Don Bluth. **CAST:** Dom DeLuise, Phillip Glasser, Madeline Kahn, Nehemiah Persoff, Christopher Plummer (voices). **1986**

AMERICAN TAIL, AN: FIEVEL GOES WEST ★★★1/2 Fievel Mousekewitz and his family leave behind the crowded city at the urgings of a conniving cat, Cat R. Waul (voiced by John Cleese). An improvement on the first film, this sequel is a straight-ahead, comedy-propelled ode to the Old West. James Stewart is wonderful as the voice of an over-the-hill law dog, and Dom DeLuise returns for more laughs as the wild and crazy Tiger. Rated G. 85m. **DIR:** Phil Nibbelink, Simon Wells. **1991**

AMERICAN TIGER ★★ A sexy and insipid tale of the return of a stolen statue to a Chinese princess who is scorned by her suitor. Set in Miami. Rated R for hot sex scenes and violence. 93m. **DIR:** Martin Dolman. **CAST:** Donald Pleasence, Mitch Gaylord, Daniel Greene. **1989**

AMERICAN WEREWOLF IN LONDON, AN ★★★1/2 Director John Landis weaves humor, violence, and the classic horror elements of suspense in the tale of the two American travelers who find more than they bargained for on the English moors. Rated R for violence, nudity, and gore. 97m. **DIR:** John Landis. **CAST:** David Naughton, Jenny Agutter, Griffin Dunne. **1981**

AMERICAN WEREWOLF IN PARIS, AN ★★ An American tourist becomes involved with a mysterious young French woman with a secret. No relation to John Landis's *An American Werewolf in London* and none of the earlier film's wit, suspense, or thrills. The trumped-up ending is especially contrived. Rated R for violence, nudity, and profanity. 97m. **DIR:** Anthony Waller. **CAST:** Tom Everett Scott, Julie Delpy, Vince Vieluf, Phil Buckman, Julie Bowen, Thierry Lhermitte. **1997 DVD**

AMERICAN YAKUZA ★★1/2 Variation on the theme features Viggo Mortensen as an FBI agent who infiltrates the American branch of the *yakuza*, only to have his loyalties waver as he rises through their ranks. Explosive finale pits the reluctant agent against former friends and new enemies. Rated R for violence, language, and adult situations. 96m. **DIR:** Frank Cappello. **CAST:** Viggo Mortensen, Michael Nouri, Franklin Ajaye, Robert Forster. **1993**

AMERICANA ★★1/2 Strange, offbeat film about a Vietnam veteran (director David Carradine) who attempts to rebuild a merry-go-round in a rural Kansas town and meets with hostility from the locals. Carradine attempts to make a statement about rebuilding America, but this gets lost in the impressionistic haze of his film. Rated PG for violence and profanity. 90m. **DIR:** David Carradine. **CAST:** David Carradine, Barbara Hershey, Michael Greene, Bruce Carradine, John Blythe Barrymore. **1981**

AMERICANIZATION OF EMILY, THE ★★★1/2 Who would think of turning the Normandy invasion into a massive publicity event? According to screenwriter

Paddy Chayefsky, the American military brass would drool over the possibilities. James Garner winningly plays the naval officer designated to be the first casualty on the beach. The script, intelligently handled by director Arthur Hiller, bristles with hard-edged humor. B&W; 117m. **DIR:** Arthur Hiller. **CAST:** James Garner, Julie Andrews, Melvyn Douglas, James Coburn, Joyce Grenfell, Keenan Wynn, Judy Carne. **1964**

AMERICANO, THE ★★1/2 Texas cowboy Glenn Ford gets embroiled with a bunch of Brazilian bad guys in this way-south-of-the-border Western. A change of scenery is commendable, but a familiar plot makes this film all but pedestrian. 85m. **DIR:** William Castle. **CAST:** Glenn Ford, Cesar Romero, Frank Lovejoy, Abbe Lane. **1954**

AMERICA'S DEADLIEST HOME VIDEO ★★★ Shot on video in a cinema verité style, this is a scathing remark on the society that has embraced reality shows like *Cops*. Here, Danny Bonaduce (?!) plays a man who inadvertently videotapes a robbery. The criminals kidnap him and then decide to have him chronicle their exploits. While the visual style becomes annoying after a half hour or so, the film still keeps a visceral punch that will leave you fascinated until the end. Not rated; contains graphic violence and profanity. 87m. **DIR:** Jack Perez. **CAST:** Danny Bonaduce. **1992**

AMERICA'S DREAM ★★★★ This compilation of three tales about the African American experience benefits from its strong cast and direction. In *Long Black Song*, Danny Glover plays a farmer whose love for his wife is tested when she falls for a traveling salesman. *The Reunion* features Lorraine Toussaint as a jazz piano player who confronts prejudices. The highlight of the trilogy, *The Boy Who Painted Christ*, stars Wesley Snipes as a small-town principal who must defend a student's painting of a black Christ. Made for cable. Rated PG-13 for profanity and adult situations. 86m. **DIR:** Bill Duke, Kevin Rodney Sullivan, Paris Barclay. **CAST:** Wesley Snipes, Danny Glover, Jasmine Guy, Lorraine Toussaint. **1995**

AMERICATHON 🐢 Abysmal comedy about a bankrupt American government staging a telethon to save itself. Rated R for profanity and sleaze. 86m. **DIR:** Neal Israel. **CAST:** John Ritter, Harvey Korman, Nancy Morgan, Peter Riegert, Zane Buzby, Fred Willard, Chief Dan George. **1979**

AMIN: THE RISE AND FALL 🐢 Idi Amin during his reign of terror in Uganda. Rated R for violence, nudity, and profanity. 101m. **DIR:** Richard Fleischer. **CAST:** Joseph Olita. **1981**

AMISTAD ★★★ An uprising aboard the Spanish slave ship *La Amistad* in 1839 boldly sets the stage to explore this real-life bloodbath and the exposure of the slaves to the American judicial system. Often riveting but runs out of intense drama well before it runs out of dry, windy speeches. Rated R for violence and nudity. 152m. **DIR:** Steven Spielberg. **CAST:** Djimon Hounsou, Anthony Hopkins, Morgan Freeman, Nigel Hawthorne, Stellan Skarsgard, Matthew McConaughey, Anna Paquin, David Paymer, Pete Postlethwaite. **1997 DVD**

AMITYVILLE HORROR, THE 🐢 A better title for this turgid mishmash would be *The Amityville Bore*.

Avoid it. Rated R. 117m. **DIR:** Stuart Rosenberg. **CAST:** James Brolin, Margot Kidder, Rod Steiger. **1979**

AMITYVILLE II: THE POSSESSION ★★ Okay, so it's not a horror classic. But thanks to tight pacing, skillful special effects, and fine acting, it is a fairly suspenseful flick. Rated R for violence, implied sex, light profanity, and adult themes. 104m. **DIR:** Damiano Damiani. **CAST:** Burt Young, Rutanya Alda, James Olson, Moses Gunn. **1982**

AMITYVILLE III: THE DEMON 🐢 In this soggy second sequel to *The Amityville Horror*, Tony Roberts plays a reporter who investigates the infamous house. Rated PG for violence and gore. 105m. **DIR:** Richard Fleischer. **CAST:** Tony Roberts, Candy Clark, Robert Joy, Tess Harper, Lori Loughlin, Meg Ryan. **1983**

AMITYVILLE 4: THE EVIL ESCAPES ★★ Rest easy: the most famous haunted house on Long Island and the subject of three earlier films is now demon-free. Unfortunately, the evil has relocated to Jane Wyatt's California homestead. Ridiculous TV movie. 95m. **DIR:** Sandor Stern. **CAST:** Patty Duke, Jane Wyatt, Norman Lloyd. **1989**

AMITYVILLE CURSE, THE ★★1/2 The famous house of hell shakes its walls and rattles its floors for the fifth time. In this chapter, three young couples have purchased the dreadful dwelling. Naturally, things aren't what they should be. Rated R. 92m. **DIR:** Tom Berry. **CAST:** Kim Coates. **1989**

AMITYVILLE 1992: IT'S ABOUT TIME 🐢 A possessed mantel clock takes its toll on an unsuspecting suburban family. This sixth installment of *The Amityville Horror* series has fair effects, but it hasn't any real suspense. Rated R for nudity, violence, and profanity. 95m. **DIR:** Tony Randel. **CAST:** Stephen Macht, Shawn Weatherly, Megan Ward, Damon Martin, Nita Talbot. **1992**

AMITYVILLE: A NEW GENERATION 🐢 Low-budget and none-too-creative. The ancient Amityville evil is now lurking behind a strange-looking mirror in the possession of a young artist. Rated R for profanity, nudity, and violence. 92m. **DIR:** John Murlowski. **CAST:** Ross Partridge, Julia Nickson, David Naughton, Richard Roundtree, Terry O'Quinn. **1993**

AMITYVILLE DOLLHOUSE ★★★ *The Amityville Horror* series continues with this direct-to-video effort about a possessed dollhouse. When a family moves into the notorious Amityville house, their young daughter is attracted to a replica dollhouse. Little does she know that the dollhouse is possessed by demons who immediately take over their entire family. Decent special effects and a constant feeling of doom keep the story moving. Rated R for language, violence, and sexuality. 97m. **DIR:** Steve White. **CAST:** Robin Thomas, Starr Andreeff. **1996**

AMNESIA ★★★ While plotting to fake his death so he can run away with his mistress, a small-town minister loses his memory after a bump on the head. This leads to complications as the plan he had been putting into effect catches up with him. A tongue-in-cheek erotic thriller that plays like a housebroken David Lynch film. Rated R for nudity, sexuality, profanity, and violence. 88m. **DIR:** Kurt Voss. **CAST:** Nicholas Walker, Dara Tomanovich, Sally Kirkland, Vin-

cent Berry, Ally Sheedy, Marthe Keller, John Savage.
1997

AMONG THE CINDERS ★★1/2 A teenager (Paul O'Shea) holds himself responsible for the accidental death of a friend, and it takes a trip to the wilds with his grandfather (Derek Hardwick) to pull him out of it. This coming-of-age drama from New Zealand has its good moments, but these are outnumbered by the unremarkable ones. Rated R for nudity, profanity, suggested sex, and brief gore. 105m. **DIR:** Rolf Haedrick. **CAST:** Paul O'Shea, Derek Hardwick. **1985**

•**AMONG THE LIVING** ★★★1/2 Unbalanced man thought long dead kills his keeper and joins the local populace, putting his twin brother in jeopardy. Strange psychological drama is a study in small-town life and mob mentality. Its earthy dialogue, frenzied action, and outstanding camera shots and composition belie its B-movie status, putting it on a par with the best productions of the day. Albert Dekker as the twin brothers and young Susan Hayward as a gutsy tart shine. B&W; 68m. **DIR:** Stuart Heisler. **CAST:** Albert Dekker, Harry Carey, Susan Hayward, Frances Farmer, Gordon Jones, Jean Phillips, Maude Eburne, Ernest Whitman. **1941**

AMONGST FRIENDS ★★★★ Writer-director Rob Weiss's compelling little study of youth led astray makes excellent use of its cast of newcomers. Steve Parlavecchio shines as one of three Long Island teenagers seduced by the easy money of organized crime. Given its humble origins, this is a far more palatable modern gangster drama than *Goodfellas*. Rated R for profanity, violence, and nudity. 88m. **DIR:** Rob Weiss. **CAST:** Steve Parlavecchio, Joseph Lindsey, Patrick McGaw, Mira Sorvino. **1993**

AMORE (1948) ★★★★ Director Roberto Rossellini's homage to actress Anna Magnani features her in two short films that showcase her brilliant talent. In "The Human Voice," based on a one-act play by Jean Cocteau, she is alone on-screen, engaged in a telephone conversation with an unseen lover. "The Miracle," inspired by a story by Federico Fellini, is a small masterpiece about a peasant woman who must defend her belief that she has given birth to the new Messiah. It was condemned by the U.S. Catholic church, which resulted in a landmark U.S. Supreme Court decision that films are protected by the First Amendment. In Italian with English subtitles. B&W; 78m. **DIR:** Roberto Rossellini. **CAST:** Anna Magnani. **1948**

AMORE! (1993) ★★★ *Cinderella* in reverse, this features a billionaire (Jack Scalia) heading for Hollywood to make it without using his wealth or connections. Succeeding only when he pretends to be an Italian stud, he must get his new girlfriend (Kathy Ireland) to love him for himself. Silly but likable time passer. Rated PG-13 for sexual situations. 93m. **DIR:** Lorenzo Doumani. **CAST:** Jack Scalia, Kathy Ireland, George Hamilton, Brenda Epperson. **1993**

AMOROUS ADVENTURES OF MOLL FLANDERS, THE ★★ Silly sex romp features a naughty Kim Novak sampling Englishmen's wares circa 1700. Howls rather than laughs result from her many sexual escapades. Not rated, this would be equivalent to a PG-13 for endless sexual situations and innuendo. 126m.

DIR: Terence Young. **CAST:** Kim Novak, Angela Lansbury, Richard Johnson, George Sanders. **1965**

AMOS & ANDREW ★★1/2 Samuel L. Jackson is a famous African-American playwright and activist who is mistaken for a burglar the first night in his new home on an exclusive New England resort island. Local sheriff Dabney Coleman forces jailed misfit Nicolas Cage to pretend to be a criminal who has taken Jackson hostage. Dumb but sometimes funny comedy full of goofy misunderstandings. Rated PG-13 for profanity and violence. 95m. **DIR:** E. Max Frye. **CAST:** Nicolas Cage, Samuel L. Jackson, Dabney Coleman, Michael Lerner, Margaret Colin, Brad Dourif, Chelcie Ross, Giancarlo Esposito. **1993**

AMOS AND ANDY (TV SERIES) ★★★ The first major television show with an all-black cast, *Amos and Andy* features sharp writing, energetic humor, and witty, memorable performances. CBS pulled the show in 1966 amid charges of racism, and rightfully so in that era. Now these surprisingly timeless comedies have been released on video, and they can be enjoyed if taken in the proper context. B&W; 30m. **DIR:** Charles Barton. **CAST:** Tim Moore, Spencer Williams Jr., Alvin Childress, Ernestine Wade, Amanda Randolph. **1951–1953**

AMSTERDAM KILL, THE ♥ Robert Mitchum stars in this dud about an international drug conspiracy. Rated R. 90m. **DIR:** Robert Clouse. **CAST:** Robert Mitchum, Bradford Dillman, Richard Egan, Leslie Nielsen, Keye Luke. **1977**

AMSTERDAMNED ♥ When a psycho killer comes up from the depths of the Amsterdam canals seeking prey, a Dutch cop and his buddy, a scuba-diving expert, try to reel him in. Rated R for violence. 114m. **DIR:** Dick Maas. **CAST:** Huub Stapel, Monique van de Ven. **1988**

AMY ★★★1/2 Disney warmth runs though this sensitive story. Jenny Agutter is Amy, a young woman who leaves her domineering husband after the death of their deaf son. She decides to teach at a school for the deaf. A film for the whole family. Rated G. 100m. **DIR:** Vincent McEveety. **CAST:** Jenny Agutter, Barry Newman, Kathleen Nolan, Chris Robinson, Margaret O'Brien, Nanette Fabray. **1981**

AMY FISHER STORY, THE ★★1/2 The best of the made-for-television movies about the Long Island Lolita, whose affair with auto mechanic Joey Buttafuoco led her to shoot Buttafuoco's wife, Mary Jo. Drew Barrymore effectively captures the spirit of the tempting teen, but steamy footage added for video features a body double. Not rated; contains adult situations. 96m. **DIR:** Andy Tennant. **CAST:** Drew Barrymore, Anthony Denison, Harley Jane Kozak. **1993**

ANACONDA ♥ A documentary-film crew, searching up the Amazon for a tribe of legendary Indians, finds instead a forty-foot killer snake. Asinine hodgepodge of monster movie clichés proves that money can't buy quality and even digital special effects can be cheesy. The wasted cast halfheartedly tries playing it for laughs. Rated PG-13 for profanity and unconvincing violence. 90m. **DIR:** Luis Llosa. **CAST:** Jennifer Lopez, Ice Cube, Jon Voight, Eric Stoltz, Jonathan Hyde, Owen C. Wilson, Kari Wuhrer. **1997 DVD**

ANALYZE THIS ★★★1/2 This very funny film, which borrows more than a little from James Coburn's 1967 counterculture hit, *The President's Analyst*, concerns what might happen if New York's toughest gangster suddenly found himself in need of therapy. When the mob boss is Robert De Niro, and the shrink is Billy Crystal, the results are quite entertaining. The supporting cast is laced with familiar character actors, none better than Joe Viterelli, simply priceless as De Niro's bodyguard. You'll be tempted into repeat viewings to catch the dialogue overshadowed the first time by the continuous laughter. Rated R for relentless profanity and considerable—albeit rather bloodless—gunfire. 106m. **DIR:** Harold Ramis. **CAST:** Robert De Niro, Billy Crystal, Lisa Kudrow, Joe Viterelli, Chazz Palminteri. **1999 DVD**

ANASTASIA (1956) ★★★1/2 Ingrid Bergman earned her second Oscar for the title role of the young woman who looks amazingly like Anastasia, Czar Nicholas's daughter. (The entire royal family was supposedly assassinated.) Is she or isn't she Anastasia? A compelling drama. 105m. **DIR:** Anatole Litvak. **CAST:** Ingrid Bergman, Yul Brynner, Helen Hayes, Akim Tamiroff. **1956**

ANASTASIA (1997) ★★★1/2 Twentieth Century Fox's first animated feature uses the Russian Revolution as a starting point for a lavish musical fairy-tale romance. This gorgeously rendered story begins in 1916 as evil sorcerer Rasputin puts a curse on the reigning Romanov family. Only the czar's daughter, Anastasia, and her grandmother survive. Ten years later the orphaned teen is struggling with amnesia when she crosses paths with her exiled grandmother in Paris. Rated G. 94m. **DIR:** Don Bluth, Gary Goldman. **CAST:** Meg Ryan, John Cusack, Angela Lansbury, Christopher Lloyd, Kelsey Grammer, Kirsten Dunst (voices). **1997 DVD**

ANASTASIA: THE MYSTERY OF ANNA ★★1/2 Star-studded cast can't compensate for the uninspired performance by Amy Irving in the title role of this TV miniseries. She plays the mysterious woman who appeared six years after the Romanov Royalty of Russia were annihilated, claiming to have survived. Rex Harrison plays her staunchest adversary as the current head of the Romanov family. Costuming and music are superior. 208m. **DIR:** Marvin J. Chomsky. **CAST:** Amy Irving, Rex Harrison, Edward Fox, Olivia de Havilland, Omar Sharif, Susan Lucci. **1986**

ANATOMY OF A MURDER ★★★★ A clever plot, realistic atmosphere, smooth direction, and sterling performances from a topflight cast make this frank and exciting small-town courtroom drama first-rate fare. Honest realism saturates throughout. B&W; 160m. **DIR:** Otto Preminger. **CAST:** James Stewart, Arthur O'Connell, Lee Remick, Ben Gazzara, Eve Arden, Kathryn Grant, George C. Scott, Joseph Welch, Orson Bean, Murray Hamilton. **1959**

ANCHORS AWEIGH ★★★ A somewhat tedious and overlong dance film that is perked up by a few truly impressive numbers, none finer than Gene Kelly's duet with an animated Jerry the mouse (of Tom and Jerry fame). Not rated; suitable for family viewing. 140m. **DIR:** George Sidney. **CAST:** Gene Kelly, Frank Sinatra, Kathryn Grayson, Dean Stockwell. **1945 DVD**

AND BABY MAKES SIX ★★★ Colleen Dewhurst is a middle-aged mother who becomes pregnant. It's too much for her loving husband (Warren Oates), who just doesn't want the responsibility of another child. A wonderful cast proved this made-for-TV movie good enough to produce a sequel, *Baby Comes Home*. 104m. **DIR:** Waris Hussein. **CAST:** Colleen Dewhurst, Warren Oates, Mildred Dunnock, Maggie Cooper, Timothy Hutton. **1979**

AND GOD CREATED WOMAN (1957) ★★1/2 Brigitte Bardot rose to international fame as the loose-moraled coquette who finds it hard to say no to an attractive male, especially a well-heeled one. Shot with as much of Bardot exposed as the law then allowed, this rather slight story works well. In French with English subtitles. 92m. **DIR:** Roger Vadim. **CAST:** Brigitte Bardot, Curt Jurgens, Jean-Louis Trintignant, Christian Marquand. **1957**

AND GOD CREATED WOMAN (1987) 🐢 Rebecca DeMornay is unbelievable as a convict who tries to go straight. Rated R for language, nudity, and simulated sex. 97m. **DIR:** Roger Vadim. **CAST:** Rebecca De-Mornay, Vincent Spano, Frank Langella, Donovan Leitch. **1987 DVD**

AND GOD SAID TO CAIN 🐢 Gary Hamilton is released from prison, and he seeks to kill the men who framed him. The climax of the film looks like it was filmed in a coal mine at midnight. Even a full-length appearance by Klaus Kinski can't save this mess. Not rated, contains violence. 99m. **DIR:** Anthony M. Dawson. **CAST:** Klaus Kinski, Peter Carsten, Calla Michelangeli, Lee Burton, Alan Collins. **1969**

... AND GOD SPOKE ★★★1/2 Frequently hilarious mock-u-mentary about the efforts to film a large-scale religious epic. Michael Riley and Stephen Rappaport are believable as the director and producer who watch as their big-budget effort is whittled down to a renegade, zero-budget production. Industry in-jokes may fly over the heads of some viewers, but you can't help but laugh at Soupy Sales playing Moses, carrying two tablets and a six-pack of soda as part of a product-placement deal. Rated R for language and nudity. 82m. **DIR:** Arthur Borman. **CAST:** Michael Riley, Stephen Rappaport, Soupy Sales, Eve Plumb. **1994**

AND HOPE TO DIE ★★★1/2 A Frenchman who is on the run from thugs hides out with an old gangster who enlists him in a kidnap scheme. Complex, well-acted crime-drama. Rated R for nudity and violence. 95m. **DIR:** René Clement. **CAST:** Robert Ryan, Tisa Farrow, Jean-Louis Trintignant, Lea Massari, Aldo Ray. **1972**

AND I ALONE SURVIVED ★★1/2 In this TV movie Blair Brown stars as Lauren Elder, the only survivor of a plane crash in California's Sierra Nevada mountains. Based on a true event, the film tends toward the overdramatic and begs for better characterizations. Still, Brown does give a fine performance. 100m. **DIR:** William A. Graham. **CAST:** Blair Brown, David Ackroyd, Vera Miles, G. D. Spradlin. **1978**

... AND JUSTICE FOR ALL ★★★1/2 This is a bristling black comedy starring Al Pacino as a lawyer who becomes fed up with the red tape of our country's legal system. It's both heartrending and darkly hilarious—but not for all tastes. Rated R. 117m. DIR: Norman Jewison. CAST: Al Pacino, Jack Warden, John Forsythe, Craig T. Nelson. **1979**

AND NOTHING BUT THE TRUTH ★★★ A British film about a TV news magazine—an Anglo *A Current Affair*. Glenda Jackson stars as a documentary filmmaker who must confront a sometimes exploitative reporter (well played by Jon Finch). Superficial but interesting. 90m. DIR: Karl Francis. CAST: Glenda Jackson, Jon Finch, Kenneth Colley. **1982**

AND NOW FOR SOMETHING COMPLETELY DIFFERENT ★★★1/2 Fitfully funny but still a treat for their fans, this was the first screen outing of the Monty Python comedy troupe. It's a collection of the best bits from the team's television series. With delightful ditties, such as "The Lumberjack Song," how can you go wrong? Rated PG. 89m. DIR: Ian McNaughton. CAST: John Cleese, Eric Idle, Terry Jones, Michael Palin, Graham Chapman, Terry Gilliam. **1972** DVD

AND NOW, MY LOVE ★★★1/2 In biography-documentary style, director Claude Lelouch juxtaposes three generations of a family while depicting the moral, political, and artistic events that shaped the members' lives. All this is wonderfully designed to show how inevitable it is for two young people (played by André Dussolier and Marthe Keller) from different backgrounds to fall in love. French, dubbed in English. 121m. DIR: Claude Lelouch. CAST: Marthe Keller, André Dussolier, Charles Denner. **1974**

AND NOW THE SCREAMING STARTS ★★★ Frightening British horror film about a young newly-wed couple moving into a house haunted by a centuries-old curse on the husband's family. Well-done, with a great cast, but occasionally a bit too bloody. Rated R. 87m. DIR: Roy Ward Baker. CAST: Peter Cushing, Stephanie Beacham, Herbert Lom, Patrick Magee, Ian Ogilvy. **1973**

AND SOON THE DARKNESS ★★1/2 Two young English college girls decide to go bicycle touring through the French countryside. But when the more vivacious of the two suddenly disappears in the same spot where a young girl was killed the year before, the foundation is laid for a tale of suspense. Rated PG. 94m. DIR: Robert Fuest. CAST: Pamela Franklin, Michele Dotrice, Sandor Eles. **1970**

AND THE BAND PLAYED ON ★★★★1/2 A gripping adaptation of journalist Randy Shilts's book about the early days of the AIDS epidemic. Matthew Modine leads an all-star cast as a scientist with the Centers for Disease Control who must battle bureaucracy and ignorance to show that AIDS is everyone's problem. Part detective thriller, part tearjerker, this film drives home its message. Rated PG-13 for adult themes. 140m. DIR: Roger Spottiswoode. CAST: Matthew Modine, Alan Alda, Phil Collins, Richard Gere, Anjelica Huston, Steve Martin, Ian McKellen, Lily Tomlin. **1993**

AND THE SHIP SAILS ON ★★ Federico Fellini's heavily symbolic parable about a luxury liner sailing the Adriatic on the eve of World War I was called by one critic "a spellbinding, often magical tribute to the illusions and delusions of art." That's one way of looking at it. We found it boring. However, Fellini fans may find it rewarding. In Italian with English subtitles. 138m. DIR: Federico Fellini. CAST: Freddie Jones, Barbara Jefford, Victor Poletti. **1984** DVD

AND THEN THERE WERE NONE ★★★★ One of the best screen adaptations of an Agatha Christie mystery. A select group of people is invited to a lonely island and murdered one by one. René Clair's inspired visual style gives this release just the right atmosphere and tension. B&W; 98m. DIR: René Clair. CAST: Barry Fitzgerald, Walter Huston, Richard Haydn, Roland Young, Judith Anderson, Louis Hayward, June Duprez, C. Aubrey Smith. **1945**

AND THEN YOU DIE ★★★★ Canadian version of *The Long Good Friday*. Kenneth Welsh is Eddie Griffin, drug czar for Canada's coke freaks. His kingdom starts unraveling around him after the Mafia don in his area is murdered. Eddie gets caught in a squeeze play between the don's successor, an up-and-coming coke dealer, and the police. The film grabs you right from the opening frame and keeps you guessing right up to the final scene. 115m. DIR: Francis Mankiewicz. CAST: Kenneth Welsh, R. H. Thomson, Wayne Robson, Tom Harvey, George Bloomfield, Graeme Campbell. **1987**

AND YOU THOUGHT YOUR PARENTS WERE WEIRD ★★ After the death of their inventor father, two brothers devote their time and energy to following in his footsteps. Celestial intervention instills the spirit of their dad into their latest invention: a robot. Thin family fare. Rated PG. 92m. DIR: Tony Goodson. CAST: Marcia Strassman, Joshua Miller, Edan Gross, Alan Thicke. **1991**

ANDERSON TAPES, THE ★★★★ Sean Connery is perfectly cast in this exciting film about an ex-con under surveillance who wants to pull off the Big Heist. Slickly done, with tight editing and direction to keep the viewer totally involved, it holds up extremely well on video. Rated PG. 98m. DIR: Sidney Lumet. CAST: Sean Connery, Dyan Cannon, Martin Balsam, Ralph Meeker, Margaret Hamilton. **1972**

ANDERSONVILLE ★★★★ Harrowing Civil War drama focuses on the inhumane conditions suffered by prisoners of war at the Confederate Andersonville compound. As told through the eyes of a young Union corporal, director John Frankenheimer's film is a testament to the human soul and spirit. Powerful, hard-hitting performances and a tough, literate script by David W. Rintels combine to make this made-for-cable film an experience that's hard to forget. Not rated; contains profanity and violence. 168m. DIR: John Frankenheimer. CAST: Jarrod Emrick, Frederic Forrest, William H. Macy, Jan Triska, Ted Marcoux. **1996**

ANDERSONVILLE TRIAL, THE ★★★★1/2 Based on MacKinley Kantor's Pulitzer Prize novel, this made-for-TV play tells the story of Andersonville, the notorious Georgia prison where 50,000 northern soldiers suffered and close to 14,000 died. This is one of the great accounts of the Civil War. 150m. DIR: George C. Scott. CAST: Martin Sheen, William Shatner, Buddy Ebsen, Richard Basehart, Cameron Mitchell, Jack Cassidy. **1970**

ANDRE ★★★★ First-class family entertainment features a bright-eyed youngster who becomes best friends with a seal, played with remarkable versatility and skill by Tory, the sea lion. Based on a true story, *Andre* details the conflict that arises when local fishermen in Rockport, Maine, and an animal-protection agency threaten to tear the twosome apart. Kids will love it, and so will their parents. Rated PG for a very brief fistfight. 94m. **DIR:** George Miller. **CAST:** Keith Carradine, Tina Majorino, Chelsea Field, Aidan Pendleton, Shane Meier, Keith Szarabajka. 1994

ANDREI RUBLEV ★★★★★ Considered by many to be the most important Russian film of the past thirty years, this epic is based on the life of Andrei Rublev, a monk and icon painter who wanders through a gruesome landscape, clinging to religious faith in the face of barbarism and pagan rituals in fifteenth-century Russia, then under the reign of Tartar invaders. Mesmerizing! In Russian with English subtitles. B&W; 185m. **DIR:** Andrei Tarkovsky. **CAST:** Andrej Mikhalkov, Andrei Tarkovsky. 1966 DVD

ANDROCLES AND THE LION ★★1/2 An incredible cast still can't save this plodding story of a mild-mannered tailor (Alan Young) whose act of kindness toward a lion helps to save a group of Christians. George Bernard Shaw's pointed retelling of an old fable loses its bite in this rambling production. B&W; 105m. **DIR:** Chester Erskine. **CAST:** Alan Young, Jean Simmons, Victor Mature, Robert Newton, Maurice Evans, Elsa Lanchester, Reginald Gardiner, Gene Lockhart, Alan Mowbray, John Hoyt, Jim Backus. 1952

ANDROID ★★★★ A highly enjoyable tongue-in-cheek sci-fi adventure takes place on a space station where a mad scientist, Dr. Daniel (played by a surprisingly subdued and effective Klaus Kinski), is trying to create the perfect android. As a group of criminal castaways arrives at the station, the doctor's current robot assistant, Max 404 (Don Opper), decides it is time to rebel. Rated PG for nudity, violence, and profanity. 80m. **DIR:** Aaron Lipstadt. **CAST:** Klaus Kinski, Don Opper, Brie Howard, Norbert Weisser. 1982

ANDROID AFFAIR, THE ★★1/2 In this made-for-cable original, a doctor falls in love with her android patient while on the run from the people who make the androids. Interesting characters, but a slow, dull plot. Not rated; contains violence. 95m. **DIR:** Richard Kletter. **CAST:** Harley Jane Kozak, Ossie Davis, Saul Rubinek, Griffin Dunne. 1995

ANDROMEDA STRAIN, THE ★★★★ A tense science-fiction thriller, this film focuses on a team of scientists attempting to isolate a deadly virus while racing against time and the possibility of nuclear war. Though not as flashy as other entries in the genre, it's highly effective. Rated G. 130m. **DIR:** Robert Wise. **CAST:** Arthur Hill, David Wayne, James Olson, Kate Reid, Paula Kelly. 1971 DVD

ANDY GRIFFITH SHOW, THE (TV SERIES) ★★★★ Six volumes of one of television's most fondly remembered situation comedies. This series takes place in fictitious Mayberry, North Carolina, a sleepy little town looked after by laid-back sheriff Andy Taylor and his manic deputy, Barney Fife (Don Knotts, winner of numerous Emmy Awards for his portrayal). Each volume contains four episodes spotlighting a particular character's most memorable moments.

B&W; 100m. **DIR:** Various. **CAST:** Andy Griffith, Don Knotts, Ron Howard, Jim Nabors, Frances Bavier, Howard McNear, George Lindsey, Hal Smith, Howard Morris. 1960–1965 DVD

ANDY HARDY GETS SPRING FEVER ★★★ Another in the long-running series about all-American life in a small town. This installment finds Andy Hardy (Mickey Rooney) saddled with the trials and tribulations of producing his high-school play. B&W; 85m. **DIR:** W. S. Van Dyke. **CAST:** Mickey Rooney, Lewis Stone, Fay Holden, Cecilia Parker, Ann Rutherford. 1939

ANDY HARDY MEETS A DEBUTANTE ★★★ Mickey Rooney again portrays the all-American teenager who dominated the long-running series. Good, wholesome family-film fare. B&W; 86m. **DIR:** George B. Seitz. **CAST:** Mickey Rooney, Lewis Stone, Cecilia Parker, Fay Holden, Judy Garland. 1940

ANDY HARDY'S DOUBLE LIFE ★★★ Fresh from championship swimming, Esther Williams got her studio start in this warm and sentimental addition to the hit series. B&W; 92m. **DIR:** George B. Seitz. **CAST:** Mickey Rooney, Lewis Stone, Cecilia Parker, Fay Holden, Ann Rutherford, Esther Williams, William Lundigan. 1942

ANDY HARDY'S PRIVATE SECRETARY ★★★ Kathryn Grayson is the focus in this slice of wholesome Americana from the innocent days just before World War II. Fun for the whole family. B&W; 101m. **DIR:** George B. Seitz. **CAST:** Mickey Rooney, Lewis Stone, Fay Holden, Ian Hunter, Kathryn Grayson, Gene Reynolds, Ann Rutherford. 1940

ANDY WARHOL: SUPERSTAR ★★★★ Thoroughly fascinating exploration of the pop icon's life and times, featuring a bevy of celebrities stepping forward with their recollections. Director Chuck Workman's film is like a time capsule filled with precious memories. 87m. **DIR:** Chuck Workman. 1991

ANDY WARHOL'S BAD ★★★1/2 Carroll Baker stars in this nasty and very sick outing from producer Andy Warhol. She plays a tough mama who runs a squad of female hit men out of her cheery suburban home. Into this strange company comes Perry King as a mysterious stranger who boards there until he completes his "mission." The film has gore, violence, and nudity. 107m. **DIR:** Jed Johnson. **CAST:** Carroll Baker, Perry King, Susan Tyrrell. 1977

ANDY WARHOL'S DRACULA 🎬 Companion piece to Andy Warhol's equally revolting version of *Frankenstein*. Rated X for excessive violence and kinky sex. 93m. **DIR:** Paul Morrissey. **CAST:** Udo Kier, Joe Dallesandro, Vittorio De Sica, Roman Polanski. 1974

ANDY WARHOL'S FRANKENSTEIN 🎬 Blood and gore gush at every opportunity. Rated R for obvious reasons. 94m. **DIR:** Paul Morrissey. **CAST:** Joe Dallesandro, Monique Van Vooren, Udo Kier. 1974

ANGEL 🎬 Bad, low-budget flick about a 15-year-old who moonlights as a Hollywood Boulevard hooker and is menaced by a psychotic killer. Rated R for nudity, violence, suggested sex, and profanity. 94m. **DIR:** Robert Vincent O'Neil. **CAST:** Cliff Gorman, Susan Tyrrell, Dick Shawn, Donna Wilkes. 1983

ANGEL 4: UNDERCOVER ★★ Darlene Vogel inherits the role of ex-hooker turned police photographer. This outing, Angel goes undercover to find out who killed one of her friends from her hooking days and gets involved with a hard-rocking band and its charismatic leader, played by Shane Fraser. Roddy McDowall chews more than scenery as the band's slimy producer who's not above blackmail. Rated R for nudity, language, and violence. 94m. DIR: George Axmith. CAST: Darlene Vogel, Shane Fraser, Mark De-Carlo, Kerrie Clark, Roddy McDowall. 1994

ANGEL AND THE BADMAN ★★★★ A fine low-budget Western with John Wayne as a gunman who sees the light through the love of Quaker girl Gail Russell. Harry Carey and Bruce Cabot also are memorable in this thoughtful action film directed by longtime Wayne screenwriter James Edward Grant. B&W; 100m. DIR: James Edward Grant. CAST: John Wayne, Gail Russell, Harry Carey, Irene Rich, Bruce Cabot. 1947 DVD

ANGEL AT MY TABLE, AN ★★★★★ New Zealand filmmaker Jane Campion's brilliant, affecting, and perceptive portrait of writer Janet Frame, detailing her emotional journey through a quirky childhood, a misdiagnosis of mental illness, and a severe, lifelong shyness. If you liked My Left Foot, you should love this story of an exceptional artist. Rated R for profanity and sexual frankness. 145m. DIR: Jane Campion. CAST: Kerry Fox, Alexia Keogh, Karen Fergusson. 1991

ANGEL BABY ★★★ Psychotic patients Harry and Kate meet at a walk-in treatment center and fall in love in this gritty Australian drama. The odds against their romance and independence skyrocket when Kate becomes pregnant and they flush their medications down the toilet to protect the health of their unborn child. This offbeat film about the power of love and inner demons has several storyline cracks but the acting is excellent. Not rated; contains graphic sex and frontal nudity. 105m. DIR: Michael Rymer. CAST: John Lynch, Jacqueline McKenzie, Colin Friels, Deborra-Lee Furness. 1995

ANGEL CITY ★★★ A family is forced to leave their West Virginia farm and travel to Florida in search of work. Exploited by a corrupt labor-camp boss, the family members open the gates for all the immigrant workers to escape and start their lives again. Made for television. 100m. DIR: Philip Leacock. CAST: Jennifer Warren, Jennifer Jason Leigh, Mitchell Ryan. 1980

ANGEL FIST ★★ This Roger Corman production combines high kicks with hot babes. In it, a beautiful policewoman goes to Manila to avenge her sister's death. Watchable, but not twice! Rated R for nudity, sex, profanity, and violence. 76m. DIR: Cirio H. Santiago. CAST: Cat Sassoon, Melissa Moore, Michael Shaner, Denise Buick, Jessica Roberts. 1993

ANGEL HEART ★★★1/2 Mickey Rourke stars as a down-and-out private investigator. The elegant, dapper, and more than slightly sinister Louis Cyphre (Robert De Niro) wants a missing singer found in order to settle a vague "debt." Absolutely not for the squeamish or for children; rated R for violence, sex, and language. 113m. DIR: Alan Parker. CAST: Mickey Rourke, Lisa Bonet, Robert De Niro, Charlotte Rampling. 1987 DVD

ANGEL IN TRAINING ★★ Low-rent family fare about a 12-year-old girl who recruits her guardian angels to help save her dad's business from an untrustworthy business partner. The film wants to be another Angels in the Outfield but lacks the imagination. Rated G. 90m. DIR: Gary Graver, Chick Vennera. CAST: Laila Dagher, Gary Imhoff, Alexis O'Keefe. 1997 DVD

ANGEL OF DEATH 💔 Even among the lowly subgenre of Nazi revival movies, this rates near the bottom of the list. Rated R for violence and profanity. 90m. DIR: Jess (Jesus) Franco. CAST: Susan Andrews, Howard Vernon. 1986

ANGEL OF DESTRUCTION ★★ When it comes to female martial arts stars, Maria Ford has a leg up on her competition. Not that she's more talented, but Ford realizes her assets and uses them accordingly. She's tracking down the serial killer who iced her sister, an undercover cop hot on the killer's trail. Plot seems overly familiar, but the presence of Ford makes the action easier to watch. Rated R for nudity, violence, and adult situations. 80m. DIR: Charles Philip Moore. CAST: Maria Ford, Charlie Spradling, Jimmy Broome, Chanda. 1994

ANGEL OF FURY 💔 Bottom-end martial arts trash, with security expert Cynthia Rothrock trying to keep a valuable computer out of enemy hands. If she could act ten times as well as she kicks ... she'd still be terrible. Rated R for violence, torture, and profanity. 76m. DIR: Ackyl Anwarv. CAST: Cynthia Rothrock, Christopher Daniel Barnes, Peter O'Brian. 1993

ANGEL OF H.E.A.T. 💔 Not enough sex and skin for the hard-core crowd, and not enough plot, good acting, or production values for the spy flick lovers. Rated R. 93m. DIR: Myrl A. Schreibman. CAST: Marilyn Chambers, Dan Jesse, Mary Woronov, Stephen Johnson. 1982

ANGEL ON MY SHOULDER (1946) ★★★★ In a break from his big-budget prestige screen biographies of the period, Paul Muni stars in this entertaining fantasy as a murdered gangster who makes a deal with the devil. He wants to return to his human form. He gets his wish and spends his time on Earth—as a judge—trying to outwit Satan. B&W; 101m. DIR: Archie Mayo. CAST: Paul Muni, Anne Baxter, Claude Rains, George Cleveland, Onslow Stevens. 1946

ANGEL ON MY SHOULDER (1980) ★★★ Remade-for-television update of the 1946 Paul Muni fantasy about a wrongly murdered gangster returned to Earth on a Satanic errand. Genial comedy-drama. 100m. DIR: John Berry. CAST: Peter Strauss, Richard Kiley, Barbara Hershey, Janis Paige. 1980

ANGEL TOWN 💔 An olympic kick-boxing trainer goes feet to head with street toughs. This anti–Mexican-American, anti-woman film is wimpy and stupid. Rated R for nudity, profanity, and violence. 102m. DIR: Eric Karson. CAST: Olivier Gruner, Theresa Saldana, Frank Aragon. 1990 DVD

ANGELA ★★ Sophia Loren's 5-month-old son is kidnapped by feisty mob king John Huston. Twenty years pass, and she falls in love with a much younger man. Could the bond be more than originally thought? Turgid. 90m. **DIR:** Boris Sagal. **CAST:** Sophia Loren, Steve Railsback, John Huston, John Vernon. **1977**

•**ANGELA'S ASHES** ★★★★ Frank McCourt's evocative memoir is realized with impressive verisimilitude in this handsome drama, which recreates every detail of the bone-grinding, heartbreaking poverty the author endured during his childhood in Ireland. Director Alan Parker and coadaptor Laura Jones retain the pragmatic, cheerful optimism that defines McCourt's book: a child's forgiving willingness to see things in their best possible light. Various compelling young actors play McCourt during his childhood years; good as they are, they're overshadowed by Emily Watson's sterling portrayal of the boy's mother. Despite humiliation and debasement most of us would find inconceivable, this woman never loses sight of her primary goal: to protect and provide for her children. This film will, in time, take its place alongside other rich period dramas and memoirs such as *Doctor Zhivago, Hope and Glory*, and *Remains of the Day* ... all films with the power to make us part of a historic setting and time that we never personally experienced. Rated R for profanity, nudity, and earthy dramatic content. 146m. **DIR:** Alan Parker. **CAST:** Emily Watson, Robert Carlyle, Michael Legge, Ciaran Owens, Joe Breen. **1999 DVD**

ANGELE ★★★1/2 Absorbing character study that blends comedy with drama in a story about a young French girl who becomes bored with life in the country and is lured into a sleazy existence in Paris with an older street hustler. A poignant drama in the tradition of Jean Renoir. In French with English subtitles. B&W; 132m. **DIR:** Marcel Pagnol. **CAST:** Orane Demazis, Fernandel, Jean Servais. **1934**

ANGELIC CONVERSATION ★★ Eclectic filmmaker and painter Derek Jarman delves into a very personal perspective of his world. A mythic figure summons his inner self to join him on a spiritual quest. Boring, heavy-handed self-indulgence saturated with personal passions and vivid visual fantasies. Liberally laced with narrations of Shakespearean sonnets by Judi Dench. 80m. **DIR:** Derek Jarman. **CAST:** Paul Reynolds, Phillip Williamson. **1985**

ANGELO, MY LOVE ★★★★ Robert Duvall wrote and directed this loosely scripted, wonderfully different movie about a streetwise 11-year-old gypsy boy. Duvall reportedly conceived the project when he spotted the fast-talking, charismatic Angelo Evans on a New York street and decided he ought to be in pictures. Rated R for profanity. 115m. **DIR:** Robert Duvall. **CAST:** Angelo Evans, Michael Evans. **1983**

ANGELS AND INSECTS ★★★★ A mild-mannered naturalist in Victorian England lives with an aristocratic family, finding ironic similarities between his hosts and the bugs he studies. The film is low-key and leisurely paced, but subtly perceptive, probing under the surface of Victorian society. Excellent performances, especially by Kristin Scott Thomas as a poor relation dependent on the generosity of her intellectual inferiors. Not rated; contains graphic simulated sex and frontal nudity. 117m. **DIR:** Philip Haas.

CAST: Mark Rylance, Patsy Kensit, Kristin Scott Thomas, Jeremy Kemp, Annette Badland, Douglas Henshall, Anna Massey. **1996**

•**ANGEL'S DANCE** ★★★1/2 James Belushi plays a skilled hit man who is hired to train a naïve would-be assassin. For the final test, a name is chosen at random from the phone book, and it's up to the novice to terminate this person as efficiently and as quickly as possible. The hit is botched, leaving Angel Chaste wondering why someone wants her dead. She in turn does a little training of her own, all the while evading the frustrated killer on her trail. The final showdown is quite satisfying and not completely predictable. Rated R primarily for violence and language. 90m. **DIR:** David L. Corley. **CAST:** James Belushi, Kyle Chandler, Sheryl Lee, Mac Davis, Jon Polito. **1999 DVD**

ANGELS DIE HARD ★★ The bikers turn out to help a community during a mining disaster. Less ridiculous than most of its predecessors and contemporaries. Look for Dan Haggerty in an early role. Violence; adult situations. Rated R. 86m. **DIR:** Richard Compton. **CAST:** William Smith, Tom Baker, R. G. Armstrong, Dan Haggerty. **1970**

ANGELS HARD AS THEY COME ★★1/2 An above-average biker gang movie. Distinguished mainly by its reasonably authentic look and feel, due largely to the contribution of Jonathan Demme, who cowrote and produced. Rated R for violence and nudity. 86m. **DIR:** Joe Viola. **CAST:** Scott Glenn, Charles Dierkop, Gary Busey. **1972**

ANGELS IN THE OUTFIELD (1951) ★★★1/2 A gruff manager of a losing baseball team is approached by an angel who beseeches him to give up his swearing and his angry attitude. In exchange, angels will help the team earn the pennant. Charming little fantasy. Not rated, but acceptable for family viewing. B&W; 102m. **DIR:** Clarence Brown. **CAST:** Paul Douglas, Janet Leigh, Keenan Wynn, Donna Corcoran, Lewis Stone, Ellen Corby. **1951**

ANGELS IN THE OUTFIELD (1994) ★★★1/2 Youngsters should fully enjoy this tale of a boy who gets some special, spiritual help in supporting his favorite baseball team, the Angels. Fans of the 1951 original may pooh-pooh, but there's certainly nothing offensive about this bit of wish fulfillment. Danny Glover, as the disbelieving-at-first coach, Christopher Lloyd, as the head angel, and the venerable Ben Johnson, as the team's Gene Autry–like owner, add class to the proceedings. Rated PG. 102m. **DIR:** William Dear. **CAST:** Danny Glover, Tony Danza, Brenda Fricker, Christopher Lloyd, Jay O. Sanders, Joseph Gordon-Levitt, Milton Davis Jr., Taylor Negron. **1994**

ANGELS OVER BROADWAY ★★★ Codirected by legendary newsmen and playwrights Ben Hecht and Lee Garmes, this tale of streetwise Douglas Fairbanks's efforts to save would-be suicide John Qualen is full of great dialogue and pithy comments on life. But it lacks the charm that would mark it as a true classic. Recommended for its dialogue, as well as its odd tone. B&W; 80m. **DIR:** Ben Hecht, Lee Garmes. **CAST:** Douglas Fairbanks Jr., Rita Hayworth, Thomas Mitchell, John Qualen. **1940**

ANGELS WITH DIRTY FACES ★★★★1/2 This is thoroughly enjoyable entertainment. The plot is that old Hollywood standby about two childhood friends, the one who goes bad (James Cagney) and the other who follows the right path (Pat O'Brien, as the priest), and the conflict between them. Yet, as directed by Warner Bros. stalwart Michael Curtiz, it often seems surprisingly fresh. B&W; 97m. **DIR:** Michael Curtiz. **CAST:** James Cagney, Pat O'Brien, Humphrey Bogart, Ann Sheridan, George Bancroft, Bobby Jordan. **1938**

ANGIE ★★★★ Emotionally involved tale of a Bensonhurst, NY, woman who becomes pregnant and begins questioning everything about her life—especially when she meets a witty, romantic Englishman (Stephen Rea) who's everything her working-class boyfriend (James Gandolfini) isn't. Geena Davis is excellent as the Italian-American heroine, who isn't always sympathetic but will touch something deep in viewers' hearts. There are some very funny moments as well. Rated R for adult subject matter. 108m. **DIR:** Martha Coolidge. **CAST:** Geena Davis, Stephen Rea, James Gandolfini, Aida Turturro, Philip Bosco, Jenny O'Hara. **1994**

ANGKOR: CAMBODIA EXPRESS 🖤 In this subpar variation on *The Killing Fields*, Robert Walker plays an American journalist who left his girlfriend (Nancy Kwan) behind in Cambodia and returns to bring her out. 86m. **DIR:** Alex King. **CAST:** Robert Walker Jr., Christopher George, Woody Strode, Nancy Kwan. **1985**

ANGRY HARVEST ★★★★ This drama from director Agnieszka Holland features Fassbinder veterans Armin Mueller-Stahl and Elisabeth Trissenaar in a mesmerizing thriller about a Jewish woman who escapes from a train bound for the Nazi death camps. The film features brilliant performances. In German with English subtitles. Not rated; contains nudity and violence. 102m. **DIR:** Agnieszka Holland. **CAST:** Armin Mueller-Stahl, Elisabeth Trissenaar. **1986**

ANGRY RED PLANET, THE ★★1/2 Entertaining (if unoriginal) science-fiction tale of an expedition to Mars running into all sorts of alien terrors, most notable of which is a terrifying kind of giant mouse/spider hybrid. A fun film, though it takes forever to get to the action. 83m. **DIR:** Ib Melchior. **CAST:** Gerald Mohr, Nora Hayden, Les Tremayne, Jack Kruschen. **1959**

ANGUISH ★★★★ This horror-thriller is actually a movie within a movie. The first portion deals with a mother and son's odd relationship that has him murdering people for their eyes, while the second portion is actually about an audience watching the film and being terrorized by an unknown killer. *Not* recommended for those with weak stomachs. Rated R. 85m. **DIR:** Bigas Luna. **CAST:** Zelda Rubinstein, Michael Lerner. **1988 DVD**

ANGUS ★★★ Throughout his formative years Angus has been the butt of mean-spirited "fat boy" jokes. In his sophomore year, he gets blindsided by a lifelong enemy's prank when he is elected winterball king and must dance with a cheerleader whom he has forever adored from afar. This gentle rite of passage is predictable, but full of genuine warmth. Rated PG-13 for language. 87m. **DIR:** Patrick Read Johnson. **CAST:** Charlie Talbert, Ariana Richards, Chris

Owen, George C. Scott, Kathy Bates, James van der Beek. **1995**

ANIMAL BEHAVIOR ★★★ This comedy features Karen Allen as a behaviorist testing a chimp named Michael. Armand Assante, as the university's new music professor, falls for Allen. Plenty of misunderstandings add to the fun. Rated PG for no apparent reason. 79m. **DIR:** H. Anne Riley. **CAST:** Armand Assante, Karen Allen, Holly Hunter, Josh Mostel. **1989**

ANIMAL CALLED MAN, AN 🖤 Based on a *They Call Me Trinity*-type character, this comic spaghetti Western fails on all counts. A rogue enters a sharpshooting contest and beats the local gunman. The next thing he knows, the gunman is after him. Surprise, surprise! Not rated, contains some violence. 83m. **DIR:** Roberto Mauri. **CAST:** Vassilli Karis, Craig Hill, Omero Capanna, Gillian Bray. **1973**

ANIMAL CRACKERS ★★★★ *Animal Crackers* is pure Marx Brothers, a total farce loosely based on a hit play by George S. Kaufman. Highlights include Groucho's African lecture—"One morning I shot an elephant in my pajamas. How he got into my pajamas, I'll never know"—and the card game with Harpo, Chico, and the ever-put-upon Margaret Dumont. B&W; 98m. **DIR:** Victor Heerman. **CAST:** The Marx Brothers, Margaret Dumont, Lillian Roth. **1930 DVD**

ANIMAL FARM ★★1/2 Serious, sincere animated adaptation of George Orwell's ingenious satire concerning the follies of government. The treatment would have benefited from greater intensity. The attempt at creating an optimistic ending was ill-advised. Keep in mind the film isn't children's fare. 72m. **DIR:** John Halas, Joy Batchelor. **1954**

ANIMAL HOUSE ★★★★1/2 Although it has spawned a seemingly relentless onslaught of inferior carbon copies, this comedy is still one of the funniest movies ever made. If you're into rock 'n' roll, partying, and general craziness, this picture is for you. We gave it a 95, because it has a good beat and you can dance to it. Rated R. 109m. **DIR:** John Landis. **CAST:** John Belushi, Tim Matheson, Karen Allen, Peter Riegert, John Vernon, Tom Hulce. **1978 DVD**

ANIMAL INSTINCTS ★★★ Maxwell Caulfield is a cop who renews his stalled relationship with his wife when he discovers that videotaping her in bed with a parade of men and women is a real turn on. Rated R for nudity, simulated sex, and language; unrated version offers much more of the same. 94m. **DIR:** Alexander Gregory Hippolyte. **CAST:** Shannon Whirry, Maxwell Caulfield, Mitch Gaylord, Delia Sheppard, David Carradine. **1992 DVD**

ANIMAL INSTINCTS 2 🖤 Somebody needs to get director Alexander Gregory Hippolyte and star Shannon Whirry out of the soft-core thriller genre; his films unfold with all the snap of drying paint, and she couldn't effectively convey sexual pleasure if her life depended on it. Rated R for nudity, simulated sex, and profanity. 92m. **DIR:** Alexander Gregory Hippolyte. **CAST:** Shannon Whirry, Woody Brown, Elizabeth Sandifer. **1994**

ANIMAL INSTINCTS: THE SEDUCTRESS 🖤 Third in the series is also the weakest. Wendy Schumacher takes over the lead role, playing a woman who finds sexual excitement in the arms of a blind musician.

Lots of kinky sex and not much more. Rated R for nudity and adult situations. Unrated version also available. 90m. DIR: Alexander Gregory Hippolyte. CAST: Wendy Schumacher, James Matthew, John Bates. 1995 DVD

ANIMAL KINGDOM, THE ★★★1/2 This filming of a Philip Barry play paved the way for his later *Holiday* and *Philadelphia Story* analyses of marriages, manners, and morals. Leslie Howard lets his hair down with bohemian girlfriend Ann Harding, but he marries snobbish Myrna Loy for appearance's sake, and it backfires. B&W; 85m. DIR: Edward H. Griffith. CAST: Leslie Howard, Myrna Loy, Ann Harding, William Gargan, Neil Hamilton, Ilka Chase, Henry Stephenson. 1932

ANIMALYMPICS ★★★ Featuring the voices of Billy Crystal, Gilda Radner, and Harry Shearer, this feature brings the Olympics to life with animals from around the world. Though the production seems somewhat overlong, there are bright spots: a news commentator called Ba Ba Wawa and a pole-vaulting hippo. 78m. DIR: Steven Lisberger. 1980

ANN VICKERS ★★★★ Rebuffed by Bruce Cabot, noble and self-sacrificing Irene Dunne scorns all men and turns to social service. Against all odds she seeks penal reform. A somewhat unique women's prison film in that the heroine is not a victimized inmate. B&W; 72m. DIR: John Cromwell. CAST: Irene Dunne, Bruce Cabot, Walter Huston, Conrad Nagel, Edna May Oliver, J. Carrol Naish. 1933

ANNA ★★★★ In this wonderfully offbeat turn on *All About Eve*, Sally Kirkland plays a former Czech film star struggling to find work in New York. Model Paulina Porizkova is fine as the refugee who remembers Kirkland's former glories and insinuates herself into the older woman's life only to surpass her successes in America. In English and Czech with subtitles. Rated PG-13 for nudity and profanity. 100m. DIR: Yurek Bogayevicz. CAST: Sally Kirkland, Paulina Porizkova, Robert Fields, Stefan Schnabel. 1987

•**ANNA AND THE KING** ★★★1/2 Pageantry and exquisite costuming reign supreme in this nonmusical version of *The King and I*. Based on Anna Leonowens's diary, this features Jodie Foster as the prim schoolteacher to the King of Siam's many children. Action star Chow Yun-Fat makes a smooth transition into his majestic role, but Foster seems to slip a bit off a tightrope between Victorian repression and attraction to the captivating king. Rated PG-13 for violence and gore. 147m. DIR: Andy Tennant. CAST: Jodie Foster, Chow Yun-Fat, Tom Felton. 1999

ANNA AND THE KING OF SIAM ★★★★ This original *King and I* boasts poignant performances that give the characters of Anna Leonowens and King Mongkut a different perspective. It's based on Margaret Landon's memoirs as a governess in the Siamese court during the last century. The story parallels the musical version, but with more details about individual family members. 128m. DIR: John Cromwell. CAST: Irene Dunne, Rex Harrison, Linda Darnell, Lee J. Cobb, Gale Sondergaard. 1946

ANNA CHRISTIE (1922) ★★ Anna (Blanche Sweet) is a former prostitute whose struggle for a new life runs her afoul of two men—her father (George F. Marion) and a sailor (Matt Burke). Don't expect any of the edgy, sordid aspects of the Eugene O'Neill original. But Henry Sharp's solid camerawork nicely conveys the dockside scenes. Silent. B&W; 75m. DIR: John Griffith Wray. CAST: Blanche Sweet, George F. Marion, Matt Burke. 1922

ANNA CHRISTIE (1930) ★★★★ Greta Garbo is mesmerizing and Marie Dressler hilariously memorable in this early sound classic adapted from Eugene O'Neill's play. The tag line for it in 1930 was "Garbo speaks!" And speak she does, uttering the famous line, "Gif me a viskey, ginger ale on the side, and don't be stingy, baby," while portraying a woman with a shady past. B&W; 90m. DIR: Clarence Brown. CAST: Greta Garbo, Charles Bickford, Marie Dressler. 1930

ANNA KARENINA (1935) ★★★★ The forever fascinating, peerless Greta Garbo, a superb supporting cast headed by Fredric March, and the masterful direction of Clarence Brown make this film one of the actress's greatest, a true film classic. B&W; 95m. DIR: Clarence Brown. CAST: Greta Garbo, Fredric March, Basil Rathbone, Freddie Bartholomew, Maureen O'Sullivan, Reginald Denny, May Robson, Reginald Owen. 1935

ANNA KARENINA (1947) ★★1/2 In this version of Tolstoy's classic story of a married woman madly in love with a military officer, Vivien Leigh is miscast as the heroine. Though she tries valiantly, she is overwhelmed by the role. An overly sentimental script doesn't help. B&W; 139m. DIR: Julien Duvivier. CAST: Vivien Leigh, Kieron Moore, Ralph Richardson, Sally Ann Howes, Michael Gough. 1947 DVD

ANNA KARENINA (1974) ★★★1/2 Based on Tolstoy's novel, this ballet was choreographed by and stars Maya Plisetskaya, the Bolshoi's great prima ballerina. Her husband, Rodion Shchedrin, composed the music. This is an imaginative and visually interesting film, as the camera and direction are creative rather than just filming a staged ballet performance. 81m. DIR: Margarita Pilichino. CAST: Bolshoi Ballet. 1974

ANNA KARENINA (1985) ★★ Tolstoy's classic suffers in this tedious remake for television. Garbo did it best in 1935. Paul Scofield as Anna's husband, however, is worth the watch. 150m. DIR: Simon Langton. CAST: Jacqueline Bisset, Paul Scofield, Christopher Reeve, Ian Ogilvy. 1985

ANNA TO THE INFINITE POWER ★★★★ Is individuality determined purely by genetic code, or by some other factor beyond the control of science? This film explores the dimensions of that question via the struggles of a brilliant, troubled child—who is also the unwitting subject of a scientific experiment to establish her own identity. Brilliant. 107m. DIR: Robert Wiemer. CAST: Martha Byrne, Dina Merrill, Mark Patton, Loretta Devine, Jack Gilford. 1982

ANNABEL TAKES A TOUR ★★1/2 A dizzy movie star and her fast-talking press agent concoct a publicity scheme. Harmless and mildly amusing, this brief programmer was the second in a series Lucille Ball and Jack Oakie did for RKO. B&W; 66m. DIR:

Lew Landers. **CAST:** Lucille Ball, Jack Oakie, Ruth Donnelly, Frances Mercer, Donald MacBride. 1938

ANNAPOLIS STORY, AN ★★ John Derek and Kevin McCarthy vie for the hand of Diana Lynn in this formula service academy yarn of rigid training, lights out, bed check, and romance. 81m. **DIR:** Don Siegel. **CAST:** John Derek, Diana Lynn, Kevin McCarthy. 1955

ANNE FRANK REMEMBERED ★★★★ Moving, Oscar-winning documentary retells the sad story of the girl whom narrator Kenneth Branagh calls "probably Hitler's most famous victim." Using the testimony of Anne Frank's friends and relatives who survived the Holocaust, director Jon Blair goes beyond the famous diary (selections from which are read by Glenn Close) to give human dimension to Anne's tragically short life. Rated PG. B&W/color; 122m. **DIR:** Jon Blair. 1995

ANNE OF AVONLEA ★★★★ Anne Shirley matures and falls in love in this sequel to *Anne of Green Gables*, which scripter-director Kevin Sullivan has helmed with the same devotion to period authenticity. 224m. **DIR:** Kevin Sullivan. **CAST:** Megan Follows, Colleen Dewhurst, Wendy Hiller. 1987

ANNE OF GREEN GABLES (1934) ★★★ L. M. Montgomery's popular juvenile book about a spunky young orphan's influence on a conservative household receives its first sound treatment in this sentimental but entertaining picture. A good version of the classic and fine family entertainment. B&W; 80m. **DIR:** George Nicholls Jr. **CAST:** Anne Shirley, Tom Brown, O. P. Heggie, Helen Westley, Sara Haden, Charley Grapewin. 1934

ANNE OF GREEN GABLES (1985) ★★★★ This delightful film, based on L. M. Montgomery's classic novel, is set in 1908 on Canada's Prince Edward Island. Anne (Megan Follows) is a foster child taken in by Matthew (Richard Farnsworth) and Marilla Cuthbert (Colleen Dewhurst), who mistakenly expect her to be a farmhand. Not rated; suitable for family viewing. 240m. **DIR:** Kevin Sullivan. **CAST:** Megan Follows, Richard Farnsworth, Colleen Dewhurst. 1985

ANNE OF THE THOUSAND DAYS ★★★ The story of Anne Boleyn, Henry VIII's second wife and mother of Queen Elizabeth I, is given the big-budget treatment. Luckily, the tragic tale of a woman who is at first pressured into an unwanted union with England's lusty king, only to fall in love with him and eventually lose her head to court intrigue, is not lost beneath the spectacle. Genevieve Bujold's well-balanced performance of Anne carries the entire production. 146m. **DIR:** Charles Jarrott. **CAST:** Genevieve Bujold, Richard Burton, Anthony Quayle. 1969

ANNIE ★★★★ A sparkling $40 million movie musical based on the Broadway production of the long-running comic strip *Little Orphan Annie*. Ten-year-old Aileen Quinn is just fine in the title role. Rated PG for brief profanity. 128m. **DIR:** John Huston. **CAST:** Albert Finney, Carol Burnett, Bernadette Peters, Edward Herrmann, Aileen Quinn, Tim Curry. 1982 **DVD**

ANNIE, A ROYAL ADVENTURE! ★★ Disappointing, nonmusical TV sequel to the 1982 smash musical *Annie*. This time "Daddy" Warbucks heads to England to be knighted and Annie and her pal go along for the ride. They meet up with scheming Lady Edwina Hogbottom (Joan Collins) who plans to blow up Buckingham Palace and become queen. Too melodramatic and unbelievable to be enjoyed. Rated G. 92m. **DIR:** Ian Toynton. **CAST:** Ashley Johnson, George Hearn, Joan Collins. 1995

ANNIE GET YOUR GUN ★★★1/2 Lavish, fast-moving transfer of Irving Berlin's stage hit to film with Annie Oaklie (Betty Hutton), Frank Butler (Howard Keel), Buffalo Bill Cody (Louis Calhern) and Sitting Bull (J. Carrol Naish) singing and shooting up a storm. "Anything You Can Do" and "There's No Business Like Show Business" are two of the musical highlights. Oscar for the score of Adolph Deutsch and Roger Edens. 107m. **DIR:** George Sidney. **CAST:** Betty Hutton, Howard Keel, Louis Calhern, Keenan Wynn, Edward Arnold, J. Carrol Naish. 1950

ANNIE HALL ★★★★★ Woody Allen's exquisite romantic comedy won the 1977 Academy Awards for best picture, actress (Diane Keaton), director (Allen), and screenplay (Allen and Marshall Brickman)—and deserved every one of them. This delightful semiautobiographical romp features Allen as Alvy Singer, a more assured version of Alan Felix, from *Play It Again, Sam*, who falls in love (again) with Keaton (in the title role). Rated PG for profanity and bedroom scenes. 94m. **DIR:** Woody Allen. **CAST:** Woody Allen, Diane Keaton, Tony Roberts, Paul Simon, Shelley Duvall, Carol Kane. 1977 **DVD**

ANNIE O ★★★ Hotshot hoopster Coco Yares has the bad luck to attend a school lacking a girls' basketball program, so she tries out for—and wins a spot on—the *boys'* varsity team. The predictable story treads no new ground, but Yares is a likable lead (her bland voiceovers notwithstanding), and the result is pleasant enough for family viewing. Suitable for all ages. 93m. **DIR:** J. Michael McClary. **CAST:** Coco Yares, Robert Stewart, Chad Willett. 1995

ANNIE OAKLEY (TV SERIES) ★★★ Annie Oakley, woman rancher and expert sharpshooter, helps Sheriff Lofty Craig maintain law and order in the 1860s town of Diablo. Two nostalgia-packed episodes on one cassette: "Trouble Shooters" and "Twisted Trails." B&W; 50m. **CAST:** Gail Davis, Brad Johnson, Jimmy Hawkins. 1953

ANNIHILATORS, THE 🖤 Another film in which Vietnam veterans reunite, organize a vigilante group, annihilate the sadistic gangs, and return to their normal lives. Rated R for grotesque violence and language. 87m. **DIR:** Charles E. Sellier Jr. **CAST:** Christopher Stone, Andy Wood, Lawrence Hilton-Jacobs, Jim Antonio, Gerrit Graham. 1985

ANOTHER CHANCE ★★ An oversexed actor (Bruce Greenwood) is allowed to return to Earth in an attempt to be faithful to one woman. Greenwood's talented large white dog and the decent special effects in Heaven and Hell make this romp watchable. Rated R for nudity and profanity. 99m. **DIR:** Jerry Vint. **CAST:** Bruce Greenwood. 1988

ANOTHER COUNTRY ★★★1/2 For this film, Julian Mitchell adapted his stage play about Guy Burgess, an Englishman who became a spy for Russia in the 1930s. Little in this story reportedly was based on fact. Still, Mitchell's postulations provide interesting viewing, and Rupert Everett's lead performance—as

Guy "Bennett"—is stunning. Rated PG for suggested sex and profanity. 90m. DIR: Marek Kanievska. CAST: Rupert Everett, Colin Firth, Cary Elwes. 1984

•ANOTHER DAY IN PARADISE ★★ Junkie teen lovers take a road trip with a veteran outlaw couple in this bleak crime story adapted from ex-convict Eddie Little's book. The film unflinchingly exposes the daily details of survival along the underbelly of America, but it mistakenly assumes that drug addicts are inherently intriguing. The gutsy R&B score is complemented with a Clarence Carter cameo. Rated R for drug use, language, sexuality, and violence. 99m. DIR: Larry Clark. CAST: James Woods, Melanie Griffith, Vincent Kartheiser, Natasha Gregson Wagner. 1999 DVD

ANOTHER 48 HRS. ★★★★ Solid sequel to the 1982 box-office smash finds director Walter Hill in top form as Eddie Murphy and Nick Nolte take on a mysterious figure known only as the Iceman. While not quite as good as the first film, *Another 48 Hrs.* nevertheless proves that the original cop/buddy team is still the best. Rated R for violence, profanity, and nudity. 95m. DIR: Walter Hill. CAST: Eddie Murphy, Nick Nolte, Brion James, Kevin Tighe, Ed O'Ross. 1990 DVD

ANOTHER MAN, ANOTHER CHANCE ★★ In 1977, director Claude Lelouch, inexplicably, decided to remake his charming film *A Man and a Woman* and set it in the American West of the late 1800s. Widow Genevieve Bujold and widower James Caan fall in love. It's light on romance and heavy on tedium. 128m. DIR: Claude Lelouch. CAST: James Caan, Genevieve Bujold, Francis Huster, Jennifer Warren, Susan Tyrrell. 1977

ANOTHER 9 WEEKS ★★ Mickey Rourke engages in more tame sadomasochistic shenanigans in this unwarranted sequel that tries but fails to deliver the visual sheen that was the only saving grace of the original *9 Weeks.* Rated R for nudity, sexual situations, and profanity. 104m. DIR: Anne Goursand. CAST: Mickey Rourke, Angie Everhart, Steven Berkoff. 1997 DVD

ANOTHER PAIR OF ACES ★★★1/2 Texas Ranger Rip Metcalf (Kris Kristofferson) enlists the aid of streetwise gambler Billy Roy Barker (Willie Nelson) in tracking down the vigilante killer of a crime lord. Engaging performances help elevate this modern-day Western/detective story, which was made for TV. 93m. DIR: Bill Bixby. CAST: Willie Nelson, Kris Kristofferson, Joan Severance, Rip Torn. 1991

ANOTHER STAKEOUT ★★★1/2 Richard Dreyfuss and Emilio Estevez are back as Seattle detectives assigned to track down an escaped federal witness. Their job is complicated by a bumbling but well-meaning assistant district attorney (played with panache by Rosie O'Donnell). Rated PG-13 for profanity and violence. 109m. DIR: John Badham. CAST: Richard Dreyfuss, Emilio Estevez, Rosie O'Donnell, Madeleine Stowe, Cathy Moriarty, Dennis Farina, Marcia Strassman, John Rubinstein, Miguel Ferrer. 1993

ANOTHER THIN MAN ★★★★ Nick and Nora Charles (William Powell and Myrna Loy) contend with a gentleman who dreams about catastrophes before they take place. As usual, the plot is sec-

ondary. Follows *After the Thin Man* (1936) and precedes *Shadow of the Thin Man* (1941). Suitable for family viewing. B&W; 105m. DIR: W. S. Van Dyke. CAST: William Powell, Myrna Loy, Virginia Grey, Otto Kruger, C. Aubrey Smith, Ruth Hussey, Nat Pendleton, Tom Neal. 1939

ANOTHER TIME, ANOTHER PLACE (1958) ★★ Hohum melodrama about American newspaperwoman whose brief affair with British journalist ends in tragedy when he dies during World War II. B&W; 98m. DIR: Lewis Allen. CAST: Lana Turner, Barry Sullivan, Glynis Johns, Sean Connery, Sidney James. 1958

ANOTHER TIME, ANOTHER PLACE (1984) ★★★ In this British import set in 1944, a woman named Janie (Phyllis Logan) lives on a small farm in Scotland with her husband, Dongal (Paul Young), fifteen years her senior. As part of a war rehabilitation program, the couple welcomes three Italian POWs onto their place, and Janie falls in love. Rated PG. 118m. DIR: Michael Radford. CAST: Phyllis Logan, Paul Young. 1984

ANOTHER WOMAN ★★★★ A subtle, purposely enigmatic yet engrossing portrait of a woman reassessing her own identity and purpose. Gena Rowlands is superb as a college professor whose life is not as solid as she assumes. When she overhears another woman (Mia Farrow) in a session with her psychoanalyst, Rowlands begins to have doubts. Rated PG. 81m. DIR: Woody Allen. CAST: Gena Rowlands, Gene Hackman, Ian Holm, Mia Farrow, John Houseman, Blythe Danner, Sandy Dennis. 1988

ANOTHER YOU ★★ In their fourth film together, Gene Wilder and Richard Pryor star in a disappointing comedy involving mistaken identities. Wilder is a pathological liar just released from a mental institution, and Pryor is a con man doing community service as his caretaker. Rated R for profanity. 100m. DIR: Maurice Phillips. CAST: Gene Wilder, Richard Pryor, Mercedes Ruehl, Stephen Lang, Vanessa L. Williams. 1991

ANTARCTICA ★★ *Antarctica* is the true story of a 1958 expedition. While in Antarctica, Japanese scientists encounter complications and are forced to return home, leaving their team of dogs behind to fend for themselves. The dogs are pretty good naturalistic actors, but you're not drawn to them as you are to the wolves of Carroll Ballard's *Never Cry Wolf.* Dubbed in English. 112m. DIR: Koreyoshi Kurahara. CAST: Ken Takakura, Tsunehiko Watase. 1984

ANTHONY ADVERSE ★★★1/2 Fredric March, in the title role, wanders around early nineteenth-century America and Mexico, sowing oats, and buckling swash, in this all-stops-out romantic blockbuster. B&W; 136m. DIR: Mervyn LeRoy. CAST: Fredric March, Olivia de Havilland, Anita Louise, Donald Woods, Edmund Gwenn, Claude Rains, Louis Hayward, Gale Sondergaard, Henry O'Neill. 1936

ANTONIA & JANE ★★★★ A perceptive British comedy about an unlikely friendship between two wildly different women. Antonia and Jane are the yin and yang of personalities, and neither has ever appreciated the turmoil in the other's life. Imagine a female and British twist on Woody Allen's comedic style. Not rated; the film contains nudity, sex, and profanity. 77m. **DIR:** Beeban Kidron. **CAST:** Imelda Staunton, Saskia Reeves. **1991**

ANTONIA'S LINE ★★★ An unmarried mother returns with her teenage daughter to her Dutch village after World War II, where she establishes a happy home—not only for her own family but for all the outcasts, misfits, and free spirits who flock to her over the next fifty years. Writer-director Marleen Gorris's sentimental feminist fairy tale is short on dramatic conflict but long on warmth—a "family values" story with 1990s attitudes. In Dutch with English subtitles. Not rated; contains nudity and simulated sex. 93m. **DIR:** Marleen Gorris. **CAST:** Willeke Van Ammelrooy, Els Dottermans, Jan Decleir, Mil Seghers, Marina de Graaf. **1995 DVD**

ANTONY AND CLEOPATRA (1973) ★★ Marginal film interpretation of Shakespeare's play. Obviously a tremendous amount of work on Charlton Heston's part, casting himself as Antony, but the film is lacking in energy. Rated PG. 160m. **DIR:** Charlton Heston. **CAST:** Charlton Heston, Hildegard Neil, Eric Porter, Fernando Rey, John Castle. **1973**

ANTONY AND CLEOPATRA (1981) ★★★1/2 Timothy Dalton and Lynn Redgrave are fine as Marc Antony and Cleopatra in Shakespeare's tale of passion, war, and betrayal in Egypt and Rome. John Carradine is outstanding as the soothsayer. A Bard Productions Ltd. release. 183m. **DIR:** Lawrence Carra. **CAST:** Timothy Dalton, Lynn Redgrave, Nichelle Nichols, John Carradine, Anthony Geary, Barrie Ingham, Walter Koenig, Brian Kerwin, Kim Miyori. **1981**

ANTS! 🎬 Just another haunting remnant of boring filmmaking from the *Movie of the Week* closet. 88m. **DIR:** Robert Sheerer. **CAST:** Robert Foxworth, Lynda Day George, Suzanne Somers, Myrna Loy, Brian Dennehy. **1977**

ANTZ ★★★1/2 In this animated feature, geared more toward adults than the kiddies, computer-generated imagery creates surprisingly real scenes such as the picnic fiasco in which worker ant Z (Woody Allen's voice) and the ants' princess (voiced by Sharon Stone) find themselves stuck in the gum on a boy's shoe. This is an animated version of *Play It Again, Sam* with Allen re-creating his role of the neurotic looking for love. Z also gets to flex his muscles and lead a revolt against a corrupt general (Gene Hackman). Rated PG for violence and profanity. 83m. **DIR:** Eric Darnell, Tim Johnson. **1998 DVD**

ANY FRIEND OF NICHOLAS NICKLEBY IS A FRIEND OF MINE ★★★1/2 A charming period piece by author Ray Bradbury. Fred Gwynne shines as a mysterious stranger who comes to a small Illinois town where he takes an imaginative schoolboy under his wing. This is a poignant and humorous drama comparable to PBS's award-winning *Anne of Green Gables*. 55m. **DIR:** Ralph Rosenblum. **CAST:** Fred Gwynne. **1981**

•**ANY GIVEN SUNDAY** ★★1/2 Pro-football coach has sacrificed wife and family for a career and a team that are now in a slump. A third-string quarterback snaps his team's losing streak and becomes the media's flavor of the month, leaving the coach to reevaluate his loyalties and choices. This flawed dra-

ma oozes passion, machismo, and spectacle as it leers at team dynamics and the inner circles of big business. Rated R for language and nudity. 160m. **DIR:** Oliver Stone. **CAST:** Al Pacino, Jamie Foxx, Cameron Diaz, Dennis Quaid, Ann-Margret, Lawrence Taylor. **1999**

ANY MAN'S DEATH ★★1/2 John Savage plays a traumatized Vietnam-vet-turned-journalist sent to Africa. He discovers a strange scientist (William Hickey) whose human experiments have killed thousands. Confusing kaleidoscope of events leaves more questions than answers. Rated R for profanity and violence. 105m. **DIR:** Tom Clegg. **CAST:** John Savage, William Hickey, Mia Sara, Ernest Borgnine. **1989**

ANY NUMBER CAN PLAY ★★★1/2 Wonderful cast in an absorbing drama revolving around the personal and professional problems of honest gambling-house owner Clark Gable. Marjorie Rambeau is a standout. Screenplay by Richard Brooks. B&W; 112m. **DIR:** Mervyn LeRoy. **CAST:** Clark Gable, Alexis Smith, Wendell Corey, Audrey Totter, Darryl Hickman, Frank Morgan, Lewis Stone, Barry Sullivan, Mary Astor, Marjorie Rambeau, Leon Ames, Edgar Buchanan, William Conrad. **1949**

ANY PLACE BUT HOME ★★★ A husband and wife wind up with a boy whom their relatives had kidnapped. Problem is, the boy has been abused, and he doesn't want to go home. No spectacular performances, and no stupendous plot twists, but this made-for-cable original is watchable. Not rated; contains violence. 95m. **DIR:** Rob Hedden. **CAST:** Joe Lando, Dale Midkiff, Mary Page Keller, Cristi Conaway, Richard Roundtree, Alan Thicke. **1997**

ANY WEDNESDAY ★★ The spiciness of the original Broadway script gets lost in this film adaptation. Jason Robards Jr. plays the New York businessman who deducts his paramour's (Jane Fonda) apartment as a business expense. A poor man's *The Apartment*. 109m. **DIR:** Robert Ellis Miller. **CAST:** Jane Fonda, Jason Robards Jr., Dean Jones, Rosemary Murphy, Ann Prentiss. **1966**

ANY WHICH WAY YOU CAN 🎬 Another comedy clinker from Clint Eastwood and company. Rated PG. 116m. **DIR:** Buddy Van Horn. **CAST:** Clint Eastwood, Sondra Locke, Geoffrey Lewis, William Smith, Ruth Gordon. **1980**

ANYTHING FOR LOVE ★★★1/2 This anthology film, composed of three entries from Showtime's *Directed By* series, allows actors to make a short film from behind the camera. In Christine Lahti's *Lieberman in Love*, which won 1995s Academy Award for live-action short film, Danny Aiello stars as a mournful widower looking for love in all the wrong places, and Lahti herself offers excellent support as an avaricious hooker. Anne Archer and William L. Petersen learn that long-dormant affairs are best left alone in Richard Dreyfuss's *Present Tense, Past Perfect*. Sadly, Christian Slater's *Museum of Love* is a complete waste of time. Rated R for profanity and simulated sex. 105m. **DIR:** Richard Dreyfuss, Christine Lahti, Christian Slater. **CAST:** Danny Aiello, Christine Lahti, Nancy Travis, Paul Mercurio, Sandra Bernhard, Samantha Mathis, Anne Archer, William L. Petersen. **1996**

•**ANYWHERE BUT HERE** ★★★ Sloppy editing and a weak script mar this predictable mother/daughter melodrama, albeit one blessed by two commanding actresses. It's yet another story about a teenage girl (Natalie Portman) alternately amused and humiliated by her free-spirited single mother (Susan Sarandon), and their attempts to find happiness in sunny California. We're left with the impression that we're watching only the high points of a much denser story. Rated PG-13 for mild profanity and sexual candor. 114m. **DIR:** Wayne Wang. **CAST:** Susan Sarandon, Natalie Portman, Eileen Ryan, Ray Baker, John Diehl, Shawn Hatosy. 1999 DVD

ANZACS ★★★★ The ANZACS (Australian/New Zealand Army Corps) join the British in World War I to stir up a few stuffed shirts among the very stiff English. Emphasis is upon the friendship and loyalty among the Australians. Paul Hogan provides a few moments of comic relief. A powerful war film that dwells on the people involved, not the machinery. Made for television, this is not rated but deals with mature subject matter. 165m. **DIR:** George Miller. **CAST:** Andrew Clark, Paul Hogan, Megan Williams. 1985

ANZIO ★★ Would-be blockbuster about the Allied invasion of Italy during World War II doesn't make the grade as either history or spectacle and ultimately wastes the talents of a great cast and an often inspired director. 117m. **DIR:** Edward Dmytryk. **CAST:** Robert Mitchum, Peter Falk, Robert Ryan, Earl Holliman, Arthur Kennedy, Patrick Magee, Mark Damon, Reni Santoni. 1968

APACHE ★★ Moralistic message Western features a hammy Burt Lancaster as an idealistic warrior who resents yet understands the encroachment of the whites and refuses to live on government reservations. Strangely typical of early-to-mid-1950s Hollywood Westerns, this entry is long on conscience and short on action. 91m. **DIR:** Robert Aldrich. **CAST:** Burt Lancaster, Jean Peters, Charles Bronson, John Dehner, Monte Blue. 1954

APACHE ROSE ★★1/2 Roy's an oil-well engineer, Dale's the skipper of a tugboat, and the fellow that's causing all the trouble runs a gambling ship. But it's still a Western because Trigger and the Sons of the Pioneers are close at hand. This is the first of the popular series to be shot in color. 75m. **DIR:** William Witney. **CAST:** Roy Rogers, Dale Evans, Bob Nolan and the Sons of the Pioneers, George Meeker, Minerva Urecal, LeRoy Mason. 1947

APACHE WOMAN 💣 Dull, awkwardly acted and directed story of an Indian affairs agent, Lloyd Bridges, investigating stagecoach holdups blamed on reservation Apaches. Released theatrically in color. B&W; 83m. **DIR:** Roger Corman. **CAST:** Lloyd Bridges, Joan Taylor, Lance Fuller, Paul Birch, Dick Miller, Chester Conklin. 1955

APARAJITO ★★★ In the second part of the chronicle of a Bengali family in the Apu trilogy, Apu's father brings the family to the holy city of Benares where his son begins his education and training. Fine ensemble acting. In Bengali with English subtitles. B&W; 108m. **DIR:** Satyajit Ray. **CAST:** Pinaki Sen Gupta, Smaran Ghosal. 1957

APART FROM HUGH ★★1/2 Two men face the difficulties of committing to a life together in this quiet, tender drama. Stylish for a debut, this low-budget effort is well written but unevenly acted. The dialogue is realistic enough to hook the viewer, but if no one hears of these actors again it will come as no surprise. Not rated; contains profanity and sexual situations. B&W; 87m. **DIR:** Jon FitzGerald. **CAST:** David Merwin, Jennifer A. Reed, Steve Arnold. 1994

APARTMENT, THE ★★★★★ Rarely have comedy and drama been satisfyingly blended into a cohesive whole. Director Billy Wilder does it masterfully in this film. With career advancement in mind, Jack Lemmon permits his boss to use his apartment for illicit love affairs. Then he gets involved with the boss's emotionally distraught girlfriend B&W; 125m. **DIR:** Billy Wilder. **CAST:** Jack Lemmon, Shirley MacLaine, Fred MacMurray, Ray Walston, Jack Kruschen, Edie Adams. 1960

APARTMENT ZERO ★★★★ A movie buff's delight, this is a whodunit, a twisted character study, and a creepy suspense-thriller. The lead character, Adrian LeDuc, is the ultimate escapist; an Argentinian who pretends to be British, he revels in movie lore and owns a run-down movie revival house. When the cinema's failure puts Adrian in a financial crunch, he decides to take in a roommate, a good-looking American who knows nothing about movies and just may be a serial killer. Rated R for violence and profanity. 124m. **DIR:** Martin Donovan. **CAST:** Hart Bochner, Colin Firth. 1989

APE, THE ★★ Boris Karloff finished out his contract with Monogram Studios with this story about a doctor who discovers a cure for polio that requires spinal fluid from a human being. Not too many thrills, but Karloff is always worth watching. B&W; 61m. **DIR:** William Nigh. **CAST:** Boris Karloff, Gertrude Hoffman. 1940 DVD

APE MAN, THE ★★ Bela Lugosi was one of the great horror film stars. However, the monster-movie boom stopped short in 1935, leaving the Hungarian actor out of work. When shockers came back in vogue four years later, Lugosi took any and every role he was offered. The result was grade-Z pictures such as this one, about a scientist (Lugosi) attempting to harness the physical power of apes for humankind. Too bad. B&W; 64m. **DIR:** William Beaudine. **CAST:** Bela Lugosi, Louise Currie, Wallace Ford, Minerva Urecal. 1943 DVD

APEX ★★★1/2 Time paradoxes have always been great sci-fi fodder, and this film is full of them. In the year 2073, a probe is sent back in time, but its interference causes a paradox that changes the future into a dying wasteland. When scientist Mitchell Cox returns from the past in an attempt to fix the future, he finds himself at war with robots bent on destroying the rest of humanity. Great special effects and a tricky screenplay. Rated R for violence. 103m. **DIR:** Phillip Roth. **CAST:** Mitchell Cox, Lisa Ann Russell, Marcus Aurelius, Adam Lawson. 1993

APHRODITE ★★ In 1914, a group of jaded aristocrats meet on a Mediterranean island to reenact a mythological tale involving Aphrodite, the goddess of beauty. Pretty but pretentious soft-core erotica.

Dubbed. Not rated; contains nudity. 96m. DIR: Robert Fuest. CAST: Horst Buchholz, Valerie Kaprisky, Capucine. 1982

APOCALYPSE, THE 🎦 Incomprehensible sci-fi with Sandra Bernhard ridiculously miscast as an outer-space salvage-ship pilot on a ship set to collide with Earth. Not rated; contains violence and profanity. 96m. DIR: Hubert de la Bouillerie. CAST: Sandra Bernhard, Cameron Dye, Frank Zagarino, Laura San Giacomo. 1996 DVD

APOCALYPSE NOW ★★★★ An exceptional war film in every sense, this work pulsates with artistic ambition. It reaches for truth, struggles for greatness—and almost succeeds. The central character, Captain Willard (Martin Sheen), tells the story of his danger-filled journey toward a fateful meeting with a man named Kurtz, a highly decorated officer whom the army contends has gone mad. Rated R. 153m. DIR: Francis Ford Coppola. CAST: Marlon Brando, Martin Sheen, Robert Duvall, Harrison Ford, Laurence Fishburne, Dennis Hopper. 1979 DVD

APOLLO 13 ★★★★ Director Ron Howard does the next to impossible with this first-rate motion picture: he turns a piece of recent history into edge-of-your-seat entertainment. Based entirely on the real-life adventures of the Apollo 13 astronauts, who came perilously close to death during their mission, this film features a topflight cast and an insightful screenplay. Rated PG. 140m. DIR: Ron Howard. CAST: Tom Hanks, Bill Paxton, Kevin Bacon, Gary Sinise, Ed Harris, Kathleen Quinlan, David Andrews, Clint Howard, Joe Spano. 1995 DVD

APOLOGY ★★★ This psycho-suspense film features Lesley Ann Warren as a bizarre artist who starts an anonymous phone service to get ideas. People call the recording and confess a sin they've committed. All goes well until a caller begins killing people in order to have something to be sorry for. Made for cable TV, this is unrated but it contains obscenities, gore, and simulated sex. 98m. DIR: Robert Bierman. CAST: Lesley Ann Warren, Peter Weller, George Loros, John Glover, Christopher Noth. 1986

APOSTLE, THE ★★★1/2 Texas Pentecostal preacher Sonny Dewey catches his wife in bed with a local youth director, beans the younger man with a baseball bat and flees to Louisiana. There he reopens a neglected country chapel and gathers a new flock. This meandering drama about a flawed, flamboyant servant of God is full of emotional and religious truth. Rated PG-13 for one scene of violence. 148m. DIR: Robert Duvall. CAST: Robert Duvall, Miranda Richardson, Farrah Fawcett, Todd Allen, John Beasley, Billy Bob Thornton, June Carter Cash. 1997 DVD

APPALOOSA, THE ★★ Slight, often boring Western follows Marlon Brando's attempts to recover an Appaloosa horse stolen by a Mexican bandit. Brando's brooding, method-acting approach to the character only makes things worse in an already slow-moving film. 98m. DIR: Sidney J. Furie. CAST: Marlon Brando, John Saxon, Anjanette Comer, Frank Silvera. 1966

APPLAUSE ★★★★1/2 This is a remarkable early sound-era movie. Filmed at actual New York locations, it tells the story of a fading vaudeville star (Helen Morgan) who loses the love of her daughter and

is jilted by her lowly boyfriend. A smashing success. B&W; 78m. DIR: Rouben Mamoulian. CAST: Helen Morgan, Joan Peers. 1929

APPLE, THE ★★1/2 In a poor section of Tehran, a devout man and his blind wife have sheltered their 12-year-old twin daughters from the outside world. Based on a true story, the film is half documentary, half fiction, with the family, and others involved in their story, all playing themselves. The situation is interesting, but the film is clumsy and plodding, and the "actors" are uncomfortable in front of the camera—all except the two sisters themselves. In Farsi with English subtitles. Not rated; suitable for general audiences. 85m. DIR: Samirah Makhmalbaf. CAST: Zahra Naderi, Massoumeh Naderi, Qorban Ali Naderi, Azize Mohammadi, Soghra Behrozi. 1998

APPLE DUMPLING GANG, THE ★★ A gambler (Bill Bixby) inherits three children who find a huge gold nugget in 1870. Tim Conway and Don Knotts trip and foul up as left-footed bad guys. Good, clean, unoriginal, predictable fare from Disney. The kids will love it. Rated G. 100m. DIR: Norman Tokar. CAST: Bill Bixby, Tim Conway, Don Knotts, Susan Clark, David Wayne, Slim Pickens, Harry Morgan. 1975

APPLE DUMPLING GANG RIDES AGAIN, THE ★★ In this sequel to the 1975 original, Tim Conway and Don Knotts again play bumbling, inept outlaws in the Old West. Rated G. 88m. DIR: Vincent McEveety. CAST: Tim Conway, Don Knotts, Harry Morgan, Jack Elam, Kenneth Mars, Ruth Buzzi, Robert Pine. 1979

APPLESEED ★★★1/2 Japanese animation. Two SWAT team officers pursue a terrorist through the experimental city of Olympus in this satisfying tale. More emphasis on story makes this fast-paced, absorbing feature a real gem. In Japanese with English subtitles. Not rated; the film has violence. 70m. DIR: Kazuyashi Katayama. 1988

APPOINTMENT, THE 🎦 Story of a father cursed by his evil daughter. Not rated, the film has some violence. 90m. DIR: Lindsey C. Vickers. CAST: Edward Woodward, Jane Merrow. 1982

APPOINTMENT IN HONDURAS ★★1/2 Good cast helps this farfetched story of an idealistic American (Glenn Ford) helping local misfits free their country from political tyranny. The actors do their best, but rather silly material gets in their way. Plot and dialogue are somewhat laughable. Ann Sheridan is highly watchable, as usual. 79m. DIR: Jacques Tourneur. CAST: Glenn Ford, Ann Sheridan, Zachary Scott, Jack Elam. 1953

APPOINTMENT WITH DEATH ★★ Standard Agatha Christie mystery made boring by poor editing and pedestrian direction. Peter Ustinov is Hercule Poirot again (bringing competency if not vivaciousness to the part), trying to unravel a murder at an archaeological dig. Rated PG for adult situations. 102m. DIR: Michael Winner. CAST: Peter Ustinov, Lauren Bacall, Carrie Fisher, John Gielgud, Piper Laurie, Hayley Mills, Jenny Seagrove, David Soul, Amber Bezer. 1988

APPOINTMENT WITH FEAR 🎦 Cancel this appointment! Not rated; contains sex, nudity, and profanity. 96m. DIR: Alan Smithee. CAST: Michelle Little, Michael Wyle, Kerry Remsen, Douglas Rowe, Garrick Dowhen. 1987

APPRENTICE TO MURDER ★★1/2 This film of the occult was inspired by a true story in Pennsylvania in 1927. Donald Sutherland appears as a religious leader with healing and mystical powers. Chad Lowe, in his desperation to get help for his alcoholic father, falls prey to Sutherland's powers. Rated PG-13 for language and violence. 97m. **DIR:** Ralph L. Thomas. **CAST:** Donald Sutherland, Chad Lowe, Mia Sara, Rutanya Alda, Eddie Jones, Mark Burton. **1987**

APPRENTICESHIP OF DUDDY KRAVITZ, THE ★★★ Richard Dreyfuss, in an early starring role, is the main attraction in this quirky little comedy about a poor Jewish lad from a Montreal ghetto. The story is full of cruel and smart-assed humor, a trait that haunts Dreyfuss to this day. Ultimately, the film is too long and too shrill. Rated PG for sexual content. 121m. **DIR:** Ted Kotcheff. **CAST:** Richard Dreyfuss, Jack Warden, Micheline Lanctot, Denholm Elliott, Randy Quaid. **1974**

APRIL FOOLS, THE 🖤 A failed attempt at a serious romantic comedy that veers too often into awkward slapstick. Rated PG for adult situations. 95m. **DIR:** Stuart Rosenberg. **CAST:** Jack Lemmon, Catherine Deneuve, Peter Lawford, Sally Kellerman, Myrna Loy, Charles Boyer. **1969**

APRIL FOOL'S DAY ★★★ A group of college kids are invited to a mansion on a desolate island by a rich girl named Muffy St. John. They read Milton, quote Boswell, play practical jokes, and get killed off in a nice, orderly fashion. Not really a horror film; more of a mystery à la *Ten Little Indians*. Rated R for violence and profanity. 90m. **DIR:** Fred Walton. **CAST:** Jay Baker, Deborah Foreman, Griffin O'Neal, Amy Steel. **1986**

APRIL IN PARIS ★★1/2 State department employee Ray Bolger mistakenly asks a chorus girl (Doris Day) to represent America at a festival of the arts in Paris, and the obvious complications arise. The often (usually) misused Bolger gets to shine in one good number, "We're Going To Ring the Bell Tonight." 101m. **DIR:** David Butler. **CAST:** Doris Day, Ray Bolger, Claude Dauphin. **1952**

APT PUPIL ★★1/2 High-school student obsessed with the Holocaust recognizes a former Nazi officer and blackmails him into sharing the details of his death-camp atrocities. This disappointing adaptation of the Stephen King novella wants to explore the contagious potential of evil but trips over contrived plot points. Rated R for violence, language, and adult themes. 112m. **DIR:** Bryan Singer. **CAST:** Ian McKellen, Brad Renfro, Bruce Davison, David Schwimmer. **1998** DVD

AQUA E SAPONE ★★1/2 Would-be teacher, desperate for a job, poses as a priest in order to get a job tutoring a young American model. Bland comedy. In Italian with English subtitles. Not rated. 100m. **DIR:** Carlo Verdone. **CAST:** Carlo Verdone, Natasha Hovey, Florinda Bolkan. **1983**

ARABESQUE ★★★1/2 Fast-paced espionage-adventure about college professor Gregory Peck and his nightmarish involvement with death-dealing secret agents is an entertaining chase film and a conscious effort to capture the 1960s. Beautiful Sophia Loren keeps Peck company. 118m. **DIR:** Stanley Do-

nen. **CAST:** Gregory Peck, Sophia Loren, Kieron Moore, Alan Badel, Carl Duering, George Coulouris. **1966**

ARABIAN KNIGHT ★★ A most voluptuous princess sings a few songs before falling for a colorless, nondescript cobbler. The two set out to save her dad's kingdom when the evil Zig Zag (one of horror legend Vincent Price's final roles) turns the kingdom over to an army of one-eyed soldiers. Director Richard Williams overwhelms the senses with nontraditional animation styles that contrast and tend to detract from the simple tale. Wee viewers will be confused. Rated G. 74m. **DIR:** Richard Williams. **1993**

ARABIAN NIGHTS (1942) ★★★ Scheherazade (Maria Montez) spends 86 minutes, not a thousand-and-one nights, as the prisoner of an evil caliph until rescued by dashing Jon Hall. No magic carpets or flying horses—but John Qualen as Aladdin and Shemp Howard as Sinbad? 86m. **DIR:** John Rawlins. **CAST:** Jon Hall, Maria Montez, Sabu, Leif Erickson, Billy Gilbert, Edgar Barrier, Richard Lane, Turhan Bey, John Qualen, Shemp Howard. **1942**

ARABIAN NIGHTS (1974) ★★1/2 Pier Paolo Pasolini re-creates some of Scheherazade's original tales in this uneven but breathtaking film. Nudity is plentiful; violence is heavy-handed. In Italian with English subtitles. Rated X. 128m. **DIR:** Pier Paolo Pasolini. **CAST:** Franco Citti. **1974**

ARACHNOPHOBIA ★★★★ Steven Spielberg protégé and longtime producer Frank Marshall does a splendid job with the *Jaws* formula in this crackerjack thriller about a small-town doctor (Jeff Daniels) and a Rambo-style exterminator (John Goodman) attempting to find and kill a huge South American spider, which has been producing a passel of deadly offspring. It's both funny and scary; a delightful roller-coaster ride of guffaws and gasps. Rated PG-13 for mild violence. 103m. **DIR:** Frank Marshall. **CAST:** Jeff Daniels, John Goodman, Harley Jane Kozak. **1990** DVD

ARCADE ★★★ Computer animation enhances this tale of a virtual-reality arcade game that actually makes players engage in mortal combat. The local teens just can't stop playing, and when they start disappearing, Megan Ward must enter the game and pull its plug. Interesting update on the *Tron* theme. Rated R for violence. 85m. **DIR:** Albert Pyun. **CAST:** Megan Ward, Peter Billingsley, John de Lancie, Sharon Farrell, Norbert Weisser. **1994**

ARCADIA OF MY YOUTH 🖤 Captain Harlock and his avengers strike back against alien invaders in this maudlin, epic-length example of Japanese animation—twice the length, twice the incoherence, and more than twice the heroic/tragic death scenes. In Japanese with English subtitles. Not rated; contains violence. 130m. **DIR:** Tomoharu Katsumata. **1982**

ARCH OF TRIUMPH ★★★ In Paris before the Nazis arrive, a refugee doctor meets and falls in love with a woman with a past in this long, slow-paced, emotionless drama. It's sad, frustrating, tedious, and sometimes murky, but fans of the principal players will forgive and enjoy. B&W; 120m. **DIR:** Lewis Milestone. **CAST:** Ingrid Bergman, Charles Boyer, Charles Laughton, Louis Calhern. **1948**

ARCHER: FUGITIVE FROM THE EMPIRE ★★ This uninspired sword-and-sorcery movie was the pilot for a television series. Lane Caudell is the young warrior of the title who must overcome numerous challenges in his quest to gain a throne. 99m. **DIR:** Nick Corea. **CAST:** Lane Caudell, George Kennedy, Belinda Bauer. 1981

ARCHER'S ADVENTURE ★★★ The two-hour running time may be a bit long for young children, but otherwise this adventure makes for good family viewing. In nineteenth-century Australia, a young man crosses the country with an untried horse that he wants to enter in a race. Plenty of engaging characters and incidents. Not rated. 120m. **DIR:** Denny Lawrence. **CAST:** Brett Climo, Robert Coleby, Tony Barry. 1985

ARCTIC BLUE ★★ Although British Columbia makes a handsome substitute for the rugged Alaskan wilderness of this snowbound, kill-or-be-killed thriller, Ross LaManna's relentlessly stupid script destroys any possible suspense. Ecologists Dylan Walsh and Rya Kihlstedt pussyfoot with amoral murderer Rutger Hauer, allowing him and his big, bad buddies to wreak all sorts of mayhem. Dumb. Rated R for violence, profanity, and brief nudity. 95m. **DIR:** Peter Masterson. **CAST:** Rutger Hauer, Dylan Walsh, Rya Kihlstedt, Richard Bradford, Kevin Cooney. 1993

ARE PARENTS PEOPLE? ★★★★ Lita (Betty Bronson) realizes she can get her estranged parents back together by indulging in some scandalous behavior. Nifty satire of 1920s social mores. Silent. B&W; 63m. **DIR:** Malcolm St. Clair. **CAST:** Betty Bronson, Florence Vidor, Adolphe Menjou. 1925

ARE YOU IN THE HOUSE ALONE? ★★1/2 In this substandard made-for-television treatment of Richard Peck's Edgar Award–winning mystery novel, a beautiful high school student becomes the target of a campaign of terror that eventually leads to a sexual attack and mental torture. It's been done better before, but Kathleen Beller is exceptional as the heroine. 96m. **DIR:** Walter Grauman. **CAST:** Kathleen Beller, Blythe Danner, Tony Bill, Robin Mattson, Dennis Quaid, Ellen Travolta, Tricia O'Neil. 1978

ARE YOU LONESOME TONIGHT ★★★ A frustrated housewife (Jane Seymour) discovers her husband is tape-recording his phone-sex conversations. Her husband disappears but leaves a clue on one of the tapes. She hires a private investigator (Parker Stevenson) and together they attempt to solve the mystery. Above-average made-for-cable thriller. Rated PG-13. 91m. **DIR:** E. W. Swackhamer. **CAST:** Jane Seymour, Parker Stevenson, Beth Broderick, Joel Brooks, Robert Pine. 1991

ARENA ★★ Dopey sci-fi version of *Rocky* features a human who must take on extraterrestrials from around the galaxy in the famed Arena. Rated PG-13 for violence. 97m. **DIR:** Peter Manoogian. **CAST:** Claudia Christian, Hamilton Camp, Marc Alaimo. 1989 DVD

ARIA ★★ High expectations are dashed in this unexpectedly boring collection of vignettes made by different directors using opera segments as a creative springboard. A few good moments, but the overall impression is about as memorable as a few hours of MTV. Rated R for nudity. 90m. **DIR:** Robert Altman, Bruce Beresford, Bill Bryden, Jean-Luc Godard, Derek Jarman, Franc Roddam, Nicolas Roeg. **CAST:** Buck Henry, John Hurt, Anita Morris, Bridget Fonda, Theresa Russell. 1988 DVD

ARIEL ★★★★ An out-of-work miner goes on a cross-country trip and encounters a mugging, false arrest, and an unexpected love affair that hints of domestic happiness. This black comedy won the National Society of Film Critics Best Foreign Film award. In Finnish with English subtitles. Not rated; the film has simulated sex. 74m. **DIR:** Aki Kaurismaki. **CAST:** Turo Pajala, Matti Pellouapaa. 1990

ARISTOCATS, THE ★★★ With Disney's twentieth animated feature film, the first to be produced in its entirety following Uncle Walt's death in 1966, the formula began to wear a bit. The original story concerns an eccentric millionairess who bequeaths her entire estate to her four cats, little realizing that the once-faithful butler (as eventual heir) will become so consumed by greed that he will attempt to orchestrate an early demise for the felines. Although the voices are wonderful—notably Phil Harris and Sterling Holloway—the songs are rather weak. Rated G. 79m. **DIR:** Wolfgang Reitherman. 1970 DVD

ARIZONA ★★★1/2 The cowgirl reigns supreme in a Western that was ahead of its time. Jean Arthur stars as an independent woman coping with male bullies and barely taking time for romance with William Holden. The black-and-white scenery is gorgeous, and the verbal battles and fistfights are spiced up with Indian attacks. B&W; 125m. **DIR:** Wesley Ruggles. **CAST:** Jean Arthur, William Holden, Warren William, Edgar Buchanan, Porter Hall, Regis Toomey, George Chandler, Byron Foulger. 1940

ARIZONA BOUND ★★★ The first of the Rough Riders movies, this entry keeps secret the fact that Buck Roberts (Buck Jones), Tim McCall (Tim McCoy), and Sandy Hopkins (Raymond Hatton) are Texas Rangers who work together—but fans of classic Westerns will be familiar with the best cowboy-trio series of them all. In this case, they're called upon to save a stagecoach line from crooks operating in Mesa City. B&W; 57m. **DIR:** Spencer Gordon Bennet. **CAST:** Buck Jones, Tim McCoy, Raymond Hatton, Dennis Moore, Luana Walters, Slim Whitaker. 1941

ARIZONA BUSHWHACKERS ❤ Howard Keel, looking as if he might break into a chorus of "Old Man River" at any moment, leads a weary cast through this dreary, formulaic Western. 86m. **DIR:** Lesley Selander. **CAST:** Howard Keel, Yvonne De Carlo, John Ireland, Marilyn Maxwell, Scott Brady, Brian Donlevy, Roy Rogers Jr. 1968

ARIZONA COWBOY ★★1/2 Rex Allen's first in a series of nineteen Westerns, giving him the distinction of being the last of the singing cowboys. Ex-GI turned rodeo star, Rex is framed for a robbery by bad guys. B&W; 67m. **DIR:** R. G. Springsteen. **CAST:** Rex Allen, Gordon Jones, Roy Barcroft. 1950

ARIZONA DAYS ★★ Entertaining shoot-'em-up as somber-voiced Tex Ritter exposes the villain while shyly wooing the girl of his dreams. Ritter's films usually contained a tune or three and healthy doses of knock-down, drag-out fighting and this early entry is no exception. B&W; 57m. **DIR:** John English. **CAST:** Tex Ritter, Eleanor Stewart, Syd Saylor, William Faversham, Snub Pollard, Forrest Taylor, Glenn Strange, William Desmond, Earl Dwire, Budd Buster. **1937**

ARIZONA DREAMS ★★1/2 Too-eccentric-for-its-own-good dark comedy has the right cast to pull it off, but ultimately fails as it is left to wander aimlessly by director Emir Kusturica. Johnny Depp is right at home as a New York hotshot who is tricked into running his uncle's Cadillac dealership in Douglas, Arizona. There, he is enchanted by an eccentric woman played by Faye Dunaway. The only fun comes in watching this May-December romance simmer in the hot Arizona sun. Rated R for adult situations and language. 119m. **DIR:** Emir Kusturica. **CAST:** Johnny Depp, Faye Dunaway, Jerry Lewis, Lili Taylor, Paulina Porizkova. **1994**

ARIZONA GUNFIGHTER ★★★1/2 Fast-draw Bob Steele takes the law into his own hands to avenge the killing of his father. To do so he becomes part of an outlaw gang. An unusual spin on the typical Bob Steele revenge motif. B&W; 57m. **DIR:** Sam Newfield. **CAST:** Bob Steele, Jean Carmen, Ted Adams, Ernie Adams. **1937**

ARIZONA HEAT 🎬 Run-of-the-mill cop story about a tough but good policeman (Michael Parks) inheriting a female partner (Denise Crosby) and tracking down a crazed cop killer. Rated R for language, violence, and sex. 91m. **DIR:** John G. Thomas. **CAST:** Michael Parks, Denise Crosby, Hugh Farrington. **1988**

ARIZONA KID ★★★1/2 Roy Rogers tracks down an outlaw guerrilla bandleader in the halcyon days before the outbreak of the Civil War. B&W; 54m. **DIR:** Joseph Kane. **CAST:** Roy Rogers, George "Gabby" Hayes. **1939**

ARIZONA LEGION ★★★★ In this energetic entry in his superior Western series for RKO Pictures, George O'Brien is a Texas Ranger who goes undercover to bring a bunch of baddies to bay. Chill Wills, as his sidekick, provides comic relief that is honestly funny. Fresh and enjoyable. B&W; 58m. **DIR:** David Howard. **CAST:** George O'Brien, Laraine Day, Chill Wills. **1939**

ARIZONA RAIDERS ★★★1/2 Two reformed Quantrill Raiders help Buster Crabbe's Arizona Rangers track down former comrades turned outlaws. Historical accuracies aside—the Arizona Rangers weren't formed until 1902—plenty of action keeps this one moving. 88m. **DIR:** William Witney. **CAST:** Audie Murphy, Ben Cooper, Buster Crabbe, Gloria Talbott. **1950**

ARIZONA RANGER ★★★1/2 The only Tim Holt Western to costar his father, onetime Western star Jack Holt, is one of Tim's best. Discharged from the Rough Riders, Tim joins the Arizona Rangers and tracks down a wife-beating outlaw. B&W; 63m. **DIR:** John Rawlins. **CAST:** Tim Holt, Jack Holt, Richard Martin, Nan Leslie, Steve Brodie. **1948**

ARIZONA STAGECOACH ★★★ A girl whose brother has been taken in by highwaymen is helped by the Range Busters when they pose as heavies themselves. Last film with the original Range Busters trio. B&W; 58m. **DIR:** S. Roy Luby. **CAST:** Ray "Crash" Corrigan, John King, Max Terhune, Nell O'Day, Charles King. **1942**

ARK OF THE SUN GOD … TEMPLE OF HELL, THE 🎬 Not only are the title and story a rip-off of *Raiders of the Lost Ark*, we are also subjected to anti-Arabic

sentiment and a hero who mutters pseudocool 007-style wisecracks. Not rated; violence. 92m. **DIR:** Anthony M. Dawson. **CAST:** David Warbeck, John Steiner, Susie Sudlow, Alan Collins. **1986**

•**ARLINGTON ROAD** ★★★ Domestic terrorism rears its ugly head in this slick, cautionary thriller. A widowed Washington, D.C., professor with a young son and a girlfriend has clean-cut neighbors who may or may not be serial bombers. The film provides plenty of nooks and crannies for conspiracy junkies to explore and gives a new deep chill to the saying "there goes the neighborhood." It pushes several social and political hot buttons on its way to a rather messy, incredulous ending. Rated R for language and violence. 117m. **DIR:** Mark Pellington. **CAST:** Jeff Bridges, Tim Robbins, Hope Davis, Joan Cusack, Spencer Treat Clark. **1999 DVD**

ARMAGEDDON ★★★1/2 The second of 1998s "destroy the world" scenarios—following *Deep Impact*—actually is better and a lot of fun, given its over-the-top performances and ultracharged macho trappings. When a rogue asteroid threatens to end Life as We Know It and conventional means fail to destroy it, deep-core driller Bruce Willis and his ragtag workers are sent through a crash course of astronaut basic training and then blasted into space to take care of things. The script is steeped with patriotic fervor, and events are anchored by the Girl Left Behind. Corny beyond words, but undeniably exciting. Rated PG-13 for violence, mild profanity, and dramatic intensity. 144m. **DIR:** Michael Bay. **CAST:** Bruce Willis, Billy Bob Thornton, Liv Tyler, Ben Affleck, Will Patton, Peter Stormare, Keith David, Steve Buscemi. **1998 DVD**

ARMED AND DANGEROUS ★★ Fired cop Frank Dooley (John Candy) and former lawyer Norman Kane (Eugene Levy), become private security guards. Rated PG-13 for language. 89m. **DIR:** Mark L. Lester. **CAST:** John Candy, Eugene Levy, Robert Loggia, Kenneth McMillan, Meg Ryan, Jonathan Banks, Brion James. **1986**

ARMED AND DEADLY ★★1/2 This mindless *Terminator* rip-off finds gutsy scientist Beth Toussaint and her young son trapped in a nuclear weapons facility, battling a cyborg in name only (just an excuse for the villain to bare his chest and still repel bullets). Only the fast pace saves it from turkeydom. Rated R for violence and profanity. 100m. **DIR:** John Eyres. **CAST:** Frank Zagarino, Gary Bynesse, Beth Toussaint. **1994**

ARMED RESPONSE ★★ In Los Angeles's Chinatown, a Vietnam vet and his family fight a Japanese mob for possession of a jade statue. *Armed Response* starts out parodying the action-adventure genre, but loses its sense of humor in the middle and bogs down for too long, becoming boring and jingoistic. Rated R. 86m. **DIR:** Fred Olen Ray. **CAST:** David Carradine, Lee Van Cleef, Mako, Lois Hamilton, Ross Hagen, Brent Huff, Laurene Landon. **1986**

ARMITAGE III: ELECTRO BLOOD ★★ A staid police detective and his sexy, loose-cannon partner, Armitage, pursue a serial killer whose victims are robots on the colonized and teeming world of Mars. This animated tale is nearly made interesting by glimpses of possible future technology. Not rated;

contains violence, nudity, and profanity. 48m. DIR: Ochi Hiroyuki. 1994

ARMORED COMMAND ★★ It's World War II, and the U.S. Tank Corps is fighting its way through the German lines. Sound familiar? Predictable programmer. 99m. DIR: Byron Haskin. CAST: Howard Keel, Tina Louise, Burt Reynolds, Warner Anderson. 1961

ARMOUR OF GOD ★★★1/2 In this big-budget, Indiana Jones–style adventure, archaeologist Jackie Chan agrees to secure the mystical "armour of God" for baddies who have kidnapped his ex-girlfriend. The stunt work and action scenes are phenomenal, even by Chan's high standards. In Cantonese with English subtitles. Not rated; contains comic violence. 98m. DIR: Jackie Chan. CAST: Jackie Chan, Alan Tam, Rosamund Kwan. 1987

ARMY OF DARKNESS ★★★1/2 This third film in writer-director Sam Raimi's *Evil Dead* series is by far the most polished. That's not to say it's the best, but the mixture of comedy and mayhem make it a good old time. Film fanatics will cherish some of Raimi's nods to famous fantastic films. Rated R for violence. 83m. DIR: Sam Raimi. CAST: Bruce Campbell, Embeth Davidtz, Marcus Gilbert, Ian Abercrombie, Richard Grove. 1993 DVD

ARMY OF ONE ★★★ Dolph Lundgren stars as a wrongly accused man who escapes from prison to exact revenge on the man who put him there. Proving his innocence is secondary, but this action-packed film entertains. Available in R-rated and unrated versions; both contain violence, profanity, and sexual situations. 106m. DIR: Vic Armstrong. CAST: Dolph Lundgren, George Segal, Kristian Alfonso. 1993 DVD

ARNOLD ★★ A delightful cast cannot save this rather muddled mess of murder and mirth. Stella Stevens, married to a corpse, suddenly discovers her costars meeting their maker in a variety of strange ways reminiscent of *The Abominable Dr. Phibes*. Rated PG for violence. 100m. DIR: Georg Fenady. CAST: Roddy McDowall, Elsa Lanchester, Stella Stevens, Farley Granger, Victor Buono, John McGiver, Shani Wallis. 1973

AROUND THE WORLD ★★1/2 Bandleader Kay Kyser entertains the troops during World War II by hamming it up with an endless number of corny puns and gags. The offstage antics of the performers are highlighted by an electrifying duel between Mischa Auer and an offended nobleman. B&W; 80m. DIR: Allan Dwan. CAST: Kay Kyser, Mischa Auer, Joan Davis. 1943

AROUND THE WORLD IN 80 DAYS (1956) ★★★★ Producer Mike Todd's opulent adaptation of Jules Verne's classic tale has dated a bit, but remains a treat for those who bask in the glow of gorgeous cinematography, lavish production values, and a whimsical script that retains the novel's essential elements. This film also features cameos by more than forty cinema legends. David Niven and Cantinflas accept the challenge to circumnavigate the globe within the prescribed time; their journey unfolds against Victor Young's stirring soundtrack and Lionel Lindon's glowing camerawork . . . most of which will be lost on a conventional television set. Hold out for a letterboxed version and find a friend with a wall-size TV

screen; the results will more than justify the trouble. 167m. DIR: Michael Anderson. CAST: David Niven, Cantinflas, Shirley MacLaine, Robert Newton. 1956

AROUND THE WORLD IN 80 DAYS (1974) ★★★A turn-of-the-century English gentleman, Phileas Fogg, undertakes a wager to go around the globe in eighty days despite endless obstacles. This is well paced for youngsters, but includes dialogue that even adults will find amusing. Made for television. 60m. DIR: Arthur Rankin Jr., Jules Bass. 1974

AROUND THE WORLD IN 80 DAYS (1989) ★★★1/2 Entertaining remake of Jules Verne's classic novel features Pierce Brosnan as the rigidly punctual Phileas Fogg. Having wagered that he would circle the globe in just eighty days, Fogg sets off with his French servant who provides the comic relief. They are followed by Peter Ustinov playing a detective who believes Fogg is a notorious bank robber. Fogg finds time to rescue and fall in love with an Indian princess. Period and ethnic costuming is impressive. Made for TV, this is not rated but contains sexual situations. 267m. DIR: Buzz Kulik. CAST: Pierce Brosnan, Eric Idle, Peter Ustinov, Julia Nickson. 1989 DVD

AROUND THE WORLD IN 80 WAYS ★★ Despite a wonderfully goofy premise, this comedy from Down Under is just not very funny. Philip Quast is a young tour guide who must take his decrepit father on a world tour, but lacks the money so he fakes it, never leaving his neighborhood. Rated R for language and crudity. 90m. DIR: Stephen MacLean. CAST: Philip Quast. 1988

AROUND THE WORLD UNDER THE SEA ★★ Volcanoes, a giant eel, a submarine, scuba gear, and a quarrel over who's in charge make this lackluster, harmless viewing. Shirley Eaton was in *Goldfinger*, in case you're a James Bond fan. 117m. DIR: Andrew Marton. CAST: Lloyd Bridges, Shirley Eaton, David McCallum, Brian Kelly, Keenan Wynn, Marshall Thompson. 1966

AROUSERS, THE ★★1/2 Tab Hunter gives a genuinely creepy performance in this sleazy thriller about a necrophiliac gym teacher with a mother complex. Not rated; features adult themes and violence. 90m. DIR: Curtis Hanson. CAST: Tab Hunter, Roberta Collins. 1970

ARRANGEMENT, THE ♥ The cast is the only real reason for watching this tedious talkfest. Rated R for language. 127m. DIR: Elia Kazan. CAST: Kirk Douglas, Deborah Kerr, Faye Dunaway, Richard Boone. 1969

ARREST BULLDOG DRUMMOND ★★1/2 Bulldog Drummond and his cronies pursue a murderer to a tropical island where he has taken refuge. Fifth in the popular series featuring John Howard. Available on a double-bill video with *Bulldog Drummond in Africa*. B&W; 57m. DIR: James Hogan. CAST: John Howard, Heather Angel, George Zucco, H. B. Warner, E. E. Clive, Reginald Denny, John Sutton. 1938

ARRIVAL, THE (1990) ★★★ Even though we learn very little about the alien and its purpose, this film manages to involve the viewer. An old man is infected with an alien and finds he is growing younger but needs to kill women for their estrogen to stay young. Rated R for profanity and violence. 107m. DIR: David

Schmoeller. **CAST:** Joseph Culp, Robin Frates, John Saxon, Robert Sampson, Michael J. Pollard. **1990**

ARRIVAL, THE (1996) ★★★ Sophisticated and engaging sci-fi thriller stars Charlie Sheen as an astronomer listening to the heavens for intelligent life. When he inadvertently intercepts a seemingly alien signal, his investigation gets him fired from his job. Refusing to give up, he stumbles into an alien conspiracy involving global warming and colonization. Rated PG-13. 119m. **DIR:** David N. Twohy. **CAST:** Charlie Sheen, Lindsay Crouse, Teri Polo, Ron Silver. **1996 DVD**

•**ARRIVAL II, THE** ★★★ Sequel to the thought-provoking sci-fi flick says Zane's half brother on the run from the aliens and trying to expose their hidden agenda. While not as well acted or intellectual as the first film, this still has a lot going for it: a complex plot, solid action, and nifty gizmos. Rated PG-13 for mild violence, profanity, and brief nudity. 101m. **DIR:** Kevin S. Tenney. **CAST:** Patrick Muldoon, Jane Sibbett. **1998 DVD**

ARROGANT, THE 💘 A waitress and a philosophy-spouting motorcyclist. There's enough profanity, violence, and nudity to earn an R rating. 86m. **DIR:** Phillippe Blot. **CAST:** Gary Graham, Sylvia Kristel. **1987**

ARROWHEAD ★★★ Charlton Heston is pitted against Jack Palance in this one-sided view of the Apache conflicts. Intense, action-packed Western. Weak script is overcome by powerful acting. 105m. **DIR:** Charles Marquis Warren. **CAST:** Charlton Heston, Jack Palance, Brian Keith. **1953**

ARROWSMITH ★★★★ Mellifluous-voiced Ronald Colman is a young, career-dedicated research doctor tempted by the profits of commercialism in this faithful rendering of Sinclair Lewis's noted novel of medicine. Helen Hayes is his first wife—doomed to die before he sees the light. This is the first film to center seriously on a doctor's career and raise the question of professional integrity and morality versus quick money and social status. B&W; 101m. **DIR:** John Ford. **CAST:** Ronald Colman, Helen Hayes, Richard Bennett, DeWitt Jennings, Beulah Bondi, Myrna Loy. **1931**

ARSENAL ★★ This imaginative, symbolic denouncement of war is rich in visual images, but takes too long to make its point. A collection of episodes that take place during the last part of World War I, this Russian offering lacks fire. B&W; 70m. **DIR:** Alexander Dovzhenko. **CAST:** Semyon Svashenko. **1929**

ARSENIC AND OLD LACE ★★★1/2 Two sweet old ladies have found a solution for the loneliness of elderly men with no family or friends—they poison them! Then they give them a proper Christian burial in their basement. Their nephew, Mortimer (Cary Grant), an obvious party pooper, finds out and wants them to stop. This delightful comedy is crammed with sparkling performances. B&W; 118m. **DIR:** Frank Capra. **CAST:** Cary Grant, Priscilla Lane, Jack Carson, James Gleason, Peter Lorre, Raymond Massey, Jean Adair, Josephine Hull. **1944 DVD**

ARSON INC. ★★ Robert Lowery is an arson-squad investigator and Anne Gwynne is his romantic interest. They perform capably, but the script is at best

predictable, and stock footage of fires is quite evident. B&W; 64m. **DIR:** William Berke. **CAST:** Robert Lowery, Anne Gwynne. **1950**

ART OF BUSTER KEATON, THE ★★★★★ The genius of silent film's unique, deadpan comic shines anew in this three-volume (ten-tape) collection of the cream of his features and short comedies, a number of which have not previously been available on cassette. 120m. per cassette. **DIR:** Buster Keaton, Roscoe Arbuckle, Eddie Cline, Charles F. Reisner. **CAST:** Buster Keaton, Roscoe "Fatty" Arbuckle, Wallace Beery, Natalie Talmadge, Kathryn McGuire. **1919–1927**

ART OF DYING, THE ★★★ The *film noir* detective meets the mad slasher in this atmospheric film about a filmmaker who steals scenes from famous slasher flicks to make his own private snuff films. Director-star Wings Hauser has created a moody film with a wonderful plot. Rated R for violence, profanity, and nudity. 96m. **DIR:** Wings Hauser. **CAST:** Wings Hauser, Kathleen Kinmont, Sarah Douglas, Michael J. Pollard. **1991**

ARTEMISIA ★★★ This controversial account of the artistic blossoming and sexual deflowering of the seventeenth-century female Italian painter is intriguing. Submerging us in the world of art, this film explores the moral, social, and political implications of the talented teen's desire to include the nude human body in her paintings. The story loses steam when her dual role as feminist warrior and amused voyeur is publicly scandalized by her father. In French with English subtitles. Rated R for nudity and sexuality. 102m. **DIR:** Agnes Merlet. **CAST:** Valentina Cervi, Miki Manojlovic, Michel Serrault. **1998**

ARTHUR ★★★★ Dudley Moore is Arthur, the world's richest (and obviously happiest) alcoholic. But all is not well in his pickled paradise. Arthur will lose access to the family's great wealth if he doesn't marry the uptight debutante picked out for him by his parents. He doesn't love her … in fact, he's in love with a wacky shoplifter (Liza Minnelli). Most of the time, it's hilarious, with John Gielgud as a sharp-tongued butler providing the majority of the laughs. Rated PG because of profanity. 97m. **DIR:** Steve Gordon. **CAST:** Dudley Moore, Liza Minnelli, Stephen Elliott, John Gielgud. **1981 DVD**

ARTHUR 2: ON THE ROCKS ★★ Some sequels simply don't take characters in the directions imagined by those who loved the original film, and *Arthur 2* is a case in point. Morose, uncomfortable, and marred by its badly contrived conclusion, call this one a good try. Rated PG for mild profanity. 99m. **DIR:** Bud Yorkin. **CAST:** Dudley Moore, Liza Minnelli, John Gielgud, Cynthia Sikes, Stephen Elliott, Paul Benedict, Geraldine Fitzgerald, Barney Martin. **1988**

ARTHUR'S HALLOWED GROUND ★★ An elderly British gent stands his ground against the system in order to protect his beloved land. A good premise, until one realizes the bit of turf in question is a field on which to play cricket! 88m. **DIR:** Freddie Young. **CAST:** Michael Elphick, Jimmy Jewel, David Swift. **1973**

•**ARTHUR'S QUEST** ★★★ In this modern twist of the classic Mark Twain story (*A Connecticut Yankee* *in King Arthur's Court*), a young Prince Arthur is sent to the twentieth century by the wizard Merlin in order to hide and train the future king of Camelot. Years pass and Arthur is now a modern teenager who has completely forgotten about his medieval lineage. When Merlin returns to reclaim the adolescent king, he must convince Arthur of who he truly is, while contending with the bad guys. This is an entertaining romp that is suitable for all ages, and will certainly appeal the most to children and young teens. Rated PG for mild violence. 92m. **DIR:** Neil Mandt. **CAST:** Catherine Oxenberg, Clint Howard, Arye Gross, Eric Christian Olsen, Brion James. **1999 DVD**

ARTICLE 99 ★★1/2 VA hospitals take it on the chin in scripter Ron Cutler's acerbic blend of *M*A*S*H* and *Catch-22*, which concerns a governmental regulation denying treatment to veterans who cannot prove their injuries are war-related. Cutler's stinging satire eventually yields to a dubiously happy ending, but getting there is a lot of fun. Rated R for profanity and graphic medical procedures. 98m. **DIR:** Howard Deutch. **CAST:** Ray Liotta, Kiefer Sutherland, Forest Whitaker, John C. McGinley, Lea Thompson, John Mahoney, Kathy Baker, Eli Wallach. **1992**

ARTISTS AND MODELS ★★★ One of the better Martin and Lewis films features Dino as a cartoonist who gets his ideas from Jerry's dreams. Cowriter and director Frank Tashlin was a former cartoonist, and brought that preposterous visual style to this movie. 109m. **DIR:** Frank Tashlin. **CAST:** Dean Martin, Jerry Lewis, Shirley MacLaine, Eva Gabor, Anita Ekberg, Eddie Mayehoff. **1955**

AS GOOD AS DEAD 🎬 Try to keep from yawning while watching this made-for-cable original about a wholesome woman who helps out a new friend, only to be mixed up in a murder. Not rated; contains violence. 95m. **DIR:** Larry Cohen. **CAST:** Judge Reinhold, Crystal Bernard, Traci Lords. **1995**

AS GOOD AS IT GETS ★★★★★ This impeccably written and performed misfit love story garnered Oscars for stars Jack Nicholson and Helen Hunt. Nicholson's a nasty, obsessive-compulsive lacking any positive redeeming values until he meets a compassionate waitress/single mom trying to raise her ailing child, and a gay artist neighbor with the most adorably ugly dog ever seen. The dialogue is tart and funny; the players couldn't be better. Rated PG-13 for profanity, violence, nudity, and sexual candor. 138m. **DIR:** James L. Brooks. **CAST:** Jack Nicholson, Helen Hunt, Greg Kinnear, Cuba Gooding Jr., Skeet Ulrich, Shirley Knight. **1997 DVD**

AS IS ★★1/2 How AIDS affects family and loved ones is dealt with in a thoughtful manner as Robert Carradine portrays a homosexual who contracts the disease. Jonathan Hadary is the lover who stands by him. Although not preachy, the film does suffer from staginess. Not rated, but the whole concept is adult in nature, and some coarse language is used. 86m. **DIR:** Michael Lindsay-Hogg. **CAST:** Robert Carradine, Jonathan Hadary, Joanna Miles, Alan Scarfe, Colleen Dewhurst. **1986**

AS SUMMERS DIE ★★★1/2 A very leisurely story set in Georgia, 1959, concerns a southern aristocrat-

ic family's attempt to wrest control of land given to a black woman years earlier, because oil deposits have been found on it. Plot line is nothing new but the performances by a veteran cast carry this HBO film. Bette Davis has some touching moments as a woman whose mental competency is challenged. 87m. **DIR:** Jean-Claude Tramont. **CAST:** Scott Glenn, Jamie Lee Curtis, Bette Davis, John Randolph, Ron O'Neal, Bruce McGill, John McIntire, Beah Richards. **1987**

AS YOU DESIRE ME ★★ Greta Garbo plays an amnesiac, and her attempt to be sexy means putting on a blond wig. It works only up to a point. Based on a play by Pirandello, the film remains resolutely stagebound. B&W; 71m. **DIR:** George Fitzmaurice. **CAST:** Greta Garbo, Erich Von Stroheim, Melvyn Douglas, Owen Moore, Hedda Hopper. **1932**

AS YOU LIKE IT ★★★ Laurence Olivier is commanding as Orlando to beautiful Elisabeth Bergner's stylized Rosalind in this early filming of Shakespeare's delightful comedy. Lovers of the Bard will be pleased. B&W; 96m. **DIR:** Paul Czinner. **CAST:** Elisabeth Bergner, Laurence Olivier, Felix Aylmer, Leon Quartermaine. **1936 DVD**

AS YOUNG AS YOU FEEL ★★1/2 Marilyn Monroe's presence in a bit part, and the fact that Paddy Chayefsky provided the original story, are the main drawing cards today in this broad spoof of big business. B&W; 77m. **DIR:** Harmon Jones. **CAST:** Monty Woolley, Thelma Ritter, David Wayne, Jean Peters, Marilyn Monroe. **1951**

ASCENT, THE ★★★ Cross between *The Great Escape* and *The Bridge on the River Kwai* minus the spellbinding acting of the two classics. Focus is on proud Italian POWs in a British concentration camp in East Africa. The men plan to leave their flag at the top of Mount Kenya in a magnificent, nose-thumbing gesture to their captors. The actual climb is death-defying with some edge-of-the-seat, hand-in-mouth moments of terror. Rated PG for violence and sexual innuendo. 96m. **DIR:** Donald Shebib. **CAST:** Vincent Spano, Ben Cross, Tony Lo Bianco, Rachel Ward. **1994**

ASCENT TO HEAVEN (MEXICAN BUS RIDE) ★★★ A young man's wedding ceremony is interrupted so he can make a two-day bus journey to get his dying mother's will ratified. On the way, he encounters a variety of hilarious adventures and delays. A good light comedy, punctuated with Luis Buñuel's great surreal touches. In Spanish with English subtitles. B&W; 85m. **DIR:** Luis Buñuel. **CAST:** Lilia Prado, Esteban Marquez. **1951**

ASH WEDNESDAY ★★1/2 Elizabeth Taylor plays an aging woman who undergoes a painful cosmetic make-over in order to make herself more appealing to husband Henry Fonda. This disjointed morality play has some good moments, but offensive close-ups of the facial operation and the melodramatic predictability of the story eventually work against it. Rated R. 99m. **DIR:** Larry Peerce. **CAST:** Elizabeth Taylor, Henry Fonda, Helmut Berger, Keith Baxter, Margaret Blye, Monique Van Vooren. **1973**

ASHANTI ★★1/2 A shopping trip turns into a tale of horror when the black wife (Beverly Johnson) of a white doctor (Michael Caine) in Africa is kidnapped and turned over to a slave trader (Peter Ustinov).

Thus begins a fairly exciting chase across various exotic locales. Rated R. 118m. **DIR:** Richard Fleischer. **CAST:** Michael Caine, Peter Ustinov, Beverly Johnson, William Holden, Omar Sharif, Rex Harrison. **1979**

ASHES AND DIAMONDS ★★★★ The conflict between idealism and instinct is explored with great intensity in this story of a Polish resistance fighter who assassinates the wrong man at the end of World War II. Director Andrzej Wajda captures all the bitterness and disillusionment of political fanaticism in this powerful testament of the Polish people during the struggle that followed the war's end. In Polish with English subtitles. B&W; 102m. **DIR:** Andrzej Wajda. **CAST:** Zbigniew Cybulski. **1958**

ASK ANY GIRL ★★★ A motivation researcher tries out his theories by helping a husband hunter to snag his playboy brother. The third male lead, lecherous Rod Taylor, steals the movie. 101m. **DIR:** Charles Walters. **CAST:** David Niven, Shirley MacLaine, Gig Young, Rod Taylor, Jim Backus. **1959**

ASPEN EXTREME ★★★1/2 Paul Gross and Peter Berg leave dead-end jobs in Detroit to hire on as Aspen ski instructors, where the former's California-style good looks make an immediate impression with predatory rich lady Finola Hughes. Rated PG-13 for profanity and suggested sex. 117m. **DIR:** Patrick Hasburgh. **CAST:** Paul Gross, Peter Berg, Finola Hughes, Teri Polo, William Russ. **1993**

ASPHALT JUNGLE, THE ★★★★1/2 One of the greatest crime films of all time. This realistic study of a jewel robbery that sours reveals early on what the outcome will be while building tension for any surprises that might pop up. Sterling Hayden and a near-perfect cast charge the film with an electric current that only increases in power as they scheme their way closer to their fate. John Huston broke new ground with this landmark drama. B&W; 112m. **DIR:** John Huston. **CAST:** Sterling Hayden, Sam Jaffe, Louis Calhern, Marilyn Monroe, Jean Hagen, James Whitmore, Marc Lawrence, Anthony Caruso. **1950**

ASSASSIN ★★1/2 Now-familiar tale of a killer cyborg running loose and out of control. Robert Conrad, retired from the Agency, is brought in from the cold to hunt and destroy the robot with the symbolic name of Golem. Originally a television movie, but released on cassette with an R rating for violence. 94m. **DIR:** Sandor Stern. **CAST:** Robert Conrad, Karen Austin, Richard Young, Robert Webber. **1986 DVD**

ASSASSIN OF YOUTH (MARIJUANA) ★★ This silly, low-budget exploitation film tells the story of a courageous young reporter who goes undercover to infiltrate the marijuana cult that has been wreaking havoc with a local town. Cornball humor gives this an extra edge on most films of this nature. B&W; 67m. **DIR:** Elmer Clifton. **CAST:** Luana Walters, Arthur Gardner, Earl Dwire. **1936**

ASSASSINATION 💔 In this predictable, poorly written action flick, Charles Bronson plays a seasoned secret service agent who is called upon to guard the first lady (Jill Ireland). Rated PG-13 for profanity and violence. 105m. **DIR:** Peter R. Hunt. **CAST:** Charles Bronson, Jill Ireland, Stephen Elliott, Jan Gan Boyd, Randy Brooks, Michael Ansara. **1987**

ASSASSINATION FILE, THE ★★★ A Secret Service agent—who resigned due to an assassination on her watch—begins an investigation into the killing. Rated R for violence, profanity, and nudity. 106m. **DIR:** John Harrison. **CAST:** Sherilyn Fenn, Paul Winfield. **1996**

ASSASSINATION GAME, THE 💔 Dismal espionage film about a rookie CIA agent teaming up with a retired KGB agent. Rated R for violence, nudity, and profanity. 89m. **DIR:** Jonathan Winfrey. **CAST:** Robert Rusler, Theodore Bikel, Denise Bixler, Doug Wert. **1992**

ASSASSINATION OF TROTSKY, THE 💔 Richard Burton as the exiled Soviet leader. A chaotic yawner. Rated R. 102m. **DIR:** Joseph Losey. **CAST:** Richard Burton, Alain Delon, Romy Schneider. **1972**

ASSASSINS ★★1/2 Professional hit man Sylvester Stallone finds himself the hunted rather than the hunter when up-and-coming shooter Antonio Banderas targets him as an unwanted rival, in this tedious, overlong action film. Only Julianne Moore, as a high-tech con woman, adds any spark to what plays like a clone of *The Gunfighter* and *The Mechanic*. Rated R for violence and profanity. 132m. **DIR:** John Badham. **CAST:** Sylvester Stallone, Antonio Banderas, Julianne Moore. **1995 DVD**

ASSASSINS DE L'ORDRE, LES (LAW BREAKERS) ★★ Marcel Carné, who directed the 1944 classic *Children of Paradise*, slips into innocuousness with this less than riveting tale. Jacques Brel plays a judge who is trying to get to the bottom of corrupt police practices. 107m. **DIR:** Marcel Carné. **CAST:** Jacques Brel, Catherine Rouvel, Michel Lonsdale, Charles Denner, Didier Haudepin. **1971**

ASSAULT, THE ★★★★1/2 This Academy Award winner for best foreign language film deserves its praise. It is a tale of war and its inevitable impact. In Holland in 1945, a Nazi collaborator is murdered and the lives of the witnesses, a small boy in particular, are changed forever. Dubbed. 126m. **DIR:** Fons Rademakers. **CAST:** Derek de Lint, Marc van Uchelen, Monique van de Ven. **1986 DVD**

ASSAULT & MATRIMONY ★★★ Likable made-for-television comedy pitting real-life husband-and-wife team Jill Eikenberry and Michael Tucker against each other as warring spouses trying to kill each other. 100m. **DIR:** James Frawley. **CAST:** Jill Eikenberry, Michael Tucker, John Hillerman, Michelle Phillips. **1987**

ASSAULT AT WEST POINT ★★★ Although based on a reprehensible actual event at West Point, the story never connects. Seth Gilliam remains too detached as Johnson Whittaker, the first black cadet accepted at West Point, whose military career was derailed after he was assaulted … and "proved" to have beaten himself unconscious. The usually excellent Sam Waterston is uncomfortably stiff as Whittaker's defense attorney. Rated PG-13 for mild profanity and brief violence. 98m. **DIR:** Harry Moses. **CAST:** Samuel L. Jackson, Sam Waterston, Seth Gilliam, John Glover, Josef Sommer, Mason Adams. **1994**

ASSAULT OF THE KILLER BIMBOS ★★ Goofy excuse for a movie has three go-go dancers running afoul of the mob and then getting mixed up with surfers. Not to be taken seriously. Rated R for nudity, violence, and profanity. 85m. **DIR:** Anita Rosenberg. **CAST:** Christina Whitaker, Elizabeth Kaitan, Nick Cassavetes, Griffin O'Neal. **1988 DVD**

ASSAULT OF THE REBEL GIRLS (CUBAN REBEL GIRLS) 💔 Errol Flynn's last film is a cheaply made bargain-basement production. B&W; 68m. **DIR:** Barry Mahon. **CAST:** Errol Flynn, Beverly Aadland, John McKay. **1959**

ASSAULT ON A QUEEN ★★★ Implausible, improbable, but sometimes fun story by Rod Serling, has Frank Sinatra and pals bluffing their way onto the *Queen Mary* for a million-dollar haul. Originally released at an overlong 146 minutes. Cuts help to move the story along. Okay family viewing. 105m. **DIR:** Jack Donohue. **CAST:** Frank Sinatra, Virna Lisi, Anthony Franciosa, Richard Conte. **1968**

ASSAULT ON AGATHON 💔 While investigating a series of robberies of Greek banks, a British and an American Interpol agent uncover a plot by a World War II underground leader to start a new revolution. 96m. **DIR:** Laslo Benedek. **CAST:** Nico Minardos, Nina Van Pallandt, John Woodvine, Marianne Faithfull. **1976**

ASSAULT ON PRECINCT 13 ★★★1/2 Here's director John Carpenter's riveting movie about a nearly deserted L.A. police station that finds itself under siege by a youth gang. It's a modern-day version of Howard Hawks's *Rio Bravo*, with exceptional performances by its entire cast. Rated R. 90m. **DIR:** John Carpenter. **CAST:** Austin Stoker, Laurie Zimmer, Tony Burton, Nancy Loomis, Darwin Joston. **1976 DVD**

ASSIGNMENT, THE ★★★★ In this superior espionage thriller, Aidan Quinn is emotionally riveting as an American naval officer who bears an uncanny resemblance to international terrorist Carlos "The Jackal" Sanchez. When he is recruited by Israeli intelligence and the CIA to impersonate the terrorist and draw him into the open, his life becomes embroiled in international intrigue and deadly consequences. Rated R for adult situations, language, nudity, and violence. 119m. **DIR:** Christian Duguay. **CAST:** Aidan Quinn, Donald Sutherland, Ben Kingsley. **1997 DVD**

ASSISI UNDERGROUND, THE ★★ Melodrama tracing the activities of a Franciscan monastery as part of the Jewish liberation network in World War II Italy. Ben Cross struggles valiantly to bring some life to this dreary fact-based tale; hard work considering the poor dialogue and unrealistic behavior of the Jews he is trying to help escape from Europe. Rated PG. 115m. **DIR:** Alexander Ramati. **CAST:** Ben Cross, James Mason, Irene Papas, Maximilian Schell, Karl Heinz Hackl, Delia Boccardo, Edmund Purdom. **1985**

ASSOCIATE, THE (1982) ★★ Disappointing comedy about an unemployed bank clerk who schemes to murder his wealthy business partner. Michel Serrault is the only bright spot in this otherwise muddled comedy. In French with English subtitles. Not rated; contains nudity and profanity. 94m. **DIR:** René Gainville. **CAST:** Michel Serrault, Claudine Auger, Catherine Alric. **1982**

ASSOCIATE, THE (1996) ★★★ Wall Street analyst Whoopi Goldberg can't catch a break in a field dominated by men, so she sets up her own partnership with a wholly fictitious male partner. Nick Thiel's

script for the most part scores with well-timed jokes about gender confusion, but things become less successful when Goldberg has to actually *become* her male counterpart. Rated PG-13 for profanity and considerable blue humor. 113m. **DIR:** Donald Petrie. **CAST:** Whoopi Goldberg, Dianne Wiest, Eli Wallach, Timothy Daly, Bebe Neuwirth, Austin Pendleton, Lainie Kazan. **1996 DVD**

ASTRO-ZOMBIES 💔 John Carradine as a mad scientist killing to obtain body parts for his new creation. 83m. **DIR:** Ted V. Mikels. **CAST:** Wendell Corey, John Carradine, Rafael Campos. **1967**

•ASTRONAUT'S WIFE, THE ★★1/2 Two American astronauts begin acting very strangely after a near-fatal deep-space accident. The wife of one of the NASA space cowboys becomes pregnant with twins and either evidence or her paranoia begins to suggest she may be an incubator for alien embryos. This sensual, extraterrestrial riff on *Rosemary's Baby* lacks gnawing suspense. Rated R for language, violence, and sexuality. 110m. **DIR:** Rand Ravich. **CAST:** Johnny Depp, Charlize Theron, Joe Morton, Nick Cassavetes. **1999 DVD**

ASYLUM (1972) ★★★★ A first-rate horror anthology from England featuring fine performances. Four seemingly unrelated stories of madness by Robert Bloch are interwoven, leading to a nail-biting climax. Rated PG. 92m. **DIR:** Roy Ward Baker. **CAST:** Barbara Parkins, Sylvia Syms, Peter Cushing, Barry Morse, Richard Todd, Herbert Lom, Patrick Magee. **1972**

ASYLUM (1996) 💔 Tired tale of a P.I. who goes undercover in a mental hospital to find out who killed his friend. Not rated; contains violence, language, and adult situations. 90m. **DIR:** James Seale. **CAST:** Robert Patrick, Malcolm McDowell, Sarah Douglas, Henry Gibson, Peter Brown, Irwin Keyes. **1996**

ASYLUM OF SATAN 💔 Girdler's first feature contains mucho sadism. Rated R. 82m. **DIR:** William Girdler. **CAST:** Charles Kissinger, Carla Borelli. **1972**

AT BERTRAM'S HOTEL ★★★1/2 Miss Marple (Joan Hickson) takes a London vacation, courtesy of her nephew Raymond, in this superior installment of the Agatha Christie series. Miss Marple encounters some old friends during her stay at Bertram's Hotel, where she discovers that surface appearances are just a little too good to be true. Costumes and set design are luxurious. Not rated; suitable for family viewing. 102m. **DIR:** Mary McMurray. **CAST:** Joan Hickson, Caroline Blakiston, Helena Michell, George Baker, James Cossins, Preston Lockwood, Joan Greenwood. **1986**

AT CLOSE RANGE ★★★★ A powerful thriller based on true events that occurred in Pennsylvania during the summer of 1978. A rural gang leader returns to the family he abandoned years ago. His two sons try to prove themselves worthy of joining the gang. Events beyond their control lead to a brutal showdown between father and sons. Rated R for violence and profanity. 115m. **DIR:** James Foley. **CAST:** Christopher Walken, Sean Penn, Christopher Penn. **1986**

AT FIRST SIGHT (1995) ★★1/2 Jonathan Silverman's knack for physical comedy and some funny dialogue help keep this slight romantic comedy afloat. He finds the woman of his dreams in Allison Smith, but allows his meddlesome, skirt-chasing best friend to knock her out of the picture. A lack of focus is a problem, as this can't decide if it's a romantic comedy, a buddy flick, or a coming-of-age story. Rated R for profanity and sexual situations. 90m. DIR: Steven Pearl. CAST: Jonathan Silverman, Dan Cortese, Allison Smith. 1995

AT FIRST SIGHT (1999) ★★ A blind masseur, at the urging of his new girlfriend, undergoes an operation to restore his vision. The theme of Oliver Sacks's original article—the dilemma of a man trying to adjust to his sense of sight after a lifetime without it— is fascinating. Unfortunately, the film concentrates on the strain that grows between the two lovers and becomes a tedious soap opera. Rated PG-13 for brief sexual scenes. 128m. DIR: Irwin Winkler. CAST: Mira Sorvino, Val Kilmer, Kelly McGillis, Steven Weber, Bruce Davison, Nathan Lane. 1999 DVD

AT GUNPOINT ★★★ Fred MacMurray plays a mild-mannered storekeeper who accidentally foils a bank robbery. The grateful town makes him sheriff, then turns to him when the outlaws return. The story is a clever reworking of *High Noon* to match MacMurray's unique screen personality, and the supporting cast is uniformly fine. Not rated, but may be too violent for young children. 81m. DIR: Alfred Werker. CAST: Fred MacMurray, Dorothy Malone, Walter Brennan, Tommy Rettig, John Qualen, Skip Homeier. 1955

AT PLAY IN THE FIELDS OF THE LORD 🖤 A boring movie without redeeming social value in spite of its high-powered cast tells a dramatic story, but Babenco's overbearing style makes it unbearable to watch. Rated R for nudity and profanity. 186m. DIR: Hector Babenco. CAST: Kathy Bates, John Lithgow, Aidan Quinn, Tom Berenger, Daryl Hannah, Tom Waits. 1991

AT SWORD'S POINT ★★1/2 The sons (and a daughter) of the fabled Three Musketeers come to the aid of the queen of France, and thwart the ambitions of a throne-hungry duke. Lighthearted adventure yarn. 81m. DIR: Lewis Allen. CAST: Cornel Wilde, Maureen O'Hara, Dan O'Herlihy, Alan Hale Jr., Robert Douglas, Blanche Yurka, Gladys Cooper. 1952

AT THE CIRCUS ★★★1/2 The Marx Brothers were running out of steam as a comedy team by this time. Still, any film with Groucho, Harpo, and Chico is worth watching, although you'll probably feel like punching the comedy's "hero" (or is that a zero?), Kenny Baker, when he sings that highly forgettable ditty "Step Up, Take a Bow." B&W; 87m. DIR: Edward Buzzell. CAST: The Marx Brothers, Margaret Dumont, Kenny Baker, Eve Arden. 1939

AT THE EARTH'S CORE ★★1/2 An Edgar Rice Burroughs adaptation benefits enormously from an inspired performance by Peter Cushing. He even manages to make Doug McClure look good occasionally. It's mostly for the kiddies, but we found ourselves clutching the arm of the chair a couple of times at the height of suspense. Rated PG. 90m. DIR: Kevin Connor. CAST: Doug McClure, Peter Cushing, Caroline Munro, Godfrey James. 1976

AT WAR WITH THE ARMY ★★★★ Dean Martin and Jerry Lewis were still fresh and funny at the time of this comedy release, but a classic it isn't (though some scenes are gems). B&W; 93m. DIR: Hal Walker. CAST: Dean Martin, Jerry Lewis, Polly Bergen, Angela Greene, Mike Kellin. 1950 DVD

ATHENA ★★ A minor musical about an eccentric family who believe regular exercise and eating all your vegetables will make your vocal chords strong. The plot is weak, but the personalities are impressive. 96m. DIR: Richard Thorpe. CAST: Jane Powell, Debbie Reynolds, Vic Damone, Edmund Purdom, Steve Reeves, Virginia Gibson, Louis Calhern, Linda Christian, Carl Benton Reid, Evelyn Varden. 1954

ATLANTIC CITY ★★★★★ This superb motion picture has all of the elements that made the films of Hollywood's golden age great—with a few appropriately modern twists tossed in. The screenplay, by John Guare—about a struggling casino worker (Susan Sarandon) who becomes involved in a drug deal—gives us powerful drama, wonderful characters, memorable dialogue, and delightfully funny situations. And the performances by Burt Lancaster, Sarandon, and Kate Reid, in particular, are top-notch. Rated R because of brief nudity and violence. 104m. DIR: Louis Malle. CAST: Burt Lancaster, Susan Sarandon, Kate Reid. 1981

ATLAS ★★ Roger Corman's obligatory entry in the sword-and-sandal genre (shot in Greece) is underpopulated (and, as Atlas, Michael Forest is a tad underfed), but it contains enough in-jokes and gore to keep Corman aficionados mildly amused. 80m. DIR: Roger Corman. CAST: Michael Forest, Barboura Morris, Frank Wolff. 1961

ATOLL K (UTOPIA) 🖤 The final screen outing of the great comedy team of Stan Laurel and Oliver Hardy is a keen disappointment. B&W; 80m. DIR: Léo Joannon. CAST: Stan Laurel, Oliver Hardy. 1950 DVD

ATOM AGE VAMPIRE 🖤 Badly dubbed Italian time-waster with cheese-ball special effects and a tired premise. B&W; 71m. DIR: Anton Giulio Masano. CAST: Alberto Lupo, Susanne Loret. 1960

ATOM MAN VS. SUPERMAN ★★ The second and final serial based on the adventures of Superman reunites most of the principal cast from the first chapterplay and throws in the Man of Steel's nemesis, Lex Luthor. Competently played by the talented and often-seen Lyle Talbot, Luthor is out to blackmail Metropolis by threatening the city with destruction. B&W; 15 chapters. DIR: Spencer Gordon Bennet. CAST: Kirk Alyn, Noel Neill, Lyle Talbot, Tommy Bond, Pierre Watkin, Jack Ingram, Don Harvey, Terry Frost. 1950

ATOMIC CAFE, THE ★★ Beyond being an interesting cultural document, this feature-length compilation of post–World War II propaganda, documentary, and newsreel footage on American attitudes toward the atomic bomb has little to offer. No MPAA rating. The film has no objectionable material, though some of the footage featuring casualties of atomic bomb explosions is quite graphic. B&W; 88m. DIR: Kevin Rafferty, Jayne Loader, Pierce Rafferty. 1982

ATOMIC DOG 🖤 Don't get burned watching this made-for-cable original about a mutant mutt bent on radioactive revenge against the family who raised his pups—the plot makes little sense, and every dog's a Lassie wannabe. Not rated; contains violence. 95m. DIR: Brian Trenchard-Smith. CAST: Daniel Hugh Kelly, Isabella Hofmann, Cindy Pickett. 1997

ATOMIC KID, THE ♥ Stupid story about prospector Mickey Rooney surviving an atomic bomb blast and attracting spies. B&W; 86m. DIR: Leslie Martinson. CAST: Mickey Rooney, Robert Strauss, Whit Bissell, Hal March. 1954

ATOMIC SUBMARINE, THE ★★★ Solid little thriller about U.S. atomic submarine and its encounter with an alien flying saucer in the Arctic suffers from budgetary limitations but benefits from a decent script, good direction, and an effective and thoroughly believable cast of fine character actors. B&W; 72m. DIR: Spencer Gordon Bennet. CAST: Arthur Franz, Dick Foran, Brett Halsey, Tom Conway, Bob Steele, Joi Lansing. 1959 DVD

ATOR: THE FIGHTING EAGLE ♥ A low-budget stupid sword-and-sorcery flick. Rated PG for violence and nudity. 98m. DIR: David Hills. CAST: Miles O'Keeffe, Sabrina Siani, Warren Hillman. 1983

•ATTACK! ★★★★ Jack Palance leads a strong cast as the leader of a platoon sent into an impossible situation by an officer who then refuses to admit his mistake by sending reinforcements to help them out. Terrific, gritty antiwar movie. B&W; 107m. DIR: Robert Aldrich. CAST: Jack Palance, Eddie Albert, Lee Marvin, Robert Strauss, Richard Jaeckel, Buddy Ebsen, Strother Martin. 1956

ATTACK FORCE Z ★★ Okay Australian film concerning a group of commandos on a secret mission against the Japanese in World War II. Most notable is a young Mel Gibson as the leader of the commandos. Not rated. 84m. DIR: Tim Burstall. CAST: John Phillip Law, Sam Neill, Mel Gibson, Chris Haywood, John Waters. 1981

ATTACK OF THE CRAB MONSTERS ★★★ Neat Roger Corman low-budget movie, seemed scarier when you were a kid, but it's still a lot of fun. A remote Pacific atoll is besieged by a horde of giant land crabs that, upon devouring members of a scientific expedition, absorb their brains and acquire the ability to speak in their voices. B&W; 64m. DIR: Roger Corman. CAST: Richard Garland, Pamela Duncan, Mel Welles, Russell Johnson, Ed Nelson. 1957

ATTACK OF THE 50-FOOT WOMAN (1958) ★★★ One of the best "schlock" films from the 1950s. Allison Hayes stars as a woman who is kidnapped by a tremendous bald alien and transformed into a giant herself. Duddy special effects only serve to heighten the enjoyment of this kitsch classic. B&W; 66m. DIR: Nathan Juran. CAST: Allison Hayes, William Hudson, Yvette Vickers. 1958

ATTACK OF THE 50-FOOT WOMAN (1993) ★★1/2 The effects look good, but everything else is pretty ho-hum in this arch remake of one of cinema's all-time turkeys. Scripter Joseph Dougherty's attempt to inject politically correct feminism is simply laughable, and it's hard to decide whether title character Daryl Hannah is less interesting before or after her transformation. Rated PG-13 for profanity and brief nudity. 90m. DIR: Christopher Guest. CAST: Daryl Hannah, Daniel Baldwin, William Windom, Cristi Conaway, Frances Fisher. 1993

ATTACK OF THE GIANT LEECHES ★★ Engagingly bad, lurid programmer—originally double-billed with *A Bucket of Blood*—about an Everglades town plagued by the title monsters. Cheesy fun from an imaginative B-movie director. B&W; 62m. DIR: Bernard Kowalski. CAST: Ken Clark, Yvette Vickers, Bruno Ve Sota. 1959

ATTACK OF THE KILLER TOMATOES ♥ In this campy cult film, the tomatoes are funnier than the actors, most of whom are rank amateurs. Rated PG. 87m. DIR: John DeBello. CAST: David Miller, Sharon Taylor, George Wilson, Jack Riley. 1980

ATTACK OF THE PUPPET PEOPLE ♥ Cheapo special effects doom this tale of a puppeteer who makes his dolls the easy way: by shrinking humans. B&W; 78m. DIR: Bert I. Gordon. CAST: John Agar, John Hoyt, June Kenney, Laurie Mitchell. 1958

ATTACK OF THE SWAMP CREATURE ♥ In one of Elvira's "Thriller Video" movies, we're subjected to the story of a mad scientist who turns himself into a giant, man-eating, walking catfish. 96m. DIR: Arnold Stevens. CAST: Frank Crowell, Patricia Robertson. 1985

ATTACK OF THE 60-FT. CENTERFOLD ♥ A model ingests a formula that causes her to grow to huge proportions in this lame comedy that mixes *Attack of the 50-Ft. Woman* with T&A. Rated R for nudity and profanity. 83m. DIR: Fred Olen Ray. CAST: J. J. North, Raelyn Saalman, Tammy Parks, Michelle Bauer, Russ Tamblyn, Ross Hagen. 1995

ATTIC, THE ★★ Rather slow-moving and routine story concerning a young woman (Carrie Snodgress) fighting to free herself from the clutches of her crippled, almost insane, father. Tries to be deep and psychological and falls flat on its face. Rated PG. 97m. DIR: George Edwards. CAST: Carrie Snodgress, Ray Milland. 1979

ATTIC: THE HIDING OF ANNE FRANK ★★★★ The true story of Anne Frank seen from the viewpoint of Miep Gies, the woman who risked everything to hide the Jewish families during World War II. William Hanley's teleplay wonderfully depicts the events outside the attic and the harsh realities of the German occupation. Great performances all around, especially from Mary Steenburgen, who portrays Gies. 95m. DIR: John Erman. CAST: Mary Steenburgen, Paul Scofield, Huub Stapel, Eleanor Bron, Frances Cuka. 1988

ATTICA ★★★★ This made-for-TV account of the horrifying Attica prison riots of 1971 is a very detailed translation of Tom Wicker's bestselling book *A Time to Die*. Screenwriter James Henerson deserves kudos for this adaptation. The performances are uniformly excellent. 100m. DIR: Marvin J. Chomsky. CAST: Charles Durning, George Grizzard, Anthony Zerbe, Glynn Turman, Henry Darrow. 1980

AU REVOIR, LES ENFANTS ★★★★★ Louis Malle may have created his masterpiece with this autobiographical account of a traumatic incident in his youth that occurred in World War II France. Certainly this heartfelt and heartbreaking work about man's inhumanity to man is likely to remain his most unforgettable creation. Rated PG for strong themes. In French with English subtitles. 104m. DIR: Louis

Malle. **CAST:** Gaspard Manesse, Raphael Fejto, Philippe Morier-Genoud, Francine Racette. **1987**

AUDREY ROSE 🎬 Plodding melodrama about a man who annoys a couple by claiming that his dead daughter has been reincarnated as their live one. Rated PG. 113m. **DIR:** Robert Wise. **CAST:** Marsha Mason, Anthony Hopkins, John Beck. **1977**

AUGUST ★★★★ Anthony Hopkins directs and stars in this lovely Victorian romance-drama. Hopkins plays Ieuan, who lives the life of Riley in his huge country estate. Ieuan loves to drink and flirt, but all that is about to come to an end when his ex-brother-in-law comes to visit with his beautiful wife, Helen, in tow. It doesn't take long before Ieuan becomes infatuated with Helen, which leads to major complications for all involved. Gorgeous production design and an excellent cast bring this little gem to life. Rated PG for language. 90m. **DIR:** Anthony Hopkins. **CAST:** Anthony Hopkins, Leslie Phillips, Kate Burton, Rhian Morgan. **1995**

AUNTIE LEE'S MEAT PIES ★★1/2 Good for Auntie Lee, played by Karen Black. Business is booming, and she sends out her four adorable niece (former *Playboy* Playmates) to fetch fresh ingredients, including motorists, highway patrolmen, hitchhikers. Tongue-in-cheek black comedy is mildly entertaining. Rated R for nudity, violence, and language. 100m. **DIR:** Joseph F. Robertson. **CAST:** Karen Black, Noriyuki "Pat" Morita, Huntz Hall, Michael Berryman. **1992**

AUNTIE MAME ★★★1/2 Rosalind Russell, in the title role, plays a free-thinking eccentric woman whose young nephew is placed in her care. Russell created the role on the stage; it was a once-in-a-lifetime showcase that she made uniquely her own. 143m. **DIR:** Morton Da Costa. **CAST:** Rosalind Russell, Forrest Tucker, Coral Browne, Fred Clark. **1958**

AURORA ENCOUNTER ★★1/2 Here's one that can be enjoyed by the whole family. Jack Elam is outstanding in a story about a small Texas town visited by aliens in the late 1800s. Rated PG. 90m. **DIR:** Jim McCullough. **CAST:** Jack Elam, Peter Brown, Carol Bagdasarian, Dottie West. **1985**

AUSTIN POWERS: INTERNATIONAL MAN OF MYSTERY ★★ This tepid spoof of the 1960s and its many spy movies drools all over itself while trying to be "groovy, baby." Powers is a Carnaby Street swinger and secret agent whose wily nemesis, Dr. Evil, is a throwback to James Bond villains of yesteryear. The two have been cryogenically frozen since 1967 and thaw out in a lame battle of (nit)wits that never comically warms up to the material it wants to skewer. Rated PG-13 for language and sexually suggestive subject matter. 88m. **DIR:** Jay Roach. **CAST:** Mike Myers, Michael York, Mimi Rogers, Elizabeth Hurley, Fabiana Udenio, Robert Wagner. **1997 DVD**

•**AUSTIN POWERS: THE SPY WHO SHAGGED ME** ★★ This limp sequel isn't really the pop-art 1960s spy spoof that its advertising campaign suggested. True, it does poke fun at the cinematic Bond, Flint, Helm, and their ilk, but only incidentally; the film really exists as a vehicle for Mike Myers's brand of slow-motion, quadruple-take humor, and an endless stream of sniggering sex and excretory jokes. If it

emanates from a bodily orifice, sooner or later it's in this film. Generously rated PG-13 for coy nudity, British profanity, raunchy sexual content, and repugnant toilet humor. 93m. **DIR:** Jay Roach. **CAST:** Mike Myers, Heather Graham, Michael York, Robert Wagner, Seth Green, Mindy Sterling, Rob Lowe. **1999 DVD**

AUTHOR! AUTHOR! ★★★ Al Pacino stars as a playwright whose wife (Tuesday Weld) leaves him with five kids (not all his) to raise in this nicely done bittersweet comedy. Dyan Cannon plays the actress with whom he falls in love. Rated PG for brief profanity. 110m. **DIR:** Arthur Hiller. **CAST:** Al Pacino, Dyan Cannon, Alan King, Tuesday Weld. **1982**

AUTOBIOGRAPHY OF A PRINCESS ★★1/2 A captivating performance by Indian actress Madhur Jaffrey dominates this mundane, British teledrama about an exiled Indian princess and her father's extutor (James Mason) sharing memories of colonial India. Unusual for a Merchant-Ivory production, this too-short film suffers from a lack of character development, uninspired dialogue, and an absence of lavish production quality. 59m. **DIR:** James Ivory. **CAST:** James Mason, Madhur Jaffrey. **1975**

AUTOBIOGRAPHY OF MISS JANE PITTMAN, THE ★★★★★ This terrific television movie traces black history in America from the Civil War years to the turbulent civil rights movement of the 1960s. All this is seen through the eyes of 110-year-old ex-slave Jane Pittman (Cicely Tyson). The entire cast is superb, but Tyson still manages to tower above the others in the title role. There is no rating, but it should be noted that there are some violent scenes. 110m. **DIR:** John Korty. **CAST:** Cicely Tyson, Richard Dysart, Odetta, Michael Murphy, Thalmus Rasulala. **1974**

AUTOMATIC ★★★1/2 This fast-paced riff on *The Terminator* is a bit more clever than the usual knockoffs. Olivier Gruner plays a compassionate android—well-versed in Asimov's Three Laws of Robotics—that accidentally kills a human superior caught raping a coworker. Fearing the bad publicity that might result, corporate exec John Glover (wonderfully slimy) orders both android and woman exterminated . . . a fate they're not about to accept quietly. Rated R for violence, rape, nudity, and profanity. 90m. **DIR:** John Murlowski. **CAST:** Olivier Gruner, Daphne Ashbrook, John Glover, Jeff Kober. **1994**

AUTOPSY 🎬 The story involves a young medical student doing graduate study in a morgue. Rated R for nudity and graphic violence. 90m. **DIR:** Armando Crispino. **CAST:** Mimsy Farmer, Raymond Lovelock, Barry Primus. **1976 DVD**

AUTUMN AFTERNOON, AN ★★★ Aging buddies discuss the fate of one of the men's daughters in this slow-moving drama. The group decides that an arranged marriage would be best for her. Although the film is dated, it is an often penetrating, insightful look into Japanese society and the era in which it is set. In Japanese with English subtitles. 112m. **DIR:** Yasujiro Ozu. **CAST:** Chishu Ryu, Shima Iwashita. **1962**

AUTUMN LEAVES ★★★1/2 Troubled middle-aged typist Joan Crawford is further anguished after marrying a younger man (Cliff Robertson) who proves to be mentally disturbed and already married. Run-of-the-mill Crawford fare. B&W; 108m. **DIR:** Robert Aldrich. **CAST:** Joan Crawford, Cliff Robertson, Vera Miles, Lorne Greene. **1956**

AUTUMN SONATA ★★★★★ Ingmar Bergman directed this superb Swedish release about the first meeting in seven years of a daughter (Liv Ullmann) with her difficult concert pianist mother (Ingrid Bergman). A great film. In Swedish and English. Rated PG. 97m. **DIR:** Ingmar Bergman. **CAST:** Ingrid Bergman, Liv Ullmann, Lena Nyman. **1978 DVD**

•AUTUMN TALE ★★★★★ A lonely winegrower is fixed up with two different men by her best friend and her son's girlfriend. French master Eric Rohmer gives us another bracing, fascinating work of art, filled with enjoyable characters and lively, intelligent conversation. It's also quite cleverly and intricately plotted, although it never feels forced or contrived. In French with English subtitles. Rated PG. 112m. **DIR:** Eric Rohmer. **CAST:** Marie Riviere, Beatrice Romand, Alain Libolt, Didier Sandre, Alexia Portal. **1998 DVD**

AVALANCHE 🐝 It's movies like this bomb that gave disaster pictures a bad name. Rated PG. 91m. **DIR:** Corey Allen. **CAST:** Rock Hudson, Mia Farrow, Robert Forster, Jeanette Nolan. **1978**

AVALON ★★★1/2 For the third film in his Baltimore trilogy, which also includes *Tin Men* and *Diner*, writer-director Barry Levinson covers fifty years in the lives of three generations of Russian-Jewish immigrants in a heart-tugging story. Armin Mueller-Stahl gives an unforgettable performance as the ultimate grandfather, whose honest values and love of family are slowly pushed out of fashion by progress. Rated PG for brief profanity. 126m. **DIR:** Barry Levinson. **CAST:** Armin Mueller-Stahl, Aidan Quinn, Elizabeth Perkins, Joan Plowright, Elijah Wood, Lou Jacobi. **1990**

AVANT GARDE PROGRAM #2 ★★★ Fascinating collection of early silent experimental films by French and German surrealists. This program features René Clair's brilliant short, "Entr'acte," with music by Erik Satie, and Eggeling's "Symphonie Diagonale." Also on this program: Man Ray's "L'Étoile de Mer." B&W; 42m. **DIR:** René Clair, Man Ray, Eggeling. **CAST:** Erik Satie, Marcel Duchamp, Man Ray. **1924–1926**

AVANTI! ★★★★ A cynical comedy in true Billy Wilder fashion with the antics of Jack Lemmon to make the ridiculous look sublime. Lemmon plays a man who goes to Europe to claim the body of his father and learns that Dad had a mistress, and the mistress had a voluptuous daughter. 144m. **DIR:** Billy Wilder. **CAST:** Jack Lemmon, Juliet Mills, Clive Revill, Edward Andrews. **1972**

AVA'S MAGICAL ADVENTURE ★★ A 10-year-old girl runs away with a two-ton friend—a circus elephant. Loads of "family fun" ensues as she is pursued by everyone from the sheriff to the bearded lady. Rated PG. 97m. **DIR:** Patrick Dempsey. **CAST:** Timothy Bottoms, Georg Stanford Brown, Patrick Dempsey. **1994**

AVENGERS, THE (TV SERIES) ★★★1/2 Patrick Macnee stars in the finest British secret agent series ever as quintessential agent John Steed. Diana Rigg

as the rugged, leather-garbed Emma Peel was followed by Linda Thorson's Tara King for the program's final year. Charming, witty, and absolutely ageless, this program will remain loved for generations to come. Suitable for family viewing. 52m. **DIR:** Don Leaver, Robert Day. **CAST:** Patrick Macnee, Diana Rigg, Linda Thorson. **1965–1969 DVD**

AVENGERS, THE ★★ Only Stuart Craig's opulent production design and a token appearance by Laurie Johnson's classic television theme save this bombastic failure from total turkeydom. It's not just that stars Ralph Fiennes (Steed) and Uma Thurman (Emma Peel) display zero chemistry and atrociously overplay the deadpan humor; the film itself doesn't seem finished. Terribly disappointing. Rated PG-13 for sexual innuendo, brief nudity, and cartoonish violence. 90m. **DIR:** Jeremiah S. Chechik. **CAST:** Ralph Fiennes, Uma Thurman, Sean Connery, Jim Broadbent, Patrick Macnee. **1998 DVD**

AVENGING, THE ★★ Michael Horse's half-Native American ancestry alienates him from his two brothers when he returns from college to take over the family ranch. Slow-moving tale of betrayal and revenge. Rated PG for violence. 100m. **DIR:** Lyman Dayton. **CAST:** Michael Horse, Efrem Zimbalist Jr., Sherry Hursey, Taylor Larcher, Joseph Running Fox. **1992**

AVENGING ANGEL (1985) 🐝 Remember *Angel*, the high school student who doubled as a Hollywood hooker? Well, she's back. Rated R for nudity, profanity, and violence. 96m. **DIR:** Robert Vincent O'Neil. **CAST:** Betsy Russell, Rory Calhoun, Susan Tyrrell, Ossie Davis. **1985**

AVENGING ANGEL, THE (1995) ★★★1/2 Tom Berenger stars as a member of a militia established by the Mormon Church to protect the members of its congregation. As one of the last of his kind, he finds himself almost an outcast among his own people—until a conspiracy to murder Brigham Young makes him both a suspect and a savior. This seldom-portrayed era in American history features strong performances and plenty of action for fans of the Western. Made for TV. 96m. **DIR:** Peter Markle. **CAST:** Tom Berenger, James Coburn, Charlton Heston, Fay Masterson, Kevin Tighe, Jeffrey Jones, Tom Bower, Leslie Hope, Daniele Quinn. **1995**

AVENGING CONSCIENCE, THE ★★1/2 Edgar Allan Poe's short stories provide the inspiration for this tale of a young writer (Henry B. Walthall) obsessed with Poe. Faced with the choice of continued patronage from his strict uncle or marriage with the "Annabel Lee" (Blanche Sweet) of his dreams, our tortured hero subjects his uncle to the tortures suggested by Poe's stories. Interesting historically, this silent feature is most effective in atmospheric chills. B&W; 78m. **DIR:** D. W. Griffith. **CAST:** Henry B. Walthall, Blanche Sweet, Mae Marsh, Robert Harron, Ralph Lewis. **1914**

AVENGING DISCO GODFATHER 🐝 Nightclub owner (Rudy Ray "Dolemite" Moore) battles angel dust pushers. Rated R for profanity, drug use, and violence. 93m. **DIR:** J. Robert Wagoner. **CAST:** Rudy Ray Moore, Carol Speed, Jimmy Lynch. **1979**

AVENGING FORCE ★★★ A better-than-average action-adventure flick about a former secret service agent forced out of retirement when his best friend, a black southern politician, is involved in an assassination attempt in which his son is killed. The acting is admittedly dry, but the action is top-notch, with plenty of opportunity to cheer for the hero. Rated R for violence and profanity. 104m. **DIR:** Sam Firstenberg. **CAST:** Michael Dudikoff, Steve James, James Booth, Bill Wallace, John P. Ryan, Marc Alaimo. **1986**

AVIATOR, THE ★★ This film, about a grumpy flyer (Christopher Reeve) during the 1920s who is forced to take a feisty passenger (Rosanna Arquette) on his mail route, is too similar to *High Road to China*. It has neither the high adventure nor the humor of the latter. Rated PG. 102m. **DIR:** George Miller. **CAST:** Christopher Reeve, Rosanna Arquette, Jack Warden, Scott Wilson, Tyne Daly, Sam Wanamaker. **1984**

AVIATOR'S WIFE, THE ★★★1/2 Not much happens in a film by French director Eric Rohmer, at least not in the traditional sense. In this typically Rohmer character study, a young law student (Philippe Marlaud) is crushed when he discovers his lover, Anne (Marie Riviere), in the company of another man and decides to spy on them. In French with English subtitles. Not rated; the film has no objectionable material. 104m. **DIR:** Eric Rohmer. **CAST:** Philippe Marlaud, Marie Riviere, Anne-Laure Marie. **1981 DVD**

AWAKENING, THE ★★1/2 In this mediocre horror flick, Charlton Heston plays an Egyptologist who discovers the tomb of a wicked queen. The evil spirit escapes the tomb and is reincarnated in Heston's newborn daughter. A bit hard to follow. Rated R for gore. 102m. **DIR:** Mike Newell. **CAST:** Charlton Heston, Susannah York, Jill Townsend, Stephanie Zimbalist. **1980**

AWAKENING OF CASSIE, THE ★★ Rather dispassionate coming-of-age film about a country girl who brings her paintings to the Big Apple where she must choose between a childish sculptor and a married man. A Romance Theatre production introduced by Louis Jourdan. Not rated, this TV production is very tame. 97m. **DIR:** Jim Drake. **CAST:** P. J. Soles, David Hedison, Patty McCormack, Richard Deacon. **1982**

AWAKENINGS ★★★★1/2 *Awakenings* is a masterpiece of characterization. In this fact-based story, a subdued Robin Williams plays a doctor who fights to use an experimental drug on a group of catatonic patients, who he believes are "alive inside." Robert De Niro is the first recipient of this medication, and his transformation is miraculous. Rated PG-13 for profanity and light violence. 121m. **DIR:** Penny Marshall. **CAST:** Robert De Niro, Robin Williams, Julie Kavner, Ruth Nelson, John Heard, Penelope Ann Miller, Max von Sydow. **1990 DVD**

AWAY ALL BOATS ★★ In this lackluster war drama, Jeff Chandler plays Captain Hanks, commander of an attack transport unit in the South Pacific during World War II. We follow Chandler and his men as they train for combat. 114m. **DIR:** Joseph Pevney. **CAST:** Jeff Chandler, George Nader, Julie Adams, Lex Barker, Keith Andes, Richard Boone, Jock Mahoney, William Reynolds, Charles McGraw, John McIntire. **1956 DVD**

AWFUL DR. ORLOFF, THE ★★★1/2 Horror classic about a demented surgeon seeking young women as unwilling skin-graft donors for his disfigured daughter. Atmospheric and creepy. Not rated, this is too strong for young viewers. 86m. **DIR:** Jess (Jesus) Franco. **CAST:** Howard Vernon, Perla Cristal. **1961**

AWFUL TRUTH, THE ★★★★ Irene Dunne and Cary Grant divorce so that they can marry others. Then they do their best to spoil one another's plans. Leo McCarey won an Oscar for directing this prime example of the screwball comedies that made viewing such a delight in the 1930s. Grant—a master of timing—is in top form, as is costar Dunne. It's hilarious all the way. B&W; 92m. **DIR:** Leo McCarey. **CAST:** Irene Dunne, Cary Grant, Ralph Bellamy, Molly Lamont. **1937**

AWFULLY BIG ADVENTURE, AN ★★★★ Hugh Grant, cast against type in one of his best performances, is the ruthlessly nasty director of a small British theater company just after World War II. Newcomer Georgina Cates is a doll as the naïve young assistant who learns a few crushing life lessons. Alan Rickman is resplendent as a leading man who knows better but still dabbles where he shouldn't. Great writing. Rated R for profanity, sexual situations, and nudity. 113m. **DIR:** Mike Newell. **CAST:** Hugh Grant, Alan Rickman, Georgina Cates, Alun Armstrong, Peter Firth, Prunella Scales, Rita Tushingham. **1994**

AY, CARMELA! ★★1/2 One of Spain's most electrifying stars, Carmen Maura, joins forces with one of her nation's most invigorating directors, Carlos Saura, in this drama about the Spanish Civil War. The film offers insight and entertainment, but it's a mystery why all that electricity generates few sparks. In Spanish with English subtitles. Not rated. 103m. **DIR:** Carlos Saura. **CAST:** Carmen Maura. **1991**

•B. MONKEY ★★1/2 British crime-drama is filled with some of the best actors on the independent scene. Deliberately paced and filled with some fine exteriors, it seems like the filmmakers were not sure what they wanted to accomplish: tell a boy-meets-girl love story or an exposé of the underworld. While it does not commit itself, the film is engaging and full of good performances. Rated R for profanity, nudity, violence, and simulated sex. 92m. **DIR:** Michael Radford. **CAST:** Asia Argento, Jared Harris, Rupert Everett. **1998 DVD**

BABAR: THE MOVIE ★★ This adaptation of the beloved *Babar* books by Jean and Laurent de Brunhoff is hampered by a formulaic story and uninspired animation. Produced by Nelvana Studios, which also makes the Care Bears movies, it is passable kiddie fare. Rated G. 75m. **DIR:** Alan Bunce. **1989**

BABE (1982) 💗 *Baywatch*'s Yasmine Bleeth would doubtless love to forget that she made her debut here as a 12-year-old orphan and Broadway wannabe who learns the tricks of the trade from homeless ex-vaudevillian Buddy Hackett. Not rated; contains mild profanity. 90m. DIR: Rafal Zielinski. CAST: Buddy Hackett, Yasmine Bleeth. 1982

BABE, THE (1992) ★★★★ In this old-fashioned, Hollywood-style bio-pic, John Goodman hits a home run as Babe Ruth. We like it better than *The Babe Ruth Story* because of its grit and seeming no-holds-barred honesty. The legend makes for a memorable motion picture. Rated PG for profanity. 115m. DIR: Arthur Hiller. CAST: John Goodman, Kelly McGillis, Trini Alvarado, Bruce Boxleitner, Peter Donat, J. C. Quinn. 1992

BABE (1995) ★★★★★ This amazing, live-action barnyard fable from Australia pushes the envelope on both animatronic effects and family storytelling. The animal stars—piglet Babe, a collie family, a nervous duck, and an elderly ewe—not only convincingly talk but what they talk about is so very fascinating! This story is about social tolerance. It's also wildly funny. Rated G. 91m. DIR: Chris Noonan. CAST: James Cromwell, Magda Szubanski. 1995 DVD

BABE: PIG IN THE CITY ★★1/2 Everything that was sweet and whimsical about 1995s *Babe* has become overblown and crass in this disappointing sequel. *Pig in the City* is forced, stupid, and littered with the slapstick nonsense that frequently hallmarks sequels. This film is scary at times, thanks to unpleasant scenes of animal cruelty, and it might well give nightmares to its target small-fry audience. The story concerns Babe's trip to a mythical metropolis (superb production design by Roger Ford) in the company of Farmer Hoggett's wife, who desperately needs money to prevent their farm from being repossessed by the bank. Everything builds to a particularly messy climax in a posh restaurant. Rated G, but be wary of exposing very young children to it. 97m. DIR: George Miller. CAST: James Cromwell, Magda Szubanski, Mary Stein, Mickey Rooney. 1998 DVD

BABE RUTH STORY, THE ★★ Bio-pic about baseball's most famous hero is long on sap and short on facts as it milks every situation for maximum sentimental value. The supporting cast is good, but William Bendix just doesn't make the grade as the immortal Bambino. B&W; 106m. DIR: Roy Del Ruth. CAST: William Bendix, Claire Trevor, Charles Bickford, Sam Levene, William Frawley, Stanley Clements. 1948

BABES IN ARMS ★★★ Richard Rodgers and Lorenz Hart wrote the musical from which this film was taken—although most of the songs they wrote are absent. But never mind; Mickey and Judy sing, dance, and prance up a storm! B&W; 96m. DIR: Busby Berkeley. CAST: Mickey Rooney, Judy Garland, June Preisser, Guy Kibbee, Charles Winninger, Henry Hull, Margaret Hamilton. 1939

BABES IN TOYLAND (1961) ★★ A disappointing Disney version of the Victor Herbert operetta. In Mother Goose Land, Barnaby (Ray Bolger) kidnaps Tom the Piper's Son (Tommy Sands) in order to marry Mary (Annette Funicello). The Toymaker (Ed Wynn) and his assistant (Tommy Kirk) eventually provide the means for Tom to save the day. Despite a good Disney cast, this film never gels. Rated G. 105m.

DIR: Jack Donohue. CAST: Ray Bolger, Tommy Sands, Ed Wynn, Annette Funicello, Tommy Kirk. 1961

BABES IN TOYLAND (1986) ★★ Disappointing film about an adultlike child who must save the mythical town of Toyland by believing in the magic of toys. Richard Mulligan creates a wonderful evil Barnaby Barnacle. Rated G. 96m. DIR: Clive Donner. CAST: Drew Barrymore, Noriyuki "Pat" Morita, Richard Mulligan, Eileen Brennan, Keanu Reeves, Jill Schoelen. 1986

BABES ON BROADWAY ★★1/2 Raising funds for underprivileged children is the excuse for this musical extravaganza showcasing Mickey Rooney and Judy Garland, both of whom shine despite a trite plot. See it for the songs. B&W; 118m. DIR: Busby Berkeley. CAST: Mickey Rooney, Judy Garland, Fay Bainter, Virginia Weidler, Richard Quine, Donna Reed. 1941

BABETTE'S FEAST ★★★★ Writer-director Gabriel Axel's Oscar-winning adaptation of Isak Dinesen's short story has the kind of wistful warmth that makes it seem like a tale told by a wise old storyteller. It also has a pixilated quality that makes it good fun. The finale is a sumptuous dinner prepared by an expatriate French chef (Stéphane Audran) for a group of devout Danish Lutherans. It may be the funniest meal ever put on screen. In French and Danish with English subtitles. Rated G. 102m. DIR: Gabriel Axel. CAST: Stéphane Audran, Jean-Philippe Lafont, Jarl Kulle, Bibi Andersson. 1987

BABY, THE ★★★ Extremely odd film by veteran director Ted Post about a teenager who has remained an infant all his life (yes, he still lives in his crib) with his insane, overprotective mother. Eerily effective chiller is entertaining, though many will undoubtedly find it repulsive and ridiculous. Rated PG. 80m. DIR: Ted Post. CAST: Ruth Roman, Marianna Hill, Anjanette Comer. 1974

BABY BOOM ★★★1/2 Yuppie fairy tale about a career woman (Diane Keaton) who finds her eighty-hour-per-week corporate job interrupted by the untimely arrival of a babe-in-arms. The laughs are frequent, but the film doesn't find any warmth until Keaton flees to the country and meets local veterinarian Sam Shepard. Rated PG for language. 103m. DIR: Charles Shyer. CAST: Diane Keaton, Harold Ramis, Sam Wanamaker, Pat Hingle, Sam Shepard. 1987

BABY CAKES ★★★★ Ricki Lake is adorable as the plump girl who sets her sights on gorgeous Craig Sheffer, even though her friends and family tell her that someone of his caliber wouldn't be interested in her. This delightful film proves that beauty is more than skin-deep. Playful and inspiring, with both stars especially likable. 93m. DIR: Paul Schneider. CAST: Ricki Lake, Craig Sheffer, Betty Buckley, John Karlen. 1989

BABY DANCE, THE ★★★★1/2 Jane Anderson's searing stage play becomes an equally compelling film, which the playwright adapted and directed herself (with a little help from producer Jodie Foster). Laura Dern and Richard Lineback are a dirt-poor southern couple who cannot afford to keep the baby currently in her womb; they contact a wealthy childless couple desperate to adopt, and already-fragile emotions quickly reach the breaking point. Both women project a level of raw desperation, while both men recognize their helpless inability to honor their "covenant" in the coldly clinical fashion of attorneys and paper-laden contracts. This tough-edged, uncompromising drama is very hard to watch. Rated R for profanity, brief nudity, and strong content. 91m. **DIR:** Jane Anderson. **CAST:** Stockard Channing, Laura Dern, Richard Lineback, Peter Riegert, Sandra Seacat. 1997

BABY DOLL ★★★★ Set in hot, humid, sleazy Mississippi, this is the story of a child bride (Carroll Baker) who sleeps in a crib, her lusting, short-on-brains husband (Karl Malden), and a scheming business rival (Eli Wallach) determined to use and abuse them both. What else but a Tennessee Williams story? When first released, the film was condemned by the Legion of Decency; Baker's skimpy pajamas became fashionable. B&W; 114m. **DIR:** Elia Kazan. **CAST:** Carroll Baker, Eli Wallach, Karl Malden, Mildred Dunnock, Lonny Chapman, Rip Torn. 1956

BABY DOLL MURDERS, THE 💔 Plodding story of a serial killer who leaves the titular toy at the scene of each crime. Rated R for violence, profanity, and sex. 90m. **DIR:** Paul Leder. **CAST:** Jeff Kober, John Saxon, Melanie Smith, Bobby DiCicco. 1993

BABY FACE ★★★ Ambitious Barbara Stanwyck uses her looks and her charms to work her way from a saloon to a fancy salon in this mildly scandalous but eventually moralistic study. Stanwyck does a standout job, and her aggressive sexuality is pretty much implied despite the furor it raised with the censors of the day. B&W; 70m. **DIR:** Alfred E. Green. **CAST:** Barbara Stanwyck, George Brent, Donald Cook, Douglass Dumbrille, Margaret Lindsay, John Wayne. 1933

BABY FACE NELSON ★★1/2 C. Thomas Howell musters up all the menace he can as the notorious gangster who terrorized the streets of Chicago and kept company with allies like John Dillinger. His reign of terror and intimidation lands him on the FBI's most-wanted list and brings down the wrath of J. Edgar Hoover. Budget-minded period piece suffers by comparison. Rated R for adult situations, language, nudity, and violence. 87m. **DIR:** Scott Levy. **CAST:** C. Thomas Howell, Lisa Zane, Doug Wert, Martin Kove, F. Murray Abraham. 1996

BABY GENIUSES 💔 Ruthless tycoon Kathleen Turner exploits a group of adorable toddlers—and this incoherent, irresponsible "comedy" does the same thing by turning them into a bunch of miniature potty-mouthed adults. Some scenes are disturbingly suggestive. Rated PG. 94m. **DIR:** Bob Clark. **CAST:** Kathleen Turner, Christopher Lloyd, Peter MacNicol, Kim Cattrall, Dom DeLuise, Ruby Dee. 1999 DVD

BABY GIRL SCOTT ★★★1/2 Emotional and tragic story of older parents forced to deal with a dangerously small premature baby and doctors who overstep their boundaries. Well acted and quite gripping, though a bit melodramatic. Not rated. 97m. **DIR:** John Korty. **CAST:** Mary Beth Hurt, John Lithgow. 1987

BABY, IT'S YOU ★★★★ Writer-director John Sayles has such an unerring sense of what's right in a

scene and such a superb ear for dialogue that his movies often seem more like intimate documentaries than simple fiction. So it is with this enjoyable movie about the trials and tribulations of high school kids in Trenton, New Jersey, circa 1966. *Baby, It's You* is not only funny and touching, but also very sexy. Rated R for violence, profanity, and nudity. 105m. **DIR:** John Sayles. **CAST:** Rosanna Arquette, Vincent Spano. 1983

BABY MAKER, THE ★★ Still timely if overwrought drama of a couple who hire Barbara Hershey to have a baby when it is discovered the wife is barren. Mediocre dialogue, too many beach scenes, and some not-so-interesting subsidiary characters drag this potentially exciting drama to a halt. One of Hershey's first roles. 109m. **DIR:** James Bridges. **CAST:** Barbara Hershey, Colin Wilcox-Horne, Scott Glenn, Sam Groom, Jeannie Berlin. 1970

BABY MONITOR: SOUND OF FEAR ★★1/2 In this made-for-cable remake, a baby-sitter overhears (via the baby monitor) two men planning her murder. Now she must somehow save the children and escape from the locked condo before the bad guys find her. This could have been a thrilling suspense film, but the characters are stupid and unlikable, and the plot is chock-full of clichés. Not rated; contains violence. 95m. **DIR:** Walter Klenhard. **CAST:** Josie Bissett, Jason Beghe, Barbara Tyson, Jeffrey Noah. 1997

BABY OF THE BRIDE 💔 Fifty-three-year-old bride Rue McClanahan finds herself pregnant at the same time as daughter Kristy McNichol, an unmarried former nun. Just too, too wacky. 93m. **DIR:** Bill Bixby. **CAST:** Rue McClanahan, Ted Shackelford, Kristy McNichol. 1991

BABY ON BOARD 💔 Only if you absolutely love chase scenes could you enjoy this extended chase between a taxi driver, the mob, a mother, and her baby. Not rated; contains violence. 95m. **DIR:** Franky Schaeffer. **CAST:** Judge Reinhold, Carol Kane, Geza Kovacs. 1991

BABY—SECRET OF THE LOST LEGEND ★★1/2 Set on the Ivory Coast of West Africa, this Disney story offers more than a cute fable about the discovery of a family of brontosauri. Violence and a hint of sex represent Disney's attempt to appeal to a wider audience. The special effects of the ancient critters make the show worth watching. Rated PG. 90m. **DIR:** B.W.L. Norton. **CAST:** William Katt, Sean Young, Patrick McGoohan. 1985

BABY TAKE A BOW ★★1/2 In Shirley Temple's first starring vehicle, she helps her dad, who's accused of stealing a valuable necklace. Shirley must outthink the investigators in order to clear Dad's name. She pouts a lot but makes up for it with her charming rendition of "On Accounta' I Love You." B&W; 76m. **DIR:** Harry Lachman. **CAST:** Shirley Temple, James Dunn, Claire Trevor. 1934

BABY THE RAIN MUST FALL ★★1/2 This confusing character study of a convict who is paroled and reunited with his family raises a lot of questions but answers none of them. B&W; 100m. **DIR:** Robert Mulligan. **CAST:** Steve McQueen, Lee Remick, Don Murray. 1965

BABYFEVER ★★★ Director Henry Jaglom's real-life wife and cowriter, Victoria Foyt, frets over a possible pregnancy with a man she's not sure she loves. The setting is a baby shower, where a roomful of women anguish over their biological clocks and the terrors and delights of mommyhood. Jaglom's trademark humor is less apparent than usual and Foyt's performance borders on shrill. Rated R for profanity and adult themes. 110m. DIR: Henry Jaglom. CAST: Victoria Foyt, Frances Fisher, Elaine Kagan, Dinah Lenney, Matt Salinger, Zack Norman, Eric Roberts. 1994

BABYLON 5 (TV SERIES) ★★★★ A landmark in TV history, this creation of J. Michael "Joe" Straczynski focuses on the last of the Babylon space stations, a meeting place and peacekeeping forum for dozens of alien races. From its shaky inception through the Shadow War and a withdrawal of allegiance to Earth, Babylon 5 is the centerpiece of a science-fiction miniseries on a par with such literary milestones as Isaac Asimov's *Foundation* trilogy, Frank Herbert's *Dune*, Robert Heinlein's *Stranger in a Strange Land*, and Ray Bradbury's *The Martian Chronicles*. Made for TV. 96m. DIR: Various. CAST: Bruce Boxleitner, Michael O'Hare, Claudia Christian, Jerry Doyle, Mira Furlan, Tracy Scoggins, Caitlin Brown. 1993–1998

BABY'S DAY OUT ★★★ Writer-producer John Hughes steals from himself, cloning the *Home Alone* formula and downsizing its youthful hero. The scion of a wealthy Chicago family, 9-month-old Baby Bink, foils his own kidnapping by gleefully crawling out a window to face the hazards of the big city. It's fast-paced and often clever, causing viewers to laugh in spite of its lack of originality. Rated PG for comic violence. 98m. DIR: Patrick Read Johnson. CAST: Joe Mantegna, Lara Flynn Boyle, Joe Pantoliano, Brian Haley, Cynthia Nixon, Fred Dalton Thompson, John Neville, Eddie Bracken. 1994

BABYSITTER, THE (1980) ★★★1/2 Outside of some glaring plot flaws, this is an effectively eerie film. Stephanie Zimbalist is Joanna, a woman hired as a housekeeper (not a baby-sitter). But Joanna is no Mary Poppins. Not rated, has violence. 96m. DIR: Peter Medak. CAST: Patty Duke, William Shatner, Quinn Cummings, David Wallace, Stephanie Zimbalist, John Houseman. 1980

BABYSITTER, THE (1995) 🎬 A baby-sitter is the fantasy object of everyone in the film. A stunningly pointless parade of erotic fantasies leads to a violent finale. Not even fans of Alicia Silverstone will get through this one. Rated R for profanity and sexuality. 90m. DIR: Guy Ferland. CAST: Alicia Silverstone, Jeremy London, J. T. Walsh, Lee Garlington, Nicky Katt, Lois Chiles, George Segal. 1995

BABY-SITTERS CLUB, THE ★★ Only a 10-year-old girl could love this simple film based on the characters who fill Ann M. Martin's preteen novels. Seven wealthy girls expand their baby-sitting service to include a day camp. Overshadowing their interactions with the little charges are the romances of three of the girls and one's dealings with her irresponsible father. Rated PG for mild profanity. 92m. DIR: Melanie

Mayron. CAST: Glenda Jackson, Bruce Davison, Schuyler Fisk, Rachael Leigh Cook, Bre Blair. 1995

BACH AND BROCCOLI ★★ Slow-moving family-fare film made in Quebec. A 12-year-old girl is forced to live with her bachelor uncle. The two establish an uneasy relationship. Not rated, but equivalent to G. 96m. DIR: André Melançon. CAST: Andrée Pelletier. 1986

BACHELOR, THE (1993) ★★★ This exquisite period piece finds turn-of-the-century doctor Keith Carradine reexamining his life after his sister, upon whom he was very dependent, dies. He eventually finds friendship and then love with a widow, wonderfully played by Miranda Richardson. Set in England, with picture-postcard scenery and dignified performances throughout. Rated PG-13 for adult situations. 105m. DIR: Roberto Faenza. CAST: Keith Carradine, Miranda Richardson, Max von Sydow, Kristin Scott Thomas. 1993

•BACHELOR, THE (1999) ★★★1/2 Charming leads and clever gags sell this romantic comedy, a remake of Buster Keaton's 1925 silent classic, *Seven Chances*. This update breathes fresh life into a tired and creaky old premise: In order to retain a whopping inheritance, a confirmed bachelor must marry a woman—*any* woman—in just slightly over a day. The fellow is Chris O'Donnell, the gal he *really* loves is Renee Zellweger, and the story goes down easily when sold by such infectiously charming performers. Everything climaxes with a uniquely riotous chase in the oft-filmed streets of San Francisco, which must have posed a particularly unusual challenge for costume designer Terry Dresbach. Rated PG-13 for profanity and mild sensuality. 101m. DIR: Gary Sinyor. CAST: Chris O'Donnell, Renee Zellweger, Hal Holbrook, James Cromwell, Edward Asner, Brooke Shields, Artie Lange. 1999 DVD

BACHELOR AND THE BOBBY-SOXER, THE ★★1/2 Lady judge Myrna Loy cleverly sentences playboy Cary Grant to baby-sit Shirley Temple, a panting nubile teenager. Some features begin to cloy. Best bit is the play on words about the Man with the Power, Voodoo and Youdo. B&W; 95m. DIR: Irving Reis. CAST: Cary Grant, Myrna Loy, Shirley Temple, Rudy Vallee. 1947

BACHELOR APARTMENT ★★1/2 Loose-living, wisecracking Lothario meets an unyielding stenographer. Oft-used plot gets special treatment from actor-director Lowell Sherman, who sacrifices anything for a great one-liner and makes this pre-Code corker remarkably fresh and fun. B&W; 74m. DIR: Lowell Sherman. CAST: Lowell Sherman, Irene Dunne, Mae Murray, Norman Kerry. 1931

BACHELOR IN PARADISE ★★1/2 Author Bob Hope rents a home to do research on suburban mores and becomes confidant and adviser to the housewives in his neighborhood. Janis Paige and Paula Prentiss steal the movie. 109m. DIR: Jack Arnold. CAST: Bob Hope, Lana Turner, Janis Paige, Paula Prentiss, Jim Hutton, Agnes Moorehead, Don Porter. 1961

BACHELOR MOTHER ★★★ The old story about a single woman who finds a baby on a doorstep and is mistaken for its mother has never been funnier than in this witty film by writer-director Garson Kanin. Ginger Rogers as the shop girl who finds her whole life upside down as a result of the confusion shows her considerable skill for comedy. David Niven, in an early starring role, is just great as the store owner's son who attempts to "rehabilitate" the fallen Rogers. B&W; 82m. DIR: Garson Kanin. CAST: Ginger Rogers, David Niven, Charles Coburn, Frank Albertson, Ernest Truex. 1939

BACHELOR PARTY ★★ Even Tom Hanks can't save this "wild" escapade into degradation when a care-free bus driver who has decided to get married is given an all-out bachelor party by his friends. Rated R for profanity and nudity. 106m. DIR: Neal Israel. CAST: Tom Hanks, Tawny Kitaen, Adrian Zmed, George Grizzard, Robert Prescott. 1984

BACK FROM ETERNITY ★★ No surprises in this re-hash of similar films about a handful of people who survive a calamity (in this case, an airplane crash) and have to learn to cope with their predicament as well as with each other. Basically a potboiler that de-pends on stock footage and phony studio sets, this tired story limps along and gives Anita Ekberg plenty of opportunity to show off her torn blouse. B&W; 97m. DIR: John Farrow. CAST: Robert Ryan, Anita Ek-berg, Rod Steiger, Phyllis Kirk. 1956

BACK HOME ★★★1/2 After spending the war years in the safety of the United States, an English girl re-turns to her family in 1945. Unfortunately, she has become too Americanized and can't fit in. Hayley Mills plays her mother, a woman too preoccupied with her husband's homecoming to notice her daughter's heartache. A Disney Channel film, this has high production values. Not rated; contains ma-ture themes. 103m. DIR: Piers Haggard. CAST: Hayley Mills, Hayley Carr, Jean Anderson, Rupert Frazer, Bren-da Bruce. 1989

BACK IN ACTION ★★1/2 Rogue cop Roddy Piper teams up with vengeful vigilante Billy Blanks, and the results look grim for the baddies. Karl Schiff-man's wafer-thin plot barely interferes with the in-cessant action scenes; if Blanks and Piper were paid by the kick, they walked off with a fortune. Rated R for violence and profanity. 93m. DIR: Steve DiMarco, Paul Ziller. CAST: Billy Blanks, Roddy Piper, Bobbie Phillips, Matt Birman, Kai Soremekun. 1994

BACK IN BUSINESS ★★ It's business as usual for former-football-player-turned-action-star Brian Bos-worth, who tries desperately not to fumble this pedestrian outing. Bosworth plays a former cop lured into a sting operation that is guaranteed to pit him against the crooked cops who got him kicked off the force. Rated R for language, nudity, and violence. 93m. DIR: Philippe Mora. CAST: Brian Bosworth, Joe Torry, Dara Tomanovich, Brion James, Alan Scarfe. 1996

BACK IN THE U.S.S.R. ★★★ Young American Frank Whaley is on a two-week tour of Moscow when he gets embroiled in the theft of a rare book stolen from the Church. First American film shot entirely in Moscow is lovely to look at, engaging in its premise. Rated PG-13 for violence. 88m. DIR: Deran Sarafian. CAST: Frank Whaley, Natalya Negoda, Andrew Divoff, Dey Young, Roman Polanski. 1992

BACK OF BEYOND ★★★1/2 This Aussie import may be disguised as a typical B action flick but is ac-tually a surreal surprise. A smoldering Paul Mercu-rio, of Strictly Ballroom fame, returns to the remote truck stop he abandoned twelve years earlier, hoping to atone for past sins. Colin Friels is the diamond smuggler whose female friend unearths a few eerie secrets. The transitions are clunky, but the ending is both original and unexpected. Rated R for profanity, violence, and nudity. 85m. DIR: Michael Robertson. CAST: Paul Mercurio, Colin Friels, John Polson, Re-bekah Elmaloglou, Dee Smart. 1995

BACK ROADS ★★★ Pug (Tommy Lee Jones) and prostitute (Sally Field) hitch and brawl down the back roads of the South in this sometimes raunchy, often hilarious romance-fantasy. Though it drags a bit, the performances by the two stars and an earthy, down-home charm make it worthwhile. Rated R. 94m. DIR: Martin Ritt. CAST: Sally Field, Tommy Lee Jones, David Keith. 1981

BACK STREET ★★★ Third version of novelist Fan-nie Hurst's romantic tearjerker about clandestine love, with Susan Hayward as the noble mistress who stands by her lover even when he stupidly marries another woman. 107m. DIR: David Miller. CAST: Su-san Hayward, John Gavin, Vera Miles. 1961

BACK STREET JANE ★★★ When a pair of thieves tries to extort drugs from a local dealer, the plan backfires and they wind up with murder on their hands. Not rated; contains nudity, sexual situations, and violence. B&W; 93m. DIR: Ronnie Cramer. CAST: Monica McFarland, Marlene Shapiro. 1989

BACK TO BACK ★★★ Two brothers clear their fa-ther, accused of an armored car robbery that hap-pened years earlier. Good performances, action, and some unforeseen twists. Rated R for violence and language. 95m. DIR: John Kincade. CAST: Bill Paxton, Ben Johnson, Susan Anspach, Apollonia Kotero. 1990 DVD

BACK TO BATAAN ★★★ A fun World War II action film with John Wayne at his two-fisted best. Good script, photography, acting, and battle action. Video quality is quite good. B&W; 95m. DIR: Edward Dmytryk. CAST: John Wayne, Anthony Quinn, Richard Loo, Beulah Bondi. 1945

BACK TO HANNIBAL: THE RETURN OF TOM SAWYER AND HUCKLEBERRY FINN ★★★ Decent guess at what Mark Twain's lovable scamps might have grown up to be. Tom, a Chicago lawyer, and Huck, a St. Louis reporter, return to their hometown when their friend, Jim, the former slave, is falsely ac-cused of murder. Lacks the wit and ingenuity of Twain but remains reasonably entertaining. Made for the Disney channel, this is family fare. 95m. DIR: Paul Krasny. CAST: Raphael Sbarge, Paul Winfield, Mitchell Anderson, Megan Follows, William Windom, Ned Beatty. 1990

BACK TO SCHOOL ★★★1/2 A true surprise from the usually acerbic Rodney Dangerfield, who sheds his lewd 'n' crude image in favor of one more sympa-thetic and controlled. He stars as the self-made own-er of a chain of "Tall and Fat" stores who decides to return to college. He selects his son's college in or-der to spend more time with the boy. Rated PG-13 for occasionally vulgar humor. 96m. DIR: Alan Metter. CAST: Rodney Dangerfield, Sally Kellerman, Burt Young, Keith Gordon, Robert Downey Jr., Ned Beatty, M. Emmet Walsh, Adrienne Barbeau, William Zabka, Severn Darden. 1986 DVD

BACK TO THE BEACH 🌹 Annette and Frankie are married, in their 40s, live in Ohio, and have two children with behavioral problems. Rated PG for language. 88m. DIR: Lyndall Hobbs. CAST: Frankie Avalon, Annette Funicello, Connie Stevens, Lori Loughlin. 1987

BACK TO THE FOREST ★★ Peter (a fairy) and his animal friends must save their home, Placid Forest, when greedy local villagers decide to level the forest for financial gain. This Japanese rendition of Scandinavian author Boy Lornsen's *Jakobus Nimmersatt* has lost something in the translation. 75m. DIR: Yoshio Koruda. 1989

BACK TO THE FUTURE ★★★★1/2 Michael J. Fox as a teenager who is zapped back in time by mad scientist Christopher Lloyd. Once there, Fox meets his parents as teenagers, an act that could result in disaster. The first fifteen minutes of this film are pretty bad, but once Fox gets back to where he doesn't belong, it's terrific entertainment. Rated PG. 116m. DIR: Robert Zemeckis. CAST: Michael J. Fox, Christopher Lloyd, Lea Thompson, Crispin Glover, Thomas F. Wilson. 1985

BACK TO THE FUTURE II ★★★ Futuristic sequel is so fast-paced and gimmick-laden that one only realizes after seeing it how essentially empty it is. The story jumps from 1985 to 2015 to 1985 to 1955, as Marty McFly attempts to save the future from the consequences of his tampering with the past. Convoluted, but it's an agreeable enough time passer. Rated PG for light violence and profanity. 105m. DIR: Robert Zemeckis. CAST: Michael J. Fox, Christopher Lloyd, Lea Thompson, Thomas F. Wilson, Elisabeth Shue, Charles Fleischer. 1989

BACK TO THE FUTURE III ★★★★1/2 Director Robert Zemeckis and screenwriter Bob Gale make up for the excesses and inadequacies of *Back to the Future II* with this rip-roaring conclusion, which has Marty McFly in the Old West attempting to get back to 1985. Rated PG for light violence. 118m. DIR: Robert Zemeckis. CAST: Michael J. Fox, Christopher Lloyd, Mary Steenburgen, Lea Thompson, Thomas F. Wilson, Elisabeth Shue, Matt Clark, Richard Dysart. 1990

BACKBEAT ★★★★ Before they became the Fab Four, the Beatles were a quintet—guitarists John Lennon, Paul McCartney, and George Harrison, backed by painter-turned-bass-player Stuart Sutcliffe and drummer Pete Best. This is an involving dramatization of the close friendship between Lennon and Sutcliffe, and how it is tested during the band's apprenticeship in seamy Hamburg, Germany. Rated R for profanity, nudity, simulated sex, and brief violence. 100m. DIR: Iain Softley. CAST: Stephen Dorff, Sheryl Lee, Ian Hart, Kai Wiesinger, Jennifer Ehle, Gary Bakewell, Chris O'Neill, Scot Williams. 1994

BACKDOOR TO HEAVEN ★★★1/2 With superb performances from a talented cast, this strong social drama is somewhat dated but still compelling. A poor young man must make a choice: a lifetime of toil

and repression or a career of crime. B&W; 86m. DIR: William K. Howard. CAST: Aline MacMahon, Wallace Ford, Stu Erwin, Van Heflin. 1939

BACKDRAFT ★★★1/2 Spectacular special effects highlight this melodramatic movie about feuding firemen brothers (well acted by Kurt Russell and William Baldwin) whose lives are endangered by the activities of a clever arsonist. Robert De Niro is typically strong as the chief investigator. Rated R for profanity, violence, and nudity. 136m. DIR: Ron Howard. CAST: Kurt Russell, William Baldwin, Robert De Niro, Donald Sutherland, Scott Glenn, Jennifer Jason Leigh, Rebecca DeMornay. 1991 DVD

BACKFIELD IN MOTION ★★★ Plenty to cheer about in this congenial comedy that makes it easy to rally behind Roseanne as the new mom-on-the-block, who organizes the local women into a football team to compete against their kids. Made-for-TV comedy, just wants to entertain, which it does. 95m. DIR: Richard Michaels. CAST: Roseanne, Tom Arnold, Colleen Camp, Conchata Ferrell. 1991

BACKFIRE (1987) ★★★★ Twisting thriller involves the carefully orchestrated psychological destruction of a rich, shell-shocked Vietnam vet. Who's the culprit? Excellent combination of whodunit and whydunit. Leads Karen Allen and Keith Carradine are oblique enough to keep the real truth neatly suspended. Rated R for nudity and violence. 90m. DIR: Gilbert Cates. CAST: Karen Allen, Keith Carradine, Jeff Fahey, Bernie Casey, Dean Paul Martin. 1987

BACKFIRE (1994) 🌹 Badly acted and written farce about a man who wants to join an all-female firefighting force. Rated PG-13 for sexual situations. 93m. DIR: A. Dean Bell. CAST: Kathy Ireland, Robert Mitchum, Telly Savalas, Shelley Winters, John Mosby, Mary McCormack. 1994

BACKGROUND TO DANGER ★★★★ Lots of action makes this one a WWII classic, with a no-nonsense cynic battling spies and attracting beautiful women right and left. Set in the neutral country of Turkey. B&W; 80m. DIR: Raoul Walsh. CAST: George Raft, Brenda Marshall, Sydney Greenstreet, Peter Lorre, Turhan Bey, Osa Massen. 1943

BACKLASH (1988) ★★★ Subtle story of two cops (David Argue, Lydia Miller) escorting an accused murderess (Gia Carides) across the Australian desert. Argue turns in a fine performance as an embittered, abrasive policeman. Rated R for language and nudity. 85m. DIR: Bill Bennett. CAST: David Argue, Gia Carides, Lydia Miller, Brian Syron. 1988

•**BACKLASH (1998)** ★★ Familiar tale of a federal prosecutor, Gina Gallagher, whose case against the Colombia drug cartel becomes deadly. Forced into protective custody, she uncovers a government conspiracy and her only hope for survival is a convicted criminal. Trite setups and lousy payoffs do little to distinguish this made-for-cable mess. Rated R for adult situations, language, and violence. 103m. DIR: Jack Ersgard. CAST: Charles Durning, Tracey Needham, JoBeth Williams, Tony Plana, James Belushi. 1998

BACKSTAB 🌹 An architect who becomes embroiled in a passionate affair that leads to murder. *Fatal At-*

traction wannabe. Rated R for nudity. 91m. DIR: James Kaufman. CAST: James Brolin, Meg Foster. 1990

BACKSTAIRS ★★★★ Superb example of the German Expressionist cinema. Its twisted sets and harsh extremes in lighting surround a grim tale of the violence that interrupts the love affair between a chambermaid and her lover. Silent. B&W; 44m. DIR: Leopold Jessner. CAST: William Dieterle. 1921

BACKSTREET DREAMS 🎬 Airheaded mush about a small-time mob enforcer. Rated R for violence and profanity. 104m. DIR: Rupert Hitzig. CAST: Brooke Shields, Jason O'Malley, Anthony Franciosa, Burt Young, Sherilyn Fenn, Nick Cassavetes, Elias Koteas. 1990

BACKSTREET JUSTICE ★★★1/2 Writer-director Chris McIntyre must have been reading a lot of Sue Grafton and Sara Paretsky, because this tough-gal–private-eye thriller borrows liberally from both authors. Linda Kozlowski is the hardened investigator trying to live down her father's reputation as a crooked cop while investigating a series of murders frightening tenants out of her inner-city apartment building. Rated R for violence, nudity, profanity, and simulated sex. 91m. DIR: Chris McIntyre. CAST: Linda Kozlowski, Hector Elizondo, John Shea, Paul Sorvino. 1993

BACKTRACK ★★★ An impressive ensemble cast, which includes uncredited cameos by Joe Pesci and Charlie Sheen, turns this quixotic, made-for-cable thriller into an intriguing curiosity. Electronic artist Jodie Foster witnesses a mob slaying, and then flees for her life from torpedo Dennis Hopper … who abandons the contract after falling in love with her. A bit overlong, but interesting. Contains profanity, violence, nudity, and kinky sexual overtones. 102m. DIR: Dennis Hopper. CAST: Dennis Hopper, Jodie Foster, Dean Stockwell, Vincent Price, John Turturro, Fred Ward, Bob Dylan. 1990

BAD AND THE BEAUTIFUL, THE ★★★★1/2 Dynamite story of a Hollywood producer (Kirk Douglas) and his turbulent relations with a studio actress (Lana Turner). Along the way there are fine performances by all of the cast. It's old Hollywood gloss, and very good, indeed. Five Oscars for this gem. B&W; 118m. DIR: Vincente Minnelli. CAST: Lana Turner, Kirk Douglas, Gloria Grahame, Dick Powell, Barry Sullivan, Walter Pidgeon, Gilbert Roland. 1952

BAD ATTITUDE ★★ Suspended after his partner is gunned down, a cop joins forces with a prostitute who turns out to be a former assassin. Together they hunt down the guys responsible for the partner's murder. Ultra-low-budget action-thriller offers nothing new but will satisfy undemanding fans of the genre. Rated R for profanity, violence, and nudity. 87m. DIR: Bill Cummings. CAST: Nathaniel de Veaux, Susan Finque, Leon, Gina Lim. 1993

BAD BEHAVIOUR ★★★1/2 There's not much plot in this slice-of-life film about the intertwining lives of several middle-class Londoners. What it lacks in story, though, it makes up for with warmth, humor, and nicely turned character touches. Improvised by the talented cast, the film takes a while to get rolling, but patience will be rewarded. Rated R for language and mature themes. 103m. DIR: Les Blair. CAST: Stephen Rea, Sinead Cusack, Philip Jackson, Phil Daniels, Saira Todd. 1993

BAD BLOOD (1988) ★★★ Absolutely terrifying thriller, thanks to Ruth Raymond's performance as the psychotic mother who lusts after her long-lost son. Linda Blair has the unfortunate role of her much-abused daughter-in-law. Rated R for nudity and violence. 103m. DIR: Chuck Vincent. CAST: Ruth Raymond, Gregory Patrick, Linda Blair. 1988

BAD BLOOD (1994) 🎬 This grotesquely violent Lorenzo Lamas slugfest, which finds our hero trying to save his younger brother from the usual goons, is offensively stupid and gory. Don't watch it on a full stomach. Rated R for violence, torture, nudity, simulated sex, and profanity. 90m. DIR: Tibor Takacs. CAST: Lorenzo Lamas, Hank Cheyne, Kimberley Kates, John P. Ryan. 1994

BAD BOYS (1983) ★★★★1/2 A grimly riveting vision of troubled youth. Sean Penn and Esai Morales are Chicago street hoods sworn to kill each other in prison. It's exciting, thought-provoking, and violent, but the violence, for once, is justified and not merely exploitative. Rated R for language, violence, and nudity. 123m. DIR: Rick Rosenthal. CAST: Sean Penn, Esai Morales, Reni Santoni, Ally Sheedy, Jim Moody, Eric Gurry. 1983 DVD•

BAD BOYS (1995) ★★★1/2 Fast-paced cop/buddy movie stars a well-matched Martin Lawrence and Will Smith as detectives assigned to investigate the theft of a large quantity of drugs from a police-evidence room. Rated R for violence, profanity, and sexual references. 118m. DIR: Michael Bay. CAST: Martin Lawrence, Will Smith, Téa Leoni, Tcheky Karyo, Theresa Randle, Joe Pantoliano. 1995 DVD

BAD CHANNELS ★★1/2 At KDUL Radio, the music, is, well, *dull!* That is, until a new DJ enters the scene. Unfortunately, he happens to be an alien, who has come to Earth to pick up chicks, shrink them, and imprison them in small bottles for the trip back home. There's plenty of off-the-wall fun when the townsfolk, including ex-MTV veejay Martha Quinn, decide to pull this guy's plug. Rated R for violence. 88m. DIR: Ted Nicolaou. CAST: Paul Hipp, Martha Quinn, Aaron Lustig, Ian Patrick Williams. 1992

BAD COMPANY (1972) ★★★★ This is a much underrated Civil War–era Western. The cultured Barry Brown and the streetwise Jeff Bridges team up as robbers. Charming performances by the leads and an intriguing, intelligent script by Robert Benton and David Newman make this well worth watching. Rated R. 94m. DIR: Robert Benton. CAST: Jeff Bridges, Barry Brown, Jim Davis, David Huddleston, John Savage, Jerry Houser, Geoffrey Lewis. 1972

BAD COMPANY (1995) ★★★ Ellen Barkin brings Laurence Fishburne into the fold of an ultrasecret corporate spy agency. She's slinky and cool, he's all self-contained swagger, and this is eye candy and attitude from beginning to end. Rated R for profanity, sexual situations, violence, and brief nudity. 108m. DIR: Damian Harris. CAST: Ellen Barkin, Laurence Fishburne, Frank Langella, Michael Beach, David Ogden Stiers, Gia Carides, Spalding Gray, Daniel Hugh Kelly. 1995

BAD DAY AT BLACK ROCK ★★★★ Spencer Tracy gives one of his greatest performances in this suspenseful, action-packed drama as a one-armed man who stirs up trouble when he arrives at a western town whose citizens have a guilty secret. Robert Ryan is superb as the main villain. Lee Marvin and Ernest Borgnine ooze menace as brutal, sadistic henchmen. 81m. **DIR:** John Sturges. **CAST:** Spencer Tracy, Robert Ryan, Anne Francis, Walter Brennan, Lee Marvin, Ernest Borgnine. 1955

BAD DREAMS 💔 Tale of a young woman awakened from a thirteen-year coma only to be haunted and hunted by the ghost of a maniacal leader of a hippie cult. Rated R for violence, gore, and profanity. 90m. **DIR:** Andrew Fleming. **CAST:** Jennifer Rubin, Bruce Abbott, Richard Lynch, Harris Yulin. 1988

BAD GIRLS (1969) ★★1/2 Weak erotic drama from Claude Chrobal about a love affair between a petty bourgeois woman and a beautiful young street artist. Poor chemistry among the characters, not one of Chabrol's better films. Lacks passion. French, dubbed in English. Rated R for mild nudity. 97m. **DIR:** Claude Chabrol. **CAST:** Stéphane Audran, Jacqueline Sassard, Jean-Louis Trintignant. 1969

BAD GIRLS (1994) ★★★1/2 Action-packed tale of four saloon gals who must elude Pinkerton bounty hunters and sadistic outlaws after one of them kills a prominent citizen in self-defense. First-rate performances by the quartet of top-billed stars and fast-paced direction by Jonathan Kaplan make this a winner. Rated R for violence and suggested sex. 81m. **DIR:** Jonathan Kaplan. **CAST:** Madeleine Stowe, Andie MacDowell, Mary Stuart Masterson, Drew Barrymore, Dermot Mulroney, James Russo, Robert Loggia, James LeGros. 1994

BAD GIRLS FROM MARS ★★1/2 Another campy exercise from no-budget auteur Fred Olen Ray, with starlet Edy Williams as the new star of a sci-fi movie whose previous stars have all been murdered. Rated R for nudity. 86m. **DIR:** Fred Olen Ray. **CAST:** Edy Williams, Oliver Darrow, Brinke Stevens. 1990

BAD GIRLS GO TO HELL ★★ Sleaze-film addict Joe Bob Briggs introduces another of Doris Wishman's Sixties drive-in weirdies. A dim-witted sexpot housewife is repeatedly ravaged by gross hairy men and lesbians amid tacky Fifties-living-room decor. Minuscule plot line features early doses of sadism and masochism with all the bawdiness of a suburban home movie. 98m. **DIR:** Doris Wishman. **CAST:** Gigi Darlene. 1965

BAD GUYS ★★ A somewhat contrived story about two police officers who are suspended indefinitely, without pay. They decide to become professional wrestlers. Rated PG. 87m. **DIR:** Joel Silberg. **CAST:** Adam Baldwin, Mike Jolly, Michelle Nicastro, Ruth Buzzi, Sgt. Slaughter. 1985

BAD INFLUENCE ★★ Rob Lowe stars as a demonic character who leads frustrated yuppie James Spader down the sleazy path to corruption. Disturbing amorality tale. Rated R for nudity, simulated sex, and violence. 100m. **DIR:** Curtis Hanson. **CAST:** Rob Lowe, James Spader, Lisa Zane. 1990

BAD JIM 💔 When an innocent man buys Billy the Kid's horse, the man, the horse, and this never-the-atrically released movie all turn bad. 90m. **DIR:** Clyde Ware. **CAST:** James Brolin, Richard Roundtree, John Clark Gable, Rory Calhoun, Ty Hardin. 1989

BAD LIEUTENANT ★★★1/2 Tough, raw, uncompromising police drama follows the last days of a crazed New York police lieutenant as he works on a rape case involving a nun. Film pulls no punches in showing the physical as well as the moral corruption of the title character. Be forewarned, some scenes are extremely tough to watch. Rated NC-17 for nudity, drug use, language, violence, and moral deprivation. 96m. **DIR:** Abel Ferrara. **CAST:** Harvey Keitel, Victor Argo, Paul Calderon. 1992 DVD

BAD LOVE ★★ Eloise has a dead-end job. Lenny is a drifter. When they meet, they ignite a passion in each other, a passion that turns to violence when they decide to rob an aging actress. Rated R for nudity, violence, adult situations, and language. 93m. **DIR:** Jill Goldman. **CAST:** Tom Sizemore, Pamela Gidley, Jennifer O'Neill, Seymour Cassel, Debi Mazar, Margaux Hemingway, Joe Dallesandro. 1992 DVD

BAD MAN OF DEADWOOD ★★★★ One of the best Roy Rogers films of this era. Trying to get away from an unlawful past, sharpshooter Roy Rogers joins a medicine show and becomes allied with a citizens group opposing a crooked conglomeration of businessmen. B&W; 54m. **DIR:** Joseph Kane. **CAST:** Roy Rogers, George "Gabby" Hayes, Sally Payne, Carol Adams, Henry Brandon. 1941

BAD MANNERS ★★ Wickedly selfish Martin Mull and Karen Black adopt a ratty little boy in the hopes of bringing some normalcy into their strange family. The idea probably looked funny on paper, but quickly turns into a sophomoric take on life. Rated R. 85m. **DIR:** Bobby Houston. **CAST:** Martin Mull, Karen Black, Anne De Salvo, Murphy Dunne. 1984

BAD MAN'S RIVER ★★ A humorous Western about the "dreaded" King gang, which robs banks along the Texas and Mexican borders. A Mexican revolutionary offers them a million dollars to blow up the arsenal used by the Mexican army, which the gang does, only to find that they have been double-crossed. 96m. **DIR:** Gene Martin. **CAST:** Lee Van Cleef, Gina Lollobrigida, James Mason. 1959 DVD

BAD MEDICINE ★★★1/2 Steve Guttenberg and Julie Hagerty play students attending a "Mickey Mouse" med school in Central America. When they find the health conditions in a nearby village unacceptable, they set up a medical clinic. The all-star cast does not disappoint. Rated PG-13 for profanity, sex, and adult situations. 97m. **DIR:** Harvey Miller. **CAST:** Steve Guttenberg, Julie Hagerty, Alan Arkin, Bill Macy, Curtis Armstrong, Julie Kavner, Joe Grifasi, Robert Romanus, Taylor Negron. 1985

BAD MOON ★★1/2 Single mom Mariel Hemingway doesn't suspect that her footloose brother is a werewolf—until he parks his trailer in her backyard. Foolish horror effort has many silly moments and phony special effects, but profits from pretty good acting and nice cinematography. Rated R for gore. 83m. **DIR:** Eric Red. **CAST:** Mariel Hemingway, Michael Paré. 1996

BAD NEWS BEARS, THE ★★★★★ An utterly hilarious comedy directed by Michael Ritchie, this film focuses on the antics of some foul-mouthed Little Leaguers, their beer-guzzling coach (Walter Matthau), and girl pitcher (Tatum O'Neal). But be forewarned, the sequels, *Breaking Training* and *The Bad News Bears Go to Japan*, are strictly no-hitters. Rated PG. 102m. **DIR:** Michael Ritchie. **CAST:** Walter Matthau, Tatum O'Neal, Vic Morrow, Alfred Lutter, Jackie Earle Haley. 1976

BAD NEWS BEARS GO TO JAPAN, THE 👎 Worst of the *Bad News Bears* trio of films, this features Tony Curtis as a small-time promoter with big ideas. Rated PG. 91m. **DIR:** John Berry. **CAST:** Tony Curtis, Jackie Earle Haley, Tomisaburo Wakayama, George Wyner, Lonny Chapman. 1978

BAD NEWS BEARS IN BREAKING TRAINING, THE ★★ Without Walter Matthau, Tatum O'Neal, and director Michael Ritchie, this sequel to *The Bad News Bears* truly is bad news … and rather idiotic. Jackie Earle Haley returns as the team star, and William Devane has a reasonable part as Haley's footloose father. Don't expect much. Rated PG for mild profanity. 100m. **DIR:** Michael Pressman. **CAST:** William Devane, Jackie Earle Haley, Clifton James. 1977

BAD RONALD ★★ Scott Jacoby lives secretly in a hidden room his mother builds for him after he kills a taunting peer. When Mama passes on, a new family moves into the place. Intriguing but tedious made-for-TV movie. 72m. **DIR:** Buzz Kulik. **CAST:** Scott Jacoby, Kim Hunter, Pippa Scott, Dabney Coleman. 1978

BAD SEED, THE ★★1/2 Despite the contrived ending and pathetically cutesy "curtain call," this story of a perfectly wicked child protected by her image is still capable of generating chills. Nancy Kelly may be more than a bit melodramatic as the concerned mother on a constant crying jag, but young Patty McCormack has that special cold beauty that makes her crimes all the more hideous. B&W; 129m. **DIR:** Mervyn LeRoy. **CAST:** Patty McCormack, Nancy Kelly, Henry Jones, Eileen Heckart, William Hopper. 1956

BAD SLEEP WELL, THE ★★★★ A man seeks revenge for the murder of his father in this suspenseful tale of corruption. Akira Kurosawa remarkably captures the spirit of Forties crime-dramas in this engrossing film, based on an Ed McBain story. In Japanese with English subtitles. B&W; 152m. **DIR:** Akira Kurosawa. **CAST:** Toshiro Mifune, Masayuki Mori, Takashi Shimura. 1960

BAD TASTE ★★★★ One of the grossest, yet most hysterically funny movies ever made. Aliens have come to Earth to harvest the new fast-food sensation of the universe—human flesh! It's up to the highly trained, if not totally adept, Alien Invasion Defense Service to save the world. Not rated; contains profanity and gore. 90m. **DIR:** Peter Jackson. **CAST:** Pete O'Herne. 1987

BADGE OF THE ASSASSIN ★★★1/2 Fine reenactment of the pursuit, capture, and trial of three radical black men who killed two policemen in Harlem in 1971. James Woods and Yaphet Kotto are intense as the assistant DA and detective who must make their case stick against the three ruthless killers. Rated R for violence and profanity. 96m. **DIR:** Mel Damski. **CAST:** James Woods, Yaphet Kotto, Alex Rocco, David Harris. 1985

BADGE 373 ★★ This police drama casts Robert Duvall as a cop out to nab his partner's killer. Pretty routine stuff is thrown together in an even more routine fashion. Rated R. 116m. **DIR:** Howard W. Koch. **CAST:** Robert Duvall, Verna Bloom, Eddie Egan, Henry Darrow. 1973

BADLANDERS, THE ★★★ Alan Ladd is a geologist, Ernest Borgnine a rancher. Both are robbed of a gold mine, so they join forces to recover their loss from an evil businessman. Mild suspense and action, but sincere performances. 83m. **DIR:** Delmer Daves. **CAST:** Alan Ladd, Ernest Borgnine, Katy Jurado, Kent Smith, Nehemiah Persoff. 1958

BAD LANDS (1939) ★★1/2 A posse chasing rapist-killer Apache Jack finds more trouble than they bargained for when their quarry reaches his friends and shifts the balance of power. Western version of RKO's own *Lost Patrol* is a somber, downbeat adventure. B&W; 70m. **DIR:** Lew Landers. **CAST:** Robert Barrat, Noah Beery Jr., Robert Coote, Guinn Williams, Andy Clyde, Francis Ford, Addison Richards, Francis McDonald. 1939

BADLANDS (1973) ★★★★ Featuring fine performances by Sissy Spacek, Martin Sheen, and Warren Oates, this is a disturbing re-creation of the Starkweather-Fugate killing spree of the 1950s. It is undeniably a work of intelligence and fine craftsmanship. However, as with Martin Scorsese's *Taxi Driver* and Bob Fosse's *Star 80*, *Badlands* is not an easy film to watch. Rated PG. 95m. **DIR:** Terence Malick. **CAST:** Martin Sheen, Sissy Spacek, Warren Oates, Ramon Bieri, Alan Vint. 1973

BADLANDS DRIFTER (CHALLENGE OF MCKENNA) ★★ An ex-priest gets caught in a range war and tries to make things right. He ends up in a battle of power, revenge, greed, and love. Exceptional performances by the entire cast make this a better-than-average spaghetti Western, with a good story to match the action and violence. Rated R for violence. 90m. **DIR:** Leon Klimovsky. **CAST:** John Ireland, Robert Woods, Daniela Giordana, Annabella Incontrera, Roberto Camardiel. 1969

BADMAN'S TERRITORY ★★★ Staunch and true marshal combats saddle scum when they flee across the border into territory beyond the government's reach. Good watching. B&W; 97m. **DIR:** Tim Whelan. **CAST:** Randolph Scott, Ann Richards, George "Gabby" Hayes, Ray Collins, Chief Thundercloud. 1946

BADMEN OF THE HILLS ★★★ A crooked sheriff tries to stop Charles Starrett's investigation into the murder of a U.S. marshal. Action-packed. B&W; 58m. **DIR:** William Berke. **CAST:** Charles Starrett, Russell Hayden, Cliff Edwards, Alan Bridge, Luana Walters. 1942

BAGDAD CAFÉ ★★★★ This delightfully offbeat comedy-drama concerns a German businesswoman who appears in the minuscule desert town in California called Bagdad. She and the highly strung owner of the town's only diner-hotel have a major culture and personality clash. Jack Palance as a bandanna-wearing artist is so perfectly weird he practically walks off with the film. Rated PG. 91m. **DIR:** Percy Adlon. **CAST:** Marianne Sägebrecht, C.C.H. Pounder, Jack Palance. 1988

BAIL JUMPER ★★★ A small-town thug and his ex-con girlfriend flee Missouri in search of the good life in New York City in this surreal love-on-the-run road movie. Bizarre romp through the American landscape that is reminiscent of David Lynch's *Wild at Heart* and Jim Jarmusch's *Mystery Train*. Not rated. 96m. **DIR:** Christian Faber. **CAST:** Eszter Balint, B. J. Spalding. **1989**

BAIL OUT ★★★ A funny, and often outright silly, action comedy about three bounty hunters who must bring the daughter of a millionaire to trial on drug charges. Lots of action and some great one-liners. Rated R. 88m. **DIR:** Max Kleven. **CAST:** Linda Blair, David Hasselhoff, John Vernon. **1988**

BAJA ★★★ Nothing is what it seems in this nifty little thriller. Molly Ringwald and Donal Logue star as Bebe and Alex, a couple on the run after a drug deal goes sour. They end up in a trailer in Baja, where they wait for Bebe's father to send them money. Instead, he sends Bebe's husband, who then attracts the attention of a hit man sent to kill Alex. How this whole horrible mess is resolved makes for a genuinely surprising finale. Not rated; contains violence and adult language. 92m. **DIR:** Kurt Voss. **CAST:** Molly Ringwald, Lance Henriksen, Donal Logue, M. A. Nickles, Corbin Bernsen. **1995**

BAJA OKLAHOMA ★★★ Lesley Ann Warren plays a tired bartender who dreams of success as a country-and-western songwriter. Willie Nelson and Emmylou Harris make cameo appearances as themselves. Made for HBO, this contains profanity, violence, and partial nudity. 100m. **DIR:** Bobby Roth. **CAST:** Lesley Ann Warren, Peter Coyote, Swoosie Kurtz, Billy Vera. **1988**

BAKER'S HAWK ★★★★ No-nonsense Westerner Clint Walker helps the local law get a group of vigilantes under control, while his son embarks on an adventure of his own involving a hawk and a mysterious hermit. An exceptional family film. Rated G. 98m. **DIR:** Lyman Dayton. **CAST:** Clint Walker, Burl Ives, Diane Baker, Lee Montgomery, Alan Young. **1976** DVD

BAKER'S WIFE, THE ★★★★ The new baker is coming to a town that has been without fresh-baked goods for too long. With great fanfare, the baker and his new wife arrive, but she has a roving eye. This comedy is a gem. In French with English subtitles. B&W; 124m. **DIR:** Marcel Pagnol. **CAST:** Raimu, Ginette Leclerc, Charles Moulin. **1938**

BALALAIKA ★★★ Cabaret singer Ilona Massey wins the heart of cossack Nelson Eddy. The plot is just a tool to introduce some wonderful musical numbers, but Massey is impressive in her American debut. B&W; 102m. **DIR:** Reinhold Schunzel. **CAST:** Nelson Eddy, Ilona Massey, Charlie Ruggles, Frank Morgan, Lionel Atwill, C. Aubrey Smith, Philip Terry, George Tobias, Joyce Compton. **1939**

BALANCE OF POWER ★★ Another in the arena-fighting genre. Here, a *sensei* must enter the underground ring to defend the world against an evil promoter of death matches. Billy Blanks puts his heart into it, which helps, but too many foul mouths and extreme violence steer this film away from the crowd at whom it would best be targeted—early teens. Rated R for profanity and violence. 92m. **DIR:** Rick Bennett. **CAST:** Billy Blanks, Mako, James Lew. **1996**

BALBOA 🐎 Tacky soap about a ruthless millionaire. Not rated; this film contains nudity. 92m. **DIR:** James Polakof. **CAST:** Tony Curtis, Carol Lynley, Steve Kanaly, Chuck Connors. **1982**

BALCONY, THE ★★★★ Jean Genet's hard-hitting surreal political fable is set in a brothel of illusion, where the customers take over real power during a revolution. Peter Falk sizzles in the role of a police chief who uses the whorehouse as a rallying point from which to suppress the revolution. Outrageous, poignant satire on the church and state, brilliantly performed by a top-notch cast. B&W; 87m. **DIR:** Joseph Strick. **CAST:** Shelley Winters, Peter Falk, Leonard Nimoy, Lee Grant. **1963**

BALL OF FIRE ★★★1/2 Stuffy linguistics professor Gary Cooper meets hotcha-cha dancer Barbara Stanwyck. He and seven lovable colleagues are putting together an encyclopedia. She's recruited to fill them in on slanguage. She does this, and more! Gangster Dana Andrews and motor-mouthed garbage man Allen Jenkins add to the madcap antics in what has been dubbed the last of the prewar screwball comedies. Good show! B&W; 111m. **DIR:** Howard Hawks. **CAST:** Gary Cooper, Barbara Stanwyck, Dana Andrews, Oscar Homolka, S. Z. Sakall, Richard Haydn, Henry Travers, Tully Marshall, Allen Jenkins. **1941** DVD

BALLAD OF A GUNFIGHTER ★★ Marty Robbins is a rough-and-ready rebel who robs stages and gives to the poor. He ends up battling guys even worse than himself. Stilted dialogue and acting interlaced with a couple of good old songs. Not rated and inoffensive. 84m. **DIR:** Bill Ward. **CAST:** Marty Robbins, Joyce Redd, Bob Barron, Nestor Paiva, Laurette Luez. **1964**

BALLAD OF A SOLDIER ★★★1/2 A soldier finds love and adventure on a ten-day pass to see his mother. This import features excellent cinematography and acting, and despite the always obvious Soviet propaganda, some piercing insights into the Russian soul. In Russian with English subtitles. B&W; 89m. **DIR:** Grigori Chukhrai. **CAST:** Vladimir Ivashov, Shanna Prokhorenko. **1959**

BALLAD OF CABLE HOGUE, THE ★★★★1/2 Jason Robards has one of his finest roles as Hogue, a loner who discovers water in the desert and becomes a successful entrepreneur by opening a stagecoach stopover. Director Sam Peckinpah's deft eye for period detail and outstanding acting by all involved make this one a winner. Rated R. 121m. **DIR:** Sam Peckinpah. **CAST:** Jason Robards Jr., Stella Stevens, Strother Martin, L. Q. Jones, David Warner. **1970**

BALLAD OF GREGORIO CORTEZ, THE ★★★1/2 This superb independent production tells the powerful story of one man's courage, pain, tragedy, and heartbreak—all of which come as the result of a simple misunderstanding. Edward James Olmos gives a haunting portrayal of the title character, who becomes a fugitive through no fault of his own. Rated PG for violence. 99m. **DIR:** Robert M. Young. **CAST:** Edward James Olmos, James Gammon, Tom Bower, Alan Vint, Timothy Scott, Barry Corbin. **1982**

BALLAD OF LITTLE JO, THE ★★★1/2 Revisionist Western stars Suzy Amis as a woman who feels trapped in a man's world, so she disguises herself as a man to get a fair shake. Amis delivers a stunning performance as she attempts to fit into a world designed for men. The usual complications arise, but Amis and a terrific supporting cast make them new and invigorating. Rated R for violence, language, and nudity. 124m. **DIR:** Maggie Greenwald. **CAST:** Suzy Amis, Bo Hopkins, David Chung, René Auberjonois, Carrie Snodgress, Ian McKellen. 1993

BALLAD OF NARAYAMA, THE ★★★★★ Based on one of the most unusual Japanese legends: a century ago in a remote mountain village in northern Japan, a local custom dictated that when a person reached 70 years old they were taken to Mount Narayama to die. A true masterpiece of Japanese cinema and a Grand Prize winner at the 1983 Cannes Film Festival. In Japanese with English subtitles. Not rated; contains nudity and violence. 129m. **DIR:** Shohei Imamura. **CAST:** Ken Ogata. 1983

BALLAD OF THE SAD CAFE, THE ★★★ Strangeness abounds in this visually appealing tale of a masochist's love for a hard, angular spinster. For its sparse content, the film has a deliberate slow-as-molasses pace, and in that time it takes many Southern stereotypes and turns them upside down. Based on the story by Carson McCullers. Rated PG-13 for violence. 100m. **DIR:** Simon Callow. **CAST:** Vanessa Redgrave, Keith Carradine, Rod Steiger. 1992

BALLISTIC ★★1/2 After a government witness is murdered while under his protection, an LAPD cop (Marjean Holden) and her father (Richard Roundtree) set out after the killers. Rated R for profanity, brief nudity, and violence. 86m. **DIR:** Kim Bass. **CAST:** Marjean Holden, Joel Beeson, Sam Jones, Richard Roundtree. 1995

BALLOT MEASURE 9 ★★★★★ This revealing documentary takes a frightening look at a persistent and growing lack of tolerance in this country. During a detailed examination of a campaign by the Oregon Citizens' Alliance, we learn of efforts to revoke "special rights" (aka equal rights) from homosexuals in 1992. Director Heather MacDonald creates a sense of urgency and tension while covering all sides of this issue, leaving us to call up pictures of Germany in the early 1930s. Not rated; contains profanity. 72m. **DIR:** Heather MacDonald. 1995

BALTIMORE BULLET, THE ★★1/2 In this tale of big-league pool hustling, clever cuesters James Coburn and Bruce Boxleitner carefully build up to scoring big in a nail-biting shoot-out with suave Omar Sharif. Rated PG. 103m. **DIR:** Robert Ellis Miller. **CAST:** James Coburn, Bruce Boxleitner, Omar Sharif, Ronee Blakley. 1980

BALTO ★★★★ This exciting animated adventure tells how wolf-dog Balto, an outcast in his Alaskan hometown, risks his life to retrieve child-saving antitoxins amid a severe epidemic and blizzard. His courage, speed, and physical strength are challenged by an avalanche, a grizzly, the icy depths of a frozen lake, and a mean sled dog. Balto's pals include a goofy snow goose and a female husky who doesn't give a hair ball whether her new friend is a half-breed or not. Rated G. 77m. **DIR:** Simon Wells. **CAST:** Kevin Bacon, Bridget Fonda, Phil Collins, Bob Hoskins, Jim Cummings (voices). 1995

BAMBI ★★★★★ This lush adaptation of Felix Salten's beloved story represents the crowning achievement of Walt Disney's animation studio. Never again would backgrounds be delineated with such realistic detail, with animation so precise that it resembled live photography. The screenplay, too, has a bit more bite than the average Disney yarn, with equal helpings of comedy and tragedy fueling a confrontation between forest animals and that most horrific of two-legged interlopers: man. 69m. **DIR:** David Hand. 1942

BAMBOO SAUCER (COLLISION COURSE) ★★1/2 America and the USSR compete with each other as they investigate reports of a UFO crash in the People's Republic of China. More concerned with plot and substance than special effects, this low-budget effort is thought-provoking and succeeds where a more gimmicky, less suspenseful approach would have failed. 100m. **DIR:** Frank Telford. **CAST:** Dan Duryea, John Ericson, Lois Nettleton, Nan Leslie. 1968

BANANA COP ★★★ Engaging comedy about an Anglo-Chinese Scotland Yard inspector assigned to investigate a Chinatown murder. His wisecracking partner is played by Teddy Robin Kwan, the Eddie Murphy of Hong Kong. In Cantonese with English subtitles. Not rated; contains violence. 96m. **DIR:** Po-Chih Leong. **CAST:** George Lam, Teddy Robin Kwan. 1984

BANANAS ★★★★ Before he started making classic comedies, such as *Annie Hall, Zelig,* and *Broadway Danny Rose,* writer-director-star Woody Allen made some pretty wild—though generally uneven—wacky movies. This 1971 comedy, with Woody's hapless hero becoming involved in a South American revolution, does have its share of hilarious moments. Rated PG. 82m. **DIR:** Woody Allen. **CAST:** Woody Allen, Louise Lasser, Carlos Montalban, Howard Cosell. 1971 DVD

BANANAS IN PAJAMAS ★★★1/2 Two episodes of the popular Australian preschool live-action television series. Two giant, colorful bananas known as B1 and B2 are joined by their friends as they teach children developmental skills. Imaginative sets and creative characters work overtime to keep kids entertained. Episodes include "Pink Spots" and "Show Business." Not rated. 27m. **DIR:** Various. 1995

BAND OF ANGELS ★★★★ Clark Gable delivers in a lavish adaptation of Robert Penn Warren's novel. He has a fiery involvement with a beautiful Southern belle and saves her from a fate worse than death when it's revealed she is really a mulatto. 127m. **DIR:** Raoul Walsh. **CAST:** Clark Gable, Yvonne De Carlo, Sidney Poitier, Efrem Zimbalist Jr. 1957

BAND OF OUTSIDERS ★★1/2 Disappointing *film noir* from director Jean-Luc Godard about a robbery that ends in the accidental death of a woman at the hands of her beautiful niece. This existential crime-drama suffers from an incoherent script. In French with English subtitles. Not rated. B&W; 97m. **DIR:** Jean-Luc Godard. **CAST:** Anna Karina, Sami Frey, Claude Brasseur. 1964

BAND OF THE HAND ★★1/2 A Vietnam vet (Stephen Lang) takes a group of incorrigible Florida teens and turns them into an anti-drug squad. That's right, it's *Mod Squad* for the 1980s and just as silly as it sounds. Rated R for profanity, brief nudity, cocaine use, and violence. 109m. **DIR:** Paul Michael Glaser. **CAST:** Stephen Lang, Michael Carmine, Lauren Holly, John Cameron Mitchell, Daniele Quinn, Leon Robinson, James Remar. 1986

BAND WAGON, THE ★★★★ One of Vincente Minnelli's best grand-scale musicals and one of Fred Astaire's most endearing roles. He plays a Hollywood has-been who decides to try his luck onstage. This is the film that gave us "That's Entertainment." Not rated—family fare. 112m. **DIR:** Vincente Minnelli. **CAST:** Fred Astaire, Cyd Charisse, Jack Buchanan, Nanette Fabray, Oscar Levant. 1953

BANDIT QUEEN ★★★★ True story of a child bride who fought against the system and sexual abuse to become the leader of a group of bandits. Set in India, film recounts how 11-year-old Phoolan Devi, sold into marriage by her family for a cow, escapes her abusive husband. Eventually, she is captured and sexually abused by a band of outlaws. Through strength and determination, Phoolan finally becomes their leader and hero. Riveting performance by Seema Biswas as Phoolan. In Hindi with English subtitles. Not rated; contains strong sexual violence. 119m. **DIR:** Shekhar Kapur. **CAST:** Seema Biswas, Nirmal Pandey, Maoj Bajpai. 1994 DVD

BANDITS (1967) 🎞 A boring horse opera about three outlaws rescued from the hangman's noose. Not rated, but equivalent to PG-13 for violence. 89m. **DIR:** Robert Conrad, Alfredo Zacharias. **CAST:** Robert Conrad, Jan-Michael Vincent, Roy Jensen, Pedro Armendariz Jr. 1967

BANDITS (1987) ★★★★ An imprisoned jewel thief sends his daughter to a Swiss boarding school while plotting to avenge his wife's murder. Once free, father and daughter reunite. The romance that develops between the charming daughter and a young thief is surprisingly moving. Superior acting and a plot that twists enough to keep viewers guessing. In French with English subtitles. Not rated; contains brief nudity and violence. 98m. **DIR:** Claude Lelouch. **CAST:** Jean Yanne, Marie-Sophie Lelouch, Patrick Bruel, Charles Gerard. 1987

◆BANDITS (1997) ★★★1/2 Four female-convict rock musicians become folk heroines and chart-toppers, when they escape from prison and go on the run. The film is a high-spirited crowd-pleaser, at once hardboiled and sentimental, and the songs (most of them sung in English) are catchy in a retro-ABBA sort of way. In German with English subtitles. Rated R for language (in subtitles), sexuality, and drug use. 110m. **DIR:** Katja von Garnier. **CAST:** Katja Riemann, Jasmin Tabatabai, Nicolette Krebitz, Jutta Hoffmann. 1997

BANDITS OF DARK CANYON ★★★1/2 Texas Ranger Rocky Lane helps escaped convict Bob Steele clear his name on a phony murder charge. The apparent victim is alive and working with Steele's best friend to cheat him out of his fortune. Above-average Lane Western—and they were all

good. B&W; 59m. **DIR:** Philip Ford. **CAST:** Allan "Rocky" Lane, Bob Steele, Eddy Waller, Roy Barcroft, Linda Johnson. 1947

BANDOLERO! ★★★ Escape south of the border with outlaw brothers James Stewart and Dean Martin (if you can buy this), who ride just a few furlongs ahead of the law (George Kennedy), taking Raquel Welch along as hostage. 106m. **DIR:** Andrew V. McLaglen. **CAST:** James Stewart, Dean Martin, Raquel Welch, Will Geer, George Kennedy, Andrew Prine. 1968

BANG BANG KID, THE ★★1/2 Goofy comedy-Western with Tom Bosley as Merriweather Newberry, the inventor of a robot gunfighter (dubbed The Bang Bang Kid). The residents of a mining community hope that they can use it to defeat Bear Bullock (Guy Madison), the town boss. Good for kids; passable for grownups in a silly mood. 90m. **DIR:** Stanley Prager. **CAST:** Guy Madison, Sandra Milo, Tom Bosley, Riccardo Garrone. 1968

BANG THE DRUM SLOWLY ★★★★ Robert De Niro and Michael Moriarty are given a perfect showcase for their acting talents in this poignant film, and they don't disappoint. The friendship of two baseball players comes alive as the team's star pitcher (Moriarty) tries to assist journeyman catcher (De Niro) in completing one last season before succumbing to Hodgkin's disease. The story may lead to death, but it is filled with life, hope, and compassion. Rated PG. 98m. **DIR:** John Hancock. **CAST:** Robert De Niro, Michael Moriarty, Vincent Gardenia. 1973

BANK DICK, THE ★★★★★ W. C. Fields is at his best in this laugh-filled comedy. In it, Fields plays a drunkard who becomes a hero. But the story is just an excuse for the moments of hilarity—of which there are many. B&W; 74m. **DIR:** Eddie Cline. **CAST:** W. C. Fields, Cora Witherspoon, Una Merkel, Shemp Howard. 1940

BANK ROBBER 🎞 Shallow, bungling thief sticks up a downtown bank and spends the rest of the movie hiding out in a seedy, nearby hotel in this offbeat but dumb comedy caper. Rated NC-17 for sex, violence, and language. 95m. **DIR:** Nick Mead. **CAST:** Patrick Dempsey, Lisa Bonet, Olivia D'Abo, Forest Whitaker, Judge Reinhold, Michael Jeter. 1993

BANK SHOT 🎞 George C. Scott as a lisping mastermind who plots to steal a bank by putting it on wheels. PG for language. 100m. **DIR:** Gower Champion. **CAST:** George C. Scott, Joanna Cassidy, Don Calfa. 1974

B.A.P.S ★★ The title stands for "Black American Princesses," two of whom (Halle Berry and Natalie Desselle) are hired to pose as the granddaughters of dying millionaire Martin Landau's long-lost love. Brainless, witless, and demeaning on every level, with nary a chuckle in the whole sad, disheveled mess. A huge disappointment from usually reliable director Robert Townsend. Landau looks plainly (and understandably) embarrassed; only Ian Richardson, as the butler, escapes with his dignity more or less intact. Rated PG-13 for mild profanity. 93m. **DIR:** Robert Townsend. **CAST:** Halle Berry, Natalie Desselle, Martin Landau, Ian Richardson. 1997

BAR GIRLS ★★ Lesbians cross paths at a Los Angeles watering hole in this sporadically funny dating game that plays like a cross between a lipsticked *Cheers* and a soap opera. Rated R for language, nudity, and simulated sex. 95m. DIR: Marita Giovanni. CAST: Nancy Allison Wolfe, Liza D'Agostino, Michael Harris, Camilla Griggs, Justine Slater. 1995

BAR-20 RIDES AGAIN ★★★ Hopalong Cassidy and Red Connors are called to Wyoming to help an old friend deal with cattle rustlers, and the Bar-20 boys and their allies wage a terrific battle. George Hayes appears as "Windy" for the first time and starts his long career as cantankerous sidekick supreme. B&W; 65m. DIR: Howard Bretherton. CAST: William Boyd, James Ellison, Jean Rouverol, George "Gabby" Hayes, Harry Worth, Paul Fix. 1935

BARABBAS ★★1/2 Early Dino De Laurentis opus is long on production, short on credibility. Standard gory religious spectacle follows the life of the thief Barabbas, whom Pilate freed when Jesus was condemned to die. Good cast of veteran character actors attempts to move this epic along, but fails. 144m. DIR: Richard Fleischer. CAST: Anthony Quinn, Jack Palance, Ernest Borgnine, Katy Jurado. 1962

BARB WIRE ★★ America's second civil war has left the nation in chaos and black-leather biker Barb—in a punk/metal nod to *Casablanca*—takes on Fascist army pigs after crossing paths with an ex-lover and his freedom-fighter wife. Rated R for nudity, language, suggested sex, and violence. 98m. DIR: David Hogan. CAST: Pamela Anderson Lee, Temuera Morrison, Victoria Rowell, Steve Railsback, Jack Noseworthy. 1996 DVD

BARBARELLA ★★1/2 Futuristic fantasy has Jane Fonda in the title role of a space beauty being drooled over by various male creatures on a strange planet. Drags at times, but Jane's fans won't want to miss it. Rated PG for partial nudity-sexual content. 98m. DIR: Roger Vadim. CAST: Jane Fonda, John Phillip Law, Anita Pallenberg, Milo O'Shea. 1968 DVD

BARBARIAN AND THE GEISHA, THE ❤ American ambassador to Japan during the nineteenth century finds romance with geisha. 105m. DIR: John Huston. CAST: John Wayne, Sam Jaffe, Eiko Ando. 1958

BARBARIAN QUEEN ❤ Another one of those lame fantasy flicks à la *Yor*, the *Conan* films, and Lou Ferrigno's *Hercules* films. Although not rated, *Barbarian Queen* has lots of nudity and violence. 75m. DIR: Hector Olivera. CAST: Lana Clarkson, Katt Shea, Frank Zagarino, Dawn Dunlap. 1985

BARBARIAN QUEEN II: EMPRESS STRIKES BACK ❤ More sword and sorcery from buxom babe Lana Clarkson, whom you might remember from the first *Barbarian Queen*, but then again: maybe not. Rated R. 87m. DIR: Joe Finley. CAST: Lana Clarkson, Greg Wrangler. 1989

BARBARIANS, THE ❤ Unconvincing fantasy film casts David and Peter Paul (wrestling's Barbarian Brothers) as twins trying to save the queen of their people. Not rated. 88m. DIR: Ruggero Deodato. CAST: Peter Paul, David Paul, Richard Lynch, Michael Berryman. 1987

BARBARIANS AT THE GATE ★★★★ The legacy of the 1980s—corporate greed—is brilliantly indicted in Larry Gelbart's adaptation of Bryan Borrough and John Helyar's mesmerizing account of the Nabisco

takeover. James Garner stars as "good ol' boy" F. Ross Johnson, the Nabisco CEO who battled the circling sharks to control the company he professed to love so dearly. Rated R for profanity. 107m. DIR: Glenn Jordan. CAST: James Garner, Jonathan Pryce, Peter Riegert, Joanna Cassidy, Fred Dalton Thompson, Mark Harelik. 1993

BARBAROSA ★★★★ Action-packed Western stars Willie Nelson and Gary Busey as a pair of outcasts on the run. Australian director Fred Schepisi has created an exciting, funny movie that combines the scenic majesty of the great John Ford Westerns with the light touch of George Roy Hill's *Butch Cassidy and the Sundance Kid*. Rated PG for violence. 90m. DIR: Fred Schepisi. CAST: Willie Nelson, Gary Busey, Isela Vega, Gilbert Roland, Danny De La Paz, George Voskovec. 1982

BARBARY COAST, THE ★★★1/2 Inspired by Herbert Asbury's colorful history of early San Francisco, this film is tailored to fit the unique talents of its great cast. This story of femme fatale Miriam Hopkins and the men in her life is fun for the whole family and a treat for film buffs who like the look of the past as created on studio back lots. B&W; 90m. DIR: Howard Hawks. CAST: Edward G. Robinson, Miriam Hopkins, Joel McCrea, Walter Brennan, Brian Donlevy, Frank Craven. 1935

BARCELONA ★★★1/2 An American sales rep in Spain and his naval-officer cousin engage in a roundrobin of romantic complications while discussing sex and politics in their exquisitely civilized monotone voices. Rated PG-13 for mature themes. 101m. DIR: Whit Stillman. CAST: Taylor Nichols, Christopher Eigeman, Tushka Bergen, Mira Sorvino, Hellena Schmied, Nuria Badia. 1994

BARE ESSENTIALS ★★ A yuppie guy and gal find themselves reevaluating their relationship after being shipwrecked on a tiny atoll. Plodding. 94m. DIR: Martha Coolidge. CAST: Mark Linn-Baker, Lisa Hartman, Gregory Harrison, Charlotte Lewis. 1990

BARE KNUCKLES ★★★ A fun martial arts thriller about a modern-day bounty hunter on the trail of a vicious killer stalking women on the streets of the city. Rated R for brief nudity, violence, and adult language. 90m. DIR: Don Edmunds. CAST: Robert Viharo, Sherry Jackson, Michael Heit, Gloria Hendry, John Daniels. 1984

BAREFOOT CONTESSA, THE ★★★ A gaggle of Hollywood vultures headed by director Humphrey Bogart picks naïve dancer Ava Gardner out of a Madrid nightclub and proceeds to mold her into a film star. A simple unpretentious soul, she marries an impotent Italian nobleman (Rossano Brazzi), dies, and is buried by her chief mentor who tells her tragic story in flashback. A cynical, bizarre tale that never delivers what it promises. 128m. DIR: Joseph L. Mankiewicz. CAST: Humphrey Bogart, Ava Gardner, Edmond O'Brien, Marius Goring, Rossano Brazzi. 1954

BAREFOOT IN THE PARK ★★★1/2 A young Robert Redford and Jane Fonda team up as newlyweds in this adaptation of Neil Simon's Broadway play. The comedy focuses on the adjustments of married life. Mildred Natwick plays the mother-in-law, and Charles Boyer is a daffy, unconventional neighbor. 105m. **DIR:** Gene Saks. **CAST:** Robert Redford, Jane Fonda, Charles Boyer, Mildred Natwick, Herb Edelman. **1967 DVD**

BARFLY ★★★★ Superb performances by Mickey Rourke and Faye Dunaway, as well as a dynamite jazz and R&B score, highlight this hip, flip, and often gruesomely funny semiautobiographical film written by Charles Bukowski. Rourke and Dunaway drink their way from one sodden, sleazy misadventure to another, and director Barbet Schroeder makes it all seem to truly take place on the street—or is that the gutter? Rated R for profanity, suggested sex, and violence. 97m. **DIR:** Barbet Schroeder. **CAST:** Mickey Rourke, Faye Dunaway, Alice Krige, J. C. Quinn, Frank Stallone. **1987**

BARITONE ★★★1/2 In 1933, a world-famous singer returns to Poland for the first time in twenty-five years. The infighting and scheming among his entourage, as well as the local officials, are meant as a parable of fascism, though this well-produced film is more enjoyable as a straightforward soap opera. In Polish with English subtitles. Not rated. 100m. **DIR:** Janusz Zaorski. **CAST:** Zbigniew Zapasiewicz. **1985**

BARJO ★★★ An oddball writer who obsessively catalogs everyday activities moves in with his sister and her husband and drives their emotional difficulties to the breaking point. Barjo's humorous investigations aren't well integrated with the black comedy of an impossible marriage between a man who wants order and a woman who wants "everything and its opposite," but both are amusing. In French with English subtitles. Rated R for sexual implications and discussions. 83m. **DIR:** Jerome Boivan. **CAST:** Hippolyte Giradot, Richard Bohringer, Anne Brochet. **1993**

BARKLEYS OF BROADWAY, THE ★★★ As a film team, Ginger Rogers and Fred Astaire parted in 1939. This final pairing, the result of Judy Garland's inability to make the picture, does not favorably compare with earlier efforts. Harry Warren's score, while augmented by a great George Gershwin number, is not up to snuff. Nevertheless, the film was a critical and commercial hit. 109m. **DIR:** Charles Walters. **CAST:** Fred Astaire, Ginger Rogers, Oscar Levant. **1949**

BARN BURNING ★★★★ A sterling adaptation of William Faulkner's short story. Oscar-winning scripter Horton Foote is responsible for this teleplay. Tommy Lee Jones is grand in a role that oozes menace. Introduced by Henry Fonda; unrated and suitable for family viewing. 40m. **DIR:** Peter Werner. **CAST:** Tommy Lee Jones, Diane Kagan, Shawn Whittington. **1980**

BARNABY AND ME ★★★ Sid Caesar's considerable comic talents aren't exactly strained in this Australian feature. Still, this lightweight story of a con man who mends his ways when he meets a young girl and her pet koala is good family viewing—a few laughs, and who can resist a koala bear? Rated G. 90m. **DIR:** Norman Panama. **CAST:** Sid Caesar, Juliet Mills. **1977**

BARNEY'S GREAT ADVENTURE ★★★ Public TV's pudgy purple dinosaur helps three children discover the joys and importance of nurturing their imagina-

tion. The wishes of Abby and her friend Marcella turn a small stuffed-toy Barney into a six-foot mentor and playmate during a visit to the farm of Abby's grandparents. Older brother Cody is skeptical of Barney's existence but then joins the fantasy. This musical romp is a rarity: an adventure for kids without bad guys. Rated G. 75m. **DIR:** Steve Gomer. **CAST:** Trevor Morgan, Kyla Pratt, Diana Rice, George Hearn, Shirley Douglas. **1998 DVD**

BARNUM (1986) ★★★ Made-for-television adaptation of Cy Coleman–Michael Stewart Broadway hit. Michael Crawford as flamboyant promoter Phineas T. Barnum is mesmerizing, tracing Barnum's life, from his humble beginnings to creating the Barnum and Bailey Circus. 113m. **DIR:** Terry Hughes. **CAST:** Michael Crawford. **1986**

BARNUM (1987) ★★★ Above-average TV film looks at the greatest showman on Earth, P. T. Barnum, played to the hilt by Burt Lancaster. Nice atmosphere and sets lend to the overall effect, but this is Lancaster's show all the way. 94m. **DIR:** Lee Philips. **CAST:** Burt Lancaster, Hanna Schygulla. **1987**

BARON MÜNCHHAUSEN (1943) ★★★ This lavish epic was intended to be a cinematic jewel in the crown of Hitler's Third Reich, a big-budget masterpiece designed to prove that Germany could compete with Hollywood. While the outlandish adventures of Baron Hieronymus Münchhausen are at times amusing and quite clever, the incredible visual spectacle—huge and chaotic sets, overly ornate costumes—often overwhelms the story. Very brief nudity; otherwise suitable for family viewing. 110m. **DIR:** Josef von Baky. **CAST:** Hans Albers, Brigitte Horney, Leo Slezak. **1943**

BARON MUNCHAUSEN (1961) ★★★ The adventures of the German folk hero, noted for the tallest tales ever told, are recounted here in a blend of live-action and inventive animation. Unfortunately, the story itself is rather boring, so kids are likely to get antsy. Also known as *The Fabulous Baron Munchausen*. In German with English subtitles. 110m. **DIR:** Karel Zeman. **CAST:** Milos Kopecky, Hana Brejchova. **1961**

BARON OF ARIZONA, THE ★★1/2 Vincent Price hams it up as a smooth con man who nearly succeeds in claiming most of the Arizona Territory as his own. This early directorial effort by Samuel Fuller lacks the edge he gave his best films, but it's well played by a good cast. Based on a real incident. B&W; 90m. **DIR:** Samuel Fuller. **CAST:** Vincent Price, Ellen Drew, Beulah Bondi, Vladimir Sokoloff, Reed Hadley, Robert Barrat. **1950**

BARRETTS OF WIMPOLE STREET, THE ★★★ Stagy but well-acted version of the romance between Robert Browning and Elizabeth Barrett under the watchful, jealous eye of her domineering father. First-rate cast triumphs over a slightly dated script. B&W; 110m. **DIR:** Sidney Franklin. **CAST:** Norma Shearer, Fredric March, Charles Laughton, Maureen O'Sullivan. **1934**

BARRY LYNDON ★★★ Although exquisitely photographed and meticulously designed, this three-hour motion picture adaptation of William Makepeace Thackeray's novel about an eighteenth-century rogue is a flawed masterpiece at best and is far too drawn out. However, it is worth watching for the lush cinematography by John Alcott. Rated PG for brief nudity and violence. 183m. DIR: Stanley Kubrick. CAST: Ryan O'Neal, Marisa Berenson, Patrick Magee, Hardy Krüger, Steven Berkoff, Gay Hamilton. 1975 DVD

BARRY MCKENZIE HOLDS HIS OWN ★★1/2 Extremely vulgar comedy based on a popular Australian comic strip about the adventures of beer-swilling Aussie Barry Crocker trying to rescue his auntie (Barry Humphries in drag as "Dame Edna Everage") from vampire Count Plasma (Donald Pleasence). You'll either be appalled or laugh yourself sick, though the impenetrable slang may make you wish the movie was subtitled. Not rated. 93m. DIR: Bruce Beresford. CAST: Barry Crocker, Barry Humphries, Donald Pleasence. 1974

BARTLEBY ★★★1/2 Herman Melville's tale of a man who "would prefer not to" seems especially timely now. Paul Scofield is the unfortunate boss who, stuck with the inert Bartleby, is forced to fire him. Superior acting makes this thought-provoking tale both moving and believable. 79m. DIR: Anthony Friedman. CAST: Paul Scofield, John McEnery. 1970

BARTON FINK ★★★★ More inspired madness from the Coen Brothers, Joel and Ethan. John Turturro stars as a New York playwright whose success on the stage, with a play celebrating the common man, leads to a lucrative screenwriting assignment. Funny but surreal. Rated R for profanity. 112m. DIR: Joel Coen. CAST: John Turturro, John Goodman, John Mahoney, Judy Davis, Jon Polito, Michael Lerner, Tony Shalhoub. 1991

•**BASE, THE** ★★ There's some action in this old war horse about an undercover military operative trying to get the goods on some bad soldiers dealing in drugs. The plot is all over the place, yet things move swiftly enough to keep logic at bay most of the time. Rated R for language, nudity, and violence. 110m. DIR: Mark L. Lester. CAST: Mark Dacascos, Tim Abell, Paula Trickey, Noah Blake. 1999 DVD

BASEBALL: A FILM BY KEN BURNS ★★★★★ The national pastime's rich and varied history, good and bad, white and black, is explored from the 1840s to the present with respect, affection, and wit. Written by Geoffrey C. Ward and Ken Burns. Narrated by John Chancellor. B&W/color. 1110m. on nine cassettes. DIR: Ken Burns. 1994 DVD

BASED ON AN UNTRUE STORY ★★ This made-for-TV movie—about a perfume maker who must find her long-lost siblings in order to save her damaged olfactory nerves—is short on laughs and long on tedium. The only funny bits involve a child trapped in a trash Dumpster in Beverly Hills, but that has nothing to do with the rest of the film. Not rated; contains suggested sex. 91m. DIR: Jim Drake. CAST: Morgan Fairchild, Dan Hedaya, Victoria Jackson, Harvey Korman, Robert Goulet, David Byron, Ricki Lake, Dyan Cannon. 1993

BASEKETBALL 💘 In their big-screen debut, Trey Parker and Matt Stone (creators of the animated hit *South Park*) play two dimwits who become overnight sports stars when they invent a game combining baseball and basketball. The game is dull and

pointless, and so is the film. Rated R for profanity and mild nudity. 98m. DIR: David Zucker. CAST: Trey Parker, Matt Stone, Yasmine Bleeth, Jenny McCarthy, Robert Vaughn, Ernest Borgnine. 1998 DVD

BASIC INSTINCT ★★ Cop Michael Douglas finds himself seduced (repeatedly) by bisexual heiress Sharon Stone, even though she's suspected of having committed a brutal ice-pick murder. Director Paul Verhoeven takes sex and violence to extremes, perhaps in an effort to cover up the TV-movie-of-the-week weakness of Joe Eszterhas's sleazy screenplay. Rated R for nudity, simulated sex, violence, and profanity. 130m. DIR: Paul Verhoeven. CAST: Michael Douglas, Sharon Stone, George Dzundza, Jeanne Triplehorn, Stephen Tobolowsky. 1992 DVD

BASIL ★★★ Handsome period production design and a high-rent cast add little to this tale based on the classic novel by Wilkie Collins. Jared Leto is the wide-eyed innocent Basil, whose strict father is grooming him to take over the family estate. Basil goes against his father's wishes and his naïveté gets the best of him when he learns too late that his new bride is in cahoots with his best friend to bring him down. Claire Forlani shines as the love of Basil's heart. Rated R for violence and adult situations. 95m. DIR: Radha Bharadwaj. CAST: Jared Leto, Christian Slater, Claire Forlani, Derek Jacobi. 1997

BASILEUS QUARTET ★★★★★ When their leader dies, the remaining members of a renowned string quartet hire a young violinist to replace him. The presence of this aggressive, virile young man forces the three older men to confront what they have made of their own lives. An intelligent, literary film, flawlessly acted. Dubbed in English. Not rated, contains nudity and sexual situations. 105m. DIR: Fabio Carpi. CAST: Hector Alterio, Omero Antonutti, Pierre Malet, François Simon. 1982

•**BASKET, THE** ★★1/2 During World War I, a new schoolmaster arrives in a small Washington town at the same time as two German war orphans. Together they teach the local yokels something about basketball, opera, and tolerance—in roughly that order. Earnest and well-meaning, the film suffers from a farfetched script and amateurish performances. Rated PG. 104m. DIR: Rich Cowan. CAST: Peter Coyote, Karen Allen, Robert Karl Burke, Amber Willenborg, Ellen Travolta, Joey Travolta. 2000

BASKET CASE ★★ Comedy and horror are mixed beautifully in this weird tale of a young man and his deformed Siamese twin out for revenge against the doctors who separated them. Gruesomely entertaining and highly recommended for shock buffs. Rated R. 91m. DIR: Frank Henenlotter. CAST: Kevin Van Hentenryck, Terri Susan Smith. 1982 DVD

BASKET CASE 2 💘 Shameless sequel. Rated R for violence and nudity. 90m. DIR: Frank Henenlotter. CAST: Kevin Van Hentenryck, Heather Rattray. 1990

BASKET CASE 3: THE PROGENY ★★★ Bad is a relative term. And with this second sequel featuring the "Times Square Freak Twins" Duane and Belial Bradley, bad means good—in a sickening sort of way. The brothers head south for the delivery of Belial's mutant offspring. Along for the ride is the weirdest bunch of creatures this side of the Cantina scene in

Star Wars. Rated R for violence, profanity, gore, and simulated mutant sex. 90m. DIR: Frank Henenlotter. CAST: Annie Ross, Kevin Van Hentenryck. 1992

BASKETBALL DIARIES, THE ★★★ This bio-pic unveils the gritty early life of poet and author Jim Carroll, a Catholic-school basketball player who quickly descends into the nightmarish world of drug addiction. Pay attention to Mark (Marky Mark) Wahlberg, whose down-and-dirty performance is all streetsmart bravura. Rated R for profanity, violence, nudity, and drug use. 102m. DIR: Scott Kalvert. CAST: Leonardo DiCaprio, Lorraine Bracco, Bruno Kirby, Ernie Hudson, Patrick McGaw, James Madio. 1995 DVD

BASQUIAT ★★★ Artist Julian Schnabel turns filmmaker with this adoring biography of Jean-Michel Basquiat, the meteoric 1980s art sensation who died of a heroin overdose at twenty-seven. Interesting and well-acted, but those unfamiliar with Basquiat's art will get little idea of it. Rated R for profanity and simulated sex. 108m. DIR: Julian Schnabel. CAST: Jeffrey Wright, Michael Wincott, Benicio Del Toro, David Bowie, Gary Oldman, Dennis Hopper. 1996

BASTARD, THE ★★★ TV miniseries ably adapts part one of John Jakes's American Revolution saga. Numerous well-known stars pop in for cameo appearances, while Andrew Stevens takes the lead as the illegitimate son of a British nobleman. His hopes of sharing the man's wealth dashed, he heads for America. 189m. DIR: Lee H. Katzin. CAST: Andrew Stevens, Tom Bosley, Kim Cattrall, Patricia Neal, Olivia Hussey. 1978

BASTARD OUT OF CAROLINA ★★★★ Dorothy Allison's harrowing novel becomes an equally gutchurning study of the casual cruelties tolerated by people in dead-end lives. Poor but proud Jennifer Jason Leigh tries to improve things for herself and her two daughters, but unwisely marries white-trash Ron Eldard, whose hair-trigger temper is matched by an unhealthy attraction to elder daughter Jena Malone. A difficult subject, well told. Rated R for child abuse, rape, profanity, and violence. 98m. DIR: Anjelica Huston. CAST: Jennifer Jason Leigh, Ron Eldard, Jena Malone, Diana Scarwid, Michael Rooker, Glenne Headly, Lyle Lovett, Dermot Mulroney, Christina Ricci. 1996 DVD

BAT, THE ★★ A mystery writer and her housemates in a creepy old mansion fall under the ominous shadow of a murderer known as "The Bat." Third filming of this creaky old play was only a moderately successful attempt to cash in on William Castle's box-office bonanzas with Vincent Price. Originally published in 1915, the 1930 film version is cited as one of Bob Kane's inspirations for *Batman.* 88m. DIR: Crane Wilbur. CAST: Agnes Moorehead, Vincent Price, Gavin Gordon, John Sutton, Darla Hood, Lenita Lane. 1959 DVD

BAT PEOPLE 💗 A young biologist on his honeymoon is bitten by a bat and is slowly transformed into a flying, blood-hungry rodent. Originally titled *It Lives by Night.* It sucks under any name. Rated R. 95m. DIR: Jerry Jameson. CAST: Stewart Moss, Marianne McAndrew, Michael Pataki. 1974

BAT 21 ★★★★ In a typically effective performance, Gene Hackman is a military mastermind who is shot down during a reconnaissance mission in Vietnam, where he is trapped behind enemy lines. It's up to pilot Danny Glover to keep Hackman safe and sane until he can be rescued. Fine telling of a heroic, true-life story guarantees to keep you on the edge of your seat. Rated R for violence and profanity. 105m. DIR: Peter Markle. CAST: Gene Hackman, Danny Glover, Jerry Reed, David Marshall Grant. 1988

BAT WHISPERS, THE ★★1/2 Mary Roberts Rinehart's venerable stage success featuring a caped killer, clutching hands, a spooky mansion, and plenty of scared females. Chester Morris made his screen debut in this slow-moving but stylish creaker about the mysterious "Bat" who informs his victims of the hour of their death and never fails to deliver. B&W; 82m. DIR: Roland West. CAST: Spencer Charters, Una Merkel, Chester Morris. 1931 DVD

BATAAN ★★★★1/2 One of the best films about World War II chronicles the exploits of an army patrol attempting to stall the Japanese onslaught in the Philippines. B&W; 114m. DIR: Tay Garnett. CAST: Robert Taylor, George Murphy, Thomas Mitchell, Lloyd Nolan, Robert Walker, Desi Arnaz Sr., Barry Nelson. 1943 DVD

BATHING BEAUTY ★★1/2 One of MGM's best-remembered musicals emerges dripping wet from the mists of time as a series of waterlogged vignettes flaunt new discovery Esther Williams. She plays a college girl who's crazy about songwriter Red Skelton, and jumps into a swimsuit as frequently as he dresses in drag in order to further the intrigue. 101m. DIR: George Sidney. CAST: Esther Williams, Red Skelton, Basil Rathbone, Margaret Dumont, Bill Goodwin, Jean Porter, Nana Bryant, Donald Meek, Harry James. 1944

BATMAN (1966) ★★★ Holy success story! The caped crusader and his youthful sidekick jump from their popular mid-1960s television series into a full-length feature film. Adam West and Burt Ward keep quip in cheek as they battle the Fearsome Foursome: the Riddler (Frank Gorshin), the Penguin (Burgess Meredith), Catwoman (Lee Meriwether), and the Joker (Cesar Romero). A lot of fun. 105m. DIR: Leslie Martinson. CAST: Adam West, Burt Ward, Frank Gorshin, Burgess Meredith, Lee Meriwether, Cesar Romero. 1966

BATMAN AND ROBIN (ADVENTURES OF BATMAN AND ROBIN) ★★1/2 The Caped Crusader and Boy Wonder swoop onto celluloid for the second time as they answer Police Commissioner Gordon's plea for help and run up against "The Wizard." Not really a great serial, but fun—and it avoids the unfortunate racism that makes the 1943 serial unpleasant. B&W; 15 chapters. DIR: Spencer Gordon Bennet. CAST: Robert Lowery, John Duncan, Lyle Talbot, Jane Adams, Ralph Graves, Don Harvey, Michael Whalen. 1949

BATMAN (1989) ★★★1/2 So much of *Batman* is awe-inspiring that one is disappointed when this ambitious production all but collapses under its own weight in the last half hour. Still, there's much to enjoy in Jack Nicholson's bizarre, over-the-top performance as the villainous Joker, Michael Keaton's underplayed but effective dual role as millionaire-playboy Bruce Wayne and Batman, and the spectacular, *Blade Runner*–like sets. Rated PG-13 for profanity and violence. 130m. **DIR:** Tim Burton. **CAST:** Jack Nicholson, Michael Keaton, Kim Basinger, Pat Hingle, Billy Dee Williams, Jack Palance, Robert Wuhl, Michael Gough. **1989 DVD**

BATMAN RETURNS ★★★1/2 Director Tim Burton turns Danny DeVito into a villainous Penguin guaranteed to produce nightmares; Michelle Pfeiffer is a seductively sensational Catwoman. Set designer Bo Welch creates a gloomy, "Machine-Age Teutonic" Gotham City. Although bound to please fans, this sequel is marred by a goofy, fright-wigged Christopher Walken—and too few appearances by its star. Rated PG-13 for violence. 130m. **DIR:** Tim Burton. **CAST:** Michael Keaton, Danny DeVito, Michelle Pfeiffer, Christopher Walken, Pat Hingle, Michael Gough. **1992 DVD**

BATMAN FOREVER ★★★1/2 A new director and a new star result in a livelier, brighter, less-brooding entry in the series. Supervillains Two-Face and the Riddler team up to unleash a reign of terror over Gotham City. Batman teams up with new sidekick, Robin, to stop them. Worth seeing for the striking visuals and playful tone, but it won't knock your socks off. Rated PG-13 for comic-book violence. 120m. **DIR:** Joel Schumacher. **CAST:** Val Kilmer, Tommy Lee Jones, Jim Carrey, Nicole Kidman, Chris O'Donnell. **1995 DVD**

BATMAN & ROBIN ★★★ In this fourth outing, Batman and Robin deal with rivalry in the realms of superhero status and female companionship, the probable death of Alfred the butler, and the possibility that Mr. Freeze might turn Gotham City into a giant, flavorless frozen treat. The determined effort to make this entry less dark than the previous films for the most part succeeds, thanks to George Clooney's attitude as Batman, and Uma Thurman's sexually charged portrayal of Poison Ivy. But Alicia Silverstone seems lost as Batgirl, and there are too many scene-ending tag lines that fall flat. Yet each installment in this series visually reinvents itself and enriches the characters. Rated PG-13 for cartoonish violence. 126m. **DIR:** Joel Schumacher. **CAST:** Arnold Schwarzenegger, George Clooney, Chris O'Donnell, Uma Thurman, Alicia Silverstone, Michael Gough, Pat Hingle. **1997 DVD**

BATMAN: MASK OF THE PHANTASM ★★★1/2 The caped crusader's slick animated series made an engaging feature-length debut with all of its *film noir* sensibilities intact. Definitely too story heavy for youngsters, this moody thriller—based strongly on Frank Miller's Dark Knight comics—finds Batman forced to defend a reputation tarnished by both the Joker (wonderfully voiced by Mark Hamill) and the title villain. Rated PG. 76m. **DIR:** Eric Radomski, Bruce W. Timm. **1993 DVD**

BATON ROUGE ★★★1/2 A gigolo and a psychiatrist team up to murder a rich man and blame his neurotic wife for the crime. One of a number of Spanish films that were released in the United States to cash in on the success of Antonio Banderas, this is one of the best, a sexy thriller filled with double and triple crosses and featuring an all-star Spanish cast. Not

rated; contains adult situations. In Spanish with English subtitles. 105m. **DIR:** Rafael Moleon. **CAST:** Antonio Banderas, Victoria Abril, Carmen Maura. **1988**

•BATS ♥ Throwback to the swarm films, this barely watchable, low-budget flick is a time waster for both Lou Diamond Phillips and potential viewers. Phillips plays a small-town Texas sheriff investigating murders in which the "perps" are mutant bats. Strictly second-rate. Rated PG-13 for profanity and gore. 91m. **DIR:** Louis Morneau. **CAST:** Lou Diamond Phillips, Dina Meyer. **1999 DVD**

BATTERED ★★1/2 This TV docudrama will have you believing there are wife beaters lurking around every corner. The script is somewhat stiff and uninventive at times, but does offer a fairly accurate picture of the few alternatives open to the women in this desperate situation. 95m. **DIR:** Peter Werner. **CAST:** Mike Farrell, LeVar Burton, Karen Grassle, Joan Blondell, Howard Duff, Diana Scarwid. **1978**

BATTERIES NOT INCLUDED ★★★ Pleasant fantasy feature about tenement dwellers who are terrorized by thugs hired by a land developer. All seems lost until a group of tiny aliens comes to their aid. Often the movie is simply too derivative and predictable. That said, the younger set will love it. Rated PG. 106m. **DIR:** Matthew Robbins. **CAST:** Hume Cronyn, Jessica Tandy, Frank McRae, Elizabeth Peña. **1987 DVD**

BATTLE ANGEL ★★★★ A young cybernetic girl becomes a successful bounty hunter in this animated tale. Outstanding artwork and bizarre characters give life to this cyberpunk adaptation of Kishiro Yukito's wildly successful comic. In Japanese with English subtitles. Not rated; contains nudity and violence. 70m. **DIR:** Hiroshi Fukutomi. **1993 DVD**

BATTLE BENEATH THE EARTH ★★1/2 Stalwart Kerwin Mathews leads the fight against the Chinese hordes who intend to invade the United States via underground tunnels. Pretty good adventure-fantasy in the comic-book/pulp magazine tradition. 91m. **DIR:** Montgomery Tully. **CAST:** Kerwin Mathews, Robert Ayres, Martin Benson, Viviane Ventura, Bessie Love. **1967**

BATTLE BEYOND THE STARS ★★★★ Here's something different; a space fantasy-comedy. Richard Thomas stars in this funny and often exciting movie as an emissary from a peaceful planet desperately searching for champions to save it from an evil warlord. It's *Star Wars* meets *The Magnificent Seven*, with fine tongue-in-cheek performances. Rated PG. 104m. **DIR:** Jimmy T. Murakami. **CAST:** Richard Thomas, John Saxon, Robert Vaughn, George Peppard. **1980**

BATTLE CIRCUS ★★ Humphrey Bogart and June Allyson are mismatched in this nonaction war picture. It's a soap opera about a military doctor arguing with and finally falling for a nurse on the Korean battlefield. Soggy. B&W; 90m. **DIR:** Richard Brooks. **CAST:** Humphrey Bogart, June Allyson, Keenan Wynn, Robert Keith, Steve Forrest, Philip Ahn, William Campbell. **1953**

BATTLE CRY ★★★ A platoon of Marines is followed into battle during World War II. The conflicts they face on the islands of the Pacific are contrasted to the emotional conflicts faced by their girlfriends at home. All in all, it is a successful piece of wartime fluff. 149m. DIR: Raoul Walsh. CAST: Van Heflin, Tab Hunter, Dorothy Malone, Anne Francis. 1955

BATTLE FOR THE PLANET OF THE APES ★★ Events come full circle in this final *Apes* film, with simian Roddy McDowall attempting peaceful coexistence with conquered humanity. Naturally, not everybody plays along with such a plan, and an impending nuclear threat adds little tension to a story whose outcome is known. Rated PG for violence. 92m. DIR: J. Lee Thompson. CAST: Roddy McDowall, Severn Darden, John Huston, Claude Akins, Paul Williams. 1973

BATTLE FORCE ★★ The effect of war on the lives of two families, one American, the other German. Passable World War II adventure. 92m. DIR: Humphrey Longon. CAST: Henry Fonda, John Huston, Stacy Keach, Helmut Berger, Samantha Eggar. 1976

BATTLE HELL ★★ More British stiff upper lip in this tale of the H.M.S. *Amethyst* battling the communist Chinese on the Yangtze River. Pretty standard war flick, overly long, but with some good battle footage. Not rated: some violence. 112m. DIR: Michael Anderson. CAST: Richard Todd, Akim Tamiroff, Keye Luke, William Hartnell, Donald Houston, Robert Urquhart, James Kenney. 1956

•**BATTLE HYMN** ★★★ Fact-based story of a World War II pilot who went on to become a minister and found an orphan's home in Korea. The script asks a bit more of star Rock Hudson than he's able to give; all in all, a decent if slightly hokey Hollywood drama. 108m. DIR: Douglas Sirk. CAST: Rock Hudson, Anna Kashfi, Dan Duryea, Don DeFore, Martha Hyer, Jock Mahoney, Alan Hale Jr. 1957

BATTLE OF ALGIERS ★★★★ This gut-wrenching Italian-Algerian pseudo-documentary about the war between Algerian citizens and their French "protectors" was released when America's involvement in Vietnam was still to reach its peak, but the parallels between the two stories are obvious. Covering the years from 1954 to 1962, this film is an emotional experience—it is not recommended for the casual viewer and is too strong for children. B&W; 123m. DIR: Gillo Pontecorvo. CAST: Yacef Saadi, Jean Martin, Brahim Haggiag. 1965

BATTLE OF AUSTERLITZ, THE 💔 This attempt to re-create the epic battle of the Napoleonic wars is slow, dull, abysmally dubbed, and generally uninspired. 123m. DIR: Abel Gance. CAST: Claudia Cardinale, Leslie Caron, Vittorio De Sica, Orson Welles. 1960

BATTLE OF BRITAIN ★★1/2 It's a shame that a film that has a $12 million budget, a cast of characters straight from the British Who's Who of film and stage, great aerial photography, and a subject matter that deals with a vital period of British history could not have been better than this semi-epic. 132m. DIR: Guy Hamilton. CAST: Michael Caine, Ralph Richardson, Robert Shaw, Trevor Howard, Susannah York, Curt Jurgens, Edward Fox, Kenneth More, Christopher Plummer, Laurence Olivier, Harry Andrews, Nigel Patrick. 1969

BATTLE OF EL ALAMEIN, THE ★★★ A re-creation of the famous twelve-day 1942 turning point clash between the artillery, tanks, and infantry of the British Eighth Army under General Montgomery and the German army's fabled Afrika Korps commanded by Field Marshal Rommel in the windswept Libyan Desert southwest of Alexandria. We know the outcome, but getting there makes for exciting watching. Rated PG. 96m. DIR: Calvin Jackson Padget. CAST: Michael Rennie, Robert Hossein, Frederick Stafford, Ettore Manni, George Hilton. 1968

BATTLE OF THE BULGE ★★ This is a fairly decent war film. It has solid acting and exciting battle sequences but suffers on video for two reasons: the small screen hurts the epic scale and 23 minutes are cut from the original print, with some important footage missing. 140m. DIR: Ken Annakin. CAST: Henry Fonda, Robert Shaw, Robert Ryan, Dana Andrews, Charles Bronson, Telly Savalas. 1965

BATTLE OF THE COMMANDOS 💔 Lots of phony battle scenes, bad acting, and a poor script all add up to a big bomb. 94m. DIR: Umberto Lenzi. CAST: Jack Palance, Curt Jurgens, Thomas Hunter, Diana Largo, Wolfgang Preiss. 1969

BATTLE OF THE SEXES, THE ★★★1/2 Peter Sellers is wonderful as an elderly Scottish Highlander bent on murder. Robert Morley, always a favorite, is simply delightful and helps keep this British comedy on a fast and funny track. B&W; 88m. DIR: Charles Crichton. CAST: Peter Sellers, Robert Morley, Constance Cummings, Jameson Clark. 1960

BATTLE SHOCK ★★ Ralph Meeker portrays an artist who becomes involved in a murder while working in Mexico. Janice Rule is his doting wife. An uneven suspenser also known under the title of *A Woman's Devotion*. 88m. DIR: Paul Henreid. CAST: Ralph Meeker, Janice Rule, Rosenda Monteros, Paul Henreid. 1956

•**BATTLEFIELD EARTH** 💔 This atrocious adaptation of L. Ron Hubbard's equally vapid book was a vanity project for star-producer John Travolta, who wanted to "honor" the Scientology founder. No chance of that; this unintentionally hilarious melee between conquering extraterrestrials and their enslaved human captives, set in the year 3000, is absolute swill. Rated PG-13 for violence. 117m. DIR: Roger Christian. CAST: John Travolta, Barry Pepper, Forest Whitaker, Kim Coates, Sabine Karsenti, Michael Byrne, Richard Tyson. 2000

BATTLEGROUND ★★★1/2 Made over the protests of MGM czar Louis B. Mayer, this rugged look at World War II's famous Battle of the Bulge has a resounding hit. Everything looks and sounds real. Oscars went to script and photography. B&W; 118m. DIR: William Wellman. CAST: Van Johnson, John Hodiak, Denise Darcel, Ricardo Montalban, George Murphy, James Whitmore. 1949

BATTLESHIP POTEMKIN, THE ★★★★★ One of a handful of landmark motion pictures. This silent classic, directed by the legendary Sergei Eisenstein, depicts the mutiny of the crew of a Russian battleship and its aftermath. The directorial technique expanded the threshold of what was then standard cinema storytelling. The massacre of civilians on the Odessa Steps remains one of the most powerful scenes in film history. Silent. B&W; 65m. DIR: Sergei

Eisenstein. **CAST:** Alexander Antonov, Vladimir Barsky. 1925 DVD

BATTLESTAR GALACTICA 💔 Adapted from the television series, this is a seventh-rate *Star Wars.* Rated PG. 125m. **DIR:** Richard A. Colla. **CAST:** Lorne Greene, Richard Hatch, Dirk Benedict, Lew Ayres, Jane Seymour. 1978 DVD

BATTLING ORIOLES, THE ★★ Baseball player's son rejuvenates his father's team and rescues his sweetheart from a fate worse than death. Of interest mainly for its re-creation of a nineteenth-century baseball game and an unbilled performance by four *Our Gang* members in a charming segment. B&W; 56m. **DIR:** Ted Wilde, Fred L. Guiol. **CAST:** Glenn Tryon, Blanche Mehaffey, John T. Prince, Noah Young. 1924

BAWDY ADVENTURES OF TOM JONES, THE 💔 This ridiculous romp features Trevor Howard as the lecherous Squire Western. Young Tom Jones (played by an innocent-looking Nick Henson) is in love with Western's daughter and spends the entire film hoping to win her hand. Rated R for nudity. 89m. **DIR:** Cliff Owen. **CAST:** Nicky Henson, Trevor Howard, Joan Collins, Arthur Lowe, Georgia Brown, Madeleine Smith, Jeremy Lloyd. 1976

BAXTER (1973) ★★1/2 Troubled schoolboy Scott Jacoby is treated by speech therapist Patricia Neal in this earnest British drama. Well-done for its type. Rated PG. 100m. **DIR:** Lionel Jeffries. **CAST:** Patricia Neal, Scott Jacoby, Jean-Pierre Cassel, Lynn Carlin, Britt Ekland. 1973

BAXTER (1988) ★★★★ In spite of the cute bull terrier on the box cover, Baxter the dog is anything but cuddly. Listening in on his thoughts as he reacts to the humans around him, we discover a creature of simple but rigid moral standards. And when he meets a young boy who worships Hitler, we learn a chilling lesson in human nature as well. In French with English subtitles. Not rated; contains adult themes and situations. 82m. **DIR:** Jerome Boivan. **CAST:** Lise Delamare, Jean Mercure, Jacques Spiesser. 1988

BAY BOY, THE ★★★★1/2 The story of a brief period in an adolescent boy's life while growing up in a small mining town on the Nova Scotia coast during the mid-1930s. This film develops the character, including the sexual awakening, guilt, and terror, of Donald Campbell (Kiefer Sutherland). Liv Ullmann is well cast as Donald's mother. 104m. **DIR:** Daniel Petrie. **CAST:** Liv Ullmann, Kiefer Sutherland, Joe MacPherson. 1985

BAYWATCH: THE MOVIE ★★ Fans of the popular syndicated television series will find this expanded episode to their liking. Unfortunately, Pamela Anderson disappears before the first act is over, leaving her small-screen costars to fill in the blanks. Plenty of sand, surf, and hot bodies as the characters head off to Hawaii for training and mystery. 90m. **DIR:** Douglas Schwartz. **CAST:** David Hasselhoff, Pamela Anderson, Alexandra Paul, David Charvet, Yasmine Bleeth. 1994

BE YOURSELF ★★1/2 Singer loves simple-minded prizefighter but loses him temporarily to a flashy blonde. A flop when it came out, this likable movie captures "funny lady" Fanny Brice's personality and performance at their best and is her earliest surviving feature. B&W; 77m. **DIR:** Thornton Freeland. **CAST:** Fanny Brice, Robert Armstrong, Gertrude Astor, Harry Green. 1930

◆**BEACH, THE** ★★ This obviously wishes to be an adult-oriented blend of *Lord of the Flies* and *The Blue Lagoon,* but the metaphor about the ephemeral nature of paradise quickly turns silly and downright stupid. Characters in possession of a "great treasure" abandon all sense of humanity and basic decency, become paranoid to a degree that is unintentionally hilarious, and literally lose their minds. Matters are not helped by having to identify with the spoiled, petulant, arrogant WASP brat-packer played with no conviction whatsoever by Leonardo DiCaprio. This is lazy filmmaking: incoherent directing, irrational scripting, and ineffectual acting, particularly by the leading man. Rated R for profanity, drug use, nudity, and violence. 119m. **DIR:** Danny Boyle. **CAST:** Leonardo DiCaprio, Tilda Swinton, Virginie Ledoyen, Guillaume Canet, Robert Carlyle. 2000 DVD

BEACH BABES FROM BEYOND 💔 The title says it all. Not worth watching even to see celebrity relatives embarrass their families. Rated R for profanity and nudity. 78m. **DIR:** Ellen Cabot. **CAST:** Joe Estevez, Don Swayze, Joey Travolta, Burt Ward, Jacqueline Stallone, Linnea Quigley, Sarah Bellomo, Tamara Landry, Nicole Posey. 1993

BEACH BABES 2: CAVE GIRL ISLAND ★★ The sequel to the bimbofest of 1993, *Beach Babes from Beyond,* is slightly better but not too much. Only Sarah Bellomo reprises her role from the original with new actresses stepping into the roles, and out of the clothes, of the other two leads. Filmed in 1995, but not released until three years later. Rated R for nudity and simulated sex. 82m. **DIR:** Ellen Cabot. **CAST:** Sarah Bellomo, Tina Holliman, Stephanie Hudson, Lenny Rose. 1998

BEACH BLANKET BINGO ★★1/2 The fifth in the series, and the last true "Beach Party" film. Basically, it's the same old stuff: stars on their way up (Linda Evans) or on their way down (Buster Keaton) or at their peak (Frankie and Annette), spouting silly dialogue and singing through echo chambers. But it's one of the best of the series, whether you're laughing with it or at it. 98m. **DIR:** William Asher. **CAST:** Frankie Avalon, Annette Funicello, Paul Lynde, Harvey Lembeck, Don Rickles, Linda Evans, Jody McCrea, Marta Kristen, John Ashley, Deborah Walley, Buster Keaton. 1965

BEACH GIRLS, THE 💔 Teenage girls throw a big party at their uncle's Malibu beach house. Rated R for nudity. 91m. **DIR:** Pat Townsend. **CAST:** Debra Blee, Val Kline, Jeana Tomasina. 1982 DVD

BEACH HOUSE 💔 Mirthless comedy about a feud between Italian kids from Brooklyn and snobs from Philadelphia. Rated PG. 75m. **DIR:** John Gallagher. **CAST:** Ileana Seidel, John Cosola. 1982

BEACH PARTY ★★1/2 Bob Cummings, a bearded, sheltered anthropologist, studies the wild dating and mating habits of beach-bound teens. He ends up courting Annette Funicello to make Frankie Avalon jealous. Cummings has his moments, as does Harvey Lembeck, as the biker Eric Von Zipper. 101m. **DIR:**

William Asher. **CAST:** Robert Cummings, Dorothy Malone, Frankie Avalon, Annette Funicello, Harvey Lembeck, Jody McCrea, John Ashley, Morey Amsterdam. **1963**

BEACHBALLS 🎗 Another sleazy teen tumble. Rated R for nudity and profanity. 79m. **DIR:** Joe Ritter. **CAST:** Phillip Paley, Heidi Helmer. **1988**

BEACHCOMBER, THE ★★★ This Somerset Maugham story of a dissolute South Seas beachcomber and the lady missionary who reforms him is sculptor's clay in the expert hands of Charles Laughton and Elsa Lanchester. He is delightful as the shiftless, conniving bum; she is clever and captivating as his Bible-toting nemesis. A scene at a bar is Laughton at his wily, eye-rolling, blustering best. B&W; 80m. **DIR:** Erich Pommer. **CAST:** Charles Laughton, Elsa Lanchester, Tyrone Guthrie, Robert Newton. **1938**

BEACHES ★★★★ Here's a terrific tearjerker that casts Bette Midler and Barbara Hershey as two unlikely friends who enjoy a thirty-year relationship that's full of ups and downs. Fans of five-handkerchief films will love it. Midler is often hilarious as the show-biz-crazy Jewish gal who both loves and competes with WASPish heiress Hershey. See it if only for the mind-boggling performance of look-alike Mayim Bialik as the 11-year-old Midler, but be prepared to suspend your disbelief. Rated PG-13 for profanity and suggested sex. 120m. **DIR:** Garry Marshall. **CAST:** Bette Midler, Barbara Hershey, John Heard, Spalding Gray. **1988**

BEAKS: THE MOVIE 🎗 Hitchcock made birds menacing. *Beaks* makes them at times unintentionally funny and at other times too gruesome to watch. 86m. **DIR:** René Cardona Jr. **CAST:** Christopher Atkins, Michelle Johnson. **1987**

BEAN ★★ The charm, manic inventiveness, and cruel hilarity of Rowan Atkinson's delightful *Mr. Bean* shorts are completely absent in this lumbering mess, which wastes the star's time and talent in a witless script (from Bean team scribes Richard Curtis and Robin Driscoll, who should know better) that sends the near-silent doofus to the United States as an "art expert" accompanying a rare painting. Rated PG-13 for vulgar gestures and blue humor. 90m. **DIR:** Mel Smith. **CAST:** Rowan Atkinson, Peter MacNicol, Pamela Reed, John Mills. **1997 DVD**

BEANSTALK ★★ There's just a bit too much "fe-fi-fo-fum" to director Michael Paul Davis's script as young J. D. Daniels tosses some seeds out the window and, surprise, up sprouts a beanstalk. This updating of the old "Jack and the Beanstalk" fairy tale is aimed at kids, but even they will groan at the bad humor and lousy makeup effects. Rated PG for mild violence. 80m. **DIR:** Michael Paul Davis. **CAST:** J. D. Daniels, Richard Moll, Margot Kidder, Patrick Renna, David Naughton, Stuart Pankin. **1994**

BEAR, THE ★★★★★ *The Bear* is a wildlife adventure film that transcends its genre. It's the *Gone with the Wind* of animal movies. Some scenes might be a little frightening for the younger set. Rated PG for violence. 93m. **DIR:** Jean-Jacques Annaud. **CAST:** Jack Wallace, Tcheky Karyo. **1989 DVD**

BEAR ISLAND 🎗 Pointlessly melodramatic tale mixing gold fever, murder, and other incidental intrigue. Rated PG for mild violence. 118m. **DIR:** Don Sharp. **CAST:** Donald Sutherland, Richard Widmark, Vanessa Redgrave, Christopher Lee, Lloyd Bridges. **1980**

BEAST, THE (1988) ★★ A clichéd war film, unique only for its adversaries: Soviet soldiers and Afghan rebels in the deserts of Afghanistan. Though the Afghans speak subtitled native language, the Soviets speak in slang-laced Americanized English. They sound more like California surfers than Russian soldiers. Rated R, with profanity and violence. 109m. **DIR:** Kevin Reynolds. **CAST:** Steven Bauer, George Dzundza. **1988**

BEAST, THE (1996) ★★★ This abbreviated version of the made-for-television miniseries actually works better. Much of the clutter has been trimmed, making for a tighter, more suspenseful tale of a tentacled killer preying on the inhabitants of a small coastal town. More underwater thrills from Peter Benchley, writer of *Jaws*. Rated PG-13 for violence. 116m. **DIR:** Jeff Bleckner. **CAST:** William L. Petersen, Karen Sillas, Charles Martin Smith, Missy Crider, Larry Drake. **1996**

BEAST FROM 20,000 FATHOMS, THE ★★★ An experimental atom bomb blast in the Arctic thaws a million-year-old giant rhedosaurus that seeks its home in the Atlantic depths off the New York coast. Based on Ray Bradbury's *Saturday Evening Post* story. B&W; 80m. **DIR:** Eugene Lourie. **CAST:** Paul Christian, Paula Raymond, Cecil Kellaway, Donald Woods, Kenneth Tobey, Lee Van Cleef. **1953**

BEAST IN THE CELLAR, THE ★★ Boring story about a pair of aging sisters (well played by veterans Beryl Reid and Flora Robson) with something to hide. Their deranged, deformed brother is down there, and he wants out! Weak. Rated R. 87m. **DIR:** James Kelly. **CAST:** Beryl Reid, Flora Robson, T. P. McKenna, John Hamill. **1971**

BEAST MUST DIE, THE ★★ A millionaire hunter invites a group of guests to an isolated mansion. One of them is a werewolf he intends to destroy. A tame, talky reworking of Agatha Christie's *Ten Little Indians*. Rated PG. 98m. **DIR:** Paul Annett. **CAST:** Calvin Lockhart, Peter Cushing, Charles Gray, Anton Diffring. **1974**

BEAST OF THE YELLOW NIGHT ★★ Having played the hero in several Filipino Blood Island, mad-scientist movies, John Ashley here takes on the mantle of the villain. This Jekyll-and-Hyde effort is as cheesy as his earlier tropical thrillers, but the sporadic mayhem may keep you amused. Rated R. 87m. **DIR:** Eddie Romero. **CAST:** John Ashley, Mary Wilcox, Eddie Garcia. **1970**

BEAST WITH FIVE FINGERS, THE ★★★ Some eerie moments with the severed hand of a deceased pianist running loose in a mansion, choking people left and right. Another high-camp, wide-eyed performance by Peter Lorre. Fine special effects. B&W; 89m. **DIR:** Robert Florey. **CAST:** Robert Alda, Peter Lorre, Andrea King, J. Carrol Naish. **1947**

BEAST WITHIN, THE 🎗 This unbelievably gory movie consists mainly of one grisly murder after another. Rated R. 90m. **DIR:** Philippe Mora. **CAST:** Ronny Cox, Bibi Besch, Paul Clemens, Don Gordon. **1982**

BEASTMASTER, THE ★★★1/2 A young medieval warrior (Marc Singer) who possesses the ability to communicate psychically with animals takes revenge—with the help of a slave (Tanya Roberts) and a master warrior (John Amos)—on the evil sorcerer (Rip Torn). It's fun for kids of all ages. Rated PG for violence and brief nudity. 118m. **DIR:** Don Coscarelli. **CAST:** Marc Singer, Tanya Roberts, Rip Torn, John Amos, Rod Loomis. **1982**

BEASTMASTER 2: THROUGH THE PORTAL OF TIME ★★★1/2 The Beastmaster (Marc Singer) travels through a hole in time to present-day Los Angeles in order to chase down his evil nemesis. More than just another stranger-in-a-strange-land tale, this film will please fans of the genre as well as those who just like a good laugh. Rated PG-13 for violence. 107m. **DIR:** Sylvio Tabet. **CAST:** Marc Singer, Wings Hauser, Kari Wuhrer, Sarah Douglas. **1991**

BEASTMASTER III: THE EYE OF BRAXUS ★★1/2 Lamely choreographed fight scenes weaken an already marginal film, but Marc Singer, as the Beastmaster, wins us over with his ease around the animals and his wry wit. This time he must save his brother from an evil lord who has ghastly ambitions. Decent special effects and above-par soundtrack by Jan Hammer (of *Miami Vice* fame). Rated PG-13 for violence. 92m. **DIR:** Gabrielle Beaumont. **CAST:** Marc Singer, David Warner, Tony Todd, Sandra Hess, Casper Van Dien, Lesley-Anne Down, Keith Coulouris. **1995**

BEAT GIRL ★★★ While American exploitation movies of previous generations are trotted out for camp value, this British "adults only" drama is actually quite well made. Gillian Hills plays a teen girl who is determined to do whatever it takes to end her father's marriage to a young Frenchwoman. Not rated; contains brief nudity. 83m. **DIR:** Edmond T. Grenville. **CAST:** Gillian Hills, David Farrar, Christopher Lee, Adam Faith, Shirley Anne Field, Oliver Reed. **1959**

BEAT STREET 🕊 A hackneyed plot, about kids breaking into show biz. Rated PG for profanity and violence. 106m. **DIR:** Stan Lathan. **CAST:** Rae Dawn Chong, Guy Davis. **1984**

BEAT THE DEVIL ★★★★ Because it's all played straight, critics and audiences alike didn't know what to make of this delightful though at times baffling satire of films in the vein of *The Maltese Falcon* and *Key Largo* when it first hit screens. Sadly, some still do not. Nonetheless, this droll comedy, cobbled on location in Italy by John Huston and Truman Capote, is a twenty-four-carat gem. B&W; 93m. **DIR:** John Huston. **CAST:** Humphrey Bogart, Robert Morley, Peter Lorre, Jennifer Jones, Gina Lollobrigida. **1954** DVD

BEATRICE ★★ In creating *Beatrice*, writer-director Bertrand Tavernier set out to demythologize the Middle Ages. He succeeds all too well with this repulsive, nightmarish movie in which the angelic title character (Julie Delpy) is raped and tortured by the demented father (Bernard Pierre Donnadieu) she once idolized. In French with English subtitles. Not rated, the film has nudity, violence, and simulated sex. 128m. **DIR:** Bertrand Tavernier. **CAST:** Bernard Pierre Donnadieu, Julie Delpy, Nils Tavernier. **1987**

BEAU BRUMMELL (1924) ★★★★ John Barrymore scores a great success as the handsome dandy who works his way into the good graces of the Prince of Wales. Mary Astor is wonderful as Lady Alvanley. This is a must-see film for admirers of the silent film nearing its peak of perfection. Silent. B&W; 92m. **DIR:** Harry Beaumont. **CAST:** John Barrymore, Mary Astor, Irene Rich, Carmel Myers. **1924**

BEAU BRUMMELL (1954) ★★★1/2 Good telling of the on-again, off-again friendship and patronage between the Prince of Wales (later George IV) and court rogue and dandy Beau Brummell. Stewart Granger is fine in the title role, and Elizabeth Taylor is beautiful, but the movie belongs to Peter Ustinov as the prince, and in a small role, Robert Morley as George III. 113m. **DIR:** Curtis Bernhardt. **CAST:** Stewart Granger, Elizabeth Taylor, Peter Ustinov, Robert Morley, James Donald, Rosemary Harris, Peter Bull. **1954**

BEAU GESTE ★★★★1/2 Gary Cooper fulfilled every idealistic boy's dream of honor, sacrifice, and brotherly love in this splendid adaptation of P. C. Wren's adventure classic. Director William Wellman painstakingly re-created the arid setting of the world's most famous Foreign Legion adventure. The action is brisk and the characters are unforgettable. B&W; 114m. **DIR:** William Wellman. **CAST:** Gary Cooper, Robert Preston, Ray Milland, Brian Donlevy, J. Carrol Naish, Susan Hayward, Broderick Crawford, Albert Dekker, Donald O'Connor, James Stephenson. **1939**

BEAU PERE ★★★★ Patrick Dewaere stars again for French director Betrand Blier (*Get Out Your Handkerchiefs*) in this film, about a stepfather who falls in love with his adopted pubescent daughter. It could have been shocking—or just plain perverse. But *Beau Pere* is a bittersweet, thoroughly charming motion picture. In French with English subtitles. Not rated; the film has nudity, profanity, and adult themes. 120m. **DIR:** Bertrand Blier. **CAST:** Patrick Dewaere, Ariel Besse, Maurice Ronet, Nicole Garcia. **1982** DVD

BEAUMARCHAIS THE SCOUNDREL ★★★1/2 An unproduced play by Sacha Guitry was the basis for this lavish and lively biography of the eighteenth-century playwright who dabbled in espionage and international politics between writing popular plays and pursuing the ladies. A first-rate cast is headed by the sly Fabrice Luchini in a film whose only drawback is that it packs too much into too little time. In French with English subtitles. Not rated; contains nudity and violence. 100m. **DIR:** Edouard Molinaro. **CAST:** Fabrice Luchini, Sandrine Kiberlain, Manuel Blanc, Michel Piccoli, Michel Serrault. **1996**

BEAUTICIAN AND THE BEAST, THE ★★★1/2 Giggle-producing combination of *The Sound of Music* and every fairy tale cliché pairs a tyrant (Timothy Dalton) with a New Yorker (Fran Drescher), and he doesn't stand a chance. When a beauty-college instructor is hired to teach the children of an Eastern European despot, she quickly turns the tiny kingdom on its ear. The two are in each other's face so often that romance inevitably blooms. Royal pageantry is a visual bonus. Rated PG for sexual innuendo. 107m.

DIR: Ken Kwapis. CAST: Fran Drescher, Timothy Dalton, Ian McNeice, Patrick Malahide, Lisa Jakub. **1997**

▶BEAUTIES OF THE NIGHT ★★★ A young music teacher in an industrial town escapes his boring life with fantasies in which the women around him become figures from history. Music and images mesh wonderfully in this lightweight concoction. Original title: *Les Belles de Nuit.* In French with English subtitles. B&W; 89m. DIR: René Clair. CAST: Gérard Philipe, Martine Carol, Gina Lollobrigida, Magali Vendeul. **1952**

BEAUTIFUL BLONDE FROM BASHFUL BEND, THE ★★1/2 Sharpshooter-schoolmarm Betty Grable has boyfriend trouble and must deal with a kidnapping and a philandering Cesar Romero in this wacky Western farce. Tolerable family fun, but not a highlight in director Preston Sturges's career. 77m. DIR: Preston Sturges. CAST: Betty Grable, Cesar Romero, Rudy Vallee, Olga San Juan, Sterling Holloway, Hugh Herbert, Porter Hall, Margaret Hamilton. **1949**

BEAUTIFUL DREAMERS ★★★1/2 Rip Torn delivers a wonderful performance as poet Walt Whitman, who accompanies a young doctor back to his small town, where the outspoken Whitman's beliefs set the local townsfolk aback. While the rest of the cast is in tune with the vision, it's Torn who paints the brightest images in this intelligent film. Rated PG-13 for language. 108m. DIR: John Kent Harrison. CAST: Rip Torn, Colm Feore, Sheila McCarthy. **1991**

BEAUTIFUL GIRLS ★★★ Another rueful comedy about commitment-shy twentysomething men and the women who are too good for them. Scott Rosenberg's script takes a condescending view of its own characters, and his dialogue is often pretentious and literary; some lines are almost literally unspeakable. Fortunately, the cast is packed with first-rate talent, and the film is much better acted than written. Rated R for profanity. 113m. DIR: Ted Demme. CAST: Timothy Hutton, Matt Dillon, Mira Sorvino, Uma Thurman, Rosie O'Donnell, Michael Rapaport, Annabeth Gish, Martha Plimpton, Natalie Portman. **1996 DVD**

▶BEAUTIFUL PEOPLE ★★★★ Chance encounters and chaos are the basic drivers of this darkly comic, cathartic story in which fallout from the ethnic cleansing in former Yugoslavia slops over to 1993 London. A Croat and a Serb share neighboring hospital beds; a junkie soccer hooligan literally becomes a human United Nations Care Package; a well-heeled woman falls in love with a destitute immigrant. These stormy stories are as emotionally messy as life itself—and brilliantly portrayed. Rated R for language, drug use, and violence. 107m. DIR: Jasmin Dizdar. CAST: Danny Nussbaum, Nicolas Farrell, Edin Dzandzanovic, Charlotte Coleman, Charles Kay, Rosalind Ayres. **2000 DVD**

BEAUTIFUL THING ★★★ It's love in bloom between two teenage boys in working-class London. Originally produced for British TV and adapted from Jonathan Harvey's play, the film is modest, likable, and competently acted. A neighbor girl's obsession with Mama Cass seems to come out of nowhere and serves mainly as an excuse for the nostalgic tunes on the soundtrack. Rated R for profanity and mature themes. 89m. DIR: Hettie Macdonald. CAST: Glen Bar-

ry, Linda Henry, Scott Neal, Tameka Empson, Ben Daniels. **1996**

BEAUTY AND THE BEAST (1946) ★★★★★ This French classic goes far beyond mere retelling of the well-known fairy tale. Its eerie visual beauty and surrealistic atmosphere mark it as a genuine original. The tragic love story between Beauty (Josette Day) and the all-too-human Beast (Jean Marais) resembles a moving painting. In French with English subtitles. B&W; 90m. DIR: Jean Cocteau. CAST: Josette Day, Jean Marais. **1946 DVD**

BEAUTY AND THE BEAST (1991) ★★★★★ A classic feature-length cartoon from Walt Disney Pictures, this adaptation of the classic fairy tale is the animated equivalent of the stage production of *Les Misérables*; a spectacular piece of musical theater complete with heartwarming moments, uproarious comedy, even suspense. Oscars went to Alan Menken for his score and to Menken and Howard Ashman for the title song. Rated G. 85m. DIR: Gary Trousdale, Kirk Wise. **1991**

BEAUTY AND THE BEAST (TV SERIES) ★★★1/2 Based on the classic legend, this popular cult television series teamed Linda Hamilton's crusading district attorney with Ron Perlman's underworld dweller. Some admire the Renaissance surroundings and unusually literate scripts; others yearn for the deep, platonic love shared by the two central characters. This much is certain: You'll either roll with the poetic dialogue or find it outrageously melodramatic. Not rated; suitable for family viewing. 100m. DIR: Richard Franklin, Victor Lobl. CAST: Ron Perlman, Linda Hamilton, Roy Dotrice, Jay Acovone. **1987**

BEAUTY FOR THE ASKING 🎔 Beautician Lucille Ball creates a skin cream that sells millions. B&W; 68m. DIR: Glenn Tryon. CAST: Lucille Ball, Patric Knowles, Frieda Inescort, Donald Woods. **1939**

BEAUTY SCHOOL 🎔 *Emmanuelle* star Sylvia Kristel seriously needs a career makeover as the owner of a beauty school who's in a desperate race to win a lucrative advertising contract. Just another lame excuse to get women naked. Rated R for nudity and adult situations. 95m. DIR: Ernest G. Sauer. CAST: Sylvia Kristel, Kevin Bernhardt, Kimberly Taylor, Jane Hamilton. **1992**

BEAVIS AND BUTT-HEAD DO AMERICA ★★★ The notorious cartoon nitwits from MTV set out to replace their stolen television set, then find themselves involved with the FBI and a stolen killer virus. Never do they understand the situation. The script neatly expands the one-gag premise to feature length, with many laughs and clever complications. The deliberately sloppy animation matches the scribbled-in-a-notebook-during-study-hall style of the humor. Rated PG-13 for mild sexual humor; not appropriate for young children. 80m. DIR: Mike Judge. CAST: Mike Judge, Robert Stack (voices). **1996 DVD**

BEAVIS AND BUTT-HEAD (TV SERIES) ★★★★ Creator Mike Judge skewers almost every facet of contemporary American society with this animated, made-for-cable series about two really dumb high-school kids with an unmatched talent for dissipation. While many consider this series to be dangerously moronic, our two "heroes" provide a slick vehicle for satire that is deceptively smart. Releases for home video, unfortunately, do not include the duo's commentary on various outrageous music videos. Not rated; contains profanity. Each 45m. **DIR:** Mike Judge. 1992–1996 DVD

BEBE'S KIDS ★★1/2 The comedy routines of the late, great black comedian Robin Harris were adapted to create this animated comedy. Harris's first date with a beautiful woman becomes a nightmare when he reluctantly agrees to take along her neighbor's troublemaking kids. Part *The Simpsons*, part *Alvin and the Chipmunks*, and part Harris, this was obviously a heartfelt project for all concerned. It just isn't that good. Rated PG-13 for profanity and violence. 93m. **DIR:** Bruce Smith. 1992

BECAUSE YOU'RE MINE ★★1/2 When an opera star is drafted into the army, his training sergeant turns out to be a fan who has (surprise!) a sister with operatic ambitions. Forget the plot, just enjoy Mario Lanza's gifted voice. 101m. **DIR:** Alexander Hall. **CAST:** Mario Lanza, James Whitmore, Doretta Morrow, Jeff Donnell, Dean Miller, Paula Corday. 1952

BECKET ★★★★ Magnificently acted spectacle of the stormy relationship between England's King Henry II (Peter O'Toole) and his friend and nemesis Archbishop Thomas Becket (Richard Burton). This visually stimulating historical pageant, set in twelfth-century England, garnered Oscar nominations for both its protagonists. 148m. **DIR:** Peter Glenville. **CAST:** Richard Burton, Peter O'Toole, Martita Hunt, Pamela Brown. 1964

BECKY SHARP ★★1/2 Well-mounted historical drama of a callous young woman who lives for social success is lovely to look at in its original three-strip Technicolor. Fine performances by a veteran cast bolster this first sound screen adaptation of Thackeray's *Vanity Fair*. 83m. **DIR:** Rouben Mamoulian. **CAST:** Miriam Hopkins, Frances Dee, Cedric Hardwicke, Billie Burke, Alison Skipworth, Nigel Bruce. 1935

BECOMING COLETTE ★★★ Beautifully photographed story chronicling the life of Colette, and the events that made her a world-famous author. From marriage to an older publisher to her introduction to decadent turn-of-the-century Paris, this film conveys a sumptuous eye for detail. Excellent performances from Mathilda May as the alluring Colette, Klaus Maria Brandauer as her husband, and Virginia Madsen as French actress Polaire. Rated R for nudity and adult situations. 97m. **DIR:** Danny Huston. **CAST:** Mathilda May, Klaus Maria Brandauer, Virginia Madsen, Paul Rhys. 1992

BED AND BREAKFAST ★★★ After a man is washed up on the beach area in front of a house in Maine inhabited by a widow and her mother-in-law, the women's lives take some unexpected turns. The film examines the tender side of human relationships in a decidedly feminine fashion, while using just enough mystery and suspense to add an edge to their tale. Rated PG-13 for brief violence, suggested sex, and profanity. 96m. **DIR:** Robert Ellis Miller. **CAST:** Roger Moore, Talia Shire, Colleen Dewhurst, Ford Rainey. 1992

BED AND SOFA ★★★ During a housing shortage in Moscow a construction worker takes in an old friend. In the ensuing ménage à trois the worker's wife, now pregnant, turns her back on both the men in her life and leaves to make a new life for herself. A startling achievement, without precedent in the Soviet cinema. Silent. B&W; 73m. **DIR:** Abram Room. **CAST:** Nikolai Batalov, Vladimir Fogel. 1927

BED OF ROSES ★★★1/2 Writer-director Michael Goldenberg's sweet little love story plays well in the hands of Christian Slater and Mary Stuart Masterson, cast as two emotionally damaged characters stumbling their way into a relationship. She's a workaholic investment banker without a past; he's a widower who delivers flowers because he enjoys bringing pleasure into strangers' lives. Rated PG for mild sexual content. 90m. **DIR:** Michael Goldenberg. **CAST:** Christian Slater, Mary Stuart Masterson, Pamela Segall, Josh Brolin. 1996 DVD

BEDAZZLED ★★★★ A cult favorite, this British comedy stars Dudley Moore as a fry cook tempted by the devil (played by his onetime comedy partner, Peter Cook). Costarring Raquel Welch, it's an often hilarious updating of the Faust legend. 107m. **DIR:** Stanley Donen. **CAST:** Peter Cook, Dudley Moore, Raquel Welch, Eleanor Bron. 1967

BEDFORD INCIDENT, THE ★★★ A battle of wits aboard a U.S. destroyer tracking Soviet submarines off Greenland during the Cold War. Richard Widmark is a skipper with an obsession to hunt and hound a particular sub. A conflict develops between the captain and Sidney Poitier, a cocky magazine reporter along for the ride. B&W; 102m. **DIR:** James B. Harris. **CAST:** Richard Widmark, Sidney Poitier, Martin Balsam, Wally Cox, Eric Portman. 1965

BEDKNOBS AND BROOMSTICKS ★★★1/2 Angela Lansbury is a witch who uses her powers to aid the Allies against the Nazis during World War II. She transports two children to faraway and strange locales during which they meet and play soccer with talking animals, among other things. This Disney film is an effective combination of special effects, animation, and live action. Rated G. 117m. **DIR:** Robert Stevenson. **CAST:** Angela Lansbury, David Tomlinson, Roddy McDowall. 1971

BEDLAM ★★★ One of the lesser entries in the Val Lewton–produced horror film series at RKO, this release still has its moments as the courageous Anna Lee tries to expose the cruelties and inadequacies of an insane asylum run by Boris Karloff, who is first-rate, as usual. B&W; 79m. **DIR:** Mark Robson. **CAST:** Boris Karloff, Anna Lee, Ian Wolfe, Richard Fraser, Jason Robards Sr. 1946

BEDROOM EYES ★★★ A young stockbroker peers into a window one evening and sees a woman so tantalizing he feels compelled to return every night. When the object of his voyeurism is murdered, the man must try to prove his innocence. A silly but undeniably erotic mystery. 90m. **DIR:** William Fruet. **CAST:** Kenneth Gilman, Dayle Haddon, Barbara Law, Christine Cattel. 1986

BEDROOM EYES II ♥ Tawdry whodunit. Rated R for nudity, profanity, and violence. 87m. **DIR:** Chuck Vincent. **CAST:** Linda Blair, Wings Hauser. 1989

BEDROOM WINDOW, THE ★★★ Upwardly mobile architect Steve Guttenberg has it made until his boss's wife (Isabelle Huppert) sees a murder being committed—from his bedroom window. When Guttenberg goes to the police in her place, he becomes the prime suspect. This is a tense thriller that manages to stay interesting despite some wildly unbelievable plot twists. Rated R for profanity, nudity, and violence. 112m. **DIR:** Curtis Hanson. **CAST:** Steve Guttenberg, Elizabeth McGovern, Isabelle Huppert, Paul Shenar. 1987 DVD

•**BEDROOMS AND HALLWAYS** ★★ Gay Londoner Leo is prodded by a heterosexual buddy to join a straight men's sensitivity group in this screwball comedy of manners. Leo's revelation that he is attracted to an Irishman in the group kicks off a domino effect of sexual exploration and exploits that includes Jane Austen dream fantasies and the skewering of New Age gurus. The film begins with comic promise but runs out of juice well before its final couplings. Not rated; contains profanity, nudity, and simulated sex. 96m. **DIR:** Rose Troche. **CAST:** Kevin McKidd, James Purefoy, Jennifer Ehle, Tom Hollander, Simon Callow, Hugo Weaving. 1999

BEDTIME FOR BONZO ★★★ This sweet-natured film is worth watching. Ronald Reagan plays a young college professor who uses a chimpanzee to prove that environment, not heredity, determines a person's moral fiber. He hires a young woman (Diana Lynn) to pose as the chimp's mom while he plays father to it. Not surprisingly, Mom and Dad fall in love. B&W; 83m. **DIR:** Frederick de Cordova. **CAST:** Ronald Reagan, Diana Lynn, Walter Slezak, Jesse White. 1951

BEDTIME STORY ★★★ A European playboy (David Niven) and a wolfish American GI (Marlon Brando, somewhat miscast), propose to settle their differences with a bet: the first to seduce naive contest winner Shirley Jones becomes King of the Cosmopolitan Hill, and the other must quietly fade away. Although often quite sexist, the result is much funnier than the shallow concept would suggest. Remade as *Dirty Rotten Scoundrels*. Suggestive themes. 99m. **DIR:** Ralph Levy. **CAST:** David Niven, Marlon Brando, Shirley Jones. 1964

BEER ★★★ Hilarious comedy that examines the seamy side of the advertising industry. Loretta Swit plays a cold-blooded advertising agent who tries to turn three ordinary guys (David Alan Grier, William Russ, and Saul Stein) into beer-drinking American heroes. Dick Shawn's impression of Phil Donahue must be seen to be believed. Rated R for profanity, sex, and adult subject matter. 83m. **DIR:** Patrick Kelly. **CAST:** Loretta Swit, Rip Torn, Kenneth Mars, David Alan Grier, William Russ, Peter Michael Goetz, Dick Shawn, Saul Stein. 1985

BEES, THE ❤ Despite all temptation to label this a honey of a picture, it's a drone that will probably give viewers the hives. Rated PG. 83m. **DIR:** Alfredo Zacharias. **CAST:** John Saxon, John Carradine. 1978

BEETHOVEN ★★★ When an adopted puppy grows up to be a 185-pound Saint Bernard, businessman Charles Grodin wishes he'd never allowed his family to take the dog in. Good family fun. Rated PG for doggy messes. 87m. **DIR:** Brian Levant. **CAST:** Charles Grodin, Bonnie Hunt, Dean Jones, Stanley Tucci, David Duchovny. 1992 DVD

BEETHOVEN'S NEPHEW ★★1/2 This surreal drama by Paul Morrissey takes an incisive look at the dark side of Beethoven's genius. It's a convoluted period piece that follows the bizarre exploits of Beethoven's young nephew, Karl. Interesting performances, beautiful settings, and great costumes carry this film over the slow spots. Rated R. 103m. **DIR:** Paul Morrissey. **CAST:** Wolfgang Reichmann, Dietmar Prinz, Jane Birkin, Nathalie Baye, Mathieu Carriere. 1985

BEETHOVEN'S 2ND ★★★ Beethoven—a massive Saint Bernard—starts a family of his own in this lightweight sequel with more charm and less slobber than the original. Beethoven's mate is owned by a modern Cruella de Vil who is holding the canine as a trump card in her divorce case—and do she and her new boyfriend ever hate dogs! Charles Grodin also returns as an air-freshener marketer who is up to his armpits in financial and domestic problems. Rated PG. 86m. **DIR:** Rod Daniel. **CAST:** Charles Grodin, Bonnie Hunt, Nicholle Tom, Christopher Castille, Sarah Rose Karr, Debi Mazar, Christopher Penn, Kevin Dunn. 1993 DVD

BEETLEJUICE ★★★ Like a cinematic trip through the Haunted Mansion, this film may require two viewings just to catch all the complex action and visual jokes. Alec Baldwin and Geena Davis play a young couple who accidentally drown and return as novice ghosts. The family that moves into their pretty little Connecticut farmhouse seems intent on destroying it aesthetically, and the ghostly couple are forced to call on the evil Betelgeuse (Michael Keaton). Rated PG for shock action and language. 93m. **DIR:** Tim Burton. **CAST:** Alec Baldwin, Geena Davis, Michael Keaton, Jeffrey Jones, Catherine O'Hara, Winona Ryder. 1988 DVD

BEFORE AND AFTER ★★★1/2 A compelling study of family dynamics, the American judicial system, and personal responsibility that is undermined by a softening of the Rosellen Brown novel. Still, this meaty drama is enhanced by Edward Furlong's sadly believable portrayal of a teenager accused of murdering his girlfriend in a small New England town. Rated PG-13 for profanity and violence. 121m. **DIR:** Barbet Schroeder. **CAST:** Meryl Streep, Liam Neeson, Edward Furlong, Alfred Molina, Ann Magnuson. 1995

BEFORE I HANG ★★★ Neat little thriller has Boris Karloff as a goodhearted doctor who creates an age-retardant serum. Trouble begins when he tests it on himself, with horrible side effects. Nicely done, the film benefits from a good supporting performance by horror veteran Edward Van Sloan. B&W; 71m. **DIR:** Nick Grindé. **CAST:** Boris Karloff, Evelyn Keyes, Bruce Bennett, Pedro De Cordoba, Edward Van Sloan. 1940

BEFORE SUNRISE ★★★★ American tourist Ethan Hawke and French student Julie Delpy meet on a Eurail train and, on the spur of the moment, hop off in Vienna to spend the day (and the night) exploring the city and getting acquainted with each other. That's all there is to it, two young people walking and talking, but the film is a lighthearted delight. The stars are immensely charming and their dialogue, as they gradually fall in love, is credible and interesting. Rated R for profanity. 101m. DIR: Richard Linklater. CAST: Ethan Hawke, Julie Delpy. 1994 DVD

BEFORE THE RAIN ★★★1/2 Macedonian filmmaker Milcho Manchevski tells a three-part story about the tragic, far-reaching effects of ancient blood feuds and modern-day civil strife in the remnants of Yugoslavia. Riveting and compellingly told. Not rated; contains violence, nudity, and mild profanity. 110m. DIR: Milcho Manchevski. CAST: Katrin Cartlidge, Rade Serbedzija, Gregoire Colin, Labina Mitevska. 1994

BEFORE THE REVOLUTION ★★★1/2 Bernardo Bertolucci made this political drama at the age of twenty-two. The plot evolves around a young man who flirts with communism, while engaging in an incestuous relationship with his aunt. Great cinematography. In Italian with English subtitles. B&W; 110m. DIR: Bernardo Bertolucci. CAST: Adriana Asti, Francesco Barilli. 1962

BEGGARS OF LIFE ★★★ Girl who kills abusive adoptive father goes on the lam with a gentle tramp and finds herself pursued by the law as well as lusting hoboes eager for her and the reward she will bring. The rest of the film doesn't quite measure up to the startling opening sequence, but it's quite a train ride as Louise Brooks tries to put some distance between herself and Wallace Beery as the head hobo who does the right thing in the last reel. B&W; 100m. DIR: William Wellman. CAST: Louise Brooks, Richard Arlen, Wallace Beery, Edgar Washington Blue, H. A. Moran. 1928

●BEGINNING OF THE END 💣 Scientist Peter Graves tries to save Chicago from the mutant grasshoppers accidentally produced in his giant vegetable experiment. Low-budget special effects. Not rated; contains comic book–type violence and destruction. 75m. DIR: Bert I. Gordon. CAST: Peter Graves, Peggie Castle, Morris Ankrum (Stepen Morris), Thomas Browne Henry. 1957

BEGOTTEN ★★★★ The entire film consists of two extended sequences, in which a godlike creature gives birth (literally) to mankind, and a solitary man is tortured by masked figures in a pit. Love it or hate it, it is utterly unique. Not rated, but not for the squeamish. B&W; 78m. DIR: Edmund Elias Merhige. CAST: Brian Salzberg, Donna Dempsey. 1991

BEGUILED, THE ★★★★ An atmospheric, daring change of pace for director Don Siegel and star Clint Eastwood, this production features the squinty-eyed actor as a wounded Yankee soldier taken in by the head (Geraldine Page) of a girls' school. He becomes the catalyst for incidents of jealousy and hatred among its inhabitants, and this leads to a startling, unpredictable conclusion. Rated R. 109m. DIR: Don Siegel. CAST: Clint Eastwood, Geraldine Page, Jo Ann Harris, Elizabeth Hartman. 1971 DVD

BEHAVE YOURSELF! ★★ A comedy written expressly for Farley Granger and Shelley Winters when they were the most popular married couple in Hollywood. They play a couple who get crossways with two different mobs, and it's all because of their pet dog—a trained smuggler who can operate between both gangs. B&W; 81m. DIR: George Beck. CAST: Shelley Winters, Farley Granger, Hans Conried, Sheldon Leonard, Lon Chaney Jr., William Demarest. 1951

BEHIND LOCKED DOORS 💣 Sleazy, near-plotless thriller about a nutcase who kidnaps young women for sexual "research." Not rated, but an R equivalent for nudity and rape. 79m. DIR: Charles Romine. CAST: Joyce Denner, Eve Reeves, Daniel Garth, Ivan Hagar. 1974

●BEHIND THE MASK ★★★ Secret-service agent infiltrates a dope-smuggling ring run by a mysterious maniac who murders his enemies with grisly abandon. Square-jawed lawmen, cold-blooded drug dealers, a beautiful heroine, and hardboiled action make this precode programmer a pulp magazine on film. B&W; 68m. DIR: John Francis Dillon. CAST: Jack Holt, Constance Cummings, Boris Karloff, Claude King, Edward Van Sloan. 1932

BEHIND THE RISING SUN ★★1/2 The versatile J. Carrol Naish plays a Japanese publisher whose political views bring him into conflict with his son, educated in the United States. It all takes place when Japan was fighting China, not long before World War II. B&W; 80m. DIR: Edward Dmytryk. CAST: Margo, Tom Neal, J. Carrol Naish, Robert Ryan. 1943

BEHOLD A PALE HORSE ★★ Gregory Peck is miscast in this slow, talky, vague drama of a Loyalist holdout in post–Civil War Spain who continues to harass the Franco regime. 118m. DIR: Fred Zinnemann. CAST: Gregory Peck, Anthony Quinn, Omar Sharif. 1963

BEING, THE 💣 Water contaminated with nuclear waste spawned a beast that likes to shove itself *through* people. Rated R for gore and nudity. 82m. DIR: Jackie Kong. CAST: Martin Landau, José Ferrer, Dorothy Malone, Ruth Buzzi. 1984

BEING AT HOME WITH CLAUDE ★★★ Complex, provocative study of the human psyche examines the murder of a young student, and the enigmatic male prostitute who confesses to the crime. During an intense interrogation, the truth about the shocking crime comes out, but not before we're subjected to a harrowing barrage of verbal abuse. In French with English subtitles. Not rated; contains adult situations and language. 86m. DIR: Jean Beaudin. CAST: Roy Dupuis, Jacques Godin, Jean-François Pinchette, Gaston Lepage. 1992

BEING HUMAN ★★1/2 -Writer-director Bill Forsyth's big-screen meditation on the plight of unexceptional men is neither funny nor dramatic. In his best sad-eyed fashion, Robin Williams plays five roles in five historical settings, ranging from the Stone Age to modern times. A brief, humorous turn by John Turturro and a touching wrap-around story make this worth watching. Rated PG-13 for light profanity, brief violence, and suggested sex. 119m. DIR: Bill Forsyth. CAST: Robin Williams, Anna Galiena, Vincent D'Onofrio, Hector Elizondo, John Turturro, Lorraine Bracco, Lindsay Crouse, Helen Miller, Charles Miller, William H. Macy. 1994

●BEING JOHN MALKOVICH ★★★★ In this surreal, original film—which explores love, identity, alternate reality, and sex—John Cusack takes a job as a filing clerk and discovers a portal that leads him into the body of actor John Malkovich. Cameron Diaz, Cusack's mousy wife, gets drawn into his bizarre discovery and finds that she, like her husband, is sexually attracted to his avaricious "partner" (Catherine Keener), who turns the portal experience into a money-making scheme. Rated R for profanity, nudity, and simulated sex. 112m. **DIR:** Spike Jonze. **CAST:** John Cusack, Cameron Diaz, Catherine Keener, Orson Bean, Mary Kay Place, John Malkovich, Charlie Sheen, Sean Penn. **1999 DVD**

BEING THERE ★★★★1/2 This sublimely funny and bitingly satiric comedy features Peter Sellers's last great screen performance. His portrayal of a simple-minded gardener—who knows only what he sees on television yet rises to great political heights—is a classic. Shirley MacLaine and Melvyn Douglas are also excellent in this memorable film, directed by Hal Ashby. Rated PG. 130m. **DIR:** Hal Ashby. **CAST:** Peter Sellers, Shirley MacLaine, Melvyn Douglas, Jack Warden. **1979**

BELARUS FILE, THE ★★1/2 Telly Savalas returns as the lollipop-sucking police detective Kojak in this made-for-television movie about a maniac murdering Russian survivors of a Nazi concentration camp. For fans of the series only. 95m. **DIR:** Robert Markowitz. **CAST:** Telly Savalas, Suzanne Pleshette, Max von Sydow, Herbert Berghof, George Savalas. **1986**

BELFAST ASSASSIN ★★1/2 This film, about an IRA hit man and a British antiterrorist who is ordered to track down the Irish assassin on his own turf, could have used a clipper-happy editor. The film takes a pro-IRA stand, yet is open-minded enough to see the other side of the story. Not rated, but the equivalent of a PG for sex, violence, and profanity. 130m. **DIR:** Lawrence Gordon Clark. **CAST:** Derek Thompson, Ray Lonnen, Benjamin Whitrow. **1982**

•**BELIEVE** ★★ Ben and Katherine, two young thrill seekers, are always intrigued by a good supernatural mystery. They decide that they should put their sleuthing to the test and investigate the haunted Wickwire House. Their brave quest turns fruitful when they encounter an actual ghost, and find themselves in the midst of a bigger mystery. The slow pace and droll plot of this movie will leave most older viewers yawning. Rated PG-13 for scariness. 95m. **DIR:** Robert Tinnell. **CAST:** Jan Rubes, Ricky Mabe, Elisha Cuthbert, Andrea Martin, Ben Gazzara. **1999 DVD**

BELIEVERS, THE ★★★1/2 Martin Sheen portrays a recently widowed father whose son is chosen as a sacrifice to a voodoo cult running rampant in New York. John Schlesinger is not the best director for a thriller of this type, but in this case the quality of the acting, the snap of the writing, and the strength of the story build the suspense nicely and provide a striking climax. Rated R for language, nudity, and nightmarism. 110m. **DIR:** John Schlesinger. **CAST:** Martin Sheen, Helen Shaver, Robert Loggia, Richard Masur, Elizabeth Wilson, Lee Richardson, Harris Yulin, Jimmy Smits. **1987**

BELIZAIRE THE CAJUN ★★★★ The Louisiana bayou of the 1850s is richly re-created in deep, dark swampland colors, along with the rhythms of Cajun accents and full-bodied folk music (score by Michael Doucet). Armand Assante is Belizaire, an herbal

doctor who finds himself in trouble because of his affection for his childhood sweetheart and his efforts to save a friend from persecution. 114m. **DIR:** Glen Pitre. **CAST:** Armand Assante, Gail Youngs, Michael Schoeffling, Stephen McHattie, Will Patton. **1986**

BELL, BOOK AND CANDLE ★★★1/2 A modestly entertaining bit of whimsy about a beautiful witch (Kim Novak) who works her magic on an unsuspecting publisher (James Stewart). Although the performances (including those in support by Jack Lemmon, Ernie Kovacs, and Hermione Gingold) are fine, this comedy is only mildly diverting. 103m. **DIR:** Richard Quine. **CAST:** James Stewart, Kim Novak, Jack Lemmon, Ernie Kovacs. **1958 DVD**

BELL JAR, THE ★★★ Based on the novel by Sylvia Plath about the mental breakdown of an overachiever in the world of big business in the 1950s, this film has a strong lead performance by Marilyn Hassett and thoughtful direction by her husband, Larry Peerce. But the overriding melancholy of the subject matter makes it difficult to watch. Barbara Barrie is also memorable in a key supporting role. Rated R. 107m. **DIR:** Larry Peerce. **CAST:** Marilyn Hassett, Julie Harris, Anne Jackson, Barbara Barrie, Robert Klein. **1979**

BELLA MAFIA ★★★ Grand soap opera adds a female twist to the *Last Don* series. Vanessa Redgrave stars as the matriarch of a large Italian family, who watches her sons grow up and get married. When a Mafia rival kills her husband and sons, she and the women gather to exact revenge. Decent cast and direction keep this made-for-television miniseries from slipping into camp. Rated R for adult situations and violence. 117m. **DIR:** David Greene. **CAST:** Vanessa Redgrave, Dennis Farina, Nastassja Kinski, Jennifer Tilly. **1997**

BELLBOY, THE ★★ A typical hour-plus of Jerry Lewis mugging and antics so dear to those who find him funny. This time around, Jerry is a bellboy at a swank hotel. Years ago, "Fatty" Arbuckle made a film of the same name that was funny. This, unfortunately, is plotless drivel seasoned with guest appearances by Milton Berle and Walter Winchell. Rated G when rereleased in 1972. B&W; 72m. **DIR:** Jerry Lewis. **CAST:** Jerry Lewis, Alex Gerry, Sonny Sands. **1960**

BELLBOY AND THE PLAYGIRLS, THE ★★ Innocuous sex comedy about a bellboy who practices to be a private eye. This would be long forgotten but for the fact that it's Francis Ford Coppola's first screen credit. He added some color sequences for the U.S. release of this 1958 German movie. Not rated, the film has nudity. 94m. **DIR:** Fritz Umgelter, Francis Ford Coppola. **CAST:** June Wilkinson. **1962**

BELLE DE JOUR ★★★★1/2 A repressed French housewife takes a day job in a bordello, where her fantasy life spins quickly out of control. This erotic classic is less scandalous now than when it was first released. Still, this witty film has aged gracefully, and some scenes retain their power to shock and perplex (a hint: italicized subtitles signify when we are watching the woman's fantasies). Deneuve has never been better. In French with English subtitles. Rated R for mature themes. 100m. **DIR:** Luis Buñuel.

CAST: Catherine Deneuve, Jean Sorel, Michel Piccoli, Geneviève Page, Pierre Clementi. 1967

BELLE EPOQUE ★★★★ An army deserter hiding out in the Spanish countryside of the 1930s becomes infatuated, one by one, with the four beautiful daughters of a crusty old artist. This eccentric, beautifully photographed movie won the 1993 Oscar for best foreign film. Delightfully ribald, strongly recommended for mature audiences only. In Spanish with English subtitles. Rated R for sexual scenes. 108m. **DIR:** Fernando Trueba. **CAST:** Jorge Sanz, Fernando Fernán-Gomez, Ariadna Gil, Penelope Cruz. 1992

BELLE OF NEW YORK, THE ★★ A fantasy set at the turn of the century, this frothy film was a box-office failure about which, in his autobiography, Fred Astaire snaps: "The less said about it the better." Harry Warren's score—assembled from earlier hits—is terrific, though none of the songs have survived as standards. 82m. **DIR:** Charles Walters. **CAST:** Fred Astaire, Vera-Ellen, Marjorie Main, Keenan Wynn. 1952

BELLE OF THE NINETIES ★★★1/2 A stereotypical Mae West vehicle, but the censors' scissors are obvious. She sings, talks back, and tangles with a boxer who wants to tame her. Some of her most famous witticisms and her better songs are in this film. Like other Mae West films, this one is a series of one-liners between clinches that spoof the battle of the sexes. B&W; 73m. **DIR:** Leo McCarey. **CAST:** Mae West, Johnny Mack Brown, Roger Pryor, John Miljan, Duke Ellington. 1934 DVD

BELLES OF ST. TRINIAN'S, THE ★★★1/2 Alastair Sim doubles as the dotty headmistress of a bonkers school for girls and her crafty bookie brother, who wants to use the place as a cover for his nefarious operations. Joyce Grenfell adds to the hilarity in this British comedy based on English cartoonist Ronald Searle's schoolgirls with a genius for mischief. B&W; 90m. **DIR:** Frank Launder. **CAST:** Alastair Sim, Joyce Grenfell, Hermione Baddeley, George Cole. 1955

BELLISSIMA ★★★ Luchino Visconti is known for such pioneering works as *Rocco and His Brothers*, *The Damned*, and *Death in Venice*. As for *Bellissima*, if you are programming an Anna Magnani festival, you might be interested in this oddly and determinedly lightweight comedy. The story is set in the Cinecitta Studios, where a search is on for the prettiest child in Rome. In Italian with English subtitles. B&W; 95m. **DIR:** Luchino Visconti. **CAST:** Anna Magnani, Walter Chiari, Tina Apicella. 1951

BELLISSIMO: IMAGES OF THE ITALIAN CINEMA ★★★ A retrospective of the Italian cinema is explored from the early 1920s to the 1980s through film clips and interviews with various directors and actors. Filmmakers include Roberto Rossellini, Vittorio De Sica, Federico Fellini, Lina Wertmuller, and Sergio Leone. In Italian with English subtitles and English narration. 110m. **DIR:** Gianfranco Mingozzi. 1978

BELLMAN AND TRUE ★★★★ This gripping crime-drama centers around a British computer genius who is forced to aid thugs in a bank heist after his son is kidnapped. Fascinating characters and suspenseful plot twists give this film depth and realism. Rated R. 114m. **DIR:** Richard Loncraine. **CAST:** Bernard Hill, Derek Newark, Richard Hope, Ken Bones, Frances Tomelty. 1988

BELLS ARE RINGING ★★ This filmed version of the Broadway musical pits answering-service operator Judy Holliday against Dean Martin in an on-again, off-again love circle. Nothing new or exciting storywise here, but Fred Clark and Eddie Foy ham it up enough to hold your interest. 127m. **DIR:** Vincente Minnelli. **CAST:** Judy Holliday, Dean Martin, Fred Clark, Eddie Foy Jr. 1960

BELLS OF CORONADO ★★1/2 Grant Withers heads an evil gang of foreign agents out to smuggle uranium to unfriendly powers. Roy Rogers plays a modern-day heroic insurance agent who is able to thwart the heavies. Comic-book story is full of fast riding and action. 67m. **DIR:** William Witney. **CAST:** Roy Rogers, Dale Evans, Pat Brady, Grant Withers. 1950

BELLS OF ROSARITA ★★1/2 Movie cowboy Roy Rogers enlists the aid of Republic Studios' top Western stars in order to save Gabby Hayes's and Dale Evans's circus. A fun Western. B&W; 54m. **DIR:** Frank McDonald. **CAST:** Roy Rogers, Dale Evans, George "Gabby" Hayes, Bob Nolan and the Sons of the Pioneers, Don Barry, Allan "Rocky" Lane, Sunset Carson, William Elliott, Robert Livingston. 1945

BELLS OF ST. MARY'S, THE ★★★★1/2 An effective sequel to *Going My Way*, also directed by Leo McCarey, this film has Bing Crosby returning as the modern-minded priest once again up against a head-strong opponent, Mother Superior (played by Ingrid Bergman). While not as memorable as his encounter with hard-headed older priest Barry Fitzgerald in the first film, this relationship—and the movie as a whole—does have its viewing rewards. B&W; 126m. **DIR:** Leo McCarey. **CAST:** Bing Crosby, Ingrid Bergman, Ruth Donnelly. 1945 DVD

BELLS OF SAN ANGELO ★★★1/2 This is a sharp and unusually violent Roy Rogers film. Roy portrays a lawman who attempts to capture a bunch of smugglers. With the help of Dale Evans and Andy Devine, he succeeds. B&W; 78m. **DIR:** William Witney. **CAST:** Roy Rogers, Dale Evans, Andy Devine, John McGuire. 1947

BELLY ★★ This low-budget, disjointed drama about two "gangsta" buddies who rob, murder, and sell drugs emphasizes gritty style over substance. By the time the two friends realize the error of their ways, it's too late to save the film from its own raunchy sensationalism. Rated R for profanity, simulated sex, nudity, violence, and drug use. 95m. **DIR:** Hype Williams. **CAST:** Nas, DMX, Taral Hicks, Lavita Raynor, Tionne "T-Boz" Watkins. 1998 DVD

BELLY OF AN ARCHITECT, THE ★★ Dreamlike, symbolism-laced story of an American architect (Brian Dennehy) trying to deal with hypocrisy in his art and in his life while working on a project in Italy. His efforts take on an urgency when he begins to suspect that he's dying of cancer. Alternately artful and pretentious, the film is most interesting as a showcase for Dennehy. 108m. **DIR:** Peter Greenaway. **CAST:** Brian Dennehy, Chloe Webb, Lambert Wilson. 1987

BELOVED ★★★1/2 Oprah Winfrey produced and stars in this dignified, reverent adaptation of Toni Morrison's Pulitzer Prize–winning novel about the scars of slavery on an African-American family in post–Civil War Ohio. Viewers unfamiliar with Morrison's evocative prose and emotionally dense story may find the film too obscure. Thandie Newton, as the mysterious title character, is oddly mannered, but the rest of the cast is excellent. Rated R for mature themes and graphic depiction of slavery. 171m. **DIR:** Jonathan Demme. **CAST:** Oprah Winfrey, Danny Glover, Thandie Newton, Kimberly Elise, Beah Richards. **1998 DVD**

BELOVED ENEMY ★★★1/2 This stylish film concerns a beautiful woman (Merle Oberon) in love with a young leader in the Irish revolution (Brian Aherne). Great supporting cast adds panache to this crackerjack Samuel Goldwyn production. B&W; 86m. **DIR:** H. C. Potter. **CAST:** Merle Oberon, Brian Aherne, Karen Morley, David Niven. **1936**

BELOVED ROGUE ★★★★★ Superb example of the heights in set design, camera work, and special effects achieved in the late American silent cinema. John Barrymore is poet Francois Villon—here more of a Robin Hood than a brooding aesthete. Unreservedly recommended. Silent. B&W; 100m. **DIR:** Alan Crosland. **CAST:** John Barrymore, Conrad Veidt. **1927**

BELOW THE BELT ★★★1/2 This agreeable low-budget feature is short on technical polish but long on heart. It's a semidocumentary about a waitress (Regina Baff) who tries to become a professional wrestler, taking advice from ex-champ Mildred Burke (playing herself). There's even a *Rocky*ish finale. Made in 1974, but not released until 1980. Rated R. 91m. **DIR:** Robert Fowler. **CAST:** Regina Baff, Mildred Burke, John C. Becher, Shirley Stoler, Dolph Sweet, Ric Mancini. **1980**

BELOW THE BORDER ★★★ Energetic Rough Riders adventure has Buck Roberts (Buck Jones) going underground as a bandit while Tim McCall (Tim McCoy) poses as a cattle buyer. It's all to trap evil Roy Barcroft and put an end to his cattle rustling. B&W; 57m. **DIR:** Howard Bretherton. **CAST:** Buck Jones, Tim McCoy, Raymond Hatton, Linda Brent, Roy Barcroft, Charles King. **1942**

BELSTONE FOX, THE ★★ An orphaned fox cub is raised in captivity and cleverly eludes both hounds and hunters. The film is worth watching for the animal photography. Not rated; contains some violence to animals. 103m. **DIR:** James Hill. **CAST:** Eric Porter, Jeremy Kemp, Bill Travers, Rachel Roberts. **1973**

BEN ★ The only thing going for this silly sequel to *Willard* is an awkwardly charming title song performed by a young Michael Jackson (a love song for a rat, no less). Rated PG for violence. 95m. **DIR:** Phil Karlson. **CAST:** Arthur O'Connell, Lee Montgomery, Rosemary Murphy. **1972**

BEN-HUR (1926) ★★★★ Colossal in every sense of the word, this greatest of silent film spectacles is still a winner today. Years in production, it cost a staggering $4 million and was two years being edited. The chariot-race and sea-battle scenes are unsurpassed. Ramon Novarro as Ben-Hur and Francis X. Bushman as Messala gave the performances of their careers. B&W; 116m. **DIR:** Fred Niblo. **CAST:** Ra-

mon Novarro, Francis X. Bushman, May McAvoy, Betty Bronson, Carmel Myers. **1926**

BEN-HUR (1959) ★★★★★ In this film, which won eleven Oscars, a wealthy Jewish nobleman during the time of Christ incurs the hostility of the Roman military governor, who was his childhood friend. He is reduced to manning an oar on a slave galley, and his family is sent to prison. Years later he returns to seek vengeance upon his Roman tormentor. This culminates in a spectacular chariot race. Charlton Heston won an Oscar for his first-rate performance in the title role. 211m. **DIR:** William Wyler. **CAST:** Charlton Heston, Jack Hawkins, Sam Jaffe, Stephen Boyd. **1959**

BEND OF THE RIVER ★★★★ James Stewart and director Anthony Mann teamed up during the early 1950s to make a series of exceptional Westerns that helped the genre return to popularity. This one deals with Stewart leading a wagon train across the country and his dealings with ex-friend Arthur Kennedy, who hijacks their supplies. Superior Western fare in every sense. 91m. **DIR:** Anthony Mann. **CAST:** James Stewart, Arthur Kennedy, Rock Hudson, Julie Adams. **1952**

●**BENEATH THE BERMUDA TRIANGLE** 🐢 An American submarine is transported to the future in this cheap-looking rip-off of *The Philadelphia Experiment*. Rated R for profanity, violence, brief nudity, and sexual situations. 84m. **DIR:** Scott Levy. **CAST:** Jeff Fahey, Richard Tyson, Jack Coleman, Chick Venera. **1996**

BENEATH THE PLANET OF THE APES ★★1/2 Charlton Heston let himself get sucked into this sequel to *Planet of the Apes*. Astronaut James Franciscus—sent to find out what happened to the first team sent to the planet—has more than simians to contend with; he also discovers a race of u-g-l-y mutants that worships an atomic bomb, since it made them what they are. . . . Some of the original's energy remains. Rated PG for violence. 95m. **DIR:** Ted Post. **CAST:** Charlton Heston, James Franciscus, Maurice Evans, Kim Hunter, Linda Harrison, James Gregory. **1970**

BENEATH THE 12-MILE REEF ★★★ Here is some good old-fashioned Hollywood entertainment. Film deals with sponge divers off the Florida coast. Light, enjoyable fluff. 102m. **DIR:** Robert D. Webb. **CAST:** Robert Wagner, Gilbert Roland, Terry Moore, Richard Boone. **1953 DVD**

BENEFICIARY, THE ★★ Suzy Amis is the cream that rises to the top of this sour exercise in stock characters and formulaic plotting. While the rest of the characters spend most of the film trying to get a clue, Amis squares off with a vengeance against a widow (Stacy Haiduk, beautiful and deadly) who plotted her tycoon husband's murder. Otherwise, the film has little to offer that hasn't been done to death. Made-for-cable. Rated R for violence, language, nudity, and adult situations. 90m. **DIR:** Marc Beinstock. **CAST:** Suzy Amis, Stacy Haiduk, Linden Ashby, Ron Silver, Robert Davi. **1997**

BENEFIT OF THE DOUBT ★★★ Donald Sutherland delivers a chilling performance as a man accused of murdering his wife and sent to prison for twenty years by the testimony of his daughter. Now Dad's out of prison, and Amy Irving believes that she and her son are due for a rather unpleasant visit. Good performances and crisp direction help maintain the suspense. Rated R for violence, language, and adult situations. 92m. **DIR:** Jonathan Heap. **CAST:** Donald Sutherland, Amy Irving, Graham Greene, Christopher McDonald. 1992

BENIKER GANG, THE ★★1/2 Pleasant family film has Andrew McCarthy as Arthur Beniker, 18-year-old orphanage inmate who leads an "orphanage break" of four other incorrigibles. Not too cutesy, and the story even makes some sense. Rated G; suitable for the entire family. 87m. **DIR:** Ken Kwapis. **CAST:** Andrew McCarthy, Jennie Dundas, Charles Fields, Jeff Alan-Lee, Danny Pintauro. 1985

BENJI ★★★★ *Benji* parallels *Lassie* and *Rin Tin Tin* by intuitively doing the right thing at the right time. In this film, a dog saves two children who get kidnapped. Unlike Lassie or Rin Tin Tin, Benji is a small, unassuming mutt, which makes him all the more endearing. Rated G. 86m. **DIR:** Joe Camp. **CAST:** Benji, Peter Breck, Deborah Walley, Edgar Buchanan, Frances Bavier, Patsy Garrett. 1974

BENJI THE HUNTED ★★★ Most kids will love this adventure featuring everyone's favorite sweet-faced mutt slogging his poor little lost way through the wilderness of the Pacific Northwest to civilization. Rated G. 90m. **DIR:** Joe Camp. **CAST:** Benji. 1987

BENNY & JOON ★★★1/2 Most viewers will enjoy this bittersweet comedy about a mentally ill artist who finds love with a quirky outsider, much to her older brother-guardian's chagrin. Folks coping with mental illness in real life will be offended by yet another film in which the problem is sanitized and trivialized. Rated PG for suggested sex and brief violence. 100m. **DIR:** Jeremiah S. Chechik. **CAST:** Johnny Depp, Mary Stuart Masterson, Aidan Quinn, Julianne Moore, Oliver Platt, C.C.H. Pounder, Dan Hedaya, Joe Grifasi, William H. Macy. 1993

BENNY GOODMAN STORY, THE ★★★ If you enjoy good big-band music and don't mind a few errors in biographical fact, then this big brassy picture is a must for you. Steve Allen as Benny Goodman does a fine job. Watch for some other great performers in cameos. 116m. **DIR:** Valentine Davies. **CAST:** Steve Allen, Donna Reed, Teddy Wilson, Herbert Anderson, Gene Krupa, Robert F. Simon. 1955

BENT ★★ Martin Sherman's provocative stage drama about the persecution of homosexuals by the Nazis during World War II loses much of its edge onscreen. The impact is further diluted on video, where the NC-17 film has been trimmed down to an R rating. The cast is fine, including Mick Jagger as a transvestite singer, but after all is said and done this is much ado about nothing. Rated R for language, violence, nudity, and adult situations. 104m. **DIR:** Sean Mathias. **CAST:** Lothaire Bluteau, Clive Owen, Brian Webber, Ian McKellen, Mick Jagger. 1996

BERETTA'S ISLAND ♥ Former Mr. Universe Franco Columbu gets weighted down in this clumsy, low-budget action effort, playing a former Interpol agent out for revenge. Not rated; contains violence. 97m.

DIR: Michael Preece. **CAST:** Franco Columbu, Ken Kercheval, Jo Campa, Arnold Schwarzenegger. 1992

BERLIN AFFAIR, THE ★★ Uneven erotic psychodrama about a Japanese art student in prewar 1938 Germany who becomes involved in a bizarre love triangle with the wife of a politically affluent German diplomat and her husband. Though heavy on eroticism, the film is lean on story and character motivation. Rated R for nudity and profanity. 97m. **DIR:** Lilliana Cavani. **CAST:** Gudrun Landgrebe, Kevin McNally, Mio Takaki. 1985

BERLIN ALEXANDERPLATZ ★★★1/2 Remember the scene in *A Clockwork Orange* in which Malcolm McDowell's eyes are wired open and he is forced to watch movies? That's how we often felt when wading through the fifteen-and-a-half hours of Rainer Werner Fassbinder's magnum opus. It has its moments of interest, and yes, even genius, but as with all of Fassbinder's films, also its excesses and false notes. In German with English subtitles. Not rated. 930m. **DIR:** Rainer Werner Fassbinder. **CAST:** Gunter Lamprecht, Hanna Schygulla, Barbara Sukowa. 1983

BERLIN CONSPIRACY, THE ♥ Separate American and East German investigations into germ warfare and Middle East terrorism are hindered by the fall of the Berlin Wall. Bland performances and bad German accents diminish this low-budget thriller. Rated R for violence and profanity. 83m. **DIR:** Terence H. Winkless. **CAST:** Marc Singer, Mary Crosby, Stephen Davies. 1991

BERLIN EXPRESS ★★★1/2 A taut, crisply edited espionage thriller from the director of the original *Cat People*. Filmed in semidocumentary style, *Berlin Express* takes full advantage of post–World War II Germany, incorporating actual footage of bombed-out Frankfurt and Berlin. Thrown together on a train to Berlin, Robert Ryan as an American nutrition expert, Paul Lukas as a marked German statesman trying to reunite his war-torn country, and Merle Oberon as Lukas's aide all give standout performances. B&W; 86m. **DIR:** Jacques Tourneur. **CAST:** Merle Oberon, Robert Ryan, Charles Korvin, Paul Lukas, Robert Coote. 1948

BERLIN TUNNEL 21 ★★ Richard Thomas stars as an American soldier in Berlin in 1961. His girlfriend cannot leave the eastern section of Berlin to join him. The solution: sneak her out. Predictable. 141m. **DIR:** Richard Michaels. **CAST:** Richard Thomas, Horst Buchholz, José Ferrer, Jacques Breuer, Nicolas Farrell, Ute Christensen. 1981

BERNADETTE ★★ This long, slow-moving French film features an almost too glamorous Sydney Penny as the impoverished young girl chosen to be the messenger at Lourdes. Rated PG for profanity. 120m. **DIR:** Jean Delannoy. **CAST:** Sydney Penny, Michelle Simonnett. 1987

BERNARD AND THE GENIE ★★★ Pleasantly amusing Christmas movie from BBC-TV stars British comedian Lenny Henry as the genie in the lamp, released by a mild-mannered London art dealer who's having a really bad day. Once the genie is freed, the fun begins. 70m. **DIR:** Paul Welland. **CAST:** Lenny Henry, Rowan Atkinson. 1991

BERNICE BOBS HER HAIR ★★★★ The perceptions of self-worth and personal integrity form the core of this droll adaptation of F. Scott Fitzgerald's ode to a shy young girl. Bernice (Shelley Duvall) sacrifices her luxuriously long hair for a shot at the inner circle of popularity jealously guarded by her hedonistic Jazz Era friends. Veronica Cartwright is wonderfully malignant as the fickle society girl who plays Pygmalion with her shy, unassuming cousin. Introduced by Henry Fonda. 49m. DIR: Joan Micklin Silver. CAST: Shelley Duvall, Veronica Cartwright, Bud Cort, Dennis Christopher, Gary Springer, Lane Binkley, Polly Holliday. 1976

BERSERK ★★★1/2 Effectively staged thriller stars Joan Crawford as the owner of a once-great circus now on its last legs—until a number of accidental deaths of the performers starts packing 'em in. Joan comes under suspicion immediately when the cops begin counting the box-office receipts. Could she be guilty? 96m. DIR: Jim O'Connolly. CAST: Joan Crawford, Ty Hardin, Michael Gough, Diana Dors, Judy Geeson. 1967

BERSERKER 🎞 Silly slasher in which a Viking demon is reincarnated in his descendants. Rated R for nudity, violence, gore, and simulated sex. 85m. DIR: Jeff Richard. CAST: Joseph Alan Johnson. 1987

BERT RIGBY, YOU'RE A FOOL ★★★ Musical-comedy star Robert Lindsay, who won a Tony for *Me and My Girl*, plays an English coal miner obsessed with the great musicals of Fred Astaire and Gene Kelly. When a strike is called at the mine, he decides to take a shot at making it as a song-and-dance man. Director Carl Reiner also scripted. There is some profanity, but the R rating seems excessive. 94m. DIR: Carl Reiner. CAST: Robert Lindsay, Cathryn Bradshaw, Robbie Coltrane, Jackie Gayle, Anne Bancroft, Corbin Bernsen. 1989

●**BESHKEMPIR, THE ADOPTED SON** ★★★1/2 Have you ever wished that they made more Kyrgyzstani movies? Well, here's one! Beshkempir is a young Kyrgyz boy who is just beginning to deal with his blossoming sexuality and raging hormones. His uncontrollable emotions lead the young man to learn that he was adopted—now making poor Beshkempir a subject of scorn and ridicule amongst his peers. This movie is beautifully shot, and gives an insight to a culture that is unfamiliar to many people. In Kyrgyzstani with English subtitles. Not rated; contains some language, violence, and nudity. B&W/color; 81m. DIR: Aktan Abdykalykov. CAST: Mirlan Abdykalykov, Albina Imasheva, Adir Abilkassimov, Bakit Dzhylkychiev, Mirlan Cinkozoev, Talai Mederov. 1998 DVD

●**BESIEGED** ★★★ English pianist in Rome is infatuated with an African medical student who lives downstairs and cleans his flat. He throws himself into her arms only to be rebuffed and told he can win her love by getting her husband released from jail. This intimate drama about love, desire, military repression, and unconditional sacrifice has uneven acting, an ambiguous ending, and relies on images for its emotional impact. But the film is saturated with sensuality. Rated R for brief nudity and sexual situations. 92m. DIR: Bernardo Bertolucci. CAST: David Thewlis, Thandie Newton, Claudio Santamaria. 1999 DVD

BEST CHRISTMAS PAGEANT EVER, THE ★★★ An engaging television movie about a group of grade-school misfits who come of age during preparation for a school Christmas play. Well-acted but already dated. 80m. DIR: George Schaefer. CAST: Dennis Weaver, Loretta Swit, Karen Grassle. 1986

BEST DEFENSE ★★★ Any movie that features the talents of Dudley Moore and Eddie Murphy has to be funny. Sometimes, however, laughs aren't enough. It's very easy to get confused in this film featuring Moore as the inept inventor of a malfunctioning piece of defense equipment, and Murphy as the hapless soldier forced to cope with it. The liberal use of profanity and several sex scenes make this R-rated romp unfit for youngsters. 94m. DIR: Willard Huyck. CAST: Dudley Moore, Eddie Murphy, Kate Capshaw, George Dzundza, Helen Shaver. 1984

BEST FOOT FORWARD ★★★1/2 Film star Lucille Ball accepts military cadet Tommy Dix's invitation to his school's annual dance. The film introduced June Allyson and Nancy Walker and gave numerous high schools a fight song by adapting its biggest hit, "Buckle Down, Winsocki." Wholesome family fun. 95m. DIR: Edward Buzzell. CAST: Lucille Ball, William Gaxton, Virginia Weidler, Tommy Dix, June Allyson, Nancy Walker, Gloria De Haven. 1943

BEST FRIENDS ★★ Burt Reynolds and Goldie Hawn star in this disappointingly tepid romantic comedy as a pair of successful screenwriters who decide to marry—thus destroying their profitable working relationship. A mess. Rated PG for profanity and adult situations. 116m. DIR: Norman Jewison. CAST: Burt Reynolds, Goldie Hawn, Ron Silver, Jessica Tandy. 1982

BEST INTENTIONS, THE ★★★★ Originally a six-hour miniseries for television, this Swedish import was cut almost in half for international theatrical distribution. However, Ingmar Bergman's story, set in 1909 and concerning the courtship and early years of his parents' marriage, remains intact, with the characterizations and situations fully explored. In Swedish with English subtitles. 186m. DIR: Bille August. CAST: Samuel Froler, Pernilla August, Max von Sydow. 1992

BEST KEPT SECRETS ★★★1/2 When a police officer is not promoted to the Special Information Unit, his wife (Patty Duke) decides to find out why. She discovers a secret file that the police department has been using for blacklisting purposes. This TV movie is guaranteed to keep your interest. 94m. DIR: Jerrold Freedman. CAST: Patty Duke, Frederic Forrest, Peter Coyote, Meg Foster. 1989

BEST LEGS IN THE 8TH GRADE, THE ★★★ Bittersweet made-for-TV comedy focusing on the complexities of modern romance. Tim Matheson is a yuppie lawyer who gets some much-needed advice on the affairs of the heart. Annette O'Toole plays his girlfriend. 48m. DIR: Tom Patchett. CAST: Tim Matheson, Annette O'Toole, James Belushi, Kathryn Harrold. 1984

BEST LITTLE GIRL IN THE WORLD, THE ★★★★1/2 This gut-wrenching teleplay about a girl, portrayed by Jennifer Jason Leigh who suffers from anorexia nervosa pulls no punches; some of the drama is hard to take, but if you can make it through the film's end, you'll feel rewarded. This was originally an after-school special. The entire cast turns in great performances. The equivalent of a PG for intense drama. 90m. DIR: Sam O'Steen. CAST: Jennifer Jason Leigh, Charles Durning, Eva Marie Saint, Jason Miller. 1986

BEST LITTLE WHOREHOUSE IN TEXAS, THE ★★1/2 Dolly Parton and Burt Reynolds in a so-so version of the Broadway play, whose title explains all. Rated R for nudity, profanity, and sexual situations. 114m. DIR: Colin Higgins. CAST: Burt Reynolds, Dolly Parton, Dom DeLuise, Charles Durning. 1982

BEST MAN, THE (1964) ★★★★ Sharp characterizations bring to life this drama of disparate political types jockeying for position and endorsement at a presidential convention. Thoroughly engrossing. B&W; 102m. DIR: Franklin J. Schaffner. CAST: Henry Fonda, Cliff Robertson, Edie Adams, Margaret Leighton, Shelley Berman, Lee Tracy, Ann Sothern. 1964

BEST MAN, THE (1997) ★★★1/2 Il Testimone Dello Sposo is a wonderfully engaging tale set during the last day of 1899 in a small Italian town. Ines Sastre is breathtaking as Francesca Babini, whose marriage to the town's wealthiest bachelor has the locals all abuzz. Unfortunately, Francesca is marrying for money, not love, but all of that changes when she sets her eyes on the best man, a world traveler named Angelo. There are laughs, hope, and lush period settings in this charming and intelligent film. In Italian with English subtitles. Rated PG. 101m. DIR: Pupi Avati. CAST: Ines Sastre, Diego Abatantuono, Dario Cantarelli. 1997

•**BEST MAN, THE (1999)** ★★★1/2 Dubbed a romantic comedy, this reunion flick has more than its share of serious moments. When a novelist (Taye Diggs) joins his former college chums for his best friend's wedding, he finds that his fictionalized account of their friendships has hit too close to home. He also must choose between his current flame and the friend he failed to romance in his youth. Multiple subplots and intrigues make this very watchable. Rated R for sex, nudity, profanity, and violence. 122m. DIR: Malcolm Lee. CAST: Taye Diggs, Nia Long, Morris Chestnut, Monica Calhoun. 1999 DVD

BEST MEN ★★★1/2 As if her wedding day weren't stressful enough, bride-to-be Hope must contend with her intended being an ex-con who can't pass up the opportunity to rob a bank. Unbeknownst to Hope and his friends, Jesse is "Hamlet," a Robin Hood–like robber who picks the day of his wedding for his latest heist. Quirky character comedy succeeds, thanks to a winning cast, spirited direction, and a script that never plays dumb. Rated R for language and violence. 89m. DIR: Tamra Davis. CAST: Dean Cain, Sean Patrick Flanery, Luke Wilson, Drew Barrymore, Andy Dick, Mitchell Whitfield. 1997

BEST OF DARK SHADOWS, THE ★★1/2 Lack of narration will leave viewers confused as this compilation jumps from one teaser to another. We meet vampires, a werewolf, a witch, ghosts, and a Jekyll and Hyde character without benefit of the back-ground leading to these shocking devlopments. B&W/color; 30m. DIR: Lela Swift, Henry Kapland, John Sedwick. CAST: Jonathan Frid, David Selby, Joan Bennett, Kate Jackson, Lara Parker, Kathryn Leigh Scott. 1965–1971

BEST OF EVERYTHING, THE ★★1/2 Soapy but interesting movie about women in business and how their work affects their private lives. 121m. DIR: Jean Negulesco. CAST: Hope Lange, Joan Crawford, Louis Jourdan, Martha Hyer, Stephen Boyd, Robert Evans, Diane Baker. 1959

BEST OF ROGER RABBIT, THE ★★★★ Three Roger Rabbit Maroon Cartoon originals shown in theaters finally make their way to home video in this minicompilation. Included are "Tummy Trouble," "Roller Coaster Rabbit," and "Trail Mix-Up." All combine live-action and animation, but due to some blue humor, "Roller Coaster Rabbit" got a PG rating. Voice talents of Charles Fleischer, Kathleen Turner, April Winchell, Corey Burton, and Lou Hirsch. Rated G/PG. 25m. DIR: Rob Minkoff, Frank Marshall, Barry Cook. 1989–1993

BEST OF THE BADMEN ★★★1/2 Another of those all-star outlaw roundups with the James Boys, Younger Brothers, Sundance Kid, and Ringo Kid—all being forced into outlawry by crooked banking and railroad interests. 84m. DIR: William D. Russell. CAST: Robert Ryan, Claire Trevor, Jack Buetel, Robert Preston, Walter Brennan, Bruce Cabot. 1951

BEST OF THE BEST ★★ An underdog U.S. national karate team battles for the world title in this martial arts Rocky. The numerous training montages, slow-motion fight scenes, and lessons in sportsmanship and courage all lead to a predictable, uplifting ending. Rated PG-13 for violence and language. 95m. DIR: Robert Radler. CAST: Eric Roberts, Phillip Rhee, Christopher Penn, James Earl Jones, Sally Kirkland, John P. Ryan. 1989 DVD

BEST OF THE BEST 2 ♥ Three martial fu buddies from the original Best battle a Schwarzeneggeresque brute in an underworld Las Vegas gladiatorial arena that caters to decadent high rollers. Rated R for violence and language. 110m. DIR: Robert Radler. CAST: Eric Roberts, Phillip Rhee, Christopher Penn, Wayne Newton, Ralph Moeller, Meg Foster. 1993 DVD

BEST OF TIMES, THE ★★★ Although this comedy starts off well, but then loses momentum right up to the ending, it benefits from likable performances by its lead players. Robin Williams and Kurt Russell star as two former football players who dropped the ball when their moment for glory came. But they get a second chance to win some games for Taft (formerly Moron), California. Rated PG-13 for profanity and suggested sex. 100m. DIR: Roger Spottiswoode. CAST: Robin Williams, Kurt Russell, Pamela Reed, Holly Palance, Donald Moffat, Margaret Whitton, M. Emmet Walsh, R. G. Armstrong, Dub Taylor. 1986 DVD

BEST REVENGE ★★1/2 Granger (John Heard), has come to Spain to team up with Bo (Levon Helm), who has promised him the contacts for a $4 million hashish deal. This fast-moving action-adventure has some good acting, but fails to rise above its pedestrian plot. 92m. DIR: John Trent. CAST: John Heard, Levon Helm, Alberta Watson, John Rhys-Davies. 1984 DVD

BEST SELLER ★★★★ James Woods and Brian Dennehy give superb performances in this gripping character study about a ruthless hit man (Woods) who convinces a Joseph Wambaugh–type cop-turned-author (Dennehy) to help him write a book. Because the book threatens to expose the illegal empire of a wealthy industrialist, the authors soon find their lives in danger. The story by Larry Cohen is outrageous at times, but the electricity generated by the stars is undeniable. Rated R for profanity and violence. 110m. **DIR:** John Flynn. **CAST:** James Woods, Brian Dennehy, Victoria Tennant, Paul Shenar. 1987

BEST YEARS OF OUR LIVES, THE ★★★★★ What happens when the fighting ends and warriors return home is the basis of this eloquent, compassionate film. William Wyler takes his time and guides a superb group of players through a tangle of postwar emotional conflicts. Harold Russell's first scene has lost none of its impact. Keep in mind World War II had just ended when this film debuted. B&W; 170m. **DIR:** William Wyler. **CAST:** Myrna Loy, Fredric March, Teresa Wright, Dana Andrews, Virginia Mayo, Harold Russell, Cathy O'Donnell. 1946 DVD

BETHUNE ★★★1/2 This biographical teleplay gets off to a slow start, but delivers an absorbing story and masterful acting. It's the biography of Norman Bethune, the Canadian hero who served as a doctor in the combat between China and Japan. 88m. **DIR:** Eric Till. **CAST:** Donald Sutherland, Kate Nelligan, David Gardner, James Hong. 1984

BETRAYAL (1978) ★★1/2 Based on a true incident, this soapy TV movie concerns a young woman who has an affair with her psychiatrist. What could have been revealing and vital breaks down into conventional melodrama. 100m. **DIR:** Paul Wendkos. **CAST:** Lesley Ann Warren, Rip Torn, Richard Masur, Peggy Ann Garner, Ron Silver, Bibi Besch. 1978

BETRAYAL (1983) ★★★★★ Harold Pinter's play about the slow death of a marriage has been turned into an intelligent and innovative film that begins with the affair breaking apart and follows it backward to the beginning. Jeremy Irons and Patricia Hodge are superb. Rated R for profanity. 95m. **DIR:** David Jones. **CAST:** Jeremy Irons, Ben Kingsley, Patricia Hodge. 1983

BETRAYAL FROM THE EAST ★★ Fast-talking, wisecracking Lee Tracy takes on imperial Japan in this biased World War II espionage programmer. Peppered with the racial slurs and stereotypes so popular during this period. B&W; 82m. **DIR:** William Berke. **CAST:** Lee Tracy, Nancy Kelly, Regis Toomey, Richard Loo, Abner Biberman, Philip Ahn. 1945

BETRAYAL OF THE DOVE ★★★ A woman and her daughter are being spooked by someone and it looks like it is her soon-to-be ex-husband. She starts to fall in love with a doctor who used to date her best friend (Kelly LeBrock), but someone is trying to kill her. The story is interesting, but LeBrock just can't act. Not rated; contains nudity, profanity, violence, and implied sex. 94m. **DIR:** Strathford Hamilton. **CAST:** Helen Slater, Billy Zane, Kelly LeBrock, Alan Thicke, Harvey Korman, Stuart Pankin, Heather Lind. 1992

BETRAYED (1954) ★★1/2 In German-occupied Holland a secret agent called "The Scarf" terrorizes underground attempts to overthrow the Nazis. A dated movie and an obviously much older Clark Gable don't add up in spite of a good supporting cast and authentic European settings. 108m. **DIR:** Gottfried Reinhardt. **CAST:** Clark Gable, Lana Turner, Victor Mature, O. E. Hasse, Louis Calhern, Wilfrid Hyde-White, Ian Carmichael, Nora Swinburne, Roland Culver, Niall MacGinnis. 1954

BETRAYED (1988) ★★★1/2 A searing performance from Debra Winger surmounts baffling inconsistencies in Joe Eszterhas's script. She's sent by mentor John Heard to infiltrate a comfortably homespun rural American community that might conceal a nest of white supremacists. Its gut-wrenching impact is repeatedly dampened by the naïve and foolish actions taken by Winger. Focus on the message and forget the story. Rated R for violence and language. 127m. **DIR:** Constantin Costa-Gavras. **CAST:** Debra Winger, Tom Berenger, John Heard, Betsy Blair, Ted Levine. 1988

BETSY, THE ★★ A classic example of how to waste loads of talent and money. The Harold Robbins novel about a wealthy family in the auto manufacturing business was trashy to start with, but after Hollywood gets done with it, not even Laurence Olivier can save this debacle. Rated R. 125m. **DIR:** Daniel Petrie. **CAST:** Laurence Olivier, Tommy Lee Jones, Robert Duvall, Katharine Ross, Lesley-Anne Down, Jane Alexander. 1978 DVD

BETSY'S WEDDING ★★★★ In this warm hearted and often uproarious comedy-drama, writer-director Alan Alda plays a down-on-his-luck dad who tries to raise money to give his daughter (Molly Ringwald) a big wedding. Ally Sheedy and newcomer Anthony LaPaglia are the standouts in a uniformly fine ensemble cast. Rated R for profanity. 106m. **DIR:** Alan Alda. **CAST:** Alan Alda, Molly Ringwald, Madeline Kahn, Joe Pesci, Ally Sheedy, Burt Young, Joey Bishop, Catherine O'Hara, Anthony LaPaglia. 1990

BETTE MIDLER—ART OR BUST ★★★★ Bette Midler exudes more talent in this hour-and-a-half special than most entertainers do in a lifetime. There are clips from her last bathhouse show and her later concert performances. Not rated; contains adult language. 82m. **DIR:** Thomas Schlamme. **CAST:** Bette Midler. 1984

BETTER LATE THAN NEVER ★★1/2 Average made-for-television comedy about nursing home inhabitants who revolt against house rules. The premise is good, the execution so-so. Theft of a train is a nice touch. Rated PG. 100m. **DIR:** Richard Crenna. **CAST:** Harold Gould, Larry Storch, Strother Martin, Tyne Daly, Harry Morgan, Victor Buono, George Gobel, Donald Pleasence, Lou Jacobi. 1979

BETTER OFF DEAD (1985) ★★ A mixture of clever ideas and awfully silly ones, this comedy focuses on the plight of teenage Everyman, Lane Meyer (John Cusack), who finds his world shattered when the love of his life, Beth (Amanda Wyss), takes up with a conceited jock. Lance figures he is "better off dead" than Beth-less. The film is at its best when writer-director Savage Steve Holland throws in little sketches that stand out from the familiar plot. Rated PG for profanity. 97m. **DIR:** Savage Steve Holland. **CAST:** John Cusack, David Ogden Stiers, Diane Franklin, Kim Darby, Amanda Wyss. **1985**

BETTER OFF DEAD (1993) ★★★ Very strong performances from Mare Winningham and Tyra Ferrell help save this familiar tale of an attorney fighting to save a death-row prisoner. The attorney who prosecuted the case now has second thoughts about the small-time thief and prostitute who killed a policeman. Not rated. 91m. **DIR:** M. Neema Bernette. **CAST:** Mare Winningham, Tyra Ferrell, Kevin Tighe, Don Harvey. **1993**

•**BETTER THAN CHOCOLATE** ★★1/2 A young college dropout gets yanked out of her lesbian closet when her uptight mother comes to visit. The film is earnest and right-minded, but it's also preachy and rather trite. Rated R for profanity and mature themes. 101m. **DIR:** Anne Wheeler. **CAST:** Wendy Crewson, Karyn Dwyer, Christina Cox, Kevin Mundy, Peter Outerbridge. **1999 DVD**

BETTER TOMORROW, A ★★★1/2 Director John Woo reinvented the Hong Kong action film and began to attract world attention with this forceful melodrama that combines the action of classic Warner Brothers gangster films with the cynical sentimentality of spaghetti Westerns. In a supporting role, future star Chow Yun-Fat steals the movie. In Cantonese with English subtitles. Not rated; contains strong violence. 104m. **DIR:** John Woo. **CAST:** Leslie Cheung, Ti Lung, Chow Yun-Fat. **1986 DVD**

BETTER TOMORROW 2, A ★★★1/2 The plot's tough to follow, and the subtitles are atrocious, but the high humor, unabashed melodrama, and roaring finale make this an action classic. Chow Yun-Fat duking it out with mafiosi in a Manhattan Chinese restaurant is a true delight. In Cantonese with English subtitles. Not rated; contains very strong violence. 100m. **DIR:** John Woo. **CAST:** Chow Yun-Fat, Leslie Cheung, Ti Lung. **1987 DVD**

BETTER TOMORROW 3, A: LOVE AND DEATH IN SAIGON ★★★1/2 This prequel set during the fall of Saigon has little to do with the two previous *Better Tomorrows*. Producer-director Tsui Hark is known for his incredible visual flamboyance and his interest in recent Asian history. This film features more of the latter, but action fans won't be displeased. In Cantonese with English subtitles. Not rated; contains strong violence. 113m. **DIR:** Tsui Hark. **CAST:** Chow Yun-Fat, Anita Mui, Tony Leung Chiu-Wai. **1989 DVD**

BETTY BLUE ★★ Betty is radically spontaneous and a bit wacky (we don't know why), Zorg is the man she inspires to continue writing. The trick is not to think too much but instead to bask in Jean-Jacques Beineix's sensuous visual flair. In French with English subtitles. Rated R. 117m. **DIR:** Jean-Jacques Beineix. **CAST:** Jean-Hugues Anglade, Beatrice Dalle. **1986**

BETWEEN FRIENDS ★★1/2 Two middle-aged divorcées meet and gradually form a life-sustaining friendship. This made-for-cable feature occasionally gets mired in melodramatic tendencies, but its two charismatic stars make it well worth watching. Not

rated. 100m. **DIR:** Lou Antonio. **CAST:** Elizabeth Taylor, Carol Burnett, Barbara Rush, Stephen Young, Henry Ramer. **1983**

BETWEEN GOD, THE DEVIL AND A WINCHESTER ❤ A treasure is stolen from a church in Texas and a band of outlaws and a holy man go on the trail to find it. 98m. **DIR:** Dario Silvester. **CAST:** Richard Harrison, Gilbert Roland. **1972**

BETWEEN HEAVEN AND HELL ❤ This one is closer to Hell, mainly because it's all talk and no action. Broderick Crawford plays a sadistic drill sergeant who browbeats spoiled recruit Robert Wagner. It's all been done before and better. 94m. **DIR:** Richard Fleischer. **CAST:** Robert Wagner, Terry Moore, Broderick Crawford, Brad Dexter, Buddy Ebsen, Scatman Crothers, Skip Homeier. **1956**

BETWEEN MEN ★★★ Johnny Mack Brown heads west to find the rejected granddaughter of the man who raised him after his own father (William Farnum) fled, mistakenly thinking he was responsible for his son's death. Complicated plot line, good performances, and competent production. Above the norm. B&W; 59m. **DIR:** Robert N. Bradbury. **CAST:** Johnny Mack Brown, William Farnum, Beth Marion. **1935**

BETWEEN THE LINES ★★★★ Very good post-Sixties film in the tradition of *Return of the Secaucus 7* and *The Big Chill*. Staff of a once-underground newspaper has to come to terms with the paper's purchase by a large publisher. Superb ensemble acting. Rated R for profanity and nudity. 101m. **DIR:** Joan Micklin Silver. **CAST:** John Heard, Jeff Goldblum, Lindsay Crouse, Stephen Collins, Jill Eikenberry, Bruno Kirby, Gwen Welles, Lewis J. Stadlen, Jon Korkes, Michael J. Pollard, Lane Smith, Joe Morton, Richard Cox, Marilu Henner. **1977**

BETWEEN TWO WOMEN ★★★★ For this TV movie Colleen Dewhurst won an Emmy as the mother-in-law from Hell. After her severe stroke, she is cared for by her much-maligned daughter-in-law (Farrah Fawcett). Remarkably moving and believable. 95m. **DIR:** Jon Avnet. **CAST:** Colleen Dewhurst, Farrah Fawcett, Michael Nouri, Steven Hill. **1986**

BETWEEN WARS ❤ Australian offering about an idealistic doctor. 97m. **DIR:** Michael Thornhill. **CAST:** Corin Redgrave, Arthur Dingham, Judy Morris. **1985**

BEULAH LAND ★★★1/2 A generational look at the life of a southern plantation family. The saga carries you through the Civil War and its aftermath. A polished TV production with a strong cast, all of whom turn in fine performances. 267m. **DIR:** Virgil Vogel, Harry Falk. **CAST:** Lesley Ann Warren, Michael Sarrazin, Eddie Albert, Hope Lange, Don Johnson, Meredith Baxter-Birney. **1980**

BEVERLY HILLS BODYSNATCHERS ❤ Dark comedy about a mortician and his mad-scientist assistant. R for nudity, profanity, and violence. 85m. **DIR:** Jonathan Mostow. **CAST:** Vic Tayback, Frank Gorshin, Art Metrano. **1989**

BEVERLY HILLS BRATS ★★ The son of a wealthy plastic surgeon convinces a would-be robber to kidnap him. Zany and outrageous situations make this watchable. PG-13 for nudity and profanity. 90m. **DIR:**

Dimitri Sotirakis. **CAST:** Peter Billingsley, Burt Young, Martin Sheen, Terry Moore. **1989**

BEVERLY HILLS COP ★★★★ In this highly entertaining cops-and-comedy caper, Eddie Murphy plays a streetwise policeman from Detroit who takes a leave of absence to track down the men who killed his best friend. This quest takes him to the unfamiliar hills of ritzy southern California, where he's greeted as anything but a hero. Rated R for violence and profanity. 105m. **DIR:** Martin Brest. **CAST:** Eddie Murphy, Lisa Eilbacher, Judge Reinhold, John Ashton. **1984**

BEVERLY HILLS COP II ★★1/2 This sequel lacks most of the charm and freshness of the first film, choosing instead to unwind as a thunderous, pounding assault on the senses. Eddie Murphy needs all his considerable talent to enliven this confusing mess, and he just manages to pull it off. Rated R for profanity and brief nudity. 102m. **DIR:** Tony Scott. **CAST:** Eddie Murphy, Judge Reinhold, Jurgen Prochnow, Ronny Cox, John Ashton, Brigitte Nielsen, Allen Garfield, Dean Stockwell. **1987**

BEVERLY HILLS COP 3 ★★★1/2 Detroit cop Axel Foley is back in Los Angeles fighting off thugs the LAPD can't handle. Eddie Murphy is in his element as the wisecracking cop and knows how to milk oneliners for laughs. Set in a California theme park with most of the characters from the first two films back on board. Rated R for language. 100m. **DIR:** John Landis. **CAST:** Eddie Murphy, Theresa Randle, Judge Reinhold, Hector Elizondo, Bronson Pinchot, Timothy Carhart, John Saxon, Alan Young, Stephen McHattie. **1994**

BEVERLY HILLS MADAM 💗 In this TV movie, Faye Dunaway is madam Lil Hutton, whose carefully cultivated reputation is being threatened by her own call girls. 97m. **DIR:** Harvey Hart. **CAST:** Faye Dunaway, Louis Jourdan, Donna Dixon, Robin Givens, Terry Farrell, Marshall Colt. **1986**

BEVERLY HILLS 90210 ★★ Pilot movie for the Fox TV series introduces America to a whole new generation of teen idols. The film explores the problems faced by the Walsh family from Minnesota when they relocate to America's city of glamour. About as socially relevant as a Clearasil commercial. 90m. **DIR:** Tim Hunter. **CAST:** Jason Priestley, Shannen Doherty, Jennie Garth, Ian Ziering, Gabrielle Carteris, Maxwell Caulfield, Josh Mostel, Richard Cummings Jr. **1990**

BEVERLY HILLS NINJA 💗 Klutzy orphan with a soft heart is raised by a Ninja clan and tangles with murderers and counterfeiters in this mirthless comedy. Rated PG-13 for language and violence. 90m. **DIR:** Dennis Dugan. **CAST:** Chris Farley, Nicollette Sheridan, Robin Sou, Chris Rock, Nathaniel Parker. **1997 DVD**

BEVERLY HILLS VAMP 💗 Writer-director Fred Olen Ray labors in vain, trying to make this vampire movie funny. Rated R for nudity, profanity, and simulated sex. 88m. **DIR:** Fred Olen Ray. **CAST:** Eddie Deezen, Tim Conway Jr., Britt Ekland. **1989**

BEVERLY HILLBILLIES, THE (TV SERIES) ★★★ Selected episodes from the long-running TV series. Corny but effective. The immensely popular series was finally canceled not because of sagging ratings but because CBS decided to upgrade its network image. Each episode 30m. **DIR:** Ralph Levy. **CAST:** Buddy Ebsen, Irene Ryan, Donna Douglas, Max Baer, Raymond Bailey, Nancy Kulp. **1962–1971**

BEVERLY HILLBILLIES GO HOLLYWOOD, THE ★★★ Enjoyable compilation of four episodes of the popular television series finds the Clampett clan with a controlling interest in Mammoth Pictures. The studio is turned head-over-heels when the Clampetts decide to take an active interest in making movies. Plenty of the corn-fed humor that made the series so popular. 104m. **DIR:** Joseph DePew. **CAST:** Buddy Ebsen, Irene Ryan, Donna Douglas, Max Baer, Nancy Culp, Raymond Bailey. **1964**

BEVERLY HILLBILLIES, THE (1993) ★★★ It's scary how much Cloris Leachman looks and sounds like Irene Ryan's Granny in this big-screen version of the backwoods Clampett family's invasion of Beverly Hills. Featuring good work from Jim Varney, Lily Tomlin, and Dabney Coleman, it's fun for adults who fondly remember the series and kids looking for a silly laugh. Rated PG for brief profanity. 93m. **DIR:** Penelope Spheeris. **CAST:** Jim Varney, Cloris Leachman, Lily Tomlin, Dabney Coleman, Lea Thompson, Diedrich Bader, Erika Eleniak, Rob Schneider, Dolly Parton, Buddy Ebsen, Zsa Zsa Gabor. **1993**

BEWARE! CHILDREN AT PLAY 💗 Monster moppets make mincemeat of the adults in a small town, setting the scene for a series of gory retaliations that look more like someone broke a ketchup bottle. Not rated; contains violence. 94m. **DIR:** Mik Cribben. **CAST:** Michael Robinson, Rich Hamilton, Robin Lilly. **1989 DVD**

BEWARE, MY LOVELY ★★★★ Robert Ryan is terrifyingly right as an amnesiac psycho who can fly into a strangling rage one minute, then return to his simpleminded handyman guise the next. Ida Lupino is also superb as the widow who hires Ryan to clean her floors, an action she soon regrets. Dark suspense remains taut right up to the ending. B&W; 77m. **DIR:** Harry Horner. **CAST:** Ida Lupino, Robert Ryan, Taylor Holmes, Barbara Whiting. **1952**

BEWARE OF A HOLY WHORE ★★★★ Rainer Werner Fassbinder's wickedly funny comedy about a movie cast and crew trying to make the best of a worsening situation. Being stranded at a seaside resort would be a dream come true for most, but turns into a nightmare here. If it can go wrong, it will. Off-screen antics will appeal to those fascinated by the movie-making process. In German with English subtitles. Not rated. 103m. **DIR:** Rainer Werner Fassbinder. **CAST:** Lou Castel, Eddie Constantine, Hanna Schygulla, Margarethe von Trotta. **1971**

BEWARE OF SPOOKS ★★★ Joe E. Brown is hilarious as a cop afraid of his own shadow. He gets mixed up with a pretty girl and some thugs in a haunted house. B&W; 76m. **DIR:** Edward Sedgwick. **CAST:** Joe E. Brown, Mary Carlisle, Clarence Kolb. **1939**

BEYOND A REASONABLE DOUBT (1956) ★★★ To reveal the faults of the justice system, novelist Dana Andrews allows himself to be incriminated in a murder. The plan is to reveal his innocence at the last minute. But the one man who can exonerate him is killed. Don't expect surprise, but shock! B&W; 80m.

DIR: Fritz Lang. **CAST:** Dana Andrews, Joan Fontaine, Sidney Blackmer, Shepperd Strudwick. **1956**

BEYOND ATLANTIS ★★ Unexciting movie about a motley bunch of adventurers looking for a fabulous treasure on an uncharted isle. Rated PG for mild violence. 89m. **DIR:** Eddie Romero. **CAST:** Patrick Wayne, John Ashley, Leigh Christian, Sid Haig. **1973**

BEYOND DARKNESS ♥ Hokey spooker about a priest and his family who move into an old house haunted by witches burned at the stake. Rated R for violence. 90m. **DIR:** Clyde Anderson. **CAST:** David Brandon. **1992**

BEYOND EVIL ♥ A luxurious mansion happens to be haunted. Rated R. 94m. **DIR:** Herb Freed. **CAST:** John Saxon, Lynda Day George, Michael Dante. **1980**

BEYOND FEAR ★★★ A man's wife and child are taken hostage by a band of outlaws, and he must work with the police to ensure the safety of his family in this compelling film. Rated R by mid-1970s standards due to violence and profanity (very little of both, actually). 92m. **DIR:** Yannick Andrei. **CAST:** Michel Bouquet, Michael Constantine, Marilu Tolo. **1975**

BEYOND JUSTICE ★★1/2 A wealthy American hires mercenaries to rescue her son. Her Arab ex-husband has taken the spoiled brat to Morocco to become the next prince of the desert. Lots of guns, explosions, and bad acting. Rated R for profanity and violence. 113m. **DIR:** Duccio Tessari. **CAST:** Rutger Hauer, Carol Alt, Omar Sharif, Elliott Gould, Kabir Bedi. **1990**

BEYOND OBSESSION ★★ Marcello Mastroianni and Eleonora Giorgi are strange bedfellows for American Tom Berenger in this confusing Italian film about hustling, obsession, and seduction. Dubbed. Not rated; has profanity and nudity. 116m. **DIR:** Lilliana Cavani. **CAST:** Tom Berenger, Marcello Mastroianni, Eleonora Giorgi, Michel Piccoli. **1982**

BEYOND RANGOON ★★★ It takes time to warm up to Patricia Arquette, who plays a tourist trying unsuccessfully to get on with her life despite haunting personal tragedy. It is the superior performance of U Aung Ko, as her guide turned adviser, that commands our undivided attention. The two are caught up in the 1988 massacre of Burmese students and monks when the military dictatorship decides to squelch the Democracy Movement. Satisfying conclusion makes up for shaky start. Rated R for violence and profanity. 96m. **DIR:** John Boorman. **CAST:** Patricia Arquette, U Aung Ko, Frances McDormand, Spalding Gray, Adelle Lutz. **1995**

BEYOND REASON ★★★ Telly Savalas shows his stuff in this sensitve film, which he wrote and directed. He plays an iconoclastic psychologist who slowly loses touch with reality. Though thought-provoking and touching throughout, the story gets a little muddy from time to time and finishes unsatisfyingly. 88m. **DIR:** Telly Savalas. **CAST:** Telly Savalas, Diana Muldaur, Marvin Laird. **1985**

BEYOND REASONABLE DOUBT (1983) ★★★ Well-crafted mystery based on the real-life conviction for double murder of an innocent New Zealand farmer. David Hemmings turns in a polished performance as a ruthless cop who engineers Thomas's conviction. 117m. **DIR:** John Laing. **CAST:** David Hemmings, John Hargreaves. **1983**

●BEYOND REDEMPTION ★★1/2 A series of gruesome murders plagues the city, and it is up to Andrew McCarthy as the lead investigator to head the quest to find the serial killer. Each murder has a biblical theme, causing McCarthy to wonder what connection the killer has with the Church. Rated R primarily for gory murder scenes. 97m. **DIR:** Chris Angel. **CAST:** Andrew McCarthy, Michael Ironside, Jayne Heitmeyer. **1999 DVD**

BEYOND SILENCE ★★★1/2 When a young girl becomes interested in music, her deaf father fears that he's losing her to a world where he can't follow. Director Caroline Link uses deafness as a metaphor for the inevitable alienation of growing children from their parents, and the film shows an uncanny insight into the undercurrents of affection and resentment that often exist side by side in families. In German with English subtitles. Rated PG-13 for mature themes. 100m. **DIR:** Caroline Link. **CAST:** Sylvie Testud, Tatjana Trieb, Howie Seago, Emmanuelle Laborit. **1996**

BEYOND THE CALL ★★★ Happily married Sissy Spacek learns that a former high-school sweetheart is about to be executed for killing a police officer, and—much to her husband's discomfort—she agrees to visit the man on death row. What follows is a series of intense conversations, during which Spacek attempts to understand what became of the gentle boy she once knew. Doug Magee's script starts well but stalls, and the conclusion is particularly dissatisfying. Rated R for violence, profanity, and dramatic intensity. 101m. **DIR:** Tony Bill. **CAST:** Sissy Spacek, David Strathairn, Arliss Howard, Janet Wright. **1996**

BEYOND THE CALL OF DUTY ★★ Another mindless adventure film, this one set on the Mekong River Delta in Vietnam. In the middle of the war, soldier Jan-Michael Vincent finds himself risking his life to save a female journalist. Pedestrian and implausible, and just a tad too late to make an impact. Rated R for violence and language. 93m. **DIR:** Cirio H. Santiago. **CAST:** Jan-Michael Vincent, Jillian McWhirter. **1992**

BEYOND THE DOOR ♥ Sick rip-off of *The Exorcist* has Juliet Mills as a woman possessed by guess what. Rated R. 94m. **DIR:** Ovidio Assonitis (Oliver Hellman). **CAST:** Juliet Mills, Richard Johnson, David Colin Jr. **1975**

BEYOND THE DOOR 2 ★★ Why, why, why? Actually, this semisequel is much better than the original mainly because its director was the famed Mario Bava. This time a young boy becomes possessed by the unseen power of hell, and many die. Alternate title: *Shock.* Rated R. 92m. **DIR:** Mario Bava. **CAST:** Daria Nicolodi, John Steiner, David Colin Jr. **1979**

BEYOND THE DOOR 3 ♥ A college student falls victim to the prince of darkness in this unscary horror yarn with laughable special effects. Rated R for profanity, nudity, and violence. 94m. **DIR:** Jeff Kwitny. **CAST:** Mary Kohnert. **1991**

BEYOND THE DOORS ♥ Jimi Hendrix, Janis Joplin, and Jim Morrison are atrociously impersonated in this docudrama that suggests they were killed by the CIA. Rated R for drug use and nudity. 117m. DIR: Larry Buchanan. CAST: Gregory Allen Chatman, Riba Meryl, Bryan Wolf. 1980

BEYOND THE FOREST ★★ Too much Bette Davis spoils this mix of greed, adultery, abortion, and murder, even if she does utter the classic line, "What a dump!" Snarling and whining, Davis gives a performance that turns the murky-plotted film into a melodramatic mess even her most devoted fans reject. B&W; 96m. DIR: King Vidor. CAST: Bette Davis, Joseph Cotten, David Brian, Ruth Roman, Minor Watson, Regis Toomey. 1949

BEYOND THE LAW (1968) 🌢 A spaghetti Western with Lee Van Cleef as a bad guy turned good. Not rated; contains adult language and some gratuitous, badly staged violence. 90m. DIR: Giorgio Stegani. CAST: Lee Van Cleef, Antonio Sabato, Lionel Stander, Bud Spencer. 1968 DVD

BEYOND THE LAW (1992) ★★ In one of those been-there-done-that roles, Charlie Sheen plays a cop who goes undercover to bust a motorcycle gang and prove to gang leader Michael Madsen that he's the stuff of which nightmares are made. Usual conflicts include Sheen's losing sight of reality as he slips into his new persona. Ho hum. Rated R for violence, language, and adult situations. 101m. DIR: Larry Ferguson. CAST: Charlie Sheen, Michael Madsen, Linda Fiorentino. 1992

BEYOND THE LIMIT ★★ Dull, unconvincing adaptation of *The Honorary Consul*, Graham Greene's novel about love and betrayal in an Argentinian town stars Michael Caine as a kidnapped diplomat and Richard Gere as the doctor in love with his wife. It'll take you beyond your limit. Rated R. 103m. DIR: John Mackenzie. CAST: Michael Caine, Richard Gere, Bob Hoskins, Elpidia Carrillo. 1983

•**BEYOND THE MAT** ★★★ Professional wrestling is the subject of this candid documentary that dives into the bloody spectacle of the World Wrestling Federation and Extreme Championship Wrestling. The film also goes backstage to examine the tryouts of two wannabe pros, the career and personal life of family man Mick "Mankind" Foley, the twilight ring years of Terry Funk, and the inner demons and rock-bottom slide of Jake "The Snake" Roberts. Rated R for language and violence. 92m. DIR: Berry Blaustein. 2000

BEYOND THE POSEIDON ADVENTURE 🌢 Michael Caine heads one of two salvage crews that race each other and time to probe the upside-down wreck of the *Poseidon*. Rated PG for mild violence and language. 114m. DIR: Irwin Allen. CAST: Michael Caine, Sally Field, Telly Savalas, Jack Warden, Peter Boyle. 1979

BEYOND THE PURPLE HILLS ★★★ Sheriff Gene Autry finds an old lawman friend murdered and arrests the victim's son, soon to be TV's Wyatt Earp, Hugh O'Brian, in his film debut. Autry realizes he can't be guilty and sets out to bring in the real killer. This film treats us to not only Autry's horse, Champion, but Little Champ as well, strutting his stuff. B&W; 70m. DIR: John English. CAST: Gene Autry, Pat

Buttram, Hugh O'Brian, James Millican, Don Beddoe. 1950

BEYOND THE RISING MOON (STAR QUEST) ★★ In the twenty-first century, a genetically created troubleshooter rebels. The same theme was handled much better in *Blade Runner*, though here the plot is secondary to the mediocre special effects and outer-space shoot-outs. 93m. DIR: Philip Cook. CAST: Tracy Davis, Hans Bachmann. 1988

BEYOND THE STARS ★★★ Troubled teen Christian Slater, spending the summer with divorced father Robert Foxworth, runs into reclusive ex-astronaut Martin Sheen, who opens up and takes the kid under his wing. They eventually form a trust that allows Sheen to introduce Slater to a secret he discovered on the moon. Rated PG. 94m. DIR: David Saperstein. CAST: Martin Sheen, Christian Slater, Robert Foxworth, Sharon Stone, Olivia D'Abo, F. Murray Abraham. 1989

BEYOND THE VALLEY OF THE DOLLS 🌢 This was rated X when it came out, but by today's standards it's an R for gratuitous nudity and profanity. 109m. DIR: Russ Meyer. CAST: Dolly Read, Cynthia Myers, Marcia McBroom. 1970

BEYOND THE WALLS ★★1/2 This Israeli film pits Jewish and Arab convicts against each other with explosive consequences. A standard prison drama. Nominated for a best foreign film Oscar, it lost to *Dangerous Moves*. 103m. DIR: Uri Barbash. CAST: Arnon Zadok, Muhamad Bakri. 1984

BEYOND THERAPY ★★ Robert Altman is a hit-and-miss director and his *Beyond Therapy* (adapted from Christopher Durang's play) qualifies as a miss. The movie, which pokes fun at psychiatrists and their patients, really is a mess filled with unconnected episodes. Most of the performances and much of the dialogue are salvageable and hilarious, however. Most notable are Tom Conti and, as a bizarre psychiatrist, Glenda Jackson. Rated R. 93m. DIR: Robert Altman. CAST: Julie Hagerty, Jeff Goldblum, Glenda Jackson, Tom Conti, Christopher Guest, Cris Campion. 1987

BEYOND TOMORROW ★★1/2 Sudden success goes to singer Richard Carlson's head. He switches his affections from fiancée Jean Parker to captivating stage star Helen Vinson. To see that right is done, three ghosts return from the grave and change his troubled mind. An interesting premise on paper, the film fails to live up to its possibilities. B&W; 84m. DIR: A. Edward Sutherland. CAST: Jean Parker, Richard Carlson, Helen Vinson, Charles Winninger, Harry Carey, C. Aubrey Smith, Maria Ouspenskaya, Rod La Rocque. 1940

BHAJI ON THE BEACH ★★★★ An assortment of women, all ethnic Indians living in England, take a day trip to the seaside resort at Blackpool, where their different stories mix and play themselves out. The film takes some getting used to, with its riotous, colorful images and thick British and Indian accents, but it's worth the effort—a charming, distinctive taste of an exotic subculture. Not rated; suitable for mature audiences. 99m. DIR: Gurinder Chadha. CAST: Kim Vithana, Lalita Ahmed, Shaheen Khan, Sarita Khajuria, Jimmi Harkishin, Zohra Segal, Peter Cellier. 1993

BHOWANI JUNCTION ★★★1/2 An exciting, often stirring drama, of the movement of passive resistance started by Mahatma Gandhi in post-World War II India. Ava Gardner stars as an Anglo-Indian being stirred by her ties to the Sikhs and their cause. Not rated, but recommended for family viewing. 110m. **DIR:** George Cukor. **CAST:** Ava Gardner, Stewart Granger, Lionel Jeffries, Bill Travers. 1956

BIBLE, THE ★★★ An overblown all-star treatment of five of the early stories in the Old Testament. Director John Huston gives this movie the feel of a Cecil B. De Mille spectacle, but there is little human touch to any of the stories. This expensively mounted production forgets that in the Bible, individual accomplishments are equally relevant to grandeur. 174m. **DIR:** John Huston. **CAST:** Michael Parks, Ulla Bergryd, Richard Harris, John Huston, Ava Gardner. 1966

•**BICENTENNIAL MAN** ★★★1/2 Isaac Asimov's classic science-fiction story gets opulent treatment in this expanded adaptation, which gives star Robin Williams another of his signature "sensitive" roles, in this case a new NDR-114 robot initially purchased as a family companion and servant. But Andrew, as he comes to be called, proves unusually creative and able to reason for himself, which over the course of several generations leads the android to remake himself in his masters' image. It's a popular sci-fi conceit: the notion that human passion, senses, and even mortality are so cherished that an android who never ages would willingly sacrifice immortality for a chance to obtain these prized abilities. The problem is that Nicholas Kazan's script has no conflict whatsoever, merely comic relief to offset the story's increasingly melancholy atmosphere. Rated PG for mild profanity and sexual candor. 132m. **DIR:** Chris Columbus. **CAST:** Robin Williams, Embeth Davidtz, Sam Neill, Oliver Platt, Keirsten Warren, Wendy Crewson, Hallie Kate Eisenberg. 1999 DVD

BICYCLE THIEF, THE ★★★★ Considered by critics an all-time classic, this touching, honest, beautifully human film speaks realistically to the heart with simple cinematic eloquence. A bill-poster's bicycle, on which his job depends, is stolen. Ignored by the police, who see nothing special in the loss, the anguished worker and his young son search Rome for the thief. In Italian with English subtitles. B&W; 90m. **DIR:** Vittorio De Sica. **CAST:** Lamberto Maggiorani, Lianella Carell, Enzo Staiola. 1949 DVD

BIG ★★★★ In this intelligent script from Gary Ross and Anne Spielberg, Tom Hanks stars as the "big person" embodiment of young David Moscow, who wishes for a creaky amusement-park fortune-telling machine to make him "big." Hanks, as the result, performs brilliantly as the 13-year-old in a 35-year-old body; he's ably assisted by spunky Elizabeth Perkins as an associate at the children's toy company where he's able to land a job. Rated PG for mild sexual themes. 102m. **DIR:** Penny Marshall. **CAST:** Tom Hanks, Elizabeth Perkins, Robert Loggia, John Heard, Jared Rushton, David Moscow. 1988 DVD

BIG BAD JOHN ★★ Bayou bad boys take leave of the swamps, setting out on a trail of violence to settle an old score. This macho masher offers a heavyweight country-and-western soundtrack. Filmed in Colorado, Texas, and New Mexico. Rated R for violence. 86m. **DIR:** Burt Kennedy. **CAST:** Jimmy Dean, Jack Elam, Ned Beatty, Romy Windsor, Jeff Osterhage, Bo Hopkins. 1990

BIG BAD MAMA ★★ Here's an okay film concerning a mother (Angie Dickinson), sort of a second-rate Ma Barker, leading her daughters on a robbery spree during the Depression. It's not a classic by any means, but the action keeps things moving along. Rated R for violence, nudity, and sex. 83m. **DIR:** Steve Carver. **CAST:** Angie Dickinson, Tom Skerritt, William Shatner, Joan Prather. 1974 DVD

BIG BAD MAMA II ♥ A shabby sequel to a so-so movie. Rated R for violence and nudity. 85m. **DIR:** Jim Wynorski. **CAST:** Angie Dickinson, Robert Culp, Danielle Brisebois, Julie McCullough, Bruce Glover. 1987

BIG BANG THEORY, THE ★★1/2 When an aspiring actress is attacked by a sleazy producer and then sexually abused by a motorcycle cop, she finds herself in the role of a lifetime. Darling Narita stars as the actress who loses her apartment, job, and dignity in one afternoon, but gains newfound power when she dons the cop's outfit and hits the streets on his motorcycle. Rated R for violence, language, and adult situations. 98m. **DIR:** Ash . **CAST:** Darling Narita, Peter Greene, Michael Newland, Eric Shrody. 1997

BIG BIRD CAGE, THE ★★ Some of the women-in-prison movies that producer Roger Corman cranked out in the Seventies were worth seeing because some talented filmmakers brought a high level of ability and excitement to them. This, however, is one of the boring ones. Rated R for nudity and violence. 88m. **DIR:** Jack Hill. **CAST:** Pam Grier, Anitra Ford, Sid Haig. 1972

BIG BLUE, THE ♥ This underwater adventure drowns largely because Rosanna Arquette attempts to re-create her ditzy *Desperately Seeking Susan* persona. Underwater shots are the only plus. Rated PG for mature themes. 118m. **DIR:** Luc Besson. **CAST:** Rosanna Arquette, Jean-Marc Barr, Jean Reno, Griffin Dunne. 1986

BIG BLUFF, THE ♥ A young woman with a terminal disease marries a gigolo who plots to murder her. B&W; 70m. **DIR:** W. Lee Wilder. **CAST:** John Bromfield, Martha Vickers, Robert Hutton, Rosemarie Bowe. 1955

•**BIG BRASS RING, THE** ★★★ This film exists thanks to an unproduced script by Orson Welles, which is further "sweetened" by Oja Kodar and F. X. Feeney; the result is yet another predictable study of corrupt politicians and their slimy secrets. William Hurt is more deadpan than usual as a candidate for governor of Missouri, a bid threatened by an old mentor (Nigel Hawthorne) with some compromising photographs and rather aberrant sexual tastes of his own. These carnal antics are displayed in a blatant manner that seems intended to shock and titillate; while such things may have been hot stuff when Welles first concocted them, they all seem trite and familiar these days. Miranda Richardson scores some points as Hurt's alcoholic and ambitious wife. Rated R for nudity, profanity, violence, and simulated sex. 104m. **DIR:** George Hickenlooper. **CAST:** William Hurt, Nigel Hawthorne, Miranda Richardson, Irène Jacob. **1999 DVD**

BIG BRAWL, THE ★★★ Director Robert Clouse again fails to reach the heights attained with his *Enter the Dragon.* Nevertheless, this kung fu comedy has its moments—most provided by star Jackie Chan. 95m. **DIR:** Robert Clouse. **CAST:** Jackie Chan, José Ferrer, Kristine DeBell, Mako. **1980**

BIG BROADCAST OF 1938, THE ★★★★ A delightful musical with a talented cast of performers who were just starting their careers. Part of the fun is watching them develop confidence and proficiency. The slight plot about ocean liners involved in a senseless race on the high seas is just an excuse for the cast members to entertain the passengers. B&W; 91m. **DIR:** Mitchell Leisen. **CAST:** W. C. Fields, Bob Hope, Martha Raye, Dorothy Lamour, Kirsten Flagstad, Shirley Ross, Ben Blue, Leif Erickson. **1938**

BIG BULLY ★★1/2 Concept and a meandering script overcome common sense in this misfired satire, which features Rick Moranis as a meek writer who returns to his small-town school to teach, only to renew ties with a much-feared childhood bully (now grown up into Tom Arnold). Older viewers are unlikely to appreciate the picture's ill-advised morals. Rated PG for slapstick violence. 93m. **DIR:** Steve Miner. **CAST:** Rick Moranis, Tom Arnold, Julianne Phillips, Carol Kane, Jeffrey Tambor, Don Knotts. **1996 DVD**

BIG BUS, THE ★★★ A superluxurious nuclear-powered bus runs into trouble while carrying a group of misfits from New York to Denver. This spoof appeared four years before *Airplane!* It's not as funny, but it does have a silly and sarcastic playfulness. One of those few films that work better on the small screen. Rated PG. 88m. **DIR:** James Frawley. **CAST:** Joseph Bologna, Stockard Channing, John Beck, Lynn Redgrave, José Ferrer, Ruth Gordon, Richard B. Shull, Sally Kellerman, Ned Beatty, Richard Mulligan, Larry Hagman, Howard Hesseman, Harold Gould. **1976**

BIG BUSINESS ★★★1/2 Bette Midler and Lily Tomlin play two sets of mismatched twins, one raised in a West Virginia country setting and another accustomed to wealth and power in New York City. Despite the unoriginal, one-joke plot, the stars manage some genuinely funny moments. Rated PG for light profanity. 95m. **DIR:** Jim Abrahams. **CAST:** Bette Midler, Lily Tomlin, Fred Ward, Edward Herrmann, Michele Placido, Daniel Gerroll, Barry Primus, Michael Gross, Deborah Rush, Nicolas Coster. **1988**

BIG BUSINESS GIRL ★★★ One of Hollywood's first career-girl movies and a star vehicle for Loretta Young and Joan Blondell. The comedy-drama mixes career problems with romantic dilemmas and is aimed primarily at a female audience with elements Hollywood still uses to appeal to women today. B&W; 75m. **DIR:** William A. Seiter. **CAST:** Loretta Young, Joan Blondell, Ricardo Cortez, Jack Albertson, Dorothy Christy, Bobby Gordon. **1931**

BIG BUST OUT, THE ★ Four female convicts escape from a prison somewhere in the Middle East when they are sent to do janitorial work at a convent. Idiotic. 75m. **DIR:** Richard Jackson. **CAST:** Vonetta McGee, Karen Carter, Linda Fox, Monica Taylor. **1973**

BIG CAT, THE ★★★ A marauding mountain lion complicates feuding between high country ranchers in this enjoyable adventure film. 75m. **DIR:** Phil Karlson. **CAST:** Lon McCallister, Preston Foster, Forrest Tucker. **1949**

BIG CHILL, THE ★★★★1/2 As with John Sayles's superb *Return of the Secaucus 7,* this equally impressive and thoroughly enjoyable film by writer-director Lawrence Kasdan concerns a weekend reunion of old friends, all of whom have gone on to varied lifestyles after once being united in the hip, committed 1960s. It features a who's who of the day's hot young stars as the friends. Rated R for nudity and profanity. 103m. **DIR:** Lawrence Kasdan. **CAST:** Tom Berenger, William Hurt, Glenn Close, Jeff Goldblum, JoBeth Williams, Kevin Kline, Mary Kay Place, Meg Tilly. **1983 DVD**

BIG COMBO, THE ★★★ A classic American gangster film done in the *film noir* style. Cornel Wilde has the starring role as a half-crazed policeman who is after gangsters and will do whatever is necessary to get them. Quite violent for its time and very well photographed, with an exciting climax. B&W; 89m. **DIR:** Joseph H. Lewis. **CAST:** Cornel Wilde, Jean Wallace, Richard Conte. **1955 DVD**

BIG COUNTRY, THE ★★★ Big-budget Western pits Gregory Peck and Charlton Heston as adversaries in an ongoing feud between rival cowmen Burl Ives and Charles Bickford. This would-be epic looks good but lacks the punch and plot of the best and most famous Westerns. 163m. **DIR:** William Wyler. **CAST:** Gregory Peck, Jean Simmons, Charlton Heston, Carroll Baker, Burl Ives, Charles Bickford. **1958**

•**BIG DADDY** ★★ This attempt to blend star Adam Sandler's two audiences—the fans of his big-screen moron comedy and the romantics pleasantly surprised by the (comparative) sensitivity of his character in *The Wedding Singer*—is uncomfortable at best, particularly because a small child is part of the package. Sandler's character, an aging adolescent who refuses to accept adult responsibility, decides to adopt a 5-year-old as a means of showing a former girlfriend that he's ready for "responsibility." Sandler's efforts to impress us as a natural father figure are clumsy at best. The boy is played by twins who certainly know how to milk pity; despite the inept direction, you can't help but adore the little guy. Too bad the same cannot be said about the film itself. Rated PG-13 for incessant vulgarity, sexual candor, and mild profanity. 95m. **DIR:** Dennis Dugan. **CAST:** Adam Sandler, Joey Lauren Adams, Jon Stewart, Allen Covert, Rob Schneider, Cole Sprouse, Dylan Sprouse. **1999 DVD**

BIG DEAL ON MADONNA STREET ★★★★ Mario Monicelli directed this tale as a classic spoof of the perfect-crime film that depicts in great detail the elaborate planning and split-second timing involved in huge thefts. Monicelli's characters—who are attempting to burglarize a safe—also formulate intricate plans and employ precise timing, but everything they do results in humiliating disaster—providing a hilarious comedy of errors. In Italian with English subtitles. B&W; 91m. DIR: Mario Monicelli. CAST: Marcello Mastroianni, Vittorio Gassman, Toto, Renato Salvatori, Claudia Cardinale. 1960

BIG EASY, THE ★★★★ Everything is easy in the Big Easy (aka New Orleans) for slick and only slightly sleazy police lieutenant Remy McSwain (Dennis Quaid). That is, until Anne Osbourne (Ellen Barkin), an upright and uptight assistant district attorney, comes along. *The Big Easy* is a wild, southern-style variation on the old-fashioned cop films of the Thirties and Forties. Rated R for violence, profanity, and sensuality. 100m. DIR: Jim McBride. CAST: Dennis Quaid, Ellen Barkin, Ned Beatty, John Goodman, Lisa Jane Persky, Ebbe Roe Smith, Tom O'Brien, Charles Ludlam. 1987 DVD

BIG FALL, THE ★★ When a femme fatale hires an L.A. detective to find her missing brother, he is surprised that the case turns out to be something quite different. Not so for viewers, who have seen this kind of Raymond Chandler parody/homage done many other times, and usually much better. Rated R for strong violence, sexual situations, and strong profanity. 94m. DIR: C. Thomas Howell. CAST: C. Thomas Howell, Sophie Ward, Jeff Kober. 1997

BIG FELLA ★★1/2 Singing dockworker in Marseilles works secretly with the police to find a rich British runaway boy. A gentle tale of missed opportunities and unrequited love. B&W; 70m. DIR: J. Elder Wills. CAST: Paul Robeson, Elisabeth Welch, Roy Emerton, James Hayter, Lawrence Brown, Eldon Grant. 1937 DVD

BIG FIX, THE ★★★1/2 Novelist Roger Simon's laidback detective, Moses Wine, comes to the screen in this flawed thriller. The setting—which harkens back to the revolutionary 1960s—has become dated, but a murder mystery of any stripe is still suspenseful. Rated PG. 108m. DIR: Jeremy Paul Kagan. CAST: Richard Dreyfuss, Susan Anspach, Bonnie Bedelia. 1978

BIG FOOT ❤ Legendary monster comes down from the hills and beats the hell out of everybody. 94m. DIR: Robert F. Slatzer. CAST: John Carradine, Joi Lansing, John Mitchum, Chris Mitchum. 1971

BIG GIRLS DON'T CRY—THEY GET EVEN ★★★1/2 Don't let the awful title (it was originally called *Stepkids*) keep you away from this low-key but charming comedy about a young teen who revolts against the revolving-door marriages of her parents that has left her part of a bizarrely extended family. Rated PG-13 for profanity. 96m. DIR: Joan Micklin Silver. CAST: Hilary Wolf, David Strathairn, Margaret Whitton, Griffin Dunne, Adrienne Shelly. 1992

BIG GREEN, THE ★★ This drab, inert comedy recycles the story from *Little Giants* and *The Mighty Ducks*. This time the sport is soccer, but nothing else has changed. Rated PG. 97m. DIR: Holly Goldberg Sloan. CAST: Steve Guttenberg, Olivia D'Abo, Jay O. Sanders, John Terry, Chauncey Leopardi. 1995

BIG HAND FOR THE LITTLE LADY, A ★★★1/2 A compulsive gambler (Henry Fonda) talks his way into a high-stakes poker game, bets everything he owns, then promptly keels over, leaving his wife (Joanne Woodward) to play out his hand. Nifty Western-comedy is a bit too padded (it was originally a one-hour TV play, *Big Deal in Laredo*), but the expert cast puts it over. 95m. DIR: Fielder Cook. CAST: Henry Fonda, Joanne Woodward, Jason Robards Jr., Charles Bickford, Burgess Meredith, Paul Ford, John Qualen, Robert Middleton. 1966

BIG HANGOVER, THE ★★1/2 One-joke movie, with Van Johnson as a veteran who almost drowned in a bombed-out wine cellar, becoming drunk at the slightest odor of alcohol. Becomes preachy when he, as a junior lawyer, turns against his employer for racial discrimination. B&W; 82m. DIR: Norman Krasna. CAST: Van Johnson, Elizabeth Taylor, Fay Holden, Leon Ames, Edgar Buchanan, Selena Royle, Gene Lockhart, Rosemary DeCamp. 1950

BIG HEAT, THE ★★★★ A crackerjack classic of crime *film noir*. Homicide detective Dave Bannion (Glenn Ford) is bent on solving the puzzle of an unexpected suicide of a fellow police officer, even though he is told by his superiors to leave bad enough alone. Exceptional acting, especially by Lee Marvin and Gloria Grahame. B&W; 90m. DIR: Fritz Lang. CAST: Glenn Ford, Gloria Grahame, Jocelyn Brando, Alexander Scourby, Lee Marvin, Jeanette Nolan, Carolyn Jones. 1953

BIG HIT, THE ★★1/2 Sweet-natured hit man wants to be liked by everyone in this outrageous action-comedy. Things fall apart when he and two assassins kidnap an Asian girl who turns out to be their boss's goddaughter. Some high energy and offbeat, dark humor, but this Hollywood–Hong Kong hybrid sometimes trips over a forced hipness. Rated R for language, violence, and nudity. 93m. DIR: Che-Kirk Wong. CAST: Mark Wahlberg, Lou Diamond Phillips, Bokeem Woodbine, China Chow, Avery Brooks, Christina Applegate, Elliott Gould, Lainie Kazan, Lela Rochon. 1998 DVD

BIG HOUSE, THE ★★★★ The granddaddy of all hard-hitting prison movies, with tough cons, abusive guards, and the inevitable doomed "bust-out." Every cliché is here, from the dim-witted gang leader and his cautious friend to the weakling snitch. But it was fresh then and still holds up. Oscar nominations for best picture and Wallace Beery's performance. B&W; 87m. DIR: George Hill. CAST: Chester Morris, Wallace Beery, Lewis Stone, Robert Montgomery, Leila Hyams. 1930

BIG JAKE ★★★ Big John Wayne takes up the trail of a gang of no-goods who kidnapped his grandson and shot up Maureen O'Hara's homestead and hired hands. One wishes there had been more scenes with Wayne and O'Hara together in this film, their last together. 110m. DIR: George Sherman. CAST: John Wayne, Richard Boone, Maureen O'Hara, Patrick Wayne, Chris Mitchum, Bobby Vinton, Bruce Cabot. 1971

BIG JIM MCLAIN ★★ This relic of the McCarthy era has John Wayne and James Arness as two-fisted investigators for the House Un-American Activities Committee. Clumsy and dull. B&W; 90m. DIR: Edward Ludwig. CAST: John Wayne, James Arness, Nancy Olson, Veda Ann Borg, Hans Conried. 1952

BIG LEBOWSKI, THE ★★ You won't care a jot for any of the characters in this deranged *film noir*, which separates this misfire from other Joel and Ethan Coen productions. Jeff Bridges, a fortysomething loser, gets mistaken for a Pasadena millionaire who shares his name; what follows involves a hoochy-coochy trophy wife, an artist who paints in the nude, a trio of mock-Nazi nihilists, a Stetson-garbed stranger, and Saddam Hussein. Rated R for nudity, drug use, violence, and profanity. 117m. DIR: Joel Coen. CAST: Jeff Bridges, John Goodman, Julianne Moore, Steve Buscemi, David Huddleston, Philip Seymour Hoffman, Tara Reid. 1998 DVD

BIG LIFT, THE ★★1/2 Montgomery Clift gives an emotionally charged performance as an air force pilot who becomes romantically involved with a young German girl in post–World War II Berlin. Excellent location photography gives a lift to this uneven melodrama. B&W; 120m. DIR: George Seaton. CAST: Montgomery Clift, Paul Douglas, Cornell Borchers, O. E. Hasse. 1950 DVD

BIG MAN ★★★ An unemployed coal miner (Liam Neeson) gets involved with illegal bare-knuckle boxing and hoodlums in this Scottish drama. The brawling is gritty and glamourless in an intriguing story that ends with a surprising turn of events. Rated R for violence. 94m. DIR: David Leland. CAST: Liam Neeson, Joanne Whalley, Ian Bannen, Billy Connolly, Hugh Grant. 1991

BIG MAN ON CAMPUS ★★★ This spoofy retelling of The Hunchback of Notre Dame story is a surprising bit of good-natured fun. Sincere comic touches by Allan Katz and Corey Parker help make this teen-marketed sexual-oriented fluff seem a little more substantial. Above average. Rated PG-13 for mild profanity. 102m. DIR: Jeremy Paul Kagan. CAST: Allan Katz, Corey Parker, Tom Skerritt, Cindy Williams. 1989

•BIG MOMMA'S HOUSE ★★ Two FBI agents are out to nab a vicious bank robber in this hokey cross-dressing comedy. They follow a female teller, who dated the dangerous fugitive, to a small southern town where one agent tries to break the case by masquerading as the teller's 300-pound grandmother. The film is fun when the phony Big Momma delivers a baby, takes karate lessons, and plays basketball, but is dull and lame for the most part. Rated PG-13 for sexual references, violence, and language. 95m. DIR: Raja Gosnell. CAST: Martin Lawrence, Nia Long, Paul Giamatti, Ella Mitchell, Terrence Howard. 2000

BIG MOUTH, THE ★★ The bloom was off the rose by this point in Jerry Lewis's solo career, and this standard gangster comedy is a profound disappointment. Title character Jerry (an apt description in a film where everybody shouts all the time) gets involved in a witless search for stolen diamonds. Lewis's character bits and attempts at disguise are pretty flimsy. For true fans only. 107m. DIR: Jerry Lewis. CAST: Jerry Lewis, Harold J. Stone. 1967

BIG NEWS ★★★ Robert Armstrong plays a boozing newspaper reporter who gets framed for the murder of his editor. Armstrong's wife, Carole Lombard, writes a women's column for a rival paper and puts in some time trying to sober up her hubby and clear him of the crime. Snappy comedy-mystery. B&W; 75m. DIR: Gregory La Cava. CAST: Robert Armstrong, Carole Lombard. 1929

BIG NIGHT ★★★★ What a delight! Immigrant brothers Tony Shalhoub and Stanley Tucci open an authentic Italian restaurant on the New Jersey shore in the late 1950s, hoping to impress customers with their exquisite cuisine. Alas, boorish Americans prefer the cheap wine and checkered tablecloths at a competitive joint just across the street. Granted the opportunity to prepare a meal for entertainer Louis Prima, the brothers empty their bank account and hope to achieve fame by serving a truly magnificent feast. This poignant character study demonstrates that art and commerce rarely mix. Rated R for profanity and sexual content. 107m. DIR: Campbell Scott, Stanley Tucci. CAST: Stanley Tucci, Tony Shalhoub, Minnie Driver, Isabella Rossellini, Ian Holm. 1995

BIG ONE, THE ★★★★ Grass-roots activist and media junkie Michael Moore films the cross-country marketing tour for his book Downsize This! Random Threats from an Unarmed American to further prove that big business is running amok. He tries to figure out why Fortune 500 companies are downsizing while posting record-breaking profits. The mischievous documentarian is in top form—like when he grills Nike CEO Phil Knight about exploiting Pacific Rim children—but his inner comedian at times overwhelms his blue-collar advocacy and investigative reporting. Rated PG-13 for language. 96m. DIR: Michael Moore. 1998

BIG PARADE, THE ★★★★ A compelling depiction of World War I, this silent film has long been recognized as King Vidor's masterpiece. As the saying goes, it has everything: romance, humor, love, tragedy, and suspense. B&W; 126m. DIR: King Vidor. CAST: John Gilbert, Renée Adorée, Hobart Bosworth. 1925

BIG PICTURE, THE ★★★★ Christopher Guest and Michael McKean spoof the film industry in this engaging, fun, and sometimes uneven story of a promising young filmmaker who finds himself thoroughly corrupted by the temptations of Hollywood. Guest and McKean hit most of their targets with skilled assistance from Martin Short as a wacked-out agent. Rated PG-13 for brief profanity and brief nudity. 100m. DIR: Christopher Guest. CAST: Kevin Bacon, Michael McKean, Martin Short, Jennifer Jason Leigh. 1989

BIG RED ★★★ This pleasant family film drawn from the beloved children's book of the same title features Walter Pidgeon as the owner of a sleek Irish setter named Big Red, which spends its formative years with young Gilles Payant. 89m. DIR: Norman Tokar. CAST: Walter Pidgeon, Gilles Payant, Emile Genest, Janette Bertrand. 1962 DVD

BIG RED ONE, THE ★★★1/2 This release gave Lee Marvin his best role in years. As a grizzled sergeant leading a platoon of "wetnoses" into the dangers of battle, he's excellent. Based on writer-director Sam Fuller's personal reminiscences of World War II. It's a terrific war movie. Rated PG. 113m. DIR: Samuel Fuller. CAST: Lee Marvin, Mark Hamill, Robert Carradine, Bobby DiCicco. 1980 DVD

BIG RIP-OFF, THE ❤ In the closing days of the Civil War, an outlaw stumbles across a dying Confederate soldier who tells him of hidden gold in the home of his blind father. Unbelievably, the outlaw passes himself off to the blind father as his son. Before he can find the gold, the blind man is killed by a gang of outlaws and our hero(?) goes after the gang. Rated R for violence. 90m. DIR: Francesco Rosi. CAST: Chip Corman, Rosemarie Dexter, Piero Lulli, Dana Ghia, Aldo Berti. 1967

BIG SCORE, THE ★★1/2 Fred Williamson breaks all the rules in going after drug king Joe Spinell. Williamson, the director, doesn't make the story move fast enough. Rated R for violence and profanity. 85m. DIR: Fred Williamson. CAST: Fred Williamson, John Saxon, Richard Roundtree, Nancy Wilson, Ed Lauter, Joe Spinell, Michael Dante. 1983

BIG SHOTS ★★★1/2 A funny and exciting film about kids, but not just for kids. After the death of his father, an 11-year-old boy from the suburbs strikes up a friendship with a young black boy who teaches him the ways of the street. Rated PG-13. 91m. DIR: Robert Mandel. CAST: Ricky Busker, Darius McCrary, Robert Joy, Robert Prosky, Paul Winfield, Jerzy Skolimowski. 1988

BIG SKY, THE ★★ Even the normally reliable director Howard Hawks can't enliven this average tale of early-day fur trappers on an expedition up the Missouri River. Action was Hawks's forte, and there just isn't enough to sustain the viewer's interest. Plenty of beautiful scenery, but that's about it. B&W; 122m. DIR: Howard Hawks. CAST: Kirk Douglas, Arthur Hunnicutt, Dewey Martin. 1952

BIG SLEEP, THE (1946) ★★★★1/2 Raymond Chandler's fans couldn't complain about this moody, atmospheric rendition of Philip Marlowe's most bizarre case. Bogart's gritty interpretation of the tough-talking P.I. is a high point in his glorious career, and sultry Lauren Bacall throws in enough spark to ignite several city blocks. Not rated, contains adult themes and violence. B&W; 114m. DIR: Howard Hawks. CAST: Humphrey Bogart, Lauren Bacall, Martha Vickers, Bob Steele, Elisha Cook Jr., Dorothy Malone. 1946 DVD

BIG SLEEP, THE (1978) ❤ Remake of the classic screen detective yarn. Rated R for violence, profanity, and nudity. 100m. DIR: Michael Winner. CAST: Robert Mitchum, James Stewart, Sarah Miles, Oliver Reed, Candy Clark, Edward Fox. 1978

BIG SLICE, THE ★★ Two writers decide to make their lives exciting. Between phone sex and police raids, the plot expands into one big mess. Rated R for violence and suggested sex. 86m. DIR: John Bradshaw. CAST: Heather Locklear, Casey Siemaszko, Leslie Hope, Justin Louis, Kenneth Welsh, Nicholas Campbell, Henry Ramer. 1990

BIG SOMBRERO, THE ★★1/2 An impoverished Gene Autry comes to the aid of Elena Verdugo and saves her from land swindlers as well as a money-grubbing fiancé in this south-of-the-border tale. This is more of a musical than a horse opera. 77m. DIR: Frank McDonald. CAST: Gene Autry, Elena Verdugo, Stephen Dunne, George J. Lewis, Martin Garralaga, Gene Roth. 1949

BIG SQUEEZE, THE ★★1/2 When she discovers her shiftless husband has secretly collected a $130,000 accident settlement, a barmaid enlists the aid of a con artist to help her get the half to which she feels entitled. Mild caper film in the Last Seduction mold is neither clever nor quirky enough to reach that level. Rated R for nudity, sexual situations, and profanity. 107m. DIR: Marcus De Leon. CAST: Lara Flynn Boyle, Peter Dobson, Danny Nucci. 1995 DVD

BIG STAMPEDE, THE ★★★1/2 In one of John Wayne's best B Westerns for Warner Bros., our hero is a deputy sheriff who goes undercover to bring a corrupt cattle baron to justice. Noah Beery Sr. is in fine form as the bad guy (black hat and all), who builds up his stock by rustling steers and killing anyone who stands in his way. Good action and suspense for the genre, with Wayne (allowed more than one take per scene) more convincing than he would be in the series of low-budget Westerns that followed. B&W; 54m. DIR: Tenny Wright. CAST: John Wayne, Noah Beery Sr., Paul Hurst, Mae Madison, Luis Alberni, Berton Churchill, Lafe McKee. 1932

BIG STEAL, THE ★★★1/2 Four sets of desperate and disparate characters chase each other over bumpy roads in the Southwest and Mexico following a robbery. An intriguing film, somewhat difficult to follow but great fun to watch. B&W; 71m. DIR: Don Siegel. CAST: Robert Mitchum, Jane Greer, William Bendix, Ramon Novarro, Patric Knowles. 1949

BIG STORE, THE ★★ Singer (and nonactor) Tony Martin inherits a department store and calls on the Marx Brothers to save him. The last and weakest of the Marx Brothers' movies for MGM, this misfire is woefully understocked in laughs. Even so, Groucho manages some good bits, often in scenes with his classic foil, Margaret Dumont, and Chico and Harpo team for a delightful piano duet. 103m. DIR: Charles F. Riesner. CAST: The Marx Brothers, Tony Martin, Virginia Grey, Margaret Dumont, Douglass Dumbrille. 1941

BIG STREET, THE ★★1/2 Though somewhat too sentimental at times, this Damon Runyon story of a busboy's (Henry Fonda) sincere devotion to a couldn't-care-less-for-him nightclub singer (Lucille Ball) is often touching and lively. Lucille Ball gives her best big-screen performance and you couldn't ask for a better gangster than Barton MacLane. B&W; 88m. DIR: Irving Reis. CAST: Henry Fonda, Lucille Ball, Hans Conried, Barton MacLane, Agnes Moorehead, Ray Collins, Sam Levene, Louise Beavers. 1942

BIG SWEAT, THE ❤ A born loser finds himself running from the law soon after his prison release. Not rated; contains profanity and violence. 85m. DIR: Ulli Lommel. CAST: Steve Molone, Robert Z'dar. 1990

•BIG TEASE, THE ★★★1/2 A Scottish hairdresser goes to Hollywood to compete in the World Freestyle Hairdressing Championship, only to learn that he's been invited merely to sit in the audience. Undaunted, he sets out to crash the competition, accompanied by a BBC film crew. Cheerful and waspishly funny, this comedy feels almost thrown together; in fact, it's quite well written and carefully crafted by people who are clearly having a wonderful time. Rated R for profanity. 86m. DIR: Kevin Allen. CAST: Craig Ferguson, Frances Fisher, Chris Langham, Mary McCormack, David Rasche, Larry Miller, Charles Napier. 1999

BIG TOP PEE-WEE ★★ Pee-wee Herman plays a country bumpkin whose greatest pleasure in life is his pet hog. The circus comes to town, and Pee-wee invites them to pitch the Big Top on his land. Film contains the longest kiss in screen history. Rated PG for hog and human love rites. 86m. **DIR:** Randal Kleiser. **CAST:** Pee-wee Herman, Kris Kristofferson, Susan Tyrrell, Valeria Golino. **1988**

BIG TOWN, THE ★★ Chicago, circa 1957. A talented small-town boy (Matt Dillon) with a penchant for crapshooting goes off to the big city. But the production loses focus and drive. Rated R for language, nudity, and sex. 110m. **DIR:** Ben Bolt. **CAST:** Matt Dillon, Diane Lane, Tommy Lee Jones, Bruce Dern, Tom Skerritt, Lee Grant, Suzy Amis. **1987**

BIG TRAIL, THE ★★★1/2 John Wayne made his starring debut in this exciting, although somewhat dated epic. Contrary to Hollywood legend, the Duke acquits himself well enough as a revenge-minded scout leading a wagon train across the wilderness. His allegedly stiff acting was long thought to be the reason for the film's box-office failure. In truth, the film was shot in wide-screen 55mm and cinema owners were unwilling to invest in the projection equipment needed to show the film in Fox Grandeur, as it was called. B&W; 110m. **DIR:** Raoul Walsh. **CAST:** John Wayne, Marguerite Churchill, El Brendel, Ian Keith, Tyrone Power Sr. **1930**

BIG TREES, THE ★★1/2 Lumberman Kirk Douglas wants the redwoods on homesteaders' land in this colorful adventure set in northwest California in 1900. A remake of 1938's *Valley of the Giants*. 89m. **DIR:** Felix Feist. **CAST:** Kirk Douglas, Eve Miller, Patrice Wymore, Edgar Buchanan, John Archer, Alan Hale Jr. **1952 DVD**

BIG TROUBLE ★★ *Big Trouble* has its moments, but alas, they are few and far between. Alan Arkin meets up with a rich married woman (Beverly D'Angelo), and the two plot against her husband (Peter Falk). Crazy plot twists abound, but none of them are all that funny. Rated R for profanity and adult subject matter. 93m. **DIR:** John Cassavetes. **CAST:** Peter Falk, Alan Arkin, Beverly D'Angelo, Charles Durning, Robert Stack, Paul Dooley, Valerie Curtin, Richard Libertini. **1985**

BIG TROUBLE IN LITTLE CHINA ★★★1/2 An adventure-fantasy with Kurt Russell as a pig trucker unwittingly swept into a mystical world underneath San Francisco's Chinatown ruled by a sinister 2,000-year-old ghost. The movie is a lighthearted special-effects showcase designed to look a bit silly, in the style of old serials. Rated PG-13. 99m. **DIR:** John Carpenter. **CAST:** Kurt Russell, Kim Cattrall, Dennis Dun, James Hong, Victor Wong, Kate Burton. **1986**

BIG VALLEY, THE (TV SERIES) ★★★ Set in Stockton, California, circa 1878, this is the TV-born saga of the Barkleys, a family of cattle ranchers. Victoria is the iron-willed widow who heads the clan. Jarrod, her oldest son, is a suave attorney. His brother Nick is a rugged cowpoke. Their half brother is Heath, whose illegitimacy has bred a rebellious streak. All three are protective of Audra, their gorgeous, haughty sister. A pair of two-part episodes are available on tape: "Legend of a General" and "Explosion."

Each tape 90m. **DIR:** Virgil Vogel. **CAST:** Barbara Stanwyck, Richard Long, Peter Breck, Lee Majors, Linda Evans. **1965–1969**

BIG WEDNESDAY ★★ Only nostalgic surfers with more than a little patience will enjoy this ode to the beach by writer-director John Milius. Rated PG. 120m. **DIR:** John Milius. **CAST:** Jan-Michael Vincent, Gary Busey, William Katt, Lee Purcell, Patti D'Arbanville. **1978**

BIG WHEEL, THE ★★1/2 Smart-mouthed Mickey Rooney rises from garage mechanic to champion racing-car driver in this well-worn story worn thinner by a poor script and poorer direction. More than 20 of the film's 92 minutes are given over to earsplitting scenes of high-speed racing. B&W; 92m. **DIR:** Edward Ludwig. **CAST:** Mickey Rooney, Thomas Mitchell, Spring Byington, Allen Jenkins, Michael O'Shea. **1949**

BIGAMIST, THE ★★★ Ida Lupino stepped behind the camera to direct several underrated *film noir* excursions in the early Fifties, of which this is among the best. Title character Edmond O'Brien is neurotic, not conventionally villainous. Lupino's only acting role in one of her directing efforts. B&W; 80m. **DIR:** Ida Lupino. **CAST:** Edmond O'Brien, Joan Fontaine, Ida Lupino, Edmund Gwenn, Jane Darwell, Kenneth Tobey. **1953**

BIGFOOT: THE UNFORGETTABLE ENCOUNTER ★★1/2 Attempt at wholesome family entertainment delivers the basics, but does nothing special with them. When a young boy meets the legendary Bigfoot creature, his encounter makes him a media star and the creature the target of some ruthless bounty hunters. Kids will enjoy this outdoor adventure that introduces such life lessons as friendship and courage into the mix. Rated PG for language. 86m. **DIR:** Corey Michael Eubanks. **CAST:** Zachery Ty Bryan, Matt McCoy, Crystal Chappell, Clint Howard, Rance Howard. **1995**

BIGGLES—ADVENTURES IN TIME ★★★★ Delightful fantasy film focuses on the adventures of a New York frozen-food merchandiser, Jim Ferguson (Alex Hyde-White), who discovers he has a time twin—a World War I British fighter ace named Biggles (Neil Dickson). Every time Biggles is in danger, Ferguson finds himself bouncing back through time to come to his twin's rescue. Rated PG for profanity and violence. 100m. **DIR:** John Hough. **CAST:** Neil Dickson, Alex Hyde-White, Peter Cushing, Fiona Hutchison, William Hootkins. **1985**

BIKINI BEACH ★★ This silly film captures Frankie Avalon and Annette Funicello in their best swim attire. A group of kids who always hang out at the beach try to prevent a man from closing it. Ho-hum. 100m. **DIR:** William Asher. **CAST:** Frankie Avalon, Annette Funicello, Keenan Wynn, Don Rickles. **1964**

BIKINI BISTRO 🖤 Videotaped rubbish starring porn queen Marilyn Chambers as herself. Rated R for nudity and profanity. 84m. **DIR:** Ernest G. Sauer. **CAST:** Marilyn Chambers, Amy Lynn Baxter, Isabelle Fortea, Joan Gerardi. **1995 DVD**

BIKINI CARWASH COMPANY, THE 🖤 When naive Midwesterner Joe Dusic agrees to take over his uncle's California car wash, he revives the failing business by employing some of the beach's best babes.

Tedious male fantasy. Two versions available: R-rated for nudity and an unrated version featuring even more of the same. 87m. **DIR:** Ed Hansen. **CAST:** Joe Dusic. 1990

BIKINI CARWASH COMPANY 2 🎬 After being tricked into selling their beloved car-wash chain to a crooked developer, the beautiful entrepreneurs launch a new business: a 24-hour lingerie shopping network. Need we say more? Available in two versions, R-rated and unrated, both with nudity and sexual situations. 94m. **DIR:** Gary Orona. **CAST:** Kristi Ducati, Suzanne Browne, Neriah Napaul, Rikki Brando. 1993

BIKINI ISLAND 🎬 Inane, low-budget T&A flick focuses on five swimsuit models stalked on an exotic location shoot. A number of likely suspects emerge but, of course, are red herrings. Rated R for nudity, violence, and profanity. 90m. **DIR:** Anthony Markes. **CAST:** Holly Floria, Jackson Robinson. 1991

BILITIS ★★★★ A surprisingly tasteful and sensitive soft-core sex film, this details the sexual awakening of the title character, a 16-year-old French girl, while she spends the summer with a family friend. Rated R for nudity and simulated sex. 93m. **DIR:** David Hamilton. **CAST:** Patti D'Arbanville, Bernard Giraudeau, Mathieu Carriere. 1982

BILL ★★★★1/2 Extremely moving drama based on the real-life experiences of Bill Sackter, a retarded adult forced to leave the mental institution that has been his home for the past forty-five years. Mickey Rooney won an Emmy for his excellent portrayal of Bill. Dennis Quaid plays a filmmaker who offers kindness to Bill as he tries to cope with life on the "outside." Not rated. 100m. **DIR:** Anthony Page. **CAST:** Mickey Rooney, Dennis Quaid, Largo Woodruff. 1981

BILL AND TED'S BOGUS JOURNEY ★★★★ This sequel, which finds our heroes traveling through Heaven and Hell rather than through time, is better than its predecessor. The special effects are first rate, and the comedy has moved up a notch. Rated PG. 90m. **DIR:** Peter Hewitt. **CAST:** Keanu Reeves, Alex Winter, Bill Sadler, Joss Ackland, Pam Grier, George Carlin. 1991

BILL AND TED'S EXCELLENT ADVENTURE ★★★ A wild romp through time with two total idiots who must find a way to pass history class. Using a time-traveling telephone booth, these two go through history enlisting the help of famous people such as Napoleon and Socrates. A good, clean, excellent way to waste an hour and a half, dude. Rated PG. 90m. **DIR:** Stephen Herek. **CAST:** Keanu Reeves, Alex Winter, George Carlin. 1989

BILL OF DIVORCEMENT, A ★★★1/2 Melodramatic weeper about a man's return to his family after confinement in a mental hospital rises above the material due to a stunning cast and deft direction by Hollywood master George Cukor. Katharine Hepburn in her first film really carries this somewhat overwrought soap opera. B&W; 70m. **DIR:** George Cukor. **CAST:** John Barrymore, Billie Burke, Katharine Hepburn, David Manners, Bramwell Fletcher, Henry Stephenson, Paul Cavanagh, Elizabeth Patterson. 1932

BILL: ON HIS OWN ★★★1/2 This is the sequel to the 1981 drama *Bill*. Mickey Rooney continues his role as Bill Sackter, a mentally retarded adult forced to live on his own after spending forty-five years in an institution. Helen Hunt costars as the college student who tutors him. It doesn't have quite the emotional impact that *Bill* carried, but it's still good. 104m. **DIR:** Anthony Page. **CAST:** Mickey Rooney, Helen Hunt, Teresa Wright, Dennis Quaid, Largo Woodruff. 1983

BILLBOARD DAD ★★ While not nearly as cloying as their current television series, this direct-to-video comedy starring the Olsen twins will most likely appeal to preteen girls who will have no problem getting past the fact that they've seen this all before. Mary-Kate and Ashley play the daughters of a single father. They take out an advertisement on a local billboard to find a new mom for Dad. Whimsical in a childish sort of way, the film should entertain its target audience. Rated G. 90m. **DIR:** Alan Metter. **CAST:** Mary-Kate Olsen, Ashley Olsen, Carl Banks. 1998

BILLIE ★★1/2 Tomboyish Patty Duke upsets everyone when she joins a boys' track team. Lightweight story with a good turn by Billy DeWolfe as the town mayor. Not rated. 87m. **DIR:** Don Weis. **CAST:** Patty Duke, Jim Backus, Warren Berlinger, Jane Greer, Billy DeWolfe, Dick Sargent, Ted Bessell. 1965

BILLION DOLLAR HOBO, THE ★★ This film has Tim Conway playing his familiar down-and-out bumpkin role, but the rest of the cast is wasted. The slow pace is a further drawback. Rated G for family viewing. 96m. **DIR:** Stuart E. McGowan. **CAST:** Tim Conway, Will Geer. 1978

BILLION FOR BORIS, A 🎬 Boris discovers that his TV set can view the future. He uses this knowledge to win big at the racetrack. Not rated; contains some foul language. 94m. **DIR:** Alex Grasshoff. **CAST:** Tim Kazurinsky, Lee Grant. 1990

BILLIONAIRE BOYS CLUB ★★1/2 Severely edited version of the miniseries starring Judd Nelson as Joe Hunt, a notorious commodities broker-cum-murderer. Nelson conveys Hunt's hypnotic personality and greed, though the production is saddled with unimaginative editing and tinny music. Based on an actual Los Angeles murder case. Made for TV. 94m. **DIR:** Marvin J. Chomsky. **CAST:** Judd Nelson, Ron Silver. 1987

BILLY BATHGATE ★★★★1/2 A compelling gangster movie with superb performances, this work, based by screenwriter Tom Stoppard on the novel by E. L. Doctorow, concerns the odyssey of young Billy Bathgate (Loren Dean) who goes from being a poor street kid in 1935 to a coveted position in the crime organization of crazy, big-time mob Dutch Schultz (Dustin Hoffman). Rated R for violence, nudity, and profanity. 106m. **DIR:** Robert Benton. **CAST:** Dustin Hoffman, Nicole Kidman, Bruce Willis, Steven Hill, Loren Dean, Steve Buscemi, Stanley Tucci. 1991

BILLY BUDD ★★★1/2 Herman Melville's brooding, allegorical novel of the overpowering of the innocent is set against a backdrop of life on an eighteenth-century British warship. The plight of a young sailor subjected to the treacherous whims of his ship's tyrannical first mate is well acted throughout. It is

werful filmmaking and succeeds in leaving its audience unsettled and questioning. B&W; 112m. DIR: Peter Ustinov. CAST: Terence Stamp, Robert Ryan, Peter Ustinov. 1962

BILLY GALVIN ★★★1/2 Surprisingly good slice-of-life drama about steelworkers in Boston. Karl Malden is excellent as Jack Galvin, a hard-bitten steelworker who doesn't want his son, Billy (Lenny Von Dohlen, also excellent), to follow in his footsteps. Rated PG for language. 99m. DIR: John Gray. CAST: Karl Malden, Lenny Von Dohlen, Toni Kalem, Keith Szarabajka, Alan North, Barton Heyman, Joyce Van Patten. 1986

BILLY JACK ★★1/2 This film that seems to suggest that a good kick in the groin will bring "peace and love" was a box-office sensation. The star, Tom Laughlin, produced and directed. Rated PG. 114m. DIR: Tom Laughlin. CAST: Tom Laughlin, Delores Taylor, Clark Howat, Bert Freed, Julie Webb. 1971 DVD

BILLY LIAR ★★★★ Poignant slices of English middle-class life are served expertly in this finely played story of a lazy young man who escapes dulling routine by retreating into fantasy. The eleven minutes Julie Christie is on screen are electric and worth the whole picture. B&W; 96m. DIR: John Schlesinger. CAST: Tom Courtenay, Julie Christie, Finlay Currie, Rachel Griffies, Mona Washbourne. 1963

BILLY MADISON 🎬 Saturday Night Live's Adam Sandler plays a rich nitwit going back to school. The filmmakers (including cowriter Sandler) still need several years of comedy school. Rated PG-13 for mild profanity and cartoon violence. 90m. DIR: Tamra Davis. CAST: Adam Sandler, Bradley Whitford, Josh Mostel, Bridgette Wilson, Darren McGavin. 1995 DVD

BILLY THE KID ★★★1/2 The legendary outlaw is romanticized, but the highlights of his life and death are straight from the history books. Predictable but fascinating, chiefly because the studio used top stars and photographed lush surroundings. Pat Garrett is missing, though. The sheriff who tangles with the kid is completely fictional. 95m. DIR: David Miller. CAST: Robert Taylor, Brian Donlevy, Chill Wills, Ethel Barrymore, Mary Howard, Gene Lockhart, Ian Hunter, Guinn Williams. 1941

BILLY THE KID MEETS THE VAMPIRES 🎬 Billy the kid takes a vacation and meets up with some of the busiest actors and actresses this side of Mars. Not rated. 118m. DIR: Steve Postal. CAST: Michael K. Saunders, Debra Orth, Angela Shepard. 1991

BILLY THE KID RETURNS ★★1/2 Roy Rogers plays look-alike to the dead Billy the Kid and restores the tranquility of Lincoln County after subduing the criminal element. Fun for fans. B&W; 58m. DIR: Joseph Kane. CAST: Roy Rogers, Smiley Burnette, Lynne Roberts (Mary Hart), Morgan Wallace, Fred Kohler Sr., Trigger. 1938 DVD

BILLY THE KID VS. DRACULA 🎬 Hokey horror film casts John Carradine as the famous vampire, on the loose in a small western town. 95m. DIR: William Beaudine. CAST: John Carradine, Chuck Courtney, Melinda Plowman, Virginia Christine, Harry Carey Jr. 1966

BILLY ZE KICK ★★1/2 Uneven comedy-mystery about a bumbling cop who discovers that the ficti-

tious tales he's been delivering to his daughter about a serial killer are beginning to spread throughout his own neighborhood as a reality. Stupid cartoon-like characters quickly become annoying and redundant. In French with English subtitles. Rated R for violence. 87m. DIR: Gérard Mordillat. CAST: Francis Perrin. 1985

BILLY'S HOLLYWOOD SCREEN KISS ★★★ A gay photographer obsesses over one of his models, a handsome young waiter who hasn't yet decided whether he likes girls or boys. Garnished with coy injokes, flamboyant drag queens, and campy fantasy sequences, the film is really an updated version of the soulful, soft-focus date movies of the 1960s and 1970s. Rated R for profanity and mature themes. 92m. DIR: Tommy O'Haver. CAST: Sean P. Hayes, Brad Rowe, Richard Ganoung, Meredith Scott Lynn, Paul Bartel, Holly Woodlawn. 1998 DVD

BILOXI BLUES ★★★★ As second in Neil Simon's loosely autobiographical trilogy (after Brighton Beach Memoirs), this witty glimpse of growing up in a Deep South World War II boot camp stars Matthew Broderick. When not clashing with the sly drill sergeant or learning about the birds and bees from an amused wartime prostitute, Broderick makes perceptive comments about life, the war, and his army buddies. Rated PG-13 for language and sexual themes. 106m. DIR: Mike Nichols. CAST: Matthew Broderick, Christopher Walken, Matt Mulhern, Casey Siemaszko. 1988

BIMBO MOVIE BASH 🎬 Directors David Parker and Mike Mendez string together a series of cheap exploitation films in order to come up with a silly plot about female aliens invading Earth. Totally worthless. Rated R for adult situations, language, nudity, and violence. 90m. DIR: David Parker, Mike Mendez. CAST: Adrienne Barbeau, Shannon Tweed, Morgan Fairchild, Julie Strain, Linnea Quigley. 1996

BIMBOS B.C. 🎬 Bimbo barbarians head to Armageddon City to find an antidote that will save their queen in this dopey film directed with a bimbo mentality. Not rated; contains violence and nudity. 75m. DIR: Todd Sheets. CAST: Gina Rydeen, Veronica Orr, Jenny Admire. 1992

BINGO 🎬 This mishmash attempt at comedy follows a dog who chases his master cross-country. The cute dog of the title can't save this film from the fleas. Rated PG for brief violence and brief profanity. 87m. DIR: Matthew Robbins. CAST: Cindy Williams, David Rasche. 1991

BINGO LONG TRAVELING ALL-STARS AND MOTOR KINGS, THE ★★★ This is a comedy-adventure of a barnstorming group of black baseball players as they tour rural America in the late 1930s. Billy Dee Williams, Richard Pryor, and James Earl Jones are three of the team's players. Only the lack of a cohesive script keeps this from receiving more stars. Rated PG. 110m. DIR: John Badham. CAST: Billy Dee Williams, James Earl Jones, Richard Pryor, Ted Ross. 1976

BIO-DOME 🎬 Two idiots (Pauly Shore, Stephen Baldwin) mistake a sealed-environment scientific experiment for a shopping mall. Cheap, stupid, and unfunny; Shore can't keep from laughing at his own antics, but you'll have no such trouble. Rated PG-13 for mild profanity. 95m. DIR: Jason Bloom. CAST: Pauly Shore, Stephen Baldwin, William Atherton, Henry Gibson, Taylor Negron, Patty Hearst. 1995

BIOHAZARD 💔 Aliens are contacted by a beautiful psychic in this low-budget *Alien* rip-off. Rated R for violence. 84m. DIR: Fred Olen Ray. CAST: Angelique Pettyjohn, Aldo Ray. 1984

BIOHAZARD: THE ALIEN FORCE ★★ Another cheesy *Alien* rip-off with slimy beasts from space bursting out of human chests. Not bad if you don't mind ultra-low-budget schlock. Rated R for violence. 88m. DIR: Steve Latshaw. CAST: Steve Zurk, Susan Fronsoe, Tom Ferguson, Patrick Moran, Katheryn Culliver, Chris Mitchum. 1994

BIONIC WOMAN, THE ★★ What we have here is the female equivalent of TV's *The Six Million Dollar Man*. Lindsay Wagner is the superwoman who annihilates the bad guys. 96m. DIR: Richard Moder. CAST: Lindsay Wagner, Lee Majors, Richard Anderson. 1975

BIRCH INTERVAL, THE ★★★ Engaging, poignant 11-year-old Susan McClung learns lessons of life and love while living with relatives in Amish Pennsylvania. An excellent cast makes this sadly neglected film a memorable viewing experience. 104m. DIR: Delbert Mann. CAST: Eddie Albert, Rip Torn, Susan McClung, Ann Wedgeworth, Anne Revere. 1976

BIRCH WOOD ★★★★ A tubercular young pianist goes to rest at the forest home of his brother. The brother cannot accept the recent death of his wife, but the pianist sees his impending death as a natural part of life. A moving story, beautifully photographed in rural Poland. In Polish with English subtitles. 99m. DIR: Andrzej Wajda. CAST: Daniel Olbrychski. 1970

BIRD ★★★★1/2 Clint Eastwood's *Bird* soars with a majesty all its own. About the life of legendary saxophonist Charlie "Bird" Parker, it is the ultimate jazz movie. It features Parker's inspired improvised solos in abundance, while telling the story of the brilliant but troubled and drug-addicted artist. Parker is solidly played by Forest Whitaker. Rated R for profanity and drug use. 140m. DIR: Clint Eastwood. CAST: Forest Whitaker, Diane Venora, Samuel E. Wright, Keith David. 1988

BIRD MAN OF ALCATRAZ ★★★★ In one of his best screen performances, Burt Lancaster plays Robert Stroud, the prisoner who became a world-renowned authority on birds. B&W; 143m. DIR: John Frankenheimer. CAST: Burt Lancaster, Karl Malden, Thelma Ritter, Telly Savalas. 1962

BIRD OF PARADISE ★★1/2 Even the reliable Joel McCrea can't save this bit of South Sea island silliness. The seafaring McCrea attempts to woo native princess Dolores Del Rio. This kind of thing looks awfully dumb today. B&W; 80m. DIR: King Vidor. CAST: Joel McCrea, Dolores Del Rio, John Halliday, Skeets Gallagher, Lon Chaney Jr. 1932 DVD

BIRD OF PREY 💔 A good cast embarrasses itself in this awful drama about a freedom fighter out to avenge the death of his father in postcommunist Bulgaria. Rated R for sexual situations, violence, and profanity. 101m. DIR: Temistocles Lopez. CAST: Boyan Milushev, Jennifer Tilly, Richard Chamberlain, Lenny

von Dohlen, Robert Carradine, Lesley Ann Warren. 1995

BIRD ON A WIRE ★★1/2 Formulaic action-comed casts Goldie Hawn as a hotshot corporate lawyer an Mel Gibson as a mystery man from her past. promising plot is eschewed in favor of madcap cha es. Rated PG-13 for profanity, violence, and nudit 106m. DIR: John Badham. CAST: Mel Gibson, Gold Hawn, David Carradine, Bill Duke, Joan Severanc 1990 DVD

BIRD WITH THE CRYSTAL PLUMAGE, THE ★★ Stylish thriller weaves a complex adventure of a American writer who witnesses a murder and drawn into the web of mystery and violence. Min cult favorite, well photographed and nicely acted t resilient Tony Musante and fashion plate Su Kendall. Rated PG. 98m. DIR: Dario Argento. CAS Tony Musante, Suzy Kendall, Eva Renzi, Enrico Mar Salerno. 1969 DVD

BIRDCAGE, THE ★★★1/2 American version of *L Cage aux Folles* lacks some of the poignance and h larity of the original; however, this remake has number of high points, particularly in the perfo mances of Robin Williams, Nathan Lane, and Ger Hackman. Williams and Lane are a gay couple wh must "go straight" to fool Hackman, a conservativ politician whose daughter is engaged to Williams son. Rated R for profanity and adult content. 118n DIR: Mike Nichols. CAST: Robin Williams, Gene Hack man, Nathan Lane, Dianne Wiest, Christine Baransk Hank Azaria, Dan Futterman, Calista Flockhart. 199 DVD

BIRDS, THE ★★★★ Alfred Hitchcock's *The Bird* is an eerie, disturbing stunner, highlighted by Eva Hunter's literate adaptation of Daphne du Maurier ominous short story. Rod Taylor and Tippi Hedre are thrown into an uneasy relationship while ou avian friends develop an appetite for somethin more substantial than bugs and berries. Hitchcock unswerving attention to character lends credibilit to the premise. Not rated, but may be too intense fc younger viewers. 120m. DIR: Alfred Hitchcock. CAS Rod Taylor, Tippi Hedren, Jessica Tandy, Suzann Pleshette, Veronica Cartwright, Ethel Griffies. 196 DVD

BIRDS II, THE: LAND'S END 💔 This idiotic seque to Hitchcock's classic is a complete mess, with inan plotting, overwrought acting, and a climax that feel like the camera just ran out of film. Director Ric Rosenthal was disgusted enough to hide behind th alias Alan Smithee. Rated R for violence and profani ty. 87m. DIR: Rick Rosenthal. CAST: Brad Johnsor Chelsea Field, James Naughton, Jan Rubes, Tippi He dren. 1994

BIRDS AND THE BEES, THE ★★ This poor remak of the 1941 Barbara Stanwyck–Henry Fonda comed hit, *The Lady Eve*, has military cardsharper Davi Niven setting daughter Mitzi Gaynor on playboy mil lionaire George Gobel in hopes of getting rich from the marriage. "Lonesome George" wiggles free, bu falls for her anyway. Don't settle for imitations. Insis on the original. 94m. DIR: Norman Taurog. CAST George Gobel, Mitzi Gaynor, David Niven. 1956

RDS OF PREY ★★★ Ex–World War II fighter lot turned peacetime Salt Lake City traffic helipter jockey (David Janssen) hears the siren song of war anew when he witnesses a bank heist in rogress and chases the robbers, who make their taway in their own 'copter. An aerial battle of wits llows. Terrific flying sequences. 81m. **DIR:** William Graham. **CAST:** David Janssen, Ralph Meeker, ayne Heilveil. 1973

RDY ★★★1/2 Matthew Modine and Nicolas age give unforgettable performances in this dark, sturbing, yet somehow uplifting study of an odd oung man named Birdy (Modine) from South iladelphia who wants to be a bird. That way he can away from all his troubles—which worsen manid after a traumatic tour of duty in Vietnam. Rated for violence, nudity, and profanity. 120m. **DIR:** Alan rker. **CAST:** Matthew Modine, Nicolas Cage, John rkins, Sandy Baron, Karen Young, Bruno Kirby. 1985 VD

RGIT HAAS MUST BE KILLED ★★★★ It is rd to imagine a more perfect film than this spell-ding, French thriller-drama. Though its plot reves around the assassination of a German terror- (Birgit Haas) by a French counterspy organizaon, this film says as much about human lationships as it does espionage. In French with nglish subtitles. Not rated; the film contains welldled violence and nudity. 105m. **DIR:** Laurent ynemann. **CAST:** Philippe Noiret, Jean Rochefort, sa Kreuzer. 1981

RTH OF A NATION, THE ★★★★ Videotape will obably be the only medium in which you will ever e this landmark silent classic. D. W. Griffith's epic ga of the American Civil War and its aftermath is day considered too racist in its glorification of the l Klux Klan ever to be touched by television or real theaters. This is filmdom's most important lestone (the first to tell a cohesive story) but uld only be seen by those emotionally prepared its disturbing point of view. B&W; 158m. **DIR:** D. Griffith. **CAST:** Lillian Gish, Mae Marsh, Henry B. althall, Miriam Cooper. 1915 DVD

RTH OF THE BLUES ★★★1/2 Although highly ctionalized, this Bing Crosby musical has the feel of ew Orleans and the unmistakable beat of the bands om New Orleans's jazz age. B&W; 85m. **DIR:** Victor hertzinger. **CAST:** Bing Crosby, Mary Martin, Brian onlevy, Eddie "Rochester" Anderson. 1941

RTHDAY BOY, THE ★★ A Cinemax Comedy Ex-riment that proves once again how difficult it is to oduce an even moderately funny film. James elushi (who also wrote the script) is a sporting-ods salesman who journeys cross-country on his rthday in an attempt to sell his old gym coach a ad of basketballs. Not rated; contains adult lan-age. 30m. **DIR:** Claude Conrad. **CAST:** James elushi, Michelle Riga, Dennis Farina, Ron Dean, Jim hnson, Ed Blatchford, Fred Kaz. 1986

SHOP'S WIFE, THE ★★★ Harmless story of an bonair angel (Cary Grant) sent to Earth to aid a shop (David Niven) in his quest for a new church. e kind of film they just don't make anymore. No ting, but okay for the whole family. B&W; 108m.

DIR: Henry Koster. **CAST:** Cary Grant, Loretta Young, David Niven, James Gleason. 1947 DVD

BITCH, THE ♥ Joan Collins has the title role in this fiasco, an adaptation of sister Jackie Collins's book. Rated R. 93m. **DIR:** Gerry O'Hara. **CAST:** Joan Collins, Kenneth Haigh, Michael Coby. 1979

BITE THE BULLET ★★★★1/2 A six-hundred-mile horse race is the subject of this magnificent adventure, an epic in every sense of the word. A real sleeper, hardly noticed during its theatrical release. Rated PG. 131m. **DIR:** Richard Brooks. **CAST:** Gene Hackman, James Coburn, Candice Bergen, Ben Johnson, Jan-Michael Vincent, Dabney Coleman, Ian Bannen. 1975

BITTER HARVEST (1981) ★★★★ In this made-for-television film based on a true incident, Ron Howard gives an excellent performance as an at-first panicky and then take-charge farmer whose dairy farm herd becomes sick and begins dying. His battle to find out the cause of the illness (chemicals in the feed), provides for scary, close-to-home drama. Good supporting cast. 104m. **DIR:** Roger Young. **CAST:** Ron Howard, Art Carney, Richard Dysart. 1981

BITTER HARVEST (1993) ★★ Strange tale about a farm boy (Stephen Baldwin) corrupted by two beautiful strangers (Patsy Kensit and Jennifer Rubin). Baldwin is good, but excessive subplots lessen the film's impact. Rated R for nudity, sex, violence, and profanity. 98m. **DIR:** Duane Clark. **CAST:** Stephen Baldwin, Patsy Kensit, Jennifer Rubin, Adam Baldwin, M. Emmet Walsh. 1993

BITTER MOON ★★ Roman Polanski again assaults audience sensibilities with this lurid psychodrama about self-destructive obsession and sexual terrorism. On a Mediterranean cruise, an unsuccessful American novelist in a wheelchair shocks and seduces a starchy Englishman with perverse details of his relationship with his French wife. This ludicrous portrait is visually seductive but not as darkly funny as intended. Rated R for simulated sex and language. 139m. **DIR:** Roman Polanski. **CAST:** Peter Coyote, Hugh Grant, Emmanuelle Seigner, Kristin Scott Thomas. 1994

BITTER RICE ★★★ A steamy temperature-raiser in its day, this Italian neorealist drama of exploited rice workers—spiced up with some sex scenes—is tame and obvious today. Well directed, though, and as a curio, worth a look. B&W; 108m. **DIR:** Giuseppe De Santis. **CAST:** Silvana Mangano, Vittorio Gassman, Raf Vallone, Doris Dowling. 1948

BITTER SUGAR ★★★ An idealistic young Cuban Communist learns that real life is quite different from the political theory on which he has been raised. Director Leon Ichaso uses trendy black-and-white photography and New Wave techniques to polish what is essentially anti-Castro propaganda. Not rated; contains sexual situations. In Spanish with English subtitles. B&W; 104m. **DIR:** Leon Ichaso. **CAST:** Rene Lavan, Mayte Vilan, Miguel Gutierrez. 1997

BITTER SWEET ★★★ Redeemed only by the lilting songs of Noel Coward, this tragic story of a violinist's romance with a dancer was the MacDonald-Eddy team's first financial failure, and it augered the end of their long reign. 92m. **DIR:** W. S. Van Dyke. **CAST:**

Jeanette MacDonald, Nelson Eddy, George Sanders, Herman Bing, Felix Bressart, Ian Hunter, Sig Ruman, Veda Ann Borg. **1940**

BITTER TEA OF GENERAL YEN, THE ★★★★ An American joins her missionary fiancé in China and finds herself drawn to a Chinese warlord who takes her prisoner. When released this movie was panned by reviewers upset by the interracial theme. A historical note: This film was chosen to open New York's Radio City Music Hall. B&W; 89m. **DIR:** Frank Capra. **CAST:** Barbara Stanwyck, Nils Asther, Gavin Gordon, Lucien Littlefield, Toshia Mori, Richard Loo, Walter Connolly. **1933**

BITTER TEARS OF PETRA VON KANT, THE ★★★ A lesbian fashion designer falls in love with another woman and is met with betrayal when her lover has an affair with an American serviceman. Overlong drama gets a lift from solid performances and great cinematography by Michael Ballhaus, (*Raging Bull, The Last Temptation of Christ*). In German with English subtitles. Not rated; contains nudity and profanity. 124m. **DIR:** Rainer Werner Fassbinder. **CAST:** Margit Carstensen, Hanna Schygulla. **1972**

BITTER VENGEANCE ★★1/2 A husband sets his wife up to look like his killer in this made-for-cable original. Weak story and sappy characters. Not rated; contains nudity, violence, and suggested sex. 90m. **DIR:** Stuart Cooper. **CAST:** Virginia Madsen, Bruce Greenwood, Kristen Hocking, Eddie Velez, Gordon Jump. **1994**

BITTERSWEET LOVE ♥ Young married couple discover that they are a half brother and sister. Rated PG. 92m. **DIR:** David Miller. **CAST:** Lana Turner, Robert Lansing, Celeste Holm, Robert Alda, Meredith Baxter-Birney. **1976**

BIZARRE, BIZARRE ★★★1/2 Frenetic farce set in Victorian England at the home of a writer of mystery novels. In French with English subtitles. 90m. **DIR:** Marcel Carné. **CAST:** Louis Jouvet, Françoise Rosay, Michel Simon, Jean-Pierre Aumont. **1937**

BIZET'S CARMEN ★★★★★ Julia Migenes-Johnson and Placido Domingo excel in this film adaptation of the opera by Georges Bizet. It is about a gypsy whose fierce independence maddens the men who become obsessed with her. In French with English subtitles. Rated PG for mild violence. 152m. **DIR:** Francesco Rosi. **CAST:** Placido Domingo, Julia Migenes-Johnson. **1985 DVD**

BLACK ADDER III (TV SERIES) ★★★★ Third in a trilogy of the *Black Adder* series, this is one of the most wicked, delightfully sardonic send-ups of British costume drama ever made. Rat-faced Rowan Atkinson is a sly former aristocrat and butler to the Prince of Wales, son of mad King George III. He's kept perpetually on his toes by the unpredictable idiocy of his twit of a prince, played with exquisite vacuousness by Hugh Laurie. Each tape 60m. **DIR:** Mandie Fletcher. **CAST:** Rowan Atkinson, Hugh Laurie. **1989**

•BLACK & WHITE (1998) ★★★ Thriller about a cop suspected of being a serial killer manages to entertain while never really growing out of its B-movie genre. Rated R for violence, nudity, sexual situations, and profanity. 97m. **DIR:** Yuri Zeltser. **CAST:**

Gina Gershon, Ron Silver, Alison Eastwood, Bari Primus. **1998**

•BLACK AND WHITE (2000) ★★ Race, class, an sexual boundaries blur in this voyeuristic tour modern Manhattan in which privileged white kic reinvent themselves as gangstas, and African Amer can thugs morph into recording artists. The film al ternates between improvised and structured scene as a documentary filmmaker, her bisexual husban and a rogue cop stir up trouble in a wannabe hip-hc version of *Nashville*. Rated R for language, drug us nudity, sex, and violence. 100m. **DIR:** James Tobac **CAST:** Alan Houston, Ben Stiller, Robert Downey Ji Brooke Shields, Mike Tyson, Claudia Schiffer, Oli "Power" Grant, Method Man, Elijah Wood, Bijc Phillips. **2000**

BLACK AND WHITE IN COLOR ★★★★ A group self-satisfied Frenchmen at a remote African traditi post become stung by patriotism at the outbreak World War I, and they organize a surprise assault on nearby German fort. This sleeper won an Oscar fc best foreign film. In French with English subtitle Not rated; contains nudity, profanity, and violenc 90m. **DIR:** Jean-Jacques Annaud. **CAST:** Jean Carme Jacques Dufilho, Catherine Rouvel, Jacques Spiesse Dora Doll. **1977**

BLACK ARROW, THE (1948) ★★★1/2 Hero Lou Hayward is in fine form as he fights the evil Georg Macready in this highly enjoyable entry into th swashbuckler genre. Some fine action scenes, with slam-bang finale. B&W; 76m. **DIR:** Gordon Dougla **CAST:** Louis Hayward, George Macready, Janet Bla Edgar Buchanan. **1948**

BLACK ARROW (1984) ★★★1/2 In this enjoyabl Disney adventure film, Sir Daniel Brackley (Olive Reed), a corrupt and wealthy landowner, is robbe by the Black Arrow, an outlaw. He then conceives o plan to marry his ward, Joanna (Georgia Slowe), an send his nephew (Benedict Taylor) to his death. Th tide turns when his nephew and the Black Arro combine forces to rescue Joanna. 93m. **DIR:** Joh Hough. **CAST:** Oliver Reed, Georgia Slowe, Benedic Taylor, Fernando Rey, Donald Pleasence. **1984**

BLACK BEAUTY (1946) ★★★ Based on Ann Sewell's novel that is about a little girl's determine effort to find her missing black colt. Though pedes trian at times, the treatment is still effective enoug to hold interest and bring a tear or two. B&W; 74n **DIR:** Max Nosseck. **CAST:** Mona Freeman, Richar Denning, Evelyn Ankers, J. M. Kerrigan, Terry Kilburr **1946**

BLACK BEAUTY (1971) ★★ One of the world most-loved children's books, *Black Beauty* has neve been translated adequately to the screen. This ve sion is passable at best. Kids who've read the boo may want to see the movie, though this movie won make anyone want to read the book. Grea Britain/Germany/Spain. 106m. **DIR:** James Hil **CAST:** Mark Lester, Walter Slezak, Patrick Mower. **197**

BLACK BEAUTY (1994) ★★★★ The Humane Soc ety should use this fine film to counter cruelty t horses. Told from the horse's point of view, every i justice is magnified tenfold. Anna Sewell would hav been proud of Caroline Thompson's sensitive scree aptation of her timeless novel. The horse carries e show, only utilizing humans to move the plot ong. Rated G for family viewing. 88m. DIR: Caroline ompson. CAST: Sean Bean, Andrew Knott, David ewlis. 1994 DVD

ACK BELT JONES ★★★ A likable kung fu action m about a self-defense school in Watts combating a lafioso"-type group. Not a classic film, but an easy ace and good humor make this a fun action movie. ated PG for violence. 87m. DIR: Robert Clouse. AST: Jim Kelly, Scatman Crothers, Gloria Hendry. 974

ACK BIRD, THE ★★★ Surprisingly enjoyable medy produced by and starring George Segal as am Spade Jr. The visual gags abound, and an air of thenticity is added by the performances of 1940s tective film regulars Lionel Stander, Elisha Cook, d Lee Patrick. The latter two costarred with mphrey Bogart in *The Maltese Falcon*, on which e film is based. It's funny, with a strong perfor-ance from Segal. Rated PG. 98m. DIR: David Giler. AST: George Segal, Stéphane Audran, Lionel Stander, e Patrick. 1975

ACK CAESAR ★★ In this passable gangster flick, ed Williamson stars as Tommy Gibbs, bloodthirsty, n-wielding Godfather of Harlem. The soundtrack the Godfather of Soul, James Brown, doesn't hurt. ated R. 92m. DIR: Larry Cohen. CAST: Fred illiamson, Art Lund, Val Avery, Julius W. Harris, illiam Wellman Jr., D'Urville Martin, Gloria Hendry. 73

ACK CAMEL, THE ★★1/2 Chan investigates mur-r on the set of a movie being shot in Hawaii. Be-use it takes place on his home turf, this early entry the series includes scenes of the wily detective at me with his ten (!) kids. B&W; 71m. DIR: Hamilton acFadden. CAST: Warner Oland, Sally Eilers, Bela Lu-si, Dwight Frye. 1931

ACK CASTLE, THE ★★★ Lightweight costume ama with gothic overtones benefits from typically rong performances by horror veterans Boris arloff and Lon Chaney Jr. in supporting roles. The lk of the story revolves around the efforts of an nglish adventurer to wrest a beautiful woman from e evil clutches of her murderous husband. B&W; m. DIR: Nathan Juran. CAST: Richard Greene, Boris arloff, Stephen McNally, Paula Corday, Lon Chaney , John Hoyt, Michael Pate. 1952

ACK CAT, THE (1934) ★★★★ A surrealistic, rikingly designed horror-thriller that has become a lt favorite thanks to its pairing of Boris Karloff and ela Lugosi. Lugosi has one of his very few good-guy les as a concerned citizen who gets drawn into a eb of evil that surrounds Karloff's black magic. vailable on a videocassette double feature with *The aven*. B&W; 70m. DIR: Edgar G. Ulmer. CAST: Boris arloff, Bela Lugosi, Jacqueline Wells. 1934

ACK CAT, THE (1981) ★★ Feline gore from Lu-o Fulci, made when he was the most prolific of the w-budget Italian exploitation-horror directors. A ry loose Poe adaptation. Rated R for violence. 92m. R: Lucio Fulci. CAST: Patrick Magee, Mimsy Farmer, avid Warbeck. 1981

•**BLACK CAT RUN** ★★ The chase is on for Patrick Muldoon, who plays a gas station attendant suspect-ed of murder and on the run. Can he rescue his kid-napped girlfriend from escaped convicts before the law catches up with him? Rated R for language and violence. 90m. DIR: D. J. Caruso. CAST: Patrick Mul-doon, Amelia Heinle, Jake Busey, Peter Greene. 1998 DVD

BLACK CAULDRON, THE ★★★ At the time, this was the most expensive animated film ever made and, for Disney, its first real failure in that field—largely due to the fact that the writers jammed all five of the *Chronicles of Prydain* into one film. Par-ents may also want to steer younger kids clear since the Horned King and his zombies seem more suited to *Lord of the Rings* than to family fare. Still, the ani-mation is dazzling. Rated PG for scary scenes and mild violence. 80m. DIR: Ted Berman, Richard Rich. 1985

BLACK CHRISTMAS ★★★ During the holiday sea-son, members of a sorority house fall victim to the homicidal obscene phone-caller living in their attic. Margot Kidder is quite convincing as a vulgar, alco-holic college kid with asthma. Atmospheric and frightening. Try to remember that it came before *Halloween* and *When A Stranger Calls*. Rated R. 99m. DIR: Bob Clark. CAST: Olivia Hussey, Keir Dullea, Margot Kidder, John Saxon. 1975

•**BLACK CIRCLE BOYS** ★★ The writers leave no cliché unturned in this lifeless thriller of a good boy who falls in with a bad crowd. Scott Bairstow stands out as the good kid who is drawn to the wrong side of the tracks, but all of his goodwill is wasted when the film becomes unexpectedly cruel. Rated R for adult situations, language, and violence. 101m. DIR: Mat-thew Carnahan. CAST: Scott Bairstow, Eric Mabius, Tara Subkoff, Donnie Wahlberg. 1997 DVD

BLACK COBRA 3 ❤ The CIA has been sending mili-tary aid to insurgent forces in a Third World country ripped by war. Rated R for violence. 89m. DIR: Dan Edwards. CAST: Fred Williamson, Forry Smith, Debra Ward. 1990

BLACK DAY BLUE NIGHT ★★1/2 Atmospheric stab at *film noir* stars Michelle Forbes and Mia Sara as two women on the run from life, whose encounter with a handsome stranger in the middle of the Ari-zona desert changes their lives forever. Rated R for nudity, profanity, violence, and adult situations. 99m. DIR: J. S. Cardone. CAST: Gil Bellows, Michelle Forbes, Mia Sara, J. T. Walsh. 1995

BLACK DEVIL DOLL FROM HELL ★★ Direct-to-video melodrama in which a miniature voodoo doll goes on a gruesome rampage. Most of the time, slug-gish and predictable. Not rated. 70m. DIR: Chester T. Turner. CAST: Rickey Roach. 1984

BLACK DOG ★★ Trucker, parolee, and stalwart family man Jack Crews has served time for vehicular manslaughter and now feels forced to drive a semi loaded with suspect cargo from Georgia to New Jer-sey to save his home from foreclosure. Road carnage piles up at a furious clip as the story's moral implica-tions grind in all gears. Rated PG-13 for language and violence. 88m. DIR: Kevin Hooks. CAST: Patrick Swayze, Randy Travis, Meat Loaf, Gabriel Casseus, Brian Vincent, Brenda Strong, Charles Dutton, Stephen Tobolowsky. **1998 DVD**

BLACK DRAGONS 🖤 A silly film about Japanese agents who are surgically altered to resemble American businessmen and chiefs of industry. B&W; 62m. **DIR:** William Nigh. **CAST:** Bela Lugosi, Joan Barclay, Clayton Moore. **1949**

BLACK EAGLE ★★1/2 A decent martial arts flick about a CIA agent (Sho Kosugi) sent to recover a top-secret laser-tracking device from a U.S. fighter downed in the Mediterranean. The KGB has also sent a man (Jean-Claude Van Damme), and the two agents do the international tango. Rated R for violence. 93m. **DIR:** Eric Karson. **CAST:** Sho Kosugi, Jean-Claude Van Damme, Vladimir Skomarovsky, Doran Clark. **1988 DVD**

BLACK FOX ★★ The first installment of the *Black Fox* trilogy. Christopher Reeve and the slave he freed, Tony Todd, are Texan pioneers in 1861 who consider themselves to be blood brothers. American Indians come across as rather savage, and Reeve is especially wooden. However, both the interracial friendship and Todd's performance are refreshing. Not rated; contains violence. 92m. **DIR:** Steven H. Stern. **CAST:** Christopher Reeve, Tony Todd, Raul Trujillo. **1993**

BLACK FRIDAY ★★★1/2 College professor Stanley Ridges is mortally wounded when he is caught in a gun battle between rival gangsters. To save his life, surgeon Boris Karloff transplants the brain of one of the wounded gangsters into Ridges's body, thus setting in motion a tragic chain of events. Karloff and Bela Lugosi are superb, but this is Ridges's showcase all the way. B&W; 70m. **DIR:** Arthur Lubin. **CAST:** Boris Karloff, Bela Lugosi, Stanley Ridges, Anne Nagel, Anne Gwynne, Paul Fix. **1940**

BLACK FURY ★★★★ Paul Muni is excellent as Joe Radek, an apolitical eastern European immigrant coal miner who unwittingly falls into the middle of a labor dispute. The acting is good, but the film doesn't reach its happy ending in a logical manner, so things just seem to fall into place without any reason. B&W; 95m. **DIR:** Michael Curtiz. **CAST:** Paul Muni, Karen Morley, William Gargan, Barton MacLane. **1935**

BLACK GESTAPO, THE 🖤 Violent blaxploitation movie set in the Watts section of L.A. during 1965, when it was the location of rioting. Rated R. 88m. **DIR:** Lee Frost. **CAST:** Rod Perry, Charles P. Robinson, Phil Hoover. **1975**

BLACK GOD (WHITE DEVIL) ★★ Uneventful tale set in the impoverished northern Brazil, about a poor peasant who changes from a fanatical preacher into an honorable bandit. Poor film-to-video transfer and hard-to-read subtitles. In Portuguese with English subtitles. Not rated; contains violence. 102m. **DIR:** Glauber Rocha. **CAST:** Yona Magalhaeds. **1964**

BLACK GODFATHER, THE ★★★ Public spirited black gangsters take time out from their more nefarious activities to keep the Mafia from selling heroin in their neighborhood. Unpretentious exploitation drama with plenty of action. Rated R for sexual situations and violence. 96m. **DIR:** John Evans. **CAST:** Rod Perry. **1974**

BLACK HAND, THE ★★ Gene Kelly offers a fine dramatic performance as a young man who must aveng- the murder of his father. He becomes embroiled i- the machinations of the Black Hand, (a.k.a. th- Mafia) at the turn of the century. 93m. **DIR:** Richar- Thorpe. **CAST:** Gene Kelly, J. Carrol Naish, Teresa Cel- **1950**

BLACK HOLE, THE 🖤 Space movie clichés. Rate- PG. 97m. **DIR:** Gary Nelson. **CAST:** Maximilian Sche- Anthony Perkins, Robert Forster, Joseph Bottom- Yvette Mimieux, Ernest Borgnine. **1979 DVD**

BLACK ICE ★★ When mystery woman Joanna Pac- la drops by for her usual rendezvous with a marrie- politician, things get out of hand and he dies. Lo- impact thriller. Rated R for nudity, violence, and la- guage. Unrated version contains more of the sam- 90m. **DIR:** Neill L. Fearnley. **CAST:** Michael Ironsid- Michael Nouri, Joanna Pacula. **1992**

BLACK JACK ★★★ George Sanders is soldier of fo- tune Michael Alexander who has a drug-smugglin- scheme in Tangiers aboard his yacht, the *Blac- Jack*. Despite the initial feeling that this is a date- film, the twists in plot will hold viewers' attention- B&W; 103m. **DIR:** Julien Duvivier. **CAST:** Georg- Sanders, Herbert Marshall, Agnes Moorehead, Patric- Roc, Marcel Dalio. **1949**

BLACK KLANSMAN, THE 🖤 This exploitative melo- drama follows the efforts of a light-skinned blac- musician to avenge the death of his daughter, kille- when the Ku Klux Klan bombed a church. Not rate- but includes violence and sexual situations. B&W- 88m. **DIR:** Ted V. Mikels. **CAST:** Richard Gilden, Rim- Kutner. **1966**

•**BLACK LEGION** ★★★1/2 Factory worker joins- terrorist group after losing a promotion to a foreign- er. Grim study of bigotry and hatred based on head- lines of the day was Humphrey Bogart's first sol- starring role, and both he and the film received crit- cal acclaim. Good example of the social conscious- ness that pervaded Warner Bros. films and set ther- apart from other studios during the 1930s. B&W- 83m. **DIR:** Archie Mayo. **CAST:** Humphrey Bogart, Eri- O'Brien-Moore, Dick Foran, Ann Sheridan, Joe Sawye- Helen Flint, Henry Brandon. **1937**

BLACK LIKE ME ★★★ Based on the book by Joh- Griffin, this film poses the question: What happen- when a white journalist takes a drug that turns hi- skin black? James Whitmore plays the reporter, wh- wishes to experience racism firsthand. Somewha- provocative at its initial release, but by today's star- dards, a lot of the punch is missing. B&W; 107m. **DIF** Carl Lerner. **CAST:** James Whitmore, Roscoe Le- Browne, Will Geer, Sorrell Booke. **1964**

BLACK LIZARD ★★★ Strange tale in which a trans- vestite kidnaps a jeweler's daughter to ransom he- for a rare jewel and to have her become one of his liv- ing dolls on his secret island. If you like the bizarr- you will enjoy this film. In Japanese with Englis- subtitles. Not rated; contains violence. 90m. **DIR:** Kinji Fukasaku. **CAST:** Akihiro Maru Yama, Yukio Mish- ma. **1968**

BLACK MAGIC (1949) ★★1/2 Orson Welles revel- in the role of famous eighteenth-century charlata- Count Cagliostro—born Joseph Balsamo, a peasan-

ith imagination and a flair for magic, hypnosis, and ne power of superstition. The story is of Cagliostro's .ttempt to gain influence and clout in Italy using his :range and sinister talents. The star codirected .without credit). B&W; 105m. **DIR:** Gregory Ratoff. **AST:** Orson Welles, Akim Tamiroff, Nancy Guild, Ray- .ond Burr, Frank Latimore. **1949**

LACK MAGIC (1992) ★★1/2 Writer-director aniel Taplitz's overly satirical tone finally mars this uirky made-for-cable tale, which turns on whether outhern seductress Rachel Ward is a witch. Al- hough the premise and performances are engaging, ne story eventually spirals out of control. Rated PG- 3. 94m. **DIR:** Daniel Taplitz. **CAST:** Rachel Ward, .udge Reinhold, Brion James, Anthony LaPaglia. **1992**

LACK MAGIC WOMAN 💘 A dreadfully boring verworking of *Fatal Attraction*. Rated R for rubbish .nd erotic scenes. 91m. **DIR:** Deryn Warren. **CAST:** lark Hamill, Amanda Wyss. **1990**

BLACK MALE ★★ Two con men, to pay off loan harks, attempt to blackmail a doctor, but their plan .ackfires when the doctor turns out to be more ruth- .ess than the mobsters. Bokeem Woodbine and .ustin Pierce star as the con men on the run from the nob, the police, and the good doctor. Rated R for .dult situations, language, nudity, and violence. 10m. **DIR:** George Baluzy, Mike Baluzy. **CAST:** Bokeem Voodbine, Roger Rees, Justin Pierce, Sascha Knopf. 999 DVD

LACK MARBLE, THE ★★★ A Los Angeles cop Robert Foxworth) and his new partner (Paula Pren- .ss) attempt to capture a dog snatcher (Harry Dean tanton) who is demanding a high ransom from a .ealthy dog lover. Along the way, they fall in love. .ased on Joseph Wambaugh's novel. Rated PG for .uage and some violence. 110m. **DIR:** Harold Becker. **AST:** Paula Prentiss, Harry Dean Stanton, Robert Fox- orth. **1980**

LACK MARKET RUSTLERS ★★1/2 The Range .usters break up a gang of rustlers that are supply- .g beef for the World War II black market. B&W; 4m. **DIR:** S. Roy Luby. **CAST:** Ray "Crash" Corrigan, .ennis Moore, Max Terhune, Glenn Strange. **1946**

LACK MASK ★★1/2 Elite, biologically engineered .ombat squad takes over the Hong Kong drug trade ·hen the government targets them for termination. . former squad member living quietly as a librarian .s forced to stop the manic activities of his past asso- .iates. The action scenes are feverish, the humor is orny, and this English-dubbed version of the 1996 ·riginal has a hip-hop soundtrack. Rated R for vio- ·nce, gore, sexual content, and language. 96m. **DIR:** ·aniel Lee. **CAST:** Jet Li, Karen Mok, Francoise Yip, Lau ·hing-wan, Patrick Lung Kang. **1999 DVD**

·LACK MOON RISING ★★ The only redeeming ·oint of this little car theft number is its occasional .ccent on humor. The cast is top-notch, but the ma- .erial is mostly pedestrian. Rated R for language, nu- .ity, sex, and some rather gruesome violence. 93m. **·IR:** Harley Cokliss. **CAST:** Tommy Lee Jones, Linda lamilton, Robert Vaughn, Richard Jaeckel, Lee Ving, .ubba Smith. **1986**

·LACK NARCISSUS ★★★1/2 Worldly temptations, .ncluding those of the flesh, create many difficulties

for a group of nuns starting a mission in the Hi- malayas. Superb photography makes this early post- war British effort a visual delight. Unfortunately, key plot elements were cut from the American prints by censors. 99m. **DIR:** Michael Powell. **CAST:** Deborah Kerr, Jean Simmons, David Farrar, Flora Robson, Sabu. **1947**

BLACK ORCHID, THE ★★1/2 Sophia Loren plays the widow of a criminal and Anthony Quinn is the businessman who is romancing her in this patchy weeper. B&W; 96m. **DIR:** Martin Ritt. **CAST:** Sophia Loren, Anthony Quinn, Ina Balin, Peter Mark Richman. **1959**

BLACK ORPHEUS ★★★★★ The Greek myth of Or- pheus, the unrivaled musician, and his ill-fated love for Eurydice has been updated and set in Rio de Janeiro during carnival for this superb film. A Por- tuguese-French coproduction, it has all the qualities of a genuine classic. Its stunning photography cap- tures both the magical spirit of the original legend and the tawdry yet effervescent spirit of Brazil. 98m. **DIR:** Marcel Camus. **CAST:** Breno Mello, Marpessa Dawn, Lea Garcia, Lourdes de Oliveira. **1959 DVD**

BLACK PANTHER, THE ★★1/2 In 1974 Donald Neil- son (Donald Sumpter), known as the Black Panther, robbed a series of post offices and killed their em- ployees. Neilson also plotted the kidnapping of a wealthy teenage heiress that went awry. *The Black Panther* portrays Neilson's actions in such a matter- of-fact fashion that it removes all the horror. Still, some good action and a few intense scenes. Not rat- ed, has violence and nudity. 90m. **DIR:** Ian Merrick. **CAST:** Donald Sumpter, Debbie Farrington, Marjorie Yates, David Swift. **1977**

BLACK PIRATE, THE ★★★1/2 One of superstar Douglas Fairbanks's most popular films, this early color production packs enough thrills for a dozen pictures. Written by Fairbanks, *Pirate* contains a duel to the death with cutlasses on the beach, a dar- ing underwater raid on a pirate ship, and one of the most famous of all movie stunts: Fairbanks's ride down the ship's sail on a knife, cleverly achieved with an apparatus hidden from the camera. Silent. B&W; 122m. **DIR:** Albert Parker. **CAST:** Douglas Fair- banks Sr., Donald Crisp, Billie Dove, Anders Randolph. **1926 DVD**

BLACK RAIN (1988) ★★★★ This winner at the Cannes Film Festival and best picture in Japan is a vivid portrait of the Hiroshima atomic bombing. It recounts the horror of the event and centers on the lives of one family five years later as they cope with radiation sickness. In Japanese with English subti- tles. Not rated; too strong for youngsters. B&W; 123m. **DIR:** Shohei Imamura. **CAST:** Yoshiko Tanaka. **1988**

BLACK RAIN (1989) ★★★★ Michael Douglas gives a solid performance in this nonstop action film as a maverick New York cop who is assigned to deliver a Yakuza gangster to the Japanese authorities, only to allow him to escape upon arrival at the airport. De- spite protests from the Japanese police, Douglas in- sists on staying on to help recapture the escaped criminal, and it is up to Ken Takakura to baby-sit the hot-tempered American detective. Rated R for violence and profanity. 110m. **DIR:** Ridley Scott. **CAST:** Michael Douglas, Andy Garcia, Ken Takakura, Kate Capshaw. **1989 DVD**

BLACK RAINBOW ★★★1/2 A father-daughter evangelical scam takes a twist when the girl (Rosanna Arquette) actually *does* develop precognitive talents. She then claims to have pinpointed a murderer. Old-world southern decadence permeates this nifty little thriller. Rated R for nudity, violence, and profanity. 103m. **DIR:** Mike Hodges. **CAST:** Rosanna Arquette, Jason Robards Jr., Tom Hulce. **1991**

BLACK RAVEN, THE ★★ Fogbound, poverty-row, old dark house cheapie about a murder-filled night at a country inn. Interesting mainly for its cast. B&W; 64m. **DIR:** Sam Newfield. **CAST:** George Zucco, Wanda McKay, Robert Livingston, Glenn Strange. **1943**

BLACK ROBE ★★★★ Thought-provoking drama follows the struggle of Jesuit priest Father LaForgue (Lothaire Bluteau) as he journeys through the frozen Canadian wilderness in 1634 with the help of Algonquian Indians who become increasingly distrustful of the strange man they call "Blackrobe." This impressive motion picture manages to examine Christianity and tribal beliefs without trivializing either. Rated R for violence, nudity, and simulated sex. 105m. **DIR:** Bruce Beresford. **CAST:** Lothaire Bluteau, Aden Young, Sandrine Holt, August Schellenberg. **1991 DVD**

BLACK ROOM, THE (1935) ★★★ Boris Karloff is excellent as twin brothers with an age-old family curse hanging over their heads. Well-handled thriller never stops moving. B&W; 67m. **DIR:** Roy William Neill. **CAST:** Boris Karloff, Marian Marsh, Robert Allen, Katherine DeMille, Thurston Hall. **1935**

BLACK ROOM, THE (1985) 💣 A philandering husband rents an apartment from a couple who kill the adulterous man's girlfriends. Rated R for nudity. 88m. **DIR:** Norman Thaddeus Vane. **CAST:** Stephen Knight, Cassandra Gavioca. **1985**

BLACK ROSE OF HARLEM ★★ Gangland romance, set in 1931, about a mobster's henchman who falls for a nightclub singer. Atmospheric but unoriginal, this period piece only comes to life when its hoodlum heroes are rubbing each other out. Rated R for violence, adult situations, and profanity. 81m. **DIR:** Fred Gallo. **CAST:** Cynda Williams, Nick Cassavetes, Joe Viterelli, Lawrence Monoson, Richard Brooks, Garrett Morris, Richard T. Jones, Maria Ford. **1995**

BLACK ROSES ★★1/2 Black Roses is the name of a hard-rock group that comes to sleepy Mill Basin for a concert. Soon, the concert hall becomes a hell on Earth. Want to see a guy get sucked into a wall-mounted speaker? It's here. Rated R for violence, nudity, and language. 90m. **DIR:** John Fasano. **CAST:** John Martin, Ken Swofford. **1988**

BLACK SABBATH ★★★1/2 Above-average trio of horror tales given wonderful atmosphere by director Mario Bava. Boris Karloff plays host and stars in the third story, a vampire opus entitled "The Wurdalak." One of the others, "A Drop of Water," is based on a story by Chekhov; the third, "The Telephone," involves dispossessed calls of the worst sort. 99m. **DIR:** Mario Bava. **CAST:** Boris Karloff, Mark Damon, Suzy Andersen. **1964**

BLACK SCORPION ★★★ Writer Craig J. Nevius's good-natured superhero saga stars sultry Joan Severance as a former cop turned black-garbed avenger of the night, whose appearance owes a lot to Michelle Pfeiffer's nasty leathers in *Batman Returns*. Joan's considerably more blatant about her sexual hunger, but the modern *noir* setting—in this case the City of Angels—is every bit as deliciously seamy. Rated R for profanity, violence, nudity, and simulated sex. 90m. **DIR:** Jonathan Winfrey. **CAST:** Joan Severance, Bruce Abbott, Stephen Lee, Rick Rossovich. **1995**

BLACK SCORPION II: AFTERSHOCK 💣 Star Joan Severance turns coproducer for this sequel to her modestly successful superhero spoof, and the result is absolutely atrocious: hammy overacting, unfinished effects shots, and a "plot" that defies description. Rated R for profanity, violence, and nudity. 85m. **DIR:** Jonathan Winfrey. **CAST:** Joan Severance, Whip Hubley, Stoney Jackson, Sherrie Rose, Stephen Lee, Garrett Morris. **1996**

BLACK SHEEP ★★ Bungling brother of a gubernatorial candidate is full of good intentions as he nearly destroys his sibling's well-oiled campaign. A low-level aide is assigned to keep the likable klutz out of trouble. The film pushes family values with schmaltzy determination and tries to camouflage its lack of fresh humor with crude comedy. Rated PG-13 for language, drug use, and violence. 87m. **DIR:** Penelope Spheeris. **CAST:** Chris Farley, David Spade, Tim Matheson, Gary Busey. **1996**

BLACK SISTER'S REVENGE ★★1/2 Shamefully, a new title and cover art imply that the movie is a blaxploitation action-adventure. In reality, it's a serious drama, originally titled *Emma Mae*, about a black girl from Georgia struggling to fit in with other kids in an L.A. ghetto. It's a low-budget movie lacking technical flair, but it deserves more attention than the misleading advertising is going to bring it. Not rated. 100m. **DIR:** Jamaa Fanaka. **CAST:** Jerri Hayes, Ernest Williams II. **1976**

BLACK STALLION, THE ★★★★★ Before taking our breath away with the superb *Never Cry Wolf*, director Carroll Ballard made an impressive directorial debut with this gorgeous screen version of the well-known children's story. Kelly Reno plays the young boy stranded on a deserted island with "The Black," a wild, but very intelligent, horse who comes to be his best friend. It's a treat the whole family can enjoy. Rated G. 118m. **DIR:** Carroll Ballard. **CAST:** Kelly Reno, Mickey Rooney, Teri Garr, Hoyt Axton, Clarence Muse. **1979 DVD**

BLACK STALLION RETURNS, THE ★★★★ A sequel to the 1979 film *The Black Stallion*, this is first rate fare for the young and the young at heart. The story, based on the novel by Walter Farley, picks up where the first film left off. Alec Ramsey (Kelly Reno) is a little older and a little taller, but he still loves his horse, "The Black." And this time, Alec must journey halfway around the world to find the stallion, which has been stolen by an Arab chieftain. Rated PG for slight violence. 93m. **DIR:** Robert Dalva. **CAST:** Kelly Reno, Vincent Spano, Teri Garr, Allen Garfield, Woody Strode. **1983**

LACK SUNDAY (1961) ★★★ Italian horror lassic about the one day each century when Satan oams the Earth. Brilliant cinematography and art irection help establish a chilling, surreal atmos- here in this tale of a witch who swears vengeance n the offspring of those who brutally killed her cen- uries ago. B&W; 83m. DIR: Mario Bava. CAST: Bar- ara Steele, John Richardson, Ivo Garrani, Andrea hecci. 1961 DVD

LACK SUNDAY (1977) ★★★ An Arab terrorist roup attempts to blow up the president at a Super owl in Miami's Orange Bowl. Tension is maintained hroughout. Rated R. 143m. DIR: John Franken- eimer. CAST: Robert Shaw, Bruce Dern, Marthe Keller, ritz Weaver. 1977

LACK SWAN, THE ★★★1/2 A pirate movie that enefits most from colorful performances by its big- ame cast. 85m. DIR: Henry King. CAST: Tyrone Pow- r, Maureen O'Hara, George Sanders, Laird Cregar, An- ony Quinn, Thomas Mitchell. 1942

LACK TIGHTS ★★★1/2 There are several attrac- ve performers in this British film that aficionados f dance should not miss: Cyd Charisse, Zizi Jean- aire, and in her last film before retirement, Moira hearer. It's a good film that even those who are not ance groupies might enjoy. The film is also known nder the French title Un, Deux, Trois, Quatre! 40m. DIR: Terence Young. CAST: Cyd Charisse, Zizi eanmaire, Moira Shearer, Roland Petit Dance Compa- y. 1960 DVD

LACK VEIL FOR LISA, A ★★ Serviceable gangster nelodrama with John Mills as the token Anglo star nported to Rome to make the movie marketable utside Italy. Tolerable action flick, if a trifle talky. ot rated. 88m. DIR: Massimo Dallamano. CAST: John ills, Luciana Paluzzi, Robert Hoffman. 1968

LACK VENUS ❤ Lavish nineteenth-century arisian costumes and settings can't salvage this ndless sex romp. Poorly dubbed. Rated R. 80m. DIR: laude Mulot. CAST: Josephine Jacqueline Jones, miliano Redondo. 1983

LACK WATER ❤ Extremely slow, boring movie bout an English lawyer who only wants to go fishing Tennessee, but ends up on the run. Not rated; con- ains profanity and nudity. 105m. DIR: Nicolas Gess- er. CAST: Julian Sands, Stacey Dash, Ned Beatty, Ed auter, Denise Crosby, Brian McNamara, Johnny Cash, od Steiger. 1989

LACK WIDOW ★★★★ A superb thriller from di- ector Bob Rafelson that recalls the best of the Bette avis–Joan Crawford "bad girl" films of earlier ecades. Debra Winger stars as an inquisitive feder- l agent who stumbles upon an odd pattern of deaths y apparently natural causes: the victims are quite ealthy, reclusive, and leave behind a young—and ery rich—widow. Rated R for nudity and adult situ- tions. 103m. DIR: Bob Rafelson. CAST: Debra Winger, heresa Russell, Sami Frey, Dennis Hopper, Nicol Williamson, Terry O'Quinn. 1987

LACK WINDMILL, THE ★★★1/2 Straightforward ory is enhanced by Don Siegel's razor-sharp direc- on and Michael Caine's engrossing performance as n intelligence agent whose son has been kid- apped. The suspense builds carefully to a satisfying

climax. Rated R. 106m. DIR: Don Siegel. CAST: Michael Caine, Joseph O'Conor, Donald Pleasence, John Vernon, Janet Suzman, Delphine Seyrig. 1974

BLACKBEARD THE PIRATE ★★★ Entertaining pi- rate yarn with some good action and fine characteri- zations. Gorgeous Linda Darnell is the charming damsel in distress. In the title role, Robert Newton is a bit overzealous at times, but puts in a fine perfor- mance. Go for it. 99m. DIR: Raoul Walsh. CAST: Robert Newton, Linda Darnell, William Bendix, Keith Andes. 1952

BLACKBEARD'S GHOST ★★★ This fun Disney comedy has Peter Ustinov playing a ghost who must prevent his ancestors' home from becoming a gam- bling casino. 107m. DIR: Robert Stevenson. CAST: Pe- ter Ustinov, Dean Jones, Suzanne Pleshette, Elsa Lan- chester. 1968

BLACKBELT ★★ A martial arts instructor protects a rising pop star from a psychopathic fan. Some good action sequences make this film stand out a little from other fight flicks. Rated R for nudity, profanity, and graphic violence. 90m. DIR: Charles Philip Moore. CAST: Don "The Dragon" Wilson, Matthias Hues, Richard Beymer. 1992

BLACKBELT 2: FATAL FORCE ★★ A wanna-be epic martial arts action film. It has Vietnam vets, heroin junkies, heavily armed elite missions forces, gunrun- ners, karate cops—one black, one white—and a strip club for good measure. Rated R for violence, profanity, and nudity. 83m. DIR: José Mari Avellana. CAST: Blake Bahner, Ronald William Lawrence, Rox- anne Baird, Michael Vlastas. 1993

BLACKBIRD, THE ★★★1/2 A murderous criminal, who masquerades as a crippled mission keeper suf- fers the fate promised by mothers to children who make faces. Silent. B&W; 70m. DIR: Tod Browning. CAST: Lon Chaney Sr., Renée Adorée, Owen Moore. 1925

BLACKBOARD JUNGLE, THE ★★★★ Glenn Ford plays a high school instructor who desperately tries to reach some emotionally turbulent youths in the New York school system. Hard-hitting, gritty drama. Excellent adaptation of Evan Hunter's powerful nov- el. B&W; 101m. DIR: Richard Brooks. CAST: Glenn Ford, Anne Francis, Vic Morrow, Sidney Poitier. 1955

BLACKENSTEIN ❤ Tasteless and grotesque entry in the subgenre of blaxploitation horror films. Rated R for violence and nudity. 92m. DIR: William A. Levey. CAST: John Hart, Joe DiSue. 1973

BLACKJACK ★★1/2 Dull, lightweight, made-for-TV action fare starring Dolph Lundgren as a mercenary suffering from a debilitating phobia acquired during a firefight who is trying to save a supermodel from the hands of a serial killer. Especially disappointing considering the combined talents of Lundgren and director John Woo. Rated R for violence and profani- ty. 112m. DIR: John Woo. CAST: Dolph Lundgren, Kate Vernon, Phillip Mackenzie, Kam Heskin, Fred William- son, Saul Rubinek. 1998 DVD

BLACKMAIL (1929) ★★★ Many bits of film busi- ness that were to become Alfred Hitchcock trade- marks are evident in this film, including the first of his cameo appearances. Story of a woman who faces the legal system as well as a blackmailer for murdering an attacker in self-defense was originally shot as a silent film but partially reshot and converted into England's first sound release. B&W; 86m. **DIR:** Alfred Hitchcock. **CAST:** Anny Ondra, Sara Allgood, John Longden, Charles Paton, Donald Calthrop, Cyril Ritchard. **1929 DVD**

BLACKMAIL (1991) ★★★ Made-for-cable thriller will keep you guessing. Miguel Tejada-Flores spins a complicated yarn of greed and betrayal—adapted from a short story by Bill Crenshaw—concerning two blackmailers who set up a rich wife. Farfetched, but entertaining. 96m. **DIR:** Reuben Preuss. **CAST:** Susan Blakely, Dale Midkiff, Beth Toussaint, Mac Davis, John Saxon. **1991**

BLACKOUT (1978) ★★★ At times, this movie, about a New York City apartment building attacked by a gang of escaped criminals during a blackout, reeks of a disaster film. Still, there are good action scenes and enough drama to make you almost forget the shortcomings. Rated R for violence. 86m. **DIR:** Eddy Matalon. **CAST:** Jim Mitchum, Robert Carradine, Belinda Montgomery, June Allyson, Jean-Pierre Aumont, Ray Milland. **1978**

BLACKOUT (1985) ★★★1/2 A police detective (Richard Widmark) becomes obsessed with an unsolved murder. Six years after the incident he begins to find valuable clues. This superior made-for-HBO movie has violence and profanity. 99m. **DIR:** Douglas Hickox. **CAST:** Richard Widmark, Keith Carradine, Kathleen Quinlan, Michael Beck. **1985**

BLACKOUT (1990) 🎞 A disturbed woman returns to her childhood home after receiving a letter from her missing father. Rated R for nudity and violence. 90m. **DIR:** Doug Adams. **CAST:** Carol Lynley, Gail O'Grady, Michael Keys-Hall, Joanna Miles. **1990**

BLACKOUT (1995) ★★★ Conservative banker Brian Bosworth suffers a concussion during a street accident, and suddenly dreams of a vastly different—and far more violent—life. Attempts to investigate this other existence unleash all sorts of goons, every one trying to kill our hero. Bosworth sells the concept and is occasionally amusing as an "ordinary" guy repeatedly astonished by his skills as a trained killer. Rated R for violence, profanity, nudity, and simulated sex. 98m. **DIR:** Allan A. Goldstein. **CAST:** Brian Bosworth, Brad Dourif, Claire Yarlett, Marta Du-Bois. **1995**

BLACKWATER TRAIL ★★★1/2 Riveting Australian thriller stars Judd Nelson as a writer who returns to his small hometown for the funeral of a close friend. When the dead man's sister suggests her brother was killed, the writer's investigation puts him on the trail of a serial killer. Creepy and effective. Not rated; contains adult situations, language, nudity, and violence. 97m. **DIR:** Ian Barry. **CAST:** Judd Nelson, Brett Climo, Gabrielle Fitzpatrick, Mark Lee, Peter Phelps, Rowena Wallace. **1995**

BLACULA ★★★1/2 An old victim (William Marshall) of Dracula's bite is loose in modern L.A. Surprisingly well-done shocker. Fierce and energetic, with a solid cast. Rated R for violence. 92m. **DIR:** William Crain. **CAST:** William Marshall, Denise Nicholas, Vonetta McGee, Thalmus Rasulala. **1972**

BLADE (1973) ★★★ Middle-aged New York detective Blade (John Marley) stalks the psycho who murdered the daughter of a powerful right-wing congressman. Along the way he uncovers a lot of other goings-on in the naked city. The story's not much, but TV addicts can count the faces that later went on hit shows (*Barney Miller*'s Steve Landesberg, *The Love Boat*'s Ted Lange, *McMillan and Wife*'s John Schuck). Rated R for violence. 90m. **DIR:** Ernest Pintoff. **CAST:** John Marley, Jon Cypher, Kathryn Walker, William Prince, Michael McGuire, Joe Santos, John Schuck, Keene Curtis, Ted Lange, Marshall Efron, Steve Landesberg. **1973**

BLADE (1998) ★★★ This gore-laden vampire flick is trashy, flashy, and outrageously violent. Wesley Snipes, starring as the character first introduced in a Marvel comic book, makes an ultracool hero with a twist: He's half vampire, a "day-walker" with superhuman strength and silver-laced weapons, who's determined to exterminate his nastier brethren. The film runs a bit long, but moves at a brisk clip. Rated R for profanity, violence, and gobs o' gore. 115m. **DIR:** Stephen Norrington. **CAST:** Wesley Snipes, Stephen Dorff, Kris Kristofferson, N'Bushe Wright, Donal Logue, Udo Kier, Traci Lords. **1998 DVD**

BLADE IN THE DARK, A ★★1/2 Fair thriller from Italian director Lamberto Bava (*Demons*) is full of psychobabble, and even though the advanced viewer will probably have the killer figured out way before the end of the movie, the film moves along nicely and keeps you interested. Rated R for violence and language. 96m. **DIR:** Lamberto Bava. **CAST:** Andrea Occhipinti, Anny Papa. **1983**

BLADE MASTER, THE 🎞 Muscleman Miles O'Keeffe chops his way across the countryside battling nasty sorcerers and spirits in a quest to conquer evil. Rated PG. 92m. **DIR:** David Hills. **CAST:** Miles O'Keeffe, Lisa Foster. **1984**

BLADE RIDER ★★ Several *Branded* TV episodes with cavalry and Indian themes loosely patched together to make up a video feature. Released to TV under the title *Ride to Glory*. Sadly, even the famous *Branded* opening theme is edited out. 102m. **DIR:** Various. **CAST:** Chuck Connors, Burt Reynolds, Lee Van Cleef, Robert Lansing, David Brian. **1966 DVD**

BLADE RUNNER ★★★★1/2 This Ridley Scott (*Alien*) production is thought-provoking and visually impressive. Harrison Ford stars as a futuristic Philip Marlowe trying to find and kill the world's remaining rebel androids in 2019 Los Angeles. The film may not be for everyone, but those who appreciate something of substance will find it worthwhile. Rated R for brief nudity and violence. 118m. **DIR:** Ridley Scott. **CAST:** Harrison Ford, Rutger Hauer, Sean Young, Daryl Hannah, Joanna Cassidy, Edward James Olmos, M. Emmet Walsh. **1982**

BLADES 🎞 Really dull slice-and-dice raunch about a power mower from hell. Rated R for violence and profanity. 101m. **DIR:** Thomas R. Randinella. **CAST:** Robert North. **1989**

BLADES OF COURAGE ★★★1/2 Christianne Hirt is a Canadian ice skater with a promising future in the Olympics. Unfortunately she is assigned a coach who employs ruthless methods to achieve what he desires. Aside from the stereotyped pushy mother, this is a realistic film that reveals the effort involved in developing a champion. It is well acted with some choice figure-skating numbers. Not rated. 98m. **DIR:** Randy Bradshaw. **CAST:** Christianne Hirt, Colm Feore, Stuart Hughes, Rosemary Dunsmore. 1988

BLAIR WITCH PROJECT, THE ❤ A fiendishly clever publicity campaign fueled the release of this ultra-low-budget quickie, which turned out to be one of the biggest swindles ever perpetrated on unsuspecting movie audiences. This "faux documentary" about three young filmmakers who meet an uncertain fate while investigating an old legend in the Maryland woods fails to deliver on all counts. Rated R for profanity. 82m. **DIR:** Daniel Myrick, Eduardo Sanchez. **CAST:** Heather Donahue, Michael C. Williams, Joshua Leonard. 1999 DVD

BLAKE'S 7 (TV SERIES) ★★★ In a postnuclear future, Earth and other populated planets are strictly controlled by the "Federation." Blake's 7, a group of escaped criminals and rebels, wanders the galaxy seeking to undercut the Federation's omnipotence. This British TV series, a cult favorite in the United States, is less campy than *Dr. Who* but not as intellectual as *The Prisoner.* Each tape includes two episodes. 105m. **DIR:** Various. **CAST:** Gareth Thomas, Sally Knyvette, Paul Darrow. 1978–1981

BLAME IT ON RIO ★★1/2 A middle-aged male sex fantasy directed by Stanley Donen (*Lucky Lady; Charade*), features Michael Caine as a befuddled fellow who finds himself involved in an affair with the teenage daughter (Michelle Johnson) of his best friend (Joseph Bologna). Although essentially in bad taste, *Blame It on Rio* does have a number of very funny moments. Rated R for nudity, profanity, and suggested sex. 110m. **DIR:** Stanley Donen. **CAST:** Michael Caine, Joseph Bologna, Valerie Harper, Michelle Johnson. 1984

BLAME IT ON THE BELLBOY ★★★★ An English-mangling Italian bellboy (Bronson Pinchot) manages to mix up the identities of a real estate salesman (Dudley Moore), a hit man (Bryan Brown), and a philandering husband (Richard Griffiths). What could have been hopelessly moronic is deliciously giddy and frequently funny. Rated PG-13 for profanity, brief violence, and silly simulated sex. 78m. **DIR:** Mark Herman. **CAST:** Dudley Moore, Bryan Brown, Richard Griffiths, Andreas Katsulas, Patsy Kensit, Alison Steadman, Penelope Wilton, Bronson Pinchot. 1992

BLAME IT ON THE NIGHT ❤ Mick Jagger cowrote the original story for this movie but wisely chose not to appear in it. It's a trite tale of a rock singer who discovers he has a 13-year-old son. Rated PG-13. 85m. **DIR:** Gene Taft. **CAST:** Nick Mancuso, Byron Thames, Leslie Ackerman, Dick Bakalyan. 1984

BLANK CHECK ★★1/2 When 11-year-old Brian Bonsall's bike is run over by mobster Miguel Ferrer, the boy ends up with a blank check. Our young hero uses it for $1 million worth of fun, only to find that money can't buy happiness. Kids will definitely enjoy Bonsall's adventures and the state-of-the-art toys. Rated PG for light violence. 93m. **DIR:** Rupert Wainwright. **CAST:** Brian Bonsall, Karen Duffy, James Rebhorn, Jayne Atkinson, Michael Faustino, Chris Deme-

tral, Miguel Ferrer, Rick Ducommun, Tone Loc, Michael Lerner, Debbie Allen, Lu Leonard. 1994

BLANKMAN ★★★ Not-bad superhero spoof suffers from too much profanity for the kids and not enough laughs for adults. Rated PG-13. 92m. **DIR:** Mike Binder. **CAST:** Damon Wayans, David Alan Grier, Robin Givens, Christopher Lawford. 1994

BLAST ★★★ When terrorists take over an international sports event and hold the women's swimming team hostage, it's up to a trapped janitor, working with the FBI, to save the day. Familiar elements find new life in this *Die Hard* repeat. Rated R for language and violence. 98m. **DIR:** Albert Pyun. **CAST:** Linden Ashby, Andrew Divoff, Kimberly Warren, Rutger Hauer, Tina Cote. 1996

BLAST FROM THE PAST ★★★★ Delightful spoof on Sixties life unfolds when a paranoid genius insists that his wife stay underground with him until the Cuban Missile Crisis passes … for 35 years! At that point, their son (Brendan Fraser), born and raised in their bomb shelter, must go above ground for some supplies. His innocence and good manners create hilarious situations as he deals with big city life in the Nineties. Rated PG-13 for sexual innuendo and language. 110m. **DIR:** Hugh Wilson. **CAST:** Brendan Fraser, Alicia Silverstone, Christopher Walken, Sissy Spacek, David Foley. 1999 DVD

BLASTFIGHTER ❤ Michael Sopkiw is a dull ex-convict trying to clean up an immoral populace. Not rated; contains violence. 93m. **DIR:** John Old Jr. **CAST:** Michael Sopkiw, Valerie Blake, George Eastman, Mike Miller. 1984

BLAZE ★★ Paul Newman stars as progressive Louisiana governor Earl Long in this late 1950s story of back-room politics and Long's affair with Bourbon Street stripper Blaze Starr. The look behind the scandalous headlines of yesteryear never really ignites. Rated R. 108m. **DIR:** Ron Shelton. **CAST:** Paul Newman, Lolita Davidovich. 1989

BLAZE STARR: THE ORIGINAL ★★ The famous stripper plays an actress who finds relief from the stresses of making movies by joining a Florida nudist camp. Campy in the extreme. Original title: *Blaze Starr Goes Nudist.* Not rated, no sexual content, but lotsa nude volleyball games (and nude checkers, too!) 79m. **DIR:** Doris Wishman. **CAST:** Blaze Starr. 1962

BLAZING SADDLES ★★★1/2 Mel Brooks directed this sometimes hilarious, mostly crude spoof of Westerns. The jokes come with machine-gun rapidity, and the stars race around like maniacs. If it weren't in such bad taste, it would be perfect for the kiddies. Rated R. 93m. **DIR:** Mel Brooks. **CAST:** Cleavon Little, Gene Wilder, Harvey Korman, Madeline Kahn, Mel Brooks, Slim Pickens. 1974 DVD

BLEAK HOUSE ★★★★ First-rate adaptation of Charles Dickens's novel was made for the BBC as a miniseries. The skilled cast is headed by Diana Rigg and Denholm Elliott. Superb sets, costumes, and photography add to the period flavor. A must-see for Dickens aficionados. Made for TV. 391m. **DIR:** Ross Devenish. **CAST:** Diana Rigg, Denholm Elliott, Peter Vaughan, T. P. McKenna. 1985

BLEEDERS ❤ Not surprisingly, the best thing about this moronic monster movie is the fake blood gel pack that adorns the box art. Rated R for violence, language, and adult situations. 92m. DIR: Peter Svatek. CAST: Rutger Hauer, Roy Dupuis, Jackie Burroughs, Kristine Lehman. 1997 DVD

BLESS THE BEASTS AND CHILDREN ♥ A group of misfit teenagers at a ranch resort rebel against their counselors to save a nearby herd of buffalo. Rated R for explicit violence. 109m. DIR: Stanley Kramer. CAST: Billy Mumy, Barry Robins, Miles Chapin, Ken Swofford, Jesse White, Vanessa Brown. 1972

BLESSED EVENT ★★★★ Lee Tracy plays a tabloid columnist whose specialty is uncovering celebrity marriages caused by pre-nuptial pregnancies. It's always fun to watch fast-talking Tracy, and here he's perfectly complemented by the delightfully grumpy Ned Sparks. B&W; 84m. DIR: Roy Del Ruth. CAST: Lee Tracy, Ned Sparks, Mary Brian, Dick Powell. 1932

BLIND DATE (1984) ★★ Not to be confused with the comedies of the same name, this *Blind Date* is about a man who gets a reprieve from his sightless existence through the miraculous effects of an experimental machine. He uses his newfound perceptions to stalk a psychotic killer through some extremely visual Greek locations. Beyond the sights and decent acting, however, the story tends to plod. Rated R for violence. 100m. DIR: Nico Mastorakis. CAST: Joseph Bottoms, Keir Dullea, Kirstie Alley, James Daughton. 1984

BLIND DATE (1987) ♥ A tasteless exercise in slapstick that sends Bruce Willis on a last-minute blind date with Kim Basinger. Rated PG-13 for adult situations. 93m. DIR: Blake Edwards. CAST: Bruce Willis, Kim Basinger, John Larroquette, William Daniels, George Coe, Mark Blum, Phil Hartman. 1987

BLIND FAITH ★★1/2 Courtney B. Vance is a resourceful attorney suddenly faced with the need to represent his nephew in a murder trial. Nothing is quite what it seems, however, and it becomes clear that the boy's father would rather see his son go to jail than acknowledge the truth. The script becomes particularly preachy in the third act, by which point the film has worn out its welcome. Rated R for profanity, violence, nudity, and dramatic intensity. 120m. DIR: Ernest R. Dickerson. CAST: Courtney B. Vance, Charles Dutton, Lonette McKee, Garland Whitt, Birdie M. Hale, Kadeem Hardison. 1998

BLIND FURY ★★★ In this outrageously violent, tongue-in-cheek martial arts movie, Rutger Hauer stars as a blind swordsman who comes to the aid of an army buddy (Terry O'Quinn) when the latter is kidnapped by gangsters and forced to make designer drugs. Directed in a completely over-the-top fashion by Phillip Noyce, *Blind Fury* is a real hoot. Rated R for violence and profanity. 86m. DIR: Phillip Noyce. CAST: Rutger Hauer, Terry O'Quinn, Brandon Call, Lisa Blount, Randall "Tex" Cobb. 1990 DVD

BLIND HUSBANDS ★★★ A doctor and his wife are in an Alpine village so that he can do some mountain climbing. His wife falls prey to the attentions of a suave Austrian army officer who seduces her. In addition to directing and starring, Erich Von Stroheim adapted the screenplay from his own story and designed the sets. A shocker when first released. Silent. B&W; 98m. DIR: Erich Von Stroheim. CAST:

Sam de Grasse, Francis Billington, Erich Von Stroheim, Gibson Gowland. 1919

BLIND JUSTICE ★★★ Writer Daniel Knauf's so-called original Western is a blatant reworking of two enduring Japanese series: the blind samurai films and the *Lone Wolf and Cub* comics. Armand Assante plays a phlegmatic, blind ex-Union soldier who briefly abandons his quest to find an infant's father ... long enough to blow away some baddies terrorizing a small town. The cast gives a lot more than the derivative script deserves. Rated R for violence, profanity, and brief nudity. 85m. DIR: Richard Spence. CAST: Armand Assante, Elisabeth Shue, Robert Davi, Adam Baldwin. 1994

BLIND RAGE ♥ If you really believe that four blind men could rob a bank during business hours, you deserve this film. Rated R for violence and profanity. 81m. DIR: Efren C. Pinion. CAST: D'Urville Martin, Leo Fong, Tony Ferrer, Dick Adair, Darnell Garcia, Charlie Davao, Leila Hermosa, Fred Williamson, Jessie Crowder. 1978

BLIND SIDE ★★★1/2 Just-plain-folks Ron Silver and Rebecca DeMornay accidentally hit and kill a Mexican cop on a deserted, fog-enshrouded highway. After panic propels them to flee the scene, their attempts to resume normal lives are sabotaged by the arrival of smooth-talking Rutger Hauer ... who seems to know far more than he openly admits. Made-for-cable psychological thriller. Rated R for profanity, violence, nudity, and simulated sex. 98m. DIR: Geoff Murphy. CAST: Rutger Hauer, Rebecca DeMornay, Ron Silver, Jonathan Banks. 1993

BLIND SPOT ★★★★ In this *Hallmark Hall of Fame* presentation, Joanne Woodward does an outstanding job of portraying a strong-headed congresswoman who must cope with the death of her drug-addicted top aide who is also her son-in-law. Laura Linney is superb as Phoebe, Woodward's drug-addicted and pregnant daughter who wants to lead her own life. The story line is quite moving and shows the viewer how each character feels. Rated PG-13 for drug use. 99m. DIR: Michael Toshiyuki Uno. CAST: Joanne Woodward, Laura Linney, Reed Edward Diamond, Fritz Weaver. 1993

BLIND TRUST (POUVOIR INTIME) ★★★★ Four misfit robbers drive away with an armored car only to find a guard locked in the back with the money. Intense and fascinating. In French with English subtitles. Rated PG-13 for profanity and violence. 86m. DIR: Yves Simoneau. CAST: Marie Tifo, Pierre Curzi, Jacques Robert Gravel. 1987

BLIND VENGEANCE ★★★1/2 Gerald McRaney plays the father of a grown son killed by smalltown white supremacist Lane Smith and two goons. Rather than blindly orchestrate a bloodbath, McRaney simply shadows his prey ... always watching, masked behind dark sunglasses, and waiting for them to panic. Intelligent made-for-cable melodrama. Rated R for violence and profanity. 93m. DIR: Lee Philips. CAST: Gerald McRaney, Lane Smith, Marg Helgenberger. 1990

BLIND VISION ★★1/2 Mail clerk Lenny Von Dohlen watches the voluptuous Deborah Shelton through a telescope, admiring her from afar. Little does Von

Dohlen realize that he's not alone, and when one of Shelton's boyfriends ends up dead, he becomes one of the main suspects in this intriguing made-for-cable thriller. 92m. DIR: Shuki Levy. CAST: Louise Fletcher, Lenny Von Dohlen, Ned Beatty, Deborah Shelton, Robert Vaughn. 1991

BLINDFOLD: ACTS OF OBSESSION ★★1/2 Only voyeurs anxious to see television star Shannen Doherty nude will enjoy this humdrum thriller. She tries to hold on to her new husband by initiating a series of progressively kinkier sexual games, while a serial killer uses the same methods on other women. Based on this evidence, Doherty won't have much of a film career. Available in R-rated and unrated versions. 93m. DIR: Lawrence I. Simeone. CAST: Judd Nelson, Shannen Doherty, Kristian Alfonso, Drew Snyder, Michael Woods. 1994

BLINDMAN'S BLUFF ★★★ Robert Urich successfully portrays a recently blind man whose former girlfriend is about to marry his best friend. A neighbor is murdered and Urich is the main suspect. Enjoyable made-for-cable whodunit. Rated PG-13. 86m. DIR: James Quinn. CAST: Robert Urich, Lisa Eilbacher, Patricia Clarkson, Ken Pogue, Ron Perlman. 1991

BLINDSIDE ★★ Only the acting talent of Harvey Keitel distinguishes this would-be suspense film yawner. Keitel stars as a former surveillance expert who discovers a murder plot. Rated R for violence and profanity. 102m. DIR: Paul Lynch. CAST: Harvey Keitel, Lori Hallier, Allen Fawcett. 1988

BLINDSIDED ★★1/2 An ex-cop turned burglar becomes blind after being shot during a setup. He goes to the ocean to recuperate and falls in love with a mysterious woman. The plot is a bit farfetched and a little hard to follow at times. Not rated, made for cable, but contains violence and suggested sex. 95m. DIR: Tom Donnelly. CAST: Jeff Fahey, Mia Sara, Rudy Ramos, Jack Kehler, Brad Hunt, Ben Gazzara. 1992

BLINK ★★★★ Superior suspense film benefits from director Michael Apted's flair for characterization and Madeleine Stowe's powerhouse performance as a musician whose sight is restored after years of blindness. Stowe witnesses a murder, but her brain is having trouble processing visual information, and this leads to sudden flashbacks of things she's seen hours and even days before. So the police think she's a crackpot. Rated R for profanity, violence, nudity, and simulated sex. 106m. DIR: Michael Apted. CAST: Madeleine Stowe, Aidan Quinn, James Remar, Peter Friedman, Bruce A. Young, Paul Dillon, Matt Roth, Laurie Metcalf. 1994

BLINK OF AN EYE ★★ Psychic soldier Michael Paré is called into action to rescue the daughter of a rich American from the grasp of Third World terrorists. Interesting premise gets so-so attention from cast and writer. Rated R for violence and language. 90m. DIR: Bob Misiorowski. CAST: Michael Paré, Janis Lee. 1992

BLISS (1986) ★★★★ In this biting black comedy from Australia, a business executive (Barry Otto) nearly dies from a heart attack. He finds himself in a hellish version of the life he once had. Not everyone will appreciate this nightmarish vision of modern life, but it is one of the most original motion pictures

of recent years. Rated R. 93m. DIR: Ray Lawrence. CAST: Barry Otto, Lynette Curran, Helen Jones, Jeff Truman. 1986

BLISS (1997) ★★★★ A young married couple endures emotional problems that are both alleviated and exacerbated when she, then he, takes instruction from the same tantric sex therapist. Amusingly aware of its own occasional ridiculousness until things take a melodramatic turn into repressed memories of child abuse. Serious about eroticism, as opposed to exploitative; you might even learn a few useful tricks here. Rated R for nudity and strong sexual content. 98m. DIR: Lance Young. CAST: Craig Sheffer, Sheryl Lee, Terence Stamp. 1997

BLISS OF MRS. BLOSSOM, THE ★★★1/2 Good farce, as only the British can produce it, with Shirley MacLaine as the discontented wife of brassiere manufacturer Richard Attenborough. Witty, adult story, with fine plot twists. Rated PG. 93m. DIR: Joseph McGrath. CAST: Shirley MacLaine, Richard Attenborough, James Booth. 1968

BLITHE SPIRIT ★★★★ Rex Harrison arranges a séance and recalls the spirit of his mischievous first wife. She decides to stick around and sabotage his second marriage. Wonderfully witty adaptation of Noel Coward's play with Margaret Rutherford hilarious as an off-base medium. 96m. DIR: David Lean. CAST: Rex Harrison, Constance Cummings, Kay Hammond, Margaret Rutherford. 1945 DVD

BLOB, THE (1958) ★★★ This was Steve McQueen's first starring role. He plays a teenager battling parents and a voracious hunk of protoplasm from outer space. Long surpassed by more sophisticated sci-fi, it's still fun to watch. 86m. DIR: Irvin S. Yeaworth Jr. CAST: Steve McQueen, Aneta Corseaut, Olin Howlin. 1958

BLOB, THE (1988) ★★★★ Frightening and occasionally comedic remake of the 1958 cult classic. This time around, Kevin Dillon and Shawnee Smith battle the gelatinous ooze as it devours the inhabitants of a small ski resort. The best horror remake since The Fly. A thrill ride for those with the stomach to take it. Rated R for profanity and state-of-the-art gruesomeness. 95m. DIR: Charles Russell. CAST: Kevin Dillon, Shawnee Smith, Donovan Leitch, Jeffrey DeMunn, Candy Clark, Joe Seneca. 1988

BLOCK-HEADS ★★★★ Twenty years after the end of World War I, Stan Laurel is discovered still guarding a bunker. He returns to a veterans' home, where Oliver Hardy comes to visit and take him to dinner. A well-crafted script provides the perfect setting for the boys' escapades. Their characters have seldom been used as well in feature films. B&W; 55m. DIR: John G. Blystone. CAST: Stan Laurel, Oliver Hardy, Patricia Ellis, Minna Gombell, Billy Gilbert, Jim Finlayson. 1938

BLOCKHOUSE, THE 🖤 Set during World War II, this hideous drama follows the exploits of a group of workers who become trapped in a German army bunker. 90m. DIR: Clive Rees. CAST: Peter Sellers, Charles Aznavour, Peter Vaughan, Jeremy Kemp. 1973

BLONDE CRAZY ★★★ An early version of The Sting, where small-time con artists James Cagney and Joan Blondell are tricked out of five grand and plot to get it back—with interest. B&W; 79m. **DIR:** Roy Del Ruth. **CAST:** James Cagney, Joan Blondell, Louis Calhern, Guy Kibbee, Ray Milland. **1931**

BLONDE HEAVEN ★★ Young girl comes to the big city with dreams of becoming an immortal star, she may just get her wish when she is drawn into a vampire coven. It's likely the erotic nature of the film will appeal to viewers most. Rated R for nudity, violence, and simulated sex. 80m. **DIR:** Ellen Cabot. **CAST:** Julie Strain, Raelyn Saalman, Joe Estevez, Michelle Bauer. **1995**

BLONDE ICE ★★ Odd, obscure melodrama about an unbalanced woman who makes a career of killing her husbands and boyfriends because she likes the attention she gets. (Not to mention the money.) Another long-forgotten curiosity revived for video. 73m. **DIR:** Jack Bernhard. **CAST:** Leslie Brooks, Robert Paige, Walter Sands, John Holland, James Griffith. 1949

BLONDE VENUS 💔 This is a rambling, incomprehensible piece of glitzy fluff. B&W; 90m. **DIR:** Josef von Sternberg. **CAST:** Marlene Dietrich, Cary Grant, Herbert Marshall. 1932

BLONDES HAVE MORE GUNS ★★1/2 Wild and wacky send-up of such thrillers as *Basic Instinct* and *Seven*. Comedian Michael McGaharin is right on the money as Detective Harry Bates, quick with the one-liners and hot on the trail of a serial killer. In true B-movie fashion, Harry falls for the prime suspect, a mysterious woman named Montana (Elizabeth Key; blonde and then some). The best part is that none of this is taken with a grain of salt. Rated R for nudity, violence, profanity, and adult situations. 84m. **DIR:** George Merriweather. **CAST:** Michael McGaharin, Elizabeth Key. 1995

BLONDIE ★★★1/2 The first and one of the best in the long-running series, this film establishes the characters by putting them in a stressful situation and letting them get some laughs out of it. Dagwood loses his job on the eve of his fifth wedding anniversary and doesn't want it to spoil the family celebration. B&W; 75m. **DIR:** Frank Strayer. **CAST:** Penny Singleton, Arthur Lake, Larry Simms, Jonathan Hale, Gene Lockhart, Ann Doran, Gordon Oliver, Kathleen Lockhart. 1938

BLONDIE TAKES A VACATION ★★★1/2 Scene-stealing character players almost take the spotlight away from the Bumstead family. Everybody takes more pratfalls than usual in a clever episode as the Bumsteads try to save a mountain lodge from bankruptcy. B&W; 75m. **DIR:** Frank Strayer. **CAST:** Penny Singleton, Arthur Lake, Donald Meek, Donald MacBride, Elizabeth Dunne, Irving Bacon. 1939

BLONDIE HAS SERVANT TROUBLE ★★★ A funny blend of comic-strip characters and haunted-house shenanigans even though the setup is more contrived than usual. Mr. Dithers wants the Bumsteads to move into a haunted house for business reasons. The outcome is predictable but still funny. B&W; 75m. **DIR:** Frank Strayer. **CAST:** Penny Singleton, Arthur Lake, Jonathan Hale, Esther Dale, Larry Simms, Irving Bacon, Fay Helm. 1940

BLONDIE IN SOCIETY ★★★1/2 A doggone cute comedy, this feature has the Bumsteads competing with a Great Dane for laughs. Dagwood brings the dog home and Blondie promptly enters the animal in a dog show. Then a very important client decides he wants the dog and causes complications. B&W; 75m. **DIR:** Frank Strayer. **CAST:** Penny Singleton, Arthur Lake, Larry Simms, Jonathan Hale, William Frawley, Garry Owen, Robert Mitchell Boys Choir. 1941

BLONDIE'S BLESSED EVENT ★★★ Blondie's daughter, Cookie, makes her first appearance in the series, making the film one of the most anxiously awaited episodes in the series. Because of Cookie, the film has more heart and personality. It also shifts the focus from Blondie and Dagwood to Cookie and Alexander. B&W; 75m. **DIR:** Frank Strayer. **CAST:** Penny Singleton, Arthur Lake, Hans Conried, Mary Wickes, Arthur O'Connell, Norma Jean Wayne. 1942

BLONDIE KNOWS BEST ★★★1/2 One of the funnier entries, chiefly due to Shemp Howard's comedic timing. Dagwood impersonates his boss, Mr. Dithers, and winds up in the care of a couple of psychologists and a half-dozen dogs. B&W; 75m. **DIR:** Abby Berlin. **CAST:** Penny Singleton, Arthur Lake, Larry Simms, Marjorie Kent, Jonathan Hale, Shemp Howard, Jerome Cowan. 1946

BLONDIE HITS THE JACKPOT ★★ This weak series entry was the next-to-last feature made in a 12-year period and boredom was setting in. Dagwood loses his job (again) and has to go to work on a construction crew. Blondie helps the family budget by entering a radio quiz show with predictable results. B&W; 75m. **DIR:** Edward L. Bernds. **CAST:** Penny Singleton, Arthur Lake, Larry Simms, Marjorie Kent, Jerome Cowan, Lloyd Corrigan. 1949

BLOOD & DONUTS ★★ Tongue-in-cheek horror film in which a vampire comes back to life and falls in love with a clerk at a donut shop. A little wild, a little funny, and a lot weird. Brief cameo by director David Cronenberg. Rated R for vampire violence and nudity. 89m. **DIR:** Holly Dale. **CAST:** Gordon Currie, Justin Lewis, Helene Clarkson, David Cronenberg. 1995

BLOOD ALLEY ★★ Humphrey Bogart was originally set to star opposite wife Lauren Bacall in this story of a merchant marine captain helping Chinese refugees make it to Hong Kong, but he dropped out. For diehard Duke Wayne fans only. 115m. **DIR:** William Wellman. **CAST:** John Wayne, Lauren Bacall, Paul Fix, Mike Mazurki. 1955

BLOOD AND BLACK LACE ★★1/2 This sometimes frightening Italian horror film features a psychotic killer eliminating members of the modeling industry with gusto. Decent entry in the genre from specialist Mario Bava. 88m. **DIR:** Mario Bava. **CAST:** Cameron Mitchell, Eva Bartok. 1964

BLOOD AND CONCRETE, A LOVE STORY ★★ A down-and-out con man gets tangled in the dirty dealings of an idiotic drug lord. Limp attempt to be an avant-garde film. Rated R for violence and profanity. 97m. **DIR:** Jeffrey Reiner. **CAST:** Billy Zane, Jennifer Beals, Darren McGavin, Harry Shearer. 1990

BLOOD AND GUNS (TEPEPA) 💔 Orson Welles's screen presence is at a loss in this dull action yarn about three men whose lives intertwine after the Mexican revolution. Rated R for profanity and violence. 90m. DIR: Giulio Petroni. CAST: Orson Welles, Tomas Milian, John Steiner. 1968

BLOOD AND ROSES ❤ The ghost of a centuries dead vampire possesses a young woman in an attempt to fulfill an ancient curse. Although artistically filmed, the script shuns almost all vampire lore. 74m. DIR: Roger Vadim. CAST: Mel Ferrer, Elsa Martinelli, Annette Vadim. 1960

BLOOD AND SAND (1922) ★★★1/2 One of Rudolph Valentino's most successful vehicles, although it lacks the action and pacing of his best pictures, *Son of the Sheik* and *The Eagle*. Silent. B&W; 80m. DIR: Fred Niblo. CAST: Rudolph Valentino, Nita Naldi, Lila Lee. 1922

BLOOD AND SAND (1941) ★★★ The "Moment of Truth" is not always just before the matador places his sword, as Tyrone Power learns in this classic story of a poor boy who rises to fame in the bullring. Linda Darnell loves him, Rita Hayworth leads him on, in this colorful remake of a 1922 Valentino starrer. 123m. DIR: Rouben Mamoulian. CAST: Tyrone Power, Rita Hayworth, Anthony Quinn, Linda Darnell, Anna Nazimova, John Carradine. 1941

BLOOD AND WINE ★★★ A Miami wine merchant (Jack Nicholson) and a small-time crook (Michael Caine) plan a jewel heist at the expense of one of the merchant's wealthy clients. Director Bob Rafelson really lays on the humid *film noir* atmosphere (Miami seems to have become one of Hollywood's favorite hotbeds of corruption). The plot, however, is never as clever or complicated as we are led to expect. Acting by the powerhouse cast is first-rate. Rated R for profanity and violence. 115m. DIR: Bob Rafelson. CAST: Jack Nicholson, Stephen Dorff, Jennifer Lopez, Judy Davis, Michael Caine. 1997

BLOOD BEACH ❤ Poor horror story of mysterious forces sucking people down into the sand. Rated R. 89m. DIR: Jeffrey Bloom. CAST: John Saxon, Marianna Hill, Otis Young. 1981

BLOOD BEAST TERROR, THE ★★ The performances of genre stalwarts Peter Cushing and Robert Flemyng—as a scientist investigating hideous murders and the doctor whose moth-woman daughter is committing them—help elevate this tepid British horror. The monster is laughable. 88m. DIR: Vernon Sewell. CAST: Peter Cushing, Robert Flemyng. 1967

BLOOD BROTHERS ★★ A boy who witnesses the gang murder of a local Asian grocer wants to go to the police but is reluctant because his older brother is one of the gang members. Unfortunately, this is a low-budget film that has nothing going for it except good intentions. Not rated; contains profanity and violence. 91m. DIR: Bruce Pittman. CAST: Mia Korf, Clark Johnson, Bill Nunn. 1996

BLOOD CASTLE (1970) ❤ Original title: *Scream of the Demon Lover*. Lamebrain hack-'em-up set against pseudogothic backdrop. Rated R. 97m. DIR: J. L. Merino. CAST: Erna Schurer, Agostina Belli. 1970

BLOOD CASTLE (1972) ★★ Adaptation of the real-life saga of Elisabeth Bathory, a seventeenth-century Hungarian countess who bathed in virgin blood in the belief it kept her young and beautiful. This Spanish-Italian coproduction inserts enough exploitable elements to ensure an R rating. Also known as *The*

Legend of Blood Castle. 87m. DIR: Jorge Grau. CAST: Lucia Bose, Ewa Aulin. 1972

BLOOD DINER ❤ Two brothers kill women to obtain body parts for a demonic ceremony. Not rated, but filled with violence, nudity, and gore. 88m. DIR: Jackie Kong. CAST: Rick Burks, Carl Crew. 1987

BLOOD FEAST ❤ First and most infamous of the drive-in gore movies bolsters practically nonexistent plot of crazed murderer with gallons of director Herschell Gordon Lewis's patented stage blood. 75m. DIR: Herschell Gordon Lewis. CAST: Connie Mason, Thomas Wood. 1963 DVD

BLOOD FEUD ★★1/2 Marcello Mastroianni, a lawyer, and Giancarlo Giannini, a sleazy hood, compete for the romantic attentions of a beautiful Sicilian widow (Sophia Loren) in this abrasive, overblown potboiler in 1920s Italy. Dubbed in English. Not rated; contains profanity and violence. B&W; 112m. DIR: Lina Wertmuller. CAST: Sophia Loren, Marcello Mastroianni, Giancarlo Giannini. 1979

BLOOD FREAK ❤ Howlingly bad Florida horror about a hippie biker who turns into—appropriately—a turkey monster. Rated R. 86m. DIR: Brad F. Grinter. CAST: Steve Hawkes. 1971

BLOOD FRENZY ★★ In this made-for-video horror-thriller, a psychotherapist takes a group of her patients into the desert for a retreat. Predictably, someone starts killing them off one by one. Who is the killer? Who cares? Not rated, the movie contains violence. 90m. DIR: Hal Freeman. CAST: Wendy MacDonald, Hank Garrett, Lisa Loring. 1987

BLOOD GAMES ❤ Dopey, misogynistic movie about an all-female traveling softball team. Rated R for violence and nudity. 90m. DIR: Tanya Rosenberg. CAST: Gregory Cummins, Laura Albert. 1990

BLOOD, GUTS, BULLETS & OCTANE ★★ Two sleazy used-car dealers go along with a shady smuggling deal to remedy their financial problems. This low-budget blend of *Pulp Fiction* and *Glengarry Glen Ross* is derivative, overdone, and ultimately pointless. Writer-director-costar Joe Carnahan shows talent, but he's a bit too much in love with the sound of his own dialogue. Rated R for violence and profanity. 86m. DIR: Joe Carnahan. CAST: Dan Leis, Joe Carnahan, Dan Harlan, Ken Rudulph, Hugh McCord. 1998 DVD

BLOOD HARVEST ❤ Tiny Tim in a slasher movie—it just doesn't get any worse than this. Not rated; contains nudity and gore. 90m. DIR: Bill Rebane. CAST: Tiny Tim, Itonia, Dean West. 1987

BLOOD HORSE ★★ In this second installment of the *Black Fox* trilogy, Christopher Reeve and the slave he freed, Tony Todd, plot to save hostages from "savage" Indians. American Indians actually get fairer treatment in this episode, as the settlers are shown to be bloody and brutal. Set in Texas in the 1860s, this has an uninspired made-for-TV look, but puts a fresh twist on the racial problems of the last century. Not rated; contains violence. 92m. DIR: Steven H. Stern. CAST: Christopher Reeve, Tony Todd, Raul Trujillo. 1993

BLOOD IN THE STREETS ★★ In this French-Italian film, a prison warden (Oliver Reed) is forced to release a prisoner as ransom for his kidnapped wife.

There are some exciting chase scenes in this overall so-so film. Rated R for sex, nudity, language, and violence. 111m. DIR: Sergio Sollima. CAST: Oliver Reed, Fabio Testi, Agostina Belli. **1974**

BLOOD LINK 🎦 All his life, a prominent physician has had strange hallucinations about older women being brutally murdered. He discovers that he is seeing through the eyes of his Siamese twin. Rated R for nudity and violence. 98m. DIR: Alberto De Martino. CAST: Michael Moriarty, Penelope Milford, Cameron Mitchell. **1983**

BLOOD MONEY ★★★ This highly engaging film features an excellent cast in a story about an underworld bail-bondsman who falls for a thrill-seeking socialite. His life becomes complicated by another female cohort. B&W; 65m. DIR: Rowland Brown. CAST: George Bancroft, Frances Dee, Judith Anderson, Chick Chandler, Blossom Seeley. **1933 DVD**

BLOOD MOON (WEREWOLF VERSUS THE VAMPIRE WOMAN, THE) ★★ Video retitling of *The Werewolf versus the Vampire Woman*, with Paul Naschy as his recurring character from Spanish horror movies, the tortured lycanthrope Waldemar. Naschy's cheapjack efforts merge Universal-style nostalgic monster ingredients with the sexploitation demands of the Seventies. Idiotic but watchable. Rated R. 86m. DIR: Leon Klimovsky. CAST: Paul Naschy, Patty Shepard. **1970**

BLOOD OF A POET ★★1/2 This pretentious and self-centered first film by France's multitalented Jean Cocteau is also intriguing, provoking, and inventive. Enrique Rivero stars in and narrates this highly personal excursion into a poet's inner life: his fears and obsessions, his relation to the world about him, and the classic poetic preoccupation with death. In French with English subtitles. B&W; 55m. DIR: Jean Cocteau. CAST: Enrique Rivero. **1930 DVD**

BLOOD OF DRACULA ★★ Okay American-international teen horror about a troubled girl who comes under the vampiric (and vaguely lesbian) influence of a sinister teacher. Occasionally atmospheric, but never scary. B&W; 68m. DIR: Herbert L. Strock. CAST: Sandra Harrison. **1957**

BLOOD OF DRACULA'S CASTLE 🎦 Quite possibly the worst Dracula movie ever made. The film has a werewolf, a hunchback, women in chains, human sacrifices, a laughable script, and a ten-dollar budget. Rated PG. 84m. DIR: Al Adamson, Jean Hewitt. CAST: John Carradine, Paula Raymond, Alex D'Arcy, Robert Dix. **1967**

BLOOD OF HEROES ★★1/2 Fairly decent hybrid of *Rollerball* and *Road Warrior* about bush-league team of wannabes playing a brutal no-holds-barred combination of hockey, squash, and football. Rutger Hauer stars as a former star of the game who takes the team to the majors. Rated R for violence, nudity, profanity, and simulated sex. 91m. DIR: David Peoples. CAST: Rutger Hauer, Joan Chen. **1989**

BLOOD OF OTHERS, THE ★★ A disappointment, considering the talent involved (in front of *and* behind the camera), this made-for-cable miniseries is a generally unconvincing adaptation of a Simone de Beauvoir novel about a doomed love affair in the occupied Paris of World War II. 176m. DIR: Claude Chabrol. CAST: Jodie Foster, Michael Ontkean, Sam Neill, Stéphane Audran, Jean-Pierre Aumont, Lambert Wilson, Micheline Presle. **1984**

BLOOD OF THE HUNTER ★★★ Location photography and decent performances heat up this Canadian thriller. Gabriel Arcand plays a trapper who is framed for murder, then must rise to the occasion when the real killer takes his wife hostage. Michael Biehn is seductively evil as the mysterious stranger. Rated R for violence. 92m. DIR: Gilles Carle. CAST: Michael Biehn, Gabriel Arcand, Alexandra Vandernoot, Edward Meeks, François-Eric Gendron. **1994**

BLOOD OF THE INNOCENT ★★★1/2 Strong supporting performances and a clever script lift this action-thriller above its brethren, although star Thomas Ian Griffith still needs to work on his line readings. He heads to Warsaw, bent on avenging the murder of his younger brother, and uncovers a corrupt scheme involving missing Russian peasants and illegal organ harvesting. Rated R for violence and profanity. 95m. DIR: Bob Misiorowski. CAST: Thomas Ian Griffith, Joanna Trzepiecinska, Rutger Hauer, John Rhys-Davies. **1994**

BLOOD OF THE VAMPIRE ★★1/2 Pretty good imitation Hammer horror flick (from the vintage period of British gothic shockers), with Donald Wolfit as the fiend. Semicampy fun, with some genuine thrills, but the direction is too flat for the film to be taken seriously. Even worse, all source prints for its video release are faded almost to sepia, robbing the film of its once gorgeous color. 87m. DIR: Henry Cass. CAST: Barbara Shelley, Donald Wolfit, Vincent Ball. **1958**

BLOOD ON SATAN'S CLAW ★★★ Fun, frightening horror film set in seventeenth-century England. A small farming community is besieged by the devil himself, who succeeds in turning the local children into a coven of witches. Familiar story is presented in a unique manner by director Piers Haggard, helped by excellent period detail and clever effects. Not for the kids, though. Rated R. 93m. DIR: Piers Haggard. CAST: Patrick Wymark, Barry Andrews, Linda Hayden, Simon Williams. **1971**

BLOOD ON THE BADGE 🎦 When a cop's partner is killed by terrorists, he goes on an unbelievable one-man campaign of revenge. A truly poor film. Not rated; contains profanity and violence. 92m. DIR: Bret McCormick. CAST: Joe Estevez, David Harrod. **1992**

BLOOD ON THE MOON ★★★1/2 Robert Mitchum is in top form in this atmospheric Western concerning cattle ranchers trying to terminate homesteaders. B&W; 88m. DIR: Robert Wise. CAST: Robert Mitchum, Barbara Bel Geddes, Robert Preston. **1948**

BLOOD ON THE SUN ★★★1/2 This hard-hitting action-drama finds James Cagney fighting Japanese military and government men in Japan just before World War II. An unusual plot and good pace make this worth watching. B&W; 98m. DIR: Frank Lloyd. CAST: James Cagney, Robert Armstrong, Wallace Ford, Sylvia Sidney. **1945 DVD**

BLOOD ORGY OF THE SHE DEVILS 🎦 Ritualistic murders. Rated PG. 73m. DIR: Ted V. Mikels. CAST: Lila Zaborin, Tom Pace. **1972**

BLOOD RAGE 🎦 When a 10-year-old boy kills a stranger at a drive-in movie, he escapes punishment by blaming his twin brother. It played movie houses and cable TV as *Nightmare at Shadow Woods*. Rated R. 83m. DIR: John Grissmer. CAST: Louise Lasser, Mark Soper. 1983

BLOOD RED 🎬 Sicilian grape farmers feud with a tycoon over land in 1850 California. Rated R for violence and nudity. 102m. DIR: Peter Masterson. CAST: Eric Roberts, Giancarlo Giannini, Dennis Hopper, Burt Young. 1989

BLOOD RELATIONS 🎬 Repugnant gorefest features three generations of a wealthy family lusting after a beautiful gold digger. Rated R for nudity, violence, and gore. 88m. DIR: Graeme Campbell. CAST: Jan Rubes, Kevin Hicks, Lynne Adams, Ray Walston. 1987

BLOOD RELATIVES ★★★1/2 Quebec inspector Donald Sutherland, investigating the murder of a teenage girl, uncovers a conspiracy involving members of the girl's family. Not one of Claude Chabrol's best, but even a lesser effort by the French Hitchcock is better than most anything else on the mystery rack. 100m. DIR: Claude Chabrol. CAST: Donald Sutherland, Aude Landry, Lisa Langlois, Stéphane Audran, Donald Pleasence, David Hemmings. 1978

BLOOD ROSE 🎬 Murky, grade-C horror from France was billed as "the first sex-horror film" for its U.S. release. Rated R. 87m. DIR: Claude Mulot. CAST: Philippe Lemaire, Anny Duperey, Howard Vernon. 1969

BLOOD SALVAGE 🎬 Psychotic family preys on distressed motorists, abducting them and then selling their vital organs to a demented doctor. Too bad the folks behind this mess couldn't give it a brain. Rated R for violence and profanity. 90m. DIR: Tucker Johnstone. CAST: Danny Nelson, Lori Birdsong, Ray Walston, John Saxon, Evander Holyfield. 1989

BLOOD SCREAMS ★★1/2 Atmospheric thriller about a sleepy Mexican village that harbors a deep, dark secret that surfaces to torment two Americans. Rated R for nudity and violence. 75m. DIR: Glenn Gebhard. CAST: Russ Tamblyn, Stacey Shaffer. 1988

BLOOD SIMPLE ★★★1/2 A slyly suspenseful, exciting (and sometimes agonizing) edge-of-your-seat story of how a bar owner (Dan Hedaya) hires a private eye (M. Emmet Walsh) to follow his wife (Frances McDormand) to find out if she's cheating on him. *Blood Simple* is defined as a "state of confusion that follows the commission of a murder, as, 'He's gone blood simple.'" Rated R for suggested sex, violence, and profanity. 96m. DIR: Joel Coen. CAST: John Getz, Frances McDormand, Dan Hedaya, M. Emmet Walsh. 1984

BLOOD SISTERS 🎬 A group of sorority girls must spend the night in a haunted house with a maniac. Rated R for nudity. 85m. DIR: Roberta Findlay. CAST: Amy Brentano, Shannon McMahon. 1987

BLOOD SONG (HAUNTED SYMPHONY) ★★ Ben Cross stars as a classical composer haunted by what appear to be spirits of the dead. Visually stunning film features fine performances but has a self-destructive sense of importance. 85m. DIR: David Tausik. CAST: Ben Cross, Beverly Garland, Jennifer Burns. 1994

BLOOD SPATTERED BRIDE, THE ★★ Sheridan Le Fanu's *Carmilla* gets another reworking in this intermittently stylish exploitation movie from Spain.

Although the climax was heavily censored by U.S. distributors, it's still R-rated. 95m. DIR: Vicente Aranda. CAST: Simon Andreu, Maribel Martin, Alexandra Bastedo. 1974 DVD

BLOOD SPELL 🎬 A modern-day evil sorcerer possesses his son in an attempt to gain immortality. Rated R for graphic violence. 87m. DIR: Deryn Warren. CAST: Anthony Jenkins. 1987

BLOOD SUCKERS FROM OUTER SPACE ★★ Low-budget horror spoof about an alien virus that causes people to vomit up their guts, turning them into sneaky zombies out to suck the innards from hapless victims. Although sometimes funny, the film is uneven. Not rated; contains profanity and partial nudity. 79m. DIR: Glenn Coburn. CAST: Thom Meyer, Pat Paulsen. 1984

●**BLOOD THIRSTY** ★★ Misleadingly promoted as a lesbian vampire movie, this is actually a more serious-minded film about a woman who becomes addicted to self-mutilation. Too poorly made to have much effect. Rated R for nudity, sex, violence, and profanity. 88m. DIR: Jeff Frey. CAST: Monique Parent, Leslie Danon, Matt Baily, Julie Strain. 1998

BLOOD TIES (1987) ★★ Brad Davis is an innocent American engineer blackmailed into assassinating his cousin, an anticrime justice in Sicily. Not rated; contains strong language, violence, and nudity. 98m. DIR: Giacomo Battiato. CAST: Brad Davis, Tony Lo Bianco, Vincent Spano, Barbara de Rossi, Ricky Tognazzi, Michael Gazzo. 1987

BLOOD TIES (1993) ★★1/2 This interesting bite on the vampire legend finds a group of former blood suckers trying to fit into society. Into their Los Angeles lair comes a teenager whose parents were murdered by vampire killers, now hot on his trail. The group must decide whether to fight back or flee, great fodder for moral arguments and exciting close calls. Rated R for sexuality, violence, and strong language. 93m. DIR: Jim McBride. CAST: Harley Venton, Patrick Bauchau, Bo Hopkins, Michelle Johnson, Jason London. 1993

BLOOD VOWS: THE STORY OF A MAFIA WIFE ★★★1/2 A fairy-tale romance between a beautiful orphan (Melissa Gilbert) and a dashing lawyer (Joe Penny) results in a nightmarish prison for her after they marry. It seems his clan needs him back home for a war between Mafia families and she can't deal with the violence or the restrictions put on mob women. Some chilling moments. Originally shown as a TV movie. 104m. DIR: Paul Wendkos. CAST: Melissa Gilbert, Joe Penny, Talia Shire, Eileen Brennan. 1987

BLOOD WARRIORS ★★ Ho-hum action epic with ex-Marine David Bradley forced to wage war against his former best friend, now a drug runner so vile and despicable that he'd molest his own sister and hold orphans hostage. Rated R for profanity, violence, and suggested sex. 96m. DIR: Sam Firstenberg. CAST: David Bradley, Frank Zagarino, Jennifer Campbell. 1993

BLOOD WEDDING ★★★ Excellent ballet adaptation of Federico Garcia Lorca's classic tragedy is impeccably performed by a great, lavishly costumed cast in an empty rehearsal hall. Carlos Saura's direction gives this production a great sense of power and beauty. In Spanish with English subtitles. 72m. DIR: Carlos Saura. CAST: Antonio Gades, Cristina Hoyos. 1981

BLOODBATH AT THE HOUSE OF DEATH ★★ Although advertised as one, this British movie is not all that much of a spoof on horror films. In the story, a team of paranormal specialists investigates a house that was the scene of a mysterious massacre. Vincent Price plays a nutty devil worshiper. Not rated, but equivalent to an R for violence, gore, sex, nudity, and profanity. 92m. DIR: Ray Cameron. CAST: Vincent Price, Kenny Everett, Pamela Stephenson, Gareth Hunt, Don Warrington, John Fortune, Sheila Steafel. 1985

BLOODBEAT 💘 This cheap supernatural flick tries to pass off the idea that a samurai ghost is haunting the backwoods of an American wilderness. 84m. DIR: Fabrice A. Zaphiratos. CAST: Helen Benton, Terry Brown. 1985

BLOODBROTHERS ★★★1/2 Richard Gere and Marilu Henner take top honors in this drama. Plot revolves around a family of construction workers and the son (Gere) who wants to do something else with his life. Rated R. 116m. DIR: Robert Mulligan. CAST: Richard Gere, Paul Sorvino, Tony Lo Bianco, Marilu Henner. 1978

BLOODFIST ★★ Typical martial arts chop-out, peopled by actual World Kickboxing Association champs, karate kings, and a wealth of other unsightly folks who just can't act. Forgettable. Rated R for ketchup. 86m. DIR: Terence H. Winkless. CAST: Don "The Dragon" Wilson, Bob Kaman. 1989 DVD

BLOODFIST 2 ★★ In this martial arts flick, lightweight kick-boxing champ Don Wilson goes to the Philippines and falls into a trap set by the ruler of an island fortress. A rip-off of the genre-classic *Enter the Dragon*. Rated R for nudity, violence, and profanity. 85m. DIR: Andy Blumenthal. CAST: Don "The Dragon" Wilson. 1989 DVD

BLOODFIST III: FORCED TO FIGHT ★★ This sequel finds star Don "The Dragon" Wilson as a new convict forced into being a target for various prison gangs. Rated R for violence and profanity. 90m. DIR: Oley Sassone. CAST: Don "The Dragon" Wilson, Richard Roundtree, Richard Paul. 1991 DVD

BLOODFIST IV—DIE TRYING ★★ Repo man Don "The Dragon" Wilson finds himself up against the CIA, FBI, and international terrorists. Plenty of martial arts action. Rated R for violence and profanity. 86m. DIR: Paul Ziller. CAST: Don "The Dragon" Wilson, Cat Sassoon, Amanda Wyss, Katie Brown, Liz Torres, James Tolkan. 1992 DVD

BLOODFIST V: HUMAN TARGET ★★ Serviceable martial arts entry features Don "The Dragon" Wilson as an undercover FBI agent who, while suffering amnesia is pegged as a double agent. He must fight for his life while fighting to regain his memory. Rated R for violence and adult language. 84m. DIR: Jeff Yonis. CAST: Don "The Dragon" Wilson, Denice Duff, Danny Lopez, Steve James. 1994

BLOODFIST VI: GROUND ZERO ★★1/2 Either Don "The Dragon" Wilson finally is learning to act, or we're simply getting used to him. This time out, he's a compassionate military courier (kind to rabbits) who gets trapped in a nuclear-missile silo with terrorists bent on targeting major North American cities. Rated R for violence, profanity, and laughably gratuitous nudity. 90m. DIR: Rick Jacobson. CAST: Don "The Dragon" Wilson, Cat Sassoon, Robin Curtis, Jonathan Fuller, Steve Garvey. 1994

BLOODHOUNDS ★★1/2 A writer (Corbin Bernsen) and a police detective (Christine Harnos) team up to track down an escaped killer. Plenty of opportunity here for witty dialogue, but it just doesn't happen, which makes this made-for-cable original nothing more than a second-rate action movie. Not rated; contains violence. 95m. DIR: Michael Katleman. CAST: Corbin Bernsen, Christine Harnos. 1996

BLOODHOUNDS II ★★★ A man is killing off rapists who escaped justice in the courts, and now he wants a famous author to help him write a manifesto about how vigilantes can solve America's problems. This made-for-cable original is a solid little thriller, sprinkled with enough wit and terror to be fun. Not rated; contains violence. 95m. DIR: Stuart Cooper. CAST: Corbin Bernsen, Nia Peeples, Ian Tracey, Suki Kaiser, Jim Byrnes, Amy Yasbeck. 1996

BLOODHOUNDS OF BROADWAY ★★★ This featherweight period comedy was stitched together by writer-director Howard Brookner from four stories by Damon Runyan. While not as hilarious as one might hope, this story has its moments, the best of which are provided by Randy Quaid as a lovesick loser and Madonna as the object of his affections. Rated PG for brief profanity and stylized violence. 90m. DIR: Howard Brookner. CAST: Matt Dillon, Jennifer Grey, Julie Hagerty, Rutger Hauer, Madonna, Esai Morales, Anita Morris, Randy Quaid. 1989

BLOODKNOT ★★★ Seductress Kate Vernon impersonates a dead man's girlfriend in order to ingratiate herself with his family, in this intriguing erotic thriller. Randy Kornfield's script remains pretty clever until the final act. Still, getting there will keep you guessing. Rated R for nudity, simulated sex, profanity, and violence. 98m. DIR: Jorge Montesi. CAST: Patrick Dempsey, Kate Vernon, Margot Kidder, Krista Bridges, Craig Sheffer. 1995

BLOODLETTING ★★★ This direct-to-video film is *Natural Born Killers* done right. Young Ariauna Albright blackmails serial killer James L. Edwards into teaching her the art of murder and soon the two are on the road, killing as they go. Performances are well done, and there is a sense of style to this tale that could easily have become exploitation. Not rated; contains violence, gore, and profanity. 96m. DIR: Matthew Jason Walsh. CAST: Ariauna Albright, James L. Edwards, Joseph Daw, Sasha Graham, Tina Krause. 1996

BLOODLINE 💘 Audrey Hepburn falls heir to a pharmaceutical fortune in this inexcusably repulsive montage of bad taste and incoherence. Rated R for sex scenes. 116m. DIR: Terence Young. CAST: Audrey Hepburn, Ben Gazzara, James Mason, Omar Sharif. 1979

BLOODLUST: SUBSPECIES III ★★ This better-than-expected continuation of the vampire series features impressive, gory special effects. Anders Hove returns as vampire Radu, pitting two sisters against each other in a battle over their souls. Rated R for language, nudity, and violence. 81m. DIR: Ted Nicolaou. CAST: Anders Hove, Melanie Shatner, Denice Duff, Kevin Blair. 1993

BLOODMATCH 🖤 Senseless vengefest as a man seeks the five people who fixed a kick-boxing contest five years earlier. Not rated; contains excessive violence and profanity as well as a sprinkling of nudity. 87m. DIR: Albert Pyun. CAST: Benny Urquidez, Thom Mathews. 1991

BLOODMOON (1989) ★★ Okay Australian slasher features a deranged private school teacher who kills couples at the nearby lovers' lane. It seems he transfers his anger at his unfaithful wife onto his promiscuous female students. Rated R for nudity, violence, and gore. 104m. DIR: Alec Mills. CAST: Loon Lissek. 1989

BLOODMOON (1997) ★★1/2 Vehicle for Australian kick boxer Gary Daniels, cast as a cop on the trail of a serial killer who specializes in martial artists. The plot is tired, but at least the action scenes are lively. Rated R for strong violence and profanity. 104m. DIR: Tony Leung. CAST: Gary Daniels, Chuck Jeffreys, Frank Gorshin. 1997 DVD

BLOODSPORT ★★ Jean-Claude Van Damme plays a martial arts master who arrives in Hong Kong to compete in the *kumite*, a violent championship contest. The fighting sequences are tremendous, but the framing story offers only clichés. Rated R for violence and language. 100m. DIR: Newt Arnold. CAST: Jean-Claude Van Damme, Donald Gibb, Leah Ayres, Normann Burton, Forest Whitaker, Bolo Yeung. 1987

BLOODSPORT II ★★ Less a sequel than a remake of the Jean-Claude Van Damme movie, with only the slightest glimmer of a plot to space out the fight scenes between contestants at an international free-form martial arts competition. Rated R for violence and profanity. 86m. DIR: Alan Mehrez. CAST: Daniel Bernhardt, Noriyuki "Pat" Morita, Donald Gibb, James Hong, Lori Lynn Dickerson, Philip Tan, Lisa McCullough, Ong Soo Han. 1996

BLOODSPORT III 🖤 Less fighting means less of what fans of this series want to see as Daniel Bernhardt is forced to compete in another *kumite* competition. Not rated; contains violence, sexual situations, and profanity. 92m. DIR: Alan Mehrez. CAST: Daniel Bernhardt, John Rhys-Davies, Amber Van Lent, James Hong, Noriyuki "Pat" Morita. 1997

•BLOODSPORT IV: THE DARK KUMITE ★★ This in-name-only sequel to the previous *Bloodsports* stars Daniel Bernhardt as an undercover cop investigating mysterious deaths at a prison. While there, he is forced to join an illegal martial arts competition. For die-hard martial arts fans only. Rated R for violence, profanity, and sex. 100m. DIR: Elvis Restaino. CAST: Daniel Bernhardt, Ivan Ivanov, Lisa Stothard, Stefanos Miltsakakis, Derek McGrath. 1998 DVD

BLOODSTONE ★★ An adventure film in the tradition of *Raiders of the Lost Ark*, this falls short of the mark. The story involves newlyweds who become involved in a jewel heist in the Middle East. Loaded with humor and lots of action, but marred by poor performances. Rated PG-13 for violence. 90m. DIR: Dwight H. Little. CAST: Brett Stimely. 1988 DVD

BLOODSTONE: SUBSPECIES II ★★1/2 A lovely college student is bitten by a vampire and spends most of the movie cringing from her shiveringly ugly master. Enjoy the comic-book sensibilities, imaginative direction, and the dark sense of humor permeating this low-budget howler. Rated R for violence and profanity. 107m. DIR: Ted Nicolaou. CAST: Anders Hove, Denice Duff. 1993

BLOODSUCKERS, THE ★★1/2 Lots of blood, gory special effects, and some good humor. Not bad for this type of film. Also known as *Return from the Past* and *Dr. Terror's Gallery of Horrors*. Not for the squeamish. 84m. DIR: David L. Hewitt. CAST: Lon Chaney Jr., John Carradine. 1967

BLOODSUCKING FREAKS (THE INCREDIBLE TORTURE SHOW) 🖤 This putrid film is an endurance test for even the most hard-core horror buffs. The scene where one of the maniacs sucks a woman's brains out with a straw has to be one of the most repulsive moments ever put on film. Rated R for nudity and violence. 89m. DIR: Joel M. Reed. CAST: Seamus O'Brian, Niles McMaster. 1978 DVD

BLOODSUCKING PHARAOHS IN PITTSBURGH ★★ Campy horror farce comparable to *Night of the Living Dead* meets *Rocky Horror Picture Show*. This time a cult killer sleazes about the city, slicing up victims with a chain saw. 89m. DIR: Alan Smithee. CAST: Jake Dengel. 1991

BLOODTHIRSTY BUTCHERS 🖤 As the title suggests, an extremely violent series of murders is committed in very gruesome fashion. Rated R. 80m. DIR: Andy Milligan. CAST: John Miranda, Annabella Wood. 1970

BLOODTIDE 🖤 Cheap horror film about bizarre rituals on a Greek isle. Rated R. 82m. DIR: Richard Jeffries. CAST: James Earl Jones, José Ferrer, Lila Kedrova. 1984

BLOODY BIRTHDAY 🖤 Three children, born during an eclipse of the moon, run amok, killing everyone in sight. Rated R. 85m. DIR: Edward Hunt. CAST: Susan Strasberg, José Ferrer, Lori Lethin, Joe Penny. 1986

BLOODY MAMA ★★1/2 Shelley Winters plays Ma Barker in this gangster flick. Her four sons share her notoriety as Depression-era bandits. Rated R. 90m. DIR: Roger Corman. CAST: Shelley Winters, Don Stroud, Pat Hingle, Robert Walden, Bruce Dern, Robert De Niro. 1970

BLOODY MOON ★★ A high-body-count exploitation horror film, this is one of the more perfunctory outings by Jess (Jesus) Franco, and thus one of his least revolting. Women are stabbed, choked, and in one memorable instance, buzz-sawed to death. A gory clip was used in Pedro Almodóvar's *Matador*. Rated R. 83m. DIR: Jess (Jesus) Franco. CAST: Olivia Pascal, Christoph Moosbrugger. 1981

BLOODY NEW YEAR ★★1/2 Five teenagers become stranded on an abandoned island resort that's caught in a time warp. Zombie ghosts begin to pop up, first taunting the kids, then terrorizing, and finally killing them. Fairly well produced and boasting some decent special effects. Rated R for violence and nudity. 90m. DIR: Norman J. Warren. CAST: Suzy Aitchison, Colin Heywood, Cathrine Roman. 1987

BLOODY PIT OF HORROR ★★ Nudie photographers and their comely models run afoul of a psycho who thinks he's the reincarnated Crimson Executioner when they visit a supposedly abandoned castle for a photo session. A laugh riot, if you've got a sick sense of humor—otherwise, steer clear. 74m. **DIR:** Max Hunter (Massimo Pupillo). **CAST:** Mickey Hargitay. 1965

BLOODY TRAIL 🖤 This Western has no plot, just an ex–Union soldier wandering through the recently defeated South. Rated R for nudity, profanity, and violence. 91m. **DIR:** Richard Robinson. **CAST:** Paul Harper, Rance Howard, John Mitchum. 1972

BLOODY WEDNESDAY ★★1/2 A peculiar psychological horror story whose prime attraction is that it never gets predictable. After a man suffers a nervous breakdown, his brother sets him up as the caretaker of a vacant hotel. Unfortunately, the story is never satisfactorily resolved. Not rated. 97m. **DIR:** Mark G. Gilhuis. **CAST:** Raymond Elmendorf, Pamela Baker. 1985

BLOW OUT ★★★★ John Travolta and Nancy Allen are terrific in this thriller by director Brian De Palma. The story concerns a motion picture sound man (Travolta) who becomes involved in murder when he rescues a young woman (Allen) from a car that crashes into a river. It's suspenseful, thrill-packed, adult entertainment. Rated R because of sex, nudity, profanity, and violence. 107m. **DIR:** Brian De Palma. **CAST:** John Travolta, Nancy Allen, John Lithgow, Dennis Franz. 1981

BLOW-UP ★★★★★ Director Michelangelo Antonioni's first English-language film was this stimulating examination into what is or is not reality. On its surface, a photographer (David Hemmings) believes he has taken a snapshot of a murder taking place. Vanessa Redgrave arrives at his studio and tries to seduce him out of the photo. 108m. **DIR:** Michelangelo Antonioni. **CAST:** Vanessa Redgrave, David Hemmings, Sarah Miles. 1966

BLOWING WILD 🖤 Wildcat Barbara Stanwyck lusts almost in vain for Gary Cooper in this foul tale of bandits in the Mexican oil fields. 90m. **DIR:** Hugo Fregonese. **CAST:** Gary Cooper, Barbara Stanwyck, Anthony Quinn, Ruth Roman, Ward Bond. 1953

BLOWN AWAY (1992) ★★ Pedestrian thriller has Corey Haim getting involved with young and dangerous Nicole Eggert, despite the warnings of older brother Corey Feldman. It's not until Eggert goes out of control that Haim sees her true colors. Haim spends half the film out of his clothes trying to prove that he's a big boy now. Rated R for nudity, language, and violence; unrated version contains more sex. 91m./93m. **DIR:** Brenton Spencer. **CAST:** Corey Haim, Corey Feldman, Nicole Eggert, Gary Farmer, Jean Leclerc. 1992

BLOWN AWAY (1994) ★★★1/2 A grudge fight turns into an explosive situation as a bomb-squad expert must deal with a mad bomber he once put away. Tommy Lee Jones holds this good, but not great film together with another strong villainous performance. Rated R for language and violence. 120m. **DIR:** Stephen Hopkins. **CAST:** Jeff Bridges, Tommy Lee Jones, Lloyd Bridges, Suzy Amis, Forest Whitaker. 1994 DVD

BLUE (1968) 🖤 God-awful, pretentious Western with Terence Stamp as a monosyllabic gunman. 113m. **DIR:** Silvio Narizzano. **CAST:** Terence Stamp, Joanna Pettet, Karl Malden, Ricardo Montalban, Sally Kirkland. 1968

BLUE (1993) ★★★1/2 A grieving French widow tries to sink into anonymity after her famous composer husband and child are killed in a car wreck. She becomes haunted by the unfinished personal and professional business of her dead spouse. Intoxicating imagery, classical music, and sensuality all induce a tracelike euphoria. For her frosty, somber performance, Juliette Binoche won the Venice Film Festival Best Actress award. In French with English subtitles. Rated R for nudity, sex, and language. 97m. **DIR:** Krzysztof Kieslowski. **CAST:** Juliette Binoche, Benoit Regent, Florence Pernel. 1993

BLUE AND THE GRAY, THE ★★★1/2 Star-studded saga dramatizes many viewpoints of the only war in history pitting American against American. Seen mostly through the eyes of an artist-correspondent, this TV miniseries is a polished, if occasionally sanitized, version of the bloodiest conflict in U.S. history. 295m. **DIR:** Andrew V. McLaglen. **CAST:** Stacy Keach, John Hammond, Lloyd Bridges, Rory Calhoun, Colleen Dewhurst, Warren Oates, Geraldine Page, Rip Torn, Robert Vaughn, Sterling Hayden, Paul Winfield, Gregory Peck. 1982

BLUE ANGEL, THE ★★★★★ This stunning tale about a straitlaced schoolteacher's obsession with a striptease dancer in Germany is the subject of many film classes. The photography, set design, and script are all top-notch, and there are spectacular performances by all. In German with English subtitles. B&W; 98m. **DIR:** Josef von Sternberg. **CAST:** Emil Jannings, Marlene Dietrich, Kurt Gerron. 1930

BLUE BIRD, THE ★★1/2 Following on the success of *The Wizard of Oz*, this extravagant fantasy features Shirley Temple as a spoiled brat who seeks true happiness by leaving her loving parents' home. Film is remarkable for the star's characterization of a spiteful little crab, which contrasts markedly with her usual sunny roles. 88m. **DIR:** Walter Lang. **CAST:** Shirley Temple, Spring Byington, Nigel Bruce. 1940

BLUE CHIPS ★★★ University-basketball coach is tempted to flush his squeaky-clean recruitment ethics down the toilet after suffering through his first losing season in a long career. Writer Ron Shelton shows a collegiate system filled with money-laundering alumni with deep pockets and blue-chip players who brazenly solicit under-the-table perks. The movie plunges deep into the aesthetics of the game and is packed with familiar NBA faces. Rated PG-13 for language. 108m. **DIR:** William Friedkin. **CAST:** Nick Nolte, Shaquille O'Neal, J. T. Walsh, Anfernee Hardaway, Alfre Woodard, Matt Nover, Mary McDonnell. 1994

BLUE CITY 🖤 Estranged son Judd Nelson returns to his hometown and learns that his father, previously the mayor, has been killed. Rated R for language and violence. 83m. **DIR:** Michelle Manning. **CAST:** Judd

Nelson, Ally Sheedy, David Caruso, Paul Winfield, Scott Wilson, Anita Morris. 1986

BLUE COLLAR ★★★1/2 This film delves into the underbelly of the auto industry by focusing on the fears, frustrations, and suppressed anger of three factory workers, superbly played by Richard Pryor, Harvey Keitel, and Yaphet Kotto. It is the social comment and intense drama that make this a highly effective and memorable film. Good music, too. Rated R for violence, sex, nudity, and profanity. 114m. DIR: Paul Schrader. CAST: Richard Pryor, Harvey Keitel, Yaphet Kotto. 1978 DVD

BLUE COUNTRY ★★★1/2 A lighthearted comedy involving a nurse who leaves the city to enjoy a free and independent life in the country. She meets up with a bachelor who equally enjoys his freedom. Their encounters with the local townspeople provide amusing glimpses of French folk life. In French with English subtitles. 90m. DIR: Jean-Charles Tacchella. CAST: Brigitte Fossey, Jacques Serres, Ginette Garcin, Armand Meffre, Ginett Mathieu. 1977

BLUE DAHLIA, THE ★★★★ In this sexy and stylish *film noir*, recently returned WWII veteran Alan Ladd is blamed for the murder of his unscrupulous wife. Mysterious and gorgeous Veronica Lake offers to help, but can he trust her? Tightly scripted by Raymond Chandler and vibrantly acted, this is a memorable effort. Not rated; contains violence. B&W; 100m. DIR: George Marshall. CAST: Alan Ladd, Veronica Lake, William Bendix, Howard DaSilva, Doris Dowling, Hugh Beaumont. 1946

BLUE DE VILLE ★★★ Engaging cross-country odyssey in which three diverse types travel together in a classic, mint blue 1959 Cadillac. Interesting characters, outrageous situations, and gorgeous scenery. 100m. DIR: Jim Johnston. CAST: Jennifer Runyon, Kimberly Pistone, Mark Thomas Miller. 1986

BLUE DESERT ★★★ Two men, one a policeman and the other a drifter, court a woman who is being terrorized in a small desert town. Solid three-person thriller that keeps the viewer intrigued with plot twists galore and solid acting. Rated R for violence. 98m. DIR: Bradley Battersby. CAST: D. B. Sweeney, Courteney Cox, Craig Sheffer. 1991

BLUE FIN ★★ The son of a commercial fisherman finds that growing up is hard to do, especially when he has to do so before he's ready. On a fishing trip with his father, the boy is caught in a storm, and must act responsibly for the first time in his life. 93m. DIR: Carl Schultz. CAST: Hardy Krüger, Greg Rowe, Liddy Clark, Hugh Keays-Byrne. 1977

BLUE FIRE LADY ★★1/2 The story of racetracks and horse racing, the trust and love between an animal and a person are well handled in this family film. It chronicles the story of Jenny (Cathryn Harrison) and her love for horses, which endures despite her father's disapproval. 96m. DIR: Ross Dimsey. CAST: Catherine Harrison, Mark Holden, Peter Cummins. 1983

BLUE FLAME ★★ Intriguing premise wears out its welcome long before the film is over. It starts off promisingly enough, with two aliens hiding out in the mind of a cop. Inside, they force the cop to face his darkest fears and desires. Brian Wimmer is OK as

the cop, but the rest of the cast isn't very arresting. Rated R for violence and sexuality. 88m. DIR: Cassian Elwes. CAST: Brian Wimmer, Jad Mager, Kerri Green, Ian Buchanan, Cecilia Peck. 1993

●**BLUE GARDENIA** ★★1/2 Woman on the lam for a murder she can't remember is befriended by the reporter sworn to bring her to justice. Standard crime film boasts a good cast and title song by Nat "King" Cole but never manages to rise above the competition. B&W; 90m. DIR: Fritz Lang. CAST: Anne Baxter, Richard Conte, Ann Sothern, Raymond Burr, Jeff Donnell, George Reeves, Ruth Storey, Richard Erdman. 1953 DVD

BLUE HAWAII ★★★1/2 In this enjoyable Elvis Presley flick, the star plays a returning soldier who works with tourists against his mom's (Angela Lansbury) wishes. 101m. DIR: Norman Taurog. CAST: Elvis Presley, Joan Blackman, Angela Lansbury, Iris Adrian. 1962 DVD

BLUE HEAVEN 🎬 New York TV executive threatened by a severe problem with alcohol. Not rated; contains violence and strong language. 100m. DIR: Kathleen Dowdey. CAST: Leslie Denniston, James Eckhouse. 1984

BLUE HOTEL ★★ Unsatisfying interpretation of Stephen Crane's short story. David Warner chews the scenery as a stranger in town who fears his life will be taken by the other guests of the hotel he occupies. The entire silly affair, which flirts with the notion of predestination, revolves around a card game. Introduced by Henry Fonda; unrated and suitable for family viewing. 55m. DIR: Ján Kadár. CAST: David Warner, James Keach, John Bottoms, Rex Everhart. 1984

BLUE HOUR, THE ★★★1/2 Bittersweet German love story about a male prostitute who falls for his female neighbor after her bullish boyfriend walks out. Excellent performances highlight this improbable love story that looks at love from both sides. In German with English subtitles. Not rated; contains nudity, sex, and frank language. 87m. DIR: Marcel Gisler. CAST: Andreas Herder, Dina Leipzig, Cristof Krix. 1991

BLUE ICE ★★★1/2 Michael Caine's engaging lead performance as retired-spy-turned-nightclub-owner Harry Anders (he's hoping to make a franchise of this character) rises smoothly above a derivative Ron Hutchinson script that borrows quite heavily from Len Deighton's *The Ipcress File* ... which also starred Caine, as another Harry (Palmer). This particular Harry, jazz lover and chef extraordinaire, gets mixed up with Sean Young, who may be more than a consul's wife. Rated R for violence, nudity, profanity, and simulated sex. 96m. DIR: Russell Mulcahy. CAST: Michael Caine, Sean Young, Ian Holm, Bob Hoskins, Bobby Short. 1993

BLUE IGUANA ★★ For his first film, writer-director John Lafia attempted a *Raising Arizona*–style spoof of the hard boiled detective story—and failed. The story concerns a "recovery specialist" (Dylan McDermott) who is coerced by IRS agents Tovah Feldshuh and Dean Stockwell into going after $40 million in contraband money. The supporting actors are allowed to overact to bizarre proportions. Rated R for violence. 90m. DIR: John Lafia. CAST: Dylan McDermott, Jessica Harper, James Russo, Tovah Feldshuh, Dean Stockwell. 1988

BLUE IN THE FACE ★★★1/2 With standing sets and numerous players left over after making *Smoke*, director Wayne Wang and scripter Paul Auster quickly put together this companion film, which once again stars Harvey Keitel as Brooklyn cigar-shop manager Auggie Wren. The free-form result is highly improvisational, with cute bits from numerous celebrity guest stars. The quirky soundtrack comes from John Lurie and the Lounge Lizards, who also appear on camera. Although not as compelling as *Smoke*, this is oddly appealing. Rated R for profanity and nudity. 98m. **DIR:** Wayne Wang. **CAST:** Harvey Keitel, Jim Jarmusch, Mel Gorham, Giancarlo Esposito, Lou Reed, Jared Harris, Lily Tomlin, Michael J. Fox, Madonna, Roseanne, Mira Sorvino. 1995

BLUE JEANS ★★ A group of French school-boys takes a trip to England to try to lose their virginity. This dull film's only redemption is that one innocent boy learns a few of life's lessons. In French with English subtitles. Not rated; contains profanity. 80m. **DIR:** Hughes des Rozier. **CAST:** Gilles Budin, Michel Gibet, Gabriel Cattand, Gerard Croce, Pierre Borizans. 1978

BLUE KITE, THE ★★★★ Once again, we have a first-rate Chinese film that has been banned in its homeland. This one tells the story of a young schoolteacher, from her first marriage in 1953 to the Cultural Revolution in 1967. Along the way she loses three husbands—and, eventually, her own freedom—to the persecutions of the communist regime. Strong, engrossing drama, balancing political tragedy with small flashes of humor and irony. In Mandarin with English subtitles. Not rated; contains mature themes and mild violence. 138m. **DIR:** Tian Zhuangzhuang. **CAST:** Tian Yi. 1994

BLUE KNIGHT, THE (1973) ★★★1/2 William Holden gives an excellent, Emmy-winning performance as the hero of Joseph Wambaugh's bestselling novel. *The Blue Knight* chronicles the last four days in the life of an aging L.A. street cop. Lee Remick is superb as Holden's girlfriend. Originally made for television and cut down from a four-part, 200-minute presentation. Not rated. 103m. **DIR:** Robert Butler. **CAST:** William Holden, Lee Remick, Joe Santos, Sam Elliott, David Moody, Jamie Farr. 1973

BLUE KNIGHT, THE (1975) ★★ This is the second made-for-TV production based on Joseph Wambaugh's bestselling book. In this rendering, George Kennedy assumes the role of tough L.A. cop Bumper Morgan, who is searching frantically for a cop killer. The story is average, but Kennedy gives a typically strong portrayal. 78m. **DIR:** J. Lee Thompson. **CAST:** George Kennedy, Alex Rocco, Verna Bloom, Glynn Turman. 1975

BLUE LAGOON, THE ★★1/2 Two things save *The Blue Lagoon* from being a complete waste: Nestor Almendros's beautiful cinematography and the hilarious dialogue. Unfortunately, the laughs are unintentional. The screenplay is a combination of *Swiss Family Robinson* and the story of Adam and Eve, focusing on the growing love and sexuality of two children stranded on a South Sea island. Rated R for nudity and suggested sex. 101m. **DIR:** Randal Kleiser. **CAST:** Brooke Shields, Christopher Atkins, Leo McKern, William Daniels. 1980 DVD

●**BLUE LIGHT, THE** ★★★1/2 After starring in a series of mountain films, a peculiarly German genre that served to celebrate nature, former dancer Leni Riefenstahl made her directorial debut with this, another in the series. The plot is little more than a folk tale about an artist who pursues a beautiful girl who is the only one who can reach the top of a local mountain. Beautifully filmed, with a rich command of film language. In German with English subtitles. B&W; 77m. **DIR:** Leni Riefenstahl. **CAST:** Leni Riefenstahl, Max Holzboer. 1932

BLUE LIGHTING, THE ★★ Lightweight action movie starring Sam Elliott as a hired gun sent to Australia to retrieve a precious gem from IRA renegade Robert Culp. Culp knows Elliott's coming and sets a series of traps for him. A passable time waster. Rated PG. 95m. **DIR:** Lee Philips. **CAST:** Sam Elliott, Robert Culp, Rebecca Gilling. 1986

BLUE MAX, THE ★★★ For those with a yen for excellent aerial-combat gymnastics, superb photography, and a fine Jerry Goldsmith music score, this is the film. The story line is quite a different matter. Seen from the eyes of Kaiser Wilhelm II, air aces, and their superior officers, the plot is very standard material. The cast is fine but somewhat restrained. See it for the marvelous dogfights. You can tolerate the story. 156m. **DIR:** John Guillermin. **CAST:** George Peppard, James Mason, Ursula Andress, Jeremy Kemp. 1966

BLUE MONEY ★★★ Larry Gormley (Tim Curry) discovers a suitcase with half a million dollars in his cab. The money turns out to belong to the mob, and they want it back. Not a very original idea, but well written, acted, and directed, this comedy provides plenty of fast-moving fun. Made for British television. 82m. **DIR:** Colin Bucksey. **CAST:** Tim Curry, Debby Bishop, Billy Connolly, Frances Tomelty. 1984

BLUE MONKEY ★★★ A small-city hospital becomes contaminated by a patient infected by an unknown insect that causes terminal gangrene as it gestates eggs. One of these insects becomes mutated and grows to huge proportions. A low-budget film, this movie sometimes has the charm, humor, and suspense of classics like *The Thing* and *Them*. Rated R for violence and language. 98m. **DIR:** William Fruet. **CAST:** Steve Railsback, Susan Anspach, Gwynyth Walsh, John Vernon, Joe Flaherty, Robin Duke. 1987

BLUE MONTANA SKIES ★★★1/2 The fur flies when Gene Autry and Smiley "Frog" Burnette discover the murder of their partner, which leads them on the trail of Canadian border pelt smugglers. Unusual snow-country Western action. B&W; 54m. **DIR:** B. Reeves "Breezy" Eason. **CAST:** Gene Autry, Smiley Burnette, June Storey, Harry Woods, Dorothy Granger. 1939

BLUE MOVIES ★★ Poorly directed, cheaply made comedy about two young entrepreneurs and their quest to make a pornographic movie. It has some funny moments. Rated R for profanity and nudity. 92m. **DIR:** Ed Fitzgerald. **CAST:** Steve Levitt, Larry

Poindexter, Lucinda Crosby, Darian Mathias, Christopher Stone, Don Calfa, Larry Linville. **1988**

BLUE MURDER AT ST. TRINIAN'S ★★★1/2 A cast of comedy veterans puts new life into a routine plot in this delightful romp. St. Trinian's is an all-girl school where the teenage students do mischief from morning to night. They have a field day when they find their new headmistress is a diamond smuggler. B&W; 87m. **DIR:** Frank Launder. **CAST:** Alastair Sim, Terry-Thomas, Lionel Jeffries, Joyce Grenfell, George Cole, Ferdinand Mayne, Eric Barker. **1955**

BLUE RIVER ★★★ Sam Elliott is the angry but highly principled man whose repressive authority is challenged by even angrier teen Jerry O'Connell. O'-Connell is quite convincing as the brilliant but troubled teen in this intimate and above-average look at the emotional glue holding a family together. Rated PG-13 for violence. 90m. **DIR:** Larry Elikann. **CAST:** Jerry O'Connell, Susan Dey, Sam Elliott, Nick Stahl, Neal McDonough, Jean Marie Barnwell, Patrick Renna. **1995 DVD**

BLUE SKIES ★★★1/2 Bing Crosby and Fred Astaire are a couple of song-and-dance men whose friendship is threatened when both fall for chorine Joan Caulfield. Plus thirty wonderful Irving Berlin songs. The newly introduced "You Keep Coming Back Like a Song" was Oscar nominated. B&W; 104m. **DIR:** Stuart Heisler. **CAST:** Bing Crosby, Fred Astaire, Joan Caulfield, Billy DeWolfe, Olga San Juan. **1946**

BLUE SKIES AGAIN ★★ A sure-fielding, solid-hitting prospect tries to break into the lineup of a minor league team. There's just one problem: The determined ball player is a female. Nothing more than a routine ball grounder. Rated PG. 96m. **DIR:** Richard Michaels. **CAST:** Harry Hamlin, Robyn Barto, Mimi Rogers, Kenneth McMillan, Dana Elcar. **1983**

BLUE SKY ★★★ Director Tony Richardson's last film before his AIDS-related death in 1991. This gutsy unforgettable film is about the pain and power of love as well as the questionable atomic-testing policies of our government during the early 1960s. A military nuclear engineer who witnesses a Nevada test-site cover-up also faces domestic problems when the scandalous behavior of his emotionally shredded wife threatens to end both their marriage and his career. Rated PG-13 for language and suggested sex. 101m. **DIR:** Tony Richardson. **CAST:** Jessica Lange, Tommy Lee Jones, Amy Locane, Powers Boothe, Anna Klemp, Chris O'Donnell. **1994**

BLUE STEEL (1934) ★★★ Fun but undistinguished B Western with a very young John Wayne as a cowpoke who saves a town from extinction when he reveals there's gold in them thar hills. B&W; 60m. **DIR:** Robert N. Bradbury. **CAST:** John Wayne, Eleanor Hunt, George "Gabby" Hayes, Ed Peil, Yakima Canutt, George Cleveland. **1934**

BLUE STEEL (1990) ★★ Female rookie cop gets involved with a Wall Street broker who turns out to be a serial killer in this lurid, visually stunning thriller. The film's high-gloss photography, however, doesn't fully compensate for the often ridiculous story line. Rated R. 102m. **DIR:** Kathryn Bigelow. **CAST:** Jamie Lee Curtis, Ron Silver, Clancy Brown, Elizabeth Peña, Louise Fletcher. **1990**

•**BLUE STREAK** ★★ After two years behind bars, the mastermind of a bungled Los Angeles jewel heist returns to the scene of his crime to retrieve a $17 million diamond that he hid in an air duct. The building has been converted into a police station so he impersonates a cop to gain access to a secured upper floor. He is mistaken for a new department transferee, assigned a partner, and gets involved in dull misadventures, shoot-outs, and chases in this progressively noisy and dumb action-comedy. Rated R for language and violence. 93m. **DIR:** Les Mayfield. **CAST:** Martin Lawrence, Luke Wilson, Peter Greene, William Forsythe. **1999 DVD**

BLUE SUNSHINE ★★1/2 Oddball mystery-thriller dealing with a series of random killings. Low-budget film is both ridiculous and terrifying at the same time. Rated PG for mild language and violence. 97m. **DIR:** Jeff Lieberman. **CAST:** Zalman King, Deborah Winters, Mark Goddard, Robert Walden, Charles Siebert. **1976**

BLUE THUNDER ★★★★1/2 A state-of-the-art helicopter is the centerpiece of this action-paced police melodrama. Piloted by Roy Scheider, the craft—a.k.a. "Blue Thunder"—battles a second rogue helicopter commanded by villain Malcolm McDowell high above the crowded streets of downtown Los Angeles. The result is a gripping and immensely entertaining—if somewhat implausible—adventure-thriller. Rated R for violence, nudity, and profanity. 109m. **DIR:** John Badham. **CAST:** Roy Scheider, Malcolm McDowell, Candy Clark, Warren Oates. **1983 DVD**

BLUE TIGER ★★★ Vengeance clashes with Japanese mysticism in this thoughtful thriller that begins as single mother Virginia Madsen helplessly watches her young son die in gunfire between warring crime factions (a *very* grim scene). She adopts a most unusual ploy to locate the killer, and soon gets more than she anticipated. Madsen brings intelligence and credibility to what might otherwise have been a ho-hum revenge saga. Rated R for violence, profanity, and simulated sex. 88m. **DIR:** Norberto Barba. **CAST:** Virginia Madsen, Toru Nakamura, Dean Hallo, Ryo Ishibashi, Harry Dean Stanton. **1994**

BLUE TORNADO ★★ Starts out wanting to be *Top Gun* and ends trying to be *E.T.—The Extra-Terrestrial*. It fails on both levels. Some impressive aerial shots save the film. Rated PG-13. 96m. **DIR:** Tony Dobb. **CAST:** Dirk Benedict, Ted McGinley, Patsy Kensit. **1990**

BLUE VELVET ★★★★1/2 In this brilliant but disturbing film, Kyle MacLachlan and Laura Dern play youngsters who become involved in the mystery surrounding nightclub singer Isabella Rossellini. It seldom lets the viewer off easy, yet it is nevertheless a stunning cinematic work. Rated R for violence, nudity, and profanity. 120m. **DIR:** David Lynch. **CAST:** Kyle MacLachlan, Isabella Rossellini, Dennis Hopper, Laura Dern, Dean Stockwell. **1986 DVD**

BLUE YONDER, THE ★★★1/2 Heartfelt tale of a boy (Huckleberry Fox) who goes back in time via a time machine to warn his late grandfather (Peter Coyote) of his unsuccessful attempt at a nonstop transatlantic flight. Good performances keep the creaky plot airborne. 89m. **DIR:** Mark Rosman. **CAST:**

Peter Coyote, Huckleberry Fox, Art Carney, Dennis Lipscomb, Joe Flood, Mittie Smith, Frank Simons. 1985

BLUEBEARD (1944) ★★★ Atmospheric low-budget thriller by resourceful German director Edgar G. Ulmer gives great character actor John Carradine one of his finest leading roles as a strangler who preys on women. B&W; 73m. **DIR:** Edgar G. Ulmer. **CAST:** John Carradine, Jean Parker, Nils Asther, Ludwig Stossel, Iris Adrian. **1944 DVD**

BLUEBEARD (1963) ★★★1/2 Claude Chabrol, justifiably known as the Gallic Hitchcock, tells the story of the Frenchman who married and murdered eleven women in order to support his real family. Chabrol approaches the material in the same manner that Chaplin did in *Monsieur Verdoux*—as a satirical parable of capitalism. Not for all tastes, obviously, but well worth a look. Screenplay by Françoise Sagan. Original title *Landru*. Dubbed in English. 114m. **DIR:** Claude Chabrol. **CAST:** Charles Denner, Michele Morgan, Danielle Darrieux, Hildegarde Neff. **1963**

BLUEBEARD (1972) ★★1/2 Richard Burton stars in this film, which has its tongue planted firmly in cheek. The legend of the multiple murderer is intermingled with Nazi lore to come out as a reasonably convincing foray into a combination of black comedy and classic horror films. Rated R. 125m. **DIR:** Edward Dmytryk. **CAST:** Richard Burton, Raquel Welch, Karin Schubert, Joey Heatherton. **1972**

BLUEBEARD'S EIGHTH WIFE ★★1/2 The first script written by Charles Brackett and Billy Wilder together, this sophisticated comedy is guilty of trying too hard. The slight story is about a seven-times-divorced millionaire who thinks he knows all about women. But he's buffaloed when he meets a nobleman's daughter. The personalities are stronger than the plot. B&W; 80m. **DIR:** Ernst Lubitsch. **CAST:** Gary Cooper, Claudette Colbert, David Niven, Edward Everett Horton, Tyler Brooke, Elizabeth Patterson, Herman Bing. **1938**

BLUEBERRY HILL ★★ Carrie Snodgress plays a neurotic mother in 1956. Her daughter finds out the truth about her deceased father and also discovers, that she has inherited his piano skills. Zzzzz. Rated R for nudity and language. 93m. **DIR:** Strathford Hamilton. **CAST:** Carrie Snodgress, Margaret Avery, Matt Lattanzi. **1987**

BLUES BROTHERS, THE ★★★1/2 Director John Landis attempted to film an epic comedy and came pretty darn close. In it, the musicians of the title, John Belushi and Dan Aykroyd, attempt to save an orphanage. The movie's excesses—too many car crashes and chases—are offset by Belushi and Aykroyd as the Laurel and Hardy of backbeat; the musical turns of Aretha Franklin, James Brown, and Ray Charles; and Landis's flair for comic timing. Rated R. 132m. **DIR:** John Landis. **CAST:** John Belushi, Dan Aykroyd, John Candy, Carrie Fisher. **1980 DVD**

BLUES BROTHERS 2000 ★★★1/2 In this follow-up to the 1980 comedy, the accent this time is on the music. Featuring a mind-boggling assemblage of blues and R&B greats, it serves not only as homage to the late Junior Wells but also as an ear-pleasing celebration of one of America's few original art forms.

From Aretha Franklin's reprise of her classic "Respect" to an eye-popping all-star finale jam featuring practically every notable performer in the blues and R&B fields, it's a real treat for fans of the music. Rated PG-13 for profanity and partial nudity. 123m. **DIR:** John Landis. **CAST:** Dan Aykroyd, John Goodman, Joe Morton, Nia Peeples, Kathleen Freeman, Frank Oz, Steve Lawrence. **1998 DVD**

BLUME IN LOVE ★★★★ Sort of the male version of *An Unmarried Woman*, this Paul Mazursky film is the heartrending, sometimes shocking tale of a lawyer (George Segal) who can't believe his wife (Susan Anspach) doesn't love him anymore. He tries everything to win her back (including rape), and the result is a drama the viewer won't soon forget. Superb performances by Segal, Anspach, and Kris Kristofferson (as the wife's new beau) help immensely. Rated R for suggested sex, profanity, and violence. 117m. **DIR:** Paul Mazursky. **CAST:** George Segal, Susan Anspach, Kris Kristofferson, Marsha Mason, Shelley Winters. **1973**

BMX BANDITS ★★★ An exciting story of young Australian kids and their BMX bikes. Features great stunts, funny East End of London villains, and a satisfying ending. Not Rated. 92m. **DIR:** Brian Trenchard-Smith. **CAST:** David Argue, John Ley, Nicole Kidman. **1983**

BOARDING SCHOOL ★★★1/2 A European boarding school for girls, located next to an all-boys' boarding school, creates the setting for sexual high jinks and young love in this sexy comedy. The 1956 theme is enhanced by some Bill Haley music. Rated R for nudity. 100m. **DIR:** André Farwagi. **CAST:** Nastassja Kinski, Gerry Sundquist, Kurt Raab. **1978 DVD**

BOAT IS FULL, THE ★★★ Markus Imhoof's film about refugees from the Nazis trying to obtain refuge in Switzerland is tragic and extraordinarily effective. It could have been a better movie, but it could hardly have been more heartbreaking. No MPAA rating. 100m. **DIR:** Markus Imhoof. **CAST:** Tina Engel, Marin Walz. **1983**

BOATNIKS, THE ★★1/2 Disney comedy in which Robert Morse plays a heroic Coast Guard officer who manages a romantic relationship with Stephanie Powers while pursuing bumbling thieves (Phil Silvers, Norman Fell, and Mickey Shaughnessy). Rated G. 99m. **DIR:** Norman Tokar. **CAST:** Stephanie Powers, Phil Silvers, Norman Fell, Robert Morse, Mickey Shaughnessy. **1970**

BOB & CAROL & TED & ALICE ★★★★1/2 In this comedy, Natalie Wood and Robert Culp (Carol and Bob) play a modern couple who believe in open marriage, pot smoking, etc. Their friends, conservative Elliott Gould and Dyan Cannon (Ted and Alice), are shocked by Bob and Carol's behavior. Meanwhile, Bob and Carol try to liven up Ted and Alice's marriage by introducing them to their way of life. Lots of funny moments. Rated R. 104m. **DIR:** Paul Mazursky. **CAST:** Natalie Wood, Robert Culp, Elliott Gould, Dyan Cannon. **1969**

BOB LE FLAMBEUR ★★★★★ This is an exquisite example of early French *film noir*. In it are all the trappings of the classic gangster movie. The most fascinating element of this import is the title charac-

...er, Bob Montagne (Roger Duchesne), who plans to rob a casino of $800 million. In French with English subtitles. B&W; 102m. **DIR:** Jean-Pierre Melville. **CAST:** Roger Duchesne, Isabel Corey, Daniel Cauchy, Howard Vernon. **1955**

BOB ROBERTS ★★★★ The writing-directing debut of star Tim Robbins is a fake documentary about a folk-singing, millionaire crypto-fascist's campaign for a seat in the Senate. Robbins's occasionally pedantic but most often clever satire features numerous cameos and his own hilarious, hate-filled compositions. (Robbins, by the way, refused to release a soundtrack album—lest real right-wing politicians appropriate the songs for their own anthems.) Rated R for profanity and sexual themes. 105m. **DIR:** Tim Robbins. **CAST:** Tim Robbins, Alan Rickman, Giancarlo Esposito, Gore Vidal. **1992**

BOBBIE JO AND THE OUTLAW ★1/2 Lynda Carter, hungry for excitement, tags along with Marjoe Gortner and his gang. An orgy of murders and robberies ensues. Lots of violence, little credibility. Rated R for nudity, violence, and profanity. 89m. **DIR:** Mark L. Lester. **CAST:** Marjoe Gortner, Lynda Carter, Jesse Vint, Merrie Lynn Ross, Belinda Balaski, Gerrit Graham. **1976**

BOBBY DEERFIELD ★★★1/2 A racing driver (Al Pacino) becomes obsessed with the cause of how a competitor was seriously injured in an accident on the track. In a visit to the hospitalized driver, he meets a strange lady (Marthe Keller) and has an affair. Rated PG. 124m. **DIR:** Sydney Pollack. **CAST:** Al Pacino, Marthe Keller, Romolo Valli. **1977**

BOBO, THE ♥ A bumbling matador (Peter Sellers) has to seduce a high-priced courtesan (Britt Ekland) in order to get employment as a singer. 105m. **DIR:** Robert Parrish. **CAST:** Peter Sellers, Britt Ekland, Rossano Brazzi. **1967**

BOCA ★★★ Dedicated journalist Rae Dawn Chong's quest—to prove that renegade Rio de Janeiro police officers are murdering street children—is mere window dressing for another of Zalman King's arty, erotic escapades. Our heroine is equally formidable in or out of her clothing. Ed Silverstein's story touches on political intrigue during Martin Sheen's brief appearances as a CIA spook. Rated R for rape, simulated sex, nudity, violence, and profanity. 91m. **DIR:** Zalman King. **CAST:** Rae Dawn Chong, Martin Kemp, Tarcisio Meira, Martin Sheen. **1994**

BOCCACCIO 70 ★★★★ As with its Renaissance namesake, this film tells stories—three of them, in fact, by three of Italy's greatest directors. Federico Fellini's entry, "The Temptation of Dr. Antonio," showcases Anita Ekberg. The second playlet, by Luchino Visconti, is "The Bet," which features Romy Schneider as a not-so-typical housewife. "The Raffle," by Vittorio De Sica, is reminiscent of a dirty joke told badly, and it tends to cheapen the panache of the first two. In Italian with English subtitles. 165m. **DIR:** Federico Fellini, Luchino Visconti, Vittorio De Sica. **CAST:** Anita Ekberg, Sophia Loren, Romy Schneider, Tomas Milian. **1962**

BODIES, REST & MOTION ★★1/2 Set in a Southwest desert city, this ponderous comedy-drama looks at the dreams and disillusionment of twentysomethings. Phoebe Cates, Bridget Fonda, and Eric Stoltz contribute a consistent charm. Rated R for adult situations and language. 93m. **DIR:** Michael Steinberg. **CAST:** Phoebe Cates, Bridget Fonda, Tim Roth, Eric Stoltz. **1993**

BODILY HARM ★★ A wife tries to clear her husband's name when he's sued for malpractice. Though his career has been ruined, her help is unappreciated. This dull-edged television movie does little justice to its Hitchcockian pretensions. 100m. **DIR:** Thomas Wright. **CAST:** Joe Penny, Lisa Hartman, Kathleen Quinlan. **1992**

BODY AND SOUL (1924) ★★1/2 Escaped convict assumes the role of a minister in a small town in the South, rapes the daughter of a loyal supporter, and steals her money. Downbeat story has a happy ending (it's all been a dream caused by a newspaper story). Paul Robeson in his first feature film is full of the devil as the brutish, drunken minister, and literally sets the congregation rolling in one of the liveliest church services on film. B&W; 79m. **DIR:** Oscar Micheaux. **CAST:** Paul Robeson, Marshall Rodgers, Lawrence Chenault, Lillian Johnson. **1924**

BODY AND SOUL (1947) ★★★★★ The best boxing film ever, this is an allegorical work that covers everything from the importance of personal honor to corruption in politics. It details the story of a fighter (John Garfield) who'll do anything to get to the top—and does, with tragic results. Great performances, gripping drama, and stark realism make this a must-see. B&W; 104m. **DIR:** Robert Rossen. **CAST:** John Garfield, Lilli Palmer, Hazel Brooks, Anne Revere, William Conrad. **1947 DVD**

BODY AND SOUL (1981) ★★★ Okay remake of the 1947 boxing classic. It's not original, deep, or profound, but entertaining. However, the original, with John Garfield, is better. Rated R for violence and profanity. 100m. **DIR:** George Bowers. **CAST:** Leon Isaac Kennedy, Jayne Kennedy, Perry Lang. **1981**

BODY ARMOR ★★★ Above-average made-for-video thriller pits hero-for-hire Ken Conway (Matt McColm) against evil Dr. Ramsey Krago (Ron Perlman), who develops deadly viruses just so he can sell the cures to the world's governments. Director Jack Gill was formerly a top stunt director and knows how to keep the bodies flying. Rated R for violence, sexual situations, nudity, and profanity. 95m. **DIR:** Jack Gill. **CAST:** Matt McColm, Annabel Schofield, Ron Perlman, Carol Alt, Morgan Brittany, Clint Howard, John Rhys-Davies. **1996 DVD**

BODY COUNT (1988) ♥ An unexceptional thriller about a man committed to a mental institution by relatives who want his money. He escapes, and the title should clue you in as to what happens next. Not rated. 93m. **DIR:** Paul Leder. **CAST:** Bernie White, Marilyn Hassett, Dick Sargent, Greg Mullavey. **1988**

BODY COUNT (1997) ★★★1/2 Tough, gripping crime-drama stars Forest Whitaker as the mastermind behind an art museum robbery. When an alarm is accidentally tripped, the police arrive and Whitaker is killed in the crossfire. His four accomplices manage to get away, but their trip is fraught with tension and further complicated when they pick up a stranded motorist. Good cast has fun being bad. Rated R for adult situations, language, and violence. 84m. DIR: Robert Patton-Spruill. CAST: David Caruso, Linda Fiorentino, John Leguizamo, Ving Rhames, Forest Whitaker, Donnie Wahlberg. 1997

BODY COUNT (1997) (DIRECT TO VIDEO) ★★1/2 *Who's the Boss?* star Alyssa Milano continues her leap into adult roles in this formulaic thriller. As Milano and her rich boyfriend make out in his parents' basement, art thieves kill the parents upstairs. When the couple is discovered, they are forced to engage in a deadly game of cat and mouse. Some menacing moments give their direct-to-video effort an edge. Rated R for adult situations, language, and violence. 88m. DIR: Kurt Voss. CAST: Alyssa Milano, Justin Theroux, Ice T. 1997

BODY DOUBLE ★★★1/2 This Brian De Palma thriller is often gruesome, disgusting, and exploitative. But you can't take your eyes off the screen. Craig Wasson is first-rate as a young actor who witnesses a brutal murder, and Melanie Griffith is often hilarious as the porno star who holds the key to the crime. Rated R for nudity, suggested sex, profanity, and violence. 110m. DIR: Brian De Palma. CAST: Craig Wasson, Melanie Griffith, Gregg Henry, Deborah Shelton. 1984 DVD

BODY HEAT ★★★1/2 This is a classic piece of *film noir,* full of suspense, characterization, atmosphere, and sexuality. Lawrence Kasdan makes his directorial debut with this topflight 1940s-style entertainment about a lustful romance between an attorney (William Hurt) and a married woman (Kathleen Turner) that leads to murder. Rated R because of nudity, sex, and murder. 113m. DIR: Lawrence Kasdan. CAST: William Hurt, Kathleen Turner, Richard Crenna, Mickey Rourke, Ted Danson. 1981 DVD

BODY IN THE LIBRARY, THE ★★★1/2 Agatha Christie's Miss Marple (Joan Hickson) stays close to home in this mystery when she is summoned by a good friend with the misfortune to have found a body in her library at Gossington Hall, St. Mary Mead. Careful armchair sleuths will find this one solvable, but red herrings abound. Not rated; suitable for family viewing. 153m. DIR: Silvio Narizzano. CAST: Joan Hickson, Gwen Watford, Andrew Cruickshank, Moray Watson, Valentine Dyall. 1984

BODY LANGUAGE (1992) ★★★ Heather Locklear doesn't quite fit the role of the first woman executive at a major corporation, but Linda Purl does a great job portraying the psychotic new secretary. Above-average made-for-cable thriller. 91m. DIR: Arthur Allan Seidelman. CAST: Heather Locklear, Linda Purl, Edward Albert. 1992

BODY LANGUAGE (1995) ★★1/2 When, oh when, will movie attorneys stop thinking with their glands? Tom Berenger is wholly unbelievable as a supposedly intelligent lawyer who gets talked by sultry Heidi Schanz into killing her husband. Naturally, things aren't quite what they seem. Costar Nancy Travis, as Berenger's perceptive partner, is much better than the rest; she makes the film watchable. Rated R for nudity, simulated sex, profanity, and violence. 100m. DIR: George Case. CAST: Tom Berenger, Nancy Travis, Robert Patrick, Eddie Jones, Dana Gladstone, Heidi Schanz. 1995

BODY MELT 🎬 Those folks down under have a thing for gross-out horror films, but the plot disintegrates faster than the people in this film. This is no *Dead Alive*—it's just dead. Rated AO; contains extreme violence, nudity, adult situations, and strong language. 82m. DIR: Philip Brophy. CAST: Gerald Kennedy, Andrew Daddo, Ian Smith, Regina Gaigalas. 1993

BODY MOVES 🎬 This dance flick is about as formulaic as you can get. Two dance troupes suffer through infighting on their way to a final showdown in the local dance contest. Rated PG-13 for profanity. 98m. DIR: Gerry Lively. CAST: Kirk Rivera. 1990

BODY OF EVIDENCE ★★1/2 Madonna's slut-in-distress is reasonably credible in Brad Mirman's flimsy erotic thriller, which finds our heroine (?) accused of murdering her elderly lover with a most unusual weapon: herself. Rated R for profanity and nudity. 99m. DIR: Uli Edel. CAST: Madonna, Willem Dafoe, Joe Mantegna, Anne Archer, Jurgen Prochnow. 1993

BODY OF INFLUENCE 🎬 A Beverly Hills psychiatrist falls in love with one of his sexy patients, who then tries to murder him. Rated R for simulated sex, nudity, profanity, and violence. 96m. DIR: Alexander Gregory Hippolyte. CAST: Nick Cassavetes, Shannon Whirry, Sandahl Bergman, Don Swayze, Richard Roundtree. 1993

BODY OF INFLUENCE 2 ★★ There's plenty of flesh on display in this familiar tale of a psychologist who falls for a new patient with some dark secrets in her past. R-rated and unrated versions; both contain nudity, adult situations, and profanity. 88/94m. DIR: Brian J. Smith. CAST: Jodie Fisher, Daniel Anderson. 1996 DVD

BODY PARTS ★★ Maurice Renard's classic short story, "The Hands of Orlac," gets hauled out one more time for this ludicrous update from gore-hound Eric Red. Criminal psychologist Jeff Fahey loses his right arm and then receives another—from a serial killer—thanks to the miracles of modern science. Rated R for profanity and outrageous gruesomeness. 88m. DIR: Eric Red. CAST: Jeff Fahey, Kim Delaney, Brad Dourif, Lindsay Duncan. 1991

BODY PUZZLE ★★ Pretty ho-hum. A serial killer collects pieces of his victims and puts them together like a puzzle. Joanna Pacula may be next on the list, or the inspiration behind the gruesome crimes. Rated R for violence, nudity, and language. 90m. DIR: Larry Louis. CAST: Joanna Pacula, Tom Aaron, Frank Quinn. 1993 DVD

BODY ROCK 🎬 A youngster from the South Bronx sees break dancing as his ticket to the big time. Rated PG-13. 93m. DIR: Marcelo Epstein. CAST: Lorenzo Lamas, Vicki Frederick, Cameron Dye, Ray Sharkey. 1984

BODY SHOT ★★ Underexposed thriller finds obsessed paparazzo Robert Patrick accused of murdering a reclusive rock star he previously harassed. Halfhearted attempt at *film noir.* Rated R for nudity, language, and violence. 98m. DIR: Dimitri Logothetis. CAST: Robert Patrick, Michelle Johnson, Ray Wise. 1993 DVD

►**BODY SHOTS** ★★ Four males and four females meet at a Los Angeles nightclub with sex predominant on the agenda. This lurid, cautionary tale then dissects date rape in *Rashomon*-like fashion while the real cancer of the film—alcoholism—feels like an afterthought. Characters talk into the camera about libido and meaningful human contact but seem more hung up on their own self-importance. Rated R for language, violence, and sexual content. 102m. DIR: Michael Cristofer. CAST: Sean Patrick Flanery, Jerry O'Connell, Tara Reid, Amanda Peet, Ron Livingston, Emily Procter, Brad Rowe, Sybil Temchen. 1999

BODY SLAM ★ A down-and-out rock 'n' roll promotional manager signs up a couple of renegade professional wrestlers to go on a barnstorming tour. Although this film is silly, it has a lot of heart. Rated PG for mild violence. 92m. DIR: Hal Needham. CAST: Dirk Benedict, Tanya Roberts, Roddy Piper, Lou Albano, Barry Gordon. 1987

BODY SNATCHER, THE (1945) ★★★★ Boris Karloff gives one of his finest performances in the title role of this Val Lewton production, adapted from the novel by Robert Louis Stevenson. Karloff is a sinister grave robber who provides dead bodies for illegal medical research and then uses his activities as blackmail to form a bond of "friendship" with the doctor he services, Henry Daniell (in an equally impressive turn). B&W; 77m. DIR: Robert Wise. CAST: Henry Daniell, Boris Karloff, Bela Lugosi. 1945

BODY SNATCHERS, THE (1993) ★★★1/2 Third screen version of Jack Finney's science-fiction tale is distinctive in its own way, although we still prefer Don Siegel's 1956 version. This time the invasion takes place on a military base, with director Abel Ferrara's stark storytelling enhanced by the atmospheric cinematography of Bojan Bazelli. Rated R for violence, nudity, and profanity. 87m. DIR: Abel Ferrara. CAST: Gabrielle Anwar, Terry Kinney, Meg Tilly, Forest Whitaker, Christine Elise, R. Lee Ermey, Reilly Murphy. 1993 DVD

BODY STROKES (SIREN'S CALL) ★★ Well, dip me in turpentine! Here's a flesh feast that doesn't involve cops turned strippers, or sex radio-talk-show hosts involved with psychos. This one's about an artist who turns to two women for inspiration—and what inspiration they provide. Not rated; contains nudity, adult situations, and language. 99m. DIR: Edward Holzman. CAST: Dixie Beck, Kristen Knittle, Catherine Weber, Bobby Johnston. 1995 DVD

BODYGUARD, THE ★★★ Lawrence Kasdan originally wrote *The Bodyguard* in 1972 with Steve McQueen in mind, and Kevin Costner attempts a homage to the charismatic action star as the protector to singer-actress Whitney Houston. The result proved extremely popular with filmgoers, so who are we to argue? While Houston is just fine in her big-screen debut, Costner's impersonation of McQueen seems cold rather than cool. So, if you're so inclined, enjoy. Rated R for profanity, suggested sex, and violence. 129m. DIR: Mick Jackson. CAST: Kevin Costner, Whitney Houston, Gary Kemp, Bill Cobbs, Ralph Waite. 1992 DVD

BOEING, BOEING ★★★ An obviously bored Jerry Lewis plays straight man to Tony Curtis's oversexed American news hound, who keeps a Parisian apartment for dalliances with stewardesses. Although it tries for the manic intensity of a 1940s screwball comedy, this mildly amusing sex farce never rises above kitsch … and is rather dated. 102m. DIR: John Rich. CAST: Jerry Lewis, Tony Curtis, Dany Saval, Thelma Ritter. 1965

BOG ✷ Unlucky group of people on an excursion into the wilderness run into the recently defrosted monster Bog. Rated PG. 87m. DIR: Don Keeslar. CAST: Gloria De Haven, Aldo Ray, Marshall Thompson. 1983

BOGGY CREEK II ★★ Pseudo-documentary schlockmaster Charles B. Pierce is at it again in this basic retelling of the search for a legendary swamp monster in southern Alabama. Cut-rate production values abound. Rated PG. 93m. DIR: Charles B. Pierce. CAST: Cindy Butler, Chuck Pierce. 1983

BOGIE ★★1/2 Boring biography of Humphrey Bogart unconvincingly enacted by Bogie and Bacall look-alikes. Too much time is spent on the drinking and temper problems of Bogie's third wife, Mayo Methot, and not enough time is spent on Lauren Bacall. Kathryn Harrold as Bacall is also bad, however, that it's probably a blessing her part is small. 100m. DIR: Vincent Sherman. CAST: Kevin O'Connor, Kathryn Harrold, Ann Wedgeworth, Patricia Barry. 1980

BOGUS ★★★ Young Haley Joel Osment delivers a surprisingly even performance as a lonely orphan forced to live with a stressed-out, career-minded Whoopi Goldberg. His imaginary friend (Gérard Depardieu) helps him deal with the recent upheaval in his young life. Remarkably, Osment is never overshadowed by the two big-name stars. Humor and tenderness play equal parts in this pleasant diversion. Rated PG. 112m. DIR: Norman Jewison. CAST: Whoopi Goldberg, Gérard Depardieu, Haley Joel Osment, Nancy Travis. 1996

BOHEMIAN GIRL, THE ★★★ Laurel and Hardy portray gypsies in this typical tale of the gypsy band versus the country officials. A variety of misadventures occur, and the film is entertaining, especially with the hilarious scene of Stan attempting to fill wine bottles and becoming more and more inebriated. B&W; 70m. DIR: James W. Horne, Charles R. Rogers. CAST: Stan Laurel, Oliver Hardy, Thelma Todd, Antonio Moreno. 1936

►**BOILER ROOM** ★★★ Promises of million-dollar incomes lure twentysomething males into a Long Island company that pushes junk stocks through high-pressure phone sales in this modern morality play. The film is fleshed out with an office romance and a tense father-son relationship in which a judge's son takes a job in the "chop shop" brokerage firm. Rated R for language and violence. 92m. DIR: Ben Younger. CAST: Giovanni Ribisi, Tom Everett Scott, Ben Affleck, Ron Rifkin, Nia Long. 2000

►**BOILING POINT (1990)** ★★★★ Riveting tale of revenge from director Takeshi Kitano, who mixes breakneck action with meaningful character development to create an exciting montage of violence and humanity. Takeshi also stars as a former Japanese gangster who teams up with a gas station attendant to take on the local *yakuza*. In Japanese with English subtitles. Not rated; contains adult situations and language. 98m. DIR: Takeshi Kitano. CAST: Masahiko Ono, Yuriko Ishida, Takahito Iguchi, Takeshi Kitano. 1990 DVD

BOILING POINT (1993) ★★★ Cop Wesley Snipes attempts to snare the crook (Dennis Hopper) who masterminded the drug-rip-off-related killing of another officer. Action buffs will be pleased by the high-octane storytelling style of filmmaker James B. Harris, who relies a bit too much on contrivance. Rated R for profanity, violence, and suggested sex. 92m. DIR: James B. Harris. CAST: Wesley Snipes, Dennis Hopper, Lolita Davidovich, Dan Hedaya, Viggo Mortensen, Seymour Cassel, Jonathan Banks, Christine Elise, Tony Lo Bianco, Valerie Perrine, James Tolkan. 1993 DVD

BOLD CABALLERO, THE ★★1/2 This little-known color film is the first sound Zorro movie and an early effort from Republic Studios, better known for their action-filled serials. Robert Livingston plays the masked avenger who sweeps tyranny out of his part of California, while clearing himself of a murder charge. 69m. DIR: Wells Root. CAST: Robert Livingston, Heather Angel, Sig Ruman, Robert Warwick, Charles Stevens, Slim Whitaker. 1936

BOLDEST JOB IN THE WEST, THE ★★ A bloodless bank robbery leads to the slaughter of a small western town and one of the gang members escaping with all the loot. Is this a comedy, a parody, or a serious action film? Veteran Spanish character-actor Fernando Sancho saves this clichéd Western from the trash can. Rated PG for violence. 100m. DIR: Joseph Loman (Jose Antonio De La Loma). CAST: Mark Edwards, Fernando Sancho, Carmen Seville. 1969

BOLERO (1982) ★★ Like American Alan Rudolph, French director Claude Lelouch is an obsessive romantic whose admirers (a small cult in this country) seem to appreciate his fervent style more than his plots. In this case, even though *Bolero* is almost three hours long, there's little plot to speak of. The film spans fifty years in the lives of a number of characters who live for music. To confuse matters, most of the cast plays multiple roles. You'll either be mesmerized or bored stiff. 173m. DIR: Claude Lelouch. CAST: James Caan, Geraldine Chaplin, Robert Hossein, Nicole Garcia, Daniel Olbrychski, Richard Bohringer. 1982

BOLERO (1984) 🐾 American heiress in the 1920s trying to lose her virginity. 106m. DIR: John Derek. CAST: Bo Derek, George Kennedy, Andrea Occhipinti, Ana Obregon, Olivia D'Abo. 1984

BOMBARDIER ★★★1/2 This is a solid action film dealing with the training of flyers during World War II. There is nothing new in the familiar formula of this film, but a good cast and fast pace make it enjoyable. B&W; 99m. DIR: Richard Wallace. CAST: Pat O'Brien, Randolph Scott, Eddie Albert, Robert Ryan, Anne Shirley, Barton MacLane. 1943

BOMBAY TALKIE ★★ An early effort from the team of producer Ismail Merchant, writer Ruth Prawer Jhabvala, and director James Ivory. (They finally hit it big in 1986 with *A Room With a View*.) In this drama, a British novelist (Jennifer Kendal) travels to India in search of romance, which she finds in the person of an Indian movie star (Shashi Kapoor). Pretty dull; the most fascinating parts have to do with the Indian film industry. 112m. DIR: James Ivory. CAST: Shashi Kapoor, Jennifer Kendal, Zia Mohyeddin. 1970

BOMBSHELL (1933) ★★★★ A fast-moving satire on Hollywood types that hasn't lost its bite or its hilarity. One reason is Jean Harlow, as she essentially plays herself in this story of a sex symbol who is used and abused. B&W; 97m. DIR: Victor Fleming. CAST: Jean Harlow, Lee Tracy, Pat O'Brien, Frank Morgan, Franchot Tone, Una Merkel, C. Aubrey Smith. 1933

BOMBSHELL (1997) ★★1/2 Young scientist Henry Thomas tries to stop his superiors from releasing a cancer-killing drug that contains a flaw that could wipe out the world. His only allies are his assistant and fiancée, who combat corporate greed and the government to stop the release. Rated R for language and violence. 95m. DIR: Paul Wynne. CAST: Henry Thomas, Frank Whaley, Madchen Amick, Pamela Gidley, Brion James. 1997

BON VOYAGE! ★★★1/2 One of Walt Disney's few adult-oriented comedies, this film combines elements of sophisticated comedy with dialogue and props from old-fashioned slapstick yarns. All the problems that could possibly befall this family on an overseas vacation is captured in pie-in-the-face detail. 130m. DIR: James Neilson. CAST: Fred MacMurray, Jane Wyman, Michael Callan, Tommy Kirk, Kevin Corcoran, Deborah Walley. 1962

BON VOYAGE, CHARLIE BROWN ★★★ An animated film starring the "Peanuts" gang, this is well suited for viewing by the younger generation. It's basically a "Peanuts" guide to world travel. Rated G. 75m. DIR: Bill Melendez. 1980

BONANZA (TV SERIES) ★★★ Western series tells the story of patriarch Ben Cartwright and his three sons, all from different mothers. Adam is suave and mature. Hoss is a big man with a bigger heart. Little Joe is earnest and hot-tempered. Together they make the Ponderosa the most prosperous ranch in the Comstock Lode country. The Cartwrights used their position, their money, their fists, and their guns to help those in distress. Volume I includes the pilot episode, "A Rose for Lotta," as well as "The Underdog," guest-starring Charles Bronson. Volume II features James Coburn in "The Dark Gate" and DeForest Kelley in "Honor of Cochise." 120m. DIR: Edward Ludwig, William F. Claxton, Robert Gordon, Don McDougall. CAST: Lorne Greene, Pernell Roberts, Dan Blocker, Michael Landon, Victor Sen Yung. 1959–1973 DVD

•**BONE COLLECTOR, THE** ★★★ Quadriplegic forensic expert with a death wish comes out of medical retirement to solve a series of abduction-murders. He enlists the aid of a female street cop to do his field work as his bedroom becomes a high-tech command post and he is fed clues to the crimes by the killer. This familiar but compelling cat-and-mouse thriller was adapted from Jeffery Deaver's 1997 novel. Rated R for grisly violence and language. 118m. DIR: Phillip Noyce. CAST: Denzel Washington,

ngelina Jolie, Queen Latifah, Michael Rooker, Luis
uzman, Ed O'Neill. **1999 DVD**

ONE DADDY ★★1/2 Grisly made-for-cable thriller
tars Rutger Hauer as a medical examiner turned
estselling novelist. Unfortunately, his book and suc-
ess have upset a killer from his past, who begins a
ew killing spree based on the doctor's book. The
rerequisite shocks (the killer likes to remove the
ones from his victims while they are still alive) are
ot nearly enough back story to make much of this or
he characters matter. Rated R for violence, lan-
uage, and adult situations. 90m. **DIR:** Mario Azzopar-
i. **CAST:** Rutger Hauer, Barbara Williams, R. H. Thom-
on. **1998**

ONEYARD, THE ★★ An aging detective and lady
sychic team up to solve some grisly goings-on at the
ocal mortuary. Their investigation leads them to the
ity morgue, where three possessed corpses plague
hem. Bizarre. 98m. **DIR:** James Cummins. **CAST:** Ed
Jelson, Norman Fell, Phyllis Diller. **1990**

ONFIRE OF THE VANITIES ★★ Tom Wolfe's novel
as been shaped into a trivial, cartoon-style movie by
irector Brian De Palma. This savage comedy about
he very rich bumping heads with the very poor in
New York City boasts great photography by Vilmos
sigmond, but the characters aren't very interesting,
specially if you liked the book. Rated R for some nu-
ity and violence. 126m. **DIR:** Brian De Palma. **CAST:**
Bruce Willis, Tom Hanks, Melanie Griffith, Saul Ru-
inek, Morgan Freeman. **1990 DVD**

ONJOUR TRISTESSE ★★★ Jean Seberg is a
poiled teenager who tries to ruin the affair between
er widowed father (David Niven) and his mistress
Deborah Kerr) in this dated soap opera. Kerr gives a
ine performance and Niven is just right as the suave
layboy, but Otto Preminger failed again to make a
tar of Seberg. Not rated. 94m. **DIR:** Otto Preminger.
CAST: Deborah Kerr, David Niven, Jean Seberg, Mylene
Demongeot. **1958**

ONNIE AND CLYDE ★★★★★ This still fresh and
nnovative gangster film was one of the first to depict
raphic violence, turning the genre inside out, com-
ining comedy, bloodshed, pathos, and social commentary with fascinating results. 111m. **DIR:** Arthur
Penn. **CAST:** Warren Beatty, Faye Dunaway, Gene Hackman, Estelle Parsons, Michael J. Pollard, Gene Wilder.
967 DVD

ONNIE PRINCE CHARLIE ★★★★ A rousing adventure about Scotland's fight to rid itself of English
ule with David Niven in one of his few appearances
as an adventurer. Not as flamboyant or as violent as
ecent films with the same theme, but rich in
ageantry and spectacle as well as talk. B&W; 118m.
DIR: Anthony Kimmins. **CAST:** David Niven, Finlay Curie, Margaret Leighton, Jack Hawkins. **1948**

ONNIE SCOTLAND ★★★ Stan Laurel and Oliver
Hardy venture to Scotland so that Stan can reap a
"major" inheritance—which turns out to be merely
bagpipes and a snuffbox. By mistake, they join the
army and are sent to India, where they help to quell a
native uprising. The thin plot offers the boys an opportunity to play off each other's strengths: Ollie's
reactions and Stan's fantasy world that keeps becoming reality. B&W; 80m. **DIR:** James W. Horne.

CAST: Stan Laurel, Oliver Hardy, James Finlayson,
June (Vlasek) Lang, William Janney. **1935**

BONNIE'S KIDS ★★1/2 Two amoral girls molested
by their stepfather kill them and move in with their
criminal uncle. Lots of action, but all rather pointless. Rated R for simulated sex, nudity, adult themes,
and violence. 105m. **DIR:** Arthur Marks. **CAST:** Tiffany
Bolling, Steve Sandor, Robin Mattson, Scott Brady.
1982

BOOGENS, THE ★★★ Effective little chiller about
miners discovering something nasty down in the
darkness. The lighting and atmosphere create a feeling of dread, and creatures are wisely kept out of
sight for the bulk of the film. Rated R for violence
and nudity. 95m. **DIR:** James L. Conway. **CAST:** Rebecca Balding, Fred McCarren, Anne-Marie Martin. **1981**

BOOGEYMAN, THE ★★★1/2 Despite the lame title, this is an inventive, atmospheric fright flick
about pieces of a broken mirror causing horrifying
deaths. Good special effects add to the creepiness.
Rated R for violence and gore. 86m. **DIR:** Ulli Lommel.
CAST: Suzanna Love, Michael Love, John Carradine.
1980 DVD

BOOGEYMAN 2, THE 🍅 Cheapo sequel. Rated R for
violence and gore. 79m. **DIR:** Bruce Star. **CAST:**
Suzanna Love, Shana Hall, Ulli Lommel. **1983**

BOOGIE BOY ★★ A recent prison parolee takes on
one more job and in predictable fashion the deal
goes sour. If we hadn't seen this one hundred times
before, this might seem like a good idea for a film. As
it stands, this plot has become a genre all its own and
this film isn't one of the better entries. Rated R for
language, violence, and excessive drug use. 98m.
DIR: Craig Hamann. **CAST:** Mark Dacascos, Jaimz
Woolvett, Emily Lloyd, Frederic Forrest, Traci Lords,
Joan Jett. **1997 DVD**

BOOGIE NIGHTS ★★★1/2 Writer-director Paul
Thomas Anderson's study of the adult film industry
tries for a definitive analysis of the 1970s, as experienced by those working at a decidedly fringe occupation. But Anderson's players often are stronger than
the words and actions he has given them. Mark
Wahlberg is excellent as a young stud delighted with
the opportunity to exploit his one natural gift who
subsequently becomes intoxicated by success,
drugs, and grandiose ambitions. Julianne Moore is
equally fine as the "veteran actress" in this porn stable, and Burt Reynolds delivers his best work in
years as the father-figure director-producer. Rated R
for nudity, simulated sex, profanity, drug use, and violence. 152m. **DIR:** Paul Thomas Anderson. **CAST:**
Mark Wahlberg, Julianne Moore, Burt Reynolds,
Heather Graham, Don Cheadle, John C. Reilly, William
H. Macy, Ricky Jay. **1997 DVD**

BOOK OF LOVE ★★ *Porky's*-like humor doesn't
help the story of a new-kid-in-town who falls for the
girlfriend of the guy who plays the front four on the
high school football team. Familiar. Rated PG-13 for
brief profanity and teenage high jinks. 85m. **DIR:**
Robert Shaye. **CAST:** Chris Young, Keith Coogan,
Michael McKean. **1991**

BOOM IN THE MOON 🍅 Buster Keaton's worst film.
It involves his being conned by villains into flying a

rocket to the moon. 83m. DIR: Jaime Salvador. CAST: Buster Keaton. 1946

BOOM TOWN ★★★★ Big-budget MGM star vehicle has buddies Clark Gable and Spencer Tracy striking it rich, going broke, and striking it rich again in the oil fields of the Southwest. Great fun. B&W; 116m. DIR: Jack Conway. CAST: Clark Gable, Spencer Tracy, Hedy Lamarr, Chill Wills, Frank Morgan, Lionel Atwill, Claudette Colbert. 1940

BOOMERANG (1947) ★★★★ Still-riveting drama, based on a true story about a prosecuting attorney who believes the man he is supposed to try for the murder of a minister is innocent. A terrific cast, expertly directed by Elia Kazan. Not rated. B&W; 88m. DIR: Elia Kazan. CAST: Dana Andrews, Jane Wyatt, Lee J. Cobb, Sam Levene, Ed Begley Sr., Karl Malden. 1947

BOOMERANG (1992) ★★1/2 Dapper advertising executive Eddie Murphy is a real ladies' man who likes to love 'em and lead 'em on—until his sexy, new boss Robin Givens gives him a taste of his own medicine. A few laughs (mostly supplied by Martin Lawrence) and a little bit of heart (courtesy of the gorgeous Halle Berry) help this predictable romantic comedy. Rated R for nudity and profanity. 118m. DIR: Reginald Hudlin. CAST: Eddie Murphy, Robin Givens, Halle Berry, David Alan Grier, Martin Lawrence, Grace Jones, Geoffrey Holder, Eartha Kitt. 1992

BOOST, THE ★★ The controversy surrounding the off-screen, *Fatal Attraction*-style relationship between James Woods and Sean Young is certainly more interesting than the movie itself. Woods gives a typically high-powered performance in this uncomfortably intense drama as a Beverly Hills investment broker who begins to use cocaine and loses control. The story lacks coherence. Rated R for nudity, profanity and drug use. 96m. DIR: Harold Becker. CAST: James Woods, Sean Young, Steven Hill. 1989

BOOT HILL ★★ Once again, Terence Hill and Bud Spencer are teamed in a spaghetti Western. This one pits them against bad guy Victor Buono. It's violent, bloody, and far from good. Rated PG. 87m. DIR: Giuseppe Colizzi. CAST: Terence Hill, Bud Spencer, Woody Strode, Lionel Stander, Victor Buono. 1969

BOOTHILL BANDITS ★★★ Top-notch Range Busters Western, as they rout Wells Fargo bandits. Glenn Strange is a standout as a lumbering, moronic killer. B&W; 58m. DIR: S. Roy Luby. CAST: Ray "Crash" Corrigan, John King, Max Terhune, Glenn Strange, John Merton, Jean Brooks. 1942

BOOTS MALONE ★★1/2 Workmanlike Western, nothing special, but with a typically solid William Holden performance in the title role of a tough guy who trains a boy to be a jockey. B&W; 103m. DIR: William Dieterle. CAST: William Holden, Johnny Stewart, Ed Begley Sr., Harry Morgan, Whit Bissell. 1952

BOOTY CALL ★★1/2 In this condom comedy, a young man who has been dating a woman for nearly two months without consummating their romance is way behind the power curve according to his streetwise buddy. The two lady hounds then double date in an evening interrupted by several late-night expeditions in search of "safe sex" protection. Rated R for nonstop sexual references, simulated sex, and language. 80m. DIR: Jeff Pollack. CAST: Tommy David-son, Jamie Foxx, Tamala Jones, Vivica A. Fox. 1997 DVD

BOPHA! ★★★1/2 Percy Mtwa's play, set during South Africa's final days under apartheid, concerns a dedicated black police officer (Danny Glover) increasingly doubtful of his servitude to white superiors. Matters come to a head with the arrival of a sadistic Special Branch liaison (Malcolm McDowell), but concluding events suggest a rather unpleasant moral: there is no atonement for past mistakes. It's a particularly unfortunate message, in light of the film's subject. Rated PG-13 for profanity, violence, and brief nudity. 120m. DIR: Morgan Freeman. CAST: Danny Glover, Malcolm McDowell, Alfre Woodard, Marius Weyers, Maynard Eziashi. 1994

BORDER, THE ★★★1/2 Jack Nicholson is first-rate in this often effective drama about a border patrol officer who rebels against the corruption in his department and the rampant greed of his wife, Valerie Perrine. Rated R. 107m. DIR: Tony Richardson. CAST: Jack Nicholson, Harvey Keitel, Valerie Perrine, Warren Oates, Elpidia Carrillo. 1982

BORDER HEAT ♥ This action flick, set in Texas, has all the excitement of a siesta. Rated R for violence. 93m. DIR: Tony Gaudioz. CAST: Darlanne Fluegel, John Vernon. 1988

BORDER PATROL ★★★ In this Hopalong Cassidy entry, Hoppy must put a stop to the criminal atrocities committed by the owner of a silver mine who is using Mexicans as virtual slaves. Robert Mitchum makes his film debut as one of the bad guys. Not the best of the series, but still good, with plenty of action. B&W; 66m. DIR: Lesley Selander. CAST: William Boyd, Andy Clyde, Russell Simpson, Duncan Renaldo Robert Mitchum. 1943

BORDER PHANTOM ★★1/2 Like all B Westerns this looks pretty creaky today, but it's entertaining thanks to Bob Steele's energetic performance and an intriguing premise, which involves mysterious murders and slavery. B&W; 59m. DIR: S. Roy Luby. CAST: Bob Steele, Harley Wood, Don Barclay, Karl Hackett. 1937

BORDER RADIO ♥ A disillusioned rock star steals a large sum of performance money owed to him by a sleazy club owner. Not rated; contains profanity and violence. B&W; 89m. DIR: Allison Anders, Dean Lent Kurt Voss. CAST: Chris D., Luana Anders. 1988

BORDER SHOOTOUT ★★★1/2 Fine actioner from an Elmore Leonard story features an honest farmer (Cody Glenn) who is suddenly appointed deputy in a corrupt town that is at the mercy of a spoiled, violent brat (Jeff Kaake). Glenn Ford portrays his usual tough-but-cool character as the sheriff out transporting a prisoner when all hell breaks loose back home. 110m. DIR: C. J. McIntyre. CAST: Cody Glenn, Glenn Ford, Jeff Kaake, Charlene Tilton, Michael Ansara. 1989

BORDER STREET ★★★★ This hard-hitting Polish film is set in the ghettos into which Nazis forced Jews during the Third Reich and where many of them died for lack of food and medicine. There are a few lapses into low-grade melodrama, but mostly this is a gripping story that retains its power. 75m. DIR: Alexander Ford. CAST: M. Cwiklinska. 1950

ORDER VIGILANTES ★★1/2 A rich silver strike pits the unscrupulous element against the honest miners and bankers in a frontier settlement, and Hopalong Cassidy and his cronies brazenly defy the crooks and start a small war. One of the most satisfying entries in the long-running series. B&W; 55m. DIR: Derwin Abrahams. CAST: William Boyd, Russell Hayden, Andy Clyde, Frances Gifford, Victor Jory, Ethel Wales, Morris Ankrum (Stepen Morris), Tom Tyler, Hank Worden. 1941

ORDERLAND ★★★1/2 Hopalong Cassidy, an outlaw! Well, sort of. In this B oater, Hoppy must pretend to be a bad guy to save the day. The characterizations are strong. The script is literate, and Morris Ankrum is great as the main outlaw. Good fun for all. B&W; 62m. DIR: Nate Watt. CAST: William Boyd, James Ellison, George "Gabby" Hayes. 1937

ORDERLINE ★★★1/2 Charles Bronson gives one of his better portrayals in this release, which got the jump on the similar The Border, with Jack Nicholson, by nearly two years. As in the later film, the central character—a border guard—becomes involved with the problems of an illegal alien and her child. The result is a watchable action film. Rated R. 105m. DIR: Jerrold Freedman. CAST: Charles Bronson, Bruno Kirby, Bert Remsen, Ed Harris, Wilford Brimley. 1980

BORIS AND NATASHA ★★★ Reasonably amusing live-action rendition of animator Jay Ward's most famous no-goodniks, the cold war klutzes from Pottsylvania who bedeviled Rocky and Bullwinkle. Our "heroes" are sent to the United States ... little knowing their beloved "Fearless Leader" has merely set them up as bait. Unbilled appearances are made by John Candy, John Travolta, and June Foray (Rocky's original cartoon voice). Originally shown on cable. 88m. DIR: Charles Martin Smith. CAST: Sally Kellerman, Dave Thomas, Paxton Whitehead, Andrea Martin, Alex Rocco, Anthony Newley. 1992

B.O.R.N. ★★ B.O.R.N. (Body Organ Replacement Network) involves the same concept as Coma. The body organ black marketeers are at it again, only this time they're kidnapping healthy, unsuspecting people right off the street. Rated R for profanity, nudity, gore. 98m. DIR: Ross Hagen. CAST: Ross Hagen, Hoke Howell, P. J. Soles, William Smith. 1988

BORN AGAIN ♥ President Nixon's special counsel Charles Colson. Rated PG. 110m. DIR: Irving Rapper. CAST: Dean Jones, Anne Francis, Jay Robinson, Dana Andrews. 1978

BORN AMERICAN ♥ Three high school buddies cross the Russian border while on summer vacation in Lapland. Rated R for sex and violence. 103m. DIR: Renny Harlin. CAST: Mike Norris, Steve Durham, David Coburn, Albert Salmi, Thalmus Rasulala. 1986

BORN BAD ★★1/2 Six teens try to rob a bank but end up trapped inside with hostages and surrounded by police. It's not Dog Day Afternoon, but as a made-for-video thriller it's not bad. Rated R for profanity, violence, and brief nudity. 84m. DIR: Jeff Yonis. CAST: James Remar, Justin Walker, Corey Feldman. 1997 DVD

BORN FREE ★★★★★ An established family classic, this is the tale of Elsa the lioness and her relationship with an African game warden and his wife.

96m. DIR: James Hill. CAST: Virginia McKenna, Bill Travers, Geoffrey Keen, Peter Lukoye. 1966

BORN IN EAST L.A. ★★★1/2 Cheech, minus Chong, had a surprise box-office hit with this comedy, which started off as a video takeoff of Bruce Springsteen's "Born in the U.S.A." While not a comedy classic, this low-budget film has a number of funny moments. Rated R for profanity. 85m. DIR: Richard "Cheech" Marin. CAST: Richard "Cheech" Marin, Daniel Stern, Paul Rodriguez, Jan-Michael Vincent. 1987 DVD

BORN INNOCENT ★★★ Rape with a broomstick marked this made-for-television film a shocker when first aired. The scene has been toned down, but the picture still penetrates with its searing story of cruelty in a juvenile detention home. Linda Blair does well as the runaway teenager. Joanna Miles is excellent as a compassionate teacher whose heart lies with her charges. It's strong stuff. 100m. DIR: Donald Wrye. CAST: Linda Blair, Kim Hunter, Joanna Miles. 1974

BORN KILLER ♥ Teenagers on an outing cross paths with two vicious convicts who torture them and leave them for dead. They're the lucky ones: they don't have to sit through this mess. 90m. DIR: Kimberley Casey. CAST: Ted Prior, Ty Hardin. 1990

BORN LOSERS ★★★ This biker exploitation movie is better than the celebrated Billy Jack, which also starred Tom Laughlin. Granted, we still have to sit through scenes with terrible amateur actors, but at least there is no girl singing off-key about her brother being dead. 112m. DIR: T. C. Frank. CAST: Tom Laughlin, Elizabeth James, Jeremy Slate, William Wellman Jr., Robert Tessier. 1967

BORN OF FIRE ★★ A classical concert flutist (Peter Firth) journeys to the Middle East in hopes of finding the reason for his father's death. The flutist only becomes embroiled in the same drama that befell his father. A boring, confusing story. Contains sex, nudity, and violence. 84m. DIR: Jamil Dehlaui. CAST: Peter Firth, Suzan Crowley, Stefan Kalipha. 1987

BORN ON THE FOURTH OF JULY ★★★1/2 Tom Cruise's superb performance is the reason to watch this overblown screen biography of Vietnam veteran and antiwar activist Ron Kovic. Characters suddenly appear and disappear. Despite all this, Kovic's tale is a powerful one, and Cruise's breakthrough performance makes it memorable. Rated R for profanity, nudity, simulated sex, and violence. 135m. DIR: Oliver Stone. CAST: Tom Cruise, Kyra Sedgwick, Willem Dafoe, Raymond J. Barry, Tom Berenger. 1989 DVD

BORN TO BE BAD ★★★ Conniving opportunist Joan Fontaine scrambles for a secure foothold in life while stepping on anything or anyone in her way. Although more than a bit melodramatic, Nicholas Ray's adult look at sexual relationships was ahead of its time and still has impact today. B&W; 94m. DIR: Nicholas Ray. CAST: Joan Fontaine, Robert Ryan, Joan Leslie, Zachary Scott, Mel Ferrer. 1950

BORN TO BE WILD ♥ Replace Free Willy's orca with a man in a gorilla suit and you've got the idea. Rated PG for the boy's defiance. 98m. DIR: John Gray. CAST: Wil Horneff, Helen Shaver, John C. McGinley, Peter Boyle. 1995

BORN TO DANCE ★★★ A curiosity piece because Jimmy Stewart croons "Easy to Love" without the help of a ghost singer on the soundtrack. The real star is Cole Porter, who wrote some of his most enduring melodies for the film. Eleanor Powell proves she has no peers when it comes to tap dancing. 105m. **DIR:** Roy Del Ruth. **CAST:** Eleanor Powell, James Stewart, Una Merkel, Buddy Ebsen, Virginia Bruce, Frances Langford, Reginald Gardiner. **1936**

BORN TO KILL ★★★1/2 Tough film about two bad apples whose star-crossed love brings them both nothing but grief is one of the best examples of American *film noir*. Lawrence Tierney's aggressive pursuit of his wife's sister (Claire Trevor) defies description. This hardboiled crime melodrama is an early surprise from director Robert Wise. B&W; 97m. **DIR:** Robert Wise. **CAST:** Lawrence Tierney, Claire Trevor, Walter Slezak, Elisha Cook Jr., Audrey Long, Philip Terry. **1947**

BORN TO RACE �-💀 This clunker of a film couldn't get off the starting line. Rated R for nudity, simulated sex, violence, and profanity. 95m. **DIR:** James Fargo. **CAST:** Joseph Bottoms, Robert Logan, Marc Singer, George Kennedy. **1988**

BORN TO RIDE ★★★1/2 A smirking, rebellious, yet likable John Stamos stars as a 1930s motorcycle pioneer with this choice: a year behind bars or an army assignment training the cavalry for a motorcycle mission in Spain. Rated PG for violence and profanity. 90m. **DIR:** Graham Baker. **CAST:** John Stamos, John Stockwell, Teri Polo, Sandy McPeak. **1991**

BORN TO RUN ★★ Acceptable made-for-TV take on teen angst is a good showcase for star Richard Grieco but little else. He's a street racer who must put everything on the line when his brother gets involved with the mob. Pretty predictable. 97m. **DIR:** Albert Magnoli. **CAST:** Richard Grieco, Joe Cortese, Jay Acovone, Shelli Lether. **1993**

BORN TO WIN ★★★1/2 In one of his best performances, George Segal plays a New York junkie with a $100-a-day habit. Ivan Passer's direction is more inventive than successful, and the film often seems to be going in several directions. But the acting makes up, including a brief appearance by a young Robert De Niro. Also known as *Addict*. Rated R for profanity. 90m. **DIR:** Ivan Passer. **CAST:** George Segal, Karen Black, Hector Elizondo, Paula Prentiss, Jay Fletcher, Robert De Niro. **1971 DVD**

BORN WILD ★★★★ Spectacular scenery and wildlife footage enhance this wonderful tale of one man's efforts to save two leopard cubs, and a fledgling photographer's efforts to bring his story to the world. Real-life conservationist John Varty portrays himself, while Brooke Shields shines as the novice photographer who finds herself drawn to Varty's cause. Rated PG for some minor violence. 98m. **DIR:** Duncan McLachlan. **CAST:** Brooke Shields, John Varty, David Keith, Martin Sheen. **1995**

BORN YESTERDAY (1950) ★★★★1/2 Judy Holliday is simply delightful as a dizzy dame who isn't as dizzy as everyone thinks she is, in this comedy directed by George Cukor. William Holden is the professor hired by a junk-dealer-made-good (Broderick Crawford) to give Holliday lessons in how to be

"high-toned." The results are highly entertaining and very funny. B&W; 103m. **DIR:** George Cukor. **CAST:** Judy Holliday, William Holden, Broderick Crawford, Howard St. John. **1950 DVD**

BORN YESTERDAY (1993) ★★★★ Updated remake of the classic 1950 George Cukor comedy works well because of the chemistry among stars Melanie Griffith, Don Johnson, and John Goodman. Married in real life, Griffith and Johnson send off all most visible sparks. Goodman adds a deceptive likability to a crooked wheeler-dealer. Rated PG for profanity. 100m. **DIR:** Luis Mandoki. **CAST:** Melanie Griffith, John Goodman, Don Johnson, Edward Herrmann, Max Perlich, Fred Dalton Thompson, Nora Dunn. **1993**

BORROWER, THE ★★ The director of *Henry: Portrait of a Serial Killer* brings us this gory tale of an alien killer sentenced to life without parole on planet Earth. Better-than-average effects help to ease us through the film's weak plot. Rated R for profanity and violence. 97m. **DIR:** John McNaughton. **CAST:** Rae Dawn Chong, Don Gordon, Antonio Fargas. **1991**

BORROWERS, THE (1993) ★★★ Quaint BBC miniseries sticks to Mary Norton's books, but lacks the visual flair necessary to suspend disbelief. The title characters are a little family who live under the floorboards of an English home and borrow items to make their living space more comfortable. When they're discovered, they flee outdoors where ever step is a new adventure. The cast rises to the occasion, but poor special effects help expose the illusion. Not rated. 199m. **DIR:** John Henderson. **CAST:** Ian Holm, Penelope Wilton, Rebecca Callard, Sian Phillips. **1993**

BORROWERS, THE (1997) ★★★★ Inventively directed, imaginatively designed, and cleverly scripted, this sterling adaptation of Mary Norton's novel has excitement to spare. The Borrowers are Norton's fabricated explanation for misplaced socks and missing jewelry; the "culprits" are mouse-sized little people who "borrow" these items for their own purposes. It's great fun for all ages. Rated PG for comic violence. 83m. **DIR:** Peter Hewitt. **CAST:** John Goodman, Jim Broadbent, Mark Williams, Hugh Laurie, Bradley Pierce, Flora Newbigin, Tom Felton. **1997 DVD**

BORSALINO ★★★1/2 Style over substance—and when the result is *this* stylish, that's a major triumph. Jean-Paul Belmondo and Alain Delon are friendly rival gangsters in 1930s Marseilles. Everything is geared to make this an eye-filling, fast-paced romp. The only liability: English dubbing of the French dialogue. Rated PG. 125m. **DIR:** Jacques Deray. **CAST:** Jean-Paul Belmondo, Alain Delon, Michel Bouquet, Catherine Rouvel. **1970**

BOSOM BUDDIES (TV SERIES) ★★★ Before achieving Oscar-winning acclaim for his acting, Tom Hanks played a cross-dressing ad man in this predictable sitcom. Peter Scolari costars as the two take on a double life. By day, they're girl-crazy stud muffins; by night they're Hildegard and Buffy living in a women-only apartment building. Gags run a bit thin but the duo is likable enough to make viewers overlook its flaws. Four volumes, each containing two episodes and lasting approximately 50m. **DIR:** Joel Zwick, Chris Thompson, Don Van Atta. **CAST:** Tom

Hanks, Peter Scolari, Wendie Jo Sperber, Donna Dixon, Holland Taylor, Telma Hopkins. **1980–1984**

BOSS ★★1/2 In the Old West, bounty hunter Fred Williamson and his sidekick D'Urville Martin ride into a town and set themselves up as the law. It's part of their plan to capture a bad guy with a hefty price on his head. Familiar but entertaining oater. Original title: *Boss Nigger*. Not rated. 87m. **DIR:** Jack Arnold. **CAST:** Fred Williamson, D'Urville Martin, R. G. Armstrong, William Smith, Barbara Leigh. **1975**

BOSS' SON, THE ★★★ Enjoyable drama about a young man's passage to adulthood. Our hero jumps at the chance to run the family factory. But when Dad decides his son must earn his way to the top, the boy learns what it truly means to earn a living. A little slow but rewarding. Not rated. 102m. **DIR:** Bobby Roth. **CAST:** Asher Brauner, Rita Moreno, Rudy Solari, Henry G. Sanders, James Darren, Piper Laurie. **1978**

BOSS' WIFE, THE ★★★1/2 After the first twenty minutes, this comedy starts rolling. Daniel Stern and Melanie Mayron play Joel and Janet, a two-career couple trying to make time for a baby. When Joel's boss (Christopher Plummer) finally notices him, he expects Joel to spend the weekend at the company resort. Laughs abound when Joel is pursued by the boss's nymphomaniac wife (beautiful Arielle Dombasle). Rated R for nudity, obscenities and sexual situations. 83m. **DIR:** Ziggy Steinberg. **CAST:** Daniel Stern, Christopher Plummer, Arielle Dombasle, Fisher Stevens, Melanie Mayron, Martin Mull. **1986**

BOSTON KICKOUT ★★1/2 One of the few films ever made with the word *kick* in the title that doesn't deal with kick boxing. John Simm rises above weak material as one of four high-school buddies who discovers reality after graduation. Simm sees the light at the end of the tunnel, and with the help of a special woman, he attempts to reach it. Rated R for adult situations, language, and violence. 107m. **DIR:** Paul Hills. **CAST:** John Simm, Emer McCourt, Marc Warren, Andrew Lincoln. **1995**

BOSTON STRANGLER, THE ★★★ True account, told in semidocumentary style, of Beantown's notorious deranged murderer, plumber Albert De Salvo. Tony Curtis gives a first-class performance as the woman killer. 120m. **DIR:** Richard Fleischer. **CAST:** Tony Curtis, Henry Fonda, Mike Kellin, Murray Hamilton, Sally Kellerman, Hurd Hatfield, George Kennedy, Jeff Corey. **1968**

BOSTONIANS, THE ★★★ A visually striking but dry production from Merchant Ivory Productions. Most of the sparks of conflict come not from the tortured love affair between Christopher Reeve and Madeleine Potter or the main theme of women's fight for equality, but from the few scenes of direct confrontation between Reeve and Vanessa Redgrave. The setting is Boston during the Centennial. 120m. **DIR:** James Ivory. **CAST:** Christopher Reeve, Vanessa Redgrave, Jessica Tandy, Madeleine Potter, Nancy Marchand, Wesley Addy, Linda Hunt, Nancy New, Jon Van Ness, Wallace Shawn. **1984 DVD**

BOTANY BAY ★★1/2 Alan Ladd stars as an unjustly accused criminal aboard a ship about to establish a penal colony in British-occupied Australia. He finds himself confronting a cruel captain (James Mason)

and romancing a beautiful young actress (Patricia Medina). Atmospheric costume drama. 94m. **DIR:** John Farrow. **CAST:** Alan Ladd, James Mason, Patricia Medina. **1953**

BOTTLE ROCKET ★★★★ Fresh out of a mental institution, twentysomething Anthony joins a misfit mastermind and a rich wimp for a robbery. While on the lam the trio bungle their way into a big heist set up by a smooth-talking con man. Rated R for language, violence, suggested sex, and nudity. 98m. **DIR:** Wes Anderson. **CAST:** Luke Wilson, Owen C. Wilson, Robert Musgrave, Lumi Cavazos, James Caan. **1996 DVD**

BOUDU SAVED FROM DROWNING ★★★★ This is the original *Down and Out in Beverly Hills*, except that the tramp (the beloved Michel Simon) is saved by an antiquarian bookseller after a suicide attempt in the Seine. Unlike the play on which it was based and unlike the Hollywood version—both of which have the bum accept his responsibilities—*Boudu* is a celebration of joyful anarchy. A masterpiece. In French with English subtitles. B&W; 88m. **DIR:** Jean Renoir. **CAST:** Michel Simon, Charles Granval, Max Dalban, Jean Dasté. **1932**

BOULEVARD ★★★ The dark side of Toronto's redlight district is brought to light in this gritty drama. Rae Dawn Chong is fine as a tough-as-nails hooker who takes in a young runaway and teaches her the ropes. They team up to bring down a vicious pimp, well played by Lou Diamond Phillips. Lance Henriksen costars as a vice cop with a mean streak. Rated R for violence, language, and nudity. 96m. **DIR:** Penelope Buitenhuis. **CAST:** Rae Dawn Chong, Lou Diamond Phillips, Lance Henriksen, Kari Wuhrer. **1994**

BOULEVARD NIGHTS ★★ Well-intentioned but dramatically dull account of a Chicano youth's desire to break out of East Los Angeles. Richard Yniguez is sincere in the lead role and Danny De La Paz is sympathetic as his brother, but the whole thing comes across like a preachy soap opera. Rated R for violence and profanity. 102m. **DIR:** Michael Pressman. **CAST:** Richard Yniguez, Marta DuBois, Danny De La Paz, Carmen Zapata, Victor Millan. **1979**

BOULEVARD OF BROKEN DREAMS ★★★1/2 A famous Hollywood screenwriter returns home to Australia to win back his wife and daughter. Good acting, a wonderful plot, interesting side plots, and superb supporting characters make this a very enjoyable film, except for several unnecessary musical interludes. Rated PG-13 for profanity and frontal nudity. 95m. **DIR:** Pino Amenta. **CAST:** John Waters, Penelope Stewart, Kim Gyngell, Nicki Paull, Andrew McFarlane, Kevin Miles. **1988**

BOUND ★★★ Ex-con Gina Gershon falls in love with gangster's moll Jennifer Tilly, and the two concoct a risky scheme to steal $2 million from the mob. First-time writers-directors Larry and Andy Wachowski mimic the *Pulp Fiction* brand of outrageous excess, but there's no denying the raw talent on hand. This may be trash, but it's trash with style. Rated R for violence, torture, profanity, nudity, and simulated sex. 108m. **DIR:** Andy Wachowski, Larry Wachowski. **CAST:** Jennifer Tilly, Gina Gershon, Joe Pantoliano, John P. Ryan, Christopher Meloni, Richard Sarafian. **1996 DVD**

BOUND AND GAGGED: A LOVE STORY ★★1/2 Ginger Lynn Allen is kidnapped by her friends, Elizabeth Saltarrelli and Chris Denton, and taken on a wild ride through backwoods Minnesota, terrorizing locals and gangsters alike. Complications really set in when Saltarrelli declares her love for Allen. Fun road trip has some potholes, but steers the course. Rated R for language, adult situations, and violence. 96m. **DIR:** Daniel Appleby. **CAST:** Ginger Lynn Allen, Elizabeth Saltarrelli, Chris Mulkey, Karen Black, Chris Denton. **1993 DVD**

BOUND BY HONOR ★★★ Taylor Hackford's often exciting and emotional drama, portraying aspects of modern Chicano immigrant life through the stories of three young East Los Angeles men, in the late 1970s and 1980s. Unfortunately, at nearly three hours, the film seems at least 30 minutes too long. The film may also remind viewers of Edward James Olmos's superior *American Me*. Jesse Borrego is memorable as a Chicano artist who finds salvation with the paintbrush. Rated R, with strong violence and profanity. 172m. **DIR:** Taylor Hackford. **CAST:** Damian Chapa, Jesse Borrego, Benjamin Bratt. **1993**

BOUND FOR GLORY ★★★★ David Carradine had one of the best roles of his career as singer-composer Woody Guthrie. Film focuses on the depression years when Guthrie rode the rails across America. Director Hal Ashby explores the lives of those hit hardest during those times. Haskell Wexler won the Oscar for his beautiful cinematography. Rated PG. 147m. **DIR:** Hal Ashby. **CAST:** David Carradine, Ronny Cox, Melinda Dillon, Randy Quaid, Gail Strickland, Ji-Tu Cumbuka, John Lehne. **1976 DVD**

BOUNTY, THE ★★★★ Mel Gibson is Fletcher Christian, and Anthony Hopkins is Captain William Bligh in this, the fourth and most satisfying screen version of *The Mutiny on the Bounty*. This sweeping seafaring epic from the director of *Smash Palace* is the first movie to present the historic events accurately—and to do so fascinatingly. Rated PG for nudity and violence. 132m. **DIR:** Roger Donaldson. **CAST:** Mel Gibson, Anthony Hopkins, Laurence Olivier, Edward Fox, Daniel Day-Lewis, Liam Neeson. **1984**

BOUNTY HUNTER ★★ Star-director Robert Ginty plays a federal bounty hunter investigating the murder of an Indian buddy. This pits him against a corrupt sheriff (Bo Hopkins). Not rated, the film has violence and profanity. 91m. **DIR:** Robert Ginty. **CAST:** Robert Ginty, Bo Hopkins. **1989**

BOUNTY HUNTER 2002 🖤 After a plague has decimated Earth, the hot commodity becomes uninfected virgins. Horrid. Not rated; contains violence, language, and adult situations. 89m. **DIR:** Sam Auster. **CAST:** Phil Nordell, Francine Lapensee, Vernon Wells, Jeff Conaway. **1992**

BOUNTY HUNTERS 🖤 Michael Dudikoff and Lisa Howard play competing bounty hunters hot on the trail of a high-priced fugitive. Lots of car chases and flying bullets do little to make this pedestrian effort worth a look. Rated R for language, nudity, and violence. 98m. **DIR:** George Erschbamer. **CAST:** Michael Dudikoff, Lisa Howard, Benjamin Ratner. **1997**

BOUNTY MAN, THE ★★★1/2 Made-for-television Western is dark, complex, and quite good. Bounty hunter Clint Walker follows a murderer into a town but is set upon by a group of outlaws. Richard Basehart is particularly good as the outlaw leader. 73m. **DIR:** John Llewellyn Moxey. **CAST:** Clint Walker, Richard Basehart, Margot Kidder, John Ericson, Arthur Hunnicutt, Gene Evans. **1972**

BOUNTY TRACKER ★★1/2 A by-the-numbers kill-or-be-killed saga, with Lorenzo Lamas reasonably adept as a licensed bounty hunter who swears vengeance on the scum who killed his brother. Good for viewers with minimal expectations. 92m. **DIR:** Kurt Anderson. **CAST:** Lorenzo Lamas, Matthias Hues, Cyndi Pass, Paul Regina. **1993**

BOURNE IDENTITY, THE ★★★1/2 Robert Ludlum's white-knuckle bestseller makes a thrilling TV miniseries starring Richard Chamberlain as an amnesiac U.S. spy dodging assassins' bullets in Europe while trying to make sense of his situation. Jaclyn Smith complicates matters as the woman he kidnaps as protection and then falls in love with. Some slow moments, but it rallies toward the end when the truth finally begins to surface. Not rated. 185m. **DIR:** Roger Young. **CAST:** Richard Chamberlain, Jaclyn Smith, Anthony Quayle, Donald Moffat, Yorgo Voyagis, Denholm Elliott. **1988**

BOWERY AT MIDNIGHT 🖤 *Very* cheaply made story about a maniac on a killing spree in the Bowery. B&W; 63m. **DIR:** Wallace Fox. **CAST:** Bela Lugosi, John Archer, Wanda McKay, Tom Neal. **1942**

BOWERY BOYS, THE (SERIES) ★★1/2 When William Wyler brought Sidney Kingsley's play, *Dead End*, to the big screen in 1937, he unknowingly created a phenomenon known over the years as The Dead End Kids, The Little Tough Guys, The East Side Kids and, finally, The Bowery Boys. While the Dead End Kids enlivened a number of terrific Warner Bros. gangster films, the Bowery Boys were the low-camp clowns of their day. Leo Gorcey and Huntz Hall led a group of (by then) middle-aged men playing teenagers hatching knuckleheaded schemes in a sweet shop run by Gorcey's father, Bernard, whom he cast, along with brother David, in the series after seizing creative control in 1946. When Bernard Gorcey died in 1956, Leo left the series, and seven films were made with Stanley Clements teaming up with Hall to lead the "boys" in their final and least interesting adventures. B&W; 60m. **DIR:** William Beaudine, Edward L. Bernds. **CAST:** Leo Gorcey, Huntz Hall, Bobby Jordan, William Benedict, David Gorcey, Gabriel Dell, Bernard Gorcey, Stanley Clements. **1946–1958**

•BOWFINGER ★★★1/2 A poverty-row filmmaker (Steve Martin) is just about to give up his dream of big-screen success when he hits upon the idea of using clandestinely shot footage of a major movie star (Eddie Murphy) unknowingly interacting with his cast members. These include a delivery boy (Murphy) who is a dead ringer for the "star" and finds himself performing a number of death-defying stunts. There are some genuinely hilarious moments in this somewhat uneven movie written and directed by Martin, with Murphy terrific in his dual role and

Heather Graham hilarious as a starlet who will do anything to get her big break. Perfect for a night of relaxed, at-home viewing. Rated PG-13 for profanity and suggested sex. 98m. DIR: Steve Martin. CAST: Steve Martin, Eddie Murphy, Heather Graham, Christine Baranski, Jamie Kennedy, Robert Downey Jr., Adam Alexi-Malle, Kohl Suddoth, Barry Newman, Terence Stamp. 1999 DVD

BOX OF MOONLIGHT ★★★★ Smart, slightly surrealistic tale of an uptight engineer's encounter with a semipathetic free spirit. Both men learn from each other's imperfect approaches to life, and writer-director Tom DiCillo (*Living in Oblivion*) is too sympathetic to both characters to presume that one knows better than the other. Sumptuously filmed in the Tennessee countryside. Rated R for profanity, nudity, and violence. 111m. DIR: Tom DiCillo. CAST: John Turturro, Sam Rockwell, Catherine Keener, Lisa Blount. 1997 DVD

BOXCAR BERTHA ★★1/2 Small-town girl (Barbara Hershey) hooks up with a gang of train robbers (led by David Carradine) in this *Bonnie and Clyde* coattailer. Martin Scorsese buffs will be disappointed. Rated R. 97m. DIR: Martin Scorsese. CAST: David Carradine, Barbara Hershey, Barry Primus, Bernie Casey, John Carradine. 1972

BOXER, THE ★★★1/2 This introspective, lean drama is set amid the seesawing sectarian violence and peace negotiations of Belfast. Danny Boy Flynn is a promising pugilist who served a fourteen-year prison sentence for his ties with the IRA. He returns to his old neighborhood, reopens a gym for Catholic and Protestant youths, and rekindles his relationship with a former girlfriend. Rated R for language and violence. 110m. DIR: Jim Sheridan. CAST: Daniel Day-Lewis, Emily Watson, Brian Cox, Ken Stott, Gerard McSorley. 1997 DVD

BOXING HELENA ★★ In this voyeuristic story of obsession, domination, and sexual inadequacy, a surgeon amputates the arms and legs of a bitchy temptress and imprisons her in his mansion. Writer-director Jennifer Chambers Lynch shoots for the same hypererotic feel that mark the films of her father, David Lynch. Rated R for nudity, sex, and profanity. 105m. DIR: Jennifer Chambers Lynch. CAST: Julian Sands, Sherilyn Fenn, Bill Paxton, Kurtwood Smith, Art Garfunkel. 1993

BOXOFFICE 🎔 From lousy nightclubs to the big time. Not rated; contains language and nudity. 92m. DIR: Josef Bogdanovich. CAST: Robin Clark, Monica Lewis, Carole Cortne, Eddie Constantine, Aldo Ray, Edie Adams, Peter Hurkos. 1981

BOY AND HIS DOG, A ★★★★1/2 Looking for intelligence and biting humor in a science-fiction satire? Try this Hugo Award–winning screen adaptation of Harlan Ellison's novel, which focuses on the adventures of a young scavenger (Don Johnson) and his telepathic dog as they roam the Earth circa 2024 after a nuclear holocaust. Rated R for violence, sexual references, and nudity. 87m. DIR: L. Q. Jones. CAST: Don Johnson, Suzanne Benton, Jason Robards Jr. 1976 DVD

BOY CALLED HATE, A ★★ Scott Caan debuted in this violent tale of a misunderstood troublemaker

and the abused young woman he rescues from a rape and then takes on a mini-crime-spree. Production values could be better, as the soundtrack sometimes drowns out the dialogue. Rated R for profanity, violence, and sexual situations. 98m. DIR: Mitch Marcus. CAST: Scott Caan, Missy Crider, James Caan, Elliott Gould, Adam Beach. 1995

BOY, DID I GET A WRONG NUMBER! 🎔 When you get a wrong number, hang up and dial again. Too bad the cast and director didn't. 99m. DIR: George Marshall. CAST: Bob Hope, Elke Sommer, Phyllis Diller. 1966

BOY FRIEND, THE ★★★ Ken Russell, at his least self-indulgent and most affectionate, provides a plucky parody of Twenties musicals. The inventiveness and opulence call to mind the work of Busby Berkeley. Twiggy's performance is engaging. Rated G. 110m. DIR: Ken Russell. CAST: Twiggy, Christopher Gable, Max Adrian, Tommy Tune, Glenda Jackson. 1971

BOY IN BLUE, THE ★★★ Nice little screen biography of Ned Hanlan (Nicolas Cage), the famed Canadian lad who owned the sport of international sculling (rowing) for ten years during the end of the nineteenth century. Although the picture plays like a thin retread of *Rocky*—particularly with respect to its music—the result is no less inspirational. Inexplicably rated R for very brief nudity and coarse language. 97m. DIR: Charles Jarrott. CAST: Nicolas Cage, Christopher Plummer, Cynthia Dale, David Naughton. 1986

BOY IN THE PLASTIC BUBBLE, THE ★★ John Travolta has his hands full in this significantly altered television adaptation of the boy who, because of an immunity deficiency, must spend every breathing moment in a sealed environment. Vapid stuff needlessly mired with sci-fi jargon. Not rated. 100m. DIR: Randal Kleiser. CAST: John Travolta, Glynnis O'Connor, Ralph Bellamy, Robert Reed, Diana Hyland, Buzz Aldrin. 1976

BOY MEETS GIRL ★★★ An early spoof of Hollywood with James Cagney and Pat O'Brien as wisecracking, irreverent studio contract writers. On the side they help a young widow with her romantic problems. B&W; 86m. DIR: Lloyd Bacon. CAST: James Cagney, Pat O'Brien, Marie Wilson, Ralph Bellamy, Frank McHugh, Dick Foran, Ronald Reagan, Penny Singleton. 1938

BOY NAMED CHARLIE BROWN, A ★★★★ Charles Schulz's "Peanuts" gang jumps to the big screen in this delightful, wistful tale of Charlie Brown's shot at fame in a national spelling bee. Rated G. 85m. DIR: Bill Melendez. 1969

BOY TAKES GIRL ★★ A young girl learns to adapt when her parents leave her at a farming cooperative one summer. Some adult themes and more romance than may be acceptable for younger viewers, but this comedy-drama is passable for older kids. 93m. DIR: Michal Bat-Adam. CAST: Gabi Eldor, Hillel Neeman, Dina Limon. 1983

BOY WHO COULD FLY, THE ★★★★ Writer-director Nick Castle has created a marvelous motion picture which speaks to the dreamer in all of us. His heroine, Milly (Lucy Deakins), is a newcomer to a small town where her neighbor, Eric (Jay Underwood), neither speaks nor responds to other people. All he does is sit on his roof and pretend to fly. Rated PG for dramatic intensity. 114m. DIR: Nick Castle. CAST: Lucy Deakins, Jay Underwood, Bonnie Bedelia, Fred Savage, Colleen Dewhurst, Fred Gwynne, Mindy Cohn. 1986

BOY WITH GREEN HAIR, THE ★★★ A young war orphan's hair changes color, makes him a social outcast, and brings a variety of bigots and narrow minds out of the woodwork in this food-for-thought fable. The medium is the message in this one. 82m. DIR: Joseph Losey. CAST: Dean Stockwell, Robert Ryan, Barbara Hale, Pat O'Brien. 1948

BOYFRIENDS AND GIRLFRIENDS ★★★★ Another of French director Eric Rohmer's delightful "Comedies and Proverbs," this import deals with two beautiful young women who become friends and have romantic adventures with various lovers. As usual, not much happens in a dramatic sense, but no one can capture the moment like Rohmer, who has us fall in love with his characters as they fall in and out of love with each other. In French with English subtitles. 102m. DIR: Eric Rohmer. CAST: Emmanuelle Chaulet, Sophie Renoir, Anne-Laure Meury, Eric Viellard, François-Eric Gendron. 1987 DVD

BOYS (1996) ★★★ A young man brings an unconscious beautiful woman back to his boardinghouse. There, he begins to fall in love with her even as her mysterious and perhaps deadly story comes to light. Unlikely but intriguing film is buoyed by its stars—Lukas Haas and Winona Ryder—who are both excellent. Based on the short story "Twenty Minutes" by James Salter. Rated PG-13 for profanity. 86m. DIR: Stacy Cochran. CAST: Winona Ryder, Lukas Haas, John C. Reilly, James LeGros, Skeet Ulrich. 1996

BOYS, THE (1997) ★★★1/2 Teamwork saves the day in this likable tale of a group of drinking buddies who play hockey. When their coach and bar owner finds himself in debt to the mob, it's up to this ragtag group of friends to play some real hockey. Released in Canada as *Les Boys*, the film has spawned two sequels and is one of Canada's highest grossing films. Not rated; contains violence. 110m. DIR: Louis Saia. CAST: Marc Messier, Remy Girard, Patrick Huard, Serge Theriault, Michelle Barrette. 1997 DVD

BOYS CLUB, THE ★★★ Satisfying thriller features Chris Penn in a harrowing performance as a psychotic stranger who takes three teenage boys hostage when he hides out in their clubhouse. As the situation becomes more intense, the boys are forced to become men in order to escape their tormentor. Atmospheric and moody. Rated R for violence and language. 92m. DIR: John Fawcett. CAST: Christopher Penn, Dominic Zamprogna, Devon Sawa, Stuart Stone. 1996 DVD

•**BOYS DON'T CRY** ★★★★ Definitely not for the faint of heart or closed of mind, this truth-is-stranger-than-fiction re-creation of actual events is a remarkably self-assured debut from director/co-scripter Kimberly Pierce, who wrote the screenplay with Andy Bienen as a graduate thesis. It blossomed into a feature-length film that is fascinating, compelling, and ultimately horrifying: the study of a re-markably brave and self-destructively foolish individual determined to construct and enjoy her own special life, no matter what the consequences. The neo-documentary, cinema verité style is amplified by its largely unrecognized cast, led by Oscar-winner Hilary Swank as a young woman determined to "pass" as a boy among the white-trash dregs of rural Nebraska. Swank's positively stunning lead performance, as captivating and mesmerizing a job of acting as you're likely to see, is a ferociously self-assured interpretation of a modern tragic heroine ... or hero, depending on one's point of view. Powerful stuff. Rated R for profanity, violence, nudity, drug use, and strong sexual content. 114m. DIR: Kimberly Pierce. CAST: Hilary Swank, Chloe Sevigny, Peter Sarsgaard, Brendan Sexton III, Alison Folland, Alicia Goranson. 1999 DVD

BOYS FROM BRAZIL, THE ★★1/2 In this thriller, Gregory Peck plays an evil Nazi war criminal with farfetched plans to resurrect the Third Reich. Laurence Olivier as a Jewish Nazi-hunter pursues him. Rated R. 123m. DIR: Franklin J. Schaffner. CAST: Gregory Peck, Laurence Olivier, James Mason, Lilli Palmer. 1978 DVD

BOYS FROM BROOKLYN, THE 🖤 Absolutely hilarious bomb with Bela Lugosi as a mad scientist turning people into apes on a forgotten island. Better known as *Bela Lugosi Meets a Brooklyn Gorilla*, a much more appropriate title. B&W; 72m. DIR: William Beaudine. CAST: Bela Lugosi, Duke Mitchell, Sammy Petrillo. 1952 DVD

BOYS IN COMPANY C, THE ★★★ The film opens with the arrival of various draftees in the Marine Corps induction center and comes close, at times, to being the powerful film the subject of the Vietnam war suggests. The combat scenes are particularly effective, and the deaths of soldiers are gory without being overdone. Rated R for violence. 127m. DIR: Sidney J. Furie. CAST: Stan Shaw, Andrew Stevens, James Canning, James Whitmore Jr. 1978

BOYS IN THE BAND, THE ★★★ Widely acclaimed film about nine men who attend a birthday party and end up exposing their lives and feelings to one another in the course of the night. Eight of the men are gay; one is straight. One of the first American films to deal honestly with the subject of homosexuality. Sort of a large-scale *My Dinner with André* with the whole film shot on one set. Rated R. 119m. DIR: William Friedkin. CAST: Kenneth Nelson, Peter White, Leonard Frey, Cliff Gorman. 1970

BOYS NEXT DOOR, THE (1985) ★★★ This story of two alienated teenage youths, Charlie Sheen and Maxwell Caulfield, going on a killing spree in Los Angeles, makes for some tense viewing. Sheen and Caulfield decide to go to L.A. Once in the city, one violent encounter spawns another. Beware: This one is extremely graphic in its depiction of violence. Rated R. 88m. DIR: Penelope Spheeris. CAST: Charlie Sheen, Maxwell Caulfield, Hank Garrett, Patti D'Arbanville, Christopher McDonald, Moon Zappa. 1985

BOYS NEXT DOOR, THE (1996) ★★★★ Powerful *Hallmark Hall of Fame* production uses humor to deliver its message about the plight of mentally ill adults. Tony Goldwyn plays the social worker to four men who are sharing a house and making a go at independent living. Their needs are endless, and Goldwyn must choose between them and keeping his marriage together. Not rated; contains mature themes. 99m. **DIR:** John Erman. **CAST:** Tony Goldwyn, Nathan Lane, Courtney B. Vance, Michael Jeter, Robert Sean Leonard, Mare Winningham. **1996**

BOYS' NIGHT OUT ★★★1/2 Three otherwise staid married men finance an apartment and set out to share a live-in girl on the one night a week they are "allowed" out. They pick Kim Novak unaware she is a sociology student studying the sexual fantasies of suburban males. Good farce, and not the least bit smutty. Well ahead of its time with a wonderful cast. 115m. **DIR:** Michael Gordon. **CAST:** Kim Novak, James Garner, Tony Randall, Howard Duff, Janet Blair, Patti Page, Jessie Royce Landis, Oscar Homolka, Howard Morris, Anne Jeffreys, Zsa Zsa Gabor, Fred Clark, William Bendix. **1962**

BOYS OF ST. VINCENT ★★★★★ This Dickensian tale of abuse and retribution, stars a mesmerizing Henry Czerny in a cold-blooded performance as a handsome, intelligent brother with a sick desire for his young charges. This is especially heart-wrenching because neither the accused nor the abused ever asks for pity. Not rated; contains profanity, violence, sexual situations, nudity, and adult themes. 186m. **DIR:** John N. Smith. **CAST:** Henry Czerny, Johnny Morina, Brian Dooley, Brian Dodd, Lise Roy, Sebastian Spence, David Hewlett. **1992**

BOYS OF THE CITY ★★ Somewhere between their incarnations as the Dead End Kids and the Bowery Boys, the Forties version of the Brat Pack turned up as the East Side Kids in low-budget movies. In this one, the gang takes a trip to the mountains, where they solve the murder of a judge by gangsters. B&W; 68m. **DIR:** Joseph H. Lewis. **CAST:** Bobby Jordan, Leo Gorcey, Dave O'Brien, Donald Haines. **1940**

BOYS ON THE SIDE ★★★1/2 To try her luck in Los Angeles, New York nightclub singer Whoopi Goldberg answers a newspaper ad and ends up as a companion to strait-laced Mary-Louise Parker on a cross-country drive. A stop in Pittsburgh adds Drew Barrymore. This road/buddy movie explores the special relationships that can develop among women. Rated R for violence, nudity, and profanity. 117m. **DIR:** Herbert Ross. **CAST:** Whoopi Goldberg, Mary-Louise Parker, Drew Barrymore, Matthew McConaughey, James Remar, Billy Wirth, Anita Gillette. **1995 DVD**

BOYS' TOWN ★★★★ Spencer Tracy gives one of his most memorable performances in this MGM classic about Father Flanagan and his struggle to give orphans and juvenile delinquents a chance at life. Overtly manipulative, but rewarding. B&W; 93m. **DIR:** Norman Taurog. **CAST:** Spencer Tracy, Mickey Rooney, Henry Hull. **1938**

BOYS WILL BE BOYS ★★★ *Home Alone* meets *Rambo* in this tale of two brothers left alone for the first time while their parents attend a company function. The brothers rise to the occasion when their father's business rival arrives to create chaos. It's up to the miniwarriors to salvage their dad's job and the house before the folks get home. Enjoyable romp benefits from large cast of recognizable faces. Rated PG for violence. 90m. **DIR:** Dom DeLuise. **CAST:** Randy Travis, Julie Hagerty, Michael DeLuise, Jon Voight, Mickey Rooney, Ruth Buzzi. **1997 DVD**

BOYZ N THE HOOD ★★★★1/2 Although *Boyz N the Hood* may appear to be an exploitation flick about gang violence, it is far from being so. This powerful drama, which marks the directing debut of 23-year-old John Singleton, is a responsible, heart-tugging tale of a modern tragedy, focusing on a group of young men and women caught in the war zone of south central Los Angeles. Rated R for profanity, violence, and nudity. 111m. **DIR:** John Singleton. **CAST:** Ice Cube, Cuba Gooding Jr., Morris Chestnut, Laurence Fishburne, Nia Long, Tyra Ferrell. **1991 DVD**

BRADDOCK: MISSING IN ACTION III ★★ After the war has ended, Colonel Braddock (Chuck Norris) returns to Vietnam to rescue a group of Amerasian children in a POW camp. A dark, grainy, low-budget film cowritten by Norris. If you liked the first two films, you'll probably enjoy this one, too. Rated R for violence. 90m. **DIR:** Aaron Norris. **CAST:** Chuck Norris, Aki Aleong. **1987**

BRADY BUNCH, THE (TV SERIES) ★★ The 1970s sitcom overdoses on bell-bottoms, polyester, and saccharine sweetness. Four-volume series features two episodes on each. The first volume features the two families merging on the honeymoon. Other highlights include a stint by Davy Jones of the Monkees, Marcia's fat nose, and Jan's identity crisis. Not hilarious in its heyday, the series has not improved with time. Each volume 50m. **DIR:** Russ Mayberry, Jack Arnold, Peter Baldwin, John Rich, Hal Cooper, Oscar Rudolph. **CAST:** Florence Henderson, Robert Reed, Ann B. Davis. **1971–1973**

BRADY BUNCH MOVIE, THE ★★★1/2 The big-screen version of the 1970s sitcom is actually a disarming parody of the old show's relentless wholesomeness, with the simple plot (the Bradys need $20,000 to save their home) serving as a framework for bits from a number of episodes. Rated PG-13 for mild profanity. 90m. **DIR:** Betty Thomas. **CAST:** Shelley Long, Gary Cole, Michael McKean, Henriette Mantel, Christine Taylor, Jennifer Elise Cox. **1995**

BRADY'S ESCAPE ★★★ A minor HBO-produced film concerning an American attempting to escape the Nazis in Europe during World War II. Nothing original is added to the familiar plot. 96m. **DIR:** Pal Gabor. **CAST:** John Savage, Kelly Reno. **1984**

BRAIN, THE (1965) ★★ Adequate remake of the oft-filmed *Donovan's Brain*, a little short on thrills and originality, but atmospheric fun nevertheless. A German-British coproduction. B&W; 85m. **DIR:** Freddie Francis. **CAST:** Peter Van Eyck, Anne Heywood, Bernard Lee, Jack MacGowran. **1965**

BRAIN, THE (1988) ★★1/2 Hokey special effects take away from this shocker about a TV psychologist (David Gale) and his alien brain. The brain (eyes, nose, and long, sharp teeth added) starts munching anyone who gets in the way. Occasionally entertaining, this is one film that never reaches its potential. Rated R for violence and mild gore. 94m. **DIR:** Edward Hunt. **CAST:** Tom Breznahan, Cyndy Preston, David Gale. **1988**

BRAIN DAMAGE ★★1/2 A wisecracking giant worm escapes from its elderly keepers and forces a teenager to kill people. Although the low budget hampers the special effects, the offbeat execution makes this worth a look for horror fans. Rated R for sexual situations and graphic violence. 90m. DIR: Frank Henenlotter. CAST: Rich Herbst, Gordon MacDonald. 1988 DVD

BRAIN DEAD ★★★ A research doctor (Bill Pullman) is pressured by his corporate sponsor to use his research on brain patterns to open a chain of attitude adjustment centers. Something snaps, and the mild-mannered doctor soon becomes the apparent victim of severe paranoia. Rated R for profanity, violence, and nudity. 85m. DIR: Adam Simon. CAST: Bill Pullman, Bud Cort, George Kennedy, Bill Paxton. 1989

BRAIN DONORS ★★★1/2 Three bumbling misfits—a shyster lawyer, a quick-witted taxi driver, and a dim-witted houseboy—join together to form a ballet company in this often hilarious take on the Marx Brothers. John Turturro steals the show as he spews out an endless stream of lightning-fast jokes à la Groucho. Rated PG for sexual innuendo and nudity. 79m. DIR: Dennis Dugan. CAST: John Turturro, Bob Nelson, Mel Smith, Nancy Marchand, John Savident, George de la Pena, Spike Alexander. 1992

BRAIN EATERS, THE ★★ Robert Heinlein's *The Puppet Masters* is the unacknowledged source for this grade-C sci-fi melodrama in the *Invasion of the Body Snatchers* tradition. It's too brief to overstay its welcome, and has earned a cult following. B&W; 60m. DIR: Bruno VeSota. CAST: Joanna Lee, Jody Fair, Ed Nelson, Leonard Nimoy. 1958

BRAIN FROM PLANET AROUS, THE ★★★ Great little film is much better than the plot or title would suggest. Giant brain from outer space takes over John Agar's body in an attempt to conquer the world. Not far behind is another brain that inhabits the body of Agar's dog and tries to prevent it. Good stuff. B&W; 70m. DIR: Nathan Juran. CAST: John Agar, Joyce Meadows, Robert Fuller. 1958

BRAIN OF BLOOD 💗 A mad doctor performs brain transplants and creates a hulking monster. 83m. DIR: Al Adamson. CAST: Kent Taylor, John Bloom, Regina Carroll, Grant Williams. 1971

BRAIN SMASHER ... A LOVE STORY ★★★ Andrew Clay is the brain smasher, a notorious professional bouncer who takes pride in his work. Teri Hatcher is an international model who recruits Clay to protect her and her sister from killer Chinese monks. Honest! Veteran character actors help levitate this one above mediocrity. Rated PG-13 for violence and profanity. DIR: Albert Pyun. CAST: Andrew Clay, Teri Hatcher, Brion James, Tim Thomerson, Charles Rocket, Nicholas Guest, Deborah Van Valkenburgh. 1993

BRAIN THAT WOULDN'T DIE, THE 💗 A doctor experiments with human limbs. B&W; 81m. DIR: Joseph Green. CAST: Jason "Herb" Evers, Virginia Leith, Adele Lamont. 1963 DVD

BRAINIAC, THE ★★★ Mexi-monster stuff about a nobleman, executed as a warlock in 1661, who comes back to life to seek revenge on the descendants of those who killed him. Every so often he transforms himself into a monster with a long, snaky tongue to suck out people's brains. With their low production values and indifferent dubbing, most Mexican horror films are good only for camp value. This one has those same flaws, but you'll also find it has some eerily effective moments. 77m. DIR: Chano Urveta. CAST: Abel Salazar. 1961

BRAINSCAN ★★ After a teenager plays a video game in which he commits murder, real killings exactly like the ones in his "game" begin to occur. This none-too-original rehash of the Freddy Krueger films is doggedly predictable, with cheap special effects and a double cop-out ending. Rated R for gore. 96m. DIR: John Flynn. CAST: Edward Furlong, Frank Langella, T. Ryder Smith, Amy Hargreaves. 1994

BRAINSTORM ★★★1/2 Christopher Walken and Natalie Wood star in this sci-fi thriller about an invention that can read and record physical, emotional, and intellectual sensations as they are experienced by an individual and allow them to be reexperienced by another human being. But what happens if it's used for evil? Rated PG for nudity and profanity. 106m. DIR: Douglas Trumbull. CAST: Christopher Walken, Natalie Wood, Louise Fletcher. 1983 DVD

BRAINWASHED ★★1/2 Disquieting psychological thriller about a man who is imprisoned by Nazis during World War II. Story documents his struggle to remain rational while being brainwashed by his captors. 102m. DIR: Gerd Oswald. CAST: Curt Jurgens, Claire Bloom, Hansjor Felmy, Albert Lieven. 1961

BRAINWAVES ★★★ A young San Francisco wife and mother undergoes brain surgery as a result of an accident. An experimental brain wave transfer is performed in an attempt to restore her to a normal life, producing startling results since the brain waves came from a murder victim. Rated R for some nudity and mild violence. 83m. DIR: Ulli Lommel. CAST: Keir Dullea, Suzanna Love, Vera Miles, Percy Rodrigues, Paul Wilson, Tony Curtis. 1982

BRAM STOKER'S BURIAL OF THE RATS 💗 Horror films just don't get worse than this cheeseball dreck, which exploits Bram Stoker's good name merely as cachet for a lot of nude women and soft-core coupling. Rated R for nudity, simulated sex, violence, and gore. 85m. DIR: Dan Golden. CAST: Adrienne Barbeau, Maria Ford, Kevin Alber. 1995

BRAM STOKER'S DRACULA ★★1/2 Vlad the Impaler, a.k.a. Dracula, becomes a tragic figure in Francis Ford Coppola's visually opulent but overwrought version of the famous vampire tale. Some offbeat casting and an overemphasis on sex and nudity. Rated R for nudity, gore, and violence. 130m. DIR: Francis Ford Coppola. CAST: Gary Oldman, Winona Ryder, Anthony Hopkins, Keanu Reeves, Richard E. Grant, Cary Elwes, Bill Campbell, Tom Waits, Sadie Frost. 1992 DVD

BRAM STOKER'S SHADOWBUILDER ★★ Modern-day adaptation of Bram Stoker's story about a demon summoned from the pits of hell and the determined priest assigned to protect a 12-year-old boy who may be the savior. The decent special effects aren't enough to hide the rudimentary acting, plotting, and direction. Rated R for violence. 101m. DIR: Jamie

Dixon. CAST: Michael Rooker, Kevin Zegers, Shawn Thompson, Steven Blum, Tony Todd. 1997 DVD

BRAM STOKER'S THE MUMMY ★★ Late entry into the classic movie monster marathon suffers from familiar plot and low budget. Lou Gossett Jr. is the Egyptologist who learns that an ancient mummy is waiting to be reincarnated. The rehash of *The Awakening* is as musty and dusty as its leading lady. Rated R for adult situations, nudity, and violence. 99m. DIR: Jeffrey Obrow. CAST: Lou Gossett Jr., Amy Locane, Eric Lutes. 1997 DVD

BRAMBLE BUSH, THE ★★ Soap opera about a doctor who pulls the plug on his terminally ill best friend while having an affair with the sick buddy's wife. There are enough subplots for an afternoon full of daytime dramas in this mildly diverting movie. 93m. DIR: Daniel Petrie. CAST: Richard Burton, Angie Dickinson, Barbara Rush, Tom Drake, James Dunn, Henry Jones. 1960

BRANDED ★★1/2 Farfetched sagebrush melodrama finds Alan Ladd and his shady sidekick hatching a plot to fleece an old rancher and his wife—as Ladd impersonates their long-missing son. Pretty creaky, but a good cast, some exciting chase scenes, and fine outdoor Technicolor photography make this worth watching. 103m. DIR: Rudolph Maté. CAST: Alan Ladd, Mona Freeman, Charles Bickford, Robert Keith, Joseph Calleia, Peter Hanson, Tom Tully, Milburn Stone. 1951

BRANNIGAN ★★1/2 John Wayne travels to London to bring back a fugitive in this enjoyable cops-and-robbers chase film. It's fun to see the Duke in jolly old England and the cast is outstanding. Rated PG. 111m. DIR: Douglas Hickox. CAST: John Wayne, Richard Attenborough, Judy Geeson, Mel Ferrer, Ralph Meeker, John Vernon. 1975

BRASS ★★ Routine made-for-TV cop thriller starring Carroll O'Connor as a top New York City police officer and a politically sensitive kidnap-murder case. The pilot for a proposed series. 94m. DIR: Corey Allen. CAST: Carroll O'Connor, Lois Nettleton, Jimmy Baio, Paul Shenar. 1985

BRASS MONKEY, THE ★★ In this British thriller we get a not-very-effective story based on a radio program. Carole Landis is a radio singer who prevents the theft of a Buddhist religious icon. The script is weak, and Landis and the other players seem bored. B&W; 84m. DIR: Thornton Freeland. CAST: Carole Landis, Carroll Levis, Herbert Lom, Avril Angers, Ernest Thesiger. 1948

BRASS TARGET ★★ Pure Hollywood hokum at its most ridiculous would ask us to believe that Gen. George Patton (George Kennedy) was murdered after World War II because of a large gold robbery committed by his staff. Not much to recommend this boring film. Rated PG for moderate language and violence. 111m. DIR: John Hough. CAST: Sophia Loren, George Kennedy, John Cassavetes, Robert Vaughn, Max von Sydow, Bruce Davison. 1978

BRASSED OFF ★★★1/2 Odd but appealing mixture of romance, comedy, class-war polemic, and marching-band musical. A coal-mining town in the north of England faces ruin when the government tries to close down its colliery. At the same time, the local miners' brass band has a shot at winning a national competition. Rated R for profanity. 107m. DIR: Mark Herman. CAST: Pete Postlethwaite, Tara Fitzgerald, Ewan McGregor, Stephen Tompkinson. 1996 DVD

BRAVADOS, THE ★★★1/2 In this revenge Western, Gregory Peck tracks down the four men who raped and killed his wife. Directors Budd Boetticher and Anthony Mann handled this theme more involvingly in their films with Randolph Scott and James Stewart, respectively, but this is nonetheless a serviceable Western. 98m. DIR: Henry King. CAST: Gregory Peck, Joan Collins, Stephen Boyd, Henry Silva, Lee Van Cleef. 1958

BRAVE LITTLE TOASTER, THE ★★★★ This delightful animated feature, based on a charming children's story by sci-fi author Thomas M. Disch, concerns a quintet of electrical appliances that journey to the big city in the hopes of finding the human master who abandoned them in a country summer cottage. Suitable for family viewing. 92m. DIR: Jerry Rees. 1987

BRAVE LITTLE TOASTER GOES TO MARS, THE ★★1/2 This tale—which concerns the efforts of our intrepid appliances—is buried beneath humdrum animation and atrocious songs. The script includes a few humorous digs at adolescence, and there's one brilliant bit of voice casting. Rated G. 73m. DIR: Robert Ramirez. 1997

BRAVE ONE, THE ★★★★ Above-average family film about a Mexican boy whose pet bull is sold. Knowing that its fate is to die in the bullfighting ring, the boy tracks his pet to Mexico City, where he does everything he can to save it. Winner of an Academy Award for best original story, which went unclaimed for almost twenty years because screenwriter "Robert Rich" was really the blacklisted Dalton Trumbo. 102m. DIR: Irving Rapper. CAST: Michel Ray, Rodolfo Hoyos, Elsa Cardenas, Joi Lansing. 1956 DVD

BRAVEHEART ★★★★★ Superb historical epic, directed by and starring Mel Gibson, has both rousing action and a strong dramatic storyline. *Braveheart* is a cinematic event. Its themes of love, honor, betrayal, remorse, and self-sacrifice are carefully sculptured into an unforgettable motion picture. Rated R for violence and nudity. 177m. DIR: Mel Gibson. CAST: Mel Gibson, Sophie Marceau, Patrick McGoohan, Brendan Gleeson, James Cosmo, David O'Hara, Angus MacFadyen. 1995

BRAZIL ★★★★ A savage blend of *1984* and *The Time Bandits* from Monty Python director Terry Gilliam. Jonathan Pryce stars as a bemused paper shuffler in a red tape–choked future society at the brink of collapsing under its own bureaucracy. Definitely not for all tastes, but a treat for those with an appreciation for social satire. Were it not for a chaotic conclusion and slightly overlong running time, this would be a perfect picture. Rated R for language and adult situations. 131m. DIR: Terry Gilliam. CAST: Jonathan Pryce, Robert De Niro, Katherine Helmond, Ian Holm, Bob Hoskins, Michael Palin, Ian Richardson. 1985 DVD

BREACH OF CONDUCT ★★ A major's wife is sexually harassed by the deranged army-base commander. Rated PG-13 for violence. 93m. DIR: Tim Matheson.

CAST: Peter Coyote, Courtney Thorne-Smith, Keith Amos, Beth Toussaint. 1994

BREACH OF TRUST ★★1/2 So-so shoot-'em-up is elevated by decent stunt work and chase scenes. A high-tech drug-money laundering scheme connects a beautiful undercover cop and a small-time hood. Mobsters follow close at their heels. Rated R for sex, nudity, profanity, and violence. 96m. DIR: Charles Wilkinson. CAST: Michael Biehn, Leilani Sarelle, Miguel Sandoval, Kim Coates, Ed Lauter. 1995

•BREAD AND CHOCOLATE ★★★★ An uneducated Italian man (Nino Manfredi in a wonderfully Chaplinesque performance) tries to provide for his family by seeking work in Switzerland, a country not kind to illegal immigrants. This bittersweet comedy was a popular favorite at art houses in the 1970s. In Italian with English subtitles. Not rated; contains no objectionable material. 109m. DIR: Franco Brusati. CAST: Nino Manfredi, Anna Karina, Johnny Dorelli. 1974

BREAD AND SALT ★★★1/2 Having left Moscow in 1985 when Russia was firmly entrenched in Communism, vivacious Irina Muravyova returns, along with a scholar of Russian studies, Richard Lourie. The two investigate the influence of capitalism on the average person in this fine documentary. On the one hand there are high prices and unemployment, and on the other hand there are choices, new freedoms, and the opportunity for some to become millionaires. Not rated; contains profanity. 95m. DIR: Jeanne Collachia. 1992

BREAK, THE ★★★ Vincent Van Patten is the most convincing thing in this Rockyesque tale of a geeky teenager hoping to become a tennis star. There are some decent moments, including a fun appearance by Martin Sheen as a bookie betting against his own son. However, we have seen too much of this before, and Ben Jorgensen is a bit too wide-eyed as the aspiring pro. Rated PG-13 for profanity and brief nudity. 104m. DIR: Lee H. Katzin. CAST: Vincent Van Patten, Ben Jorgensen, Martin Sheen, Rae Dawn Chong, Valerie Perrine, Gerrit Graham. 1994

BREAK OF DAWN ★★★1/2 Based on a true story, this chronicles Pedro J. Gonzalez's entry to the United States in 1928 and his rapid rise to popularity as the first Mexican radio show host. When his influence over the East L.A. population threatens the racist DA, he's framed for rape. Low-budget, yet convincing. In English and Spanish with English subtitles when needed. Not rated, contains mature themes. 100m. DIR: Isaac Artenstein. CAST: Oscar Chavez, Tony Plana, Maria Rojo, Pepe Serna. 1988

BREAK OF HEARTS ★★1/2 Mediocre drama about a struggling composer and her troubled marriage to a highly acclaimed symphony conductor. Some good acting makes up for the predictable script. B&W; 80m. DIR: Phillip Moeller. CAST: Katharine Hepburn, Charles Boyer, John Beal. 1935

•BREAK UP ★★★ Direct-to-video suspense thriller gets a major boost from a top-notch cast and sharp direction. A battered wife is suspected of killing her womanizing husband and a good cop/bad cop duo is assigned to protect her, then track her down when she's accused of the murder. Director Paul Marcus gets plenty of mileage out of the formulaic script,

while the cast more than rises to the challenge. Rated R for adult situations, language, nudity, and violence. 101m. DIR: Paul Marcus. CAST: Bridget Fonda, Kiefer Sutherland, Steven Weber, Penelope Ann Miller, Hart Bochner. 1998 DVD

BREAKAWAY ★★ A mob messenger tries to stay one step ahead of a professional killer long enough to enjoy the money she stole from her former boss. Aside from the casting of scandal-ridden ice skater Tonya Harding in a supporting role, there's nothing memorable here. Rated R for violence, nudity, sexual situations, and profanity. 95m. DIR: Sean Dash. CAST: Teri Thompson, Joe Estevez, Tonya Harding, Tony Noakes. 1996

BREAKDOWN ★★★★ This creepy thriller turns a stranded-motorist scenario into a seamless blend of panic, anguish, and crackerjack action scenes. Jeff and Amy Taylor, who have car trouble while taking a scenic route through the Southwest, are relieved when a polite trucker stops to help. Their relief is short-lived when Amy accepts a ride to a nearby diner and then apparently melts into the desolate landscape. Rated R for language, violence, and terror. 96m. DIR: Jonathan Mostow. CAST: Kurt Russell, Kathleen Quinlan, J. T. Walsh, M. C. Gainey, Jack Noseworthy, Rex Linn. 1997 DVD

BREAKER! BREAKER! 🎬 A quickie thrown together to cash in on the CB craze. Rated PG. 86m. DIR: Don Hulette. CAST: Chuck Norris, George Murdock, Terry O'Connor, Don Gentry. 1977

BREAKER MORANT ★★★★★ This is one Australian import you won't want to miss. Imagine the high adventure of the original Gunga Din, the wise-cracking humor of To Have and Have Not, and the character drama of The Caine Mutiny all rolled into one supermovie. Rated PG. 107m. DIR: Bruce Beresford. CAST: Edward Woodward, Jack Thompson, John Waters, Bryan Brown, Charles Tingwell. 1979 DVD

BREAKFAST AT TIFFANY'S ★★★★ An offbeat yet tender love story of a New York writer and a fey party girl. Strong performances are turned in by George Peppard and Audrey Hepburn. Hepburn's Holly Golightly is a masterful creation that blends the sophistication of a Manhattan "escort" with the childish country girl of her roots. Henry Mancini's score is justly famous, as it creates much of the mood for this wistful story. 115m. DIR: Blake Edwards. CAST: Audrey Hepburn, George Peppard, Patricia Neal, Buddy Ebsen, Mickey Rooney, Martin Balsam. 1961 DVD

BREAKFAST CLUB, THE ★★★★ A group of assorted high school misfits gets to be friends while serving weekend detention in this terrific comedy, directed by John Hughes, the king of watchable teen films. Rated R. 100m. DIR: John Hughes. CAST: Emilio Estevez, Molly Ringwald, Paul Gleason, Judd Nelson, Anthony Michael Hall, Ally Sheedy. 1985 DVD

BREAKFAST IN HOLLYWOOD ★★ This is a romantic comedy based on the radio series of the same name. The plot is thin, but there are some nice musical moments from Nat King Cole and Spike Jones. B&W; 91m. DIR: Harold Schuster. CAST: Bonita Granville, Beulah Bondi, Tom Breneman. 1946

BREAKHEART PASS ★★★ Charles Bronson is a government agent on the trail of gunrunners in the

Old West. Most of the action of this modest Western takes place aboard a train, so the excited pitch needed to fully sustain viewers' interest is never reached. Rated PG—some violence and rough language. 95m. DIR: Tom Gries. CAST: Charles Bronson, Ben Johnson, Ed Lauter, Richard Crenna, Charles Durning, Jill Ireland, John Mitchum. 1976

BREAKIN' ★★ The dancing scenes are wonderful but as a whole, this is pretty lame. The film would have us believe that jazz dancer Kelly (Lucinda Dickey) could hook up with street dancers Ozone ("Shabba-Doo") and Turbo ("Boogaloo Shrimp") to win dance contests and finally break (no pun intended) into big-time show biz. Rated PG for profanity and violence. 90m. DIR: Joel Silberg. CAST: Lucinda Dickey, Adolfo Quinones, Michael Chambers, Ben Lokey. 1984

BREAKIN' 2 ELECTRIC BOOGALOO ★★1/2 This sometimes exhilarating break-dancing movie is better than the original. This time, Kelly (Lucinda Dickey), Ozone (Adolfo "Shabba-Doo" Quinones), and Turbo (Michael "Boogaloo Shrimp" Chambers) put on a show to save a local arts center for children. Rated PG for brief violence and suggested sex. 90m. DIR: Sam Firstenberg. CAST: Lucinda Dickey, Adolfo Quinones, Michael Chambers. 1984

BREAKING ALL THE RULES ♥ Teenagers look for love (translation: lust) and adventure on the last day of summer vacation. 91m. DIR: James Orr. CAST: Carl Marotte, Thor Bishopric, Carolyn Dunn. 1984

BREAKING AWAY ★★★★★ There comes a time in every young man's life when he must loose the ties of home, family, and friends and test his mettle. Dennis Christopher is the young man who retains an innocence we too often mistake for naïveté; Paul Dooley and Barbara Barrie are the often humorously confused parents who offer subtle, sure guidance. This is a warm portrayal of family life and love, of friendships, of growing up and growing away. Rated PG for brief profanity. 100m. DIR: Peter Yates. CAST: Dennis Christopher, Dennis Quaid, Daniel Stern, Jackie Earle Haley, Paul Dooley, Barbara Barrie. 1979

BREAKING FREE ★★1/2 A fledgling juvenile delinquent finds the right path when he is put to work at a summer camp for blind children. Made for the Disney Channel, this is an earnest drama whose honest characters are more compelling than the predictable story. Rated PG. 100m. DIR: David Mackay. CAST: Christine Taylor, Jeremy London, Gina Phillips, Nicolas Surovy. 1995

BREAKING GLASS ★★1/2 British film about a new wave singer's rise to the top, at the expense of personal relationships. Hazel O'Connor's heavy music isn't for all tastes, and the plot line is as old as film itself, but the actors are sincere. 104m. DIR: Brian Gibson. CAST: Phil Daniels, Hazel O'Connor, Jon Finch, Jonathan Pryce. 1980

REAKING HOME TIES ★★★ Texas farm family drama, set in the 1950s, in which the proud father sends his only son off to college in the big city. Well-written TV drama with believable characters and good acting. 95m. DIR: John Wilder. CAST: Jason Robards Jr., Eva Marie Saint, Doug McKeon, Erin Gray, Claire Trevor. 1987

BREAKING IN ★★★★ This low-key character comedy comes from director Bill Forsyth and screenwriter John Sayles. Burt Reynolds, in one of his finest screen performances, is a professional thief who becomes the mentor for a crazy housebreaker (Casey Siemaszko). A fascinating slice of life. Rated R for profanity. 95m. DIR: Bill Forsyth. CAST: Burt Reynolds, Casey Siemaszko, Albert Salmi, Harry Carey Jr. 1989

BREAKING POINT (1989) ★★★1/2 Decent World War II espionage thriller, this remake of *36 Hours* features Corbin Bernsen as a top U.S. intelligence officer who becomes the victim of an elaborate Nazi plot. Made for cable, this is unrated but contains mature themes. 90m. DIR: Peter Markle. CAST: Corbin Bernsen, Joanna Pacula, John Glover, David Marshall Grant. 1989

BREAKING POINT (1993) ★★★ Solid performances and British Columbia locales highlight this slick little thriller, with Gary Busey well cast as a former cop who reluctantly rejoins the force after the return of a nasty serial killer dubbed "the surgeon." Since we quickly learn the maniac's identity, it's more a *Columbo*-style procedural than a mystery, but Busey makes it work. Rated R for violence, profanity, and suggested sex. 95m. DIR: Paul Ziller. CAST: Gary Busey, Kim Cattrall, Darlanne Fluegel. 1993

BREAKING THE ICE ★★ In this improbable meld of music and ice skating, Bobby Breen gets a job singing at a Philadelphia rink, and meets skating moppet Irene Dare. B&W; 79m. DIR: Eddie Cline. CAST: Bobby Breen, Charlie Ruggles, Dolores Costello, Billy Gilbert, Margaret Hamilton. 1938

BREAKING THE RULES ★★★1/2 Three friends reunite and learn that one of them is dying of cancer. They take a cross-country trip to California and meet an unusual woman along the way. Annie Potts is brilliant as Mary, the wacky artist who wants to beautify the country. Rated PG-13 for profanity and suggested sex. 100m. DIR: Neal Israel. CAST: Jason Bateman, C. Thomas Howell, Jonathan Silverman, Annie Potts, Krista Tesreau. 1991

BREAKING THE SURFACE: THE GREG LOUGANIS STORY ★★ Unlike diving, a movie is meant to make a big splash. But this made-for-cable original about diver Greg Louganis barely makes a ripple. Uninspired acting and scarce plot are just a few of the problems here. Not rated; contains violence. 95m. DIR: Steven H. Stern. CAST: Mario Lopez, Michael Murphy, Rosemary Dunsmore, Bruce Weitz. 1996

BREAKING THE WAVES ★★★1/2 Exquisite, thought-provoking tale of a young woman whose marriage to a strong and handsome oil-rig worker is jeopardized when he's paralyzed due to an accident. Encouraged by her husband to seek out other lovers, Bess's quest to heal her husband opens a world of emotions inside her. Rated R for adult situations, language, and nudity. 159m. DIR: Lars von Trier. CAST: Emily Watson, Stellan Skarsgard, Katrin Cartlidge, Jean-Marc Barr, Udo Kier. 1996 DVD

BREAKING UP ★★★ Russell Crowe and Salma Hayek star as a couple struggling to end a once-good relationship now held together by nothing more than sex and force of habit. Adapted from Michael

Cristofer's two-character play, this never escapes its theatrical origins but provides a good showcase for its two talented stars. Rated R for sexual situations, profanity, and nudity. 89m. DIR: Robert Greenwald. CAST: Russell Crowe, Salma Hayek. 1995

BREAKING UP IS HARD TO DO ★★ Superficial made-for-TV movie about six men, all recently divorced, going through the usual trials and tribulations as they try to heal the wounds. 96m. DIR: Lou Antonio. CAST: Ted Bessell, Jeff Conaway, Robert Conrad, Billy Crystal, Tony Musante, David Ogden Stiers. 1979

BREAKOUT (1975) ★★★ While not exactly Charles Bronson at his best, this action-adventure film does have its moments as the star, playing a devil-may-care helicopter pilot, rescues Robert Duvall, an American businessman framed for murder and held captive in a Mexican jail. Rated PG. 96m. DIR: Tom Gries. CAST: Charles Bronson, Robert Duvall, Jill Ireland, John Huston, Sheree North, Randy Quaid. 1975

BREAKOUT (1998) 🎬 Totally inept family comedy about an inventor whose son and his friends are kidnapped to force him to abandon his invention. The film turns into a low-rent *Home Alone* clone of the worst order. Not rated. 86m. DIR: John Bradshaw. CAST: Robert Carradine, Evan Bonifant, James Hong. 1998

•**BREAKS, THE** ★★★ Hip-hop comedy about an Irish boy raised by an African American family in the hood. Mitch Mullany, who wrote the script and stars as Derrick, is a fish out of water as his attempts to fit in create one hysterical moment after another. Rated R for adult situations and language. 86m. DIR: Eric Meza. CAST: Mitch Mullany, Carl Anthony Payne III, Paula Jai Parker, Clifton Powell, Loretta Devine. 1999 DVD

BREAKTHROUGH 🎬 Richard Burton as a heroic German officer who saves the life of an American colonel (Robert Mitchum) after the Nazis thwart an attempt on Hitler's life. Rated PG. 115m. DIR: Andrew V. McLaglen. CAST: Richard Burton, Robert Mitchum, Rod Steiger, Curt Jurgens. 1978

BREATH OF SCANDAL, A ★★ This intended high-style romantic comedy set in Austria in the gossip-rife court of Franz Joseph has little going for it. The script, taken from the Molnar play that poor John Gilbert adapted for his disastrous first talkie, is uninspired. The casting is uninspired. The directing is uninspired. But the scenery and costumes are nice. 98m. DIR: Michael Curtiz. CAST: Sophia Loren, John Gavin, Maurice Chevalier, Angela Lansbury. 1960

BREATHING FIRE ★★1/2 Better-than-average kickboxing effort teams brothers Jonathan Ke Quan and Jerry Trimble against their father, the mastermind behind a bank robbery. Good action and decent performances. Rated R for violence. 92m. DIR: Lou Kennedy. CAST: Jonathan Ke Quan, Jerry Trimble. 1991

BREATHING LESSONS ★★★★ Joanne Woodward steals the show in this, the 180th *Hallmark Hall of Fame*. Woodward plays a whimsical, meddling woman who tries to make things right but usually makes matters worse. James Garner, excellent as her long-suffering husband, resigns himself to their unpredictable but lasting relationship. Based on Anne Tyler's novel, this film focuses on relationships rather than actions and events and has a surprisingly powerful effect on viewers. 93m. DIR: John Erman. CAST: James Garner, Joanne Woodward, Paul Winfield, Joyce Van Patten. 1994

•**BREATHING ROOM** ★★ The usual complications plague a couple in this look at a relationship in jeopardy. The writing and direction are flaccid as the film examines a one-month period in the couple's lives as they attempt to find common ground in their relationship. Not very exciting or original. Rated R for adult situations and language. 90m. DIR: Jon Sherman. CAST: Susan Lloyd, Dan Futterman, Nadia Dajani, Stryker Hardwicke, David Thornton. 1996

BREATHLESS (1959) ★★★★★ Richard Gere or Jean-Paul Belmondo? The choice should be easy after you see the Godard version of this story of a carefree crook and his "along for the ride" girlfriend. See it for Belmondo's performance as the continent's most charming crook, but while you're along for the ride, note just how well made a film can be. B&W 89m. DIR: Jean-Luc Godard. CAST: Jean-Paul Belmondo, Jean Seberg. 1959

BREATHLESS (1983) 🎬 Richard Gere plays a thief hunted by police. Rated R for nudity, profanity, and violence. 100m. DIR: Jim McBride. CAST: Richard Gere, Valerie Kaprisky, Art Metrano, John P. Ryan. 1983 DVD

BREED APART, A ★★★1/2 When a billionaire collector hires an adventurous mountain climber to steal the eggs of an endangered pair of nesting eagles, the result is a nicely paced film that manages to combine drama, suspense, romance, and even a touch of post-Vietnam commentary. Rutger Hauer plays the strange recluse who lives in a tent-palace in the loneliest reaches of the Blue Ridge Mountains. Rated R for sex, nudity, and violence. 95m. DIR: Philippe Mora. CAST: Rutger Hauer, Kathleen Turner, Powers Boothe, Donald Pleasence. 1984

BREEDERS (1986) 🎬 Aliens come to Earth yet again to mate with women in this lurid sci-fi chiller. Not rated; contains nudity, violence, rape, gore, and profanity. 77m. DIR: Tim Kincaid. CAST: Teresa Farley, Lance Lewman, Frances Raines, Jennifer Delora, Ed French. 1986

BREEDERS (1996) 🎬 Aliens from a dying planet battle college students in this tired made-for-video feature. Rated R for violence, nudity, and sexual situations. 93m. DIR: Paul Matthews. CAST: Todd Jenser, Samantha Janus, Oliver Tobias. 1996 DVD

BRENDA STARR 🎬 Spoof of long-running comic strip character features an unconvincing Brooke Shields. This was completed in 1987 but not released until 1992. Rated PG for profanity. 94m. DIR: Robert Ellis Miller. CAST: Brooke Shields, Timothy Dalton, Tony Peck, Diana Scarwid. 1992 DVD

BREWSTER McCLOUD ★★★ If you liked Robert Altman's *M*A*S*H* (the movie) and *Harold and Maude*, and your humor takes a few degrees off-center, you'll enjoy this "flight of fantasy" about a boy (Bud Cort) who wants to make like a bird. Rated R. 104m. DIR: Robert Altman. CAST: Bud Cort, Sally Kellerman. 1970

BREWSTER'S MILLIONS (1945) ★★1/2 This is the fifth of seven film versions of the 1902 novel and stage success about a young man who will inherit millions if he is able to spend $1 million quickly and quietly within a set period of time. Dennis O'Keefe and company perform this Tinsel Town stalwart in fine fashion, making for a bright, entertaining comic romp. B&W; 79m. DIR: Allan Dwan. CAST: Dennis O'-Keefe, Helen Walker, June Havoc, Mischa Auer, Eddie "Rochester" Anderson, Gail Patrick. 1945

BREWSTER'S MILLIONS (1985) ★★★ It took director Walter Hill to bring Richard Pryor out of his movie slump with this unspectacular, but still entertaining, comedy about a minor-league baseball player who stands to inherit $300 million if he can fulfill the provisions of a rather daffy will. It's no classic, but still much, much better than *The Toy* or *Superman III*. Rated PG for profanity. 97m. DIR: Walter Hill. CAST: Richard Pryor, John Candy, Lonette McKee, Stephen Collins, Pat Hingle, Tovah Feldshuh, Hume Cronyn. 1985 DVD

BRIAN'S SONG ★★★★★ This is one of the best movies ever made originally for television. James Caan is Brian Piccolo, a running back for football's Chicago Bears. His friendship with superstar Gale Sayers (Billy Dee Williams) becomes a mutually stimulating rivalry on the field and inspirational strength when Brian is felled by cancer. As with any quality film that deals with death, this movie is buoyant with life and warmth. Rated G. 73m. DIR: Buzz Kulik. CAST: James Caan, Billy Dee Williams, Jack Warden, Judy Pace, Shelley Fabares. 1970

BRIDE, THE ★1/2 This remake of James Whale's classic 1935 horror-comedy of the macabre, *Bride of Frankenstein*, has some laughs. But these, unlike in the original, are unintentional. Rock singer Sting makes a rather stuffy, unsavory Dr. Charles (?!) Frankenstein, and Jennifer Beals is terribly miscast as his second creation. Rated PG-13 for violence, suggested sex, and nudity. 119m. DIR: Franc Roddam. CAST: Sting, Jennifer Beals, Geraldine Page, Clancy Brown, Anthony Higgins, David Rappaport. 1985

BRIDE AND THE BEAST, THE ♥ Stock jungle footage is used to pad out this tale of the new bride of a big-game hunter who, under hypnosis, discovers that she lived a past life as a gorilla. 78m. DIR: Adrian Weiss. CAST: Charlotte Austin, Lance Fuller, Johnny Roth, Steve Calvert, William Justine. 1958

BRIDE CAME C.O.D., THE ★★★ Bette Davis plays a runaway bride, and James Cagney goes after her on behalf of her rich father. A fun comedy in spite of an overused plot line. B&W; 92m. DIR: William Keighley. CAST: Bette Davis, James Cagney, Jack Carson, Eugene Pallette, George Tobias. 1941

BRIDE OF CHUCKY ★★ Playing Chucky's old flame, Jennifer Tilly uses witchcraft to bring him back to life. Instead, she winds up inside a bride doll. Using teen lovebirds, the odd couple head back to Chucky's grave to make the transformation complete. Excessive gore and senseless violence is sprinkled with moments of comic relief. Facial expressions on both dolls are disturbing and oddly impressive. Brad Dourif voices the devilish Chucky. Rated R for gore, profanity, violence, and sexual situations.

89m. DIR: Ronny Yu. CAST: Jennifer Tilly, Nick Stabile, Katherine Heigl. 1999 DVD

BRIDE OF FRANKENSTEIN ★★★★★ This is a first-rate sequel to *Frankenstein*. This time, Henry Frankenstein (Colin Clive) is coerced by the evil Dr. Praetorius (Ernest Thesiger in a delightfully weird and sinister performance) into creating a mate for the monster. B&W; 75m. DIR: James Whale. CAST: Boris Karloff, Colin Clive, Valerie Hobson, Dwight Frye, Ernest Thesiger, Elsa Lanchester. 1935 DVD

BRIDE OF RE-ANIMATOR ★★★ Not as effective but just as bloodily wacked-out, this sequel brings back most of the cast and crew behind the first film to wreak more havoc at Miskatonic University. Fans of the first *Re-Animator* won't want to miss it. Not rated; contains profanity, nudity, and gore. 99m. DIR: Brian Yuzna. CAST: Bruce Abbott, Jeffrey Combs, David Gale, Claude Earl Jones. 1989 DVD

BRIDE OF THE GORILLA ★★ Love and marriage on a jungle plantation give Raymond Burr more than he bargained for as he falls victim to an evil curse. Intermittently engrossing. B&W; 65m. DIR: Curt Siodmak. CAST: Raymond Burr, Barbara Payton, Lon Chaney Jr., Tom Conway, Paul Cavanagh, Woody Strode. 1951

BRIDE OF THE MONSTER ★★ Another incredibly inept but hilarious film from Ed Wood Jr., this stinker uses most of the mad scientist clichés and uses them poorly as a cadaverous-looking Bela Lugosi tries to do fiendish things to an unconscious (even while alert) Loretta King. This bottom-of-the-barrel independent monstrosity boasts possibly the worst special-effects monster of all time, a rubber octopus that any novelty store would be ashamed to stock. B&W; 69m. DIR: Edward D. Wood Jr. CAST: Bela Lugosi, Tor Johnson, Tony McCoy, Loretta King. 1955 DVD

BRIDE WALKS OUT, THE ★★★ This fast-paced comedy relies more on the dialogue and personalities of the supporting cast than on the stars or the story. Newlyweds Barbara Stanwyck and Gene Raymond can't get along on the amount of money he makes, and her spending estranges them. Lots of fun. B&W; 75m. DIR: Leigh Jason. CAST: Barbara Stanwyck, Gene Raymond, Robert Young, Ned Sparks, Helen Broderick, Billy Gilbert, Ward Bond, Hattie McDaniel. 1936

BRIDE WITH WHITE HAIR, THE ★★★★ A swordsman and a witch join forces during China's Mo Dynasty to battle the evil supernatural powers of a pair of bisexual Siamese twins. Like many of the astonishing fantasy-adventures coming out of Hong Kong, this one can be hard to follow. But when it's this gorgeous, fast, and furious, you don't mind watching it a few times. Not rated; contains violence and sexual situations. In Chinese with English subtitles; dubbed version also available. 92m. DIR: Ronny Yu. CAST: Brigitte Lin, Leslie Cheung, Elaine Lui. 1993 DVD

BRIDE WORE BLACK, THE ★★★★ François Truffaut pays homage to Alfred Hitchcock in this suspenseful drama about a woman who tracks down and kills a group of men who killed her husband on their wedding day. Fine Bernard Herrmann score. 95m. DIR: François Truffaut. CAST: Jeanne Moreau, Claude

Rich, Jean-Claude Brialy, Michel Bouquet, Michel Lonsdale, Charles Denner. **1968**

BRIDE WORE RED, THE ★★ A trampy club singer pretends to be a society debutante, and all the rich guys fall in love with her. Joan Crawford played so many street girls who posed as classy ladies, her movies became a cliché. This is probably the definitive one. B&W; 103m. **DIR:** Dorothy Arzner. **CAST:** Joan Crawford, Franchot Tone, Robert Young, Billie Burke, Reginald Owen, Dickie Moore, George Zucco. **1937**

BRIDES OF CHRIST ★★★★ Set during the 1960s, this Australian miniseries centers on a group of Catholic women—nuns, novices, and schoolgirls—and their life choices. The high quality of this production draws you into their insular world, as well as a time of immense social change. Made for Australian TV. Not rated. Each tape 100m. **DIR:** Ken Cameron. **CAST:** Brenda Fricker, Josephine Byrnes, Sandy Gore, Kym Wilson, Naomi Watts. **1991**

BRIDES OF DRACULA ★★★1/2 The depraved son of a debauched noblewoman is held prisoner by her to spare the countryside his blood lust. When a pretty young teacher sets him free, his mother is the first victim of his reign of terror. David Peel is the blond vampire and Peter Cushing reprises his role as Dr. Van Helsing in this nicely acted Hammer Films horror entry. 85m. **DIR:** Terence Fisher. **CAST:** Peter Cushing, David Peel, Martita Hunt, Yvonne Monlaur, Freda Jackson, Miles Malleson, Mona Washbourne. **1960**

BRIDES OF THE BEAST 🌑 First entry in a dreadful trio of Filipino Blood Island, mad-scientist potboilers. Original title: *Brides of Blood.* 85m. **DIR:** Eddie Romero, Gerardo de Leon. **CAST:** John Ashley, Kent Taylor, Beverly Hills. **1968**

BRIDESHEAD REVISITED ★★★★ Evelyn Waugh's novel of British upper-class decadence gets royal treatment in this adaptation from John Mortimer. Jeremy Irons stars as the impressionable Oxford youth bedazzled by Sebastian Flyte (Anthony Andrews), youngest of the ill-fated Marchmain family. Not rated; includes frank sexual themes and brief nudity. 388m. **DIR:** Charles Sturridge, Michael Lindsay-Hogg. **CAST:** Jeremy Irons, Anthony Andrews, Diana Quick, Laurence Olivier, Claire Bloom, John Gielgud, Stéphane Audran, Mona Washbourne, John Le Mesurier, Simon Jones. **1981**

•**BRIDGE, THE** ★★★1/2 Just before the end of World War II, a small group of schoolboys are drafted by the German army and assigned to defend a worthless bridge against the approaching Americans. Nominated for an Academy Award as Best Foreign Language Film, this is one of the great antiwar movies. B&W; 106m. **DIR:** Bernhard Wicki. **CAST:** Folker Bohnet, Fritz Wepper, Michael Hinz. **1959**

BRIDGE AT REMAGEN, THE ★★★ Solid World War II drama concerns the German attempt to hold or blow up one of the last remaining bridges leading into the fatherland. Well-done action sequences keep things moving along at a good pace. Not a great film, but it should fill the bill for fans of the genre. 115m. **DIR:** John Guillermin. **CAST:** George Segal, Ben Gazzara, Robert Vaughn, E. G. Marshall, Bradford Dillman, Peter Van Eyck. **1969 DVD**

•**BRIDGE OF DRAGONS** ★★★ Dolph Lundgren stars as a warrior who must decide between loyalty to his increasingly evil leader and the life of a young princess who is being forced into becoming the leader's bride. Lundgren fans should eat up the action and ignore the other outright silliness. Rated R for violence. 95m. **DIR:** Isaac Florentine. **CAST:** Dolph Lundgren, Cary-Hiroyuki Tagawa, Rachel Shane. **1999 DVD**

BRIDGE OF SAN LUIS REY, THE ★★1/2 Five people meet death when an old Peruvian rope bridge collapses. This snail's-pace, moody version of Thornton Wilder's fatalistic 1920s novel traces their lives. Not too hot, and neither was the 1929 version. B&W; 85m. **DIR:** Rowland V. Lee. **CAST:** Lynn Bari, Anna Nazimova, Louis Calhern, Akim Tamiroff, Francis Lederer, Blanche Yurka, Donald Woods. **1944 DVD**

BRIDGE ON THE RIVER KWAI, THE ★★★★★ This powerful, dramatic story centers around the construction of a bridge by British and American prisoners of war under the command of Japanese colonel Sessue Hayakawa. Alec Guinness is the stiff-upper-lipped British commander who uses the task as a way of proving British superiority. 161m. **DIR:** David Lean. **CAST:** William Holden, Alec Guinness, Jack Hawkins, Sessue Hayakawa, James Donald. **1957**

BRIDGE TO HELL ★1/2 After a group of World War II POWs escape, a bridge is their last obstacle and they decide to take it out after crossing. (Sound familiar?) Lots of shooting and explosions. Unfortunately not much of a plot. Not rated; contains violence and profanity. 94m. **DIR:** Umberto Lenzi. **CAST:** Andy J. Forest. **1989**

BRIDGE TO NOWHERE ★★1/2 Five streetwise city kids head to the rough-and-rugged country for a fun-filled weekend. Once they trespass on the land of an extremely vicious and violent man (Bruno Lawrence), they are forced to fight for survival. Parental discretion advised. 87m. **DIR:** Ian Mune. **CAST:** Bruno Lawrence, Alison Routledge, Margaret Umbers, Philip Gordon. **1986**

BRIDGE TO SILENCE ★1/2 Sincere performances by a talented cast, including Marlee Matlin in her first speaking role, cannot quite overcome a melodramatic story in which a deaf woman (Matlin) nearly loses custody of her daughter to the mother (Lee Remick) who never understood her. Made for television. 95m. **DIR:** Karen Arthur. **CAST:** Marlee Matlin, Lee Remick, Josef Sommer, Michael O'Keefe. **1989**

BRIDGE TOO FAR, A ★★★1/2 Here's another story of a famous battle with the traditional all-star cast. In this case it's World War II's "Operation Market Garden," a disastrous Allied push to get troops behind German lines and capture an early bridgehead on the Rhine. Rated PG. 175m. **DIR:** Richard Attenborough. **CAST:** Dirk Bogarde, James Caan, Michael Caine, Sean Connery, Laurence Olivier, Robert Redford. **1977 DVD**

BRIDGES AT TOKO-RI, THE ★★★★1/2 With this picture, screenwriter Valentine Davies and director Mark Robson created one of the cinema's most authentic depictions of war. It is certainly the best motion picture about the Korean War. James Michener's novel, as adapted here, centers on a bomber pi

...t and his crew, part of an aircraft-carrier force assigned to destroy vital North Korean bridges. 103m. DIR: Mark Robson. CAST: William Holden, Fredric March, Grace Kelly, Mickey Rooney, Earl Holliman, Charles McGraw, Robert Strauss, Willis Bouchey, Gene Reynolds. 1954

BRIDGES OF MADISON COUNTY, THE ★★★★ Touching story of a brief romantic encounter between a free-spirited photographer for *National Geographic* magazine and an emotionally neglected wife of an Iowa farmer. Clint Eastwood and Meryl Streep are superb as the two kindred spirits who find themselves thrown together for four unforgettable hot summer days in 1965. Rated PG-13 for suggested sex and profanity. 135m. DIR: Clint Eastwood. CAST: Clint Eastwood, Meryl Streep, Annie Corley, Victor Slezak, Jim Haynie. 1995 DVD

BRIEF ENCOUNTER (1945) ★★★★1/2 In this evergreen classic, a chance meeting in a railroad station results in a doomed, poignant love affair between two lonely people married to others. Celia Johnson is the woman, Trevor Howard the man. A compassionate look at the innocence of sudden, unforeseen romance. David Lean's direction results in a moving, memorable film for all time. B&W; 86m. DIR: David Lean. CAST: Celia Johnson, Trevor Howard, Stanley Holloway, Joyce Carey, Cyril Raymond. 1945 DVD

BRIEF ENCOUNTER (1974) ★★1/2 This is a remake of the 1945 classic film that was based on Noel Coward's play *Still Life*. It tells the story of two married strangers who meet in a British train terminal and fall into a short-lived but intense romance. This made-for-television production suffers in comparison. 103m. DIR: Alan Bridges. CAST: Richard Burton, Sophia Loren. 1974

BRIG, THE ★★1/2 One of the more self-conscious efforts of the American New Cinema of the 1960s, adapted from a stage play set in a Marine Corps prison. With almost no dialogue, the film conveys the dehumanizing aspects of life as a prisoner. But even at this abbreviated length (it was originally 120m.), it's hard to watch. B&W; 57m. DIR: Jonas Mekas, Adolfas Mekas. CAST: Warren Finnerty. 1965

BRIGADOON ★★★★ Enchanting musical stars Van Johnson and Gene Kelly as two Americans who discover Brigadoon, a Scottish village with a life span of only one day for every hundred years. In the village, Kelly meets Cyd Charisse, and they naturally dance up a storm. 108m. DIR: Vincente Minnelli. CAST: Gene Kelly, Van Johnson, Cyd Charisse, Elaine Stewart, Barry Jones. 1954 DVD

BRIGHT ANGEL ★★★1/2 Thoroughly engrossing film follows a young woman's attempt to free her brother from jail. A real sleeper that grabs hold and refuses to let go right up to its uncompromising conclusion. Rated R for language, nudity, and violence. 94m. DIR: Michael Fields. CAST: Dermot Mulroney, Lili Taylor, Mary Kay Place, Bill Pullman, Burt Young, Valerie Perrine, Sam Shepard. 1991

BRIGHT EYES ★★★1/2 Delicious melodrama finds Shirley Temple living in a fine mansion as the maid's daughter. After her mom's untimely death, three people vie for her adoption rights. Curly Shirley is irresistible as the ever-cheerful little Bright Eyes. 83m. DIR: David Butler. CAST: Shirley Temple, James Dunn, Jane Withers, Judith Allen. 1934

BRIGHT LIGHTS, BIG CITY ★★ Films grappling with the evils of substance abuse run the risk of glamorizing the subject they intend to criticize, and that is precisely the problem with this adaptation of Jay McInerney's novel (even though he wrote his own screenplay). Rated R for language and graphic drug emphasis. 110m. DIR: James Bridges. CAST: Michael J. Fox, Kiefer Sutherland, Phoebe Cates, Swoosie Kurtz, Frances Sternhagen, John Houseman, Jason Robards Jr., Dianne Wiest, William Hickey. 1988

BRIGHT SHINING LIE, A ★★★1/2 In this controversial exposé of the Vietnam War, Bill Paxton dominates the screen as John Paul Vann, a shrewd strategist and career soldier sent into Vietnam in 1962 as one of the American "advisors." His subsequent candor about the corrupt South Vietnamese torpedoes his military career; he later returns and continues to lock horns with higher-ups over the "right" way to fight the war. Terry George's film paints a grim picture of a war America clearly didn't understand. Rated R for profanity, violence, and nudity. 120m. DIR: Terry George. CAST: Bill Paxton, Amy Madigan, Vivian Wu, Donal Logue, James Rebhorn, Kurtwood Smith, Eric Bogosian. 1998 DVD

BRIGHTON BEACH MEMOIRS ★★★1/2 Neil Simon's reminiscences of his adolescence make for genuinely enjoyable viewing. Refreshingly free of Simon's often too-clever dialogue, it aims for the heart and, more often than not, hits its mark. Rated PG-13 for sexual references. 110m. DIR: Gene Saks. CAST: Jonathan Silverman, Blythe Danner, Bob Dishy, Brian Drillinger, Stacey Glick, Judith Ivey, Lisa Waltz. 1986 DVD

BRIGHTON STRANGLER, THE ★★1/2 John Loder runs amok after a Nazi bomb destroys the London theater where he has been playing a murderer in a drama. Stunned in the explosion, he confuses his true identity with the character he has been playing. A chance remark by a stranger sends him off to the seaside resort of Brighton, where he performs his stage role for real! B&W; 67m. DIR: Max Nosseck. CAST: John Loder, June Duprez, Miles Mander, Rose Hobart, Ian Wolfe. 1945

BRIGHTY OF THE GRAND CANYON ★★ Acceptable little film for the family. Brighty is a desert mule who teams up with Dick Foran, a prospector who has discovered a large vein of gold in the Grand Canyon. The photography is quite good. 89m. DIR: Norman Foster. CAST: Joseph Cotten, Dick Foran, Karl Swenson, Pat Conway. 1967

BRILLIANT DISGUISE, A ★★ Anthony Denison plays sportswriter Andy Manola, who falls for Michelle, a woman with seemingly multiple personalities. According to psychiatrist Corbin Bernsen, she's dangerous and it doesn't surprise him when Manola's friends and colleagues start dropping like flies. Or is someone setting her up? The search for the truth provides plenty of steamy opportunity for Lysette Anthony to take off her clothes. Rated R for nudity, violence, and strong language. 97m. DIR: Nick

Vallelonga. **CAST:** Lysette Anthony, Anthony Denison, Corbin Bernsen, Gregory McKinney. 1993

BRILLIANT LIES ★★1/2 Adapted from a play by David Williamson, this Australian drama starts out as a he-said, she-said tale of sexual harassment in which a secretary suing for wrongful dismissal and her macho ex-boss both appear to be unscrupulous liars. But the script abuses the audience by withholding important story points until the finale, rendering the whole thing dishonest. Not rated; contains strong profanity. 88m. **DIR:** Richard Franklin. **CAST:** Anthony LaPaglia, Gia Carides, Zoe Carides, Ray Barrett. 1996

BRIMSTONE ★★★★ Undercover lawman Rod Cameron breaks up a cattle-rustling family headed by Walter Brennan. Solid performances and direction make this one of Cameron's best Westerns. 90m. **DIR:** Joseph Kane. **CAST:** Rod Cameron, Walter Brennan, Forrest Tucker, Jack Holt, Adrian Booth, Jim Davis. 1949

BRIMSTONE AND TREACLE ★★★ Sting plays an angelic-diabolic young drifter who insinuates himself into the home lives of respectable Denholm Elliott and Joan Plowright in this British-made shocker. Rated R. 85m. **DIR:** Richard Loncraine. **CAST:** Denholm Elliott, Joan Plowright, Suzanna Hamilton, Sting. 1982

BRING ME THE HEAD OF ALFREDO GARCIA ★★1/2 Warren Oates gives an outstanding performance as a piano player in Mexico who becomes mixed-up with vicious bounty hunters. Hard-core Sam Peckinpah fans will appreciate this one more than the casual viewer. Rated R. 112m. **DIR:** Sam Peckinpah. **CAST:** Warren Oates, Isela Vega, Gig Young, Robert Webber, Emilio Fernandez, Kris Kristofferson, Helmut Dantine. 1974

●**BRINGING OUT THE DEAD** ★★1/2 If the point of a story is a character's redemption, but redemption occurs in a doomed environment, then what have we gained? That's the problem facing this dreary, unsettling, and ultimately overwhelming indictment of big-city emergency medicine. Plainly reminiscent of *Taxi Driver*, this reunion by director Martin Scorsese and scripter Paul Schrader (adapting Joe Connelly's novel) starts off in what seems like a realistic universe, but ultimately drifts into the heightened realm of exaggerated, *film noir* farce. Nicolas Cage stars as a battered and burned-out EMS paramedic lately plagued by the ghost of a young woman he failed to save. True, the horror is presented with Scorsese's characteristically energized, often balletic grace, but eventually the trick camerawork and throbbing pop soundtrack become tiresome. Rated R for profanity, violence, medical gore, and drug use. 118m. **DIR:** Martin Scorsese. **CAST:** Nicolas Cage, Patricia Arquette, John Goodman, Ving Rhames, Tom Sizemore. 1999 DVD

BRINGING UP BABY ★★★★★ A classic screwball comedy, this Howard Hawks picture has lost none of its punch even after fifty years. Katharine Hepburn plays a daffy rich girl who gets an absentminded professor (Cary Grant) into all sorts of trouble. *Bringing Up Baby* is guaranteed to have you falling out of your seat with helpless laughter. B&W; 102m. **DIR:**

Howard Hawks. **CAST:** Cary Grant, Katharine Hepburn, Charlie Ruggles, May Robson. 1938

BRINK OF LIFE ★★★ Early Ingmar Bergman film set entirely in a hospital maternity ward, where three women ponder their pregnancies and the relationships that preceded them. Rather bleak and naturalistic, this is an actors' piece, though Bergman still controls the film emotionally in subtle ways. In Swedish with English subtitles. B&W; 82m. **DIR:** Ingmar Bergman. **CAST:** Eva Dahlbeck, Ingrid Thulin, Bibi Andersson, Max von Sydow, Erland Josephson. 1957

BRINKS JOB, THE ★★1/2 Peter Falk stars in this enjoyable release in which a gang of klutzy crooks pulls off "the crime of the century." It's a breezy caper film reminiscent of George Roy Hill's *Butch Cassidy and the Sundance Kid* and *The Sting*. Rated PG. 103m. **DIR:** William Friedkin. **CAST:** Peter Falk, Peter Boyle, Allen Garfield, Warren Oates, Paul Sorvino, Gena Rowlands. 1978

BRITANNIA HOSPITAL ★★★ A wildly inadequate hospital serves as a metaphor for a sick society in this okay black comedy by British director Lindsay Anderson (*If; O Lucky Man*). Rated R. 115m. **DIR:** Lindsay Anderson. **CAST:** Leonard Rossiter, Graham Crowden, Malcolm McDowell, Joan Plowright. 1982

BROADCAST BOMBSHELLS 🎬 Tedious titillation about an envious TV-news producer who tries to undermine a sexy anchorwoman. Rated R for adult situations, nudity, and strong language. 83m. **DIR:** Ernest G. Sauer. **CAST:** Amy Lynn Baxter, Debbie Rochon, John Richardson, Elizabeth Heyman, Joseph Pallister, Scott Baker. 1995

BROADCAST NEWS ★★★★★ Writer-director-producer James L. Brooks tackles the flashy emptiness of contemporary television journalism. William Hurt stars as the coming trend in news anchors—all enthusiasm and no education—who clashes amiably with Albert Brooks as the reporter's reporter, blessed with insight and a clever turn of phrase, but no camera presence. Both are attracted to dedicated superproducer Holly Hunter, an overachiever who schedules brief nervous breakdowns into her work day. Rated R for profanity. 131m. **DIR:** James L. Brooks. **CAST:** William Hurt, Albert Brooks, Holly Hunter, Jack Nicholson, Robert Prosky, Joan Cusack. 1987 DVD

BROADWAY BILL ★★★ One of Frank Capra's favorite films and one of the few he remade in later years. Warner Baxter stars as a horse owner who cares more about animals than his superficial family. He shirks family responsibility and his inheritance to train his favorite horse, Broadway Bill. Capra's remake was called *Riding High* and starred Bing Crosby. B&W; 90m. **DIR:** Frank Capra. **CAST:** Warner Baxter, Myrna Loy, Helen Vinson, Walter Connolly, Frankie Darro, Jason Robards Sr., Lucille Ball, Ward Bond, Dennis O'Keefe, Margaret Hamilton, Alan Hale Sr., Lynne Overman, Douglass Dumbrille. 1934

BROADWAY DANNY ROSE ★★★1/2 The legendary talent agent Broadway Danny Rose (Woody Allen) takes on an alcoholic crooner (Nick Apollo Forte) and carefully nurtures him to the brink of stardom in this hilarious comedy, also written and directed by Allen. Mia Farrow is delightful as a gang-ter's moll who inadvertently gets Rose in big trouble. Rated PG for brief violence. B&W; 86m. DIR: Woody Allen. CAST: Woody Allen, Mia Farrow, Milton Berle, Sandy Baron. 1984

ROADWAY MELODY, THE ★★ Prototype of all the backstage musical romances. Two sisters (Anita Page and Bessie Love) run afoul of big-city corruption when they leave the sticks to pursue their destinies in New York. Stolid acting and awkward sound-recording techniques are mostly unrelieved, although the "Singin' in the Rain" number (the first of many times the song will be heard in MGM musicals) still packs a rough kind of charm. Somehow it won an Oscar as the year's best picture. B&W; 104m. DIR: Harry Beaumont. CAST: Anita Page, Bessie Love, Charles King. 1929

ROADWAY MELODY OF 1936 ★★★ Backstage musical comedy. Obnoxious gossip columnist Jack Benny tries to use dancer Eleanor Powell to harass producer Robert Taylor. Forget the plot and enjoy the singing and dancing—including Taylor's rendition of "I've Got a Feelin' You're Foolin'," the only time he sang on-screen in his own voice. B&W; 110m. DIR: Roy Del Ruth. CAST: Jack Benny, Eleanor Powell, Robert Taylor, Una Merkel, Buddy Ebsen. 1935

ROADWAY MELODY OF 1938 ★★1/2 Fifteen-year-old Judy Garland stops the show in this tuneful musical anthology when she sings the now legendary "Dear Mr. Gable" version of "You Made Me Love You." The finale stretches credibility until it snaps as Eleanor Powell, in top hat and tails, dances with a division of chorus boys before a neon skyline. B&W; 110m. DIR: Roy Del Ruth. CAST: Robert Taylor, Eleanor Powell, George Murphy, Binnie Barnes, Sophie Tucker, Judy Garland, Buddy Ebsen, Willie Howard, Billy Gilbert. 1937

ROADWAY MELODY OF 1940 ★★★ Fine performances redeem this otherwise tired tale of friendship and rivalry between dancing partners. The dancing of course, is flawless; the Cole Porter songs are outstanding. B&W; 102m. DIR: Norman Taurog. CAST: Fred Astaire, Eleanor Powell, George Murphy, Frank Morgan, Ian Hunter. 1940

ROADWAY RHYTHM ★★1/2 A reworking of Jerome Kern's last Broadway musical, Very Warm for May, with one of the finest songs Kern ever wrote, "All the Things You Are." The routine plot pits ex-vaudevillian performers against the new breed of singers. B&W; 114m. DIR: Roy Del Ruth. CAST: George Murphy, Ginny Simms, Gloria De Haven, Lena Horne, Hazel Scott, Tommy Dorsey, Charles Winninger, Ben Blue. 1943

ROADWAY SERENADE ★★★ A musical aimed strictly at Jeanette MacDonald fans. She does all the singing as a woman at odds with her husband and her career. The splashy finale was directed by Busby Berkeley. B&W; 113m. DIR: Robert Z. Leonard. CAST: Jeanette MacDonald, Lew Ayres, Ian Hunter, Frank Morgan, Virginia Grey, Rita Johnson, William Gargan. 1929

ROADWAY TO CHEYENNE ★★1/2 A New York mob moves west to set up a cattlemen's protection association, but a New York cop on vacation breaks up their racket. This was Rex Bell's first Western,

and it set the formula for many of his pictures. B&W; 60m. DIR: Harry Fraser. CAST: Rex Bell, George "Gabby" Hayes, Marceline Day. 1932

•BROKEDOWN PALACE ★★★ Two female mid-western high-school graduates take a trip to Bangkok where they meet a seductive Australian who offers them a free flight to Hong Kong. At the airport, they are arrested for drug trafficking; an expatriate Yankee lawyer and his Thai wife come to their rescue. Similar material has been covered with much more tension, but the acting is excellent and the photography is stunning. Rated PG-13 for language, violence, and drug use. 100m. DIR: Jonathan Kaplan. CAST: Claire Danes, Kate Beckinsale, Bill Pullman, Jacqueline Kim. 1999 DVD

BROKEN ANGEL ★★ Distraught parents find their world turned upside down when their daughter disappears after a gang fight during her senior prom. Made for TV movie that superficially skims the surface of parental trust and love. 94m. DIR: Richard T. Heffron. CAST: William Shatner, Susan Blakely, Roxann Biggs, Brock Peters. 1992

BROKEN ARROW (1950) ★★★ Jeff Chandler is the Apache chief Cochise and James Stewart is a cavalry scout in this sympathetic look at Indians and white settlers struggling to coexist on the Western frontier in the 1870s. The film was the first to treat the Indian with respect and understanding. 93m. DIR: Delmer Daves. CAST: James Stewart, Jeff Chandler, Debra Paget, Will Geer, Arthur Hunnicutt, Basil Ruysdael, Jay Silverheels. 1950

BROKEN ARROW (1996) ★★★★ In this thrill-packed film, Christian Slater, a copilot on top-secret B-3 Stealth bombers, is shocked when his mentor, John Travolta, uses a practice mission as a way to steal nuclear weapons. Angered over being passed up for promotions, Travolta plans to use the threat of widespread destruction to blackmail the U.S. government. Rated R for violence and profanity. 108m. DIR: John Woo. CAST: John Travolta, Christian Slater, Samantha Mathis, Delroy Lindo, Frank Whaley, Bob Gunton, Howie Long, Jack Thompson. 1996 DVD

BROKEN BLOSSOMS ★★★1/2 The tragic story of a young Chinese boy's unselfish love for a cruelly mistreated white girl. Lillian Gish is heart-twisting as the girl; Richard Barthelmess's portrayal of the Chinese boy made him an overnight star. Donald Crisp, later famous in warm and sympathetic roles, is the unfortunate girl's evil tormentor. Silent. B&W; 68m. DIR: D. W. Griffith. CAST: Lillian Gish, Richard Barthelmess, Donald Crisp. 1919 DVD

BROKEN CHAIN, THE ★★★ Solid action film looks at the quandary the Indian Nations faced during the American Revolution. With all sides vying for their help, the Nation is placed in a no-win situation eventually pitting tribe against tribe. Made for TV. 94m. DIR: Lamont Johnson. CAST: Eric Schweig, Wes Studi, Buffy Sainte-Marie, Pierce Brosnan, J. C. White Shirt, Graham Greene. 1993

BROKEN ENGLISH ★★★1/2 The Romeo and Juliet theme is played out amidst racial tension among ethnic groups immigrating to modern New Zealand. Aleksandra Vujcic plays a young Croatian waitress who falls in love with a Maori coworker, in defiance of her volatile, possessive father. Rated NC-17 for profanity, nudity, and graphic simulated sex. 91m. DIR: Gregor Nicholas. CAST: Aleksandra Vujcic, Julian Arahanga, Rade Serbedzija. 1996

BROKEN HARVEST ★★★★ A sad family drama set in 1950s rural Ireland, this is played out against a larger theme of a country and its people in turmoil. Warm family love and simmering rivalries are intensified by parochial values, an oppressive church, and bitterness reaching back to the Irish Civil War. This effective-looking period piece is extremely atmospheric and evocative, but sometimes too slow and overly dramatized. Still, it is the natural follow-up to *Michael Collins*. Not rated; contains violence. 106m. DIR: Maurice O'Callaghan. CAST: Colin Lane, Marian Quinn, Niall O'Brien, Darren McHugh. 1995

BROKEN LANCE ★★★★ Spencer Tracy's superb performance as a cattle baron at odds with his Indian wife and bickering sons is but one of the pleasures in this first-rate adult Western. The screenplay, based on 1949's *House of Strangers*, won an Oscar, and Katy Jurado was nominated for best supporting actress. 97m. DIR: Edward Dmytryk. CAST: Spencer Tracy, Richard Widmark, Jean Peters, Robert Wagner, Katy Jurado, Earl Holliman, Hugh O'Brian. 1954

BROKEN TRUST (1992) 💘 Only fans of daytime television may be able to find something to salvage in this laughable story of a woman terrorized by her sister and business rivals. Rated R for nudity. 84m. DIR: Ralph Portillo. CAST: Kimberly Foster, Kathryn Harris, Nick Cassavetes, Don Swayze, Edward Arnold. 1992

BROKEN TRUST (1995) ★★★ Tom Selleck is a judge dedicated to upholding judicial standards. What weakens the film is the unbelievable plot that has him setting up a corruption sting that lays waste to both family and friends before he questions his strictly right-or-wrong world. Not rated; contains violence. 90m. DIR: Geoffrey Sax. CAST: Tom Selleck, William Atherton, Marsha Mason, Elizabeth McGovern. 1995

•**BROKEN VESSELS** ★★★1/2 Powerful tale of two ambulance drivers who find common ground on the mean streets. Unlike Martin Scorsese's *Bringing Out the Dead*, director Scott Ziehl's film is filled with memorable characters, explosive situations, and a reality that benefits the performers. Jason London and Todd Field are excellent as the new paramedic and the veteran who rely on each other even though the odds are against them. Rated R for adult situations, language, violence, and nudity. 91m. DIR: Scott Ziehl. CAST: Jason London, Todd Field, Roxana Zal, Susan Traylor, James Hong, Patricia Cranshaw. 1998 DVD

BROKEN VOWS ★★★1/2 Effective made-for-television melodrama stars Tommy Lee Jones as a priest caught between his vows and the love of a woman. Delicately handles the moral dilemma of the priest, who must decide to give up a job he does extremely well or give up the woman who brings solace to his life. Not rated. 95m. DIR: Jud Taylor. CAST: Tommy Lee Jones, Annette O'Toole, Milo O'Shea, David Groh, Madeleine Sherwood. 1986

BRONCO (TV SERIES) ★★★1/2 Originally tapped to take over the role of *Cheyenne* when Clint Walker walked out during a salary dispute, Ty Hardin became *Bronco* in a series that drew many of its stories from historic events. In "Shadow of Jesse James," Bronco must arrest the famed outlaw (James Coburn). In "Death of an Outlaw," Bronco Layne finds himself involved in the Lincoln County War alongside Billy the Kid and Pat Garrett. Each 49m. DIR: Leslie Goodwins, Robert L. Strock. CAST: Ty Hardin, James Coburn, Allan "Rocky" Lane, Rhodes Reason. 1958–1962

BRONCO BILLY ★★★ This warmhearted character study centers around Clint Eastwood as Bronco Billy, the owner of a run-down Wild West show. Sondra Locke is deserted on her honeymoon by her husband (Geoffrey Lewis). Desperate, she agrees to join the show as Eastwood's assistant and that's when the lightweight tale takes a romantic turn. Rated PG. 119m. DIR: Clint Eastwood. CAST: Clint Eastwood, Sondra Locke, Geoffrey Lewis, Scatman Crothers, Sam Bottoms, Bill McKinney, Dan Vadis. 1980 DVD

BRONX EXECUTIONER, THE 💘 A group of humans battle for their lives against cyborgs bent on their destruction. Not rated; contains violence. 88m. DIR: Bob Collins. CAST: Margie Newton, Chuck Valent, Woody Strode. 1989

BRONX TALE, A ★★★★ Robert De Niro makes an impressive directorial debut with this atmospheric, exquisitely detailed character study of a youngster torn between his hardworking, bus-driver dad (De Niro) and the flashy mobster (played superbly by screenwriter Chazz Palminteri) who rules their Bronx neighborhood. It's hard-edged at times—disturbingly so in segments on racial hatred—but ultimately rewarding. Rated R for violence and profanity. 122m. DIR: Robert De Niro. CAST: Robert De Niro, Chazz Palminteri, Joe Pesci, Lillo Brancato, Francis Capra, Taral Hicks. 1993 DVD

BRONX WAR, THE ★★★ Two drug-dealing factions—one black, one Hispanic—declare war and nonstop bloodfest ensues. A capable actor (who is credited only as Joseph) leads the Hispanics. Not rated, but equivalent to an R for violence, profanity, and nudity. 91m. DIR: Joseph B. Vasquez. CAST: Fabio Urena, Charmain Cruz, Andre Brown. 1989

BRONZE BUCKAROO ★★1/2 Singing cowboy Bob Blake and his harmonizing henchmen ride to the rescue of a brother and sister victimized by a crooked neighbor. Plenty of music and humor fill out this "all-colored cast" shoot-'em-up. B&W; 58m. DIR: Richard C. Kahn. CAST: Herbert Jeffrey (Herbert Jeffries), Spencer Williams Jr., Clarence Brooks, Lucius Brooks, Artie Young. 1938

BROOD, THE ★★ Fans of director David Cronenberg will no doubt enjoy this offbeat, grisly horror tale about genetic experiments. Others need not apply. Rated R. 90m. DIR: David Cronenberg. CAST: Oliver Reed, Samantha Eggar, Art Hindle. 1979

•**BROOKLYN STATE OF MIND, A** ★★ Paint-by-numbers portrait of an Italian-American neighborhood in New York and the denizens who live there. Director Frank Rainone paints a superficial picture life on the streets, allowing clichés rather than characters to inhabit his frame. There isn't one honest moment in this tale of a young man who falls under the intimidation of the local mob boss. Rated PG-3 for language and violence. 92m. DIR: Frank Raine. CAST: Danny Aiello, Vincent Spano, Rick Aiello, ony Danza, Jennifer Esposito. 1997

ROTHER FROM ANOTHER PLANET, THE ★★★ In this thoughtful comic fantasy, a dark-kinned extraterrestrial (Joe Morton) on the lam rom alien cops crash-lands his spaceship in New ork harbor, staggers ashore on Ellis Island, then nakes his way to Harlem. Not rated, the film has profanity and violence. 110m. DIR: John Sayles. CAST: oe Morton, Darryl Edwards, Steve James. 1984 DVD

ROTHER JOHN ★★ In this not-so-heavenly melorama, Sidney Poitier stars as an angel who returns o his Alabama hometown to see how things are going. He steps into bigotry and labor troubles. Not one f Poitier's best. Rated PG. 94m. DIR: James Goldtone. CAST: Sidney Poitier, Paul Winfield, Will Geer, everly Todd, Bradford Dillman. 1971

ROTHER OF SLEEP ★★ In a remote village in ineteenth-century Austria, a self-taught musical enius is an outcast among his brutish, stupid neighors. Overwrought and Wagnerian, the film is often udicrous and outlandish. As the supposed artistic enius, Andre Eiserman's performance is unconvincing. In German with English subtitles. Rated R for udity. 127m. DIR: Joseph Vilsmaier. CAST: Andre Eisrmann, Dana Vavrova, Ben Becker. 1996

ROTHER ORCHID ★★★ Comedy, action, sentinentality, and social comment are intertwined in his generally enjoyable gangster movie about a good-natured hood (Edward G. Robinson) who goes roke in Europe trying to get a little class. Old-fashioned fun. B&W; 91m. DIR: Lloyd Bacon. CAST: Edward G. Robinson, Humphrey Bogart, Ann Sothern, onald Crisp, Ralph Bellamy, Allen Jenkins, Cecil Kellway, Morgan Conway, Paul Guilfoyle, Tom Tyler. 1940

ROTHER SUN, SISTER MOON ★★★★ Alec uinness stars as the Pope in this movie about religious reformation. The film shows a young Francis of Assisi starting his own church. He confronts the ope and rejects the extravagant and pompous ceremonies of the Catholic Church, preferring simple religious practices. Rated PG. 121m. DIR: Franco Zefirelli. CAST: Graham Faulkner, Judi Bowker, Alec Guinness. 1973

ROTHERHOOD, THE ★★ A *Godfather* predecessor, *The Brotherhood* stars Kirk Douglas and Alex Cord as Italian brothers who inherit their father's criminal empire. Douglas doesn't make a convincing talian, but the story is good and overcomes the poor casting and cinematography. Not rated, contains violence and mild profanity. 96m. DIR: Martin Ritt. CAST: Kirk Douglas, Alex Cord, Irene Papas, Luther Adler, Susan Strasberg, Murray Hamilton. 1968

ROTHERHOOD OF DEATH ♥ Satanic Ku Klux Klansmen battle gun-toting black Vietnam veterans n the pre–civil rights movement South. Rated R for violence and language. 85m. DIR: Bill Berry. CAST: Roy Jefferson, Le Tari, Haskell V. Anderson. 1976

BROTHERHOOD OF JUSTICE ★★ Rich teenagers decide to band together after their high school is vandalized. Yuppie *Death Wish*. Ninety minutes of bad dialogue, but the message is worth something. Rated PG for violence. 97m. DIR: Charles Braverman. CAST: Keanu Reeves, Kiefer Sutherland, Lori Loughlin, Billy Zane. 1986

BROTHERHOOD OF SATAN ♥ Ridiculous thriller about a small town taken over by witches and devil worshipers. Rated PG. 92m. DIR: Bernard McEveety. CAST: Strother Martin, L. Q. Jones, Charles Bateman, Ahna Capri. 1971

BROTHERHOOD OF THE ROSE ★★1/2 Lifelong friends Peter Strauss and David Morse become CIA operatives, with Morse betraying his friend. Originally a made-for-television miniseries, this film works better in its abbreviated version. Rated PG-13. 103m. DIR: Marvin J. Chomsky. CAST: Robert Mitchum, Peter Strauss, Connie Sellecca, David Morse. 1989

BROTHERLY LOVE ★★★1/2 A revenge melodrama. Judd Hirsch plays twin brothers, one a respectable businessman, the other a sociopath. When the latter is released from a mental ward, he vows to ruin his brother. This TV movie is not rated, but contains some violence. 94m. DIR: Jeff Bleckner. CAST: Judd Hirsch, Karen Carlson, George Dzundza, Barry Primus, Lori Lethin, Josef Sommer. 1985

BROTHERS IN ARMS ★★ Adequate slasher features backwoods crazies hunting humans as part of their religious rituals. A terrifying, suspense-filled chase with plenty of bloodshed. Rated R for extreme violence. 95m. DIR: George Jay Bloom III. CAST: Todd Allen, Jack Starrett. 1988

BROTHERS IN LAW ★★★★ Callow young lawyer Ian Carmichael learns how the British courts really work when an elder barrister takes him under his wing. A most enjoyable British satire, with Terry-Thomas particularly funny as a perennial defendant. 94m. DIR: Roy Boulting. CAST: Ian Carmichael, Richard Attenborough, Terry-Thomas, Jill Adams, John Le Mesurier. 1957

BROTHERS IN THE SADDLE ★★★ Steve Brodie is the ne'er-do-well brother of straight shooter Tim Holt in this above-average Western. Uncommonly hard-edged for a series Western of the late 1940s, when interest in the genre was flagging and most cowboy movies were lifeless remakes. B&W; 60m. DIR: Lesley Selander. CAST: Tim Holt, Richard Martin, Steve Brodie. 1949

BROTHERS IN TROUBLE ★★★ The tribulations of a loose family of Pakistani emigrants living in England are explored with honesty in this often compelling drama, produced for the BBC. Not rated; contains nudity, violence, sexual situations, and profanity. 102m. DIR: Udayan Prasad. CAST: Om Puri, Angeline Ball, Pavan Malhotra. 1995

BROTHERS KARAMAZOV, THE ★★★ Director Richard Brooks, who also scripted, and a fine cast work hard to give life to Russian novelist Fyodor Dostoyevski's turgid account of the effect of the death of a domineering father on his disparate sons: a fun-lover, a scholar, a religious zealot, and an epileptic. Studio promotion called it absorbing and exciting. It is, but only in flashes. 146m. DIR: Richard Brooks.

CAST: Yul Brynner, Claire Bloom, Lee J. Cobb, Maria Schell, Richard Basehart, William Shatner, Albert Salmi. 1957

BROTHER'S KEEPER ★★★ The strange case of upstate New York's Ward brothers makes for an intriguing documentary. The four aged brothers lived and worked together on a small dairy farm. When one of the brothers is found dead in bed, and one of the remaining three is charged with murder, their lives change forever. Joe Berlinger and Bruce Sinofsky make their feature-film debut with this impressively detailed examination of the case, and of the brothers' incredible lifestyle. 116m. **DIR:** Joe Berlinger, Bruce Sinofsky. 1992

BROTHERS LIONHEART, THE ★★1/2 This slow-moving children's fantasy filmed in Sweden, Denmark, and Finland features two brothers who are reunited after death in a medieval world where they fight dragons and villains in an attempt to free their war leader, Ulva, who will rid the country of tyrants. If you don't fall asleep within the first forty-five minutes, you will be rewarded with a fine fairy tale. Rated G. 108m. **DIR:** Olle Hellbron. **CAST:** Staffan Gotestam, Lars Soderdahl, Allan Edwall. 1977

BROTHERS MCMULLEN, THE ★★★ Writer-director-star Edward Burns's low-budget comedy about the romantic entanglements of three Irish-American brothers—one happily married, one unhappily engaged, one footloose and commitment shy—was the surprise hit of the 1995 Sundance Film Festival. The film was somewhat overpraised; the female characters are shallow, and the male bonding is a bit hackneyed. Still, it's a promising debut; Burns may yet prove to be a major talent. Rated R for profanity and mature themes. 98m. **DIR:** Edward Burns. **CAST:** Edward Burns, Jack Mulcahy, Mike McGlone, Connie Britton, Maxine Bahns. 1995

BROTHERS OF THE WEST ★★1/2 Standard plot in which the hero (Tom Tyler) must clear his framed brother. B&W; 58m. **DIR:** Sam Katzman. **CAST:** Tom Tyler, Lois Wilde. 1937

•**BROWN'S REQUIEM** ★★★ Hardboiled story about a private investigator, hired by a suspiciously wealthy golf caddie to watch over his younger sister, who uncovers a perverse conspiracy. Adequate telling of the James Ellroy novel. Rated R for profanity, violence, and nudity. 97m. **DIR:** Jason Freeland. **CAST:** Michael Rooker, Kevin Corrigan, Selma Blair, Tobin Bell, Brad Dourif, Jack Conley, Brion James, Valerie Perrine, Harold Gould, Barry Newman. 1998 DVD

BROWNING VERSION, THE (1951) ★★★★ Michael Redgrave, in perhaps his greatest performance, is an aging teacher betrayed by his wife and disliked by his students, forced into early retirement by illness. He feels his whole life has been a failure. Fine adaptation by Terence Rattigan of his play. B&W; 90m. **DIR:** Anthony Asquith. **CAST:** Michael Redgrave, Jean Kent, Nigel Patrick, Wilfrid Hyde-White, Ronald Howard, Bill Travers. 1951

BROWNING VERSION, THE (1994) ★★★ This updated remake of the 1951 Michael Redgrave classic is a nice try, but it loses something by moving the action into the 1990s. Albert Finney is fine as usual, although he's better at portraying the old teacher's gruffness than his sensitivity, and his final I'm-a-failure speech doesn't quite ring true. Good supporting cast. Rated R for profanity. 97m. **DIR:** Mike Figgis. **CAST:** Albert Finney, Greta Scacchi, Matthew Modine, Julian Sands, Michael Gambon, Ben Silverston. 1994

BRUBAKER ★★★ Robert Redford stars as Henry Brubaker, a reform-minded penologist who takes over a decrepit Ohio prison only to discover the state prison system is even more rotten than its facilities. The film begins dramatically enough, with Redford masquerading as one of the convicts. After that, its dramatic impact lessens. Rated R. 132m. **DIR:** Stuart Rosenberg. **CAST:** Robert Redford, Yaphet Kotto, Jane Alexander, Murray Hamilton. 1980

BRUCE LEE: CURSE OF THE DRAGON ★★★ Rare footage and a slick style will appeal to Lee fans. The focus is on his work and his athletic prowess, although his childhood and untimely death are probed. Addendum about Lee's deceased son, Brandon, seems slightly tacky. Narrated by George Takei. Not rated. 90m. **DIR:** Fred Weintraub, Tom Khun. **CAST:** Bruce Lee, James Coburn, Linda Emery Lee, Brandon Lee, Chuck Norris. 1993

•**BRUTAL TRUTH, THE** ★★★ Friends who haven't seen each other in a long time gather at a secluded mountain cabin to celebrate their ten year high school reunion. Everything seems to be just dandy until one of them turns up dead, and everyone else must figure out if the death was the result of a suicide or a homicide. Dark secrets that had been suppressed for a decade come to light, and the finger of guilt revolves to point at each person in turn. Basically, this movie is *The Big Chill* for a twenty-something crowd. The acting is decent, but the story tends to drag at times. Rated R for violence, language, and sexual situations. 89m. **DIR:** Cameron Thor. **CAST:** Christina Applegate, Molly Ringwald, Johnathon Schaech, Justin Lazard, Moon Zappa, Paul Gleason. 1999 DVD

BRUTE FORCE ★★★ Hardened convict and sadistic correctional officer bring down a prison when they collide. An insider's look at the lives of cellmates via dialogue and flashbacks humanizes them but they all take part in an almost cartoonishly gruesome murder. Not rated, but suggested for mature audiences. B&W; 98m. **DIR:** Jules Dassin. **CAST:** Burt Lancaster, Hume Cronyn, Charles Bickford, Howard Duff, Whit Bissell, Sam Levene, John Hoyt. 1947 DVD

BRUTE MAN, THE ★★ A homicidal maniac escapes from an asylum. Unmemorable, standard B-movie stuff, notable mainly as a showcase for actor Rondo Hatton. This was Hatton's last film. He died in the year of its release, at the age of 42. B&W; 60m. **DIR:** Jean Yarbrough. **CAST:** Tom Neal, Rondo Hatton, Jane Adams. 1946 DVD

BRYLCREEM BOYS, THE ★★★1/2 Handsome love story set in Ireland during World War II. Bill Campbell plays a downed Canadian pilot who finds himself interned in a POW camp with German pilot Angus MacFayden. When the men are allowed to go to the local town, they both fall in love with the same woman. Gorgeous scenery and an interesting take on the war. Rated PG-13 for language and violence.

06m. DIR: Terence Ryan. CAST: Bill Campbell, William McNamara, Angus MacFadyen, Jean Butler. **1996 DVD**

BUBBLEGUM CRASH, VOLS. 1–3 ★★★ Japanese animation. The Knight Sabers, unofficial superhero protectors of Mega Tokyo, are back in continuing new adventures based on the popular *Bubblegum Crisis* series. Though they have gotten on with their lives, the resourceful women reunite to meet the evil Voice and his nefarious minions. In Japanese with English subtitles. Not rated; contains violence and nudity. 45m. each. DIR: Noda Yasuyuki, Kiyotsumu Toshifumi, Fukushima Hiroyuki, Ishiodori Hiroshi. **1991**

BUBBLEGUM CRISIS, VOLS. 1–8 ★★★ Eight-part Japanese animated epic. Compelling stories with some visually stunning (albeit graphically violent) sequences involving the Knight Sabers and archenemies, the Boomers, genetically altered, Terminator-like mutants. This stylish series owes more than a passing nod to Ridley Scott's *Blade Runner*. In Japanese with English subtitles. Not rated with profanity and violence. 30–53m. each DIR: Akiyama Katsuhito, Hayashi Hiroki, Oobari Masami, Takayama Fumihiko, Gooda Hiroaki. **1987–90**

BUCCANEER, THE ★★ Studio-bound remake of C. B. De Mille's 1938 romance of pirate Jean Lafitte. A cast capable of hamming *and* acting, but that's not enough to make this stiff color creaker come alive. 121m. DIR: Anthony Quinn. CAST: Yul Brynner, Charlton Heston, Claire Bloom, Charles Boyer, Douglass Dumbrille, Lorne Greene, Ted de Corsia. **1958**

BUCCANEERS, THE ★★★★ An exquisite adaptation of Edith Wharton's final novel, this atmospheric drama conveys the high fashion and simmering emotions of the nineteenth-century aristocracy. Best of all, it costars Mira Sorvino as one of four New World teenagers who conquer Old World London with their high spirits. Packaged with *A Lady Does Not Write*, an uninspired but informative sixty-minute documentary about Wharton. Not rated; contains sexual situations. 288m. DIR: Philip Saville. CAST: Carla Gugino, Mira Sorvino, Alison Elliott, Rya Kihlstedt, Cherie Lunghi. **1995**

BUCK AND THE PREACHER ★★1/2 Harry Belafonte and director Sidney Poitier play two escaped slaves heading west. On the way, they meet up with "bad guy" Cameron Mitchell and lovely Ruby Dee. So-so Western. Rated PG. 102m. DIR: Sidney Poitier. CAST: Sidney Poitier, Harry Belafonte, Ruby Dee, Cameron Mitchell. **1972 DVD**

BUCK BENNY RIDES AGAIN ★★★ A Western spoof made to capitalize on Jack Benny's popular radio program. Most of his radio colleagues join him as he tries to impersonate a wild and woolly cowboy. Benny's humor hasn't dated nearly as much as some of his contemporaries. B&W; 82m. DIR: Mark Sandrich. CAST: Jack Benny, Eddie "Rochester" Anderson, Ellen Drew, Phil Harris, Dennis Day, Andy Devine, Virginia Dale. **1940**

BUCK PRIVATES ★★★ Abbott and Costello are at their best in their first starring film, but it's still no classic. On the lam, the two are forced to enlist during World War II. B&W; 82m. DIR: Arthur Lubin. CAST: Bud Abbott, Lou Costello, Lee Bowman, Alan Curtis, Jane Frazee. **1941 DVD**

BUCK PRIVATES COME HOME ★★ Bud Abbott and Lou Costello reprise their roles from their first big hit, this time mustering out of the service and bringing an orphan with them. B&W; 77m. DIR: Charles Barton. CAST: Bud Abbott, Lou Costello, Beverly Simmons, Nat Pendleton, Tom Brown, Don Beddoe, Donald MacBride. **1947 DVD**

BUCK ROGERS: DESTINATION SATURN (PLANET OUTLAWS) ★★1/2 Edited-down version of the popular serial loses much of the continuity of the twelve-episode chapterplay, but still proves to be great fun as ideal hero Buster Crabbe enthusiastically goes after the vile Killer Kan. B&W; 91m. DIR: Ford Beebe, Saul Goodkind. CAST: Buster Crabbe, Constance Moore, Jackie Moran, Jack Mulhall, Anthony Warde, C. Montague Shaw, Philip Ahn. **1939**

BUCK ROGERS IN THE 25TH CENTURY ★★ Updating of the Buck Rogers legend finds Buck (Gil Gerard), after years of suspended animation, awakened in a future society under attack by the power-mad Princess Ardala (Pamela Hensley). Substandard space fare was originally made as a TV pilot. Rated PG. 89m. DIR: Daniel Haller. CAST: Gil Gerard, Erin Gray, Pamela Hensley, Tim O'Connor, Henry Silva. **1979**

BUCKET OF BLOOD, A ★★★ A funny beatnik spoof—and horror-movie lampoon—in the style of the original *Little Shop of Horrors*, put together by the same creative team. Dick Miller is a nerdy sculptor whose secret is pouring wet clay over the bodies of murder victims; the resulting, contorted sculptures make him a superstar among the cognoscenti. B&W; 66m. DIR: Roger Corman. CAST: Dick Miller, Barboura Morris, Ed Nelson, Anthony Carbone. **1959**

BUCKEYE AND BLUE ★★ Disappointing *Bonnie and Clyde*–style Western featuring Robin Lively and Jeff Osterhage as a couple of desperadoes who engage in a crime spree after the Civil War. No new twists on this tired theme. Rated PG. 94m. DIR: J. C. Compton. CAST: Robyn Lively, Jeff Osterhage, Rick Gibbs, Will Hannah. **1988**

BUCKSKIN ★★1/2 Trite, overwritten, A. C. Lyles-produced Western featuring a score of familiar-face, long-in-the-tooth actors—which is the best feature of this film about a heroic marshal battling a domineering cattle baron. 97m. DIR: Michael Moore. CAST: Barry Sullivan, Wendell Corey, Joan Caulfield, Bill Williams, John Russell, Barbara Hale, Lon Chaney Jr., Barton MacLane. **1968**

BUCKSKIN FRONTIER ★★★ Railroad representative Richard Dix and freight-line owner Lee J. Cobb fight over business and a crucial mountain pass in this big-budget, fast-action Western. B&W; 82m. DIR: Lesley Selander. CAST: Richard Dix, Jane Wyatt, Lee J. Cobb, Albert Dekker, Joe Sawyer, Victor Jory, Lola Lane. **1943**

BUCKTOWN 🐢 This mindless blaxploitation flick finds Fred Williamson journeying to a southern town to bury his brother, who has been killed by corrupt cops. Rated R. 95m. DIR: Arthur Marks. CAST: Fred Williamson, Pam Grier, Thalmus Rasulala, Tony King, Bernie Hamilton, Art Lund. **1975**

BUD AND LOU ★★★ Made-for-TV movie explores the tensions between comedians Bud Abbott (Harvey Korman) and Lou Costello (Buddy Hackett). Based, we assume, on the excellent book of the same name by Bob Thomas, this film is at its best when examining the poignant offscreen relationship between the two funnymen. Its greatest flaw is that the stars are unable to make the duo's most celebrated routines even amusing. 99m. **DIR:** Robert C. Thompson. **CAST:** Harvey Korman, Buddy Hackett, Michele Lee, Arte Johnson, Robert Reed. 1978

BUDDY ★★1/2 Based on the true story of an animal-loving 1920s socialite who tried to raise a baby gorilla as if he were her own, this film is an awkward mix of cute and creepy. Youngsters will be enthralled by the first section, featuring dozens of cuddly animals, but they may be shocked when Buddy rebels against his forced humanization. Adults may admire the sociological quandaries of the climax, yet find the setup much too cloying. Rated PG for gorilla-related fits. 84m. **DIR:** Caroline Thompson. **CAST:** René Russo, Robbie Coltrane, Alan Cumming, Irma P. Hall, Paul Reubens. 1997

BUDDY, BUDDY ★★ Jack Lemmon is a clumsy would-be suicide who decides to end it all in a hotel. Walter Matthau is a hit man who rents the room next door and finds the filling of his contract difficult. The results are less than hilarious but do provoke a few smiles. Rated R because of profanity and brief nudity. 96m. **DIR:** Billy Wilder. **CAST:** Jack Lemmon, Walter Matthau, Paula Prentiss, Klaus Kinski. 1981

BUDDY HOLLY STORY, THE ★★★★1/2 Gary Busey's outstanding performance as Buddy Holly makes this one of the few great rock 'n' roll movies. Not only does he convincingly embody the legend from Lubbock, Texas, he also sings Holly's songs—including "That'll Be the Day," "Not Fade Away," and "It's So Easy"—with style and conviction. Backed by Don Stroud and Charles Martin Smith, who also play and sing impressively. Rated PG. 114m. **DIR:** Steve Rash. **CAST:** Gary Busey, Don Stroud, Charles Martin Smith, Dick O'Neill. 1978 DVD

BUDDY SYSTEM, THE ★★ In the middle of this movie, the would-be novelist (Richard Dreyfuss) takes his unbound manuscripts to the edge of the sea and lets the wind blow the pages away. He should have done the same thing with the screenplay for this mediocre romantic comedy. The plot is that old chestnut about a fatherless little kid (Wil Wheaton) who helps his mom (Susan Sarandon) and an eligible man (Dreyfuss) get together. Rated PG for profanity. 110m. **DIR:** Glenn Jordan. **CAST:** Richard Dreyfuss, Susan Sarandon, Nancy Allen, Wil Wheaton. 1984

BUDDY'S SONG ★★★1/2 Roger Daltrey delivers a surprisingly strong performance as a loser who takes hope in his son's singing career. Very watchable albeit painfully so at times. Rated R for nudity, profanity, and violence. 107m. **DIR:** Claude Whatham. **CAST:** Roger Daltrey, Chesney Hawkes, Sharon Duce, Michael Elphick. 1991

•**BUENA VISTA SOCIAL CLUB, THE** ★★★★1/2 German director Wim Wenders films the efforts of American guitarist Ry Cooder to reunite a group of long-forgotten Cuban musicians who flourished during Havana's tourist heyday in the 1940s and 1950s. Though their ages range from sixty-five to over ninety, they've lost little of their talent for music and none of their joy in making it, and the film is a wonderful record of both. In Spanish with English subtitles. Rated G. 102m. **DIR:** Wim Wenders. **CAST:** Ry Cooder, Joachim Cooder, Rubén González, Ibrahim Ferrer, Compay Segundo, Omara Portuondo, Eliades Ochoa. 1999 DVD

BUFFALO '66 ★★★★ Teen tap dancer Layla is kidnapped by freshly paroled Billy in this gritty, moody drama. The greasy sociopath vaguely apologizes to his victim, then bullies her into posing as his wife during a visit to the home of his creepy parents in Buffalo. When the charade ends, Billy plans to kill a former Bills place-kicker, but finds Layla harder to shake than the emotional demons from his past. Rated R for profanity, nudity, sexual situations, and violence. 110m. **DIR:** Vincent Gallo. **CAST:** Vincent Gallo, Christina Ricci, Anjelica Huston, Ben Gazzara. 1998 DVD

BUFFALO BILL ★★★1/2 The famed frontiersman William Cody gets the Hollywood biography treatment in this slick, but sometimes bland motion picture. Joel McCrea brings his usual dignity to the role. 90m. **DIR:** William Wellman. **CAST:** Joel McCrea, Maureen O'Hara, Linda Darnell, Thomas Mitchell, Anthony Quinn, Edgar Buchanan. 1944

BUFFALO BILL AND THE INDIANS ★★1/2 In this offbeat Western, Paul Newman, Burt Lancaster, Harvey Keitel, Geraldine Chaplin, Joel Grey, Kevin McCarthy, and Will Sampson are fun to watch as they interact like jazz musicians jamming on the theme of distorted history and the delusion of celebrity. Rated PG. 120m. **DIR:** Robert Altman. **CAST:** Paul Newman, Joel Grey, Kevin McCarthy, Burt Lancaster, Harvey Keitel, Geraldine Chaplin, Will Sampson. 1976

BUFFALO GIRLS ★★★1/2 As the hard-fightin', hard-drinkin', and hard-lovin' Calamity Jane, Anjelica Huston rides herd over a sprawling, enjoyable tale of the last days of the West. Obviously a labor of love by all concerned. Made for TV; contains profanity and violence. 192m. **DIR:** Rod Hardy. **CAST:** Anjelica Huston, Melanie Griffith, Sam Elliott, Gabriel Byrne, Peter Coyote, Jack Palance, Reba McEntire, Tracey Walter, Floyd Red Crow Esterman, Charlayne Woodard, John Diehl, Andrew Bicknell, Paul Lazar, Russell Means. 1995

BUFFALO JUMP ★★★1/2 Enjoyable, family-oriented Canadian drama stars Wendy Crewson as a young woman who inherits a ranch in the middle of nowhere. She rises to the challenge and learns some very valuable lessons about growing up. Pleasant affair. Not rated. 97m. **DIR:** Eric Till. **CAST:** Wendy Crewson, Paul Gross. 1989

BUFFALO SOLDIERS ★★★ Danny Glover rides tall in the saddle in this semifactual tale of the legendary African American Calvary Corp. and their mission to track down Apache warrior Victorio. Even though the script plays loose with the facts, a decent cast and strong direction helps this action-adventure achieve full gallop. Not rated; contains violence. 94m. **DIR:** Charles Haid. **CAST:** Danny Glover, Bob Gun-

...on, Carl Lumbly, Glynn Turman, Mykelti Williamson. 1997

BUFFALO STAMPEDE ★★★ Zane Grey story has buffalo hunter Randolph Scott in love with the daughter of an outlaw stirring up Indian trouble. B&W; 59m. **CAST:** Randolph Scott, Harry Carey, Buster Crabbe, Noah Beery Sr. 1933

BUFFET FROID (COLD CUTS) ★★★★ Outrageously funny surreal black comedy about three hapless murderers. This whimsical study in madness is laced with brilliant performances and great direction by Bertrand Blier. Highly engaging. In French with English subtitles. Not rated; contains nudity, profanity, and violence. 95m. **DIR:** Bertrand Blier. **CAST:** Gérard Depardieu, Bernard Blier, Jean Carmet. 1979 DVD

BUFFY, THE VAMPIRE SLAYER ★★★1/2 A high school cheerleader has to put down her pom-poms and forgo hanging out at the mall when she discovers that she's the latest in a long line of women whose job it is to kill vampires. It's better than it sounds. Rated PG-13 for violence and profanity. 100m. **DIR:** Fran Rubel Kuzui. **CAST:** Kristy Swanson, Donald Sutherland, Rutger Hauer, Luke Perry. 1992

BUFORD'S BEACH BUNNIES ★★ Harry Buford, owner of the Bunny Hole, offers a large reward to whichever Bunny employee can make his son Cheeter lose his virginity. Extremely bad acting and dialogue. The background action is funnier than the plot. Rated R for nudity, profanity, and graphic sex. 94m. **DIR:** Mark Pirro. **CAST:** Jim Hanks, Rikki Brando, Monique Parent, Amy Page, Barrett Cooper, Ina Rogers, Charley Rossman, David Robinson. 1992

BUG ★★1/2 Weird horror film with the world, led by Bradford Dillman, staving off masses of giant mutant beetles with the ability to commit arson, setting fire to every living thing they can find. Rated PG for violence. 100m. **DIR:** Jeannot Szwarc. **CAST:** Bradford Dillman, Joanna Miles, Richard Gilliland. 1975

▶**BUG BUSTER** ★★ Time how long it takes you to be reminded of *Arachnophobia*. This time instead of spiders it's cockroaches terrorizing people, but nothing else has changed plot-wise. A nasty-spirited film that lacks any likable characters. Rated R for violence, gore, and simulated sex. 93m. **DIR:** Lorenzo Doumani. **CAST:** Randy Quaid, Katherine Heigl, Meredith Salenger, James Doohan, George Takei. 1998

BUGGED! ★★★ Delightfully refreshing and goofy, this big bug flick is probably the best film to ever come out of Troma. Director Ronald K. Armstrong plays a clueless exterminator out to save the world from an invasion of—wait for it—giant grasshoppers. So sit back and enjoy this quirky spoof. Rated PG-13 for gore, violence, and profanity. 90m. **DIR:** Ronald K. Armstrong. **CAST:** Priscilla K. Basque, Ronald K. Armstrong. 1996

BUGLES IN THE AFTERNOON ★★1/2 In this modest Western a young army officer is made a victim by a jealous rival. Set in the time of Custer's last stand, it has fairly good scenery and cinematography. 85m. **DIR:** Roy Rowland. **CAST:** Ray Milland, Hugh Marlowe, Helena Carter, Forrest Tucker, Barton MacLane, George Reeves. 1952

BUGS BUNNY/ROAD RUNNER MOVIE, THE ★★★★ Classic cartoons made by Chuck Jones for Warner Bros. are interwoven into this laughfest; the first and best of the 1970s and '80s feature-length compilations. Includes such winners as "Duck Amuck" and "What's Opera, Doc?" Rated G. 92m. **DIR:** Chuck Jones, Phil Monroe. 1979

BUGS BUNNY, SUPERSTAR ★★★★ A delightful collection of nine classic Warner Bros. cartoons from the Thirties and Forties. Produced mainly as a tribute to director Bob Clampett, this tape is a must-see if only for the hilarious *Fantasia* parody "Corny Concerto." Rated G. 90m. **DIR:** Larry Jackson. 1975

BUG'S LIFE, A ★★★★★ The story features an industrious worker ant whose inventive talents place his colony in peril from a band of marauding grasshoppers. Determined to compensate for the trouble he has caused, the little fellow undertakes a dangerous journey to "the city," where he hopes to find some resourceful "warrior bugs" for a final reckoning with the grasshoppers. This film is witty, luxuriously animated, and lots of fun. Rated G; suitable for all ages. 94m. **DIR:** John Lasseter. 1998 DVD

BUGSY ★★★1/2 Charming, shrewd, and given to fits of uncontrollable temper and violence, gangster Benjamin-"Bugsy" Siegel becomes obsessed with the creation of Las Vegas, an expensive project that puts him dangerously at odds with his partners. Rated R for violence, brief profanity, and nudity. 135m. **DIR:** Barry Levinson. **CAST:** Warren Beatty, Annette Bening, Harvey Keitel, Ben Kingsley, Elliott Gould, Joe Mantegna, Bebe Neuwirth, Wendy Phillips, Richard Sarafian, Bill Graham. 1991 DVD

BUGSY MALONE ★★★1/2 The 1920s gangsters weren't really as cute as these children, who run around shooting whipping cream out of their pistols. But if you can forget that, this British musical provides light diversion. Rated G. 93m. **DIR:** Alan Parker. **CAST:** Scott Baio, Florrie Augger, Jodie Foster, John Cassisi, Martin Lev. 1976

BULL DURHAM ★★★★ Tim Robbins plays a rookie pitcher for a minor league baseball team. He has a lightning-fast throw, but he's apt to hit the team mascot as often as the strike zone. Kevin Costner is a dispirited catcher brought in to "mature" Robbins. A quirky, intelligent comedy with plenty of surprises, the film contains some of the sharpest jabs at sports since *Slap Shot*. Rated R for profanity and sexual content. 104m. **DIR:** Ron Shelton. **CAST:** Kevin Costner, Susan Sarandon, Tim Robbins, Trey Wilson, Robert Wuhl. 1988 DVD

BULLDOG COURAGE ★★1/2 Tim McCoy is excellent in the dual role of father and son in this slow-paced series Western. When Slim Braddock is killed, it's up to his son, Tim, to avenge his death after a period of several years. This was one of McCoy's last starring films. B&W; 66m. **DIR:** Sam Newfield. **CAST:** Tim McCoy, Joan Woodbury, Paul Fix, Eddie Buzzard. 1935

BULLDOG DRUMMOND ★★★ Ronald Colman smoothly segued from silent to sound films playing the title's ex–British army officer adventurer in this exciting, witty, definitive first stanza of what became a popular series. B&W; 89m. **DIR:** F. Richard Jones.

CAST: Ronald Colman, Joan Bennett, Lilyan Tashman. 1929

BULLDOG DRUMMOND COMES BACK ★★★ The first of seven films starring John Howard as the adventurer-sleuth is an atmospheric tale of revenge. The crazed widow of one of Bulldog Drummond's former enemies makes off with our hero's girl, Phyllis. A gem available on tape with *Bulldog Drummond Escapes*. B&W; 59m. **DIR:** Louis King. **CAST:** John Howard, John Barrymore, Louise Campbell, E. E. Clive, Reginald Denny, J. Carrol Naish. 1937

BULLDOG DRUMMOND ESCAPES ★★ Famed ex–British army officer Bulldog Drummond comes to the aid of his ladylove when she becomes embroiled in an international espionage ring. Young Ray Milland stars in his only outing as the World War I hero in this okay series entry. Paired on tape with *Bulldog Drummond Comes Back*. B&W; 65m. **DIR:** James Hogan. **CAST:** Ray Milland, Guy Standing, Heather Angel, Porter Hall, Reginald Denny, E. E. Clive, Fay Holden. 1937

BULLDOG DRUMMOND IN AFRICA ★★1/2 An international spy ring has struck again. This time they've kidnapped Colonel Neilson and hidden him somewhere in North Africa, and Hugh "Bulldog" Drummond isn't going to stand for it. Good fun. Double-billed with *Arrest Bulldog Drummond* on tape. B&W; 58m. **DIR:** Louis King. **CAST:** John Howard, Heather Angel, J. Carrol Naish, H. B. Warner, Anthony Quinn. 1938

BULLDOG DRUMMOND'S BRIDE ★★1/2 The last of Paramount's Bulldog Drummond series. A crack bank robber uses Drummond's honeymoon flat as a hideout for himself and his explosives. Not the best of the series, but it's still a rousing adventure. On tape with *Bulldog Drummond's Secret Police*. B&W; 56m. **DIR:** James Hogan. **CAST:** John Howard, Heather Angel, Reginald Denny, H. B. Warner, Eduardo Ciannelli. 1939

BULLDOG DRUMMOND'S PERIL ★★★ Bulldog Drummond has a personal stake in a chase that takes him from London to Switzerland—the synthetic diamond that was stolen is a wedding gift intended for our hero and his patient fiancée, Phyllis. Full of close calls, witty dialogue, and an injection of controlled lunacy by the great John Barrymore. On tape with *Bulldog Drummond's Revenge*. B&W; 66m. **DIR:** James Hogan. **CAST:** John Howard, John Barrymore, Louise Campbell, H. B. Warner, Reginald Denny. 1938

BULLDOG DRUMMOND'S REVENGE ★★★ The second film in Paramount's Drummond series featuring John Howard, this entry focuses on the hero's attempts to recover a powerful explosive. Aided by the colorful Colonel Neilson (John Barrymore at his most enjoyable), Drummond fights evildoers at every turn. Released on a double bill with *Bulldog Drummond's Peril*. B&W; 55m. **DIR:** Louis King. **CAST:** John Howard, John Barrymore, Louise Campbell, Reginald Denny, E. E. Clive. 1937

BULLDOG DRUMMOND'S SECRET POLICE ★★1/2 Stylish entry in the long-running series finds gentleman adventurer Bulldog Drummond searching a forbidding castle for hidden treasure while matching wits with a crazed murderer. Double billed with *Bulldog Drummond's Bride* on videotape. B&W; 54m. **DIR:** James Hogan. **CAST:** John Howard, Heather Angel, Reginald Denny, Leo G. Carroll, H. B. Warner. 1939

BULLET ★★1/2 Flashy but empty crime-drama pits an ex-con (Mickey Rourke) against the drug lord (Tupac Shakur) who framed him. Ted Levine steals the show as Rourke's uncontrollable brother. Quite a step down for the director, former music-video whiz Julien Temple. Rated R for violence and profanity. 96m. **DIR:** Julien Temple. **CAST:** Mickey Rourke, Tupac Shakur, Ted Levine. 1996

BULLET FOR SANDOVAL, A ★★1/2 A gritty story of Warner, a rebel soldier who deserts to be with his fiancée at childbirth. When he arrives at the Sandoval hacienda he finds her dead and her father blames him for his daughter's death. Warner is given his baby son and thrown out. He assembles a band of renegades to seek vengeance on Sandoval. Good acting from Ernest Borgnine and George Hilton. Rated PG. 96m. **DIR:** Julio Buchs. **CAST:** Ernest Borgnine, George Hilton, Annabella Incontrera, Alberto De Mendoza, Leo Anchoriz. 1969

BULLET FOR THE GENERAL, A ★★★ A spaghetti Western with a social conscience. Gian Maria Volonté hams it up as a Mexican revolutionary explaining his cause to Lou Castel, who unbeknownst to him is really an American mercenary hired to assassinate him. Dubbed in English. 95m. **DIR:** Damiano Damiani. **CAST:** Gian Maria Volonté, Lou Castel, Martine Beswick, Klaus Kinski. 1967

BULLET IN THE HEAD ★★★★ In 1967, three childhood friends are forced to leave Hong Kong and head for Vietnam, where they believe they can make enough money to buy their way out of their troubles. Instead, they find a land operating under the rules of insanity. John Woo considers this to be his best film, a sprawling epic of loyalty and betrayal in wartime, even though it is not a conventional war film (i.e., none of the characters are soldiers). Not rated; contains strong violence. 136m. **DIR:** John Woo. **CAST:** Tony Leung Chiu-Wai, Jacky Cheung, Waise Lee, Simon Yam. 1990 DVD

BULLET TO BEIJING ★★★ Michael Caine revives British agent Harry Palmer in this involving made-for-cable espionage thriller. A victim of government downsizing, Palmer ends up helping a Russian tycoon and his assistant keep a dangerous weapon from falling into the hands of the North Koreans. Rated R for language, nudity, and violence. 105m. **DIR:** George Mihalka. **CAST:** Michael Caine, Jason Connery, Mia Sara, Michael Gambon, Michael Sarrazin. 1995

BULLETPROOF (1988) ★★1/2 Gary Busey plays a one-man army named Frank "Bulletproof" McBain, an ex-CIA agent who single-handedly takes on a band of multinational terrorists. It's silly, but fun—thanks to Busey and a strong cast of character actors. Rated R for profanity, nudity, and violence. 95m. **DIR:** Steve Carver. **CAST:** Gary Busey, Darlanne Fluegel, Henry Silva, Thalmus Rasulala, L. Q. Jones, Rene Enriquez, R. G. Armstrong, Luke Askew. 1988

BULLETPROOF (1996) ★★ This action-comedy buddy picture is a less-than-satisfying mix of raunchy humor and pedestrian shoot-outs. A small-time crook is hired to finalize a big drug deal, but his best friend and partner in crime turns out to be a cop. The two squabble and survive with only a few bright comic moments in this generally mean-spirited mess. Rated R for violence, nudity, and language. 84m. **DIR:** Ernest R. Dickerson. **CAST:** Damon Wayans, Adam Sandler, James Caan, Kristen Wilson, James Farentino. **1996 DVD**

BULLETPROOF HEART ★★★ A hardened, emotionless hit man is contracted to kill a female socialite and takes along a buddy. The men find themselves transformed by an eerie brush with the doomed woman who is expecting them. This provocative *film noir* leer into the face of impending death is given a compelling edge by its excellent cast. Rated R for language, sex, and violence. 98m. **DIR:** Mark Malone. **CAST:** Anthony LaPaglia, Mimi Rogers, Peter Boyle, Matt Craven. **1995**

BULLETS OR BALLOTS ★★★1/2 A hard-nosed cop (Edward G. Robinson), after being unceremoniously fired from the police force, joins up with the big-time crime boss (Barton MacLane) who has long been his friendly enemy. William Keighley's high-spirited direction helps put over this action-packed but melodramatic gangster movie. B&W; 81m. **DIR:** William Keighley. **CAST:** Edward G. Robinson, Joan Blondell, Barton MacLane, Humphrey Bogart, Frank McHugh. **1936**

BULLETS OVER BROADWAY ★★★★ During the Roaring Twenties, a playwright-turned-director finds his artistic vision compromised when much-needed backing for his latest production is secured from a big-time gangster, who insists that his no-talent mistress be featured in an important role. Rated PG. 99m. **DIR:** Woody Allen. **CAST:** John Cusack, Chazz Palminteri, Dianne Wiest, Mary-Louise Parker, Jennifer Tilly, Jim Broadbent, Tracey Ullman, Jack Warden, Joe Viterelli, Harvey Fierstein, Rob Reiner. **1994 DVD**

BULLFIGHTER AND THE LADY, THE ★★★★ Many of the themes explored in the superb series of low-budget Westerns director Budd Boetticher later made with Randolph Scott (*Decision at Sundown; The Tall T*) are evident in this first-rate drama. A skeet-shooting champ (Robert Stack) decides to become a bullfighter. B&W; 123m. **DIR:** Budd Boetticher. **CAST:** Robert Stack, Joy Page, Gilbert Roland, Katy Jurado. **1951**

BULLFIGHTERS, THE ★★★ While not a classic, this latter-day Laurel and Hardy film is surprisingly good—especially when you consider that the boys had lost all control over the making of their pictures by this time. The story has Laurel resembling a famous bullfighter, and, of course, this leads to chaos in the ring. B&W; 61m. **DIR:** Malcolm St. Clair. **CAST:** Stan Laurel, Oliver Hardy, Margo Woode, Richard Lane, Carol Andrews. **1945**

BULLIES 🖤 A family moves to a small town that happens to be run by a murderous family of moonshiners. Rated R for graphic violence and profanity. 96m. **DIR:** Paul Lynch. **CAST:** Jonathan Crombie, Janet Laine Green, Olivia D'Abo. **1985**

BULLITT ★★★★ Although a bit dated now, this police drama directed by Peter Yates still features one of star Steve McQueen's best screen performances. The San Francisco car-chase sequence is still a corker. 113m. **DIR:** Peter Yates. **CAST:** Steve McQueen, Robert Vaughn, Jacqueline Bisset, Norman Fell, Don Gordon, Suzanne Somers. **1968 DVD**

BULLSEYE ★★★ In this surprisingly entertaining—albeit featherweight—caper comedy from director Michael Winner, Michael Caine and Roger Moore essay dual roles as two identical pairs of con men. Sally Kirkland costars as the brains (and body) of the organization. Rated PG-13 for profanity. 95m. **DIR:** Michael Winner. **CAST:** Michael Caine, Roger Moore, Sally Kirkland. **1990**

BULLSHOT (BULLSHOT CRUMMOND) ★★1/2 A movie can be fun for a while, then overstay its welcome. Such is the case with this spoof of Herman Cyril "Scapper" McNiele's *Bulldog Drummond* mystery-spy adventures. Everything is played to the hilt, and the characters become caricatures. Although this is occasionally irritating, the star-screenwriters do create some funny moments. Rated PG for profanity, sex, and violence. 95m. **DIR:** Dick Clement. **CAST:** Alan Shearman, Diz White, Ron House, Frances Tomelty, Michael Aldridge. **1985**

BULLWHIP ★★1/2 In this agreeable movie, Guy Madison avoids the hangin' tree by agreeing to marry a fiery half-breed (Rhonda Fleming). If the plot sounds familiar, it should. Jack Nicholson saw a similar one in *Goin' South*. 80m. **DIR:** Harmon Jones. **CAST:** Rhonda Fleming, Guy Madison, James Griffith, Don Beddoe. **1958**

BULWORTH ★★★1/2 Warren Beatty is a disillusioned senator who jump-starts his moribund reelection campaign by biting the hand that feeds him. It's pretty damn funny to watch ol' Warren outfit himself in gang-banger togs while delivering his eye-opening political messages . . . in rap, no less. Rated R for profanity and drug use. 107m. **DIR:** Warren Beatty. **CAST:** Warren Beatty, Halle Berry, Oliver Platt, Paul Sorvino, Jack Warden, Don Cheadle, Sean Astin. **1998 DVD**

•**BUMBLEBEE FLIES ANYWAY, THE** ★★★ Touching tale of a young man suffering from amnesia, who befriends the other children in a hospital for the terminally ill. Elijah Wood, as Barney Snow, slowly tries to reconstruct his memories after an accident. Snow finds time to make friends with cancer patient Mazzo, played with dignity by Joseph Perrino, and fall in love with Mazzo's sister Cassie, played by Rachael Leigh Cooke. Janeane Garofalo shines as the only doctor who sees Snow as a person and not a patient. Rated PG-13 for language. 95m. **DIR:** Martin Duffy. **CAST:** Elijah Wood, Janeane Garofalo, Rachael Leigh Cook, Joseph Perrino, Roger Rees. **2000**

BUNCO ★★1/2 Passable made-for-television crime thriller that has Robert Urich and Tom Selleck as a pair of police detectives out to bust a confidence ring. Typical TV fare. 90m. **DIR:** Alexander Singer. **CAST:** Robert Urich, Tom Selleck, Donna Mills, Michael Sacks, Will Geer, Arte Johnson, James Hampton, Bobby Van. **1976**

BUNDLE OF JOY ★★★ In this breezy remake of Ginger Rogers's *Bachelor Mother*, Debbie Reynolds portrays a department-store salesgirl who takes custody of an infant. (Eddie Fisher is suspected of being the father.) A scandal ensues. 98m. DIR: Norman Taurog. CAST: Debbie Reynolds, Eddie Fisher, Adolphe Menjou, Tommy Noonan. 1956

•BUNKER, THE ★★★★ Based on *Newsweek* reporter James P. O'Donnell's book about the fall of Hitler's regime, this HBO movie reveals a confused, unsteady leader (Anthony Hopkins at his Emmy-winning best) surrounded by his top men. Aware of his mental demise, some of his men dare to defy his orders. Glory-days flashbacks make a stark contrast to his final days. Susan Blakely's Eva Braun comes across as a complete airhead. Piper Laurie's chilling performance as Goebbels's wife will inspire a few nightmares. Not rated; contains mature themes, profanity, and animal cruelty. 151m. DIR: George Schaefer. CAST: Anthony Hopkins, Richard Jordan, Piper Laurie, Susan Blakely. 1980

BUNNY'S TALE, A ★★★ Engaging comedy-drama stars Kirstie Alley as feminist author Gloria Steinem, who became a Bunny at a Playboy Club in order to get the real story behind the Hugh Hefner empire. Her experiences make for major entertainment, and this made-for-TV film never slips into the peekaboo trap it easily could have. 97m. DIR: Karen Arthur. CAST: Kirstie Alley, Cotter Smith, Deborah Van Valkenburgh, Joanna Kerns, Delta Burke. 1985

BUONA SERA, MRS. CAMPBELL ★★★1/2 Great farce, with Gina Lollobrigida having convinced three World War II soldiers that they fathered her child, collecting support payments from each. Then she learns the ex-GIs are returning to Italy for a twenty-year reunion. 113m. DIR: Melvin Frank. CAST: Gina Lollobrigida, Peter Lawford, Phil Silvers, Telly Savalas, Shelley Winters, Lee Grant. 1968

'BURBS, THE ★★ In this weird and ultimately unsatisfying comedy, Tom Hanks plays a suburbanite who becomes more and more concerned about the bizarre family who has moved in next door. Essentially it's *Neighbors* all over again, with Hanks, Carrie Fisher, Rick Ducommun, and Bruce Dern turning in strong performances. Despite some inspired touches from director Joe Dante, it falls flat in the final third. Rated PG for violence and profanity. 102m. DIR: Joe Dante. CAST: Tom Hanks, Bruce Dern, Carrie Fisher, Rick Ducommun, Corey Feldman, Wendy Schaal, Henry Gibson. 1989

BURDEN OF DREAMS ★★★★★ Documentary specialist Les Blank unearthed a rare treasure in Ecuador, where Werner Herzog labored for years to make *Fitzcarraldo*, a lavish film depicting a man's obsessive quest to bring opera to the jungle. Shooting on location, among fighting tribes, Herzog's task becomes a parallel quest of compulsion. Blank makes the metaphors meaningful, more powerful even than Herzog did. Not rated. 94m. DIR: Les Blank. CAST: Werner Herzog, Klaus Kinski, Mick Jagger, Jason Robards Jr., Claudia Cardinale. 1982

BUREAU OF MISSING PERSONS ★★★ Pat O'Brien is the whole show as a rough, wisecracking police detective, helping fugitive Bette Davis prove she is innocent of murder. Fast-paced. B&W; 75m. DIR: Roy Del Ruth. CAST: Bette Davis, Pat O'Brien,

Lewis Stone, Glenda Farrell, Allen Jenkins, Hugh Herbert. 1933

BURGLAR (U.S.) ★★★ Whoopi Goldberg stars in this amiable but unspectacular caper comedy as a retired cat burglar forced back into a life of crime by a crooked cop (G. W. Bailey). She ends up the prime suspect in a rather messy murder case. Goldberg does well in a role originally written for Bruce Willis. Rated R for profanity and violence. 91m. DIR: Hugh Wilson. CAST: Whoopi Goldberg, Bob Goldthwait, G. W. Bailey, Lesley Ann Warren. 1987 DVD

BURGLAR (RUSSIAN) ★★★ Two unemployed brothers, beset by family problems, find an outlet in Leningrad's punk-rock scene. Nothing special, but worth seeing for a look at an underground musical culture that's not dominated by commercial interests. In Russian with English subtitles. Not rated. 101m. DIR: Valery Ogorodnikov. CAST: Konstantin Kinchev, Oleg Yelykomov. 1987

•BURGLAR FROM HELL ❤ This low-budget independent film lacks decent acting, dialogue, cinematography, and sound, but it does have something of a plot, sort of—a burglar killed and buried comes back to life when a group of young adults rents a house for the weekend. Not rated; contains profanity, violence, nudity, and gore. 100m. DIR: Chip Herman. CAST: Matt O'Connor, Ben Stanski, Barry Gaines. 1999

BURIED ALIVE (1979) ★★ If *Psycho*'s Norman Bates wasn't lonely enough for you, here's another demented taxidermist who takes necrophilia to extremes that are gross even for Italian gore films. This is probably the slickest, most compulsively watchable effort by bad-taste auteur Joe D'Amato. Rated R. 90m. DIR: Joe D'Amato (Aristide Massaccesi). CAST: Sam Modesto, Ann Cardin. 1979

BURIED ALIVE (1990) ★★★★ Nice guy Tim Matheson is poisoned by his greedy wife (Jennifer Jason Leigh, at her nastiest) and her lover; believed dead, Matheson is buried in a cheap casket (having fortunately bypassed technicalities such as embalming). Excellent contemporary take on Poe's "Premature Burial." Made for cable. Rated R for mild violence. 93m. DIR: Frank Darabont. CAST: Tim Matheson, Jennifer Jason Leigh, William Atherton, Hoyt Axton. 1990

BURIED ALIVE II ★★1/2 An unfaithful husband poisons his wife and buries her so he can run off with his mistress. But the poison only puts his wife in a deep coma, and when she wakes up, she's not very happy. The plot in this made-for-cable original is full of holes, and the acting is buried under bad lines. Not rated; contains profanity. 95m. DIR: Tim Matheson. CAST: Ally Sheedy, Stephen Caffrey, Tracey Needham, Tim Matheson. 1997

BURKE AND WILLS ★★ Like most Australian period movies, this historical drama about a failed attempt to travel through the uncharted interior of nineteenth-century Australia is meticulously produced, but ends up being more exhausting than entertaining. It's also about 45 minutes too long. It's rated PG-13 for language and brief nudity. 140m. DIR: Graeme Clifford. CAST: Jack Thompson, Nigel Havers, Greta Scacchi. 1987

BURMESE HARP, THE ★★★★ A haunting Japanese antiwar film about a soldier who, at the end of World War II, disguises himself as a monk and embarks on a soul-searching journey back to a mountain fortress where his comrades met their death. In Japanese with English subtitles. B&W; 116m. **DIR:** Kon Ichikawa. **CAST:** Shoji Yasui, Rentaro Mikuni. 1956

BURN! ★★★★ Marlon Brando's performance alone makes *Burn!* worth watching. Seldom has a star so vividly and memorably lived up to his promise as acting great, and that's what makes this film a must-see. Brando plays Sir William Walker, an egotistical mercenary sent by the British to instigate a slave revolt on a Portuguese-controlled sugar-producing island. He succeeds all too well by turning José Dolores (Evaristo Marquez) into a powerful leader and soon finds himself back on the island, plotting the downfall of his Frankenstein monster. Rated PG. 112m. **DIR:** Gillo Pontecorvo. **CAST:** Marlon Brando, Evaristo Marquez, Renato Salvatori. 1969

BURN UP! ★★ Nothing overly original about this Japanese animated story. Three female police officers get embroiled in the investigation of a notorious white slaver, but obvious plotting undermines fair animation. Not rated; contains nudity and violence. 50m. **DIR:** Yasunori Ide. 1991

BURN, WITCH, BURN ★★★★ A college psychology professor sets out to debunk the occult only to find himself under attack by a practitioner of the supernatural. A superb screenplay by Charles Beaumont and Richard Matheson helps make this British film one of the best on the subject of witchcraft. 90m. **DIR:** Sidney Hayers. **CAST:** Peter Wyngarde, Janet Blair, Margaret Johnson, Anthony Nicholls. 1962

BURNDOWN ★★★ This is a murder mystery with the killer the victim of radioactivity. Peter Firth is the police chief trying to solve the murders, and Cathy Moriarty is a news reporter trying to find the far more complex problem of a nuclear leak and cover-up that could be deadly to the entire town. Rated R for violence. 87m. **DIR:** James Allen. **CAST:** Peter Firth, Cathy Moriarty. 1989

BURNING, THE 💣 Similar to many other blood feasts, it's the story of a summer camp custodian who, savagely burned as a result of a teenage prank, comes back years later for revenge. Rated R. 90m. **DIR:** Tony Maylam. **CAST:** Brian Matthews, Leah Ayres, Brian Backer. 1981

BURNING BED, THE ★★★★ Farrah Fawcett is remarkably good in this made-for-TV film based on a true story. She plays a woman reaching the breaking point with her abusive and brutish husband, well played by Paul LeMat. Fawcett not only proves she can act, but that she has the capacity to pull off a multilayered role. Believable from start to finish, this is a superior television film. 105m. **DIR:** Robert Greenwald. **CAST:** Farrah Fawcett, Paul LeMat, Richard Masur, Grace Zabriskie. 1984

BURNING COURT, THE ★★★ Variation on the haunted-house theme, with a family gathered at their cursed estate by a dying uncle. More stylized than scary. French, dubbed in English. Not rated. B&W; 102m. **DIR:** Julien Duvivier. **CAST:** Jean-Claude Brialy, Nadja Tiller, Perrette Pradier. 1962

BURNING HILLS, THE ★★1/2 Average revenge tale of wounded homesteader Tab Hunter pursued by a cattleman's posse. Natalie Wood, terribly miscast as a Mexican half-breed, comes to his side. Screenplay by Irving Wallace from a Louis L'Amour novel. 94m. **DIR:** Stuart Heisler. **CAST:** Tab Hunter, Natalie Wood, Skip Homeier, Eduard Franz, Earl Holliman, Claude Akins, Ray Teal. 1956

BURNING SEASON, THE ★★★★ This absorbing docudrama traces the meteoric rise of Brazil's Chico Mendes, played with quiet dignity by Raul Julia. Mendes's story is of a small-town rubber tapper who reluctantly opposes rapacious businessmen determined to raze the Amazon forest and create cattle-grazing country. Rated R for profanity, violence, torture, and brief nudity. 125m. **DIR:** John Frankenheimer. **CAST:** Raul Julia, Carmen Argenziano, Esai Morales, Edward James Olmos, Sonia Braga, Nigel Havers. 1994

BURNING SECRET ★★ A cool, overly restrained mystery-romance, set in an Austrian health spa in the years between the world wars. Faye Dunaway and Klaus Maria Brandauer star as emotionally crippled strangers who meet when Brandauer befriends her young son. Remarkably short on passion. Rated PG. 110m. **DIR:** Andrew Birkin. **CAST:** Faye Dunaway, Klaus Maria Brandauer. 1988

BURNT BY THE SUN ★★★★ Deserving Best Foreign Language Film Academy Award winner about a Russian revolutionary hero (director Nikita Mikhalkov) whose quiet country holiday is upset by the arrival of his young wife's former lover and, more alarmingly, Stalin's purges of the 1930s. In Russian with English subtitles. Rated R for nudity, sex, and violence. 134m. **DIR:** Nikita Mikhalkov. **CAST:** Nikita Mikhalkov, Oleg Menchikov, Ingeborga Dapkounaite, Nadia Mikhalkov. 1994

BURNT OFFERINGS ★★ Good acting cannot save this predictable horror film concerning a haunted house. Rated PG. 115m. **DIR:** Dan Curtis. **CAST:** Oliver Reed, Karen Black, Burgess Meredith, Bette Davis, Lee Montgomery, Eileen Heckart. 1976

BUS IS COMING, THE ★★★ The message of this production is: racism (both black and white) is wrong. In this film, Billy Mitchell (Mike Sims) is a young black soldier who returns to his hometown after his brother is murdered. Billy's white friend encourages him to investigate the death of his brother, while his black friends want to tear the town down. The acting is not the greatest, but the film does succeed in making its point. Rated PG for violence. 102m. **DIR:** Wendell J. Franklin. **CAST:** Mike Simms, Stephanie Faulkner, Burl Bullock. 1971

BUS STOP ★★★★1/2 Marilyn Monroe plays a show girl who is endlessly pursued by an oaf of a cowboy named Bo (Don Murray). He even kidnaps her when she refuses to marry him. Lots of laughs as Bo mistreats his newly found "angel." Arthur O'Connell is excellent as Verg, Bo's older and wiser friend who advises Bo on the way to treat women. 96m. **DIR:** Joshua Logan. **CAST:** Marilyn Monroe, Don Murray, Arthur O'Connell, Betty Field, Casey Adams. 1956

BUSHIDO BLADE 💣 Richard Boone gives an outrageously hammy performance as Commander Matthew Perry, whose mission is to find a valuable sword. Rated R for violence. 104m. **DIR:** Tom Kotani. **CAST:** Richard Boone, Frank Converse, James Earl Jones, Toshiro Mifune, Mako. 1979

BUSHWHACKED 🖤 Incompetent delivery man is framed for murder and poses as a Ranger Scout leader to six woodland tenderfoots (one of them a girl) while trying to clear himself. Rated PG-13 for language. 96m. **DIR:** Greg Beeman. **CAST:** Daniel Stern, Jon Polito, Brad Sullivan. 1995

BUSHWHACKERS ★★★ Ex-Confederate John Ireland tries to hang up his guns, but a ruthless land baron forces him to buckle 'em on again. Routine range-war tale saved by a better-than-competent cast. B&W; 70m. **DIR:** Rod Amateau. **CAST:** John Ireland, Dorothy Malone, Wayne Morris, Lawrence Tierney, Lon Chaney Jr. 1951

BUSINESS AFFAIR, A ★★★ A flawed, if enjoyable, reversal on the old *Taming of the Shrew* theme. The focus grows a little blurry around the halfway mark, but there are some fine performances and strong characters in this romantic European comedy. A gorgeous model irritates her famous, badly behaved novelist husband when she writes a bestseller. Christopher Walken, in one of his more controlled performances, is the publisher who woos her professionally and personally. Rated R for profanity and nudity. 105m. **DIR:** Charlotte Brandstrom. **CAST:** Jonathan Pryce, Carole Bouquet, Christopher Walken, Sheila Hancock. 1993

BUSINESS AS USUAL ★★ Glenda Jackson plays a dress-shop manager fired after going to bat for an employee who's been sexually harrassed by a higher-up. Writer-director Lezli-An Barrett's script covers a wide range of issues but never develops any dramatic tension or strong characters. Rated PG. 89m. **DIR:** Lezli-An Barrett. **CAST:** Glenda Jackson, John Thaw, Cathy Tyson, Mark McGann, James Hazeldine. 1987

•**BUSINESS FOR PLEASURE** ★★ Kinky but unsatisfactory erotic drama about a businessman who likes to watch. That's the plot of writer Zalman King's sexual cavalcade that finds a businesswoman so desperate to save her company that she's willing to procure sexual entertainment for an investor. Like all King escapades, there is enough soft-core to heat up a chilly night, but not nearly enough plot to make it matter. Not rated; contains adult situations, language, and nudity. 97m. **DIR:** Rafael Eisenman. **CAST:** Caron Bernstein, Gary Stretch, Jeroen Krabbé, Joanna Pacula. 1996

BUSTED UP ★★1/2 A story about a local-circuit bare-fisted fighter and a nightclub singer. Typical plot, average acting, but professionally produced and technically polished. Rated R for violence and language. 93m. **DIR:** Conrad E. Palmisano. **CAST:** Irene Cara, Paul Coufos, Tony Rosato, Stan Shaw. 1986

BUSTER ★★★ Pop star Phil Collins makes his film debut in this enjoyable story about the Great Train Robbery of 1963. Collins is Buster Edwards, who became a folk hero after he and his cronies pulled off the greatest robbery in the history of England. It's enjoyable fare and an interesting character study. Rated R for language and brief nudity. 93m.

DIR: David Greene. **CAST:** Phil Collins, Julie Walters, Sheila Hancock. 1988

BUSTER AND BILLIE ★★ A handsome high school boy falls in love with a homely but loving girl in the rural South. Set in the 1940s, the film has an innocent, sweet quality until it abruptly shifts tone and turns into a mean-spirited revenge picture. Rated R for violence and nudity. 100m. **DIR:** Daniel Petrie. **CAST:** Jan-Michael Vincent, Joan Goodfellow, Pamela Sue Martin, Clifton James. 1974

BUSTER AND FATTY ★★★ Two of silent film's greatest comedy stars, Buster Keaton and Roscoe "Fatty" Arbuckle, cavort in five hilarious examples of the art of slapstick: *Coney Island*, *The Butcher Boy* (Keaton's film debut), *Good Night Nurse*, *Out West*, and the long-thought-lost *Back Stage*. B&W; 94m. **DIR:** Roscoe Arbuckle. **CAST:** Roscoe "Fatty" Arbuckle, Buster Keaton, Al St. John, Alice Lake, Agnes Neilson, Joe Bordeaux. 1917–19

BUSTER KEATON: A HARD ACT TO FOLLOW ★★★★★ Offered in three parts, this is a truly superb narrative study of Buster Keaton's matchless stone-faced comic genius. The episodes, titled "From Vaudeville to Movies," "Star without a Studio," and "A Genius Recognized," chronicle Buster Keaton's amazing and mercurial career from near start to close with compassion, insight, and captivating accuracy. A unique opportunity to see one of the greats of the silent screen at work. B&W/color; each part. 52m. **DIR:** Kevin Brownlow, David Gill. 1987

BUSTER KEATON FESTIVAL VOL. 1–3 ★★★★ Hilarious collection of silent shorts from the legendary comic genius. Includes such priceless gems as: *The Paleface*, *The Boat*, *Daydreams*, *The Balloonatic*, and *The Blacksmith*. Silent. B&W; 55m. **DIR:** Buster Keaton, Eddie Cline, Malcolm St. Clair. **CAST:** Buster Keaton, Virginia Fox, Joe Roberts, Eddie Cline, Sybil Seely, Bonnie Hill, Freeman Wood, Joseph Keaton, Myra Keaton, Louise Keaton, Phyllis Haver, Renée Adorée. 1921–1922

BUSTIN' LOOSE ★★1/2 Take superbad ex-con Richard Pryor, stick him on a school bus with goody-two-shoes teacher Cicely Tyson and eight ornery schoolchildren, and what have you got? A cross-country, comic odyssey as long as Pryor is up to his madcap antics. But *Bustin' Loose* bogs down in its last half hour. Rated R for profanity and violence. 94m. **DIR:** Oz Scott. **CAST:** Richard Pryor, Cicely Tyson, Robert Christian, Alphonso Alexander, Janet Wong. 1981 DVD

BUT NOT FOR ME ★★1/2 Clark Gable does a credible job as an aging Broadway producer who feels the ravages of time in both his professional career and private life. Predictable comedy-drama but the leading players (especially Lilli Palmer) and a title song by Ella Fitzgerald help. B&W; 105m. **DIR:** Walter Lang. **CAST:** Clark Gable, Carroll Baker, Lilli Palmer, Lee J. Cobb, Barry Coe, Thomas Gomez, Charles Lane. 1959

BUTCH AND SUNDANCE: THE EARLY DAYS ★★ Director Richard Lester has made better films (see *A Hard Day's Night* and *Superman II*), and because his usual film is a comedy, this outing is especially disappointing. Nearly all of the jokes fall flat despite a screenplay that hints at the original film with Paul Newman and Robert Redford. Rated PG for some mildly crude language and (very little) violence. 111m. **DIR:** Richard Lester. **CAST:** William Katt, Tom Berenger, Brian Dennehy, John Schuck, Jeff Corey. **1979**

BUTCH CAMP 💔 Embarrassing tale of a meek gay office worker who enrolls in Commandant Samantha Rottweiler's "Butch Camp" and finds the whole experience humiliating. He's not the only one. Poor production values and an eat-all-of-the-scenery performance by comedian Judy Tenuta seal the film's fate. Not rated; contains nudity, language, and adult situations. 85m. **DIR:** Alessandro de Gaetano. **CAST:** Paul Denniston, Judy Tenuta, Jordan Roberts, Bill Ingraham. **1998**

BUTCH CASSIDY AND THE SUNDANCE KID ★★★★1/2 George Roy Hill directed this gentle Western spoof featuring personal-best performances by Paul Newman, Robert Redford, and Katharine Ross. A spectacular box-office success, and deservedly so, the release deftly combines action with comedy. Rated PG. 112m. **DIR:** George Roy Hill. **CAST:** Paul Newman, Robert Redford, Katharine Ross. **1969** DVD

BUTCHER BOY, THE ★★ Imagine *Tom Sawyer* transplanted to Ireland and set in the early 1960s, then mixed with the walking-nightmare hallucinations of Roman Polanski's *Repulsion*. Toss in thick Irish accents, blend with a shrieking directorial style, and you've got this savage, blackly comic study of a feisty kid losing his mind. Rated R for profanity, violence, and just about every perversion you could imagine. 105m. **DIR:** Neil Jordan. **CAST:** Stephen Rea, Fiona Shaw, Eamonn Owens, Alan Boyle, Milo O'Shea, Sinead O'Connor. **1998**

BUTCHER'S WIFE, THE ★★ You don't have to be clairvoyant to know what's going to happen in this comedy about a North Carolina psychic who weds a New York City butcher because she thinks he's the man of her dreams. Apart from isolated moments of inspiration, *The Butcher's Wife* is comparable with a so-so episode of *Bewitched*. Rated PG-13 for profanity. 105m. **DIR:** Terry Hughes. **CAST:** Demi Moore, Jeff Daniels, George Dzundza, Mary Steenburgen, Frances McDormand, Margaret Colin. **1991**

BUTTERFIELD 8 ★★★ Severe illness helped sway votes her way when Elizabeth Taylor copped an Oscar for her by-the-numbers portrayal of a big-ticket call girl who wants to go straight after finding someone she thinks is Mr. Right. Adapted from the John O'Hara novel. 109m. **DIR:** Daniel Mann. **CAST:** Elizabeth Taylor, Laurence Harvey, Eddie Fisher, Dina Merrill, Mildred Dunnock, Betty Field. **1960**

BUTTERFLIES ARE FREE ★★★★ Edward Albert is a blind youth determined to be self-sufficient in spite of his overbearing mother and the distraction of his will-o'-the-wisp next-door neighbor (Goldie Hawn). This fast-paced comedy benefits from some outstanding performances, none better than that by Eileen Heckart. Her concerned, protective, and sometimes overloving mother is a treasure to behold. Rated PG. 109m. **DIR:** Milton Katselas. **CAST:** Goldie Hawn, Edward Albert, Eileen Heckart, Mike Warren. **1972**

BUTTERFLY ★★ Sex symbol Pia Zadora starts an incestuous relationship with her father (Stacy Keach). Orson Welles, as a judge, is the best thing about this film. Rated R. 107m. **DIR:** Matt Cimber. **CAST:** Pia Zadora, Stacy Keach, Orson Welles, Lois Nettleton. **1982**

BUTTERFLY KISS ★★★ Amanda Plummer frantically hams it up as a crazed lesbian serial killer, with Saskia Reeves as her simpering, stupid girlfriend. The actresses do good work, but their characters are unconvincingly written, and the film is extremely unpleasant. There's no real suspense, just grisly tension while waiting for the next victim to be clubbed to death. Rated R for profanity, violence, and simulated sex. 88m. **DIR:** Michael Winterbottom. **CAST:** Amanda Plummer, Saskia Reeves, Kathy Jamieson, Desmond McAteer, Lisa Jane Riley. **1994**

BUY AND CELL 💔 A Wall Street broker takes the rap for his boss's insider trading. Rated R. 91m. **DIR:** Robert Boris. **CAST:** Robert Carradine, Michael Winslow, Randall "Tex" Cobb, Fred Travalena, Ben Vereen, Malcolm McDowell. **1989**

BUYING TIME ★★1/2 A young man goes undercover to procure evidence that will convict a drug-dealing killer, but he finds his own life in jeopardy. Rated R for nudity, profanity, violence, and animal abuse. 97m. **DIR:** Mitchell Gabourie. **CAST:** Jeff Schultz, Laura Cruickshank, Page Fletcher, Dean Stockwell. **1989**

BY DAWN'S EARLY LIGHT ★★★ This slick adaptation of William Prochnau's *Trinity's Child*, unfolds like an updated *Fail-Safe*. Nuclear terrorists trick the Soviet Union into believing the U.S. has struck first, and the reprisal is launched before the mistake is detected. Not rated made-for-cable film; contains profanity. 104m. **DIR:** Jack Sholder. **CAST:** Powers Boothe, Rebecca DeMornay, James Earl Jones, Martin Landau, Darren McGavin, Jeffrey DeMunn, Peter MacNicol, Rip Torn. **1990**

BY DESIGN ★★1/2 Patty Duke plays a lesbian fashion designer who decides she'd like to have a baby. She attempts to get pregnant by a heterosexual man. Interesting subject matter gets an uneven result. Rated R. 88m. **DIR:** Claude Jutra. **CAST:** Patty Duke, Sara Botsford, Saul Rubinek. **1981**

BY LOVE POSSESSED ★★1/2 Problems among the upper crust of a small New England town include alcoholism, impotence, and rape charges. It all adds up to dull soap opera with so-so performances. Very loosely based on the novel by James Gould Cozzens. 115m. **DIR:** John Sturges. **CAST:** Lana Turner, Efrem Zimbalist Jr., Jason Robards Jr., Barbara Bel Geddes, George Hamilton, Susan Kohner, Thomas Mitchell, Everett Sloane, Carroll O'Connor. **1961**

BY THE BLOOD OF OTHERS ★★★ The town fathers of a small village search for a plan to rescue two women held hostage by a mentally disturbed young man. Like his father, novelist Georges Simenon, director Marc Simenon brings psychological depth to this suspense drama. In French with English subtitles. 95m. **DIR:** Marc Simenon. **CAST:** Mariangela Melato, Yves Beneyton, Bernard Blier. **1973**

BY THE LAW ★★★★ Adapted from Jack London's short story, "The Unexpected," this is a grim story of three trappers isolated by Alaskan storms and floods. Silent. Russian. B&W; 90m. **DIR:** Lev Kuleshov. **CAST:** Alexandra Khokhlova, Sergei Komarov, Vladimir Fogel. 1926

BY THE LIGHT OF THE SILVERY MOON ★★★ More trouble for the Winfield family in this sequel to *On Moonlight Bay*, with innocent Leon Ames suspected by his family of being involved with a French actress. Post–WWI setting, with many familiar songs from that period. 102m. **DIR:** David Butler. **CAST:** Doris Day, Gordon MacRae, Leon Ames, Rosemary DeCamp, Billy Gray, Mary Wickes, Russell Arms. 1953

BY THE SWORD ★★1/2 Plenty of swordplay fails to sharpen this standard tale of revenge set in the professional world of sword fighting. F. Murray Abraham is the old pro, Eric Roberts the Olympic star and son of the man killed by Abraham years earlier in the heat of passion. Abraham plays a dangerous cat-and-mouse game with Roberts as he insinuates himself into his life, and then must face off against him when the truth is revealed. Rated R for language and violence. 91m. **DIR:** Jeremy Paul Kagan. **CAST:** F. Murray Abraham, Eric Roberts, Mia Sara, Christopher Rydell. 1991

BY WAY OF THE STARS ★★★1/2 Breathtaking outdoor adventure stars Zachary Bennett as young Lucas Bienman, a nineteenth-century Prussian teen who heads to the New World to find his father. When Luke arrives in the untamed Canadian West, his trek is filled with adventure and close calls, not to mention Indians, and a killer hot on his trail. Gorgeous scenery and decent cast make this *Hallmark Hall of Fame* presentation an adventure for the entire family. Rated PG. 150m. **DIR:** Allan Winton King. **CAST:** Zachary Bennett, Tantoo Cardinal, Gema Zamprogna, Jan Rubes. 1992

BYE-BYE ★★★ Two French-Arab brothers move from Paris to Marseilles to live with their uncle, where they experience hostility toward "foreigners" and the hardships of the street. Writer-director Karim Dridi's film has persuasive acting and quiet, slice-of-life realism. In translation, unfortunately, it is marred by clumsy English subtitles. In French and Arabic with English subtitles. Not rated; contains mature themes, mild profanity (in subtitles), and one sexual episode. 102m. **DIR:** Karim Dridi. **CAST:** Sami Bouajila, Nozha Khouadra, Philippe Ambrosini, Ouassini Embarek. 1995

BYE BYE, BABY 🎦 Bizarre twist on Noel Coward's *Private Lives*. The film was clearly shot simultaneously in English and Italian, with dialogue that sounds like badly translated Esperanto. Rated R for nudity. 90m. **DIR:** Enrico Oldoini. **CAST:** Carol Alt, Luca Barbareschi, Brigitte Nielsen, Jason Connery. 1989

BYE BYE BIRDIE ★★★ A rock star's approaching appearance in a small town turns several lives upside down in this pleasant musical-comedy. Based on the successful Broadway play, this is pretty lightweight stuff, but a likable cast and good production numbers make it worthwhile. No rating; okay for the whole family. 112m. **DIR:** George Sidney. **CAST:** Dick Van Dyke, Ann-Margret, Janet Leigh, Paul Lynde, Bobby Rydell. 1963 DVD

BYE BYE BRAZIL ★★★1/2 This is a bawdy, bizarre, satiric, and sometimes even touching film that follows a ramshackle traveling tent show—the Caravana Rolidei—through the cities, jungle, and villages of Brazil. In Portuguese with English subtitles. Rated R. 110m. **DIR:** Carlos Diegues. **CAST:** José Wilker, Betty Faria. 1980

BYE BYE, LOVE ★★ Three divorced male buddies—all child-custody weekend warriors—get a forty-eight-hour crash course in single parenting and dating. Rated PG-13 for language. 105m. **DIR:** Sam Weisman. **CAST:** Matthew Modine, Randy Quaid, Paul Reiser, Janeane Garofalo, Rob Reiner. 1995

CABARET ★★★★★ This classic musical-drama takes place in Germany in 1931. The Nazi party has not yet assumed complete control, and the local cabaret unfolds the story of two young lovers, the ensuing mood of the country, and the universal touch of humanity. Everything is handled with taste—bisexual encounters, the horrors of the Nazi regime, and the bawdy entertainment of the nightclub. "Host" Joel Grey is brilliant. Michael York and Liza Minnelli are first-rate. So is the movie. Rated PG. 128m. **DIR:** Bob Fosse. **CAST:** Liza Minnelli, Michael York, Helmut Griem, Joel Grey. 1972 DVD

•CABARET BALKAN ★★★1/2 During one night in Belgrade, the lives of a number of characters intertwine in a series of chance encounters. The film paints a harrowing picture of a society about to self-destruct, suffused with rage and despair, yet lit by flashes of bitter humor that underscore the characters' humanity. It's an unforgettable descent into something very much like Dante's *Inferno* right here on earth. In Serbo-Croatian with English subtitles. Rated R for violence and profanity (in subtitles). 100m. **DIR:** Goran Paskaljevic. **CAST:** Lazar Ristovski, Miki Manojlovic, Nikola Ristanovski, Nebojsa Glogovac. 1998

CABEZA DE VACA ★★★★ Director Nicolas Echevarria draws on his experience as a documentary filmmaker for this engrossing study of Spanish explorer Alvar Nunez Cabeza de Vaca, who landed in Florida in 1528 and rose from an Indian slave to a respected shaman with another tribe. In Spanish with English subtitles. Rated R for violence and profanity. 112m. **DIR:** Nicolas Echevarria. **CAST:** Juan Diego. 1992

CABIN BOY 🎦 Pathetic, filthy-rich geek mistakes a grungy fishing trawler for a cruise ship in this lame fantasy-comedy version of *Captains Courageous*. Rated PG-13 for language. 80m. **DIR:** Adam Resnick. **CAST:** Chris Elliott, Ritch Brinkley, Brian Doyle-Murray,

James Gammon, Brion James, Melora Walters, Andy Richter. 1994

•CABIN BY THE LAKE ★★ Judd Nelson plays a screenwriter working on a movie about a serial killer who drowns his victims and tends to their submerged bodies every day. Although he says he's just researching his next film, Nelson *is* the serial killer. This made-for-cable original tries to be a black comedy, but suffers from extreme seriousness at times, and extreme silliness at others. Not rated; contains violence. 95m. DIR: Po-Chih Leong. CAST: Judd Nelson, Hedy Burress, Michael Weatherly, Susan Gibney. 2000

CABIN IN THE COTTON ★★★ An ambitious young sharecropper is educated by, and then works for, a rich landowner. His loyalties are challenged when he learns of widespread theft by tenant farmers. Worth the price of rental to hear vixen Bette Davis utter the immortal, and often misquoted line: "Ah'd *like* ta' kiss ya, but ah jus' washed mah hair." B&W; 78m. DIR: Michael Curtiz. CAST: Richard Barthelmess, Bette Davis, Dorothy Jordan, Russell Simpson. 1932

CABIN IN THE SKY ★★★ One of Hollywood's first general-release black films and Vincente Minnelli's first feature. Eddie Anderson shows acting skill that was sadly and too long diluted by his playing foil for Jack Benny. Ethel Waters, as always, is superb. The film is a shade racist, but bear in mind that it was made in 1943, when Tinsel Town still thought blacks did nothing but sing, dance, and love watermelon. B&W; 100m. DIR: Vincente Minnelli. CAST: Eddie "Rochester" Anderson, Lena Horne, Ethel Waters, Rex Ingram, Louis Armstrong. 1943

CABINET OF DOCTOR CALIGARI, THE ★★★1/2 A nightmarish story and surrealistic settings are the main ingredients of this early German classic of horror and fantasy. Cesare, a hollow-eyed sleepwalker (Conrad Veidt), commits murder while under the spell of the evil hypnotist Dr. Caligari (Werner Krauss). Ordered to kill Jane, a beautiful girl (Lil Dagover), Cesare defies Caligari, and instead abducts her. Silent. B&W; 51m. DIR: Robert Wiene. CAST: Werner Krauss, Conrad Veidt, Lil Dagover. 1919 DVD

CABIRIA ★★ This feature purportedly had a decisive influence on D. W. Griffith's epic ambitions. It made an international star out of Bartolomeo Pagano, whose role of strongman Maciste predated Schwarzenegger by many decades. Italian playwright Gabriele D'Annunzio lent his name—and some subtitles—to the picture. Silent. Italian. B&W; 95m. DIR: Giovanni Pastrone. CAST: Bartolomeo Pagano. 1914

CABLE GUY, THE ★★★ Jim Carrey's first attempt to project "serious" isn't exactly dramatic; it's like his usual antic slapstick in a more irritating vein. The basic idea is frightening: What if Ace Ventura wanted to be your friend and wouldn't take no for an answer? Director Ben Stiller tries to turn this tale of an obsessive pay-TV installer into a satire of both stalker movies and television culture in general, but it's still too much of a silly Carrey vehicle to work out its more intelligent ideas. Rated PG-13. 91m. DIR:

Ben Stiller. CAST: Jim Carrey, Matthew Broderick, Leslie Mann. 1996

CABO BLANCO ♥ A miserable suspense-thriller remake of *Casablanca*. As good as he can be when he wants to, Charles Bronson is no Humphrey Bogart. Rated R. 87m. DIR: J. Lee Thompson. CAST: Charles Bronson, Dominique Sanda, Jason Robards Jr. 1982 DVD

CACTUS ★★★1/2 Have patience with this warm and witty tale of a French lady (Isabelle Huppert) injured in an auto accident while visiting Australia. A young blind man helps her adjust to her diminishing eyesight. The supporting cast and Australian locale add to this story of growth and awareness. 96m. DIR: Paul Cox. CAST: Isabelle Huppert, Robert Menzies, Norman Kaye. 1986

CACTUS FLOWER ★★★ Watch this one for Goldie Hawn's performance that earned her an Academy Award as best supporting actress. She's the slightly wonky girlfriend of dentist Walter Matthau, who actually loves his nurse (Ingrid Bergman). Although adapted from a hit Broadway play by Abe Burrows, this film version is pretty short on laughs. Ingrid Bergman is far too serious in her role, and Matthau simply doesn't make a credible dentist. Rated PG for adult situations. 103m. DIR: Gene Saks. CAST: Walter Matthau, Ingrid Bergman, Goldie Hawn. 1969

CADDIE ★★★★ This is an absorbing character study of a woman who struggles to support herself and her children in Australia in the 1920s. Thanks greatly to the star's performance, it is yet another winner from down under. MPAA unrated, but contains mild sexual situations. 107m. DIR: Donald Crombie. CAST: Helen Morse, Takis Emmanuel, Jack Thompson, Jacki Weaver. 1976

CADDY, THE ★★★ In this lesser comedy from the Martin and Lewis team, the fellas enter the world of golf. Jerry plays a would-be golf pro. Strictly formulaic, but highlighted by several entertaining clashes between the two stars. 95m. DIR: Norman Taurog. CAST: Dean Martin, Jerry Lewis, Donna Reed, Fred Clark. 1953

CADDYSHACK ★★ Only Rodney Dangerfield, as an obnoxious refugee from a leisure-suit collectors' convention, offers anything of value in this rip-off of the *Animal House* formula. Chevy Chase and Bill Murray sleepwalk through their poorly written roles, and Ted Knight looks a little weary. Rated R for nudity and sex. 99m. DIR: Harold Ramis. CAST: Chevy Chase, Rodney Dangerfield, Ted Knight, Michael O'Keefe, Bill Murray. 1980 DVD

CADDYSHACK II ♥ Deciding to pass on this abysmal sequel may be the smartest career move Rodney Dangerfield ever made. Rated PG for profanity. 103m. DIR: Allan Arkush. CAST: Jackie Mason, Chevy Chase, Dan Aykroyd, Robert Stack, Dyan Cannon, Randy Quaid, Jonathan Silverman. 1988 DVD

CADENCE ★★1/2 Well-meant film about the evils of racism is skewed by director Martin Sheen's overly sympathetic portrait of a prejudiced stockade commander who attempts to use newcomer Charlie Sheen to spy on his cell mates, all of whom are black. More notable for good intentions than dramatic power. Rated PG-13 for profanity and violence. 97m. DIR:

Martin Sheen. **CAST:** Charlie Sheen, Martin Sheen, Laurence Fishburne, Michael Beach, Ramon Estevez. 1991

CADILLAC MAN ★★★ Philandering car salesman Robin Williams embarks on the worst few days of his life when his wife (Pamela Reed) demands more alimony, a gangster wants payment on a $20,000 gambling debt, and his boss demands that he sell a month's worth of cars in one day—then distraught husband Tim Robbins comes roaring into the dealership with an automatic weapon looking for the man who has been bedding his wife. Well acted and often hilarious. Rated R for violence, profanity, and nudity. 95m. **DIR:** Roger Donaldson. **CAST:** Robin Williams, Tim Robbins, Pamela Reed, Fran Drescher, Zack Norman. 1990

CADILLAC RANCH ★★★1/2 Three estranged sisters reunite to search for their father's hidden legacy in this offbeat action-comedy. Suzy Amis, Renee Humphrey, and Caroleen Feeney have little in common except a desire to find what's buried at the famous Cadillac Ranch in Texas. Rated R for language, violence, and sexuality. 95m. **DIR:** Lisa Gottlieb. **CAST:** Suzy Amis, Renee Humphrey, Caroleen Feeney, Christopher Lloyd, Linden Ashby. 1996 **DVD**

CAESAR AND CLEOPATRA ★★1/2 George Bernard Shaw's wordy play about Rome's titanic leader and Egypt's young queen. Claude Rains and Vivien Leigh are brilliant. 127m. **DIR:** Gabriel Pascal. **CAST:** Claude Rains, Vivien Leigh, Stewart Granger, Francis L. Sullivan, Flora Robson. 1946

CAFE AU LAIT ★★ Visually lively but shallow look at racial relations in Paris, where a pregnant young woman refuses to tell her two boyfriends—one Jewish, one black—which is the prospective father. Not rated; contains some nudity. 94m. **DIR:** Mathieu Kassovitz. **CAST:** Mathieu Kassovitz, Julie Mauduech, Hubert Kounde. 1994

CAFE EXPRESS ★★★1/2 Chaplinesque comedy starring Nino Manfredi, best known in this country for *Bread and Chocolate*. He plays a similar character here, a vendor selling coffee on a commuter train. Because such sales are illegal, he is hounded by conductors and other petty types. A bit lightweight, but Manfredi is always fun to watch. 105m. **DIR:** Nanni Loy. **CAST:** Nino Manfredi, Adolfo Celi, Vittorio Mezzogiorno. 1980

CAFE ROMEO ★★★ Raised with old-world traditions that no longer apply to them, six lifelong friends seek out a niche in the world as they venture from their neighborhood coffeehouse. Second-generation Italian-Americans are the focus of this somewhat uneven romantic comedy. Rated R for profanity. 93m. **DIR:** Rex Bromfield. **CAST:** Catherine Mary Stewart, Jonathan Crombie. 1991

CAFE SOCIETY ★★★ New York's 1950s nightclub scene was laced with sin and wealthy ne'er-do-wells having more cash than common sense, and this nasty little melodrama follows the very public scandal that destroyed one young man, brought temporary fame to a naïve party girl, and forever changed the salacious environment. Deeper characterization would have been nice. Rated R for profanity, nudity, simulated sex, and drug use. 108m. **DIR:** Raymond DeFelitta. **CAST:** Frank Whaley, Peter Gallagher, Lara Flynn Boyle, John Spencer, Anna Thomson, David Patrick Kelly. 1995

CAGE ★★★ Fine actioner features Lou Ferrigno as a brain-damaged Vietnam vet drawn into an underworld gambling arena. Although the dialogue is uninspired, Ferrigno shines. Rated R for violence and profanity. 101m. **DIR:** Lang Elliott. **CAST:** Lou Ferrigno, Reb Brown, Michael Dante. 1988

CAGE II: ARENA OF DEATH, THE 🦃 Absolutely ludicrous tale of a muscle man (Lou Ferrigno) who is kidnapped and made to fight in the infamous "cage" battles to the death. When his partner comes looking for him, you know it won't be long until they're in the ring facing each other. No-budget doldrums with only Ferrigno's undeniable muscled screen presence to give it any life. Rated R for violence and profanity. 94m. **DIR:** Lang Elliott. **CAST:** Lou Ferrigno, Reb Brown, James Shigeta, Shannon Lee. 1994

CAGED FEAR 🦃 Innocent woman gets thrown behind bars. Not even good trash. Rated R for nudity, violence, language. 93m. **DIR:** Bobby Houston. **CAST:** David Keith, Ray Sharkey, Deborah May, Karen Black. 1991

CAGED HEART, THE (L'ADDITION) ★★★ This absorbing French film has Bruno Winkler (Richard Berry) arrested for shoplifting when he tries to help a beautiful young woman (Victoria Abril). Once behind bars, he's accused of aiding a crime lord in his escape and shooting a guard. One can't help but get caught up in the story. Rated R for violence and profanity. 85m. **DIR:** Denis Amar. **CAST:** Richard Berry, Richard Bohringer, Victoria Abril. 1985

CAGED HEAT ★★ A typical R-rated women's-prison-break picture from Roger Corman's New World Pictures. For a change, this one is set in the United States. Otherwise its distinctions are marginal, despite direction by Jonathan Demme. 84m. **DIR:** Jonathan Demme. **CAST:** Juanita Brown, Erica Gavin, Barbara Steele. 1974

CAGED HEAT 2: STRIPPED OF FREEDOM 🦃 It's hard to believe they still make these women-behind-bars movies, but what's even harder to believe is that nothing has changed. Same script, same lecherous inmates and guards, same young innocent thrown in with the wolves. Rated R for nudity, adult situations, violence, and language. 84m. **DIR:** Cirio H. Santiago. **CAST:** Jewel Shepard, Pamela D'Pella, Chanel Akiko Hirai. 1994

CAGED HEAT 3000 🦃 The makers of this film take the women-in-prison genre into the future with the same results: an excuse to get women naked. Not rated; contains nudity, violence, and adult language. 85m. **DIR:** Aaron Osborne. **CAST:** Cassandra Leigh, Kena Land, Bob Ferrelli. 1995

CAHILL—US MARSHAL ★★1/2 John Wayne was still making B Westerns in the 1970s—to the disappointment of those who (rightly) expected better. Although still enjoyable, this film about a lawman (Wayne) whose son (Gary Grimes) becomes a bank robber is routine at best. Still, the performances by the Duke and George Kennedy (as the chief baddie) do bring pleasure. Rated PG. 103m. **DIR:** Andrew V.

McLaglen. CAST: John Wayne, George Kennedy, Gary Grimes, Neville Brand. 1973

CAINE MUTINY, THE ★★★★ Superb performances by Humphrey Bogart, Van Johnson, José Ferrer, and Fred MacMurray, among others, make this adaptation of Herman Wouk's classic novel an absolute must-see. This brilliant film concerns the hard-nosed Captain Queeg (Bogart), who may or may not be slightly unhinged, and the subsequent mutiny by his first officer and crew, who are certain he is. Beautifully done, a terrific movie. 125m. DIR: Edward Dmytryk. CAST: Humphrey Bogart, José Ferrer, Van Johnson, Robert Francis, Fred MacMurray. 1954 DVD

CAINE MUTINY COURT MARTIAL, THE ★★★★ Splendid adaptation of Herman Wouk's brilliant Pulitzer Prize–winning novel. Brad Davis comes aboard in the Humphrey Bogart role as Queeg, whose unorthodox actions aboard the U.S.S. *Caine* forced his crew to mutiny. Director Robert Altman keeps everything shipshape, and evokes outstanding performances from the enlisted men. Rated PG. 100m. DIR: Robert Altman. CAST: Brad Davis, Eric Bogosian, Jeff Daniels, Peter Gallagher, Michael Murphy. 1988

CAIRO ★★★1/2 One of Jeanette MacDonald's last films, and she gets to warble with a woman singer instead of her leading man. Ethel Waters costars in this spoof of wartime spy melodramas. Robert Young provides the obligatory romantic interest, but the chief highlight is the music. B&W; 101m. DIR: W. S. Van Dyke. CAST: Jeanette MacDonald, Ethel Waters, Robert Young, Dooley Wilson, Reginald Owen. 1942

CAL ★★★★ Superb Irish film, which focuses on "the troubles" in Northern Ireland, stars John Lynch as Cal, a teenage boy who wants to sever his ties with the IRA. Cal tries to be anything but easy, as the leader tells him, if he isn't for them, he's against them. Cal hides out at the home of Marcella (Helen Mirren, in a knockout of a performance). She's the widow of a policeman he helped murder. Nevertheless, they fall in love. Rated R for sex, nudity, profanity, and violence. 102m. DIR: Pat O'Connor. CAST: Helen Mirren, John Lynch, Donal McCann. 1984

CALAMITY JANE (1953) ★★★ A legend of the Old West set to music for Doris Day, who mends her rootin', tootin' ways in order to lasso Howard Keel. The song "Secret Love" copped an Oscar. Cute 'n' perky. 101m. DIR: David Butler. CAST: Doris Day, Howard Keel, Allyn Ann McLerie, Philip Carey. 1953

CALAMITY JANE (1984) ★★★★ Director James Goldstone provides more than just the story of Calamity Jane, which is fascinating in itself as a tale of one of America's early feminists. His unglamorous production and straightforward storytelling give a true feeling of the Old West. Jane Alexander, in an Emmy-nominated performance, shows the many sides of this spirited lady. A made-for-TV movie. 100m. DIR: James Goldstone. CAST: Jane Alexander, Frederic Forrest, David Hemmings, Ken Kercheval, Talia Balsam. 1984

CALENDAR GIRL ★★ Three teenage Nevada boys head for Hollywood to meet Marilyn Monroe. Clearly intended as both a tribute to Monroe and a warm memoir of adolescence, the film fails on both counts as it swings between dumb slapstick and even dumber sentimentality. Anyone old enough to remember Monroe is too old to fall for this. Rated PG-13 for mild profanity. 90m. DIR: John Whitesell. CAST: Jason Priestley, Gabriel Olds, Jerry O'Connell. 1993

CALIFORNIA CASANOVA ★★ Tyrone Power Jr. is delightful as a bumbling nerd who is transformed by a charming count. Best scenes: when Power receives advice from a number of sources on how to be irresistible. Rated R for nudity and profanity. 94m. DIR: Nathaniel Christian. CAST: Jerry Orbach, Audrey Landers, Tyrone Power. 1991

CALIFORNIA DREAMING ★★ Wimpy film about a dork from Chicago trying to fit into the California lifestyle. The cast is good, but the story is maudlin and slow-moving. Rated R for partial nudity. 93m. DIR: John Hancock. CAST: Glynnis O'Connor, Seymour Cassel, Dennis Christopher, Tanya Roberts. 1979

CALIFORNIA GOLD RUSH ★★ The writer Bret Harte (Robert Hays) is in the right place at the right time to chronicle the gold rush days of California from Sutter's Fort. Rated PG. 100m. DIR: Jack B. Hively. CAST: Robert Hays, John Dehner, Ken Curtis, Henry Jones, Dan Haggerty. 1985

CALIFORNIA SUITE ★★★1/2 This enjoyable adaptation of the Neil Simon play features multiple stars. The action revolves around the various inhabitants of a Beverly Hills hotel room. We are allowed to enter and observe the private lives of the various guests in the room during the four watchable short stories within this film. Rated PG. 103m. DIR: Herbert Ross. CAST: Jane Fonda, Alan Alda, Maggie Smith, Richard Pryor, Bill Cosby. 1978

CALIGULA ❤ A $15 million porno flick with big stars. Rated X for every excess imaginable. 156m. DIR: Tinto Brass. CAST: Malcolm McDowell, Peter O'Toole, Teresa Ann Savoy, Helen Mirren. 1980 DVD

CALIGULA, THE UNTOLD STORY ❤ Cheesy English-dubbed Italian movie is even worse than the big-budget *Caligula* that it tries to rip off. Not rated; contains nudity and violence. 90m. DIR: David Hills. CAST: David Haughton, Laura Gemser. 1988

CALL HER SAVAGE ★★ Clara Bow no longer had "it" by the time she attempted to make a comeback in this ludicrous melodrama. She plays a half-white, half-native girl who tries to fit into proper society. B&W; 80m. DIR: John Francis Dillon. CAST: Clara Bow, Monroe Owsley, Gilbert Roland, Thelma Todd. 1932

CALL ME ★★ In this silly suspense-thriller, a New York newspaper columnist (Patricia Charbonneau) mistakenly believes an obscene phone caller to be her boyfriend and soon finds herself involved with murder and mobsters. Rated R for violence, profanity, nudity, and simulated sex. 96m. DIR: Sollace Mitchell. CAST: Patricia Charbonneau, Patti D'Arbanville, Sam Freed, Boyd Gaines, Stephen McHattie, Steve Buscemi. 1988

CALL ME BWANA ★★1/2 A bogus writer of safari books sent to Africa to locate a downed space capsule encounters Russian agents. Too few one-liners by the past master. 103m. DIR: Gordon Douglas. CAST: Bob Hope, Anita Ekberg, Edie Adams, Lionel Jefferies. 1963

CALL NORTHSIDE 777 ★★★★ A Chicago reporter digs into the 11-year-old murder of a policeman and the life sentence of a possibly innocent man. Based on fact. Outstanding on-location filming. Also released as *Calling Northside 777*. B&W; 111m. **DIR:** Henry Hathaway. **CAST:** James Stewart, Richard Conte, Lee J. Cobb, Helen Walker, Betty Garde, Howard Smith, John McIntire, Paul Harvey. 1948

CALL OF THE PRAIRIE ★★1/2 The Bar-20s Johnny Nelson has gotten too chummy with the wrong crowd. Hoppy, away selling cattle, returns to clean out the vermin. B&W; **DIR:** Howard Bretherton. **CAST:** William Boyd, James Ellison, George "Gabby" Hayes, Muriel Evans, Chester Conklin, Hank Mann, Al Bridges. 1936

CALL OF THE WILD (1972) ★★★1/2 Charlton Heston stars in this adaptation of Jack London's famous novel. A domesticated dog is stolen and forced to pull a snow sled in Alaska as John (Charlton Heston) searches for gold. Some profanity and violence. Rated PG. 100m. **DIR:** Ken Annakin. **CAST:** Charlton Heston, Michele Mercier, Maria Rohm, Rik Battaglia. 1972

CALL OF THE WILD (1992) ★★★ Fairly loyal to Jack London's best-selling novel, this drama focuses on the many changes a domesticated dog must undergo after being stolen for arctic sledding. Rick Schroder is the only human to show him genuine kindness after his ordeal begins. High production values and authentic location shots are a plus. Not rated, contains simulated animal abuse. 97m. **DIR:** Alan Smithee. **CAST:** Rick Schroder, Gordon Tootoosis, Duncan Fraser, Mia Sara. 1992

CALL OF THE WILD: THE DOG OF THE YUKON ★★★★ Rousing *Hallmark Hall of Fame* adaptation of Jack London's wilderness adventure stars Rutger Hauer as the miner who inherits Buck, a wild dog who becomes his best friend. The bond is sealed when they save each other, but Buck is forced to decide whether to stay with Thornton or return to the wild. Outstanding production values and stirring narration by Richard Dreyfuss complement this handsome production. Rated PG. 91m. **DIR:** Peter Svatek. **CAST:** Rutger Hauer, Bronwen Booth, Charles Powell, John Novak. 1996

CALL OUT THE MARINES ★★1/2 The prime attraction here is the team of Victor McLaglen and Edmund Lowe in their last comedy together. As always, they play a pair of battling marine buddies, this time engaged in a rivalry over saloon singer Binnie Barnes. Several songs (by Mort Greene and Harry Revel) are no great shakes. 66m. **DIR:** Frank Ryan. **CAST:** Victor McLaglen, Edmund Lowe, Binnie Barnes, Paul Kelly, Robert Smith, Franklin Pangborn. 1942

CALL TO GLORY ★★★1/2 Engrossing pilot episode for a short-lived TV series. Set in the early 1960s, it follows an air force officer's family through the events of the Kennedy presidency. The taut script ably balances the story of their struggle to deal with military life and still retains the flavor of a historical chronicle of the times. This uniformly well-acted and -directed opening show promised much quality that was unfortunately unfulfilled in later episodes. 97m. **DIR:** Thomas Carter. **CAST:** Craig T. Nelson, Cindy Pickett, Keenan Wynn, Elisabeth Shue, David Hollander. 1984

CALL TO REMEMBER, A ★★★★ Poignant drama about a Holocaust survivor who receives a call that one of her children—who she thought was killed in Nazi Germany—may be alive. The complexity of her family's past and present lives threatens to overwhelm them all. Rated R for profanity. 111m. **DIR:** Jack Bender. **CAST:** Blythe Danner, Joe Mantegna, David Lascher. 1997

CALLER, THE ★ Sci-fi thriller about a man and a woman playing a cat-and-mouse game of mind trips. Rated R for violence and profanity. 97m. **DIR:** Arthur Allan Seidelman. **CAST:** Malcolm McDowell, Madolyn Smith. 1987

CALLIE AND SON ★★1/2 Syrupy drama about a poor waitress who becomes the queen of a Texas publishing empire. On the way, she is reunited with her long-lost son. Sometimes halfway engrossing; sometimes really disturbing. 150m. **DIR:** Waris Hussein. **CAST:** Lindsay Wagner, Jameson Parker, Dabney Coleman, Andrew Prine, Michelle Pfeiffer, James Sloyan. 1981 DVD

CALLING DR. DEATH ★★1/2 The first in a series of six B features inspired by the then-popular *Inner Sanctum* radio series, each featuring Lon Chaney Jr. as a man who may or may not be guilty of a crime. Here he's a neurologist suspected of murdering his cheating wife. B&W; 62m. **DIR:** Reginald LeBorg. **CAST:** Lon Chaney Jr., Patricia Morison, J. Carrol Naish, David Bruce. 1943

CALLING WILD BILL ELLIOTT ★★1/2 In his first assignment in an A picture for Republic Studios, Wild Bill Elliott pals up with Gabby Hayes to fight off evil robbers harassing the lovely Anne Jeffreys. Gabby Hayes is supposed to be a funny sidekick, but here he is more of an anvil around the neck. Average. B&W; 78m. **DIR:** Spencer Gordon Bennet. **CAST:** William Elliott, Anne Jeffreys, George "Gabby" Hayes. 1943

CALM AT SUNSET ★★★★ Powerful study of a father-son relationship stars Michael Moriarty as the father who makes every attempt to steer his son away from the fishing business. When the son disregards and signs up on another boat, he sets the stage for a confrontation that eventually brings the family together. Excellent performances and an intelligent script make this *Hallmark Hall of Fame* production a winner. Rated PG. 98m. **DIR:** Daniel Petrie. **CAST:** Michael Moriarty, Peter Facinelli, Kevin Conway, Melvin Van Peebles, Christopher Orr, Kate Nelligan. 1996

CALTIKI, THE IMMORTAL MONSTER ★★ Explorers find an ancient bloblike monster living under a Mayan temple. They kill it but bring a sample back to the city, where it starts to regenerate and grow. Although cut for United States release and atrociously dubbed, this Italian monster movie isn't half bad thanks to atmospheric photography by future horror director Mario Bava (who also directed some of the film). B&W; 76m. **DIR:** Robert Hampton (Riccardo Freda). **CAST:** John Merivale, Didi Sullivan, Gerard Herter. 1959

CAME A HOT FRIDAY ★★ Mildly amusing film set in 1949 New Zealand, where two con men make their rtune cheating bookmakers all across the country. ated PG for language and adult situations. 101m. R: Ian Mune. CAST: Peter Bland, Philip Gordon, Billy James, Michael Lawrence. 1985

AMELOT ★★★ The legend of King Arthur and the ound Table—from the first meeting of Arthur Richard Harris) and Guinevere (Vanessa Redgrave) the affair between Guinevere and Lancelot (Fran- Nero), and finally the fall of Camelot—is brought life in this enjoyable musical. 178m. DIR: Joshua gan. CAST: Richard Harris, Vanessa Redgrave, Fran- Nero, David Hemmings, Lionel Jeffries. 1967 DVD

AMERAMAN, THE ★★★★ This silent casts uster Keaton as a freelance news cameraman try- g desperately to impress a girl and earn his spurs ith a scoop. He finally gets in the thick of a Chinese ng war, filming his way to success in a hail of bul- ts. A superb example of Keaton comedy genius. lent. B&W; 70m. DIR: Edward Sedgwick. CAST: uster Keaton, Marceline Day, Edward Brophy. 1928

AMERON'S CLOSET ★★★ A young boy with psy- nic powers unwittingly unleashes a demon in his oset. The above-par special effects, by Oscar win- er Carlo Rambaldi (*E.T.* and *Alien*), and an ever- owing tension makes this a neat little supernatu- thriller. Not rated; contains violence. 90m. DIR: Ar- and Mastroianni. CAST: Cotter Smith, Mel Harris, Tab unter, Chuck McCann, Leigh McCloskey. 1989

AMILA (1984) ★★★1/2 A romantic and true story f forbidden love in the classic tradition. Susu Peco- aro is Camila O'Gorman, the daughter of a wealthy ristocrat in Buenos Aires in the mid-1800s. Imanol rias plays Ladislao Gutierrez, a Jesuit priest. In panish with English subtitles. Not rated, but with ex, nudity, and violence. 105m. DIR: Maria Luisa emberg. CAST: Susu Pecoraro, Imanol Arias, Hector tterio, Mona Maris. 1984

AMILLA (1994) ★★1/2 A female bonding/road icture. Jessica Tandy is an eccentric retired violin- t who heads for Toronto with her tenant, composer ridget Fonda. The characters are fun, but their sit- ation is implausible and the script too cutesy. Rated G-13 for profanity and brief nudity. 101m. DIR: eepa Mehta. CAST: Jessica Tandy, Bridget Fonda, ias Koteas, Maury Chaykin, Hume Cronyn. 1994

AMILLE ★★★★ Metro-Goldwyn-Mayer's lavish roduction of the Dumas classic provided screen oddess Greta Garbo with one of her last unqualified ccesses and remains the consummate adaptation f this popular weeper. The combined magic of the tudio and Garbo's presence legitimized this archaic reaker about a dying woman and her love affair with younger man (Robert Taylor, soon to be one of IGM's biggest stars). B&W; 108m. DIR: George ukor. CAST: Greta Garbo, Robert Taylor, Lionel Barry- nore, Henry Daniell, Laura Hope Crews, Elizabeth Al- an, Lenore Ulric, Jessie Ralph. 1936

AMILLE CLAUDEL ★★★★ Poignant, romantic ragedy based on the life of sculptor Camille Claudel. sabelle Adjani gives an emotion-charged perfor- nance as the 21-year-old artist who becomes roman- ically involved with the great French sculptor Au- uste Rodin in Paris during the late 1800s. In French ith English subtitles. Not rated; contains nudity

and is recommended for adults. 149m. DIR: Bruno Nuytten. CAST: Isabelle Adjani, Gérard Depardieu, Lau- rent Grevill, Alain Cuny. 1990

CAMORRA ★★ Lina Wertmuller lacks her usual bite in this well-intentioned but conventional crime story. The movie details the efforts of an ex-prosti- tute to band the women of Naples together against the mobsters. Rated R for violence and sexual situa- tions. 115m. DIR: Lina Wertmuller. CAST: Angela Moli- na, Francisco Rabal, Harvey Keitel. 1986

CAMOUFLAGE ★★★★ Biting satire of Polish intel- lectuals focuses on a middle-aged professor and his callow young colleague. While much of the sting will be lost on non-Polish-speaking audiences, the hu- mor comes across well. In Polish with English subti- tles. Not rated; B&W; 106m. DIR: Krzysztof Zanussi. CAST: Zbigniew Zapasiewicz, Piotr Garlicki. 1977

CAMP NOWHERE ★★1/2 Affluent teens rent their own summer hideaway to get away from the night- marish theme camps (such as Camp Broadway and Camp Micro Chippewa) offered by their parents in this mild, disposable romp. There are no adults, no counselors, and no rules. But the folks at home push for a Parents' Day that nearly drags the kids' secret out of the woods. Rated PG. 94m. DIR: Jonathan Price. CAST: Jonathan Jackson, Christopher Lloyd, M. Emmet Walsh, Wendy Makkena. 1994

CAMPUS MAN ★★ In this well-intended and gener- ally watchable movie, a college student (John Dye) produces an all-male pinup calendar and strikes it rich. Rated PG. 95m. DIR: Ron Casden. CAST: John Dye, Kim Delaney, Kathleen Wilhoite, Steve Lyon, Mor- gan Fairchild, Miles O'Keeffe. 1987

CAN IT BE LOVE ❤ Run-of-the-mill teen sex comedy about two horny guys looking to do something about it. Dreadful. Rated R for nudity and language. 90m. DIR: Peter Maris. CAST: Charles Klausmeyer, Richard Beaumont. 1992

CAN SHE BAKE A CHERRY PIE? ★★★ Karen Black plays a woman whose husband leaves her before she has fully awakened one morning. She meets Eli, played by Michael Emil, a balding character actor whose body is slowly sliding into his knees. This is a small film, and its appeal is quiet. It also is an exam- ple of what can be right with American movie-mak- ing, even when the money isn't there. No rating, but considerable vulgar language, sexual situations. 90m. DIR: Henry Jaglom. CAST: Karen Black, Michael Emil. 1984

CAN YOU HEAR THE LAUGHTER? THE STORY OF FREDDIE PRINZE ★★1/2 Freddie Prinze was a Puerto Rican comedian who rose from the barrio to television stardom in a relatively brief time. His pre- mier achievement was a starring role in *Chico and the Man*, with Jack Albertson. Sympathetic, but no punches are pulled on the facts surrounding his death. 106m. DIR: Burt Brinckerhoff. CAST: Ira Angus- tain, Kevin Hooks, Randee Heller, Julie Carmen. 1979

CANADIAN BACON ★★ What begins as a funny and savvy political comedy quickly dissolves into the kind of sophomoric drivel writer-director Michael Moore would normally lampoon. Neither Moore's script nor his direction keeps up the pace as Ameri- ca tries to improve the national economy by waging war on Canada. Unfortunately, there is nothing special about John Candy's final performance. Rated PG for profanity. 95m. DIR: Michael Moore. CAST: John Candy, Rhea Perlman, Kevin Pollak, Bill Nunn, Rip Torn, Alan Alda, Dan Aykroyd. **1995**

CAN'T HARDLY WAIT ★★★ Well-crafted teen party movie that has amusingly torn away the facades of typical characters and replaced them with more natural personas over the course of one really bitchin' graduation party. The film has an appropriate woozy look, fine pacing, and a good sense of humor. Rated PG-13 for substance abuse, sex, and language. 96m. DIR: Deborah Kaplan, Harry Elfont. CAST: Jennifer Love Hewitt, Ethan Embry, Seth Green, Lauren Ambrose, Peter Facinelli, Charlie Korsmo, Jenna Elfman. **1998**

CAN-CAN ★★★ Frank Sinatra plays an 1890s French attorney defending Shirley MacLaine's right to perform the risqué cancan in a Parisian nightclub. The stars appear, at times, to be walking through their roles. Cole Porter songs include "I Love Paris," "C'est Magnifique" and the wonderful "Just One of Those Things." 131m. DIR: Walter Lang. CAST: Shirley MacLaine, Frank Sinatra, Maurice Chevalier, Juliet Prowse, Louis Jourdan. **1960**

CANCEL MY RESERVATION ★★ Tired reworking of a Bob Hope formula comedy is slow going despite a pretty good cast and a plot lifted from a Louis L'Amour novel. Hope plays a popular TV show host who heads to Arizona for a rest and gets mixed up with crooks. Highlight of the film is a nightmare sequence with cameos of celebrities including John Wayne and Bing Crosby. 99m. DIR: Paul Bogart. CAST: Bob Hope, Eva Marie Saint, Ralph Bellamy, Forrest Tucker, Anne Archer, Keenan Wynn, Chief Dan George. **1972**

CANDIDATE, THE ★★★1/2 Michael Ritchie expertly directed this incisive look at a political hopeful (Robert Redford) and the obstacles and truths he must confront on the campaign trail. Rated PG. 109m. DIR: Michael Ritchie. CAST: Robert Redford, Peter Boyle, Don Porter, Allen Garfield. **1972** DVD

CANDIDE ★★★ Voltaire's classic tale of the wanderer trying to see the best in everything is updated to the World War II era with mixed results. Clever, but more talky than funny despite a top-flight French cast. Dubbed in English. B&W; 93m. DIR: Norbert Carbonnaux. CAST: Jean-Pierre Cassel, Daliah Lavi, Pierre Brasseur, Michel Simon, Jean Richard, Louis de Funes. **1960**

CANDLES AT NINE ★★ Old-dark-house mystery about a young woman who inherits a fortune from a great-uncle she hardly knew, with the stipulation that she has to spend a month living in his gloomy mansion. Musical star Jessie Matthews was the draw for this British film that is competently made but unexceptional. B&W; 84m. DIR: John Harlow. CAST: Jessie Matthews, John Stuart, Beatrix Lehmann. **1944**

CANDLESHOE ★★1/2 Confused Disney comedy about a street kid (Jodie Foster) duped by shady Leo McKern into posing as an heir to Helen Hayes. Marred by typically excessive Disney physical "humor" (read: slapstick). Rated G. 101m. DIR: Norman

Tokar. CAST: David Niven, Helen Hayes, Jodie Fost Leo McKern, Vivian Pickles. **1977** DVD

CANDY MOUNTAIN ★★★★ Mediocre musici (Kevin J. O'Connor) takes to the highway in sear of legendary guitar craftsman Elmore Silk. Celebra ed photographer and underground filmmak Robert Frank joins screenwriter Rudy Wurlitzer create an engaging, offbeat, visually beautiful fil Rated R for nudity and profanity. 90m. DIR: Robe Frank, Rudy Wurlitzer. CAST: Kevin J. O'Connor, Har Yulin, Tom Waits, Bulle Ogier, David Johansen, Le Redbone, Joe Strummer, Dr. John. **1987**

CANDYMAN, THE (1968) 🦃 English drug peddl in Mexico City plots to kidnap the child of an Ame can movie star. 98m. DIR: Herbert J. Leder. CAS George Sanders, Leslie Parrish. **1968**

CANDYMAN (1992) ★★★★ A very scary flick s in the slums of Chicago, it concerns a mythical hoo handed killer who can be called forth by looking i mirror and chanting his name five times. Virgin Madsen researches the Candyman's story and fin out he is all too real. Rated R for violence, profan and nudity. 101m. DIR: Bernard Rose. CAST: Virgin Madsen, Tony Todd, Xander Berkeley, Kasi Lemmor Vanessa L. Williams, Michael Culkin. **1992** DVD

CANDYMAN: FAREWELL TO THE FLESH ★★ Mu dered slave turned artist returns from the dead prey upon the denizens of modern New Orleans. Th gruesome sequel flashes back to the slave's allege "crime" against a plantation owner and his horrif dispatch by a frenzied mob. Rated R for violenc gore, and language. 94m. DIR: Bill Condon. CAS Tony Todd, Kelly Rowan, Veronica Cartwright, Timot Carhart. **1995**

●**CANDYMAN 3: DAY OF THE DEAD** ★★ In this, th obligatory third installment of the series, the Cand man returns from the grave to wreak vengean upon those who have uttered his name five tim while gazing into a reflective surface. Donna D'Err co of *Baywatch* fame plays the femme fatale and d scendant of the original Candyman. It is up to her send the Candyman back to hell for him to wait un Candyman 4 comes along. This film has an occasio ally entertaining murder scene but mostly it's just waste of time. Rated R for grisly murders and tidbi of other questionable material. 93m. DIR: Turi Mey CAST: Tony Todd, Donna D'Errico, Nick Corri, Alex Robinson, Lupe Ontiveros. **1999** DVD

CANNERY ROW ★★★ It's hard to dislike th film, starring Nick Nolte and Debra Winger. Despi its artificiality, halting pace, and general uneve ness, there are so many marvelous moments—mo provided by Frank McRae as the lovable simpl ton Hazel—that you don't regret having seen it. Ra ed PG for slight nudity, profanity, and violenc 120m. DIR: David S. Ward. CAST: Nick Nolte, Deb Winger, Audra Lindley, M. Emmet Walsh, Frank McRa **1982**

CANNIBAL 🦃 Originally titled *The Last Surviv* this stomach churner is among the first (and wors Italian exploitation potboilers about safaris that ru afoul of Amazon cannibals. Rated R. 90m. DIR: Rug gero Deodato. CAST: Massimo Foschi, Me Me Lai, Ivan Rassimov. **1976**

ANNIBAL HOLOCAUST ★★ An expedition follows previous safari of filmmakers into the Amazon. hey find some film cans near a village and view the orrific contents in New York. The farthest reaches f exploitation are explored in this most extreme— ad disturbing—entry in the late-Seventies canni- al movie subgenre, directed by the field's pioneer uteur. Not rated, but with graphic violence. 95m. **IR:** Ruggero Deodato. **CAST:** Francesca Ciardi, Luca arbareschi, Robert Kerman. **1979**

ANNIBAL! THE MUSICAL 🦃 The title is about as ntertaining as this typical Troma turkey gets. Rated for gruesome violence. 105m. **DIR:** Trey Parker. **AST:** Ian Hardin, Jason McHugh. **1995 DVD**

ANNIBAL WOMEN IN THE AVOCADO JUNGLE OF EATH ★★1/2 *Playboy* playmate Shannon Tweed ars in this comedic adventure about a feminist an- ropologist in search of the infamous cannibal omen, a group of ultraleft feminists who eat their ates. Some great sight gags, with most of the funny its belonging to semimacho guide Bill Maher. Rated G-13 for nudity. 90m. **DIR:** J. D. Athens. **CAST:** Shan- on Tweed, Adrienne Barbeau, Bill Maher, Barry rimus. **1988 DVD**

ANNONBALL ★★ David Carradine plays an un- leasant antihero out to beat the rest of the cast in n exotic race. Rated R for violence. 93m. **DIR:** Paul artel. **CAST:** David Carradine, Veronica Hamel, Gerrit raham, Sylvester Stallone, Robert Carradine, Carl ottlieb, Belinda Balaski. **1976**

ANNONBALL RUN 🦃 This star-studded bore is the tory of an unsanctioned, totally illegal cross-coun- y car race in which there are no rules and few sur- ivors. Rated PG for profanity. 95m. **DIR:** Hal Need- am. **CAST:** Burt Reynolds, Roger Moore, Farrah Faw- ett, Dom DeLuise, Dean Martin, Sammy Davis Jr. **981**

ANNONBALL RUN II 🦃 Awful rehash of *Cannon- all Run*. Rated PG. 108m. **DIR:** Hal Needham. **CAST:** urt Reynolds, Dom DeLuise, Shirley MacLaine, Marilu enner, Telly Savalas, Dean Martin, Sammy Davis Jr., rank Sinatra. **1984 DVD**

AN'T BUY ME LOVE ★★ The title song is the Bea- les' classic tune. Unfortunately, this film is all down- ill from there. Patrick Dempsey plays a nerd who arns that popularity isn't all it's cracked up to be. he message is delivered in heavy-handed style. till, teens will love it. Rated PG-13 for profanity. 4m. **DIR:** Steve Rash. **CAST:** Amanda Peterson, atrick Dempsey, Courtney Gains, Tina Caspary, Seth reen, Sharon Farrell, Dennis Dugan, Ami Dolenz, teve Franken. **1987**

AN'T HELP SINGING ★★★★1/2 A spirited West- rn with music by Jerome Kern, this is the only Tech- icolor film Deanna Durbin made. Songs include the tle number, "Californi-yay," "More and More," and Swing Your Sweetheart." All told, a delight. 89m. **IR:** Frank Ryan. **CAST:** Deanna Durbin, Robert Paige, kim Tamiroff, David Bruce, June Vincent, Clara Bland- k, Ray Collins, Leonid Kinskey. **1944**

AN'T STOP THE MUSIC 🦃 Despite the title, the usic of the Village People was stopped cold by this asically awful musical about show biz. Rated PG. 18m. **DIR:** Nancy Walker. **CAST:** The Village People, Valerie Perrine, Bruce Jenner, Steve Guttenberg, Paul Sand, Tammy Grimes, June Havoc, Jack Weston, Barbara Rush, Leigh Taylor-Young. **1980**

CANTERBURY TALES, THE ★★★1/2 Four of Chaucer's stories are adapted by Pier Paolo Pasolini in his inimitable style—gleefully offensive satire, with the Church the first of many targets. Not for the genteel. Rated X for nudity and simulated sex. 109m. **DIR:** Pier Paolo Pasolini. **CAST:** Hugh Griffith, Laura Betti, Tom Baker, Josephine Chaplin, Pier Paolo Pasolini. **1971**

CANTERVILLE GHOST, THE (1944) ★★★ It's a battle of two of filmdom's most notorious scene stealers: Charles Laughton as a 300-year-old ghost and oh-so-cute pigtailed little Margaret O'Brien. The fantasy tale of American soldiers in a haunted English castle during World War II takes second place to these two scenery munchers. B&W; 92m. **DIR:** Jules Dassin. **CAST:** Charles Laughton, Robert Young, Margaret O'Brien, William Gargan, Reginald Owen. **1944**

CANTERVILLE GHOST, THE (1986) ★★★ Modern retelling of the classic Oscar Wilde short story, with John Gielgud as the blowhard ghost who tries to terrorize a spunky American family. Gielgud is excellent as the ghost, but Ted Wass is highly unsatisfactory as the father, and the ghostly shenanigans have a dangerous quality about them that was not present in the original. Not rated; suitable for older children. 96m. **DIR:** Paul Bogart. **CAST:** John Gielgud, Ted Wass, Andrea Marcovicci, Alyssa Milano, Harold Innocent, Lila Kaye. **1986**

CANVAS ★★1/2 Artist turns to a life of crime to make good on a deal his brother had with the mob. Pedestrian but watchable. Rated R for language and violence. 94m. **DIR:** Alain Zaloum. **CAST:** Gary Busey, John Rhys-Davies, Cary Lawrence. **1992**

CAPE FEAR (1962) ★★★★ Great cast in a riveting tale of a lawyer (Gregory Peck) and his family menaced by a vengeful ex-con (Robert Mitchum), who Peck helped to send up the river eight years earlier. Now he's out, with big plans for Peck's wife and especially his daughter. B&W; 106m. **DIR:** J. Lee Thompson. **CAST:** Gregory Peck, Polly Bergen, Robert Mitchum, Lori Martin, Martin Balsam, Telly Savalas, Jack Kruschen. **1962**

CAPE FEAR (1991) ★★ A profound disappointment from Martin Scorsese, this remake of J. Lee Thompson's suspense classic seems to have everything going for it: a great cast, a story by John D. MacDonald, and even cameos by stars of the original. But somehow it all boils down to Robert De Niro doing an impression of Freddy Krueger from *A Nightmare on Elm Street*. Rated R for violence and profanity. 130m. **DIR:** Martin Scorsese. **CAST:** Robert De Niro, Nick Nolte, Jessica Lange, Joe Don Baker, Robert Mitchum, Gregory Peck, Juliette Lewis, Martin Balsam, Illeana Douglas, Fred Dalton Thompson. **1991**

CAPER OF THE GOLDEN BULLS, THE 🦃 Stephen Boyd plays a wealthy American who is blackmailed into robbing the Royal Bank of Spain. Not rated, has some violence. 106m. **DIR:** Russell Rouse. **CAST:** Stephen Boyd, Yvette Mimieux, Giovanna Ralli, Vito Scotti, J. G. Devlin, Arnold Moss, Walter Slezak. **1966**

•**CAPITOL CONSPIRACY, THE** ★★1/2 Don "The Dragon" Wilson stars as a government agent who, as a child, was part of a program to instill clairvoyant abilities. Now someone is trying to kill everyone associated with that program. Silly plot made bearable by Wilson's martial artistry and a rare appearance by horror icon Barbara Steele. Also known as *The Prophet.* Rated R for violence and nudity. 83m. **DIR:** Fred Olen Ray. **CAST:** Don "The Dragon" Wilson, Barbara Steele, Wendy Schumacher, Paul Michael Robinson. **1999 DVD**

CAPONE ★★ Made-for-TV gangster effort brings nothing new to the formula. Behind bars for tax evasion, notorious mobster Al Capone still manages to run Chicago. It's up to FBI agent Keith Carradine to put an end to Capone's reign of terror. Additional footage added for video. Rated R for violence and nudity. 97m. **DIR:** Michael Pressman. **CAST:** Keith Carradine, Ray Sharkey, Debrah Farentino, Charles Haid. **1989 DVD**

CAPRICORN ONE ★★★★ In this suspenseful release, the government stages a mock flight to Mars in a television studio, with astronauts James Brolin, Sam Waterston, and O. J. Simpson pretending to be in outer space and landing on the planet. Then the news is released by the Pentagon that the ship crashed upon reentry and all aboard were killed, which puts the lives of the astronauts in danger. Rated PG. 124m. **DIR:** Peter Hyams. **CAST:** Elliott Gould, James Brolin, Hal Holbrook, Sam Waterston, Karen Black, O. J. Simpson, Telly Savalas. **1978 DVD**

CAPTAIN AMERICA (1944) ★★★ Joe Simon and Jack Kirby's comic-book character is brought to movie life to tangle with the fiendishly refined Lionel Atwill, who has not only a destructive ray machine but a machine capable of bringing dead animals back to life! Two-fisted District Attorney Dick Purcell manfully pursues Atwill. B&W; 15 chapters. **DIR:** John English, Elmer Clifton. **CAST:** Dick Purcell, Lorna Gray, Lionel Atwill, Charles Trowbridge, Russell Hicks, John Davidson, Frank Reicher, Hugh Sothern. **1944**

CAPTAIN AMERICA (1979) ★★ A criminal genius plots to extort millions from the government with a stolen nuclear device. Of course the only man who can stop him is the star-spangled avenger. This is average TV fare with a disappointingly simple plot. Not rated, but suitable for all viewers. 90m. **DIR:** Rod Holcomb. **CAST:** Reb Brown, Len Birman, Heather Menzies, Steve Forrest. **1979**

CAPTAIN AMERICA (1990) ❤ The golden-age comic-book character tries to make the leap to the big screen with disastrous results. In 1941, America's supersoldier is defeated by the Red Skull, and accidentally thrown into suspended animation. Fifty years later, he awakens in time to foil a scheme by his old enemy. Rated PG-13 for violence and profanity. 104m. **DIR:** Albert Pyun. **CAST:** Matt Salinger, Ronny Cox, Ned Beatty, Darren McGavin, Melinda Dillon, Scott Paulin. **1990**

CAPTAIN AMERICA II: DEATH TOO SOON ❤ Ridiculous made-for-television adventure of the comic-book hero. Plodding. 100m. **DIR:** Ivan Nagy.

CAST: Reb Brown, Christopher Lee, Connie Sellecc[...] Len Birman. **1979**

CAPTAIN APACHE ★★ Muddled Western has Le[...] Van Cleef in title role gunning down dozens of one-d[...] mensional characters who cross his path or appe[...] likely to. Rated PG for violence. 94m. **DIR:** Alexand[...] Singer. **CAST:** Lee Van Cleef, Stuart Whitman, Carr[...] Baker, Percy Herbert. **1971**

CAPTAIN BLOOD ★★★1/2 Errol Flynn's youthf[...] enthusiasm, great character actors, realistic mini[...] ture work, and Erich Wolfgang Korngold's score a[...] meld together under Michael Curtiz's direction an[...] provide audiences with perhaps the best pirate fil[...] of all time. B&W; 95m. **DIR:** Michael Curtiz. **CAST:** E[...] rol Flynn, Olivia de Havilland, Basil Rathbone, Lion[...] Atwill, Ross Alexander, Guy Kibbee, Henry Stephe[...] son. **1935**

CAPTAIN CAUTION ★★1/2 In command of a sh[...] during the War of 1812 with England, Victor Matur[...] in the title role, is taken for a coward when he urge[...] prudence. Richard Wallace's fast-paced, cannon-be[...] lowing direction quells all restlessness, howeve[...] B&W; 85m. **DIR:** Richard Wallace. **CAST:** Victor Ma[...] ture, Louise Platt, Bruce Cabot, Leo Carrillo, Vivien[...] Osborne, El Brendel, Robert Barrat, Miles Mande[...] Roscoe Ates. **1940**

CAPTAIN HORATIO HORNBLOWER ★★★★ An e[...] joyable adventure film that is faithful to the C. [...] Forester novels and to the reputation of the rugge[...] British seacoast where it was filmed. Gregory Peck[...] wooden acting style serves the character well, an[...] he warms up when Virginia Mayo's Lady Wellesle[...] becomes an unwanted passenger aboard his shi[...] 117m. **DIR:** Raoul Walsh. **CAST:** Gregory Peck, Virgin[...] Mayo, Dennis O'Dea, James Robertson Justice, Robe[...] Beatty. **1951**

CAPTAIN JANUARY ★★★ Orphan Shirley Temp[...] is taken in by a lonely lighthouse keeper (Gu[...] Kibbee). The incredible dance number featurin[...] Shirley and a local fisherman (Buddy Ebsen) [...] worth the price of the rental. B&W; 75m. **DIR:** Dav[...] Butler. **CAST:** Shirley Temple, Guy Kibbee, Buddy E[...] sen, Jane Darwell. **1936**

CAPTAIN KIDD ★★ Not even Charles Laughtor[...] mugging and posturing can redeem this swashbuc[...] ling yarn about the pirate whose treasure is still be[...] ing sought. 89m. **DIR:** Rowland V. Lee. **CAST:** Charle[...] Laughton, Randolph Scott, Reginald Owen, John Ca[...] radine, Sheldon Leonard, Barbara Britton, Gilbe[...] Roland. **1945**

CAPTAIN KRONOS: VAMPIRE HUNTER ★★★1/[...] British film directed by the producer of *Th[...] Avengers* television show. It's an unconventiona[...] horror tale about a sword-wielding vampire killer. A[...] interesting mix of genres. Good adventure, with hig[...] production values. Rated PG for violence. 91m. **DIF** Brian Clemens. **CAST:** Horst Janson, John David Ca[...] son, Caroline Munro, Shane Briant. **1974**

CAPTAIN NEWMAN, M.D. ★★★ The movie fluctu[...] ates between meaningful laughter and heavy drama[...] An excellent ensemble neatly maintains the ba[...] ance. Gregory Peck is at his noble best as a sympa[...] thetic army psychiatrist. The film's most grippin[...] performance comes from Bobby Darin, who plays sychotic. 126m. DIR: David Miller. CAST: Gregory eck, Angie Dickinson, Tony Curtis, Eddie Albert, Jane ithers, Bobby Darin, Larry Storch. 1963

APTAIN NUKE AND THE BOMBER BOYS ★★★ mior-high fantasy about three youths who ditch hool in order to avoid punishment. They hide out a burnt-out pizza parlor, where they discover what oks like a nuclear bomb. When they send a picture the device to the FBI for confirmation, they are egged as terrorists, and the chase begins. Rated G-13 for language. 90m. DIR: Charles Gale. CAST: pe Mantegna, Joanna Pacula, Joe Piscopo, Martin neen, Rod Steiger, Ryan Thomas Johnson. 1995

APTAIN RON ★★★ A lighthearted comedy about Chicago businessman (Martin Short) who inherits is uncle's yacht and drags his family to the aribbean. In search of someone to pilot the boat— ctually a broken-down hulk—the group finds Cap- ain Ron (Kurt Russell), a less than skilled skipper. me hilarious bits. Rated PG-13 for profanity. 100m. IR: Thom Eberhardt. CAST: Kurt Russell, Martin hort, Mary Kay Place, Paul Anka. 1992

APTAIN SCARLETT ★★1/2 A dashing hero nought to be dead returns to France after the apoleonic Wars to discover his estate has been con- scated by a nasty nobleman. Saving ladies in dis- ess and righting wrongs becomes his life. Simple, redictable, and good clean fun. 75m. DIR: Thomas arr. CAST: Richard Greene, Leonora Amar, Nedrick oung. 1953

APTAIN SINBAD ★★1/2 This whimsical fantasy ts Sinbad against the evil El Kerim. There's plenty color and magic to enthrall younger audiences. 5m. DIR: Byron Haskin. CAST: Guy Williams, Heidi ruhl, Pedro Armendariz, Abraham Sofaer, Henry andon, Geoffrey Toone. 1963

APTAINS COURAGEOUS (1937) ★★★★★ This an exquisite adaptation of Rudyard Kipling's story bout a spoiled rich kid who falls from an ocean liner nd is rescued by fishermen. Through them, the lad arns about the rewards of hard work and genuine iendship. Spencer Tracy won a well-deserved best- ctor Oscar for his performance as the fatherly fish- rman. B&W; 116m. DIR: Victor Fleming. CAST: pencer Tracy, Freddie Bartholomew, Lionel Barry- ore, Melvyn Douglas, Mickey Rooney. 1937

APTAINS COURAGEOUS (1995) ★★★ Made-for- able movie is a watchable if inaccurate version of udyard Kipling's classic. Setting has been changed om the late 1800s to 1934 and it is the captain's son ho seems to have the greatest impact on the de- anding young heir who spends three months at sea n a no-frills fishing boat learning about hard work nd friendship. 99m. DIR: Michael Anderson. CAST: obert Urich, Kenny Vadas, Kaj-Erik Eriksen, Eric Snei- er, Duncan Fraser, Robert Wisden. 1995

APTAINS OF THE CLOUDS ★★★ Set in Canada in 940, this enjoyable film stars a typically robust ames Cagney as a bush pilot who joins the Royal anadian Air Force. Lots of romance and humor add the fun. Good color photography, too, but not uch action. 113m. DIR: Michael Curtiz. CAST: James agney, Dennis Morgan, Alan Hale Sr., Brenda Mar- all, George Tobias. 1942

CAPTAIN'S PARADISE, THE ★★★ From the opening shot, in which he is "shot," Alec Guinness displays the seemingly artless comedy form that marked him for stardom. He plays the bigamist skip- per of a ferry, a wife in each port, flirting with deli- cious danger. Timing is all, and close shaves—in- cluding a chance meeting of the wives—yields edge of seat entertainment. Lotsa fun. B&W; 77m. DIR: Anthony Kimmins. CAST: Alec Guinness, Celia John- son, Yvonne De Carlo, Bill Fraser. 1953

CAPTAIN'S TABLE ★★1/2 This is a delightful come- dy about a skipper of a cargo liner who is given trial command of a luxury liner. Has some wildly funny moments. Not rated. B&W; 90m. DIR: Jack Lee. CAST: John Gregson, Peggy Cummins, Donald Sinden, Nadia Gray. 1960

CAPTIVE ★★1/2 A rich man's daughter is kid- napped by a trio of young European anarchists whose only purpose is to convert her to their way of thinking. Arty but obscure. Not rated; contains nudi- ty, suggested sex, and violence. 95m. DIR: Paul May- ersberg. CAST: Irina Brook, Oliver Reed. 1986

CAPTIVE HEART ★★★★1/2 Exciting, well-written, marvelously performed story that examines the plight of British POWs and their Nazi captors. A su- perior job by all involved. B&W; 108m. DIR: Basil Dearden. CAST: Michael Redgrave, Rachel Kempson, Basil Radford, Jack Warner. 1948

CAPTIVE HEARTS ★★1/2 Quiet little drama about two bomber crewmen (Chris Makepeace and Michael Sarrazin) shot down over a small Japanese town in the waning days of World War II. Makepeace is in over his head with this role, but Pat Morita, as the village elder, and Sarrazin carry the picture. Rat- ed PG for language and violence. 102m. DIR: Paul Al- mond. CAST: Noriyuki "Pat" Morita, Chris Makepeace, Michael Sarrazin. 1988

CAPTIVE IN THE LAND, A ★★★ The first U.S.-Sovi- et production in thirteen years, this drama gives new meaning to the term Cold War. Sam Waterston is an American meteorologist leaving the Arctic when he parachutes down to a marooned Alexander Potapov. An intense psychological drama ensues when a storm leaves both men trapped in the icy desolation of an endless winter. Though the acting is emotional- ly charged and their dueling philosophies are in- triguing, the film feels claustrophobic. Rated PG for profanity. 98m. DIR: John Berry. CAST: Sam Water- ston, Alexander Potapov. 1991

CAPTIVE PLANET ❤ Earth is once again besieged by alien invaders in this very missable movie. 105m. DIR: Al Bradley. CAST: Sharon Baker, Chris Avran. 1986

CAPTIVE RAGE ❤ A plane carrying American citi- zens is hijacked. Rated R for violence, profanity, and nudity. 99m. DIR: Cedric Sundstrom. CAST: Oliver Reed, Robert Vaughn. 1988

CAPTIVE WILD WOMAN ★★ John Carradine uses "glandular treatments" to transform an ape into the curvy Acquanetta (!!), who sleepwalks instead of acts. So bad it translates into good grade-B fun. Spawned sequels *Jungle Woman* and *Jungle Cap- tive*. Not rated. B&W; 61m. DIR: Edward Dmytryk.

CAST: John Carradine, Acquanetta, Evelyn Ankers, Milburn Stone, Martha Vickers. **1943**

CAPTIVES ★★★ Julia Ormond plays a dentist who rebounds from a painful divorce by falling in love with a patient (Tim Roth)—one of the inmates she treats at a high-security prison. Low-key drama made for the BBC resembles a cross between *Brief Encounter* and *The Crying Game*, though not quite as good. Still, worthwhile for fans of the two stars. Rated R for violence and adult situations. 100m. **DIR:** Angela Pope. **CAST:** Tim Roth, Julia Ormond, Richard Hawley, Peter Capaldi. **1994**

CAPTURE OF GRIZZLY ADAMS, THE ★★1/2 Like an 1850s version of *The Fugitive*'s Richard Kimble, Grizzly Adams hides in the woods with his animal friends to avoid punishment for a murder he didn't commit. In this TV movie, a sequel to the popular series, he risks capture to visit his orphanage-bound daughter. Not rated; contains no objectionable material. 96m. **DIR:** Don Keeslar. **CAST:** Dan Haggerty, Kim Darby, Noah Beery Jr., Keenan Wynn, June Lockhart, Chuck Connors, G. W. Bailey. **1982**

●**CAPTURED ALIVE** ❤ Really amateurish film has a plane crashing and a bunch of hillbillies subsequently kidnapping the survivors to help them transport toxic waste. Rated R for violence, profanity, and nudity. 90m. **DIR:** Chris McIntyre. **CAST:** Dan Pinto. **1995**

●**CAR, THE** ★★ A black luxury sedan terrorizes a small New Mexico town in this none-too-scary film. The car is supposedly possessed by the devil, but you'll be possessed by the urge to go to sleep. Rated PG for mild violence. 95m. **DIR:** Elliot Silverstein. **CAST:** James Brolin, Kathleen Lloyd, John Marley, John Rubinstein. **1977 DVD**

CAR 54 WHERE ARE YOU? (TV SERIES) ★★★1/2 Early-'60s television series about the comic misadventures of Bronx policemen Gunther Toody and Francis Muldoon. The laugh track is annoyingly loud but the shows are quite funny, with outrageous situations and memorable characters. Each cassette contains two episodes; there were sixty in all. B&W; 50m. **DIR:** Nat Hiken, Stanley Prager. **CAST:** Joe E. Ross, Fred Gwynne, Paul Reed, Al Lewis, Charlotte Rae. **1961–1963**

CAR 54, WHERE ARE YOU? (1991) ❤ David Johansen, as Officer Toody, is hilarious, but this goofy comedy can't hold it together. Lingering too long on numerous sight gags costs them their punch and several musical scenes seem very out of place. The fragile plot about catching a gangster is overshadowed by numerous unimportant subplots. Original TV-series cast members make cameo appearances. Rated PG-13 for comic-book violence. 85m. **DIR:** Bill Fishman. **CAST:** David Johansen, John C. McGinley, Fran Drescher, Nipsey Russell, Al Lewis, Rosie O'Donnell. **1991**

CAR WASH ★★★1/2 This is an ensemble film that features memorable bits from Richard Pryor, George Carlin, Franklin Ajaye, Ivan Dixon, and the Pointer Sisters. There are plenty of laughs, music, and even a moral in this fine low-budget production. Rated PG. 97m. **DIR:** Michael Schultz. **CAST:** Richard Pryor, Franklin Ajaye, Sully Boyar, Ivan Dixon. **1976 DVD**

CARAVAGGIO ★★★★ Derek Jarman's extraordinary and revealing film is based on the life and art of Caravaggio, perhaps the greatest of Italian post-Renaissance painters. This controversial biography explores the artist's life, which was troubled by extremes of passion and artistic radicalism. Not rated; contains nudity, profanity, and violence. 97m. DIR: Derek Jarman. **CAST:** Nigel Terry, Sean Bean, Tilda Swinton, Spencer Leigh, Michael Gough. **1986**

CARAVAN TO VACCARES ❤ If this cliché-ridden film had followed the plot of Alistair MacLean's novel, it might have been exciting. Read the book instead. Rated PG. 98m. **DIR:** Geoffrey Reeve. **CAST:** David Birney, Charlotte Rampling, Michel Lonsdale, Marcel Bozzuffi. **1974**

CARAVAN TRAIL ★★★★ The leader (Eddie Dean) of a wagon train of settlers takes the job of marshal to restore homesteaders' land being stolen by outlaws. He enlists the aid of some not-so-bad outlaws to stop the land grabbers. Lash LaRue (in his second supporting role to Dean) steals the picture. LaRue went on to star in his own series of well-received B's. 57m. **DIR:** Robert Emmett Tansey. **CAST:** Eddie Dean, Lash LaRue, Charles King. **1946**

CARAVANS ★★ An American diplomat is sent to the Middle East to bring back the daughter of an American politician. Rated PG. 123m. **DIR:** James Fargo. **CAST:** Anthony Quinn, Michael Sarrazin, Jennifer O'Neill, Christopher Lee, Joseph Cotten, Barry Sullivan, Jeremy Kemp. **1978**

CARBON COPY ★★★1/2 This amiable lightweight comedy of racial manners stars George Segal as a white corporate executive who suddenly discovers he has a teenage black son just itching to be adopted in lily-white San Marino, California. Rated PG. 92m. **DIR:** Michael Schultz. **CAST:** George Segal, Susan Saint James, Denzel Washington, Jack Warden, Dick Martin. **1981**

CARDIAC ARREST ★★ Garry Goodrow, maverick detective, investigates a series of grisly murders that has the cops puzzled and the citizens of San Francisco living in fear. Rated R for violence and adult situations. 90m. **DIR:** Murray Mintz. **CAST:** Garry Goodrow, Mike Chan, Max Gail. **1980 DVD**

CARDINAL, THE ★★★ Director Otto Preminger's epic view of a vital and caring young Catholic priest's rise from a backwoods clergyman to cardinal. Alternately compelling and shallow. Watch for the late Maggie McNamara in her last role. 175m. **DIR:** Otto Preminger. **CAST:** Tom Tryon, Romy Schneider, Carol Lynley, John Huston. **1963**

CARE BEARS MOVIE, THE ★★★ Poor animation mars this children's movie about bears who cheer up a pair of kids. Rated G, no objectionable material. 80m. **DIR:** Aran Selznick. **CAST:** Mickey Rooney, Georgia Engel (voices). **1985**

CAREER ★★★★ Anthony Franciosa delivers a surprisingly powerful performance as an actor for whom success is always just beyond reach. In his pursuit for the one big part, he sacrifices his personal happiness and youth. Exemplary supporting performances by Dean Martin and Carolyn Jones. B&W; 105m. **DIR:** Joseph Anthony. **CAST:** Anthony Franciosa, Dean Martin,

, Shirley MacLaine, Carolyn Jones, Joan Blackman.
59

AREER GIRLS ★★1/2 Two former roommates, w successful businesswomen, get together for a eekend reunion and have flashbacks to their hun- y college days. Writer-director Mike Leigh's noted yle of semi-improvisational scripting comes up npty this time. In the course of two days, the men run into far too many of their old friends and vers, greeting each contrivance with cries of "What coincidence!" Rated R for profanity and some sexu- ity. 87m. **DIR:** Mike Leigh. **CAST:** Katrin Cartlidge, nda Steadman, Kate Byers, Mark Benton. 1997

AREER OPPORTUNITIES ★★ The town liar is cked in a department store overnight with the wn beauty and two bumbling burglers in this just ssable film written and coproduced by John Hugh- . Rated PG-13 for brief profanity and violence. m. **DIR:** Bryan Gordon. **CAST:** Frank Whaley, Jennifer onnelly, Barry Corbin, Noble Willingham, William rsythe, Dermot Mulroney, Kieran Mulroney, John ndy. 1991 DVD

AREFREE ★★★ In this blend of music, slapstick tuations, and romantic byplay, Ginger Rogers is a azy, mixed-up girl-child who goes to psychiatrist ed Astaire for counsel. His treatment results in er falling in love with him. While trying to stop this, e falls in love with her. Of course they dance! It's ore screwball comedy than musical. B&W; 80m. **R:** Mark Sandrich. **CAST:** Fred Astaire, Ginger ogers, Ralph Bellamy, Jack Carson. 1938

AREFUL ★★★★ *Careful* is set in a candy-colored ountain village where avalanches are so common at no one speaks above a whisper. This makes for a ychological tension that drives its inhabitants to xtremes that are equally bizarre and amusing. Not ted; contains brief nudity. 96m. **DIR:** Guy Maddin. **AST:** Kyle McCulloch, Gosia Dobrowolska, Paul Cox. 92

AREFUL HE MIGHT HEAR YOU ★★★★1/2 A ild's-eye view of the harsh realities of life, this Aus- alian import is a poignant, heartwarming, sad, and metimes frightening motion picture. A young boy amed P.S. (played by 7-year-old Nicholas Gledhill) ts caught up in a bitter custody fight between his vo aunts. While the movie does tend to become a arjerker on occasion, it does so without putting off e viewer. Rated PG for suggested sex and violence. 6m. **DIR:** Carl Schultz. **CAST:** Robyn Nevin, Nicholas edhill, Wendy Hughes, John Hargreaves. 1983

ARIBBEAN MYSTERY, A ★★★1/2 In this BBC- oduced Agatha Christie mystery, the quiet atmos- here of a tropical-island resort is shattered by in- igue and murder, and Miss Marple is soon on the ene. Although quite elderly, she shows awareness nd vitality with a turn of her head and the sparkle in er eyes. The theme music, characterizations, and nematography make this story enjoyable. Not rat- l; suitable for family viewing. 100m. **DIR:** Christo- er Petit. **CAST:** Joan Hickson, Donald Pleasence, T. P. cKenna, Michael Feast, Sheila Ruskin. 1989

ARIBE ★★ In this bland spy thriller, CIA agent ara Glover and her partner arrange a weapons sale r their own personal gain. But the contact, Stephen McHattie, has no intention of fulfilling his part of the bargain. He kills Glover's partner and confiscates the weapons. Beautiful photography of the Belize jungles and mountains rescues this tired spy thriller. 90m. **DIR:** Michael Kennedy. **CAST:** John Savage, Kara Glover, Stephen McHattie. 1987

CARIBOO TRAIL ★★★★ Cattleman Randolph Scott finds gold in Canada but has to fight off Victor Jory's claim jumpers. Gorgeous Colorado scenery stands in for the Canadian wilderness. 81m. **DIR:** Edwin L. Marin. **CAST:** Randolph Scott, George "Gabby" Hayes, Bill Williams, Victor Jory, Douglas Kennedy, Dale Robertson, Jim Davis. 1950

CARLA'S SONG ★★★1/2 Glasgow bus driver experiences a political awakening in this angry, melancholy look at the Nicaraguan war between right-wing U.S.-backed Contras and the leftist Sandanista government. In 1987, he befriends a female Nicaraguan refugee and they travel to her homeland where they cross paths with a blunt, outspoken former CIA operative. In English and Spanish with English subtitles. Not rated; contains adult themes and language. 127m. **DIR:** Kenneth Loach. **CAST:** Robert Carlyle, Oyanka Cabezas, Scott Glenn. 1998 DVD

CARLITO'S WAY ★★★★ Al Pacino, a former drug dealer trying to go straight, finds himself being pulled back into the criminal underworld when his best friend and attorney asks for his help. It's trash, but great trash. Rated R for nudity, profanity, violence, simulated sex, and drug use. 141m. **DIR:** Brian De Palma. **CAST:** Al Pacino, Sean Penn, Penelope Ann Miller, John Leguizamo, Ingrid Rogers, Luis Guzman, James Rebhorn, Viggo Mortensen, Richard Foronjy, Adrian Pasdar. 1993 DVD

CARLTON-BROWNE OF THE F.O. ★★1/2 A British foreign-office secretary is assigned to a small island nation, formerly of the empire. For serious buffs this is an interesting, but not classic, bit of movie history. Not rated and only mildly ribald. B&W; 88m. **DIR:** Jeffrey Dell. **CAST:** Terry-Thomas, Peter Sellers, Luciana Paluzzi. 1958

CARMEN JONES ★★★★ An exceptionally well-staged adaptation of Oscar Hammerstein's updating of the famous opera with Georges Bizet's music intact. As in the opera, a flirt causes a soldier to go off the deep end because of his passion for her, but the main event is the music. The cast includes celebrity singers, but their voices were dubbed to suit the operatic range of the music. 105m. **DIR:** Otto Preminger. **CAST:** Dorothy Dandridge, Harry Belafonte, Pearl Bailey, Diahann Carroll, Brock Peters, Roy Glenn, Olga James. 1954

CARMEN MIRANDA: BANANAS IS MY BUSINESS ★★★1/2 To Yanks she was the lady with the fruit on her head, but in Brazil, Carmen Miranda was huge. Brazilian filmmaker Helena Solberg nearly explains the cult of personality surrounding a woman who tried to use the Hollywood system, but found it ate her up. This merely whets the appetite since Solberg's mistake was to interject a personal but mostly inane narrative that never moves past broad generalizations. U.S.-Brazilian production. Not rated. B&W/color; 91m. **DIR:** Helena Solberg. 1994

CARMILLA ★★★★ This tale from the cable TV series *Nightmare Classics* features a lonely southern girl (Ione Skye) befriending a stranger (Meg Tilly) who just happens to be a vampire. Some positively chilling scenes!! Not rated, contains gore and violence. 52m. DIR: Gabrielle Beaumont. CAST: Ione Skye, Meg Tilly, Roddy McDowall, Roy Dotrice. 1989

CARNAL CRIMES 💙 When a bored housewife meets a kinky photographer, she ends up taking a walk on the wild side that threatens her life and marriage. Rated R for simulated sex, nudity, violence, and profanity. 92m. DIR: Alexander Gregory Hippolyte. CAST: Linda Carol, Martin Hewitt, Rich Crater, Paula Trickey, Alex Kubik. 1992 DVD

CARNAL KNOWLEDGE ★★★★ The sexual dilemmas of the modern American are analyzed and come up short in this thoughtful film. Jack Nicholson and singer Art Garfunkel are college roommates whose lives are followed through varied relationships with the opposite sex. Nicholson is somewhat of a stinker, and one finds oneself more in sympathy with the women in the cast. Rated R. 96m. DIR: Mike Nichols. CAST: Jack Nicholson, Candice Bergen, Art Garfunkel, Ann-Margret. 1971 DVD

CARNIVAL IN FLANDERS ★★★★ This sly drama is about a village that postpones its destruction by collaborating with its conquerors. A clever, subtle work, this classic tries to re-create the great paintings of the masters depicting village life during carnival time. In French with English subtitles. B&W; 92m. DIR: Jacques Feyder. CAST: Françoise Rosay, Andre Alerme, Jean Murat, Louis Jouvet, Micheline Cheirel. 1936

CARNIVAL OF BLOOD 💙 Boring horror mystery about a series of murders committed at New York's Coney Island. 87m. DIR: Leonard Kirman. CAST: Earle Edgerton, Judith Resnick, Burt Young. 1976

CARNIVAL OF SOULS ★★★1/2 Creepy film made on a shoestring budget in Lawrence, Kansas, concerns a girl who, after a near-fatal car crash, is haunted by a ghoulish, zombielike character. Extremely eerie, with nightmarish photography, this little-known gem has a way of getting to you. Better keep the lights on. B&W; 80m. DIR: Herk Harvey. CAST: Candace Hilligoss, Sidney Berger. 1962 DVD

CARNIVAL ROCK 💙 This tedious tale about a nightclub offers little enjoyment. Great music, though, by the Platters and David Houston. 80m. DIR: Roger Corman. CAST: Susan Cabot, Dick Miller, Brian Hutton. 1958

CARNIVAL STORY ★★ Familiar story of rivalry between circus performers over the affections of the girl they both love. No real surprises. Filmed in Germany. 95m. DIR: Kurt Neumann. CAST: Anne Baxter, Steve Cochran, Jay C. Flippen, George Nader. 1954

CARNOSAUR ★★1/2 Writer-director Adam Simon's unpleasantly bleak, end-of-the-world chiller winds up as nothing more than a laughably crude *Jurassic Park* rip-off. Mad scientist Diane Ladd genetically alters chicken eggs so that human females will give birth to dinosaurs, effectively terminating our reign on Earth. Has Colonel Sanders heard about this one? Rated R for gore and profanity. 83m. DIR: Adam Si-

mon. CAST: Diane Ladd, Raphael Sbarge, Jennif Runyon, Clint Howard. 1993 DVD

CARNOSAUR 2 ★★1/2 Superior sequel dredg up several familiar formulas and uses them to go advantage. You'll recognize which films are bei ripped off in good, gory fashion in this exciting tale a group of technicians who find more than they ba gained for when they attempt to restore power to top-secret mining facility. Confined setting, hone suspense, and decent special effects keep the chi coming. Rated R for gore. 83m. DIR: Louis Mornea CAST: John Savage, Cliff De Young, Rick Dean, Rya Thomas Johnson, Don Stroud. 1994 DVD

CARNOSAUR 3: PRIMAL SPECIES ★★1/2 Rog Corman's dinosaur franchise continues with th predictable sequel about a team of antiterrorist sp cial forces whose latest assignment is to elimina some escaped man-eating carnosaurs. Scott Vale tine plays the team leader who discovers that th carnosaurs are practically indestructible. Fans the first two films will find plenty to like, while tho looking for something different will be disappointe Rated R for violence and language. 85m. DI Jonathan Winfrey. CAST: Scott Valentine, Jane Gun Morgan Englund, Rick Dean. 1995 DVD

CARNY ★★★★ This film takes us behind the brig lights into the netherworld of the "carnies," peop who spend their lives cheating, lying, and stealin from others yet consider themselves superior their victims. Gary Busey, Jodie Foster, Robb Robertson are all outstanding. The accent in *Carn* is on realism with disenchanted losers who live on from day to day. Rated R. 107m. DIR: Robert Kayl CAST: Gary Busey, Jodie Foster, Robbie Robertso Meg Foster, Bert Remsen. 1980

CARO DIARIO ★★1/2 Three stories related by ar starring Nanni Moretti, who has been called Italy Woody Allen. The third story, where Moretti's myst rious skin disorder baffles a series of doctors, is th funniest. The others—Moretti tooling around Ron on his motor scooter and cruising the islands off th Italian coast—are self-indulgent, and laughs a rare. Not rated; suitable for general audience 128m. DIR: Nanni Moretti. CAST: Nanni Moretti, Je nifer Beals. 1993

CAROLINA SKELETONS ★★★ Lou Gossett J adept as usual, stars in this fact-based story about war hero's return to a southern town in search of th truth behind his brother's execution years earlie Quality performances from Gossett and Bruce Der Made for cable. Rated R for profanity and violenc 94m. DIR: John Erman. CAST: Lou Gossett Jr., Bru Dern. 1992 DVD

CAROLINE? ★★★★ *Hallmark Hall of Fame* pr sentation is an excellent exercise in sustained su pense. Stephanie Zimbalist is the question mark i question, the long-lost daughter who has been pr sumed dead for the past fifteen years. When Carolir suddenly shows up to claim the family inheritanc her very presence raises suspicions and doubt Pamela Reed is especially effective as the newe family member who begins to realize that things ar not exactly what they seem. 100m. DIR: Joseph Sa gent. CAST: Stephanie Zimbalist, Pamela Reed, George Grizzard, Patricia Neal. 1989

CAROLINE AT MIDNIGHT ★★★★ Here's an erotic thriller with a surprising finish. Timothy Daly's a journalist who receives a phone call from a deceased girlfriend and finds himself involved with the frightened wife of a dirty cop who may have been responsible for the girlfriend's death. Rated R for nudity, rape, simulated sex, profanity, and violence. 89m. DIR: Scott McGinnis. CAST: Timothy Daly, Mia Sara, Paul LeMat, Clayton Rohner, Zach Galligan, Virginia Madsen, Judd Nelson. 1993

CAROUSEL ★★★★★ A unique blend of drama and music with the eloquent Rodgers and Hammerstein score performed by the best of both Hollywood and opera. Molnar's famous story of *Liliom*, the carnival barker who gets one day to prove he's worthy of Heaven, is transferred to Maine, where majestic backdrops add emotional emphasis. Exceptional. 128m. DIR: Henry King. CAST: Gordon MacRae, Shirley Jones, Gene Lockhart, Cameron Mitchell, Barbara Ruick, Claramae Turner, Robert Rounseville, Jacques d'Amboise. 1956 DVD

CARPATHIAN EAGLE ★★ Murdered men begin popping up with their hearts cut out. A police detective scours the town and racks his brain looking for the killer, not realizing how close he is. What all this has to do with the title is never resolved in this addition to Elvira's "Thriller Video." 60m. DIR: Francis Megahy. CAST: Anthony Valentine, Suzanne Danielle, Sian Phillips. 1982

CARPENTER, THE ★★★ Once you realize writer Doug Taylor and director David Wellington had their tongues planted firmly in cheek, you will enjoy this tale of a neglected wife, after a mental breakdown, moving into an unfinished country home where a mysterious night carpenter becomes her protector. Not a spoof, just handled with style and wit. Not rated, but has gore, profanity, and nudity. 87m. DIR: David Wellington. CAST: Wings Hauser, Lynne Adams. 1989

CARPETBAGGERS, THE ★★★ Howard Hughes–like millionaire George Peppard makes movies, love, and enemies in the Hollywood of the 1920s and 1930s. Alan Ladd, as a Tom Mix clone, helps in this, his last picture. Carroll Baker is steamy. Very tame compared with the porno-edged Harold Robbins novel. 150m. DIR: Edward Dmytryk. CAST: George Peppard, Alan Ladd, Audrey Totter, Carroll Baker, Robert Cummings, Lew Ayres, Martin Balsam, Archie Moore. 1964

CARPOOL ★★ A workaholic father (David Paymer) and his children are kidnapped on their way to school by would-be robber Tom Arnold. Arnold and Paymer might make a good team (one blusters, the other cringes), but they're stuck with a script mixing corny jokes and even cornier family values sermons. The kids are all straight from a Hollywood casting office, and Arthur Hiller's arthritic direction doesn't help. Rated PG-13 for mild profanity and cartoon violence. 105m. DIR: Arthur Hiller. CAST: Tom Arnold, David Paymer, Rhea Perlman, Rachel Leigh Cook, Rod Steiger. 1996

CARRIE (1952) ★★★★ Theodore Dreiser's *Sister Carrie*: Jennifer Jones in the title role and Laurence Olivier as her morally blinded married lover make this tale a classic. Basil Ruysdael is perfect in a bit as Olivier's unyielding employer. B&W; 118m. DIR: William Wyler. CAST: Jennifer Jones, Laurence Olivier, Eddie Albert, Basil Ruysdael, Miriam Hopkins. 1952

CARRIE (1976) ★★★1/2 The ultimate revenge tale for anyone who remembers high school as a time of rejection and ridicule. The story follows the strange life of Carrie White (Sissy Spacek), a student severely humiliated by her classmates and stifled by the Puritan beliefs of her mother (Piper Laurie), a religious fanatic. Rated R for nudity, violence, and profanity. 97m. DIR: Brian De Palma. CAST: Sissy Spacek, Piper Laurie, John Travolta, Nancy Allen, Amy Irving. 1976 DVD

CARRIED AWAY ★★★ Dennis Hopper is superb as a middle-aged man whose comfortable life is coming to an end. His mother is dying, his teaching career is nearly over, and his longtime girlfriend Rosealee wants a lifelong commitment. Joseph is at a crossroads, and the crossing guard turns out to be new 17-year-old student Catherine, who sets her sights on the vulnerable Joseph. Rated R for nudity, adult situations, and profanity. 108m. DIR: Bruno Barreto. CAST: Dennis Hopper, Amy Irving, Amy Locane, Julie Harris, Gary Busey, Hal Holbrook. 1996

CARRIER 🖤 Small-town teenage outcast suddenly becomes a carrier of an unknown disease that consumes living organisms on contact. Rated R for violence and profanity. 99m. DIR: Nathan J. White. CAST: Gregory Fortescue, Steve Dixon. 1987

CARRINGTON ★★★1/2 The unorthodox relationship between painter Dora Carrington and homosexual writer Lytton Strachey, from their meeting in 1915 to his death (and her suicide) in 1932. Jonathan Pryce makes the eccentric Strachey a genuinely magnetic figure. Rated R for profanity, nudity, and simulated sex. 122m. DIR: Christopher Hampton. CAST: Emma Thompson, Jonathan Pryce, Steven Waddington, Rufus Sewell, Samuel West, Penelope Wilton. 1995

CARRINGTON, V. C. ★★★ Everybody's Englishman David Niven gives one of the finest performances of his career. A stalwart British army officer, accused of stealing military funds, undertakes to conduct his own defense. This is a solid, engrossing drama. Filmed in England and released heavily cut in the United States under the title *Court Martial*. B&W; 105m. DIR: Anthony Asquith. CAST: David Niven, Margaret Leighton, Noelle Middleton, Laurence Naismith, Victor Maddern, Maurice Denham. 1955

CARRY ON ADMIRAL ★★ His Majesty's navy suffers semi-hilariously at the hands of a madcap crew tangled in ribald high jinks, double identity, and comic cuts. Originally titled *The Ship Was Loaded*. 81m. DIR: Val Guest. CAST: David Tomlinson, Peggy Cummins, Alfie Bass, Ronald Shiner. 1957

CARRY ON AT YOUR CONVENIENCE ★★ The British *Carry On* comedy players were still carrying on in 1971, but they were starting to run out of breath. Not rated, but full of innuendoes. 86m. DIR:

Gerald Thomas. **CAST:** Sidney James, Kenneth Williams, Charles Hawtrey, Joan Sims. 1971

CARRY ON BEHIND ♥ Archaeologists and holiday campers stumble over each other while trying to share the same location. Not rated. 90m. **DIR:** Gerald Thomas. **CAST:** Elke Sommer, Kenneth Williams, Sidney James, Joan Sims. 1975

CARRY ON CLEO ★★★1/2 It's a matter of personal taste, but we find this to be the funniest of the *Carry On* series. (Of course, you might not find any of them funny.) It's designed as a spoof of the then-current Burton-Taylor *Cleopatra. Dr. Who* fans will spot Jon Pertwee in a small role. 92m. **DIR:** Gerald Thomas. **CAST:** Amanda Barrie, Sidney James, Kenneth Williams, Kenneth Connor, Joan Sims, Charles Hawtrey, Jim Dale, Jon Pertwee. 1965

CARRY ON COWBOY ★★1/2 Another in a very long, and weakening, line of British farces, many of them spoofs of highly popular films. Replete with the usual double-entendre jokes and sight gags, this one sends up *High Noon.* 91m. **DIR:** Gerald Thomas. **CAST:** Sidney James, Kenneth Williams, Joan Sims, Angela Douglas, Jim Dale. 1966

CARRY ON CRUISING ★★★ One of the earlier, and therefore better, entries in the long-lived British series. The jokes are more energetic, less forced. In this one, the players try desperately to fill in for the regular crew of a Mediterranean cruise ship. Not rated. B&W; 99m. **DIR:** Gerald Thomas. **CAST:** Sidney James, Kenneth Williams, Kenneth Connor, Liz Fraser. 1962

CARRY ON DOCTOR ★★★ Adding veteran British comic Frankie Howerd to the cast helped perk up this *Carry On* entry a bit. The usual gang plays the bumbling staff of a hospital, caught up in a battle over a secret weight-loss formula. Not rated. 95m. **DIR:** Gerald Thomas. **CAST:** Frankie Howerd, Sidney James, Kenneth Williams, Charles Hawtrey, Jim Dale, Hattie Jacques, Joan Sims, Peter Butterworth. 1968

CARRY ON EMMANUELLE ♥ The last of the *Carry On* series, and not a moment too soon. Not rated. 88m. **DIR:** Gerald Thomas. **CAST:** Suzanne Danielle, Kenneth Williams, Kenneth Connor, Joan Sims, Peter Butterworth, Beryl Reid. 1978

CARRY ON NURSE ★★★ Daffy struggle between patients and hospital staff. It's one of the most consistently amusing entries in this British comedy series. 90m. **DIR:** Gerald Thomas. **CAST:** Kenneth Connor, Kenneth Williams, Charles Hawtrey, Terence Longden. 1960

CARS THAT EAT PEOPLE (THE CARS THAT ATE PARIS) ★★★ Peter Weir began with this weird black comedy-horror film about an outback Australian town where motorists and their cars are trapped each night. Rated PG. 90m. **DIR:** Peter Weir. **CAST:** John Meillon, Terry Camilleri, Kevin Miles. 1975

CARSON CITY CYCLONE ★★★★ Donald "Red" Barry plays a cocky young defense attorney framed for the murder of his father (a judge and banker). Intricate plot that proves how good B Westerns can be. B&W; 55m. **DIR:** Howard Bretherton. **CAST:** Don Barry, Noah Beery Sr., Roy Barcroft. 1943

CARSON CITY KID ★★★★ Top-notch Roy Rogers period Western dominated by Bob Steele in an off-beat villainous role. Roy Rogers, in the title role, pursues a cunning gambler who murdered his brother. B&W; 54m. **DIR:** Joseph Kane. **CAST:** Roy Rogers, George "Gabby" Hayes, Bob Steele, Noah Beery Jr., Pauline Moore. 1940

CARTIER AFFAIR, THE ♥ Less than funny comic romance that involves a male secretary falling in love with his soap-opera-legend boss. 96m. **DIR:** Rod Holcomb. **CAST:** Joan Collins, David Hasselhoff, Telly Savalas, Jay Gerber, Hilly Hicks. 1985 DVD

CARTOONS GO TO WAR ★★★★ An extremely tight and well-made look at the use of cartoons during World War II as a way to lift morale among civilians and train soldiers without preaching. Though brief, this A&E documentary clearly puts the war effort into a new context while entertaining us. Rare footage is blended with sharp revelations by historians and several well-spoken animators such as Chuck Jones. Not rated. B&W/color; 50m. **DIR:** Sharon R. Baker. 1995

CARTOUCHE ★★★★ Great stuff: an eighteenth-century swashbuckler done with wit, incredible style, and an intoxicating passion for action and romance. Jean-Paul Belmondo and Claudia Cardinale head a band of brigands. In French with English subtitles. 115m. **DIR:** Philippe de Broca. **CAST:** Jean-Paul Belmondo, Claudia Cardinale, Odile Versois, Marcel Dalio, Philippe Lemaire. 1964

CASABLANCA ★★★★★ A kiss may be just a kiss and a sigh just a sigh, but there is only one *Casablanca.* This feast of romance and World War II intrigue is an all-time classic. B&W; 102m. **DIR:** Michael Curtiz. **CAST:** Humphrey Bogart, Ingrid Bergman, Claude Rains, Paul Henreid, Peter Lorre, Sydney Greenstreet. 1942 DVD

CASANOVA (1976) ★★★1/2 Federico Fellini's account of the sexually bogus Venetian nobleman is a surreal journey into self-obsession and deviance. Casanova is depicted as a tedious braggart. In English and Italian with subtitles. Not rated; contains nudity and profanity and is recommended for adult viewing. 139m. **DIR:** Federico Fellini. **CAST:** Donald Sutherland. 1976

CASANOVA (1987) ★★ After infamous eighteenth century ladies' man Richard Chamberlain is arrested as an undesirable, the viewer—unfortunately—suffers through his entire life story. A drag. Not rated; contains nudity and sexual situations. 122m. **DIR:** Simon Langton. **CAST:** Richard Chamberlain, Faye Dunaway, Sylvia Kristel, Ornella Muti, Hanna Schygulla, Sophie Ward. 1987

CASANOVA BROWN ★★★ Gary Cooper's plans to remarry are complicated when he learns his recently divorced ex-wife (Teresa Wright) is about to have a baby. Mild laughs but good performances. Frank Morgan steals the show. B&W; 94m. **DIR:** Sam Wood. **CAST:** Gary Cooper, Teresa Wright, Frank Morgan, Anita Louise, Jill Esmond. 1944

CASANOVA'S BIG NIGHT ★★1/2 The evergreen Bob Hope is a lowly tailor's assistant masquerading as the great lover Casanova in this costume comedy set in plot-and-intrigue-ridden Venice. Old Ski Nose is irrepressible, sets are sumptuous, and costumes lavish, but the script and direction don't measure up.

Funny, but not *that* funny. 86m. **DIR:** Norman Z. McLeod. **CAST:** Bob Hope, Joan Fontaine, Basil Rathbone, Audrey Dalton, Frieda Inescort, Hope Emerson, Hugh Marlowe, John Carradine, John Hoyt, Robert Hutton, Raymond Burr, Lon Chaney Jr. 1954

•**CASBAH** ★★1/2 Oft-filmed story of a charismatic thief who loses himself in the underworld gets the musical treatment this time. The tunes are good, but it's difficult to erase the image of Charles Boyer as the tragic romantic who followed his heart rather than his instincts. B&W; 93m. **DIR:** John Berry. **CAST:** Tony Martin, Yvonne De Carlo, Peter Lorre, Marta Toren, Hugo Haas, Thomas Gomez, Douglas Dick, Virginia Gregg. 1948

CASE FOR MURDER, A ★★1/2 From the beginning, it's easy to spot the murderer in this plotless suspense thriller. A lawyer in a prestigious firm is murdered, and all the evidence points to his wife, who can't remember where she was that evening. The acting is decent, but the story is boring. Rated R for violence and suggested sex. 94m. **DIR:** Duncan Gibbins. **CAST:** Jennifer Grey, Peter Berg, Belinda Bauer, Eugene Roche, Robert Do Qui. 1993

CASE OF DEADLY FORCE, A ★★★★ Richard Crenna plays a determined attorney who helps a victim's family win the first-ever "wrongful death" suit against the Boston Police Department after an innocent black man is shot to death. Based on a true story of police corruption and violence, this drama is surprisingly taut and packs an emotional punch. Made for TV. 95m. **DIR:** Michael Miller. **CAST:** Richard Crenna, John Shea, Tate Donovan. 1986

CASE OF LIBEL, A ★★★★★ Slick, superb made-for-cable adaptation of Henry Denker's famed Broadway play. The story closely follows the legendary Westbrook Pegler–Quentin Reynolds libel suit, wherein columnist Pegler had attempted to smear Reynolds's reputation with a series of vicious lies. Ranks with the finest courtroom dramas on film. Not rated. 92m. **DIR:** Eric Till. **CAST:** Edward Asner, Daniel J. Travanti, Gordon Pinsent, Lawrence Dane. 1984

CASE OF THE BLACK CAT, THE ★★1/2 In his only film as Perry Mason, Ricardo Cortez takes over from Warren William to investigate the death of a man who was killed after changing his will. One of the better entries in the series. B&W; 66m. **DIR:** William McGann. **CAST:** Ricardo Cortez, June Travis, Jane Bryan. 1936

CASE OF THE CURIOUS BRIDE, THE ★★ Perry Mason is dragged away from his new hobby—gourmet cooking—to investigate the cause of a woman being blackmailed by her "dead" husband. Look fast for Errol Flynn as a corpse. B&W; 74m. **DIR:** Michael Curtiz. **CAST:** Warren William, Margaret Lindsay, Claire Dodd, Allen Jenkins, Warren Hymer, Errol Flynn, Mayo Methot. 1935

CASE OF THE HOWLING DOG, THE ★★ Suave Warren William is a far cry from Raymond Burr in this, the first of a half-dozen Perry Mason movies made shortly after Erle Stanley Gardner created the character. Mary Astor is a suspect in a murder case that begins when two men claim to be married to her.

B&W; 75m. **DIR:** Alan Crosland. **CAST:** Warren William, Mary Astor, Helen Trenholme, Allen Jenkins. 1934

CASE OF THE LUCKY LEGS, THE ★★★★ Best entry in the Warner Bros. series of Perry Mason pictures, this has the wisecracking lawyer (Warren William) battling a perennial hangover, doctor's orders, and pesky police officers as he tries to find the murderer of a con man. B&W; 61m. **DIR:** Archie Mayo. **CAST:** Warren William, Genevieve Tobin, Patricia Ellis, Lyle Talbot, Allen Jenkins, Barton MacLane, Porter Hall, Henry O'Neill. 1935

CASE OF THE STUTTERING BISHOP, THE ★★ Donald Woods is Perry Mason number three in the last film of the series. His job: ascertain whether a woman who claims to be the heiress to a dead man's fortune is an impostor. B&W; 70m. **DIR:** William Clemens. **CAST:** Donald Woods, Ann Dvorak, Anne Nagel. 1937

CASE OF THE VELVET CLAWS, THE ★★1/2 Perry Mason's honeymoon with new wife Della Street(!) is interrupted by one of those pesky murders, this one involving the publisher of a sleazy tabloid. One of the better entries, though it was Warren William's last time as Mason. B&W; 60m. **DIR:** William Clemens. **CAST:** Warren William, Claire Dodd, Winifred Shaw. 1936

CASEY'S SHADOW ★★1/2 Only the droll playing of star Walter Matthau makes this family film watchable. Matthau is a horse trainer deserted by his wife and left to raise three sons. Only the star's fans will want to ride it out. Rated PG. 116m. **DIR:** Martin Ritt. **CAST:** Walter Matthau, Alexis Smith, Robert Webber, Murray Hamilton. 1978

CASH McCALL ★★★ James Garner is great as a fast-moving financial wizard who must slow down his plan to take over a plastic factory when he pauses to woo the owner's daughter. Lightweight—but the stars shine. 102m. **DIR:** Joseph Pevney. **CAST:** James Garner, Natalie Wood, Dean Jagger, Nina Foch, Henry Jones, E. G. Marshall. 1959

CASINO (1980) ★★ This pedestrian telemovie features former *Mannix* star Mike Connors as the action-oriented owner of a plush hotel and casino. 100m. **DIR:** Don Chaffey. **CAST:** Mike Connors, Gene Evans, Barry Van Dyke, Gary Burghoff, Joseph Cotten, Lynda Day George, Robert Reed, Barry Sullivan. 1980

CASINO (1995) ★★★★ Teaming with scripter Nicholas Pileggi, Martin Scorsese gives us a record of the events that transformed Las Vegas from sin-laden mecca to family-oriented Disneyland, as experienced by casino owner Robert De Niro and best friend Joe Pesci, a hair-trigger mob assassin. The only sour note comes from Sharon Stone, who simply doesn't have the acting chops required by her role. Rated R for violence, profanity, drug use, and nudity. 182m. **DIR:** Martin Scorsese. **CAST:** Robert De Niro, Joe Pesci, Sharon Stone, Kevin Pollak, James Woods, John Bloom. 1995 DVD

CASINO ROYALE (1954) ★★★★ 007 fans who believe Sean Connery to have been the first screen incarnation of their favorite secret agent will be surprised and thrilled by this Bonded treasure, originally aired live on an American television anthology series. Barry Nelson stars as an Americanized "Jimmy" Bond who faces the menacing Le Chiffre (Peter Lorre, in a deliciously evil role) across a gambling table. From the Ian Fleming novel, this remains a surprisingly faithful adaptation of its source material. B&W; 55m. **DIR:** William H. Brown. **CAST:** Barry Nelson, Peter Lorre, Linda Christian. **1954**

CASINO ROYALE (1967) ★★ This is the black sheep of the James Bond family of films. Not wanting to compete with the Sean Connery vehicles, this film was intended to be a stylish spoof. For the most part, it's an overblown bore. 130m. **DIR:** John Huston, Ken Hughes, Robert Parrish, Joseph McGrath, Val Guest. **CAST:** Peter Sellers, Ursula Andress, David Niven, Orson Welles, Joanna Pettet, Woody Allen, Deborah Kerr, William Holden, Charles Boyer, John Huston, George Raft, Jean-Paul Belmondo. **1967**

CASPER ★★★ Casper the friendly ghost redefines "friendly" as the adolescent spirit develops a crush on the young daughter of a ghost therapist. Mainly for kids, but parents should take note: A twist in the story may lead impressionable children to believe it's possible to bring dead parents back to life. Rated PG. 96m. **DIR:** Brad Silberling. **CAST:** Christina Ricci, Bill Pullman, Cathy Moriarty, Eric Idle. **1995**

CASPER: A SPIRITED BEGINNING ★★★ Family-friendly, direct-to-video prequel to the theatrical *Casper*, this film tells the story of Casper's arrival in the world of ghosts and of one teacher's fight to prevent a historic landmark from being demolished. Voices of James Earl Jones, Jeremy Foley, Pauly Shore. Rated PG. 90m. **DIR:** Sean McNamara. **CAST:** Steve Guttenberg, Lori Loughlin, Rodney Dangerfield, Michael McKean, Brendon Ryan Barrett. **1997**

CASS TIMBERLANE ★★ Sinclair Lewis's story of a prominent judge married to a voluptuous younger woman turns into a silly, superficial soap opera. Spencer Tracy and Lana Turner are mismatched as the judge and his wife. B&W; 119m. **DIR:** George Sidney. **CAST:** Spencer Tracy, Lana Turner, Zachary Scott, Mary Astor, Tom Drake, Albert Dekker. **1947**

CASSANDRA 🖤 Lifeless psychic thriller about an Australian woman plagued by a nightmare of her mother's gruesome suicide. Rated R for violence and nudity. 94m. **DIR:** Colin Eggleston. **CAST:** Tessa Humphries, Shane Briant. **1987**

CASSANDRA CROSSING, THE 🖤 A plague-infested train heads for a weakened bridge. Rated PG. 127m. **DIR:** George Pan Cosmatos. **CAST:** Richard Harris, Sophia Loren, Burt Lancaster, Ava Gardner, Martin Sheen. **1977 DVD**

CAST A DEADLY SPELL ★★★1/2 Scriptwriter Joseph Dougherty's premise is hard to resist: that, in a slightly altered Los Angeles of 1948, *everybody* would use magic as a means to get ahead ... except one lone private detective named H. Phillip Lovecraft (Fred Ward), last of the truly honest men. This made-for-cable *noir* fantasy is often wry and always entertaining. Rated R for violence and profanity. 93m. **DIR:** Martin Campbell. **CAST:** Fred Ward, David Warner, Julianne Moore, Clancy Brown. **1991**

CAST A GIANT SHADOW ★★ The early history of Israel is told through the fictionalized biography of American Col. Mickie Marcus (Kirk Douglas). Mar-

cus, an expatriate army officer, is cajoled into aiding Israel in its impending war to wrest independence from its hostile Arab neighbors. Highly romanticized piece of historical fluff. 142m. **DIR:** Melville Shavelson. **CAST:** Kirk Douglas, Senta Berger, Angie Dickinson. **1966**

CAST THE FIRST STONE ★★★ When schoolteacher Jill Eikenberry is raped and becomes pregnant, she decides to keep the baby despite public protest. When school officials doubt her version of the story, they dismiss her. Eikenberry fights back by hiring lawyer Richard Masur, who not only helps her win the case, but helps restore her dignity as well. Riveting made-for-television movie. 94m. **DIR:** John Korty. **CAST:** Jill Eikenberry, Lew Ayres, Richard Masur, Elizabeth Ruscio, Joe Spano. **1990**

CASTAWAY ★★ Nicolas Roeg adds some surreal touches to this otherwise mediocre film about a wealthy publisher (Oliver Reed) who advertises for a woman to live with him for a year on a deserted tropical island. His dreams of animal passion turn into domestic doldrums when his companion (Amanda Donohoe) opts for celibacy. Rated R for profanity, nudity, and simulated sex. 118m. **DIR:** Nicolas Roeg. **CAST:** Oliver Reed, Amanda Donohoe. **1987**

CASTAWAY COWBOY, THE ★★★1/2 James Garner plays a Texas cowboy in Hawaii during the 1850s. There he helps a lovely widow (Vera Miles) start a cattle ranch despite problems created by a land-grabbing enemy (Robert Culp). Good family entertainment. Rated G. 91m. **DIR:** Vincent McEveety. **CAST:** James Garner, Vera Miles, Robert Culp, Eric Shea. **1974 DVD**

CASTLE FREAK ★★ Disappointing bogeyman movie from Stuart Gordon, who should know better. When a couple (genre favorites Jeffrey Combs and Barbara Crampton) inherit a castle in Italy, they pack up everything and move. The castle comes with all the modern conveniences, including a blood-thirsty creature who preys on the locals. Gory special effects are no substitute for suspense. Rated R for gore, nudity, and adult language. 90m. **DIR:** Stuart Gordon. **CAST:** Jeffrey Combs, Barbara Crampton, Jonathan Fuller, Jessica Dollarhide. **1995 DVD**

CASTLE IN THE DESERT ★★★ Charlie Chan travels to the Mojave Desert as the guest of a millionaire whose wife is descended from the infamous Borgias. By some odd coincidence, people begin to die by poison. Full of secret panels, mysterious shadows, and close-ups of gloved hands, this is one of the most satisfying of the later Chans. B&W; 61m. **DIR:** Harry Lachman. **CAST:** Sidney Toler, Arleen Whelan, Richard Derr, Douglass Dumbrille, Henry Daniell. **1942**

CASTLE OF BLOOD (CASTLE OF TERROR) ★★★ Grand fun: the best of the black-and-white Italian horrors ground out in the Sixties following Mario Bava's wild *Black Sunday*. A stranger (George Riviere) meets Edgar Allan Poe in a tavern, and the author bets him he can't spend the night alone in a haunted mansion. Who could resist? U.S. TV title: *Castle of Terror*. B&W; 84m. **DIR:** Anthony M. Dawson. **CAST:** Barbara Steele, George Riviere. **1964**

CASTLE OF CAGLIOSTRO, THE ★★★★ Japanese animation with wider appeal than most Japanese animated features. International thief Wolf and his partners in crime attempt to rescue a young princess from a marriage to the wicked Count Cagliostro. Memorable animation, story, and characters. 100m. **DIR:** Hayao Miyazaki. **1980**

CASTLE OF EVIL ♥ Take an electronic humanoid, a dead scientist, some faulty wiring, what appears to be a good cast, and throw them together with a budget that must have run into the tens of dollars and you get this pathetic suspense movie. 81m. **DIR:** Francis D. Lyon. **CAST:** Virginia Mayo, Scott Brady, David Brian, Hugh Marlowe. **1966**

CASTLE OF FU MANCHU ♥ The worst Fu Manchu film ever made. 92m. **DIR:** Jess (Jesus) Franco. **CAST:** Christopher Lee, Richard Greene, Maria Perschy. **1968**

CASTLE OF THE CREEPING FLESH ♥ Knee-slapper of a bad Eurotrash horror opus, witlessly enlivened by open-heart surgery footage. Once (incorrectly) credited to director Jess Franco, rather than the actual culprit—leading man Adrian Hoven. Not rated. 90m. **DIR:** Percy G. Parker. **CAST:** Adrian Hoven, Janine Reynaud, Howard Vernon. **1968**

CASTLE OF THE LIVING DEAD ★★1/2 What makes this otherwise run-of-the-mill horror yarn worth watching are some impressive scenes toward the end. They were added by Michael Reeves, a young Englishman who directed several powerful horror films before his suicide. Christopher Lee plays a count who preserves people with an embalming formula. Donald Sutherland, in his film debut, plays two parts, including an old witch woman! B&W; 90m. **DIR:** Herbert Wise. **CAST:** Christopher Lee, Philippe Leroy, Donald Sutherland. **1964**

CASTLE, THE (1963) ★★★1/2 This highly metaphorical story from Franz Kafka's incomplete novel is translated literally here and makes for a very strange and humorous affair. Maximilian Schell is a land surveyor who is employed by the mysterious inhabitants of a castle, only to be denied access to the place once he arrives there. Not rated, has sex and nudity. 89m. **DIR:** Rudolf Noelte. **CAST:** Maximilian Schell, Cordula Trantow, Trudik Daniel. **1983**

CASTLE, THE (1997) ★★★ The head of a cheerful, lowbrow Australian family decides to put up a fight when the airport next door wants to expand by demolishing his ramshackle home. An unexpected smash hit in Australia, this goofy, eccentric, low-budget comedy is hard to resist. Performances are appealing, and the writing has some of the droll spirit of a well-made Monty Python skit. Rated R for profanity. 82m. **DIR:** Rob Sitch. **CAST:** Michael Caton, Anne Tenney, Stephen Curry, Anthony Simko, Charles Tingwell. **1997 DVD**

CASUAL SEX? ★★★ Oddball, likable comedy about two single girls (Lea Thompson and Victoria Jackson) who go hunting for men at a health resort. Although not providing roll-in-the-aisles laughter, *Casual Sex?* is a real attempt at making some sense of the safe-sex question. Rated R for sexual frankness, language and nudity. 90m. **DIR:** Genevieve Robert. **CAST:** Lea Thompson, Victoria Jackson, Stephen Shellen, Mary Gross, Andrew Clay. **1988 DVD**

CASUALTIES ★★★ Better-than-average revenge thriller stars Caroline Goodall as a woman trapped in a violent marriage to a vicious cop who won't let her leave. Mark Harmon plays the stranger who convinces her to turn the tables on her spouse. Intense situations and thoughtful characters create a heightened level of suspense. Rated R for adult situations, language, and violence. 85m. **DIR:** Alex Graves. **CAST:** Mark Harmon, Caroline Goodall, Jonathan Gries, Michael Beach. **1997**

CASUALTIES OF LOVE: THE LONG ISLAND LOLITA STORY ★★ One of a trio of made-for-TV movies that exploited the alleged affair between teenager Amy Fisher and auto mechanic Joey Buttafuoco. The acting by the two leads is surprisingly good. 94m. **DIR:** John Herzfeld. **CAST:** Jack Scalia, Alyssa Milano, Leo Rossi, Phyllis Lyons. **1993**

CASUALTIES OF WAR ★★★★ Michael J. Fox turns in an exceptional performance in this thought-provoking Vietnam War drama as the lone dissenter during his squad's rape and murder of a Vietnamese girl. Director Brian De Palma graphically brings home the horror of a war without purpose and heroes without valor. Rated R for violence, simulated sex, and profanity. 106m. **DIR:** Brian De Palma. **CAST:** Michael J. Fox, Sean Penn, Don Harvey, John C. Reilly. **1989**

CAT, THE (1966) ♥ Poor story of a lost boy who is rescued by a wildcat. 87m. **DIR:** Ellis Kadison. **CAST:** Peggy Ann Garner, Barry Coe, Roger Perry, Dwayne Rekin. **1966**

CAT, THE (1971) (LE CHAT) ★★★ Adaptation of the Georges Simenon novel about a long-married couple. Somewhere along the line their love turned to mutual loathing, and the husband transferred his affections to their pet cat. Not much happens, but watching Jean Gabin and Simone Signoret convey their feelings with almost no dialogue can be fascinating. In French with English subtitles. 88m. **DIR:** Pierre Granier-Deferre. **CAST:** Jean Gabin, Simone Signoret. **1971**

CAT AND MOUSE ★★★1/2 Written, produced, and directed by Claude Lelouch, *Cat and Mouse* is a deliciously urbane and witty whodunit guaranteed to charm and deceive while keeping you marvelously entertained. The plot has more twists and turns than a country road, and the characters are ... well ... just slightly corrupt and totally fascinating. In French with English subtitles. Rated PG. 107m. **DIR:** Claude Lelouch. **CAST:** Michele Morgan, Jean-Pierre Aumont, Serge Reggiani, Valerie Lagrange. **1975**

CAT AND THE CANARY, THE (1927) ★★★1/2 An exceptional silent version of a mystery that has been subsequently remade several times. The entire cast is wonderful as a spooky group that spends the night in a mysterious old house. Laura LaPlante is in top form. B&W; 75m. **DIR:** Paul Leni. **CAST:** Laura La-Plante, Tully Marshall, Flora Finch, Creighton Hale. **1927 DVD**

•CAT AND THE CANARY, THE (1939) ★★★ A group of relatives gather at a creepy old mansion to read the will of a rich man ten years after his death. Sliding panels, portraits with eyes that move, and a knife-wielding maniac in a fright mask make this comedy-chiller a real winner. Bob Hope, in this third version of a silent classic, initiates his successful teaming with Paulette Goddard. Brash, fun, and genuinely spooky. B&W; 74m. DIR: Elliott Nugent. CAST: Bob Hope, Paulette Goddard, Douglass Montgomery, Gale Sondergaard, George Zucco, John Beal. 1939

CAT AND THE CANARY, THE (1978) ★★★1/2 A surprisingly entertaining remake of the 1927 period thriller about a group of people trapped in a British mansion and murdered one by one. Rated PG. 90m. DIR: Radley Metzger. CAST: Honor Blackman, Michael Callan, Edward Fox, Wendy Hiller, Carol Lynley, Olivia Hussey. 1978 DVD

CAT AND THE FIDDLE, THE ★★★★ Jeanette Mac-Donald sings "The Night Was Made for Love," and the screen comes alive with romance. Ramon Novarro costars in a tuneful rendition of a Jerome Kern operetta about a struggling composer who gets upset because MacDonald sings "She Didn't Say Yes" in response to his romantic overtures. B&W; 90m. DIR: William K. Howard. CAST: Jeanette MacDonald, Ramon Novarro, Frank Morgan, Jean Hersholt, Charles Butterworth. 1934

CAT BALLOU ★★★ In this offbeat, uneven but fun comedy-Western, Jane Fonda plays Cat, a former schoolteacher out to avenge her father's death. Michael Callan is her main romantic interest. Lee Marvin outshines all with his Oscar-winning performance in the dual roles of the drunken hired gun and his evil look-alike. 96m. DIR: Elliot Silverstein. CAST: Jane Fonda, Lee Marvin, Michael Callan, Jay C. Flippen. 1965

CAT CHASER ★★ Peter Weller gives a stiff performance as an ex-Marine who gets mixed up in love, revenge, and murder. Rated R for violence, language, nudity, simulated sex, and rape. 97m. DIR: Abel Ferrara. CAST: Peter Weller, Kelly McGillis, Charles Durning, Frederic Forrest, Tomas Milian. 1988

CAT FROM OUTER SPACE, THE ★★1/2 Disney comedy–sci-fi about a cat from outer space with a magical collar. The cat needs the United States to help it return to its planet. Rated G. 103m. DIR: Norman Tokar. CAST: Ken Berry, Sandy Duncan, Harry Morgan, Roddy McDowall. 1978 DVD

CAT GIRL ★★ Dreary British B movie recommended only to fans of Barbara Shelley, who plays a young girl linked by a family curse to the spirit of a murderous panther. B&W; 70m. DIR: Alfred Shaughnessy. CAST: Barbara Shelley. 1957

•CAT IN THE BRAIN, A 💙 No real plot to tell of in this tepid entry from Italian gore master Lucio Fulci in which he plays himself, a horror film director growing sick of it all. Rated R for violence, gore, nudity, and simulated sex. 87m. DIR: Lucio Fulci. CAST: Lucio Fulci, David L. Thompson, Brett Halsey. 1990

CAT O'NINE TAILS ★★1/2 One of Italian horror maestro Dario Argento's least memorable films gets bogged down in tedious plotting. Blind Karl Malden and newspaperman James Franciscus team up to find a murderer. Dubbed in English. Rated PG. 112m. DIR: Dario Argento. CAST: Karl Malden, James Franciscus, Catherine Spaak, Carlo Alighiero. 1971

CAT ON A HOT TIN ROOF (1958) ★★★★ This heavy drama stars Elizabeth Taylor as the frustrated Maggie and Paul Newman as her alcoholic, ex-athlete husband. They've returned to their father's (Big Daddy, played by Burl Ives) home upon hearing he's dying. They are joined by Newman's brother, Gooper, and his wife, May, and their many obnoxious children. 108m. DIR: Richard Brooks. CAST: Elizabeth Taylor, Paul Newman, Burl Ives, Jack Carson. 1958 DVD

CAT ON A HOT TIN ROOF (1985) ★★★1/2 Updated rendition of the famed Tennessee Williams play strikes to the core in most scenes but remains oddly distanced in others. The story itself is just as powerful as it must have been in 1955, with its acute examination of a family under stress. Jessica Lange is far too melodramatic as Maggie the Cat. Things really come alive, though, when Big Daddy (Rip Torn) and Brick (Tommy Lee Jones) square off. A near miss. Unrated, has sexual situations. 140m. DIR: Jack Hofsiss. CAST: Jessica Lange, Tommy Lee Jones, Rip Torn, Kim Stanley, David Dukes, Penny Fuller. 1985 DVD

CAT PEOPLE (1942) ★★★★ Simone Simon, Kent Smith, and Tom Conway are excellent in this movie about a shy woman (Simon) who believes she carries the curse of the panther. Jacques Tourneur knew the imagination was stronger and more impressive than anything filmmakers could show visually and played on it with impressive results. B&W; 73m. DIR: Jacques Tourneur. CAST: Simone Simon, Kent Smith, Tom Conway. 1942

CAT PEOPLE (1982) ★★ While technically a well-made film, Cat People spares the viewer nothing—incest, bondage, bestiality. It makes one yearn for the films of yesteryear, which achieved horror through implication. Rated R for nudity, profanity, and gore. 118m. DIR: Paul Schrader. CAST: Nastassja Kinski, Malcolm McDowell, John Heard, Annette O'Toole, Ed Begley Jr., Ruby Dee, Scott Paulin. 1982 DVD

CAT WOMEN OF THE MOON 💙 Another ludicrous entry in the travel-to-a-planet-of-barely-dressed-women subgenre. 64m. DIR: Arthur Hilton. CAST: Sonny Tufts, Marie Windsor, Victor Jory. 1954

CATAMOUNT KILLING, THE 💙 Choppy and clichéd film about the perfect crime gone sour. 82m. DIR: Krzysztof Zanussi. CAST: Horst Buchholz, Ann Wedgeworth, Polly Holliday. 1985

CATCH AS CATCH CAN ★★ Vittorio Gassman plays a television-commercial actor who finds the animal kingdom out to get him. The dubbed English makes it worse. Not rated, has sex and nudity. 92m. DIR: Franco Indovina. CAST: Vittorio Gassman, Martha Hyer, Gila Golan, Claudio Gora, Massimo Serato. 1968

CATCH ME A SPY ★★★ This is a good suspense-thriller with, surprisingly, a few laughs. The story is built around an East-West espionage theme in which both sides trade for their captured spies. Rated PG. 93m. DIR: Dick Clement. CAST: Kirk Douglas, Marlene Jobert, Trevor Howard. 1971

CATCH ME IF YOU CAN ★★★ When financially troubled Cathedral High is threatened with closure, the student council resorts to gambling on illegal car races. Above average teen action flick. Rated PG. 105m. DIR: Stephen Sommers. CAST: Matt Lattanzi, M. Emmet Walsh, Geoffrey Lewis. 1989

CATCH THE HEAT ★★ Tiana Alexander is a narcotics cop in San Francisco sent undercover to South America to bust Rod Steiger. Even Alexander's kung fu prowess is routine with these cardboard characters. Rated R. 88m. **DIR:** Joel Silberg. **CAST:** David Dukes, Tiana Alexander, Rod Steiger, Brian Thompson, Jorge Martinez, John Hancock. 1987

CATCH-22 ★★★ This release stars Alan Arkin as a soldier in World War II most interested in avoiding the insanity of combat. Its sarcasm alone is enough to sustain interest. Rated R. 121m. **DIR:** Mike Nichols. **CAST:** Alan Arkin, Martin Balsam, Richard Benjamin, Anthony Perkins, Art Garfunkel. 1970

CATERED AFFAIR, THE ★★1/2 Bette Davis portrays a woman from the Bronx who is determined to give her daughter a big wedding. This Paddy Chayefsky drama, which he and Gore Vidal adapted from Chayefsky's teleplay, has much of the realistic flavor of his classic *Marty*. B&W; 93m. **DIR:** Richard Brooks. **CAST:** Bette Davis, Ernest Borgnine, Debbie Reynolds, Barry Fitzgerald, Rod Taylor. 1956

CATHERINE & CO. ★★1/2 British-born Jane Birkin is one of France's most popular actresses, though this, one of her typical soft-core sex comedies, hardly shows why. She plays a young woman who, having drifted into an innocent sort of prostitution, decides to incorporate herself with four regular "stockholders." Rated R. 99m. **DIR:** Michel Boisrone. **CAST:** Jane Birkin, Patrick Dewaere, Jean-Claude Brialy, Jean-Pierre Aumont. 1975

CATHERINE THE GREAT ★★ Stodgy spectacle from Great Britain is sumptuously mounted but takes its own time in telling the story of the famed czarina of Russia and her (toned-down) love life. Elisabeth Bergner in the title role lacks a real star personality, and dashing Douglas Fairbanks Jr. and sage Flora Robson provide the only screen charisma evident. Fair for a historical romance, but it won't keep you on the edge of your seat. B&W; 92m. **DIR:** Paul Czinner. **CAST:** Elisabeth Bergner, Douglas Fairbanks Jr., Flora Robson, Joan Gardner, Gerald Du Maurier. 1934

CATHOLICS ★★★★1/2 This film has Martin Sheen playing the representative of the Father General (the Pope). He comes to Ireland to persuade the Catholic priests there to conform to the "new" teachings of the Catholic Church. The Irish priests and monks refuse to discard traditional ways and beliefs. Trevor Howard is excellent as the rebellious Irish abbot. 78m. **DIR:** Jack Gold. **CAST:** Trevor Howard, Martin Sheen, Raf Vallone, Andrew Keir. 1973

CATHY'S CURSE 🐱 A young girl is possessed by the spirit of her aunt, who died in an automobile accident as a child. 90m. **DIR:** Eddy Matalon. **CAST:** Alan Scarfe, Randi Allen. 1976

CATLOW ★★ A Louis L'Amour yarn is the basis for this minor Western about a gold robbery. Typical effort by formerly blacklisted Sam Wanamaker. Rated PG. 103m. **DIR:** Sam Wanamaker. **CAST:** Yul Brynner, Richard Crenna, Leonard Nimoy, Daliah Lavi, Jeff Corey, Jo Ann Pflug. 1971

CATS ★★★1/2 While not as personal or as exciting as seeing it live, this videotaped performance of Andrew Lloyd Webber's musical is still enjoyable. Restaged and cast for this special performance, *Cats* comes alive with colorful characters, memorable tunes (one specially written for this performance), and a sense of awe. Even though it has been playing for more than ten years onstage, this is the perfect

opportunity for fans in small towns to appreciate the myth and the magic. Not rated. 115m. **DIR:** David Mallet. **CAST:** Elaine Paige, John Mills, Ken Page. 1998 DVD

CATS DON'T DANCE ★★★ Song-and-dance cat Danny ventures from Kokomo, Indiana, to 1939 Hollywood in search of stardom in this animated musical. Danny, a relentless optimist, can't understand why animals are cast only as animals—and never in leading roles. His career dreams are threatened by a ruthless child actress. Rated G. 76m. **DIR:** Mark Dindal. 1997

CAT'S EYE ★★★1/2 Writer Stephen King and director Lewis Teague, who brought us *Cujo*, reteam for this even better horror release: a trilogy of terror in the much-missed *Night Gallery* anthology style. It's good, old-fashioned, tell-me-a-scary-story fun. Rated PG-13 for violence and gruesome scenes. 98m. **DIR:** Lewis Teague. **CAST:** James Woods, Robert Hays, Kenneth McMillan, Drew Barrymore, Candy Clark, Alan King. 1985

CAT'S PLAY ★★★★ A chaste friendship between a widow and a retired music teacher runs into trouble when one of her friends makes romantic gestures toward the man. A deliberately paced but lovely film. In Hungarian with English subtitles. 115m. **DIR:** Karoly Maak. **CAST:** Margit Dayka, Samu Balasz. 1974

CATTLE QUEEN OF MONTANA ★★ Barbara Stanwyck gives a strong performance in this otherwise routine Western. Plot revolves around Stanwyck trying to protect her farm from land grabbers, who also murdered her father. Meanwhile, the Indians are out to wipe out everybody. 88m. **DIR:** Allan Dwan. **CAST:** Barbara Stanwyck, Ronald Reagan, Gene Evans, Jack Elam. 1954

CATWALK 🐱 Do we really need a 95-minute documentary on model Christy Turlington as she models, shops, and falls asleep in various hotels? The answer is no. Not rated; contains profanity. 95m. **DIR:** Robert Leacock. **CAST:** Christy Turlington. 1995

CAUGHT (1949) ★★★ Starry-eyed model Barbara Bel Geddes marries neurotic millionaire Robert Ryan, who proceeds to make her life miserable. His treatment drives her away and into the arms of young doctor James Mason. B&W; 88m. **DIR:** Max Ophüls. **CAST:** Robert Ryan, Barbara Bel Geddes, James Mason, Natalie Schafer, Ruth Brady, Curt Bois, Frank Ferguson. 1949

CAUGHT (1996) ★★★1/2 A young drifter, after being "adopted" by a New Jersey fish merchant and his wife, begins a torrid affair with the woman. When the couple's weasel-like son moves back home unexpectedly, the unstable atmosphere spins toward an appalling climax. Not rated; contains profanity, simulated sex, and brief but intense violence. 109m. **DIR:** Robert M. Young. **CAST:** Edward James Olmos, Maria Conchita Alonso, Arie Verveen, Steven Schub. 1996

CAUGHT IN THE ACT ★★1/2 Gregory Harrison stars as a drama teacher in this made-for-cable original. He finds an extra $10 million in his bank account and then is arrested for murder. Unfortunately, the viewer can figure out the entire plot in the first ten minutes. Rated PG-13 for violence and suggested sex. 93m. **DIR:** Deborah Reinisch. **CAST:** Gregory Harrison,

Leslie Hope, Patricia Clarkson, Kimberly Scott, Kevin Tighe. **1993**

CAUGHT IN THE DRAFT ★★★1/2 A gun-shy movie idol attempts to avoid the draft and mistakenly enlists in the army. Some very good gags; even the (then) topical ones stand up. B&W; 82m. **DIR:** David Butler. **CAST:** Bob Hope, Dorothy Lamour, Eddie Bracken, Lynne Overman, Irving Bacon. **1941**

CAULDRON OF BLOOD ✹ Boris Karloff plays a blind sculptor who uses the skeletons of women his wife has murdered as the foundations for his projects. 95m. **DIR:** Edward Mann (Santos Alocer). **CAST:** Boris Karloff, Viveca Lindfors, Jean-Pierre Aumont. **1968**

CAUSE OF DEATH ★★ A college student and his girlfriend become entangled in a drug lord's attempt to retrieve an illicit fortune. A cut-rate remake (rip-off?) of *Marathon Man*. Rated R for violence and nudity. 86m. **DIR:** Philip J. Jones. **CAST:** Michael Barak, Sydney Coale Phillips, Daniel Martine. **1991 DVD**

CAVALCADE ★★★★1/2 A richly detailed pageant of life in London between 1900 and 1930, this film is as innovative as it was when it was declared best picture of 1933. The drama of relationships focuses on the way World War I affected their lives. A truly remarkable film. B&W; 111m. **DIR:** Frank Lloyd. **CAST:** Clive Brook, Diana Wynyard, Ursula Jeans, Margaret Lindsay, Bonita Granville, Billy Bevan, Una O'Connor, Beryl Mercer, Frank Lawton. **1933**

CAVE GIRL ✹ A high school student gets lost in a cave during a field trip and pops up in prehistoric times. Rated R for nudity and profanity. 85m. **DIR:** David Oliver. **CAST:** Daniel Roebuck, Cindy Ann Thompson. **1985**

CAVE OF THE LIVING DEAD ✹ An Interpol inspector and a witch join forces to locate some missing girls. 89m. **DIR:** Akos von Ratony. **CAST:** Adrian Hoven, Karin Field, Erika Remberg, Wolfgang Preiss, John Kitzmiller. **1964**

CAVEMAN ★★ Ex-Beatle Ringo Starr plays the prehistoric hero in this spoof of *One Million Years B.C.* Because of the amount of sexual innuendo, it is definitely not recommended for kids. Rated PG. 92m. **DIR:** Carl Gottlieb. **CAST:** Ringo Starr, Barbara Bach, John Matuszak, Shelley Long, Dennis Quaid. **1981**

CB4 ★★ This attempt to parody the rap music industry has some very funny moments, but overall it fails as a satire and becomes a silly sex comedy full of profanity and misogyny. Rated R for violence, profanity, and nudity. 88m. **DIR:** Tamra Davis. **CAST:** Chris Rock, Allen Payne, Deezer D, Phil Hartman, Art Evans, Theresa Randle, Willard E. Pugh, Richard Gant, Charlie Murphy, Chris Elliott. **1993**

C.C. & COMPANY ★★1/2 Basically idiotic action film has Broadway Joe Namath (in his first feature) cast as C.C. Ryder, misfit member of a rowdy biker gang, attempting to "split" when he falls for top fashion photographer Ann-Margret. Rated R for mild language and nudity. 90m. **DIR:** Seymour Robbie. **CAST:** Joe Namath, Ann-Margret, William Smith, Sid Haig, Jennifer Billingsley, Greg Mullavey. **1970**

CEASE FIRE ★★★1/2 An answer to the comic book–style heroism of *Rambo* and the *Missing in Action* movies, *Cease Fire* is a heartfelt, well-acted,

and touching drama about the aftereffects of Vietnam and the battle still being fought by some veterans. Don Johnson stars as Tim Murphy, a veteran whose life begins to crumble after fifteen years of valiant effort at fitting back into society. Rated R for profanity and violence. 97m. **DIR:** David Nutter. **CAST:** Don Johnson, Lisa Blount, Robert F. Lyons, Richard Chaves, Chris Noel. **1985**

CEILING ZERO ★★★★ Once again, director Howard Hawks focuses on a group of professionals: pilots battling thick fog and crude ground-to-air communications to get the mail through. Cocky flier James Cagney joins old friend Pat O'Brien's crew only to neglect his duties in favor of seducing a fellow flier June Travis. Fast-paced and riveting; one of the finest of the Cagney-O'Brien teamings. B&W; 95m. **DIR:** Howard Hawks. **CAST:** James Cagney, Pat O'Brien, June Travis, Stu Erwin, Barton MacLane, Isabel Jewell. **1935**

CELEBRATING BIRD: THE TRIUMPH OF CHARLIE PARKER ★★★★ Fascinating documentary that chronicles jazz legend Charlie Parker's career through interviews and live performances. Parker, nicknamed Bird, created a new style of jazz before his untimely death at 34. Other jazz greats—Dizzy Gillespie, Charles Mingus, and Thelonius Monk—add to the pleasure. 58m. **DIR:** Gary Giddins, Kendrick Simmons. **CAST:** Charlie Parker. **1987**

CELEBRATION, THE ★★1/2 A Danish clan gathers for the patriarch's sixtieth birthday party—and if you can't guess what "shocking" secrets will come out, then you probably haven't seen many dysfunctional-family-reunion pictures lately. The film has the novelty of its documentary style (shot on video with available light) to compensate for trite characters and monotonous predictability. In Danish with English subtitles. Rated R for profanity and sexual scenes. 101m. **DIR:** Thomas Vinterberg. **CAST:** Ulrich Thomsen, Henning Moritzen, Thomas Bo Larsen, Paprika Steen. **1998**

CELEBRITY ★★★1/2 Three high school buddies go too far on a drunken binge, with one of them raping a country girl. This crime binds the three as they go on with their lives. Each gains fame in a different medium (writing, acting, and preaching). Twenty-five years later, they're reunited in a highly publicized trial. This sudsy TV miniseries will have you glued to your set. 313m. **DIR:** Paul Wendkos. **CAST:** Michael Beck, Joseph Bottoms, Ben Masters. **1984**

CELEBRITY (1998) ★★1/2 In trendy Manhattan, a journalist (Kenneth Branagh) skids down the ladder of fame while his neurotic ex-wife (Judy Davis) climbs up. The black-and-white photography is the tip-off that writer-director Woody Allen is on his high horse again, making sour jokes about the shallowness of celebrity worship. Many stars do cute little two-scene bits, like guests at a show-biz party taking turns entertaining. Rated R for profanity. B&W; 114m. **DIR:** Woody Allen. **CAST:** Kenneth Branagh, Judy Davis, Charlize Theron, Leonardo DiCaprio, Famke Janssen, Winona Ryder. **1998 DVD**

CELESTE ★★ Ponderously pedestrian, spasmodically amusing and touching, this tale concerns the blooming fondness between the author Marcel

Proust and his maid, who says of him, "At times I feel like his mother, and at times his child." This movie is historically interesting, but ultimately bleak and lackluster. In German with English subtitles. Not rated. 107m. **DIR:** Percy Adlon. **CAST:** Eva Mattes, Jurgen Arndt. **1981**

CELESTIAL CLOCKWORK ★★1/2 This comic Cinderella story about a Venezuelan opera singer who moves to France to become a movie musical star is alternately charming and dull. In a mix of old-fashioned storytelling, performance art, and fantasy, immigrant Ana is tricked by a jealous roommate and prevented from meeting an opera producer. Ana's teacher, a clairvoyant gay waiter, and a lesbian psychoanalyst conspire to secure her an audition. In French and Spanish with English subtitles. Not rated, but appropriate for adults. 86m. **DIR:** Fina Torres. **CAST:** Ariadna Gil, Arielle Dombasle, Evelyne Didi, Frederic Longbois, Lluis Homar. **1996**

CELIA, CHILD OF TERROR ★★ Misleadingly promoted on video as a horror movie (the original title was simply *Celia*), this Australian import is about a 9-year-old girl having trouble adjusting to life in a conservative suburb after her beloved grandmother dies. Not rated, but not suitable for young children. 110m. **DIR:** Ann Turner. **CAST:** Rebecca Smart. **1989**

•**CELINE AND JULIE GO BOATING** ★★★★★ Described by one critic as "the most important film since *Citizen Kane,*" this entertaining movie succeeds both as an intellectual inquiry (into the nature of fiction) and as sheer cinematic fun. Two women—a librarian and a magician—visit a mysterious house only to forget what they observed every time they leave. As they gradually reconstruct the story, they realize that a little girl is in danger within. In French with English subtitles. 192m. **DIR:** Jacques Rivette. **CAST:** Dominique Labourier, Juliet Berto, Bulle Ogier, Marie-France Pisier, Barbet Schroeder. **1974**

CELLAR, THE ★★★ An ancient Indian demon, called upon to rid the world of the white man, resides in the basement of a rural farmhouse. When a young boy comes to visit his divorced father, no one believes his story about the hideous creature. A relatively scary monster movie directed by the man who brought us the wonderful *Night of the Demons.* Rated PG-13 for violence. 90m. **DIR:** Kevin S. Tenney. **CAST:** Patrick Kilpatrick, Suzanne Savoy, Ford Rainey. **1990**

CELLAR DWELLER 🎬 Typical junk about a hideous, satanic monster. Not rated; contains violence. 78m. **DIR:** John Carl Buechler. **CAST:** Deborah Mullowney, Vince Edwards, Yvonne De Carlo. **1987**

CELLBLOCK SISTERS 🎬 If there's a women-in-prison cliché missing here, it can't have been for lack of trying. Rated R for violence, profanity, nudity, and sexual situations. 96m. **DIR:** Henri Charr. **CAST:** Annie Wood, Gail Harris, Jenna Bodner. **1995**

CELLULOID CLOSET, THE ★★★★ Oscar-nominated documentary about the portrayal of homosexuals and lesbians in film history is charming and informative on any level. It's a feast of clips for film buffs, with thoughtful narration (written by Armistead Maupin, read by Lily Tomlin) and illuminating commentary by a variety of writers, actors, and filmmak-

ers (Harvey Fierstein, Paul Rudnick, Susan Sarandon, Tom Hanks, Arthur Laurents, etc). Rated R for mature themes. B&W/color; 102m. **DIR:** Robert Epstein, Jeffrey Friedman. **1995**

CELTIC PRIDE ★★★ During the NBA play-offs, two fanatical followers of the Boston Celtics, Daniel Stern and Dan Aykroyd, accidentally kidnap Damon Wayans, the star player from the opposing Utah Jazz team. While never laugh-out-loud funny, this comedy does have its moments, thanks to fine character turns from the stars. Rated PG-13 for humorous violence and profanity. 90m. **DIR:** Tom DeCerchio. **CAST:** Daniel Stern, Damon Wayans, Dan Aykroyd, Gail O'-Grady, Adam Hendershott, Paul Guilfoyle. **1996**

CEMENT GARDEN, THE ★★ This oddball little film is definitely not for everyone. Four children in working-class England find themselves suddenly orphaned and, to avoid being separated, the kids bury Mama's corpse in concrete in the basement. Sixteen-year-old Jack (Andrew Robertson) has decidedly unbrotherly feelings about his nubile older sister (Charlotte Gainsbourg). It's dreary, spiritless, and extremely ugly to look at. Not rated; contains profanity, incest, and other sexual activity. 101m. **DIR:** Andrew Birkin. **CAST:** Andrew Robertson, Charlotte Gainsbourg, Sinead Cusack, Alice Coulthard, Ned Birkin. **1993**

CEMETERY CLUB, THE ★★★1/2 Ellen Burstyn, Olympia Dukakis, and Diane Ladd are excellent as three widows who have trouble adjusting to life without their husbands. Screenwriter Ivan Menehell, who penned the original play, is not entirely successful in translating his snappy bits of stage repartee into screen action. Rated PG-13 for profanity. 107m. **DIR:** Bill Duke. **CAST:** Ellen Burstyn, Olympia Dukakis, Diane Ladd, Danny Aiello, Lainie Kazan, Jeff Howell, Christina Ricci, Bernie Casey, Wallace Shawn. **1993**

CEMETERY HIGH 🎬 This is one high school you won't want to attend. Not rated; contains violence, nudity, gore, and simulated sex. 80m. **DIR:** Gorman Bechard. **CAST:** Debi Thibeault. **1987**

CENTER OF THE WEB 🎬 Threadbare plot about an undercover agent for the Justice Department who's framed for the assassination of a state governor. Rated R for violence, nudity, and profanity. 90m. **DIR:** David A. Prior. **CAST:** Ted Prior, Tony Curtis, Charlene Tilton, Robert Davi, Bo Hopkins, Charles Napier. **1992**

•**CENTER STAGE** ★★1/2 This film, which spotlights the ballet world, is something of a mess, from the stereotypic characters to the mix of classical scores with bubblegum pop tunes. Although the picture deserves credit for casting actual dancers and showcasing their athletic grace, the script lacks pizzazz. Rated PG-13 for profanity and sexual candor. 113m. **DIR:** Nicholas Hytner. **CAST:** Amanda Schull, Zoe Saldana, Susan May Pratt, Peter Gallagher, Donna Murphy, Debra Monk, Ethan Stiefel. **2000**

CENTERFOLD GIRLS 🎬 Insane brute spends his time killing beautiful, exotic models. Rated R. 93m. **DIR:** John Peyser. **CAST:** Andrew Prine, Tiffany Bolling, Aldo Ray, Ray Danton, Jeremy Slate. **1974**

CENTRAL STATION ★★★1/2 A crusty old woman in Rio de Janeiro finds herself saddled with an orphan boy. When she reluctantly agrees to escort him cross-country to find his father, her maternal instincts come unbidden to the surface. This foreign-language variation on John Cassavetes's *Gloria* is predictable but well acted by the two principals, with a fascinating look at parts of Brazil tourists seldom see. In Portuguese with English subtitles. Rated R for profanity (in subtitles). 115m. **DIR:** Walter Salles Jr. **CAST:** Fernanda Montenegro, Vincius de Oliveira, Marilia Pera, Soia Lira. 1998 DVD

CENTURY ★★★★ Luscious turn-of-the-century drama set in London. Clive Owen is excellent as an idealistic doctor on the verge of a major breakthrough concerning diabetes. Robert Stephens is his mentor, a seasoned doctor who is threatened. Miranda Richardson shines as the lab assistant who stands by the young doctor's side. Gorgeous scenery and excellent production values take us back to a time and place that no longer exists. Not rated. 115m. **DIR:** Stephen Poliakoff. **CAST:** Miranda Richardson, Charles Dance, Clive Owen, Robert Stephens. 1993

CERTAIN FURY ★★ Tatum O'Neal is Scarlet ("Scar")—a dumb white street woman; Irene Cara is Tracy—a dumb pampered black woman. They're thrown together and run for their lives from police and drug dealers. Rated R for violence. 87m. **DIR:** Stephen Gyllenhaal. **CAST:** Tatum O'Neal, Irene Cara, Nicholas Campbell, George Murdock, Moses Gunn, Peter Fonda. 1985

CÉSAR ★★★1/2 The final and best part of the Marseilles trilogy that includes *Marius* and *Fanny*. You can watch it on its own, but you won't enjoy it nearly as much unless you see all three parts; the cumulative effect is resoundingly emotional. In French with English subtitles. B&W; 117m. **DIR:** Marcel Pagnol. **CAST:** Raimu, Orane Demazis, Pierre Fresnay. 1933

CÉSAR AND ROSALIE ★★★1/2 Beautifully orchestrated story of human passion about a woman (Romy Schneider) and her relationship with two lovers over a period of years. Excellent cast and a subtle screenplay and direction give strength to this comedy-drama. In French with English subtitles. Not rated. 104m. **DIR:** Claude Sautet. **CAST:** Yves Montand, Romy Schneider, Sami Frey, Umberto Orsini, Eva Marie Meineke. 1972

CHAIN LIGHTNING ★★ A slow-moving story about a World War II veteran who volunteers to test-fly a new jet during peacetime. But Bogart isn't the type to play a wimp, so the movie is not very credible. B&W; 94m. **DIR:** Stuart Heisler. **CAST:** Humphrey Bogart, Eleanor Parker, Raymond Massey, Richard Whorf, James Brown, Fay Baker, Morris Ankrum (Stepen Morris). 1950

CHAIN OF COMMAND 🎬 Mindless violence as an ex–Green Beret witnesses a war crime and is then forced to take on his superiors when they try to quiet him. Rated R for violence, nudity, and adult language. 98m. **DIR:** David Worth. **CAST:** Michael Dudikoff, Todd Curtis, Keren Tishman, R. Lee Ermey. 1993

CHAIN OF DESIRE 🎬 Intended as a message film about AIDS, this fails to engage or involve the viewer on any level. The film consists of just one sexual encounter after another. Not rated; contains profanity,

sex, and drug use. 107m. **DIR:** Temistocles Lopez. **CAST:** Linda Fiorentino, Elias Koteas, Malcolm McDowell, Tim Guinee, Grace Zabriskie. 1993

CHAIN REACTION (1980) ★★★ Engrossing drama following a nuclear power plant employee (Ross Thompson) accidentally exposed to a lethal dose of radiation during a near meltdown. Rated R for some explicit sex, nudity, and violence. 87m. **DIR:** Ian Barry, George Miller. **CAST:** Steve Bisley, Anna-Maria Winchester. 1980

CHAIN REACTION (1996) ★★★ When water is proven to be a clean source of energy via some inventive technology, the dark forces of the capitalistic status quo move in, leaving the scientists working on the project either dead or on the run from the authorities. Star Keanu Reeves doesn't bring this one quite up to *Speed*, but it's diverting enough as an evening's viewing. Rated PG-13 for profanity and violence. 106m. **DIR:** Andrew Davis. **CAST:** Keanu Reeves, Morgan Freeman, Rachel Weisz, Fred Ward, Kevin Dunn, Brian Cox, Joanna Cassidy, Chelcie Ross. 1996 DVD

CHAIN, THE ★★★ Obsessed American cop Gary Busey loses his job while pursuing gunrunner Victor Rivers, who leads our hero on a merry chase in the wilds of Central America. Alas, both men are captured by brutish soldiers, and the film turns into a modern echo of *The Defiant Ones*. Better than average for this sort of stuff. Rated R for profanity and violence. 96m. **DIR:** Luca Bercovici. **CAST:** Gary Busey, Victor Rivers, Rez Cortez, Joonee Gamboa, Craig Judd, James Rose. 1996

CHAINED ★★★ A typical potboiler from the 1930s that still radiates the vibes between Clark Gable and Joan Crawford. In this one he plays a macho South American rancher. The swimming scene with Gable and Crawford has as much sex appeal as an R-rated movie without nudity, just knowing looks. B&W; 75m. **DIR:** Clarence Brown. **CAST:** Clark Gable, Joan Crawford, Otto Kruger, Stu Erwin, Mickey Rooney, Akim Tamiroff, Una O'Connor. 1934

CHAINED FOR LIFE 🎬 This murder drama featuring Siamese twins Daisy and Violet Hilton is certainly one of the saddest and most exploitative feature films of all. Cheap and embarrassing, this tawdry attempt to cash in on a physical deformity is long, boring, and in terrible taste. B&W; 81m. **DIR:** Harry Fraser. **CAST:** Daisy Hilton, Violet Hilton. 1951

CHAINED HEAT 🎬 The story of women in prison, this cheapo offers few surprises. Rated R. 95m. **DIR:** Paul Nicholas. **CAST:** Linda Blair, John Vernon, Nita Talbot, Stella Stevens, Sybil Danning, Tamara Dobson. 1983

CHAINS 🎬 Schmaltzy clone of the cult favorite *The Warriors*. Violence and seminudity. 93m. **DIR:** Roger J. Barski. **CAST:** Jimi Jourdan. 1990

CHAINS OF GOLD ★★★1/2 A crusading social worker combs Los Angeles to find a young friend kidnapped by a particularly nasty drug-running street gang. The somewhat chaotic script comes from four hands (including John Travolta's), but director Rod Holcomb maintains a snappy pace that circumvents a few glaring inconsistencies. Made for cable; rated R for language and violence. 95m. **DIR:** Rod Holcomb.

CAST: John Travolta, Marilu Henner, Bernie Casey, Hector Elizondo, Joey Lawrence. 1991 DVD

CHAIR, THE ★★1/2 Atmospheric movie about a psychologist (James Coco) who sets up shop in an abandoned prison and runs tests on a select group of inmates. More spooky than scary. Rated R for profanity, violence, and gore. 94m. DIR: Waldemar Korzeniowsky. CAST: James Coco, Trini Alvarado, Paul Benedict, John Bentley, Stephen Geoffreys. 1989

CHAIRMAN OF THE BOARD 🎦 Wacky prop comedian Carrot Top tries to weave his high-energy live act into a lame comedy about a surf geek and inventor who inherits a corporation. Rated PG-13 for language and sex-related humor. 95m. DIR: Alex Zamm. CAST: Carrot Top (Scott Thompson), Jack Warden, Raquel Welch, Larry Miller, Courtney Thorne-Smith, Estelle Harris, Mystro Clark, Jack Plotnick, M. Emmet Walsh. 1998 DVD

CHALK GARDEN, THE ★★★ Adapted from the play of the same name by Enid Bagnold. The plot centers around a spoiled brat (Hayley Mills) who is the bane of her grandmother's (Edith Evans) life until she is made to see the light of day by the new governess (Deborah Kerr). Sensational acting all around. 106m. DIR: Ronald Neame. CAST: Deborah Kerr, Edith Evans, Hayley Mills, John Mills, Elizabeth Sellars. 1964

CHALLENGE, THE ★★★1/2 An American (Scott Glenn) gets caught in the middle of a decades-old private war between two brothers in modern-day Japan. This movie has ample rewards for both samurai film aficionados and regular moviegoers. Rated R for profanity and violence. 112m. DIR: John Frankenheimer. CAST: Scott Glenn, Toshiro Mifune, Calvin Young. 1982

CHALLENGE OF A LIFETIME ★★★ A depressed middle-aged woman decides to pick herself up by training for the Hawaiian Ironman competition. Worth seeing for the always-fun Penny Marshall and underground star Mary Woronov in a rare TV appearance. Not rated; contains no objectionable material. 95m. DIR: Russ Mayberry. CAST: Penny Marshall, Richard Gilliland, Mary Woronov, Jonathan Silverman, Paul Gleason, Cathy Rigby, Mark Spitz. 1985

CHALLENGE TO BE FREE ★★ This forgettable film features a fur trapper being chased across one thousand miles of frozen Arctic wasteland by twelve men and one hundred dogs. Rated G. 88m. DIR: Tay Garnett, Ford Beebe. CAST: Mike Mazurki, Vic Christy, Jimmy Kane. 1974

CHALLENGE TO LASSIE ★★ A Disney-type tale rewritten to suit Lassie at the height of her fame. The Disney remake (Greyfriar's Bobby) is more believable and better suited to family tastes. This one is strictly for Lassie buffs. 76m. DIR: Richard Thorpe. CAST: Edmund Gwenn, Donald Crisp, Alan Webb, Alan Napier, Henry Stephenson, Sara Allgood, Geraldine Brooks, Reginald Owen. 1949

CHALLENGE TO WHITE FANG 🎦 White Fang is a German shepherd running loose in the Yukon trying to stop crooks from cheating an old man out of his gold mine. Not rated. 89m. DIR: Lucio Fulci. CAST: Franco Nero, Virna Lisi, Harry Carey Jr. 1986

CHALLENGERS, THE ★★★1/2 Strong coming-of-age drama about a young girl, terrifically played by Gema Zamprogna, addresses important issues about growing up without seeming preachy. After her father dies, and she's forced to move to a small town, Mackie (Zamprogna) decides that the only way to fit into a local group of boys is to become one of them. Her masquerade works, but provides complications that force her to realize her own self-worth. Girls and boys alike will enjoy Mackie's adventures and realizations. Rated PG. 97m. DIR: Eric Till. CAST: Gema Zamprogna, Eric Christmas, Gwynyth Walsh. 1993

CHAMBER OF FEAR ★ Another of the Mexican films featuring footage of Boris Karloff shot in Los Angeles just before his death (see Sinister Invasion). 87m. DIR: Juan Ibanez, Jack Hill. CAST: Boris Karloff. 1968

•CHAMBER OF HORRORS (1940) ★★1/2 Breezy British thriller about a mysterious crypt and the search for the keys to unlock its secrets. Popular melodrama penned by Edgar Wallace boasts a torture chamber as well as a spooky mansion complete with creepy servants and all the trimmings. Fun but familiar fare. B&W; 80m. DIR: Norman Lee. CAST: Lilli Palmer, Leslie Banks, Romilly Lange, Gina Malo. 1940

CHAMBER OF HORRORS (1966) ★★1/2 A mad killer stalks 1880s Baltimore. Two wax-museum owners attempt to bring him to justice. Originally produced as a television pilot titled House of Wax, but it was considered too violent. Tame and silly. 99m. DIR: Hy Averback. CAST: Patrick O'Neal, Cesare Danova, Wilfrid Hyde-White, Suzy Parker, Tony Curtis, Jeanette Nolan. 1966

CHAMBERMAID ON THE TITANIC, THE ★★1/2 To get even with the wife he thinks has been unfaithful, a French coal miner invents a one-night stand with a maid from the Titanic the night before its ill-fated voyage. The tale grows in the telling, making him a sort of celebrity—until the chambermaid turns up alive. In French with English subtitles. Not rated; contains mature themes and sexual situations. 96m. DIR: Bigas Luna. CAST: Olivier Martinez, Romane Bohringer, Aitana Sanchez-Gijon. 1997

CHAMELEON (1995) ★★1/2 Latter-day "super cop" outing involving a revenge-obsessed DEA agent (Anthony LaPaglia) who's a master of disguise. His superiors unwittingly help him out when they assign him to bust a drug cartel—whose head just happens to be responsible for the murder of the lawman's wife and child. LaPaglia has a field day in the central role, but the film's plot is just a bit too derivative. Rated R for violence. 108m. DIR: Michael Pavone. CAST: Anthony LaPaglia, Kevin Pollak, Wayne Knight, Melora Hardin, Derek McGrath, Andy Romano, Robin Thomas, Richard Brooks. 1997

•CHAMELEON (1998) ★★1/2 Cheesy sci-fi actioner about an androidlike warrior battling the evil corporations. Entertaining if not outstanding. Rated R for nudity, sexual situations, violence, and profanity. 90m. DIR: Stuart Cooper. CAST: Bobbie Phillips, Eric Lloyd, John Adam. 1998

CHAMELEON STREET ★★★★ Chameleon Street is not an address; he's a man: a real-life Detroit imposter named William Douglas Street. And this quirky, entertaining film tells his story. A fascinating, offbeat screen portrait by writer-director-star

Wendell B. Harris Jr., it details how Street successively poses as a *Time* magazine reporter, a physician who actually performs surgery, an attorney who befriends Detroit Mayor Coleman Young, a foreign-exchange college student from France, and other purely bogus individuals. Rated R. 98m. **DIR:** Wendell B. Harris Jr. **CAST:** Wendell B. Harris Jr. **1989**

CHAMP, THE (1931) ★★★★ Wallace Beery is at his absolute best in the Oscar-winning title role of this tearjerker, about a washed-up fighter and his adoring son (Jackie Cooper) who are separated against their will. King Vidor manages to make even the hokiest bits of hokum work in this four-hankie feast of sentimentality. B&W; 87m. **DIR:** King Vidor. **CAST:** Wallace Beery, Jackie Cooper, Irene Rich. **1931**

CHAMP, THE (1979) ★★★1/2 This remake is a first-class tearjerker. Billy Flynn (Voight), a former boxing champion, works in the backstretch at Hialeah when not drinking or gambling away his money. His son, T.J. (Schroder), calls him "Champ" and tells all his friends about his father's comeback, which never seems to happen. Rated PG. 121m. **DIR:** Franco Zeffirelli. **CAST:** Jon Voight, Faye Dunaway, Rick Schroder, Jack Warden. **1979**

CHAMPAGNE 🎬 Alfred Hitchcock regarded this silent feature as one of his worst films, and who are we to disagree? B&W; 69m. **DIR:** Alfred Hitchcock. **CAST:** Betty Balfour, Gordon Harker. **1928**

CHAMPAGNE FOR CAESAR ★★★★ Satire of early television and the concept of game shows is funnier now than when it was originally released. A treasure trove of trivia and great one-liners, this intelligent spoof features actor Ronald Colman as Beauregarde Bottomley, self-proclaimed genius and scholar who exacts his revenge on soap tycoon Vincent Price by appearing on his quiz show and attempting to bankrupt his company by winning all their assets. B&W; 99m. **DIR:** Richard Whorf. **CAST:** Ronald Colman, Celeste Holm, Vincent Price, Barbara Britton, Art Linkletter. **1950**

CHAMPAGNE SAFARI, THE ★★★1/2 Fascinating documentary about Charles Bedaux, one of the world's richest men in the 1930s. This film is built around the footage of a lavish "safari" he took through the Canadian Rockies in a fleet of Citroëns bearing all the luxuries he and his party could want. (He even hired Oscar-winning cinematographer Floyd Crosby to film it.) B&W/color; 100m. **DIR:** George Ungar. **1995**

CHAMPION ★★★★ One of Hollywood's better efforts about the fight game. Kirk Douglas is a young boxer whose climb to the top is accomplished while forsaking his friends and family. He gives one of his best performances in an unsympathetic role. B&W; 100m. **DIR:** Mark Robson. **CAST:** Kirk Douglas, Arthur Kennedy, Ruth Roman. **1949**

CHAMPIONS ★★★★ The touching true story of English steeplechase jockey Bob Champion (John Hurt), who fought a desperate battle against cancer to win the 1981 Grand National. Rated PG. 113m. **DIR:** John Irvin. **CAST:** John Hurt, Edward Woodward, Jan Francis, Ben Johnson. **1984 DVD**

CHAN IS MISSING ★★★★ In this delightful independent production, filmed in San Francisco's Chi-

natown, two cab drivers attempt to track down a friend who disappeared after they gave him $5,000 to purchase a taxi license. Although in form a mystery, this comedy is also a gentle jab at racial stereotypes and a revealing study of problems faced by members of the Asian-American community. Not rated, the film has some profanity. 81m. **DIR:** Wayne Wang. **CAST:** Wood Moy, Marc Hayashi. **1982**

CHANCES ARE ★★★1/2 In this derivative but generally charming romantic comedy, a surprisingly effective Robert Downey Jr. plays the reincarnated soul of Cybill Shepherd's husband (Christopher McDonald). Downey has retained a dormant memory of his past life. It returns during a visit to Shepherd's home just as he is about to seduce "their" daughter (Mary Stuart Masterson). It's good silly fun from then on—even if you've seen *Here Comes Mr. Jordan* or *Heaven Can Wait*. Rated PG for mild profanity. 108m. **DIR:** Emile Ardolino. **CAST:** Cybill Shepherd, Robert Downey Jr., Ryan O'Neal, Mary Stuart Masterson, Christopher McDonald, Josef Sommer. **1989 DVD**

CHANDU THE MAGICIAN ★★1/2 Stylishly produced and full of exotic sets, sleight of hand, and special effects, this imaginative fantasy suffers from a stolid performance by Edmund Lowe. Bela Lugosi, however, is in rare form as the gleefully maniacal Roxor, master of the black arts. An enjoyable curiosity. B&W; 70m. **DIR:** William Cameron Menzies, Marcel Varnel. **CAST:** Edmund Lowe, Bela Lugosi, Irene Ware, Henry B. Walthall. **1932**

CHANEL SOLITAIRE ★★ This halfhearted rendering of the rise to prominence of French designer Coco Chanel (played by fragile Marie-France Pisier) is long on sap and short on plot. For the terminally romantic only. Rated R. 120m. **DIR:** George Kaczender. **CAST:** Marie-France Pisier, Timothy Dalton, Rutger Hauer, Karen Black, Brigitte Fossey. **1981**

CHANG ★★★★ "Chang" means elephant, and in this remarkable pseudo-documentary by the explorers-filmmakers who later teamed to make *King Kong*, the threat of a rampaging herd of the beasts looms over daily life among villagers in primitive Thailand. This is a restored version, from first-rate source prints, of one of the most vivid location adventures of its day. B&W; 67m. **DIR:** Merian C. Cooper, Ernest B. Schoedsack. **1927**

CHANGE OF HABIT ★★ In direct contrast to the many comedy-musicals that Elvis Presley starred in, this drama offers a more substantial plot. Elvis plays a doctor helping the poor in his clinic. Mary Tyler Moore plays a nun who is tempted to leave the order to be with Elvis. Rated G. 93m. **DIR:** William A. Graham. **CAST:** Elvis Presley, Mary Tyler Moore, Barbara McNair, Jane Elliot, Edward Asner. **1970**

CHANGE OF SEASONS, A 🎬 Poor Shirley MacLaine. The only difference between this and *Loving Couples*, which closely followed it into release, is that Anthony Hopkins and Bo Derek costar as the ultramodern mate swappers. Rated R. 102m. **DIR:** Richard Lang. **CAST:** Shirley MacLaine, Anthony Hopkins, Bo Derek, Michael Brandon. **1980**

CHANGELING, THE ★★★ This ghost story is blessed with everything a good thriller needs: a suspenseful story, excellent performances by a top-name cast, and well-paced solid direction by Peter Medak. The story centers around a composer whose wife and daughter are killed in a tragic auto accident. Rated R. 109m. DIR: Peter Medak. CAST: George C. Scott, Trish Van Devere, Melvyn Douglas, Jean Marsh, Barry Morse. 1979

CHANGING HABITS ★★1/2 Estranged from her father, an aspiring young artist supports herself by shoplifting art supplies and working at a nunnery in exchange for room and board. That this character is more appealing than obnoxious is due to the charms of star Moira Kelly. Rated R for profanity and sexual situations. 92m. DIR: Lynn Roth. CAST: Moira Kelly, Christopher Lloyd, Dylan Walsh, Eileen Brennan, Teri Garr, Shelley Duvall, Frances Bay, Anne Haney, Taylor Negron, Annabelle Gurwitch. 1997 DVD

CHANTILLY LACE ★★★1/2 This modern spin on Clare Boothe's *The Women* gets considerable mileage from its high-octane ensemble cast but ultimately disappoints because of its improvisational nature. Director-coplotter Linda Yellen encouraged her seven stars to develop their own dialogue but failed to provide enough structure. It's entertaining to watch these ladies discuss men, relationships, and jobs, but the third act is self-indulgently maudlin. Rated R for profanity, brief nudity, simulated sex. 105m. DIR: Linda Yellen. CAST: Lindsay Crouse, Jill Eikenberry, Martha Plimpton, Ally Sheedy, Talia Shire, Helen Slater, JoBeth Williams. 1993

CHAPAYEV ★★★ Although this was obviously designed as propaganda for the Bolshevik revolution, it is still well-made and entertaining, with a minimum of proselytizing. The film follows the overthrow of the czar from the point of view of Chapayev, a Russian general. In Russian with English subtitles. B&W; 95m. DIR: Sergei Vasiliev, Georgi Vasiliev. CAST: Boris Bobochkin. 1934

CHAPLIN ★★★1/2 Richard Attenborough takes almost a scandal-sheet approach in this bio-pic of Charlie Chaplin, forgetting what made Chaplin so important was the movies he made. Worth seeing for Robert Downey Jr.'s impersonation of Chaplin. Rated PG-13 for profanity and nudity. 145m. DIR: Richard Attenborough. CAST: Robert Downey Jr., Dan Aykroyd, Geraldine Chaplin, Kevin Dunn, Anthony Hopkins, Milla Jovovich, Moira Kelly, Kevin Kline, Diane Lane, Penelope Ann Miller, Paul Rhys, John Thaw, Marisa Tomei, Nancy Travis, James Woods. 1992 DVD

CHAPLIN REVUE, THE ★★★★ Assembled and scored by Charlie Chaplin for release in 1959, this revue is composed of three of his longer, more complex and polished films: *A Dog's Life*, which established Chaplin's reputation as a satirist; *Shoulder Arms*, a model for *The Great Dictator*; and *The Pilgrim*, in which escaped convict Chaplin assumes the garb of a minister. B&W; 121m. DIR: Charles Chaplin. CAST: Charlie Chaplin, Edna Purviance, Tom Wilson, Sydney Chaplin. 1959

CHAPTER TWO ★★★1/2 Writer Neil Simon examines the problems that arise when a recently widowed author courts and marries a recently divorced actress. George Schneider (James Caan) is recovering from the death of his wife when he strikes up a whirlwind courtship with actress Jennie MacLaine

(Marsha Mason). They get married, but George is tormented by the memory of his first, beloved wife. Rated PG. 124m. DIR: Robert Moore. CAST: James Caan, Marsha Mason, Valerie Harper, Joseph Bologna. 1979

CHARACTER (KARAKTER) ★★★ In 1920s Rotterdam, a young man struggles to succeed against both the stigma of his illegitimate birth and the machinations of his biological father, a heartless, petty government official. This 1997 Oscar winner for best foreign film has relentless pacing, attractive actors, and handsome cinematography to recommend it, but the melodrama is rather bombastic and overwrought. In Dutch with English subtitles. Rated R for mature themes. 114m. DIR: Mike van Diem. CAST: Fedja van Huet, Jan Decleir, Betty Schuurman, Victor Low. 1997

CHARADE ★★★★1/2 A comedy-mystery directed in the Alfred Hitchcock suspense style featuring the ever-suave Cary Grant helping widow Audrey Hepburn find the fortune stashed by her late husband. Walter Matthau, George Kennedy, and James Coburn are first-rate in support. 114m. DIR: Stanley Donen. CAST: Cary Grant, Audrey Hepburn, Walter Matthau, James Coburn, George Kennedy. 1963 DVD

CHARGE OF THE LIGHT BRIGADE, THE (1936) ★★★★ October 25, 1854: Balaclava, the Crimea; military minds blunder, and six hundred gallant Britishers, sabers flashing, ride to their deaths. The film, which climaxes with one of the most dramatic cavalry charges in history, is based on Tennyson's famous poem. B&W; 116m. DIR: Michael Curtiz. CAST: Errol Flynn, Olivia de Havilland, Patric Knowles, Donald Crisp, David Niven, Henry Stephenson. 1936

CHARGE OF THE LIGHT BRIGADE, THE (1968) ★★★1/2 Good depiction of the events leading up to the ill-fated 1854 Crimea engagement of the famed British unit that was controlled and directed by a glory-seeking and incompetent gentry. The climactic charge is moviemaking at its best. Rated PG-13 for violence. 128m. DIR: Tony Richardson. CAST: Trevor Howard, John Gielgud, Vanessa Redgrave, Harry Andrews, Jill Bennett, David Hemmings. 1968

CHARIOTS OF FIRE ★★★★★ Made in England, this is the beautifully told and inspiring story of two runners who competed for England in the 1924 Olympics. Rated PG, the film has no objectionable content. 123m. DIR: Hugh Hudson. CAST: Ben Cross, Ian Charleson, Nigel Havers, Nicolas Farrell, Alice Krige, Cheryl Campbell, Ian Holm, John Gielgud, Dennis Christopher, Brad Davis, Nigel Davenport. 1981 DVD

CHARIOTS OF THE GODS ★★ Based on Erich Von Daniken's bestselling book, this German production presents the theory that centuries ago Earth was visited by highly advanced space folks. The film is a nice travelogue, but its theories are never proved. Of minor interest only. Rated G. 98m. DIR: Harald Reinl. 1974 DVD

CHARLEY AND THE ANGEL ★★ Time-worn plot about a guardian angel who teaches an exacting man (Fred MacMurray) a few lessons in kindness and humility. The kids won't mind, but chances are you've seen a better version already. 93m. DIR: Vincent

McEveety. **CAST:** Fred MacMurray, Cloris Leachman, Harry Morgan, Kurt Russell, Vincent Van Patten. **1973**

CHARLEY VARRICK ★★★★ A bank robber (Walter Matthau) accidentally steals money from the mob (he hits a bank where its ill-gotten gains are laundered). Matthau is superb as Varrick, the "last of the independents," and Joe Don Baker sends chills up the spine as the hit man relentlessly pursuing him. Rated PG. 111m. **DIR:** Don Siegel. **CAST:** Walter Matthau, Joe Don Baker, Felicia Farr, Andrew Robinson, John Vernon. **1973**

CHARLIE BOY 🎬 Charlie Boy is an African fetish, inherited by a young British couple, that will take care of all your problems—usually by killing them. 60m. **DIR:** Robert Young. **CAST:** Leigh Lawson, Angela Bruce. **1982**

CHARLIE CHAN IN SHANGHAI ★★1/2 On what is supposed to be a vacation in his homeland of China, Charlie is drawn into a murder involving a ring of drug smugglers. Costar Charles Locher later changed his name to Jon Hall. B&W; 70m. **DIR:** James Tinling. **CAST:** Warner Oland, Irene Hervey, Keye Luke, Jon Hall. **1935**

CHARLIE CHAN IN CITY IN DARKNESS ★★ None of the younger Chans are on hand as Charlie, at a reunion with his war buddies in Paris, looks into the murder of an arms dealer who was selling to the Germans. Average entry with a touch of war propaganda. B&W; 75m. **DIR:** Herbert Leeds. **CAST:** Sidney Toler, Lynn Bari, Richard Clarke, Leo G. Carroll, Lon Chaney Jr. **1939**

CHARLIE CHAN AND THE CURSE OF THE DRAGON QUEEN ★★ Although there are moments in this tongue-in-cheek send-up of the 1930s Charlie Chan mystery series that recapture the fun of yesteryear, overall it's just not a very good movie. Rated PG. 97m. **DIR:** Clive Donner. **CAST:** Peter Ustinov, Lee Grant, Angie Dickinson, Richard Hatch. **1981**

CHARLIE CHAN AT MONTE CARLO ★★ Warner Oland's last appearance as the Asian detective was this below-average entry. Charlie and son investigate the murder of a messenger and the theft of a million dollars' worth of bonds. B&W; 71m. **DIR:** Eugene Ford. **CAST:** Warner Oland, Keye Luke, Virginia Field, Sidney Blackmer. **1937**

CHARLIE CHAN AT THE OLYMPICS ★★★ In one of the better series entries, Charlie helps track a stolen device that can fly a plane by remote control. The film features footage from the Berlin Olympics and of the *Hindenburg*, which exploded before this was released. B&W; 71m. **DIR:** H. Bruce Humberstone. **CAST:** Warner Oland, Katherine DeMille, Allan "Rocky" Lane, Keye Luke. **1937**

CHARLIE CHAN AT THE OPERA ★★★1/2 Charlie Chan is called in to help solve the mysterious disappearance of a mental patient. Crazed baritone Boris Karloff chews up the scenery magnificently as the odds-on killer, but sly Warner Oland as Chan and Keye Luke as his number-one son hold their own in this often confusing mystery. The thirteenth film in the Fox series, this is one of the best. B&W; 68m. **DIR:** H. Bruce Humberstone. **CAST:** Warner Oland, Boris Karloff, Charlotte Henry, Keye Luke, Thomas Beck, William Demarest. **1936**

CHARLIE CHAN AT THE RACETRACK ★★1/2 On a ship from Honolulu to Los Angeles, Charlie investigates the death of an old friend who was about to expose a racetrack-swindling operation. One of three Chan mysteries made in 1936. B&W; 70m. **DIR:** H. Bruce Humberstone. **CAST:** Warner Oland, Keye Luke, Helen Wood, Thomas Beck. **1936**

CHARLIE CHAN AT THE WAX MUSEUM ★★★ A radio broadcast from a wax museum means murder—as Charlie Chan weaves his way through false clues, false faces, and poison darts to unravel the eerie goings-on. Spooky settings and top character actors like Marc Lawrence make this one of the best of the Sidney Toler Chans made for 20th Century Fox. This one is compact and tantalizing. B&W; 64m. **DIR:** Lynn Shores. **CAST:** Sidney Toler, C. Henry Gordon, Marc Lawrence, Marguerite Chapman. **1949**

CHARLIE CHAN AT TREASURE ISLAND ★★1/2 San Francisco's 1939 World's Fair is the setting for this Chan entry, as Charlie (Sidney Toler) is aided by sideshow magician Cesar Romero in finding out who killed a mystery novelist. B&W; 72m. **DIR:** Norman Foster. **CAST:** Sidney Toler, Cesar Romero, Victor Sen Yung, Pauline Moore. **1939**

CHARLIE CHAN IN EGYPT ★★★ In one of the better Charlie Chan films, the Oriental detective investigates when the body of an archaeologist is found inside a pharaoh's tomb. Worth seeing for some effective chills and an early appearance by Rita Hayworth (still billed as "Rita Casino.") B&W; 65m. **DIR:** Louis King. **CAST:** Warner Oland, Pat Paterson, Thomas Beck, Rita Hayworth, Stepin Fetchit. **1935**

CHARLIE CHAN IN HONOLULU ★★1/2 Sidney Toler and Victor Sen Yung make their debut as Charlie Chan and son Jimmy, here trying to keep anyone from leaving a ship docked at Honolulu while they investigate an onboard murder. B&W; 67m. **DIR:** H. Bruce Humberstone. **CAST:** Sidney Toler, Phyllis Brooks, Victor Sen Yung, George Zucco. **1939**

CHARLIE CHAN IN LONDON ★★★ Chan visits an English country estate in order to prove that a man about to be executed for murder is innocent. A superior series entry, written by detective novelist Philip MacDonald. B&W; 79m. **DIR:** Eugene Forde. **CAST:** Warner Oland, Drue Leyton, Douglas Walton, Alan Mowbray, Ray Milland, E. E. Clive. **1934**

CHARLIE CHAN IN PANAMA ★★1/2 Charlie Chan races to expose an enemy agent who plans to blow up the Panama Canal in order to keep U.S. Navy ships from passing through. Still pretty good, despite the once-topical war references. B&W; 67m. **DIR:** Norman Foster. **CAST:** Sidney Toler, Jean Rogers, Lionel Atwill, Victor Sen Yung. **1940**

CHARLIE CHAN IN PARIS ★★1/2 Former Fu Manchu Warner Oland drew on almost twenty years of cinematic experience playing Oriental menaces to make the character of Charlie Chan uniquely his own. This seventh entry in the series shows why he succeeded so well. The Honolulu sleuth seeks the knife-wielding killer who murdered one of his agents. Chan's oldest son Lee (Keye Luke) makes his initial appearance and aids his father. B&W; 72m. **DIR:** Lewis Seiler. **CAST:** Warner Oland, Mary Brian, Erik Rhodes, John Miljan, Thomas Beck, Keye Luke. **1935**

CHARLIE CHAN IN RENO ★★1/2 While staying at a Reno hotel for women seeking divorces, a Honolulu woman is accused of murder. This gives Charlie another excuse to travel, although the emphasis in this series entry is on good, old-fashioned mystery instead of location. B&W; 70m. **DIR:** Norman Foster. **CAST:** Sidney Toler, Ricardo Cortez, Phyllis Brooks, Victor Sen Yung, Slim Summerville. **1939**

CHARLIE CHAN IN RIO ★★1/2 The last of the better-budgeted Charlie Chans was an improvement over the previous efforts. Chan (Sidney Toler) arrives in Rio de Janeiro to bring back a murderess, only to discover that she has been killed. Chan brings the killer to bay with the aid of a psychic. B&W; 60m. **DIR:** Harry Lachman. **CAST:** Sidney Toler, Mary Beth Hughes, Cobina Wright Jr., Victor Jory, Harold Huber, Richard Derr. **1941**

CHARLIE CHAN IN THE SECRET SERVICE ★★ First of Monogram Pictures's *Charlie Chan* programmers, as the poverty-row studio picked up the series from 20th Century Fox. A scientist working on a new explosive is murdered, and the secret service calls upon Charlie to find his killer. For die-hard fans only. B&W; 65m. **DIR:** Phil Rosen. **CAST:** Sidney Toler, Mantan Moreland, Gwen Kenyon, Benson Fong. **1944**

CHARLIE CHAN ON BROADWAY ★★★ A nightclub singer plans to publish her diary, revealing all she knows about some of New York's shadiest characters. When she is murdered, it's Charlie Chan to the rescue. One of the better Chan films, with a good use of Manhattan nightlife setting. B&W; 68m. **DIR:** Eugene Ford. **CAST:** Warner Oland, Keye Luke, Joan Marsh, J. Edward Bromberg, Lon Chaney Jr. **1937**

CHARLIE CHAN'S MURDER CRUISE ★★ Unmemorable mystery has the Oriental sleuth investigating the murder of a Scotland Yard detective on a cruise ship. Not the worst of the series, but for Chan completists only. B&W; 75m. **DIR:** Eugene Forde. **CAST:** Sidney Toler, Marjorie Weaver, Lionel Atwill, Victor Sen Yung, Leo G. Carroll. **1940**

CHARLIE CHAN'S SECRET ★★1/2 Charlie Chan travels from Honolulu to San Francisco in search of a missing heir. When the heir is murdered and then mysteriously appears during a séance, Chan nabs the culprit. Sliding panels, supernatural overtones, and plenty of red herrings highlight this tenth entry in the long-running series. B&W; 72m. **DIR:** Gordon Wiles. **CAST:** Warner Oland, Rosina Lawrence, Charles Quigley, Astrid Allwyn, Jonathan Hale. **1936**

CHARLIE CHAPLIN ... OUR HERO ★★★ Another trio of slapstick comedies starring Charlie Chaplin, who also scripted and directed the first two: *A Night at the Show* and *In the Park*. The third, *Hot Finish*, was originally titled *Mabel At the Wheel*. B&W; 58m. **DIR:** Charles Chaplin, Mabel Normand, Mack Sennett. **CAST:** Charlie Chaplin, Edna Purviance, Lloyd Bacon, Mabel Normand, Chester Conklin, Al St. John. **1914–15**

CHARLIE CHAPLIN—THE EARLY YEARS VOL. 1–4 ★★★★ Outstanding series of silent shorts features classic masterpieces: *The Immigrant, Easy Street, The Count, The Pawnbroker, The Floorwalker, The Vagabond, Behind the Screen,* and *The Ring*. Silent. B&W; 61–64m. **DIR:** Charles Chaplin. **CAST:** Charlie Chaplin, Edna Purviance, Eric Campbell, Albert Austin,

Henry Bergman, Lloyd Bacon, Charlotte Mineau, James T. Kelly, Leo White. **1915–1917**

CHARLIE CHAPLIN CARNIVAL ★★★ One of a number of anthologies made up of two-reel Chaplin films, this one is composed of *The Vagabond, The Count, Behind the Screen,* and *The Fireman*. Charlie Chaplin, Edna Purviance (forever his leading lady), and the giant Eric Campbell provide most of the hilarious, romantic, touching moments. Bedrock fans will find *The Vagabond* a study for the longer films that followed in the 1920s—*The Kid*, in particular. B&W; 80m. **DIR:** Charles Chaplin. **CAST:** Charlie Chaplin, Edna Purviance, Eric Campbell, Lloyd Bacon. **1916**

CHARLIE CHAPLIN CAVALCADE ★★★ Another in a series of anthologies spliced up out of two- and three-reel Chaplin comedies. This features four of his best: *One a.m., The Pawn-shop, The Floorwalker, The Rink*. As in most of Chaplin's short comedies, the sidesplitting action results mainly from underdog Chaplin clashing with the short-fused giant Eric Campbell. B&W; 81m. **DIR:** Charles Chaplin. **CAST:** Charlie Chaplin, Henry Bergman, Edna Purviance, John Rand, Wesley Ruggles, Frank J. Coleman, Albert Austin, Eric Campbell, Lloyd Bacon, Leo White. **1916**

CHARLIE CHAPLIN FESTIVAL ★★★ The third in a number of Chaplin film anthologies. Featuring *Easy Street*, one of his best-known hits, this group contains *The Cure, The Adventurer,* and *The Immigrant*, and gives viewers the full gamut of famous Chaplin emotional expressions. The coin sequence in the latter is sight-gag ingenuity at its best. B&W; 80m. **DIR:** Charles Chaplin. **CAST:** Charlie Chaplin, Eric Campbell, Edna Purviance, Albert Austin, Henry Bergman. **1917**

CHARLIE, THE LONESOME COUGAR ★★★ A misunderstood cougar comes into a lumber camp in search of food and companionship. After adopting the animal, the men are not certain whether it will adapt back to its wild habitat, or even if they want it to. More believable than the story line would suggest. Rated G. 75m. **DIR:** Not credited. **CAST:** Ron Brown, Bryan Russell, Linda Wallace, Jim Wilson, Rex Allen. **1968 DVD**

CHARLIE'S GHOST ★★★★ Engaging comedy, based on a story by Mark Twain, stars young Trenton Knight as the much-put-upon Charlie. His archaeologist father unearths the legendary Coronado's grave, thus unleashing his spirit. Lots of fun delivered by a strong cast. Rated PG for some minor violence. 92m. **DIR:** Anthony Edwards. **CAST:** Richard "Cheech" Marin, Anthony Edwards, Trent Knight, Charles Rocket, Linda Fiorentino, Daphne Zuniga. **1994**

CHARLOTTE'S WEB ★★ Disappointing adaptation of E. B. White's beloved children's book. Charlotte the spider, Wilbur the pig, and Templeton the rat lose all their charm and turn into simpering participants in a vacuous musical. For kids only. Rated G. 85m. **DIR:** Charles A. Nichols, Iwao Takamoto. **1973**

CHARLY ★★★★ Cliff Robertson won the best-actor Oscar for his role in this excellent science-fiction film as a retarded man turned into a genius through scientific experiments. Claire Bloom is also excellent as the caseworker who becomes his friend. Rated PG. 103m. **DIR:** Ralph Nelson. **CAST:** Cliff Robertson, Claire Bloom, Lilia Skala, Dick Van Patten. **1968**

CHARRO! ★★ Nonmusical Western was intended to introduce Elvis Presley, serious actor. However, the only thing this misfire proved was that its star could go without shaving. Try Don Siegel's *Flaming Star* instead. 98m. **DIR:** Charles Marquis Warren. **CAST:** Elvis Presley, Ina Balin, Victor French. 1969

CHASE, THE (1946) ★★ If the tempo were faster and the writing tighter, this film might have been interesting. As it is, it staggers along. The plot is quite predictable as Michele Morgan runs away from her husband. B&W; 86m. **DIR:** Arthur Ripley. **CAST:** Robert Cummings, Michele Morgan, Peter Lorre, Steve Cochran. 1946

CHASE, THE (1966) ★★1/2 Convoluted tale of prison escapee (Robert Redford) who returns to the turmoil of his Texas hometown. The exceptional cast provides flashes of brilliance, but overall, the film is rather dull. Redford definitely showed signs of his superstar potential here. 135m. **DIR:** Arthur Penn. **CAST:** Robert Redford, Jane Fonda, Marlon Brando, Angie Dickinson, Janice Rule, James Fox, Robert Duvall, E. G. Marshall, Miriam Hopkins, Martha Hyer. 1966

CHASE, THE (1994) ★★ Avoid this frivolous action-comedy unless you want to spend nearly 90 minutes in the front seat of a red BMW. Charlie Sheen plays a wrongly convicted prison escapee who takes the daughter of California's richest man hostage. They feud for several miles and then fall in love with the cops in hot pursuit. Wild action scenes include front-seat sex and cadavers bouncing down the freeway. A predictable yarn. Rated PG-13 for nudity, sex, and language. 88m. **DIR:** Adam Rifkin. **CAST:** Charlie Sheen, Kristy Swanson, Ray Wise, Cary Elwes, Henry Rollins. 1994

CHASERS ★★1/2 The misadventures of two Navy Shore Patrol lawmen (Tom Berenger, William McNamara) escorting a female prisoner (Erika Eleniak) to Charleston, SC. The premise is borrowed from *The Last Detail*, but the drawn out story never really gets rolling. Still, the stars are attractive, and the supporting cast is good; it might be worth a look on a slow night. Rated R for profanity, nudity, and sexual scenes. 103m. **DIR:** Dennis Hopper. **CAST:** Tom Berenger, William McNamara, Erika Eleniak, Gary Busey, Crispin Glover, Dean Stockwell, Marilu Henner, Dennis Hopper. 1994

CHASING AMY ★★★ Love blossoms between two young comic-book artists, even though she's a lesbian. The real obstacle to their happiness is the hero's sulky immaturity and his business partner, who seems jealous and possessive for more than platonic reasons. Rated R for profanity and nudity. 105m. **DIR:** Kevin Smith. **CAST:** Ben Affleck, Joey Lauren Adams, Jason Lee, Dwight Ewell, Jason Mewes. 1997 DVD

CHASING DREAMS ★★★ Here's another film made before a current top-billed player's stardom. In this case Kevin Costner is in and out of the story within the first five minutes. We're left with a low-budget, but very appealing, tearjerker. While Costner's away at college, his slightly younger brother must work on the farm, care for their ill youngest brother, and somehow sneak in baseball practice.

Rated PG for profanity. 96m. **DIR:** Sean Roche, Therese Conte. **CAST:** David Brown, Jim Shane, Kevin Costner. 1981

CHATO'S LAND ★★1/2 Unjustly accused of murdering a lawman, a half-breed Apache (the top-billed, but seldom seen Charles Bronson) must fight off a posse bent on killing him. Overly violent Western substitutes types for characters and bloodshed for story structure. Rated R. 110m. **DIR:** Michael Winner. **CAST:** Charles Bronson, Jack Palance, Jill Ireland, Richard Basehart, James Whitmore, Simon Oakland, Richard Jordan. 1972

CHATTAHOOCHEE ★★★★ British actor Gary Oldman gives a brilliant performance as an American war hero who attempts a bizarre suicide and ends up in the nightmarish Chattahoochee State Mental Hospital. Once inside, he devotes himself to exposing the horrific treatment of the patients. Rated R for brutality, nudity, and profanity. 98m. **DIR:** Mick Jackson. **CAST:** Gary Oldman, Dennis Hopper, Frances McDormand, Pamela Reed, Ned Beatty, M. Emmet Walsh. 1990

CHATTANOOGA CHOO CHOO ★★ The story deals with a bet to make a New York-to-Chattanooga train trip within a deadline. George Kennedy plays the comedy villain and owner of a football team of which Joe Namath is the coach. Rated PG for mild profanity. 102m. **DIR:** Bruce Bilson. **CAST:** George Kennedy, Barbara Eden, Joe Namath, Melissa Sue Anderson. 1984

CHEAP DETECTIVE, THE ★★★ Follow-up to *Murder By Death* from director Robert Moore and writer Neil Simon is an affectionate parody of the Humphrey Bogart classics. Generally enjoyable. Rated PG. 92m. **DIR:** Robert Moore. **CAST:** Peter Falk, Ann-Margret, Eileen Brennan, Sid Caesar, Stockard Channing, James Coco, Dom DeLuise, Louise Fletcher, John Houseman, Madeline Kahn, Fernando Lamas, Marsha Mason, Phil Silvers, Vic Tayback, Abe Vigoda, Paul Williams, Nicol Williamson. 1978

CHEAP SHOTS ★★ An aging Greek proprietor tries to save his motel from ruin. Urged by a full-time boarder, he makes blue films of a couple staying in one of his cabins. Not rated. The film includes some profanity and nudity. 90m. **DIR:** Jeff Ureles, Jerry Stoeffhaas. **CAST:** Louis Zorich, David Patrick Kelly, Mary Louise Wilson, Patience Moore. 1991

CHEAPER TO KEEP HER ♥ A sexist private detective tracks down ex-husbands who haven't paid their alimony. Rated R. 92m. **DIR:** Ken Annakin. **CAST:** Mac Davis, Tovah Feldshuh, Art Metrano, Ian McShane. 1980

CHEAT, THE ★★★★ A socialite gambles heavily on Wall Street, loses, and borrows money from a rich Oriental. Sensational melodrama in its time, and it holds up well today. Silent. B&W; 60m. **DIR:** Cecil B. DeMille. **CAST:** Sessue Hayakawa, Fannie Ward. 1915

CHEATIN' HEARTS ★★★★ Gorgeously photographed, multilayered story of three strong women and the men in their lives, in the "new" West. Sally Kirkland must come to terms with her philandering husband (James Brolin) and a new life as her two daughters make their own way in the world. Intriguing look, if a bit slow, at adult choices and the result-

...g consequences. Rated R for profanity and nudity. 8m. **DIR:** Rod McCall. **CAST:** Sally Kirkland, James rolin, Kris Kristofferson, Pamela Gidley. **1993**

HECK AND DOUBLE CHECK 🎬 This sad comedy tarring radio's Amos 'n' Andy in blackface was KO's biggest hit for the 1930 season and made Freenan Gosden and Charles Correll the top stars for hat year—but they never made another film. B&W; 0m. **DIR:** Melville Brown. **CAST:** Freeman Gosden, Charles Correll, Sue Carol, Charles Norton. **1930**

HECK IS IN THE MAIL, THE 🎬 Story of a man who s tired of the capitalist system. Rated R for profanity. 88m. **DIR:** Joan Darling. **CAST:** Brian Dennehy, Anne Archer, Hallie Todd, Chris Herbert, Michael Bowen, Dick Shawn, Beau Starr. **1986**

HECKERED FLAG ★★1/2 A race car driver must ace his ex-friend after stealing his girlfriend. An overdose of macho get-even feats serve as annoying distractions until the two learn to work together on a winning team. Not rated, contains nudity, profanity, and violence. 100m. **DIR:** John Glen, Michael Levine. **CAST:** Bill Campbell, Rob Estes, Amanda Wyss, Carrie Hamilton, Pernell Roberts. **1990**

HECKING OUT 🎬 A nervous fellow believes his own fatal heart attack is mere hours away. Rated R for language. 95m. **DIR:** David Leland. **CAST:** Jeff Daniels, Melanie Mayron, Michael Tucker, Ann Magnuson. **1989**

HEECH AND CHONG'S NEXT MOVIE ★★ This is Cheech and Chong's (Richard Marin and Thomas Chong) in-between movie—in between *Up in Smoke*, their first, and *Nice Dreams*, number three. If you liked either of the other two, you'll like *Next Movie*. But if you didn't care for the duo's brand of humor there, you won't in this one either. Rated R for nudity and profanity. 99m. **DIR:** Thomas Chong. **CAST:** Cheech and Chong, Evelyn Guerrero, Betty Kennedy. **1980**

HEERLEADER CAMP ★ Another dumb teenage slasher flick, this time set at a resort for cheerleaders. Rated R for nudity and violence. 89m. **DIR:** John Quinn. **CAST:** Betsy Russell, Leif Garrett, Lucinda Dickey. **1987**

HEERS FOR MISS BISHOP ★★★ Nostalgic, poignant story of a schoolteacher in a midwestern town who devotes her life to teaching. A warm reassuring film in the tradition of *Miss Dove* and *Mr. Chips*. B&W; 95m. **DIR:** Tay Garnett. **CAST:** Martha Scott, William Gargan, Edmund Gwenn, Sterling Holloway, Sidney Blackmer. **1941**

HEETAH ★★★ Two L.A. teens journey to Kenya to spend six months with their parents. A chance encounter with a cheetah cub sets the stage for a well-handled version of the old-fashioned Disney adventure movies for kids. Rated G. 83m. **DIR:** Jeff Blyth. **CAST:** Keith Coogan, Lucy Deakins. **1989**

HEF IN LOVE, A ★★★ Gourmet French chef Pascal searches the Soviet Union in the 1920s for gastronomic delights. He then opens a restaurant, which is invaded by the Red Army. The chef faces abuse and even the loss of his princess lover to a sourpuss army officer, but will not abandon his eatery. In French with English subtitles. Rated PG-13 for nudity and sexual situations. 98m. **DIR:** Nan Dzhordzhadze.

CAST: Pierre Richard, Micheline Presle, Nino Kirtadze, Teimour Kahmhadze, Jean-Yves Gautier, Ramaz Tchkhikvadze. **1996**

CHERNOBYL: THE FINAL WARNING ★★★ Well-intended look at the Chernobyl nuclear power plant disaster in Russia. This telefilm takes a close look at one family affected by the accident, as well as the broad impact it had and continues to have on the entire world. 94m. **DIR:** Anthony Page. **CAST:** Jon Voight, Jason Robards Jr., Sammi Davis, Annette Crosbie, Ian McDiarmid. **1991**

CHEROKEE FLASH ★★★ Old-time outlaw Roy Barcroft tries to go straight, but his old henchmen don't intend to allow him to do so. Barcroft's foster son, Sunset Carson, comes to his rescue. B&W; 58m. **DIR:** Thomas Carr. **CAST:** Sunset Carson, Roy Barcroft, Linda Stirling, Tom London, John Merton. **1945**

CHEROKEE KID, THE ★★★1/2 Sinbad makes an engaging gunslinger in this amiable, made-for-HBO Western spoof, which sends him through numerous low-key adventures that help him develop the skill to challenge heartless railroad tycoon James Coburn. A Martinez is quite funny as the loquacious companion who tells the Kid's story during a somber funeral, and Burt Reynolds is a hoot as a tale-spinning mountain man. Rated PG-13 for violence and profanity. 91m. **DIR:** Paris Barclay. **CAST:** Sinbad, James Coburn, Gregory Hines, A Martinez, Ernie Hudson, Mark Pellegrino, Burt Reynolds. **1996**

CHERRY 2000 ★★1/2 Made before she graduated to better roles in *Stormy Monday* and *Working Girl*, Melanie Griffith starred in this barely released movie as a sort of female Mad Max. Set in the year 2017, the semiparody casts Griffith as a mercenary who guides yuppie David Andrews through the deserts of the Southwest, now the domain of psychotic terrorists, in search of a robot warehouse. Rated PG-13. 93m. **DIR:** Steve De Jarnett. **CAST:** Melanie Griffith, David Andrews, Ben Johnson, Tim Thomerson, Brion James, Harry Carey Jr., Michael C. Gwynne. **1988**

CHEYENNE (TV SERIES) ★★★★ This Western series ranks with *Gunsmoke*, *Rawhide*, and *Maverick* as one of the best of its kind. Clint Walker plays Cheyenne Bodie, who roams the West in episodes that explore every possible theme in the genre. In "White Warrior," one of two shows released so far on video, Michael Landon plays a white man raised by Indians who causes problems for wagon master Cheyenne. In "The Iron Trail," Cheyenne must stop outlaw Dennis Hopper, who is out to kidnap President Ulysses S. Grant. B&W; Each 49m. **DIR:** Leslie Martinson, Lee Sholem. **CAST:** Clint Walker, Michael Landon, Dennis Hopper. **1955–1962**

CHEYENNE AUTUMN ★★★1/2 John Ford brings us this story of the mistreatment of the American Indian. His standard heroes, the U.S. cavalry, play the role of the villains as they try to stop a group of Cheyenne Indians from migrating back to their Wyoming homeland from a barren reservation in Oklahoma. 160m. **DIR:** John Ford. **CAST:** Richard Widmark, Karl Malden, Carroll Baker, James Stewart, Edward G. Robinson, Ricardo Montalban, Sal Mineo. **1964**

CHEYENNE SOCIAL CLUB, THE ★★★ This Western-comedy has a number of pleasing moments. James Stewart, an itinerant cowhand, and his low-key cohort Henry Fonda inherit some property in Cheyenne—which turns out to be a bordello. The premise is good, but at times director Gene Kelly doesn't have a firm grip on the script or on these hugely talented actors. Rated PG. 103m. DIR: Gene Kelly. CAST: James Stewart, Henry Fonda, Shirley Jones, Sue Ane Langdon. 1970

CHEYENNE TAKES OVER ★★★ Lash LaRue's long-needed vacation at the Lobos ranch is anything but restful as he discovers it's been taken over by an impersonator who claims birthright to the land. B&W; 58m. DIR: Ray Taylor. CAST: Lash LaRue, Al St. John, Nancy Gates. 1947

CHEYENNE WARRIOR ★★★ Against the backdrop of the Civil War, expectant mother Rebecca Carver and her husband are making the long trek west when a gang of vicious marauders kill her husband and leave her stranded in a remote trading post. There she teams with a Cheyenne warrior who also encountered the marauders, and was left for dead. Message of tolerance is well presented without seeming preachy. Rated PG-13 for violence. 86m. DIR: Mark Griffiths. CAST: Kelly Preston, Pato Hoffman, Bo Hopkins, Dan Haggerty, Rick Dean. 1994 DVD

CHICAGO JOE AND THE SHOWGIRL ★★ Based on the real-life Cleft Chin Murder Case in 1944 London, this disappointing thriller stars Kiefer Sutherland as a U.S. serviceman who teams up with an English dancer (Emily Lloyd) for a crime spree that ends in one murder and another attempted murder. Rated R for violence and profanity. 103m. DIR: Bernard Rose. CAST: Kiefer Sutherland, Emily Lloyd, Patsy Kensit, Liz Fraser, Alexandra Pigg. 1990

CHICKEN CHRONICLES, THE 💔 The carnal pursuits of a high school senior. Rated PG. 95m. DIR: Francis Simon. CAST: Steve Guttenberg, Ed Lauter, Lisa Reeves, Meredith Baer, Phil Silvers. 1977

CHICKEN RANCH ★★★ This documentary about the brothel that was the setting for the musical *The Best Little Whorehouse in Texas* presents a different picture of prostitution. Although shot in a cinema verité style—the workers and customers speak for themselves, with no passing of judgment by the filmmakers—the movie paints a relentlessly grim picture of the oldest profession. Not rated. 84m. DIR: Nick Broomfield, Sandi Sissel. 1983

•**CHICKEN RUN** ★★★1/2 This wry, wacky, egg-farm version of *The Great Escape* is a clever claymation adventure set on a 1950s English poultry ranch. Stern, greedy Mrs. Tweedy and her hen-pecked husband run the farm like a prisoner-of-war camp. Ginger is a scrappy, determined hen that asks a cocky rooster to help all her feathered friends escape before the Tweedys process them into pot pies. The film includes many of the mood swings that made Babe so richly rewarding, and an exciting rescue inside a pot pie factory (think *Modern Times* crossed with Indiana Jones heroics). Rated G. 85m. DIR: Nick Park, Peter Lord. 2000

CHIEFS ★★★★ A string of unsolved murders in 1920 in a small southern town is at the base of this engrossing suspense-drama. The story follows the various police chiefs from the time of the murders to 1962 when the town's first black police chief is intrigued by the case and the spell it casts over the town and its political boss (Charlton Heston). 200m. DIR: Jerry London. CAST: Charlton Heston, Wayne Rogers, Billy Dee Williams, Brad Davis, Keith Carradine, Stephen Collins, Tess Harper, Paul Sorvino, Victoria Tennant. 1985

CHIKAMATSU MONOGATARI ★★★★★ Because of a misunderstanding, a clerk and the wife of his employer are forced to flee their homes. One of Kenji Mizoguchi's masterpieces, a tragedy of ill-fated love in seventeenth-century Japan. In Japanese with English subtitles. Not rated. 110m. DIR: Kenji Mizoguchi. CAST: Kazuo Hasegawa, Kyoko Kagawa. 1954

CHILD BRIDE OF SHORT CREEK ★★ Based on a true account, this is the story of a polygamist community in Arizona disbanded by the police. Made for TV. 100m. DIR: Robert Michael Lewis. CAST: Christopher Atkins, Diane Lane, Conrad Bain, Dee Wallace. 1981

CHILD IN THE NIGHT ★★1/2 With all the devices of a murder mystery in place, the new twist to the theme in this TV movie involves *Peter Pan's* Captain Hook. A boy swears that the pirate villain had a hand in killing his father. 93m. DIR: Mike Robe. CAST: Jo-Beth Williams, Tom Skerritt, Elijah Wood, Darren McGavin, Season Hubley. 1990

CHILD IS WAITING, A ★★★ Difficult to watch but emotionally satisfying. Judy Garland, in a brilliant performance, is a worker at a hospital treating mentally retarded children. 102m. DIR: John Cassavetes. CAST: Burt Lancaster, Judy Garland, Gena Rowlands, Steven Hill, Paul Stewart. 1963

CHILD OF DARKNESS, CHILD OF LIGHT ★★ Two American teenage girls become pregnant while remaining virgins; according to Church prophecy, one will bear the child of God and the other will spawn the son of Satan ... but which is which? What hath *The Omen* wrought? Dedicated performances save this produced-for-TV Catholic chiller from complete turkeydom. Rated PG-13. 85m. DIR: Marina Sargenti. CAST: Anthony Denison, Brad Davis, Paxton Whitehead, Sydney Penny, Sela Ward. 1991

CHILD OF GLASS ★★ When a boy's parents buy an old New Orleans mansion, he discovers that it's haunted. Inoffensive Disney made-for-TV movie with a hammy performance by Olivia Barash as the ghost. 93m. DIR: John Erman. CAST: Steve Shaw, Katy Kurtzman, Barbara Barrie, Biff McGuire, Nina Foch, Anthony Zerbe, Olivia Barash. 1978

CHILDREN, THE 💔 Terrible film about kids marked by a radioactive accident while they were on a school bus. Rated R. 89m. DIR: Max Kalmanowicz. CAST: Martin Shaker, Gil Rogers, Gale Garnett. 1980

CHILDREN OF A LESSER GOD ★★★★ Based on the Tony Award–winning play by Mark Medoff, this superb film concerns the love that grows between a teacher (William Hurt) for the hearing-impaired and a deaf woman (Oscar-winner Marlee Matlin). The performances are impeccable, the direction inspired, and the story unforgettable. Considering the problems inherent in telling its tale, this represents phenomenal achievement for first-time film direcor Randa Haines. Rated R for suggested sex, profanity, and adult themes. 118m. **DIR:** Randa Haines. **CAST:** William Hurt, Marlee Matlin, Piper Laurie, Philip osco. **1986**

CHILDREN OF AN LAC, THE ★★★★ Just before the fall of Saigon in 1975, three women did the next o impossible: They managed the escape of hundreds perhaps thousands) of Vietnamese children. One of hese women was actress Ina Balin, who plays herelf here. The performances and production values f this made-for-television film are very good. 100m. **DIR:** Ina Balin, Shirley ones, Beulah Quo, Alan Fudge, Ben Piazza. **1980**

CHILDREN OF FURY ★★1/2 FBI agents try to capure a group of religious fanatics without harming he children in their care. Based on the true story of ne of the longest standoffs in FBI history, this nade-for-TV movie is pretty familiar stuff, with heroc good guys and cardboard villains. Not rated; conains violence. 85m. **DIR:** Charles Haid. **CAST:** Dennis ranz, Tess Harper, Kyle Secor, Paul LeMat, Ed Begley r. **1995**

CHILDREN OF HEAVEN ★★★★ Young boy in ehran picks up his sister's pink shoes from the cobler and loses them while running errands in this gentle, languid drama. The siblings devise a plan to keep their money-strapped parents from discovering he loss by sharing a lone pair of sneakers that they each must wear to school. This simple story of sibling nity and resourcefulness quietly becomes a poetic, motionally rich fable as modern Iran is filtered hrough children's eyes. In Farsi with English subtiles. Rated PG. 88m. **DIR:** Majid Madjidi. **CAST:** Amir Naji, Mir Farrokh Hashemian, Bahare Seddiqi. **1998**

CHILDREN OF NATURE ★★★★ This enthralling ook at old age was the first film from Iceland to reeive an Oscar nomination for best foreign-language novie. It details the story of an elderly couple, abanloned by families into a nursing home. They escape one night, and head for the woman's homeland in Northern Iceland. In Icelandic with English subtiles. Not rated. 85m. **DIR:** Fridrik Thor Fridriksson. **CAST:** Gisli Halldorsson, Sigridur Hagalin, Bruno Ganz. **1991**

CHILDREN OF NOISY VILLAGE, THE ★★★★ *My Life as a Dog* director Lasse Hallstrom adapted stories by Swedish writer Astrid Lindgren (best known for her *Pippi Longstocking* series). The stories are inked as tales created by the children of a small, happy town for the amusement of themselves and their neighbors. Children may need a little encouragement to sit through this the first time, but as a family film it can be pleasantly habit-forming. Not rated. Dubbed in English. 88m. **DIR:** Lasse Hallstrom. **CAST:** Linda Bergstrom, Anna Sahlin, Ellem Demercus. **1986**

CHILDREN OF PARADISE, THE ★★★★★ Long beloved by connoisseurs the world over is this rich and rare film of infatuation, jealousy, deception, grief, murder, and true love lost forever—set in pre-1840 Paris. Brilliant performances carefully controlled by superb direction make this fascinating account of the timeless foibles of men and women a true cinema classic. As Baptiste, the mime, in love with an unattainable beautiful woman, Jean-Louis Barrault is matchless. In French with English subtitles. B&W; 188m. **DIR:** Marcel Carné. **CAST:** Jean-Louis Barrault, Arletty, Maria Casares, Pierre Brasseur, Albert Remay, Leon Larive. **1944**

CHILDREN OF RAGE ★★1/2 This little-seen film deserves credit for doing something that few were willing to do at the time it was made: look beyond the actions of Palestinian terrorists to try to understand their motives. Unfortunately, good intentions don't compensate for lack of drama in this talky story about an Israeli doctor who attempts to open lines of communications with terrorists. Not rated; contains violence. 106m. **DIR:** Arthur Allan Seidelman. **CAST:** Helmut Griem, Olga Georges-Picot, Cyril Cusack, Simon Ward. **1975**

CHILDREN OF SANCHEZ, THE ★★★ Anthony Quinn stars as a poor Mexican worker who tries to keep his large family together. This well-intentioned film is slightly boring. Rated PG. 126m. **DIR:** Hall Bartlett. **CAST:** Anthony Quinn, Dolores Del Rio. **1978**

CHILDREN OF THE CORN 🐱 Yet another adaptation of a Stephen King horror story. A young couple come to a midwestern farming town where a young preacher with mesmerizing powers has instructed all the children to slaughter adults. Rated R for violence and profanity. 93m. **DIR:** Fritz Kiersch. **CAST:** Peter Horton, Linda Hamilton, R. G. Armstrong, John Franklin. **1984**

CHILDREN OF THE CORN II: THE FINAL SACRIFICE 🐱 A sour-pussed teen cult leader instigates more violence in this follow-up to Stephen King's original short story. Rated R for violence, simulated sex, and the world's most gruesome nosebleed. 94m. **DIR:** David F. Price. **CAST:** Terence Knox, Paul Scherrer, Rosalind Allen, Ned Romero. **1993**

CHILDREN OF THE CORN III: URBAN HARVEST ★★★1/2 After their father is killed by a deadly force in the cornfield, brothers Eli and Joshua are adopted by a young couple in Chicago. Eli brings along some corn from home, and while Joshua attempts to fit in, Eli summons the evil spirit to do his bidding. Rated R for gore and language. 91m. **DIR:** James Hickox. **CAST:** Daniel Cerny, Ron Melendez, Michael Ensign. **1995**

CHILDREN OF THE CORN IV: THE GATHERING ★★ Those nasty children from the cornfield return in this fourth chapter. This time the return of the corn beastie causes the children of a small town to develop horrendous fevers and zombielike personas while the adults just die, die, die. More of the same for people who liked the first three. Rated R for violence. 85m. **DIR:** Greg Spence. **CAST:** Naomi Watts, Brent Jennings, Samaria Graham, William Windom, Karen Black. **1996**

CHILDREN OF THE CORN V: FIELDS OF TERROR ★★ A group of college kids passes through the town where the title children live and kill for a satanic beastie who lives in the corn rows. Not one of the best of the series. Rated R for violence and horror. 83m. **DIR:** Ethan Wiley. **CAST:** Stacy Galina, Alexis Arquette, Adam Wylie, Greg Vaughan, Eva Mendez, Ahmet Zappa, Fred Williamson, David Carradine. **1998**

•**CHILDREN OF THE CORN 666: ISAAC'S RETURN** ★★ More of the same from the continuing direct-to-video franchise that has nothing to do with Stephen King's original story. This outing, a young woman returns to Nebraska in search of her birth mother and discovers her family has ties to the devil. Hokum from beginning to end. Rated R for adult situations, language, and violence. 78m. DIR: Kari Skogland. CAST: Natalie Ramsey, John Franklin, Stacy Keach, Nancy Allen, Alix Koromzay. **1999 DVD**

CHILDREN OF THE DAMNED ★★1/2 Inevitable, but disappointing, sequel to the 1960 sleeper, *Village of the Damned*. Worldwide, only six of the alien children have survived, so the children band together. B&W; 90m. DIR: Tony Leader. CAST: Ian Hendry, Alan Badel, Barbara Ferris, Alfred Burke. **1963**

CHILDREN OF THE DUST ★★★★ Superior miniseries is based on actual events and people of the nineteenth-century American West. Former gunfighter Gypsy Smith (Sidney Poitier) is all guts and compassion and hero to both Indians and African Americans. Not rated; contains violence and sexual situations. 180m. DIR: David Green. CAST: Sidney Poitier, Michael Moriarty, Regina Taylor, Billy Wirth, Joanna Going, Farrah Fawcett. **1995**

CHILDREN OF THE FULL MOON ❤ Even the curvaceous horror hostess Elvira and her off brand of humor can't salvage this cross between *Rosemary's Baby* and *The Wolfman*. 60m. DIR: Tom Clegg. CAST: Christopher Cazenove, Celia Gregory, Diana Dors. **1982**

CHILDREN OF THE NIGHT ★★★ Stylish horror-thriller goes right for the jugular in grand fashion. Peter DeLuise stars as a teacher who's summoned to the small town of Allburg when one of his friends claims that he has two female vampires locked up in a bedroom. Plenty of great, gory effects, and some splendid, campy acting. Rated R for violence and language. 92m. DIR: Tony Randel. CAST: Peter DeLuise, Karen Black, Maya McLaughlin, Ami Dolenz. **1992**

CHILDREN OF THE REVOLUTION ★★★ A fanatical Australian Communist has a one-night stand in 1949 Russia with Joseph Stalin and a double agent. She returns Down Under pregnant, marries a sweet-natured party associate, and raises a son who parlays an infatuation with prison into a lucrative position as a police-rights activist. Rated R for sexuality and language. 101m. DIR: Peter Duncan. CAST: Judy Davis, Sam Neill, Richard Roxburgh, F. Murray Abraham, Rachel Griffiths, Geoffrey Rush. **1996**

CHILDREN OF TIMES SQUARE, THE ★★★ A baby-faced teenage runaway is suddenly confronted with the pimps and drug dealers who prey on the desperate newcomers to New York City. Violent, powerful, made-for-TV message film. 95m. DIR: Curtis Hanson. CAST: Howard Rollins Jr., Joanna Cassidy, David Ackroyd, Larry B. Scott. **1986**

CHILDREN SHOULDN'T PLAY WITH DEAD THINGS ❤ Typical "evil dead" entry; amateur filmmakers work in a spooky graveyard and make enough noise to, well, wake the dead. Rated PG. 85m. DIR: Bob Clark. CAST: Alan Ormsby, Anya Ormsby, Jeffrey Gillen. **1972 DVD**

CHILDREN'S HOUR, THE ★★★1/2 Originally this was a moderately well-received play by Lillian Hellman, which director William Wyler filmed in 1937 (as *These Three*). Not satisfied with his first attempt, Wyler directed this remake about rumored lesbianism in a school for girls. Good performances from a veteran cast. B&W; 107m. DIR: William Wyler. CAST: Audrey Hepburn, Shirley MacLaine, James Garner, Miriam Hopkins, Veronica Cartwright, Fay Bainter. **1962**

CHILD'S CHRISTMAS IN WALES, A ★★ Dylan Thomas's holiday classic gets a tasteful but disappointingly clumsy treatment in this made-for-public-television special. Director Don McBrearty's images do not complement Thomas's brilliantly evocative words, and often actually contradict them. More like Walton Mountain than Thomas's mythical Welsh town of Llareggub. Not rated. 55m. DIR: Don McBrearty. CAST: Denholm Elliott, Mathonwy Reeves. **1987**

CHILD'S PLAY ★★1/2 Hokey, violent horror film finds a dying criminal putting his soul into a doll. When a mother buys the doll for her son's birthday, predictable mayhem occurs. Good special effects and some humorous dialogue keep this one from becoming routine. Rated R. 87m. DIR: Tom Holland. CAST: Catherine Hicks, Chris Sarandon, Brad Dourif. **1988 DVD**

CHILD'S PLAY 2 ★★★ Chucky, the psychopathic doll from the 1988 original, returns to wreak more havoc as he attempts to transfer his demented soul into the body of a little boy. Effects wizard Kevin Yagher's new Chucky puppet adds to the terror. Rated R for violence and profanity. 88m. DIR: John Lafia. CAST: Alex Vincent, Jenny Agutter, Gerrit Graham, Christine Elise, Grace Zabriskie, Brad Dourif. **1990 DVD**

CHILD'S PLAY 3 ★★ A mess of molten plastic at the end of *Child's Play 2*, Chucky the killer doll is resurrected eight years later when the new CEO of the toy company that manufactured the Good Guys dolls resumes production. Chucky once again sets out to trade souls with Andy, now a teenaged cadet at a state-run military school. Rated R for violence and profanity. 89m. DIR: Jack Bender. CAST: Justin Whalin, Brad Dourif. **1991**

•**CHILL FACTOR** ★★ A short-order cook (Skeet Ulrich) and an ice-cream truck driver (Cuba Gooding Jr.) go on the lam with a deadly biological weapon to keep it out of the hands of a demented arms dealer. They need the ice-cream truck because the weapon will detonate if the temperature rises above fifty degrees. Stitched together from pieces of better movies (*Speed*, *Raiders of the Lost Ark*, *The Wages of Fear*) and hammered across with clumsy enthusiasm, the film quickly becomes noisy and overbearing. Rated R for profanity and violence. 105m. DIR: Hugh Johnson. CAST: Cuba Gooding Jr., Skeet Ulrich, Peter Firth, David Paymer, Daniel Hugh Kelly. **1999 DVD**

CHILLER ★★★ A wealthy corporate widow's heir prematurely thaws out at a cryogenics facility. This made-for-TV sci-fi-horror film sketchily explores the possibility of life after death. Fright-master Wes Craven does a fair job of building suspense. 100m.

IR: Wes Craven. **CAST:** Michael Beck, Paul Sorvino, Jill Schoelen, Beatrice Straight, Laura Johnson. **1985**

CHILLERS ★★ Bored travelers at a bus depot exchange scary stories while waiting for a bus that never seems to come. Not that scary. Not rated; contains violence. 90m. **DIR:** Daniel Boyd. **CAST:** Jesse Emery, Marjorie Fitzsimmons, Jim Wolff. **1988**

CHILLING, THE 🎬 Frozen bodies in a cryogenics facility are charged back to life during a lightning storm. A truly horrible experience. Rated R for profanity. 91m. **DIR:** Jack A. Sunseri, Deland Nuse. **CAST:** Linda Blair, Dan Haggerty, Troy Donahue. **1991**

CHILLY SCENES OF WINTER ★★★★ You'll probably find this excellent little film in the comedy section of your local video store, but don't be fooled; it's funny all right, but it has some scenes that evoke the true pain of love. John Heard plays a man in love with a married woman (Mary Beth Hurt). She also loves him, but is still attached to her husband. Rated PG for language and sex. 96m. **DIR:** Joan Micklin Silver. **CAST:** John Heard, Mary Beth Hurt, Peter Riegert, Kenneth McMillan, Gloria Grahame. **1979**

CHIMES AT MIDNIGHT (FALSTAFF) ★★★1/2 This arresting film combines parts of five of the Bard's plays in which the popular, indelible Sir John Falstaff appears. Orson Welles as the famous roly-poly tosspot is superb, but the film is hampered by its anemic budget. Ralph Richardson narrates. B&W; 115m. **DIR:** Orson Welles. **CAST:** Orson Welles, Jeanne Moreau, Margaret Rutherford, John Gielgud, Keith Baxter, Alan Webb, Walter Chiari. **1967**

CHINA BEACH (TV SERIES) ★★★1/2 Television pilot film for Emmy Award–winning dramatic series. Set at a medical base in Vietnam, this is basically *M*A*S*H* without the laughs. Dana Delaney shines as a nurse who has seen so much that she's becoming numb. Sixties songs are a plus. 97m. **DIR:** Rod Holcomb. **CAST:** Dana Delany, Nan Woods, Michael Patrick Boatman, Tim Ryan, Chloe Webb. **1988**

CHINA CRY ★★★★ Based on the autobiography by Nora Lamm, this gripping drama is the story of one woman's struggle for justice in 1950s Communist China. Julia Nickson gives an outstanding performance as the adult version of the lead character, whose idyllic, privileged life as the daughter of a doctor (James Shigeta) is all but destroyed after the Japanese invade Shanghai in 1941. Rated PG-13. 103m. **DIR:** James F. Collier. **CAST:** Julia Nickson, Russell Wong, James Shigeta, France Nuyen. **1991**

CHINA GATE ★★1/2 A romantic triangle develops in North Vietnam in the late Fifties. Not bad, but Angie Dickinson and Lee Van Cleef as Asians just don't cut it. B&W; 95m. **DIR:** Samuel Fuller. **CAST:** Angie Dickinson, Gene Barry, Nat King Cole, Lee Van Cleef. **1957**

CHINA GIRL 🎬 Romeo and Juliet on Friday the 13th. Rated R for violence and profanity. 90m. **DIR:** Abel Ferrara. **CAST:** James Russo, David Caruso, Richard Panebianco, Sari Chang, Russell Wong, Joey Chin, James Hong. **1987**

CHINA IS NEAR ★★1/2 Marco Bellocchio, infamous for the tiresome *Devil in the Flesh*, displays a talent for both sardonic humor and political satire in this early film. The main characters plot against

each other to gain political office, sexual satisfaction, and financial security. Their various connivings eventually bring them together as a sort of large, squabbling family. In Italian with English subtitles. B&W; 110m. **DIR:** Marco Bellocchio. **CAST:** Glauco Mauri, Elda Tattoli. **1968**

CHINA LAKE MURDERS, THE ★★★ Made-for-cable TV movie centers around the killings committed by a man masquerading as a California highway patrolman. Michael Parks is the killer who befriends tormented sheriff Tom Skerritt. 89m. **DIR:** Alan Metzger. **CAST:** Tom Skerritt, Michael Parks, Lauren Tewes, Nancy Everhard. **1990**

CHINA MOON ★★★★ Hotshot Florida detective Ed Harris falls in love with femme fatale Madeleine Stowe, and finds himself a suspect when her brutal husband is murdered. It's hard-boiled detective fiction in the classic vein with terrific performances and atmospheric direction. Rated R for profanity, nudity, simulated sex, and violence. 99m. **DIR:** John Bailey. **CAST:** Ed Harris, Madeleine Stowe, Benicio Del Toro, Pruitt Taylor Vince, Roger Aaron Brown, Charles Dance. **1994**

CHINA, MY SORROW ★★★ In communist China, a mischievous boy is sent to a wilderness reeducation camp where he struggles with hardship and penalties for nonconformity. A satisfying blend of tension and unexpected humor. In Mandarin with English subtitles. 86m. **DIR:** Dai Sijie. **CAST:** Guo Liang-Yi, Tieu Quan Nghieu, Vuong Han Lai, Sam Chi-Vy. **1989**

CHINA O'BRIEN ★★ A former cop returns home to avenge her father's murder, using kung fu on the drug-dealing perpetrators. Rated R for violence and profanity. 90m. **DIR:** Robert Clouse. **CAST:** Cynthia Rothrock. **1990 DVD**

CHINA O'BRIEN 2 ★★ When a vengeful kingpin is sprung from jail, the streets aren't safe in a lady sheriff's town. Rated R for profanity. 85m. **DIR:** Robert Clouse. **CAST:** Cynthia Rothrock, Richard Norton. **1985**

CHINA SEAS ★★★1/2 Clark Gable is the captain of a Chinese river steamer in pirate-infested waters. Jean Harlow is once again the lady with a spotted past, who we all know is the perfect mate for Gable if he'd only realize it himself. An enjoyable screen romp. B&W; 90m. **DIR:** Tay Garnett. **CAST:** Clark Gable, Jean Harlow, Wallace Beery, Lewis Stone. **1935**

CHINA SKY ★★ Heroic doctor Randolph Scott puts down his stethoscope long enough to pick up a carbine and help Chinese guerrillas knock off hundreds of Japanese soldiers in this potboiler based on a Pearl Buck story. B&W; 78m. **DIR:** Ray Enright. **CAST:** Randolph Scott, Ruth Warrick, Anthony Quinn, Ellen Drew, Richard Loo. **1945**

CHINA SYNDROME, THE ★★★★★ This taut thriller, about an accident at a nuclear power plant, features strong performance and solid direction. It's superb entertainment with a timely message. Rated PG. 123m. **DIR:** James Bridges. **CAST:** Jane Fonda, Jack Lemmon, Michael Douglas, Scott Brady. **1979 DVD**

CHINA WHITE ★★ Shoot-'em-up takes place in Amsterdam's Chinatown when two Chinese drug lords threaten the Italian Mafia's profit margin. Add a romantic liaison and you have a just-watchable actioner. Rated R for violence and profanity. 99m. DIR: Ronny Yu. CAST: Russell Wong, Steven Vincent Leigh, Lisa Schrage, Billy Drago. 1990

CHINATOWN ★★★★★ Robert Towne's fascinating, Oscar-winning script fuels this complicated thriller. Jack Nicholson is a seedy private investigator hired for what seems a simple case of spousal infidelity, but rapidly escalates into a complex affair of mistaken identity and investment schemes. Faye Dunaway is the mysterious woman who may—or may not—know more than she admits. Rated R for language, violence, and brief nudity. 131m. DIR: Roman Polanski. CAST: Jack Nicholson, Faye Dunaway, John Huston, Perry Lopez, Diane Ladd, John Hillerman, Burt Young. 1974 DVD

CHINATOWN MURDERS, THE: MAN AGAINST THE MOB ★★★ L.A. cop George Peppard and his partners battle a prostitution ring operating out of Chinatown. Made-for-TV movie is most effective at recreating the sights and sounds of the 1940s, though the story is average TV fare. 102m. DIR: Michael Pressman. CAST: George Peppard, Richard Bradford, Charles Haid, Julia Nickson, Ursula Andress. 1989

CHINESE BOX ★★1/2 A dying journalist and author moons over his unconsummated love for a former prostitute and in between cocktail parties becomes fascinated by a scarred street hustler. This tepid, metaphorical meditation on affairs of the heart and the return of Hong Kong to Chinese rule is only partially satisfying. Rated R for language and mature themes. In English and Mandarin with English subtitles. 109m. DIR: Wayne Wang. CAST: Jeremy Irons, Gong Li, Maggie Cheung, Rubén Blades, Michael Hui. 1998 DVD

CHINESE BOXES ★★★ Arty thriller about an innocent American caught up in murderous intrigue in West Berlin. The plot is as puzzling as the game of the title. Thoughtful, patient viewers may enjoy it. Not rated; the film has violence and profanity. 87m. DIR: Christopher Petit. CAST: Will Patton, Gottfried John, Robbie Coltrane. 1984

CHINESE CAT, THE ★★ Second entry in the Monogram run of *Charlie Chan* mystery B features. Made just as the series was running out of energy. The red herrings drop like flies as rivals battle for possession of a statuette bearing a rare diamond. B&W; 65m. DIR: Phil Rosen. CAST: Sidney Toler, Benson Fong, Joan Woodbury, Mantan Moreland, Ian Keith. 1944

CHINESE CONNECTION, THE ★★★ This action-packed import, in which Bruce Lee plays a martial arts expert out to avenge the death of his mentor, is good, watchable fare. But be forewarned: It's dubbed, and not all that expertly. Rated R. 107m. DIR: Lo Wei. CAST: Bruce Lee, Miao Ker Hsio. 1979 DVD

CHINESE GHOST STORY, A ★★★1/2 Atmospheric supernatural love story in ancient China where a young student takes shelter from a storm in a haunted temple where he falls for a beautiful ghost. Impressive special effects are laced with comical situations. In Cantonese with English subtitles. 93m. DIR:

Ching Siu Tung. CAST: Leslie Cheung, Wong Tsu Tsien, Wu Ma. 1987 DVD

CHINESE ROULETTE ★★★ A businessman, his wife, and their lovers are forced into an intense psychological game of truth telling by the couples' paraplegic daughter in this fascinating social satire. In German with English subtitles. Not rated; contains nudity and profanity. 96m. DIR: Rainer Werner Fassbinder. CAST: Anna Karina, Margit Carstensen, Ulli Lommel, Brigitte Mira. 1976

CHINESE WEB, THE 🖤 Peter Parker (alias Spiderman) wards off a corrupt businessman. 95m. DIR: Don McDougall. CAST: Nicholas Hammond, Robert F. Simon, Benson Fong, John Milford, Ted Danson. 1978

CHINO ★★ A surprisingly low-key Charles Bronson Western about a horse breeder who attempts to live a peaceful life. An above-average performance by Bronson and an adequate one by his wife, Jill Ireland, as Chino's love interest. Rated PG. 98m. DIR: John Sturges. CAST: Charles Bronson, Jill Ireland, Vincent Van Patten. 1973 DVD

CHIPMUNK ADVENTURE, THE ★★ Alvin, Simon, and Theodore go on a round-the-world adventure in this uninspired feature-length cartoon. What made the original, scruffy chipmunks so appealing is missing here, replaced by a sort of ersatz Disney plot about jewel-smuggling villains. The kids may get a kick out of this, but anyone over the age of nine is advised to find something else to do. Rated G. 76m. DIR: Janice Karman. 1987

CHIPS, THE WAR DOG ★★★1/2 This heart-wrenching account of the Dogs for Defense program formed during World War II focuses on the incredible bond formed between a lonely private and a heroic German shepherd. William Devane plays the military leader determined to train donated family pets to accompany soldiers on dangerous missions. Made for the Disney Channel, the only objectionable scenes take place on the battlefield. 95m. DIR: Ed Kaplan. CAST: Brandon Douglas, William Devane, Ned Vaughn, Paxton Whitehead, Ellie Cornell, Robert Miranda. 1989

CHISHOLMS, THE ★★★ This made-for-TV oater is a vast saga of a family's trek west from Virginia to California. A bit talky, but worth a viewing. 300m. DIR: Mel Stuart. CAST: Robert Preston, Rosemary Harris, Ben Murphy, Brian Kerwin. 1979

CHISUM ★★★1/2 The best of the John Wayne Westerns directed by Andrew V. McLaglen, this sprawling epic centers around the revenge sought by Billy the Kid (Geoffrey Duel) after his mentor (Patric Knowles) is murdered by the corrupt, land-grabbing bad guys. Rated G. 111m. DIR: Andrew V. McLaglen. CAST: John Wayne, Forrest Tucker, Christopher George, Ben Johnson, Patric Knowles, Bruce Cabot, Glenn Corbett. 1970

CHITTY CHITTY BANG BANG ★★1/2 This musical extravaganza, based on a book by Ian Fleming, is aimed at a children's audience. In it, a car flies, but the flat jokes and songs leave adult viewers a bit seasick as they hope for a quick finale. However, the kiddies will like it. Rated G. 142m. DIR: Ken Hughes. CAST: Dick Van Dyke, Sally Ann Howes, Anna Quayle, Lionel Jeffries, Benny Hill. 1968 DVD

CHLOE IN THE AFTERNOON ★★★★ This film concludes director Eric Rohmer's series of "moral fables." It is a trifle featherweight and utterly charming. Will the faithful hero have an affair with bohemian Chloe (played deftly by singer-actress Zouzou)? In French with English subtitles. No rating. 97m. DIR: Eric Rohmer. CAST: Bernard Verley, Zouzou, Françoise Verley, Françoise Fabian, Beatrice Romand. 1972 DVD

CHLOE: LOVE IS CALLING YOU ★★1/2 Strange little bayou romance about a vengeful voodoo woman and the child she stole from a white family fifteen years before. Young Chloe is raised to believe herself the daughter of spell-casting Mandy, so when she falls in love with a wealthy white man she's warned off. Mandy breaks up the engagement party and kidnaps Chloe to be used as a human sacrifice in a voodoo ritual. Lots of atmospheric location footage and local players lend this curio its reality and heighten the frenzied finale. B&W; 54m. DIR: Marshall Neilan. CAST: Olive Borden, Reed Howes, Mollie O'Day, Frank Joyner, Georgette Harvey, Philip Ober. 1934

CHOCOLAT ★★★★ A subtle, sophisticated, remarkably restrained French look at the colonial life of the past in Africa, as viewed from the innocent perspective of an 8-year-old girl. Cecile Ducasse is memorable as the girl, whose story of growing racial awareness is told in flashback. In French with English subtitles. Rated PG-13 for profanity. 105m. DIR: Claire Dennis. CAST: Cecile Ducasse. 1989

CHOCOLATE SOLDIER, THE ★★ Nelson Eddy and Rise Stevens play husband and wife opera stars whose marriage is skidding in this clever, winning remake of the Lunt-Fontanne hit, *The Guardsman*. Delightful. B&W; 102m. DIR: Roy Del Ruth. CAST: Nelson Eddy, Rise Stevens, Florence Bates, Nigel Bruce. 1941

CHOCOLATE WAR, THE ★★★1/2 Actor Keith Gordon makes an impressive directorial debut with this comedy-drama about a bereaved student (Ilan Mitchell-Smith) facing the horrors of a sadistic teacher (John Glover) and a secret society of students at his Catholic high school. Some excellent performances and a story that keeps you fascinated. Rated R for profanity and violence. 103m. DIR: Keith Gordon. CAST: John Glover, Ilan Mitchell-Smith, Wally Ward, Adam Baldwin, Bud Cort. 1989

CHOICE, THE ★★ Abortion is the controversy in this made-for-television film. Susan Clark stars as a mother who must help her daughter make the critical decision on whether to have an abortion or not. Too sentimental, but the performances are commendable. 100m. DIR: David Greene. CAST: Susan Clark, Mitchell Ryan, Jennifer Warren. 1981

CHOICE OF ARMS, A ★★★ Yves Montand is a retired gangster who has chosen a peaceful life raising stud horses and giving his beautiful wife, Catherine Deneuve, all she could hope for. Gérard Depardieu is the convict who arrives seeking asylum. In French with subtitles; this film is unrated. 114m. DIR: Alain Corneau. CAST: Yves Montand, Gérard Depardieu, Catherine Deneuve, Michel Galabru, Gerard Lanvin. 1983

CHOIRBOYS, THE 🎬 Despite its stellar ensemble cast, this remains one of the worst police dramas ever lensed. Rated R for profanity and raunch. 119m. DIR: Robert Aldrich. CAST: Charles Durning, Lou Gossett Jr., Perry King, Randy Quaid, Burt Young, James Woods, Blair Brown. 1977

CHOKE CANYON 🎬 A two-fisted physicist takes on an evil industrialist in this absurd action-adventure movie. Rated PG. 96m. DIR: Chuck Bail. CAST: Stephen Collins, Janet Julian, Lance Henriksen, Bo Svenson. 1986

C.H.O.M.P.S. ★★ A small-town enterprise is saved from bankruptcy with a young engineer (Wesley Eure) designs a computer-controlled watchdog. *C.H.O.M.P.S.* has a lot of the absurdity of a cartoon. Kids under twelve may enjoy it, but the profanity thrown in for the PG rating is purely gratuitous. 90m. DIR: Don Chaffey. CAST: Wesley Eure, Valerie Bertinelli, Conrad Bain, Chuck McCann, Red Buttons, Jim Backus. 1979

CHOOSE ME ★★★★ A feast of fine acting and deliciously different situations, this stylish independent film works on every level and proves that inventive, nonmainstream entertainment is still a viable form. Written and directed by Alan Rudolph, the film is a funny, quirky, suspenseful, and surprising essay on love, sex, and the wacky state of male-female relationships in the 1980s. Rated R for violence and profanity. 110m. DIR: Alan Rudolph. CAST: Lesley Ann Warren, Keith Carradine, Genevieve Bujold. 1984

CHOPPER CHICKS IN ZOMBIETOWN ★★1/2 A mad mortician is killing people and reanimating their bodies to work in a mine. A parody of both biker movies and zombie flicks from the crazies at Troma Inc. Rated R for profanity and violence. 84m. DIR: Dan Hoskins. CAST: Jamie Rose, Vicki Frederick, Ed Gale, Don Calfa, Martha Quinn. 1991

CHOPPING MALL ★★1/2 A group of teenagers hold the ultimate office party at the local shopping mall. At midnight it is impenetrably sealed and security droids, armed with high-tech weaponry, go on patrol, incapacitating any unauthorized personnel. This film has a good sense of humor and good visual effects. Rated R for nudity, profanity, and violence. 77m. DIR: Jim Wynorski. CAST: Kelli Maroney, Tony O'Dell, John Terlesky, Russell Todd. 1986

CHORUS LINE, A ★★★★ The screen version of Michael Bennett's hit Broadway musical allows the viewer to experience the anxiety, struggle, and triumph of a group of dancers auditioning for a stage production. Director Richard Attenborough gracefully blends big production numbers with intimate moments. Rated PG for profanity and sexual descriptions. 120m. DIR: Richard Attenborough. CAST: Michael Douglas, Alyson Reed, Terrence Mann, Audrey Landers, Jan Gan Boyd. 1985

CHORUS OF DISAPPROVAL, A ★★★ Film version of the hilarious Alan Ayckbourn play. Jeremy Irons is fun to watch as the protagonist, who stirs up intrigue in a small town when he joins its little theatre company, and Anthony Hopkins is truly bizarre as its domineering director. Rated PG for profanity and suggested sex. 92m. DIR: Michael Winner. CAST: Jeremy Irons, Anthony Hopkins, Jenny Seagrove. 1989

CHOSEN, THE ★★★★★ A flawless, arresting drama illustrating the conflict between friendship and family loyalty experienced by two young men. Based on the novel of the same name by Chaim Potok, the story, centering on Jewish issues, transcends its setting to attain universal impact. Rated G. 105m. **DIR:** Jeremy Paul Kagan. **CAST:** Robby Benson, Rod Steiger, Maximilian Schell. **1978**

CHRIST STOPPED AT EBOLI ★★ Based on a renowned Italian novel about Carlo Levi, a political exile who was punished in 1935 for his antifascist writings and exiled to a village in southern Italy. Irene Papas livens things up with her resounding laugh, but ultimately this quiet tale is forgettable. In Italian with English subtitles. 118m. **DIR:** Francesco Rosi. **CAST:** Gian Maria Volonté, Irene Papas, Alain Cuny, Lea Massari, François Simon. **1983**

CHRISTIAN THE LION ★★1/2 A lion born in a London zoo is returned to the wilds in Kenya. This pleasant film is also interesting for the real-life drama. Bill Travers portrayed George Adamson, the wildlife expert, in *Born Free*. Now, Adamson is seen helping Christian adapt to his natural habitat. Rated G for family viewing. 89m. **DIR:** Bill Travers, James Hill. **CAST:** Bill Travers, Virginia McKenna, George Adamson. **1976**

CHRISTIANE F. ★★ Although quite interesting in places, this West German film dealing with young heroin addicts ultimately becomes a bore. In German with English subtitles. 124m. **DIR:** Uli Edel. **CAST:** Natja Brunkhorst, Thomas Haustein. **1981**

CHRISTINA ★★ Contrived mystery film about a wealthy foreigner (Barbara Parkins) who pays an unemployed aircraft engineer (Peter Haskell) twenty-five thousand dollars to marry her so she can acquire a U.S. passport … or so we think. 95m. **DIR:** Paul Krasny. **CAST:** Barbara Parkins, Peter Haskell, James McEachin, Marlyn Mason. **1974**

CHRISTINE ★★★1/2 Novelist Stephen King and director John Carpenter team up for topflight, tasteful terror with this movie about a 1958 Plymouth Fury with spooky powers. It's scary without being gory; a triumph of suspense and atmosphere. Rated R for profanity and violence. 111m. **DIR:** John Carpenter. **CAST:** Keith Gordon, John Stockwell, Alexandra Paul, Harry Dean Stanton, Robert Prosky, Christine Belford, Roberts Blossom. **1983 DVD**

CHRISTMAS CAROL, A (1938) ★★★1/2 This film version of Charles Dickens's Christmas classic is a better-than-average retelling of Ebenezer Scrooge's transformation from a greedy malcontent to a generous, compassionate businessman. Reginald Owen is fine as Scrooge, and so is the rest of the cast. B&W; 69m. **DIR:** Edwin L. Marin. **CAST:** Reginald Owen, Gene Lockhart, Kathleen Lockhart, Leo G. Carroll, Terry Kilburn. **1938**

CHRISTMAS CAROL, A (1951) ★★★★★ Starring Alastair Sim as Ebenezer Scrooge, the meanest miser in all of London, this is a wondrously uplifting story—as only Charles Dickens could craft one. Recommended for the whole family, *A Christmas Carol* is sure to bring a tear to your eye and joy to your heart. B&W; 86m. **DIR:** Brian Desmond Hurst. **CAST:** Alastair Sim, Kathleen Harrison, Jack Warner, Michael Hordern. **1951 DVD**

CHRISTMAS CAROL, A (1984) ★★★★ This solid rendition of Dickens's classic follows the text and style of the original story more closely than previous versions. Only George C. Scott's performance keeps this from being the best realization of Dickens's story; he makes an excellent, crotchety Scrooge, but as the reformed Scrooge he is simply gruff, not at all like Alastair Sim's dramatic transformation in the earlier version. Good cinematography and grand settings. Rated PG. 100m. **DIR:** Clive Donner. **CAST:** George C. Scott, Frank Finlay, Angela Pleasence, David Warner, Edward Woodward, Susannah York. **1984**

•**CHRISTMAS CAROL, A (1999)** ★★★★ Dickens's much redone classic is infused with new life in this TNT/Hallmark Entertainment collaboration. Naturally, the special effects have improved over earlier efforts but more impressive than that is what Patrick Stewart brings to the part of Ebenezer Scrooge. Having performed dramatic readings from Dickens's masterpiece for a decade, he seems to embody the author's antigreed theme and his transformation from ogre to benefactor is nothing short of miraculous. Not rated; suitable for family viewing. 89m. **DIR:** David Jones. **CAST:** Patrick Stewart, Richard E. Grant, Joel Grey. **1999**

CHRISTMAS COAL MINE MIRACLE, THE ★★★ In this made-for-television film a crew of striking coal miners, threatened by their union-busting bosses, enter a mine and are trapped by an explosion. The action is good, but the tone is too sweet. Also known as *Christmas Miracle in Caulfield, U.S.A.* 100m. **DIR:** Jud Taylor. **CAST:** Mitchell Ryan, Kurt Russell, Andrew Prine, John Carradine, Barbara Babcock, Melissa Gilbert, Don Porter, Shelby Leverington. **1977**

CHRISTMAS EVIL 🖤 A toy factory employee goes slowly insane. Not rated, but the equivalent of an R rating for sex and violence. 91m. **DIR:** Lewis Jackson. **CAST:** Brandon Maggart, Jeffrey DeMunn. **1983**

CHRISTMAS IN CONNECTICUT (1945) ★★★1/2 In this spirited comedy, a successful newspaper family-advice columnist (Barbara Stanwyck) arranges a phony family for herself—all for the sake of publicity. The acting is good and the pace is quick, but the script needs polishing. Nonetheless, it's a Christmas favorite. B&W; 101m. **DIR:** Peter Godfrey. **CAST:** Barbara Stanwyck, Dennis Morgan, Sydney Greenstreet, S. Z. Sakall, Reginald Gardiner, Una O'Connor. **1945**

CHRISTMAS IN CONNECTICUT (1992) ★★ A New York cooking show host, Dyan Cannon, actually knows nothing about the culinary arts and a national park ranger, Kris Kristofferson, hailed a hero for his rescue of a little boy during a snowstorm, are brought together and fall in love. This lightweight, syrupy romance farce is strictly by the numbers. Cannon tries hard but Kristofferson is as wooden as ever. Directorial debut of Arnold Schwarzenegger. No rating. 93m. **DIR:** Arnold Schwarzenegger. **CAST:** Dyan Cannon, Kris Kristofferson, Tony Curtis, Richard Roundtree, Kelly Cinnante. **1992**

CHRISTMAS IN JULY ★★★1/2 Touching, insightful comedy-drama about a young couple's dreams and aspirations. Dick Powell is fine as the young man who mistakenly believes that he has won a contest and finds all doors opening to him—until the error is discovered. This one is a treat for all audiences. Once you've seen it, you'll want to see all of Preston Sturges's films. B&W; 67m. DIR: Preston Sturges. CAST: Dick Powell, Ellen Drew, Raymond Walburn, William Demarest, Ernest Truex, Franklin Pangborn. 1940

CHRISTMAS KID, THE ★★ A woman dies on Christmas Eve while giving birth to a son who is christened "The Christmas Kid" and raised by the town. He becomes a gunman and is hired by the town boss but switches sides when his girlfriend is killed. He becomes the sheriff and cleans up the lawlessness. A good story and acting. Filmed in Spain. Rated G. 87m. DIR: Sidney Pink. CAST: Jeffrey Hunter, Louis Hayward, Gustavo Rojo, Perla Cristal, Luis Prendes, Jack Taylor. 1966

CHRISTMAS LILIES OF THE FIELD ★★★ A handyman (Billy Dee Williams) returns to help nuns and orphans once again, in this sequel to the award-winning 1963 film. A solid, well-intentioned movie, yet not quite achieving the charm of the original. Not rated, but suitable for all ages. 98m. DIR: Ralph Nelson. CAST: Billy Dee Williams, Maria Schell, Fay Hauser. 1984

CHRISTMAS REUNION, A ★★★★ A good tearjerker in which a boy, unwanted by his grandfather, hears a story told by a man who looks like Santa Claus about a grandson and grandfather who must learn to accept each other. Good acting and writing. Not rated, but suitable for all audiences. 92m. DIR: David Hemmings. CAST: Edward Woodward, Meredith Edwards, James Coburn, Gweirydd Gwyndaf. 1993

CHRISTMAS STORY, A ★★★★ Both heartwarming and hilarious, this is humorist Jean Shepherd's recollections of being a kid in the 1940s and the monumental Christmas that brought the ultimate longing—for a regulation Red Ryder air rifle. Problem is, his parents don't think it's such a good idea. Peter Billingsley is marvelous as the kid. Melinda Dillon and Darren McGavin also shine as the putupon parents. A delight for young and old. Rated PG. 98m. DIR: Bob Clark. CAST: Peter Billingsley, Darren McGavin, Melinda Dillon, Ian Petrella. 1983 DVD

CHRISTMAS TO REMEMBER, A ★★★★ Grandpa Larson (Jason Robards), who never got over his son's death, resents his grandson's visit. His unkind manner toward the boy convinces the youngster that he must run away. Eva Marie Saint plays Grandma Larson, who rebukes her husband for his cruelty. Joanne Woodward makes a cameo appearance. Not rated, this provides fine family entertainment comparable with a G rating. 96m. DIR: George Englund. CAST: Jason Robards Jr., Eva Marie Saint, Joanne Woodward. 1979

CHRISTMAS WIFE, THE ★★★1/2 Jason Robards delivers his usual superior performance as a newly widowed man who goes to a lonely hearts agency. Julie Harris, as his arranged date, has quite a little secret to hide. Fine seasonal heart-warmer created for HBO. 73m. DIR: David Jones. CAST: Jason Robards Jr., Julie Harris, Don Francks. 1988

CHRISTMAS WITHOUT SNOW, A ★★★★ John Houseman and the entire cast shine in this beautiful made-for-TV story about a dictatorial choirmaster, a newly divorced woman, a church choir, and their combined problems while rehearsing for a performance of Handel's *Messiah* oratorio. Definitely worth viewing. 100m. DIR: John Korty. CAST: John Houseman, Ramon Bieri, James Cromwell, Valerie Curtin. 1980

CHRISTOPHER COLUMBUS (1985) 🎗 Stinkeroo travelogue-as-history, edited down from a lethally boring and misbegotten miniseries. 128m. DIR: Alberto Lattuada. CAST: Gabriel Byrne, Faye Dunaway, Oliver Reed, Max von Sydow, Eli Wallach, Nicol Williamson, José Ferrer, Virna Lisi, Raf Vallone. 1985

CHRISTOPHER COLUMBUS: THE DISCOVERY (1992) 🎗 For all we care, this lamebrained movie about the famous Italian explorer can remain undiscovered. Tom Selleck as King Ferdinand is the worst casting since John Wayne as Genghis Khan. Rated PG-13 for violence and nudity. 120m. DIR: John Glen. CAST: Marlon Brando, Tom Selleck, George Corraface, Rachel Ward, Robert Davi. 1992

CHRISTOPHER STRONG ★★1/2 Katharine Hepburn's second film, this one gave her her first starring role. She is a record-breaking flyer who falls passionately in love with a married man she cannot have. High-plane soap opera. Kate's legions of fans will love it, however. B&W; 77m. DIR: Dorothy Arzner. CAST: Katharine Hepburn, Colin Clive, Billie Burke, Helen Chandler, Jack LaRue. 1933

CHROME SOLDIERS ★★★ Gary Busey returns home from Desert Storm to find his brother dead. Busey and four other Vietnam veterans take on a corrupt sheriff in this surprisingly good made-for-cable movie. 91m. DIR: Thomas Wright. CAST: Gary Busey, Ray Sharkey, William Atherton, Nicholas Guest, Yaphet Kotto. 1992

CHRONOPOLIS ★★★★ Highly original and imaginative science-fiction animation feature about a city lost in space where strange pharaoh-like immortals put an end to their deathless state by fabricating time, represented by metamorphosing white balls. Filmmaker Piotr Kamler took five years to complete this project. Not rated. In French with English subtitles. 70m. DIR: Piotr Kamler. 1982

CHU CHU AND THE PHILLY FLASH ★★ This is another bittersweet comedy about a couple of losers. It's supposed to be funny. It isn't. The stars, Alan Arkin and Carol Burnett, do manage to invest it with a certain wacky charm, but that isn't enough to make up for its shortcomings. Rated PG. 100m. DIR: David Lowell Rich. CAST: Alan Arkin, Carol Burnett, Jack Warden, Ruth Buzzi. 1981

CHUCK AMUCK: THE MOVIE ★★★★ Released in tandem with Warner Bros. animator Chuck Jones's lighthearted autobiography, this equally compelling documentary provides ample evidence of the artist's impressive work on shorts such as "What's Opera, Doc?" and "Duck Dodgers in the 24th Century." Richly informative anecdotes unfold while Jones, pencil in hand, effortlessly demonstrates the conceptual origins of beloved characters such as Bugs Bunny, the Road Runner, and Pepe Le Pew. Jones is quite witty and charming in his own right. Not rated. 52m. DIR: John Needham. 1989

CHUCK BERRY HAIL! HAIL! ROCK 'N' ROLL ★★★★★ Put simply, this is the greatest rock 'n' roll concert movie ever made. Keith Richards, Eric Clapton, Julian Lennon, and Linda Ronstadt are just some of the singers and players who back Berry during his sixtieth-birthday-tribute concert at St. Louis's Fox Theatre. Rated PG. 120m. **DIR:** Taylor Hackford. **CAST:** Chuck Berry, Keith Richards, Bo Diddley, Little Richard, Eric Clapton, Linda Ronstadt, Johnnie Johnson. **1987**

C.H.U.D. ★★ The performances by John Heard and Daniel Stern make this cheapo horror film watchable. C.H.U.D. (Cannibalistic Humanoid Underground Dwellers) are New York City bag people who have been exposed to radiation and start treating the other inhabitants of the city as lunch. Rated R for violence, profanity, and gore. 88m. **DIR:** Douglas Cheek. **CAST:** John Heard, Daniel Stern, Christopher Curry. **1984**

C.H.U.D. II (BUD THE C.H.U.D.) 🐝 This is not a sequel at all, but a thinly disguised *Return of the Living Dead III*. Rated R for violence. 84m. **DIR:** David Irving. **CAST:** Brian Robbins, Gerrit Graham, Robert Vaughn, Bianca Jagger, June Lockhart, Norman Fell. **1989**

CHUKA ★★ A hard-bitten gunfighter and a disgraced cavalry officer try to keep marauding Indians from getting to the voluptuous Italian beauty who happened to end up in the Southwest in full makeup. Ho hum. 105m. **DIR:** Gordon Douglas. **CAST:** Rod Taylor, John Mills, Ernest Borgnine, Luciana Paluzzi, James Whitmore, Louis Hayward. **1967**

CHUMP AT OXFORD, A ★★★ Stan Laurel receives a scholarship to Oxford, and Oliver Hardy accompanies him. They are the butt of pranks and jokes until Stan receives a blow on the head and becomes a reincarnation of a college hero. A fair script, but the Stan and Ollie characters never seem to fit well into it. B&W; 63m. **DIR:** Alf Goulding. **CAST:** Stan Laurel, Oliver Hardy, Wilfred Lucas, Forrester Harvey, James Finlayson, Anita Garvin. **1940**

CHUNGKING EXPRESS ★★★ This mildly intoxicating slice of Hong Kong romance *noir* is split into two faintly connected stories. A cop gets dumped by his girlfriend and tries to fall in love with the next woman he encounters. Next, a cop gets dumped by a stewardess and is harmlessly stalked by a daffy food-counter clerk. In Mandarin and Cantonese with English subtitles. Rated PG-13 for language and violence. 103m. **DIR:** Wong Kar-Wai. **CAST:** Tony Leung Chiu-Wai, Faye Wang, Brigitte Lin, Takeshi Kaneshiro, Valerie Chow. **1995**

CHURCH, THE ★★1/2 Horror impresario Dario Argento wrote this tale of demons entombed under a Gothic cathedral who are let loose during a renovation project. Not rated; contains violence, profanity, and gore. 110m. **DIR:** Michele Soavi. **CAST:** Hugh Quarshie, Tomas Arana, Feodor Chaliapin. **1991**

CIA CODENAME ALEXA 🐝 An intelligence agent and a gung-ho cop reprogram a terrorist to turn against her boss. Ridiculous. Rated R for violence and profanity. 90m. **DIR:** Joseph Merhi. **CAST:** Lorenzo Lamas, O. J. Simpson, Kathleen Kinmont, Alex Cord. **1992**

CIA II: TARGET: ALEXA 🐝 The CIA tries to recover a stolen microchip in this very violent, plotless film.

Rated R for violence. 90m. **DIR:** Lorenzo Lamas. **CAST:** Lorenzo Lamas, Kathleen Kinmont, Pamela Dixon, John Savage. **1993**

CIAO FEDERICO! ★★★ A revealing portrait of Federico Fellini at work, directing the actors who populate the unreal world of *Satyricon*. Immersed in the creative process, Fellini is captured by documentary filmmaker Gideon Bachmann. In English and Italian with English subtitles. Not rated. 55m. **DIR:** Gideon Bachmann. **CAST:** Federico Fellini, Martin Potter, Hiram Keller, Roman Polanski, Sharon Tate. **1971**

CIAO! MANHATTAN 🐝 Far more pornographic than any skin flick, this sleazy, low-budget release features Edie Sedgwick, a onetime Andy Warhol "superstar," in a grotesque parody of her life. 84m. **DIR:** John Palmer, David Weisman. **CAST:** Edie Sedgwick, Isabel Jewell, Baby Jane Holzer, Roger Vadim, Viva, Paul America. **1983**

CIAO PROFESSORE ★★1/2 *To Sir with Love* goes Italian when a pompous, uptight teacher is accidentally assigned to a poor school in a tough neighborhood. The setting is unusual and the kids are cute, but all the clichés are trotted out with dull predictability. In Italian with English subtitles. Rated R for profanity. 91m. **DIR:** Lina Wertmuller. **CAST:** Paolo Villaggio, Isa Danieli, Gigio Morra, Ester Carloni, Sergio Solli. **1993**

•CIDER HOUSE RULES, THE ★★★★ A young man (Tobey Maguire) leaves the orphanage where he grew up, working in an apple orchard, and falling for his best friend's girl while the friend is off fighting World War II. John Irving's novel becomes a sincere, sagacious film about lessons taught and learned among the forests and orchards of Maine. Irving won a well-deserved Oscar for his smooth, intelligent script, as did Michael Caine, equally deserving for his performance as the compassionate doctor who runs the orphanage. Rated PG-13 for mature themes of abortion and incest. 131m. **DIR:** Lasse Hallstrom. **CAST:** Tobey Maguire, Michael Caine, Charlize Theron, Delroy Lindo, Paul Rudd, Kate Nelligan. **1999**

CIGARETTE GIRL FROM MOSSELPROM, THE ★★1/2 A man falls in love with a cigarette girl who unwittingly becomes a movie star, and in turn falls for the cameraman. Charming, quirky tale of unrequited love and unattained dreams. A clever ending makes this silent movie worth a look if your tastes are eclectic enough. Silent. B&W; 78m. **DIR:** Yuri Zhelyabuzhsky. **CAST:** Yulia Solntseva. **1924**

CIMARRON (1931) ★★★ One of the panoramic, expensive early sound films, this Western based on Edna Ferber's novel presents the story of a pioneer family bent on building an empire out of the primitiveness of early Oklahoma. It won the Academy Award for best picture, but some scenes now seem dated. B&W; 124m. **DIR:** Wesley Ruggles. **CAST:** Richard Dix, Irene Dunne, Estelle Taylor, William Collier Jr., Roscoe Ates. **1931**

CIMARRON (1960) ★★★ Overlong Western opens with a spectacular re-creation of the 1889 Oklahoma land rush, but bogs down into a familiar building-of-the-West tale. Tries for epic status but misses the mark. 147m. **DIR:** Anthony Mann. **CAST:** Glenn Ford, Maria Schell, Anne Baxter, Arthur O'Connell, Mercedes

McCambridge, Russ Tamblyn, Vic Morrow, Robert Keith, Aline MacMahon, Harry Morgan, Charles McGraw, Royal Dano, Edgar Buchanan. **1960**

CINCINNATI KID, THE ★★★★ Steve McQueen had one of his earliest acting challenges in this study of a determined young poker player on his way to the big time. He lets nothing stand in his way, especially not the reigning king of the card tables, Edward G. Robinson. 113m. DIR: Norman Jewison. CAST: Steve McQueen, Ann-Margret, Edward G. Robinson, Karl Malden, Tuesday Weld. **1965**

CINDERELLA (1950) ★★★★ In this underappreciated Disney delight, a pretty youngster, who is continually betrayed and abused by her stepmother and stepsisters, is given one night to fulfill her dreams by a fairy godmother. The mice characters are among the studio's best, and the story moves along at a good clip. Almost in the league of *Snow White and the Seven Dwarfs* and *Pinocchio*, this animated triumph is sure to please the young and the young-at-heart. Rated G. 75m. DIR: Wilfred Jackson, Hamilton Luske, Clyde Geronimi. **1950**

CINDERELLA (1964) ★★★ This film is a reworking of the live 1957 CBS broadcast of the Rodgers and Hammerstein musical that featured the young Julie Andrews. The score is unchanged with the exception of an additional "Loneliness of Evening," which had been cut from *South Pacific*. A charming show for the entire family. 100m. DIR: Charles S. Dubin. CAST: Lesley Ann Warren, Stuart Damon, Ginger Rogers, Walter Pidgeon, Celeste Holm. **1964**

CINDERELLA (1976) ★★★ Imagine the classic fairy tale retold by way of sex comedy and you have this generally harmless piece of fluff, tame by modern standards. The film was a hit and followed shortly thereafter by the sequel *Fairy Tales*. Not rated; contains nudity and suggested sex. 94m. DIR: Michael Pataki. CAST: Cheryl Smith, Kirk Scott, Sy Richardson. **1976**

CINDERELLA (1985) ★★★★ This is one of the most entertaining of producer Shelley Duvall's *Faerie Tale Theatre* entries. Jennifer Beals is a shy, considerate, and absolutely gorgeous Cinderella; Matthew Broderick does his aw-shucks best as the smitten Prince Henry. Sweetly romantic, a treat for all. Not rated—family fare. 60m. DIR: Mark Cullingham. CAST: Jennifer Beals, Matthew Broderick, Jean Stapleton, Eve Arden, Edie McClurg. **1985**

CINDERELLA (1987) ★★★★ The immortal fairy tale is set to music by Sergei Prokofiev and performed by the world-acclaimed Berlin Comic Opera Ballet. The beautiful Hannelore Bey and Roland Gawlick as the principals provide a balance to the comedy of the rest of the ballet corps. 75m. DIR: Tom Schilling. CAST: Berlin Comic Opera Ballet. **1987**

CINDERELLA LIBERTY ★★★1/2 Marsha Mason earned an Oscar nomination as a feisty Seattle hooker with a worldly-wise 11-year-old son in this quirky little romance, which also stars James Caan as a sailor who learns to love them both. The plot is predictable, but the performances are genuinely touching. Rated R for profanity and sexual themes. 117m. DIR: Mark Rydell. CAST: James Caan, Marsha Mason, Eli Wallach. **1973**

CINDERFELLA ★★ Musical version of the oft-told fairy tale has little to recommend it. Adapted for the talents of star Jerry Lewis, it will only appeal to his fans. 91m. DIR: Frank Tashlin. CAST: Jerry Lewis, Anna Maria Alberghetti, Ed Wynn. **1960**

CINEMA PARADISO ★★★★ A pleasant sense of nostalgia pervades this Oscar winner for best foreign language film. Giuseppe Tornatore's story focuses on the love of a young boy—and indeed the entire Sicilian village where he lives—for movies. In Italian with English subtitles. Not rated, the film has profanity and suggested sex. 123m. DIR: Giuseppe Tornatore. CAST: Philippe Noiret, Jacques Perrin, Salvatore Cascio, Marco Leonardi. **1989 DVD**

CIRCLE OF DANGER ★★★ An American in England investigates his brother's death during a commando raid. Survivors of the raid offer clues in this murky, moody, talky mystery. B&W; 86m. DIR: Jacques Tourneur. CAST: Ray Milland, Patricia Roc, Marius Goring, Hugh Sinclair. **1951**

•CIRCLE OF DECEIT ★★★ A reporter troubled by his failing marriage accepts an assignment in war-torn Lebanon, where he hopes to find some meaning to the questions of life that trouble him. If that description sounds pretentious, it's because this film more than occasionally is. Still, location shooting in Lebanon and strong performances make this better than it deserves to be. In German with English subtitles. Not rated; contains violence and sexuality. 108m. DIR: Volker Schlöndorff. CAST: Bruno Ganz, Hanna Schygulla, Jean Carmet, Jerzy Skolimowski. **1981**

CIRCLE OF FEAR ★★1/2 Disgruntled Vietnam vet personally biffs almost every Filipino in Manila, searching for the nasties who kidnapped his daughter and sold her into sex slavery. Passable macho-actioner. Patrick Dollaghan does a shameless Michael Douglas impression. Rated R. 87m. DIR: Clark Henderson. CAST: Patrick Dollaghan, Wesley Penning, Joey Aresco, Vernon Wells. **1989**

CIRCLE OF FRIENDS ★★★★ Minnie Driver contributes a career-making lead performance as a college-age Irish woman—circa 1957—coming to grips with earthly love and Catholic fidelity in this charming adaptation of Maeve Binchy's bestseller. Rated PG-13 for candid sexuality. 96m. DIR: Pat O'Connor. CAST: Minnie Driver, Chris O'Donnell, Geraldine O'Rawe, Saffron Burrows, Alan Cumming, Colin Firth. **1995 DVD**

CIRCLE OF IRON ★★★ Bruce Lee was preparing the screenplay for this martial arts fantasy shortly before he died. Ironically, the lead role fell to David Carradine, who had also been chosen over Lee for the lead in the television series *Kung Fu*. Fans of the genre will love it. Rated R for violence. 102m. DIR: Richard Moore. CAST: David Carradine, Jeff Cooper, Christopher Lee, Roddy McDowall, Eli Wallach, Erica Creer. **1979**

CIRCLE OF LOVE 🎔 This is a terrible rehash of Max Ophuls's *La Ronde*. 105m. DIR: Roger Vadim. CAST: Jane Fonda, Jean-Claude Brialy, Maurice Ronet, Jean Sorel, Anna Karina. **1964**

CIRCLE OF PASSION ★★★ French-Canadian production features director Charles Finch as a banker trapped in a loveless marriage. Passion returns to his life when he takes a business trip to Paris and romances hat maker Sandrine Bonnaire. When he falls in love with her, he must confront the reality of his marriage. Jane March is wonderful as the emotionally deprived wife. In English and French. Rated R for adult situations and language. 94m. DIR: Charles Finch. CAST: Charles Finch, Jane March, Sandrine Bonnaire, Julian Sands, James Fox. 1996

CIRCLE OF TWO 💔 Eccentric artist develops a romantic—but somehow platonic—relationship with a teenage girl. Rated PG for nudity. 105m. DIR: Jules Dassin. CAST: Richard Burton, Tatum O'Neal, Kate Reid, Robin Gammell. 1980

CIRCONSTANCES ATTENUANTES ★★★ A hard-nosed, retired judge and his wife are stranded in an auberge filled with criminals. The ending is a bit far-fetched, but the film is enjoyable. In French with English subtitles. B&W; 90m. DIR: Jean Boyer. CAST: Michel Simon, Arletty, Dorville, Andrex, Robert Ozanne, Georges Lannes. 1955

CIRCUITRY MAN ★★★ Kinky tale of a futuristic world where computer chips simulate drugs and sex. A beautiful bodyguard must smuggle the chips across the country through an elaborate underground maze. Dennis Christopher steals the show as a scummy subterranean dweller who helps her get there. Rated R for violence and profanity. 85m. DIR: Steven Lovy. CAST: Dana Wheeler-Nicholson, Jim Metzler, Lu Leonard, Dennis Christopher, Vernon Wells. 1989

CIRCUITRY MAN II: PLUGHEAD REWIRED ★★ Sequel misses the mark with the belief that more is better. Vernon Wells returns as the notorious Plughead, a villain who loves to tap into people's minds and then give them a dose of his twisted sense of pain. It's up to hero Circuitry Man (Jim Metzler) to put an end to Plughead's reign of terror. Rated R for violence, language, and adult situations. 97m. DIR: Steven Lovy, Robert Lovy. CAST: Jim Metzler, Deborah Shelton, Vernon Wells, Traci Lords, Dennis Christopher. 1993

CIRCUMSTANCES UNKNOWN ★★★ Suspenseful made-for-cable original about a deranged jeweler who likes to kill happily married couples. Judd Nelson is very good at portraying the psycho killer. Not rated; contains violence. 95m. DIR: Robert Lewis. CAST: Judd Nelson, Isabel Glasser, William R. Moses. 1995

CIRCUS, THE/A DAY'S PLEASURE ★★★ This double feature admirably showcases Charlie Chaplin's world-famous gifts for comedy and pathos. In the first, vagabond Charlie hooks up with a traveling circus and falls for the bareback rider, who loves a muscle-bound trapeze artist. In the second feature, Charlie and his family try in vain to have Sunday fun. Silent. B&W; 105m. DIR: Charles Chaplin. CAST: Charlie Chaplin, Allan Garcia, Merna Kennedy, Harry Crocker, Betty Morrisey, George Davis, Henry Bergman. 1928

CIRCUS OF FEAR 💔 For its U.S. theatrical release, this tired Edgar Wallace mystery was shorn of half an hour, retitled *Psycho Circus*, and issued in black and white—but don't expect its video restoration to do anything but make its flaws more obvious. B&W; 90m. DIR: John Llewellyn Moxey. CAST: Christopher Lee, Suzy Kendall, Klaus Kinski. 1967

CIRCUS OF HORRORS ★★★ British thriller about a renegade plastic surgeon using a circus as a front. After making female criminals gorgeous, he enslaves them in his Temple of Beauty. When they want out, he colorfully offs them. Well made with good performances. This is the more violent European version. 87m. DIR: Sidney Hayers. CAST: Anton Diffring, Erika Remberg, Yvonne Romain, Donald Pleasence. 1960

CIRCUS WORLD 💔 Even John Wayne can't help this sappy soap opera set under the big top. 135m. DIR: Henry Hathaway. CAST: John Wayne, Rita Hayworth, Claudia Cardinale, John Smith, Lloyd Nolan, Richard Conte. 1964

CISCO KID, THE ★★★ The Cisco Kid and his faithful companion, Pancho, battle the French Occupation Army and American gunners in Mexico. Enjoyable, lighthearted Western is spiced with humor and enthusiastic performances by Jimmy Smits and Richard "Cheech" Marin. Made for TV. 95m. DIR: Luis Valdez. CAST: Jimmy Smits, Richard "Cheech" Marin, Sadie Frost, Ron Periman, Bruce Payne. 1994

CISCO KID (TV SERIES) ★★★ The Cisco Kid, O'Henry's Robin Hood of the Old West, and his English language mangling sidekick Pancho, rode the TV range for 176 episodes. The only series of its type filmed entirely in color. Volume one features two of the best episodes: "Quarter Horse" and "Postmaster." 50m. DIR: Eddie Davis. CAST: Duncan Renaldo, Leo Carrillo. 1951

CITADEL, THE ★★★1/2 Superb acting by a fine cast marks this adaptation of novelist A. J. Cronin's story of an impoverished doctor who temporarily forsakes his ideals. B&W; 112m. DIR: King Vidor. CAST: Robert Donat, Rosalind Russell, Ralph Richardson, Rex Harrison, Emlyn Williams, Francis L. Sullivan, Felix Aylmer, Mary Clare, Cecil Parker. 1938

CITIZEN COHN ★★★★ James Woods is the ultimate unstoppable force in this mesmerizing made-for-cable account of attorney Roy Cohn's meteoric rise to power. Blessed with a viciously prideful mother (Lee Grant), the anti-Semitic and blatantly homophobic Cohn (who was both Jewish and gay) quickly learned how to dominate by intimidation. David Franzoni's fascinating script unfolds in flashback, as Cohn lies dying of AIDS in a hospital bed. 110m. DIR: Frank Pierson. CAST: James Woods, Joe Don Baker, Joseph Bologna, Ed Flanders, Frederic Forrest, Lee Grant, Pat Hingle. 1992

CITIZEN KANE ★★★★★ The story of a reporter's quest to find the "truth" about the life of a dead newspaper tycoon closely parallels the life of William Randolph Hearst. This picture is an enjoyable experience for first-time viewers, as well as for those who have seen it ten times. B&W; 119m. DIR: Orson Welles. CAST: Orson Welles, Joseph Cotten, Everett Sloane, Agnes Moorehead, Ray Collins, George Coulouris, Ruth Warrick, Dorothy Comingore. 1941

CITIZEN RUTH ★★★1/2 This stinging social satire, about the battle over abortion rights, wisely balances its skewering of both pro-life and pro-choice camps. Ruth Stoops is a derelict who has abandoned her children and is arrested for criminal endangerment of a fetus. She then becomes a media pawn for opposing camps of moral crusaders. Rated R for language, simulated sex, and mature subject matter. 104m. DIR: Alexander Payne. CAST: Laura Dern, Swoosie Kurtz, Kurtwood Smith, Mary Kay Place, Kelly Preston, Burt Reynolds, M. C. Gainey. 1996

CITIZEN X ★★★★★ In this brilliant thriller, based on the actual events surrounding a Soviet serial killer who operated for most of a decade before finally being caught, Stephen Rea stars as the forensic-analyst-turned-detective assigned to the case in 1982. With party official Donald Sutherland as his clandestine ally, Rea doggedly builds a case against the unknown specter responsible for scores of murders. Rated R for violence, profanity, and brief nudity. 102m. DIR: Chris Gerolmo. CAST: Stephen Rea, Donald Sutherland, Jeffrey DeMunn, Joss Ackland, John Wood, Max von Sydow. 1995 DVD

CITIZEN'S BAND ★★★★ Delightful character study centers around a group of people who use citizens band radios. Screenwriter Paul Brickman and director Jonathan Demme turn this slight premise into a humorous and heartwarming collection of vignettes with Paul LeMat appealing as the central character and Charles Napier screamingly funny as a philandering truck driver. Rated PG. 98m. DIR: Jonathan Demme. CAST: Paul LeMat, Candy Clark, Ann Wedgeworth, Marcia Rodd, Charles Napier, Alix Elias, Roberts Blossom, Bruce McGill, Ed Begley Jr. 1977

CITY FOR CONQUEST ★★★1/2 James Cagney gives another outstanding performance as a self-sacrificing man who gives his all in the boxing ring to advance the career of his musician brother. Everyone shines in this curious blend of beautiful music and crime melodrama. B&W; 101m. DIR: Anatole Litvak. CAST: James Cagney, Ann Sheridan, Arthur Kennedy, Frank Craven, Donald Crisp, Frank McHugh, George Tobias, Jerome Cowan, Anthony Quinn, Lee Patrick, Blanche Yurka, Elia Kazan. 1940

CITY GIRL ★★★ A Minnesota wheat farmer marries a waitress during a visit to Chicago and brings her back to his farm. A fragmentary, tantalizing glimpse at what was almost a Murnau masterpiece. Before the film's completion Murnau was pulled from the project, and the continuity, accordingly, is choppy. Silent. B&W; 89m. DIR: F. W. Murnau. CAST: Charles Farrell, Mary Duncan, David Torrence. 1930

CITY HALL ★★★★ A memorable performance by Al Pacino as the world-weary mayor of New York City is but one of the highlights of this involving drama. When a 6-year-old child is killed after being caught in the crossfire between a police detective and a gangster, it's up to deputy mayor John Cusack to supervise damage control. However, his investigation uncovers a trail of corruption that could bring down the entire power structure of the city. First-rate work by all involved. Rated R for violence and profanity. 117m. DIR: Harold Becker. CAST: Al Pacino, John Cusack, Bridget Fonda, Danny Aiello, Martin Landau, David Paymer, Anthony Franciosa. 1996 DVD

CITY HEAT ★★★ Clint Eastwood and Burt Reynolds portray a cop and a private eye, respective-

ly, in this enjoyable action-comedy, directed by Richard Benjamin. It's fun for fans of the stars. Rated PG for violence. 94m. DIR: Richard Benjamin. CAST: Clint Eastwood, Burt Reynolds, Jane Alexander, Madeline Kahn, Irene Cara, Richard Roundtree, Rip Torn, Tony Lo Bianco. 1984

CITY IN FEAR ★★★ David Janssen is excellent in his last role, a burned-out writer goaded by a ruthless publisher (Robert Vaughn). The plot concerns a mad killer on the loose in a big city. High-quality made-for-TV feature. 150m. DIR: Jud Taylor. CAST: David Janssen, Robert Vaughn, Susan Sullivan, William Prince, Perry King, William Daniels. 1980

CITY IN PANIC ❤ A brutal killer stalks the city streets, murdering homosexuals. Not rated; contains nudity and graphic violence. 85m. DIR: Robert Bouvier. CAST: Dave Adamson. 1987

CITY LIGHTS ★★★★★ In his finest film, Charlie Chaplin's little tramp befriends a blind flower seller, providing her with every kindness he can afford. Charlie develops a friendship with a drunken millionaire and takes advantage of it to help the girl even more. Taking money from the millionaire so the girl can have an eye operation, he is arrested and sent to jail. His release from jail and the subsequent reunion with the girl may well be the most poignant ending of all his films. B&W; 81m. DIR: Charles Chaplin. CAST: Charlie Chaplin, Virginia Cherrill, Harry Myers, Hank Mann. 1931 DVD

CITY LIMITS ❤ Another in the endless parade of life-after-the-apocalypse, Mad Max rip-off films. Rated PG-13 for brief nudity, violence, and language. 85m. DIR: Aaron Lipstadt. CAST: Darrell Larson, John Stockwell, Kim Cattrall, Rae Dawn Chong, Robby Benson, James Earl Jones. 1984

CITY OF ANGELS ★★★★ Nicolas Cage is a heavenly messenger who falls in love with Earth-bound surgeon Meg Ryan in this melodramatic fairy tale; their hesitant, sensuous relationship unfolds against the actual West Coast "city of angels"—teeming with dark-cloaked apparitions perched on billboards and tall buildings. Rated PG-13 for profanity, operating room intensity, and sensuality. 114m. DIR: Brad Silberling. CAST: Nicolas Cage, Meg Ryan, Dennis Franz, Andre Braugher. 1998 DVD

CITY OF HOPE ★★★★1/2 Divided into two main stories, writer-director-star John Sayles's brilliant screenplay is about modern-day city life and the corruption found therein. There are no good guys or bad guys, just folks who are trying to survive. With a superb cast enlivening even the smallest parts, the result is a motion picture with uncommon resonance. Rated R for profanity and violence. 129m. DIR: John Sayles. CAST: Vincent Spano, Tony Lo Bianco, Joe Morton, John Sayles, Angela Bassett, David Strathairn, Maggie Renzi, Anthony Denison, Kevin Tighe, Barbara Williams. 1991

CITY OF INDUSTRY ★★★ Scripter Ken Solarz and director John Irvin spin a moody, modern film noir around a robbery that turns sour only after its perfect execution. When the twitchy, psychopathic driver decides to keep everything himself, he kills all but one of his partners. That one survivor becomes almost superhuman in his quest for vengeance. Rated R for violence, profanity, and nudity. 97m. DIR: John Irvin. CAST: Harvey Keitel, Stephen Dorff, Famke Janssen, Timothy Hutton, Wade Dominguez. 1997

CITY OF JOY ★★★★ A disillusioned American surgeon (Patrick Swayze) goes to India and discovers purpose in life in poverty-stricken Calcutta. Swayze's character and story are a bit contrived, but the film is saved by Om Puri's superb performance as a fearful farmer who becomes a hero. Rated PG-13 for profanity and violence. 134m. DIR: Roland Joffe. CAST: Patrick Swayze, Pauline Collins, Om Puri, Art Malik. 1992

CITY OF LOST CHILDREN, THE ★★★ A mad scientist, unable to have dreams of his own, kidnaps children in order to steal their dreams. This oddball fairy tale never really becomes as compelling as it intends to be; it's more a collection of visual and dramatic effects than a unified, forceful story. Many of those effects, however, are striking and make the film fascinating. In French with English subtitles. Rated R for mild violence and general nightmarish atmosphere. 112m. DIR: Marc Caro, Jean-Pierre Jeunet. CAST: Ron Perlman, Daniel Emilfork, Judith Vittet, Dominique Pinon. 1995 DVD

CITY OF SHADOWS ★★ It's the old story of Cain and Abel, set in the not-so-distant future. The first brother is a cop who lives by his own rules and deals out justice in like fashion, and the other is a maniac outlaw who kidnaps little boys and kills them. Some good action sequences along with satisfactory acting make this a passable film. 92m. DIR: David Mitchell. CAST: John P. Ryan, Paul Coufos, Tony Rosato. 1986

CITY OF THE VAMPIRES 🎬 Sort of a *Night of the Living Dead* with vampires instead, this film fails to live up to the promise of its premise. Not rated; contains violence and gore. 83m. DIR: Ron Bonk. CAST: Matthew Jason Walsh, Anne-Marie O'Keefe. 1995

CITY OF WOMEN ★★1/2 Marcello Mastroianni plays a middle-aged womanizer who follows a beautiful woman to a mansion, where he is held hostage. Federico Fellini's controversial film has been criticized as antifeminist, although it is really anti-everything. MPAA not rated, but contains profanity and nudity. 139m. DIR: Federico Fellini. CAST: Marcello Mastroianni, Ettore Manni. 1981

CITY ON FIRE ★★★ Violent crime-drama about an undercover cop out to bust a syndicate of jewel thieves in Hong Kong. Pretty impressive screen action with an explosive climactic shoot-out. In Cantonese with English subtitles. Not rated; contains violence and nudity. 98m. DIR: Ringo Lam. CAST: Chow Yun-Fat. 1989 DVD

CITY SLICKERS ★★★★ Three buddies experiencing individual midlife crises decide that going on a cattle drive will be just the thing to cure their collective depression. The result is a comedy guaranteed to cheer anyone up, with great one-liners and hilarious physical comedy. Jack Palance is outstanding as the leathery trail boss who terrifies his city-bred drovers. Rated PG-13 for profanity. 109m. DIR: Ron Underwood. CAST: Billy Crystal, Bruno Kirby, Daniel Stern, Patricia Wettig, Helen Slater, Jack Palance, Tracey Walter, Josh Mostel. 1991

CITY SLICKERS II ★★★★ The city slickers look for a lost treasure and trip all over themselves. The often funny screenplay has the same flavor as the first film with a different slant on the personalities—Jon Lovitz replaces Bruno Kirby, but the rest of the cast is the same, with Jack Palance playing his original character's twin brother. Rated PG-13 for language. 110m. DIR: Paul Weiland. CAST: Billy Crystal, Jack Palance, Daniel Stern, Jon Lovitz, Patricia Wettig, Bill McKinney, Noble Willingham, Josh Mostel, Bob Balaban. 1994

CITY THAT NEVER SLEEPS ★★★1/2 Dated but delectable film about a Chicago policeman (Gig Young) who decides to leave his wife and the force to run away with a cheap show girl. In a corny device, the city talks to us—via an offscreen narrator—to introduce its citizens and explain its purpose in society. Not rated, it contains violence. B&W; 90m. DIR: John H. Auer. CAST: Gig Young, Mala Powers, Edward Arnold, William Talman. 1953

CITY WAR ★★★ The stars of John Woo's *A Better Tomorrow* are reteamed as a pair of cops stalked by a vengeful gangster. Neither the script nor the direction are up to Woo's standards, but the actors make this a satisfying thriller. In Cantonese with English subtitles. Not rated; contains strong violence. 100m. DIR: Sun Chung. CAST: Chow Yun-Fat, Danny Lee. 1988 DVD

CITY WITHOUT MEN ★★ Wan drama of women who live in a boardinghouse near the prison where their husbands are serving time. Good cast, but otherwise forgettable. B&W; 75m. DIR: Sidney Salkow. CAST: Linda Darnell, Michael Duane, Sara Allgood, Glenda Farrell, Margaret Hamilton. 1943

CIVIL ACTION, A ★★★★ This legal drama boasts an intelligent script and a dynamite supporting performance from Robert Duvall, superbly cast as a seasoned attorney, wholly unmindful of the moral bankruptcy of the side he represents. This is a true story about personal-injury attorney Jan Schlichtmann, who went to bat against Beatrice Foods and W. R. Grace & Co. in the hopes of proving that corporate negligence was responsible when an unnaturally high number of children in tiny Woburn, Massachusetts, died of leukemia in the 1970s. A small band of local parents suspected poisoned drinking water due to industrial dumping. The film demonstrates our current legal system's inability to extract truth or justice from demons with deep pockets. Rated PG for profanity. 118m. DIR: Steven Zaillian. CAST: John Travolta, Robert Duvall, Tony Shalhoub, William H. Macy, John Lithgow, Kathleen Quinlan. 1998 DVD

CIVIL WAR, THE ★★★★★ Weaving an eloquent tapestry of letters, diaries, war dispatches, and contemporary newspaper reports, with academic opinion, award-winning director-producer Ken Burns brings the Civil War of 1861–1865 vividly to life in epic proportion. A brilliant tour de force. Unforgettable. B&W/color; 660m. DIR: Ken Burns. 1990

CIVIL WAR DIARY ★★★1/2 This low-budget family film is a fairly realistic account of a Civil War-era clan, as told by its youngest member. The story centers on the home front at a time when the older males are choosing sides and leaving the farm. Not rated, but with violence. 82m. DIR: Kevin Meyer. CAST: Todd Duffey, Miriam Byrd-Nethery, Hollis McCarthy. 1990

CIVILIZATION ★★★ Though little-known today, Thomas Ince was one of the first great American film producers and Civilization was his crowning effort. Seeing the overwhelming response to D. W. Griffith's epic Birth of a Nation, Ince abandoned the short Westerns and dramas that made him wealthy and he put all his efforts into this moralistic antiwar blockbuster. But America entered World War I and Civilization died at the box office. Silent with intertitles. B&W; 102m. DIR: Thomas Ince. CAST: Howard Hickman, Enid Markey, Lola May. 1916

CLAIRE OF THE MOON ★★1/2 Two women with conflicting points of view are roommates at a writers' retreat. They get on each other's nerves until a seminar conducted by a congenial, openly gay lecturer launches them into a sexual relationship. Controversial film is well acted and directed, but not for all tastes. Not rated; contains nudity, simulated sex, and profanity. 92m. DIR: Nicole Conn. CAST: Trisha Todd, Karen Trumbo, Daimon Craig, Faith DeVitt. 1992 DVD

CLAIRE'S KNEE ★★★★★ There is no substitute for class, and director Eric Rohmer exhibits a great deal of it in this fifth film in a series entitled Six Moral Tales. The plot is simplicity itself. Jerome (Jean-Claude Brialy) renews his friendship with a writer (Aurora Cornu) whose roommate has two daughters; one is Claire. Jerome is intrigued by Claire but is obsessed with her knee—her right knee, to be specific. In French with English subtitles. PG rating. 103m. DIR: Eric Rohmer. CAST: Jean-Claude Brialy, Aurora Cornu, Beatrice Romand. 1971 DVD

CLAMBAKE ★★★ Typical Elvis Presley musical-romance has a Prince and the Pauper scenario. Elvis, an oil baron's son, trades places with Will Hutchins, a penniless water-ski instructor, in order to find a girl who'll love him for himself and not his money. When Elvis falls for a gold-digging Shelley Fabares, he must compete with Bill Bixby, the playboy speedboat racer. 100m. DIR: Arthur H. Nadel. CAST: Elvis Presley, Shelley Fabares, Will Hutchins, Bill Bixby, Gary Merrill, James Gregory. 1967

CLAN OF THE CAVE BEAR 🎬 In this dreadfully dumb adaptation of Jean M. Auel's bestselling fantasy novel, a Cro-Magnon child is grudgingly adopted by a tribe of Neanderthals. Rated R. 100m. DIR: Michael Chapman. CAST: Daryl Hannah, Pamela Reed, Thomas Waites. 1986 DVD

CLARA'S HEART ★★1/2 Despite a wonderful performance by Whoopi Goldberg, this is a strangely unaffecting drama about a Jamaican maid who helps a youngster (Neil Patrick Harris) come to terms with life. The characters are so unsympathetic, though, that the viewer cannot help but lose interest. PG-13 for profanity. 107m. DIR: Robert Mulligan. CAST: Whoopi Goldberg, Michael Ontkean, Kathleen Quinlan, Spalding Gray, Beverly Todd, Neil Patrick Harris. 1988

CLARENCE ★★★ Clarence, the angel who guided Jimmy Stewart through It's A Wonderful Life, is back for more fun in this charming (made-for-TV) sequel that finds the guardian angel assisting a young mother headed for tragedy. Not a classic, but filled with the best of intentions. Rated G. 92m. DIR: Eric Till. CAST: Robert Carradine, Kate Trotter. 1990

CLARENCE DARROW ★★★★ This television adaptation of the stage play is a tour de force for Henry Fonda. Highlights from the career of one of the most gifted legal minds ever to pace the courtrooms of America. 81m. DIR: John Rich. CAST: Henry Fonda. 1978

CLARENCE, THE CROSS-EYED LION ★★ A family comedy that plays like a TV sitcom because that's basically what it is. Writer-star Marshall Thompson wrote this story about an adult lion with a focus problem and an American family in Africa with soft hearts. The story and characters were immortalized on TV in Daktari. 98m. DIR: Andrew Marton. CAST: Marshall Thompson, Betsy Drake, Richard Haydn, Cheryl Miller. 1965

CLASH BY NIGHT ★★★1/2 Intense, adult story is a dramatist's dream but not entertainment for the masses. Barbara Stanwyck gives another of her strong characterizations as a woman with a past who marries amiable Paul Douglas only to find herself gravitating toward tough but sensual Robert Ryan. Gritty realism and outstanding performances make this a slice-of-life tragedy that lingers in the memory. B&W; 105m. DIR: Fritz Lang. CAST: Barbara Stanwyck, Paul Douglas, Robert Ryan, Marilyn Monroe, Keith Andes, J. Carrol Naish. 1952

CLASH OF THE TITANS ★★1/2 Perseus (Harry Hamlin), the son of Zeus (Laurence Olivier), mounts his flying horse, Pegasus, and fights for the hand of Andromeda (Judi Bowker). Plagued by corny situations and stilted dialogue, only the visual wonders by special-effects wizard Ray Harryhausen make this movie worth seeing. Rated PG for violence and gore. 118m. DIR: Desmond Davis. CAST: Laurence Olivier, Harry Hamlin, Judi Bowker, Burgess Meredith, Maggie Smith. 1981

CLASS 🎬 Unfunny comedy about two preppies, one of whom falls in love with the other's alcoholic mother. Rated R for nudity, profanity, sex, and violence. 98m. DIR: Lewis John Carlino. CAST: Rob Lowe, Jacqueline Bisset, Andrew McCarthy, Stuart Margolin. 1983

CLASS ACT ★★★ Rap singers Kid 'N Play follow up their House Party successes with this ingratiating, lightweight teen comedy. Kid (Christopher Reid, the one with the mile-high hair) plays a brilliant, straight-A student who moves to a new school. Unfortunately, his official record gets switched with those belonging to a nonachieving, streetwise troublemaker (played by Christopher Martin). Rated PG-13, with profanity and sexual references. 98m. DIR: Randall Miller. CAST: Christopher Reid, Christopher Martin, Lamont Jackson, Doug E. Doug. 1992

CLASS ACTION ★★★1/2 When a crusading lawyer agrees to represent a group of people whose cars had the habit of exploding on impact, he discovers his daughter is handling the defense. Rated R for profanity and violence. 106m. DIR: Michael Apted. CAST: Gene Hackman, Mary Elizabeth Mastrantonio, Colin Friels, Joanna Merlin, Laurence Fishburne, Jonathan

Silverman, Jan Rubes, Matt Clark, Fred Dalton Thompson. 1991

CLASS OF '44 ★★★ Sequel to the very popular *Summer of '42* proves once again it's tough to top the original. Gary Grimes and Jerry Houser are back again. This time we follow the two through college romances. No new ground broken, but Grimes is very watchable. Rated PG. 95m. **DIR:** Paul Bogart. **CAST:** Gary Grimes, Jerry Houser, William Atherton, Deborah Winters. 1973

CLASS OF MISS MACMICHAEL, THE ★★ British film about obnoxious students battling obnoxious teachers. Mixes *The Blackboard Jungle*, *To Sir with Love*, and *Teachers* without expanding on them. Loud and angry, but doesn't say much. Rated R for profanity. 91m. **DIR:** Silvio Narizzano. **CAST:** Glenda Jackson, Oliver Reed, Michael Murphy. 1978

CLASS OF 1984 ★★1/2 Violent punkers run a school. A new teacher arrives and tries to change things, but his pregnant wife is raped. He takes revenge by killing all the punkers. Rated R for violence. 93m. **DIR:** Mark L. Lester. **CAST:** Perry King, Merrie Lynn Ross, Roddy McDowall, Timothy Van Patten. 1982

CLASS OF 1999 ★★1/2 Exciting sequel to *Class of 1984*. High school has become a battleground in 1999, forcing the administration to rely on android faculty to teach the kids. When the new teachers malfunction, they initiate a killer curriculum. Rated R for violence. 96m. **DIR:** Mark L. Lester. **CAST:** Bradley Gregg, Traci Lin, John P. Ryan, Pam Grier, Stacy Keach, Malcolm McDowell. 1990

CLASS OF 1999 II: THE SUBSTITUTE ★★1/2 Agreeable sequel finds rogue android soldier Sasha Mitchell posing as a high-school teacher to rid the school of human vermin. He's programmed to kill and finds plenty of prey among the thugs and gangs that rule the halls, but a mysterious stranger is out to force Mitchell to do his dirty work. Rated R for violence, language, and nudity. 90m. **DIR:** Spiro Razatos. **CAST:** Sasha Mitchell, Nick Cassavetes, Caitlin Dulany, Jack Knight. 1993

CLASS OF NUKE 'EM HIGH ✿ The makers of *The Toxic Avenger* strike again in this poor black comedy-monster movie. Rated R for nudity, profanity, and graphic violence. 84m. **DIR:** Richard W. Haines, Samuel Weil. **CAST:** Janelle Brady, Gilbert Brenton. 1987 DVD

CLASS OF NUKE 'EM HIGH 2: SUBHUMANOID MELTDOWN ★★ Bad acting, scantily clad women, gross special effects, and a totally off-the-wall plot are all parts of this tongue-in-cheek flick from the wackos at Troma Inc. Remember, it's *supposed* to be this bad. Rated R for violence, profanity, and nudity. 96m. **DIR:** Eric Louzil. **CAST:** Brick Bronsky, Lisa Gaye. 1991

CLASS OF NUKE 'EM HIGH III ✿ These students flunk out in reading, writing, and radiation. More of the same, but worse. Rated R for violence and language. 97m. **DIR:** Eric Louzil. **CAST:** Lisa Gaye, Brick Bronsky, Leesa Rowland. 1995

CLASS OF '61 ★★ When the Civil War erupted, friendly West Point cadets found themselves donning opposing uniforms. This made-for-TV production is effectively poignant and surprisingly stylish. Oscar-winning cinematographer Janusz Kaminski (*Schindler's List*) uses strong visuals and montages to explain the chaos and confusion of the war, and it generally works on an emotional level. However, it ends too abruptly. Not rated; contains mild profanity and violence. 95m. **DIR:** Gregory Hoblit. **CAST:** Dan Futterman, Joshua Lucas, Clive Owen, Sophie Ward, Niall O'Brien, Christien Anholt, Andre Braugher. 1992

CLASSIC FOREIGN SHORTS: VOLUME 2 ★★★1/2 Excellent collection of foreign-film shorts by Europe's hottest movie directors. Featured in this collection is François Truffaut's early "Les Mistons," Jean-Luc Godard's first short, "All the Boys Named Patrick," Roman Polanski's "The Fat and the Lean," and "Two Men and a Wardrobe." Also: early featurettes by Michelangelo Antonioni ("U.N.") and Orson Welles ("Hearts of Age"). B&W; 100m. **DIR:** Jean-Luc Godard, Roman Polanski, Michelangelo Antonioni, François Truffaut, Orson Welles. 1989

CLAUDIA ★★ Tame British soaper concerning the traumatized wife of a wealthy control-freak who escapes her husband's dominance. She starts a new life and falls in love with a young musician, but hubby tracks her down. Not rated, but equivalent to PG-13. 88m. **DIR:** Anwar Kawadri. **CAST:** Deborah Raffin, Nicholas Ball. 1985

CLAY PIGEON, THE ★★★ It is just after World War II. Sailor Bill Williams comes out of a coma to find he is going to be court-martialed for treason. When he is also accused of murder, he gets on the trail of the real killer. Tight plot and taut direction make this a seat-edge thriller. B&W; 63m. **DIR:** Richard Fleischer. **CAST:** Bill Williams, Barbara Hale, Richard Quine, Richard Loo, Frank Fenton, Frank Wilcox, Martha Hyer. 1949

CLAY PIGEONS ★★1/2 An auto mechanic in a small Montana town gets tangled in a murderous web spun by a seemingly amiable truck driver, played with reptilian charm by Vince Vaughn. Scott Wilson as a folksy sheriff and the delightful Janeane Garofalo as a sarcastic FBI agent add class to the film, but director David Dobkin keeps tripping over the holes in the needlessly complicated script. Rated R for profanity, nudity, violence, and sexual scenes. 104m. **DIR:** David Dobkin. **CAST:** Joaquin Phoenix, Janeane Garofalo, Vince Vaughn, Georgina Cates, Scott Wilson. 1998 DVD

CLEAN AND SOBER ★★★★ Michael Keaton gives a brilliant performance in this highly effective drama as a hotshot executive who wakes up one morning to find that his life is totally out of control. He checks into a drug rehabilitation center to dry out and discovers the shocking truth about himself. An impressive filmmaking debut for Glenn Gordon Caron, creator of television's *Moonlighting*. Rated R for violence and profanity. 124m. **DIR:** Glenn Gordon Caron. **CAST:** Michael Keaton, Morgan Freeman, M. Emmet Walsh, Kathy Baker. 1988 DVD

CLEAN SHAVEN ★★★ To call a film schizophrenic is not usually a compliment, but it best describes this stylish concoction that bucks conventionality. Writer-director Lodge Kerrigan pushes us inside the head of a recently released mental patient searching

r his young daughter. This minimalist and creepy
ick loses points for being just a little too different.
etter-boxed. Not rated; contains violence, profani-
, and sexual situations. 80m. DIR: Lodge Kerrigan.
AST: Peter Greene, Robert Albert, Jennifer McDonald,
egan Owen, Molly Castelloe. 1993 DVD

LEAN SLATE (COUP DE TORCHON) (1981)
★★★ Set during 1938 in a French West African
olonial town, this savage and sardonic black come-
y is a study of the circumstances under which
acism and fascism flourish. Philippe Noiret stars as
simple-minded sheriff who decides to wipe out cor-
uption. In French with English subtitles. Not rated;
e film has nudity, implied sex, violence, profanity,
d racial epithets. 128m. DIR: Bertrand Tavernier.
AST: Philippe Noiret, Isabelle Huppert, Stéphane Au-
ran. 1981

LEAN SLATE (1994) ★★★1/2 Private eye Dana
arvey starts each day fresh—with no idea of who he
. This strange form of amnesia means trouble,
nce he's supposed to testify against a powerful
rime boss who commited a murder our hero doesn't
member. Carvey is fun to watch in a movie that is
ily occasionally funny. The best scenes involve Car-
y's comic canine co-star, Barkley. Rated PG-13 for
olence and profanity. 107m. DIR: Mick Jackson.
AST: Dana Carvey, Valeria Golino, James Earl Jones,
evin Pollak, Michael Murphy, Michael Gambon. 1994

LEAR AND PRESENT DANGER ★★★1/2 Tom
lancy's principled, thoughtful hero, Jack Ryan, is
rced to take on the president of the United States
hen he steps in for his ailing boss to lead the fight
gainst the Colombian drug cartels and corruption
 the ranks. The result is a first-rate spy thriller.
ated PG-13 for violence, profanity, and nudity.
41m. DIR: Phillip Noyce. CAST: Harrison Ford, Willem
afoe, Anne Archer, James Earl Jones, Joaquim de
meida, Henry Czerny, Harris Yulin, Donald Moffat,
ean Jones, Hope Lange. 1994 DVD

LEARCUT ★★★ Native American Graham Greene
nds the destruction of Indian land by a Canadian
aper mill an injustice, and to make his point, kid-
aps the mill manager. Interesting message comple-
ented by above-average acting and some gorgeous
notography. Rated R for language and violence.
3m. DIR: Richard Bugajski. CAST: Graham Greene,
oyd Red Crow Westerman, Raul Trujillo, Michael
ogan. 1992

LEO FROM 5 TO 7 ★★★1/2 Filmed in real time,
is new wave film follows 90 minutes in the life of a
ightclub singer awaiting the results of a critical
edical test. Sharp-eyed viewers can look for Jean-
uc Godard, Anna Karina, Sami Frey, Jean-Claude
rialy, and others as performers in a comedy film
ewed by the protagonist. In French with English
ubtitles. Not rated. 90m. DIR: Agnes Varda. CAST:
orinne Marchand, Antoine Bourseiller, Michel
egrand. 1962 DVD

LEO/LEO ♥ This *Goodbye Charlie* rip-off becomes
nwatchable due to its many toilet jokes and sex
ags. Rated R for nudity. 92m. DIR: Chuck Vincent.
AST: Jane Hamilton. 1989

LEOPATRA (1934) ★★★★ One of the most opu-
nt and intelligent films Cecil B. De Mille ever di-

rected. Its success arises in large part from historical accuracy and the superb peformances by all the
principals. B&W; 95m. DIR: Cecil B. DeMille. CAST:
Claudette Colbert, Warren William, Henry Wilcoxon, C.
Aubrey Smith. 1934

CLEOPATRA (1963) ★★★★ This multimillion-dollar, four-hour-long extravaganza created quite a sen-
sation when released. Its all-star cast includes Eliza-
beth Taylor (as Cleopatra) and Richard Burton (as
Marc Antony). The story begins when Caesar meets
Cleopatra in her native Egypt and she has his son.
Later she comes to Rome to join Caesar when he be-
comes the lifetime dictator of Rome. Marc Antony
gets into the act as Cleopatra's Roman lover. 243m.
DIR: Joseph L. Mankiewicz. CAST: Elizabeth Taylor,
Richard Burton, Rex Harrison, Roddy McDowall,
Pamela Brown. 1963

CLEOPATRA JONES ♥ Secret agent Cleopatra
Jones returns from an overseas assignment to save
her old neighborhood. Rated PG for violence. 80m.
DIR: Jack Starrett. CAST: Tamara Dobson, Shelley Winters, Bernie Casey, Brenda Sikes. 1973 DVD

CLEOPATRA JONES AND THE CASINO OF GOLD
★★ Tamara Dobson stars as a U.S. agent out to shut
down a drug empire run by the Dragon Lady (Stella
Stevens). A big budget saves this yawner from
turkeydom. Rated R for violence, profanity, and nudity. 96m. DIR: Chuck Bail. CAST: Tamara Dobson, Stella
Stevens, Norman Fell. 1975

CLERKS ★★★ Convenience-store clerk Dante
Hicks spends a day in Quick Stop purgatory when he
reluctantly opens shop for a no-show coworker. He
develops shell shock from sexual revelations by his
girlfriend, mopes over the marriage of a high-school
flame, plays street hockey on the store rooftop,
trades psychobabble with a cynical video-store
clerk, and deals with a parade of weird customers.
Rated R due to language. B&W; 99m. DIR: Kevin
Smith. CAST: Brian O'Halloran, Jeff Anderson, Marilyn
Ghigliotti, Lisa Spoonauer. 1994 DVD

CLIENT, THE ★★★★ Outstanding thriller, based
on a John Grisham novel, stars a highly effective Susan Sarandon as a no-nonsense New Orleans lawyer
who becomes the only person to stand between a
young murder witness and a politically ambitious
district attorney. Rated PG-13 for violence and profanity. 120m. DIR: Joel Schumacher. CAST: Susan
Sarandon, Tommy Lee Jones, Mary-Louise Parker, Anthony LaPaglia, Anthony Edwards, Ossie Davis, Brad
Renfro, David Speck, J. T. Walsh, Will Patton, William
H. Macy, Kimberly Scott, William Sanderson. 1994
DVD

CLIFFHANGER ★★ Expert mountain climber
Sylvester Stallone attempts to rescue his girlfriend
from the clutches of criminal John Lithgow, who is
holding her hostage in the Rockies. Action fans may
enjoy this one, but its preponderance of clichés will
turn off more discriminating viewers. Rated R for violence and profanity. 115m. DIR: Renny Harlin. CAST:
Sylvester Stallone, John Lithgow, Michael Rooker, Janine Turner. 1993 DVD

CLIFFORD ♥ The novelty of seeing the full-grown
Martin Short playing a malevolent 10-year-old wears
off *very* quickly. Rated PG, but not suitable for small

children. 90m. DIR: Paul Flaherty. CAST: Martin Short, Charles Grodin, Dabney Coleman, Mary Steenburgen. 1994

CLIMATE FOR KILLING, A ★★1/2 Effective murder mystery about a headless and handless corpse that may be linked to a murder-suicide from sixteen years before. John Beck is the dedicated sheriff's captain and Steven Bauer is the big-city detective sent to evaluate him. Rated R for violence, profanity, and nudity. 104m. DIR: J. S. Cardone. CAST: John Beck, Steven Bauer, Mia Sara, John Diehl, Katharine Ross. 1991

CLIMAX, THE ★★★ Boris Karloff plays the house physician of Vienna's Royal Theater with an obsessive crush on opera star June Vincent. When she has no time for the good doctor, he kills her. Years later, when a new star appears on the scene, the madness continues in this eerie and atmospheric thriller. Not rated. 86m. DIR: George Waggner. CAST: Boris Karloff, Susanna Foster, Turhan Bey, Gale Sondergaard, June Vincent. 1944

CLIMB, THE ★★★ Straightforward account of the 1953 German assault on Nanga Parbat, the world's fifth highest peak. Bruce Greenwood is Herman Buhl, the arrogant climber who reached the summit alone. Rated PG, but suitable for the whole family. 86m. DIR: Donald Shebib. CAST: Bruce Greenwood, James Hurdle, Kenneth Walsh, Ken Pogue, Thomas Hauff. 1988 DVD

CLINTON AND NADINE ★★★ Andy Garcia and Ellen Barkin enliven this otherwise routine cable-TV revenge thriller. He's determined to learn who killed his brother, and she's a sympathetic call girl in the right place at the right time. Violence and brief nudity. 108m. DIR: Jerry Schatzberg. CAST: Andy Garcia, Ellen Barkin, Morgan Freeman, Michael Lombard. 1987

•CLIVE BARKER'S SALOME AND THE FORBIDDEN ★★★ The famous horror scribe presents two short films based on classic tales made early in his career. The first tells the tale of the famous dancer, while the second re-creates *Faust*. Of the two, *The Forbidden* is the more entertaining segment with its negative-image photography. While far from the best work in Barker's oeuvre, this anthology serves as a fine example of some of the themes that would later dominate his work. Made between 1972 and 1978, these were not released until 1995. Not rated; contains violent images. B&W; 70m. DIR: Clive Barker. CAST: Doug Bradley, Clive Barker, Julie Blake, Peter Atkins. 1995 DVD

CLOAK AND DAGGER (1946) ★★1/2 Director Fritz Lang wanted to make this as a warning about the dangers of the atomic age. But Warner Bros. reedited the film into a standard spy melodrama. The story has American scientist Gary Cooper, working for the OSS, sneaking into Nazi Germany to grab an Italian scientist who is helping the Nazis build the atom bomb. B&W; 106m. DIR: Fritz Lang. CAST: Gary Cooper, Lilli Palmer, Robert Alda, James Flavin, J. Edward Bromberg, Marc Lawrence. 1946

CLOAK AND DAGGER (1984) ★★★ A highly imaginative boy (Henry Thomas, of *E.T.*) who often plays pretend games of espionage with his fantasy friend, Jack Flack (Dabney Coleman), finds himself involved in a real life-and-death situation when he stumbles on to the evil doings of a group of spies (led by Michael Murphy). It's suspenseful and fast-paced but not so scary and violent as to upset the kiddies. Rated PG. 101m. DIR: Richard Franklin. CAST: Henry Thomas, Dabney Coleman, Michael Murphy, John McIntire, Shelby Leverington. 1984

CLOCK, THE ★★★ Dated but still entertaining film directed by Judy Garland's then-husband, Vincente Minnelli. Judy stars as a working girl who meets and falls in love with soldier Robert Walker. He's on a forty-eight-hour leave, so they decide to make the most of the time they have together. 90m. DIR: Vincente Minnelli. CAST: Judy Garland, Robert Walker, James Gleason, Keenan Wynn. 1945

CLOCKERS ★★★★ Novelist Richard Price's gritty thought-provoking examination of the modern world of drug dealing gets first-class treatment from co-scripter-director Spike Lee. Occasional moralizing is offset by some riveting performances, especially that of Delroy Lindo as a remorseless drug kingpin. Apart from the grisly opening scenes—centering on the examination of a street-killing victim—there is surprisingly little violence or exploitation. Rated R for profanity and violence. 128m. DIR: Spike Lee. CAST: Harvey Keitel, John Turturro, Delroy Lindo, Mekhi Phifer, Keith David, Mike Starr. 1995 DVD

CLOCKMAKER, THE (1973) ★★★★ A small-town clock maker is stunned to learn that his son, whom he raised after the death of his wife, has committed a murder and is on the run from the police. Examining his life, he realizes how little he actually knows the boy. This strong, confident first film from Bertrand Tavernier, based on a Georges Simenon novel, features one of Philippe Noiret's finest performances. In French with English subtitles. Not rated. 105m. DIR: Bertrand Tavernier. CAST: Philippe Noiret, Jean Rochefort, Christine Pascal. 1973

•CLOCKMAKER (1998) ★★ Imaginative low-budget time-travel fantasy about three kids sneaking into a clockmaker's home and messing with a machine, resulting in the computer age coming almost a hundred years too soon. The efforts of the filmmakers are hampered, however, by the poor acting of the young lead. Rated PG for mild violence. 90m. DIR: Christopher Rémy. CAST: Anthony Medwetz, Katie Johnston, Pierrino Mascarino. 1998

CLOCKWATCHERS ★★ First-time director Jill Sprecher's corrosive little picture wants to be an indictment of a sterile, small-minded office environment, but it's difficult to appreciate this tedious little drama, even as an object lesson. Basically, this is a one-act theater exercise stretched to interminable lengths. Rated PG-13 for profanity. 96m. DIR: Jill Sprecher. CAST: Toni Collette, Parker Posey, Lisa Kudrow, Alanna Ubach. 1998 DVD

CLOCKWISE ★★★1/2 No one plays a pillar of pomposity better than John Cleese. In *Clockwise*, he gets a perfect role for his patented persona. Brian Stimpson, a headmaster, runs everything by the clock—in the extreme. However, his complete control is soon shattered by a misunderstanding—and hilarity is the result. Rated PG. 96m. DIR: Christopher Morahan.

AST: John Cleese, Penelope Wilton, Alison Steadman, Stephen Moore, Sharon Maiden, Joan Hickson. **1987**

CLOCKWORK ORANGE, A ★★★★ Not for every taste, this is a stylized, "ultraviolent" black comedy. Malcolm McDowell stars as the number-one malchick, Alex, who leads his "droogs" through "a bit of the old ultraviolence" for a real "horror show." Rated R. 137m. **DIR:** Stanley Kubrick. **CAST:** Malcolm McDowell, Patrick Magee, Adrienne Corri. **1971 DVD**

CLONES, THE ★★1/2 In a sinister plot to control the weather, several government scientists are duplicated and placed in strategic meteorological stations. Basically silly film is made watchable by the believable performances of Michael Greene and Gregory Sierra, and there's a terrific roller coaster–chase finale. Rated PG for language and violence. 86m. **DIR:** Paul Hunt, Lamar Card. **CAST:** Michael Greene, Bruce Bennett, Gregory Sierra, John rew Barrymore. **1973**

CLONUS HORROR, THE ★★1/2 Government scientists are hard at work creating a master race of superhumans in a laboratory. One of them breaks free to warn the world. Not a bad time waster for science-fiction fans. Also known as *Parts: The Clonus Horror.* Rated R. 90m. **DIR:** Robert S. Fiveson. **CAST:** Tim Donnelly, Dick Sargent, Peter Graves, Keenan Wynn, Lurene Tuttle. **1979**

CLOSE ENCOUNTERS OF THE THIRD KIND ★★★★ This is director Steven Spielberg's enchanting, pre-*E.T.* vision of an extraterrestrial visit to Earth. The movie goes against many long-nurtured conceptions about space aliens. The humans, such as Richard Dreyfuss, act more bizarre than the nonthreatening childlike visitors. Spielberg never surrenders his role as storyteller to the distractions of special effects. Rated PG. 132m. **DIR:** Steven Spielberg. **CAST:** Richard Dreyfuss, François Truffaut, Teri Garr, Melinda Dillon. **1977**

CLOSE MY EYES ★★1/2 Love triangles don't get much more startling than this alternately cold, itchy, sensitive, and beguiling British drama about incest between a brother and his older, married sister. The acting is superb, with Alan Rickman stealing scenes as the filthy rich husband who suspects his wife is having an affair. Rated R for nudity, profanity, and sexual themes. 109m. **DIR:** Stephen Poliakoff. **AST:** Alan Rickman, Saskia Reeves, Clive Owen. **1991**

CLOSE TO EDEN ★★★★ A visiting Russian's encounter with a family of farmers, descended from Genghis Khan, is the device director Nikita Mikhalkov uses to study the effects of modernization in Inner Mongolia. As this slow-moving film goes on, the events become increasingly surreal. In Mongol, Chinese, and Russian with English subtitles. Not rated, the film has violence and profanity. 106m. **DIR:** Nikita Mikhalkov. **CAST:** Badema, Bayaertu, Vladimir Gostukhin. **1991**

CLOSE TO HOME ★★1/2 Canadian docudrama focuses on the link between child abuse and neglect to teen runaways and prostitution. A bit heavy-handed but still an effective message to parents. 93m. **DIR:** Rick Beairsto. **CAST:** Daniel Allman. **1985**

CLOSELY WATCHED TRAINS ★★★★1/2 A bittersweet coming-of-age comedy-drama against a back-

drop of the Nazi occupation of Czechoslovakia. A naïve young train dispatcher is forced to grow up quickly when asked to help the Czech underground. This gentle film is one of the more artistic efforts to come from behind the Iron Curtain. B&W; 91m. **DIR:** Jiri Menzel. **CAST:** Vaclav Neckar, Jitka Bendova. **1966**

CLOSER, THE ★★1/2 Danny Aiello reprises his stage role as a businessman whose pending retirement sets into motion an evening of high stakes for those anxious to succeed him. Aiello is the one to watch here. Rated R for profanity. 86m. **DIR:** Dimitri Logothetis. **CAST:** Danny Aiello, Michael Paré, Justine Bateman, Diane Baker, Joe Cortese. **1990**

●**CLOSER YOU GET, THE ★★★**1/2 The battle of the sexes takes an eccentric turn in this gentle Irish comedy, in which a group of men in a rugged village on the Donegal coast decide to improve their romantic prospects by "fooling" some gorgeous American gals into thinking their town is a tourist destination. ("Ideal age range between twenty and twenty-one," their *Miami Herald* ad reads. "Must be fit and sporty.") This little community doesn't exactly lack for good female companionship, however, and the village ladies are justifiably annoyed. The ensuing gender sparring plays out whimsically with fresh and unmannered characters. Rated PG-13 for fleeting profanity and sexual candor. 92m. **DIR:** Aileen Ritchie. **CAST:** Niamh Cusack, Sean McGinley, Ian Hart, Ewan Stewart, Sean McDonagh, Cathleen Bradley, Pat Shortt. **2000**

CLOSET LAND ★★ A writer of innocuous children's books is taken from her bed and tortured by a government representative. This bizarre suspense tale is, unfortunately, message-laden. Rated R for profanity and violence. 93m. **DIR:** Radha Bharadwaj. **CAST:** Madeleine Stowe, Alan Rickman. **1991**

CLOUD DANCER ★★★1/2 This film features one of David Carradine's best performances. As the king of daredevil pilots, he struggles to keep ahead of his ambitious protégé (Joseph Bottoms) as well as fighting his love for Jennifer O'Neill. Rated PG. 108m. **DIR:** Barry Brown. **CAST:** David Carradine, Jennifer O'Neill, Joseph Bottoms, Colleen Camp. **1980**

CLOUD WALTZING ★★★ Beautiful photography and a respectable performance by Kathleen Beller are the highlights of this telefilm. The story is only marginal. Beller stars as an American journalist who is sent to France to do an exclusive interview with a hard-nosed French wine maker. She uses many ploys, including a hot-air balloon ride, to get her interview and finally her man. 103m. **DIR:** Gordon Flemyng. **CAST:** Kathleen Beller, François-Eric Gendron. **1987**

CLOUDED YELLOW, THE ★★★1/2 Near misses and a suspenseful chase across the English countryside are made all the more enjoyable by a superior cast. Accused murderer Jean Simmons goes on the lam with retired spy Trevor Howard. Nothing, of course, is as it seems. Not rated; contains implied violence. B&W; 96m. **DIR:** Ralph Thomas. **CAST:** Jean Simmons, Trevor Howard, Sonia Dresdel, Barry Jones. **1951**

CLOUDS OVER EUROPE ★★★1/2 Handsome test pilot Laurence Olivier teams up with a man from Scotland Yard to discover why new bombers are disappearing in this on-the-verge-of-war thriller. B&W; 82m. DIR: Tim Whelan. CAST: Laurence Olivier, Valerie Hobson, Ralph Richardson. 1939

CLOVER ★★★ On their wedding night, a couple are in a car accident, and the husband dies. His wife must deal not only with her grief but with a daughter from her husband's previous union, and with his family, who were not too thrilled about the interracial marriage. Add to this the ghost of the husband, who keeps popping up to open old wounds. This made-for-cable original is a good little drama. Not rated. 95m. DIR: Jud Taylor. CAST: Elizabeth McGovern, Ernie Hudson, Loretta Devine, Zelda Harris. 1997

CLOWN, THE ★★★ Red Skelton in a dramatic role? Yes, it's true. In this film, a reworking of *The Champ*, he portrays a comedian who wins the love of his estranged son. Skelton is commendable and Tim Considine is excellent as the son. This film has an average story line but is well performed. B&W; 91m. DIR: Robert Z. Leonard. CAST: Red Skelton, Jane Greer, Tim Considine, Loring Smith. 1953

CLOWN AT MIDNIGHT, THE ★★ A group of teenagers helping restore an old Canadian opera house finds itself the target of a demented killer dressed like the clown from Pagliacci's opera. Some atmosphere and costarring roles by Margot Kidder and Christopher Plummer do little to make this more than a routine exercise. Rated R for violence, language, nudity, and adult situations. 92m. DIR: Jean Pellerin. CAST: James Duval, Sarah Lassez, Tatyana Ali, Margot Kidder, Christopher Plummer. 1998

CLOWN MURDERS, THE ★ Confusing mess about a Halloween prank. Not rated, but equivalent to an R for violence, profanity, and nudity. 94m. DIR: Martyn Burke. CAST: Stephen Young, John Candy, Lawrence Dane, Al Waxman. 1975

CLOWNHOUSE ★★1/2 Novices willing to try a relatively bloodless horror flick might give this little programmer a try. Writer-director Victor Salva's script is strictly by the numbers as it sets the stage for three brothers to fight for their lives against three clowns (actually lunatics from a local asylum). Rated R for profanity and mild violence. 81m. DIR: Victor Salva. CAST: Nathan Forrest Winters. 1989

CLOWNS, THE ★★★★1/2 Federico Fellini's television documentary is a three-ring spectacle of fun and silliness, too. Here, style is substance, and the only substance worth noting is the water thrown onto the journalist who asks the cast of circus crazies, "What does it all mean?" In Italian with English subtitles. 90m. DIR: Federico Fellini. CAST: Mayo Morin, Lima Alberti. 1971

CLUB, THE (1985) ★★★ A highly paid rookie joins an Australian football team whose last championship was twenty years ago. A powerful story of winning and losing, of business and loyalty, and of determination. Intense and polished. Rated PG for profanity and violence. 98m. DIR: Bruce Beresford. CAST: Jack Thompson, Harold Hopkins, Graham Kennedy, John Howard. 1985

CLUB, THE (1993) ★★ At their high-school prom six teens' deepest, darkest fears become reality. They'll have the devil to pay as they are initiated into

a deadly club. Nifty special effects help save this routine shocker. Rated R for violence, language, and adult situations. 88m. DIR: Brenton Spencer. CAST: Joel Wyner, Kim Coates, Andrea Roth, Rino Romano, Kelli Taylor. 1993

CLUB DES FEMMES ★★★ The romantic adventures of three young women who live in a plush mansion where no men are allowed were fairly shocking by 1930s American standards, but this lightweight import is just a diverting curio today. In French with English subtitles. B&W; 88m. DIR: Jacques Deval. CAST: Danielle Darrieux, Valentine Tessier. 1936

CLUB EXTINCTION 💣 A grim, depressing movie—ostensibly set in twenty-first-century Berlin—that fails on all levels. The plot revolves around apparent suicides that one cop believes are murders. Rated R for violence and gore. 112m. DIR: Claude Chabrol. CAST: Alan Bates, Jennifer Beals, Andrew McCarthy, Jan Niklas. 1990

CLUB FED ★★ Gangster's moll Judy Landers framed on a murder charge, is sent to a minimum security prison run by a corrupt warden. There are more "guest stars" than laughs in this too-familiar comedy. Rated PG-13 for double entendre humor. 91m. DIR: Nathaniel Christian. CAST: Judy Landers, Burt Young, Lance Kinsey, Karen Black, Sherman Hemsley, Allen Garfield, Joseph Campanella, Lyle Alzado, Mary Woronov. 1991

CLUB LIFE ★★ Neon lovers! May we have your attention please. This is just the film for you. The neon used in the disco surpasses anything you've ever seen. Rated R. 93m. DIR: Norman Thaddeus Vane. CAST: Tony Curtis, Dee Wallace, Michael Parks, Yana Nirvana. 1987

CLUB MED ★1/2 Another tired retread of the *Fantasy Island/Love Boat/Hotel* scenario. 104m. DIR: Bob Giraldi. CAST: Jack Scalia, Linda Hamilton, Patrick Macnee, Bill Maher. 1986

CLUB PARADISE ★★ Robin Williams and Jimmy Cliff start their own little Club Med–style resort. PG-13 for language and drug humor. 104m. DIR: Harold Ramis. CAST: Robin Williams, Peter O'Toole, Jimmy Cliff, Twiggy, Rick Moranis, Adolph Caesar, Eugene Levy, Joanna Cassidy. 1986

CLUB VAMPIRE 💣 Sleazy, would-be vampire chiller from the Corman factory is not a film, but a thin excuse to wallow in depravity. Rated R for violence, gore, profanity, and nudity. 76m. DIR: Andy Ruben. CAST: John Savage, Starr Andreeff. 1997

CLUBHOUSE DETECTIVES ★★ When a boy believes he has witnessed a murder, he turns to his clubhouse buddies for help in solving the crime. Definitely geared for the *Hardy Boys* crowd. Rated PG for violence. 85m. DIR: Eric Henoershot. CAST: Michael Ballam, Michael Galeota, Jimmy Galeota, Suzanne Barnes. 1995

CLUE ★★1/2 Inspired by the popular board game, the movie is a pleasant spoof of whodunits. The delightful ensemble establishes a suitably breezy style. Silliness eventually overwhelms the proceedings. As a gimmick, the film was originally shown in theatres with three different endings. All versions are included on the videocassette. Rated PG. 100m. DIR: Jonathan Lynn. CAST: Eileen Brennan, Tim Curry,

Madeline Kahn, Christopher Lloyd, Michael McKean, Martin Mull, Lesley Ann Warren. **1985 DVD**

CLUELESS ★★★1/2 Delightful spoof of spoiled Beverly Hills brats features adorably petulant Alicia Silverstone as the leader of the pack. In her efforts to manipulate the romances of her peers, she puts her own love life on hold ... temporarily. What's great about this film is the hilarious spin on teen fads and slang. Unlike most teen flicks, this can be enjoyed by adults as well. Rated PG-13 for profanity and drug use. 92m. **DIR:** Amy Heckerling. **CAST:** Alicia Silverstone, Paul Rudd, Stacey Dash, Brittany Murphy, Dan Hedaya. **1995 DVD**

COACH 🦴 A root-for-the-underdog basketball saga without heart. 100m. **DIR:** Bud Townsend. **CAST:** Cathy Lee Crosby, Michael Biehn, Keenan Wynn. **1978 DVD**

COAL MINER'S DAUGHTER ★★★★1/2 Sissy Spacek gives a superb, totally believable performance in this film biography of country singer Loretta Lynn. The title role takes Spacek from Lynn's impoverished Appalachian childhood through marriage at thirteen up to her mid-thirties and reign as the "First Lady of Country Music." Rated PG. 125m. **DIR:** Michael Apted. **CAST:** Sissy Spacek, Tommy Lee Jones, Beverly D'Angelo, Levon Helm. **1980**

COAST PATROL, THE ★★ Set on the Maine coast and shot on the Pacific off Long Beach, this lively melodrama of smugglers and speedboat chases is Fay Wray's first film of record. If you're a fan, enjoy. Silent with musical score. B&W; 76m. **DIR:** Bud Barsky. **CAST:** Fay Wray, Kenneth McDonald. **1925**

COAST TO COAST ★★ Dyan Cannon stars as a wacko blonde who's been railroaded into a mental hospital by her husband. Cannon escapes by bopping her psychiatrist over the head with a bust of Freud, and the chase is on. A trucker (Robert Blake) gives Cannon a lift, and they romp from Pennsylvania to California. Rated PG for profanity. 95m. **DIR:** Joseph Sargent. **CAST:** Dyan Cannon, Robert Blake, Quinn Redeker, Michael Lerner, Maxine Stuart, Bill Lucking. **1980**

COBB ★★★★ Ty Cobb, the most despised and possibly greatest player in the history of baseball, is seen as a belligerent bigot and beater of women as he slides into the final throes of cancer, heart disease, diabetes, and alcoholism. Rated R for language, sex, and violence. 128m. **DIR:** Ron Shelton. **CAST:** Tommy Lee Jones, Robert Wuhl, Lolita Davidovich. **1994**

COBRA, THE (1967) 🦴 Dana Andrews battles communist drug smugglers in this stultifying spy stinker. Not rated. 97m. **DIR:** Mario Sequi. **CAST:** Dana Andrews, Anita Ekberg, Peter Martell. **1967**

COBRA (1986) ★★ Sylvester Stallone comes back for more *Rambo*-like action as a tough city cop on the trail of a serial killer in this unrelentingly grim and gruesome thriller. It is packed with action and violence. Rated R for violence, gore, and profanity. 45m. **DIR:** George Pan Cosmatos. **CAST:** Sylvester Stallone, Brigitte Nielsen, Reni Santoni, Andrew Robinson. **1986 DVD**

COBRA WOMAN ★★★★1/2 A cult classic. Maria Montez is so bad she's good as twin sisters, one evil

and one good. 70m. **DIR:** Robert Siodmak. **CAST:** Maria Montez, Jon Hall, Sabu, Mary Nash, Lon Chaney Jr., Moroni Olsen, Edgar Barrier. **1944**

COCA COLA KID, THE ★★★ A nude scene between Eric Roberts and Greta Scacchi in a bed covered with feathers is enough to make anyone's temperature rise, but as a whole this little film doesn't have enough bite to it. Roberts plays a gung-ho troubleshooter from the popular beverage company who comes to Australia to sell the drink to a hard-nosed businessman (Bill Kerr) who has a monopoly on a stretch of land with his own soft drink. Worth a look. Rated R for nudity. 90m. **DIR:** Dusan Makavejev. **CAST:** Eric Roberts, Greta Scacchi, Bill Kerr. **1985**

COCAINE COWBOYS 🦴 This inept thriller concerns a struggling rock band whose members resort to drug smuggling in order to finance their music career. Rated R for nudity and graphic violence. 86m. **DIR:** Ulli Lommel. **CAST:** Jack Palance, Tom Sullivan, Andy Warhol, Suzanna Love. **1979**

COCAINE: ONE MAN'S SEDUCTION ★★★1/2 Though this is not another *Reefer Madness*, the subject could have been handled a little more subtly. Still, the melodrama is not obtrusive enough to take away from Dennis Weaver's brilliant performance as a real estate salesman who gets hooked. Not rated, but the equivalent of a PG for adult subject matter. 97m. **DIR:** Paul Wendkos. **CAST:** Dennis Weaver, Karen Grassle, Pamela Bellwood, James Spader, David Ackroyd, Jeffrey Tambor. **1983**

COCAINE WARS 🦴 John Schneider plays an undercover agent in a South American country who takes on a drug lord's empire. Rated R for violence, profanity, and nudity. 82m. **DIR:** Hector Olivera. **CAST:** John Schneider, Kathryn Witt, Federico Luppi, Royal Dano. **1986**

COCKEYED CAVALIERS ★★★ One of the better Wheeler and Woolsey vehicles, a costume comedy set in sixteenth-century Britain with the wacky duo posing as the king's physicians. Funniest bit is a parody of Garbo's *Queen Christina*. B&W; 72m. **DIR:** Mark Sandrich. **CAST:** Bert Wheeler, Robert Woolsey, Thelma Todd, Noah Beery Sr. **1934**

COCKFIGHTER ★★ Title says it all. Warren Oates and Harry Dean Stanton can't breathe life into this simplistic look at the illegal sport of cockfighting. For Oates fans only. Rated R. 83m. **DIR:** Monte Hellman. **CAST:** Warren Oates, Harry Dean Stanton, Richard B. Shull, Troy Donahue, Millie Perkins. **1974**

COCKTAIL 🦴 Tom Cruise, as the fast-rising newcomer of the glass-and-bottle set. Rated R for language and brief nudity. 104m. **DIR:** Roger Donaldson. **CAST:** Tom Cruise, Bryan Brown, Elisabeth Shue, Laurence Luckinbill. **1988**

COCOANUTS ★★★1/2 The Marx Brothers' first movie was one of the earliest sound films and suffers as a result. Notice how all the maps and newspapers are sopping wet (so they wouldn't crackle into the supersensitive, primitive microphones). The romantic leads are laughably stiff, and even the songs by Irving Berlin are forgettable. However, the Marxes—all four of them, Groucho, Harpo, Chico, and Zeppo—supply some classic moments, making the picture well worth watching. B&W; 96m. **DIR:** Joseph

Santley, Robert Florey. **CAST:** The Marx Brothers, Kay Francis, Margaret Dumont. **1929 DVD**

COCOON ★★★★★ *Cocoon* is a splendid entertainment about a group of people in a retirement home who find what they believe is the fountain of youth. Only trouble is the magic place belongs to a group of extraterrestrials, who may or may not be friendly. Rated PG-13 for suggested sex, brief nudity, and light profanity. 118m. **DIR:** Ron Howard. **CAST:** Don Ameche, Wilford Brimley, Hume Cronyn, Brian Dennehy, Jack Gilford, Steve Guttenberg, Barret Oliver, Maureen Stapleton, Jessica Tandy, Gwen Verdon, Tahnee Welch. **1985**

COCOON: THE RETURN ★★★1/2 Daniel Petrie pulls off something of a minor miracle in this sequel, which has the elderly Earthlings returning home to help their alien friends rescue some cocoons that have been endangered by an earthquake. Petrie keeps our interest by concentrating on the characters and getting uniformly splendid performances. Rated PG for slight profanity. 112m. **DIR:** Daniel Petrie. **CAST:** Don Ameche, Wilford Brimley, Courteney Cox, Hume Cronyn, Brian Dennehy, Jack Gilford, Steve Guttenberg, Maureen Stapleton, Jessica Tandy, Gwen Verdon, Tahnee Welch. **1988**

CODE NAME: CHAOS ★★ Stellar cast works desperately to save this misguided comedy about former CIA spooks gathering their resources on a tropical island in order to send the rest of the world into chaos. Rated R for profanity. 96m. **DIR:** Antony Thomas. **CAST:** Diane Ladd, Robert Loggia, David Warner, Alice Krige, Brian Kerwin. **1989**

CODE NAME: DANCER ★★★ Kate Capshaw plays a former CIA agent living a quiet married life in L.A., when she's called back to Cuba to settle an old score. TV movie originally titled *Her Secret Life.* 93m. **DIR:** Buzz Kulik. **CAST:** Kate Capshaw, Jeroen Krabbé, Gregory Sierra, Cliff De Young. **1987**

CODE NAME: EMERALD ★★★1/2 Better-than-average World War II espionage film about a double agent (Ed Harris) who attempts to rescue a U.S. Army officer (Eric Stoltz) held for interrogation in a French prison. The plot moves along at a good clip despite the lack of action. Rated PG for violence and sex. 95m. **DIR:** Jonathan Sanger. **CAST:** Ed Harris, Max von Sydow, Horst Buchholz, Helmut Berger, Cyrielle Claire, Eric Stoltz. **1985**

CODE NAME: WILD GEESE ★★ Marginal action-adventure is set in the Golden Triangle of Asia. A group of mercenaries hire out as a task force to destroy the opium trade for the Drug Enforcement Administration. Rated R. 101m. **DIR:** Anthony M. Dawson. **CAST:** Lewis Collins, Lee Van Cleef, Ernest Borgnine, Mimsy Farmer, Klaus Kinski. **1984**

CODE OF SILENCE ★★★★ With this film, Chuck Norris proved himself the heir to Charles Bronson as the king of the no-nonsense action movie. In *Code of Silence,* the star gives a right-on-target performance as tough cop Sgt. Eddie Cusack, who takes on warring mob families and corrupt police officers. Rated R for violence and profanity. 102m. **DIR:** Andrew Davis. **CAST:** Chuck Norris, Henry Silva, Bert Remsen, Dennis Farina, Mike Genovese, Ralph Foody, Nathan Davis. **1985**

CODENAME: KYRIL ★★★1/2 When the Kremlin discovers that someone has been leaking secrets to British intelligence, an assassin (Ian Charleson) is dispatched to England to discover the traitor's identity. Edward Woodward is the laconic agent on his trail in this splendidly acted, tautly directed spy film. Made for cable. Rated R for violence. 115m. **DIR:** Ian Sharp. **CAST:** Edward Woodward, Ian Charleson, Denholm Elliott, Joss Ackland, Richard E. Grant. **1988**

COFFY 🖤 Pam Grier is wasted in this feeble blaxploitation action flick. Rated R. 91m. **DIR:** Jack Hill. **CAST:** Pam Grier, Booker Bradshaw, Sid Haig, Allan Arbus, Robert DoQui. **1973**

COHEN AND TATE ★★ Roy Scheider stars as a burned-out Mafia hit man. He contracts for one last job: the kidnapping of a 9-year-old boy (Harley Cross) who has witnessed the murder of his informant parents by the mob. Rated R for violence and profanity. 86m. **DIR:** Eric Red. **CAST:** Roy Scheider, Adam Baldwin, Harley Cross. **1989**

COLD AROUND THE HEART ★★★ Writer John Ridley takes a stab at directing with this "neo-noir" tale of double-crossing lovers on the run from the law and each other. David Caruso and Kelly Lynch are fine as the untrustworthy lovers who turn on each other when they heist some stolen diamonds. Rated R for adult situations, language, nudity, and violence. 96m. **DIR:** John Ridley. **CAST:** David Caruso, Kelly Lynch, Stacey Dash, Christopher Noth, John Spencer. **1996**

COLD-BLOODED ★★★1/2 Unusual comedy starring Jason Priestley as a slightly simpleminded bookie promoted to hit man. Tutored under the exacting and sometimes doting eyes of Peter Riegert, Priestley learns he is finally good at something. The twist comes in the form of Kimberly Williams, turning this into a humorously weird, if overwrought, love story. Rated R for profanity and violence. 93m. **DIR:** M. Wallace Wolodarsky. **CAST:** Jason Priestley, Peter Riegert, Robert Loggia, Janeane Garofalo, Michael J. Fox, Kimberly Williams. **1994**

COLD COMFORT ★★ A traveling salesman is rescued from certain death only to be kept prisoner by a madman as a gift to his eighteen-year-old daughter. Rated R for profanity and nudity. 88m. **DIR:** Vic Sarin. **CAST:** Maury Chaykin, Margaret Langrick. **1989**

COLD COMFORT FARM ★★★★ Triumphant, droll film adaptation of Stella Gibbons's 1932 English literary satire. A sophisticated young Londoner goes to live with her grim, rustic relatives. Rather than being terrified or intimidated, she self-confidently sets about arranging fulfilling lives for one and all. A small masterpiece of amused British mockery with a delightful generosity at its heart. Rated PG. 105m. **DIR:** John Schlesinger. **CAST:** Kate Beckinsale, Eileen Atkins, Rufus Sewell, Ian McKellen, Sheila Burrell, Joanna Lumley. **1995**

COLD FEET (1984) ★★★1/2 This enjoyable low-key romance features a film writer (Griffin Dunne) who has just left his complaining, childlike wife (Blanche Baker) and vowed to go it alone. Enter an attractive scientist (Marissa Chibas) who has just dumped her overbearing boyfriend. Rated PG for slight profanity.

1m. DIR: Bruce Van Dusen. CAST: Griffin Dunne, Marissa Chibas, Blanche Baker. 1984

COLD FEET (1989) ★★★1/2 The scheme is to smuggle emeralds from Mexico into the United States inside a horse that is being imported for stud purposes. Offbeat fun. Rated R for nudity and language. 94m. DIR: Robert Dornhelm. CAST: Keith Carradine, Sally Kirkland, Tom Waits, Rip Torn. 1989

COLD FEVER ★★★1/2 Viewers with a taste for the offbeat should hunt for this gentle comedy about a Japanese businessman who unwillingly journeys to Iceland to perform a memorial ceremony for his deceased parents. The odd locations and odder characters are reminiscent of the films of Jim Jarmusch. In Japanese and Icelandic with English subtitles. Not rated; contains profanity. 85m. DIR: Fridrik Thor Fridriksson. CAST: Masatochi Nagase, Lili Taylor, Fisher Stevens, Seijun Suzuki. 1995

COLD FRONT ★★★1/2 Martin Sheen is an L.A. cop on assignment in Vancouver who is teamed up with Michael Ontkean to solve a murder that involves a hit man who has gone berserk. Fast-paced thriller. Not rated, with violence and strong language. 94m. DIR: Paul Bnarbic. CAST: Martin Sheen, Beverly D'Angelo, Michael Ontkean, Kim Coates. 1989

COLD HEAT ♥ This farfetched film is basically about abuse—how two selfish parents abuse their son. Not rated, though there is some profanity and violence. 85m. DIR: Ulli Lommel. CAST: John Phillip Law, Britt Ekland, Robert Sacchi. 1990

COLD HEAVEN ★★1/2 In this moody, murky melodrama, the unfaithful wife of a physician watches in horror as her mate is run over by a speedboat near Acapulco. His body then disappears from a hospital autopsy slab! Rated R for profanity and nudity. 105m. DIR: Nicolas Roeg. CAST: Theresa Russell, Mark Harmon, James Russo, Talia Shire, Will Patton, Richard Bradford. 1992

COLD JUSTICE ★★1/2 There's plenty of bare-fisted action in this tale of a priest who is actually a con man with an unsaintly agenda. Rated R for violence. 106m. DIR: Terry Green. CAST: Dennis Waterman, Roger Daltrey, Ron Dean, Penelope Milford. 1989

COLD LIGHT OF DAY, THE ★★★★ Chilling crime-drama stars Richard E. Grant as a hard-nosed detective on the trail of a serial killer of little girls. When all of his avenues run out, the detective decides to use a little girl as live bait with disastrous results. Atmospheric, hard-hitting thriller works on many levels. Not rated; contains profanity and violence. 101m. DIR: Rudolf Van Den Berg. CAST: Richard E. Grant, Lynsey Baxter, Simon Cadell, James Laurenson. 1995

COLD RIVER ★★★★ In the autumn of 1932, an experienced guide takes his 14-year-old daughter and his 12-year-old stepson on an extended camping trip. Far out in the wilderness, the father dies of a heart attack, and the children must survive a blizzard, starvation, and an encounter with a wild mountain man. A fine family movie. Rated PG. 94m. DIR: Fred G. Sullivan. CAST: Suzanna Weber, Pete Teterson, Richard Jaeckel. 1981

COLD ROOM, THE ♥ This made-for-television movie is a waste of good material. Amanda Pays accompanies father George Segal to East Germany only to find she has fallen into a time-warp and now faces Gestapo agents and mysteries about her own life. 95m. DIR: James Dearden. CAST: George Segal, Amanda Pays, Warren Clarke, Anthony Higgins. 1984

COLD SASSY TREE ★★★ Small-town drama reflects on the lives of residents of Cold Sassy Tree—a rural community built on the site of a former sassafras grove, and still isolated with a post–Civil War mentality in the early 1900s. Good performances and well-meaning sentimentality abound. This cable TV-movie is not rated. 97m. DIR: Joan Tewkesbury. CAST: Faye Dunaway, Richard Widmark, Frances Fisher, Neil Patrick Harris. 1989

COLD STEEL ♥ Brainless rehash about a cop out for revenge for the murder of his father. Rated R for violence, nudity, and profanity. 91m. DIR: Dorothy Ann Puzo. CAST: Brad Davis, Adam Ant, Sharon Stone, Jonathan Banks. 1988

COLD SWEAT (1970) ♥ Dated, offensively sexist piece of machismo. Rated R. 94m. DIR: Terence Young. CAST: Charles Bronson, Liv Ullmann, Jill Ireland, James Mason, Gabriele Ferzetti, Michael Constantine. 1970 DVD

COLD SWEAT (1993) ★★ A hit man (Ben Cross) decides to quit the business after he kills an innocent bystander. Persuaded to do one more job, he goes after the ambitious, double-crossing partner of a ruthless businessman, whose wife is cheating on him with his partner and Cross's contact. A good idea overcome by the film's sexual content. Rated R for simulated sex, nudity, violence, and profanity. 93m. DIR: Gail Harvey. CAST: Ben Cross, Adam Baldwin, Shannon Tweed, Dave Thomas. 1993

COLD TURKEY ★★ This comedy, about a small town in Iowa where the whole populace tries to give up smoking at once, sat on the shelf for two years, and understandably—despite the knockout cast and a few funny scenes, the humor is mean-spirited and decidedly unpleasant. Rated PG. 99m. DIR: Norman Lear. CAST: Dick Van Dyke, Pippa Scott, Tom Poston, Bob Newhart, Edward Everett Horton, Vincent Gardenia, Barnard Hughes. 1971

COLDFIRE ♥ Lots of action and violence and zero personality in this tale of a dedicated cop trying to stop the flow of a deadly designer drug. Not rated; contains violence and adult situations. 90m. DIR: Wings Hauser. CAST: Wings Hauser, Michael Easton. 1992

COLDITZ STORY, THE ★★★1/2 Tight direction, an intelligent script, and a terrific cast make this one of the most compelling British dramas of the 1950s and one of the best prison films of all time. John Mills is outstanding as the glue that keeps the escape plans together, but the entire crew works well together. B&W; 97m. DIR: Guy Hamilton. CAST: John Mills, Eric Portman, Lionel Jeffries, Bryan Forbes, Ian Carmichael, Theodore Bikel, Anton Diffring, Richard Wattis. 1957

COLLECTION, THE ★★★★ A superb cast shines in this British television adaptation of the Harold Pinter play about the consequences of an unusual romantic triangle. The stars bring a professional elegance and extra viewer interest to the downbeat story. Made for TV. 64m. **DIR:** Michael Apted. **CAST:** Alan Bates, Malcolm McDowell, Helen Mirren, Laurence Olivier. 1975

COLLECTOR, THE ★★★★1/2 In this chiller, Terence Stamp plays a disturbed young man who, having no friends, collects things. Unfortunately, one of the things he collects is beautiful Samantha Eggar. He keeps her as his prisoner and waits for her to fall in love with him. Extremely interesting profile of a madman. 119m. **DIR:** William Wyler. **CAST:** Terence Stamp, Samantha Eggar, Maurice Dallimore, Mona Washbourne. 1965

COLLECTOR'S ITEM ★★★1/2 This erotic suspense-drama is a surprise sleeper. Tony Musante meets up with gorgeous Laura Antonelli whom he had seduced sixteen years earlier. The actors give intense performances and Antonelli just may have found a role model in Glenn Close of *Fatal Attraction* fame. Not rated, but strictly adult fare with nudity and profanity. 99m. **DIR:** Giuseppe Patroni Griffi. **CAST:** Tony Musante, Laura Antonelli, Florinda Bolkan. 1988

COLLEGE ★★★1/2 An anti-athletics bookworm, Buster Keaton, goes to college on a scholarship. His girl falls for a jock, and Keaton decides to succeed in athletics to win her back. He fails hilariously in every attempt, but finally rescues her by unwittingly using every athletic skill. B&W; 65m. **DIR:** James W. Horne. **CAST:** Buster Keaton, Anne Cornwall, Flora Bramley, Grant Winters. 1927 DVD

COLLEGE SWING ★★★1/2 One of Betty Grable's first major musicals, this film kids collegiates and intellectual attitudes by showing what happens when Gracie Allen inherits a small-town college and staffs it with vaudeville performers. Some hummable tunes by Frank Loesser, a witty Preston Sturges script. B&W; 86m. **DIR:** Raoul Walsh. **CAST:** Bob Hope, Betty Grable, George Burns, Gracie Allen, Martha Raye, Ben Blue, Robert Cummings, John Payne, Jerry Colonna. 1938

COLLISION COURSE (1989) ★★ A tough Detroit cop gets mixed up with a Japanese police officer as they track the smugglers of an experimental car part. Some nice bits of comedy can't save this mishmash of action and Japan bashing. Rated PG for violence and profanity. 99m. **DIR:** Lewis Teague. **CAST:** Noriyuki "Pat" Morita, Jay Leno, Chris Sarandon, Ernie Hudson, John Hancock, Al Waxman, Randall "Tex" Cobb, Tom Noonan. 1989

COLONEL EFFINGHAM'S RAID ★★1/2 Slight small-town story about Charles Coburn's efforts to preserve a local monument is pleasant enough and has marvelous characters. Not a great film, but harmless fun and at times thought-provoking. B&W; 70m. **DIR:** Irving Pichel. **CAST:** Charles Coburn, Joan Bennett, William Eythe, Allyn Joslyn, Elizabeth Patterson, Donald Meek. 1945

COLONEL REDL ★★1/2 The ponderous and deliberate nature of this film, which tells the story of a pawn in a struggle for power in the Austro-Hungarian Empire just prior to World War I, keeps it from becoming fully satisfying. In German with English subtitles. Rated R for profanity, nudity, simulated sex,

and violence. 144m. **DIR:** Istvan Szabo. **CAST:** Klaus Maria Brandauer, Armin Mueller-Stahl. 1985

COLONY (1996) ★★★ Effective chiller about the body in rebellion picks up some of the themes from the works of David Cronenberg (the new flesh being the most prevalent) and becomes a triumph of originality over budget. While the film stumbles here and there, the overall picture shines in telling its tale of body parts taking on a mind of their own. Some versions list the title on the box as *Colony Mutation.* Rated R for violence, profanity, gore, and simulated sex. 83m. **DIR:** Thomas Berna. **CAST:** Dave Rommel, Susan Cane. 1996

COLONY, THE (1995) ★★ John Ritter moves his family into an idyllic, high-tech neighborhood, only to blanch at the price they must pay for security. Sad to see Ritter in such poorly written, made-for-TV tripe. Rated PG-13 for violence and profanity. 93m. **DIR:** Rob Hedden. **CAST:** John Ritter, Hal Linden, Mary Page Keller, Marshall Teague, Todd Jeffries, Alexander Picatto, Cody Dorkin, June Lockhart. 1995

COLOR ME BARBRA ★★ Streisand's second TV special doesn't hold a candle to her first, *My Name Is Barbra.* 60m. **DIR:** Dwight Hemion. **CAST:** Barbra Streisand. 1966

COLOR ME BLOOD RED 🦃 An artist discovers the perfect shade of red for his paintings. Not rated; the film has violence. 70m. **DIR:** Herschell Gordon Lewis. **CAST:** Don Joseph. 1965 DVD

COLOR ME DEAD ★★1/2 An innocent accountant (Tom Tryon) gets caught in the middle of an illegal uranium robbery and is poisoned with a deadly slow-working drug. He tries to find out why he was murdered. Carolyn Jones is effective as Tryon's girl friend-secretary and gives the story poignancy; but the screenplay is wanting. Not rated; contains violence. 91m. **DIR:** Eddie Davis. **CAST:** Tom Tryon, Carolyn Jones, Rick Jason. 1969

COLOR OF COURAGE, THE ★★★1/2 The Supreme Court case from the 1940s, *Sipes v. McGhee,* comes alive in this made-for-cable movie, where a black family moves into a neighborhood with a restrictive covenant in place. While the McGhee family fight the restriction, Mrs. McGhee befriends Mrs. Sipes in spite of their differences. With only a glimpse of the real violence and hate generated by this case, the film focuses on the improbable friendship of the two women. Rated PG. 91m. **DIR:** Lee Rose. **CAST:** Linda Hamilton, Lynn Whitfield, Bruce Greenwood, Roger Guenveur Smith. 1998

COLOR OF JUSTICE ★★ Writer-director Lionel Chetwynd's strident drama, intended to reflect our legal system's unfair treatment of black suspects quickly deteriorates into an insulting, moronic indictment of liberals, Christians, feminists, opportunistic politicians, and the media. The acting—by performers capable of much better—is laughably over-the-top. Rated R for profanity and violence. 93m. **DIR:** Lionel Chetwynd. **CAST:** F. Murray Abraham, Bruce Davison, Gregory Hines, Judd Hirsch, Saul Rubinek. 1997

COLOR OF MONEY, THE ★★★★ A sequel to *The Hustler,* this film features outstanding performances by Paul Newman as the now-aging pool hampion and Tom Cruise as his protégé. The story may be predictable, even clichéd, but the actors make it worth watching. Rated R for nudity, profanity, and violence. 117m. **DIR:** Martin Scorsese. **CAST:** Paul Newman, Tom Cruise, Mary Elizabeth Mastrantonio, Helen Shaver, John Turturro. **1986 DVD**

COLOR OF NIGHT ❤ Anguished psychiatrist Bruce Willis takes over a murdered colleague's therapy group, only to encounter death threats and the sultry advances of pouty Jane March, whose image as an erotic seductress vanishes with every poorly delivered line of vapid dialogue. This mess comes from the director who gave us *The Stunt Man?* Rated R for profanity, nudity, simulated sex, and violence. 121m. **DIR:** Richard Rush. **CAST:** Bruce Willis, Jane March, Rubén Blades, Lesley Ann Warren, Scott Bakula, Brad Dourif, Lance Henriksen. **1994 DVD**

COLOR OF POMEGRANATES, THE ★★★★ Visually rich but difficult film is best viewed as a mosaic epic of the spiritual history of Armenia, a nation long persecuted by its neighbors for its Christianity. The film, which went unseen for years while its creator was in a Soviet jail, is structured around incidents in the life of the eighteenth-century poet Sayat Nova. In Armenian with English subtitles. 73m. **DIR:** Sergi Parajanov. **CAST:** Sofico Chiaureli. **1969**

COLOR PURPLE, THE ★★★★ Steven Spielberg's adaptation of Alice Walker's Pulitzer Prize–winning novel about the growth to maturity and independence of a mistreated black woman is one of those rare brings a tear to the eye and joy to the heart. Walker's story, set between 1909 and 1947 in a small town in Georgia, celebrates the qualities of kindness, compassion, and love. Rated PG-13 for violence, profanity, and suggested sex. 130m. **DIR:** Steven Spielberg. **CAST:** Whoopi Goldberg, Danny Glover, Adolph Caesar, Margaret Avery, Oprah Winfrey, Rae Dawn Chong, Akosua Busia. **1985 DVD**

COLORADO SERENADE ★★★ Eddie Dean and stuntman extraordinaire Dave Sharpe help a crusading judge clean out a nest of outlaws. More trouble arises when the judge learns his long lost son is the leader of the gang. 68m. **DIR:** Robert Emmett Tansey. **CAST:** Eddie Dean, Roscoe Ates, David Sharpe, Forrest Taylor, Dennis Moore. **1946**

COLORADO SUNSET ★★★ A phony protective association causes a milk war among ranchers until they vote Gene Autry in as sheriff. B&W; 61m. **DIR:** George Sherman. **CAST:** Gene Autry, Smiley Burnette, June Storey, Buster Crabbe. **1939**

COLORS ★★★★ Robert Duvall gives a powerhouse performance in this hard-hitting police drama. He's a cool, experienced cop who attempts to teach his young, hotheaded partner (Sean Penn) how to survive in East Los Angeles. Penn manages to match Duvall and director Hopper holds it all together, although he does go overboard in the sex and violence department. Rated R for language, profanity, suggested sex, and nudity. 119m. **DIR:** Dennis Hopper. **CAST:** Sean Penn, Robert Duvall, Maria Conchita Alonso, Randy Brooks, Don Cheadle. **1988**

COLOSSUS OF NEW YORK, THE ★★1/2 When a brilliant scientist is killed in a car crash, his father transplants his brain into a giant robot, with pre-

dictably dire results. Unlike most cheapo 1950s horror films, this studio production at least takes itself seriously, but genre fans will find it drab. B&W; 70m. **DIR:** Eugene Lourie. **CAST:** John Baragrey, Otto Kruger, Charles Herbert, Mala Powers, Ross Martin. **1958**

COLOSSUS: THE FORBIN PROJECT ★★1/2 Low-key thriller about a supercomputer designed for defense that becomes too big for its bytes. Colossus launches its own plan for world domination. This intelligent production is disturbing and very well made. Lack of stars and a downbeat story kept it from becoming the box-office hit it deserved. Rated PG. 100m. **DIR:** Joseph Sargent. **CAST:** Eric Braeden, Susan Clark, William Schallert. **1969**

COLUMBO: MURDER BY THE BOOK ★★★1/2 Steven Spielberg steers a winning cast through a provoking "perfect crime" script by writer Steven Bochco (*Hill Street Blues, L.A. Law*). As homicide detective Columbo, Peter Falk is hard-pressed to trip up smug murderer Jack Cassidy. One of the best episodes of the long-running television series. 79m. **DIR:** Steven Spielberg. **CAST:** Peter Falk, Jack Cassidy, Martin Milner, Rosemary Forsyth. **1971**

COMA ★★★1/2 A doctor (Genevieve Bujold) becomes curious about several deaths at a hospital where patients have all lapsed into comas. Very original melodrama keeps the audience guessing. One of Michael Crichton's better film efforts. Rated PG for brief nudity and violence. 113m. **DIR:** Michael Crichton. **CAST:** Genevieve Bujold, Michael Douglas, Richard Widmark, Rip Torn, Elizabeth Ashley. **1978 DVD**

COMANCHE TERRITORY ★★★ An old-fashioned Western that tampers with history to cover loopholes in the plot, this cowboy tale shows Jim Bowie helping Indians cope with the greed of settlers who should have known better. Good action and colorful sets make the movie work. 76m. **DIR:** George Sherman. **CAST:** Maureen O'Hara, Macdonald Carey, Charles Drake, James Best, Will Geer. **1950**

COMANCHEROS, THE ★★★ Big John Wayne is the laconic Texas Ranger assigned to bring in dandy gambler Stuart Whitman for murder. Along the way, Wayne bests bad guy Lee Marvin, and Whitman proves himself a hero by helping the big guy take on the ruthless gun- and liquor-running villains of the title, led by Nehemiah Persoff. It's a fine Western with lots of nice moments. 107m. **DIR:** Michael Curtiz. **CAST:** John Wayne, Stuart Whitman, Lee Marvin, Ina Balin, Bruce Cabot, Nehemiah Persoff, Bob Steele. **1961**

COMBAT KILLERS ★★ The captain of an American platoon in the Philippines during the closing days of World War II puts his men through unnecessary dangers in fighting Japanese forces. Straightforward adventure will please war fans, though others may find it routine. The movie is unrated and contains some violence and profanity. 96m. **DIR:** Ken Loring. **CAST:** Paul Edwards, Marlene Dauden. **1980**

COMBINATION PLATTER ★★★ Delightfully engaging film about the mostly illegal immigrant employees of a Chinese restaurant in New York and their bid to stay in the United States. Explored herein are their bouts with love, money, racism, and honor. Winner of the best screenplay award at the 1993 Sundance Festival. Not rated; contains some profanity (mostly in Chinese). 85m. DIR: Tony Chan. CAST: Jeff Lau, Colleen O'Brien, Colin Mitchell, Kenneth Lu. 1993

COME ALONG WITH ME ★★★ Rather high-brow amusement is provided by this adaptation of Shirley Jackson's unfinished novel. Estelle Parsons portrays an eccentric widow who sells everything before moving on to a new town. With a new name she begins her career as a dabbler in the supernatural. Not rated, but suitable for all ages. 60m. DIR: Joanne Woodward. CAST: Estelle Parsons, Barbara Baxley, Sylvia Sidney. 1981

COME AND GET IT ★★★1/2 Based on Edna Ferber's novel, this involving film depicts life in Wisconsin's lumber country. It captures the robust, resilient nature of the denizens. Edward Arnold is perfectly cast as the grasping capitalist who needs to have his eyes opened. Walter Brennan's performance earned an Oscar for best supporting actor. B&W; 105m. DIR: Howard Hawks, William Wyler. CAST: Edward Arnold, Joel McCrea, Frances Farmer, Walter Brennan. 1936 DVD

COME AND SEE ★★★★ During World War II, a provincial teenager experiences the horrors of war as the Nazis ravage Byelorussia. In Russian with English subtitles. Not rated, but far too upsetting for children. 146m. DIR: Elem Klimov. CAST: Alexei Kravchenko, Olga Mironova. 1985

COME BACK, AFRICA ★★★1/2 Lionel Rogosin, director of the extraordinary On the Bowery, has created another overwhelming portrait of human tragedy in this drama about a black South African who loses a series of jobs while trying to keep his residency in Johannesburg. Exploited by a racist bureaucracy, the central character is forced to endure the horrible conditions of the hazardous coal mines. Not rated, but recommended for adult viewers. B&W; 83m. DIR: Lionel Rogosin. 1959

COME BACK, LITTLE SHEBA ★★★★ A maudlin, emotionally anguished housewife dreams of long past, happier days while her small world and drunken husband are upset by a younger woman. Shirley Booth made her screen debut and won an Oscar for her work here. Cast against type, Burt Lancaster as the husband matches her all the way. B&W; 99m. DIR: Daniel Mann. CAST: Shirley Booth, Burt Lancaster, Terry Moore, Richard Jaeckel. 1952

COME BACK TO THE FIVE AND DIME, JIMMY DEAN, JIMMY DEAN ★★★1/2 This film concerns the twenty-year reunion of the Disciples of James Dean, a group formed by high school friends from a small Texas town after Giant was filmed on location nearby. Their get-together forces the members to confront the lies they have been living since those innocent days. Not rated; contains profanity and mature subject matter. 110m. DIR: Robert Altman. CAST: Sandy Dennis, Cher, Karen Black, Sudie Bond, Kathy Bates, Marta Heflin. 1982

COME BLOW YOUR HORN ★★★1/2 Frank Sinatra looks very much at home as a bachelor playboy, teaching his younger brother how to live the good life. Based on Neil Simon's hit play, coproduced by director Bud Yorkin and screenwriter Norman Lear.

Not rated, with (now) innocent sexual innuendo. 112m. DIR: Bud Yorkin. CAST: Frank Sinatra, Lee J Cobb, Molly Picon, Barbara Rush, Jill St. John, Tony Bill, Dan Blocker. 1963

COME ON TARZAN ★★★★ Wild horses are being sold for dog food. Ken Maynard and steed Tarzan must stop it. Top-notch. B&W; 61m. DIR: Alan James CAST: Ken Maynard, Kate Campbell, Roy Stewart. 1932

COME SEE THE PARADISE ★★★ One of the great tragedies of World War II was the internment of American citizens who were of Japanese descent British writer-director Alan Parker attempts to put a human face on this regrettable piece of U.S. history but he isn't wholly successful. Rated R for violence nudity, and profanity. 133m. DIR: Alan Parker. CAST Dennis Quaid, Tamlyn Tomita, Sab Shimono. 1990

COME SEPTEMBER ★★★ A generational war be tween "elderly" Rock Hudson and young Bobby Darin, with Gina Lollobrigida and Sandra Dee as the love interests. Pretty Italian settings and bouncy energy make for a fun, if dated, light comedy. Not rated 114m. DIR: Robert Mulligan. CAST: Rock Hudson, Gina Lollobrigida, Sandra Dee, Bobby Darin, Joel Grey, Walter Slezak. 1961

COMEBACK ★★★1/2 Real-life rock singer Eric Burdon (lead singer of the Animals) stars in this rock'n'roll drama. Burdon plays a white blues singer trying to get back on top. 96m. DIR: Christel Buschmann. CAST: Eric Burdon. 1982

COMEBACK KID, THE ★★ John Ritter plays a down-and-out major leaguer who ends up coaching a group of street kids. Mediocre made-for-TV movie. 97m. DIR: Peter Levin. CAST: John Ritter, Doug McKeon, Susan Dey, Jeremy Licht, James Gregory. 1980

COMEDIAN, THE ★★★★★ Originally aired live as a Playhouse 90 drama, this film features Mickey Rooney as Sammy Hogarth, a ruthless, egomaniacal comedy star. His insatiable desire for unconditional adoration and obedience from those closest to him makes life a nightmare for his humiliated brother Lester (Mel Torme) and gag writer (Edmond O'Brien). Rod Serling's tight screenplay and the outstanding performances combine to make this an undated classic. B&W; 90m. DIR: John Frankenheimer. CAST: Mickey Rooney, Mel Torme, Edmond O'Brien, Kim Hunter. 1957

COMEDIANS, THE ★★ In this drama, Elizabeth Taylor and Richard Burton inadvertently become involved in the political violence and unrest of Haiti under Papa Doc Duvalier. The all-star cast does little to improve an average script—based on Graham Greene's novel. 160m. DIR: Peter Glenville. CAST: Elizabeth Taylor, Richard Burton, Alec Guinness, Peter Ustinov, Paul Ford, Lillian Gish, James Earl Jones, Cicely Tyson. 1967

COMEDY OF TERRORS ★★★ Screenwriter Richard Matheson's horror-comedy follow-up to his big-screen riff on Poe's The Raven lacks its predecessor's punch. However, there's much to be said for any film featuring the combined talents of Vincent Price, Peter Lorre, Boris Karloff, and Basil Rathbone. The plot has Price hamming it up as a funeral director who aggressively pursues customers to bolster his business—the fact that they haven't died yet doesn't seem to dissuade him. 88m. DIR: Jacques Tourneur. CAST: Vincent Price, Peter Lorre, Boris Karloff, Basil Rathbone, Joe E. Brown, Joyce Jameson. 1963

COMES A HORSEMAN ★★★ Dark, somber, but haunting Western set in the 1940s about the efforts of a would-be land baron (Jason Robards Jr.) to cheat his long-suffering neighbor (Jane Fonda) out of her land. She fights back with the help of a World War II veteran (James Caan) and a crusty old-timer (Richard Farnsworth). Rated PG for violence. 118m. DIR: Alan J. Pakula. CAST: Jane Fonda, James Caan, Jason Robards Jr., George Grizzard, Richard Farnsworth, Jim Davis. 1978

COMFORT AND JOY ★★★1/2 Scottish filmmaker Bill Forsyth scores again with this delightful tale of a disc jockey (Bill Paterson) whose life is falling apart. His girlfriend walks out on him, taking nearly everything he owns. Birds seem to like decorating his pride and joy: a red BMW. And what's worse, he gets involved in a gangland war over—are you ready for this?—the control of ice-cream manufacturing and sales. It's one you'll want to see. Rated PG. 90m. DIR: Bill Forsyth. CAST: Bill Paterson, Eleanor David, C. P. Grogan, Alex Norton. 1984

COMFORT OF STRANGERS, THE ★★★ Disturbing thriller follows a British couple on vacation in Venice. Film takes its time about getting to the heart of matters, but Christopher Walken's performance is especially delicious as a crazed stranger. Rated R for nudity and violence. 117m. DIR: Paul Schrader. CAST: Christopher Walken, Natasha Richardson, Rupert Everett, Helen Mirren. 1991

COMIC, THE (1985) 💣 Set in a police state of the near future, an aspiring comic kills a popular entertainer in order to get a chance to perform in his stead. Not rated; brief nudity. 90m. DIR: Richard Driscoll. CAST: Steve Munroe. 1985

COMIN' ROUND THE MOUNTAIN ★★★1/2 One of Abbott and Costello's best offerings, this one has the sexy Dorothy Shay and a cute plot about a shy country gal from the Ozarks trying to have a romantic liaison with Lou Costello to unite two feuding families. B&W; 77m. DIR: Charles Lamont. CAST: Bud Abbott, Lou Costello, Dorothy Shay, Kirby Grant, Robert Easton, Joe Sawyer. 1951

COMING HOME ★★★1/2 Jane Fonda, Jon Voight, and Bruce Dern give superb performances in this thought-provoking drama about the effect the Vietnam War has on three people. Directed by Hal Ashby, it features a romantic triangle with a twist: Fonda, the wife of a gung-ho officer, Dern, finds real love when she becomes an aide at a veteran's hospital and meets a bitter but sensitive paraplegic, Voight. Rated R. 127m. DIR: Hal Ashby. CAST: Jane Fonda, Jon Voight, Bruce Dern, Robert Carradine, Robert Ginty, Penelope Milford. 1978

COMING OUT ALIVE ★★★ Enjoyable suspense chiller involving one mother's search for her child after he's abducted by her estranged husband. Scott Hylands is wonderful in his role as a soldier-for-hire who helps her out. 77m. DIR: Don McBrearty. CAST: Helen Shaver, Scott Hylands, Michael Ironside, Anne Ditchburn, Monica Parker. 1984

COMING OUT OF THE ICE ★★★1/2 An engrossing made-for-television movie based on a true story. An American spends thirty-eight years in a Soviet prison camp for not renouncing his American citizenship. 97m. DIR: Waris Hussein. CAST: John Savage, Willie Nelson, Ben Cross, Francesca Annis. 1987

COMING OUT UNDER FIRE ★★★★ Arthur Dong's compelling and award-winning documentary examines the lives of nine homosexuals and lesbians during World War II. Utilizing archive film, photographs, and present-day interviews, this amazing documentary exposes the hypocrisy of the armed forces "don't ask, don't tell" policy as it pertained to the soldiers and sailors who chose recruitment over branding as sexual deviates. Come face-to-face with the men and women who served their country in silence. Not rated; contains nudity. B&W; 71m. DIR: Arthur Dong. 1994

COMING TO AMERICA ★★★1/2 Eddie Murphy deserves credit for trying to do something different in *Coming to America*. Murphy, who also wrote the story, stars as a pampered African prince who refuses to marry the pretty and pliable queen his father (James Earl Jones) has picked for him, opting instead to journey to New York City to find an intelligent, independent woman to be his lifelong mate. The film is a little slow at times, but the laughs are frequent enough to hold one's interest. Rated R for profanity, nudity, and suggested sex. 116m. DIR: John Landis. CAST: Eddie Murphy, Arsenio Hall, James Earl Jones, John Amos, Madge Sinclair. 1988 DVD

•COMING UNGLUED ★★1/2 Kids try to interfere with the plans of their father to get a promotion that would require the whole family to move to a different city. Despite the "Daddy knows least" stereotype, this is inoffensive family entertainment. Not rated. 93m. DIR: Fred Gerber. CAST: Judge Reinhold, Joely Fisher. 1999

COMING UP ROSES ★★1/2 This offbeat comedy is about the efforts of a projectionist in a small mining village in south Wales to keep a local movie theatre open. Endearing characters performed with zest by an all-Welsh-speaking cast but the movie never rises above the poor film direction. In Welsh with English subtitles. Not rated. 90m. DIR: Stephen Bayly. CAST: Dafydd Hywel, Lola Gregory, Bill Paterson. 1986

COMMAND DECISION ★★★1/2 Tense, gripping look at the psychology and politics of waging war under pressure. Confrontation and anguish color this engrossing drama, based on the stage hit. B&W; 112m. DIR: Sam Wood. CAST: Clark Gable, Walter Pidgeon, Van Johnson, Brian Donlevy, Charles Bickford, John Hodiak, Edward Arnold, John McIntire. 1948

COMMANDMENTS ★★★ Aidan Quinn stars as a man who thinks God is out to get him. To get even, he decides to break all ten commandments. In the midst of his sinning, he finds love. Rated R for language and nudity. 92m. DIR: Daniel Taplitz. CAST: Aidan Quinn, Courteney Cox, Anthony LaPaglia. 1996

COMMANDO ★★★1/2 "Commando" John Matrix makes Rambo look like a wimp. As played by big, beefy Arnold Schwarzenegger, he "eats Green Berets for breakfast." He soon goes on the warpath when his 11-year-old daughter is kidnapped by a South American dictator (Dan Hedaya) he once helped depose. Rated R for violence and profanity. 90m. DIR: Mark L. Lester. CAST: Arnold Schwarzenegger, Rae Dawn Chong, Dan Hedaya, James Olson, Alyssa Milano. 1986 DVD

COMMANDO SQUAD ★★ Lots of action but no substance in this standard tale of American drug agents operating undercover in Mexico. Kathy Shower is a tough female agent who tries to rescue her lover/co-agent (Brian Thompson). Rated R for strong language and violence. 90m. DIR: Fred Olen Ray. CAST: Brian Thompson, Kathy Shower, William Smith, Sid Haig, Robert Quarry, Ross Hagen, Mel Welles. 1987

COMMANDOS 🗣 Italian World War II film with dubbed English and not enough action. Rated PG for violence. 89m. DIR: Armando Crispino. CAST: Lee Van Cleef, Jack Kelly, Marino Masé. 1968

COMMANDOS STRIKE AT DAWN ★★1/2 Okay WWII tale of underground fighter Paul Muni, who goes up against the Nazis after they invade his Norwegian homeland. The great cast deserved a better script than this, though it is nice to watch Muni and Lillian Gish practice their art. Some good action sequences keep things moving. B&W; 96m. DIR: John Farrow. CAST: Paul Muni, Lillian Gish, Cedric Hardwicke, Anna Lee, Alexander Knox, Ray Collins. 1942

COMMISSAR, THE ★★★★ A cinematic gift from Glasnost, it's a long-repressed Soviet film about a female Soviet officer and her relationship with a family of Jewish villagers. Challenging and innovative, it's a pro-Semitic film from the mid-Sixties that languished on a shelf for two decades before being freed by changing times. It surfaced in the U.S. in 1988. In Russian with English subtitles. 115m. DIR: Aleksandr Askoldov. CAST: Nonna Mordyukova. 1988

COMMITMENTS, THE ★★★★ The music is wonderful in this R&B musical about a Dublin promoter (Robert Arkins) who decides to put together the ultimate Irish soul band. Andrew Strong is particularly amazing as the soulful lead vocalist. Rated R for profanity. 125m. DIR: Alan Parker. CAST: Robert Arkins, Michael Aherne, Angeline Ball, Maria Doyle, Dave Finnegan, Bronagh Gallagher, Felim Gormley, Glen Hansard, Dick Massey, Johnny Murphy, Kenneth McCluskey, Andrew Strong. 1991 DVD

COMMITTED ★★★ Jennifer O'Neill stars as a nurse who is tricked into committing herself into a mental institution. O'Neill is reasonably convincing as the single sane person in a sea of insanity. Rated R for violence. 101m. DIR: William A. Levey. CAST: Jennifer O'Neill, Robert Forster, Ron Palillo. 1990

COMMON BONDS ★★ The prison system helps rehabilitate a born loser by chaining him to a handicapped man's wheelchair. Airheaded message drama. Not rated, but with profanity and violence. 109m. DIR: Allan A. Goldstein. CAST: Rae Dawn Chong, Michael Ironside, Brad Dourif. 1991

COMMON LAW, THE ★★1/2 Constance Bennett has a field day as a kept woman who dumps her older lover and becomes painter Joel McCrea's model. True love wins out in the end, naturally. Predictable melodrama. B&W; 72m. DIR: Paul Stein. CAST: Constance Bennett, Joel McCrea, Hedda Hopper, Marion Shilling. 1931

COMMON THREADS: STORIES FROM THE QUILT ★★★★ In *Common Threads: Stories from the Quilt*, AIDS becomes a shared ground for survivors of loved ones. They fashion a giant quilt with the names of the deceased stitched into each design. This stirring documentary is not only a tribute to the dead and dying, it is a study of how parents, lovers, and friends of victims have learned to deal constructively with loss—and to bring the impact of AIDS to the public. Not rated. 80m. DIR: Robert Epstein, Jeffrey Friedman. 1990

COMMUNION ★★★1/2 Science-fiction author Whitley Strieber based this remarkable movie on his alleged real-life close encounters of the third kind. Unlike Steven Spielberg's fantasy-like film about the first mass-human contact with aliens, Strieber's story, directed by his longtime friend Philippe Mora, is an often terrifying movie. And it's all the more powerful because of Strieber's insistence that the events depicted are true. Rated R for profanity. 100m. DIR: Philippe Mora. CAST: Christopher Walken, Lindsay Crouse, Frances Sternhagen, Andreas Katsulas. 1989 DVD

COMPANION, THE ★★ Made-for-cable movie, about a woman writer who buys a perfect male android, starts out interestingly enough, but you'll soon tire of the empty plot. Rated R for violence and suggested sex. 94m. DIR: Gary Fleder. CAST: Kathryn Harrold, Bruce Greenwood, Talia Balsam, Joely Fisher, Brion James. 1994

COMPANY BUSINESS ★★★ In what may be the first post–Cold War spy thriller, Gene Hackman plays an ex-CIA agent who is enlisted to escort an imprisoned KGB agent (Mikhail Baryshnikov) back to Russia. The two spies must band together to escape double-crossers on both sides of the parting Iron Curtain. Rated PG-13 for violence and profanity. 96m. DIR: Nicholas Meyer. CAST: Gene Hackman, Mikhail Baryshnikov, Kurtwood Smith, Terry O'Quinn. 1991

COMPANY OF WOLVES, THE ★★★1/2 Neither a horror film nor a fantasy for the kiddies, this dark, psychologically oriented rendering of the "Little Red Riding Hood" story is for thinking viewers only. Angela Lansbury stars as Grandmother, who turns the dreams of her granddaughter (Sarah Patterson) into tales of spooky terror. Rated R for violence and gore. 95m. DIR: Neil Jordan. CAST: Angela Lansbury, David Warner, Sarah Patterson. 1985

COMPETITION, THE ★★★1/2 Richard Dreyfuss and Amy Irving star in this exquisitely crafted and completely enjoyable romance about two classical pianists who, while competing for top honors in a recital program, fall in love. Lee Remick and Sam Wanamaker add excellent support. Watch it with someone you love. Rated PG. 129m. DIR: Joel Oliansky. CAST: Richard Dreyfuss, Amy Irving, Lee Remick, Sam Wanamaker. 1980

COMPLEAT BEATLES, THE ★★★★ Even experts on the life and times of the Fab Four are likely to find something new and enlightening. Furthermore, while not a consistent work, this film provides something of interest for fans and nonfans. 119m. DIR: Patrick Montgomery. CAST: Malcolm McDowell, the Beatles. 1982

COMPROMISING POSITIONS ★★ In the first half hour, this is a hilarious and innovative takeoff on murder mysteries and a devastatingly witty send-up of suburban life. However, it soon descends into the clichés of the mystery genre. That's too bad, because the plot, about an overly amorous dentist who is murdered, has great possibilities. Rated R for nudity, profanity, and violence. 98m. DIR: Frank Perry. CAST: Susan Sarandon, Raul Julia, Edward Herrmann, Judith Ivey, Mary Beth Hurt, Anne De Salvo, Josh Mostel. 1985

COMPULSION ★★★1/2 Superb characterizations add up to first-rate melodrama in this retelling of the infamous 1924 Leopold-Loeb murder case. Orson Welles is brilliant as the brooding defense attorney. B&W; 103m. DIR: Richard Fleischer. CAST: Orson Welles, Bradford Dillman, Dean Stockwell, Diane Varsi, Martin Milner, E. G. Marshall. 1959

COMPUTER WORE TENNIS SHOES, THE ★★ A student becomes a genius after being short-circuited with a computer. The movie is weak, with the "excitement" provided by mobsters and gamblers. 87m. DIR: Robert Butler. CAST: Kurt Russell, Cesar Romero, Joe Flynn, William Schallert. 1969

COMRADE X ★★★ American reporter Clark Gable pursues Russian streetcar conductor Hedy Lamarr in this fair reworking of the *Ninotchka* theme. Eve Arden is a standout. B&W; 90m. DIR: King Vidor. CAST: Clark Gable, Hedy Lamarr, Oscar Homolka, Felix Bressart, Eve Arden, Sig Ruman. 1940 ♥

COMRADES IN ARMS 🚫 Extremely bad dialogue kills this film in which a Russian and an American join forces to combat an international drug cartel. Rated R for violence and profanity. 91m. DIR: J. Christian Ingvordsen. CAST: Lyle Alzado, Lance Henriksen, Rick Washburne. 1991

COMRADES OF SUMMER, THE ★★★1/2 Sports fans will get a kick out of this amiable made-for-cable fairy tale that finds washed-up player Joe Mantegna sent to help the Russians field a baseball team for the 1992 Olympics. Although patterned after a slew of similar underdog fantasies, this one works thanks to Mantegna's enthusiasm and Robert Rodat's script. Rated R for profanity and suggested sex. 90m. DIR: Tommy Lee Wallace. CAST: Joe Mantegna, Natalya Negoda, Mark Rolston, Michael Lerner. 1992

CON, THE ★★1/2 To pay off a large debt, a con artist pretends to fall in love with a very nerdy—but soon to be rich—guy in this made-for-cable original. Unconvincing characters and a predictable plot make the viewer lose interest. Rated PG-13 for violence. 95m. DIR: Steven Schachter. CAST: Rebecca DeMornay, William H. Macy, Frances Sternhagen, Mike Nussbaum, Don Harvey, Angela Paton. 1997

CON AIR ★★★★ Although improbable and predictable, this thriller from British director Simon West is an impressive big-screen debut. Nicolas Cage is a decent guy who winds up in prison on a bad rap and dutifully serves eight years. Cage finally catches a flight home on a rather special C-123K transport. Rated R for violence and profanity. 115m. DIR: Simon West. CAST: Nicolas Cage, John Cusack, John Malko-

vich, Steve Buscemi, Ving Rhames, Colm Meaney, Mykelti Williamson, Rachel Ticotin. 1997 DVD

CON ARTISTS, THE ♥ What could have been a lark turns into a ho-hum caper. 87m. DIR: Sergio Corbucci. CAST: Anthony Quinn, Capucine. 1977 DVD

CONAGHER ★★★1/2 Katharine Ross is a lonely widow with two children running a stagecoach way station and Sam Elliott is a cowhand she's attracted to, in this made-for-cable Western. Elliott seems to have been born to play cowboys. A welcome addition to a fading genre. 118m. DIR: Reynaldo Villalobos. CAST: Sam Elliott, Katharine Ross, Barry Corbin, Billy Green Bush, Ken Curtis, Paul Koslo, Gavan O'Herlihy, Pepe Serna, Dub Taylor. 1991

CONAN THE BARBARIAN ★★★1/2 Featuring Arnold Schwarzenegger in the title role, this sword-and-sorcery epic is just as corny, raunchy, sexist, and unbelievably brutal as the original tales by Robert E. Howard. Therefore, it seems likely Conan fans will be delighted. Rated R for nudity, profanity, and violence. 129m. DIR: John Milius. CAST: Arnold Schwarzenegger, Sandahl Bergman, James Earl Jones, Mako. 1982 DVD

CONAN THE DESTROYER ★★★ In this lightweight, violent sequel, Conan (Arnold Schwarzenegger) bests beasts and bloodthirsty battlers at every turn with the help of his sidekick (Tracey Walter), a wizard (Mako), a staff-wielding thief (androgynous Grace Jones), and a giant warrior (Wilt Chamberlain) as they go on a perilous mission to find a sacred stone. Rated PG for violence. 103m. DIR: Richard Fleischer. CAST: Arnold Schwarzenegger, Grace Jones, Wilt Chamberlain, Tracey Walter. 1984 DVD

CONCEALED WEAPON ★ Cheap thriller about an actor who lands the role of a lifetime, then finds the script coming to life. Rated R for nudity, violence, and adult language. 85m. DIR: David Payne, Milas Zivkovich. CAST: Daryl Haney, Suzanne Wouk, Monica Simpson, Mark Driscoll. 1994

CONCEIVING ADA ★★ A computer genius develops a software program that enables her to establish contact with Ada Lovelace, the daughter of Lord Byron, who was herself an early experimenter in the mathematical principles that would one day lead to computer science. The film has a tantalizing premise, but the execution is haphazard. Not rated; contains brief nudity and sexual scenes. 85m. DIR: Lynn Hershman Leeson. CAST: Tilda Swinton, Franchesca Faridany, Karen Black, Timothy Leary, John O'Keefe. 1997 DVD

CONCRETE ANGELS ★★ Set in 1964 Toronto, this downbeat teen drama revolves around several friends trying to put together a band to enter in a competition. Separate stories of the boys are spun off, told with more realism than most teen films about the early Sixties. Not rated, but an R equivalent. 97m. DIR: Carlo Liconti. CAST: Joseph Dimambro, Luke McKeehan. 1987

CONCRETE JUNGLE, THE (1962) (CRIMINAL, THE) ★★★ Grim, claustrophobic prison drama is tightly directed and well acted (especially by the underrated Stanley Baker), and remains one of the best films of its kind as well as one of director Joseph Losey's most satisfying works. Often referred to in filmographies as *The Criminal*, this uncompromising look at life "inside" boasts gutsy, believable performances. B&W; 86m. DIR: Joseph Losey. CAST: Stanley Baker, Margit Saad, Sam Wanamaker, Gregoire Aslan, Jill Bennett, Laurence Naismith, Edward Judd. 1962

CONCRETE JUNGLE, THE (1982) ★★ This women's-prison melodrama has it all: an innocent girl who learns the ropes the hard way, an evil matron in collusion with the head bad girl, gratuitous shower and mud-wrestling scenes, and plentiful overacting. In short, a trash classic. Rated R for violence, nudity, and profanity. 99m. DIR: Tom DeSimone. CAST: Tracy Bregman, Jill St. John, Barbara Luna, Peter Brown, Nita Talbot. 1982

CONDITION RED ★★ James Russo stands out in an otherwise unbelievable piece of jailhouse drivel. Playing a guard who is sick of his job, he becomes involved with a female inmate and helps her escape. Plot, dialogue, and other actors are not credible. Rated R for nudity, sex, violence, gore, and profanity. 85m. DIR: Mika Kaurismaki. CAST: James Russo, Cynda Williams, Paul Calderon, Victor Argo. 1995

CONDORMAN ★★ This Disney film has everything you've ever seen in a spy film—but it was better the first time. A comic-book writer (Michael Crawford) gets his chance to become a spy when he goes after a beautiful Russian defector (Barbara Carrera). Rated PG. 90m. DIR: Charles Jarrott. CAST: Michael Crawford, Oliver Reed, James Hampton, Barbara Carrera. 1981 DVD

•CONDUCT UNBECOMING ★★★ When the wife of a Bengal Lancer is raped, a secret trial of the accused man is conducted by the officers at an outpost in India. Good performances from a star cast are the main reason to see this stagy drama with a disappointing ending. Rated PG. 107m. DIR: Michael Anderson. CAST: Michael York, Richard Attenborough, Trevor Howard, Stacy Keach, Christopher Plummer, Susannah York. 1975

CONEHEADS ★★★ Critically lambasted comedy based on the old *Saturday Night Live* sketch is bound to be a hit with preteens. Dan Aykroyd and Jane Curtin reprise their roles as Beldar and Prymaat, aliens from the planet Remulac who are forced to masquerade as humans after being stranded on Earth. Rated PG for brief profanity and some gross comedy bits. 87m. DIR: Steve Barron. CAST: Dan Aykroyd, Jane Curtin, Michelle Burke, Michael McKean, Jason Alexander, Lisa Jane Persky, Laraine Newman, Chris Farley, Dave Thomas, Sinbad, Jan Hooks, Phil Hartman, Jon Lovitz, David Spade, Michael Richards. 1993

•CONFESSION, THE ★★1/2 A high-profile cast is wasted in this meandering courtroom drama. Ben Kingsley overcomes the hysterics, playing a man on trial for killing the doctors responsible for letting his son die. Unfortunately, Alec Baldwin has little to work with as the attorney defending him. More melodrama than drama, the film tackles important issues, but drops the ball halfway to the goal. Rated R for violence and language. 114m. DIR: David Hugh Jones. CAST: Ben Kingsley, Alec Baldwin, Amy Irving, Jay O. Sanders. 1999 DVD

•CONFESSIONAL, THE ★★1/2 An insane priest blackmails young women who have confessed to "impure" actions, and resorts to murder when his activities are threatened to be exposed. This British thriller is distasteful but also luridly inventive, if you're not easily offended. Rated R for gruesome violence and nudity. 104m. DIR: Pete Walker. CAST: Anthony Sharp, Susan Penhaligon, Stephanie Beacham. 1977

CONFESSIONS OF A HITMAN ♥ Extremely boring. A dying hit man is being chauffeured to Las Vegas to avenge the death of his father; along the way he telephones people to confess past transgressions. Rated R for violence and profanity. 93m. DIR: Larry Leahy. CAST: James Remar, Michael Wright, Emily Longstreth. 1992

CONFESSIONS OF A POLICE CAPTAIN ♥ Heavy-handed melodrama wastes a fine performance by Martin Balsam as a good cop amid an avalanche of corruption. This Italian-made film is given to excess. Rated PG. 102m. DIR: Damiano Damiani. CAST: Martin Balsam, Franco Nero, Marilu Tolo. 1971

CONFESSIONS OF A SERIAL KILLER ★★1/2 Based on the exploits of serial killer Henry Lee Lucas, this shocker shot in semidocumentary form is realistically gritty and hard to watch, but compelling nonetheless. The film manages to repulse with every murder. Robert A. Burns is appropriately creepy as the person confessing. Not rated; contains violence, nudity, and strong language. 85m. DIR: Mark Blair. CAST: Robert A. Burns, Dennis Hill. 1987

CONFIDENTIAL ★★ A film that starts off well but quickly strangles on its own *film noir* style. A newspaper reporter investigating an old murder in 1949 Los Angeles is slain, and a hard-bitten detective tries to find the reasons why. Rated R for nudity, language, and violence. 95m. DIR: Bruce Pittman. CAST: August Schellenberg, Chapelle Jaffe, Neil Munro. 1988

CONFIDENTIALLY YOURS ★★1/2 François Truffaut's last film is a stylized murder mystery in the tradition of Hitchcock, but it's only a lighthearted soufflé. Jean-Louis Trintignant plays a real estate agent framed for murder. Rated PG. In French with English subtitles. B&W; 110m. DIR: François Truffaut. CAST: Fanny Ardant, Jean-Louis Trintignant, Jean-Pierre Kalfon. 1983 DVD

CONFLICT ★★ Humphrey Bogart wants to get rid of his wife so he can marry his mistress in this reverse rip-off of *The Postman Always Rings Twice*. A suspense film that should have been better considering the talent involved. B&W; 86m. DIR: Curtis Bernhardt. CAST: Humphrey Bogart, Alexis Smith, Rose Hobart, Sydney Greenstreet, Charles Drake, Grant Mitchell. 1945 DVD

CONFLICT OF INTEREST ♥ Gratuitously sleazy cop thriller. Noteworthy only to watch Judd Nelson put another nail in the coffin of his once-promising career. Rated R for violence, nudity, and profanity. 87m. DIR: Gary Davis. CAST: Christopher McDonald, Alyssa Milano, Dey Young, Judd Nelson. 1993

CONFORMIST, THE ★★★★ Fascinating character study of Marcello Clerici (Jean-Louis Trintignant), a follower of Mussolini. He becomes increasingly obsessed with conformity as he tries to suppress a traumatic homosexual experience suffered as a youth. He is forced to prove his loyalty to the fascist state by murdering a former professor who lives in exile. In French with English subtitles. Rated R for language and subject matter. 107m. DIR: Bernardo Bertolucci. CAST: Jean-Louis Trintignant, Stefania Sandrelli, Dominique Sanda, Pierre Clementi. 1971

CONGO ★★★ A field expedition to an uncharted jungle locale, featuring characters with diverse ulterior motives, runs into a pack of vicious gray-haired gorillas protecting a legendary diamond mine. Rated PG-13 for violence. 102m. DIR: Frank Marshall. CAST: Dylan Walsh, Laura Linney, Ernie Hudson, Joe Don Baker, Tim Curry. 1995 DVD

CONNECTICUT YANKEE, A ★★★1/2 Based on Mark Twain's famous 1889 fantasy of a "modern man" thrust back to King Arthur's Court in a dream caused by a blow to the head. In the title role, Will Rogers happily helps young love in both the story and the story within the story. B&W; 96m. DIR: David Butler. CAST: Will Rogers, William Farnum, Frank Albertson, Maureen O'Sullivan, Myrna Loy. 1931

CONNECTION, THE (1961) ★★★★ A group of junkies await the arrival of their heroin dealer while a documentary filmmaker records their withdrawal symptoms. A classic of the American avant-garde cinema, filmed in real time and featuring a topflight jazz score. B&W; 103m. DIR: Shirley Clarke. CAST: William Redfield, Warren Finnerty, Garry Goodrow, Roscoe Lee Browne. 1961

CONNECTION (1973) ★★★1/2 Charles Durning steals the show in this made-for-television movie. As an out-of-work newspaperman desperately in need of money, he becomes the intermediary between an insurance company and a high-priced jewel thief. Taut direction and a literate script help. 73m. DIR: Tom Gries. CAST: Charles Durning, Ronny Cox, Zohra Lampert, Dennis Cole, Dana Wynter. 1973

CONQUEROR, THE 🖤 John Wayne plays Genghis Khan, and the results are unintentionally hilarious. 111m. DIR: Dick Powell. CAST: John Wayne, Susan Hayward, Pedro Armendariz, Agnes Moorehead. 1956 DVD

CONQUEROR WORM, THE ★★★ In this graphic delineation of witch-hunting in England during the Cromwell period, Vincent Price gives a sterling performance as Matthew Hopkins, a self-possessed and totally convincing witch finder. The production values are very good considering the small budget. A must-see for thriller fans. 88m. DIR: Michael Reeves. CAST: Vincent Price, Ian Ogilvy, Hilary Dwyer. 1968

CONQUEST ★★★ A better-than-average Greta Garbo picture because she isn't the whole show. Charles Boyer plays Napoleon—and Garbo is Marie Walewska, his Polish mistress. This is the story of how they met and why he deserted Josephine for her. B&W; 112m. DIR: Clarence Brown. CAST: Greta Garbo, Charles Boyer, May Whitty, Reginald Owen, Alan Marshal, Henry Stephenson, Leif Erickson. 1937

CONQUEST OF THE PLANET OF THE APES ★★ Having been rescued by Ricardo Montalban at the end of his previous film adventure, simian Roddy McDowall matures and leads his fellow apes—now domesticated—in a freedom revolt that sets the stage for the events in the very first film. Very melodramatic and formulaic, with few clichés left unused. Rated PG for violence. 87m. DIR: J. Lee Thompson. CAST: Roddy McDowall, Ricardo Montalban, Don Murray, Severn Darden. 1972

CONRACK ★★★★ In this sleeper, based on a true story, Jon Voight plays a dedicated white teacher determined to bring the joys of education to deprived blacks inhabiting an island off the coast of South Carolina. Rated PG. 107m. DIR: Martin Ritt. CAST: Jon Voight, Paul Winfield, Hume Cronyn, Madge Sinclair. 1974

CONSENTING ADULTS (1985) ★★★1/2 Based on a bestselling novel by Laura Z. Hobson, this made-for-TV film tells the story of an all-American family when their son proclaims his homosexuality. It is told with taste and style. 100m. DIR: Gilbert Cates. CAST: Marlo Thomas, Martin Sheen, Talia Balsam, Barry Tubb, Ben Piazza. 1985

CONSENTING ADULTS (1992) 🖤 Almost every scene in this film is telegraphed, leaving little suspense. A name cast is wasted. Rated R for profanity, nudity, and violence. 99m. DIR: Alan J. Pakula. CAST: Kevin Kline, Mary Elizabeth Mastrantonio, Kevin Spacey, Rebecca Miller, E. G. Marshall, Forest Whitaker. 1992

CONSOLATION MARRIAGE ★★★ Slow-moving but well-made (for early talkie) soap opera about two jilted sweethearts (Irene Dunne and Pat O'Brien) who marry each other on the rebound, then their old lovers come back. Stilted dialogue is a drawback, but the film remains interesting for the early performances of the stars. Not rated, but suitable for all audiences. B&W; 81m. DIR: Paul Sloane. CAST: Irene Dunne, Pat O'Brien, John Halliday, Myrna Loy. 1931

CONSPIRACY OF FEAR, THE ★★★ After the death of his father, a young man tries to figure out why everyone is so interested in a mysterious package his father was supposed to have had. This made-for-cable thriller might have been a better film, but the cinematography and editing, which give us something of a cross between a music video and a home movie, distract the viewer from the action. Not rated; contains profanity and violence. 110m. DIR: John Eyres. CAST: Geraint Wyn Davies, Leslie Hope, Andrew Lowery, Christopher Plummer. 1996

CONSPIRACY: THE TRIAL OF THE CHICAGO 8 ★★★ Docudrama-style made-for-cable-TV movie about the notorious court proceedings that followed the riots of the 1968 Democratic convention. Solid performances by a top-notch cast. 118m. DIR: Jeremy Paul Kagan. CAST: Robert Carradine, Elliott Gould, Martin Sheen, Robert Loggia. 1987 DVD

CONSPIRACY THEORY ★★★★ Being paranoid doesn't mean that they *aren't* out to get you, Mel Gibson is a terrified little man with fuzzy memories of something related to the "them" he blames for everything from fluoridated water to NASA's plans to assassinate the U.S. president. Gibson's role turns serious quickly; Julia Roberts supports him well as a sympathetic Justice Department attorney who gradually realizes he isn't just imagining things. Rated R for violence and profanity. 140m. DIR: Richard Donner. **CAST:** Mel Gibson, Julia Roberts, Patrick Stewart, Cylk Cozart. 1997 DVD

CONSPIRATOR ★★1/2 A bride, who comes to realize her British army officer husband is a Soviet spy, is torn between love and loyalty. Wooden performances by the stars. B&W; 85m. **DIR:** Victor Saville. **CAST:** Robert Taylor, Elizabeth Taylor, Robert Flemyng, Honor Blackman, Wilfrid Hyde-White. 1949

CONSUMING PASSIONS ★★ Morbid, gross, and sometimes amusing movie about a nerdish junior executive who discovers a "secret ingredient"—human beings—that saves a sagging candy company. Adapted from a play written by Michael Palin and Terry Jones of *Monty Python's Flying Circus* fame, the film suffers from the one-joke premise. Rated R for language, sexual situations, and overall grossness. 95m. **DIR:** Giles Foster. **CAST:** Tyler Butterworth, Jonathan Pryce, Freddie Jones, Sammi Davis, Prunella Scales, Vanessa Redgrave, Thora Hird. 1988

CONTACT ★★★★ In this adaptation of Carl Sagan's sole novel, Jodie Foster is self-absorbed astronomer Ellie Arroway, who rejects blind faith and spiritualism while believing strongly in the possibility of life in other galaxies and that such beings would communicate with Earth. Indeed such contact is established. Naturally, government officials interfere, and there's considerable political intrigue prior to a heady final act reminiscent of the "stargate" sequel in *2001: A Space Odyssey.* We need more thoughtful science fiction like this. Rated PG. 150m. **DIR:** Robert Zemeckis. **CAST:** Jodie Foster, Matthew McConaughey, James Woods, John Hurt, Tom Skerritt, Angela Bassett, William Fichtner, David Morse. 1997 DVD

CONTAGION ★★ When a traveling salesman is trapped in a rural mansion for a night, he comes under the influence of its reclusive owner. First, he must prove himself worthy by committing a murder. Rambling, unsatisfying thriller. Not rated. 90m. **DIR:** Karl Zwicky. **CAST:** John Doyle, Nicola Bartlett. 1988

CONTAGIOUS ★★1/2 This insipid little made-for-cable thriller features an epidemic of cholera sweeping across parts of the United States. Lindsay Wagner plays a doctor who tries to find the source, save her family, and deal with hundreds of patients. All very predictable. Not rated. 95m. **DIR:** Joe Napolitano. **CAST:** Lindsay Wagner, Elizabeth Peña, Tom Wopat, Ken Pogue. 1997

CONTEMPT ★★★1/2 A cult film to be, if it isn't already, this one takes a tongue-in-cheek, raised-eyebrow look at European moviemaking. Jack Palance is a vulgar producer; Fritz Lang, playing himself, is his director; Jean-Luc Godard plays Lang's assistant, and in directing this film turned it into an inside joke—in real (not reel) life, he held the film's producer Joseph E. Levine in contempt. 103m. **DIR:** Jean-Luc Godard. **CAST:** Brigitte Bardot, Jack Palance, Fritz Lang, Jean-Luc Godard, Michel Piccoli. 1963

CONTINENTAL DIVIDE ★★★1/2 As lighthearted romantic comedies go, this one is tops. John Belushi stars as Ernie Souchak, a Chicago newspaper columnist unexpectedly sent into the Rockies to write a story about an ornithologist (Blair Brown). Just as unexpectedly, they fall in love. Rated PG because of slight amounts of nudity. 103m. **DIR:** Michael Apted.

CAST: John Belushi, Blair Brown, Allen Garfield, Carlin Glynn. 1981

CONTRABAND ★★ A mediocre Italian gangster movie, dubbed into English. This time the main vice is contraband goods rather than hard drugs or prostitution. But the story is the same. 87m. **DIR:** Lucio Fulci. **CAST:** Fabio Testi, Ivana Monti. 1980

CONTRACT ★★★★ Enjoyable and provocative satire takes place at the wedding party of the son of a well-to-do doctor. The arranged marriage is already off to a bad start, and things get steadily worse. In Polish with English subtitles. Not rated, the film features nudity. 111m. **DIR:** Krzysztof Zanussi. **CAST:** Leslie Caron, Maja Komorowska, Tadeusz Lomnicki. 1980

CONTRACT FOR LIFE: THE S.A.D.D. STORY ★★★1/2 Based on the work of real-life hockey coach Bob Anastas, this chronicles the creation of Students Against Drunk Driving. After two of his all-stars are killed while driving drunk, Anastas (beautifully played by Stephen Macht) inspires his students to band together to prevent similar tragedies. Well done! 46m. **DIR:** Joseph Pevney. **CAST:** Stephen Macht. 1984

CONUNDRUM ★★★1/2 Writer-director Douglas Barr's twisty little thriller should keep you guessing, while cops Michael Biehn and Marg Helgenberger pursue the baddies who brutally killed the former's wife. The supporting characters are unusually well developed for this genre, and the plot remains credible to the very end. Rated R for violence, profanity, nudity, and simulated sex. 98m. **DIR:** Douglas Barr. **CAST:** Marg Helgenberger, Michael Biehn, Ron White, Peter MacNeill, Dan Lett. 1995

CONVENT, THE ★★★★ Sweltering tale of an American professor and his French wife, whose visit to the ancient convent Arrabida sparks a classic tale of seduction and betrayal. While Michael works on his thesis, Helene is swept away by Baltar, the guardian of the archives. In English, French, and Portuguese with English subtitles. Not rated. 90m. **DIR:** Manoel de Oliveira. **CAST:** John Malkovich, Catherine Deneuve, Lenor Silveira, Luis Miguel Cintra. 1995

CONVERSATION, THE ★★★★★ Following his box-office and artistic triumph with *The Godfather,* director Francis Ford Coppola made this absorbing character study about a bugging-device expert (Gene Hackman) who lives only for his work but finds himself developing a conscience. Although not a box-office hit when originally released, this is a fine little film. Rated PG. 113m. **DIR:** Francis Ford Coppola. **CAST:** Gene Hackman, John Cazale, Allen Garfield, Cindy Williams, Harrison Ford. 1974

CONVERSATION PIECE ★★ Burt Lancaster portrays a bewildered, reclusive professor whose life changes direction when he encounters a countess and her children. In Italian with English subtitles. 122m. **DIR:** Luchino Visconti. **CAST:** Burt Lancaster, Silvana Mangano, Helmut Berger, Claudia Cardinale. 1974

CONVICT COWBOY ★★★★ An honorable lifer finds fame and inner peace on the prison rodeo circuit. The entire cast is excellent, including cameo player Ben Gazzara as the warden who believes in "rehabilitation through ranching." Rick Way and Jim Lindsay's script suggests that some men might better their lives through honest repentance. Rated R for profanity and violence. 106m. **DIR:** Rod Holcomb. **CAST:** Jon Voight, Kyle Chandler, Marcia Gay Harden, Stephen McHattie, Ben Gazzara. **1995**

CONVICTED ★★★ Fact-based drama focuses on inadequacies in the judicial system when family man John Larroquette is accused of being a rapist and sentenced to five years in prison. Wife Lindsay Wagner spends five years searching for the truth in this inspiring made-for-TV tale of truth and justice. 94m. **DIR:** David Lowell Rich. **CAST:** John Larroquette, Lindsay Wagner, Carroll O'Connor, Burton Gilliam. **1990**

CONVOY (1940) ★★★1/2 Excellent documentary-style, stiff-upper-lip British film about the daily danger faced by the officers and crew of cargo convoys and the warships that protect them. Producer Michael Balcon gave this movie his customary stamp of authenticity and humanity. B&W; 95m. **DIR:** Pen Tennyson. **CAST:** Clive Brook, John Clements, Judy Campbell, Edward Chapman, Michael Wilding, Charles Farrell, Albert Lieven. **1940**

CONVOY (1978) ★★ Truckers, led by Kris Kristofferson, go on a tri-state protest over police brutality, high gas prices, and other complaints. An uneven script and just fair acting mar this picture. Rated PG. 110m. **DIR:** Sam Peckinpah. **CAST:** Kris Kristofferson, Ali MacGraw, Ernest Borgnine, Madge Sinclair, Burt Young. **1978**

COOGAN'S BLUFF ★★★★ Clint Eastwood and director Don Siegel in their first collaboration. The squinty-eyed star hunts down a murderous fugitive (Don Stroud) in the asphalt jungle. Rated PG. 100m. **DIR:** Don Siegel. **CAST:** Clint Eastwood, Lee J. Cobb, Susan Clark, Tisha Sterling, Don Stroud, Betty Field, Tom Tully. **1968**

COOK, THE THIEF, HIS WIFE & HER LOVER, THE ★★★★ British film about a long-suffering wife who carries on an affair in a restaurant owned by her sadistic, obnoxious husband. Gorgeously crafted yet explicit and sometimes distressingly brutal. A dark, haunting comedy with few bodily functions ignored, but the story is about excessive behavior—so nothing seems gratuitous. Rated NC-17 for nudity, violence, profanity, and simulated sex … you name it. 123m. **DIR:** Peter Greenaway. **CAST:** Michael Gambon, Helen Mirren, Richard Bohringer, Alan Howard. **1990**

COOKIE ★★★1/2 In this frothy piece of fluff, Emily Lloyd stars as the rebellious daughter of a gangster (Peter Falk) who cannot figure out how to keep his offspring in line. It's entertaining but forgettable. Rated R for profanity and violence. 93m. **DIR:** Susan Seidelman. **CAST:** Emily Lloyd, Peter Falk, Dianne Wiest, Jerry Lewis, Michael Gazzo, Brenda Vaccaro, Adrian Pasdar. **1989**

COOKIE'S FORTUNE ★★★★ Southern eccentrics are alive and well in this quirky character comedy from director Robert Altman and scripter Anne Rapp. The story, laced with Gothic overtones and a small-town Mississippi setting, concerns the aftermath of a suicide by one of the community's leading citizens. Tempers flare, libidos soar into hyperdrive,

and some rather unexpected family secrets are revealed. Events are dominated by Glenn Close's Camille Dixon, a fussy, bossy, and unapologetically nasty shrike who believes that rules were made solely for the common herd. Rated PG-13 for profanity, sexual candor, and brief violence. 118m. **DIR:** Robert Altman. **CAST:** Glenn Close, Julianne Moore, Liv Tyler, Chris O'Donnell, Charles Dutton, Patricia Neal, Ned Beatty, Courtney B. Vance, Donald Moffat, Lyle Lovett. **1999 DVD**

COOL AS ICE 🐝 Vanilla Ice's first starring role as a motorcycle rider who woos a small-town girl proves he is an even worse actor than he is a rap singer. If that's possible. Rated PG for profanity. 91m. **DIR:** David Kellogg. **CAST:** Vanilla Ice, Kristin Minter, Michael Gross, Sidney Lassick, Dody Goodman, Candy Clark. **1991**

COOL BLUE ★★ Bumbling artist meets mysterious siren in urban bohemia. Miscast, labored, and pitifully unbelievable, *Cheers* star Woody Harrelson looks as if he needs a few belts. Rated R. 90m. **DIR:** Mark Mullen, Richard Shepard. **CAST:** Woody Harrelson. **1988**

•COOL, DRY PLACE, A ★★★ After his wife leaves him, a small-town lawyer is forced to spend more time with his five-year-old son in this engaging but somewhat meandering comedy-drama. Young Bobby Moat, who plays the son, is a real scene-stealer. Rated PG-13 for sexual situations and mild profanity. 97m. **DIR:** John N. Smith. **CAST:** Vince Vaughn, Monica Potter, Joey Lauren Adams, Bobby Moat. **1998**

COOL HAND LUKE ★★★★★ One of Paul Newman's greatest creations is the irrepressible Luke. Luke is a prisoner on a southern chain gang and not even the deprivations of these subhuman conditions will break his spirit. George Kennedy's performance is equally memorable and won him a supporting Oscar. 126m. **DIR:** Stuart Rosenberg. **CAST:** Paul Newman, George Kennedy, J. D. Cannon, Lou Antonio, Robert Drivas, Strother Martin. **1967 DVD**

COOL RUNNINGS ★★★★ Inspired by the phenomenal popularity of the 1988 Olympics' Jamaican bobsled team, this is a wildly fictionalized *Rocky*-type comedy. Four black tropical sportsmen (a soapbox-derby racer and three sprinters) take the Calgary Winter Olympics by storm while overcoming physical, social, and personal adversity. Their misadventures produce an avalanche of infectious belly laughs. One of John Candy's last films. Rated PG. 95m. **DIR:** Jon Turteltaub. **CAST:** Doug E. Doug, Leon, Malik Yoba, Rawle D. Lewis, John Candy. **1993 DVD**

COOL SURFACE, THE ★★★ In this quirky thriller, aspiring screenwriter Robert Patrick bases his new screenplay on a neighbor, an actress played by Teri Hatcher. Things really start snowballing when Hatcher attempts to land the lead in Patrick's movie and life. Change-of-pace role for Patrick, who plays a mouse ready to roar. Rated R for nudity, violence, and language. 88m. **DIR:** Erik Anjou. **CAST:** Robert Patrick, Teri Hatcher, Matt McCoy, Ian Buchanan, Cyril O'Reilly. **1993**

COOL WORLD ★★ Cartoonist Gabriel Byrne is lured by his sexy creation Kim Basinger into a bizarre animated world that came from his imagination. Brad Pitt is the detective who attempts to bring Byrne back. Like no feature-length cartoon you've ever seen before. Rated PG-13 for sexual content. 98m. **DIR:** Ralph Bakshi. **CAST:** Kim Basinger, Gabriel Byrne, Brad Pitt. **1992**

•**COOLER CLIMATE, A** ★★1/2 Scripter Marsha Norman delivers a respectable adaptation of Zena Collier's novel about two lonely, dissimilar women eventually becoming allies and friends. Sally Field is a naïve wife who, out of humiliation, foolishly abandons her former life after learning that her husband is having an affair; Judy Davis is a brittle, wealthy socialite suffering through her own loveless marriage. Field, determined to turn herself around, accepts a job as the condescending Davis's housekeeper ... a position that everybody in the local community warns is likely to be brief. But the resolute Field—always best playing plucky characters—digs in her heels, and the eventual thaw and bonding is no less entertaining for its predictability. Rated PG-13 for profanity, brief nudity, and simulated sex. 99m. **DIR:** Susan Seidelman. **CAST:** Sally Field, Judy Davis, Winston Rekert, Jerry Wasserman, Carly Pope. **1999**

COOLEY HIGH ★★★★ Highly enjoyable comedy-drama set in an inner-city Chicago high school in the early 1960s. This is probably the only *American Graffiti* clone that doesn't suffer by comparison. Featuring a first-rate soundtrack of vintage Motown tunes. Rated PG for mild profanity and sexual concerns. 107m. **DIR:** Michael Schultz. **CAST:** Glynn Turman, Lawrence Hilton-Jacobs, Garrett Morris, Cynthia Davis. **1975 DVD**

COOPERSTOWN ★★★★ Superior baseball fantasy focuses on a bitter ex-ball player, who is unhappy because he hasn't been inducted into the hall of fame. He is visited by the ghost of a friend who died on the eve of his own induction. Film captures the essence of baseball. 108m. **DIR:** Charles Haid. **CAST:** Alan Arkin, Hope Lange, Graham Greene, Ed Begley Jr., Josh Charles, Ann Wedgeworth. **1992**

COP ★★ This crime thriller quickly goes from being a fascinating character study to just another sleazy and mindless slasher flick. Rated R for violence, gore, simulated sex, nudity, and profanity. 110m. **DIR:** James B. Harris. **CAST:** James Woods, Lesley Ann Warren, Charles Durning, Charles Haid, Raymond J. Barry, Randi Brooks. **1988**

COP AND A HALF ★★★1/2 When youngster Norman D. Golden witnesses a gang-style murder, he uses his knowledge to coerce the authorities into making him a police officer. Burt Reynolds is in his element as the gruff detective assigned to take care of the boy. A predictable but fun romp. Rated PG for brief profanity and violence. 93m. **DIR:** Henry Winkler. **CAST:** Burt Reynolds, Ray Sharkey, Ruby Dee, Holland Taylor, Frank Sivero, Norman D. Golden II. **1993 DVD**

COP AND THE GIRL, THE 🐝 Something is lost in the translation of this dubbed German film. Not rated; contains profanity and violence. 95m. **DIR:** Peter Keglevic. **CAST:** Jurgen Prochnow, Annette Von Klier. **1987**

COP FOR THE KILLING, A ★★ Typical crime-drama fails to present a credible case. James Farentino

plays a Los Angeles police lieutenant out to avenge the murder of his partner by a vicious drug lord. Nothing new in this made-for-television effort. Rated R for intense situations. 87m. **DIR:** Dick Lowry. **CAST:** James Farentino, Steven Weber, Susan Walters, Charles Haid, Harold Sylvester. **1994**

COP IN BLUE JEANS, THE 🐝 An undercover cop (Thomas Milian) tries to take out an underworld boss. (Jack Palance). Not rated; contains violence. 92m. **DIR:** Bruno Corbucci. **CAST:** Tomas Milian, Jack Palance, Maria Rosaria Omaggio, Guido Mannari. **1978**

COPACABANA 🐝 Not even Groucho Marx can save this slight comedy about the problems caused by a woman applying for two jobs at the same nightclub. B&W; 92m. **DIR:** Alfred E. Green. **CAST:** Groucho Marx, Carmen Miranda, Andy Russell, Steve Cochran, Abel Green. **1947**

COPLAND ★★★1/2 Sylvester Stallone's the power in name only for sleepy Garrison, N.J.—a "bedroom community" for New York City cops hoping to leave behind the danger of their jobs. But Garrison's bucolic streets conceal a cesspool of corruption. James Mangold's moody direction is better than his plot, but this remains a noteworthy stretch for an actor trying to leave *Rocky* and *Rambo* behind. Rated R for violence and profanity. 100m. **DIR:** James Mangold. **CAST:** Sylvester Stallone, Harvey Keitel, Ray Liotta, Robert De Niro, Peter Berg, Janeane Garofalo, Robert Patrick, Michael Rapaport, Annabella Sciorra. **1997 DVD**

COP-OUT ★★ In this ambitious but shoestring-budgeted murder mystery, a detective tries to get his incarcerated brother off the hook. The resolution of this whodunit comes as no real surprise. Not rated, though there is partial nudity, violence, and considerable profanity. 102m. **DIR:** Lawrence L. Simeone. **CAST:** David D. Buff. **1991**

COPPER CANYON ★★ A gunslinger helps homesteaders stake their claims after the Civil War. This would have been a more believable picture with a different cast. Milland's British accent and Lamarr's Austrian one are completely out of place in the American Southwest. 83m. **DIR:** John Farrow. **CAST:** Ray Milland, Hedy Lamarr, Macdonald Carey, Mona Freeman, Harry Carey Jr., Frank Faylen, Hope Emerson, Ian Wolfe, Peggy Knudsen. **1950**

COPS AND ROBBERS ★★ This mediocre cops-on-the-take caper features two burned-out New York cops who decide to use all they've learned to pull off the perfect crime. Rated PG for violence. 89m. **DIR:** Aram Avakian. **CAST:** Joseph Bologna, Cliff Gorman. **1973**

COPS AND ROBBERSONS ★★1/2 Mild-mannered suburban dad Chevy Chase is a wannabe detective who gets a taste of the real thing. Hardboiled cop Jack Palance moves in to set up surveillance on Chase's new neighbor (Robert Davi), a counterfeiter with the nasty habit of murdering his customers. The few chuckles almost make it worthwhile. Rated PG for violence. 95m. **DIR:** Michael Ritchie. **CAST:** Chevy Chase, Jack Palance, Dianne Wiest, Robert Davi, David Barry Gray, Jason James Richter, Fay Masterson, Miko Hughes, M. Emmet Walsh. **1994**

COPYCAT ★★★★ Impressive suspense-thriller about a criminal psychologist who develops agoraphobia after a serial killer makes an attempt on her life. She is forced out of her hiding place when a detective seeks her help in solving a recent series of murders, not knowing that the psychologist may be next on the killer's list. Rated R for violence, nudity, and profanity. 123m. DIR: Jon Amiel. CAST: Sigourney Weaver, Holly Hunter, Dermot Mulroney, Will Patton, John Rothman, J. E. Freeman, Harry Connick Jr., William McNamara. 1996 DVD

COQUETTE ★★★ A sticky soap opera that looks hokey today, but it wowed audiences in 1929. Mary Pickford won an Oscar for the role of a college girl who lies in court to get her father off. He was charged with murder, and the film itself is a Flapper Age melodrama that set a pattern for so-called women's movies. B&W; 81m. DIR: Sam Taylor. CAST: Mary Pickford, Matt Moore, Johnny Mack Brown, Louise Beavers. 1929

CORLEONE ★★ Dull Italian drama about two childhood friends in Sicily who decide to fight the powerful landowners who control their homeland. Aside from the title, which is the name of the Sicilian town where they live, this has no connection to the *Godfather* movies. Rated R for profanity, violence. 115m. DIR: Pasquale Squiteri. CAST: Giuliano Gemma, Claudia Cardinale, Francisco Rabal. 1985

CORN IS GREEN, THE (1945) ★★★★ Bette Davis leads a winning cast in this well-mounted film of British playwright-actor Emlyn Williams's drama of education vs. coal in a rough-edged Welsh mining village. John Dall is the young miner whom schoolteacher Davis grooms to win a university scholarship. B&W; 114m. DIR: Irving Rapper. CAST: Bette Davis, John Dall, Joan Lorring, Nigel Bruce, Rhys Williams, Mildred Dunnock. 1945

CORN IS GREEN, THE (1979) ★★★1/2 Based on Emlyn Williams's play and directed by George Cukor, this telefilm stars Katharine Hepburn. She gives a tour-de-force performance as the eccentric spinster-teacher who helps a gifted young man discover the joys of learning. 100m. DIR: George Cukor. CAST: Katharine Hepburn, Ian Saynor, Bill Fraser, Patricia Hayes, Anna Massey. 1979

CORNBREAD, EARL AND ME ★★1/2 A fine cast of black performers is ill served by this overdone drama about racism. A gifted basketball player is mistakenly killed by the police. It's a familiar plot directed with little inspiration by Joseph Manduke. Rated R. 95m. DIR: Joseph Manduke. CAST: Moses Gunn, Bernie Casey, Rosalind Cash, Madge Sinclair. 1975

CORNERED ★★★ Fresh from his success as hard-boiled sleuth Philip Marlowe in *Murder, My Sweet*, former song-and-dance man Dick Powell continued to score as a dramatic actor in this thriller about a discharged Canadian airman on the trail of Nazi collaborators who murdered his French wife. The hunt takes him from France to Switzerland to Argentina. B&W; 102m. DIR: Edward Dmytryk. CAST: Dick Powell, Walter Slezak, Micheline Cheirel, Luther Adler, Morris Carnovsky. 1946

•CORONER, THE ♥ The city coroner, rather than waiting for folks to die, likes to kidnap people and drag them down to his basement to conduct vicious experiments on them. Either that, or he bores them to death. The acting and effects are downright abysmal. Rated R primarily for violence. 79m. DIR: Juan A. Mas. CAST: Jane Longenecker, Dean St. Louis. 1999 DVD

CORONER CREEK ★★★★ Solid Western marks the first film in the series produced by the company set up by Randolph Scott and Harry Brown. Their collaboration culminated in the superb series directed by Budd Boetticher (*Ride Lonesome, The Tall T*). Even so, this film is no slouch, with Scott attempting to track down the man responsible for the murder of his fiancée. 90m. DIR: Ray Enright. CAST: Randolph Scott, Marguerite Chapman, George Macready, Forrest Tucker, Edgar Buchanan. 1948

CORPORATE AFFAIRS ★★ Short on laughs, sex comedy focuses on the sexcapades of corporate executives, each clawing his or her way to the top. Rated R for nudity, profanity, and violence. 82m. DIR: Terence H. Winkless. CAST: Peter Scolari, Mary Crosby, Chris Lemmon, Ken Kercheval. 1990

CORPORATE LADDER ★★ Tired tale of backstabbing vixen who is willing to do anything in her attempt to reach the top. Kathleen Kinmont is appropriately menacing, but she's constantly fighting an uphill battle thanks to trite writing and uninspired direction. Rated R for language, nudity, and violence. 112m. DIR: Nick Vallelonga. CAST: Kathleen Kinmont, Anthony John Denison, Talisa Soto, Jennifer O'Niell, Ben Cross. 1996

CORPSE GRINDERS, THE ♥ This silly horror comedy about two cat-food makers who use human corpses in their secret recipe has a cult reputation as one of those so-bad-it's-good movies. 72m. DIR: Ted V. Mikels. CAST: Sean Kenney, Monika Kelly. 1972

CORPSE VANISHES, THE ♥ Hokey pseudoscientific thriller about crazed scientist Bela Lugosi and his efforts to keep his elderly wife young through transfusions from young girls. B&W; 64m. DIR: Wallace Fox. CAST: Bela Lugosi, Luana Walters, Tristram Coffin, Minerva Urecal, Elizabeth Russell. 1942 DVD

CORREGIDOR ♥ An early World War II movie made on the cheap, and it shows. Elissa Landi is the girl in a romantic triangle. There isn't any action whatever. B&W; 73m. DIR: William Nigh. CAST: Elissa Landi, Donald Woods, Otto Kruger, Frank Jenks, Ian Keith, Wanda McKay. 1943

CORRIDOR OF MIRRORS ★★★1/2 A nail-biter about an artist obsessed with the painting of a Renaissance-era woman. He convinces himself that he is the reincarnation of her lover and seeks her modern counterpart. Lushly photographed and suspensefully produced to make every goose pimple count. Directed by England's foremost action-film specialist who later went on to direct James Bond movies. B&W; 94m. DIR: Terence Young. CAST: Christopher Lee, Eric Portman, Lois Maxwell, Edana Romney, Barbara Mullen, Hugh Sinclair. 1948

CORRIDORS OF BLOOD ★★★ Kindly surgeon (Boris Karloff) in nineteenth-century London tries to perfect anesthesia and becomes addicted to narcotics. In a mental fog, he is blackmailed by grave robbers. A suprisingly effective thriller originally withheld from release in the United States for five years. 86m. **DIR:** Robert Day. **CAST:** Boris Karloff, Francis Matthews, Adrienne Corri, Betta St. John, Nigel Green, Christopher Lee. **1957 DVD**

CORRINA, CORRINA ★★★1/2 Set in the 1950s, Whoopi Goldberg goes to work as a maid for jingle writer Ray Liotta, who has recently lost his wife to cancer and all but lost his little daughter to her self-imposed world of silence. Writer-producer-director Jessie Nelson imbues spirit-lifting entertainment with deft insights into the human condition. Rated PG. 114m. **DIR:** Jessie Nelson. **CAST:** Whoopi Goldberg, Ray Liotta, Tina Majorino, Wendy Crewson, Larry Miller, Erica Yohn, Jenifer Lewis, Joan Cusack, Harold Sylvester, Steven Williams, Don Ameche. **1994 DVD**

CORRUPT ★★ Turtle-paced psychological thriller featuring Harvey Keitel as a corrupt narcotics officer. Not rated, but equivalent to an R for violence and profanity. 99m. **DIR:** Roberto Faenza. **CAST:** Harvey Keitel, John Lydon, Sylvia Sidney, Nicole Garcia. **1984 DVD**

CORRUPT ONES, THE ★★★ Robert Stack plays a photographer who receives the key to a Chinese treasure. Not surprisingly, he soon finds that he's not alone in his search for the goodies. This is a good—but not great—adventure film. 92m. **DIR:** James Hill. **CAST:** Robert Stack, Nancy Kwan, Elke Sommer, Werner Peters. **1966**

CORRUPTOR, THE ★★★1/2 Chow Yun-Fat is the primary attraction in this 1990s *noir* tale of a Chinatown cop who believes he can mix with forces on the Dark Side without becoming tainted. The story concerns our hero's ethical awakening, when it becomes clear that the underworld Tongs are determined to corrupt his naïve and likable younger partner. The result is a slick and suspenseful B film. Rated R for violence, profanity, nudity, sexual content, and drug use. 111m. **DIR:** James Foley. **CAST:** Chow Yun-Fat, Mark Wahlberg, Ric Young, Paul Ben-Victor, Andrew Pang, Brian Cox. **1999 DVD**

CORSICAN BROTHERS, THE (1941) ★★★1/2 Alexandre Dumas's classic story of twins who remain spiritually tied, though separated, crackles in this lavish old Hollywood production. Intrigue and swordplay abound. Douglas Fairbanks Jr. is fine, backed by two of the best supporting players ever: J. Carrol Naish and Akim Tamiroff. B&W; 112m. **DIR:** Gregory Ratoff. **CAST:** Douglas Fairbanks Jr., Ruth Warrick, J. Carrol Naish, Akim Tamiroff, H. B. Warner, Henry Wilcoxon. **1941**

CORSICAN BROTHERS, THE (1984) 🐝 Loosely based on the book by Alexandre Dumas, this forgettable film features Tommy Chong and Richard "Cheech" Marin as twins. Rated R. 90m. **DIR:** Thomas Chong. **CAST:** Cheech and Chong, Roy Dotrice. **1984**

CORVETTE SUMMER 🐝 This mindless car-chase film finds Mark Hamill in Las Vegas hunting car thieves who have ripped off his Corvette. Rated PG. 105m. **DIR:** Matthew Robbins. **CAST:** Mark Hamill, Kim Melford, Annie Potts. **1978**

COSI ★★★★ An amateur stage director's first real assignment is to stage a version of Mozart's *Cosi Fan Tutte* with the occupants of an Australian mental home. His job is complicated because the patients can't sing, read Italian, or memorize lines and the head of the institute is dead set against the idea. When he falls for his troubled leading lady, the stage is set for a wild evening of fun. Bright, cheery Australian import. Rated R for adult situations and language. 100m. **DIR:** Mark Joffe. **CAST:** Ben Mendelsohn, Barry Otto, Toni Collette, Rachel Griffiths, Aden Young, Colin Friels. **1996**

COSMIC MAN, THE 🐝 An invisible alien comes to this planet in a giant levitating Ping-Pong ball. B&W; 72m. **DIR:** Herbert Greene. **CAST:** John Carradine, Bruce Bennett, Angela Greene. **1959**

COSMIC MONSTERS, THE ★★ Low-budget horror from Great Britain. Giant carnivorous insects invade our planet. An alien in a flying saucer arrives to save the day. The effects are cheap. B&W; 75m. **DIR:** Gilbert Gunn. **CAST:** Forrest Tucker, Gaby André. **1958**

COSMIC SLOP ★★1/2 You could almost agree with the blurb on the box that this is a "multicultural *Twilight Zone*," except it is too preachy and the special effects are pathetic. However, the first episode in this three-story, sci-fi anthology, executive produced by directors Reginald and Warrington Hudlin (*House Party*), has the kind of mind-numbing impact that will stay with you for days. Made for HBO. Rated R for violence and profanity. 87m. **DIR:** Reginald Hudlin, Warrington Hudlin, Kevin Sullivan. **CAST:** Robert Guillaume, Nicholas Turturro, George Clinton, Paula Jai Parker, Chi McBride. **1994**

COTTON CLUB, THE ★★★★ The story about two pairs of brothers, one black and one white, is set at Harlem's most famous nightclub. Cornet player Gere and moll Diane Lane make love while Gregory Hines dances his way into the heart of songbird Lonette McKee. Rated R for violence, nudity, profanity, and suggested sex. 128m. **DIR:** Francis Ford Coppola. **CAST:** Richard Gere, Diane Lane, James Remar, Gregory Hines, Lonette McKee. **1984**

COTTON COMES TO HARLEM ★★★★ The comedy-drama based on Chester Himes's book introduces Coffin Ed and Gravedigger Jones, two cops who accuse a local clergyman of swindling the citizens. The movie was filmed in Harlem and started a trend of serio-comic films with all-black casts that exploited stereotypical characters but still pleased audiences. Excellent cast and fine production values. Rated R. 97m. **DIR:** Ossie Davis. **CAST:** Godfrey Cambridge, Raymond St. Jacques, Calvin Lockhart, Redd Foxx, Cleavon Little, Emily Yancy, Judy Pace. **1970**

COUCH IN NEW YORK, A 🐝 Could a film be more boring? Sophisticated Manhattan shrink William Hurt decides on a change of scenery, and—sight unseen—swaps apartments with Parisian Juliette Binoche. She proves more successful than he at "treating" his clients (who seem not to care about switching "therapists" in midtreatment); he grows curious, returns to New York, and poses as a new "patient." Utterly ludicrous, and a total yawn. Rated PG-13 for profanity. 108m. **DIR:** Chantal Akerman. **CAST:** William Hurt, Juliette Binoche, Stephanie Buttle, Paul Guilfoyle, Richard Jenkins. **1996 DVD**

COUCH TRIP, THE ★★1/2 Dan Aykroyd and Walter Matthau offer a few moments of mirth in this middling comedy about a computer hacker (Aykroyd) who escapes from a mental institution and becomes a hugely successful media shrink. Charles Grodin is exceptional as the neurotic radio doctor Aykroyd replaces, and Mary Gross has some terrific scenes as Grodin's wacky wife. Rated R for profanity and suggested sex. 95m. DIR: Michael Ritchie. CAST: Dan Aykroyd, Walter Matthau, Charles Grodin, Donna Dixon, Richard Romanus, Mary Gross, David Clennon, Arye Gross. 1988

COUNT DRACULA ★★1/2 Christopher Lee dons the cape once again in this mediocre version of the famous tale about the undead fiend terrorizing the countryside. Rated R. 98m. DIR: Jess (Jesus) Franco. CAST: Christopher Lee, Herbert Lom, Klaus Kinski. 1970

COUNT OF MONTE CRISTO, THE (1912) ★★★ The famous Irish actor James O'Neill, father of playwright Eugene, is captured for posterity in his popular interpretation of the Alexandre Dumas story. An unmoving camera is focused onstage, and O'Neill is supremely hammy, but this is an invaluable record of a bygone time. Silent. B&W; 90m. DIR: Edwin S. Porter. CAST: James O'Neill. 1912

COUNT OF MONTE CRISTO, THE (1934) ★★★★ In the title role, Robert Donat heads a superb, fine-tuned cast in this now-classic film of Dumas's great story. Innocent sailor Edmond Dantes, falsely accused of aiding the exiled Napoleon and infamously imprisoned for fifteen years, escapes to levy revenge on those who framed him. A secret cache of treasure makes it all very sweet. B&W; 119m. DIR: Rowland V. Lee. CAST: Robert Donat, Elissa Landi, Irene Hervey, Louis Calhern, Sidney Blackmer, Raymond Walburn, O. P. Heggie. 1934

COUNT OF MONTE CRISTO, THE (1975) ★★★1/2 Solid TV adaptation of the Alexandre Dumas classic. Richard Chamberlain cuts a dashing figure as the persecuted Edmond Dantes. The casting of Tony Curtis as the evil Mondego works surprisingly well. 100m. DIR: David Greene. CAST: Richard Chamberlain, Tony Curtis, Louis Jourdan, Donald Pleasence, Taryn Power. 1975

COUNT YORGA, VAMPIRE ★★★ Contemporary vampire terrorizes Los Angeles. Somewhat dated, but a sharp and powerful thriller. Stars Robert Quarry, an intense, dignified actor who appeared in several horror films in the early 1970s, then abruptly left the genre. Rated R for violence. 91m. DIR: Bob Kelljan. CAST: Robert Quarry, Roger Perry, Donna Anders, Michael Murphy. 1970

COUNTDOWN ★★★ This lesser-known Robert Altman film finds James Caan and Robert Duvall as American astronauts preparing for a moon shot. Realistic scenes and great acting—well worth watching. Not rated. 101m. DIR: Robert Altman. CAST: James Caan, Robert Duvall, Charles Aidman. 1968

COUNTERFEIT TRAITOR, THE ★★★★ A spy story based on a real-life character. William Holden is exceptionally good as the Swedish-American businessman who poses as a Nazi sympathizer. Authentic location work and good production values give this one an edge. 141m. DIR: George Seaton. CAST: William Holden, Lilli Palmer, Klaus Kinski, Hugh Griffith, Eva Dahlbeck. 1962

COUNTERFORCE 🎬 An elite special missions force is hired to protect an exiled Middle East democratic leader. A bore. Rated R. 98m. DIR: J. Anthony Loma. CAST: George Kennedy, Jorge Rivero, Andrew Stevens, Isaac Hayes, Louis Jourdan, Robert Forster. 1987

COUNTESS FROM HONG KONG, A 🎬 Charlie Chaplin's final and most disappointing effort, this pits stowaway Sophia Loren against extremely dull Marlon Brando in a shipboard love story that lacks laughs, coherence, and romance. Rated G. 108m. DIR: Charles Chaplin. CAST: Marlon Brando, Sophia Loren, Sydney Chaplin, Tippi Hedren, Patrick Cargill, Bill Nagy, Geraldine Chaplin, Margaret Rutherford, Charlie Chaplin. 1967

COUNTRY ★★★★ A quietly powerful movie about the plight of farmers struggling to hold on while the government and financial institutions seem intent on fostering their failure. *Country* teams Jessica Lange and Sam Shepard on-screen, for the first time since the Oscar-nominated *Frances*, in a film as topical as today's headlines. Rated PG. 109m. DIR: Richard Pearce. CAST: Jessica Lange, Sam Shepard, Wilford Brimley, Matt Clark. 1984

COUNTRY GENTLEMEN ★★ Fast-talking confidence men Ole Olsen and Chic Johnson sell shares in a worthless oil field to a group of World War I veterans, then learn thar's oil in them thar hills! Humorous, but what a weary plot! This flick did little for the comic duo, who always fared better on the stage. B&W; 54m. DIR: Ralph Staub. CAST: Ole Olsen, Chic Johnson, Joyce Compton, Lila Lee. 1936

COUNTRY GIRL, THE (1954) ★★★1/2 Bing Crosby and Grace Kelly give terrific performances in this little-seen production. Crosby plays an alcoholic singer who wallows in self-pity until he seizes a chance to make a comeback. Kelly won an Oscar for her sensitive portrayal of his wife. B&W; 104m. DIR: George Seaton. CAST: Bing Crosby, Grace Kelly, William Holden, Anthony Ross. 1954

COUNTRY GIRL, THE (1982) ★★★1/2 Cable TV remake of Clifford Odets's tragic play pales somewhat compared to the Bing Crosby–Grace Kelly rendition. In this filmed stage-play version Dick Van Dyke is the alcoholic actor who has one last chance at a comeback. Ken Howard is the brash young director who blames Van Dyke's wife (Faye Dunaway) for the actor's decline. 137m. DIR: Gary Halvorson. CAST: Faye Dunaway, Dick Van Dyke, Ken Howard. 1982

COUNTRY LIFE ★★★★ Chekhov's play *Uncle Vanya*, about family squabbles on a Russian country estate, is transplanted to an Australian sheep ranch shortly after World War I. This film is almost as faithful as *Vanya on 42nd Street*, and considerably funnier, with a boisterous and hearty spirit of which Chekhov would approve. As the dissolute country doctor, Sam Neill is in top form. Rated PG-13 for mild profanity and adult situations. 103m. DIR: Michael Blakemore. CAST: Sam Neill, Greta Scacchi, John Hargreaves, Kerry Fox, Patricia Kennedy, Maurie Fields, Googie Withers, Michael Blakemore. 1994

COUNTRYMAN ★★★1/2 A strange and fun film following the adventures of a young marijuana-smuggling woman (Kristian Sinclair) whose airplane crash-lands in Jamaica. She is rescued by Countryman and led to safety. Lots of Rasta humor and supernatural happenings keep the viewer entertained. *Countryman* also has a great reggae music soundtrack. Rated R for nudity and adult themes. 103m. DIR: Dickie Jobson. CAST: Hiram Keller, Kristian Sinclair. 1984

COUP DE GRACE ★★ In 1920, the daughter of a once-wealthy family falls in love with the militaristic leader of a group of soldiers. Mostly impenetrable pontificating on sex and politics, poorly adapted from a novel by Marguerite Yourcenar. In German with English subtitles. Not rated. 95m. DIR: Volker Schlöndorff. CAST: Margarethe von Trotta, Matthias Habich, Mathieu Carriere. 1976

COUPE DE VILLE ★★★1/2 It's 1963, the last glorious months before the fall of Kennedy's Camelot, and three estranged brothers are recruited to bring a 1954 Cadillac from Michigan to Florida as a surprise gift for their mother's fiftieth birthday. Delightful comedy. Rated PG-13 for profanity and brief violence. 110m. DIR: Joe Roth. CAST: Daniel Stern, Patrick Dempsey, Arye Gross, Alan Arkin. 1990

COURAGE MOUNTAIN ★★★★ Ignore all those highfalutin critics who gave this well-made family film a thumbs-down. Director Christopher Leitch has done a marvelous job in turning this quasi-sequel to *Heidi* into compelling entertainment. Plenty of suspense, strong characterizations, and an edge-of-your-seat ending. Rated PG for brief violence. 120m. DIR: Christopher Leitch. CAST: Juliette Caton, Charlie Sheen, Leslie Caron. 1990

COURAGE OF LASSIE ★★1/2 Everybody's favorite collie is called Bill and suffers postwar trauma in this unusual entry into the popular series. Bill leaves his wilderness home to become Elizabeth Taylor's dog, but is injured and somehow ends up in the canine corps. 92m. DIR: Fred M. Wilcox. CAST: Elizabeth Taylor, Frank Morgan, Tom Drake, Selena Royle, Harry Davenport, George Cleveland. 1946

COURAGE UNDER FIRE ★★★★ Decorated Gulf War hero Denzel Washington investigates the background of a medevac pilot scheduled to receive a Medal of Honor. Unfortunately, the award is posthumous, and Washington is battling his own demons, having given the order that killed his best friend during "friendly fire." Rated R for violence and profanity. 116m. DIR: Edward Zwick. CAST: Denzel Washington, Meg Ryan, Lou Diamond Phillips, Michael Moriarty, Matt Damon, Seth Gilliam, Bronson Pinchot, Scott Glenn. 1996

COURAGEOUS DR. CHRISTIAN, THE ★★1/2 In this episode of the Dr. Christian series, Jean Hersholt again plays the saintlike physician. Predictable but pleasing. B&W; 67m. DIR: Bernard Vorhaus. CAST: Jean Hersholt, Dorothy Lovett, Robert Baldwin, Tom Neal. 1940

COURAGEOUS MR. PENN ★★ Stilted title of this bloodless biography of religious leader William Penn is indicative of the mediocrity of the entire production. B&W; 79m. DIR: Lance Comfort. CAST: Clifford Evans, Deborah Kerr. 1943

COURT JESTER, THE ★★★ Romance, court intrigue, a joust, and in the middle of it all the one and only Danny Kaye as a phony court jester full of double-takes and double-talk. This is one funny film of clever and complicated comic situations superbly brought off. 101m. DIR: Norman Panama, Melvin Frank. CAST: Danny Kaye, Glynis Johns, Basil Rathbone, Angela Lansbury, Mildred Natwick, Robert Middleton. 1956 DVD

COURTESANS OF BOMBAY ★★★★ Fascinating mix of documentary and fiction explores the lives of impoverished Indian women who support themselves through a combination of performing and prostitution. Made for British television, the film is chiefly concerned with the social context of a society that encourages such life-styles. Not rated; the subject matter is discreetly handled but too frank for young children. 73m. DIR: Ismail Merchant, James Ivory, Ruth Prawer Jhabvala. CAST: Saeed Jaffrey. 1983

COURT-MARTIAL OF BILLY MITCHELL, THE ★★★ In 1925, Army General Billy Mitchell was court-martialed for calling the army and the navy almost treasonous for their neglect of military air power after World War I. Gary Cooper is marvelous as Mitchell, but the show is almost stolen by prosecuting attorney Rod Steiger. 100m. DIR: Otto Preminger. CAST: Gary Cooper, Rod Steiger, Charles Bickford, Ralph Bellamy, Elizabeth Montgomery, Jack Lord, Peter Graves, Darren McGavin. 1955

COURT-MARTIAL OF JACKIE ROBINSON, THE ★★★1/2 Well-made television drama examines racism in the army from 1942 to 1944. Andre Braugher is very good as the young Robinson, with veterans Ruby Dee and Bruce Dern lending stellar support in small but important roles. 94m. DIR: Larry Peerce. CAST: Andre Braugher, Daniel Stern, Ruby Dee, Stan Shaw, Paul Dooley, Bruce Dern. 1990

COURTNEY AFFAIR, THE ★★★ British family saga stretching across four and a half decades: 1900–1945. Classy soap opera in which a housemaid marries money and trades the backstairs for the drawing room. B&W; 112m. DIR: Herbert Wilcox. CAST: Anna Neagle, Michael Wilding, Coral Browne. 1947

COURTSHIP ★★★★ A touching and engrossing period play (set in 1915) from the pen of Horton Foote, whose superb dialogue makes this tale of a young woman's coming-of-age easy to believe. A wonderful transport back to the more chivalrous days of yesteryear. No rating. 85m. DIR: Howard Cummings. CAST: Hallie Foote, Amanda Plummer, Rochelle Oliver, Michael Higgins, William Converse-Roberts. 1987

COURTSHIP OF EDDIE'S FATHER, THE ★★★ A delightful blend of sophisticated romance and family idealism that inspired a successful TV series in the 1960s. Little Ronny Howard is exceptional as the motherless son who gives Dad, Glenn Ford, advice on his love life. 117m. DIR: Vincente Minnelli. CAST: Glenn Ford, Ron Howard, Stella Stevens, Dina Merrill, Shirley Jones, Jerry Van Dyke, Roberta Sherwood. 1963

COURTYARD, THE ★★★1/2 An architect moves into an apartment complex in Los Angeles, and within a week finds himself embroiled in a murder investigation. Between repeated attempts to find the murderer, he falls in love with the dead man's sister. Credible performances from Andrew McCarthy and Madchen Amick shore up the complex plot in this made-for-cable original. Rated R for profanity, violence, and nudity. 105m. **DIR:** Fred Walton. **CAST:** Andrew McCarthy, Madchen Amick, David Packer, Bonnie Bartlett, Vincent Schiavelli, Richard "Cheech" Marin. 1995

COUSIN BETTE ★★★★ Set in France during the nineteenth century, director Des McAnuff's film is filled with juicy performances and a wicked screenplay based on Balzac's novel. Jessica Lange, as Bette, gets even with her extended family through a plan involving greed, sexual temptation, and loyalty. Elisabeth Shue is the saucy temptress who sets Bette's plan into motion. Rated R for language, adult situations, and nudity. 110m. **DIR:** Des McAnuff. **CAST:** Jessica Lange, Elisabeth Shue, Bob Hoskins, Hugh Laurie, Aden Young, Kelly MacDonald. 1997 DVD

COUSIN BOBBY ★★★★ Filmmaker Jonathan Demme hadn't seen his second cousin, the Reverend Robert Castle, for thirty years until a family reunion inspired him to make this film. A socially conscious minister, Castle believes that one man can make a difference: in modern footage, we see him leading a congregation in Harlem and fighting institutionalized racism. A small gem. Not rated; no objectionable material. 70m. **DIR:** Jonathan Demme. 1992

COUSIN, COUSINE ★★★1/2 Marie-Christine Barrault and Victor Lanoux star in this beloved French comedy in the U.S., remade as *Cousins*. Married to others, they become cousins. Once the kissing starts, their relationship expands beyond the boundaries of convention. In French with English subtitles. 95m. **DIR:** Jean-Charles Tacchella. **CAST:** Marie-Christine Barrault, Victor Lanoux, Marie-France Pisier, Guy Marchand. 1975

COUSINS ★★★★1/2 *Cousins* is an utter delight; a marvelously acted, written, and directed romance. Ted Danson, Isabella Rossellini, Sean Young, and William Petersen star as star-crossed spouses, cousins, and lovers in this Americanized takeoff on the 1975 French comedy hit, *Cousin, Cousine*. *Cousins* is about love rather than sex, making it a rare modern movie with heart. Rated PG-13 for profanity and suggested sex. 109m. **DIR:** Joel Schumacher. **CAST:** Ted Danson, Isabella Rossellini, Sean Young, William L. Petersen, Lloyd Bridges, Norma Aleandro, Keith Coogan. 1989

COVER GIRL ★★★ Beautiful Rita Hayworth, a performer in Gene Kelly's nightclub act, must choose between a fabulous gig as a *Vanity* magazine cover girl—which may lead to a future with a millionaire producer—or life with an extremely petulant, chauvinistic Kelly. Let's-put-on-a-show scenario works well. 107m. **DIR:** Charles Vidor. **CAST:** Rita Hayworth, Gene Kelly, Phil Silvers, Eve Arden. 1944

COVER GIRL MURDERS, THE ★★1/2 If you like to see beautiful women in skimpy bathing suits, you'll love this made-for-cable original—just don't expect much of a plot or great acting. During a remote-island photo shoot, the cover girls are murdered one by one. Rated PG-13 for violence and an attempted rape. 87m. **DIR:** James A. Contner. **CAST:** Lee Majors, Jennifer O'Neill, Adrian Paul, Beverly Johnson, Vanessa Angel, Arthur Taxier, Bobbie Phillips, Fawna MacLaren, Mowava Pryor. 1993

COVER ME ★★ When a female cop is fired for shooting a bad guy, she has one chance to get her job back—take off her clothes and go undercover as a centerfold model. Silly thriller is helped by performers who give it the old college try despite the fact the material is ridiculous. Rated R for sexuality, language, and violence. 94m. **DIR:** Michael Schroeder. **CAST:** Rick Rossovich, Elliott Gould, Corbin Bernsen, Courtney Taylor, Paul Sorvino. 1995

COVER STORY 💔 Inane tale of a man who falls in love with a dead woman's picture. But wait! Is she really dead? If this sounds intriguing, forgive us—it's really a time waster. Senseless with some of the most ridiculous dialogue on film. Not rated; contains nudity, sex, violence, and profanity. 93m. **DIR:** Gregg Smith. **CAST:** William Wallace, Tuesday Knight, Leland Orser, Dale Dye. 1994

COVERED WAGON, THE ★★★1/2 Touted as "the biggest thing the screen has had since *The Birth of A Nation*," this epic pioneer saga broke audience attendance records all over the world and remained in circulation for many years. Love, adventure, humor, danger, and despair overlap each other in this somewhat dated but still exciting blockbuster. A landmark Western. Silent. B&W; 83m. **DIR:** James Cruze. **CAST:** J. Warren Kerrigan, Lois Wilson, Alan Hale Sr., Ernest Torrence, Tully Marshall. 1923

COVERED WAGON DAYS ★★1/2 The Three Mesquiteers have until sunset to prove a friend innocent of a murder actually committed by silver smugglers. B&W; 54m. **DIR:** George Sherman. **CAST:** Robert Livingston, Duncan Renaldo, Raymond Hatton. 1940

COVERT ASSASSIN ★★★ Roy Scheider is in fine form in this action-thriller that features him as ex-NATO antiterrorist task-force commander Peter Stride. After he's asked to resign, Stride accepts an offer from a beautiful baroness to track down the terrorists who killed her husband. Exotic locations, exciting action sequences, and sympathetic characters work in this low-budget film's favor. Rated R for violence and adult language. 114m. **DIR:** Tony Wharmby. **CAST:** Roy Scheider, Sam Wanamaker, Ted McGinley, Patricia Millardet, Christopher Buchholz. 1993

COVER-UP ★★ Reporters flock to Israel after an American military base is bombed. Violence begets violence in this confusing espionage thriller. Not rated; contains violence, profanity, and nudity. 89m. **DIR:** Manny Coto. **CAST:** Dolph Lundgren, Lou Gossett Jr., John Finn. 1990

COW TOWN ★★1/2 Action and stunts as well as a good crew of familiar faces make this, Gene Autry's seventy-second film, as fun-filled, better than many of his earlier efforts. Grazing rights, stampedes, gunplay, and a song or two (or three) are packed into the film. B&W; 70m. **DIR:** John English. **CAST:** Gene Autry, Gail Davis, Harry Shannon, Jock Mahoney. 1950

COWARD OF THE COUNTY ★★★ This made-for-TV film is based on Kenny Rogers's hit song. He plays a World War II Georgia preacher with a pacifist nephew. When the nephew's girlfriend is raped, he's put to the ultimate test of his nonviolent beliefs. The acting and setting are believable, making this a film worth viewing. 110m. DIR: Dick Lowry. CAST: Kenny Rogers, Fredric Lehne, Largo Woodruff, Mariclare Costello, Ana Alicia. 1981

COWBOY AND THE BALLERINA, THE ★★ This telemovie is romance at its most basic. Lee Majors plays a former world-champion rodeo rider who meets a Russian ballerina (Leslie Wing) who is attempting to defect. Corny but adequate time passer. 100m. DIR: Jerry Jameson. CAST: Lee Majors, Leslie Wing, Christopher Lloyd, Anjelica Huston. 1984

COWBOY AND THE LADY, THE ★★ Offbeat casting did not help in this slow comedy about a city girl who falls for a rodeo star. The Oscar-nominated title song is by Lionel Newman and Arthur Quenzer. B&W; 91m. DIR: H. C. Potter. CAST: Gary Cooper, Merle Oberon, Walter Brennan, Patsy Kelly, Harry Davenport. 1938

COWBOY MILLIONAIRE ★★★ The accent is on humor in this series Western, which has two-fisted George O'Brien and sidekick Edgar Kennedy acting as "colorful cowboy types" at a hotel out west. It's just a way to raise money to finance their mining operation. B&W; 65m. DIR: Eddie Cline. CAST: George O'Brien, Edgar Kennedy. 1935

COWBOY WAY, THE ★★★ Two New Mexico rodeo ropers—one a keeper of near civility, the other part crude clown and part prairie Peter Pan—put their personal feud aside while rescuing a friend's Cuban daughter from New York City immigrant smugglers. This comic if unenlightened fish-out-of-water story about squabbling saddle rats who kiss and make up and help someone out along the way has a rousing finale. Rated PG-13 for language and violence. 102m. DIR: Gregg Champion. CAST: Kiefer Sutherland, Woody Harrelson, Cara Buono, Dylan McDermott, Ernie Hudson. 1994 DVD

COWBOYS, THE ★★★★1/2 Along with Don Siegel's *The Shootist*, this is the best of John Wayne's latter-day Westerns. The Duke plays a rancher whose wranglers get gold fever. He's forced to recruit a bunch of green kids in order to take his cattle to market. Bruce Dern is on hand as the outlaw leader who fights our hero in one of the genre's most memorable (and violent) scenes. Rated PG. 128m. DIR: Mark Rydell. CAST: John Wayne, Roscoe Lee Browne, Bruce Dern, Colleen Dewhurst, Slim Pickens. 1972 DVD

CRACK HOUSE ★★ Okay exploitation film about the tragic world of crack cocaine. Two young lovers from the barrio are swept into the nightmare when the boyfriend avenges the murder of his cousin by a rival gang. Rated R for nudity, violence, and profanity. 97m. DIR: Michael Fischa. CAST: Richard Roundtree, Jim Brown, Anthony Geary. 1990

CRACK-UP ★★1/2 Cast against type, Pat O'Brien does a commendable job portraying an art critic investigating a forgery ring in this taut low-budget suspense-thriller. B&W; 93m. DIR: Irving Reis. CAST: Pat O'Brien, Claire Trevor, Herbert Marshall. 1946

CRACKER FACTORY ★★★★ This made-for-TV drama features Natalie Wood as Cassie Barrett, an alcoholic housewife who loses her grip on reality. Her long-suffering husband, Charlie (Peter Haskell), silently offers support while she spends her rehabilitation in the Cracker Factory, a mental institution. Not rated, but the mature topic warrants parental discretion. 95m. DIR: Burt Brinckerhoff. CAST: Natalie Wood, Peter Haskell, Shelley Long, Vivian Blaine, Perry King. 1979

CRACKER (TV SERIES) ★★★★★ In this British crime series, Robbie Coltrane is dazzling as Fitz, a forensic psychologist blessed with shrewd insight and the ability to think just like the sickos in these grim stories. Fitz is far from admirable; he smokes, drinks, and gambles too much, pays scant attention to his wife and children, and lacks the diplomacy to suffer fools gladly. But his talent is impossible to ignore. Not rated, but equivalent to PG-13 for violence, explicit dialogue, and strong sexual content. Each tape 135m. DIR: Roy Battersby. CAST: Robbie Coltrane, Barbara Flynn, Geraldine Somerville. 1993–95

CRACKERJACK ★★★ This *Die Hard*-in-a-mountain-chalet would be even better if star Thomas Ian Griffith were a better actor; his reactions of surprised horror cannot be distinguished from his lady-killing smiles. He's a suicidal cop still grieving over the loss of his family, who gets a chance at atonement when deranged neo-Nazi Christopher Plummer attacks an ice-bound resort filled with guests ... including our hero's brother. Rated R for violence, profanity, and nudity. 96m. DIR: Michael Mazo. CAST: Thomas Ian Griffith, George Touliatos, Lisa Bunting, Nastassja Kinski, Christopher Plummer. 1994

CRACKERS 🎬 A bunch of down-and-out San Franciscans decide to turn to crime in order to survive. Rated PG. 92m. DIR: Louis Malle. CAST: Donald Sutherland, Jack Warden, Sean Penn, Wallace Shawn. 1984

CRACKING UP 🎬 No laughs here. Rated R. 83m. DIR: Jerry Lewis. CAST: Jerry Lewis, Herb Edelman, Zane Buzby, Dick Butkus, Milton Berle. 1983

CRADLE WILL FALL, THE ★★ This made-for-television suspense movie falls flat. Lauren Hutton is an attorney who gets entangled with a doctor (Ben Murphy). Along comes another doctor—straight out of Dachau, one would think—who turns things upside down. The story is silly and the direction uninspired. 100m. DIR: John Llewellyn Moxey. CAST: Lauren Hutton, Ben Murphy, James Farentino, Charlita Bauer, Carolyn Ann Clark. 1983

●**CRADLE WILL ROCK** ★★★★ This ambitious, fact-based ensemble drama is set during the Depression, when a rather unique blend of desperation and innovation prompted yet another clash between art and politics. The U.S. government's Federal Theatre Project, designed to lift national spirits by bringing low-cost theater to millions of Americans, is "co-opted" by composer-playwright Marc Blitzstein and the flamboyant Orson Welles, who hope to produce a play revolving around the rise of unions in response to onerous working conditions. Much of writer-director Tim Robbins's film, a captivating brew of fact and fancy, is advocacy filmmaking in the same manner at the original *Cradle Will Rock* was advocacy theater. The result is energetic, important, and fun to watch. Rated R for profanity, nudity, and sexual content. 132m. DIR: Tim Robbins. CAST: Hank Azaria, Rubén Blades, Joan Cusack, John Cusack, Cary Elwes, Cherry Jones, Angus MacFadyen, Bill Murray, Vanessa Redgrave, Susan Sarandon, John Turturro, Emily Watson. 1999 DVD

CRAFT, THE ★★ Four high-school misfits form a coven of witches and cast black-magic spells on their tormenting peers. A promisingly mischievous idea and good leading performances are frittered away in a standard special-effects marathon. There are a few good, creepy moments, but the story doesn't hold together from scene to scene. Rated R for profanity and violence. 100m. DIR: Andrew Fleming. CAST: Robin Tunney, Fairuza Balk, Neve Campbell, Rachel True, Skeet Ulrich. 1996 DVD

CRAIG'S WIFE ★★★ In her first film success, Rosalind Russell is brilliant as Harriet Craig, the wife of the title, a heartless domestic tyrant whose neurotic reference for material concerns over human feelings alienates all around her. John Boles is her long-suffering, slow-to-see-the-light husband. B&W; 75m. DIR: Dorothy Arzner. CAST: Rosalind Russell, John Boles, Billie Burke, Jane Darwell, Thomas Mitchell, Emma Kruger. 1936

CRANES ARE FLYING, THE ★★★★ During World War II, a young woman is so shattered at the news of her lover's death that she agrees to marry a man she doesn't care for. Sublime, moving, and beautifully filmed, this little gem was named Best Film at Cannes. In Russian with English subtitles. B&W; 94m. DIR: Mikhail K. Kalatozov. CAST: Tatyana Samoilova, Alexei Batalov. 1957

CRASH! (1977) 🦃 Made quickly to cash in on the big-budget *The Car*, released the same year, this low-budget film will leave the viewer dozing. Rated PG for violence. 89m. DIR: Charles Band. CAST: José Ferrer, Sue Lyon, John Carradine. 1977

CRASH (1996) ★★1/2 After a near-fatal auto accident, a film producer is drawn into a shadowy cult of people who are turned on by vehicular mayhem. Based on J. G. Ballard's 1973 novel, the film is neither credible nor involving, as no link exists between sex and car crashes, and the characters' emotionally sterile lives are tiresome to watch. Rated NC-17 for profanity, nudity, and graphic simulated sex. 98m. DIR: David Cronenberg. CAST: James Spader, Holly Hunter, Deborah Unger, Elias Koteas, Rosanna Arquette. 1996 DVD

CRASH AND BURN ★★1/2 Futuristic tale of a rebel television station infiltrated by an android from the corporation that now runs the world. Fast-paced, with above-par special effects, this film is directed with uncommon grace by B-movie king Charles Band. Rated R for violence and profanity. 85m. DIR: Charles Band. CAST: Paul Ganus, Megan Ward, Ralph Waite. 1990 DVD

CRASH DIVE ★★ An American nuclear submarine becomes the staging ground for suspense when terrorists invade, holding the crew hostage and threatening to blow up Washington, D.C. Standard action are held back by low budget and lackluster direc-

tion. Rated R for language and violence. 90m. DIR: Andrew Stevens. CAST: Michael Dudikoff, Frederic Forrest, Jay Acovone. 1996

CRASH OF FLIGHT 401 ★★ Based on fact, this made-for-television movie tells the story of the disastrous airliner crash in the Florida Everglades in December of 1972 and the eventful rescue of seventy-three survivors. Routine. 100m. DIR: Barry Shear. CAST: William Shatner, Eddie Albert, Adrienne Barbeau. 1978

CRASHOUT ★★1/2 Okay story about the odyssey of six convicts who crash out of prison. Unfortunately, the fine character development is hurt by a sometimes static plot and disappointing climax. William Bendix, however, is wonderfully unsympathetic as the self-serving ringleader. B&W; 82m. DIR: Lewis R. Foster. CAST: William Bendix, Arthur Kennedy, Luther Adler, William Talman, Marshall Thompson. 1955

CRATER LAKE MONSTER, THE 🦃 Inexpensive, unimpressive film about a prehistoric creature emerging from the usually quiet lake of the title and raising hell. Rated PG. 89m. DIR: William R. Stromberg. CAST: Richard Cardella, Glenn Roberts. 1977

CRAVING, THE 🦃 A witch burned at the stake hundreds of years ago comes back to life and resurrects her werewolf henchman to do her dirty work. Rated R for violence and nudity. 93m. DIR: Jack Molina. CAST: Paul Naschy. 1980

CRAWLERS 🦃 Dreadful, low-budget effort. Tree roots exposed to toxic chemicals change into vicious vines. Rated R for sex, violence, and language. 94m. DIR: Martin Newlin. CAST: Jason Saucier, Mary Sellers. 1993

CRAWLING EYE, THE ★★★ Acceptable horror-thriller about an unseen menace hiding within the dense fog surrounding a mountaintop. A nice sense of doom builds throughout, and the monster remains unseen (always the best way) until the very end. B&W; 85m. DIR: Quentin Lawrence. CAST: Forrest Tucker, Janet Munro. 1958

CRAWLING HAND, THE 🦃 Low-budget tale of a dismembered hand at large in a small town. B&W; 89m. DIR: Herbert L. Strock. CAST: Peter Breck, Rod Lauren, Kent Taylor. 1963

CRAWLSPACE 🦃 Terrible imitation of the classic *Peeping Tom*, with Klaus Kinski as a sadistic landlord who engages in murder and voyeurism. Rated R. 82m. DIR: David Schmoeller. CAST: Klaus Kinski, Talia Balsam. 1986

CRAZED 🦃 A demented man living in a boardinghouse becomes obsessed with a young woman. Not rated; contains violence and profanity. 88m. DIR: Richard Cassidy. CAST: Laslo Papas, Belle Mitchell, Beverly Ross. 1984

CRAZIES, THE ★★ A military plane carrying an experimental germ warfare virus crashes near a small midwestern town, releasing a plague of murderous madness. George Romero attempts to make a statement about martial law while trying to capitalize on the success of his cult classic, *Night of the Living Dead*. Rated R. 103m. DIR: George A. Romero. CAST: Lane Carroll, W. G. McMillan, Lynn Lowry, Richard Liberty. 1975

CRAZY FOR LOVE ★★1/2 Village-idiot Bourvil will come into an inheritance, but only if he can finish his grade-school education. Naturally, other family members try to ensure that he will fail. Innocuous slapstick comedy with Brigitte Bardot, in her first film, giving no indication of being a star in the making. In French with English subtitles. B&W; 80m. DIR: Jean Boyer. CAST: Bourvil, Jane Marken, Brigitte Bardot. 1953

CRAZY FROM THE HEART ★★★ Made-for-cable comedy-drama looks at the relationship between a Texas high school principal and a Mexican janitor. As they become more of each other, the pressures of an interracial affair come to bear. A little sugary at times, but still manages to keep focused on the main issues. 96m. DIR: Thomas Schlamme. CAST: Christine Lahti, Rubén Blades, William Russ, Louise Latham, Mary Kay Place, Tommy Muniz. 1991

CRAZY HORSE ★★★1/2 Fine Turner Network production chronicles the rise and fall of the Lakota warrior renowned for taking down Custer. Among the Indians, he had a humble start, and his greatest battles would be waged within his tribe in the name of love and loyalty. Throughout the film there are dreamlike sequences in which Crazy Horse is channeled advice from a murdered chief. Michael Greyeyes is very believable as the legendary hero. Not rated; contains nudity and violence. 90m. DIR: John Irvin. CAST: Michael Greyeyes, Irene Bedard, Lorne Cardinal, John Finn. 1996

•**CRAZY IN ALABAMA** ★★★1/2 Small-town southern housewife kills her husband, leaves her seven kids with relatives and lugs her husband's head to Hollywood in a hatbox in this bizarre, comic tale about racism, freedom, spousal abuse, and personal growth. The lady becomes an actress while back home her 13-year-old nephew is engulfed by a civil rights storm stirred up by a muddled sheriff. The film's infectious passion offsets a muddled start and several plot spasms. Rated PG-13 for violence, language, and sensuality. 104m. DIR: Antonio Banderas. CAST: Melanie Griffith, Lucas Black, Meat Loaf Aday, David Morse, Cathy Moriarty. 1999 DVD

CRAZY IN LOVE ★★★ Holly Hunter shares an island home with her mother and grandmother, whose bitter experiences with men may be a bad influence on Hunter's marriage. Minor but enjoyable romantic drama. Not rated; contains no objectionable material. 93m. DIR: Martha Coolidge. CAST: Holly Hunter, Gena Rowlands, Bill Pullman, Julian Sands, Herta Ware, Frances McDormand. 1992

CRAZY MAMA ★★★ Vibrant film blends crime, comedy, and finely drawn characterizations in this story of three women on a crime spree from California to Arkansas and their experiences with the various men they pick up along the way. Successful mixture of music and atmosphere of the 1950s, coupled with a 1970s attitude, makes this an enjoyable film. Rated PG. 82m. DIR: Jonathan Demme. CAST: Stuart Whitman, Cloris Leachman, Ann Sothern, Jim Backus. 1975

CRAZY MOON ★★ This is another entry in the *Harold and Maude* genre: neurotic, alienated young man gets his act together when he falls in love with a spunky disabled woman who is managing to cop with real problems. Rated PG-13. 89m. DIR: Alla Eastman. CAST: Kiefer Sutherland, Vanessa Vaugha 1986

CRAZY PEOPLE ★★★1/2 Dudley Moore is an a writer who grows weary of lying to people. His "honest" ad campaigns get him confined to a mental inst tution. Pure formula, but the ads are often hilariou Rated R for profanity and scatological humor. 91r DIR: Tony Bill. CAST: Dudley Moore, Daryl Hanna Paul Reiser, J. T. Walsh. 1990

CRAZY RAY, THE ★★★1/2 René Clair's classic fa tasy about a scientist's paralyzing ray is basically a experimental film. A handful of people who have n been affected by the ray take advantage of the situ tion and help themselves to whatever they want b eventually begin to fight among themselves. B&W 60m. DIR: René Clair. CAST: Henri Rollan, Madelir Rodrigue, Albert Préjean. 1923

CRAZYSITTER, THE ★★ Very dark premise, of a ex-con turned nanny (Beverly D'Angelo) who tries sell her spoiled charges, is a comic hard sell. The ol noxious children choose the broken-down D'Angel when their self-centered parents finally decide t hire a disciplinarian. Few light moments. Whimsica musical intro by David and Eric Wurst promise more than the film delivers. Rated PG-13 for profan ty and criminal activity. 92m. DIR: Michael James M Donald. CAST: Beverly D'Angelo, Brady Bluhm, Rach Duncan, Ed Begley Jr., Carol Kane. 1994

CREATION OF THE HUMANOIDS ★★ In this futu istic parable, Don Megowan plays a cop who is para noid about the development of near-perfect an droids. This low-budget vision of the future is long o talk, short on action, and hard to take seriously. 75n DIR: Wesley E. Barry. CAST: Don Megowan. 1962

CREATOR ★★ This film, about a scientist (Pete O'Toole) who is attempting to bring back to life th wife who died thirty years before, during childbirt is, at first, a very witty and occasionally heart-tu ging comedy. However, in its last third, it turns int sort of second-rate tearjerker. Rated R for nudit profanity, and simulated sex. 108m. DIR: Ivan Passe CAST: Peter O'Toole, Mariel Hemingway, Vincer Spano, Virginia Madsen, David Ogden Stiers, Joh Dehner. 1985 DVD

CREATURE 🐕 The reawakening of human-devou ing life on one of Jupiter's moons. Rated R for vic lence. 97m. DIR: William Malone. CAST: Stan Iva Wendy Schaal, Klaus Kinski, Marie Laurin, Lyma Ward. 1985

CREATURE FROM BLACK LAKE ★★ This is anoth er forgettable, cliché-ridden horror film. Denni Fimple and John David Carson play two college stu dents who go to the swamps of Louisiana in search the missing link. Through the reluctant help of th locals, they come face-to-face with a man in an ap suit. Rated PG. 97m. DIR: Joy N. Houck Jr. CAST: Jac Elam, Dub Taylor, Dennis Fimple, John David Carso 1979

CREATURE FROM THE BLACK LAGOON ★★★1/ In the remote backwaters of the Amazon, member of a scientific expedition run afoul of a vicious pre historic man-fish inhabiting the area and are force fight for their lives. Excellent film (first in a trilo-) features true-to-life performances, a bone-chill-g score by Joseph Gershenson, and beautiful, lush otography that unfortunately turns to mud in the rky 3-D video print. 79m. DIR: Jack Arnold. CAST: chard Carlson, Julie Adams, Richard Denning, stor Paiva, Antonio Moreno, Whit Bissell. 1954

REATURE FROM THE HAUNTED SEA, THE 🖤 A uddled horror-comedy about a Bogart-type crook anning to steal a treasure with the help of a mythi-l sea monster. B&W; 60m. DIR: Roger Corman. AST: Anthony Carbone, Betsy Jones-Moreland. 1960

REATURE WALKS AMONG US, THE ★★1/2 Sur-isingly imaginative, intermittently scary second quel to *Creature from the Black Lagoon* shows at would happen if the Amazon gill man were sur-cally altered to enable him to breathe on land. For ce, the lengthy passages between monster attacks en't boring. B&W; 78m. DIR: John Sherwood. CAST: ff Morrow, Rex Reason, Leigh Snowden. 1956

REATURES THE WORLD FORGOT 🖤 Migrating vemen battle for superiority of the tribe. Rated , but contains some nudity. 95m. DIR: Don Chaffey. AST: Julie Ege, Tony Bonner. 1970

REEP 🖤 Director Tim Ritter attempted to boost e production of this film by casting nymphomaniac thy Willets as a sexy serial killer, but alas, notori-y does not a good film make. Not rated; contains vi-ence, profanity, gore, nudity, and incest. 90m. DIR: m Ritter. CAST: Kathy Willets, Joel Wynkoop, Patricia aul, Tom Karr. 1995

REEPER, THE ★★ A feline phobia almost sends e daughter of a research scientist clawing up the alls. Dad's conducting experiments on cats—that's ght, cats—for a mysterious miracle serum. Silly lm. DIR: Jean Yarbrough. CAST: Onslow Stevens, Ed-ardo Ciannelli. 1948

REEPERS ★★ Plodding Italian production casts ennifer Connelly as a young girl with the ability to mmunicate with, and control, insects. Use her little friends to track down the maniac who's een murdering students at the Swiss girls' school e's attending. Rated R for gore. 82m. DIR: Dario Ar-ento. CAST: Jennifer Connelly, Donald Pleasence, aria Nicolodi, Dalila Di Lazzaro. 1985

REEPING FLESH, THE ★★★ Peter Cushing and iristopher Lee are top-notch in this creepy tale out an evil entity accidentally brought back to life y an unsuspecting scientist. While not as good as e stars' Hammer Films collaborations this will still rove pleasing to their fans. Rated PG. 91m. DIR: eddie Francis. CAST: Peter Cushing, Christopher Lee, orna Heilbron. 1972

REEPING TERROR, THE ★★ A so-bad-it's-good lassic. Lake Tahoe is terrorized by a pair of outer-pace monsters, played by extras dressed in old car-ets. One of the cheapest movies you'd ever want to ee. B&W; 75m. DIR: Art J. Nelson. CAST: Vic Savage, hannon O'Neill. 1964

REEPOZOIDS 🖤 A post-apocalyptic sci-fi-horror arn about military deserters who find an aban-oned science lab that has a bloodthirsty monster andering in the halls. Rated R for violence, nudity,

and profanity. 72m. DIR: David DeCoteau. CAST: Lin-nea Quigley, Ken Abraham. 1987

CREEPS, THE ★★ A mad scientist finds a way to bring back to life the fictional creatures Dracula, Frankenstein's monster, the wolfman, and the mum-my. Trouble is, his process didn't work properly, and they're all only three feet tall. That ridiculous premise actually makes for a fairly amusing horror spoof, although non-horror buffs probably will miss the in-jokes that fuel this made-for-video flick. Rated R for violence and nudity. 80m. DIR: Charles Band. CAST: Rhonda Griffin, Justin Lauer, Phil Fondacaro, Bill Moynihan. 1997 DVD

CREEPSHOW ★★★★ Stephen King, the modern master of printed terror, and George Romero, the di-rector who frightened unsuspecting moviegoers out of their wits with *Night of the Living Dead*, teamed for this funny and scary tribute to the E.C. horror comics of the 1950s. Like *Vault of Horror* and *Tales from the Crypt*, two titles from that period, it's an anthology of ghoulish bedtime stories. Rated R for profanity and gore. 120m. DIR: George A. Romero. CAST: Hal Holbrook, Adrienne Barbeau, Fritz Weaver, Leslie Nielsen, Stephen King. 1982 DVD

CREEPSHOW 2 ★★ Three tales of horror and terror based on short stories by Stephen King and a screen-play by George Romero that should have turned out a lot better than this. "Ol' Chief Wooden Head" stars George Kennedy and Dorothy Lamour as senior citi-zens in a slowly dying desert town. "The Raft" con-cerns four friends whose vacation at a secluded lake turns into a nightmare. "The Hitchhiker" features Lois Chiles as a hit-and-run driver. Rated R for nudi-ty, violence, and profanity. 92m. DIR: Michael Gor-nick. CAST: Lois Chiles, George Kennedy, Dorothy Lamour. 1987

CREMATORS, THE 🖤 Semipro effort by the cosce-narist for *It Came from Outer Space*, with a nearly identical premise. Not rated. 90m. DIR: Harry Essex. CAST: Maria Di Aragon, Marvin Howard. 1972

CREW, THE ★★★★ Five people on a weekend cruise stop to rescue a couple on a burning boat, only to find themselves tossed into a sexual soup pep-pered with cattiness and pop psychology. Not the *Dead Calm* rip-off you'd expect. In fact, surprises float from all directions in this outrageous little flick. Unfortunately, you have to close your eyes to a major plot hole that keeps this bunch together—but it's a forgivable sin. Rated R for profanity and vio-lence. 99m. DIR: Carl Colpaert. CAST: Viggo Mortensen, Donal Logue, Jeremy Sisto, Pamela Gidley, Laura Del Sol, John Philbin, Sam Jenkins. 1994

•¡CRIA! ★★★★ In this haunting and sometimes surreal film, a 9-year-old girl is obsessed with her mother's death. She blames her father, and then feels responsible when he dies as well. Psychological depth and a mesmerizing performance from young Ana Torrent save the melodramatic story. In Spanish with English subtitles. 115m. DIR: Carlos Saura. CAST: Ana Torrent, Geraldine Chaplin. 1975

CRICKET, THE ★★★1/2 A roadside café is the set-ting for this James M. Cain–like triangle involving an older woman, her new husband, and the woman's grown daughter. Although marketed as a steamy sex drama, it's considerably better than that, thanks to fine performances and probing direction by Alberto Lattuada. In Italian with English subtitles. Not rated; contains nudity and violence. 130m. **DIR:** Alberto Lattuada. **CAST:** Anthony Franciosa, Clio Goldsmith. 1982

CRIER, THE ★★1/2 There's a bit of *The Evil Dead* in this film based on the Mexican legend of La Llorona, a woman who cries over the loss of her children. First-time director Glynn Beard focuses on the chills and puts makeup effects to good use at key moments. Rated R for violence and profanity. 82m. **DIR:** Glynn Beard. **CAST:** Glynn Beard, Margaret Erin-Easley, Lorena Guitierrez. 1995

CRIES AND WHISPERS ★★★★★ Directed and written by Ingmar Bergman and hauntingly photographed by Sven Nykvist, this Swedish-language film tells a story of a dying woman, her two sisters, and a servant girl. Faultless performances make this an unforgettable film experience. Rated R. 106m. **DIR:** Ingmar Bergman. **CAST:** Harriet Andersson, Liv Ullmann, Ingrid Thulin, Kari Sylwan. 1972

CRIES OF SILENCE ★★ Somber tale of a 15-year-old girl who is discovered in the marshes of Mississippi after a devastating hurricane in 1969. It's up to a kindly doctor to break the girl's silence and discover her dark secret. This tale of child abuse is too heavy-handed to be effective. Not rated. 109m. **DIR:** Avery Crounse. **CAST:** Kathleen York, Karen Black, Ed Nelson, Erin Buchanan. 1996

CRIME & PASSION ★★ A weak comedy of sex and money that gives us Omar Sharif as a rich businessman who becomes sexually aroused when bad things happen to him. Karen Black provides some moments of zing with her particular brand of oddness. Her seduction of Joseph Bottoms is a classic. Weird and wild. Rated R. 92m. **DIR:** Ivan Passer. **CAST:** Omar Sharif, Karen Black, Joseph Bottoms, Bernhard Wicki. 1975

CRIME AND PUNISHMENT (1935) ★★★★ The most faithful film version of the Dostoyevski novel, this film makes good use of atmospheric lighting, dramatic shadows, and eerie mood music. Peter Lorre stars as Raskolnikov, a mild-mannered man who unwittingly becomes a murderer. He successfully escapes the police, but his conscience takes over. Thought-provoking as well as entertaining. B&W; 88m. **DIR:** Josef von Sternberg. **CAST:** Peter Lorre, Edward Arnold, Marian Marsh, Elisabeth Risdon, Mrs. Patrick Campbell. 1935

CRIME AND PUNISHMENT (1935) ★★★★ Excellent screen adaptation of Dostoyevski's complex, brooding novel. Director Pierre Chenal's poetic, surreal touch adds to the climate of dark realism in this tragedy about a murderer who struggles with his conscience after commiting a brutal, senseless crime. In French with English subtitles. B&W; 110m. **DIR:** Pierre Chenal. **CAST:** Harry Baur, Pierre Blanchar. 1935

CRIME AND PUNISHMENT (1970) ★★★★ Another fine adaptation of Dostoyevski's story about an impoverished student living in squalor in a rooming house and murdering an old pawnbroker. Solid performances and a fine script. In Russian with English

subtitles. B&W; 220m. **DIR:** Lev Kulijanov. **CAS** Georgi Taratorkin. 1970

CRIME KILLER, THE ♥ A confusing plot has a n nonsense cop getting suspended, teaming up wi two of his ex–Vietnam buddies, and smashing guns-and-airplane deal with an Arab connection. I sipid. Not rated. 90m. **DIR:** George Pan-Andrea **CAST:** George Pan-Andreas, Leo Morrell, Athan Karra 1985

CRIME LORDS ★★ Wayne Crawford directs ar stars in this cop-buddy drama that originates in L Angeles and ends on the streets of Hong Kong. Bo story and stars are predictable. Rated R for violenc 96m. **DIR:** Wayne Crawford. **CAST:** Wayne Crawfor Martin Hewitt. 1990

CRIME OF DR. CRESPI, THE ★★ Moody povert row item whose main distinction is its casting, pri cipally Erich Von Stroheim as a vengeful surgeo B&W; 63m. **DIR:** John H. Auer. **CAST:** Erich Von Str heim, Dwight Frye, Paul Guilfoyle. 1935

CRIME OF MONSIEUR LANGE, THE ★★★★ Jea Renoir's compelling masterpiece sprang from the d rector's belief that the common man, by united a tion, could overcome tyranny. When the head of printing press disappears with all of the firm's fund the employees band together and raise enough mo ey to go into business as a publisher of popular nove ettes. In French with English subtitles. B&W; 90n **DIR:** Jean Renoir. **CAST:** René Lefèvre, Jules Berr 1935

CRIME OF PASSION ★★1/2 The story of a toug newspaperwoman who will do anything to hold on her man is a good showcase for Barbara Stanwyc But it's a contrived and predictable movie, the typ she made many times during her long career. Th film has more suggestive scenes than usual for i era. B&W; 85m. **DIR:** Gerd Oswald. **CAST:** Barbar Stanwyck, Sterling Hayden, Raymond Burr, Fay Wra Royal Dano, Stuart Whitman. 1957

CRIME OF THE CENTURY ★★★★ This HBO orig nal explores the 1932 Lindbergh baby kidnappin and murder. Stephen Rea stars as Bruno Richar Hauptmann, the illegal immigrant scapegoated fo the heinous crime that shocked the entire natio Scripter William Nicholson makes it clear tha Hauptmann had some peripheral involvement to th case … but was nowhere near the mastermin painted by impatient police officers pressured for re sults. Rated PG for dramatic intensity. 120m. **DIR:** Mark Rydell. **CAST:** Stephen Rea, Isabella Rossellini, T. Walsh, Joe Mantegna, Allen Garfield, Joh Harkins, Barry Primus, David Paymer. 1996

CRIME STORY ★★★ Something more serious fro action star Jackie Chan, who this time plays a detec tive investigating a kidnapping while wrestling wit police corruption. While Chan gets to display hi trademark stunt work, this film is darker and mor complicated than his other outings. Rated R for vic lence. 104m. **DIR:** Che-Kirk Wong. **CAST:** Jackie Char Kent Chang, Law Kang, Ken Lo, Christine Ng. 199 DVD

CRIME ZONE ♥ A young couple struggles to escap a futuristic society turned police state. Rated R fo idity and profanity. 96m. DIR: Luis Llosa. CAST: avid Carradine, Peter Nelson, Sherilyn Fenn. 1988

RIMEBROKER ★★1/2 Jacqueline Bisset stars as a dge by day—bank robber by night—in this enterlining but absurd thriller. Rated R for nudity and violence. 98m. DIR: Ian Barry. CAST: Jacqueline Bisset, lasaya Kato, Gary Day, John Bach. 1993

RIMES AND MISDEMEANORS ★★★★★ Martin landau plays a successful doctor who attempts to nd a foolish affair. However, his emotionally unstale mistress refuses to let him go. On the periphery re Woody Allen's antics as a documentary filmmakr hired by his egotistical brother-in-law to make a novie about the latter's career as a TV sitcom king. ated PG-13 for adult themes. 104m. DIR: Woody llen. CAST: Martin Landau, Woody Allen, Alan Alda, ia Farrow, Anjelica Huston, Jerry Orbach, Sam Warston. 1989 DVD

RIMES AT THE DARK HOUSE ★★ Wilkie Collins's he Woman in White served as the source material or this typically florid, over-the-top outing for ritain's Tod Slaughter, the king of eye-rolling camp. &W; 61m. DIR: George King. CAST: Tod Slaughter. 940

RIMES OF PASSION ❤ By day she's a highly paid ashion designer; by night, she's a kinky high-priced ooker. Rated R for nudity, simulated sex, profanity, nd violence. 107m. DIR: Ken Russell. CAST: Kathleen urner, Anthony Perkins, John Laughlin. 1984 DVD

RIMES OF STEPHEN HAWKE, THE ★★ The cast a bit better than usual for this, one of Tod Slaughr's early outings, in which a serial killer and a charable moneylender share a deadly secret. But daughter's grandiosely overdone style is, as ever, an cquired taste. B&W; 65m. DIR: George King. CAST: od Slaughter, Marjorie Taylor, Eric Portman. 1936

RIMES OF THE HEART ★★★★1/2 In this superb creen adaptation of Beth Henley's Pulitzer rize–winning play, Diane Keaton, Jessica Lange, nd Sissy Spacek star as three eccentric sisters who tick together despite an onslaught of extraordinary roblems. It is a film of many joys. Not the least of which are the performances of the stars, fine bits by am Shepard and Tess Harper in support, the biting umor, and the overall intelligence. Rated PG-13 for ubject matter. 105m. DIR: Bruce Beresford. CAST: Dine Keaton, Jessica Lange, Sissy Spacek, Sam Shepd, Tess Harper, David Carpenter, Hurd Hatfield. 1986

RIMETIME ★★★ The fine line between reality nd fantasy begins to blur for Bobby, an actor who ortrays a serial killer on a television show that rereates true crimes. As the bodies add up, so do the atings. When the killer stops, Bobby is out of a job. he two meet and produce a solution that guaranees them both work. Rated R for adult situations, anguage, nudity, and violence. 95m. DIR: George uizer. CAST: Stephen Baldwin, Pete Postlethwaite, eraldine Chaplin, Karen Black, Sadie Frost. 1997

RIMEWAVE ★★★ Hired assassins try to silence a ousewife in this hyperkinetic slapstick comedy. Too cattered to be satisfying (and too low-budget for its mbition), it nevertheless has many inventive and ilarious moments. Cowritten by Sam Raimi and oel and Ethan Coen. Rated PG-13 for violence. 83m.

DIR: Sam Raimi. CAST: Louise Lasser, Brion James, Bruce Campbell. 1985

CRIMINAL CODE, THE ★★★★ A powerful performance by Boris Karloff as a revenge-minded convict, elevates this Howard Hawks release from interesting to memorable. It's a lost classic that deserves its release on video. The story involves a district attorney (impressively played by Walter Huston) who overzealously pursues his job, with the result that an innocent man (Phillips Holmes) is sent to prison. B&W; 83m. DIR: Howard Hawks. CAST: Boris Karloff, Walter Huston, Phillips Holmes. 1931

CRIMINAL HEARTS ★★ Low-rent road movie features Amy Locane as the jilted lover out to teach her ex-boyfriend a lesson when she picks up hitchhiker Kevin Dillon. It doesn't take long before these two are on the run from the cops and their pasts. Rated R for adult situations, language, and violence. 92m. DIR: David Payne. CAST: Kevin Dillon, Amy Locane, Morgan Fairchild, M. Emmet Walsh, Don Stroud. 1995

CRIMINAL JUSTICE ★★ Writer-director Andy Wolk's disagreeably vague and stridently preachy telescript is partly salvaged by Forest Whitaker's masterful lead performance as a felon accused of robbing and knifing a young woman, whose veracity (as the only witness) is never sufficiently questioned. Not rated, but with considerable profanity. 90m. DIR: Andy Wolk. CAST: Forest Whitaker, Anthony LaPaglia, Rosie Perez, Jennifer Grey. 1990

CRIMINAL LAW ★★1/2 Gary Oldman gives a strong performance in this suspense-thriller as an attorney who successfully defends accused killer Kevin Bacon. It is only after proving his client's innocence by discrediting eyewitnesses, that Oldman discovers Bacon is guilty—and intends to kill again. At first, the film bristles with tension and intelligence, yet it goes on to become predictable and ludicrous. Rated R for violence, simulated sex, and profanity. 112m. DIR: Martin Campbell. CAST: Gary Oldman, Kevin Bacon, Karen Young, Tess Harper, Joe Don Baker. 1989

CRIMINAL LIFE OF ARCHIBALDO DE LA CRUZ, THE ★★★★ Luis Buñuel's violently erotic satire about a perverted young aristocrat who believes a music box he owned as a child has the power to kill. This surreal black comedy is an uncompromising attack on the social, religious, and political ramifications of contemporary society. A must-see! In Spanish with English subtitles. Not rated. B&W; 91m. DIR: Luis Buñuel. CAST: Ernesto Alonso, Miroslava Stern. 1955

CRIMINAL MIND, THE ★★1/2 A decent cast saves this tired thriller about two brothers who wind up on opposite sides of the law—one becomes a district attorney, the other a mob member. When his brother is killed, the district attorney gets it from all sides, including the mob and the FBI. Rated R for violence, language, and sexuality. 93m. DIR: Joseph Vittorie. CAST: Ben Cross, Frank Rossi, Tahnee Welch, Lance Henriksen, Mark Davenport. 1993

CRIMINAL PASSION ★★1/2 A homicide detective teams with her ex-lover to nab a senator's son suspected of being a serial killer. When privilege distances the suspect from the cops, she decides the only way to get her man is to go undercover and insinuate herself into his life. R-rated and unrated versions available; both contain nudity, adult situations, violence, and strong language. 96m. **DIR:** Donna Deitch. **CAST:** Joan Severance, Anthony Denison, Wolfgang Bodison, Henry Darrow, John Allen Nelson. 1994

CRIMINALLY INSANE ★★ This debut outing for Priscilla Alden's obese psychopath, Crazy Fat Ethel, should cure any compulsive overeaters in the audience. A sequel followed thirteen years later (*Crazy Fat Ethel II*). Not rated. 61m. **DIR:** Nick Phillips. **CAST:** Priscilla Alden. 1974

CRIMSON PIRATE, THE ★★★1/2 One of the all-time great swashbucklers, this follow-up to *The Flame and the Arrow* features the incredibly agile Burt Lancaster besting villains and winning fair maids in high style. Lancaster's partner from his circus days, Nick Cravat, joins in for some rousing action scenes. It's part adventure story, part spoof, and always entertaining. 104m. **DIR:** Robert Siodmak. **CAST:** Burt Lancaster, Nick Cravat, Eva Bartok, Torin Thatcher, Christopher Lee. 1952

CRIMSON TIDE ★★★1/2 Top-notch undersea adventure explodes with star power, as by-the-book captain Gene Hackman finds himself at odds with new executive officer Denzel Washington. An American submarine carrying nuclear weapons is galvanized into action when Russian rebels steal a similarly armed vessel. Director Tony Scott's best film by far. Rated R for violence and profanity. 115m. **DIR:** Tony Scott. **CAST:** Denzel Washington, Gene Hackman, George Dzundza, Viggo Mortensen, James Gandolfini, Matt Craven, Lillo Brancato, Rick Schroder. 1995 DVD

•**CRINOLINE HEAD** ★★ Made in the wake of the superior *Scream*, this indie film attempts to give viewers more of the same but falls shy of the mark. The plot has a kook wearing a crinoline on his head and butchering the local teens in some decidedly gross ways. Not rated; contains gore, violence, and profanity. 90m. **DIR:** Tommy Faircloth. **CAST:** Brian Kelly, Tracy Powlas. 1997

CRIPPLED MASTERS, THE ★★★ Standard martial arts–revenge film with one difference: the heroes are an armless man and a legless man, who combine to form an unbeatable fighting machine. Despite the exploitative nature of the film, the two fighters are worthy of this showcase. Rated R for violence. 90m. **DIR:** Joe Law. **CAST:** Frankie Shum, Jack Conn. 1982

CRISIS AT CENTRAL HIGH ★★★1/2 In the late Fifties Little Rock, Arkansas, was rocked by the integration of the school system. This television film is a retelling of those events as seen through the eyes of teacher Elizabeth Huckaby, one of the principal characters involved. Joanne Woodward is simply wonderful as the caught-in-the-middle instructor. 125m. **DIR:** Lamont Johnson. **CAST:** Joanne Woodward, Charles Durning, Henderson Forsythe, William Russ. 1981

CRISS CROSS (1948) ★★★ A less than riveting plot mars this otherwise gritty *film noir*. Burt Lancaster plays an armored-car guard who, along with his less than trustworthy wife, gets involved with a bunch of underworld thugs. B&W; 87m. **DIR:** Robert

Siodmak. **CAST:** Burt Lancaster, Yvonne De Carlo, Da Duryea, Stephen McNally, Richard Long. 1948

CRISSCROSS (1992) ★★★ Some fine perfo mances highlight this slice-of-life character stuc about a 12-year-old boy who discovers the shockir truth about his mother's nighttime job. Screenwrite Scott Sommer adds some interesting touches to th tale set in the Sixties, but director Chris Menges d rects in too laid-back a fashion. Rated R for profan ty, nudity, and violence. 100m. **DIR:** Chris Menge: **CAST:** Goldie Hawn, Arliss Howard, James Gammo Keith Carradine, David Arnott, J. C. Quinn, Steve Bu: cemi. 1992

CRITICAL CARE ★★★ Although there's plenty t attack in the world of managed care and insuranc industry meddling, *Critical Care* tiptoes around th lofty subject and instead becomes the tale of a your doctor seeking an epiphany, an understanding (what all those years of study and hospital rotation re ally meant. Rated R for profanity and mild sexu; content. 105m. **DIR:** Sidney Lumet. **CAST:** Jame Spader, Kyra Sedgwick, Helen Mirren, Margo Martir dale, Albert Brooks, Wallace Shawn, Anne Bancrot 1997 DVD

CRITICAL CHOICES ★★1/2 This made-for-cabl original focuses on both sides (pro-life and prc choice) of the protest at an abortion clinic. Unfortu nately, the movie straddles the fence so much, an ends so abruptly, we hardly know what to make of i Uninspired acting and minimal plot only muddy th waters further. Not rated; contains profanity and vio lence. 88m. **DIR:** Claudia Weill. **CAST:** Betty Buckle' Pamela Reed, Diana Scarwid, Liisa Repo-Martell, Bria Kerwin. 1996

CRITICAL CONDITION ★★1/2 Mishmash of a come dy has some funny moments but ultimately tests th viewer's patience. Richard Pryor stars as a hustle who must feign insanity to stay out of prison. Whil under observation in a psychiatric ward of a big hos pital, Pryor surprisingly finds himself in charge c the institution. Rated R for profanity, violence, an scatological humor. 105m. **DIR:** Michael Apted. **CAS** Richard Pryor, Rachel Ticotin, Rubén Blades, Joe Mar tegna, Bob Dishy, Joe Dallesandro, Garrett Morris Randall "Tex" Cobb. 1987

CRITIC'S CHOICE ★★ A disappointment in spite its cast, the film is a superficial version of Ira Levin successful Broadway play. The contrivances begi when a theater critic has to review his wife's ne play, then goes to his first wife for advice. Good cas tries to make the best of poor script and uninspire direction. 100m. **DIR:** Don Weis. **CAST:** Bob Hope, Lt cille Ball, Rip Torn, Marilyn Maxwell, Jim Backus, Mar Windsor, Jerome Cowan. 1963

CRITTERS ★★★1/2 This mild horror film with it hilarious spots could become a cult classic. In i eight ravenous critters escape from a distant plane and head for Earth. Two futuristic bounty hunter: pursue them, and the fun begins. Rated PG-13 fc gore and profanity. 90m. **DIR:** Stephen Herek. **CAST** Dee Wallace, M. Emmet Walsh, Scott Grimes, Don Op per, Terrence Mann. 1986

CRITTERS 2: THE MAIN COURSE ★★ *Critters* takes off where the first one ended, but dwells mc uch on a dopey subplot. Rated PG-13 for violence and profanity. 87m. **DIR:** Mick Garris. **CAST:** Scott rimes, Liane Curtis, Don Opper, Barry Corbin, Terence Mann. **1987**

RITTERS 3 🖤 Those ferocious fur balls from outer ace are back for more, this time inhabiting an artment building. Low rent all the way. Rated PG-3 for violence. 86m. **DIR:** Kristine Peterson. **CAST:** ristopher Cousins, Joseph Cousins, Don Opper. **991**

RITTERS 4 ★★ Ferocious fur balls are back for a gger bite of the pie. Go figure! Rated PG-13 for violence. 94m. **DIR:** Rupert Harvey. **CAST:** Don Opper, aul Whitthorne, Angela Bassett, Brad Dourif. **1991**

ROCODILE 🖤 An island paradise is turned into a ellhole by a giant crocodile. Not rated; contains rofanity and violence. 95m. **DIR:** Sompote Sands. **AST:** Nat Puvanai. **1981**

CROCODILE" DUNDEE ★★★★1/2 In this hilarius Australian import, Paul Hogan plays the title naracter, a hunter who allegedly crawled several iles for help after a king-size crocodile gnawed off leg. This slight exaggeration persuades an American newspaper reporter to seek him out and persuade him to join her on a trip to New York, where ne naive outbacker faces a new set of perils. Rated G-13 for profanity and violence. 98m. **DIR:** Peter aiman. **CAST:** Paul Hogan, Linda Kozlowski, John eillon, Mark Blum, David Gulpilil, Michael Lombard. **986**

CROCODILE" DUNDEE II ★★★1/2 This follow-up the wildly successful release from Down Under dds action to the winning formula of laughs, surrises, romance, and adventure. Mick Dundee (Paul ogan) and Sue Charlton (Linda Kozlowski) are living a relatively quiet life in New York City until some olombian drug dealers step in. The results should lease fans of the first film. Rated PG for violence nd light profanity. 110m. **DIR:** John Cornell. **CAST:** aul Hogan, Linda Kozlowski, John Meillon, Charles utton, Hector Ubarry, Juan Fernandez. **1988**

ROMWELL ★★ Richard Harris hams it up again in is overblown historical melodrama. A fine cast sunders amid tradition-soaked locations and beautiful backgrounds. The accoutrements and design re splendid, but the story is lacking and Harris's erformance is inept. 145m. **DIR:** Ken Hughes. **CAST:** ichard Harris, Alec Guinness, Robert Morley, Frank inlay, Dorothy Tutin, Timothy Dalton, Patrick Magee. **970**

RONOS ★★★★ In this atmospheric Mexican ampire movie, a kindly old antique dealer discovers n alchemist's ancient, eternal-life device—and the nirst for blood that comes from using it. Rife with lever religious symbolism, satiric wit, and some tender family values, this subtle, intelligent chiller arks back to the Hammer horrors of the 1960s and oger Corman's best Edgar Allan Poe pictures. In nglish and Spanish with English subtitles. Not rated, with limited graphic effects and gore. 92m. **DIR:** uillermo del Toro. **CAST:** Federico Luppi, Ron Perlaan, Claudio Brook, Tamara Shanath. **1993**

ROOKED HEARTS ★★ The talents of an ensemble ast are showcased in this slow-paced story of a fam-

ily's struggle to give each other room to grow. The film resembles movies adapted from John Irving novels, only here, the surreal humor and irony are missing. Rated R for profanity and partial nudity. 113m. **DIR:** Michael Bortman. **CAST:** Vincent D'Onofrio, Jennifer Jason Leigh, Peter Berg, Cindy Pickett, Juliette Lewis, Marg Helgenberger, Peter Coyote. **1991**

CROOKLYN ★★★1/2 As low key as Spike Lee gets, this episodic movie focuses on an African-American family in 1970s Brooklyn. It's filled with shouting matches, but it's also a warm and well-observed character comedy, featuring a tough, natural performance by young Zelda Harris as the only girl in a brood full of rambunctious boys. Rated PG-13. 132m. **DIR:** Spike Lee. **CAST:** Zelda Harris, Alfre Woodard, Delroy Lindo, David Patrick Kelly, Carlton Williams. **1994 DVD**

CROOKS AND CORONETS (SOPHIE'S PLACE) ★★ This picture had only a limited release in the United States and for good reason. It wasn't cunning and bold enough for a good crime picture, and certainly not funny enough for a quality comedy. Dame Edith Evans owns a large estate and the other characters are villains trying to steal the valuable property from her. Not rated. 102m. **DIR:** Jim O'Connolly. **CAST:** Edith Evans, Telly Savalas, Cesar Romero, Warren Oates, Harry H. Corbett. **1970**

CROSS COUNTRY ★★ Michael Ironside plays Detective Ed Roersch, who pursues Richard Beymer following the murder of an expensive call girl. Although this movie involves prostitution, blackmail, murder, and deceit, it still manages to bore. Rated R for nudity, sex, profanity, and violence. 95m. **DIR:** Paul Lynch. **CAST:** Richard Beymer, Nina Axelrod, Michael Ironside, Brent Carver. **1983**

CROSS CREEK ★★★1/2 About the life of 1930s author Marjorie Kinnan Rawlings (Mary Steenburgen), this watchable release illustrates how Rawlings's relationships with backwoods folks inspired her novels, particularly *The Yearling* and *Jacob's Ladder*. Rated PG for brief violence. 122m. **DIR:** Martin Ritt. **CAST:** Mary Steenburgen, Rip Torn, Peter Coyote, Dana Hill. **1983**

CROSS MISSION ★★ There's lots of shooting, some martial arts, even a little voodoo in this predictable tale about a pretty photographer and a handsome soldier of fortune in a banana republic. They are taken prisoner by the rebels, then converted to the cause. Rated R. 90m. **DIR:** Al Bradley. **CAST:** Richard Randall. **1989**

CROSS MY HEART (1987) ★★ Interminable comedy about the disastrous third date of two vulnerable people trying to keep silly secrets from each other. Martin Short and Annette O'Toole are unmemorable as the couple. Rated R for nudity and language. 88m. **DIR:** Armyan Bernstein. **CAST:** Martin Short, Annette O'Toole, Paul Reiser, Joanna Kerns. **1987**

CROSS MY HEART (1991) ★★★★★ Jacques Fansten's bittersweet film spotlights the innocence, the pain, the insecurities, and the resilience of children. With surprising humor and rare sensitivity, the film examines the efforts of a group of children to comfort one of their own. In French with English subtitles. Not rated. 105m. DIR: Jacques Fansten. 1991

CROSS OF IRON ★★★1/2 With this action-packed war film, director Sam Peckinpah proved that he hadn't lost the touch that made *Ride the High Country* and *The Wild Bunch* such memorable movies. Still, *Cross of Iron* did not receive much acclaim when released. Perhaps it was the theme: the heroics of weary German soldiers in World War II. A precursor of *Das Boot*, this film is an interesting work by one of Hollywood's more original directors. Rated R. 119m. DIR: Sam Peckinpah. CAST: James Coburn, Maximilian Schell, James Mason, David Warner. 1977

CROSSCUT ★★1/2 Hard-edged action and gorgeous Pacific Northwest scenery enhance this gritty crime-thriller about a New York mobster who has made a fatal mistake: he killed a rival's son. The mobster hightails it to logging country, where his cover is jeopardized by the local loggers, who play just as rough as the mob. Rated R for violence, profanity, and adult situations. 90m. DIR: Paul Raimondi. CAST: Costas Mandylor, Megan Gallagher, Casey Sander, Jay Acovone. 1995

CROSSFIRE (1947) ★★★1/2 While on leave from the army, psychopathic bigot Robert Ryan meets Sam Levene in a nightclub and later murders him during an argument. An army buddy is blamed; another is also murdered. Often billed as a *film noir*, this interesting film is more of a message indicting anti-Semitism, and it was the first major Hollywood picture to explore racial bigotry. B&W; 86m. DIR: Edward Dmytryk. CAST: Robert Ryan, Robert Mitchum, Robert Young, Sam Levene, Gloria Grahame, Paul Kelly, Steve Brodie. 1947

CROSSFIRE (1986) 🎬 Outlaws are saved from execution by a gang of Mexican freedom fighters. 82m. DIR: Robert Conrad, Alfredo Zacharias. CAST: Robert Conrad, Jan-Michael Vincent, Manuel Ochoa Lopez. 1986

CROSSING, THE ★★ Australian melodrama about a young woman in a romantic triangle forced into choosing between life in a small town with her current boyfriend or with his best friend who left town to pursue a career in the art world. Clichéd. Rated R for nudity and profanity. 92m. DIR: Russell Crowe. CAST: Russell Crowe, Robert Mammone, Danielle Spencer. 1992

CROSSING DELANCEY ★★★★1/2 Amy Irving has the role of her career as the independent New Yorker scrutinized by Susan Sandler's deft and poignant screenplay. Irving has a bookstore job that brings her into close contact with the Big Apple's literary scene; she fulfills deeper needs with visits to her feisty grandmother (Reizl Bozyk). Grandmother has matchmaking plans, involving street vendor Peter Riegert, whose flawless timing is one of the many highlights here. Rated PG for language and mild sexual themes. 97m. DIR: Joan Micklin Silver. CAST: Amy Irving, Peter Riegert, Reizl Bozyk, Jeroen Krabbé, Sylvia Miles. 1988

CROSSING GUARD, THE ★★★ A jeweler is shredded by grief after his young daughter is killed by a drunk driver. He resolutely tells his estranged wife that he plans to shoot the culprit now that he has been released from prison. It's an unpleasant but riveting story about strained moral responsibility, the licking of emotional wounds, the contradictions of masculinity, and the tragic cracks into which whole families can tumble. Rated R for violence, nudity, and language. 114m. DIR: Sean Penn. CAST: Jack Nicholson, David Morse, Anjelica Huston, Robin Wright, Piper Laurie. 1995 DVD

CROSSING THE BRIDGE ★★★ Gutsy, credible performances give this 1970s coming-of-age story a raw edge as three Detroit buddies get jolted into adulthood when a plan to smuggle hash across the Canadian border goes sour. Written and directed with apparent autobiographical clarity by Mike Binder. Rated R for language and violence. 103m. DIR: Mike Binder. CAST: Josh Charles, Jason Gedrick, Stephen Baldwin, Cheryl Pollack, Richard Edson. 1992

CROSSING THE LINE (1990) ★★1/2 When a motorcycle accident puts his best friend in a coma, rich kid Rick Hearst takes the heat. Exciting race footage sets the pace for this domestic drama about sibling rivalry. Rated R for strong language. 94m. DIR: Gary Graver. CAST: John Saxon, Rick Hearst, Jon Stafford, Cameron Mitchell. 1990

CROSSOVER DREAMS ★★★★ Rubén Blades plays a popular Latino musician who tries his talent at the big time. The price he pays for his efforts is high. And while this may all sound like one big movie cliché, it's now time to add that the cast put in performances that redefine the story, giving this first tale a bite that will surprise the viewer. 85m. DIR: Leon Ichaso. CAST: Rubén Blades, Shawn Elliot, Elizabeth Peña, Tom Signorelli, Frank Robles. 1985

CROSSROADS ★★★1/2 A superb blues score by guitarist Ry Cooder highlights this enjoyable fantasy about an ambitious young bluesman (Ralph Macchio) who "goes down to the crossroads," in the words of Robert Johnson, to make a deal with the devil for fame and fortune. Most viewers will enjoy the performances, the story, and the music in this all-too-rare big-screen celebration of the blues and its mythology. Rated R for profanity, suggested sex and violence. 105m. DIR: Walter Hill. CAST: Ralph Macchio, Joe Seneca, Jami Gertz, Joe Morton, Dennis Lipscomb, Harry Carey Jr. 1986

CROSSWORLDS ★★★1/2 Good and evil collide in this imaginative science-fiction adventure. Josh Charles stars as Joe Talbot, a young man whose peaceful existence is disrupted when he's swept into the mystical valley of "Crossworld," a place where all dimensions of the universe converge. When Talbot' bedroom is invaded by aliens looking for a magic crystal, he escapes with the crystal. Talbot is joined by a mercenary and a beautiful woman from another galaxy in his attempt to keep the crystal from the forces of evil. Interesting premise and likable cast distinguish this made-for-cable effort from the rest of the pack. Rated PG-13 for violence. 91m. DIR: Krishna Rao. CAST: Josh Charles, Rutger Hauer, Stuart Wilson, Andrea Roth. 1996 DVD

CROW: CITY OF ANGELS, THE ★★ Not a sequel but a virtual remake of the 1994 film, with French actor Vincent Perez (struggling with English) as a motorcycle mechanic back from the dead to avenge his own murder. This time, the urban-hell atmosphere is even darker and dirtier—even the cocaine is black. The chic despair and morbid obsession with death is overwrought, and at times unintentionally comic. Rated R for violence, profanity, and drug use. 80m. **DIR:** Tim Pope. **CAST:** Vincent Perez, Mia Kirshner, Richard Brooks, Iggy Pop. **1996 DVD**

CROW, THE ★★★★ The accidental death of Brandon Lee during production did not prevent director Alex Proyas from making a genuinely gripping, comic-book horror-thriller. Lee plays a musician who comes back from the dead to wreak vengeance on the urban criminals who killed him and his fiancée. Looking like the Joker and distributing bloody justice, our hero stalks a darkly lit hellscape of decaying tenements, maddening noise, and sadistic sociopathy. Rated R for violence, language, brief nudity, and drug use. 97m. **DIR:** Alex Proyas. **CAST:** Brandon Lee, Ernie Hudson, Michael Wincott, David Patrick Kelly, Jon Polito. **1994 DVD**

CROWD, THE ★★★★1/2 Director King Vidor's pioneering slice-of-life story of a working-class family in a big city during the Jazz Age still holds up beautifully after sixty years. James Murray, in his only major movie, gives an extraordinary performance as a hardworking clerk who never seems to get ahead. Not rated; suitable for all but the youngest children. B&W; 90m. **DIR:** King Vidor. **CAST:** James Murray, Eleanor Boardman. **1928**

CRUCIBLE OF HORROR ★★★1/2 Intense story of a violent, domineering man (Michael Gough in one of his better roles) who drives his passive wife and nubile daughter to murder. The suspense and terror build unrelentingly. Keep the lights on! Rated R. 91m. **DIR:** Viktors Ritelis. **CAST:** Michael Gough, Yvonne Mitchell. **1971**

CRUCIBLE OF TERROR 💜 A demented sculptor coats his female victims with molten bronze in this lame British offering. Rated R. 79m. **DIR:** Ted Hooker. **CAST:** Mike Raven, Mary Maude, James Bolam. **1971**

CRUCIBLE, THE ★★★★★ In 1692 Massachusetts, nineteen Salem Puritans were hanged by their peers after a clique of young girls accused them of witchcraft. Arthur Miller turned the incident into a 1953 stage play that was—among other interpretations—an indictment of McCarthy-era communist hunts. Miller has now turned his play into a crisp, volcanic film about repressed sexuality, collective evil, and mass hysteria. Rated PG-13 for brief nudity, intense adult situations, and brief violence. 115m. **DIR:** Nicholas Hytner. **CAST:** Winona Ryder, Daniel Day-Lewis, Joan Allen, Paul Scofield, Bruce Davison. **1996**

CRUCIFER OF BLOOD ★★1/2 Charlton Heston is far from believable as Sherlock Holmes in this melodramatic, yet atmospheric cable movie about a thirty-year-old curse involving a stolen treasure. Written and directed by Heston's son, Fraser. Richard Johnson fares a bit better as Dr. Watson, while Susannah Harker steals the film as their client. 105m. **DIR:** Fraser Heston. **CAST:** Charlton Heston, Richard Johnson, Susannah Harker, John Castle, Clive Wood, Simon Callow, Edward Fox. **1991**

CRUDE OASIS, THE ★★1/2 A bored young housewife escapes her small-town blues through her dreams. When she discovers her husband is having an affair, she finds solace in the arms of a stranger. Rated R for profanity and adult situations. 82m. **DIR:** Alex Graves. **CAST:** Jennifer Taylor, Aaron Shields, Robert Peterson. **1995**

CRUEL INTENTIONS 💜 This hilarious update of Choderlos de Laclos's *Les Liaisons Dangereuses* is a travesty from start to finish: a lackluster comedy-drama, which must have resulted from a wager among cast members to see who could deliver the most inept performance. They all win. Rated R for profanity, base sexual behavior, drug use, and brief nudity. 97m. **DIR:** Roger Kumble. **CAST:** Ryan Phillippe, Sarah Michelle Gellar, Reese Witherspoon, Selma Blair, Louise Fletcher, Joshua Jackson. **1999 DVD**

CRUEL SEA, THE ★★★1/2 The ever-changing and unpredictable wind-lashed sea is the star of this gripping documentary-style adventure about a stalwart British warship during World War II. B&W; 121m. **DIR:** Charles Frend. **CAST:** Jack Hawkins, Virginia McKenna, Stanley Baker, Donald Sinden. **1953**

CRUEL STORY OF YOUTH ★★★ Two bored middle-class teenagers set up a scheme to extort money from businessmen. Nagisa Oshima is clearly more interested in exploring Godardian techniques than in his emotionally bereft characters (though the approach is suited to them). An interesting but chilly film. In Japanese with English subtitles. B&W; 97m. **DIR:** Nagisa Oshima. **CAST:** Yusuke Kawazu, Miyuji Kuwano. **1960**

CRUISE, THE ★★★ Real-life double-decker bus guide Timothy "Speed" Levitch bares his love/hate relationship with all things Manhattan and eloquently chats about the chaos of the universe in this grainy black-and-white documentary. The film is a sort of "My Tour with Andre," with the passionate Levitch providing a running commentary on New York City's colorful history and inhabitants, always in quest of a fascinating story or enlightenment. Not rated. B&W; 76m. **DIR:** Bennett Miller. **1998**

CRUISE INTO TERROR 💜 Dreadful suspense flick made for the tube. 100m. **DIR:** Bruce Kessler. **CAST:** Dirk Benedict, John Forsythe, Lynda Day George, Christopher George, Stella Stevens, Ray Milland, Frank Converse, Lee Meriwether, Hugh O'Brian. **1977**

CRUISING 💜 A horror in the real sense of the word. Rated R. 106m. **DIR:** William Friedkin. **CAST:** Al Pacino, Paul Sorvino, Karen Allen, Richard Cox, Don Scardino. **1980**

CRUMB ★★★★1/2 If you think your family is strange, wait until you get a glimpse into the tortured, dysfunctional Crumb clan. Director Terry Zwigoff cleverly uses others to reveal the sexual and psychological demons of Robert Crumb, the creator of Fritz the Cat. Psychically damaged family members, candid ex-lovers, and Crumb himself reveal humorous, creepy, and startling secrets about this talented, offbeat artist. Rated R for profanity and nudity. 119m. **DIR:** Terry Zwigoff. **CAST:** Robert Crumb. **1994 DVD**

CRUSADES, THE (1935) ★★1/2 A Cecil B. DeMille epic that improves with time, this sword-sandal-andshmaltz dramatization of the Third Crusade takes too many liberties with history to ring completely true. Loretta Young stars as Berengaria of Navarre, the hapless lady in love with Richard the Lion-Hearted. The movie is more about their touch-and-go romance than the pursuit of the Holy Grail. But it has moments of excitement. B&W; 123m. **DIR:** Cecil B. DeMille. **CAST:** Loretta Young, Henry Wilcoxon, Ian Keith, Joseph Schildkraut, Mischa Auer, Montagu Love. **1935**

CRUSADES, THE (1995) ★★★★ Monty Pythoner and medieval expert Terry Jones has found a new way to educate—by making us laugh. This four-tape set presents a complete history of the Crusades and breaks new ground as a documentary with a style that blends paintings, location footage, reenactments, and computer imagery. Always amusing, host Jones springs to life in the midst of a mural, or pokes his head onto the edge of the screen to make humorous asides or biting bon mots. Made for A&E. Not rated. 200m. **DIR:** Alan Ereira, David Wallace. **CAST:** Terry Jones. **1995**

CRUSH, THE (1993) 🎬 Trash from the very start, a teen tart from hell becomes obsessed with the hunkish, nice-guy journalist who rents her parents' guest house. Rated R for language, sexual themes, and violence. 90m. **DIR:** Alan Shapiro. **CAST:** Alicia Silverstone, Cary Elwes, Jennifer Rubin. **1993 DVD**

CRUSH (1994) ★★★ When Marcia Gay Harden flees the car accident that leaves her best friend in a coma, she heads straight for the writer her pal was to have interviewed. Harden's character seduces the writer and befriends his teenage daughter. This Australian tale of obsession is told with a weirdness that almost excuses its predictability. Not rated; contains profanity, nudity, and sexual situations. 97m. **DIR:** Alison Maclean. **CAST:** Marcia Gay Harden, William Zappa, Donough Rees, Caitlin Bossley. **1993**

CRUSOE ★★1/2 This film by noted cinematographer-turned-director Caleb Deschanel is an attractive but incomplete examination of *Robinson Crusoe* updated to the early nineteenth century. Crusoe is now a young slave trader in Virginia. Aidan Quinn makes an appealing title character. Rated PG-13. 97m. **DIR:** Caleb Deschanel. **CAST:** Aidan Quinn, Ade Sapara. **1989**

CRY-BABY 🎬 John Waters's flimsy remake of *Hairspray* features Johnny Depp as a *drape* from the bad side of town. Rated PG-13 for violence and profanity. 89m. **DIR:** John Waters. **CAST:** Johnny Depp, Amy Locane, Polly Bergen, Susan Tyrrell, Iggy Pop, Ricki Lake, Traci Lords, Troy Donahue, Joey Heatherton, David Nelson, Patty Hearst, Joe Dallesandro, Willem Dafoe. **1990**

CRY BLOOD, APACHE ★★1/2 Joel McCrea, in a cameo appearance as a favor to his son, tells in flashback how he and a bunch of prospectors slaughtered a band of Indians. A girl, the lone survivor of the massacre, promises to lead them to a secret gold mine. 85m. **DIR:** Jack Starrett. **CAST:** Jody McCrea, Dan Kemp, Jack Starrett, Joel McCrea. **1970**

CRY DANGER ★★★ Dick Powell plays a wisecracking ex-con who has been framed for a robbery. Upon his release, he sets out to take revenge on the people

who set him up. Rhonda Fleming is the woman he loves. Not bad! Not rated, this contains violence. B&W; 80m. **DIR:** Robert Parrish. **CAST:** Dick Powell, Rhonda Fleming, William Conrad, Richard Erdman. **1950**

CRY FOR LOVE, A ★★★1/2 Taut teledrama about two people—one an alcoholic, the other addicted to uppers—who, through some very real difficulties, fall in love. Their attempts to help each other over the crises of substance abuse draw them closer together. 100m. **DIR:** Paul Wendkos. **CAST:** Susan Blakely, Powers Boothe, Gene Barry, Edie Adams, Lainie Kazan, Charles Siebert. **1980**

CRY FREEDOM ★★★★1/2 Director Richard Attenborough and screenwriter John Briley's superb film about South African apartheid begins by chronicling the growing friendship between nonviolent black leader Steve Biko (Denzel Washington) and white newspaperman Donal Woods (Kevin Kline). When Biko is brutally murdered, Woods must fight to tell the truth to the rest of the world. Rated PG for violence. 130m. **DIR:** Richard Attenborough. **CAST:** Kevin Kline, Penelope Wilton, Denzel Washington, Ian Richardson. **1987 DVD**

CRY FROM THE MOUNTAIN ★★1/2 A man takes his preteen son on a camping trip, during which he plans to reveal that he and the boy's mother are getting divorced. Created by the Billy Graham Ministry, this film features attractive Alaskan scenery but is extremely preachy. Rated PG; no objectionable material. 88m. **DIR:** James F. Collier. **CAST:** Chris Kidd, Wes Parker, Rita Walter. **1985**

CRY IN THE DARK, A ★★★★1/2 A chilling, superbly acted true-life drama set in 1980 Australia, this film features Meryl Streep and Sam Neill as the parents of an infant who is stolen by a wild dog while they are camping out—or so they say. The authorities begin to doubt their story and the Australian people begin spreading rumors that the baby was killed in a sacrificial rite. Thus begins this harrowing motion picture. Rated PG-13 for mature themes. 120m. **DIR:** Fred Schepisi. **CAST:** Meryl Streep, Sam Neill, Charles Tingwell. **1988 DVD**

CRY IN THE NIGHT, A ★★ Based on the Mary Higgins Clark bestseller, this begins as a decent mystery-thriller and soon descends into campy melodrama. Perry King is a wealthy Canadian who falls for Carol Higgins Clark, a dead ringer for his dead mama. Apt to leave you giggling. Rated PG-13 for violence. 99m. **DIR:** Robin Spry. **CAST:** Perry King, Carol Higgins Clark. **1992**

CRY IN THE WILD, A ★★★1/2 En route to visit his father, an embittered teenager must crash-land a small plane over the Canadian forest when the pilot suddenly dies. Poignant boy-against-nature film. Rated PG for profanity and violence. 81m. **DIR:** Mark Griffiths. **CAST:** Jared Rushton, Ned Beatty, Pamela Sue Martin. **1990 DVD**

CRY IN THE WIND ★★★ David Morse is a bitterly lonely mountain man who kidnaps shy and pretty schoolgirl Megan Follows. Though effectively harsh, the flick only touches the surface of what was the largest manhunt in Pennsylvania history. 95m. **DIR:**

Charles Correll. **CAST:** David Morse, Megan Follows, David Soul. **1991**

CRY OF BATTLE ★★ The son (James MacArthur) of a wealthy businessman gets caught in the Philippines during the Japanese occupation and has to resort to guerrilla warfare. Poorly directed, but does address the ethical questions of racism and the conduct of war. Not rated; with violence. B&W; 99m. **DIR:** Irving Lerner. **CAST:** James MacArthur, Van Heflin, Rita Moreno, Leopoldo Salcedo, Sidney Clute. **1957**

CRY OF THE BANSHEE ★★ Uninspired film casts Vincent Price as a witch-hunting magistrate whose family is threatened when a curse is placed upon his house by practitioners of the old religion. Price fared much better in the similar *The Conqueror Worm*. Rated R for violence and nudity. 87m. **DIR:** Gordon Hessler. **CAST:** Vincent Price, Elisabeth Bergner, Hugh Griffith. **1970**

CRY OF THE INNOCENT ★★★1/2 Exciting made-for-TV suspense-thriller has Rod Taylor playing the grieving husband and father who loses his wife and children when a plane crashes into their summer home in Ireland. When a Dublin detective tells Taylor the crash was no accident, Taylor is determined to find out who planted the bomb in the plane. 93m. **DIR:** Michael O'Herlihy. **CAST:** Rod Taylor, Joanna Pettet, Nigel Davenport, Cyril Cusack, Jim Norton, Alexander Knox. **1980**

CRY TERROR ★★ Disappointingly slow, but well-acted BBC teleplay about a recently paroled ex-con being hounded by a vicious gang. The gang holds his brother and the patrons of a roadside garage hostage until they get the loot from a bank job the ex-con pulled. 71m. **DIR:** Robert Tronson. **CAST:** Bob Hoskins, Susan Hampshire. **1974**

CRY, THE BELOVED COUNTRY (1952) ★★★★ A touching film about the problems of apartheid in South Africa with Sidney Poitier and Canada Lee exceptionally good as preachers fighting prejudice in their homeland. Based on Alan Paton's controversial novel of the same name and the inspiration for the Kurt Weill musical drama, *Lost in the Stars*. B&W; 105m. **DIR:** Zoltán Korda. **CAST:** Sidney Poitier, Canada Lee, Joyce Carey, Charles Carson, Geoffrey Keen. **1952**

CRY, THE BELOVED COUNTRY (1995) ★★★1/2 In 1940s South Africa, a black minister (James Earl Jones) and a bigoted white farmer (Richard Harris) are forced by a shared tragedy to search for some common ground. This third film version of Alan Paton's modern classic novel is solemn and rather plodding, but deeply and sincerely felt, with towering, heartrending performances by Jones and Harris. Rated PG-13 for mature themes. 108m. **DIR:** Darrell Roodt. **CAST:** James Earl Jones, Richard Harris. **1995**

CRY UNCLE! ★★ This is a sometimes very funny spoof of private eye yarns. Allen Garfield is good as a detective who gets involved in all sorts of trouble, but the script is next to tasteless. 87m. **DIR:** John G. Avildsen. **CAST:** Allen Garfield. **1971** DVD

CRY WOLF ★★ A muddled murder mystery that wastes the talents of its stars. But their personalities still glow. The idea of a feisty woman like Barbara Stanwyck fighting her brother-in-law for her late husband's estate is a good premise, especially with

suave, self-confident Errol Flynn as the brother-in-law. Unfortunately, the script lets them both down before the finish. B&W; 83m. **DIR:** Peter Godfrey. **CAST:** Errol Flynn, Barbara Stanwyck, Geraldine Brooks, Richard Basehart, Jerome Cowan. **1947**

CRYING CHILD, THE ★★★ This fascinating supernatural thriller about a woman who loses a child, but still hears a baby crying in the night. Several chilling scenes and good performances all around in this made-for-cable original. Not rated. 95m. **DIR:** Robert Lewis. **CAST:** Mariel Hemingway, Finola Hughes, George Del Hoyo, Kin Shriner. **1996**

CRYING FREEMAN, VOLS. 1–3 ★★★★ Very faithful adaptation of the Japanese comic book about a young artist forced into a life of violence as chief assassin and eventual leader of a secret criminal society. Fine animation captures the original (and much admired) artwork of creators Koike and Ikegami. Dubbed in English. Not rated; contains violence and nudity. 50m. each **DIR:** Johei Matsuura. **1991–1992**

CRYING GAME, THE ★★★★★ Brilliant, adult-oriented motion picture by writer-director Neil Jordan casts sad-eyed Stephen Rea as an IRA volunteer assigned to guard British soldier Forest Whitaker, and that's when the plot's ingenious twists and turns begin. Newcomer Jaye Davidson makes a startling film debut. This evocative exploration of the human condition should be on every serious film buff's must-see list. Rated R for violence, profanity, and nudity. 113m. **DIR:** Neil Jordan. **CAST:** Stephen Rea, Miranda Richardson, Forest Whitaker, Jaye Davidson, Jim Broadbent, Ralph Brown, Adrian Dunbar. **1992** DVD

CRYPT OF THE LIVING DEAD ★ Arguably the worst of a trilogy of horror films directed by Ray Danton, this modern vampire opus—originally titled *Hannah, Queen of Vampires*—is cheap and predictable. Rated R. 83m. **DIR:** Ray Danton. **CAST:** Andrew Prine, Mark Damon, Patty Sheppard. **1972**

CRYSTAL FORCE 🦃 Distraught over the death of her father, a woman buys a crystal centerpiece that turns out to be the gateway for a rather troublesome, antisocial demon. Rated R for violence and nudity. 82m. **DIR:** Laura Keats. **CAST:** Katherine McCall, John Serrdakue, Tony C. Burton. **1990**

CRYSTAL HEART 🦃 A young man with a rare illness falls in love with an aspiring rock singer. Rated R. 103m. **DIR:** Gil Bettman. **CAST:** Tawny Kitaen, Lee Curreri, Lloyd Bochner. **1987**

CRYSTAL TRIANGLE 🦃 Animated tale of an archaeologist who becomes involved in the search for "the message of God" while battling demons and Soviet and American spies. Truly inane. In Japanese with English subtitles. Not rated; contains violence and nudity. 86m. **DIR:** Seiji Okuda. **1987**

CRYSTALSTONE ★★1/2 Although it has a magical undercurrent, *Crystalstone* is more about the very down-to-earth adventures of two children escaping from a wicked guardian than about the fantastical Crystalstone. A good film for older children, with just enough action and ghoulishness to amuse them. Rated PG. 103m. **DIR:** Antonio Pelaez. **CAST:** Frank Grimes, Kamlesh Gupia. **1987**

CTHULHU MANSION 🦃 A magician unleashes the devil's foot soldiers on a group of thugs hiding out at his home. Probably the world's worst adaptation of an H. P. Lovecraft concept. Rated R for profanity and violence. 92m. DIR: Juan Piquer Simon. CAST: Frank Finlay, Marcia Layton, Brad Fisher. 1990

CUBA ★★★ A thinly veiled remake of *Casablanca*, this Richard Lester film is nonetheless far superior to J. Lee Thompson's similar *Cabo Blanco* (which starred Charles Bronson). Sean Connery and Brooke Adams play one-time lovers renewing their passion during the fall of Batista in 1959. As usual, Lester invests his tale with memorable bits. Rated R. 121m. DIR: Richard Lester. CAST: Sean Connery, Brooke Adams, Jack Weston, Hector Elizondo, Denholm Elliott, Chris Sarandon, Lonette McKee. 1979

CUBE ★★★1/2 Suspenseful tale of six strangers who wake up and find themselves trapped in a prison made out of rotating, booby-trapped cubes. After a rather gruesome vivisection, you never know what to expect as the strangers try to make sense of their environment and escape. Rated R for violence and language. 90m. DIR: Vincenzo Natali. CAST: Maurice Dean Wint, Nikki De Boer, Nicky Guadagni, David Hewlett, Andrew Miller, Wayne Robson, Julian Richings. 1997 DVD

CUJO ★★★1/2 Stephen King's story of a mother and son terrorized by a rabid Saint Bernard results in a movie that keeps viewers on the edge of their seats. Rated R for violence and language. 91m. DIR: Lewis Teague. CAST: Dee Wallace, Danny Pintauro, Daniel Hugh-Kelly, Christopher Stone. 1983 DVD

CUL-DE-SAC ★★★ Early Roman Polanski black comedy, about hoods on the lam who briefly victimize a man and his luscious young wife. Early Polanski is just like later Polanski ... an acquired taste. One of the director's first films in English. B&W; 111m. DIR: Roman Polanski. CAST: Donald Pleasence, Françoise Dorleac, Lionel Stander, Jack MacGowran, Jacqueline Bisset. 1966

CULPEPPER CATTLE CO., THE ★★★1/2 A strong supporting cast makes this coming-of-age story set in the Old West into a real treat for fans of shoot-'em-ups. Gary Grimes is a 16-year-old farm boy who dreams of becoming a cowboy. Rated R for violence. 92m. DIR: Dick Richards. CAST: Gary Grimes, Billy Green Bush, Luke Askew, Bo Hopkins, Geoffrey Lewis, Royal Dano. 1972

CULT OF THE COBRA ★★ An Asian high priestess goes to Manhattan to seek vengeance on the American soldiers who defiled her temple. Don't confuse this drab thriller with the camp favorite *Cobra Woman*. B&W; 80m. DIR: Francis D. Lyon. CAST: Faith Domergue, Richard Long, Marshall Thompson, Kathleen Hughes, Jack Kelly. 1955

•CUP, THE ★★★1/2 In an Indian monastery of exiled Tibetan monks, a group of the younger monks search for a TV set so they can watch the World Cup soccer finals. This gentle little slice-of-monastic-life drama has a great deal of simple charm, showing that these exotic characters are not as foreign or strange as they may seem at first glance. In Hindi and Tibetan with English subtitles. Rated G. 94m. DIR: Khyentse Norbu. CAST: Orgyen Tobgyal, Neten Chokling, Jamyang Lodro, Lama Chonjor, Godu Lama, Thinley Nudi. 1999

CUP FINAL ★★★ This drama caused a stir in its native Israel, thanks to its refreshingly evenhanded examination of the relationship between an Israeli prisoner and a squad of PLO soldiers in 1982. The Israeli is taken prisoner, and then is shuttled across war-torn Lebanon along with the PLO. In Hebrew with English subtitles. 107m. DIR: Eran Riklis. CAST: Moshe Ivgi. 1992

CUPID 🖤 While waiting for Cupid to bring him true love, a young psycho murders all the women who fail to make the grade. Rated R for violence and profanity. 95m. DIR: Doug Campbell. CAST: Zach Galligan, Ashley Laurence, Mary Crosby. 1997

•CUPID AND CATE ★★★1/2 Mary-Louise Parker plays the oddball in what seems to be a normal family. Her engagement to a bore is threatened by her attraction to a hunk and she is forced to confront her own self-centered and childish perceptions of the world. Comic moments are outweighed by high drama in this intriguing coming-of-age film. Not rated; contains mature themes. 95m. DIR: Brent Shields. CAST: Mary-Louise Parker, Peter Gallagher, Philip Bosco. 2000

CURDLED ★★1/2 Gore hound Angela Jones decides her life calling is to become a postforensic maid and mop up after gruesome crimes. William Baldwin is the blue-blood killer who fascinates her with his serial decapitations. Lacking enough reason behind the rhyme, this is too strange to embrace, either as black comedy or thriller. Rated R for profanity, gore, and implied violence. 94m. DIR: Reb Braddock. CAST: William Baldwin, Angela Jones, Mel Gorham, Daisy Fuentes, Barry Corbin. 1995

CURE, THE ★★★ An 11-year-old boy who contracted AIDS from a blood transfusion is rescued from peer isolation by a young neighbor. The ravaging physical effects of AIDS are too slickly packaged, but the story is filled with credible compassion. Rated PG-13 for language. 95m. DIR: Peter Horton. CAST: Joseph Mazzello, Brad Renfro, Diana Scarwid, Annabella Sciorra, Bruce Davison. 1995

CURIOSITY KILLS ★★★ C. Thomas Howell and Rae Dawn Chong help make an improbable story fascinating. He's a photographer paying the rent by working as handyman in his inner-city warehouse-turned-apartment complex; she's a neighbor who joins him to learn why a new tenant showed up so quickly after the apparent suicide of another neighbor. Rated R for violence and gore. Made for cable. 86m. DIR: Colin Bucksey. CAST: C. Thomas Howell, Rae Dawn Chong, Courteney Cox, Paul Guilfoyle. 1990

CURLY SUE ★★ Writer-director John Hughes pours on the syrupy sweetness again with this tale of a homeless father-daughter duo who con their way into the life of a beautiful attorney. A diabetic's nightmare. Rated PG for brief profanity. 98m. DIR: John Hughes. CAST: James Belushi, Kelly Lynch, Alisan Porter, John Getz, Fred Dalton Thompson. 1991

CURLY TOP ★★★ Millionaire songwriter John Boles adopts moppet Shirley Temple who plays matchmaker when he falls in love with her sister Rochelle Hudson. Almost-too-cute Shirley sings "Animal Crackers in My Soup." Arthur Treacher provides his usual droll humor. B&W; 74m. DIR: Irving Cummings. **CAST:** Shirley Temple, John Boles, Rochelle Hudson, Jane Darwell, Arthur Treacher. **1935**

CURSE, THE ❤ A meteor crashes and infects the water of a small town with alien parasites. Rated R for violence. 92m. **DIR:** David Keith. **CAST:** Wil Wheaton, John Schneider, Claude Akins. **1987**

CURSE II—THE BITE ❤ Not even closely related to the first movie. Not rated; contains violence and gore. 97m. **DIR:** Fred Goodwin. **CAST:** Jill Schoelen, J. Eddie Peck, Jamie Farr, Bo Svenson. **1988**

CURSE III: BLOOD SACRIFICE ★★ After her sister interrupts the ritual killing of a goat by a group of African natives, a farmer's wife (Jenilee Harrison) must face a curse placed on her by the village's witch doctor. Christopher Lee portrays a local doctor who may or may not have something to do with it. Too bad. Rated R for profanity, nudity, and violence. 91m. **DIR:** Sean Burton. **CAST:** Christopher Lee, Jenilee Harrison. **1990**

CURSE IV: THE ULTIMATE SACRIFICE ★★★ This pseudosequel, originally called *Catacombs*, is a surprisingly stylish low-budget thriller. The memorable Feodor Chaliapin has a supporting role here. He's an aging patriarch who befriends his aide, a young priest troubled by a premature mid-life crisis. To make matters worse, a beautiful schoolteacher has invaded the brotherly order, and there's an ancient evil lurking below in the catacombs. Rated R, but fairly tame except for some blood, violence, and subject matter. 84m. **DIR:** David Schmoeller. **CAST:** Timothy Van Patten, Laura Schaefer, Jeremy West, Ian Abercrombie, Feodor Chaliapin. **1993**

CURSE OF FRANKENSTEIN, THE ★★★1/2 Hammer Films' version of the Frankenstein story about a scientist who creates a living man from the limbs and organs of corpses. Peter Cushing gives a strong performance as the doctor, with Christopher Lee his equal as the sympathetic creature. Some inspired moments are peppered throughout this well-handled tale. 83m. **DIR:** Terence Fisher. **CAST:** Peter Cushing, Christopher Lee, Robert Urquhart. **1957**

•CURSE OF INFERNO, THE ★★ A pair of bumbling bankrobbers match wits with a rich and very crooked businessman. The presence of Janine Turner is the film's only saving grace. Rated R for profanity. 87m. **DIR:** John Warren. **CAST:** Pauly Shore, Janine Turner, Ned Beatty. **1997**

CURSE OF KING TUT'S TOMB, THE ❤ Made-for-TV misfire concerning the mysterious events surrounding the opening of King Tut's tomb. 100m. **DIR:** Philip Leacock. **CAST:** Eva Marie Saint, Robin Ellis, Raymond Burr, Harry Andrews, Tom Baker. **1980**

CURSE OF THE BLACK WIDOW ★★ Made-for-TV movie with a recycled script and a cast that seems to have been plucked from an unshot *Love Boat* installment. Who's the killer that's leaving victims draped in gooey webbing? Only director Dan Curtis's familiarity with the genre gives this telefilm some bounce. 100m. **DIR:** Dan Curtis. **CAST:** Anthony Franciosa, Donna Mills, Patty Duke, June Allyson. **1977**

CURSE OF THE BLUE LIGHTS ❤ Teenagers must find a way to escape from an underground world populated by demons. Not rated, but gory enough for an R rating. 96m. **DIR:** John H. Johnson. **CAST:** Brent Ritter. **1989**

CURSE OF THE CAT PEOPLE, THE ★★★ When Val Lewton was ordered by the studio to make a sequel to the successful *Cat People*, he came up with this gentle fantasy about a child who is haunted by spirits. Not to be confused with the 1980s version of *Cat People*. B&W; 70m. **DIR:** Gunther Von Fritsch, Robert Wise. **CAST:** Simone Simon, Kent Smith, Jane Randolph, Elizabeth Russell. **1944**

CURSE OF THE CRYING WOMAN, THE ★★1/2 One of the better Mexican monster movies released straight to TV by American International Pictures in the 1960s. The film's visual style appears to have been influenced by *Nosferatu* and *Black Sunday*. B&W; 74m. **DIR:** Rafael Baledon. **CAST:** Rosita Arenas, Abel Salazar. **1961**

CURSE OF THE CRIMSON ALTAR ❤ Supposedly based on H. P. Lovecraft's "Dreams in the Witch-House," this film bears no resemblance to that classic. Rated PG for violence. 87m. **DIR:** Vernon Sewell. **CAST:** Boris Karloff, Christopher Lee, Michael Gough, Barbara Steele. **1970**

CURSE OF THE CRYSTAL EYE ★★★1/2 Better-than-average update of the Saturday-morning serial obviously owes a debt to *Raiders of the Lost Ark*. Jameson Parker and Cynthia Rhodes attempt to retrieve the infamous Crystal Eye from a hidden desert fortress while fighting off friends and foes alike. Impressive action sequences and a rousing sense of adventure elevate this one above the many low-budget affairs that followed *Raiders*. Rated R for violence. 82m. **DIR:** Joe Tornatore. **CAST:** Jameson Parker, Cynthia Rhodes, Mike Lane, David Sherwood, André Jacobs. **1993**

CURSE OF THE DEMON ★★★★1/2 Horrifying tale of an American occult expert, Dr. Holden (Dana Andrews), traveling to London to expose a supposed devil cult led by sinister Professor Karswell (Niall MacGinnis). Unfortunately for Holden, Karswell's cult proves to be all too real as a demon from hell is dispatched by the professor to put an end to the annoying investigation. Riveting production is a true classic of the genre. B&W; 96m. **DIR:** Jacques Tourneur. **CAST:** Dana Andrews, Peggy Cummins, Niall MacGinnis, Maurice Denham. **1958**

CURSE OF THE FLY ★★1/2 British-made film has only the slightest connection to the original *The Fly* and *The Return of the Fly*, as scientist Brian Donlevy tries to perfect his matter-teleportation machine that mutates living tissue. B&W; 86m. **DIR:** Don Sharp. **CAST:** Brian Donlevy, George Baker, Carole Gray, Burt Kwouk. **1965**

CURSE OF THE HOUSE SURGEON, THE ❤ This tripe—about a pseudoexorcist for homes—makes *Plan 9 from Outer Space* look like *Citizen Kane*. Not rated. 113m. **DIR:** Steve Postal. **CAST:** Kendrick Kaufman, Jennifer Tuck, Angela Shepard, Angel Langley, Maurice Postal. **1991**

CURSE OF THE LIVING DEAD (KILL, BABY, KILL) ★★★ More commonly available on video as *Kill, Baby, Kill*. It's the great Mario Bava's closing essay in gothic horror, a tremendously atmospheric supernatural mystery about a Transylvanian village and the doctor who tries to free it from a hideous curse in which murder victims are found with gold coins imbedded in their hearts. Slow-paced, but stay with it. 75m. DIR: Mario Bava. CAST: Giacomo Rossi-Stuart. 1966

CURSE OF THE MUMMY'S TOMB, THE 🐝 Wholly unmemorable flapping-bandage horror. An atypically dull effort from England's Hammer Studios. 80m. DIR: Michael Carreras. CAST: Terence Morgan, Fred Clark, Ronald Howard, Jeanne Roland, Michael Ripper. 1964

CURSE OF THE PINK PANTHER, THE ★★★ No, this isn't another trashy compilation of outtakes featuring the late Peter Sellers. Instead, series producer-writer-director Blake Edwards has hired Ted Wass to play a bumbling American detective searching for the still-missing Jacques Clouseau, and he's a delight. When Wass is featured, *Curse* is fresh and diverting—and, on a couple of memorable occasions, it's hilarious. Rated PG for nudity, profanity, violence, and scatological humor. 109m. DIR: Blake Edwards. CAST: Ted Wass, David Niven, Robert Wagner, Harvey Korman, Herbert Lom. 1983

CURSE OF THE PUPPET MASTER ★★ The durable direct-to-video franchise is showing its age with this sixth entry. This one deals with another mad scientist trying to create a perfect race of puppet people. Obviously the filmmakers have never seen Congress in action. Time to cut the strings on this franchise. Rated R for violence and language. 90m. DIR: David DeCoteau. CAST: George Peck, Emily Harrison, Josh Green, Michael Guerin, Marc Newburger. 1998 DVD

•**CURSE OF THE QUEERWOLF** ★★1/2 Once you get past the juvenile humor of this film, there are some genuine laughs to be found in this horror-comedy. Here, a man is bitten on the tush by a transsexual lycanthrope (a queerwolf) and finds himself becoming one as well. The only thing that seems to help slow his transformation is a photo of John Wayne. Go figure. Not rated; contains sexual humor and profanity. 90m. DIR: Mark Pirro. CAST: Michael Palazzolo, Kent Butler, Forrest J. Ackerman, Conrad Brooks. 1987

CURSE OF THE STARVING CLASS ★★1/2 Sam Shepard's play-turned-film has his customarily dreary tone and is far too symbolic for its own good. Stars James Woods and Kathy Bates never fully realize their roles as destitute farmers about to lose their property (poetic license aside, just-plain-folks don't *talk* like this). Rated R for profanity and brief nudity. 102m. DIR: J. Michael McClary. CAST: James Woods, Kathy Bates, Randy Quaid, Henry Thomas, Kristin Fiorella, Lou Gossett Jr. 1994

CURSE OF THE UNDEAD ★★★ Horror-Western starring Michael Pate as a mysterious gunslinger who's immune to bullets. John Hoyt plays the town doctor, baffled when several young girls end up dead, all with puncture wounds in their necks, and Eric Fleming is the preacher who suspects there's evil in town. Not rated. B&W; 89m. DIR: Edward Dein. CAST: Eric Fleming, Michael Pate, Kathleen Crowley, John Hoyt, Bruce Gordon. 1959

CURSE OF THE WEREWOLF, THE ★★★1/2 After being brutally raped in a castle dungeon by an imprisoned street beggar, a young woman gives birth to a son with a strange appetite for blood. His heritage remains a mystery until adulthood, whereupon he begins transforming into a wolf as the full moon rises. Oliver Reed is fine in the role of the werewolf, one of his earliest screen performances. 91m. DIR: Terence Fisher. CAST: Oliver Reed, Clifford Evans, Yvonne Romain, Anthony Dawson. 1961

CURSE OF THE YELLOW SNAKE, THE ★★ An Oriental death cult is on the rampage in this lively comic-strip fantasy from the pen of the incredibly prolific pulp author Edgar Wallace, whose hundreds of yarns were the foundation for a cottage industry in West German exploitation movies from the Fifties through the Seventies. B&W; 98m. DIR: Franz Gottlieb. CAST: Joachim Fuchsberger. 1963

CURTAINS 🐝 A movie actress gets herself committed to a mental institution as preparation for an upcoming film. Rated R. 89m. DIR: Jonathan Stryker. CAST: John Vernon, Samantha Eggar, Linda Thorson, Anne Ditchburn. 1983

CUSTODIAN, THE ★★★1/2 An Australian cop decides he's had it with corruption in the police force, so he tackles the problem in a very unconventional way. He's also dealing with his own problems, including being thrown out of his house by his alcoholic wife. Very well-acted, with an intriguing plot. Not rated; contains nudity, violence, and profanity. 96m. DIR: John Dingwall. CAST: Anthony LaPaglia, Hugo Weaving, Barry Otto, Kelly Dingwall, Bill Hunter, Gosia Dobrowolska. 1993

CUT AND RUN 🐝 A television journalist in South America covering a bloody cocaine war. Rated R for violence, profanity, and nudity. 87m. DIR: Ruggero Deodato. CAST: Lisa Blount, Leonard Mann, Willie Aames, Richard Lynch, Richard Bright, Michael Berryman, John Steiner, Karen Black. 1985

CUT THROATS NINE 🐝 More slasher movie than Western, this brutal film tells the story of a cavalry officer and his daughter who accompany a wagon load of convicts. The wagon overturns and the guards are killed, and a gruesome tale of violence, rape, and murder follows. Only for the strong of stomach. Rated R for violence and nudity. 90m. DIR: Joaquin Romero Marchent. CAST: Robert Hundar, Emma Cohen, Manuel Tejada, Alberto Dalbes, Antonio Itanzo. 1973

CUTTER'S WAY ★★★★ This comes very close to being a masterpiece. The screenplay, by Jeffrey Alan Fiskin, adapted from the novel *Cutter and Bone* by Newton Thornburg, is a murder mystery. The three lead performances are first-rate. Rated R because of violence, nudity, and profanity. 105m. DIR: Ivan Passer. CAST: Jeff Bridges, John Heard, Lisa Eichhorn, Ann Dusenberry. 1981

CUTTHROAT ISLAND ★★★ A pirate's scrappy daughter scalps her father to honor his dying request and finds part of a treasure map tattooed on his skull. She then must wrest other pieces of the map from a scam artist and a notorious sea villain to locate a fabulous isle booty. The film's slow-motion effects are overdone and its humor is often too cute, but this sprawling swashbuckler develops a sportive seediness and rich, atmospheric funk. Rated PG-13 for language and violence. 123m. DIR: Renny Harlin.

CAST: Geena Davis, Matthew Modine, Frank Langella, Maury Chaykin, Harris Yulin, Stan Shaw. **1995 DVD**

CUTTING CLASS ★★ A mass murderer is on the loose at a local high school. Sound familiar? Well … it is. Rated R for violence and profanity. 91m. **DIR:** Raspo Pallenberg. **CAST:** Donovan Leitch, Jill Schoelen, Brad Pitt, Roddy McDowall, Martin Mull. **1989**

CUTTING EDGE, THE ★★★1/2 Ice-hockey player D. B. Sweeney reluctantly becomes the figure-skating partner of ice queen Moira Kelly. Few surprises, but those who thaw at the idea of a love story will find it entertaining. Rated PG for profanity. 101m. **DIR:** Paul Michael Glaser. **CAST:** D. B. Sweeney, Moira Kelly, Roy Dotrice, Dwier Brown, Terry O'Quinn. **1992**

•CUTTING MOMENTS ★★★ Fueled by pure imagination and a hard-core attitude, this highly enjoyable anthology film hits the mark far more often than it misses. The best is the title segment, although wise viewers will fast-forward past *Don't Nag Me.* The special effects of gore guru Tom Savini are also on hand in the film, a special treat for fans. Not rated; contains gore, violence, profanity, and nudity. 76m. **DIR:** Douglas Buck, Casey Kehoe, Timothy Healy, Gino Panaro, Craig Wallace. **CAST:** Nica Ray, Gary Betsworth, Jared Barsky. **1998**

CYBER BANDITS ★★ Secret plans for a virtual-reality weapon are tattooed onto a heroic sailor's back in order to prevent world domination by a megalomaniac millionaire. Farfetched action outing that uses high technology as camouflage for its own lack of invention. Rated R for violence and adult situations. 86m. **DIR:** Erik Fleming. **CAST:** Martin Kemp, Alexandra Paul, Robert Hays, Adam Ant, Grace Jones, Henry Gibson, James Hong. **1995**

CYBER CITY OEDO 808 ★★1/2 Three convicts are offered early release in exchange for service as "Cyber Police"—investigators charged with solving crimes of a technological nature. Above-average animation makes this one more watchable than some, but the lack of character detail leaves much to be desired. In Japanese with English subtitles. Not rated; contains profanity. 46m. **DIR:** Yoshiaki Kawajiri. **1990**

CYBER NINJA ★★★1/2 Eye-popping special effects and elaborate set design highlight this Japanese space opera reminiscent of *Star Wars.* Saki, a warrior/princess, has been abducted and taken to the Dark Overlord, who plans to use her as a sacrifice to unleash a powerful evil that will sweep the land. It's up to Cyber Ninja and a small band of rebels to battle the Overlord and save the princess. Dubbed. Not rated; contains fantasy-type violence. 80m. **DIR:** Keita Amamiya. **CAST:** Hanbei Kawai, Hiroki Ida, Eri Morishita, Makoto Yokoyama. **1988**

CYBER TRACKER ★★ Don "The Dragon" Wilson stars as a government agent who suddenly finds himself framed for murder and targeted for elimination by lethal androids called cyber trackers. These androids are commissioned by the government to execute violent criminals on the spot. Rated R for violence, nudity, and profanity. 91m. **DIR:** Richard Pepin. **CAST:** Don "The Dragon" Wilson, Richard Norton, Stacie Foster, Steve Burton, Abby Dalton, Jim Maniaci. **1994 DVD**

CYBER TRACKER 2 ★★1/2 A secret-service agent and his TV-news-anchor wife are forced to prove their innocence when cyborgs created to resemble them go on a killing spree. Some high-energy shootouts and explosion scenes galore distinguish this routine but competent high-tech testosterone-fest. Rated R for violence and strong language. 97m. **DIR:** Richard Pepin. **CAST:** Don "The Dragon" Wilson, Stacie Foster, Tony Burton, Jim Maniaci, Anthony DeLongis, John Kessir, Stephen Rowe, Steve Burton. **1995**

CYBERNATOR ❤ In the near future, a police detective (Lonnie Schuyler) has his hands full battling a group of evil cyborg assassins developed by the military. Rated R for violence and nudity. 84m. **DIR:** Robert Rundle. **CAST:** Lonnie Schuyler, Christina Peralta, James K. Williams, William Smith. **1991 DVD**

CYBERZONE ★★1/2 Sporadically effective *Blade Runner* rip-off about a twenty-first-century bounty hunter searching for four female "pleasure 'droids" hijacked by a corporate mogul. The movie's offbeat combination of titillation and low-rent sci-fi is undeniably cheesy but nonetheless entertaining. Rated R for sexual situations and violence. 80m. **DIR:** Fred Olen Ray. **CAST:** Marc Singer, Matthias Hues, Rochelle Swanson, Robin Clark, Kin Shriner, Cal Bartlett, Robert Quarry, Ross Hagen, Brinke Stevens. **1995**

CYBORG ❤ A study in bad. Bad script. Bad acting. Bad directing. Bad special effects. A soldier of the future (Jean-Claude Van Damme) seeks vengeance against the savage gang that killed his family. Rated R for violence. 90m. **DIR:** Albert Pyun. **CAST:** Jean-Claude Van Damme, Deborah Richter, Dayle Haddon. **1989 DVD**

CYBORG 2 ❤ This turgid sequel-in-name-only steals profusely from *Blade Runner* and *Max Headroom.* A martial-arts instructor (Elias Koteas) does the unthinkable by falling in love with a pouting cyborg (Angelina Jolie). Rated R for violence, profanity, nudity, and simulated sex. 99m. **DIR:** Michael Schroeder. **CAST:** Elias Koteas, Angelina Jolie, Allen Garfield, Billy Drago, Jack Palance. **1993 DVD**

CYBORG 3: THE RECYCLER ★★ Outrageous situations and campy performances save the day for this tired sequel about a cyborg who discovers she is pregnant. It's actually quite fun to watch Malcolm McDowell chew the scenery as the bad guy. Rated R for violence. 90m. **DIR:** Michael Schroeder. **CAST:** Zach Galligan, Khrystyne Haje, Richard Lynch, Malcolm McDowell. **1994**

CYBORG COP ★★ Convoluted concoction borrows from several different genres, but can't come to grips with its own identity. A former DEA agent locates his brother on a Caribbean island, but learns that his sibling has become a cyborg in a cruel experiment. John Rhys-Davies is cheerfully villainous, while the rest of the cast must grin and bear tiresome clichés. Rated R for violence and language. 94m. **DIR:** Sam Firstenberg. **CAST:** David Bradley, Todd Jensen, Alonna Shaw, John Rhys-Davies. **1993**

CYBORG SOLDIER ★★ A renegade cop is assigned the duty of wiping out a series of berserk cyborg slaves. Plenty of action and just enough storyline. Rated R for violence. 97m. **DIR:** Sam Firstenberg.

CAST: David Bradley, Morgan Hunter, Jill Pierce, Dale Cutts, Victor Mellaney. 1993

CYBORG: THE SIX MILLION DOLLAR MAN ★★★ Pilot for the long-running ABC series is more serious and subdued than the episodes to follow. Col. Steve Austin (Lee Majors), after flying an experimental jet that crashes, is turned into a superman with powerful robotic limbs. Very good. 73m. **DIR:** Richard Irving. **CAST:** Lee Majors, Darren McGavin, Martin Balsam. 1973

CYCLO ★★★1/2 Innocence, evil, poverty, and wealth all rub shoulders amid Ho Chi Minh City's teeming downtown streets soon after the Vietnam War in this hallucinogenic drama about the fragility of life and family. A teen bicycle-taxi driver is intoxicated with a false sense of power when he and his older sister are sucked into the city's cruel criminal underworld. In Vietnamese and French with English subtitles. Not rated; contains sexual content, adult themes, and violence. 124m. **DIR:** Tran Anh Hung. **CAST:** Le Van Loc, Tony Leung Chiu-Wai, Tran Nu Yen-Khe, Nguyen Nhu Quynh. 1996

CYCLONE 💣 Stupid action flick about a top-secret military experiment. Rated R for violence and profanity. 89m. **DIR:** Fred Olen Ray. **CAST:** Heather Thomas, Martin Landau, Jeffrey Combs, Troy Donahue, Martine Beswick, Robert Quarry, Hurst Hall. 1986

CYCLONE IN THE SADDLE 💣 Absolute bottom-of-the-barrel wagon train oater. B&W; 52m. **DIR:** Elmer Clifton. **CAST:** Rex Lease, Bobby Nelson, William Desmond, Yakima Canutt. 1935

CYCLOPS, THE ★★1/2 Low-budget whiz Bert I. Gordon does it again with this cheaply made but effective film about a woman (Gloria Talbott) whose brother is transformed into a big, crazy monster by—what else?—radiation. Neat little movie. B&W; 75m. **DIR:** Bert I. Gordon. **CAST:** James Craig, Lon Chaney Jr., Gloria Talbott. 1957

CYRANO DE BERGERAC (1925) ★★★★ This silent French version of the classic drama may seem stagy to modern viewers, especially in comparison to the 1990 version starring Gérard Depardieu. But the story is still gripping, and new English intertitles and the original hand tinting make this restored version a pleasure to watch for viewers who have suffered through hard-to-view silent films. 114m. **DIR:** Augusto Genina. **CAST:** Pierre Magnier, Linda Mogila, Angelo Ferrari. 1925

CYRANO DE BERGERAC (1950) ★★★★ Charming, touching story of steadfast devotion and unrequited love done with brilliance and panache. As the fearless soldier of the large nose, José Ferrer superbly dominates this fine film. Mala Powers is beautiful as his beloved Roxanne. William Prince, who now often plays heavies, makes Christian a proper, handsome, unimaginative nerd. B&W; 112m. **DIR:** Michael Gordon. **CAST:** José Ferrer, Mala Powers, William Prince. 1950

CYRANO DE BERGERAC (1990) ★★★★★ This lavish French production is both ethereal and earthy, poetic and robust, a quintessential, cinematic new version of the classic play about an unattractive cavalier with the soul of perfect romance. The most charismatic and fascinating Gallic actor of the day—Gérard Depardieu—creates the definitive Cyrano. Rated PG. 135m. **DIR:** Jean-Paul Rappeneau. **CAST:** Gérard Depardieu, Anne Brochet, Vincent Perez, Jacques Weber. 1990

D2: THE MIGHTY DUCKS ★★★ Just a notch below the original. Coach Emilio Estevez and his youthful team of hockey players and misfits represent America in an international competition. Sure it's contrived, but kids won't care. Rated PG. 107m. **DIR:** Sam Weisman. **CAST:** Emilio Estevez, Michael Tucker, Jan Rubes, Kathryn Erbe, Cartsen Norgaard. 1994

D3: THE MIGHTY DUCKS ★★ If you saw either of the first two Ducks movies, here we go again. This time the gang takes on the stuck-up snobs at a high-class prep school and has to prove itself against the school's cutthroat varsity hockey team. Guess who wins. Both the kids and the formula are getting too old to retain the series' original charm. Rated PG. 104m. **DIR:** Robert Lieberman. **CAST:** Emilio Estevez, Jeffrey Nordling, Heidi Kling, Joss Ackland. 1996

DA ★★★★ New York City playwright Martin Sheen returns to his Irish home when his adoptive father (Barnard Hughes) dies. While in the house in which he was raised, Sheen relives his less-than-idyllic youth with the help of his father's cantankerous ghost. Both sentimental and uncompromising, this special film benefits from a performance of a lifetime by Hughes and one of nearly equal merit by Sheen. Rated PG for profanity. 96m. **DIR:** Matt Clark. **CAST:** Barnard Hughes, Martin Sheen, William Hickey, Doreen Hepburn. 1988

DAD ★★★★ In this wonderful weeper, Ted Danson is a successful businessman who attempts to make an emotional connection with his 75-year-old father (Jack Lemmon) before it is too late. Writer-director Gary David Goldberg, who adapted the novel by William Wharton, doesn't let us off easy. Rated PG. 116m. **DIR:** Gary David Goldberg. **CAST:** Jack Lemmon, Ted Danson, Olympia Dukakis, Kathy Baker, Kevin Spacey, Ethan Hawke. 1989

DADDY LONG LEGS ★★★1/2 The oft-told tale of the wealthy playboy secretly arranging the education of a poor orphaned waif, is, as expected, secondary to the song and dance. Leslie Caron has a natural grace not seen in many of Fred Astaire's partners; their dances seem to flow. A highlight is Fred's drumstick solo in "History of the Beat." Academy Award nominations for Johnny Mercer's "Something's Got to Give" and the scoring by Alfred Newman. 126m. **DIR:** Jean Negulesco. **CAST:** Fred Astaire, Leslie Caron, Terry Moore, Thelma Ritter. 1955 DVD

DADDY NOSTALGIA ★★★ Enjoyable exploration of the relationship between a daughter and her dy-ng father. Dirk Bogarde and Jane Birkin are magical as they try to work out their differences and come to understand and respect each other. Director Bertrand Tavernier scores again. In French with English subtitles. Rated PG. 105m. **DIR:** Bertrand Tavernier. **CAST:** Dirk Bogarde, Jane Birkin, Odette Laure. 1990

DADDY'S BOYS ★★ Depression-era crime-drama about an ex-farmer turned bank robber. Typical Roger Corman production has a few surprises but is basically familiar stuff. Rated R for violence and sexual situations. 84m. **DIR:** Joe Minion. **CAST:** Daryl Haney, Laura Burkett. 1988

DADDY'S DYIN' AND WHO'S GOT THE WILL ★★1/2 Mildly enjoyable comedy about a group of southern eccentrics who just may be rich—if they can find the last will and testament of their nearly dearly departed dad. Entertaining, although the feudin' and fussin' does get to be a bit much. Rated PG-13 for profanity. 117m. **DIR:** Jack Fisk. **CAST:** Beau Bridges, Beverly D'Angelo, Tess Harper, Judge Reinhold, Amy Wright, Keith Carradine, Bert Remsen. 1990

DADDY'S GIRL ★★ Gabrille Boni is effective as Jody, a psychotic 11-year-old who will do anything to stop anyone who comes between her and her father. Don Mitchell (William Katt) adores his adopted daughter Jody so much that he is blind to her deceptive ways. When Karen, the girl's older cousin, moves in with the family, she uncovers Jody's dark side. Paint-by-the-numbers plotting and lackluster direction do little to make this exercise in horror more than it is. Rated R for violence and language. 95m. **DIR:** Martin Kitrosser. **CAST:** William Katt, Michele Greene, Roxana Zal, Gabrille Boni. 1996

DADDY'S GONE A-HUNTING ★★★ Veteran director Mark Robson knows how to get the best out of the material he has to work with. And this is an exciting, neatly crafted psychological drama—in which Carol White gets involved with a psychotic photographer (Scott Hylands). If you get a chance to go a-hunting for this one at your local video store, you won't go unrewarded. Not rated, but with some violent content. 108m. **DIR:** Mark Robson. **CAST:** Carol White, Paul Burke, Scott Hylands, Mala Powers. 1969

DAENS ★★★★ Powerful, moving tribute to the human will. Jan DeCleir delivers a stunning performance as Father Daens, a man of the cloth who puts everything on the line in order to improve the wretched working conditions in the local factories. Pitting himself against church officials, local government, and big business, Father Daens discovers the difference between what's right and what's popular. Nominated for Best Foreign Language Film. In Flemish and French with English subtitles. Not rated; contains strong images. 134m. **DIR:** Jan DeCleir. **CAST:** Jan DeCleir, Gerard Desarthe, Antje De Boeck, Michael Pas. 1992

DAFFY DUCK'S MOVIE: FANTASTIC ISLAND ★ This pedestrian compilation is for Warner Bros. cartoon fanatics and toddlers only. Chunks of fairly funny shorts are strung together with a weak, dated parody of TV's *Fantasy Island*. Daffy deserved better. Rated G. 78m. **DIR:** Friz Freleng. 1983

DAFFY DUCK'S QUACKBUSTERS ★★★★★ The best feature-length compilation of Warner Bros. cartoons since Chuck Jones's *The Bugs Bunny/Road Runner Movie*, this release features two new cartoons—"Quackbusters" and "Night of the Living Duck"—as well as classics from Jones ("Claws for Alarm," "Transylvania 6-5000," and "The Abominable Snow Rabbit") and Friz Freleng ("Hyde and Go Tweet"). The wraparound story is animated with as much care as the original cartoons, and the result is a delight for young and old. 80m. **DIR:** Greg Ford, Terry Lennon. 1988

DAGGER OF KAMUI, THE ★★★ The beautifully animated film from veteran director Rin Taro is wounded by a somewhat overlong (and sometimes terribly corny) story. Jiro, a young Ninja, is bent on discovering the secret that caused the death of his parents and threatens the destruction of the Tokugawa shogunate. In Japanese with English subtitles. Not rated; contains violence. 132m. **DIR:** Rin Taro. 1985

DAGORA, THE SPACE MONSTER 🎬 A cache of gems stolen by Japanese gangsters is ripped off by a giant, flying, diamond-eating jellyfish. Probably a true story. 80m. **DIR:** Inoshiro Honda. **CAST:** Yosuke Natsuki. 1964

DAIN CURSE, THE 🎬 A poor, two-hour version of a just passable TV miniseries based on the Dashiell Hammett classic. 123m. **DIR:** E. W. Swackhamer. **CAST:** James Coburn, Hector Elizondo, Jason Miller, Jean Simmons. 1978

DAISIES IN DECEMBER ★★★★ Joss Ackland and Jean Simmons shine as a pair of senior citizens who tentatively grope their way into a relationship, in this charming story from scripter Jenny Paschall. Ackland initially resents being dumped at a seaside enclave for seniors while the rest of his family enjoys a skiing vacation, but he's eventually won over by longtime resident Simmons's obvious joy in every little delight that each morning provides. Watch for Ian Crowe, charming in a small role as a solicitous taxi driver. Rated PG for mild profanity. 97m. **DIR:** Mark Haber. **CAST:** Joss Ackland, Jean Simmons, Pippa Guard, Judith Barker, Barbara Lott, Ian Crowe. 1995

DAISY MILLER ★★ This limp screen adaptation of a story by the great novelist Henry James is more a study on rambling dialogue than on the clashing of two cultures. Rated G. 93m. **DIR:** Peter Bogdanovich. **CAST:** Cybill Shepherd, Barry Brown, Cloris Leachman, Mildred Natwick, Eileen Brennan. 1974

DAKOTA (1945) ★★1/2 Any Western with John Wayne, Walter Brennan, and Ward Bond has to be a winner, right? Wrong. This substandard film may be interesting to see for their performances, but you also have to put up with the incredibly untalented Vera Ralston (she was the wife of Republic Studio head Herbert Yates). It's almost worth it. B&W; 82m. **DIR:** Joseph Kane. **CAST:** John Wayne, Vera Hruba Ralston, Walter Brennan, Ward Bond. 1945

DAKOTA (1988) ★★★ Outstanding cinematography highlights this run-of-the-mill story of a troubled teen on the run. Lou Diamond Phillips is the teen who works off a debt by training horses on a Texas farm. In the process he learns he must also face his past. Rated PG-13. 90m. **DIR:** Fred Holmes. **CAST:** Lou Diamond Phillips, Dee Dee Morton. **1988**

DAKOTA INCIDENT ★★1/2 It's a fight to the finish in this fairly good Western as the Indians attack a stagecoach rolling through Dakota Territory in those thrilling days of yesteryear. 88m. **DIR:** Lewis R. Foster. **CAST:** Dale Robertson, Linda Darnell, John Lund. **1956**

DALEKS—INVASION EARTH 2150 A.D. ★★★ The always watchable Peter Cushing revives his distinctive interpretation of the ever-popular Dr. Who in this honorable sequel to *Dr. Who and the Daleks*. This time, the title creatures are attempting to take over Earth. 84m. **DIR:** Gordon Flemyng. **CAST:** Peter Cushing, Bernard Cribbins, Andrew Keir, Ray Brooks. **1966**

DALEY: THE LAST BOSS ★★★ Hal Holbrook narrates this PBS documentary about Richard J. Daley, mayor of Chicago for more than twenty years. While he is best remembered as a proponent of law and order at any cost (demonstrated by his reaction to antiwar protests at the 1968 Democratic Convention), this documentary presents him as one of the last of the old-style "machine" politicians who built Chicago into the major urban center it is today. B&W/color; 112m. **DIR:** Barak Goodman. **1995**

DAM BUSTERS, THE ★★★★1/2 Richard Todd and Michael Redgrave star in this British film about the development and use of a specially designed bomb to destroy a dam in Germany during World War II. An outstanding cast and great script. 205m. **DIR:** Michael Anderson. **CAST:** Richard Todd, Michael Redgrave, Ursula Jeans, Basil Sydney. **1954**

DAMAGE ★★ When Stephen Fleming—a respected British Parliament member—meets his son's new girlfriend, he's overcome by a sexual obsession that sends his entire world into a tragic tailspin. A highgloss soap that is as cold and detached as the enigmatic woman at its lurid core. Rated R for language, nudity, and violence. 100m. **DIR:** Louis Malle. **CAST:** Jeremy Irons, Juliette Binoche, Miranda Richardson, Rupert Graves, Leslie Caron, Ian Bannen. **1993 DVD**

DAMES ★★★ Music, songs, dancing, great Busby Berkeley numbers. Plot? Know the one about backing a Broadway musical? But, gee, it's fun to see and hear Joan Blondell, Dick Powell, Ruby Keeler, ZaSu Pitts, Guy Kibbee, and Hugh "Woo-woo" Herbert again. B&W; 90m. **DIR:** Ray Enright. **CAST:** Joan Blondell, Dick Powell, Ruby Keeler, ZaSu Pitts, Guy Kibbee, Hugh Herbert. **1934**

DAMIEN: OMEN II ★★★1/2 In this first sequel to *The Omen*, William Holden plays the world's richest man, Richard Thorn. In the previous picture, Richard's brother is shot by police while attempting to kill his son, who he believed to be the Antichrist, son of Satan. *Damien: Omen II* picks up seven years later. Rated R. 107m. **DIR:** Don Taylor. **CAST:** William Holden, Lee Grant, Lew Ayres, Sylvia Sidney. **1978**

DAMN THE DEFIANT! ★★★★ Authenticity is the hallmark of this saga of the Napoleonic period. This British production pits the commanding officer of a British warship against a hated second officer. The performances are superb. 101m. **DIR:** Lewis Gilbert. **CAST:** Alec Guinness, Dirk Bogarde, Maurice Denham, Anthony Quayle. **1962**

DAMN YANKEES ★★★1/2 A torrid, wiggling vamp teams with a sly, hissing devil to frame the Yankees by turning a middle-aged baseball fan into a wunderkind and planting him on the opposing team, the Washington Senators. Gwen Verdon is sensational as the temptress Lola, who gets whatever she wants. Hollywood called on her to reprise her role in the original Broadway musical hit. Lots of pep and zing in this one. 110m. **DIR:** George Abbott, Stanley Donen. **CAST:** Gwen Verdon, Ray Walston, Tab Hunter. **1958**

DAMNATION ALLEY (SURVIVAL RUN) ★★ The nuclear holocaust movie, which disappeared after its heyday in the 1950s, is revived, complete with giant mutations and roaming survivors. While it's not a bad movie, it's not particularly good, either. The laser effects are awful. Rated PG. 91m. **DIR:** Jack Smight. **CAST:** Jan-Michael Vincent, George Peppard, Dominique Sanda, Jackie Earle Haley, Paul Winfield. **1977**

DAMNED, THE ★★★1/2 Deep, heavy drama about a German industrialist family that is destroyed under Nazi power. This film is difficult to watch, as the images are as bleak as the story itself. In German with English subtitles. Rated R for sex. 155m. **DIR:** Luchino Visconti. **CAST:** Dirk Bogarde, Ingrid Thulin, Helmut Griem, Helmut Berger. **1969**

DAMNED RIVER ★★★ Four Americans take a rafting adventure vacation down the Zambezi River in Zimbabwe. Things get out of hand when their guide turns out to be a psychopath and a *Deliverance* game of survival is played out. Rated R for violence. 96m. **DIR:** Michael Schroeder. **CAST:** Stephen Shellen, John Terlesky. **1989**

DAMSEL IN DISTRESS, A ★★★ By choice, Fred Astaire made this one without Ginger, who complemented him, but with Joan Fontaine—then a beginner—who could not dance. Fred's an American popular composer in stuffy London. He mistakenly thinks heiress Joan is a chorus girl. B&W; 98m. **DIR:** George Stevens. **CAST:** Fred Astaire, Joan Fontaine, Gracie Allen, George Burns, Constance Collier, Reginald Gardiner. **1937**

DAN CANDY'S LAW (ALIEN THUNDER) ★★ The Royal Canadian Mounted Police always get their man. So where's the suspense? Not in this movie, that's for sure. The most appealing element is the glorious Canadian scenery. Rated PG. 90m. **DIR:** Claude Fournier. **CAST:** Donald Sutherland, Kevin McCarthy, Chief Dan George, Francine Racette. **1973**

DANCE ★★ Mediocre story of a group of dancers, working with a high-pressure new choreographer, who are polishing their toe shoes for the National New York Ballet auditions. An interesting soundtrack, with IAM IAM, but the only star is black dancer, Carlton Wilborn. Not rated. 92m. **DIR:** Robin Murray. **CAST:** Johan Renvall, Ellen Troy, Carlton Wilborn. **1988**

DANCE, FOOLS, DANCE ★★1/2 Joan Crawford plays a determined young woman who becomes a crime reporter and tries to make her reputation by bringing gangster Clark Gable to justice. The sparks fly—and their torrid teaming and some risqué bits of business rescue this precode melodrama from the stale plot line. B&W; 81m. **DIR:** Harry Beaumont.

CAST: Joan Crawford, Clark Gable, Cliff Edwards, Natalie Moorehead. **1931**

DANCE, GIRL, DANCE ★★★1/2 Lucille Ball doing a striptease! That's just one of the highlights of this RKO comedy-drama about a couple of ambitious chorus girls who struggle to make it big on Broadway. B&W; 89m. **DIR:** Dorothy Arzner. **CAST:** Maureen O'Hara, Louis Hayward, Lucille Ball. **1940**

DANCE HALL ★★ This is a minor musical about a nightclub owner (Cesar Romero) who falls in love with one of his employees (Carole Landis). Not great. The cast saves this film from being a dud. B&W; 74m. **DIR:** Irving Pichel. **CAST:** Carole Landis, Cesar Romero, William Henry, June Storey. **1941**

DANCE HALL RACKET 🎬 Lenny Bruce plays creepy killer Vincent, bodyguard to a vice lord. B&W; 60m. **DIR:** Phil Tucker. **CAST:** Lenny Bruce. **1953**

DANCE ME OUTSIDE ★★★★ Original and provocative, this film strips away preconceptions to show us that life on the reservation is not what you'd expect. Based on W. P. Kinsella's book, it's a surprisingly dense coming-of-age story peppered with savvy humor. A small Canadian production, it features four teenagers trying to deal with the murder of a friend, as well as their own growing pains, all the while addressing racial tensions from the native perspective. Rated R for profanity and violence. 87m. **DIR:** Bruce McDonald. **CAST:** Ryan Black, Adam Beach, Lisa LaCroix, Michael Greyeyes, Jennifer Podemski, Kevin Hicks, Sandrine Holt. **1994**

DANCE OF DEATH 🎬 Don't waste your time. Not rated. 75m. **DIR:** Juan Ibanez. **CAST:** Boris Karloff, Andres Garcia. **1971 DVD**

DANCE OF THE DAMNED ★★ Well-made but ultimately boring tale about a suicidal stripper and her chance meeting with a vampire. They spend the night discussing life, death, and the feel of the sun, but that's about it. Producer Roger Corman remade this as the much better *To Sleep with a Vampire*. Rated R for profanity, nudity, and violence. 83m. **DIR:** Katt Shea Ruben. **CAST:** Cyril O'Reilly, Starr Andreeff, Maria Ford. **1989**

DANCE OR DIE ★★ Another listless made-for-video thriller. This one pits a drug-addicted Las Vegas choreographer against mob drug dealers and federal drug agents. 81m. **DIR:** Richard W. Munchkin. **CAST:** Ray Kieffer, Rebecca Barrington. **1988**

DANCE 'TIL DAWN 🎬 Typical teen tripe traps vapid rich kids in the same room as geeky teens with their chaperoning, shallow parents. Blech. Rated PG for sexual innuendo. 96m. **DIR:** Paul Schneider. **CAST:** Christina Applegate, Tempestt Bledsoe, Tracey Gold, Kelsey Grammer, Edie McClurg, Alyssa Milano, Alan Thicke. **1988**

DANCE WITH A STRANGER ★★★★1/2 A superbly acted, solidly directed import, this British drama is a completely convincing tale of tragic love. Miranda Richardson makes a stunning film debut as the platinum-blonde hostess in a working-class nightclub who falls in love with a self-indulgent, upper-class snob (Rupert Everett). The screenplay was based on the true story of Ruth Ellis, who, on July 13, 1955, was hanged at London's Holloway prison for shooting her lover outside a pub. Rated R for profanity, nudity,

sex, and violence. 102m. **DIR:** Mike Newell. **CAST:** Miranda Richardson, Rupert Everett, Ian Holm, Matthew Carroll. **1985**

DANCE WITH DEATH ★★1/2 Sordid thriller with Barbara Alyn Woods as a cop who goes undercover as a stripper to flush out a killer. Getting naked was obviously a prerequisite to getting a role. Rated R for nudity, violence, and strong language. 90m. **DIR:** Charles Philip Moore. **CAST:** Maxwell Caulfield, Martin Mull, Barbara Alyn Woods, Drew Snyder. **1991**

DANCE WITH ME ★★★ This conventional love story makes an agreeable showcase for Latin superstar Chayanne, whose smile could light an auditorium. That's good, because scripter Daryl Matthews's tale is formulaic: A jaded dance pro is reawakened to life's possibilities after meeting a kind, attractive stranger. Ironically, the two stars spend little time dancing with each other. Rated PG for mild sensual content. 126m. **DIR:** Randa Haines. **CAST:** Vanessa L. Williams, Chayanne, Kris Kristofferson, Jane Krakowski, Beth Grant, Joan Plowright. **1998 DVD**

DANCER, TEXAS: POP. 81 ★★★★ A group of friends—who promised themselves that they would leave their small town when they graduated from high school—wrestles with that promise as the time finally arrives. Excellent performances, writing, and direction. Rated PG. 97m. **DIR:** Tim McCanlies. **CAST:** Breckin Meyer, Peter Facinelli, Ethan Embry, Eddie Mills. **1998 DVD**

DANCERS ★★1/2 Only lovers of ballet will enjoy this wafer-thin drama, since its latter half is devoted solely to an American Ballet Theatre production of *Giselle*. The minimal attempt at parallel storytelling concerns the conceited company star-director and the dancer who falls under his spell. Rated PG for sexual themes. 99m. **DIR:** Herbert Ross. **CAST:** Mikhail Baryshnikov, Leslie Browne. **1987**

DANCES WITH WOLVES ★★★★★ Heartfelt, thoroughly involving saga of a disillusioned Union soldier's flight from the Civil War, and his eventual finding of inner peace in harmony with nature and the Lakota Sioux. A brilliant filmmaking debut from director-star Kevin Costner, this epic reestablished the Western's viability at the box office. In English and Lakota Sioux with subtitles. Rated PG-13 for violence and brief nudity. 185m. **DIR:** Kevin Costner. **CAST:** Kevin Costner, Mary McDonnell, Graham Greene, Rodney A. Grant. **1990 DVD**

DANCING AT LUGHNASA ★★1/2 Five sisters and the out-of-wedlock son of one of them eke out a hardscrabble existence in rural Ireland of the 1930s. Brian Friel's play won numerous awards and has a devoted following, but on film it plays like a self-conscious rehash of *The Glass Menagerie*, gloomy, predictable, and a little dreary. However, acting is the strong cast is first-rate. Rated PG. 92m. **DIR:** Pat O'Connor. **CAST:** Meryl Streep, Michael Gambon, Kathy Burke, Catherine McCormack, Sophie Thompson. **1998 DVD**

DANCING IN THE DARK ★★1/2 Interesting drama about Edna Cormick (Martha Henry) who—after twenty years of being the ideal housewife, finds her life torn apart in a few short hours. From her hospital bed, Edna reconstructs the events that led up to her act of vengeance. Although this film is extremely slow-moving, feminists are likely to appreciate it. Rated PG-13. 93m. DIR: Leon Marr. CAST: Martha Henry, Neil Munro, Rosemary Dunsmore. 1986 DVD

DANCING LADY ★★★ Joan Crawford goes from burlesque dancer to Broadway star in this backstage drama set to music. A good film, this was also one of her early money-makers. Fred Astaire made his screen debut in one dance number. B&W; 94m. DIR: Robert Z. Leonard. CAST: Joan Crawford, Clark Gable, Fred Astaire, Franchot Tone, May Robson, Grant Mitchell, Sterling Holloway, Ted Healy, The Three Stooges. 1933

DANCING MOTHERS ★★★ Bee-sting-lipped Jazz Age flapper Clara Bow romps through this verge-of-sound silent about flaming youth. Enthusiastic performances offset the simple plot. B&W; 60m. DIR: Herbert Brenon. CAST: Clara Bow, Alice Joyce, Dorothy Cumming, Norman Trevor. 1926

DANCING WITH DANGER ❤ A scissor-wielding maniac is on the loose in this poorly acted and directed, made-for-cable, so-called mystery movie. Rated PG-13 for violence. 90m. DIR: Stuart Cooper. CAST: Cheryl Ladd, Ed Marinaro, Miguel Sandoval, Pat Skipper, Stanley Kamel. 1994

DANDELIONS ❤ This German-made soft-porn film stars Rutger Hauer as a cold, sadistic leather boy. Made in 1974. Dubbed in English. 92m. DIR: Adrian Hoven. CAST: Rutger Hauer, Dagmar Lassander. 1987

DANDY IN ASPIC, A ★★ Who's on whose side? That's the question that pops up most often in this confusing, rather flat spy thriller. Laurence Harvey plays a double agent based in Berlin who is ordered to kill himself. This was director Anthony Mann's last film; he died during production and Harvey completed the direction. 107m. DIR: Anthony Mann. CAST: Laurence Harvey, Tom Courtenay, Mia Farrow, Lionel Stander, Harry Andrews. 1968

DANGAIO ★★★1/2 Japanese animation. Four psionically enhanced warriors learn to work together against an evil space pirate and his minions. Strong characterization and visuals add much to this above-average story. In Japanese with English subtitles. Not rated violence. 45m. DIR: Toshihiro Hirano. 1990

DANGER ★★★ Three *film noir* episodes created for television: "The Lady on the Rock," "The System," and "Death Among the Relics." Sophisticated Alfred Hitchcock–like suspense chillers. Turn down the lights. B&W; 77m. DIR: Sidney Lumet. CAST: Don Hammer, Olive Deering, Kim Stanley, Eli Wallach. 1952

DANGER: DIABOLIK ★★★ Director Mario Bava departed from the horror genre he normally specialized in, and staged this pop-art fantasy, based on an Italian comic strip of the time. Master criminal Diabolik outwits the police and government agents assigned to catch him in a garishly colored, playful spoof that sometimes is worthy of silent serial master Louis Feuillade. 105m. DIR: Mario Bava. CAST: John Phillip Law, Marisa Mell, Michel Piccoli, Terry-Thomas, Adolfo Celi. 1967

DANGER LIGHTS ★★★ Louis Wolheim plays a tough-as-nails rail-yard boss who befriends hobo Robert Armstrong and jeopardizes his chances with a young Jean Arthur, who is "almost" a fiancée. This story, done many times before and since, works well against the backdrop of a railroad world that is now largely gone. B&W; 73m. DIR: George B. Seitz. CAST: Louis Wolheim, Jean Arthur, Robert Armstrong, Hugh Herbert. 1930

DANGER MAN (TV SERIES) ★★★1/2 CBS-TV imported this British-produced thriller, the first of three spy-flavored dramas to star Patrick McGoohan (see additional entries under *Secret Agent* and *The Prisoner*). The series debuted in May, 1961, and quietly went off the air after an undistinguished run of 24 episodes. McGoohan starred as the "Danger Man," a freelancer named John Drake, who worked as a security investigator in affiliation with NATO. A bit violent, but suitable for family viewing. B&W; 55m. DIR: Various. CAST: Patrick McGoohan. 1961

DANGER OF LOVE ★★ Truth is duller than fiction in this made-for-TV *Fatal Attraction* clone based on the true story of a suburban New York woman who murders her lover's wife. Rated R for violence and sexual situations. 97m. DIR: Joyce Chopra. CAST: Joe Penny, Jenny Robertson, Deborah Benson, Joseph Bologna, Fairuza Balk. 1992

DANGER ZONE, THE (1986) ❤ Contrived low-budget flick about a psychopathic murderer on the loose. Rated R for language, nudity, and violence. 90m. DIR: Henry Vernon. CAST: Michael Wayne, Jason Williams, Suzanne Tara, Robert Canada, Juanita Ranney. 1986

DANGER ZONE (1995) ★★★ Billy Zane, our charming hero, gets mixed up with mercenaries trying to recover stolen plutonium, which is disguised as toxic waste and hidden somewhere within the jungles of South Africa. The stunts are a lot of fun. Rated R for profanity, violence, and nudity. 92m. DIR: Allan Eastman. CAST: Billy Zane, Ron Silver, Cary-Hiroyuki Tagawa, Robert Downey Jr., Lisa Collins. 1995

DANGEROUS (1935) ★★ One of the weakest movies to earn its star an Oscar. Bette Davis plays a former stage-star-turned-alcoholic rescued by an idealistic architect (Franchot Tone). B&W; 78m. DIR: Alfred E. Green. CAST: Bette Davis, Franchot Tone, Alison Skipworth, Margaret Lindsay, John Eldredge, Dick Foran. 1935

DANGEROUS, THE (1994) ★★★ Rod Hewitt's overly complicated plot concerns a bad guy turned good, a good cop turned rogue, the usual seedy drug barons, two knife-wielding psychopaths, Ninja assassins bent on revenge, and a couple of Hollywood veterans slumming as colorful snitches. The squalid New Orleans setting is appropriate for the tough-guy heroics, and the script achieves brief moments of poetic grace. Rated R for profanity, violence, nudity, and simulated sex. 92m. DIR: Rod Hewitt. CAST: Robert Davi, Michael Paré, Cary-Hiroyuki Tagawa, Elliott Gould, John Savage, Joel Grey. 1994

DANGEROUS BEAUTY ★★★★1/2 Catherine McCormack shines as sixteenth-century Venice courtesan Veronica Franco, who becomes legendary with her verbal and sexual skills, and ability to sway the heads of foreign diplomats. Her pursuit of a married man, the oncoming plague, and persecution by the Church threaten her existence. *Dangerous Beauty* is filled with visual and verbal splendor. Rated R for nudity, adult situations, and language. 112m. DIR: Marshall Herskovitz. CAST: Catherine McCormack, Rufus Sewell, Oliver Platt, Jacqueline Bisset, Fred Ward, Moira Kelly. **1998 DVD**

DANGEROUS CHARTER ❤ Three fishermen find an abandoned yacht with a corpse on board. B&W; 74m. DIR: Robert Gottschalk. CAST: Chris Warfield, Sally Fraser, Chick Chandler. **1962**

DANGEROUS COMPANY ★★ The true story of convict Ray Johnson, who lived in and out of prison for years until his reform. Excellent acting saves what would otherwise be a tedious biography. 100m. DIR: Lamont Johnson. CAST: Beau Bridges, Carlos Brown, Karen Carlson, Kene Holiday, Ralph Macchio. **1982**

DANGEROUS CURVES ★★★1/2 A college senior gets a chance to earn a position with a corporation if he can deliver a birthday present to the boss's daughter. The present is a bright red Porsche. This zany comedy, aimed at the younger set, actually has a wider appeal. The young leads are appealing, and the support of Robert Klein and Robert Stack add to the enjoyment. Rated PG. 93m. DIR: David Lewis. CAST: Tate Donovan, Danielle von Zerneck, Robert Stack, Robert Klein, Robert Romanus. **1988 DVD**

DANGEROUS GAME (1990) ★★1/2 Group of adventurous kids break into a large department store, but a vengeful cop enters the picture and decides to teach the rowdy youths a lesson in blue light specials. Rated R for violence. 102m. DIR: Stephen Hopkins. CAST: Steven Grives, Marcus Graham, Miles Buchanan, Kathryn Walker. **1990**

DANGEROUS GAME, A (1993) ★★★1/2 Manipulation is the name of this game when a director (Harvey Keitel) plays mind games with the cast in the movie he's making. Keitel's life is out of control as he crosses all boundaries between real life and reel life on his volatile set. The movie seems to be going nowhere for an hour and then explodes with passion and violence. Madonna is in top form as an actress playing an actress. Rated R for violence, profanity, sexual situations, nudity, and drug use. Not rated director's cut also available. 107m. DIR: Abel Ferrara. CAST: Harvey Keitel, Madonna, James Russo. **1993**

DANGEROUS GROUND ★★1/2 South African exile Vusi travels home to bury his father after thirteen years in America. His younger brother is a malcontent soldier and another brother is missing. Vusi teams up with a stripper to save his brother and dent South Africa's new urban drug problems. Rated R for violence, drug use, and brief nudity. 92m. DIR: Darrell Roodt. CAST: Ice Cube, Elizabeth Hurley, Ving Rhames, Sechaba Morajele, Eric Miyeni. **1997 DVD**

DANGEROUS HEART ❤ In this made-for-cable original, the widow of a cop unwittingly starts dating the drug dealer who killed her husband. He only wants the money her husband stole from them. Boring, unbelievable, badly acted, and poorly written. Not rated; contains violence and sexual situations. 95m. DIR: Michael Scott. CAST: Timothy Daly, Lauren Holly, Jeffrey Nordling, Alice Carter, Bill Nunn. **1993**

DANGEROUS INDISCRETION ★★★ Entertaining B-movie thriller stars C. Thomas Howell as an advertising executive who beds the beautiful Joan Sever-

ance. When her husband discovers the indiscretion, however, he sets out to make Howell's life a living hell. Engrossing, sexy, and well made. Howell's performance here can be counted among his best. Rated R for nudity, sexual situations, and profanity. 81m. DIR: Richard Kletter. CAST: C. Thomas Howell, Malcolm McDowell, Sue Mathew, Joan Severance. **1994**

DANGEROUS LIAISONS ★★★★ Based on the classic French novel *Les Liaisons Dangereuses*, this exquisitely filmed story of competitive sexual gamesmanship between two ex-lovers is charged with sensual energy. The cast, led by a marvelously brittle Glenn Close and John Malkovich, is first-rate. There's a sumptuous rhythm to the language and a lush setting that beautifully captures upper-class, eighteenth-century France. Rated R. 120m. DIR: Stephen Frears. CAST: Glenn Close, John Malkovich, Michelle Pfeiffer, Mildred Natwick, Swoosie Kurtz, Uma Thurman. **1989 DVD**

DANGEROUS LIFE, A ★★1/2 Interesting made-for-cable portrayal of the Philippine uprising against Ferdinand and Imelda Marcos during the mid-Eighties. Gary Busey plays a reporter stationed in Manila when all hell breaks loose. Not rated, but some violence. 163m. DIR: Robert Markowitz. CAST: Gary Busey, Rebecca Gilling, James Handy. **1988**

DANGEROUS LOVE ❤ A maniac killer with a camera begins murdering his dates and taping their deaths. Rated R for nudity, profanity, and violence. 96m. DIR: Marty Ollstein. CAST: Elliott Gould, Lawrence Monoson, Anthony Geary. **1988**

DANGEROUS MINDS ★★1/2 High-school instructor LouAnne Johnson's inner-city memoirs are transformed into a dissatisfying film, with Michelle Pfeiffer miscast as an ex-Marine who demonstrates the true value of education to a bunch of "bad kids." The characters lack depth, the tone is inconsistent, and the story is all over the map. If you want motivation, stick with *Stand and Deliver*. Rated R for profanity and violence. 99m. DIR: John N. Smith. CAST: Michelle Pfeiffer, George Dzundza, Courtney B. Vance, Robin Bartlett, Bruklin Harris. **1995 DVD**

DANGEROUS MISSION ★★ In this below-average movie, Piper Laurie witnesses a mob killing in New York City and has to flee the city because the killers are after her. The chase ends at Glacier National Park. A good cast but an overdone plot. 75m. DIR: Louis King. CAST: Victor Mature, Piper Laurie, Vincent Price, William Bendix. **1954**

DANGEROUS MOONLIGHT (SUICIDE SQUADRON) ★★★ Polish pianist Anton Walbrook stops tickling the ivories and starts squeezing the trigger as he climbs into the cockpit as a bomber pilot for the RAF during World War II. Excellent aerial sequences. B&W; 83m. DIR: Brian Desmond Hurst. CAST: Anton Walbrook, Sally Gray, Derrek de Marney. **1941**

DANGEROUS MOVES ★★★★1/2 Worthy of its Oscar for best foreign film of 1984, this French film about a chess match between two grand masters in Geneva is not just for fans of the game. Indeed, the real intensity that is created here comes from the sidelines: the two masters' camps, the psych-out attempts, the political stakes, and the personal dramas. Rated PG for adult situations and language.

95m. **DIR:** Richard Dembo. **CAST:** Michel Piccoli, Leslie Caron, Alexandre Arbatt, Liv Ullmann. **1984**

DANGEROUS PASSAGE ★★ Routine adventure-drama finds Robert Lowery in Central America, where he discovers that an inheritance awaits him back in the States. Phyllis Brooks provides the love interest. Mysterious shadows and attempts on Lowery's life provide the tension. B&W; 61m. **DIR:** William Burke. **CAST:** Robert Lowery, Phyllis Brooks, Jack LaRue, Victor Kilian. **1944**

DANGEROUS PASSION ★★ Good cast brings life to this pedestrian crime-drama. Carl Weathers wins the respect of mob boss Billy Dee Williams when he takes the rap for a murder. Then he beats the rap, is recruited into the family, and soon falls for his boss's sultry wife. Lonette McKee is quite good as the femme fatale in this made-for-television film. Not rated; contains adult situations. 94m. **DIR:** Michael Miller. **CAST:** Carl Weathers, Billy Dee Williams, Lonette McKee. **1989**

DANGEROUS PLACE, A ★★1/2 The *Karate Kid* formula still has some juice, particularly in the hands of young martial arts star Ted Jan Roberts. This time out, he infiltrates a gang of kids believed responsible for the death of his older brother. Sean Dash's story is strictly a fairy tale, but the result should be reasonably appealing to younger fans. Rated R for violence and profanity. 97m. **DIR:** Jerry P. Jacobs. **CAST:** Ted Jan Roberts, Corey Feldman, Erin Gray, Marshall Teague, Mako, Dick Van Patten. **1994**

DANGEROUS PREY ★★ An outlandish premise helps keep this otherwise unremarkable outing afloat. As a result of getting romantically involved with a Russian gunrunner, a stuntwoman (Shannon Whirry) is abducted and sent to an institute where a troop of seductive hit women are trained. Whirry makes a wooden *macha* heroine, but fans of fast-paced shoot-outs and explosions won't be disappointed. Rated R. 92m. **DIR:** Lloyd A. Simandl. **CAST:** Shannon Whirry, Ciara Hunter, Joseph Laufer, Beatrice De Borg, Carlo Cartier, Michael Rogers. **1995**

DANGEROUS PURSUIT ★★ A nightclub waitress sleeps with a stranger for money and then realizes he is a contract killer. Three years later, after running to the other side of the United States and getting married to a cop, she discovers the stranger in her new town and that he is going to kill again. Mediocre made-for-cable thriller. 96m. **DIR:** Sandor Stern. **CAST:** Gregory Harrison, Alexandra Powers, Brian Wimmer, Scott Valentine, Robert Prosky. **1989**

DANGEROUS RELATIONS ★★★1/2 This apparently lurid prison drama is actually a thoughtful tale about an estranged father and son attempting to make peace while forced to serve their parole under the same roof. Made for TV. 93m. **DIR:** Georg Stanford Brown. **CAST:** Lou Gossett Jr., Blair Underwood, Rae Dawn Chong, David Harris, Clarence Williams III. **1993**

DANGEROUS SUMMER, A ♥ Set in Australia, this film deals with a posh resort damaged by fire and the subsequent investigation. Not rated; the film has violence and profanity. 100m. **DIR:** Quentin Masters. **CAST:** James Mason, Tom Skerritt, Ian Gilmour, Wendy Hughes. **1984**

DANGEROUS TOUCH ★★ Kate Vernon stars as a radio sex therapist who finds herself falling in lust with mysterious stranger Lou Diamond Phillips. Before long, she realizes there's something amiss and finds herself knee-deep in a quagmire of blackmail, revenge, and murder. Loaded with action and steamy sex but could have used a more cohesive plot. Not rated, but the equivalent of an R for nudity and sexual situations. 99m. **DIR:** Lou Diamond Phillips. **CAST:** Lou Diamond Phillips, Kate Vernon, Max Gail. **1993** DVD

DANGEROUS VENTURE ★★1/2 Better-than-average Hopalong Cassidy adventure finds our heroes searching for Aztec ruins in the Southwest. B&W; 55m. **DIR:** George Archainbaud. **CAST:** William Boyd, Andy Clyde, Rand Brooks. **1947**

DANGEROUS WHEN WET ★★ Fame and fortune await she who swims the English Channel. Esther Williams plays a corn-fed wholesome who goes for it; Fernando Lamas cheers her on. Semisour Jack Carson and high-kicking Charlotte Greenwood clown. Good music and a novel underwater Tom and Jerry cartoon sequence. 95m. **DIR:** Charles Walters. **CAST:** Esther Williams, Fernando Lamas, Jack Carson, Charlotte Greenwood, Denise Darcel. **1953**

DANGEROUS WOMAN, A ★★1/2 Debra Winger stars as a mentally impaired but well-meaning woman whose life begins falling apart. An affair with a new handyman brings romance, while an unjust accusation of stealing calls up more volatile emotions. The film lacks a cohesive dramatic structure and distinct point of view. Rated R for profanity, violence, and simulated sex. 99m. **DIR:** Stephen Gyllenhaal. **CAST:** Debra Winger, Barbara Hershey, Gabriel Byrne, David Strathairn, Laurie Metcalf, Chloe Webb, John Terry, Jan Hooks, Paul Dooley, Viveka Davis, Richard Riehle. **1993**

DANGEROUSLY CLOSE ★★ In this disappointing modern-day vigilante film, a group of students, led by a Vietnam veteran teacher, tries to purge their school of "undesirable elements" by any means necessary—including murder. Film starts out promising enough but soon loses focus with its rambling script and stereotypical situations. Rated R for profanity, violence, and brief nudity. 95m. **DIR:** Albert Pyun. **CAST:** John Stockwell, Carey Lowell, Bradford Bancroft, Madison Mason. **1986**

DANGERS OF THE CANADIAN MOUNTED ★★ A rumored horde of Genghis Khan's treasure trove inspires the mysterious "Chief" into a frenzy of territorial railway sabotage along the Alaskan-Canadian boundary. The battle for the security of the border escalates until the ringleaders and the treasure are plucked from a sunken Chinese junk and placed in the hands of authorities. B&W; 12 chapters **DIR:** Fred Brannon, Yakima Canutt. **CAST:** Jim Bannon, Virginia Belmond, Anthony Warde, Dorothy Granger, Tom Steele, Dale Van Sickel, I. Stanford Jolley. **1948**

DANIEL ★★1/2 Sidney Lumet directed this disappointing and ultimately depressing screen version of E. L. Doctorow's thinly veiled account of the Rosenberg case of thirty years ago, in which the parents of two young children were electrocuted as spies. If it weren't for Timothy Hutton's superb performance in the title role (as one of the children), *Daniel* would be much less effective. Rated R for profanity and violence. 130m. DIR: Sidney Lumet. CAST: Timothy Hutton, Mandy Patinkin, Lindsay Crouse, Edward Asner, Amanda Plummer. 1983

DANIEL BOONE ★★★★ Action-packed story of the early American frontier features rugged outdoor star George O'Brien in the title role and evil John Carradine as a renegade who aids the Indians. This rousing film is great schoolboy adventure stuff. B&W; 77m. DIR: David Howard. CAST: George O'Brien, Heather Angel, John Carradine. 1936

DANIEL BOONE, TRAIL BLAZER ★★1/2 This is a slightly better-than-average Western that has Daniel Boone (Bruce Bennett) not only pathfinding for settlers but fighting off what seems to be the entire population of Native Americans. Good performances and lots of action save it from being mundane. 76m. DIR: Albert C. Gannaway. CAST: Bruce Bennett, Lon Chaney Jr., Faron Young. 1956

DANIELLA BY NIGHT ★★1/2 A relic from the days when "art film" was a code term for extra "ooh-la-la," this murder mystery was a hit in 1962 because it offered Elke Sommer (in her last pre-Hollywood film) in a brief nude scene. In French with English subtitles. Not rated; contains sexual situations. 83m. DIR: Max Pecas, Radley Metzger. CAST: Elke Sommer, Ivan Desny. 1962

DANIELLE STEEL'S DADDY ★★1/2 Made-for-television movie based on Danielle Steel's best-selling book. Patrick Duffy plays Oliver Watson, whose seemingly perfect life takes a tailspin when his wife takes a powder on him and their three children. Forced to juggle single parenthood with a burgeoning career as an advertising executive, Watson moves to L.A. and falls for an actress. 95m. DIR: Michael Miller. CAST: Patrick Duffy, Lynda Carter, Kate Mulgrew. 1990

DANIELLE STEEL'S FINE THINGS ★★ Condensed television miniseries based on bestseller by author Danielle Steel. Too much soap and not enough opera in this tale of newlyweds, D. W. Moffett and Tracy Pollan, who discover she suffers from the most incurable of miniseries diseases. Ho-hum, but costar Cloris Leachman has some nice moments. 145m. DIR: Tom Moore. CAST: D. W. Moffett, Tracy Pollan, Noley Thornton, Cloris Leachman, Darrell Larson. 1990

DANIELLE STEEL'S KALEIDOSCOPE ★★★ Tearjerker about three sisters who were separated at a young age and eventually reunited. If you like Danielle Steel's work, you'll like this movie. Not rated, but suitable for all audiences. 96m. DIR: Jud Taylor. CAST: Jaclyn Smith, Perry King, Colleen Dewhurst, Patricia Kalember, Claudia Christian. 1992

DANIELLE STEEL'S ONCE IN A LIFETIME ★★★ After being struck by a car, an unconscious writer (Lindsay Wagner) replays her losses and mistakes. Having lost her husband and daughter in a fire, she has failed to recognize her second chance for happiness. Perhaps more compelling than her love life are her attempts to help her deaf son. Passable melodramatic fare. Not rated, contains sexual situations. 90m. DIR: Michael Miller. CAST: Lindsay Wagner, Barry Bostwick, Rex Smith, Amy Aquino, Darrell Thomas Utley. 1994

DANNY ★★★ A warm, touching, predictable story of an unhappy little girl who obtains a horse that has been injured and then sold off by the spoiled daughter of the wealthy stable owners. A fine family film. Rated G. 90m. DIR: Gene Feldman. CAST: Rebecca Page, Janet Zarish. 1977

DANNY BOY (1941) ★★ Estranged from her husband and small son, a singer searches for them, only to find that they have become street musicians. Overly sentimental, but the music is nice enough. B&W; 80m. DIR: Oswald Mitchell. CAST: Ann Todd, Wilfrid Lawson. 1941

DANNY BOY (1982) ★★★★ A young saxophone player witnesses the brutal murder of two people and becomes obsessed with understanding the act. Set in Ireland, this movie is enhanced by haunting musical interludes that highlight the drama of the people caught up in the Irish "troubles." There are flaws, most notably in some of the coincidences, but the overall effect is mesmerizing. Rated R. 92m. DIR: Neil Jordan. CAST: Stephen Rea, Marie Kean, Ray McAnally, Donal McCann. 1982

DANNY, THE CHAMPION OF THE WORLD ★★★🅐 ★★ This smashing adaptation of Roald Dahl's children's story benefits from the inspired casting of Jeremy Irons and his precocious son, Samuel, as the only two people standing up to would-be land baron Robbie Coltrane. The elder Irons won't allow his property to become part of a local tycoon's ever-expanding haven for big-city bird hunters. Young Samuel Irons fiercely loves and believes in his father and helps to win the day while fighting his own battles. Suitable for all ages. 99m. DIR: Gavin Millar. CAST: Jeremy Irons, Robbie Coltrane, Samuel Irons, Cyril Cusack, Lionel Jeffries, Ronald Pickup, Jean Marsh, Michael Hordern. 1989

DANNY THOMAS SHOW, THE (TV SERIES) ★★★★ Also known as *Make Room for Daddy*. These early episodes featured Jean Hagen as Danny's wife. Thomas, a nightclub entertainer, spends a lot of time away from his family—but even when he's home, the family goes on without him. Hilarious bits arise as he tries to reclaim his place as head of the household. Rusty Hamer steals every scene he appears in as Thomas's precocious son. 110m. DIR: Sheldon Leonard. CAST: Danny Thomas, Jean Hagen, Rusty Hamer, Sherry Jackson. 1953–56

DANSE MACABRE ★★ Filmed on location in the Soviet Union, this horror film features Robert Englund as an American choreographer working at a world-renowned ballet college. When girls from around the world are allowed to enroll, trouble begins. One by one they are murdered. Rated R for nudity, violence, and profanity. 97m. DIR: Greydon Clark. CAST: Robert Englund. 1991

DANTE'S INFERNO ★★1/2 This early film by director Ken Russell exhibits great cinematic style but falls short in dramatic execution. The movie focuses on the morose and brilliant poet and painter Dante Gabriel Roth, played by Oliver Reed with comic pathos. Not very engaging. Not rated, but recommended for adult viewers. B&W; 90m. DIR: Ken Russell. CAST: Oliver Reed. 1968

DANTE'S PEAK ★★1/2 Pierce Brosnan is an intuitive volcanologist who believes that the Pacific Northwest community of Dante's Peak is endangered by a local volcano. Naturally, nobody believes him; yet he's eventually proven correct. In fairness, Brosnan and his colleagues seem like authentic scientists. Some of the hair's-breadth escapes are preposterous, but the film definitely knows how to keep your adrenaline running. Rated PG-13 for profanity and violence. 108m. DIR: Roger Donaldson. CAST: Pierce Brosnan, Linda Hamilton, Charles Hallahan, Grant Heslov, Elizabeth Hoffman, Jamie Renée Smith, Jeremy Foley. 1997 DVD

DANTON ★★★1/2 Polish director Andrzej Wajda takes the French revolutionary figure (well played by Gérard Depardieu) and the events surrounding his execution by onetime comrades and turns it into a parable of modern life. It may not be good history, but the film does provide food for thought. In French. Rated PG. 136m. DIR: Andrzej Wajda. CAST: Gérard Depardieu, Wojiech Pszoniak, Patrice Chereau. 1982

DANZON ★★★★ Completely agreeable romantic drama about a thirty-something telephone operator who lives a shielded life with her teenage daughter in Mexico City. Her only foray into the world comes every Wednesday night when she dances the seductive *Danzon* with Carmello, her dance partner of six years. When he fails to appear one evening, she embarks on a journey of self-discovery and awakening in search of him. In Spanish with English subtitles. Rated PG. 103m. DIR: Maria Novaro. CAST: Maria Rojo, Blanca Guerra, Tito Vasconcelos, Carmen Salinas. 1992

DARBY O'GILL AND THE LITTLE PEOPLE ★★★1/2 Darby O'Gill is an Irish storyteller who becomes involved with some of the very things he talks about, namely leprechauns, the banshee, and other Irish folk characters. This wonderful tale is one of Disney's best films and a delightful fantasy film in its own right. It features a young and relatively unknown Sean Connery as Darby's future son-in-law. 93m. DIR: Robert Stevenson. CAST: Albert Sharpe, Janet Munro, Sean Connery, Jimmy O'Dea. 1959

DARING DOBERMANS, THE ★★1/2 Fun sequel to *The Doberman Gang* is a little more kiddy-oriented, but it's still okay, featuring another well-planned caper for the canine stars. Rated PG for very light violence and language. 90m. DIR: Byron Chudnow. CAST: Charles Knox Robinson, Tim Considine, David Moses, Joan Caulfield. 1973

DARING GAME ★★1/2 Ivan Tors, producer of TV's *Sea Hunt* and *Flipper*, heads back into the water for this unsuccessful series pilot. It's about a team of commandos nicknamed The Flying Fish who are proficient on land, air, and sea. No better or worse than a lot of stuff that *did* make it to TV. 101m. DIR: Laslo Benedek, Ricou Browning. CAST: Lloyd Bridges, Nico Minardos, Michael Ansara, Joan Blackman, Shepperd Strudwick. 1968

DARING YOUNG MAN, THE ★★★ Above-average comedy featuring Joe E. Brown as a bumbling serviceman who becomes mixed up with foreign spies and a radio-controlled bowling ball. B&W; 73m. DIR: Frank Strayer. CAST: Joe E. Brown, Marguerite Chapman, William Wright. 1942

DARK, THE (1979) ★★ A deadly alien. Rated R. 92m. DIR: John "Bud" Cardos. CAST: William Devane, Cathy Lee Crosby, Richard Jaeckel, Keenan Wynn, Vivian Blaine. 1979

DARK, THE (1994) 💟 Beneath a graveyard lives a subterranean creature with the power to destroy or heal. It is pursued by a vindictive cop out to destroy it and a scientist who wants to save it. Rated R for violence, nudity, and profanity. 87m. DIR: Craig Pryce. CAST: Stephen McHattie, Cynthia Belliveau, Jaimz Woolvett, Brion James. 1994

DARK ADAPTED EYE, A ★★★★ Secrets and skulduggery abound in this BBC mystery based on a Ruth Rendell novel written under her nom de plume, Barbara Vine. The past constantly overlaps the present in this fictional account of one of the last female murderers to be hanged in Great Britain. Not rated; contains mild profanity, violence, sexual situations, and adult themes. 152m. DIR: Tim Fywell. CAST: Helena Bonham Carter, Sophie Ward, Celia Imrie. 1994

DARK AGE ★★1/2 What begins as a blatant *Jaws* rip-off becomes an entertaining thriller about a giant killer crocodile. A bit tough to follow due to Australian accents, but this flick offers a tolerable way to kill an hour and a half. Rated R for violence. 90m. DIR: Arch Nicholson. CAST: John Jarratt, Nikki Coghill, Max Phipps. 1987

DARK ANGEL, THE ★★★1/2 This episode of the PBS series *Mystery!* is eerie, edgy, and atmospheric. Based on an 1864 Sheridan Le Fanu novel which is said to have influenced Bram Stoker, this Gothic piece explores the darker side of familial ties, focusing on vices, decay, and misplaced trust. The melodrama is made memorable by the deliciously creepy performance of Peter O'Toole. 150m. DIR: Peter Hammond. CAST: Peter O'Toole, Jane Lapotaire, Alan MacNaughton, Tim Woodward. 1992

DARK ANGEL: THE ASCENT ★★1/2 All hell breaks loose when a particularly nasty she-devil gets bored torturing the eternally damned and decides to take her skills to the surface. Angela Featherstone triumphs as the bewitching demon who finds plenty to punish. Gory special effects and lots of tongue-out-of-cheek humor make this low-budget exercise worth a look. Rated R for gore and adult situations. 80m. DIR: Linda Hassani. CAST: Angela Featherstone, Daniel Markel, Mike Genovese, Nicholas Worth, Milton James. 1994

DARK BACKWARD, THE ★★ A self-professed comedian can't get a laugh from his audience. Eventually, he is given a hand—a third one, growing from an arm in the middle of his back. Likely to become a cult film. Rated R for profanity. 100m. DIR: Adam Rifkin. CAST: Judd Nelson, Bill Paxton, Wayne Newton, James Caan, Lara Flynn Boyle. 1991

DARK BREED ★★★ A space mission returns to Earth bearing some uninvited guests, monstrous parasites bent on taking over our planet. It's up to Agent Nick Saxon (Jack Scalia) to save us. About what one would expect from a sci-fi thriller where the hero's name is Nick Saxon, though it's lively enough. Rated R for strong violence. 104m. DIR: Richard Pepin. CAST: Jack Scalia, Jonathan Banks, Robin Curtis. 1996

DARK CITY ★★★ This hypnotic nightmare blends gothic comic-book fantasy with science-fiction *noir*. John Murdoch awakens in a hotel room bathtub and discovers he is wanted for murders he can't remember committing. While pursued by police, he learns that bald extraterrestrials called the Strangers are controlling the minds of the city's entire populace as they study the human soul and try to avert their own extinction. The story is muddled but the visuals are absolutely stunning. Rated R for language, nudity, and violence. 103m. DIR: Alex Proyas. CAST: Rufus Sewell, Kiefer Sutherland, Jennifer Connelly, William Hurt, Richard O'Brien. 1998 DVD

DARK COMMAND ★★★1/2 Raoul Walsh, who directed John Wayne's first big Western, *The Big Trail*, was reunited with the star after the latter's triumph in *Stagecoach* for this dynamic shoot-'em-up. Walter Pidgeon is Quantrill, a once-honest man who goes renegade and forms Quantrill's Raiders. It's up to the Duke, with help from his *Stagecoach* costar Claire Trevor, Roy Rogers, and Gabby Hayes, to set things right. B&W; 94m. DIR: Raoul Walsh. CAST: John Wayne, Claire Trevor, Walter Pidgeon, Roy Rogers, George "Gabby" Hayes. 1940 DVD

DARK CORNER, THE ★★★1/2 Released from prison after being framed by his partner, private eye Mark Stevens finds he is being dogged by a man in a white suit. Before he can fathom why, he finds his ex-partner's body under his bed, and the police once again closing in. His secretary, Lucille Ball, helps unravel the sinister murder scheme. Above-average *film noir*. B&W; 99m. DIR: Henry Hathaway. CAST: Mark Stevens, Clifton Webb, Lucille Ball, William Bendix, Kurt Kreuger. 1946

DARK CRYSTAL, THE ★★★ Jim Henson of "The Muppets" fame created this lavish fantasy tale in the style of J.R.R. Tolkien (*The Lord of the Rings*), using the movie magic that brought E.T. and Yoda (*The Empire Strikes Back*) to life. It's a delight for children of all ages. Rated PG. 93m. DIR: Jim Henson, Frank Oz. 1983 DVD

DARK EYES ★★★1/2 Based on several short stories by Anton Chekhov, this film takes its title from a Russian ballad that fills the soundtrack. Marcello Mastroianni is wonderfully endearing as a dapper, love-struck Italian who meets a young Russian woman at a spa and later in her village. The Russian scenery, replete with rolling hills at dawn and singing Gypsies, is a tourist's dream. In Italian with English subtitles. 118m. DIR: Nikita Mikhalkov. CAST: Marcello Mastroianni, Marthe Keller, Silvana Mangano. 1987

DARK FORCES ★★★ Robert Powell plays a modern-day conjurer who gains the confidence of a family by curing their terminally ill son; or does he? The evidence stacks up against Powell as we find he may be a foreign spy and stage magician extraordinaire. While uneven, this film is decent entertainment. Rated PG for brief nudity and some violence. 96m. DIR: Simon Wincer. CAST: Robert Powell, Broderick

Crawford, David Hemmings, Carmen Duncan, Alyson Best. 1984

DARK HABITS ★★ This surreal comedy features Carmen Maura as a nightclub singer. Director Pedro Almodóvar has a touch of Luis Buñuel without the depth or intelligence. This is fitfully funny, self-indulgent, and overlong. In Spanish with English subtitles. Not rated, but recommended for adults. 116m. DIR: Pedro Almodóvar. CAST: Carmen Maura. 1984

DARK HALF, THE ★★★1/2 Based on Stephen King's tale of a writer and his homicidal pseudonym. When threatened with the exposure of his literary alter ego, writer Timothy Hutton sees his chance to rid himself and his family of that dark side. But his alter ego manifests itself as a nasty killer bent on revenge. Rated R for violence and profanity. 115m. DIR: George A. Romero. CAST: Timothy Hutton, Amy Madigan, Michael Rooker, Julie Harris, Robert Joy, Kent Broadhurst, Beth Grant, Rutanya Alda, Tom Mardirosian. 1993 DVD

▶DARK HARBOR ★★ In this complex but unfulfilling thriller, a couple, disillusioned with each other, find a wounded man on the side of the road. The brief encounter leads to an emotional showdown when the stranger shows up at their secluded Maine house. The film attempts to be a sexually charged thriller, but lacks conviction and stamina. Rated R for adult situations, language, nudity, and violence. 89m. DIR: Adam Coleman Howard. CAST: Alan Rickman, Polly Walker, Norman Reedus. 1999 DVD

DARK HORSE ★★★1/2 Inspirational tale of a lonely teenage girl who gets into trouble and is sentenced to ten weekends of community service at a horse ranch. Great family entertainment, played out in heart-tugging, sentimental fashion. Not rated. 98m. DIR: David Hemmings. CAST: Ed Begley Jr., Mimi Rogers, Ari Meyers, Donovan Leitch, Samantha Eggar, Tab Hunter. 1992

DARK JOURNEY ★★★ Espionage with a twist. A British and a German spy fall in love in Stockholm during World War I. B&W; 82m. DIR: Victor Saville. CAST: Vivien Leigh, Conrad Veidt, Joan Gardner, Anthony Bushell. 1937

DARK MIRROR, THE ★★★1/2 Olivia de Havilland, who did this sort of thing extremely well, plays twin sisters—one good, one evil—enmeshed in murder. Lew Ayres is the shrink who must divine who is who. Good suspense. B&W; 85m. DIR: Robert Siodmak. CAST: Olivia de Havilland, Lew Ayres, Thomas Mitchell, Richard Long. 1946

DARK NIGHT OF THE SCARECROW ★★★ Despite its hasty beginning that fails to set up a strong premise for the pivotal scene of the movie, this is a chilling film that mixes the supernatural with a moral message. Borrows some ideas from such films as *To Kill a Mockingbird* and *Of Mice and Men*. 100m. DIR: Frank DeFelitta. CAST: Charles Durning, Tonya Crowe, Jocelyn Brando. 1981

DARK OBSESSION ★★ Painful to watch and ultimately pointless, this focuses on a sadistic husband's obsession with controlling his wife. Released with two ratings; NC-17 and R, this contains nudity, profanity, and violence. 97m. DIR: Nick Broomfield.

CAST: Amanda Donohoe, Gabriel Byrne, Douglas Hodge, Ian Carmichael, Michael Hordern. 1990

DARK OF THE SUN (MERCENARIES) (1968) ★★★★ Tough-as-nails mercenary Rod Taylor and his friend Jim Brown lead troops-for-hire deep into hostile guerrilla territory to retrieve a fortune in diamonds, and to rescue (if possible) the inhabitants of a remote European settlement in the Congo. Not rated, but violent and unsettling. 101m. **DIR:** Jack Cardiff. **CAST:** Rod Taylor, Yvette Mimieux, Jim Brown, Peter Carsten, Kenneth More, Andre Morell, Calvin Lockhart. 1968

DARK PASSAGE ★★★ This is an okay Humphrey Bogart vehicle in which the star plays an escaped convict who hides out at Lauren Bacall's apartment while undergoing a face change. The stars are watchable, but the uninspired direction (including some disconcerting subjective camera scenes) and the outlandish plot keep the movie from being a real winner. B&W; 106m. **DIR:** Delmer Daves. **CAST:** Humphrey Bogart, Lauren Bacall, Bruce Bennett, Agnes Moorehead. 1947

DARK PAST, THE ★★ A psychotic killer escapes from prison and a psychologist attempts to convince the hood to give himself up. Lee J. Cobb is marvelous as the psychiatrist and William Holden is wonderful as the bad guy. Nina Foch is top-notch as Holden's moll. A remake of *Blind Alley.* 75m. **DIR:** Rudolph Maté. **CAST:** William Holden, Lee J. Cobb, Nina Foch, Adele Jergens. 1948

DARK PLACES ★★★1/2 Christopher Lee and Joan Collins play two fortune hunters trying to scare away the caretaker (Robert Hardy) of a dead man's mansion so they can get to the bundle of cash stashed in the old house. The film has a sophisticated psychological twist to it that is missing in most horror films, but the cardboard bats on clearly visible wires have got to go! Rated PG for gore and profanity. 91m. **DIR:** Don Sharp. **CAST:** Christopher Lee, Joan Collins, Herbert Lom, Robert Hardy, Jane Birkin, Jean Marsh. 1973

DARK PLANET 🐝 Cheap, poorly written sci-fi featuring a cast that presumably wasn't aware what it was getting into. Rated R for violence. 96m. **DIR:** Albert Magnoli. **CAST:** Paul Mercurio, Michael York, Harley Jane Kozak, Maria Ford. 1996 DVD

DARK PRINCE: THE INTIMATE DIARY OF THE MARQUIS DE SADE 🐝 Ridiculous and boring sleaze from the Roger Corman factory. Available in R and not-rated versions. Both with nudity, sexual situations, and violence. 87/96m. **DIR:** Gwyneth Gibby. **CAST:** Nick Mancuso, Janet Gunn, John Rhys-Davies. 1997

DARK PRINCE: THE INTIMATE TALES OF MARQUIS DE SADE ★★ Nick Mancuso atrociously overacts as the infamous marquis, whose life and writings have been so loosely treated over the years that there's no point even comparing them to the real person. This Roger Corman production is recommended only to die-hard trash addicts. Rated R for nudity, sexual situations, and violence. 88m. **DIR:** Gwyneth Gibby. **CAST:** Nick Mancuso, Janet Gunn, John Rhys-Davies, Charlotte Nielsen. 1996

DARK RIDER 🐝 A corny chase film about a guy on a bike who saves a desert town from small-time gang-

sters. Not rated; contains violence and profanity. 94m. **DIR:** Bob Ivy. **CAST:** Joe Estevez, Doug Shanklin. 1991

DARK RIVER: A FATHER'S REVENGE ★★★ When his daughter dies, a man stands alone to prove the town's leading industry is to blame. This better-than-average TV film covers some familar territory, but contains some exceptional performances. 95m. **DIR:** Michael Pressman. **CAST:** Mike Farrell, Tess Harper, Helen Hunt. 1989

DARK SANITY 🐝 A formerly institutionalized housewife comes home and begins to have dark psychic visions of doom. Not rated; contains violence. 89m. **DIR:** Martin Greene. **CAST:** Aldo Ray. 1982

DARK SECRET OF HARVEST HOME, THE ★★1/2 Novelist-actor Tom Tryon's bewitching story of creeping horror gets fair treatment in this dark and foreboding film of Janus personalities and incantations in picturesque New England. 118m. **DIR:** Leo Penn. **CAST:** Bette Davis, Rosanna Arquette, David Ackroyd, Michael O'Keefe. 1978

DARK SECRETS 🐝 A reporter researching an exposé of a Hugh Hefner–like figure is seduced by his hedonistic world. Heavy-breathing trash. Rated R for nudity, sexual situations, violence, and profanity. 90m. **DIR:** John Bowen. **CAST:** Monique Parent, Justin Carroll, Julie Strain, Joe Estevez. 1996 DVD

DARK SHADOWS (TV SERIES) ★★★ A truly different soap opera, this includes a bona fide vampire—one Barnabas Collins (convincingly portrayed by Jonathan Frid). Volumes 1 to 4, for example, begin with a greedy grave robber who gives the vampire new life, and culminate with the vampire's choosing a local girl for his bride. Mysterious, frightening, and atmospheric. B&W; each. 105–120m. **DIR:** John Sedwick, Lela Swift. **CAST:** Jonathan Frid, Joan Bennett, Kathryn Leigh Scott, John Karlen, Alexandra Moltke. 1966–1967

DARK SIDE, THE ★★★ Extremely seedy street thriller in which a naïve New York cabbie falls for a pretty girl on the run from a pair of ruthless porn-film merchants who specialize in snuff movies. Rated R for brutality and language. 95m. **DIR:** Constantino Magnatta. **CAST:** Tony Galati, Cyndy Preston. 1987

DARK SIDE OF GENIUS ★★1/2 The L.A. art scene is the backdrop of this erotic thriller about a paroled murderer whose recent nude paintings have made him the toast of the town. Finola Hughes stars as an art reporter who senses something more diabolical, delves deeper into the art world, and unleashes a desire within her that might end up costing her life. Rated R for nudity, violence, and adult language. 86m. **DIR:** Phedon Papamichael. **CAST:** Finola Hughes, Glenn Shadix, Patrick Richwood, Moon Zappa. 1994

DARK SIDE OF THE MOON, THE 🐝 A lunar mission crew sheds some light on the moon's shaded half and its relationship to the Bermuda Triangle. Rated R. 96m. **DIR:** D. J. Webster. **CAST:** Will Bledsoe, Alan Blumenfeld, John Diehl, Robert Sampson. 1989

DARK STAR ★★★1/2 This is one of the strangest sci-fi films you are likely to run across. Four astronauts have been in space entirely too long as they seek and destroy unstable planets. Director John Carpenter's first film is very funny in spurts and always crazy. Rated PG because of language. 83m. DIR: John Carpenter. CAST: Dan O'Bannon, Brian Narelle. 1974 DVD

DARK TIDE ★★1/2 Brigitte Bako's atrocious acting mars what might have been a reasonably taut erotic thriller containing—for once—a nice balance between dramatic tension and soft-core groping. She's the catalyst who turns island thugs against researcher Chris Sarandon, who ignores imminent danger while collecting venom from incredibly malicious sea snakes. Rated R for profanity, nudity, violence, rape, and simulated sex. 94m. DIR: Luca Bercovici. CAST: Brigitte Bako, Richard Tyson, Chris Sarandon. 1993

DARK TOWER 💔 A supernatural entity starts killing people. Rated R for violence and profanity. 91m. DIR: Ken Barnett. CAST: Michael Moriarty, Jenny Agutter, Theodore Bikel, Carol Lynley, Anne Lockhart, Kevin McCarthy. 1987

DARK UNIVERSE, THE 💔 Just another *Alien* rip-off as a group of scientists prevent some nasty creatures from turning Earth into their very own intergalactic fast-food franchise. Not rated; contains nudity, violence, and profanity. 83m. DIR: Steve Latshaw. CAST: Blake Pickett, Cherie Scott, Bently Tittle, John Maynard, Paul Austin Sanders. 1993

DARK VICTORY ★★★★ This Warner Bros. release gave Bette Davis one of her best roles, as a headstrong heiress who discovers she has a brain tumor. A successful operation leads to a love affair with her doctor (George Brent). In the midst of all this bliss, Davis learns the tragic truth: surgery was only a halfway measure, and she will die in a year. Sure it's corny. But director Edmund Goulding, Davis, and her costars make it work. B&W; 106m. DIR: Edmund Goulding. CAST: Bette Davis, George Brent, Humphrey Bogart, Ronald Reagan, Geraldine Fitzgerald. 1939 DVD

DARK WATERS ★★1/2 Muddled story of orphaned girl(?), Merle Oberon, and her strange and terrifying experiences in the bayou backwaters of Louisiana is atmospheric, but fails to deliver enough of a story to justify its moody buildup. But the supporting players (along with the misty bogs) really carry the ball in this film. B&W; 90m. DIR: André de Toth. CAST: Merle Oberon, Franchot Tone, Thomas Mitchell, Fay Bainter, Rex Ingram, John Qualen, Elisha Cook Jr. 1944 DVD

DARK WIND ★★★ Investigating a murder on his reservation, Navajo cop Lou Diamond Phillips finds a mystery involving rival tribes, drug smugglers, and government agents. Documentary filmmaker Errol Morris approaches his material matter-of-factly, but a capable cast maintains the suspense and intrigue. Rated R for language and violence. 111m. DIR: Errol Morris. CAST: Lou Diamond Phillips, Gary Farmer, Fred Ward, Guy Boyd. 1991

DARKMAN ★★★★ Sam Raimi's *Darkman* borrows elements from *The Invisible Man, The Phantom of the Opera*, and the Marvel Comics line of brooding superheroes. Liam Neeson is just right as the horribly disfigured scientist who becomes a crime fighter. Some of the sequences in this ultraviolent but inventive movie are so outrageous, they'll make your jaw drop. Rated R for violence and profanity. 96m. DIR:

Sam Raimi. CAST: Liam Neeson, Frances McDormand, Colin Friels, Larry Drake. 1990 DVD

DARKMAN II: THE RETURN OF DURANT ★★ He's back, only without Liam Neeson or a credible plot. Though decidedly brutal and occasionally nonsensical, this has a certain comic-book stylishness that keeps it from completely sinking. Arnold Vosloo steps into the role of the disfigured scientist matching wits against Larry Drake as Durant, the man who messed him up. Released directly to video. Rated R for profanity and violence. 93m. DIR: Bradford May. CAST: Larry Drake, Arnold Vosloo, Kim Delaney, Renee O'Connor. 1995 DVD

DARKMAN III: DIE, DARKMAN, DIE ★★1/2 Any ongoing series potential has been eradicated by this quickie entry, which turns Sam Raimi's tragic superhero into just another wisecracking killer-for-vengeance. Without the outrageous stunts and hyperkinetic visuals that made the first film so memorable, viewers are far more likely to cheer for villain Jeff Fahey. At least he has the talent to properly deliver his florid dialogue! Rated R for violence, profanity, and gore. 87m. DIR: Bradford May. CAST: Jeff Fahey, Darlanne Fluegel, Roxann Biggs, Arnold Vosloo. 1995

•**DARKNESS** ★★ Poor lighting and sound bring down this amateurish film in which vampires overrun a small town. Famed genre director John Carpenter edited the film under a pseudonym. Not rated; contains violence and gore. 90m. DIR: Leif Jonker. CAST: Gary Miller, Michael Gisick. 1994

DARKSIDE, THE ★★ A rookie cab driver picks up a porn star who is being pursued by thugs. There's some good suspense here, but melodramatic acting holds it back. Rated R for nudity, violence, and profanity. 95m. DIR: Constantino Magnatta. CAST: Tony Galati, Cyndy Preston. 1987

DARLING ★★★★ John Schlesinger's direction is first-rate, and Julie Christie gives an Oscar-winning portrayal of a ruthless model who bullies, bluffs, and claws her way to social success, only to find life at the top meaningless. B&W; 122m. DIR: John Schlesinger. CAST: Julie Christie, Dirk Bogarde, Laurence Harvey, Jose Luis de Villalonga. 1965

DARLING LILI ★★★ Dismissed out of hand on original release, and a box office flop to boot, this actually is a charming WWI romance with a Mata Hari–style narrative. Johnny Mercer and Henry Mancini provide the bouncy score. The planes later turned up in Roger Corman's *Von Richthofen and Brown*. Rated G. 136m. DIR: Blake Edwards. CAST: Julie Andrews, Rock Hudson, Jeremy Kemp, Lance Percival. 1970

•**DARWIN CONSPIRACY, THE** ★★ Yet another campy sci-fi outing in which an experiment to increase the intelligence of man is tested on an unwilling human guinea pig. More of the same. Rated PG. 90m. DIR: Winrich Kolbe. CAST: Jason Brooks, Robert Floyd, Stacy Haiduk, Kevin Tighe. 1998

D.A.R.Y.L. ★★★★ In this delightful science-fiction film, Barret Oliver stars as a boy adopted by Mary Beth Hurt and Michael McKean. He turns out to be a perfect little fellow ... maybe a little too perfect. *D.A.R.Y.L.* is a film the whole family can enjoy. Rated PG for violence and light profanity. 99m. DIR:

Simon Wincer. **CAST:** Barret Oliver, Mary Beth Hurt, Michael McKean, Josef Sommer. **1985**

DAS BOOT (THE BOAT) ★★★★ During World War II, forty thousand young Germans served aboard Nazi submarines. Only ten thousand survived. This West German film masterpiece re-creates the tension and claustrophobic conditions of forty-three men assigned to a U-boat in 1941. This is the English-dubbed version. 150m. **DIR:** Wolfgang Petersen. **CAST:** Jurgen Prochnow, Herbert Gronemeyer. **1981 DVD**

DATE WITH AN ANGEL ★ A beautiful angel loses control of her wings and lands in the arms of a mortal. Rated PG for profanity. 105m. **DIR:** Tom McLoughlin. **CAST:** Michael E. Knight, Phoebe Cates, Emmanuelle Beart, David Dukes. **1987**

DATE WITH JUDY, A ★★1/2 Ho-hum musical comedy about rival teenagers Jane Powell and Elizabeth Taylor fighting for the affections of Robert Stack. High point is Carmen Miranda teaching Wallace Beery to dance. 113m. **DIR:** Richard Thorpe. **CAST:** Jane Powell, Wallace Beery, Elizabeth Taylor, Carmen Miranda, Robert Stack, Xavier Cugat, Scotty Beckett, Leon Ames. **1948**

DAUGHTER OF DARKNESS ★★★1/2 Lovely Mia Sara follows her bad dreams back to her hometown of Budapest, where she learns that her relatives actually hang from the family tree. They're vampires. Rated R for horror and violence. 93m. **DIR:** Stuart Gordon. **CAST:** Mia Sara, Anthony Perkins, Jack Coleman, Robert Reynolds. **1987**

DAUGHTER OF DR. JEKYLL ★ Okay horror film about a girl (Gloria Talbott) who thinks she's inherited the famous dual personality. B&W; 71m. **DIR:** Edgar G. Ulmer. **CAST:** Gloria Talbott, John Agar, Arthur Shields, John Dierkes. **1957**

DAUGHTER OF HORROR 🙋 The longest sixty minutes of your life. B&W; 60m. **DIR:** John Parker. **CAST:** Adrienne Barrett, Bruno Ve Sota. **1955**

•**DAUGHTER OF THE DRAGON** ★★1/2 Dr. Fu Manchu returns yet again to wreak vengeance on his enemies, but this time he forces his daughter Ling Moy to assist him. After the evil mastermind's death Ling Moy embraces her father's hate-driven ways and continues in his murderous footsteps until permanently stopped by a lover. Sliding panels, torture, sacrifice, and hairbreadth escapes plus touching performances by Anna May Wong and Sessue Hayakawa highlight this last Paramount entry into the saga of Sax Rohmer's twisted genius. B&W; 70m. **DIR:** Lloyd Corrigan. **CAST:** Anna May Wong, Warner Oland, Bramwell Fletcher, Sessue Hayakawa, Frances Dade. **1931**

DAUGHTERS OF DARKNESS ★★★ Slick, handsomely mounted, and often genuinely eerie updating of the Elisabeth Bathory legend. Amid kinky trappings and soft-focus camera work, a wealthy woman vampire seduces a young couple at a European spa. Dated, but still striking and original. Rated R. Available in 87- and 96-m. versions of varying explicitness. **DIR:** Harry Kumel. **CAST:** Delphine Seyrig, Daniele Ouimet, John Karlen, Fons Rademakers. **1971 DVD**

DAUGHTERS OF SATAN 🙋 Modern-day witches. Rated R for nudity and violence. 96m. **DIR:** Hollingsworth Morse. **CAST:** Tom Selleck, Barra Grant. **1972**

DAUGHTERS OF THE DUST ★★★★ Writer-director Julie Dash's absolutely gorgeous motion picture is set in 1902 on one of the sea islands off Georgia and North Carolina. It plays like a series of vintage photographs set to music combined with dramatic sequences. The story centers around a final ceremony being held prior to an African-American family's journey North. Fascinating. Not rated, the film has no objectionable material. 113m. **DIR:** Julie Dash. **CAST:** Adisa Anderson, Cheryl Lynn Bruce, Cora Lee Day. **1992**

DAVE ★★★★ Moments of sheer hilarity elevate this Capra-esque fantasy, in which an actor is hired to impersonate the president. When the chief executive has a heart attack, our hero is coerced into continuing the masquerade—and this allows him to start turning the country around. Kevin Kline is superb in a dual role. This one will tickle your funny bone and warm your heart. Rated PG for profanity and suggested sex. 100m. **DIR:** Ivan Reitman. **CAST:** Kevin Kline, Sigourney Weaver, Frank Langella, Kevin Dunn, Ving Rhames, Ben Kingsley, Charles Grodin, Arnold Schwarzenegger, Jay Leno, Oliver Stone. **1993 DVD**

DAVID AND BATHSHEBA ★★ Mediocre biblical epic with a polished cast nearly defeated by mundane script. Normally reliable director Henry King can't breathe life into this soporific soap opera. 116m. **DIR:** Henry King. **CAST:** Gregory Peck, Susan Hayward, Raymond Massey, Kieron Moore. **1951**

DAVID AND LISA ★★★1/2 Mentally disturbed teenagers (Keir Dullea and Janet Margolin) meet and develop a sensitive emotional attachment while institutionalized. Abetted by Howard DaSilva as their understanding doctor, Dullea and Margolin make this study highly watchable. Independently produced, this one was a sleeper. B&W; 94m. **DIR:** Frank Perry. **CAST:** Keir Dullea, Janet Margolin, Howard DaSilva, Neva Patterson, Clifton James. **1962 DVD**

DAVID COPPERFIELD ★★★★1/2 A first-rate production of Charles Dickens's rambling novel about a young man's adventures in nineteenth-century England. W. C. Fields and Edna May Oliver are standouts in an all-star cast. B&W; 100m. **DIR:** George Cukor. **CAST:** Freddie Bartholomew, Frank Lawton, Lionel Barrymore, W. C. Fields, Edna May Oliver, Basil Rathbone. **1935**

•**DAVID HOLZMAN'S DIARY** ★★★★ Viewers who think that indie films were invented in the 1990s should run, not walk, to see this little gem. In a parody of cinema verité, a young filmmaker in New York decides to put his entire life on camera in the hope that it will become clearer to him. Instead, he only infuriates everyone around him. It's so well done that you may find yourself thinking it's real, but it's all scripted and acted. Not rated; contains no objectionable material. B&W; 74m. **DIR:** Jim McBride. **CAST:** L. M. "Kit" Carson, Eileen Dietz, Louise Levine. **1968**

DAVINCI'S WAR ★★ Ex–Special Services agent recruits a hit man to help rout the CIA-sponsored drug smuggling ring responsible for the death of his sister. Standard shoot-'em-up with a bit of a message. Rated R for violence, sex, and profanity. 94m. **DIR:** Raymond Martino. **CAST:** Joey Travolta, Michael Nouri, Vanity, James Russo, Sam Jones. 1993 DVD

DAVY CROCKETT AND THE RIVER PIRATES ★★★ Fess Parker, as idealized Davy Crockett, takes on Big Mike Fink (Jeff York) in a keelboat race and tangles with Indians in the second Walt Disney–produced Davy Crockett feature composed of two television episodes. Thoroughly enjoyable and full of the kind of boyhood images that Disney productions evoked so successfully in the late 1940s and '50s. Fun for the whole family. 81m. **DIR:** Norman Foster. **CAST:** Fess Parker, Buddy Ebsen, Kenneth Tobey, Jeff York. 1956

DAVY CROCKETT, KING OF THE WILD FRONTIER ★★★1/2 Finely played by all involved, this is actually a compilation of three episodes that appeared originally on television and were then released theatrically. 88m. **DIR:** Norman Foster. **CAST:** Fess Parker, Buddy Ebsen, Hans Conried, Kenneth Tobey. 1955

DAWN OF THE DEAD ★★★★ This film is the sequel to *Night of the Living Dead.* The central characters are three men and one woman who try to escape from man-eating corpses. As a horror movie, it's a masterpiece, but if you have a weak stomach, avoid this one. Rated R. 126m. **DIR:** George A. Romero. **CAST:** David Emge, Ken Foree, Scott Reiniger, Tom Savini. 1979 DVD

DAWN OF THE MUMMY 🎬 Archaeologists open up an accursed tomb. Not rated; contains graphic violence. 93m. **DIR:** Frank Agrama. **CAST:** Brenda King. 1981

DAWN ON THE GREAT DIVIDE ★★★ With a bigger budget than usual and a story with more plot twists than the average B Western, the result is a good shoot-'em-up in the series vein. Buck Jones, of course, dominates as the two-fisted leader of a wagon train who takes on Indians, bad guys, and corrupt officials with equal aplomb. It was the last movie made by Jones, who died heroically trying to save lives during a fire at Boston's Coconut Grove on November 28, 1942. B&W; 63m. **DIR:** Howard Bretherton. **CAST:** Buck Jones, Raymond Hatton, Rex Bell, Mona Barrie. 1942

DAWN PATROL, THE ★★★★ Basil Rathbone is excellent as a commanding officer of a frontline British squadron during World War I who has no choice but to order raw replacements into the air against veteran Germans. Errol Flynn and David Niven shine as gentlemen at war. A fine film. B&W; 103m. **DIR:** Edmund Goulding. **CAST:** Errol Flynn, Basil Rathbone, David Niven, Melville Cooper, Barry Fitzgerald, Donald Crisp. 1938

DAWN RIDER ★★ John Wayne is out for revenge in this formula B Western. His loving father is killed during a robbery, and it's up to a gangly, slightly stilted Wayne to get the bad guys. B&W; 56m. **DIR:** Robert N. Bradbury. **CAST:** John Wayne, Marion Burns, Yakima Canutt, Reed Howes. 1935 DVD

DAWNING, THE ★★★1/2 Leisurely paced coming-of-age film focuses on a naïve Irish girl whose life changes when she meets a renegade IRA leader. Seaside shots are spectacular as well as haunting. Equivalent to a PG for violence. 97m. **DIR:** Robert

Knights. **CAST:** Anthony Hopkins, Rebecca Pidgeon, Trevor Howard, Jean Simmons. 1988

DAWSON PATROL, THE ★ A Royal Canadian Mounted Police dogsled expedition turns tragic in this feeble docudrama set at the turn of the century. Not rated; contains violence. 75m. **DIR:** Peter Kelly. **CAST:** George R. Robertson, Tim Henry, Neil Dainaro, James B. Douglas. 1985

DAY AFTER, THE ★★★★ Excellent made-for-TV movie special received much advance publicity because of its timely topic: the effects of a nuclear war. Jason Robards Jr. plays a hospital doctor who treats many of the victims after the nuclear attack. 126m. **DIR:** Nicholas Meyer. **CAST:** Jason Robards Jr., JoBeth Williams, Steve Guttenberg, John Cullum, John Lithgow. 1983

DAY AND THE HOUR ★★ Drab war drama, set in Nazi-occupied France, has widow Simone Signoret involved with American paratrooper Stuart Whitman. B&W; 115m. **DIR:** René Clement. **CAST:** Simone Signoret, Stuart Whitman, Genevieve Page, Michel Piccoli, Reggie Nalder. 1963

•**DAY AT THE BEACH** ★★★ A group of friends travels to an empty beach house and breaks in, helping themselves to its luxurious accommodations. The resident returns and is held hostage. The group finds out that their tied-up host is a member of the mob, and they have a lot more on their hands than they expected. Darkly humorous at times, this movie is only hindered by low production values, and the occasionally dragging plot. Not rated; may be inappropriate for children. 93m. **DIR:** Nick Veronis. **CAST:** Jane Adams, Patrick Fitzgerald, Neal Jones, Catherine Kellner, Joe Ragno, Paul Gleason, Nick Veronis. 1998

DAY AT THE RACES, A ★★★1/2 The Marx Brothers—Groucho, Harpo, and Chico, that is—were still at the peak of their fame in this MGM musical-comedy. Though not as unrelentingly hilarious and outrageous as the films they made at Paramount with Zeppo, it is nonetheless enjoyable. B&W; 111m. **DIR:** Sam Wood. **CAST:** The Marx Brothers, Allan Jones, Maureen O'Sullivan, Margaret Dumont. 1937

DAY FOR NIGHT ★★★★★ One of the best of the film-within-a-film movies ever made, this work by the late François Truffaut captures the poetry and energy of the creative artist at his peak. In French with English subtitles. Beware of the badly dubbed English version. Rated PG. 120m. **DIR:** François Truffaut. **CAST:** Jacqueline Bisset, Jean-Pierre Léaud, François Truffaut. 1973

DAY IN OCTOBER, A ★★1/2 WWII drama set in Nazi-occupied Denmark, about efforts to evacuate Danish Jews into neutral Sweden. Competently made film seems overly familiar, despite the efforts of a strong cast. Rated PG. 97m. **DIR:** Kenneth Madsen. **CAST:** D. B. Sweeney, Kelly Wolf, Tovah Feldshuh. 1992

DAY IN THE COUNTRY, A ★★★★ A young girl seduced on an afternoon outing returns to the scene fourteen years later, an unhappily married woman. Jean Renoir's lyrical impressionistic tragedy is based on a story by Guy de Maupassant. Mesmerizing cinematography by Claude Renoir and Henri Cartier-Bresson. In French with English subtitles. 40m.

DIR: Jean Renoir. **CAST:** Sylvia Bataille, George Darnoux. **1935**

DAY IN THE DEATH OF JOE EGG, A ★★★ This competent British production features the wonderful Alan Bates and Janet Suzman as a married couple whose small son, physically and mentally disabled since birth, causes them to consider euthanasia. Doesn't sound too funny, but in a strange way it is. 106m. **DIR:** Peter Medak. **CAST:** Alan Bates, Janet Suzman, Peter Bowles. **1972**

DAY MY PARENTS RAN AWAY, THE ★★★ Bobby Jacoby plays a teen who has been abandoned by parents in search of a better life. Left to his own devices and their credit cards, he indulges in his wildest fantasies, throwing parties, letting the laundry pile up, and feasting on TV dinners. Then reality hits, and he decides that he wants his folks back, but they don't want to come home. Rated PG for some adult situations. 95m. **DIR:** Martin Nicholson. **CAST:** Matt Frewer, Bobby Jacoby, Brigid Conley Walsh, Blair Brown, Martin Mull. **1993**

DAY OF ATONEMENT ★★ A complicated plot, derivative situations, and cardboard characters do little to distinguish this weak mobster effort about warring factions in Miami. Even the high-caliber cast can't save it, despite a noble effort from Christopher Walken as a vicious drug lord. Rated R for violence and language. 119m. **DIR:** Alexandre Arcady. **CAST:** Christopher Walken, Jennifer Beals, Jill Clayburgh, Richard Berry, Roger Hanin. **1993**

DAY OF JUDGMENT, A ★★1/2 After the local preacher leaves for lack of a congregation (maybe because none of them can act), the nasties of a small town are taught their lesson by the grim reaper. Not rated; contains violence. 101m. **DIR:** C.D.H. Reynolds. **CAST:** William T. Hicks. **1981**

DAY OF THE ANIMALS ♥ Nature goes nuts after the Earth's ozone layer is destroyed. Rated R for violence, profanity, and gore. 98m. **DIR:** William Girdler. **CAST:** Christopher George, Lynda Day George, Richard Jaeckel, Leslie Nielsen, Michael Ansara, Ruth Roman. **1977 DVD**

DAY OF THE ASSASSIN ♥ Chuck Connors plays a James Bond–type hero in this dull action film. Not rated; contains violence and profanity. 94m. **DIR:** Brian Trenchard-Smith, Carlos Vasallo. **CAST:** Chuck Connors, Glenn Ford, Richard Roundtree, Jorge Rivero, Henry Silva, Andres Garcia. **1979**

DAY OF THE DEAD ★★ The third film in George A. Romero's *Dead* series doesn't hold up to its predecessors. Like earlier films in the series, *Day of the Dead* portrays graphic scenes of cannibalism, dismemberment, and other gory carnage. Unlike the other films, this one has no truly likable characters to root for. Not rated; contains scenes of violence. 100m. **DIR:** George A. Romero. **CAST:** Lori Cardille, Terry Alexander, Richard Liberty, Joseph Pilato. **1985 DVD**

DAY OF THE DOLPHIN, THE ★★★ Fine film centering on a research scientist (George C. Scott) who teaches a pair of dolphins to speak, and how they're kidnapped and used in an assassination attempt. Rated PG for language. 104m. **DIR:** Mike Nichols.

CAST: George C. Scott, Trish Van Devere, Paul Sorvino, Fritz Weaver. **1973**

DAY OF THE JACKAL, THE ★★★★ Edward Fox is a cunning assassin roaming Europe in hopes of a crack at General Charles de Gaulle. High suspense and a marvelous performance by Fox underscore a strong story line. Rated PG. 141m. **DIR:** Fred Zinnemann. **CAST:** Edward Fox, Alan Badel, Tony Britton, Cyril Cusack. **1973 DVD**

DAY OF THE LOCUST, THE ★★★★1/2 This drama is both extremely depressing and spellbinding. It shows the unglamorous side of Hollywood in the 1930s. The people who don't succeed in the entertainment capital are the focus of the film. Rated R. 144m. **DIR:** John Schlesinger. **CAST:** Donald Sutherland, Karen Black, Burgess Meredith, Bo Hopkins, William Atherton. **1975**

DAY OF THE TRIFFIDS, THE ★★★1/2 This British film has triffids—alien plants—arriving on Earth during a meteor shower. The shower blinds most of the Earth's people. Then the plants grow, begin walking, and eat humans. This one will grow on you. 95m. **DIR:** Steve Sekely. **CAST:** Howard Keel, Nicole Maurey, Janette Scott, Kieron Moore, Mervyn Johns. **1963**

DAY OF THE WARRIOR ♥ Impenetrably overplotted and underdressed sex-and-action nonsense from Andy Sidaris, the poor man's Russ Meyer. Rated R for nudity, sexual situations, violence, and profanity. 97m. **DIR:** Andy Sidaris. **CAST:** Kevin Light, Cristian Letelier, Julie Strain, Julie K. Smith, Shae Marks, Marcus Bagwell. **1997**

DAY OF WRATH ★★★1/2 Slow-moving, intriguing story of a young woman who marries an elderly preacher but falls in love with his son. Visually effective and well acted by all the principals, this film relies too much on symbolism but is still worthy as a study of hysteria and the motivations behind fear. B&W; 98m. **DIR:** Carl Dreyer. **CAST:** Lisbeth Movin, Thorkild Roose. **1944**

DAY ONE ★★★ Television tackles the creation of the atomic bomb as American scientists work on the Manhattan Project. Stellar cast helps this true story, which is rich in production values and benefits from a riveting screenplay. Not rated. 141m. **DIR:** Joseph Sargent. **CAST:** Brian Dennehy, David Strathairn, Michael Tucker, Richard Dysart, David Ogden Stiers. **1989**

DAY THAT SHOOK THE WORLD, THE ★★★ A slow start can't reduce one's fascination with the shocking incident—the assassination of Austria's Archduke Ferdinand and his wife—that resulted in World War I. Rated R for violence, including disturbing hunting scenes and graphic torture footage. 111m. **DIR:** Veljko Bulajic. **CAST:** Christopher Plummer, Maximilian Schell, Florinda Bolkan. **1978**

DAY THE EARTH CAUGHT FIRE, THE ★★★★ Veteran director Val Guest helmed this near-classic film concerning the fate of the Earth following simultaneous nuclear explosions at both poles, sending the planet on a collision course with the sun. Incredibly realistic production is unsettling, with Edward Judd perfectly cast as an Everyman caught up in the mass panic and hysteria. B&W; 99m. DIR: Val Guest. CAST: Edward Judd, Janet Munro, Leo McKern. 1962

DAY THE EARTH STOOD STILL, THE ★★★★ *The Day the Earth Stood Still* is one of the better science-fiction films. Even though some of the space gimmicks are campy and not up to today's standards of special effects, the film holds up well because of a good adult script and credible performances by Michael Rennie and Patricia Neal. B&W; 92m. DIR: Robert Wise. CAST: Michael Rennie, Patricia Neal, Hugh Marlowe, Sam Jaffe, Billy Gray. 1951

DAY THE SUN TURNED COLD, THE ★★★1/2 Intriguing mystery-drama about the police captain in a bleak town in northern China trying to investigate a 10-year-old case when a young man accuses his mother of having murdered his father. Well-filmed tale may be too somber for casual viewers, but rewarding for the patient. Not rated. In Chinese with English subtitles. 99m. DIR: Yim Ho. CAST: Siqin Gowa, Tuo Zhong Hua, Li Hu. 1994

DAY THE WORLD ENDED, THE ★★ After a nuclear holocaust, a handful of survivors battle each other and the local mutant monster. Minor melodrama featuring one of Roger Corman's cheaper monster suits. B&W; 82m. DIR: Roger Corman. CAST: Richard Denning, Lori Nelson, Mike Connors. 1956

DAY TIME ENDED, THE ♥ Grade-Z sci-fi clunker, about nature gone wild. 79m. DIR: John "Bud" Cardos. CAST: Jim Davis, Dorothy Malone, Chris Mitchum. 1980

DAYBREAK (1993) ★★★★ Writer-director Stephen Tolkin's cautionary drama, based on Alan Bowne's play *Beirut*, takes place in a decrepit New York City of the near future, controlled by a fascistic government that has made social outcasts of those stricken with an AIDS-like plague. One young woman (Moira Kelly), dismayed by the Orwellian youth patrols, contacts underground rebels who spirit diseased victims to safer quarters. Rated R for nudity, simulated sex, profanity, and violence. 91m. DIR: Stephen Tolkin. CAST: Cuba Gooding Jr., Moira Kelly, Omar Epps, Alice Drummond, Martha Plimpton, John Savage. 1993

DAYDREAMER, THE (1966) ★★★ This *Children's Treasures* presentation combines live action with puppetry to bring a young Hans Christian Andersen and his tales to life. 80m. DIR: Jules Bass. CAST: Paul O'Keefe, Burl Ives, Tallulah Bankhead, Terry-Thomas, Victor Borge, Ed Wynn, Patty Duke, Boris Karloff, Ray Bolger, Hayley Mills, Jack Gilford, Margaret Hamilton. 1966

DAYDREAMER, THE (1970) (LE DISTRAIT) ★★★ This early vehicle for popular French comedian Pierre Richard, who also wrote and directed, is a hodgepodge of gags in varying comic styles. He plays a bumbler who lands a job at an ad agency and nearly destroys the place. In French with English subtitles. 80m. DIR: Pierre Richard. CAST: Pierre Richard, Bernard Blier, Maria Pacome, Marie-Christine Barrault. 1970

DAYLIGHT ★★★ Working-class Sylvester Stallone, once an emergency-medical-services chief, happens to be on hand when a spectacular accident traps people inside New York's Holland Tunnel. The survivors overcome numerous obstacles while trying to find a way out before the tunnel collapses. Rated PG-13 for violence, profanity, and dramatic intensity. 115m. DIR: Rob Cohen. CAST: Sylvester Stallone, Amy Brenneman, Viggo Mortensen, Dan Hedaya, Jay O. Sanders, Karen Young, Claire Bloom. 1996 DVD

•DAYS AND NIGHTS IN THE FOREST ★★★★ In one of his best films, Satyajit Ray presents a deceptively simple tale of four city men vacationing in the country, where they meet a variety of women who draw out their personalities. Delicately woven, this is a rewarding film for those up to its deliberate pace. In Hindi with English subtitles. B&W; 115m. DIR: Satyajit Ray. CAST: Soumitra Chatterjee, Sharmila Tagore. 1969

DAYS OF GLORY ★★ A young Gregory Peck (in his first film) and a cast of practically unknown European actors try their darndest to make this story of guerrilla warfare on the Russian front work, but the end result is limp and unconvincing. B&W; 86m. DIR: Jacques Tourneur. CAST: Gregory Peck, Tamara Toumanova, Alan Reed, Maria Palmer. 1944

DAYS OF HEAVEN ★★★★1/2 Each frame looks like a page torn from an exquisitely beautiful picture book. The film begins in the slums of Chicago, where Bill (Richard Gere) works in a steel mill. He decides to take Abby (Brooke Adams), his girl, and Linda (Linda Manz), his young sister, to the Texas Panhandle to work in the wheat fields at harvest time. That's the beginning of an idyllic year that ends in tragedy. Rated PG. 95m. DIR: Terence Malick. CAST: Richard Gere, Brooke Adams, Sam Shepard, Linda Manz. 1978 DVD

DAYS OF OLD CHEYENNE ★★★★ Don Barry accepts the job of town marshal from Big Bill Harmon (William Haade) in the belief Harmon is interested in maintaining law and order. Above-average oater. B&W; 56m. DIR: Elmer Clifton. CAST: Don Barry, Emmet Lynn, Lynn Merrick, William Haade. 1943

DAYS OF THRILLS AND LAUGHTER ★★★1/2 An homage to classic silent-film comedians and daredevils, this collection of clips includes, among other winners, Charlie Chaplin's dinner-roll dance from *Gold Rush*. A worthwhile nostalgia film. B&W; 93m. DIR: Robert Youngson. CAST: Buster Keaton, Stan Laurel, Oliver Hardy, Charlie Chaplin, Harold Lloyd, Douglas Fairbanks Sr., The Keystone Kops. 1961

DAYS OF THUNDER ★★★★ Star Tom Cruise and director Tony Scott take their *Top Gun* tactics to the racetrack in this fast-car fantasy set during the Daytona 500, and the result is remarkably satisfying. Screenwriter Robert Towne takes the standard story and infuses it with a richness that recalls the golden age of Hollywood. Rated PG-13 for profanity and violence. 108m. DIR: Tony Scott. CAST: Tom Cruise, Robert Duvall, Nicole Kidman, Randy Quaid, Michael Rooker, Cary Elwes. 1990 DVD

DAYS OF WINE AND ROSES, THE (1958) ★★★1/2 Unpolished but still excellent television original from which the 1962 film was adapted. Cliff Robertson is the up-and-coming executive and Piper Laurie, his pretty wife, whose lives are shattered by alcoholism. Written for the *Playhouse 90* series, it is introduced by Julie Harris and framed with interviews with the featured players. B&W; 90m. DIR: John

Frankenheimer. **CAST:** Cliff Robertson, Piper Laurie. **1958**

DAYS OF WINE AND ROSES (1962) ★★★1/2 In this saddening film, Jack Lemmon and Lee Remick shatter the misconceptions about middle-class alcoholism. B&W; 117m. **DIR:** Blake Edwards. **CAST:** Jack Lemmon, Lee Remick, Charles Bickford, Jack Klugman. **1962**

DAYS OF WRATH ★★★ One of the best non-Leone spaghetti Westerns. A veteran gunfighter teaches the town bastard how to use a gun. He gains his self-respect and the fear of the townspeople. All goes well until the gunfighter kills his student's only friend, the town sheriff. The student turns on the teacher, putting to use all that he's been taught. A strong performance by veteran Hollywood heavy Lee Van Cleef. Rated PG. 97m. **DIR:** Tonino Valerii. **CAST:** Lee Van Cleef, Giuliano Gemma, Walter Rilla, Crista Linder, Piero Lulli, Andrea Bosic. **1967**

DAYTON'S DEVILS ★★ Leslie Nielsen leads a group of has-beens and ex-cons—or, as the video box says, "a melting pot of losers"—in a robbery of an air force base bank. 107m. **DIR:** Jack Shea. **CAST:** Leslie Nielsen, Rory Calhoun, Lainie Kazan, Barry Sadler, Georg Stanford Brown. **1968**

DAYTRIPPERS, THE ★★★1/2 After a Long Island housewife finds an apparent love note to her husband, she wedges herself into the family station wagon with her mother, father, sister, and sister's boyfriend to search Manhattan for the suspect spouse. Their misadventures provide plenty of comic relief. The closer they get to solving their mystery, the more they learn the truth about themselves. Rated R for language and mature themes. 87m. **DIR:** Greg Mottola. **CAST:** Hope Davis, Anne Meara, Parker Posey, Pat McNamara, Liev Schreiber, Stanley Tucci. **1996 DVD**

DAZED AND CONFUSED ★★★1/2 Writer-director Richard Linklater shows how the final day of high school in 1976 affects the outgoing seniors and incoming freshmen. Contains occasional truths and a lot of heart. Rated R for profanity and drug use. 103m. **DIR:** Richard Linklater. **CAST:** Jason London, Rory Cochrane, Adam Goldberg, Anthony Rapp, Sasha Jenson, Milla Jovovich, Michelle Burke. **1993 DVD**

D.C. CAB 🖤 Take the bus. Rated R. 99m. **DIR:** Joel Schumacher. **CAST:** Gary Busey, Mr. T, Adam Baldwin, Max Gail. **1983**

D-DAY THE SIXTH OF JUNE ★★ Slow-moving account of the Normandy invasion in World War II. Story concentrates on Allied officers Robert Taylor's and Richard Todd's romantic and professional problems. 106m. **DIR:** Henry Koster. **CAST:** Robert Taylor, Richard Todd, Dana Wynter, Edmond O'Brien. **1956**

DEAD, THE ★★★★★ John Huston's final bow is an elegant adaptation of James Joyce's short story about a party given by three women for a group of their dearest friends. During the evening, conversation drifts to those people, now dead, who have had a great influence on the lives of the guests and hostesses at the party. Huston, who died before the film was released, seems to be speaking to us from beyond the grave. This is one of his best. Rated PG. 81m. **DIR:** John Huston. **CAST:** Anjelica Huston, Donal

McCann, Ingrid Craigie, Dan O'Herlihy, Marie Kean, Donal Donnelly, Sean McClory. **1987**

DEAD AGAIN ★★★★★ A highly stylized suspense thriller in which a Los Angeles detective is hired to uncover the identity of a woman who has lost her memory. He enlists the aid of a hypnotist, who discovers that the woman may have led a previous life that may have involved the detective. Either way, someone is out to kill them both. Rated R for violence. 107m. **DIR:** Kenneth Branagh. **CAST:** Kenneth Branagh, Emma Thompson, Andy Garcia, Derek Jacobi, Hanna Schygulla, Robin Williams, Campbell Scott. **1991 DVD**

DEAD AHEAD ★★★ In this made-for-cable original, a woman's son is taken hostage, and she stalks the band of criminals through the wilderness. Good action and plot, but the acting is a little stiff. Not rated; contains violence. 95m. **DIR:** Stuart Cooper. **CAST:** Stephanie Zimbalist, Peter Onorati, Sarah Chalke. **1996**

DEAD AHEAD: THE EXXON VALDEZ DISASTER ★★★★ First-rate advocacy cinema from scripter Michael Baker, who documents the ecological disaster that resulted when the Exxon Valdez dumped 11 million gallons of oil into Alaska's Prince William Sound. John Heard, as the site's leading environmental champion, is appropriately outraged; Christopher Lloyd has the tougher role as the Exxon bureaucrat sacrificed as the incident's scapegoat. 88m. **DIR:** Paul Seed. **CAST:** John Heard, Christopher Lloyd, Ron Frazier, Michael Murphy, Rip Torn. **1992**

DEAD AIR ★★★1/2 A disc jockey receives harassing phone calls, then several female acquaintances turn up dead, and he is the prime suspect. A well-scripted mystery that will keep you guessing until the end. Not rated; contains violence and suggested sex. 93m. **DIR:** Fred Walton. **CAST:** Gregory Hines, Debrah Farentino, Beau Starr, Gloria Reuben, Laura Harrington, Michael Harris. **1994**

DEAD ALIVE ★★★1/2 Over-the-top New Zealand gorefest is so disgusting, it's hilarious. When shy and introverted Timothy Balme's doting mother is bitten by a Sumatran rat monkey, she begins to exhibit zombielike traits, including eating the flesh of the undead. Before you know it, the house is zombie central, and the lengths Balme must go through to alleviate the problem are extreme, to say the least. Rated R for violence, gore, and language; unrated version contains buckets more gore. 85m. /97m. **DIR:** Peter Jackson. **CAST:** Timothy Balme, Diana Penalver, Elizabeth Moody. **1992 DVD**

DEAD AND BURIED ★★ This muddled venture by the creators of *Alien* (Ronald Shusett and Dan O'Bannon) involves a series of gory murders, and the weird part is that the victims seem to be coming back to life. The puzzle is resolved during the suspenseful, eerie ending—definitely the high point of the movie. Rated R for violence. 92m. **DIR:** Gary A. Sherman. **CAST:** James Farentino, Melody Anderson, Jack Albertson, Dennis Redfield. **1981**

DEAD BADGE ★★★ Intense made-for-cable thriller about a rookie cop who is assigned a dead cop's badge. It's supposed to be an honor, but rookie Dan Sampson (Brian Wimmer) finds it a curse. When he begins to look into the circumstances behind the cop's death, Sampson's investigation is cut short by some crooked cops who suggest that he leave things alone. Good cast pumps life into this good cop–bad cop scenario. Rated R for violence. 95m. DIR: Douglas Barr. CAST: Brian Wimmer, M. Emmet Walsh, James B. Sikking, Yaphet Kotto, Olympia Dukakis. 1994

DEAD-BANG ★★1/2 Don Johnson stars as real-life L.A. detective Jerry Buck, whose investigation into the murder of a police officer leads to the discovery of a chilling conspiracy. Johnson's strong performance is supported by an excellent cast. John Frankenheimer directs with authority and adds texture to the familiar plot. Rated R for violence, profanity, nudity, and simulated sex. 109m. DIR: John Frankenheimer. CAST: Don Johnson, Penelope Ann Miller, William Forsythe, Bob Balaban, Tim Reid. 1988 DVD

DEAD BEAT ★★★ Dead girls tell no tales—at least that is what local heartthrob Kit and his former girl-friend are hoping. When a female high-school student disappears, Kit knows what happened to her. Keeping it a secret from Kit's new girlfriend is going to be murder. Sara Gilbert and Natasha Gregson Wagner shine as the two women in Kit's life, while Bruce Ramsay shows a flair for dark comedy as Kit. Rated R for language. 94m. DIR: Adam Dubov. CAST: Bruce Ramsay, Natasha Gregson Wagner, Sara Gilbert, Balthazar Getty. 1994

DEAD BOYZ CAN'T FLY 🐝 This absolute nonsense about a pathetic gang of hoodlums tries to make a statement about violence and urban decay but gets lost in its own chaos. Not rated; contains violence. 102m. DIR: Howard Winters. CAST: David John, Brad Friedman, Delia Sheppard. 1990

DEAD CALM ★★★1/2 A married couple (Sam Neill and Nicole Kidman) are terrorized at sea by a maniac (Billy Zane) in this intelligent, stylish thriller from Australian director Phillip Noyce. Although impressive overall, the movie has some unnecessarily explicit scenes. A near classic. Rated R for violence, profanity, nudity, and simulated sex. 95m. DIR: Phillip Noyce. CAST: Sam Neill, Nicole Kidman, Billy Zane. 1989 DVD

DEAD CENTER ★★ Derivative thriller finds punk Justin Lazard caught between some rock and a hard place when a drug deal turns sour. He agrees to be trained by the government as a professional assassin. The only twist here is that Lazard is being set up for a fall. Rated R for violence, language, and nudity. 90m. DIR: Steve Carver. CAST: Justin Lazard, Rachel York, Eb Lottimer. 1994

DEAD CERTAIN ★★ A psycho killer (Brad Dourif yet again) is tracked by an equally seedy cop. Better made than average, but that doesn't help the tired plot. Not rated, but an R equivalent for violence and sexuality. 93m. DIR: Anders Palm. CAST: Francesco Quinn, Brad Dourif, Karen Russell. 1990

DEAD COLD ★★ When a couple travels to a snowy wilderness to celebrate their second honeymoon, they are surprised by a mysterious traveler who arrives at their door. Ludicrous suspense film is low on surprises and high on camp. Rated R for violence,

profanity, and nudity. 91m. DIR: Kurt Anderson. CAST: Lysette Anthony, Chris Mulkey, Peter Dobson. 1995

DEAD CONNECTION ★★1/2 Pedestrian thriller fails to live up to its pedigree. Instead, this is just another shaggy-dog story about a phone-sex killer and the hard-as-nails detective (Michael Madsen) intent on catching him. Lisa Bonet is the reporter who knows a hot story when she sees one. Madsen's moody performance is a treat. Rated R for violence, nudity, and language. 93m. DIR: Nigel Dick. CAST: Michael Madsen, Lisa Bonet, Gary Stretch. 1993

DEAD DON'T DIE, THE 🐝 George Hamilton must take on the Zombie Master in order to clear his dead brother's name. Made for TV. 76m. DIR: Curtis Harrington. CAST: George Hamilton, Ray Milland, Joan Blondell, Linda Cristal, Ralph Meeker. 1975

DEAD EASY ★★★1/2 George, Alexa, and Armstrong are three friends who anger a crime boss whose overreaction sets off a chain of events that results in every small-time hood and paid killer chasing them. Well-done contemporary crime-thriller. Rated R for nudity, violence, language. 90m. DIR: Bert Diling. CAST: Scott Burgess, Rosemary Paul, Tim McKenzie. 1978

DEAD END ★★★ Many famous names combined to film this story of people trying to escape their oppressive slum environment. Humphrey Bogart is cast in one of his many gangster roles from the 1930s. Joel McCrea conforms to his Hollywood stereotype by playing the "nice guy" architect, who dreams of rebuilding New York's waterfront. B&W; 93m. DIR: William Wyler. CAST: Humphrey Bogart, Sylvia Sidney, Joel McCrea, Claire Trevor. 1937

DEAD END (1997) ★★ Overly familiar tale of a police sergeant who is framed for his ex-wife's murder. Forced to flee with his son, the cop finds he has to befriend the criminals he once busted in order to survive the streets. Nothing new. Rated R for violence, language, nudity, and adult situations. 93m. DIR: Douglas Jackson. CAST: Eric Roberts, Jacob Tierney, Eliza Roberts, Jayne Heitmeyer. 1997 DVD

DEAD-END DRIVE-IN ★★ It's the year 1990. After widespread economic collapse, the world is in chaos. The Dead-End Drive-In is a relocation camp for the undesirable element. Rated R for language, violence, and nudity. 92m. DIR: Brian Trenchard-Smith. CAST: Ned Manning, Natalie McCurry. 1986

DEAD EYES OF LONDON ★★1/2 A German remake of the Bela Lugosi chiller *The Human Monster*. Once again the director of a home for the blind uses the place as a front for criminal activities. Interesting vehicle for Klaus Kinski, who gives a great maniacal performance. Even so, the film lacks the eerie atmosphere of the original. B&W; 104m. DIR: Alfred Vohrer. CAST: Klaus Kinski, Karin Baal. 1961

DEAD FOR A DOLLAR ★★ Three double-crossing gunmen try to hunt down a $200,000 bank-robbery cache, but a woman outsmarts them all. A good performance by John Ireland is all that holds the film together. Not rated; contains violence. 92m. DIR: Osvaldo Civirani. CAST: George Hilton, John Ireland, Sandra Milo, Piero Vida. 1968

DEAD FUNNY ★★★ Offbeat black comedy about two women deciding what to do with the body of one of their boyfriends when he's found dead in the kitchen. Andrew McCarthy plays the obnoxious boyfriend who likes practical jokes, Elizabeth Peña and Paige Turco the women who use the moment to reminisce about the events leading up to the discovery. Good performances and a twisted sense of humor help the proceedings along. Rated R for language and violence. 91m. DIR: John Feldman. CAST: Elizabeth Peña, Paige Turco, Andrew McCarthy. 1995

•DEAD HATE THE LIVING, THE ★★★1/2 Highly amusing horror film filled to the brim with nods to genre films past and present. Director David Parker has concocted a tale of indie filmmakers making their own no-budget zombie film in an abandoned hospital. While there, they accidentally unleash real zombies and their master Eibon. The film manages to be a horror fan's kind of film without sinking into the aren't-we-smug kind of mugging so prevalent in many of today's horror teen films. Highly recommended for horror buffs. Rated R for gore, violence, and profanity. 90m. DIR: David Parker. CAST: Eric Clawson, Matt Stephens. 2000 DVD

DEAD HEART ★★ Bryan Brown stars in this Australian film as a rural lawman faced with the duty of imposing government justice on aboriginal elders who, he believes, have committed murder to avenge the desecration of their sacred grounds. While the film may have deeper impact in its native land, to American eyes it seems merely grim and nasty. Not rated; contains violence, nudity, sexual situations, and profanity. 107m. DIR: Nicholas Parsons. CAST: Bryan Brown, Ernie Dingo, Angie Milliken, Gnarnay Yarrahe Waitaire. 1996 DVD

DEAD HEAT ★★ In this so-so but gory spoof of the living-dead genre, Treat Williams and Joe Piscopo star as a pair of L.A. police detectives who find the mastermind behind a group of robberies that are being committed by criminals brought back from the dead. The special effects are pretty good, but 60 percent of the jokes fall flat. Rated R for violence and profanity. 86m. DIR: Mark Goldblatt. CAST: Treat Williams, Joe Piscopo, Lindsay Frost, McGavin, Vincent Price, Keye Luke. 1988

DEAD HEAT ON A MERRY-GO-ROUND ★★★1/2 Thoroughly engrossing film depicts the heist of an airport bank. Not a breezy caper flick, it unfolds a complex plot in a darkly intelligent manner. The cast is impeccable. James Coburn delivers one of his most effective performances. 104m. DIR: Bernard Girard. CAST: James Coburn, Camilla Sparv, Aldo Ray, Ross Martin, Severn Darden, Robert Webber. 1966

DEAD HUSBANDS ★★1/2 This black comedy takes inspiration from the ubiquitous chain letter, but the difference is, the wife at the bottom of the list must kill the husband at the top. One woman has to work doubly hard to get her husband added to the list. The film would have worked, if the plot weren't too silly (even for a farce), and if they hadn't cast bumbling John Ritter as the troublesome husband. At least the music in this made-for-cable original is a real kick. Rated PG-13 for violence. 95m. DIR: Paul Shapiro. CAST: John Ritter, Nicollette Sheridan, Sonja Smits, Amy Yasbeck. 1998

DEAD IN THE WATER ★★★1/2 Bryan Brown energizes this droll little made-for-cable thriller, as an amoral womanizer determined to plot the perfect murder—of his wife—so he can retire in comfort with his sexy secretary. Things naturally go awry, and our poor antihero finds himself suspected in a murder he *didn't* commit. Rated PG-13. Mild violence and sexual themes. 90m. DIR: Bill Condon. CAST: Bryan Brown, Teri Hatcher, Anne De Salvo, Veronica Cartwright. 1991

DEAD IS DEAD ★★1/2 A scientist must locate the drug he created when he discovers it turns the user into a zombie. Low-budget take on *Return of the Living Dead*. Not rated; contains violence and gore. 75m. DIR: Mike Stanley. CAST: Mike Stanley, Connie Cocquyt, Rob Binge. 1993

DEAD MAN ★★★1/2 A strange but poetic art-house Western, strictly for fans of enigmatic metaphors, literary allusions, and dream-state storytelling. Johnny Depp stars as a wanderer in the old West. He may be a misplaced eastern dude or the ghost of English poet William Blake, and his guide through the badlands is a philosophical Indian named Nobody. Meanwhile, a disgruntled industrialist has hired three gunfighters to hunt him down. B&W; 120m. DIR: Jim Jarmusch. CAST: Johnny Depp, Gary Farmer, Robert Mitchum, Lance Henriksen, Michael Wincott, John Hurt, Alfred Molina, Gabriel Byrne. 1996

DEAD MAN ON CAMPUS ★★ MTV production about college roommates facing failure who turn to an old school code that awards a 4.0 GPA to the surviving roommates of a suicide victim. They set out on a search for the most likely candidate. Bad taste abounds yet some incidents are hilarious. Rated R for drug use, language, and sexual situations. 94m. DIR: Alan Cohn. CAST: Tom Everett Scott, Mark Paul Gosselaar, Corey Page, Lochlyn Munro. 1998 DVD

DEAD MAN OUT ★★ Awaiting execution, an inmate on Death Row (Rubén Blades) goes mad. This creates a problem for the state, since an insane man cannot be executed. The state-appointed psychiatrist (Danny Glover) contemplates whether or not he should declare Ben sane again in time for him to die. Ron Hutchinson's teleplay is riveting, and Glover and Blades deliver fine performances. Not rated. 87m. DIR: Richard Pearce. CAST: Danny Glover, Rubén Blades, Larry Block, Samuel L. Jackson, Sam Stoner, Maria Ricossa, Ali Giron, Val Ford. 1988

DEAD MAN WALKING (1987) ★★★ Surprisingly well-done low-budget science fiction in which a disease has divided the world's population into the haves and the have-nots. A young man (Jeffrey Combs) hires a daredevil mercenary (Wings Hauser) to rescue his girlfriend (Pamela Ludwig) from the plague zone. Rated R for violence. 90m. DIR: Gregory Brown. CAST: Wings Hauser, Brion James, Jeffrey Combs, Pamela Ludwig. 1987

DEAD MAN WALKING (1995) ★★★★ Sister Helen Prejean's 1993 bestseller is the basis for this compelling account of her life's work: as spiritual adviser for condemned killers awaiting execution on death row in New Orleans's Angola Prison. Susan Sarandon contributes a superb performance as the dedicated but often overwhelmed Sister Prejean, while Sean

Penn is memorable as her first "client." The film wishes to demonstrate the evils of capital punishment. Rated R for profanity, violence, rape, and nudity. 120m. **DIR:** Tim Robbins. **CAST:** Susan Sarandon, Sean Penn, Robert Prosky, Raymond J. Barry, R. Lee Ermey. **1995 DVD**

DEAD MAN'S CURVE ★★ Based on the urban myth that if your college roommate commits suicide you get a 4.0 for that semester, this made-for-cable original examines what happens when two roommates decide to improve their grades by killing their other roommate and making it look like suicide. While the movie starts out okay, it ultimately fails because it's filled with scenes too strange to be credible, plot twists that only seem to confuse, and odd camera shots. Rated R for profanity and violence. 95m. **DIR:** Dan Rosen. **CAST:** Matthew Lillard, Michael Vartan, Randall Batinkoff, Keri Russell, Dana Delany. **1997**

DEAD MAN'S EYES ★★1/2 Blinded by jealous model Acquanetta, artist Lon Chaney Jr. is suspected of murdering the man who provides eye tissue to restore his sight. Average entry in the *Inner Sanctum* mystery series. B&W; 64m. **DIR:** Reginald LeBorg. **CAST:** Lon Chaney Jr., Acquanetta, Jean Parker, Paul Kelly. **1944**

DEAD MAN'S GULCH ★★★ Story of two former pony express riders. One becomes an outlaw, the other a lawman. B&W; 56m. **DIR:** John English. **CAST:** Don Barry, Lynn Merrick. **1943**

DEAD MAN'S WALK ★★★1/2 The high caliber of Western drama that began with the adaptation of Larry McMurtry's *Lonesome Dove* continues with his prequel, in which a young Gus McCrae and Woodrow Call have their first encounter with adventure and the Texas Rangers. Like the other films in the series, it's a dusty and perilous vision of the Old West made all the more poignant by the naïveté of its protagonists. Made for TV. 271m. **DIR:** Yves Simoneau. **CAST:** F. Murray Abraham, Keith Carradine, Patricia Childress, Brian Dennehy, Edward James Olmos, Harry Dean Stanton, David Arquette, Jonny Lee Miller. **1997**

DEAD MEN CAN'T DANCE ★★ Interesting premise can't rise above the exploitation roots of this gender-bender war film featuring Kathleen York as a CIA agent in South Korea training as a combat army ranger. York and her female comrades are called into action when York's boyfriend tries to steal nuclear warheads from the enemy. This gung-ho effort suffers from poor execution. Rated R for adult situations, language, and violence. 97m. **DIR:** Stephen Anderson. **CAST:** Michael Biehn, Kathleen York, Adrian Paul, R. Lee Ermey. **1997**

DEAD MEN DON'T DIE ★★1/2 Nosy television newscaster Elliott Gould stumbles across a story most reporters would die for. Unfortunately, Gould does, but is resurrected through a voodoo spell. Now a zombie, he sets out to solve his own murder. Somewhat funny, proves that for television anchors there is life after death. Rated R for violence and language. 94m. **DIR:** Malcolm Marmorstein. **CAST:** Elliott Gould, Melissa Sue Anderson, Mark Moses, Mabel King. **1991**

DEAD MEN DON'T WEAR PLAID ★★★★ In this often hilarious and always entertaining comedy, Steve Martin plays a private eye who confronts the suspicious likes of Humphrey Bogart, Burt Lancaster, Alan Ladd, Bette Davis, and other stars of Hollywood's Golden Age, with the help of tricky editing and writer-director Carl Reiner. Rachel Ward co-stars as Martin's sexy client. Rated PG for adult themes. B&W; 89m. **DIR:** Carl Reiner. **CAST:** Steve Martin, Rachel Ward, Reni Santoni, Carl Reiner, George Gaynes. **1982 DVD**

DEAD MEN TELL ★★1/2 When an old lady is killed just before setting sail to find a rumored pirate treasure worth $60 million, Charlie Chan investigates. A spooky atmosphere helps cover up the obvious low budget. B&W; 61m. **DIR:** Harry Lachman. **CAST:** Sidney Toler, Sheila Ryan, Victor Sen Yung. **1941**

DEAD MEN WALK ★★ Master character actor George Zucco makes the most of one of his few leading roles, a dual one at that, in this grade-Z cheapie about vampires and zombies. B&W; 67m. **DIR:** Sam Newfield. **CAST:** George Zucco, Mary Carlisle, Nedrick Young, Dwight Frye. **1943 DVD**

DEAD NEXT DOOR, THE ★★★ Though he receives no credit, Sam Raimi produced and financed this low-budget zombie film that marked the debut of cult director J. R. Bookwalter. As a virus sweeps the world and turns people into zombies, the government creates a zombie squad to take care of the problem. Not rated; contains violence, gore, and profanity. 84m. **DIR:** J. R. Bookwalter. **CAST:** Peter Ferry, Bogdan Pecic, Scott Spiegel. **1989**

DEAD OF NIGHT (1945) ★★★★1/2 The granddaddy of the British horror anthologies still chills today, with the final sequence—in which ventriloquist Michael Redgrave fights a losing battle with his demonic dummy—rating as an all-time horror classic. The other stories are told almost as effectively. B&W; 104m. **DIR:** Alberto Cavalcanti, Basil Dearden, Robert Hamer, Charles Crichton. **CAST:** Mervyn Johns, Michael Redgrave, Sally Ann Howes, Miles Malleson, Googie Withers, Basil Radford. **1945**

DEAD OF NIGHT (1977) ★★ This trilogy of shockers written by Richard Matheson has some interesting twists, but is far inferior to his other achievements. Elvira is host on this, another in her "Thriller Video" series. 76m. **DIR:** Dan Curtis. **CAST:** Ed Begley Jr., John Hackett, Patrick Macnee. **1977**

DEAD OF WINTER ★★★ When aspiring actress Mary Steenburgen steps in at the last minute to replace a performer who has walked off the set of a film in production, she is certain it is the chance of a lifetime. But once trapped in a remote mansion with the creepy filmmakers, she begins to believe it may be the last act of her lifetime. The story is a bit contrived, but one only realizes it after the film is over. Rated R for profanity and violence. 98m. **DIR:** Arthur Penn. **CAST:** Mary Steenburgen, Roddy McDowall, Jan Rubes, William Russ, Ken Pogue. **1987**

DEAD ON ★★ A woman has an affair with a man and then suggests that they kill each other's spouses. If you like all sex and no plot, you'll love this. Available in R and unrated versions, both with nudity, graphic sex, violence, and profanity. 90m. **DIR:** Ralph

Hemecker. **CAST:** Matt McCoy, Tracy Scoggins, Shari Shattuck, David Ackroyd, Thomas Wagner. **1993**

DEAD ON SIGHT ★★1/2 Jennifer Beals stars as a woman who is seeing visions of horrible violence in her sleep. Then she awakens and discovers the vicious dream murders have actually occurred. Joined by an unbelieving detective (Daniel Baldwin), Beals decides she must stop the murderer herself—or become his next victim. So-so mystery-thriller works more often than not, but borrows heavily from other films and you're never quite sure you haven't seen it before. Rated R for violence and profanity. 96m. **DIR:** Reuben Pruess. **CAST:** Jennifer Beals, Daniel Baldwin, Kurtwood Smith. **1994**

DEAD ON THE MONEY ★★1/2 Clever made-for-cable thriller has debonair Corbin Bernsen and John Glover vying for the affections of Amanda Pays, who always wanted a man who would love her to death. Too bad one of her suitors is willing to accommodate that request. 92m. **DIR:** Mark Cullingham. **CAST:** Corbin Bernsen, Amanda Pays, John Glover, Kevin McCarthy, Eleanor Parker. **1990**

DEAD PIT, THE ★★1/2 A woman at a mental asylum accidentally unleashes the spirit of a crazed surgeon and the hordes of lobotomized zombies on whom he experimented. The film treads on familiar ground but has a sense of stylishness. Rated R for violence and profanity. 95m. **DIR:** Brett Leonard. **CAST:** Jeremy Slate, Cheryl Lawson. **1989**

DEAD POETS SOCIETY ★★★1/2 Robin Williams offers an impressive change-of-pace as an unorthodox English teacher. He inspires a love of poetry and intellectual freedom in his students at a strict, upscale New England prep school. Though not entirely satisfying in its resolution, the film offers much of the heart and mood of *Goodbye, Mr. Chips* and *The Prime of Miss Jean Brodie*. Richly textured by Australian filmmaker Peter Weir. Rated PG. 124m. **DIR:** Peter Weir. **CAST:** Robin Williams, Robert Sean Leonard, Norman Lloyd, Ethan Hawke. **1989 DVD**

DEAD POOL, THE ★★★★ Clint Eastwood's fifth Dirty Harry adventure is a surprisingly strong entry in the long-running series. Action and chuckles are in abundance as our hero tracks down a weirdo who is murdering celebrities on a list that also carries Harry's name. It's good fun for fans. Rated R for violence and profanity. 92m. **DIR:** Buddy Van Horn. **CAST:** Clint Eastwood, Patricia Clarkson, Liam Neeson, Evan Kim. **1988**

DEAD PRESIDENTS ★★★★ Three New York kids—two African Americans and a Puerto Rican—grow up to be Marines in the late 1960s and return from Vietnam to a decaying neighborhood short on jobs and teeming with drugs and criminal temptations. The film crackles with all the adrenal temperament of a soul-music opera. Rated R for violence, nudity, and language. 125m. **DIR:** Allen Hughes, Albert Hughes. **CAST:** Larenz Tate, Bokeem Woodbine, Chris Tucker, Keith David, N'Bushe Wright, Freddy Rodriguez. **1995 DVD**

DEAD RECKONING (1947) ★★★ World War II veteran Humphrey Bogart is caught in a web of circumstance when he seeks the solution to an old army buddy's disappearance. Lizabeth Scott and Morris

Carnovsky tell too many lies trying to cover it all up. A brutal yet sensitive example of *film noir*. Bogart is excellent. B&W; 100m. **DIR:** John Cromwell. **CAST:** Humphrey Bogart, Lizabeth Scott, Morris Carnovsky, Charles Cane, Marvin Miller, Wallace Ford, George Chandler. **1947**

DEAD RECKONING (1990) ★★★ Cliff Robertson enlivens this cat-and-mouse thriller, as the doting husband of a younger wife (Susan Blakely) who may—or may not—be conspiring with her ex-lover (Rick Springfield) to kill him. At times faintly reminiscent of Roman Polanski's *Knife in the Water* (though nowhere as subtle), this made-for-cable tale kicks into gear once our uneasy trio is stranded in an abandoned lighthouse. Rated R for considerable violence. 95m. **DIR:** Robert Lewis. **CAST:** Cliff Robertson, Susan Blakely, Rick Springfield. **1990**

DEAD RINGER ★★★ Proof positive that nobody's as good as Bette Davis when she's bad. She plays twins—one good, one bad. The bad one gets the upper hand. Bette chews the scenery with so much relish that the movie is fun to watch in spite of its ghoulish plot. B&W; 116m. **DIR:** Paul Henreid. **CAST:** Bette Davis, Peter Lawford, Karl Malden, Jean Hagen, Estelle Winwood, George Macready, Ben Remsen. **1964**

DEAD RINGERS ★★1/2 Director and coscripter David Cronenberg toys intriguingly with the connective link between identical twins until the film sinks into a gruesome spiral of depravity and gratuitous gore. Jeremy Irons is superb as both halves of twin gynecologists specializing in fertility. Rated R for graphic medical procedures, sexual themes, and unsettling violence. 115m. **DIR:** David Cronenberg. **CAST:** Jeremy Irons, Genevieve Bujold, Heidi Von Palleske, Stephen Lack. **1988 DVD**

DEAD SILENCE (1989) 🎬 When a financially strapped film director is sponsored by a mob leader, he must use the mobster's no-talent son in the lead. What could have been hilarious and clever falls short. Rated R for profanity and violence. 90m. **DIR:** Harrison Ellenshaw. **CAST:** Clete Keith, Doris Anne Soyka, Joseph Scott, Craig Fleming. **1989**

DEAD SILENCE (1996) ★★★1/2 This gripping thriller turns on a clever premise: a trio of violent psychopaths hold a busload of deaf-mute girls hostage in a standoff with the police. James Garner, the hostage negotiator who takes charge of the case, and Marlee Matlin, as the girls' teacher, is a plucky, young woman with more courage than common sense. Donald Stewart's script has a few surprises and is guaranteed to keep viewers at the edges of their seats. Rated R for violence, profanity, and strong sexual content. 100m. **DIR:** Daniel Petrie Jr. **CAST:** James Garner, Marlee Matlin, Kim Coates, Charles Martin Smith, Kenneth Welsh, James Villemaire, Mimi Kuzyk, Lolita Davidovich. **1996**

DEAD SLEEP ★★★ Australian thriller features Linda Blair as a nurse in a rather peculiar psychiatric hospital. It seems that the head doctor (Tony Bonner) keeps patients comatose to "cure" them of their day-to-day anxieties. If this weren't bad enough, he resorts to murder on the rebellious ones. Rated R for nudity, profanity, and violence. 92m. **DIR:** Alec Mills. **CAST:** Linda Blair, Tony Bonner, Andrew Booth. **1990**

DEAD SOLID PERFECT ★★★★ Dan Jenkins's witty golf fable becomes an equally engaging made-for-cable film, with Randy Quaid starring as a second-stringer desperate to have his shot at success. Jenkins and coscripter-director Bobby Roth deftly capture the boring routine of cross-country tours. 97m. DIR: Bobby Roth. CAST: Randy Quaid, Kathryn Harrold, Larry Riley, Corinne Bohrer, Jack Warden. 1988

DEAD SPACE ❤ A galactic lawman answers a distress signal from a space lab. Everyone associated with this film exhibits dead space from the shoulders up. Rated R for violence and nudity. 72m. DIR: Fred Gallo. CAST: Marc Singer, Laura Tate, Bryan Cranston, Judith Chapman. 1990

DEAD TIDES ★★ Murky action-adventure pits boat captain Roddy Piper against a drug dealer, the Coast Guard, and the DEA. Has its moments, but not enough of them. Rated R for violence, language, and nudity. 100m. DIR: Serge Rodnunsky. CAST: Roddy Piper, Tawny Kitaen, Trevor Goddard, Miles O'Keeffe. 1996

DEAD TIRED (GROSSE FATIGUE) ★★★ Michel Blanc, France's answer to Woody Allen, plays himself and his dead ringer in this strange parody on success. Bored with making personal appearances, he trades places with his look-alike for a temporary reprieve. Unfortunately, his double refuses to step aside. Cameo appearances by Philippe Noiret and Roman Polanski at the end of the film are worth waiting for. In French with English subtitles. Rated R for nudity, profanity, and violence. 85m. DIR: Michel Blanc. CAST: Michel Blanc, Carole Bouquet, Philippe Noiret, Roman Polanski. 1994

DEAD TO RIGHTS ★★1/2 Charles Bronson and Dana Delany make for an unlikely father-daughter team of police officers tracking the killer of another family member. It's better as a thriller than as a drama, with the domestic arguments simply getting in the way of the plot. Made for television. Rated R for violence and profanity. 93m. DIR: Rod Holcomb. CAST: Charles Bronson, Dana Delany, Xander Berkeley, Louis Giambalvo, Jenette Goldstein. 1993

DEAD WEEKEND ❤ This infantile, $1.98 quickie about a shape-shifting alien visitor is merely a thin excuse for star Stephen Baldwin to have his way with five different women. Rated R for nudity, simulated sex, profanity, and violence. 82m. DIR: Amos Poe. CAST: Stephen Baldwin, David Rasche, Alexis Arquette, Nicholas Worth. 1995

DEAD ZONE, THE ★★★★ This is an exciting adaptation of the Stephen King suspense novel about a man who uses his psychic powers to solve multiple murders and perhaps prevent the end of the world. Rated R for violence and profanity. 103m. DIR: David Cronenberg. CAST: Christopher Walken, Brooke Adams, Tom Skerritt, Herbert Lom, Martin Sheen. 1983

DEADBOLT ★★★ Effective thriller finds student Justine Bateman looking for a roommate to share share expenses. Enter Adam Baldwin, who seems perfect. Then his true colors start shining through, and Bateman finds herself a captive in her own apartment. Baldwin is appropriately creepy. Not rated; contains adult language and violence. 95m. DIR: Douglas Jackson. CAST: Justine Bateman, Adam Baldwin, Chris Mulkey, Michele Scarabelli. 1992 DVD

DEADFALL ★★★ Gimmicky tale of con artists has plenty going for it, most notably director Christopher Coppola's over-the-top approach to the material. Young con artist Michael Biehn mistakenly kills his father during a sting, then teams up with his uncle and gets involved in a series of double crosses. High-rent cast keeps this one interesting. Rated R for nudity, violence, and language. 99m. DIR: Christopher Coppola. CAST: Michael Biehn, Sarah Trigger, Nicolas Cage, James Coburn, Charlie Sheen, Peter Fonda, Talia Shire. 1993

DEADLINE (1987) ★★★ Christopher Walken is good as a reporter covering the conflict in Beirut, finding himself becoming personally involved when he falls for a German nurse working for the rebels. This film is very much in the vein of *Salvador* and *Under Fire*, but cannot duplicate their tension. Rated R. 100m. DIR: Nathaniel Gutman. CAST: Christopher Walken, Hywel Bennett. 1987

DEADLINE (1988) ★★★ John Hurt gives a moving performance as an alcoholic British journalist who becomes involved in a doomed love affair with a beautiful noblewoman (Imogen Stubbs). Together they weather a revolution on an island estate in the Persian Gulf. Rated R for nudity, profanity, and graphic violence. 110m. DIR: Richard Stroud. CAST: John Hurt, Imogen Stubbs, Robert McBain, Greg Hicks. 1988

DEADLINE AT DAWN ★★ Penned by Clifford Odets, this film is predictable and anticlimactic. While on liberty, sailor Bill Williams is slipped a mickey by Lola Lane and, upon awakening, he finds her dead. With the help of a dancer (Susan Hayward) and a cabbie (played flatly by Paul Lukas), he sets out to clear himself. B&W; 83m. DIR: Harold Clurman. CAST: Susan Hayward, Paul Lukas, Lola Lane, Bill Williams, Jerome Cowan. 1946

DEADLINE USA ★★★★ In this hard-hitting newspaper drama, Humphrey Bogart plays an editor who has to fight the city's underworld while keeping the publisher (superbly portrayed by Ethel Barrymore) from giving in to pressure and closing the paper down. While Kim Hunter is wasted in the small role as Bogart's ex-wife, the picture has much to recommend it. B&W; 87m. DIR: Richard Brooks. CAST: Humphrey Bogart, Kim Hunter, Ethel Barrymore. 1952

DEADLOCK ★★★★ High marks to this high-tech update of *The Defiant Ones*, which pairs Rutger Hauer and Mimi Rogers (both superb) as convicts linked by futuristic collars necessitating their remaining in close proximity … at the risk of impromptu decapitations. Broderick Miler's clever scene script blends perfectly with Lewis Teague's wry direction. Rated R for violence and sexual content. 95m. DIR: Lewis Teague. CAST: Rutger Hauer, Mimi Rogers, Joan Chen, James Remar. 1991

DEADLOCK 2 ★★ Another sequel in which none of the originals appears. To keep their exploding collars from detonating, Esai Morales and Nia Peeples must stick together while breaking out of the "Playland" prison. There is a spark between these two, but

Morales is too good an actor for such cheesy entertainments. Made for TV. Not rated; contains violence and profanity. 120m. DIR: Graeme Campbell. CAST: Esai Morales, Nia Peeples. 1995

•DEADLOCKED ★★★1/2 Charles S. Dutton is spellbinding as a distraught father determined to free a son convicted of rape and murder. Taking the jury hostage, he commands the prosecutor (David Caruso) to find out what really happened. Tense moments and a generous sprinkling of surprises will keep viewers enthralled in this TNT Original. Not rated; contains sex, violence, and profanity. 89m. DIR: Michael Watkins. CAST: Charles Dutton, David Caruso, Jo D. Jonz. 2000

DEADLY ADVICE ★★★1/2 A Greek chorus of dead British murderers dish up advice and a skewed morality to Jane Horrocks, who has found a decisive way of dealing with her oppressive, sharp-tongued mother. There aren't as many surprises as there should be, but the dialogue is humorously understated and Horrocks is a gleeful comedian. Rated R for violence, profanity, brief nudity, and sexual situations. 91m. DIR: Mandie Fletcher. CAST: Jane Horrocks, Brenda Fricker, Imelda Staunton, Jonathan Pryce. 1993

DEADLY ALLIANCE 🎦 Two shoestring filmmakers get caught up in the dealings of a secret cartel composed of the world's seven largest oil companies. 90m. DIR: Paul Salvatore Parco. CAST: Mike Lloyd Gentry. 1975

DEADLY BET ★★1/2 A compulsive gambler and alcoholic almost loses everything, including his girlfriend, to a ruthless kick boxer. Watchable if unmemorable little film. Rated R for profanity and seemingly endless violence. 93m. DIR: Richard W. Munchkin. CAST: Jeff Wincott, Charlene Tilton, Steven Vincent Leigh. 1992

DEADLY BLESSING 🎦 A strange religious sect. Rated R because of nudity and bloody scenes. 102m. DIR: Wes Craven. CAST: Maren Jensen, Susan Buckner, Sharon Stone, Lois Nettleton, Ernest Borgnine, Jeff East. 1981

DEADLY COMPANION 🎦 Slow-moving, confusing film has Michael Sarrazin trying to find his wife's killer. Not rated; contains violence and nudity. 90m. DIR: George Bloomfield. CAST: Anthony Perkins, Michael Sarrazin, Susan Clark, Howard Duff. 1986

DEADLY COMPANIONS, THE ★★1/2 When gunfighter Brian Keith accidentally kills the son of dance-hall hostess Maureen O'Hara, he attempts to make amends by escorting her through hostile Indian Territory. A less than grade-A Western made notable because it was director Sam Peckinpah's first feature. 90m. DIR: Sam Peckinpah. CAST: Brian Keith, Maureen O'Hara, Chill Wills, Steve Cochran. 1961

DEADLY CURRENTS ★★★ Exiled CIA agent William L. Petersen finds himself in a political hotbed when he befriends stranger George C. Scott on the small island of Curaçao. Things heat up when several factions arrive on the island to settle an old score with Scott. Exotic locales and double and triple crosses add color and suspense to this thriller, made for cable under the title Curaçao. Rated R for language and violence. 93m. DIR: Carl Schultz. CAST:

William L. Petersen, George C. Scott, Julie Carmen Trish Van Devere, Philip Anglim. 1993

DEADLY DAPHNE'S REVENGE 🎦 Troma, masters of the no-budget cheapie, have taken a standard rape drama and tacked on scenes of a mental patient to create an utterly confusing film. Rated R for violence. 98m. DIR: Richard Harding Gardner. CAST: Laurie Tait Partridge, Anthony Holt, Richard Harding Gardner. 1993

DEADLY DESIRE ★★★ Greed and lust rear their ugly heads in this made-for-cable thriller, about a cop-turned-private investigator (Jack Scalia) lured into a web woven by sexpot Kathryn Harrold. Nothing new here, but the performances are strong. Rated R for violence and sex. 93m. DIR: Charles Correll. CAST: Jack Scalia, Kathryn Harrold, Will Patton, Joe Santos. 1991

DEADLY DREAMS ★★ Run-of-the-mill suspenser about a writer who dreams that the psychotic murderer who slew his parents is coming after him. Soon his dreams spill over into reality. Rated R for violence, nudity, and language. 79m. DIR: Kristine Peterson. CAST: Mitchell Anderson. 1988

DEADLY EMBRACE 🎦 Sexual decadence ends in murder. Soft-core porn dud. 82m. DIR: Ellen Cabot. CAST: Jan-Michael Vincent, Jack Carter, Ken Abraham 1988

DEADLY ENCOUNTER (1972) ★★★1/2 Hounded by mobsters, Susan Anspach enlists the aid of her old lover Larry Hagman, an ex–combat helicopter pilot. Great aerial stunts are a treat and help keep the action moving right along. Pretty good for television. 100m. DIR: William A. Graham. CAST: Larry Hagman, Susan Anspach, James Gammon, Michael C. Gwynne. 1972 DVD

DEADLY ENCOUNTER (1975) 🎦 A rich woman schemer. Rated R for sexual talk. 90m. DIR: R. John Hugh. CAST: Dina Merrill, Carl Betz, Leon Ames. 1975

DEADLY EYES ★★ Grain full of steroids creates rats the size of small dogs. Rated R for gore, nudity, and simulated sex. 87m. DIR: Robert Clouse. CAST: Sam Groom, Sara Botsford, Scatman Crothers. 1982

DEADLY FORCE ★★★ Wings Hauser (Vice Squad) plays "Stony" Jackson Cooper, an ex-cop who returns to his old Los Angeles stomping grounds to stomp people until he finds the maniac who stomped a buddy's daughter to death. Rated R for violence, nudity, and profanity. 95m. DIR: Paul Aaron. CAST: Wings Hauser, Joyce Ingalls, Paul Shenar. 1983

DEADLY FRIEND ★★ A teenage whiz revives his murdered girlfriend by inserting a computer chip into her brain. The girl becomes a robot-zombie and kills people. This would-be thriller has much in common with its title character. It's cold, mechanical, and brain-dead. Rated R for violence. 99m. DIR: Wes Craven. CAST: Matthew Laborteaux, Michael Sharrett, Kristy Swanson. 1986

DEADLY GAME ★★1/2 What hath Richard Connell wrought? Scripter Wes Claridge is merely the latest to borrow liberally from "The Most Dangerous Game," this time pitting seven virtual strangers against a masked (and well-armed) maniac. Made for cable TV. Rated R for profanity and violence. 93m. DIR: Thomas Wright. CAST: Michael Beck, Jenny Seagrove.

rove, Roddy McDowall, Mitchell Ryan, Marc Singer. 1991

EADLY GAMES ★★ The central motif of this goofy lasher drama is a board game. Sam Groom is excellent as the small-town cop-protagonist. R rating. 5m. **DIR:** Scott Mansfield. **CAST:** Sam Groom, Steve ailsback, Alexandra Morgan, Colleen Camp, June ockhart, Jo Ann Harris, Dick Butkus. 1982

EADLY HARVEST 🎬 Mankind's unrelenting industrialization of arable land and subsequent cold winters (and summers!) wreak havoc with America's cological system. Rated PG. 86m. **DIR:** Timothy ond. **CAST:** Clint Walker, Nehemiah Persoff, Kim Cattall, David Brown. 1976

EADLY HERO ★★★1/2 Strange yet engaging badop film with Don Murray as a New York police officer struggling to stay on the force after an incident's repercussions threaten his upcoming pension. The lm is dated by the trendy mid-Seventies fashions nd popular art, yet that is ironically one of its more teresting qualities. Rated PG for violence and proanity. 102m. **DIR:** Ivan Nagy. **CAST:** Don Murray, Dan Williams, Lilia Skala, George S. Irving, Conchata errell, Ron Weyand, James Earl Jones, Treat Williams. 975

EADLY HEROES 🎬 Ludicrous action-thriller bout a pair of American agents who must hunt own a team of terrorists who kidnapped one of their ives. Virtually unwatchable except for the occaonal line of dialogue that's so bad it's good. Rated R r profanity, violence, and brief nudity. 104m. **DIR:** enahem Golan. **CAST:** Michael Paré, Jan-Michael ncent, Billy Drago, Claudette Mink. 1993

EADLY IMPACT ★★ Fred Williamson and Bo venson work well together in this otherwise conived, Italian-made action film about an attempt to p off Las Vegas gambling houses. Rated R. 90m. **R:** Larry Ludman. **CAST:** Fred Williamson, Bo Svenon. 1985

EADLY INTENT ★★ A murderous archaeologist rerns from an expedition with a priceless jewel and ood on his hands. He's soon murdered and everyody who knew him is after the jewel. Although the ast is talented, the film is flawed by poor pacing and ad logic. Rated R for violence and language. 83m. **R:** Nigel Dick. **CAST:** Lisa Eilbacher, Steve Railsback, aud Adams, Lance Henriksen, Fred Williamson. 1988

EADLY MANTIS, THE ★★1/2 Can heroic scients head off a mammoth praying mantis winging its ay from the North Pole to New York City? Okay speal effects, though even at 78 minutes it seems too ng. B&W; 78m. **DIR:** Nathan Juran. **CAST:** Craig evens, William Hopper. 1957

EADLY OBSESSION ★★ This contrived, uneven riller is about a disfigured psychopath who dwells the tunnels and caves beneath a wealthy private ollege. He terrorizes the campus inhabitants in an fort to extort large sums of money. Rated R, conins nudity and violence. 93m. **DIR:** Jeno Hodi. **AST:** Jeffrey R. Iorio. 1988

EADLY OUTBREAK ★★★ Action star Jeff Speakan stands between terrorists and a deadly chemil in this moderately suspenseful action film. eakman stars as a U.S. Embassy first sergeant as-

signed to a chemical facility outside Tel Aviv where a visiting team of scientists turns out to be terrorists. Some spectacular stunts and decent acting make this direct-to-video effort better than the norm. Rated R for violence and profanity. 94m. **DIR:** Rick Avery. **CAST:** Jeff Speakman, Ron Silver, Rochelle Swanson. 1995

DEADLY PAST ★★ A paroled man is drawn into a murder conspiracy when his ex-girlfriend first seduces, then recruits him to help her. Good performance by Dedee Pfeiffer in this otherwise turgid thriller. Rated R for nudity, profanity, and violence. 90m. **DIR:** Tibor Takacs. **CAST:** Carol Alt, Dedee Pfeiffer, Ron Marquette, Mark Dacascos. 1994

DEADLY POSSESSION ★★ Aussie thriller presents two college students on the trail of a masked slasher plaguing downtown Adelaide. Low-budget chiller picks up pace halfway through, and then leaves several burning questions. Not rated. 99m. **DIR:** Craig Lahiff. **CAST:** Penny Cook, Anna-Maria Winchester, Olivia Hamnett. 1987

DEADLY PREY 🎬 Absolutely wretched piece of celluloid about a secret mercenary boot camp. Rated R for violence and profanity. 87m. **DIR:** David A. Prior. **CAST:** Cameron Mitchell, Troy Donahue. 1987

DEADLY RIVALS 🎬 Emerald smuggling and corporate espionage in this confusing thriller. Rated R for nudity, profanity, and violence. 93m. **DIR:** James Dodson. **CAST:** Andrew Stevens, Cela Wise, Margaux Hemingway, Joseph Bologna, Richard Roundtree. 1992

DEADLY SANCTUARY 🎬 Two newly orphaned sisters fall prey to prison, prostitution, murder, and a torturous hellfire club. 93m. **DIR:** Jess (Jesus) Franco. **CAST:** Sylva Koscina, Mercedes McCambridge, Jack Palance, Klaus Kinski, Akim Tamiroff. 1970

DEADLY SPYGAMES ★★1/2 A government agent and his ex-lover are sent to destroy a Cuban radar station and prevent World War III. James Bond fans may enjoy this spy spoof, but it could be too silly for others. Not rated; contains mild sexual situations. 86m. **DIR:** Jack M. Sell. **CAST:** Jack M. Sell, Adrianne Richmond, Troy Donahue, Tippi Hedren. 1989

DEADLY STRANGER ★1/2 A drifter (Michael J. Moore) takes a job on a plantation where the owner and a local union leader are conspiring to exploit migrant workers. Clichéd movie wastes the talents of Darlanne Fluegel and the time of the viewer. Not rated; nudity. 93m. **DIR:** Max Kleven. **CAST:** Darlanne Fluegel, Michael J. Moore, John Vernon. 1988

DEADLY SURVEILLANCE ★★★★ An unexpected treat. What could have been another tired and gory struggle between good cops and nasty drug lords emerges as fresh, witty, and engaging, thanks to a deft script from Hal Salwen and director Paul Ziller. Michael Ironside plays against type as a dedicated cop. Rated R for nudity, violence, and profanity. 92m. **DIR:** Paul Ziller. **CAST:** Michael Ironside, Christopher Bondy, Susan Almgren, David Carradine. 1991

DEADLY TARGET ★★ After being captured in Los Angeles, a Chinese gangster gets away with the help of a Chinese triad. Hong Kong detective Gary Daniels enlists the aid of a maverick cop and a Chinese card dealer to zero in on his prey. This one misses the mark. Rated R for violence, nudity, and profanity. 92m. DIR: Charla Driver. CAST: Gary Daniels, Ken McLeod, Max Gail, Byron Mann. 1994

DEADLY TRACKERS, THE ★★1/2 Extremely violent Western follows sheriff Richard Harris's attempt to track down the outlaw gang responsible for killing his family during a bank robbery. Film starts out well, but quickly becomes a standard revenge tale and is far too long. Be warned: There are some truly brutal scenes throughout. Rated R. 110m. DIR: Barry Shear. CAST: Richard Harris, Rod Taylor, Neville Brand, William Smith, Al Lettieri, Isela Vega. 1973

DEADLY TWINS 🎬 A typical revenge flick about twin sisters who are gang raped. Not rated; contains adult themes. 87m. DIR: Joe Oaks. CAST: Judy Landers, Audrey Landers. 1985

DEADLY VENGEANCE 🎬 The poor acting, editing, and lighting in this insipid film make one wonder if it was planned by a couple of beginning film students over a keg of beer. Contains obscenities, simulated sex scenes, and violence. 84m. DIR: A. C. Qamar. CAST: Arthur Roberts, Alan Marlowe, Bob Holden. 1985

DEADLY VOYAGE ★★★★ This gripping, fact-based drama concerns events that took place in 1992, when a Russian container ship left Ghana, West Africa, with a handful of stowaways on board. This very ship had recently been fined for the same infraction. The first mate takes charge when the new stowaways are discovered; the result is brutal and incredibly compelling ... because one man gets away. But how long can he elude capture on a ship at sea? Rated R for profanity, nudity, and violence. 90m. DIR: John Mackenzie. CAST: Omar Epps, Joss Ackland, Sean Pertwee, David Suchet, Andrew Divoff. 1996

DEADLY WEAPON ★★★ Producer Charles Band remakes his own *Laserblast* with this improved version. Writer-director Michael Miner gives the film a sense of comic bookishness that allows the viewer to sit back and enjoy the silliness of a boy finding a laser gun and using it to his own ends. Rated PG-13 for violence and profanity. 89m. DIR: Michael Miner. CAST: Rodney Easton, Kim Walker, Joe Regalbuto, William Sanderson. 1988

DEADMAN'S CURVE ★★★ This made-for-TV biopic recounts the true story of Fifties rock stars Jan and Dean. An endearing sense of humor and their engaging surf sound propels them to the top. Then a near-fatal auto accident brings their career to a screeching halt. Richard Hatch and Bruce Davison deliver strong performances as Jan Berry and Dean Torrence. The use of Jan and Dean's original hits adds spark to the film. 100m. DIR: Richard Compton. CAST: Richard Hatch, Bruce Davison, Pamela Bellwood, Susan Sullivan, Dick Clark, Wolfman Jack. 1978

DEADMAN'S REVENGE ★★★1/2 Suspenseful and humorous tale about an evil railroad man who steals people's property and has them arrested for crimes they did not commit. One innocent man is after the crook to collect what is rightfully his, and along the way meets his long-lost son. Well acted and fun to watch. Rated PG-13 for mild violence. 92m. DIR: Alan J. Levi. CAST: Bruce Dern, Michael Ironside, Vondie Curtis-Hall, Keith Coulouris, Daphne Ashbrook, Tobin

Bell, John M. Jackson, Doug McClure, Randy Travis. 1994

DEADMATE ★★1/2 Writer-director Straw Weisman concocts a spooky and bizarre tale about a woman who marries a mortician unaware that he, and most of the town, like to do strange things to dead bodies. Not rated; contains violence and nudity. 93m. DIR: Straw Weisman. CAST: Elizabeth Manning, David Gregory, Lawrence Brockius, Adam Wahl, Judith Mayes, Kelvin Keraga. 1988

DEADTIME STORIES 🎬 Bizarre, ghoulish version of fairy tales. 89m. DIR: Jeffrey S. Delman. CAST: Scott Valentine. 1987

DEAL OF THE CENTURY ★★ A two-bit arms hustler (Chevy Chase) peddles an ultrasophisticated super weapon to a Central American dictator. This black comedy ends up in that nether world of the near misses. Rated PG for violence and profanity. 99m. DIR: William Friedkin. CAST: Chevy Chase, Sigourney Weaver, Gregory Hines, Vince Edwards. 1983

DEALERS 🎬 Boring British rip-off of *Wall Street*. Rated R for violence and profanity. 92m. DIR: Colin Bucksey. CAST: Rebecca DeMornay, Paul McGann, Derrick O'Connor. 1989

DEAR AMERICA: LETTERS HOME FROM VIETNAM ★★★★ This docudrama traces the Vietnam conflict from 1964 to 1973 through the eyes of America's soldiers writing to their loved ones at home. The live footage has been so carefully selected that you forget that the letter you are hearing is being read by an actor instead of the person on the screen. Offscreen narration by a *Who's Who* of actors, including Robert De Niro, Ellen Burstyn, Tom Berenger, Michael J. Fox, Sean Penn, Martin Sheen, and Robin Williams. Rated PG. 86m. DIR: Bill Couturie. 1988

DEAR BRIGITTE ★★1/2 A clever premise goes wrong. Boy genius who handicaps horses won't play unless he gets to go to meet Brigitte Bardot. What could have been charming comes across as contrived pap. 100m. DIR: Henry Koster. CAST: James Stewart, Fabian, Glynis Johns, Billy Mumy, Cindy Carol, Jesse White, Ed Wynn, Brigitte Bardot. 1965

DEAR DEAD DELILAH 🎬 Delilah (Agnes Moorehead) is about to die, but there's a fortune buried somewhere on her property that her loony relatives will do anything to get ahold of. Rated R for blood. 90m. DIR: John Farris. CAST: Agnes Moorehead, W. Geer, Michael Ansara, Dennis Patrick. 1972

DEAR DETECTIVE ★★1/2 A lighthearted film with moments of quality about a female homicide detective involved in a series of murdered local government officials, counterpointed by an amusing love interest with a mild-mannered university professor. Not rated with mild violence. Made for TV. 92m. DIR: Dean Hargrove. CAST: Brenda Vaccaro, Arlen Dean Snyder, Ron Silver, Michael MacRae, Jack Ging, M. Emmet Walsh. 1979

DEAR GOD ★★★ This inoffensive comedy serves as a starring debut for Greg Kinnear, cast as an amiable con artist forced into honest labor as a means of cleaning his criminal record. He winds up in the post office's dead dead-letter section, where he takes an interest in the pleas of citizens desperate enough to write—and mail—letters to God. Rated PG for mild profanity. 112m. DIR: Garry Marshall. CAST: Greg Kinnear, Laurie Metcalf, Maria Pitillo, Tim Conway, Hector Elizondo, Roscoe Lee Browne, Jon Seda. 1996

●DEAR HEART ★★★1/2 Very likable comedy about a romance between two middle-aged people. She's a small-town postmistress in Manhattan for a convention, he's a salesman already engaged to another woman. B&W; 114m. DIR: Delbert Mann. CAST: Glenn Ford, Geraldine Page, Michael Anderson Jr., Angela Lansbury. 1964

DEAR SANTA 🎦 Obviously the filmmakers behind this low-budget effort saw *The Santa Clause*. When a husband and father neglects his family for work at Christmas, he's recruited to be the next Santa Claus by a magical elf. Standard issue and dull as dishwater. Rated G. 87m. DIR: Peter Stewart. CAST: D. L. Green, Debra Rich, Harrison Myers. 1998 DVD

DEAR WIFE ★★1/2 The second of three amusing films involving the same cast of characters, and mostly the same players. This sequel to *Dear Ruth* has fresh-faced younger sister (to Joan Caulfield) Mona Freeman conniving to elect heartthrob William Holden to the state senate seat sought by her politician father Edward Arnold. Billy DeWolfe fills it all out with his peculiar brand of haughty humor. B&W; 88m. DIR: Richard Haydn. CAST: Joan Caulfield, William Holden, Mona Freeman, Edward Arnold, Billy DeWolfe. 1949

DEATH AND THE MAIDEN ★★★1/2 In an unnamed South American country, a woman (Sigourney Weaver) terrorizes the man (Ben Kingsley) who she says raped and tortured her under the former fascist regime. Chilean writer Ariel Dorfman's play examines the fine line between justice and vengeance. A taut and fascinating film, very well acted and tensely directed by suspense veteran Roman Polanski. Rated R for profanity and violence. 103m. DIR: Roman Polanski. CAST: Sigourney Weaver, Ben Kingsley, Stuart Wilson. 1994

DEATH ARTIST 🎦 If you don't believe executive producer Roger Corman could do a word-for-word remake of his classic black comedy *A Bucket of Blood* without a single laugh, see this. But that's the only reason to see it. Rated R for violence, nudity, sexual situations, substance abuse, and profanity. 79m. DIR: Michael James McDonald. CAST: Anthony Michael Hall, Justine Bateman, Shadoe Stevens, Sam Lloyd. 1996

DEATH AT LOVE HOUSE ★★ Much tamer than the lurid title would suggest. Robert Wagner plays a writer who becomes obsessed with a movie queen who died years earlier. This mildly suspenseful hokum is made palatable by the engaging cast. Made for TV. 78m. DIR: E. W. Swackhamer. CAST: Robert Wagner, Kate Jackson, Sylvia Sidney, Joan Blondell, Dorothy Lamour, John Carradine, Bill Macy, Marianna Hill. 1976

DEATH BECOMES HER ★★★1/2 Meryl Streep and Goldie Hawn seem to have a ball clowning around in this marvelously entertaining, special-effects-laden fantasy about the secret of eternal life and the war between two women. There are scenes in this very, very twisted comedy guaranteed to make your jaw drop, and it is most definitely not for children. That

said, open-minded adults and older teenagers will get a real kick out of it. Rated PG-13 for profanity, nudity, and violence. 104m. DIR: Robert Zemeckis. CAST: Meryl Streep, Goldie Hawn, Bruce Willis, Isabella Rossellini, Ian Ogilvy. 1992 DVD

DEATH BEFORE DISHONOR 🎦 Grade Z war film. Rated R for violence and profanity. 112m. DIR: Terry Leonard. CAST: Fred Dryer, Brian Keith, Joanna Pacula, Paul Winfield. 1986

DEATH BENEFIT ★★★ A young woman falls off a cliff, but was it an accident, or was she murdered to collect on her life insurance? This made-for-cable original, based on a true story, follows an attorney's investigation into the mysterious death. Rated PG-13 for suggested sex. 89m. DIR: Mark Piznarski. CAST: Peter Horton, Carrie Snodgress, Wendy Makkena, Elizabeth Ruscio, Penny Johnson. 1996

DEATH CHASE ★★ An innocent jogger is caught up in a shoot-out, given a gun by a dying man, and suddenly finds himself in the midst of an elaborate chase. The premise is intriguing, but the execution is uninspired in this shoddily made thriller. 88m. DIR: David A. Prior. CAST: William Zipp, Paul Smith, Jack Starrett, Bainbridge Scott. 1988

DEATH DREAMS ★★★ The ghost of a little girl tries to communicate the identity of her killer to her grieving mother. No one believes her. A well-acted, made-for-TV mystery. 94m. DIR: Martin Donovan. CAST: Christopher Reeve, Fionnula Flanagan, Marg Helgenberger. 1992

DEATH DRUG ★★ A truthful yet cliché-filled movie about a promising young musician who starts using angel dust. Although the drug PCP deserves any bad rap it gets, this movie is a mediocre effort. Not rated, but fairly inoffensive. 73m. DIR: Oscar Williams. CAST: Philip Michael Thomas, Vernee Watson, Rosalind Cash. 1986

DEATH HOUSE 🎦 Framed for murder by the mob, Dennis Cole discovers that prisoners are being used for dangerous scientific experiments with nasty side effects. Give this one life without parole. Not rated; contains nudity, violence, and profanity. 92m. DIR: John Saxon. CAST: Dennis Cole, John Saxon, Anthony Franciosa. 1992

DEATH HUNT ★★★1/2 Based on the true story of a hazardous manhunt in the Canadian Rockies, *Death Hunt* pits trapper Charles Bronson against Mountie Lee Marvin. This gritty adventure film, directed by Peter Hunt, also features vicious dogfights and bloody shoot-outs set against the spectacular scenery of the Yukon Territory. Rated R. 97m. DIR: Peter R. Hunt. CAST: Charles Bronson, Lee Marvin, Andrew Stevens, Angie Dickinson, Carl Weathers, Ed Lauter. 1981

DEATH IN BRUNSWICK ★★1/2 Short-order cook and all-around loser Sam Neill (in an endearing performance) falls for a much younger Greek barmaid who already has a fiancé. Rowdy and fast-moving, but the plot is ludicrous. Rated R for profanity, violence, nudity, and sexual situations. 106m. DIR: John Ruane. CAST: Sam Neill, Zoe Carides, John Clarke, Yvonne Lawley. 1990

DEATH IN THE GARDEN ★★★1/2 A disparate group of refugees flees a Central American riot by escaping into the jungle. One of cinema master Luis Buñuel's most obscure films, this strikingly photographed adventure contains little of his usual satirical edge, though it offers a fairly gripping story. Also known as *Evil Eden*. In Spanish with English subtitles. Not rated. 90m. DIR: Luis Buñuel. CAST: Georges Marchal, Simone Signoret, Michel Piccoli, Charles Vanel. 1956

DEATH IN VENICE ★★ Slow, studied film based on Thomas Mann's classic novel about an artist's quest for beauty and perfection. The good cast seems to move through this movie without communicating with one another or the audience. Visually absorbing, but lifeless. Adult language, adult situations throughout. Rated PG. 130m. DIR: Luchino Visconti. CAST: Dirk Bogarde, Marisa Berenson, Mark Burns, Silvana Mangano. 1971

DEATH KING, THE 🎭 From the director of the similarly disturbing *Nekromantik* comes this slightly better tale of a deadly chain letter. In German with English subtitles. Not rated; contains violence, profanity, gore, and nudity. 80m. DIR: Jorg Buttgereit. CAST: Herman Kopp, Eva Kurz. 1989

DEATH KISS, THE ★★★ Entertaining movie-within-a-movie whodunit is a treat for fans of early 1930s films and a pretty well-paced mystery to boot as Bela Lugosi (in fine, hammy form) is embroiled in the investigation of a murder that took place during filming. B&W; 75m. DIR: Edwin L. Marin. CAST: Bela Lugosi, David Manners, Adrienne Ames, John Wray, Vince Barnett, Edward Van Sloan. 1933

DEATH MACHINE ★★ Claustrophobic thriller about a psychotic genius who unleashes his killing machine on the female boss that axed his project and fired him. Some futuristic thrills evolve as the prey is joined by two friends in a desperate attempt to terminate the "Death Machine." Rated R for violence and language. 99m. DIR: Stephen Norrington. CAST: Brad Dourif, Ely Pouget, William Hootkins. 1994 DVD

DEATH OF A BUREAUCRAT ★★★ An entertaining black comedy about a man's struggle with the red tape of bureaucracy. He attempts to replace his dead relative in a graveyard after having to have him illegally exhumed. Delightful farce. In Spanish with English subtitles. Not rated. B&W; 87m. DIR: Tomas Gutierrez Alea. CAST: Salvador Wood. 1966

DEATH OF A CENTERFOLD ★★ This made-for-TV film chronicles the brutal murder of Playboy playmate Dorothy Stratten. Bob Fosse's *Star 80* does a much better job. Not rated. 100m. DIR: Gabrielle Beaumont. CAST: Jamie Lee Curtis, Robert Reed, Bruce Weitz. 1981

DEATH OF A GUNFIGHTER ★★★ Any time you see the name Alan Smithee in the directorial slot, that means the real director had his name taken off the credits. In this case, Don Siegel and Robert Totten were alternately at the helm of what still emerges as a sturdy Western. Richard Widmark is very good as the sheriff who has outlived his usefulness to the town but refuses to change, thus setting the stage for tragic results. Rated PG. 100m. DIR: Alan Smithee. CAST: Richard Widmark, Lena Horne, Carroll O'Connor, John Saxon, Kent Smith. 1969

DEATH OF A PROPHET ★★1/2 Docudrama combines live footage of Sixties civil rights movement among black Americans as well as interviews with people who were close to Malcolm X. Morgan Freeman reenacts Malcolm X during the twenty-four hours prior to his assassination. Freeman portrays Malcolm X as a patient, religious man who believed there was an African connection with the quality of life black Americans could enjoy. Not rated, contains violence. 60m. DIR: Woodie King Jr. CAST: Morgan Freeman, Yolanda King, Mansoor Najee-ullah, Sam Singleton. 1991

DEATH OF A SALESMAN ★★★★ Impressive TV version of the Arthur Miller play. Dustin Hoffman is excellent as the aging, embittered Willy Loman, who realizes he has wasted his life and the lives of his family. Kate Reid is his long-suffering wife and Charles Durning is the neighbor. Thoughtful and well produced. 135m. DIR: Volker Schlöndorff. CAST: Dustin Hoffman, Kate Reid, John Malkovich, Stephen Lang, Charles Durning. 1985

DEATH OF A SCOUNDREL ★★★ If anyone could portray a suave, debonair, conniving, ruthlessly charming, amoral, despicable, notorious, manipulating cad, it was George Sanders. He does so to a *tee* in this portrait of the ultimate rake—based on the life of financier Serge Rubenstein. 119m. DIR: Charles Martin. CAST: George Sanders, Zsa Zsa Gabor, Tom Conway, Yvonne De Carlo, Nancy Gates, Coleen Gray, Victor Jory, John Hoyt. 1956

DEATH OF A SOLDIER ★★1/2 Based on a true story. In 1942 an American GI stationed in Australia murdered three Melbourne women. The incident aggravated U.S.-Australian relations, and General MacArthur ordered the execution of the serviceman to firm up Allied unity. James Coburn plays a major who believes the GI isn't sane enough to stand trial. Rated R for profanity, violence, and nudity. 93m. DIR: Philippe Mora. CAST: James Coburn, Bill Hunter, Reb Brown, Maurie Fields. 1985

DEATH OF ADOLF HITLER, THE ★★★ Made-for-British-television dramatization of the last ten days of the dictator's life, all spent in the underground bunker where he received the news of Germany's defeat. Frank Finlay is excellent as Hitler, avoiding the usual stereotypes. The low-key nature of the production renders it eerie, but strangely unmoving. Not rated. 107m. DIR: Rex Firkin. CAST: Frank Finlay, Caroline Mortimer, Ray McAnally. 1972

DEATH OF THE INCREDIBLE HULK, THE ★★★ Supposedly dead David Banner (Bill Bixby) works as a janitor at a laboratory where a world-renowned scientist is creating a formula that could free Banner from the monster within him. Unfortunately, an international spy ring also wants the formula. Made for TV. 96m. DIR: Bill Bixby. CAST: Bill Bixby, Lou Ferrigno, Philip Sterling, Andreas Katsulas. 1990

DEATH ON THE NILE ★★★1/2 The second in the series of films based on the Hercule Poirot mysteries, written by Agatha Christie, is good, but nothing special. Peter Ustinov stars as the fussy Belgian detective adrift in Africa with a set of murder suspects. Despite a better-than-average Christie plot, this film, directed by John Guillermin, tends to sag here and there. Rated PG. 140m. DIR: John Guillermin. CAST: Peter Ustinov, Bette Davis, David Niven, Mia Farrow, Angela Lansbury, George Kennedy, Jack Warden. 1978

DEATH RACE 2000 ★★★ Futuristic look at what has become our national sport: road racing where points are accumulated for killing people with the race cars. David Carradine and Sylvester Stallone star in this tongue-in-cheek sci-fi action film. Stallone is a howl as one of the competitors. Rated R—violence, nudity, and language. 78m. DIR: Paul Bartel. CAST: David Carradine, Sylvester Stallone, Louisa Moritz, Mary Woronov, Joyce Jameson, Fred Grandy. 1975 DVD

DEATH RIDES A HORSE ♥ Needlessly tedious spaghetti Western about a young boy who witnesses the butchery of his family and then grows up to take his revenge. Rated PG for violence. 114m. DIR: Giulio Petroni. CAST: Lee Van Cleef, John Phillip Law, Mario Brega, Anthony Dawson. 1969 DVD

DEATH RIDES THE PLAINS ★★★ The Lone Rider must stop a rancher who sells his land and then kills the multiple buyers. Offbeat land-grab plot. A class act. B&W; 56m. DIR: Sam Newfield. CAST: Robert Livingston, Al St. John, I. Stanford Jolley. 1943

DEATH RING ♥ A cast of star relatives do nothing to freshen this umpteenth update of "The Most Dangerous Game." Rated R for violence, sexual situations, and profanity. 91m. DIR: R. J. Kizer. CAST: Mike Norris, Billy Drago, Chad McQueen, Don Swayze. 1992

DEATH SPA ★★1/2 A disturbing gore flick about the dead wife of a health-spa owner who makes things unbearable for him and the patrons of his state-of-the-art spa. Not rated; contains violence, nudity, profanity, and gore. 89m. DIR: Michael Fischa. CAST: William Bumiller, Brenda Bakke, Merritt Butrick, Robert Lipton, Alexa Hamilton, Rosalind Cash, Shari Shattuck. 1990

DEATH SQUAD, THE ★★ A self-appointed coterie of cops is rubbing out criminals beating the rap on legal technicalities. A former officer is given the job of finding out who's doing it and cleaning house. Clint Eastwood did it all infinitely better in *Magnum Force*. Made for television. 78m. DIR: Harry Falk. CAST: Robert Forster, Michelle Phillips, Claude Akins, Melvyn Douglas. 1974

DEATH TAKES A HOLIDAY ★★★ Strange story of Death forsaking its duty for three days wrapped up in a love story. Intriguing concept gets "the works" from matinee idol Fredric March and ethereal beauty Evelyn Venable, and some eerie scenes make this one worth a watch. B&W; 80m. DIR: Mitchell Leisen. CAST: Fredric March, Evelyn Venable, Henry Travers, Kent Taylor, Guy Standing, Gail Patrick. 1934

DEATH TARGET ★★ Three soldiers for hire reunite in one last bid for fortune. But when one of the guys falls for a drug-addict hooker, her loony pimp gets into the act, putting a wrench in the works for everyone. Macho. No rating. 72m. DIR: Peter Hyams. CAST: Jorge Montesi, Elaine Lakeman. 1983

DEATH TRAIN ★★★★ An excellent adaptation of an Alistair MacLean story about a renegade Soviet general who terrorizes the world with two nuclear bombs. One bomb is aboard a hijacked train travel-ing through Europe. A blend of fine acting, editing, and suspense makes for a top-notch film. Not rated; acceptable for cable, but contains violence. 95m. DIR: David S. Jackson. CAST: Pierce Brosnan, Patrick Stewart, Alexandra Paul, Ted Levine, Christopher Lee. 1992

DEATH VALLEY ★★ Paul LeMat and Catharine Hicks star in this okay horror film about a vacation that turns into a nightmare. Rated R for violence and gore. 87m. DIR: Dick Richards. CAST: Paul LeMat, Catherine Hicks, Stephen McHattie, Stephen Brimley. 1982

DEATH VALLEY MANHUNT ★★★ Wild Bill Elliott routs the efforts of swindlers to take over Gabby Hayes and the homesteaders' oil well. Ingenue Anne Jeffreys later gained fame on TV's *Topper*. B&W; 55m. DIR: John English. CAST: William Elliott, George "Gabby" Hayes, Anne Jeffreys. 1943

DEATH WARMED UP ★★ In this winner of the 1984 Grand Prix International Festival of Fantasy and Science Fiction Films, a psycho doctor is transforming patients into mutant killers, until a former patient comes after revenge. Rated R for violence, nudity, and profanity. 83m. DIR: David Blyth. CAST: Michael Hurst, Margaret Umbers, David Leitch. 1983

DEATH WARRANT ★★ Action-fu star Jean-Claude Van Damme has plenty to kick about as he plays an undercover cop sent into the slammer to investigate a series of inmate deaths. Before the final showdown, there are beatings and big-house clichés galore. Rated R for language and violence. 89m. DIR: Deran Sarafian. CAST: Jean-Claude Van Damme, Robert Guillaume, Cynthia Gibb, George Dickerson. 1990

DEATH WATCH ★★★★ A thought-provoking look at the power and the misuse of the media in a future society. Harvey Keitel has a camera implanted in his brain. A television producer (Harry Dean Stanton) uses Keitel to film a documentary of a terminally ill woman (Romy Schneider) without her knowledge. Suspenseful science-fiction drama. Rated R for profanity and suggested sex. 117m. DIR: Bertrand Tavernier. CAST: Romy Schneider, Harvey Keitel, Harry Dean Stanton, Max von Sydow. 1980

DEATH WEEKEND ★★ Don Stroud is chillingly convincing as a vicious sadist who, with the help of two demented pals, terrorizes lovers Brenda Vaccaro and Chuck Shamata at their *House by the Lake*, which was the film's theatrical title. Director William Fruet dwells too much on the cruelty. As a result, the film is uncomfortable to watch. Rated R for violence and profanity. 89m. DIR: William Fruet. CAST: Brenda Vaccaro, Don Stroud, Chuck Shamata. 1977

DEATH WISH ★★★★ Charles Bronson gives an excellent performance as Paul Kersey, a mild-mannered New Yorker moved to violence when his daughter is raped and his wife killed by sleazy muggers. It's a gripping story of one man's revenge. Rated R because of nudity and violence (includes a graphic rape scene). 93m. DIR: Michael Winner. CAST: Charles Bronson, Hope Lange, Vincent Gardenia, Jeff Goldblum. 1974

DEATH WISH II ♥ This carbon-copy sequel to the successful *Death Wish* is a revolting, violent crime chiller. Rated R because of nudity and violence. 93m.

DIR: Michael Winner. **CAST:** Charles Bronson, Jill Ireland, Vincent Gardenia, J. D. Cannon, Anthony Franciosa. **1982**

DEATH WISH III 🗡 Paul Kersey (Charles Bronson) loses a loved one and then goes on another rampage. Rated R for violence, profanity, drug use, nudity, and sex. 99m. **DIR:** Michael Winner. **CAST:** Charles Bronson, Deborah Raffin, Ed Lauter, Martin Balsam. **1985**

DEATH WISH IV: THE CRACKDOWN 🗡 Charles Bronson is back as the vigilante, but this time he's hired to destroy two drug families operating in Los Angeles. Rated R for violence and language. 98m. **DIR:** J. Lee Thompson. **CAST:** Charles Bronson, Kay Lenz, John P. Ryan, Perry Lopez, Soon-Teck Oh, George Dickerson, Dana Barron. **1987**

DEATH WISH V: THE FACE OF DEATH ★★1/2 Vigilante Charles Bronson returns to hunt a ruthless mobster who just happens to be his fiancée's ex-husband. The story is quite captivating, and the film doesn't contain too much gore or violence. Rated R for nudity, profanity, and violence. 95m. **DIR:** Allan A. Goldstein. **CAST:** Charles Bronson, Lesley-Anne Down, Robert Joy, Michael Parks, Chuck Shamata, Kenneth Welsh. **1993 DVD**

DEATHDREAM ★★★1/2 The underrated director Bob Clark made some interesting low-budget movies in his native Canada before gaining commercial success (and critical scorn) with the *Porky's* series. This unsettling horror tale, an update of "The Monkey's Paw" as a comment on the Vietnam War and modern family life, is one of his best. It's a creepy mood piece, also known as *Dead of Night*. Rated R. 88m. **DIR:** Bob Clark. **CAST:** John Marley, Richard Backus, Lynn Carlin, Anya Ormsby. **1972**

DEATHFIGHT ★★ Brother battles brother in this decent martial arts flick that features the art of shoot boxing. When the patriarch of the family selects his adopted son to run the family smuggling business, the natural son frames his brother for murder. Rated R for nudity, violence, and profanity. 92m. **DIR:** Anthony Maharaj. **CAST:** Richard Norton, Karen Moncrieff, Chuck Jeffreys, Ron Vreeken, Franco Guerrero, José Mari Avellana, Tetchie Agbayani. **1992**

DEATHGAME ★★ Timothy Bottoms wastes his time and talent in this rip-off of *Escape from L.A.*, as a weary police investigator who searches for a missing young woman and winds up as prey in an enclosed arena. The cheap sets and gratuitous nudity brand it as yet another quickie from producer Roger Corman. Rated R for violence, profanity, nudity, and simulated sex. 80m. **DIR:** Randolph Cheveldave. **CAST:** Timothy Bottoms, Alfonso Quijada, Vince Murdocco, Nicholas Hill, David McCallum, Jody Thompson. **1996**

DEATHMASK ★★ This talky, confusing screenplay is interesting in concept but is never sure where it's going. The plot involves a medical investigator who, after his daughter drowns, pours all his energy into investigating the death of a young boy. Not rated. 103m. **DIR:** Richard Friedman. **CAST:** Farley Granger, Lee Bryant, Arch Johnson. **1984**

DEATHMOON 🗡 A simple-minded telefilm about a businessman who is cursed by an old crone and turns into a werewolf. Not rated. 90m. **DIR:** Bruce Kessler.

CAST: Robert Foxworth, Charles Haid, France Nuyen. **1985**

DEATHROW GAMESHOW 🗡 Incredibly dull comedy about a detestable game show host who's on the run from mobsters. Rated R. 78m. **DIR:** Mark Pirro. **CAST:** Robin Blythe, John McCafferty. **1988**

DEATHSHIP ★★ This story of a modern-day lost *Flying Dutchman* involves a World War II battleship—haunted by those who died on it. The ship destroys any seagoing vessels it can find because it needs blood. There are a few chills along the way, but not enough. Rated R for violence and brief nudity. 91m. **DIR:** Alvin Rakoff. **CAST:** George Kennedy, Richard Crenna, Nick Mancuso, Sally Ann Howes, Kate Reid, Saul Rubinek. **1980**

DEATHSHOT 🗡 Two Illinois detectives will stop at nothing to break up a drug ring. 90m. **DIR:** Mitch Brown. **CAST:** Richard C. Watt, Frank Himes. **1973**

DEATHSPORT ★★ Not really a sequel to *Death Race 2000*, but cut from the same cloth. Both are low-budget action films centered around futuristic no-holds-barred road races. The first film, though, was a lot more fun. Rated R for violence and nudity. 82m. **DIR:** Henry Suso, Allan Arkush. **CAST:** David Carradine, Claudia Jennings, Richard Lynch. **1978 DVD**

DEATHSTALKER 🗡 This film has a muscle-bound warrior attempting to save a beautiful princess (Barbi Benton) from an evil wizard. Rated R for nudity, profanity, simulated rape, and violence. 80m. **DIR:** John Watson. **CAST:** Richard Hill, Barbi Benton, Lana Clarkson. **1984**

DEATHSTALKER II: DUEL OF THE TITANS ★★1/2 Deathstalker and a feisty deposed princess battle the evil magician who has taken over her kingdom. Lowbrow fun is too busy making fun of itself to be taken seriously. The R rating is for nudity and violence. 85m. **DIR:** Jim Wynorski. **CAST:** John Terlesky, Monique Gabrielle. **1987**

DEATHSTALKER III—THE WARRIORS FROM HELL ★★1/2 Tongue-in-cheek sword-and-sorcery tale about the search for three magical stones that will lead to the riches of the world. You have so much fun with this one, you forget how hokey it really is. Rated R for nudity and violence. 85m. **DIR:** Alfonso Corona. **CAST:** John Allen Nelson, Carla Herd, Thom Christopher, Terri Treas. **1988**

DEATHSTALKER IV: MATCH OF THE TITANS 🗡 Unbelievably bad sword-and-sorcery flick finds all the greatest warriors gathered for a tournament. Acting is nonexistent and fight scenes are poorly staged. Rated R for nudity and violence. 85m. **DIR:** Howard R. Cohen. **CAST:** Richard Hill, Maria Ford, Michelle Moffett, Brett Clark. **1992**

DEATHTRAP ★★★ An enjoyable mystery-comedy based on the Broadway play, this Sidney Lumet film stars Michael Caine, Christopher Reeve, and Dyan Cannon. Caine plays a once-successful playwright who decides to steal a brilliant murder mystery just written by one of his students (Reeve), murder the student, and collect the royalties. Rated PG for violence and adult themes. 116m. **DIR:** Sidney Lumet. **CAST:** Michael Caine, Christopher Reeve, Dyan Cannon, Irene Worth, Henry Jones. **1982 DVD**

DEBAJO DEL MUNDO (UNDER EARTH) ★★★★ A Polish family's prosperous life is shattered when the German army invades their small farming community. This Spanish film captures the spirit of a family torn apart by war. A great cast gives compelling performances in this poignant drama. Dubbed in English. Rated R for profanity and graphic violence. 100m. DIR: Beda Docampo Feijoo, Juan Bautista Stagnaro. CAST: Sergio Renan. 1988

DECAMERON, THE ★★★★ Earthy, vibrant adaptation of eight stories from the fourteenth-century work by Boccaccio. Probably Pier Paolo Pasolini's most purely enjoyable film. Dubbed in English. 111m. DIR: Pier Paolo Pasolini. CAST: Franco Citti. 1971

DECAMERON NIGHTS ★★★ Louis Jourdan is Boccaccio, the poet, storyteller, and humanist best known for *The Decameron*. Three of his tales are told within the overall frame of his trying to win the love of a recent widow (Joan Fontaine). Each story features the cast members as various characters. The sets and costumes add greatly to this period comedy. 75m. DIR: Hugo Fregonese. CAST: Joan Fontaine, Louis Jourdan, Joan Collins, Binnie Barnes, Marjorie Rhodes, Godfrey Tearle. 1953

DECEIT ★★★ Alien sex fiends sent to destroy Earth find a little time to sample its women. When one of them chooses a street-smart prostitute she proves to be more than a match for them. Original, offbeat story is amusing as well as thought-provoking, if somewhat erratic. Rated R for nudity, profanity, and violence. 92m. DIR: Albert Pyun. CAST: Norbert Weisser, Samantha Phillips, Diane DeFoe, Christian Andrews, Scott Paulin. 1993

DECEIVED ★★★1/2 In this suspense thriller, Goldie Hawn finds out what happens when Mr. Right (John Heard) turns out to be the bogeyman. Director Damian Harris keeps the screws turned tight. Rated PG-13 for violence and profanity. 104m. DIR: Damian Harris. CAST: Goldie Hawn, John Heard, Robin Bartlett, Amy Wright, Jan Rubes, Kate Reid. 1991

DECEIVER ★★★ An unemployed, alcoholic, epileptic textile heir takes several polygraph tests after his phone number is found in the pocket of a murdered hooker. Cops grill him until he turns the tables and makes several seamy accusations about their personal lives and taunts them to tell the truth. This lurid mind game about displaced hostility and personal demons is a triumph of style over substance. Rated R for language, violence, and sexual content. 102m. DIR: Jonas Pate, Josh Pate. CAST: Tim Roth, Michael Rooker, Renee Zellweger, Christopher Penn, Ellen Burstyn, Michael Parks. 1998

DECEIVERS, THE ★★1/2 Melodramatic yarn set in 1820s India and based on the true story of the murderous Thuggee cult. Pierce Brosnan goes undercover and joins the cult. This slow-going film has its moments. Rated PG-13. 103m. DIR: Nicholas Meyer. CAST: Pierce Brosnan, Shashi Kapoor, Saeed Jaffrey. 1988

DECEMBER ★★★ Intelligent, thoughtful drama unfolds on the day after Pearl Harbor has been bombed by the Japanese. Five New England prep school friends gather to discuss the implications of the event, and how it will affect them. Compelling. Rated PG. 92m. DIR: Gabe Torres. CAST: Wil Wheaton, Brian Krause, Balthazar Getty, Chris Young. 1991

DECEMBER 7TH: THE MOVIE ★★★ Cinematographer Gregg Toland, commissioned by the Navy Department to prepare a documentary on the Pearl Harbor attack, instead made this feature-length film where the military, in the form of Walter Huston as Uncle Sam, was criticized for being unprepared in the Pacific. The navy suppressed the film, editing it to a 34-minute short, which, on its own, won an Oscar as best documentary. A curiosity and, as such, recommended. B&W; 82m. DIR: John Ford, Gregg Toland. CAST: Walter Huston, Harry Davenport. 1943

DECEMBER BRIDE ★★★1/2 Suppressed desire flies in the face of a shocked society in this oddly beautiful love story. Strong-willed Saskia Reeves is a servant who takes up with two brothers, defying all convention in their rural Irish village at the turn of the century. Director Thaddeus O'Sullivan uncovers the tremulous eroticism beneath a stony emotional landscape. It takes true talent to reveal such passion when everyone keeps his clothes on. Not rated; contains adult themes. 90m. DIR: Thaddeus O'Sullivan. CAST: Saskia Reeves, Donal McCann, Ciaran Hinds. 1994

DECEPTION (1946) ★★★1/2 A better-than-average Bette Davis melodrama, with Claude Rains as a domineering orchestra conductor who imposes his will on musician Davis. The leads make this detergent drama work with their intensity and apparent desire to one-up each other in front of the camera. 110m. DIR: Irving Rapper. CAST: Bette Davis, Paul Henreid, Claude Rains. 1946

DECEPTION (1993) ★★1/2 Postcard gorgeous but empty-headed exotic pseudothriller is amazingly fun because it makes so little sense. When an aviation-supply vendor is burned beyond recognition in a plane crash, his wife tries to keep their business afloat. While settling bills, she finds a packet of coded baseball cards that leads to clandestine bank accounts around the world. Rated PG-13 for profanity. 95m. DIR: Graeme Clifford. CAST: Andie MacDowell, Liam Neeson, Viggo Mortensen. 1993

DECISION AT SUNDOWN ★★★★ Full of hate, Randolph Scott arrives in town to avenge himself and kill the man responsible for his wife's death. Many surprises in the brooding script. A class act. 77m. DIR: Budd Boetticher. CAST: Randolph Scott, John Carroll, Karen Steele, Noah Beery Jr., Bob Steele. 1957

DECLINE OF THE AMERICAN EMPIRE, THE ★★★★ Writer-director Denys Arcand focuses on two groups, one male and one female. Both reveal secrets about their lives. Rated R for profanity, nudity, and simulated sex. In French with English subtitles. 101m. DIR: Denys Arcand. CAST: Dominique Michel, Dorothee Berryman, Louise Portal. 1986

DECLINE OF WESTERN CIVILIZATION, THE ★★★★ The L.A. punk scene captured at its 1979 peak, before MTV and the music industry sanitized it into oblivion (and made the stinging title seem sarcastic). Director Penelope Spheeris is both a fan of the music and an objective observer of the scene, which she depicts in engrossing detail. Not rated; the film contains profanity. 100m. DIR: Penelope Spheeris. 1981

DECONSTRUCTING HARRY ★★★ Woody Allen strays into Ingmar Bergman territory with a familiar writer's conceit—the notion of fictional characters "coming to life" and confronting their creator. The result is a film in which it's occasionally difficult to determine whether we're watching this story's central character, his fictional alter egos, or an amalgam of both. Allen stars as Harry Block, an aptly named writer suffering from the ultimate writer's block: an inability to survive in the real world. Harry has put himself, and all the people he knows, into his fiction. His latest novel is so thinly disguised that it has egregiously insulted, alienated, and infuriated nearly everybody he knows. Rated R for nudity, sexual content, and profanity. 95m. DIR: Woody Allen. CAST: Woody Allen, Kirstie Alley, Bob Balaban, Billy Crystal, Judy Davis, Amy Irving, Elisabeth Shue, Robin Williams. 1997 DVD

DECORATION DAY ★★★★★ This superior adaptation of John William Corrington's novel finds retired judge James Garner investigating a mystery when an old friend (Bill Cobbs) refuses to accept a long overdue Medal of Honor. Originally produced as a television *Hallmark Hall of Fame* special, this stirring character study benefits from superb performances—particularly by Garner—and first-rate production values. 91m. DIR: Robert Markowitz. CAST: James Garner, Bill Cobbs, Judith Ivey, Ruby Dee, Laurence Fishburne. 1991

DECOY ★★★ This otherwise average kill-or-be-killed saga is highlighted by its unusual characters, notably Peter Weller as a bald disciple of Cree mysticism. He and his best friend agree to shelter flighty Darlene Vogel from baddies intending to kidnap her as a means of pressuring dear ol' Dad. Naturally, things get a little complicated. Rated R for violence, torture, and profanity. 97m. DIR: Vittorio Rambaldi. CAST: Peter Weller, Robert Patrick, Charlotte Lewis, Darlene Vogel. 1995

DEDEE D'ANVERS ★★1/2 Simone Signoret's first starring role was as a prostitute in this melodrama. She works the docks but tries to get out of the life with the help of a kindly sailor. Pretty gloomy. In French with English subtitles. B&W; 95m. DIR: Yves Allegret. CAST: Simone Signoret, Marcel Pagliero, Bernard Blier. 1949

DEDICATED MAN, A ★★ Haunting British romance about a workaholic who asks a lonely spinster to pose as his wife. All goes well until she starts asking questions about his past. The *Romance Theatre* presentation will disappoint viewers hoping for high passions. 50m. DIR: Robert Knights. CAST: Alec McCowen, Joan Plowright, Christopher Irving. 1982

DEE SNIDER'S STRANGELAND 🌶 Exercise in futility as former Twisted Sister lead singer Dee Snider writes and costars in this sleazy thriller about a psychopath who lures young people to his lair over the Internet and then subjects them to all kinds of horrible torture. Amateurishly acted and directed. Rated R for violence, language, nudity, and adult situations. 91m. DIR: John Pipelow. CAST: Dee Snider,

Michael Gage, Brett Harrelson, Elizabeth Peña, Linda Cardellini. 1998

DEEP, THE ★★ The success of *Jaws* prompted this screen adaptation of another Benchley novel, but the results weren't nearly as satisfying. A good cast founders in this waterlogged tale of treasure hunting. Rated PG. 123m. DIR: Peter Yates. CAST: Robert Shaw, Jacqueline Bisset, Nick Nolte, Lou Gossett Jr., Eli Wallach, Robert Tessier. 1977 DVD

•**DEEP BLUE SEA** ★★ At a midocean research station where scientists are experimenting on sharks, the creatures develop superhuman intelligence and turn on their captors. The script is almost idiotic, with one cornball line after another, as if the writers never even expected us to believe it. The special effects, like the story, are flashy but unconvincing, and the actors are a mixed bag—generally, the better they are the sooner they get munched. Rated R for violence and profanity. 106m. DIR: Renny Harlin. CAST: Saffron Burrows, Samuel L. Jackson, Thomas Jane, LL Cool J, Jacqueline McKenzie, Michael Rapaport, Stellan Skarsgard, Aida Turturro. 1999 DVD

DEEP COVER (1980) 🌶 A Soviet spy poses as a Cambridge professor. Rated R for nudity, violence, and profanity. 81m. DIR: Richard Loncraine. CAST: Tom Conti, Donald Pleasence, Denholm Elliott. 1980

DEEP COVER (1992) ★★★★ With this no-nonsense action film about a straitlaced cop (brilliantly played by Laurence Fishburne) who goes undercover for the DEA, Bill Duke hits his stride as a director. Duke tells his story of Fishburne's descent into decadence, danger, and disillusionment in a compelling, in-your-face fashion. Rated R for violence, profanity, and nudity. 112m. DIR: Bill Duke. CAST: Laurence Fishburne, Jeff Goldblum, Victoria Dillard, Charles Martin Smith, Sidney Lassick, Clarence Williams III, Gregory Sierra. 1992 DVD

DEEP CRIMSON ★★★ Middle-aged, toupee-obsessed Raymond hustles money from Mexican widows and spinsters after answering their lonely hearts ads. He dates an overweight nurse with two children who sympathizes with his scam. She then abandons her two children and accompanies him on a multiple-murder spree. This lushly photographed crime-thriller is both grisly and perversely fascinating. In Spanish with English subtitles. Not rated; contains violence, profanity, and sexual themes. 109m. DIR: Arturo Ripstein. CAST: Regina Orozco, Daniel Giminez-Cacho, Marisa Paredes, Veronica Merchant. 1996

DEEP END ★★★1/2 A young man working in a London bathhouse becomes obsessed with a beautiful female coworker. Offbeat drama with realistic performances by the cast. Rated R. 88m. DIR: Jerzy Skolimowski. CAST: John Moulder-Brown, Jane Asher, Diana Dors. 1970

DEEP END OF THE OCEAN, THE ★★★1/2 Based on Jacqueline Mitchard's weepy bestseller about family catastrophe, this melodrama begins when the family's youngest child disappears, with the parents not knowing whether he was kidnapped or simply wandered off, and an older brother who feels responsible for having "failed" to properly watch after the little guy. Flash-forward nine years, to the moment when a kid shows up to mow the lawn ... and is immediately recognized as the long-missing boy. The inevitable questions and answers cut to the core of human relationships, and the desperate need for healing among these players: husband and wife, parent and child, brother and brother. Rated PG-13 for profanity. 148m. DIR: Ulu Grosbard. CAST: Michelle Pfeiffer, Treat Williams, Jonathan Jackson, John Kapelos, Ryan Merriman, Whoopi Goldberg. 1999 DVD

DEEP IMPACT ★★★ This standard-issue sci-fi melodrama dilutes its cataclysmic premise with too much talk and too little action, and when the climactic "money shots" finally *do* arrive, they're over before viewers can adjust to the results. The film only really comes alive during its exciting outer-space sequences, when veteran astronaut Robert Duvall leads a crew in an effort to destroy the rogue comet that threatens to annihilate all life on Earth. Rated PG-13 for dramatic intensity and brief profanity. 115m. DIR: Mimi Leder. CAST: Robert Duvall, Téa Leoni, Elijah Wood, Vanessa Redgrave, Maximilian Schell, Morgan Freeman. 1998 DVD

DEEP IN MY HEART ★★ Most of the films presenting the lives of great composers have been tepid and silly. This biography of Sigmund Romberg is no exception. The songs are wonderful, but the rest is pure drivel. Along the way, Gene Kelly, Tony Martin, and Ann Miller drop by for brief musical visits, and that's it. Only fair. 132m. DIR: Stanley Donen. CAST: José Ferrer, Merle Oberon, Paul Henreid, Walter Pidgeon, Helen Traubel. 1954

DEEP IN THE HEART OF TEXAS ★★★1/2 This is a well-directed, finely photographed film about post–Civil War land snatching. It's the first in a series of seven films to co-star the two great Western stars, Johnny Mack Brown and Tex Ritter. This one has lots of black hats, a few white hats, and plenty of action. B&W; 74m. DIR: Elmer Clifton. CAST: Johnny Mack Brown, Tex Ritter. 1942

DEEP RED (1975) ★★★ Another stylish and brutal horror-mystery from Italian director Dario Argento. His other works include *The Bird with the Crystal Plumage* and *Suspiria*. Like those, this film is slim on plot and a bit too talky, but Argento builds tension beautifully with rich atmosphere and driving electronic music. Rated R for violence. 98m. Original running time 122m. DIR: Dario Argento. CAST: David Hemmings, Daria Nicolodi, Gabriele Lavia. 1975 DVD

DEEP RED (1994) ★★★★ This well-made thriller casts Michael Biehn as a private investigator in the near future who agrees to track down a missing husband. When the man, a scientist working on a top-secret project called "Deep Red," is killed just as Biehn finds him, our hero realizes he's being used. Flashback style is disconcerting at first, but the acting and premise hold the viewer's interest. Made for cable. 86m. DIR: Craig R. Baxley. CAST: Michael Biehn, Joanna Pacula, Lisa Collins, John de Lancie, Tobin Bell, John Kapelos, Steven Williams, Michael Des Barres. 1994

DEEP RISING ★★ A gang of modern-day pirates intercepts a cruise ship in midocean to plunder the superrich passengers—but a swarm of sea serpents has beaten them to it, devouring everyone on board. Writer-director Stephen Sommers throws everything he can think of into this waterlogged thriller, but the special effects and sets aren't credible, the action isn't exciting, and the comic relief isn't funny. Rated R for profanity and gore. 106m. DIR: Stephen Sommers. CAST: Treat Williams, Famke Janssen, Kevin J. O'Connor, Anthony Heald, Wes Studi. 1997 DVD

DEEP SIX, THE ★★★1/2 Good action and the magnetism of popular Alan Ladd as a WWI naval officer who doesn't know the meaning of the word *fear*. 105m. DIR: Rudolph Maté. CAST: Alan Ladd, William Bendix, Efrem Zimbalist Jr., Dianne Foster, Joey Bishop. 1958

DEEP SPACE 🦃 A creature created by the air force runs amok, and two rebel policemen track it down. Rated R for violence and language. 90m. DIR: Fred Olen Ray. CAST: Charles Napier, Ann Turkel, Ron Glass, Julie Newmar, James Booth, Anthony Eisley, Bo Svenson. 1988

DEEP TROUBLE ★★ In this made-for-cable original, Robert Wagner plays a deep-sea diver who happens upon an armored car, filled with diamonds, under the waves. Now he must hide the jewels, save a beautiful woman, and avenge the death of his partner. Too unbelievable to be enjoyed. Not rated; contains violence. 95m. DIR: Armand Mastroianni. CAST: Robert Wagner, Isabelle Pasco, Jean-Yves Berteloot, Frederic Darie, Jean-François Pages, Ben Cross. 1993

DEEPSTAR SIX 🦃 A secret navy underwater colonization project goes awry. Rated R for violence and profanity. 105m. DIR: Sean S. Cunningham. CAST: Taurean Blacque, Nancy Everhard, Greg Evigan, Miguel Ferrer, Nia Peeples, Matt McCoy, Cindy Pickett. 1989

DEER HUNTER, THE ★★★★★ Five friends work at the dangerous blast furnace in a steel mill in the dingy town of Clairton, Pennsylvania, in 1968. At quitting time, they make their way to their favorite local bar to drink away the pressures of the day. For three of the friends, it is the last gathering before they leave for Vietnam, where they find horror and death. A gripping study of heroism and the meaning of friendship. Rated R for profanity and violence. 183m. DIR: Michael Cimino. CAST: Robert De Niro, John Cazale, John Savage, Meryl Streep, Christopher Walken. 1978 DVD

DEERSLAYER (1920) ★★1/2 Silent German version of Fenimore Cooper's frontier stories was trimmed by more than half for American release in 1923, but what's left is pretty good. Bela Lugosi is an impressive Chingachgook and is able to maintain his dignity despite the hoary plot machinations. Idyllic settings, realistic costuming, and a charming framework of scouts being read this story around a campfire engage a viewer and make one hope for the eventual discovery of the whole film. B&W; 60m. DIR: Arthur Wellin. CAST: Emil Mamelok, Bela Lugosi, Herten Heden, Gottfried Krause. 1920

DEERSLAYER, THE (1978) ★★1/2 Made-for-TV movie, based on James Fenimore Cooper's classic, is a film of adventure in early America. The heroes, Hawkeye (Steve Forrest) and Chingachgook (Ned Romero), attempt to save a Mohican princess and avenge the death of Chingachgook's son. 98m. DIR: Dick Friedenberg. CAST: Steve Forrest, John Anderson, Ned Romero, Joan Prather. 1978

DEF BY TEMPTATION ★★★ A divinity student is tempted by a seductive succubus who wants his soul. This independently produced horror-comedy is entertaining and well-acted by its all-black cast. Rated R for profanity and violence. 95m. DIR: James Bond III. CAST: James Bond III, Kadeem Hardison, Melba Moore. 1990 DVD

DEF-CON 4 ★★1/2 The first half of this film contains special effects the equal of any in modern science fiction, an intelligent script, and excellent acting. The second half is one postholocaust yawn. The overall impression is that perhaps the filmmakers ran out of time or money or both. Rated R for language and violence. 85m. DIR: Paul Donovan. CAST: Maury Chaykin, Kate Lynch, Tim Choate, Lenore Zann. 1985

DEFENDERS, THE ★★★ Reginald Rose's 1961–1965 television show gets an update in this made-for-cable original series, but one of the faces remains the same: E. G. Marshall as patriarch Lawrence Preston, head of the legal firm that bears his name. Unfortunately, time and countless subsequent film and TV lawyers have blunted what once had a dramatic edge. Rated R for profanity and violence. 100m. DIR: Andy Wolk. CAST: Beau Bridges, E. G. Marshall, Martha Plimpton, Roma Maffia, Mark Blum, John Larroquette. 1997

•DEFENDERS, THE: TAKING THE FIRST ★★1/2 A lot of interesting ideas get lost in this made-for-cable movie based on the television series of the same name. It's easy to admire where the writers were going, but we never warm up to the protagonists, an uncle-niece lawyer team, and the plot doesn't make much sense. Rated PG. 96m. DIR: Andy Wolk, Peter Wolk. CAST: Beau Bridges, Martha Plimpton, Philip Casnoff, Jeremy London. 1998

DEFENDING YOUR LIFE ★★★1/2 Once again, star-writer-director Albert Brooks has come up with that increasing rarity: an intelligent comedy. Brooks plays an advertising executive who dies in a car accident and finds himself in Judgment City, where he must defend the cowardly, self-involved life he led on Earth. Fine support from Meryl Streep, Rip Torn, Lee Grant and Buck Henry. Rated PG for brief profanity. 100m. DIR: Albert Brooks. CAST: Albert Brooks, Meryl Streep, Rip Torn, Lee Grant, Buck Henry. 1991

DEFENSE OF THE REALM ★★★★ In London, two reporters (Gabriel Byrne and Denholm Elliott) become convinced that a scandal involving a government official (Ian Bannen) may be a sinister cover-up. Acting on this belief puts both their lives in danger. A tough-minded British thriller that asks some thought-provoking questions. Rated PG for suspense. 96m. DIR: David Drury. CAST: Gabriel Byrne, Greta Scacchi, Denholm Elliott, Ian Bannen, Bill Paterson, Fulton MacKay. 1986

DEFENSE PLAY 🅦 Substandard spy story about a group of newly graduated high school geniuses. Not rated; contains profane language, violence, and nudity. 95m. DIR: Monte Markham. CAST: David Oliver, Monte Markham. 1988

DEFENSELESS ★★★ A successful attorney (Barbara Hershey) becomes involved with a sleazy landlord (J. T. Walsh) who is a child pornographer. Sus-

penseful whodunit, with Sam Shepard as a detective who investigates the landlord's mysterious murder. Rated R for violence, profanity, and murder. 104m. DIR: Martin Campbell. CAST: Barbara Hershey, Sam Shepard, Mary Beth Hurt, J. T. Walsh. 1991

DEFIANCE ★★★ Potent story depicts savage New York street gang terrorizing helpless neighborhood. Outsider Jan-Michael Vincent reluctantly gets involved. This well-directed film packs quite a wallop. Rated R for violence and profanity. 102m. DIR: John Flynn. CAST: Jan-Michael Vincent, Art Carney, Theresa Saldana, Danny Aiello, Fernando Lopez. 1980

DEFIANT ONES, THE ★★★★ Director Stanley Kramer scored one of his few artistic successes with this compelling story about two escaped convicts (Tony Curtis and Sidney Poitier) shackled together—and coping with mutual hatred—as they run from the authorities in the South. B&W; 97m. DIR: Stanley Kramer. CAST: Tony Curtis, Sidney Poitier, Theodore Bikel, Charles McGraw, Lon Chaney Jr. 1958

DEJA VU (1984) 🅦 Stupid story about reincarnation. Rated R. 91m. DIR: Anthony Richmond. CAST: Jaclyn Smith, Shelley Winters, Claire Bloom, Nigel Terry. 1984

DEJA VU (1998) ★★1/2 A young woman about to be married finds herself inexplicably attracted to another man—almost as if they had met somewhere before. The familiar plot has a clever O. Henry–style twist at the end, but the jabbering talkiness of the script is a drawback. Noel Harrison (son of Rex) and Anna Massey (daughter of Raymond) easily steal the show as the couple's staid British hosts. Rated PG-13 for mature themes. 116m. DIR: Henry Jaglom. CAST: Victoria Foyt, Stephen Dillane, Vanessa Redgrave, Glynis Barber, Noel Harrison, Anna Massey, Rachel Kempson. 1998

DELI, THE ★★★1/2 À la *Clerks* and *Smoke*, this film set in a Brooklyn deli is less interested in plot than in displaying a gallery of neighborhood characters. Plenty of familiar faces and some snappy dialogue makes this a winning if slight independent comedy. Not rated; contains profanity. 98m. DIR: John Gallagher. CAST: Mike Starr, Matt Kesslar, Frank Vincent, Burt Young, Heather Matarazzo, Judith Malina. 1997

DELIBERATE STRANGER, THE ★★★ Mark Harmon is impressive in his first major role as serial killer Ted Bundy in this better-than-average TV movie. The script for all the time it spends depicting Bundy's crimes doesn't provide enough insight into what made Bundy tick. 192m. DIR: Marvin J. Chomsky. CAST: Mark Harmon, Frederic Forrest, George Grizzard, Ben Masters, Glynnis O'Connor, M. Emmet Walsh, John Ashton. 1986

DELICATE DELINQUENT, THE ★★★ Jerry Lewis stars on his own for the first time in this surprisingly agreeable story about a goofball delinquent who ends up as a policeman. B&W; 100m. DIR: Don McGuire. CAST: Jerry Lewis, Darren McGavin, Horace McMahon, Martha Hyer. 1957

DELICATESSEN ★★★1/2 In a post-apocalyptic world, a former circus clown comes to a town that has advertised for a butcher's assistant. What our hero doesn't know is that it's a short-term job, during which he'll be well fed until it's time for the boss to stock his shelves. Inventive black comedy will appeal enormously to some and offend others. In French with English subtitles. Not rated; the film has violence and nudity. 95m. **DIR:** Jean-Pierre Jeunet, Marc Caro. **CAST:** Marie-Laure Dougnac, Dominique Pinon, Karen Viard, Jean Claude Dreyfus. 1991

DELINQUENT DAUGHTERS ★1/2 A reporter and a cop decide to find out just what's going on with today's kids after a high school girl commits suicide. Slow-moving cheapie that is merely a hyped-up dud. B&W; 71m. **DIR:** Albert Herman. **CAST:** June Carlson, Fifi D'Orsay, Teala Loring. 1944

DELINQUENT SCHOOL GIRLS 💔 Ridiculously racist and sexist sleaze-a-thon features three cons on the run. Rated R for profanity, violence, and nudity. 89m. **DIR:** Gregory Corarito. **CAST:** Michael Pataki, Bob Minor, Stephen Stucker. 1974

DELIRIOUS ★★★1/2 In this frequently funny, albeit outrageous, fantasy, soap-opera writer John Candy has a car accident and wakes up to find himself in the fictional town of his television show. *Delirious* was not a critical or box-office success, but we found it clever, surprising, and amiably goofy. Rated PG. 94m. **DIR:** Tom Mankiewicz. **CAST:** John Candy, Mariel Hemingway, Raymond Burr, David Rasche, Charles Rocket, Dylan Baker, Jerry Orbach, Renee Baker. 1991

DELIVERANCE ★★★★★ Jon Voight, Burt Reynolds, and Ned Beatty are superb in this first-rate film about a canoe trip down a dangerous river that begins as a holiday but soon turns into a weekend of sheer horror. Based on the novel by James Dickey. Rated R for profanity, sex, and violence. 109m. **DIR:** John Boorman. **CAST:** Jon Voight, Burt Reynolds, Ned Beatty, Ronny Cox, James Dickey. 1972 DVD

DELIVERY BOYS ★★1/2 This average teen comedy features pizza delivery boys who break dance during their time off. They plan to compete in a break dance contest that offers a $10,000 prize but encounter problems in getting there on time. Rated R. 94m. **DIR:** Ken Handler. **CAST:** Jody Olivery, Joss Marcano, Mario Van Peebles. 1984

DELLAMORTE, DELLAMORE ★★★1/2 Former Dario Argento acolyte Michele Soavi comes into his own with this strange horror-comedy whose plot keeps making abrupt shifts every reel or so. Rupert Everet is the groundskeeper of a cemetery where the dead just won't stay put. Highly recommended for horror buffs. Rated R for considerable gruesome behavior. 105m. **DIR:** Michele Soavi. **CAST:** Rupert Everett, François Hadji-Lazaro, Mickey Knox. 1994

DELOS ADVENTURE, THE 💔 Scientists stumble on a secret Soviet military operation. Rated R for gratuitous nudity and excessive violence and gore. 99m. **DIR:** Joseph Purcell. **CAST:** Roger Kern, Jenny Neuman, Kurtwood Smith, Kevin Brophy. 1987

DELTA FORCE, THE ★★ In this disappointing action film, which is perhaps best described as "The Dirty Dozen at the Airport," Chuck Norris and Lee Marvin are leaders of an antiterrorist group charged with saving the passengers on a hijacked airliner. Rated R for profanity and violence. 126m. **DIR:** Mena-

hem Golan. **CAST:** Chuck Norris, Lee Marvin, Martin Balsam, Joey Bishop, Robert Forster, Lainie Kazan, George Kennedy, Hanna Schygulla, Susan Strasberg, Bo Svenson, Robert Vaughn, Shelley Winters. 1986

DELTA FORCE 2 ★★ An outrageously exciting sky-diving sequence highlights this otherwise routine and overly cold-blooded action-adventure about a commando leader (Chuck Norris) who goes after a Colombian drug lord (Billy Drago). Rated R for language and violence. 115m. **DIR:** Aaron Norris. **CAST:** Chuck Norris, Billy Drago, John P. Ryan, Richard Jaeckel. 1990

DELTA FORCE 3 ★★1/2 Platoon of second-generation stars fill in for Chuck Norris in this adequate third entry for the action-seeking Delta Force. Rated R for violence and profanity. 97m. **DIR:** Sam Firstenberg. **CAST:** Nick Cassavetes, Eric Douglas, Mike Norris, Matthew Penn, John P. Ryan. 1990

DELTA FORCE, COMMANDO TWO 💔 An enemy government tricks a military official in order to steal nuclear weapons, and impending global disaster has to be halted by the Delta Force. A complete mess throughout. Rated R for violence. 100m. **DIR:** Frank Valenti. **CAST:** Richard Hatch, Fred Williamson, Van Johnson. 1991

DELTA FOX 💔 A hired assassin finds that he himself has been set up to be killed. Rated R. 92m. **DIR:** Ferd Sebastian, Beverly Sebastian. **CAST:** Priscilla Barnes, Richard Lynch, Stuart Whitman, John Ireland, Richard Jaeckel. 1977

DELTA HEAT ★★★ An LAPD police officer teams up with a New Orleans ex-cop-turned-swamp-rat to track down a killer drug dealer. At first this looks like a boring movie, but keep watching; it actually gets better. Rated R for violence and profanity. 91m. **DIR:** Michael Fischa. **CAST:** Anthony Edwards, Lance Henriksen, Betsy Russell, Linda Dona, Rod Masterson. 1992

DELTA OF VENUS ★★1/2 Arty smutmeister Zalman King's take on Anaïs Nin's carnal classic is about as exciting as watching paint dry. Pouty Marek Vasut plays an American writer caught in France during the early years of World War II who proceeds to live out the erotic tales she pens for an unknown benefactor. As usual, King's camera work is far too deliberately self-conscious. Rated R for considerable nudity, simulated sex, profanity, and drug use. 102m. **DIR:** Zalman King. **CAST:** Costas Mandylor, Eric Da Silva, Marek Vasut, Zette, Audie England. 1995

DELUGE (1933) ★★ The destruction of much of New York by earthquakes and a tidal wave. B&W; 70m. **DIR:** Felix Feist. **CAST:** Peggy Shannon, Sidney Blackmer, Lois Wilson, Matt Moore, Edward Van Sloan, Fred Kohler Sr., Samuel S. Hinds. 1933

DELUGE, THE (POTOP) (1973) ★★★ Overlong period piece set in the seventeenth century during the turbulent Polish-Swedish war. The story evolves around the stormy relationship between a barbaric soldier and a young gentlewoman. Based on the novel by Nobel Prize–winning author Henryk Sienkiewicz. In Polish with English subtitles. Not rated; contains violence. 185m. **DIR:** Jerzy Hoffman. **CAST:** Daniel Olbrychski. 1973

DELUSION (1980) 💔 A nurse relates a series of murders that occurred while she cared for an elderly invalid. Rated R for violence and gore. 83m. **DIR:** Alan Beattie. **CAST:** Patricia Pearcy, David Hayward, John Dukakis, Joseph Cotten. **1980**

DELUSION (1991) ★★★ A computer whiz, having just embezzled $480 thousand, heads for Reno, picks up a Las Vegas show girl and her boyfriend (who is a hit man for the mob). Very odd little movie, but some will find this a real gem. Rated R for profanity, nudity, and violence. 99m. **DIR:** Carl Colpaert. **CAST:** Jim Metzler, Jennifer Rubin, Kyle Secor, Robert Costanzo, Jerry Orbach, Tracey Walter. **1991**

DELUSIONS OF GRANDEUR ★★★ In seventeenth-century Spain, a valet is given the job of royal tax collector and uses his position to boost taxes on the rich and give the money to the poor. Likable slapstick farce. In French with English subtitles. Not rated; contains no objectionable material. 85m. **DIR:** Gerard Oury. **CAST:** Yves Montand, Louis de Funes. **1971**

DEMENTIA 13 ★★★ Early Francis Coppola film is a low-budget shocker centering on a family plagued by violent ax murders that are somehow connected with the death of the youngest daughter many years before. Acting is standard, but the photography, creepy locations, and weird music are what make this movie click. Produced by Roger Corman. B&W; 75m. **DIR:** Francis Ford Coppola. **CAST:** William Campbell, Luana Anders, Patrick Magee. **1963 DVD**

DEMETRIUS AND THE GLADIATORS 🎬 Film centers on the search for the robe that Christ wore before he was crucified. Overblown. 101m. **DIR:** Delmer Daves. **CAST:** Victor Mature, Susan Hayward, Debra Paget, Michael Rennie, Anne Bancroft, Ernest Borgnine, Richard Egan, Jay Robinson. **1954**

DEMOLITION MAN ★★1/2 High-concept action-thrillers just don't get much dumber than this, which attempts to argue that society is much better with heapin' helpings of exaggerated violence. Renegade cop Sylvester Stallone goes into the deep freeze for several decades, and then wakes in an insipid future civilization which cannot handle the mayhem of crazed psychotic Wesley Snipes. Stallone has said it himself—he just can't play comedy. Rated R for profanity and violence. 114m. **DIR:** Marco Brambilla. **CAST:** Sylvester Stallone, Wesley Snipes, Sandra Bullock, Nigel Hawthorne. **1993 DVD**

DEMOLITIONIST, THE ★★1/2 Nicole Eggert plays "Robo-Babe" in this cheesy yet satisfying futuristic action-thriller set in the near future. When an undercover cop is killed by a vicious mobster, her body is reconstructed into a one-woman fighting machine with superhuman strength. Rated R for violence, profanity, and nudity. 100m. **DIR:** Robert Kurtzman. **CAST:** Nicole Eggert, Richard Grieco, Bruce Abbott, Susan Tyrrell. **1995 DVD**

DEMON (GOD TOLD ME TO) ★★★1/2 A minor masterpiece, this movie opens with several mass murders. The only thing that connects these incidents is they are committed by pleasant, smiling people who explain their acts by saying, "God told me to." Rated R for nudity, profanity, and violence. 95m. **DIR:** Larry Cohen. **CAST:** Tony Lo Bianco, Sandy Dennis, Sylvia Sidney, Deborah Raffin, Sam Levene, Mike Kellin. **1977**

DEMON BARBER OF FLEET STREET, THE ★★1/2 Long before Vincent Price was the embodiment of evil, there was Tod Slaughter, master of the Grand Guignol school of lip-smacking villainy and star of many bloody thrillers. Partially based on a true occurrence, this popular folktale tells the story of Sweeney Todd, an amoral barber who cuts the throats of his clients. Seldom seen in America since World War II, this influential film was a great success for the flamboyant Slaughter and provides the basis for the musical theater hit. B&W; 76m. **DIR:** George King. **CAST:** Tod Slaughter, Bruce Seton. **1936**

DEMON CITY SHINJUKU ★★★ Evil threatens to overrun the Earth in this sometimes-scary tale that unfortunately has all the usual elements of animation cliché: the beautiful heroine, the mystic guy with a sword, and demons, demons, demons. Yet surprisingly good. In Japanese with English subtitles. Not rated; contains violence, nudity, and profanity. 81m. **DIR:** Yoshiaki Kawajiri. **1993 DVD**

DEMON IN MY VIEW, A ★★★ One of Anthony Perkins' last roles was a psycho. But this time his reign of terror takes place in Europe, where he is a mild apartment dweller who is hiding a murderous past. A fine, edgy performance by Perkins highlights this intelligent thriller. Rated R for violence. 98m. **DIR:** Petra Hafter. **CAST:** Anthony Perkins. **1992**

DEMON KEEPER ★★ Creaky, haunted-house thriller. Fake medium Edward Albert summons up a real spirit and unleashes a demon. The special effects are better than usual, but the dialogue is frightfully unfunny. Rated R for horror, violence and language. 90m. **DIR:** Joe Tornatore. **CAST:** Dirk Benedict, Edward Albert, Katrina Maltby, Mike Lane. **1994**

DEMON LOVER, THE 🎬 College kids and bikers get involved with a Satanist. Rated R for nudity, profanity, and violence. 87m. **DIR:** Donald G. Jackson. **CAST:** Christmas Robbins, Gunnar Hansen, Sonny Bell. **1976**

DEMON OF PARADISE 🎬 An ancient sea creature awakened from its slumber. Rated R for brief nudity and violence. 84m. **DIR:** Cirio H. Santiago. **CAST:** Kathryn Witt, William Steis, Laura Banks. **1987**

DEMON SEED ★★★ Good, but not great, science-fiction film about a superintelligent computer designed by scientist Fritz Weaver to solve problems beyond the scope of man. The computer, however, has other ideas. Weaver's wife (Julie Christie) becomes its unwilling guinea pig and, eventually, mate. Rated R. 94m. **DIR:** Donald Cammell. **CAST:** Julie Christie, Fritz Weaver, Gerrit Graham. **1977**

DEMON WIND ★★★ After one of the dumbest reasons ever to go to a spooky house, a group of young people are systematically dispatched. Some great one-liners and slimy special effects. Rated R for violence, nudity, and gore. 97m. **DIR:** Charles Philip Moore. **CAST:** Eric Larson, Francine Lapensee, Bobby Johnson. **1990**

DEMONIAC 🎬 Director Jess Franco plays the lead himself in this dreary affair (originally titled *Ripper of Notre Dame* and, in a hard-core-porn version, *Exorcism & Black Masses*). Rated R. 87m. **DIR:** Jess (Jesus) Franco. **CAST:** Jess Franco, Lina Romay, Oliver Mathot. **1979**

DEMONIC TOYS 🎬 An army of toys is brought to life by a demon. A plastic baby doll's wisecracks are the only highlight of this film. Not rated, but has profanity and violence. 86m. **DIR:** Peter Manoogian. **CAST:** Tracy Scoggins, Bentley Mitchum. 1991

DEMONOID ✿ A couple unearth a severed hand while working in a Mexican mine. Rated R for graphic violence. 78m. **DIR:** Alfredo Zacharias. **CAST:** Samantha Eggar, Stuart Whitman. 1981

DEMONS ★★★ Selected at random, people on the street are invited to an advance screening of a new horror film. When the members of the audience try to escape, they find themselves trapped. Although much of the acting is poor and some story elements are plain stupid, this actually is a very frightening movie. Not rated, but features graphic violence and adult language. 89m. **DIR:** Lamberto Bava. **CAST:** Urbano Barberini. 1986 DVD

DEMONS 2 ✿ Cross between George Romero's zombies and *The Evil Dead* attacking the inhabitants of a high-rise apartment building. Not rated, but an R equivalent for violence and gore. 88m. **DIR:** Lamberto Bava. **CAST:** David Knight, Nancy Brilli. 1987 DVD

DEMONS IN THE GARDEN ★★★★ Fascinating portrait of a family damaged by fratricidal rivalries and morally wasted by corruption, as seen through the eyes of a young boy during post–Civil War Spain. Breathtaking cinematography by José Luis Alcaine. In Spanish with English subtitles. Not rated; contains adult themes. 100m. **DIR:** Manuel Gutierrez Aragon. **CAST:** Angela Molina, Imanol Arias. 1982

DEMONS OF THE MIND ★★1/2 One of the last significant Hammer films before the British horror factory's demise in 1976. A Bavarian nobleman, fearing his children are possessed, keeps them locked away. Gillian Hills, in a role intended for Marianne Faithfull, is especially effective. Rated R. 89m. **DIR:** Peter Sykes. **CAST:** Paul Jones, Yvonne Mitchell, Gillian Hills. 1972

DEMONSTONE ★★ In Manila a beautiful woman is possessed by an evil spirit bent on frying assorted gang members. Throw in Jan-Michael Vincent as an ex-Marine and all hell breaks loose. Rated R for adult language, violence, and nudity. 90m. **DIR:** Andrew Prowse. **CAST:** R. Lee Ermey, Jan-Michael Vincent, Nancy Everhard. 1989

DEMPSEY ★★★ Treat Williams plays Jack Dempsey, World Heavyweight Champion boxer from 1919 to 1926. Stylish and with riveting plot twists. As Dempsey's first wife, Sally Kellerman is particularly effective. Not rated, contains violence and profanity. 110m. **DIR:** Gus Trikonis. **CAST:** Treat Williams, Sam Waterston, Sally Kellerman, Victoria Tennant, Peter Mark Richman, Jesse Vint. 1983

DENIAL ★★★ Erotic tale of free-spirited young woman Robin Wright whose chance encounter with hunky artist Jason Patric turns her life upside down. Wright leaves to regain her identity, only to be consumed by Patric's memory. Rated R for nudity. 103m. **DIR:** Erin Dignam. **CAST:** Jason Patric, Robin Wright, Barry Primus, Rae Dawn Chong. 1991

DENISE CALLS UP ★★★1/2 A circle of New York friends and acquaintances carry on their complicated relationships by phone, fax, and modem, unable or unwilling to meet face-to-face. Director Hal Salwen's script is witty and complicated, and the acting

is first-rate—especially considering that virtually the entire film is composed of close-ups of people talking on the phone, with no two of them ever on screen at the same time. Rated PG-13 for mature themes and mild profanity. 80m. **DIR:** Hal Salwen. **CAST:** Timothy Daly, Dana Wheeler-Nicholson, Caroleen Feeney, Liev Schreiber, Alanna Ubach, Sylvia Miles. 1996

DENNIS POTTER: THE LAST INTERVIEW ★★★★ Talking heads are rarely as compelling as this chatfest filmed by the BBC in June of 1994, a few weeks before Potter died of cancer. Swigging champagne and morphine, freed from the constraints of consequence, Potter is revealed as the intelligent wag he was. Not only does Potter discuss his work, such as *The Singing Detective* and *Pennies from Heaven*, but he opens up about his life. Rarely are such barebones, low-budget films this fascinating. Not rated; contains profanity. 70m. **DIR:** Tom Poolew. **CAST:** Dennis Potter, Melvyn Bragg. 1994

DENNIS THE MENACE ★★★★ The first movie to be made from the famous comic strip has the advantage of a John Hughes script to give it wit and style. The story centers on the relationship between 6-year-old Dennis Mitchell and his grouchy neighbor, Mr. Wilson. An affable mixture of talents in a classy family-oriented movie. Rated PG. 101m. **DIR:** Nick Castle. **CAST:** Walter Matthau, Christopher Lloyd, Joan Plowright, Lea Thompson, Mason Gamble, Robert Stanton. 1993

DENNIS THE MENACE: DINOSAUR HUNTER ★★1/2 Dennis unearths a dinosaur bone in the front yard. A friend of his father's, who majored in paleontology, comes to live with the family and causes chaos for the entire neighborhood. The story is predictable and viewers will wish the father would just get a backbone. Rated G. 95m. **DIR:** Doug Rogers. **CAST:** William Windom, James W. Jansen, Patricia Estrinn, Patsy Garrett, Victor DiMattia, Barton Tinapp. 1987

DENTIST, THE ★★ This tedious horror film cuts to the nerve only because of the relentless soundtrack of dentist-office noises and endless close-ups of dental equipment. Otherwise, this made-for-cable original about an obsessive and violent dentist is as dull as an overused drill. Rated R for profanity, violence, nudity, and suggested sex. 89m. **DIR:** Brian Yuzna. **CAST:** Corbin Bernsen, Linda Hoffman, Earl Boen. 1996 DVD

DENTIST 2, THE: BRACE YOURSELF ★★ It's the same old drill for psychopath dentist Dr. Allan Feinstone, once again played by Corbin Bernsen. Having escaped from prison, Feinstone finds himself in a small town where he kills the local dentist and sets up shop in this made-for-cable sequel. Rated R for violence, language, and adult situations. 99m. **DIR:** Richard Dana Smith. **CAST:** Corbin Bernsen, Clint Howard, Jillian McWhirter. 1998 DVD

DENVER AND RIO GRANDE, THE ★★1/2 A fairly routine Western about railroad men and their rivalries. Enlivened by a spectacular train crash staged by outdoor specialist Byron Haskin. 89m. **DIR:** Byron Haskin. **CAST:** Edmond O'Brien, Sterling Hayden, Dean Jagger, ZaSu Pitts, J. Carrol Naish. 1952

DENVER KID ★★★ Border patrolman Rocky Lane joins an outlaw gang to solve a brutal massacre. B&W; 60m. DIR: Philip Ford. CAST: Allan "Rocky" Lane, Eddy Waller, William Henry, Douglas Fowley. 1948

DERANGED ★★★1/2 Based on the life of serial killer Ed Gein, this little-seen but much-adored film is a true gem. The film's cutting-edge use (at the time) of intrusion into the narrative by a reporter gives it a documentary feel. Generally well acted, this is a chilling look at one man's depraved lifestyle. Rated R for violence and profanity. 82m. DIR: Alan Ormsby, Jeff Gillen. CAST: Roberts Blossom, Cosette Lee, Leslie Carlson. 1974

DERSU UZALA ★★★1/2 This epic about the charting of the Siberian wilderness (circa 1900) is surprisingly as intimate in relationships and details as it is grand in vistas and scope. A Japanese-Russian coproduction, the second half of this Oscar winner is much better than the first. In Russian and Japanese with English subtitles. 140m. DIR: Akira Kurosawa. CAST: Maxim Munzuk, Yuri Solomin. 1974

DESCENDING ANGEL ★★★ First-rate made-for-cable thriller about a resourceful fellow (Eric Roberts) who begins to suspect his fiancée's Romanian father (George C. Scott) might have aided himself with Hitler's Nazis during World War II. The theme may be a bit shopworn, but the execution is superb. Not rated, but with violence, profanity, and brief nudity. 98m. DIR: Jeremy Paul Kagan. CAST: George C. Scott, Eric Roberts, Diane Lane, Jan Rubes. 1990

DESERT BLOOM ★★★ This poignant study of awakening adolescence and family turmoil is effectively set against a backdrop of 1950 Las Vegas, as the atomic age dawns. The story unfolds slowly but sensitively. Thirteen-year-old Annabeth Gish gives a remarkably complex performance as a brilliant girl who must cope with an abusive stepfather, an ineffectual mother, and a sexpot aunt. Rated PG. 106m. DIR: Eugene Corr. CAST: Jon Voight, JoBeth Williams, Ellen Barkin, Allen Garfield, Annabeth Gish. 1986

DESERT FOX, THE ★★★★ A tour-de-force performance by James Mason marks this film biography of German Field Marshal Rommel. His military exploits are glossed over in favor of the human story of the disillusionment and eventual involvement in the plot to assassinate Hitler. B&W; 88m. DIR: Henry Hathaway. CAST: James Mason, Jessica Tandy, Cedric Hardwicke, Luther Adler, Desmond Young. 1951

DESERT HEARTS ★★★1/2 A sensitive portrayal of the evolving relationship between a young, openly lesbian woman and a quiet university professor ten years her senior in 1959. Patricia Charbonneau and Helen Shaver superbly set off the development of their individual and joint characters. Some may find the explicit love scenes upsetting, but the humor and characterization entirely overrule any objection, and the bonus of 1950s designs and sets is a treat. Rated R for profanity and sex. 90m. DIR: Donna Deitch. CAST: Helen Shaver, Patricia Charbonneau, Audra Lindley, Gwen Welles, Dean Butler. 1986

•**DESERT HEAT** ★★ The kind of heat that usually causes an uncomfortable rash. Totally predictable revenge fantasy stars Jean-Claude Van Damme as a loner willing to call it a day when he is attacked by a biker gang. He finds a new reason for living when he vows to get even. This direct-to-video effort is tired and full of clichés. Rated R for violence and language. 95m. DIR: John G. Avildsen. CAST: Jean-Claude Van Damme, Noriyuki "Pat" Morita, Danny Trejo, Larry Drake. 1999 DVD

DESERT KICKBOXER ★★ More kick-boxing action, with John Haymes Newton as a border guard who takes on a ruthless drug dealer and his drug empire. You've seen it all before. Rated R for violence. 86m. DIR: Isaac Florentine. CAST: John Haymes Newton, Paul Smith, Judie Aronson. 1992

•**DESERT PHANTOM** ★★★ Tenderfoot sharpshooter drumming up business for an ammunition firm turns out to be a tough hombre looking for the man who murdered his sister and her husband. In between throwing lead and punches he helps a girl save her ranch and unmasks the "phantom" who's been murdering cowhands to keep them off the trail of a rich mine. Rich characterizations, lots of action, and good pacing make this independent oater a winner. B&W; 65m. DIR: S. Roy Luby. CAST: Johnny Mack Brown, Sheila Manners, Ted Adams, Karl Hackett, Hal Price, Charles King. 1936

DESERT RATS, THE ★★★★ Very good World War II drama focuses on the British North African campaign against the German forces, led by Field Marshal Rommel. Richard Burton heads a small, outnumbered unit charged with holding a strategic hill while facing the enemy onslaught. Tough, realistic. B&W; 88m. DIR: Robert Wise. CAST: Richard Burton, Robert Newton, James Mason, Chips Rafferty. 1953

DESERT SONG, THE ★★★★ This version of Sigmund Romberg's popular romance has colorful settings in the desert and the charming voices of Kathryn Grayson and Gordon MacRae. It's also highly enjoyable with glorious music. 110m. DIR: H. Bruce Humberstone. CAST: Kathryn Grayson, Gordon MacRae, William Conrad, Raymond Massey. 1953

DESERT WARRIOR 🖤 After World War III, two warring factions fight for dominance. Rated PG-13 for violence and nudity. 89m. DIR: Jim Goldman. CAST: Lou Ferrigno, Shari Shattuck. 1988

DESERTER, THE 🖤 Arid, interminable spaghetti Western (a U.S.-Italian-Yugoslavian coproduction) with an absolute stiff for a leading man, and a bewildered supporting cast. Rated PG. 99m. DIR: Burt Kennedy. CAST: Bekim Fehmiu, John Huston, Richard Crenna, Chuck Connors, Ricardo Montalban, Woody Strode, Slim Pickens, Ian Bannen, Brandon de Wilde, Patrick Wayne. 1971

DESIGNING WOMAN ★★★1/2 Diverting comedy with sportswriter Gregory Peck and successful dress designer Lauren Bacall marrying after a whirlwind romance. Mickey Shaughnessy, as Peck's bodyguard, steals the show. 118m. DIR: Vincente Minnelli. CAST: Gregory Peck, Lauren Bacall, Sam Levene, Dolores Gray, Mickey Shaughnessy, Chuck Connors. 1957

DESIRE ★★ Dull story about a common Scottish fisherman and a globe-trotting feminist. They fall in love when they were young, and whenever they meet again, their love is always rekindled. Not rated; contains profanity and simulated sex. 108m. DIR: Andrew Birkin. **CAST:** Greta Scacchi, Vincent D'Onofrio, Anais Jeanneret, Hanns Zischler, Barbara Jones. 1993

DESIRE AND HELL AT SUNSET MOTEL ★★★ When hot and sultry Sherilyn Fenn checks into the Sunset Motel with her husband, Whip Hubley, they get more room service than they bargained for. She wants her husband, who thinks she's fooling around, dead, and her lover, David Johansen, is willing to oblige. Director Alien Castle's film debut is a handsome, lush stab at *film noir*. Rated PG-13 for profanity and violence. 87m. **DIR:** Allen Castle. **CAST:** Sherilyn Fenn, Whip Hubley, David Hewlett, David Johansen, Paul Bartel. 1990

DESIRE UNDER THE ELMS ★★ A hard-hearted New England farmer (Burl Ives) brings home an immigrant bride (Sophia Loren), who promptly falls into the arms of his weakling son (Anthony Perkins). Eugene O'Neill's play was already ponderously dated by the time it was filmed, and Loren (whose command of English was still shaky) is miscast. B&W; 114m. **DIR:** Delbert Mann. **CAST:** Burl Ives, Sophia Loren, Anthony Perkins, Frank Overton, Pernell Roberts, Anne Seymour. 1958

DESIRÉE ★★ A romantic tale of Napoleon's love for 17-year-old seamstress Desirée Clary. Marlon Brando bumbles about as Napoleon in this torpid travesty of history. 110m. **DIR:** Henry Koster. **CAST:** Marlon Brando, Jean Simmons, Merle Oberon, Michael Rennie, Cameron Mitchell, Isobel Elsom, John Hoyt, Cathleen Nesbitt. 1954

DESK SET ★★★1/2 Robert Fryer and Lawrence Carr's Broadway play benefits from the chemistry between Tracy and Hepburn. This isn't their best movie, but it's still fun to watch. Hepburn bucks Tracy's attempts to rework the research department of a TV network. Joan Blondell steals her every scene as a wisecracking coworker. 103m. **DIR:** Walter Lang. **CAST:** Spencer Tracy, Katharine Hepburn, Joan Blondell, Dina Merrill, Neva Patterson. 1957

DESOLATION ANGELS ★★1/2 Male egos take it on the chin in this low-budget, partly improvised film whose credits include thanks to "the makers of Prozac." Writer-director Tim McCann is good with both his actors and his camera, but the characters in this story of sexual violence are too clichéd to have any real impact. Rated R for violence, profanity, and sexual situations. 94m. **DIR:** Tim McCann. **CAST:** Michael Rodrick, Jennifer Thomas, Peter Bassett. 1995 DVD

DESPAIR ★★★★ Karlovich (Dirk Bogarde), a Russian living in Germany in 1930, runs an unsuccessful chocolate factory. The stock market crash in America pushes his business into even deeper trouble, and he begins to lose touch with himself in a major way. Black comedy at its blackest. Rated R. 119m. **DIR:** Rainer Werner Fassbinder. **CAST:** Dirk Bogarde, Klaus Lowitsch. 1979

DESPERADO ★★ A traveling Mexican musician uses an arsenal of weapons stashed in his guitar case to avenge the death of his lover. This sequel to *El Mariachi* is bigger, bolder, bloodier, steamier, and more cartoonish than the original, but its endless waves of balletic shoot-outs soon become tiring. Rat-ed R for violence, nudity, sex, and language. 106m. **DIR:** Robert Rodriguez. **CAST:** Antonio Banderas, Steve Buscemi, Salma Hayek, Richard "Cheech" Marin, Joaquim de Almeida, Quentin Tarantino. 1995 DVD

DESPERADOS, THE ★★ After the Civil War, a paranoid parson heads a gang of cutthroats and outlaws, including his three sons, in a violent crime spree. Roughly made (in Spain) and quite savage. Rated PG. 90m. **DIR:** Henry Levin. **CAST:** Vince Edwards, Jack Palance, Neville Brand, George Maharis, Sylvia Syms, Christian Roberts. 1969

DESPERATE ★★★ Tidy little chase film finds Steve Brodie and his wife Audrey Long on the lam from the law and a gang of thieves after he witnesses a warehouse robbery that results in the death of a police officer. The story is anything but new, yet director Anthony Mann breathes some life into it and keeps the level of suspense up. B&W; 73m. **DIR:** Anthony Mann. **CAST:** Steve Brodie, Audrey Long, Raymond Burr, Douglas Fowley. 1947

DESPERATE CRIMES 🏆 Aptly titled, this movie *is* a crime as it desperately attempts to tell the tale of a man searching for the murderers of his girlfriend. Rated R for nudity, simulated sex, violence, and profanity. 92m. **DIR:** Andreas Marfori. **CAST:** Denise Crosby, Van Quattro, Rena Niehaus, Franco Columbu, Nicoletta Boris, Elizabeth Kaitan, Randi Ingerman, Traci Lords. 1993 DVD

DESPERATE HOURS, THE (1955) ★★★★ Three escaped convicts terrorize a suburban Indiana family; based on Joseph Hayes's novel and play. Humphrey Bogart is too old for the part that made a star of Paul Newman on Broadway, but the similarity to the The Petrified Forest must have been too good to pass up. Fredric March takes top acting honors. Not rated. B&W; 112m. **DIR:** William Wyler. **CAST:** Humphrey Bogart, Fredric March, Arthur Kennedy, Martha Scott, Gig Young. 1955

DESPERATE HOURS (1990) ★★1/2 Desperate remake of William Wyler's 1955 suspense classic, with Mickey Rourke taking over the Humphrey Bogart role. Rourke's pointless posturing and director Michael Cimino's tendency toward overkill make it more campy than chilling. Rated R for violence and profanity. 106m. **DIR:** Michael Cimino. **CAST:** Mickey Rourke, Anthony Hopkins, Mimi Rogers, Lindsay Crouse, Kelly Lynch, Elias Koteas, David Morse, Shawnee Smith. 1990

DESPERATE JOURNEY ★★1/2 Average WWII propaganda film follows the exploits of an RAF bomber crew that is shot down while on a special mission over Poland. They escape and begin a treacherous and sometimes humorous journey across Germany, trying to return to England. B&W; 106m. **DIR:** Raoul Walsh. **CAST:** Errol Flynn, Ronald Reagan, Alan Hale Sr., Arthur Kennedy, Raymond Massey. 1942

DESPERATE LIVING ★★ A "monstrous fairy tale," director John Waters calls it. This story is about a murderess (played by Mink Stole) and her escapades through a village of criminals who are ruled by a demented queen (Edith Massey). But various scenes provide enough humor and wit for anyone with a taste for the perverse and a yen for some good old-fashioned misanthropy. Not rated, but the equivalent of an X, due to violence, nudity, and unbridled gore. 95m. **DIR:** John Waters. **CAST:** Mink Stole, Edith Massey, Jean Hill, Liz Renay, Susan Lowe. **1977**

DESPERATE MEASURES ★★ This so-called thriller concerns a cop, trying to save his son's life, who must deal with a homicidal sociopath who happens to be the only suitable bone-marrow donor in the entire civilized world. Yeah, right. Rated R for profanity and violence. 100m. **DIR:** Barbet Schroeder. **CAST:** Andy Garcia, Michael Keaton, Brian Cox, Marcia Gay Harden, Erik King. **1998 DVD**

DESPERATE MOTIVE ★★★1/2 Creepy David Keith moves into his long-lost cousin's home with hopes of moving into his life. Chilling because it seems so plausible, although successful adman William Katt is a little too trusting. Keith's economic and intent performance foils Marg Helgenberger's edgy destructiveness. Rated R for violence and profanity. 92m. **DIR:** Andrew Lane. **CAST:** David Keith, Marg Helgenberger, Mel Harris, William Katt. **1991**

DESPERATE MOVES ★★★ Steve Tracy plays a young nerd from a small Oregon town traveling to California to pursue his dreams. Touching and amusing, if occasionally silly. Good effort by supporting cast. Not rated, but would probably fall near the PG-13 category. 106m. **DIR:** Oliver Hellman. **CAST:** Steve Tracy, Eddie Deezen, Isabel Sanford, Paul Benedict, Christopher Lee. **1986**

DESPERATE PREY ★★★ After accidentally capturing the murder of a prominent lawyer on videotape, a woman becomes the target of a brutal killer. Rated R for violence and nudity. 102m. **DIR:** Danny Vendramini. **CAST:** Claudia Karvan, Catherine McClements, Alexander Petersons. **1992**

DESPERATE REMEDIES ★★ Utterly bizarre film loaded with outrageous costumes, lush imagery, surreal sets, and twisted performances. A pair of women work together to save the crumbling life of a third—at any cost. Rated R for nudity and sexuality. 92m. **DIR:** Stewart Main, Peter Wells. **CAST:** Jennifer Ward-Leland, Kevin Smith, Lisa Chappell, Clifford Curtis, Michael Hurst, Kiri Mills. **1994**

DESPERATE TRAIL ★★★1/2 In this offbeat, intense Western, revenge-minded marshal Sam Elliott relentlessly tracks down daughter-in-law Linda Fiorentino, whom he blames for the death of his son. She falls in with a con man, which leads to some comic misadventures and even love, but this Old West Bonnie and Clyde are forced to continually look over their shoulders, often seeing what they fear most. Made for TV. 96m. **DIR:** P. J. Pesce. **CAST:** Sam Elliott, Craig Sheffer, Linda Fiorentino, Frank Whaley. **1995**

DESPERATE WOMEN ★★ Three convicted women crossing a desert on their way to prison meet up with an ol' softy (Dan Haggerty) who takes them under his wing. 98m. **DIR:** Earl Bellamy. **CAST:** Dan Haggerty, Susan Saint James, Ronee Blakley, Ann Dusenberry. **1978**

DESPERATELY SEEKING SUSAN ★★★★1/2 A delightfully daffy, smart, and intriguing comedy made from a feminine perspective. Rosanna Arquette stars as a bored housewife who adds spice to her life by following the personal column love adventures of the mysterious Susan (Madonna). One day, our heroine decides to catch a glimpse of her idol and, through a set of unlikely but easy-to-take plot convolutions, ends up switching places with her. Rated PG-13 for violence. 104m. **DIR:** Susan Seidelman. **CAST:** Rosanna Arquette, Madonna, Robert Joy, Mark Blum, Laurie Metcalf, Aidan Quinn. **1985 DVD**

DESTINATION MOON ★★★1/2 Story involves the first American spaceship to land on the moon. Even though the sets are dated today, they were what scientists expected to find when people did land on the moon. This film boasts the classic pointed spaceship and bubble helmets on the space travelers, but it is still great fun for fans of the genre. Rated PG-13. 99m. **DIR:** Irving Pichel. **CAST:** Warner Anderson, John Archer, Tom Powers, Dick Wesson. **1950 DVD**

DESTINATION TOKYO ★★★★ Superior World War II adventure focuses on a submarine crew as they attempt to penetrate Tokyo Bay and destroy Japanese vessels. Cary Grant's fine performance as the commander is complemented by a crackling script and assured direction by Delmer Daves. B&W; 135m. **DIR:** Delmer Daves. **CAST:** Cary Grant, John Garfield, Alan Hale Sr., Dane Clark, Warner Anderson. **1943**

DESTINY ★★★1/2 Fritz Lang's first important success is a triumph of style that delves into the nature of love. Consisting of interlocking stories, dream sequences, and nightmarish associations, Lang's fable tells the story of a young woman who challenges Death for the life of her lover but cannot bring herself to offer the sacrifices the grim one demands. Silent. B&W; 114m. **DIR:** Fritz Lang. **CAST:** Lil Dagover, Walter Janssen, Bernhard Goetzke, Rudolf Klein-Rogge. **1921**

DESTINY TO ORDER ★★1/2 A writer's creations come to life to haunt him in this strange love story. A bit disjointed, this is nonetheless a fun film. Not rated; contains violence and profanity. 93m. **DIR:** Jim Purdy. **CAST:** Stephen Quimette, Alberta Watson, Michael Ironside. **1990**

DESTINY TURNS ON THE RADIO ★★1/2 Quentin Tarantino portrays a godlike creature playing with the fates of Las Vegas losers in this arch, rather precious comedy. Rated R for profanity. 102m. **DIR:** Jack Baran. **CAST:** James LeGros, Dylan McDermott, Nancy Travis, Quentin Tarantino, James Belushi. **1995**

DESTROYER 🚫 Lyle Alzado has the title role as a maniacal serial killer that the electric chair can't stop. Rated R for gratuitous violence, language, and nudity. 93m. **DIR:** Robert Kirk. **CAST:** Lyle Alzado, Anthony Perkins, Deborah Foreman, Clayton Rohner. **1988**

DESTRUCTORS, THE ★★ Anthony Quinn plays a narcotics agent who just can't seem to get the goods on a major drug dealer (James Mason). Dated. Not rated. 89m. **DIR:** Robert Parrish. **CAST:** Michael Caine, Anthony Quinn, James Mason. **1974**

DESTRY RIDES AGAIN ★★★★ *Destry*'s plot may seem a trifle clichéd, but it is the classic Western that copycats imitate. The story of a mild-mannered citizen who finds himself grudgingly forced to stand up against the bad guys may seem familiar, especially with Jimmy Stewart in the lead. But this is the original. B&W; 95m. **DIR:** George Marshall. **CAST:**

James Stewart, Marlene Dietrich, Brian Donlevy, Mischa Auer, Una Merkel. **1939**

DETECTIVE, THE (1954) ★★★1/2 The versatile Alec Guinness is sublime in this deft film presentation of G. K. Chesterton's priest-detective in action. Here Father Brown seeks out purloined art treasures and the culprits responsible. Joan Greenwood, of the ultrathroaty voice, and the rest of the cast fit like Savile Row tailoring. Intelligent, highly entertaining fare from Britain. B&W; 91m. **DIR:** Robert Hamer. **CAST:** Alec Guinness, Joan Greenwood, Peter Finch, Bernard Lee, Sidney James. **1954**

DETECTIVE, THE (1968) ★★★ A disgusted NYPD detective (Frank Sinatra), railroads the wrong man into the electric chair while seeking a homosexual's killer. He loses his job and leaves his nympho wife (Lee Remick). Filmed on location in New York, this is one of the first hard-look-at-a-cop's-life films. 114m. **DIR:** Gordon Douglas. **CAST:** Frank Sinatra, Lee Remick, Al Freeman Jr., Jacqueline Bisset, Ralph Meeker, Jack Klugman, Robert Duvall, William Windom. **1968**

DETECTIVE SADIE AND SON ★★★ Debbie Reynolds plays a rough-and-ready street cop forced into early retirement by her yuppie boss. She becomes a neighborhood vigilante, and her heroic deeds land her back on the force—training her less-than-dedicated son. A few funny moments are found among the encounters with numerous assailants and muggers. Made for TV, this contains considerable violence. 94m. **DIR:** John Llewellyn Moxey. **CAST:** Debbie Reynolds, Brian McNamara, Sam Wanamaker. **1988**

DETECTIVE SCHOOL DROPOUTS ★★★★ David Landsberg and Lorin Dreyfuss co-star in this hilarious comedy. (The two wrote the screenplay as well.) Landsberg plays Wilson, whose obsession with detective stories loses him a string of jobs. Finally, he goes to P.I. Miller (Dreyfuss) for lessons in investigation. The two accidentally become involved in an intrigue with star-crossed lovers. Rated PG for obscenities. 92m. **DIR:** Filippo Ottoni. **CAST:** David Landsberg, Lorin Dreyfuss, Christian De Sica, Valeria Golino, George Eastman. **1985**

DETONATOR II: NIGHT WATCH ★★ Pierce Brosnan reprises his international action hero in this, his last role before becoming James Bond. A team of experts goes toe-to-toe with international terrorists. Passable entertainment with Brosnan playing a much grittier hero. Rated R for violence and profanity. 99m. **DIR:** David S. Jackson. **CAST:** Pierce Brosnan, Alexandra Paul, William Devane. **1995**

DETOUR (1945) ★★★ Routine story about a drifter enticed into crime is skillfully constructed, economically produced, and competently acted; it has long been considered one of the best (if not *the* best) low-budget films ever made. Ann Savage as the beguiling, destructive enchantress playing off Tom Neal's infatuation rings just as true in this bargain-basement production as it does in the highly acclaimed adult crime-dramas produced by the major studios. B&W; 69m. **DIR:** Edgar G. Ulmer. **CAST:** Tom Neal, Ann Savage, Claudia Drake, Tim Ryan. **1945**

•**DETOUR (1999)** ★★★ After a failed attempt to rip off a fortune in mob drug money, Jeff Fahey hopes to lay low in his boyhood small-town home—until the vengeful gangsters track him down. Made to order for action fans, this is a bit livelier than the usual made-for-video product. Rated R for profanity, violence, and nudity. 93m. **DIR:** Joey Travolta. **CAST:** Jeff Fahey, Gary Busey, Michael Madsen, James Russo, Tim Thomerson. **1999**

DETROIT 9000 (DETROIT HEAT) ★★1/2 Two Detroit cops, one black and one white, look for the vicious hoods who robbed a political rally. Tamer than usual blaxploitation thriller. Rated R for violence, profanity, and brief nudity. 106m. **DIR:** Arthur Marks. **CAST:** Alex Rocco, Hari Rhodes, Vonetta McGee, Scatman Crothers. **1973**

•**DETROIT ROCK CITY** ★★ Four Cleveland "stoners" set out on an odyssey to see the heavy metal band Kiss in Detroit. Everything that can go wrong does, but between fights and muggings the guys manage to find romance. Focusing on sex, drugs, and rock 'n' roll, this R-rated film is meant to exclude viewers under 17. Unfortunately, few over 17 would want to see it. Rated R for drug use, sex, violence, and profanity. 98m. **DIR:** Adam Rifkin. **CAST:** Edward Furlong, Giuseppe Andrews, James DeBello, Sam Huntington. **1999 DVD**

•**DEUCE BIGALOW: MALE GIGOLO** ★★★ Wacky career-change flick features Rob Schneider as a scruffy fish-tank cleaner who falls into a gig as a gigolo. Each of his "dates" turns out to be bizarre and offbeat and he finds himself boosting their self-esteems rather than their libidos. One-liners play second fiddle to Schneider's hilarious facial reactions throughout the film. Rated R for sexual innuendo, profanity, and violence. 90m. **DIR:** Mike Mitchell. **CAST:** Rob Schneider, Arija Bareikis, William Forsythe, Eddie Griffin, Oded Fehr. **1999**

DEVASTATOR, THE 🎬 Lousy acting and writing ravage this movie about an evil marijuana plantation owner. Rated R for violence and language. 89m. **DIR:** Cirio H. Santiago. **CAST:** Richard Hill, Katt Shea, Crofton Hardester, Kaz Garas, Terence O'Hara, Bill McLaughlin. **1985**

DEVI (THE GODDESS) ★★★★ Excellent social satire from India's gifted Satyajit Ray. A deeply religious landowner becomes convinced that his beautiful daughter-in-law is the incarnation of the Hindu goddess Kali, to whom he becomes fanatically devoted. In Bengali with English subtitles. B&W; 96m. **DIR:** Satyajit Ray. **CAST:** Chhabi Biswas, Soumitra Chatterjee. **1960**

DEVIL AND DANIEL WEBSTER, THE ★★★★ This wickedly witty tale, based on a Stephen Vincent Benét story, delivers some potent messages. Edward Arnold, so often cast as a despicable villain, is riveting as the noble Webster. This eloquent hero must defend ingenuous James Craig in a bizarre courtroom. Both of their immortal souls are at stake. Opposing Webster is Mr. Scratch, also known as the Devil. Walter Huston gives a dazzling performance in the role. B&W; 85m. **DIR:** William Dieterle. **CAST:** Edward Arnold, Walter Huston, James Craig, Anne Shirley, Jane Darwell, Simone Simon, Gene Lockhart. **1941**

DEVIL AND MAX DEVLIN, THE ★★ This is visible proof that it takes more than just a few talented people to create quality entertainment. Despite Elliott Gould, Bill Cosby, and Susan Anspach, this Disney production—another takeoff on the Faustian theme of a pact made with the devil—offers little more than mediocre fare. It's basically a waste of fine talent. Rated PG. 96m. DIR: Steven H. Stern. CAST: Elliott Gould, Bill Cosby, Susan Anspach, Adam Rich. 1981

DEVIL AND MISS JONES, THE ★★★★ One of those wonderful comedies Hollywood used to make. Witty, sophisticated, poignant, and breezy, this one has millionaire Charles Coburn going undercover as a clerk in his own department store in order to probe employee complaints and unrest. Delightful doings. B&W; 92m. DIR: Sam Wood. CAST: Jean Arthur, Robert Cummings, Charles Coburn, Spring Byington, S. Z. Sakall, William Demarest. 1941

DEVIL AT 4 O'CLOCK, THE ★★★ This script may be weak and predictable, but the acting of Spencer Tracy and Frank Sinatra make this a watchable motion picture. Tracy is a priest who is in charge of an orphanage. When their island home is endangered by an impending volcanic eruption, he seeks the aid of a group of convicts headed by Sinatra. 126m. DIR: Mervyn LeRoy. CAST: Spencer Tracy, Frank Sinatra, Kerwin Mathews, Jean-Pierre Aumont. 1961

DEVIL BAT, THE ★★ Pretty fair thriller from PRC gives us Bela Lugosi as yet another bloodthirsty mad scientist who trains oversize rubber bats to suck blood from selected victims by use of a scent. B&W; 69m. DIR: Jean Yarbrough. CAST: Bela Lugosi, Suzanne Kaaren, Dave O'Brien, Guy Usher. 1941 DVD

DEVIL BAT'S DAUGHTER ★★ Unimaginative sequel to *Devil Bat* finds heroine Rosemary La Planche fearing for her sanity as her father spends more and more of his time experimenting with those darn bats ... . Low-budget bore. B&W; 66m. DIR: Frank Wisbar. CAST: Rosemary La Planche, Michael Hale, Molly Lamont. 1946 DVD

DEVIL COMMANDS, THE ★★★ Good entry in Boris Karloff's mad-doctor series for Columbia Pictures has the star attempting to communicate with his dead wife by using brain waves and corpses. Karloff's performance is the main asset here, although director Edward Dmytryk deserves credit for creating a strong atmosphere of forboding and moving the story along at a good clip. B&W; 65m. DIR: Edward Dmytryk. CAST: Boris Karloff, Amanda Duff, Richard Fiske, Anne Revere, Ralph Penny. 1941

DEVIL DOG: THE HOUND OF HELL 🎔 Made-for-television movie is even more ridiculous than the title implies. 95m. DIR: Curtis Harrington. CAST: Richard Crenna, Yvette Mimieux, Victor Jory, Ken Kercheval, Nick Esposito. 1976

DEVIL DOGS OF THE AIR ★★★ James Cagney is a hotshot barnstormer who joins the Marine Air Corps and refuses to conform to tradition and the authority of Pat O'Brien. Familiar roles for the stars but they play them so well. Great aerial stunt work is a plus. B&W; 86m. DIR: Lloyd Bacon. CAST: James Cagney,

Pat O'Brien, Margaret Lindsay, Frank McHugh, Russell Hicks, Ward Bond. 1935

DEVIL DOLL, THE (1936) ★★★1/2 Imaginative fantasy-thriller pits crazed Lionel Barrymore and his tiny "devil dolls" against those who have done him wrong. Although not as original an idea now as it was then, the acting, special effects, and director Tod Browning's odd sense of humor make this worth seeing. B&W; 79m. DIR: Tod Browning. CAST: Lionel Barrymore, Maureen O'Sullivan, Frank Lawton, Henry B. Walthall. 1936

DEVIL DOLL (1963) ★★ Isn't it amazing how many horror movies have been made with the same story of a ventriloquist's dummy occupied by a human soul? This low-key British version has some creepy moments as Hugo the dummy stalks his victims with a knife, but lackadaisical direction holds the movie back. B&W; 80m. DIR: Lindsay Shonteff. CAST: Bryant Halliday, William Sylvester, Yvonne Romain. 1963

DEVIL GIRL FROM MARS 🎔 Messenger (the Devil Girl) sent from her native planet to kidnap Earth men for reproductive purposes. B&W; 76m. DIR: David MacDonald. CAST: Patricia Laffan, Hazel Court, Hugh McDermott. 1955 DVD

DEVIL HORSE, THE ★★★ One of the best Mascot serials and a real audience favorite, this top-notch adventure features Harry Carey as a man tracking his brother's killer, evil Noah Beery. Codirector Richard Talmadge was one of the most famous and popular of silent stuntmen, and his apt hand as well as a fine cast, good photography, and exciting stunts make this a memorable serial. B&W; 12 chapters. DIR: Otto Brower, Richard Talmadge. CAST: Harry Carey, Noah Beery Sr., Frankie Darro, Greta Granstedt, Barrie O'Daniels, Yakima Canutt, Lane Chandler. 1932

DEVIL HUNTER YOHKO ★★ Japanese animation. Imagine schoolgirl Yohko's surprise when she finds out that she is the next in a long line of Devil Hunters. This one is definitely not for children. In Japanese with English subtitles. Not rated; contains violence and nudity. 45m. DIR: Tetsuro Aoki. 1990

DEVIL IN A BLUE DRESS ★★★★ This old-fashioned murder mystery is about an ex-G.I., Easy Rawlins, who finds himself forced out of a job in the aircraft industry in post-WWII Los Angeles. In order to make his house payments, Easy agrees to find the missing mistress of a mayoral candidate, thus embarking on his first case as a private eye. Based on the popular detective series by Walter Mosley, this film gives a rare glimpse of the African American culture of the time against a superb, jump-blues soundtrack. Rated R for violence, profanity, nudity, and simulated sex. 102m. DIR: Carl Franklin. CAST: Denzel Washington, Tom Sizemore, Jennifer Beals, Don Cheadle, Maury Chaykin, Terry Kinney. 1995 DVD

DEVIL IN THE FLESH (1946) ★★★1/2 Story of an adulterous love affair between a young man and the wife of a soldier during World War I is moving and tragic. The mutual attraction of the two turns to passion after the girl's husband leaves for the front, and the growing guilt that they feel turns their love into torment. French with English subtitles. B&W; 110m.

DIR: Claude Autant-Lara. **CAST:** Micheline Presle, Gérard Philipe, Denise Grey. 1946

DEVIL IN THE FLESH (1987) 🎬 A story of two young lovers—a lanky student and a *Betty Blue*–like madwoman. In Italian with English subtitles. Rated X. 120m. **DIR:** Marco Bellocchio. **CAST:** Maruschka Detmers, Federico Pitzalis. 1987

DEVIL IN THE FLESH (1998) ★★ You can always count on video to keep the sex thriller genre alive. This one stars Rose McGowan as the new girl in school who makes the life of a caring male teacher a living nightmare. Rated R for language, violence, nudity, and adult situations. 92m. **DIR:** Steve Cohen. **CAST:** Rose McGowan, Alex McArthur, Sherrie Rose. 1998

DEVIL IN THE HOUSE OF EXORCISM, THE ★★ Originally titled *House of Exorcism*. Not as crummy as everybody says it is, but no Oscar candidate, either. Producer Alfred Leone took some footage from *Lisa and the Devil* and footage shot by Mario Bava, added some scenes shot by himself, and cobbled together this noisy *Exorcist* rip-off. Bava hides behind the pseudonym Mickey Lion. Rated R. 93m. **DIR:** Mario Bava. **CAST:** Elke Sommer, Robert Alda, Telly Savalas. 1975

DEVIL, PROBABLY, THE ★★★ If you've never seen a film by French director Robert Bresson, this isn't the one to start with. A young Frenchman is unable to find any meaning in life, and his friends try to persuade him that life is worth living. Bresson's stark staging and unblinking camera enhance the gloom in a film that will seem merely pessimistic to those not on his wavelength. Not rated; contains nudity and adult situations. In French with English subtitles. 95m. **DIR:** Robert Bresson. **CAST:** Antoine Monnier, Tina Irissari. 1977

●**DEVIL RIDES OUT, THE** ★★★1/2 Adapted from Dennis Wheatley's witchcraft novel, this is one of the finest films to come out of Britain's Hammer Films. The direction by Terence Fisher is top-notch and the scenes of mounting terror are still effective today. 95m. **DIR:** Terence Fisher. **CAST:** Christopher Lee, Charles Gray. 1967

DEVIL THUMBS A RIDE, THE ★★★1/2 After murdering an innocent citizen during a robbery, a cold-blooded killer hitches a ride with a tipsy, unsuspecting salesman, picks up two female riders, and continues his murderous path. Nifty *noir*. B&W; 62m. **DIR:** Felix Feist. **CAST:** Lawrence Tierney, Ted North, Nan Leslie. 1947

DEVIL WITHIN HER, THE 🎬 Hilariously bad at times, plodding the rest. Rated R for violence, nudity, and profanity. 90m. **DIR:** Peter Sasdy. **CAST:** Joan Collins, Donald Pleasence, Eileen Atkins, Ralph Bates, Caroline Munro, John Steiner. 1975

DEVILFISH ★★1/2 That's actually Lamberto Bava hiding behind the director credit and what we have here is actually a *Jaws* rip-off hiding in plain sight. The film concerns a government-created monster shark terrorizing Florida. The script has many layers to it, but poor acting and a woefully bad creature sink this film. Not rated; contains violence, gore, simulated sex, and profanity. 92m. **DIR:** John Old Jr. **CAST:** Michael Sopkiw, Valentine Monnier. 1984

DEVILMAN VOL. 1–2 ★★ Vaguely reminiscent of the works of H. P. Lovecraft, this animated film has only a few points of interest. In order to defend the world from an impending demon invasion, two young men gain supernatural powers by becoming demons themselves. In Japanese with English subtitles. Not rated; contains violence and nudity. 55m. each. **DIR:** Tsutomu Iida. 1987–1990 DVD

DEVILS, THE ★★★★ Next to *Women in Love*, this is director Ken Russell's best film. Exploring witchcraft and politics in France during the seventeenth century, it's a mad mixture of drama, horror, camp, and comedy. Ugly for the most part (with several truly unsettling scenes), it is still fascinating. Rated R. 109m. **DIR:** Ken Russell. **CAST:** Oliver Reed, Vanessa Redgrave, Dudley Sutton, Max Adrian, Gemma Jones. 1971

DEVIL'S ADVOCATE ★★★1/2 Al Pacino dominates this intriguing fantasy, as the charismatic head of a New York City law firm that woos cocky Florida defense attorney Keanu Reeves and his sexpot wife. Our young hero has never lost a case, a talent not lost on his new mentor, whose hypnotic appeal speaks of greater-than-average powers ... and, indeed, as the title suggests, this particular firm is controlled by Satan himself. Although the script plays somewhat fast and loose with actual biblical content, Pacino's portrayal of Pure Evil is a thrill ride unto itself. Rated R for violence, profanity, nudity, simulated sex, and perverse sexual content. 138m. **DIR:** Taylor Hackford. **CAST:** Keanu Reeves, Al Pacino, Charlize Theron, Jeffrey Jones, Judith Ivey, Craig T. Nelson. 1997 DVD

●**DEVIL'S ARITHMETIC, THE** ★★★1/2 Self-absorbed modern teen Kirsten Dunst gets a painful lesson in her own Jewish heritage, when she opens the door for Elijah during a Passover celebration and finds herself inexplicably catapulted back in time, into the body of a relative who survived incarceration in a WWII Nazi death camp. Robert J. Avrech's script, adapted from Jane Yolen's novel, is honorable, even though this film clearly is intended as a family experience, and thus mutes the story's worst atrocities. Although tough going at times, this one should be watched by all; the lessons here must never be forgotten ... as Dunst's character learns. Rated PG-13 for violence, brief nudity, and dramatic intensity. 95m. **DIR:** Donna Deitch. **CAST:** Kirsten Dunst, Brittany Murphy, Paul Freeman, Mimi Rogers, Louise Fletcher. 1999

DEVIL'S BRIGADE, THE ★★1/2 During World War II, a disciplined Canadian troop is sent to Utah to train with a ragtag gang of American army misfits for a planned joint operation. Not rated, but has graphic battle scenes. 130m. **DIR:** Andrew V. McLaglen. **CAST:** William Holden, Cliff Robertson, Vince Edwards, Michael Rennie, Dana Andrews, Claude Akins, Carroll O'Connor, Richard Jaeckel. 1968

DEVIL'S BROTHER, THE ★★★1/2 Opera star Dennis King makes a formidable lead, and Laurel and Hardy make hearty helpers with his romantic problems with Thelma Todd. Auber's operetta gets glowing treatment with its musical numbers produced with big budgets and lots of pizazz. The original title was *Fra Diavolo*, and it confused audiences on first release, so it was anglicized for a reissue and became an instant hit. B&W; 88m. DIR: Charles R. Rogers. CAST: Stan Laurel, Oliver Hardy, Dennis King, Thelma Todd, James Finlayson, Henry Armetta. 1933

DEVIL'S CANYON ★★ Essentially a prison-break movie dressed up in cowboy clothes. Lawman Dale Robertson is railroaded into the Arizona State Pen at the turn of the century after killing two men in self-defense. Static, claustrophobic, set-bound—originally made in 3-D. 92m. DIR: Alfred Werker. CAST: Dale Robertson, Virginia Mayo, Stephen McNally, Arthur Hunnicutt. 1953

DEVIL'S COMMANDMENT, THE ★★★ Serious horror fans should make an effort to find this movie, which marked the beginning of the revival of the gothic horror film in Europe. Another version of the story of Countess Bathory, who tried to salvage her youth with the blood of young women, the film was sliced up by both its Italian and American distributors. The distinctive visual sense of director Riccardo Freda (assisted by cinematographer Mario Bava) is still compelling. Dubbed in English. B&W; 71m. DIR: Riccardo Freda. CAST: Gianna Maria Canale, Antoine Balpetre, Paul Muller. 1956

DEVIL'S DISCIPLE, THE ★★★1/2 An amusing romp through the American Revolution, by way of George Bernard Shaw. The movie follows a strait-laced pastor (Burt Lancaster) and an engaging rogue (Kirk Douglas), who suspend their differences long enough to outwit a British garrison. B&W; 82m. DIR: Guy Hamilton. CAST: Burt Lancaster, Kirk Douglas, Laurence Olivier, Janette Scott, Eva LeGallienne, Harry Andrews, George Rose. 1959

DEVIL'S EYE, THE ★★ Disappointing comedy. In order to cure the sty in his eye, the devil sends Don Juan (Jarl Kulle) from hell to breach a woman's chastity. Bibi Andersson plays Britt-Marie, the pastor's virgin daughter. 90m. DIR: Ingmar Bergman. CAST: Jarl Kulle, Bibi Andersson, Gunnar Björnstrand. 1960

DEVIL'S GIFT, THE ♥ Ultra-low-budget and uncredited rip-off of Stephen King's short story "The Monkey." Not rated. 112m. DIR: Kenneth Berton. CAST: Bob Mendlesolin. 1984

DEVIL'S MESSENGER, THE ★★ A film of note for its curio value only. Lon Chaney plays the devil (in a dark, short-sleeved sport shirt!), who takes pity on a young suicide victim and sends her back to Earth to lure sinners to their doom. An uncredited Curt Siodmak (*Donovan's Brain*) worked on the script. B&W; 72m. DIR: Herbert L. Strock. CAST: Lon Chaney Jr., Karen Kadler, John Crawford. 1961

DEVIL'S OWN, THE ★★★1/2 Undercover IRA soldier Brad Pitt comes to the United States on a mission to secure missiles for the lads back home, and as part of his "deep cover" moves in with salt-of-the-earth Irish cop Harrison Ford and his family … who know nothing of their visitor's background. The secret leaks when events go predictably awry. The complex script does a good job of humanizing a character we'd normally dismiss as a monster, and the central metaphor is laced with irony: "Don't look for a happy ending; it's not an American story, it's an Irish one." Rated R for violence and profanity. 110m.

DIR: Alan J. Pakula. CAST: Harrison Ford, Brad Pitt, Margaret Colin, Rubén Blades, Treat Williams. 1997 DVD

DEVIL'S RAIN, THE ★★1/2 Great cast in a fair shocker about a band of devil worshipers at large in a small town. Terrific makeup, especially Ernest Borgnine's! Rated PG for language and violence. 85m. DIR: Robert Fuest. CAST: Ernest Borgnine, Ida Lupino, William Shatner, Eddie Albert, Tom Skerritt, Keenan Wynn, John Travolta. 1975 DVD

DEVIL'S UNDEAD, THE ★★★1/2 A surprisingly entertaining and suspenseful release starring the two kings of British horror, Christopher Lee and Peter Cushing, as a sort of modern-day Holmes and Watson in a tale of demonic possession. Rated PG. 91m. DIR: Peter Sasdy. CAST: Christopher Lee, Peter Cushing, Georgia Brown, Diana Dors. 1979

DEVIL'S WEDDING NIGHT, THE ★★ Say this for the Italians: even when their movies stink, they pack them with exploitable ingredients. Here, it's vampire queen Sara Bay (Rosalba Neri before she Anglicized her name), disrobing at every opportunity just as she did in *Lady Frankenstein*, and seducing knuckle-headed twin brothers, both played by Mark Damon. Rated R. 85m. DIR: Paul Solvay. CAST: Sara Bay, Mark Damon, Frances Davis. 1973

DEVLIN ★★★ Dedicated cop Bryan Brown takes quite a pounding in scripter David Taylor's twisty adaptation of Roderick Thorp's book, which finds our hero set up as the prime suspect in a highly visible political slaying. Devlin gradually works his way into a complex scheme involving departmental corruption. Totally preposterous made-for-cable mystery, but entertaining. 110m. DIR: Rick Rosenthal. CAST: Bryan Brown, Roma Downey, Lloyd Bridges, Lisa Eichhorn, Jan Rubes. 1992

DEVLIN CONNECTION III, THE ★★ One of the *Devlin Connection* TV episodes entitled "Love, Sex, Sin and Death at Point Dume" features Rock Hudson and Jack Scalia as a father-son duo who try to find a murderer before he kills their friend (Leigh Taylor-Young). Nothing special here, folks. 50m. DIR: Christian I. Nyby II. CAST: Rock Hudson, Jack Scalia, Leigh Taylor-Young, Tina Chen. 1982

DEVONSVILLE TERROR, THE ★★★ Three witches are killed in Devonsville in 1683, and one of them places a curse on the townspeople. Flash forward to the present. This film has good performances, high production values, and a scary script that is not based on special effects. Rated R for nudity, violence, mild gore. 97m. DIR: Ulli Lommel. CAST: Paul Wilson, Suzanna Love, Donald Pleasence. 1983 DVD

DEVOTION ★★1/2 Watchable but farfetched tale about a rich young woman who poses as a dowdy nanny in order to get close to the man of her dreams. All goes well until his wife comes between them. B&W; 81m. DIR: Robert Milton. CAST: Ann Harding, Leslie Howard, O. P. Heggie. 1931 DVD

D.I., THE ★★★ Jack Webb embodies the tough, nononsense drill instructor so commonly associated with the Marine Corps in this straightforward story of basic training and the men that it makes (or breaks). Don Dubbins plays the troublesome recruit who makes life miserable for Webb; many other roles are played by real-life members of the armed services. B&W; 106m. DIR: Jack Webb. CAST: Jack Webb, Don Dubbins, Lin McCarthy, Monica Lewis, Jackie Loughery, Virginia Gregg. 1957

DIABOLICALLY YOURS ★★★ How would you like to wake up after an accident to find a beautiful wife and a luxurious mansion that you have no recollection of? Sound great? Unfortunately, it's the start of a nightmare. This French film is unrated, but contains violence. 94m. DIR: Julien Duvivier. CAST: Alain Delon, Senta Berger. 1967

DIABOLIQUE (1955) ★★★★ Classic thriller builds slowly but rapidly gathers momentum along the way. Both wife and mistress of a headmaster conspire to kill him. The twisted plot of murder has since been copied many times. In French with English subtitles. B&W; 107m. DIR: Henri-Georges Clouzot. CAST: Simone Signoret, Vera Clouzot, Charles Vanel, Paul Meurisse. 1955 DVD

DIABOLIQUE (1996) ★★1/2 Deliver us from remakes that attempt to "improve" on the original! Sharon Stone's delightfully slinky outfits are the only genuine attraction in this updated so-called thriller, which pairs her with Isabelle Adjani as the mistress and wife who decide to murder abusive school headmaster Chazz Palminteri. What was fresh and genuinely frightening in French director Henri-Georges Clouzot's original is old hat here. Rated R for violence, nudity, profanity, and simulated sex. 108m. DIR: Jeremiah S. Chechik. CAST: Sharon Stone, Isabelle Adjani, Chazz Palminteri, Kathy Bates, Spalding Gray, Allen Garfield. 1996 DVD

DIAL: HELP ★★1/2 While at times a bit contrived, this film has an ease about it as a young woman gets hooked up with a dead operator and begins to see her friends dying. Rated R for violence and profanity. 96m. DIR: Ruggero Deodato. CAST: Charlotte Lewis, William Berger. 1988

DIAL M FOR MURDER ★★★★ Alfred Hitchcock imbues this classic thriller with his well-known touches of sustained suspense. Ray Milland is a rather sympathetic villain whose desire to inherit his wife's fortune leads him to one conclusion: murder. His plan for pulling off the perfect crime is foiled temporarily. Undaunted, he quickly switches to Plan B, with even more entertaining results. 105m. DIR: Alfred Hitchcock. CAST: Grace Kelly, Robert Cummings, Ray Milland, John Williams. 1954

•DIAL M FOR MURDER (1981) ★★1/2 This made-for-TV remake of the Alfred Hitchcock film isn't truly awful—if nothing else, it has a good cast going through the familiar paces. But you'd want to see it only if you can't get the original. 100m. DIR: Boris Sagal. CAST: Christopher Plummer, Angie Dickinson, Anthony Quayle, Ron Moody, Michael Parks. 1981

DIAMOND FLEECE, THE ★★1/2 An ex-convict who is a master at security systems is hired to protect a $5 million diamond. All the actors, especially Brian Dennehy, do a wonderful job, but the plots lacks depth. Made for cable. 91m. DIR: Al Waxman. CAST: Ben Cross, Kate Nelligan, Brian Dennehy, Tony Rosato. 1992

DIAMOND HEAD ★★ Domineering Hawaiian plantation boss Charlton Heston comes close to ruining his family with his dictatorial ways. The lush scenery is the only credible thing in this pineapple opera. 107m. DIR: Guy Green. CAST: Charlton Heston, Yvette Mimieux, George Chakiris, France Nuyen, James Darren. 1963

DIAMOND TRAP, THE ★★1/2 A stubborn New York detective follows the trail of a femme fatale. Touches of lighthearted comedy liven this droll made-for-TV film about a $12-million diamond heist. Otherwise, this mystery has little in the way of genuine plot twists. 93m. DIR: Don Taylor. CAST: Howard Hesseman, Brooke Shields, Ed Marinaro, Darren McGavin. 1992

•DIAMONDBACKS ★★ A lone engineer at a remote NASA outpost battles the members of a right-wing militia. Plot takes a backseat to stunts and pyrotechnics, which are average but plentiful. Not rated; contains violence and profanity. 91m. DIR: Barnard Salzman. CAST: Miles O'Keeffe, Eb Lottimer, Timothy Bottoms, Chris Mitchum. 1999 DVD

DIAMONDS ★★★ Well-planned plot and good chemistry between Robert Shaw and Richard Roundtree make this an enjoyable film of action and intrigue. When a British entrepreneur hires an excon and his girlfriend to assist him in a $100 million diamond heist the stage is set for an amazing number of plot twists. 108m. DIR: Menahem Golan. CAST: Robert Shaw, Richard Roundtree, Barbara Hershey, Shelley Winters. 1975 DVD

DIAMONDS ARE FOREVER ★★★★ This release was supposed to be Sean Connery's last appearance as James Bond before he decided to return for Never Say Never Again. It's good fun for 007 fans and far superior to most of the Roger Moore films that followed it. Rated PG. 119m. DIR: Guy Hamilton. CAST: Sean Connery, Jill St. John, Charles Gray, Bruce Cabot. 1971

DIAMOND'S EDGE ★★★1/2 When his detective older brother is thrown in jail, a young teen takes over his current case. Though it was made for younger viewers, adults will enjoy this private eye spoof's clever homages to classic mystery films. Rated PG. 83m. DIR: Stephen Bayly. CAST: Dursley McLinden, Colin Dale, Susannah York, Patricia Hodge, Roy Kinnear, Bill Paterson, Jimmy Nail, Saeed Jaffrey. 1988

DIAMONDS ON WHEELS ★★ Subpar Disney adventure pits a group of teenage auto-racing enthusiasts against a mob of jewel thieves. Strictly formula; even toddlers will realize they've seen it before. Rated G. 87m. DIR: Jerome Courtland. CAST: Peter Firth, Patrick Allen. 1973

DIANE ★★ Lana Turner's swan song at MGM, the studio that developed her star power, and Roger Moore's Hollywood debut. She plays the mistress of a sixteenth-century French king, and he plays the king. Lots of court intrigue, pageantry, and aimless talk. 110m. DIR: David Miller. CAST: Lana Turner, Roger Moore, Marisa Pavan, Henry Daniell, Taina Elg, Cedric Hardwicke, Torin Thatcher, Ian Wolfe, Gene Reynolds. 1956

DIARY OF A CHAMBERMAID (1946) ★★ Octave Mirbeau's once daring novel had most of its quirky and sensational elements watered down for this Hollywood version directed by Jean Renoir during his

American sojourn in the 1940s. Not one of his better American films. B&W; 86m. **DIR:** Jean Renoir. **CAST:** Burgess Meredith, Paulette Goddard. 1946

DIARY OF A CHAMBERMAID (1964) ★★★★ Excellent remake of Jean Renoir's 1946 film concerns the personal dilemma of a maid (Jeanne Moreau) caught in the grip of fascism in 1939 France. Director Luis Buñuel paints a cynical portrait of the bourgeoisie—a stunning character study. French dialogue with English subtitles. B&W; 95m. **DIR:** Luis Buñuel. **CAST:** Jeanne Moreau, Michel Piccoli, Georges Geret, Daniel Ivernel. 1964

DIARY OF A COUNTRY PRIEST ★★★★1/2 The slow pace at the beginning of this tale about a priest trying to minister to his parish might tend to put some viewers off. However, with Bresson's poetic style and camera work, the wait is well worth it. In French with English subtitles. B&W; 120m. **DIR:** Robert Bresson. **CAST:** Claude Laydu, Nicole Ladmiral, Nicole Maurey. 1950

DIARY OF A HITMAN 🖤 A hired killer struggles with his conscience when asked to perform his last hit on a young wife and her baby. Laughable dialogue, Forest Whitaker's Italian accent, and Sherilyn Fenn's awful acting are just three contributing factors to this mess. Rated R for violence, profanity, and nudity. 90m. **DIR:** Roy London. **CAST:** Forest Whitaker, Sherilyn Fenn, James Belushi, Lois Chiles, Sharon Stone. 1991

DIARY OF A LOST GIRL ★★★★ In this silent classic, Louise Brooks plays a young girl who is raped by her father's business partner (Fritz Rasp). Banished to a girls' reformatory, she eventually escapes, falling prey to the false sanctuary provided by a whorehouse madame. Those who maintain there is a docility to silent films may be surprised by the relatively mature subject matter in this film. B&W; 99m. **DIR:** G. W. Pabst. **CAST:** Louise Brooks, Joseph Rovensky, Fritz Rasp, André Roanne, Valeska Gert. 1929

DIARY OF A MAD HOUSEWIFE ★★★ Most women will detest Jonathan (Richard Benjamin), the self-centered, social climber husband of Tina (Carrie Snodgress). He has had an affair and also lost all their savings in a bad investment. Tina, a college graduate, has been unhappily stuck at home for years with their two children. She finally finds happiness in an affair with George (Frank Langella). Profanity, sex, and nudity are included in this film. 94m. **DIR:** Frank Perry. **CAST:** Richard Benjamin, Carrie Snodgress, Frank Langella. 1970

DIARY OF A MAD OLD MAN ★★★1/2 An old man in failing health is rejuvenated by his growing obsession with his beautiful daughter-in-law. Delicate, tastefully handled film adapted from a Japanese novel. Rated PG-13 for brief nudity. In English. 93m. **DIR:** Lili Rademakers. **CAST:** Ralph Michael, Beatie Edney, Derek de Lint. 1987

DIARY OF A MADMAN 🖤 Unatmospheric adaptation of Guy de Maupassant's *The Horla*—with Vincent Price as a murderous sculptor. 96m. **DIR:** Reginald LeBorg. **CAST:** Vincent Price, Nancy Kovack, Ian Wolfe. 1963

DIARY OF A SEDUCER ★★★1/2 Darkly comic tale of a young French female student whose mundane life is brightened when a fellow student lends her a copy of a rare book that has a strange sexual hold over its readers. How the written word drives readers to extremes to fulfill their romantic wishes makes for a funny, offbeat film. In French with English subtitles. Not rated; contains adult situations. 95m. **DIR:** Daniele Dubroux. **CAST:** Chiara Mastroianni, Melvil Poupaud, Jéan-Pierre Leaud. 1996

DIARY OF A SERIAL KILLER ★★★ Gary Busey and Arnold Vosloo dish up delicious performances as a reporter and the serial killer who grants him an exclusive. At first, reporter Busey is enthralled with the offer, but when the body count begins to climb, he decides to cancel the killer. Good take on an interesting premise misses the mark due to clumsy plotting and silly dialogue. Rated R for adult situations, language, and violence. 92m. **DIR:** Joshua Wallace. **CAST:** Gary Busey, Arnold Vosloo, Michael Madsen, Julia Campbell. 1997 DVD

DIARY OF A TEENAGE HITCHHIKER ★★ Trite dialogue and an inappropriate score lessen the impact of this made-for-TV drama documenting the dangers of hitchhiking for young women. Inferior. 96m. **DIR:** Ted Post. **CAST:** Charlene Tilton, Dick Van Patten, Katherine Helmond, James Carroll Jordan, Katy Kurtzman, Dominique Dunne, Craig T. Nelson. 1979

DIARY OF ANNE FRANK, THE ★★★1/2 Excellent adaptation of the Broadway play dealing with the terror Jews felt during the Nazi raids of World War II. Two families are forced to hide in a Jewish sympathizer's attic to avoid capture by the Nazis. Anne (Millie Perkins) is the teenage girl who doesn't stop dreaming of a better future. Shelley Winters won an Oscar for her role as the hysterical Mrs. Van Daan, who shares sparse food and space with the Frank family. B&W; 170m. **DIR:** George Stevens. **CAST:** Millie Perkins, Joseph Schildkraut, Shelley Winters. 1959

DIARY OF FORBIDDEN DREAMS ★★1/2 A bizarre variation on the classic fantasy *Alice In Wonderland*, this concerns a beautiful young woman (Sydne Rome) who becomes lost in a remote area of the Italian Riviera. The film suffers from too many diversions that create a complete mess. Rated R for nudity and language. 94m. **DIR:** Roman Polanski. **CAST:** Hugh Griffith, Marcello Mastroianni, Sydne Rome. 1981

•**DICK** ★★★ Spoof of the Watergate break-in features two unlikely teens as the leak to the press. A delightful start, with the girls exuding a charming combination of innocence and joy as Nixon's Secret Youth Advisors and dog walkers, takes rather a nasty turn in the latter half. The dramatic change in the duo hits a low in the final cheesy scene that is unforgettably bad. Rated PG-13 for language, obscene gestures, and drug use. 94m. **DIR:** Andrew Fleming. **CAST:** Kirsten Dunst, Michelle Williams, Dan Hedaya, Will Ferrell. 1999 DVD

DICK TRACY (1937) ★★★ Chester Gould's comic-strip detective Dick Tracy (Ralph Byrd) chases a mysterious criminal known as *The Spider* who has kidnapped his brother and turned him into a slave. Great stunts and plenty of action in this one. B&W; 15 chapters. **DIR:** Ray Taylor, Alan James. **CAST:** Ralph

Byrd, Kay Hughes, Smiley Burnette, Lee Van Atta, Francis X. Bushman. 1937

DICK TRACY (1990) ★★★★ Chester Gould's comic-strip detective (Warren Beatty) takes on a bevy of baddies while fending off the affections of the sultry Breathless (Madonna) in this stylish, old-fashioned piece of screen entertainment. Al Pacino has a field day as the main heavy, Big Boy Caprice, while other big-name stars and character actors do cameo bits. Rated PG for violence. 120m. **DIR:** Warren Beatty. **CAST:** Warren Beatty, Madonna, Glenne Headly, Al Pacino, Dustin Hoffman, James Caan, Mandy Patinkin, Paul Sorvino, Charles Durning, Dick Van Dyke, R. G. Armstrong, William Forsythe. 1990

DICK TRACY MEETS GRUESOME ★★1/2 Everybody's favorite Dick Tracy, Ralph Byrd, returns to the role he originated in serials for Republic Studios just in time to do battle with Gruesome, played with style by the great Boris Karloff. B&W; 65m. **DIR:** John Rawlins. **CAST:** Ralph Byrd, Boris Karloff, Anne Gwynne, Edward Ashley, June Clayworth. 1947 DVD

DICK TRACY RETURNS ★★★ Ralph Byrd's second outing as comic-strip detective Dick Tracy finds the unbeatable G-man hot on the trail of the murderous Stark gang, an evil family that has killed one of Tracy's men. B&W; 15 chapters. **DIR:** William Witney, John English. **CAST:** Ralph Byrd, Lynne Roberts (Mary Hart), Charles Middleton, David Sharpe, Jerry Tucker, Ned Glass. 1938

DICK TRACY VS. CRIME INC. ★★★ Dick Tracy is called in to help stop the mysterious "Ghost," a ruthless member of the Council of Eight, a group of influential citizens attempting to rid the city of crime. B&W; 15 chapters. **DIR:** William Witney, John English. **CAST:** Ralph Byrd, Michael Owen, Jan Wiley, John Davidson, Ralph Morgan. 1941

DICK TRACY VERSUS CUEBALL ★★ Dick Tracy chases a bald strangler who made off with a fortune in jewelry in this low-budget feature film. Morgan Conway's anemic Dick Tracy holds this one back, but Dick Wessel as Cueball peps up this modest programmer. B&W; 62m. **DIR:** Gordon Douglas. **CAST:** Morgan Conway, Anne Jeffreys, Lyle Latell, Rita Corday, Dick Wessel. 1946 DVD

DICK TRACY'S DILEMMA ★★1/2 Two-fisted detective Dick Tracy (Ralph Byrd) finds himself up against a maniacal killer with an iron hook. B&W; 60m. **DIR:** John Rawlins. **CAST:** Ralph Byrd, Lyle Latell, Kay Christopher, Jack Lambert, Ian Keith. 1947 DVD

DICK TRACY'S G-MEN ★★★ FBI agent Dick Tracy is forced to pursue the evil Zarnoff, the head of an international spy ring, after already capturing him and witnessing his execution. The ruthless spy lord is revived by drugs and redoubles his efforts at sabotage, putting Tracy and his men in one tight spot after another. B&W; 15 chapters. **DIR:** William Witney, John English. **CAST:** Ralph Byrd, Irving Pichel, Ted Pearson, Jennifer Jones, Walter Miller. 1939

DICK TURPIN ★★ Tom Mix exchanges chaps and six-guns for cape and sword in this rather stolid portrayal of the legendary English highwayman. Good production values and crisp photography, but this one's no match for Mix's more traditional Western

adventures. Silent. B&W; 70m. **DIR:** John G. Blystone. **CAST:** Tom Mix, Kathleen Myers. 1925

DICK VAN DYKE SHOW, THE (TV SERIES) ★★★★ Comedy writer Dick Van Dyke spends his days devising jokes with quipsters Morey Amsterdam and Rose Marie for "The Alan Brady Show" and his nights in suburbia with well-meaning wife Mary Tyler Moore and their son, Larry Matthews. Inevitably, some complication comes along to upset the delicate balance, but matters are soon resolved. Hilarious in its day, this sitcom still works. B&W; 58m. **DIR:** Carl Reiner, Various. **CAST:** Dick Van Dyke, Mary Tyler Moore, Rose Marie, Morey Amsterdam, Larry Matthews, Richard Deacon, Jerry Paris, Ann Morgan Guilbert, Carl Reiner. 1961–1966

DIE! DIE! MY DARLING! ★★1/2 This British thriller was Tallulah Bankhead's last movie. She plays a crazed woman who kidnaps her late son's fiancée for punishment and salvation. Grisly fun for Bankhead fans, but may be too heavy-handed for others. Not rated, the film has violence. 97m. **DIR:** Silvio Narizzano. **CAST:** Tallulah Bankhead, Stefanie Powers, Peter Vaughan, Donald Sutherland. 1965

DIE HARD ★★★★1/2 If this rip-roaring action picture doesn't recharge your batteries, you're probably dead. Alan Rickman and Alexander Godunov play terrorists who invade an L.A. high-rise. The direction of John McTiernan packs a wallop. Bruce Willis is more human, not to mention chattier, than most action heroes. Rated R for violence, nudity, profanity, and drug use. 131m. **DIR:** John McTiernan. **CAST:** Bruce Willis, Alan Rickman, Bonnie Bedelia, Alexander Godunov, Paul Gleason, William Atherton, Hart Bochner, James Shigeta, Reginald Vel Johnson. 1988 DVD

DIE HARD 2: DIE HARDER ★★★★ In this solid sequel, maverick cop Bruce Willis takes on terrorists into a Washington D.C. airport, while his wife (Bonnie Bedelia) circles overhead in a plane which is running out of fuel. Willis does a fine job of reprising his wisecracking hero. Rated R for violence and profanity. 124m. **DIR:** Renny Harlin. **CAST:** Bruce Willis, Bonnie Bedelia, William Atherton, Reginald Vel Johnson, Franco Nero, John Amos, Dennis Franz, Art Evans, Fred Dalton Thompson. 1990 DVD

DIE HARD WITH A VENGEANCE ★★★1/2 In this third entry in the series, it's Bruce Willis versus a mad bomber who terrorizes New York City to divert attention from a massive break-in at the federal reserve bank. It's a nonstop chase with spectacular stunts, but if you need a bit of logic with your thrills you had better pass it by. Rated R for violence and profanity. 130m. **DIR:** John McTiernan. **CAST:** Bruce Willis, Jeremy Irons, Samuel L. Jackson, Graham Greene, Colleen Camp. 1995 DVD

DIE LAUGHING ❤ Robby Benson stars as Pinsky, a young cabbie with aspirations of becoming a rock recording star. Rated PG. 108m. **DIR:** Jeff Werner. **CAST:** Robby Benson, Linda Grovenor, Charles Durning, Bud Cort. 1980

DIE, MONSTER, DIE! ❤ A slow-moving H. P. Lovecraft adaptation about a young man (Nick Adams) visiting his fiancée's family estate. 80m. **DIR:** Daniel

Haller. **CAST:** Boris Karloff, Nick Adams, Suzan Farmer. 1965

DIE SCREAMING, MARIANNE 🎬 Graphic horror film concerns a young girl (Susan George) who is pursued by numerous crazies. Rated R. 90m. **DIR:** Pete Walker. **CAST:** Susan George, Barry Evans. 1972

DIE WATCHING 🎬 An emotionally scarred video director lures women to fake auditions where he gives them scenes worth dying for. They should have left the lens cap on. Rated R for nudity, violence, and language. 92m. **DIR:** Charles Davis. **CAST:** Christopher Atkins, Vali Ashton, Tim Thomerson. 1993 DVD

DIFFERENT FOR GIRLS ★★★1/2 Overgrown adolescent Paul Prentice (Rupert Graves) meets the shy youth he protected from bullies when they were both in school—but Karl has had a sex change and is now Kim (Steven Mackintosh). Still as repressed as Paul is pugnacious, Kim lets herself be drawn out of her shell by his well-meaning but troublesome attempts at understanding. Two excellent performances and a sharply observed script make this British comedy-drama worth seeing. Rated R for nudity, sexual situations, and profanity. 96m. **DIR:** Richard Spence. **CAST:** Steven Mackintosh, Rupert Graves, Miriam Margolyes, Saskia Reeves, Neil Dudgeon, Ian Dury. 1996 DVD

DIFFERENT STORY, A ★★★1/2 Perry King and Meg Foster play homosexuals who realize their romances are just not clicking. They fall in love with each other, marry, grow rich, and, eventually, dissatisfied. King and Foster are genuinely funny and appealing. Rated PG. 107m. **DIR:** Paul Aaron. **CAST:** Perry King, Meg Foster, Valerie Curtin, Peter Donat. 1979

DIGGER ★★★★ Wonderful coming-of-age tale about a 12-year-old boy named Digger, well played by Adam Hann-Byrd, who goes to stay with his grandmother on an island in the Pacific Northwest while his parents work out problems back home. At first a stranger in a strange land, Digger eventually warms up to his surroundings and the people of the island. Leslie Nielsen is a delight as the man trying to woo Digger's grandmother, played by Olympia Dukakis. Rated PG. 92m. **DIR:** Robert Turner. **CAST:** Adam Hann-Byrd, Joshua Jackson, Barbara Williams, Timothy Bottoms, Olympia Dukakis, Leslie Nielsen. 1994

DIGGING TO CHINA ★★★1/2 Timothy Hutton makes his director's debut with this winning drama about a mentally challenged man (Kevin Bacon) who befriends a young girl. Both dream of escaping from their dreary existence, and together they form a bond that makes their families suspicious. How the two overcome prejudice and find happiness makes for engaging viewing. The screenplay by Karen Janszen is filled with emotional heart tugs and whimsy. Rated PG for language. 103m. **DIR:** Timothy Hutton. **CAST:** Kevin Bacon, Mary Stuart Masterson, Cathy Moriarty, Evan Rachel Wood. 1997 DVD

DIGGSTOWN ★★★★1/2 Imagine the best parts of *The Sting* and *Rocky* combined in one terrific movie, and you get a good idea how supremely entertaining *Diggstown* is. James Woods and Lou Gossett work wonderfully together as a pair of con men who attempt to scam crook Bruce Dern, at his slimy best. Rated R for profanity and violence. 97m. **DIR:** Michael Ritchie. **CAST:** James Woods, Lou Gossett Jr.,

Bruce Dern, Oliver Platt, Heather Graham, Randall "Tex" Cobb. 1992 DVD

DIGITAL MAN ★★ Special effects are the only saving grace of this low-budget effort about a high-tech killing machine and the team of commandos sent to destroy it. Rated R for violence and language. 95m. **DIR:** Phillip Roth. **CAST:** Ken Olandt, Kristen Dalton, Adam Baldwin, Ed Lauter, Matthias Hues. 1994

DILLINGER (1945) ★★★ This look at the life and style of archetypal American gangster-antihero John Dillinger bids fair to be rated a *film noir*. Tough guy off-screen Lawrence Tierney is perfect in the title role. B&W; 89m. **DIR:** Max Nosseck. **CAST:** Edmund Lowe, Anne Jeffreys, Lawrence Tierney, Eduardo Ciannelli, Marc Lawrence, Elisha Cook Jr. 1945

DILLINGER (1973) ★★★★ John Milius made an explosive directorial debut with this rip-roaring gangster film featuring Warren Oates in his best starring role. As a jaunty John Dillinger, he has all the charisma of a Cagney or a Bogart. Rated R for profanity and violence. 96m. **DIR:** John Milius. **CAST:** Warren Oates, Ben Johnson, Cloris Leachman, Michelle Phillips, Richard Dreyfuss, Harry Dean Stanton, Geoffrey Lewis, Steve Kanaly, Frank McRae. 1973

DILLINGER (1990) ★★★ Shallow but often stylish look at the famous gangster's life. Mark Harmon makes for a suave, cool John Dillinger but an acid jazz background score and a superficial screenplay detract from the film's overall effect. Not rated; contains mild profanity and violence. 95m. **DIR:** Rupert Wainwright. **CAST:** Mark Harmon, Sherilyn Fenn, Will Patton, Bruce Abbott, Tom Bower, Patricia Arquette, Vince Edwards, Lawrence Tierney. 1990

DILLINGER & CAPONE ★★ Martin Sheen and F. Murray Abraham are wasted in this crime-drama about an unholy alliance forged between the famous gangsters. Five years after being presumed dead, John Dillinger reemerges and is recruited by Al Capone to pull off a bank heist. Low budget and hokey dialogue keep this one from reaching for more. Rated R for violence and language. 95m. **DIR:** Jon Purdy. **CAST:** Martin Sheen, F. Murray Abraham, Sasha Jenson, Don Stroud. 1995

DIM SUM: A LITTLE BIT OF HEART ★★★★ An independently made American movie about the tension and affection between a Chinese mother and daughter living in San Francisco's Chinatown. The film moves quietly, but contains many moments of humor. The restraint of the mother, who wants her daughter to marry, and the frustration of the daughter, who wants to live her life as she chooses, are beautifully conveyed by real-life mother and daughter Laureen and Kim Chew. Victor Wong, as a rambunctious uncle, is a gas. Rated PG. 88m. **DIR:** Wayne Wang. **CAST:** Laureen Chew, Kim Chew, Victor Wong. 1985

DIMPLES ★★★ Dimpled darling Shirley Temple tries to care for her lovable rogue grandfather Frank Morgan, a street pickpocket who works the crowds she gathers with her singing and dancing. A rich patron takes her in hand, gets her off the street, and on the stage. B&W; 79m. **DIR:** William A. Seiter. **CAST:** Shirley Temple, Frank Morgan, Helen Westley, Stepin Fetchit, John Carradine. 1936

DINER ★★★★1/2 Writer-director Barry Levinson's much-acclaimed bittersweet tale of growing up in the late 1950s, unlike *American Graffiti*, is never cute or idealized. Instead, it combines insight, sensitive drama, and low-key humor. Rated R for profanity and adult themes. 110m. **DIR:** Barry Levinson. **CAST:** Steve Guttenberg, Daniel Stern, Mickey Rourke, Kevin Bacon, Ellen Barkin. 1982 DVD

DINGAKA ★★★1/2 Cultures collide in this South African film as Masai warrior Ken Gampu tracks his daughter's killer to a metropolis and comes face-to-face with civilized justice. Spectacularly filmed by writer-producer Jamie Uys, this impressive movie features knockout performances by African film star Gampu as the accused and Stanley Baker as his attorney. 98m. **DIR:** Jamie Uys. **CAST:** Stanley Baker, Juliet Prowse, Ken Gampu, Bob Courtney. 1965

DINGO ★★★1/2 Jazz legend Miles Davis has his only acting role in this winning tale of an Australian man whose life's ambition is to play the trumpet like his idol. Colin Friels costars as John "Dingo" Anderson, a family man who is willing to throw it all away in order to pursue his dreams. A trip to Paris and to the great jazz clubs helps Dingo make up his mind. Offbeat and original, director Rolf de Heer's film is a celebration of music and life. Not rated. 108m. **DIR:** Rolf De Heer. **CAST:** Colin Friels, Miles Davis, Helen Buday. 1992

DINNER AT EIGHT (1933) ★★★★★ A sparkling, sophisticated, and witty comedy of character written by George S. Kaufman and Edna Ferber for the Broadway stage, this motion picture has a terrific all-star cast and lots of laughs. It's an all-time movie classic. B&W; 113m. **DIR:** George Cukor. **CAST:** John Barrymore, Jean Harlow, Marie Dressler, Billie Burke, Wallace Beery. 1933

DINNER AT EIGHT (1990) ★★★ Commendable television remake of MGM's classic comedy. Socialite Marsha Mason has nothing but problems while planning a dinner party for visiting English dignitaries. The lives of those on her guest list are equally explored as the night of the party arrives. 92m. **DIR:** Ron Lagomarsino. **CAST:** John Mahoney, Marsha Mason, Stacy Edwards, Joel Brooks, Tim Kazurinsky, Harry Hamlin, Ellen Greene, Lauren Bacall, Charles Durning. 1990

DINNER AT THE RITZ ★★★1/2 Good cast makes British whodunit about Annabella seeking her father's murderer an enjoyable diversion. Well-produced, with just a light enough touch to balance out all the familiar elements of crime melodrama. Early David Niven effort displays his unique qualities at comedy and light drama. B&W; 77m. **DIR:** Harold Schuster. **CAST:** David Niven, Paul Lukas, Annabella, Romney Brent. 1937

●**DINNER GAME, THE** ★★★★ A boorish cad gets his just desserts in this delightful French romp, which efficiently sets up a provocative underdog scenario and then turns richly comical as the tables are turned most efficiently. A condescending publisher and his equally obnoxious friends regularly meet for a dinner party where each is responsible for bringing an "idiot" as a guest. The victims have no idea that they're on hand merely to be humiliated, and their boorish yuppie "sponsors" compare notes later in the evening and award points to whoever brought the "best idiot." Our boorish publisher learns of a lowly—and lonely—accountant who reproduces famous monuments with matchsticks, and will discuss the topic with the zeal of a soccer fanatic. Fortunately for us, things don't work out quite as expected, and the resulting farce—punctuated by some truly inspired telephone humor—becomes increasingly hilarious. Unfairly rated PG-13 for minor profanity and sexual content. 82m. **DIR:** Francis Verber. **CAST:** Thierry Lhermitte, Jacques Villeret, Francis Huster, Daniel Prevost, Alexandra Vandernoot, Catherine Frot. 1998 DVD

DINO ★★ Sal Mineo plays a troubled teen. Brian Keith is the savvy psychologist who helps him understand his emotions in this utterly predictable film. The street jargon is strained. B&W; 96m. **DIR:** Thomas Carr. **CAST:** Sal Mineo, Brian Keith, Susan Kohner, Frank Lovejoy, Joe De Santis. 1957

●**DINOSAUR** ★★★★ Although very small fry may be frightened by the story's grimmer elements, this magnificent achievement will play superbly for all remaining ages: an exciting, animated epic with equal measures of character detail and survival-at-all-costs thrills. The visual experience is enchanting: a mix of digitally enhanced, live-action backgrounds on which the computer-animated characters frolic and fight. The protagonist, a peaceful Iguanodon, is "adopted" by a family of lemurs; these unlikely heroes prove their value after joining a massive herd of similarly herbivorous dinosaurs, all being led across a scarred desert wasteland to find a lush nesting ground that may no longer exist. Directors Ralph Zondag and Eric Leighton orchestrate the various adventures with breathtaking ferocity. James Newton Howard's dynamic symphonic score amplifies the excitement. Rated PG for violent and dramatic story content. 84m. **DIR:** Ralph Zondag, Eric Leighton.

●**DINOSAUR BABES** ★★ They don't get much campier than this hilariously bad dinosaur movie in which some of the highlights include Amazons hunting for male sacrifices, and a man on a UFO using a laser to kill a T-Rex. Not rated; contains nudity and violence. 90m. **DIR:** Brett Piper. **CAST:** Jeff Corniello, Mike Whitehead, Melissa Ann, Kelly Lynn. 1991

DINOSAUR ISLAND ♥ Extremely low-budget effort uses rubber prehistoric beasts to get women out of their clothes. Absolutely horrid. Rated R for nudity and violence. 85m. **DIR:** Jim Wynorski, Fred Olen Ray. **CAST:** Ross Hagen, Richard Gabi, Antonia Dorian, Toni Naples. 1994

●**DINOSAUR VALLEY GIRLS** ♥ Take a look at the title and you'll get the idea of what's in store from this dull T&A fantasy. Not rated; contains nudity. 94m. **DIR:** Donald F. Glut. **CAST:** William Marshall, Griffen Drew, Karen Black. 1996 DVD

DINOSAURUS! ★★1/2 Workers at a remote construction site accidentally stumble upon a prehistoric brontosaurus, tyrannosaurus rex, and a caveman (all quite alive) while excavating the area. Sure, the monsters look fake, and most of the humor is unintentional, but this film is entertaining nonetheless. 85m. **DIR:** Irvin S. Yeaworth Jr. **CAST:** Ward Ramsey, Paul Lukather. **1960**

DIPLOMANIACS ★★1/2 In this preposterous romp, Bert Wheeler and Robert Woolsey play Indian-reservation barbers sent to a peace convention in Switzerland. This is a musical comedy, so don't expect too much plot. Hugh Herbert is a delight. Woo-woo! B&W; 63m. **DIR:** William A. Seiter. **CAST:** Bert Wheeler, Robert Woolsey, Marjorie White, Hugh Herbert, Louis Calhern, Edgar Kennedy. **1933**

DIPLOMATIC IMMUNITY ★★ A slipshod actioner about a marine (Bruce Boxleitner) who pursues his daughter's killer to Paraguay. Rated R for violence, profanity, and nudity. 95m. **DIR:** Peter Maris. **CAST:** Bruce Boxleitner, Billy Drago, Tom Breznahan, Christopher Neame, Robert Forster, Meg Foster. **1991**

•**DIPLOMATIC SIEGE** ★★ This totally preposterous political thriller features Peter Weller and Daryl Hannah as bomb experts sent to disarm a nuclear warhead hidden inside the U.S. embassy in Bucharest. When terrorists take over the embassy, the two find themselves racing against time to save the day. The filmmaker's attempt to juggle too many balls creates chaos rather than suspense. Rated R for language and violence. 94m. **DIR:** Gustavo Graef-Marino. **CAST:** Peter Weller, Daryl Hannah, Tom Berenger. **1999 DVD**

DIRECT HIT ★★ The assassin with a heart of gold has become a genre unto itself, and this entry brings nothing new to the party. William Forsythe plays a CIA hit man who wants out of the business but agrees to one last hit. When he finds out that the woman is an innocent victim, he turns the tables and becomes her bodyguard. The usual chaos ensues. Rated R for violence, language, and adult situations. 91m. **DIR:** Joseph Merhi. **CAST:** William Forsythe, John Champa, Richard Norton, George Segal. **1993**

DIRT BIKE KID, THE ★★ A boy buys an old dirt bike that turns out to have a life of its own. Rated PG for vulgarity. 91m. **DIR:** Hoite C. Caston. **CAST:** Peter Billingsley, Stuart Pankin, Anne Bloom, Patrick Collins. **1985**

DIRTY DANCING ★★★★ A surprise hit. Jennifer Grey stars as a teenager poised at the verge of adulthood in the early Sixties. She accompanies her family on a Catskills vacation and meets up with rhythm-and-blues in the form of dancers Patrick Swayze and Cynthia Rhodes. Nothing new, but the players present the material with exuberant energy. Rated PG-13 for language and sexual themes. 97m. **DIR:** Emile Ardolino. **CAST:** Jennifer Grey, Patrick Swayze, Cynthia Rhodes, Jerry Orbach, Jack Weston. **1987 DVD**

DIRTY DISHES ★★ The American-born daughter-in-law of Luis Buñuel makes her directorial debut with this mediocre comedy. A beautiful French housewife finds herself trapped in an uneventful marriage. This leads to an explosive encounter with a lecherous neighbor. Takes its theme from the superior *Diary of a Mad Housewife*. In French with English subtitles. Not rated. 99m. **DIR:** Joyce Buñuel. **CAST:** Pierre Santini, Liliane Roveryre, Liza Braconnier. **1982**

DIRTY DOZEN, THE ★★★★1/2 Lee Marvin is assigned to take a group of military prisoners behind

German lines and strike a blow for the Allies. It's a terrific entertainment—funny, star-studded, suspenseful, and even touching. 145m. **DIR:** Robert Aldrich. **CAST:** Lee Marvin, Ernest Borgnine, Charles Bronson, Jim Brown, John Cassavetes, Donald Sutherland, Clint Walker. **1967 DVD**

DIRTY DOZEN, THE: THE NEXT MISSION ★★ This disappointing made-for-TV sequel brings back Lee Marvin as the hard-as-nails Major Reisman; Ernest Borgnine and Richard Jaeckel also reprise their roles. This time the Dozen are sent to assassinate a German general who is plotting to kill Hitler. Not rated. 99m. **DIR:** Andrew V. McLaglen. **CAST:** Lee Marvin, Ernest Borgnine, Richard Jaeckel, Ken Wahl, Larry Wilcox. **1985**

DIRTY DOZEN, THE: THE DEADLY MISSION ★★ Second TV sequel to the 1967 classic has none of the style or suspense of the original, although some situations were lifted directly from it. The battle scenes are well staged. Telly Savalas, whose character died in the original, is now the commander of twelve new misfits. 100m. **DIR:** Lee H. Katzin. **CAST:** Telly Savalas, Ernest Borgnine, Randall "Tex" Cobb, Vince Edwards, Gary Graham, Wolf Kahler. **1987**

DIRTY DOZEN, THE: THE FATAL MISSION ★★ Telly Savalas again leads a reluctant ragtag gang in this third TV sequel to the 1967 hit. Welcome plot twists include both a Nazi agent and a woman officer among the Dozen. Okay battle scenes. 100m. **DIR:** Lee H. Katzin. **CAST:** Telly Savalas, Ernest Borgnine, Jeff Conaway, Alex Cord, Erik Estrada, Ernie Hudson, James Carroll Jordan, Ray "Boom Boom" Mancini, John Matuszak, Natalija Nogulich, Heather Thomas, Anthony Valentine, Richard Yniguez. **1988**

DIRTY GAMES 💔 The daughter of a murdered scientist tries to prevent terrorists from blowing up a nuclear dump site. Not rated; contains violence. 97m. **DIR:** Gary Hofmeyr. **CAST:** Jan-Michael Vincent, Valentina Vargas, Ronald France, Michael McGovern. **1993**

DIRTY HARRY ★★★★1/2 This is the original and still the best screen adventure of Clint Eastwood's maverick San Francisco detective. Outfoxed by a maniacal killer (Andy Robinson), "Dirty Harry" Callahan finally decides to deal out justice in his own inimitable and controversial fashion for an exciting, edge-of-your-seat climax. Rated R. 102m. **DIR:** Don Siegel. **CAST:** Clint Eastwood, Harry Guardino, John Mitchum, Reni Santoni, Andrew Robinson, John Vernon. **1971 DVD**

DIRTY LAUNDRY 💔 Stupid chase film involving a young man and a group of drug-dealing thugs. Rated PG-13 for profanity. 81m. **DIR:** William Webb. **CAST:** Leigh McCloskey, Jeanne O'Brien, Frankie Valli, Sonny Bono. **1987**

DIRTY LITTLE SECRET ★★1/2 A woman and three other criminals kidnap a young boy, who is really the woman's son. She wants him back, but the others just want the money. A few plot surprises spice up this made-for-cable original, but flat acting and uninspired lines dull the overall flavor. Rated R for violence. 95m. **DIR:** Rob Fresco. **CAST:** Tracey Gold, Jack Wagner, Mary Page Keller, Ian Tracey, Michal Suchanek. **1998**

DIRTY MARY, CRAZY LARRY ★★★ Race-car driver Peter Fonda and his two accomplices lead Vic Morrow and a small army of law enforcement officers on a frantic, nonstop chase in this satisfying low-budget action film. Rated R for language and violence. 93m. DIR: John Hough. CAST: Peter Fonda, Susan George, Vic Morrow, Adam Roarke, Roddy McDowall. 1974

DIRTY PAIR: AFFAIR ON NOLANDIA 🎬 A ridiculously contrived and poorly animated story has two scantily clad female intergalactic troubleshooters investigating cases with very little brain power. Japanese, dubbed in English. Not rated; contains nudity, profanity, and violence. 57m. DIR: Masahara Okuwaki. 1985

DIRTY ROTTEN SCOUNDRELS ★★★★1/2 This remake of *Bedtime Story,* is a genuine laugh riot. Michael Caine plays a sophisticated con man whose successful bilking of wealthy female tourists is endangered by upstart Steve Martin. Their battle of wits reaches comic highs when they duel over the fortune and affections of American heiress Glenne Headly. Rated PG for profanity. 110m. DIR: Frank Oz. CAST: Steve Martin, Michael Caine, Glenne Headly, Barbara Harris. 1988 DVD

DIRTY TRICKS 🎬 This Canadian-made movie brings the comedy-thriller genre to an all-time low. Rated PG. 91m. DIR: Alvin Rakoff. CAST: Elliott Gould, Kate Jackson, Rich Little, Arthur Hill, Nicholas Campbell. 1980

DIRTY WORK ★★1/2 A gambling, crooked bail bondsman murders a drug dealer and steals his money. He doesn't realize the money is marked by a crime boss. Rated R for violence and profanity. 88m. DIR: John McPherson. CAST: Kevin Dobson, John Ashton, Donnelly Rhodes, Jim Byrnes, Mitchell Ryan. 1992

DIRTY WORK (1998) ★★ Mouthy loser and his chubby lifelong buddy are tired of "taking crap" and become so good at revenge that they begin charging people to do their dirty work. This outrageous, mean-spirited comedy is occasionally hilarious but generally trashy. Rated PG-13 for crude sexual humor and language. 81m. DIR: Bob Saget. CAST: Norm MacDonald, Artie Lange, Jack Warden, Christopher McDonald. 1998 DVD

DISAPPEARANCE, THE ★★★★ This exciting film has Donald Sutherland portraying a professional hit man who can't do his job properly after his wife disappears. He pursues a top man in the organization (Christopher Plummer) because he believes that he is responsible for his wife's disappearance. Rated R for sex and violence. 80m. DIR: Stuart Cooper. CAST: Donald Sutherland, Francine Racette, David Hemmings, John Hurt, Christopher Plummer. 1977

DISAPPEARANCE OF AIMEE, THE ★★★1/2 Strong performers and taut direction made this one made-for-television movie that is way above average. Faye Dunaway plays preacher Aimee Semple McPherson, whose mysterious disappearance in 1926 gave rise to all sorts of speculation. A literate script, solid supporting performances by Bette Davis and James Woods, and plenty of period flavor make this one a winner. 110m. DIR: Anthony Harvey. CAST: Faye Dunaway, Bette Davis, James Woods, Severn Darden. 1976

DISAPPEARANCE OF CHRISTINA, THE ★★★ In this made-for-cable original, an unhappy, wealthy wife disappears during a boating trip. The police think her husband killed her, while he is sure that she's still alive and is trying to drive him crazy. Interesting plot with an unexpected ending. Rated PG-13 for violence. 92m. DIR: Karen Arthur. CAST: John Stamos, Kim Delaney, C.C.H. Pounder, Robert Carradine. 1993

DISAPPEARANCE OF GARCIA LORCA, THE ★★1/2 A Spanish youth meets the famous poet and playwright Federico Garcia Lorca; years later he braves the terrors of Francois fascist regime to investigate Lorca's death during the Spanish Civil War. The mystery is so drawn out and the solution so wholly fictitious that it gives us no insight into Lorca's fate. Rated R for violence and some sexual content. 142m. DIR: Marcos Zurinaga. CAST: Esaí Morales, Andy Garcia, Jeroen Krabbé, Giancarlo Giannini, Miguel Ferrer, Edward James Olmos, Marcela Walerstein. 1997

DISASTER AT SILO 7 ★★★ An actual incident suggested the events in this occasionally absorbing drama that follows the aftermath of a disastrous fuel leak in an eastern Texas nuclear-missile silo. The script's reach is bigger than its grasp; an abrupt conclusion leaves numerous plot points and character antagonisms unresolved. The made-for-television restrictions just don't permit the story to be properly gritty. Rated PG for mild profanity. 94m. DIR: Larry Elikann. CAST: Michael O'Keefe, Joe Spano, Patricia Charbonneau, Ray Baker, Perry King, Peter Boyle, Dennis Weaver. 1988

DISCLOSURE ★★★★ Intelligent and gripping drama about a male business executive who files sexual harassment charges against his female superior, a former flame. Once Paul Attanasio's screenplay—based on the novel by Michael Crichton—gets past this role-reversal plot twist, the film really hits its stride, keeping the viewer guessing until the end. Although it appears to be another sex thriller à la Douglas's previous hits, *Basic Instinct* and *Fatal Attraction, Disclosure* is closer to a clever corporate-intrigue variation on *All the President's Men.* Rated R for simulated sex and profanity. 120m. DIR: Barry Levinson. CAST: Michael Douglas, Demi Moore, Donald Sutherland, Caroline Goodall, Dennis Miller, Roma Maffia, Dylan Baker, Rosemary Forsyth. 1994 DVD

DISCOVERY PROGRAM ★★★★ Marvelous collection of four short stories including the 1987 Oscar winner for best short film, "Ray's Male Heterosexual Dance Hall," which spoofs networking executives. "The Open Window" is also a comedy featuring a would-be actor who goes off the deep end when he can't get a good night's sleep. Not rated, contains profanity, violence, and nudity. 106m. DIR: Bryan Gordon, Damian Harris, Rupert Wainwright, Stephen Anderson. CAST: Eric Stoltz, James Spader. 1987

DISCREET CHARM OF THE BOURGEOISIE, THE ★★★★ Dinner is being served in this Luis Buñuel masterpiece, but the food never gets a chance to arrive at the table. Every time the hosts and guests try to begin the meal, some outside problem rises. Typically French, typically Buñuel, typically hilarious. Winner of the best foreign film Oscar for 1972. 100m. **DIR:** Luis Buñuel. **CAST:** Fernando Rey, Delphine Seyrig, Stéphane Audran, Bulle Ogier, Jean-Pierre Cassel, Michel Piccoli. 1972

DISEMBODIED, THE ★★ Ridiculous jungle horror worth seeing for Allison (*Attack of the 50-Foot Woman*) Hayes as Tonda, a bored doctor's wife who moonlights as a voodoo priestess. B&W; 66m. **DIR:** Walter Grauman. **CAST:** Paul Burke, Allison Hayes, Eugenia Paul, John E. Weingraf. 1957

DISHONORED ★★★1/2 Sin and sex are the real stars of this Marlene Dietrich movie. She plays a World War I Austrian spy who tangles with an overly amorous Russian agent. Dietrich's second Hollywood vehicle was the first to make good use of her mystique. B&W; 91m. **DIR:** Josef von Sternberg. **CAST:** Marlene Dietrich, Victor McLaglen, Lew Cody, Gustav von Seyffertitz, Warner Oland. 1931

DISHONORED LADY 🎬 Beautiful magazine executive is accused of killing her former boyfriend. Ponderous adaptation of a successful Broadway drama. B&W; 85m. **DIR:** Robert Stevenson. **CAST:** Hedy Lamarr, Dennis O'Keefe, John Loder, William Lundigan. 1947

DISORDERLIES 🎬 Ralph Bellamy and a few rap songs by The Fat Boys are all there are to recommend this embarrassingly bad film. Rated PG. 87m. **DIR:** Michael Schultz. **CAST:** The Fat Boys, Tony Plana, Ralph Bellamy, Anthony Geary. 1987

DISORDERLY ORDERLY, THE ★★★ Jerry Lewis is out of control at a nursing home in a good solo effort directed by comedy veteran Frank Tashlin, who reached his peak here. Comic gems abound in this film, which isn't just for fans. In fact, if you've never been one of Jerry's faithful, give this one a try to see if you can't be swayed. You just might be surprised. 90m. **DIR:** Frank Tashlin. **CAST:** Jerry Lewis, Glenda Farrell, Susan Oliver, Everett Sloane, Jack E. Leonard, Kathleen Freeman. 1964

DISORGANIZED CRIME ★★ Misadventures of five ex-cons trying to pull a bank heist in a small Montana town. Some fine performances are wasted in this disorganized mess that can't decide whether it's a comedy or an action-drama. Rated R for violence and profanity. 98m. **DIR:** Jim Kouf. **CAST:** Hoyt Axton, Corbin Bernsen, Rubén Blades, Ed Gwynne, Ed O'Neill, Lou Diamond Phillips, Daniel Roebuck, William Russ. 1989

DISPLACED PERSON, THE ★★★★ Man's cruel, ugly side is exposed in this adaptation of Flannery O'Connor's brutal short story. Irene Worth is a struggling Georgia farm widow who allows a Polish World War II refugee and his family to live and work on her land. The woman's initially sympathetic feelings gradually mirror those of her other worthless laborers, who fear that their lives of relative laziness are jeopardized by this "unwanted foreigner." Introduced by Henry Fonda; unrated and suitable for family viewing. 58m. **DIR:** Glenn Jordan. **CAST:** Irene Worth, John Houseman, Shirley Stoler, Lane Smith, Robert Earl Jones. 1976

DISRAELI ★★★1/2 Worth seeing solely for George Arliss's Oscar-winning performance, *Disraeli* shows how pretentious movies became when the talkies arrived. He plays the wily English prime minister who outwits the Russians in a fight over the Suez Canal. B&W; 89m. **DIR:** Alfred E. Green. **CAST:** George Arliss, Florence Arliss, Joan Bennett, Anthony Bushell. 1929

DISTANT DRUMS ★★ Good old laconic Gary Cooper tracks down gun smugglers who are selling fire sticks to renegade Seminole Indians in the Everglades. A tired story and screenplay manage to get by on Cooper, good photography, and music. 101m. **DIR:** Raoul Walsh. **CAST:** Gary Cooper, Mari Aldon, Richard Webb, Ray Teal, Arthur Hunnicutt, Robert Barrat, Clancy Cooper. 1951

DISTANT JUSTICE ★★ George Kennedy rises above the material in this tale of a dedicated police chief who takes the law into his own hands and helps a friend find out who killed his wife and kidnapped his daughter. Rated R for violence and adult language. 91m. **DIR:** Toru Murakawa. **CAST:** George Kennedy, David Carradine, Bunta Sugawara, Eric Lutes. 1992

DISTANT THUNDER (1974) ★★★★ Outstanding drama by Satyajit Ray about the effects of a famine on the lives of various family members in World War II India. Beautiful cinematography sweeps the viewer through the desert landscapes of India. In Bengali with English subtitles. 92m. **DIR:** Satyajit Ray. **CAST:** Soumitra Chatterjee. 1974

DISTANT THUNDER (1988) ★★1/2 After roaming the wilds of the Pacific Northwest with his Vietnam-vet buddies for several years, ex-soldier John Lithgow decides to return to civilization and find the son (Ralph Macchio) he hasn't seen in over a decade. Lithgow struggles valiantly with the downbeat material, but Macchio is miscast and no help at all. Rated R for violence and profanity. 114m. **DIR:** Rick Rosenthal. **CAST:** John Lithgow, Ralph Macchio. 1988

DISTANT VOICES/STILL LIVES ★★★★★ An impressionistic memory film, based on the director's family memories and history. Set in England in the late 1940s, it explores the relationships and emotions of a middle-class family as they undergo domestic brutality, failed marriages, and the pains of life. The film's rich humanity and its unique use of a robust musical score overcome its cynicism. Offbeat and original. 85m. **DIR:** Terence Davies. **CAST:** Freda Dowie, Pete Postlethwaite, Angela Walsh, Dean Williams. 1988

DISTINGUISHED GENTLEMAN, THE ★★★1/2 Con man–style takeoff on *Mr. Smith Goes to Washington*. Eddie Murphy is a street hustler who hustles a seat in the House of Representatives. The first two-thirds of the movie, with an accent on comedy, are the best. Rated R for profanity, suggested sex, and nudity. 100m. **DIR:** Jonathan Lynn. **CAST:** Eddie Murphy, James Garner, Sheryl Lee Ralph, Lane Smith, Joe Don Baker, Grant Shaud, Kevin McCarthy, Charles Dutton. 1992 DVD

DISTORTIONS ★★1/2 The crazy plot developments in the final fifteen minutes of the film—about a widow (Olivia Hussey) being held captive by her wicked aunt (Piper Laurie)—make this rather contrived film interesting. Rated PG for violence. 98m. **DIR:** Armand Mastroianni. **CAST:** Steve Railsback, Olivia Hussey, Piper Laurie, Rita Gam, Edward Albert, Terence Knox, June Chadwick. **1987**

DISTURBANCE, THE ♥ Perfectly dreadful tale of a psychotic trying to come to grips with himself while slaughtering the requisite nubile young women. Not rated, the film has violence and profanity. 81m. **DIR:** Cliff Guest. **CAST:** Timothy Greeson. **1989**

DISTURBED ★★1/2 At first glance this film looks quite hokey, but soon the viewer starts to wonder if sex-obsessed Sandy Ramirez (Pamela Gidley) really *is* dead, or if Dr. Russell (Malcolm McDowell) is actually just going crazy. Rated R for nudity, profanity, and violence. 96m. **DIR:** Charles Winkler. **CAST:** Malcolm McDowell, Geoffrey Lewis, Priscilla Pointer, Clint Howard, Pamela Gidley. **1990**

DISTURBING BEHAVIOR ★★ High-school rebels and misfits are turning one by one into squeaky-clean overachievers in Stepford wives fashion. These model citizens wear letter sweaters, get great grades, hold bake sales—and fly into homicidal rages. It is up to a new student, a punkish sexpot and a stoner, to put an end to all this hellish conformity. This indictment of adults as grim reapers of free thinking is neither chilling nor suspenseful. Rated R for drug use, violence, and nudity. 83m. **DIR:** David Nutter. **CAST:** James Marsden, Katie Holmes, Nick Stahl, Bruce Greenwood, Bill Sadler. **1998 DVD**

DIVA ★★★★ In this stunningly stylish suspense film by first-time director Jean-Jacques Beineix, a young opera lover unknowingly becomes involved with the underworld. Unbeknownst to him, he's in possession of some very valuable tapes—and the delightful chase is on. In French with English subtitles. Rated R for profanity, nudity, and violence. 123m. **DIR:** Jean-Jacques Beineix. **CAST:** Frederic Andrei, Wilhemenia Wiggins Fernandez. **1982 DVD**

DIVE, THE ★★★ This Norwegian-British production tells of two veteran divers who are asked to return for an emergency dive to fix a broken oil pipeline. Outstanding performances and photography. Not rated but suitable for family viewing. 97m. **DIR:** Tristan DeVere Cole. **CAST:** Bjorn Sundquist, Frank Grimes. **1990**

DIVE BOMBER ★★★ The planes and acting styles date this one pretty badly, but the story line, about a military doctor working on ways to prevent blackouts while flying, is still intriguing. 133m. **DIR:** Michael Curtiz. **CAST:** Errol Flynn, Fred MacMurray, Ralph Bellamy, Alexis Smith, Craig Stevens, Robert Armstrong, Regis Toomey. **1941**

DIVIDED BY HATE ★★1/2 A deluded preacher lures a woman and her children into a white-supremacist hate group. Her husband tries everything to get his family back, with little success. This made-for-cable drama, based on a true story, is a chilling examination of hate groups, but the acting is lackluster and the film is more message than entertainment. Not rated; contains violence. 95m. **DIR:** Tom Skerritt. **CAST:** Dylan Walsh, Andrea Roth, Jim Beaver, Tom Skerritt. **1997**

DIVINE ♥ Filmmaker John Waters's special tribute to the famous transvestite comic features Divine in a rare, early short "The Diane Linkletter Story" and

the only existing performance of the famous "The Neon Woman" show. Unless you're a die-hard fan of John Waters or Divine, this exercise in cinema of the absurd could be torture. Not rated; contains profanity and nudity. 110m. **DIR:** John Waters. **CAST:** Divine. **1990**

DIVINE MADNESS ★★★1/2 Here's the sassy, unpredictable Bette Midler as captured in concert by director Michael Ritchie. Some of it is great; some of it is not. It helps if you're a Midler fan. Rated R for profanity. 95m. **DIR:** Michael Ritchie. **CAST:** Bette Midler. **1980 DVD**

DIVINE NYMPH, THE ★★1/2 This story of love and passion resembles an Italian soap opera at best. Laura Antonelli is the young beauty who is unfaithful to her fiancé. In Italian with English subtitles. Rated R for nudity. 89m. **DIR:** Giuseppe Patroni Griffi. **CAST:** Laura Antonelli, Terence Stamp, Marcello Mastroianni. **1977**

DIVING IN ★★ A feel-good movie about a teenager's ambition to make his high school diving team and overcome a fear of heights. Predictable. Rated PG-13. 92m. **DIR:** Strathford Hamilton. **CAST:** Burt Young, Matt Lattanzi, Matt Adler, Kristy Swanson. **1990**

•**DIVORCE AMERICAN STYLE** ★★★1/2 Delightfully daffy comedy about a couple going through divorce. What would normally be fertile ground for melodrama is actually a breeding ground for lively insights about the human condition. Dick Van Dyke and Debbie Reynolds are wonderful as the couple who realize that the only thing left in their marriage is their routine. How they go about rectifying this makes for engaging viewing. Not rated. 109m. **DIR:** Bud Yorkin. **CAST:** Dick Van Dyke, Debbie Reynolds, Jason Robards Jr., Jean Simmons, Van Johnson, Joe Flynn, Tom Bosley. **1967**

DIVORCE HIS: DIVORCE HERS ★★1/2 This less-than-exceptional TV movie follows the breakup of a marriage in which both partners explain what they think led to the failure of their marriage. The talents of Elizabeth Taylor and Richard Burton are barely tapped. 144m. **DIR:** Waris Hussein. **CAST:** Richard Burton, Elizabeth Taylor, Carrie Nye, Barry Foster, Gabriele Ferzetti. **1972 DVD**

DIVORCE—ITALIAN STYLE ★★★1/2 Considered naughty in its day, now this Italian black comedy about a philandering husband's plans to rid himself of his wife simply plays as the fast, racy romp it is. Endlessly imitated in later, lesser rip-offs. Oscar for original screenplay. B&W; 104m. **DIR:** Pietro Germi. **CAST:** Marcello Mastroianni, Daniela Rocca, Stefania Sandrelli. **1962**

DIVORCE OF LADY X, THE ★★★★ In this British comedy, Laurence Olivier plays a lawyer who allows Merle Oberon to spend the night at his place. Although nothing actually happened that night, Olivier finds himself branded "the other man" in her divorce. A series of hilarious misunderstandings are the result. 90m. **DIR:** Tim Whelan. **CAST:** Merle Oberon, Laurence Olivier, Binnie Barnes, Ralph Richardson. **1938**

DIVORCEE, THE ★★ Dated melodrama about a woman with loose morals. Silly by today's standards, this was racy when made and earned Norma Shearer a best-actress Oscar. A curiosity piece with a good cast. B&W; 83m. DIR: Robert Z. Leonard. CAST: Norma Shearer, Robert Montgomery, Chester Morris, Conrad Nagel, Florence Eldridge. 1930

DIXIANA ★★ Slow-moving musical about a pretty young performer and her affairs of the heart just meanders about with tepid numbers and heavy-handed humor. Bill "Bojangles" Robinson does a cameo tap routine, but the rest of the entertainment is uninspired. B&W; 100m. DIR: Luther Reed. CAST: Bebe Daniels, Everett Marshall, Bert Wheeler, Robert Woolsey, Joseph Cawthorn. 1930 DVD

DIXIE CHANGING HABITS ★★★1/2 Suzanne Pleshette plays Dixie, who runs a highly successful prostitution ring. When she's busted, she must spend time in a convent directed by Cloris Leachman as the Mother Superior. All in all, this made-for-TV comedy is highly entertaining. 96m. DIR: George Englund. CAST: Suzanne Pleshette, Cloris Leachman, Kenneth McMillan, John Considine. 1982

DIXIE DYNAMITE 🎔 Imagine one of those cheesy Burt Reynolds good-ol'-boys movies, where he and some buddies raise heck in revenge for mistreatment from the local deputy. Now imagine it without Burt Reynolds. The ever-watchable Warren Oates isn't enough. Rated PG. 89m. DIR: Lee Frost. CAST: Warren Oates, Christopher George, Jane Anne Johnstone, R. G. Armstrong. 1976

DIXIE JAMBOREE ★★ Another B movie from lowly PRC Studios. The action takes place on the showboat *Ellabella* and the characters range from con men to various musicians and roustabouts. B&W; 80m. DIR: Christy Cabanne. CAST: Guy Kibbee, Lyle Talbot, Eddie Quillan, Frances Langford, Fifi D'Orsay, Charles Butterworth. 1945

DIXIE LANES 🎔 Chaotic comedy revolving around the bad luck of a family named Laid Law. Not rated, but equivalent to a PG-13. 90m. DIR: Don Cato. CAST: Hoyt Axton, Karen Black, Art Hindle, Tina Louise, Ruth Buzzi, Moses Gunn, John Vernon. 1988

DJANGO ★★ Spaghetti Western lacks convincing performances. A border town is about to explode, and the stranger, Django (Franco Nero), lights the fuse. 90m. DIR: Sergio Corbucci. CAST: Franco Nero. 1965 DVD

DJANGO SHOOTS FIRST ★★★ One of the better comic spaghetti Westerns. Django's son inherits half a town. The only problem is he must share it with his old man's crooked partner. Good performances by Glenn Saxon and veteran European character actor Fernando Sancho highlight this funny, entertaining film. Not rated. 96m. DIR: Alberto De Martino. CAST: Glenn Saxon, Fernando Sancho, Evelyn Stewart, Erica Blanc, Alberto Lupo. 1966

DNA ★★1/2 A young scientist and a CIA agent battle a monster created with DNA stolen from the scientist's jungle lab. Decent special effects somewhat compensate for a confusing plot in this made-for-video monster movie that borrows equally from *Alien* and *Predator*. Rated R for profanity and violence. 94m. DIR: William Mesa. CAST: Mark Dacascos, Jurgen Prochnow, Robin McKee. 1997

DO THE RIGHT THING ★★★1/2 Writer-director-star Spike Lee's controversial study of the deep-rooted racism in America starts off as a hilarious multi-character comedy and evolves into a disturbing, thought-provoking, and timely drama. The events take place during the hottest day of the year in a one-block area of the Brooklyn neighborhood of Bedford-Stuyvesant, where tensions exist among the blacks, Italians, and Koreans who live and work there. Rated R for violence, profanity, and nudity. 120m. DIR: Spike Lee. CAST: Danny Aiello, Ossie Davis, Ruby Dee, Richard Edson, Giancarlo Esposito, Spike Lee, Bill Nunn, John Savage, John Turturro. 1989 DVD

DO YOU REMEMBER DOLLY BELL? ★★★1/2 Delightful coming-of-age story set in 1960s Sarajevo, when stable political circumstances brought a flood of Western culture to Yugoslavia. In Serbo-Croatian with English subtitles. Not rated; mild sexual content. B&W; 106m. DIR: Emir Kusturica. CAST: Slavko Stimac, Mira Banjac. 1981

D.O.A. (1949) ★★★1/2 CPA Edmond O'Brien, slowly dying from radiation poisoning, seeks those responsible in this fast-paced, stylized *film noir* thriller. Most unusual is the device of having the victim play detective and hunt his killers as time runs out. Neville Brand takes honors as a psychopath who tries to turn the tables on the victim before he can inform the police. B&W; 83m. DIR: Rudolph Maté. CAST: Edmond O'Brien, Pamela Britton, Luther Adler, Lynne Baggett, Neville Brand. 1949 DVD

D.O.A. (1988) ★★ This failed update of the 1949 *film noir* classic makes the crippling mistake of hauling its Chandleresque story line into the 1980s. Dennis Quaid is the hard-drinking college professor who wakes to find he's been fatally poisoned; with mere hours to live, he drags love-struck college student Meg Ryan along on the hunt for his killer. Rated R for language and violence. 96m. DIR: Rocky Morton, Annabel Jankel. CAST: Dennis Quaid, Meg Ryan, Charlotte Rampling, Daniel Stern, Jane Kaczmarek. 1988

DOBERMAN GANG, THE ★★1/2 A vicious pack of Doberman pinschers are trained as bank robbers in this implausible but well-made action tale. Rated PG for language, mild violence. 87m. DIR: Byron Chudnow. CAST: Byron Mabe, Julie Parrish, Simmy Bow, Hal Reed. 1972

DOC HOLLYWOOD ★★★ En route to Beverly Hills, Dr. Benjamin Stone (Michael J. Fox) has a car accident in South Carolina, where the local residents are in need of an M.D. Doc Stone persists in his hopes for fame and fortune until he meets the pretty Lou (Julie Warner) and falls in love. Good formula fun. Rated PG-13 for nudity and profanity. 110m. DIR: Michael Caton-Jones. CAST: Michael J. Fox, Julie Warner, Bridget Fonda, Woody Harrelson, George Hamilton. 1991 DVD

DOC SAVAGE. . . , THE MAN OF BRONZE ★★★ Perfectly acceptable—although campy—first appearance by the famed hero of pulp novels, Doc Savage. Ron Ely makes a suitable Savage, complete with torn shirt and deadpan delivery. Special effects and set design are minimal, a true shame since this is the last film produced by science-fiction pioneer George Pal. Rated PG—some violence. 100m. DIR: Michael

Anderson. **CAST:** Ron Ely, Pamela Hensley, Darrell Zwerling, Michael Miller, Paul Gleason. **1975**

DOCKS OF NEW YORK, THE ★★★★ A solid drama of love and death on a big-city waterfront. Rough-edged George Bancroft rescues would-be suicide Betty Compson, marries her, clears her of a murder charge, and goes to jail for her. The direction is masterful, the camera work and lighting superb in this, one of the last silent films to be released. B&W; 60m. **DIR:** Josef von Sternberg. **CAST:** George Bancroft, Betty Compson, Olga Baclanova, Mitchell Lewis. **1928**

DOCTOR, THE ★★★★ A doctor discovers the sore throat that's been bothering him is actually cancer, and, in becoming a patient, experiences the dehumanizing effects of the medical establishment. An effective drama with a superlative star performance by William Hurt. Rated PG-13 for profanity and scenes of surgery. 128m. **DIR:** Randa Haines. **CAST:** William Hurt, Christine Lahti, Elizabeth Perkins, Mandy Patinkin, Adam Arkin, Charlie Korsmo, Wendy Crewson, Bill Macy. **1991**

•DR. AKAGI ★★★★ This sort of Japanese Damon Runyon story is filled with erotic undertows, raw vitality, and oddball, multishaded characterizations. The title physician is obsessed with battling a hepatitis epidemic in Japan just before World War II. He is supported by his village's most in-demand whore, a drug-addicted surgeon, and other outcasts when his activities land him in trouble with military authorities. A compelling blend of drama, melodrama, comedy, and carnality intermingles the outrageous with the restrained. In Japanese with English subtitles. Not rated. 128m. **DIR:** Shohei Imamura. **CAST:** Akira Emoto, Kumiko Aso, Jacques Gamblin. **1999**

DR. ALIEN ✓ Aliens assume human form and conduct experiments on a high school boy. Rated R for nudity and profanity. 90m. **DIR:** David DeCoteau. **CAST:** Billy Jacoby, Judy Landers, Arlene Golonka, Troy Donahue. **1988 DVD**

DOCTOR AND THE DEVILS, THE ★★★ This film, based on a true story, with an original screenplay by Dylan Thomas, is set in England in the 1800s. Dr. Cook (Timothy Dalton) is a professor of anatomy, who doesn't have enough corpses to use in class demonstrations. Not for the squeamish. Rated R for language, simulated sex, and violence. 93m. **DIR:** Freddie Francis. **CAST:** Timothy Dalton, Jonathan Pryce, Twiggy, Julian Sands, Stephen Rea, Phyllis Logan, Beryl Reid, Sian Phillips. **1985**

DOCTOR AT LARGE ★★★ Young Dr. Simon Sparrow wants to join the hospital staff, but the grumpy superintendent isn't buying. Comic conniving ensues as Sparrow seeks a place. Third in a series of seven films featuring Dr. Sparrow. 98m. **DIR:** Ralph Thomas. **CAST:** Dirk Bogarde, James Robertson Justice, Shirley Eaton. **1957**

DOCTOR AT SEA ★★★ Fed up with the myriad complications of London life and romance, young, handsome Dr. Simon Sparrow seeks a rugged man's world by signing up on a passenger-carrying freighter as ship's doctor. He goes from the frying pan into the fire when he meets Brigitte Bardot on the high seas! Second in the highly successful British

comedy series. 92m. **DIR:** Ralph Thomas. **CAST:** Dirk Bogarde, Brigitte Bardot, Brenda de Banzie, James Robertson Justice. **1955**

DR. BETHUNE ★★★★ Big-budget story of the Canadian doctor who is revered in China for the many lives he saved when that country fought Japan. Donald Sutherland played the same character in the TV-movie *Bethune* (also on video), and he emphasizes the man's larger-than-life qualities, both positive and negative, in this unusually absorbing biography. Not rated; contains adult themes. 115m. **DIR:** Phillip Borsos. **CAST:** Donald Sutherland, Helen Mirren, Helen Shaver, Colm Feore, Anouk Aimée. **1990**

DR. BLACK AND MR. HYDE ✓ Dr. Black develops a serum to cure his kidney ailment that turns him into a monster with white skin. Rated R. 88m. **DIR:** William Crain. **CAST:** Bernie Casey, Rosalind Cash. **1976**

DR. BUTCHER, M.D. (MEDICAL DEVIATE) ✓ Italian cannibal-zombie movie, and you know what that means—gore galore. Rated R. Dubbed in English. 80m. **DIR:** Francesco Martino. **CAST:** Ian McCulloch, Alexandra Cole. **1979**

DR. CALIGARI ✓ Purportedly an update-parody of the German classic, this self-consciously bizarre movie is all gaudy art design and no plot. Rated R for sexual obsessions. 80m. **DIR:** Stephen Sayadian. **CAST:** Madeleine Reynal. **1989 DVD**

DR. CHRISTIAN MEETS THE WOMEN ✓ Kindly old Dr. Christian takes on a diet charlatan in this stanza of the film series. B&W; 60m. **DIR:** William McGann. **CAST:** Jean Hersholt, Dorothy Lovett, Edgar Kennedy, Frank Albertson, Veda Ann Borg, Rod La Rocque. **1940**

DR. CYCLOPS ★★★ Oscar-nominated special effects dominate this tale of a brilliant physicist (Albert Dekker) in the remote jungles of Peru. He shrinks a group of his colleagues to miniature size in order to protect his valuable radium discovery. Entertaining film is best remembered as one of the earliest Technicolor horror movies, with lush photography and an effective performance by Dekker. 75m. **DIR:** Ernest B. Schoedsack. **CAST:** Albert Dekker, Janice Logan, Charles Halton, Thomas Coley, Victor Kilian. **1940**

DR. DEATH: SEEKER OF SOULS ★★1/2 Dr. Death discovered how to cheat death one thousand years ago by periodically transferring his soul into another body. He's willing to share his talents with others, too. The makers of this low-rent terror tale had a tongue-in-cheek sense of humor, and it shows. Look for a cameo by head Stooge Moe Howard. Rated R, though pretty tame by current standards. 87m. **DIR:** Eddie Saeta. **CAST:** John Considine, Barry Coe, Cheryl Miller, Florence Marly, Jo Morrow. **1973**

DOCTOR DETROIT ★★1/2 Dan Aykroyd stars in this comedy as a soft-spoken English professor who becomes a comic book–style pimp. Aykroyd has some genuinely funny moments, but the movie is uneven overall. Rated R for profanity, nudity, and violence. 89m. **DIR:** Michael Pressman. **CAST:** Dan Aykroyd, Howard Hesseman, Nan Martin, T. K. Carter. **1983**

DOCTOR DOLITTLE ★★1/2 Rex Harrison plays the title role in this children's tale, about a man who finds more satisfaction being around animals than people. Children may find this film amusing, but for the most part, the acting is weak, and any real script is nonexistent. 152m. DIR: Richard Fleischer. CAST: Rex Harrison, Samantha Eggar, Anthony Newley, Richard Attenborough. 1967 DVD

DR. DOLITTLE (1998) ★★★1/2 An MD discovers he can talk to the animals, but he would rather not. Eddie Murphy's restrained performance only adds to this funny film. Not as noble or feel-good as *Babe* but on its own level just as amazing that the filmmakers could pull this off as well as they do. This film is truly for the entire family. Rated PG-13 for language. 110m. DIR: Betty Thomas. CAST: Eddie Murphy, Ossie Davis, Oliver Platt, Peter Boyle, Norm MacDonald, Albert Brooks, Chris Rock, Reni Santoni, John Leguizamo, Julie Kavner, Garry Shandling, Ellen DeGeneres, Brian Doyal-Murray, Philip Proctor, . . 1998

DR. FAUSTUS ★★ Richard Burton is the man who sells his soul and Elizabeth Taylor is Helen of Troy in this weird adaptation of Christopher Marlowe's retelling of the ancient legend. Strictly for Taylor and Burton fans. 93m. DIR: Richard Burton. CAST: Richard Burton, Elizabeth Taylor. 1968

DR. FRANKENSTEIN'S CASTLE OF FREAKS ❤ Italian exploitation film with Rossano Brazzi, Michael Dunn, and Edmond Purdom at the nadir of their careers. Rated R. 89m. DIR: Robert H. Oliver. CAST: Rossano Brazzi, Michael Dunn, Edmund Purdom. 1973

DR. GIGGLES ❤ An escaped lunatic with a medical fixation employs stainless-steel technology to dispatch the usual libidinous teenagers. Tiresome lowrent shocker. Malpractice all the way. Rated R for violence and gore. 95m. DIR: Manny Coto. CAST: Larry Drake, Holly Marie Combs, Glenn Quinn, Cliff De Young, Richard Bradford. 1992 DVD

DR. GOLDFOOT AND THE BIKINI MACHINE ★★ Camp appeal saves this low-budget drive-in fare, as mad scientist Vincent Price creates an army of seductive female robots in an attempt to gain power and wealth. Silliness ensues. 88m. DIR: Norman Taurog. CAST: Vincent Price, Frankie Avalon, Susan Hart, Dwayne Hickman, Fred Clark. 1965

DR. GOLDFOOT AND THE GIRL BOMBS ❤ Vincent Price returns as the notorious mad scientist Dr. Goldfoot, this time turning his female robots into bombs. 85m. DIR: Mario Bava. CAST: Vincent Price, Fabian, Laura Antonelli, Franco Franchi. 1966

DOCTOR GORE ❤ Cheap horror movie about a demented surgeon who, after the death of his wife, sets about assembling the perfect woman with parts taken from other women. Rated R. 91m. DIR: Pat Patterson. CAST: J. G. "Pat" Patterson. 1975

DOCTOR HACKENSTEIN ❤ Boring rip-off of *Re-Animator*, as well as all those Frankenstein flicks. Rated R for nudity and violence. 88m. DIR: Richard Clarke. CAST: David Muir, Stacey Travis. 1988

DR. HECKYL AND MR. HYPE ★★★1/2 Oh, no, not another *Dr. Jekyll and Mr. Hyde* parody! But this is quite funny, right up there with Jerry Lewis's *The Nutty Professor*. Oliver Reed is hilarious as both an ugly podiatrist and his alter ego, a handsome stud. Writer-director Charles B. Griffith, who wrote the original *Little Shop of Horrors*, has a field day here.

Rated R for nudity. 99m. DIR: Charles B. Griffith. CAST: Oliver Reed, Sunny Johnson, Mel Welles, Jackie Coogan, Corinne Calvet, Dick Miller. 1980

DOCTOR IN DISTRESS ★★★ In this high jinks-jammed British comedy of medical student and young physician trials and tribulations, head of hospital Sir Lancelot Spratt reveals he is human when he falls in love. Hero Dr. Simon Sparrow has trouble romancing a beautiful model. It's all fast-pace and very funny. Fourth in a series of seven that began with *Doctor in the House*. B&W; 103m. DIR: Ralph Thomas. CAST: Dirk Bogarde, Samantha Eggar, James Robertson Justice. 1963

DOCTOR IN THE HOUSE ★★★1/2 This well-paced farce features a superb British cast. It's about the exploits of a group of medical students intent on studying beautiful women and how to become wealthy physicians. This low-key comedy of manners inspired six other *Doctor* movies and eventually led to a TV series. Not rated. 92m. DIR: Ralph Thomas. CAST: Dirk Bogarde, Muriel Pavlow, Kenneth More, Donald Sinden, Kay Kendall, James Robertson Justice, Donald Houston. 1954

DR. JEKYLL AND MR. HYDE (1920) ★★★1/2 Still considered one of the finest film versions of Robert Louis Stevenson's story, this features John Barrymore in a bravura performance as the infamous doctor who becomes a raging beast. Barrymore always prided himself on changing into the dreadful Hyde by contorting his body rather than relying on heavy makeup. Silent. B&W; 63m. DIR: John S. Robertson. CAST: John Barrymore, Martha Mansfield, Nita Naldi, Louis Wolheim, Charles Lane. 1920 DVD

DR. JEKYLL AND MR. HYDE (1932) ★★★★1/2 Fredric March's Oscar-winning performance is the highlight of this terrific horror film, which is also the best of the many versions of Robert Louis Stevenson's classic tale of good and evil. The direction by Rouben Mamoulian is exquisite. B&W; 98m. DIR: Rouben Mamoulian. CAST: Fredric March, Miriam Hopkins, Rose Hobart. 1932

DR. JEKYLL AND MR. HYDE (1941) ★★★ A well-done version of Robert Louis Stevenson's classic story about a good doctor who dares to venture into the unknown. The horror of his transformation is played down in favor of the emotional and psychological consequences. Spencer Tracy and Ingrid Bergman are excellent, the production lush. B&W; 114m. DIR: Victor Fleming. CAST: Spencer Tracy, Ingrid Bergman, Lana Turner, Donald Crisp, C. Aubrey Smith, Sara Allgood. 1941

DR. JEKYLL AND MR. HYDE (1973) ❤ Kirk Douglas stars in this major misfire, a made-for-television musical based on Robert Louis Stevenson's classic tale. 90m. DIR: David Winters. CAST: Kirk Douglas, Susan George, Stanley Holloway, Michael Redgrave, Donald Pleasence. 1973

DR. JEKYLL AND MS. HYDE ★★ Disappointing spoof on the well-known horror story features Tim Daly as the obsessed scientist. Adding estrogen to his life-altering formula, he creates a beautiful but evil alter ego (Sean Young). Humor is coarse, relying heavily on the anatomy and eliciting groans and guffaws rather than genuine belly laughs. Rated PG-13 for nudity, profanity, and sexual situations. 90m. DIR: David F. Price. CAST: Timothy Daly, Sean Young, Lysette Anthony, Stephen Tobolowsky, Harvey Fierstein. 1995

DR. JEKYLL AND SISTER HYDE ★★ One of many variations on a Jack the Ripper theme, this one has a mad scientist driven to terrible deeds with slightly different results. Contains far too many midnight scenes in foggy old London Town. No rating, but contains violence and nudity. 94m. DIR: Roy Ward Baker. CAST: Ralph Bates, Martine Beswick, Gerald Sim. 1971

DR. JEKYLL'S DUNGEON OF DEATH 💔 The great-grandson of the original Dr. Jekyll spends the entire movie in his basement, injecting the family serum into unwilling specimens. Rated R. 88m. DIR: James Wood. CAST: James Mathers. 1982

DR. KILDARE'S STRANGE CASE ★★★ Friendly old Dr. Gillespie and his medical whiz junior, Dr. Kildare, are featured in this tale of the deranged. Lew Ayres deals with a cuckoo. Nurse Laraine Day provides love interest; Lionel Barrymore is at the ready to counsel as Dr. Gillespie. This is one of the best of the Kildare series. B&W; 76m. DIR: Harold S. Bucquet. CAST: Lew Ayres, Lionel Barrymore, Laraine Day, Nat Pendleton, Samuel S. Hinds, Emma Dunn. 1940

DR. MABUSE, THE GAMBLER (PARTS I AND II) ★★★★ This is it—the granddaddy of all criminal mastermind films. The pacing, though slow and deliberate, pays off in a spectacular climax, with the evil and elusive Mabuse gone mad in a counterfeiter's cellar. Silent. B&W; Pt. One, 120m; Pt. Two, 122m. DIR: Fritz Lang. CAST: Rudolf Klein-Rogge. 1922–1923

DOCTOR MORDRID ★★★1/2 Jeffrey Combs is Doctor Mordrid, a sorcerer biding his time in a New York brownstone. He keeps watch over the portal to another dimension, a dimension that is reigned over by his mortal enemy. Fanciful special effects. Rated R for violence and nudity. 102m. DIR: Albert Band, Charles Band. CAST: Jeffrey Combs, Yvette Nipar, Brian Thompson, Jay Acovone. 1992

DR. NO ★★★★ The first of the James Bond movie sensations, it was in this film that Sean Connery began his ascent to stardom as the indomitable British secret agent 007. Bond is sent to Jamaica to confront the evil Dr. No, a villain bent on world domination. Ursula Andress was the first of the (now traditional) sensual Bond heroines. As with most of the series' films, there is a blend of nonstop action and tongue-in-cheek humor. 111m. DIR: Terence Young. CAST: Sean Connery, Ursula Andress, Jack Lord, Bernard Lee, Joseph Wiseman. 1962 DVD

DR. OTTO AND THE RIDDLE OF THE GLOOM BEAM ★★★ A fun and wacky journey into the mind of Jim Varney. Dr. Otto has a deranged plan and Lance Sterling is the only person who can stop him. Varney plays both Otto and Sterling in this refreshingly strange comedy. A must for Varney fans. Rated PG. 97m. DIR: John R. Cherry III. CAST: Jim Varney. 1986

DR. PETIOT ★★★1/2 Michel Serrault delivers a chilling performance as the monstrous French doctor who murdered the desperate Jews he was paid to protect. After receiving all their valuables, he never

gave them the promised safe passage to Argentina. Based on fact, this WWII horror story is all the more haunting as we witness the fiendish glee he takes with each new victim. Not rated, but definitely not for family viewing. In French with English subtitles. 102m. DIR: Christian de Chalonge. CAST: Michel Serrault, Pierre Romans, Zbigniew Horoks, Berangere Bonvoisin. 1990

DR. PHIBES RISES AGAIN ★★★1/2 Good-natured terror abounds in this fun sequel to *The Abominable Dr. Phibes*, with Vincent Price reprising his role as a disfigured doctor desperately searching for a way to restore his dead wife to life. Entertaining. Rated PG for mild violence. 89m. DIR: Robert Fuest. CAST: Vincent Price, Robert Quarry, Peter Jeffrey, Fiona Lewis, Peter Cushing, Hugh Griffith, Terry-Thomas, Beryl Reid. 1972

DR. QUINN MEDICINE WOMAN ★★★ This pilot film for Jane Seymour's TV series is surprisingly riveting. Seymour convincingly plays a Boston doctor who goes west to start her practice. Scorned by the rugged pioneers she encounters, she must seek ways to prove her talents to them. Not rated; contains violence. 94m. DIR: Jeremy Paul Kagan. CAST: Jane Seymour, Joe Lando, Diane Ladd, Guy Boyd, Colm Meaney. 1992

DR. STRANGE ★★ Another Marvel Comics super-hero comes to life. Dr. Strange is chosen by the guardian of the spirit world to protect Earth from the evil villainess who is set on invading. The adventures of our hero are high on magic and sorcery for a fair rendition of the comic-book hero. 94m. DIR: Philip DeGuere. CAST: Peter Hooten, Clyde Kusatsu, Jessica Walter, Eddie Benton, John Mills. 1978

DR. STRANGELOVE OR HOW I LEARNED TO STOP WORRYING AND LOVE THE BOMB ★★★★★ Stanley Kubrick's black comedy masterpiece about the dropping of the "bomb." Great performances from an all-star cast, including Peter Sellers in three hilarious roles. Don't miss it. B&W; 93m. DIR: Stanley Kubrick. CAST: Peter Sellers, Sterling Hayden, George C. Scott, Slim Pickens, Keenan Wynn, James Earl Jones. 1964 DVD

DR. SYN ★★1/2 Master character actor George Arliss's final film has him playing a traditional English vicar who blossoms into a pirate when the sun goes down. Nothing earthshaking here, but direction and rich atmosphere make it all palatable. B&W; 80m. DIR: Roy William Neill. CAST: George Arliss, Margaret Lockwood, John Loder, Roy Emerton, Graham Moffatt. 1937

DR. SYN, ALIAS THE SCARECROW ★★1/2 Showcased in America as a three-part television program in 1964, colorful tale of a man who poses as a minister by day and a champion of the oppressed by night. Patrick McGoohan brings style and substance to the legendary Dr. Syn. 129m. DIR: James Neilson. CAST: Patrick McGoohan, George Cole, Tony Britton, Geoffrey Keen, Kay Walsh. 1962

DOCTOR TAKES A WIFE, THE ★★★1/2 This delightful comedy employs an oft-used plot. Through a series of misadventures, Ray Milland is incorrectly identified as Loretta Young's handsome husband. So he takes advantage of the misunderstanding. All ends happily. B&W; 89m. DIR: Alexander Hall. CAST: Ray Milland, Loretta Young, Reginald Gardiner, Edmund Gwenn, Gail Patrick. 1940

DR. TARR'S TORTURE DUNGEON ★★1/2 A reporter investigating an insane asylum in nineteenth-century France discovers that the director, whose therapy includes having patients act out their obsessions, is really one of the inmates. Much better than the usual Marcus schlock. Rated R for sex and violence. 88m. DIR: Juan Lopez Moctezuma. CAST: Claudio Brook, Ellen Sherman. 1972

DR. TERROR'S HOUSE OF HORRORS ★★★ Good anthology horror entertainment about a fortune teller (Peter Cushing) who has some frightening revelations for his clients. A top-flight example of British genre moviemaking. 98m. DIR: Freddie Francis. CAST: Peter Cushing, Christopher Lee, Roy Castle, Donald Sutherland. 1965

DR. WHO AND THE DALEKS ★★★ In this feature film derived from the BBC television series, an eccentric old scientist takes his friends to a planet that has been devastated by nuclear war, where they help a peace-loving people fight a race of war-mongering mutants who have encased their fragile bodies in robot shells. This juvenile science-fiction adventure should please youngsters. Rated G. 83m. DIR: Gordon Flemyng. CAST: Peter Cushing, Roy Castle, Jennie Linden, Barrie Ingham. 1965

DR. WHO: REVENGE OF THE CYBERMEN ★★★ This is the first video from the popular British TV series and stars the fourth Dr. Who, Tom Baker. In this film, the evil Cybermen attempt to destroy the planet Voga, which is made of solid gold, the only item that can kill them. A good introduction to *Dr. Who*, the longest-running science-fiction TV series. 92m. DIR: Michael E. Briant. CAST: Tom Baker, Elizabeth Sladen. 1986

DR. WHO (TV SERIES) ★★★★ Created in Britain in the early Sixties, *Dr. Who* is the longest-running science-fiction television series ever. Although marketed as a kids' show, *Dr. Who* appealed mostly to adults who understood the humor and the references. The first year left the viewers in the dark as to who the doctor and his niece really were, but gradually revealed the secret of their past (the good doctor and his niece were time lords of alien ancestry). Not rated, but suitable for kids. 95m. each tape DIR: Various. CAST: William Hartnell, Patrick Troughton, Jon Pertwee, Tom Baker, Peter Davison, Colin Baker, Sylvester McCoy, William Russell, Jacqueline Hill, Carol Ann Ford. 1963–1989

DOCTOR X ★★★1/2 From mayhem to murder, from cannibalism to rape—this picture offers it all. Dr. X is played with panache by Lionel Atwill. Lee Tracy is the reporter who tries valiantly to uncover and expose the mysterious doctor. This piece of vintage horror is a sure bet. 80m. DIR: Michael Curtiz. CAST: Lionel Atwill, Preston Foster, Fay Wray, Lee Tracy. 1932

DR. ZHIVAGO ★★★★ In this epic film, Omar Sharif is Zhivago, a Russian doctor and poet whose personal life is ripped apart by the upheaval of the Russian Revolution. The choppy and lengthy screenplay is often sacrificed to the spectacle of vast panoramas, detailed sets, and impressive costumes,

but these artistic elements, along with a beautiful musical score, make for cinema on a grand scale. 176m. DIR: David Lean. CAST: Omar Sharif, Julie Christie, Geraldine Chaplin, Rod Steiger, Alec Guinness, Tom Courtenay. 1965

DOCTORS' WIVES ✇ Trashy film that focuses on the seedy side of being a doctor's wife. Rated PG. 100m. DIR: George Schaefer. CAST: Gene Hackman, Richard Crenna, Carroll O'Connor, Janice Rule, Dyan Cannon, Cara Williams. 1971

DODES 'KA-DEN ★★★★ Akira Kurosawa's first color film is a spellbinding blend of fantasy and reality. The film chronicles the lives of a group of Tokyo slum dwellers that includes children, alcoholics, and the disabled. Illusion and imagination are their weapons as they fight for survival. In Japanese with English subtitles. 140m. DIR: Akira Kurosawa. CAST: Yoshitaka Zushi. 1970

DODGE CITY ★★★★ Swashbuckler Errol Flynn sets aside his sword for a pair of six-guns to clean up the wild, untamed frontier city of the title. The best of Flynn's Westerns, this release is beautifully photographed in color with an all-star supporting cast. 105m. DIR: Michael Curtiz. CAST: Errol Flynn, Olivia de Havilland, Ann Sheridan, Bruce Cabot, Alan Hale Sr., Ward Bond. 1939

DODSWORTH ★★★★ Walter Huston, in the title role, heads an all-star cast in this outstanding adaptation of the Sinclair Lewis novel. Auto tycoon Samuel Dodsworth is the epitome of the classic American self-made man. His wife is an appearance-conscious nouveau riche snob. An intelligent, mature script, excellent characterizations, and sensitive cinematography make this film a modern classic. B&W; 101m. DIR: William Wyler. CAST: Walter Huston, Ruth Chatterton, Mary Astor, David Niven, Spring Byington, Paul Lukas, John Payne, Maria Ouspenskaya. 1936 DVD

DOES THIS MEAN WE'RE MARRIED? ★★1/2 Romantic comedy contains a sprinkling of bittersweet moments as an American comedienne earns her French green card by marrying an irresponsible playboy. Rated PG-13 for profanity, nudity, and violence. 93m. DIR: Carol Wiseman. CAST: Patsy Kensit, Stephane Freiss. 1990

DOG DAY ✇ Lee Marvin is an American fugitive on the run in this maudlin and often offensive tale of intrigue set in France. Sex, profanity, and violence. 101m. DIR: Yves Boisset. CAST: Lee Marvin, Jean Carmet, Victor Lanoux, Miou-Miou, Tina Louise. 1985

DOG DAY AFTERNOON ★★★★1/2 A masterpiece of contemporary commentary. Al Pacino once again proves himself to be in the front rank of America's finest actors. Director Sidney Lumet scores high with masterful pacing and real suspense. This is an offbeat drama about a gay man who's involved in bank robbing. Highly recommended. Rated R. 130m. DIR: Sidney Lumet. CAST: Al Pacino, John Cazale, Charles Durning, Carol Kane, Chris Sarandon. 1975 DVD

DOG EAT DOG ★★ Moll Jayne Mansfield and sundry gangsters, hiding out on a Greek island, fight over $1 million in cash. It's a dog all right, though the dialogue is good for some cheap laughs. B&W; 86m.

DIR: Ray Nazarro. **CAST:** Cameron Mitchell, Jayne Mansfield, Isa Miranda. 1963

DOG OF FLANDERS, A (1960) ★★★★ Ouida's world-famous 1872 tear jerking novel about a boy and his dog and their devotion to each other tastefully filmed in its European locale. Nello (David Ladd) delivers milk from a cart pulled by the dog Patrasche. Donald Crisp and Theodore Bikel shine in character roles, but the picture belongs to Ladd and the scene-stealing mutt fans will recall from *Old Yeller*. Have Kleenex handy. 96m. **DIR:** James B. Clark. **CAST:** David Ladd, Donald Crisp, Theodore Bikel. 1960

•**DOG OF FLANDERS, A (1999)** ★★1/2 The venerable children's classic about a poor boy and his dog gets a well-intentioned but lackluster retelling. The dog takes a backseat to the puppy-love romance between the boy and a neighbor girl, and the film's authentic look clashes badly with the too-modern dialogue; still, the strong supporting cast helps. An interesting sidelight: the 1960 version starred David Ladd, whose ex-wife Cheryl Ladd plays the girl's mother here. Rated PG. 100m. **DIR:** Kevin Brodie. **CAST:** Jeremy James Kissner, Jack Warden, Jesse James, Madylin Sweeten, Jon Voight, Cheryl Ladd. 1999

DOG SOLDIER: SHADOWS OF THE PAST ★★ Japanese animation. A troubled ex-Green Beret and his buddy are enlisted by the government to take on a supervillain who has stolen a virus with a potential for biological warfare. Only for die-hard animation fans. In Japanese with English subtitles. Not rated; contains violence. 45m. **DIR:** Hiroyuki Ebata. 1989

DOG STAR MAN ★★★★ An abstract vision of the creation of the universe—an epic work consisting of a prelude and four parts, making brilliant use of superimpositions, painting on film, distorting lenses, and rhythmic montage. This feature makes for hypnotic experimenting in silent filmmaking. 78m. **DIR:** Stan Brakhage. 1964

DOG TROUBLE ★★1/2 This television fantasy, based on T. Ernesto Bethancourt's *The Dog Days of Arthur Cane*, borrows heavily from the Disney *Shaggy Dog* series. Here, selfish behavior causes young Arthur to be cursed by a very unusual spell. Now an Australian sheepdog (adeptly played by the expressive Bandit), Arthur must somehow redeem himself to become a boy again. The lack of originality and a cliché-ridden plot override the moral: children should be generous and giving. Rated G. 40m. **DIR:** Robert C. Thompson. **CAST:** Ross Harris, John Scott Clough, Linda Henning, Alex Henteloff. 1984

•**DOGFIGHT** ★★1/2 River Phoenix is one of a group of Marines who stage an "ugly date" contest on the eve of their departure for Vietnam. Even though the premise is incredibly mean-spirited, this is actually a fairly entertaining flick. Rated R for profanity and brief violence. 95m. **DIR:** Nancy Savoca. **CAST:** River Phoenix, Lili Taylor, Richard Panebianco, Anthony Clark, Mitchell Whitfield, Holly Near. 1991

DOGFIGHTERS, THE ★★ These "Top Guns" are stuck in a bottom-feeder movie that lacks originality and a budget to make a difference. Robert Davi is totally miscast as a fighter pilot sent to destroy a pluto-

nium plant in Eastern Europe. Unspectacular special effects and ho-hum aerial sequences do little to pick things up. Rated R for profanity and violence. 96m. **DIR:** Barry Zetlin. **CAST:** Robert Davi, Alexander Godunov, Ben Gazzara, Lara Harris. 1995

•**DOGMA** ★★1/2 Two fallen angels (Matt Damon, Ben Affleck) may trigger the Apocalypse if they succeed in reentering Heaven, so a lapsed Catholic (Linda Fiorentino) is recruited to stop them. Writer-director Kevin Smith's doomsday comedy sparked protests for its supposed blasphemy, but it is more irreverent (and certainly profane) than sacrilegious. It also has a high percentage of misfired gags and a poor performance by Fiorentino weighing it down. Rated R for profanity. 125m. **DIR:** Kevin Smith. **CAST:** Ben Affleck, Matt Damon, Linda Fiorentino, Salma Hayek, Jason Lee, Alan Rickman, Chris Rock. 1999 DVD

DOGPOUND SHUFFLE ♥ Ron Moody and David Soul as two drifters who rescue a dog from the pound. Rated PG for language. 98m. **DIR:** Jeffrey Bloom. **CAST:** Ron Moody, David Soul, Raymond Sutton, Pamela McMyler, Ray Stricklyn. 1974

DOGS IN SPACE ★★ Michael Hutchence, the lead singer of the Australian rock group INXS, stars in this film about the pop culture in Melbourne in 1978. This is a trip through the sexually permissive commune that merely serves as a setting for the singing performances of Hutchence. This is really only for the enjoyment of his fans and not the general public. Rated R for profanity, nudity, and suggested sex. 109m. **DIR:** Richard Lowenstein. **CAST:** Michael Hutchence, Saskia Post, Chris Haywood. 1988

DOGS OF HELL ♥ Low-budget thriller about a rural sheriff and a pack of rottweilers. Originally filmed in 3-D, the movie is rated R for profanity and graphic violence. 90m. **DIR:** Worth Keeter. **CAST:** Earl Owensby. 1982

DOGS OF WAR, THE ★★ A graphic account of the coup d'etat of a West African dictatorship (starring Christopher Walken as the leader of a band of mercenaries). Unfortunately, this movie doesn't quite hold together. Rated R for violence. 102m. **DIR:** John Irvin. **CAST:** Christopher Walken, Tom Berenger, Colin Blakely, Hugh Millais. 1980

DOIN' TIME ♥ *Doin' Time* is a bum rap. Rated R for profanity and sex. 84m. **DIR:** George Mendeluk. **CAST:** Jeff Altman, Dey Young, Richard Mulligan, John Vernon, Judy Landers, Colleen Camp, Melanie Chartoff, Graham Jarvis, Pat McCormick, Eddie Velez, Jimmie Walker. 1984

DOIN' TIME ON PLANET EARTH ★★1/2 A teenage nerd living in Sunnydale, Arizona ("Prune Capital of the World"), feels so out of place that he wonders if he isn't really from another planet. His unique "adoption fantasy" is fed by the arrival of two weirdos (Adam West and Candace Azzara). First-time director Charles Matthau (son of Walter) makes the most of a meager budget and an uneven cast. Rated PG. 83m. **DIR:** Charles Matthau. **CAST:** Nicholas Strouse, Adam West, Candy Azzara, Martha Scott, Matt Alden, Andrea Thompson. 1988

DOLEMITE ★★ Nightclub owner tracks down the drug dealers who framed him. Supposedly a parody of blaxploitation movies, you'll be laughing at this rather than with it. Rated R for nudity, sexual situations, violence, and profanity. 89m. DIR: D'Urville Martin. CAST: Rudy Ray Moore, D'Urville Martin, Jerry Jones. 1975 DVD

DOLL ★★★★ Per Oscarsson gives a remarkable performance as a lonely, depraved night watchman who steals a mannequin from a department store and engages in bizarre fantasies with it. Psychologically unsettling film. In Swedish with English subtitles. B&W; 94m. DIR: Arne Mattson. CAST: Per Oscarsson. 1962

DOLL FACE ★★★ "Hubba Hubba Hubba." That's the song that launched Perry Como, and it was in this movie that it was first sung. Vivian Blaine is fine as a burlesque dancer who shoots to the top with the help of her boyfriend. It's one of those nice, often overlooked movies. B&W; 80m. DIR: Lewis Seiler. CAST: Vivian Blaine, Dennis O'Keefe, Perry Como, Carmen Miranda. 1945

•DOLL IN THE DARK, A ♥ A Japanese tourist is kidnapped by a florist who is obsessed with Asian women in this weak rip-off of The Collector. Not rated; contains profanity, sexual situations, and violence. 94m. DIR: Philip Scarpaci. CAST: Billy Drago, Naomi Kawashima, Josh Brauer. 1998

DOLLAR ★★ Three married couples bicker, flirt, separate, and unite all in one overblown weekend at a ski lodge. Noteworthy only for the radiant presence of a young Ingrid Bergman. In Swedish with English subtitles. B&W; 74m. DIR: Gustav Molander. CAST: Ingrid Bergman. 1938

$ (DOLLARS) ★★★★★ Simply one of the best heist capers ever filmed. Warren Beatty, bank employee, teams with Goldie Hawn, hooker, to duplicate critical safe deposit keys for a cool $1.5 million. Intriguing concept, deftly directed in a fashion that reveals continuous unexpected plot twists. Rated R for violence and sexual situations. 119m. DIR: Richard Brooks. CAST: Warren Beatty, Goldie Hawn, Gert Fröbe, Robert Webber. 1972

DOLLMAKER, THE ★★★★ Jane Fonda won an Emmy for her intensely quiet portrayal of a mother of five in 1940s Kentucky. As a devoted mother, her only personal happiness is sculpting dolls out of wood. When her husband is forced to take work in Detroit, their relocation causes many personal hardships and setbacks. The story is beautifully told. This made-for-TV movie is unrated, but it provides excellent family entertainment. 140m. DIR: Daniel Petrie. CAST: Jane Fonda, Levon Helm, Amanda Plummer, Susan Kingsley, Ann Hearn, Geraldine Page. 1984

DOLLMAN ★★1/2 Futuristic cop chases a suspect through a time warp, crash landing on present-day Earth, where the bigger-than-life hero finds himself only thirteen inches tall—but with an attitude. The carnage that permeates this film is vicious. Rated R for violence. 87m. DIR: Albert Pyun. CAST: Tim Thomerson, Jackie Earle Haley, Nicholas Guest. 1991

DOLLMAN VS. DEMONIC TOYS ★★ In this high-concept, low-budget jumble, several drive-in regulars meet for one final, lackluster showdown. Dollman (Tim Thomerson) teams up with Tracy Scoggins and shrunken nurse Melissa Behr (so reduced in

Bad Channels) to fight possessed toys. Rated R for violence, language, and brief nudity. 84m. DIR: Charles Band. CAST: Tim Thomerson, Tracy Scoggins, Melissa Behr, Phil Brock, Phil Fondacaro. 1993

DOLLS ★★1/2 During a fierce storm, six people are stranded at the home of a kindly old doll maker and his wife. One by one, they are attacked by malevolent little creatures in funny outfits. (No, not Campfire Girls.) From the same people who made Re-Animator and From Beyond. Rated R for violence. 77m. DIR: Stuart Gordon. CAST: Stephen Lee, Guy Rolfe, Hilary Mason. 1987

DOLL'S HOUSE, A (1973) ★★★ Jane Fonda is quite good in this screen version of Henrik Ibsen's play about a liberated woman in the nineteenth century, and her struggles to maintain her freedom. Pacing is a problem at times, but first-class acting and beautiful sets keep the viewer interested. 103m. DIR: Joseph Losey. CAST: Jane Fonda, David Warner, Trevor Howard. 1973

DOLL'S HOUSE, A (1989) ★★★★ A spoiled housewife (Claire Bloom), confident that her husband adores her, is in for a rude awakening when a past transgression resurfaces and threatens her carefree existence. Fine rendition of Ibsen's masterpiece. Rated G. 96m. DIR: Patrick Garland. CAST: Claire Bloom, Anthony Hopkins, Ralph Richardson, Denholm Elliott. 1989

DOLLY DEAREST ★★1/2 When an American family takes ownership of a run-down Mexican doll factory, they find that their new lease in life is no Child's Play. As luck would have it, the factory sits next to an ancient burial ground. Rated R for violence. 94m. DIR: Maria Lease. CAST: Rip Torn, Sam Bottoms, Denise Crosby. 1991

DOLLY SISTERS, THE ★★★★ A rare case of a fictionalized movie biography that offers style and truth. 114m. DIR: Irving Cummings. CAST: Betty Grable, June Haver, John Payne, Reginald Gardiner, Frank Latimore, S. Z. Sakall. 1945

DOLORES CLAIBORNE ★★★★ This thoughtful Stephen King adaptation is drawn from another of the terror master's straight dramas and benefits from Kathy Bates's performance as a Maine housekeeper accused of murdering her employer and now reluctantly reunited with her estranged daughter. Rated R for profanity, violence, and deviant sexual behavior. 131m. DIR: Taylor Hackford. CAST: Kathy Bates, Jennifer Jason Leigh, Judy Parfitt, Christopher Plummer, David Strathairn, Eric Bogosian, John C. Reilly. 1995 DVD

DOMINICK AND EUGENE ★★★★1/2 Fraternal twin brothers Dominick and Eugene Luciano have big plans for the future. Eugene (Ray Liotta), an ambitious medical student, plans to take care of Dominick (Tom Hulce), who is considered "slow" but nonetheless has been supporting them by working as a trash collector. All "Nicky" wants is to live in a house by a lake where he and his brother can be together. This is a deeply touching film; superbly directed and acted. Rated PG-13. 103m. DIR: Robert M. Young. CAST: Tom Hulce, Ray Liotta, Jamie Lee Curtis, Todd Graff, Robert Levine. 1988

DOMINION (1989) ★★★ Presented as a four-part story, this animated action-comedy chronicles the "Tank Police," an ultraviolent futuristic next-step-up from police SWAT teams. In Japanese with English subtitles. Not rated; contains violence, profanity, and illustrated nudity. 160m. DIR: Mashimo Koichi. 1989

DOMINION (1994) 💔 Kids are a pain in the neck in this horror flick about pint-sized vampires. Not rated; contains violence and profanity. 70m. DIR: Todd Sheets. CAST: Carol Barta, Frank Dunlay, Auggi Alvarez, Tonia Monahan, Jenny Admire. 1994

DOMINIQUE IS DEAD ★★1/2 Weird film from England about a greedy man attempting to rid himself of his wife in order to get his hands on her money. Of course, things don't quite work out as planned. Mildly interesting movie, also known as Dominique. Rated PG. 98m. DIR: Michael Anderson. CAST: Cliff Robertson, Jean Simmons, Jenny Agutter, Flora Robson, Judy Geeson. 1978

DOMINO ★★ Artsy Italian film delves into the surreal as it follows Brigitte Nielsen in her quest for love. She's been looking in all the wrong places and now thinks she's found it in the voice of an obscene caller. Rated R for nudity and countless sexual situations. 96m. DIR: Ivana Massetti. CAST: Brigitte Nielsen. 1989

DOMINO PRINCIPLE, THE 💔 Assassination/double-cross/conspiracy thriller. R for violence. 100m. DIR: Stanley Kramer. CAST: Gene Hackman, Richard Widmark, Candice Bergen, Eli Wallach, Mickey Rooney. 1977

DON IS DEAD, THE ★★★1/2 Director Richard Fleischer gives us yet another story of a Mafia family struggling for control of Las Vegas interests (à la The Godfather). Well-acted performances make for better-than-average viewing. Rated R for violence. 115m. DIR: Richard Fleischer. CAST: Anthony Quinn, Frederic Forrest, Robert Forster, Al Lettieri, Angel Tompkins, Charles Cioffi. 1973

DON JUAN ★★★ The now-legendary Great Profile John Barrymore is at the top of his hand-kissing, cavalier womanizing form in this entertaining romantic adventure. The first silent released with canned music and sound effects. Silent. B&W; 111m. DIR: Alan Crosland. CAST: John Barrymore, Mary Astor, Estelle Taylor, Myrna Loy. 1926

DON JUAN DEMARCO ★★★ Johnny Depp plays a mental patient who imagines himself the descendant of the famous lover; Marlon Brando is his aging psychiatrist, envying "Don Juan's" romantic outlook. Depp's personal charm keeps the soggy nonsense afloat. Rated PG-13 for mildly sexual situations. 90m. DIR: Jeremy Leven. CAST: Johnny Depp, Marlon Brando, Faye Dunaway, Rachel Ticotin, Bob Dishy, Talisa Soto, Richard Sarafian, Franc Luz, Geraldine Pailhas. 1995 DVD

DON KING: ONLY IN AMERICA ★★★★ Boxing promoter and entrepreneur Don King uses his flamboyant style and questionable business practices to rise to the top of the boxing game only to encounter numerous pitfalls along the way. Outstanding biography benefits immensely from Ving Rhames, who virtually becomes this man. Made for cable. Rated R for adult situations, language, nudity, and violence. 112m. DIR: John Herzfeld. CAST: Ving Rhames, Vondie Curtis-Hall, Jeremy Piven, Loretta Devine. 1997

DON Q, SON OF ZORRO ★★★1/2 Derring-do in old California as the inimitable Douglas Fairbanks fights evildoers and greedy oppressors while saving ladylove Mary Astor from a fate worse than death. Well-mounted, inventive, and fast-paced. Silent. B&W; 111m. DIR: Donald Crisp. CAST: Douglas Fairbanks Sr., Mary Astor, Jack McDonald, Donald Crisp. 1925

DON QUIXOTE (1933) ★★★ A strange amalgam of Cervantes' novel and a quasi-operatic treatment by composer Jacques Ibert. Of interest primarily to opera purists and G. W. Pabst buffs, it is a splendid document of the great opera basso, Feodor Chaliapin. Pabst's moody visuals nicely complement the singing. In French with English subtitles. B&W; 82m. DIR: G. W. Pabst. CAST: Feodor Chaliapin. 1933

DON QUIXOTE (1988) ★★★★★ A thrilling and gorgeous production of the tale of the old knight who dreams of chivalry and fighting windmills. Critics hailed this performance as one of the greatest large-cast ballets ever recorded. A must for a grand night at the ballet. 120m. DIR: Marius Petipa, Alexander Gorsky. CAST: Kirov Ballet. 1988

•DON QUIXOTE (2000) ★★★1/2 This TNT/Hallmark Entertainment collaboration allows John Lithgow to brilliantly adapt Miguel de Cervantes's aging Everyman into a noble knight. The most mundane scene takes on an exciting aura as he sets out to right imagined wrongs. As his devoted sidekick, Bob Hoskins provides first-rate comic relief. Not rated; contains comic-book violence. 120m. DIR: Peter Yates. CAST: John Lithgow, Bob Hoskins, Isabella Rossellini, Vanessa Williams. 2000

DONA FLOR AND HER TWO HUSBANDS ★★★★ A ribald Brazilian comedy about a woman (Sonia Braga) haunted by the sexy ghost of her first husband (José Wilker), who's anything but happy about her impending remarriage, this film inspired the Sally Field vehicle Kiss Me Goodbye. The original is better all around. In Portuguese with English subtitles. Not rated; the film has nudity. 106m. DIR: Bruno Barreto. CAST: Sonia Braga, José Wilker, Mauro Mendonca. 1978

DONKEY SKIN (PEAU D'ANE) ★★★★ Looking for a fairy tale for an adult audience? A princess, about to be forced to marry her own father, hides out as a scullery maid. Before long, the local Prince Charming sees through her drab disguise. A delightful combination of the real and the dreamlike that could have been unbearably cute in less skilled hands. Okay for kids, but not really intended for them. In French with English subtitles. 90m. DIR: Jacques Demy. CAST: Catherine Deneuve, Jean Marais, Jacques Perrin, Delphine Seyrig. 1984

DONNA HERLINDA AND HER SON ★★★ This highly enjoyable, raunchy comedy explores the bizarre relationship a mother has with her sexually liberated homosexual son. It's a delightful comedy of manners featuring a memorable cast and a director with a great touch for deadpan humor. In Spanish with English subtitles. 90m. DIR: Jaime Humberto

Hermosillo. **CAST:** Guadalupe Del Toro, Marco Antonio Trevino. 1986

DONNER PASS: THE ROAD TO SURVIVAL ★★ This fair made-for-TV retelling of the true story of the Donner party is based on historical accounts and tells of the snowstorm that traps the party and the physical hardship and starvation that lead to the infamous conclusion. Made for TV. 98m. **DIR:** James L. Conway. **CAST:** Robert Fuller, Diane McBain, Andrew Prine, John Anderson, Michael Callan. 1978

DONNIE BRASCO ★★★1/2 In this crime-drama, the title character, an FBI agent has burrowed so deep into the Mafia that he becomes "a made guy." It's a seductive life, one based on loyalty and trust. Brasco is particularly fond of Lefty Ruggiero, his mentor. Still, the question remains, is he a hood called Brasco or an agent named Joe Pistone? Based on a true story, this film is enthralling throughout. Rated R for profanity and violence. 121m. **DIR:** Mike Newell. **CAST:** Al Pacino, Johnny Depp, Michael Madsen, Bruno Kirby, James Russo, Anne Heche. 1997

DONOR, THE ★★ Action star Jeff Wincott plays Billy Castle, a professional stuntman who is a specimen of perfect health. That's good for his job, but bad for his private life, as Billy becomes an unwitting donor for an illegal organ bank. Rated R for violence, language, and nudity. 94m. **DIR:** Damien Lee. **CAST:** Jeff Wincott, Michelle Johnson, Gordon Thompson. 1994

DONOR UNKNOWN ★★1/2 A wealthy man suffers a heart attack and wakes up to find he's had a heart transplant. As he attempts to learn about the donor, he uncovers a sinister conspiracy in this slow-moving but sometimes interesting made-for-cable original. Not rated; contains violence and suggested sex. 93m. **DIR:** John Harrison. **CAST:** Peter Onorati, Alice Krige, Clancy Brown, Richard Portnow, Sam Robards. 1995

DONOVAN'S BRAIN ★★★ After his death in a plane crash, a powerful business magnate has his brain removed by a research scientist (Lew Ayres) who hopes to communicate with the organ by feeding it electricity. Before you know it, the brain is in control, forcing the doctor to obey its ever-increasing demands. Credible acting and tight pacing. B&W; 83m. **DIR:** Felix Feist. **CAST:** Lew Ayres, Nancy Davis, Gene Evans, Steve Brodie. 1953

DONOVAN'S REEF ★★★ Director John Ford's low, knock-about style of comedy prevails in this tale of two old drinking, seafaring buddies—John Wayne and Lee Marvin—forced to aid another pal, Jack Warden, in putting on an air of respectability to impress the latter's visiting daughter (Elizabeth Allen). 109m. **DIR:** John Ford. **CAST:** John Wayne, Lee Marvin, Elizabeth Allen, Jack Warden, Dorothy Lamour. 1963

DON'S ANALYST, THE ★★1/2 A therapist gives a Mafia don a new look at life in this mildy entertaining comedy. Great cast gives it a shot, though. Rated R for language and nudity. 103m. **DIR:** David Jablin. **CAST:** Kevin Pollak, Robert Loggia, Joseph Bologna, Angie Dickinson, Sherilyn Fenn. 1997

DON'S PARTY ★★★1/2 *Don's Party* is a hilarious, and at times vulgar, adult comedy. Like the characters in *Who's Afraid of Virginia Woolf?*, the eleven revelers at Don's party lose all control, and the

evening climaxes in bitter hostilities and humiliating confessions. With no MPAA rating, the film has nudity and profanity. 91m. **DIR:** Bruce Beresford. **CAST:** John Hargreaves, Pat Bishop, Graham Kennedy. 1976 DVD

DON'T ANSWER THE PHONE ★★ Also known as *The Hollywood Strangler*, this unpleasantly brutal exploitation quickie might have been better in more competent hands. Rated R for violence and nudity. 94m. **DIR:** Robert Hammer. **CAST:** James Westmoreland. 1981 DVD

DON'T BE A MENACE TO SOUTH CENTRAL WHILE DRINKING YOUR JUICE IN THE 'HOOD ♥ Unfunny, stereotypical, stupid, and crass. The Wayans family should have known better. Rated R for profanity and mock violence. 89m. **DIR:** Paris Barclay. **CAST:** Shawn Wayans, Marlon Wayans, Suli McCullough, Chris Spencer, Darrell Heath. 1996 DVD

DON'T BE AFRAID OF THE DARK ★★★ Scary TV movie as newlyweds Kim Darby and Jim Hutton move into a weird old house inhabited by eerie little monsters who want Kim for one of their own. The human actors are okay, but the creatures steal the show. 74m. **DIR:** John Newland. **CAST:** Kim Darby, Jim Hutton, Pedro Armendariz Jr., William Demarest. 1973

DON'T BOTHER TO KNOCK ★★★ An early and very effective performance by Marilyn Monroe as a neurotic baby-sitter who goes over the edge. Will hold your interest. Anne Bancroft's film debut. B&W; 76m. **DIR:** Roy Ward Baker. **CAST:** Richard Widmark, Marilyn Monroe, Anne Bancroft, Elisha Cook Jr. 1952

DON'T CRY, IT'S ONLY THUNDER ★★★★ Here is one of those "little" movies that slipped by without much notice yet is so satisfying when discovered by adventurous video renters. A black market wheeler-dealer (Dennis Christopher), lining his pockets behind the lines during the Vietnam War is forced to aid some Asian nuns and their ever-increasing group of Saigon street orphans. The results are predictably heartwarming and occasionally heartbreaking, but the film never drifts off into sentimental melodrama. Rated PG. 108m. **DIR:** Peter Werner. **CAST:** Dennis Christopher, Susan Saint James. 1982

DON'T DO IT ★★ This supposed comedy takes a cold look at love among the Generation X crowd as three couples right out of central casting change their moods as often as their partners. Rated R for profanity, adult themes, and sexual situations. 90m. **DIR:** Eugene Hess. **CAST:** Alexis Arquette, Balthazar Getty, Heather Graham, James LeGros, Sheryl Lee, James Marshall, Esai Morales. 1995 DVD

DON'T DRINK THE WATER ★★★★1/2 Jackie Gleason plays a caterer on a vacation with his wife and daughter. When the plane taking them to Greece is hijacked behind the Iron Curtain, Gleason is accused of spying and finds asylum in the U.S. embassy. Based on Woody Allen's wacky play. Rated G. 100m. **DIR:** Howard Morris. **CAST:** Jackie Gleason, Estelle Parsons, Ted Bessell, Joan Delaney, Michael Constantine, Howard St. John, Danny Meehan, Richard Libertini. 1969

DON'T FENCE ME IN ★★★★1/2 Outstanding Roy Rogers film. Fans rate it one of his five best. Reporter Dale Evans comes west seeking legendary gunslinger Wildcat Kelly, who turns out to be Gabby Hayes. Hayes steals the film, which includes the Sons of the Pioneers' classic "Tumbling Tumbleweeds" as well as the Cole Porter title song. B&W; 71m. **DIR:** John English. **CAST:** Roy Rogers, George "Gabby" Hayes, Dale Evans, Robert Livingston, Marc Lawrence, Bob Nolan and the Sons of the Pioneers. 1945

DON'T GO NEAR THE WATER ★★★ World War II navy public-relations personnel try to grab the glory away from the other services. Mickey Shaughnessy's role as a foul-mouthed enlisted man is one of the greatest jokes ever played on movie censors. Turn up the sound and pay attention—they apparently didn't. 107m. **DIR:** Charles Walters. **CAST:** Glenn Ford, Gia Scala, Earl Holliman, Anne Francis, Keenan Wynn, Fred Clark, Eva Gabor, Russ Tamblyn, Mickey Shaughnessy, Mary Wickes, Jack Albertson. 1957

DON'T GO IN THE HOUSE 💗 A mom-obsessed killer grows up wanting to set pretty young women on fire. Rated R. 82m. **DIR:** James Ellison. **CAST:** Dan Grimaldi. 1980 DVD

DON'T GO TO SLEEP ★★1/2 Supernatural thriller goes the distance but comes up short as the deceased daughter of a couple returns from the grave in order to reunite her family—on the other side. Made-for-television suspense works because of above-average cast. 100m. **DIR:** Richard Lang. **CAST:** Dennis Weaver, Valerie Harper, Ruth Gordon, Robert Webber. 1982

DON'T HANG UP ★★★1/2 Wonderful transcontinental romance features Rosanna Arquette and David Suchet as two lonely people on opposite continents who discover friendship and then love via a series of long-distance phone calls. Arquette plays a handicapped New York actress who is embarrassed by her crutches. Suchet plays a man who suffers from agoraphobia, and finds solace in his London apartment through his conversations with the actress. It's a sentimental, poignant tale of blind love and faith. Not rated. 84m. **DIR:** Barry Davis. **CAST:** Rosanna Arquette, David Suchet. 1990

DON'T LET YOUR MEAT LOAF ★★ Three Brooklyn friends who want to be professional comics try to raise money to open their own comedy club. Filmmaker Leander Sales deserves credit for making a movie on an apparently nonexistent budget, but the amateurish result hardly seems worth the effort. Not rated; contains mild violence, brief nudity, sexual situations, substance abuse, and profanity. 81m. **DIR:** Leander Sales. **CAST:** Leander Sales, Dana S. Hubbard, Brad Albright, Khadijah Karriem. 1995

DON'T LOOK BACK (1967) ★★★ A documentary account directed by D. A. Pennebaker of folksinger/poet ("guitarist," he calls himself) Bob Dylan on a 1965 tour of England. The tedium of travel and pressures of performing are eased by relaxing moments with fellow travelers Joan Baez, Alan Price, and (briefly) Donovan. Shot in striking black and white, with excellent sound quality. Not rated, it contains some vulgarity. B&W; 96m. **DIR:** D. A. Pennebaker. **CAST:** Bob Dylan, Joan Baez, Donovan, Alan Price. 1967

DON'T LOOK BACK: THE STORY OF LEROY "SATCHEL" PAIGE ★★ Made-for-television docudrama about legendary baseball player Leroy "Satchel" Paige and his crusade to get black ball players out of the Negro leagues and into the majors. Despite a good cast and inspiring subject matter, film comes up short. 89m. **DIR:** Richard A. Colla. **CAST:** Lou Gossett Jr., Cleavon Little, Clifton Davis, Jim Davis, Hal Williams, Beverly Todd, Ernie Barnes, Ossie Davis. 1981

DON'T LOOK BACK (1996) ★★★ It's awfully hard to like this story's protagonist, a drunk and drug user who steals money from the mob, then involves childhood friends by leading the bad guys to his small hometown. Although star Eric Stoltz doesn't do anything to make this guy endearing, there's plenty of suspense while worrying about his completely innocent buddies. Rated R for profanity, violence, and drug use. 90m. **DIR:** Geoff Murphy. **CAST:** Eric Stoltz, John Corbett, Josh Hamilton, Billy Bob Thornton, Annabeth Gish, Dwight Yoakam, Amanda Plummer, Peter Fonda. 1996

DON'T LOOK IN THE BASEMENT ★★1/2 When the director of an insane asylum is murdered by one of the inmates, his assistant takes over. But that doesn't put an end to the murders. This is one horror movie in which the low budget actually helps; the lack of professionalism in the production gives it a disturbingly eerie aura. Rated R for violence. 95m. **DIR:** S. F. Brownrigg. **CAST:** William McGee. 1973 DVD

DON'T LOOK NOW ★★★★ Excellent psychic thriller about a married couple who, just after the accidental drowning of their young daughter, start having strange occurrences in their lives. Beautifully photographed by director Nicolas Roeg. Strong performances by Julie Christie and Donald Sutherland make this film a must-see. Rated R. 110m. **DIR:** Nicolas Roeg. **CAST:** Julie Christie, Donald Sutherland. 1973

DON'T MESS WITH MY SISTER 💗 A young man trapped in a forced marriage. Not rated; contains profanity, violence, and sexual situations. 85m. **DIR:** Meir Zarchi. **CAST:** Joe Perce, Jeannine Lemay. 1985 DVD

DON'T OPEN TILL CHRISTMAS ★★1/2 A crazed maniac mutilates and kills bell-ringing Santas, and no one has a clue to the killer's identity, not even the filmmakers. But even with this problem, there is still a good bit of suspense. Not rated; contains graphic violence and profanity. 86m. **DIR:** Edmund Purdom. **CAST:** Edmund Purdom, Caroline Munro, Gerry Sundquist. 1985

DON'T RAISE THE BRIDGE, LOWER THE RIVER 💗 Weak vehicle for Jerry Lewis concerns his efforts to keep his marriage alive. Rated G. 99m. **DIR:** Jerry Paris. **CAST:** Jerry Lewis, Terry-Thomas, Jacqueline Pearce, Bernard Cribbins. 1968

DON'T SLEEP ALONE 💗 Sleazy thriller about a pretty young woman who may be killing her lovers. Rated R for adult situations, language, nudity, and violence. 81m. **DIR:** Tim Andrew. **CAST:** Lisa Welti, Doug Jeffry, Robert Donovan. 1997

DON'T TALK TO STRANGERS ★★★ In this made-for-cable original, a woman remarries and, on her way to California, her son is kidnapped. Her ex-husband is suspected, but people are not always what they appear to be. Suspenseful and enjoyable. Rated R for violence. 94m. DIR: Robert Lewis. CAST: Pierce Brosnan, Shanna Reed, Terry O'Quinn, Keegan MacIntosh, Michael MacRae. 1994

DON'T TELL HER IT'S ME ★★★ A syrupy-sweet romantic comedy about a cancer patient (Steve Guttenberg) who can't get back into dating after his recovery has left him with no hair and a bloated face. His sister (Shelley Long) comes to his aid and turns him into the type of man the girl of his dreams (Jami Gertz) would want. Rated PG-13 for mild violence and brief profanity. 103m. DIR: Malcolm Mowbray. CAST: Steve Guttenberg, Jami Gertz, Shelley Long, Kyle MacLachlan, Madchen Amick. 1991

DON'T TELL MOM THE BABYSITTER'S DEAD ★★ After their baby-sitter drops dead, four rowdy kids rely on their 17-year-old sister to put food on the table. Unfortunately, the funniest line in this adolescent comedy is the film's title. Rated PG-13 for language. 142m. DIR: Stephen Herek. CAST: Christina Applegate, Joanna Cassidy, John Getz, Keith Coogan, Josh Charles. 1991

DOOLINS OF OKLAHOMA ★★★★1/2 Oklahoma outlaw Bill Doolin attempts to go straight when he meets the right girl, only to be hounded by his own gang and an unrelenting marshal. Historically inaccurate, but well staged and action packed. B&W; 90m. DIR: Gordon Douglas. CAST: Randolph Scott, Louise Allbritton, George Macready, John Ireland, Noah Beery Jr. 1949

DOOM ASYLUM 🎬 A man responsible for his wife's accidental death inhabits an old abandoned asylum. Not rated; contains nudity and graphic violence. 77m. DIR: Richard Friedman. CAST: Patty Mullen, Ruth Collins. 1987

DOOM GENERATION, THE ★★ Three teen slackers go on a cross-country sex-and-violence spree, meeting various bizarre characters and gaining a reputation as dangerous outlaws. Writer-director Gregg Araki's low-rent knockoff of Natural Born Killers has energy and anarchic spirit, but the jokes are lame and the shocks are sophomoric. Rated R for profanity, violence, nudity, and simulated sex. 85m. DIR: Gregg Araki. CAST: James Duval, Rose McGowan, Johnathon Schaech, Cress Williams, Parker Posey, Heidi Fleiss. 1995 DVD

DOOMED CARAVAN ★★1/2 A crook with dreams of empire tries to take over a tough widow's freighting business and Hopalong Cassidy and his pals come to her rescue. B&W; 61m. DIR: Lesley Selander. CAST: William Boyd, Russell Hayden, Andy Clyde, Minna Gombell, Morris Ankrum (Stepen Morris), Georgia Hawkins. 1941

DOOMED MEGALOPOLIS, PARTS 1–4 ★★★ The evil, adept Kato wars with the forces of good as he seeks to unleash the slumbering spirit that guards Tokyo in this nicely executed animated horror story with strong, original visuals and a suspenseful plot. Fine animation. Dubbed in English. Not rated; contains violence and nudity. Each 50m. DIR: Rin Taro. 1992

DOOMED TO DIE ★★ Monogram's popular series about the aged Chinese detective, Mr. Wong, was running out of steam by the time this film, the fourth in the series, was released. Wong (Boris Karloff) is called in by hardboiled homicide captain Grant Withers after a millionaire is murdered and his ship is sunk. B&W; 68m. DIR: William Nigh. CAST: Boris Karloff, Grant Withers, Marjorie Reynolds, Melvin Lang, Guy Usher. 1940 DVD

DOOMSDAY FLIGHT, THE ★★★ Rod Serling wrote the script for this made-for-television movie, the first to depict the hijacking of an airliner. A distraught Edmond O'Brien blackmails an airline company by planting a bomb aboard a passenger plane. May not be as provocative today. Still, good acting is on hand as the search for the bomb is carried out. 100m. DIR: William A. Graham. CAST: Jack Lord, Edmond O'Brien, Van Johnson, John Saxon, Michael Sarrazin. 1966

DOOMSDAY GUN ★★★★ Slick drama with Frank Langella cast as genius inventor Gerald Bull, the wholly amoral scientist determined to develop the world's biggest gun. And that's just what he did—for Saddam Hussein, with the tacit approval of U.S. and British intelligence agencies. Rated PG-13 for profanity. 106m. DIR: Robert Young. CAST: Frank Langella, Alan Arkin, Kevin Spacey, Michael Kitchen, Francesca Annis, Tony Goldwyn, James Fox. 1994

DOOMWATCH ★★1/2 Sci-fi for the Masterpiece Theatre crowd, with plenty of British reserve. A scientist aids the army in investigating an island where pollution has turned the population into mutants. Thoughtful, though not very scary. Based on a BBC miniseries. Not rated. 92m. DIR: Peter Sasdy. CAST: George Sanders, Ian Bannen, Judy Geeson. 1972

DOOR TO DOOR ★★★1/2 An aspiring salesman learns the ropes from a veteran who has a variety of other ways of augmenting his income (very few of them legal). A gentle, offbeat comedy. Rated PG. 85m. DIR: Patrick Bailey. CAST: Ron Leibman, Arliss Howard, Jane Kaczmarek. 1984

DOORS, THE ★★★1/2 Writer-director Oliver Stone's screen biography of rock group The Doors is a lot like the band it portrays: outrageous, exciting, boring, insightful, silly, and awfully pretentious. Nevertheless, Val Kilmer gives an inspired, spookily accurate performance as Jim Morrison. Rated R for simulated sex, profanity, and violence. 135m. DIR: Oliver Stone. CAST: Val Kilmer, Meg Ryan, Frank Whaley, Kevin Dillon, Kyle MacLachlan, Billy Idol, Dennis Burkley, Josh Evans, Kathleen Quinlan. 1991 DVD

DOORS, THE SOFT PARADE ★★ For diehard Doors fans this tape is sheer heaven. Directed by Doors member Ray Manzarek, it's a collection of backstage clips and performances by the band, including the infamous Miami concert. Songs include "The Changeling," "Wishful Sinner," "Wild Child," "Build Me a Woman," "The Unknown Soldier," "The Soft Parade," and "Hello I Love You." Not rated. 50m. DIR: Ray Manzarek. 1969

DOPPELGANGER: THE EVIL WITHIN ★★ Drew Barrymore is either a schizoid murderer or actually has the evil counterpart she claims. A few chills before it deteriorates into drive-in hell. Rated R for profanity, violence, and nudity. 105m. DIR: Avi Nesher. CAST: Drew Barrymore, George Newbern. 1992

DORIAN GRAY 🦃 Horrid updating of the Oscar Wilde classic novel. Fascinating story has never been more boring, with some good actors wasted. Alternate title: *The Secret of Dorian Gray*. Rated R. 93m. DIR: Massimo Dallamano. CAST: Helmut Berger, Richard Todd, Herbert Lom. 1970

DORM THAT DRIPPED BLOOD, THE (PRANKS) 🦃 The only good thing about this film is the title. Rated R for violence. 84m. DIR: Jeffrey Obrow, Stephen Carpenter. CAST: Pamela Holland, Stephen Sachs. 1981

DOT AND THE BUNNY ★★★ A little girl falls asleep, dreaming of her adventures with a lop-eared rabbit as they search for a missing baby kangaroo. Real-life backgrounds make this a unique production that involves animated characters parading about the Australian jungle. 79m. DIR: Yoram Gross. 1982

DOUBLE AGENTS ★★★ A German agent tries to smuggle war secrets from England to France, while British intelligence tries to discover her identity and stop her. Intricate World War II suspense-drama. Dubbed. B&W; 81m. DIR: Robert Hossein. CAST: Marina Vlady, Robert Hossein. 1959

DOUBLE BLAST ★★1/2 Action-packed kick-boxing film finds 10-year-old Lorne Berfield and his 13-year-old sister (Crystal Summer) tracking down the kidnappers of a noted scientist (Linda Blair). Kung-fu action mixed with *Indiana Jones*–like adventure makes this a pleasant diversion. Things really kick in when their father, kick-boxing champion Dale "Apollo" Cook, gets involved. Rated PG for violence. 89m. DIR: Tim Spring. CAST: Linda Blair, Dale "Apollo" Cook, Joe Estevez, Lorne Berfield, Crystal Summer. 1993

DOUBLE CROSS ★★1/2 A small fender bender, a seductive blonde, and a simple little white lie prove disastrous for new stranger-in-town Patrick Bergin. When he locks fenders with ravishing Kelly Preston, Bergin is all too happy to forget about his car when he gets the chance to race Preston's engine. His life is in need of a tune-up when his sexual tryst implicates him in a small-town murder. Rated R for violence, adult situations, and language. 96m. DIR: Michael Keusch. CAST: Patrick Bergin, Kelly Preston, Jennifer Tilly, Kevin Tighe. 1994

DOUBLE DEAL 🦃 Casual direction and a poor adaptation of a story that wasn't very good in the first place resulted in this dull programmer from RKO. B&W; 83m. DIR: Abby Berlin. CAST: Richard Denning, Marie Windsor, Carleton Young, Fay Baker, Taylor Holmes, Paul E. Burns, James Griffith. 1950

DOUBLE DRAGON 🦃 Cheesy clash of good and evil based on the wildly popular video game in which a crime lord tries to snatch the second half of a magical medallion from three teens and rule the world. Rated PG-13 for language and violence. 95m. DIR: Jim Yukich. CAST: Robert Patrick, Mark Dacascos, Scott Wolf, Kristina Malandro Wagner, Julia Nickson. 1994 DVD

DOUBLE DYNAMITE ★★1/2 Disappointing comedy about a bank teller (Frank Sinatra) who receives a generous reward for saving a gangster's life completely by accident. Sinatra and Groucho Marx can't rise above the weak script and direction. B&W; 80m. DIR: Irving Cummings. CAST: Frank Sinatra, Jane Russell, Groucho Marx. 1951

DOUBLE EDGE ★★ Faye Dunaway plays an aggressive New York reporter on assignment in Jerusalem. She realizes that there are no clear-cut answers. Dunaway is believable as she struggles with both her toughness and vulnerability. Not rated; contains sex and violence. 96m. DIR: Amos Kollek. CAST: Faye Dunaway, Amos Kollek, Shmuel Shiloh, Muhamad Bakri. 1992

DOUBLE EXPOSURE (1982) ★★★1/2 This psychological thriller about a photographer (Michael Callan) who has nightmares of murders that come true has some pretty ghoulish scenes. The cast puts in solid performances. Not rated; contains violence, profanity, nudity, and adult subject matter. 95m. DIR: Wiliam Byron Hillman. CAST: Michael Callan, Joanna Pettet, James Stacy, Pamela Hensley, Cleavon Little, Seymour Cassel, Robert Tessier. 1982

DOUBLE EXPOSURE (1987) ★★★ Two aspiring Venice Beach photographers divide their time between trying to impress the local bathing beauties and solving a murder that they accidentally photographed (shades of *Blow-up!*). Standard comedy thriller done with a little panache. Rated R for nudity. 100m. DIR: Nico Mastorakis. CAST: Mark Hennessy, Scott King, John Vernon. 1987

DOUBLE EXPOSURE (1989) ★★★ This biographical film about Depression-era photographer Margaret Bourke-White has a familiar plot: strong woman fights for equality in a man's profession. Exceptional performances save this telefilm from mediocrity. 94m. DIR: Lawrence Schiller. CAST: Farrah Fawcett, Frederic Forrest, David Huddleston, Jay Patterson. 1989

DOUBLE EXPOSURE (1993) ★★ Abusive, obsessive husband Ian Buchanan believes his lovely wife (Jennifer Gatti) is having an affair, and hires private detective Ron Perlman to investigate. When the news comes back positive, Buchanan plots to do away with his wife. When Gatti turns up dead, the plot blows up in Buchanan's face. But did he really do it? Rated R for nudity, violence, and language. 93m. DIR: Claudia Hoover. CAST: Ron Perlman, Ian Buchanan, Jennifer Gatti, Dedee Pfeiffer, James McEachin, William R. Moses. 1993

DOUBLE HAPPINESS ★★★ A 22-year-old aspiring actress struggles to balance her life while living in Canada with her overprotective parents who are immigrants from Hong Kong. She has trouble negotiating her ethnicity with the world: her thespian goals do not meet the Old World expectations of her folks, and—even more horrific—she is secretly dating a white man. Partly in Chinese with English subtitles. Rated PG-13 for language, nudity, and suggested sex. 87m. DIR: Mina Shum. CAST: Sandra Oh, Alannah Ong, Stephen Chang, Frances You. 1995

DOUBLE IMPACT ★★★ Jean-Claude Van Damme gets a chance to strut his acting stuff in the dual role of twin brothers—one a Beverly Hills aerobic instructor, the other a Hong Kong smuggler—who join forces to avenge their parents' murder. Enough action for Van Damme fans, coupled with a surprising amount of comedy. Rated R for violence, profanity, and simulated sex. 118m. **DIR:** Sheldon Lettich. **CAST:** Jean-Claude Van Damme, Geoffrey Lewis, Alan Scarfe. 1991

DOUBLE INDEMNITY ★★★★ This is one of the finest suspense films ever made. Fred MacMurray is an insurance salesman who, with Barbara Stanwyck, concocts a scheme to murder her husband and collect the benefits. The husband's policy, however, contains a rider that states that if the husband's death is caused by a moving train the policy pays double face value. Edward G. Robinson is superb as MacMurray's suspicious boss. B&W; 106m. **DIR:** Billy Wilder. **CAST:** Fred MacMurray, Barbara Stanwyck, Edward G. Robinson, Porter Hall. 1944 DVD

DOUBLE JEOPARDY (1992) ★★ Romantic thrillers don't earn much dumber than this mess, which finds Salt Lake City schoolmaster Bruce Boxleitner the sole witness to ex-girlfriend Rachel Ward's justifiable (?) murder of her violent boyfriend. Made for cable. 100m. **DIR:** Lawrence Schiller. **CAST:** Rachel Ward, Bruce Boxleitner, Sela Ward, Sally Kirkland, Jay Patterson. 1992

•**DOUBLE JEOPARDY (1999)** ★★★ Framed for a murder she didn't commit, Ashley Judd eludes her determined parole officer (Tommy Lee Jones) as she hunts down her rotten husband. To really enjoy this film, reality must be suspended and the improbable accepted as possible. The worst thing a viewer can do, in terms of enjoying this flick, is to wage a debate over the double jeopardy statute. Some tense moments lead to a satisfying confrontation. Rated R for sex, violence, and language. 93m. **DIR:** Bruce Beresford. **CAST:** Tommy Lee Jones, Ashley Judd, Benjamin Weir, Jay Brazeau, Bruce Greenwood I. 1999 DVD

DOUBLE LIFE, A ★★★★ Ronald Colman gives an Oscar-winning performance as a famous actor whose stage life begins to take over his personality and private life, forcing him to revert to stage characters, including Othello, to cope with everyday situations. Brilliantly written by Garson Kanin and Ruth Gordon, and impressively acted by a standout cast. Top treatment of a fine story. B&W; 104m. **DIR:** George Cukor. **CAST:** Ronald Colman, Edmond O'Brien, Shelley Winters, Ray Collins. 1947

DOUBLE LIFE OF VERONIQUE, THE ★★★★ In this exquisite adult fairy tale, the luminous Irène Jacob plays the dual role of two identical women, one Polish and one French, who live parallel lives. It is an enigmatic but gorgeous film; one that often seems like a series of paintings come to life on-screen. In French and Polish with English subtitles. Not rated; the film has nudity and suggested sex. 105m. **DIR:** Krzysztof Kieslowski. **CAST:** Irène Jacob, Halina Gryglaszewska, Kalina Jedrusik. 1991

DOUBLE MCGUFFIN, THE ★★★1/2 Here's another family (as opposed to children's) movie. It's full of Hitchcock references in a story about some smart kids who uncover a plot to kill the leader of a Middle Eastern country. The three nominal stars only have supporting parts; they get top billing just for marquee value. From Joe Camp, the one-man movie factory who created the *Benji* films. Rated PG. 101m.

DIR: Joe Camp. **CAST:** Ernest Borgnine, George Kennedy, Elke Sommer, Rod Browning, Lisa Whelchel, Vincent Spano, Lyle Alzado. 1979

DOUBLE-O KID, THE ★★ During a summer internship for the CIA, an obnoxious teenager stumbles across a terrorist who plans to make a plane full of scientists disappear into the Bermuda Triangle. Too many chase scenes and unbelievable getaways ruin this film. Rated PG-13 for violence and profanity. 95m. **DIR:** Duncan McLachlan. **CAST:** Corey Haim, Brigitte Nielsen, Wallace Shawn, Nicole Eggert, Basil Hoffman, John Rhys-Davies, Karen Black, Anne Francis. 1992

DOUBLE OBSESSION ★★ *Fatal Attraction* meets *Single White Female* as college coed Margaux Hemingway falls for roommate Maryam d'Abo. When d'Abo falls in love with someone else, the fun begins. Vindictive roommates have become a genre all their own, and this entry tries to punch the right buttons, but to no avail. Over-the-top acting erases any hope. Rated R for violence, language, and nudity. 88m. **DIR:** Eduardo Montes. **CAST:** Margaux Hemingway, Maryam D'Abo, Frederic Forrest, Scott Valentine. 1992

DOUBLE REVENGE ★★1/2 Tough Guy Joe Dallesandro bungles a small-town robbery, resulting in the death of a local businessman's wife. You guessed it— everybody wants revenge. Rated R. 96m. **DIR:** Armand Mastroianni. **CAST:** Leigh McCloskey, Joe Dallesandro, Nancy Everhard, Theresa Saldana, Richard Rust. 1988

DOUBLE STANDARD ❤ A prolific circuit-court justice gets caught leading a double family life. Made for TV. 95m. **DIR:** Louis Rudolph. **CAST:** Robert Foxworth, Pamela Bellwood, Michele Greene. 1988

DOUBLE SUICIDE ★★★★ Stunning portrait of erotic obsession and passion in turn-of-century Japan. Director Masahiro Shinoda explores sexual taboos in his story of a merchant and a geisha whose ill-fated love affair is orchestrated entirely by outside forces. This poignant drama is presented in the style of a Bunraku puppet play. In Japanese with English subtitles. Not rated. B&W; 105m. **DIR:** Masahiro Shinoda. **CAST:** Kichiemon Nakamura, Shima Iwashita. 1969

DOUBLE TAKE ★★★ A struggling writer witnesses a murder and testifies, sending the accused to jail. But when he sees the real murderer running around free, he realizes he's made a terrible mistake. Or has he? Predictable but entertaining. Rated R for profanity, violence, and nudity. 86m. **DIR:** Mark L. Lester. **CAST:** Craig Sheffer, Brigitte Bako, Costas Mandylor. 1997

•**DOUBLE TAP** ★★1/2 An undercover FBI agent falls in love with a hit man and they find themselves the target of an evil drug lord. Entertaining but nothing spectacular. Rated R for profanity and violence. 87m. **DIR:** Greg Yaitanes. **CAST:** Stephen Rea, Heather Locklear, Peter Greene, Kevin Gage, A Martinez. 1997

DOUBLE TEAM ★★1/2 CIA operative balks at gunning down an international terrorist in front of a child and is exiled to a swank island. He later escapes and teams up with a weapons specialist to hunt down his missed target. The film's exhilarating showdown in a Rome coliseum involves a prowling tiger, land mines, martial arts combat, and a new-born baby tucked into a handbasket. The action is impressively choreographed, but the script stinks. Rated R for violence. 91m. **DIR:** Tsui Hark. **CAST:** Jean-Claude Van Damme, Dennis Rodman, Mickey Rourke, Natacha Lindinger. **1997 DVD**

DOUBLE THREAT ★★ An aging screen queen (Sally Kirkland) becomes concerned when her gigolo/costar gets interested in her young body double. Tricky behind-the-scenes thriller boasts a few unexpected twists. Available in R and unrated versions; both feature profanity, nudity, and sexual situations. 94m./96m. **DIR:** David A. Prior. **CAST:** Sally Kirkland, Andrew Stevens, Sherrie Rose, Chick Vennera, Richard Lynch, Anthony Franciosa. **1992**

DOUBLE TROUBLE (1967) ★★ Typical Elvis Presley musical. This time he plays a rock 'n' roll singer touring England. When a teenage heiress (whose life is constantly threatened) falls for him, he gets caught up in the action. 92m. **DIR:** Norman Taurog. **CAST:** Elvis Presley, Annette Day. **1967**

DOUBLE TROUBLE (1991) ★★ Inane actioner features muscle-bound twins (wrestling duo Peter Paul and David Paul) on either side of the law. They team up to pursue a deadly diamond thief. Rated R for violence and profanity. 87m. **DIR:** John Paragon. **CAST:** Peter Paul, David Paul, Roddy McDowall, Steve Kanaly. **1991**

DOUBLE VISION 💔 A prudish identical twin steps into her naughty sister's shoes to retrace the last days before her death. Despite a fine supporting cast, sexy Kim Cattrall can't wade through this murky murder mystery. Not rated; contains profanity. 92m. **DIR:** Robert Knights. **CAST:** Kim Cattrall, Gale Hansen, Christopher Lee, Macha Meril. **1992**

DOUBLE WEDDING ★★★★ William Powell as a painter and Myrna Loy as a dress designer play Cupid in an effort to get Florence Rice married to John Beal. But the plan backfires. A delightful slapstick comedy. Lots of fun. B&W; 87m. **DIR:** Richard Thorpe. **CAST:** William Powell, Myrna Loy, Florence Rice, Edgar Kennedy, Sidney Toler, Jessie Ralph, Mary Gordon, John Beal. **1937**

DOUBLECROSSED ★★★1/2 Dennis Hopper is a casting agent's dream come true as a drug smuggler-turned-DEA informant in this fascinating fact-based study. Hopper's beguiling con artist is impossible to dislike. Rated R for violence and relentlessly foul language. 111m. **DIR:** Roger Young. **CAST:** Dennis Hopper, Robert Carradine, Richard Jenkins, Adrienne Barbeau, G. W. Bailey. **1991**

DOUBTING THOMAS ★★★ Wealthy manufacturer Will Rogers foils his stagestruck wife's acting ambition in this moderately amusing but outdated comedy. B&W; 78m. **DIR:** David Butler. **CAST:** Will Rogers, Billie Burke, Alison Skipworth, Sterling Holloway, Frank Albertson, John Qualen. **1935**

DOUGH AND DYNAMITE/KNOCKOUT, THE ★★★ Two of the best slapstick two-reelers Mack Sennett's famous Keystone Studios churned out during the heyday of fast-and-furious, rough-and-tumble comedies. *The Knockout,* actually a Fatty Arbuckle film, has Charlie Chaplin playing the referee, the third man in the ring, in a fight sequence between behemoths (to him) Edgar Kennedy and Arbuckle. *Dough and Dynamite* is set in a French restaurant. B&W; 54m. **DIR:** Mack Sennett, Charles Chaplin. **CAST:** The Keystone Kops. **1914**

DOUGHBOYS ★★ Buster Keaton mistakenly enlists in the army and in spite of himself becomes a hero. His second sound film, and a letdown from start to finish. B&W; 79m. **DIR:** Edward Sedgwick. **CAST:** Buster Keaton, Sally Eilers, Cliff Edwards, Edward Brophy. **1930**

DOUGHGIRLS, THE ★★ The setting is crowded Washington D.C. during World War II when a hotel room could hardly be had. Not even for honeymooners who find they have to share their suite with an assortment of military men and women. A comedy that relies on the wartime era for its laughs, and the personalities take a backseat to the dated dialogue. B&W; 102m. **DIR:** James V. Kern. **CAST:** Ann Sheridan, Jane Wyman, Eve Arden, Alexis Smith, Jack Carson, Craig Stevens, Charlie Ruggles, Alan Mowbray, Regis Toomey. **1944**

DOUG'S 1ST MOVIE ★★ This artlessly animated version of the cartoon show is a bland riff on *E.T.* Doug Funny is a middle schooler in a town populated with green-, blue-, and purple-faced kids with either monotone or whiny voices. He is harassed by a bully, competes for the attention of a girl, and discovers that a prominent citizen is covering up pollution problems. Rated G. 77m. **DIR:** Maurice Joyce. **1999**

DOWN AMONG THE "Z" MEN 💔 Before there was a Monty Python there were the Goons, a British comedy team that featured Peter Sellers, among others (see cast). B&W; 82m. **DIR:** Maclean Rogers. **CAST:** Peter Sellers, Harry Secombe, Michael Bentine, Spike Milligan, Carol Carr. **1961**

DOWN AND DIRTY ★★★ Brutal but brilliant black comedy about a slumlord of a shantytown in Rome. Nino Manfredi is excellent as a money-hoarding patriarch whose obsession with his stash leads to a plot by his wife and delinquent sons to kill him. In Italian with English subtitles. Not rated; contains violence, profanity, and nudity. 115m. **DIR:** Ettore Scola. **CAST:** Nino Manfredi, Francesco Anniballi. **1976**

DOWN AND OUT IN AMERICA ★★★★ Oscar-winning documentary about the "new poor," working-class people who have been caught on the downward spiral into poverty. Actress-turned-director Lee Grant makes it clear that these people are not isolated cases, but victims of conditions that affect more and more American families every year. Not rated. 60m. **DIR:** Lee Grant. **1985**

DOWN AND OUT IN BEVERLY HILLS ★★★1/2 When a Los Angeles bum (Nick Nolte) loses his dog to a happy home, he decides to commit suicide in a Beverly Hills swimming pool. The pool's owner (Richard Dreyfuss) saves the seedy-looking character's life and thereby sets in motion a chain of events that threatens to destroy his family's rarefied existence. Rated R. 102m. **DIR:** Paul Mazursky. **CAST:** Nick Nolte, Bette Midler, Richard Dreyfuss, Little Richard, Tracy Nelson, Elizabeth Peña, Evan Richards. **1986**

DOWN ARGENTINE WAY ★★★ Tuneful Technicolor extravaganza is the granddaddy of all the fruit-filled South American musical–comedy–romances cranked out in the 1940s. The incredible production numbers feature the rubber-jointed Nicholas Brothers and the incredible Carmen Miranda. 92m. DIR: Irving Cummings. CAST: Don Ameche, Betty Grable, Carmen Miranda, Charlotte Greenwood, J. Carrol Naish, Henry Stephenson. 1940

DOWN BY LAW ★★★1/2 *Stranger Than Paradise* director Jim Jarmusch improves on his static deadpan style by allowing his *Down by Law* characters a bit more life. In fact, he appears to be leaning more optimistically toward activity. He gives the film an energetic Italian comedian (Roberto Benigni), who looks like a dark-haired Kewpie doll. This lively imp inspires his lethargic companions (John Lurie, Tom Waits) to speak, sing, and generally loosen up a little. Rated R for nudity and profanity. 90m. DIR: Jim Jarmusch. CAST: John Lurie, Tom Waits, Roberto Benigni, Ellen Barkin. 1986

DOWN CAME A BLACKBIRD ★★★ Journalist Laura Dern, a pill-popping alcoholic forever scarred by her experiences in a war-torn country, profiles the saintly counselor who runs a clinic for torture survivors. Before long, the writer is less an observer and more a patient. Kevin Droney's sensitive script concludes with a real surprise. Rated R for nudity, torture, violence, rape, and profanity. 112m. DIR: Jonathan Sanger. CAST: Raul Julia, Laura Dern, Vanessa Redgrave, Cliff Gorman, Sarita Choudhury, Jay O. Sanders. 1995

DOWN DAKOTA WAY ★★1/2 Roy Rogers takes a harder line with the bad guys in this exciting B Western, tracking down the no-goods responsible for the death of his friend, a veterinarian who could finger the man responsible for flooding the market with diseased meat. 67m. DIR: William Witney. CAST: Roy Rogers, Dale Evans, Pat Brady, Monte Montana, Roy Barcroft. 1949

DOWN IN THE DELTA ★★★★ A Chicago grandmother, desperate to save her daughter and grandchildren from the dangers of the streets, bundles them off to live with her brother-in-law in rural Mississippi. Poet Maya Angelou, directing her first film, lacks the finesse to smooth out the rough edges in Myron Goble's episodic script, but she's sensitive enough to emphasize its family-values message, and smart enough not to interfere with her first-rate cast. Rated PG-13 for mild profanity. 107m. DIR: Maya Angelou. CAST: Alfre Woodard, Al Freeman Jr., Loretta Devine, Wesley Snipes, Esther Rolle, Mary Alice. 1998 DVD

DOWN, OUT & DANGEROUS ★★1/2 Mildly suspenseful made-for-cable original about a successful businessman who makes the mistake of helping a homeless psychotic killer. Rated R for violence and profanity. 90m. DIR: Noel Nosseck. CAST: Richard Thomas, Bruce Davison, Cynthia Ettinger. 1995

DOWN PERISCOPE ★★★ Kelsey Grammer stars as a maverick submarine commander whose unorthodox behavior lands him a sad diesel-powered sub and a crew of navy misfits. Their mission: outmaneuver the cream of the U.S. Navy's nuclear fleet. Standard-issue military screwball comedy made palatable by a strong ensemble cast. Rated PG for mild profanity. 92m. DIR: David S. Ward. CAST: Kelsey Grammer, Lauren Holly, Rob Schneider, Harry Dean Stanton, Bruce Dern, William H. Macy, Rip Torn, Harland Williams. 1995

DOWN TEXAS WAY ★★1/2 An agreeable if undistinguished entry in the Rough Riders series, this feature has Rangers Buck Jones and Tim McCoy coming to the aid of their pal, Raymond Hatton, when he is accused of murder. B&W; 57m. DIR: Howard Bretherton. CAST: Buck Jones, Tim McCoy, Raymond Hatton, Luana Walters, Harry Woods, Glenn Strange. 1942

DOWN THE DRAIN ★★ A criminal lawyer sets up a big heist. Standard cross, no-honor-among-thieves story. Rated R for nudity, language, and violence. 105m. DIR: Robert C. Hughes. CAST: Andrew Stevens, Teri Copley, John Matuszak, Joseph Campanella, Don Stroud. 1990

DOWN TO EARTH ★★★★ One of the brightest of the early Douglas Fairbanks social comedies. All the "big guns" are here—scenarist Anita Loos; her husband, director John Emerson; and some sparkling camerawork by Victor Fleming (before he turned full-time director). Silent. B&W; 52m. DIR: John Emerson. CAST: Douglas Fairbanks Sr., Eileen Percy, Gustav von Seyffertitz. 1917

DOWN TO THE SEA IN SHIPS ★★★ The plot involving a family of whalers has appeal, but vivid scenes filmed at sea aboard real New England whalers out of Bedford make it worthwhile. B&W; 83m. DIR: Elmer Clifton. CAST: William Walcott, Marguerite Courtot, Clara Bow. 1922

DOWN TWISTED ★★ Stylish *Romancing the Stone*–type thriller about an innocent waitress who agrees to help her roommate out of a jam. Before she knows it, she's stuck in Central America with a disreputable soldier of fortune and people shooting at her. The convoluted plot gets better as it goes along, though you may not find it worth the effort. Rated PG-13. 88m. DIR: Albert Pyun. CAST: Carey Lowell, Charles Rocket, Thom Mathews, Linda Kerridge. 1987

DOWN UNDER ❤ Patrick Macnee narrates this crudely shot tale of two southern California surfers in Australia. Stale and pointless. 90m. DIR: Not credited. CAST: Don Atkinson, Donn Dunlop, Patrick Macnee. 1984

DOWNDRAFT ★★1/2 There's absolutely no logic to this action thriller, but it certainly moves. Vincent Spano leads a military-assault team into an impregnable mountain bunker, which has been commandeered by a mad scientist and his bloodthirsty cyborg surrogate. The dialogue is ludicrous, but the stunts are pretty slick. Rated R for violence and profanity. 92m. DIR: Michael Mazo. CAST: Vincent Spano, Kate Vernon, Paul Koslo, John Novak, William Taylor, John Pyper-Ferguson. 1996

DOWNHILL RACER ★★★1/2 Robert Redford struggles with an unappealing character, in this study of an Olympic skier. But Gene Hackman is excellent as the coach, and the exciting scenes of this snow sport hold the film together. Rated PG. 101m. DIR: Michael Ritchie. CAST: Robert Redford, Gene Hackman, Camilla Sparv. 1969

DOWNHILL WILLIE ★★★ Amiable comedy about a clueless guy who may be short on brain cells but is a pro on skis. When Willie decides to enter the notorious "Kamikaze Run," he's pitted against a slew of hot-shot skiers, including an egotistical ski instructor and an alcoholic ex-Olympian. Typical teen-comedy high jinks ensue in this fun but tame underdog story filled with exciting skiing sequences and beautiful ski bunnies. Rated PG for language and sexual innuendo. 90m. DIR: David Mitchell. CAST: Keith Coogan, Lochlan Monroe, Staci Keanan, Estelle Harris, Fred Stoller. **1996 DVD**

DOWNTOWN ★★ Anthony Edwards plays a rookie cop who is transferred to a hard-core inner-city neighborhood. An uneven attempt to balance comedy and violent action. The excellent cast outstrips the project. Rated R. 96m. DIR: Richard Benjamin. CAST: Anthony Edwards, Forest Whitaker, Penelope Ann Miller, Joe Pantoliano. **1990**

D.P. ★★★★ The shattering loss of innocence by war's true victims—children—is examined in this Emmy-winning adaptation of Kurt Vonnegut's poignant story. Julius Gordon is one of many orphans cared for by nuns in post–World War II Germany, a truly "displaced person" because he is the only boy with black skin. Not rated; suitable for family viewing. 60m. DIR: Alan Bridges. CAST: Stan Shaw, Rosemary Leach, Julius Gordon. **1985**

DRACULA (1931) ★★★★ Bela Lugosi found himself forever typecast after brilliantly bringing to life the bloodthirsty Transylvanian vampire of the title in this 1931 genre classic, directed by Tod Browning. His performance and that of Dwight Frye as the spider-eating Renfield still impress even though this early talkie seems somewhat dated today. B&W; 75m. DIR: Tod Browning. CAST: Bela Lugosi, Dwight Frye, David Manners, Helen Chandler, Edward Van Sloan. **1931 DVD**

DRACULA (SPANISH) ★★★ The familiar tale of the bloodthirsty Count Dracula is enacted by a Spanish-speaking cast in this sister production to the famous 1931 American counterpart. The count actually rises from his coffin on camera, and the women (especially the unholy brides) are erotic and enticing. Bela Lugosi is still the consummate Dracula, but this overlong production has some memorable moments. In Spanish with English subtitles. B&W; 104m. DIR: George Melford. CAST: Carlos Villarias, Lupita Tovar, Pablo Alvarez Rubio. **1931**

DRACULA (1973) ★★★★ Surprisingly effective made-for-television version of Bram Stoker's classic tale has Jack Palance as a sympathetic count trapped by his vampirism. Director Dan Curtis and scripter Richard Matheson had previously collaborated on the excellent *The Night Stalker* telefilm and work together equally well here. 99m. DIR: Dan Curtis. CAST: Jack Palance, Simon Ward, Nigel Davenport, Pamela Brown, Fiona Lewis. **1973**

DRACULA (1979) ★★1/2 This *Dracula* is a film of missed opportunities. Frank Langella makes an excellent Count Dracula. It's a pity he has so little screen time. The story, for the uninitiated, revolves around the activities of a bloodthirsty vampire who leaves his castle in Transylvania for fresh hunting in London. Rated R. 109m. DIR: John Badham. CAST: Frank Langella, Laurence Olivier, Donald Pleasence, Jan Francis. **1979 DVD**

DRACULA A.D. 1972 ★★★ A spectacular opening sequence featuring Dr. Van Helsing (Peter Cushing) and Count Dracula (Christopher Lee) fighting atop a runaway coach is the high point in this Hammer film that jumps from a period setting to modern-day London. Things go a bit downhill from there as a wannabe vampire leads a band of hippies into the clutches of the ageless count. The San Francisco band, Stoneground, plays two songs in a party scene. Rated PG. 100m. DIR: Alan Gibson. CAST: Peter Cushing, Christopher Lee, Stephanie Beacham, Michael Coles, Christopher Neame. **1972**

DRACULA AND SON ★★ French vampire spoof was probably much funnier before the inane English dubbing was added. The Dracula family looks for a new home after the Communists run them out of their Transylvanian home. Rated PG. 88m. DIR: Edouard Molinaro. CAST: Christopher Lee, Bernard Ménez. **1976**

DRACULA: DEAD AND LOVING IT ★★★ Perhaps we're too generous toward this silly send-up by director Mel Brooks; however, it does make a fine viewing companion to the filmmaker's superior *Young Frankenstein*. While Brooks pokes fun at Coppola's pompous *Bram Stoker's Dracula*, he also pays homage to Lugosi's interpretation of the title character and the innovations brought to the familiar story by Hammer Films in *Horror of Dracula*. Rated PG-13 for comic gore and scatological humor. 90m. DIR: Mel Brooks. CAST: Leslie Nielsen, Peter MacNicol, Steven Weber, Amy Yasbeck, Lysette Anthony, Harvey Korman, Mel Brooks, Mark Blankfield, Chuck McCann, Anne Bancroft, Avery Schreiber. **1996**

DRACULA HAS RISEN FROM THE GRAVE ★★1/2 Freddie Francis took over the directorial reins from Terence Fisher for Hammer Films's third Dracula–Christopher Lee vehicle, and the result, while visually striking (Francis is an Oscar-winning cinematographer), is a major step down dramatically. A tepid revenge plot has the Count going after the niece of a monsignor. Rated G. 92m. DIR: Freddie Francis. CAST: Christopher Lee, Veronica Carlson, Rupert Davies, Barry Andrews. **1968**

DRACULA—PRINCE OF DARKNESS ★★★ Christopher Lee returns in his most famous role with mixed results. This first sequel to *Horror of Dracula* lacks the vigor and tension of its predecessor as the revived count stalks a group of travelers. 90m. DIR: Terence Fisher. CAST: Christopher Lee, Barbara Shelley, Andrew Keir, Suzan Farmer. **1966 DVD**

DRACULA RISING ♥ After 500 years, a reincarnated woman is saved from an evil vampire by the wonderful vampire who loved her before; a good idea sucked dry by poor acting. Rated R for violence and nudity. 85m. DIR: Fred Gallo. CAST: Christopher Atkins, Stacey Travis, Doug Wert, Tara McCann. **1992**

DRACULA VS. FRANKENSTEIN ♥ Dracula's eternal search for blood. Pretty bad. Rated R. 90m. DIR: Al Adamson. CAST: J. Carrol Naish, Lon Chaney Jr., Jim Davis. **1971**

DRACULA'S DAUGHTER ★★★1/2 The lady in the title tries to break her addiction to human blood after she exorcises and burns the remains of her dead sire—but the cure doesn't take. This brooding film is stylish and creates its own strange mood through imaginative sets, art design, music, and compelling performances by Gloria Holden as the unhappy undead and Irving Pichel as her dour but dedicated servant. B&W; 69m. DIR: Lambert Hillyer. CAST: Gloria Holden, Otto Kruger, Marguerite Churchill, Edward Van Sloan, Irving Pichel. 1936

DRACULA'S GREAT LOVE ★★ Anyone who isn't familiar with the cinematic exploits of Spanish horror film star Paul Naschy (Jacinto Molina to all you bilingual fans) may not want to begin here. Barrel-chested, hirsute Pablo is better suited to werewolves—in such romps as *Fury of the Wolfman*—than Transylvania's seducer. Some of this film's extensive nudity was cut, but it's still R-rated. 83m. DIR: Javier Aguirre. CAST: Paul Naschy, Haydee Politoff. 1972

DRACULA'S LAST RITES (1980) ♥ The vampires here (none named Dracula) are the mortician, police chief, and doctor in a small town. Originally called *Last Rites*. Rated R. 88m. DIR: Domonic Paris. CAST: Patricia Lee Hammond, Gerald Fielding. 1980

DRACULA'S WIDOW ★★ The bloodsucking lord of Transylvania is dead, but his estranged wife doesn't believe it. She tracks down the last remaining descendant of Jonathan Harker, who assures her of her spouse's demise. She then goes on a rampage, slaughtering a satanic vampire cult in hopes of finding Dracula's remains. Rated R for violence and nudity. 86m. DIR: Christopher Coppola. CAST: Josef Sommer, Sylvia Kristel, Lenny Von Dohlen, Stefan Schnabel. 1988

DRAGNET (1947) ★★1/2 This low-budget feature focuses on international jewelry thievery, with Henry Wilcoxon of Scotland Yard tracking crooks from London to New York, aided by airline hostess Mary Brian. Chock-full of action and skulduggery. B&W; 71m. DIR: Leslie Goodwins. CAST: Henry Wilcoxon, Mary Brian, Douglass Dumbrille, Virginia Dale. 1947

DRAGNET (1954) ★★★★ The feature-length (color!) version of the popular detective series with director-star Jack Webb as the no-nonsense Sgt. Joe Friday, and Ben Alexander as his original partner, Frank Smith. In the story, based as always on a true case, Friday and Smith are assigned to solve the murder of a mobster. All clues seem to lead to his former associates. 89m. DIR: Jack Webb. CAST: Jack Webb, Ben Alexander, Richard Boone, Ann Robinson, Dennis Weaver. 1954

DRAGNET (1987) ★★1/2 Dan Aykroyd's deliriously funny impersonation of Jack Webb can only carry this comedy so far. While Tom Hanks adds some moments of his own, the screenplay about political double-dealing tends to bog down. Rated PG-13 for profanity and violence. 107m. DIR: Tom Mankiewicz. CAST: Dan Aykroyd, Tom Hanks, Alexandra Paul, Harry Morgan, Christopher Plummer, Dabney Coleman, Elizabeth Ashley, Jack O'Halloran, Kathleen Freeman. 1987 DVD

DRAGON CHOW ★★★ Humorous and touching film about a Pakistani man living in West Germany. He lands a job in a mediocre Chinese restaurant where he strikes up a friendship with an Oriental waiter. Good slice-of-life character study. In German, Urdu, and Mandarin with English subtitles. Not rat-

ed. B&W; 75m. DIR: Jan Schuttes. CAST: Bhaskar, Ric Young. 1987

DRAGON KNIGHT ★★ Based on a popular Japanese video game, the film doesn't achieve much beyond the usual titillation. The animation is fair, but the story of a mischievous swordsman rescuing a castleful of helpless women is doomed from the start. In Japanese with English subtitles. Not rated; contains nudity, sexual situations and violence. 40m. DIR: Jun Fukuda. 1991

DRAGON SEED ★★1/2 This study of a Chinese town torn asunder by Japanese occupation is taken from the novel by Nobel Prize winner Pearl S. Buck. It's occasionally gripping but in general too long. B&W; 145m. DIR: Jack Conway, Harold S. Bucquet. CAST: Katharine Hepburn, Walter Huston, Turhan Bey, Hurd Hatfield. 1944

DRAGON: THE BRUCE LEE STORY ★★★★ The life of martial arts superstar Bruce Lee is given first-class treatment, in this mixture of fact and fantasy. The fight scenes are spectacular, and the acting of Jason Scott Lee and Lauren Holly is excellent. Look for Van Williams, Lee's costar in the *Green Hornet* series, in a brief bit as the director of that TV show. Rated PG-13 for violence, profanity, nudity, and simulated sex. 120m. DIR: Rob Cohen. CAST: Jason Scott Lee, Lauren Holly, Michael Learned, Nancy Kwan, Robert Wagner. 1993 DVD

DRAGONHEART ★★★★ In tenth-century England, swordsman Dennis Quaid vows to slay all dragons when his young charge, a prince and future king, turns to evil after his life is saved by dragon magic. A marvelously entertaining film filled with surprises, this is one sword-and-sorcery epic that won't disappoint fans of the genre or casual viewers. Sean Connery supplies the voice of Draco, "the last of the dragons." Rated PG-13 for violence. 106m. DIR: Rob Cohen. CAST: Dennis Quaid, Sean Connery, Dina Meyer, Julie Christie, David Thewlis, Pete Postlethwaite. 1996 DVD

DRAGONS FOREVER ★★★1/2 A lawyer is persuaded to work against chemical plant owners who want to take over a site used by local fishermen. Amazing martial arts highlight this exciting comedy featuring Hong Kong's talented director-actor Jackie Chan. In Cantonese with English subtitles. Not rated; contains violence. 88m. DIR: Sammo Hung. CAST: Jackie Chan. 1986

DRAGONSLAYER ★★1/2 Peter MacNicol plays a sorcerer's apprentice who, to save a damsel in distress, must face a fearsome fire-breathing dragon. While the special effects are spectacular, the rest of the film doesn't quite live up to them. It's slow, and often too corny for older viewers. Rated PG for violence. 110m. DIR: Matthew Robbins. CAST: Peter MacNicol, Caitlin Clarke, Ralph Richardson. 1981

DRAGONWORLD ★★1/2 A touch of whimsy and a sense of fun make this modern-day fairy tale excellent for children. The target audience will forgive the cheesy special effects and poor production values, and instead concentrate on the tale of a young man who stumbles across a real dragon in Scotland. When finances become scarce, he's forced to sell the dragon to an evil promoter. It's a fairy tale, so you know it has a happy ending. Rated PG. 84m. DIR: Ted Nicolaou. CAST: Sam MacKenzie, Brittney Powell, John Calvin, Lila Kaye, Courtland Mead, Andrew Keir. 1994

DRAUGHTMAN'S CONTRACT, THE ★★★1/2 Set in 1964 in the English countryside, this stylish British production is about a rich lady (Janet Suzman) who hires an artist to make detailed drawings of her house. Then strange things begin to happen—a murder not being the least. Rated R for nudity, profanity, and violence. 103m. DIR: Peter Greenaway. CAST: Anthony Higgins, Janet Suzman. 1982 DVD

DRAW ★★1/2 Kirk Douglas and James Coburn play outlaw and lawman respectively. Both appear on a collision course for a gunfight but, alas, what we are treated to is a trick ending. Lots of missed chances in this one. Made for HBO cable television. 98m. DIR: Steven H. Stern. CAST: James Coburn, Kirk Douglas. 1984

DREAM A LITTLE DREAM ★★ An obnoxious teen has the hots for Miss Unattainable (Meredith Salenger). When the two get caught up in Jason Robards Jr.'s dream, he gets his chance to be with her. Mediocre. Rated PG-13 for language. 115m. DIR: Marc Rocco. CAST: Jason Robards Jr., Corey Feldman, Corey Haim, Meredith Salenger, Piper Laurie. 1989

DREAM A LITTLE DREAM 2 💔 Like the first one really deserved a sequel? This one involves spies, special glasses, and the two Coreys! Rated PG-13 for language and adult situations. 91m. DIR: James Lemmo. CAST: Corey Haim, Corey Feldman, Robyn Lively, Stacie Randall. 1994

DREAM DATE ★★1/2 Single father Clifton Davis remembers what he was like when he started dating, and doesn't like it when his daughter is ready for her first date. Made-for-TV farce enlivened by an effective cast. Not rated. 96m. DIR: Anson Williams. CAST: Clifton Davis, Tempestt Bledsoe, Kadeem Hardison, Anne-Marie Johnson, Richard Moll, Pauly Shore. 1989

DREAM FOR CHRISTMAS, A ★★ Overwhelmed by a soundtrack far too dramatic for its simple settings, this tale of a black pastor and his family who move to California to start a congregation is full-fledged Americana. A very basic production that parallels the television hit, The Waltons. And it came from the very same creator: Earl Hamner. 100m. DIR: Ralph Senensky. CAST: George Spell, Hari Rhodes, Beah Richards. 1973

•DREAM HOUSE ★★1/2 Silly sci-fi story in which a futuristic, computerized house decides that its occupants are detrimental to its safety requirements. Rated R for profanity. 90m. DIR: Graeme Campbell. CAST: Timothy Busfield, Lisa Jakub, Jennifer Dale, Cameron Graham. 1998

DREAM LOVER (1986) 💔 A struggling musician suffers bloodcurdling nightmares. Rated R for violence. 104m. DIR: Alan J. Pakula. CAST: Kristy McNichol, Ben Masters, Paul Shenar, Justin Deas, John McMartin, Gayle Hunnicutt. 1986

DREAM LOVER (1994) ★★1/2 Rebounding from a divorce, Ray (James Spader) marries Lena (Madchen Amick), who seems to be the woman of his dreams. Then he finds out that her name isn't really Lena—and that's just the beginning. This psychological thriller is rather coldly calculated, but slickly

made and unpredictable—it will certainly hold your interest, though you may hate yourself in the morning. Rated R for profanity and nudity. 103m. DIR: Nicholas Kazan. CAST: James Spader, Madchen Amick, Bess Armstrong, Fredric Lehne, Larry Miller, Clyde Kusatsu. 1994

DREAM MACHINE 💔 Macho male teen fantasy has Corey Haim securing the automobile of his dreams by being in the right place at the right time. This comedy starts to run on empty long before it reaches the finishing line. Rated PG. 85m. DIR: Lyman Dayton. CAST: Corey Haim, Evan Richards, Susan Seaforth Hayes, Jeremy Slate. 1990

DREAM MAN 💔 Patsy Kensit plays a cop with psychic powers who can't tell if the man she loves killed his wife. Go figure. Rated R for nudity, violence, and language. 94m. DIR: René Bonniere. CAST: Patsy Kensit, Bruce Greenwood, Andrew McCarthy, Jim Byrnes, Denise Crosby. 1994

DREAM OF KINGS, A ★★★★ Anthony Quinn turns in an unforgettable performance in this powerful and touching drama set in Chicago's Greek community. He plays an earthy, proud father determined to raise enough money to flee from America to Greece with his ailing young son. A moving character study. Not rated. 111m. DIR: Daniel Mann. CAST: Anthony Quinn, Irene Papas, Inger Stevens, Sam Levene, Val Avery. 1969

DREAM OF PASSION, A ★★★1/2 Melina Mercouri plays a Greek actress who is preparing to play Medea. As a publicity stunt, she goes to a prison to meet a real-life Medea. Ellen Burstyn is brilliant as the American prisoner who has killed her three children in order to take revenge on her husband. Rated R. 106m. DIR: Jules Dassin. CAST: Melina Mercouri, Ellen Burstyn, Andreas Voutsinas, Despo Diamantidou. 1978

DREAM STREET ★★ Good struggles with evil in this sentimental morality tale of London's infamous Limehouse slum. Two brothers, in love with the same girl, vie for her attentions. Good eventually wins. Silent. B&W; 138m. DIR: D. W. Griffith. CAST: Carol Dempster, Charles Emmett Mack, Ralph Graves, Tyrone Power Sr., Morgan Wallace. 1921

DREAM TEAM, THE ★★★1/2 When a psychiatrist (Dennis Boutsikaris) takes four mental patients on a field trip to Yankee Stadium, he is unexpectedly waylaid and his quartet of lovable loonies is let loose in the Big Apple. This gem of a comedy features terrific ensemble performances. It'll steal your heart—guaranteed. Rated PG for profanity and violence. 113m. DIR: Howard Zieff. CAST: Michael Keaton, Christopher Lloyd, Peter Boyle, Stephen Furst, Lorraine Bracco, Dennis Boutsikaris. 1989

DREAM TO BELIEVE ★★★ If you like Flashdance, Rocky, and the World Gymnastics Competition, you'll love this Cinderella story. It's the soap drama of a teenage girl who, against physical odds, turns herself into an accomplished gymnast. No rating. 96m. DIR: Paul Lynch. CAST: Olivia D'Abo, Rita Tushingham, Keanu Reeves. 1985

DREAM WITH THE FISHES ★★★1/2 An odd, rocky friendship develops between a suicidal voyeur (David Arquette) and the dying neighbor he's been spying on (Brad Hunt); each is intrigued by the other, and they agree to spend their last few days together. Offbeat and appealing, this eccentric comedy keeps surprising you just as you think you've got it all figured out. Not rated; contains profanity and mature themes. 97m. DIR: Finn Taylor. CAST: Finn Arquette, Brad Hunt, Kathryn Erbe, Cathy Moriarty. 1997

DREAMANIAC 🎬 A heavy-metal composer teams up with a succubus to kill teens in this tired picture that doesn't break any new ground. Not rated; contains gore, violence, profanity, and nudity. 82m. DIR: David DeCoteau. CAST: Thomas Bern, Kim McKamy, Sylvia Summers. 1986

DREAMCHILD ★★★★ Some of those familiar with *Alice's Adventures in Wonderland* may be surprised to learn that there was a real Alice. Lewis Carroll first told his fanciful stories to 10-year-old Alice Liddel on a summer boat ride on July 1, 1862. In 1932, Alice went to New York City to participate in a Columbia University tribute to Carroll. These facts provide the basis for this rich and thought-provoking film. Rated PG. 94m. DIR: Gavin Millar. CAST: Coral Browne, Peter Gallagher, Ian Holm, Jane Asher, Nicola Cowper. 1986

DREAMER ★★ Small-towner Tim Matheson pursues his dream: to become a champion bowler. As exciting as a film about bowling can be. (Which is to say, not very.) Rated PG. 86m. DIR: Noel Nosseck. CAST: Tim Matheson, Susan Blakely, Jack Warden. 1979

•**DREAMING OF JOSEPH LEES** ★★1/2 Eva, a young woman in Somerset, England, falls in love with her second cousin, Joseph Lees. Afraid to commit to him, Eva marries another and tries to wipe Lees from her memory. When Lees and Eva are reunited at a family wedding, Eva finds herself trapped in a loveless marriage to a man who will do anything to keep her. The film fails to explore the depth of the love triangle that threatens Eva's happiness. Nice 1950s period detail and handsome performances, but not much else. Rated R for adult situations, language, and nudity. 92m. DIR: Eric Styles. CAST: Samantha Morton, Lee Ross, Rupert Graves. 1999

DREAMING OUT LOUD ★★1/2 Chester Lauck and Norris Goff, better known as radio's Lum and Abner, fare well in this first of a film series based on their misadventures at the Jot-em Down Store in Pine Ridge, Arkansas. The cracker-barrel philosophers quietly, and with humor, exert a variety of influences on their fellow citizens. It's corn, but clean corn. B&W; 65m. DIR: Harold Young. CAST: Chester Lauck, Norris Goff, Frances Langford, Robert Wilcox, Irving Bacon, Frank Craven, Phil Harris. 1940

DREAMLIFE OF ANGELS, THE ★★★1/2 Director Erick Zonca examines the unconventional friendship that develops between two young women: a friendly, cheerful drifter and a beautiful blonde with hidden depths of anger and self-loathing. The film is low-key but fascinating, revealing subtle psychological impulses that first draw the two women together, then drive them apart in anger and confusion. In French with English subtitles. Rated R for nudity and sexual scenes. 113m. DIR: Erick Zonca. CAST:

Elodie Bouchez, Natacha Regnier, Gregoire Colin, Jo Prestia, Patrick Mercado. 1998 DVD

DREAMS ★★1/2 Fascinating but confusing drama about a photo agency head and her top model. In Swedish with English subtitles. B&W; 86m. DIR: Ingmar Bergman. CAST: Eva Dahlbeck, Harriet Andersson, Gunnar Björnstrand, Ulf Palme. 1955

DREAMS COME TRUE 🎬 A restless young factory worker meets a young woman with whom he shares an unusual power, the ability to control and live in their dreams. Rated R. 95m. DIR: Max Kalmanowicz. CAST: Michael Sanville, Stephanie Shuford. 1984

DREAMS LOST, DREAMS FOUND ★★1/2 Decent Harlequin Romance movie takes place in scenic Scotland. Kathleen Quinlan stars as a widow who buys a cursed castle. She meets a handsome lord but can't decide if he's worthy of her love. Soap opera-ish but location shots are a plus. Not rated; contains sexual situations. 102m. DIR: Willi Patterson. CAST: Kathleen Quinlan, David Robb, Colette O'Neil, Charles Gray, Betsy Brantley. 1987

DREAMSCAPE ★★★★ If you can go along with its intriguing but farfetched premise—that trained psychics can enter other people's nightmares and put an end to them—this film will reward you with topflight special effects, thrills, chills, and surprises. Rated PG-13 for suggested sex, violence, and profanity. 99m. DIR: Joseph Ruben. CAST: Dennis Quaid, Max von Sydow, Christopher Plummer, Eddie Albert, Kate Capshaw. 1984 DVD

DRESS GRAY ★★★★★ Extremely well-made TV miniseries about the closing of ranks at a military academy after an unpopular plebe is murdered. Alec Baldwin is the beleaguered cadet who refuses to be the scapegoat or let the investigation die. Compelling Gore Vidal script is enhanced by a stellar cast. Not rated; contains mild profanity. 192m. DIR: Glenn Jordan. CAST: Alec Baldwin, Hal Holbrook, Eddie Albert, Lloyd Bridges, Susan Hess. 1986

DRESSED TO KILL (1941) ★★1/2 Private eye Michael Shayne attempts to solve a confusing multiple murder that centers around an acting troupe and a very old grudge. Fun, tongue-in-cheek mystery involves a subplot about Shayne's doomed efforts to marry a burlesque queen and boasts a very clever murder plot and device. B&W; 75m. DIR: Eugene Forde. CAST: Lloyd Nolan, Mary Beth Hughes, Sheila Ryan, William Demarest, Ben Carter, Erwin Kaiser, Henry Daniell, Mantan Moreland. 1941

DRESSED TO KILL (1946) ★★★ Final entry in Universal's popular Rathbone/Bruce Sherlock Holmes series. This one involves counterfeiting, specifically a Bank of England plate hidden in one of three music boxes. After filming was completed, Rathbone—fearing typecasting—had had enough; his concerns clearly were genuine, as he did not work again for nearly nine years. Not rated—suitable for family viewing. B&W; 72m. DIR: Roy William Neill. CAST: Basil Rathbone, Nigel Bruce, Patricia Morison, Edmund Breon, Frederic Worlock, Harry Cording. 1946 DVD

DRESSED TO KILL (1980) ★★★1/2 Director Brian De Palma again borrows heavily from Alfred Hitchcock in this story of sexual frustration, madness, and murder set in New York City. Angie Dickinson plays a sexually active housewife whose affairs lead to an unexpected conclusion. Rated R for violence, strong language, nudity, and simulated sex. 105m. DIR: Brian De Palma. CAST: Michael Caine, Angie Dickinson, Nancy Allen, Keith Gordon. 1980

DRESSER, THE ★★★★★ Peter Yates directed this superb screen treatment of Ronald Harwood's play about an eccentric stage actor (Albert Finney) in wartime England and the loyal valet (Tom Courtenay) who cares for him, sharing his triumphs and tragedies. Rated PG for language. 118m. DIR: Peter Yates. CAST: Albert Finney, Tom Courtenay, Edward Fox, Zena Walker. 1983

DRESSMAKER, THE ★★★1/2 In London during World War II, a teenage girl lives with two maiden aunts, one who tries to insulate her and one who encourages her to enjoy herself. Worth seeing for the performances of three superb actresses (including Jane Horrocks in her debut), though the ending is a bit perfunctory. Not rated, with sexual discussions that put this above the heads of young children. 90m. DIR: Jim O'Brien. CAST: Joan Plowright, Billie Whitelaw, Jane Horrocks, Tim Ransom. 1988

DRIFTER, THE ★★ A successful businesswoman picks up a hitchhiker and they have a one-night stand. Afterward he refuses to leave her alone and her life is in jeopardy. Perhaps with a better script this could have been a reverse Fatal Attraction. Rated R for violence, nudity, and profanity. 89m. DIR: Larry Brand. CAST: Kim Delaney, Timothy Bottoms, Miles O'Keeffe. 1988

DRIFTIN' KID ★★1/2 It seems every B-Western star was required to make at least one oater wherein he played a dual role. Tom Keene does it here—but it's all been done better elsewhere. Outlaws after government grazing contracts. B&W; 57m. DIR: Robert Emmett Tansey. CAST: Tom Keene, Betty Miles, Frank Yaconelli, Stanley Price. 1941

DRIFTING WEEDS ★★★★★ The leader of a troupe of traveling actors visits an old lover and his illegitimate son when the actors pass through a distant village. An exquisitely simple but moving drama from the master Japanese director Yasujiro Ozu. Also known as Floating Weeds. In Japanese with English subtitles. 119m. DIR: Yasujiro Ozu. CAST: Ganjiro Nakamura, Machiko Kyo. 1959

DRILLER KILLER, THE 🎬 A maniac named Reno falls for his roommate. When rejected by her, he goes crazy. Not rated; contains violence, gore, and profanity. 84m. DIR: Abel Ferrara. CAST: Carolyn Mare, Jimmy Laine. 1979 DVD

DRIVE-IN ★★★ Enjoyable film about a day in the life of a small Texas town. At dusk all the citizens head off for the local drive-in theater. With as many as three plots developing, Drive-In is like a Southern American Graffiti. Rated PG. 96m. DIR: Rod Amateau. CAST: Lisa Lemole, Glen Morshower, Gary Cavagnaro, Trey Wilson. 1976

DRIVE-IN MASSACRE ★★1/2 If you're in the mood for a slasher movie, you could do worse than this ultralow-budget gorefest. The title says it all: Psycho killer bumps off patrons at a drive-in movie, but there are some bits that will please anyone who has ever spent summer nights at an outdoor cinema. Rated R for gore and nudity. 78m. DIR: Stuart Segall. CAST: Jake Barnes, Adam Lawrence. 1976

DRIVE LIKE LIGHTNING ★★★ A guilt-ridden ex-daredevil is hired to drive a stunt car to Los Angeles. At first this looks like just another bad cross-country truck driving movie, but don't let first impressions fool you. A nice surprise. Not rated; made for cable. 96m. DIR: Bradford May. CAST: Steven Bauer, Cynthia Gibb, William Russ, Paul Koslo. 1991

•DRIVE ME CRAZY ★★★1/2 This teen Pygmalion is a cut above most high-school caste comedies. A girl social climber gets dumped by a popular jock just before the big dance. She then dates and initiates the makeover of a grungy boy neighbor who has been dumped by his punkette girlfriend. Romance and several surprises blossom in a solidly written film that develops characters rather than just caricatures. Rated PG-13 for language and teen drug and alcohol use. 94m. DIR: John Schultz. CAST: Melissa Joan Hart, Adrien Grenier, Ali Larter, Gabriel Carpenter. 1999 DVD

DRIVER, THE ★★★★ High-energy crime drama focuses on a professional getaway driver (Ryan O'Neal) and his police pursuer (Bruce Dern). Walter Hill's breakneck pacing and spectacular chase scenes make up for the lack of plot or character development. It's an action movie pure and simple. Rated PG for violence and profanity. 90m. DIR: Walter Hill. CAST: Ryan O'Neal, Bruce Dern, Isabelle Adjani, Ronee Blakley, Matt Clark. 1978

DRIVER'S SEAT, THE ★★ Tedious Italian-made drama featuring Elizabeth Taylor in one of her less memorable performances as a psychotic woman with a death wish. Rated PG. 101m. DIR: Giuseppe Patroni Griffi. CAST: Elizabeth Taylor, Ian Bannen, Mona Washbourne, Andy Warhol. 1973

DRIVING ME CRAZY ★★★1/2 Charming comedy stars German actor Thomas Gottschalk as the inventor of a car that runs on turnips. He discovers capitalism and Los Angeles with the help of Billy Dee Williams. Predictable, but fun in a low-key way. Rated PG-13. 88m. DIR: Jon Turteltaub. CAST: Billy Dee Williams, Thomas Gottschalk, Dom DeLuise, Michelle Johnson, George Kennedy. 1991

DRIVING MISS DAISY ★★★★★ Alfred Uhry's stage play is brought to stunning, emotionally satisfying life by director Bruce Beresford and his superb cast. The story concerns the twenty-five-year relationship of the feisty Miss Daisy (Jessica Tandy) and a wise, wily chauffeur, Hoke (Morgan Freeman). Dan Aykroyd is remarkably effective as Daisy's doting son. Rated PG for profanity. 99m. DIR: Bruce Beresford. CAST: Morgan Freeman, Jessica Tandy, Dan Aykroyd, Patti LuPone, Esther Rolle. 1989 DVD

DROP DEAD FRED ★★1/2 A young woman has a childhood imaginary friend who reappears to help her through a crisis. A wild romp with stunning visual effects that some viewers may find offensive. Rated PG-13 for profanity and brief nudity. 98m. DIR: Ate De Jong. CAST: Phoebe Cates, Rik Mayall, Marsha Mason, Tim Matheson, Carrie Fisher, Ron Eldard. 1991

DROP DEAD GORGEOUS (1991) 🎬 Sally Kellerman's career remains in the toilet with this disaster. Made for cable. 88m. DIR: Paul Lynch. CAST: Jennifer

Rubin, Peter Outerbridge, Stephen Shellen, Sally Kellerman, Michael Ironside. 1991

●DROP DEAD GORGEOUS (1999) ★★1/2 Spoofed documentary of a teen pageant in "small mindedville" Minnesota pits sweet, economically challenged Kirsten Dunst against spoiled brat Denise Richards. The "documentary" crew captures innumerable "let's offend everybody" comments before expanding its scope to include the mysterious accidents of some of the contestants. Only the very thick-skinned will find this amusing. Rated PG-13 for religious and ethnic jokes and profanity. 95m. DIR: Michael Patrick. CAST: Kirsten Dunst, Denise Richards, Kirstie Alley, Ellen Barkin. 1999 DVD

DROP SQUAD, THE ★★★ Intriguing idea that needed a more sophisticated execution. DROP is an acronym for Deprogramming and Restoration of Pride. Eriq La Salle, an African-American advertising exec selling questionable products to a black market, finds himself kidnapped and brutally reprogrammed. Too many characters and a subplot involving dissension within the squad blur the lines and divert the dramatic tension. Rated R for profanity and violence. 88m. DIR: David C. Johnson. CAST: Eriq La Salle, Vondie Curtis-Hall, Ving Rhames, Vanessa L. Williams, Spike Lee, Michael Ralph. 1994 DVD

DROP ZONE ★★★1/2 When two brothers are assigned by their superiors at U.S. marshal headquarters to guard an important witness, they are caught off guard by a midair kidnapping of their charge—with deadly consequences. The government writes the witness off as dead and blame the brothers. Plenty of action and stunts, and a commanding performance by Wesley Snipes make this one a winner. Rated R for violence and profanity. 101m. DIR: John Badham. CAST: Wesley Snipes, Gary Busey, Yancy Butler, Michael Jeter, Malcolm Jamal-Warner, Corin Nemec, Kyle Secor, Luca Bercovici. 1994 DVD

DROWNING BY NUMBERS ★★ Director Peter Greenaway brings us another exercise in excess and esoteric glibness. Three women, all friends and all three with the same first name, exact revenge on their sadistic husbands by drowning them. Rated R for violence, profanity, and nudity. 121m. DIR: Peter Greenaway. CAST: Joan Plowright, Juliet Stevenson, Joely Richardson. 1988

●DROWNING MONA ★★★1/2 This dark, tasteless, and cynical comedy is funny as hell, although the suggestively violent segments may repel mainstream viewers. It's a warped murder mystery involving a roster of nitwit suspects so hilariously feeble-minded that they can't *help* but look guilty ... particularly since everybody in the entire hamlet of Verplanck, New York, loathed the victim. Peter Steinfeld aptly calls his script a "white-trash *Murder on the Orient Express*." Rated PG-13 for crude humor, violence, and a bit of eccentric sexual behavior. 95m. DIR: Nick Gomez. CAST: Danny DeVito, Bette Midler, Neve Campbell, Jamie Lee Curtis, Casey Affleck, William Fichtner, Marcus Thomas, Peter Dobson. 2000

DROWNING POOL, THE ★★1/2 Disappointing follow-up to *Harper*, with Paul Newman re-creating the title role. Director Stuart Rosenberg doesn't come up with anything fresh in this stale entry into the detective genre. Rated PG—violence. 108m. DIR: Stuart Rosenberg. CAST: Paul Newman, Joanne Woodward, Anthony Franciosa, Richard Jaeckel, Murray Hamilton, Melanie Griffith, Gail Strickland, Linda Haynes. 1976

DRUGSTORE COWBOY ★★★1/2 A gritty, often shocking examination of life on the edge, this superb character study features Matt Dillon in a terrific performance as the leader of a gang of drug users in the 1960s. Dillon and his cohorts keep their habits fed by robbing drugstores until their luck runs out. Rated R for profanity and violence. 100m. DIR: Gus Van Sant. CAST: Matt Dillon, Kelly Lynch, James Remar, William S. Burroughs, James LeGros, Heather Graham. 1989 DVD

DRUM ♥ Sweaty, sexed-up continuation of *Mandingo*, Kyle Onstott's lurid tale of plantation life in the pre–Civil War South. 110m. DIR: Steve Carver. CAST: Ken Norton, Warren Oates, Pam Grier, John Colicos, Yaphet Kotto. 1976

DRUM BEAT ★★1/2 Indian fighter Alan Ladd is detailed to ensure peace with marauding Modocs on the California-Oregon border in 1869. His chief adversary, in beads and buckskins, is Charles Bronson. As usual, white man speaks with forked tongue, but everything ends well. 111m. DIR: Delmer Daves. CAST: Alan Ladd, Audrey Dalton, Marisa Pavan, Robert Keith, Anthony Caruso, Warner Anderson, Elisha Cook Jr., Charles Bronson. 1954

DRUM TAPS ★★★ Ken Maynard and the Boy Scouts drive land grabbers from the range. Only time Kermit Maynard (who had his own Western series) ever appears in one of his brother's Westerns. B&W; 61m. DIR: J. P. McGowan. CAST: Ken Maynard, Frank Coghlan Jr., Kermit Maynard. 1933

DRUMS ★★★1/2 Stiff-upper-lip British Empire epic starts slow but builds to an exciting climax as soldiers of the queen aid young Prince Sabu in his struggle against usurping uncle Raymond Massey. 99m. DIR: Zoltán Korda. CAST: Sabu, Raymond Massey, Valerie Hobson, Roger Livesey, David Tree. 1938

DRUMS ALONG THE MOHAWK ★★★★ Claudette Colbert and Henry Fonda are among a group of sturdy settlers of upstate New York during the Revolutionary War. Despite the episodic nature of its story, this emerges as another richly detailed film from director John Ford. Beautifully photographed in color, the work benefits from vibrant supporting performances by Edna May Oliver, Jessie Ralph, John Carradine, and Ward Bond. 103m. DIR: John Ford. CAST: Claudette Colbert, Henry Fonda, Edna May Oliver, John Carradine, Jessie Ralph, Robert Lowery, Ward Bond. 1939

DRUMS IN THE DEEP SOUTH ★★1/2 Two friends, both in love with the same girl, find themselves on opposite sides in the Civil War. 87m. DIR: William Cameron Menzies. CAST: James Craig, Guy Madison, Barbara Payton, Craig Stevens. 1951

DRUMS OF FU MANCHU ★★★1/2 This exciting serial presents the definitive Fu Manchu with smooth, sinister Henry Brandon splendidly cast as the greatest of all Far Eastern menaces. Sir Dennis Nayland Smith and his associates tackle the deadly doctor to p him from finding the scepter of the great nghis Khan. B&W; 15 chapters. **DIR:** William Witt-, John English. **CAST:** Henry Brandon, Robert Kel-, Gloria Franklin, Olaf Hytten, Tom Chatterton, Lua-Walters, George Cleveland, Dwight Frye. **1940**

UMS OF JEOPARDY ★★1/2 Russian scientist Karlov blames his daughter's death on the royal ily and vows revenge. Each of Karlov's intended tims receives a piece of the jewels known as the ums of Jeopardy before dying. There are plenty of ases and wild fights, good laboratory scenes, and a rpet-chewing performance by Warner Oland as a lshevik Dr. Fu Manchu. B&W; 105m. **DIR:** George Seitz. **CAST:** Warner Oland, June Collyer, Lloyd ghes, Mischa Auer, Clara Blandick. **1931**

RUNKEN ANGEL ★★★★ Master director Akira rosawa shows an early interest in good ys and bad guys. Toshiro Mifune is a petty gangster o learns from an idealistic slum doctor (Takashi imura) that he is dying of tuberculosis. In Japan-e with English subtitles. B&W; 102m. **DIR:** Akira rosawa. **CAST:** Toshiro Mifune, Takashi Shimura. 49

RUNKS ★★★ Gary Lennon's stageplay makes an easy transition to film, mostly because director eter Cohn does little beyond pointing his camera d shooting. Members of Alcoholics Anonymous tell eir individual stories; some are interesting, but ost go nowhere. Richard Lewis holds our attention the one fully fleshed character. Interesting idea, ful execution. Rated R for profanity and nudity.)m. **DIR:** Peter Cohn. **CAST:** Richard Lewis, Faye Dun-way, Spalding Gray, Lisa Gay Hamilton, George Mar-, Amanda Plummer, Parker Posey, Howard Rollins , Dianne Wiest. **1997 DVD**

RY CLEANING ★★★ A middle-class married uple takes in a young bisexual drifter who disrupts eir blandly comfortable existence. Director Anne ontaine keeps the domestic drama low-key and nvincing, avoiding melodrama and soap-opera ex-ess. Character relationships are ambiguous and uzzling, with dangerous undercurrents, and the esolution is both unexpected and inevitable. In ench with English subtitles. Not rated; contains ature themes and sexual scenes. 97m. **DIR:** Anne ontaine. **CAST:** Miou-Miou, Charles Berling, Stanislas erhar, Mathilde Seigner. **1997 DVD**

RY WHITE SEASON, A ★★★★ A white school-eacher in South Africa slowly becomes aware of what apartheid means to black people. Based on the ovel by André Brink, this adaptation occasionally ecomes melodramatic. Overall, however, this pow-rful story riveting. Rated R for violence and profani-y. 106m. **DIR:** Euzhan Palcy. **CAST:** Donald Sutherland, anet Suzman, Jurgen Prochnow, Zakes Mokae, Susan arandon, Marlon Brando. **1989**

RYING UP THE STREETS ♥ Canadian exposé of rugs and prostitution. Not rated. 90m. **DIR:** Robin pry. **CAST:** Sarah Torgov, Don Francks, Len Cariou, alvin Butler. **1984**

DU BARRY WAS A LADY ★★ A slow-moving adap-ation of a popular stage hit minus most of the music hat made it popular. Set in the court of Louis XIV, his musical romp gives Red Skelton a chance to mug

and Gene Kelly a chance to dance. 101m. **DIR:** Roy Del Ruth. **CAST:** Red Skelton, Lucille Ball, Gene Kelly, Zero Mostel, Virginia O'Brien, Donald Meek, Louise Beavers, Tommy Dorsey. **1943**

DU-BEAT-E-O ★★ More of a pastiche than a feature movie, *du-BEAT-e-o* has the air of something thrown together by a bunch of guys goofing around in a film-editing room. The skeleton plot has underground L.A. filmmaker Dubeateo (Ray Sharkey) and his edi-tor (Derf Scratch of the punk band Fear) trying to turn some scattered footage of rocker Joan Jett into a movie. Not rated, there is nudity and profanity. 84m. **DIR:** Alan Sacks. **CAST:** Ray Sharkey, Derf Scratch. **1984**

DUCHESS AND THE DIRTWATER FOX, THE ♥ This Western-comedy romp never clicks. Rated PG. 103m. **DIR:** Melvin Frank. **CAST:** George Segal, Goldie Hawn, Conrad Janis, Thayer David. **1976**

DUCHESS OF IDAHO ★★1/2 Esther Williams at-tempts to have businessman John Lund become in-terested in her friend, lovesick Paula Raymond, only leading to Esther being pursued by him and a band-leader, Van Johnson. A badly arranged appearance by 40-year-old Eleanor Powell—her swan song. 99m. **DIR:** Robert Z. Leonard. **CAST:** Esther Williams, Van Johnson, John Lund, Paula Raymond, Lena Horne, Eleanor Powell. **1950**

DUCK SOUP ★★★★★ Groucho, Harpo, Chico, and Zeppo in their best film: an antiestablishment come-dy that failed miserably at the box office at the time of its release. Today, this Leo McCarey–directed romp has achieved its proper reputation as the quin-tessential Marx Brothers classic. B&W; 70m. **DIR:** Leo McCarey. **CAST:** The Marx Brothers, Margaret Du-mont, Louis Calhern, Raquel Torres, Edgar Kennedy. **1933 DVD**

DUCKTALES: THE MOVIE—TREASURE OF THE LOST LAMP ★★★ Adapted from a Disney cartoon series for television, this is a *Raiders of the Lost Ark*–style animated adventure in which Uncle Scrooge McDuck and his three great-nephews set out after lost treasure. In the style of the classic Don-ald Duck comic books by Carl Barks. Rated G. 106m. **DIR:** Bob Hathcock. **1990**

DUDE RANGER ★★★★ In this sturdy, well-played, and skillfully directed adaptation of the Zane Grey story, George O'Brien is a city boy who heads west to claim his inheritance: a ranch he fully intends to sell the first chance he gets. As it turns out, rustlers have been depleting his stock, and O'Brien stays on to find the culprits. B&W; 65m. **DIR:** Eddie Cline. **CAST:** George O'Brien, Irene Hervey. **1934**

DUDES ★★★ Billed as the first punk-rock Western, this film starts off well as a comedy about three New York City rockers (Jon Cryer, Daniel Roebuck and Flea) who decide to go to California in hopes of find-ing a better life. After the first goofy 20 minutes, *Dudes* abruptly turns violent. Rated R for violence and profanity. 90m. **DIR:** Penelope Spheeris. **CAST:** Jon Cryer, Catherine Mary Stewart, Daniel Roebuck, Flea, Lee Ving. **1988**

•DUDLEY DO-RIGHT ★★★ This film is silly and un-relentingly corny, but it's also rather fun. It will res-onate best with older viewers who fondly remember the Jay Ward cartoon series on which it's based; writer-director Hugh Wilson has retained all the key elements, from the raised-eyebrow double takes to the melodramatically deadpan announcer (Corey Burton) who provides ironic commentary about all on-screen events. Brendan Fraser is properly stalwart and virtuous as the square-shouldered Canadian Mountie who genuinely deserves to wear a medal that reads "pretty good conduct," and Alfred Molina is ideal as the black-garbed, black-mustached Snidely Whiplash, the very epitome of comic villainy. The two spar over Sarah Jessica Parker's fair and true Nell Fenwick, in an amusing story line that elevates Canadian values at the expense of boorish American behavior. Rated PG for comic violence and slightly suggestive sensuality. 76m. DIR: Hugh Wilson. CAST: Brendan Fraser, Sarah Jessica Parker, Alfred Molina, Eric Idle, Robert Prosky, Alex Rocco. 1999 DVD

DUEL ★★★★ Early Spielberg film was originally a 73-minute ABC made-for-TV movie, but this full-length version was released theatrically overseas. The story is a simple one: a mild-mannered businessman (Dennis Weaver) alone on a desolate stretch of highway suddenly finds himself the unwitting prey of the maniacal driver of a big, greasy oil tanker. 91m. DIR: Steven Spielberg. CAST: Dennis Weaver, Eddie Firestone. 1971

DUEL AT DIABLO ★★1/2 Overly complicated Western stars James Garner as a revenge-minded scout helping a cavalry troop transport guns and ammunition through Indian Territory. Subplots abound in this well-meant but unnecessarily dreary indictment of racism. The performances are good, however. 103m. DIR: Ralph Nelson. CAST: James Garner, Sidney Poitier, Bibi Andersson, Dennis Weaver, Bill Travers, John Hoyt. 1966

DUEL IN THE SUN ★★★ Sprawling, brawling Western has land baron Lionel Barrymore's sons, unbroken, short-fused Gregory Peck, and solid-citizen Joseph Cotten vying for the hand of hot-blooded, half-breed Jennifer Jones. Peck and Jones take a lusty love-hate relationship to the max in the steaming desert. A near epic with a great musical score. 130m. DIR: King Vidor. CAST: Jennifer Jones, Gregory Peck, Joseph Cotten, Lionel Barrymore, Walter Huston, Lillian Gish, Harry Carey. 1946 DVD

DUEL OF CHAMPIONS ❤ Alan Ladd is a weary centurion leader in ancient Rome fighting for the glory that once was. Forgettable. 105m. DIR: Ferdinando Baldi. CAST: Alan Ladd, Robert Keith, Franco Fabrizi. 1961

DUEL OF HEARTS ★★ Lush TV adaptation of Barbara Cartland's bestseller. A free-spirited woman falls for a handsome lord and takes a position as his mother's companion. Dim romantic adventure, but the cast rises to the occasion. 95m. DIR: John Hough. CAST: Alison Doody, Michael York, Geraldine Chaplin, Benedict Taylor, Richard Johnson. 1990

DUELLISTS, THE ★★★★ The Duellists traces a long and seemingly meaningless feud between two soldiers in the Napoleonic Wars. This fascinating study of honor among men is full of irony and heroism. Rated R. 101m. DIR: Ridley Scott. CAST: Keith Carradine, Harvey Keitel, Albert Finney, Edward Fe Cristina Raines, Robert Stephens, Tom Conti. 1977

DUET FOR ONE ★★★ As an English virtuoso viol ist with multiple sclerosis, Julie Andrews gives outstanding performance in this high-class tearje er. Alan Bates is her sympathetic but philanderi husband. Max von Sydow is the psychiatrist who a tempts to help her. And Rupert Everett plays her pr tégé who shuns the classical world for big-time sho biz. Rated R. 110m. DIR: Andrei Konchalovsky. CAS Julie Andrews, Alan Bates, Max von Sydow, Rupe Everett. 1987

DUMB AND DUMBER ★★★★ Jim Carrey and Je Daniels work extremely well together in this hila ous story of two dim bulbs who unwittingly becon involved in a high-stakes kidnapping scheme. It's a low humor—with plenty of time for the toilet—y you laugh in spite of yourself. Rated PG-13 for h morous violence, scatological humor, and nudi 106m. DIR: Peter Farrelly. CAST: Jim Carrey, Je Daniels, Lauren Holly, Teri Garr, Karen Duffy, Mi Starr, Charles Rocket, Victoria Rowell, Cam Neely, Fe ton Perry. 1994 DVD

DUMB WAITER, THE ★★ This TV adaptation Harold Pinter's absurdist drama will probably n appeal to general audiences. Two hit men (John Tr volta and Tom Conti) await their latest assignmen in a deserted restaurant's basement. 60m. DIF Robert Altman. CAST: John Travolta, Tom Conti. 198

DUMBO ★★★★ Disney's cartoon favorite abou the outcast circus elephant with the big ears is family classic. It has everything: personable animal a poignant story, and a happy ending. It is good fu and can still invoke a tear or two in the right places 64m. DIR: Ben Sharpsteen. 1941

DUNE ❤ The only good thing about the movie ver sion of Dune is it makes one want to read (or reread the book. Otherwise, it's a $47 million mess. Rate PG-13 for gore, suggested sex, and violence. 145m DIR: David Lynch. CAST: Sting, Kyle MacLachlan, Ma von Sydow, Jurgen Prochnow, Sean Young, Kennet McMillan, Richard Jordan, Dean Stockwell, Patric Stewart, José Ferrer, Brad Dourif, Francesca Annis 1984 DVD

DUNE WARRIORS ★★ Rip-off of The Magnificen Seven set in an apocalyptic future stars David Carra dine as the head honcho of a band of mercenaries Plenty of action to cover up the familiar plot. Rated for violence, profanity, and nudity. 77m. DIR: Cirio H Santiago. CAST: David Carradine, Richard Hill, Luke Askew, Jillian McWhirter. 1991

DUNERA BOYS, THE ★★★★ Bob Hoskins is sensa tional in this harrowing war drama about a group o Jewish refugees who are ironically suspected of be ing German informants by the British army. They are shipped to a prison camp in Australia on the HM! Dunera. A film of great intelligence and humanity Rated R for violence and profanity. 150m. DIR: Greg Snedon. CAST: Joe Spano, Bob Hoskins, Warren Mitchell. 1987

DUNGEONMASTER, THE ❤ It's corny, it's bad, it's simplistic. Rated PG-13 for mild violence. 73m. DIR: Rosemarie Turko, John Carl Buechler, Charles Band, id Allen, Steve Ford, Peter Manoogian, Ted Nic. ST: Jeffrey Byron, Richard Moll. 1985

NSTON CHECKS IN ★★★ Dunston is a small ngutan who has been trained to steal jewels from nk hotel rooms. The hairy bandit tires of his an master, befriends a mischievous teen at the r-star hotel they are plundering, and turns a huge mal ball into chaos. This dose of energetic silli- ss is given a big boost from its impressive cast. ed PG. 90m. DIR: Ken Kwapis. CAST: Jason Alexan- , Faye Dunaway, Eric Lloyd, Rupert Everett, Glenn adix, Paul Reubens. 1995

NWICH HORROR, THE ❤ Torpid horror-thriller de when folks didn't know that it's impossible to apt H. P. Lovecraft. Dean Stockwell foreshadowed s hammy role in *Dune* with this laughable portray- of a warlock. Rated PG for violence. 90m. DIR: niel Haller. CAST: Sandra Dee, Dean Stockwell, Sam fe, Ed Begley Sr., Talia Shire. 1970

PLICATES ★★★1/2 Surprisingly good made-for- ble movie. A hospital in upstate New York is really government research facility for altering criminal nds. Good acting by all—and a well-written script. m. DIR: Sandor Stern. CAST: Gregory Harrison, Kim eist, Cicely Tyson, Lane Smith, Bill Lucking, Kevin Carthy. 1992

JRANGO ★★★★ Based on Irish author John B. ane's autobiographical novel, this delightful Hall- ark Hall of Fame features Matt Keeslar as a head- ong cattle man who defies the local buyers. In or- r to get a fair price, he attempts a cattle drive. ong the way, he grows up, takes on the thugs sent thwart him, and matures in his feelings for a lovely ss. Unrated, contains violence. 92m. DIR: Brent ields. CAST: Matt Keeslar, Patrick Bergin, George earn, Nancy St. Alban, Brenda Fricker. 1999

UST ★★ A Bergmanesque tale of a lonely South rican farmer's daughter and her descent into mad- ss after she kills her abusive father. Jane Birkin es a commendable job as the bitter farm maid, but e film is very moody, with lots of mumbled lines d long still shots. Not rated; contains violence and ggested sex. 87m. DIR: Marion Hansel. CAST: Jane rkin, Trevor Howard. 1985

UST DEVIL ★★★ A South African devil arises om the desert to stalk hapless (and hopeless) vic- ms. Moody and gory, this great-looking horror flick too slow and artsy for its own good, and disjointed diting undermines creepy ritualism and eye-catch- g settings. Rated R for strong violence, sexuality, nd language. 87m. DIR: Richard Stanley. CAST: obert Burke, Chelsea Field, Zakes Mokae, Rufus wart. 1992

USTY ★★★ An emotional story of a retired, lonely nepherd in Australia who is adopted by Dusty, a tray sheepdog. 89m. DIR: John Richardson. CAST: ill Kerr, Noel Trevarthen, Carol Burns, Nicholas Hol- nd, John Stanton. 1985

UTCH ★★★ Dutch Dooley (Ed O'Neill) agrees to hat seems like a simple task: picking up his girl- riend's son from an Atlanta boarding school and riving him home to Chicago. Written by John Hugh- s, isn't quite *Planes, Trains and Automobiles*. Rat-

ed PG-13 for profanity. 95m. DIR: Peter Faiman. CAST: Ed O'Neill, JoBeth Williams, Ethan Randall. 1991

DUTCH GIRLS ❤ British field-hockey team grap- pling with rites of puberty. Rated R for suggested sex. 83m. DIR: Giles Foster. CAST: Bill Paterson, Colin Firth, Timothy Spall. 1985

D. W. GRIFFITH TRIPLE FEATURE ★★★ Kentucky dreamer and failed playwright David Wark Griffith was the American film industry's first great mover and shaker. Three fine examples of his early short films make up this feature: *The Battle of Elderbush Gulch*, *Iola's Promise*, and *The Goddess of Sage- brush Gulch*. Silent. B&W; 50m. DIR: D. W. Griffith. CAST: Mae Marsh, Lillian Gish, Charles West, Blanche Sweet, Mary Pickford. 1922

DYBBUK, THE ★★★1/2 Eerie film version of a pop- ular folktale set in nineteenth-century Poland. A stu- dent kills himself when the father of the girl to whom he has been pledged in marriage breaks the promise in order to marry her into a rich family. The girl is then possessed by the spirit of the dead boy. A well- made film for its time and place. In Yiddish with En- glish subtitles. 122m. DIR: Michael Wasynski. CAST: Abraham Morevski. 1938

DYING TO REMEMBER ★★★ A fashion designer dreams about a former life in which she was murdered. She goes to San Francisco looking for an- swers and finds the man who may have killed her. The movie has a good suspenseful plot and is also well-acted. Rated PG-13 for violence. 87m. DIR: Arthur Allan Seidelman. CAST: Melissa Gilbert, Ted Shackelford, Scott Plank, Christopher Stone, Jay Ro- binson. 1993

DYING YOUNG ★★1/2 A free-spirited, working- class woman finds herself falling in love with the scion of a wealthy San Francisco family after she's hired to help him recover from the side effects of chemotherapy treatments. Julia Roberts and Camp- bell Scott elevate this uninspired *Love Story* clone. Rated R for profanity. 110m. DIR: Joel Schumacher. CAST: Julia Roberts, Campbell Scott, Vincent D'Ono- frio, Colleen Dewhurst, David Selby, Ellen Burstyn. 1991

DYNAMITE AND GOLD ★★1/2 Passable made-for- television effort teams Willie Nelson and Delta Burke as two fortune seekers looking for buried cache of gold. Also known as *Where the Hell's That Gold?* 91m. DIR: Burt Kennedy. CAST: Willie Nelson, Delta Burke, Jack Elam, Gerald McRaney. 1990

DYNAMITE CANYON ★★1/2 Tom Keene infiltrates an outlaw gang that is attempting to grab Evelyn Fin- ley's ranch for its copper deposits. It's a bit slower than other Keene oaters. B&W; 58m. DIR: Robert Em- mett Tansey. CAST: Tom Keene, Evelyn Finley, Kenne Duncan. 1941

DYNAMITE PASS ★★1/2 Unconventional shoot- 'em-up has cowpoke Tim Holt and sidekick Richard Martin helping a construction engineer battle a tyrannical toll-road operator and his hired guns. All of the principals and supporting players give it their best shot, and this modest little oater has a nice edge to it. B&W; 61m. DIR: Lew Landers. CAST: Tim Holt, Richard Martin, Regis Toomey, Lynne Roberts (Mary

Hart), John Dehner, Robert Shayne, Cleo Moore, Denver Pyle, Ross Elliott. **1950**

DYNAMO 💔 Miserable rip-off of the Bruce Lee legend. Rated R for violence, nudity, and simulated sex. 93m. **DIR:** Hwa I. Hong. **CAST:** Bruce Li, Mary Han, James Griffith, Steve Sandor. **1978**

DYNASTY OF FEAR ★★ A slow-paced British murder mystery. An emotionally disturbed young lady is set up with psychological traps to take the blame for murder by a devious and greedy pair of lovers. Rated PG for relatively mild violence. 93m. **DIR:** Jimmy Sangster. **CAST:** Joan Collins, Peter Cushing, Judy Geeson, Ralph Bates. **1985**

EACH DAWN I DIE ★★★★ Energetic Warner Bros. film occasionally slips the bounds of believability but never fails to be entertaining. James Cagney is terrific as the youthful reporter who is framed for murder after exposing a crooked district attorney. B&W; 92m. **DIR:** William Keighley. **CAST:** James Cagney, George Raft, George Bancroft, Jane Bryan, Maxie Rosenbloom. **1939**

EAGLE, THE ★★★ Produced to boost the legendary Rudolph Valentino's then-sagging popularity, this satirical romance of a Russian Cossack lieutenant who masquerades as a do-gooder bandit to avenge his father's death proved a box-office winner for the star. Valentino is at his romantic, swoon-inducing, self-mocking best in the title role. Silent. B&W; 72m. **DIR:** Clarence Brown. **CAST:** Rudolph Valentino, Vilma Banky, Louise Dresser, Clark Ward, Spottiswoode Aitken. **1925**

EAGLE HAS LANDED, THE ★★★ Michael Caine is a Nazi agent who is given orders to plan and carry out the kidnapping or murder of Prime Minister Churchill. This movie gets started on a promising note, but it is sabotaged by a weak, contrived ending. Rated PG. 123m. **DIR:** John Sturges. **CAST:** Michael Caine, Donald Sutherland, Robert Duvall. **1977**

EAGLE'S BROOD ★★★ Hopalong Cassidy and Johnny Nelson aid an old Mexican outlaw whose son has been killed and grandson kidnapped. Second in the long-running series, this fine entry has a maturity and edge to it that would be rounded off within the next few years as the target audience changed. B&W; 59m. **DIR:** Howard Bretherton. **CAST:** William Boyd, James Ellison, William Farnum, George "Gabby" Hayes, Joan Woodbury, Paul Fix. **1935**

EAGLE'S WING ★★ When an Indian brave steals a magnificent white stallion from a fur trapper, a struggle of wits, courage, and endurance begins for the horse. Magnificent scenery highlights this British production. Rated PG. 100m. **DIR:** Anthony Harvey. **CAST:** Martin Sheen, Sam Waterston, Harvey Keitel, Stéphane Audran, Caroline Langrishe. **1980**

EARLY FROST, AN ★★★★1/2 This timely, tremely effective drama focuses on a family's tempt to come to grips with the fact that their son not only gay but has AIDS as well. Gena Rowlan one of Hollywood's most neglected actresses, a Aidan Quinn take the acting honors as mother a son. One of those rare television movies that wo on all levels, it is highly recommended. 100m. **DIR:** John Erman. **CAST:** Gena Rowlands, Ben Gazza Aidan Quinn, Sylvia Sidney, John Glover. **1985**

EARLY RUSSIAN CINEMA: BEFORE THE REVOL TIONS (VOL. 1–10) ★★★★ Soviet cinema did emerge fully formed from the heads of Eisenste Vertov, and Dovzhenko. Russia enjoyed a boom film industry prior to the revolution, but the Sovi found many of these films too cosmopolitan and moved them from circulation. This collection twenty-eight works unearthed by Glasnost provid a fascinating look at a wide spectrum of pre-Sov society. Silent. B&W; 695m. **DIR:** Evgenii Bauer, Lad law Starewicz, Yakov Protázanov. **1908–1918**

EARLY SUMMER ★★★1/2 Involved and involvi story about a young woman rebelling against arranged marriage in post–World War II Tokyo. Yas jiro Ozu, one of Japan's most respected directo deftly presents this tale of culture clash, which w the Japanese Film of the Year Award in 1951. Japanese with English subtitles. B&W; 135m. **D** Yasujiro Ozu. **CAST:** Setsuko Hara. **1951**

EARRINGS OF MADAME DE. . . , THE ★★★★ giddily romantic roundelay sparked by a pair of di mond earrings. They keep changing hands but a ways come back to haunt the fickle countess wi owned them first. The style is a bit too lighthearte for what is ultimately a tragic story, but Max Ophü imbues it with wit and technical flash. In Fren with English subtitles. 105m. **DIR:** Max Ophüls. **CAS** Charles Boyer, Danielle Darrieux, Vittorio De Sica. **19** **EARTH (1930)** ★★★★ One of the last class silent films, this short homage to the spirit of the co lective farmer and his intangible ties to the land er ploys stunning camera shots. Certain scenes fro the original print no longer exist, but what remai of this film tells a beautiful, moving story. Russia silent. B&W; 56m. **DIR:** Alexander Dovzhenko. **CAS** Semyon Svashenko. **1930**

•**EARTH (1998)** ★★★★ As India nears indepe dence from Great Britain in 1947, long-simmerin ethnic hatred among Hindus, Moslems, and Sikh begins to boil to the surface. Writer-director Deep Mehta tells her story from the viewpoint of an eigh year-old girl whose governess has admirers of all pe suasions, and the romantic dilemma symbolizes th conflicts in the country as a whole. The film is mela choly, elegiac, and quite moving. In Hindi with En glish subtitles. Not rated; deals with mature theme and contains brief scenes of violence and sexualit 104m. **DIR:** Deepa Mehta. **CAST:** Aamir Khan, Nandi Das, Rahul Khanna, Kitu Gidwani, Maia Sethna. **1998**

EARTH GIRLS ARE EASY ★★★ A wacky but con sistently funny musical comedy is based on the bizarre premise of some extraterrestrial visitor crash-landing in the swimming pool behind Valle girl Geena Davis's house. Davis and friend Juli

wn decide to shave the hairy intruders, discover
/ are hunks, and acquaint the visitors with the
lifestyle. Rated PG for mild profanity. 100m.
: Julien Temple. CAST: Geena Davis, Jeff Goldblum,
e Brown, Jim Carrey, Damon Wayans, Michael Mc-
n, Charles Rocket. 1989 DVD

RTH VS. THE FLYING SAUCERS ★★★★ Stun-
g special effects by Ray Harryhausen enhance
familiar 1950s plot about an invasion from outer
ce. After misinterpreting a message for peace
n the initially easygoing aliens, the military
ns fire—and then all hell breaks loose! B&W;
. DIR: Fred F. Sears. CAST: Hugh Marlowe, Joan
lor, Donald Curtis, Morris Ankrum (Stepen Morris).
6

RTH VS. THE SPIDER ★★ A giant spider invades
nountain community in this American-Interna-
nal rip-off of Bert Arnold's *Tarantula*. Special ef-
ts are so-so; one of Bert I. Gordon's more tolerable
e wasters. B&W; 72m. DIR: Bert I. Gordon. CAST:
Kemmer, June Kenney, Gene Roth. 1958

RTHLING, THE ★★★1/2 A dying man (William
den) and an orphaned boy (Rick Schroder) meet
the Australian wilderness in this surprisingly ab-
bing family film. A warning to parents: There is a
nor amount of profanity, and a scene in which the
's mother and father are killed may be too shock-
for small children. Rated PG. 102m. DIR: Peter
linson. CAST: William Holden, Rick Schroder, Jack
mpson, Olivia Hamnett, Alwyn Kurts. 1980

RTHLY POSSESSIONS ★★★1/2 Novelist Anne
er's always loopy characters strike again in this
l little tale, which concerns a mildly repressed
usewife whose desire to "see more of the world"
mes true in a wholly unexpected manner: She is
ken hostage by a rather inept bank robber.
ripter Steven Roberts isn't able to get the neces-
y depth in this adaptation and your willingness to
ept these unlikely events therefore rests solely
th the two stars. While both do their best, you're
ely to remain somewhat dissatisfied. Rated PG-13
profanity and gunplay. 103m. DIR: James Lapine.
ST: Susan Sarandon, Stephen Dorff, Elizabeth
ss, Jay O. Sanders. 1999 DVD

RTHQUAKE ★★ Once you get past the special-ef-
ts mastery of seeing Los Angeles destroyed,
u've got a pretty weak film on your hands. The clas-
San Francisco did it better. Rated PG. 129m. DIR:
ark Robson. CAST: Charlton Heston, Genevieve Bu-
d, Lorne Greene, Ava Gardner, Walter Matthau,
eorge Kennedy. 1974 DVD

RTHWORM TRACTORS ★★★ Big mouth Joe E.
rown plays braggart salesman Alexander Botts for
the comedy he can squeeze out of tractor jokes.
sed on the noted *Saturday Evening Post* stories
the 1930s, this is one of Brown's better efforts.
n stuff. B&W; 63m. DIR: Ray Enright. CAST: Joe E.
own, Gene Lockhart, Guy Kibbee, Dick Foran.
936

EAST IS EAST ★★1/2 Though he's been living thir-
years in England, a Pakistani father tries to im-
se the old-country ways on his seven children, who
nsider themselves English. Intended as a comedy
clashing cultures, the film suffers from two differ-

ent styles: Om Puri plays the father as if he were doing *King Lear*, while his kids seem to have wandered
in from some BBC sitcom. Rated R for profanity.
101m. DIR: Iain Softley. CAST: Om Puri, Linda Bassett,
Jordan Routledge, Archie Panjabi, Emil Marwa. 1999

EAST OF BORNEO ★★★ Intrepid and tenacious
Rose Hobart searches the teeming Borneo jungle for
her supposedly lost doctor husband Charles Bickford, who isn't lost at all but living it up as personal
physician to native prince Georges Renavent. Filled
with wildlife, this jungle adventure is lots of fun and
ends with a bang. B&W; 77m. DIR: George Melford.
CAST: Rose Hobart, Charles Bickford, Georges Renavent, Noble Johnson. 1931

EAST OF EDEN (1955) ★★★★★ The final portion
of John Steinbeck's renowned novel of miscommuni-
cation and conflict between a father and son was
transformed into a powerful, emotional movie.
James Dean burst onto the screen as the rebellious
son in his first starring role. Jo Van Fleet received an
Oscar for her role as Kate, a bordello madam and
Dean's long-forgotten mother. 115m. DIR: Elia Kazan.
CAST: James Dean, Jo Van Fleet, Julie Harris, Raymond Massey, Burl Ives. 1955

EAST OF EDEN (1982) ★★★1/2 This above-average television miniseries maintains the integrity of
the source material by John Steinbeck without dip-
ping too far into pathos. One major change: the focus
shifts from the two sons who crave Papa's affection,
to the deliciously evil woman—Jane Seymour—who
twists them all around her little finger. Stick with the
1955 original. Not rated. 240m. DIR: Harvey Hart.
CAST: Jane Seymour, Timothy Bottoms, Bruce Boxleitner, Warren Oates, Anne Baxter, Lloyd Bridges, Howard
Duff. 1982

EAST OF ELEPHANT ROCK ★★ This story of the
1948 British struggle to maintain a Far Eastern
colony focuses on a new governor general's takeover
after his predecessor is murdered by terrorists. The
film is slow-paced and burdened with soap-opera
overtones. Rated R. 93m. DIR: Don Boyd. CAST: John
Hurt, Jeremy Kemp, Judi Bowker. 1981

EAST OF KILIMANJARO ★★ A deadly virus has affected the cattle of the area in Africa east of Kilimanjaro. A daring photographer throws his weight into
the fight against the microbe. Routine adventure.
75m. DIR: Arnold Belgard. CAST: Marshall Thompson,
Gaby André. 1957

EAST SIDE, WEST SIDE ★★1/2 A middling adaptation of Marcia Davenport's bestseller, with Barbara
Stanwyck married to James Mason who is fooling
around with Ava Gardner, but Stanwyck hangs in
there trying to win back his love. This is a rare
chance to see Nancy Davis (Reagan) in action. B&W;
108m. DIR: Mervyn LeRoy. CAST: Barbara Stanwyck,
James Mason, Van Heflin, Ava Gardner, Cyd Charisse,
Nancy Davis, Gale Sondergaard. 1949

•EAST-WEST ★★★1/2 At the end of World War II,
refugees from the Russian Revolution are invited
back to help rebuild their homeland, but it's all a
sham—most of them are immediately killed or imprisoned. The film follows one of the few families allowed to live in relative peace, and shows how their
humanity suffers as the oppressive life under Stalin

wears them down. The solemn and drab film is disjointed in its last half hour, but the story remains engrossing. In French and Russian with English subtitles. Rated R for sexual scenes. 121m. **DIR:** Regis Wargnier. **CAST:** Sandrine Bonnaire, Oleg Menchikov, Sergei Bodrov Jr., Catherine Deneuve. 1999

EASTER PARADE ★★★★ Judy Garland and Fred Astaire team up for this thoroughly enjoyable musical. Irving Berlin provided the songs for the story, about Astaire trying to forget ex–dance partner Ann Miller as he rises to the top with Garland. The result is an always watchable—and repeatable—treat. 104m. **DIR:** Charles Walters. **CAST:** Judy Garland, Fred Astaire, Peter Lawford, Jules Munshin, Ann Miller. 1948

EASTERN CONDORS ★★★★ À la *The Dirty Dozen*, a group of hardened criminals are sent to Vietnam on a suicide mission. Star-director Sammo Hung, who usually plays comical parts, may be built like a cannonball, but he can move like one, too! In Cantonese with English subtitles. Not rated; contains strong violence. 100m. **DIR:** Sammo Hung. **CAST:** Sammo Hung, Yuen Biao, Haing S. Ngor. 1986 DVD

EASY COME, EASY GO ★★ For Elvis Presley fans only. Elvis sings some snappy songs, but the plot is not going to be filed under great scripts—our star is a frogman searching for treasure on behalf of the United States Navy. 95m. **DIR:** John Rich. **CAST:** Elvis Presley, Elsa Lanchester, Dodie Marshal, Pat Priest. 1967

EASY LIVING ★★★1/2 Shorn of the clichés one usually expects from movies about over-the-hill athletes, this picture offers a realistic account of an aging professional football player (Victor Mature) coming to terms with the end of a long career and a stormy home life. Lucille Ball and Lizabeth Scott are wonderful as the understanding secretary and shrewish wife, respectively. B&W; 77m. **DIR:** Jacques Tourneur. **CAST:** Victor Mature, Lucille Ball, Lizabeth Scott, Sonny Tufts. 1949

EASY MONEY ★★ In this fitfully funny comedy, slob Rodney Dangerfield attempts to clean up his act, with the help of pal Joe Pesci, to qualify for a large inheritance. Rated R for profanity and suggested sex. 95m. **DIR:** James Signorelli. **CAST:** Rodney Dangerfield, Joe Pesci, Geraldine Fitzgerald, Candy Azzara. 1983 DVD

EASY RIDER ★★★1/2 Time has not been kind to this 1969 release, about two drifters (Peter Fonda and Dennis Hopper) motorcycling their way across the country only to be confronted with violence and bigotry. Jack Nicholson's keystone performance, however, still makes it worth watching. Rated R. 94m. **DIR:** Dennis Hopper. **CAST:** Peter Fonda, Dennis Hopper, Jack Nicholson, Karen Black, Luana Anders. 1969 DVD

EASY TO LOVE ★★1/2 Tony Martin and Van Johnson vie for the love of mermaid Esther Williams in this most lavish of her numerous water spectacles. A toe-curling, high-speed sequence performed on water skis tops the Busby Berkeley numbers staged in lush Cypress Gardens at Winter Haven, Florida. 96m. **DIR:** Charles Walters. **CAST:** Esther Williams, Tony Martin, Van Johnson, Carroll Baker, John Bromfi[...] 1953

EASY VIRTUE ★★ In this melodrama, based loo[...] on a Noel Coward play, the wife of an alcoholic f[...] in love with a younger man who commits suicide. [...] past life prevents her from leading a normal [...] Considering the directorial credit, this is close[...] dull. A British production. B&W; 73m. **DIR:** Al[...] Hitchcock. **CAST:** Isabel Jeans, Franklyn Dyall, Hunter. 1927 DVD

EASY WHEELS ★★★ Life, love, and the pursuit [...] better draft beer with the leather-bound unshav[...] Dumb fun. Rated R. 94m. **DIR:** David O'Malley. **CA**[...] Paul LeMat, Eileen Davidson, Barry Livingston, Geo[...] Plimpton. 1989

EAT A BOWL OF TEA ★★★★ This little dome[...] charmer, set in New York's post–World War II Chi[...] town, concerns the trouble that brews betwee[...] young Chinese-American veteran (Russell Wo[...] and the girl (Cora Miao) he meets and marries d[...] ing a brief visit to China. Scripter Judith Rascoe [...] faithfully adapted Louis Chu's novel. Rated PG-13[...] sexual themes. 114m. **DIR:** Wayne Wang. **CAST:** C[...] Miao, Russell Wong, Victor Wong, Lau Siu Ming. 19[...]

EAT AND RUN 💋 Science-fiction spoof is abou[...] four-hundred pound alien named Murry Creatu[...] Rated R for nudity. 85m. **DIR:** Christopher Hunt. **CA**[...] Ron Silver, R. L. Ryan. 1986

EAT DRINK MAN WOMAN ★★★★ This comic fe[...] about food, fatherhood, and frayed family ties foc[...] es on the delicate balancing acts required to ma[...] the most of both great meals and life itself. Whil[...] widowed master Taipei chef is losing his sense [...] taste, his three modern, unmarried daughters wi[...] their way through the mine fields of independen[...] and man-woman relationships. Their ritual Sund[...] dinners become stormy buffets of battered feelin[...] and surprise announcements. In Mandarin w[...] English subtitles. No MPAA rating. 123m. **DIR:** A[...] Lee. **CAST:** Sihung Lung, Kuei-Mei Yang, Chien-L[...] Wu, Yu-Wen Wang. 1994

EAT MY DUST ★★ A low-budget 1976 race yarn [...] table only for the fact that it gave Ron Howard t[...] power to direct his next starring vehicle, *Gra*[...] *Theft Auto*, which, in turn, led to such treats as *Nig*[...] *Shift* and *Splash*. Rated PG. 90m. **DIR:** Charles [...] Griffith. **CAST:** Ron Howard, Christopher Norris, Da[...] Madden, Warren Kemmerling. 1976 DVD

EAT OR BE EATEN ★★★ This spoof centers arou[...] newscasters Haryll Hee and Sharyll Shee as they co[...] er the crisis in Labyrinth County. Between news co[...] erage we see clever commercials that poke fun [...] those we normally see, as well as takeoffs on [...] evangelists and sitcoms. This one has lots of laugh[...] Not rated, it deals with adult topics and is compar[...] ble to a PG. 30m. **DIR:** Phil Austin. **CAST:** Firesign Th[...] atre Players. 1985

EAT THE PEACH ★★ *Eat the Peach* takes place [...] an Irish village and tells the story of Vinnie a[...] Arthur, two friends who see the Elvis Presley fil[...] *Roustabout* in which a cyclist rides the carnival Wa[...] of Death, and decide to create their own. A slight a[...] subtle movie. You want to like it, but it just nev[...] kicks in. Rated PG. 90m. **DIR:** Peter Ormrod. **CAS**[...]

hen Brennan, Eamon Morrissey, Catherine Byrne, Toibin. **1987**

THE RICH ♥ This ludicrous exercise in bad e uses profanity, violence, and toilet jokes to elic-ughs. Rated R. 92m. **DIR:** Peter Richardson. **CAST:** h Pellay, Ronald Allen, Sandra Dorne. **1987**

EN ALIVE ★★ Director Tobe Hooper's follow-up *'he Texas Chainsaw Massacre* has a similar ne but is less successful. The owner of a run-Louisiana motel kills whoever wanders into his her of the swamp, with the aid of a large, hungry ator. This horror flick is often sloppy, but buffs want to see it, anyway, for its cast. Rated R for ng violence. 97m. **DIR:** Tobe Hooper. **CAST:** Neville d, Mel Ferrer, Carolyn Jones, Marilyn Burns, iam Finley, Stuart Whitman, Robert Englund. **1976**

ING ★★★★ A group of women talk about food, and self-esteem. A highly entertaining social ma evocative of some of Woody Allen's more seri-work. 110m. **DIR:** Henry Jaglom. **CAST:** Nelly , Lisa Richards, Frances Bergen, Mary Crosby, n Welles. **1991**

ING PATTERN ★★ This film traces the further entures of the *Lexx*, a living, breathing, feeding ceship, and her crew. Bizarre, sometimes silly fi flick is like a story from the pages of *Heavy Met-* Rated R for some sci-fi gore and violence. 93m. : Rainer Matsutani. **CAST:** Brian Downey, Eva ermann, Michael McManus, Doreen Jacobi, Rutger er. **1996**

ING RAOUL ★★★★ A hilarious black comedy ritten and directed by Paul Bartel, this low-bud-film presents an inventive but rather bizarre so-on to the recession. When Mary Bland (Mary ronov) is saved by her frying-pan-wielding hus-d, Paul (Bartel), from a would-be-rapist, the hap-y married couple happily discover that the now-ceased attacker was rolling in dough—so they roll n and hit on a way to end their economic woes. ed R for nudity, profanity, sexual situations, and lence. 83m. **DIR:** Paul Bartel. **CAST:** Paul Bartel, ry Woronov, Robert Beltran, Susan Saiger. **1982**

BTIDE ★★ Harry Hamlin, who has become a fa-iar face in this genre, plays an attorney who be-es involved with his main suspect's wife. Their li-on drags him into a web of clichés and through a ze of stock sex-thriller characters, all who do ir thing and then make a hasty exit. There's very le suspense and the usual dose of direct-to-video . Not rated; contains nudity, adult situations, vio-ce, and strong language. 94m. **DIR:** Craig Lahiff. ST: Harry Hamlin, Judy McIntosh, John Waters, Su-n Lyons. **1994**

ENEZER ★★★1/2 This Wild West version of arles Dickens's *A Christmas Carol* rides tall in e saddle thanks to Jack Palance's Scrooge. When oon owner Scrooge cheats a young man out of his d and lays off his bartender on Christmas Eve, he ts the stage for the traditional visit from three ristmas ghosts. While this made-for-television vie is slow going at the beginning, it does pick up the second act and even delivers a shoot-out for e third. Rated PG for mild violence. 94m. **DIR:** Ken

Jubenvill. **CAST:** Jack Palance, Rick Schroder, Amy Lo-cane, Albert Schultz, Joshua Silberg. **1997**

EBONY TOWER, THE ★★★ Sir Laurence Olivier is well cast as an aging artist who shields himself from the world outside his estate in this fine screen adap-tation of the John Fowles novel. This absorbing British TV drama is not rated, but it contains some partial nudity. 80m. **DIR:** Robert Knights. **CAST:** Lau-rence Olivier, Greta Scacchi. **1986**

ECHO OF THUNDER, THE ★★★★ Filmed in Aus-tralia, this moving *Hallmark Hall of Fame* reveals a "bare bones" family struggling against the elements of the outback as well as financial disaster. When her husband's oldest daughter comes to live with them, a woman must learn to accept her or destroy the whole family. Not rated; contains adult themes. 90m. **DIR:** Simon Wincer. **CAST:** Judy Davis, Jamey Sheridan, Lauren Hewett, Emily Jane Browning. **1998**

ECHO PARK ★★★ Tom Hulce, Susan Dey, and Michael Bowen star as three young show-biz hope-fuls living in one of Los Angeles's seedier neighbor-hoods. Director Robert Dornhelm and screenwriter Michael Ventura have some interesting things to say about the quest for fame, and the stars provide some memorable moments. Rated R for nudity, profanity, and violence. 93m. **DIR:** Robert Dornhelm. **CAST:** Su-san Dey, Tom Hulce, Michael Bowen, Christopher Walker, Shirley Jo Finney, John Paragon, Richard "Cheech" Marin, Cassandra Peterson (Elvira). **1986**

ECHOES IN THE DARKNESS ★★★1/2 This Joseph Wambaugh crime-drama is based on the 1979 true-life murder of schoolteacher Susan Reinert (Stockard Channing). It's a toned-down TV movie devoid of most of the usual Wambaugh grit. At just under four hours, it takes quite a commitment for one night's viewing. Not rated. 234m. **DIR:** Glenn Jor-dan. **CAST:** Peter Coyote, Robert Loggia, Stockard Channing, Peter Boyle, Gary Cole, Treat Williams, Cindy Pickett. **1987**

ECLIPSE, THE ★★★1/2 A woman dissolves an af-fair with an older man, only to become involved with a self-centered young stockbroker in Rome's fren-zied Borsa. Michelangelo Antonioni's meditation on doomed love has some good moments. Winner of the Grand Prize at Cannes. In Italian with English subti-tles. B&W; 123m. **DIR:** Michelangelo Antonioni. **CAST:** Alain Delon, Monica Vitti, Francisco Rabal. **1962**

ECSTASY ★★1/2 Completely overshadowed since its release by the notoriety of Hedy Lamarr's nude scenes, this new packaging in video should shift the emphasis back to the film itself, which is basically a romance of illicit love. Filmed in pre-Hitler Czecho-slovakia, this version is subtitled in English. B&W; 88m. **DIR:** Gustav Machaty. **CAST:** Hedy Lamarr, Arib-ert Mog. **1933**

ED ★★1/2 This disposable but entertaining comedy features a baseball-playing chimp. Ed is a smart-aleck primate who becomes the mascot for the de-moralized minor league Santa Rosa Rockets. He not only wears the pants on the team (and uses toilets, too), but also snaps the losing streak—both on the field and off—of a demoralized fastball pitcher. The familiar ballpark story is written by David Mickey Evans (*The Sandlot*). Rated PG. 97m. **DIR:** Bill Couturie. **CAST:** Matt LeBlanc, Jayne Brook, Bill Cobbs, Jack Warden. 1996

ED & HIS DEAD MOTHER ★★★1/2 Goofy fun finds mamma's boy Steve Buscemi so desperate to get dear old Mom back that he pays shyster salesman John Glover to bring her back from the dead. Well, *Guess Who's Coming to Dinner*? One problem: Mom now eats bugs and has other undead habits as well. Traditional havoc ensues. Rated PG-13 for language, adult situations, and horror violence. 93m. **DIR:** Jonathan Wacks. **CAST:** Steve Buscemi, Ned Beatty, Miriam Margolyes, John Glover, Sam Jenkins. 1992

ED WOOD ★★★★1/2 Director Tim Burton's brilliant black-and-white study of "the worst filmmaker in Hollywood history" features unforgettable performances by Johnny Depp, in the title role, and Martin Landau, as Bela Lugosi. Although not for all tastes, this loving tribute to grade-Z movies and the campy pleasures they provide is a film buff's delight. Rated R for profanity, drug use, and men in women's clothing. B&W; 124m. **DIR:** Tim Burton. **CAST:** Johnny Depp, Martin Landau, Sarah Jessica Parker, Bill Murray, Patricia Arquette, Jeffrey Jones, G. D. Spradlin, Vincent D'Onofrio, Mike Starr. 1994

EDDIE ★★1/2 Vocal female basketball fan Eddie Franklin enters a free-throw contest and winds up coaching a fictitious New York Knicks team. The Knicks are languishing at the hoop and turnstile, so it's up to Eddie to improve their court performance, smooth out their personal affairs, and stand up to the team's flamboyant billionaire owner. The film's fan-appreciation messages are a nice touch, but the real NBA—with its eccentric superstars and tabloid melodrama—is a much bigger scream. Rated PG-13 for language. 88m. **DIR:** Steve Rash. **CAST:** Whoopi Goldberg, Frank Langella, Dennis Farina, Lisa Ann Walter. 1996 DVD

EDDIE AND THE CRUISERS ★★★1/2 Long after his death, rock 'n' roll singer Eddie Wilson's (Michael Paré) songs become popular all over again. This revives interest in a long-shelved concept album. The tape for it has been stolen, and it's up to Wilson's onetime collaborator (Tom Berenger) to find them. Only other people want the tapes, too, and they may be willing to kill to get them. The songs are great! Rated PG. 92m. **DIR:** Martin Davidson. **CAST:** Tom Berenger, Michael Paré, Ellen Barkin. 1983

EDDIE AND THE CRUISERS II: EDDIE LIVES! ★★★ Solid sequel to *Eddie and the Cruisers* finds Eddie (Michael Paré) hiding out in Montreal while his songs enjoy new popularity. This prompts him to try music again and, of course, puts him on the inevitable road back to stardom. Thoughtful, well-intentioned film. Rated PG-13 for profanity and suggested sex. 100m. **DIR:** Jean-Claude Lord. **CAST:** Michael Paré, Marini Orsini, Bernie Coulson. 1989

EDDIE MACON'S RUN ★★1/2 John Schneider as a prison escapee who manages to stay one step ahead of the law. Kirk Douglas costars as the hard-nosed policeman on his trail. It's a predictable, lightweight movie. Rated PG for vulgar language and violence.

95m. **DIR:** Jeff Kanew. **CAST:** John Schneider, Douglas, Lee Purcell, Leah Ayres. 1983

EDDY DUCHIN STORY, THE ★★1/2 Overly s⌷ mental telling of the troubled professional and f⌷ ly life of pianist-bandleader Eddy Duchin. Many piano renditions of the standards of the era ("⌷ and Soul," "Sweet Sue"), and Duchin's theme s⌷ "Chopin Nocturne in E Flat," all dubbed by Car⌷ Cavallaro. 123m. **DIR:** George Sidney. **CAST:** Ty Power, Kim Novak, Victoria Shaw, James Whitm⌷ Rex Thompson. 1956

EDEN (1993 TV SERIES) ★★ This erotic soap o⌷ is brought to you by the folks at *Playboy* and feat⌷ one of the best-looking casts on the small scr⌷ The story (such as it is) centers on Eden, a beac⌷ sort where guests, staff, and hormones run wild. rated, contains nudity and sexual situations. F⌷ tape 98m. **DIR:** Victor Lobl. **CAST:** Barbara Woods, Steve Chase, Darcy DeMoss. 1993

EDEN ★★★★ Joanna Going is exceptiona⌷ writer-director Howard Goldberg's touching tale⌷ 1960s housewife named Helen, who is quickly ti⌷ of the constraints placed on her by a dominee⌷ husband and a degenerating illness. When the ⌷ ple takes in a student, Helen finds a soul mate ⌷ understands her desire to be free. With the stude⌷ encouragement, Helen begins to have out-of-b⌷ experiences that leave her physically weak but ⌷ vide the freedom she seeks. Both heartfelt ⌷ haunting, *Eden* is a film of hope and desire. Rate⌷ for language and adult situations. 106m. D⌷ Howard Goldberg. **CAST:** Joanna Going, Dylan Wa⌷ Sean Patrick Flanery. 1996 DVD

EDGAR ALLAN POE'S MADHOUSE 🎬 The film⌷ nothing to do with Poe and only manages to degr⌷ his name. Not rated; contains violence, profan⌷ and nudity. 75m. **DIR:** Todd Sheets. **CAST:** Tonia M⌷ ahan, Jenny Admire, Kim Adler, Matt Lewis, Mike ⌷ man. 1992

EDGE, THE ★★★1/2 Writer David Mamet a⌷ director Lee Tamahori have combined forces ⌷ produce a genuinely muscular thriller and con⌷ of wills between a reclusive billionaire and ⌷ hotshot fashion photographer who may have desi⌷ on the other man's wife. Both become stran⌷ in the Alaskan wilderness and subsequently ⌷ forced to cooperate in order to survive. Rated R ⌷ profanity, violence, and gore. 121m. **DIR:** Lee Tar⌷ hori. **CAST:** Anthony Hopkins, Alec Baldwin, ⌷ Macpherson, Harold Perrineau Jr., L. Q. Jones. 1⌷ DVD

EDGE OF DARKNESS (1943) ★★★1/2 Power⌷ acting by a stage-trained cast make this a bett⌷ than-average war picture. The plot focuses on eff⌷ of the Norwegian underground to run off the Na⌷ during World War II. B&W; 120m. **DIR:** Lewis M⌷ stone. **CAST:** Errol Flynn, Ann Sheridan, Walter Hust⌷ Judith Anderson, Helmut Dantine, Nancy Colem⌷ Morris Carnovsky, John Beal. 1943

EDGE OF DARKNESS (1986) ★★★★1/2 A co⌷ plex mystery produced as a miniseries for Brit⌷ television. The story revolves around a nuclear p⌷ cessing plant and its covert government relatio⌷

Bob Peck offers an intense portrayal of a British police detective who, step-by-step, uncovers the truth as he investigates the murder of his daughter. 307m. DIR: Martin Campbell. CAST: Bob Peck, Joe Don Baker, Jack Woodson, John Woodvine, Joanne Whalley. 1986

EDGE OF HONOR ★★★ Group of Explorer Scouts on an expedition come across a cache of high-tech weapons belonging to a group of smugglers. This one gets a merit badge for exciting action and ingenuity. Rated R for language and violence. 92m. DIR: Michael Spence. CAST: Corey Feldman, Meredith Salenger, Scott Reeves, Ken Jenkins, Don Swayze, Christopher Neame. 1991

EDGE OF SANITY ★★ Anthony Perkins is retooling his psychopathic screen persona again in this handsome-looking but mediocre British production of *Dr. Jekyll and Mr. Hyde*. No new twists on this old theme, but plenty of sexy girls and sordid violence. Rather forgettable. Not rated, this uncensored version is recommended for adults only. 86m. DIR: Gerard Kikoine. CAST: Anthony Perkins, Glynis Barber, David Lodge. 1989

•EDGE OF SEVENTEEN ★★ This candid coming-out story of a gay teen in 1984 Sandusky, Ohio, is an uneven mix of poignant drama, heartbreaks, comic pop-culture nostalgia, soap-opera schlock, and unsavory sex. Gangly, dewy-eyed Eric is attracted to a fellow amusement-park buffet server. He wrestles with self-identity, enters a predatory gay bar scene, and is befriended by a lesbian nightclub manager. Not rated; contains simulated sex, profanity, and violence. 100m. DIR: David Moreton. CAST: Chris Stafford, Gabrych Anderson, Tina Holmes, Stephanie McVay, Lea DeLaria, Stephanie McVay, Lea DeLaria. 1999

EDIE & PEN ★★★1/2 Victoria Tennant's engaging script explores the relationship between two dissimilar women who meet in Reno while getting quickie divorces, then become fast friends. Conservative Stockard Channing has been humiliated by a cheating husband who dumped her, while party-hardy Jennifer Tilly is all set to become a bride again ... the very next day! Skirt-chasing Scott Glenn saves the film from nonstop girl talk. Rated PG-13 for profanity and simulated sex. 98m. DIR: Matthew Irmas. CAST: Stockard Channing, Jennifer Tilly, Scott Glenn, Stuart Wilson, Michael McKean, Martin Mull, Michael O'Keefe, Joanna Gleason. 1996

EDISON, THE MAN ★★★1/2 The second half of MGM's planned two-part tribute to Thomas Alva Edison (following by months the release of *Young Tom Edison*). Spencer Tracy is perfect as the great inventor from young manhood through age 82. Great family viewing. B&W; 107m. DIR: Clarence Brown. CAST: Spencer Tracy, Rita Johnson, Lynne Overman, Charles Coburn, Gene Lockhart, Henry Travers. 1940

EDITH AND MARCEL ★★★★ Based on the real life of famous torch singer Edith Piaf (Evelyn Bouix), this powerful musical-drama follows the passionate affair she had with champion boxer Marcel Cerdan (Marcel Cerdan Jr.). Director Claude Lelouch brings to life the stormy romance that captured the attention of the world. In French with English subtitles. 170m. DIR: Claude Lelouch. CAST: Evelyne Bouix, Marcel Cerdan Jr., Jacques Villeret, Francis Huster. 1983

ED'S NEXT MOVE ★★★ A naïve young geneticist moves from the Midwest to Manhattan and strikes up a tentative courtship with a struggling musician. Writer-director John Walsh crams in every idea he can think of for his first film, and not all of them work. Still, the performances are likable and the film is briskly paced. Rated R for profanity. 88m. DIR: John Walsh. CAST: Matt Ross, Callie Thorne, Kevin Carroll. 1996

EDTV ★★★1/2 Perhaps the spookiest thing about this film is that it *doesn't* seem all that far-fetched. The notion of turning one ordinary fellow's life into an ongoing TV show makes this film more prophet than parody. And no, scripters Lowell Ganz and Babaloo Mandel aren't guilty of blatant theft; where Andrew Niccol's *The Truman Show* was elegant and ferociously clever, this effort is down 'n' dirty, like the macabre spontaneity of homegrown local-access cable programming. The programmer of a struggling cable channel, who at first is pleased by the success of her idea, realizes that she has contributed to the destruction of a really nice guy: a goofy San Francisco video-store clerk with no immediate concept of his pending loss of dignity. It all works because the unwitting celebrity is understated, deceptively unaffected, and wholly endearing. Rated PG-13 for profanity and sexual candor. 122m. DIR: Ron Howard. CAST: Matthew McConaughey, Jenna Elfman, Woody Harrelson, Sally Kirkland, Martin Landau, Ellen DeGeneres, Rob Reiner, Dennis Hopper, Elizabeth Hurley. 1999

EDUCATING RITA ★★★★1/2 A boozing, depressed English professor (Michael Caine) takes on a sharp-witted, eager-to-learn hairdresser (Julie Walters) for Open University tutorials and each educates the other, in this delightful romantic comedy based on a London hit play. Rated PG for profanity. 110m. DIR: Lewis Gilbert. CAST: Michael Caine, Julie Walters, Michael Williams. 1983

EDUCATION OF LITTLE TREE, THE ★★★★ Orphaned 8-year-old boy is nurtured by his grandparents in backwoods East Tennessee. His white grandfather and Cherokee grandmother teach him what they call the "Indian way" of relating to nature, moonshining, church, neighbors, and the encroachment of a hypocritical civilization. This adaptation of Forrest Carter's 1986 novel has a cleansing sense of decency and dignity. Rated PG. 117m. DIR: Dick Friedenberg. CAST: Joseph Ashton, James Cromwell, Tantoo Cardinal, Graham Greene, Mika Boorem. 1998

EDUCATION OF SONNY CARSON, THE ★★★ This grim but realistic movie is based on the autobiography of Sonny Carson, a ghetto-raised black youth whose life was bounded by gangs, drugs, and crime. There's no upbeat happy ending and no attempt to preach, either; the film simply shows ghetto life for the frightening hell it is. Rated R. 104m. DIR: Michael Campus. CAST: Rony Clanton, Don Gordon, Joyce Walker, Paul Benjamin. 1974

EDWARD AND MRS. SIMPSON ★★★ This mini-series does a commendable, if overlong, job of capturing the romance between a manipulative American divorcée and a rather simpleminded king. Talky in that inimitable *Masterpiece Theatre* style, but by the end we are quite convinced Mrs. Simpson saved the future of the English monarchy by keeping Edward VIII off the throne. Originally aired as seven episodes on PBS, it has been released in a truncated version on video. Not rated. 270m. **DIR:** Waris Hussein. **CAST:** Edward Fox, Cynthia Harris. **1980**

EDWARD SCISSORHANDS ★★★ A mean-spirited, violent ending irrevocably mars what might have been a charming fantasy. Through the character of Edward Scissorhands (Johnny Depp), a sweet-natured android whose exposure to civilization is anything but pleasant, cowriter-director Tim Burton seems to be exorcising the pain of his own adolescence. Rated PG-13 for violence and profanity. 89m. **DIR:** Tim Burton. **CAST:** Johnny Depp, Winona Ryder, Dianne Wiest, Anthony Michael Hall, Alan Arkin, Vincent Price, Kathy Baker, Conchata Ferrell. **1990**

EDWARD II ★★★ This bizarre, medieval costume drama—the characters speak in rich Elizabethan prose while wearing mostly modern attire—grabs Christopher Marlowe's sixteenth century play (*The Troublesome Reign of Edward II*) by the throat and heaves it into the 1990s. The story about the downfall of England's openly gay king skewers sexual obsessions, repression, and politics with an intriguing sense of timelessness and moral decay. Rated R for profanity, nudity, and violence. 90m. **DIR:** Derek Jarman. **CAST:** Steven Waddington, Andrew Tiernan, Tilda Swinton, Nigel Terry. **1992**

EEGAH! 🎗 Teenage caveman gets the hots for brain-dead babe. 90m. **DIR:** Nicholas Merriwether (Arch Hall Sr.). **CAST:** Arch Hall Jr., Richard Kiel, Marilyn Manning, William Watters (Arch Hall Sr.). **1962**

•EEL, THE ★★★1/2 An office worker spends eight years in prison for killing his wife and her lover. After he is released, he tries to begin life anew as a barber in a small fishing village. Winner of the grand prize at the Cannes Film Festival, this meandering character study may try the patience of viewers unaccustomed to Japanese films. In Japanese with English subtitles. Not rated; contains strong violence, nudity, and sexual situations. 117m. **DIR:** Shohei Imamura. **CAST:** Koji Yakusho, Misa Shimizu, Fujio Tsuneta. **1997**

EFFECT OF GAMMA RAYS ON MAN-IN-THE-MOON MARIGOLDS, THE ★★★ Toxic drama based on Paul Zindel's Pulitzer Prize–winning play about an eccentric, widowed mother and her two daughters. Joanne Woodward is excellent as Beatrice, whose dreams of a better life have taken a toll on her reality. Her youngest daughter, Matilda, escapes her dreary existence through her animals and school, where her science project (the title of the film) serves as a metaphor for her mother's relationship with her and her sister. Rated PG. 100m. **DIR:** Paul Newman. **CAST:** Joanne Woodward, Nell Potts, Roberta Wallach, Judith Lowry, David Spielberg. **1972**

•EFFI BRIEST ★★★ In the late 1800s, a young girl seeks to escape her stifling marriage to a much older man by having an affair with a soldier. Rainer Werner Fassbinder faithfully adapted this film from a novel that is Germany's equivalent of *Madame Bovary* or *Anna Karenina*. His intention is to evoke the stifling domesticity of German society of the time, a goal that may not entertain all viewers. In German with English subtitles. B&W; 140m. **DIR:** Rainer Werner Fassbinder. **CAST:** Hanna Schygulla, Wolfgang Schenck, Ulli Lommel. **1974**

EFFICIENCY EXPERT, THE (SPOTSWOOD) ★★★ Echoes of *Local Hero* are present in this offbeat film about British efficiency expert Anthony Hopkins plying his trade in 1960s Australia and beginning to question his own efficacy. While this film doesn't have the charm and truly off-the-wall humor of director Bill Forsyth's cult comedy, it is generally enjoyable. Rated PG for violence. 96m. **DIR:** Mark Joffe. **CAST:** Anthony Hopkins, Ben Mendelsohn, Toni Collette, Bruno Lawrence, Rebecca Rigg. **1992**

EGG ★★★ Delightful, bittersweet comedy from Holland about a quiet, illiterate baker who romances an awkward and lonely schoolteacher. In Dutch with English subtitles. 58m. **DIR:** Danniel Danniel. **CAST:** Johan Leysen, Marijke Veugelers. **1988**

EGG AND I, THE ★★★ Hayseed Fred MacMurray spirits his finishing-school bride Claudette Colbert away from Boston to cope with chicken farming in the rural Pacific Northwest. Everything goes wrong. Marjorie Main and Percy Kilbride as Ma and Pa Kettle made comic marks bright enough to earn them their own film series. Not a laugh riot, but above-average funny. B&W; 108m. **DIR:** Chester Erskine. **CAST:** Claudette Colbert, Fred MacMurray, Louise Allbritton, Marjorie Main, Percy Kilbride, Donald MacBride, Samuel S. Hinds, Fuzzy Knight. **1947**

EGYPTIAN, THE ★★1/2 With the exception of Edmund Purdom, most of the cast is ill-used in this highly atmospheric, bumpy biblical spectacle centering on a physician. 140m. **DIR:** Michael Curtiz. **CAST:** Jean Simmons, Edmund Purdom, Victor Mature, Gene Tierney, Peter Ustinov, Michael Wilding. **1954**

EIGER SANCTION, THE ★★1/2 Laughable but entertaining adaptation of Trevanian's equally laughable but entertaining novel. Clint Eastwood is a college professor by day and supersecret agent by night. Outrageously overblown characters and plenty of opportunities for Eastwood to strut his macho stuff. Rated R for violence and sex. 128m. **DIR:** Clint Eastwood. **CAST:** Clint Eastwood, George Kennedy, Jack Cassidy, Thayer David, Vonetta McGee. **1975 DVD**

8 1/2 ★★★★★ Perhaps one of Federico Fellini's strongest cinematic achievements. *8 1/2* is the loose portrayal of a film director making a personal movie and finding himself trapped in his fears, dreams, and irresolutions. This brilliant exercise features outstanding performances, especially by Marcello Mastroianni. Dubbed into English. Not rated. B&W; 135m. **DIR:** Federico Fellini. **CAST:** Marcello Mastroianni, Anouk Aimée, Claudia Cardinale, Barbara Steele, Sandra Milo. **1963**

•**EIGHT DAYS A WEEK** ★★1/2 Likable but not very significant romantic comedy about a young man so in love with his next-door neighbor that he camps out under her balcony until she becomes his. Writer-director Michael Davis's attempt at a lighthearted *Romeo and Juliet* has some funny, almost human moments dealing with teenage dating, but ultimately slips into situation comedy territory. Rated R for language. 92m. **DIR:** Michael Davis. **CAST:** Joshua Schaffer, Keri Russell, R. D. Robb, Mark L. Taylor, Catherine Hicks. **1999**

8 HEADS IN A DUFFEL BAG ★★ Mafia courier Joe Pesci is transporting the title package (proof that the victims of a mob hit are dead) when an airport switcheroo sends the grisly stash on a Mexican vacation with a college student. The premise is ghoulish but not very original, and the frantic, hammy performances elicit only a few scattered laughs. Rated R for profanity and grisly humor. 93m. **DIR:** Tom Schulman. **CAST:** Joe Pesci, Andy Comeau, Kristy Swanson, George Hamilton, Dyan Cannon, David Spade, Todd Louiso. **1997**

8MAN 🐄 After a Tokyo detective is murdered, his body is turned into a cyborg cop in this extremely slow, boring film. Not rated; contains violence. 91m. **DIR:** Yasuhiro Horiuchi. **CAST:** Kai Shishido, Etsushi Takahashi, Sachiko Ayashi, Osamu Ohtomo, Joe Shishido. **1992**

EIGHT MEN OUT ★★★1/2 Writer-director John Sayles scores a home run with this baseball drama about the 1919 Black Sox scandal—when members of the Chicago White Sox conspired to throw the World Series. A superb ensemble cast, which includes Sayles as Ring Lardner, shines in this true-life shocker, with David Strathairn and John Cusack giving standout performances. Rated PG for profanity. 120m. **DIR:** John Sayles. **CAST:** Charlie Sheen, John Cusack, Christopher Lloyd, D. B. Sweeney, David Strathairn, Michael Lerner, Clifton James, John Sayles, Studs Terkel. **1988**

8MM ★★1/2 Ostensibly a murder mystery but actually a deliberate attempt to test the tolerance of mainstream viewers who hope they don't know anyone this depraved. The desultory pacing fails to involve us in the mystery that sends surveillance expert Nicolas Cage in search of a missing young woman who may have participated (as victim) in an authentic snuff film. Our hero's subsequent descent into human slime, however, remains as detached as Cage's often somnambulant performance. Rated R for violence, profanity, nudity, and sexual deviancy. 123m. **DIR:** Joel Schumacher. **CAST:** Nicolas Cage, Joaquin Phoenix, James Gandolfini, Peter Stormare, Anthony Heald, Chris Bauer, Catherine Keener. **1999** DVD

8 SECONDS ★★1/2 This sanitized story of real-life bull rider Lane Frost—the youngest cowboy ever inducted into the Rodeo Hall of Fame—needs more grit. Lane's meteoric rise to superstardom, his showdown with the notorious bull, Red Rock, and the toll of the circuit on his marriage to a championship barrel racer is promising material, but the story—in rodeo lingo—doesn't quite cowboy up. Rated PG-13 for language. 97m. **DIR:** John G. Avildsen. **CAST:** Luke

Perry, Cynthia Geary, Stephen Baldwin, Red Mitchell, Carrie Snodgress. **1994** DVD

18 AGAIN 🐄 Yet another unsuccessful attempt to portray the older man magically switching into a young man's body. Rated PG for language and sexual suggestion. 100m. **DIR:** Paul Flaherty. **CAST:** George Burns, Charlie Schlatter, Tony Roberts, Anita Morris, Miriam Flynn, Jennifer Runyon, Red Buttons. **1988**

EIGHTEENTH ANGEL, THE ★★★ In this chiller from the writer of *The Omen*, a teacher and his daughter move to Rome where they become mixed up with the Etruscan order, a monastery that believes Satan will return to Earth in the form of an innocent child. Cloning, Satanism, and the death of a child are all thrown into the mix and the film moves along with a momentum all its own. Similarities to the older film, however, are undeniable. Rated R for gore, profanity, and violence. 90m. **DIR:** William Bindley. **CAST:** Christopher McDonald, Rachel Leigh Cook, Maximilian Schell. **1997**

EIGHTH DAY, THE ★★★1/2 A corporate workaholic is taught to enjoy life by a man with Down's syndrome (Pascal Duquenne). When writer-director Jaco Van Dormael borrows shamelessly from *Rain Man*, *Forrest Gump*, *King of Hearts*, and *One Flew over the Cuckoo's Nest*, his film is trite and superficial. When he uses his own imagination, though, the film soars. Duquenne, who has Down's syndrome in real life, gives a performance of amazing range and variety. In French with English subtitles. Not rated; contains mature themes and mild profanity. 114m. **DIR:** Jaco Van Dormael. **CAST:** Daniel Auteuil, Pascal Duquenne, Miou-Miou, Isabelle Sadoyan, Henri Garcin, Michele Maes. **1996**

EIGHTIES, THE ★★ A somewhat disjointed, tepid film about the making of a musical. If you're suddenly seized by an uncontrollable urge to attend an experimental French acting workshop, then snap this one up. In French with English subtitles. Not rated; the film has nudity. 82m. **DIR:** Chantal Akerman. **CAST:** Aurore Clement, Magali Noel. **1983**

84 CHARING CROSS ROAD ★★1/2 Anne Bancroft manages to act manic even while reading books in this true story based on the life of Helene Hanff, a writer and reader who begins a twenty-year correspondence with a London bookseller (Anthony Hopkins). Along with her orders for first editions, Hanff sends witty letters and care packages to the employees during the hard postwar times. Hanff and the bookseller begin to rely on the correspondence, yet never get to meet. Rated PG for language. 99m. **DIR:** David Jones. **CAST:** Anne Bancroft, Anthony Hopkins, Judi Dench, Maurice Denham. **1986**

84 CHARLIE MOPIC ★★★1/2 Powerfully realistic tour of Vietnam, circa 1969. A reconnaissance patrol sets out "in country" with an army motion picture (MOPIC) cameraman recording everything he can. What begins as a routine mission soon turns into a nightmare of terror and survival. A compelling and engrossing experience. Rated R for violence and profanity. 95m. **DIR:** Patrick Duncan. **CAST:** Richard Brooks, Christopher Borgard. **1989**

800 LEAGUES DOWN THE AMAZON ★★ Exotic locations and capable stars can't save this Jules Verne story from sinking twenty thousand leagues under the sea. Barry Bostwick floats through this tiresome yawner about a falsely accused man who risks capture and execution when he attempts to return home for his daughter's wedding. Adventuresome trip down the Amazon is the only high point. Rated PG-13 for violence. 85m. DIR: Luis Llosa. CAST: Barry Bostwick, Adam Baldwin, Daphne Zuniga, Tom Verica, E. E. Bell. 1993

8 MILLION WAYS TO DIE ★★ An alcoholic ex-cop, Jeff Bridges, attempts to help a high-priced L.A. prostitute get away from her crazed Colombian coke-dealer boyfriend, Andy Garcia. Considering the talent involved, this one should have been a real killer, but there are holes in the script and dead spots throughout. Rated R for violence, nudity, and language. 115m. DIR: Hal Ashby. CAST: Jeff Bridges, Rosanna Arquette, Alexandra Paul, Andy Garcia. 1986

EIJANAIKA (WHY NOT?) ★★★★ Set in the 1860s when Japan opened up to world trade after a military dictatorship, in power more than 700 years, was toppled, putting the emperor back in power and causing a rebellion by his subjects. Fascinating. In Japanese with English subtitles. Not rated, the film has nudity, profanity, and violence. 151m. DIR: Shohei Imamura. CAST: Shigeru Izumiya, Kaori Momoi, Ken Ogata, Mitsuko Baisho. 1981

EL (THIS STRANGE PASSION) ★★★★ Surreal portrait of a wealthy and devout middle-aged man, who is driven to madness by his pathological jealousy and obsession with religious ritual. Director Luis Buñuel has created an ironic dramatization of the destructive effect obsession can have on marriage and sexuality. In Spanish with English subtitles. B&W; 82m. DIR: Luis Buñuel. CAST: Arturo De Cordova. 1952

EL AMOR BRUJO ★★ This occasionally brilliant big-screen production of Manuel de Falla's ballet will appeal primarily to flamenco fans. The cast is excellent but overall the movie fails to fascinate. In Spanish with English subtitles. Rated PG for brief, stylized violence and references to sex in lyrics. 100m. DIR: Carlos Saura. CAST: Antonio Gades, Cristina Hoyos, Laura Del Sol. 1986

EL BRUTO (THE BRUTE) ★★★1/2 Exceptional surreal drama from Luis Buñuel about a tough slaughterhouse laborer who is exploited by a tyrannical landowner. Some strange melodramatic twists laced with moments of irony make this Mexican film one of Buñuel's stronger efforts. In Spanish with English subtitles. Not rated. B&W; 83m. DIR: Luis Buñuel. CAST: Pedro Armendariz, Katy Jurado, Andres Soler. 1952

EL CID ★★★ Some of the best battle action scenes ever filmed are included in this 1961 spectacle about the medieval Spanish hero El Cid. Unfortunately, on smaller home screens much of the splendor will be lost. You will be left with the wooden Charlton Heston and the beautiful Sophia Loren in a love story that was underdeveloped due to the movie's emphasis on spectacle. 184m. DIR: Anthony Mann. CAST: Charlton Heston, Sophia Loren, Raf Vallone, Hurd Hatfield. 1961

EL CONDOR ★★ A disappointing Western, this features cardboard performances by Jim Brown and Lee Van Cleef as two adventurers determined to take a fortress of gold called El Condor. Not rated, but equivalent to an R for nudity and violence. 102m. DIR: John Guillermin. CAST: Jim Brown, Lee Van Cleef, Patrick O'Neal. 1970

EL DIABLO ★★★1/2 When one of his students is kidnapped by outlaws, schoolteacher Anthony Edwards joins forces with gunfighter Lou Gossett to bring her back. This cable-produced Western adds offbeat plot twists and oddball bits of comedy to the shoot-'em-up formula. It's entertaining, if not particularly believable. 115m. DIR: Peter Markle. CAST: Anthony Edwards, Lou Gossett Jr., John Glover, M. C. Gainey, Sarah Trigger, Robert Beltran, Joe Pantoliano. 1990

EL DORADO ★★★1/2 Few stars could match John Wayne's ability to dominate a scene—and one of those few, Robert Mitchum, costars in this tale of a land war between Edward Asner and R. G. Armstrong. Mitchum plays the drunk, and Wayne is the gunfighter with whom he forms an uneasy alliance. It's an upscale B Western with some of the best scenes ever in a cowboy movie. 126m. DIR: Howard Hawks. CAST: John Wayne, Robert Mitchum, James Caan, Arthur Hunnicutt, Edward Asner, Michele Carey, Christopher George, Charlene Holt, Jim Davis, Paul Fix, R. G. Armstrong, Johnny Crawford. 1967 DVD

EL MARIACHI ★★★ This contemporary shoot-'em-up semi-spoofs spaghetti Westerns and Mexican action flicks. It's a visually choppy, grungy gem—shot on a fourteen-day, $7,000 schedule and cleaned up somewhat by Columbia Pictures before release—about a wandering Mexican musician who is pursued by thugs when he's mistaken for a rival hit man. In Spanish with English subtitles. Rated R for violence. 80m. DIR: Robert Rodriguez. CAST: Carlos Gallardo, Consuelo Gomez, Jaime de Hoyos, Peter Marquardt, Reinol Martinez. 1993 DVD

EL NORTE ★★★★★ A rewarding story about two Guatemalans, a young brother and sister, whose American dream takes them on a long trek to El Norte—the United States. This American-made movie is funny, frightening, poignant, and sobering—a movie that stays with you. In Spanish with subtitles. Rated R for profanity and violence. 139m. DIR: Gregory Nava. CAST: Zaide Silvia Gutierrez, David Villalpando. 1983

EL PASO KID ★★★ Ex-outlaw Sunset Carson becomes a lawman through a series of coincidences, eventually redeeming himself for his past. B&W; 54m. DIR: Thomas Carr. CAST: Sunset Carson, Hank Patterson. 1946

EL PROFESSOR HIPPIE ★★1/2 Veteran comedian Luis Sandrini plays a college professor who, because of his freethinking attitudes and concerns for moral questions over matters of business, has more in common with his students than his colleagues. This gentle comedy is a real audience pleaser. In Spanish. 91m. DIR: Fernando Ayala. CAST: Luis Sandrini. 1969

EL SUPER ★★★★ A funny and touching view of Cuban exiles living in a basement apartment during a cold winter in New York City. Raymundo Hidalgo-

Gato turns in a strong performance as the superintendent who dreams of his homeland while struggling with the conditions of his new culture. In Spanish with English subtitles. Not rated. 80m. DIR: Leon Ichaso. CAST: Raymundo Hidalgo-Gato, Elizabeth Peña. 1979

ELEANOR: FIRST LADY OF THE WORLD ★★★ Jean Stapleton's Eleanor Roosevelt will either charm you or grate on your nerves in this made-for-TV movie. But either way, you'll be inspired by the story of Mrs. Roosevelt's determination. 102m. DIR: John Erman. CAST: Jean Stapleton, E. G. Marshall, Coral Browne, Joyce Van Patten. 1982

•**ELEANOR ROOSEVELT STORY, THE** ★★★★ Hillary Rodham Clinton provides a special introduction to the video of this film that won the Oscar for best documentary. Using newsreel footage and photographs, it focuses on the years following the death of Eleanor's husband, Franklin, as she overcame personal tragedy to devote her life to public service. An inspirational film. Narrated by Achibald MacLeish. B&W; 90m. DIR: Richard Kaplan. 1965

ELECTRA GLIDE IN BLUE ★★★★ Robert Blake plays an Arizona cop with aspirations of being a detective. This extremely violent melodrama features good performances by the entire cast with several twists and turns to keep the viewer guessing. Rated R. 106m. DIR: James William Guercio. CAST: Robert Blake, Billy Green Bush, Mitchell Ryan, Elisha Cook Jr., Jeannine Riley, Royal Dano. 1973

ELECTRIC DREAMS ★★★ An ingenious blending of the motion picture with the rock music video, this release deals with the complications that arise when an absentminded architect, Miles (Lenny Von Dohlen), buys his first home computer. It isn't long before the computer (the voice is Bud Cort, of *Harold and Maude* fame) begins to develop a rather feisty personality. Rated PG for profanity. 96m. DIR: Steve Barron. CAST: Lenny Von Dohlen, Virginia Madsen, Bud Cort (voice). 1984

ELECTRIC GRANDMOTHER, THE ★★★★ Heartwarming TV adaptation of Ray Bradbury's "Sing the Body Electric" features Maureen Stapleton as a loving grandmother hired to raise three motherless children. She has some rather magical powers and only one drawback: she must be plugged in each night in order to recharge. 35m. DIR: Noel Black. CAST: Maureen Stapleton, Edward Herrmann. 1981

ELECTRIC HORSEMAN, THE ★★★ Directed by Sydney Pollack, this film brought the third teaming of Jane Fonda and Robert Redford on the screen. The result is a winsome piece of light entertainment. Redford plays Sonny Steele, a former rodeo star who has become the unhappy spokesman for Ranch Breakfast, a brand of cereal. He's always in trouble and in danger of blowing the job—until he decides to rebel. Rated PG. 120m. DIR: Sydney Pollack. CAST: Robert Redford, Jane Fonda, Valerie Perrine, Willie Nelson, John Saxon, Nicolas Coster, Wilford Brimley. 1979 DVD

ELEGANT CRIMINAL, THE ★★★★ Handsomely produced true story of a nineteenth century intellectual who rebelled against his loveless upbringing by embarking on a life of crime, one designed to lead to

his execution. In the title role, Daniel Auteuil is both charming and brutal, seductive and cold. Not rated, the film has violence and sexual situations. In French with English subtitles. 120m. DIR: Francis Girod. CAST: Daniel Auteuil, Jean Poiret, Marie-Armelle Deguy. 1990

ELEKTRA ★★★ This *Live from the Met* production is the Greek legend of Elektra and her obsession with revenge. Overly dramatic performances and operatic theatrics. Only opera buffs and Birgit Nilsson fans need to view this one. In German with English subtitles. 112m. DIR: Brian Large. CAST: Birgit Nilsson. 1980

ELEMENT OF CRIME, THE ★★★ Uneven attempt at *film noir*, about an ex-cop who returns to a postnuclear Europe to uncover the mystery of a serial killer who preys on young girls. Brilliant camera work shot entirely in sepia tone is not enough to sustain interest. Not rated; contains nudity and violence. 105m. DIR: Lars von Trier. CAST: Michael Elphick, Esmond Knight. 1988

ELEMENTARY SCHOOL, THE ★★★★ In post-WWII Prague, a pair of mischievous schoolboys are fascinated by their new schoolteacher, a former soldier who brings military discipline to his new job. This Oscar-nominated film from the director of *Kolya* is a comical but knowing portrait of small-town life that is in a class with the work of such Czech masters as Jiri Menzel and Milos Forman. In Czech with English subtitles. Not rated; contains sexual situations. 100m. DIR: Jan Sverak. CAST: Vaclav Jakoubek, Jan Triska, Zdenek Sverak, Radoslav Budac. 1990

ELENA AND HER MEN ★★★ One of Jean Renoir's personal favorites, this musical fantasy is about the power of love, and the evil of dictators. Ingrid Bergman is supported by a fine cast in this enjoyable comedy-drama. Originally released in America as *Paris Does Strange Things*. In French with English subtitles. 98m. DIR: Jean Renoir. CAST: Ingrid Bergman, Jean Marais, Mel Ferrer, Juliette Greco. 1956

ELENI ★★★ Interesting film adaptation of Nicholas Gage's factual book *Eleni*. In 1948, during the civil war in Greece, a small mountain village is terrorized by a group of Communist guerrillas. Eleni Gatzoyiannis (Kate Nelligan) defies the Communists and their attempts to abduct her children and is subsequently tortured and executed in cold blood. Eleni's son Nicholas Gage (John Malkovich) returns to Greece after many years as a reporter for the *New York Times*, devoting his life there to unmasking her killers. Rated PG for language and violence. 116m. DIR: Peter Yates. CAST: Kate Nelligan, John Malkovich, Linda Hunt. 1985

ELEPHANT BOY ★★★ Sabu made his film debut and became a star in this drama about a boy who claims to know where elephants go to die. Robert Flaherty's codirection gives the film a travelogue quality, but it interests and delights just the same. B&W; 80m. DIR: Robert Flaherty, Zoltán Korda. CAST: Sabu, W. E. Holloway, Walter Hudd, Bruce Gordon. 1937

ELEPHANT MAN, THE (1980) ★★★★ Though it has its flaws, this film is a fascinating and heartbreaking study of the life of John Merrick, a hopelessly deformed but kind and intelligent man who struggles for dignity. John Hurt is magnificent in the title role. Rated PG. B&W; 125m. **DIR:** David Lynch. **CAST:** Anthony Hopkins, John Hurt, Anne Bancroft, Wendy Hiller, Freddie Jones. **1980**

ELEPHANT MAN, THE (1982) ★★★★ Unlike the David Lynch film, this is a straight adaptation (made for television) of the Broadway play about the hideously deformed Victorian John Merrick. Philip Anglim plays Merrick without makeup, using only pantomime to suggest his appearance, and his performance is tremendously moving. 112m. **DIR:** Jack Hofsiss. **CAST:** Philip Anglim, Kevin Conway, Penny Fuller. **1982**

ELEPHANT WALK ★★ Elizabeth Taylor plays the bride of a Ceylon tea planter (Peter Finch) bewildered by her new home and carrying on with the hired hand (Dana Andrews). Dull, unconvincing drama; the climactic elephant stampede is too little, too late. 103m. **DIR:** William Dieterle. **CAST:** Elizabeth Taylor, Peter Finch, Dana Andrews, Abraham Sofaer. **1954**

ELEVATOR TO THE GALLOWS ★★★★ Marvelously twisted tale of murder and deceit features Jeanne Moreau as a wealthy woman plotting to have her husband killed by her lover. Her lover's getaway car is stolen by two teenagers who fit murder into their joyride, leaving the lover to take the rap. Jazz score by Miles Davis is perfect backdrop to nonstop decadence. (Also known as *Frantic.*) Not rated, in French with English subtitles. B&W; 87m. **DIR:** Louis Malle. **CAST:** Jeanne Moreau, Maurice Ronet, Georges Poujouly. **1957**

11 HARROWHOUSE ★★1/2 Confused heist caper vacillates wildly between straight drama and dark comedy. Diamond salesman Charles Grodin is talked into stealing valuable gems. Too farfetched to be taken seriously. An excellent cast goes to waste. Rated PG—mild sexual overtones. 95m. **DIR:** Aram Avakian. **CAST:** Charles Grodin, Candice Bergen, James Mason, John Gielgud. **1974**

ELFEGO BACA: SIX GUN LAW ★★1/2 Two-fisted lawyer Elfego Baca is charismatically portrayed by top actor Robert Loggia in compilation of episodes from *Walt Disney Presents* originally aired from 1958 to 1962. Defending justice in Tombstone, Arizona, Elfego Baca fights for the lives of an Englishman framed for murder and a rancher charged with bank robbery. 77m. **DIR:** Christian Nyby. **CAST:** Robert Loggia, James Dunn, Lynn Bari, James Drury, Jay C. Flippen, Kenneth Tobey, Annette Funicello, Patric Knowles, Audrey Dalton. **1962**

ELIMINATORS, THE ♥ A mad scientist creates the perfect weapon, the "Mandroid." Rated PG. 95m. **DIR:** Peter Manoogian. **CAST:** Andrew Prine, Denise Crosby, Patrick Reynolds, Roy Dotrice. **1986**

ELIZABETH ★★★★1/2 England's sixteenth-century royal highness is given a modern blast of bravado as she is jerked from dungeon to throne amidst bloody Catholic and Protestant feuding. Elizabeth becomes both pawn and power broker in a series of scandals and conspiracies before crowning herself England's Virgin Queen. This visually lush, revisionist lesson in survival and self-empowerment excel-lently captures physical details of the past as well as the fire of the queen's soul. Rated R for violence and sexuality. 124m. **DIR:** Shekhar Kapur. **CAST:** Cate Blanchett, Joseph Fiennes, Geoffrey Rush, Chris Eccleston. **1998 DVD**

ELIZABETH R ★★★★★ Double oscar winner Glenda Jackson won an Emmy Award for her brilliant, multihued portrayal of England's queen Elizabeth I in this six-part BBC-TV *Masterpiece Theater* dramatic chronicle of the forty-six-year reign of history's most heralded monarch. Engrossing and superb in every aspect, this ranks as one of public television's most outstanding miniseries. 540m. **DIR:** Claude Whatham, Herbert Wise, Richard Martin, Donald McWhinnie. **CAST:** Glenda Jackson, Ronald Hines, Vivian Pickles, Nicholas Selby, Robin Ellis. **1972**

ELLA CINDERS ★★★ Solid vehicle for comedienne Colleen Moore (then approaching the peak of her screen fame). It's an update on the Cinderella story, locating the fairy tale's events in contemporary Hollywood. The best scenes satirize moviemaking and the big studios of the day. Silent. B&W; 60m. **DIR:** Alfred E. Green. **CAST:** Colleen Moore, Lloyd Hughes. **1926**

ELLEN FOSTER ★★★1/2 This *Hallmark Hall of Fame* production questions the wisdom of keeping biological families together when neglect and abuse are present. Jena Malone is superb as a 10-year-old forced to run the household while Mom dies and Dad drinks. Things get even worse when her steely-hearted grandmother (chillingly portrayed by Julie Harris) forces her to live in her mansion. Not rated; contains adult themes. 90m. **DIR:** John Erman. **CAST:** Jena Malone, Julie Harris, Ted Levine, Glynnis O'Connor, Debra Monk, Kate Burton, Barbara Garrick. **1997**

ELLIS ISLAND ★★★ This TV miniseries, of the soap-opera variety, follows the lives of three immigrants who come to the United States at the turn of the century. All struggle to find acceptance, happiness, and success in the promised land. 310m. **DIR:** Jerry London. **CAST:** Richard Burton, Faye Dunaway, Ben Vereen, Melba Moore, Ann Jillian, Greg Martyn, Peter Riegert. **1984**

ELMER GANTRY ★★★★ Burt Lancaster gives one of his most memorable performances in this release as a phony evangelist who, along with Jean Simmons, exploits the faithful with his fire-and-brimstone sermons. Arthur Kennedy is the reporter out to expose their operation in this screen version of Sinclair Lewis's story set in the Midwest of the 1920s. 145m. **DIR:** Richard Brooks. **CAST:** Burt Lancaster, Jean Simmons, Dean Jagger, Arthur Kennedy, Shirley Jones. **1960**

ELUSIVE CORPORAL, THE ★★★★1/2 Twenty-five years after he made his greatest masterpiece, *La Grande Illusion*, Renoir reexamines men in war with almost equally satisfying results. This time the soldiers are Frenchmen in a World War II prison camp. This is a delicate drama infused with considerable wit. In French with English subtitles. 108m. **DIR:** Jean Renoir. **CAST:** Jean-Pierre Cassel, Claude Brasseur, Claude Rich. **1962**

ELUSIVE PIMPERNEL, THE ★★1/2 Lesser remake of the 1934 swashbuckling adventure, *The Scarlet*

Pimpernel. David Niven pales in comparison to Leslie Howard's portrayal of the death-defying savior. Not enough action to sustain viewer interest. 107m. DIR: Michael Powell. CAST: David Niven, Margaret Leighton, Cyril Cusack, Jack Hawkins. 1950

ELVES 🖤 Santa's little helpers are genetically mutated by former Nazi scientists. Not rated; the film has violence, nudity, and profanity. 89m. DIR: Jeff Mandel. CAST: Dan Haggerty, Deanna Lund. 1989

ELVIRA MADIGAN ★★★★ A simple and tragic story of a young Swedish officer who falls in love with a beautiful circus performer. Outstanding photography makes this film. Try to see the subtitled version. 89m. DIR: Bo Widerberg. CAST: Pia Degermark, Thommy Berggren. 1967 DVD

ELVIRA, MISTRESS OF THE DARK ★★★1/2 The late-night TV scream queen of B-film horror makes her debut as a movie star. It was well worth the wait! Elvira descends upon a midwestern town to sell her late aunt's estate. What ensues is a laugh riot, albeit with more breast jokes than you can count. You'll scream when you see Elvira as a baby. Rated PG-13 for profanity. 90m. DIR: James Signorelli. CAST: Elvira (Cassandra Peterson), Morgan Shepherd, Daniel Greene, Jeff Conaway, Susan Kellerman. 1988

ELVIS '56 ★★★★ Impressive documentary traces the evolution of Elvis Presley from naïve teenage rocker to jaded superstar—all in the space of one year. Narrated by Levon Helm (of The Band), the film uses television appearances, newsreel footage, publicity stills, and recordings to re-create the pivotal year in Elvis's career and life. 60m. DIR: Alan Raymond, Susan Raymond. CAST: Documentary. 1987 DVD

ELVIS AND ME 🖤 Originally a TV miniseries, this film version of Priscilla Presley's biography is disturbingly one-sided. 192m. DIR: Larry Peerce. CAST: Dale Midkiff, Susan Walters, Billy Green Bush. 1988

ELVIS MEETS NIXON ★★1/2 Alan Rosen's satiric script takes an actual event and uses it to outrageously parody both individuals in this made-for-cable production. While the meeting itself did occur (Presley wanted to become an undercover agent in the war against drugs), this overly broad dramatization gets most of its mileage from pithy commentary by Dick Cavett and other amused spectators. Rated R for profanity and mild violence. 95m. DIR: Allan Arkush. CAST: Rick Peters, Curtis Armstrong, Richard Beymer, Bob Gunton. 1997

ELVIS—THAT'S THE WAY IT IS ★★★★1/2 Col. Tom Parker insisted that Elvis make this documentary about his concert at the International Hotel in Las Vegas. It was one of Col. Parker's wisest decisions because it showcased Elvis's personality better than any of his thirty-one feature-length films. 107m. DIR: Denis Sanders. 1970

ELVIS: THE LOST PERFORMANCES ★★★ Only if you like Elvis would you enjoy these outtakes from two of his live-concert movies, *Elvis—That's the Way It Is* (1970) and *Elvis on Tour* (1972). Also included is footage of Elvis rehearsing at a sound studio in 1970. 60m. DIR: Patrick Michael Murphy. CAST: Elvis Presley. 1992

ELVIS—THE MOVIE ★★★★ A fictional account of Elvis Presley's rise to stardom, it probes deeply into the family life of rock 'n' roll's king. This TV movie should rate highly with fans of Elvis, as well as those just interested in a good story. Excellent voice re-creation by Ronnie McDowell. 117m. DIR: John Carpenter. CAST: Kurt Russell, Shelley Winters, Pat Hingle, Melody Anderson, Season Hubley, Charlie Hodge, Ellen Travolta, Ed Begley Jr. 1979

EMANON 🖤 The Messiah comes to New York City. Rated PG-13 for minor obscenities. 98m. DIR: Stuart Paul. CAST: Stuart Paul, Cheryl M. Lynn, Jeremy Miller. 1986

EMBRACE OF THE VAMPIRE ★★ Alyssa Milano has it hot and heavy for vampire hunk Martin Kemp, the man of her dreams. Problems arise when she's forced to choose between her human boyfriend and her dreamy bloodsucker. The film plods along with steamy but predictable results. Not rated; contains nudity, violence, and profanity. 93m. DIR: Anne Goursand. CAST: Martin Kemp, Alyssa Milano, Harrison Puett, Charlotte Lewis, Jennifer Tilly. 1994 DVD

EMBRYO ★★1/2 Rock Hudson plays a scientist who succeeds in developing a fetus into a full-grown woman in record time. But something isn't quite right. Adequate thriller with a good ending. Rated PG. 104m. DIR: Ralph Nelson. CAST: Rock Hudson, Barbara Carrera, Diane Ladd. 1976

EMERALD FOREST, THE ★★★★ In this riveting adventure film based on a true story, Powers Boothe stars as Bill Markham, an American engineer who, with his family, goes to the Amazon jungle to build a dam. There, his 5-year-old son is stolen by a native tribe known as the Invisible People. Markham spends the next ten years trying to find his son. Rated R for nudity, suggested sex, profanity, and violence. 110m. DIR: John Boorman. CAST: Powers Boothe, Meg Foster, Charley Boorman. 1985

EMERALD JUNGLE ★★ Originally titled *Eaten Alive by Cannibals,* this fitfully entertaining entry in the Italian cannibal parade was given its video moniker in the hope it would steal some of the thunder from John Boorman's unrelated *The Emerald Forest.* Heavily cut for U.S. release, but still plenty gross. Rated R. 90m. DIR: Umberto Lenzi. CAST: Robert Kerman, Janet Agren, Mel Ferrer. 1980

EMIGRANTS, THE ★★★★1/2 Completely absorbing but at times disturbingly sad saga of a group of impoverished farmers leaving mid-1800s Sweden to search for instant riches in America. The hardships and the resulting doubts suffered en route are graphically told and spellbinding. When this English-dubbed version was released in the United States in 1972, it garnered many Oscar nominations including best picture, director, and actress (Liv Ullmann). Rated PG for adult language and content. 151m. DIR: Jan Troell. CAST: Max von Sydow, Liv Ullmann, Allan Edwall. 1971

EMIL AND THE DETECTIVES ★★★1/2 One of the better live-action adventures made by the Disney Studios in the early 1960s, this grand little tale follows the escapades of a young boy who hires a gang of young, amateur sleuths after he's been robbed. Wholly improbable, but neatly constructed from the classic children's novel by Erich Kastner. 99m. DIR: Peter Tewksbury. CAST: Roger Mobley, Walter Slezak, Bryan Russell, Heinz Schubert. 1964

EMILY ★★ This British film was Koo Stark's premiere in soft-core porn. She plays a teenager returning home from boarding school who finds out that her mother is a well-paid prostitute. This bit of news upsets Emily momentarily, but she manages to create her own sexual world with a female painter, the painter's husband, and her boyfriend, James. Lots of nudity and sex. Rated R. 87m. DIR: Henry Herbert. CAST: Koo Stark. 1982

EMILY BRONTE'S WUTHERING HEIGHTS ★★★1/2 Based on the 1847 book, this features gorgeous Juliette Binoche as the somewhat schizophrenic Cathy. Physically and emotionally she's bound to Heathcliff (Ralph Fiennes), yet she longs to belong to her neighbor's upper-crust society. Fiennes adopts a devilish persona as he wreaks his revenge on all who have hurt her. A notch above a soap but equally compelling. Not rated; contains violence. 104m. DIR: Peter Kosminsky. CAST: Juliette Binoche, Ralph Fiennes, Janet McTeer, Sophie Ward. 1992

EMINENT DOMAIN ★★1/2 Unsettling political thriller with Donald Sutherland as a high-ranking official in Poland who is stripped of his power, only to get stonewalled when he attempts to find out the reason. Plenty of suspense. Rated PG-13 for profanity. 102m. DIR: John Irvin. CAST: Donald Sutherland, Anne Archer, Jodhi May, Paul Freeman. 1991

EMMA ★★★★ The legendary Marie Dressler was Oscar nominated for this comedy-drama about an aging, dowdy housekeeper who falls in love with and marries the rich widower who hired her. B&W; 73m. DIR: Clarence Brown. CAST: Marie Dressler, Myrna Loy, Jean Hersholt, John Miljan, Richard Cromwell, Leila Bennett. 1932

EMMA (1996) ★★★★ The A&E team behind *Pride and Prejudice* created a lavish and wry comedy with a markedly different flavor than Gwyneth Paltrow's frothy theatrical version. A crisp, fast pace is enhanced by Kate Beckinsale's precise delivery, though she's occasionally too brittle in the title role. Especially intriguing are the amusing enactments of Emma's meddlesome daydreams and flights of fancy. Not rated. 107m. DIR: Diarmuid Lawrence. CAST: Kate Beckinsale, Mark Strong, Prunella Scales, Bernard Hepton, Raymond Coulthard, Samantha Morton, Olivia Williams, Dominic Rowan, Lucy Robinson. 1996 DVD

EMMA (1996) ★★★★ Jane Austen's novel of a charming young meddler (Gwyneth Paltrow) arranging everyone's romantic lives while neglecting her own makes a charming, well-acted film. Director Douglas McGrath makes it all look a little too candied and idealized, and Jeremy Northam is a bit too young and handsome for his role as Emma's older friend, but those are only minor drawbacks in a breezy and engaging entertainment. Rated PG. 111m. DIR: Douglas McGrath. CAST: Gwyneth Paltrow, Jeremy Northam, Toni Collette, Greta Scacchi, Juliet Stevenson, Sophie Thompson. 1996 DVD

EMMANUELLE ★★★ Sylvia Kristel became an international star as a result of this French screen adaptation of Emmanuelle Argan's controversial

book about the initiation of a diplomat's young wife into the world of sensuality. In the soft-core sex film genre, this stands out as one of the best. Rated R for nudity. 92m. DIR: Just Jaeckin. CAST: Sylvia Kristel, Marika Green, Daniel Sarky, Alain Cuny. 1974 DVD

EMMA'S SHADOW ★★★★ Enchanting story of an 11-year-old girl from wealthy parents who fakes her own kidnapping in the 1930s. Winner of the Danish best film award. In Danish with English subtitles. Not rated. 93m. DIR: Soeren Kragh-Jacobsen. CAST: Line Kruse, Borje Ahlstedt. 1988

•EMPEROR AND THE ASSASSIN, THE ★★★1/2 In third century bc, a warlord obsessed with becoming China's first emperor discovers that his bloodline is tainted; an assassin vows never to kill again only to seek redemption through his sword. A court concubine becomes the link between both men, and an ancestral mandate to unify the seven dominant kingdoms of China brings massive human suffering to a country scarred by 550 years of bloodshed. The narrative of this lavish, bloody epic about royal egos, lust, and revenge drags at times, but its visual sweep is staggering. In Mandarin with English subtitles. Rated R for violence and language. 161m. DIR: Chen Kaige. CAST: Gong Li, Zhang Fengyi, Li Xuejian. 2000 DVD

EMPEROR JONES, THE ★★★1/2 This liberal version of Eugene O'Neill's prize-winning play invents entire sections that were written to capitalize on star Paul Robeson's fame as a singer as well as an introductory piece that provides a background for Robeson's character, the doomed Jones. This is still an interesting and sometimes strong film despite the drastic changes. Surviving prints that have been transferred to tape are not always in the best of condition, so quality will vary on this title. B&W; 72m. DIR: Dudley Murphy. CAST: Paul Robeson, Dudley Digges, Frank Wilson. 1933

EMPEROR WALTZ, THE ★★★1/2 Bing Crosby is a traveling phonograph salesman who attempts to make a sale and obtain an endorsement from Austria's Emperor Franz Josef. Continuously witty and at times hilarious screenplay by producer Charles Brackett and director Billy Wilder. Not many songs but lots of fun. 116m. DIR: Billy Wilder. CAST: Bing Crosby, Joan Fontaine, Roland Culver, Lucile Watson, Richard Haydn, Sig Ruman. 1948

EMPEROR'S SHADOW, THE ★★★1/2 In the third century B.C., the first emperor of China tries to unite his squabbling realm in the face of opposition from a childhood friend, now a revered musician. This lavish historical epic has something for everyone: cast-of-thousands spectacle, political intrigue, sexual scheming, and psychological insight, all superbly acted and beautifully photographed against stunning scenery. In Mandarin with English subtitles. Not rated; contains violence and brief sexual scenes. 123m. DIR: Zhou Xiaowen. CAST: Jiang Wen, Ge You, Xu Qing. 1996 DVD

EMPIRE CITY ★★ Standard fare features Michael Paré as a hard-as-nails detective who is paired with a female cop to help solve a murder in this attempt at *film noir.* Not rated; contains violence, adult situations, and language. 71m. DIR: Mark Rosner. CAST:

Michael Paré, Mary Mara, Beau Starr, Peter Frechette. 1991

EMPIRE OF THE ANTS ♥ H. G. Wells must somersault in his grave every time somebody watches this insulting adaptation of one of his more intriguing sci-fi stories. Rated PG for violence. 90m. **DIR:** Bert I. Gordon. **CAST:** Joan Collins, Robert Lansing, Albert Salmi, Robert Pine. 1977

EMPIRE OF THE DARK ★★ Run-of-the-mill devil flick concerning a Los Angeles police officer (writer-director-star Steve Barkett) who saves his baby son from a demonic cult. Twenty years later he and the now grown-up son must battle the cult again. Not rated; contains violence and profanity. 93m. **DIR:** Steve Barkett. **CAST:** Steve Barkett, Richard Harrison. 1991

EMPIRE OF THE SUN ★★★1/2 J. G. Ballard's harrowing autobiographical examination of life in a World War II Japanese prison camp has been given the Hollywood treatment by director Steven Spielberg, who filmed on location in Shanghai. Christian Bale, as Young Ballard, winds up in a concentration camp for four years. Too much surface gloss prevents this from being a classic, but it nonetheless contains scenes of surprising power and poignancy. Rated PG for language and intensity. 145m. **DIR:** Steven Spielberg. **CAST:** Christian Bale, John Malkovich, Miranda Richardson, Nigel Havers. 1987

EMPIRE RECORDS ★★ A day in the life of a group of record-store employees. Filled with eccentric characters and hard-driving music, this film is annoying but funny often enough. Features songs by the Gin Blossoms, the Cranberries, Toad the Wet Sprocket, and Evan Dando. Rated PG-13 for sexual situations, profanity, and drugs. 89m. **DIR:** Alan Moyle. **CAST:** Anthony LaPaglia, Maxwell Caulfield, Debi Mazar, Rory Cochrane, Johnny Whitworth, Robin Tunney. 1995

EMPIRE STATE ♥ Powerful real estate magnate becomes involved with some shady dealings in London. Rated R for nudity and violence. 104m. **DIR:** Ron Peck. **CAST:** Martin Landau, Ray McAnally, Catherine Harrison. 1987

EMPIRE STRIKES BACK, THE ★★★★★ In George Lucas's follow-up to *Star Wars*, Billy Dee Williams joins Mark Hamill (Luke Skywalker), Harrison Ford (Han Solo), Carrie Fisher (Princess Leia), and the gang in their fight against the forces of the Empire led by Darth Vader. It's more action-packed fun in that faraway galaxy a long time ago. Rated PG. 124m. **DIR:** Irvin Kershner. **CAST:** Billy Dee Williams, Harrison Ford, Carrie Fisher, Mark Hamill, Anthony Daniels, Dave Prowse, James Earl Jones (voice). 1980

EMPLOYEES' ENTRANCE ★★★1/2 Warren William is especially sleazy as the manager of a department store who takes advantage of the fact that jobs are scarce due to the Depression. Surprisingly frank comedy-drama made before the Hays Office started to clamp down. B&W; 75m. **DIR:** Roy Del Ruth. **CAST:** Warren William, Loretta Young, Wallace Ford, Allen Jenkins. 1933

EMPTY CANVAS, THE ★★ Would-be painter Horst Buchholz falls for gold-digging model Catherine Spaak. Maudlin pap. B&W; 118m. **DIR:** Damiani. **CAST:** Bette Davis, Horst Buchholz, Catherine Spaak, Daniela Rocca, Georges Wilson. 1964

EMPTY HOLSTERS ★★★ Cowboy crooner Dick Foran is framed for murder and sent up the river. Once out of prison, Foran is forced to prove his innocence and defend the townsfolk without the aid of his six-shooters. Veteran heavy Glenn Strange, in a nice twist, is a good-guy sidekick. B&W; 58m. **DIR:** B. Reeves "Breezy" Eason. **CAST:** Dick Foran, Glenn Strange. 1937

ENCHANTED APRIL ★★★1/2 In order to escape their boring lives and demanding husbands, two female friends hatch a plot, with the help of two women they've never met, to rent a luxurious mansion on the Italian Riviera. For all four of them, their little getaway turns out to be full of surprises, delights, and life-changing realizations. A warm-hearted romp that is as magical as its setting. Rated PG. 97m. **DIR:** Mike Newell. **CAST:** Miranda Richardson, Joan Plowright, Josie Lawrence, Polly Walker, Alfred Molina, Michael Kitchen, Jim Broadbent. 1992

ENCHANTED COTTAGE, THE ★★★1/2 An engrossing blend of romance, fantasy, and melodrama. Robert Young gives one of his best big-screen performances as a battle-scarred World War II veteran. Dorothy McGuire offers a beautifully realized portrayal of a young woman whose inner loveliness is hidden beneath a painfully plain exterior. As the blind friend who sees so much more than everyone else, Herbert Marshall is as suave as ever. B&W; 91m. **DIR:** John Cromwell. **CAST:** Dorothy McGuire, Robert Young, Herbert Marshall, Spring Byington, Hillary Brooke. 1945

ENCHANTED FOREST, THE ★★★ Pleasant fantasy about an old hermit who teaches a young boy to love the forest and its creatures lacks a big-studio budget but is fine family fare. 77m. **DIR:** Lew Landers. **CAST:** Edmund Lowe, Harry Davenport, Brenda Joyce, Billy Severn, John Litel. 1945 DVD

ENCHANTED ISLAND ♥ Dull adaptation of Herman Melville's *Typee*. 95m. **DIR:** Allan Dwan. **CAST:** Dana Andrews, Jane Powell, Arthur Shields, Don Dubbins. 1958

ENCHANTMENT ★★★1/2 An enchanting fantasy that bubbles over with romantic intentions. An old man watches his grandniece make some of the same mistakes he made in his romantic life and finds a way for her to benefit from those mistakes. Light entertainment made enjoyable by a strong cast. B&W; 101m. **DIR:** Irving Reis. **CAST:** David Niven, Teresa Wright, Evelyn Keyes, Farley Granger, Jayne Meadows, Leo G. Carroll, Shepperd Strudwick. 1948

ENCINO MAN ★★★ This teen comedy—about a couple of misfits who find a caveman frozen in their backyard—is surprisingly funny. Sean Astin and Pauly Shore are best friends who defrost the prehistoric man. Rated PG for mild sexual innuendos. 88m. **DIR:** Les Mayfield. **CAST:** Sean Astin, Brendan Fraser, Pauly Shore, Megan Ward, Michael DeLuise, Mariette Hartley, Richard Masur. 1992 DVD

ENCORE ★★★ Somerset Maugham introduces three of his short stories in this sequel to *Trio*. The best of the three is "Gigolo and Gigolette" in which trapeze artist Glynis Johns begins to feel used by her husband as he promotes her death-defying act. The other two ("The Ant and the Grasshopper" and "Winter Cruise") are more humorous. B&W; 85m. DIR: Harold French, Pat Jackson, Anthony Pelissier. CAST: Glynis Johns, Nigel Patrick, Kay Walsh, Roland Culver, Ronald Squire, Peter Graves. 1952

ENCOUNTER AT RAVEN'S GATE ★★★1/2 A small Australian town is stricken by unusual occurrences: electrical faults, violent and psychotic human behavior. Solid acting, vivid characterizations, a refreshing atmosphere of alternative cinema, and a sedately haunting soundtrack make this one worth a watch. Rated R for violence. 85m. DIR: Rolf De Heer. CAST: Ritchie Singer, Steven Vidler, Vincent Gil, Saturday Rosenberg. 1988

ENCOUNTER WITH THE UNKNOWN ★★★1/2 Rod Serling narrates a series of true events in psychic phenomena. The episodes are based on studies made by Dr. Jonathan Rankin between 1949 and 1970. Each deals with a person's encounter with the unknown or supernatural. Rated PG. 90m. DIR: Harry Thomason. CAST: Rod Serling, Rosie Holotik, Gene Ross. 1973

END, THE ★★★1/2 The blackest of black comedies, this stars Burt Reynolds (who also directed) as an unfortunate fellow who is informed he's dying of a rare disease. Poor Burt can hardly believe it. So he decides to end it all. In the process, he meets a maniac (Dom DeLuise) who is more than willing to lend a hand. It's surprisingly funny. Rated R. 100m. DIR: Burt Reynolds. CAST: Burt Reynolds, Sally Field, Dom DeLuise, Joanne Woodward, David Steinberg, Pat O'Brien, Myrna Loy, Kristy McNichol, Robby Benson. 1978

•END OF DAYS ★★1/2 When Satan comes to New York City to mate and gain control of the world for the next millenium, he takes over the body of a financial executive to prey on a young woman that the Vatican is protecting. But the priests fail to stop ol' Scratch, so it's up to one-man-army Arnold Schwarzenegger to take him on. Terrific opening scenes slide into a where-do-we-go-from-here dilemma for director Peter Hyams, who is forced to top himself once too often. The result is an overreliance on special effects at the expense of strong storytelling. Rated R for violence, profanity, nudity, and simulated sex. 120m. DIR: Peter Hyams. CAST: Arnold Schwarzenegger, Gabriel Byrne, Kevin Pollak, Robin Tunney, C.C.H. Pounder, Rod Steiger, Derrick O'Connor, Miriam Margolis, Udo Kier, Mark Margolis. 1999 DVD

END OF INNOCENCE, THE ★★ Seriocomic story of a woman, driven over the edge who "finds herself" only after a drug overdose. All that saves the film are occasional flashes of style and self-mockery from first-time feature director Dyan Cannon (who also wrote). Rated R for profanity and sexual situations. 92m. DIR: Dyan Cannon. CAST: Dyan Cannon, John Heard, George Coe, Rebecca Schaeffer, Billie Bird, Viveka Davis. 1990

END OF ST. PETERSBURG, THE ★★★1/2 The story of a worker who gradually becomes aware of his duty to his class. He becomes a part of the 1917 Revolution. Although pure propaganda, this powerful indictment of czarist Russia has a fervor and sweep that transcends its message. Silent, with English intertitles. B&W; 75m. DIR: V. I. Pudovkin. CAST: Ivan Chuvelov. 1927

END OF SUMMER 🎗 Positively laughable exercise in turn-of-the-century bodice ripping, with artist Jacqueline Bisset unable to pledge her love to randy Peter Weller; it's the sort of oh-so-melodramatic treacle that gives romance novels a bad name. Rated R for nudity, simulated sex, and drug use. 95m. DIR: Linda Yellen. CAST: Jacqueline Bisset, Peter Weller, Julian Sands, Amy Locane. 1995

•END OF THE AFFAIR, THE ★★1/2 From production designer Anthony Pratt's impeccable re-creation of WWII London, to the convincing yet unassuming manner with which director Neil Jordan populates every scene, The End of the Affair looks and feels like a product of the era it simulates. But the story—adapted from one of Graham Greene's most tortured novels of guilt and Catholic angst—is a sluggish, ponderous, three-character melodrama so much a product of its very British origins that it becomes a parody of the clipped, unemotional atmosphere that we always associate with our cousins across the pond. In a word, it's boring, and you won't care a whit about the adulterous affair that ultimately destroys all three of these self-absorbed boors. Rated R for nudity and strong sexual content. 105m. DIR: Neil Jordan. CAST: Ralph Fiennes, Julianne Moore, Stephen Rea, Ian Hart, Jason Isaacs, James Bolam, Sam Bould. 1999 DVD

END OF THE LINE ★★★ Financed as a labor of love by executive producer and costar Mary Steenburgen, this first film by director Jay Russell features Wilford Brimley as a railroad worker who, with buddy Levon Helm, steals a train engine to protest the closing of the freight depot where he has worked for thirty-eight years. The skilled performances will keep you interested right to the end of the line. Rated PG for profanity. 105m. DIR: Jay Russell. CAST: Wilford Brimley, Levon Helm, Kevin Bacon, Bob Balaban, Barbara Barrie, Mary Steenburgen, Holly Hunter, Bruce McGill, Howard Morris. 1988

END OF THE ROAD ★★ Stacy Keach plays a college graduate who falls out of society, receives help from an unorthodox psychotherapist named Doctor D (James Earl Jones), then becomes intimately involved with a married couple. The imagery can be compelling, but the finale is too graphic. Rated X (by 1960s standards) but more like a hard R for sex, nudity, and adult themes. 110m. DIR: Aram Avakian. CAST: Stacy Keach, Harris Yulin, Dorothy Tristan, James Earl Jones. 1969

END OF THE TRAIL ★★★★ The great Western star Colonel Tim McCoy was a lifelong champion of the American Indian. This is his magnum opus, a movie sympathetic to Native Americans made nearly twenty years before Broken Arrow. It's an ambitious, somewhat dated story of a cavalry officer (McCoy) falsely accused of treason and forced to prove his innocence by uncovering the true villain. B&W; 62m. DIR: D. Ross Lederman. CAST: Tim McCoy, Luana Walters, Wheeler Oakman. 1932

END OF THE WORLD 🎗 Aliens plot to destroy the Earth while disguised as religious figures. Rated PG.

7m. DIR: John Hayes. CAST: Christopher Lee, Sue yon, Lew Ayres, Dean Jagger, Macdonald Carey. 1977

ND OF VIOLENCE, THE ★★★ Director Wim Wenders attempts to address the state of life in Los Angeles through the eyes of numerous spy cameras situated throughout the city, and the kidnapping of a popular Hollywood producer. It's a melting pot of ideas that never comes to a full boil, and by tackling so much in so little time, Wenders hasn't delivered more than an interesting idea. Rated R for language. 22m. DIR: Wim Wenders. CAST: Andie MacDowell, Bill Pullman, Gabriel Byrne, Traci Lind, Loren Dean. 1997 DVD

NDANGERED ❤ A relentlessly stupid and badly acted riff on Richard Connell's "Most Dangerous Game," with mewling Sandra Hess trying to evade some psychopathic drug runners. Rated R for violence, drug use, profanity, and nudity. 91m. DIR: Nick Jellis. CAST: Sandra Hess, Rick Aiello, Martin Kove. 1994

NDANGERED SPECIES ★★★1/2 Everything about this nifty science-fiction suspense-thriller is well-done. The story deals with bizarre incidents involving cattle mutilation and is based on fact. In it, a country sheriff (JoBeth Williams) and a hard-boiled New York detective (Robert Urich) join forces to find out who or what is responsible. Rated R for discreetly handled nudity, violence, and profanity. 97m. DIR: Alan Rudolph. CAST: Robert Urich, JoBeth Williams, Paul Dooley, Hoyt Axton. 1982

NDLESS DESCENT ❤ A group of otherworldly genetic mutants in a subaquarian chamber. Not rated; contains violence, profanity, and gore. 79m. DIR: Juan Piquer Simon. CAST: Jack Scalia, R. Lee Ermey, Ray Wise, Deborah Adair. 1989

NDLESS GAME, THE ★★ With a creakily indifferent tone, writer-director Bryan Forbes's cold war–styled spy thriller overdoses on the residual cynicism of a once-vibrant genre. Albert Finney stars as a retired agent summoned back to learn why aged members of a disbanded European operation are being killed. Not rated; explicit dialogue, brief nudity, and violence. 120m. DIR: Bryan Forbes. CAST: Albert Finney, George Segal, Anthony Quayle, Nanette Newman. 1990

NDLESS LOVE ★★ Though this story of a teenage love affair has all the elements of a great romance, it is marred by implausibility and inconsistency. The film improves as it progresses and even offers some compelling moments, but not enough to compensate for its flaws. Rated R because of sex and nudity. 115m. DIR: Franco Zeffirelli. CAST: Brooke Shields, Martin Hewitt, Shirley Knight, Don Murray. 1981

NDLESS NIGHT ❤ Routine suspense from the pen of Agatha Christie. Not rated; contains slight nudity and some violence. 95m. DIR: Sidney Gilliat. CAST: Hayley Mills, Hywel Bennett, Britt Ekland, George Sanders. 1972

NDLESS SUMMER, THE ★★★★ The only surfing documentary ever to gain an audience outside the Beach Boys set, this is an imaginatively photographed travelogue that captures the joy, danger, and humor of searching for the perfect wave. Much of the success is attributable to the whimsical narra-

tion. 95m. DIR: Bruce Brown. CAST: Mike Hynson, Robert August. 1966 DVD

ENDLESS SUMMER II ★★★ Bruce Brown's long-delayed sequel to his 1966 cult hit about surfing around the world is basically more of the same. This time, superior 1990s technology makes much of the footage truly spectacular. Brown again narrates with hokey charm. A must-see for surfing fans, a pleasant diversion for others. Rated PG for brief glimpses of some topless beaches. 107m. DIR: Bruce Brown. CAST: Patrick O'Connell, Robert "Wingnut" Weaver. 1994

ENDURANCE (1985) ❤ Grown Japanese men subject themselves to all kinds of torture and humiliation in this Japanese game show aimed at American audiences. Not rated, but not for the squeamish. 90m. DIR: Edward Simons, Peter McRae. CAST: None Credited. 1985

ENDURANCE ★★1/2 This film about Ethiopian runner Haile Gebrsellasie, a gold medalist at the 1996 Atlanta Olympics, is an uneasy mix of documentary race footage (directed by Bud Greenspan) and awkward reenactments of events from Gebrsellasie's life, with the runner and family playing themselves. Director Leslie Woodhead concentrates more on atmosphere than events, and the result is often tedious, with important facts tossed off in the closing credits rather than dramatized during the film itself. Rated PG. 83m. DIR: Leslie Woodhead. CAST: Haile Gebrsellasie, Yonas Zergaw, Shawananness Gebrsellasie, Tedesse Haile. 1998

ENEMIES—A LOVE STORY ★★★★ Director Paul Mazursky achieves a delicate mixture of drama and comedy in his adaptation of the novel by Isaac Bashevis Singer. Set in New York in 1949, the film focuses on the hectic life of Holocaust survivor and womanizer Herman Broder (Ron Silver). Rated R for profanity, nudity, and simulated sex. 120m. DIR: Paul Mazursky. CAST: Ron Silver, Anjelica Huston, Lena Olin, Margaret Sophie Stein, Alan King, Paul Mazursky. 1989

●ENEMY ACTION ★★1/2 Low-budget Roger Corman production about officers trying to stop a terrorist plan to detonate stolen bombs in Washington, DC. Standard thriller fare enlivened by Randolph Mantooth as a scene-stealing villain. Rated R for violence and profanity. 84m. DIR: Brian Katkin. CAST: C. Thomas Howell, Lisa Thornhill, Randolph Mantooth, Richard Lynch. 1999

ENEMY BELOW, THE ★★★1/2 Robert Mitchum as the captain of a U.S. Navy destroyer and Curt Jurgens as the commander of a German submarine play a deadly game of chess as they pursue each other across the South Atlantic during World War II. This little-seen aquatic duel is well worth viewing. 98m. DIR: Dick Powell. CAST: Robert Mitchum, Curt Jurgens, David Hedison, Theodore Bikel, Russell Collins, Kurt Kreuger, Frank Albertson, Doug McClure. 1957

ENEMY FROM SPACE ★★★★ Brian Donlevy makes his second appearance as Professor Quatermass, a scientist hero who discovers that aliens are slowly taking over the governments of Earth—starting with Britain. It's an uncommonly powerful film. The first entry in the theatrical trilogy was The

Creeping Unknown and the last was *Five Million Years to Earth.* B&W; 85m. DIR: Val Guest. CAST: Brian Donlevy, William Franklyn. 1957 DVD

ENEMY MINE ★★ A would-be outer-space epic. Two futuristic foes, an Earthman (Dennis Quaid) and a reptilian alien (Louis Gossett Jr.), are stranded on a hostile planet and forced to rely on each other for survival. Rated PG-13 for violence and profanity. 108m. DIR: Wolfgang Petersen. CAST: Dennis Quaid, Lou Gossett Jr., Brion James, Richard Marcus, Lance Kerwin. 1985

ENEMY OF THE LAW ★★★★ The Texas Rangers track down an outlaw gang who, years before, robbed a safe and hid the money. There are some hilarious escapades in this well-above-average oater. Tex Ritter's songs are always good. B&W; 59m. DIR: Harry Fraser. CAST: Tex Ritter, Dave O'Brien, Guy Wilferson, Charles King. 1945

ENEMY OF THE STATE ★★★ If it's possible for a film to be too visually dynamic, then this is it. Director Tony Scott, obsessed with unbridled technology and rapid-fire style-for-its-own-sake, nearly overwhelms the intriguing story at the heart of this disturbing commentary on the fragility of personal privacy. Will Smith stars as a lawyer who gets sucked into a conspiracy case involving a rogue NSA dirty-trickster who killed a U.S. congressman. Our hero's life is turned upside down until he meets up with a former agent with lots of answers. When all is said and done, credibility isn't so much stretched as mangled beyond recognition. But it does succeed on a "kick-ass" level. Rated R for violence and profanity. 127m. DIR: Tony Scott. CAST: Will Smith, Gene Hackman, Jon Voight, Regina King, Loren Dean, Jake Busey, Barry Pepper. 1998 DVD

ENEMY TERRITORY ★★ This film features a good premise but suffers from poor acting, writing, and production values. Gary Frank is an insurance salesman trapped inside a ghetto apartment building and battling a vicious gang. Rated R for language, extreme violence, and brief nudity. 89m. DIR: Peter Manoogian. CAST: Gary Frank, Ray Parker Jr., Jan-Michael Vincent, Frances Foster. 1987

ENEMY UNSEEN ★★1/2 Mercenary tracks down the kidnapped daughter of a wealthy industrialist through the darkest regions of Africa, where she is about to be sacrificed in a ritual in the crocodile spirits. Rated R for violence. 90m. DIR: Elmo De Witt. CAST: Vernon Wells, Stack Pierce. 1991

ENEMY WITHIN, THE ★★★1/2 This remake of *Seven Days in May* lacks the earlier film's urgency—and Rod Serling's taut script—but it's still a riveting idea. When an unpopular U.S. president decides to severely trim the military budget, a retaliatory coup is initiated by the vice president, the secretary of defense and a hawkish general. Only one honorable soldier stands in their way. This low-budget film still turns on a terrifying (and all too credible) concept. Rated PG-13 for profanity and violence. 86m. DIR: Jonathan Darby. CAST: Forest Whitaker, Sam Waterston, Dana Delany, Josef Sommer, George Dzundza, Jason Robards Jr. 1994

ENFORCER, THE (1951) ★★★1/2 A big-city district attorney, Humphrey Bogart, attempts to break up the mob in this effective crime drama. At unde 90 minutes, it moves like lightning and is refreshing ly devoid of most of the clichés of the genre. B&W 87m. DIR: Bretaigne Windust. CAST: Humphrey Bo gart, Zero Mostel, Everett Sloane, Ted de Corsia, Ro Roberts. 1951

ENFORCER, THE (1976) ★★★★ A step up fror the muddled *Magnum Force* and a nice companio piece to *Dirty Harry*, this third entry in the popula series has detective Harry Callahan grudgingly tear with a female cop (Tyne Daly) during his pursuit of band of terrorists. John Mitchum gives a standou performance in his final series bow as tough co Frank DiGeorgio. It'll make your day. Rated R. 96n DIR: James Fargo. CAST: Clint Eastwood, Tyne Daly Harry Guardino, Bradford Dillman, John Mitchun 1976

ENGLISH PATIENT, THE ★★★★ Even before th ceremonies were held, this old-style, David Lean—es que epic had Oscar written all over it. Set durin World War II, the film begins with a spectacular, fier plane crash in which there is one survivor, known t his caretaker only as "The English Patient." Ralpl Fiennes, as the mysterious title character, carries u through flashbacks, conspiracies, and the properl slower pace of the character-driven storytelling. A involved are to be commended for this modern, hig class fare. Rated R for sex and violence. 160m. DIF Anthony Minghella. CAST: Ralph Fiennes, Juliett Binoche, Willem Dafoe, Kristin Scott Thomas, Navee Andrews, Colin Firth, Jurgen Prochnow, Kevin Whatel 1996 DVD

ENGLISHMAN ABROAD, AN ★★★★ Much ac claimed BBC production dramatizing actress Cora Browne's actual Moscow encounter with an exile British diplomat accused of spying for the Russians Alan Bates is witty, sarcastic, and ultimately tragi as the infamous Guy Burgess—longing for som taste of the England now so unattainable to him. A superb script by Alan Bennett. 63m. DIR: Joh Schlesinger. CAST: Alan Bates, Coral Browne, Charle Gray. 1988

ENGLISHMAN WHO WENT UP A HILL BUT CAM! DOWN A MOUNTAIN, THE ★★★★ Charming British fluff, set during World War I, about a cartogra pher who, after declaring "the first mountain i Wales" to be sixteen feet short of official Britis! mountain height, is delayed by eccentric locals unti they can build it up from lowly hill status. Rated P for language and some sexual innuendo. 99m. DIR Christopher Monger. CAST: Hugh Grant, Tara Fitzger ald, Colm Meaney, Kenneth Griffith. 1995 DVD

ENIGMA ★★ Espionage yarn succumbs to letharg The KGB sics an elite group of assassins on five Sovi et dissidents. A CIA agent (Martin Sheen) attempt to thwart the insidious scheme by entangling his for mer lover with the top Russian agent. Rated PG 101m. DIR: Jeannot Szwarc. CAST: Martin Sheen Brigitte Fossey, Sam Neill, Derek Jacobi, Michel Lons dale, Frank Finlay. 1982

•**ENJO** ★★★★ Like many of the best Japanese films, this is a simple story told with unerring prec sion. Adapted from a novel by Yukio Mishima, it i the story of a religious young man who decides to de roy a sacred temple in Kyoto in order to keep it from being defiled by tourists. The black-and-white photography is breathtaking. In Japanese with English subtitles. B&W; 96m. DIR: Kon Ichikawa. CAST: Kaizo Ichikawa. 1958

NOLA GAY: THE MEN, THE MISSION, THE ATOMIC BOMB ★★★ In this made-for-TV drama, Patrick Duffy plays Paul Tibbets, the man in charge of the plane that dropped the atomic bomb over Hiroshima. The film delves into the lives and reactions of the crew members in a fairly effective manner. 150m. DIR: David Lowell Rich. CAST: Billy Crystal, Kim Darby, Patrick Duffy, Gary Frank, Gregory Harrison. 1980

ENSIGN PULVER ★★★ This sequel to *Mr. Roberts* doesn't quite measure up. The comedy, which takes place aboard a World War II cargo ship, can't stay afloat despite the large and impressive cast. Robert Walker Jr. is no match for Jack Lemmon, who played the original Ensign Pulver in 1955. 104m. DIR: Joshua Logan. CAST: Robert Walker Jr., Burl Ives, Walter Matthau, Tommy Sands, Millie Perkins, Kay Medford, Larry Hagman, Jack Nicholson. 1964

ENTANGLED ★★ Judd Nelson overacts his way through this thriller about a jealous American novelist involved in a romantic triangle and murder. Pierce Brosnan's charismatic performance deserves better than this amazingly transparent plot. Rated R for profanity, nudity, and violence. 98m. DIR: Max Fischer. CAST: Judd Nelson, Pierce Brosnan, Laurence Treil. 1992

ENTER LAUGHING ★★1/2 Carl Reiner's semiautobiographical comedy, about a young man who shucks his training and ambitions as a pharmacist to become a comedian, is studded with familiar faces and peopled by engaging personalities—but doesn't really leave a lasting memory. 112m. DIR: Carl Reiner. CAST: Reni Santoni, José Ferrer, Shelley Winters, Elaine May, Jack Gilford, Janet Margolin, Michael J. Pollard, Don Rickles, Rob Reiner, Nancy Kovack. 1967

ENTER THE DRAGON ★★★★ Bruce Lee soared to international superstardom with this fast-paced, tongue-in-cheek kung fu film. A big-budget American version of the popular Chinese genre, it has a good plot and strong performances—from Lee, John Saxon, and Jim Kelly. Rated R, due to violence. 97m. DIR: Robert Clouse. CAST: Bruce Lee, John Saxon, Jim Kelly, Ahna Capri, Yang Tse, Angela Mao. 1973 DVD

ENTER THE NINJA ★★ A passable martial arts adventure about practitioners of an ancient Oriental art of killing. Rated R. 94m. DIR: Menahem Golan. CAST: Franco Nero, Susan George, Sho Kosugi, Alex Courtney. 1981

ENTERTAINER, THE ★★★★ Laurence Olivier is brilliant as Archie Rice, a self-deceiving, low-moraled, small-talent vaudeville song-and-dance man in this slice-of-life drama based on the play written especially for him by John Osborne. Constantly nagged about his failures, insulted by audiences, and careless of all who love him, Archie is finally brought down by a raging ego that demands unreserved admiration. Olivier reveled in the role, declaring, "It's what I really am. I am not Hamlet." 97m. DIR: Tony Richardson. CAST: Laurence Olivier,

Brenda de Banzie, Joan Plowright, Roger Livesey, Alan Bates, Albert Finney. 1960

ENTERTAINING ANGELS ★★★★ This biography of Dorothy Day, who devoted her life to helping the poor and homeless beginning in the Great Depression, is inspirational in the best sense of the word. Although produced by a religious group, this film shows how one person truly can make a difference. This is an excellent family film. Rated PG-13 for adult situations and a little profanity. 111m. DIR: Michael Ray Rhodes. CAST: Moira Kelly, Martin Sheen, Heather Graham, Lenny Von Dohlen, Melinda Dillon, Paul Lieber, Brian Keith, Tracey Walter, Allyce Beasley. 1996

ENTERTAINING MR. SLOANE ★★ Joe Orton, the young British playwright whose short life formed the basis of *Prick Up Your Ears*, wrote the play from which this film was made. Neither play nor film has aged well. An amoral young man is taken in at a house where both a grotesque middle-aged woman and her brother, a latent homosexual, have romantic designs on him. Well performed, but no longer shocking enough to be effective. Not rated. 94m. DIR: Douglas Hickox. CAST: Beryl Reid, Peter McEnery, Harry Andrews, Alan Webb. 1970

ENTITY, THE ♥ Barbara Hershey stars as a woman who is sexually molested by an invisible, sex-crazed demon. Rated R for nudity, profanity, violence, and rape. 115m. DIR: Sidney J. Furie. CAST: Barbara Hershey, Ron Silver, Jacqueline Brooks. 1983

ENTRAPMENT ★★ Disappointing thriller wastes the talents of Sean Connery, a world-class thief who appears to be ensnared in the web of a sexy insurance investigator (Catherine Zeta-Jones). Slow start and preposterous ending can't be salvaged by decent special effects. Rated PG-13 for violence, language, and partial nudity. 112m. DIR: Jon Amiel. CAST: Sean Connery, Catherine Zeta-Jones, Ving Rhames, Maury Chaykin, Will Patton. 1999 DVD

ENTRE NOUS (BETWEEN US) ★★★★★ This down-to-earth, highly human story by director Diane Kurys concentrates on the friendship between two women, Madeline (Miou-Miou) and Lena (Isabelle Huppert), who find they have more in common with each other than with their husbands. It is an affecting tale the viewer won't soon forget. Rated PG for nudity, suggested sex, and violence. 110m. DIR: Diane Kurys. CAST: Miou-Miou, Isabelle Huppert, Guy Marchand. 1983 DVD

•ENTROPY ★★1/2 Stephen Dorff plays a very demanding new director who keeps having problems with the production, cast, and crew of his inaugural film. While bringing his movie together, Dorff's social life begins to fall apart, too. This movie is full of fine performances, but suffers from a plot and pace that quickly atrophy. Rated R. 110m. DIR: Phil Joanou. CAST: Stephen Dorff, Judith Godreche, Kelly MacDonald, Lauren Holly, Hector Elizondo. 1999

EQUALIZER, THE: "MEMORIES OF MANON" ★★★ Edward Woodward's commanding performance as *The Equalizer* gives weight to this made-for-TV release about a New York avenger and his discovery of danger stalking the daughter (Melissa Anderson) he didn't know he had. Fans of Woodward will enjoy a second look. 96m. **DIR:** Tony Wharmby. **CAST:** Edward Woodward, Melissa Sue Anderson, Anthony Zerbe, Robert Lansing, Jon Polito, Keith Szarabajka. 1988

EQUINOX (1971) (THE BEAST) ★★ Good special effects save this unprofessional movie about college students searching for their archaeology professor. On their search, they must face monsters and the occult. Rated PG. 82m. **DIR:** Jack Woods. **CAST:** Edward Connell, Barbara Hewitt. 1971

EQUINOX (1993) ★★1/2 Oodles of glossy style and a fine Matthew Modine performance aren't quite enough to maintain intense interest in this enigmatic, surreal tale of twin brothers—timid, shy writer, Henry, and mean-spirited criminal, Freddy. Lara Flynn Boyle costars as a woman who draws the brothers together. Though writer-director Rudolph offers intriguing ideas, he's never quite clear or passionate enough to bring the ideas home. Rated R, with profanity. 100m. **DIR:** Alan Rudolph. **CAST:** Matthew Modine, Lara Flynn Boyle, Fred Ward. 1993

EQUINOX FLOWER ★★★★ An interesting look at the Japanese custom of arranged marriages. Setsuko's parents had an arranged marriage and want the same for her; she, having found her own true love, rebels. In Japanese with English subtitles. Not rated, but suitable for all audiences. 115m. **DIR:** Yasujiro Ozu. **CAST:** Shin Saburi. 1958

EQUUS ★★★★ Peter Firth plays a stable boy whose mysterious fascination with horses results in an act of meaningless cruelty and violence. Richard Burton plays the psychiatrist brought in to uncover Firth's hidden hostilities. The expanding of Peter Shaffer's play leaves the film somewhat unfocused but the scenes between Burton and Firth are intense, riveting, and beautifully acted. This was Burton's last quality film role; he was nominated for best actor. Rated R for profanity and nudity. 137m. **DIR:** Sidney Lumet. **CAST:** Richard Burton, Peter Firth, Colin Blakely, Joan Plowright, Harry Andrews, Eileen Atkins, Jenny Agutter. 1977

ER: THE SERIES PREMIERE ★★★★★ The pilot for the high-rated television series created by Michael Crichton features the adventures, both inspiring and tragic, of the employees of an emergency room. Brilliantly acted, tautly directed, and expertly written, this is network television at its best. Not rated. 90m. **DIR:** Rod Holcomb. **CAST:** Anthony Edwards, George Clooney, Sherry Stringfield, Noah Wyle, Eriq La Salle, Miguel Ferrer. 1995

•**ERASABLE YOU** ★★★ Black comedy about a divorced man who lives in poverty with his new wife because the first one claims his entire salary in alimony. They hire a hit man to kill her, unleashing a flood of unforeseeable complications. A sleeper with funny twists. Not rated; contains profanity and violence. 85m. **DIR:** Harry Bromley-Davenport. **CAST:** Timothy Busfield, M. Emmet Walsh, Melora Hardin. 1998

ERASER ★★★ Arnold Schwarzenegger plays a federal marshal working for the Witness Protection Program. To protect his witness—a defense-contractor employee who discovers illegal sales of superweapons to foreign buyers—and maintain world peace, Schwarzenegger wipes out half the planet. Lots of shoot-outs and explosions, but only two or three scenes display the grand-scale fun and inventiveness we have come to expect from an Arnold actioner. Rated R for violence and profanity. 107m. **DIR:** Charles Russell. **CAST:** Arnold Schwarzenegger, James Caan, Vanessa L. Williams, James Coburn, Robert Pastorelli. 1996 DVD

ERASERHEAD ★★ Weird, weird movie ... Director David Lynch created this nightmarish film about Henry Spencer (Jack Nance), who, we assume, lives in the far (possibly post-apocalyptic) future when everyone is given a free lobotomy at birth. Nothing else could explain the bizarre behavior of its characters. B&W; 90m. **DIR:** David Lynch. **CAST:** Jack Nance, Charlotte Stewart, Jeanne Bates. 1978

ERENDIRA ★★1/2 In this disturbing and distasteful black comedy, Irene Papas stars as a wealthy older woman who loses everything in a fire accidentally set by her sleepwalking granddaughter, Erendira (Claudia Ohana). The grandmother turns her charge into a prostitute and insists that she earn back over $1 million. In Spanish with English subtitles. Not rated, the film has nudity, profanity, simulated sex, and violence. 103m. **DIR:** Ruy Guerra. **CAST:** Irene Papas, Claudia Ohana, Michel Lonsdale. 1983

ERIC ★★★★ This made-for-TV movie is the true story of Eric Lund, a teenager with a promising athletic future who becomes terminally ill. John Savage, in the title role, gives a meaningful portrayal of a young man who refuses to give up. Patricia Neal, as the mother, gives the kind of warm, sensitive performance she is noted for, and there is a fine supporting cast. 100m. **DIR:** James Goldstone. **CAST:** Patricia Neal, John Savage, Claude Akins, Sian Barbara Allen, Mark Hamill, Nehemiah Persoff. 1975

ERIK THE VIKING ★★★ The first half hour of this account of the exploits of Erik the Red is so awful one is tempted to hit the reject button. However, perseverance pays off in this movie from ex-Monty Python crazy Terry Jones. It actually gets to be fun. Rated PG-13 for profanity and suggested sex. 106m. **DIR:** Terry Jones. **CAST:** Tim Robbins, Mickey Rooney, Eartha Kitt, Terry Jones, Imogen Stubbs, John Cleese, Antony Sher. 1989

•**ERIN BROCKOVICH** ★★★★1/2 Part legal drama and part advocacy cinema, and fueled throughout by Julia Roberts's most personal performance to date, this engaging film is smart, sassy, and quietly chilling, the latter because it's based on frankly horrifying events that occurred in an isolated California desert community early in the 1990s. Susannah Grant's deft script turns Roberts into an unlikely heroine: a single mother, with three young children, who we meet as she's trying to obtain yet another job. Circumstances finally bring her to the offices of an independent attorney (Albert Finney, also excellent), where Erin's natural curiosity and intelligence flame after coming across a "routine" real estate transaction laced with medical records. Watch for the actual Erin Brockovich early on, in a brief appearance as a waitress. Rated R for profanity. 130m. **DIR:** Steven Soderbergh. **CAST:** Julia Roberts, Albert

...nney, Aaron Eckhart, Marg Helgenberger, Cherry ...nes. 2000

...KMO ★★1/2 A provincial Chinese noodle seller en-...es her neighbor's color TV—not to mention the ...eighbor's virile young husband. This domestic com-...y has appealing players, but a leaden pace and far ...o many shots of noodles being squeezed out of an ...cient pasta maker. In Mandarin with English sub-...les (which are often unintentionally amusing). ...t rated; suitable for general audiences. 93m. DIR: ...ou Xiaowen. CAST: Alia, Liu Pei Qi, Ge Zhijun, Zhang ...aiyan. 1994

...RNEST GOES TO AFRICA ★★ The lovable oaf ...eads to Africa, where he finds adventure and ro-...ance. Even though this outing was filmed entirely ...i that continent, it's strictly for die-hard fans who ...aven't grown tired of his mugging. Rated PG. 90m. ...R: John Cherry. CAST: Jim Varney, Linda Kash, ...mie Bartlett. 1997

...RNEST GOES TO CAMP ♥ Could have been called ...eatballs XI for all the originality it contains. Rated ...G for profanity and scatological humor. 95m. DIR: ...hn R. Cherry III. CAST: Jim Varney, Victoria Racimo, ...hn Vernon, Iron Eyes Cody, Lyle Alzado. 1987

...RNEST GOES TO JAIL ★★★ Comic gem in ...hich the indisputably talented Jim Varney plays not ...ly the well-meaning and dim-witted Ernest P. Wor-...ll but also the crafty villain of the piece. Rated PG ...r brief violence. 82m. DIR: John R. Cherry III. CAST: ...m Varney, Gailard Sartain, Randall "Tex" Cobb, ...arles Napier. 1990

...RNEST GREEN STORY, THE ★★★★1/2 This true ...ory of the first black graduate of Little Rock, ...kansas's Central High School in 1958 shows ...cism at its ugliest and determination at its most ...agnificent. Ernest Green, along with eight other ...ave black students, withstood taunts, threats, and ...tacks to enforce the 1954 Supreme Court decision ...pposing segregated schools. Superb acting and an ...utstanding musical score. Not rated; contains vio-...nce and racial slurs. 101m. DIR: Eric Laneuville. ...AST: Morris Chestnut, C.C.H. Pounder, Gary Grubbs, ...na Lifford, Avery Brooks, Ruby Dee. 1992

...RNEST IN THE ARMY ★★ In order to fulfill his ...ream of driving tanks, Ernest P. Worrell joins the ...rmy Reserves, where he creates havoc for his supe-...ors and a disgruntled Middle East dictator who is ...o match for the goofy grunt. Pretty much what you ...ould expect from this franchise. Rated PG. 85m. ...IR: John Cherry. CAST: Jim Varney, Hayley Tyson, ...avid Miller. 1997

...RNEST RIDES AGAIN ★★ Ernest Rides Again, ...nd again, and again. The series has almost run out ...f steam in this weak entry, as Ernest discovers a ...ng-lost Revolutionary War cannon, rumored to hold ...e real Crown Jewels of England. It's a race to see ...ho can get to the cannon first, but no one crosses ...e finish line in terms of evoking laughs. Tape con-...ains featurette, Mr. Bill Goes to Washington. Rated ...G for mild innuendo. 100m. DIR: John R. Cherry III. ...AST: Jim Varney, Ron K. James, Duke Ernsberger, ...nda Kash, Jeffrey Pillars. 1993

...RNEST SAVES CHRISTMAS ★★★ In this family ...ovie, a vast improvement over Ernest Goes to

Camp, TV pitchman Jim Varney returns as Ernest P. Worrell. This time the obnoxious but well-meaning Ernest attempts to help Santa Claus (Douglas Seale) find a successor. The script is funny without being moronic, and sentimental without being maudlin. Rated PG. 95m. DIR: John R. Cherry III. CAST: Jim Varney, Douglas Seale, Oliver Clark, Billie Bird. 1988

ERNEST SCARED STUPID ★★★1/2 Ernest P. Worrell accidentally reawakens a troll from its 200-year-old tomb and puts the town's children in danger. While those with an aversion to slapstick may not enjoy it, this horror spoof is old-fashioned movie fun. Rated PG for scary stuff. 91m. DIR: John R. Cherry III. CAST: Jim Varney, Eartha Kitt. 1991

ERNIE KOVACS: TELEVISION'S ORIGINAL GENIUS ★★★★ This tribute to the late Ernie Kovacs, produced for cable television, is a series of clips from Kovacs's television career along with comments from friends and family. Those familiar with Kovacs's work will fondly remember his innovative creations: Percy Dovetonsils, Eugene, and the Nairobi Trio. For others, this serves as an introduction to Kovacs's comic genius. 86m. DIR: Keith Burns. CAST: Ernie Kovacs, Edie Adams, Jack Lemmon, Steve Allen, Chevy Chase, John Barbour. 1982

EROTIKILL ★★ The indefatigable Spanish director Jess Franco—who's made so many cheap exploitation pictures, even he can't remember them all—is at the helm, and, briefly, in the cast of this raunchy opus about a female bloodsucker (Lina Romay) prowling the decadent Riviera. Definitely not for the kiddies, or the easily offended. You can find an even more explicit U.S. video edition under the title Loves of Irina. Rated R. 90m. DIR: Jess (Jesus) Franco. CAST: Lina Romay, Jack Taylor, Alice Arno. 1981

EROTIQUE ★★★ Four internationally known female directors contribute a segment each to this collection of short films. Best is Taiwanese Clara Law's story of young lovers restrained by cultural barriers, but all of the stories are intriguing, despite the obvious low budgets. Not rated; contains nudity, profanity, and sexual situations. 120m. DIR: Lizzie Borden, Monika Treut, Ana Maria Magalhaes, Clara Law. CAST: Priscilla Barnes, Camilla Soeberg, Claudia Ohana. 1995 DVD

ERRAND BOY, THE ★★★ One of Jerry Lewis's better solo efforts, as he proceeds (in his own inimitable style) to make a shambles of the Hollywood movie studio where he is employed as the local gofer. Very funny. B&W; 92m. DIR: Jerry Lewis. CAST: Jerry Lewis, Brian Donlevy, Sig Ruman. 1961

•ERUPTION ★★ An American photojournalist in a South American country is endangered by both rebel attempts to unseat the country's dictator and a volcano that's about to blow. Typical slapdash Roger Corman production that seems to exist mostly as an excuse to use some volcano footage. Rated R for profanity and violence. 106m. DIR: Gwyneth Gibby. CAST: F. Murray Abraham, Cyril O'Reilly, Patricia Velasquez. 1998

ESCAPADE IN FLORENCE ♥ Uninspired story about two young men and their misadventures in picturesque Italy. 80m. DIR: Steve Previn. CAST: Ivan

Desny, Tommy Kirk, Annette Funicello, Nino Castelnuovo. 1962

ESCAPADE IN JAPAN ★★★1/2 Little Jon Provost, his friend Roger Nakagawa, and Japan itself are the stars of this charming film about a young boy who survives an airplane crash in Japan and is taken in by a family of isolated fishers. This is one of the all-time best kids-on-the-run films. 93m. DIR: Arthur Lubin. CAST: Jon Provost, Roger Nakagawa, Cameron Mitchell, Teresa Wright. 1957

ESCAPE ARTIST, THE ★★ Confusing, rambling account of a boy (Griffin O'Neal, who might be appealing with better material) who uses a love of magic and escape artistry to frame the city politicos responsible for killing his father. Rated PG—mild violence and profanity. 96m. DIR: Caleb Deschanel. CAST: Griffin O'Neal, Raul Julia, Teri Garr, Joan Hackett, Desi Arnaz Sr. 1982

ESCAPE CLAUSE ★★★ Insurance actuary Andrew McCarthy is stunned to learn he's the target of a killer, supposedly hired by his wife … and then his wife turns up dead! Scripter Danilo Bach's clever little thriller rises above the usual genre melodrama and should keep you guessing until the very end. Rated R for violence, nudity, profanity, and simulated sex. 95m. DIR: Brian Trenchard-Smith. CAST: Andrew McCarthy, Paul Sorvino, Connie Britton, Kate McNeil, Kenneth Welsh. 1996

ESCAPE FROM ALCATRAZ ★★★★ Any movie that combines the talents of star Clint Eastwood and director Don Siegel is more than watchable. This is a gripping and believable film about the 1962 breakout from the supposedly perfect prison. Patrick McGoohan is also excellent as the neurotic warden. Rated PG. 112m. DIR: Don Siegel. CAST: Clint Eastwood, Patrick McGoohan, Roberts Blossom, Jack Thibeau. 1979 DVD

ESCAPE FROM ATLANTIS ★★★ Escapist family adventure stars Jeff Speakman as a father who treats his family to a cruise in the Bahamas. When they enter the Bermuda Triangle, they are transported to the mythical land of Atlantis. The ooh-and-aah factor wears off when his daughter is mistaken for the long-lost queen and an evil king refuses to let her leave the island. Lots of fun and imagination in this made-for-cable effort. Rated PG-13 for violence. 93m. DIR: Strathford Hamilton. CAST: Jeff Speakman, Tim Thomerson, Justin Burnette, Mercedes McNab, Breck Wilson, Brian Bloom. 1997

ESCAPE FROM FORT BRAVO ★★★1/2 Union officer William Holden is in charge of a wilderness outpost holding Confederate prisoners. He must keep them in while trying to keep out marauding Indians. Good suspense and action scenes. B&W; 98m. DIR: John Sturges. CAST: William Holden, Eleanor Parker, John Forsythe, William Demarest, William Campbell, John Lupton, Richard Anderson, Polly Bergen. 1953

•**ESCAPE FROM MARS** ★★ Plodding sci-fi flick about the first manned trip to Mars. Rated PG. 88m. DIR: Neill L. Fearnley. CAST: Christine Elise, Peter Outerbridge, Allison Hossack, Michael Shanks. 1999

ESCAPE FROM NEW YORK ★★★1/2 The year is 1997. *Air Force One*—with the president (Donald Pleasence) on board—is hijacked by a group of revo-

lutionaries and sent crashing into the middle [of] Manhattan, which has been turned into a top-secu[rity] ty prison. It's up to Snake Plissken (Kurt Russell), former war hero gone renegade, to get him out [in] twenty-four hours. It's fun, surprise-filled entertai[n]ment. Rated R. 99m. DIR: John Carpenter. CAST: Ku[rt] Russell, Lee Van Cleef, Ernest Borgnine, Dona[ld] Pleasence, Adrienne Barbeau. 1981

ESCAPE FROM SAFEHAVEN 🐢 Futuristic fil[m] about a family that is terrorized by a ruthless gover[n]ment. Rated R. 87m. DIR: Brian Thomas Jones, Jam[es] McCalmont. CAST: Rick Gianasi. 1988

ESCAPE FROM SOBIBOR ★★★★ Inspiring tru[e] life tale of the largest prisoner escape from a Na[zi] death camp, with a superior cast led by Alan Arki[n]. Harrowing prison camp scenes elevate the suspen[se] as the prisoners plan and then execute their dari[ng] escape. Edited for video, this made-for-television e[ffort] try rises to the occasion with a tight script by Re[gi]nald Rose. 120m. DIR: Jack Gold. CAST: Rutger Hau[er], Alan Arkin, Joanna Pacula. 1987 DVD

ESCAPE FROM SURVIVAL ZONE ★★ On the eve [of] World War III, a trio of television journalists take [a] course in survival training, only to face a whacke[d] out former Marine commander. Predictable mel[o]drama. Not rated; contains violence and profanit[y]. 85m. DIR: Chris Jones. CAST: Terrence Ford, Paris Je[f]ferson, Raymond Johnson. 1991

ESCAPE FROM THE KGB 🐢 A jet-setting CIA age[nt] is sent to infiltrate a Siberian spaceport. Insipid. N[ot] rated. 99m. DIR: Harald Phillipe. CAST: Thoma[s] Hunter, Marie Versini, Ivan Desny, Walter Barnes. 198[?]

ESCAPE FROM THE PLANET OF THE APES ★★ [?] Escaping the nuclear destruction of their own wor[ld] and time, intelligent simians Roddy McDowall a[nd] Kim Hunter arrive on ours. This third *Apes* ent[ry] makes wonderful use of the *Strangers in a Stran[ge] Land* theme, which turns ugly all too quickly as h[u]manity decides to destroy the apes. Rated PG for vi[o]lence. 98m. DIR: Don Taylor. CAST: Roddy McDowa[ll], Kim Hunter, Eric Braeden, Bradford Dillman, Willia[m] Windom, Ricardo Montalban. 1971

ESCAPE: HUMAN CARGO ★★★1/2 This fact-base[d] thriller concerns the frustrating series of events th[at] began in 1977, when Texan John McDonald (Tre[at] Williams) contracted to build prefab housing in Sa[u]di Arabia. Williams is credible as the headstro[ng] American unwilling to tolerate dishonesty or abus[e] who only gradually realizes that he's in over his hea[d] and must outwit his "hosts" if he is to survive. Rate[d] R for nudity, profanity, and violence. 110m. DIR: S[i]mon Wincer. CAST: Treat Williams, Stephen Lang, Sa[m]son Gabay, Zeev Revach. 1997

ESCAPE ME NEVER ★★★ A blend of colorful pe[r]sonalities keeps this one afloat. Since it isn't typic[al] of any of the major stars involved, it's interesting [to] see how a sophisticated composer handles his lov[e]less marriage and his passionate love of music. B&[W]; 105m. DIR: Peter Godfrey. CAST: Errol Flynn, I[da] Lupino, Eleanor Parker, Gig Young, Reginald Denn[y], Isobel Elsom, Albert Basserman, Ludwig Stossel. 194[?]

ESCAPE, THE ★★ A convict escapes from pris[on] and falls in love with a young woman. Then the a[u]thorities catch up with him. Not rated, but contai[ns]

nudity, violence, and profanity. 91m. DIR: Stuart Gillard. CAST: Patrick Dempsey, Brigitte Bako, Colm Feore, Vincent Gale, W. Morgan Sheppard. **1995**

ESCAPE TO ATHENA ★★★ Roger Moore as a Nazi officer? Sonny Bono as a member of the Italian Resistance? Elliott Gould as a hippie in a World War II concentration camp? Sound ridiculous? It is. It's a *Hogan's Heroes* for the big screen but, in a dumb sort of way, entertaining. Rated PG. 101m. DIR: George Pan Cosmatos. CAST: Roger Moore, Telly Savalas, David Niven, Claudia Cardinale, Stefanie Powers, Richard Roundtree, Elliott Gould, Sonny Bono. **1979**

ESCAPE TO BURMA 🖤 A tea plantation, wild animals, and a hunted man seeking refuge. B&W; 87m. DIR: Allan Dwan. CAST: Barbara Stanwyck, Robert Ryan, David Farrar, Murvyn Vye. **1955**

ESCAPE TO LOVE ★★★ This adventurous romance pits a beautiful American student (Clara Perryman) and her lover against the Polish KGB as they speed on a train toward Paris. Their passion increases to a point where they must both reach a life-changing decision. 105m. DIR: Herb Stein. CAST: Clara Perryman. **1982**

ESCAPE TO THE SUN ★★★ Two young university students try to escape from the oppressive Soviet Union under the watchful eyes of the KGB. They try first for an exit visa; only one visa is issued, and one of the students is taken into custody. The two are forced to make a heroic escape to the West. Rated PG for violence. 94m. DIR: Menahem Golan. CAST: Laurence Harvey, Josephine Chaplin, John Ireland, Jack Hawkins. **1972**

ESCAPE TO WHITE MOUNTAIN ★★ Hard-to-like teenager runs away from his father and their junkyard. When a kindly Apache man gives him a lift, he introduces the teen to Apache beliefs, which is the only highlight to an otherwise poorly acted, low-budget film. When the Apaches speak among themselves, English subtitles are used. Not rated; contains profanity and violence. 80m. DIR: Rob Sabal. CAST: Caleb Smith, Ethelbah Midnite, Caesar Del Trecco, Mike Minjarez. **1994**

ESCAPE TO WITCH MOUNTAIN ★★★1/2 In this engaging Disney mystery-fantasy, two children with strange powers are pursued by men who want to use them for evil purposes. It's good! Rated G. 97m. DIR: John Hough. CAST: Eddie Albert, Ray Milland, Kim Richards, Ike Eisenmann. **1975**

ESCAPE 2000 🖤 A nauseating science-fiction film from Britain, this consists of a series of close-ups of people in the throes of death. Rated R. 92m. DIR: Brian Trenchard-Smith. CAST: Steve Railsback, Olivia Hussey, Michael Craig, Carmen Duncan, Roger Ward. **1981**

ESCAPES ★★★ Low-budget anthology in the *Twilight Zone* vein, featuring six stories of the bizarre and done with great style by director David Steensland. Top honors go to "A Little Fishy," a grimly funny tale, and "Who's There?," a neat yarn about an escaped laboratory experiment and a Sunday jogger. 71m. DIR: David Steensland. CAST: Vincent Price, Michael Patton-Hall, John Mitchum, Todd Fulton, Jerry Grisham, Ken Thorley. **1985**

E.T.—THE EXTRA-TERRESTRIAL ★★★★★ The most entertaining science-fiction film of all time, this is Steven Spielberg's gentle fairy tale about what happens when a young boy meets up with a very special fellow from outer space. Sheer wonder is joined with warmth and humor in this movie classic. Rated PG. 115m. DIR: Steven Spielberg. CAST: Dee Wallace, Henry Thomas, Peter Coyote, Robert MacNaughton, Drew Barrymore. **1982**

●**ETERNAL, THE** ★★ Murky supernatural thriller about an American woman haunted by memories of her ancestral home in Ireland. When her hallucinations start controlling her life she packs up her husband and son to return home. Instead of a warm welcome from her creepy uncle, she gets chills from what he has stored down in the basement. Despite its eerie look, the film fails to generate anything more than an occasional jump moment. Rated R for adult situations, language, and violence. 95m. DIR: Michael Almereyda. CAST: Alison Elliott, Jared Harris, Lois Smith, Rachel O'Rourke, Christopher Walken, Jason Miller. **1998 DVD**

●**ETERNAL EVIL** ★★★ This mystical thriller has a filmmaker experimenting with astral projection and running afoul of souls who jump from one body to another when one is used up. Intriguing film with slick production values. Rated R for violence. 86m. DIR: George Mihalka. CAST: Winston Rekert, Karen Black. **1986 DVD**

ETERNAL RETURN, THE ★★★ Interesting modern adaptation of the Tristan and Isolde legend from a script by Jean Cocteau. In French with English subtitles. B&W; 110m. DIR: Jean Delannoy. CAST: Jean Marais, Madeleine Sologne, Jean Murat. **1943**

ETERNALLY YOURS ★★★ A stellar cast of accomplished scene stealers deftly brings off this iffy story of a magician (David Niven) and his wife (Loretta Young), who thinks his tricks are overshadowing their marital happiness. B&W; 95m. DIR: Tay Garnett. CAST: Loretta Young, David Niven, C. Aubrey Smith, ZaSu Pitts, Billie Burke, Eve Arden, Hugh Herbert, Broderick Crawford. **1939**

ETERNITY 🖤 A reincarnated goodie-two-shoes battling his greedy brother. Rated R for nudity and simulated sex. 122m. DIR: Steven Paul. CAST: Jon Voight, Armand Assante, Wilford Brimley, Eileen Davidson. **1990**

ETHAN FROME ★★★★ Edith Wharton's austere novel about nineteenth-century Puritan values and doomed love is given an equally austere film treatment in this longish but well-acted drama. Liam Neeson is memorable as the title character, a deformed recluse. Joan Allen plays Frome's bitter wife while Patricia Arquette steals his heart and seals his fate. A bit severe, chilly, and static for some viewers—others will love its literary purity. Rated PG. 147m. DIR: John Madden. CAST: Liam Neeson, Patricia Arquette, Joan Allen, Katharine Houghton. **1993**

EUBIE! ★★★★ Originally a Broadway tribute to legendary composer Eubie Blake, this is nonstop song, dance, and vaudeville entertainment. Gregory Hines and Maurice Hines are outstanding with their toe-stomping tap routines. About twenty of Blake's tunes are performed on this tape—including "I'm

Just Wild About Harry," "I've Got the Low Down Blues," and "In Honeysuckle Time." Not rated. 85m. DIR: Julianne Boyd. CAST: Gregory Hines, Terri Burrell, Maurice Hines, Leslie Dockery. 1981

EUREKA ★★★1/2 Another stunner from Nicolas Roeg is about an ambitious gold miner (Gene Hackman) who makes his fortune in the snowbound Canadian wilderness, then retires to his very own Caribbean island. Rated R for sex, nudity, violence, and profanity. 130m. DIR: Nicolas Roeg. CAST: Gene Hackman, Theresa Russell, Rutger Hauer, Jane Lapotaire, Mickey Rourke, Ed Lauter, Joe Pesci. 1983

EUROPA, EUROPA ★★★ Based on the autobiography of Solomon Perel, this stunning film traces the author's real-life death-defying adventures during World War II in war-torn Europe. A Jewish teenager who first masquerades as a Communist and later is accepted into the Nazi Youth Party, Perel sees the war from all sides in this ironic, spine-tingling story. In German and Russian with English subtitles. Rated R for nudity. 115m. DIR: Agnieszka Holland. CAST: Marco Holschneider, Delphine Forest. 1990

EUROPEANS, THE ★★★★ This intelligent, involving adaptation of the Henry James novel is another wonder from director James Ivory. Lee Remick is one of two freethinking, outspoken foreigners who descend on their Puritan relatives in nineteenth-century New England. The result is a character-rich study of a clash of cultures. Rated PG. 90m. DIR: James Ivory. CAST: Lee Remick, Robin Ellis, Wesley Addy, Tim Choate, Lisa Eichhorn, Tim Woodward, Kristin Griffith. 1979

EVE OF DESTRUCTION 🎦 Gregory Hines is a counterinsurgency expert battling a state-of-the-art female robot. Rated R for violence, nudity, and profanity. 90m. DIR: Duncan Gibbins. CAST: Gregory Hines, Renee Soutendijk, Michael Greene. 1991

EVE'S BAYOU ★★★★ This languid, episodic Southern Gothic drama ventures into an African-American family closet and immediately begins rattling skeletons. "The summer I killed my father, I was 10 years old," begins the narration of Eve Baptiste as she nuzzles the film into early 1960s backwater Louisiana, where her affluent family is up to its eyeballs in voodoo, adultery, and emotional turmoil. Rated R for suggested sex, language, and violence. 109m. DIR: Kasi Lemmons. CAST: Jurnee Smollett, Samuel L. Jackson, Lynn Whitfield, Debbi Morgan, Diahann Carroll. 1997 DVD

EVEL KNIEVEL ★★1/2 Autobiography of motorcycle stuntman Evel Knievel. George Hamilton is surprisingly good as Knievel. Some nice stunts. Rated PG. 90m. DIR: Marvin J. Chomsky. CAST: George Hamilton, Sue Lyon, Rod Cameron. 1972

EVELYN PRENTICE ★★★ Myrna Loy kills a blackmailer and her unknowing lawyer husband defends another woman accused of the crime. Strangely remote movie saved by a twist ending and the debut of Rosalind Russell. B&W; 80m. DIR: William K. Howard. CAST: William Powell, Myrna Loy, Una Merkel, Rosalind Russell, Harvey Stephens, Isabel Jewell, Edward Brophy, Jessie Ralph. 1934

EVEN COWGIRLS GET THE BLUES ★★ Born with unusually large thumbs, Sissy Hankshaw becomes the world's greatest hitchhiker, a passion she pu[rsues] when not hanging out at a health spa with [a] band of nonconformist cowgirls. An incoherent, un[dramatic] and humorless adaptation of Tom Rob[bins's] popular, counterculture novel. Rated R fo[r] profanity, violence, and suggested sex. 102m. DIR: Gus Van Sant. CAST: Uma Thurman, John Hurt, Rai[n] Phoenix, Noriyuki "Pat" Morita, Keanu Reeves, Lo[r]raine Bracco, Angie Dickinson, Sean Young, Crispi[n] Glover, Ed Begley Jr., Carol Kane, Roseanne, Buck Her[r], Grace Zabriskie, Udo Kier. 1994

EVENING STAR, THE ★★★1/2 The central cas[t] members of 1983's *Terms of Endearment* reunite fo[r] this sequel, adapted from the novel by Larry M[c]Murtry. The results aren't quite as successful, if onl[y] because Shirley MacLaine's feisty Aurora isn't give[n] a sparring partner to match Debra Winger's fiery de[-]livery as Emma, in the first film. A few characters vi[e] for that position: Miranda Richardson, as a divorce[d] Houston socialite jealous because she wasn't give[n] custody of Emma's children; and Juliette Lewis, a[s] the most tempestuous of those kids. Marion Ros[s] shines, as Aurora's long-devoted housekeeper, an[d] Jack Nicholson briefly returns as astronaut Garret[t] Breedlove. MacLaine holds the film together as th[e] true "evening star," who appears first, burns bright[-]est, and lasts longest. Rated PG-13 for profanity[,] earthy dialogue, and brief nudity. 129m. DIR: Robe[rt] Harling. CAST: Shirley MacLaine, Jack Nicholson, Mar[-]ion Ross, Miranda Richardson, Mackenzie Astir[n], George Newbern, Juliette Lewis, Bill Paxton, Ben John[-]son, Donald Moffat. 1996

EVENT HORIZON ★★ Dreary sci-fi flick just can'[t] seem to gather any kind of momentum. A team of in[-]terplanetary rescuers discovers a derelict ship take[n] over by supernatural forces and then proceeds to di[e] one by one. It's a regrettable waste of a fine cast an[d] intriguing premise. Rated R for violence, profanity[,] nudity, and suggested sex. 95m. DIR: Paul Anderso[n]. CAST: Laurence Fishburne, Sam Neill, Kathleen Quin[-]lan, Joely Richardson, Richard T. Jones, Jack Nose[-]worthy. 1997 DVD

EVER AFTER ★★★★1/2 Exquisite retelling of th[e] *Cinderella* story with a luminous Drew Barrymore a[s] the young charmer who rises above her station t[o] steal the heart of the prince. Anjelica Huston is ex[-]cellent as the wicked stepmother who schemes t[o] keep Barrymore away from her true love, the crow[n] prince of France. Director Andy Tennant delivers [a] live-action fairy tale filled with heart and humor, an[d] just the right amount of magic. Rated PG-13 for lan[-]guage. 100m. DIR: Andy Tennant. CAST: Drew Barry[-]more, Anjelica Huston, Dougray Scott, Jeanne Moreau[.] 1998 DVD

EVERGREEN ★★★★ Superb showcase for the leg[-]endary Jessie Matthews spans two generations in its['] story of a British music-hall entertainer and her tal[-]ented daughter (both roles played by Jessi[e] Matthews). The captivating Rodgers and Hart score includes "Dancing on the Ceiling" and the rousing showstopper "Over My Shoulder." B&W; 85m. DIR: Victor Saville. CAST: Jessie Matthews. 1934

EVERLASTING SECRET FAMILY, THE ★★1/2 Strange Australian film about a secret society of powerful men who choose teenage boys to be their possessions. Not rated; contains nudity and sexual situations. 93m. DIR: Michael Thornhill. CAST: Arthur Dignam, Mark Lee, Heather Mitchell, John Meillon. 1988

EVERSMILE NEW JERSEY 💔 Daniel Day-Lewis shows little of the talent he displayed in *My Left Foot*. Here he plays a traveling dentist. As exciting as getting teeth pulled. Rated PG. 103m. DIR: Carlos Sorin. CAST: Daniel Day-Lewis, Mirjana Jokovic. 1989

EVERY BREATH ★★ Weak thriller runs out of breath well before the race is over. Judd Nelson stars as a young man who is seduced by a couple's looks, money, and kinky games. As he plays, he finds out that its hosts have some very weird ideas. What might have been decadent is merely docile. Rated R for nudity, adult situations, and language. 89m. DIR: Steve Bing. CAST: Judd Nelson, Joanna Pacula, Patrick Bauchau. 1993

EVERY DAY'S A HOLIDAY ★★★1/2 A heavily censored script weakens the Mae West allure, but she still gives us a fascinating picture of highly suggestive sex. West is the only woman in the movie (which she wrote) about a shady lady who impersonates a French singer to get the cops off her back. Most of the movie is just an excuse for her to sing some of her trademark songs. B&W; 80m. DIR: A. Edward Sutherland. CAST: Mae West, Edmund Lowe, Charles Winninger, Lloyd Nolan, Walter Catlett, Chester Conklin, Charles Butterworth, Louis Armstrong. 1938

EVERY GIRL SHOULD BE MARRIED ★★1/2 A bit of light comic froth balanced mostly on Cary Grant's charm and polish. He plays a baby doctor. Betsy Drake, who later got him offscreen, plays a salesgirl bent on leading him to the altar. The title is irksome, but the picture's diverting, innocent fun. B&W; 85m. DIR: Don Hartman. CAST: Cary Grant, Betsy Drake, Franchot Tone, Diana Lynn, Alan Mowbray. 1948

EVERY MAN FOR HIMSELF AND GOD AGAINST ALL ★★★★ Based on a real incident, the story of Kasper Hauser (Bruno S.) tells of a man who had been kept in confinement since birth. Hauser's appearance in Nuremberg in the 1820s was a mystery. He tried to adjust to a new society while maintaining his own vision. Also released as *The Mystery of Kaspar Hauser*. In German with English subtitles. No MPAA rating. 110m. DIR: Werner Herzog. CAST: Bruno S., Walter Ladengast, Brigitte Mira. 1975

EVERY MOTHER'S WORST FEAR ★★★ In this made-for-cable original, a 16-year-old girl is lured from home by someone she meets on the Internet. Her mother frantically follows a tenuous thread of clues to track her down. The story is inspired by true events, but this script stretches the credibility a little too thin, despite the valiant acting efforts of Cheryl and Jordan Ladd. Rated PG-13 for violence. 91m. DIR: Bill L. Norton. CAST: Cheryl Ladd, Jordan Ladd, Robert Wisden, Ted McGinley. 1998

EVERY OTHER WEEKEND ★★★★ Upset that both her career and her two young children are slipping away from her, a divorced actress kidnaps the children from their father (who has custody) and takes them on the road in the hope of reforging a connection with them. Worth seeing for a typically strong

performance by French actress Nathalie Baye, who excels at bringing difficult characters to full life. Not rated; contains adult situations. 100m. DIR: Nicole Garcia. CAST: Nathalie Baye, Miki Manojlovic. 1990

EVERY TIME WE SAY GOODBYE ★★★ A change-of-pace role for Tom Hanks, who stars as an American pilot in WWII Jerusalem who falls in love with a young Jewish girl. Hanks brings a certain well-rounded realism to this dramatic part, injecting the seriousness with humor, and Cristina Marsillach is very subtle as the Jewish girl. Rated PG-13 for mild profanity, brief nudity, and mature themes. 97m. DIR: Moshe Mizrahi. CAST: Tom Hanks, Cristina Marsillach, Benedict Taylor. 1987

EVERY WHICH WAY BUT LOOSE ★★★ After *Smokey and the Bandit* cleaned up at the box office, Clint Eastwood decided to make his own modern-day cowboy movie. This 1978 release proved to be one of the squinty-eyed star's biggest money-makers. The film is far superior to its sequel, *Any Which Way You Can*. Rated R. 114m. DIR: James Fargo. CAST: Clint Eastwood, Sondra Locke, Geoffrey Lewis, Clyde (the ape), Ruth Gordon. 1978

EVERYBODY SING ★★ Judy Garland is the focus in this let's-put-on-a-show musical. The movie offers a rare performance by Fanny Brice singing comedy songs. The best is "Quainty, Dainty Me." Judy Garland sings swing, and Allan Jones sings love songs in this minor tunefest. B&W; 80m. DIR: Edwin L. Marin. CAST: Judy Garland, Fanny Brice, Allan Jones, Billie Burke, Monty Woolley, Reginald Gardiner, Henry Armetta. 1938

EVERYBODY WINS ★★1/2 Private eye Nick Nolte meets woman of mystery Debra Winger and finds himself drawn into her efforts to clear a man convicted of murder. The script by playwright Arthur Miller (his first since *The Misfits* in 1960) has a clever enough plot, but the dialogue is stiff, and director Karel Reisz paces the film at a reckless gallop. Rated R. 94m. DIR: Karel Reisz. CAST: Nick Nolte, Debra Winger, Will Patton, Judith Ivey, Kathleen Wilhoite, Jack Warden. 1990

EVERYBODY'S ALL-AMERICAN ★★★1/2 Though a bit long-winded at times, this story (based on a book by *Sports Illustrated*'s Frank Deford) is a must-see for anyone who believes professional athletes have it made. Dennis Quaid is the college football hero who believes he can go on catching passes as a professional forever. He soon finds himself unable to cope. Jessica Lange (as Quaid's wife) and Timothy Hutton round out an unnecessary love triangle. Rated R for profanity and suggested sex. 122m. DIR: Taylor Hackford. CAST: Dennis Quaid, Jessica Lange, Timothy Hutton, John Goodman. 1988

EVERYBODY'S FINE ★★★★ Giuseppe Tornatore followed up his international sensation, *Cinema Paradiso*, with this more cynical, more complex, but quite affecting work. Marcello Mastroianni corrals a fabulous late-in-his-career role as an elderly widower who decides to travel about Italy, seeing his grown children. He's under the delusion that "everybody's fine," when in reality they've all gotten into various kinds of trouble or financial difficulty. In Italian with English subtitles. Not rated. 108m. DIR: Giuseppe

Tornatore. **CAST:** Marcello Mastroianni, Michele Morgan. **1991**

EVERYONE SAYS I LOVE YOU ★★★ Old-fashioned musical/comedy about what we all go through when we fall in love is filtered through the romances of an extended, affluent, Upper East Side family. Love-struck people—played by usually nonsinging and nondancing actors—suddenly stop their daily routines to croon and shuffle their feet to romantic and exuberant pop chestnuts all over New York, Venice, and Paris. Rated R for language. 101m. **DIR:** Woody Allen. **CAST:** Woody Allen, Natasha Lyonne, Drew Barrymore, Edward Norton, Lukas Haas, Gaby Hoffman, Natalie Portman, Alan Alda, Goldie Hawn, Julia Roberts, Tim Roth. **1996 DVD**

EVERYTHING HAPPENS AT NIGHT ★★★ A Sonja Henie movie with a minimum of ice-skating scenes, this film is largely a vehicle for then newcomers Ray Milland and Robert Cummings. Both fall for Henie, a skater they meet in Europe while trying to uncover the mystery behind a political assassination. It's rather contrived, but it works. B&W; 76m. **DIR:** Irving Cummings. **CAST:** Sonja Henie, Ray Milland, Robert Cummings, Maurice Moscovich, Leonid Kinskey, Alan Dinehart, Fritz Feld, Victor Varconi. **1939**

EVERYTHING RELATIVE ★★★★ You won't find a better or more relevant film about lesbians than this striking independent effort that features top-notch production values, a thoughtful and witty script, plus outstanding performances. The film follows seven female college friends who reunite fifteen years later to reminisce about old times and update their lives. Available in R-rated and not-rated versions; both contain adult situations, language and nudity. 105m. **DIR:** Sharon Pollack. **CAST:** Monica Bell, Gabriella Messina, Stacey Nelkin, Ellen McLaughlin, Olivia Negron, Andrea Weber, Carol Schneider. **1996**

EVERYTHING THAT RISES ★★★★ Dennis Quaid directs and stars in this fine TNT original. His character is a macho cowboy who must confront his own fears when his son is paralyzed. Slow start gives way to riveting emotion so keep the Kleenex handy. Not rated; contains adult themes and violence. 90m. **DIR:** Dennis Quaid. **CAST:** Dennis Quaid, Ryan Merriman, Mare Winningham, Harve Presnell, Meat Loaf. **1998**

EVERYTHING YOU ALWAYS WANTED TO KNOW ABOUT SEX BUT WERE AFRAID TO ASK ★★★★ This gave Woody Allen, scriptwriter, star, and director, an opportunity to stretch out without having to supply all the talent himself. Several sequences do not feature Woody at all. The film is broken up into vignettes supposedly relating to questions asked. Rated R. 87m. **DIR:** Woody Allen. **CAST:** John Carradine, Woody Allen, Lou Jacobi, Louise Lasser, Anthony Quayle, Lynn Redgrave, Tony Randall, Burt Reynolds, Gene Wilder. **1972**

EVIDENCE OF BLOOD ★★★ This small-town mystery reunited *Passion Fish* costars Mary McDonnell and David Strathairn. Dalene Young's script (based on the book by Thomas H. Cook) is filled with genuine plot twists and turns as a Pulitzer Prize–winning author returns to his small hometown for a little rest and relaxation but finds himself drawn to a 40-year-old mystery haunting the locals. Filled with atmosphere and interesting characters, *Evidence of Blood* is a better-than-average made-for-cable thriller that delivers the goods. Rated PG-13 for language and violence. 120m. **DIR:** Andrew Mondshein. **CAST:** Mary McDonnell, David Strathairn. **1997**

EVIL, THE ★★★ Psychologist Richard Crenna, his wife, and some of his students are trapped in an old mansion where an unseen force kills them off one by one. It's your basic haunted-house story with one added twist: the devil himself makes a memorable appearance in the person of Victor Buono, a choice bit of casting. Rated R for violence and nudity. 89m. **DIR:** Gus Trikonis. **CAST:** Richard Crenna, Joanna Pettet, Andrew Prine, Cassie Yates, Victor Buono, Mary Louise Weller. **1978**

EVIL CLUTCH 🖤 She's a babe, she's a beast, she's a good time, until you get her aroused, and then the monster in her comes out. Most men wouldn't know the difference. Rated R for violence and nudity. 88m. **DIR:** Andreas Marfori. **CAST:** Caralina C. Tassoni, Diego Ribon, Luciano Crovato. **1988**

EVIL DEAD, THE ★★★★ Five college students spending the weekend at a cabin in the Tennessee woods accidentally revive demons who possess their bodies. This low-budget wonder isn't much in the plot department, but it features lots of inventive camera work and gruesome special effects. Most of the violence is committed against unfeeling demons so it's not that hard to take, though a sequence in which a woman is molested by a tree (!) is in poor taste. Not rated, but the black-humored violence isn't for children. 86m. **DIR:** Sam Raimi. **CAST:** Bruce Campbell, Ellen Sandweiss. **1982 DVD**

EVIL DEAD 2 ★★★1/2 The original *Evil Dead* didn't have a lot of plot, and the sequel has even less. Ash, the survivor of the first film, continues to battle demons in the cabin in the woods. A few lost travelers happen by to provide additional demon fodder. It's more of a remake than a sequel, except that this time director Sam Raimi has explicitly fashioned it as a tribute to one of his greatest influences: the Three Stooges. The overt slapstick may turn off some horror fans. Not rated, it contains nonstop violence and gore. 85m. **DIR:** Sam Raimi. **CAST:** Bruce Campbell, Sarah Barry. **1987 DVD**

EVIL ED ★★★ A quiet film editor becomes a little too involved with his job when he is assigned to work on a gory horror series. This Swedish import (shot in English) may appeal to those with a taste for dry humor as well as die-hard horror buffs, but be forewarned—it is extremely gruesome. Rated R for strong violence, gore, and nudity. 90m. **DIR:** Anders Jacobsson. **CAST:** Johan Ruebeck, Olof Rhodin, Peter Lofberg. **1995 DVD**

EVIL HAS A FACE ★★1/2 Stiff acting and a predictable plot stunt what could have been an interesting made-for-cable thriller about a police sketch artist who discovers a terrible secret about her own past when she sketches the picture of a child molester. Not rated; contains violence. 95m. **DIR:** Rob Fresco. **CAST:** Sean Young, William R. Moses, Joe Guzaldo. **1996**

EVIL LAUGH 🖤 A typical slasher film about college students spending the weekend in an abandoned house while a crazed serial killer stalks and kills them. Rated R for violence and nudity. 90m. DIR: Dominick Brascia. CAST: Steven Bad, Dominick Brascia. 1986

•EVIL LIVES ★★ Supernatural silliness about an immortal man who stalks college coeds for the life force necessary to bring his dead lover back to life. Couple of moments of clarity are blurred by flat acting and lifeless direction. Rated R for adult situations, language, nudity, and violence. 90m. DIR: Thunder Levin. CAST: Tristan Rodgers, Arabella Holzbog, Tyrone Power, Sonia Curtis, Griffin O'Neal, Paul Ben-Victor. 1997

EVIL MIND, THE (THE CLAIRVOYANT) ★★★ Nicely mounted story of fake mentalist who realizes that his phony predictions are actually coming true. The elegant Claude Rains gives a fine performance as a man who has inexplicably acquired a strange power and finds himself frightened by it. Interesting and fun. B&W; 80m. DIR: Maurice Elvey. CAST: Claude Rains, Fay Wray, Mary Clare. 1934

EVIL OBSESSION ★★ Homer (Corey Feldman) joins an acting class to get closer to the supermodel with whom he is obsessed. Is he the one who is brutally murdering other models? You'll have no trouble guessing the identity of the killer in this average erotic thriller. Rated R for nudity, sexual situations, violence, and profanity. 95m. DIR: Richard W. Munchkin. CAST: Corey Feldman, Kimberly Stevens, Mark Derwin, Brion James. 1995

EVIL OF DRACULA ★★★ The new teacher at a prestigious girls' school discovers that the headmaster is a vampire. Once you get over seeing Asian actors in a Dracula story, this is a surprisingly good vampire movie. Dubbed in English. Not rated; contains mild violence. 82m. DIR: Michio Yamamoto. CAST: Toshio Kurosawa, Kunie Tanaka. 1974

EVIL OF FRANKENSTEIN, THE ★★1/2 A weaker entry in Hammer Films's popular Frankenstein series pits Dr. Frankenstein (Peter Cushing) against an underhanded hypnotist (Peter Woodthorpe). Good production values and handsome set pieces, but the monster makeup is silly and the script convoluted. 98m. DIR: Freddie Francis. CAST: Peter Cushing, Duncan Lamont, Peter Woodthorpe. 1964

•EVIL ROY SLADE ★★★ Westerns take a beating in this entertaining spoof as bad guy supreme swaps bullets and clichés with his rival and encounters just about every stock character the genre has to offer. One of the best sagebrush satires. Made for TV as a pilot for a proposed series. 97m. DIR: Jerry Paris. CAST: John Astin, Dick Shawn, Mickey Rooney, Edie Adams, Henry Gibson, Dom DeLuise, Milton Berle. 1972

EVIL SPAWN ❤ An antiaging serum turns a vain actress into a giant werebug. Not rated, with nudity, violence, and sexual situations. 88m. DIR: Kenneth J. Hall. CAST: Bobbie Bresee, John Carradine. 1987

EVIL SPIRITS ❤ Tongue-in-cheek humor fails to save this low-budget shocker about a landlady whose backyard is overcrowded with the buried bodies of her tenants. Rated R for nudity and violence. 95m. DIR: Gary Graver. CAST: Arte Johnson, Karen Black, Robert Quarry. 1991

EVIL THAT MEN DO, THE ★★1/2 Believe it or not, Charles Bronson has made a watchable film for a change. He plays a professional killer who comes out of retirement to avenge the brutal murder of an old friend. Rated R for violence and profanity. 90m. DIR: J. Lee Thompson. CAST: Charles Bronson, Theresa Saldana, José Ferrer, Joseph Maher. 1984

EVIL TOONS ❤ Silly slasher spoof features an animated beast possessing the cleaning lady's body. Rated R for nudity, profanity, and violence. 88m. DIR: Fred Olen Ray. CAST: Madison Stone, David Carradine, Arte Johnson, Dick Miller. 1990

EVIL TOWN ❤ In a quaint mountain town, a mad doctor is keeping the citizens from aging at the expense of young tourists. Rated R for violence, nudity, and language. 88m. DIR: Edward Collins. CAST: James Keach, Dean Jagger, Robert Jr. Walker, Michele Marsh. 1987

EVIL UNDER THE SUN ★★★★ This highly entertaining mystery, starring Peter Ustinov as Agatha Christie's Belgian detective Hercule Poirot, is set on a remote island in the Adriatic Sea where a privileged group gathers at a luxury hotel. Of course, someone is murdered and Poirot cracks the case. Rated PG because of a scene involving a dead rabbit. 102m. DIR: Guy Hamilton. CAST: Peter Ustinov, Jane Birkin, Colin Blakely, James Mason, Roddy McDowall, Diana Rigg, Maggie Smith, Nicholas Clay. 1982

EVIL WITHIN, THE ★★★ Gory fun as a parasitic creature crawls out of the bowels of hell and into the womb of an unsuspecting woman who then slaughters every guy she can get into the sack. Rated R for gore, violence, adult situations, and language. 88m. DIR: Alain Robak. CAST: Emmanuelle Escourrou, Jean-François Gallotte, Christina Sinniger. 1994

EVILS OF THE NIGHT ❤ Vampires from outer space hire two idiot mechanics to kidnap teenagers for them. Rated R for nudity, simulated sex, and violence. 85m. DIR: Mardi Rustam. CAST: Neville Brand, Aldo Ray, John Carradine, Tina Louise, Julie Newmar, Karrie Emerson, Tony O'Dell. 1985

EVILSPEAK ❤ A devil-worshiping medieval Spanish priest is brought into modern times by a student on a computer. Rated R for nudity, violence, and gore. 89m. DIR: Eric Weston. CAST: Clint Howard, R. G. Armstrong, Joe Cortese, Claude Earl Jones. 1982

EVITA ★★★1/2 The long-awaited film of Andrew Lloyd Webber and Tim Rice's pop opera about the legendary first lady of Argentina (who died of cancer at thirty-three) is musically impressive, well-photographed, and spectacularly staged and edited. Madonna is poised and confident (with the score modified to suit her voice), but the film really belongs to Antonio Banderas, robust and riveting (and with a surprisingly strong singing voice), as the omnipresent narrator swaggering through Evita's life. Rated PG. 134m. DIR: Alan Parker. CAST: Madonna, Antonio Banderas, Jonathan Pryce, Jimmy Nail. 1996 DVD

•EVOLUTION'S CHILD ★★★ Scientists discover a three-thousand-year-old man frozen in the Italian Alps, and ask a fertility doctor to extract the corpse's frozen sperm for a more complete DNA analysis. As you might expect, the sample somehow winds up in one of the doctor's patients, and a unique child is born. At times touching, at times stretching credibility too thin, this made-for-cable original entertains but doesn't seem to offer any new ideas, despite the emphasis on the science of the situation. Not rated. 95m. **DIR:** Jeffrey Reiner. **CAST:** Ken Olin, Taylor Nichols, Heidi Swedberg, Susan Gibney, Jacob Smith. 1999

EVOLVER ★★★ Engaging high-tech thriller about a new interactive game that begins to think for itself. Teen Ethan Randall is excited when he wins the chance to try out the new "Evolver" in his home. Excitement turns to terror when the family learns the game, a robot that hunts, was actually a prototype for a government weapon. Now it has reverted back to its original program, and the game becomes real. Lots of fun and good special effects make this thriller a good bet. Rated R for violence and language. 90m. **DIR:** Mark Rosman. **CAST:** Ethan Randall, Cindy Pickett, John de Lancie, Cassidy Rae, Paul Dooley. 1994 DVD

EWOK ADVENTURE, THE ★★ Two children use the help of the friendly Ewok people to find their kidnapped parents in this dull entry in the *Star Wars* family of films. Subpar special effects. Not rated, but would probably rank a PG for mild violence. 96m. **DIR:** John Korty. **CAST:** Eric Walker, Warwick Davis, Fionnula Flanagan, Guy Boyd. 1984

EWOKS: THE BATTLE FOR ENDOR ★★ Those almost too lovable, diminutive rascals from *Return of the Jedi* appear in their own adventure as they try to help two orphans stop an evil entity from destroying them all. Hokey and a bit cutesy. Contains some scenes that may be too intense for children. 98m. **DIR:** Jim Wheat, Ken Wheat. **CAST:** Wilford Brimley, Warwick Davis, Paul Gleason. 1986

EX, THE ★★1/2 Yancy Butler delivers a deliciously over-the-top performance as a woman who sets out to destroy her ex-husband and his new family. Dierdre (Butler) is definitely psychotic and uses her wiles to infiltrate the family and tear it apart from within. Some genuine moments of suspense can't hide the fact we've seen it all before. Rated R for violence, language, and nudity. 87m. **DIR:** Mark L. Lester. **CAST:** Yancy Butler, Nick Mancuso, Suzy Amis. 1996

EX-LADY ★★ Early women's lib, with Bette Davis reluctantly marrying her lover, knowing it will take the romance out of their relationship. Nothing much. B&W; 67m. **DIR:** Robert Florey. **CAST:** Bette Davis, Gene Raymond, Frank McHugh. 1933

EX-MRS. BRADFORD, THE ★★★★ Appealing story about physician William Powell and ex-wife Jean Arthur "keeping company" again is fast and funny. Arthur has a taste for murder mysteries and wants to write them, and Powell is attempting to help the police solve a series of murders. The pace is quick and the dialogue sparkles in this vintage gem. B&W; 80m. **DIR:** Stephen Roberts. **CAST:** William Powell, Jean Arthur, James Gleason, Eric Blore, Robert Armstrong, Lila Lee, Grant Mitchell. 1936

EXCALIBUR ★★★★ Swords cross and magic abounds in this spectacular, highly enjoyable version of the Arthurian legend. A gritty, realistic view of the rise to power of King Arthur, the forbidden love of Queen Guinevere and Sir Lancelot and the quest of the Knights of the Round Table for the Holy Grail. Highlighted by lush photography and fine performances. Rated R. 140m. **DIR:** John Boorman. **CAST:** Nicol Williamson, Nigel Terry, Helen Mirren, Nicholas Clay, Cherie Lunghi, Corin Redgrave, Paul Geoffrey, Liam Neeson, Patrick Stewart. 1981 DVD

●**EXCALIBUR, THE** ★ Boring tale of yet another teen being sent to the time of King Arthur in order to help out in some grand task that apparently only he can achieve. This time out the teen must help Merlin and Arthur recover Excalibur before an evil witch can take over the kingdom. You'll have a case of déjà vu. Rated PG for mild violence and profanity. 90m. **DIR:** James Head. **CAST:** Jason McSkimming, Mak Fyfe, Natalie Ester. 1998

●**EXCELLENT CADAVERS** ★★★1/2 Chazz Palminteri delivers an impassioned and wholly credible performance as Judge Giovanni Falcone, one of the few individuals who stood up to the increasingly violent Mafia in the 1980s, in this absorbing but inexplicably truncated adaptation of Alexander Stille's fascinating book. Falcone's assignment was tantamount to a death wish in a country where such government crusaders routinely were killed (and thus turned into "excellent cadavers"), but the judge got his big break when a career mafioso (F. Murray Abraham), appalled by his younger colleagues' lack of honor, spilled his guts in a mass trial that became a national sensation. This would have made a superb miniseries, but the film screams of compromise and considerable eleventh-hour trimming. Rated R for violence and profanity. 86m. **DIR:** Ricky Tognazzi. **CAST:** Chazz Palminteri, F. Murray Abraham, Anna Galiena, Andy Luotto, Lina Sastri. 1999 DVD

EXCESS BAGGAGE ♥ Neglected rich girl Alicia Silverstone fakes her own kidnapping to get Daddy's attention, then winds up missing for real when thief Benicio Del Toro hijacks her car. Sloppy, witless would-be-romantic comedy suffers from moronic dialogue, lurching direction, and an ugly, disheveled look. Rated PG-13 for mild violence and profanity. 101m. **DIR:** Marco Brambilla. **CAST:** Alicia Silverstone, Benicio Del Toro, Christopher Walken, Harry Connick Jr., Nicholas Turturro, Michael Bowen, Jack Thompson. 1997

EXCESSIVE FORCE ★★★ Good cast and an unexpected, eleventh-hour snap of the tail enliven this otherwise standard kill-or-be-killed actionfest. Van Damme wannabe Thomas Ian Griffith scripts himself a heroic role as a cop determined to nail syndicate boss Burt Young. Plenty o' kicks and licks and enough intelligent plotting to furrow a few brows. Rated R for profanity, nudity, simulated sex, and excessive violence. 87m. **DIR:** Jon Hess. **CAST:** Thomas Ian Griffith, Lance Henriksen, Tom Hodges, James Earl Jones, Charlotte Lewis, Burt Young. 1993

EXCESSIVE FORCE II: FORCE ON FORCE ★★ Stacie Randall plays special agent Harly Cordell, who is determined to bring down her ex-boyfriend, a former Navy SEAL turned terrorist. When a series of assassinations rocks Los Angeles, Cordell suspects it's the work of Francis Lydell (Dan Gauthier), the man who left her for dead. Now it's payback time. Rated R for violence, language, and adult situations. 88m. DIR: Jonathan Winfrey. CAST: Stacie Randall, Dan Gauthier, Jay Patterson, John Mese. 1995

EXECUTION, THE ★★ Five women survivors of the Holocaust, now living in Los Angeles, have a chance meeting with a former Nazi doctor from their camp. They plot to seduce and then kill him. There is some suspense in this made-for-TV movie, but it is too melodramatic to be believable. 100m. DIR: Paul Wendkos. CAST: Jessica Walter, Barbara Barrie, Sandy Dennis, Valerie Harper, Michael Lerner, Robert Hooks. 1985

EXECUTION OF PRIVATE SLOVIK, THE ★★★★ Superior made-for-television film chronicles the fate of American soldier Eddie Slovik, who was executed for desertion during World War II. Intelligent teleplay, powerful performances, and sensitive direction. 120m. DIR: Lamont Johnson. CAST: Martin Sheen, Ned Beatty, Gary Busey, Charles Haid, Mariclare Costello. 1974

EXECUTIONER, THE ★★ This British spy picture features George Peppard as an intelligence agent who believes he is being compromised by fellow spy Keith Michell. Joan Collins is the love interest. Average. Rated PG. 107m. DIR: Sam Wanamaker. CAST: George Peppard, Joan Collins, Judy Geeson, Oscar Homolka, Keith Michell, Nigel Patrick. 1970

EXECUTIONER'S SONG, THE ★★★1/2 Pulitzer Prize novelist Norman Mailer's made-for-television adaptation of his engrossing account of convicted killer Gary Gilmore's fight to get Utah to carry out his death sentence. The performances of Tommy Lee Jones and Rosanna Arquette are electrifying. Not rated. 200m. DIR: Lawrence Schiller. CAST: Tommy Lee Jones, Rosanna Arquette, Christine Lahti, Eli Wallach. 1982

EXECUTIVE ACTION ★★★★ This forceful film, based on Mark Lane's book *Rush to Judgment*, features a fascinating look at possible reasons for the assassination of John F. Kennedy. Rated PG. 91m. DIR: David Miller. CAST: Burt Lancaster, Robert Ryan, Will Geer, Gilbert Green, John Anderson. 1973

EXECUTIVE DECISION ★★★★ Kurt Russell, a U.S. government expert on Middle East terrorism, finds himself out of his office and on a do-or-die mission with gung ho commando leader Steven Seagal when an American airliner is taken hostage in midair. Even though this movie runs over two hours, its suspense never flags. Excellent writing, direction, and performances. Rated R for violence and profanity. 135m. DIR: Stuart Baird. CAST: Kurt Russell, Steven Seagal, Halle Berry, John Leguizamo, Oliver Platt, Joe Morton, David Suchet, Len Cariou, B. D. Wong, Marla Maples Trump. 1996 DVD

•**EXECUTIVE POWER** ★★ A good cast is wasted in this tired political thriller about an ex–Secret Service agent investigating whether the death of a presidential adviser was really suicide. Rated R for violence and profanity. 97m. DIR: David R. Corley. CAST: Craig Sheffer, John Heard, Andrea Roth, Joanna Cassidy, William Atherton, Denise Crosby. 1997

EXECUTIVE SUITE ★★★★ An all-star cast is topnotch in this film about the world of corporate life. Based on Cameron Hawley's novel, the drama examines the intense power struggles in big business with honesty and panache. B&W; 104m. DIR: Robert Wise. CAST: William Holden, June Allyson, Barbara Stanwyck, Fredric March, Louis Calhern, Walter Pidgeon, Shelley Winters, Dean Jagger, Nina Foch, Paul Douglas. 1954

EXECUTIVE TARGET ★★★ Not much more than a ninety-five-minute car chase, but it's not a bad one. The cast is adequate with the exception of Angie Everhart, who seems hopelessly lost in the role of a killer. If car chases are your thing, this is just the movie for you. Rated R for profanity and violence. 95m. DIR: Joseph Merhi. CAST: Michael Madsen, Keith David, Angie Everhart, Dayton Callie, Kathy Christopherson, Roy Scheider. 1996

EXILED IN AMERICA 🎭 Extremely bad acting and a poor script kill this film, in which a revolutionary hero is hunted by Central American terrorists. Not rated; contains violence. 85m. DIR: Paul Leder. CAST: Maxwell Caulfield, Edward Albert, Wings Hauser, Viveca Lindfors, Stella Stevens. 1990

EXISTENZ ★★★1/2 A designer of virtual reality computer games goes on the run, pursued by terrorists out to destroy her. David Cronenberg's sciencefiction thriller takes us into a world where the line between fantasy and reality grows dangerously thin—puzzles within puzzles, games within games—right up to the very last shot. Rated R for profanity and violence. 97m. DIR: David Cronenberg. CAST: Jennifer Jason Leigh, Jude Law, Ian Holm, Willem Dafoe, Don McKellar, Sarah Polley. 1999 DVD

EXIT ★★ Shannon Whirry plays one of a group of strippers taken hostage by a pair of criminals. She breaks loose and joins forces with bodyguard Joe Bucci. This is one preposterous, silly movie with dialogue so bad it's actually quite funny. Rated R for violence, profanity, and nudity. 90m. DIR: Ric Roman Waugh. CAST: Shannon Whirry, David Bradley, Larry Manetti, Joe Bucci. 1996

EXIT IN RED ★★1/2 Psychiatrist Mickey Rourke finds himself framed for murder after having an affair with one of his patients. So-so little thriller is full of plot holes, but performances and style keep it afloat. Rated R for language, violence, and nudity. 96m. DIR: Yurek Bogayevicz. CAST: Mickey Rourke, Annabel Schofield, Anthony Michael Hall, Carré Otis. 1996

EXIT TO EDEN 🎭 The usually reliable Garry Marshall directs the worst film of his career, an offensive, witless mess about love and intrigue at a sex fantasy resort. Rated R for profanity, nudity, and simulated sex. 113m. DIR: Garry Marshall. CAST: Dana Delany, Paul Mercurio, Rosie O'Donnell, Dan Aykroyd, Hector Elizondo, Iman. 1994

EXODUS ★★1/2 The early days of Israel are seen through the eyes of various characters, in this epic, adapted from the novel by Leon Uris. Directed by the heavy-handed Otto Preminger, its length and plodding pace caused comic Mort Sahl to quip, "Otto, let my people go," at a preview. 213m. DIR: Otto Preminger. CAST: Paul Newman, Eva Marie Saint, Ralph Richardson, Peter Lawford, Lee J. Cobb, Sal Mineo, Jill Haworth. 1960

EXORCIST, THE ★★★1/2 A sensation at the time of its release, this horror film—directed by William Friedkin (*The French Connection*)—has lost some of its punch because of the numerous imitations it spawned. An awful sequel, *Exorcist II: The Heretic*, didn't help much either. Rated R. 121m. DIR: William Friedkin. CAST: Ellen Burstyn, Max von Sydow, Linda Blair, Jason Miller, Lee J. Cobb. 1973 DVD

EXORCIST II: THE HERETIC 🖤 The script is bad, the acting poor, and the direction lacking in pace or conviction. Rated R for violence and profanity. 110m. DIR: John Boorman. CAST: Richard Burton, Linda Blair, Louise Fletcher, James Earl Jones, Max von Sydow. 1977

EXORCIST III: LEGION ★★ This time priests discover some unutterable evil and turn to detective George C. Scott for help. Rated R for all sorts of ghastly stuff. 108m. DIR: William Peter Blatty. CAST: George C. Scott, Ed Flanders, Brad Dourif. 1990 DVD

EXOTICA ★★★ Strange characters—an emotionally shredded tax auditor, a gay pet-store owner, a young lap dancer, the pregnant owner of the title's plush strip club, and the club's sleazy emcee—wallow neck deep in fixations, mysterious pasts, tragedy, fantasies, and lust. Not rated; contains nudity, adult situations, and profanity. 103m. DIR: Atom Egoyan. CAST: Bruce Greenwood, Elias Koteas, Mia Kirshner, Don McKellar, Arsinée Khanjian. 1994 DVD

EXPECT NO MERCY 🖤 Federal agent gets trapped inside a virtual-reality facility, where he must do battle against virtual-reality assassins. The results are virtually stupid. Rated R for violence and adult language. 91m. DIR: Zale Dalen. CAST: Billy Blanks, Jalal Merhi, Wolf Larson, Laurie Holden. 1995

EXPERIENCE PREFERRED ... BUT NOT ESSENTIAL ★★★★★ This delightful British import, which is somewhat reminiscent of Scottish director Bill Forsyth's *Gregory's Girl* and *Local Hero*, follows the awkward and amusing adventures of a young woman during her first summer job at a Welsh coastal resort in 1962. She comes to town insecure and frumpy and leaves at the end of the summer pretty, sexy, and confident. Rated PG for language. 80m. DIR: Peter Duffell. CAST: Elizabeth Edmonds, Sue Wallace, Geraldine Griffith, Karen Meagher, Ron Bain, Alun Lewis, Robert Blythe. 1983

EXPERIMENT IN TERROR ★★★1/2 A sadistic killer (Ross Martin) kidnaps the teenage sister (Stefanie Powers) of a bank teller (Lee Remick). An FBI agent is hot on the trail, fighting the clock. The film crackles with suspense. The acting is uniformly excellent. Martin paints an unnerving portrait of evil. B&W; 123m. DIR: Blake Edwards. CAST: Glenn Ford, Lee Remick, Stefanie Powers, Ross Martin, Ned Glass. 1962

EXPERT, THE ★★★ Special-forces expert Jeff Speakman decides to settle a blood feud by breaking into the prison where his nemesis waits. An otherwise routine kickfest is enlivened by a better-than-average script. Rated R for violence and profanity. 92m. DIR: Rick Avery. CAST: Jeff Speakman, James Brolin, Michael Shaner, Alex Datcher, Jim Varney. 1994

EXPERTS, THE ★★ John Travolta and Arye Gross star as two hip nightclub entrepreneurs from New York City. Charles Martin Smith is a KGB agent who whisks the boys off to a secret American-like community in Russia. Top-notch cast. Rated PG-13 for violence and profanity. 94m. DIR: Dave Thomas. CAST: John Travolta, Arye Gross, Kelly Preston, Deborah Foreman, James Keach, Charles Martin Smith. 1988

EXPLORERS ★★★1/2 The young and the young at heart are certain to have a grand time watching *Explorers*. It's a just-for-fun fantasy about three kids (Ethan Hawke, River Phoenix, and Jason Presson) taking off on the greatest adventure of all: a journey through outer space. Rated PG for minor violence and light profanity. 109m. DIR: Joe Dante. CAST: Ethan Hawke, River Phoenix, Jason Presson, Dick Miller, Robert Picardo. 1985

EXPOSE 🖤 A political payoff to a congressman's daughter sets the stage for further extortion in this sleazy and tawdry tale of lust and revenge. Not rated; contains adult situations, language, nudity, and violence. 76m. DIR: B. A. Rudnick. CAST: Tracy Tutor, Kevin West, Daneen Boone, Libby George. 1997

EXPOSED ★★ Nastassja Kinski stars in this mediocre and confusing film as a high-priced fashion model whose constant exposure in magazines and on television has made her the target for the sometimes dangerous desires of two men. Former ballet star Rudolph Nureyev is also featured. Rated R. 100m. DIR: James Toback. CAST: Nastassja Kinski, Rudolf Nureyev, Harvey Keitel, Ian McShane. 1983

EXPOSURE 🖤 Passive photojournalist (Peter Coyote) working in Brazil learns a gruesome art form of knife fighting in this exotic and senseless thriller. Rated R for profanity, nudity, and violence. 106m. DIR: Walter Salles Jr. CAST: Peter Coyote, Tcheky Karyo, Amanda Pays. 1992

EXPRESS TO TERROR ★★ This mystery set on a superpertrain will come in handy for those times when you're missing those old NBC *Wednesday Night at the Movies* flicks. 120m. DIR: Dan Curtis. CAST: George Hamilton, Steve Lawrence, Stella Stevens, Don Meredith, Fred Williamson, Don Stroud. 1979

EXTERMINATING ANGEL, THE ★★★★★ Luis Buñuel always did love a good dinner party. In *The Discreet Charm of the Bourgeoisie*, the dinner party never could get under way, and here the elite *après-opéra* diners find they cannot escape the host's sumptuous music room. This is a very funny film—in a very black key. In Spanish with English subtitles. B&W; 95m. DIR: Luis Buñuel. CAST: Silvia Pinal, Enrique Rambal. 1962

EXTERMINATOR, THE ★★ A vigilante who takes the law into his own hands when the law refuses to punish the gang members who made a cripple of his best friend. Rated R. 101m. DIR: James Glickenhaus. CAST: Christopher George, Samantha Eggar, Robert Ginty, Steve James, Tony DiBenedetto. 1980 DVD

EXTERMINATOR 2, THE 🖤 In this disgusting cheapo, Robert Ginty returns as the one-man vigilante force. 104m. DIR: Mark Buntzman. CAST: Robert Ginty, Deborah Gefner, Frankie Faison, Mario Van Peebles. 1984

EXTERMINATORS OF THE YEAR 3000 🖤 This one rips off George Miller's *The Road Warrior* almost to the letter. Rated R for violence and profanity. 101m.

DIR: Jules Harrison. **CAST:** Robert Jannucci, Alicia Moro, Alan Collins, Fred Harris, Beryl Cunningham, Luca Venantini. 1983

EXTRA GIRL, THE ★★★ Madcap silent comedienne Mabel Normand's last film—and a winner! Normand plays a naïve, star-struck midwestern girl who fantasizes about fame in films. She wins a beauty contest, goes to Hollywood, and winds up a no-name extra. Silent with music score. B&W; 87m. **DIR:** Dick Jones. **CAST:** Mabel Normand, Ralph Graves. 1923

EXTRAORDINARY ADVENTURES OF MR. WEST IN THE LAND OF THE BOLSHEVIKS, THE ★★ An American tourist (Podobed) finds some of the realities beyond the stereotypes of Soviet Russia. Offbeat and uneven. Silent. B&W; 55m. **DIR:** Lev Kuleshov. **CAST:** Podobed, Vsevolod Pudovkin. 1924

EXTREME JUSTICE ★★★ Intelligent performances and a disturbing story line ripped from current headlines are nearly sabotaged by director Mark L. Lester's emphasis on ludicrous violence and gratuitous mayhem. Bad-boy cop Lou Diamond Phillips gets assigned to an LAPD "Death Squad" headed by old buddy Scott Glenn; our heroes then watch and wait while slimeballs jeopardize innocent civilians. Rated R for rape, violence, profanity, nudity, and drug use. 95m. **DIR:** Mark L. Lester. **CAST:** Lou Diamond Phillips, Scott Glenn, Chelsea Field, Yaphet Kotto, Ed Lauter. 1993 DVD

EXTREME MEASURES ★★1/2 Farfetched thriller, which exploits the sort of medical nightmares usually found in Robin Cook novels. Hugh Grant's an emergency-room doctor puzzled by a homeless man's bizarre symptoms; the subsequent investigation eventually leads to a revered surgeon (Gene Hackman). Grant simply isn't convincing as a reluctant detective, and it's inconceivable that such a charming fellow wouldn't find somebody to believe him. Dumb, dumb, dumb. Rated R for violence, profanity, and nudity. 117m. **DIR:** Michael Apted. **CAST:** Hugh Grant, Gene Hackman, Sarah Jessica Parker, David Morse, Bill Nunn. 1996 DVD

EXTREME PREJUDICE ★★★★ Nick Nolte in peak form in this modern-day Western as a two-fisted Texas Ranger whose boyhood friend, Powers Boothe, has become a drug kingpin across the border in Mexico. The federal government sends six high-tech agents to nail Boothe with "extreme prejudice." Rated R for profanity, drug use, nudity, and violence. 96m. **DIR:** Walter Hill. **CAST:** Nick Nolte, Powers Boothe, Maria Conchita Alonso, Michael Ironside, Rip Torn, Clancy Brown, William Forsythe. 1987

EXTREMITIES ★★1/2 This well-meant but difficult-to-watch thriller casts Farrah Fawcett (in a first-rate performance) as a single woman who is brutalized in her own home by a homicidal maniac (James Russo). When she manages to outwit her attacker, she must decide between bloody revenge and human compassion. Robert M. Young directs this adaptation by William Mastrosimone of his play with authority and realism. Rated R for violence. 100m. **DIR:** Robert M. Young. **CAST:** Farrah Fawcett, James Russo, Diana Scarwid, Alfre Woodard. 1986

EYE FOR AN EYE (1981) ★★1/2 This surprisingly entertaining kung fu movie features Chuck Norris as Shawn Kane, an ex-cop trying to crack a narcotics-smuggling ring. With the help of a lovely news editor (Maggie Cooper) and a martial arts master (Mako) who doubles as a walking fortune cookie, Kane confronts a sinister Christopher Lee and, finally, a human tank called The Professor. Rated R. 106m. **DIR:** Steve Carver. **CAST:** Chuck Norris, Christopher Lee, Richard Roundtree, Mako, Maggie Cooper. 1981

EYE FOR AN EYE (1995) ★★1/2 Sally Field plays a suburbanite whose daughter is raped and murdered. When the killer gets off on a technicality, Mama decides to go after him herself. The film is slickly made and suspenseful, but manipulative and unpleasant; under the lynch-mob surface there are hints of a more honest, thoughtful film about grief, loss, and anger. Rated R for profanity and two brutal rape scenes. 101m. **DIR:** John Schlesinger. **CAST:** Sally Field, Kiefer Sutherland, Ed Harris, Joe Mantegna, Alexandra Kyle. 1996

●**EYE OF THE BEHOLDER** ✦ Our brief critique can't do justice to this failed thriller's excessive shortcomings, starting with the unintentionally hilarious premise and directorial flourishes too heavy-handed and silly for words. Rated R for nudity, violence, and profanity. 101m. **DIR:** Stephan Elliott. **CAST:** Ewan McGregor, Ashley Judd, Jason Priestley, k. d. lang, Patrick Bergin, Genevieve Bujold. 1999 DVD

EYE OF THE DEMON ✦ A yuppie couple relocates to a New England island. TV movie originally titled *Bay Coven*. 92m. **DIR:** Carl Schenkel. **CAST:** Tim Matheson, Pamela Sue Martin, Barbara Billingsley, Woody Harrelson, Susan Ruttan. 1987

EYE OF THE EAGLE ✦ Cheap shoot-'em-up focuses on three do-gooders who combat a renegade band of U.S. soldiers. 84m. **DIR:** Cirio H. Santiago. **CAST:** Brett Clark, Robert Patrick, Ed Crick, William Steis. 1987

EYE OF THE EAGLE 2 ✦ This lousy sequel features a corrupt army major plotting against an honest private. Rated R for nudity and profanity. 79m. **DIR:** Carl Franklin. **CAST:** Todd Field, Andy Wood. 1988

EYE OF THE EAGLE 3 ✦ A maverick squadron of soldiers takes a stand against enemy Vietnamese troops. More or less the A-team before they went to work in the public sector. Rated R for profanity and nudity. 90m. **DIR:** Cirio H. Santiago. **CAST:** Steve Kanaly, Ken Wright, Peter Nelson, Carl Franklin. 1991

EYE OF THE NEEDLE ★★★1/2 In this adaptation of Ken Follett's novel, Donald Sutherland stars as the deadly Nazi agent who discovers a ruse by the Allies during World War II. Plenty of suspense and thrills for those new to the story. Rated R because of nudity, sex, and violence. 112m. **DIR:** Richard Marquand. **CAST:** Donald Sutherland, Ian Bannen, Kate Nelligan, Christopher Cazenove. 1981 DVD

EYE OF THE SNAKE ✦ They don't make them any worse than this. Not rated; contains adult language and situations. 91m. **DIR:** Max Reid. **CAST:** Sydney Penny, Malcolm McDowell, Lois Chiles, Jason Cairns. 1990

EYE OF THE STORM ★★ After witnessing his parents' brutal murder, a boy is blinded by the trauma. Raised by his older brother, the two run a Bates-type hotel. The latest unlucky boarders are an abusive drunk (Dennis Hopper) and his glitzy wife (Lara Flynn Boyle). Rated R for profanity and violence. 98m. DIR: Yuri Zeltser. CAST: Craig Sheffer, Lara Flynn Boyle, Bradley Gregg, Leon Rippy, Dennis Hopper. 1991

EYE OF THE TIGER ★★★ Buck Mathews (Gary Busey) stands up against a motorcycle gang and the corrupt law enforcement that have plagued a small town in Texas. Busey and Yaphet Kotto give quality performances that save this formula vengeance film. Rated R for violence and language. 90m. DIR: Richard C. Sarafian. CAST: Gary Busey, Yaphet Kotto, Seymour Cassel. 1986

EYE OF THE WOLF ★★ Jeff Fahey plays a zoologist who takes the only witness to a murder, a wild wolf, into protective custody. Forget the hokey plot and just enjoy the gorgeous Canadian scenery. Rated PG-13 for violence. 96m. DIR: Arnaud Selignac. CAST: Jeff Fahey, Sophie Duez, Lorne Brass. 1994

EYE ON THE SPARROW ★★★ Mare Winningham and Keith Carradine star in this fact-based made-for-TV drama about a blind couple trying to buck the system and become adoptive parents. Winningham's performance is especially forceful, but both actors are amazingly convincing. 94m. DIR: John Korty. CAST: Mare Winningham, Keith Carradine, Conchata Ferrell. 1987

EYEBALL 🖤 Vacationers on a tour bus are murdered. Rated R for violence and nudity. 87m. DIR: Umberto Lenzi. CAST: John Richardson. 1977

EYES BEHIND THE STARS 🖤 A reporter and a UFO specialist investigate reports that extraterrestrial beings have landed on Earth. Not rated. 95m. DIR: Roy Garrett. CAST: Robert Hoffman, Nathalie Delon, Martin Balsam. 1972

EYES OF A STRANGER ★★ The Love Boat's Julie, Lauren Tewes, plays a reporter who decides to track down a psychopathic killer. Lots of blood and some sexual molestation. Rated R. 85m. DIR: Ken Wiederhorn. CAST: Lauren Tewes, Jennifer Jason Leigh. 1981

EYES OF A WITNESS ★★1/2 Mildly engaging drama about an American businessman whose attempt to rescue his daughter from the Kenya bush lands him in deep trouble when he's accused of murdering a high-ranking official. Daniel J. Travanti and Jennifer Grey play the father and daughter whose lives are thrown into jeopardy in the made-for-television drama shot on location. Not rated; contains some violence. 90m. DIR: Peter R. Hunt. CAST: Daniel J. Travanti, Jennifer Grey, Carl Lumbly, Daniel Gerroll. 1994

EYES OF AN ANGEL ★★★1/2 Heart-tugger about a man at the end of his rope, who finds renewed hope through his daughter and an injured Doberman. After his wife dies of a drug overdose and he's left with his 10-year-old daughter, Bobby Allen (well played by John Travolta) decides to pick up stakes and start new in another city. When he fails to realize his daughter's emotional attachment to a dog they left behind, he sets into motion a cross-country odyssey that touches the heart and soul. Rated PG-13 for language and adult themes. 91m. DIR: Robert Harmon. CAST: John Travolta, Ellie Raab. 1989

EYES OF FIRE ★★★ Old-West settlers accused of witchcraft are surrounded by woods made from the souls of earlier settlers—and the witch who cast the spell upon them. Above-average special-effects highlight this original tale. Rated R for violence and nudity; 90m. DIR: Avery Crounse. CAST: Dennis Lipscomb Rebecca Stanley, Guy Boyd. 1983

EYES OF LAURA MARS, THE ★★ Laura Mars (Faye Dunaway) is a kinky commercial photographer whose photographs, which are composed of violent scenes, somehow become the blueprints for a series of actual killings. It soon becomes apparent the maniac is really after her. Although well acted and suspenseful, this is an unrelentingly cold and gruesome movie. Rated R. 103m. DIR: Irvin Kershner. CAST: Faye Dunaway, Tommy Lee Jones, Brad Dourif, René Auberjonois. 1978 DVD

EYES OF TEXAS ★★★1/2 Villainess Nana Bryant out to acquire valuable ranch land at any cost, including using vicious killer dogs to discourage prospective landowners. Director William Witney brought much-needed action and a harder, often brutal, edge to the Rogers films in the late 1940s after they had stagnated into overblown musicals in the mid-1940s. B&W; 70m. DIR: William Witney. CAST: Roy Rogers, Andy Devine, Nana Bryant, Lynne Roberts (Mary Hart), Roy Barcroft, Bob Nolan and the Sons of the Pioneers. 1948

EYES OF THE AMARYLLIS ★★1/2 A young girl goes to Nantucket to care for her grandmother, an invalid awaiting the return of her long-dead husband. This well-intended low-budget film is likely to bore kids, though it may interest adults who recall the Natalie Babbitt novel on which it was based. Not rated; contains no objectionable material. 84m. DIR: Frederick King Keller. CAST: Ruth Ford, Martha Byrne. 1982

EYES OF THE BEHOLDER ★★ Okay thriller about a doctor who performs a new radical surgery on disturbed Lenny Von Dohlen, who escapes and wreaks havoc. Pretty pedestrian, but an interesting cast keeps things merrily rolling along. Rated R for violence. 89m. DIR: Lawrence L. Simeone. CAST: Joanna Pacula, Matt McCoy, George Lazenby, Charles Napier, Lenny Von Dohlen. 1992

EYES OF THE BIRDS ★★★★ Powerful fact-based psychological drama set in a supposedly model South American prison. A Red Cross investigation into prison conditions leads to reprisals. Unlike most prison movies, this film's effect comes from what it implies rather than what it shows. In French with English subtitles. 89m. DIR: Gabriel Auer. CAST: Roland Amastutz, Philippe Clevot. 1983

EYES OF THE SERPENT 🖤 Long ago and far away, two sisters, one good, one evil, vie for control of a pair of magical swords. It's obvious no one in this film fought over acting lessons. Not rated; contains nudity, violence, and adult situations. 86m. DIR: Ricardo Jacques Gale. CAST: Diana Frank, Lenore Andriel, Tom Schultz, David Michael Sterling. 1994

EYES WIDE SHUT ★★★ Kubrick enthusiasts will love this stylized descent into rampant sensual excess, which makes a striking epitaph for one of the greatest film directors of all time. Tom Cruise and Nicole Kidman heat up the screen as a happily married New York couple who come apart at the seams after she shares one of her sexual fantasies. The notion that his wife betrayed him—if only in her mind—proves more than Cruise can handle, and he spends the next forty-eight hours in a whirlwind of sexual temptation that becomes more improbable by the hour. With an adapted script heavily influenced by the Freudian content in Arthur Schnitzler's source novel, we must consider that our hero's misadventures may occur solely in his mind. Mainstream viewers are apt to find it a lot of fuss, with very little payoff. But it sure is interesting to watch. Rated R for nudity, simulated sex, strong sexual content, profanity, and drug use. 159m. **DIR:** Stanley Kubrick. **CAST:** Tom Cruise, Nicole Kidman, Sydney Pollack, Marie Richardson, Rade Serbedzija, LeeLee Sobieski, Alan Cumming. **1999 DVD**

EYES WITHOUT A FACE ★★★★1/2 Georges Franju, one of the underrated heroes of French cinema, creates an austerely beautiful horror film about a plastic surgeon who, in systematic experiments, removes the faces of beautiful young women and tries to graft them onto the ruined head of his daughter. Imaginative cinematography by Eugen Shuftan with music by Maurice Jarre. Subtitled, not rated. (Originally released in America as *The Horror Chamber of Dr. Faustus*.) B&W; 102m. **DIR:** Georges Franju. **CAST:** Pierre Brasseur, Alida Valli, Edith Scob, Juliette Mayniel. **1960**

EYEWITNESS ★★★★ A humdinger of a movie. William Hurt plays a janitor who, after discovering a murder victim, meets the glamorous television reporter (Sigourney Weaver) he has admired from afar. In order to prolong their relationship, he pretends to know the killer's identity—and puts both their lives in danger. Rated R for violence and profanity. 102m. **DIR:** Peter Yates. **CAST:** William Hurt, Sigourney Weaver, Christopher Plummer, James Woods. **1981**

F FOR FAKE ★★ This sad and sloppy film by Orson Welles supposedly chronicles the exploits of several famous fakers. Quick cuts and a rambling narrative do nothing to enhance this vanity piece. Not rated; contains brief nudity. 98m. **DIR:** Orson Welles. **CAST:** Orson Welles, Elmyr de Hory, Clifford Irving, Oja Kodar. **1973**

FABULOUS BAKER BOYS, THE ★★★★1/2 This deliciously sultry character study concerns a pair of mildly contentious piano-playing brothers (played by offscreen brothers Jeff and Beau Bridges) who, in an effort to revitalize a lounge act mired in tired old standards, hire a feisty singer (Michelle Pfeiffer). She becomes the catalyst that prompts age-old regrets to surface. Rated R for language. 113m. **DIR:**

Steve Kloves. **CAST:** Jeff Bridges, Michelle Pfeiffer, Beau Bridges, Jennifer Tilly. **1989 DVD**

FABULOUS DORSEYS, THE ★★ A mildly musical, plotless dual biography of the Dorsey brothers as they fight their way to the top while fighting with each other, trombone and clarinet at the ready. Janet Blair is cute, William Lundigan is personable, and Paul "Pops" Whiteman is along for the ride. B&W; 88m. **DIR:** Alfred E. Green. **CAST:** Tommy Dorsey, Jimmy Dorsey, Janet Blair, William Lundigan, Paul Whiteman. **1947**

FABULOUS FLEISCHER FOLIO, THE (VOLUME FIVE) ★★ The Christmas cartoons of Max and Dave Fleischer are featured in this Disney video release, which is for animation buffs and youngsters only. Included are: "Rudolph the Red-Nosed Reindeer," "The Ski's the Limit," "Peeping Penguins," "Bunny Mooning," "Snow Fooling," and "Christmas Comes But Once a Year." 43m. **DIR:** Dave Fleischer. **1937–1949**

FABULOUS TEXAN, THE ★★★ Upon returning from the Civil War, Confederate officers Wild Bill Elliott and John Carroll find their part of Texas to be under the dictatorial rule of carpetbagger Albert Dekker. While not directed with much inspiration, this benefits from earnest performances. B&W; 95m. **DIR:** Edward Ludwig. **CAST:** William Elliott, John Carroll, Albert Dekker, Catherine McLeod, Andy Devine, Jim Davis. **1947**

FABULOUS VILLAINS, THE ★★1/2 From the first filming of the Frankenstein monster in 1906 to Batman's villainous enemy The Joker, and Freddy Kruger, this mixture of silent and sound clips, publicity stills, and trailers, documents the famous and infamous villains and monsters of motion pictures. Even Popeye's Bluto is included. 58m. **DIR:** James Gordon. **1992**

◆**FACADE** 🖤 Absolutely shoddy tale about a murder and the attempt to cover it up. Also known as *Death Valley*. Rated R for profanity and sexual situations. 93m. **DIR:** Carl Colpaert. **CAST:** Daniella Elle, Brad Garrett, Angus MacFadyen, Dawn Radenburgh, Eric Roberts, Camilla Overbye Roos, Roger Guenveur Smith, Joe Viterelli. **1997**

FACE AT THE WINDOW, THE ★★1/2 Tod Slaughter produced and starred in a number of lurid gothic plays that barnstormed through the English provinces in the 1920s and eventually were made into low-budget horror films. This one, about a fiendish killer in 1880s Paris, was the most cinematic, and thus probably the best. Worth seeing as a curio, but it still drags, even at barely an hour. B&W; 65m. **DIR:** George King. **CAST:** Tod Slaughter, Marjorie Taylor, John Warwick. **1939**

FACE BEHIND THE MASK, THE ★★★★ An excellent B movie that anticipates the better-known *films noir* of the later 1940s. Peter Lorre gives one of his best performances as an immigrant watchmaker. When his face is scarred in an accident, he is unable to find work and bitterly turns to crime. B&W; 69m. **DIR:** Robert Florey. **CAST:** Peter Lorre, Evelyn Keyes, Don Beddoe. **1941**

FACE DOWN ★★★ A detective finds himself embroiled in a murder case that leads him back to the police department he was ejected from years earlier.

Stylish, well-written *film noir*. Rated R for sexuality, violence, and profanity. 107m. DIR: Thom Eberhardt. CAST: Joe Mantegna, Peter Riegert, Cameron Thor, Kelli Maroney, Adam Ant. **1997**

FACE IN THE CROWD, A ★★★★ A sow's ear is turned into a silk purse in this Budd Schulberg story, scripted by the author, of a television executive who discovers gold in a winsome hobo she molds into a tube star. But all that glitters is not gold. A fine cast makes this a winning film, which brought Andy Griffith and Lee Remick to the screen for the first time. B&W; 125m. DIR: Elia Kazan. CAST: Andy Griffith, Patricia Neal, Lee Remick, Anthony Franciosa, Walter Matthau, Kay Medford. **1957**

FACE OF ANOTHER, THE ★★★★ Excellent surreal drama that explores the dehumanization and identity crisis of a man disfigured in an accident. A great parable of the Frankenstein theme, with hauntingly erotic overtones. In Japanese with English subtitles. B&W; 124m. DIR: Hiroshi Teshigahara. CAST: Tatsuya Nakadai. **1966**

FACE OF MARBLE, THE 💔 Mad scientist John Carradine revives the dead in this typical entry from the poverty-row studio Monogram. B&W; 72m. DIR: William Beaudine. CAST: John Carradine, Claudia Drake, Robert Shayne, Willie Best. **1946**

FACE THE EVIL ★★ Former Playmate Shannon Tweed manages to keep her clothes on in this unimaginative, derivative thriller. Tweed apes Bruce Willis, playing an actress on a location shoot at a museum attempting to stop bad guy Lance Henriksen from getting his hands on some nasty nerve gas. Rated R for language and violence. 92m. DIR: Paul Lynch. CAST: Shannon Tweed, Bruce Payne, Lance Henriksen, Jayne Heitmeyer. **1996 DVD**

FACE THE MUSIC ★★1/2 Molly Ringwald and Patrick Dempsey are divorced songwriters forced to write one last ditty together. The plot is contrived and Ringwald just can't sing, but this romance is pleasant enough, if predictable. Rated PG-13 for profanity and sexual situations. 93m. DIR: Carol Wiseman. CAST: Molly Ringwald, Patrick Dempsey, Lysette Anthony. **1992**

•FACE TO KILL FOR, A ★★ At times predictable, at times outrageous, this made-for-cable original just doesn't satisfy. A woman with disfiguring facial scars goes to prison for a crime she didn't commit. After she serves her time, she gets cosmetic surgery and a new identity, then seeks revenge on the man who framed her. Not rated; contains violence. 95m. DIR: Michael Toshiyuki Uno. CAST: Crystal Bernard, Doug Savant, Billy Dean, Claire Rankin, Barry Corbin. **1998**

FACE/OFF ★★★★ This outrageous thriller pits FBI agent Sean Archer against terrorist Castor Troy. The two mortal enemies surgically swap faces in a story that wallows in barbaric lunacy. The emotional connection between the two men—one a hero and the other a villain—becomes a seductive creep show as they become trapped not only in each other's body but also in each other's daily life. Rated R for language and violence. 138m. DIR: John Woo. CAST: John Travolta, Nicolas Cage, Joan Allen, Alessandro Nivola, Dominique Swain, Gina Gershon. **1997 DVD**

FACES OF WOMEN ★★★★ A novel comedy about the roles of women in contemporary African society. Despite amateurish touches, it is overall a delightful, original work. Not rated; contains nudity and sexual situations. In African tribal dialects with English subtitles. 105m. DIR: Desire Ecare. CAST: Eugenie Cisse Roland, Albertine Guessan. **1985**

•FACTS OF LIFE ★★★ Dated comedy vehicle for Bob Hope and Lucille Ball as suburbanites trying to have an affair because their respective spouses take them for granted. Pretty wan as satire, but there are enough bright lines and bits of slapstick to keep fans of the stars happy. 103m. DIR: Melvin Frank. CAST: Bob Hope, Lucille Ball, Ruth Hussey, Don DeFore, Louis Nye. **1960**

FACULTY, THE ★★ This science-fiction thriller about conformity versus individualism is an *Invasion of the Body Snatchers* update with gruesome special effects and plenty of splatter. High-school misfits are stalked and butchered by teachers who are oddly preoccupied with more than just missing homework. Rated R for violence, gore, drug use, nudity, and language. 116m. DIR: Robert Rodriguez. CAST: Elijah Wood, Clea DuVall, Shawn Hatosy, Josh Harnett, Robert Patrick, Laura Harris, Piper Laurie, Bebe Neuwirth, Salma Hayek, Jon Stewart. **1998 DVD**

FADE TO BLACK (1980) ★★★ Movie buffs and horror fans will especially love this funny, suspenseful, and entertaining low-budget film that features Dennis Christopher in a tour-de-force performance. Christopher plays Eric Binford, an odd young man who spends most of his time absorbing films. His all-night videotaping sessions and movie orgies only make him out of step with other people his age, and soon Eric goes over the edge. Rated R. 100m. DIR: Vernon Zimmerman. CAST: Dennis Christopher, Linda Kerridge, Tim Thomerson, Morgan Paull, Marya Small. **1980 DVD**

FADE TO BLACK (1993) ★★ A professor of social anthropology videotapes a murder from his window, but the police won't believe him. He decides he must play detective with the help of his wheelchair-bound friend. A bad attempt at remaking Alfred Hitchcock's brilliant *Rear Window*. Not rated, made for cable, but contains violence. 95m. DIR: John McPherson. CAST: Timothy Busfield, Heather Locklear, Michael Beck, Louis Giambalvo, David Byron, Cloris Leachman. **1993**

FAHRENHEIT 451 ★★★★ Still the best adaptation of a Ray Bradbury book to hit the screen (big or small). Oskar Werner is properly troubled as a futuristic "fireman" responsible for the destruction of books, who begins to wonder about the necessity of his work. This is director François Truffaut's first English-language film, and he treats the subject of language and literature with a dignity not found in most American films. Not rated—family fare. 111m. DIR: François Truffaut. CAST: Oskar Werner, Julie Christie, Cyril Cusack, Anton Diffring. **1967 DVD**

FAIL-SAFE ★★★★ In this gripping film, a United States aircraft is mistakenly assigned to drop the big one on Russia, and the leaders of the two countries grapple for some kind of solution as time runs out. B&W; 111m. DIR: Sidney Lumet. CAST: Henry Fonda,

Walter Matthau, Fritz Weaver, Larry Hagman, Dom DeLuise, Frank Overton. 1964

FAIR GAME (1995) ★★1/2 A Miami lawyer is stalked by ex-KGB renegades after she tries to reposses their command-post freighter. She's protected by a homicide detective and the two face all sorts of danger as they go on the run and fall in lust. The action is exhilarating, but the script for supermodel Cindy Crawford's coming-out party as lead actress is amateurish. Rated R for violence, nudity, suggested sex, and language. 90m. DIR: Andrew Sipes. CAST: Cindy Crawford, William Baldwin, Steven Berkoff, Christopher McDonald. 1995 DVD

FAIRY TALE: A TRUE STORY ★★★★ The infamous "Cottingley Fairy Hoax," perpetrated by two young girls on a credulous British public shortly after World War I, is the basis for this enchanting, family-oriented fantasy. Precocious Frances and Elise, living at the edge of a beck they know is inhabited by fairies, fabricate some photos of the camera-shy creatures in a misguided effort to "share" their discovery. These photos come to the attention of Sir Arthur Conan Doyle, whose enthusiastic acceptance of same becomes an embarrassment to his best friend Harry Houdini, who routinely debunks such nonsense. Michael Howells's production design is gorgeous and impeccably true to its setting and era. Rated PG for no particular reason. 99m. DIR: Charles Sturridge. CAST: Florence Hoath, Elizabeth Earl, Paul McGann, Phoebe Nicholls, Peter O'Toole, Harvey Keitel. 1997

FAIRY TALES 🕊 Sequel to the equally adult *Cinderella* has a prince trying to find his bride. Not rated; contains nudity, profanity, and simulated sex. 83m. DIR: Harry Tampa. CAST: Don Sparks, Professor Irwin Corey, Sy Richardson, Linnea Quigley. 1977

FAITHFUL ★★ Depressed housewife Cher matches wits with the hit man (Chazz Palminteri) hired by husband Ryan O'Neal. The interplay between Cher and Palminteri can't overcome the basic implausibility of the entire plot, and the film's origin as a talky stage play (written by Palminteri) is all too clear. O'Neal's performance seems like an afterthought. Rated R for profanity. 88m. DIR: Paul Mazursky. CAST: Cher, Ryan O'Neal, Chazz Palminteri, Paul Mazursky, Amber Smith. 1996

FAKEOUT ★★ A Las Vegas singer goes to jail instead of ratting on her boyfriend. Later, agreeing to falsely testify in exchange for her freedom, she becomes a target for death. Not rated; contains violence. 89m. DIR: Matt Cimber. CAST: Telly Savalas, Pia Zadora, Desi Arnaz Jr., Larry Storch. 1982

FALCON AND THE SNOWMAN, THE ★★★★★ In this powerful motion picture, Timothy Hutton and Sean Penn give stunning performances as two childhood friends who decide to sell United States secrets to the Russians. Based on a true incident, this release makes no judgments. The viewer is left to decide right and wrong, and whether Boyce met with justice. Rated R for violence and profanity. 131m. DIR: John Schlesinger. CAST: Timothy Hutton, Sean Penn, Pat Hingle, Lori Singer, Richard Dysart. 1985 DVD

FALCON IN MEXICO, THE ★★ The ninth film in the long-running series finds the suave sleuth south of the border as he tries to recover a woman's portrait. The owner of the gallery where the painting was displayed has been murdered and the artist responsible for the painting was reportedly killed fifteen years earlier, but Tom Conway as the smooth Falcon untangles the mystery. B&W; 70m. DIR: William Berke. CAST: Tom Conway, Mona Maris, Nestor Paiva, Bryant Washburn. 1944

FALCON TAKES OVER, THE ★★★ Early entry in the popular *Falcon* mystery-film series sets star George Sanders in a search for a missing woman. He encounters a good many of Hollywood's favorite character actors and actresses as well as much of the plot from Raymond Chandler's *Farewell My Lovely*, of which this is the first filmed version. B&W; 63m. DIR: Irving Reis. CAST: George Sanders, James Gleason, Ward Bond, Hans Conried, Lynn Bari. 1942

FALCON'S BROTHER, THE ★★★ The sophisticated Falcon (played by former Saint, George Sanders) races against time to prevent the assassination of a South American diplomat. Aided by his brother (in fact Sanders's real-life brother, Tom Conway), the Falcon realizes his goal but pays with his life at the end. Brother Tom vows to continue the work his married sibling has left undone. This well-made, nicely acted little detective film is a true oddity. B&W; 63m. DIR: Stanley Logan. CAST: George Sanders, Tom Conway, Don Barclay, Jane Randolph, Amanda Varela. 1942

FALL ★★★ When a cabbie picks up a stunning supermodel, an unlikely romance blooms. Charming and sexy love story with rich, attractive characters. Not rated; contains profanity and strong sexual situations. 90m. DIR: Eric Schaeffer. CAST: Eric Schaeffer, Amanda De Cadanet, Francie Swift, Lisa Vidal, Rudolf Martin. 1996

FALL FROM GRACE ★★★★ Enthralling espionage thriller made its debut on television, but is best served here without the annoying commercial breaks. The tension is high as military forces convene to trick Hitler and his advisors with misinformation in order to pull off the attack on D day. Filled with vibrant performances, exquisite production detail, and a taut script, the film is exciting and suspenseful. Not rated; contains some violence. 180m. DIR: Waris Hussein. CAST: James Fox, Michael York, Patsy Kensit, Tara Fitzgerald, Gary Cole. 1994

FALL OF THE HOUSE OF USHER, THE (1949) ★★ Low-budget, semiprofessional adaptation of the famous horror tale. Produced in England, it is by turns amateurish, tedious, and genuinely scary. B&W; 74m. DIR: Ivan Barnett. CAST: Gwen Watford, Kaye Tendeter, Irving Steen. 1949

FALL OF THE HOUSE OF USHER, THE (1960) ★★★1/2 Imagination and a chilling sense of the sinister make this low-budget Roger Corman version of Edgar Allan Poe's famous haunted-house story highly effective. Vincent Price is without peer as Usher. 79m. DIR: Roger Corman. CAST: Vincent Price, Mark Damon, Myrna Fahey. 1960

FALL OF THE HOUSE OF USHER, THE (1979) 🕊 Edgar Allan Poe tale is tacky, inept, and dull. Rated

PG. 101m. DIR: Stephen Lord. CAST: Martin Landau, Robert Hays, Charlene Tilton, Ray Walston. 1979

FALL OF THE ROMAN EMPIRE, THE ★★★★ During the early and mid-1960s, Hollywood looked to the history books for many of its films. Director Anthony Mann has fashioned an epic that is a feast for the eyes and does not insult the viewers' intelligence. *The Fall of the Roman Empire* has thrilling moments of action and characters the viewer cares about. 149m. DIR: Anthony Mann. CAST: Sophia Loren, James Mason, Stephen Boyd, Alec Guinness, Christopher Plummer, John Ireland, Mel Ferrer. 1964

FALL TIME ★★1/2 A direct-to-video release starring Mickey Rourke as a none-too-believable criminal philosopher masterminding a bank heist in a small, 1950s Wisconsin town. Three high-school kids accidentally get in on the action when a ghoulish prank is mistaken for part of the heist. Stephen Baldwin's performance and a surprising ending are the only things going for this muddled story. Rated R for profanity and violence. 88m. DIR: Paul Warner. CAST: Mickey Rourke, Stephen Baldwin, Sheryl Lee, David Arquette, Jason London, Jonah Bleachman. 1993 DVD

FALLEN ★★★ When homicide cop Denzel Washington finds himself framed for copycat murders by the vengeful spirit of a recently executed serial killer, it seems that our hero has no chance of defeating this malevolent entity. Washington brings considerable depth to his character, but it's not enough to wholly save a film that runs half an hour too long. Rated R for profanity and violence. 124m. DIR: Gregory Hoblit. CAST: Denzel Washington, John Goodman, Donald Sutherland, Embeth Davidtz, James Gandolfini, Elias Koteas. 1998 DVD

FALLEN ANGEL ★★★1/2 This made-for-television drama deals with the controversial topic of child pornography. A young girl, Jennifer (played by Dana Hill), is pushed into pornography by a so-called adult friend, Howard (played by Richard Masur). Jennifer sees no hope of getting out of her predicament, because she can't communicate with her mother (played by Melinda Dillon). Very timely topic! 100m. DIR: Robert Michael Lewis. CAST: Dana Hill, Richard Masur, Melinda Dillon, Ronny Cox, David Hayward. 1981

FALLEN ANGELS ★★★★ High marks to this two-volume anthology series that adapts some of the moodiest short fiction of the 1940s. Each tale is set in or near seamy World War II–era Los Angeles locales and involves the sort of characters made famous by Raymond Chandler and Cornell Woolrich. The private eyes talk tough, the women are hard as nails, and the cops are always on the take or on the lam. Not rated, with considerable violence and strong sexual content. 90m. DIR: Steven Soderbergh, Jonathan Kaplan, Phil Joanou, Tom Hanks, Tom Cruise, Alfonso Cuaron. CAST: Laura Dern, Gary Busey, Bonnie Bedelia, James Woods, Tom Hanks, Peter Gallagher, Gary Oldman, Joe Mantegna, Bruno Kirby, Isabella Rossellini, Alan Rickman. 1993 DVD

FALLEN IDOL, THE ★★★★ A small boy hero-worships a household servant suspected of murdering his wife in this quiet Graham Greene thriller. Largely told from the child's point of view, this one is pulse-raising. As always, the late Ralph Richardson is great. Bernard Lee later became "M" in the Bond films. B&W; 94m. DIR: Carol Reed. CAST: Ralph Richardson, Michele Morgan, Bobby Henrey, Jack Hawkins, Bernard Lee. 1948

FALLEN SPARROW, THE ★★★ In this sometimes confusing but generally engrossing film, John Garfield is a veteran of the Spanish Civil War whose wartime buddy is later murdered by Fascists in New York City. Many powerful scenes and strong performances make this one of Garfield's best films. 94m. DIR: Richard Wallace. CAST: John Garfield, Maureen O'Hara, Walter Slezak, Patricia Morison, Martha O'Driscoll. 1943

FALLING DOWN ★★★ Defense worker Michael Douglas is mad as hell, and he's not going to take it anymore. So he goes on an impromptu reign of terror in East Los Angeles. *Falling Down* has been misinterpreted as endorsing violence, but it is, above all, a thoughtful and believable character study. Rated R for violence and profanity. 112m. DIR: Joel Schumacher. CAST: Michael Douglas, Robert Duvall, Barbara Hershey, Rachel Ticotin, Frederic Forrest, Tuesday Weld, Lois Smith. 1993 DVD

FALLING FROM GRACE ★★★★ Famous country singer finds that going home again may not be such a good idea after all. During a family visit to his rural Indiana hometown, he rekindles a relationship with an old girlfriend who not only married his brother, but also is having an affair with their dad. This opens a Pandora's box of festering regrets and emotional wounds that writer Larry McMurtry instills with a sense of truth rarely found in films today. Rated PG-13 for profanity. 101m. DIR: John Mellencamp. CAST: John Mellencamp, Mariel Hemingway, Kay Lenz, Claude Akins, Dub Taylor. 1992

FALLING IN LOVE ★★★ Robert De Niro and Meryl Streep are fine as star-crossed lovers who risk their marriages for a moment of passion. Thanks to the uneven direction of Ulu Grosbard and an unbelievable story by Michael Cristofer, the stars' performances are the only outstanding features in this watchable love story. Rated PG for profanity and adult situations. 107m. DIR: Ulu Grosbard. CAST: Robert De Niro, Meryl Streep, Harvey Keitel. 1984

FALLING IN LOVE AGAIN ★★1/2 Elliott Gould stars as a middle-aged dreamer who is obsessed with his younger days in the Bronx. Gould and wife (Susannah York) are on vacation and headed east to recapture the past. The film suffers from countless long flashbacks of his youthful romance with a WASP princess (Michelle Pfeiffer) and is a poor attempt at romantic comedy. Rated R. 103m. DIR: Steven Paul. CAST: Elliott Gould, Susannah York, Michelle Pfeiffer, Stuart Paul. 1980 DVD

FALSE ARREST ★★★ Based on a 1981 Arizona case, this features Donna Mills being falsely accused of killing her husband's partner. Perjuring witnesses land her in the slammer. Her only hope is proving that even the DA lied to get her convicted. Believable and well-done with Mills at her best. Not rated; contains nudity and violence. 102m. DIR: Bill L. Norton. CAST: Donna Mills, Robert Wagner, Steven Bauer, James Handy, Lane Smith. 1991

FALSE COLORS ★★1/2 Typical entry in the Hopalong Cassidy series places Hoppy on the side of the innocent people who are being terrorized and murdered by ace heavy Douglass Dumbrille, who wants their property and water rights. B&W; 65m. **DIR:** George Archainbaud. **CAST:** William Boyd, Andy Clyde, Jimmy Rogers, Claudia Drake, Douglass Dumbrille, Robert Mitchum. 1943

FALSE IDENTITY ★★★ Stacy Keach returns to his home after seventeen years in prison and cannot remember many prior events. A clumsy finale is the one shortcoming of this otherwise interesting suspense-drama. Rated PG-13. 97m. **DIR:** James Keach. **CAST:** Stacy Keach, Genevieve Bujold, Veronica Cartwright. 1990

FAME ★★★1/2 Today everybody wants to be a star. *Fame* addresses that contemporary dream in a most charming and lively fashion. By focusing on the aspirations, struggles, and personal lives of a group of talented and ambitious students at New York City's High School for the Performing Arts, it manages to say something about all of us and the age we live in. Rated R. 130m. **DIR:** Alan Parker. **CAST:** Irene Cara, Lee Curreri, Eddie Barth, Laura Dean, Paul McCrane, Barry Miller, Gene Anthony Ray, Maureen Teefy. 1980

FAMILY, THE (1970) ★★★ Charles Bronson is mad. Some creep framed him and, what's worse, stole his girl! Bronson is out for revenge. This film has plenty of action, but nothing new to offer. Rated R. 100m. **DIR:** Sergio Sollima. **CAST:** Charles Bronson, Jill Ireland, Telly Savalas, Michael Constantine, George Savalas. 1970

FAMILY, THE (1987) ★★★ This bustling, good-natured film, thick with anecdotes, covers the life of a man growing up in Italy from the turn of the century to the present. It is a celebration of family life. In Italian with English subtitles. The film has no objectionable material. 140m. **DIR:** Ettore Scola. **CAST:** Vittorio Gassman, Fanny Ardant, Stefania Sandrelli. 1987

FAMILY BUSINESS ★★1/2 Despite the high-powered cast of Sean Connery, Dustin Hoffman, and Matthew Broderick, this is a disappointing drama about a three-generation crime family from director Sidney Lumet. Rated R for profanity and violence. 116m. **DIR:** Sidney Lumet. **CAST:** Sean Connery, Dustin Hoffman, Matthew Broderick. 1989

FAMILY GAME, THE ★★★1/2 This is a very funny film about a modern Japanese family faced with the same problems as their Western counterparts. A teen with school problems, a father striving for middle-class affluence, and a new tutor who shakes things up result in what was voted best film of 1983 in Japan. With English subtitles. 107m. **DIR:** Yoshimitsu Morita. **CAST:** Yusaku Matsuda, Juzo Itami. 1983

FAMILY JEWELS, THE ★★1/2 Jerry Lewis tries to outperform Alec Guinness (in *Kind Hearts and Coronets*) in this syrupy tale of a wealthy young heiress (Donna Butterworth) forced to select a guardian from among six uncles. Lewis plays all six, but his seventh—the family chauffeur—is the only one with any credibility. It's a long stretch for this material. 100m. **DIR:** Jerry Lewis. **CAST:** Jerry Lewis, Donna Butterworth, Sebastian Cabot. 1965

FAMILY LIFE ★★★1/2 A middle-class British girl strives to break free of her parents, who resort to increasingly severe measures to keep her under their control. Powerful drama filmed in a near-documentary style. Not rated. 95m. **DIR:** Kenneth Loach. **CAST:** Sandy Ratcliff, Bill Dean. 1971

FAMILY MATTER, A ★★★ Handsome production values elevate this standard Mafia soap opera. Supermodel Carol Alt plays a Mafia princess bent on revenge, not realizing that the man she loves is the same one who killed her father. Syndicated television feature also known as *Vendetta.* Not rated. 112m. **DIR:** Stuart Margolin. **CAST:** Carol Alt, Eric Roberts, Burt Young, Eli Wallach, Nick Mancuso. 1990

•**FAMILY OF COPS** ★★1/2 Charles Bronson is okay as a police commander investigating a murder involving his daughter, but this made-for-television suspense drama lacks conviction. Instead, it's a by-the-numbers exercise for Bronson, whose character tries to balance the work and family sides of his character but never delivers the goods. Rated PG-13 for violence. 93m. **DIR:** Ted Kotcheff. **CAST:** Charles Bronson, Daniel Baldwin, Barbara Williams, Angela Featherstone, John Vernon. 1995 DVD

FAMILY PLOT ★★★★ Alfred Hitchcock's last film proved to be a winner. He interjects this story with more humor than his other latter-day films. A seedy medium and her ne'er-do-well boyfriend (Barbara Harris and Bruce Dern) encounter a sinister couple (Karen Black and William Devane) while searching for a missing heir. They all become involved in diamond theft and attempted murder. Rated PG. 120m. **DIR:** Alfred Hitchcock. **CAST:** Karen Black, Bruce Dern, Barbara Harris, William Devane, Ed Lauter, Cathleen Nesbitt, Katherine Helmond. 1976

FAMILY PRAYERS ★★★1/2 Poignant coming-of-age drama introduces Tzvi Ratner-Stauber as a 13-year-old trying to make sense of his life. When his parents (Joe Mantegna and Anne Archer) start questioning their marriage, he must discard youth for adulthood. In the process he learns some valuable lessons, especially from his eccentric aunt, wonderfully played by Patti LuPone. Rated PG for language. 109m. **DIR:** Scott Rosenfelt. **CAST:** Joe Mantegna, Anne Archer, Paul Reiser, Allen Garfield, Patti LuPone, Tzvi Ratner-Stauber. 1991

FAMILY THING, A ★★★★ Arkansas redneck Robert Duvall gets the shock of his life after his mother dies, and a sealed letter reveals that he's actually the result of his father having "been with" a black servant who subsequently died during childbirth. Worse yet, our hero learns of an older half brother living in urban Chicago, and curiosity leads him to a meeting with genial cop James Earl Jones. The two men interact wonderfully in this balanced script, which only stumbles during Duvall's weird exodus through downtown Chicago. Irma P. Hall steals the film as a blind, irascible aunt who emphasizes the strength and value of family ties. Rated PG-13 for profanity and mild violence. 109m. **DIR:** Richard Pearce. **CAST:** Robert Duvall, James Earl Jones, Michael Beach, Irma P. Hall, David Keith. 1996

FAMILY UPSIDE DOWN, A ★★★ A touching, all too real drama about a previously self-sufficient couple whose age makes them dependent on their grown children. Hayes, Duke, and Zimbalist were nominated, and Astaire won an Emmy for this affecting made-for-television film. 100m. **DIR:** David Lowell Rich. **CAST:** Helen Hayes, Fred Astaire, Efrem Zimbalist Jr., Patty Duke. 1978

FAMILY VIEWING ★★★★ Canadian filmmaker Atom Egoyan has created a brilliant surreal portrait of a dysfunctional family in this absorbing character study. The story centers around a troubled young man who attempts to piece together the events that led to the disappearance of his mother. Not rated, but recommended for adults. 86m. **DIR:** Atom Egoyan. **CAST:** David Hemblen. 1988

FAN, THE ★★★1/2 In this fast-moving suspense yarn, a young fan is obsessed with a famous actress (Lauren Bacall). When his love letters to her are ignored, he embarks on a murder spree. *The Fan* is an absorbing thriller. The acting is first-rate and the camera work breathtaking. Rated R. 95m. **DIR:** Edward Bianchi. **CAST:** Lauren Bacall, James Garner, Maureen Stapleton, Michael Biehn. 1981

FAN, THE (1996) ★★1/2 Traveling knife salesman Robert De Niro's devotion to baseball gets out of hand when favorite player Wesley Snipes goes into a slump. High-octane action director Tony Scott isn't comfortable with the thriller genre, and Phoef Sutton's script is just plain stupid. Legitimate concerns about celebrities stalked by psychotic fans are lost in this disorganized mess. Rated R for violence and profanity. 120m. **DIR:** Tony Scott. **CAST:** Robert De Niro, Wesley Snipes, Ellen Barkin, John Leguizamo, Benicio Del Toro, Patti D'Arbanville. 1996 DVD

FANCY PANTS ★★★1/2 Bob Hope and Lucille Ball in their prime were an unbeatable comic team. Here they specialize in slapstick with Hope posing as a British earl to impress the locals in her New Mexican town. 92m. **DIR:** George Marshall. **CAST:** Bob Hope, Lucille Ball, Bruce Cabot. 1950

FANDANGO ★★ This is an unfunny comedy about a group of college chums (led by Kevin Costner and Judd Nelson) going on one last romp before being inducted into the army—or running away from the draft—in 1971. *Fandango* seems as if it's going to get better any minute, but it doesn't. Rated PG for profanity. 91m. **DIR:** Kevin Reynolds. **CAST:** Kevin Costner, Judd Nelson, Sam Robards, Chuck Bush, Brian Cesak. 1984

●**FANFAN THE TULIP** ★★★1/2 In this affectionate parody of swashbucklers, a French soldier in Louis XV's army has more adventures than Errol Flynn had in any three movies. Not only does he defeat the enemy army virtually single-handedly, but also wins the hand of the princess while doing so. An international hit that first brought Gina Lollobrigida to world attention. In French with English subtitles. 104m. **DIR:** Christian Jaque. **CAST:** Gérard Philipe, Gina Lollobrigida, Noël Roquevert. 1951

FANNY (1932) ★★★★ The middle part of a trilogy that began with *Marius* and ended with *César*, this can be viewed on its own. Young Marius leaves Marseilles to become a sailor, not knowing that his fiancée, Fanny, is pregnant. In his absence, she marries another man, who agrees to raise the child as his

own. The film itself is static—it was conceived for the stage—but the performances are superb, particularly Raimu as Marius's father. In French with English subtitles. B&W; 120m. **DIR:** Marc Allegret. **CAST:** Raimu, Orane Demazis, Pierre Fresnay. 1932

FANNY (1961) ★★★★ Leslie Caron is a beautiful and lively Fanny in this 1961 film. She plays a young girl seeking romance with the boy she grew up with. Unfortunately, he leaves her pregnant as he pursues a life at sea. 133m. **DIR:** Joshua Logan. **CAST:** Leslie Caron, Maurice Chevalier, Charles Boyer, Horst Buchholz, Baccaloni, Lionel Jeffries. 1961

FANNY AND ALEXANDER ★★★★★ Set in Sweden around the turn of the century, this movie follows the adventures of two children. Some have called this Ingmar Bergman's first truly accessible work. It is undeniably his most optimistic. In Swedish with English subtitles. Rated R for profanity and violence. 197m. **DIR:** Ingmar Bergman. **CAST:** Pernilla Allwin, Bertil Guve. 1983

FANTASIA ★★★★★ Originally intended as the first in a series of projects blending animation with classical music, *Fantasia* proved disappointing for Walt Disney (although its box-office take still made it the year's second most popular picture). Plans for a sequel were abandoned, but the original grew steadily more popular during subsequent rereleases … particularly with the counterculture crowd, which embraced the new 70mm prints and Dolby sound of its 1970s reissue. *Fantasia* was first conceived as a feature-length vehicle for Mickey Mouse, but his comedic segment is far from the film's most popular sequence. Fans generally cite the delicacy of various movements from Tchaikovsky's "The Nutcracker Suite," or the genuine terror inflicted by the dark figure of evil in Mussorgsky's "Night on Bald Mountain." 120m. **DIR:** Walt Disney. 1940

●**FANTASIA 2000** ★★★★ Call this another of those rare seminal moments in the history of celluloid enchantment; nothing less can describe the sheer exhilaration of watching *Fantasia 2000*, although it'll lose much of its punch when divorced from the IMAX screen on which it debuted. Fans of the original are certain to enjoy this spectacular follow-up, and even those who find the 1940 classic to be somewhat tedious will have to admire the economical pacing here. Its eight sequences—one old, seven new—move crisply to their musical selections, and the music itself is livelier than the original; highlights are the sequences set to Gershwin's "Rhapsody in Blue" and Elgar's "Pomp and Circumstance," both superbly edited and absolutely delightful. Rated G and suitable for all ages. 75m. **DIR:** Pixote Hunt, Hendel Butoy, Eric Goldberg, James Algar, Francis Glebas, Gaetan Brizzi, Paul Brizzi. 2000

FANTASIES ❤ A female Walter Mitty. Rated R for brief nudity. 81m. **DIR:** John Derek. **CAST:** Bo Derek, Peter Hooten, Anna Alexiadis. 1984

FANTASIST, THE ❤ A psychotic killer in Dublin sets up his victims with provocative phone calls, then kills them. Rated R for violence and nudity. 98m. **DIR:** Robin Hardy. **CAST:** Christopher Cazenove, Timothy Bottoms. 1986

FANTASTIC PLANET ★★★ This French-Czechoslo-akian production is an animated metaphor concerning the class struggles—and, eventually, war—between two races on an alien planet. Lovely animation and a non-preachy approach to the story combine to produce a fine little film that makes its points and sticks in the memory. Short, but sincere and effective. Voices of Barry Bostwick, Nora Heflin. Rated PG—intense subject matter and some violence. 71m. DIR: René Laloux. 1973 DVD

FANTASTIC VOYAGE ★★★ Scientists journey into inner space—the human body—by being shrunk to microscopic size. They then are threatened by the system's natural defenses. This Richard Fleischer film still packs an unusually potent punch. 100m. DIR: Richard Fleischer. CAST: Stephen Boyd, Raquel Welch, Edmond O'Brien, Donald Pleasence, Arthur O'Connell, William Redfield, Arthur Kennedy. 1966

FANTASY ISLAND ★★1/2 Dreams and fantasies come true and then some on a mysterious millionaire's island paradise in this sub-average TV-er that spawned the hit series. Yawn. 100m. DIR: Richard Lang. CAST: Ricardo Montalban, Bill Bixby, Sandra Dee, Peter Lawford, Carol Lynley, Hugh O'Brian. 1977

FAR AND AWAY ★★★★ Director Ron Howard's sweeping tale of Irish immigrants who come to America in search of land in the late 1800s is truly an entertaining saga. Tom Cruise and his real-life wife Nicole Kidman play a bickering couple from different social classes who find themselves adrift in the New World. Look for the letter-boxed edition to more fully enjoy Howard's grand vision. Rated PG-13 for violence and profanity. 140m. DIR: Ron Howard. CAST: Tom Cruise, Nicole Kidman, Thomas Gibson, Robert Prosky, Barbara Babcock, Colm Meaney, Eileen Pollock, Michelle Johnson. 1992 DVD

FAR COUNTRY, THE ★★★1/2 James Stewart is a tough-minded cattleman intent on establishing himself in Alaska during the Klondike gold rush of 1896. The result is fine Western fare. 97m. DIR: Anthony Mann. CAST: James Stewart, Ruth Roman, Walter Brennan, Corinne Calvet, John McIntire, Jay C. Flippen, Steve Brodie, Harry Morgan. 1955

FAR FROM HOME ★★★ On vacation, pubescent Drew Barrymore and divorced dad Matt Frewer make the mistake of stopping at a trailer camp where a mad killer is at work. Off-kilter thriller with some interesting twists. Rated R for violence and nudity. 86m. DIR: Meiert Avis. CAST: Matt Frewer, Drew Barrymore, Richard Masur, Karen Austin, Susan Tyrrell, Jennifer Tilly, Dick Miller. 1988

FAR FROM HOME: THE ADVENTURES OF YELLOW DOG ★★★ Heartwarming film shortchanges viewers by depriving us of more of Yellow Dog's adventures with his young master (Jesse Bradford) and on his own. The boy and his faithful companion make a treacherous journey through gorgeous but uncivilized Canadian forests after their boat capsizes. Bruce Davison and Mimi Rogers are fine as the boy's distraught parents who refuse to give up the search. Rated PG for some gross bug-eating and hunting scenes. 81m. DIR: Phillip Borsos. CAST: Bruce Davison, Mimi Rogers, Jesse Bradford, Tom Bower. 1994

FAR FROM THE MADDING CROWD ★★★★ The combination of the world-class director and a stellar British cast makes this Thomas Hardy adaptation a lovely, intelligent epic. Julie Christie plays a country girl who becomes entangled in the lives of three diverse men. Cinematographer-now-director Nicolas Roeg beautifully captured the rustic countryside. 169m. DIR: John Schlesinger. CAST: Julie Christie, Terence Stamp, Alan Bates, Peter Finch. 1967

FAR FRONTIER ★★★★ Top-of-the-line, hard-edged, later Roy Rogers oater as desperadoes smuggle deported owl hoots back into the U.S. in oil drums. Border patrolman Rogers makes the vicious scheme a losing venture. Action-packed. B&W; 67m. DIR: William Witney. CAST: Roy Rogers, Gail Davis, Andy Devine, Roy Barcroft, Clayton Moore, Riders of the Purple Sage. 1948

FAR NORTH ★★★ Actor-playwright Sam Shepard's first film as a director is a surprisingly funny comedy-drama about three generations of a farming family. Yet underlying the humor is a typically Shepardian sense of tragedy as wayward daughter Jessica Lange comes home after her father is hurt in a farming accident. Rated PG-13 for profanity and sexy scenes. 87m. DIR: Sam Shepard. CAST: Jessica Lange, Charles Durning, Tess Harper, Donald Moffat, Ann Wedgeworth, Patricia Arquette. 1988

FAR OFF PLACE, A ★★★1/2 Disney adventure film is an awkward blend of *The Gods Must Be Crazy* and *The Rescuers Down Under*. In order to escape the ivory poachers who killed their parents, two teenagers must cross the treacherous Kalahari Desert with the aid of a young Bushman. Two scenes of extreme violence make this film a bit too strong for children under 10. Rated PG for violence and brief profanity. 107m. DIR: Mikael Salomon. CAST: Reese Witherspoon, Ethan Randall, Jack Thompson, Sarel Bok, Maximilian Schell. 1993

FAR OUT MAN 🎦 A bad script, worse acting, frequent play on gastric distress. Rated R. 85m. DIR: Thomas Chong. CAST: Tommy Chong, Martin Mull, Rae Dawn Chong, C. Thomas Howell, Judd Nelson, Richard "Cheech" Marin. 1990

FAR PAVILIONS, THE ★★★ In this romantic adventure, Ben Cross plays Ash, a young British officer in imperial India. Oddly enough, he had been raised as an Indian until he was eleven. As an adult, he is reunited with his childhood friend the Princess Anjuli (Amy Irving). Despite her impending marriage to the elderly Rajaha (Rossano Brazzi), Ash and Anjuli fall in love. Rated PG for sex and violence. 108m. DIR: Peter Duffell. CAST: Ben Cross, Amy Irving, Omar Sharif, Christopher Lee, Benedict Taylor, Rossano Brazzi. 1983

FARAWAY, SO CLOSE ★★★★ Sequel to *Wings of Desire* focuses on the seriocomic adventures of the second angel as he follows Bruno Ganz into the corporeal realm and falls prey to earthly temptation. Offbeat but heartwarming and thought-provoking. In English and German with English subtitles. Rated PG-13 for violence and profanity. 140m. DIR: Wim Wenders. CAST: Otto Sanders, Peter Falk, Horst Buchholz, Willem Dafoe, Nastassja Kinski, Heinz Ruhmann,

Bruno Ganz, Solveig Dommartin, Rudiger Volger, Lou Reed. 1993

FAREWELL MY CONCUBINE ★★★1/2 This emotionally engorged, visually staggering epic is about a pair of male Peking opera stars whose commitment to art and each other is challenged throughout fifty years of civil war, foreign invasion, social revolution, political convulsions, and private squabbling. One performer, forced to forsake his true sexual identity, becomes the odd player out in a volatile love triangle when his mentor marries a courtesan. This exotic backstage pass to the theatrical and political growing pains of China loses momentum but should not be missed. In Mandarin with English subtitles. Rated R. 154m. **DIR:** Chen Kaige. **CAST:** Leslie Cheung, Zhang Fengyi, Gong Li. 1993 DVD

FAREWELL MY LOVELY ★★★1/2 This superb film adaptation of Raymond Chandler's celebrated mystery novel stands as a tribute to the talents of actor Robert Mitchum who makes a perfect, world-weary Philip Marlowe, private eye. The detective's search for the long-lost love of a gangster takes us into the netherworld of pre–World War II Los Angeles for a fast-paced period piece. Rated R. 97m. **DIR:** Dick Richards. **CAST:** Robert Mitchum, Charlotte Rampling, John Ireland, Sylvia Miles, Harry Dean Stanton. 1975 DVD

FAREWELL TO ARMS, A ★★★★ Ernest Hemingway's well-crafted story of doomed love between a wounded ambulance driver and a nurse in Italy during World War I. Adolphe Menjou is peerless, Helen Hayes dies touchingly, and Gary Cooper strides away in the rain. B&W; 78m. **DIR:** Frank Borzage. **CAST:** Helen Hayes, Gary Cooper, Adolphe Menjou, Mary Philips, Jack LaRue. 1932 DVD

FAREWELL TO THE KING ★★★1/2 In this old-fashioned, boy's-eye-view adventure epic from writer-director John Milius, Nick Nolte plays a World War II soldier who deserts following Gen. Douglas MacArthur's retreat from Corregidor. Nolte ends up in the jungles of Borneo, where he becomes a king. Nigel Havers is excellent as the British officer who incites the natives to battle. Rated PG-13 for profanity and violence. 114m. **DIR:** John Milius. **CAST:** Nick Nolte, Nigel Havers, Frank McRae, James Fox. 1989

FARGO ★★★★1/2 In this remarkable *film noir*, a soft-spoken car salesman arranges for his wife to be kidnapped with the idea of keeping most of the ransom provided by her wealthy father. Unfortunately, nothing goes quite as he plans. It's hilarious, twisted, and sometimes shocking—in other words, a must-see. Rated R for violence, gore, and profanity. 97m. **DIR:** Joel Coen. **CAST:** Frances McDormand, William H. Macy, Steve Buscemi, Peter Stormare, Harve Presnell, Jose Feliciano. 1996

FARINELLI IL CASTRATO ★★ The life of eighteenth-century castrato singer Farinelli becomes a low-camp melodrama, sumptuously mounted but dramatically unbelievable and funny in the wrong places. Farinelli's "voice" is electronically synthesized from a tenor and soprano; the effect is interesting, but the lip-synching is so unconvincing that it destroys the credibility of the music scenes. In Italian and French with English subtitles. Rated R for

nudity and simulated sex. 110m. **DIR:** Gerard Corbia **CAST:** Stefano Dionisi, Enrico Lo Verso, Elsa Zylbe stein, Javier Bardem, Jeroen Krabbé. 1994

FARMER AND CHASE ★★★ Aging bank robb Ben Gazzara reluctantly agrees to let his callow so accompany him on what he intends to be his last jo But the job goes bad, leaving the pair with a bank fu of hostages and no way out. Credit first-time write director Michael Seitzman with keeping his foc sharp and picking a first-rate cast. Rated R for stror profanity, violence, and sexual situations. 97m. **DI** Michael Seitzman. **CAST:** Ben Gazzara, Lara Flyr Boyle, Todd Field. 1997

FARMER TAKES A WIFE, THE ★★ Tiresome mus cal remake of a 1935 Janet Gaynor–Henry Fonc drama (filmed under the same title). This depictic of life along the Erie Canal in the early nineteen century is a mistake from word one. 81m. **DIR:** Hen Levin. **CAST:** Betty Grable, Dale Robertson, Thelma Ri ter, John Carroll, Eddie Foy Jr., Merry Anders. 1953

FARMER'S DAUGHTER, THE ★★★ Loretta Your won the best actress Oscar for her delightful perfo mance in this charming comedy about a Swedis woman who clashes with the man she loves over congressional election. B&W; 97m. **DIR:** H. C. Potte **CAST:** Loretta Young, Joseph Cotten, Ethel Barrymor Charles Bickford, Lex Barker, Keith Andes, James A ness. 1947

FARMER'S OTHER DAUGHTER, THE ♥ Incredib lame film about a family trying to save their fari from foreclosure. 84m. **DIR:** John Patrick Haye **CAST:** Judy Pennebaker, Bill Michael, Ernest Ashwort 1965

•**FARMER'S WIFE, THE** ★★★ Alfred Hitchco toyed with slapstick comedy in this early silent fea ture about a farmer who seeks high and low for a ne bride after his wife dies. Naturally, he overlooks h housekeeper, who has loved him from afar for year Unusual point-of-view shots feature characters tall ing to other people by looking directly into the cam era. B&W; 97m. **DIR:** Alfred Hitchcock. **CAST:** Jameso Thomas, Lillian Hall-Davies, Gordon Harker, Gib McLaughlin, Maud Gill, Louise Pounds. 1928

FAST BREAK ★★1/2 As a basketball coach, Gab Kaplan resurrects some of the laughs he got with h sweathogs on *Welcome Back, Kotter*. Kaplan plays New York deli worker who quits to coach a colleg basketball team in Nevada. Kaplan must beat tough rival team in order to get a contract at the un versity, so he whips the unpromising team int shape. Rated PG. 107m. **DIR:** Jack Smight. **CAS** Gabe Kaplan, Harold Sylvester, Mike Warren, Bernar King, Reb Brown. 1979

FAST, CHEAP AND OUT OF CONTROL ★★★ Docu mentary filmmaker Errol Morris profiles a wild-an mal tamer, a topiary gardener, a robot builder, and man who studies the naked mole rat of Africa. A first the men appear to have nothing in common bu enthusiasm for their work—then Morris begins t draw odd little connections between them that kee catching the viewer off guard. On the down sid though, he also seems at times be poking mean-spir ited fun at them; a little less condescension migh have made this interesting film far more compelling

0m. DIR: Errol Morris. CAST: Dave Hoover, George Mendonca, Ray Mendez, Rodney Brooks. 1997

AST FOOD 🖤 Typical inane college sex comedy. ated PG-13 for sexual situations. 91m. DIR: Michael Simpson. CAST: Jim Varney, Traci Lords. 1989

AST FORWARD ★★ An undisguised variation on ne cliché of "let's put on a show so we can make it in how biz." In it, eight high school kids from San- usky, Ohio, journey to New York for a promised audi- on. A bubbly bit of fluff that relies on sheer energy o patch up its plot and make up for the lack of an in- pired score. Sometimes, it works. Rated PG. 100m. IR: Sidney Poitier. CAST: John Scott Clough, Don ranklin. 1985

AST GETAWAY 🖤 Spectacular stunts aren't enough o save this mindless tale of a 16-year-old kid who obs banks with his dad. There's not enough here to nake a wholehead. Rated PG-13 for violence. 85m. IR: Spiro Razatos. CAST: Corey Haim, Cynthia othrock, Leo Rossi, Marcia Strassman. 1990

AST GETAWAY II ★★ Direct-to-video trash stars orey Haim as a former bank-robber-turned-securi- y-adviser who discovers that all of the banks he's upposed to be protecting are being robbed—and hat someone is trying to set him up to take the fall. udicrous storyline, sloppy direction, and a particu- arly annoying performance by Haim make this one o avoid. Rated PG-13 for profanity. 94m. DIR: Oley assone. CAST: Corey Haim, Cynthia Rothrock, Leo ossi. 1993

AST LANE FEVER ★★1/2 A street gang with ouped-up streetcars bullies others into racing for noney. An underdog good guy loses to the bad guys, hen comes back against all odds. Interesting take nd a fascinating look at Australia through the cam- ra lens. Rated R for profanity, sex, and violence. 4m. DIR: John Clark. CAST: Terry Serio, Deborah Con- vay, Max Cullen, Graham Bond. 1982

AST MONEY (1996) ★★ Yancy Butler and Matt McCoy play star-crossed lovers on the run from the aw and the mob when they find themselves in pos- ession of a suitcase full of mob money. Familiar. ated R for violence, profanity, and nudity. 93m. DIR: lexander Wright. CAST: Yancy Butler, Matt McCoy, ohn Ashton, Trevor Goddard, Patrika Darbo. 1996

AST TALKING ★★ This Australian comedy stars od Zuanic as a little punk that you'd love to shake nd put on the straight and narrow. The fact that he as a miserable home life that doesn't hold much of future for him doesn't make this fast talker any nore endearing. 93m. DIR: Ken Cameron. CAST: Rod uanic, Steve Bisley, Tracy Mann, Dennis Moore, Toni llaylis, Chris Truswell. 1984

AST TIMES AT RIDGEMONT HIGH ★★1/2 In 1979, ameron Crowe went back to high school to discover what today's teens are up to and wrote about his ex- eriences. Youngsters will love it, but adults will robably want to skip the movie and read the book. ated R for nudity, profanity, and simulated sex. 2m. DIR: Amy Heckerling. CAST: Sean Penn, Jennifer ason Leigh, Judge Reinhold, Brian Backer, Phoebe ates, Ray Walston, Forest Whitaker, Eric Stoltz, Nico- as Cage, Eric Stoltz, Forest Whitaker. 1982 DVD

FAST-WALKING ★★★1/2 This one is definitely not for everyone, but if you are adventurous, it may surprise you. James Woods plays a prison guard whose yearning for the good life leads him into a jail- break scheme. Film plays for black comedy and gen- erally succeeds. Rated R for violence, language, nu- dity. 116m. DIR: James B. Harris. CAST: James Woods, Kay Lenz, Tim McIntire, Robert Hooks, Susan Tyrrell. 1983

FASTEST GUITAR ALIVE, THE ★★ Weak action yarn about Confederate spies who steal a fortune. Worth a viewing, mainly for Roy Orbison's appear- ance. 87m. DIR: Michael Moore. CAST: Roy Orbison, Sammy Jackson, Maggie Pierce, Joan Freeman. 1968

FASTEST GUN ALIVE, THE ★★★ Serviceable Western casts Glenn Ford as a mild-mannered store- keeper who gets unwanted fame as a fast draw. After beating a string of cowpokes seeking a reputation, Ford must face a miscast Broderick Crawford, a bad- man who doesn't relish the idea of being thought of as second best. 92m. DIR: Russell Rouse. CAST: Glenn Ford, Broderick Crawford, Jeanne Crain, Leif Erickson, Russ Tamblyn, Rhys Williams, Noah Beery Jr., Chubby Johnson, J. M. Kerrigan, Allyn Joslyn. 1956

FAT CITY ★★★★1/2 This neglected treasure is per- haps the best film ever made about boxing. Tank- town matches between hopefuls and has-beens along California's Central Valley keep Stacy Keach and Jeff Bridges in hamburger and white port. A classic piece of Americana and one of John Huston's greatest achievements. Rated PG. 96m. DIR: John Huston. CAST: Stacy Keach, Jeff Bridges, Susan Tyrrell, Nicholas Colasanto, Candy Clark. 1972

FAT MAN AND LITTLE BOY ★★1/2 In spite of its historically significant story line—the World War II development of the atomic bomb—this film remains curiously flat and distanced. The clash between military chief General Leslie R. Groves (Paul New- man) and scientific genius J. Robert Oppenheimer (Dwight Schultz) seems mannered and forced. Rat- ed PG-13 for intensity. 126m. DIR: Roland Joffe. CAST: Paul Newman, Dwight Schultz, Bonnie Bedelia, John Cusack, Laura Dern, Natasha Richardson. 1989

FATAL ATTRACTION (1985) ★★★1/2 In this sus- penseful film, two people get caught up in sexual fan- tasy games so intense that they begin to act them out—in public. Fatal Attraction would receive a higher rating if it had a smoother transition from the innocent flirting to the heavy-duty sexual activity that leads to the film's ironic and tragic close. Rat- ed R for nudity, violence, and profanity. 90m. DIR: Michael Grant. CAST: Sally Kellerman, Stephen Lack, Lawrence Dane, John Huston. 1985

FATAL ATTRACTION (1987) ★★★★ This adult shocker works beautifully as a nail-biting update of Play Misty for Me. It's the married man's ultimate nightmare. Glenn Close chews up the screen as Michael Douglas's one-night stand; when he (very married, to Anne Archer, an underappreciated tal- ent) backs away and tries to resume his ordinary routine, Close becomes progressively more danger- ous. Rated R for nudity and language. 119m. DIR:

Adrian Lyne. **CAST:** Glenn Close, Michael Douglas, Anne Archer. 1987

FATAL BEAUTY 🎬 Whoopi Goldberg stars as an improbably resourceful cop pursuing several smarmy drug pushers. Rated R for language and excessive violence. 104m. **DIR:** Tom Holland. **CAST:** Whoopi Goldberg, Sam Elliott, Rubén Blades, Harris Yulin, John P. Ryan, Jennifer Warren, Brad Dourif. 1987

FATAL BOND 🎬 Linda Blair doesn't turn any heads in this fatally flawed thriller about a woman who suspects her lover is a serial killer. Rated R for nudity, violence, and language. 89m. **DIR:** Phil Avalon. **CAST:** Linda Blair, Jerome Elhers, Stephen Leeder, Joe Bugner, Donal Gibson. 1991

FATAL CHARM ★★1/2 Teenager Amanda Peterson initiates a relationship-by-mail with beguiling Christopher Atkins, sentenced and jailed for the brutal murders of numerous young women. Although Nicolas Niciphor's script tosses in a few clever twists, the ho-hum execution (director Fritz Kiersch, hiding behind a pseudonym) turns this made-for-cable production into a standard thriller. Rated R for violence, nudity, and profanity. 90m. **DIR:** Alan Smithee. **CAST:** Christopher Atkins, Amanda Peterson, Mary Frann, James Remar, Andrew Robinson, Peggy Lipton. 1992

FATAL COMBAT ★★1/2 Stop me if you've heard this one before: A billionaire broadcaster holds death matches between top athletes. His audience: wealthy aristocrats bored with the dullness of everyday life. But when a top martial artist is kidnapped and forced to fight for that audience, the billionaire may have bitten off more than he can chew. Ultimately tedious *Mortal Kombat/Street Fighter* rip-off is buoyed somewhat by the undeniable video presence of star Jeff Wincott. Rated R for profanity and violence. 93m. **DIR:** Damien Lee. **CAST:** Jeff Wincott, Phillip Jarrett, Richard Fitzpatrick, Guylaine St-Onge, Joseph Dimambro, Sven-Ole Thorsen. 1995

FATAL EXPOSURE ★★1/2 Mare Winningham partially salvages this routine made-for-cable thriller—as a resourceful single parent whose photo order gets mixed up at the processing lab ... which sends her home with pictures originally intended for a hired killer. Nick Mancuso is engaging as a neighbor with a mysterious past. Rated PG-13. 89m. **DIR:** Alan Metzger. **CAST:** Mare Winningham, Nick Mancuso, Christopher McDonald, Geoffrey Blake. 1991

FATAL GAMES 🎬 In a school for young athletes, a murderer begins eliminating the students, using a javelin. Not rated; contains explicit nudity and violence. 88m. **DIR:** Michael Elliot. **CAST:** Sally Kirkland, Lynn Banashek, Teal Roberts. 1984

FATAL HOUR, THE ★★1/2 Boris Karloff is cast as homicide detective Mr. Wong in this suspenseful thriller about murder and jewel smuggling. Grant Withers is solid as Police Captain Street. B&W; 68m. **DIR:** William Nigh. **CAST:** Boris Karloff, Grant Withers, Marjorie Reynolds, Charles Trowbridge. 1940 DVD

FATAL IMAGE, THE ★★★ Watchable made-for-TV film features a Philadelphia mother-daughter team (Michele Lee and Justine Bateman) as they find romance, murder, and each other on a Parisian vacation. Bateman's obsession with her camcorder en-

ables her to inadvertently film a murder. Now the murderer and her henchman want the videotape and are willing to kill the American tourists to get it. 96m. **DIR:** Thomas Wright. **CAST:** Michele Lee, Justin Bateman, François Dunoyer. 1990 DVD

FATAL INSTINCT (1992) ★★1/2 Sexy thriller ready-made for video, throwing sex and violence in a sordid tale of a private detective who jeopardize everything in his life to prove the woman he loves isn't guilty. Rated R for nudity, language, and violence unrated version contains more sexual content. 95m **DIR:** John Dirlam. **CAST:** Michael Madsen, Laura Johnson, Tony Hamilton. 1992

FATAL INSTINCT (1993) ★★★ Carl Reiner send up a bevy of thrillers in this hit-and-miss spoof. Armand Assante is a dumb-as-dirt detective who ge mixed up with a femme fatale. This goofy movie has its share of laughs. Rated PG-13 for light profanit silly violence, and wacky sex. 89m. **DIR:** Carl Reine **CAST:** Armand Assante, Sean Young, Sherilyn Fen Kate Nelligan, Christopher McDonald, James Rema Tony Randall, Clarence Clemmons, Eartha Kitt, Ronn Schell, Carl Reiner. 1993

FATAL INVERSION, A ★★★★★ The most impres sive of the psychological thrillers adapted by th BBC from a Ruth Rendell novel written under he nom de plume, Barbara Vine. An eerie script and e citing direction befits her strange tale of a bacchanalian summer shared by five young adults who late learn that a corrosive past can ooze into the presen This has an ending you won't be able to shake. No rated; contains nudity, drug use, and sexual situations. 150m. **DIR:** Tim Fywell. **CAST:** Jeremy Northan Douglas Hodge, Gordon Warnecke, Saira Todd, Jul Ford. 1991

FATAL MISSION ★★ It took five screenwriters, in cluding Peter Fonda, to bring this formulaic jung action film to the screen. Fonda portrays a Speci Forces agent during the Vietnam War. Rated R for v olence. 84m. **DIR:** George Rowe. **CAST:** Peter Fond Mako, Jim Mitchum, Tia Carrere. 1990

FATAL PAST ★★ Hokum about a gangster's mistres and bodyguard, reincarnated tragic figures from a cient Japan, doomed to live out their fate once agai in modern-day Los Angeles. Unbeknownst to the they are about to play out a dangerous re-creation their previous lives, and only one woman, a snoop newspaper reporter, can bring the events full circl Too confusing for its own good. Rated R for nudity, v olence, and adult language. 85m. **DIR:** Clive Fleur **CAST:** Costas Mandylor, Kasia Figura, Terence Coope Steven Grimes. 1993

FATAL PULSE 🎬 A house full of sorority girls. No rated; contains nudity, violence, and profanity. 90m **DIR:** Anthony Christopher. **CAST:** Michelle McCormic Ken Roberts. 1988

FATAL VISION ★★★★1/2 This excellent TV mini eries is based on the actual case of convicted mu derer, Dr. Jeffrey MacDonald. In 1970, MacDona (Gary Cole) murdered his pregnant wife and tw daughters. Although he denies the charges, his fa ther-in-law (Karl Malden) becomes suspicious an helps to convict him. 198m. **DIR:** David Greene. **CAST:**

Karl Malden, Gary Cole, Eva Marie Saint, Gary Grubbs, Mitchell Ryan, Andy Griffith. **1984**

FATALLY YOURS ★★ Bad acting and editing erase the entertainment value of this tired reincarnation tale. When a writer is drawn to a vacant and crumbling house, he immediately fashions a novel mirroring past events that, surprisingly, connect him to the house. Rated EM for violence, profanity, nudity, and sexual situations. 90m. **DIR:** Tim Everitt. **CAST:** Rick Rossovich, George Lazenby, Roddy McDowall, Sage Stallone, John Capodice, Sarah MacDonell, Robert Gentile. **1995**

FATE 🖤 The last of the good guys searches for the woman who deserves him in this strange, self-proclaimed romantic comedy. Rated PG-13. 114m. **DIR:** Stuart Paul. **CAST:** Stuart Paul, Cheryl M. Lynn, Kaye Ballard, Susannah York. **1990**

FATHER (1966) ★★★ Istvan Szabo, best known for the Oscar-winning *Mephisto*, directed this drama. A boy creates an elaborate fantasy about the heroism of his father, who was killed in World War II. As an adult, he is led to abandon his fantasies and examine the reality of his heritage. Slow-moving but provocative. In Hungarian with English subtitles. B&W; 89m. **DIR:** Istvan Szabo. **CAST:** Andras Balint, Miklos Gabor. **1966**

FATHER (1990) ★★★★ A small, intense Australian drama starring Max Von Sydow as a popular pub owner and doting granddad who may have been a vicious Nazi officer. This is propelled by riveting performances from Sydow and Carol Drinkwater as the daughter who absolutely does not want to think the worst, even when reality begins to tear away her defenses. Rated PG-13 for profanity and implied violence. 106m. **DIR:** John Power. **CAST:** Max von Sydow, Carol Drinkwater, Julia Blake, Steve Jacobs. **1990**

FATHER & SCOUT ★★1/2 Somewhat amusing made-for-television comedy about a nerdy dad who is forced to take his Eagle Scout son on a camping trip. Of course Dad knows nothing about the great outdoors, but before the trip is done, both father and son will have bonded. Rated PG. 92m. **DIR:** Richard Michaels. **CAST:** Bob Saget, Brian Bonsall, Heidi Swedberg, Stuart Pankin. **1994**

FATHER GOOSE ★★★ A bedraggled, unshaven, and unsophisticated Cary Grant is worth watching even in a mediocre comedy. Grant plays a hard-drinking Australian coast watcher during the height of World War II. His reclusive life-style on a remote Pacific island is interrupted when he is forced to play nursemaid to a group of adolescent schoolgirls and their prudish teacher (Leslie Caron). 115m. **DIR:** Ralph Nelson. **CAST:** Cary Grant, Leslie Caron. **1964 DVD**

FATHER HOOD ★★1/2 A con man finds his latest big score sabotaged by the unexpected arrival of his runaway daughter, who wants him to save his son from the same institution that brutalized her. Not all of the movie works, but Patrick Swayze is funny and believable in a role that seems to have been fashioned out of cardboard. Rated PG-13 for brief profanity and violence. 95m. **DIR:** Darrell Roodt. **CAST:** Patrick Swayze, Halle Berry, Sabrina Lloyd, Brian Bon-

sall, Michael Ironside, Diane Ladd, Bob Gunton, Adrienne Barbeau. **1993**

FATHER OF THE BRIDE (1950) ★★★1/2 Spencer Tracy's proud and frantic papa is the chief attraction in this droll examination of last-minute preparations prior to daughter Elizabeth Taylor's wedding. Writers Frances Goodrich and Albert Hackett include a few too many scenes of near-slapstick hysteria, but the quieter moments between father and daughter are wonderful (if a bit dated). 93m. **DIR:** Vincente Minnelli. **CAST:** Spencer Tracy, Elizabeth Taylor, Joan Bennett, Leo G. Carroll, Don Taylor, Billie Burke. **1950**

FATHER OF THE BRIDE (1991) ★★★1/2 Steve Martin is the father who becomes increasingly aghast at the costs and craziness involved in his daughter's marriage. With this remake of the 1950 Spencer Tracy film, director Charles Shyer and the star create a heartwarming comedy the whole family can enjoy. Rated PG for brief profanity. 105m. **DIR:** Charles Shyer. **CAST:** Steve Martin, Diane Keaton, Martin Short, Kimberly Williams, George Newbern, B. D. Wong. **1991 DVD**

FATHER OF THE BRIDE PART II ★★★★ With their spin on *Father's Little Dividend*, married moviemakers Charles Shyer and Nancy Meyers outdo their first entry in the updated series. Of course, Steve Martin's comic timing—both physical and verbal—deserves much of the credit for the effectiveness of this heartwarming and hilarious sequel that centers around the consequences of having a baby. Rated PG. 106m. **DIR:** Charles Shyer. **CAST:** Steve Martin, Diane Keaton, Martin Short, Kimberly Williams, George Newbern, B. D. Wong, Peter Michael Goetz, Jane Adams, Eugene Levy. **1995 DVD**

FATHERLAND ★★★1/2 Nazi Germany defeated Western Europe in this thoughtful adaptation of Robert Harris's book, which opens in the early 1960s, with an aging Hitler anxious to begin negotiations with U.S. President Joseph Kennedy. But a visiting American journalist uncovers evidence suggesting that Germany perpetrated a horrible atrocity during World War II. Dedicated sci-fi readers won't find anything new here, but the drama unfolds with intelligence and conviction. Rated PG-13 for violence, profanity, and brief nudity. 106m. **DIR:** Chris Menaul. **CAST:** Rutger Hauer, Miranda Richardson, Peter Vaughan, Michael Kitchen, Jean Marsh. **1994**

FATHERS & SONS ★★★1/2 Mystical overtones enhance this drama of a teenager in jeopardy (Rory Cochrane) and his widower dad (Jeff Goldblum), who tries to shield his son from life's more painful lessons as the boy becomes entangled with a local drug dealer. Slow going, but atmospheric, well-acted, and artfully directed. Rated PG for profanity, sexuality, and brief nudity. 109m. **DIR:** Paul Mones. **CAST:** Jeff Goldblum, Rory Cochrane, Rosanna Arquette, Joie Lee. **1992**

FATHER'S DAY ★★ Overly rational Los Angeles attorney Billy Crystal and insecure ex-hippy Robin Williams chase after a teenager with questionable parentage, thanks to a former girlfriend who—years earlier—dallied with both our heroes. This misfired remake of Francis Veber's *Les Compères* proves, once again, that Hollywood hasn't a clue how to match the style and humor of French sex comedies. Rated PG-13 for profanity and mild sexual content. 98m. DIR: Ivan Reitman. CAST: Robin Williams, Billy Crystal, Julia Louis-Dreyfus, Nastassja Kinski, Charlie Hofheimer, Bruce Greenwood. 1997 DVD

FATHER'S LITTLE DIVIDEND ★★★ In *Father of the Bride*, the marriage of daughter Elizabeth Taylor to Don Taylor made a wreck out of Spencer Tracy. Now, in the sequel, she's expecting. This play off of a winner doesn't measure up to the original, but it's entertaining fare anyway. Spencer Tracy could bluster and be flustered with the best. 82m. DIR: Vincente Minnelli. CAST: Spencer Tracy, Elizabeth Taylor, Joan Bennett, Don Taylor, Billie Burke. 1951 DVD

FATHER'S REVENGE, A ★★★★ When his daughter, a flight assistant, is taken hostage in Germany by terrorists, a high school basketball coach (Brian Dennehy) decides to take matters into his own hands. The often-seen Dennehy is given one of his better-written roles in this TV movie, and he does a terrific job with it. 93m. DIR: John Herzfeld. CAST: Brian Dennehy, Ron Silver, Joanna Cassidy, Anthony Valentine. 1987

FATSO ★★1/2 Too many juvenile toilet jokes mar what might have been a humorous study of a man's confrontation with his own obesity. Dom DeLuise stars as the chubby Italian-American who wrestles with a variety of diets. Messages get lost amid the shrill performances. Rated PG for language and questionable humor. 94m. DIR: Anne Bancroft. CAST: Dom DeLuise, Anne Bancroft, Candy Azzara, Ron Carey. 1980

FATTY FINN ★★★ This film seems to borrow from the Little Rascals comedy series. In it, young Fatty Finn is desperately trying to earn money to buy a radio. But the neighborhood bully and his gang sabotage Fatty's efforts. The happy ending makes up for all the hardships 10-year-old Fatty has endured. 91m. DIR: Maurice Murphy. CAST: Ben Oxenbould, Bert Newton. 1984

FAUST ★★★★★ The undisputed master of early German cinema, Friedrich W. Murnau triumphs once again with the legendary story of Faust. Gosta Ekman gives an excellent performance as Faust and Emil Jannings plays the Devil with comic pathos. Silent with English intertitles. B&W; 100m. DIR: F. W. Murnau. CAST: Emil Jannings, Gosta Ekman, Camilla Horn. 1926 DVD

FAVOR, THE ★★★ Although this romantic comedy desperately wants to be a ribald sex farce, it's just not played with the proper tone. Harley Jane Kozak, pining for a long-unseen high-school sweetheart, emerges as an unsympathetic busybody when she persuades best friend Elizabeth McGovern to meet and sleep with the guy. Despite a rather amusing climax, we never really like any of these people. Rated R for profanity and frank sexuality. 97m. DIR: Donald Petrie. CAST: Harley Jane Kozak, Elizabeth McGovern, Bill Pullman, Brad Pitt, Ken Wahl, Larry Miller. 1994

FAVOR, THE WATCH AND THE VERY BIG FISH, THE ★★ In this muddled madcap comedy, Bob Hoskins tries hard as a photographer who gets distracted by the mysterious Natasha Richardson while searching for the perfect model to portray Jesus Christ—whom he finally finds in Jeff Goldblum. An noyingly frantic. Rated R for profanity, nudity, and violence. 89m. DIR: Ben Lewin. CAST: Bob Hoskins, Jeff Goldblum, Natasha Richardson, Michel Blanc, Jean Pierre Cassel, Angela Pleasence. 1992

FAWLTY TOWERS (TV SERIES) ★★★★ This British television series is a true comedy classic. Written by Monty Python's John Cleese and his ex wife, Connie Booth, the show is a situation comedy about the problems of running a small seaside inn. The characters are typical and the story lines mundane, but in the hands of Cleese and company, each episode is a near-perfect ballet of escalating frustration. For sheer, double-over belly laughs, this series has never been equaled. Each episode 75m. DIR: John Cleese, Connie Booth. CAST: John Cleese, Prunella Scales, Connie Booth. 1975

FBI MURDERS, THE ★★★1/2 Superior made for-TV drama focuses on the manhunt for two thrill killers, played with penetrating menace by Michael Gross and David Soul. When these two family men go on a robbing rampage, the FBI gets involved. Intelligent screenplay and inspired casting make this a must-see. 95m. DIR: Dick Lowry. CAST: Ronny Cox, Bruce Greenwood, Michael Gross, Doug Sheehan, David Soul. 1988

FBI STORY, THE ★★★ A glowing history of the FBI from Prohibition to the cold war, through the career of a fictitious agent (James Stewart). Some good episodes reminiscent of Warner Bros.' G-Man pictures of the Thirties, but with too many forays into Stewart's family life. Not rated, but with lots of gunplay. 149m. DIR: Mervyn LeRoy. CAST: James Stewart, Vera Miles, Larry Pennell, Nick Adams, Murray Hamilton, Diane Jergens. 1959

FEAR (1955) ★★ Neither star Ingrid Bergman nor her then-husband director Roberto Rossellini are able to save this tired drama of an indiscreet wife being blackmailed by her lover's ex. As ever, Bergman scores personally. B&W; 91m. DIR: Roberto Rossellini. CAST: Ingrid Bergman, Kurt Kreuger, Mathias Wieman. 1955

FEAR (1988) ★★★ Vicious, brutal story of four escaped convicts who go on a rampage of murder and kidnapping. Cliff De Young and Kay Lenz star as a married couple whose vacation is terrifyingly interrupted when the cons take them hostage. A surprisingly fine performance by Frank Stallone highlights this impressive study in terror. Rated R for violence and profanity. 96m. DIR: A. Ferretti. CAST: Cliff De Young, Kay Lenz, Frank Stallone. 1988

FEAR (1990) ★★★1/2 Until a rather rushed climax, which culminates in a maze of mirrors, this made-for-cable thriller makes a slick showcase for Ally Sheedy. As a psychic who "tunes in" to the thoughts of serial killers, she assists skeptical police and then pens bestsellers based on her exploits . . . until she encounters a deranged killer who's *also* a psychic. Rated R for violence and nudity. 98m. DIR: Rockne S. O'Bannon. CAST: Ally Sheedy, Lauren Hutton, Michael O'Keefe, Stan Shaw. 1990

FEAR, THE (1994) ★★ This by-the-numbers drivein movie with characters right out of central casting is especially misogynist and uneventful. Rated R for violence, profanity, and sexual situations. 98m. DIR: Vincent Robert. CAST: Eddie Bowz, Ann Turkel, Leland Hayward, Darin Heames, Vince Edwards, Anna Karin, Wes Craven. 1994 DVD

FEAR (1996) ★★1/2 A 16-year-old girl ventures into a seamy Seattle pool hall where she meets her Prince Charming. We all know he is dirt. So does her dad, who wedges himself between the two young lovers until the psychotic suitor storms the family's house with his scum buddies. Family dynamics are developed with stings of truth, but the ending is a sensationalized thrillfest. Rated R for language, gore, nudity, violence, and suggested sex. 95m. DIR: James Foley. CAST: Reese Witherspoon, Mark Wahlberg, William L. Petersen, Alyssa Milano, Amy Brenneman. 1996 DVD

•FEAR, THE: HALLOWEEN NIGHT 🐾 More unsuspecting young people face off against the wooden creature named Morty, who is as stiff as the plot and direction. Rated R for violence and language. 95m. DIR: Chris Angel. CAST: Gordon Currie, Stacy Grant, Phillip Rhys, Betsy Palmer. 1999 DVD

FEAR AND LOATHING IN LAS VEGAS 🐾 Director-cowriter Terry Gilliam's adaptation of Hunter S. Thompson's infamous, pseudobiographical epic of gonzo-journalistic social commentary is a veritable mess from start to finish: an absolutely unwatchable jumble of surrealistic images and uncontrolled, self-indulgent performances by leads Johnny Depp (fitfully funny as Thompson surrogate Raoul Duke) and Benicio Del Toro (utterly loathsome as bestial "Dr. Gonzo"). Rated R for profanity, drug use, and incessant deviant behavior. 119m. DIR: Terry Gilliam. CAST: Johnny Depp, Benicio Del Toro, Tobey Maguire, Mark Harmon, Cameron Diaz, Gary Busey, Ellen Barkin. 1998 DVD

FEAR, ANXIETY AND DEPRESSION ★★ Todd Solondz wrote and directed this Woody Allen-ish vehicle for himself. He plays a nerdish playwright who pursues an outrageously punk performer and his best friend's girl while being relentlessly chased by his female counterpart. Rated R for profanity and violence. 84m. DIR: Todd Solondz. CAST: Todd Solondz, Jill Wisoff. 1989

FEAR CITY ★★ After a promising directorial debut with Ms. 45, Abel Ferrara backslid with this all-too-familiar tale about a psychopath killing prostitutes in New York City. Some good performances and action sequences still can't save this one. Rated R for violence, nudity, and profanity. 93m. DIR: Abel Ferrara. CAST: Tom Berenger, Billy Dee Williams, Rae Dawn Chong, Melanie Griffith, Rossano Brazzi, Jack Scalia. 1985

FEAR IN THE NIGHT (DYNASTY OF FEAR) ★★★1/2 Effective British shocker about a teacher and his off-balance bride at a desolate boys' school. Another suspenseful offering from Hammer Films. Rated PG. 94m. DIR: Jimmy Sangster. CAST: Ralph Bates, Judy Geeson, Peter Cushing, Joan Collins. 1972

FEAR INSIDE, THE ★★★ Christine Lahti's gripping performance lends credibility to this otherwise routine made-for-cable shocker. She plays a frantic agoraphobic (fear of open spaces) unable to flee her home after it's invaded by a pair of nasty psychopaths. The cat-and-mouse games wear thin after a while, but Lahti definitely puts us in her corner. 105m. DIR: Leon Ichaso. CAST: Christine Lahti, Dylan McDermott, Jennifer Rubin. 1992

FEAR NO EVIL 🐾 The story of the satanic high school student hell-bent on destroying a senior class. Rated R. 96m. DIR: Frank LaLoggia. CAST: Stephan Arngrim, Elizabeth Hoffman. 1981

FEAR OF A BLACK HAT ★★★ This rap film chronicles a year on the road with the group N.W.H. (Niggaz With Hats) as they wax pseudophilosophically about their lives and songs, squabble with recording rivals, split up, and reunite. Just as rap seems to be forever coupled to drive-by shootings, misogyny, and street life, along comes a comic mockumentary reminding us that there's no business like show business. Rated R for language and nudity. 87m. DIR: Rusty Cundieff. CAST: Mark Christopher Lawrence, Larry B. Scott, Rusty Cundieff, Kasi Lemmons. 1994

FEAR STRIKES OUT ★★1/2 Anthony Perkins stars in this compelling, if melodramatic, biography of baseball player Jim Piersall, whose dramatic mental breakdown during the season was played to a national audience. Elmer Bernstein's music is particularly effective, but a little more baseball and a bit less psychology would have helped this film. B&W; 81m. DIR: Robert Mulligan. CAST: Anthony Perkins, Karl Malden, Norma Moore, Adam Williams, Perry Wilson, Peter J. Votrian. 1957

FEARLESS (1978) 🐾 This confusing, raunchy Italian film features Joan Collins as a rather inept striptease artist in Vienna. Not rated; it contains violence and nudity. 89m. DIR: Stelvio Massi. CAST: Joan Collins, Maurizio Merli. 1978

FEARLESS (1993) ★★★★ This offbeat exploration of mankind's spiritual side focuses on Jeff Bridges's inability to resume his normal, day-to-day life after surviving a plane crash. This fascinating and rewarding movie may pose more questions than it answers, but it's highly satisfying. Rated R for profanity and violence. 124m. DIR: Peter Weir. CAST: Jeff Bridges, Isabella Rossellini, Rosie Perez, Tom Hulce, John Turturro, Benicio Del Toro, Deirdre O'Connell. 1993 DVD

FEARLESS TIGER 🐾 When his brother dies from a drug overdose, a wealthy man goes to Hong Kong and learns martial arts to avenge him. Toothless nonsense. Rated R for violence and profanity. 88m. DIR: Ron Hulme. CAST: Jalal Mehri, Jamie Farr, Monika Schnarre, Bolo Yeung. 1993

FEARLESS VAMPIRE KILLERS, OR, PARDON ME, BUT YOUR TEETH ARE IN MY NECK, THE ★★★★ Roman Polanski playfully revamps Transylvanian folklore as an elderly, nutty professor and his mousy protégé hunt down a castle-dwelling bloodsucker who has kidnapped the buxom daughter of a lecherous innkeeper. This misadventure of two of the most unlikeliest of heroes gushes with ghoulish, offbeat humor. 111m. DIR: Roman Polanski. CAST: Roman Polanski, Jack MacGowran, Alfie Bass, Sharon Tate, Ferdinand Mayne. 1966

FEAST OF JULY ★★★1/2 Fans of Greek tragedy and doomed love affairs will have plenty to sink their teeth into, as this tale of a nineteenth-century woman betrayed by her lover is a downer of classic dimensions. Embeth Davidtz brings texture and complexity to a difficult role. Director Christopher Menaul has a couple of tricks we haven't seen before, and the attention to setting and scenery is unsurpassed. The ending, however, will surprise no one. Rated R for violence, sexual situations, and adult themes. 116m. DIR: Chris Menaul. CAST: Embeth Davidtz, Ben Chaplin, Tom Bell, James Purefoy, Greg Wise, Kenneth Anderson. 1995

FEATHERED SERPENT, THE ♥ Charlie Chan mystery—with Roland Winters the least convincing of the movie Chans—is unwatchable. B&W; 61m. DIR: William Beaudine. CAST: Roland Winters, Keye Luke, Victor Sen Yung. 1948

FEDERAL HILL ★★★ Set in the Federal Hill district of Providence, R.I., this portrait of five friends and gang members explores the options open to one gang member when he decides he wants out. Strong performances help the script along, but not enough to make this an important movie. Rated R for language and violence. B&W; 100m. DIR: Michael Corrente. CAST: Nicholas Turturro, Jason Andrews, Libby Langdon, Michael Raynor, Robert Turano. 1994

•FEDERAL OPERATOR 99 ★★★ Topflight action serial pits government agent against piano-playing villain and his henchmen (and one mean henchwoman) who deal in theft, death, destruction, and extortion. Great stunts, ingenious perils and escapes—plus good acting—make what passed as a routine chapterplay in its day a top entry in the genre. This stands as a perfect example of the quality Saturday-afternoon entertainment that died with the advent of television. 12 episodes. B&W; DIR: Spencer Gordon Bennet, Wallace Grissell, Yakima Canutt. CAST: Marten Lamont, George J. Lewis, Helen Talbot, Lorna Gray, LeRoy Mason, Hal Taliaferro, Bill Stevens. 1945

FEDORA ★★★★ This marvelous ball-of-twine mystery is writer-director Billy Wilder's bookend to his 1950 classic Sunset Boulevard. Down-on-his-luck producer William Holden flies to a Greek isle to lure a Garbo-like actress out of retirement. This is not an old man's dismissal of Hollywood as many believe; in fact, it is Wilder's last great film. 114m. DIR: Billy Wilder. CAST: William Holden, Marthe Keller, Hildegarde Neff, José Ferrer. 1978

FEDS ★★ A second-string comedy about two women (Mary Gross and Rebecca DeMornay) who work to beat the odds and graduate from the FBI's training academy. Some good laughs, but not enough. Rated PG-13 for mild language. 83m. DIR: Dan Goldberg. CAST: Mary Gross, Rebecca DeMornay, Ken Marshall. 1988

FEEL MY PULSE ★★1/2 Silent screwball comedy boasts a hypochondriac heiress who inherits a sanitarium that is used by bootleggers as a front and a hideout. Bebe Daniels does a fine job as the germwary, sheltered young girl who encounters a life she didn't dream existed. Silent. B&W; 86m. DIR: Gregory La Cava. CAST: Bebe Daniels, Richard Arlen, William Powell. 1928

FEELING MINNESOTA ★★ Sibling rivalry goes wild when black sheep Keanu Reeves shows up at his brother's wedding and runs off with bride Cameron Diaz. Steven Baigelman's film is coarse and oafish, arch and leaden, with a condescension toward its blue-collar characters that leaves an ugly aftertaste. Rated R for profanity and violence. 95m. DIR: Steven Baigelman. CAST: Keanu Reeves, Cameron Diaz, Vincent D'Onofrio, Delroy Lindo, Dan Aykroyd, Courtney Love, Tuesday Weld. 1996 DVD

•FELICIA'S JOURNEY ★★★1/2 Bob Hoskins shines during this sluggish psychological drama, as a malevolent nightmare concealed within a figure so benign and charming, that we're unlikely to credit the danger … until it's too late. This fussy, prissy catering manager crosses paths with a despondent 17-year-old girl who has left Ireland and journeyed to England's industrial midlands in search of the young man who said that he would cherish her forever. What follows is revealed with impressive narrative skill by director Atom Egoyan, who skillfully manipulates past and present, weaving current events with flashbacks and even some of the girl's dreams. But this film lacks the larger character tapestry and layered density of The Sweet Hereafter, which better justified the director's somber, protracted pacing. Ultimately, the payoff isn't nearly as interesting as the setup, and the final scenes are laced with too much contrivance and coincidence. Rated PG-13 for dramatic intensity. 114m. DIR: Atom Egoyan. CAST: Bob Hoskins, Elaine Cassidy, Arsinée Khanjian, Peter McDonald, Gerard McSorley. 1999 DVD

FELLINI SATYRICON ★★★1/2 Federico Fellini's visionary account of ancient Rome before Christ is a bizarre, hallucinatory journey. Imaginative art direction, lavish costumes, and garish makeup create a feast for the eyes. Composer Nino Rota's brilliant score is another plus. Italian dialogue with English subtitles. Not rated; contains nudity and violence. 129m. DIR: Federico Fellini. CAST: Martin Potter, Hiram Keller, Gordon Mitchell, Capucine. 1969

FELLINI'S ROMA ★★★★ Federico Fellini's odyssey through Rome is the director's impressionistic account of the city of his youth. With the help of a small film crew, Fellini explores the Italian capital with his own unique brand of visionary wit. A brilliant piece of moviemaking. In Italian with English subtitles. Not rated. 128m. DIR: Federico Fellini. CAST: Peter Gonzales, Marne Maitland, Federico Fellini. 1972

FELLOW TRAVELER ★★1/2 What could have been a gripping drama, set amid the horror and persecution of Hollywood's McCarthyesque witch-hunts, loses its momentum when Michael Eaton's script descends into pop psychobabble. Ron Silver stars as a screenwriter who, while hiding in England (where he fled, rather than testify before the House Un-American Activities Committee), learns that his best friend has committed suicide—after some dealings with HUAC. Made for HBO. 91m. DIR: Philip Saville. CAST: Ron Silver, Hart Bochner, Imogen Stubbs, Daniel J. Travanti. 1989

FELONY ★★1/2 Relentless action keeps this low-budget crime-thriller from hitting the skids. A renegade CIA agent sets up an ambush that leaves twelve cops dead. When the ambush is recorded by one of those television-reality shows, the agent orders that the tape be retrieved and the witnesses killed. The only one willing to stand up to him is a detective on the edge. Rated R for violence and adult language. 90m. DIR: David A. Prior. CAST: Jeffrey Combs, Lance Henriksen, Leo Rossi, Ashley Laurence, David Warner, Joe Don Baker. 1995

FEMALE ★★★ The lady president of an automobile manufacturing company, used to having things her own way, falls in love with a man who won't bend. Amusing romantic comedy with a feminist undercurrent. B&W; 60m. DIR: Michael Curtiz. CAST: Ruth Chatterton, George Brent, Johnny Mack Brown, Ruth Donnelly, Douglass Dumbrille. 1933

FEMALE JUNGLE ★★ A suitably sleazy, low-rent crime potboiler that was one of Jayne Mansfield's first movies. Lawrence Tierney is a police detective stalking a killer. One of the few features directed by Roger Corman stock-company actor Bruno VeSota. Alternate title: *The Hangover.* B&W; 56m. DIR: Bruno VeSota. CAST: Jayne Mansfield, Lawrence Tierney, John Carradine, Kathleen Crowley. 1956

FEMALE PERVERSIONS ★★ A dynamic attorney (Tilda Swinton) seems on the fast track to professional success, but she's plagued by troubling romantic relationships, and tormented by unresolved feelings for her father and her kleptomaniac sister (Amy Madigan). Director Susan Streitfeld's film isn't as interesting as it sounds; it's pretentious, obscure, grating, and poorly acted all around—even by the usually reliable Madigan. Rated R for profanity, nudity, and graphic sex. 119m. DIR: Susan Streitfeld. CAST: Tilda Swinton, Amy Madigan, Karen Sillas, Frances Fisher, Laila Robins, Clancy Brown. 1997

FEMALE TROUBLE ★★ The story of Dawn Davenport (Divine) from her days as a teenage belligerent through her rise to fame as a criminal and then to her death as a convicted murderer. As in other films by Waters, the theme here is the Jean Genet–like credo "crime equals beauty." Though it is unrated, this film is the equivalent of an X, due to sex, nudity, and violence. 90m. DIR: John Waters. CAST: Divine, Edith Massey, Cookie Mueller, David Lochary, Mink Stole, Michael Potter. 1973

FEMALIEN 🎬 Science-fiction nonsense about aliens who have evolved into pure light energy and must rely on the reports of a female scout sent to Earth for their sexual pleasure. Just another excuse to get people out of their clothes. Rated R and unrated versions both contain nudity and adult situations. 80/90m. DIR: Cybil Richards. CAST: Jacqueline Lovell, Matt Schue, Vanesa Talor. 1996 DVD

FEMME FATALE ★★ Colin Firth plays a newlywed who travels to Los Angeles to track down his runaway bride. A sordid look at L.A. nightlife is the main attraction in this otherwise routine suspense film. Rated R for nudity and violence. 96m. DIR: Andre Guttfreund. CAST: Colin Firth, Lisa Zane, Billy Zane, Scott Wilson. 1990

FEMME FONTAINE: KILLER BABE FOR THE CIA ★★ The only thing missing from this retread of spy movies is the kitchen sink. Professional assassin Drew Fontaine's latest assignment is personal: She's out to avenge the murder of her father. She has her work cut out for her, including doing battle with a

gang of lesbian "feminazis." Don't ask. Rated R for nudity, violence, and profanity. 93m. DIR: Margot Hope. CAST: Margot Hope, James Hong, Catherine Dao, Arthur Roberts. 1995

FENCE, THE ★★1/2 Bill Wirth plays Terry Griff, a 29-year-old who has been incarcerated since the age of fifteen. Now on parole, he attempts to get his life together. His efforts are short-lived when his parole officer frames him for a crime he didn't commit. Film eventually dwindles down to predictable subplots, all nicely wrapped up by the final frame. Not rated. 90m. DIR: Peter Pistor. CAST: Billy Wirth, Marc Alaimo, Erica Gimpel, Paul Benjamin. 1994 DVD

FER-DE-LANCE ★★ Made-for-TV suspense film is mildly entertaining as a cargo of poisonous snakes escape aboard a crippled submarine at the bottom of the sea, making life unpleasant for all concerned. 100m. DIR: Russ Mayberry. CAST: David Janssen, Hope Lange, Jason "Herb" Evers, Ivan Dixon. 1974

FERNANDEL THE DRESSMAKER ★★ Using Fernandel as the hub, the film is a bit of whimsy about a gentleman's tailor who desires to become a world-famous couturier. Even with a lightweight plot, watching this famous comedian is certainly worth the time and effort to wade through the nonsense. In French with English subtitles. B&W; 84m. DIR: Jean Boyer. CAST: Fernandel, Suzy Delair, Françoise Fabian. 1957

FERNGULLY 2: THE MAGICAL RESCUE ★★ Direct-to-video sequel lacks the appeal and voice talent of the first film, although younger children probably won't care. Batty Koda, Crysta, Pips, and the Beetle Boys must rise to the occasion when humans cart off three baby animals from the forest. Rated G. 75m. DIR: Phil Robinson. CAST: James Baker, Jamie Baker, Kevin Beachwood, Erik Bergmann. 1997 DVD

FERNGULLY—THE LAST RAINFOREST ★★★ A fairy discovers the ugly truth about the human race, which once worked alongside her magical peoples in nurturing the rain forest but is now destroying it. Robin Williams's inspired voice work (as Batty) elevates this environmental plea aimed at children. Other voices are provided by Tim Curry, Samantha Mathis, Christian Slater, Grace Zabriskie, Richard "Cheech" Marin, and Tommy Chong. Rated G. 76m. DIR: Bill Kroyer. 1992

FEROCIOUS FEMALE FREEDOM FIGHTERS ★★ À la Woody Allen's *What's Up Tiger Lily?*, this is a junky martial arts movie redubbed by a Los Angeles comedy troupe. The spotty results tend toward the sophomoric, though you'll probably laugh at some of it. Not rated; the film contains violence and crude humor. 74m. DIR: Jopi Burnama. CAST: Eva Arnez, Barry Prima. 1989

FERRIS BUELLER'S DAY OFF ★★★★ Writer-director John Hughes strikes again, this time with a charming tale of a high school legend in his own time (Matthew Broderick, playing the title character) who pretends to be ill in order to have a day away from school. The expressive Broderick owns the film, although he receives heavy competition from Jeffrey Jones, whose broadly played dean of students has been trying to nail Ferris Bueller for months. Rated PG-13 for mild profanity. 104m. DIR: John Hughes. CAST: Matthew Broderick, Alan Ruck, Mia Sara, Jeffrey

Jones, Jennifer Grey, Charlie Sheen, Cindy Pickett, Lyman Ward. **1986 DVD**

FEUD, THE ★★★ Two families in neighboring small towns are drawn into a feud that neither wants—but which neither will be the first to quit. This film isn't as satirical as the Thomas Berger novel on which it is based, but it's an agreeable farce nonetheless. Rated R. 96m. **DIR:** Bill D'Elia. **CAST:** René Auberjonois, Ron McLarty, Joe Grifasi. **1988**

FEVER ★★1/2 Ex-con Armand Assante wants only to go straight and reunite with former girlfriend Marcia Gay Harden, who has set up housekeeping with compassionate lawyer Sam Neill. Macho sparring between the two men is interrupted when Harden is kidnapped by one of Assante's enemies. Lurid and violent made-for-cable fodder. Rated R for violence and language. 99m. **DIR:** Larry Elikann. **CAST:** Sam Neill, Armand Assante, Marcia Gay Harden, Joe Spano. **1991**

FEVER LAKE ★★ This slickly made picture has production values equal to any big-budget film, but it is unemotionally involving and never develops a sense of terror. What could have been *The Shining* for the teen set instead steers toward mediocrity. Not rated; contains violence. 95m. **DIR:** Ralph Portillo. **CAST:** Corey Haim, Mario Lopez, Bo Hopkins. **1997**

FEVER PITCH ★★ Ryan O'Neal plays a sports journalist writing about gambling. To research his story, O'Neal becomes a gambler, loses his wife, endangers his job, and becomes involved with a sleazy bookie. Rated R for profanity and violence. 95m. **DIR:** Richard Brooks. **CAST:** Ryan O'Neal, Catherine Hicks, Giancarlo Giannini, Bridgette Anderson, Chad Everett, John Saxon, William Smith. **1985**

FEW GOOD MEN, A ★★★★ Calling this film the best Perry Mason movie ever made may sound like a put-down, but it isn't. Director Rob Reiner keeps the viewer guessing throughout this courtroom-based drama, which features Tom Cruise as a wisecracking navy defense lawyer whose clients have been accused of murder. The acting is first-rate. Rated R for violence and profanity. 134m. **DIR:** Rob Reiner. **CAST:** Tom Cruise, Jack Nicholson, Demi Moore, Kevin Bacon, Kiefer Sutherland, Kevin Pollak, James Marshall, J. T. Walsh, Christopher Guest, Matt Craven, Wolfgang Bodison, Cuba Gooding Jr. **1992 DVD**

FFOLKES ★★★ Of course, no movie with Roger Moore is a classic, but this tongue-in-cheek spy thriller with the actor playing against his James Bond stereotype provides some good, campy entertainment. This film features Moore as a woman-hating, but cat-loving, gun for hire who takes on a band of terrorists. Rated PG. 99m. **DIR:** Andrew V. McLaglen. **CAST:** Roger Moore, James Mason, Anthony Perkins, Michael Parks, David Hedison. **1980**

FIANCÉ, THE ★★ Dull erotic thriller with Lysette Anthony as a wife who becomes the focus of a stranger after they have a brief but personal conversation. Rated R for profanity, violence, and sexual situations. 94m. **DIR:** Martin Kitrosser. **CAST:** William R. Moses, Lysette Anthony, Patrick Cassidy. **1997**

FIDDLER ON THE ROOF ★★★★ A lavishly mounted musical, this 1971 screen adaptation of the long-running Broadway hit, based on the stories of Sholem Aleichem, works remarkably well. This is primarily thanks to Topol's immensely likable portrayal of Tevye, the proud but put-upon father clinging desperately to the old values. Rated G. 181m. **DIR:** Norman Jewison. **CAST:** Topol, Norman Crane, Leonard Frey, Molly Picon, Paul Mann, Rosalind Harris. **1971 DVD**

FIDDLIN' BUCKAROO ★★★ Secret service agent Ken Maynard, on the trail of outlaw Fred Kohler, is mistakenly arrested for a crime Kohler's gang committed. One of several Maynard Westerns he directed himself, this one is heavy on the music end. B&W; 65m. **DIR:** Ken Maynard. **CAST:** Ken Maynard, Fred Kohler Sr., Frank Rice. **1933**

FIELD, THE ★★★★ Richard Harris gives a superb performance in this drama, which is not unlike the dark side of John Ford's *The Quiet Man.* Tom Berenger plays an American who comes to Ireland in search of his roots and with plans to modernize the country, which include buying and paving a piece of fertile land lovingly tended by Harris and his son (Sean Bean). Rated PG-13 for violence and profanity. 107m. **DIR:** Jim Sheridan. **CAST:** Richard Harris, John Hurt, Sean Bean, Tom Berenger, Brenda Fricker, Frances Tomelty. **1990 DVD**

FIELD OF DREAMS ★★★★★ A must-see motion picture, this spirit-lifting work stars Kevin Costner as an Iowa farmer who hears a voice telling him to build a baseball diamond in the middle of his corn field. Against all common sense, he does so and sets in motion a chain of wonderful events. Costner gets strong support from Amy Madigan, Burt Lancaster, James Earl Jones, and Ray Liotta in this all-ages delight adapted from the novel, *Shoeless Joe,* by W. P. Kinsella. Rated PG for brief profanity. 106m. **DIR:** Phil Alden Robinson. **CAST:** Kevin Costner, Amy Madigan, James Earl Jones, Burt Lancaster, Ray Liotta, Timothy Busfield. **1989 DVD**

FIELD OF FIRE 🎬 Battling behind enemy lines in Cambodia, a special combat squad attempts to retrieve a downed military expert. Hokey heroics. Rated R for profanity and nudity. 100m. **DIR:** Cirio H. Santiago. **CAST:** David Carradine. **1992**

FIELD OF HONOR (1986) ★★ Tale of a Dutch infantryman in the Korean War left for dead after a surprise attack by the Chinese. Everett McGill is the survivor who hides out with two shell-shocked kids. Rated R for violence, profanity, and nudity. 93m. **DIR:** Hans Scheepmaker. **CAST:** Everett McGill, Ron Brandsteder, Hey Young Lee. **1986**

FIELD OF HONOR (1988) ★★ A nineteenth-century French saga about young men at war, with aspirations to the classic status of *The Red Badge of Courage.* Despite its aim at tragic symmetry, the film's muddled and meandering script causes it to fall short. Strangely uninvolving. In French with English subtitles. 89m. **DIR:** Jean-Pierre Denis. **CAST:** Cris Campion. **1988**

FIEND WITHOUT A FACE ★★★1/2 Surprisingly effective little horror chiller with slight overtones of the "Id" creature from *Forbidden Planet.* Scientific thought experiment goes awry and creates nasty creatures that look like brains with coiled tails. Naturally, they eat people. Story builds to a great climax

B&W; 74m. **DIR:** Arthur Crabtree. **CAST:** Marshall Thompson, Kim Parker, Terry Kilburn. 1958

FIENDISH PLOT OF DR. FU MANCHU, THE 💖 Peter Sellers plays a dual role of "insidious Oriental villain" Fu Manchu, who is out to rule the world, and his arch-enemy, the Holmes-like Nayland Smith of Scotland Yard. Rated PG. 108m. **DIR:** Piers Haggard. **CAST:** Peter Sellers, Helen Mirren, Sid Caesar, David Tomlinson. 1980

FIERCE CREATURES ★★★ The cast from *A Fish Called Wanda* obviously had fun making this nonsensequel, but its broader tone provides less of the deft British wit that made their first effort so entertaining. John Cleese plays a stuffy civil servant sent to increase a zoo's profit margin, a task he embraces by suggesting to relocate all cuddly animals and concentrate solely on "fierce" creatures. Jamie Lee Curtis is the corporate shark sent to help Cleese; Michael Palin is one of the flustered keepers. Kevin Kline plays two roles, neither very successfully. The plot essentially disappears midway through the disjointed film, although the rising sexual tension between Cleese and Curtis is pretty funny. Rated PG-13 for strong sexual content. 93m. **DIR:** Robert Young, Fred Schepisi. **CAST:** John Cleese, Jamie Lee Curtis, Kevin Kline, Michael Palin, Ronnie Corbett, Carey Lowell. 1997 DVD

FIESTA ★★1/2 One of Esther Williams's lesser movies, helped by the scenery of Mexico, the excitement of bullfighting, and the dancing skills of Cyd Charisse. Esther Williams poses as her brother in the bullring so he can slip away to compose music. Only Williams swims better than she bullfights, and there's no water in the ring. A novelty that's mildly entertaining. 104m. **DIR:** Richard Thorpe. **CAST:** Esther Williams, Ricardo Montalban, Cyd Charisse, Mary Astor, Fortunio Bonanova, John Carroll. 1947

FIG LEAVES ★★★ The age-old problem facing a woman who has "nothing to wear" is the subject of this amusing fluff. Adam and Eve Smith start out in the Garden of Eden, and then progress to the big city in 1926, living as plumber and wife. Eve secretly gets a job as a fashion model and has the chance to wear all the new styles she wants and rekindle her romance with Adam. Lots of fun, and a visual feast. B&W; 68m. **DIR:** Howard Hawks. **CAST:** George O'Brien, Olive Borden, Phyllis Haver, Andre de Beranger, William Austin, Heinie Conklin. 1926

●**FIGHT CLUB** 💖 If director David Fincher and screenwriter Jim Uhls intended to make us believe that we haven't advanced a jot from the putrescent slime that once may have spawned mankind, they succeeded brilliantly. This appalling, grotesque, and interminable endurance test is fairy-tale fiction for serial killers, imbeciles who succumb to road rage, and frustrated white guys: all the morons who seek excuses to justify their increasingly bad behavior and hair-trigger tempers. Proceed with caution. Rated R for profanity, violence, torture, nudity, and sexual content. 139m. **DIR:** David Fincher. **CAST:** Brad Pitt, Edward Norton, Helena Bonham Carter, Meat Loaf, Jared Leto. 1999 DVD

FIGHT FOR US ★★ After the fall of the Marcos regime in the Philippines, right-wing death squads terrorize the countryside. Poor production values, amateur-night actors, and pedestrian direction take the fight out of this one. Rated R for violence, profanity, and simulated sex. 92m. **DIR:** Lino Brocka. **CAST:** Phillip Salvador. 1990

FIGHTER ATTACK ★★ An American pilot (Sterling Hayden) shot down in Italy joins up with an Italian terrorist group to block off a Nazi supply tunnel. Familiar World War II melodrama. 80m. **DIR:** Lesley Selander. **CAST:** Sterling Hayden, Joy Page, J. Carrol Naish. 1953

FIGHTING BACK ★★★ A deli owner decides to organize a neighborhood committee against crime after his wife and mother are victims of violence. You can't help but cheer him on. A rapid succession of violent acts, profanity, and occasional nudity make this R-rated film questionable for young audiences. 98m. **DIR:** Lewis Teague. **CAST:** Tom Skerritt, Patti LuPone, Michael Sarrazin, Yaphet Kotto, David Rasche, Ted Ross. 1982

FIGHTING CARAVANS ★★★1/2 Despite the title, this is a Zane Grey Western—and a good one, full of intrigue, action, and, for leavening, a smattering of comedy. Lanky, taciturn Gary Cooper, wanted by the law, avoids arrest by conning a wagon-train girl to pose as his wife. Romance blooms as the train treks west, into the sights of hostile forces. B&W; 80m. **DIR:** Otto Brower, David Burton. **CAST:** Gary Cooper, Lily Damita, Ernest Torrence, Eugene Pallette, Charles Winninger. 1931

FIGHTING CODE ★★1/2 Buck Jones impersonates a girl's dead brother in order to solve a murder and save the ranch from a scheming lawyer. A young Ward Bond shows why he later became such a star and fine actor. B&W; 65m. **DIR:** Lambert Hillyer. **CAST:** Buck Jones, Ward Bond. 1933

FIGHTING FATHER DUNNE ★★★1/2 Inspirational, at times tearjerking, tale of one priest's effort to care for the homeless boys of St. Louis in 1905. You'll be amazed by the clever priest's ability to acquire supplies and services with goodwill instead of hard cash. B&W; 93m. **DIR:** Ted Tetzlaff. **CAST:** Pat O'Brien, Barry Fitzgerald, Darryl Hickman. 1948

FIGHTING KENTUCKIAN, THE ★★★ Worth seeing if only for the rare and wonderful on-screen combination of John Wayne and Oliver Hardy, this period adventure casts the duo as frontiersmen who come to the aid of the homesteading Napoleonic French. If only Vera Hruba Ralston weren't the Duke's love interest, this could have been a real winner. B&W; 100m. **DIR:** George Waggner. **CAST:** John Wayne, Vera Hruba Ralston, Philip Dorn, Oliver Hardy. 1949 DVD

FIGHTING MAD ★★★ A quiet, unassuming farmer (Peter Fonda) is driven to distraction by a ruthless businessman who wants to assume his property. Instead of a free-for-all of violence and car crashes (as in other Fonda films of the time), this ranks as an in-depth character study. Rated R for violence. 90m. **DIR:** Jonathan Demme. **CAST:** Peter Fonda, Lynn Lowry, John Doucette, Philip Carey, Scott Glenn, Kathleen Miller. 1976

FIGHTING MARINES, THE ★★ U.S. Marines run up against a modern-day pirate. The plot's thin, the acting forced, but the special effects are remarkable.

Pieced together from twelve serial chapters. B&W; 69m. **DIR:** Joseph Kane, B. Reeves "Breezy" Eason. **CAST:** Grant Withers, Adrian Morris, Ann Rutherford, Jason Robards Sr., Pat O'Malley. **1936**

FIGHTING PRINCE OF DONEGAL, THE ★★★1/2 A rousing adventure-action film set in sixteenth-century Ireland. When Peter McEnery succeeds to the title of Prince of Donegal, the Irish clans are ready to fight English troops to make Ireland free. This is a Disney British endeavor that is definitely worth watching. 110m. **DIR:** Michael O'Herlihy. **CAST:** Peter McEnery, Susan Hampshire, Tom Adams, Gordon Jackson. **1966**

FIGHTING RANGER, THE ★★★ Entertaining but predictable piece has Buck Jones and sidekick Frank Rice chasing down a killer. Good cast and production values. B&W; 60m. **DIR:** George B. Seitz. **CAST:** Buck Jones, Frank Rice, Ward Bond, Frank La Rue. **1934**

FIGHTING SEABEES, THE ★★★ John Wayne and Dennis O'Keefe are construction workers fighting the Japanese in their own way while each attempts to woo Susan Hayward away from the other. This 1944 war film, which costars William Frawley, is actually better than it sounds. B&W; 100m. **DIR:** Edward Ludwig. **CAST:** John Wayne, Dennis O'Keefe, Susan Hayward, William Frawley, Duncan Renaldo. **1944** DVD

FIGHTING SHADOWS ★★★ Royal Canadian Mountie Tim O'Farrell (Tim McCoy) returns to his former home to find out who is terrorizing fur trappers there. Standard fare is made watchable by the stars. B&W; 57m. **DIR:** David Selman. **CAST:** Tim McCoy, Ward Bond. **1935**

FIGHTING 69TH, THE ★★★ Tough-guy James Cagney does a good job as a loner who buckles under fire and causes the death of some of his comrades in this all-male World War I story. Based partly on fact, this virile Warner Brothers blockbuster boasts good cinematography and great battle scenes. B&W; 89m. **DIR:** William Keighley. **CAST:** James Cagney, Pat O'Brien, George Brent, Jeffrey Lynn, Alan Hale Sr., Frank McHugh, Dennis Morgan, Dick Foran, William Lundigan. **1940**

FIGHTING SULLIVANS, THE (SULLIVANS, THE) ★★★★ This fact-based story of five brothers who died together when the cruiser *Juneau* was torpedoed by the Germans emotionally devastated World War II moviegoers. The early scenes of the boys growing up in Waterloo, Iowa, is fine Americana, but be forewarned: the ending has some of the saddest, most heart-wrenching moments ever filmed. B&W; 111m. **DIR:** Lloyd Bacon. **CAST:** Thomas Mitchell, Anne Baxter, Selena Royle, Ward Bond, Bobby Driscoll. **1944** DVD

FIGHTING WESTERNER, THE ★★★ Rugged mining engineer Randolph Scott works undercover to learn who is responsible for murders at a radium mine. Tense mystery-Western. B&W; 54m. **DIR:** Charles Barton. **CAST:** Randolph Scott, Kathleen Burke, Ann Sheridan, Chic Sale. **1935**

FINAL ALLIANCE ♥ Will Colton (David Hasselhoff) returns to a hometown that has been overrun by gangs. Rated R for violence and language. 93m. **DIR:**

Mario Di Leo. **CAST:** David Hasselhoff, Bo Hopkins, John Saxon. **1990**

FINAL ANALYSIS ★★ Hitchcock meets Ken and Barbie in this silly suspense movie about a psychiatrist who becomes a murder suspect. Too serious to be funny and too campy to be believable. Rated R for violence, profanity, and nudity. 122m. **DIR:** Phil Joanou. **CAST:** Richard Gere, Kim Basinger, Uma Thurman, Eric Roberts, Paul Guilfoyle, Keith David. **1992** DVD

FINAL APPEAL ★★★ Decent thriller stars JoBeth Williams as a wife who thinks she has it all until she walks in on her abusive husband and his mistress. When she's forced to kill him in self-defense, no one will believe her, including her attorney brother. When she's arrested for murder, it begins to look like someone is out to frame her. Likable cast makes this made-for-television thriller watchable. Rated PG-13 for violence. 94m. **DIR:** Eric Till. **CAST:** JoBeth Williams, Brian Dennehy. **1993**

FINAL APPROACH ★★ Confusing, muddled sci-fi entry has test pilot James B. Sikking trying to recall the moments before a fateful crash. Virtual reality effects are film's only saving grace, which attempts to surprise viewers with a twist ending, but one that comes too little, too late. Rated PG-13. 101m. **DIR:** Eric Steven Stahl. **CAST:** James B. Sikking, Hector Elizondo, Madolyn Smith, Kevin McCarthy. **1992**

FINAL CHAPTER—WALKING TALL ♥ Garbage. Rated R for violence. 112m. **DIR:** Jack Starrett. **CAST:** Bo Svenson, Margaret Blye, Forrest Tucker, Lurene Tuttle, Morgan Woodward, Libby Boone. **1977**

FINAL COMBAT, THE ★★★★ In a post-apocalypse world, a lonely man makes an attempt to break away and find a kind of happiness. He soon discovers that he must fight for what he desires rather than try to run away. The good performances and the compelling story are accentuated by the fact that there is no dialogue in the movie. Rated R for violence. B&W; 93m. **DIR:** Luc Besson. **CAST:** Pierre Jolivet, Fritz Wepper, Jean Bouise, Jean Reno. **1984**

FINAL COMEDOWN, THE ♥ Dated, heavy-handed film about a black man who becomes involved with a group of militants. Rated R for violence, profanity, and nudity. 84m. **DIR:** Oscar Williams. **CAST:** Billy Dee Williams, D'Urville Martin, Celia Kaye, Raymond St. Jacques. **1972**

FINAL CONFLICT, THE ★★ The third and last in the *Omen* trilogy, this disturbing but passionless film concerns the rise to power of the son of Satan, Damien Thorn (Sam Neill), and the second coming of the Saviour. It depends more on shocking spectacle than gripping tension for its impact. Rated R. 108m. **DIR:** Graham Baker. **CAST:** Sam Neill, Rossano Brazzi, Don Gordon, Lisa Harrow, Mason Adams. **1981**

FINAL COUNTDOWN, THE ★★1/2 Farfetched but passable story about an aircraft carrier traveling backward in time to just before the start of World War II. The crew must then decide whether or not to change the course of history. Some good special effects and performances by the leads manage to keep this one afloat. Rated PG. 104m. **DIR:** Don Taylor. **CAST:** Kirk Douglas, Martin Sheen, Katharine Ross. **1980**

FINAL CUT, THE ★★★1/2 You can't beat following a bomb-disposal squad for edge-of-the-seat suspense, and this slick little thriller keeps the screws properly tightened. Sam Elliott puts his world-weary charm to good use as a former demolition expert summoned when local cops are stymied by a serial bomber whose devices are never wired the same way twice. Rated R for profanity, violence, and simulated sex. 99m. DIR: Roger Christian. CAST: Sam Elliott, Charles Martin Smith, Anne Ramsey, Ray Baker, Matt Craven, John Hannah, Amanda Plummer. 1995

•**FINAL DAYS, THE** ★★★1/2 Solid made-for-television dramatization of the last days of Richard M. Nixon's presidency. Based on the bestselling novel by Bob Woodward and Carl Bernstein, the reporters who uncovered the Watergate scandal, the drama features a powerful performance by Lane Smith as Nixon. Handsome production values and a sense of time and place go a long way, but it's the fine-tuned writing, direction, and acting that bring this historical flashback to life. Rated PG. 150m. DIR: Richard Pearce. CAST: Lane Smith, Richard Kiley, David Ogden Stiers, Ed Flanders, Theodore Bikel. 1989

FINAL DEFEAT, THE ★★ After the Civil War, Guy Madison leads a group of ex-Confederate rebels on a rampage through the West. He unknowingly takes on a government undercover agent who tricks him into believing that he knows the whereabouts of a buried treasure. A good score and the presence of Madison make this a nice film. Rated PG. 90m. DIR: E. G. Rowland. CAST: Guy Madison, Edd Byrnes, Louise Barrett, Enio Girolami, Pedro Sanchez. 1968

•**FINAL DESTINATION** ★★ A teenager's premonition saves him and several others from a plane crash; then, some mysterious force begins killing the survivors one by one. What starts out like *The Sixth Sense* quickly turns into an unimaginative variation on the standard teen-slasher formula, with cruel fate this time taking the place of the usual serial killer. Rated R for violence and profanity. 90m. DIR: James Wong. CAST: Devon Sawa, Ali Larter, Kerr Smith, Kristen Cloke, Daniel Roebuck, Chad E. Donella, Seann William Scott. 2000

FINAL EMBRACE ★★1/2 Video director Oley Sassone treads on familiar turf, a seamy tale of murder in the music video business. Attractive cast, but there's more plot and energy in a music video. Rated R for nudity, violence, and adult language. 88m. DIR: Oley Sassone. CAST: Robert Rusler, Nancy Valen, Dick Van Patten, Linda Dona. 1992

FINAL EQUINOX 🖤 Government agent tries to save the Earth's people from being turned into vegetables. Not rated; contains profanity, nudity, violence, and substance abuse. 93m. DIR: Serge Rodnunsky. CAST: Joe Lara, Tina May Simpson, Gary Kasper, Martin Kove, David Warner. 1996

FINAL EXAM 🖤 A mad slasher hacks his way through a college campus. Rated R. 90m. DIR: Jimmy Huston. CAST: Joel S. Rice. 1981

FINAL EXECUTIONER, THE 🖤 Following a nuclear holocaust, a small undamaged elite hunt down the contaminated human leftovers. Not rated; contains violence and sex. 95m. DIR: Romolo Guerrieri. CAST:

William Mang, Marina Costa, Harrison Muller, Woody Strode. 1983

FINAL EXTRA, THE ★★ After a star reporter is shot by an arch-criminal known as The Shadow, the case is taken over by his sister and an eager cub reporter. Obscure silent mystery will appeal only to nostalgia buffs. B&W; 75m. DIR: James Hogan. CAST: Marguerite de la Motte, Grant Withers. 1927

FINAL IMPACT ★★ Ex-world kick-boxing champ (Lorenzo Lamas) trains an innocent kid (Mike Worth) for the finals in an effort to avenge his own defeat. Reasonably watchable. Rated R for violence and profanity. 97m. DIR: Joseph Merhi, Stephen Smoke. CAST: Lorenzo Lamas, Michael Worth, Jeff Langton, Kathleen Kinmont. 1991

FINAL JUDGMENT 🖤 Brad Dourif stars as a Hollywood priest whose shady past catches up with him when he becomes the prime suspect in the murder of a stripper. Rated R for violence, nudity, and profanity. 90m. DIR: Louis Morneau. CAST: Brad Dourif, Isaac Hayes, Karen Black, Maria Ford, Orson Bean, David Ledingham. 1992

FINAL JUSTICE (1984) 🖤 Joe Don Baker plays a rural sheriff who travels to Italy to take on the Mafia and halt criminal activities. Rated R for nudity, violence, and language. 90m. DIR: Greydon Clark. CAST: Joe Don Baker, Venantino Venantini, Helena Abella, Bill McKinney. 1984 DVD

FINAL JUSTICE (1994) 🖤 Repulsive revenge melodrama pitting three suburban couples against a pair of vicious backwoodsmen. Rated R for rape, strong violence, nudity, sexual situations, and profanity. 92m. DIR: Brent Huff. CAST: James Brolin, Brent Huff, Shawn Huff, Rob Roy Fitzgerald. 1994

FINAL MISSION (1984) 🖤 *First Blood* rip-off. Not rated, but with profanity, violence, and nudity. 101m. DIR: Cirio H. Santiago. CAST: Richard Young, John Dresden, Kaz Garas, Christine Tudor. 1984

FINAL MISSION (1994) ★★ OK attempt at creating a virtual-reality thriller is sabotaged by inane dialogue and tired direction. Fighter pilots are being brainwashed during flight simulations and then turn kamikaze when they get inside the real thing. Young hotshot pilot (Billy Wirth) investigates and runs up against the standard-issue plot complications and stock villains. Good idea gone awry. Rated R for language and violence. 92m. DIR: Lee Redmond. CAST: Billy Wirth, Corbin Bernsen, Elizabeth Gracen, Steve Railsback. 1994

FINAL NOTICE 🖤 Failed TV pilot with Gil Gerard as a romantic private eye who has help from a stuffy yet sexy librarian (Melody Anderson). Boring made-for-cable fodder. 91m. DIR: Steven H. Stern. CAST: Gil Gerard, Melody Anderson, Jackie Burroughs, Kevin Hicks, Louise Fletcher, David Ogden Stiers, Steve Landesberg. 1989

FINAL OPTION, THE ★★★★ Judy Davis stars in this first-rate British-made suspense-thriller as the leader of a fanatical antinuclear group that takes a group of U.S. and British officials hostage and demands that a nuclear missile be launched at a U.S. base in Scotland. If not, the hostages will die. And it's up to Special Air Services undercover agent Peter Skellen (Lewis Collins) to save their lives. Rated

R for violence and profanity. 125m. DIR: Ian Sharp. CAST: Judy Davis, Lewis Collins, Richard Widmark, Robert Webber, Edward Woodward. 1982

FINAL ROUND ★★ Undiscriminating action fans may tolerate this low-rent translation of Richard Connell's "The Most Dangerous Game," but there's little appeal for mainstream viewers. Thanks to poor lighting, Lorenzo Lamas's fight scenes are barely visible ... no doubt to hide the $1.98 sets. Rated R for violence, profanity, and nudity. 90m. DIR: George Erschbamer. CAST: Lorenzo Lamas, Anthony De Longis, Kathleen Kinmont. 1993

FINAL TERROR, THE ★★ Rachel Ward and Daryl Hannah weren't big stars when they made this mediocre low-budget slasher flick for onetime B-movie king Sam Arkoff and now they probably wish they hadn't. Rated R for brief nudity and violence. 82m. DIR: Andrew Davis. CAST: Rachel Ward, Daryl Hannah, John Friedrich, Adrian Zmed. 1981

FINAL VERDICT ★★★ Based on true events, this is a slow-paced account of one girl's adoration of her lawyer father (Treat Williams). Set in Los Angeles circa 1919, this made-for-TV film does an above-average job. 93m. DIR: Jack Fisk. CAST: Treat Williams, Glenn Ford, Olivia Burnette, Ashley Crow, Raphael Sbarge. 1991

FIND THE LADY ★★★ In this slapstick rendition of a cops-and-robbers spoof, John Candy, as the cop, and Mickey Rooney, as a kidnapper, create lots of laughs on the way to a very funny finish. 90m. DIR: John Trent. CAST: John Candy, Mickey Rooney, Peter Cook, Lawrence Dane, Alexandra Bastedo. 1986

•FINDING GRACELAND ★★ Whimsical tale of a hitchhiking Elvis and his effects on a young motorist crumbles under its own weight. At first the film shows lots of promise. Johnathon Schaech stars as a young man heading to Memphis who picks up a hitchhiker (played by Harvey Keitel) who claims to be Elvis. Both men have reasons to reach Memphis, but it is the road trip there that is most telling. Lots of plot holes force this comedy-drama off the road long before the characters reach their destination. Bridget Fonda costars as a Marilyn Monroe lookalike who tags up with the two men. Rated PG-13 for language. 97m. DIR: David Winkler. CAST: Harvey Keitel, Johnathon Schaech, Bridget Fonda. 1998 DVD

FINE MADNESS, A ★★★ Whimsical story of a daffy, radical poet, well portrayed by Sean Connery (proving that, even in the 1960s, he could stretch further than James Bond). Many of the laughs come from his well-developed relationship with wife Joanne Woodward, although the film occasionally lapses into lurid slapstick. Not rated; adult themes. 104m. DIR: Irvin Kershner. CAST: Sean Connery, Joanne Woodward, Jean Seberg. 1966

FINE MESS, A ❤ Supposedly inspired by the Laurel and Hardy classic, The Music Box. Gag after gag falls embarrassingly flat. Rated PG. 100m. DIR: Blake Edwards. CAST: Ted Danson, Howie Mandel, Richard Mulligan, Stuart Margolin, Maria Conchita Alonso, Jennifer Edwards, Paul Sorvino. 1986

FINE ROMANCE, A ★★★ This is a lovely little romantic comedy with Julie Andrews and Marcello Mastroianni as a couple of discarded lovers whose spouses have left them. Thrust together to contemplate their options, both go through emotional withdrawal and loss, eventually finding happiness with each other. Rated PG-13 for profanity. 83m. DIR: Gene Saks. CAST: Julie Andrews, Marcello Mastroianni. 1993

FINEST HOUR, THE ★★1/2 Two new navy SEAL recruits form an alliance after trying to outdo one another. After being separated for a couple of years, they team up again during the Persian Gulf War. Very dull plot that could have been shorter. Rated R for profanity, violence, and nudity. 105m. DIR: Shimon Dotan. CAST: Rob Lowe, Gale Hansen, Tracy Griffith, Eb Lottimer. 1991

FINGER MAN (1955) ★★ Captured crook saves his hide by helping the Internal Revenue get the goods on crime kingpin Forrest Tucker. Frank Lovejoy as the reluctant informer does a credible job, but crazy Timothy Carey as Tucker's top enforcer steals the show. B&W; 81m. DIR: Harold Schuster. CAST: Frank Lovejoy, Forrest Tucker, Peggie Castle, Timothy Carey. 1955

FINGER ON THE TRIGGER ★★ Ex-Union and ex-Confederate soldiers band together to defeat a party of Indians on the warpath. They must make bullets out of the only source available, a stash of golden horseshoes. This B Western filmed in Spain is Rory Calhoun's only European Western. Not rated; contains violence. 89m. DIR: Sidney Pink. CAST: Rory Calhoun, James Philbrook, Todd Martin, Leo Anchoriz, Silvia Solar. 1965

FINGERS ★★★★ Harvey Keitel gives an electric performance as a would-be concert pianist who is also a death-dealing collector for his loan-sharking dad. Extremely violent and not for all tastes, but there is an undeniable fascination toward the Keitel character and his tortured life. Rated R. 91m. DIR: James Toback. CAST: Harvey Keitel, Jim Brown, Tisa Farrow, Michael Gazzo. 1978

•FINGERS AT THE WINDOW ★★★ An evil schemer employs a series of weak-willed men to hack to death witnesses who threaten his impersonation of a wealthy medical specialist. Entertaining and engaging, this breezy thriller from MGM's B unit takes some swipes at the psychiatric profession and features two of the oddest protagonists ever found in the ax-murder film. Offbeat and funny. B&W; 80m. DIR: Charles Lederer. CAST: Lew Ayres, Laraine Day, Basil Rathbone, Walter Kingsford, James Flavin, Miles Mander. 1942

FINIAN'S RAINBOW ★★1/2 Those who believe Fred Astaire can do no wrong haven't seen this silly oddity. Francis Coppola's heavy direction is totally inappropriate for a musical and the story's concerns about racial progress, which were outdated when the film first appeared, are positively embarrassing now. Rated G. 145m. DIR: Francis Ford Coppola. CAST: Fred Astaire, Petula Clark, Tommy Steele, Keenan Wynn, Barbara Hancock, Don Francks. 1968

FINISH LINE ★★ Pressured by his coach-father to excel, a high school athlete begins using steroids. Well-meaning drama, made for cable TV, is as predictable as most TV movies. Not rated. 96m. DIR:

John Nicolella. **CAST:** James Brolin, Josh Brolin, Mariska Hargitay, Billy Vera. **1989**

FINISHING SCHOOL ★★1/2 A poor little rich girl finds true love with a med student. Surprisingly progressive, this film was codirected and written by a woman—Wanda Tuchock—rare, indeed, for the 1930s. Some scenes are melodramatic and attitudes are dated, but overall the film remains engrossing. B&W; 73m. **DIR:** Wanda Tuchock, George Nicholls Jr. **CAST:** Frances Dee, Billie Burke, Ginger Rogers, Bruce Cabot, John Halliday. **1934**

FINISHING TOUCH, THE ★★1/2 Soon-to-be-divorced husband-and-wife detectives are assigned to the same case, a psychotic killer who sells the videotapes of the murders. The viewer knows exactly what will happen in the unimaginative plot. Rated R for nudity, profanity, and graphic sex. 82m. **DIR:** Fred Gallo. **CAST:** Michael Nader, Shelley Hack, Arnold Vosloo, Art Evans. **1991**

FINNEGAN BEGIN AGAIN ★★★★ In this endearing romance, Robert Preston plays Michael Finnegan, an eccentric retired advice columnist who befriends schoolteacher Elizabeth (Mary Tyler Moore) after learning of her secret affair with a married undertaker (Sam Waterston). Their eventual romance becomes a warm, funny, and tender portrayal of love blossoming in later life. Made for cable. 97m. **DIR:** Joan Micklin Silver. **CAST:** Mary Tyler Moore, Robert Preston, Sam Waterston, Sylvia Sidney. **1985**

FIRE! ★★ Another of producer Irwin Allen's suspense spectaculars involving an all-star cast caught in a major calamity. This one concerns a mountain town in the path of a forest fire set by an escaped convict. Worth watching once. 100m. **DIR:** Earl Bellamy. **CAST:** Ernest Borgnine, Vera Miles, Alex Cord, Donna Mills, Lloyd Nolan, Ty Hardin, Neville Brand, Gene Evans, Erik Estrada. **1977**

FIRE AND ICE (1983) ★★★★ Animated film is geared more to adults than children. Sword-and-sorcery fantasy keeps the action moving. The plot begins with evil sorcerer Nekron planning world domination. It thickens when he kidnaps the princess, Teegra, to force her father to turn his kingdom over to him as his daughter's ransom. Rated PG. 81m. **DIR:** Ralph Bakshi. **1983**

FIRE AND ICE (1987) 🦃 When the musical theme of a film offers only the words of the title sung over and over again, you know you're in for an ordeal. No rating. 80m. **DIR:** Willy Bogner. **CAST:** John Eaves, Suzy Chaffee. **1987**

FIRE AND SWORD 🦃 Tristan and Isolde. Not rated; contains violence and nudity. 84m. **DIR:** Vieth von Furstenborug. **CAST:** Christopher Waltz, Antonia Presser, Peter Firth, Leigh Lawson. **1985**

FIRE BIRDS 🦃 Lame revision of *Top Gun*. Rated PG-13 for violence and language. 85m. **DIR:** David Greene. **CAST:** Nicolas Cage, Sean Young, Tommy Lee Jones. **1990**

FIRE DOWN BELOW ★★★1/2 Steven Seagal goes after some nasty corporate types who are covertly dumping toxic waste in Kentucky's Appalachian hills while the locals suffer at their hands. It's the old save-the-ranch cowboy B-movie formula with extra kicks, and fun for fans of no-brainer entertainment.

Rated R for violence and profanity. 105m. **DIR:** Felix Enriquez Alcala. **CAST:** Steven Seagal, Marg Helsenberger, Kris Kristofferson, Harry Dean Stanton, Stephen Lang, Levon Helm, Ed Bruce, Brad Hunt, Richard Masur, Randy Travis. **1997 DVD**

FIRE, ICE & DYNAMITE 🦃 Stunt director Willy Bogner oversees ex–James Bond star Roger Moore in this stunt-filled yet ultimately boring crime caper. Rated PG for violence. 105m. **DIR:** Willy Bogner. **CAST:** Roger Moore, Shari Belafonte. **1990**

FIRE IN THE SKY ★★ UFO buffs might get a lift out of this dramatization of the alleged abduction of Travis Walton (D. B. Sweeney) in 1975, but most viewers will be disappointed. Rated PG-13 for profanity and nudity. 110m. **DIR:** Robert Lieberman. **CAST:** D. B. Sweeney, Robert Patrick, James Garner, Craig Sheffer, Peter Berg, Henry Thomas, Noble Willingham, Kathleen Wilhoite. **1993**

FIRE NEXT TIME, THE ★★★ Preachy futuristic disaster film repeatedly delivers a heavy-handed environmental message. As a result of global warming, coastal towns are flooding while plains dry up. Amidst this, Craig T. Nelson tries to reunite his estranged family. Unbelievable plot twists and occasional lectures weaken the film's overall effectiveness. Not rated; contains profanity and suggestive comments. 180m. **DIR:** Tom McLoughlin. **CAST:** Craig T. Nelson, Bonnie Bedelia, Richard Farnsworth, Jurgen Prochnow. **1992**

FIRE OVER ENGLAND ★★★ A swashbuckling adventure of Elizabethan England's stand against the Spanish Armada. Made in the 1930s, it wasn't released in this country until 1941, in order to evoke American support and sympathy for Britain's plight against the Nazi juggernaut during its darkest days. This is only one of the three films that united husband and wife Laurence Olivier and Vivien Leigh. B&W; 92m. **DIR:** Alexander Korda. **CAST:** Laurence Olivier, Vivien Leigh, Flora Robson. **1936**

FIRE WITH FIRE ★★ What hath Shakespeare wrought? The true story of a girl's Catholic school that invited the residents of a neighboring boy's reform school to a dance. Another good girl/bad boy melodrama wherein misunderstood teens triumph against all odds. Craig Sheffer and Virginia Madsen are appealing, but the plot is laughable. Rated PG-13 for mild sex and language. 103m. **DIR:** Duncan Gibbins. **CAST:** Craig Sheffer, Virginia Madsen, Jon Polito, Kate Reid, Jean Smart. **1986**

FIRE WITHIN, THE ★★★★ After his release from a sanatorium, a suicidal alcoholic looks for reasons not to kill himself. What sounds like a terribly depressing movie becomes a sharp study of a complex character in the hands of Louis Malle (who also scripted). In French with English subtitles. B&W; 121m. **DIR:** Louis Malle. **CAST:** Maurice Ronet, Lena Skerla, Jeanne Moreau, Alexandra Stewart. **1963**

FIREBIRD 2015 AD 🦃 In the near future, gas is so scarce that the government outlaws private ownership of automobiles and sets up an agency to destroy them. Rated PG. 97m. **DIR:** David Robertson. **CAST:** Darren McGavin, Doug McClure, George Touliatos. **1981**

FIRECREEK ★★★ When an easygoing farmer accepts the job of sheriff in a small town, he finds himself forced to stand up to a gang of ruthless outlaws. Like *The Cheyenne Social Club* before it, this downbeat Western is of interest only for the interplay of its top-billed stars—for some of us this is more than enough to make it worth watching. 104m. DIR: Vincent McEveety. CAST: James Stewart, Henry Fonda, Inger Stevens, Dean Jagger, Ed Begley Sr., Gary Lockwood, Jack Elam, Jay C. Flippen, Barbara Luna, James Best, Brooke Bundy, Morgan Woodward, John Quaien. 1968

FIREFLY, THE ★★★1/2 One of Jeanette MacDonald's most popular movies even though her perennial costar, Nelson Eddy, is not in it. This is the only film they made separately that clicked. Allan Jones gets to sing the film's best song, "Donkey Serenade." MacDonald gets to sing most of the others, including "Giannina Mia" and "Love Is Like a Firefly" from Rudolf Friml's 1912 operetta. B&W; 137m. DIR: Robert Z. Leonard. CAST: Jeanette MacDonald, Allan Jones, Warren William, Douglass Dumbrille, Billy Gilbert, George Zucco, Henry Daniell. 1937 .

FIREFOX ★★★1/2 Clint Eastwood doffs his contemporary cowboy garb to direct, produce, and star in this action-adventure film about an American fighter pilot assigned to steal a sophisticated Russian aircraft. The film takes a while to take off, but when it does, it's good, action-packed fun. Rated PG for violence. 124m. DIR: Clint Eastwood. CAST: Clint Eastwood, Freddie Jones, David Huffman, Warren Clarke, Ronald Lacey, Stefan Schnabel. 1982

FIREHAWK ★★ Walk through the park as survivors of a downed American helicopter platoon must contend with the oncoming Vietcong, plus the traitor among them with his own agenda. Plenty of action keeps this from being a total disaster. Rated R for violence and adult language. 92m. DIR: Cirio H. Santiago. CAST: Martin Kove, Vic Trevino, Matt Salinger, Terrence "T. C." Carson. 1992

FIREHEAD 🎬 A dopey Russian/CIA plot that sags even in the middle of low-budget telekinetic special effects. Rated R for language. 88m. DIR: Peter Yuval. CAST: Brett Porter, Gretchen Becker, Martin Landau, Christopher Plummer, Chris Lemmon. 1990

FIREHOUSE (1972) ★★ Rookie flame fighter Richard Roundtree saves face and his marriage amid the hostile big-city firehouse environment of racism. 80m. DIR: Alex March. CAST: Richard Roundtree, Andrew Duggan, Richard Jaeckel, Val Avery, Paul LeMat, Vince Edwards, Sheila Frazier. 1972

FIREHOUSE (1987) 🎬 *Charlie's Angels* clone set in a firehouse. Rated R. 91m. DIR: J. Christian Ingvordsen. CAST: Barrett Hopkins, Shannon Murphy, Violet Brown, John Anderson, Peter Onorati. 1987 DVD

FIRELIGHT ★★★★ This lush, haunting Victorian romance is a sort of Baby M meets *Jane Eyre*. It's about surrogate motherhood, parenting, and—rather bizarrely—euthanasia. In the 1830s, 22-year-old Swiss governess Elizabeth makes a secret pact with a British landowner to bear him an heir. Emotional and moral dilemmas emerge as Elizabeth discovers she cannot renounce her love for her child, and pragmatic life-shaping decisions begin bouncing like bad checks. Rated R for simulated sex, nudity, and language. 104m. DIR: William Nicholson. CAST: Sophie Marceau, Stephen Dillane, Dominique Belcourt. 1998

FIREMAN'S BALL, THE ★★1/2 Highly acclaimed comedy of a small-town firemen's gathering that turns into a sprawling, ludicrous disaster. Fairly weak considering direction by Milos Forman. In Czech with English subtitles. 73m. DIR: Milos Forman. CAST: Jan Vostricil. 1968

FIREPOWER (1979) ★★ *Firepower* is a muddled, mindless mess. A research chemist is blown up by a letter bomb while his wife, Sophia Loren, watches helplessly. The chemist was about to prove that a company owned by the third-richest man in the world, Carl Stegner (George Touliatos), has been distributing drugs responsible for causing the cancerous deaths of many people. The widow joins Justice Department agent James Coburn in trying to bring Stegner out of seclusion. Rated R. 104m. DIR: Michael Winner. CAST: Sophia Loren, James Coburn, O. J. Simpson, Eli Wallach, Vincent Gardenia, Anthony Franciosa, George Touliatos. 1979

FIREPOWER (1993) 🎬 Two cops infiltrate a crime-ridden section of twenty-first-century Los Angeles on the trail of a crime lord who arranges no-holds-barred death matches. Rated R for violence. 94m. DIR: Richard Pepin. CAST: Chad McQueen, Gary Daniels, Joseph Ruskin, Jim Hellwig. 1993

FIRES ON THE PLAIN ★★★★ Kon Ichikawa's classic uses World War II and soldiers' cannibalism as symbols for the brutality of man. This film is uncomplicated and its emotion intensely focused, giving it a stark and disturbing vision. In Japanese with English subtitles. 105m. DIR: Kon Ichikawa. CAST: Eiji Funakoshi. 1959

FIRES WITHIN ★★ Boring love triangle involving an American fisherman, a Cuban refugee, and a Cuban political prisoner. Writer Cynthia Cidre failed to create a film with either believable characters and/or an engaging plot. 90m. DIR: Gillian Armstrong. CAST: Jimmy Smits, Greta Scacchi, Vincent D'Onofrio, Luis Avalos. 1991

FIRESTARTER ★★★1/2 Stephen King writhes again. This time, Drew Barrymore stars as the gifted (or is that haunted) child of the title, who has the ability—sometimes uncontrollable—to ignite objects around her. David Keith is the father who tries to protect her from the baddies. Suspenseful, poignant, and sometimes frightening entertainment that goes beyond its genre. Rated R for violence. 115m. DIR: Mark L. Lester. CAST: David Keith, Drew Barrymore, George C. Scott, Martin Sheen. 1984 DVD

FIRESTORM ★★ This gloriously hokey disaster-action movie is an unintentional hoot. Smoke-jumper Jesse Graves parachutes into forests with an elite squad of firefighters armed with shovels, axes, and chain saws. Oozing more sap than the surrounding pines, the story begins with the rescue of a little girl and her dog from a doomed rural cabin. It lamely shifts into thriller mode as Jesse tries to save a female ornithologist from a prison escapee and a rampant forest inferno. Rated R for language and violence. 89m. DIR: Dean Semler. CAST: Howie Long, William Forsythe, Suzy Amis, Scott Glenn. 1998 DVD

FIREWALKER 🗨 Two soldiers of fortune search for hidden treasure and end up in a Mayan temple of doom. Rated PG. 96m. DIR: J. Lee Thompson. CAST: Chuck Norris, Lou Gossett Jr., Melody Anderson, John Rhys-Davies. 1986

FIREWORKS ★★★★ Japanese cop Nishi splits his time between *yakuza* stakeouts and vigils at his cancer-stricken wife's hospital bed before fine-tuning his own destiny. Nishi retires from the police force after a shoot-out leaves fellow officers dead and crippled. The incident and its aftermath are revisited in flashbacks as he takes his spouse on a doctor-prescribed vacation. This combination crime-thriller and melodrama is tender, savage, explosive, languid, comic, and poetic. In Japanese with English subtitles. Not rated; contains violence and profanity. 103m. DIR: Takeshi Kitano. CAST: Takeshi Kitano, Kayoko Kishimoto, Ren Osugi, Susumu Terajima, Tetsu Watanabe. 1997 DVD

FIRING LINE, THE ★★ Amateurish effort from writer-director John Gale about a rebel uprising in a South American country. Rated R for violence. 98m. DIR: John Gale. CAST: Reb Brown, Shannon Tweed, Carl Terry. 1991 DVD

FIRM, THE ★★★★ Director Sydney Pollack takes the old-style Hollywood approach in this adaptation of John Grisham's bestselling suspense-thriller by surrounding star Tom Cruise with a top-flight cast of supporting actors—and it works. Cruise plays an ambitious young lawyer who joins a law firm in Memphis only to find that his high salary and impressive perks come with a price: either go along with the company's corrupt dealings or become its next victim. Gripping. Rated R for profanity, violence, and suggested sex. 154m. DIR: Sydney Pollack. CAST: Tom Cruise, Gene Hackman, Jeanne Tripplehorn, Ed Harris, Holly Hunter, Hal Holbrook, David Strathairn, Wilford Brimley, Gary Busey. 1993 DVD

FIRST AFFAIR ★★★ Melissa Sue Anderson stars as a naïve Harvard scholarship student. She finds herself romantically inclined toward her English professor's husband. A strong entourage of actors helps make this an insightful commentary about the difficulties of keeping a marriage together, and the pain of losing one's innocence. Made for television. 100m. DIR: Gus Trikonis. CAST: Loretta Swit, Melissa Sue Anderson, Joel Higgins, Charley Lang, Kim Delaney, Amanda Bearse. 1983

FIRST AND TEN ★★1/2 A pilot for the Home Box Office series of the same name, this football satire chronicles the hapless exploits of a West Coast team. Its locker room humor may limit it to an adult audience, but there are sufficient laughs. 97m. DIR: Donald Kushner. CAST: Fran Tarkenton, Geoffrey Scott, Reid Shelton, Ruta Lee, Delta Burke. 1985

FIRST BLOOD ★★★1/2 Sylvester Stallone is top-notch as a former Green Beret who is forced to defend himself from a redneck cop (Brian Dennehy) in the Oregon mountains. The action never lets up. A winner for fans. Rated R for violence and profanity. 97m. DIR: Ted Kotcheff. CAST: Sylvester Stallone,

Richard Crenna, Brian Dennehy, David Caruso, Jack Starrett. 1982 DVD

FIRST DEADLY SIN, THE ★★ Lawrence Sanders's excellent mystery is turned into a so-so cop flick with Frank Sinatra looking bored as aging Detective Edward X. Delaney, on the trail of a murdering maniac (David Dukes). Costar Faye Dunaway spends the entire picture flat on her back in a hospital bed. Rated R. 112m. DIR: Brian G. Hutton. CAST: Frank Sinatra, Faye Dunaway, James Whitmore, David Dukes, Brenda Vaccaro, Martin Gabel, Anthony Zerbe. 1980 DVD

FIRST DEGREE ★★ Rob Lowe is actually pretty good as a charming cop who wins the affections of a gorgeous widow when he investigates her husband's murder. Questions surface about possible suspects including the mob, the not-very-grief-stricken wife, and even the investigator. The plot takes a few extra zags, leaving us merely perplexed, and the ending creates just one more puzzle. Rated R for nudity, violence, and profanity. 98m. DIR: Jeff Woolnough. CAST: Rob Lowe, Leslie Hope, Tom McCamus, Joseph Griffin. 1995

... FIRST DO NO HARM ★★1/2 A Midwestern couple nearly lose everything they have when their 4-year-old son develops epilepsy. Director Jim Abrahams made this TV movie inspired by his own son's experience with epilepsy and with doctors whose reliance on debilitating drugs causes more harm than good. But too much of the story plays like a self-righteous indictment of doctors and an infomercial for the ketogenic diet. Not rated. 94m. DIR: Jim Abrahams. CAST: Meryl Streep, Fred Ward, Seth Adkins, Allison Janney. 1997

FIRST FAMILY 🗨 Unfunny farce about an inept president, his family, and his aides. Rated R. 104m. DIR: Buck Henry. CAST: Bob Newhart, Gilda Radner, Madeline Kahn, Richard Benjamin, Harvey Korman, Bob Dishy, Rip Torn. 1980

FIRST KID ★★ Sinbad's larger-than-life persona is wasted on this inert fluff fest. The contrast between his electric personality and the somberness of his fellow secret agents provides the film's running joke. A heartwarming relationship develops between him and his young charge as Sinbad provides the fathering the president has neglected to do. Oddly, it takes Timothy Busfield's dramatic pathos to wake up viewers, which says little for a comedy. Rated PG for violence. 97m. DIR: David Mickey Evans. CAST: Sinbad, Brock Pierce, Timothy Busfield, Robert Guillaume, Zachery Ty Bryan. 1996

FIRST KNIGHT ★★★★ Apart from the anachronistic performance by Richard Gere as a kung-fu-fighting(!) Lancelot, this is a memorable retelling of the King Arthur legend, with its emphasis on a historical, romantic approach as opposed to fantasy. Director Jerry Zucker keeps it big and impressive, developing his characters in a believable fashion. Rated PG-13 for violence. 133m. DIR: Jerry Zucker. CAST: Sean Connery, Richard Gere, Julia Ormond, Ben Cross, John Gielgud. 1995 DVD

FIRST LOVE (1939) ★★★ Cute Deanna Durbin take on a "modern" Cinderella story. She's the orphaned and unwanted niece forced to live with wealthy relatives; Robert Stack is the rich kid who steals her heart and gives Deanna her first screen kiss. Funnier than you'd expect, but some viewers may find Durbin's brand of music annoyingly dated. Not rated. B&W; 85m. **DIR:** Henry Koster. **CAST:** Deanna Durbin, Robert Stack, Eugene Pallette, Helen Parrish. **1939**

FIRST LOVE (1977) ★★ A somber movie about a college student who is unlucky in love. While the film has an interesting cast, sharp dialogue, and a refreshingly honest story, it's basically muddleheaded. Rated R for nudity and language. 92m. **DIR:** Joan Darling. **CAST:** William Katt, Susan Dey, John Heard, Beverly D'Angelo, Robert Loggia. **1977**

FIRST MAN INTO SPACE, THE ★★1/2 An arrogant test pilot is mutated, by cosmic rays, into a blood-hungry monster. Although it's dated and scientifically incorrect, this sci-fi chiller still has some B-film fun. Not rated, but suitable for all viewers. B&W; 78m. **DIR:** Robert Day. **CAST:** Marshall Thompson. **1958 DVD**

FIRST MEN *IN* THE MOON ★★★1/2 This whimsical adaptation of an H. G. Wells novel benefits greatly from the imaginative genius of Ray Harryhausen, who concocts the critters—stop-motion and otherwise—that menace some turn-of-the-century lunar explorers who arrive via a Victorian-era spaceship. Although the tone is initially tongue-in-cheek, this adventurous plot eventually develops some rather chilling teeth. Not rated, but great fun for the entire family. 103m. **DIR:** Nathan Juran. **CAST:** Edward Judd, Martha Hyer, Lionel Jeffries, Peter Finch. **1964**

FIRST MONDAY IN OCTOBER ★★★ This is a Walter Matthau picture, with all the joys that implies. As he did in *Hopscotch*, director Ronald Neame allows Matthau, who plays a crusty Supreme Court justice, to make the most of every screen moment. Jill Clayburgh plays the first woman appointed to the Supreme Court. Rated R for nudity and profanity. 98m. **DIR:** Ronald Neame. **CAST:** Walter Matthau, Jill Clayburgh, Barnard Hughes, Jan Sterling. **1981**

FIRST NAME: CARMEN ★★★ Jean-Luc Godard does a fabulous job portraying an eccentric filmmaker whose niece has hired him to direct a movie; actually, she is using him as a front for a terrorist attack. Slow-moving at times. In French with English subtitles. Not rated; contains profanity and nudity. 85m. **DIR:** Jean-Luc Godard. **CAST:** Maruschka Detmers, Jacques Bonnaffe, Myriem Roussel, Jean-Luc Godard. **1983 DVD**

FIRST 9 WEEKS, THE ★★ Prequel in name only, this is a somber tale of a New York currency trader who winds up in New Orleans to seal a deal with a billionaire. Instead, he strikes up an affair with the billionaire's wife, and is then framed for murder by the jealous husband. Ho hum. People don't rent these for the plot; the performances aren't much better. Malcolm McDowell delivers his trademark sneer as the bad guy. Rated R for adult situations, nudity, language, and violence. 104m. **DIR:** Alexander Wright. **CAST:** Malcolm McDowell, Paul Mercurio, Clara Bellar. **1998 DVD**

FIRST NUDIE MUSICAL, THE ★★★ A struggling young director saves the studio by producing the world's first pornographic movie musical à la Busby Berkeley. Pleasant but extremely crude little romp. Not as bad as it sounds, but definitely for the very open-minded, and that's being generous. Rated R for nudity. 100m. **DIR:** Mark Haggard. **CAST:** Bruce Kimmel, Stephen Nathan, Cindy Williams, Diana Canova. **1979**

FIRST POWER, THE 🖤 Repulsive thing-that-wouldn't-die trash. Rated R. 100m. **DIR:** Robert Resnikoff. **CAST:** Lou Diamond Phillips, Tracy Griffith, Jeff Kober, Mykelti Williamson, Dennis Lipscomb. **1990**

FIRST TIME, THE ★★★ With parents pushing poor Charlie into a relationship with a girl—any girl!—he resists. But when he gets into filmmaking, the opposite sex goes mad for him. This campus comedy is rated PG-13 for mature situations and language. 96m. **DIR:** Charlie Loventhal. **CAST:** Tim Choate, Krista Erickson, Wallace Shawn, Wendie Jo Sperber. **1982**

FIRST TIME FELON ★★★1/2 Daniel Thierrault's script is a fact-based account of an insolent gangbanger who, arrested on a minor charge and given the opportunity to avoid jail by attending a rehabilitation boot camp, learns personal integrity but then finds that the world at large still dismisses him as an ex-convict. It's tough sledding for the first fifteen minutes, during which you won't care at all for the violent thugs, but the story quickly improves. Rated R for profanity, drug use, and violence. 105m. **DIR:** Charles S. Dutton. **CAST:** Omar Epps, Delroy Lindo, Rachel Ticotin, Justin Pierce, William Forsythe. **1997**

FIRST TURN-ON, THE 🖤 This cheapie features four campers and their counselor trapped in a cave seeking amusement. Not rated; contains nudity and profanity and sexual situations. 88m. **DIR:** Michael Herz, Samuel Weil. **CAST:** Michael Sanville. **1983**

FIRST WIVES CLUB, THE ★★★★ The ladies get their revenge in this delightful adaptation of Olivia Goldsmith's bestselling novel. Well-heeled Manhattanites Bette Midler, Goldie Hawn, and Diane Keaton all have been left by husbands now squiring much younger bimbos. Refusing to roll over and play dead, the spurned women concoct elaborate schemes to regain financial control from their ex-husbands. Overall this is gender humor at its funniest, with Midler positively stealing the show. Rated PG for mild profanity. 104m. **DIR:** Hugh Wilson. **CAST:** Bette Midler, Goldie Hawn, Diane Keaton, Maggie Smith, Dan Hedaya, Bronson Pinchot, Jennie Dundas, Eileen Heckart, Stephen Collins, Elizabeth Berkeley, Marcia Gay Harden, Sarah Jessica Parker. **1996 DVD**

FIRST WORKS, VOLUMES 1 & 2 ★★1/2 Each volume contains commercial film clips, candid interviews, and the student films of top Hollywood directors. While the interviews are old, and many of the clips and photographs are faded, it's worth watching for the student films, if you can stand the bargain-basement production values. Not rated; contains profanity. B&W/color; 120m. each **DIR:** Robert Kline. **CAST:** Roger Corman, Taylor Hackford, Spike Lee, Paul Mazursky, Oliver Stone, Robert Zemeckis, John Carpenter, Richard Donner, Ron Howard, John Milius, Martin Scorsese, Susan Seidelman. **1995**

FIRST YANK INTO TOKYO 🖤 Tom Neal has plastic surgery so he can pose as a Japanese soldier and help an American POW escape. B&W; 82m. **DIR:** Goron Douglas. **CAST:** Tom Neal, Barbara Hale, Richard Loo, Keye Luke, Benson Fong. **1945**

FIRSTBORN ★★★★ An emotionally charged screen drama that deftly examines some topical, thought-provoking themes, this stars Teri Garr as a divorced woman who gets involved with the wrong man (Peter Weller) to the horror of her two sons. Rated PG for profanity and violence. 100m. **DIR:** Michael Apted. **CAST:** Teri Garr, Peter Weller. **1984**

FISH CALLED WANDA, A ★★★★1/2 Monty Python veteran John Cleese wrote and starred in this hilarious caper comedy. Jamie Lee Curtis and Kevin Kline are American crooks who plot to double-cross their British partners in crime (Michael Palin and Tom Georgeson) with the unwitting help of barrister Cleese. Be forewarned: *Wanda* has something in it to offend everyone. Rated R for profanity and violence. 108m. **DIR:** Charles Crichton. **CAST:** John Cleese, Jamie Lee Curtis, Kevin Kline, Michael Palin, Tom Georgeson, Patricia Hayes. **1988 DVD**

FISH HAWK ★★★ Excellent drama about an Indian (Will Sampson) who befriends a young farm boy in turn-of-the-century rural America. Sampson has a drinking problem, which he kicks in an effort to return to his former life. Rated G; contains very mild profanity. 95m. **DIR:** Donald Shebib. **CAST:** Will Sampson, Don Francks, Charles Fields, Chris Wiggins. **1984**

FISH THAT SAVED PITTSBURGH, THE ★★1/2 Curious mixture of disco, astrology, and comedy. A failing basketball team turns to a rather eccentric medium for help, and the resulting confusion makes for a few amusing moments. Features a veritable smorgasbord of second-rate actors, from Jonathan Winters to basketball great Julius Irving (Dr. J.). Proceed at your own risk. Rated PG for profanity. 102m. **DIR:** Gilbert Moses. **CAST:** Stockard Channing, Flip Wilson, Jonathan Winters, Julius Erving. **1979**

FISHER KING, THE ★★★★1/2 Jack Lucas is a radio talk-show host whose irreverent manner indirectly causes a tragedy; his remorse plunges him into an alcoholic haze. Enter a street person named Parry, who involves Jack in a quest for the Holy Grail in New York City. This adult-oriented fairy tale will win the hearts of those who haven't lost their sense of wonder. Rated R for profanity, nudity, and violence. 137m. **DIR:** Terry Gilliam. **CAST:** Robin Williams, Jeff Bridges, Mercedes Ruehl, Amanda Plummer, Michael Jeter. **1991 DVD**

F.I.S.T. ★★ It's too bad that *F.I.S.T.* is so predictable and cliché-ridden, because Sylvester Stallone gives a fine performance. As Johnny Kovak, leader of the Federation of Interstate Truckers, he creates an even more poignant character than Rocky Balboa. It is ironic that Stallone, after being favorably compared with Marlon Brando, should end up in a film so similar to *On the Waterfront* ... and with Rod Steiger yet! Rated PG. 145m. **DIR:** Norman Jewison. **CAST:** Sylvester Stallone, Rod Steiger, Peter Boyle, Melinda Dillon, David Huffman, Tony Lo Bianco. **1978**

FIST FIGHTER ★★ A drifter (Jorge Rivero) heads to Central America to avenge a friend's murder. For fans of two-fisted action-oriented movies. Rated R

for violence. 99m. **DIR:** Frank Zuniga. **CAST:** Jorge Rivero, Mike Connors, Edward Albert. **1988**

FIST OF IRON ★★ Strictly for the kick-boxing and martial arts set. There's enough mayhem in this tale of a fight-to-the-death match and the men who enter to satisfy fans of the genre. Rated R for extreme violence. 94m. **DIR:** Richard W. Munchkin. **CAST:** Michael Worth, Matthias Hues, Sam Jones, Marshall Teague, Jenilee Harrison. **1994**

FIST OF STEEL ♥ A futuristic gladiator battles rivals for survival in a postapocalyptic world. Not rated; contains violence, profanity, nudity, substance abuse, and sexual situations. 97m. **DIR:** Irvin Johnson. **CAST:** Dale "Apollo" Cook, Gregg Douglass, Cynthia Khan, Don Nakaya Nielsen. **1993**

FIST OF THE NORTH STAR (1986) ★★1/2 Japanese animation. Extreme violence is the main plot ingredient in this animated post-apocalyptic kung fu epic wherein a trio of brothers vie for the title of "Fist of the North Star." Released in some U.S. theatrical markets, probably because of the unrivaled spectacle of animated carnage. 110m. **DIR:** Toyoo Ashida. **1986 DVD**

FIST OF THE NORTH STAR (1995) ♥ Ultraviolent and incoherent live-action adaptation of the postapocalyptic Japanese animated series; if this stuff appeals to you, stick with the original. Rated R for violence, profanity, and gore. 88m. **DIR:** Tony Randel. **CAST:** Gary Daniels, Costas Mandylor, Christopher Penn, Isako Washio, Melvin Van Peebles, Malcolm McDowell. **1995 DVD**

FISTFUL OF DOLLARS, A ★★★ Clint Eastwood parlayed his multi-year stint on television's *Rawhide* into international fame with this film, a slick remake of Akira Kurosawa's *Yojimbo*. Eastwood's laconic "Man With No Name" blows into a town nearly blown apart by two feuding families; after considerable manipulation by all concerned, he moves on down the road. 96m. **DIR:** Sergio Leone. **CAST:** Clint Eastwood, Mario Brega, Gian Maria Volonté. **1964 DVD**

FISTFUL OF DYNAMITE, A ★★★ After his success with Clint Eastwood's "Man with No Name" Westerns, Sergio Leone made this sprawling, excessive film set during the Mexican revolution. A thief, played by Rod Steiger, is drawn into the revolution by Irish mercenary James Coburn. Soon both are blowing up everything in sight and single-handedly winning the war. 121m. **DIR:** Sergio Leone. **CAST:** Rod Steiger, James Coburn, Maria Monti, Romolo Valli. **1972**

FISTS OF FURY ★★★ Bruce Lee's first chop-socky movie (made in Hong Kong) is corny, action-filled, and violent. It's no *Enter the Dragon*, but his fans—who have so few films to choose from—undoubtedly will want to see it again. Rated R. 102m. **DIR:** Lo Wei. **CAST:** Bruce Lee, Maria Yi, James Tien, Nora Miao. **1972 DVD**

FIT TO KILL ♥ Filmmaker Andy Sidaris continues his series of female spy movies, which usually serve as just an excuse to get women out of their clothes. This one has less flesh than usual, so there's nothing to watch at all. Rated R for nudity, violence, and adult situations. 94m. **DIR:** Andy Sidaris. **CAST:** Dona

Speir, Roberta Vasquez, Julie Strain, Cynthia Brimhall. 1993

FITZCARRALDO ★★★1/2 For Werner Herzog, the making of this film was reportedly quite an ordeal. Watching it may be an ordeal for some viewers as well. In order to bring Caruso, the greatest voice in the world, to the backwater town of Iquitos, the title character (Klaus Kinski) decides to haul a large boat over a mountain. Not rated; this film has profanity. In German with English subtitles. 157m. **DIR:** Werner Herzog. **CAST:** Klaus Kinski, Claudia Cardinale. 1982 DVD

FIVE BLOODY GRAVES ★★ Somewhat imaginative as Death narrates the tale of an odd mix of travelers pursued across the desert by a savage band of Indians. Extreme violence. Also titled: *Gun Riders* and *Lonely Man.* 81m. **DIR:** Al Adamson. **CAST:** Robert Dix, Scott Brady, Jim Davis, John Carradine. 1969

FIVE CAME BACK ★★★ A plane carrying the usual mixed bag of passengers goes down in the jungle. Only five of the group will survive. The cast, fine character players all, makes this melodrama worthwhile, though it shows its age. B&W; 75m. **DIR:** John Farrow. **CAST:** Chester Morris, Wendy Barrie, John Carradine, Allen Jenkins, Joseph Calleia, C. Aubrey Smith, Patric Knowles, Lucille Ball. 1939

FIVE CARD STUD ★★1/2 Muddled Western with a whodunit motif. Gambler-gunfighter Dean Martin attempts to discover who is systematically murdering the members of a lynching party. Robert Mitchum adds some memorable moments as a gun-toting preacher, but most of the performances are lifeless, with Roddy McDowall's gunslinger the most ludicrous of all. This is far from top-notch Henry Hathaway. 103m. **DIR:** Henry Hathaway. **CAST:** Dean Martin, Robert Mitchum, Inger Stevens, Roddy McDowall, Katherine Justice, Yaphet Kotto, Denver Pyle. 1968

FIVE CORNERS ★★★1/2 Most viewers will feel a little *Moonstruck* after watching this bizarre comedy-drama written by John Patrick Shanley. Jodie Foster stars as a young woman who attempts to get help from the tough-guy-turned-pacifist (Tim Robbins) who saved her from being raped by an unhinged admirer (John Turturro) when the latter is released from prison. Moments of suspense and hard-edged realism are effectively mixed with bits of offbeat comedy. Rated R for violence and adult themes. 92m. **DIR:** Tony Bill. **CAST:** Jodie Foster, Tim Robbins, John Turturro. 1988 DVD

◆5 DARK SOULS ★★1/2 Modest little chiller tells of three wannabes who are led into the woods by the high school's most popular clique, a group of five teens with plans of putting the trio in a snuff movie. This risqué film treads the line between trash and respectability, and manages to come across fairly well. Not rated; contains violence. 90m. **DIR:** Jason Paul Collum. **CAST:** Tina Ona Paukstelis, Matthew Winkler, Christopher D. Harder. 1996

FIVE DAYS ONE SUMMER ★★★ This is an old-fashioned romance, with Sean Connery as a mountain climber caught in a triangle involving his lovely niece and a handsome young guide. Two handkerchiefs and a liking for soap operas are suggested.

Rated PG for adult situations. 108m. **DIR:** Fred Zinnemann. **CAST:** Sean Connery, Anna Massey, Betsy Brantley, Lambert Wilson. 1983

5 DEAD ON THE CRIMSON CANVAS ★★ Ambitious production tries to pay homage to the Italian *giallo* films but doesn't succeed. The pieces are all there, but nothing seems to work well together. Not rated; contains violence and profanity. 96m. **DIR:** Joseph A. Parda. **CAST:** Liz Haverty, Joseph Zaso, Mony Damevsky. 1996

FIVE EASY PIECES ★★★★1/2 Shattering drama concerns Jack Nicholson's return to his family home after years of self-imposed exile. Playing a once promising pianist who chose to work in the oil fields, Nicholson has rarely been better; his fully shaded character with its explosions of emotion are a wonder to behold. One of the gems of the Seventies. The chicken-salad scene in the diner is now a classic. Rated R. 90m. **DIR:** Bob Rafelson. **CAST:** Jack Nicholson, Karen Black, Susan Anspach, Billy Green Bush, Sally Struthers, Ralph Waite, Fannie Flagg. 1970 DVD

FIVE FINGERS ★★★1/2 James Mason, the trusted valet to the British ambassador in World War II Ankara, sells government secrets to the Germans. He gets rich but does no harm as the Germans mistakenly think he is a double agent and take no action on the material he gives them. It seems farfetched, but it's based on fact. Wonderful suspense. Also released as *Operation Cicero.* B&W; 108m. **DIR:** Joseph L. Mankiewicz. **CAST:** James Mason, Danielle Darrieux, Michael Rennie, Walter Hampden. 1952

FIVE GOLDEN DRAGONS 🎬 An innocent man runs into an international crime ring in Hong Kong. Boring, poorly made adventure. 93m. **DIR:** Jeremy Summers. **CAST:** Robert Cummings, Rupert Davies, Margaret Lee, Brian Donlevy, Christopher Lee, George Raft, Dan Duryea. 1967

FIVE GOLDEN HOURS ★★★ Ernie Kovacs is hilarious as a professional mourner who lives off the generosity of grieving widows. Things become complicated when he falls for penniless Italian baroness Cyd Charisse. B&W; 89m. **DIR:** Mario Zampi. **CAST:** Ernie Kovacs, Cyd Charisse, Dennis Price, John Le Mesurier, Kay Hammond, George Sanders. 1961

FIVE GRAVES TO CAIRO ★★★ A British officer schemes to outwit Field Marshall Rommel by posing as a waiter at a desert outpost where Rommel is visiting. The great Billy Wilder's second film as a director is a fairly standard espionage tale that seems out of place in his body of work, though traces of his usual themes can be spotted. B&W; 96m. **DIR:** Billy Wilder. **CAST:** Franchot Tone, Anne Baxter, Erich Von Stroheim. 1943

FIVE HEARTBEATS, THE ★★★★★ Everything is just right with writer-director Robert Townsend's musical–comedy–drama about the rise and fall of a 1960s soul group. Townsend gets excellent performances from his actors (especially Michael Wright) and always manages to put an unexpected twist on the often-too-familiar show-biz story. Rated R for profanity and violence. 120m. **DIR:** Robert Townsend. **CAST:** Robert Townsend, Michael Wright, Leon, Harry J. Lennix, Tico Wells, Diahann Carroll, Harold Nicholas, Tressa Thomas, John Terrell. 1991

FIVE PENNIES, THE ★★★ A lively biography of jazzman Red Nichols with his contemporaries playing themselves in the jam sessions. The story line is a little sticky as it deals with family tragedies as well as triumphs. But the music is great, and there are twenty-five musical numbers. Red Nichols dubbed the soundtrack, and that's a bonus when he and Louis Armstrong are duetting. 117m. DIR: Melville Shavelson. CAST: Danny Kaye, Barbara Bel Geddes, Tuesday Weld, Louis Armstrong, Bob Crosby, Ray Anthony, Shelley Manne, Bobby Troup, Harry Guardino. 1959

FIVE WEEKS IN A BALLOON ★★★ Up, up, and away on a balloon expedition to Africa, or, Kenya here we come! Author Jules Verne wrote the story. Nothing heavy here, just good, clean fun and adventure in the mold of *Around the World in Eighty Days*. 101m. DIR: Irwin Allen. CAST: Red Buttons, Barbara Eden, Fabian, Cedric Hardwicke, Peter Lorre, Herbert Marshall, Billy Gilbert, Reginald Owen, Henry Daniell, Barbara Luna, Richard Haydn. 1962

FIFTY/FIFTY ★★★ Peter Weller and Robert Hays star as former CIA operatives, now mercenaries on opposite sides of a bloody civil war. Treachery and betrayal soon force them to trust only each other, especially when the CIA sends troubleshooter Charles Martin Smith to get them to organize a rebellion. Rated R for nudity, violence, and profanity. 101m. DIR: Charles Martin Smith. CAST: Peter Weller, Robert Hays, Charles Martin Smith. 1993

52 PICK-UP ★1/2 Generally unentertaining tale of money, blackmail, and pornography, as adapted from Elmore Leonard's story. Roy Scheider's secret fling with Kelly Preston leads to big-time blackmail and murder. It's more cards than Scheider could ever pick up, and a more mean and nasty movie than most people will want to watch. Rated R for nudity, profanity, simulated sex, and violence. 111m. DIR: John Frankenheimer. CAST: Roy Scheider, Ann-Margret, Vanity, John Glover, Clarence Williams III, Kelly Preston. 1986 DVD

54 ★★ The rise and fall of Studio 54, the trendy Manhattan disco of the 1970s and 1980s, provides the background for a timid rehash of *Saturday Night Fever*. The story is trite, the characters are uninteresting, even the disco music on the soundtrack is boring. The film's only asset is Mike Myers as club owner Steve Rubell; too bad the film wasn't about him instead. Rated R for profanity, drug use, and sexual scenes. 89m. DIR: Mark Christopher. CAST: Ryan Phillippe, Salma Hayek, Neve Campbell, Mike Myers. 1998

55 DAYS AT PEKING ★★ A lackluster big-screen adventure about the Boxer Revolt in 1900. Charlton Heston, David Niven, and the rest of the large cast seem made of wood. 150m. DIR: Nicholas Ray. CAST: Charlton Heston, Ava Gardner, David Niven, John Ireland. 1963

FIFTH AVENUE GIRL ★★ Limp social comedy features Ginger Rogers as a homeless but levelheaded young lady who is taken in by Walter Connolly, one of those unhappy movie-land millionaires who is just dying to find someone to lavish gifts on. B&W; 83m. DIR: Gregory La Cava. CAST: Ginger Rogers, Walter Connolly, Verree Teasdale, Tim Holt, James Ellison, Kathryn Adams. 1939

FIFTH ELEMENT, THE ★★★1/2 This hyperkinetic sci-fi thriller doesn't score for logic or coherence, but it sure knows how to dazzle and excite. Twenty-third-century cabbie Bruce Willis gets involved with a gorgeous extraterrestrial who holds the key to saving the universe. The two dodge nasty aliens, befriend a befuddled priest and a manic media talk-show host, all while staying one step ahead of the dangerously insane villain. You may hate yourself in the morning, but you'll have to admit this is a lot of fun. Rated PG-13 for nudity, violence, and profanity. 127m. DIR: Luc Besson. CAST: Bruce Willis, Gary Oldman, Ian Holm, Milla Jovovich, Chris Tucker, Luke Perry, Brion James. 1997 DVD

FIFTH FLOOR, THE 🐝 College lass is mistakenly popped into an insane asylum. Rated R for violence and nudity. 90m. DIR: Howard Avedis. CAST: Bo Hopkins, Dianne Hull, Patti D'Arbanville, Mel Ferrer, Sharon Farrell. 1980

FIFTH MONKEY, THE ★★★ Ben Kingsley is upstaged by four chimpanzees in this uplifting adventure. Kingsley plays a Brazilian peasant desperately trying to earn enough money to marry the woman he loves by selling snakeskins. Rated PG-13 for violence. 93m. DIR: Eric Rochat. CAST: Ben Kingsley. 1990

FIFTH MUSKETEER, THE ★★ An uninspired retelling of *The Man in the Iron Mask*. Beau Bridges is watchable enough as King Louis XIV and his twin brother, Philipe, who was raised as a peasant by D'Artagnan (Cornel Wilde) and the Three Musketeers (Lloyd Bridges, José Ferrer, and Alan Hale Jr.). The film never springs to life. Rated PG. 103m. DIR: Ken Annakin. CAST: Beau Bridges, Sylvia Kristel, Ursula Andress, Cornel Wilde, Olivia de Havilland, José Ferrer, Rex Harrison, Lloyd Bridges, Alan Hale Jr. 1979

FIVE THOUSAND FINGERS OF DR. T, THE ★★★★ A delightful fantasy about children. Tommy Rettig would rather play baseball than practice the piano. Hans Conried plays Dr. Terwilliker, the piano teacher who gives the kid nightmares. Dr. Seuss cowrote the script. 89m. DIR: Roy Rowland. CAST: Hans Conried, Mary Healy, Peter Lind Hayes, Henry Kulky, Tommy Rettig. 1952

FIVE MILLION YEARS TO EARTH ★★★★ The best of the big-screen *Quatermass* adventures has the professor and his colleagues investigating the discovery of an alien craft buried in London. While the special effects may appear somewhat quaint today, the solid writing and performances make it rewarding for open-minded viewers. This sequel to *The Creeping Unknown* and *Enemy from Space* was released as *Quatermass and the Pit* in England. The series ends with the made-for-TV *Quatermass Conclusion*. Rated PG. 98m. DIR: Roy Ward Baker. CAST: James Donald, Barbara Shelley, Andrew Keir, Julian Glover, Maurice Good. 1968

FIX, THE 🐝 Tedious film about drug dealers. Not rated, has violence. 95m. DIR: Will Zens. CAST: Vince Edwards, Tony Dale, Richard Jaeckel, Julie Hill, Byron Cherry, Charles Dierkop, Don Dubbins, Leslie Leah, Robert Tessier. 1984

FIXER, THE ★★1/2 Writer-director Charles Robert Carner's saga of high-level corruption and political intrigue in Chicago is nothing new and seems to exist only because star-producer Jon Voight wanted a project that would allow him to blossom from an evil man into a repentant hero. He plays a longtime "arranger" of corrupt deals who experiences an epiphany after a near-crippling accident. Rated R for profanity, violence, nudity, simulated sex, and gore. 105m. **DIR:** Charles Robert Carner. **CAST:** Jon Voight, Brenda Bakke, J. J. Johnston, Miguel Sandoval, Brent Jennings. 1997

FLAME AND THE ARROW, THE ★★★★ Burt Lancaster is at his acrobatic, tongue-in-cheek best in this film as a Robin Hood–like hero in Italy leading his oppressed countrymen to victory. It's a rousing swashbuckler. 88m. **DIR:** Jacques Tourneur. **CAST:** Burt Lancaster, Virginia Mayo, Nick Cravat. 1950

FLAME OF THE BARBARY COAST ★★1/2 John Wayne plays a Montana rancher who fights with a saloon owner (Joseph Schildkraut) over the affections of a dance hall girl (Ann Dvorak). It's watchable, nothing more. B&W; 91m. **DIR:** Joseph Kane. **CAST:** John Wayne, Ann Dvorak, William Frawley, Joseph Schildkraut. 1945

FLAME OVER INDIA ★★★★1/2 Rip-snorting adventure film has British officer Kenneth More and American governess Lauren Bacall escorting a young Hindu prince to safety during a political and religious uprising. J. Lee Thompson's flawless direction, a fine script, and terrific performances make this little-known film a classic. 130m. **DIR:** J. Lee Thompson. **CAST:** Lauren Bacall, Kenneth More, Herbert Lom, Wilfrid Hyde-White, I. S. Johar, Ian Hunter. 1959

FLAME TO THE PHOENIX, A ★★ On the eve of Hitler's invasion of Poland, British diplomats plan their strategy while the Polish underground prepares for a long, bloody struggle. This talky drama is hard to follow, with characters of various nationalities all speaking with British accents. Not rated, the movie contains brief nudity and sexual situations. 80m. **DIR:** William Brayne. **CAST:** Frederick Treves, Ann Firbank. 1983

FLAMENCO ★★1/2 This concert performance of flamenco song and dance is superbly photographed, and there are moments when it blazes with startling, ferocious grace. Unfortunately, the singing dominates the dance and guitar playing, and the sparse subtitles give only a brief opening narration and the names of the songs being performed. As a result, the film soon grows monotonous for those who can't understand the language. In Spanish with English subtitles. Not rated; suitable for general audiences. 100m. **DIR:** Carlos Saura. **CAST:** Enrique Morente, Jose Menese, Jose Merce, Marlo Maya, Matilde Coral. 1995

FLAMING STAR ★★★★ A solid Western directed by Don Siegel (*Dirty Harry*), this features Elvis Presley in a remarkably effective performance as a half-breed Indian who must choose sides when his mother's people go on the warpath. 92m. **DIR:** Don Siegel. **CAST:** Elvis Presley, Barbara Eden, Steve Forrest, Dolores Del Rio, John McIntire. 1960

FLAMINGO KID, THE ★★★1/2 A teen comedy-drama with more on its mind than stale sex jokes. Matt Dillon stars as Jeffrey Willis, a Brooklyn kid who discovers how the other half lives when he takes a summer job at a beach resort. A good story that explores the things (and people) that shape our values as we reach adulthood. A genuine pleasure, and you'll be glad you tried it. Rated PG-13 for frank sexual situations. 100m. **DIR:** Garry Marshall. **CAST:** Matt Dillon, Richard Crenna, Jessica Walter, Janet Jones, Hector Elizondo. 1984 **DVD**

FLAMINGO ROAD ★★★1/2 A typical Joan Crawford soap opera with her dominating the weak men in her life. In this one she plays a carnival dancer who intrigues Zachary Scott and David Brian in a small town where the carnival stops. Fast-moving melodrama. B&W; 94m. **DIR:** Michael Curtiz. **CAST:** Joan Crawford, David Brian, Sydney Greenstreet, Zachary Scott, Gladys George. 1949

FLASH, THE ★★★1/2 DC comic-book hero is accurately portrayed in this TV movie that piloted a short-lived series. Highly watchable with decent special effects and a light touch of good humor. Not rated; contains violence. 94m. **DIR:** Robert Iscove. **CAST:** John Wesley Shipp, Amanda Pays, Michael Nader, Tim Thomerson, Alex Desert. 1990

FLASH AND THE FIRECAT 🦃 Flash (Roger Davis) and Firecat (Tricia Sembera) blaze across the California beaches, stealing cars and robbing banks. 94m. **DIR:** Ferd Sebastian, Beverly Sebastian. **CAST:** Richard Kiel, Roger Davis, Tricia Sembera. 1975

FLASH GORDON ★★★1/2 If you don't take it seriously, this campy film based on the classic Alex Raymond comic strip of the 1930s is a real hoot. Sam Jones, as Flash, and Melody Anderson, as Dale Arden, race through the intentionally hokey special effects to do battle with Max von Sydow, who makes an excellent Ming the Merciless. Rated PG. 110m. **DIR:** Mike Hodges. **CAST:** Sam Jones, Topol, Max von Sydow, Melody Anderson, Timothy Dalton. 1980 **DVD**

FLASH GORDON CONQUERS THE UNIVERSE ★★★ The third and last of Universal's landmark Flash Gordon serials finds the Earth in jeopardy again as Ming the Merciless spreads an epidemic known as the Plague of the Purple Death in yet another attempt to rule the universe. This serial was a strong competitor in that great period from 1937 to 1945 when the chapterplay market was important. B&W; 12 chapters. **DIR:** Ford Beebe, Ray Taylor. **CAST:** Buster Crabbe, Carol Hughes, Charles Middleton, Frank Shannon, Lee Powell. 1940 **DVD**

FLASH GORDON: ROCKETSHIP (SPACESHIP TO THE UNKNOWN; PERILS FROM PLANET MONGO) ★★★ Original feature version of the first *Flash Gordon* serial is one of the best reedited chapterplays ever released. Boyish Buster Crabbe is the perfect Flash Gordon; Jean Rogers is one of the loveliest of all serial queens; and classic character heavy Charles Middleton becomes the embodiment of malevolent villainy as the infamous Ming the Merciless. B&W; 97m. **DIR:** Frederick Stephani. **CAST:** Buster Crabbe, Jean Rogers, Frank Shannon, Charles Middleton, Priscilla Lawson. 1936

FLASH OF GREEN, A ★★★1/2 This is a compelling adaptation of John D. MacDonald's novel about a small-town Florida reporter (Ed Harris) whose boredom, lust, and curiosity lead him into helping an ambitious, amoral county official (Richard Jordan) win approval for a controversial housing project. The acting is superb. 118m. **DIR:** Victor Nunez. **CAST:** Ed Harris, Blair Brown, Richard Jordan, George Coe, Isa Thomas, William Mooney, Joan Goodfellow, Helen Stenborg, John Glover. 1984

FLASHBACK ★★ Straitlaced FBI agent Kiefer Sutherland is assigned to take hippie prankster Dennis Hopper to Oregon, where he is to stand trial. On the way Hopper switches places with Sutherland, and the chase is on. Clichés abound in this mushy mishmash. Rated R for profanity and violence. 106m. **DIR:** Franco Amurri. **CAST:** Dennis Hopper, Kiefer Sutherland, Carol Kane, Cliff De Young, Paul Dooley, Richard Masur, Michael McKean. 1990

FLASHDANCE ★★★ Director Adrian Lyne explodes images on the screen with eye-popping regularity while the spare screenplay centers on the ambitions of Alex Owens (Jennifer Beals), a welder who dreams of making the big time as a dancer. Alex finds this goal difficult to attain—until contractor Nick Hurley (Michael Nouri) decides to help. Rated R for nudity, profanity, and implied sex. 96m. **DIR:** Adrian Lyne. **CAST:** Jennifer Beals, Michael Nouri, Lilia Skala. 1983

FLASHFIRE ★★1/2 John Warren and Dan York's sloppily scripted cop thriller lurches to such an abrupt halt, you'll wonder who pulled the financial plug. Billy Zane is barely credible as a detective trying to solve his partner's murder with the help of a gregarious hooker who saw the killers. Routine stuff, handled with very little wit. Rated R for profanity, nudity, violence, and simulated sex. 89m. **DIR:** Elliot Silverstein. **CAST:** Billy Zane, Lou Gossett Jr., Kristin Minter. 1993 DVD

FLASHPOINT ★★★1/2 Kris Kristofferson and Treat Williams star in this taut, suspenseful, and action-filled thriller as two Texas-border officers who accidentally uncover an abandoned jeep containing a skeleton, a rifle, and $800,000 in cash—a discovery that puts their lives in danger. Rated PG-13 for profanity and violence. 95m. **DIR:** William Tannen. **CAST:** Kris Kristofferson, Treat Williams, Rip Torn, Kevin Conway, Tess Harper. 1984

FLAT TOP ★★ A mediocre World War II action film following the exploits of an aircraft carrier battling the Japanese forces in the Pacific. Most of the battle scenes are taken from actual combat footage. B&W; 83m. **DIR:** Lesley Selander. **CAST:** Richard Carlson, Sterling Hayden, Keith Larsen, Bill Phillips. 1952

FLATBED ANNIE AND SWEETIE PIE: LADY TRUCKERS ★★1/2 Annie Potts is Flatbed Annie, a veteran trucker who trains a novice named Sweetie Pie (Kim Darby). The two team up in an effort to support their costly rig. Mildly entertaining diversion. Made for TV. 104m. **DIR:** Robert Greenwald. **CAST:** Annie Potts, Kim Darby, Harry Dean Stanton, Arthur Godfrey, Rory Calhoun. 1979

FLATLINERS ★★★ In this morbid but compelling thriller a group of medical students experiment with death. They kill each other one by one and then are brought back to life. But things don't work out as they expect. Rated R. 111m. **DIR:** Joel Schumacher. **CAST:** Kiefer Sutherland, Julia Roberts, Kevin Bacon, William Baldwin, Oliver Platt. 1990 DVD

•**FLAWLESS** ★★1/2 Manhattan's seedy East Village is the setting for this fractured tale about a hate-love relationship between former security guard Walt and flamboyant drag queen Rusty. The film begins as Walt tries to stop a robbery and has a stroke. He then reluctantly takes singing lessons from Rusty to improve his slurred speech. The film works when it sticks to the volatile relationship of its two main characters, but often strays to messy subplots involving drug thugs and a gay beauty contest. Rated R for language and violence. 111m. **DIR:** Joel Schumacher. **CAST:** Robert De Niro, Philip Seymour Hoffman. 1999 DVD

FLED ★★ Two convicts—one black and one white—flee a Georgia chain-gang massacre while cuffed together at the wrist and spend the rest of the movie trying not to get killed by the Cuban mob and corrupt FBI agents. Typical, overly vicious odd couple action-comedy. Rated R for language, violence, and brief nudity. 105m. **DIR:** Kevin Hooks. **CAST:** Laurence Fishburne, Stephen Baldwin, Will Patton, Robert Hooks, David Dukes, Salma Hayek, Michael Nader, Victor Rivers, Robert Burke. 1996 DVD

FLESH ♥ Joe Dallesandro as a street hustler who can't stay away from transvestites, sleazy women, and drugs. Not rated, contains nudity and profane language. 90m. **DIR:** Paul Morrissey. **CAST:** Joe Dallesandro, Geraldine Smith, Patti D'Arbanville, Candy Darling. 1968 DVD

FLESH AND BLOOD (1922) ★★1/2 Prison escapee, disguised as a crippled violin player, discovers his daughter is in love with his enemy's son. True to the melodramatic sentiment of the time, Lon Chaney Sr. hobbles back to prison a cripple but throws his crutches away at the gates and enters a proud man. B&W; 73m. **DIR:** Irving Cummings. **CAST:** Lon Chaney Sr., DeWitt Jennings, Noah Beery Sr., Ralph Lewis, Jack Mulhall. 1922

FLESH AND BLOOD (SWORD AND THE ROSE, THE (1985)) ★★★1/2 Set in medieval Europe, *Flesh and Blood* follows the lives of two men—mercenary soldier Rutger Hauer and the son of a feudal lord (Tom Burlinson)—and their love for the same woman (Jennifer Jason Leigh). The cast is stellar, the sets are lavish, and the plot turns will keep the viewer guessing, but not in the dark. Rated R for violence, sex, nudity, profanity. 126m. **DIR:** Paul Verhoeven. **CAST:** Rutger Hauer, Jennifer Jason Leigh, Tom Burlinson, Susan Tyrrell, Ronald Lacey, Jack Thompson. 1985

FLESH AND BLOOD SHOW, THE ♥ Sluggish, gory British horror about a failed actor. Rated R. 96m. **DIR:** Pete Walker. **CAST:** Ray Brooks. 1972

FLESH AND BONE ★★★1/2 In the prologue to this suspenseful, thought-provoking film, a young boy named Arliss becomes an unwilling accomplice to murder when his father uses him in a robbery that goes awry. Years later, the adult Arliss drifts from place to place, seemingly to avoid memories of his dark past. An act of kindness toward a pretty stranger leads to a day of reckoning. The offbeat drama is not for all tastes. Rated R for violence, profanity, nudity, and simulated sex. 127m. **DIR:** Steve Kloves. **CAST:** Dennis Quaid, Meg Ryan, James Caan, Gwyneth Paltrow, Scott Wilson, Christopher Rydell. 1993

FLESH AND THE DEVIL ★★★ Story of a woman who flouts moral conventions by pursuing a third man while married to two others. The sensual pairing of sultry Greta Garbo with suave John Gilbert electrifies this film. B&W; 103m. **DIR:** Clarence Brown. **CAST:** Greta Garbo, John Gilbert. 1927

FLESH EATERS, THE ★★ This is the notorious cult horror epic—rarely available, even on video, in its uncut form—about a mad scientist (Martin Kosleck) who unleashes voracious organisms into the waters surrounding his tropical island laboratory. A seminal gore film, scripted by comics writer Arnold Drake, it'll have you chuckling at its amateurish performances one minute, then gagging at its surprisingly vivid special effects in the next. B&W; 87m. **DIR:** Jack Curtis. **CAST:** Martin Kosleck, Rita Morley. 1964

FLESH EATING MOTHERS ★★ Tepid mix of gore and gags in a suburb where adulterous mothers become infected with a virus that turns them into cannibalistic zombies. Not rated, comic violence. 90m. **DIR:** James Aviles Martin. **CAST:** Robert Lee Oliver, Donatella Hecht. 1988

FLESH FEAST 🐢 Veronica Lake was working as a waitress in Florida when she coproduced and starred in this film about a plastic surgeon who uses maggots as a unique form of dermabrasion. Rated R. 72m. **DIR:** Brad F. Grinter. **CAST:** Veronica Lake. 1970

FLESH GORDON ★★1/2 Porno version of the famed serial *Flash Gordon*, this fitfully amusing parody's main point of interest is the often excellent miniature work and dimensional animation by Jim Danforth and other special-effects pros. The story, about a sex ray aimed at Earth by Emperor Wang of the planet Porno, is obvious and amateurish. Rated X for nudity, language, and overall content. 70m. **DIR:** Howard Ziehm, Michael Benveniste. **CAST:** Jason Williams, Suzanne Fields, John Hoyt. 1974

FLESH GORDON 2: FLESH GORDON MEETS THE COSMIC CHEERLEADERS ★★★ A surprisingly good set design makes this tasteless sequel entertaining. Flesh is kidnapped by cosmic cheerleaders and taken to their home planet where a villain has sapped the collective libido of the male population. Filled with gratuitous nudity and bad jokes, this one is not for everybody. Available in R-rated and unrated versions, both with nudity and sexual situations. 101m. **DIR:** Howard Ziehm. **CAST:** Vince Murdocco, Robyn Kelly, Tony Travis, Morgan Fox. 1993

FLESHBURN ★★★1/2 An Indian who left five men in the desert to die breaks out of an insane asylum to hunt down and wreak his revenge against the psychiatrists who sentenced him. This film promises to be more than exploitation, and it does not let you down. Rated R for profanity and violence. 91m. **DIR:** George Gage. **CAST:** Sonny Landham, Steve Kanaly, Karen Carlson. 1983

FLESHTONE ★★ Eccentric artist gets involved in phone sex to ease his loneliness, only to become the main suspect when his phone date ends up dead. Is there just one script out there being remade over and over again? R-rated and unrated versions; both contain nudity, adult situations, and violence. 89/91m. **DIR:** Harry Hurwitz. **CAST:** Martin Kemp, Lise Cutter, Tim Thomerson. 1994

FLETCH ★★★★ Chevy Chase is first-rate as Gregory McDonald's wisecracking reporter, I. M. "Fletch" Fletcher, who starts out doing what seems to be a fairly simple exposé of drug dealing in Los Angeles and ends up taking on a corrupt cop (Joe Don Baker), a tough managing editor (Richard Libertini), and a powerful millionaire (Tim Matheson) who wants Fletch to kill him. The laughs are plenty and the action almost nonstop. Rated PG for violence and profanity. 96m. **DIR:** Michael Ritchie. **CAST:** Chevy Chase, Joe Don Baker, Tim Matheson, Dana Wheeler-Nicholson, Richard Libertini, M. Emmet Walsh. 1985 DVD

FLETCH LIVES ★★★1/2 Chevy Chase returns to the role of I. M. Fletcher and scores another triumph. In this one, Fletch finds himself heir to a southern plantation and quits his newspaper job—only to become both a murder suspect and a target for unscrupulous villains. If you enjoyed the original *Fletch*, this sequel is guaranteed to satisfy. Rated PG. 98m. **DIR:** Michael Ritchie. **CAST:** Chevy Chase, Cleavon Little, Hal Holbrook, Julianne Phillips, Richard Libertini, Randall "Tex" Cobb, George Wyner. 1989

FLIGHT FROM VIENNA ★★★ Theodore Bikel gets to demonstrate the range of his acting abilities as a Hungarian official trying to defect to the West. B&W; 54m. **DIR:** Denis Kavanagh. **CAST:** Theodore Bikel, John Bentley, Donald Gray. 1956

FLIGHT OF BLACK ANGEL ★★1/2 This potentially intriguing made-for-cable thriller, about a renegade fighter pilot with a stolen tactical nuclear weapon, turns unsavory and relentlessly stupid at the halfway point. Training instructor Peter Strauss takes it personally when one of his former students, believing himself a self-styled "Angel of the Lord," uses real missiles on trainees and then heads out on a mission to annihilate Las Vegas. Rated R for language and violence. 102m. **DIR:** Jonathan Mostow. **CAST:** Peter Strauss, William O'Leary. 1991

FLIGHT OF DRAGONS, THE ★★★★ Stop-motion animation and the voices of John Ritter, James Earl Jones, Harry Morgan, and James Gregory bring this fantasy to life. Good wizards select a man to stop the evil reign of the Red Wizards. Grade-schoolers will be fascinated by this tale. 98m. **DIR:** Arthur Rankin Jr., Jules Bass. 1982

FLIGHT OF RAINBIRDS, A ★★★ Fun bedroom farce features Jeroen Krabbé as both an endearing, innocent klutz and his sexy alter ego/mentor. He must analyze his stern Calvinist upbringing before he can enjoy life and find romance. In Dutch with English subtitles. Not rated; contains nudity and sexual situations. 94m. **DIR:** Ate De Jong. **CAST:** Jeroen Krabbé, Marijke Merckens, Henriette Tol, Huib Rooymans, Claire Wauthion. 1981

FLIGHT OF THE EAGLE ★★★1/2 This Swedish production presents the true adventure of three foolhardy 1897 polar explorers (one played by Max von Sydow) who tried to conquer the Arctic in a balloon. In Swedish with English subtitles. Not rated; the film has some gore. 139m. DIR: Jan Troell. CAST: Max von Sydow. 1982

FLIGHT OF THE INNOCENT ★★★★ When his family is murdered, a sweet-natured 10-year-old boy miraculously escapes, only to be pursued by the killers. This emotionally involving film examines a modern-day phenomenon: the kidnapping of children from well-to-do families in northern Italy by their southern neighbors, who hold their victims for ransom. In Italian with English subtitles. Rated R for violence and profanity. 115m. DIR: Carlo Carlei. CAST: Manuel Colao, Federico Pacifici, Sal Borgese, Giusi Cataldo, Lucio Zagaria, Massimo Lodolo, Francesca Neri, Jacques Perrin. 1993

FLIGHT OF THE INTRUDER, THE ★★ Spectacular aerial-action sequences almost salvage this jingoistic, one-dimensional war film in which navy fliers Brad Johnson and Willem Dafoe ignore orders and bomb a restricted area in Hanoi. Based on the novel by Stephen Coonts. Rated PG-13 for profanity and violence. 115m. DIR: John Milius. CAST: Danny Glover, Willem Dafoe, Brad Johnson, Rosanna Arquette. 1991

FLIGHT OF THE NAVIGATOR ★★★ This all-ages Disney delight concerns a youngster (Joey Kramer) who has the unique ability to communicate with machines and uses this to help a UFO find its way home. Kids will love its crazy creatures, special effects, and action-packed conclusion, while parents will appreciate its nice balance of sense and nonsense. Rated PG for mild cussing. 90m. DIR: Randal Kleiser. CAST: Joey Kramer, Veronica Cartwright, Cliff De Young, Sarah Jessica Parker, Howard Hesseman, Matt Adler. 1986

FLIGHT OF THE PHOENIX, THE ★★★★ An all-star international cast shines in this gripping adventure about the desert crash of a small plane and the grueling efforts of the meager band of passengers to rebuild and repair it against impossible odds, not the least of which are starvation and/or heat prostration. 143m. DIR: Robert Aldrich. CAST: James Stewart, Richard Attenborough, Peter Finch, Ernest Borgnine, Hardy Krüger, Ronald Fraser, Christian Marquand, Ian Bannen, George Kennedy, Dan Duryea. 1966

FLIGHT TO FURY ★★1/2 Jack Nicholson wrote the screenplay for this clever low-budget thriller. Nicholson plays a member of a group of conniving thieves smuggling diamonds out of the Philippines. B&W; 73m. DIR: Monte Hellman. CAST: Dewey Martin, Fay Spain, Jack Nicholson. 1964

FLIGHT TO MARS ★★1/2 Scientists and newsmen crash on Mars during a space voyage and discover a race of humans living beneath the surface of the planet. Although slow, a fairly effective plea for international and intergalactic harmony. 72m. DIR: Lesley Selander. CAST: Cameron Mitchell, Arthur Franz, Marguerite Chapman, Morris Ankrum (Stepen Morris), John Litel, Virginia Huston. 1951

FLIM-FLAM MAN, THE ★★★ A con man (George C. Scott) teaches an army deserter (Michael Sar-razin) the art of fleecing yokels. Scott is an altogether charming, wry, winning rascal in this improbable, clever film, which is highlighted by a spectacular car-chase scene. 104m. DIR: Irvin Kershner. CAST: George C. Scott, Michael Sarrazin, Sue Lyon, Harry Morgan, Jack Albertson. 1967

FLINCH ★★1/2 OK thriller offers a pair of live store mannequins who witness a murder while working the window of a popular department store. Of course, the police won't believe them so it's up to them to find the killer. Live-mannequin angle is the only new trick up this film's sleeve, though it is fascinating to watch costar Nick Mancuso give the most over-the-top performance of his career. Rated R for violence and nudity. 93m. DIR: George Erschbamer. CAST: Judd Nelson, Gina Gershon, Nick Mancuso. 1994

FLINTSTONES, THE ★★★ Yuppie nostalgia and the amazing efforts of Jim Henson's Creature Shop are this film's major attractions, but the appeal wears thin pretty quickly. In spite of—or because of—the efforts of a rumored thirty-five writers, this live-action re-creation of the 1960s animated series lurches awkwardly from one scene to the next. Very small children will love it, but they won't understand the topical references or the occasionally risqué humor. Rated PG for cartoonish violence and mild sexuality. 105m. DIR: Brian Levant. CAST: John Goodman, Elizabeth Perkins, Rick Moranis, Rosie O'Donnell, Elizabeth Taylor, Kyle MacLachlan, Halle Berry. 1994 DVD

•FLINTSTONES IN VIVA ROCK VEGAS, THE ★★ Fred and Barney are bachelors seeking the perfect woman. Problems arise when Wilma's mother snubs Fred and an unscrupulous suitor vies for Wilma's hand in marriage. Endless wordplays make the most of the prehistoric angle. Kids will enjoy the sights and adults can giggle over the clever lines. Rated PG for scatological humor and comic-book violence. 90m. DIR: Brian Levant. CAST: Mark Addy, Stephen Baldwin, Kristen Johnston, Jane Krakowski. 2000

FLIPPER (1963) ★★★ America's love of dolphins took root in this gentle adventure. After Luke Halpin saves a wounded dolphin, he must convince his fisherman father (Chuck Connors) that dolphins help man and should not be destroyed. Filmed in the Florida Keys. 85m. DIR: James B. Clark. CAST: Chuck Connors, Luke Halpin. 1963

FLIPPER (1996) ★★★ Amiable Paul Hogan is the brightest spot in this ordinary update of the 1960s television series. City kid Elijah Wood learns how to become a man while spending the summer with his uncle and a mirthful dolphin, but Alan Shapiro makes a serious mistake with the degenerate nature of his story's villain, who more properly belongs in an Arnold Schwarzenegger thriller. Rated PG for a surprising level of violence. 96m. DIR: Alan Shapiro. CAST: Paul Hogan, Elijah Wood, Chelsea Field, Isaac Hayes, Jonathan Banks, Jason Fuchs, Jessica Wesson. 1996

FLIPPER'S NEW ADVENTURE ★★★ One of the better sequels shows the affection and teamwork enjoyed by a young boy and his pet dolphin when they outwit blackmailers. Filmed in the Bahamas and released less than a year after, Flipper made a sensational movie debut. The sequel led to a TV series. 103m. DIR: Leon Benson. CAST: Luke Halpin, Brian Kelly, Pamela Franklin, Francesca Annis, Tom Helmore. 1964

FLIPPER'S ODYSSEY ★★1/2 Rin Tin Tin with fins heroically saves a photographer, a lonely fisherman's dog, and his own young master. Flipper outacts the rest of the cast. Underwater shots are the highlight. 77m. DIR: Paul Landres. CAST: Brian Kelly, Luke Halpin, Tommy Norden. 1965

FLIPPING ★★★ Intense crime-thriller set in Hollywood stars David Amos as Mike Moore, who yearns to be a wiseguy with a lot of power. Until then, Mike works as a collector for crime boss Leo (Keith David). Mike's partners are a tight-knit group until Leo orders them to kill a rival crime boss. Their loyalties to each other and Leo are severely tested. Rated R for adult situations, language, and violence. 102m. DIR: Gene Mitchell. CAST: David Amos, David Proval, Keith David, Barry Primus, Tony Burton. 1996

FLIRT ★★★1/2 Independent filmmaker Hal Hartley (Trust, Amateur) goes for something a bit more experimental in this film which is actually three short films, each telling the same story with a different cast, different location (Manhattan, Berlin, and Tokyo), and a different perspective. The results are both intriguing and provocative, though more so for Hartley fans than newcomers. Not rated; contains sexual themes. 85m. DIR: Hal Hartley. CAST: Bill Sage, Martin Donovan, Karen Sillas, Michael Imperioli, Hal Hartley. 1996

FLIRTATION WALK ★★1/2 Dull story of romantic mix-ups and misunderstandings between a West Point cadet and the commanding officer's daughter. Surprisingly few songs, all forgettable. Nominated for best picture, but, in 1934, so were eleven other movies. B&W; 98m. DIR: Frank Borzage. CAST: Dick Powell, Ruby Keeler, Pat O'Brien, Guinn Williams, Ross Alexander, John Eldredge. 1934

FLIRTING ★★★★ This Australian comedy-drama is the second film in a projected coming-of-age trilogy. In the first film, The Year My Voice Broke, we meet Danny in a small town in the Australian outback. In Flirting, Danny is at an all-boys boarding school, across a lake from an all-girls school. Amid the typical prep school studies, socials, and antics, Danny is surprised to find himself falling for a young Ugandan girl. These two Duigan films are genuine sleepers. 96m. DIR: John Duigan. CAST: Noah Taylor, Thandie Newton, Nicole Kidman. 1992

FLIRTING WITH DISASTER ★★★★1/2 Neurotic yuppie Ben Stiller goes on a cross-country search for his biological parents (Lily Tomlin, Alan Alda), leaving adoptive parents Mary Tyler Moore and George Segal sulking back home in New York. Hilariously original and inventive comedy is reminiscent of Preston Sturges at his madcap best; the star-studded cast is in peak form. Rated R for profanity and brief nudity. 92m. DIR: David O. Russell. CAST: Ben Stiller, Patricia Arquette, Téa Leoni, Mary Tyler Moore, George Segal, Lily Tomlin, Alan Alda. 1996 DVD

FLOATING AWAY ★★★ Rosanna Arquette tries hard to lift this saga above ordinary cliché, but she's not able to surmount Tim Sandlin's by-the-numbers script, adapted from his book Sorrow Floats. She plays a young mother who turns to alcohol after her beloved father's death, and who loses everything— home, child, friends—when she has had enough. Unfortunately, some of this story's incidental characters are just too bizarre for words. Rated R for profanity, nudity, rape, and violence. 105m. DIR: John Badham. CAST: Rosanna Arquette, Paul Hogan, Judge Reinhold, Brendan Fletcher. 1998

FLOOD! ★★★ Bureaucratic peevishness is responsible for a small town being caught short when a dam bursts. Slick and predictable, but interesting just the same. If you like this, you'll like its sister film, Fire! 100m. DIR: Earl Bellamy. CAST: Robert Culp, Martin Milner, Barbara Hershey, Richard Basehart, Carol Lynley, Roddy McDowall, Cameron Mitchell, Teresa Wright. 1976

FLOOD: A RIVER'S RAMPAGE ★★★ Torrential rains set the stage for this Hallmark production take on the disastrous floods that took their toll on the Midwest. Richard Thomas, Kate Vernon, and Jan Rubes are among those downriver from the pending natural disaster, hoping to salvage their homesteads. Predictable, but it's easy to rally around these characters. Rated PG-13. 92m. DIR: Bruce Pittman. CAST: Richard Thomas, Kate Vernon, Jan Rubes. 1997

FLOR SYLVESTRE ★★★1/2 Mexican-born beauty Dolores Del Rio made many schlocky movies in America but had to return to her native country to appear in quality productions. This tale of two families torn apart by the Mexican revolution is one of the best. The story is a little corny, but beautifully photographed and directed. In Spanish with English subtitles. B&W; 94m. DIR: Emilio Fernandez. CAST: Dolores Del Rio, Pedro Armendariz, Emilio Fernandez. 1945

FLORIDA STRAITS ★★1/2 Raul Julia is a Cuban refugee who enlists the aid of charter boaters Fred Ward and Daniel Jenkins to help him get back to Cuba and rescue the woman he loves. Although a bit contrived in spots, this is watchable. An unrated HBO production that contains some violence and rough language. 98m. DIR: Mike Hodges. CAST: Raul Julia, Fred Ward, Daniel H. Jenkins, Jaime Sanchez, Victor Argo, Ilka Tanya Payan, Antonio Fargas. 1986

FLOUNDERING ★★★ James LeGros is the hero, of sorts, in this black, and sometimes bleak, comedic look at life in Los Angeles for the less-than-privileged. LeGros's life spirals downhill until he is literally sleeping in the gutter, but a cynical outlook and sharp writing keep this off-kilter comedy on track. Rated R for profanity, adult themes, drug use, sexual situations, and profanity. 97m. DIR: Peter McCarthy. CAST: James LeGros, John Cusack, Ethan Hawke, Steve Buscemi, Kim Wayans. 1994 DVD

FLOWER DRUM SONG ★★ Set in San Francisco's colorful Chinatown, this Rodgers and Hammerstein musical rings sour. It has its bright moments, but the score is largely second-rate. The plot is conventional: a modern son's views versus those of an old-fashioned father. Ingredients include the usual Oriental cliché of an arranged marriage. 131m. DIR: Henry

Koster. **CAST:** Jack Soo, Nancy Kwan, Benson Fong, Miyoshi Umeki, Juanita Hall, James Shigeta. **1962**
FLOWER OF MY SECRET, THE ★★★★ Pedro Almodóvar goes light on camp and deeper into emotional empathy with this tale of a middle-aged romance novelist. As her marriage crumbles, she comes to hate her work—and a big part of herself. One of the Spanish bad boy's more compelling character studies. In Spanish with English subtitles. Rated R. 108m. **DIR:** Pedro Almodóvar. **CAST:** Marisa Paredes, Juan Echanove, Imanol Arias, Rossy De Palma. **1995**
FLOWERS IN THE ATTIC ★★1/2 After the death of their father, four children are taken (by their mother) to live with their religious-zealot grandmother and dying grandfather. The kids are locked into the attic of the family mansion because of some dark family secrets. Louise Fletcher chews up the scenery as the domineering grandmother in this adaptation of V. C. Andrews's gothic horror novel. Rated PG-13. 92m. **DIR:** Jeffrey Bloom. **CAST:** Louise Fletcher, Victoria Tennant, Kristy Swanson, Jeb Adams. **1987**
FLUBBER ★★1/2 Disappointing remake of Disney's *The Absent-Minded Professor* is aptly retitled. Special-effects advancements, as well as particular innovations provided by Industrial Light & Magic, make the invention rather than the inventor the film's star. Robin Williams simply reacts to the hyperactive green goo, allowing it to steal every scene. Rated PG for comic-book violence. 94m. **DIR:** Les Mayfield. **CAST:** Robin Williams, Marcia Gay Harden, Clancy Brown, Ted Levine, Wil Wheaton, Edie McClurg. **1997 DVD**
FLUKE ★★★ This odd little film about reincarnation and karma has a distinctively European flavor that is strangely appealing. Rated PG for violence and mild profanity. 105m. **DIR:** Carlo Carlei. **CAST:** Matthew Modine, Nancy Travis, Eric Stoltz, Max Pomeranc, Samuel L. Jackson. **1995**
FLUNKY, WORK HARD! ★★★ This short feature is the earliest surviving work of Japanese filmmaker Mikio Naruse. It's an odd mix about an insurance salesman struggling to provide for his wife and son. But it provides a priceless look at Japanese life before World War II. In Japanese with English subtitles. B&W; 28m. **DIR:** Mikio Naruse. **CAST:** Isamu Yamaguchi. **1931**
FLUSTERED COMEDY OF LEON ERROL, THE ★★★ When he wasn't portraying a rubber-legged drunk in features, former vaudeville and burlesque comic Leon Errol scored big in dozens of comedy shorts. This compilation—"Crime Rave," "Man I Cured," and "A Panic in the Parlor"—shows why. B&W; 56m. **DIR:** Hal Yates. **CAST:** Leon Errol, Virginia Vale, Frank Faylen. **1939–1941**
FLY, THE (1958) ★★★★ Classic horror film builds slowly but really pays off. A scientist (Al Hedison, soon to become David) experimenting with unknown forces turns himself into the hideous title character. Impressive production with top-notch acting and real neat special effects. 94m. **DIR:** Kurt Neumann. **CAST:** David Hedison, Patricia Owens, Vincent Price, Herbert Marshall. **1958**

FLY, THE (1986) ★★★1/2 A brilliant research scientist, Seth Brundle (Jeff Goldblum), has developed a way to transport matter. One night, thoroughly gassed, he decides to test the device on himself. Unfortunately, a pesky housefly finds its way into the chamber with the scientist. It must also be said that this otherwise entertaining update simply falls apart at the conclusion. Rated R for gore and slime. 100m. **DIR:** David Cronenberg. **CAST:** Jeff Goldblum, Geena Davis, John Getz. **1986**
FLY II, THE ★★1/2 This sequel to David Cronenberg's masterfully crafted 1986 horror remake of *The Fly* doesn't have the right chemistry. The weak, unbelievable story centers around the birth of an heir (Eric Stoltz) to the original fly. This one doesn't fly. Rated R for violence, adult situations, and profanity. 104m. **DIR:** Chris Walas. **CAST:** Eric Stoltz, Daphne Zuniga, Lee Richardson, John Getz. **1989**
FLY AWAY HOME ★★★★ Uplifting musical score by Mark Isham enhances this heartwarming, fact-based adventure. An eccentric inventor (Jeff Daniels) is reunited with his withdrawn daughter (Anna Paquin) following her mother's death. When a flock of Canadian geese bond to the girl, father and daughter share an incredible journey to restore the natural migration patterns of the geese. Terry Kinney, as Daniels's brother, injects delightfully comic moments. Rated PG for mild profanity. 105m. **DIR:** Carroll Ballard. **CAST:** Jeff Daniels, Anna Paquin, Dana Delany, Terry Kinney. **1996 DVD**
•**FLY BOY** ★★★ Better-than-average direct-to-video family adventure about a 10-year-old boy who finds joy and comfort spending time with his grandfather, a former WWII flying ace. James Karen is wonderful as the grandfather, a kindly man who dreams of flying one more time before his death. How his last wish comes true is at the heart of this winning, respectful film. Rated PG. 86m. **DIR:** Richard Stanley. **CAST:** Miko Hughes, James Karen, Kathleen Lloyd, Gregory Itzin. **1999**
FLY BY NIGHT ★★1/2 Two rappers join forces and achieve success when they take on the guise of gangsta rappers, but find themselves trapped by their newfound success. Little real insight and poor execution. Rated R for language and adult situations. 93m. **DIR:** Steve Gomer. **CAST:** Jeffrey Sams, Ron Brice, MC Lyte, Leo Burmester, Todd Graff. **1992**
FLYING BLIND ★★★ This is the third release of upscale B pictures from the William H. Pine–William C. Thomas production unit that operated at Paramount Pictures from 1941 through 1945. The previous films were *Power Dive* and *Forced Landing*, and all three share the same topic: aviation. The script here is by Maxwell Shane and deals with heroes versus evil foreign agents in the United States. B&W; 70m. **DIR:** Frank McDonald. **CAST:** Richard Arlen, Jean Parker. **1941**
FLYING DEUCES ★★★ Stan Laurel and Oliver Hardy join the foreign legion to help Ollie forget his troubled romantic past. Many laugh-filled situations, although the script has weak areas and the movie occasionally drags. B&W; 65m. **DIR:** A. Edward Sutherland. **CAST:** Stan Laurel, Oliver Hardy, Jean Parker. **1939 DVD**

FLYING DOWN TO RIO ★★1/2 We're sure the joy of watching Fred Astaire and Ginger Rogers dance is the only thing that has prevented the negatives of this embarrassing movie from being burned. The climactic dance number, in which chorus girls perform on airplane wings, is so corny it has now passed into the realm of camp. B&W; 89m. **DIR:** Thornton Freeland. **CAST:** Dolores Del Rio, Ginger Rogers, Fred Astaire. 1933

FLYING FOOL, THE ★★1/2 The story about the protective older brother and his kid brother falling for the same girl was old when this vintage talkie was released, but top-notch dialogue and good aviation sequences make this breezy programmer good entertainment. B&W; 73m. **DIR:** Tay Garnett. **CAST:** William Boyd, Marie Prevost, Russell Gleason, James Gleason. 1929

FLYING LEATHERNECKS ★★★1/2 John Wayne is the apparently heartless commander of an airborne fighting squad, and Robert Ryan is the caring officer who questions his decisions in this well-acted war film. The stars play off each other surprisingly well, and it's a shame they didn't do more films together. 102m. **DIR:** Nicholas Ray. **CAST:** John Wayne, Robert Ryan, Jay C. Flippen. 1951

FLYING SAUCER, THE 🎗 American agent sent to Alaska to investigate a report of an unidentified flying object. B&W; 69m. **DIR:** Mikel Conrad. **CAST:** Mikel Conrad, Denver Pyle, Russell Hicks. 1950

FLYING SERPENT, THE ★★ Mad doctor Zucco keeps mythological Mexican bird Quetzalcoatl (the same monster that turns up, much bigger, in Larry Cohen's *Q*) in a cage, periodically letting it out to attack his enemies. One of the all-time great, unintentional laugh riots from poverty-row studio PRC, directed by Sam Newfield under one of his many pseudonyms, Sherman Scott. B&W; 59m. **DIR:** Sam Newfield. **CAST:** George Zucco, Ralph Lewis. 1946 DVD

FLYING TIGERS, THE ★★1/2 Exciting dogfight action scenes make this low-budget John Wayne World War II vehicle watchable, but the story sags a bit. B&W; 102m. **DIR:** David Miller. **CAST:** John Wayne, John Carroll, Mae Clarke, Gordon Jones. 1942 DVD

FM ★★★ Before television's *WKRP in Cincinnati* spoofed hip radio, there was this enjoyable comedy, with Martin Mull stealing scenes as a crazed disc jockey. Fans of Seventies rock will enjoy the soundtrack and live appearances by the era's superstars. Rated PG for profanity. 104m. **DIR:** John A. Alonzo. **CAST:** Michael Brandon, Martin Mull, Eileen Brennan, Cleavon Little, Cassie Yates, Alex Karras, Norman Lloyd, James Keach. 1978 DVD

FOG, THE ★★★ This is one of those *almost* movies. Director John Carpenter is on familiar ground with this story of nineteenth-century colonists back from the dead, terrorizing a modern-day fishing village. The lack of any real chills or surprises makes this one a nice try but no cigar. Rated R. 91m. **DIR:** John Carpenter. **CAST:** Adrienne Barbeau, Jamie Lee Curtis, John Houseman, Hal Holbrook, Janet Leigh. 1980

FOG ISLAND ★★ This *Old Dark House* rip-off from poverty row's Monogram Pictures never takes off, but mystery and suspense buffs should enjoy its rare teaming of genre veterans George Zucco and Lionel Atwill. B&W; 72m. **DIR:** Terry Morse. **CAST:** George Zucco, Veda Ann Borg, Lionel Atwill, Jerome Cowan. 1945

FOLKS ★★1/2 Comedy about a stock-exchange whiz who finds his perfect life turned upside down. Depending on your mood, this can be entertaining, or tasteless, and unfunny. Rated PG-13 for violence and profanity. 108m. **DIR:** Ted Kotcheff. **CAST:** Tom Selleck, Don Ameche, Anne Jackson, Christine Ebersole, Wendy Crewson, Michael Murphy. 1992

FOLLOW ME, BOYS! ★★★1/2 Heartwarming Disney film in which Fred MacMurray plays the new Boy Scout leader in a small 1930s town. 131m. **DIR:** Norman Tokar. **CAST:** Vera Miles, Fred MacMurray, Lillian Gish, Kurt Russell. 1966

FOLLOW ME QUIETLY ★★★ Low-budget thriller about a deranged killer who strangles people when it rains. Tight, fast-moving detective drama with standout performances. B&W; 60m. **DIR:** Richard Fleischer. **CAST:** William Lundigan, Dorothy Patrick, Jeff Corey. 1949

FOLLOW THAT CAMEL ★★★1/2 This British comedy, part of the *Carry On* series, features Phil Silvers as the conniving Sgt. Knockers. Lots of laughs, mostly derived from puns and sexist jokes. Some dialogue is a bit racy for young children. Not rated. 91m. **DIR:** Gerald Thomas. **CAST:** Phil Silvers, Jim Dale, Peter Butterworth, Charles Hawtrey, Anita Harris, Joan Sims, Kenneth Williams. 1967

FOLLOW THAT CAR 🎗 Typical good-ol'-boy action-adventure. Rated PG for language and violence. 96m. **DIR:** Daniel Haller. **CAST:** Dirk Benedict, Tanya Tucker, Teri Nunn. 1980

FOLLOW THAT DREAM ★★★1/2 Elvis is almost too sweet as the naive hillbilly who, along with his family, moves to a Florida beach. Some laughs result from their inability to fit in. The story is based on Richard Powell's novel *Pioneer Go Home*. Not rated; contains no objectionable material. 110m. **DIR:** Gordon Douglas. **CAST:** Elvis Presley, Arthur O'Connell, Joanna Moore, Anne Helm, Jack Kruschen. 1962

FOLLOW THE BOYS ★★★1/2 A World War II morale builder that still works as entertainment. The story is trite, but the star turns are terrific, particularly Orson Welles's magic act with Marlene Dietrich. George Raft heads the cast as a Hollywood star organizing a USO tour and putting it ahead of his private life. B&W; 110m. **DIR:** A. Edward Sutherland. **CAST:** George Raft, Vera Zorina, Marlene Dietrich, Orson Welles, Jeanette MacDonald, W. C. Fields, Sophie Tucker, The Andrews Sisters, Maria Montez, Nigel Bruce. 1944

FOLLOW THE FLEET ★★★★ Fred Astaire and Ginger Rogers are at their best as a dance team separated by World War II. However, sailor Astaire still has time to romance Rogers while shipmate Randolph Scott gives the same treatment to her screen sister Harriet Hilliard (Mrs. Ozzie Nelson). Look for Lucille Ball in a small part. B&W; 110m. **DIR:** Mark Sandrich. **CAST:** Fred Astaire, Ginger Rogers, Randolph Scott, Harriet Nelson, Betty Grable. 1936

FOOD OF THE GODS 🎗 H. G. Wells's story is trashed in this Bert I. Gordon bomb. After ingesting an unknown substance, various animals become giants and threaten the occupants of a remote mountain cabin. Rated PG. 88m. DIR: Bert I. Gordon. CAST: Marjoe Gortner, Ida Lupino, Pamela Franklin, Ralph Meeker. 1976

FOOD OF THE GODS PART II 💔 Disgusting sequel. Rated R for violence, profanity, and nudity. 90m. DIR: Damien Lee. CAST: Paul Coufos. 1989

FOOL AND HIS MONEY, A ★★★ A fool and his money may soon be parted, and that's exactly what advertising executive Morris Codman is counting on. Jonathan Penner plays Morris, who is looking for the next big thing. When God speaks to him through his television set, he's inspired to invent a new religion. Heaven help the poor flock who are about to get fleeced in this frequently funny comedy. Rated R for language. 84m. DIR: Daniel Adams. CAST: Jonathan Penner, Sandra Bullock, George Plimpton, Wendy Adams. 1988

FOOL FOR LOVE ★★★1/2 Writer-star Sam Shepard's disturbing, thought-provoking screenplay is about people who, as one of his characters comments, "can't help themselves." Shepard plays a cowboy-stuntman who is continuing his romantic pursuit of Kim Basinger in spite of her objections. For open-minded adults who appreciate daring, original works. Rated R for profanity and violence. 107m. DIR: Robert Altman. CAST: Sam Shepard, Kim Basinger, Harry Dean Stanton, Randy Quaid. 1986

FOOL KILLER, THE ★★ Set in the 1800s, this is a tale of a mischievous young runaway who learns about a legendary killer—who may well be his new traveling companion. A shivery variation on *Huckleberry Finn*. Not rated. B&W; 100m. DIR: Servando Gonzalez. CAST: Anthony Perkins, Edward Albert, Dana Elcar, Salome Jens, Henry Hull. 1967

FOOLIN' AROUND ★★★ Gary Busey went from his acclaimed title performance in *The Buddy Holly Story* to starring in this amiable rip-off of *The Graduate* and *The Heartbreak Kid*. Still, Busey, as a working-class boy who falls in love with rich girl Annette O'Toole, is always watchable. He and O'Toole make the movie's lack of originality easier to take. Rated PG. 111m. DIR: Richard T. Heffron. CAST: Gary Busey, Annette O'Toole, John Calvin, Eddie Albert, Cloris Leachman, Tony Randall. 1980

FOOLISH ★★ Stand-up comedian Foolish Waise and his hustler brother Fifty Dollah run afoul of a scary mobster while chasing their very personalized visions of the American Dream. Sidebars of this profanity-laced, muddled comic melodrama include a family death, romantic conflicts, and both domestic and street violence. Rated R for language, nudity, and sexual content. 86m. DIR: Dave Meyers. CAST: Eddie Griffin, Master P, Andrew Clay, Jonathan Banks, Amy Petersen, Marla Gibbs. 1999 DVD

FOOLISH WIVES ★★★★ Anticipating Orson Welles by two decades, director and star Erich Von Stroheim also wrote, produced, codesigned, and co-costumed this stark and unsettling account of a sleazy rogue's depraved use of women to achieve his aims. Von Stroheim is brilliant as the oily, morally corrupt, bogus nobleman plying his confidence game against the naïve rich in post–World War I Monaco

and Monte Carlo. The final scene is a masterful simile. Silent. B&W; 107m. DIR: Erich. Von Stroheim. CAST: Erich Von Stroheim, Mae Busch, Rudolph Christians. 1921–1922

FOOLS 💔 An aging star of horror pictures falls in love with the beautiful wife of an attorney. Rated PG. 97m. DIR: Tom Gries. CAST: Jason Robards Jr., Katharine Ross, Scott Hylands. 1970

FOOLS OF FORTUNE ★★ The troubles in Northern Ireland turn the idyllic childhood of Willie Clinton into a nightmare, and as an adult he plots his revenge. Based on the novel by William Trevor, this is a profoundly disturbing drama that features good performances but is of an intensity that makes it nearly unwatchable. Rated PG-13 for violence. 109m. DIR: Pat O'Connor. CAST: Mary Elizabeth Mastrantonio, Iain Glen, Julie Christie, Michael Kitchen, Sean McClory. 1990

FOOLS RUSH IN ★★★ East meets West in this pleasant comedy about a New York builder and a Las Vegas photographer (whose roots are in central Mexico) and the rocky marriage they create out of their one-night stand. Both in-laws step in to complicate matters and to allow the culture-clash jokes to accelerate. The few serious scenes take a backseat to humor. Rated PG-13 for sexual situations and language. 105m. DIR: Andy Tennant. CAST: Matthew Perry, Salma Hayek, Jon Tenney, Carlos Gomez, Jill Clayburgh, John Bennett Perry. 1997 DVD

FOOTLIGHT PARADE ★★★1/2 Brash and cocksure James Cagney is a hustling stage director bent upon continually topping himself with Busby Berkeley–type musical numbers, which, not surprisingly, are directed by Busby Berkeley. Another grand-scale musical from the early days of sound films. B&W; 100m. DIR: Lloyd Bacon. CAST: James Cagney, Ruby Keeler, Joan Blondell, Dick Powell, Guy Kibbee, Hugh Herbert, Frank McHugh. 1933

FOOTLIGHT SERENADE ★★ Heavyweight boxing champion Victor Mature means trouble for Broadway entertainers John Payne and Betty Grable when he joins their stage show. So-so musical. One of a series Grable made to boost morale during World War II. B&W; 80m. DIR: Gregory Ratoff. CAST: John Payne, Betty Grable, Victor Mature, Jane Wyman, James Gleason, Phil Silvers. 1942

FOOTLOOSE ★★★★ A highly entertaining film that combines the rock beat exuberance of *Flashdance* and *Risky Business* with an entertaining— and even touching—story. This features Kevin Bacon as a Chicago boy who finds himself transplanted to a small rural town where rock music and dancing are banned—until he decides to do something about it. Rated PG for slight profanity and brief violence. 107m. DIR: Herbert Ross. CAST: Kevin Bacon, Lori Singer, John Lithgow, Dianne Wiest, Christopher Penn, Sarah Jessica Parker. 1984

FOOTSTEPS IN THE DARK ★★1/2 A dated but interesting blend of comedy and crime with Errol Flynn at his self-mocking best. He is a mystery novelist who plays amateur detective and finds out he's bitten off more than he can chew. He gets out of it by laughing at it. One of Flynn's first modern-dress adventure roles. B&W; 96m. DIR: Lloyd Bacon. CAST: Errol Flynn, Brenda Marshall, Ralph Bellamy, William Frawley, Alan Hale Sr., Lucile Watson, Lee Patrick, Grant Mitchell, Allen Jenkins. **1941**

FOR A FEW DOLLARS MORE ★★1/2 Plot-heavy and overlong sequel to *A Fistful of Dollars* finds Clint Eastwood's "Man With No Name" partnered with shifty Lee Van Cleef, with both in pursuit of bad guy Gian Maria Volonté. Eastwood has his hands full, but the story contains few surprises. 130m. DIR: Sergio Leone. CAST: Clint Eastwood, Lee Van Cleef, Gian Maria Volonté, Klaus Kinski. **1965 DVD**

FOR A LOST SOLDIER ★★1/2 During World War II, a 12-year-old Dutch boy has an affair with a Canadian soldier in this film adapted from the autobiographical novel by Rudi van Dantzig. This Dutch import, one of the most professionally directed and acted of gay love stories, handles the subject matter with taste but is definitely not for everyone. In English and Dutch with subtitles. Not rated, the film has profanity, nudity, and simulated sex. 92m. DIR: Roeland Kerbosch. CAST: Jeroen Krabbé, Maarten Smit, Andrew Kelly. **1993**

FOR BETTER AND FOR WORSE ★★ A mixture of misguided "slapschtick" and unfunny lines sinks this otherwise passable comedy in which the pope is invited to a wedding—and accepts. Rated PG-13 for mild profanity. 94m. DIR: Paolo Barzman. CAST: Patrick Dempsey, Kelly Lynch, Gerard Rinaldi. **1992**

FOR BETTER OR WORSE ★★★ Jason Alexander directed and stars in this lightweight comedy about a hapless loser (his fiancée has left him; he attends twelve-step programs just for the company) whose life is turned upside down when his criminal brother shows up. Before Alexander can protest, he's on the run with his no-good brother and beautiful new sister-in-law, fleeing thugs and falling in love. Rated PG-13 for violence and profanity. 95m. DIR: Jason Alexander. CAST: Jason Alexander, James Woods, Lolita Davidovich, Joe Mantegna, Jay Mohr. **1995**

●**FOR HIRE** ★★ An author's latest book sets into motion a tale of murder for hire. When his source is threatened by exposure, the author turns to a terminally ill cabdriver to take care of his problem. The relationship between author Joe Mantegna and cabdriver Rob Lowe shows promise, but once the setup has been established, it's all downhill. Rated R for language and violence. 93m. DIR: Jean Pellerin. CAST: Joe Mantegna, Rob Lowe. **1997 DVD**

FOR KEEPS 🖤 The serious issue of teen pregnancy is irresponsibly trivialized. Rated PG-13 for frank language. 98m. DIR: John G. Avildsen. CAST: Molly Ringwald, Randall Batinkoff, Kenneth Mars, Brenda Vaccaro, Conchata Ferrell, Miriam Flynn. **1988**

FOR LADIES ONLY ★★★ A young, good-looking farm-belt guy goes to New York to become a star. He finally turns to stripping to make more money. This stale, TV film is a predictable morality play made fresher with the role reversal. 94m. DIR: Mel Damski. CAST: Gregory Harrison, Lee Grant, Louise Lasser, Dinah Manoff. **1981**

FOR LOVE ALONE ★★★1/2 An Australian girl is frustrated by the romantic double standard of the 1930s. Helen Buday plays the lovelorn student willing to waste her life on her selfish professor (Hugo

Weaving) until she meets a dashing banker (Sam Neill). Buday and Neill are excellent, but Weaving offers a very wooden performance. Rated PG for partial nudity and simulated sex. 102m. DIR: Stephen Wallace. CAST: Helen Buday, Sam Neill, Hugo Weaving. **1985**

FOR LOVE OF ANGELA ★★ A beautiful jewelry clerk falls in love with the store owner's son. His meddling mom tries to break them up. Originally made for commercial TV, this film has numerous cuts and breakaways that are most distracting. 105m. DIR: Rudy Vejar. CAST: Sarah Rush, Barbara Mallory, David Winn, Margaret Fairchild, Dr. Joyce Brothers. **1982**

FOR LOVE OF IVY ★★★★ Sidney Poitier delivers a terrific performance as Jack Parks, trucking company owner by day and gambling operator by night. Ivy (Abbey Lincoln) is a maid for a wealthy family. When she decides to leave their employ, the family's children (Beau Bridges and Lauri Peters) connive to get Parks to take her out and make her happy. Carroll O'Connor and Nan Martin play Ivy's employers. This is a fine comedy-drama with a wonderful ending. 101m. DIR: Daniel Mann. CAST: Sidney Poitier, Abbey Lincoln, Beau Bridges, Nan Martin, Carroll O'Connor, Lauri Peters. **1968 DVD**

●**FOR LOVE OF THE GAME** ★★★★ While not quite up to the heroic status of 1984's *The Natural*—although it certainly *wants* to be—this is a worthy crescendo to what history undoubtedly will term the Costner Baseball Trilogy. This, from the Michael Shaara novel, finally, is *his* character's story: no mere observer of sanctified events (*Field of Dreams*) or witness to another player's rise to success (*Bull Durham*), Costner's Billy Chapel is a well-respected and much-honored veteran pitcher who has spent his entire professional career with the Detroit Tigers ... and now faces the tumultuous decision whether to allow himself to be traded when the team is sold, or leave the game entirely. On top of this, in a subplot that isn't quite as successful, the love of his life has decided to abandon him. Events leading up to both these catastrophes are played out in flashback between the innings of a climactic, season-ending game. Fans disenchanted by what baseball has become need look no further than the films that have portrayed it best, and this one deserves placement in their company. Rated PG-13 for mild sensuality and profanity. 137m. DIR: Sam Raimi. CAST: Kevin Costner, Kelly Preston, John C. Reilly, Jena Malone, Brian Cox. **1999 DVD**

FOR LOVE OR MONEY ★★★1/2 An ambitious, fast-talking hotel concierge is on the way to realizing his ultimate dream until romance conflicts with finance. This movie is the kind of thing Michael J. Fox does best and could have been titled *The Secret of My Success, Part II*. That's not a put-down, either; this entertaining comedy should be popular with Fox's fans. Rated PG for brief profanity and suggested sex. 95m. DIR: Barry Sonnenfeld. CAST: Michael J. Fox, Gabrielle Anwar, Anthony Higgins, Bob Balaban, Michael Tucker, Udo Kier, Dan Hedaya, Isaac Mizrahi, Patrick Breen, Simon Jones. **1993**

FOR ME AND MY GAL ★★★ A colorful tribute to the great and grand days of vaudeville before World War I, this tuneful trip down memory lane boosted Judy Garland's stock out of sight and made a star of Gene Kelly, he of the fleet-footed and beguiling smile. Flaws aside—the predictable plot needs a shave—this is a generally warm, invigorating picture rife with the nostalgia of happy times. B&W; 104m. **DIR:** Busby Berkeley. **CAST:** Judy Garland, Gene Kelly, George Murphy, Stephen McNally, Keenan Wynn. **1942**

FOR PETE'S SAKE ★★★ Lightweight comedy vehicle tailor-made to fit the talents of Barbra Streisand. In this one she plays the wife of cabdriver Michael Sarrazin, trying to raise money for him while becoming involved with underworld thugs. Strictly for Streisand fans. Rated PG. 90m. **DIR:** Peter Yates. **CAST:** Barbra Streisand, Michael Sarrazin, Estelle Parsons, Molly Picon. **1974**

FOR QUEEN AND COUNTRY ★★★1/2 A taut, tragic combination of social commentary and ghetto thriller focusing on racism in contemporary England. American actor Denzel Washington is superb as a black working-class British soldier who returns home from military service to find himself restricted to a second-class life. Rated R. 108m. **DIR:** Martin Stellman. **CAST:** Denzel Washington, Amanda Redman, George Baker. **1989**

FOR RICHER, FOR POORER ★★ Self-made millionaire Jack Lemmon despairs when son Jonathan Silverman seems content to do little beyond spending Dad's money. The solution? Give it all away, thus *forcing* the bum to pull his own weight. Lame made-for-cable comedy. Rated PG. 90m. **DIR:** Jay Sandrich. **CAST:** Jack Lemmon, Talia Shire, Jonathan Silverman, Joanna Gleason, Madeline Kahn. **1992**

FOR RICHER OR POORER ★★ A wacky businessman with a penchant for theme parks and his spoiled wife go on the lam after a ballistic IRS agent decides to take them down. Things pick up when the couple hides out in an Amish colony. The running joke is the contrast between the overly indulged city slickers and the simple world they've entered. Unfortunately, only half the gags really work. Rated PG-13 for language and sexual situations. 118m. **DIR:** Bryan Spicer. **CAST:** Tim Allen, Kirstie Alley, Jay O. Sanders, Michael Lerner, Wayne Knight, Larry Miller. **1997 DVD**

FOR ROSEANNA ★★★1/2 In a small Italian village, devoted husband Marcello (Jean Reno) is desperate to fulfill the wish of his dying wife, Roseanna (Mercedes Ruehl), to be buried next to her dead daughter. Problem is, there are only a few sites left in the graveyard, so while Roseanna is busy trying to find a new wife to take her place, Marcello desperately tries to keep everyone else in town alive. This rather dark premise masks a sweetly romantic film. Rated PG-13 for sexual situations. 95m. **DIR:** Paul Weiland. **CAST:** Jean Reno, Mercedes Ruehl, Polly Walker, Mark Frankel. **1997**

FOR THE BOYS ★★★1/2 Show-biz pseudobiography is an ambitious, larger-than-life examination of the impact on America of the last three major wars. The story is told through the experiences of two USO entertainers, the brash Dixie Leonard (Bette Midler) and the egotistical Eddie Sparks (James Caan). Not all of its ambitions are met, but this musical still succeeds as an emotional experience. Rated R for profanity and violence. 148m. **DIR:** Mark Rydell. **CAST:** Bette Midler, James Caan, George Segal, Patrick O'Neal, Christopher Rydell, Arliss Howard, Arye Gross, Norman Fell, Rosemary Murphy, Bud Yorkin. **1991**

FOR THE FIRST TIME ★★★ An opera star on tour in Europe meets and falls in love with a deaf girl. More substance than usual for a Mario Lanza movie. Sadly the last film in his short career. 97m. **DIR:** Rudolph Maté. **CAST:** Mario Lanza, Johanna Von Koszian, Kurt Kasznar, Zsa Zsa Gabor. **1959**

FOR THE LOVE OF BENJI ★★★1/2 The adorable mutt cleverly saves the day again when he takes on a spy ring in Athens. The whole family can enjoy this one together. Rated G. 85m. **DIR:** Joe Camp. **CAST:** Benji, Patsy Garrett, Cynthia Smith, Allen Fuizat, Ed Nelson. **1977**

FOR THE LOVE OF IT ★★1/2 This would-be wacky comedy is so confusing, you'll find yourself absorbed. Don Rickles wants the Russians' secret plans to take over the Middle East to create a new video game called "Doom's Day," but the CIA and FBI are also interested in them. Some of the chase scenes become so involved that the viewer forgets this is a comedy. Rated PG for violence and adult themes. 98m. **DIR:** Hal Kanter. **CAST:** Don Rickles, Deborah Raffin, Jeff Conaway, Tom Bosley, Henry Gibson, Barbi Benton, Adam West, Norman Fell, Noriyuki "Pat" Morita. **1980**

FOR THE MOMENT ★★1/2 Promoted as a nostalgic romance, this wartime drama is a fairly downbeat affair. Two airmen undergoing training in Canada early in World War II fall in love with married women whose husbands have already left for the war. Rated PG-13 for adult situations, profanity, and violence. 120m. **DIR:** Aaron Kim Johnston. **CAST:** Russell Crowe, Christianne Hirt, Wanda Cannon. **1995**

FOR US THE LIVING: THE MEDGAR EVERS STORY ★★★★ Assassinated civil-rights activist Medgar Evers is profiled in this inspirational drama. Adapted from Evers's wife's biography, this film gives a look at the total person, not just the legends surrounding him. Originally made for television, thus is unrated. 90m. **DIR:** Michael Schultz. **CAST:** Howard Rollins Jr., Irene Cara, Margaret Avery, Roscoe Lee Browne. **1983**

FOR WHOM THE BELL TOLLS ★★★1/2 The film version of Ernest Hemingway's story about patriots and outsiders fighting side by side during the Spanish Civil War. The pace is slow, and the purpose of the fight is never made clear. Greek actress Katina Paxinou won a supporting Oscar and her performance is still fiery and entertaining but Gary Cooper is listless and Ingrid Bergman self-conscious. 174m. **DIR:** Sam Wood. **CAST:** Gary Cooper, Ingrid Bergman, Katina Paxinou, Akim Tamiroff, Joseph Calleia, Arturo De Cordova, Mikhail Rasumny. **1943 DVD**

FOR YOUR EYES ONLY ★★★1/2 For the first time since Roger Moore took over the role of 007 from Sean Connery, we have a film in the style that made the best Bond films—*From Russia with Love* and *Goldfinger*—so enjoyable. *For Your Eyes Only* is genuine spy adventure, closer in spirit to the novels by Ian Fleming. Rated PG. 127m. **DIR:** John Glen.

CAST: Roger Moore, Carole Bouquet, Lynn-Holly Johnson, Topol. 1981 DVD

FOR YOUR HEIGHT ONLY ★★1/2 Filipino spoof of James Bond movies starring midget actor Weng Weng as Agent 003. Not rated; has mild sexual implications. 90m. DIR: Not credited. CAST: Weng Weng. 1983 DVD

FOR YOUR LOVE ONLY ★★ European beauty Nastassja Kinski stars as a young student who has an affair with her teacher, which leads to murder and blackmail. Pretty dull soap opera made for German television and released theatrically in 1982. Not rated; contains sexual situations and violence. 97m. DIR: Wolfgang Petersen. CAST: Nastassja Kinski, Christian Quadflieg. 1976

FORBIDDEN ★★★ Made-for-cable film about a gentile woman who falls in love with a Jewish man during World War II: a crime in Hitler's Germany. Enough suspense here to keep the viewer attentive, but not enough atmosphere to make it as intense as the melodramatic soundtrack assumes it to be. Not rated, but the equivalent of a PG for some violence and light sex. 114m. DIR: Anthony Page. CAST: Jacqueline Bisset, Jurgen Prochnow, Irene Worth, Peter Vaughan. 1984

FORBIDDEN CHOICES ★★1/2 This superficial adaptation of Carolyn Chute's The Beans of Egypt, Maine misses the novel's rich texture and emerges as little more than an unsympathetic, episodic study of a young stud who can't keep his pants zipped. Martha Plimpton does nice work as the narrator, who falls for this fellow from the wrong side of the tracks, and eventually regrets this choice. Rated R for profanity, nudity, simulated sex, and rape. 109m. DIR: Jennifer Warren. CAST: Martha Plimpton, Kelly Lynch, Rutger Hauer, Patrick McGaw. 1994

FORBIDDEN DANCE, THE ♥ The Lambada, the sensuous Brazilian dance craze. Rated PG-13. 90m. DIR: Greydon Clark. CAST: Laura Herring, Jeff James, Richard Lynch. 1990 DVD

•FORBIDDEN FRUIT ★★★1/2 Usually known as a comedian, Fernandel plays it straight in this drama based on a novel by Georges Simenon. He's a middle-aged country doctor who tries to break out of his bourgeois life by having an affair with a young prostitute. Once-scandalous film is no longer shocking, but still a compelling story. In French with English subtitles. Not rated; contains brief nudity. B&W; 97m. DIR: Henri Verneuil. CAST: Fernandel, Françoise Arnoul, Sylvie. 1952

FORBIDDEN GAMES (1951) ★★★★★ It has been said that Forbidden Games is to World War II what Grand Illusion is to World War I. The horror of war has never been more real than as portrayed here against the bucolic surroundings of the French countryside. At the nucleus of the plot is Paulette, played by 5-year-old Brigitte Fossey. Witnessing German troops kill her parents twists the girl, who acquires an attraction to the symbols of death. A truly tragic, must-see work. In French with English subtitles. B&W; 87m. DIR: René Clement. CAST: Brigitte Fossey, Georges Poujouly. 1951

FORBIDDEN GAMES (1995) ♥ Private investigator looks into the death of a modeling-agency director in

a soft-core erotic thriller that should be forbidden. Not rated; contains nudity, violence, and profanity. 89m. DIR: Edward Holzman. CAST: Jeff Griggs, Lesli Kay Sterling, Gail Harris. 1995

FORBIDDEN PLANET ★★★★1/2 This is the most highly regarded sci-fi film of the 1950s. Its special-effects breakthroughs are rather tame today, but its story remains interesting. As a space mission from Earth lands on the Planet Altair-4 in the year 2200, they encounter a doctor (Walter Pidgeon) and his daughter (Anne Francis) who are all that remain from a previous colonization attempt. It soon becomes apparent that some unseen force on the planet does not bid them welcome. 98m. DIR: Fred M. Wilcox. CAST: Walter Pidgeon, Anne Francis, Leslie Nielsen, Jack Kelly. 1956 DVD

FORBIDDEN QUEST ★★★★ Filmmaker Peter Delpeut mixed documentary footage taken by polar explorers of the early twentieth century with a fictional story about one such failed expedition to create this fascinating piece of history. Although some viewers might prefer to see the real-life scenes by themselves, this method is much more accessible (and provides a use for those cases when only fragments of film have survived). Not rated. B&W/color; 75m. DIR: Peter Delpeut. 1995

•FORBIDDEN SINS ★★1/2 Shannon Tweed stars as an attorney who falls in love with the rich client she's defending on a murder case. Of course, all is not as it seems. Rated R for profanity, nudity, violence, and sexual situations. 90m. DIR: Robert Angelo. CAST: Shannon Tweed, Corbin Timbrook, Timothy Vahle, Myles O'Brien. 1998

FORBIDDEN SUN ♥ Lauren Hutton as an ex-Olympian who coaches a group of young female hopefuls on the isle of Crete. Rated R for violence and adult situations. 88m. DIR: Zelda Barron. CAST: Lauren Hutton, Cliff De Young, René Estevez. 1989

FORBIDDEN TRAIL ★★★1/2 In this superior series Western, one of several Buck Jones made for Columbia Pictures in the 1930s, the star and Al Smith play a couple of happy-go-lucky cowboys who find themselves in the middle of a range war. Jones, usually the stalwart, square-jawed defender of justice, takes a comedic approach to his part, and the results are quite pleasing. B&W; 71m. DIR: Lambert Hillyer. CAST: Buck Jones, Barbara Weeks, Mary Carr, Al Smith. 1932

FORBIDDEN TRAILS ★★ In this, the least interesting of the Rough Riders Westerns, a pair of hardened criminals (Charles King and Bud Osborne) force a youngster (Dave O'Brien) to take part in their evil schemes. Robert N. Bradbury's direction lacks the energy brought to the series by Howard Bretherton, but the stars are as watchable as ever. B&W; 55m. DIR: Robert N. Bradbury. CAST: Buck Jones, Tim McCoy, Raymond Hatton, Dave O'Brien, Tristram Coffin, Charles King. 1941

FORBIDDEN WORLD ★★ Jesse Vint was rescued from the obscurity of his deep-space death in Silent Running, and his reward was a starring role in this rip-off of Alien in which an experimental foodstuff starts killing the inhabitants of a space colony. Rated R for violence. 77m. DIR: Allan Holzman. CAST: Jesse

Vint, Dawn Dunlap, June Chadwick, Linden Chiles. **1982**

FORBIDDEN ZONE 🎬 Absurd, would-be "cult" film has Herve Villechaize as the ruler of a bizarre kingdom located in the "Sixth Dimension." A sort-of comedy, this should be avoided by all means. Rated R for nudity and adult content. B&W; 76m. **DIR:** Richard Elfman. **CAST:** Herve Villechaize, Susan Tyrrell, Marie-Pascale Elfman, Viva. **1980**

FORBIDDEN ZONE: ALIEN ABDUCTION 🎬 Science-fiction trappings do little to hide the fact that this film is just an excuse to get women out of their clothes. Three women discover they've each been abducted by an alien and used for sexual experiments. Not rated; contains nudity and adult situations. 90m. **DIR:** Lucian S. Diamonde. **CAST:** Darcy De Moss, Pia Reyes, Dmitri Bogmaz, Carmen Lacatus. **1996**

FORCE, THE ★★1/2 OK crime-drama about a rookie cop who crosses paths with a hardboiled homicide detective who winds up dead. When he begins to investigate the circumstances behind the death, he's met with resistance by everyone on the force, including his superiors, who suggest he drop the matter. No surprises here, but enough close calls to warrant a look. Rated R for violence, language, and nudity. 94m. **DIR:** Mark Rosman. **CAST:** Jason Gedrick, Kim Delaney, Gary Hudson. **1994**

FORCE FIVE ★★ In this action-packed but predictable martial arts film, a soldier of fortune and his four buddies rescue a woman held on a remote island. Rated R for violence, nudity, and profanity. 78m. **DIR:** Robert Clouse. **CAST:** Gerald Gordon, Nick Pryor, Bradford Dillman, Tom Villard. **1981**

FORCE OF ARMS ★★ A war drama with more talk than action, this film steals some of Hemingway's *A Farewell to Arms* and adds modern wartime philosophy. A soldier feels responsible when his buddies are killed in battle but regains self-esteem when he falls in love with a WAC. B&W; 99m. **DIR:** Michael Curtiz. **CAST:** William Holden, Nancy Olson, Gene Evans, Frank Lovejoy. **1951**

FORCE OF EVIL ★★★ A lawyer (John Garfield) abandons his principles and goes to work for a racketeer in this somber, downbeat story of corruption and loss of values. Compelling story and acting compensate for some of the heavy-handedness of the approach. A good study of ambition and the different paths it leads the characters on. B&W; 78m. **DIR:** Abraham Polonsky. **CAST:** John Garfield, Thomas Gomez, Roy Roberts, Marie Windsor. **1948**

FORCE OF ONE ★★★ This is the follow-up to *Good Guys Wear Black*. In this karate film, Chuck Norris cleans up a California town that has drug problems. As always, it only takes one good guy (Norris) to kick and/or punch some sense into the bad guys. Rated PG. 90m. **DIR:** Paul Aaron. **CAST:** Chuck Norris, Jennifer O'Neill, James Whitmore, Pepe Serna. **1979**

FORCE TEN FROM NAVARONE 🎬 Poor sequel to the classic *Guns of Navarone*. 118m. **DIR:** Guy Hamilton. **CAST:** Robert Shaw, Harrison Ford, Edward Fox, Franco Nero, Barbara Bach, Carl Weathers, Richard Kiel. **1978 DVD**

FORCED MARCH ★★★ Chris Sarandon is a deteriorating American Method actor portraying Miklos Radnoti, in a movie about the Hungarian poet's ordeal at a Jewish labor camp. As a film about the making of a film it is engaging at times—especially as it relates each character's dedication to the project. Not rated. 104m. **DIR:** Rick King. **CAST:** Chris Sarandon, Renee Soutendijk, Josef Sommer, John Seitz. **1989**

FORCED VENGEANCE ★★1/2 Even pacing and a somewhat suspenseful plot are not enough to make this film a must-see—unless you're a die-hard Chuck Norris fan, that is. This time, our martial arts master plays a casino security chief living in the Far East. Rated R for violence, nudity, and profanity. 90m. **DIR:** James Fargo. **CAST:** Chuck Norris, Mary Louise Weller, Camilla Griggs, Michael Cavanaugh, David Opatoshu, Seiji Sakaguchi. **1982**

FORCES OF NATURE ★★★1/2 The path to true love gets rocky in this engaging and occasionally wild tale. Poor Ben Affleck just wants to reach Savannah in time for his own wedding, but the journey is punctuated by countless examples of marriages gone bad, not to mention the delectable distraction of free-spirited Sandra Bullock. Although rainstorms and hurricanes impede our hero's progress, the script never loses sight of the primary quandary: Ben's a nice guy, and nice guys don't dump their soon-to-be wives ... no matter how sparkling the temptation. Rated PG-13 for profanity and mild sexual content. 102m. **DIR:** Bronwen Hughes. **CAST:** Sandra Bullock, Ben Affleck, Maura Tierney, Steve Zahn, Blythe Danner, Ronny Cox, David Strickland, Meredith Scott Lynn. **1999 DVD**

FORD: THE MAN & THE MACHINE ★★1/2 This TV biography of Henry Ford runs out of gas long before the film does. Canadian effort stars Cliff Robertson as the grandfather of the automobile, only to let senility slip in and affect the script. Episodic storytelling revs its engine for those interested in such fare, but doesn't flesh out the story enough for a full road trip. 210m. **DIR:** Allan Eastman. **CAST:** Cliff Robertson, Hope Lange, Michael Ironside, Heather Thomas, R. H. Thomson. **1987**

FOREIGN AFFAIRS ★★★ Opposites attract in this light, warm story of a college professor and a sanitation engineer who meet in England and fall in love. Stars rise above familiar story line and keep interest level up. 106m. **DIR:** Jim O'Brien. **CAST:** Joanne Woodward, Brian Dennehy, Eric Stoltz, Stephanie Beacham, Ian Richardson. **1993**

FOREIGN BODY ★★★ An Indian émigré in London, longing to make a fortune and lose his virginity, makes both wishes come true by posing as a doctor to upper-class hypochondriacs. So-so script benefits from perky performances by a superior British cast. Rated PG-13 for ribald humor. 108m. **DIR:** Ronald Neame. **CAST:** Victor Banerjee, Warren Mitchell, Amanda Donohoe, Trevor Howard. **1986**

FOREIGN CORRESPONDENT ★★★★★ Classic Alfred Hitchcock thriller still stands as one of his most complex and satisfying films. Joel McCrea stars as an American reporter in Europe during the war, caught up in all sorts of intrigue, romance, etc., in his dealings with Nazi spies, hired killers, and the like as he attempts to get the truth to the American public. B&W; 120m. DIR: Alfred Hitchcock. CAST: Joel McCrea, Laraine Day, Herbert Marshall, George Sanders, Edmund Gwenn. 1940

FOREIGN FIELD, A ★★★★ Three Allied soldiers, determined to revisit the spot that most changed their lives, return to Normandy nearly fifty years after D day. Memories, ranging from bitter to bittersweet, flood them as they discover the past was not quite as they remembered. A spirited and weathered cast brings a touching and unexpectedly funny perspective to that bloody chapter of World War II. Made for British and American TV. Not rated; contains profanity. 90m. DIR: Charles Sturridge. CAST: Alec Guinness, Leo McKern, John Randolph, Jeanne Moreau, Lauren Bacall, Geraldine Chaplin, Edward Herrmann. 1993

FOREIGN STUDENT ★★1/2 In 1956 at a small Virginia university, a visiting French student (Marco Hofschneider) falls in love with a young black woman (Robin Givens). This low-budget drama has sincere performances, sensitive direction, and pretty photography, but the script is trite and predictable, and the dialogue is often unintentionally funny. Rated R for nudity. 93m. DIR: Eva Sereny. CAST: Marco Hofschneider, Robin Givens, Rich Johnson, Charlotte Ross, Edward Herrmann, Jack Coleman, Charles Dutton, Hinton Battle, Anthony Herrera. 1994

FOREST, THE 🎬 Waste of time. Not rated. 90m. DIR: Don Jones. CAST: Dean Russell, Michael Brody. 1983

FOREST WARRIOR ★★★★ Surprisingly enjoyable family film in which Chuck Norris stars as a forest spirit who joins a group of kids to defend the forest from a greedy lumber mogul. Excellent performances make for an entertaining and inspirational adventure. Instead of *Walker, Texas Ranger* think *Walker, Power Ranger*, and you'll get the general idea. 98m. DIR: Aaron Norris. CAST: Chuck Norris, Terry Kiser, Max Gail, Roscoe Lee Browne, Trent Knight, Megan Paul, Josh Wolford, Jordan Brower, Michael Friedman, William Sanderson, Loretta Swit, Michael Beck. 1996

FOREVER ★★ How long does this movie seem to last? The title says it all. Once the filmmakers get past the initial plot device—a music-video director moves into a haunted house and falls in love with a ghost—the film seems to fall apart. There's way too much going on for the film's own good, and the hammy performances don't lend credibility to the serious undercurrents. Rated R for sexuality. 93m. DIR: Thomas Palmer Jr. CAST: Sean Young, Keith Coogan, Diane Ladd, Sally Kirkland. 1992

FOREVER AMBER ★★★1/2 After much tampering by censors, Kathleen Winsor's (then) lusty bestseller made it to the screen. Linda Darnell plays ambitious tavern wench Amber St. Clare, who seduces all in sight until she becomes the mistress of Charles II. First-rate production and cast. 140m. DIR: Otto Preminger. CAST: Linda Darnell, Cornel Wilde, Richard Greene, George Sanders, Glenn Langan, Richard Haydn, Jessica Tandy, Anne Revere, John Russell, Leo G. Carroll, Margaret Wycherly. 1947

FOREVER AND A DAY ★★★★ A morale builder during World War II and worth seeing for its cast, this film is a series of episodes linked together by a regal house in war-torn London. An American with British ancestry (Kent Smith) visits the house with plans to take it over. B&W; 104m. DIR: René Clair, Robert Stevenson, Herbert Wilcox, Victor Saville, Cedric Hardwicke, Edmund Goulding. CAST: Kent Smith, Charles Laughton, Anna Neagle, Ray Milland, Claude Rains, Ida Lupino, Merle Oberon, Brian Aherne, Victor McLaglen, Robert Cummings, Buster Keaton, Elsa Lanchester. 1943 DVD

FOREVER DARLING ★★1/2 Lucille Ball's marriage to chemist Desi Arnaz is in trouble. Her guardian angel (James Mason) tries to put things right. Mild romantic comedy with too few of the *I Love Lucy*–style antics. 96m. DIR: Alexander Hall. CAST: Lucille Ball, Desi Arnaz Sr., James Mason, Louis Calhern, Marilyn Maxwell. 1956

FOREVER JAMES DEAN ★★★★ Anyone remotely interested in the mercurial star James Dean will want to see this documentary—tracing Dean's career from his first Pepsi commercial to the final scene in *Giant*. From Emmy-winning filmmaker Ara Chekmayan. 69m. DIR: Ara Chekmayan. 1988

FOREVER LULU 🎬 Ridiculous rip-off of *Desperately Seeking Susan*. Rated R for nudity, profanity, and violence. 86m. DIR: Amos Kollek. CAST: Hanna Schygulla, Deborah Harry, Alec Baldwin, Paul Gleason, Annie Golden, Dr. Ruth Westheimer, Charles Ludlam. 1987

FOREVER MARY ★★★ A teacher in between assignments accepts a position at a notorious boys' reform school. His students are tough street kids with little hope of redemption. Updated version of *To Sir With Love*, Italian style. In Italian with English subtitles. Not rated; contains violence and profanity. 100m. DIR: Marco Risi. CAST: Michele Placido, Claudio Amendola. 1989

FOREVER YOUNG (1983) ★★ This slow-moving British soap opera features a handsome priest who is idolized by a lonely boy. Not rated, but brief nudity and mature themes would make it comparable with a PG. 85m. DIR: David Drury. CAST: James Aubrey, Nicholas Gecks, Alec McCowen. 1983

FOREVER YOUNG (1992) ★★★ In a charming performance, Mel Gibson plays a test pilot who has himself cryogenically frozen in 1939 only to wake up in 1992—alone. Gibson and his costars give this piece of fluff a buoyancy. Rated PG for profanity. 104m. DIR: Steve Miner. CAST: Mel Gibson, Jamie Lee Curtis, Elijah Wood, Isabel Glasser, Joe Morton, David Marshall Grant. 1993 DVD

FORGET MOZART ★★ Poorly paced, surreal whodunit revolving around Mozart. But who killed him? In German with English subtitles. Not rated, contains nudity. 93m. DIR: Salvo Luther. CAST: Armin Mueller-Stahl. 1986

FORGET PARIS ★★★1/2 A romantic comedy with more comedy than romance focusing on what happens after the honeymoon ends and the marriage begins. Billy Crystal's sly, observant humor elicits some good belly laughs, and, as usual, Debra Winger brings a sassy intelligence to her character that adds emo-ional depth missing from the script. Rated PG-13. 100m. **DIR:** Billy Crystal. **CAST:** Billy Crystal, Debra Winger, Joe Mantegna, Cynthia Stevenson, Richard Masur, Julie Kavner, William Hickey. **1995 DVD**

FORGOTTEN, THE ★★1/2 Six Vietnam Green Beret POWs are released after seventeen years only to be put through more torture by U.S. officials. A disturbing psychological thriller, this made-for-cable TV movie has violence and some strong language. 96m. **DIR:** James Keach. **CAST:** Keith Carradine, Steve Railsback, Stacy Keach. **1989**

FORGOTTEN ONE, THE ★★1/2 Unusual romantic triangle, in which novelist Terry O'Quinn moves into a house haunted by a ghost from his past life. The ghost attempts to have O'Quinn kill himself, so that they may be together in the afterlife. Kristy McNichol contributes a fine performance. Rated R for nudity and profanity. 89m. **DIR:** Phillip Badger. **CAST:** Terry O'Quinn, Kristy McNichol. **1989**

FORGOTTEN PRISONERS ★★★ The horrors of life in a Turkish prison are vividly depicted in this gutwrenching made-for-cable drama that focuses on human rights. Ron Silver is excellent as a lawyer hired by Amnesty International. 92m. **DIR:** Robert Greenwald. **CAST:** Ron Silver, Hector Elizondo, Roger Daltrey. **1990**

FORGOTTEN SILVER ★★★1/2 Director Peter Jackson explores the life and career of forgotten New Zealand cinema pioneer Colin McKenzie, who invented sound movies in 1908 and color film in 1914. The only catch is that the film is a hilarious hoax; McKenzie never existed. Still, the "vintage" footage and the on-camera comments by actor Sam Neill and historian Leonard Maltin were so convincing that, when it was shown without a disclaimer on New Zealand TV, 80 percent of the audience believed it. This one is an absolute must for film buffs. Not rated; suitable for all audiences. 53m. **DIR:** Peter Jackson. **CAST:** Costa Botes, Marguerite Hurst, Peter Jackson, Leonard Maltin, Sam Neill. **1996**

FORGOTTEN TUNE FOR THE FLUTE, A ★★★ This Glasnost romantic comedy is a little long and stumbles with a somewhat contrived ending, but it's a joy otherwise. It introduces to the West the vivacious and talented Tatyana Dogileva and is a perfect remedy for American movie watchers who think all Russian films are solemn enterprises at best, epic drags at worst. In Russian with English subtitles. 131m. **DIR:** Eldar Ryazanov. **CAST:** Tatyana Dogileva. **1988**

FORLORN RIVER ★★★ Exciting Zane Grey story has horse thieves trying to buy army mounts with sixguns. Good photography, literate script. B&W; 56m. **DIR:** Charles Barton. **CAST:** Buster Crabbe, June Martel, Harvey Stephens. **1937**

FORMULA, THE ★★ Take a plot to conceal a method of producing enough synthetic fuel to take care of the current oil shortage and add two superstars like George C. Scott and Marlon Brando. Sounds like the formula for a real blockbuster, doesn't it? Unfortunately, it turns out to be the formula for a major disappointment. Rated R. 117m. **DIR:** John G. Avildsen. **CAST:** George C. Scott, Marlon Brando, Marthe Keller, John Gielgud, G. D. Spradlin. **1980**

FORREST GUMP ★★★★★ Based on the novel by Winston Groom, the feel-good movie of 1994 boasts a magnificent performance by Tom Hanks and remarkable special effects. Despite his 75 I.Q., Hanks's title character finds himself a major player in events from the 1950s to the 1980s as director Robert Zemeckis's wizardry places him in context with everyone from Elvis Presley to President John F. Kennedy by using stand-ins and actual documentary footage. Somehow, this sleight of hand becomes anything but a slight piece of entertainment. Rated PG-13 for violence and profanity. 142m. **DIR:** Robert Zemeckis. **CAST:** Tom Hanks, Sally Field, Robin Wright, Gary Sinise, Mykelti Williamson, Michael Connor Humphreys. **1994**

FORSAKING ALL OTHERS ★★★ Offbeat casting with Clark Gable as the nice guy, for years secretly in love with Joan Crawford, while she allows herself to be manipulated by a cad. The movie is stolen by lovely Billie Burke and droll Charles Butterworth. B&W; 84m. **DIR:** W. S. Van Dyke. **CAST:** Joan Crawford, Clark Gable, Robert Montgomery, Charles Butterworth, Billie Burke, Rosalind Russell. **1934**

FORT APACHE ★★★★1/2 The first entry in director John Ford's celebrated cavalry trilogy stars Henry Fonda as a post commandant who decides to make a name for himself by starting a war with the Apaches, against the advice of an experienced soldier (John Wayne). Great film. B&W; 127m. **DIR:** John Ford. **CAST:** John Wayne, Henry Fonda, Shirley Temple, Ward Bond, John Agar, George O'Brien. **1948**

FORT APACHE—THE BRONX ★★★1/2 Jarring violence surfaces throughout this story about New York's crime-besieged South Bronx, but absorbing dramatic elements give this routine cops-and-criminals format gutsy substance. Paul Newman, as an idealistic police veteran, proves his screen magnetism hasn't withered with time. The supporting cast is top-notch. Rated R for violence, profanity, and sexual references. 125m. **DIR:** Daniel Petrie. **CAST:** Paul Newman, Ken Wahl, Edward Asner, Kathleen Beller, Rachel Ticotin. **1981**

FORT OSAGE ★★★ Nefarious businessmen cause an Indian uprising while taking money from settlers. Compact oater is better than one would expect. B&W; 72m. **DIR:** Lesley Selander. **CAST:** Rod Cameron, Jane Nigh, Morris Ankrum (Stepen Morris) Douglas Kennedy. **1951**

FORT SAGANNE ★★★★ Gérard Depardieu stars as a young peasant who dreams of being an officer in the French Foreign Legion but is forced to join as a lowly enlisted man. Stationed at a forgotten desert outpost in Algeria, his subsequent adventures and personal tragedies make for engrossing viewing. In French with English subtitles. Not rated; contains nudity and violence. 180m. **DIR:** Alain Corneau. **CAST:** Gérard Depardieu, Catherine Deneuve, Philippe Noiret, Sophie Marceau. **1984**

FORTRESS (1985) ★★1/2 In this drawn-out story of a mass kidnapping in the Australian outback, Rachel Ward is passable as a teacher in a one-room school. She is abducted along with her students, ranging in age from about 6 to 14. The story centers around their attempts to escape. 90m. **DIR:** Arch

Nicholson. **CAST:** Rachel Ward, Sean Garlick, Rebecca Rigg. 1985

FORTRESS (1993) ★★1/2 Grim science-fiction thriller about a married couple thrown into a monstrous, underground prison for having a second child. Inmates are controlled by small explosive devices that are blasted into the digestive system via the throat. The couple must escape before their baby is delivered and turned into a "kidbot" that is half human and half gadgetry. Another cultish, ghoulish, deadpan joke from the maker of *Re-Animator*. Rated R for violence and profanity. 92m. **DIR:** Stuart Gordon. **CAST:** Christopher Lambert, Loryn Locklin, Kurtwood Smith. 1993 DVD

•**FORTRESS 2: RE-ENTRY** ★★ Christopher Lambert returns to reprise his role as the father that had one too many children and was incarcerated as a result. This time around, the fortress is an impenetrable coed prison orbiting Earth from which Lambert must figure out how to escape. Plagued by halfhearted performances and below-par effects, *Fortress 2* cannot escape from its own inconsistencies. Rated R for nudity, violence, and profanity. 92m. **DIR:** Geoff Murphy. **CAST:** Christopher Lambert, Pam Grier. 1999 DVD

FORTRESS OF AMERIKKKA ★★ Murderous mercenaries battle the residents of a small California town. Campy Troma nonsense with plenty of gratuitous nudity and bad acting, as promised. Rated R. 97m. **DIR:** Eric Louzil. **CAST:** Gene Le Brock. 1989

FORTUNE AND MEN'S EYES ★★1/2 Well acted but unpleasant and ultimately an exploitative look at homosexuality in prison. Rated R for violence and suggested sex. 102m. **DIR:** Harvey Hart. **CAST:** Wendell Burton, Michael Greer, Zooey Hall. 1971

FORTUNE COOKIE, THE ★★★★1/2 Jack Lemmon is accidentally injured by a player while filming a football game from the sidelines. His brother-in-law, Walter Matthau, sees this as an ideal attempt to make some lawsuit money. So starts the first of the usually delightful Lemmon-Matthau comedies. Matthau is at his scene-stealing best in this Oscar-winning role. B&W; 125m. **DIR:** Billy Wilder. **CAST:** Jack Lemmon, Walter Matthau, Ron Rich, Cliff Osmond. 1966

FORTUNE DANE ★★1/2 Originally a pilot for a TV series, this fair action film features Carl Weathers as a cop out to find who corrupted his banker father. Rated PG for violence. 83m. **DIR:** Nicholas Sgarro, Charles Correll. **CAST:** Carl Weathers, Adolph Caesar. 1986

FORTUNE, THE ★★1/2 Two would-be criminals bungle an attempt to kidnap and murder a young heiress. The great look and sound of this film can't compensate for story problems and lack of real comedy (despite an outlandish performance by Jack Nicholson). 88m. **DIR:** Mike Nichols. **CAST:** Jack Nicholson, Warren Beatty, Stockard Channing, Florence Stanley, Richard B. Shull, Tom Newman. 1975

FORTUNE'S FOOL ★★1/2 Best known for his dramatic roles, Emil Jannings hams it up in this German comedy about a profiteering meat-packer. Jannings displays the gifts that made him a dominating screen figure. Silent. B&W; 60m. **DIR:** Reinhold Schunzel.

CAST: Emil Jannings, Daguey Servaes, Reinhold Schunzel. 1925

FORTUNES OF WAR (1987) ★★★ Based on Olivia Manning's novels *Balkan Trilogy* and *Levant Trilogy*, this BBC epic focuses on the effects of World War II on a nonmilitary British couple living in Romania. The husband is attracted to rebel factions and lofty ideals, while his wife must focus on daily life and reality. Slow-moving and overlong. 335m. **DIR:** James Cellan Jones. **CAST:** Kenneth Branagh, Emma Thompson, Ronald Pickup, Rupert Graves. 1987

FORTUNES OF WAR (1993) ★★★ When a desperate American relief worker takes a risky smuggling job, he doesn't realize how big a risk he's taking. As he makes his way to the delivery point with a shipment of drugs, he learns it's not just imprisonment that's awaiting him, but also a violent death. Rated R for violence and profanity. 107m. **DIR:** Thierry Notz. **CAST:** Matt Salinger, Michael Ironside, Haing S. Ngor, Michael Nouri. 1993

FOUL PLAY ★★★ Gloria Mundy (Goldie Hawn) accidentally becomes involved in a plot to assassinate the Pope. Detective Tony Carlson (Chevy Chase) tries to protect and seduce her. Hawn is good as the damsel in distress, but Chase is hardly the Cary Grant type. Still it's fun. Rated PG. 116m. **DIR:** Colin Higgins. **CAST:** Goldie Hawn, Chevy Chase, Dudley Moore, Burgess Meredith, Marilyn Sokol. 1978

FOUNTAINHEAD, THE ★★1/2 Gary Cooper tries his best in this Ayn Rand novel, brought to the screen without any of the book's vitality or character development. "Coop" is cast as Howard Roark, a Frank Lloyd Wright-type architect whose creations are ahead of their time and therefore go unappreciated. Patricia Neal is the love interest. B&W; 114m. **DIR:** King Vidor. **CAST:** Gary Cooper, Patricia Neal, Raymond Massey, Kent Smith, Robert Douglas. 1949

4:50 FROM PADDINGTON ★★★1/2 Agatha Christie's spinster detective, Miss Marple, is more challenged than usual when she must find the murderer *and* the corpse. A railway traveler witnesses a woman being strangled on a passing train, and reports the murder ... but the body can't be found! Strong performances, picturesque set designs, and moody score bring this 1950s mystery to life. Not rated; suitable for family viewing. 110m. **DIR:** Martyn Friend. **CAST:** Joan Hickson, David Horovitch, David Waller, Jill Meager, Maurice Denham. 1987

FOUR ADVENTURES OF REINETTE AND MIRABELLE ★★★1/2 French film that is actually slices of everyday life for two different girls—one naïve and one sophisticated. Not much plot; this is more of a character study. Slow-moving but pleasant. In French with English subtitles. 95m. **DIR:** Eric Rohmer. **CAST:** Joelle Miguel, Jessica Forde. 1986

FOUR BAGS FULL ★★★★ In Nazi-occupied Paris, two scoundrels attempt to transport a contraband slaughtered pig across town. But when word of their cargo gets out, the Nazis are the least of their worries. First-rate comic thriller with a refreshingly cynical look at Frenchmen during the war. In French with English subtitles. Not rated. B&W; 90m. **DIR:** Claude Autant-Lara. **CAST:** Jean Gabin, Bourvil, Louis de Funes. 1956

D MAN ★★★ A scientist (Robert Lansing) learns
f a method of moving through objects (walls, doors,
ink vaults, etc.), without realizing the terrible con-
equences, which eventually lead to madness and
urder. Eerie sci-fi film hampered only by often
rash music. From the director of *The Blob*. 85m.
IR: Irvin S. Yeaworth Jr. CAST: Robert Lansing, Lee
leriwether, James Congdon, Robert Strauss, Patty
uke. **1959 DVD**

OUR DAUGHTERS ★★★1/2 Widower Claude
ains helps his daughters through the ups and
owns of small-town romance in this irresistible
earjerker from a Fannie Hurst novel. Great cast,
ith John Garfield a standout in his first film. B&W;
Om. DIR: Michael Curtiz. CAST: Claude Rains, Rose-
ary Lane, Lola Lane, Priscilla Lane, Gale Page, John
arfield. **1938**

OUR DAYS IN JULY ★★★ A stark, cold realistic
iew of war-torn Northern Ireland, concentrating on
vo couples: one Catholic, and one Protestant. Irish
ccents may be difficult, but the almost intrusive na-
ure of this "fly-on-the-wall" directorial style makes
worth the effort. 99m. DIR: Mike Leigh. CAST: Brid
rennan, Desmond McAleer, Charles Lawson, Paula
amilton. **1984**

OUR DAYS IN SEPTEMBER ★★★★ Brazilian
larxist students kidnap the American ambassador
protest their oppressive military government,
hen argue among themselves about their next move
s the secret police swing into action against them.
act-based docudrama lets the narrative speak for
self and shows a satisfying grasp of the dramatic
uances of the story. In Portuguese with English sub-
tles. Rated R for profanity (in subtitles) and vio-
ence. 106m. DIR: Bruno Barreto. CAST: Alan Arkin,
edro Cardoso, Claudia Abreu, Matheus Nachtergaele.
997

OUR DEUCES, THE ★★ Jack Palance is a gang
eader during Prohibition times in this high-camp
ction film about gangsters. The movie is poorly con-
eived, with an odd mixture of blood and spoof. The
our Deuces does not have an MPAA rating, but it
ontains sex, nudity, violence, and profanity. 87m.
IR: William H. Bushnell Jr. CAST: Jack Palance, Carol
ynley, Warren Berlinger, Adam Roarke, Gianni Russo,
. B. Haggerty, John Haymer, Martin Kove, E. J. Peaker.
975

OUR EYES AND SIX GUNS ★★1/2 Fairly amusing
omedy-Western about an optometrist who goes west
run a store and ends up helping Wyatt Earp clean
p Tombstone. Made for TV. 92m. DIR: Peter Markle.
AST: Judge Reinhold, Patricia Clarkson, Fred Ward,
an Hedaya, M. Emmet Walsh, Dennis Burkley, John
chuck, Jonathan Gries, Austin Pendleton. **1992**

OUR FACES WEST ★★★ A small-scale Western
hat tends to be overlooked, it uses a standard for-
ula (an outlaw is pursued by a determined sheriff).
ut the writing, acting, and direction find those nu-
nces that can make a story fresh. B&W; 90m. DIR:
lfred E. Green. CAST: Joel McCrea, Frances Dee,
harles Bickford, Joseph Calleia. **1948**

OUR FEATHERS, THE (1939) ★★★★ A young
nan (John Clements) from a military background is
randed a coward when he forsakes military duty for

a home and family during time of war. Rejected by
his family, friends, and fiancée, he sets out to prove
his manhood. This motion picture was one of the few
English productions of its era to gain wide acceptance. It still holds up well today. 115m. DIR: Zoltan
Korda. CAST: Ralph Richardson, John Clements, June
Duprez, C. Aubrey Smith. **1939**

FOUR FEATHERS, THE (1978) ★★★ Solid television retelling of the A. E. W. Mason story, with plenty
of action and derring-do. Beau Bridges portrays the
Britisher fighting against Sudanese tribesmen in
nineteenth-century Africa. Although the transition
of the story from British to American ideals is shaky,
the story itself is powerful. 110m. DIR: Don Sharp.
CAST: Beau Bridges, Robert Powell, Simon Ward, Jane
Seymour, Harry Andrews. **1978**

FOUR FOR TEXAS ★★ Nonsensical story about
tough-guy Frank Sinatra teaming up with fast-shoot-
ing Dean Martin to operate a floating gambling casino. Long and pretty silly. 124m. DIR: Robert Aldrich.
CAST: Frank Sinatra, Dean Martin, Anita Ekberg, Ursula
Andress, Victor Buono, Charles Bronson, Mike Mazurki, Richard Jaeckel. **1963**

FOUR FRIENDS ★★ Arthur Penn directed and
Steve Tesich (*Breaking Away*) wrote this interesting but ultimately disappointing film about America
as seen through the eyes of a young immigrant (Craig
Wasson) and the love he shares with two friends for a
freethinking young woman (Jodi Thelen). Rated R
because of violence, nudity, and profanity. 114m.
DIR: Arthur Penn. CAST: Craig Wasson, James Leo
Herlihy, Jodi Thelen. **1981**

FOUR HORSEMEN OF THE APOCALYPSE ★★ The
1921 silent version of this complex antiwar tale of
two brothers who fight on opposite sides during
World War I is still the best. When Rudolph Valentino
played Julio, you cared. This one, updated to World
War II, falls flat, despite a fine cast. 153m. DIR: Vincente Minnelli. CAST: Glenn Ford, Ingrid Thulin,
Charles Boyer, Lee J. Cobb, Paul Henreid, Paul Lukas.
1961

FOUR IN A JEEP ★★1/2 Just after World War II, Vienna was nationally divided into four zones. This picture deals with a police patrol made up of American,
Soviet, British, and French troops who clash over
cases with which they must deal. It's not a terribly
exciting film, but it does evoke some emotion about
this tragic episode in postwar history. B&W; 96m.
DIR: Leopold Lindtberg. CAST: Viveca Lindfors, Ralph
Meeker. **1951**

FOUR JACKS AND A JILL ★★ Four broke but big-
hearted musicians take in a young singer who manages to tangle them up with gangsters and the law.
Full of tunes and silly coincidences, this typical low-
budget studio B film is short on story and shorter still
on credibility. B&W; 68m. DIR: Jack B. Hively. CAST:
Ray Bolger, Anne Shirley, June Havoc, Desi Arnaz Sr.,
Eddie Foy Jr., Fritz Feld, Henry Daniell. **1942**

FOUR JILLS IN A JEEP ★★★1/2 A typical morale-
builder from World War II, and a curiosity. It dramatizes the real-life tour of four Hollywood actresses as
they cheer the troops with song and dance. The
movie includes the talents of other Hollywoodites
who symbolized the best show business had to offer

during the war years. B&W; 89m. **DIR:** William A. Seiter. **CAST:** Kay Francis, Carole Landis, Martha Raye, Mitzi Mayfair, Betty Grable, Alice Faye, Carmen Miranda, Phil Silvers, Dick Haymes, Jimmy Dorsey. **1944**

FOUR JUNIOR DETECTIVES ★★ Cheap production values and ham-bone acting beleaguer this obviously dubbed adventure about four youths who uncover a legendary sword that serves as a clue to lost treasure. Rated PG-13 for some violence. 81m. **DIR:** Ulrich King. **1994**

FOUR MUSKETEERS, THE ★★★★ In this superb sequel to Richard Lester's *The Three Musketeers*, the all-star cast is remarkably good, and the director is at the peak of his form. The final duel between Michael York and Christopher Lee is a stunner. Rated PG. 108m. **DIR:** Richard Lester. **CAST:** Oliver Reed, Raquel Welch, Richard Chamberlain, Frank Finlay, Michael York, Christopher Lee, Faye Dunaway, Charlton Heston. **1975 DVD**

FOUR RODE OUT ♥ U.S. marshall in pursuit of a Mexican bank robber. 90m. **DIR:** John Peyser. **CAST:** Pernell Roberts, Sue Lyon, Julian Mateos, Leslie Nielsen. **1968**

FOUR ROOMS ♥ Four pointless, painfully unfunny black comedies are tied together at a decayed hotel on New Year's Eve. Rated R for language, nudity, drug use, and violence. 95m. **DIR:** Quentin Tarantino, Alexandre Rockwell, Allison Anders, Robert Rodriguez. **CAST:** Tim Roth, Antonio Banderas, Jennifer Beals, Valeria Golino, Madonna, Quentin Tarantino, Marisa Tomei. **1995 DVD**

FOUR SEASONS, THE ★★★1/2 Written and directed by Alan Alda, this film focuses on the pains and joys of friendship shared by three couples who are vacationing together. Despite a flawed and uneven script, the characters have been skillfully drawn and convincingly played by an excellent cast. *Four Seasons* is by no means perfect, yet it is an appealing, uplifting piece of entertainment. Rated PG. 117m. **DIR:** Alan Alda. **CAST:** Alan Alda, Carol Burnett, Len Cariou, Sandy Dennis, Rita Moreno, Jack Weston. **1981**

FOUR SKULLS OF JONATHAN DRAKE, THE ★★★ A family is haunted by a 200-year-old curse in which the men are decapitated on their sixtieth birthdays. Could it involve villainous Dr. Zurich (Henry Daniell), whose hobby is head shrinking? Good-looking horror-thriller with a fun performance by Daniell. B&W; 70m. **DIR:** Edward L. Cahn. **CAST:** Eduard Franz, Henry Daniell, Valerie French, Grant Richards. **1959**

FOUR WEDDINGS AND A FUNERAL ★★★★ A reserved Englishman meets an attractive American at a wedding and falls in love with her, but his inability to express his feelings seems to forestall any possibility of a relationship—until they meet again and again. The ensemble cast give this clever film true charm. Rowan Atkinson is hilarious as a nervous novice priest. Rated R for profanity, suggested sex, and adult themes. 118m. **DIR:** Mike Newell. **CAST:** Hugh Grant, Andie MacDowell, Kristin Scott Thomas, Simon Callow, James Fleet, John Hannah, Charlotte Coleman, David Bower, Corin Redgrave, Rowan Atkinson, Anna Chancellor. **1994 DVD**

FOUR CARATS ★★★1/2 This comedy has Liv Ullmann playing a 40-year-old divorcée being pursued by a rich 22-year-old, Edward Albert. Laughs abound as Ullmann's grown daughter (Deborah Raffin) and ex-husband (Gene Kelly) react to her latest suitor. Rated PG. 110m. **DIR:** Milton Katselas. **CAST:** Liv Ullmann, Edward Albert, Gene Kelly, Nancy Walker, Deborah Raffin. **1973**

FORTY POUNDS OF TROUBLE ★★★1/2 Thoroughly enjoyable retread of *Little Miss Marker* finds casino manager Tony Curtis saddled with adorable moppet Claire Wilcox after her father takes leave. In an effort to impress visiting songstress Suzanne Pleshette, Curtis assumes the father role, and then must decide what course to take when the girl's father dies in an accident. Wilcox is a little charmer, and the chemistry between Curtis and Pleshette is magical. 106m. **DIR:** Norman Jewison. **CAST:** Tony Curtis, Suzanne Pleshette, Claire Wilcox, Howard Morris, Phil Silvers, Larry Storch. **1963**

FORTY THIEVES ★★★ An ex-convict comes to town paroled into the custody of Sheriff Hopalong Cassidy. Unhappy about Hoppy's control, he rounds up his old gang, the Forty Thieves. B&W; 61m. **DIR:** Lesley Selander. **CAST:** William Boyd, Andy Clyde, Jimmy Rogers, Louise Currie. **1944**

42ND STREET ★★★★ Every understudy's dream is to get a big chance and rise to stardom. Such is the premise of *42nd Street*. This Depression-era musical of 1933 is lifted above cliché by its vitality and sincerity. B&W; 98m. **DIR:** Lloyd Bacon. **CAST:** Dick Powell, Ruby Keeler, Ginger Rogers, Warner Baxter, Una Merkel. **1933**

FORTY SEVEN RONIN ★★★1/2 A fascinating glimpse into the mentality of the Japanese during World War II, this two-volume cassette rates complete watching by completists only. The first volume is made from an old, scratchy print and is a slow-paced account of how an insult to a powerful lord's honor brings terrible and unjust punishment. The second tape, made from a pristine 35mm. print, recaps most of the events from part one as the lord's retainers plot a daring revenge. In Japanese with English subtitles. Not rated; the film has brief violence. 112m. **DIR:** Kenji Mizoguchi. **CAST:** Chojuro Kawarsaki, Knemon Nakamura. **1942**

48 HRS. ★★★★1/2 Add *48 Hrs.* to the list of the best cops-and-robbers movies ever made. It's so action-packed, it'll keep you on the edge of your seat. There's more good news: It's funny too. In the story, a cop (Nick Nolte) goes looking for a psychotic prison escapee (James Remar) with the help of a fast-talking con man (Eddie Murphy). There's never a dull moment. Rated R for violence, profanity, and nudity. 96m. **DIR:** Walter Hill. **CAST:** Eddie Murphy, Nick Nolte, Annette O'Toole, Frank McRae, James Remar, David Patrick Kelly. **1982 DVD**

•**FORTY-NINERS** ★★1/2 A frontiersman saves a group of settlers on their way to California during the great gold rush from a thieving wagonmaster and marauding Indians. Good-natured, if familiar, pioneer film. B&W; 53m. **DIR:** John P. McCarthy. **CAST:** Tom Tyler, Betty Mack, Alan Bridge, Fern Emmett, Gordon Wood. **1932**

9TH PARALLEL, THE ★★★ Rich suspense drama about a World War II German U-boat sunk off the coast of Canada whose crew makes it to shore and tries to reach safety in neutral territory. The cast is first-rate, the characterizations outstanding. Original story won an Oscar. B&W; 105m. **DIR:** Michael Powell. **CAST:** Laurence Olivier, Anton Walbrook, Eric Portman, Leslie Howard, Raymond Massey, Finlay Currie, Glynis Johns. 1941

400 BLOWS, THE ★★★★★ Poignant story of a boy and the world that seems to be at odds with him is true and touching as few films have ever been. Powerful, tender, and at times overwhelmingly sad, this great film touches all the right buttons without being exploitative. In French with English subtitles. B&W; 99m. **DIR:** François Truffaut. **CAST:** Jean-Pierre Léaud, Patrick Auffay, Claire Maurier, Albert Remy. 1959 DVD

1492: THE CONQUEST OF PARADISE ★★ Gérard Depardieu, so effective in character studies, is miscast as Christopher Columbus in this bloated epic. Beautifully filmed by director Ridley Scott and well acted by a strong cast. Rated PG-13 for violence and nudity. 152m. **DIR:** Ridley Scott. **CAST:** Gérard Depardieu, Armand Assante, Sigourney Weaver, Angela Molina, Fernando Rey, Tcheky Karyo, Frank Langella, Michael Wincott, Loren Dean, Kevin Dunn. 1992

FOURTH MAN, THE ★★★1/2 Jeroen Krabbé plays gay alcoholic writer prone to hallucinations. Invited to lecture at a literary society, he meets a mysterious woman who he becomes convinced intends to kill him. This emerges as an atmospheric, highly original chiller. In Dutch with English subtitles. Not rated; the film has nudity, simulated sex, violence, and profanity. 128m. **DIR:** Paul Verhoeven. **CAST:** Jeroen Krabbé, Renee Soutendijk. 1984

FOURTH PROTOCOL, THE ★★★ Michael Caine is the best component of this stiff screen version of Frederick Forsyth's thriller. Caine is a British agent who suspects "something big" is being smuggled into England; his guess is accurate, and he discovers an atomic-bomb delivery is being supervised by ultra-cool Russian agent Pierce Brosnan. Rated R for violence, nudity, and language. 119m. **DIR:** John Mackenzie. **CAST:** Michael Caine, Pierce Brosnan, Joanna Cassidy, Ned Beatty. 1987

FOURTH STORY ★★★ Mark Harmon's amiable private detective lands a most intriguing case when a puzzled woman (Mimi Rogers) hires him to find her husband ... who simply vanished after breakfast one morning. Although the finale is somewhat clumsy in this made-for-cable thriller, getting there is quite fun. Rated PG-13 for brief nudity. 91m. **DIR:** Ivan Passer. **CAST:** Mark Harmon, Mimi Rogers, Paul Gleason, Michael Patrick Boatman, Cliff De Young, M. Emmet Walsh. 1991

FOURTH WAR, THE ★★ Old war-horse Roy Scheider can't adjust to a peaceful, politicized new army—especially when he confronts a Soviet colonel (Jurgen Prochnow) of similiar persuasions. Fine performances by Scheider and Prochnow are wasted in this mediocre thriller. Rated R for violence and profanity. 95m. **DIR:** John Frankenheimer. **CAST:** Roy Scheider, Jurgen Prochnow, Harry Dean Stanton, Tim Reid. 1990

FOURTH WISE MAN, THE ★★★1/2 A surprisingly well-done fable about a physician who sets out to join three other notables in a quest to witness the birth of the Messiah, but this fourth wise man (Martin Sheen) encounters stumbling blocks along the way. Stylishly produced TV movie. 72m. **DIR:** Michael Ray Rhodes. **CAST:** Martin Sheen, Alan Arkin, Eileen Brennan, Ralph Bellamy, Richard Libertini, Harold Gould, Lance Kerwin, Adam Arkin. 1985

FOURTH WISH, THE ★★★★ This moving Australian tearjerker features a 12-year-old boy dying of leukemia. His father's desire to grant his final wishes gets progressively harder to arrange. Wonderful story of a father's love, but be prepared with a box of Kleenex nearby. Not rated. 120m. **DIR:** Don Chaffey. **CAST:** John Meillon, Robert Bettles, Robyn Nevin. 1976

FOX AND HIS FRIENDS ★★1/2 Filmmaker Rainer Werner Fassbinder has the starring role as a lower-class carnival entertainer known as Fox, the Talking Head, who strikes it rich after a hard life by winning the lottery. His wealth attracts an elegant, bourgeois homosexual lover who proceeds to take advantage of him. In German with English subtitles. Not rated; contains nudity and is recommended for adult viewers. 123m. **DIR:** Rainer Werner Fassbinder. **CAST:** Rainer Werner Fassbinder, Peter Chatel, Karlheinz Böhm, Harry Baer. 1975

FOX AND THE HOUND ★★★1/2 Gorgeous animation in the classic Disney style elevates this not-so-classic children's film in which a little fox and a puppy become friends. Later, when they've grown up, their bond clashes with their natural instincts. The younger set will enjoy this lightweight film, but it falls squarely in the void between the studio's two great eras of feature-length cartoons. Rated G. 83m. **DIR:** Art Stevens, Ted Berman, Richard Rich. 1981 DVD

FOXES ★★★ Adrian Lyne directed this fitfully interesting film, about four young women who share an apartment in Los Angeles. The cast is good but somehow it all falls flat. Rated R. 106m. **DIR:** Adrian Lyne. **CAST:** Jodie Foster, Sally Kellerman, Cherie Currie, Randy Quaid, Scott Baio. 1980

FOXFIRE ★★★★1/2 Jessica Tandy is mesmerizing in this *Hallmark Hall of Fame* presentation. She plays an elderly Appalachian woman who must choose between her beloved mountaintop cabin and a new home with her son and his children. Hume Cronyn is the ghost of her late husband whom Tandy keeps very much alive, and John Denver is the singing son who wants to care for her. The Blue Ridge Mountains are as much a part of this lovely film as Tandy's thoughtful performance. Rated PG. 118m. **DIR:** Jud Taylor. **CAST:** Jessica Tandy, Hume Cronyn, John Denver. 1987

FOXFIRE (1996) ★★ Angelina Jolie, a pouty stranger with only a nickname, drifts into the unhappy lives of four teenage girls, and naturally changes their lives forever. This adaptation of a Joyce Carol Oates novel begins on strong footing as Jolie teaches the girls to fight against sexual and social abuse. However, it suffers greatly from slipshod direction, semideveloped characters, and enough dangling plot threads to weave a sequel. Rated R for nudity, profanity, sexual situations, and violence. 102m. DIR: Annette Haywood-Carter. CAST: Angelina Jolie, Hedy Buress, Jenny Shimizu, Jenny Lewis, Sarah Rosenberg. 1996 DVD

FOXFIRE LIGHT 🎬 A love triangle in the Ozarks. Badly written. Rated PG for adult situations. 102m. DIR: Allen Baron. CAST: Leslie Nielsen, Tippi Hedren, Lara Parker, Barry Van Dyke, Burton Gilliam. 1982

FOXTRAP 🎬 Fred Williamson plays a bodyguard sent to Europe to find a missing heiress. Rated R for violence, drug use, and sexual situations. 88m. DIR: Fred Williamson. CAST: Fred Williamson, Christopher Connelly, Arlene Golonka. 1986

FOXTROT ★★1/2 Peter O'Toole plays a European aristocrat who escapes World War II when he takes a yacht to a deserted island and sets up residence with his wife (Charlotte Rampling), his ship's captain (Max von Sydow), and his servant (Jorge Luke). Foxtrot centers on the wastes of the leisure class even in a time of war. Rated R for sex, nudity, and violence. 91m. DIR: Arturo Ripstein. CAST: Peter O'Toole, Charlotte Rampling, Max von Sydow, Jorge Luke, Helena Rojo, Claudio Brook. 1975

FOXY BROWN ★★ Pam Grier takes on the mobsters who butchered her boyfriend. Grier and Jack Hill—the man who directed her in several Filipino sexploitation prison flicks—are reteamed for this wildly sadistic urban-crime melodrama. A richly deserved R rating. 94m. DIR: Jack Hill. CAST: Pam Grier, Peter Brown, Terry Carter. 1974

FRAME BY FRAME ★★★ Michael Biehn and Marg Helgenberger stand out in this made-for-cable crime-thriller. They play undercover cops Stash and Ekberg, devoted to their jobs and each other. When Stash's wife is brutally murdered in a mob-style hit, all evidence points back to them. Now the two cops are the chief suspects in the murder, and it doesn't take long for them to suspect each other as well. Rated R for violence, profanity, and adult situations. 97m. DIR: Douglas Barr. CAST: Michael Biehn, Marg Helgenberger. 1995

FRAME UP ★★ A watchable mishmash about a sheriff's investigation of a boy's murder. Rated R for rape scenes and language. 90m. DIR: Paul Leder. CAST: Wings Hauser, Bobby DiCicco, Frances Fisher. 1990

FRAMED (1930) ★★★ Atmospheric melodrama that makes the most of lighting, shadows, and sexy situations. The story is your basic melodrama: girl wants revenge on the man who shot her father but falls for the killer's son instead. One of the first gangster melodramas of the 1930s. B&W; 71m. DIR: George Archainbaud. CAST: Evelyn Brent, Regis Toomey, Ralf Haralde. 1930

FRAMED (1975) 🎬 Thoroughly nauseating and graphically violent story of a man framed for a crime he did not commit. Rated R for gory violence and language. 106m. DIR: Phil Karlson. CAST: Joe Don Baker, Conny Van Dyke, Gabriel Dell, Brock Peters, John Marley. 1975

FRAMED (1990) ★★★ This wry little caper comedy plunges Jeff Goldblum, as a talented art forger, into the realm of bewilderment and uncertainty he occupied so well with Into the Night. Gary Rosen's script goes for chuckles rather than belly laughs, but the tricky finale will be enjoyed by those who appreciate the genre. Not rated, with mild profanity and sexual situations. 90m. DIR: Dean Parisot. CAST: Jeff Goldblum, Kristin Scott Thomas, Todd Graff, Michael Lerner, James Hong. 1990

FRANCES ★★★★1/2 This chilling, poignant motion picture explains why Frances Farmer was never allowed to reign as a star in Hollywood. Jessica Lange is superb as the starlet who snubs the power structure and pays a horrifying price for it. Kim Stanley is also impressive as Frances's mother, a money-and fame-hungry hag who uses her daughter. Sam Shepard is the one person who loves Frances for who she really is. An unforgettable film. Rated R. 139m. DIR: Graeme Clifford. CAST: Jessica Lange, Kim Stanley, Sam Shepard, Jeffrey DeMunn. 1982 DVD

FRANCESCO ★★★ Mickey Rourke may seem an odd choice to play a monk, but playing against type is what makes his performance as the real-life Francesco so believable. Set in Italy during the thirteenth century, the film chronicles the spiritual awakening of Francesco, the decadent son of a wealthy merchant who abandons his past and sets forth to help the poor and needy of his town. Shot on location, the film features an appealing supporting cast who help bring this remarkable story to life. Rated PG-13 for adult situations. 105m. DIR: Lilliana Cavani. CAST: Mickey Rourke, Helena Bonham Carter, Andrea Ferreol, Hanns Zischler. 1989 DVD

FRANCIS GARY POWERS: THE TRUE STORY OF THE U-2 SPY INCIDENT ★★★1/2 In this made-for-television movie, the infamous 1960 U-2 spy plane shot down over Russia is dramatized. The best performances in this true story are supplied by the supporting cast. Based on U-2 pilot Francis Gary Powers's book, it's worth viewing. 120m. DIR: Delbert Mann. CAST: Lee Majors, Noah Beery Jr., Nehemiah Persoff, Brooke Bundy, William Daniels, James Gregory, Lew Ayres. 1976

FRANCIS GOES TO THE RACES ★★★ Francis the talking mule teaches another mule how to win races so he can help Donald O'Connor cope with some crooks at the track. Enjoyable in spite of a very hokey plot. B&W; 88m. DIR: Arthur Lubin. CAST: Donald O'Connor, Piper Laurie, Cecil Kellaway, Larry Keating, Jesse White. 1951

FRANCIS IN THE HAUNTED HOUSE ★★★ Last entry in the series of seven Francis, the Talking Mule films. This time Mickey Rooney (replacing Donald O'Connor as the savvy mule's confidant) and Francis find themselves involved with a gang of murdering thieves in a creepy castle. When Rooney goes to the police with the mule's rendition of events, he finds himself pursued by both police and crooks. 80m. DIR: Charles Lamont. CAST: Mickey Rooney, Virginia Welles, Paul Cavanagh. 1956

FRANCIS IN THE NAVY ★★★ Sixth of the seven-picture series starring Francis, the talking mule. (Chill Wills provides his voice.) Silly, but the kids will enjoy it. B&W; 80m. DIR: Arthur Lubin. CAST: Donald O'Connor, Martha Hyer, Jim Backus, David Janssen, Clint Eastwood, Martin Milner, Paul Burke. **1955**

FRANCIS JOINS THE WACS ★★★ Chill Wills appears in person and does the voice of the talking mule. He competes with himself for laughs in a comedy that sends Francis and his human pal to the WACS by mistake. B&W; 94m. **DIR:** Arthur Lubin. **CAST:** Donald O'Connor, Chill Wills, Mamie Van Doren, ZaSu Pitts, Lynn Bari, Julie Adams, Joan Shawlee. **1954**

FRANCIS, THE TALKING MULE ★★★1/2 First in a series from Universal, this delightful comedy tells the story of how a dimwitted student at West Point (Donald O'Connor) first met up with the famous talking mule of the title. The gags really fly as Francis proceeds to get O'Connor in all sorts of outrageous predicaments, consistently pulling him out just in the nick of time. Some screamingly funny scenes. Chill Wills (voice). Followed by six sequels. B&W; 91m. **DIR:** Arthur Lubin. **CAST:** Donald O'Connor, Patricia Medina, ZaSu Pitts, Tony Curtis, Ray Collins. **1950**

FRANCOIS TRUFFAUT: STOLEN MOMENTS ★★★ You have to have seen many of Truffaut's films to appreciate this letter-boxed homage to the late director-writer-actor. The glitterati of the French cinema came out in force to praise and dissect Truffaut, but too many assumptions were made regarding the audience's knowledge. Occasionally there is so much going on that you can barely take it all in while reading the subtitles. Interesting, but not what it could have been. Not rated; contains profanity. 93m. **DIR:** Serge Toubiana, Michel Pascal. **CAST:** Fanny Ardant, Nathalie Baye, Gérard Depardieu, Marcel Ophuls, Marie-France Pisier, Eric Rohmer, Bertrand Tavernier, Ewa Truffaut, Laura Truffaut, Madeleine Morgenstern. **1993**

FRANK & JESSE ★★★1/2 Yet another revisionist retelling of the infamous outlaws, with star-coproducer Rob Lowe turning his character (Jesse James) into a martyred hero of the Deep South. Script is outrageously politically correct, but the earnest performances will grow on you. Rated R for violence and brief nudity. 105m. **DIR:** Robert Boris. **CAST:** Rob Lowe, Bill Paxton, Randy Travis, Dana Wheeler-Nicholson, Maria Pitillo, William Atherton. **1995 DVD**

FRANK AND OLLIE ★★★★ A warmhearted documentary portrait of Frank Thomas and Ollie Johnston, two of the so-called Nine Old Men, the legendary original Disney animators. Thomas and Johnston also happen to be the best of friends and have been since they joined Disney in the 1930s. The film explores the nature of great animation and of enduring friendship. Rich humor and cartoon clips abound. Rated PG for mild profanity. 89m. **DIR:** Theodore Thomas. **CAST:** Frank Thomas, Ollie Johnston. **1995**

FRANKENHOOKER ★★ In order to replace his girlfriend, a budding scientist decides to place her head on the various body parts of unfortunate streetwalkers in this low-budget gorefest. Not rated; contains violence, profanity, nudity, and gore. 85m. **DIR:** Frank Henenlotter. **CAST:** James Lorinz, Patty Mullen, Louise Lasser, Shirley Stoler. **1990 DVD**

FRANKENSTEIN (1931) ★★★★ Despite all the padding, grease paint, and restrictive, awkward costuming, Boris Karloff gives a strong, sensitive performance in this 1931 horror classic—with only eyes and an occasional grunt to convey meaning. It still stands as one of the great screen performances. B&W; 71m. **DIR:** James Whale. **CAST:** Colin Clive, Mae Clarke, Boris Karloff, John Boles. **1931 DVD**

FRANKENSTEIN (1958) 🎬 Boris Karloff as the great-grandson of the famous doctor, attempting to create a monster of his own. B&W; 83m. **DIR:** Howard W. Koch. **CAST:** Boris Karloff, Tom Duggan, Jana Lund, Don Barry. **1958**

FRANKENSTEIN (1973) ★★1/2 Bo Svenson's sympathetic portrayal of the monster is the one saving grace of this essentially average made-for-TV retelling of Mary Wollstonecraft Shelley's horror tale. 130m. **DIR:** Glenn Jordan. **CAST:** Robert Foxworth, Susan Strasberg, Bo Svenson, Willie Aames. **1973**

FRANKENSTEIN (1984) ★★★ Solid made-for-TV adaptation of Mary Shelley's often-filmed tale. Robert Powell gives a believable performance as a young Dr. Frankenstein, whose creation (David Warner) runs amok. Fine period flavor, crisp direction, and an excellent cast headed by Warner and John Gielgud. 81m. **DIR:** James Ormerod. **CAST:** Robert Powell, David Warner, Carrie Fisher, John Gielgud, Terence Alexander, Susan Wooldridge. **1984**

FRANKENSTEIN (1992) ★★★ Taking some liberties with Mary Shelley's classic tale, this film at least portrays the creature sympathetically. Randy Quaid is the much hunted being who implores his creator (Patrick Bergin) to help him find peace in a threatening world. Lush forest footage is a plus; plot inconsistencies a minus. Made for cable; contains violence, gore, and nudity. 117m. **DIR:** David Wickes. **CAST:** Patrick Bergin, Randy Quaid, John Mills, Lambert Wilson, Fiona Gillies. **1992**

FRANKENSTEIN AND ME ★★1/2 An orphaned boy obsessed with movie monsters thinks he has found the answer to his problems when a traveling carnival comes to town, displaying what they claim is the real Frankenstein monster. Bland kiddie movie may also entertain parents who grew up with classic horror movies. Rated PG for mild violence. 91m. **DIR:** Robert Tinnell. **CAST:** Jamieson Boulanger, Burt Reynolds, Louise Fletcher. **1996**

FRANKENSTEIN AND THE MONSTER FROM HELL ★★ The release of Hammer Films veteran Terence Fisher's final directorial effort would be a major event, but for one thing: this is a censored TV print, not the R-rated original. But the out-of-print Japanese Laserdisc merits three stars. 93m. **DIR:** Terence Fisher. **CAST:** Peter Cushing, Shane Briant, Madeleine Smith, Dave Prowse, Patrick Troughton, Bernard Lee. **1974**

●**FRANKENSTEIN CREATED WOMAN** ★★★ The doctor captures the spirit of a man through a new technique he has discovered and places it into the body of beautiful Susan Denberg. It's not long before Denberg is out and about killing people. High production values and a superb cast help an otherwise mediocre story line. 92m. **DIR:** Terence Fisher. **CAST:** Peter Cushing, Susan Denberg. 1967

FRANKENSTEIN GENERAL HOSPITAL ★★ Horror fans will appreciate some of the in-jokes in this parody, set in a hospital where the original Dr. Frankenstein's great-great-grandson is at work on the usual monster. Mark Blankfield has some funny bits as Bob Frankenstein, but the rest is thin going. Rated R for nudity. 92m. **DIR:** Deborah Roberts. **CAST:** Mark Blankfield. 1988

FRANKENSTEIN ISLAND 🎬 A group of men stranded on a remote island stumble upon a colony of young women in leopard-skin bikinis. Rated PG. 89m. **DIR:** Jerry Warren. **CAST:** John Carradine, Robert Clarke, Steve Brodie, Cameron Mitchell, Andrew Duggan. 1981

FRANKENSTEIN MEETS THE SPACE MONSTER 🎬 The Frankenstein here is actually an android named Frank sent into outer space by NASA. Also known as *Mars Invades Puerto Rico.* B&W; 75m. **DIR:** Robert Gaffney. **CAST:** James Karen, Nancy Marshall, Robert Reilly. 1965

FRANKENSTEIN MEETS THE WOLF MAN ★★★1/2 As the title suggests, two of Universal's most famous monsters clash in this series horror film. Very atmospheric, with beautiful photography, music, set design, and special effects. Only drawback is Bela Lugosi's overblown portrayal of the Frankenstein monster. B&W; 73m. **DIR:** Roy William Neill. **CAST:** Lon Chaney Jr., Patric Knowles, Bela Lugosi, Ilona Massey, Maria Ouspenskaya. 1943

•**FRANKENSTEIN REBORN!** ★★1/2 Unaired pilot for a potential television series called *Filmonsters* in the *Goosebumps* tradition from producer Charles Band. The cast is game and the story stays close to its source material with decent makeup effects, but the film seems confused as to whether it is set in the 1800s or present day. Rated PG for mild violence. 70m. **DIR:** Julian Breen. **CAST:** Haven Burton, Ben Gould, Jaason Simmons. 1998

FRANKENSTEIN SINGS ★★★ Absolutely ridiculous but somehow charming musical horror film that has more in common with the "Monster Mash" than with *The Rocky Horror Picture Show.* Based on the stage play *I'm Sorry but the Bridge Is Out, You'll Have to Spend the Night* by Sheldon Allman and Bobby "Boris" Pickett. Directors Cohen and Sokolow were also partially responsible for Disney's *Toy Story.* Rated PG. 83m. **DIR:** Joel Cohen, Alec Sokolow. **CAST:** Candace Cameron, Ian Bohen, Sarah Douglas, John Kassir, Bobby Pickett, Jimmie Walker. 1995

FRANKENSTEIN UNBOUND ★★1/2 Director Roger Corman makes his comeback with this twisted retelling of the Frankenstein legend in which a scientist from the year 2031 is sucked back in time and meets up with author Mary Godwin (soon to be Mary Shelley), as well as the infamous Dr. Victor Frankenstein. Rated R for violence and gore. 90m. **DIR:** Roger Corman. **CAST:** John Hurt, Raul Julia, Bridget Fonda, Jason Patric. 1990

FRANKENSTEIN'S DAUGHTER 🎬 The makeup is ridiculous, the sets are cheap, and the performers need to be oiled. B&W; 85m. **DIR:** Richard Cunha.

CAST: John Ashley, Sandra Knight, Donald Murphy, Harold Lloyd Jr. 1958

FRANKENWEENIE ★★★★ Young Barret Oliver brings his dog Sparky back to life. Director Tim Burton's first live-action short subject, made during his tenure at Walt Disney Studios, reworks the classic Mary Shelley tale of life after death into an affectionate tribute to the style of James Whale. Exquisite! Rated PG. 28m. **DIR:** Tim Burton. **CAST:** Daniel Stern, Shelley Duvall, Joseph Maher, Barret Oliver. 1984

FRANKIE AND JOHNNY (1934) 🎬 Poorly acted costume drama inspired by the now-legendary love-triangle song. B&W; 66m. **DIR:** Chester Erskine. **CAST:** Helen Morgan, Chester Morris, Lilyan Tashman. 1934

FRANKIE AND JOHNNY (1966) ★★★ As the song goes, Elvis, as a Mississippi riverboat singer-gambler, betrays his lady (Donna Douglas) with his roving heart. He easily captures the attention of beautiful young ladies but must suffer the consequences. Elvis fans won't be disappointed. 87m. **DIR:** Frederick de Cordova. **CAST:** Elvis Presley, Donna Douglas, Sue Ane Langdon, Harry Morgan, Nancy Kovack, Audrey Christie. 1966

FRANKIE AND JOHNNY (1991) ★★★1/2 It's the supporting characters in this angst-ridden Terrence McNally drama who make it such a treat. Set primarily in a diner, *Frankie and Johnny* offers occasionally deft and delicious servings of one-liners; but Al Pacino and Michelle Pfeiffer are somehow not quite right in their roles as unlikely lovers. Rated R for profanity and nudity. 117m. **DIR:** Garry Marshall. **CAST:** Al Pacino, Michelle Pfeiffer, Hector Elizondo, Kate Nelligan, Nathan Lane, Jane Morris. 1991

FRANKIE STARLIGHT ★★★★ In this gentle Irish import, Anne Parillaud is the French emigré who flees her native country after World War II, only to find she never quite fits into her new life. Corban Walker shines in the title role of an adult dwarf writing the story of his unusual mother. Rated R for profanity, brief nudity, and sexual situations. 100m. **DIR:** Michael Lindsay-Hogg. **CAST:** Anne Parillaud, Matt Dillon, Gabriel Byrne, Corban Walker, Alan Pentony, Rudi Davis, Georgina Cates. 1995

FRANTIC (1988) ★★★1/2 Director Roman Polanski bounces back with this clever and often darkly funny Hitchcockian thriller, which makes Harrison Ford a stranger in the very strange underbelly of Paris. He's a surgeon visiting the city to lecture at a medical conference; when his wife (Betty Buckley) vanishes from their hotel room, he confronts indifference through official channels before trying to puzzle things out on his own. Inexplicably rated R for minimal violence. 120m. **DIR:** Roman Polanski. **CAST:** Harrison Ford, Emmanuelle Seigner, Betty Buckley, John Mahoney, David Huddleston. 1988 **DVD**

FRANZ 🎬 Leon falls in love with a woman named Leonie. He is tortured by his oppressive mother and his war memories. In French with English subtitles. 88m. **DIR:** Jacques Brel. **CAST:** Jacques Brel. 1972

FRASIER THE LOVABLE LION (FRASIER THE SENSUOUS LION) ★★1/2 Cute film about a zoology professor who discovers he can talk with Frasier, the oversexed lion at the Lion Country Safari Theme Park in Irvine, California. It is a children's film, even though the subject matter does border on being adult. 97m. DIR: Pat Shields. CAST: Michael Callan, Katherine Justice. 1973

FRATERNITY DEMON ✔ A college student comes across the incantation that frees Isha, demon of lust and sex, just in time for a big frat house party. Rated R for nudity and sexual situations. 85m. DIR: C. B. Rubin. CAST: Trixxie Bowie, Charles Laurette, Al Darrough, Deborah Carlin. 1992 DVD

FRATERNITY VACATION ✔ A teen-lust comedy with no laughs, no imagination, and no point. Rated R for profanity and nudity. 95m. DIR: James Frawley. CAST: Stephen Geoffreys, Sheree Wilson, Cameron Dye, Leigh McCloskey. 1985

FRAUDS ★★1/2 Demented insurance-investigator Phil Collins turns a young couple's claim into a deadly game of cat and mouse. Teetering between black comedy and chills, this is an artistic jumble, though its very weirdness gives it a curious appeal. The plot slips past the realm of plausibility in the final act. Rated R for violence and profanity. 94m. DIR: Stephan Elliott. CAST: Phil Collins, Hugo Weaving, Josephine Byrnes. 1992

•FREAK CITY ★★★1/2 Natalie Cole shines in this drama, as one of several disabled or disturbed residents in a care facility that becomes a new home for a bitter young woman (Samantha Mathis) confined to a wheelchair. The parts are somewhat stereotyped—Jonathan Silverman as a blind man unwilling to stand up to his domineering mother, Marlee Matlin as a developmentally disabled woman who nonetheless remains spirited and cheerful—but the execution is warm and engaging; Jane Shepard's script carefully maintains the dignity of all these characters. But Cole owns the film, as a former singer who has retreated from reality, a scene wherein she emerges from her shell and croons one ballad is a throat-catching grabber. Rated R for profanity. 104m. DIR: Lynne Littman. CAST: Natalie Cole, Samantha Mathis, Marlee Matlin, Peter Sarsgaard, Jonathan Silverman, Estelle Parsons. 1999

FREAKED ★★★1/2 Hilariously demented comedy about a sideshow proprietor who uses toxic waste to create custom-made freaks. Like *Gremlins* made by the *Airplane!* team with an MTV-rude attitude: loud, fast, gross, and obnoxious—and we mean that in a good way. Rated R for profanity and general tastelessness. 80m. DIR: Alex Winter, Tom Stern. CAST: Alex Winter, Randy Quaid, Bill Sadler, Megan Ward, Mr. T, Bob Goldthwait, Brooke Shields. 1993

FREAKMAKER ★★ Retitled video version of a badly washed-out print of the British horror shocker, *Mutations*. Mad doctor Donald Pleasence botches one experiment in genetics after another. This wildly sadistic movie is buoyed by its own tastelessness, which includes exploiting some real sideshow performers in a way Tod Browning never imagined. Rated R. 92m. DIR: Jack Cardiff. CAST: Donald Pleasence, Tom Baker, Michael Dunn. 1973

FREAKS ★★★★ This legendary "horror" movie by Tod Browning is perhaps the most unusual film ever made and certainly one of the most unsettling. Based on Tod Robbins's *Spurs*, this is the story of a circus midget who falls in love with a statuesque trapeze artist and nearly becomes her victim as she attempts to poison him for his money. Incensed by her betrayal of their little friend, the armless, legless, pinheaded "freaks" exact their revenge. B&W; 64m. DIR: Tod Browning. CAST: Wallace Ford, Leila Hyams, Olga Baclanova, Roscoe Ates. 1932

FREAKSHOW ✔ Z-grade anthology boasts five terror tales narrated by the "Freakmaster" (Gunnar Hansen), and the lowest production values this side of a student film. Rated R for violence, sexual situations, and strong language. 102m. DIR: William Cooke, Paul Talbot. CAST: Gunnar Hansen, Shannon Michelle Parsons, Brian D. Kelly, Jennifer Peluso, Gene Aimone, Josh Craig. 1995

FREAKY FRIDAY ★★★1/2 One of Disney's better comedies from the 1970s, this perceptive fantasy allows mom Barbara Harris and daughter Jodie Foster to share a role-reversing out-of-body experience. Adapted with wit by Mary Rodgers from her own book. Rated G. 95m. DIR: Gary Nelson. CAST: Jodie Foster, Barbara Harris, John Astin, Ruth Buzzi, Kaye Ballard. 1977

FREDDIE AS F.R.O.7 ★★1/2 The British fascination with secret agents and magical kingdoms has been fused somewhat awkwardly in this kiddies-only animated film. The cast supplying voices is impressive, however, with Ben Kingsley, Billie Whitelaw, Michael Hordern, and Jonathan Pryce among the participants. Rated G. 90m. DIR: Jon Acevski. 1992

FREDDY'S DEAD: THE FINAL NIGHTMARE ★★★ In what has been promised as the last in the *Nightmare on Elm Street* series of films, the audience gets just what is expected. A new batch of teenagers is served up for slaughter, only this time they are led by an adult who just happens to be Freddy Krueger's daughter. The finale was in 3-D in the theaters and something is lost in the video transfer. Rated R for violence and profanity. 96m. DIR: Rachel Talalay. CAST: Robert Englund, Lisa Zane, Yaphet Kotto. 1991 DVD

FREE AND EASY ★★★ Buster Keaton's first sound movie has him chaperoning a beauty pageant winner to Hollywood, and stumbling into the movies himself. A good transition from silents to talkies for this wonderful clown. B&W; 92m. DIR: Edward Sedgwick. CAST: Buster Keaton, Anita Page, Robert Montgomery, Dorothy Sebastian. 1930

•FREE ENTERPRISE ★★★ Wonderfully engaging romp about two wannabe filmmakers who literally worship the ground that William Shatner walks on. When they get a chance to meet their hero, their lives are dramatically changed. Told with its tongue definitely in cheek, director Robert Meyer Burnett's comedy is filled with enough hip commentary and references to please most fans of the genre. Eric McCormack and Rafer Weigel are hilarious as the two fans who find that there is life after *Star Trek*. Rated R for adult situations, language, and nudity. 114m. DIR: Robert Meyer Burnett. CAST: William Shatner, Eric McCormack, Audie England, Rafer Weigel, Patrick Van Horn. 1998 DVD

•FREE MONEY ★★★★ Outrageously campy and quirky comedy will leave you gasping for breath in mirth and amazement. Marlon Brando stars as the crooked sheriff, Mira Sorvino as the FBI agent who's out to put him behind bars, and Charlie Sheen and Thomas Haden Church as his two luckless sons-in-law. Rated R for profanity and sexuality. 91m. DIR: Yves Simoneau. CAST: Marlon Brando, Donald Sutherland, Thomas Haden Church, Mira Sorvino, Charlie Sheen, David Arquette. 1998 DVD

FREE OF EDEN ★★★1/2 A young woman growing up in Brooklyn decides to get an education and rise above the poverty and dead-end fate for which she's destined. She convinces a former teacher—now a high-powered, cutthroat executive—to tutor her, and both teacher and pupil learn more than they expected. Only a few contrived scenes mar this fascinating made-for-cable original. Not rated; contains profanity and violence. 98m. DIR: Leon Ichaso. CAST: Sidney Poitier, Phylicia Rashad, Robert Hooks, Sydney Tamiia Poitier. 1998

FREE RIDE ★★ Disjointed rip-off of *Animal House*, with Gary Herschberger playing a supercool professional student, and Reed Rudy as his bunkie. Fitfully funny. Rated R for language and nudity. 92m. DIR: Tom Trbovich. CAST: Gary Herschberger, Reed Rudy, Dawn Schneider, Peter DeLuise, Warren Berlinger, Mamie Van Doren, Frank Campanella. 1986

FREE SOUL, A ★★1/2 Primarily a showcase for Lionel Barrymore, who won an Oscar for his role of a cantankerous attorney. The character is based on Adela Rogers St. John's father, a lawyer known for his colorful but irascible ways. Remade as *The Girl Who Had Everything*. With Elizabeth Taylor. B&W; 89m. DIR: Clarence Brown. CAST: Clark Gable, Lionel Barrymore, Norma Shearer, Leslie Howard, James Gleason. 1931

FREE, WHITE, AND 21 ★★ A southern black man is accused of raping a white woman who is working for the civil rights movement. The main attraction of this dated movie is that it is made in a pseudodocumentary style—as a trial during which the testimony is shown in the form of flashbacks. Interesting, though very overlong. B&W; 102m. DIR: Larry Buchanan. CAST: Frederick O'Neal, Annalena Lund. 1963

FREE WILLY ★★★★ Family entertainment about a friendship between a troubled boy and an endangered killer whale has a true dramatic edge. Strong character development and a staunch avoidance of clichés make this a treat for the entire family. Rated PG for brief profanity. DIR: Simon Wincer. CAST: Jason James Richter, Lori Petty, Jayne Atkinson, August Schellenberg, Michael Madsen, Michael Ironside, Richard Riehle. 1993 DVD

FREE WILLY 2: THE ADVENTURE HOME ★★★ Willy the whale—with a new animatronic double and stock footage replacing original star Keiko—returns for another wild, wet adventure that tests his friendship with the teen orphan Jesse. The two pals and their families meet and frolic in the Pacific Northwest before an offshore oil spill cuts short their happy reunion and leads to several tight scrapes. Rated PG. 96m. DIR: Dwight H. Little. CAST: Jason James Richter, Michael Madsen, August Schellenberg, Francis Capra, Jayne Atkinson, Mary Kate Schellhardt. 1995

FREE WILLY 3: THE RESCUE ★★★ The majestic whale's buddy from previous Willy films returns as a research tech. His team must determine why whale populations are decreasing. Befriending the young son of an illegal whaler, the duo determines to thwart the threat to Willy's pod. Parents should be prepared to discuss the film parents' lawlessness and appropriate consequences for their actions. Great underwater photography. Rated PG for violence. 85m. DIR: Sam Pillsbury. CAST: Jason James Richter, August Schellenberg, Annie Corley, Vincent Berry, Patrick Kilpatrick. 1997

FREEBIE AND THE BEAN ★★★ Before astounding filmgoers with the outrageous black comedy *The Stunt Man*, director Richard Rush twisted the cop genre around with this watchable (but not spectacular) release. James Caan and Alan Arkin play San Francisco detectives who wreak havoc while on the trail of gangster Jack Kruschen. Rated R. 113m. DIR: Richard Rush. CAST: Alan Arkin, James Caan, Valerie Harper, Loretta Swit. 1974

●FREEDOM SONG ★★★★ Powerfully emotional film about the civil rights movement. Told with sly humor and emotional intensity, *Freedom Song* focuses on the young (mostly teenagers) and is bolstered by a terrific cast and Phil Alden Robinson's usual meticulous direction. Not rated; contains profanity. 150m. DIR: Phil Alden Robinson. CAST: Danny Glover, Vondie Curtis-Hall, Vicellous Reon Shannon, Glynn Turman, Stan Shaw, Michael Jai White, David Strathairn. 2000

FREEFALL ★★★1/2 Although this thriller eventually becomes too tricky for its own good, John Irvin's slick direction doesn't let you ponder apparent plot inconsistencies. Wildlife photographer Pamela Gidley goes to Africa to shoot a rare bird, and winds up involved with assassins and Interpol agents who seem convinced she has something they desire. Plot twists abound, and most of them work. Rated R for violence, nudity, and suggested sex. 96m. DIR: John Irvin. CAST: Eric Roberts, Pamela Gidley, Jeff Fahey. 1994

FREEJACK ★★★ Technology in the year 2009, when the haves have more and the have-nots are destitute, has made it possible for the ultrarich to extend their lives—by finding a donor from the past. Emilio Estevez is the race-car driver who, after a spectacular crash, wakes up to find himself eighteen years in the future and runnng from those who want to erase his mind. It's not great, but not bad. Rated R for violence and profanity. 101m. DIR: Geoff Murphy. CAST: Emilio Estevez, Mick Jagger, René Russo, Anthony Hopkins, Jonathan Banks, David Johansen. 1992 DVD

FREEWAY (1988) ★★★ A fad film mirroring the real-life series of freeway killings in the Los Angeles area. A nurse (Darlanne Fluegel), dissatisfied with the police investigation of the murder of her boyfriend by a freeway sniper, pursues the killer on her own. Good acting, exciting direction, and some great action sequences make up for the threadbare plot. Rated R for violence, profanity, and nudity. 95m. DIR: Francis Delia. CAST: Darlanne Fluegel, James Russo, Richard Belzer, Michael Callan. 1988

FREEWAY (1996) ♥ Bent, punk retelling of *Little Red Riding Hood*—which concerns a shrill teenager's clash with a serial killer—is gratuitously violent, numbingly profane, and utterly without redeeming value. Rated R for profanity, violence, drug use, and strong sexual content. 101m. DIR: Matthew Bright. CAST: Kiefer Sutherland, Reese Witherspoon, Wolfgang Bodison, Dan Hedaya, Amanda Plummer, Brooke Shields. 1996 DVD

•**FREEWAY 2: CONFESSIONS OF A TRICKBABY** ★★★1/2 This sequel to the cult hit *Freeway* (by the same writer-director) has nothing in common with its predecessor but the notion of updating a Brothers Grimm story to a modern setting. In this case, Hansel and Gretel are a pair of female career criminals on the run from prison and in search of Sister Gomez, a witch in a candy house. Bizarre and imaginative, with a perverse performance by Vincent Gallo as the wicked witch. Rated R for violence, profanity, sexual situations, and drug use. 97m. DIR: Matthew Bright. CAST: Natasha Lyonne, Maria Celedonio, Vincent Gallo. 1999 DVD

FREEWAY MANIAC 💖 Matricidal maniac escapes from an insane asylum, not once but twice. *Playboy* cartoonist Gahan Wilson wrote this turkey. 94m. DIR: Paul Winters. CAST: Loren Winters, James Courtney. 1988

FREEZE—DIE—COME TO LIFE ★★★★ Vitaly Kanevski's gritty, uncomfortable look at the hard life in a part of the Soviet Union that's about as far from Moscow as one can get and still be in the USSR. The depressing, evocatively filmed story of two youngsters trying to overcome poverty and brutality in the bleak frozen terrain of the Soviet Orient. In Russian with English subtitles. Not rated. 105m. DIR: Vitaly Kanevski. 1990

FREEZE FRAME ★★1/2 This totally unbelievable tale of how a team of would-be high school reporters expose corporate corruption is just the right confection for younger, after-school viewers. The idea comes across loud and clear: it's okay to be a smart young woman. Not rated, but with mild violence. 78m. DIR: William Bindley. CAST: Shannen Doherty, Charles Haid, Robyn Douglass, Seth Michaels. 1992

FRENCH CAN CAN ★★★ Jean Renoir's rich cinematic style is evident in this comedy-drama starring Jean Gabin as a nightclub owner. Renoir tosses his can-can artists at the viewer, seducing us with the consuming spectacle. In French with English subtitles. 93m. DIR: Jean Renoir. CAST: Jean Gabin. 1955

FRENCH CONNECTION, THE ★★★★★ Gene Hackman is an unorthodox New York narcotics cop in this Oscar-winning performance. He and his partner (Roy Scheider) are investigating the flow of heroin coming into the city from France. The climactic chase is the best in movie history. Rated R. 104m. DIR: William Friedkin. CAST: Gene Hackman, Fernando Rey, Roy Scheider, Eddie Egan, Sonny Grosso. 1971

FRENCH CONNECTION II, THE ★★ Disappointing sequel to the 1971 winner for best picture has none of the thrills, chills, and action of the original. Instead, New York detective Popeye Doyle (Gene Hackman), who has journeyed to Paris to track the drug trafficker who eluded him in the States, finds himself addicted to heroin and suffering withdrawal. He isn't the only one who suffers. ... There's the viewer,

too. Rated R. 119m. DIR: John Frankenheimer. CAST: Gene Hackman, Fernando Rey, Bernard Fresson, Jean-Pierre Castaldi, Charles Milot. 1975

FRENCH DETECTIVE, THE ★★★★ Suspenseful police drama featuring Lino Ventura as a tough, independent veteran cop who pursues a hood working for a corrupt politician. Solid performances by Ventura and Patrick Dewaere. In French with English subtitles. 93m. DIR: Pierre Granier-Deferre. CAST: Lino Ventura, Patrick Dewaere, Victor Lanoux, Jacques Serres. 1975

FRENCH EXIT ★★★★ Entertaining and charismatic love story about two competing screenwriters who fall in love despite the fact they're complete opposites and are often fighting over the same job. Rated R for profanity. 88m. DIR: Daphina Kastner. CAST: Jonathan Silverman, Madchen Amick, Molly Hagan, Vince Grant, Craig Vincent. 1996

FRENCH KISS ★★★1/2 When her fiancé falls in love during a business trip to Paris and cancels their wedding plans, jilted Meg Ryan decides to fly from Canada to France and win him back. Along the way, she meets French jewel thief Kevin Kline, who, for reasons unknown to her, can't seem to let her out of his sight. Fans of the stars will enjoy this frothy romp. Rated PG-13 for profanity and suggested sex. 111m. DIR: Lawrence Kasdan. CAST: Meg Ryan, Kevin Kline, Timothy Hutton, Jean Reno, François Cluzet, Susan Anbeh. 1995 DVD

FRENCH LESSONS ★★★1/2 Romantic comedy about an English teenager who goes to Paris to study French for the summer. She is determined to fall in love and learns more out of the classroom than in. Rated PG. 90m. DIR: Brian Gilbert. CAST: Jane Snowden, Diana Blackburn, Françoise Brion. 1986

FRENCH LIEUTENANT'S WOMAN, THE ★★★★★ A brilliant adaptation of John Fowles' bestseller, starring Meryl Streep as the enigmatic title heroine and Jeremy Irons as her obsessed lover. Victorian and modern attitudes on love are contrasted in this intellectually and emotionally engrossing film. Rated R because of sexual references and sex scenes. 123m. DIR: Karel Reisz. CAST: Meryl Streep, Jeremy Irons, Leo McKern, Hilton McRae, Emily Morgan. 1981

FRENCH LINE, THE ★★ This is a dull musical with forgettable songs. Ultrarich heroine Jane Russell can't find true love. She masquerades as a fashion model during a voyage, hoping her money won't show while she snags a man. Despite presenting Miss Russell in 3-D, the film was a bust. 102m. DIR: Lloyd Bacon. CAST: Jane Russell, Gilbert Roland, Mary McCarty, Craig Stevens, Steven Geray, Arthur Hunnicutt. 1954

FRENCH POSTCARDS ★★★1/2 This film benefits from the skillful supporting performances by two noted French film stars, Marie-France Pisier and Jean Rochefort. The younger set of characters are well played by David Marshall Grant, Miles Chapin, Valerie Quennessen, and Blanche Baker. *French Postcards* is an enjoyable way to spend a couple of hours. Rated PG. 92m. DIR: Willard Huyck. CAST: David Marshall Grant, Blanche Baker, Miles Chapin, Debra Winger, Marie-France Pisier, Valerie Quennessen, Jean Rochefort. 1979

FRENCH QUARTER ★★1/2 Everyone in the cast plays two characters, one in modern times and one at the turn of the century, in this drama set in New Orleans. Both stories are connected by voodoo magic, as a woman discovers she is the reincarnation of a prostitute. Slow-moving but intriguing. Rated R for sexual situations. 101m. DIR: Dennis Kane. CAST: Bruce Davison, Virginia Mayo. 1977

FRENCH SILK ★★ Cheesy world of lingerie modeling is platform for a hack made-for-television thriller about a CEO of a lingerie company (Susan Lucci) who is framed for murder. Shari Belafonte plays a supermodel who holds the key to the mystery. Rated PG-13 for adult situations. 90m. DIR: Noel Nosseck. CAST: Susan Lucci, Lee Horsley, Shari Belafonte, Jim Metzler. 1993

FRENCH TWIST ★★1/2 A good-hearted lesbian (director Josiane Balasko) disrupts the lives of a not-so-happily-married couple in this earnest but clumsy sex farce. The three stars try hard, but their characters are selfish, unsympathetic dolts, and there's not much they can do to redeem them. In French with English subtitles. Rated R for nudity and mature content. 107m. DIR: Josiane Balasko. CAST: Josiane Balasko, Victoria Abril, Alain Chabat. 1995

FRENCH WAY, THE ★★ Famed burlesque dancer Josephine Baker appears as a café singer in this underdressed comedy about a boy and a girl who want to marry but can't. Baker begins to do her famous feather dance, but the ending is edited out. In French with English subtitles. B&W; 73m. DIR: Jacques De Baroncelli. CAST: Josephine Baker, Micheline Presle, Georges Marshall. 1952

FRENCH WOMAN, THE ★★ Laughable erotic thriller loosely based on the bestselling memoirs of Madame Claude, who operated a "modeling agency" of high-priced hookers. Rated R for nudity. 97m. DIR: Just Jaeckin. CAST: Françoise Fabian, Murray Head, Dayle Haddon, Klaus Kinski, Robert Webber. 1977

FRENCHMAN'S FARM ★★1/2 A fairly tame Australian import about a female law student who has a psychic experience and witnesses a murder that took place forty years earlier. Some good suspense, but the psychic-encounter scene is overdone. Rated R for language and violence. 86m. DIR: Ron Way. CAST: Tracy Tainsh, Ray Barrett, Norman Kaye, John Meillon. 1986

FRENZY ★★★★1/2 Marks a grand return to one of Hitchcock's favorite themes: that of a man accused of a murder he did not commit and all but trapped by the circumstantial evidence. Rated R. 116m. DIR: Alfred Hitchcock. CAST: Jon Finch, Barry Foster, Barbara Leigh-Hunt, Anna Massey, Alec McCowen. 1972

•**FREQUENCY** ★★★1/2 The beguiling premise behind this clever sci-fi yarn concerns a modern-day cop who would give anything to undo the past, particularly the chain of events that resulted in his father's death thirty years earlier. Thanks to a ham radio and "the mother of all sunspots," the two men are able to communicate with each other, across the barrier of time; both discover that things *can* be changed, although not always for the better. The result is a clever "What if?" tale, well worth your time. Rated PG-13 for violence and mild profanity. 118m. DIR:

Gregory Hoblit. CAST: Dennis Quaid, Jim Caviezel, Andre Braugher, Elizabeth Mitchell, Noah Emmerich. 2000

FRESH ★★★★ A 12-year-old Brooklyn dope runner named Fresh attempts to rescue his sister from the squalor of addiction and avenge a school friend's death. This harrowing urban drama about survival and redemption in inner-city America plays like a coiled spring that could snap at any moment. Rated R for language and violence. 110m. DIR: Boaz Yakin. CAST: Sean Nelson, Samuel L. Jackson, Giancarlo Esposito, N'Bushe Wright. 1994

FRESH HORSES ★★ Adult version of *Pretty in Pink*. Molly Ringwald continues as the kid from the wrong side of the tracks, only this time there's nothing upbeat about her. Andrew McCarthy is once again typecast as a middle-class nice guy. Rated PG-13 for profanity and violence. 106m. DIR: David Anspaugh. CAST: Molly Ringwald, Andrew McCarthy, Patti D'Arbanville. 1988

•**FRESHMAN, THE (1925)** ★★★ If you've never seen the great silent comedian Harold Lloyd, here's the place to start. In this entertaining film, he plays a college freshman who will do anything to become popular. B&W; 76m. DIR: Sam Taylor, Fred Newmeyer. CAST: Harold Lloyd, Jobyna Ralston. 1925

FRESHMAN, THE (1990) ★★★★ This offbeat comedy stars Matthew Broderick as a film student who gets a job with an Italian-American importer who looks suspiciously like Don Corleone. Marlon Brando gets a wonderful opportunity to parody his Oscar-winning *Godfather* performance. Brando and Broderick are superb. Rated PG. 102m. DIR: Andrew Bergman. CAST: Marlon Brando, Matthew Broderick, Bruno Kirby, Penelope Ann Miller, Maximilian Schell. 1990 DVD

FRIDA ★★ Tedious, disjointed account of the life of Mexican painter Frida Kahlo, considered to be the most important woman artist of the twentieth century. The film desperately fails to give any insight into the artist's life, which was laced with human tragedy and self-obsession. In Spanish with English subtitles. Not rated; contains mild nudity. 108m. DIR: Paul Leduc. CAST: Ofelia Medina. 1984

FRIDAY ★★ This uneven comedy is about a day of stoop life in south central Los Angeles. The film has an appealing low-key tone, ends with an antigun message, and introduces some oddball neighborhood characters. Rated R for language, drug use, and violence. 101m. DIR: F. Gary Gray. CAST: Ice Cube, Chris Tucker, Nia Long, Tiny Lester, Bernie Mac, John Witherspoon, Regina King. 1995 DVD

FRIDAY FOSTER ★★1/2 In this blaxploitation effort, Pam Grier plays the title character, a fashion photographer who doubles as a two-fisted avenger—this time taking on antiblack terrorists. A strong supporting cast helps. Rated R. 90m. DIR: Arthur Marks. CAST: Pam Grier, Julius W. Harris, Thalmus Rasulala, Carl Weathers, Eartha Kitt, Godfrey Cambridge, Yaphet Kotto. 1975

FRIDAY THE 13TH: THE ORPHAN ❤ No relation to the popular slasher series, this one has a disturbed youth killing everyone around him. Rated R for violence and language. 88m. **DIR:** John Ballard. **CAST:** Mark Owens, Joanna Miles. **1979**

FRIDAY THE 13TH ★★★ The original slasher flick. A group of Crystal Lake camp counselors are systematically murdered by a maniac. Not much of a plot, just the killer hacking and slashing his way through the dwindling counselor population. Fine makeup effects by master Tom Savini highlight this spatterfest that has fostered many imitations and a series of eight Jason Voorhees slice-and-dicers. Rated R for gore. 95m. **DIR:** Sean S. Cunningham. **CAST:** Betsy Palmer, Adrienne King, Harry Crosby, Kevin Bacon. **1980 DVD**

FRIDAY THE 13TH, PART II ★★ This sequel to the box-office hit of the same name is essentially the *Psycho* shower scene repeated ad nauseam. A group of young people are methodically sliced and diced by Jason, the masked maniac. Though the makeup effects in this rehash were reportedly toned down, there is still enough blood for gore hounds. Rated R for gruesomeness, no matter how toned-down. 87m. **DIR:** Steve Miner. **CAST:** Amy Steel, John Furey, Adrienne King, Betsy Palmer. **1981 DVD**

FRIDAY THE 13TH, PART III ★★ More gruesome ax, knife, and meat-cleaver murders occur at sunny Crystal Lake. Works the same as the first two, though for the theatrical release it had the hook of being in 3-D. The video isn't in 3-D, so Jason is just his old two-dimensional self hacking and hewing his way through another unlucky group of campers. Won't they ever learn? Rated R for obvious reasons. 96m. **DIR:** Steve Miner. **CAST:** Dana Kimmel, Paul Kratka. **1982**

FRIDAY THE 13TH—THE FINAL CHAPTER ★★★ It has been said that the only reason makeup master Tom Savini agreed to work on this film was that it gave him a chance to kill Jason, the maniacal killer whom he created in the original film. Well, Jason does die. Oh, boy! Does he ever! But not before dispatching a new group of teenagers. Savini's work is the highlight of this flick, which is really just a rehash of the first three. Rated R for extreme gruesomeness. 90m. **DIR:** Joseph Zito. **CAST:** Kimberly Beck, Corey Feldman, Peter Barton, Joan Freeman. **1984**

FRIDAY THE 13TH, PART V—A NEW BEGINNING 🖤 Well, they did it. The producers promised *Friday the 13th—The Final Chapter* would be the last of its kind. They lied. Rated R for graphic violence and simulated sex. 92m. **DIR:** Danny Steinmann. **CAST:** John Shepherd, Melanie Kinnaman, Richard Young. **1985**

FRIDAY THE 13TH, PART VI: JASON LIVES ★★★ It may be hard to believe, but this fifth sequel to the unmemorable *Friday the 13th* is actually better than all those that preceded it. Of course this thing is loaded with violence, but it is also nicely buffered by good comedy bits and one-liners. Rated R for language and violence. 85m. **DIR:** Tom McLoughlin. **CAST:** Thom Mathews, Jennifer Cooke. **1986**

FRIDAY THE 13TH, PART VII: THE NEW BLOOD ★★1/2 Jason returns, only this time someone's waiting for him: a mentally disturbed teenage girl with telekinetic powers. The result is a bloodbath as the two battle to decide who will star in Part VIII. A decent sequel with a little less gore than usual. Rated R for violence, language, and nudity. 90m. **DIR:** John Carl Buechler. **CAST:** Lar Park Lincoln, Terry Kiser. **1988**

FRIDAY THE 13TH, PART VIII: JASON TAKES MANHATTAN ★★ Fans of the series may be disappointed with the lack of blood in this seventh sequel. Jason torments a group of teenagers aboard a cruise ship and then takes to the streets of the Big Apple. Rated R for violence and profanity. 100m. **DIR:** Rob Hedden. **CAST:** Jensen Daggett, Scott Reeves, Peter Mark Richman. **1989**

FRIED GREEN TOMATOES ★★★★ Adapted from Fannie Flagg's novel, *Fried Green Tomatoes at the Whistle Stop Café*, this touching motion picture is the story of friendships between two sets of women. Kathy Bates is the put-upon, overweight housewife who finds herself in the rec room of a senior citizens' home listening to Jessica Tandy's tales of the Depression-era adventures of two young women. It's wonderful. Rated PG-13 for profanity and violence. 120m. **DIR:** Jon Avnet. **CAST:** Kathy Bates, Mary Stuart Masterson, Mary-Louise Parker, Jessica Tandy, Cicely Tyson, Chris O'Donnell, Stan Shaw, Gailard Sartain, Lois Smith. **1991 DVD**

FRIEND OF THE DECEASED, A ★★★ A Ukrainian intellectual, unable to find work, hires a hit man to kill him, then changes his mind and hires another hit man to protect him from the first. Despite the low-comedy premise, this sardonic drama explores the social and emotional dislocation of life in the former Soviet Union. In Russian with English subtitles. Rated R for nudity and profanity (in subtitles). 100m. **DIR:** Vyacheslav Krishtofovich. **CAST:** Alexander Lazarev, Tatiana Krvitska, Yevgeni Pashin, Yelena Korikova, Constantin Kosyshin. **1997**

FRIEND OF THE FAMILY 🖤 She's friendly all right, as she seduces everyone in the family, including mom and daughter. Just an excuse to get everyone naked. Not rated; contains nudity and profanity. 102m. **DIR:** Edward Holzman. **CAST:** Shauna O'Brien, Annelyn Griffin Drew, C. T. Miller, Lissa Boyle. **1993 DVD**

FRIEND OF THE FAMILY II 🖤 Ludicrous, derivative *Fatal Attraction* rip-off in which a successful businessman has a one-night affair that turns into a never-ending nightmare. Notable only for its steamy sexual sequences, of which there are plenty. Available in R and not-rated versions, both of which contain profanity, nudity, and strong sexual situations. 89m. **DIR:** Nicholas Medina. **CAST:** Shauna O'Brien, Paul Michael Robinson, Jenna Bodner, Jeff Rector, Arthur Roberts. **1996 DVD**

FRIENDLY FIRE ★★★★ A gripping account of an American couple who run into government indifference when they attempt to learn the truth about their son's death—by American artillery fire—in Vietnam. Based on a true story. Both Carol Burnett and Ned Beatty give smashing performances as the grieved couple. Picture won four Emmy awards. Not rated; made for TV. 180m. **DIR:** David Greene. **CAST:**

Carol Burnett, Ned Beatty, Sam Waterston, Timothy Hutton. 1979

FRIENDLY PERSUASION ★★★ Jessamyn West's finely crafted novel of a Quaker family beset by the realities of the Civil War in southern Indiana is superbly transferred to film by an outstanding cast guided by gifted direction. 140m. **DIR:** William Wyler. **CAST:** Gary Cooper, Dorothy McGuire, Marjorie Main, Anthony Perkins, Robert Middleton, Richard Eyer. 1956

FRIENDS ★★1/2 The friendship between three South African women is threatened when one uses terrorism against the oppressive government still ruling the country in the late 1980s. The atmosphere, chilling in the face of institutionalized racism, and strong performances nearly overcome the narrative's basic flaws. Not rated; contains profanity, violence, nudity, and sexual situations. 109m. **DIR:** Elaine Proctor. **CAST:** Kerry Fox, Dambisa Kente, Michele Burgers. 1994

FRIENDS, LOVERS & LUNATICS ★★ Chaos abounds as six different relationships evolve. Everything comes to a head when the title characters all arrive at a cabin on the same weekend. Listless attempt at screwball comedy. Rated R. 87m. **DIR:** Stephen Withrow. **CAST:** Daniel Stern, Sheila McCarthy, Page Fletcher, Deborah Foreman. 1989

FRIENDSHIP IN VIENNA, A ★★★ So-so Disney Home Video does not do justice to its weighty subject. Two schoolgirl friends are suddenly torn apart in 1938 because one is Jewish and the other the daughter of a Hitler supporter. They vow to remain friends despite outside forces. This film lacks the sincere passion the subject demands. Not rated; contains violence. 94m. **DIR:** Arthur Allan Seidelman. **CAST:** Jenifer Lewis, Kamie Harper, Edward Asner, Jane Alexander, Stephen Macht, Rosemary Forsyth. 1993

FRIGHT HOUSE 💘 Two films are worse than one in this production that is actually two movies edited together to make a supposedly new film. Rated R for violence. 110m. **DIR:** Len Anthony. **CAST:** Al Lewis, Duane Jones, Jennifer Delora. 1989

FRIGHT NIGHT ★★★★1/2 Charley Brewster (William Ragsdale) is a fairly normal teenager save one thing: he's convinced his neighbor, Jerry Dandrige (Chris Sarandon), is a vampire—and he is! So Charley enlists the aid of former screen vampire hunter Peter Vincent (Roddy McDowall), and the result is a screamingly funny horror spoof. Rated R for nudity, profanity, and gore. 105m. **DIR:** Tom Holland. **CAST:** Chris Sarandon, William Ragsdale, Roddy McDowall, Amanda Bearse, Stephen Geoffreys. 1985 **DVD**

FRIGHT NIGHT II ★★★ Charley Brewster (William Ragsdale) is back, after undergoing some psychiatric counseling from his original *Fright Night* encounter with the vampire next door. Like its predecessor, this one takes a fang-in-cheek attitude toward horror flicks, but it isn't the certifiable spoof the original was. Rated R for profanity, violence, and brief nudity. 90m. **DIR:** Tommy Lee Wallace. **CAST:** William Ragsdale, Roddy McDowall, Traci Lynn, Julie Carmen, Jonathan Gries. 1989

FRIGHTENERS, THE ★★★ After suffering a near-death experience, Frank Bannister finds himself caught between two worlds: the living and the dead. So, with the help of some ghostly compatriots, he sets up a scam as an exorcist and battles an evil creature haunting both worlds. Diverting. Rated R for violence and profanity. 109m. **DIR:** Peter Jackson. **CAST:** Michael J. Fox, Trini Alvarado, Peter Dobson, John Astin, Jeffrey Combs, Dee Wallace, Jake Busey, R. Lee Ermey. 1996 **DVD**

FRIGHTMARE 💘 An eccentric horror-movie star is called back from the dead. Not rated; this film contains some violence. 86m. **DIR:** Norman Thaddeus Vane. **CAST:** Luca Bercovici, Jennifer Starret, Nita Talbot. 1982

FRINGE DWELLERS, THE ★★★★ This Australian production, which follows the domestic problems of a family of Aborigines who move from a shantytown to a proper suburban neighborhood, is an intriguing, touching, but nonsentimental look at a face of people unfamiliar to most Americans. It's rated PG for language. 98m. **DIR:** Bruce Beresford. **CAST:** Justine Saunders, Kristina Nehm, Bob Maza. 1987

FRISCO KID, THE ★★★ Gene Wilder and Harrison Ford make a surprisingly effective and funny team as a rabbi and outlaw, respectively, making their way to San Francisco. Good fun. Rated PG. 122m. **DIR:** Robert Aldrich. **CAST:** Gene Wilder, Harrison Ford, William Smith, Penny Peyser. 1979

FRITZ THE CAT ★★★ This is an X-rated rendition of Robert Crumb's revolutionary feline, and it's the most outrageous cartoon ever produced. Fritz the Cat has appeared in Zap Comix and Head Comix, as well as in other underground mags. It's sometimes funny and sometimes gross, but mostly just so-so. 77m. **DIR:** Ralph Bakshi. 1972

FROGS ★★ In this fair horror film, Ray Milland has killed frogs, so frogs come to kill his family. The whole cast dies convincingly. Rated PG. 91m. **DIR:** George McCowan. **CAST:** Ray Milland, Sam Elliott, Joan Van Ark. 1972

FROGS FOR SNAKES ★★★ Low-echelon criminals compete for roles in a theater group run by a loan shark in a strange, seedy Manhattan neighborhood. The characters spout their favorite monologues between bouts of sex, maiming, and murder. Rated R for language, violence, nudity, and sexual content. 92m. **DIR:** Amos Poe. **CAST:** Barbara Hershey, Robbie Coltrane, Lisa Marie, Harry Hamlin, Ron Perlman, Clarence Williams III, John Leguizamo, Debi Mazar, Ian Hart. 1999

FROM A FAR COUNTRY ★★★ Polish biography of Pope John Paul II features a winning performance by Warren Clark and stunning location footage. Made-for-television drama spans several decades, from his days as a small boy in 1926 Poland, through the turbulent years of World War II, and finally his appointment to the Vatican. Self-serving but fascinating nonetheless. Also known as *Zdalekiego Kraju*. Not rated. 120m. **DIR:** Krzysztof Zanussi. **CAST:** Warren Clarke, Sam Neill, Robert Frazer, Lisa Harrow, Carol Gilles. 1981

FROM BEYOND ★★★ A lecherous scientist and his assistant create a machine that stimulates a gland in the brain that allows one to see into another dimension. Then the fun begins—with better-than-average special effects, scary-looking monsters, and suspenseful horror. Made by the creators of *Re-Animator*. Rated R for graphic violence and nudity. 89m. **DIR:** Stuart Gordon. **CAST:** Jeffrey Combs, Barbara Crampton, Ken Foree. **1986**

FROM BEYOND THE GRAVE ★★★ One of the best Amicus horror anthologies, this features Peter Cushing as the owner of a curio shop, Temptations Ltd., where customers get more than they bargain for. A strong cast of character actors enlivens this fine adaptation of four R. Chetwynd-Hayes stories: "The Gate Crasher," "An Act of Kindness," "The Elemental," and "The Door." Rated PG. 97m. **DIR:** Kevin Connor. **CAST:** Peter Cushing, Margaret Leighton, Ian Bannen, David Warner, Donald Pleasence, Lesley-Anne Down, Diana Dors. **1973**

FROM DUSK TILL DAWN 2: TEXAS BLOOD MONEY ★1/2 This direct-to-video sequel lacks the bite and ferociousness of the original, and is sorely missing the on-screen presence of original stars Quentin Tarantino and George Clooney. All hell breaks loose when one of a team of bank robbers is bitten by a vampire, thus turning most of the crew into invincible blood suckers. The special effects are hit-and-miss. Rated R for violence, language, and adult situations. 88m. **DIR:** Scott Spiegel. **CAST:** Robert Patrick, Bo Hopkins, Duane Whitaker, Muse Watson, Danny Trejo, Brett Harrelson. **1999 DVD**

FROM DUSK TILL DAWN ★★ This vampire opus has everything—except believable characters, a coherent storyline, and a sense of style. Still, fans of the horror genre may get a kick out of what happens when a pair of bank-robbing brothers hook up with a family on vacation and end up at the nightclub from hell. Rated R for violence, gore, profanity, and nudity. 110m. **DIR:** Robert Rodriguez. **CAST:** Harvey Keitel, George Clooney, Quentin Tarantino, Juliette Lewis, Eric Liu, Fred Williamson, Richard "Cheech" Marin, Tom Savini. **1996 DVD**

FROM HELL IT CAME ★★ The murdered prince of a South Seas tribe returns as a vengeful walking tree. A so-bad-it's-good classic featuring the only monster in screen history who would lose a footrace with the Mummy. B&W; 71m. **DIR:** Dan Milner. **CAST:** Tod Andrews, Tina Carver, Linda Watkins, Gregg Palmer. **1957**

FROM HELL TO BORNEO ★★ George Montgomery owns an island. Crooks and smugglers want it. He defends it. Sweat and jungle. 96m. **DIR:** George Montgomery. **CAST:** George Montgomery, Torin Thatcher, Julie Gregg, Lisa Moreno. **1964**

FROM HELL TO VICTORY 🖤 This hokey story of a bunch of strangely allied friends during World War II has nothing to offer. Rated PG. 100m. **DIR:** Hank Milestone. **CAST:** George Peppard, George Hamilton, Capucine, Horst Buchholz, Sam Wanamaker. **1979**

FROM HERE TO ETERNITY (1953) ★★★★★ This smoldering drama, depicting the demands of military life just before America's involvement in World War II, earned the Academy Award for best picture of 1953. This riveting classic includes the historic on-the-beach love scene that turned a few heads during its time. And no wonder! Director Fred Zinnemann

took chances with this realistic portrait of the U.S. military. B&W; 118m. **DIR:** Fred Zinnemann. **CAST:** Burt Lancaster, Montgomery Clift, Deborah Kerr, Frank Sinatra, Donna Reed, Ernest Borgnine. **1953**

FROM HERE TO ETERNITY (1979) ★★★ William Devane and Natalie Wood find playtime during wartime in this watchable TV remake of the 1953 movie classic. This glossy melodrama depicts army-base life and a general sense of moral chaos brought on by World War II. 110m. **DIR:** Buzz Kulik. **CAST:** Natalie Wood, William Devane, Steve Railsback, Kim Basinger. **1979**

FROM HOLLYWOOD TO DEADWOOD ★★★ Two loser detectives need to score a case or give it up. Finding a missing starlet leaving a trail of blackmail and murder may be too much for them. Offbeat mystery. Rated R for violence and language. 96m. **DIR:** Rex Pickett. **CAST:** Scott Paulin, Jim Haynie, Barbara Schock. **1989**

FROM RUSSIA WITH LOVE ★★★★1/2 The definitive James Bond movie. Sean Connery's second portrayal of Agent 007 is right on target. Lots of action, beautiful women, and great villains. Connery's fight aboard a passenger train with baddy Robert Shaw is as good as they come. 118m. **DIR:** Terence Young. **CAST:** Sean Connery, Lotte Lenya, Robert Shaw, Daniela Bianchi. **1963**

FROM THE DEAD OF NIGHT ★★1/2 After a near-death experience, Lindsay Wagner is pursued by spirits of the dead. For a made-for-TV movie, this one has some pretty scary moments—if only it didn't take so long to get to them. 190m. **DIR:** Paul Wendkos. **CAST:** Lindsay Wagner, Bruce Boxleitner, Robin Thomas, Diahann Carroll, Robert Prosky. **1989**

FROM THE EARTH TO THE MOON ★★★ Entertaining tale based on Jules Verne's story of a turn-of-the-century trip to the Moon led by Joseph Cotten and sabotaged by George Sanders. 100m. **DIR:** Byron Haskin. **CAST:** Joseph Cotten, George Sanders, Debra Paget, Don Dubbins. **1958 DVD**

FROM THE HIP ★★★ Thoroughly unrealistic but nonetheless entertaining courtroom comedy that works in spite of director Bob Clark's tendency to forget that he's no longer making *Porky's*. Judd Nelson stars as a brash young attorney. John Hurt delivers a particularly fine, high-powered performance as a ruthless egomaniac who considers himself better than the rest of humanity. Rated PG for language. 111m. **DIR:** Bob Clark. **CAST:** Judd Nelson, Elizabeth Perkins, John Hurt, Ray Walston, Darren McGavin. **1987**

FROM THE JOURNALS OF JEAN SEBERG ★★★★ Mary Beth Hurt is both sensational and heartbreaking as the celebrated actress whose immediate rise to fame and eventual downfall are chronicled in director Mark Rappaport's incisive and challenging film. Be prepared as you go behind the scenes and witness the relationship between film and those who inhabit its frames. Funny, touching, and ultimately sad. Not rated. 97m. **DIR:** Mark Rappaport. **CAST:** Mary Beth Hurt. **1995 DVD**

FROM THE LIVES OF THE MARIONETTES ★★ This Ingmar Bergman film, which details the vicious sex murder of a prostitute by an outwardly compassionate and intelligent man, is a puzzle that never really resolves itself. Nevertheless, fans will no doubt consider it another triumphant essay on the human condition. B&W; 104m. **DIR:** Ingmar Bergman. **CAST:** Robert Atzorn, Christine Buchegger, Heinz Bennent. **1980**

FROM THE MIXED-UP FILES OF MRS. BASIL E. FRANKWEILER ★★★★ Two children run away from home and hide out in the Metropolitan Museum, dodging security guards and the police. When they come across a mysterious statue, their curiosity leads them to the statue's former owner, Mrs. Basil E. Frankweiler. Now the real adventure begins in this charming and delightful film. Rated PG. 92m. **DIR:** Marcus Cole. **CAST:** Lauren Bacall, Jean Marie Barnwell, Jesse Lee. **1995**

FROM THE TERRACE ★★ Overblown denouncement of the struggle for success and the almighty dollar is just so much Technicolor trash despite the luminous presence of Paul Newman and Joanne Woodward. 144m. **DIR:** Mark Robson. **CAST:** Paul Newman, Joanne Woodward, Myrna Loy, Ina Balin, Leon Ames, Elizabeth Allen, Barbara Eden, George Grizzard, Patrick O'Neal, Felix Aylmer. **1960**

FRONT, THE ★★★★ Focusing on the horrendous blacklist of entertainers in the 1950s, this film manages to drive its point home with wit and poignance. This film is about writers who find a man to submit their scripts to after they have been blacklisted. Woody Allen plays the title role. Rated PG. 94m. **DIR:** Martin Ritt. **CAST:** Woody Allen, Zero Mostel, Andrea Marcovicci, Joshua Shelley, Georgann Johnson. **1976**

FRONT PAGE, THE (1931) ★★★★ A newspaper editor and his ace reporter do battle with civic corruption and each other in the first version of this oft-filmed hit comedy. The fast-paced, sparkling dialogue and the performances of the Warner Bros. stable of character actors have not aged after more than sixty years. This classic movie retains a great deal of charm. B&W; 99m. **DIR:** Lewis Milestone. **CAST:** Pat O'Brien, Adolphe Menjou, Mary Brian, Edward Everett Horton. **1931**

FRONT PAGE, THE (1974) ★★★1/2 Third version (of four to date) of the Ben Hecht–Charles MacArthur play is not quite as frantic as its predecessors, but retains some flavor of the era. Rated PG for profanity. 105m. **DIR:** Billy Wilder. **CAST:** Jack Lemmon, Walter Matthau, Carol Burnett, Charles Durning, Herb Edelman, Vincent Gardenia, Allen Garfield, Harold Gould, Susan Sarandon, David Wayne. **1974 DVD**

FRONTIER HORIZON ★★★ In this modern-day Western, the Three Mesquiteers ride to the rescue when a group of ranchers battle unscrupulous land grabbers. Jennifer Jones makes an early screen appearance here under the name Phyllis Isley. B&W; 56m. **DIR:** George Sherman. **CAST:** John Wayne, Ray "Crash" Corrigan, Raymond Hatton, Jennifer Jones. **1939**

FRONTIER PONY EXPRESS ★★1/2 Good action-packed Western finds Roy Rogers (in one of his early starring roles) coming to the aid of pony express riders who have been preyed on by robbers. B&W; 54m.

DIR: Joseph Kane. **CAST:** Roy Rogers, Lynne Roberts (Mary Hart), Raymond Hatton, Edward Keane. **1939**

FROZEN ASSETS 🎬 About what you'd expect from a comedy about a sperm bank. The plot is even worse than the performances by Shelley Long and Corbin Bernsen. Rated PG-13 for profanity and sexual themes. 92m. **DIR:** George Miller. **CAST:** Corbin Bernsen, Shelley Long. **1992**

FROZEN GHOST, THE ★★ Unsurprising *Inner Sanctum* mystery in which a stage hypnotist is suspected of causing the death of a member of his audience. B&W; 61m. **DIR:** Harold Young. **CAST:** Lon Chaney Jr., Evelyn Ankers, Martin Kosleck, Milburn Stone, Elena Verdugo. **1945**

FROZEN LIMITS, THE ★★1/2 In this mediocre slapstick comedy, six British men accidentally read a 40-year-old news story about a gold rush in Alaska. They pack their bags and head to the United States, only to run into trouble. Not rated, but suitable for all audiences. B&W; 82m. **DIR:** Marcel Varnel. **CAST:** Jimmy Nervo, Teddy Knox, Bud Flanagan, Chesney Allen, Charlie Naughton, Jimmy Gold, Moore Marriott. **1939**

FROZEN TERROR ★★1/2 Pretty good spaghetti horror from the son of the late horror maestro, Mario Bava. Bava *fils* unfortunately hasn't lived up to the promise displayed here. The video title (the film's original moniker was *Macabro*) refers to the unbalanced leading lady's prize possession: the head of her departed lover, stored in the refrigerator. Rated R. 91m. **DIR:** Lamberto Bava. **CAST:** Bernice Stegers. **1980**

FUGITIVE, THE (1947) ★★★ Intriguing John Ford version of Graham Greene novel is a flawed minor masterpiece. Complex story about a self-doubting priest escaping a relentless police lieutenant in Mexico where the government strives to control the Catholic church. B&W; 99m. **DIR:** John Ford. **CAST:** Henry Fonda, Dolores Del Rio, Pedro Armendariz, J. Carrol Naish, Leo Carrillo, Ward Bond, Robert Armstrong, John Qualen. **1947**

FUGITIVE, THE (TV SERIES) ★★★★ Wildly popular TV series that featured an innocent man falsely convicted of murdering his wife and sentenced to death. Escaping, he becomes both pursuer and pursued as he seeks the one-armed man he saw at the scene of the crime while evading a single-minded police lieutenant. Each episode features well-known stars. Volumes 1 to 5, 105m. each. **DIR:** Richard Donner, William A. Graham, Jerry Hopper. **CAST:** David Janssen, Barry Morse, Bill Raisch, Mickey Rooney, Suzanne Pleshette, Susan Oliver, Ron Howard, Kurt Russell, John McIntire. **1963–1966**

FUGITIVE, THE: THE LAST EPISODE (TV SERIES) ★★★1/2 Dr. Richard Kimble is sentenced to death for the murder of his wife. He escapes from Indiana police lieutenant Philip Gerard and goes in search of the one-armed man he believes was the real culprit. After four outstanding seasons, the series ends in run-of-the-mill fashion when Kimble finally encounters the one-armed man. Though somewhat disappointing, this two-part episode is a must for fans. 120m. **DIR:** Don Medford. **CAST:** David Janssen, Barry Morse, Bill Raisch, Diane Brewster. **1967**

FUGITIVE, THE (1993) ★★★★ In a riveting performance, Harrison Ford stars as Dr. Richard Kimble, an innocent man accused of murdering his wife. Tracked by the relentless U.S. Marshal Sam Girard, Kimble tries to prove his innocence by finding the one-armed man he believes committed the crime. Rated PG-13 for profanity and violence. 133m. **DIR:** Andrew Davis. **CAST:** Harrison Ford, Tommy Lee Jones, Sela Ward, Joe Pantoliano, Jeroen Krabbé, Andreas Katsulas, Daniel Roebuck. **1993 DVD**

FUGITIVE GIRLS 💙 Here's a video treasure for camp buffs—a women's prison movie written by Ed (*Plan 9 from Outer Space*) Wood! Rated R for nudity and sexual situations. 90m. **DIR:** A. C. Stephen. **CAST:** Jabee Abercrombie, Rene Bond, Edward D. Wood Jr. 1975

FUGITIVE KIND, THE ★★ This picture takes Tennessee Williams's stage play *Orpheus Descending*, shakes it up, and lets a new story line fall out. Marlon Brando is a wanderer who woos southern belles while strumming a guitar. As one of the wooed, Joanne Woodward gives a fine performance. B&W; 135m. **DIR:** Sidney Lumet. **CAST:** Marlon Brando, Joanne Woodward, Anna Magnani, Victor Jory. 1959

FUGITIVE RAGE ★★ Babes break out of prison to battle the mob, corrupt cops, and a secret government agency. Of course, they have time for a shower first. ... Director Fred Olen Ray has done so many of these he could probably shoot them in his sleep— and this time it looks like he did. Rated R for nudity, sexual situations, violence, and profanity. 90m. **DIR:** Fred Olen Ray. **CAST:** Wendy Schumacher, Shauna O'Brien, Jay Richardson. 1996

FUGITIVE ROAD ★★ Erich Von Stroheim as a border guard helping immigrants escape to America. 69m. **DIR:** Frank Strayer. **CAST:** Erich Von Stroheim. 1934

FUGITIVE VALLEY ★★★ An outlaw gang led by "The Whip" terrorizes the West until the Range Busters infiltrate the outlaws and uncover several surprises, including a lady Robin Hood. B&W; 61m. **DIR:** S. Roy Luby. **CAST:** Ray "Crash" Corrigan, John King, Max Terhune, Julie Duncan, Glenn Strange. 1941

FULFILLMENT ★★ When an impotent farmer senses his wife's attraction to his visiting brother, he suggests that she sleep with the other man to conceive the child they can't have. Self-serious made-for-TV drama, originally shown as *The Fulfillment of Mary Gray*. Not rated, the film features sexual situations. 96m. **DIR:** Piers Haggard. **CAST:** Cheryl Ladd, Ted Levine, Lewis Smith. 1989

FULL BODY MASSAGE ★★★ When a worldly masseuse begins working for a wealthy businesswoman, the two aren't sure their differing worlds are compatible. However, after several appointments, it becomes apparent that each has much to learn from the other. Talky yet engrossing drama is enhanced by near-perfect performances from both Rogers and Brown and taut direction by Roeg. Rated R for profanity and nudity. 93m. **DIR:** Nicolas Roeg. **CAST:** Mimi Rogers, Bryan Brown. 1995

FULL CONTACT 💙 Watch this movie if you want to see 90 minutes of kick-boxing, bad acting, and no plot. Rated R for profanity, violence, and nudity. 96m. **DIR:** Rick Jacobson. **CAST:** Jerry Trimble, Gerry

Blanck, Denise Buick, Marcus Aurelius, Raymond Storti. 1992 DVD

FULL ECLIPSE ★★★ This horror yarn never quite takes off, in spite of a clever premise. Dedicated cop Mario Van Peebles is recruited by an elite assault squad comprised of—surprise!—drug-induced werewolves, who really put the bite on bad guys. Unresolved moral conflicts and a sloppy finale ultimately sabotage what could have been a great thriller. Rated R for violence, profanity, and strong sexual content. 98m. **DIR:** Anthony Hickox. **CAST:** Mario Van Peebles, Patsy Kensit, Anthony Denison, Jason Beghe, Bruce Payne. 1993

FULL EXPOSURE ★★ Seedy, made-for-TV crime-drama features Anthony Denison as a police detective on a case involving a murdered call girl and her missing video diary of clients. He's teamed with rookie Lisa Hartman, and things really heat up when she goes undercover as a call girl and finds herself attracted to the lifestyle. Not rated. 95m. **DIR:** Noel Nosseck. **CAST:** Lisa Hartman, Anthony Denison, Jennifer O'Neill, Vanessa L. Williams. 1989

FULL FATHOM FIVE ★★1/2 Adequate actioner focuses on Panamanian countermeasures to an American invasion. Michael Moriarty is the captain of an American submarine ordered to destroy a Soviet nuclear sub. Rated PG for violence. 82m. **DIR:** Carl Franklin. **CAST:** Michael Moriarty, Maria Rangel, Michael Cavanaugh. 1990

FULL HEARTS AND EMPTY POCKETS ★★ A German youth in Rome begins with nothing and, through luck and happy coincidence, rises to a position of wealth and power. Forgettable European production will appeal only to those who can't resist another look at the streets of Rome. Dubbed in English. B&W; 88m. **DIR:** Camillo Mastrocinque. **CAST:** Thomas Fritsch, Alexandra Stewart, Gino Cervi, Senta Berger, Linda Christian, Françoise Rosay. 1963

FULL METAL JACKET ★★★★ Stanley Kubrick and Vietnam? How can that combination miss? Well, it does and it doesn't. Kubrick scores higher in smaller moments than in scenes seemingly intended to be climactic. Don't be surprised if days later, fragments are still with you. Rated R for violence and some inventive and colorful profanity. 120m. **DIR:** Stanley Kubrick. **CAST:** Matthew Modine, Adam Baldwin, Vincent D'Onofrio, R. Lee Ermey, Dorian Harewood, Arliss Howard, Ed O'Ross. **1987 DVD**

FULL MONTY, THE ★★★★ You won't soon find a better comedy than this delightful study of the extremes to which unemployment will drive desperate men. Strapped for cash and respect and inspired by a visit from the Chippendales dancers to their small town, six average fellows decide to turn themselves into lean, mean dancing machines. To secure an audience for their decidedly unbuff bodies, they declare that they'll take their act all the way to "the full monty" ... a complete onstage strip. Life is all about respect, and this ranks as one of the most hilarious ways of achieving that goal. Rated R for profanity and nudity. 95m. **DIR:** Peter Cattaneo. **CAST:** Robert Carlyle, Mark Addy, William Snape, Steve Huison, Tom Wilkinson, Paul Barber, Hugo Speer. **1996 DVD**

FULL MOON IN BLUE WATER ★★ Gene Hackman and Teri Garr bring wonderful moments to this offbeat comedy-drama. Otherwise, the film is corny and uneven. Rated R for profanity and light violence. 94m. DIR: Peter Masterson. CAST: Gene Hackman, Teri Garr, Burgess Meredith, Elias Coteas, Kevin Cooney. 1988

FULL MOON IN PARIS ★★ French film from Eric Rohmer does not sustain its momentum with this tale of a young girl's disillusionment with her live-in lover. Perhaps the problem is her self-absorption and lack of commitment, but you just don't seem to care about what happens. In French with English subtitles. 102m. DIR: Eric Rohmer. CAST: Pascale Ogier, Fabrice Luchini, Tcheky Karyo. 1984 DVD

FULLER BRUSH GIRL, THE ★★★ Lucy's in typical form as a dizzy cosmetics salesgirl up to her mascara in murder and hoodlums. Wisecracking dialogue and familiar character faces help this one out. Harmless fun. B&W; 85m. DIR: Lloyd Bacon. CAST: Lucille Ball, Eddie Albert, Jerome Cowan, Lee Patrick. 1950

FULLER BRUSH MAN, THE ★★★ Red Skelton slapsticks along his route as a door-to-door salesman and gets involved with murder. Sadly unsung master gagster Buster Keaton deserves a lot of credit for the humor he adds to many other Skelton films. B&W; 93m. DIR: S. Sylvan Simon. CAST: Red Skelton, Janet Blair, Don McGuire, Adele Jergens, Buster Keaton. 1948

FUN ★★★ *Heavenly Creatures* meets *Natural Born Killers* in this story of two misfits who cement their unnaturally close bond with an act of murder. Products of tabloid-TV America, the two girls titillate each other with stories of the (fictional) abuses they've endured and wonder who will play them in the TV movie based on their exploits. Well-acted, but the script seems familiar and the direction is showoffishly busy. Rated R for violence and adult situations. 105m. DIR: Rafal Zielinski. CAST: Alicia Witt, Renee Humphrey, William R. Moses. 1993

FUN AND FANCY FREE ★★1/2 The first segment of this Disney feature is the story of Bongo, a circus bear who runs away and falls for a female bear. It's a moderately entertaining tale. When Edgar Bergen narrates the clever version of "Jack and the Beanstalk," pitting Mickey, Donald, and Goofy against Willie the Giant, things pick up considerably. 96m. DIR: Walt Disney. CAST: Edgar Bergen, Luana Patten, Dinah Shore. 1947 DVD

FUN IN ACAPULCO ★★1/2 Beautiful Acapulco sets the stage for this sun-filled Elvis Presley musical. This time he's a lifeguard by day and a singer by night at a fancy beachfront resort. Typical of Elvis's bits. 97m. DIR: Richard Thorpe. CAST: Elvis Presley, Ursula Andress, Paul Lukas, Alejandro Rey, Elsa Cardenas. 1963

FUN WITH DICK AND JANE ★★★★ How does one maintain one's life-style after a sacking from a highly paid aerospace position? George Segal and Jane Fonda have a unique solution. They steal. This comedy caper is well named, because some quality fun is in store for the audience. Rated PG. 95m. DIR: Ted Kotcheff. CAST: Jane Fonda, George Segal, Ed McMahon. 1977

FUNERAL, THE (1987) ★★★1/2 An old man's sudden death creates hilarious havoc for his surviving family members in this engagingly offbeat comedy directed by Juzo Itami. The Japanese burial ritual becomes the stage where the younger generation struggles with the complex rituals of the traditional Buddhist ceremony. In Japanese with English subtitles. 124m. DIR: Juzo Itami. CAST: Nobuko Miyamoto, Tsutomu Yamazaki. 1987 DVD

FUNERAL, THE (1996) ★★1/2 Two 1930s gangsters (Christopher Walken, Chris Penn) gather to bury their kid brother, while plotting revenge on the presumed killer (Benicio Del Toro, in the film's best performance). Atmospheric and well-acted but marred by pretentious dialogue and an unconvincing, ultraviolent climax. The endless flood of profanity seems out of place in the 1930s. Rated R for violence, profanity, and simulated sex. 98m. DIR: Abel Ferrara. CAST: Christopher Walken, Christopher Penn, Vincent Gallo, Benicio Del Toro, Annabella Sciorra, Isabella Rossellini. 1996

FUNERAL HOME ★★ This film doesn't quite know what it wants to be—a character study with horrific overtones or a grim film. Either way, William Fruet's direction is too laid back to matter. Rated R for violence and profanity. 93m. DIR: William Fruet. CAST: Lesleh Donaldson, Kay Hawtrey, Barry Morse. 1981

FUNERAL IN BERLIN ★★★1/2 Second in Michael Caine's series of three "Harry Palmer" films, following *The Ipcress File* and preceding *The Billion-Dollar Brain*. This time, working-class spy Palmer assists in the possible defection of a top Russian security chief (Oscar Homolka). As usual, Caine can do no wrong; his brittle performance and the authentic footage of the Berlin Wall add considerably to the film's bleak tone. Not rated; suitable for family viewing. 102m. DIR: Guy Hamilton. CAST: Michael Caine, Oscar Homolka, Eva Renzi, Paul Hubschmid, Guy Doleman. 1967

FUNHOUSE, THE ★★1/2 Looking for a watchable modern horror film? Then welcome to this film about a group of teens trapped in the carnival attraction of the title proves that buckets of blood and severed limbs aren't essential elements to movie terror. Rated R. 96m. DIR: Tobe Hooper. CAST: Elizabeth Berridge, Cooper Huckabee, Miles Chapin, Largo Woodruff, Sylvia Miles. 1981 DVD

FUNLAND ★★1/2 Schizophrenic comedy about a family amusement park taken over by the mob. Although scripted by two *Saturday Night Live* writers, this flick doesn't know whether it wants to be a comedy, a drama, or a thriller. It does offer some weird and funny bits, though. Rated PG-13. 98m. DIR: Michael A. Simpson. CAST: William Windom, David L. Lander, Bruce Mahler, Jan Hooks, Lane Davies. 1986

FUNNY ABOUT LOVE ★★ We love Gene Wilder, but he's neither lovable nor funny in this misbegotten movie about a cartoonist who feels his "biological clock" ticking and attempts to have a baby with a caterer (Christine Lahti). Rated PG-13 for suggested sex and profanity. 92m. DIR: Leonard Nimoy. CAST: Gene Wilder, Christine Lahti, Mary Stuart Masterson, Stephen Tobolowsky, Robert Prosky, Susan Ruttan, Anne Jackson. 1990

FUNNY DIRTY LITTLE WAR (NO HABRA MAS PE-
LAS NI OLVIDO) ★★★ This allegorical, comedic
piece begins in the small town of Colonia Vela. The
comedy centers around the struggle between the
Marxists and the Peronistas in 1974, shortly before
the death of Juan Perón. The action quickly builds
from a series of foolish misunderstandings to a very
funny confrontation. Spanish with English subtitles.
Not rated. 80m. DIR: Hector Olivera. CAST: Federico
Luppi, Hector Bidonde. 1985

FUNNY FACE ★★★1/2 One of the best of Fred Astaire's later pictures. This time he's a fashion photographer who discovers naïve Audrey Hepburn and
turns her into a sensation. Typical fairy-tale plot, enlivened by Astaire's usual charm and a good score
based on the works of George Gershwin. 103m. DIR:
Stanley Donen. CAST: Fred Astaire, Audrey Hepburn,
Kay Thompson, Michel Auclair, Ruta Lee. 1957

FUNNY FARM ★★ Chevy Chase and Madolyn Smith
star as Andy and Elizabeth Farmer who give up the
city life for greener pastures in Vermont. Their idyllic country life goes awry with a series of predictable
disasters, laboriously dramatized. Rated PG for
adult language and situations. 101m. DIR: George
Roy Hill. CAST: Chevy Chase, Madolyn Smith, Joseph
Maher, Brad Sullivan, MacIntyre Dixon. 1988 DVD

FUNNY GIRL ★★★★ The early years of Ziegfeld
Follies star Fanny Brice were the inspiration for a
superb stage musical. Barbra Streisand re-created
her Broadway triumph in as stunning a movie debut
in 1968 as Hollywood ever witnessed. She sings,
roller-skates, cracks jokes, and tugs at your heart in
a tour-de-force performance. Rated G. 155m. DIR:
William Wyler. CAST: Barbra Streisand, Omar Sharif,
Walter Pidgeon, Kay Medford. 1968

FUNNY LADY ★★★ The sequel to Funny Girl is
not the original, but still worth seeing. We follow
comedienne Fanny Brice after she became a stage
luminary only to continue her misfortunes in private
life. James Caan plays her second husband, producer Billy Rose, and Omar Sharif returns in his role of
Fanny's first love. But Streisand's performance and a
few of the musical numbers carry the day. 149m. DIR:
Herbert Ross. CAST: Barbra Streisand, James Caan,
Omar Sharif, Ben Vereen. 1975

FUNNY THING HAPPENED ON THE WAY TO THE
FORUM, A ★★★★ Ancient Rome is the setting for
this fast-paced musical comedy. Zero Mostel is a never-ending source of zany plots to gain his freedom
and line his toga with loot as a cunning slave. He is
ably assisted by Phil Silvers and Jack Gilford in this
bawdy romp through classic times. Look for Buster
Keaton in a nice cameo. 99m. DIR: Richard Lester.
CAST: Zero Mostel, Phil Silvers, Jack Gilford, Michael
Crawford, Buster Keaton. 1966 DVD

FUNNYBONES ★★★★1/2 Oliver Platt is the unfunny son of a successful comedian who travels to Blackpool, England, in search of new material and family
roots. Platt brings just the right edginess and desire
to the film, and Jerry Lewis does a surprisingly good
dramatic turn as his dad. Watch for Lee Evans, whose
physical comedy is amazing, but ignore the lame
subplot involving wax eggs and Oliver Reed. Rated R
for profanity and violence. 128m. DIR: Peter Chelsom.

CAST: Oliver Platt, Leslie Caron, Jerry Lewis, Lee
Evans, Richard Griffiths, Oliver Reed, George Carl,
Freddie Davies. 1995

FUNNYMAN 🎬 Despite his star billing, Christopher
Lee only has a cameo role in this impenetrable horror nonsense about visitors to an old mansion being
killed in Freddie Krueger–like ways by a demon harlequin. Rated R for graphic violence, nudity, sexual
situations, adult situations, substance abuse, and
profanity. 89m. DIR: Simon Sprackling. CAST: Tim
James, Christopher Lee, Benny Young, Ingrid Lacey,
Pauline Black. 1995

FURTHER ADVENTURES OF TENNESSEE BUCK,
THE ★★ Yet another cheap imitation of Indiana
Jones, with David Keith playing an incorrigible jun-
gle adventurer hired as a guide by a young couple.
Kathy Shower, a 1987 Playboy playmate, is the fe-
male side of the couple; she can't act worth a lick.
Rated R for violence, language, nudity, and simulat-
ed sex. 90m. DIR: David Keith. CAST: David Keith,
Kathy Shower, Sidney Lassick. 1988

FURY (1936) ★★★★ A stranger in a small town
(Spencer Tracy) becomes the innocent victim of a
lynch mob and turns into a one-man mob himself
when he luckily survives. The script gets a bit contrived toward the end, but it's still powerful stuff,
brutally well directed by Fritz Lang. B&W; 94m. DIR:
Fritz Lang. CAST: Sylvia Sidney, Spencer Tracy, Walter
Abel, Edward Ellis, Bruce Cabot, Walter Brennan. 1936

FURY, THE (1978) ★★★ A contemporary terror
tale that utilizes the average-man-against-the-un-
known approach that made Hitchcock's suspense
films so effective. In the story, Kirk Douglas is forced
to take on a super-powerful government agency that
kidnapped his son (Andrew Stevens) who has psychic powers. It's a chiller. Rated R. 118m. DIR: Brian
De Palma. CAST: Kirk Douglas, Andrew Stevens, Amy
Irving, Fiona Lewis, John Cassavetes, Charles Durning.
1978

FURY OF HERCULES, THE ★★ Some Yugoslavian
exteriors and the presence of Brad Harris, one of the
more formidable post-Steve Reeves sword-and-sandal stars, boost this battle-filled saga about a corrupt
kingdom. And, for once, the English dubbing is decent. 97m. DIR: Gianfranco Parolini. CAST: Brad Harris, Bridgette Corey. 1962

FURY OF THE CONGO 🎬 There's no fury and pre-
cious little Congo in this dull jungle filler. B&W; 69m.
DIR: William Berke. CAST: Johnny Weissmuller, Sherry
Moreland, William Henry, Lyle Talbot. 1951

FURY OF THE WOLF MAN ★★ Fifth of a popular
Spanish series featuring the sympathetic werewolf
Waldemar Daninsky. Badly dubbed, but high produc-
tion values make it watchable. Not rated; the film
has violence. 85m. DIR: José Maria Zabalza. CAST:
Paul Naschy. 1971

FURY WITHIN, THE ★★1/2 A family in the middle
of a separation is also being terrorized by a poltergeist. A few deaths and other strange occurrences
add to the confusion about who's behind the haunting, but overzealous acting and overblown dialogue
make this made-for-cable original more silly than
scary. Rated PG-13 for violence. 95m. DIR: Noel

Nosseck. **CAST:** Ally Sheedy, Costas Mandylor, Vincent Berry. **1998**

•**FUTURE FEAR** ♥ Producer Roger Corman cannibalizes his own library to flesh out this weak thriller about a scientist who creates an antidote to a deadly virus. So bad calling it a B movie would be an insult to B movies. Rated R for adult situations, language, and violence. 80m. **DIR:** Lewis Baumander. **CAST:** Jeff Wincott, Maria Ford, Stacy Keach, Shawn Thompson. **1997**

FUTURE HUNTERS ♥ A warrior from the future travels back to the present. Rated R for violence, profanity, and nudity. 96m. **DIR:** Cirio H. Santiago. **CAST:** Robert Patrick. **1985**

FUTURE-KILL ♥ Frat boys run into a gang of punks—one of whom has been exposed to radiation. Rated R for profanity, nudity, and gore. 83m. **DIR:** Ronald W. Moore. **CAST:** Edwin Neal, Marilyn Burns. **1984**

FUTURE SHOCK ★★ In this hit-or-miss episodic thriller, three patients face their worst fears when doctor Martin Kove subjects them to virtual-reality therapy. The best bit features Bill Paxton as a roommate from hell. Rated PG-13 for violence and sexual situations. 93m. **DIR:** Eric Parkinson. **CAST:** Vivian Schilling, Martin Kove, Carrot Top (Scott Thompson), Brion James, Bill Paxton. **1993**

FUTURE ZONE ♥ David Carradine stars as a modern-day cop whose son time travels into the past to rescue him from death. Rated R for violence and profanity. 90m. **DIR:** David A. Prior. **CAST:** David Carradine, Ted Prior, Charles Napier. **1990**

FUTUREKICK ♥ A kung fu kick-boxing mystery set in a bleak futuristic technocratic society. Low-budget rip-off. Rated R for nudity, profanity, and violence. 80m. **DIR:** Damian Klaus. **CAST:** Meg Foster, Christopher Penn, Eb Lottimer. **1991**

FUTURESPORT ★★ Okay, who ordered the *Rollerball* remake? Proving that there's nothing new under the sun, this made-for-television science-fiction drama stars Dean Cain as Tre, the undisputed champion of Futuresport. When assassins threaten the life of Tre and his girlfriend, they turn to the creator of the game, Orbike Fixx, who convinces the opposing side to play one final game that will decide definitively world domination. Mundane and familiar plot elements do little to make any of this exciting. The video contains additional footage not shown on television. Rated R for language and violence. 89m. **DIR:** Ernest R. Dickerson. **CAST:** Dean Cain, Vanessa L. Williams, Wesley Snipes, Rachel Shane, Bill Smitrovich. **1998 DVD**

FUTUREWORLD ★★★ An amusement park of the future caters to any adult fantasy. Lifelike androids carry out your every whim. A fun place, right? Not so, as reporter Peter Fonda finds out in this sequel to *Westworld*. This is okay escapist fare. Rated PG. 104m. **DIR:** Richard T. Heffron. **CAST:** Peter Fonda, Blythe Danner, Arthur Hill, Yul Brynner, Stuart Margolin, John P. Ryan. **1976**

FUTZ ★★ Once controversial, now merely a curiosity piece, this film adaptation of an avant-garde play by New York's famed La Mama troupe is like something out of a time capsule. There's no real plot, but it's set in a farm community where one farmer is ostracized for falling in love with his prize pig Amanda. Not rated, contains nudity and sexual situations. 92m. **DIR:** Tom O'Horgan. **CAST:** Seth Allen, Sally Kirkland. **1969**

FUZZ ★★★ Raquel Welch and Burt Reynolds star as police in this comedy-drama. Yul Brynner plays a bomb-happy villain. It has a few good moments, but you'd have to be a member of the Burt Reynolds fan club to really love it. Rated PG. 92m. **DIR:** Richard A. Colla. **CAST:** Raquel Welch, Burt Reynolds, Yul Brynner, Tom Skerritt. **1972**

F/X ★★★1/2 In this fast-paced, well-acted suspense-thriller, Bryan Brown plays special-effects wizard Rollie Tyler, who accepts thirty thousand dollars from the Justice Department's Witness Relocation Program to stage the fake assassination of a mob figure who has agreed to name names. After he successfully fulfills his assignment, Tyler is double-crossed and must use his wits and movie magic to survive. Rated R for profanity, suggested sex, and violence. 110m. **DIR:** Robert Mandel. **CAST:** Bryan Brown, Brian Dennehy, Diane Venora, Cliff De Young, Mason Adams, Jerry Orbach. **1986 DVD**

F/X 2: THE DEADLY ART OF ILLUSION ★★★ Special-effects expert Bryan Brown gets himself into trouble again when he agrees to help a police officer catch a serial killer. With the help of ex-cop Brian Dennehy and some of his own movie magic, Brown outwits the bad guys in this fast-paced, enjoyable, and never-believable-for-a-minute sequel. Rated PG-13 for violence, nudity, and profanity. 104m. **DIR:** Richard Franklin. **CAST:** Bryan Brown, Brian Dennehy, Rachel Ticotin, Joanna Gleason, Philip Bosco, Kevin J. O'Connor, Tom Mason. **1991**

GABBEH ★★★★ This magical, beautifully colored fable begins as a woman emerges from the rug being washed in a stream by an old couple. She tells the story of her life in a tribe of desert nomads, waiting for her father to give permission for her to marry the lover who follows the tribe at a distance. An utterly delightful (if sometimes confusing) film that is a real eye-opener to viewers unfamiliar with Arab cultures. In Farsi with English subtitles. Not rated; contains no offensive material. 72m. **DIR:** Mohsen Makhmalbaf. **CAST:** Shaghayegh Jodat. **1996**

GABE KAPLAN AS GROUCHO ★★★ Even avid Grouchophiles will enjoy this one-man made-for-cable show about everyone's favorite Marx brother. Gabe Kaplan does a comfortable impersonation, and the script mixes laughs with honest (but never spiteful) biography. 89m. **DIR:** John Bowab. **CAST:** Gabe Kaplan. **1982**

GABRIEL OVER THE WHITE HOUSE ★★★ A corrupt politician becomes president and then experiences a change of heart, soul, and mind. A highly moralistic fable intended as a tribute to FDR and a condemnation of the presidents who preceded him. Acted with sincerity and directed with a sentimental hand. B&W; 87m. **DIR:** Gregory La Cava. **CAST:** Walter Huston, Franchot Tone, Jean Parker, Karen Morley, Dickie Moore, C. Henry Gordon, Samuel S. Hinds. 1933

GABRIELA ★★★ Sexy Sonia Braga is both cook and mistress for bar owner Marcello Mastroianni in this excellent adaptation of Brazilian novelist Jorge Amado's comic romp *Gabriela, Clove and Cinnamon*. In Portuguese with English subtitles. Rated R. 102m. **DIR:** Bruno Barreto. **CAST:** Sonia Braga, Marcello Mastroianni, Antonio Cantafora. 1983

GABY, A TRUE STORY ★★★★ Rachel Levin gives a smashing portrayal of a brilliant young woman trapped in a body incapacitated by cerebral palsy. Based on the true-life drama of Gabriela Brimmer. Assisted by a screenplay that steers clear of maudlin situations, the cast delivers powerful performances. Rated R for profanity and sexual frankness. 120m. **DIR:** Luis Mandoki. **CAST:** Liv Ullmann, Norma Aleandro, Robert Loggia, Rachel Levin, Lawrence Monoson, Robert Beltran. 1987

GADJO DILO ★★★★1/2 Amiable young Frenchman armed with a music recorder and bootlegged cassette searches bleak, wintry Romania for the gypsy singer adored by his deceased father. He is befriended by a gypsy elder, smitten by a foul-mouthed dancer, and eyed with contempt by villagers. Subtitled *The Crazy Stranger*, this rambling tale of pride, prejudice, passion, and reciprocated violence embraces us more like long-lost relatives than armchair tourists. In Romany and French with English subtitles. Rated R for profanity, simulated sex, nudity, and violence. 100m. **DIR:** Tony Gatlif. **CAST:** Romain Duris, Isidor Serban, Rona Hartner, Florin Moldovan. 1998

GAL YOUNG 'UN ★★★ Set in the early 1900s, this charming low-budget film focuses on a young man who woos a lonely, elderly (and comparatively rich) widow. He cons her into marriage with his boyish charm and uses her money to set up his own moonshine still. Featuring fine performances and good use of locations, this film is not rated. 105m. **DIR:** Victor Nunez. **CAST:** Dana Peru, David Peck, J. Smith-Cameron. 1986

GALACTIC GIGOLO ★★ Brainless, relentlessly silly movie about an alien (Carmine Capobianco) who wins a trip to Prospect, Connecticut. Rated R for language and nudity. 80m. **DIR:** Gorman Bechard. **CAST:** Carmine Capobianco, Debi Thibeault, Frank Stewart, Ruth Collins. 1987

GALAXIES ARE COLLIDING ★★★ Some hilarious insights await a man so afraid of marriage that he walks out on his bride-to-be. Looking for the meaning of life, he and his best friend head to the desert, where they encounter all sorts of social misfits. How these strangers help him focus on his real feelings provide writer-director John Ryman numerous opportunities to explore the human condition. Rated R for adult language. 97m. **DIR:** John Ryman. **CAST:**

Kelsey Grammer, Dwier Brown, Karen Medak, Susan Walters, Rick Overton. 1992

GALAXINA ★★ See Captain Cornelius Butt (Avery Schreiber), of the spaceship *Infinity*, consume a raw egg and regurgitate a rubbery creature that later calls him "Mommy." Visit an intergalactic saloon that serves humans (they're on the menu, not the guest list). Low-budget space spoof. Rated R. 95m. **DIR:** William Sachs. **CAST:** Avery Schreiber, Dorothy Stratten, Stephen Macht. 1980 DVD

GALAXIS 💔 Brigitte Nielsen is on a mission to save her planet from evil ruler Richard Moll. Who cares? Rated R for violence. 91m. **DIR:** William Mesa. **CAST:** Brigitte Nielsen, Richard Moll, John H. Brennan, Craig Fairbrass. 1995

GALAXY OF TERROR ★★1/2 In this movie, which was also known as *Planet of Horrors*, the crew of a spaceship sent to rescue a crash survivor finds itself facing one horror after another on a barren planet. This chiller wastes no time in getting to the thrills. Rated R because of profanity, nudity, and violence. 82m. **DIR:** B. D. Clark. **CAST:** Erin Moran, Edward Albert, Ray Walston. 1981

GALAXY OF THE DINOSAURS 💔 Uncredited rip-off of Ray Bradbury's "A Sound of Thunder." Not rated; contains violence. 70m. **DIR:** Lance Randas. **CAST:** James Black, Christine Morrison, Tom Hoover. 1998

•GALAXY QUEST ★★★★ Delightful send-up of *Star Trek* has the cast of a canceled, 20-year-old television show attending a sci-fi convention only to be beamed up by real aliens who want their help in defeating a powerful, intergalactic enemy. Screenwriters David Howard and Robert Gordon mine every possible aspect of ground-breaking TV production for humor. There's the egotistical actor (Tim Allen) idolized for his role as the ship's captain, the classically trained actor (Alan Rickman) who feels his "alien" character is beneath him, a busty blonde (Sigourney Weaver) whose only function is to repeat the computer's announcements. Highly entertaining and even heartwarming. Rated PG. 104m. **DIR:** Dean Parisot. **CAST:** Tim Allen, Sigourney Weaver, Alan Rickman, Tony Shalhoub, Sam Rockwell, Daryl Mitchell, Enrico Colantoni. 1999 DVD

GALL FORCE ★★ Japanese animation. A wandering, boorish plot acts as a thin disguise for yet another "prepubescent-girls-get-naked-in-space" story. Occasional cleverness saves this from the turkey bin. In Japanese with English subtitles. Not rated; contains nudity. 86m. **DIR:** Katsuhito Akiyama. 1986

GALL FORCE 2 ★★1/2 While marginally better than the original, this animated sequel still has little to recommend it other than some vivid artwork. In this one, Lufy, one of the heroines from the original, is brought back to life only to face the dilemma of continuing a bitter war or trying to save the last habitable world, Earth. In Japanese with English subtitles. Not rated; contains violence and nudity. 50m. **DIR:** Katsuhito Akiyama. 1987

GALLAGHER'S TRAVELS ★★ An English reporter teams up with an Australian photographer to track down an animal-smuggling ring. There's not much adventure. 94m. **DIR:** Michael Caulfield. **CAST:** Ivar

Kants, Joanne Samuel, Stuart Campbell, Jennifer Hagan. 1987

GALLANT HOURS, THE ★★★1/2 This is not an action epic, but a thoughtful view of the ordeal of command, with James Cagney in a fine performance as Fleet Admiral William F. Halsey Jr. Done in semidocumentary style, following Halsey's command from 1942 through the battle of Guadalcanal. B&W; 111m. **DIR:** Robert Montgomery. **CAST:** James Cagney, Dennis Weaver, Ward Costello, Richard Jaeckel. 1960

GALLIPOLI ★★★★1/2 Add this to the list of outstanding motion pictures from Australia and the very best films about war. Directed by Peter Weir this appealing character study, which is set during World War I, manages to say more about life on the battlefront than many of the more straightforward pictures in the genre. Rated PG because of violence. 110m. **DIR:** Peter Weir. **CAST:** Mark Lee, Mel Gibson, Robert Grubb, Tim McKenzie, David Argue. 1981 DVD

GALLOPING GHOST, THE ★★ College football melodrama starring real-life football legend Red Grange. Antiquated. B&W; 12 chapters. **DIR:** B. Reeves "Breezy" Eason. **CAST:** Harold "Red" Grange, Dorothy Gulliver. 1931

GALLOWGLASS ★★1/2 Not one of the better BBC adaptations of a Ruth Rendell novel written under her nom de plume, Barbara Vine. Lacking a much-needed edginess and complexity, this is merely nasty. The main characters in this mystery about damaging obsessiveness are so odious that one feels no sympathy for them, and thus no attachment to the story. Not rated; contains brief nudity and sexual situations. 150m. **DIR:** Tim Fywell. **CAST:** Arkie Whitely, John McArdle, Michael Sheen, Paul Rhys, Claire Hackett. 1992

GAMBIT ★★★1/2 An engaging caper comedy that teams Michael Caine's inventive but unlucky thief with Shirley MacLaine's mute and mysterious woman of the world … or *is* she? The target is a valuable art treasure, jealously guarded by ruthless owner Herbert Lom, and Caine's plan is—to say the least—unusual. Caine and MacLaine make a grand pair; it's a shame they didn't get together for another film of this sort. Not rated; suitable for family viewing. 108m. **DIR:** Ronald Neame. **CAST:** Michael Caine, Shirley MacLaine, Herbert Lom. 1966

GAMBLE, THE ♥ Matthew Modine plays an impoverished nobleman who loses in a bet. Rated R for nudity and violence. 108m. **DIR:** Carlo Vanzina. **CAST:** Matthew Modine, Faye Dunaway, Jennifer Beals. 1988

GAMBLE ON LOVE ♥♥ Las Vegas provides the backdrop for this slow-moving film. Liz (Beverly Garland) inherits a casino from her father and falls in love with the brash casino manager. This relationship leads to an explosive climax. 105m. **DIR:** Jim Balden. **CAST:** Beverly Garland. 1982

GAMBLER, THE (1974) ★★★1/2 This gritty film features James Caan in one of his best screen portrayals as a compulsive, self-destructive gambler. Director Karel Reisz keeps the atmosphere thick with tension. Always thinking he's on the edge of a big score, Caan's otherwise intelligent college professor character gets him deeper and deeper into trouble. It's a downer, but still worth watching. Rated R.

111m. **DIR:** Karel Reisz. **CAST:** James Caan, Paul Sorvino, Lauren Hutton, Jacqueline Brooks, Morris Carnovsky. 1974

GAMBLER, THE (1980) ★★★ Bringing his late 1970s hit record to life, Kenny Rogers teams with Bruce Boxleitner in this story of a drifting cardplayer, his lost son, a shady railroad magnate, and the usual bunch of black-hatted villains. This made-for-TV movie spawned two equally entertaining sequels. 95m. **DIR:** Dick Lowry. **CAST:** Kenny Rogers, Bruce Boxleitner, Christine Belford, Harold Gould, Clu Gulager. 1980

GAMBLER, PART II—THE ADVENTURE CONTINUES, THE ★★★ Reprising his role as gambler Brady Hawks, Kenny Rogers ambles his way farther west with sidekick Bruce Boxleitner—toward the poker game to end all poker games in San Francisco. Fans loved how to fold 'em the first time around, so here it is again. Made for TV. 190m. **DIR:** Dick Lowry. **CAST:** Kenny Rogers, Bruce Boxleitner, Linda Evans, Johnny Crawford, Cameron Mitchell, Mitchell Ryan, Harold Gould, Gregory Sierra, Ken Swofford. 1983

GAMBLER, PART III—THE LEGEND CONTINUES, THE ★★★ Again playing gambler Brady Hawks, Kenny Rogers nearly comes a cropper on the end of a rope when he's hung by a zealous Mexican army officer. Made for TV. 185m. **DIR:** Dick Lowry. **CAST:** Kenny Rogers, Bruce Boxleitner, Melanie Chartoff, Matt Clark, George Kennedy, Charles Durning, Jeffrey Jones. 1987

GAMBLER RETURNS, THE: LUCK OF THE DRAW ★★1/2 A high-stakes, winner-take-all poker game is held in San Francisco, but the main draw is cameo appearances by the stars of classic TV-Western series. Overlong, but fun for fans. Made for TV. 180m. **DIR:** Dick Lowry. **CAST:** Kenny Rogers, Rick Rossovich, Reba McEntire, Claude Akins, Gene Barry, Paul Brinegar, David Carradine, Chuck Connors, Johnny Crawford, James Drury, Linda Evans, Brian Keith, Jack Kelly, Patrick Macnee, Doug McClure, Hugh O'Brian, Park Overall, Mickey Rooney, Dub Taylor, Clint Walker. 1991

GAME, THE (1988) ★★1/2 *The Game* is what the rich and powerful play once a year, a high-tech hunting party in which humans are the prey. Joseph Campanella infiltrates the group to seek revenge on the men who killed his family, while soldier of fortune Craig Alan gives them a run for their money on the battlefield. Not rated; contains violence. 96m. **DIR:** Cole McKay. **CAST:** Joseph Campanella, Craig Alan. 1988

GAME, THE (1997) ★★★★★ Corporate executive Michael Douglas has lost focus; he's successful, but just going through the motions—both at home and at work. Then brother Sean Penn comes up with a surprise birthday present that sends Douglas on a trip straight to his own personal hell. This clever, thought-provoking film packs the kind of punch evidenced by so few of its brethren and invites second and third viewings. The cast is marvelous and the "game" unforgettable. Rated R for violence and profanity. 128m. **DIR:** David Fincher. **CAST:** Michael Douglas, Sean Penn, Deborah Unger, James Rebhorn, Peter Donat, Carroll Baker, Anna Katarina, Armin Mueller-Stahl. 1997 DVD

GAME FOR VULTURES ★★ A long, dusty, and violent trek through the agonies of South Africa's ongoing conflict. Strong cast, strong theme, weak movie. Rated R for lots of machine-gun violence. 113m. DIR: James Fargo. CAST: Joan Collins, Richard Harris, Richard Roundtree, Ray Milland. 1986

GAME IS OVER, THE ★★★ Emile Zola's novel *La Curée* was the basis for this adult story of a young woman who marries an older man but finds herself attracted to (and eventually sharing a bed with) his son. Well-acted, this film by Jane Fonda's then-husband Roger Vadim holds up well for today's audiences. In French. 96m. DIR: Roger Vadim. CAST: Jane Fonda, Peter McEnery, Michel Piccoli, Tina Marquand. 1966

GAME OF DEATH 🎬 The climactic twenty minutes of Bruce Lee in action fighting Kareem Abdul-Jabbar and Danny Inosanto are thrilling. The rest of the film is not. Rated R. 102m. DIR: Robert Clouse. CAST: Bruce Lee, Kareem Abdul-Jabbar, Danny Inosanto, Gig Young, Hugh O'Brian, Colleen Camp, Dean Jagger, Chuck Norris. 1979 DVD

GAME OF LOVE, THE ★★1/2 A group of people (young, old, single, married, and divorced) congregate at a local night spot in this routine romantic drama. Ken Olin is the bar owner who oversees the whole scene and gives out advice. Rated PG for adult themes. 94m. DIR: Bobby Roth. CAST: Ken Olin, Ed Marinaro, Max Gail, Robert Rusler, Belinda Bauer, Tracy Nelson, Jack Blessing, Gerrit Graham, Janet Margolin, Brynn Thayer. 1987

GAME OF SEDUCTION ★★ A professional killer accepts a bet that he cannot seduce a proper married woman. Tired continental erotica with a cast that should know better. Dubbed. Not rated; contains nudity and sexual situations. 81m. DIR: Roger Vadim. CAST: Sylvia Kristel, Nathalie Delon, Jon Finch. 1985

GAMERA: GUARDIAN OF THE UNIVERSE ★★★ Gamera helps a team of scientists battle flying monsters that are attacking Japan in this first of a new series of Gamera movies. While a bigger budget and computer effects make this far superior to the cheesy 1960s movies, at heart it remains true to the spirit of the originals (unlike many such revivals). Not rated; contains monster violence. 99m. DIR: Shusuke Kaneko. CAST: Tsuyoshi Ihara, Akira Onodera. 1995

GAMERA THE INVINCIBLE ★★ Typical cheesy Japanese giant-monster movie starring a prehistoric fire-breathing turtle. (It flies, too.) Neither as silly nor as campy as its sequels, this features clumsily spliced-in footage of Albert Dekker and Brian Donlevy that was added for the U.S. market. B&W; 86m. DIR: Noriyaki Yuasa. CAST: Albert Dekker, Brian Donlevy. 1965

GAMERA VERSUS BARUGON ★★ In this first sequel, the giant flying turtle becomes a good guy, as he was to remain for the rest of the series. The bad guy, Barugon, is a giant dinosaur. Of course, several Japanese cities are leveled as the two battle, but no problem—civilization was reconstructed in time for the next sequel. 101m. DIR: Shigeo Tanaka. CAST: Kojiro Hongo. 1966

GAMERA VERSUS GAOS ★★ Ever the friend of little children, Gamera does his giant flaming Frisbee impression once again to save his little pals from Gaos, another giant monster. Opinion differs as to whether Gaos more closely resembles a bat or a fox, as if it mattered at all to the poor stuntman sweating it out inside that rubber suit. 87m. DIR: Noriyaki Yuasa. CAST: Kojiro Hongo. 1967

GAMERA VERSUS GUIRON ★★ Flame on! The twirling turtle battles spearheaded Guiron, an evil giant (of course) monster from outer space. Does Japan have a Ministry of Giant Monsters responsible for naming all these behemoths? 82m. DIR: Noriyaki Yuasa. 1969

GAMERA VERSUS ZIGRA 🎬 Fans of this kind of stuff will be disappointed to note that, in the last of the Gamera movies, the titanic turtle battles a silly Transformer-style swordfish. Some film student should do a paper comparing this with *Godzilla vs. the Smog Monster*. 87m. DIR: Noriyaki Yuasa. CAST: Reiko Kasahara. 1971

GAMES OF COUNTESS DOLINGEN OF GRATZ, THE ★★1/2 Baffling drama concerning a schizoid woman (Carol Kane). She indulges in an exercise in reality and fantasy that centers around a little girl's erotic experience. The film's uneven narrative structure only adds to the confusion. In French with English subtitles. Not rated; contains nudity. 110m. DIR: Catherine Binet. CAST: Georges Perec, Michel Lonsdale, Carol Kane. 1981

GAMMA PEOPLE, THE 🎬 Weak science-fiction tale about children being transformed into homicidal monsters or geniuses. B&W; 79m. DIR: John Gilling. CAST: Paul Douglas, Eva Bartok, Leslie Phillips, Walter Rilla. 1956

GANDHI ★★★★★ One of the finest screen biographies ever, this film chronicles the life of the Indian leader. Running three hours, it is an old-style "big" picture, with spectacle, great drama, superb performances, and an enormous cast. Yet for all its hugeness, *Gandhi* achieves a remarkable intimacy. Viewers will feel as if they have actually known the man Indians called the "Great Soul." Rated PG for violence. 188m. DIR: Richard Attenborough. CAST: Ben Kingsley, Candice Bergen, Edward Fox, John Gielgud, Martin Sheen, John Mills, Trevor Howard, Saeed Jaffrey, Roshan Seth. 1982

GANG BUSTERS 🎬 As a film about prison life and various attempts at breakout, this picture simply doesn't measure up. B&W; 78m. DIR: Bill Karan. CAST: Myron Healey, Sam Edwards, Don Harvey, Frank Gerstle. 1955

GANG IN BLUE ★★1/2 Dedicated cop Mario Van Peebles suffers racist taunts from a secret squad of rogue officers with a white supremacist agenda. Naturally, our hero is determined to expose every last one of the miscreants. Rick Natkin and David Fuller's script is needlessly shrill and lopsided, and paints nearly all Caucasian characters as vicious, unrepentant swine. Rated R for violence and profanity. 100m. DIR: Melvin Van Peebles. CAST: Mario Van Peebles, Josh Brolin, Melvin Van Peebles, Cynda Williams, Stephen Lang, J. T. Walsh. 1996

GANG RELATED ★★1/2 Two corrupt New York homicide cops rob and kill drug dealers and then blame their crimes on street gangs in this unconventional, uneven police thriller. One victim turns out to be an undercover DEA agent, and two outlaw detectives dig themselves deeper into trouble when they are assigned to the murder they committed. Rated R for violence, language, and nudity. 106m. **DIR:** Jim Kouf. **CAST:** James Belushi, Tupac Shakur, Dennis Quaid, Lela Rochon, David Paymer, James Earl Jones. 1997

GANG'S ALL HERE, THE ★★★1/2 A good example of the pizazz of wartime musicals, this is one of the most colorful. Credit goes to Carmen Miranda's dancing style, Busby Berkeley's imaginative choreography, Alice Faye's songs of love, and Benny Goodman's music. That's still entertainment! 103m. **DIR:** Busby Berkeley. **CAST:** Alice Faye, Carmen Miranda, James Ellison, Sheila Ryan, Benny Goodman, Phil Baker, Eugene Pallette, Edward Everett Horton. 1943

GANGS, INC. (PAPER BULLETS) ★★ Low-budget crime drama about an anguished woman with an unhappy past who seeks justification in a life of crime. B&W; 72m. **DIR:** Phil Rosen. **CAST:** Joan Woodbury, Jack LaRue, Alan Ladd, John Archer, Vince Barnett. 1941

GANGS OF SONORA ★★★ The Three Mesquiteers aid a lady newspaper editor opposing a corrupt official trying to prevent Wyoming's entrance into the Union. B&W; 56m. **DIR:** John English. **CAST:** Robert Livingston, Bob Steele, Rufe Davis, Robert Frazer. 1941

GANGSTER, THE ★★1/2 Slow-moving film about a gang boss with an attitude just doesn't make the grade despite a great cast and realistic locales. B&W; 82m. **DIR:** Gordon Wiles. **CAST:** Barry Sullivan, Belita, Joan Lorring, Akim Tamiroff, Harry Morgan, John Ireland, Sheldon Leonard, Elisha Cook Jr., Leif Erickson, Charles McGraw. 1947

GANGSTER STORY ★★★ Walter Matthau ventured behind the camera for the first and only time to make this B movie about a smooth operator who gets in over his head with a treacherous mobster. Just as you'd expect from Matthau, this quirky *noir* exercise has a strong vein of dry humor (beginning with the theme song, "The Itch for Scratch"). B&W; 66m. **DIR:** Walter Matthau. **CAST:** Walter Matthau, Carol Grace. 1960

GANGSTER WARS ★★1/2 This movie traces the lives of mobsters "Lucky" Luciano, "Bugsy" Siegel, and Meyer Lansky from their childhood friendship to becoming the most powerful leaders in organized crime during the 1920s. This is an action-packed gangster movie, which at times is difficult to follow and tends to lead the viewer down some dead ends. Rated PG for violence. 121m. **DIR:** Richard C. Sarafian. **CAST:** Michael Nouri, Brian Benben, Joe Penny. 1981

GANGSTER'S BOY ★★1/2 Jackie Cooper's first dramatic role uses every cliché possible to showcase his boyish appeal. His role of the school valedictorian ostracized by his classmates when they learn that his father was a bootlegger was intended to make him the James Dean of his day. It didn't. B&W; 79m. **DIR:** William Nigh. **CAST:** Jackie Cooper, Robert Warwick, Betty Blythe. 1938

GANGSTER'S LAW ❤ Mafia story filmed in Italy. Dubbed. 89m. **DIR:** Siro Marcellini. **CAST:** Klaus Kinski, Maurice Poli, Suzy Andersen, Max Delys. 1986

GANJASAURUS REX ❤ A prodrug propaganda film about a prehistoric monster that awakens when the authorities begin burning marijuana crops. Not rated. 88m. **DIR:** Ursi Reynolds. **CAST:** Paul Bassis, Dave Fresh, Rosie Jones. 1988

GARBAGE PAIL KIDS MOVIE, THE ❤ Disgusting would-be comedy. Rated PG-13. 100m. **DIR:** Rod Amateau. **CAST:** Anthony Newley, Mackenzie Astin, Katie Barberi. 1987

GARBO TALKS ★★★★ In this often funny and touching contemporary comedy, Anne Bancroft is delightful as an outspoken crusader against the small injustices in the world. But she has her fantasies, too, and enlists the aid of her son (Ron Silver) in finding Greta Garbo, who at age 79 could occasionally be spotted walking around New York. Rated PG for profanity. 103m. **DIR:** Sidney Lumet. **CAST:** Anne Bancroft, Ron Silver, Carrie Fisher, Howard DaSilva, Dorothy Loudon, Hermione Gingold. 1984

GARDEN, THE ★★★ Uncompromising film from controversial director Derek Jarman tackles the Church's persecution of homosexuality by depicting the passion play as a celebration of life between two male lovers. Jarman's juxtaposition of traditional events and those experienced by the lovers makes for a visual feast, but some may find the comparison sacrilegious. Not rated; contains nudity and adult situations. 90m. **DIR:** Derek Jarman. **CAST:** Tilda Swinton, Johnny Mills, Phillip MacDonald, Roger Cook, Kevin Collins. 1990

GARDEN OF ALLAH, THE ★★ Gloriously photographed, yawnable yarn of romance in the Algerian boondocks. However, the early Technicolor—which won a special Oscar—is outstanding. Could be retitled: *Marlene's Manhunt.* 80m. **DIR:** Richard Boleslawski. **CAST:** Marlene Dietrich, Charles Boyer, Tilly Losch, John Carradine, Basil Rathbone, Joseph Schildkraut. 1936

GARDEN OF DELIGHTS, THE ★★★ Surreal comedy about a wealthy industrialist who suffers amnesia after a car accident. His greedy family attempts to gain the number of his Swiss bank account. In Spanish with English subtitles. 99m. **DIR:** Carlos Saura. **CAST:** José Luis Lopez Vasquez. 1970

GARDEN OF REDEMPTION, THE ★★★ Thoughtful drama concerning a Tuscan priest who, during the waning days of World War II, struggles against cowardice while the Nazis play merry hell with his fellow villagers. Anthony LaPaglia is properly tortured as the nervous central character, but the script—adapted from a short story by Anthony DiFranco—just dribbles to a close. Rated PG-13 for profanity, violence, and simulated sex. 100m. **DIR:** Thomas Michael Donnelly. **CAST:** Anthony LaPaglia, Embeth Davidtz, Dan Hedaya, Peter Firth, Felix Knyphausen. 1997

GARDEN OF THE FINZI-CONTINIS, THE ★★★★ Vittorio De Sica's adaptation of a Giorgio Bassani novel views the life of an aristocratic Jewish family's misfortune in Fascist Italy. Flawless acting by Dominique Sanda and Helmut Berger. One of De Sica's best. Rated R. 95m. DIR: Vittorio De Sica. CAST: Dominique Sanda, Helmut Berger, Lino Capolicchio, Fabio Testi. 1971

GARDENS OF STONE ★★★1/2 A poignant drama examining the self-described toy soldiers who officiate at military funerals at Virginia's Fort Myer. The setting is the Vietnam 1960s, and James Caan stars as a disillusioned sergeant. D. B. Sweeney shines as a young recruit, but James Earl Jones steals his every scene as the poetically foulmouthed Sergeant Major "Goody" Nelson. Rated R for profanity. 111m. DIR: Francis Ford Coppola. CAST: James Caan, Anjelica Huston, James Earl Jones, D. B. Sweeney, Dean Stockwell, Mary Stuart Masterson, Dick Anthony Williams, Lonette McKee, Sam Bottoms. 1987

•**GARGOYLES** (1972) ★★ Cornel Wilde plays a professor who discovers gargoyles in the Carlsbad Caverns and sets them free. Stephen King claims this is one of his favorite films despite the horrendous effects work. Made for television. Rated PG for intense scares. 74m. DIR: Bill L. Norton. CAST: Cornel Wilde, Jennifer Salt. 1972 DVD

GARGOYLES: THE MOVIE (1994) ★★★1/2 Above-average animation and well-scripted storyline make this enjoyable for animation fans of all ages. Gargoyles who protected a Scottish castle in A.D. 994 were placed under a spell for a thousand years. 80m. DIR: Kazuo Terada, Saburo Hashimoto, Takamitsu Kawamura. 1994

GAS ★★ Tasteless, tedious comedy about an artificial gas crisis in a Midwest city. Rated R. 94m. DIR: Les Rose. CAST: Sterling Hayden, Peter Aykroyd, Susan Anspach, Donald Sutherland, Howie Mandel, Helen Shaver. 1981

GAS, FOOD, LODGING ★★★★1/2 Richard Peck's insightful coming-of-age novel gets first-rate treatment from scripter-director Allison Anders, who has fashioned a superb study of three women frustrated by their dead-end lives in a small New Mexico town. Harried single mom Brooke Adams works as a waitress while trying to find time for her two daughters. Great performances all around. Rated R for profanity and simulated sex. 100m. DIR: Allison Anders. CAST: Brooke Adams, Ione Skye, Fairuza Balk, James Brolin. 1992

GAS PUMP GIRLS 💗 This teen comedy features four beautiful girls who take on a big oil company. Rated PG for nudity. 102m. DIR: Joel Bender. CAST: Kirsten Baker, Dennis Bowen, Huntz Hall, Rikki Marin, William Smith. 1978

GASLIGHT (1940) ★★★★ The first version of Patrick Hamilton's play is much tighter and more suspenseful than the version starring Ingrid Bergman. Diana Wynyard isn't as good as Bergman, but Anton Walbrook is much more sinister than Charles Boyer as the scheming husband trying to drive his wife insane. This British-made version was supposedly destroyed so as not to compete with the Hollywood version. Bits and pieces of surviving prints were edited together and a new negative made. B&W. 84m. DIR: Thorold Dickinson. CAST: Anton Walbrook, Diana Wynyard, Robert Newton. 1940

GASLIGHT (1944) ★★★★ Ingrid Bergman won her first Academy Award as the innocent young bride who, unfortunately, marries Charles Boyer. Boyer is trying to persuade her she is going insane. Many consider this the definitive psychological thriller. B&W; 114m. DIR: George Cukor. CAST: Ingrid Bergman, Joseph Cotten, Charles Boyer, Angela Lansbury. 1944

GAS-S-S-S 💗 A gas accidentally escapes from a chemical company doing military work and everyone in the world over the age of thirty dies, creating a society that is a twisted parody of certain aspects of the destroyed civilization. Rated PG for language and sexual situations. 78m. DIR: Roger Corman. CAST: Robert Corff, Elaine Giftos, Bud Cort, Ben Vereen, Cindy Williams, Country Joe and the Fish. 1970

GATE, THE ★★ A film that insists that children shouldn't play heavy-metal records with satanic messages. The kids in this film do and so unlock a gate to an ancient netherworld. Not very scary, this film exhibits outstanding special effects. Rated PG-13 for mild violence and profanity. 85m. DIR: Tibor Takacs. CAST: Stephen Dorff. 1987

GATE II ★★ Special effects and acting lift this film above its mediocre story. Basically a rehash of the original: teenagers open the door to the netherworld and then must fight evil spirits. Rated R for violence, profanity, and suggested sex. 90m. DIR: Tibor Takacs. CAST: Louis Tripp, Simon Reynolds, James Villemaire, Pamela Segall. 1992

GATE OF HELL ★★★★ Beautiful, haunting tale about a samurai who becomes a monk in twelfth-century Japan in order to atone for his crime of driving a married woman to suicide. Winner of the Academy Award for best foreign film. Director Teinosuke Kinugasa brilliantly re-creates medieval Japan. In Japanese with English subtitles. 86m. DIR: Teinosuke Kinugasa. CAST: Machiko Kyo. 1953

GATES OF HELL ★★1/2 Veteran Italian horror-film director Lucio Fulci strikes again with this tale of one of the gates to Hell being opened in a small town. As with most other Fulci productions, this one focuses too much on the gore and not enough on the story. Rated X for gore and violence. 90m. DIR: Lucio Fulci. CAST: Christopher George, Katherine MacColl, Robert Sampson. 1983

•**GATES OF HELL PART II: DEAD AWAKENING** 💗 Extremely poor sequel in name only to director Lucio Fulci's original gore epic has absolutely nothing to do with that superior film. Not rated; contains violence. 87m. DIR: G. D. Marcum. CAST: Tamera Hext, Tom Campitelli. 1997

GATEWAY TO THE MIND ★★★ Age has not diminished the entertainment value of this Bell science series. Through live action and Chuck Jones's animation, this episode explains the five senses. 58m. DIR: Owen Crump. CAST: Dr. Frank Baxter. 1958

GATHERING, THE ★★★★ Winner of the Emmy for outstanding TV drama special of 1977–1978, this powerful tearjerker features Ed Asner as Adam Thornton. He returns to the family he abandoned after learning that he's dying. The reunion with his family occurs at Christmas and succeeds mainly because his estranged wife (Maureen Stapleton) encourages her children to forgive and forget the past.

104m. **DIR:** Randal Kleiser. **CAST:** Edward Asner, Maureen Stapleton, Lawrence Pressman. **1977**

GATHERING, PART II, THE ★★★1/2 Picking up two years after *The Gathering*, this sequel opens with Kate (Maureen Stapleton) managing her late husband's business. When she falls in love with a business tycoon, she decides to break the news to her grown children over Christmas dinner. 104m. **DIR:** Charles S. Dubin. **CAST:** Maureen Stapleton, Rebecca Balding, Efrem Zimbalist Jr., Jameson Parker. **1979**

GATHERING STORM 🐛 Winston Churchill's life from 1937 to the start of World War II. 72m. **DIR:** Herbert Wise. **CAST:** Richard Burton, Virginia McKenna, Robert Hardy, Ian Bannen. **1974**

GATOR ★★ Burt Reynolds directed this mildly entertaining sequel to *White Lightning*. In it, Burt plays an ex-con out to get revenge—with the help of undercover agent Jack Weston—on some nasty southern politicians. Rated PG. 116m. **DIR:** Burt Reynolds. **CAST:** Burt Reynolds, Jack Weston, Lauren Hutton, Jerry Reed, Alice Ghostley, Mike Douglas, Dub Taylor. **1976**

GATOR BAIT II—CAJUN JUSTICE ★★ A revenge flick with a twist: a happy ending. Cajun newlyweds are ravaged by a group of bayou inbreds. The low-budget look and poor acting rate only two stars, but this is a decent entry in the revenge category. Rated R for violence. 95m. **DIR:** Ferd Sebastian, Beverly Sebastian. **CAST:** Jan MacKenzie. **1988**

GATTACA ★★★★ Fascinating fable about a frightening future where the citizens are genetically engineered to be perfect. Into this world comes Vincent, an in-valid, one bred through conventional means. To fulfill his dreams of space travel, Vincent assumes the identity of a genetically perfect worker. Vincent's ploy goes unnoticed until a murder disrupts the training facility where he works. Well made and executed. Rated PG-13 for adult situations, language, nudity, and violence. 106m. **DIR:** Andrew Niccol. **CAST:** Ethan Hawke, Uma Thurman, Alan Arkin, Jude Law, Loren Dean, Gore Vidal. **1997 DVD**

GAUNTLET, THE ★★ One of actor-director Clint Eastwood's few failures, this release features the squinty-eyed star as an alcoholic, barely capable cop assigned to bring a prostitute (Sondra Locke) to trial. Rated R. 109m. **DIR:** Clint Eastwood. **CAST:** Clint Eastwood, Sondra Locke, Pat Hingle, William Prince. **1977 DVD**

GAY DIVORCÉE, THE ★★★★ This delightful musical farce was the only Fred Astaire/Ginger Rogers film to be nominated for a best-picture Oscar. The outstanding score includes "Night and Day" and "The Continental." B&W; 107m. **DIR:** Mark Sandrich. **CAST:** Fred Astaire, Ginger Rogers, Edward Everett Horton, Alice Brady, Erik Rhodes, Eric Blore, Betty Grable. **1934**

GAY PURR-EE ★★★ Feature-length cartoon about the adventures of three country cats in the big city of Paris. Okay for kids, though it's really meant for adults who enjoy musicals, with some good Harold Arlen songs. Not rated. 86m. **DIR:** Abe Levitow. **CAST:** Judy Garland, Robert Goulet, Red Buttons, Morey Amsterdam, Hermione Gingold, Mel Blanc. **1962**

GAZEBO, THE ★★★★ Hilarious dark comedy about blackmail, murder, and a body that keeps coming back. Many plot twists add to the fun. There is a lot more, but worth renting if only to see Glenn Ford make elaborate preparations to commit a murder. 102m. **DIR:** George Marshall. **CAST:** Glenn Ford, Debbie Reynolds, Carl Reiner, John McGiver, Bert Freed, Martin Landau, Dick Wessel. **1959**

GEISHA, A ★★★★ An aging geisha reluctantly agrees to train the daughter of her old patron. The two women initially do not get along, but the realization that theirs is a dying way of life unites them. A small-scale gem from one of Japan's finest directors. In Japanese with English subtitles. Not rated. B&W; 100m. **DIR:** Kenji Mizoguchi. **CAST:** Michiyo Kogure, Ayako Wakao. **1953**

GENE KRUPA STORY, THE ★★ A fictionalized biography of the late great drummer Gene Krupa. The film borrows facts when needed. Krupa's addiction to drugs is handled with delicacy. B&W; 101m. **DIR:** Don Weis. **CAST:** Sal Mineo, Susan Kohner, Susan Oliver, James Darren, Yvonne Craig, Red Nichols. **1959**

GENEALOGIES OF A CRIME ★★★ Conspiracies involving the French-Belgian Psychoanalytic Society run rampant in this strange, comic slice of suspense. A female lawyer known for taking limelight cases—and losing them—defends and becomes infatuated with a young man who murdered his psychiatrist aunt. A series of flashbacks indicate that his Freudian guardian had not really raised the lad from childhood, but rather used him as a research experiment. In French with English subtitles. Not rated. 113m. **DIR:** Raúl Ruiz. **CAST:** Catherine Deneuve, Michel Piccoli, Melvil Poupaud. **1998**

GENERAL, THE (1927) ★★★★★ *The General* is a film based on an incident in the Civil War. Buster Keaton is an engineer determined to recapture his stolen locomotive. Magnificent battle scenes are mere backdrops for Keaton's inspired acrobatics and comedy. Solid scripting, meticulous attention to detail, and ingenious stunt work make this picture excellent. B&W; 74m. **DIR:** Buster Keaton. **CAST:** Buster Keaton, Marion Mack, Glen Cavender, Jim Farley, Joseph Keaton. **1927 DVD**

GENERAL, THE (1998) ★★★★ It's impossible not to enjoy the bravura filmmaking here, even with its reprehensible central character: Martin Cahill. Although ruthless and brutally efficient when it came to his aptitude for crime—during a 20-year career, Cahill is credited with having stolen over $60 million—the notorious Dublin gangster acquired populist favor, mostly because of how he kept befuddling the police. John Boorman presents all these shenanigans, no matter how felonious, with the enthusiastic elan of a contemporary swashbuckling epic. The result is unexpectedly engaging: a celebration of often-nasty behavior that turns ugly only when Cahill finally gets too brazen even for his own reputation. Rated R for profanity and violence. 129m. **DIR:** John Boorman. **CAST:** Brendan Gleeson, Adrian Dunbar, Sean McGinley, Jon Voight, Maria Doyle Kennedy, Angeline Ball. **1998 DVD**

GENERAL DELLA ROVERE ★★★★ Vittorio De Sica gives a first-rate performance as a small-time windler who is arrested by the occupying German army and blackmailed into impersonating an executed Italian general. Brilliantly directed by Roberto Rossellini. In Italian with English subtitles. B&W; 130m. **DIR:** Roberto Rossellini. **CAST:** Vittorio De Sica, Hannes Messemer, Sandra Milo, Giovanna Ralli. 1957

GENERAL DIED AT DAWN, THE ★★★ Nicely turned story of adventurer Gary Cooper battling Chinese warlord Akim Tamiroff. Film is a bit short on action but draws some fine character studies. Madeleine Carroll is good as Cooper's love interest, but it is Tamiroff who steals the show. B&W; 97m. **DIR:** Lewis Milestone. **CAST:** Gary Cooper, Akim Tamiroff, Madeleine Carroll, Porter Hall, Dudley Digges. 1936

GENERAL IDI AMIN DADA ★★★★ Barbet Schroeder often makes films about people you wouldn't want to spend much time with—*Barfly, Reversal of Fortune*—but never more so than in this documentary about murderous Ugandan dictator Idi Amin. Amin cooperated fully in the making of this film, which nevertheless shows him to be an extremely bizarre, self-inflated despot. Mesmerizingly weird. Not rated. 90m. **DIR:** Barbet Schroeder. 1975

GENERAL SPANKY ★★ A feature-length version of the *Our Gang* series, later popular on TV as *The Little Rascals*. A good attempt to give new life to the characters, but it just proved that audiences can sit still just so long while kids get mischief out of their systems. B&W; 71m. **DIR:** Fred Newmeyer, Gordon Douglas. **CAST:** Spanky McFarland, Buckwheat Thomas, Carl "Alfalfa" Switzer, Phillips Holmes, Rosina Lawrence, Louise Beavers, Hobart Bosworth, Ralph Morgan, Irving Pichel. 1936

GENERAL'S DAUGHTER, THE ★★★1/2 Nelson DeMille's novel serves as a good blueprint for this engaging conspiracy thriller, which gives us a fiercely capable hero in the form of Warrant Officer Paul Brenner a CID investigator with the "special power" to interrogate and arrest any military person anywhere in the world. The story concerns the grotesque murder of Captain Elisabeth Campbell, whose naked body is found in the middle of the military base commanded by her own father, a highly decorated general. Our hero quickly discovers no shortage of suspects. Rated R for profanity, violence, rape, nudity, and deviant sexual behavior. 115m. **DIR:** Simon West. **CAST:** John Travolta, Madeleine Stowe, James Cromwell, Timothy Hutton, Clarence Williams III, James Woods. 1999 DVD

GENERATION ★★★ Remember the generation gap? If not, then you're not likely to enjoy this dated but modestly amusing comedy about a businessman (David Janssen) trying to cope with his pregnant daughter and hippie son-in-law, who want to have their baby at home. Rated PG. 104m. **DIR:** George Schaefer. **CAST:** David Janssen, Kim Darby, Peter Duel, Carl Reiner, Andrew Prine, James Coco, Sam Waterston. 1969

GENERATION, A ★★★ During World War II, two young men in occupied Warsaw join the Resistance. While Andrzej Wajda's first feature film was somewhat restrained by government involvement, it questions the difference between the official and appar-

ent versions of Polish life. In Polish with English subtitles. Not rated. B&W; 90m. **DIR:** Andrzej Wajda. **CAST:** Tadeusz Lomnicki, Tadeusz Janezar, Roman Polanski. 1954

GENEVIEVE ★★★1/2 Captivating, low-key comedy about friendly rivals who engage in a race after finishing a vintage car rally in England. No pretenses or false claims in this charming film, just great performances, beautiful countryside, and a spirit of fun and camaraderie. This stylish feature gave Kenneth More one of his best roles and showcased the charm and comedy flair of Kay Kendall, one of Britain's top talents. 86m. **DIR:** Henry Cornelius. **CAST:** Kenneth More, Kay Kendall, Dinah Sheridan, John Gregson, Arthur Wontner. 1954

GENGHIS COHN ★★★★ Extremely creative and unusual, this supernatural black comedy turns the tables on racial stereotyping. Antony Sher plays the ghost of a Jewish comedian who comes back to haunt the former SS officer who killed him at Dachau. No rattling chains here, as the dead comic has a revenge scheme that is both hysterically twisted and deadly somber. The very weirdness inherent to this flick is what makes it work. Made for British television. Not rated; contains profanity, violence, and nudity. 100m. **DIR:** Elijah Moshinsky. **CAST:** Robert Lindsay, Diana Rigg, Antony Sher. 1993

GENTLE GIANT ★★★ A touching, Disneyesque story of a lonely boy and an orphaned black bear cub. Mildly awkward acting and editing, but the film's heart is pure and the animal scenes are very good. Not rated, with only minimal violence. 93m. **DIR:** James Neilson. **CAST:** Dennis Weaver, Vera Miles, Clint Howard, Ralph Meeker. 1967

GENTLE SAVAGE ★★★1/2 In this well-paced Western, William Smith portrays an American Indian framed for the rape and beating of a white girl in a small town. The girl's stepfather, who actually committed the crime, incites the townsmen to go after the innocent man. When the townsmen kill the hapless fellow's brother, the American Indian community retaliates. Rated R for violence. 85m. **DIR:** Sean MacGregor. **CAST:** William Smith, Gene Evans, Barbara Luna, Joe Flynn. 1978

GENTLEMAN BANDIT, THE ★★★ Ralph Waite gives a convincing portrait of Father Pagano, who was accused of a series of armed robberies in 1978. This made-for-TV biography chronicles his ordeal when mistakenly identified by seven eyewitnesses. Good viewing. 96m. **DIR:** Jonathan Kaplan. **CAST:** Ralph Waite, Julie Bovasso, Jerry Zaks, Joe Grifasi, Estelle Parsons, Vincent Spano. 1981

GENTLEMAN FROM CALIFORNIA ★★1/2 Ricardo Cortez returns from Spain to find his California homeland being robbed and plundered by unscrupulous newcomers. He soon becomes the Robin Hood of the Californians. B&W; 58m. **DIR:** Gus Meins. **CAST:** Ricardo Cortez, Marjorie Weaver, Katherine DeMille, Helen Holmes. 1937

GENTLEMAN JIM ★★★★1/2 Errol Flynn has a field day in this beautifully filmed biography of heavyweight champion Jim Corbett. Always cocky and light on his feet, Flynn is a joy to behold and will make those who considered him a star instead of an actor think twice. Ward Bond is equally fine as John L. Sullivan. Said to have been Flynn's favorite role. B&W; 104m. DIR: Raoul Walsh. CAST: Errol Flynn, Jack Carson, Alan Hale Sr., Alexis Smith, Ward Bond. 1942

GENTLEMAN KILLER ★★ The brother of a murdered army officer takes revenge on the outlaws who have taken over a small border town. A better than average Western with a surprise ending and good performances by Anthony Steffen and Eduardo Fajardo. Not rated; contains violence. 97m. DIR: George Finley. CAST: Anthony Steffen, Eduardo Fajardo, Silvia Solar, Mariano Vidal Molina. 1969

GENTLEMEN PREFER BLONDES ★★ Howard Hawks gets surprisingly good performances from his stars, Jane Russell and Marilyn Monroe, in this 1953 musical comedy. As usual, Hawks does his best to make good scenes, but this time the silly plot—about two women searching for husbands—thwarts his estimable talents. 91m. DIR: Howard Hawks. CAST: Jane Russell, Marilyn Monroe, Charles Coburn, Tommy Noonan, Elliott Reid, George Winslow. 1953

GENTLEMEN'S AGREEMENT ★★1/2 A writer doing a feature on anti-Semitism passes himself off as a Jew. Along with the anticipated problems, he gets surprising reactions from friends and coworkers. With 1947's Crossfire this was a Hollywood pace-setter in attacking bigotry, but it has lost some bite. Oscars for the best picture, director Elia Kazan, and supporting actress Celeste Holm. B&W; 118m. DIR: Elia Kazan. CAST: Gregory Peck, Dorothy McGuire, John Garfield, Celeste Holm, Anne Revere, June Havoc, Albert Dekker, Jane Wyatt, Dean Stockwell, Sam Jaffe. 1947 DVD

GENUINE RISK ★★★1/2 Losers caught in a love triangle tangle in this neat homage to Forties crime-boss pictures. The film is ragged, but it's also erotic and occasionally funny. Rated R for profanity, nudity, and violence. 86m. DIR: Kurt Voss. CAST: Terence Stamp, Michelle Johnson. 1990

•GEN-X COPS ★★1/2 The Gen-X Cops are almost as unpredictable and dangerous as the criminals they hunt, and it is up to them and their flashy style to capture the vile Akatura who has gotten hold of a shipment of smuggled explosives. The Gen-X Cops will either save the day or get kicked off the force trying. Gen-X Cops is full of martial arts action, but nothing too impressive. Rated R for violence. 113m. DIR: Benny Chan. CAST: Nicholas Tse, Stephen Fung, Sam Lee, Grace Ip, Toru Nakamura, Eric Tsang, Daniel Wu. 1999 DVD

GEORGE BALANCHINE'S THE NUTCRACKER ★★★ Despite the presence of Macaulay Culkin, this is a rather stage-bound filming of the New York City Ballet's annual production of Tchaikovsky's masterpiece. Not very cinematic, but luscious to look at and glorious to listen to. Plus, the dancing is often marvelous. Narrated by Kevin Kline. Rated G. 93m. DIR: Emile Ardolino. CAST: Macaulay Culkin, Darci Kistler, Kyra Nichols, Wendy Whelan. 1993

GEORGE BURNS AND GRACIE ALLEN SHOW, THE (TV SERIES) ★★★1/2 In this classic series, George Burns plays a nearly imperturbable entertainer, married to madcap Gracie Allen. Allen turns every-

day life into a nonstop adventure by innocently causing a whirlwind of confusion. She's endlessly endearing. Burns is dryly delightful, puffing on his cigar and looking into the camera, commenting on the developing plot. B&W; 120m. DIR: Ralph Levy. CAST: George Burns, Gracie Allen, Harry Von Zell, Ronnie Burns, Bea Benaderet, Hal March, Bob Sweeney, Fred Clark, Larry Keating. 1950–1958

GEORGE CARLIN: JAMMIN' IN NEW YORK ★★★★ More irreverent humor from the master of wordplay. Comedian George Carlin disburses hilarious words of wisdom on everything from the Persian Gulf War to airline announcements. Taped at The Paramount in Madison Square Garden, New York City. Not rated, contains adult language. 60m. DIR: Rocco Urbishi. CAST: George Carlin. 1992

GEORGE MCKENNA STORY, THE ★★★1/2 Based on a true story, a new principal tries to make a gang-ridden high school a better place to learn. He gains the respect of the students and most of the faculty, but a few teachers try to have him removed. Denzel Washington does a nice job of portraying the compassionate principal, and Lynn Whitfield is wonderful as his neglected wife. Not rated; contains violence. 93m. DIR: Eric Laneuville. CAST: Denzel Washington, Lynn Whitfield, Akosua Busia, Richard Masur. 1986

GEORGE OF THE JUNGLE ★★★ Winning Brendan Fraser plays the lucky if unintelligent jungle boy in Disney's faithful live-action adaptation of Jay Ward's 1960s cartoon character. Off-beat humor alternately annoys and amuses as Fraser pursues romance with a daffy heiress. Jim Henson's Creature Shop does wonders with animatronics and computer-generated images. Particularly impressive stunt on the San Francisco–Oakland Bay Bridge is a must-see. Rated PG for comic-book violence. 92m. DIR: Sam Weisman. CAST: Brendan Fraser, Leslie Mann, Holland Taylor, Sinbad. 1997 DVD

GEORGE WALLACE ★★★★ Powerful performance by Gary Sinise as Alabama's controversial governor portrays a complicated man more concerned with being elected than with preserving racial inequities. Based on Marshall Frady's book Wallace, this fine TNT miniseries goes beyond the inflammatory headlines into the planning stage of each incident that warranted national attention and, at times, intervention. An interesting use of black-and-white newsreels as well as new footage at key historic moments in the film is very effective. Not rated; contains sexual situations, violence, and profanity. 180m. DIR: John Frankenheimer. CAST: Gary Sinise, Mare Winningham, Clarence Williams III, Angelina Jolie, Joe Don Baker, Terry Kinney, William Sanderson. 1997

GEORGE WASHINGTON ★★★1/2 Sweeping made-for-TV chronicle of George Washington as surveyor and fighter in the French and Indian Wars through his years as commander of the victorious colonial army. Some dull home scenes at Mount Vernon but there are ample battles and fascinating revelations of the infighting among the "professional" generals who surrounded him. Based on the books of James Thomas Flexner. 408m. DIR: Buzz Kulik. CAST: Barry Bostwick, Patty Duke, David Dukes, Jaclyn Smith, Lloyd Bridges, Robert Stack, Anthony Zerbe. 1984

GEORGE WASHINGTON: THE FORGING OF A NA-TION ★★★1/2 A fine made-for-TV sequel to 1984s *George Washington*. The film covers Washington's two terms in office and the myriad problems he faced as the leader of a new nation. 210m. **DIR:** William A. Graham. **CAST:** Barry Bostwick, Patty Duke, Jeffrey Jones, Richard Bekins, Penny Fuller, Lise Hilboldt. **1986**

GEORGE WASHINGTON SLEPT HERE ★★★ Some mild laughs when Jack Benny and Ann Sheridan buy a run-down Colonial house and are frustrated at every attempt to make it habitable. Many of the situations were repeated, to better advantage, in *Mr. Blandings Builds His Dream House*. B&W; 91m. **DIR:** William Keighley. **CAST:** Jack Benny, Ann Sheridan, Charles Coburn, Percy Kilbride, Hattie McDaniel. **1942**

GEORGE WHITE'S SCANDALS ★★ Joan Davis saves this fairly minor musical from collapsing. B&W; 95m. **DIR:** Felix Feist. **CAST:** Joan Davis, Jack Haley, Jane Greer, Philip Terry. **1945**

GEORGE'S ISLAND ★★★1/2 Adventure looms for 10-year-old orphan George when he's taken away from his grandfather and placed in a foster home. Escaping in a boat, he comes across an island that's a virtual playground, if it weren't for the ghosts of swashbuckling pirates guarding a treasure. Rated PG for some pirate violence that might scare younger children. 89m. **DIR:** Paul Donovan. **CAST:** Ian Bannen, Sheila McCarthy, Maury Chaykin. **1991**

GEORGIA (1987) ★★★1/2 Intense psychological drama. Judy Davis stars in dual roles as a successful attorney investigating her own mother's accidental drowning and as the mother, a photographer. While attempting to find out more, she runs into some deadly roadblocks. Davis is powerfully mesmerizing as both a professional woman and a free spirit whose acquaintances are at the core of this mystery. Not rated; contains violence and adult situations. 90m. **DIR:** Ben Lewin. **CAST:** Judy Davis, John Bach, Julia Blake, Alex Menglet, Marshall Naper. **1987**

GEORGIA (1995) ★★ At the core of the film's waning narrative is the volatile relationship between Sadie, a wannabe rock singer with an anguished, grating voice, and her nightingale folk-rock older sister Georgia. Leaving muddy footprints all over the ladies' frayed domestic canvas are the tics, lures, hassles, and glamour of show business. Rated R for language, simulated sex, substance abuse, and nudity. 117m. **DIR:** Ulu Grosbard. **CAST:** Jennifer Jason Leigh, Mare Winningham, Ted Levine, John Doe, Max Perlich, John C. Reilly. **1995 DVD**

GEORGIA, GEORGIA ★★ This film, adapted by Maya Angelou from one of her stories, is a dated but fairly interesting study of racism. The story centers around the relationship between a white photographer and a black singer. If you get mildly involved with this movie, stay with it. Rated R. 91m. **DIR:** Stig Bjorkman. **CAST:** Diana Sands, Dirk Benedict, Minnie Gentry, Roger Furman. **1972**

GEORGY GIRL ★★★1/2 Generations clash as suave, patient fairy godfather James Mason works to make chubby London mod girl Lynn Redgrave his mistress in this totally engaging British comedy.

Charlotte Rampling is a standout as the chubby's tough-bitch roommate. Mason, of course, gives another of his flawless characterizations. B&W; 100m. **DIR:** Silvio Narizzano. **CAST:** Lynn Redgrave, James Mason, Alan Bates, Charlotte Rampling. **1966**

GERMANY IN AUTUMN ★★★ Dense political anthology that includes contributions by a dozen filmmakers, collectively inspired by two notorious events involving terrorists that took place in Germany in 1977. Some episodes will have no resonance for non-German viewers, but two command special attention: a sly skit about TV executives by novelist Heinrich Boll; and Rainer Werner Fassbinder's painfully realistic segment in which he berates his then-lover and argues politics with his mother. In German with English subtitles. Not rated; contains adult themes and nudity. 124m. **DIR:** Heinrich Boll, Alf Brustellin, Bernhard Sinkel, Hans Peter Cloos, Katja Rupe, Rainer Werner Fassbinder, Alexander Kluge, Beate Mainka-Jellinghaus, Maximiliane Mainka, Peter Schubert, Edgar Reitz, Volker Schlöndorff. **CAST:** Hannelore Hoger, Katja Rupe, Hans Peter Cloos, Rainer Werner Fassbinder. **1978**

GERONIMO (1993) ★★1/2 This superficial account of the great Apache leader tries to cover too much ground within its limited time frame. Not to be confused with the theatrical film *Geronimo: An American Legend*. Made for cable television. 92m. **DIR:** Roger Young. **CAST:** Joseph Running Fox, Ryan Black, Jimmy Herman, Nick Ramus, Michelle St. John. **1993**

GERONIMO: AN AMERICAN LEGEND (1994) ★★★1/2 Strong performances and a thought-provoking screenplay add grit to this powerhouse Western about the Apache warrior. Told through the eyes of an idealistic officer, this near epic is a collection of what Howard Hawks called "good scenes" that will please fans of the genre. Rated PG-13 for profanity and violence. 110m. **DIR:** Walter Hill. **CAST:** Jason Patric, Gene Hackman, Robert Duvall, Wes Studi, Matt Damon, Rodney A. Grant, Kevin Tighe, Steve Reevis, Scott Wilson, Carlos Palomino. **1994 DVD**

GERTRUDE ★★★★1/2 A woman leaves her husband for a younger man. When her lover proves equally unsatisfying, she embarks on a series of affairs before realizing that true happiness lies within herself. Danish director Carl Dreyer's last film almost completely eliminates camera movement in order to force our attention onto what is happening between the characters. In Danish with English subtitles. 116m. **DIR:** Carl Dreyer. **CAST:** Nina Pens Rede, Bendt Rothe. **1963**

GERVAISE ★★★ Soap-opera fans will be the best audience for this adaptation of an Emile Zola novel. Set in 1850 Paris, the movie follows the sad life of a woman who is abandoned by her lover, unlucky in business, and sent into penury by her drunken husband. In French with English subtitles. B&W; 120m. **DIR:** René Clement. **CAST:** Maria Schell, François Perier, Suzy Delair. **1956**

•**GET CARTER** ★★★★ Michael Caine is memorable as Jack Carter, a vicious London gangster whose search for his brother's killer leads him down a trail of lies, deceit, and death, and through New-castle looking for the man who gave the order. Director Mike Hodges is Caine's best friend, allowing him the opportunity to create an unlikable character with no apologies. Brutal and tough, the film remains a classic of its kind. Rated R for adult situations, language, and violence. 111m. DIR: Mike Hodges. CAST: Michael Caine, Ian Hendry, Britt Ekland, John Osborne. 1971

GET CHRISTIE LOVE! ★★ A television entry in the blaxploitation genre, this adventure centers on a female police detective (Teresa Graves) who tracks drug dealers on the streets of Los Angeles in the 1970s. Fairly tame when compared to others in its genre. 75m. DIR: William A. Graham. CAST: Teresa Graves, Harry Guardino, Louise Sorel, Paul Stevens. 1974

GET CRAZY ★★★1/2 Here's the wildest, weirdest, and most outrageous rock 'n' roll comedy any of us is likely to see. It's a story about a rock concert on New Year's Eve. Malcolm McDowell plays a Mick Jagger–style rock singer, Allen Goorwitz is a Bill Graham–ish promoter, and Daniel Stern is his lovesick stage manager. Rated R for nudity, profanity, violence, and suggested sex. 92m. DIR: Allan Arkush. CAST: Malcolm McDowell, Allen Garfield, Daniel Stern, Ed Begley Jr., Miles Chapin, Lou Reed, Stacey Nelkin, Bill Henderson, Franklin Ajaye, Bobby Sherman, Fabian. 1983

GET ON THE BUS ★★★1/2 A mixed bag of African American characters sets out for Washington, D.C., and the Million Man March. The script and characters are cliché-ridden, but director Spike Lee and a superb cast, all working at the top of their considerable powers, give the film its urgency of conviction and a patina of documentary realism. Things bog down in the last few minutes, when the bombastic speeches defeat even these fine actors. Rated R for profanity. 122m. DIR: Spike Lee. CAST: Charles Dutton, Andre Braugher, Ossie Davis, Richard Belzer. 1996

GET OUT YOUR HANDKERCHIEFS ★★★1/2 Winner of the 1978 Academy Award for best foreign film, this stars Gérard Depardieu as a clumsy husband so desperate to make his melancholic wife happy and pregnant that he provides her with a lover (Patrick Dewaere). A mostly improbable existential drama. In French. Not rated, contains nudity. 108m. DIR: Bertrand Blier. CAST: Gérard Depardieu, Patrick Dewaere, Carole Laure. 1978

•GET REAL ★★★ A gay teenager falls in love with his school's most handsome athlete, who furtively returns his affections but won't speak to him in the halls. The story is familiar, even a little trite, and at times it's as solemn and moony as most teenagers in love, straight or gay. It could have used a little more humor, perhaps, but the appealing cast puts it over with conviction. Rated R for language and sexual content. 110m. DIR: Simon Shore. CAST: Ben Silverstone, Brad Gorton, Charlotte Brittain, Stacy Hart. 1998 DVD

GET SHORTY ★★★★★ John Travolta solidified his status as the comeback king of the 1990s with his performance in this smart, often outrageous screen adaptation of the Elmore Leonard novel. Travolta plays Chili Palmer, a collector for the mob who, after being sent to Hollywood to collect some outstanding

debts, decides to go into business for himself—specifically, the movie business. This is the best insider's look at the sleazy side of Tinsel Town since Robert Altman's *The Player*. Rated R for profanity and violence. 105m. DIR: Barry Sonnenfeld. CAST: John Travolta, Gene Hackman, René Russo, Danny DeVito, Bette Midler, Dennis Farina, Delroy Lindo, James Gandolfini, David Paymer, Martin Ferrero, Miguel Sandoval, Jonathan Gries, Linda Hart. 1995 DVD

GET SMART AGAIN ★★1/2 This pleasant trip down memory lane reunites the cast of the TV sitcom for one last go at the creeps of KAOS. Breezy, pleasant, and funnier than you'd expect, in a silly way. Made for TV. 93m. DIR: Gary Nelson. CAST: Don Adams, Barbara Feldon. 1989

GET TO KNOW YOUR RABBIT ★★★ This cute comedy won't appeal to everyone but will captivate fans of the Smothers Brothers' brand of offbeat humor. Tom Smothers wants to be a magician so he takes lessons from Orson Welles. But it's a lost cause. The satire hurts, but the laughs help. Rated R. 91m. DIR: Brian De Palma. CAST: Tom Smothers, Orson Welles, John Astin, Katharine Ross, Samantha Jones, M. Emmet Walsh. 1972

GETAWAY, THE (1972) ★★★★ Top-notch adventure and excitement occur when convict Steve McQueen has his wife seduce the Texas Parole Board chairman (Ben Johnson) in exchange for his early freedom. McQueen becomes jealous and resentful after the deal is consummated and kills the chairman, setting off a shotgun-charged chase. Rated PG. 122m. DIR: Sam Peckinpah. CAST: Steve McQueen, Ali MacGraw, Ben Johnson, Sally Struthers. 1972 DVD

GETAWAY, THE (1994) ★★1/2 Surprisingly effective scene-for-scene remake of director Sam Peckinpah's flawed but sometimes brilliant action film. Alec Baldwin lacks the charisma of Steve McQueen as a convict who secures his release from prison with the help of his wife, but Kim Basinger outdoes Ali MacGraw as the other half of this modern-day outlaw couple. Rated R for violence, profanity, nudity and simulated sex. 115m. DIR: Roger Donaldson. CAST: Alec Baldwin, Kim Basinger, James Woods, Michael Madsen, David Morse, Jennifer Tilly, James Stephens, Burton Gilliam, Richard Farnsworth. 1994 DVD

GETTING AWAY WITH MURDER ★★ A fabulous cast is wasted on this unfunny stab at black comedy. When Jack Lambert (Dan Aykroyd) suspects his neighbor is actually a Nazi war criminal, he decides to take the law into his own hands. After killing poor Max Mueller (Jack Lemmon), Lambert realizes it's a case of mistaken identity. Okay, you can laugh now. Rated R for profanity. 92m. DIR: Harvey Miller. CAST: Dan Aykroyd, Jack Lemmon, Lily Tomlin, Bonnie Hunt, Brian Kerwin. 1996

GETTING EVEN ★★ This is a fast-paced but unspectacular action-adventure film. The hero is a wealthy industrialist with a passion for danger. Rated R for violence and nudity. 89m. DIR: Dwight H. Little. CAST: Edward Albert, Audrey Landers, Joe Don Baker. 1986

GETTING EVEN WITH DAD ★★★1/2 421An enjoyable, lightweight comedy that serves mainly as a showcase for its big-name Hollywood players. An 11-year-old boy blackmails his con man father into going straight in an effort to bond with him. Rated PG. 110m. **DIR:** Howard Deutch. **CAST:** Ted Danson, Macaulay Culkin, Glenne Headly, Hector Elizondo, Gailard Sartain, Saul Rubinek. **1994**

GETTING GOTTI ★★★1/2 The high-profile crime trial of reputed mob boss John Gotti gets the made-for-television treatment in this absorbing, hard-hitting courtroom drama. Lorraine Bracco stars as the assistant U.S. attorney who grew up with Gotti, and now wants to put him behind bars. Anthony Denison is both appropriately charming and volatile as Gotti, whose Teflon alibi is about to get the acid test. Director Robert Young convincingly separates high drama from fact to deliver a film that packs quite a punch. 93m. **DIR:** Robert Young. **CAST:** Lorraine Bracco, Anthony Denison, Ellen Burstyn. **1994**

GETTING IN ★★ Medical thriller desperately in need of a transfusion. Med student Gabriel Higgs failed to make the cut to attend Johns Hopkins Medical School. Sixth on the waiting list, he attempts to bribe students ahead of him in order to improve his chances. No need: Someone is murdering the candidates, and it looks like Higgs is the guilty party. Rated R for violence, adult situations, and language. 94m. **DIR:** Doug Liman. **CAST:** Kristy Swanson, Andrew McCarthy, Stephen Mailer, Dave Chappelle. **1993**

GETTING IT RIGHT ★★★1/2 Surrounded by a wonderful cast of endearing eccentrics, Jesse Birdsall sails through his role as a 31-year-old virgin who becomes a sensitive lover (to Lynn Redgrave's madcap neglected socialite). Something of an updated version of the British social comedies of the Sixties (*Georgy Girl*, *Alfie*). Highly recommended. Rated R for nudity and sexual situations. 102m. **DIR:** Randal Kleiser. **CAST:** Jesse Birdsall, Helena Bonham Carter, Peter Cook, John Gielgud, Jane Horrocks, Lynn Redgrave. **1989**

GETTING OF WISDOM, THE ★★★★ Out of Australia, this better-than-average rites-of-passage story of an unrefined country girl (Susannah Fowle) who gets sent off to school in the city displays all the qualities of top-notch directing. The girl is easy prey for her more sophisticated, yet equally immature classmates. The story takes place in the mid-1800s and is taken from the classic Australian novel by Henry Handel Richardson. Not rated, but the equivalent of a G. 100m. **DIR:** Bruce Beresford. **CAST:** Susannah Fowle, Sheila Helpmann, Patricia Kennedy, Hilary Ryan. **1980**

GETTING OUT ★★★1/2 An intense performance from Rebecca DeMornay knocks this right out of the usual range of made-for-TV flicks. She plays a tough troubled woman trying to turn her life around, without much help from her nightmare of a mother. The script has some depth to it, but the real treasure is DeMornay. Not rated; contains violence and sexual situations. 92m. **DIR:** John Korty. **CAST:** Rebecca De-Mornay, Ellen Burstyn, Robert Knipper, Carol Mitchell-Leon, Richard Jenkins. **1993**

GETTING OVER 🖤 This low-budget black exploitation flick is so poorly lit that it's hard to discern the facial expressions of the actors. Not rated; it contains profanity. 108m. **DIR:** Bernie Rollins. **CAST:** John Daniels, Gwen Brisco, Paulette Gibson. **1980**

GETTING PHYSICAL ★★★1/2 Alexandra Paul plays Nadine, a pudgy junk-food addict who decides to toughen up after her purse is stolen. Couch potatoes can vicariously experience the joy of Nadine's transformation from chubby wimp to lean bodybuilder. A must-see for everyone who dreams about a fitter life-style. Made for television, this is unrated and very mild. 95m. **DIR:** Steven H. Stern. **CAST:** Alexandra Paul, Sandahl Bergman, David Naughton. **1984**

GETTING STRAIGHT ★★1/2 During the campus riots of the 1960s, Hollywood jumped on the bandwagon with such forgettable films as *The Strawberry Statement* and *R.P.M.* Add *Getting Straight* to the list. Elliott Gould plays a "hip" graduate student caught up in campus unrest. It now seems like an odd curio. Rated PG. 124m. **DIR:** Richard Rush. **CAST:** Elliott Gould, Candice Bergen, Max Julien, Jeff Corey, Robert F. Lyons. **1970**

GETTYSBURG ★★ Civil War buffs will revel in the authenticity writer-director Ronald F. Maxwell brings to this epic film, while all others will find it overlong and lethargic. That said, the sections in the first half of the movie featuring Jeff Daniels and Sam Elliott are superb. Rated PG for violence. 248m. **DIR:** Ronald F. Maxwell. **CAST:** Tom Berenger, Jeff Daniels, Sam Elliott, Martin Sheen, Richard Jordan, Stephen Lang, C. Thomas Howell, Kevin Conway, Andrew Prine, John Diehl, Richard Anderson, Maxwell Caulfield, Timothy Scott, George Lazenby. **1993**

GHASTLY ONES, THE 🖤 Members of a family, reunited for the reading of their dead father's will, are murdered by a mysterious killer. Not rated; the movie has lots of fake-looking gore. 81m. **DIR:** Andy Milligan. **CAST:** Don Williams, Maggie Rogers. **1969**

GHETTO BLASTER ★ Another war vet returns home to find it overrun by gangs and decides to do something about it. Rated R for violence, nudity, and profanity. 82m. **DIR:** Alan A. Stewart. **CAST:** Richard Hatch, R. G. Armstrong, Richard Jaeckel. **1988**

GHIDRAH, THE THREE-HEADED MONSTER ★★★ A giant egg from outer space crashes into Japan and hatches the colossal three-headed flying monster of the title. It takes the combined forces of Godzilla, Rodan, and Mothra to save Tokyo. Good Japanese monster movie is marred only by dumb subplot of evil agent out to kidnap a Martian princess. 85m. **DIR:** Inoshiro Honda. **CAST:** Yosuke Natsuki, Yuriko Hoshi, Hiroshi Koizumi. **1965**

GHOST AND MR. CHICKEN, THE ★★★ OK, so you can spot the stunt double and Don Knotts's twitches are a little, well, obvious. Still, fans of Knotts's familiar routine will enjoy watching their skinny underdog hero solve a ghost story while winning the prettiest girl in town. One of the better of Knotts's benign, yet entertaining, comedies. Not rated. 90m. **DIR:** Alan Rafkin. **CAST:** Don Knotts, Joan Staley, Dick Sargent, Liam Redmond, Skip Homeier, Philip Ober. **1966**

GHOST AND MRS. MUIR, THE ★★★★ Romantic comedy at its best in this heartwarming tale about a young widow who decides to live in the lighthouse home of a long-dead sailor, setting the stage for a perfect love story. 104m. **DIR:** Joseph L. Mankiewicz.

CAST: Gene Tierney, Rex Harrison, Edna Best, George Sanders, Anna Lee, Natalie Wood. **1947**

GHOST AND THE DARKNESS, THE ★★★★ A thrilling, chilling yarn about the endangerment of Great Britain's building of a railway through eastern Africa by a pair of clever, man-eating lions. Despite his success against difficult odds, army engineer Val Kilmer has never encountered such a situation. So he joins forces with a great white hunter to put an end to this almost unworldly duo. Rated R for violence and profanity. 109m. **DIR:** Stephen Hopkins. **CAST:** Michael Douglas, Val Kilmer, Tom Wilkinson, John Kani, Bernard Hill, Brian McCardle, Om Puri. **1996 DVD**

GHOST BREAKERS ★★★1/2 Amusing Bob Hope romp finds him investigating the eerie mansion inherited by Paulette Goddard. The laughs mix evenly with the thrills in this hilarious blend of gags and mayhem. Often imitated (film was inspiration for Martin-Lewis vehicle *Scared Stiff*) but never equaled. Great atmosphere. 85m. **DIR:** George Marshall. **CAST:** Bob Hope, Paulette Goddard, Richard Carlson, Anthony Quinn, Paul Lukas. **1940**

GHOST BRIGADE ★★ A band of ghost soldiers is trying to take over Earth. An interesting concept, but the story moves way too slowly. Rated R for violence and profanity. 80m. **DIR:** George Hickenlooper. **CAST:** Corbin Bernsen, Martin Sheen, Adrian Pasdar, Ray Wise, Cynda Williams. **1992**

GHOST CATCHERS, THE ★★★ Nightclub performers Ole Olsen and Chic Johnson help a southern colonel and his two daughters rid their mansion of ghosts. Typically wacky shenanigans from the *Hellzapoppin* duo. Look carefully for Mel Torme as a jazz drummer, and Morton Downey Sr., who sings "These Foolish Things." B&W; 69m. **DIR:** Eddie Cline. **CAST:** Ole Olsen, Chic Johnson, Gloria Jean, Martha O'Driscoll, Leo Carrillo, Lon Chaney Jr., Andy Devine. **1944**

GHOST CHASE ★★ Teen filmmakers are taken on by a ruthless movie mogul after one of the boys inherits some seemingly worthless trinkets from his grandfather. Decent special effects, but acting and dialogue are lifeless. Rated PG for profanity. 89m. **DIR:** Roland Emmerich. **CAST:** Jason Lively, Tim McDaniel, Jill Whitlow, Paul Gleason. **1988**

GHOST DAD ★★1/2 This family-oriented, *Topper*-style comedy casts Bill Cosby as a daddy (what else?) who continues to provide for his family—even after he's dead. The story's serious underpinnings give resonance to this comic delight. Rated PG. 95m. **DIR:** Sidney Poitier. **CAST:** Bill Cosby, Denise Nicholas, Kimberly Russell. **1990 DVD**

•GHOST DOG: THE WAY OF THE SAMURAI ★★★★ Contract killer adheres to the tenets of an 18th-century Samurai handbook in this gangster hip-hop Eastern Western. His best friend is a Haitian ice cream vendor who does not understand a word he says. His enemies are twilight-year Italian-American hoods whose boss watches TV cartoons. This violent, often wildly funny spin on Sam Peckinpah's infatuation with men on the brink of extinction is set on a seedy Sopranos turf and fueled by music from Wu-Tang Clan's RZA, "the Thelonious Monk of hip-hop."

Rated R for language and violence. 116m. **DIR:** Jim Jarmusch. **CAST:** Forest Whitaker, Henry Silva, Trissa Vessey, John Tormey, Isaach de Bankole. **2000**

GHOST FEVER ♥ Southern cops investigate strange happenings at Magnolia Mansion. Director Alan Smithee doesn't exist; it's a fake name applied when the real director (in this case, Lee Madden) doesn't want his name on the final product. Rated PG. 86m. **DIR:** Alan Smithee. **CAST:** Sherman Hemsley, Luis Avalos. **1985**

GHOST GOES WEST, THE ★★★★ A millionaire buys a Scottish castle and transports it stone by stone to America only to discover that it comes complete with a ghost. Robert Donat gives a memorable performance in this bit of whimsy. B&W; 100m. **DIR:** René Clair. **CAST:** Robert Donat, Jean Parker. **1935**

GHOST IN MONTE CARLO, A ★★ Weak, flimsy period piece mystery concerns revenge and intrigue among the royalty in beautiful Monte Carlo. 93m. **DIR:** John Hough. **CAST:** Sarah Miles, Oliver Reed, Christopher Plummer, Samantha Eggar, Ron Moody, Fiona Fullerton, Lysette Anthony. **1990**

GHOST IN THE MACHINE ★★1/2 Fans of the *Nightmare on Elm Street* films should enjoy this high-tech variation, where a dying serial killer infiltrates a mainframe computer. No surprises, and the special effects are a bit cheap, but the film is efficiently packaged. Rated R for violence. 95m. **DIR:** Rachel Talalay. **CAST:** Karen Allen, Chris Mulkey, Ken Thorley. **1993**

GHOST IN THE NOONDAY SUN ♥ Too silly pirate parody. Not rated. 90m. **DIR:** Peter Medak. **CAST:** Peter Sellers, Anthony Franciosa, Peter Boyle, Spike Milligan, Clive Revill. **1974**

GHOST IN THE SHELL ★★★ In a vast Asian city of the future, a female cyborg investigates the sinister doings of a mysterious supercriminal invading the twenty-first century's information highways. This engrossing Japanese animated feature is definitely not for small children. The confusing plot and dull American voices are drawbacks, but the visual style is fascinating and the action often brilliantly executed. Not rated; contains some nudity and much violence. 82m. **DIR:** Oshii Mamoru. **1995 DVD**

GHOST OF FRANKENSTEIN ★★★1/2 Dr. Frankenstein's second son takes a crack at monster rehabilitation and all's well until Ygor shares his thoughts (literally). This was the fourth Frankenstein film from Universal Studios and the beginning of the series' skid to programmer status. Luckily, Bela Lugosi is back as Ygor, the supporting cast is good, the music score is first-rate, and there are enough dynamic set pieces to liven up the story. B&W; 67m. **DIR:** Erle C. Kenton. **CAST:** Lon Chaney Jr., Cedric Hardwicke, Ralph Bellamy, Lionel Atwill, Bela Lugosi. **1942**

GHOST PATROL ★★ Colonel Tim McCoy takes a commanding lead in this low-budget film about a government agent investigating the strange crashes of airplanes carrying top-secret information. An effort to cash in on the unexpected success of Gene Autry's *Phantom Empire* and Tom Mix's *Miracle Rider*. B&W; 57m. **DIR:** Sam Newfield. **CAST:** Tim McCoy, Claudia Dell, Walter Miller, Wheeler Oakman, Slim Whitaker. **1936**

GHOST SHIP ★★1/2 Creaky but occasionally spooky British tale of a couple who buy a ship only to discover it is haunted by the ghosts of some unhappy previous owners. Not rated. B&W; 69m. DIR: Vernon Sewell. CAST: Dermot Walsh, Hazel Court, Joss Ackland. 1951

GHOST STORY 💌 This film, based on the bestselling novel by Peter Straub, is about as frightening as an episode of *Sesame Street*. Rated R because of shock scenes involving rotting corpses and violence. 110m. DIR: John Irvin. CAST: John Houseman, Douglas Fairbanks Jr., Melvyn Douglas, Fred Astaire, Alice Krige, Craig Wasson, Patricia Neal. 1981 DVD

GHOST TOWN ★★ A passable time waster mixing two genres, the horror film and the Western. Modern-day deputy (Franc Luz) with a penchant for the Old West stumbles into a satanic netherworld: ghost town in the middle of the Arizona desert. Rated R for nudity, violence, and profanity. 85m. DIR: Richard Governor. CAST: Franc Luz, Catherine Hickland, Bruce Glover. 1988

GHOST TOWN LAW ★★★ Atmospheric B Western has the Rough Riders on the trail of a gang that murdered two of their colleagues. The gang, in a nice touch, hides out in a ghost town, where there might be more than just outlaws for our heroes to contend with. B&W; 62m. DIR: Howard Bretherton. CAST: Buck Jones, Tim McCoy, Raymond Hatton, Charles King. 1942

GHOST TOWN RENEGADES ★★★ Outlaws try to take over an abandoned mining town from its rightful owners. Lash's bullwhip dispenses its usual fast justice. B&W; 57m. DIR: Ray Taylor. CAST: Lash LaRue, Jack Ingram, Terry Frost. 1947

GHOST WALKS, THE ★★1/2 Actors rehearsing a play in a spooky old house get more than they planned on as an escaped lunatic is thrown into the mix. B&W; 65m. DIR: Frank Strayer. CAST: John Miljan, June Collyer, Richard Carle, Henry Kolker, Johnny Arthur. 1935

GHOST WARRIOR ★★1/2 In Japan, two skiers exploring a cave find a 400-year-old samurai warrior entombed in ice. He is taken to the United States in a hush-hush operation and revived. Although slow at times, this film is an entertaining, though violent, diversion. Rated R for violence. 86m. DIR: Larry Carbol. CAST: Hiroshi Fujioka, John Calvin, Janet Julian, Andy Wood. 1984

GHOST WRITER ★★ Harmless piece of fluff about a writer who moves into her new home only to find it haunted by an actress who was murdered and wants to find her killer. Lightweight. Rated PG for adult situations. 94m. DIR: Kenneth J. Hall. CAST: Audrey Landers, Judy Landers, Jeff Conaway, Joey Travolta, Dick Miller. 1989

GHOST, THE (1963) ★★★ Barbara Steele is a faithless wife who poisons her husband, only to have him return and exact revenge. Entertaining Italian gothic that's a sequel of sorts to the same director's *The Horrible Dr. Hitchcock*. A must for devotees of Italian chillers, with splendidly atmospheric camera work. 93m. DIR: Robert Hampton (Riccardo Freda). CAST: Barbara Steele, Peter Baldwin. 1963

GHOST (1990) ★★★ This generally diverting romantic-fantasy-comedy-drama casts Patrick Swayze as a murder victim who tries to protect his wife (Demi Moore) from his killers with the help of a psychic (Whoopi Goldberg). The scenes between Swayze and Moore are designed to be ultraromantic, Goldberg's scenes are played for laughs, and the crimes are hard-edged. Director Jerry Zucker isn't always successful in balancing so many elements and tones. Rated PG-13 for violence, suggested sex, and profanity. 105m. DIR: Jerry Zucker. CAST: Patrick Swayze, Demi Moore, Whoopi Goldberg, Tony Goldwyn. 1990

GHOSTBUSTERS ★★★★ Bill Murray, Dan Aykroyd, Sigourney Weaver, and Harold Ramis are terrific in this very funny and often frightening comedy-horror film about a special organization that fights evil spirits. Is it *The Exorcist* meets *Saturday Night Live*? That's pretty close—but it's better. Rated PG for profanity and scary scenes. 107m. DIR: Ivan Reitman. CAST: Bill Murray, Dan Aykroyd, Sigourney Weaver, Harold Ramis, Annie Potts, Ernie Hudson, William Atherton, Rick Moranis. 1984 DVD

GHOSTBUSTERS II ★★1/2 In this watchable sequel to the 1984 box-office blockbuster, the original cast returns to take on an explosion of evil spirits on a fateful New Year's Eve. The formula now seems fairly tired, despite some funny moments at the outset. Older kids are more likely to enjoy the shenanigans than adults. Rated PG. 110m. DIR: Ivan Reitman. CAST: Bill Murray, Dan Aykroyd, Sigourney Weaver, Harold Ramis, Rick Moranis, Ernie Hudson, Annie Potts. 1989 DVD

GHOSTRIDERS ★★ Just before being hanged in 1886, a notorious criminal puts a curse on the preacher responsible for his execution. One hundred years later he and his gang return to wreak vengeance on the preacher's descendants. Rated R for violence and language. 85m. DIR: Alan L. Stewart. CAST: Bill Shaw. 1987

GHOSTS CAN'T DO IT ★★ Bo knows breast exposure. Too bad hubby-director John doesn't know anything about making a coherent or even moderately funny movie. Anthony Quinn is Bo's dead husband who appears to her somewhere in the sky, which is a guess because the two only appear on the screen together at the very beginning. Poor ghost effects don't help. Rated R for nudity and profanity. 95m. DIR: John Derek. CAST: Bo Derek, Anthony Quinn, Don Murray, Julie Newmar, Leo Damian. 1990

GHOSTS OF BERKELEY SQUARE ★★1/2 After accidentally killing themselves while plotting to murder a superior officer, two British officers are condemned to haunt an old mansion until it is visited by royalty. Routine ghost comedy made palatable by a good cast. B&W; 85m. DIR: Vernon Sewell. CAST: Robert Morley, Felix Aylmer, Ernest Thesiger, Wilfrid Hyde-White. 1947

GHOSTS OF MISSISSIPPI ★★ This rehash of the 1963 slaying of civil-rights activist Medgar Evers and the trial 30 years later that puts accused killer Byron De La Beckwith behind bars is more pat and dry than dramatic. The film is not so much about the NAACP official who was shot in the back in his own driveway, but rather the white district attorney who reopens the case just as his marriage to an old money southern belle collapses. Rated PG-13 for violence and language. 123m. **DIR:** Rob Reiner. **CAST:** Alec Baldwin, James Woods, Whoopi Goldberg, Craig T. Nelson, William H. Macy, Susann Thompson. **1996 DVD**

GHOSTS ON THE LOOSE ✔ Silly movie pits moronic East Side Kids against a bored Bela Lugosi and his German henchmen in this pallid variation on the "old haunted house" theme. B&W; 65m. **DIR:** William Beaudine. **CAST:** The East Side Kids, Bela Lugosi, Ava Gardner, Rick Vallin. **1943**

GHOUL, THE (1933) ★★1/2 Trading on the success he achieved in *Frankenstein* and *The Mummy*, Boris Karloff plays an Egyptologist seeking eternal life through a special jewel. He dies and the jewel is stolen, bringing him back from the dead to seek revenge on the thief. B&W; 73m. **DIR:** T. Hayes Hunter. **CAST:** Boris Karloff, Cedric Hardwicke, Ernest Thesiger, Ralph Richardson, Kathleen Harrison. **1933**

GHOUL, THE (1975) ★★1/2 "Stay out of the garden, dear, there's a flesh-eating monster living there." One of Peter Cushing's many horror films. No gore, but not boring, either. Rated R. 88m. **DIR:** Freddie Francis. **CAST:** Peter Cushing, John Hurt, Gwen Watford. **1975**

GHOUL SCHOOL ✔ Move over, Ed Wood; this could just be the worst movie ever made as students are turned into zombies. Not rated; contains violence, nudity, profanity, gore, and simulated sex. 90m. **DIR:** Tim O'Rawe. **CAST:** Joe Franklin, Nancy Sirianni, Jackie Martling. **1990**

GHOULIES ✔ Gruesome. Rated PG-13 for violence and sexual innuendo. 87m. **DIR:** Luca Bercovici. **CAST:** Peter Liapis, Lisa Pelikan, John Nance. **1985**

GHOULIES II ✔ Dreadful sequel that dramatizes the further adventures of those mischievous little demons. Rated PG-13 for violence. 89m. **DIR:** Albert Band. **CAST:** Damon Martin, Royal Dano. **1987**

GHOULIES III ✔ Third chapter in the series finds the ghoulish slime-balls creating havoc at a local university. Like this movie, they flunk out! Rated R for violence. 94m. **DIR:** John Carl Buechler. **CAST:** Kevin McCarthy, Evan Mackenzie. **1989**

GHOULIES IV ✔ This series about pesky little creatures summoned up by black magic got real old even before the first chapter came out. Rated R for mayhem. 84m. **DIR:** Jim Wynorski. **CAST:** Peter Liapis, Barbara Alyn Woods, Stacie Randall, Bobby DiCicco. **1993**

GIANT ★★★1/2 The third part of director George Stevens's American Trilogy, which also included *Shane* and *A Place in the Sun*, this 1956 release traces the life of a cattle rancher through two generations. Although the lead performances by Elizabeth Taylor, Rock Hudson, and James Dean are unconvincing when the stars are poorly "aged" with makeup, *Giant* is still a stylish, if overlong movie that lives up to its title. 198m. **DIR:** George Stevens. **CAST:** James Dean, Rock Hudson, Elizabeth Taylor, Carroll Baker, Dennis Hopper. **1956**

GIANT BEHEMOTH, THE ★★1/2 A dinosaur attacks London in what is a virtual remake of the same director's *Beast from 20,000 Fathoms*. The animated

monster by Willis O'Brien (the original *King Kong*) isn't bad, but he was clearly working with a low budget. B&W; 79m. **DIR:** Eugene Lourie. **CAST:** Gene Evans, Andre Morell, Jack MacGowran. **1959**

GIANT CLAW, THE ✔ A must-see for bad-movie buffs, this sci-fi thriller pitting air force jets against a prehistoric bird features a puppet monster so tacky you'll love it. 76m. **DIR:** Fred F. Sears. **CAST:** Jeff Morrow, Mara Corday, Morris Ankrum (Stepen Morris). **1957**

GIANT FROM THE UNKNOWN ✔ Legendary conquistador buried for centuries in the mountains of California comes to life and continues his cruel ways until archaeologists devise a way to end him. B&W; 77m. **DIR:** Richard Cunha. **CAST:** Ed Kemmer, Sally Fraser, Buddy Baer, Morris Ankrum (Stepen Morris), Bob Steele. **1958**

GIANT GILA MONSTER, THE ✔ Slimy, slow-moving monster lizard prowls the Texas countryside. B&W; 74m. **DIR:** Ray Kellogg. **CAST:** Don Sullivan. **1959**

GIANT OF METROPOLIS, THE ★★1/2 This above-average sword-and-sandal adventure has nothing to do with Fritz Lang's silent classic, *Metropolis*, despite title similarities. Set in 10,000 B.C., it's about a mythical strongman (Gordon Mitchell) who emerges from the desert to battle a sadistic despot. 82m. **DIR:** Umberto Scarpelli. **CAST:** Gordon Mitchell. **1962**

GIANT ROBO ★★★★ Broadly played and beautifully drawn, this Japanese animated series blends the feel of traditional Saturday matinee serials with today's best animation. Super villains and heroes (including the radio-controlled Giant Robo and his boy master) clash over the fate of the world. Absolutely stunning animation with delightful characters and action. Dubbed in English. Not rated, but suitable for most audiences. 55m. each **DIR:** Yasuhiro Imagawa. **1992**

GIDEON'S TRUMPET ★★★★ Henry Fonda is the chief delight in this factual account of Clarence Earl Gideon, who was thrown into prison in the early 1960s for a minor crime—and denied a legal counsel because he could not afford to pay for one. Gideon boned up on the laws of our land and concluded that everybody was entitled to a lawyer, whether or not such was affordable. This made-for-TV movie accurately follows Anthony Lewis's source book. Not rated; suitable for family viewing. 104m. **DIR:** Robert Collins. **CAST:** Henry Fonda, John Houseman, José Ferrer. **1980**

GIDGET ★★1/2 The eternal beach bunny, Gidget (Sandra Dee), becomes involved with Cliff Robertson in order to make the man she's infatuated with (James Darren) notice her. This is the first and the best of a subpar surfer series. 95m. **DIR:** Paul Wendkos. **CAST:** Sandra Dee, James Darren, Arthur O'Connell, Cliff Robertson, Doug McClure. **1959**

GIDGET GOES HAWAIIAN ★★ Everyone's favorite "girl-midget" (played here by Deborah Walley, taking over from Sandra Dee) returns to the screen in this inoffensive, brainless sequel to the 1959 box-office hit. 102m. **DIR:** Paul Wendkos. **CAST:** Deborah Walley, James Darren, Michael Callan, Carl Reiner, Peggy Cass, Eddie Foy Jr. **1961**

GIDGET GOES TO ROME ★★ The irrepressible beach bunny presses onward, if not upward, in this below-average sequel to *Gidget*. 101m. **DIR:** Paul Wendkos. **CAST:** Cindy Carol, James Darren, Jeff Donnell, Jessie Royce Landis. **1963**

GIFT, THE ★★★ A 55-year-old bank worker (Pierre Mondy) decides to take early retirement. So his coworkers give him an unusual gift, an expensive hooker (Clio Goldsmith), who is asked to seduce him without his knowing her profession. An amiable sex comedy that most adult viewers will find diverting. In French with English subtitles. Rated R for nudity and profanity. 105m. **DIR:** Michel Lang. **CAST:** Clio Goldsmith, Pierre Mondy, Claudia Cardinale. **1982**

•**GIFT OF LOVE: THE DANIEL HUFFMAN STORY** ★★★ This heartwarming tale chronicles the tough decision made by 17-year-old Daniel Huffman: to donate one of his kidneys to save his grandmother's life. Unfortunately, that also means the high-school football star will never play the game again; and may never get a scholarship to attend college. While the story is inspiring, there's not enough to make a decent movie, and so this made-for-cable effort winds up being a ninety-minute commercial for organ donation. Not rated; contains mild profanity. 93m. **DIR:** John Korty. **CAST:** Debbie Reynolds, Ed Marinaro, John Bourgeois, Dan MacDonald, Elden Henson. **2000**

GIFT OF LOVE, THE ★★ Inspired by, but bearing very little resemblance to, O. Henry's short-story masterpiece "The Gift of the Magi," this fluffy TV special features Marie Osmond and Timothy Bottoms as star-crossed lovers. Osmond's acting skills are minimal, but her turn-of-the-century gowns are splendid. 96m. **DIR:** Don Chaffey. **CAST:** Marie Osmond, Timothy Bottoms, James Woods, June Lockhart. **1978**

GIG, THE ★★★ Very nicely done comedy-drama concerning a group of men who get together once a week to play Dixieland jazz. Film admirably avoids the clichés associated with this type of buddy film. Nice ensemble acting, with Cleavon Little and Joe Silver leading the way. Give this one a try. 92m. **DIR:** Frank D. Gilroy. **CAST:** Wayne Rogers, Cleavon Little, Joe Silver, Andrew Duncan, Daniel Nalbach. **1985**

GIGASHADOW ★★ The further adventures of the *Lexx*, a gigantic living spaceship, and its bizarre crew. For fans of the *Lexx* series only. Rated R for violence and sexuality. 93m. **DIR:** Robert Sigl. **CAST:** Malcolm McDowell, Brian Downey, Eva Habermann, Michael McManus, Michael Habeck. **1997**

GIGI ★★★★ Young Leslie Caron, being groomed as a courtesan, has more serious romance (with Louis Jourdan) on her mind. This exquisite Lerner-Loewe confection won nine Oscars and was the last nugget from the Golden Age of MGM Musicals. Maurice Chevalier and Hermione Gingold lend an unforgettable touch of class. 116m. **DIR:** Vincente Minnelli. **CAST:** Leslie Caron, Louis Jourdan, Maurice Chevalier, Hermione Gingold, Jacques Bergerac, Eva Gabor. **1958** **DVD**

G.I. BLUES ★★★1/2 Juliet Prowse improves this otherwise average Elvis Presley film. The action takes place in Germany, where Elvis makes a bet with his GI buddies he can date the aloof Prowse, who plays a nightclub dancer. 104m. **DIR:** Norman Taurog. **CAST:** Elvis Presley, Juliet Prowse. **1960** **DVD**

G.I. JANE ★★★★ Demi Moore demonstrates true grit in this testosterone-laden tale of Lt. Jordan O'Neil, the nation's first female officer allowed to participate in Navy SEAL training. Minimizing this character's stridency or "Joan of Arc" tendencies, results in a well-balanced story about a capable and intelligent young woman fighting for the chance to demonstrate her skills. While hardly the last word on basic training, this film introduces several intriguing characters, from a poetry-quoting training chief to a foxy U.S. senator, who may not be as dedicated a sponsor as O'Neil believes. Rated R for profanity, violence, and brief nudity. 125m. **DIR:** Ridley Scott. **CAST:** Demi Moore, Viggo Mortensen, Anne Bancroft, Jason Beghe, Daniel Von Bargen, John Michael Higgins. **1997** **DVD**

GILDA ★★★★ Glenn Ford plays a small-time gambler who goes to work for a South American casino owner and his beautiful wife, Gilda (Rita Hayworth). When the casino owner disappears and is presumed dead, Ford marries Hayworth and proceeds to make her life miserable. Then the husband returns, seeking revenge against them. There is some violence in this film. B&W; 110m. **DIR:** Charles Vidor. **CAST:** Glenn Ford, Rita Hayworth, George Macready, Joseph Calleia, Steven Geray. **1946**

GILDA LIVE ★★ We've always loved Gilda Radner's characters from *Saturday Night Live*, and they're all represented in *Gilda Live*. But something is missing in her live show. The result is very few laughs. Rated R. 96m. **DIR:** Mike Nichols. **CAST:** Gilda Radner, Don Novello, Paul Shaffer. **1980**

GIMME AN "F" 💣 Blame *Flashdance* for this tawdry little teen-exploitation flick concerned with a cheerleaders' competition. Rated R for nudity and language. 100m. **DIR:** Paul Justman. **CAST:** Stephen Shellen, Mark Keyloun, Jennifer Cooke, John Karlen, Daphne Ashbrook. **1984**

GIMME SHELTER ★★★★ This documentary chronicles the events leading up to and including the now-infamous free Rolling Stones concert in 1969 at the Altamont Speedway outside San Francisco. It's the dark side of Woodstock, with many unforgettable scenes, including the actual murder of a spectator by the Hell's Angels in front of the stage as the Stones are playing. Rated R for violence, language, and scenes of drug use. 91m. **DIR:** David Maysles, Albert Maysles, Charlotte Zwerin. **CAST:** The Rolling Stones, Melvin Belli. **1970**

GIN GAME, THE ★★★1/2 A sensitive, insightful, and touchingly funny, award-winning Broadway play taped live in London with its two original stars. The enchanting performances are highlighted with superb simplicity in this two-character play that explores the developing relationship between two senior citizens. Not rated, but freely sprinkled with profanity. 82m. **DIR:** Mike Nichols. **CAST:** Jessica Tandy, Hume Cronyn. **1984**

GINGER 💣 We don't want to say this is the best of the three films starring Cheri Caffaro as a socialite turned crime fighter—let's just say it's the least repulsive. Rated R for violence and nudity. 89m. DIR: Don Schain. CAST: Cheri Caffaro, Cindy Barnett. 1971

GINGER ALE AFTERNOON ❤ Tedious would-be comedy about a bickering couple. Rated R for profanity and brief nudity. 88m. DIR: Rafal Zielinski. CAST: Dana Andersen, John M. Jackson, Yeardley Smith. 1989

GINGER AND FRED ★★★ Set in the bizarre world of a modern-television supernetwork, this Fellini fantasy presents Giulietta Masina and Marcello Mastroianni as Ginger and Fred—a dance couple of the late Forties who copied the style of Fred Astaire and Ginger Rogers. The two are reunited for *Here's to You*, a television extravaganza. This is a brilliant satire of television and modern life. Rated PG-13 for profanity and adult themes. 127m. DIR: Federico Fellini. CAST: Marcello Mastroianni, Giulietta Masina, Franco Fabrizi. 1986

GINGER IN THE MORNING ★★1/2 A lonely salesman, Monte Markham, picks up a hitchhiker, Sissy Spacek, and romance blossoms in this okay romantic comedy. No great revelations about human nature will be found in this one, just harmless fluff that will be forgotten soon after it's been viewed. 89m. DIR: Gordon Wiles. CAST: Sissy Spacek, Monte Markham, Slim Pickens, Susan Oliver, Mark Miller. 1973

GINGERBREAD MAN, THE ★★1/2 Southern defense attorney Rick Magruder is hired by a sultry waitress to get her father committed to a mental institution. The apparently deranged elder escapes from custody and stalks Magruder's family. The acting in this atmospheric, melodramatic thriller about manipulation and lust is excellent. Rated R for language, violence, and nudity. 115m. DIR: Robert Altman. CAST: Kenneth Branagh, Embeth Davidtz, Robert Downey Jr., Robert Duvall, Daryl Hannah, Mae Whitman, Famke Janssen, Tom Berenger. 1998 DVD

GIRL, THE ★★★ A strange and disturbing European film analyzing the seduction of a powerful attorney by a 14-year-old schoolgirl. Lust, passion, and murder become the norm. Unfortunately, what might have been a very powerful film becomes slow and plods to the finish. Though no rating is available, there is ample sex and nudity throughout the film. 104m. DIR: Arne Mattson. CAST: Franco Nero, Bernice Stegers, Clare Powney, Christopher Lee. 1986

GIRL, A GUY AND A GOB, A ★★★ A silly, predictable comedy that tends to grow on you; it focuses on a working girl, her happy-go-lucky sailor boyfriend, and an upper-crust executive. Dated, of course, but cute and polished. Movie buffs will be interested to note the producer was legendary Harold Lloyd. Not rated; contains nothing offensive. B&W; 90m. DIR: Richard Wallace. CAST: Lucille Ball, George Murphy, Edmond O'Brien, Henry Travers. 1941

GIRL CAN'T HELP IT, THE ★★★ Tom Ewell is given the task of turning squealing Jayne Mansfield into a singer on the clear understanding that he keep his hands to himself, a tough request when faced with the would-be singer's winning ways and obvious charms. Great rock 'n' roll by some of its premier interpreters is the real reason for watching this film. 99m. DIR: Frank Tashlin. CAST: Tom Ewell, Jayne Mansfield, Edmond O'Brien, Julie London, Henry

Jones, Fats Domino, The Platters, The Treniers, Little Richard, Gene Vincent and His Blue Caps, Eddie Cochran, Barry Gordon, Ray Anthony, Nino Tempo, The Chuckles. 1957

GIRL CRAZY ★★★ Girls are driving the ever-ebullient Mickey Rooney bonkers. His family sends him to a small southwestern college, hoping the "craze" will fade, but he meets Judy Garland, and away we go into another happy kids-give-a-show musical with glorious George and Ira Gershwin tunes. B&W; 99m. DIR: Busby Berkeley, Norman Taurog. CAST: Mickey Rooney, Judy Garland, June Allyson, Rags Ragland, Guy Kibbee, Nancy Walker, Henry O'Neill. 1943

GIRL FROM HUNAN ★★★ At the turn of the century, a Chinese woman's arranged marriage and her place in decent society are threatened by her opposition to the accepted moral standards of her community. In Cantonese with English subtitles. Not rated. 99m. DIR: Xie Fei, U Lan. CAST: Na Renhua, Liu Qing, Deng Xiaotuang. 1988

GIRL FROM MISSOURI, THE ★★★★1/2 A delightful comedy that shows Jean Harlow's comedic style to advantage, this is the movie that gave censors headaches because it boldly and bluntly said that some women will do anything for money. B&W; 74m. DIR: Jack Conway. CAST: Jean Harlow, Franchot Tone, Patsy Kelly, Lewis Stone, Lionel Barrymore, Alan Mowbray, Nat Pendleton, Clara Blandick. 1934

GIRL FROM PETROVKA, THE ★★★ American journalist Hal Holbrook falls in love with Russian Goldie Hawn while on assignment in the Soviet Union. The manipulative script often becomes overly melodramatic, but the film still works as an effective tearjerker. Something about Hawn's guileless, resourceful character is impossible to resist, and the story's conclusion packs a surprising punch. Rated PG for adult situations. 104m. DIR: Robert Ellis Miller. CAST: Goldie Hawn, Hal Holbrook, Anthony Hopkins. 1974

GIRL FROM PHANTASIA ★★★ The title character is gatekeeper of another world who mistakenly crosses into ours in hopes of finding that love has finally returned. Instead, she finds a lecherous young man and a sorcerer sworn to destroy her world. A decent entry in the Japanese-animation genre. In Japanese with English subtitles. Not rated; contains violence and nudity. 40m. DIR: Jun Kamiya. 1994

GIRL HAPPY ★★★ This is *Where the Boys Are* in reverse, as Elvis plays chaperon to a Chicago mobster's daughter in Fort Lauderdale, Florida. While Elvis romances vixenish Mary Ann Mobley, his nerdish charge (Shelley Fabares) constantly gets into trouble with a sexy Italian. 96m. DIR: Boris Sagal. CAST: Elvis Presley, Shelley Fabares, Mary Ann Mobley. 1964

GIRL HUNTERS, THE ★★1/2 Mickey Spillane plays his creation Mike Hammer in this unusual detective film about a private eye who pulls himself together after a seven-year binge, when he discovers that the woman he thought he sent to her death might still be alive. Lloyd Nolan and Shirley Eaton are the only real actors in this uneven production—the rest of the cast are Spillane's cronies, and many of his favorite bars and hangouts are carefully re-created in this British-made film. 103m. DIR: Roy Rowland. CAST:

Mickey Spillane, Shirley Eaton, Lloyd Nolan, Hy Gardner, Scott Peters. **1963 DVD**

GIRL IN A SWING, THE ★★★1/2 In this atmospheric and sensual suspense-thriller, a young executive travels to Amsterdam, where he falls in love with a woman who may be a murderer. Rated R for nudity, profanity, and violence. 119m. **DIR:** Gordon Hessler. **CAST:** Meg Tilly, Rupert Frazer. **1989**

GIRL IN BLACK STOCKINGS, THE ★★1/2 Who's the mad killer stalking women at a Utah resort? So-so mystery. B&W; 71m. **DIR:** Howard W. Koch. **CAST:** Anne Bancroft, Lex Barker, Mamie Van Doren, John Dehner, Marie Windsor, Stuart Whitman. **1957**

GIRL IN BLUE, THE ★★1/2 Trifling romantic drama about a man obsessed with a woman he glimpsed fleetingly years before. Filmed in Montreal. Not rated, the movie contains brief nudity and sexual situations. 105m. **DIR:** George Kaczender. **CAST:** David Selby, Maud Adams. **1973**

GIRL IN EVERY PORT, A (1928) ★★★ Tough sailor with an eye for the ladies discovers a swaggering rival has been beating his time at all ports of call. Louise Brooks has quite a decision to make but she takes it in stride and follows her heart. Breezy, adult comedy-drama is fun to watch and filled with the little touches and interesting interplay between characters that would come to distinguish director Howard Hawks's sound films. B&W; 79m. **DIR:** Howard Hawks. **CAST:** Victor McLaglen, Robert Armstrong, Louise Brooks, Leila Hyams, Francis McDonald. **1928**

GIRL IN EVERY PORT, A (1952) ★★ Silly film about sailors involved in horse-racing scheme milks the old hide-the-horse-on-the-ship gag for all that it's worth (which isn't much) and then some. B&W; 86m. **DIR:** Chester Erskine. **CAST:** Groucho Marx, William Bendix, Marie Wilson, Don DeFore, Gene Lockhart. **1952**

GIRL IN THE CADILLAC ★★ An innocent woman inadvertently becomes involved with a trio of bank robbers, falling for one of them. Tolerable if unexceptional comedy-action-romance. Rated R for profanity, violence, and brief nudity. 89m. **DIR:** Lucas Platt. **CAST:** Erika Eleniak, William McNamara, Michael Lerner, Bud Cort. **1995**

GIRL IN THE PICTURE, THE ★★★ A slight but charming movie from Scotland. John Gordon Sinclair plays a Glasgow photographer who's feeling stagnant in his relationship with his design-student girlfriend. The problems they face are never dealt with, but it doesn't seem to matter because the going with this amusing pair is so enjoyable. Rated PG. 90m. **DIR:** Cary Parker. **CAST:** Gordon John Sinclair, Irina Brook, David McKay, Gregor Fisher, Paul Young, Rikki Fulton. **1985**

•GIRL, INTERRUPTED ★★★1/2 This adaptation of Susanna Kaysen's memoir aspires to be a feminine response to *One Flew Over the Cuckoo's Nest*, and to the degree that it involves stars Winona Ryder and Angelina Jolie (Oscar winner), that ambition is fulfilled. But the other residents of fictitious Claymore Institute, which stands in for the facility where Kaysen voluntarily committed herself in the 1960s, emerge as little more than stereotypes and stick fig-

ures; and some of these women are even held up for the ridicule of cheap laughs. This film should be a quiet classic along the lines of *I Never Promised You a Rose Garden*, but Mangold's superficial handling and the "girls just wanna have fun" atmosphere prove damaging. Rated R for profanity, brief nudity, and dramatic intensity. 125m. **DIR:** James Mangold. **CAST:** Winona Ryder, Angelina Jolie, Clea DuVall, Brittany Murphy, Elizabeth Moss, Jared Leto, Jeffrey Tambor. **1999 DVD**

GIRL MOST LIKELY, THE ★★★1/2 This musical, a remake of *Tom, Dick and Harry*, succeeds because it's light and breezy. The choreography is by the late Gower Champion and is wonderful to watch. This is a fine film for the entire family. 98m. **DIR:** Mitchell Leisen. **CAST:** Jane Powell, Cliff Robertson, Tommy Noonan, Una Merkel. **1957**

GIRL OF THE GOLDEN WEST, THE ★★1/2 Jeanette MacDonald is an 1850s saloon owner attracted to bold bandit Nelson Eddy in this sloppy, hitless musical version of a 1905 play (better done by Puccini). B&W; 120m. **DIR:** Robert Z. Leonard. **CAST:** Jeanette MacDonald, Nelson Eddy, Walter Pidgeon, Leo Carrillo, Buddy Ebsen, Monty Woolley, H. B. Warner, Charley Grapewin. **1938**

GIRL RUSH ★★1/2 Mildly amusing comedy about vaudeville performers who attempt to stage a show called *The Frisco Follies* for a group of miners. Their efforts are met with resistance by a menacing gambler played by Robert Mitchum. B&W; 65m. **DIR:** Gordon Douglas. **CAST:** Robert Mitchum, Frances Langford, Wally Brown. **1944**

GIRL 6 ★★ Out-of-work actress Theresa Randle takes a job as a phone-sex operator and becomes obsessed with the work and some of her unseen clients. There are good performances, with several star cameos, but the film staggers back and forth between melodrama and racy comedy, never settling on a style or clearly developing a theme. Rated R for profanity and suggested sex. 109m. **DIR:** Spike Lee. **CAST:** Theresa Randle, Isaiah Washington, Spike Lee, Debi Mazar, Peter Berg. **1996**

GIRL TO KILL FOR, A ❤🗡 A sociopathic heiress manipulates a naïve college student into killing her strict guardian. Rated R for nudity, profanity, and violence. 89m. **DIR:** Richard Oliver. **CAST:** Karen Medak, Sasha Jeason, Karen Austin, Alex Cord, Rod McCary. **1990**

GIRL WHO HAD EVERYTHING, THE ★★ A dated melodrama obviously produced to capitalize on Elizabeth Taylor's beauty. She plays the daughter of a lawyer, and she falls in love with a criminal her father is slated to defend in court. Good performances; weak script. B&W; 69m. **DIR:** Richard Thorpe. **CAST:** Elizabeth Taylor, William Powell, Fernando Lamas, Gig Young, James Whitmore. **1953**

GIRL WHO SPELLED FREEDOM, THE ★★★★1/2 Disney does an excellent job of adapting the Yann family's true story, dramatizing their flight from Cambodia to find refuge with a Tennessee family. Made for TV, this fine film is unrated. 90m. **DIR:** Simon Wincer. **CAST:** Wayne Rogers, Mary Kay Place, Jade Chinn, Kathleen Sisk. **1985**

•**GIRL WITH A SUITCASE** ★★★★ A singer quits her job to follow her lover, who eventually jilts her. She then falls in love with his teenage brother, who returns her affection even though she knows it can never work. This hackneyed plot succeeds thanks to sensitive writing and first-rate performances by Claudia Cardinale and Jacques Perrin as the young lovers. In Italian with English subtitles. B&W; 111m. **DIR:** Valerio Zurlini. **CAST:** Claudia Cardinale, Jacques Perrin, Gian Maria Volontè. 1961

GIRL WITH THE HATBOX, THE ★★ A greedy big-faced employer gives his employee a lottery ticket instead of wages. She wins and is then plagued with advances from her boss. Slapstick, postrevolution esoterica. Silent. B&W; 67m. **DIR:** Boris Barnet. **CAST:** Anna Sten, Vladimir Fogel. 1927

GIRL WITH THE HUNGRY EYES, THE ★★ Annoyingly ambiguous thriller tells the story of a dead model (she committed suicide thirty years earlier) who returns to drain the blood of the living. Rated R for nudity, violence, and horror. 85m. **DIR:** Jon Jacobs. **CAST:** Christina Fulton, Isaac Turner, Leon Herbert, Bret Carr. 1993

GIRLFRIEND FROM HELL ★★★1/2 A painfully shy girl becomes the life—and death—of the party when she is possessed by the devil. Inventive low-budget comedy. Rated R for sexual situations and profanity. 92m. **DIR:** Daniel M. Paterson. **CAST:** Liane Curtis, Dana Ashbrook, James Daughton. 1989

GIRLFRIENDS ★★★★ Realistic film about a young Jewish woman who learns to make it on her own after her best friend/roommate leaves to get married. Melanie Mayron's performance is the highlight of this touching and offbeat comedy drama. Rated PG. 88m. **DIR:** Claudia Weill. **CAST:** Melanie Mayron, Anita Skinner, Eli Wallach, Christopher Guest, Viveca Lindfors. 1978

GIRLS ARE FOR LOVING 💔 The last of the *Ginger* films, with stripper Ginger (Cheri Caffaro) battling international bad guys in her spare time. Rated R for nudity, violence, and simulated sex. 90m. **DIR:** Don Schain. **CAST:** Cheri Caffaro, Timothy Brown. 1973

GIRLS! GIRLS! GIRLS! ★★ In this musical-comedy, Elvis Presley is chased by an endless array of beautiful girls. Sounds like the ideal situation? Not for poor Elvis as he tries to choose just one. 105m. **DIR:** Norman Taurog. **CAST:** Elvis Presley, Stella Stevens, Benson Fong, Laurel Goodwin, Jeremy Slate. 1962

GIRLS IN PRISON ★★ Pointless remake of the 1956 film that has only the slithery performance of Anne Heche to recommend it. Otherwise, it's just bad camp noir. Rated R for profanity, violence, and nudity. 83m. **DIR:** John McNaughton. **CAST:** Anne Heche, Ione Skye, Missy Crider. 1994

GIRLS JUST WANT TO HAVE FUN 💔 Sarah Jessica Parker stars as a young woman who just *lovoves* to dance. Rated PG for profanity. 90m. **DIR:** Alan Metter. **CAST:** Sarah Jessica Parker, Lee Montgomery, Morgan Woodward, Jonathan Silverman. 1985

GIRLS OF HUNTINGTON HOUSE ★★ With Shirley Jones as the teacher in a halfway house for unwed young mothers-to-be, this made-for-TV story explores the plight of a group of young women trying to

make a most difficult decision. Simplistic dialogue and plot developments help to water down the impact of this one. 73m. **DIR:** Alf Kjellin. **CAST:** Shirley Jones, Sissy Spacek, Mercedes McCambridge, Pamela Sue Martin. 1973

GIRLS TOWN (1959) ★★ It overstays its welcome by about 15 minutes, but this trash opus about a bad girl (Mamie Van Doren) sent to a prison farm is otherwise a laugh riot. And what a cast! The Platters supply some musical numbers. B&W; 92m. **DIR:** Charles Haas. **CAST:** Mamie Van Doren, Mel Torme, Paul Anka, Ray Anthony, Maggie Hayes, Cathy Crosby, Gigi Perreau, Gloria Talbott, Jim Mitchum, Elinor Donahue, Sheilah Graham. 1959

GIRLS TOWN (1996) ★★1/2 Three high-school classmates react with shock and anger to the suicide of a fourth friend. Director Jim McKay and Denise Casano developed the script from improvisations with the three lead actresses, and their scenes have energy and bite. Minor characters, though, are not so well developed, and scenes involving them seem forced and lack conviction. Rated R for profanity. 90m. **DIR:** Jim McKay. **CAST:** Lili Taylor, Bruklin Harris, Anna Grace, Aunjanue Ellis. 1996

GIRLY 💔 A bizarre tale about the killing exploits of a demented English family. Rated R for suggested sex. 101m. **DIR:** Freddie Francis. **CAST:** Vanessa Howard, Michael Bryant, Ursula Howells, Pat Heywood, Robert Swann. 1987

GIT ALONG, LITTLE DOGIES ★★ Typical of Gene Autry's prewar films, this thin story of a spoiled, willful girl who is eventually tamed and socialized by the silver-voiced cowboy is heavy on the music and singing stars. B&W; 60m. **DIR:** Joseph Kane. **CAST:** Gene Autry, Smiley Burnette, Judith Allen, William Farnum. 1937

GIVE A GIRL A BREAK ★★ This somewhat hackneyed story of three would-be's vying to replace a star when she quits a Broadway show is nice, passes the time, but lacks stature. 82m. **DIR:** Stanley Donen. **CAST:** Debbie Reynolds, Marge Champion, Gower Champion, Kurt Kasznar, Bob Fosse, Helen Wood, Lurene Tuttle. 1953

GIVE 'EM HELL, HARRY! ★★★★ This is the film version of James Whitmore's wonderful portrayal of President Harry S. Truman. Taken from the stage production, the film is a magnificent tribute and entertainment. Rated PG. 102m. **DIR:** Steve Binder. **CAST:** James Whitmore. 1975

GIVE ME A SAILOR ★★★ Light and breezy romantic comedy starring Bob Hope and Jack Whiting as two sailors in love with the same woman. The woman's ugly-duckling sister agrees to help Hope land her, in exchange for Hope's helping the sister land Whiting. Lots of lunacy and slapstick follow as the ugly duckling becomes a swan, turning the tables on everyone. B&W; 78m. **DIR:** Elliott Nugent. **CAST:** Bob Hope, Martha Raye, Betty Grable, Jack Whiting. 1938

GIVE MY REGARDS TO BROAD STREET ★★ Paul McCartney wrote and stars in this odd, but not really offensive, combination of great rock music and a truly insipid story as a rock singer who loses the master tapes for his album and finds his future seriously threatened. Forget the story and enjoy the songs. Rated PG for mild violence. 108m. DIR: Peter Webb. CAST: Paul McCartney, Ringo Starr, Barbara Bach, Linda McCartney. 1984

GLADIATOR, THE (1986) (TELEVISION) ★★ Competent but attenuated TV film about a mechanic (Ken Wahl) who goes on the vengeance trail after his younger brother is killed by a deranged DUI. Some of the drama works, but often the narrative becomes repetitious. 94m. DIR: Abel Ferrara. CAST: Ken Wahl, Nancy Allen, Robert Culp, Stan Shaw, Rosemary Forsyth, Bart Braverman. 1986

GLADIATOR (1992) ★★★ A middle-class kid moves to the tough South Side of Chicago, where he gets involved with the world of illegal underground boxing. Some down-and-dirty fight scenes and the presence of character actors Brian Dennehy, Robert Loggia, and Ossie Davis make this film more than a clone of *Rocky*. Rated R for violence, profanity, and nudity. 98m. DIR: Rowdy Herrington. CAST: James Marshall, Cuba Gooding Jr., Robert Loggia, Ossie Davis, Brian Dennehy, John Heard. 1992

•GLADIATOR (2000) ★★★★ This ambitious Roman Empire action epic recounts the tale of a virtuous and earnest fighting man, devoted to his country and its ideals, who is betrayed by those loyal only to themselves and political ambition. Russell Crowe stars as the wronged Maximus, who is made a slave after his noble emperor is murdered by the man's greedy son, who then appoints himself emperor and initiates the events that will lead to the fall of Rome. Maximus wants only to return to Rome, where he hopes to kill the vile and depraved creep. The gladitorial games are sensational, the computer-enhanced re-creation of Rome's glory breathtaking. Rated R for constant, bloody violence and strongly suggested sexual deviancy. 154m. DIR: Ridley Scott. CAST: Russell Crowe, Joaquin Phoenix, Connie Nielsen, Oliver Reed, Richard Harris, Derek Jacobi, Djimon Hounsou. 2000

•GLADIATOR COP II: THE SWORDSMAN ★★ An ex-cop and a man who believes himself to be Alexander the Great among others battle for control of a mythical sword. Passable action-fantasy is held up by decent acting and stunt work, but holds little interest in the way of story. Rated R for violence. 85m. DIR: Nick Rotundo. CAST: Lorenzo Lamas, Frank Alexander, James Hong. 1995

GLASS BOTTOM BOAT, THE ★★★ Doris Day is hired by amorous scientist Rod Taylor as his biographer. Slapstick complications arise when she is suspected of being a Russian spy. 110m. DIR: Frank Tashlin. CAST: Doris Day, Rod Taylor, Arthur Godfrey, Paul Lynde, Dom DeLuise. 1966

GLASS CAGE, THE ★★★ Erotic thriller is the story of a former CIA agent (Richard Tyson) who finds himself in New Orleans, searching for his ex-lover. He finds her but winds up enmeshed with nasty mob types and corrupt cops. Stylish. Rated R for violence, nudity, and sexual situations. 96m. DIR: Michael Schroeder. CAST: Charlotte Lewis, Richard Tyson, Stephen Nichols, Joseph Campanella, Richard Moll, Eric Roberts. 1996

GLASS HOUSE, THE ★★★★ This powerful prison drama is based on a story by Truman Capote. An idealistic new prison guard (Clu Gulager) is overwhelmed by the gang violence within the prison. Alan Alda plays a new prisoner who becomes the target of a violent gang leader (Vic Morrow). R for sex and violence. 89m. DIR: Tom Gries. CAST: Vic Morrow, Clu Gulager, Billy Dee Williams, Dean Jagger, Alan Alda. 1972 DVD

GLASS KEY, THE ★★★★ Solid version of Dashiell Hammett's excellent novel has Alan Ladd as the bodyguard to politician Brian Donlevy, who is accused of murder. It's up to Ladd to get him off, and he has to take on vicious gangsters to get the job done. Fine work by everyone involved makes this a cinematic gem. B&W; 85m. DIR: Stuart Heisler. CAST: Brian Donlevy, Alan Ladd, Veronica Lake, William Bendix. 1942

GLASS MENAGERIE, THE ★★★★ Director Paul Newman made this impressive screen drama to immortalize wife Joanne Woodward's excellent portrayal of faded southern belle Amanda Winfield, whose strong opinions tend to make her adventure-hungry son (John Malkovich) miserable, and drive her shy daughter (Karen Allen) deeper within herself. This is the best film version to date of Tennessee Williams's semiautobiographical play. Rated PG. 134m. DIR: Paul Newman. CAST: Joanne Woodward, John Malkovich, Karen Allen, James Naughton. 1987

GLASS SHIELD, THE ★★★ An ambitious yet over-obvious and uninvolving look at corruption in a southern California sheriff's station, as seen through the conflicted, morally compromised eyes of a naive black rookie. Rated PG-13 for violence. 107m. DIR: Charles Burnett. CAST: Michael Patrick Boatman, Lori Petty, Ice Cube, Elliott Gould, Richard Anderson, Michael Ironside, Bernie Casey. 1995

GLASS SLIPPER, THE ★★1/2 The supporting players steal the spotlight from the leads, throwing this musical version of *Cinderella* off balance. The ballet scenes are beautifully staged to make it worth seeing for dance enthusiasts, but others may be bored. Estelle Winwood is especially good as the fairy godmother. An unusual musical, but not a memorable one. 94m. DIR: Charles Walters. CAST: Leslie Caron, Michael Wilding, Estelle Winwood, Keenan Wynn, Elsa Lanchester, Barry Jones, Lurene Tuttle, Amanda Blake, Lisa Daniels. 1955

GLEAMING THE CUBE ★★★ Better-than-average murder-mystery aimed at the teenage crowd. Christian Slater stars as a skateboard ace who kick starts a murder investigation when his adopted Vietnamese brother is found hanged in a motel. Spectacular, exciting skateboard stunts and an appealing performance by Slater help glide over the holes in the plot. Rated PG-13. 104m. DIR: Graeme Clifford. CAST: Christian Slater, Steven Bauer, Richard Herd, Ed Lauter. 1989 DVD

GLEN AND RANDA ★★★ As with all cult films, this will not appeal to everyone. The film, at times thought-provoking, is both depressing and satirical. Two young people, Glen (Steve Curry) and Randa (Shelley Plimpton), set out on a search for knowledge across postholocaust America. Rated R for nudity and violence. 94m. **DIR:** Jim McBride. **CAST:** Steven Curry, Shelley Plimpton, Woodrow Chambliss, Garry Goodrow. 1986

GLEN OR GLENDA ★★ Incredible film by the incomparably *inept* Edward D. Wood Jr., tells the powerful story of a young transvestite who finally summons up the courage to come out of the closet and ask his fiancée if he can wear her sweater. B&W; 67m. **DIR:** Edward D. Wood Jr. **CAST:** Bela Lugosi, Dolores Fuller, Daniel Davis, Lyle Talbot, Timothy Farrell, George Weiss. 1953 DVD

GLENGARRY GLEN ROSS ★★★★★ Powerhouse performances and a blistering script highlight David Mamet's adaptation of his own Pulitzer-winning stage play, set during 24 frantic hours in the lives of four rapacious real estate salesmen. Al Pacino and Jack Lemmon are the two central players, the former a relaxed "closer" able to entice anybody into anything, the latter increasingly frantic over a lengthy bad streak. Rated R for relentless profanity. 120m. **DIR:** James Foley. **CAST:** Al Pacino, Jack Lemmon, Ed Harris, Alan Arkin, Kevin Spacey, Jonathan Pryce, Alec Baldwin. 1992

GLENN MILLER STORY, THE ★★★1/2 Follows the life story of famous trombonist and bandleader Glenn Miller, who disappeared in a plane during World War II. Jimmy Stewart delivers a convincing portrayal of the popular bandleader whose music had all of America tapping its feet. Miller's appearances is the highlight of the film, with guest appearances by Louis Armstrong and Gene Krupa. 113m. **DIR:** Anthony Mann. **CAST:** James Stewart, June Allyson, Charles Drake, Harry Morgan, Frances Langford, Gene Krupa, Louis Armstrong. 1954

GLIMMER MAN, THE ★★★1/2 Steven Seagal is a student of Eastern philosophy and a top-notch detective imported from New York to Los Angeles to help catch a serial killer known as the Family Man. Keenen Ivory Wayans is the local detective assigned to the case, who resents being teamed with a mysticism-spouting know-it-all. Their chemistry makes the convoluted story work. Rated R for profanity and violence. 92m. **DIR:** John Gray. **CAST:** Steven Seagal, Keenen Ivory Wayans, Bob Gunton, Brian Cox, Michelle Johnson, John Jackson, Stephen Tobolowsky. 1996 DVD

GLITCH! 💗 Inane comedy features two bumbling burglars posing as sleazy filmmakers. Rated R for nudity and profanity. 88m. **DIR:** Nico Mastorakis. **CAST:** Julia Nickson, Will Egan, Steve Donmyer, Dick Gautier, Ted Lange. 1988 DVD

GLITTER DOME, THE ★★1/2 Made-for-HBO cable version of Joseph Wambaugh's depressingly downbeat story concerning two police detectives in Los Angeles, James Garner and John Lithgow, out to solve a murder. Both cops appear on the edge of losing control. 90m. **DIR:** Stuart Margolin. **CAST:** James Garner, Margot Kidder, John Lithgow, Colleen Dewhurst, John Marley. 1985

GLITZ 💗 Drearily botched TV adaptation of excellent Elmore Leonard crime novel, with Jimmy Smits ineffective as Miami Beach detective. 96m. **DIR:** Sandor Stern. **CAST:** Jimmy Smits, Markie Post, John Diehl. 1988

GLOBAL AFFAIR, A ★★1/2 When a child is abandoned at the United Nations, all nation members put in a claim for custody. Nothing much. B&W; 84m. **DIR:** Jack Arnold. **CAST:** Bob Hope, Michele Mercier, Robert Sterling, Lilo Pulver, Elga Andersen, Yvonne De Carlo. 1964

GLORIA (1980) ★★★1/2 After his family is executed by the Mafia, a little boy hides out with a female neighbor. Together they must flee or be killed. Gena Rowlands is very good in the title role as the streetwise Gloria, whose savvy and brains keep the two alive. Rated R—language, violence. 121m. **DIR:** John Cassavetes. **CAST:** Gena Rowlands, Buck Henry, John Adames, Julie Carmen, Lupe Guarnica. 1980

GLORIA (1999) ★★1/2 A gangster's moll shelters a boy when his parents are murdered and both wind up running from the mob. This tolerable but unnecessary remake of John Cassavetes's 1980 melodrama showcases a cheerfully hammy Sharon Stone trying to fill the shoes of the redoubtable Gena Rowlands. Rated R for profanity and violence. 108m. **DIR:** Sidney Lumet. **CAST:** Sharon Stone, Jeremy Northam, Cathy Moriarty, Jean-Luke Figueroa, Mike Starr, George C. Scott, Sarita Choudhury. 1999 DVD

GLORIANA ★★★1/2 Written by Benjamin Britten to celebrate the coronation of Queen Elizabeth II, this opera is the love story of Elizabeth I and the Earl of Essex. A beautiful production filmed for TV. 146m. **DIR:** Derek Bailey. **CAST:** Sarah Walker, Anthony Rolfe Johnson. 1984

GLORIFYING THE AMERICAN GIRL ★★1/2 The only film produced by legendary showman Florenz Ziegfeld, this dreary backstage rags-to-riches story reeked of mothballs even in 1929. Recognizing that, Ziegfeld padded it out with Follies production numbers that provide the only reason to watch this. Highlights are an Eddie Cantor skit, a bevy of celebrity cameos, and torch singer Helen Morgan giving her all on "What I Wouldn't Do for That Man." B&W; 95m. **DIR:** Millard Webb. **CAST:** Mary Eaton, Edward Crandall, Eddie Cantor, Helen Morgan. 1929

GLORY ★★★★★ If nothing else, *Glory* rights a terrible wrong. It brings to light the fact that black soldiers fought valiantly on the side of the Union during the Civil War. Yet this excellent film is more than an important lesson in history; it is also a fully involving antiwar movie blessed with unforgettable scenes and scintillating actors (including Oscar recipient Denzel Washington). Rated R for violence and brief profanity. 202m. **DIR:** Edward Zwick. **CAST:** Matthew Broderick, Denzel Washington, Cary Elwes, Morgan Freeman. 1989 DVD

GLORY AT SEA ★★ Typical British salute to those who fought in World War II—Trevor Howard, the captain of a decrepit battleship, wins the respect of his men while under fire. B&W; 90m. **DIR:** Compton Bennett. **CAST:** Trevor Howard, Richard Attenborough, Sonny Tufts, James Donald. 1952

GLORY BOYS, THE ★★1/2 A many-sided Middle Eastern, terrorist/counterterrorist plot and counterplot. Solid production values, but the overfamiliar scenario is a waste. No rating but contains violence and profanity. 130m. **DIR:** Michael Ferguson. **CAST:**

Rod Steiger, Anthony Perkins, Alfred Burke, Joanna Lumley. 1984

GLORY! GLORY! ★★★1/2 Marvelously irreverent spoof of television evangelism features Richard Thomas as the dedicated but boring successor to his father's multi-million-dollar church. Thomas hires delightfully saucy Ellen Greene, a hard-core rock 'n' roll singer, to be Sister Ruth. Made for cable. 152m. DIR: Lindsay Anderson. CAST: Richard Thomas, Ellen Greene, James Whitmore, Winston Rekert. 1989

GLORY STOMPERS, THE 💔 Silly cycle movie, about rival biker clubs. Not rated, some violence. 81m. DIR: Anthony M. Lanza. CAST: Dennis Hopper, Jody McCrea, Chris Noel, Jock Mahoney, Casey Kasem. 1967

GLORY YEARS ★★ Three old high school buddies on their twenty-year reunion use their alumni fund to gamble in Las Vegas. The whole film reeks of a bad *Big Chill* rip-off. Originally an HBO miniseries. Not rated, has profanity, sex, and nudity. 150m. DIR: Arthur Allan Seidelman. CAST: George Dzundza, Archie Hahn, Tim Thomerson, Tawny Kitaen, Michael Fairman, Sandy Simpson, Beau Starr, Donna Pescow. 1987

G-MEN VS. THE BLACK DRAGON ★★1/2 The British, Chinese, and American secret service team up to fight the deadly Black Dragon Society of Japan. The action and stunts are top-notch in this serial. B&W; 15 chapters. DIR: William Witney. CAST: Rod Cameron, Constance Worth, George J. Lewis. 1943

GNOME-MOBILE, THE ★★1/2 This one is kid city. From Disney, of course. Walter Brennan doubles as a wealthy businessman and a gnome who must find a wife for his grandson-gnome. The Gnome-Mobile is one fancy Rolls-Royce. 104m. DIR: Robert Stevenson. CAST: Walter Brennan, Ed Wynn, Matthew Garber, Karen Dotrice. 1967

GO ★★★★ The events of a single night are traced from the viewpoints of three interlocking sets of characters: a supermarket clerk, her friends and coworkers, and two young actors. The complicated, sometimes raunchy story is well acted by a cast of rising young stars, and moves at a lightning pace, with an audacious surprise around every corner. Rated R for profanity, nudity, drug use, and sexual scenes. 103m. DIR: Doug Liman. CAST: Sarah Polley, Katie Holmes, Desmond Askew, Jay Mohr, Scott Wolf, William Fichtner, Timothy Olyphant, Jane Krakowski, Taye Diggs. 1999 DVD

GO FISH ★★1/2 A low-budget amateur film about courtship and love in Chicago's lesbian community. Shot on weekends over most of a year, the film is lighthearted and playful, but it's also rather primitive and clumsy. The acting is especially awkward and camera conscious. Not rated; contains lesbian love scenes and frank discussions of sex. B&W; 85m. DIR: Rose Troche. CAST: Guinevere Turner, V. S. Brodie. 1994

GO FOR BROKE! ★★★1/2 This a paean to the grit and guts of the Japanese-Americans who comprised the 442nd Regiment during World War II. Their gallantry and team spirit, in the face of homefront prejudice and battlefront horror, earned them a nation's respect and presidential citation for outstanding accomplishments in combat. 90m. DIR: Robert Pirosh. CAST: Van Johnson, Warner Anderson. 1951

GO INTO YOUR DANCE ★★★ The only film to costar husband and wife Al Jolson and Ruby Keeler is a charming curiosity piece. Besides Jolson's singing and Keeler's dancing, this backstage drama has exotic Helen Morgan singing some of the torch songs she made famous. B&W; 89m. DIR: Archie Mayo. CAST: Al Jolson, Ruby Keeler, Helen Morgan, Glenda Farrell, Benny Rubin, Phil Regan, Patsy Kelly, Barton MacLane. 1935

GO, JOHNNY, GO! 💔 Despite the presence of some great rock 'n' roll and R&B acts, this story of a boy plucked from anonymity to become a star is about as dull as they come. B&W; 75m. DIR: Paul Landres. CAST: Jimmy Clanton, Alan Freed, Sandy Stewart, Chuck Berry, Jo-Ann Campbell, Eddie Cochran, Ritchie Valens, The Cadillacs, Jackie Wilson, The Flamingos. 1958

GO KILL AND COME BACK ★★ Unique opening, but routine viewing, as a bounty hunter tracks a notorious bandit hoping to locate a treasure of buried gold. Only the always-fine acting of veteran Gilbert Roland and a great musical score by Francesco De Masi make this worthwhile. Rated PG; contains violence. 98m. DIR: Enzo G. Castellari. CAST: George Hilton, Gilbert Roland, Edd Byrnes, Kareen O'Hara, Gerard Herter, Pedro Sanchez. 1968

GO-MASTERS, THE ★★★★ An impressive coproduction from Japan and China. Set primarily during the Sino-Japanese War, it details the odyssey of a young man who becomes a champion player in the ancient art of Go at a heartrending price. A fascinating tale of obsession, heartbreak, and the tragedies of war. In Chinese and Japanese with English subtitles. Not rated, the film has violence. 123m. DIR: Junya Sato, Duan Ji-Shun. CAST: Sun Dao-Lin. 1984

GO NOW ★★1/2 Better than average disease-of-the-week movie that emphasizes character and relationships over "ain't that a pity" symptom voyeurism. *The Full Monty*'s Robert Carlyle is excellent as a happy-go-lucky Scottish bloke who isn't so happy once he's struck with multiple sclerosis. Juliet Aubrey has the less showy but equally challenging part of his physically active girlfriend, torn between loyalty and her own conflicting needs. Not rated; contains language, nudity, sex, drug use, and mild violence. 88m. DIR: Michael Winterbottom. CAST: Robert Carlyle, Juliet Aubrey, James Nesbitt. 1995

GO TELL THE SPARTANS ★★★★ In one of the best Vietnam war films, Burt Lancaster is a commander who begins to wonder "what we're doing over there." It's a very honest portrayal of America's early days in Vietnam with Lancaster giving an excellent performance. Rated R. 114m. DIR: Ted Post. CAST: Burt Lancaster, Craig Wasson, Marc Singer. 1978

GO WEST ★★★1/2 Far from prime-screen Marx Brothers, this is still one of their best MGM movies and a treat for their fans. Good comedy bits combine with a rip-roaring climax (stolen by screenwriter Buster Keaton from *The General*) for a highly watchable star comedy. B&W; 81m. DIR: Edward Buzzell. CAST: The Marx Brothers, John Carroll, Diana Lewis, Walter Woolf King. 1940 DVD

GO WEST, YOUNG MAN ★★ No Mae West movie is all bad, but this one comes close. West based her screenplay on someone else's story so it doesn't fit very well. The censors snipped her usual one-liners and diluted the humor. She plays a glamorous movie star who falls for a handsome stranger and decides to steal him from his girlfriend with predictable results. B&W; 80m. DIR: Henry Hathaway. CAST: Mae West, Randolph Scott, Warren William, Alice Brady, Lyle Talbot, Isabel Jewell, Jack LaRue, Margaret Perry. 1936

GOALIE'S ANXIETY AT THE PENALTY KICK ★★★ An athlete suffering from alienation commits a senseless murder for no apparent reason in this slow-moving, existential thriller. Arthur Brauss gives a moody performance. Excellent adaptation by Wim Wenders of the Peter Handke novel. In German with English subtitles. B&W; 101m. DIR: Wim Wenders. CAST: Arthur Brauss, Erika Pluhar. 1971

GO-BETWEEN, THE ★★★★ In class-distinction-ruled Edwardian England, a high-society lady and an aloof, mysterious farmer use an innocent boy to carry their messages and assist their clandestine romance behind her fiancé's back. A delicate, haunting film, winner of the 1971 Cannes Grand Prix. Rated PG. 116m. DIR: Joseph Losey. CAST: Julie Christie, Alan Bates, Edward Fox, Margaret Leighton, Michael Redgrave. 1970

GOBLIN 🖤 Sloppily made direct-to-video chiller has a couple besieged by the title demon. Not rated; contains violence, profanity, and gore. 75m. DIR: Todd Sheets. CAST: Jenny Admire, Tonia Monahan, Bobby Westrick. 1993

GOD BLESS THE CHILD ★★★★ Inspiring made-for-TV drama about one man's fight to insure that a homeless mother and her daughter get the help and find the dignity they deserve. Mare Winningham delivers a heartbreaking performance as the woman abandoned in a new city by her husband. Winningham struggles to raise her daughter under extreme circumstances, and social worker Dorian Harewood changes their lives in this roller coaster of emotions. Grace Johnston will steal your heart as the understanding daughter. Not rated. 93m. DIR: Larry Elikann. CAST: Mare Winningham, Dorian Harewood, Grace Johnston. 1988

GOD IS MY WITNESS ★★★★ Although India is second only to the U.S. in the number of movies it produces every year, *God Is My Witness* is the sole mainstream Indian film that has been distributed here. But it's a doozy. Gloriously overstuffed with action, melodrama, musical numbers, and broad heroics that harken back to the heyday of John Wayne, this is like a dozen movies all rolled into one. Not rated; contains mild violence. In Hindu with English subtitles. 193m. DIR: Mukul S. Anand. CAST: Amitabh Bachchan, Sridevi, Danny Denzongpa. 1992

•**GOD SAID, HA!** ★★★★ Julia Sweeney brings her touching and courageous one-woman show to the screen, and the results are equally affecting. The former *Saturday Night Live* comedian explores the struggles she went through when her brother died of cancer, and her subsequent struggle when she learned she also had cancer. There's a sweet poignancy to every word she speaks, which she delivers with honesty. Frequently funny, sometimes sad, always entertaining. Rated PG-13 for language. 86m. DIR: Julia Sweeney. CAST: Julia Sweeney. 1998

•**GOD'S ARMY** ★★★ A young Mormon grapples with his faith while serving a mission in Los Angeles under the tutelage of an older mentor. The boy's faith is never really in danger, though; the film is a mixture of reverent Sunday school lesson and vanity production for writer-producer-director-costar Richard Dutcher (whose character literally works miracles). Non-Mormons may remain unmoved, but will appreciate the film's skilled production and sincere performances. Rated PG. 118m. DIR: Richard Dutcher. CAST: Matthew Brown, Richard Dutcher, DeSean Terry, Michael Buster. 2000

GODDESS, THE ★★★ A lonely girl working in a Maryland five-and-dime dreams of film stardom, goes to Hollywood, clicks in a minor role, and makes the big time, only to find it all bittersweet. Stage star Kim Stanley, largely ignored by Hollywood, does well in the title role, though she was far from suited for it. Paddy Chayefsky supposedly based his screenplay on Marilyn Monroe. B&W; 105m. DIR: John Cromwell. CAST: Kim Stanley, Lloyd Bridges, Betty Lou Holland, Joyce Van Patten, Steven Hill. 1958

GODFATHER, THE ★★★★★ Mario Puzo's popular novel comes to life in artful fashion. Filmed in foreboding tones, the movie takes us into the lurid world of the Mafia. Marlon Brando won an Oscar for his performance, but it's Al Pacino who grabs your attention with an unnerving intensity. Rated R. 175m. DIR: Francis Ford Coppola. CAST: Marlon Brando, Al Pacino, James Caan, Richard Castellano, John Cazale, Diane Keaton, Talia Shire, Robert Duvall, Sterling Hayden, John Marley, Richard Conte, Al Lettieri. 1972

GODFATHER, PART II, THE ★★★★★ This gripping sequel equals the quality of the original, an almost unheard-of circumstance in Hollywood. Francis Ford Coppola skillfully meshes past and present, intercutting the story of young Don Corleone, an ambitious, immoral immigrant, and his son Michael, who lives up to his father's expectations, turning the family's crime organization into a sleek, cold, modern operation. Winner of seven Academy Awards. Rated R. 200m. DIR: Francis Ford Coppola. CAST: Al Pacino, Robert Duvall, Diane Keaton, Robert De Niro, John Cazale, Talia Shire, Lee Strasberg, Michael Gazzo. 1974

GODFATHER, PART III, THE ★★★★1/2 From the first frame of this Shakespeare-influenced final chapter in the screen's finest gangster epic, we are thrust back into the world of the Corleone family. It is two decades after the "modern-day" events in *Part II*, and Michael has moved the family interests out of crime and into legitimate enterprises. But sinister forces lurking within his empire compel him to revert to the old, violent ways. Rated R for violence and profanity. 163m. DIR: Francis Ford Coppola. CAST: Al Pacino, Diane Keaton, Talia Shire, Andy Garcia, Eli Wallach, Joe Mantegna, Sofia Coppola, George Hamilton, Richard Bright, Helmut Berger, Don Novello, John Savage. 1990

GODFATHER EPIC, THE ★★★★ Few screen creations qualify as first-class entertainment and cinematic art. Francis Ford Coppola's *The Godfather* series unquestionably belongs in that category. Yet as good as *The Godfather* and *The Godfather, Part II* are, they are no match for *The Godfather Epic*. By editing the two films together in chronological order, or the videotape release of *The Godfather Epic*, Coppola has created a master work. See it! Rated R. 380m. **DIR:** Francis Ford Coppola. **CAST:** Marlon Brando, Talia Shire, James Caan, Robert Duvall, John Cazale, Al Pacino, Diane Keaton, Robert De Niro. 1977

GODS AND MONSTERS ★★★★ This fact-based character drama contains a mesmerizing portrait of bleak, frustrated old age. Ian McKellen's sensational lead performance explores the final sad days of classic horror-film director James Whale, who took his own life in 1957. The retired filmmaker's empty days, highlighted only by the promise of interviews that become no more than fan-boy queries about working with Boris Karloff, change with the arrival of a strapping new gardener who becomes companion, confessor, and … but that would be telling. Carter Burwell's sound track is haunting and unforgettable. Rated R for nudity and sexual candor. 105m. **DIR:** Bill Condon. **CAST:** Ian McKellen, Brendan Fraser, Lynn Redgrave. 1998 DVD

GOD'S LITTLE ACRE ★★★★ This is a terrific little film focusing on poor Georgia farmers. Robert Ryan gives one of his best performances as an itinerant farmer. Aldo Ray, Jack Lord, and Buddy Hackett lend good support. B&W; 110m. **DIR:** Anthony Mann. **CAST:** Robert Ryan, Aldo Ray, Tina Louise, Jack Lord, Fay Spain, Buddy Hackett. 1958

GODS MUST BE CRAZY, THE ★★★★ This hilarious, poignant, exciting, thought-provoking, violent, slapstick concoction involves three separate stories. One is about a Bushman whose tribe selects him to get rid of an evil thing sent by the gods: a Coke bottle. The second features the awkward love affair of a teacher and a klutzy scientist. The last involves a band of terrorists fleeing for their lives. These all come together for a surprising and satisfying climax. Not rated, the film has violence. 109m. **DIR:** Jamie Uys. **CAST:** Marius Weyers, Sandra Prinsloo. 1980

GODS MUST BE CRAZY II, THE ★★★★ Those who loved the original *Gods Must Be Crazy* will find more to enjoy in this gentle tale, which has the Bushman hero trying to find his two children after they've been carried away in a poacher's truck. Rated PG for brief profanity and light violence. 97m. **DIR:** Jamie Uys. **CAST:** N!Xau, Lena Farugia, Hans Strydom. 1990

GODS OF THE PLAGUE ★★ Incredibly boring drama about a professional killer who eludes a police manhunt with the help of his underworld friends. Hard-to-read subtitles. In German with English subtitles. Not rated; contains graphic nudity. B&W; 92m. **DIR:** Rainer Werner Fassbinder. **CAST:** Hanna Schygulla, Margarethe von Trotta. 1970

GODSEND, THE ❤ Cheaply rips off *The Exorcist* and *The Omen* in its tale of a demented daughter. Rated R. 93m. **DIR:** Gabrielle Beaumont. **CAST:** Cyd Hayman, Malcolm Stoddard, Angela Pleasence. 1979

GODSON, THE ★★ Rodney Dangerfield costars in this lame mob comedy that doesn't get any respect even as it attempts to spoof previous gangster films. Here, the number-three son of a notorious mafioso is being groomed for the family business, much to the dismay of the rest of the family. The cast doesn't have much to score with, and the humor is scattershot, with only a couple of gags hitting the bull's-eye. Rated PG-13 for language, cartoon violence, and adult situations. 89m. **DIR:** Bob Hoge. **CAST:** Kevin McDonald, Rodney Dangerfield, Dom DeLuise, Fabiana Udenio, Lou Ferrigno, Irwin Keyes. 1998 DVD

GODZILLA (1998) ★★★★ This take on the "Big G" is an engaging update of classic 1950s monster movies, highlighted by an amazingly streamlined, lifelike huge creature as well as the trashing of New York City. The dialogue occasionally is corny, particularly that between a plucky biologist hero and his estranged girlfriend, but her weaknesses are eclipsed by the gung-ho news cameraman, and the resourceful French secret agent who knows more about the giant scaly monster than he's telling. It all builds to a manic chase sequence that never loses its momentum. Rated PG-13 for monster-scale carnage. 139m. **DIR:** Roland Emmerich. **CAST:** Matthew Broderick, Jean Reno, Maria Pitillo, Hank Azaria, Kevin Dunn, Michael Lerner, Harry Shearer. 1998 DVD

GODZILLA, KING OF THE MONSTERS ★★★½ First, and by far the best, film featuring the four-hundred-foot monstrosity that was later reduced to a superhero. Here he's all death and destruction, and this movie really works, thanks to some expert photographic effects and weird music. B&W; 80m. **DIR:** Inoshiro Honda, Terry Morse. **CAST:** Raymond Burr, Takashi Shimura. 1956 DVD

GODZILLA 1985 ❤ Once again, the giant Japanese lizard tramples cars and crushes tall buildings in his search for radioactive nutrition. Rated PG. 91m. **DIR:** Kohji Hashimoto, R. J. Kizer. **CAST:** Raymond Burr, Keiji Kobayashi. 1985

GODZILLA VERSUS BIOLLANTE ★★½ Resurrected after more than a decade and given an A-movie budget, Godzilla is still just a big lug in a green monster suit. This time he battles a giant slime mold. Well-made but overlong. Rated PG for (and we quote the MPAA) "traditional Godzilla violence." 104m. **DIR:** Kazuki Omori. 1989

GODZILLA VS. GIGAN ❤ A basic rehash of previous Godzilla movies, only this time much more boring. 89m. **DIR:** Jun Fukuda. **CAST:** Hiroshi Ishikawa. 1972

GODZILLA VS. MECHAGODZILLA ★★ For Godzilla fans only. An enemy from space builds a metal Godzilla in an effort to take over the world. Godzilla is pressed into action to destroy the beast. Rated PG. 82m. **DIR:** Jun Fukuda. **CAST:** Masaaki Daimon. 1975

GODZILLA VS. MONSTER ZERO ★★★ Pretty good monster movie has an alien civilization "borrowing" Godzilla and Rodan to help defeat the hometown menace Monster Zero (known previously and since as Ghidrah). 90m. **DIR:** Inoshiro Honda. **CAST:** Nick Adams, Akira Takarada. 1966 DVD

GODZILLA VS. MOTHRA ★★★ Fine Godzilla movie pits the "king of the monsters" against archenemy Mothra for its first half, later has him taking on twin caterpillars recently hatched from the moth's giant egg. Excellent battle scenes in this one, with Godzilla's first appearance a doozy. 90m. **DIR:** Inoshiro Honda. **CAST:** Akira Takarada, Yuriko Hoshi, Hiroshi Koizumi. **1964 DVD**

GODZILLA VS. THE SEA MONSTER 🎬 Godzilla must tackle a giant, rotten-looking crab monster. 85m. **DIR:** Jun Fukuda. **CAST:** None Credited. **1966**

GODZILLA VS. THE SMOG MONSTER 🎬 In this ecology-minded disaster flick, the big guy takes on an amorphous, pollution-belching monstrosity spawned by the excesses of industrial waste. 87m. **DIR:** Yoshimitu Banno. **CAST:** Akira Yamauchi. **1972**

GODZILLA'S REVENGE ★★ In his dreams, a young boy visits Monster Island and learns about self-respect from Godzilla's son. Goofy kid's movie, assembled from scenes made for other Godzilla films. Rated G. 92m. **DIR:** Inoshiro Honda. **CAST:** Kenji Sahara. **1969 DVD**

GOIN' SOUTH ★★★ Star Jack Nicholson also directed this odd little Western tale of an outlaw (Nicholson) saved from the gallows by a spinster (Mary Steenburgen). The catch is he must marry her and work on her farm. Lots of attempts at comedy, but only a few work. Look for John Belushi in a small role as a Mexican cowboy. Rated PG, contains some violence and language. 109m. **DIR:** Jack Nicholson. **CAST:** Jack Nicholson, Mary Steenburgen, John Belushi. **1978**

GOIN' TO TOWN ★★★ A Mae West comedy that poses the idea that there are men who can resist La West. That's farfetched, even for Hollywood. She plays a cattle queen who inherits an oil field and falls hard for the British engineer who surveys her property. He rebuffs her. She does a Pygmalion twist on herself and becomes a sophisticated lady and even sings opera to impress the guy. Good one-liners and enjoyable songs, but Mae West is the only impressive player. B&W; 74m. **DIR:** Alexander Hall. **CAST:** Mae West, Paul Cavanagh, Ivan Lebedeff, Marjorie Gateson, Monroe Owsley, Grant Withers. **1935**

GOING ALL THE WAY ★★★ Nostalgic romantic drama about two soldiers returning to their small hometown after the Korean War. Athletic Gunner and shy photographer Sonny become mismatched allies as they look for purpose in their lives. Quaint slice of Americana benefits from a superb cast and excellent direction. Rated R for adult situations, language, and nudity. 103m. **DIR:** Mark Pellington. **CAST:** Ben Affleck, Jeremy Davies, Amy Locane, Rachel Weisz, Rose McGowan. **1997 DVD**

GOING APE! ★★ Tony Danza plays the heir to a million-dollar fortune-with-a-catch: he has to care for three unpredictable simians. Because the film is padded with familiar material, little fun shines through. Rated PG. 87m. **DIR:** Jeremy Joe Kronsberg. **CAST:** Tony Danza, Jessica Walter, Stacey Nelkin, Danny DeVito, Art Metrano, Joseph Maher. **1981**

GOING BANANAS 🎬 Idiotic safari film. Rated PG. 95m. **DIR:** Boaz Davidson. **CAST:** Dom DeLuise, Jimmie Walker, David Mendenhall, Herbert Lom. **1988**

GOING BERSERK 🎬 This is an unfunny comedy starring former *SCTV* regulars John Candy, Joe Flaherty, and Eugene Levy. Rated R. 85m. **DIR:** David

Steinberg. **CAST:** John Candy, Joe Flaherty, Eugene Levy, Alley Mills, Pat Hingle, Richard Libertini. **1983**

GOING HOLLYWOOD ★★1/2 The music is better than the story. Marion Davies plays a hometown girl who is determined to have both Crosby and a career in that order. The best song is "Temptation" sung by Crosby in his inimitable crooning fashion. Very brisk pace; very enjoyable staging of musical numbers. B&W; 80m. **DIR:** Raoul Walsh. **CAST:** Bing Crosby, Marion Davies, Fifi D'Orsay, Patsy Kelly, Ned Sparks, Stu Erwin. **1933**

GOING IN STYLE ★★★★ Three retirees who gather daily on a park bench need to add some spice to their empty existence. So they decide to rob a bank. This crime caper has some unexpected plot twists with a perfect sprinkling of humor. A delight throughout. Rated PG. 96m. **DIR:** Martin Brest. **CAST:** George Burns, Art Carney, Lee Strasberg, Charles Hallahan, Pamela Payton-Wright. **1979**

GOING MY WAY ★★★½ Bing Crosby won the best-actor Oscar in 1944 for his delightful portrayal of the easygoing priest who finally wins over his strict superior (Barry Fitzgerald, who also won an Oscar for his supporting role). Leo McCarey wrote and directed this funny, heartwarming character study and netted two Academy Awards for his efforts as well as crafting the year's Oscar-winning best picture. B&W; 130m. **DIR:** Leo McCarey. **CAST:** Bing Crosby, Barry Fitzgerald, Rise Stevens, Gene Lockhart, Frank McHugh. **1944**

GOING OVERBOARD 🎬 Lame comedy about a cruise-ship waiter who yearns to be a stand-up comic. The jokes are all wet. Rated PG-13. 97m. **DIR:** Valerie Breman. **CAST:** Adam Sandler, Tom Hodges, Lisa Collins, Billy Zane, Ricky Paul Goldin, Burt Young. **1989 DVD**

GOING PLACES ★★ Memorable only as one of Gérard Depardieu's first screen appearances. He and Patrick Dewaere play amiable low-lifes who dabble in petty thievery. Contains one of filmdom's most acutely uncomfortable scenes, when one of the young lads gets shot in the testicles. In French with English subtitles. Rated R for sex. 117m. **DIR:** Bertrand Blier. **CAST:** Gérard Depardieu, Patrick Dewaere, Miou-Miou, Jeanne Moreau, Isabelle Huppert, Brigitte Fossey. **1974**

GOING UNDER ★★ The wacky crew of the sub *Standard* set sail for *Airplane*-style high jinx on the open sea. The jokes are seaworthy, but the execution is all wet. Rated PG. 81m. **DIR:** Mark W. Travis. **CAST:** Bill Pullman, Wendy Schaal, Ned Beatty, Robert Vaughn, Bud Cort, Michael Winslow. **1991**

GOING UNDERCOVER 🎬 Chris Lemmon plays an airhead gumshoe hired by Jean Simmons to protect her stepdaughter. Rated PG-13 for violence. 89m. **DIR:** James Keneim Clarke. **CAST:** Jean Simmons, Lea Thompson, Chris Lemmon. **1988**

GOLD COAST ★★★ Yet another Elmore Leonard novel hits the screen, this one a mostly serious story about a crime lord's widow who discovers she can keep her inherited millions only if she remains faithful to her husband's memory ... which is to say, she avoids contact with all other men. For the rest of her life. Alas, she and a small-potatoes grifter fall in love, and both explore various avenues to shake the attention of the vicious cowboy killer watching to ensure the lady's fidelity. The script doesn't really do justice to the book. Rated R for violence, profanity, nudity, and suggested sex. 111m. **DIR:** Peter Weller. **CAST:** David Caruso, Marg Helgenberger, Jeff Kober, Barry Primus, Wanda de Jesus. **1997**

GOLD DIGGERS OF 1933 ★★★★ Typical 1930s song-and-dance musical revolves around a Broadway show. Notable tunes include: "We're in the Money," sung by Ginger Rogers; "Forgotten Man," sung by Joan Blondell; and "Shadow Waltz," by the chorus girls. Enjoyable fare if you like nostalgic musicals. B&W; 96m. **DIR:** Mervyn LeRoy. **CAST:** Joan Blondell, Ruby Keeler, Dick Powell, Aline MacMahon, Ginger Rogers, Sterling Holloway. **1933**

GOLD DIGGERS OF 1935 ★★★ Classic Busby Berkeley musical production numbers dominate this absurd story of mercenary schemers swarming around the rich at a posh resort. Though the film sags and lags, the kitsch director's staging of "Lullaby of Broadway" is a piece of cinematic brilliance. B&W; 95m. **DIR:** Busby Berkeley. **CAST:** Dick Powell, Adolphe Menjou, Winifred Shaw, Glenda Farrell. **1935**

GOLD DIGGERS: THE SECRET OF BEAR MOUNTAIN ★★ Disappointing attempt to create a female version of Tom Sawyer and Huckleberry Finn's adventures. Preteens may enjoy the watery cave but David Keith's abusive character make this inappropriate viewing for the very audience at which it's aimed. Rated PG for violence. 95m. **DIR:** Kevin James Dobson. **CAST:** Christina Ricci, Anna Chlumsky, David Keith, Brian Kerwin, Polly Draper. **1995**

GOLD OF NAPLES, THE ★★★1/2 A charming quartet of vignettes: Sophia Loren as a wife who cheats on her pizza-baker husband; demon cardplayer Vittorio De Sica being put down by a clever child; Toto as a henpecked husband; and Silvana Mangano playing a married whore whose marital arrangement is more than passing strange. B&W; 107m. **DIR:** Vittorio De Sica. **CAST:** Sophia Loren, Vittorio De Sica, Toto, Silvana Mangano. **1954**

GOLD RUSH, THE ★★★★★ Charlie Chaplin's classic comedy is immortal for the scrumptious supper of a boiled boot, the teetering Klondike cabin, and the dance of the dinner rolls. Some parts are very sentimental, but these give the viewer time to catch his or her breath after laughing so much. B&W; 100m. **DIR:** Charles Chaplin. **CAST:** Charlie Chaplin, Mack Swain, Georgia Hale. **1925 DVD**

GOLDEN AGE OF COMEDY, THE ★★★★ This compilation introduced new generations of moviegoers to the great years of silent comedy and continues to do so. Many of the shorts with Laurel and Hardy will be familiar to viewers, but the segments with Will Rogers spoofing silent-film greats Douglas Fairbanks and Tom Mix, and the footage with Harry Langdon (once considered a comedic equal to Charlie Chaplin, Buster Keaton, and Harold Lloyd) are seldom seen and well worth the wait. B&W; 78m. **DIR:** Robert Youngson. **CAST:** Stan Laurel, Oliver Hardy, Will Rogers, Harry Langdon, Ben Turpin, Carole Lombard, Snub Pollard. **1957**

GOLDEN BOY ★★★★ William Holden made a strong starring debut in this screen adaptation of Clifford Odet's play about a musician who becomes a boxer. Though a bit dated today, Holden and costar Barbara Stanwyck still shine. B&W; 100m. **DIR:** Rouben Mamoulian. **CAST:** William Holden, Barbara Stanwyck, Adolphe Menjou, Lee J. Cobb. **1939**

GOLDEN CHILD, THE ★★ Eddie Murphy stars as a Los Angeles social worker who is stunned when members of a religious sect call him "The Chosen One" and expect him to save a magical child from the forces of evil. You'll be even more stunned when you watch this cheesy comedy-adventure and realize it was one of the biggest hits of its year. Rated PG-13 for violence and profanity. 96m. **DIR:** Michael Ritchie. **CAST:** Eddie Murphy, Charlotte Lewis, Charles Dance, Randall "Tex" Cobb, Victor Wong, James Hong. **1986 DVD**

GOLDEN COACH, THE ★★★★ Jean Renoir's little-known Franco-Italian masterpiece features Anna Magnani in a stunning performance as the leading lady of an eighteenth-century acting troupe touring South America. Magnani finds herself caught in a complex love triangle with a soldier, a vain bullfighter, and a viceroy who gives her a golden coach. In English. 95m. **DIR:** Jean Renoir. **CAST:** Anna Magnani. **1952**

GOLDEN DEMON ★★★ As a rule, most Japanese love stories are sad. This story of true love broken by pride, tradition, and avarice is an exception. The story of a poor young man, in love with his adopted parents' daughter, who loses her to a rich entrepreneur (an arranged marriage), is richly entertaining. In Japanese with English subtitles. 91m. **DIR:** Koji Shima. **CAST:** Jun Negami. **1953**

GOLDEN EARRINGS ★★★★ An enjoyable romantic romp that wouldn't have worked with a different cast. Marlene Dietrich plays a gypsy who becomes a spy to help British officer Ray Milland escape the Nazis in Germany's Black Forest. The story sounds silly and contrived, but Dietrich's performance makes it compelling. B&W; 95m. **DIR:** Mitchell Leisen. **CAST:** Marlene Dietrich, Ray Milland, Murvyn Vye, Quentin Reynolds, Reinhold Schunzel, Bruce Lester, Dennis Hoey, John Dehner. **1947**

GOLDEN GATE ★★★ Good cast, good idea, lousy direction. Matt Dillon is a young, cocky FBI agent who spins a case out of air against a Chinese laundry worker in 1962. Trouble is, Dillon's got a conscience and tries to make amends to the man's daughter, played by the sensuous Joan Chen. The metaphysical slant is interesting, but this is turgid going, as the plot just about ceases midway through the story. Rated R for profanity and sexual situations. 101m. **DIR:** John Madden. **CAST:** Matt Dillon, Joan Chen, Bruno Kirby. **1993**

GOLDEN HONEYMOON, THE ★★★★ Delightful adaptation of Ring Lardner's deft and biting story. James Whitmore steals the show as talkative Charley Tate, a crusty old windbag married fifty happy years to his patient wife, Lucy (Teresa Wright). While celebrating their golden anniversary in Florida, she meets up with an old flame, and Charley feels the need to prove that Lucy didn't choose the wrong fella fifty years back. Introduced by Henry Fonda; unrated and suitable for family viewing. 52m. **DIR:** Noel Black. **CAST:** James Whitmore, Teresa Wright, Stephen Elliott, Nan Martin. **1980**

GOLDEN SEAL, THE ★★★1/2 A young boy (Torquil Campbell) living with his parents (Steven Railsback and Penelope Milford) on the Aleutian Islands makes friends with a rare golden seal and her pup. It's a good story, predictably told. Rated PG. 95m. **DIR:** Frank Zuniga. **CAST:** Torquil Campbell, Steve Railsback, Penelope Milford. **1983**

GOLDEN STALLION, THE ★★1/2 Offbeat entry to the Roy Rogers series places the emphasis on Trigger and his efforts to save a cute palomino mare from a life of crime. Absolute hooey, but fun to watch, for kids and animal lovers. 67m. **DIR:** William Witney. **CAST:** Roy Rogers, Dale Evans, Estelita Rodriguez, Pat Brady. **1949**

GOLDEN VOYAGE OF SINBAD, THE ★★★★ First-rate Arabian Nights adventure pits Captain Sinbad (John Phillip Law) against the evil Prince Koura (Tom Baker) for possession of a magical amulet with amazing powers. This is a superb fantasy, with some truly incredible effects by master animator Ray Harryhausen. Rated G. 105m. **DIR:** Gordon Hessler. **CAST:** John Phillip Law, Tom Baker, Caroline Munro, Gregoire Aslan, John Garfield Jr. **1974 DVD**

GOLDENEYE ★★★★ The James Bond franchise roared back to life with the dapper Pierce Brosnan as the newest actor carrying 007s License to Kill. Teamed with a gorgeous computer programmer, Bond battles a renegade Soviet military officer planning to wreak worldwide havoc with a lethal orbiting satellite. Slick pacing, deliciously evil villains, and audacious stunts prove once again that Bond can more than hold his own. Rated PG-13 for violence and sexual content. 130m. **DIR:** Martin Campbell. **CAST:** Pierce Brosnan, Sean Bean, Izabella Scorupco, Famke Janssen, Joe Don Baker, Judi Dench, Robbie Coltrane. **1995 DVD**

GOLDENGIRL 🎬 This modern retread of *Frankenstein* fails on all counts. Rated PG. 104m. **DIR:** Joseph Sargent. **CAST:** Susan Anton, James Coburn, Curt Jurgens, Robert Culp, Leslie Caron, Jessica Walter. **1979**

GOLDFINGER ★★★★ So enjoyable to watch that it's easy to forget the influence of the film on the spy-adventure genre. From the precredits sequence (cut out of most TV versions) to the final spectacular fight with Goldfinger's superhuman henchman, Oddjob (Harold Sakata), the film firmly establishes characters and situations that measured not only future Bond films but all spy films to follow. Sean Connery is the ultimate 007, John Barry's music is unforgettable, and Oddjob made bowler hats fashionable for heavies. 108m. **DIR:** Guy Hamilton. **CAST:** Sean Connery, Gert Fröbe, Honor Blackman, Harold Sakata. **1964 DVD**

GOLDWYN FOLLIES, THE 🎬 Goldwyn's folly is a better title for this turkey. 120m. **DIR:** George Marshall. **CAST:** Adolphe Menjou, Andrea Leeds, Kenny Baker, The Ritz Brothers, Vera Zorina, Edgar Bergen. **1938 DVD**

GOLDY, THE LAST OF THE GOLDEN BEARS 🎬 Low production values, inane dialogue, and inconsistent

time jumps make a mess of this let's-save-a-bear programmer. 91m. **DIR:** Trevor Black. **CAST:** Jeff Richards. **1984**

GOLEM, THE (HOW HE CAME INTO THE WORLD) (DER GOLEM, WIE ER IN DIE WELT) ★★★★ Director Paul Wegener plays the lead role as the Golem, an ancient clay figure from Hebrew mythology that is brought to life by means of an amulet activated by the magic word "Aemaet" (the Hebrew word for truth). In a story similar to *Frankenstein*, the man of clay roams through medieval Prague in a mystic atmosphere created by the brilliant cameraman Karl Freund. Silent. B&W; 70m. **DIR:** Paul Wegener. **CAST:** Paul Wegener. **1920 DVD**

GOLGOTHA ★★ Early, seldom-seen depiction of the passion of Jesus Christ was reverently filmed in France, where it was a big box-office success. Adapted from the four gospels of the New Testament, using only direct quotes for the lines spoken by Jesus. In French with English subtitles. B&W; 100m. **DIR:** Julien Duvivier. **CAST:** Robert le Vigan, Jean Gabin, Harry Baur. **1935**

GOLIATH AND THE BARBARIANS ★★ Steve Reeves plays Goliath in this so-so Italian action film. In this episode, he saves Italy from invading barbaric tribes. As in many of Reeves's films, the only object of interest is the flexing of his muscles. 86m. **DIR:** Carlo Campogalliani. **CAST:** Steve Reeves, Bruce Cabot, Giulia Rubini, Chelo Alonso. **1960**

GOLIATH AND THE DRAGON ★★ The original, Italian version of this film had Maciste (Italy's mythological hero, renamed Goliath by U.S. distributors) fighting a three-headed, fire-breathing dog and other horrors—but *not* a dragon. So the Americans had a life-size dragon's head built for Mark Forest to swing his sword at, and hired Jim Danforth to animate a miniature dragon thrashing about for the long shots—and spliced the whole thing, lasting a couple of minutes, into the existing film. 87m. **DIR:** Vittorio Cottafavi. **CAST:** Mark Forest, Broderick Crawford, Gaby André. **1960**

GOLIATH AND THE VAMPIRES ★★ A horde of barbarians who drink blood, torture their victims, and dissolve amid puffs of blue smoke are the formidable adversaries for Goliath (actually, Maciste) in this colorful, mindlessly enjoyable sword-and-sandal fantasy. U.S. television title: *The Vampires*. 91m. **DIR:** Giacomo Gentilomo. **CAST:** Gordon Scott, Jacques Sernas, Gianna Maria Canale. **1964**

GOLIATH AWAITS ★★1/2 This undersea adventure is about the discovery of a sunken ocean liner, many of whose original passengers are still alive after years on the bottom. It was much better as a two-part (200-minute) miniseries on TV. 95m. **DIR:** Kevin Connor. **CAST:** Mark Harmon, Robert Forster, Eddie Albert, Emma Samms, Christopher Lee, John Carradine, Frank Gorshin, Jean Marsh. **1981**

GONE ARE THE DAYS ★★★ After witnessing a shooting, the Daye family is assigned to a witness relocation agent (Harvey Korman), who is creatively unsuccessful in a long-distance game of hide-and-seek. This wacky comedy is pleasantly acted and well photographed. A Disney made-for-cable production.

good fun for the family. 90m. **DIR:** Gabrielle Beaumont. **CAST:** Harvey Korman, Susan Anspach, Robert Hogan. **1984**

GONE FISHIN' 🎬 This *Ishtar* for the 1990s throws together two great actors and lets them sink under the weight of slow-moving shtick. Danny Glover and Joe Pesci are two slow thinkers who manage to wreak havoc wherever they go. Rated PG for violence. 92m. **DIR:** Christopher Cain. **CAST:** Danny Glover, Joe Pesci, Nick Brimble, Rosanna Arquette. **1997**

GONE IN 60 SECONDS (1974) 🎬 Stuntman-turned-film-auteur H. B. Halicki wrecks a bunch of cars faster than you can say Hal Needham. Rated PG for violence. 97m. **DIR:** H. B. Halicki. **CAST:** H. B. Halicki, Marion Busia, George Cole, James McIntire, Jerry Daugirda. **1974**

GONE IN 60 SECONDS (2000) ★★ Producer Jerry Bruckheimer's bombastic action epics are known to be long on visual glitz and short on plot and characterization, but this one's shabby even by his usual standards. Based loosely on H. B. Halicki's much-admired 1974 original, this remake lacks its predecessor's raw energy … rather crippling for a project that should exude an aura of danger and radiate sheer speed. It does neither, instead idling and stalling precisely when better filmmakers would understand how to kick it into gear. Blame director Dominic Sena, whose experience with TV commercials and music videos serves him poorly here; he thinks in short bursts and thus helms an overly edited mess that can't even deliver one decent car chase. Rated PG-13 for violence, profanity, and mild sensuality. 119m. **DIR:** Dominic Sena. **CAST:** Nicolas Cage, Giovanni Ribisi, Angelina Jolie, Will Patton, Delroy Lindo, Robert Duvall, Timothy Olyphant. **2000**

GONE TO TEXAS ★★★ Sam Elliott plays frontier hero Sam Houston in this sprawling, action-packed, but overlong biography. 144m. **DIR:** Peter Levin. **CAST:** Sam Elliott, Michael Beck, James Stephens, Devon Ericson. **1986**

GONE WITH THE WEST ★★ With this excellent cast, one would expect more, but this is a confusing and vague tale about an Old West ex-con on the vengeance trail. 92m. **DIR:** Bernard Gerard. **CAST:** James Caan, Stefanie Powers, Aldo Ray, Barbara Werle, Robert Walker Jr., Sammy Davis Jr., Michael Conrad. **1972 DVD**

GONE WITH THE WIND ★★★★★ The all-time movie classic with Clark Gable and Vivien Leigh as Margaret Mitchell's star-crossed lovers in the final days of the Old South. Need we say more? 222m. **DIR:** Victor Fleming. **CAST:** Clark Gable, Vivien Leigh, Leslie Howard, Olivia de Havilland, Thomas Mitchell, Hattie McDaniel. **1939**

GONIN ★★ Five desperate men of varied backgrounds band together to steal a huge amount of money from a Tokyo crime boss. The enraged hoodlum hires two gay assassins to hunt them down. This bloody thriller has a seductive visual pull, especially during the action scenes, but weak character development and plotting. In Japanese with English subtitles. Not rated; contains violence, profanity, rape,

nudity, and torture. 109m. **DIR:** Takashi Ishii. **CAST:** Koichi Sato, Naoto Takenaka, Jimpachi Nezu, Masahiro Motoki, Kippei Shiina, Takeshi Kitano, Kazuya Kimura, Megumi Yokoyama. **1998**

GONZA THE SPEARMAN ★★★★ Powerful, classic tale of love, honor, and tragedy set in the early 1700s in Japan. Director Masahiro Shinoda's brilliant adaptation of well-known bunkaru playwright Monzaemon Chikamatsu's story features an equally impressive score by composer Toru Takemitsu. In Japanese with English subtitles. Not rated; contains nudity and violence. 126m. **DIR:** Masahiro Shinoda. **CAST:** Hiromi Go. **1986**

GOOD BURGER ★★1/2 Nickelodeon teams sweet-natured Kel Mitchell with an exasperated Kenan Thompson to create goofy Abbott-and-Costello–ish knockoffs. The two, working at a small hamburger stand, must compete with a flashy new mega-burger haven. Corny and unbelievable with endless sight gags and physical humor to break down one's natural groan response. Aimed at preteens, adults may catch themselves laughing as well. Rated PG for wreckless driving without a license and comic-book violence. 90m. **DIR:** Brian Robbins. **CAST:** Kel Mitchell, Kenan Thompson, Sinbad, Abe Vigoda, Dan Schneider, Shar Jackson. **1997**

GOOD EARTH, THE ★★★★ Nobel Prize novelist Pearl Buck's engrossing, richly detailed story of a simple Chinese farm couple whose lives are ruined by greed is impressively brought to life in this milestone film. Luise Rainer won the second of her back-to-back best-actress Oscars for her portrayal of the ever-patient wife. The photography and special effects are outstanding. B&W; 138m. **DIR:** Sidney Franklin. **CAST:** Paul Muni, Luise Rainer, Keye Luke, Walter Connolly, Jessie Ralph. **1937**

GOOD EVENING MR. WALLENBERG ★★★★ Truly harrowing account of Raoul Wallenberg, the Swedish businessman ultimately responsible for protecting thousands of Jews in Budapest during the final hours of World War II. While this film is often difficult to bear, Stellan Skarsgard's compelling portrayal of Wallenberg shines complete with all the madness, frustration, and sheer horror of the world around him. In Swedish, German, and Hungarian with English subtitles. Not rated; contains violence and nudity. 115m. **DIR:** Kjell Grede. **CAST:** Stellan Skarsgard, Katharina Thalbach, Karoly Eperjes. **1990**

GOOD FATHER, THE ★★★1/2 In this brilliant British import, Anthony Hopkins is a walking time bomb. A separation from his wife has left him on the outside of his son's life. Hopkins's reaction is so extreme that he is haunted by nightmares. Director Mike Newell lays on the suspense artfully with this device while detailing the revenge Hopkins plots against the wife of a friend who is in similar circumstances. Rated R for profanity, suggested sex, and stylized violence. 90m. **DIR:** Mike Newell. **CAST:** Anthony Hopkins, Jim Broadbent, Harriet Walter, Simon Callow, Joanne Whalley. **1986**

GOOD FIGHT, THE ★★1/2 Christine Lahti and Terry O'Quinn elevate this courtroom drama above the clichés as divorced attorneys drawn back together after she takes on an impossible case. The chemistry between the two explodes when their love of the law clears the way for a rekindled romance. The best moments take place in the courtroom and not the bedroom. Not rated. 91m. **DIR:** John David Coles. **CAST:** Christine Lahti, Terry O'Quinn, Kenneth Welsh, Lawrence Dane. 1992

GOOD GUYS AND THE BAD GUYS, THE ★★★ Watchable comedy-Western gets better as it gets older, primarily because "they don't make 'em like they used to." Robert Mitchum and George Kennedy play two former foes who join forces to thwart the plans of young upstart David Carradine and his gang. Rated PG. 90m. **DIR:** Burt Kennedy. **CAST:** Robert Mitchum, George Kennedy, David Carradine, John Carradine, Tina Louise, Martin Balsam, Lois Nettleton, Douglas Fowley, Marie Windsor, John Davis Chandler. 1969

GOOD GUYS WEAR BLACK ★★ This Chuck Norris action film starts out well but quickly dissolves into a routine political action-thriller that really goes nowhere. Lightweight entertainment. Rated PG. 96m. **DIR:** Ted Post. **CAST:** Chuck Norris, Anne Archer, James Franciscus, Lloyd Haynes, Jim Backus, Dana Andrews. 1979

GOOD IDEA ★★ Odd characters abound in this anarchic comedy. Anthony Newley tries to win his ex-wife back from her new husband, a crooked architect. John Candy is funny as a daft cop, but it's only a small role, although the video packaging makes him look like the star. Original title: *It Seemed Like a Good Idea at the Time*. Rated PG. 106m. **DIR:** John Trent. **CAST:** Anthony Newley, Stefanie Powers, Isaac Hayes, Lloyd Bochner, Yvonne De Carlo, Lawrence Dane, John Candy. 1975

GOOD LUCK ★★1/2 Paraplegic dental technician Bernard Lemley asks blind former Seattle Seahawks receiver "Olee" Olezniak to help him change society's image of the disabled. Lem's first challenge is to break through Olee's unhealthy preoccupation with impotency, bowel movements, and self-pity while the bitter ex-jock sits in jail. The squabbling new buddies then test each other's trust and team up to enter a white-water rafting race. Most of the movie follows their amusing, raunchy, but often awkwardly staged road trip. Rated R for profanity and suggested sex. 98m. **DIR:** Richard LaBrie. **CAST:** Gregory Hines, Vincent D'Onofrio, Max Gail. 1997 DVD

GOOD MAN IN AFRICA, A ★★1/2 The film never achieves the right satirical tone in this story about a bumbling, boozy, British bureaucrat in a fictional African nation. Colin Friels is rendered almost invisible by the strong performances of Sean Connery, John Lithgow, and Lou Gossett Jr. As a comedy, it simply isn't very funny; as a drama, it's too irreverent. Rated R for profanity, nudity, and sex. 95m. **DIR:** Bruce Beresford. **CAST:** Colin Friels, Joanne Whalley, Sean Connery, Lou Gossett Jr., John Lithgow, Diana Rigg, Sarah Jane Fenton. 1994

GOOD MEN AND BAD ★★ The final episode of the *Black Fox* trilogy starring Christopher Reeve and Tony Todd, set in Texas in the 1860s. An extremely stiff Reeve, crushed by the murder of his wife, threatens to cross the line from good to evil while seeking

revenge. Todd is the freed slave who tries to find justice for blood brother Reeve within the boundaries of the law. As with the other episodes, the only intriguing aspects are Todd's performance and the interracial aspects of the story. Not rated; contains violence. 92m. **DIR:** Steven H. Stern. **CAST:** Christopher Reeve, Tony Todd, Raul Trujillo. 1993

GOOD MORNING, BABYLON ★★★ This follows the misadventures of two brothers who come to America to find their fortunes as artists and find jobs on the production of D. W. Griffith's silent classic, *Intolerance*. The movie has moments of lyrical beauty and its story is sweet. But the dialogue has been translated from Italian in an occasionally awkward fashion. Rated PG-13 for nudity and profanity. 115m. **DIR:** Paolo Taviani, Vittorio Taviani. **CAST:** Vincent Spano, Joaquim de Almeida, Greta Scacchi, Charles Dance. 1987

GOOD MORNING, VIETNAM ★★★1/2 Robin Williams stars as disc jockey Adrian Cronauer, who briefly ruled Saigon's Armed Forces Radio in 1965. Williams's improvisational monologues are the high points in a film that meanders too much, but Forest Whitaker also shines. Rated R for language and violence. 120m. **DIR:** Barry Levinson. **CAST:** Robin Williams, Forest Whitaker, Tung Thanh Tran, Chintara Sukapatana, Bruno Kirby, Robert Wuhl, J. T. Walsh. 1987 DVD

GOOD MOTHER, THE ★★ Single mom Anna (Diane Keaton) finds romance with an irresistible Irish artist (Liam Neeson). Anna's ex-husband accuses the artist of sexually abusing his daughter. This film will make you speculate on the rightness or wrongness of Anna's sexually open child-rearing techniques. Rated R for nudity and obscenities. 104m. **DIR:** Leonard Nimoy. **CAST:** Diane Keaton, Jason Robards Jr., Ralph Bellamy, Liam Neeson, James Naughton. 1988

GOOD NEIGHBOR SAM ★★★ This comedy is similar to many of the lightweight potboilers given to Jack Lemmon in the 1960s. It is an overlong farce about a married advertising designer who pretends marriage to his foreign neighbor next door so she can secure an inheritance. 130m. **DIR:** David Swift. **CAST:** Jack Lemmon, Romy Schneider, Dorothy Provine, Edward G. Robinson. 1964

GOOD NEWS ★★★ Football hero Peter Lawford resists the class vamp and wins the big game and the campus cutie who loves him in this quintessential musical of college life. The dialogue is painfully trite and trying, but energy and exuberance abound. 95m. **DIR:** Charles Walters. **CAST:** June Allyson, Peter Lawford, Patricia Marshall, Joan McCracken, Mel Tormé. 1948

GOOD NIGHT, MICHELANGELO ★★1/2 In this bizarre but whimsical film, we see the intertwined lives of four Italian families. Confusing but ultimately rewarding. Rated R for profanity. 91m. **DIR:** Carlo Liconti. **CAST:** Lina Sastri, Kim Cattrall, Tony Nardi. 1989

GOOD OLD BOYS, THE ★★★★★ Hewey Calloway is as wild as the country in which he's lived, a fact that adds tension during his visit to the west Texas homestead of his soft-spoken brother. Not only does lewey lock horns with a pompous lawman along the rail, but he renews a long-standing feud with his strong-willed sister-in-law. An awkward romance with schoolmarm Spring Refro adds charm to this story in which the brothers must save the Calloway ranch from a scheming banker. Familiar conventions of the genre avoid cliché, and the result is extremely satisfying. Made for TV. 110m. **DIR:** Tommy Lee Jones. **CAST:** Tommy Lee Jones, Sissy Spacek, Terry Kinney, Frances McDormand, Sam Shepard, Wilford Brimley, Matt Damon, Blayne Weaver, Bruce McGill, Larry Mahan, Richard Jones. **1995**

GOOD SAM ★★ Gary Cooper plays a guy who can't say no in this barely watchable "comedy." He's Mr. Nice-Guy to everyone but his own family. He feels he has to help everyone, so he lends all his money to "friends" and the "needy." B&W; 114m. **DIR:** Leo McCarey. **CAST:** Gary Cooper, Ann Sheridan, Edmund Lowe. **1948**

GOOD SON, THE ★★★ Against-the-grain casting makes this updated *Bad Seed* a kinky hoot. Cutie-pie Macaulay Culkin stars in his first R-rated movie as a wicked, psychotic child whose cousin temporarily moves in after his mother dies. This psychological thriller delivers some creepy chills as Culkin escorts his new pal to the edge of hell. Going *Home Alone* again will never be the same. Rated R for profanity and violence. 87m. **DIR:** Joseph Ruben. **CAST:** Macaulay Culkin, Elijah Wood, Quinn Culkin, Wendy Crewson. **1993**

GOOD THE BAD AND THE UGLY, THE ★★★★ The best of Italian director Sergio Leone's spaghetti Westerns with Clint Eastwood, this release features the latter in the dubiously "good" role, with Lee Van Cleef as "the bad" and Eli Wallach as "the ugly." All three are after a cache of gold hidden in a Confederate army graveyard. For Leone fans, it's full of what made his movies so memorable. Others might find it a bit long, but no one can deny its sense of style. 161m. **DIR:** Sergio Leone. **CAST:** Clint Eastwood, Eli Wallach, Lee Van Cleef. **1966 DVD**

GOOD WIFE, THE 🖤 One woman's yearning for sexual fulfillment. Rated R. 97m. **DIR:** Ken Cameron. **CAST:** Rachel Ward, Bryan Brown, Sam Neill, Steven Vidler. **1987**

GOOD WILL HUNTING ★★★★1/2 When a janitor at MIT is discovered to be a natural mathematical genius, he and the powers-that-be turn to a troubled psychologist to sort out the boy's problems. Surprisingly straightforward direction with a few quirky touches, and superb performances result in a near masterpiece of cinema that can be enjoyed by viewers of all ages and backgrounds. Damon co-wrote the Oscar-winning screenplay with friend and co-star Ben Affleck. This is one not to miss. Rated R for profanity and violence. 126m. **DIR:** Gus Van Sant. **CAST:** Matt Damon, Robin Williams, Ben Affleck, Minnie Driver, Stellan Skarsgard, Casey Affleck, Cole Hauser. **1997 DVD**

GOODBYE AGAIN ★★1/2 Françoise Sagan melodrama starring Ingrid Bergman as a fashion designer who uses callow Tony Perkins to make noncommittal boyfriend Yves Montand jealous. The Paris settings and capable cast make it painless. Look for Diahann Carroll. 120m. **DIR:** Anatole Litvak. **CAST:** Ingrid Bergman, Anthony Perkins, Yves Montand, Jessie Royce Landis, Peter Bull, Diahann Carroll. **1961**

GOODBYE BIRD, THE ★★ A teenage boy having a difficult time coping with his parents' divorce gets in trouble at school and is assigned to a work program at the local pound. He decides to rescue the unwanted creatures therein by setting up an animal shelter in a deserted barn. Sentimental, farfetched story may still please youngsters. Rated G. 91m. **DIR:** William Clark. **CAST:** Christopher Pettiet, Cindy Pickett, Wayne Rogers. **1992**

GOODBYE COLUMBUS ★★★★ This film marked the start of Ali MacGraw's and Richard Benjamin's movie careers. Ali plays a rich, spoiled Jewish-American princess who meets a college dropout (Benjamin) at her country club. They have an affair, and we get to see her flaws through his "average guy" eyes. Rated R. 105m. **DIR:** Larry Peerce. **CAST:** Richard Benjamin, Ali MacGraw, Jack Klugman. **1969**

GOODBYE EMMANUELLE ★★ One of the *Emmanuelle* soft-core series, this one takes place on a tropical island and concerns a succession of personal and sexual relationships among half a dozen men and women. The dubbing is tolerable. Rated R for sexual situations. 92m. **DIR:** François Letterier. **CAST:** Sylvia Kristel, Umberto Orsini, Jean Pierre Bouvier. **1979**

GOODBYE GIRL, THE ★★★★1/2 Neil Simon's sparkling screenplay and the acting of Marsha Mason and Richard Dreyfuss combine to produce one of the best pure comedies since Hollywood's golden '30s. Mason and Dreyfuss are a mismatched pair of New Yorkers forced to become roommates. Rated PG. 110m. **DIR:** Herbert Ross. **CAST:** Richard Dreyfuss, Marsha Mason, Quinn Cummings. **1977 DVD**

GOODBYE LOVER ★★★1/2 This thoroughly demented drama is a macabre bit of *modern noir* that faithfully retains the atmosphere of classic 1950s B flicks, while injecting the wincing, ghastly humor that made *Pulp Fiction* and *Fargo* such guilty pleasures (credit Joel Coen's contributions to the script). A very bad girl has plenty of company in a Machiavellian murder scheme that starts as she dallies with two brothers, with murderous results. Mary-Louise Parker is superb as the other woman in this complex romantic rhombus, and Ellen DeGeneres steals the show as a cynical police detective forever belittling her Bible-thumping partner. Rated R for violence, profanity, nudity, and strong sexual content. 115m. **DIR:** Roland Joffe. **CAST:** Patricia Arquette, Dermot Mulroney, Ellen DeGeneres, Mary-Louise Parker, Don Johnson, Ray McKinnon. **1999 DVD**

GOODBYE, MISS 4TH OF JULY ★★★1/2 Inspirational true story of a young Greek immigrant who refuses to let her American dream be tarnished by bigotry in 1917 West Virginia. Roxana Zal plays spunky Niki Janus, who befriends Big John Creed (Lou Gossett Jr.) and thus attracts the wrath of the Ku Klux Klan. Made for the Disney Channel, this has high production values. Not rated; contains frightening scenes of night riders in action. 89m. **DIR:** George Miller. **CAST:** Roxana Zal, Lou Gossett Jr., Chris Sarandon, Chantal Contouri, Chynna Phillips, Mitchell Anderson. 1988

GOODBYE, MR. CHIPS (1939) ★★★1/2 Robert Donat creates one of filmdom's most heartwarming roles as Chips, the Latin teacher of an English boys' school. The poignant movie follows Chips from his first bumbling, early teaching days until he becomes a beloved school institution. Greer Garson was introduced to American audiences in the rewarding role of Chips's loving wife. B&W; 114m. **DIR:** Sam Wood. **CAST:** Robert Donat, Greer Garson, John Mills. 1939

GOODBYE, MR. CHIPS (1969) ● Cash in this *Chips.* Rated G. 151m. **DIR:** Herbert Ross. **CAST:** Peter O'Toole, Petula Clark, Michael Redgrave, George Baker, Sian Phillips. 1969

GOODBYE, MY LADY ★★★ A young boy in the bayou country finds a lost dog and takes it to his heart, knowing that it probably belongs to someone else and that he might have to give it up. Director William Wellman transforms James Street's novel into a warm, enduring film. This uncluttered little gem features standout performances by Brandon de Wilde and Walter Brennan as the youngster and his uncle. B&W; 94m. **DIR:** William Wellman. **CAST:** Walter Brennan, Phil Harris, Brandon de Wilde, Sidney Poitier, William Hopper, Louise Beavers. 1956

GOODBYE NEW YORK ★★★ In this amusing comedy, an insurance salesperson (Julie Hagerty) becomes fed up with her job and husband and leaves for Paris. After falling asleep on the plane, she wakes up in Israel with no money and no luggage. Rated R for language and very brief nudity. 90m. **DIR:** Amos Kollek. **CAST:** Julie Hagerty, Amos Kollek, David Topaz, Shmuel Shiloh. 1984

GOODBYE, NORMA JEAN ★★★ A depiction of Norma Jean Baker's travels along the rocky road to superstardom as Marilyn Monroe. Her only motivation in life is her dream of becoming a star. Rated R for nudity. 95m. **DIR:** Larry Buchanan. **CAST:** Misty Rowe, Terrence Locke, Patch Mackenzie. 1975

GOODBYE PEOPLE, THE ★★★★ This unashamedly sentimental film is a delight. Martin Balsam is memorable as a man attempting to realize the dream of many years by rebuilding his Coney Island hot dog stand. Pamela Reed and Judd Hirsch, as the young people who help him, turn in outstanding performances, and the hot dog stand itself is a fantastic structure. 104m. **DIR:** Herb Gardner. **CAST:** Judd Hirsch, Martin Balsam, Pamela Reed, Ron Silver, Michael Tucker, Gene Saks. 1984

GOODFELLAS ★★★★★ No punches are pulled in this violent, mesmerizing movie, which covers thirty years in the life of a Mafia family. Based on the book by Nicholas Pileggi, it features Ray Liotta as a half-Irish, half-Sicilian kid from Brooklyn who achieves his life's ambition of being a gangster when he is adopted by a local "family" headed by Paul Sorvino. Rated R for violence, profanity, and depictions of drug use. 148m. **DIR:** Martin Scorsese. **CAST:** Robert De Niro, Joe Pesci, Ray Liotta, Lorraine Bracco, Paul Sorvino. 1990 DVD

GOODNIGHT, GOD BLESS ● British entry in the slasher sweepstakes has a maniacal killer dressed in priest's garb. Not rated; contains violence and sexual suggestion. 100m. **DIR:** John Eyres. **CAST:** Emma Sutton, Frank Rozelaar Goleen. 1988

GOOF BALLS ● This lame comedy opens with a bungled robbery performed by a bunch of inept losers. Gangsters, oil sheiks, bikinied girls, and a number of other stupid characters abound. No rated. 89m. **DIR:** Brad Turner. **CAST:** Ben Gordon. 1987

GOOFY MOVIE, A ★★★1/2 Single parent Goofy tries some male bonding with teenage son Max. Kids will enjoy this slapstick-filled feature-length cartoon that attempts to address the frequent misunderstandings between teens and their parents. Rated G. 78m. **DIR:** Kevin Lima. 1995 DVD

GOONIES, THE ★★★ This "Steven Spielberg production" is a mess. But it's sometimes an entertaining mess. The screenplay, taken from a story by Spielberg, concerns a feisty group of underprivileged kids—whose housing project is about to be destroyed—who find a treasure map, which could be the solution to all their problems. Rated PG for profanity. 111m. **DIR:** Richard Donner. **CAST:** Sean Astin, Josh Brolin, Jeff Cohen, Corey Feldman, Kerri Green, Martha Plimpton, Ke Huy-Quan. 1985

GOOSE WOMAN, THE ★★★ Unusual drama, based on a novel by Rex Beach: a famous opera star, after giving birth to an illegitimate son, loses her standing and is reduced to poverty and drink. A contrived ending mars an otherwise sensitive outing for Louise Dresser and then-young director Clarence Brown. Silent. B&W; 90m. **DIR:** Clarence Brown. **CAST:** Louise Dresser, Jack Pickford, Constance Bennett. 1925

GOOSEBUMPS: THE HAUNTED MASK ★★★★ Perfectly realized Halloween story based on R. L. Stine's popular series of books. Carly Beth is so proud of her new Halloween mask that she never takes it off. Then on Halloween night, she learns that she can't take it off—she has become a monster. Plenty of chills and mayhem ensue as Carly Beth seeks help for her unusual problem. Not rated. 44m. **DIR:** Timothy Bond. **CAST:** Kathryn Long, Cody Jones, Kathryn Short, Brenda Bazinet. 1995

GOR ★★ A mild-mannered college professor is thrust through time and space to help a simple tribe recover its magical stone in this Conan-inspired sword-and-sorcery flick. Elaborate costumes and sets don't make up for the second-rate story. Rated PG for violence. 95m. **DIR:** Fritz Kiersch. **CAST:** Urbano Barberini, Rebecca Ferratti, Jack Palance, Paul Smith, Oliver Reed. 1987

GORATH ● An out-of-control planet headed for Earth is the subject of this Japanese science-fiction flick. 77m. **DIR:** Inoshiro Honda. **CAST:** None Credited. 1964

GORDON'S WAR ★★1/2 Competent but uninspiring variation on *Death Wish* with an all-black cast. Paul Winfield is a Vietnam vet who avenges his wife's drug death. Rated R for violence, language, graphic drug use, and nudity. 90m. **DIR:** Ossie Davis. **CAST:** Paul Winfield, Carl Lee, David Downing, Tony King, Gilbert Lewis. 1978

GORDY ★★ This live-action tale about a talking pig who becomes a tabloid celebrity and CEO of a rich conglomerate is slow-paced and the film's slaughterhouse finale may upset younger viewers. Rated G.

89m. DIR: Mark Lewis. CAST: Justin Garms, Doug Stone, Deborah Hobart, Kristy Young, Michael Roescher, Tom Lester, Ted Manson. 1995

GORE VIDAL'S BILLY THE KID ★★ Uninspired retelling of the last years of Billy the Kid. Fine location cinematography enhance the realism, but the script and direction all but sink this TV movie. 92m. DIR: William A. Graham. CAST: Val Kilmer, Wilford Brimley. 1989

GORE VIDAL'S LINCOLN ★★★★ Fine made-for-TV adaptation of Gore Vidal's novel depicting Lincoln as more of a politician than an idealist. Sam Waterston makes a decent Lincoln but Mary Tyler Moore delivers the performance of a lifetime as a mentally unstable Mary Todd Lincoln. The film focuses on the four years between Lincoln's presidential election and his assassination. Not rated; contains violence and gore in multiple Civil War battle scenes. 118m. DIR: Lamont Johnson. CAST: Sam Waterston, Mary Tyler Moore, Richard Mulligan, Ruby Dee, Steven Culp, Tom Brennan, Gregory Cooke. 1988

GORGEOUS HUSSY ★★ This tale of an innkeeper's daughter who wins the hearts of various political guests is the kind of movie that flickers in the bedrooms of insomniacs at three in the morning. B&W; 103m. DIR: Clarence Brown. CAST: Joan Crawford, Lionel Barrymore, Robert Taylor, Franchot Tone, Melvyn Douglas, James Stewart. 1936

GORGO ★★★1/2 Unpretentious thriller from England has a dinosaur-type monster captured and put on display in London's Piccadilly Circus, only to have its towering two-hundred-foot parent destroy half the city looking for it. Brisk pacing and well-executed effects. 76m. DIR: Eugene Lourie. CAST: Bill Travers, William Sylvester, Vincent Winter, Martin Benson. 1961

GORGON, THE ★★★ Peter Cushing and Christopher Lee take on a Medusa-headed monster in this British Hammer Films chiller. A good one for horror buffs. 83m. DIR: Terence Fisher. CAST: Peter Cushing, Christopher Lee, Richard Pasco, Barbara Shelley. 1964

GORILLA, THE ★★ This is another one of those horror comedies that takes place in an old mansion and again wastes poor Bela Lugosi's acting talents. The Ritz Brothers were an acquired taste, to be sure. B&W; 66m. DIR: Allan Dwan. CAST: The Ritz Brothers, Bela Lugosi, Lionel Atwill. 1939 DVD

GORILLA AT LARGE ★★ Silly murder mystery set against a carnival background came at the end of the 3-D craze. A cast of familiar faces looks properly embarrassed by the inane goings-on, thus making it fun to watch. 84m. DIR: Harmon Jones. CAST: Cameron Mitchell, Anne Bancroft, Lee J. Cobb, Raymond Burr, Charlotte Austin, Lee Marvin. 1954

GORILLAS IN THE MIST ★★★★ Sigourney Weaver stars in this impressive biopic about Dian Fossey, the crusading primatologist whose devotion to the once nearly extinct mountain gorillas of central Africa led to her murder. Rather than present Fossey as a saint, the film takes great pains to show her complexity. Fossey's interaction with the gorillas provides unforgettable scenes. Rated PG-13 for profanity, suggested sex, and violence. 129m. DIR: Michael Apted.

CAST: Sigourney Weaver, Bryan Brown, Julie Harris, John Omirah Miluwi. 1988 DVD

GORKY PARK ★★1/2 In this maddeningly uninvolving screen version of Martin Cruz Smith's bestselling mystery novel, three mutilated bodies are found in the Moscow park, and it's up to Russian policeman Arkady Renko (a miscast William Hurt) to find the maniacal killer. Lee Marvin is quite good as a suave bad guy, as are Joanna Pacula and Brian Dennehy. Rated R for nudity, sex, violence, and profanity. 128m. DIR: Michael Apted. CAST: William Hurt, Lee Marvin, Joanna Pacula, Brian Dennehy, Ian Bannen, Alexander Knox. 1983

GORP ✔ Particularly unfunny summer-camp flick. Rated R for nudity and profanity. 91m. DIR: Joseph Ruben. CAST: Michael Lembeck, Philip Casnoff, Dennis Quaid, David Huddleston, Rosanna Arquette. 1980

GOSHOGUN—THE TIME STRANGER ★★★ Six friends defy death in this animated story of sacrifice and loyalty among a group of elite government agents. Don't let the shifting time lines throw you—there's more here than meets the eye. In Japanese with English subtitles. Not rated; contains violence, nudity, and profanity. 90m. DIR: Kunihiko Yuyama. 1985

GOSPEL ★★★★ Featuring many of the top stars of black gospel music, this is a joyous, spirit-lifting music documentary that contains the highlights of a five-and-a-half-hour concert filmed in June 1981 at Oakland Paramount Theater. The spirited performances might even make a believer out of you—that is, if you aren't already. Rated G. 92m. DIR: David Levick, Frederick A. Rizenberg. CAST: Mighty Clouds of Joy, Clark Sisters, Walter Hawkins and the Hawkins Family, Shirley Caesar, Rev. James Cleveland. 1982

GOSPEL ACCORDING TO SAINT MATTHEW, THE ★★★★ Pier Paolo Pasolini's visionary account of Jesus Christ's spiritual struggle against the afflictions of social injustice. Shot on location throughout southern Italy with a cast of nonprofessional actors who possess a natural quality. This highly acclaimed film received a special jury prize at the Venice Film Festival. In Italian with English subtitles. B&W; 136m. DIR: Pier Paolo Pasolini. CAST: Enrique Irazoque. 1964

GOSPEL ACCORDING TO VIC, THE ★★★1/2 In this delightful comedy from Scotland, a teacher (Tom Conti) at a Glasgow parochial school finds that he can create miracles—even though he doesn't believe in them. Those who have reveled in the subtle, sly humor of Gregory's Girl, Local Hero, and other Scottish films will find similar joys in this. Rated PG-13 for adult content. 92m. DIR: Charles Gormley. CAST: Tom Conti, Helen Mirren, David Hayman, Brian Pettifer, Jennifer Black. 1986

•GOSSIP ★★1/2 Three college students start a nasty rumor as an exercise for a communications class, then the rumor gets out of hand and the innocent begin to suffer. The film has a kind of sinister energy, but it's shallow, casually vicious, and unconvincing, as if we're not expected to believe it but merely enjoy the trendy MTV-age hipness of it all. Rated R for profanity, sexual scenes, and brief violence. 90m. DIR: Davis Guggenheim. CAST: James

Marsden, Lena Headey, Norman Reedus, Kate Hudson, Edward James Olmos, Eric Bogosian. **2000**

GOTCHA! ★★★ In this entertaining mixture of coming-of-age comedy and suspense-thriller, a college boy (Anthony Edwards) goes to Paris in search of romance and adventure. He gets both when he meets a beautiful, mysterious woman (Linda Fiorentino) who puts both of their lives in danger. Rated PG-13 for slight nudity, suggested sex, profanity, and violence. 97m. **DIR:** Jeff Kanew. **CAST:** Anthony Edwards, Linda Fiorentino, Alex Rocco, Nick Corri, Marla Adams, Klaus Lowitsch. **1985**

GOTHAM ★★ A *film noir* thriller that's confusing, slow, and tediously melodramatic. Tommy Lee Jones is a Marlowesque detective hired as a go-between for a well-to-do husband and his murdered wife (Virginia Madsen). Romantically atmospheric and beautifully photographed, the film is marred by terrible dialogue and anemic acting. Rated R for nudity, simulated sex, violence, and profanity. 92m. **DIR:** Lloyd Fonvielle. **CAST:** Tommy Lee Jones, Virginia Madsen, Frederic Forrest. **1988**

GOTHIC ★★ Director Ken Russell returns to his favorite subject—the tortured artist—for this look at what may have happened that spooky evening in 1816 when Lord Byron, poet Percy Shelley, his fiancée Mary, her stepsister Claire, and Byron's ex-lover Dr. Polidori spent the evening together, attempting to scare each other. What the viewer gets is the usual Russell bag of tricks: insane hallucinations, group sex, scenes of gruesome murders, and much, much more. Rated R. 90m. **DIR:** Ken Russell. **CAST:** Gabriel Byrne, Julian Sands, Natasha Richardson, Timothy Spall. **1986 DVD**

GOTTI ★★★★ Armand Assante embraces the title role in this absorbing docudrama, as the Mafia "Teflon Don" who was just as loved by blue-collar New Yorkers as he was despised by the FBI. Based on *Gotti, Rise and Fall*, by Jerry Capeci and Gene Mustain, the story loosely follows Gotti's career from 1973 to the betrayal from within that finally brought him down. Assante convincingly sells Gotti as a suave clotheshorse, with a hair-trigger temper matched only by the savvy that maintained his growing power base. Compelling viewing. Rated R for violence and profanity. 116m. **DIR:** Robert Harmon. **CAST:** Armand Assante, William Forsythe, Richard Sarafian, Frank Vincent, Dominic Chianese, Anthony Quinn. **1996**

GOVERNESS, THE ★★1/2 Although you're bound to sympathize with an intelligent and well-bred nineteenth-century Jewish woman prompted to conceal her heritage due to a repressive environment, it's hard to get beyond this gal's self-destructive stupidity. The woman in question (Minnie Driver) takes a job as a governess but quickly initiates an affair with the child's father. Pretty tiresome for most of us. Rated R for nudity and strong sexual content. 114m. **DIR:** Sandra Goldbacher. **CAST:** Minnie Driver, Tom Wilkinson, Harriet Walter, Florence Hoath, Bruce Myers, Jonathan Rhys Meyers. **1998 DVD**

GRACE AND GLORIE ★★★1/2 Having left the fast-paced city life, Diane Lane plays a woman who finds hospice work very satisfying and peaceful. That peace is shattered by a new patient (Gena Rowlands) who forces her to confront her attraction to death and dying. Rowlands's scenes are more inspiring than depressing in this *Hallmark Hall of Fame* production. Smiles and tears are virtually guaranteed. Not rated; contains adult themes. 99m. **DIR:** Arthur Allan Seidelman. **CAST:** Gena Rowlands, Diane Lane, Neal McDonough, Chris Beetem. **1998**

GRACE OF MY HEART ★★1/2 Give writer-director Allison Anders credit: she obviously tried to take us inside the music business with this film about the career of a Carole King–style singer-songwriter. Indeed it is pretty much King's story up until she leaves New York for Los Angeles and starts up an affair with a surf-music genius/recluse. It is here that the film loses its pace and credibility. Illeana Douglas shines throughout, even when the screenplay begins to border on parody. Rated R for suggested sex and profanity. 116m. **DIR:** Allison Anders. **CAST:** Illeana Douglas, Matt Dillon, Eric Stoltz, John Turturro, Bruce Davison, Patsy Kensit, Chris Isaak, Bridget Fonda. **1996 DVD**

GRACE QUIGLEY ★★1/2 After witnessing the murder of her landlord, spinster Katharine Hepburn enlists the aid of freelance hit man Nick Nolte. Hepburn wants Nolte to end her life, but not before he puts to rest some of her elderly friends who feel it is time for them to die. Extremely black comedy doesn't have enough humor and warmth to rise above its gruesome subject matter. Rated R. 87m. **DIR:** Anthony Harvey. **CAST:** Katharine Hepburn, Nick Nolte, Elizabeth Wilson, Chip Zien, Christopher Murney. **1985**

GRADUATE, THE ★★★★1/2 Mike Nichols won an Academy Award for his direction of this touching, funny, unsettling, and unforgettable release about a young man (Dustin Hoffman, in his first major role) attempting to chart his future and develop his own set of values. He falls in love with Katharine Ross, but finds himself seduced by her wily, sexy mother, Anne Bancroft (as Mrs. Robinson). Don't forget the superb soundtrack of songs by Paul Simon and Art Garfunkel. 105m. **DIR:** Mike Nichols. **CAST:** Dustin Hoffman, Anne Bancroft, Katharine Ross. **1967 DVD**

GRADUATION DAY ★★ A high school runner dies during a competition. Soon someone begins killing all her teammates. Plenty of violence in this one. Rated R. 96m. **DIR:** Herb Freed. **CAST:** Christopher George, Michael Pataki, E. J. Peaker. **1981**

GRAFFITI BRIDGE ★★ Prince's hollow fantasy sequel to *Purple Rain* is about the conflicting values (artistic integrity versus commercial success) that ignite a power struggle between two nightclub co-owners (funksters Prince and Morris Day). Rated PG-13 for profanity and sexual themes. 111m. **DIR:** Prince. **CAST:** Prince, Morris Day, Jerome Benton, Ingrid Chavez. **1990**

GRAIN OF SAND, THE ★★★1/2 A struggling woman retreats to her hometown to search for an old love. Delphine Seyrig's strong performance is the highlight of this moving drama. In French with English subtitles. 90m. **DIR:** Pomme Meffre. **CAST:** Delphine Seyrig, Genevieve Fontanel. **1982**

GRAND CANYON ★★★★1/2 Writer-director Lawrence Kasdan picks up ten years later with the baby-boom generation he first examined in *The Big*

Chill. Through a collection of vignettes of daily life, a superb cast portrays what it's like to be 40 in the Nineties. No motion picture is flawless, but this funny, touching, and insightful character study comes pretty close. Rated R for profanity, nudity, and violence. 134m. **DIR:** Lawrence Kasdan. **CAST:** Danny Glover, Kevin Kline, Steve Martin, Mary McDonnell, Mary-Louise Parker, Alfre Woodard. **1991**

GRAND HOTEL ★★★★ World War I is over. Life in the fast lane has returned to Berlin's Grand Hotel, crossroads of a thousand lives, backdrop to as many stories. This anthology of life at various levels won an Oscar for best picture. B&W; 113m. **DIR:** Edmund Goulding. **CAST:** John Barrymore, Greta Garbo, Wallace Beery, Joan Crawford, Lionel Barrymore, Lewis Stone. **1932**

GRAND ILLUSION ★★★★★ Shortly before Hitler plunged Europe into World War II, this monumental French film tried to examine why men submit to warfare's "grand illusions." We are taken to a German prison camp in World War I, where it becomes quite easy to see the hypocrisy of war while watching the day-to-day miniworld of camp life. This classic by Jean Renoir is a must-see for anyone who appreciates great art. B&W; 95m. **DIR:** Jean Renoir. **CAST:** Jean Gabin, Pierre Fresnay, Erich Von Stroheim, Marcel Dalio, Julien Carette. **1937 DVD**

GRAND ISLE ★★★ While on vacation on an island paradise, Kelly McGillis discovers the passion inside of her reawakened when she encounters several men. Handsome production features a gorgeous cast and scenery. Contains nudity and simulated sex. 94m. **DIR:** Mary Lambert. **CAST:** Kelly McGillis, Julian Sands, Glenne Headly, Ellen Burstyn. **1991**

GRAND LARCENY ★★ A miscast Marilu Henner brings low this caper comedy about the American-raised daughter of a French thief, whose death results in her having to take over the "family business." Only the presence of debonair Ian McShane saves this from being a complete failure. Made for TV. 95m. **DIR:** Jeannot Szwarc. **CAST:** Marilu Henner, Ian McShane, Louis Jourdan, Omar Sharif. **1988**

GRAND PRIX ★★1/2 The cars, the drivers, and the race itself are the real stars of this international epic, beautifully filmed on locations throughout Europe. The four interrelated stories of professional adversaries and their personal lives intrude on the exciting footage of the real thing. Yves Montand, though, does a credible job in what is basically a big-budget soap opera with oil stains. 179m. **DIR:** John Frankenheimer. **CAST:** James Garner, Eva Marie Saint, Yves Montand, Toshiro Mifune, Brian Bedford, Jessica Walter, Antonio Sabato, Adolfo Celi. **1966**

GRAND THEFT AUTO ★★1/2 The basic plot of *It's a Mad Mad Mad Mad World* is given a retread by first-time director—and star—Ron Howard in this frantic 1977 car-chase comedy. Sadly, little of the style that made *Night Shift* and *Splash* such treats is evident here. Rated PG. 89m. **DIR:** Ron Howard. **CAST:** Ron Howard, Nancy Morgan. **1977 DVD**

GRAND TOUR: DISASTER IN TIME ★★★ Lawrence O'Donnell and C. L. Moore's classic science-fiction novella, *The Vintage Season*, is the basis of this intriguing made-for-cable drama, which finds

innkeeper Jeff Daniels rather puzzled over the strange behavior of some new tourists … who, for example, clearly don't understand the principle behind tying shoes. Unfortunately, writer-director David N. Twohy ruins a good thing with his needlessly upbeat conclusion. Rated PG-13. 99m. **DIR:** David N. Twohy. **CAST:** Jeff Daniels, Ariana Richards, Emilia Crow, Jim Haynie. **1992**

•**GRANDMA'S BOY** ★★★ Shy, young man wins the girl of his dreams with the help of his loving grandmother. Through some time-worn plot devices, the timid fellow captures a local terror and takes on the bully who has plagued him most of his life, but it's satisfying fun and still holds up. Harold Lloyd scored his feature-length bull's-eye with this release and joined the pantheon of great silent comedians that included Charlie Chaplin and Buster Keaton. B&W; 49m. **DIR:** Fred Newmeyer. **CAST:** Harold Lloyd, Mildred Davis, Anna Townsend, Charles Stevenson, Dick Sutherland. **1922**

GRANDMA'S HOUSE ★★★1/2 Two orphaned teens sent to live with their grandparents suspect that this seemingly kindly old couple have a few skeletons in the closet. Cleverly written thriller has more than its share of surprises. Not rated, but violence makes this unsuitable for kids. 89m. **DIR:** Peter Rader. **CAST:** Eric Foster, Kim Valentine, Brinke Stevens. **1989**

GRANDVIEW, U.S.A. ★★ A coming-of-age study lacking in depth and characterization. Rated R for nudity, violence, and profanity. 97m. **DIR:** Randal Kleiser. **CAST:** Jamie Lee Curtis, C. Thomas Howell, Patrick Swayze, Jennifer Jason Leigh, Ramon Bieri, Carole Cook, Troy Donahue, William Windom. **1984**

GRANNY, THE ★★★ Stella Stevens chews up the scenery in this hilarious horror spoof, as a miserable, spiteful, wealthy old battle-ax whose conniving family hastens her departure for her fortune. Granny, though, has plans of her own. She acquires a mythical potion for eternal life that doesn't quite produce the results she expected. Rated R for nudity, violence, and profanity. 85m. **DIR:** Luca Bercovici. **CAST:** Stella Stevens, Shannon Whirry. **1994**

GRAPES OF WRATH, THE ★★★★★ Henry Fonda stars in this superb screen adaptation of the John Steinbeck novel about farmers from Oklahoma fleeing the Dust Bowl and poverty of their home state only to be confronted by prejudice and violence in California. It's a compelling drama beautifully acted by the director's stock company. B&W; 129m. **DIR:** John Ford. **CAST:** Henry Fonda, John Carradine, Jane Darwell, Russell Simpson, Charley Grapewin, John Qualen. **1940**

GRASS HARP, THE ★★1/2 This is based on Truman Capote's bittersweet memoir detailing a boyhood spent with his two maiden aunts. A strong supporting cast helps to define his eccentric southern family, but Edward Furlong is too understated as Capote's alter ego. There are some charming moments, but cloying sentimentalism undermines all. Rated PG for mild profanity. 107m. **DIR:** Charles Matthau. **CAST:** Walter Matthau, Jack Lemmon, Sissy Spacek, Piper Laurie, Mary Steenburgen, Edward Furlong, Charles Durning, Nell Carter, Roddy McDowall. **1995**

GRASS IS ALWAYS GREENER OVER THE SEPTIC TANK, THE ★★★1/2 Carol Burnett and Charles Grodin shine in this tale of the domestic horrors of suburban life taken from Erma Bombeck's bestseller. The comedy doesn't always work, but when it does it rivals Grodin's *The Heartbreak Kid* and some of the best moments of Burnett's TV show. No rating, but the equivalent of a PG for language. 98m. **DIR:** Robert Day. **CAST:** Carol Burnett, Charles Grodin, Alex Rocco, Linda Gray. 1978

GRASS IS GREENER, THE ★★★1/2 Cary Grant and Deborah Kerr star as a married couple experimenting with extramarital affairs in this comedy. Some funny moments, but it's not hilarious. 105m. **DIR:** Stanley Donen. **CAST:** Cary Grant, Deborah Kerr, Jean Simmons, Robert Mitchum. 1960

GRASSHOPPER, THE ★★★1/2 Jacqueline Bisset is riveting in this little-known film. She plays a young woman who abandons the security of her family for the glamour and excitement of the entertainment world. Unfortunately, her career hopes are shattered as each man in her life robs her of self-respect. Quirky ending warns viewers of the rapid descent one might take after rejecting morality. Equivalent to an R for sexual situations and seedy lifestyle. 95m. **DIR:** Jerry Paris. **CAST:** Jacqueline Bisset, Jim Brown, Joseph Cotten. 1970

GRAVE, THE ★★★1/2 You'll have fun with this nasty little thriller. After hearing about a treasure supposedly buried beneath a grave, two good ol' boys bust out of prison, connect with some particularly dim-witted friends. Although warped and vicious, this will please viewers with a macabre sense of humor. Good twist ending, too. Rated R for profanity, violence, and simulated sex. 90m. **DIR:** Jonas Pate. **CAST:** Craig Sheffer, Gabrielle Anwar, Anthony Michael Hall, Josh Charles, Donal Logue, Keith David, Eric Roberts. 1995

GRAVE INDISCRETION ★★★ A stuffy British archaeologist finds his world infiltrated and eventually overrun by a mysterious and ultimately menacing butler. Outstanding performances throughout. Also known as *Gentlemen Don't Eat Poets*. Rated R for nudity. 98m. **DIR:** John-Paul Davidson. **CAST:** Alan Bates, Theresa Russell, Sting, John Mills. 1996

GRAVE OF THE FIREFLIES ★★★★ Those who doubt that animation can successfully tell serious, meaningful stories should watch this wonderful animated feature. Young Seita and his little sister, homeless and orphaned during the final days of World War II, try desperately to survive in a time when food and aid are scarce. This story will break your heart. In Japanese with English subtitles. Not rated, but suitable for most audiences. 88m. **DIR:** Isao Takahata. 1988 DVD

GRAVE OF THE VAMPIRE ❤ Baby bloodsucker grows up to search for his father and discover his birthright. 95m. **DIR:** John Hayes. **CAST:** William Smith, Michael Pataki. 1972

GRAVE SECRETS ★★ A woman, tormented by what she believes are ghosts, hires a parapsychologist in this not-too-scary supernatural flick. Rated R for violence and profanity. 90m. **DIR:** Donald P. Borchers.

CAST: Paul LeMat, Renee Soutendijk, David Warner, Lee Ving, John Crawford. 1989

GRAVE SECRETS: THE LEGACY OF HILLTOP DRIVE ★★ The paranormal goings-on in this made-for-TV movie are pretty mild. Too much of a resemblance to the ghost story classic *Poltergeist*. 94m. **DIR:** John Patterson. **CAST:** Patty Duke, David Soul, David Selby, Keirsten Warren, Kimberly Cullum. 1992

GRAVESEND ★★1/2 Young director Salvatore Stabile makes an impressive debut with this gritty tale of four Brooklyn teenagers trying to dispose of a body. Unfortunately, the cast isn't nearly as committed as the director, and they fail to command the situation or our attention. Rated R for language and violence. 86m. **DIR:** Salvatore Stabile. **CAST:** Thomas Brandise, Tom Malloy, Michael Parducci, Tony Tucci. 1997 DVD

GRAVEYARD SHIFT (1987) ❤ New York cabbie expects more than a tip. Rated R. 90m. **DIR:** Gerard Ciccoritti. **CAST:** Silvio Oliviero, Helen Papas. 1987

GRAY LADY DOWN ★★★1/2 This adventure film starring Charlton Heston is action-packed and well-acted. The story concerns a two-man rescue operation of a sunken nuclear sub that has collided with a freighter. Beautiful photography and special effects. 111m. **DIR:** David Greene. **CAST:** Charlton Heston, David Carradine, Stacy Keach, Ned Beatty, Ronny Cox, Rosemary Forsyth. 1977 DVD

GRAYEAGLE ★★ Disappointing reworking of John Wayne's *The Searchers*, with Alex Cord as the Cheyenne warrior Grayeagle, who kidnaps Lana Wood and is pursued by the girl's father, Ben Johnson. Rated PG for violence and mild nudity. 104m. **DIR:** Charles B. Pierce. **CAST:** Ben Johnson, Iron Eyes Cody, Lana Wood, Alex Cord, Jack Elam, Paul Fix. 1977

GREASE ★★★ After they meet and enjoy a tender summer romance, John Travolta and Olivia Newton-John tearfully part. Surprisingly, they are reunited when she becomes the new girl at his high school. Around his friends, he must play Mr. Tough Guy, and her goody-two-shoes image doesn't quite fit in. Slight, but fun. Rated PG. 110m. **DIR:** Randal Kleiser. **CAST:** John Travolta, Olivia Newton-John, Stockard Channing, Jeff Conaway, Didi Conn, Eve Arden, Sid Caesar. 1978

GREASE 2 ★★★ A sequel to the most successful screen musical of all time, *Grease 2* takes us back to Rydell High. The result is a fun little movie that seems to work almost in spite of itself. Rated PG for suggestive gestures and lyrics. 115m. **DIR:** Patricia Birch. **CAST:** Maxwell Caulfield, Michelle Pfeiffer, Adrian Zmed, Lorna Luft, Didi Conn. 1982

GREASED LIGHTNING ★★★ *Greased Lightning* is a funny and exciting film. Richard Pryor is a knock-out in the lead role, and the film is a real audience pleaser. Because the story is true, it carries a punch even *Rocky* couldn't match. Wendell Scott's story is more dramatic. Scott was the first black man to win a NASCAR Grand National stock car race. Rated PG. 96m. **DIR:** Michael Schultz. **CAST:** Richard Pryor, Pam Grier, Beau Bridges, Cleavon Little, Richie Havens. 1977

GREASER'S PALACE ★★1/2 You'll either love or hate this one, a retelling of the passion of Christ set n a small western town. Sometimes inventive, sometimes maddening. Not rated. 91m. DIR: Robert Downey. CAST: Allan Arbus, Luana Anders, Herve Villechaize, Don Calfa. 1972 DVD

GREAT ADVENTURE, THE ★★ Spin-off of *Call of the Wild* has an orphan boy, his dog, and a dance-hall queen take on a Yukon bully in gold-rush Dawson. Good family story with veterans Jack Palance and Joan Collins in prime form. Rated PG. 90m. DIR: Paul Elliotts. CAST: Joan Collins, Jack Palance, Fred Romer, Elisabetta Virgili. 1976

GREAT ALLIGATOR, THE 🦃 Italian exploitation cheapie about a resort community and the monster alligator that dines on its inhabitants. Rated R. 91m. DIR: Sergio Martino. CAST: Barbara Bach, Mel Ferrer, Claudio Cassinelli. 1979

GREAT AMERICAN SEX SCANDAL, THE ★★★ Enjoyable, made-for-television romp about a sex trial that has the whole world talking, especially the sequestered jury. When a nebbish accountant is brought to trial for embezzlement, the facts behind his case intrigue the media, his attorney, the jury, and even the accountant himself. While the world waits patiently to find out the facts, the jury members grapple with personal problems of their own. Likable cast of familiar faces. Rated PG-13 for adult situations. 94m. DIR: Michael Schultz. CAST: Stephen Baldwin, Barbara Bosson, Heather Locklear, Bronson Pinchot, Lynn Redgrave, Tracy Scoggins, Alan Thicke, Reginald Vel Johnson. 1989

GREAT BALLS OF FIRE ★★★★ A landmark music bio. It's obvious how hard talented Dennis Quaid has worked on his piano playing (with hands, feet, head, and tail) and on his Jerry Lee Lewis hellion-touched-by-God mannerisms and he's sublime in the role. So is Alec Baldwin, playing it straight and righteous as Jerry Lee's famous cousin, Jimmy Swaggart. Some miraculous moments. Rated PG-13 for profanity and sexual themes. 110m. DIR: Jim McBride. CAST: Dennis Quaid, Winona Ryder, Alec Baldwin, Trey Wilson. 1989

GREAT BANK HOAX, THE ★★1/2 It is doubtful that viewers today will think of Watergate when watching this comedy caper, but it was originally intended as a parable. When the pillars of the community find out that the bank has been embezzled, they decide to rob it. Great characterizations by all-star cast. Rated PG. 89m. DIR: Joseph Jacoby. CAST: Richard Basehart, Burgess Meredith, Paul Sand, Ned Beatty, Michael Murphy, Arthur Godfrey. 1977

GREAT CARUSO, THE ★★★★ A number of factual liberties are taken in this lavish screen biography of the great Italian tenor, but no matter. Mario Lanza's voice is magnificent; Ann Blyth and Dorothy Kirsten sing like birds. Devotees of music will love the arias. 109m. DIR: Richard Thorpe. CAST: Mario Lanza, Ann Blyth, Dorothy Kirsten. 1950

GREAT CHASE, THE ★★★★ Silent-film chases from several classics comprise the bulk of this compilation, including the running acrobatics of Douglas Fairbanks Sr. in *The Mark of Zorro*, the escape of Lillian Gish over the ice floes in *Way Down East*, and car chases and stunts of all descriptions from silent comedies. A large part of the film is devoted to

Buster Keaton's locomotive chase from *The General*. B&W; 79m. DIR: Frank Gallop. CAST: Buster Keaton, Douglas Fairbanks Sr., Lillian Gish, Pearl White. 1963 DVD

GREAT DAN PATCH, THE ★★★ The story of the greatest trotting horse of them all. Good racing scenes. An opera for horse lovers. B&W; 94m. DIR: Joseph M. Newman. CAST: Dennis O'Keefe, Gail Russell, Ruth Warrick, Charlotte Greenwood. 1949

GREAT DAY ★★1/2 Eleanor Roosevelt's impending trip to Great Britain is the background for this tribute to England's women during wartime. Effective quasi-documentary. B&W; 94m. DIR: Lance Comfort. CAST: Eric Portman, Flora Robson, Sheila Sim. 1945

GREAT DAY IN HARLEM, A ★★★★ In the summer of 1958, fifty-seven hard-core, nocturnal jazz musicians gathered in front of a Harlem brownstone stoop. The photograph taken that morning for *Esquire* magazine, which included such giants as Thelonious Monk, Count Basie, Gene Krupa, Marian McPartland, Charles Mingus, and Art Blakey, has become the most famous snapshot in jazz history. The event has been shaped into a warm valentine using home-movie footage, archival performances, interviews, and stills. Not rated. 60m. DIR: Jean Bach. 1995 DVD

GREAT DICTATOR, THE ★★★★★ Charlie Chaplin stars in and directs this devastating lampoon of the Third Reich. The celebrated clown's first all-talking picture, it casts him in two roles—as his famous Little Tramp and as Adenoid Hynkel, the Hitler-like ruler of Tomania. As with the similarly themed *Duck Soup*, starring the Marx Brothers, the comedy was a little too whimsical for wartime audiences. But it has to be regarded as a classic. B&W; 128m. DIR: Charles Chaplin. CAST: Charlie Chaplin, Jack Oakie, Paulette Goddard. 1940 DVD

GREAT ELEPHANT ESCAPE, THE ★★★ Plenty of adventure in this tale of a boy who joins his mother in Africa. There, he meets a local boy, and together they attempt to save a baby elephant from poachers. The two youths and the baby elephant set out on a trek across the Dark Continent, finding all kinds of adventure, fun, and danger. Exotic locale, likable characters, and a good story make this an enjoyable romp. Rated PG for violence. 95m. DIR: George Miller. CAST: Stephanie Zimbalist, Joseph Gordon-Levitt, Julian Sands. 1995

GREAT ESCAPE, THE ★★★★★ If ever there was a movie that could be called pure cheer-the-heroes entertainment, it's *The Great Escape*. The plot centers around a German prison camp in World War II. The commandant has received the assignment of housing all the escape-minded Allied prisoners. The Germans are obviously playing with fire with this all-star group, and, sure enough, all hell breaks loose with excitement galore. 168m. DIR: John Sturges. CAST: Steve McQueen, James Garner, Charles Bronson, Richard Attenborough, James Coburn. 1963 DVD

GREAT ESCAPE II, THE ★★ In World War II, seventy-five American and British soldiers tunnel themselves out of prison. This star-studded, made-for-television two-parter has been shortened considerably for video, but still plays well. 93m. DIR: Paul

Wendkos, Jud Taylor. **CAST:** Christopher Reeve, Judd Hirsch, Donald Pleasence, Charles Haid. **1988**

GREAT EXPECTATIONS (1946) ★★★1/2 A penniless orphan becomes a gentleman through the generosity of a mysterious patron. The second of three film versions of Charles Dickens's classic story. Made at the close of World War II, this version is by far the finest from all standpoints: direction, script, cast, photography, art direction. B&W; 118m. **DIR:** David Lean. **CAST:** John Mills, Alec Guinness, Valerie Hobson, Bernard Miles, Finlay Currie, Martita Hunt, Jean Simmons. **1946 DVD**

GREAT EXPECTATIONS (1983) ★★ Spotty though interesting-enough animated adaptation of Charles Dickens's classic tale about a young man's lessons in maturity. There's a lot of tragedy here (as expected), which may catch the attention of older children, but small youngsters will no doubt find this too low-key. 72m. **DIR:** Jean Tych. **1983**

GREAT EXPECTATIONS (1988) ★★★★ Fine BBC production of Charles Dickens's classic tale about a boy named Pip. This broadcast takes special care to include every plot convolution (and there are many!). While literary enthusiasts will rejoice in this, most casual viewers will be fidgeting with impatience. Best to watch this in two sittings! 300m. **DIR:** Julian Amyes. **CAST:** Stratford Johns, Gerry Sundquist, Joan Hickson. **1988**

GREAT EXPECTATIONS (1989) ★★★★1/2 First-rate, British-made miniseries of the Charles Dickens classic features outstanding performances, especially by Anthony Hopkins as Magwitch and Jean Simmons (Estella in director David Lean's 1946 version) as the mysterious and poignant Miss Haversham. Recommended for the whole family. 310m. **DIR:** Kevin O'Connor. **CAST:** Anthony Hopkins, Jean Simmons, John Rhys-Davies, Ray McAnally, Kim Thomson. **1989**

GREAT EXPECTATIONS (1998) ★★★1/2 Of all Dickens's best-known books, this one has the most timeless elements: a penniless, unsophisticated boy falls in love with a worldly, wealthy, slightly older girl who regards him as a toy. With the boy's subsequent efforts to level the playing field by "rising" to her station, he discovers that he has left behind those portions of his personality that defined him. This rendition begins in a small Florida town and eventually moves to New York City. Anne Bancroft has a field day as demented old Ms. Dinsmoor. Rated R for profanity, nudity, and strong sexual content. 111m. **DIR:** Alfonso Cuaron. **CAST:** Ethan Hawke, Gwyneth Paltrow, Chris Cooper, Anne Bancroft, Robert De Niro, Hank Azaria, Josh Mostel. **1998 DVD**

GREAT EXPECTATIONS—THE UNTOLD STORY ★★1/2 This story should *never* have been told. We follow Magwitch, the escaped convict who befriends the little boy in Charles Dickens's *Great Expectations*, as he changes to a rich gentleman in Australia. Not rated. 102m. **DIR:** Tim Burstall. **CAST:** John Stanton, Sigrid Thornton, Robert Coleby, Noel Ferrier. **1987**

GREAT FLAMARION, THE ★★★ Schemer Mary Beth Hughes suckers vaudeville trick-shot artist Erich Von Stroheim into murdering her husband and leaves him to take the fall while she flees with Dan

Duryea. Nothing new in the plot line, but Von Stroheim's performance is reward enough. B&W; 78m. **DIR:** Anthony Mann. **CAST:** Erich Von Stroheim, Mary Beth Hughes, Dan Duryea. **1945**

GREAT GABBO, THE ★★★1/2 Cinema giant Erich Von Stroheim gives a tour-de-force performance as a brilliant but cold ventriloquist whose disregard for the feelings of others comes back to haunt him when he realizes that he has lost the affection of a girl he has come to love. This is a film that lingers in the memory and rates with other fine films about ventriloquism like *Dead Of Night* and *Magic*. B&W; 89m. **DIR:** James Cruze. **CAST:** Erich Von Stroheim, Betty Compson, Don Douglas. **1929**

GREAT GATSBY, THE ★★★ This is a well-mounted, well-acted film that is, perhaps, a bit overlong. However, Robert Redford, the mysterious title character, is marvelous as Gatsby. Bruce Dern is equally memorable as the man who always has been rich and selfish. Rated PG. 144m. **DIR:** Jack Clayton. **CAST:** Robert Redford, Mia Farrow, Karen Black, Sam Waterston, Bruce Dern. **1974**

GREAT GUNS ★★ Although it's a cut below their classics, *Sons of the Desert* fans will love it, and so will most—especially the young. Stan and Ollie have jobs guarding a rich man's playboy son. He gets drafted; the fellows join up to continue their work. The playboy gets along just fine in khaki. The boys get up to their ears in trouble with an archetypical sergeant. B&W; 74m. **DIR:** Monty Banks. **CAST:** Stan Laurel, Oliver Hardy, Sheila Ryan, Dick Nelson. **1941**

GREAT GUY ★★ Depression film about a feisty inspector crusading against corruption in the meatpacking business. Not vintage James Cagney ... but okay. B&W; 75m. **DIR:** John G. Blystone. **CAST:** James Cagney, Mae Clarke, Edward Brophy. **1936**

GREAT IMPOSTOR, THE ★★★1/2 The amazing story of Ferdinand Demara is told in engrossing style by director Robert Mulligan. Demara, with natural charm and uncanny adaptability, successfully managed to pose as everything from a clergyman to a doctor. The role is a tour de force for Tony Curtis. Compelling and seasoned with dark humor. 112m. **DIR:** Robert Mulligan. **CAST:** Tony Curtis, Edmond O'Brien, Arthur O'Connell, Gary Merrill. **1960**

GREAT INDIAN RAILWAY, THE ★★★★ Gorgeous photography and extensive research turned this National Geographic production into a true enticement for armchair travelers. It leaves one with an understanding of the machinations of the largest train system in the world and its effects on Indian society. However, there is too much material for one film—occasionally there are dropped snippets of information leave one hungering for more. Narrated by Linda Hunt. Not rated. 111m. **DIR:** William Livingston. **1995**

GREAT LAND OF SMALL, THE ★★ Beautifully photographed but slightly disjointed tale of a magical dwarf who can only be seen by children. Rated G; should appeal to children, but nothing in it for adults. 94m. **DIR:** Vojta Jasny. **CAST:** Karen Elkin, Michael Blouin, Michael J. Anderson, Ken Roberts. **1987**

GREAT LIE, THE ★★★ Prime soap opera in the tradition of Bette Davis's *The Old Maid*, but this time he is the bitchy one who takes over someone else's child. Mary Astor (an Oscar winner for supporting ctress) plays a concert pianist who marries Davis's ormer lover, George Brent. The marriage turns out o be illegal, and, before they can get married again Brent crashes in the jungle. B&W; 102m. **DIR:** Edmund Goulding. **CAST:** Bette Davis, George Brent, Mary Astor, Hattie McDaniel, Lucile Watson, Jerome Cowan, Grant Mitchell. **1941**

GREAT LOCOMOTIVE CHASE, THE ★★★1/2 Fess Parker and his band of spies infiltrate the South and abscond with a railroad train. Jeffrey Hunter is the conductor who chases them to regain possession of the train. This is a straightforward telling of actual events, emphasizing action and suspense. 85m. **DIR:** Francis D. Lyon. **CAST:** Fess Parker, Jeffrey Hunter, Jeff York, John Lupton. **1956**

GREAT LOS ANGELES EARTHQUAKE, THE ★★1/2 The big one hits Los Angeles in this condensed version of the television miniseries. Characters get lost in the trim, leaving only victims of the overblown special effects. Joe Spano is especially embarrassing as the city official afraid to cry wolf. 106m. **DIR:** Larry Elikann. **CAST:** Joanna Kerns, Dan Lauria, Alan Autry, Ed Begley Jr., Joe Spano. **1990**

GREAT LOVE EXPERIMENT, THE ★★ This HBO Family Playhouse special features a nerdy teen who becomes the guinea pig for the in group. To her surprise, she is suddenly pursued by three cool guys and made over by the most popular girl in the senior class. For teens only. 45m. **DIR:** Claudia Weill. **CAST:** Tracy Pollan. **1982**

GREAT LOVER, THE ★★★★ This is top-notch Bob Hope. The story, as usual, is simple. While on a transatlantic steamship, a timid Boy Scout leader romances lovely Rhonda Fleming and tracks down a strangler. Comedic suspense is well played. B&W; 80m. **DIR:** Alexander Hall. **CAST:** Bob Hope, Rhonda Fleming, Roland Young, Jim Backus, Roland Culver, George Reeves. **1949**

GREAT MADCAP, THE ★★1/2 To cure a rich man of his profligate ways, his family tricks him into thinking that his fortune has been lost. One of director Luis Buñuel's least interesting films, this features satirical themes that he would later redo. In Spanish with English subtitles. B&W; 90m. **DIR:** Luis Buñuel. **CAST:** Fernando Soler, Ruben Rojo. **1949**

GREAT MAN VOTES, THE ★★★1/2 Drunken widower raises his two spunky kids in a rather unorthodox home. They are constantly harassed by the children of the more successful fathers until the party relies on Barrymore's vote to set the tone for other precincts. B&W; 72m. **DIR:** Garson Kanin. **CAST:** John Barrymore, Peter Holden, Virginia Weidler, Katharine Alexander. **1939**

GREAT MAN'S LADY, THE ★★1/2 It's all a bit much as Barbara Stanwyck stoically dedicates her life to a city founder who really doesn't deserve all that devotion. Stanwyck is her usual feisty self, but the film's structure suffers from trying to cover too much round. Not rated. B&W; 91m. **DIR:** William Wellman. **CAST:** Barbara Stanwyck, Joel McCrea, Brian Donlevy, Thurston Hall, K. T. Stevens, Lloyd Corrigan. **1942**

GREAT MCGINTY, THE ★★★1/2 The ups and downs of hobo Brian Donlevy and his crooked cohort Akim Tamiroff make for very funny satire in this refreshing gem from the inventive Preston Sturges. The action is secondary to the great dialogue. The leads are fine and the rapport they share on screen is truly engaging. B&W; 83m. **DIR:** Preston Sturges. **CAST:** Brian Donlevy, Akim Tamiroff, Muriel Angelus, Louis Jean Heydt, Arthur Hoyt. **1940**

GREAT MISSOURI RAID, THE ★★ Another depiction of Frank and Jesse James and their pals the Younger brothers. This picture is good for a latenight view or while you're microwaving your dinner. Passable, but better accounts of the James boys are available. 83m. **DIR:** Gordon Douglas. **CAST:** Wendell Corey, Macdonald Carey, Ellen Drew, Ward Bond. **1950**

GREAT MOMENT, THE ★★ A nineteenth-century dentist promotes the use of ether as an anesthetic. Confusing blend of comedy and drama makes this bio-pic very uneven. B&W; 83m. **DIR:** Preston Sturges. **CAST:** Joel McCrea, Betty Field, William Demarest, Harry Carey, Grady Sutton, Franklin Pangborn, Jimmy Conlin, Louis Jean Heydt, Thurston Hall, Porter Hall. **1944**

GREAT MOUSE DETECTIVE, THE ★★★1/2 Disney's charming adaptation of Eve Titus's *Basil of Baker Street* involves a diminutive consulting detective's efforts to rescue a master toy maker from the evil clutches of dastardly Professor Ratigan. Sherlock Holmes riffs abound, as Basil and his faithful companion, Dr. Dawson, scour London streets in search of clues. Take note of the climactic battle between Basil and Ratigan in the thrashing gear works of Big Ben, Disney's first serious experiment with computer animation. Rated G. 73m. **DIR:** John Musker, Ron Clements, Dave Michener, Bunny Mattison. **1986**

GREAT MUPPET CAPER, THE ★★★★ Miss Piggy, Kermit the Frog, Fozzie Bear, and the Great Gonzo attempt to solve the mysterious theft of the fabulous Baseball Diamond in this, the second feature-length motion picture Muppet outing. Rated G. 95m. **DIR:** Jim Henson. **CAST:** Muppets, Diana Rigg, Charles Grodin, Peter Falk, Peter Ustinov, Jack Warden, Robert Morley. **1981**

GREAT, MY PARENTS ARE DIVORCING ★★★★ The French have a talent for dramatizing stories from a child's point of view. In this film, love and marriage and divorce are explored through the reactions of a group of children who unite as their real families are dissolving. Warmhearted film, offering laughs and wisdom in equal portions. In French with English subtitles. Not rated. 98m. **DIR:** Patrick Braoude. **CAST:** Patrick Braoude, Clementine Celarie, Patrick Bouchitey. **1992**

GREAT NORTHFIELD MINNESOTA RAID, THE ★★★ A strong cast of character actors propels this offbeat Western, which chronicles the exploits of the James-Younger gang. Cliff Robertson is an effectively world-weary and witty Cole Younger, and Robert Duvall sets off sparks as a crafty, calculating Jesse James. The film never quite satisfies as a whole though there are some terrific moments. Rated R for violence and profanity. 91m. **DIR:** Phil

Kaufman. **CAST:** Cliff Robertson, Robert Duvall, Luke Askew, R. G. Armstrong, Dana Elcar, Donald Moffat, Jack Pearce, Matt Clark, Elisha Cook Jr. **1972**

GREAT OUTDOORS, THE ★★1/2 Another screwball comedy featuring former members of *Saturday Night Live* and *SCTV*, this stars Dan Aykroyd and John Candy as brothers-in-law battling to take charge of a family vacation in the country, where almost everything goes wrong. Aside from Aykroyd, all the characters are shallow. Rated PG for profanity. 90m. **DIR:** Howard Deutch. **CAST:** Dan Aykroyd, John Candy, Stephanie Faracy. **1988 DVD**

GREAT RACE, THE ★★★1/2 Set in the early 1900s, this film comically traces the daily events of the first New York–to–Paris car race. Unfortunately, two-and-a-half hours of silly spoofs will have even the most avid film fan yawning. 147m. **DIR:** Blake Edwards. **CAST:** Tony Curtis, Natalie Wood, Jack Lemmon, Peter Falk, Keenan Wynn, Larry Storch, Arthur O'Connell, Vivian Vance. **1965**

GREAT RIVIERA BANK ROBBERY, THE ★★★1/2 In 1976, a group of French right-wing terrorists called "The Chain," with the assistance of a gang of thieves, pulled off one of the largest heists in history. The step-by-step illustration of this bold operation proves to be interesting, and the fact that this incident really happened makes this film all the more enjoyable. 98m. **DIR:** Francis Megahy. **CAST:** Ian McShane, Warren Clarke, Stephen Greif, Christopher Malcolm. **1979**

GREAT ROCK AND ROLL SWINDLE, THE ★★★★ Free-form pseudodocumentary about legendary punk-rock band the Sex Pistols is just an excuse for promoter Malcolm McLaren to blow his own horn, though he does that quite entertainingly. Not rated; contains profanity. 103m. **DIR:** Julien Temple. **CAST:** Malcolm McLaren, Sid Vicious, John Lydon, Paul Cook, Steve Jones. **1980**

GREAT ST. LOUIS BANK ROBBERY, THE ★★★1/2 Underrated crime-drama in the *Asphalt Jungle* vein, featuring 19-year-old Steve McQueen as a college athlete on the skids who joins a trio of experienced criminals planning to rob a bank. The film's modest budget works in its favor, lending a note of gritty realism (some of the extras were people who were at the real-life robbery who actually inspired this film!). B&W; 87m. **DIR:** Charles Guggenheim, John Stix. **CAST:** Steve McQueen, Crahan Denton, David Clarke. **1959 DVD**

GREAT ST. TRINIAN'S TRAIN ROBBERY, THE ★★★ The last in the series of British comedies based on Ronald Searle's cartoons depicting a girls' school populated by monstrously awful brats. In this one, the students prove more than a match for thieves who have hidden loot on the school premises. Not the best of the series, but fun nonetheless. 94m. **DIR:** Frank Launder, Sidney Gilliat. **CAST:** Frankie Howerd, Reg Varney, Dora Bryan. **1966**

GREAT SANTINI, THE ★★★★ Robert Duvall's superb performance in the title role is the most outstanding feature of this fine film. The story of a troubled family and its unpredictable patriarch (Duvall), it was released briefly in early 1980 and then disappeared. But thanks to the efforts of the New York film critics, it was rereleased with appropriate hoopla and did well at the box office. Rated PG for profanity and violence. 116m. **DIR:** Lewis John Carlino. **CAST:** Robert Duvall, Blythe Danner, Michael O'Keefe. **1980 DVD**

GREAT SCOUT AND CATHOUSE THURSDAY, THE ★★★ Eccentric Western-comedy involving a variety of get-rich-quick schemes concocted by an amusing band of rogues. Oliver Reed steals the show as a wacky American Indian whose double-crosses usually backfire. Not much plot and considerable silliness, but fun nonetheless. Rated PG for sexual situations. 102m. **DIR:** Don Taylor. **CAST:** Lee Marvin, Oliver Reed, Elizabeth Ashley, Robert Culp, Strother Martin, Kay Lenz. **1976**

GREAT SMOKEY ROADBLOCK, THE ★★1/2 Entertaining if somewhat hokey comedy-drama casts Henry Fonda as a trucker on the verge of losing his rig, when along comes a homeless entourage of prostitutes (led by Eileen Brennan), who persuade Henry to take them for a ride. Rated PG for language. 84m. **DIR:** John Leone. **CAST:** Henry Fonda, Eileen Brennan, John Byner, Dub Taylor, Susan Sarandon, Austin Pendleton. **1976**

GREAT TEXAS DYNAMITE CHASE, THE ★★ Bullets and bodies fly in this low-budget cult film about two female bank robbers who blast their way across the countryside. Look for Johnny Crawford, of *The Rifleman* fame, in a featured role. Violence and some nudity. Rated R. 90m. **DIR:** Michael Pressman. **CAST:** Claudia Jennings, Jocelyn Jones, Johnny Crawford, Chris Pennock. **1977**

GREAT TRAIN ROBBERY, THE ★★★★ Based on a true incident, this suspense-filled caper has plenty of hooks to keep you interested. Sean Connery is dashing and convincing as mastermind Edward Pierce. Lesley-Anne Down is stunning as his mistress, accomplice, and disguise expert. Add a pinch of Donald Sutherland as a boastful pickpocket and cracksman, and you have a trio of crooks that can steal your heart. Rated PG. 111m. **DIR:** Michael Crichton. **CAST:** Sean Connery, Lesley-Anne Down, Donald Sutherland, Alan Webb. **1979 DVD**

GREAT WALDO PEPPER, THE ★★★ The daredevil barnstorming pilots of the era between the world wars are sent a pleasant valentine by director George Roy Hill in this flying film. Robert Redford, in a satisfying low-key performance, is Waldo Pepper, a barnstormer who yearns for the action of the World War I dogfights. Rated PG. 108m. **DIR:** George Roy Hill. **CAST:** Robert Redford, Bo Svenson, Susan Sarandon, Bo Boundin. **1975 DVD**

GREAT WALL, A ★★★1/2 Not a documentary about the 1,500-mile structure that rolls wavelike through northern China. Instead, it is a warm comedy about the clash of cultures that results when a Chinese-American family returns to its homeland. It is also the first American movie to be made in the People's Republic of China. As such, it gives some fascinating insights into Chinese culture and often does so in a marvelously entertaining way. Rated PG. 100m. **DIR:** Peter Wang. **CAST:** Peter Wang, Sharon Iwai, Kelvin Han Yee. **1986**

GREAT WALLENDAS, THE ★★★ In this made-for-television movie, Lloyd Bridges stars as the head of the Wallenda family of high-wire artists. Bridges gives one of his most convincing performances as he keeps the spirit and determination of the family alive through their many tragedies. 104m. **DIR:** Larry Elikann. **CAST:** Lloyd Bridges, Britt Ekland, Taina Elg, John van Dreelen, Cathy Rigby, Michael McGuire. **1978**

GREAT WALTZ, THE ★★★★ This biography of Viennese waltz king Johann Strauss II may have no factual bearing whatever (and it doesn't), but it's great fun and cinematically quite stunning. Unfortunately, Oscar Hammerstein's new lyrics to the waltzes are entrusted to diva Miliza Korjus, whose weak voice and inept bel canto technique are quite awful. B&W; 103m. **DIR:** Julien Duvivier. **CAST:** Fernand Gravet, Luise Rainer, Miliza Korjus. **1938**

GREAT WHITE HOPE, THE ★★★ Compelling, emotional character study of the first black heavyweight champion, Jack Johnson, with a supercharged performance by James Earl Jones in the main role. Jones is supported by an equally great cast in this portrait of a man doomed by the prejudice of his society. Rated PG. 101m. **DIR:** Martin Ritt. **CAST:** James Earl Jones, Jane Alexander, Lou Gilbert, Hal Holbrook. **1970**

GREAT WHITE HYPE, THE ★★1/2 It's hard to satirize a blood sport that has already become an ugly parody of itself, but this chaotic boxing comedy produces a few laughs. When fight fans tire of watching two black boxers punch each other, a slippery promoter slyly markets a Caucasian challenger to battle the world's African American champ. The film wants to be the *Spinal Tap* of pugilism but misses many punches. Rated R for language and violence. 91m. **DIR:** Reginald Hudlin. **CAST:** Damon Wayans, Peter Berg, Samuel L. Jackson, Jeff Goldblum, Jon Lovitz, Richard "Cheech" Marin, Jamie Foxx. **1996**

GREAT ZIEGFELD, THE ★★★★ This Academy Award–winning best picture is a marvelous film biography of legendary showman Florenz Ziegfeld. William Powell is perfect in the title role and Oscar winner Luise Rainer is tremendous as the fabulous Anna Held. The sets, costumes, and production design are superb. This is Hollywood at its finest. B&W; 176m. **DIR:** Robert Z. Leonard. **CAST:** William Powell, Myrna Loy, Luise Rainer, Frank Morgan, Fanny Brice, Virginia Bruce, Reginald Owen, Dennis Morgan. **1936**

GREATEST, THE ★★ Muhammad Ali plays himself in this disjointed screen biography, which is poorly directed by Tom Gries. Even the supporting performances don't help much. Rated PG. 101m. **DIR:** Tom Gries. **CAST:** Muhammad Ali, Ernest Borgnine, John Marley, Robert Duvall, James Earl Jones, Roger E. Mosley. **1977**

GREATEST MAN IN THE WORLD, THE ★★★★ A droll adaptation of James Thurber's tale. Brad Davis is an uncouth amateur barnstormer who outperforms Charles Lindbergh by flying nonstop around the world ... aided by a brilliant method of fuel conservation, and fortified—during the four-day trip—by a hunk of salami and a gallon of gin. Introduced by Henry Fonda; suitable for family viewing. 51m. **DIR:** Ralph Rosenblum. **CAST:** Brad Davis, Reed Birney, John McMartin, Howard DaSilva, Carol Kane, William Prince, Sudie Bond. **1980**

GREATEST SHOW ON EARTH, THE ★★★★ The 1952 Oscar winner for best picture succeeds in the same manner as its subject, the circus; it's enjoyable family entertainment. Three major stories of backstage circus life all work and blend well in this film. 153m. **DIR:** Cecil B. DeMille. **CAST:** Betty Hutton, James Stewart, Charlton Heston, Cornel Wilde, Dorothy Lamour, Gloria Grahame. **1952**

GREATEST STORY EVER TOLD, THE ★★★ Although this well-meant movie is accurate to the story of Jesus, the viewer tends to be distracted by its long running time and the appearance of Hollywood stars in unexpected roles. 141m. **DIR:** George Stevens. **CAST:** Max von Sydow, Charlton Heston, Carroll Baker, Angela Lansbury, Sidney Poitier, Telly Savalas, José Ferrer, Van Heflin, Dorothy McGuire, John Wayne, Ed Wynn, Shelley Winters. **1965**

GREED ★★★★★ One of the greatest silent films, this is the stark, brilliant study of the corruption of a decent, simple man by the specter of poverty and failed dreams. Gibson Gowland is superb as the bumbling self-taught dentist who marries spinster ZaSu Pitts, loses his trade, and succumbs to avarice-based hatred leading to murder. A masterpiece. Silent. B&W; 133m. **DIR:** Erich Von Stroheim. **CAST:** Gibson Gowland, ZaSu Pitts, Jean Hersholt. **1924**

GREEDY ★★★1/2 An aging Kirk Douglas is typically robust in this aptly named comedy. A group of scheming relatives recruit Douglas's favorite nephew, Michael J. Fox, to keep the rich old coot from throwing his millions away on a young mistress. It's only occasionally funny, but never boring. Phil Hartman is terrific as the nastiest family member. Rated PG-13 for profanity and suggested sex. 113m. **DIR:** Jonathan Lynn. **CAST:** Michael J. Fox, Kirk Douglas, Olivia D'Abo, Phil Hartman, Ed Begley Jr., Jere Burns, Colleen Camp, Bob Balaban, Joyce Hyser, Mary Ellen Trainor, Kevin McCarthy. **1994 DVD**

GREEK TYCOON, THE ★★1/2 When this film was first shown, it stimulated much controversy and interest, because it promised to tell all about the Aristotle Onassis and Jackie Kennedy romance. Anthony Quinn borrows from his *Zorba the Greek* role to be a convincingly macho and callous Greek shipping tycoon. Unfortunately, the plot was neglected and the story comes across as grade-B soap. Rated R. 106m. **DIR:** J. Lee Thompson. **CAST:** Anthony Quinn, Jacqueline Bisset, Raf Vallone, Edward Albert, Charles Durning, Camilla Sparv, James Franciscus. **1978**

GREEN ARCHER ★★ Detective Spike Holland tries to unravel the mystery of Garr Castle after he is called in to investigate the disappearance of Valerie Howett's sister, Elaine. Lots of sliding panels and silhouettes of the phantom bowman in this slow-moving chapterplay. B&W; 15 chapters. **DIR:** James W. Horne. **CAST:** Victor Jory, Iris Meredith, James Craven, Robert Fiske. **1940**

GREEN BERETS, THE ★★★ John Wayne's Vietnam war movie is better than its reputation would suggest. We were fully prepared to hate the film after having avoided it when originally released. However, it turned out to be an exciting and enjoyable (albeit typical) Wayne vehicle. Rated G. 141m. **DIR:** John Wayne, Ray Kellogg. **CAST:** John Wayne, David Janssen, Jim Hutton, Aldo Ray, Raymond St. Jacques, Bruce Cabot, Jack Soo, George Takei, Patrick Wayne. **1968 DVD**

GREEN CARD ★★★★ Delightful old-fashioned comedy-romance from Australian writer-director Peter Weir. Gérard Depardieu plays a French immigrant-songwriter who attempts to stay in America by marrying Andie MacDowell, who needs a husband to land a choice apartment in Manhattan. Hilarious and heartwarming. Rated PG-13 for brief profanity. 108m. **DIR:** Peter Weir. **CAST:** Gérard Depardieu, Andie MacDowell, Bebe Neuwirth. **1990**

GREEN DOLPHIN STREET ★★ Plodding drama about two sisters, Lana Turner and Donna Reed, in romantic pursuit of the same man, Van Heflin. Special effects, including a whopper of an earthquake, won an Oscar, but do not a film make. B&W; 141m. **DIR:** Victor Saville. **CAST:** Lana Turner, Donna Reed, Van Heflin, Edmund Gwenn, Frank Morgan, Richard Hart. **1947**

●**GREEN FOR DANGER** ★★★★ Mystery fans shouldn't miss this classic British whodunit, written and filmed with a dry sense of humor. Alastair Sim is a delight as the Scotland Yard detective trying to solve the riddle of a man who was murdered in a hospital—while he was being operated on! B&W; 91m. **DIR:** Sidney Gilliat. **CAST:** Alastair Sim, Sally Gray, Trevor Howard. **1946**

GREEN HORNET, THE (TV SERIES) ★★★ Based on the 1930s radio series created by George W. Trendle, this TV show was an attempt to cash in on the *Batman* phenomenon and is more compelling, less campy. Van Williams ably portrayed the heroic Britt Reid, crime fighter extraordinaire. This short-lived series showcased the martial arts wizardry and unique charisma of Bruce Lee, who played Reid's trusty sidekick, Kato. Two episodes are included per tape. All twenty-six episodes of the series are available. 60m. each tape. **DIR:** Various. **CAST:** Van Williams, Bruce Lee, Wende Wagner, Lloyd Gough, Walter Brooke. **1966–1967**

GREEN ICE ★★ Unconvincing tale of an emerald theft in Colombia. Ryan O'Neal engineers the robbery. Rated PG. 115m. **DIR:** Ernest Day. **CAST:** Ryan O'Neal, Anne Archer, Omar Sharif. **1981**

GREEN MAN, THE ★★★1/2 Albert Finney chews up the scenery in great style as an alcoholic innkeeper who tantalizes guests by suggesting that his bed-and-breakfast is haunted ... and then discovers, with shock, that his unlikely yarns may have come true. A darkly comic novel by Kingsley Amis is the inspiration for this made-for-TV tale. Definitely not for the prudish. 150m. **DIR:** Elijah Moshinsky. **CAST:** Albert Finney, Michael Hordern, Sarah Berger, Linda Marlowe. **1991**

GREEN MANSIONS ★★★ Anthony Perkins is a South American aristocrat, fleeing a revolution, who is befriended by a native tribe. He is sent by them to a rain forest to hunt and kill a mystical vengeful goddess, Rima, the Bird Girl, but finds instead a young innocent (Audrey Hepburn) and her secretive grandfather (Lee J. Cobb). Starts off well but is over-

all a rather shallow working of William Henry Hudson's romantic novel. Location filming helps. 104m. **DIR:** Mel Ferrer. **CAST:** Audrey Hepburn, Anthony Perkins, Lee J. Cobb, Sessue Hayakawa, Henry Silva, Nehemiah Persoff. **1959**

●**GREEN MILE, THE** ★★★★ Excellent acting keeps this overly long adaptation of Stephen King's 1996 serial novel from eroding into an emotionally sticky parable about racism, justice, resurrection, and the spiritual value of a pet death row mouse. Set mostly in a Depression-era penitentiary, the film slowly builds power as a cell-block superintendent bonds with a gentle-giant African American convicted of child murder. It's a rather old-fashioned story of good versus evil as shaped by some very surprising supernatural events. Rated R for profanity, violence, and a grisly execution. 180m. **DIR:** Frank Darabont. **CAST:** Tom Hanks, Michael Clarke Duncan, Michael Jeter, David Morse, Sam Rockwell, James Cromwell, Doug Hutchison, Barry Pepper, Bonnie Hunt. **1999 DVD**

GREEN PASTURES ★★★★ A fine all-black cast headed by Rex Ingram as de Lawd brings Marc Connelly's classic fable of life in heaven vividly to the screen. A unique viewing experience. B&W; 90m. **DIR:** William Keighley, Marc Connelly. **CAST:** Rex Ingram, Eddie "Rochester" Anderson. **1936**

GREEN PROMISE, THE ★★★ The hard life of farmers and their families is explored in this surprisingly involving and well-acted film. Walter Brennan gives his usual first-rate performance as the patriarch who toils over and tills the land. B&W; 93m. **DIR:** William D. Russell. **CAST:** Marguerite Chapman, Walter Brennan, Robert Paige, Natalie Wood. **1949**

GREEN ROOM, THE ★★ Based on the writings of Henry James, this is a lifeless and disappointing film by François Truffaut about a writer who turns a dilapidated chapel into a memorial for World War I soldiers. Not the French filmmaker at his best. In French with English subtitles. Rated PG. 93m. **DIR:** François Truffaut. **CAST:** François Truffaut, Nathalie Baye, Jean Dasté. **1978**

GREEN SLIME, THE 🎦 A bit of alien green guck makes its way onto a space station, multiplies itself into ookie monsters. Laughable, with such poor special effects that no one asked to be listed in the credits. Not rated, but it won't scare the kids. 88m. **DIR:** Kinji Fukasaku. **CAST:** Robert Horton, Richard Jaeckel, Luciana Paluzzi. **1969**

GREEN WALL, THE ★★★★1/2 A young family, determined to escape the pressure of life in Lima, struggles against overwhelming obstacles to survive in the exotic, overgrown Peruvian jungle. Stunning cinematography by Mario Robles Godoy. In Spanish with English subtitles. 110m. **DIR:** Armando Robles Godoy. **CAST:** Julio Aleman. **1970**

GREETINGS ★★★ Robert De Niro shines in his starring debut, an offbeat comedy about a young man's sexual odyssey through New York City. Director Brian De Palma takes a satirical overview on free love, the JFK assassination, and Vietnam. Made on a shoestring budget. Rated R for nudity and profanity. 85m. **DIR:** Brian De Palma. **CAST:** Robert De Niro, Jonathan Warden, Gerrit Graham, Allen Garfield. **1968**

GREGORY'S GIRL ★★★1/2 In this utterly delightful movie from Scotland, a gangly, good-natured kid named Gregory—who has just gone through a five-inch growth spurt that has left him with the physical grace of a drunken stilt walker and made him a problem player on the school's winless soccer team—falls in love with the team's newest and best player: a girl named Dorothy. Not rated, the film has no objectionable content. 91m. **DIR:** Bill Forsyth. **CAST:** Gordon John Sinclair, Dee Hepburn, Chic Murray, Jake D'Arcy, Alex Norton, John Bett, Clare Grogan. 1981

GREMLINS ★★★★ "Steven Spielberg Presentation" is highly wacky. It's one part *E.T.—The Extra-Terrestrial*, one part scary-funny horror film, one part Muppet movie, and one part Bugs Bunny–Warner Bros. cartoon. Sound strange? You got it. In the story, Billy Peltzer (Zach Galligan) gets a cute little pet from his inventor-father (Hoyt Axton) for Christmas. But there's a catch. Rated PG for profanity and stylized violence. 111m. **DIR:** Joe Dante. **CAST:** Zach Galligan, Phoebe Cates, Hoyt Axton, Frances Lee McCain, Polly Holliday, Glynn Turman, Dick Miller, Keye Luke, Scott Brady. 1984 DVD

GREMLINS 2: THE NEW BATCH ★★★★ Those mischievous mutating creatures are back. This time they invade a futuristic New York office complex run by a Donald Trump–like billionaire. Playful, energetic, and much like the first movie in its use of visual gags, social satire, cartoonish mayhem, surprise in-jokes for film fans. Rated PG-13 for cartoon violence. 114m. **DIR:** Joe Dante. **CAST:** Zach Galligan, Phoebe Cates, John Glover, Robert Prosky, Robert Picardo, Christopher Lee, Dick Miller, Jackie Joseph. 1990

GRENDEL, GRENDEL, GRENDEL ★★★ Charming animated feature that recasts the legend of Beowulf from the point of view of the monster, depicted sympathetically as a peaceable sort with the bad habit of munching on the occasional villager. Adapted from John Gardner's novel, this is fine for kids and grownups. Not rated. 88m. **DIR:** Alexander Stitt. **CAST:** Peter Ustinov, Keith Michell. 1979

GREY FOX, THE ★★★★★ Richard Farnsworth (*Comes a Horseman*) stars in this marvelously entertaining Canadian feature as the gentleman bandit Bill Miner who, as the movie poster proclaimed, "on June 17, 1901, after thirty-three years in San Quentin Prison for robbing stagecoaches, was released into the twentieth century." Rated PG for brief violence. 92m. **DIR:** Phillip Borsos. **CAST:** Richard Farnsworth, Jackie Burroughs, Ken Pogue, Timothy Webber. 1982

GREY MATTER ★★ This metaphysical horror film is thought-provoking but hampered by bad acting and a small budget. Not rated; contains violence. 89m. **DIR:** Joy N. Houck Jr. **CAST:** James Best, Barbara Burgess, Gerald McRaney. 1973

GREYFRIARS BOBBY ★★★ Somewhat lethargic tale of a dog that is befriended by an entire town after his owner dies. The plot drags, but the cast and the atmosphere of the settings make it worth watching. 91m. **DIR:** Don Chaffey. **CAST:** Donald Crisp, Laurence Naismith, Alex Mackenzie, Kay Walsh. 1961

GREYSTOKE: THE LEGEND OF TARZAN, LORD OF THE APES ★★★1/2 Director Hugh Hudson made one of the few Tarzan movies to remain faithful to the books and original character created by Edgar Rice Burroughs. Tarzan in one dramatic leap, goes from the dank, dangerous rain forests of West Africa to claim his rightful heritage—a baronial mansion in Scotland and a title as the seventh Earl of Greystoke. Rated PG for nudity and violence. 129m. **DIR:** Hugh Hudson. **CAST:** Christopher Lambert, Andie MacDowell, Ian Holm, Ralph Richardson, James Fox, Cheryl Campbell. 1984

GRIDLOCK'D ★★★★ This character-driven comedy-drama features Tupac Shakur and Tim Roth, as a pair of junkies who decide to get clean after a friend nearly dies of an overdose. Of course, our somewhat sullied heroes' path to a better life is fraught with problems. Not only can they not get into a rehab program without an immense hassle, but being in the wrong place at the wrong time puts them on the bad side of a group of gangsters. Rated R for nudity, profanity, and violence. 91m. **DIR:** Vondie Curtis-Hall. **CAST:** Tim Roth, Tupac Shakur, Thandie Newton, Charles Fleischer, Howard Hesseman, James Pickens Jr., John Sayles, Eric Payne. 1997 DVD

GRIEF ★★★ A hectic, behind-the-scenes comedy about a week in the life of the people who bring *The Love Judge* to daytime television. Like *Soapdish*, director-writer Richard Glatzer's comedy is a pointed, hilarious exposé of the trials and tribulations that befall the people who get the show on the air every day. Alexis Arquette shines as the up-and-coming producer whose sexual preference gets him into hot water with a straight coworker. Not rated; contains adult language and situations. 86m. **DIR:** Richard Glatzer. **CAST:** Alexis Arquette, Jackie Beat, Craig Chester, Illeana Douglas. 1994

GRIEVOUS BODILY HARM ★★1/2 This Australian drama is a well-woven tale about a police detective trying to find his missing wife. The acting is first-rate, as is the script, but director Mark Joffe lets the pace drag from time to time. Rated R. 135m. **DIR:** Mark Joffe. **CAST:** Colin Friels, John Waters, Bruno Lawrence, Shane Briant. 1988

GRIFFIN AND PHOENIX: A LOVE STORY ★★★1/2 Strange, haunting tearjerker about two dying people in love with one another and with life. Jill Clayburgh and Peter Falk in the title roles win hearts handsdown and lift spirits as gloom and doom close in. Made for TV. 100m. **DIR:** Daryl Duke. **CAST:** Peter Falk, Jill Clayburgh, Dorothy Tristan. 1976

GRIFTERS, THE ★★★★ A savagely funny and often shocking adaptation by Donald E. Westlake of Jim Thompson's hardboiled novel, this black comedy is like a grotesque version of *The Sting*. Anjelica Huston, John Cusack, and Annette Bening are clever crooks who cheat their way through life until the inevitable catches up with them. Rated R for violence, nudity, and profanity. 119m. **DIR:** Stephen Frears. **CAST:** Anjelica Huston, John Cusack, Annette Bening, Pat Hingle, Henry Jones, J. T. Walsh, Charles Napier, Stephen Tobolowsky, Gailard Sartain. 1990 DVD

GRIM 🐢 A small town is menaced by a menacing-looking rubber monster that lives under their sleepy little suburb. Rated R for violence and adult language. 86m. DIR: Paul Matthews. CAST: Emmanuel Xuereb, Tres Handley, Peter Tregloan. 1995 DVD

GRIM PRAIRIE TALES ★★★ Two plains travelers, one a city dweller and the other a trail-weary bounty hunter, exchange stories of horror while they camp on the open prairie. Their freaky tales will test your ability to suspend belief, but all are fun to watch. Rated R for violence, profanity, and gore. 87m. DIR: Wayne Coe. CAST: James Earl Jones, Brad Dourif, William Atherton, Lisa Eichhorn, Marc McClure, Scott Paulin. 1990

GRIM REAPER, THE (1962) ★★★ Absorbing crime-drama about the violent death of a prostitute—as told through three different people. Pier Paolo Pasolini's script recalls *Rashomon*, with its series of flashbacks. Bernardo Bertolucci's first feature film. In Italian with English subtitles. B&W; 100m. DIR: Bernardo Bertolucci. CAST: Francesco Rulu. 1962

GRIM REAPER, THE (1980) 🎬 The cannibal and zombie subgenres are combined in a single cheap movie by a director—Joe D'Amato (née Aristide Massaccesi) who has dabbled in each. Rated R. 87m. DIR: Joe D'Amato (Aristide Massaccesi). CAST: Tisa Farrow, Saverio Vallone. 1980 DVD

GRIND ★★1/2 A young man who cares more about racing cars than his dead-end job at a factory is drawn into an affair with his brother's frustrated wife. Some good performances and a feel for life in suburban New Jersey aren't enough to recommend this dreary melodrama. Rated R for profanity and sexual situations. 96m. DIR: Chris Kentis. CAST: Billy Crudup, Adrienne Shelly, Paul Schulze, Frank Vincent. 1996

•**GRISBI** ★★★★ A gangster classic that concentrates less on violence than on character. Jean Gabin plays an aging gangster who has stolen a fortune in gold bars that he hopes will allow him to live out the rest of his life in style. The problem is, hanging on to the loot proves to be harder than getting it. Look for Jeanne Moreau in a small part. Dubbed in English. B&W; 90m. DIR: Jacques Becker. CAST: Jean Gabin, Rene Dary, Dora Doll, Lino Ventura. 1953

GRISSOM GANG, THE ★★★ Lurid crime-drama set in the 1920s. A wealthy heiress (Kim Darby) is kidnapped by a family of grotesque rednecks whose leader (Scott Wilson) falls in love with her. This gritty, violent film receives comically uneven direction from Robert Aldrich. Rated R. 127m. DIR: Robert Aldrich. CAST: Kim Darby, Scott Wilson, Irene Dailey, Tony Musante, Robert Lansing. 1971

GRIZZLY ★★ Another "nature runs amok" film with Christopher George going up against an eighteen-foot killer bear this time out. Some taut action, but the movie has no style or pizzazz. Rated PG for violence. 92m. DIR: William Girdler. CAST: Christopher George, Andrew Prine, Richard Jaeckel. 1976 DVD

GRIZZLY MOUNTAIN ★★1/2 *Grizzly Adams* star Dan Haggerty heads up this family fantasy about two kids who stumble into a cave and travel back in time. There, they meet mountain man Haggerty, who is trying to save the surrounding area from developers. Even though the film has a made-for-television look,

it's lots of fun, especially for younger children who will appreciate the silly humor and kid angle. Rated G. 96m. DIR: Jeremy Haft. CAST: Dan Haggerty, Kim Morgan Greene, Nicole Lund, Martin Kove, Dyland Haggerty, Megan Haggerty. 1997

GROOVE TUBE, THE ★★1/2 A sometimes funny and most times just silly—or gross—1974 takeoff on television by writer-director Ken Shapiro. The V.D. commercial is a classic, however. Look for Chevy Chase in his first, brief screen appearance. Rated R. 75m. DIR: Ken Shapiro. CAST: Ken Shapiro, Lane Sarasohn, Chevy Chase, Richard Belzer. 1974

GROSS ANATOMY ★★★ Sort of a *Paper Chase* for med school, this focuses on the very likable son of a fisherman who must accept or reject the cutthroat competition among his peers. A bit contrived but still watchable. Rated PG-13 for profanity. 107m. DIR: Thom Eberhardt. CAST: Matthew Modine, Daphne Zuniga, Christine Lahti. 1989

GROSS JOKES ★★ A group of comedians tell off-color and somewhat gross jokes culled from the book by Julius Alvin. Moderately funny. Not rated; contains adult language and humor. 53m. DIR: Bob Williams. CAST: George Wallace, Tommy Sledge, Sheryl Bernstein, Tim Jones, Barry Diamond, Joe Alaskey, Budd Friedman. 1985

GROSSE POINTE BLANK ★★★★ This dark-hued romp is a career-maker for star John Cusack, a meticulous assassin who finds business conflicting with pleasure while attending his ten-year high-school reunion. When not dodging bullets, Cusack tries to patch things up with the girl he jilted long ago at the high-school prom. The script is sharp and sassy, the action fast and furious, and the comic tone too funny for words. Rated R for violence and profanity. 107m. DIR: George Armitage. CAST: John Cusack, Minnie Driver, Dan Aykroyd, Alan Arkin, Joan Cusack, Jeremy Piven, Hank Azaria. 1997 DVD

GROTESQUE 🎬 Psychotic punks looking for a treasure. Rated R for violence and nudity. 80m. DIR: Joe Tornatore. CAST: Linda Blair, Tab Hunter, Charles Dierkop. 1987

GROUND CONTROL ★★★1/2 In this direct-to-video drama, Jack Harris, a former controller still haunted by the crash of a plane, is called back into action when a storm takes out the tower in Phoenix, and he's forced to land the planes with no radar or contact. Gripping one moment, melodramatic the next, the film ultimately wins us over with decent performances and a traveler's common fear. Rated PG-13 for language. 98m. DIR: Richard Howard. CAST: Kiefer Sutherland, Robert Sean Leonard, Kelly McGillis, Henry Winkler, Kristy Swanson, Michael Gross, Margaret Cho. 1998 DVD

GROUND ZERO ★★1/2 Political thriller that lacks the strike capability to give it a dramatic victory. While a cameraman investigates his father's death, he stumbles onto a cover-up by the British and Australian governments involving nuclear testing in the Fifties. Aborigines, political influence, corruption, murder, and genocide are just some of the fallout from his investigation. Just enough to keep you interested, but ultimately misses the target. Rated PG-13 for violence and profanity. 100m. DIR: Michael Pattinson, Bruce Myles. **CAST:** Colin Friels, Jack Thompson, Donald Pleasence. **1988**

GROUNDHOG DAY ★★★1/2 Arrogantly self-centered TV weatherman Phil Connors (Bill Murray), practically convinced he *creates* the weather, stumbles into a time warp and winds up repeating the most insipid day of his life: twenty-four hours in Punxsutawney, Pennsylvania, during its annual Groundhog Day festivities. The film actually displays some heart in its last act. Rated PG for profanity. 103m. **DIR:** Harold Ramis. **CAST:** Bill Murray, Andie MacDowell, Chris Elliott, Stephen Tobolowsky. **1993** **DVD**

GROUNDSTAR CONSPIRACY, THE ★★★1/2 This nifty thriller has gone unrecognized for years. George Peppard stars as a government investigator sent to uncover the security leak that led to the destruction of a vital—and secret—space laboratory, and the amnesia-stricken Michael Sarrazin is his only lead. The clever plot and excellent character interactions build to a surprising climax. Rated PG. 103m. **DIR:** Lamont Johnson. **CAST:** George Peppard, Michael Sarrazin, Christine Belford. **1972**

GROUP, THE ★★★ Based on the book by Mary McCarthy about the lives and loves of eight female college friends. Overlong, convoluted semi-sleazy fun. The impressive cast almost makes you forget it's just a catty soap opera. So watch it anyway. 150m. **DIR:** Sidney Lumet. **CAST:** Joan Hackett, Elizabeth Hartman, Shirley Knight, Joanna Pettet, Jessica Walter, James Broderick, Larry Hagman, Richard Mulligan, Hal Holbrook. **1966**

GROWN-UPS ★★ Originally made for cable TV, this theatre piece by cartoonist Jules Feiffer revolves around a writer (Charles Grodin) and his difficulties with his family. Feiffer's dialogue is sharply observed, but there's no real story, and the characters' continual bickering never leads anywhere. 106m. **DIR:** John Madden. **CAST:** Charles Grodin, Martin Balsam, Marilu Henner, Jean Stapleton. **1985**

GRUESOME TWOSOME 💣 *Sweeney Todd*–style parody about a wig maker and her homicidal son. 72m. **DIR:** Herschell Gordon Lewis. **CAST:** Elizabeth David, Chris Martel. **1967**

GRUMPIER OLD MEN ★★★★ The second teaming of Jack Lemmon and Walter Matthau as cranky, lifelong neighbors provides—surprisingly—as many chuckles and guffaws as their first outing. This time, the two codgers agree on a temporary truce when newcomer Sophia Loren threatens to turn the local bait shop into an Italian restaurant. Once again, Burgess Meredith, as Lemmon's sex-obsessed father, gets most of the belly laughs. Rated PG-13 for vulgarity and suggested sex. 100m. **DIR:** Howard Deutch. **CAST:** Jack Lemmon, Walter Matthau, Ann-Margret, Sophia Loren, Burgess Meredith, Kevin Pollak, Daryl Hannah, Ann Guilbert. **1995** **DVD**

GRUMPY OLD MEN ★★★★ A howlingly funny tale of two longtime rivals (Walter Matthau and Jack Lemmon) fighting over the affections of sexy new neighbor Ann-Margret. Lemmon and Matthau are in top form, but 84-year-old Burgess Meredith, as Lemmon's irascible father, has the film's funniest lines. Be sure to catch the outtakes shown during the clos-

ing credits for a laugh-filled capper to this comic gem. Rated PG-13 for sexual references. 105m. **DIR:** Donald Petrie. **CAST:** Jack Lemmon, Walter Matthau, Ann-Margret, Daryl Hannah, Burgess Meredith, Kevin Pollak, Ossie Davis, Buck Henry. **1993** **DVD**

GUADALCANAL DIARY ★★★★ Timely story of the U.S. Marine Corp's deadly struggle for this South Pacific island is one of the best wartime adventure films. B&W; 93m. **DIR:** Lewis Seiler. **CAST:** Preston Foster, Lloyd Nolan, William Bendix, Richard Conte, Anthony Quinn, Richard Jaeckel. **1943**

GUANTANAMERA! ★★★ Famous singer Yoyita returns to her hometown after fifty years and rekindles a passionate relationship with her first love. She dies in his arms, and the rest of this whimsical romantic comedy chronicles the journey of her coffin back to Havana under the escort of her lover, her unhappily married niece, and her niece's husband. In Spanish with English subtitles. Not rated; contains sexual references. 104m. **DIR:** Tomas Gutierrez Alea, Juan Carlos Tabio. **CAST:** Mirta Ibarra, Jorge Perugorria, Raul Eguren, Carlos Cruz, Conchito Brando, Pedro Fernandez. **1994**

GUARDIAN, THE (1984) ★★★1/2 When the tenants of an upper-class New York City apartment house become fed up with the violence of the streets intruding on their building, they hire a live-in guard (Louis Gossett Jr.). While he does manage to rid the building of lawbreakers, some begin to question his methods. This HBO made-for-cable film is notches above most cable fare. Profanity and violence. 102m. **DIR:** David Greene. **CAST:** Martin Sheen, Lou Gossett Jr., Arthur Hill. **1984**

GUARDIAN, THE (1990) 💣 Los Angeles couple finds out the hard way that the attractive, charming nanny they've hired is a tree-worshiping druid. Rated R for language, violence, and nudity. 93m. **DIR:** William Friedkin. **CAST:** Jenny Seagrove, Dwier Brown. **1990** **DVD**

GUARDIAN ANGEL ★★ Martial arts expert Cynthia Rothrock is back in this pedestrian effort about an ex-cop out to avenge the deaths of her partner and lover. She gets her chance when the killer breaks out of jail, and Rothrock is hired to protect the killer's next target. Novelty here is the killer is a woman. Anyone for a good cat fight? Rated R for violence, language, and adult situations. 98m. **DIR:** Richard W. Munchkin. **CAST:** Cynthia Rothrock, Daniel McVicar, Lydie Denier, Marshall Teague. **1993** **DVD**

GUARDIAN OF THE ABYSS 💣 Uneventful devil-worship flick from England. 50m. **DIR:** Don Sharp. **CAST:** Ray Lonnen. **1985**

GUARDING TESS ★★★★ Secret service agent Nicolas Cage wants out of his current assignment—looking after feisty former first lady Shirley MacLaine—but she has other ideas in this highly entertaining comedy-drama. MacLaine and Cage do not immediately spring to mind as a perfect pairing, but they work extremely well together. Intriguing characters, some genuine laughs, a few tears, and even a sprinkle of suspense. Rated PG-13 for profanity and light violence. 98m. **DIR:** Hugh Wilson. **CAST:** Shirley MacLaine, Nicolas Cage, Austin Pendleton, Edward Albert, James Rebhorn, Richard Griffiths, Harry J. Lennix. **1994 DVD**

GUARDSMAN, THE ★★★★ A movie landmark since it is the only film to costar Broadway's Alfred Lunt and Lynn Fontanne. This film also recorded their most successful roles for posterity. Ferenc Molnar wrote the original play about a man who tests his wife's faithfulness by posing as a macho, romantic Russian guardsman. B&W; 83m. **DIR:** Sidney Franklin. **CAST:** Alfred Lunt, Lynn Fontanne, Roland Young, ZaSu Pitts, Maude Eburne, Herman Bing. **1931**

GUESS WHO'S COMING TO DINNER ★★★ This final film pairing of Spencer Tracy and Katharine Hepburn was one of the first to deal with interracial marriage. Though quite daring at the time, this movie seems rather quaint today. Still, Tracy and Hepburn are fun to watch, and Sidney Poitier and Katharine Houghton make an appealing young couple. 108m. **DIR:** Stanley Kramer. **CAST:** Spencer Tracy, Katharine Hepburn, Sidney Poitier, Katharine Houghton, Cecil Kellaway, Beah Richards, Virginia Christine. **1967 DVD**

GUEST IN THE HOUSE ★★★ This grim melodrama features Anne Baxter as an emotionally disturbed girl who turns an idyllic household into a chaotic nightmare. An engrossing psychological thriller. B&W; 121m. **DIR:** John Brahm. **CAST:** Anne Baxter, Ralph Bellamy, Aline MacMahon, Ruth Warrick, Jerome Cowan. **1944**

GUEST WIFE ★★1/2 Claudette Colbert poses as foreign correspondent Don Ameche's wife to fool the boss, who thinks he's married. Funny and cute but not that funny and cute. B&W; 90m. **DIR:** Sam Wood. **CAST:** Claudette Colbert, Don Ameche, Dick Foran, Charles Dingle, Grant Mitchell, Irving Bacon. **1945**

GUIDE FOR THE MARRIED MAN, A ★★★1/2 Worldly Robert Morse tries to teach reluctant Walter Matthau the fundamentals of adultery. His lessons are acted out by a dazzling roster of top comedy stars. This episodic film provides a steady stream of laughs. The bit in which Joey Bishop is caught redhanded and practices the "deny, deny, deny" technique is a classic. 89m. **DIR:** Gene Kelly. **CAST:** Walter Matthau, Inger Stevens, Robert Morse, Sue Ane Langdon, Lucille Ball, Jack Benny, Joey Bishop, Art Carney, Jayne Mansfield, Carl Reiner, Sid Caesar, Phil Silvers, Jeffrey Hunter, Sam Jaffe. **1967**

GUIDE FOR THE MARRIED WOMAN, A ★★1/2 In this made-for-television movie, Cybill Shepherd plays a frustrated housewife who decides that life must hold more excitement than her current predictable situation. Though the cast includes many big names, this film never really takes off and is no match for the earlier *Guide for the Married Man.* 100m. **DIR:** Hy Averback. **CAST:** Cybill Shepherd, Charles Frank, John Hillerman, Elaine Joyce, Peter Marshall, Eve Arden. **1978**

GUILTY AS CHARGED ♥ Black comedy fans are in for a shock with this unfunny tale of a vigilante who tracks down criminals and gives them the hot seat in his homemade electric chair. Pull the plug on this puppy before it short-circuits. Rated R for violence. 93m. **DIR:** Sam Irvin. **CAST:** Rod Steiger, Lauren Hutton, Isaac Hayes, Heather Graham. **1991**

GUILTY AS SIN ★★ A courtroom melodrama about a lady lawyer who falls for her handsome client. But the movie is an uneven blend of star power and director's disinterest. 120m. **DIR:** Sidney Lumet. **CAST:** Rebecca DeMornay, Don Johnson, Stephen Lang, Jack Warden. **1993**

GUILTY BY SUSPICION ★★★★ Robert De Niro is marvelous as a Hollywood director who loses his home and ability to make a living after refusing to testify against his friends at a hearing of the House Un-American Activities Committee during the blacklist period of the Fifties. Riveting film by producer-turned-writer-director Irwin Winkler. Rated PG-13 for profanity. 105m. **DIR:** Irwin Winkler. **CAST:** Robert De Niro, Annette Bening, George Wendt, Patricia Wettig, Sam Wanamaker, Ben Piazza, Gailard Sartain, Stuart Margolin, Martin Scorsese. **1991 DVD**

•**GUINEVERE** ★★★ An insecure young woman has an affair with a middle-aged alcoholic who makes a practice of seducing and abandoning sweet young things. Writer-director Audrey Welles draws sincere, layered performances from her cast that compensate for the familiarity of the story and the patently false ending. Rated R for profanity and sexual scenes. 104m. **DIR:** Audrey Welles. **CAST:** Stephen Rea, Sarah Polley, Jean Smart, Gina Gershon, Paul Dooley. **1999 DVD**

GULAG ★★1/2 This engrossing tale of an American athlete shipped to a Soviet prison camp works at odd moments in spite of a preposterous script. On the other hand, the escape sequence is clever and quite exciting. 120m. **DIR:** Roger Young. **CAST:** David Keith, Malcolm McDowell. **1985**

GULLIVER IN LILLIPUT ★★ This British TV movie stays fairly close to the Jonathan Swift classic satire of small-minded people. Probably too close because it's not long before these bickering people stop being funny and start getting on your nerves. Not rated; contains no objectionable material. 107m. **DIR:** Barry Letts. **CAST:** Andrew Burt, Elizabeth Sladen. **1982**

GULLIVER'S TRAVELS (1939) ★★1/2 Made and issued as an answer to Disney's *Snow White and the Seven Dwarfs,* this full-length cartoon of the famous Jonathan Swift satire about an English sailor who falls among tiny people in a land called Lilliput is just so-so. Lanny Ross, Jessica Dragonette (voices). 74m. **DIR:** Dave Fleischer. **1939 DVD**

GULLIVER'S TRAVELS (1977) ★★ Richard Harris seems lost in this meager retelling of the Jonathan Swift satire. The combination of live action and animation further detracts from the version. Rated G. 80m. **DIR:** Peter R. Hunt. **CAST:** Richard Harris, Catherine Schell. **1977**

GULLIVER'S TRAVELS (1996) (TELEVISION) ★★★★ This made-for-TV miniseries cuts no corners in majestic sets, special effects, and an all-star cast. Remaining loyal to Jonathan Swift's satiric classic, we travel not only to the lands of giants and little people but also to a flying island of pseudointellectuals and an island ruled by horses. Ted Danson is superb as Gulliver. His adventures are told in flashbacks from an English insane asylum where he is committed for his "ravings." Not rated; not really suitable for small children due to violence and a scene in which Danson urinates to put out a fire. 175m. **DIR:** Charles Sturridge. **CAST:** Ted Danson, Mary Steenburgen, James Fox, Geraldine Chaplin, Edward Woodward, Ned Beatty, Peter O'Toole, Omar Sharif. **1996**

GUMBALL RALLY, THE ★★1/2 First film based on an anything-goes cross-country road race. Featuring some excellent stunt driving, with occasional laughs, it's much better than *Cannonball Run*. Rated PG for language. 107m. **DIR:** Chuck Bail. **CAST:** Michael Sarrazin, Gary Busey, Tim McIntire, Raul Julia, Normann Burton. **1976**

GUMBY THE MOVIE ★★★ Even die-hard Gumby fans will find this too much of a good thing. Unanswered plot questions will bother all but the youngest tots who will just enjoy watching Gumby and his pals. Dozens of new characters have been added to the cast from the 1960s TV show, but Gumby and Pokey are still the stars as they take on the greedy Blockheads. Rated G. 90m. **DIR:** Art Clokey. **1995**

GUMMO ♥ A perfect example of why overhyped, precocious teenage directors should not be allowed to make films. There's nothing entertaining or redeeming about the two teenage slackers who need to get a life. Rated R for language, violence, and adult situations. 89m. **DIR:** Harmony Korine. **CAST:** Jacob Reynolds, Nick Sutton, Linda Manz, Max Perlich, Chloe Sevigny. **1997**

GUMSHOE ★★★1/2 Every hard-bitten private-eye film and *film noir* is saluted in this crime-edged comedy. Liverpool bingo caller Albert Finney finds himself in deep, murky water when he tries to live his fantasy of being a Humphrey Bogart–type shamus. Raymond Chandler and Dashiell Hammett fans will love every frame. Rated PG. 88m. **DIR:** Stephen Frears. **CAST:** Albert Finney, Billie Whitelaw, Frank Finlay, Janice Rule, Caroline Seymour. **1972**

GUMSHOE KID, THE ★★1/2 Wannabe gumshoe Jay Underwood quits school to join the family private eye business. Rated R for nudity and violence. 98m. **DIR:** Joseph Manduke. **CAST:** Jay Underwood, Tracy Scoggins, Vince Edwards. **1990**

GUN CODE ★★★ When the residents of Miller's Flats find themselves being coerced into paying protection money, Tim Haines (Tim McCoy) rides to the rescue, guns ablazing. Even the minuscule budgets of Producers Releasing Corporation couldn't stop McCoy from turning out above-average Westerns. B&W; 52m. **DIR:** Peter Stewart. **CAST:** Tim McCoy, Dave O'Brien. **1940**

GUN CRAZY (1950) ★★★1/2 Young man obsessed by guns teams up with a carnival sharpshooter who leads him into a life of robbery and murder. This odd little cult classic is fast and lean. MacKinlay Kantor wrote the original story and cowrote the screenplay. B&W; 86m. **DIR:** Joseph H. Lewis. **CAST:** Peggy Cummins, John Dall, Morris Carnovsky. **1950**

GUN FURY ★★★ Donna Reed is kidnapped. Rock Hudson chases the bad men and saves her from a fate worse than death in Arizona's mesmerizing Red Rock country. Villainy abounds. 83m. **DIR:** Raoul Walsh. **CAST:** Rock Hudson, Donna Reed, Lee Marvin, Philip Carey, Neville Brand. **1953**

GUN IN BETTY LOU'S HANDBAG, THE ★★1/2 In order to get into the spirit of this generally predictable screwball comedy, one has to accept screenwriter Grace Cary Bickley's premise that a neglected wife would claim to be a murderer to get her police-detective husband's attention. Breathlessly sincere performances by Penelope Ann Miller and Eric Thal make it as entertaining as it is dumb. Rated PG-13 for profanity and violence. 90m. **DIR:** Alan Moyle. **CAST:** Penelope Ann Miller, Eric Thal, Alfre Woodard, William Forsythe, Cathy Moriarty. **1992**

GUN IN THE HOUSE, A ★★★1/2 This TV movie stars Sally Struthers as a woman being tried for the handgun murder of a man who broke into her house. Struthers excels in the role. An above-average drama. 100m. **DIR:** Ivan Nagy. **CAST:** Sally Struthers, David Ackroyd, Jeffrey Tambor, Dick Anthony Williams, Millie Perkins. **1981**

GUN IS LOADED, THE ♥ Avant-garde poet and rock performer Lydia Lunch's angst-ridden look at New York City. Not rated; contains profanity and nudity. 65m. **DIR:** Lydia Lunch. **CAST:** Lydia Lunch. **1989**

GUN RIDERS, THE ★★ Genre fans may enjoy this violent adult Western, though others will find it nihilistic and sleazy. A sadistic gunman, nicknamed the Messenger of Death, is the center of a story pitting Indians, gunrunners, and settlers against each other. Photographed by Vilmos Zsigmond. Rated PG. 88m. **DIR:** Al Adamson. **CAST:** Robert Dix, Scott Brady, Jim Davis, John Carradine, Paula Raymond. **1969**

•**GUN SHY (2000)** ★★ A stressed-out, undercover drug agent is persuaded to stay on the job for one more sting against a Colombian drug lord; meanwhile, he falls for a wisecracking nurse. This inane, confused comedy rambles in circles until the climax, where it all but disintegrates before your eyes. Rated R for violence, profanity, and brief nudity. 101m. **DIR:** Eric Blakeney. **CAST:** Liam Neeson, Oliver Platt, Sandra Bullock, Jose Zuniga. **2000** DVD

GUN SMUGGLERS ★★★1/2 When an entire shipment of Gatling guns is stolen, Tim Holt must act fast. B&W; 61m. **DIR:** Frank McDonald. **CAST:** Tim Holt, Richard Martin, Martha Hyer, Paul Hurst, Gary Gray, Douglas Fowley. **1948**

GUNBUSTER—VOLS. 1–3 ★★ Japanese animation. A tedious, overwrought tale of duty and sacrifice in the Space Force. Quality animation. In Japanese with English subtitles. Not rated violence and illustrated nudity. 55–60m. **DIR:** Hideaki Anno. **1989**

GUNCRAZY (1992) ♥ Small-town bad girl Drew Barrymore's love letters to young convict James LeGros brings him to town upon parole, whereupon the two shoot up the locals. Growin' up sure is hard to do. Rated R for violence, suggested sex, and profanity. 96m. **DIR:** Tamra Davis. **CAST:** Drew Barrymore, James LeGros, Rodney Harvey, Joe Dallesandro, Michael Ironside, Ione Skye. **1992**

GUNDOWN AT SANDOVAL ★★★ Texas John Slaughter faces overwhelming odds when he vows to avenge a friend's death and goes against the inhabitants of Sandoval, an infamous outlaw hideout. Featuring lots of hard riding and gunplay, this Disney television show was originally shown in Europe as a feature film. 72m. DIR: Harry Keller. CAST: Tom Tryon, Dan Duryea, Beverly Garland, Lyle Bettger, Harry Carey Jr. 1959

GUNFIGHT, A ★★ Lifeless Western features the acting debut of country singer Johnny Cash. He is teamed with Kirk Douglas in a story of two long-in-the-tooth gunslingers. 90m. DIR: Lamont Johnson. CAST: Kirk Douglas, Johnny Cash, Jane Alexander, Karen Black, Raf Vallone. 1971

GUNFIGHT AT THE O.K. CORRAL ★★★★ The Wyatt Earp–Doc Holliday legend got another going-over in this rather good Western. Burt Lancaster and Kirk Douglas portray these larger-than-life gunfighters, who shoot it out with the nefarious Clanton family in 1881 Tombstone. The movie effectively builds up its tension until the climactic gunfight. 122m. DIR: John Sturges. CAST: Burt Lancaster, Kirk Douglas, Rhonda Fleming, Jo Van Fleet, John Ireland, Lee Van Cleef, Frank Faylen. 1957

GUNFIGHTER, THE (1950) ★★★★★ A notorious gunslinger (Gregory Peck) tries to settle down, but his reputation dogs him wherever he goes. Peck (though almost too young for his role) gives one of his best performances in this neglected classic. There's not much action, but it's an engrossing character study. B&W; 84m. DIR: Henry King. CAST: Gregory Peck, Helen Westcott, Millard Mitchell, Skip Homeier, Jean Parker, Karl Malden. 1950

GUNFIGHTER (1997) ★★1/2 Old West gunslinger tale is more likely to cause saddle sores than jubilation for Western fans. Robert Carradine plays The Kid, a singer looking for work, who encounters The Stranger, who relates his deadly and colorful past, including a shoot-out with a bad guy named Tex. Now Tex wants revenge, and The Stranger must face down his old nemesis one more time. At least Carradine doesn't break out in song. Rated R for violence. 95m. DIR: Christopher Coppola. CAST: Martin Sheen, Robert Carradine, Clu Gulager. 1997 DVD

GUNFIGHTER'S MOON ★★1/2 Gunfighter Frank Morgan (Lance Henriksen) returns to the town where he once lived to help the new sheriff. Complications ensue with the sheriff's wife (Morgan's former lover), and her daughter, who doesn't know that Morgan is her real father. Mix of Western and soap opera doesn't really work, despite a good performance by Henriksen. Rated PG-13 for violence. 95m. DIR: Larry Ferguson. CAST: Lance Henriksen, Kay Lenz. 1997

GUNFIGHTERS, THE ★★ The Everett Boys (Art Hindle, Reiner Schoene, and Tony Addabbo) are forced to become outlaws when a powerful rancher sets his sights on their land. The Western suffers from erratic storytelling and so-so acting. 96m. DIR: Clay Borris. CAST: Art Hindle, Reiner Schoene, Tony Addabbo, George Kennedy. 1987

GUNFIRE ★★★ More story than action in this tale of an outlaw who is pardoned on the condition he kill a rancher whose land the railroad wants. Problems set in when the gunfighter sympathizes with the rancher and falls in love with his wife. Convincing performances by Warren Oates, Fabio Testi, and Jenny Agutter make this better than average. Not rated; contains violence. 90m. DIR: Monte Hellman.

CAST: Warren Oates, Jenny Agutter, Fabio Testi, Carlos Bravo, Sam Peckinpah. 1978

GUNG HO! (1943) ★★1/2 Although not meant to be funny, this ultrapatriotic war film has its truly outrageous moments. It must have been a real booster for wartime filmgoers in America. Today it's almost embarrassing—particularly during the scene in which a recruit is accepted into a special team of commandos simply because he "hates Japs." B&W; 88m. DIR: Ray Enright. CAST: Randolph Scott, Grace McDonald, Alan Curtis, Noah Beery Jr., J. Carrol Naish, David Bruce, Robert Mitchum, Sam Levene. 1943

GUNG HO (1985) ★★★★ Another winner from director Ron Howard and writers Lowell Ganz and Babaloo Mandel, who previously teamed on *Night Shift* and *Splash*. This is a pointed study of the cultural chaos that occurs when small-town Hadleyville's automobile plant is rescued by imported Japanese management. Rated PG-13 for language. 111m. DIR: Ron Howard. CAST: Michael Keaton, Gedde Watanabe, George Wendt, Mimi Rogers, John Turturro, Clint Howard. 1985

GUNGA DIN ★★★★★ An acknowledged classic, this release has it all: laughs, thrills, and chills. Howard Hawks was originally set to direct it and played a large part in its creation. Plot: Three soldiers in nineteenth-century India put down a native uprising with the help of an Indian water carrier. B&W; 117m. DIR: George Stevens. CAST: Cary Grant, Victor McLaglen, Douglas Fairbanks Jr., Joan Fontaine, Sam Jaffe, Eduardo Ciannelli. 1939

GUNMAN FROM BODIE ★★★1/2 The best of the many trio series Westerns of the 1930s and 40s, *The Rough Riders* teamed two of the genre's most charismatic stars, Buck Jones and Tim McCoy, with one of the best sidekicks in the business, Raymond Hatton. The second film in the series, *Gunman from Bodie*, is considered by most aficionados to be the best. The plot, about a trio of marshals who set out to capture a gang of cattle thieves, may be worn-out, but the star power makes this first-rate. B&W; 60m. DIR: Spencer Gordon Bennet. CAST: Buck Jones, Tim McCoy, Raymond Hatton, Dave O'Brien. 1941

GUNMEN ★★★ Action-packed movie stars Mario Van Peebles as a New York detective who turns bounty hunter to bring down South American drug lord Patrick Stewart. Top-billed Christopher Lambert is the wacko brother of a drug runner, whose whereabouts may be the key to the mission. An oddball cop/buddy movie with touches of the spaghetti Western, it's weird and uneven, but entertaining. Rated R for violence, profanity, nudity, and simulated sex. 97m. DIR: Deran Sarafian. CAST: Christopher Lambert, Mario Van Peebles, Denis Leary, Patrick Stewart, Sally Kirkland, Kadeem Hardison, Richard Sarafian. 1994

GUNRUNNER, THE ★★ Kevin Costner plans to make a fortune bootlegging liquor in order to buy guns for China's downtrodden masses. Poor editing destroys the continuity of what might have been an intriguing film. Rated R for violence and a hint of sex. 92m. DIR: Nardo Castillo. CAST: Kevin Costner, Sara Botsford. 1989

GUNS FOR DOLLARS ★★ Every gimmick is used in this comedy-spaghetti Western about a bounty hunter hired by Mexican revolutionaries, a Russian spy, and a female American spy disguised as a nun seeking the missing jewels of Emperor Maximilian. Plenty of action and humor are weaved throughout the plot. Not rated; contains violence. 94m. **DIR:** Anthony Ascot. **CAST:** George Hilton, Charles Southwood, Agata Flory, Roberto Camardiel, Paolo Gozlino, Rick Boyd. **1971**

GUNS OF DIABLO ★★★ Wagon train guide Charles Bronson, accompanied by young Kurt Russell, rides into a strange town where he unexpectanly rekindles an old romance and is ambushed by ruthless outlaws. Edited from two episodes of the TV series *Travels of Jamie McPheeters*. 91m. **DIR:** Boris Ingster. **CAST:** Charles Bronson, Kurt Russell, Susan Oliver, Jan Merlin. **1964**

GUNS OF FORT PETTICOAT ★★★1/2 Cavalry officer Audie Murphy trains a group of women to defend their settlement against marauding Indians. Unusual twist on a tired plot. 82m. **DIR:** George Marshall. **CAST:** Audie Murphy, Kathryn Grant, Hope Emerson, Jeff Donnell, James Griffith. **1957**

GUNS OF HATE ★★ When a prospector finds the fabled Lost Dutchman mine, outlaws try to steal it from him and his daughter. Tim Holt to the rescue in one of his best RKO outings. B&W; 62m. **DIR:** Lesley Selander. **CAST:** Tim Holt, Richard Martin, Steve Brodie, Nan Leslie, Myrna Dell. **1948**

GUNS OF NAVARONE, THE ★★★★ Along with *The Great Escape*, this film is one of the best World War II adventure yarns. Gregory Peck, David Niven, and Anthony Quinn are part of a multinational task force that is sent to Greece with a mission to destroy two huge German batteries that threaten a fleet of Allied troop transports. 145m. **DIR:** J. Lee Thompson. **CAST:** Gregory Peck, David Niven, Anthony Quinn, Stanley Baker, Anthony Quayle, James Darren, Irene Papas. **1961 DVD**

GUNS OF THE MAGNIFICENT SEVEN ★★★ George Kennedy, fresh from his success with *Cool Hand Luke*, steps in for Yul Brynner as Chris, a well-meaning gunfighter who has a bad habit of getting his friends killed while defending the downtrodden. This second sequel has some fine performances—particularly by Kennedy and James Whitmore—and some rousing action scenes, but the original *Seven* has yet to be equaled. Rated PG. 106m. **DIR:** Paul Wendkos. **CAST:** George Kennedy, Monte Markham, James Whitmore, Bernie Casey, Joe Don Baker, Michael Ansara. **1969**

•**GUNSHY (1998)** ★★ The friendship between a writer and an Atlantic City mobster, who agree to share their knowledge with each other, fuels this pedestrian dramatic thriller. Their mutual interests also include the mobster's girlfriend. Things get complicated, but not enough to make the film more than it is. Rated R for adult situations, language, and violence. 105m. **DIR:** Jeff Celentano. **CAST:** William L. Petersen, Jeff Wincott, Diane Lane, Kevin Gage, Eric Schaeffer. **1998 DVD**

GUNSLINGER ★★★ Outlaw John Ireland is hired by land-grabbing saloon boss Allison Hayes to kill female sheriff, Beverly Garland. An early one from director Roger Corman, who has become somewhat of a cult figure. 83m. **DIR:** Roger Corman. **CAST:** John Ireland, Beverly Garland, Allison Hayes, Chris Alcaide, Dick Miller. **1956**

GUNSMOKE (TV SERIES) ★★★★ Television's finest Western series most important asset was the exquisite cast ensemble: James Arness as Marshal Matt Dillon, Amanda Blake as Kitty the saloon keeper, Dennis Weaver and Ken Curtis as well-meaning deputies, and Milburn Stone as the irascible Doc Adams. The best episodes are the half hours, which feature some of the tightest, most evocative storytelling ever to be presented. 60m. per tape. **DIR:** Various. **CAST:** James Arness, Milburn Stone, Amanda Blake, Dennis Weaver, Ken Curtis, Burt Reynolds, Glenn Strange, Buck Taylor. **1955–1975**

GUNSMOKE: RETURN TO DODGE ★★★ When Matt Dillon (James Arness), now retired from the job of town marshal, is badly wounded in a fight, Miss Kitty (Amanda Blake) leaves her new home in New Orleans to be at his side in Dodge, where an old enemy of theirs is also headed to exact revenge. Buoyed by a series of flashbacks from the series' twenty years of episodes. 96m. **DIR:** Vincent McEveety. **CAST:** James Arness, Amanda Blake, Buck Taylor, Steve Forrest, Earl Holliman. **1987**

GUS ★★★1/2 This Disney comedy has a mule named Gus delivering the winning kicks for a losing football team. Naturally, the rival team kidnaps the mule before the big game, and the search is on. Lots of slapstick comedy for the kids to enjoy in this one. Rated G. 96m. **DIR:** Vincent McEveety. **CAST:** Edward Asner, Don Knotts, Gary Grimes, Dick Van Patten. **1976**

GUY: AWAKENING OF THE DEVIL ★★ Our heroes in this animated tribute to sex and violence are a pair of hard-boiled soldiers of fortune, one of whom gains the ability to mutate into a giant, apparently invulnerable creature. In Japanese with English subtitles. Available rated R or unrated, both with nudity and violence; the unrated version contains explicit sex. 40m. **DIR:** Yorihisa Uchida. **1990**

GUY II: SECOND TARGET ★★1/2 Guy and Raina, the terrible twosome of fortune hunters, go after a fortune hidden in the temple of a bizarre cult in this animated feature. Fans of the transforming-monster subgenre will enjoy this one. In Japanese with English subtitles. Not rated; contains violence, profanity, and brief nudity. 33m. **DIR:** Yorihisa Uchida. **1992**

GUY NAMED JOE, A ★★★★ Enchanting film has a dead WWII pilot (Spencer Tracy) coming back to Earth from heaven to aid a young aviator (Van Johnson) with his love life and combat missions. MGM pulls out all the stops with a blockbuster cast and high production values. Tracy's performance is sublime. B&W; 120m. **DIR:** Victor Fleming. **CAST:** Spencer Tracy, Van Johnson, Irene Dunne, Ward Bond, Lionel Barrymore, James Gleason. **1943**

•**GUYANA TRAGEDY, THE: THE STORY OF JIM JONES** ★★★★ Powers Boothe won an Emmy award for his gripping portrayal of the Reverend Jim Jones, whose growing megalomania led him to establish a camp in South America. There, in 1978, Jones led more than nine hundred followers in a mass suicide. Though made for television, this well-documented story features a conclusion that will shock most viewers, and is not suitable for younger children. 192m. **DIR:** William A. Graham. **CAST:** Powers Boothe, Ned Beatty, Irene Cara, Veronica Cartwright, Rosalind Cash, Brad Dourif, Meg Foster, Michael C. Gwynne, Diane Ladd, Ron O'Neal, Randy Quaid, Diana Scarwid, Brenda Vaccaro, LeVar Burton. **1980**

GUYS AND DOLLS ★★★ This passable musical stars Marlon Brando and Frank Sinatra as New York gamblers with a gangster-like aura. Brando and Sinatra bet on whether or not a lovely Salvation Army soldier (Jean Simmons) is date bait. 150m. **DIR:** Joseph L. Mankiewicz. **CAST:** Marlon Brando, Frank Sinatra, Jean Simmons, Vivian Blaine, Stubby Kaye, Veda Ann Borg. **1955 DVD**

GUYVER, THE ★★1/2 Japanese comic-book superhero jumps to the big screen in a film that's truly comic book in look and style. Jack Armstrong is a college student who stumbles across a helmet that transforms him into a superhero. Hot on his tail are a gang of mutants and a CIA agent. Outrageous special effects and tongue-in-cheek humor make this adventure film worthy of continuation. Rated PG-13 for violence. 92m. **DIR:** Screaming Mad George, Steve Wang. **CAST:** Mark Hamill, David Gale, Michael Berryman, Jack Armstrong. **1992**

GUYVER 2: DARK HERO ★★ Gooey monsters do battle with a metallic hero in this comic-book–like film based on the popular comic-book series. The convoluted story is about thirty minutes too long, despite very entertaining battle choreography, some fine visual effects, and great monster makeup. Rated R for profanity, violence, and gore. 127m. **DIR:** Steve Wang. **CAST:** David Hayter, Kathy Christopherson, Christopher Michael. **1994**

GUYVER: OUT OF CONTROL ★★1/2 An early look at the origin of the Guyver superhero, this animated story tries to make up for its lack of detail with violent action but doesn't quite succeed. In Japanese with English subtitles. Not rated; contains violence and nudity. 55m. **DIR:** Hiroshi Watanabe. **1987**

GYMKATA 🦃 Disappointing fist-and-foot actioner. Rated R for violence. 90m. **DIR:** Robert Clouse. **CAST:** Kurt Thomas, Tetchie Agbayani, Richard Norton. **1985**

GYPSY (1962) ★★★ Tries to surpass its hackneyed situation with an energetic musical score and a story about real people. In this case, the characters are stripper Gypsy Rose Lee and her backstage mother supreme, Rose. The music is excellent, but the characters are weakly defined. 149m. **DIR:** Mervyn LeRoy. **CAST:** Natalie Wood, Rosalind Russell, Karl Malden. **1962 DVD**

GYPSY (1993) ★★★★ Bette Midler struts her stuff in this engaging TV adaptation of the Broadway musical. She's Mama Rose, the boisterous, driven stage mother of June Havoc and Gypsy Rose Lee. It's a show-stopping performance, and Midler deftly shades her hard-edged but endearing character while belting out Jule Styne's memorable tunes with élan. Made for TV. 150m. **DIR:** Emile Ardolino. **CAST:** Bette Midler, Cynthia Gibb, Peter Riegert, Edward Asner. **1993 DVD**

GYPSY ANGELS 🦃 Even die-hard fans eager to see Vanna White in a blink-and-you'll-miss-it topless scene won't care about this romance between an Atlanta stripper and a stunt pilot. Rated R. 92m. **DIR:** Alan Smithee. **CAST:** Vanna White, Gene Bicknell, Richard Roundtree, Tige Andrews, Marilyn Hassett, Lyle Waggoner. **1989**

GYPSY BLOOD ★★1/2 This adaptation of the Prosper Merimee story *Carmen* vaulted both director Ernst Lubitsch and star Pola Negri to the front rank of the European film scene. It has been called the first major postwar German release on the international scene. The title was changed to *Gypsy Blood* for American distribution. Silent. B&W; 104m. **DIR:** Ernst Lubitsch. **CAST:** Pola Negri. **1918**

GYPSY COLT ★★★ A good Americanized updating of *Lassie Come Home* with a girl and her horse. The exciting and well-filmed scenes of the horse, Gypsy, alone and in peril will hold the interest of children and adults. Fine Western scenery is a plus. 72m. **DIR:** Andrew Marton. **CAST:** Donna Corcoran, Ward Bond, Frances Dee, Larry Keating, Lee Van Cleef. **1954**

GYPSY WARRIORS, THE ★★ James Whitmore Jr. and Tom Selleck are two American soldiers in World War II who go behind enemy lines to capture a formula for germ warfare. The humor is bland and the action is déjà vu. Not rated. Has violence. 77m. **DIR:** Lou Antonio. **CAST:** James Whitmore Jr., Tom Selleck, Joseph Ruskin, Lina Raymond, Michael Lane, Ted Gehring, Albert Paulsen, Kenneth Tigar. **1978**

GYPSY WILDCAT ★★★ A colorful adventure set in medieval times with a plot similar to Westerns of the 1940s and a cast of once-popular Hollywood sex objects. 77m. **DIR:** Roy William Neill. **CAST:** Maria Montez, Jon Hall, Douglass Dumbrille, Leo Carrillo, Gale Sondergaard, Nigel Bruce, Curt Bois. **1944**

HABIT ★★★ Rich in atmosphere and ambiguity, this tale of a man on the rebound who falls into the arms of a mysterious woman keeps you guessing. Close friends fear for his life: they suspect that the woman is a vampire. The film captures a dark underground world where nothing is what it seems. Not rated; contains violence, language, nudity, and adult situations. 112m. **DIR:** Larry Fessenden. **CAST:** Larry Fessenden, Meredith Snaider, Aaron Beall, Patricia Coleman, Heather Woodbury, Jesse Hartman. **1997 DVD**

HABITAT ★★★ The greenhouse effect really takes its toll on one family in this made-for-cable, science-fiction morality play about the evil mankind inflicts on the Earth and one another. A high-school student watches his father's accelerated evolution experiment spiral out of control. Then Dad disappears, Mom turns into Mother Nature, and the house grows into a forest fortress. Rated R for adult situations, language, nudity, and violence. 103m. **DIR:** Renee Daalder. **CAST:** Balthazar Getty, Alice Krige, Tcheky Karyo, Lara Harris, Kenneth Walsh. **1996 DVD**

HABITATION OF DRAGONS, THE ★★★ Horton Foote's moving play about one family's secrets and cruelty. Frederic Forrest plays the complacent older brother whose life is about to fall apart when his wife's affair is revealed. Younger brother (Brad Davis) finally is allowed to reach out to him despite the strained years between them. Slow pace matches the painful effort the family makes in order to face the past and deal with the present. Not rated; contains adult themes. 94m. **DIR:** Michael Lindsay-Hogg. **CAST:** Frederic Forrest, Brad Davis, Jean Stapleton, Hallie Foote. **1992**

HACKERS ★★ Manhattan high-school cyberpunks surfing the net stumble onto an industrial extortion conspiracy. The leather-clad, rock 'n' roll hackers are framed for the crime but enlist the aid of the information-highway underground to make things right. Cyberspace becomes a neon wonderland, but the film's visual sizzle is dampened by a clumsy plot and awkward acting. Rated PG-13 for language and suggested sex. 95m. **DIR:** Iain Softley. **CAST:** Jonny Lee Miller, Angelina Jolie, Fisher Stevens, Lorraine Bracco. **1995 DVD**

HADLEY'S REBELLION ★★★ Low-key drama of the growing pains encountered by a country boy as he tries to adjust to a new life in California. Well-intentioned script lacks impact, and Griffin O'Neal makes for a bland hero. Rated PG. 96m. **DIR:** Fred Walton. **CAST:** Griffin O'Neal, William Devane, Charles Durning, Adam Baldwin. **1984**

HAIL CAESAR ★ Director-star Anthony Michael Hall tries to prove his worth to his girlfriend's father so that he may pursue his first love: rock and roll. This *Caesar* takes a stab at comedy and misses. Rated PG for language and adult situations. 93m. **DIR:** Anthony Michael Hall. **CAST:** Anthony Michael Hall, Robert Downey Jr., Judd Nelson, Samuel L. Jackson, Frank Gorshin. **1994**

HAIL, HERO! ★★ Dated, uneven film features an overly rambunctious Michael Douglas (in his first film) returning home to announce his enlistment during the Vietnam War. Rated PG. 100m. **DIR:** David Miller. **CAST:** Michael Douglas, Arthur Kennedy, Peter Strauss, Teresa Wright. **1969**

HAIL MARY ★★★★ This story of the coming of Christ in modern times will offend only the most dogmatic Christians, or narrow-minded religious zealots. Godard's eye for the aesthetic gives this film a compassionate feel. *The Book of Mary*, a film by Anne-Marie Mieville, is the prologue and is equally beautiful. In French with English subtitles. Not rated; the equivalent of an R for nudity. 107m. **DIR:** Jean-Luc Godard. **CAST:** Myriem Roussel, Thierry Lacoste, Philippe Lacoste. **1985**

HAIL THE CONQUERING HERO ★★★★1/2 Defense plant worker Eddie Bracken is passed off by Marine buddies as the hero of Guadalcanal and his hometown goes overboard in adulation and tribute.

Another winning satire from writer-director Preston Sturges. Fine family viewing. B&W; 101m. **DIR:** Preston Sturges. **CAST:** Eddie Bracken, Ella Raines, William Demarest, Raymond Walburn, Franklin Pangborn. **1944**

HAIR ★★★1/2 Neglected adaptation of the hit Broadway play about 1960s unrest. John Savage is the uptight Midwesterner who pals up with a group of (shudder) hippies celebrating the Age of Aquarius. Grand musical moments, due to Twyla Tharp's impressive choreography. Rated PG for nudity. 121m. **DIR:** Milos Forman. **CAST:** Treat Williams, John Savage, Beverly D'Angelo, Annie Golden, Charlotte Rae. **1979 DVD**

HAIRDRESSER'S HUSBAND, THE ★★★★ A 12-year-old boy has his first experience with sensuality in the chair of a local hairdresser. The warmth of the shampoo and the closeness of her body give birth to a romantic notion that leads the adult Antoine (Jean Rochefort) to marry a hairdresser (Anna Galiena). French writer-director Patrice Leconte takes a whimsical approach to the story. In French with English subtitles. Not rated, the film has simulated sex. 84m. **DIR:** Patrice Leconte. **CAST:** Jean Rochefort, Anna Galiena, Roland Bertin. **1992**

HAIRSPRAY ★★★ Writer-director John Waters's ode to the dance craze of the Sixties features some outrageously campy performances. The story revolves around the desire of a pudgy teen (Ricki Lake) to be one of the featured stars on a Baltimore TV show in 1963. Rated PG. 87m. **DIR:** John Waters. **CAST:** Sonny Bono, Divine, Colleen Fitzpatrick, Deborah Harry, Ricki Lake, Leslie Ann Powers, Clayton Prince, Jerry Stiller, Mink Stole, Shawn Thompson, Pia Zadora. **1988**

HAIRY APE, THE ★★★ Eugene O'Neill's play about an animal-like coal stoker on an ocean liner. The hairy ape falls in love with a heartless socialite passenger who at once is captivated and repulsed by his coarse approach to life. William Bendix is fascinating in the title role. B&W; 90m. **DIR:** Alfred Santell. **CAST:** William Bendix, Susan Hayward, John Loder. **1944**

HALF A SIXPENCE ★★ A tuneful musical incarnation of H. G. Wells' novel, *Kipps*, as presented on Broadway with most of the original Broadway cast. The story of a British boy winning and losing a fortune, and winning, losing, and re-winning a girlfriend, is flashy and tuneful, but a mite long for one sitting. 149m. **DIR:** George Sidney. **CAST:** Tommy Steele, Julia Foster, Cyril Ritchard, Pamela Brown, James Villiers, Hilton Edwards, Penelope Horner. **1967**

HALF BAKED ♥ Dopey comedy about three New York City potheads who sell stolen laboratory marijuana to raise bail for their jailed roommate. Rated R for drug use, language, nudity, and sexual content. 82m. **DIR:** Tamra Davis. **CAST:** Dave Chappelle, Guillermo Diaz, Jim Breuer, Harland Williams, Rachel True, Clarence Williams III. **1998 DVD**

HALF-BREED, THE ★★1/2 Predictable oater about a saloon owner determined to drive Apaches off their land so he can mine the gold he's sure is there. 81m.

DIR: Stuart Gilmore. **CAST:** Robert Young, Janis Carter, Jack Buetel, Reed Hadley, Barton MacLane. 1952

HALF HUMAN 🖤 From the director of *Godzilla* comes an abominable snowman terrorizing Mount Fuji. B&W; 78m. **DIR:** Inoshiro Honda. **CAST:** John Carradine, Morris Ankrum (Stepen Morris). 1958

HALF-MOON STREET ★★ Half-baked adaptation of Paul Theroux's *Doctor Slaughter*, which was equally flawed as a novel. Sigourney Weaver stars as an American abroad who decides to supplement her academic (but low-paid) government position by moonlighting as a sophisticated "escort." Rated R for nudity and sexual themes. 90m. **DIR:** Bob Swaim. **CAST:** Sigourney Weaver, Michael Caine, Patrick Kavanagh. 1986

HALF OF HEAVEN ★★★★ A woman works her way up from poverty to power in this unusual import from Spain. Rosa (Angela Molina) almost seems to drift her way to the top as Madrid's most successful restaurateur, but there are deeper meanings in this often funny and always fascinating mix of magic, politics, and romance. Not rated, the film has brief violence. In Spanish with English subtitles. 127m. **DIR:** Manuel Gutierrez Aragon. **CAST:** Angela Molina, Margarita Lozano, Fernando Fernán-Gomez. 1987

HALFBACK OF NOTRE DAME, THE ★★★ Clumsy Gabriel Hogan is a hulking school misfit in this family-oriented spin on Victor Hugo, with Emmanuelle Vaugier positively sparkling as the French exchange student who persuades him that piano lessons might be more fulfilling than football. It's a sweet little story, capably told. Rated PG for minor end-zone violence. 97m. **DIR:** René Bonniere. **CAST:** Gabriel Hogan, Scott Hylands, Allen Cutler, Sandra Nelson, Emmanuelle Vaugier. 1995

HALFMOON ★★1/2 From his study in Tangiers, American author Paul Bowles (*The Sheltering Sky*) introduces three short films adapted from his work. All set in North Africa, the tales are mesmerizingly filmed even though their meanings may be hard to grasp. Not rated. 90m. **DIR:** Frieder Schlaich, Irene von Alberti. **CAST:** Samir Guesmi, Khaled Ksouri, Veronica Quilligan. 1995

HALLELUJAH! ★★★★ Dated in technique but up-to-date in story and acting, this is the first major movie with an all-black cast. The plot revolves around a preacher who has lost his fight with temptation too many times. Irving Berlin wrote the song, "Waiting at the End of the Road," expressly for the film. B&W; 106m. **DIR:** King Vidor. **CAST:** Nina Mae McKinney, Daniel Hayner. 1929

HALLELUJAH, I'M A BUM ★★★★ A charming Depression-day comedy and one of the few films with dialogue delivered in rhymed stanzas, this film boasts a name cast headed by Al Jolson as a hobo who tries to reform after he meets a beautiful woman. Rodgers and Hart wrote "You Are Too Beautiful" expressly for this film. The composer-lyricist team also appears as photographers. B&W; 82m. **DIR:** Lewis Milestone. **CAST:** Al Jolson, Madge Evans, Frank Morgan, Harry Langdon, Tyler Brooke, Edgar Connor. 1933

HALLELUJAH TRAIL, THE ★★★ Those who fondly remember television's *F Troop* should adore this cavalry comedy, which finds Burt Lancaster and Jim Hutton leading a wagon-train load of liquor through Indian territory. Temperance leader Lee Remick wants it all destroyed. Overlong, but fun nonetheless. 167m. **DIR:** John Sturges. **CAST:** Burt Lancaster, Lee Remick, Jim Hutton, Brian Keith, Martin Landau, Donald Pleasence. 1965

HALLOWEEN ★★★★1/2 This is a surprisingly tasteful and enjoyable slasher film. Director John Carpenter puts the accent on suspense and atmosphere rather than blood and guts, as in other films of this kind. The story revolves around the escape of a souless maniac who returns to the town where he murdered his sister. Rated R. 93m. **DIR:** John Carpenter. **CAST:** Jamie Lee Curtis, Donald Pleasence, Nancy Loomis, P. J. Soles, Charles Cyphers. 1978 DVD

HALLOWEEN II ★★★ This respectable sequel picks up where the original left off: with the boogeyman on the prowl and Jamie Lee Curtis running for her life. Rated R because of violence and nudity. 92m. **DIR:** Rick Rosenthal. **CAST:** Jamie Lee Curtis, Donald Pleasence, Charles Cyphers, Jeffrey Kramer, Lance Guest. 1981 DVD

HALLOWEEN III: SEASON OF THE WITCH ★★1/2 A maniacal mask manufacturer in northern California provides kiddies with devilishly designed pumpkin masks. Not a true sequel to the gruesome *Halloween* twosome, but still watchable. Rated R. 96m. **DIR:** Tommy Lee Wallace. **CAST:** Tom Atkins, Stacey Nelkin, Dan O'Herlihy. 1983 DVD

HALLOWEEN IV: THE RETURN OF MICHAEL MYERS ★★★ The makers of this third sequel to John Carpenter's ground-breaking *Halloween* obviously tried to create a quality horror film and for the most part they've succeeded. Director Dwight H. Little commendably puts the accent on atmosphere and suspense in detailing the third killing spree of Michael Myers (a.k.a. The Shape). Donald Pleasence returns as Myers's nemesis, Dr. Loomis, to hunt down this fiendish foe. Rated R for violence and profanity. 88m. **DIR:** Dwight H. Little. **CAST:** Donald Pleasence, Ellie Cornell, Danielle Harris. 1988 DVD

HALLOWEEN V: THE REVENGE OF MICHAEL MYERS ★★ What started off as the story of a truly frightening killer (the unstoppable Michael Myers) has become a run-of-the-mill slasher series. Tedious. Rated R for violence. 89m. **DIR:** Dominique Othenin-Girard. **CAST:** Donald Pleasence, Ellie Cornell, Danielle Harris, Beau Starr. 1989

HALLOWEEN: THE CURSE OF MICHAEL MYERS ★★★ Realizing this is the last outing for Michael Myers, the filmmakers have upped the ante in terms of suspense and gore. Michael returns to his old stomping grounds to put an end to his lineage. There are all kinds of subplots about devil worshipers and kids in trouble, plus enough scares to give even the strongest of wills a jolt. Rated R for violence, profanity, adult situations, and nudity. 88m. **DIR:** Joe Chappelle. **CAST:** Paul Stephen Rudd, Marianne Hagan, Mitchell Ryan, Donald Pleasence. 1995

HALLOWEEN: H20 ★★ This seventh entry in the slasher series has a knockout climax but focuses more on false alarms than true terror. Unstoppable zombie Michael Myers returns twenty years after his first murderous rampage as a child to stalk his sister Laurie, who is now the alcoholic headmistress of a private school. Rated R for violence, gore, profanity, and sexual situations. 85m. **DIR:** Steve Miner. **CAST:** Jamie Lee Curtis, Josh Harnett, Adam Arkin, LL Cool J, Joseph Gordon Levitt, Michelle Williams, Adam Hann-Byrd, Jodi Lyn O'Keefe. 1998 DVD

HALLOWEEN TREE, THE ★★★★ Delightful animated version of the Ray Bradbury tale. A group of trick-or-treaters embark on an incredible journey as they chase the soul of a friend through Halloween's history. Written and narrated by Bradbury. Not rated, but suitable for all ages. 70m. **DIR:** Mario Piluso. **CAST:** Ray Bradbury, Leonard Nimoy, Annie Baker, Alex Greenwald, Edan Gross, Lindsay Crouse (voices). 1993

HALLS OF MONTEZUMA ★★★1/2 There's a minimum of romance and lots of action in this oft-told story of American Marines at war in the South Pacific during World War II. Realistic adventure yarn. 113m. **DIR:** Lewis Milestone. **CAST:** Richard Widmark, Jack Palance, Jack Webb, Robert Wagner, Karl Malden, Reginald Gardiner, Philip Ahn. 1950

HAMBONE AND HILLIE ★★★ A delightful story of love and loyalty between an old woman (Lillian Gish) and her dog and constant companion, Hambone. While boarding a flight in New York to return to Los Angeles, Hambone is accidentally lost. And so begins a three-thousand-mile cross-country trip filled with perilous freeways, wicked humans, and dangerous animals. Rated PG. 97m. **DIR:** Roy Watts. **CAST:** Lillian Gish, Timothy Bottoms, Candy Clark, O. J. Simpson, Robert Jr. Walker. 1984

HAMBURGER—THE MOTION PICTURE 💔 A very funny comedy could be made about the fast-food industry, but this isn't it. Rated R for profanity, nudity, suggested sex, and violence. 90m. **DIR:** Mike Marvin. **CAST:** Leigh McCloskey, Sandy Hackett, Randi Brooks, Charles Tyner, Chuck McCann, Dick Butkus. 1986

HAMBURGER HILL ★★1/2 In dealing with one of the bloodiest battles of the Vietnam War, director John Irvin and screenwriter Jim Carabatsos have made a film so brutally real that watching it is an endurance test. Although well-acted and well made, it is more like a shocking documentary than a work of fiction. Rated R for violence and profanity. 112m. **DIR:** John Irvin. **CAST:** Anthony Barrile, Michael Patrick Boatman, Don Cheadle, Michael Dolan, Don James, Dylan McDermott, M. A. Nickles, Harry O'Reilly, Tim Quill, Courtney B. Vance, Steven Weber, Daniel O'Shea. 1987 DVD

HAMLET (1948) ★★★★★ In every way a brilliant presentation of Shakespeare's best-known play masterminded by England's foremost player. Superb in the title role, Laurence Olivier won the 1948 Oscar for best actor, and (as producer) won for best picture. A high point among many is Stanley Holloway's droll performance as the First Gravedigger. B&W; 150m. **DIR:** Laurence Olivier. **CAST:** Laurence Olivier, Basil Sydney, Eileen Herlie, Jean Simmons, Felix Aylmer, Terence Morgan, Peter Cushing, Stanley Holloway. 1948

HAMLET (1996) ★★★★★ This is the most impressive version of *Hamlet* ever to appear on the big screen. Filming William Shakespeare's play in its entirety, Kenneth Branagh added the depth long missing from previous screen versions. Each character springs to full life while Branagh brings the vitality and inventiveness to *Hamlet* that made his *Henry V* and *Much Ado About Nothing* so memorable. The story, of course, involves murder, incest, and revenge in the royal Danish court. Rated PG-13. 242m. **DIR:** Kenneth Branagh. **CAST:** Kenneth Branagh, Julie Christie, Derek Jacobi, Kate Winslet, Billy Crystal, Robin Williams, Jack Lemmon, Gérard Depardieu, Charlton Heston, Rufus Sewell, Brian Blessed. 1996

HAMLET (1969) ★★★ Nicol Williamson gives a far more energetic portrayal of the famous Dane than the noted Oscar-winning performance of Laurence Olivier. Worth seeing for comparison of interpretations. An exceptional supporting cast adds to the allure of this low-budget adaptation. 113m. **DIR:** Tony Richardson. **CAST:** Nicol Williamson, Gordon Jackson, Anthony Hopkins, Judy Parfitt, Marianne Faithfull, Mark Dignam. 1969

HAMLET (1990) ★★★★1/2 Kenneth Branagh's *Henry V* proved that Shakespeare adaptations could be accessible to mainstream audiences and still remain faithful to the source. Director Franco Zefirelli's *Hamlet* continues this tradition, with Mel Gibson bringing great vitality and physicality to the role of the Bard's most poignant hero. Rated PG for violence. 135m. **DIR:** Franco Zeffirelli. **CAST:** Mel Gibson, Glenn Close, Alan Bates, Ian Holm, Paul Scofield, Helena Bonham Carter. 1990

HAMMERED: THE BEST OF SLEDGE ★★ Well-intentioned but flat takeoff of tough cop movies and TV shows, *Hammered* stars David Rasche as Detective Sledge Hammer, a man who talks to his gun and loves extreme and senseless violence. This is a compilation of four *Sledge Hammer* TV shows. 104m. **DIR:** Jackie Cooper, Gary Walkow, Martha Coolidge. **CAST:** David Rasche, Anne-Marie Martin, Harrison Page, John Vernon. 1986

HAMMERSMITH IS OUT ★★★1/2 In this black comedy an insane criminal is sprung from an asylum by an ambitious attendant. Gaining strength and polish as the plot unfolds, the film promises a bit more than it actually offers. Rated R for profanity, sexual situations, and mild violence. 108m. **DIR:** Peter Ustinov. **CAST:** Elizabeth Taylor, Richard Burton, Peter Ustinov, Beau Bridges, George Raft, John Schuck. 1971

HAMMETT ★★ A disappointing homage to mystery writer Dashiell Hammett, this Wim Wenders–directed and Francis Ford Coppola–meddled production was two years in the making and hardly seems worth it. The plot is nearly incomprehensible, something that could never be said of the real-life Hammett's works (*The Maltese Falcon, The Thin Man,* etc.). Rated PG. 97m. **DIR:** Wim Wenders. **CAST:** Frederic Forrest, Peter Boyle, Marilu Henner, Elisha Cook Jr., R. G. Armstrong. 1982

HAND, THE 💔 Thumbs down on this dull film. Rated R. 104m. **DIR:** Oliver Stone. **CAST:** Michael Caine, Andrea Marcovicci, Annie McEnroe, Bruce McGill. 1981

HAND GUN ★★ The story of a bad guy (Seymour Cassel) and his son (Treat Williams) and the cops that are out to stop them. With an atmosphere just like that of TV's *NYPD Blue*, *Hand Gun* lacks the intelligence and depth that make the program work. Rated R for violence, profanity, and nudity. 90m. **DIR:** Whitney Ransick. **CAST:** Treat Williams, Seymour Cassel, Paul Schulze. **1994 DVD**

HAND THAT ROCKS THE CRADLE, THE ★★★1/2 Once you get past the utterly disgusting first ten minutes, this becomes an effective little suspense tale of a woman who gets revenge for her husband's death by posing as a nanny. Rebecca DeMornay is chilling as the menacing cradle rocker. Rated R for violence, profanity, and nudity. 110m. **DIR:** Curtis Hanson. **CAST:** Annabella Sciorra, Rebecca DeMornay, Matt McCoy, Ernie Hudson, John de Lancie. **1992 DVD**

HANDFUL OF DUST, A ★★★★ Based on Evelyn Waugh's masterpiece, this is a deliciously staged drama of actions and fate. Set in post–World War I England and the jungles of South America, the film presents two aristocrats searching along different paths for happiness. Superb ensemble playing. 118m. **DIR:** Charles Sturridge. **CAST:** James Wilby, Rupert Graves, Kristin Scott Thomas, Anjelica Huston, Alec Guinness. **1988**

HANDMAID'S TALE, THE ★★★★ Adapted from Margaret Atwood's chilling cautionary novel, this feminist horror story stars Natasha Richardson as one of the few remaining fertile women in a futuristic United States where ultraconservatives rule and mandate that all such women must "serve" to provide children for carefully selected members of the upper crust. Rated R for language and explicit sexual themes. 109m. **DIR:** Volker Schlöndorff. **CAST:** Natasha Richardson, Robert Duvall, Faye Dunaway, Aidan Quinn, Elizabeth McGovern, Victoria Tennant. **1990**

HANDS ACROSS THE TABLE ★★★1/2 Carole Lombard is charismatic and witty as a manicurist who must choose between charming-but-poor Fred MacMurray or wealthy-but-dull Ralph Bellamy. Lots of silly plot complications but sparkling performances. Not rated. B&W; 80m. **DIR:** Mitchell Leisen. **CAST:** Carole Lombard, Fred MacMurray, Ralph Bellamy, William Demarest, Astrid Allwyn, Ruth Donnelly, Marie Prevost. **1935**

HANDS OF A STRANGER ★★ Mediocre remake of *The Hands of Orlac*, the old chestnut about a pianist who receives the hands of a murderer after his own are mangled in an accident. The preposterously purple dialogue is a hoot. B&W; 86m. **DIR:** Newt Arnold. **CAST:** Paul Lukather, Joan Harvey, Irish McCalla, Barry Gordon. **1962**

HANDS OF ORLAC ★★★ In one of his finest roles, Conrad Veidt stars in this oft-filmed story of a concert pianist who is led to believe a killer's hands have been grafted onto his own after an accident. This Austrian silent is a top competitor in a field dominated by German terror films and remains a riveting entry. B&W; 82m. **DIR:** Robert Wiene. **CAST:** Conrad Veidt, Fritz Kortner, Carmen Cartellieri, Alexandra Sorina, Paul Askonas, Fritz Strassny. **1925**

HANDS OF STEEL 🎞 A cyborg assassin goes wrong and is pursued by police and baddies. Rated R for language and violence. 94m. **DIR:** Martin Dolman.

CAST: Daniel Greene, Janet Agren, Claudio Cassinelli, George Eastman, John Saxon. **1986**

HANDS OF THE RIPPER ★★★1/2 First-rate period horror—the last great offering of Britain's Hammer Films—speculates what might have happened if Jack the Ripper had had a daughter who grew up unknowingly emulating her murderous dad. A literate script, fine performances, and astute direction by then-promising Peter Sasdy. Rated R. 85m. **DIR:** Peter Sasdy. **CAST:** Eric Porter, Angharad Rees, Jane Merrow. **1971**

HANG 'EM HIGH ★★★ Clint Eastwood's first stateside spaghetti Western is a good one, with the star out to get the vigilantes who tried to hang him for a murder he didn't commit. Pat Hingle is the hangin' judge who gives Clint his license to hunt, and Ben Johnson is the marshal who saves his life. Ed Begley Sr. is memorable as the leader of the vigilantes. Rated PG. 114m. **DIR:** Ted Post. **CAST:** Clint Eastwood, Inger Stevens, Ed Begley Sr., Pat Hingle, Arlene Golonka, Ben Johnson. **1968 DVD**

HANGAR 18 🎞 The story revolves around an alien spaceship that is accidentally disabled by a U.S. satellite. Rated PG. 93m. **DIR:** James L. Conway. **CAST:** Darren McGavin, Robert Vaughn, Gary Collins, Joseph Campanella, James Hampton. **1980**

HANGIN' WITH THE HOMEBOYS ★★★★ A multicultural *Wayne's World*, this features four young men—two black, two Puerto Rican—on the brink of nowhere. All unsuccessful, they gather for a boys' night out. Bittersweet, with both hilarious and tragic scenes. A low-budget gem. Rated R for nudity, violence, and profanity. 89m. **DIR:** Joseph B. Vasquez. **CAST:** Doug E. Doug, Mario Joyner, John Leguizamo. **1991**

•HANGING GARDEN, THE ★★★ A man returns home after years of separation from his family to attend his sister's wedding, and is reminded why he left in the first place. He is constantly haunted by visions of a rotund, teenage boy dangling from a noose, and he struggles to make sense of what it means. The acting is good, and the themes are respectable, but the film has a habit of plodding along. Rated R for language and some violence. 91m. **DIR:** Thom Fitzgerald. **CAST:** Chris Leavins, Kerry Fox, Seana McKenna, Peter MacNeill. **1996**

HANGING ON A STAR 🎞 Deborah Raffin is the persistent and savvy road agent for a promising group of unknown musicians. Rated PG. 93m. **DIR:** Mike MacFarland. **CAST:** Lane Caudell, Deborah Raffin, Wolfman Jack. **1978**

HANGING TREE, THE ★★★★ A strange, haunting tale, with Gary Cooper as a withdrawn and secretive doctor in a mining town. When he cares for a blinded traveler (Maria Schell), the jealousy of the miners brings about violence and tragedy. All but ignored when released, this is worth a look. George C. Scott's movie debut. 106m. **DIR:** Delmer Daves. **CAST:** Gary Cooper, Maria Schell, Karl Malden, George C. Scott, Ben Piazza, Virginia Gregg, Guy Wilkerson, Karl Swensen, King Donovan, John Dierkes. **1956**

•HANGING UP ★★1/2 Buried somewhere inside this mess is a poignant, often shattering story of a woman who dearly loves her father, despite his having sunk into the babbling of senile dementia. Alas, director-costar Diane Keaton treats her film like a screwball comedy, which is at odds with the heart-breaking tragedies to be found in Delia and Nora Ephron's screenplay. The result, a mishmash of conflicting moods, will please nobody. Don't take this call. Rated PG-13 for profanity. 92m. DIR: Diane Keaton. CAST: Meg Ryan, Diane Keaton, Lisa Kudrow, Walter Matthau, Adam Arkin, Cloris Leachman. 2000 DVD

HANGMAN'S KNOT ★★★1/2 Randolph Scott as a Confederate officer who hijacks a Union gold shipment and then learns the Civil War is over. While he decides what to do with their bounty, outlaws attack them at an isolated way station. 81m. DIR: Roy Huggins. CAST: Randolph Scott, Donna Reed, Lee Marvin, Richard Denning, Claude Jarman Jr. 1952

HANGMEN ★★ Extremely violent, poorly acted, and poorly written time killer. An ex–CIA operative (Rick Washburne) is hunted by another agency man (Jake La Motta) who has gone bad. Washburne's family is dragged into the mess. Rated R for violence and language. 88m. DIR: J. Christian Ingvordsen. CAST: Rick Washburne, Jake La Motta, Doug Thomas. 1987 DVD

HANGMEN ALSO DIE ★★★★ Brian Donlevy plays the assassin charged with killing a Nazi stooge in Prague. Gene Lockhart is the scapegoat. One of Fritz Lang's best movies. B&W; 134m. DIR: Fritz Lang. CAST: Brian Donlevy, Walter Brennan, Anna Lee, Gene Lockhart, Dennis O'Keefe. 1943 DVD

HANGOVER SQUARE ★★★1/2 The director and star of The Lodger reunite for this similar tale of a schizophrenic composer who kills under the influence of certain sounds. An above-average thriller with strong music (by Bernard Herrmann), atmospheric photography, and a gripping performance by star Laird Cregar, who died before the film was released. B&W; 77m. DIR: John Brahm. CAST: Laird Cregar, Linda Darnell, George Sanders, Glenn Langan, Alan Napier. 1945

HANK AARON: CHASING THE DREAM ★★★★1/2 Not what you expect, as "Hammerin' Hank" the sports hero is only part of the story. This encompasses the insidious pervasiveness of racism in American life by focusing on one athlete who helped break down the color lines. Interviews with sports figures, Aaron family members, and political leaders are seamlessly blended with reenactments and memorable archival footage. The result is both an exciting document of sports history and a searing comment on cultural bigotry. Not rated. B&W/color; 95m. DIR: Mike Tollin. CAST: Hank Aaron. 1995

HANKY PANKY ★★ In an obvious takeoff on the Hitchcock suspense formula, this seldom funny comedy features Gene Wilder as an innocent man caught up in international intrigue and murder. Rated PG for violence and gore. 110m. DIR: Sidney Poitier. CAST: Gene Wilder, Gilda Radner, Richard Widmark, Kathleen Quinlan, Robert Prosky. 1982

HANNA K. 🗡 Jill Clayburgh is an Israeli lawyer appointed to defend a man who entered the country illegally in an attempt to reclaim the land where he grew up. Rated R for coarse language. 110m. DIR: Constantin Costa-Gavras. CAST: Jill Clayburgh, Jean Yanne, Gabriel Byrne, David Clennon. 1984

HANNAH AND HER SISTERS ★★★★★ A two-year study of a family held together by house-mother Mia Farrow. Hannah is best friend, trusted confidante, and sympathetic peacemaker for sisters Barbara Hershey and Dianne Wiest, husband Michael Caine, and parents Maureen O'Sullivan and Lloyd Nolan. Woody Allen is a hypochondriac who may get his fondest wish: a fatal disease. Rated PG-13 for sexual situations. 106m. DIR: Woody Allen. CAST: Woody Allen, Michael Caine, Mia Farrow, Carrie Fisher, Barbara Hershey, Maureen O'Sullivan, Dianne Wiest, Max von Sydow, Daniel Stern, Lloyd Nolan, Sam Waterston. 1986

HANNA'S WAR ★★★1/2 Powerful true story of a brave Jewish girl who is recruited by the British to rescue captured British fliers during WWII. Maruschka Detmers plays the brave Hanna who, though tortured brutally after her own capture, refuses to divulge military secrets. Rated PG-13 for violence. 148m. DIR: Menahem Golan. CAST: Maruschka Detmers, Ellen Burstyn, Anthony Andrews, Donald Pleasence. 1988

HANNIE CAULDER ★★1/2 Revenge Western has Raquel Welch learning to be a gunslinger with the help of laid-back Robert Culp, so that she can hunt down and kill the three maniacs (Ernest Borgnine, Jack Elam, and Strother Martin) who murdered her husband. Rated R for violence. 85m. DIR: Burt Kennedy. CAST: Raquel Welch, Robert Culp, Ernest Borgnine, Jack Elam, Strother Martin, Christopher Lee. 1972

HANOI HILTON, THE 🗡 A prisoner-of-war camp during the Vietnam War. Rated R for profanity and extreme violence. 130m. DIR: Lionel Chetwynd. CAST: Michael Moriarty, Paul LeMat, David Soul, Jeffrey Jones, Lawrence Pressman. 1987

HANOVER STREET ★★ Action director Peter Hyams is out of his element with this melodramatic World War II drama, which consists mostly of an unlikely tryst between American soldier Harrison Ford and (married) British nurse Lesley-Anne Down. Overblown and mawkish. Rated PG. 109m. DIR: Peter Hyams. CAST: Harrison Ford, Lesley-Anne Down, Christopher Plummer, Alec McCowen. 1979

HANS BRINKER ★★★ This is the well-known tale of Hans Brinker and his silver skates. Made this time as a musical, it stars Robin Askwith as Hans with Eleanor Parker and John Gregson as his mother and invalid father, and there are some pleasant skating sequences. This film would make particularly good family viewing for the holidays. It is not rated, but would be considered a G. 103m. DIR: Robert Scheerer. CAST: Robin Askwith, Eleanor Parker, Richard Basehart, Roberta Torey, John Gregson, Cyril Ritchard. 1979

HANS CHRISTIAN ANDERSEN ★★★1/2 Danny Kaye is superb as the famous storyteller, and Frank Loesser composed some wonderful songs for this glossy oversweet musical. Ballet great Jeanmaire is a knockout. This is top-notch family entertainment. 120m. DIR: Charles Vidor. CAST: Danny Kaye, Farley Granger, Zizi Jeanmaire, John Qualen. 1952 DVD

HANS CHRISTIAN ANDERSEN'S THUMBELINA ★★★ Perhaps we've been spoiled by recent Disney works like *The Little Mermaid, Beauty and the Beast,* and *Aladdin,* but this telling of the famous children's tale seems awfully slight in the story and song departments. The animation is fine, although not up to Don Bluth's highest standards, but the adventures of its tiny heroine are a bit on the ho-hum side. That said, little girls will adore it. Rated G. 83m. **DIR:** Don Bluth, Gary Goldman. **1994**

HANUSSEN ★★★★ In this German import based on a true story, Klaus Maria Brandauer is at the peak of his powers as a clairvoyant whose hypnotic, frightening talent for predicting the future both shocks and arouses the apathetic German public in the 1920s and 1930s. When his prophecies bring him to the attention of Adolf Hitler and the Nazi party, he finds his life in danger. In German with English subtitles. Rated R for violence and nudity. 117m. **DIR:** Istvan Szabo. **CAST:** Klaus Maria Brandauer, Erland Josephson, Walter Schmidinger. **1989**

HAPPIEST MILLIONAIRE, THE ★★★ The Disney version of a factual memoir of life in the Philadelphia household of eccentric millionaire Anthony J. Drexel Biddle. Lively light entertainment that hops along between musical numbers. 118m. **DIR:** Norman Tokar. **CAST:** Fred MacMurray, Tommy Steele, Greer Garson, Geraldine Page, Gladys Cooper, John Davidson. **1967**

HAPPILY EVER AFTER ★★ For some unknown reason, a seemingly happy wife and mother takes off with a bisexual male prostitute in this Brazilian film. After *Dona Flor and Her Two Husbands,* director Bruno Barreto again presents a woman who seems to need two very different men in her life. In Portuguese with English subtitles. Not rated; contains nudity and simulated sex. 108m. **DIR:** Bruno Barreto. **CAST:** Regina Duarte, Paulo Castelli. **1986**

HAPPINESS ★★★ This perverse *Father Knows Best* as filtered through shock cinema is dangerously ambiguous and overwrought. It tries to turn the moral sewage of a pathetic extended New Jersey family (pedophilia, rape, murder, phone sex, mutilation, stalking) into a dark comedy. Not rated; contains graphic sexual situations, profanity, and nudity. 140m. **DIR:** Todd Solondz. **CAST:** Jane Adams, Dylan Baker, Justin Elvin, Cynthia Stevenson, Lara Flynn Boyle, Jared Harris, Philip Seymour Hoffman, Elizabeth Ashley, Camryn Manheim, Ben Gazzara, Louise Lasser. **1998 DVD**

HAPPY BIRTHDAY, GEMINI ★★ A strong play about a sexual-identity crisis becomes a weak movie when the sexuality is toned down too much. The movie doesn't need graphic sex scenes, just some intelligent dialogue so the characters can communicate with each other. The story is about a newly graduated Harvard man who thinks he may be gay. The sparkling supporting cast keeps the movie moving. Rated R. 107m. **DIR:** Richard Benner. **CAST:** Madeline Kahn, Rita Moreno, David Marshall Grant, Robert Viharo. **1980**

HAPPY BIRTHDAY TO ME ★★ After surviving a tragic car accident that killed her mother, a young woman (Melissa Sue Anderson) suffers recurrent blackouts. During these lapses of consciousness, other students at her exclusive prep school are murdered in bizarre and vicious ways. Story coherence and credibility take a backseat to all the bloodletting. Rated R. 108m. **DIR:** J. Lee Thompson. **CAST:** Melissa Sue Anderson, Glenn Ford, Matt Craven. **1981**

HAPPY GILMORE ★★ A wannabe ice hockey player can scrap with the big boys better than he can skate. He discovers he can use his power puck swat to drive golf balls record distances and tries to win enough money on the PGA Tour to save his grandmother from the IRS. The laughs are patchy and Adam Sandler's sociopathic tantrums slice wildly off course. Rated PG-13 for language and violence. 92m. **DIR:** Dennis Dugan. **CAST:** Adam Sandler, Christopher McDonald, Julie Bowen, Frances Bay, Carl Weathers. **1996 DVD**

HAPPY GO LOVELY ★★★ Perky Vera-Ellen is a dancing darling in this lightweight musical with a very tired plot about a producer who hires a chorus girl with the idea that her boyfriend has money to invest in his show. It's all cute, but nothing startling. 87m. **DIR:** H. Bruce Humberstone. **CAST:** David Niven, Vera-Ellen, Cesar Romero. **1951 DVD**

HAPPY HOOKER, THE ★★★ After Xaviera Hollander's novel became a bestseller, Lynn Redgrave was cast as Hollander in this offbeat comedy. Redgrave recounts Hollander's rise from free-lance prostitute to one of New York's most infamous madams. Viewers get a peek at the kinky scenes when they play the sex-for-hire game. Rated R for nudity and sex. 96m. **DIR:** Nicholas Sgarro. **CAST:** Lynn Redgrave, Jean-Pierre Aumont, Elizabeth Wilson, Tom Poston, Lovelady Powell, Nicholas Pryor. **1975**

HAPPY HOOKER GOES HOLLYWOOD, THE ★★ If you've ever wanted to see Adam (*Batman*) West in drag, here's your chance. Lots of other people embarrass themselves as well in this comedy that certainly tries hard for laughs (though it gets very few). Rated R, but it's all talk and no action. 85m. **DIR:** Alan Roberts. **CAST:** Martine Beswick, Chris Lemmon, Adam West, Phil Silvers, Richard Deacon, Edie Adams, Dick Miller. **1980**

HAPPY HOOKER GOES TO WASHINGTON, THE 🎬 Xaviera Hollander (Joey Heatherton) is called to Washington. Rated R. 89m. **DIR:** William A. Levey. **CAST:** Joey Heatherton, George Hamilton, Ray Walston, Jack Carter. **1977**

HAPPY HOUR ★★ Blah comedy about a chemist's discovery of a secret ingredient that makes beer irresistible. A lot of T&A, and a good peformance by Rich Little as a supersmy, but the premise keeps the film's comedic stock low. Not rated, coarse language. 88m. **DIR:** John DeBello. **CAST:** Richard Gilliland, Jamie Farr, Tawny Kitaen, Rich Little. **1986**

HAPPY LANDING ★★★1/2 One of Sonja Henie's most popular movies, and her costars get most of the credit. Two men compete for her affections between songs, dancing, and ice-skating routines. The songs are especially good, and the singers—Don Ameche, Ethel Merman, Peters Sisters, and Condos Brothers—are outstanding. B&W; 102m. **DIR:** Roy Del Ruth. **CAST:** Sonja Henie, Don Ameche, Cesar Romero,

Ethel Merman, Lon Chaney Jr., Jean Hersholt, Wally Vernon, Billy Gilbert, El Brendel, Raymond Scott. **1938**

HAPPY NEW YEAR (1973) (LA BONNE ANNÉE) ★★★★ Delightful French crime caper mixed with romance and comedy. As two thieves plot a jewel heist, one (Lino Ventura) also plans a meeting with the lovely antique dealer (Françoise Fabian) who runs the shop next door to their target. Director Claude Lelouch's film blends suspense with engaging wit. Rated PG for profanity and sex. Available in French version or dubbed. 114m. **DIR:** Claude Lelouch. **CAST:** Lino Ventura, Françoise Fabian, Charles Gerard. **1974**

HAPPY NEW YEAR (1987) ★★★1/2 Another film that was the victim of the studio system; it received only a marginal theatrical release. Peter Falk deserves to be seen in his multirole performance. He and Charles Durning are a couple of con men planning a jewel heist in Florida. (Based on Claude Lelouch's 1973 French film of the same name.) Rated PG. 86m. **DIR:** John G. Avildsen. **CAST:** Peter Falk, Charles Durning, Tom Courtenay, Wendy Hughes. **1987**

•**HAPPY, TEXAS** ★★★1/2 Two escaped convicts pose as a gay couple traveling the rural South organizing small-town beauty pageants. Their plans to rob a bank go awry when they both fall for local women. The film is modest, easygoing, and likable, just like the town of the title, with many amusing performances—especially Steve Zahn as a dim bulb who suddenly discovers his talent for choreography. Rated PG-13 for mild profanity and violence. 98m. **DIR:** Mark Illsley. **CAST:** Jeremy Northam, Steve Zahn, Ally Walker, Illeana Douglas, William H. Macy. **1999**

HAPPY TOGETHER ★★1/2 This college romance is basically a 1990s retread of *The Sterile Cuckoo*, with Helen Slater taking a spirited whirl at the Liza Minnelli role. Slater is a charming, underrated actress, but she tries too hard—as does the film as a whole. Rated PG-13. 102m. **DIR:** Mel Damski. **CAST:** Patrick Dempsey, Helen Slater. **1990 DVD**

HARD BOILED ★★★1/2 Nobody stages gun battles better than director John Woo, whose relentless scenes of violence have a lyrical, almost poetic style. With Woo's trademark character development we get to know tough cop Chow Yun-Fat before he's sent into the eye of the storm with a renegade cop in an attempt to stop a gun-smuggling operation and find the killer who iced his partner. Explosive action and carnage ensue. Not rated; contains graphic violence and adult situations. 127m. **DIR:** John Woo. **CAST:** Chow Yun-Fat, Tony Leung Chiu-Wai, Teresa Mo. **1988**

HARD BOUNTY ★★ Jim Wynorski, possibly the busiest B-movie director working today, has corralled a better-than-usual cast for this Old West tale of murder and revenge with a female attitude. Rated R for violence, language, and adult situations. 90m. **DIR:** Jim Wynorski. **CAST:** Matt McCoy, Kelly LeBrock, Rochelle Swanson. **1995 DVD**

HARD CHOICES ★★★ Independently made low-budget feature starts out as a drama about a social worker's efforts to free a boy she believes has been unjustly imprisoned. But it loses plausibility when she falls in love with him and helps him escape. Not

rated; contains nudity, violence, and profanity. 90m. **DIR:** Rick King. **CAST:** Margaret Klenck, Gary McCleery, John Seitz, John Sayles, Martin Donovan, Spalding Gray. **1984**

•**HARD CORE LOGO** ★★★★ Frolicking, high-octane pseudodocumentary in the vein of *This Is Spinal Tap*. Here, director Bruce MacDonald chronicles a last-gasp reunion of punk band Hard Core Logo. It is up to front man Joe Dick to keep the band together, but the tensions and pitfalls of life on the road soon begin to take their toll on the band and anarchy results. The cast is uniformly good, but it is Hugh Dillon who takes the spotlight as Dick. A delight. Rated R for profanity, simulated sex, violence, and substance abuse. 92m. **DIR:** Bruce McDonald. **CAST:** Hugh Dillon, Callum Keith Rennie, Terry David Mulligan. **1996**

HARD COUNTRY ★★★1/2 Though it tries to make a statement about the contemporary cowboy lost in the modern world and feminism in the boondocks, this is really just lighthearted entertainment. A rockabilly love story of the macho man (Jan-Michael Vincent) versus the liberated woman (Kim Basinger). Rated PG. 104m. **DIR:** David Greene. **CAST:** Jan-Michael Vincent, Michael Parks, Kim Basinger, Tanya Tucker, Ted Neeley, Daryl Hannah. **1981**

HARD DAY'S NIGHT, A ★★★★★ Put simply, this is the greatest rock 'n' roll comedy ever made. Scripted by Alan Owen as a sort of day in the life of the Beatles, it's fast-paced, funny, and full of great Lennon-McCartney songs. Even more than thirty years after its release, it continues to delight several generations of viewers. B&W; 85m. **DIR:** Richard Lester. **CAST:** The Beatles, Wilfred Brambell, Victor Spinetti, Anna Quayle. **1964**

HARD DRIVE ★★1/2 In this Internet thriller, Leo Damian plays a former child star now resigned to communicating to the world through his computer. He begins an E-mail affair with a mysterious woman with a kinky sexual appetite, and they decide to meet. The mystery woman ends up dead; the former child star becomes the main suspect. Some plot twists keep this high-tech thriller from crashing. Not rated; contains nudity, violence, and strong language. 92m. **DIR:** James Meredino. **CAST:** Matt McCoy, Leo Damian, Christina Fulton, Edward Albert. **1994 DVD**

HARD EIGHT ★★★1/2 Casinos and hotel and motel rooms are the key settings of this seductive character study of two love-starved gamblers and a hooker. Seasoned high roller Sydney takes homeless lug John underwing and teaches him about gambling and personal style. When an extortion scam backfires on his rather dumb new friend, Sydney intervenes. The film crackles with superb dialogue, quiet desperation, and impending tragedy. Rated R for violence, language, and sexuality. 101m. **DIR:** Paul Thomas Anderson. **CAST:** Philip Baker Hall, John C. Reilly, Gwyneth Paltrow, Samuel L. Jackson. **1997 DVD**

HARD EVIDENCE ★★ Gregory Harrison stands out in this tired action film about a married man who learns that his mistress's business is drug smuggling. Before he knows it, he shoots a DEA agent in self-defense. Then his wife is dragged into the mess. Rated

R for nudity, violence, and language. 100m. **DIR:** Michael Kennedy. **CAST:** Gregory Harrison, Joan Severance, Cali Timmins, Andrew Airlie. 1994

•**HARD HOMBRE** ★★1/2 Easygoing cowpoke who promised his mother not to fight takes a job on a beautiful señorita's ranch and is mistaken for a notorious outlaw. Lots of humor with some riding and even a tussle or two thrown in for good measure. B&W; 65m. **DIR:** Otto Brower. **CAST:** Hoot Gibson, Lina Basquette, Skeeter Bill Robbins, Mathilde Comont, Jesse Arnold, Raymond Nye. 1931

HARD JUSTICE ★★ Despite Greg Yaitanes's stylish direction, this tale of a cop who goes undercover in a prison to avenge his partner's death is just another mindless exercise in nonstop action. No surprises here. Rated R for strong violence and adult language. 95m. **DIR:** Greg Yaitanes. **CAST:** David Bradley, Charles Napier, Yuji Okumoto. 1995

HARD PROMISES ★★★ A woman divorces her husband while he is away on a twelve-year trip, only to have him turn up right before she remarries. Rated PG for profanity. 95m. **DIR:** Martin Davidson. **CAST:** Sissy Spacek, William L. Petersen, Brian Kerwin, Mare Winningham, Jeff Perry. 1991

HARD RAIN ★★ This shallow disaster-heist flick is not convincingly written or acted. A security guard is accosted by bandits when his armored car becomes stuck in a flooded small Midwestern town that is threatened by possible collapse of a nearby dam. The guard takes his $3 million cargo and sloshes into the night with a way-too-nice villain and his white-trash cronies pursuing on Jet-Skis and in motorboats. Rated R for language and violence. 98m. **DIR:** Mikael Salomon. **CAST:** Christian Slater, Morgan Freeman, Minnie Driver, Randy Quaid, Betty White. 1998 DVD

HARD ROCK NIGHTMARE 🖤 Is a werewolf responsible for killing the members of a heavy metal band? Not rated; contains violence and brief nudity. 89m. **DIR:** Dominick Brascia. **CAST:** Martin Hansen, Gregory Joujon-Roche, Troy Donahue. 1989

HARD ROCK ZOMBIES ★★1/2 The title pretty much says it all: After being murdered while on the road, the members of a heavy-metal band are brought back from the dead as zombies. Amusing in a goofy way, though shoddy special-effects makeup brings it down a notch. Rated R for violence and gore. 94m. **DIR:** Krishna Shah. **CAST:** E. J. Curcio, Sam Mann. 1985

HARD TARGET ★★★1/2 For his first American film, Hong Kong film legend John Woo delivers an action movie that will please both fans of the genre and serious film buffs. Vietnam veteran Jean-Claude Van Damme comes up against bloodthirsty millionaires whose ultimate thrill is to hunt human game. Reminiscent of Walter Hill's earlier films—*The Driver*, for example—this thriller is somewhat short on character development, but for nonstop excitement it has few peers. Rated R for extreme violence and profanity. 92m. **DIR:** John Woo. **CAST:** Jean-Claude Van Damme, Lance Henriksen, Yancy Butler, Wilford Brimley, Arnold Vosloo, Kasi Lemmons. 1993 DVD

HARD TICKET TO HAWAII 🖤 Drug enforcement in Hawaii. Rated R for plentiful nudity and sexual situations. 96m. **DIR:** Andy Sidaris. **CAST:** Dona Speir, Hope Marie Carlton, Ronn Moss. 1987

HARD TIME ★★ Talk about retro! Burt Reynolds returns to his favorite role: the tough-talking, world-weary investigator who never plays by the rules. This time he's a Florida cop framed for a murder he didn't commit. Mia Sara is laughably miscast as the attorney who agrees to defend our hero. Reynolds remains watchable but it's a shame to see him return to this fluff after proving his greater capabilities in *Boogie Nights*. Rated PG-13 for violence and drug use. 95m. **DIR:** Burt Reynolds. **CAST:** Burt Reynolds, Charles Durning, Mia Sara, Billy Dee Williams, Robert Loggia, Michael Buie. 1998

HARD TIMES ★★★1/2 This release is far and away one of Charles Bronson's best starring vehicles. In it he plays a bare-knuckles fighter who teams up with a couple of hustlers, James Coburn and Strother Martin, to "sting" some local hoods. Bronson's wife, Jill Ireland, is surprisingly good as the love interest. Rated PG. 97m. **DIR:** Walter Hill. **CAST:** Charles Bronson, James Coburn, Jill Ireland, Strother Martin. 1975 DVD

HARD TO DIE 🖤 "Hard to watch" is a more appropriate title for this silly slashfest. Five girls taking inventory don sexy lingerie then become victims. Pictures on video box include two women who weren't even in the film. Rated R for nudity, profanity, violence, and gore. 81m. **DIR:** Jim Wynorski. **CAST:** Orville Ketchum, Robyn Harris, Melissa Moore, Debra Dare, Forrest J. Ackerman, Lindsay Taylor. 1990

HARD TO HOLD ★★ In this highly forgettable film, Rick Springfield plays a music superstar who has everything except the woman (Janet Eilber) he loves. The first half hour is quite good, but from there it goes downhill into soap opera. Rated PG for brief nudity and profanity. 93m. **DIR:** Larry Peerce. **CAST:** Rick Springfield, Janet Eilber, Patti Hansen, Albert Salmi. 1984

HARD TO KILL ★★★1/2 Solid action film stars martial arts expert Steve Seagal as an honest cop who falls prey to corruption. Crisply directed by Bruce Malmuth, this is a definite cut above most movies in its genre. Rated R for violence, profanity, and nudity. 95m. **DIR:** Bruce Malmuth. **CAST:** Steven Seagal, Kelly LeBrock. 1990 DVD

HARD TRAVELING ★★ California, 1940. A struggling farm couple battle the odds to survive. Slow-moving saga. Rated PG. 99m. **DIR:** Dan Bessie. **CAST:** J. E. Freeman, Ellen Geer, Barry Corbin. 1985

HARD TRUTH ★★ Cop Michael Rooker and safe-cracker Eric Roberts team up to intercept a mob cash payment being made to a city councilman. But who is double-crossing whom, and who will get the girl (Lysette Anthony) both want? Better-than-average video thriller, with a plot that keeps you guessing right up to the end. Not rated; contains violence, nudity, sexual situations, and profanity. 100m. **DIR:** Kristine Peterson. **CAST:** Eric Roberts, Michael Rooker, Lysette Anthony, Ray Baker. 1994

HARD WAY, THE (1942) ★★★★ Ida Lupino proved she could carry the whole show as a disgruntled woman who hates her life and wants to make sure her sister has a better one. She manipulates her sister's life and destroys just about everyone else around them. Hardcore melodrama and exceptionally good. B&W; 108m. **DIR:** Vincent Sherman. **CAST:** Ida Lupino, Joan Leslie, Dennis Morgan, Jack Carson, Roman Bohnen, Faye Emerson, Gladys George, Julie Bishop. **1942**

HARD WAY, THE (1979) ★★ Patrick McGoohan is an international terrorist who wants out of the business. Unfortunately for him, a former associate (Lee Van Cleef) wants him to do one more job and will have him killed if he doesn't. 88m. **DIR:** Michael Dryhurst. **CAST:** Patrick McGoohan, Lee Van Cleef, Donal McCann, Edna O'Brien. **1979**

HARD WAY, THE (1991) ★★★1/2 Formulaic buddy movie about a movie star attempting to research a cop role by hanging out with the real thing. Engaging performances by Michael J. Fox and James Woods. Rated R for profanity and violence. 95m. **DIR:** John Badham. **CAST:** Michael J. Fox, James Woods, Penny Marshall, Stephen Lang, Annabella Sciorra. **1991 DVD**

HARDBODIES 💗 Three middle-aged men rent a summer beach house in hopes of seducing teenage girls. Rated R for nudity, simulated sex, and profanity. 90m. **DIR:** Mark Griffiths. **CAST:** Grant Cramer, Teal Roberts, Gary Wood, Michael Rapaport, Roberta Collins. **1984**

HARDBODIES 2 💗 Sexual antics of a group of students on an academic cruise. Rated R for nudity and profanity. 89m. **DIR:** Mark Griffiths. **CAST:** Brad Zutaut, James Karen. **1986**

HARDCORE ★★ This film stars George C. Scott as Jake Van Dorn, whose family leads a church-oriented life in their home in Grand Rapids, Michigan. When the church sponsors a youth trip to California, Van Dorn's daughter Kristen (Ilah Davis) is allowed to go. She disappears, so Van Dorn goes to Los Angeles and learns she's now making porno flicks. *Hardcore* is rated R, but is closer to an X. 108m. **DIR:** Paul Schrader. **CAST:** George C. Scott, Peter Boyle, Season Hubley, Dick Sargent, Ilah Davis. **1979**

HARDER THEY COME, THE ★★★★ Made in Jamaica by Jamaicans, this film has become an underground cult classic. In it, a rural boy comes to the big city to become a singer. There, he is forced into a life of crime. Rated R. 98m. **DIR:** Perry Henzell. **CAST:** Jimmy Cliff, Janet Barkley. **1973**

HARDER THEY FALL, THE ★★★1/2 This boxing drama is as mean and brutal as they come. A gentle giant is built up, set up, and brought down by a collection of human vultures while sportswriter Humphrey Bogart flip-flops on the moral issues. The ring photography is spectacular. Don't expect anything like *Rocky*. B&W; 109m. **DIR:** Mark Robson. **CAST:** Humphrey Bogart, Rod Steiger, Jan Sterling, Mike Lane, Max Baer, Jersey Joe Walcott. **1956**

HARDHAT AND LEGS ★★★ The scene is New York City. Kevin Dobson is a horseplaying Italian construction worker who whistles at nice gams. Sharon Gless is democratic upper class. The twain meet, and sparks fly. It's all cheerful and upbeat and works because of first-rate acting. Made for television. 104m. **DIR:** Lee Philips. **CAST:** Kevin Dobson, Sharon Gless. **1980**

HARDLY WORKING ★★ Jerry Lewis's 1980s screen comeback is passable family fare. As a middle-aged, out-of-work clown, he tries his hand at a number of jobs and flubs them all. His fans will love it; others need not apply. Rated PG. 91m. **DIR:** Jerry Lewis. **CAST:** Jerry Lewis, Susan Oliver, Roger C. Carmel, Deanna Lund, Harold J. Stone, Steve Franken. **1981**

HARDWARE 💗 A post-apocalypse salvage expert gives the remains of a robot to his lady friend unaware that the mechanical creature was programmed to kill humans. Rated R for violence, gore, nudity, and profanity. 95m. **DIR:** Richard Stanley. **CAST:** Dylan McDermott, Stacey Travis, John Lynch, Iggy Pop. **1990**

HAREM ★★★1/2 Nastassja Kinski is a stockbroker who is abducted by a wealthy OPEC oil minister (Ben Kingsley) and becomes a part of his harem. A bittersweet tale of a lonely dreamer and his passion for a modern woman. Not rated, but has violence, profanity, and nudity. 107m. **DIR:** Arthur Joffe. **CAST:** Nastassja Kinski, Ben Kingsley, Robbin Zohra Segal. **1985**

HARLAN COUNTY, U.S.A. ★★★★1/2 This Oscar-winning documentary concerning Kentucky coal miners is both tragic and riveting. Its gripping scenes draw the audience into the world of miners and their families. Superior from start to finish. Rated PG. 103m. **DIR:** Barbara Kopple. **1977**

HARLEM NIGHTS ★★★ This gangster movie has taken a tremendous critical beating, but we found it enjoyable. Not only has writer-producer-director-star Eddie Murphy created an old-fashioned melodrama that, save for the continuous profanity, could just as easily have starred Humphrey Bogart or James Cagney but he has given fine roles to some of the industry's finest black performers. Rated R for profanity, violence, and suggested sex. 119m. **DIR:** Eddie Murphy. **CAST:** Eddie Murphy, Richard Pryor, Redd Foxx, Danny Aiello, Michael Lerner, Della Reese, Stan Shaw, Arsenio Hall. **1989**

HARLEM RIDES THE RANGE ★★1/2 Stale plot about stolen mine rights (to a radium mine this time) is secondary to the limited action and uniqueness of seeing an all-black cast in what had traditionally been the territory of white actors and actresses. B&W; 58m. **DIR:** Richard Kahn. **CAST:** Herbert Jeffrey (Herbert Jeffries), Lucius Brooks. **1939**

HARLEY ★★ Lou Diamond Phillips stars as Harley, an L.A. motorcycle hood who gets sent to a Texas ranch instead of a juvenile detention center. Good family film. Rated PG. 80m. **DIR:** Fred Holmes. **CAST:** Lou Diamond Phillips. **1985**

HARLEY DAVIDSON AND THE MARLBORO MAN ★★ Mickey Rourke is the hog-riding hero, Don Johnson the cowboy in 1996, when a drug called Crystal Dream is killing addicts by the thousands. So our heroes go to war with the pushers. It's hard to believe that the director who helmed the exquisite *Lonesome Dove* was responsible for this post-apocalyptic hogwash. Rated R for violence, profanity, and nudity. 98m. **DIR:** Simon Wincer. **CAST:** Mickey Rourke, Don Johnson, Chelsea Field, Giancarlo Esposito, Vanessa L. Williams, Julius W. Harris, Robert Ginty. **1991**

HARLOW ★★ One of two films made in 1965 that dealt with the life of the late film star and sex goddess Jean Harlow. Carroll Baker simply is not the actress to play Harlow, and the whole thing is a trashy mess. 125m. DIR: Gordon Douglas. CAST: Carroll Baker, Peter Lawford, Red Buttons, Mike Connors, Raf Vallone, Angela Lansbury, Martin Balsam, Leslie Nielsen. 1965

HARMONISTS, THE ★★★1/2 As persecution in Hitler-era Europe spreads, the Comedian Harmonists—five Berlin singers and their pianist—were scrutinized by the Nazis for including Jews in their group. This fascinating musical biography about love, tolerance, patriotism, mass denial, and the tentacles of bigotry is both sweeping and intimate. In German with English subtitles. Rated R for brief nudity. 115m. DIR: Joseph Vilsmaier. CAST: Aldrich Noethen, Ben Becker, Meret Becker, Heino Firch, Henrich Schafmeister, Max Tidof. 1999

HARMONY CATS ★★ Mediocre morality play about an out-of-work symphony violinist who, as a last resort, teams up with a country and western group. Obviously out of his league, Jim Byrnes begins to get into the swing of things. Hee-haw! Not rated; contains strong language and adult situations. 104m. DIR: Sandy Wilson. CAST: Kim Coates, Jim Byrnes, Lisa Brokop. 1993

HARMONY LANE ★★ Only the music saves this halfhearted account of composer Stephen Foster's tragic life from being classed a turkey. The sets are shoddy, the camera rarely moves, most of the acting is insipid, and the screenplay is one long string of music cues. B&W; 89m. DIR: Joseph Santley. CAST: Douglass Montgomery, Evelyn Venable, Adrienne Ames, William Frawley. 1935

HAROLD AND MAUDE ★★★★★ Hal Ashby directed this delightful black comedy about an odd young man named Harold (Bud Cort) who devises some rather elaborate fake deaths to jar his snooty, manipulative mother (Vivian Pickles). Soon his attention turns to an octogenarian named Maude (Ruth Gordon), with whom he falls in love. Featuring a superb soundtrack of songs by Cat Stevens, this is one of the original cult classics—and deservedly so. Rated PG. 90m. DIR: Hal Ashby. CAST: Bud Cort, Vivian Pickles, Ruth Gordon, Cyril Cusack, Charles Tyner, Ellen Geer. 1972

HAROLD LLOYD'S COMEDY CLASSICS ★★★ This nostalgic retrospective combines four of Harold Lloyd's prestardom shorts: *The Chef, The Cinema Director, Two Gun Gussie,* and *I'm On My Way.* Silent with musical score. Compiled after Lloyd's death. B&W; 47m. DIR: Harold Lloyd. CAST: Harold Lloyd, Bebe Daniels, Snub Pollard. 1919

HARPER ★★★★1/2 Ross MacDonald's detective, Lew Archer, undergoes a name change but still survives as a memorable screen character in the capable hands of Paul Newman. This one ranks right up there with *The Maltese Falcon, The Big Sleep* (the Humphrey Bogart version), *Farewell My Lovely,* and *The Long Goodbye* as one of the best of its type. 121m. DIR: Jack Smight. CAST: Paul Newman, Lauren Bacall, Shelley Winters, Arthur Hill, Julie Harris, Janet Leigh, Robert Wagner. 1966

HARPER VALLEY P.T.A. ★★ Based on the popular country song, this silly piece of fluff features Barbara Eden as the sexy woman who gives her gossiping neighbors their proper comeuppance. Rated PG. 102m. DIR: Richard Bennett. CAST: Barbara Eden, Ronny Cox, Nanette Fabray, Susan Swift, Ron Masak. 1978

HARRAD EXPERIMENT, THE ★★ Uninvolving adaptation of Robert Rimmer's well-intentioned bestseller about an experimental college that makes sexual freedom the primary curriculum. The film is attractive as a novelty item because of erotic scenes between Don Johnson and Laurie Walters. Rated R. 88m. DIR: Ted Post. CAST: Don Johnson, James Whitmore, Tippi Hedren, Bruno Kirby, Laurie Walters. 1973

HARRIET THE SPY ★★ Nickelodeon's maiden theatrical release disappoints by gearing itself directly to 10-year-olds rather than to general audiences. That said, it does make some points about being different and how parents need to be actively involved in their children's lives. The sixth-grade sleuth follows her nanny's (Rosie O'Donnell) advice, writing down everything she sees and thinks. When her private notebook is exposed she must face the ostracism of her peers. Rated PG for cruelty. 97m. DIR: Bronwen Hughes. CAST: Michelle Trachtenberg, Rosie O'Donnell, Vanessa Lee Chester, Gregory Edward Smith, Eartha Kitt, J. Smith-Cameron. 1996

HARRISON BERGERON ★★★1/2 Although it owes as much to C. M. Kornbluth's "The Marching Morons" as to Kurt Vonnegut's original short story, this intriguing thriller says a lot about the perils of enforced conformity. Sean Astin stars as a futuristic kid whose congenital intelligence cannot be suppressed by the gadgets all people wear to be "truly equal." Rated R for violence, profanity, simulated sex, and graphic newsreel footage. 99m. DIR: Bruce Pittman. CAST: Sean Astin, Miranda de Pencier, Christopher Plummer, Buck Henry, Eugene Levy, Howie Mandel, Andrea Martin. 1995

HARRY AND SON ★★★ A widower (Paul Newman) can land a wrecking ball on a dime but can't seem to make contact with his artistically inclined son, Howard (Robby Benson), in this superb character study. Directed, coproduced, and cowritten by Newman, it's sort of a male *Terms of Endearment.* Rated PG for nudity and profanity. 117m. DIR: Paul Newman. CAST: Paul Newman, Robby Benson, Joanne Woodward, Ellen Barkin, Ossie Davis, Wilford Brimley. 1984

HARRY AND THE HENDERSONS ★★★ A shaggy *E.T.* story, this focuses on the plight of a family (headed by John Lithgow and Melinda Dillon) that just happens to run into Bigfoot one day. It's silly, outrageously sentimental, and a gentle poke in the ribs of Steven Spielberg, whose Amblin Productions financed the film. Rated PG for profanity and violence. 110m. DIR: William Dear. CAST: John Lithgow, Melinda Dillon, Don Ameche, Lainie Kazan, David Suchet. 1987

HARRY AND TONTO ★★★★ Art Carney won an Oscar for his tour-de-force performance in this character study, directed by Paul Mazursky. In a role that's a far cry from his Ed Norton on Jackie Gleason's *The*

Honeymooners, the star plays an older gentleman who, with his cat, takes a cross-country trip and lives life to the fullest. Rated R. 115m. **DIR:** Paul Mazursky. **CAST:** Art Carney, Ellen Burstyn, Chief Dan George, Geraldine Fitzgerald, Larry Hagman, Arthur Hunnicutt. 1974

HARRY AND WALTER GO TO NEW YORK ★★1/2 James Caan and Elliott Gould appear to be having the time of their lives portraying two inept con men. Michael Caine and Diane Keaton are, as always, excellent. *Harry and Walter* is sort of like Chinese food—an hour later, you feel as if you haven't had anything. Rated PG. 123m. **DIR:** Mark Rydell. **CAST:** James Caan, Elliott Gould, Michael Caine, Diane Keaton, Charles Durning. 1976

HARRY TRACY ★★★1/2 Bruce Dern plays the title role in this surprisingly amiable little Western, with the star as the last of a gentlemanly outlaw breed. Although he's a crafty character, Harry always seems to get caught. His mind is all too often on other things—in particular, a well-to-do woman (Helen Shaver). Rated PG. 100m. **DIR:** William A. Graham. **CAST:** Bruce Dern, Helen Shaver, Michael C. Gwynne, Gordon Lightfoot. 1982

HARRY'S WAR ★★ In this cornball comedy, Harry Johnson (Edward Herrmann) takes on the Internal Revenue Service, which made a mistake on his return. Rated PG. 98m. **DIR:** Kieth Merrill. **CAST:** Edward Herrmann, Geraldine Page, Karen Grassle, David Ogden Stiers, Salome Jens, Elisha Cook Jr. 1981

HARUM SCARUM ★★★ When a swashbuckling film star (Elvis Presley) visits a primitive Arabian country, he is forced to aid assassins in their bid to destroy the king. Simultaneously, he falls in love with the king's beautiful daughter (Mary Ann Mobley). Elvis manages to belt out nine tunes, including "Shake That Tambourine" and "Harem Holiday." His fans won't be disappointed. 86m. **DIR:** Gene Nelson. **CAST:** Elvis Presley, Mary Ann Mobley, Michael Ansara, Billy Barty. 1965

HARVEST ★★★★ Simple but touching story of a man and woman struggling to survive in a deserted village. One of the great director's best loved films, though it does drag on a bit too long. In French with English subtitles. B&W; 129m. **DIR:** Marcel Pagnol. **CAST:** Gabriel Gabrio, Fernandel, Orane Demazis. 1937

HARVEST OF FIRE ★★★1/2 A series of barn burnings, presumed to be hate crimes against the Amish in Iowa, brings a modern FBI agent into the Mennonite world in this moving *Hallmark Hall of Fame* production. An Amish widow opens her home and insights to the agent. More than a good mystery, this is a relationship film in which the two women find common ground. Compelling viewing on an enlightening topic. Made-for-TV, this is not rated, but contains violence. 90m. **DIR:** Arthur Allan Seidelman. **CAST:** Patty Duke, Lolita Davidovich, J. A. Preston, Jean Louisa Kelly, Eric Mabius, James Read. 1996

HARVEST, THE ★★1/2 While in Mexico investigating a series of killings, screenwriter Miguel Ferrer is abducted and drugged. When he awakens he finds out that one of his kidneys has been removed. Now black-market organ dealers want his second kidney.

Interesting idea gets only a modicum of suspense from writer-director David Marconi, while familiar faces do their best to flesh out the background. Rated R for violence and language. 97m. **DIR:** David Marconi. **CAST:** Miguel Ferrer, Harvey Fierstein, Leilani Sarelle, Anthony Denison, Tim Thomerson, Henry Silva. 1992

HARVEY ★★★★1/2 James Stewart has one of his best screen roles as Elwood P. Dowd, a delightful drunk whose companion is a six-foot rabbit named Harvey. Josephine Hull is the concerned relative who wants Elwood committed to a mental institution, and Cecil Kellaway is the psychiatrist who discovers there's more magic than madness to our hero's illusion. B&W; 104m. **DIR:** Henry Koster. **CAST:** James Stewart, Josephine Hull, Peggy Dow, Charles Drake, Cecil Kellaway. 1950

HARVEY GIRLS, THE ★★★ Rousing fun marks this big, bustling musical, which is loosely tied to the development of pioneer railroad-station restaurateur Fred Harvey's string of eateries along the Santa Fe right-of-way. Judy Garland is the innocent who goes west to grow up, Angela Lansbury is the wise bad girl, and John Hodiak is the requisite gambler. 102m. **DIR:** George Sidney. **CAST:** Judy Garland, John Hodiak, Ray Bolger, Preston Foster, Virginia O'Brien, Angela Lansbury, Marjorie Main, Chill Wills, Cyd Charisse, Kenny Baker. 1945

HASTY HEART ★★★1/2 Made for Showtime pay cable, this version of the 1949 movie with Ronald Reagan is corny as all get-out, but is still pretty effective. In an army hospital in Burma during WWII, a proud Scottish soldier (Gregory Harrison) doesn't know that he has only a few weeks to live. He refuses to accept the hospitality of the other soldiers in the ward, all of whom know of his approaching death. Get out your handkerchiefs! 135m. **DIR:** Martin Speer. **CAST:** Gregory Harrison, Cheryl Ladd, Perry King. 1983

HATARI! ★★★ If only Howard Hawks had been able to do as he wanted and cast Clark Gable along with John Wayne in this story of zoo-supplying animal hunters in Africa, this could have been a great film. As it is, it's still enjoyable, with a fine blend of action, romance, and comedy. 159m. **DIR:** Howard Hawks. **CAST:** John Wayne, Elsa Martinelli, Red Buttons, Hardy Krüger. 1962

HATBOX MYSTERY, THE ★★ In a scant 44 minutes private detective Tom Neal saves his secretary from prison, brings the guilty party to bay, and still has time to explain just what happened. Not great but a real curio, perhaps the shortest detective film ever sold as a feature. B&W; 44m. **DIR:** Lambert Hillyer. **CAST:** Tom Neal, Pamela Blake, Allen Jenkins, Virginia Sale. 1947

HATE ★★★★1/2 Three youths of diverse backgrounds team up to fight gangs and police in the Paris suburbs. When one friend ends up in the hospital thanks to police brutality, another takes the law into his own hands and cements the destiny of all three. Gritty and unrelenting, the film packs quite a punch. In French with English subtitles. Not rated; contains violence and profanity. 95m. **DIR:** Mathieu

Kassovitz. **CAST:** Vincent Cassel, Hubert Kounde, Said Taghmaoui. **1995**

HATFIELDS AND THE MCCOYS, THE ★★1/2 The great American legend of backwoods feuding long celebrated in song and story. Jack Palance and Steve Forrest make the most of portraying the clan patriarchs. The feud was reason enough to leave the hills and head west in the 1880s. Made for TV. 74m. **DIR:** Clyde Ware. **CAST:** Jack Palance, Steve Forrest, Richard Hatch, Joan Caulfield. **1975**

HAUNTED ★★★★ Aidan Quinn is a renowned debunker of spirit mediums and ghost stories who travels to a remote British estate at the request of a terrified elderly woman. Nothing is what it seems, but you probably won't be able to figure out the mystery before he does. Set in the Roaring Twenties, this beautifully shot adaptation of James Herbert's novel is rife with a sexuality and horror underscored by subtle direction. Rated R for nudity, sexual situations, and adult themes. 107m. **DIR:** Lewis Gilbert. **CAST:** Aidan Quinn, Kate Beckinsale, Anthony Andrews, John Gielgud, Anna Massey, Victoria Shalet. **1995**

HAUNTED CASTLE ★★★ Based on the novel by Rudolf Stratz, this complex chiller takes place in a northern German castle shrouded in a mysterious, haunting atmosphere. Great cinematography and set design make for an impressive spectacle. Silent. B&W; 56m. **DIR:** F. W. Murnau. **CAST:** Paul Hartmann, Olga Tschechowa. **1921**

HAUNTED GOLD ★★★1/2 John Wayne gives one of his best early performances in this enjoyable Warner Bros. B Western, in which a gold mine is haunted by a mysterious figure known as "The Phantom." Wayne and his saddle pal, Blue Washington, ride to the rescue of Sheila Terry, who is threatened by both the spooky villain and a gang of outlaws led by veteran heavy Harry Woods. An effective mix of genres. B&W; 58m. **DIR:** Mack V. Wright. **CAST:** John Wayne, Sheila Terry, Harry Woods, Erville Anderson, Otto Hoffman, Martha Mattox, Blue Washington, Slim Whitaker. **1932**

HAUNTED HONEYMOON 💔 Limp chiller spoof. Rated PG. 90m. **DIR:** Gene Wilder. **CAST:** Gene Wilder, Gilda Radner, Dom DeLuise, Jonathan Pryce, Paul Smith, Peter Vaughan. **1986**

HAUNTED PALACE, THE ★★★1/2 Although the title of this horror film, one of the best in a series of American-International Pictures releases directed by Roger Corman, was taken from a poem by Edgar Allan Poe, Charles Beaumont's screenplay was based on a story, "The Case of Charles Dexter Ward," written by H. P. Lovecraft. It's better than average Corman, with Vincent Price nicely subdued as the descendant of an ancient warlock. 85m. **DIR:** Roger Corman. **CAST:** Vincent Price, Debra Paget, Lon Chaney Jr., Elisha Cook Jr., Leo Gordon. **1963**

HAUNTED SEA, THE ★★ When a sea captain and his crew come across a deserted ship carrying Aztec treasure, they think their ship has come in. Unfortunately, the treasure is being guarded by an ancient creature that doesn't take kindly to looters. Silliness on the high seas. Rated R for language and violence. 73m. **DIR:** Daniel Patrick. **CAST:** Joanna Pacula, Krista Allen, James Brolin. **1997**

HAUNTED STRANGLER, THE ★★★1/2 Boris Karloff is well cast in this effective story of a writer who develops the homicidal tendencies of a long-dead killer he's been writing about. Gripping horror film. B&W; 81m. **DIR:** Robert Day. **CAST:** Boris Karloff, Anthony Dawson, Elizabeth Allan. **1958 DVD**

HAUNTED SUMMER ★★ Though visually stunning, this story of the meeting between Lord Byron and Percy Shelley (that eventually led to Mary Shelley's tale *Frankenstein*) is just too weird to be taken seriously. Full of sexual innuendo and drug-induced tripping, this is definitely one for fans of period pieces only. Rated R. 106m. **DIR:** Ivan Passer. **CAST:** Philip Anglim, Laura Dern, Alice Krige, Eric Stoltz, Alex Winter. **1988**

HAUNTING, THE (1963) ★★★★ Long considered one of the most masterly crafted tales of terror ever brought to the screen, this gripping triumph for Robert Wise still packs a punch. Julie Harris and Claire Bloom are outstanding as they recognize and finally confront the evil that inhabits a haunted house. Based on Shirley Jackson's classic *The Haunting of Hill House*. B&W; 112m. **DIR:** Robert Wise. **CAST:** Julie Harris, Claire Bloom, Richard Johnson, Russ Tamblyn, Fay Compton, Lois Maxwell. **1963**

HAUNTING, THE (1999) ★★★ Scientist Liam Neeson lures three insomniacs to a haunted house under the pretense of studying sleep deprivation when he's actually testing reactions to fear. Forget Robert Wise's classic film and Shirley Jackson's gripping, original story—both of which allowed the viewer to imagine the terror—and you may get a few thrills out of this blatant, special-effects-laden scarefest. Rated PG-13 for scary stuff and mild profanity. 113m. **DIR:** Jan De Bont. **CAST:** Liam Neeson, Catherine Zeta-Jones, Lili Taylor, Owen C. Wilson, Bruce Dern. **1999 DVD**

HAUNTING OF JULIA, THE ★★ A vague, confused story of a young mother whose daughter chokes to death. In this otherwise pedestrian film there are sporadic spots of quality, mostly in Tom Conti's scenes. Rated R for profanity. 96m. **DIR:** Richard Loncraine. **CAST:** Mia Farrow, Keir Dullea, Tom Conti. **1981**

HAUNTING OF MORELLA, THE 💔 Bad acting and directing help to mutilate this movie in which a mother's curse is placed upon her baby daughter. Rated R for violence and nudity. 82m. **DIR:** Jim Wynorski. **CAST:** David McCallum, Nicole Eggert, Christopher Halsted. **1989**

HAUNTING OF SARAH HARDY, THE ★★★ A suspense story of a recently married heiress who returns to her estate after a fifteen-year absence. Fairly standard TV film. 92m. **DIR:** Jerry London. **CAST:** Sela Ward, Michael Woods, Roscoe Born, Morgan Fairchild, Polly Bergen. **1989**

HAUNTING OF SEA CLIFF INN, THE ★★1/2 A not-very-scary, made-for-cable original about a husband and wife who buy an old Victorian and start to convert it into a bed and breakfast, only to discover the house is haunted. Passable acting, but not much plot. Rated PG-13 for violence. 94m. **DIR:** Walter Klenhard. **CAST:** Ally Sheedy, William R. Moses, Louise Fletcher, Lucinda Weist, Tom McCleister. **1994**

AUNTING PASSION, THE ★★ An uneven made-for-TV supernatural romance in which a ghost seduces housewife Jane Seymour. There are a few chills, but more often than not, it falls short of the mark. 98m. DIR: John Korty. CAST: Jane Seymour, Gerald McRaney, Millie Perkins, Ruth Nelson. 1983

JAUNTS OF THE VERY RICH ★★ This TV movie brings together a handful of people who have had close calls with death. It's sort of a low-quality *Twilight Zone* version of *Fantasy Island*. 72m. DIR: Paul Wendkos. CAST: Lloyd Bridges, Donna Mills, Edward Asner, Cloris Leachman, Anne Francis, Tony Bill, Robert Reed, Moses Gunn. 1972

JAV PLENTY ★★★ Lee Plenty is an aspiring novelist who comes to terms with his relationship with naughty New York businesswoman Havilland Savage. This profanity-laced visit with upwardly mobile African-American professionals begins clumsily before establishing a fresh, seductive comic charm. Rated R for profanity. 91m. DIR: Christopher Scott Cherot. CAST: Christopher Scott Cherot, Chenoa Maxwell, Tammi Jones, Robinne Lee, Reginald James. 1998

HAVANA ★★ Despite a very promising and involving first hour, this *Casablanca*, Cuban style, bogs down in political polemics and a predictable plot as out-for-himself gambler Robert Redford finds himself falling in love with a politically involved widow (Lena Olin). Rated R for profanity, violence, and nudity. 130m. DIR: Sydney Pollack. CAST: Robert Redford, Lena Olin, Alan Arkin, Raul Julia, Tomas Milian, Tony Plana. 1990 DVD

HAVE A NICE FUNERAL ★★★ Is Sartana a ghost or a magician? Whatever, he's an avenging angel who goes after an evil banker and his devious daughter. An over-the-top performance by John Garko makes this one of the best of the Sartana series. Not rated; contains violence. 90m. DIR: Anthony Ascot. CAST: John Garko, Antonio Vilar, Daniela Giordana, George Wang, Frank Ressel, Franco Pesce. 1971

HAVE GUN, WILL TRAVEL (TV SERIES) ★★★★ One of the most popular TV Westerns of its day, this excellent series has been out of the public eye for nearly three decades. The erudite, black-clad Paladin (Richard Boone) is a hired gun with a conscience. Boone brings a precise, understated mix of strength, tenderness, menace, and irony to what remains his greatest role. Made for TV. B&W; 58m. DIR: Andrew V. McLaglen, Various. CAST: Richard Boone, Kam Tong, Lisa Lu. 1957–63

HAVING A WONDERFUL CRIME ★★★ Pat O'Brien plays a lawyer who gets together with amateur sleuths Carole Landis and George Murphy to find out why a magician mysteriously disappeared. A murder mystery played for laughs with a cast who can put it across. B&W; 71m. DIR: A. Edward Sutherland. CAST: Pat O'Brien, Carole Landis, George Murphy, Gloria Holden, George Zucco. 1945

HAVING A WONDERFUL TIME 💔 Based on a Broadway stage hit, this was *supposed* to be romance and comedy at a famed Catskills resort hotel. B&W; 71m. DIR: Alfred Santell. CAST: Ginger Rogers, Douglas Fairbanks Jr., Red Skelton, Lucille Ball, Eve Arden, Lee Bowman, Jack Carson. 1938

HAVING IT ALL ★★★ Dyan Cannon makes up for any script deficiencies with sheer exuberance. In this remake of *The Captain's Paradise*, the roles are reversed, and Cannon plays the bigamist. As a fashion designer, she is constantly traveling between New York and Los Angeles. She has a home and husband in each and manages to juggle the two. Made for TV, this is unrated. 100m. DIR: Edward Zwick. CAST: Dyan Cannon, Hart Bochner, Barry Newman, Sylvia Sidney, Melanie Chartoff. 1982

HAWAII ★★★★ All-star epic presentation of Part III of James Michener's six-part novel of the same title. Excellent performances by Max von Sydow and Julie Andrews as the early 1800s missionaries to Hawaii, as well as by Richard Harris as the sea captain who tries to woo Andrews away. 171m. DIR: George Roy Hill. CAST: Julie Andrews, Max von Sydow, Richard Harris, Gene Hackman, Carroll O'Connor. 1966

HAWK, THE ★★★ A wife who was once institutionalized starts to think her husband is a serial killer. Is she going crazy again, or is she right? The plot has a few good twists, but it's too easy to figure out. Rated R for profanity and violence. 84m. DIR: David Hayman. CAST: Helen Mirren, George Costigan, Rosemary Leach, Owen Teale, Melanie Hill. 1992

HAWK OF THE WILDERNESS ★★★ Wonderful nonsense about the son of a scientist who is shipwrecked on an unknown island and raised and protected by a giant native. The film is filled with earthquakes, exploding volcanoes, bloodthirsty manhunters, and greedy treasure seekers. The most exciting elements of the 1930s jungle/tropical paradise films mixed with the best self-sacrifice and revenge traditions of the day make this a grand serial. B&W; 12 chapters. DIR: William Witney, John English. CAST: Herman Brix, Noble Johnson, Mala, Monte Blue, Jill Martin, William Royle. 1938

HAWK THE SLAYER ★★ In this sword-and-sorcery adventure, John Terry plays the good Hawk, who, with his band of warriors—a dwarf and an elf among them—fights Jack Palance, his evil older brother. Palance's performance saves the film from mediocrity. Not rated; has violence. 90m. DIR: Terry Marcel. CAST: Jack Palance, John Terry. 1980

HAWKS ★★★★ This neglected treasure concerns a couple of feisty patients—Timothy Dalton and Anthony Edwards—in a hospital terminal ward. The macabre gallows humor may be difficult for mainstream tastes, but Dalton's often enraged battle with life is utterly compelling. With music by the Bee Gees (and Barry Gibb takes cocredit for the story idea). Rated R for profanity and brief nudity. 103m. DIR: Robert Ellis Miller. CAST: Timothy Dalton, Anthony Edwards. 1989

HAWKS AND THE SPARROWS, THE ★★1/2 A father and his rambunctious son take a stroll that soon becomes a religious pilgrimage in this poetic comedy. The famous Italian comic Toto gives this lifeless story its brightest moments. In Italian with English subtitles. B&W; 90m. DIR: Pier Paolo Pasolini. CAST: Toto, Davoli Ninetto. 1966

HAWK'S VENGEANCE ★★ Run-of-the-mill action film is the story of a soldier avenging the death of his brother. Rated R for violence and language. 96m.

DIR: Marc Voizard. **CAST:** Gary Daniels, Jayne Heitmeyer, Vlasta Vrana, Cass Magda, Catherine Blythe. 1996

HAWMPS! 💘 Old West cavalry unit uses camels instead of horses. Rated G. 120m. **DIR:** Joe Camp. **CAST:** James Hampton, Christopher Connelly, Slim Pickens, Denver Pyle, Jack Elam. 1976

HAZEL CHRISTMAS SHOW, THE (TV SERIES) ★★1/2 The know-it-all housekeeper celebrates the Yuletide in two special episodes from the 1961–1966 series. "Just 86 Shopping Minutes Left Till Christmas" finds her employer, Mr. Baxter, deciding that the family should have an austere, noncommercialized Christmas. "Hazel's Christmas Shopping" has the spunky maid working part-time in a department store to save up money to buy gifts for the Baxters. Not rated. 60m. **DIR:** William D. Russell. **CAST:** Shirley Booth, Don DeFore, Whitney Blake, Bobby Buntrock, Karen Steele, Lauren Gilbert, Molly Dodd, Byron Foulger, Eleanor Andley, Helen Spring. 1961; 1965

HE GOT GAME ★★1/2 This uneven drama is about ethnic pride, urban survival, and the corruption of American sports. Jake Shuttlesworth, an Attica inmate on a one-week furlough, can shave time off his manslaughter sentence by convincing his basketball-star son Jesus to enroll at the governor's alma mater. There's one problem: Jesus hates his dad. The film's often brilliant cinematic flourishes are undercut by a contrived script. Rated R for language, nudity, simulated sex, drug use, and domestic violence. 137m. **DIR:** Spike Lee. **CAST:** Denzel Washington, Ray Allen, Milla Jovovich, Rosario Dawson, Hill Harper. 1998 DVD

HE KNOWS YOU'RE ALONE ★★ There's a killer on the loose, specializing in brides-to-be. His current target for dismemberment is pretty Amy (Caitlin O'Heaney). While stalking his special prey, the killer keeps his knife sharp by decimating the population of Staten Island. Rated R. 94m. **DIR:** Armand Mastroianni. **CAST:** Don Scardino, Caitlin O'Heaney, Elizabeth Kemp, Tom Hanks. 1981

HE SAID, SHE SAID ★★★1/2 When telling friends how they got together, married directors Ken Kwapis and Marisa Silver were surprised to hear how much their stories differed. So they decided to make a movie about a courting couple (Kevin Bacon, Elizabeth Perkins) and the male/female opposing views of the romance. Slight, but charming. Rated PG-13 for profanity. 115m. **DIR:** Ken Kwapis, Marisa Silver. **CAST:** Kevin Bacon, Elizabeth Perkins, Sharon Stone, Nathan Lane, Anthony LaPaglia. 1990

HE WALKED BY NIGHT ★★★★1/2 Richard Basehart is superb in this documentary-style drama as a killer stalked by methodical policemen. A little-known cinematic gem, it's first-rate in every department and reportedly inspired Jack Webb to create *Dragnet.* B&W; 79m. **DIR:** Alfred Werker, Anthony Mann. **CAST:** Richard Basehart, Scott Brady, Jack Webb, Roy Roberts, Whit Bissell. 1948

HE WHO GETS SLAPPED ★★★1/2 One of Lon Chaney Sr.'s best performances as a brilliant scientist who becomes a circus clown after a personal tragedy. The very first film produced by MGM. Silent.

B&W; 80m. **DIR:** Victor Sjöström. **CAST:** Lon Chaney Sr., Norma Shearer, John Gilbert. 1924

HEAD (1968) ★★★ They get the funniest looks from everyone they meet. And it's no wonder. This film is truly bizarre. The Monkees were hurtled to fame in the aftershock of the Beatles' success. Their ingratiating series was accused of imitating *A Hard Day's Night,* but their innovative feature-film debut, *Head,* was ahead of its time. A free-form product of the psychedelic era. 86m. **DIR:** Bob Rafelson. **CAST:** Mickey Dolenz, David Jones, Mike Nesmith, Peter Tork, Teri Garr, Vito Scotti, Timothy Carey, Logan Ramsey. 1968

HEAD, THE (1959) ★★ Magnificently atmospheric and surreal West German mad scientist shocker with a much stronger plot than most films of its ilk—notably the Edgar Wallace series—could boast. Classically gothic and fogbound, this fascinating oddity follows the horrific events that result when a mad scientist becomes victim of his most daring experiment. B&W; 92m. **DIR:** Victor Trivas. **CAST:** Horst Frank, Michel Simon. 1959 DVD

HEAD AGAINST THE WALL ★★★ An unruly boy who blames his father for his mother's accidental death is sent to a mental hospital. Director Georges Franju shot much of this (his first feature-length film) in an actual insane asylum, and the sense of fatalistic foreboding may be a bit too oppressive for many viewers. In French with English subtitles. B&W; 98m. **DIR:** Georges Franju. **CAST:** Jean-Pierre Mocky, Pierre Brasseur, Anouk Aimée, Charles Aznavour. 1958

HEAD OF THE FAMILY ★★ Cheesy horror movie about mutant quadruplets controlled by their other brother, a giant disembodied head. More sexy than scary, thanks to a subplot about a cheating wife looking to have the clan murder her husband. Rated R for nudity, sexual situations, and violence. 82m. **DIR:** Robert Talbot. **CAST:** Blake Bailey, J. W. Perra, Jacqueline Lowell. 1996 DVD

HEAD OFFICE ★★ A sometimes funny comedy about the son of an influential politician who upon graduating from college gets a high-paying job with a major corporation. Rated PG-13. 90m. **DIR:** Ken Finkleman. **CAST:** Judge Reinhold, Lori-Nan Engler, Eddie Albert, Merritt Butrick, Ron Frazier, Richard Masur, Rick Moranis, Jane Seymour, Danny DeVito. 1985

HEADIN' HOME ★★ A small-town lad smitten with the baseball bug earns the enmity of his community when his play helps a visiting team defeat the locals. Years later he returns to his family and best girl a baseball star. Well on his way to becoming a legend, Babe Ruth basically plays himself in his first film. Though missing enough footage to make the story hazy, it is a fabulous opportunity to see one of the great baseball figures of the twentieth century playing at the legendary Polo Grounds. B&W; 56m. **DIR:** Lawrence Windom. **CAST:** Babe Ruth, Ruth Taylor, William Sheer, Margaret Sedden, Francis Victory, James Marcus. 1920

HEADLESS BODY IN TOPLESS BAR 💘 The first film based on a *New York Post* headline and about as good as the source would indicate. Cheap, dreary, and unconvincing, it's about a deranged gunman ho takes the pathetic denizens of a Manhattan rip bar hostage and the degrading psychological mes he makes them play. Not rated; contains lots nudity, violence, language, and erotic subject mat-r. 106m. **DIR:** James Bruce. **CAST:** Raymond J. Barry, nnifer MacDonald, Taylor Nichols, David Selby, Paul illiams. 1996

EADLESS HORSEMAN, THE ★★1/2 The time-nnored (but worn) story of lanky Yankee school-aster Ichabod Crane's rube-ish efforts to wed ealthy Katrina Van Tassel. Will Rogers looks the art of the homespun Crane and gives a fair impres-on of the character. Silent. B&W; 52m. **DIR:** Edward enturini. **CAST:** Will Rogers, Lois Meredith. 1922

EADS ★★★ Talk about disappointments! This arkly satirical slice of small-town somnambulism ens brilliantly, but fails to fulfill its potential. Jon ryer is perfect as a rookie reporter for the mori-nd *Dry Falls Daily Document*, the newspaper for community brought to life when decapitated wnsfolk start popping up. Sadly, events quickly col-pse into a conventional (and boring) murder mys-ry. Rated R for gore, profanity, and simulated sex. 2m. **DIR:** Paul Shapiro. **CAST:** Jon Cryer, Edward As-er, Jennifer Tilly, Shawn Thompson, Roddy Mc-owall. 1994

EAR MY SONG ★★★★ A gentle satire in the style *Local Hero* and *Gregory's Girl*, this English im-ort tells the sly story of a promoter (Adrian Dunbar, ho cowrote the screenplay) who attempts to fool e public one time too many. It's charming, heart-arming, and funny. Rated R for profanity, nudity, d brief violence. 104m. **DIR:** Peter Chelsom. **CAST:** ed Beatty, Adrian Dunbar, Shirley Anne Field, Tara tzgerald, William Hootkins. 1991

EAR NO EVIL ★★★1/2 A deaf athletic trainer nds herself living a nightmare after a client plants a re coin on her. Restaurant owner D. B. Sweeney ies to help while becoming sensitized to her handi-ap. The deaf angle gives this thriller a decent edge, it it's too predictable to be totally gripping. Rated for violence and profanity. 98m. **DIR:** Robert Green-ald. **CAST:** Marlee Matlin, D. B. Sweeney, Martin neen. 1993

EARSE, THE ❤ This film is about a satanic pact tween an old woman and her lover. Rated PG. 00m. **DIR:** George Bowers. **CAST:** Trish Van Devere, seph Cotten, David Gautreaux, Donald Hotton. 1980

EARST AND DAVIES AFFAIR, THE ★★★ From illiam Randolph Hearst's and Marion Davies's first eeting at the Ziegfeld Follies to his death, this ade-for-TV original takes the viewer through their ntire affair—told from Davies's point of view. The ise-en-scène is beautiful, since the film was shot location at Hearst Castle. Both Robert Mitchum d Virginia Madsen deliver fine performances as e title couple. Not rated. 95m. **DIR:** David Lowell ch. **CAST:** Robert Mitchum, Virginia Madsen, Fritz eaver, Doris Belack. 1985

EART ★★ A down-and-out boxer (Brad Davis) akes a comeback. This is well-worn territory and *eart* has little new to offer. Rated R for violence and rofanity. 93m. **DIR:** James Lemmo. **CAST:** Brad

Davis, Jesse Doran, Sam Gray, Robinson Frank Adu, Steve Buscemi, Frances Fisher. 1987

HEART AND SOULS ★★★1/2 Sentimental fantasy follows the misadventures of Robert Downey Jr., who, at the moment of his birth, is "adopted" by a quartet of ghosts. The spirits cut off all communication with him when he's ten, breaking the boy's heart. So he's not exactly happy to see them again when he's an adult and they're asking for help. Rated PG-13 for brief profanity, one sexy scene, and light violence. 104m. **DIR:** Ron Underwood. **CAST:** Robert Downey Jr., Charles Grodin, Alfre Woodard, Kyra Sedgwick, Elisabeth Shue, Tom Sizemore, David Paymer. **1993 DVD**

HEART BEAT ★★★★ *Heart Beat* is a perfect title for this warm, bittersweet visual poem on the beat generation by writer-director John Byrum. It pulses with life and emotion, intoxicating the viewer with a rhythmic flow of stunning images and superb performances by Nick Nolte, Sissy Spacek, and John Heard. The story begins with the cross-country adventure that inspired Jack Kerouac's *On the Road*. Rated R. 109m. **DIR:** John Byrum. **CAST:** Nick Nolte, Sissy Spacek, John Heard, Ray Sharkey, Ann Dusenberry. 1980

HEART CONDITION ★★★ By sheer force of talent, Bob Hoskins and Denzel Washington turn this formulaic movie into something worth watching. Hoskins is a racist cop who has a heart attack and is given recently deceased Washington's heart in a transplant operation. Rent this one on discount night, and it just may put a smile on your face. Rated R for profanity, sexual situations, and violence. 90m. **DIR:** James D. Parriott. **CAST:** Bob Hoskins, Denzel Washington, Chloe Webb, Roger E. Mosley. 1990

HEART IS A LONELY HUNTER, THE ★★★★ This release features Alan Arkin in a superb performance, which won him an Academy Award nomination. In it, he plays a sensitive and compassionate man who is also a deaf-mute. Rated G. 125m. **DIR:** Robert Ellis Miller. **CAST:** Alan Arkin, Sondra Locke, Laurinda Barrett, Stacy Keach, Chuck McCann, Cicely Tyson. 1968

HEART LIKE A WHEEL ★★★★ This top-notch film biography of racing-champion Shirley Muldowney features a marvelous performance by Bonnie Bedelia as the first woman to crack the National Hot Rod Association's embargo against female competitors. Rated PG for profanity. 113m. **DIR:** Jonathan Kaplan. **CAST:** Bonnie Bedelia, Beau Bridges, Leo Rossi, Hoyt Axton, Bill McKinney, Dean Paul Martin, Dick Miller. 1983

HEART OF A CHAMPION: THE RAY MANCINI STORY ★★★ Made-for-TV movie of the life of Ray "Boom Boom" Mancini focuses on his quest for the lightweight boxing title. His drive is intensified by his desire to bring pride to his father, who could have had a shot at the title had he not been called to serve in World War II. Fight sequences staged by Sylvester Stallone. 100m. **DIR:** Richard Michaels. **CAST:** Robert Blake, Doug McKeon, Mariclare Costello. 1985

HEART OF ARIZONA ★★ Belle Starr and daughter Jackie move near the Bar-20, and Hopalong Cassidy has his hands full. Belle and Jackie are pinned down by rustlers who are using her ranch. The outlaw queen bravely walks into a hail of bullets with her guns blazing before help arrives. B&W; 68m. **DIR:** Lesley Selander. **CAST:** William Boyd, George "Gabby" Hayes, Russell Hayden, Natalie Moorhead, John Elliot, Lane Chandler. **1938**

HEART OF DARKNESS ★★1/2 Slow-moving and sometimes incoherent made-for-TV interpretation of Joseph Conrad's novel concerning an ivory company representative who may or may not have gone mad at his isolated African outpost, and the steamboat captain sent to find him. Conrad's novel is served far better by director Francis Ford Coppola's *Apocalypse Now.* 104m. **DIR:** Nicolas Roeg. **CAST:** Tim Roth, John Malkovich, Isaach De Bankee, James Fox, Morten Faldaas, Iman. **1994**

HEART OF DIXIE, THE ★★ With its heart in the right place but its head lost in the clouds this film only manages to satisfy on two levels: its 1957 period details of the South, which is struggling to maintain its slipping grip on antebellum grandeur; and a small, tight performance by Treat Williams. The film centers on the activities of a group of sorority sisters at Alabama's Randolph University and their Big-Daddy-in-training lugs of boyfriends. Rated PG for mild violence and reasonably oblique sexual discussions. 110m. **DIR:** Martin Davidson. **CAST:** Ally Sheedy, Virginia Madsen, Phoebe Cates, Don Michael Paul, Treat Williams. **1989**

HEART OF DRAGON ★★★ Jackie Chan, in a departure from his usually good-natured hero, employs less humor and more pathos as a policeman unwillingly burdened by his retarded brother's daily antics. Director Sammo Hung costars, creating to perfection the childish sibling. Blood proves thicker than water when Chan's brother is falsely accused of a robbery, and Chan risks his life and career to protect him. In Chinese with English subtitles. Not rated; contains violence. 85m. **DIR:** Sammo Hung. **CAST:** Jackie Chan, Emily Chu, Sammo Hung. **1985 DVD**

HEART OF GLASS ★★★★1/2 One of director Werner Herzog's most haunting and mystifying films. In a small village in preindustrial Germany, a glassblower dies, and the secret for his unique ruby glass is lost forever leaving the townspeople in hysteria. A remarkable, visionary film. In German with English subtitles. Not rated. 93m. **DIR:** Werner Herzog. **CAST:** Josef Bierbichler. **1976**

HEART OF JUSTICE ★★★1/2 Engrossing drama follows a reporter's attempt to piece together the reason a popular author was murdered by a wealthy socialite. Film plays like an Alfred Hitchcock movie with very fine performances by all involved. 108m. **DIR:** Bruno Barreto. **CAST:** Dennis Hopper, Eric Stoltz, Jennifer Connelly, Bradford Dillman, William H. Macy, Dermot Mulroney, Vincent Price, Joanna Miles, Harris Yulin. **1993**

HEART OF MIDNIGHT ★★★ What begins as a disturbing haunted-house movie becomes a chilling whodunit. Jennifer Jason Leigh inherits a dilapidated ballroom with a steamy past. Grippingly weird. Rated R. 95m. **DIR:** Matthew Chapman. **CAST:** Jennifer Jason Leigh, Peter Coyote, Frank Stallone, Brenda Vaccaro. **1989**

HEART OF THE GOLDEN WEST ★★1/2 This modern-day adventure pits Roy Rogers and his fellow ranchers against cheating city slickers intent on defrauding the cowboys and putting them out of business. Enjoyable Western hokum. B&W; 65m. **DIR:** Joseph Kane. **CAST:** Roy Rogers, Smiley Burnette, George "Gabby" Hayes, Ruth Terry. **1942**

HEART OF THE ROCKIES ★★★★ Possibly the best of the Three Mesquiteers series as the trio find a vicious mountain family behind cattle rustling and the illegal trapping of game. B&W; 56m. **DIR:** Joseph Kane. **CAST:** Robert Livingston, Ray "Crash" Corrigan, Max Terhune, Yakima Canutt, Lynne Roberts (Mary Hart). **1937**

HEART OF THE STAG ★★★★ The shocking subject matter—forced incest—could have resulted in an uncomfortable film to watch. However, New Zealander Michael Firth, who directed the movie and conceived the story, handles it expertly, and the result is a riveting viewing experience. Rated R for violence, profanity, and sexual situations. 94m. **DIR:** Michael Firth. **CAST:** Bruno Lawrence, Terence Cooper, Mary Regan. **1983**

HEARTACHES ★★★ A touching, yet lighthearted, film about love, friendship, and survival follows the trials and tribulations of a young pregnant woman (Annie Potts), who is separated from her husband (Robert Carradine), and the kooky girlfriend she meets on the bus (Margot Kidder). The Canadian film is rated R for a minimal amount of sex, which is handled discreetly. 93m. **DIR:** Donald Shebib. **CAST:** Robert Carradine, Margot Kidder, Annie Potts, Winston Rekert, George Touliatos. **1981**

HEARTBEEPS ★★★ Andy Kaufman and Bernadette Peters play robots who fall in love and decide to explore the world around them. It's a good family film, and the kids will probably love it. Rated PG. 79m. **DIR:** Allan Arkush. **CAST:** Andy Kaufman, Bernadette Peters, Randy Quaid. **1981**

HEARTBREAK HOTEL ★★★ In this bit of none-too-convincing whimsy, Charlie Schlatter plays an aspiring rock guitarist who kidnaps Elvis Presley (David Keith). Keith does a terrific job of impersonating Presley, and director Chris Columbus's script has some warmly funny moments, but the movie cannot overcome its preposterous premise. Rated PG-13 for profanity and violence. 100m. **DIR:** Chris Columbus. **CAST:** David Keith, Tuesday Weld, Charlie Schlatter, Chris Mulkey. **1988**

HEARTBREAK HOUSE ★★★1/2 Rex Harrison is ideally cast as George Bernard Shaw's Captain Shotover. At Shotover's house the guests include his two daughters and a visiting young woman, each in the grip of romantic trauma. What is presented is essentially an ongoing collision of philosophies, but the able cast keeps the debate lively. Not rated, but with no objectionable material. 122m. **DIR:** Anthony Page. **CAST:** Rex Harrison, Amy Irving, Rosemary Harris. **1985**

HEARTBREAK KID, THE ★★★★ The lack of care or commitment in the modern marriage is satirized in this comedy. Charles Grodin plays a young man who's grown tired of his wife while driving to their honeymoon in Florida. By the time he sees beautiful Cybill hepherd on the beach, his marriage has totally disintegrated. Jeannie Berlin, director Elaine May's aughter, is the big scene stealer as Grodin's whining bride. Rated PG. 104m. **DIR:** Elaine May. **CAST:** Charles Grodin, Cybill Shepherd, Jeannie Berlin, Eddie Ibert, Audra Lindley. **1972**

HEARTBREAK RIDGE ★★★ Whoever thought Grenada would be the subject of cinematic war heroics? Though the film could use some trimming, the tory of a hard-nosed Marine sergeant whipping a opeless-looking unit into a crack fighting team is till compelling. Rated R. 126m. **DIR:** Clint Eastwood. **AST:** Clint Eastwood, Marsha Mason, Everett McGill, Mo Svenson, Mario Van Peebles, Moses Gunn, Tom Villard. **1986**

HEARTBREAKERS ★★★1/2 Two men in their thirties, Arthur Blue (Peter Coyote) and Eli Kahn (Nick Mancuso), friends since childhood, find their relationship severely tested when each is suddenly caught up in his own fervent drive for success. Rated R for simulated sex and profanity. 106m. **DIR:** Bobby Roth. **CAST:** Peter Coyote, Nick Mancuso, Max Gail, Kathryn Harrold. **1984**

HEARTBURN ★★★1/2 Uneven adaptation of Nora Ephron's novel (she also wrote the screenplay) and a thinly disguised account of her own separation from Watergate journalist Carl Bernstein. Jack Nicholson and Meryl Streep fall in love, get married, and drift apart. Its strength comes from the superb performances by the stars and an incredible supporting cast. Needlessly rated R for language. 108m. **DIR:** Mike Nichols. **CAST:** Meryl Streep, Jack Nicholson, Jeff Daniels, Maureen Stapleton, Stockard Channing, Richard Masur, Catherine O'Hara, Milos Forman. **1986**

HEARTLAND ★★★★ This is an excellent and deceptively simple story, of a widow (Conchata Ferrell) who settled, with her daughter and a homesteader (Rip Torn), in turn-of-the-century Wyoming. The film deals with the complex problems of surviving in nature and society. It's well worth watching. Rated PG. 96m. **DIR:** Richard Pearce. **CAST:** Conchata Ferrell, Rip Torn, Lilia Skala, Megan Folsom. **1979**

HEARTLESS ★★ Heartless, gutless, and brainless, this made-for-cable original is about a young woman who receives a heart transplant. Little does she know, the heart came from a murdered woman, and the story goes into a terminal coma from there. Not rated; contains violence and suggested sex. 95m. **DIR:** Judith Vogelsang. **CAST:** Madchen Amick, Louise Fletcher, David Packer, Tom Schanley, Pamela Bellwood, Bo Svenson. **1997**

HEARTS ADRIFT ★★ A woman and her daughter take a trip to San Diego, one to find love and the other to rekindle an old flame. This made-for-cable original has an artificial, soap-opera feel to it, and (considering the cast) it's no wonder. Not rated; contains suggested sex. 95m. **DIR:** Vic Sarin. **CAST:** Sydney Penny, Scott Reeves, Kathleen Noone, Nicolas Coster, Don Murray. **1996**

HEARTS AND ARMOUR ★★1/2 Warrior Orlando (Rick Edwards) seeks victory over the Moors and the rescue of his love (Tanya Roberts), while his female comrade-in-arms, Bradamante (Barbara de Rossi), falls in love with Ruggero (Ron Moss), the Moor

whom Orlando is fated to kill. Unfortunately, the script is not strong enough to do justice to the complex plot. Not rated; has violence and nudity. 101m. **DIR:** Giacomo Battiato. **CAST:** Zenda Araya, Barbara de Rossi, Rick Edwards, Ronn Moss, Tanya Roberts. **1983**

HEARTS AND MINDS ★★★★★ Unforgettable Oscar-winning documentary about the effects of the Vietnam War on the people of that country. Without narration or commentary, filmmaker Peter Davis juxtaposes scenes of the ruined country with interviews of military leaders. Rated R. 112m. **DIR:** Peter Davis. **1974**

HEART'S DESIRE ★★ Richard Tauber, a popular tenor in British operetta, stars in this ho-hum musical as a Viennese waiter who becomes a star in London. In the end, true love brings him back home. B&W; 79m. **DIR:** Paul Stein. **CAST:** Richard Tauber, Leonora Corbett. **1935**

HEARTS OF DARKNESS ★★★★★ Draws on 60 hours of footage shot by Eleanor Coppola during the 238 days of principal photography in the Philippines for husband Francis's *Apocalypse Now* (as well as after-the-fact interviews with its cast and crew). Unprecedented insight into the moviemaking process and the on-location madness. A must-see for film buffs. Not rated; the film has profanity and graphic scenes of native rituals during which animals are slain. 96m. **DIR:** Fax Bahr, George Hickenlooper. **1992**

HEARTS OF FIRE ✿ A girl who dreams of becoming a rock star. Rated R for brief nudity and profanity. 95m. **DIR:** Richard Marquand. **CAST:** Fiona, Bob Dylan, Rupert Everett, Julian Glover. **1987**

HEARTS OF THE WEST ★★★ Pleasant little comedy-drama about an aspiring writer from Iowa (Jeff Bridges) who, determined to pen masterful Westerns, winds up in Hollywood as a most reluctant cowboy. The setting is the early 1920s, and the story playfully explores many classic Western myths. Rated PG. 103m. **DIR:** Howard Zieff. **CAST:** Jeff Bridges, Alan Arkin, Blythe Danner, Andy Griffith. **1975**

HEARTS OF THE WORLD ★★★ This World War I epic, a propaganda film, was made to convince the United States to enter the conflict and aid Britain and France. Actual battle footage from both sides in the conflict is interwoven with the story of a young man going to war and the tragic effects on his family and village. Silent. B&W; 122m. **DIR:** D. W. Griffith. **CAST:** Lillian Gish, Dorothy Gish, Robert Harron, Ben Alexander. **1918**

HEARTSTOPPER ★★★ In this film based on his novel *The Awakening*, John Russo spins a fascinating tale of a surgeon accused and hanged for vampirism who returns from the grave as a real vampire. Acting is top-notch, as Russo paints an exciting story. 96m. **DIR:** John Russo. **CAST:** Kevin Kindlon, John Hall, Moon Zappa, Tom Savini. **1991**

HEAT (1972) ★★★ One of Andy Warhol's better film productions is this steamy tale of an unemployed actor (Joe Dallesandro) whose involvement with a neurotic has-been actress (Sylvia Miles) has tragicomic results. A low-budget homage to *Sunset Boulevard* that even non-Warhol fans may enjoy. Excellent music score composed and performed by John Cale. Rated R for nudity and language. 100m.

DIR: Paul Morrissey. **CAST:** Sylvia Miles, Joe Dallesandro, Andrea Feldman, Pat Ast. 1972

HEAT (1987) ★★1/2 A good try at an action thriller that doesn't succeed because of awkward pacing, uneven direction, and a mood that swings wildly from raw violence to good-buddy playfulness. Burt Reynolds is a Las Vegas–based troubleshooter with two problems: an old girlfriend who craves revenge and a mousy young executive (Peter MacNicol, stealing every scene he shared with Reynolds) who craves the ability to protect himself. Rated R for language and violence. 101m. **DIR:** Dick Richards. **CAST:** Burt Reynolds, Karen Young, Peter MacNicol, Howard Hesseman, Neill Barry, Diana Scarwid. 1987

HEAT (1995) ★★★1/2 If this cops-and-robbers tale had concentrated solely on the professional rivalry between police detective Al Pacino and thief Robert De Niro, *Heat* would have been a hands-down winner; however, too much screen time is allotted to their private lives. Nevertheless, the excellent cast makes it worth watching and the action scenes are top-notch. Rated R for violence, simulated sex, and profanity. 172m. **DIR:** Michael Mann. **CAST:** Al Pacino, Robert De Niro, Val Kilmer, Jon Voight, Tom Sizemore, Diane Venora, Amy Brenneman, Ashley Judd, Mykelti Williamson, Wes Studi, Natalie Portman. 1995 DVD

HEAT AND DUST ★★★★ Two love stories—one from the 1920s and one from today—are entwined in this classy, thoroughly enjoyable soap opera about two British women who go to India and become involved in its seductive mysteries. Julie Christie stars as a modern woman retracing the steps of her great-aunt (Greta Scacchi), who fell in love with an Indian ruler (played by the celebrated Indian star Shashi Kapoor). Rated R for nudity and brief violence. 130m. **DIR:** James Ivory. **CAST:** Julie Christie, Greta Scacchi, Shashi Kapoor, Christopher Cazenove, Julian Glover, Susan Fleetwood. 1983

HEAT AND SUNLIGHT ★★★★ Electrifying, narratively risky drama featuring director Rob Nilsson as a photographer who is overwhelmed with jealousy and obsession. Visually stunning, with a great soundtrack by David Byrne and Brian Eno. Rated R for nudity and profanity. B&W; 98m. **DIR:** Rob Nilsson. **CAST:** Rob Nilsson. 1987

HEAT OF DESIRE ★★ So many sex comedies are about married men who discover adultery brings new vitality, this plot has become a cinematic cliché. But this didn't stop director Luc Beraud from using it again in this disappointing film. In French with English subtitles. Not rated; the film has nudity and suggested sex. 91m. **DIR:** Luc Beraud. **CAST:** Patrick Dewaere, Clio Goldsmith, Jeanne Moreau, Guy Marchand. 1984

HEATED VENGEANCE ★★ A U.S. serviceman (Richard Hatch) returns to Southeast Asia years after the Vietnam War to bring back his old flame (Jolina Mitchell-Collins). Former enemies abduct him and bring him back to their camp, where he finds that they are dealing with drugs. Not rated, has violence, profanity, sex, and nudity. 91m. **DIR:** Edward Murphy. **CAST:** Richard Hatch, Michael J. Pollard,

Dennis Patrick, Mills Watson, Cameron Dye, Robert Walker Jr. 1987

HEATHCLIFF—THE MOVIE 🎬 An example of everything that is wrong with cartoons today, this release is sloppily drawn, poorly scripted, and generally pointless. Rated G. 89m. **DIR:** Bruno Bianchi. 1986

HEATHERS ★★★★ A *Dr. Strangelove* or *Blue Velvet* of the teen set, this brash black comedy tackles such typically adolescent issues as peer pressure, high school cliques, heterosexuality, and homosexuality—and even teen suicide—in ways that are inventive, irreverent, startling, and occasionally offensive. Rated R; with violence and profanity. 110m. **DIR:** Michael Lehmann. **CAST:** Winona Ryder, Christian Slater, Kim Walker. 1989 DVD

HEAT'S ON, THE ★★1/2 After a three-year absence Mae West returned to the screen as a Broadway star caught between two rival producers. She shouldn't have bothered, since the firmly entrenched Hays Office knocked out the double entendres for which she was noted. Her last film until 1970s dismal *Myra Breckenridge*. B&W; 80m. **DIR:** Gregory Ratoff. **CAST:** Mae West, Victor Moore, William Gaxton, Lloyd Bridges, Lina Romay, Xavier Cugat, Hazel Scott. 1943

HEATSEEKER ★★ Having beaten to death the kick-boxing formula in the here and now, the filmmakers behind this effort take the sport to the year 2019 when cyborgs rule the kick-boxing arena. There's only one human opponent left, and he refuses to fight. Yeah, right. Rated R for violence. 91m. **DIR:** Albert Pyun. **CAST:** Keith Cooke, Thom Mathews, Norbert Weisser, Gary Daniels. 1995

HEATWAVE (1983) ★★★ Judy Davis plays an idealistic liberal opposed to proposed real estate developments. Davis's crusade leads to her involvement in a possible kidnap-murder and a love affair with the young architect of the housing project she's protesting. Not rated. 99m. **DIR:** Phillip Noyce. **CAST:** Judy Davis, Richard Moir, Chris Haywood, Bill Hunter, Anna Jemison. 1983

HEAT WAVE (1990) ★★★1/2 Cable television film depicting the Watts riots of the early Seventies. Blair Underwood plays a young black *L.A. Times* employee given his chance at reporting when it becomes apparent that white journalists cannot get into the Watts area to cover the riots. Engrossing fact-based account. 96m. **DIR:** Kevin Hooks. **CAST:** Blair Underwood, Cicely Tyson, James Earl Jones, Margaret Avery. 1990

HEAVEN (1987) ★★★ Weird collage assembled by actress Diane Keaton mixes footage from old movies with interviews of assorted oddballs who talk about what they think Heaven will be like. Love it or hate it, it's certainly different. Not rated. 80m. **DIR:** Diane Keaton. 1987

•HEAVEN (1998) ★★★★ Gruesomely violent and almost unbearably intense thriller scores on almost every level—from its fine performances to its tight editing to its gutsy dare-to-turn-your-eyes away direction. Recommended but not for everybody. Rated R for violence, profanity, and nudity. 103m. **DIR:** Scott Reynolds. **CAST:** Martin Donovan, Joanna Going, Patrick Malahide, Richard Schiff, Karl Urban, Danny

Edwards, Michael Langley, Jeremy Birchall, Clint Sharplin. **1998 DVD**

HEAVEN AND EARTH (1991) ★★★ Imagine the battles of the great Akira Kurosawa samurai epics, but without the rich philosophical dimension or tragic aura. This film lacks the emotional staying power of the master's work, but it is still rich in splendor. In Japanese with English subtitles. Rated PG-13. 106m. **DIR:** Haruki Kadokawa. **CAST:** Takaaki Enoki. **1991**

HEAVEN AND EARTH (1993) ★★★ Oliver Stone returns to Vietnam to focus on one woman's Dickensian ordeals. She survives the French and American invasions, and then tackles life in the gluttonous United States after marrying a war-weary sergeant who, in a bit of near comical overkill, becomes violently homicidal. Actors in lead roles are sensational, but their characters are lost amid Stone's bombastic visual diatribes. Rated R for violence, profanity, nudity, and rape. 140m. **DIR:** Oliver Stone. **CAST:** Hiep Thi Le, Tommy Lee Jones, Joan Chen, Haing S. Ngor, Debbie Reynolds. **1993**

HEAVEN BEFORE I DIE ★★★ Likable low-budget feature about a Middle Easterner who comes to Toronto to pursue his dream of becoming a Charlie Chaplin impersonator. Giancarlo Giannini (*Swept Away*) steals the film as a petty thief who helps him get the hang of life in the New World. Rated PG. 98m. **DIR:** Izidore K. Musallam. **CAST:** Andy Velasquez, Giancarlo Giannini, Joanna Pacula. **1997**

HEAVEN CAN WAIT (1943) ★★★★★ Newly deceased Don Ameche meets "Your Excellency" (the devil) and reviews his roguish life. If ever you wondered what was meant by "the Lubitsch touch," *Heaven Can Wait* explains it. Quite simply this is the most joyful fantasy–love story ever filmed. 112m. **DIR:** Ernst Lubitsch. **CAST:** Don Ameche, Gene Tierney, Charles Coburn, Laird Cregar, Spring Byington, Eugene Pallette, Marjorie Main, Louis Calhern, Signe Hasso, Allyn Joslyn, Florence Bates. **1943**

HEAVEN CAN WAIT (1978) ★★★★1/2 In this charming remake of *Here Comes Mr. Jordan* (1941), Warren Beatty plays quarterback Joe Pendleton, who meets a premature demise when an overzealous angel takes the athlete's spirit out of his body after an accident. As it turns out, it wasn't Joe's time to die. However, in the interim, his body is cremated. Thus begins a quest to find a proper earthly replacement. Rated PG. 100m. **DIR:** Warren Beatty, Buck Henry. **CAST:** Warren Beatty, Julie Christie, Jack Warden, Dyan Cannon, Charles Grodin, James Mason, Buck Henry, Vincent Gardenia. **1978 DVD**

HEAVEN HELP US ★★ Donald Sutherland, John Heard, Wallace Shawn, and Kate Reid support the youthful cast of this comedy about a group of schoolboys (played by Andrew McCarthy, Kevin Dillon, Malcolm Dunarie, and Stephen Geoffreys) discovering the opposite sex and other adolescent pursuits. Rated R. 90m. **DIR:** Michael Dinner. **CAST:** Andrew McCarthy, Kevin Dillon, Malcolm Dunarie, Stephen Geoffreys, Donald Sutherland, John Heard, Wallace Shawn, Kate Reid. **1985**

HEAVEN IS A PLAYGROUND ★★★1/2 A Chicago slum has one thing going for it: a basketball coach determined to take kids off the streets and onto college campuses. Enter a young white lawyer who helps the coach vanquish an unethical promoter. Rated R for profanity and violence. 104m. **DIR:** Randall Fried. **CAST:** Mike Warren, D. B. Sweeney, Richard Jordan. **1991**

HEAVEN ON EARTH ★★★★ Scripters Margaret Atwood and Peter Pearson pay tribute to a bit of Canadian history with this poignant look at the thousands of orphaned "home children" shipped from England to work as indentured slaves . . . or, if they were lucky, to be adopted into loving families. Suitable for family viewing. 82m. **DIR:** Allan Kroeker. **CAST:** R. H. Thomson, Sian Leisa Davies. **1986**

HEAVEN OR VEGAS ★★ Life is a gamble, but this misguided tale of love and redemption comes up snake eyes. Richard Grieco is the high-rent gigolo and Yasmine Bleeth the part-time call girl looking for a better life and redemption in Montana. Things heat up when her younger sister threatens their newfound happiness. This direct-to-video effort is nothing more than a soap opera that leaves a nasty ring around the tub. Rated R for language and adult situations. 110m. **DIR:** Gregory C. Haynes. **CAST:** Richard Grieco, Yasmine Bleeth, Andy Romano, Monica Potter, Geoffrey Blake, Sarah Schaub. **1996**

HEAVEN TONIGHT ★★★1/2 This British import is a slick contemporary retelling of *A Star Is Born*, with John Waters as an aging rocker frustrated by his inability to generate the headlines he did twenty years earlier, and Guy Pearce as his capable, soft-spoken son, whose musical star is on the rise. Frank Howson and Alister Webb's script contains considerable truth and a lot of heart. Rated R for profanity and drug use. 97m. **DIR:** Pino Amenta. **CAST:** John Waters, Rebecca Gilling, Kim Gyngell, Guy Pearce. **1993**

HEAVENLY BODIES 🖤 More sweaty dancing bodies à la *Flashdance*. Rated R for nudity, profanity, and sexual innuendo. 90m. **DIR:** Lawrence Dane. **CAST:** Cynthia Dale, Richard Rebiere, Laura Henry. **1985**

HEAVENLY CREATURES ★★★★★ Two New Zealand schoolgirls conspire to murder one girl's mother in the mid-1950s when parental concerns about their obsessive friendship threaten to separate them forever. Surreal scenes set in an alternate universe inhabited by unicorns, giant butterflies, castles, and claymation-type knights are used to reimagine the emotional slide of the two teens into chilling action. This tragic, mesmerizing, and grisly character study is based on a true story about author Anne Perry. Rated R for language and violence. 99m. **DIR:** Peter Jackson. **CAST:** Melanie Lynskey, Kate Winslet. **1994**

HEAVENLY KID, THE ★★ *The Heavenly Kid* is earthbound. Cocky Bobby Fontana (Lewis Smith) bit the big one in a chicken race seventeen years ago: which would make it 1968, but the soundtrack and the wardrobe are definitely 1955—a basic problem rendering this otherwise simply stupid film completely unintelligible. Rated PG-13 for language, situations, and bare body parts. 90m. **DIR:** Cary Medoway. **CAST:** Lewis Smith, Jason Gedrick, Jane Kaczmarek, Richard Mulligan. **1985**

HEAVEN'S A DRAG ★★ This so wants to be the gay version of *Truly, Madly, Deeply*, but it's merely a pale copy. Ian Williams is too weak an actor to carry off his haunting of a former lover (Thomas Arklie) in this bittersweet love story. Makes a good point about facing your emotions, warts and all, but the script and the presentation buckle under their good intentions. Not rated; contains profanity and brief nudity. 96m. **DIR:** Peter Mackenzie Litten. **CAST:** Ian Williams, Thomas Arklie, Dillie Keane, Tony Slattery. **1994**

HEAVENS ABOVE ★★★1/2 Another low-key gem from the late Peter Sellers, this irreverent story of a clergyman with the common touch spoofs just about everything within reach, some of it brilliantly. Sellers shows his congregation the error of their selfish ways and engages them in some odd charities, often with hilarious results. B&W; 105m. **DIR:** John Boulting, Roy Boulting. **CAST:** Peter Sellers, Cecil Parker, Isabel Jeans, Eric Sykes. **1963**

HEAVEN'S BURNING ★★★1/2 Excitement abounds in this twisted tale of a young, bored Japanese bride honeymooning in Australia who fakes her own kidnapping only to be taken for real during a bank robbery. When the getaway-car driver kidnaps her from his accomplices to keep them from killing her, they head to the Outback to hide out. Clever *film noir* with lots of twists. Rated R for adult situations, language, and violence. 99m. **DIR:** Craig Lahiff. **CAST:** Russell Crowe, Youki Kudoh, Kenji Isomura, Ray Barrett. **1997**

HEAVEN'S GATE ★★1/2 Written and directed by Michael Cimino (*The Deer Hunter*), this $36 million epic Western about the land wars in Wyoming between the cattle barons and immigrant farmers, is awkward and overlong but at least makes sense in the complete video version. Rated R for nudity, sex, and violence. 219m. **DIR:** Michael Cimino. **CAST:** Kris Kristofferson, Christopher Walken, Isabelle Huppert, John Hurt, Sam Waterston, Brad Dourif, Jeff Bridges, Joseph Cotten. **1980 DVD**

HEAVEN'S PRISONERS ★★★★ Alec Baldwin gives an outstanding performance as ex-cop Dave Robicheaux, who finds himself drawn back into the sleazy underworld of New Orleans when a plane crashes in the waters near his bait shop. Adapted from the hardboiled detective novel by James Lee Burke, the film is deliberate in its pace and may disappoint some viewers, but excellent performances, stylish direction, and a blues-powered soundtrack make it a rich character study in a mystery setting. Rated R for violence, profanity, nudity, and sex. 132m. **DIR:** Phil Joanou. **CAST:** Alec Baldwin, Kelly Lynch, Mary Stuart Masterson, Eric Roberts, Teri Hatcher. **1996**

HEAVY ★★★ This moody, low-key drama is a *Marty* for the 1990s. Introverted, overweight pizza chef Victor lives with his mom and works at her dingy diner. He is befriended by a pretty college dropout with boyfriend problems who jump-starts his stagnant personal life. The film lays bare the insecurities and fantasies of a physically large but socially invisible loser and looks at the world through his wildly darting eyes. Not rated; contains strong language, nudity, and sex. 119m. **DIR:** James Mangold. **CAST:** Pruitt Tay-

lor Vince, Liv Tyler, Shelley Winters, Deborah Harry, Evan Dando, Joe Grifasi. **1996 DVD**

HEAVY METAL ★★★ While this animated film, based on the French science-fiction comic book of the same name, has not aged particularly well, there are still some high points in its anthology of stories. Combining the sexy sci-fi art style pioneered by Frank Frazetta with an updated E. C. Comics approach to storytelling, it also features the rock music of Blue Oyster Cult, Black Sabbath, Cheap Trick, and others. Voices by John Candy, John Vernon, Harold Ramis, Eugene Levy, and Joe Flaherty. Rated R for sex and violence. 90m. **DIR:** Gerald Potterton. **1981 DVD**

HEAVY TRAFFIC ★★★ Ralph Bakshi's follow-up to *Fritz the Cat* is a mixture of live action and animation. Technically outstanding, but its downbeat look at urban life is rather unpleasant to watch. Rated R for profanity, nudity, and violence. 76m. **DIR:** Ralph Bakshi. **CAST:** Animated. **1973**

HEAVYWEIGHTS ★★ Chubby boys attending summer fat camp seeking sanctuary from the weight-conscious world are greeted with a jolt. The camp's new owner, a health guru, initiates a rigorous fitness regime that he wants to film for an infomercial. Rated PG. 103m. **DIR:** Steven Brill. **CAST:** Ben Stiller, Tom McGowan, Leah Lail, Aaron Schwartz, Kenan Thompson, Tom Hodges, Shaun Weiss, Jerry Stiller, Anne Meara. **1995**

HECK'S WAY HOME ★★★1/2 After losing "his people" during a move from Winnipeg to Vancouver (in preparation for a sea voyage to Australia), a resourceful dog hits the road in a determined effort to find them again. Chris Haddock's script is a charmer all the way, and Alan Arkin lends considerable comic relief as a dogcatcher on the verge of retirement ... but not before *finally* dealing with his long-term nemesis. Rated G. 92m. **DIR:** Michael Scott. **CAST:** Chad Krowchuk, Michael Riley, Shannon Lawson, Don Francks, Alan Arkin. **1995**

HEDD WYN ★★★★ Haunting, true tale of how a young Welsh farmer's dreams of winning a poetry contest are dashed when he signs up to fight in World War I. Before he goes off to fight in the war, Ellis Evans (Huw Garmon) submits a poem into competition under the pseudonym Hedd Wyn. Lying mortally wounded in a trench, Evans examines his life, his loves, and ultimately, his death. Lyrical, almost epic in proportion. In Welsh with English subtitles. Not rated. 123m. **DIR:** Paul Turner. **CAST:** Huw Garmon, Sue Roderick, Judith Humphreys, Nia Dryhurst. **1992**

HEDDA ★★★★ Screenwriter-director Trevor Nunn creates a fine adaptation of Henrik Ibsen's *Hedda Gabler*. Glenda Jackson presides as a coldhearted, power-hungry manipulator who toys with the lives and emotions of those around her. Jackson's costars—members of the Royal Shakespeare Company—match her fine performance. 103m. **DIR:** Trevor Nunn. **CAST:** Glenda Jackson, Timothy West, Peter Eyre, Patrick Stewart. **1975**

HEIDI (1937) ★★★★ This classic stars a spunky Shirley Temple as the girl who is taken away from her kind and loving grandfather's home in the Swiss Alps and forced to live with her cruel aunt. B&W; 88m.

DIR: Allan Dwan. **CAST:** Shirley Temple, Jean Hersholt, Arthur Treacher. **1937**

HEIDI (1965) ★★★★ Shirley Temple fans will disagree, but we think that the beautiful location scenes filmed in the Swiss Alps and the generally high level of production and performances make this the best version on video of the classic children's tale. It's been updated to the present day, but otherwise it is faithful to Johanna Spyri's book. Dubbed in English. 95m. **DIR:** Werner Jacobs. **CAST:** Eva Maria Singhammer. **1965**

HEIDI CHRONICLES, THE ★★★ Wendy Wasserstein adapted her Pulitzer Prize–winning play for cable, but it never loses that stagy feeling. Jamie Lee Curtis and Tom Hulce are fun and believable as college students whose friendship spans thirty years. Wasserstein makes a strong case for feminism and the dialogue is intelligent and witty, but the supporting roles are stereotypical and there are no dramatic surprises. Not rated; contains profanity and sexual situations. 94m. **DIR:** Paul Bogart. **CAST:** Jamie Lee Curtis, Tom Hulce, Kim Cattrall, Peter Friedman. **1995**

HEIDI FLEISS, HOLLYWOOD MADAME ★★★★ Award-winning documentary filmmaker Nick Broomfield turns his cameras on infamous Beverly Hills madam Heidi Fleiss, and the result is a fascinating look at a woman's fall from fame. Utilizing family home movies, news clips, and personal interviews, Broomfield depicts a woman on the fast track in Hollywood, serving a clientele of the rich and infamous. Neither pretty nor flattering, it's always engaging and juicy. Not rated; contains nudity, profanity, and adult situations. 106m. **DIR:** Nick Broomfield. **1995 DVD**

HEIDI'S SONG ★★ Only those 5 years old and younger will enjoy this feature-length cartoon adaptation of Johanna Spyri's classic children's tale. Rated G. 94m. **DIR:** Robert Taylor. **1982**

HEIRESS, THE ★★★★1/2 This moving drama takes place in New York City in the mid-1800s. Olivia de Havilland is excellent (she won an Oscar for this performance) as a plain but extraordinarily rich woman who is pursued by a wily gold digger (played by Montgomery Clift). Ralph Richardson is great as her straitlaced father. B&W; 115m. **DIR:** William Wyler. **CAST:** Olivia de Havilland, Montgomery Clift, Ralph Richardson, Miriam Hopkins, Vanessa Brown, Mona Freeman, Ray Collins. **1949**

HEIST, THE ★★★1/2 Fun revenge film features Pierce Brosnan as a framed con seeking to even the score with his former racetrack partner (Tom Skerritt). There are so many twists and turns in the plot that you will be guessing the final outcome until the closing shot. Not rated HBO film features violence. 97m. **DIR:** Stuart Orme. **CAST:** Pierce Brosnan, Tom Skerritt, Wendy Hughes. **1989 DVD**

•**HELD UP** ★★ Chicago smart aleck and his fiancée stop at a rural convenience store while touring the Grand Canyon area in his vintage Studebaker Hawk. When she discovers he spent their house nest egg on the car, she hitches a ride to Las Vegas and he becomes a hostage of Mexican bandits in a poorly executed robbery. This comedy about a black man stranded in redneck country (locals mistake the lead character for Mike Tyson and Puff Daddy) is more flat than funny. Rated PG-13 for language and sexual innuendo. 89m. **DIR:** Steve Rash. **CAST:** Jamie Foxx, Nia Long, Eduardo Yanez, Barry Corbin, John Cullum. **2000**

•**HELEN MORGAN STORY, THE** ★★★ Largely fictional biography of the singing star of the 1920s, with Ann Blyth as the torch singer and Paul Newman as the hood who does her wrong. Ripe melodrama that at least provides more than a dozen great songs (actually sung by Gogi Grant). B&W; 118m. **DIR:** Michael Curtiz. **CAST:** Ann Blyth, Paul Newman, Richard Carlson, Gene Evans. **1959**

HELEN OF TROY ★★★ This Greek myth, about the woman whose face launched a thousand ships, is bogged down with 1950s attitudes but manages to entertain through sheer extravagance. A cast of thousands wages war over the illicit affair between Queen Helen and Prince Paris. Plenty of grand-scale battles. 141m. **DIR:** Robert Wise. **CAST:** Rossana Podesta, Jacques Sernas, Cedric Hardwicke, Stanley Baker, Niall MacGinnis. **1955**

HELL COMES TO FROGTOWN �› This laughable poverty-row quickie is set in one of those post-apocalyptic futures that allow a minimum of set design. Rated R for nudity, language, and violence. 88m. **DIR:** R. J. Kizer, Donald G. Jackson. **CAST:** Roddy Piper, Sandahl Bergman, Rory Calhoun. **1987**

HELL HARBOR ★★1/2 Sleazy descendant of a pirate wants to sell his daughter to the harbor's moneylender, but she has eyes for a handsome skipper and passage to Havana. B&W; 83m. **DIR:** Henry King. **CAST:** Lupe Velez, Jean Hersholt, Gibson Gowland, John Holland, Al St. John. **1930**

HELL HIGH �› Students playing cruel practical jokes pick on the wrong victim, who summons demons from her past to do her bidding. The real cruel joke is having to sit through this film. Rated R for violence. 84m. **DIR:** Douglas Grossman. **CAST:** Christopher Stryker, Christopher Cousins, Jason Brill, Maureen Mooney. **1986**

HELL HOUNDS OF ALASKA ★★ Action tale taking place in Alaska during the gold rush. Outlaws ambush and murder a miner and kidnap his son. When the deed is discovered, a friend of the slain man tries to rescue the boy. Beautiful scenery and direction make this a fine family film. Rated G. 90m. **DIR:** Harald Reinl. **CAST:** Doug McClure, Harold Leipnitz, Angelica Ott, Roberto Blanco. **1973**

HELL IN THE PACIFIC ★★★1/2 John Boorman directed this moody, somewhat trying drama about an American and a Japanese conducting their own private war on a deserted island at the end of World War II. Well acted. 103m. **DIR:** John Boorman. **CAST:** Lee Marvin, Toshiro Mifune. **1968 DVD**

HELL IS FOR HEROES ★★★★ This tense, gritty World War II drama is heaven for action fans. Director Don Siegel is at his riveting best, drawing the viewer into the claustrophobic, nightmarish atmosphere. B&W; 90m. **DIR:** Don Siegel. **CAST:** Steve McQueen, Bobby Darin, Fess Parker, James Coburn, Harry Guardino, Mike Kellin, Nick Adams, Bob Newhart. **1962**

HELL NIGHT ★★ Linda Blair (*The Exorcist*) returns to the genre that spawned her film career in this low-budget horror flick about fraternity and sorority pledges spending the night in a mansion "haunted" by a crazed killer. Rated R. 101m. DIR: Tom DeSimone. CAST: Linda Blair, Vincent Van Patten, Peter Barton, Jenny Neuman. 1981 DVD

HELL ON FRISCO BAY ★★★ A 1930s-type hard-boiled crime story of a framed cop who does his time, is released from prison, and goes after the bigwig gangster who set him up. Lots of action on San Francisco's streets and its famous bay. 98m. DIR: Frank Tuttle. CAST: Alan Ladd, Joanne Dru, Edward G. Robinson, William Demarest, Fay Wray. 1955

HELL SHIP MUTINY ★★ South Seas programmer with captain Jon Hall battling smugglers who are exploiting island natives. Watchable only for the cast. B&W; 66m. DIR: Lee Sholem, Elmo Williams. CAST: Jon Hall, John Carradine, Peter Lorre, Roberta Haynes, Mike Mazurki. 1957

HELL SQUAD (1985) 💗 Las Vegas show girls are recruited by the CIA. Rated R for nudity and gore. 88m. DIR: Kenneth Hartford. CAST: Bainbridge Scott, Glen Hartford, William Bryant, Marvin Miller. 1985

HELL TO ETERNITY ★★★ A trimly told and performed antiprejudice, antiwar drama based on the life of World War II hero Guy Gabaldon, a Californian raised by Japanese-American parents. Jeffrey Hunter and Sessue Hayakawa share acting honors as the hero and the strong-minded Japanese commander who confronts him in the South Pacific. Lots of battle scenes. B&W; 132m. DIR: Phil Karlson. CAST: Jeffrey Hunter, David Janssen, Vic Damone, Patricia Owens, Sessue Hayakawa. 1960

HELL TOWN ★★1/2 Stepping up from his low-budget programmers for Republic and Monogram, John Wayne was cast in the last of Paramount's series of films based on the stories of Zane Grey. He plays a happy-go-lucky cowhand who falls in with rustlers. Also known as *Born to the West*. B&W; 50m. DIR: Charles Barton. CAST: John Wayne, Marsha Hunt, Johnny Mack Brown, Alan Ladd, James Craig, Monte Blue, Lucien Littlefield. 1938

HELL UP IN HARLEM 💗 Violent, cheaply made sequel to *Black Caesar*. Rated R. 98m. DIR: Larry Cohen. CAST: Fred Williamson, Julius W. Harris, Gloria Hendry, Margaret Avery, D'Urville Martin. 1973

HELLBENDERS, THE 💗 Story of a washed-out Confederate and his band of sons. 92m. DIR: Sergio Corbucci. CAST: Joseph Cotten, Norma Bengell, Julian Mateos, Angel Aranda. 1967

HELLBORN 💗 Only the most masochistic Ed Wood fans will want to sit through this tape. B&W; 50m. DIR: Edward D. Wood Jr. CAST: Edward D. Wood Jr., Mona McKinnon. 1952–1993

HELLBOUND ★★ Only Chuck Norris and his fists of steel can stop a Beelzebub clone set free in modern society. Rated R for violence, nudity, and language. 97m. DIR: Aaron Norris. CAST: Chuck Norris, Calvin Levels, Sheree Wilson, Christopher Neame. 1993

●**HELLCAB** ★★★ Will Kern's stage play becomes a film with most of its emotional core intact. Paul Dillon does an excellent job of steering this human-interest drama through the mean streets of Chicago, playing a cabdriver whose day is filled with all sorts of adventures, and interesting characters and situa-tions. But we hardly get to know the man behind the wheel and this keeps the film from becoming complete. Rated R for adult situations and language. 96m. DIR: Mary Cybulski, John Tintori. CAST: Paul Dillon, Gillian Anderson, John Cusack, Moira Harris, Michael Ironside, Laurie Metcalf, Julianne Moore, Kevin J. O'Connor. 1998

HELLCATS, THE 💗 Even within the lowly subgenre of biker movies, this one is the pits. Not rated, it features violence. 90m. DIR: Robert F. Slatzer. CAST: Ross Hagen, Dee Duffy. 1967

HELLCATS OF THE NAVY ★★★ This none-too-exciting drama has one thing to attract viewers: President Ronald Reagan and First Lady Nancy co-star. B&W; 82m. DIR: Nathan Juran. CAST: Ronald Reagan, Nancy Davis, Arthur Franz, Harry Lauter. 1957

HELLDORADO (1934) ★★ A penniless hitchhiker discovers a ghost town with a gold mine. The picture boasts an acclaimed director and a highly professional cast, but it is unpersuasively produced. B&W; 75m. DIR: James Cruze. CAST: Richard Arlen, Madge Evans, Henry B. Walthall, Ralph Bellamy, James Gleason, Helen Jerome Eddy. 1934

HELLDORADO (1946) ★★ Roy and the boys exercise their fists and tonsils while breaking up a gang of black-market racketeers in postwar Las Vegas. The popular rodeo forms the backdrop as Roy, Dale, and Gabby entertain the likes of singer Eddie Acuff and future Lone Ranger Clayton Moore. B&W; 70m. DIR: William Witney. CAST: Roy Rogers, George "Gabby" Hayes, Dale Evans, Bob Nolan and the Sons of the Pioneers, LeRoy Mason, Paul Harvey, Rex Lease, Eddie Acuff, Clayton Moore. 1946

HELLER IN PINK TIGHTS ★★1/2 Legendary nineteenth-century actress and love goddess Adah Issacs Menken inspired this odd film about a ragtag theatrical troupe wandering the West in the 1880s. Colorful but air-filled, it offers a busty blonde Sophia Loren with lusty Tony Quinn. 100m. DIR: George Cukor. CAST: Sophia Loren, Anthony Quinn, Margaret O'Brien, Edmund Lowe, Steve Forrest, Eileen Heckart, Ramon Novarro. 1960

HELLFIGHTERS ★★ Once again the talents of John Wayne have been squandered. The Duke is cast as a high-priced fireman sent around the world to put out dangerous oil rig fires. Even hard-core Wayne fans may wince at this one. Rated PG. 121m. DIR: Andrew V. McLaglen. CAST: John Wayne, Katharine Ross, Vera Miles, Jim Hutton, Bruce Cabot. 1969 DVD

HELLFIRE ★★★1/2 Solid, offbeat Western in which a ne'er-do-well gambler, William ("Wild Bill") Elliott, is shoved onto the path of righteousness when a preacher saves his life. A bit preachy at times, it still packs a solid wallop of entertainment. 79m. DIR: R. G. Springsteen. CAST: William Elliott, Marie Windsor, Forrest Tucker, Jim Davis, Grant Withers, Paul Fix, Denver Pyle. 1949

HELLFIRE CLUB, THE ★★ Tepid historical swashbuckler, made in England, about a dashing swordsman who is the grown-up son of one of the founders of royalty's legendary sex-and-sin fellowship. Doesn't devote enough screen time to the title organization's nefarious activities. 88m. DIR: Robert S. Baker, Monty

Berman. **CAST:** Keith Michell, Adrienne Corri, Peter Cushing. **1960**

HELLGATE ★★ A band of badly scripted teenagers on holiday search for adventure in a legendary ghost town—unfortunately peopled by the nasty living dance-hall dead. Feeble camp humor and tepid special effects sink this lightly erotic post-teen horror. Rated R. 96m. **DIR:** William A. Levey. **CAST:** Ron Palillo, Abigail Wolcott, Evan J. Klisser. **1989**

HELLHOLE 💔 A young woman witnesses her mother's murder and psychosomatically loses her memory. Rated R for violence and nudity. 90m. **DIR:** Pierre DeMoro. **CAST:** Ray Sharkey, Judy Landers, Marjoe Gortner, Edy Williams. **1985**

HELLMASTER 💔 Long-thought-dead professor John Saxon returns to his alma mater to continue his experiments turning students into mutants. The final exam has got to be a bummer. Not rated; contains horror violence. 99m. **DIR:** Douglas Schulze. **CAST:** John Saxon, David Emge. **1990**

HELLO AGAIN ★★1/2 Suburban housewife Shelley Long chokes to death on a Korean meatball only to find herself brought back to life via a magic spell cast by her wacky sister (Judith Ivey). Screenplay by Susan Isaacs. Rated PG for profanity. 95m. **DIR:** Frank Perry. **CAST:** Shelley Long, Judith Ivey, Gabriel Byrne, Corbin Bernsen, Sela Ward, Austin Pendleton. **1987**

HELLO, DOLLY! 💔 Barbra Streisand as an intrepid matchmaker. Rated G. 146m. **DIR:** Gene Kelly. **CAST:** Barbra Streisand, Walter Matthau, Michael Crawford, E. J. Peaker, Marianne McAndrew. **1969**

HELLO, FRISCO, HELLO ★★1/2 John Payne is a selfish Barbary Coast saloon owner who buys and marries his way to Nob Hill, deserting friends and a true love. A best-song Oscar for Harry Warren and Mack Gordon's "You'll Never Know." 99m. **DIR:** H. Bruce Humberstone. **CAST:** Alice Faye, John Payne, Jack Oakie, Lynn Bari, June Havoc, Laird Cregar, Ward Bond. **1943**

HELLO, MARY LOU: PROM NIGHT II 💔 Another tedious exploitation flick about a girl who returns from the grave to get revenge on her killers. Rated R for violence, nudity, and language. 96m. **DIR:** Bruce Pittman. **CAST:** Lisa Schrage, Wendy Lyon, Michael Ironside. **1987**

HELLRAISER ★★1/2 In his directing debut, Clive Barker adapts his short story and proves even the author can't necessarily bring his work to life on the screen. The story is about a man who acquires a demonic Rubik's Cube. Although imbued with marvelous visuals, the film has little of the intensity of a Barker novel. Rated R for violence, sex, and adult language. 90m. **DIR:** Clive Barker. **CAST:** Andrew Robinson, Clare Higgins, Ashley Laurence. **1987**

HELLRAISER II: HELLBOUND ★★1/2 People without skin! If that doesn't either pique your interest or turn you away, nothing will. A psychiatric patient, who is lost in a world of puzzles, unleashes the nasty Cenobites (introduced in *Hellraiser*). Clive Barker protégé Tony Randel makes everything a bit overwhelming, but it's all good, clean, gruesome fun. Rated R for gore. 96m. **DIR:** Tony Randel. **CAST:** Clare Higgins, Ashley Laurence, Kenneth Cranham. **1988**

HELLRAISER 3: HELL ON EARTH ★★★ Pinhead returns, only this time he's brought some new friends and they don't want to go back where they came from. Combine gory and (very imaginative) special effects and a slightly off-center story and you have one that should please fans, but make others sick. Rated R for profanity, simulated sex, and graphic violence. 90m. **DIR:** Anthony Hickox. **CAST:** Terry Ferrell, Doug Bradley, Paula Marshall, Kevin Bernhardt, Ashley Laurence. **1992**

HELLRAISER: BLOODLINE ★★ This fourth installment in Clive Barker's highly successful series about the dark prince of Hell was controversial before it even came out. What is left is a by-the-numbers exercise in skinnings and death that treads none of the daring ground of its predecessors. Director Alan Smithee is really special-effects artist Kevin Yagher. Rated R for violence, profanity, and gore. 86m. **DIR:** Alan Smithee. **CAST:** Doug Bradley, Bruce Ramsey, Valentina Vargas. **1996**

HELL'S ANGELS '69 ★★ Two rich kids devise a plan to rob a gambling casino by infiltrating the Hell's Angels and then using the gang to create a diversion. The plan works until the bikers retaliate. Mediocre. 97m. **DIR:** Lee Madden. **CAST:** Tom Stern, Jeremy Slate, Conny Van Dyke, Sonny Barger, Terry the Tramp. **1969**

HELL'S ANGELS FOREVER ★★1/2 A documentary on the notorious biker organization; mostly a feature-length endorsement rather than an objective profile. Early portion, tracing the Hells Angels' origins in post–World War II, working-class California, is best. Rated R for profanity. 87m. **DIR:** Richard Chase, Kevin Keating, Leon Gast. **1983**

HELL'S ANGELS ON WHEELS ★★1/2 This is one of the better 1960s biker films, most notably because Jack Nicholson has a big role in it. Not a great work by any means, but if you like biker movies. 95m. **DIR:** Richard Rush. **CAST:** Adam Roarke, Jack Nicholson, Sabrina Scharf, John Garwood, Jana Taylor. **1967**

HELL'S BRIGADE 💔 Rotten film concerning a commando raid on Hitler's Germany during World War II. 99m. **DIR:** Henry Mankiewirk. **CAST:** Jack Palance, John Douglas. **1980**

HELL'S HINGES ★★★ William S. Hart's trademark character, the good-bad man, loses his heart to the new minister's sister when she arrives in Hell's Hinges. The minister is corrupted and the church burned down, causing Hart to seek revenge. This grim story is perhaps Hart's best film, and certainly his most imitated. Silent. B&W; 65m. **DIR:** William S. Hart, Charles Swickard. **CAST:** William S. Hart, Clara Williams, Robert McKim. **1916**

HELL'S HOUSE 💔 Gangster and prison films in the 1930s had their junior counterparts. In this barely so-so example, an innocent boy does time in a harsh reformatory because he won't rat on an adult crook friend. Junior Durkin is the poor kid, Pat O'Brien is the crook—a bootlegger—and Bette Davis is his girl. B&W; 72m. **DIR:** Howard Higgin. **CAST:** Junior Durkin, Bette Davis, Pat O'Brien, Frank Coghlan Jr., Charley Grapewin, Emma Dunn. **1932**

HELLSTROM CHRONICLE, THE ★★★★ This 1971 pseudodocumentary features fantastic close-up cinematography of insects and their ilk underpinning a story line by Dr. Hellstrom (Lawrence Pressman), which contends the critters are taking over. Despite the dumb premise, *The Hellstrom Chronicle* remains a captivating film. Rated G. 90m. DIR: Walon Green. CAST: Lawrence Pressman. 1971

HELLZAPOPPIN ★★★ Olsen and Johnson's famously frantic Broadway show was filmed with inconsistent results. Like the Marx Brothers' MGM films, this is hurt by the introduction of a vapid romantic subplot, and while the two comics take every possible opportunity to make fun of it on-screen, it constantly bogs down the film. B&W; 84m. DIR: H. C. Potter. CAST: Ole Olsen, Chic Johnson, Robert Paige, Jane Frazee, Lewis Howard, Martha Raye, Mischa Auer, Elisha Cook Jr., Richard Lane, Hugh Herbert, Shemp Howard, Billy Curtis. 1941

HELP! ★★★★ Though neither as inventive nor as charming as *A Hard Day's Night*, this second collaboration between director Richard Lester and the Fab Four has energy, fun, and memorable songs. The slim plot has a bizarre religious cult trying to retrieve a sacrificial ring from Ringo. From the reverberating opening chord of the title tune, the movie sweeps you up in its irresistibly zesty spirit. 90m. DIR: Richard Lester. CAST: The Beatles, Leo McKern, Eleanor Bron, Victor Spinetti. 1965 DVD

HELTER SKELTER ★★★★ The story of Charles Manson's 1969 murder spree is vividly retold in this excellent TV movie. Steve Railsback is superb as the crazed Manson. Based on prosecutor Vincent Bugliosi's book, this is high-voltage stuff. Not rated and too intense for the kids. 114m. DIR: Tom Gries. CAST: George DiCenzo, Steve Railsback, Nancy Wolfe, Marilyn Burns. 1976

HELTER-SKELTER MURDERS, THE 🖤 Sensationalistic account of the Tate murders. Rated R for graphic violence. B&W/color; 83m. DIR: Frank Howard. CAST: Debbie Duff. 1988

HENNESSY ★★★ After his family is killed by a bomb, an Irishman plots to assassinate the Queen of England in revenge. Fairly suspenseful thriller with a sympathetic performance by Rod Steiger, though the fact that we know the queen is still alive tends to ruin the suspense. Rated PG. 103m. DIR: Don Sharp. CAST: Rod Steiger, Lee Remick, Richard Johnson, Trevor Howard, Eric Porter. 1975

HENRY IV ★★★ This Italian TV film is based on a Luigi Pirandello play. A modern aristocrat is thrown from his horse and then believes he is Emperor Henry IV. Twenty years pass and his past lover and a psychiatrist devise a plan to shake him back to reality. It's interesting, but seems long. In Italian with English subtitles. 95m. DIR: Marco Bellocchio. CAST: Marcello Mastroianni, Claudia Cardinale, Leopoldo Trieste. 1984

HENRY V (1944) ★★★★★ The first of Olivier's three major film forays into Shakespeare (the others are *Hamlet* and *Richard III*), this production blazed across screens like a meteor. A stirring, colorful film, full of sound and fury, and all the pageantry one expects from English history brought to vivid life. Olivier won an honorary Oscar for acting, directing, and producing. In a word: superb. 137m. DIR: Lau-

rence Olivier. CAST: Laurence Olivier, Robert Newton, Leslie Banks, Felix Aylmer, Renée Asherson, Leo Genn. 1944 DVD

HENRY V (1989) ★★★★★ What star-adapter-director Kenneth Branagh has done with Shakespeare's *Henry V* on screen is nothing short of miraculous. Not better, but different, than Laurence Olivier's 1944 production, Branagh's version truly does "ascend the brightest heaven of invention," as promised in the film's stunning prologue. In chronicling young King Henry's war against France, Branagh has created a Shakespearean adaptation on an epic scale and one of the best films of its kind. Rated PG for violence. 138m. DIR: Kenneth Branagh. CAST: Kenneth Branagh, Derek Jacobi, Paul Scofield, Judi Dench, Ian Holm, Emma Thompson, Robert Stephens, Geraldine McEwan, Alec McCowen. 1989 DVD

HENRY & JUNE ★★1/2 Good direction doesn't offset mediocre acting and an excruciatingly boring script in this oft-melodramatic story about expatriate author Henry Miller and his personal problems with sex. Based on Anaïs Nin's memoirs, it was the first release under the NC-17 rating code, though could have squeaked through with an R. 136m. DIR: Phil Kaufman. CAST: Fred Ward, Uma Thurman, Maria de Medeiros, Kevin Spacey, Richard E. Grant. 1990 DVD

HENRY FOOL ★★★★1/2 Henry is an unkempt, self-deluded ex-convict who moves into the basement of a home inhabited by geeky garbageman Simon Grim, his slutty sister, and their despondent mother. He is writing a lengthy "confession" and convinces Simon to capture his own thoughts on paper. Simon does and becomes a media sensation in this profane seriocomic myth about friendship, artistic license, celebrity, and cultural trends. Rated R for language, sexuality, and adult themes. 137m. DIR: Hal Hartley. CAST: Thomas Jay Ryan, James Urbaniak, Parker Posey, Maria Porter, Kevin Corrigan. 1998

HENRY MILLER ODYSSEY ★★★★ This film biography is regulation for all fans and those who would know more about one of America's most controversial writers. Alive with Miller and close friends, it is a finely photographed documentary revealing his opinions and reflections, innate gentleness, beguiling charm, and vigorous lust for living. 60m. DIR: Robert Snyder. CAST: Henry Miller, Lawrence Durrell, Anaïs Nin, Alfred Perles. 1969

HENRY: PORTRAIT OF A SERIAL KILLER ★★★★ Chillingly real and brutally explicit, this profile of a murderous drifter and his former prison pal emerges as a quasi-documentary that dwells so deep in the psychopathic mind of its title character one almost expects disclaimers to parade across the screen. Not rated, but filled with violence and raw brutality. 90m. DIR: John McNaughton. CAST: Michael Rooker. 1990 DVD

HER ALIBI ★★★ This clever comedy-mystery presents Tom Selleck as a suspense writer who provides an alibi for a beautiful murder suspect (Paulina Porizkova). Fans of director Bruce Beresford may think this ditty is beneath him, but only a curmudgeon can resist its daffy charms. Rated PG for proanity and comic violence. 110m. DIR: Bruce Beresford. CAST: Tom Selleck, Paulina Porizkova, William Daniels, Tess Harper, Patrick Wayne, Hurd Hatfield. 1989 DVD

HERBIE GOES BANANAS ★★1/2 This is the corniest and least funny of Disney's "Love Bug" series. This time Herbie is headed for Brazil to compete in the Grand Primio. Rated G. 93m. DIR: Vincent McEveety. CAST: Cloris Leachman, Charles Martin Smith, John Vernon, Stephan W. Burns, Harvey Korman. 1980

HERBIE GOES TO MONTE CARLO ★★★1/2 Herbie the VW falls in love with a sports car as they compete in a race from Paris to Monte Carlo. There are lots of laughs in this one. Rated G. 104m. DIR: Vincent McEveety. CAST: Dean Jones, Don Knotts, Julie Sommars, Eric Braeden, Roy Kinnear, Jacque Marin. 1977

HERBIE RIDES AGAIN ★★★1/2 This Disney comedy-adventure is a sequel to *The Love Bug*. This time, Helen Hayes, Ken Berry, and Stephanie Powers depend on Herbie, the magical Volkswagen, to save them from an evil Keenan Wynn. Rated G. 88m. DIR: Robert Stevenson. CAST: Helen Hayes, Ken Berry, Stefanie Powers, Keenan Wynn. 1974

HERCULES (1959) ★★1/2 The first and still the best of the Italian-made epics based on the mythical superhero. Steve Reeves looks perfect in the part as Hercules out to win over his true love, the ravishing Sylva Koscina. Some nice action scenes. 107m. DIR: Pietro Francisci. CAST: Steve Reeves, Sylva Koscina, Ivo Garrani. 1959

HERCULES (1983) 🎬 Lou Ferrigno as the most famous muscle man of them all. Rated PG for violence. 98m. DIR: Lewis Coates. CAST: Lou Ferrigno, Sybil Danning, Brad Harris, Rossana Podesta. 1983

HERCULES AND THE LOST KINGDOM ★★★ First of the four TV movies that led to the hit series *Hercules: The Legendary Journeys*, this film introduces the son of Zeus to a new generation by adding wacky camera angles and modern views to the proceedings. Here, Hercules must save a lost kingdom from the tyrannous rule of his stepmother Hera. Mindless but enjoyable fun that the whole family can watch. Rated PG for violence. 91m. DIR: Harley Cokliss. CAST: Kevin Sorbo, Anthony Quinn, Renee O'Connor, Eric Close. 1994

HERCULES AND THE AMAZON WOMEN ★★★ Second of the TV movies based on the adventures of the legendary strongman introduces Herc to the feminist ways of the Amazons, a race of warrior women. It's a battle of the sexes with Hercules in the middle trying to prove that men and women can live together. Once again, Anthony Quinn is a delight to watch as Zeus, the king of the gods. Rated PG for violence and suggested sex. 87m. DIR: Bill L. Norton. CAST: Kevin Sorbo, Anthony Quinn, Roma Downey, Lucy Lawless, Michael Hurst. 1994

HERCULES AND THE CIRCLE OF FIRE ★★★1/2 Exciting, old-fashioned adventure tale finds Hercules fighting to save humanity lest the torch of life be extinguished by Hera. For the third outing as Hercules, Kevin Sorbo really slips into the role and makes it his own, combining just the right amount of heroics, humor, and charm. The special effects and

fight scenes are superb, and the influence of producer Sam Raimi shows in what is probably the best of the four movies. Rated PG for violence. 89m. DIR: Doug Lefler. CAST: Kevin Sorbo, Anthony Quinn, Tawny Kitaen. 1994

HERCULES IN THE UNDERWORLD ★★★ Fourth and final installment in the TV movies about the exploits of the legendary strongman pits Hercules against medusas and Cerberus in the underworld. Kevin Sorbo really gets the hang of his role as Hercules here, and Anthony Quinn is a wonderful Zeus. Rated PG for violence and some frightening scenes. 91m. DIR: Bill L. Norton. CAST: Kevin Sorbo, Anthony Quinn, Tawny Kitaen, Marley Shelton, Timothy Balme, Michael Hurst. 1994

HERCULES AND THE CAPTIVE WOMEN ★★1/2 Hercules, his stowaway son, the King of Thebes, and a midget sail toward the lost city of Atlantis searching for the answers to a string of mysterious occurrences. Cornball, campy, and a good deal of fun. An Italian and French production, but dubbed in English. Not rated. 95m. DIR: Vittorio Cottafavi. CAST: Reg Park, Fay Spain. 1963

HERCULES (ANIMATED) (1997) ★★★★ Hercules is very much the hero of his finger-snapping signature tune and a larger-than-life archetype who demands hyperbole and excess. Sensational contribution by lyricist David Zippel, who teams with composer and Academy Award magnet Alan Menken. Credit also goes to James Woods, tremendous with his vocal characterization of the villain, Hades. He's matched by Broadway star Susan Egan as Meg, a slinky femme fatale with husky radiance and sex appeal. Rated G; suitable for all ages. 86m. DIR: John Musker, Ron Clements. 1997 DVD

HERCULES GOES BANANAS 🎬 Ridiculous piece of celluloid starring a very young Arnold Schwarzenegger as Hercules. 73m. DIR: Arthur Allan Seidelman. CAST: Arnold Schwarzenegger, Arnold Stang. 1972

HERCULES IN THE HAUNTED WORLD ★★★ Easily the best of the many *Hercules* sequels, because it was designed and directed by famed Italian genre master Mario Bava (*Black Sabbath*). Ignore the brief, dopey comic relief and enjoy the escapist, action-filled plot, which sends Hercules on a journey through Hades. Breathtaking visuals. 83m. DIR: Mario Bava. CAST: Reg Park, Christopher Lee. 1961

HERCULES, PRISONER OF EVIL ★★ Not bad for its type, this sword-and-sandal action spectacle is really part of the *Ursus* subgenre of Italian muscleman movies; the Hercules moniker was slapped on when it was dubbed and released straight to U.S. TV. 90m. DIR: Anthony M. Dawson. CAST: Reg Park, Ettore Manni. 1964

HERCULES UNCHAINED ★★ When the god of muscles sets his little mind on something, don't get in his way! In this one, he's out to rescue his lady fair. It's a silly but diverting adventure. Steve Reeves is still the best Hercules on film, dubbed voice and all. 101m. DIR: Pietro Francisci. CAST: Steve Reeves, Sylva Koscina, Primo Carnera, Sylvia Lopez. 1960

HERE COME THE CO-EDS ★★1/2 Standard-issue Abbott and Costello romp of the mid-1940s, with our heroes cast as custodians of a prim girls' academy.

High energy, low IQ comedy. B&W; 87m. **DIR:** Jean Yarbrough. **CAST:** Bud Abbott, Lou Costello, Peggy Ryan, Martha O'Driscoll, Lon Chaney Jr. **1945**

HERE COME THE GIRLS ★★★ Bumbling Bob Hope is taken from the chorus and made the star of a Broadway show, unaware he is a decoy for a jealous slasher infatuated with the leading lady. Some good gags and lots of musical numbers. 78m. **DIR:** Claude Binyon. **CAST:** Bob Hope, Arlene Dahl, Tony Martin, Rosemary Clooney, Millard Mitchell, William Demarest, Fred Clark, Robert Strauss. **1953**

HERE COME THE WAVES ★★★1/2 Bing Crosby stars as a famous singer who enlists in the navy with best friend Sonny Tufts. A fun musical that features Betty Hutton as twins—so that both leading men get the girl. "Accentuate the Positive" was written for this film. B&W; 100m. **DIR:** Mark Sandrich. **CAST:** Bing Crosby, Betty Hutton, Sonny Tufts. **1944**

HERE COMES MR. JORDAN ★★★★★ We all know that bureaucracy can botch up almost anything. Well, the bureaucrats of heaven can really throw a lulu at boxer Joe Pendleton (Robert Montgomery). The heavenly administrators have called Joe up before his time, and they've got to set things straight. B&W; 93m. **DIR:** Alexander Hall. **CAST:** Robert Montgomery, Evelyn Keyes, Claude Rains, Rita Johnson, Edward Everett Horton, James Gleason. **1941**

HERE COMES SANTA CLAUS 🎬 Two kids visit Santa at the North Pole to make a personal plea for the return of the boy's parents on Christmas. 78m. **DIR:** Christian Gion. **CAST:** Karen Cheryl, Armand Meffre. **1984**

HERE COMES THE GROOM ★★★ Bing Crosby stars as a reporter returning from France with two war orphans. Jane Wyman finds herself torn between Crosby and wealthy Franchot Tone. Director Frank Capra keeps the pace brisk and adds to an otherwise familiar tale. 114m. **DIR:** Frank Capra. **CAST:** Bing Crosby, Jane Wyman, Alexis Smith, Franchot Tone. **1951**

HERE COMES TROUBLE ★★★ Jewel thief Mona Barrie mistakenly involves Paul Kelly in a crime when she gives him a cigarette case containing some loot. A mixture of comedy and crime—a perfect hour-long time filler. B&W; 62m. **DIR:** Lewis Seiler. **CAST:** Paul Kelly, Arline Judge, Mona Barrie, Gregory Ratoff. **1936**

◆**HERE ON EARTH** ★★1/2 A rich kid at an East Coast prep school falls for a working-class girl despite the disapproval of his father. If that sounds familiar, it's because the film is a blatant rip-off of *Love Story*, right down to the mysterious fatal disease. The appealing young stars, a good supporting cast, and nice scenery make the film a tolerable tearjerker. Rated PG-13 for mild profanity. 97m. **DIR:** Mark Piznarski. **CAST:** Chris Klein, LeeLee Sobieski, Josh Hartnett, Bruce Greenwood, Annette O'Toole, Annie Corley, Stuart Wilson, Elaine Hendrix, Michael Rooker. **2000**

HERITAGE OF THE DESERT ★★★ Donald Woods comes West to claim an inheritance and is soon mixed up with outlaws. Best of three screen versions based on the Zane Grey novel. B&W; 74m. **DIR:** Lesley Selander. **CAST:** Donald Woods, Russell Hayden, Evelyn Venable, Sidney Toler. **1939**

HERO, THE (1971) ★★ Richard Harris distinguishes himself neither as actor nor as director in this mawkish sports drama. He plays a soccer star getting on in years who agrees to throw a game for money. Not the freshest of story lines. Not rated. 97m. **DIR:** Richard Harris. **CAST:** Richard Harris, Romy Schneider, Kim Burfield. **1971**

HERO (1992) ★★★★1/2 This saucy spin on Frank Capra's *Meet John Doe* is an acerbic—and often tremendously funny—indictment of American heroworship. Andy Garcia is revered for having rescued passengers from a stricken airplane; unfortunately, he's taking credit for an act actually performed by small-potatoes criminal Dustin Hoffman (who, looking more ferret-like than ever, is simply priceless). Rated PG-13 for profanity. 116m. **DIR:** Stephen Frears. **CAST:** Dustin Hoffman, Geena Davis, Andy Garcia, Joan Cusack, Chevy Chase, Tom Arnold. **1992 DVD**

HERO AIN'T NOTHIN' BUT A SANDWICH, A ★★1/2 Heartfelt, uneven black soap opera—a typical latter-day Ralph Nelson production. The director of *Lilies of the Field* lays it on thick in this sentimental adaptation of Alice Childress's book about a black ghetto teen's drug problem. 105m. **DIR:** Ralph Nelson. **CAST:** Cicely Tyson, Paul Winfield, Larry B. Scott, Glynn Turman. **1978**

HERO AND THE TERROR ★★1/2 Chuck Norris gives a good performance in this otherwise disappointing thriller. He's a police officer suffering from deep trauma after confronting a brutal, demented killer called the Terror (Jack O'Halloran). When the Terror escapes from a mental ward, our hero must battle the monster again. Rated R for violence and profanity. 90m. **DIR:** William Tannen. **CAST:** Chuck Norris, Jack O'Halloran, Brynn Thayer, Jeffrey Kramer, Steve James. **1988**

HERO AT LARGE ★★★1/2 In this enjoyably lightweight film, John Ritter plays Steve Nichols, an out-of-work actor who takes a part-time job to promote a movie about a crusading superhero, *Captain Avenger*. Rated PG. 98m. **DIR:** Martin Davidson. **CAST:** John Ritter, Anne Archer, Bert Convy, Kevin McCarthy. **1980**

HEROES ★★★1/2 Henry Winkler is excellent in this compelling story of a confused Vietnam vet traveling cross-country to meet a few of his old war buddies. MCA Home Video has elected to alter the film's closing theme for this release. Removing the emotionally charged "Carry on Wayward Son" by Kansas in favor of a teary generic tune somewhat diminishes the overall impact of the movie. Rated PG for mild language and violence. 113m. **DIR:** Jeremy Paul Kagan. **CAST:** Henry Winkler, Sally Field, Harrison Ford, Val Avery. **1977**

HEROES DIE YOUNG 🎬 A suicide squad goes behind enemy lines to knock out an oil field in German-occupied Romania. Not rated. B&W; 76m. **DIR:** Gerald S. Shepard. **CAST:** Erika Peters, Scott Borland. **1960**

HEROES FOR SALE ★★★ Warner Bros., noted for gangster films, also turned out many social conscience dramas during the Great Depression, and this is a good one. Richard Barthelmess, more a Poor Soul than an Everyman, suffers morphine addiction caused by war injuries, the loss of a business in the industrial revolution, the death of his wife in a labor riot, and unjust imprisonment as a radical. Grim going, but fine performances. B&W; 71m. **DIR:** William Wellman. **CAST:** Richard Barthelmess, Aline MacMahon, Loretta Young. **1933**

HEROES OF DESERT STORM ★★1/2 Flag-waving, made-for-TV movie looks at the men (and women) who fought in Desert Storm. Pedestrian effort shows how quick it was made to cash in on patriotism. 93m. **DIR:** Don Ohlmeyer. **CAST:** Daniel Baldwin, Angela Bassett, Marshall Bell, Kris Kamm, Tim Russ. **1992**

HEROES OF THE HEART ★★★ When an old woman tells the residents of a trailer park she has been given the power by God to make their dreams come true, they discuss with each other just what their dreams are. Odd but intriguing comedy-drama. Not rated; contains profanity. 101m. **DIR:** Daniel Boyd. **CAST:** Lina Basquette, Larry Groce, John McIntire. **1995**

HEROES STAND ALONE ★★★ A plane on a secret mission is shot down behind enemy lines. The not so distant future is the setting for this Vietnam-style war movie. Not rated but contains violence and nudity. 83m. **DIR:** Mark Griffiths. **CAST:** Chad Everett, Bradford Dillman. **1990**

HEROIC LEGEND OF ARISLAN ★★★ An interesting tale and appealing characters blend well in this East-meets-West animated hybrid where European-style knights (with Japanese-style hearts) pit their swords against evil. Very good animation. Dubbed in English. Not rated; contains violence. 59m. each. **DIR:** Mamoru Hamatsu. **1992 DVD**

HESTER STREET ★★★★ Beautifully filmed look at the Jewish community in nineteenth-century New York City. Film focuses on the relationship of a young couple, he turning his back on the old Jewish ways while she fights to hold on to them. Fine performances and great attention to period detail make this very enjoyable. Rated PG. B&W; 92m. **DIR:** Joan Micklin Silver. **CAST:** Carol Kane, Steven Keats, Mel Howard. **1975**

HEXED ★★ A hotel desk clerk with pathological liar tendencies gets mixed up in a bizarre twist of mistaken identity. This wannabe curiosity comedy from the creator of the TV series *Sledge Hammer* doesn't quite know the difference between being outrageous and being absolutely tasteless. Rated R for violence, simulated sex, and language. 100m. **DIR:** Alan Spencer. **CAST:** Arye Gross, Claudia Christian, Adrienne Shelly, Norman Fell, Michael E. Knight, Ray Baker. **1993**

HEY ABBOTT! ★★★★ This is a hilarious anthology of high points from Abbott and Costello television programs. Narrated by Milton Berle, the distillation includes the now-legendary duo's classic routines: "Who's on First?," "Oyster Stew," "Floogle Street," and "The Birthday Party." B&W; 76m. **DIR:** Jim Gates. **CAST:** Bud Abbott, Lou Costello, Joe Besser, Phil Silvers, Steve Allen. **1978**

HEY, BABU RIBA ★★★1/2 Yugoslav version of *American Graffiti*. Poignant, funny reminiscence of four boys and a girl growing up in the early Fifties. The film has an easy charm. In Serbo-Croatian with English subtitles. Rated R for mild profanity, violence, and sex. 109m. **DIR:** Javan Acin. **CAST:** Gala Videnovic. **1986**

HEY GOOD LOOKIN' 🖤 Boring animated film about street gangs of New York City during the 1950s. Rated R. 86m. **DIR:** Ralph Bakshi. **1983**

HEY, I'M ALIVE! ★★1/2 TV movie based on a true story of two people who survived a plane crash in the Yukon, then struggled to stay alive until rescuers could locate them. Well-acted, though nothing you haven't seen before. 74m. **DIR:** Lawrence Schiller. **CAST:** Edward Asner, Sally Struthers. **1975**

HEY THERE, IT'S YOGI BEAR ★★★ With this movie, Hanna-Barbera Studios made the jump from TV to feature-length cartoon. The result is consistently pleasant. Mel Blanc, J. Pat O'Malley, Julie Bennett, Daws Butler, Don Messick (voices). Rated G. 89m. **DIR:** William Hanna, Joseph Barbera. **1964**

HI LIFE ★★ Eric Stoltz plays an unemployed actor who desperately needs $900 to pay off a loan shark or have his legs broken. A lie he creates in order to get the money from his girlfriend takes on a life all its own, putting the actor in an unwelcome spotlight. Quaint, but not as Runyonesque as writer-director Roger Hedden wants us to believe. Rated R for language. 82m. **DIR:** Roger Hedden. **CAST:** Eric Stoltz, Daryl Hannah, Campbell Scott, Charles Durning, Peter Riegert, Moira Kelly. **1998 DVD**

HI MOM ★★★ Robert De Niro reprises his role as a Vietnam vet in this award-winning comedy under the direction of a young Brian De Palma. In this semi-sequel to *Greetings*, De Niro continues his adventures as an amateur filmmaker in Greenwich Village. Rated R for nudity and profanity. 87m. **DIR:** Brian De Palma. **CAST:** Robert De Niro, Jennifer Salt, Allen Garfield. **1970**

HIDDEN, THE ★★★1/2 When a bizarre series of crimes wreaks havoc in Los Angeles, police detective Michael Nouri finds himself paired with an FBI agent (Kyle MacLachlan) whose behavior becomes increasingly strange as they pursue what may be an alien intruder. This hybrid science-fiction–adventure will delight those who like their entertainment unpredictable. Rated R for violence, nudity, and profanity. 97m. **DIR:** Jack Sholder. **CAST:** Michael Nouri, Kyle MacLachlan, Ed O'Ross, Clu Gulager, Claudia Christian, Clarence Felder. **1987 DVD**

HIDDEN II, THE ★★ Poor sequel stars Raphael Sbarge as an intergalactic cop tracking down a particularly nasty alien who likes to jump from body to body, leaving behind a pile of corpses and a frustrated police force. While the special effects are up to par, film takes way too long to get up to speed, relying on a cameo by original star Michael Nouri to tie the two films together. Rated R for violence, language, and nudity. 95m. **DIR:** Seth Pinsker. **CAST:** Raphael Sbarge, Kate Hode, Michael Nouri. **1993**

HIDDEN AGENDA ★★★★ Frances McDormand is a member of a panel investigating British atrocities in Northern Ireland who is caught up in the cover-up of the death of her boyfriend at the hands of British soldiers. This is a wonderful conspiracy flick concerning the rise to power of British Prime Minister Margaret Thatcher. An added touch of realism is supplied by director Kenneth Loach's documentary-style filmmaking. Rated R for violence and profanity. 105m. **DIR:** Kenneth Loach. **CAST:** Frances McDormand, Brian Cox, Brad Dourif, Mai Zetterling. **1990 DVD**

HIDDEN ASSASSIN ★★ Action fans will most appreciate this routine thriller about a U.S. marshal sent to Prague to apprehend an assassin. He immediately suspects a professional hit woman and before long begins to fall for his prey. Rated R for violence, profanity, and nudity. 88m. **DIR:** Ted Kotcheff. **CAST:** Dolph Lundgren, Maruschka Detmers, John Ashton, Assumpta Serna. **1994**

HIDDEN FEARS ★★ After she witnesses her husband's murder, a woman (Meg Foster) tries to block it out, but those memories have come back to haunt her, forcing her to remember what she saw. And she realizes that the killers are still looking for her. A mundane exercise in make-believe. Not rated; contains violence. 90m. **DIR:** Jean Bodon. **CAST:** Meg Foster, Frederic Forrest, Bever-Leigh Banfield, Wally Taylor. **1992**

HIDDEN FORTRESS, THE ★★★★★ Toshiro Mifune stars in this recently reconstructed, uncut, and immensely entertaining 1958 Japanese period epic directed by Akira Kurosawa. George Lucas has openly admitted the film's influence on his *Star Wars* trilogy. *Hidden Fortress* deals with a strong-willed princess (à la Carrie Fisher in the space fantasy) and her wise, sword-wielding protector (Mifune in the role adapted for Alec Guinness). In Japanese with English subtitles. Not rated, the film has violence. B&W; 126m. **DIR:** Akira Kurosawa. **CAST:** Toshiro Mifune, Minoru Chiaki. **1958**

HIDDEN GOLD ★★★ Hopalong Cassidy takes the job of ranch foreman for a girl to stop a crook who wants to steal a gold mine. B&W; 61m. **DIR:** Lesley Selander. **CAST:** William Boyd, Russell Hayden, Britt Wood, Roy Barcroft, Ruth Rogers. **1940**

HIDDEN IN AMERICA ★★★★ Beau Bridges gives a devastatingly real performance as a blue-collar single father of two trying to make ends meet after losing his job. Too proud to accept help from a compassionate doctor, Bridges obsesses on the role of besieged martyr ... until malnutrition threatens his young daughter. Both kids are superb. Coproducer Jeff Bridges orchestrated this film to help raise awareness of a growing problem. Rated PG for intensity. 95m. **DIR:** Martin Bell. **CAST:** Beau Bridges, Bruce Davison, Shelton Dane, Jena Malone, Alice Krige, Josef Sommer, Frances McDormand, Jeff Bridges. **1996**

HIDDEN OBSESSION ★★ A news anchorwoman, stalked by an obsessive fan, falls for the likable deputy next door, but is he really what he seems? Slow. Rated R for nudity, violence, and simulated sex. 92m. **DIR:** John Stewart. **CAST:** Jan-Michael Vincent, Heather Thomas, Nicholas Celozzi. **1993**

HIDDEN VALLEY OUTLAWS ★★★★ Marshall Bill Elliott is duped by an outlaw leader—but only for a while—as he searches for the Whistler, an unemotional killer who whistles while he robs and plunders. B&W; 54m. **DIR:** Howard Bretherton. **CAST:** William Elliott, George "Gabby" Hayes, Anne Jeffreys, Roy Barcroft, LeRoy Mason. **1944**

HIDE AND GO SHRIEK ★★ Slasher film that's a cut above the others because of the acting. Eight high school seniors, four boys and four girls, celebrate their graduation by partying in a deserted furniture store. Their plans are interrupted by a psychotic killer. Not rated, contains nudity and extreme violence. 94m. **DIR:** Skip Schoolnik. **CAST:** George Thomas, Brittain Frye. **1987**

•**HIDE & SEEK** ♦ Daryl Hannah and Bruce Greenwood play a couple whose idyllic life is turned upside down when a deranged couple kidnap the pregnant Hannah to raise her child as their own. Absolutely zero thrills or emotional payoffs in this direct-to-video stiff. Rated R for adult situations, language, and violence. 100m. **DIR:** Sidney J. Furie. **CAST:** Daryl Hannah, Bruce Greenwood, Jennifer Tilly, Vincent Gallo. **1999**

HIDE IN PLAIN SIGHT ★★★1/2 James Caan is a tire factory laborer whose former wife marries a two-bit hoodlum. The hood turns informant and, under the Witness Relocation Program, is given a secret identity. Caan's former wife and their two children are spirited off to points unknown. Caan's subsequent quest for his kids becomes a one-man-against-the-system crusade in this watchable movie. Rated PG. 98m. **DIR:** James Caan. **CAST:** James Caan, Jill Eikenberry, Robert Viharo, Joe Grifasi. **1980**

HIDEAWAY ★★★ Good cast gets lost in this special effects–heavy thriller. What starts off promisingly enough succumbs to director Brett Leonard's obsession with computer imagery. Those images are used to convey the psychic link Jeff Goldblum shares with a serial killer. Thanks to a life-after-death experience, Goldblum sees everything the killer sees, including the stalking of his daughter, played by Alicia Silverstone. Rated R for violence, language, and nudity. 103m. **DIR:** Brett Leonard. **CAST:** Jeff Goldblum, Christine Lahti, Alicia Silverstone, Rae Dawn Chong, Jeremy Sisto, Alfred Molina. **1995**

HIDEAWAYS, THE ★★★ Two bored suburban kids spend a week hiding out in the Metropolitan Museum of Art. Interested in one of the statues, the duo tracks down its donor, an eccentric rich woman (Ingrid Bergman) who lives in a mansion in New Jersey. Fanciful tale won't appeal to all children, but it has a legion of admirers. Originally titled *From the Mixed-Up Files of Mrs. Basil E. Frankweiler*. Rated G. 105m. **DIR:** Fielder Cook. **CAST:** Ingrid Bergman, Sally Prager, Johnny Doran, George Rose, Richard Mulligan, Madeline Kahn. **1973**

HIDEOUS ★★ A monster born from toxic waste becomes the prize for a collector of oddities, who finds his latest acquisition is capable of mutating into little ferocious monsters who don't take kindly to strangers. Sick special effects and a sense of morbid fun save this from becoming an extended joke. Rated R for language, nudity, and violence. 82m. **DIR:** Charles Band. **CAST:** Michael Citriniti, Rhonda Griffin, Mel Johnson Jr., Tracie May. **1997 DVD**

HIDEOUS KINKY ★★★1/2 Single mother and her two young daughters swap a bleak existence in London for the wonders of 1972 Morocco in this exotic drama. The mother seeks self-discovery and wants her daughters to embrace a life of adventure, even as they struggle with abandonment issues. Then a street performer becomes lover, father figure, and mentor to the clan. Rated R for language, nudity, and sexual content. 101m. **DIR:** Gillies MacKinnon. **CAST:** Kate Winslet, Carrie Mullan, Bella Riza, Said Taghmaoui. **1999 DVD**

HIDEOUS SUN DEMON, THE 🎞 Robert Clarke directed and also stars as the scientist turned into a lizard-like monster by radiation. B&W; 74m. **DIR:** Robert Clarke. **CAST:** Robert Clarke, Patricia Manning. **1959 DVD**

HIDER IN THE HOUSE ★★ Unfortunately Gary Busey's wonderful portrayal of an ex-convict who builds a secret room in a stranger's house is not enough to save this poorly written film. Good cast, but just too unbelievable. Rated R for violence. 109m. **DIR:** Matthew Patrick. **CAST:** Gary Busey, Mimi Rogers, Michael McKean, Elizabeth Ruscio, Bruce Glover. **1989**

HIDING OUT ★★ Jon Cryer does some top-notch acting in this comedy-drama, and screenwriters Joe Menosky and Jeff Rothberg avoid the obvious clichés in their story of a Boston stockbroker (Cryer) hiding from the mob in a suburban Delaware high school. The result, however, is a collection of bits and pieces rather than a cohesive whole. Rated PG-13 for profanity and violence. 98m. **DIR:** Bob Giraldi. **CAST:** Jon Cryer, Keith Coogan, Annabeth Gish, Oliver Cotton, Claude Brooks, Ned Eisenberg. **1987**

HIDING PLACE, THE ★★1/2 A professional cast gives depth and feeling to this true story of two Dutch women who are sent to a concentration camp for hiding Jews from the Nazis during World War II. This film was produced by Reverend Billy Graham's Evangelistic Association. 145m. **DIR:** James F. Collier. **CAST:** Julie Harris, Eileen Heckart, Arthur O'Connell. **1975**

HIGH AND LOW ★★★★★ From a simple but exquisitely devised detective story, Akira Kurosawa builds a stunning work of insight, humor, suspense, and social commentary. Toshiro Mifune is the businessman who must decide if he will pay a ransom to kidnappers who have taken his chauffeur's young son by mistake. A masterwork, featuring superb acting by two of the giants of Japanese cinema, Mifune and Tatsuya Nakadai. Based on Ed McBain's 87th Precinct novel *King's Ransom*. In Japanese with English subtitles. B&W; 143m. **DIR:** Akira Kurosawa. **CAST:** Toshiro Mifune, Tatsuya Nakadai, Tatsuya Mihashi, Tsutomu Yamazaki, Takashi Shimura. **1963 DVD**

HIGH AND THE MIGHTY, THE ★★★1/2 John Wayne stars as Dan Roman, a veteran pilot with a tragic past. Although slow-going at times, this *Grand Hotel* in the air has more than enough fine moments generated by a cast of familiar faces to keep the viewer's interest. 147m. **DIR:** William Wellman. **CAST:** John Wayne, Claire Trevor, Laraine Day, Robert Stack, Jan Sterling, Phil Harris, Robert Newton, David Brian, Paul Kelly, Sidney Blackmer, Julie Bishop, John Howard, Wally Brown, Ann Doran, John Qualen, Paul Fix, George Chandler, Douglas Dowley, Regis Toomey,

Carl "Alfalfa" Switzer, William Schallert, Karen Sharpe, John Smith. **1954**

HIGH ANXIETY ★★ Mel Brooks successfully spoofed the horror film with *Young Frankenstein* and the Western with *Blazing Saddles*. However, this takeoff of the Alfred Hitchcock suspense movies falls miserably flat. Rated PG. 94m. **DIR:** Mel Brooks. **CAST:** Mel Brooks, Madeline Kahn, Cloris Leachman, Harvey Korman, Dick Van Patten, Ron Carey. **1977**

HIGH ART ★★★★ A devastating yet natural performance by Ally Sheedy makes this a worthwhile movie, even for some not normally enchanted by skinny lesbian junkies talking about semiotics. Sheedy, the once-great photographer for whom art and love are unbearably painful, is seduced back to work by a young magazine editor, with dire consequences for both women and anyone who cares for either of them. Rated R for skinny lesbian junkie stuff. 101m. **DIR:** Lisa Cholodenko. **CAST:** Ally Sheedy, Radha Mitchell, Patricia Clarkson. **1998**

HIGH-BALLIN' ★★ Peter Fonda and Jerry Reed are good old boys squaring off against the bad boss of a rival trucking company. The film has enough action and humor to make it a passable entertainment. Helen Shaver is its most provocative element. Rated PG. 100m. **DIR:** Peter Carter. **CAST:** Peter Fonda, Jerry Reed, Helen Shaver, Chris Wiggins, David Ferry. **1978**

HIGH COMMAND, THE ★★★ Rebellion, a new murder, and a 16-year-old killing absorb the interest of officers and men at an isolated British outpost on an island off the coast of Africa during the fading days of the British empire. B&W; 84m. **DIR:** Thorold Dickinson. **CAST:** Lionel Atwill, Lucie Mannheim, James Mason. **1937**

HIGH COUNTRY, THE ★★ So-so production values drag down this tale of an escaping convict (Timothy Bottoms) and a wide-eyed girl (Linda Purl) in the Canadian Rockies. It's a clichéd story, although Bottoms turns in his usual accomplished performance. Not rated, but has violence and brief nudity. 99m. **DIR:** Harvey Hart. **CAST:** Timothy Bottoms, Linda Purl, George Sims, Jim Lawrence, Bill Berry, Walter Mills. **1980**

HIGH CRIME ★★ Narcotics cop vs. Mafia kingpin in the picturesque Italian seaport of Genoa. Full of action, but no surprises. Rated PG. 100m. **DIR:** Enzo G. Castellari. **CAST:** Franco Nero, James Whitmore, Fernando Rey. **1973**

HIGH DESERT KILL ★★ A group of deer hunters are stalked, a la *Predator*, in this third-rate knockoff. Marc Singer and Anthony Geary meet old man Chuck Connors in the high desert of Arizona and soon find the only animals left in their area are themselves. Made for cable. 93m. **DIR:** Harry Falk. **CAST:** Marc Singer, Anthony Geary, Chuck Connors, Micah Grant. **1989**

◆HIGH FIDELITY ★★★★ Spin this baby! *High Fidelity* is both a primer on the agonies of modern love and a keenly observed examination of music geeks and their universe. In this stream-of-consciousness study of one man's attempt to determine why his relationships never last, John Cusack is mocking, analytical, and self-deprecating. He becomes a turn-of-the-new-century Everyman: a likable cad in a comfortable rut, who wonders if life is moving on without him. Rarely has a late-entry approach to adulthood been portrayed so engagingly and convincingly. The screenplay, adapted by D. V. DeVincentis, Steve Pink, and Cusack, is based on Nick Hornby's novel. Rated R for profanity. 107m. **DIR:** Stephen Frears. **CAST:** John Cusack, Iben Hjejle, Todd Louiso, Jack Black, Lisa Bonet, Catherine Zeta-Jones, Joan Cusack, Tim Robbins, Lili Taylor, Sara Gilbert. **2000**

HIGH HEELS (1972) ★★★ A French comedy to make you chuckle more often than not. A medical student marries the homely daughter of a hospital president to ensure himself a job. In French with English subtitles. Not rated, but recommended for viewers over 18 years of age. 90m. **DIR:** Claude Chabrol. **CAST:** Laura Antonelli, Jean-Paul Belmondo, Mia Farrow. **1972**

HIGH HEELS (1992) ★★★★ In this black comedy, the incandescent Victoria Abril plays the neurotic daughter of a self-absorbed film and stage star. When the mother returns to Spain after several years in Mexico, both women find themselves suspects in a murder investigation. It's funny, suspenseful, and oh-so-sexy. In Spanish with English subtitles. Not rated; the film has nudity, simulated sex, and violence. 115m. **DIR:** Pedro Almodóvar. **CAST:** Victoria Abril, Marisa Paredes, Miguel Bosé. **1991**

HIGH HOPES ★★★★★ A biting satire of Margaret Thatcher's England, as viewed by three distinct, combative couples in modern London. Ruth Sheen and Philip Davis are memorable as two latter-day hippie leftists who name their cactus Thatcher because it's a pain in the you-know-where. 100m. **DIR:** Mike Leigh. **CAST:** Ruth Sheen, Philip Davis. **1989**

HIGH NOON ★★★★★ Gary Cooper won his second Oscar for his role of the abandoned lawman in this classic Western. It's the sheriff's wedding day, and the head of an outlaw band, who has sworn vengeance against him, is due to arrive in town at high noon. When Cooper turns to his fellow townspeople for help, no one comes forward. The suspense of this movie keeps snowballing as the clock ticks ever closer to noon. B&W; 84m. **DIR:** Fred Zinnemann. **CAST:** Gary Cooper, Grace Kelly, Lloyd Bridges, Thomas Mitchell, Katy Jurado, Otto Kruger, Lon Chaney Jr. **1952 DVD**

HIGH NOON, PART TWO 💔 This is a poor attempt at a sequel. 100m. **DIR:** Jerry Jameson. **CAST:** Lee Majors, David Carradine, J. A. Preston, Pernell Roberts, M. Emmet Walsh. **1980**

HIGH PLAINS DRIFTER ★★★ Star-director Clint Eastwood tried to revive the soggy spaghetti Western genre one more time, with watchable results. Eastwood comes to a frontier town just in time to make sure its sleazy citizens are all but wiped out by a trio of revenge-seeking outlaws. Although atmospheric, it's also confusing and sometimes just downright nasty. Rated R for violence, profanity, and suggested sex. 105m. **DIR:** Clint Eastwood. **CAST:** Clint Eastwood, Verna Bloom, Marianna Hill, Mitchell Ryan, Jack Ging, Geoffrey Lewis, John Mitchum. **1973 DVD**

HIGH RISK ★★1/2 While snatching $5 million from a South American drug smuggler (James Coburn), four amateur conspirators (James Brolin, Cleavon Little, Bruce Davison, and Chick Vennera) cross paths with a sleazy bandit leader (Anthony Quinn), hordes of Colombian soldiers, and plenty of riotous trouble. This preposterous adventure offers diversion, but a lot of it is just plain awful. Rated R. 94m. **DIR:** Stewart Raffill. **CAST:** James Brolin, Cleavon Little, Bruce Davison, Chick Vennera, Anthony Quinn, James Coburn, Ernest Borgnine, Lindsay Wagner. **1981 DVD**

HIGH ROAD TO CHINA ★★★ Tom Selleck stars as a World War I flying ace who, with the aid of his sidekick/mechanic, Jack Weston, helps a spoiled heiress (Bess Armstrong) track down her missing father (Wilford Brimley). It's just like the B movies of yesteryear: predictable, silly, and fun. Rated PG for violence. 120m. **DIR:** Brian G. Hutton. **CAST:** Tom Selleck, Bess Armstrong, Jack Weston, Wilford Brimley, Robert Morley, Brian Blessed. **1983**

HIGH ROLLING 💔 Two out-of-work carnival workers hitchhike through Australia until they are picked up by a drug runner. Rated PG for profanity and brief nudity. 88m. **DIR:** Igor Auzins. **CAST:** Joseph Bottoms, Grigor Taylor, Sandy Hughs, Judy Davis, John Clayton. **1977**

HIGH SCHOOL CAESAR 💔 A rich high school kid (John Ashley) is ignored by the father he idolizes, so he spends his time running a protection racket, selling exams, and rigging school elections. Neither good nor bad enough to be memorable. B&W; 72m. **DIR:** O'Dale Ireland. **CAST:** John Ashley, Gary Vinson, Lowell Brown. **1960**

HIGH SCHOOL CONFIDENTIAL! ★★1/2 A narcotics officer sneaks into a tough high school to bust hopheads. Incredibly naïve treatment of drug scene is bad enough, but it's the actors' desperate attempts to look "hip" that make the film an unintentional laugh riot. B&W; 85m. **DIR:** Jack Arnold. **CAST:** Russ Tamblyn, Jan Sterling, John Drew Barrymore, Mamie Van Doren. **1958**

HIGH SCHOOL HIGH ★★1/2 Producer David Zucker of *Naked Gun* and *Airplane!* fame returns with his trademark, rapid-fire, hit-and-miss sight gags and wacky one-liners. This time, optimistic Jon "That's the ticket!" Lovitz leaves a private academy to teach in a bleak inner-city high. Attempt to resolve social issues is a bit ambitious for this spoof. Rated PG-13 for profanity and violence. 85m. **DIR:** Hart Bochner. **CAST:** Jon Lovitz, Tia Carrere, Mekhi Phifer, Malinda Williams, Louise Fletcher. **1996 DVD**

HIGH SCHOOL, USA ★★ The fact that the dancing robot is the best actor in this film should tell you something. This made-for-TV feature is your typical teen flick, which is exceptional only because it doesn't rely on nudity and foul language to hold its audience's attention. 96m. **DIR:** Rod Amateau. **CAST:** Michael J. Fox, Dwayne Hickman, Angela Cartwright. **1983**

HIGH SEASON ★★★★ This delightfully pixilated comedy-mystery presents a group of people feuding, faking, laughing, and loving on a breathtaking Greek isle. Cowritten and directed by Clare Peploe, the wife of Bernardo Bertolucci, *High Season* offers Jacqueline Bisset as a photographer and James Fox as her sculptor husband. Rated R for brief nudity and adult themes. 104m. DIR: Clare Peploe. CAST: Jacqueline Bisset, Irene Papas, James Fox, Kenneth Branagh, Sebastian Shaw, Robert Stephens. 1988

HIGH SIERRA ★★★1/2 Humphrey Bogart is at his best as a bad guy with a heart of gold in this 1941 gangster film. Bogart pays for the operation that corrects pretty Joan Leslie's crippled foot, but he finds his love is misplaced. One of the finest of the Warner Bros. genre entries. B&W; 100m. DIR: Raoul Walsh. CAST: Humphrey Bogart, Ida Lupino, Alan Curtis, Arthur Kennedy, Joan Leslie, Henry Hull. 1941

HIGH SOCIETY ★★★1/2 The outstanding cast in this film is reason enough to watch this enjoyable musical remake of The Philadelphia Story. The film moves at a leisurely pace, helped by some nice songs by Cole Porter. 107m. DIR: Charles Walters. CAST: Bing Crosby, Frank Sinatra, Grace Kelly, Louis Armstrong, Celeste Holm. 1956

HIGH SPIRITS ♥ Peter O'Toole tries to generate revenue for the ancient family castle by proclaiming it a haunted tourist trap. Rated PG-13 for language and mild sexual themes. 97m. DIR: Neil Jordan. CAST: Peter O'Toole, Steve Guttenberg, Daryl Hannah, Beverly D'Angelo, Jennifer Tilly, Liam Neeson. 1988

HIGH STAKES (1986) ★★ Hoping to become a star reporter, a young daydreamer gets his chance when he uncovers a criminal plot to unearth a hidden Nazi treasure. His Walter Mitty–ish fantasies are the least appealing part of the movie, but some funny supporting characters and one-liners compensate. Not rated. 82m. DIR: Larry Kent. CAST: David Foley, Roberta Weiss, Winston Rekert. 1986

HIGH STAKES (1989) ★★★ Sally Kirkland turns in a convincing portrayal as a burned-out hooker who meets a financial whiz dealing with his own personal crises. His fascination with Kirkland sweeps him into her sleazy world. Rated R for violence and profanity. 86m. DIR: Amos Kollek. CAST: Sally Kirkland, Robert LuPone, Richard Lynch. 1989

HIGH STRUNG ♥ Steve Oedekerk bombards his audience with screaming complaints about everything. About as much fun as sitting in the dentist chair and listening to the guy in the next cubicle having his teeth drilled. Megastar Jim Carrey appears mostly in brief flashes. Rated R for profanity. 93m. DIR: Roger Nygard. CAST: Steve Oedekerk, Thomas F. Wilson, Denise Crosby, Fred Willard, Jim Carrey. 1994

HIGH TIDE ★★★★ Judy Davis gives a superb performance as a rock 'n' roll singer stranded in a small Australian town when she loses her job in a band and her car breaks down all in the same day. She winds up staying in a trailer park only to encounter by accident the teenage daughter she deserted following the death of her husband. The offbeat but moving film reunites Davis with her My Brilliant Career director, Gillian Armstrong, for some truly impressive results. Rated PG. 102m. DIR: Gillian Armstrong. CAST: Judy Davis, Jan Adele, Claudia Karvan, Colin Friels. 1987

HIGH VELOCITY ★★ Run-of-the-mill feature made in Manila about two ex-Vietnam buddies hired to rescue the head of a big corporation from Asian terrorists. Rated PG. 106m. DIR: Remi Kramer. CAST: Ben Gazzara, Britt Ekland, Paul Winfield, Keenan Wynn, Alejandro Rey, Victoria Racimo. 1977

HIGH VOLTAGE (1929) ★★1/2 Elements of Stagecoach are evident in this early Pathé sound film (made ten years before John Ford's classic) that teams a pre–Hopalong Cassidy William Boyd and a lovely young Carole Lombard as a world-wise couple who fall for each other while snowbound during a bus trip in California's Sierra Nevada. Worth watching for Lombard's fine performance. B&W; 57m. DIR: Howard Higgin. CAST: William Boyd, Carole Lombard, Owen Moore, Diane Ellis, Billy Bevan. 1929

HIGH VOLTAGE (1997) ★★ This throwback to Bruce Lee martial arts films stars his daughter Shannon, who plays the girlfriend of an Asian crime lord and falls for a thief who has stolen her boyfriend's money. The attempt to infuse style falls flat as does the rest of the film. Rated R for language and violence. 92m. DIR: Isaac Florentine. CAST: Antonio Sabato Jr., Shannon Lee, George Cheung, William Zabka. 1997 DVD

HIGHER AND HIGHER ★★ Frank Sinatra and the entire cast do a wonderful job in this practically plotless picture about a once-rich man teaming up with his servants in his quest to be wealthy once again. This is Sinatra's first major film effort, and he does a fine job with the first-rate songs. B&W; 90m. DIR: Tim Whelan. CAST: Frank Sinatra, Michele Morgan, Jack Haley, Leon Errol, Victor Borge, Mel Torme. 1943

HIGHER LEARNING ★★ Date rape. Racism. Sexism. Neo-Nazism. Elitism. This ambitious, issue-packed look at the social turbulence of a fictional college campus gets an A for effort while expounding on the waywardness of the modern world. The film's flurry of sociopolitical punches, however, is amateurishly strung together. Rated R for language and violence. 127m. DIR: John Singleton. CAST: Omar Epps, Kristy Swanson, Tyra Banks, Jennifer Connelly, Laurence Fishburne, Ice Cube, Michael Rapaport. 1995

HIGHEST HONOR, THE ★★★★★ A World War II story of a unique friendship between two enemies: Captain Robert Page, an Australian army officer, and Winoyu Tamiya, a security officer in the Japanese army. This great war film, packed with high adventure and warm human drama, is also a true story. Rated R. 99m. DIR: Peter Maxwell. CAST: John Howard, Atsuo Nakamura, Stuart Wilson. 1984

HIGHLANDER ★★ A sixteenth-century Scottish clansman discovers he is one of a small group of immortals destined to fight each other through the centuries. The movie is a treat for the eyes, but you'll owe your brain an apology. Rated R for violence. 110m. DIR: Russell Mulcahy. CAST: Christopher Lambert, Clancy Brown, Sean Connery. 1986 DVD

HIGHLANDER 2: THE QUICKENING ★★1/2 Christopher Lambert and Sean Connery reprise their roles as the Highlander and his mentor Ramirez who have been banished to Earth. Great special effects can't keep one from thinking that something is missing from the film—like a cohesive plot. Rated R for violence. 91m. DIR: Russell Mulcahy. CAST: Christopher Lambert, Virginia Madsen, Michael Ironside, Sean Connery, John C. McGinley. 1991 DVD

HIGHLANDER: THE GATHERING ★★ This is a combination of two episodes from the TV series, which is why the plot seems disjointed. Duncan and Connor must battle the evil immortals. Mind-numbing. Rated PG-13 for nudity and violence. 98m. **DIR:** Thomas Wright, Ray Austin. **CAST:** Adrian Paul, Alexandra Vandernoot, Stan Kirsch, Christopher Lambert, Richard Moll, Vanity. 1992

HIGHLANDER: THE FINAL DIMENSION ★★ That sixteenth-century Scottish clansman (Christopher Lambert) is still roaming through time, still fighting the forces of evil (represented by Mario Van Peebles), and still speaking with an inexplicable French accent. The third entry in the series has no discernible plot and suffers greatly from the absence of Sean Connery as the Highlander's mentor. Rated R for violence. 99m. **DIR:** Andy Morahan. **CAST:** Christopher Lambert, Mario Van Peebles, Deborah Unger, Mako, Marc Neufield, Raul Trujillo. 1994 DVD

HIGHPOINT 💔 Confusing comedy-thriller about an accountant who becomes mixed up in a CIA plot. Rated R; contains profanity and violence. 88m. **DIR:** Peter Carter. **CAST:** Richard Harris, Christopher Plummer, Beverly D'Angelo, Kate Reid, Peter Donat, Saul Rubinek. 1980

HIGHWAY 61 ★★★ A wacky, somewhat surreal road comedy about a small-town Canadian barber whose claim to fame is finding a dead body. When the corpse's sister—a refugee from a rock 'n' roll crew—appears, they go on a journey down one of North America's most famous highways. Rated R for profanity, simulated sex, and nudity. 105m. **DIR:** Bruce McDonald. **CAST:** Valerie Buhagiar, Don McKellar, Earl Pastko. 1992

HIGHWAY TO HELL ★★★★ Two young lovers get caught in an inter-dimensional speed trap, and are sent straight to hell. Fast-paced writing and action, as well as large dashes of humor and sight gags, make this an entertaining thriller. Rated R for violence and profanity. 100m. **DIR:** Ate De Jong. **CAST:** Patrick Bergin, Chad Lowe, Kristy Swanson, Richard Farnsworth. 1991

HIJACKING HOLLYWOOD ★★★ Henry Thomas is a boyish filmmaker who takes the abuse of being a production assistant. When he can't take it anymore, he steals a reel of expensive special-effects footage and holds it ransom. Small, low-budget independent effort works magic with its charm and spunk. Rated R for adult situations, language, and nudity. 93m. **DIR:** Neil Mandt. **CAST:** Henry Thomas, Carrot Top (Scott Thompson), Mark Metcalf. 1997 DVD

HILARY AND JACKIE ★★★★ The need to separate the artist from the art is key to this fascinating drama, which concerns the life of celebrated English cellist Jacqueline du Pre. Jackie could do no wrong in the eyes of her fans, who were more than willing to forgive her shocking candor and her tendency, during performances, to sensuously embrace her cello as one might a paramour. But she also was a monster: insecure, selfish, self-centered, capriciously cruel and spiteful. We cannot possibly like this woman. Yet we can at least begin to understand her in this absorbing and thoughtful study of talent's fragility. Rated R for profanity, nudity, and sexual content.

125m. **DIR:** Anand Tucker. **CAST:** Emily Watson, Rachel Griffiths, David Morrissey, James Frain, Charles Dance, Celia Imrie. 1998 DVD

HILL, THE ★★★★ Powerful drill-sergeant-from-hell film, this zeroes in on the psychological and mental agony faced by a group of British military prisoners. Sean Connery is excellent as the latest victim of the break-their-spirits program. 122m. **DIR:** Sidney Lumet. **CAST:** Sean Connery, Harry Andrews, Ian Hendry, Ossie Davis, Michael Redgrave. 1965

HILL STREET BLUES (TV SERIES) ★★★★ Steven Bochco's landmark 1980s police drama forever redefined the way we view cop shows. Daniel J. Travanti collected a pair of well-deserved Emmy awards as Captain Frank Furillo, the precinct captain who served as the show's rock-hard anchor. No matter how grim the day's events, he'd usually wind up at home in the evening, sharing a bathtub with lover Veronica Hamel, who occasionally busted his chops by day fulfilling her duties as public defender. Mike Post's catchy theme became a top-forty hit, and the ensemble cast grew to include considerably more than two dozen ongoing roles. Michael Conrad, as Sergeant Esterhaus, always spoke the series' signature line: "Let's be careful out there." Each episode 47m. **DIR:** Various. **CAST:** Daniel J. Travanti, Michael Conrad, Michael Warren, Charles Haid, Veronica Hamel, Bruce Weitz, Rene Enriquez, Keil Martin, Taurean Blacque, James B. Sikking, Joe Spano, Betty Thomas. 1981–87

HILLBILLYS IN A HAUNTED HOUSE 💔 Unbelievably bad mishmash of country corn and horror humor. 88m. **DIR:** Jean Yarbrough. **CAST:** Ferlin Husky, Joi Lansing, Don Bowman, John Carradine, Lon Chaney Jr., Basil Rathbone, Molly Bee, Merle Haggard, Sonny James. 1967 DVD

HILLS HAVE EYES, THE 💔 City folk have inherited a silver mine and are stopping on their way to California to check it out. That's when a ghoulish family comes crawling out of the rocks. Rated R for violence and profanity. 89m. **DIR:** Wes Craven. **CAST:** Susan Lamer, Robert Houston, Virginia Vincent, Russ Grieve, Dee Wallace. 1977

HILLS HAVE EYES, THE: PART TWO 💔 This really lame sequel wouldn't scare the most timid viewer. Rated R for violence and profanity (mild by horror standards). 86m. **DIR:** Wes Craven. **CAST:** John Laughlin, Michael Berryman. 1984

HILLS OF HOME ★★★★ Effective family fare about an aging doctor and his devoted collie, Lassie. While tending to the townspeople, the kindly physician attempts to cure his dog's fear of water only to need help himself. A satisfying tearjerker, in the mold of *All Creatures Great and Small.* 97m. **DIR:** Fred M. Wilcox. **CAST:** Edmund Gwenn, Tom Drake, Janet Leigh, Donald Crisp, Rhys Williams, Reginald Owen, Alan Napier, Eileen Erskine. 1948

HILLS OF OLD WYOMING ★★1/2 Cattle rustlers plaguing the local ranchers have been traced back to the Indian reservation by Hopalong Cassidy and his pals. With the law, rustlers, and the local Indians all after the Bar-20 boys, Hoppy saves their hides when he finds proof to convict the murdering thieves.

B&W; 80m. DIR: Nate Watt. CAST: William Boyd, George "Gabby" Hayes, Russell Hayden, Morris Ankrum (Stepen Morris), Gail Sheridan, Chief Big Tree, Steve Clemento. 1937

HILLS OF UTAH, THE ★★1/2 Harking back to a classic theme, Gene returns to the town where his father was killed and manages to settle a local feud as well as uncover the truth about his father's murder. Even with Pat Buttram, this is somber for a Gene Autry film. B&W; 70m. DIR: John English. CAST: Gene Autry, Pat Buttram, Elaine Riley, Onslow Stevens, Donna Martell. 1951

HILLSIDE STRANGLERS, THE ★★★ A video release of a made-for-television flick concerning two of California's most wanted criminals. Richard Crenna is the hard-nosed detective. Dennis Farina and Billy Zane are the cousins holding Los Angeles in a stranglehold of fear. 95m. DIR: Steven Gethers. CAST: Richard Crenna, Dennis Farina, Billy Zane, Tony Plana. 1989

HI-LO COUNTRY, THE ★★★ Two cowboys (Woody Harrelson, Billy Crudup) raise hell and defy the tides of progress in post–World War II New Mexico, while one of them carries on with the married woman they both love. Based on a novel by Max Evans, good performances and atmospheric detail redeem the overfamiliar story and slow pacing. Rated R for profanity, violence, and sexual scenes. 114m. DIR: Stephen Frears. CAST: Woody Harrelson, Billy Crudup, Patricia Arquette, Penelope Cruz, Sam Elliott, Cole Hauser, James Gammon. 1999 DVD

HIMATSURI ★★★★1/2 Metaphysical story about man's lustful and often destructive relationship with nature. Kinya Kitaoji plays a lumberjack in a beautiful seaboard wilderness which is about to be marred by the building of a marine park. Rated R for nudity and violence. 120m. DIR: Mitsuo Yanagimachi. CAST: Kinya Kitaoji. 1985

HINDENBURG, THE ♥ Another disaster movie whose major disaster is its own script. Rated PG. 125m. DIR: Robert Wise. CAST: George C. Scott, Anne Bancroft, William Atherton, Roy Thinnes, Burgess Meredith, Charles Durning. 1975 DVD

HIPS, HIPS, HOORAY ★★★ Clowns Bert Wheeler and Robert Woolsey liven up this early, somewhat blue, comedy-musical. The pair play havoc as they invade Thelma Todd's ailing cosmetic business. B&W; 68m. DIR: Mark Sandrich. CAST: Bert Wheeler, Robert Woolsey, Thelma Todd, Ruth Etting, George Meeker, Dorothy Lee. 1934

HIRED HAND, THE ★★★1/2 This low-key Western follows two drifters, Peter Fonda and Warren Oates, as they return to Fonda's farm and the wife, Verna Bloom, he deserted seven years earlier. While working on the farm, Fonda and Bloom begin to rekindle their relationship. Beautiful cinematography and fine performances, especially by Oates, add greatly to this worthy entry in the genre. Rated R. 93m. DIR: Peter Fonda. CAST: Peter Fonda, Warren Oates, Verna Bloom, Severn Darden. 1971

HIRED TO KILL ★★ Aimless violence permeates this action film concerning a soldier of fortune and his efforts to infiltrate a Third World island and free a prisoner. Trite and just plain silly. Rated R for violence, nudity, and adult language. 91m. DIR: Nico Mastorakis, Peter Rader. CAST: Brian Thompson, Oliver Reed, George Kennedy, José Ferrer. 1990

•HIROSHIMA ★★★★ A fascinating, ambitious film (made for cable TV) that provides both the American and Japanese perspective on the creation, use, and aftermath of the atomic bombs dropped on two Japanese cities in 1945. Archival footage increases the feeling that one is watching history, a feeling that the well-researched script deserves. In English and Japanese with English subtitles. Rated PG for violence. 190m. DIR: Koreyoshi Kurahara, Roger Spottiswoode. CAST: Wesley Addy, Jeffrey DeMunn, David Gow, Richard Masur. 1995 DVD

HIROSHIMA, MON AMOUR ★★★★ A mind-boggling tale about two people: one, a Frenchwoman, the other, a male survivor of the blast at Hiroshima. They meet and become lovers. Together they live their pasts, present, and futures in a complex series of fantasies, and nightmares. In French with English subtitles. B&W; 88m. DIR: Alain Resnais. CAST: Emmanuelle Riva, Bernard Fresson, Eiji Okada. 1959

HIROSHIMA: OUT OF THE ASHES ★★★★ This superior TV-movie rendition of the atomic bombing of Hiroshima allows us to see things from the perspective of those who were among the ruins. An ironic twist of fate places freed POWs among the ruins. Rated PG-13 for violence. 98m. DIR: Peter Werner. CAST: Max von Sydow, Judd Nelson, Noriyuki "Pat" Morita, Mako, Ben Wright. 1990

HIS BODYGUARD ★★1/2 Industrial spies break into a research lab to steal a biomedical prototype and a deaf scientist and the female head of security are caught up in it all. This made-for-cable original features decent acting, but too much of the story is pointless chasing around. Rated PG-13 for violence. 95m. DIR: Artie Mandelberg. CAST: Mitzi Kapture, Anthony Natale, Michael Copeman, Robin Gammell, Robert Guillaume. 1998

HIS BROTHER'S GHOST ★★★1/2 Sturdy entry in the Billy Carson series has Buster Crabbe as a two-fisted rancher bent on capturing the gang that killed his best friend. It's much better than it sounds, one of the best Crabbe made in the series, which originally starred Bob Steele as a whitewashed Billy the Kid. B&W; 54m. DIR: Sam Newfield. CAST: Buster Crabbe, Al St. John, Charles King, Karl Hackett. 1945

HIS BUTLER'S SISTER ★★★★1/2 A delightful Deanna Durbin singfest with a stellar performance by Pat O'Brien as the butler of the title. Durbin sings both modern and classical opera every time there's a lull in the comic high jinks about a composer chasing a girl until she catches him. B&W; 94m. DIR: Frank Borzage. CAST: Deanna Durbin, Pat O'Brien, Franchot Tone, Akim Tamiroff, Evelyn Ankers. 1943

HIS DOUBLE LIFE ★★★ Edwardian novelist Arnold Bennett's comedy about a wealthy recluse who finds a better life by becoming a valet when his valet dies and is buried under his name. Remade with Monty Woolley and Gracie Fields as Holy Matrimony in 1943. B&W; 67m. DIR: Arthur Hopkins, William C. de Mille. CAST: Lillian Gish, Roland Young. 1933

HIS GIRL FRIDAY ★★★★ Based on Ben Hecht and Charles MacArthur's *The Front Page*, Howard Hawks converted this gentle spoof of newspapers and reporters into a hilarious battle of the sexes. Rosalind Russell is the reporter bent on retirement, and Cary Grant is the editor bent on maneuvering her out of it—and winning her heart in the process. B&W; 92m. **DIR:** Howard Hawks. **CAST:** Cary Grant, Rosalind Russell, Ralph Bellamy, Gene Lockhart, Helen Mack, Ernest Truex. **1940 DVD**

HIS KIND OF WOMAN ★★★1/2 Entertaining chase film as two-fisted gambler Robert Mitchum breezes down to South America to pick up $50 thousand only to find out he's being set up for the kill. Jane Russell is in fine shape as the worldly gal with a good heart, and Vincent Price steals the show as a hammy Hollywood actor. B&W; 120m. **DIR:** John Farrow. **CAST:** Robert Mitchum, Jane Russell, Vincent Price, Tim Holt, Charles McGraw, Raymond Burr, Jim Backus, Marjorie Reynolds. **1951**

HIS MAJESTY O'KEEFE ★★★1/2 A rip-snortin' adventure movie with Burt Lancaster furnishing all the energy as the nineteenth century American businessman who sails to the South Seas and finds a fortune in copra waiting for him. He also teaches the natives how to use gunpowder, and the result is both exciting and hilarious. 92m. **DIR:** Byron Haskin. **CAST:** Burt Lancaster, Joan Rice, Abraham Sofaer, Philip Ahn. **1954**

HIS NAME WAS KING ★★ Spaghetti Western about a bounty hunter named King (Richard Harrison) who tracks down a ring of gunrunners near the Mexican border. Not rated, but equal to a PG. 90m. **DIR:** Don Reynolds. **CAST:** Richard Harrison, Klaus Kinski. **1983**

HIS PICTURE IN THE PAPERS ★★★1/2 This clever film has Douglas Fairbanks performing a variety of Herculean feats—all aimed at getting his picture on the front pages of the New York papers. This comedy helped to define Fairbanks's motion-picture persona as the boisterous, buoyant, devil-may-care, ultra-athletic young go-getter. Silent. B&W; 68m. **DIR:** John Emerson. **CAST:** Douglas Fairbanks Sr. **1916**

HIS PRIVATE SECRETARY ★★ Playboy son of a bill collector is put to work by his father but falls for the daughter of his first deadbeat, an impoverished cleric. John Wayne is long on enthusiasm and short on technique as he tackles the lead in his only independent film for Showmen's Pictures, a visible step beneath the Mascot serials and Monogram Westerns he was toiling in at the time. B&W; 61m. **DIR:** Philip H. Whitman. **CAST:** John Wayne, Evalyn Knapp, Reginald Barlow, Arthur Hoyt, Natalie Kingston, Al St. John. **1933**

HISTORY IS MADE AT NIGHT ★★★ A preposterous film, but ... Colin Clive is a sadistic jealous husband whose wife, Jean Arthur, falls for Parisian headwaiter Charles Boyer. He tries to frame the headwaiter for a murder he himself committed. He fails. Insanely determined to destroy the lovers, he arranges for his superliner to hit an iceberg! B&W; 97m. **DIR:** Frank Borzage. **CAST:** Charles Boyer, Jean Arthur, Colin Clive, Leo Carrillo. **1937**

HISTORY OF THE WORLD, PART ONE, THE ❤ Mel Brooks is lost in this collection of bits that emerge like unused footage from *Monty Python's The Meaning of Life*. Rated R for crude language. 86m. **DIR:** Mel Brooks. **CAST:** Mel Brooks, Dom DeLuise, Madeline Kahn, Harvey Korman, Gregory Hines, Cloris Leachman. **1981 DVD**

HIT! (1973) ★★1/2 This is a praiseworthy attempt to bring some legitimacy to the blaxploitation genre. Billy Dee Williams plays an American police detective who tracks drug dealers to Marseilles. Rated R for nudity, violence, and profanity. 134m. **DIR:** Sidney J. Furie. **CAST:** Billy Dee Williams, Paul Hampton, Richard Pryor, Gwen Welles. **1973**

HIT, THE (1984) ★★★★ The British seem to have latched on to the gangster film with a vengeance. First, they made the superb film *The Long Good Friday*, and now they've scored again with this gripping character study. John Hurt gives an unusually restrained (and highly effective) performance as a hit man assigned to take care of a squealer (Terence Stamp) who has been hiding in Spain after testifying against the mob. Rated R for violence. 97m. **DIR:** Stephen Frears. **CAST:** John Hurt, Terence Stamp, Tim Roth, Fernando Rey, Laura Del Sol, Bill Hunter. **1984**

HIT AND RUN ★★1/2 A New York cabdriver, obsessed with the death of his wife in a hit-and-run accident, becomes a pawn in a murder plot. Mystery fans will appreciate the nighttime atmosphere and carefully (if slowly) developed plot. Rated PG. 96m. **DIR:** Charles Braverman. **CAST:** Paul Perri, Claudia Cron, Bart Braverman. **1982**

HIT LADY ★★1/2 Entertaining twist on an old story has Yvette Mimieux as a hit lady who tries to retire, only to be blackmailed into taking on just one more job. Television movie; contains some cleaned-up violence. 74m. **DIR:** Tracy Keenan Wynn. **CAST:** Yvette Mimieux, Dack Rambo, Clu Gulager, Joseph Campanella, Keenan Wynn. **1974**

HIT LIST (1988) ★★ The Mafia hires a hit man (Lance Henriksen) to stifle a key witness. The hit man gets the address wrong and ends up kidnapping Jan-Michael Vincent's son. Some familiar faces pop up in the supporting cast of this not-so-bad suspense-drama. Rated R for violence and profanity. 87m. **DIR:** William Lustig. **CAST:** Jan-Michael Vincent, Rip Torn, Lance Henriksen, Leo Rossi. **1988**

HIT LIST, THE (1992) ★★★★ High marks to this twisty thriller from scripter Reed Steiner. Jeff Fahey stars as an implacable assassin whose professional routine goes awry after meeting client Yancy Butler. Post-dubbing is inexplicably awful for an American-made film. Rated R for extreme violence, profanity, simulated sex, and nudity. 97m. **DIR:** William Webb. **CAST:** Jeff Fahey, Yancy Butler, James Coburn, Michael Beach, Jeff Kober. **1992**

HIT THE DECK ★★1/2 Fancy-free sailors on shore leave meet girls, dance, sing, and cut up in this updated 1920s Vincent Youmans film from Broadway. Good, time-filling eyewash. 112m. **DIR:** Roy Rowland. **CAST:** Jane Powell, Tony Martin, Debbie Reynolds, Vic Damone, Ann Miller, Russ Tamblyn, Walter Pidgeon, Gene Raymond. **1955**

HIT THE DUTCHMAN ★★1/2 A Jewish ex-convict wants to become involved with gangster Legs Diamond, but must first change his name. This run-of-the-mill gangster film drags on way too long. Rated R for profanity, violence, and nudity. 116m. DIR: Menahem Golan. CAST: Bruce Nozick, Will Kempe, Sally Kirkland. 1992

HIT THE ICE ★★★ Abbott and Costello play a pair of photographers in this outing, eluding assorted crooks. Gags abound, but so do musical numbers, which always seem to grind these films to a halt. On a par with most of their other efforts, it guarantees a great time for A&C fans. B&W; 82m. DIR: Charles Lamont. CAST: Bud Abbott, Lou Costello, Patric Knowles, Elyse Knox. 1943

HIT THE SADDLE ★★★ A gold digging fandango dancer (Rita Hayworth, née Cansino) comes between two of the Three Mesquiteers while they battle a sinister outlaw gang. B&W; 54m. DIR: Mack V. Wright. CAST: Robert Livingston, Ray "Crash" Corrigan, Max Terhune, Rita Hayworth. 1937

HIT WOMAN: THE DOUBLE EDGE ★★1/2 Soap star Susan Lucci plays dual roles as an assassin and the FBI agent out to find her. The story is quite dull, but Lucci does a fine job portraying two radically different people. Rated R for violence. 94m. DIR: Stephen Stafford. CAST: Susan Lucci, Robert Urich, Michael Woods, Kevin Dunn, Paul Freeman, Kari Lizer, Robert Prosky. 1992

HITCHER, THE ★★★ C. Thomas Howell plays a young, squeamish, California-bound motorist who picks up a hitchhiker, played by Rutger Hauer, somewhere in the desert Southwest. What transpires is action that will leave you physically and emotionally drained. If you thought *The Terminator* was too violent, this one will redefine the word for you. Rated R. 96m. DIR: Robert Harmon. CAST: Rutger Hauer, C. Thomas Howell, Jeffrey DeMunn, Jennifer Jason Leigh. 1986 DVD

HITCHHIKER, THE (SERIES) ★★★ Stories culled from HBO anthology series are included in this compilation of tapes. The stories always have a supernatural background and a moral but sometimes are a bit shallow. Not rated; contains adult language, violence, and nudity. Each tape 90m. DIR: Roger Vadim, Paul Verhoeven, Carl Schenkel, Phillip Noyce, Mai Zetterling, Richard Rothstein, David Wickes, Mike Hodges. CAST: Page Fletcher, Harry Hamlin, Karen Black, Gary Busey, Geraldine Page, Margot Kidder, Darren McGavin, Susan Anspach, Peter Coyote, Barry Bostwick, Willem Dafoe, M. Emmet Walsh, Tom Skerritt, Steve Collins, Shannon Tweed, Robert Vaughn, Sybil Danning, Michael O'Keefe. 1985

HITCHHIKERS 🎗 Female hitchhikers rob the motorists who stop to pick them up. Rated R for nudity, profanity, and simulated sex. 87m. DIR: Ferd Sebastian. CAST: Misty Rowe, Norman Klar, Linda Avery. 1971

HITCHHIKER'S GUIDE TO THE GALAXY, THE ★★★★ While perhaps the least successful adaptation (behind the book and LP) of Douglas Adam's now-classic BBC radio series, this television incarnation nonetheless succeeds quite well. Simon Jones is perfect as bathrobe-garbed Arthur Dent, an insignificant ordinary citizen thrown into the adventure of his life after narrowly escaping the Earth's destruction by aliens annoyed at how our planet

blocked their proposed spatial thoroughfare. 194m. DIR: Alan Bell. CAST: Peter Jones, Simon Jones, David Dixon, Joe Melia, Martin Benson. 1985

HITLER ★★ Richard Basehart plays Adolf Hitler in this rather slow-moving, shallow account of *der Führer's* last years. You're better off watching a good documentary on the subject. 107m. DIR: Stuart Heisler. CAST: Richard Basehart, Cordula Trantow, Maria Emo, John Mitchum. 1962

HITLER—DEAD OR ALIVE 🎗 Paroled gangster and his henchmen accept a $1 million offer to assassinate Hitler. B&W; 72m. DIR: Nick Grindé. CAST: Ward Bond, Warren Hymer, Paul Fix. 1942

HITLER, THE LAST TEN DAYS ★★ This film should hold interest only for history buffs. It is a rather dry and tedious account of the desperate closing days of the Third Reich. Alec Guinness gives a capable, yet sometimes overwrought, performance as the Nazi leader from the time he enters his underground bunker in Berlin until his eventual suicide. Rated PG. 108m. DIR: Ennio DeConcini. CAST: Alec Guinness, Simon Ward, Adolfo Celi, Diane Cilento. 1973

HITLER'S CHILDREN ★★★★ A great love story is created with the horror of Nazi Germany as a background. This film shows a young German boy who falls in love with an American girl. The boy gets caught up in Hitler's enticing web of propaganda, while his girlfriend resists all of Hitler's ideas. B&W; 83m. DIR: Edward Dmytryk, Irving Reis. CAST: Tim Holt, Bonita Granville, Kent Smith, Otto Kruger. 1942

HITLER'S DAUGHTER 🎗 Made-for-cable drama suggests one of Hitler's mistresses produced a girl-child, who was then trained by Nazi-nasties to revive the Fourth Reich in our United States. Rated R for language and violence. 88m. DIR: James A. Contner. CAST: Patrick Cassidy, Melody Anderson, Veronica Cartwright, Kay Lenz. 1990

HITMAN, THE ★★★1/2 A police officer goes underground after being betrayed and shot by his crooked partner. Officially listed as dead, he becomes the "hit man" for a Seattle crime boss in order to bring down a sophisticated drug operation. Rated R for violence and profanity. 96m. DIR: Aaron Norris. CAST: Chuck Norris, Michael Parks, Al Waxman, Alberta Watson. 1991 DVD

HITZ ★★ Melodramatic dramatization of kids killing kids among L.A. gangs loses credibility in the courtroom, with judges taking their work too personally. Muddled message film. Rated R for nudity, violence, and profanity. 90m. DIR: William Sachs. CAST: Emilia Crow, Richard Coca, Elliott Gould. 1992

•**HI-YO SILVER** ★★1/2 A tyrant operating under government protection in the old Southwest is brought to justice by a masked rider and his companions. Feature version of the serial has five potential Lone Rangers, and the audience has to guess along with the bad guys which one it is. Only about one-third of the film remains after editing down fifteen episodes so the storyline is pretty jumpy, but a framing device with new footage added helps a bit. B&W; 69m. DIR: William Witney, John English. CAST: Lee Powell, Chief Thundercloud, Herman Brix, Hal Taliaferro, George Letz, Lane Chandler, Lynne Roberts (Mary Hart), Stanley Andrews. 1940

H-MAN, THE ★★★ Unintentional humor makes this low-budget Japanese monster movie a near comedy classic. A boat wanders into a nuclear-test zone, mutating a crew member into a horrible water monster. With some of the lamest special effects ever filmed, this is guaranteed to make even the most humorless individual crack a smile. Not rated, but suitable for all ages. 79m. **DIR:** Inoshiro Honda. **CAST:** Yumi Shirakawa. **1959**

HOBBIT, THE ★★ Disappointing cartoon version of the classic J. R. R. Tolkien fantasy. Orson Bean provides the voice of the dwarflike Hobbit, Bilbo Baggins, and John Huston, at his stentorian best, is the wizard Gandalf. Unfortunately, all the creatures have a cutesy look, which doesn't gel with the story. An unrated TV movie. 78m. **DIR:** Arthur Rankin Jr., Jules Bass. **1978**

HOBSON'S CHOICE (1954) ★★★★ Charles Laughton gives one of his most brilliant performances as a turn-of-the-century London shoemaker whose love for the status quo and his whiskey is shattered by the determination of his daughter to wed. This is the original 1954 movie version of the British comedy. Laughton is expertly supported by John Mills and Brenda de Banzie as the two who wish to marry. B&W; 107m. **DIR:** David Lean. **CAST:** Charles Laughton, John Mills, Brenda de Banzie, Daphne Anderson. **1954**

HOBSON'S CHOICE (1983) ★★★1/2 Sharon Gless is the main attraction in this quaint period drama, set in 1914 New Orleans. She's the spirited and capable eldest daughter of the irascible Henry Horatio Hobson (Jack Warden), seller of shoes and self-proclaimed "pillar of the community." Gless methodically arranges a marriage with his finest shoemaker (Richard Thomas). Not rated; suitable for family viewing. 100m. **DIR:** Gilbert Cates. **CAST:** Sharon Gless, Jack Warden, Richard Thomas, Bert Remsen, Robert Englund, Lillian Gish. **1983**

HOCUS POCUS ★★★1/2 While not much of a box-office hit, this cauldron's brew of thrills and laughs will delight children. Three witches, revived after 300 years, wreak havoc in modern-day Salem, Massachusetts. The movie is scary enough to involve youngsters but not so frightening as to give them nightmares. Rated PG for brief vulgarity and scary stuff. **DIR:** Kenny Ortega. **CAST:** Bette Midler, Sarah Jessica Parker, Kathy Najimy, Omri Katz, Thora Birch, Vinessa Shaw, Amanda Shepherd. **1993 DVD**

HOFFA ★★★★ Though it leaves several questions about its subject's past and family life unaddressed, this screen biography of labor leader Jimmy Hoffa is a tour de force. The film does not whitewash the events that led to Hoffa's rise to power but maintains a moral ambiguity. Screenplay by David Mamet. Rated R for profanity, violence, and nudity. 140m. **DIR:** Danny DeVito. **CAST:** Jack Nicholson, Danny De-Vito, Armand Assante, J. T. Walsh, John C. Reilly, Frank Whaley, Kevin Anderson, John P. Ryan, Robert Prosky, Natalija Nogulich, Nicholas Pryor, Paul Guilfoyle, Karen Young, Cliff Gorman. **1992**

HOGAN'S HEROES (TV SERIES) ★★★ One of the better sitcoms from the late 1960s. During World War II, Col. Robert Hogan leads an international band of resistance fighters composed of prisoners of war interned in a Nazi POW camp, right under the noses of their bumbling German captors. Good writing, directing, and ensemble acting made the idea work for 168 shows. Made for TV. 50m. per tape **DIR:** Various. **CAST:** Bob Crane, Werner Klemperer, John Banner, Robert Clary, Richard Dawson, Larry Hovis, Ivan Dixon, Kenneth Washington. **1965–70**

HOLCROFT COVENANT, THE ★★ In the closing days of World War II, three infamous Nazi officers deposit a large sum of money into a Swiss bank account to be withdrawn years later by their children. This slow but intriguing film, based on the novel by Robert Ludlum, will undoubtedly please spy-film enthusiasts, although others may find it tedious and contrived. Rated R for adult situations. 105m. **DIR:** John Frankenheimer. **CAST:** Michael Caine, Anthony Andrews, Victoria Tennant, Mario Adorf, Lilli Palmer. **1985**

HOLD 'EM JAIL ★★★ Fast-moving Wheeler and Woolsey burlesque puts them in prison with a warden (slow-burning Edgar Kennedy) whose passion is football. To get on his good side, they put together a prison football team and challenge a rival prison to a gridiron battle. B&W; 74m. **DIR:** Norman Taurog. **CAST:** Bert Wheeler, Robert Woolsey, Betty Grable, Robert Armstrong, Edgar Kennedy. **1932**

HOLD ME, THRILL ME, KISS ME ★★★1/2 Offbeat, slightly sleazy comedy about a drifter who hooks up with a sex-obsessed stripper and her sweet-natured sister only to find violence, depravity, and danger. Writer-director Joel Hershman set out to, in his words, "make a movie just as tasteless, vulgar and tacky as Hollywood for a lot less money." He's succeeded. Not rated, the film has profanity, nudity, simulated sex, and violence. 97m. **DIR:** Joel Hershman. **CAST:** Adrienne Shelly, Max Parrish, Sean Young, Diane Ladd, Andrea Naschak, Bela Lehoczky, Timothy Leary. **1993**

HOLD THAT GHOST ★★★1/2 Abbott and Costello score in this super comedy about two goofs (guess who) inheriting a haunted house where all kinds of bizarre events occur. You may have to watch this one a few times to catch all the gags. B&W; 86m. **DIR:** Arthur Lubin. **CAST:** Bud Abbott, Lou Costello, Richard Carlson, Joan Davis. **1941**

HOLD THE DREAM ★★★ This made-for-TV sequel to *A Woman of Substance* finds an aging Emma Harte (Deborah Kerr) turning over her department-store empire to her granddaughter, Paula (Jenny Seagrove). The rest of the family has plans to steal the business for themselves. Not as captivating as *Woman of Substance*, this sequel will still manage to entertain patrons of the soaps. 180m. **DIR:** Don Sharp. **CAST:** Jenny Seagrove, Deborah Kerr, Stephen Collins, James Brolin. **1986**

HOLD YOUR MAN ★★★★ One of the best examples of a movie that succeeds because of the vibes between its stars, this one holds your attention from start to finish. The two leads play a gangster and a gun moll who trade barbs, insults, and kisses with equal displays of passion. B&W; 87m. **DIR:** Sam Wood. **CAST:** Jean Harlow, Clark Gable, Dorothy

Burgess, Guy Kibbee, Stu Erwin, Elizabeth Patterson. 1933

HOLE IN THE HEAD, A ★★★ Frank Sinatra plays a Florida motel owner who never quite manages to get his life together, torn between his adoring son (Eddie Hodges) and his nagging brother (Edward G. Robinson). The veteran cast keeps this wispy comedy afloat, and its virtues include the Oscar-winning song "High Hopes." Not rated; suitable for the whole family. 120m. DIR: Frank Capra. CAST: Frank Sinatra, Edward G. Robinson, Eleanor Parker, Eddie Hodges, Carolyn Jones, Thelma Ritter, Keenan Wynn, Joi Lansing. 1959

HOLES, THE ★★ Obscure French satire about a group of misanthropes who live in the Paris sewers. Francophiles will want to see it for the cast, but there's little else to recommend it. Dubbed in English. Not rated. 94m. DIR: Pierre Tchernia. CAST: Michel Serrault, Michel Galabru, Charles Denner, Philippe Noiret, Gérard Depardieu. 1973

HOLIDAY ★★★1/2 This delightful film was adapted from the Broadway play by Phillip Barry and features Cary Grant as a nonconformist, who, for love's sake, must confront New York City's upper-class society. Indeed, he must make the ultimate sacrifice to please his fiancée (Doris Nolan) and join her father's banking firm. Only her sister (Katharine Hepburn) seems to understand Grant's need to live a different kind of life. B&W; 93m. DIR: George Cukor. CAST: Katharine Hepburn, Cary Grant, Doris Nolan, Lew Ayres, Edward Everett Horton, Binnie Barnes, Henry Daniell. 1938

HOLIDAY AFFAIR (1949) ★★★ Two highly different men court a pretty widow with a young son in this Christmas season story. A warm and friendly film for devotees of romantic melodrama. B&W; 87m. DIR: Don Hartman. CAST: Janet Leigh, Robert Mitchum, Wendell Corey. 1949

HOLIDAY AFFAIR (1996) ★★★ This made-for-cable remake is not much of an improvement on the story of two men vying for the attentions of one woman during the Christmas season. From the start, it's obvious whom Cynthia Gibb will end up with, and her barely credible performance gives no indication she is in emotional turmoil. The result is just dull. Not rated. 95m. DIR: Alan Myerson. CAST: Cynthia Gibb, David James Elliott, Tom Irwin. 1996

HOLIDAY HOTEL ★★★ It's August, and all of France is going on vacation for the entire month. The cast of this fast-paced comedy is heading toward the Brittany coast. Michel Lang keeps the tempo moving with clever farcical bits and dialogue. Partially in English, the movie has an R rating due to nudity and profanity. 109m. DIR: Michel Lang. CAST: Sophie Barjac, Daniel Ceccaldi, Michel Grellier, Guy Marchand. 1978

HOLIDAY IN MEXICO ★★★1/2 Song-filled feast, with widowed Walter Pidgeon as the Ambassador to Mexico. He and his daughter, Jane Powell, find the loves of their lives. Powell sings the "Italian Street Song" and a moving version of "Ave Maria." Jose Iturbi plays Chopin's "Polonaise." 127m. DIR: George Sidney. CAST: Walter Pidgeon, José Iturbi, Roddy Mc-

Dowall, Ilona Massey, Jane Powell, Xavier Cugat, Hugo Haas, Linda Christian. 1946

HOLIDAY INN ★★★★ Irving Berlin's music and the delightful teaming of Bing Crosby and Fred Astaire are the high points of this wartime musical. The timeless renditions of "White Christmas" and "Easter Parade" more than make up for a script that at best could be called fluff. B&W; 101m. DIR: Mark Sandrich. CAST: Bing Crosby, Fred Astaire, Marjorie Reynolds, Virginia Dale. 1942 DVD

HOLLOW POINT ★★1/2 Here's a switch: action hero Thomas Ian Griffith abandons his usual "style" and plays this explosive shoot-'em-up strictly for cartoon-style laughs. Unfortunately, neither Griffith nor costar Tia Carrere can manage the proper tongue-in-cheek tone; both are overshadowed by costar Donald Sutherland, who steals the film as an assassin with principles. Rated R for violence, profanity, and drug use. 103m. DIR: Sidney J. Furie. CAST: Thomas Ian Griffith, Tia Carrere, John Lithgow, Donald Sutherland. 1995

HOLLOW REED ★★★1/2 A gay father's attempt to gain custody of his son after he suspects the child is being abused sparks controversy in this intense and topical drama. Martin Donovan is sensational as the father trying to start his new life after divorce only to have his lifestyle scrutinized when he attempts to investigate his son's abuse. Rated R for adult situations and language. 105m. DIR: Angela Pope. CAST: Martin Donovan, Joely Richardson, Ian Hart, Jason Flemyng, Sam Bould. 1995

HOLLYWOOD BOULEVARD ★★★ A would-be actress goes to work for inept moviemakers in this comedy. This is the first film that Joe Dante (*Gremlins*) directed. Rated R. 83m. DIR: Joe Dante, Allan Arkush. CAST: Candice Rialson, Mary Woronov, Rita George, Jeffrey Kramer, Dick Miller, Paul Bartel. 1976

HOLLYWOOD BOULEVARD II 🎭 Sleazoid trash takes place on a movie set. Rated R for nudity, profanity, and violence. 82m. DIR: Steve Barnett. CAST: Ginger Lynn Allen, Kelly Monteith, Eddie Deezen. 1989

HOLLYWOOD CANTEEN ★★★ An all-star tribute to soldiers, sailors, and Marines who frequented the famed Hollywood Canteen during World War II. Bette Davis and John Garfield founded the USO haven, and just about everybody in show business donated his and her time to make the servicemen feel at ease. The slim storyline is about the one millionth soldier to visit the Canteen. B&W; 125m. DIR: Delmer Daves. CAST: Bette Davis, John Garfield, Joan Crawford, Ida Lupino, Errol Flynn, Olivia de Havilland, Joan Leslie, Jack Benny, Roy Rogers, Robert Hutton, Dane Clark, Sydney Greenstreet, Peter Lorre, Barbara Stanwyck, Alexis Smith, Eddie Cantor, Janis Paige. 1944

HOLLYWOOD CAVALCADE ★★★★ A highly fictionalized history of early Hollywood with several comic veterans from the silent days on hand to do what they do best. 96m. DIR: Irving Cummings. CAST: Don Ameche, Alice Faye, Jed Prouty, Alan Curtis, Chick Chandler, Donald Meek, Al Jolson, Buster Keaton, Ben Turpin, Chester Conklin, Mack Sennett, The Keystone Kops. 1939

HOLLYWOOD CHAINSAW HOOKERS ★★ Easily Fred Olen Ray's best film (which admittedly is saying very little), this is not the rip-off its title suggests. Ray delivers a campy, sexy, *very* bloody parody about attractive prostitutes who dismember their unsuspecting customers. Both gory and tedious. Rated R. 90m. DIR: Fred Olen Ray. CAST: Gunnar Hansen, Linnea Quigley. 1988

HOLLYWOOD CONFIDENTIAL ★★ Mediocre mystery thriller about a team of detectives who clean up celebrity "messes." Plays like a failed television-series pilot. Rated R for sexual content and violence. 92m. DIR: Reynaldo Villalobos. CAST: Edward James Olmos, Charlize Theron, Rick Aiello. 1995 DVD

HOLLYWOOD COP 🎬 Undercover cop battles the mob. Rated R for nudity and violence. B&W; 100m. DIR: Amir Shervan. CAST: David Goss, Jim Mitchum, Cameron Mitchell, Troy Donahue, Aldo Ray, Lincoln Kilpatrick. 1987

HOLLYWOOD DETECTIVE, THE ★★1/2 This chatty thriller bears all the earmarks of a failed television pilot, with Telly Savalas starring as a has-been TV actor rather improbably hired by jittery Helene Udy to find her missing boyfriend. Christopher Crowe's script is cute but nothing special; his few topical references to Malathion and Medflies do not a *Chinatown* make. 93m. DIR: Kevin Connor. CAST: Telly Savalas, Helene Udy, George Coe, Joe Dallesandro. 1991

HOLLYWOOD DREAMS 🎬 Casting couches, lecherous agents, and plenty of sleazy stereotypes await a Midwest starlet hoping to make it big in Hollywood. Not rated; contains strong sexual content. 90m. DIR: Ralph Portillo. CAST: Kelly Cook, Danny Smith, Debra Beatty, Rick Scandlin. 1993 DVD

HOLLYWOOD HARRY ★★★1/2 Robert Forster stars in this comedy about a down-and-out detective who is forced to take his runaway niece on his investigations. Rated PG-13 for profanity. 99m. DIR: Robert Forster. CAST: Robert Forster, Joe Spinell, Shannon Wilcox, Kathrine Forster, Marji Martin, Mallie Jackson, Read Morgan. 1985

HOLLYWOOD HEARTBREAK ★★1/2 Decent, but all too familiar, tale of a Hollywood hopeful. This time the twist is that instead of a gorgeous starlet, the protagonist is a male writer. Not rated; contains profanity. 80m. DIR: Lance Dickson. CAST: Mark Moses, Carol Mayo Jenkins, Ron Karabatsos. 1990

HOLLYWOOD HIGH 🎬 Four girls in their quest for a place to "get it on." Rated R for profanity and nudity. 81m. DIR: Patrick Wright. CAST: Marcy Albrecht, Sherry Hardin. 1976

HOLLYWOOD HIGH, PART II 🎬 Teen sexploitation at its worst. Rated R for profanity and nudity. 86m. DIR: Caruth C. Byrd, Lee Thornburg. CAST: April May, Donna Lynn, Camille Warner, Drew Davis, Bruce Dobos. 1981

HOLLYWOOD HOT TUBS 🎬 A young man wangles a job at a local hot tub firm in L.A. Rated R for nudity. 103m. DIR: Chuck Vincent. CAST: Paul Gunning, Donna McDaniel. 1984

HOLLYWOOD HOTEL ★★ Saxophonist Dick Powell wins a talent contest, gets a film contract, but gets the boot because he won't cozy up to bitchy star Lola Lane, preferring her sister instead. Songs by Johnny Mercer and Richard Whiting, including "Hooray for Hollywood," help bolster this otherwise average musical mishmash. B&W; 109m. DIR: Busby Berkeley. CAST: Dick Powell, Rosemary Lane, Lola Lane, Ted Healy, Alan Mowbray, Frances Langford, Hugh Herbert, Louella Parsons, Glenda Farrell, Edgar Kennedy. 1937

•**HOLLYWOOD KNIGHTS, THE** ★★★★ Despite the lowbrow antics, this nostalgic chestnut says a lot about male bonding. With their hamburger hangout ready to close on Halloween Eve, 1965, a local car club decides to have one last blowout to retaliate against the snobs. Funny, romantic, and emotionally in touch with the spirit of the era, the film includes many memorable moments and a soundtrack that keeps the joint jumping. Rated R for adult situations and language. 92m. DIR: Floyd Mutrux. CAST: Tony Danza, Michelle Pfeiffer, Robert Wuhl, Fran Drescher, Stuart Pankin, Richard Schaal, Leigh French. 1980 DVD

HOLLYWOOD MEATCLEAVER MASSACRE 🎬 Cheesy hack-'em-up about a vengeful demon. Amateurish and inept. Rated R. 87m. DIR: Evan Lee. CAST: Christopher Lee, Larry Justin. 1975

HOLLYWOOD OR BUST ★★1/2 One of Dean Martin and Jerry Lewis's lesser efforts concerns the boys' misadventures on a trip to Hollywood where movie nut Jerry hopes to meet his dream girl, Anita Ekberg (who plays herself). Starts off well, but stalls as soon as the musical interludes begin. The final teaming of Martin and Lewis. 95m. DIR: Frank Tashlin. CAST: Jerry Lewis, Dean Martin, Pat Crowley, Anita Ekberg. 1956

HOLLYWOOD PARTY ★★★ Jimmy Durante's jungle series as "Schnarzan, the Conqueror" are box-office failures, so he hosts a large party to generate interest in them. That's it, but it opens the door for some lavish musical numbers and cameo appearances by Stan Laurel, Oliver Hardy, the Three Stooges, Jack Pearl (as Baron Muenchausen), and Mickey Mouse. A Walt Disney cartoon short is in color. B&W/color; 69m. DIR: Allan Dwan, Roy Rowland. CAST: Jimmy Durante, Stan Laurel, Oliver Hardy, Lupe Velez. 1934

HOLLYWOOD SAFARI ★★1/2 A family of animal trainers tries to find their escaped mountain lion before it is killed by a trigger-happy deputy eager to substitute it for a lion that has been attacking local tourists. Adventure aimed at kids, who may not mind the jumpy plot and cheapo special effects. Rated PG for mild violence. 89m. DIR: Henri Charr. CAST: Ted Jan Roberts, Ryan J. O'Neill, David Leisure, Don "The Dragon" Wilson, Debby Boone. 1997

HOLLYWOOD SHUFFLE ★★★1/2 In the style of *Kentucky Fried Movie*, writer-director-star Robert Townsend lampoons Hollywood's perception of blacks—and racial stereotypes in general. It's not always funny, but some scenes are hilarious. A private-eye spoof called "Death of a Break Dancer," and something entitled "Black Acting School" are the standouts. Rated R for profanity and adult content. 82m. DIR: Robert Townsend. CAST: Robert Townsend, Anne-Marie Johnson, Starletta Dupois. 1987

HOLLYWOOD STRANGLER MEETS THE SKID ROW SLASHER 🖤 Psycho wanders around L.A. taking photos of amateur models and then strangling them. Rated R for nudity, violence, and gore. 72m. **DIR:** Wolfgang Schmidt. **CAST:** Pierre Agostino, Carolyn Brandt. **1982**

HOLLYWOOD VICE SQUAD 🖤 A tepid affair about a runaway in the sleazoid areas of Hollywood. Rated R for nudity, profanity, and violence. 93m. **DIR:** Penelope Spheeris. **CAST:** Ronny Cox, Frank Gorshin, Leon Isaac Kennedy, Trish Van Devere, Carrie Fisher. **1986**

HOLOCAUST ★★★1/2 This Emmy-winning miniseries is one of the finest programs ever produced for television. The story follows the lives of two German families during the reign of Hitler's Third Reich. Everyone in front of and behind the camera does a stunning job. This is a must-see. 570m. **DIR:** Marvin J. Chomsky. **CAST:** Tom Bell, Michael Moriarty, Tovah Feldshuh, Meryl Streep, Fritz Weaver, David Warner. **1978**

HOLOCAUST 2000 🖤 The Antichrist plans to destroy the world, using nuclear reactors. Rated R. 96m. **DIR:** Alberto De Martino. **CAST:** Kirk Douglas, Agostina Belli, Simon Ward, Anthony Quayle. **1978**

HOLY INNOCENTS ★★★★ This moving drama explores the social class struggles in a remote farming community during Franco's rule in Spain. It's a sensitive and compelling look into the struggle of the rural lower class against the wealthy landowners. This critically acclaimed film earned acting awards at the Cannes Film Festival for Alfredo Landa and Francisco Rabal. In Spanish with English subtitles. 108m. **DIR:** Mario Camus. **CAST:** Alfredo Landa, Francisco Rabal. **1984**

HOLY MAN ★★ This comedy misfire is an unfocused assortment of half-baked ideas without the benefit of a star to hold it all together, since Eddie Murphy's participation is as vapid as the concept itself. He plays a spiritual innocent—or so we're led to believe—trying to save network executive Jeff Goldblum's soul, not that you're likely to care, since the stars have zero chemistry. Rated PG for mildly tasteless humor. 114m. **DIR:** Stephen Herek. **CAST:** Eddie Murphy, Jeff Goldblum, Kelly Preston, Robert Loggia, Jon Cryer. **1998 DVD**

HOLY MATRIMONY ★★1/2 Well-intentioned comedy has a moral and some good performances, but a formulaic chase story keeps it mired in mediocrity. Patricia Arquette dreams of becoming a star in Hollywood, so she helps her ne'er-do-well boyfriend rob a carnival owner only to find herself hiding out in a strict, religious Hutterite settlement. This leads to all sorts of rarely hilarious complications. Rated PG-13 for profanity, violence, and suggested nudity. 93m. **DIR:** Leonard Nimoy. **CAST:** Patricia Arquette, Armin Mueller-Stahl, Joseph Gordon-Levitt, Tate Donovan, John Schuck. **1994**

•**HOLY SMOKE** ★★ An Australian family hires a deprogrammer (Harvey Keitel) to rescue their daughter (Kate Winslet) from an Indian religious cult. Director Jane Campion's over-the-top film flails around madly without ever lighting on a coherent idea; the age gap and lack of chemistry between Winslet and Keitel don't help. Rated R for nudity, profanity, and sexual scenes. 120m. **DIR:** Jane Campion. **CAST:** Kate Winslet, Harvey Keitel, Julie Hamilton, Sophie Lee, Pam Grier. **1999**

HOMAGE ★★1/2 The odd-couple friendship between a reclusive older woman (Blythe Danner) and the young man she hires to tend her estate (Frank Whaley) is disrupted when he becomes obsessed with her daughter, a sexy actress (Sheryl Lee). Quirky drama that never fully delivers on all the issues it raises. Rated R for profanity and sexual situations. 100m. **DIR:** Ross Kagan Marks. **CAST:** Blythe Danner, Frank Whaley, Sheryl Lee, Bruce Davison. **1996**

HOMBRE ★★★★ Paul Newman gives a superb performance as a white man raised by Indians who is enticed into helping a stagecoach full of settlers make its way across treacherous country. Richard Boone is the baddie who makes this chore difficult, but the racism Newman encounters in this Martin Ritt film provides the real—and thought-provoking—thrust. 111m. **DIR:** Martin Ritt. **CAST:** Paul Newman, Fredric March, Richard Boone, Diane Cilento, Cameron Mitchell, Barbara Rush, Martin Balsam. **1967**

HOME ALONE ★★★★ A child's eye view of *It's a Wonderful Life* in which youngsters are reminded of the importance of family and real values. It all begins when 8-year-old Kevin McAllister (Macaulay Culkin) wishes his family would just go away, and they, unbeknownst to him, accidentally go on vacation without him. From there on it's a roller-coaster ride of chuckles and chills. Rated PG for brief vulgarity and silly violence. 100m. **DIR:** Chris Columbus. **CAST:** Macaulay Culkin, Joe Pesci, Daniel Stern, John Heard, Catherine O'Hara, Roberts Blossom, John Candy. **1990 DVD**

HOME ALONE 2: LOST IN NEW YORK ★★★★ Essentially a bigger-budgeted remake of the first film, this sequel is filled with belly laughs. Writer-producer John Hughes does tend to get a bit maudlin, but Macaulay Culkin's misadventures in the Big Apple, after being more believably separated from his parents this time, are more consistently entertaining than his first time *Home Alone*. Rated PG for profanity and slapstick violence. 113m. **DIR:** Chris Columbus. **CAST:** Macaulay Culkin, Joe Pesci, Daniel Stern, Catherine O'Hara, John Heard, Tim Curry, Brenda Fricker, Eddie Bracken. **1992 DVD**

HOME ALONE 3 ★★★1/2 Alex D. Linz fills in nicely as Alex Pruitt, who has to fend off a band of international crooks intent on retrieving a computer chip hidden inside one of his toys. Home with the chicken pox, Alex is forced to become resourceful when his mom steps out to get his medicine, and the crooks step in. Funny, endearing stuff. Rated PG. 102m. **DIR:** Raja Gosnell. **CAST:** Alex D. Linz, Haviland Morris, Lenny Von Dohlen, Olek Krupa, Kevin Kilner, Rya Kihlstedt. **1997 DVD**

HOME AND THE WORLD ★★★★ Satyajit Ray's critically acclaimed, harrowing account of the coming-of-age of an Indian woman. She falls in love with her husband's best friend, an organizer against British goods. This fascinating portrait of Bengali life was based on the Nobel Prize–winning novel by Rabindranath Tagore. In Bengali with English subtitles. Not rated. 130m. **DIR:** Satyajit Ray. **CAST:** Soumitra Chatterjee, Victor Banerjee. **1984**

HOME FOR CHRISTMAS ★★★ Unbelievable, yet touching, made-for-TV tale of a young girl's desire to receive a grandfather for Christmas. Mickey Rooney plays the homeless man she's chosen. 96m. **DIR:** Peter McCubbin. **CAST:** Mickey Rooney, Chantellese Kent, Simon Richards, Lesley Kelly. **1990 DVD**

HOME FOR THE HOLIDAYS (1972) (TELEVISION) ★★★ This TV movie focuses on a family that gathers for Christmas, only to learn they're being stalked by a psycho with a pitchfork. A chilling whodunit. 90m. **DIR:** John Llewellyn Moxey. **CAST:** Sally Field, Jessica Walter, Eleanor Parker, Julie Harris, Jill Haworth, Walter Brennan. **1972**

HOME FOR THE HOLIDAYS (1995) ★★1/2 The stressful, crisis-laden Thanksgiving weekend of a "typical" American family makes for a film with a split personality. The first half is overbearing and obnoxious, while the second half turns suddenly mushy and sentimental. The quiet moments are the best, but they're too few and too late. Rated PG-13 for mild profanity. 103m. **DIR:** Jodie Foster. **CAST:** Holly Hunter, Robert Downey Jr., Anne Bancroft, Dylan McDermott, Charles Durning, Geraldine Chaplin, Steve Guttenberg, Claire Danes. **1995**

HOME FRIES ★★★ Two brothers, after killing their philandering stepfather, decide to go after Dad's teenage mistress (Drew Barrymore)—until one brother falls in love with her. The amiably offbeat premise and the sweet, vulnerable performances of Barrymore and Luke Wilson help to offset the meandering contrivances of the script and Dean Parisot's uneasy direction. Catherine O'Hara has some eerie moments as the boys' demented mother. Rated PG-13 for mild profanity. 96m. **DIR:** Dean Parisot. **CAST:** Drew Barrymore, Luke Wilson, Jake Busey, Catherine O'Hara, Shelley Duvall. **1998 DVD**

HOME FROM THE HILL ★★★★ Melodramatic film focuses on a wealthy but dysfunctional southern family. Robert Mitchum is the philandering patriarch. George Hamilton and George Peppard debut as Mitchum's grown sons. Downbeat but well acted and directed. 151m. **DIR:** Vincente Minnelli. **CAST:** Robert Mitchum, Eleanor Parker, George Hamilton, George Peppard, Luana Patten. **1959**

HOME IS WHERE THE HART IS 🐝 Lethargic, unfunny attempt at a black comedy. Rated PG-13. 85m. **DIR:** Rex Bromfield. **CAST:** Valri Bromfield, Stephen E. Miller, Eric Christmas, Leslie Nielsen, Martin Mull. **1987**

HOME MOVIES ★★ A little film produced with the help of Brian De Palma's filmmaking students at Sarah Lawrence College. A director, played by Kirk Douglas, gives "star therapy" to a young man who feels he is a mere extra in his own life. The film is quirky and fun at times, but as entertainment, it's quite tedious. Rated PG. 90m. **DIR:** Brian De Palma. **CAST:** Nancy Allen, Keith Gordon, Kirk Douglas, Gerrit Graham, Vincent Gardenia. **1980**

HOME OF OUR OWN, A ★★★ A single mother (Kathy Bates) and her six kids move into an abandoned farmhouse in Idaho, making a deal with the owner to fix it up and eventually buy it from him.

There's a crisis every ten minutes, and not much happens that you haven't seen before, but the actors carry the film, especially Edward Furlong and Clarissa Lessig as the two older children. Rated PG. 102m. **DIR:** Tony Bill. **CAST:** Kathy Bates, Edward Furlong, Clarissa Lessig, Soon-Teck Oh, Tony Campisi. **1993**

HOME OF THE BRAVE ★★★ This is one of the first films dealing with blacks serving in the military during World War II. The story finds James Edwards on a mission in the Pacific and deals with the racial abuse that he encounters from his own men. The good plot of this film could use some more action, yet it is still worth watching. B&W; 85m. **DIR:** Mark Robson. **CAST:** James Edwards, Steve Brodie, Jeff Corey, Douglas Dick. **1949**

HOME REMEDY ★★★ A young New Jersey man retreats into his suburban house, where the noisy woman next door is his only obstacle to complete and blissful inertia. Odd, talky black comedy. Not rated, mild sexual situations. 92m. **DIR:** Maggie Greenwald. **CAST:** Seth Barrish, Maxine Albert. **1988**

HOME, SWEET HOME (1914) ★★1/2 Henry B. Walthall is John Howard Payne in this fanciful biography of the famous composer. Lillian Gish is his faithful, long-suffering sweetheart. Denied happiness in life, the lovers are united as they "fly" to heaven. Silent. B&W; 80m. **DIR:** D. W. Griffith. **CAST:** Henry B. Walthall, Lillian Gish, Dorothy Gish, Mae Marsh, Spottiswoode Aitken, Miriam Cooper, Robert Harron, Donald Crisp, Blanche Sweet, Owen Moore. **1914**

HOME SWEET HOME (1982) ★★★★ One in a series of films made by Mike Leigh in the 1970s and early 1980s for British television. A low-budget, bitter black comedy, it is an incisive bit of snoopery. Leigh reveals the isolation of the English working class by focusing on three postal workers who find their lives mingled, as one of them is sleeping with the wives of the other two. Leigh makes it clear that the Monty Pythoners didn't have to look far for their parodies. Not rated; contains profanity and adult themes. 90m. **DIR:** Mike Leigh. **CAST:** Eric Richard, Timothy Spall, Kay Stonham, Lorraine Brunning. **1982**

HOMEBODIES ★★★ A cast of aging screen veterans liven up this offbeat thriller about a group of senior citizens who turn into a hit squad when faced with eviction. Director Larry Yust keeps things moving at a lively pace and even manages a few bizarre twists in the final scenes. Rated PG for violence, language. 96m. **DIR:** Larry Yust. **CAST:** Douglas Fowley, Ruth McDevitt, Ian Wolfe. **1974**

HOMEBOY ★★ This slow-moving, moody drama about a washed-up cowboy prizefighter is engorged with down-and-out characters. Mickey Rourke stars as the maverick boxer who drinks, smirks, and mumbles his way to one last shot as a top middleweight contender. The raunchy, atmospheric soundtrack is by Eric Clapton and Michael Kamen. Rated R for profanity and violence. 118m. **DIR:** Michael Seresin. **CAST:** Mickey Rourke, Christopher Walken, Debra Feuer, Kevin Conway. **1988**

HOMEBOYS ★★ Mexican-Americans are portrayed as ruthless drug dealers in this urban piece about how a cop can be torn between his job and his love for his brother. The young cast does a fair job in this low-budget production. Not rated, but with nudity and profanity. 91m. **DIR:** Lindsay Norgard. **CAST:** Todd Bridges, David Garrison. **1992**

HOMEBOYS II: CRACK CITY ★★ A good kid falls in with a bad crowd when he moves to Harlem from the suburbs. Well-intentioned message movie is weighed down by too many ridiculous plot elements. It has nothing to do with *Homeboys*. Not rated, but an R equivalent for violence and nudity. 90m. **DIR:** Daniel Matmor. **CAST:** Brian Paul Stewart, Delia Sheppard. **1989**

HOMECOMING (1948) ★★ In this post–WWII melodrama, Clark Gable, Lana Turner, and Anne Baxter are glamorous. If they had something to do other than talk and stare, they might have had a better movie. It's about an army surgeon who has a romance with his nurse while both are in the trenches. Even with Gable and Turner as the illicit lovers, the movie isn't as good as it should have been. B&W; 113m. **DIR:** Mervyn LeRoy. **CAST:** Clark Gable, Lana Turner, Anne Baxter, John Hodiak, Ray Collins, Cameron Mitchell, Gladys Cooper, Marshall Thompson. **1948**

HOMECOMING, THE (1973) ★★★★ Michael Jayston brings his wife, Vivien Merchant, home to meet the family after several years of separation. His father and two brothers are no-holds-barred Harold Pinter characters. If you like drama and Pinter, you'll want to check out this American Film Theater production, which has outstanding direction by Peter Hall. 111m. **DIR:** Peter Hall. **CAST:** Cyril Cusack, Ian Holm, Michael Jayston, Vivien Merchant, Terrence Rigby, Paul Rogers. **1973**

HOMECOMING (1996) ★★★1/2 When their mentally unstable mother simply wanders off one day, adolescent Kimberlee Peterson takes charge of three younger siblings and eventually guides them to an eccentric grandmother who scarcely knows them. Anne Bancroft steals the show as that estranged relative, but director Mark Jean wisely doesn't let her go over the top. Heartwarming entertainment, perfect for the entire family. Rated G. 105m. **DIR:** Mark Jean. **CAST:** Anne Bancroft, Kimberlee Peterson, Trever O'Brien, Hanna Hall, William Greenblatt, Bonnie Bedelia. **1996**

HOMEGROWN ★★★ Enjoyable film with a terrific cast about a group of illicit marijuana farmers who decide to take over the business when their boss is gunned down. In order to do that, however, they have to pretend he's still alive. Rated R for profanity and nudity. 103m. **DIR:** Stephen Gyllenhaal. **CAST:** Billy Bob Thornton, Hank Azaria, Kelly Lynch, Jon Bon Jovi, Judge Reinhold, Ted Danson, John Lithgow, Jamie Lee Curtis. **1998 DVD**

HOMER AND EDDIE ★★★ Outstanding performance by James Belushi as a retarded man trying to return to his dying father despite the fact that his father has disowned him. Whoopi Goldberg plays a sociopathic woman who gives Belushi the ride of a lifetime. Rated R for profanity and violence. 102m. **DIR:** Andrei Konchalovsky. **CAST:** James Belushi, Whoopi Goldberg, Karen Black, Anne Ramsey. **1989**

HOMETOWN BOY MAKES GOOD ★★★ Waiter Anthony Edwards returns home to Minnesota for a visit and finds out that the little white lie he told his mother has spread. It seems the whole town thinks he's a famous psychiatrist, and pretty soon he's Doc Minnesota. Half the fun is watching Edwards cover his bases while continuing the sham. Good supporting cast pitches in to make this a fun outing. Not rated; contains adult language. 88m. **DIR:** David Burton Morris. **CAST:** Anthony Edwards, Grace Zabriskie, Chris Mulkey. **1993**

HOMEWARD BOUND: THE INCREDIBLE JOURNEY ★★★1/2 The folks at Walt Disney Pictures take the animal adventure to artistic heights. A remake of Disney's *The Incredible Journey*, this highly entertaining movie gives voices (supplied by Sally Field, Michael J. Fox, and Don Ameche) and hilarious dialogue to two dogs and a cat, who attempt to make their way home through the untamed wilderness of a national forest. A delight for all ages. Rated G. 84m. **DIR:** Duwayne Dunham. **CAST:** Robert Hays, Kim Greist, Jean Smart, Veronica Lauren, Kevin Chevalia, Benj Thall. **1993 DVD**

HOMEWARD BOUND II: LOST IN SAN FRANCISCO ★★ American bulldog Chance, golden retriever Shadow, and Himalayan cat Sassy once again are separated from their family. This time they need to survive the bully pooches, pet nappers, and mean streets of San Francisco while trying to find their way back to their new Marin digs. Lacks the original film's breathtaking nature thrills and warm humor. Rated G. 97m. **DIR:** David R. Ellis. **CAST:** Robert Hays, Kim Greist, Veronica Lauren, Kevin Chevalia, Benj Thall. **1996**

HOMEWORK 🖤 High school teacher seduces one of her students. Rated R for nudity. 90m. **DIR:** James Beshears. **CAST:** Joan Collins, Shell Kepler, Wings Hauser, Betty Thomas. **1982**

HOMEWRECKER ★★★1/2 Scientist Robby Benson suffers a breakdown after accidentally killing a family during a military defense test. When he privately rebuilds his computer, he adds human traits, and the computer (voiced by Kate Jackson) takes on a very human, and jealous, persona. An imaginative plot, tight editing, and Benson's performance overcome the low budget. Rated PG-13 for profanity. 88m. **DIR:** Fred Walton. **CAST:** Robby Benson, Sydney Walsh, Sarah Rose Karr. **1992**

HOMICIDAL ★★★ Schlockmeister William Castle's best movie is this blatant *Psycho* takeoff that, unlike most such imitations, at least manages to add a few new twists. B&W; 87m. **DIR:** William Castle. **CAST:** Glenn Corbett, Patricia Breslin, Jean Aless, Eugenie Leontovich. **1961**

HOMICIDAL IMPULSE ★★1/2 Derivative thriller stars Scott Valentine as an assistant district attorney who gets involved with scheming intern Vanessa Angel, who's willing to do anything to rise to the top, including murder. Rated R for nudity and violence. 86m. **DIR:** David Tausik. **CAST:** Scott Valentine, Vanessa Angel, Charles Napier. **1992**

HOMICIDE ★★★1/2 A detective is assigned against his will to investigate the murder of an older Jewish woman killed at her shop in a predominantly black neighborhood. Crackling dialogue and a suspenseful atmosphere make up for a plot twist that doesn't quite ring true in this Chinese puzzle of a movie. Rated R for profanity and violence. 102m. **DIR:** David Mamet. **CAST:** Joe Mantegna, William H. Macy, Natalija Nogulich, Ving Rhames. 1991

HONDO ★★★★ One of John Wayne's best films and performances, this 3-D Western overcomes the gimmicky process with excellent performances, plenty of action, and an uncommonly strong screenplay from frequent Wayne collaborator James Edward Grant. The Duke plays an army scout who adopts a widowed frontierswoman (Geraldine Page in her Oscar-nominated film debut) and her son. 84m. **DIR:** John Farrow. **CAST:** John Wayne, Geraldine Page, Ward Bond, Lee Aaker, James Arness, Michael Pate, Leo Gordon, Paul Fix. 1953

HONDO AND THE APACHES ★★★ Based on the John Wayne film. Ralph Taeger is Indian scout, Hondo Lane. Three episodes of the *Hondo* TV series edited into feature form. 85m. **DIR:** Lee H. Katzin. **CAST:** Ralph Taeger, Robert Taylor, Noah Beery Jr., Michael Rennie, John Smith, Kathie Browne. 1967

HONEY, I BLEW UP THE KID ★★★★ This is a delightful sequel to *Honey, I Shrunk the Kids.* The new adventure once again finds scientist Rick Moranis working on an experiment, only this time it's an enlargement ray that blows up his kid to 112 feet tall! The special effects are remarkable. Rated PG. 89m. **DIR:** Randal Kleiser. **CAST:** Rick Moranis, Marcia Strassman, Lloyd Bridges, Robert Oliveri, John Shea. 1992

HONEY, I SHRUNK THE KIDS ★★★1/2 Old-fashioned Disney fun in the *Absent-Minded Professor* tradition gets contemporary special effects and solid bits of comedy. Rick Moranis is the scientist who invents a machine that, when accidentally triggered, shrinks his and the neighbors' kids to ant-size. Rated PG for slight profanity. 100m. **DIR:** Joe Johnston. **CAST:** Rick Moranis, Jared Rushton, Matt Frewer. 1989

HONEY POT, THE ★★ Rex Harrison summons three of his former loves to his deathbed for the reading of his will. This bloated, star-studded extravaganza could lose thirty minutes from its first half and become an entertaining little whodunit. 131m. **DIR:** Joseph L. Mankiewicz. **CAST:** Rex Harrison, Susan Hayward, Cliff Robertson, Maggie Smith, Capucine, Edie Adams. 1967

HONEY, WE SHRUNK OURSELVES ★★ Third, and weakest, entry in Disney's *Honey* series, this wisely was passed over for theatrical release, going straight to video. For a film that relies on special effects, there are too many computer graphics that just don't measure up. Rick Moranis, who shrinks himself and his brother (Stuart Pankin), seems to sleepwalk through his part of nutty invention. Rated PG for juvenile misbehavior. 75m. **DIR:** Dean Cundey. **CAST:** Rick Moranis, Stuart Pankin, Eve Gordon, Bug Hall, Robin Bartlett. 1996

HONEYBOY ★★ Erik Estrada is the boy, Morgan Fairchild the honey, in this watered-down compilation of every boxing cliché ever employed in the poor-boy-makes-good genre. Not rated and suitable for viewing by families with relatively strong stomachs. 100m. **DIR:** John Berry. **CAST:** Erik Estrada, Morgan Fairchild, Hector Elizondo, James McEachin, Phillip R. Allen. 1982

HONEYMOON ★★★1/2 A Frenchwoman (Nathalie Baye) goes on what appears to be a carefree New York vacation with her boyfriend (Richard Berry). However, he is busted for smuggling cocaine, and she is set for deportation. She goes to an agency that arranges marriages of convenience. She is assured that she will never see her new American "husband"—only to have him show up and refuse to leave her alone. Rated R for profanity, nudity, and violence. 98m. **DIR:** Patrick Jamain. **CAST:** Nathalie Baye, John Shea, Richard Berry, Peter Donat. 1987

HONEYMOON ACADEMY ★★ A secret agent (Kim Cattrall) marries unsuspecting Robert Hays. Reliance on sight gags and slapstick for laughs doesn't pan out. Rated PG-13 for violence. 94m. **DIR:** Gene Quintano. **CAST:** Robert Hays, Kim Cattrall, Leigh Taylor-Young, Jonathan Banks. 1990

HONEYMOON IN VEGAS ★★★★ Private detective Nicolas Cage finally overcomes his fear of commitment and agrees to marry longtime love Sarah Jessica Parker. On their honeymoon, they go to Las Vegas where everything begins going wrong, and they end up in the clutches of gangster James Caan. More inspired madcap madness from writer-director Andrew Bergman. Rated PG-13. 100m. **DIR:** Andrew Bergman. **CAST:** James Caan, Nicolas Cage, Sarah Jessica Parker, Anne Bancroft, Peter Boyle, Noriyuki "Pat" Morita. 1992 DVD

HONEYMOON KILLERS, THE ★★★ Grim story of a smooth-talking Lothario and his obese lover who befriend and murder vulnerable older women for their money is based on the infamous "lonely hearts killers" of the 1940s and 1950s. Not for the squeamish, but a solid entry in the growing file of true-crime films. 108m. **DIR:** Leonard Kastle. **CAST:** Tony Lo Bianco, Shirley Stoler, Mary Jane Higby. 1970

HONEYMOON MACHINE, THE ★★1/2 Three sailors use the master computer of their cruiser in an attempt to beat the roulette at a casino in Venice. Dean Jagger is fun as a bellowing admiral. 87m. **DIR:** Richard Thorpe. **CAST:** Steve McQueen, Brigid Bazlen, Jim Hutton, Paula Prentiss, Dean Jagger, Jack Weston, Jack Mullaney. 1961

HONEYMOON MURDERS 🖤 A couple honeymoons at a possessed country cottage in this inept attempt at a horror movie. Not rated. 114m. **DIR:** Steve Postal. **CAST:** Dave Knapp, Angela Shepard. 1990

HONEYMOONERS, THE (TV SERIES) ★★★★★ A tacky apartment in Bensonhurst, Brooklyn, is the setting for the misadventures of bus driver Ralph Kramden, his wife Alice, and their best friends, the Nortons. When Alice derides Ralph's get-rich-quick schemes, he's apt to bellow, "One of these days—Pow! Right in the kisser!" But, Gleason tempers the bluster with childlike appeal and, by the end of the episode, contrite Ralph embraces Alice and proclaims, "Baby, you're the greatest!" Each of the thirty-nine filmed episodes is a comic gem. Two episodes per tape. B&W; 50m. each tape. **DIR:** Frank Satenstein. **CAST:** Jackie Gleason, Art Carney, Audrey Meadows, Joyce Randolph. 1955–1956

HONEYMOONERS, THE: LOST EPISODES (TV SERIES) ★★★1/2 For years, the thirty-nine filmed episodes of *The Honeymooners*, all created during the 1955–1956 season, were the only ones the public could view. Then, with a dramatic flourish, Jackie Gleason announced that he had uncovered dozens of other episodes, preserved on kinescope. The skits often matched the classic thirty-nine in the categories of heart and hilarity. At their worst, these sketches surpass ninety-nine percent of what passes for comedy on television today. Twenty-two volumes; two or three episodes per tape. B&W; 47–55m. each tape. **DIR:** Frank Satenstein. **CAST:** Jackie Gleason, Art Carney, Audrey Meadows, Joyce Randolph. 1952–1957

HONEYSUCKLE ROSE ★★1/2 For his first starring role, country singer Willie Nelson is saddled with a rather stodgy film that all but sinks in the mire of its unimaginative handling and sappy story. Rated PG. 119m. **DIR:** Jerry Schatzberg. **CAST:** Willie Nelson, Dyan Cannon, Amy Irving, Slim Pickens. 1980

HONG KONG '97 ❤ Dismal, low-budget thriller about an assassin trying to unravel China's takeover of Hong Kong in 1997 from Great Britain. Rated R for nudity, violence, and adult language. 91m. **DIR:** Albert Pyun. **CAST:** Robert Patrick, Tim Thomerson, Brion James, Ming-Na Wen. 1994

HONKY TONK ★★★ A gambler fleeing tar and feathers meets a Boston beauty and her con man father on the train going to a new frontier town. He grows rich from graft and marries the beauty. Clark Gable and Lana Turner clicked as a team in this lively, lusty oater. B&W; 105m. **DIR:** Jack Conway. **CAST:** Clark Gable, Lana Turner, Frank Morgan, Claire Trevor, Marjorie Main, Albert Dekker, Henry O'Neill, Chill Wills, Veda Ann Borg. 1941

HONKY TONK FREEWAY ★★★ Director John Schlesinger captures the comedy of modern American life in a small Florida town. The stars keep you laughing. Rated R. 107m. **DIR:** John Schlesinger. **CAST:** William Devane, Beverly D'Angelo, Beau Bridges, Geraldine Page, Teri Garr. 1981

HONKYTONK MAN ★★★★ Clint Eastwood stars as an alcoholic, tubercular country singer headed for an audition at the Grand Ole Opry during the depths of the Depression. A bittersweet character study, it works remarkably well. You even begin to believe Eastwood in the role. The star's son, Kyle Eastwood, makes an impressive film debut. Rated PG for strong language and sexual content. 122m. **DIR:** Clint Eastwood. **CAST:** Clint Eastwood, Kyle Eastwood, John McIntire. 1982

HONOLULU ★★★★ More comedy than musical, this film was the last film George Burns made before his comeback in *The Sunshine Boys* more than a quarter of a century later. Robert Young plays a movie star and his twin brother, who change places and cause all sorts of mix-ups. Burns and Gracie Allen fill most of the time with choice one-liners. B&W; 83m. **DIR:** Edward Buzzell. **CAST:** Eleanor Powell, George Burns, Gracie Allen, Robert Young, Rita Johnson, Sig Ruman, Ruth Hussey, Eddie "Rochester" Anderson, Ann Morris, Clarence Kolb. 1939

HONOR AMONG THIEVES ★★1/2 Charles Bronson plays a mercenary who is locked in a French bank over the weekend with Alain Delon, a doctor. Bronson is there to rob the bank of its 200 million francs, while Delon is there to replace some misappropriated securities. This is a little different type of picture for Bronson—a bit more subtle, a little slower-paced, and with more dialogue than action. Rated R. 93m. **DIR:** Jean Herman. **CAST:** Charles Bronson, Alain Delon, Brigitte Fossey. 1983

HONOR AND GLORY ❤ Below-average actioner features kung fu expert Cynthia Rothrock as an FBI agent out to protect a nuclear arsenal from an evil banker. It turns into a family affair ... yawn: zzzz. Not rated; contains profanity and violence. 87m. **DIR:** Godfrey Hall. **CAST:** Cynthia Rothrock, Donna Jason, Chuck Jeffreys, Gerald Klein. 1992

HONOR THY FATHER ★★ A movie version of the real-life internal Mafia war that took place during the late 1960s among members of the Bonanno crime family. Weak. Not rated; contains violence. 97m. **DIR:** Paul Wendkos. **CAST:** Joseph Bologna, Brenda Vaccaro, Raf Vallone. 1973

HONOR THY FATHER & MOTHER: THE MENENDEZ KILLINGS ★★ The better (and that's not saying much) of two made-for-television docudramas chronicling the murders of Jose and Kitty Menendez (James Farentino and Jill Clayburgh), who were allegedly murdered by their sons Erik and Lyle in order to inherit the family fortune. Film fails to add anything new to the tragic events that gripped America when the sons were brought to trial. Not rated; contains strong images of violence. 97m. **DIR:** Paul Schneider. **CAST:** James Farentino, Jill Clayburgh, Billy Warlock, David Beron. 1993

HOODLUM ★★★1/2 When gangster Dutch Schultz begins to yank control of the Harlem numbers racket from its black caretakers, he steps on the toes of his organized crime associates. Bumpy Johnson then joins forces with the mob's Lucky Luciano to exterminate the greedy, swaggering renegade. This predictable, violent melodrama benefits from its 1930s Harlem setting and excellent cast. Rated R for violence, language, nudity, and suggested sex. 142m. **DIR:** Bill Duke. **CAST:** Laurence Fishburne, Tim Roth, Andy Garcia, Cicely Tyson, Vanessa L. Williams, Clarence Williams III, Richard Bradford. 1997 DVD

HOODLUM EMPIRE ★★ A racketeer's nephew decides to go straight after a tour of duty in World War II but runs into problems from both sides of the law. A very thinly disguised filmic depiction of the famous Estes Kefauver investigation into Frank Costello and his ties with organized crime, this docudrama is long on talent but short on style. B&W; 98m. **DIR:** Joseph Kane. **CAST:** Brian Donlevy, Claire Trevor, Forrest Tucker, Vera Hruba Ralston, Luther Adler, John Russell, Gene Lockhart, Grant Withers, Taylor Holmes, Richard Jaeckel. 1952

HOODLUM PRIEST, THE ★★★1/2 Don Murray gives a sincere performance as Father Charles Dismis Clark, a Jesuit priest who devotes himself to helping newly released convicts reenter society. The focus is on one young parolee (Keir Dullea, in his debut) who has trouble finding his way. Murray coproduced. B&W; 101m. DIR: Irvin Kershner. CAST: Don Murray, Keir Dullea, Larry Gates, Logan Ramsey, Don Joslyn, Cindi Wood. 1961

●HOODS ★★1/2 A small group of gangsters is commissioned to put a hit out on a fellow that they've never heard of. When they finally track down the elusive target, the assassins discover that their target is just a kid. The group is thrown into confusion by this unexpected turn of affairs, but they soon find out that there is a lot to this kid that they do not know about. The cast is full of recognizable faces, but the film cannot decide whether it is a dark satire or a slapstick farce—it doesn't work as either. Rated R for language, violence, and sexual situations. 92m. DIR: Mark Malone. CAST: Joe Mantegna, Kevin Pollak, Joe Pantoliano, Jennifer Tilly. 1998 DVD

HOOK ★★★1/2 For all its minor flaws, director Steven Spielberg's heartfelt continuation of James M. Barrie's *Peter Pan* is fine family entertainment. There are some dull spots, but it's doubtful they'll be as glaring on the small screen. Look for Glenn Close and singer David Crosby in brief bits as pirates on Hook's ship. Rated PG for vulgar language. 137m. DIR: Steven Spielberg. CAST: Robin Williams, Dustin Hoffman, Julia Roberts, Bob Hoskins, Maggie Smith, Charlie Korsmo, Phil Collins, Glenn Close, David Crosby. 1991 DVD

HOOK, LINE AND SINKER ★★ Silly story of two nitwits who woo a mother and daughter. The popular comedy team of Wheeler and Woolsey did better work than this sort of a watered-down version of The Marx Brothers'. B&W; 71m. DIR: Eddie Cline. CAST: Bert Wheeler, Robert Woolsey, Dorothy Lee, Hugh Herbert, Natalie Moorhead. 1930

HOOP DREAMS ★★★★★ This rich slice of the American Dream stretches into the realm of exhilarating Hollywood drama. Three white guys with a camera talked their way into the lives of two black youths in 1987 and emerged nearly five years later with a staggering urban saga. Hoping to eventually play in the NBA, the two 14-year-olds accept sports scholarships to a high-profile Catholic high school. The recruitment is sweet, but the kids are faced with escalating pressures that alter their lives. Rated PG-13 for language. 171m. DIR: Steve James. CAST: William Gates, Arthur Agee. 1994

HOOPER ★★★★ Fresh from their success with *Smokey and the Bandit*, director Hal Needham and stars Burt Reynolds and Sally Field are reunited in this humorous, knockabout comedy about Hollywood stuntmen. Jan-Michael Vincent adds to the film's impact as an up-and-coming fall guy out to best top-of-the-heap Reynolds. Good fun. Rated PG. 99m. DIR: Hal Needham. CAST: Burt Reynolds, Sally Field, Jan-Michael Vincent, Brian Keith. 1978 DVD

HOOSIER SCHOOLBOY ★★★ A Depression-era melodrama that's as timely today as it was in the 1930s. The story is told through the eyes of a young schoolboy who sees how many WWI veterans are treated by businessmen after the war is over. He realizes that's one reason why his father is an alcoholic. Good story despite maudlin treatment. B&W; 62m. DIR: William Nigh. CAST: Mickey Rooney, Anne Nagel, Frank Sheilds, Edward Pawley. 1937

HOOSIERS ★★★★1/2 The most satisfying high school basketball movie in years. Gene Hackman is the new coach—with a mysterious past—at Hickory High. His unorthodox methods rankle the locals, his fellow teachers, and the undisciplined team members. But before you can say hoosiermania, the team is at the 1951 state championships. It doesn't hurt that the realistic script is based on a true Indiana Cinderella story. Rated PG. 114m. DIR: David Anspaugh. CAST: Gene Hackman, Barbara Hershey, Dennis Hopper, Sheb Wooley. 1986 DVD

HOPALONG CASSIDY RETURNS ★★★ Cassidy pins on a sheriff's badge and lines up miners and ranchers to stop Blackie, a gang enforcer and murderer. Hoppy guns him down and bestows a last kiss on the dying saloon owner, Lilly. B&W; 74m. DIR: Nate Watt. CAST: William Boyd, George "Gabby" Hayes, Evelyn Brent, Stephen Morris, William Janney, Gail Sheridan. 1936

HOPALONG RIDES AGAIN ★★★ Spring is in the air but with it comes danger for Hopalong Cassidy. A herd was stolen and friends murdered near Black Mesa and that's where the Bar-20 gang is now headed. Hoppy likes a woman there whose brother, an eccentric scientist, is actually the cold-blooded murderer. B&W; 65m. DIR: Lesley Selander. CAST: William Boyd, George "Gabby" Hayes, Russell Hayden, William Duncan, Lois Wilde, Billy King, Harry Worth. 1937

HOPE ★★★★ This TNT original is about racial injustice in a small Mississippi town. The mouthpiece for the message is a spunky young girl (Jena Malone) who must choose between family and fairness. The subject matter is somber, but Malone and her sidekick (Lee Norris) inject mirthful moments as youthful outsiders. Not rated; contains profanity and racist remarks. 90m. DIR: Goldie Hawn. CAST: Jena Malone, Jeffrey Sams, J. T. Walsh, Christine Lahti, Catherine O'Hara, Lee Norris. 1997

HOPE AND GLORY ★★★★1/2 Writer-producer-director John Boorman's much-praised film chronicles his boyhood experiences during the London blitz. Rather than the horror story one might expect, it is a marvelously entertaining, warm, and thoughtful look backward. Blessed with vibrant characters, cultural richness, and a fresh point of view, it never fails to fascinate. Rated PG-13 for profanity and suggested sex. 113m. DIR: John Boorman. CAST: Sarah Miles, David Hayman, Derrick O'Connor, Susan Wooldridge, Sammi Davis, Ian Bannen, Sebastian Rice Edwards, Jean-Marc Barr. 1987

HOPE FLOATS ★★1/2 Housewife Birdee appears on a national TV talk show, where her best friend confesses she is having an affair with her husband. Humiliated, heartbroken, and in shock, Birdee moves into her eccentric mother's Texas home with her distraught daughter, where she mopes in her bathrobe before landing a job and dating a hayseed hunk. Rated PG-13 for mature themes and language. 110m. DIR: Forest Whitaker. CAST: Sandra Bullock, Harry Connick Jr., Gena Rowlands, Mae Whitman, Michael Paré. 1998 DVD

HOPPITY GOES TO TOWN ★★★ Max and Dave Fleischer, of Betty Boop and Popeye fame, brought their distinctive style of animation to this feature about the insect residents of Bugtown. The Fleischers were better at making short cartoons—there's not enough plot or characterization here to justify a feature—but their style is always delightful. Adults may enjoy it more than kids. Kenny Gardner, Gwen Williams, Jack Mercer, Ted Pierce (voices). 77m. **DIR:** Dave Fleischer. 1941

HOPPY SERVES A WRIT ★★1/2 Hopalong Cassidy in Oklahoma Territory. Strictly a formula series Western, but well mounted, breezy, and moves along at a fast clip with a good cast. B&W; 67m. **DIR:** George Archainbaud. **CAST:** William Boyd, Andy Clyde, Victor Jory, George Reeves, Robert Mitchum, Byron Foulger. 1943

HOPSCOTCH ★★★★ Walter Matthau is wonderful in this fast-paced and funny film as a spy who decides to extract a little revenge on the pompous supervisor (Ned Beatty) who demoted him. Glenda Jackson has a nice bit as Matthau's romantic interest. Rated R. 104m. **DIR:** Ronald Neame. **CAST:** Walter Matthau, Ned Beatty, Glenda Jackson. 1980

HORIZONTAL LIEUTENANT, THE ★★★ A bumbling World War II junior officer is assigned to catch an elusive supplies thief at a Pacific island storage base. Mild service comedy with likable stars. 90m. **DIR:** Richard Thorpe. **CAST:** Jim Hutton, Paula Prentiss, Jack Carter, Jim Backus, Charles McGraw, Miyoshi Umeki, Marty Ingels. 1962

HORN BLOWS AT MIDNIGHT, THE ★★★ A comedy classic that has improved with age. Jack Benny ridiculed it because it flopped when first released. But his kidding elevated it to a cult status, and it is delightful to watch today. The plot about an angel sent to Earth to blow his trumpet and end the world may be a cliché, but Benny gives it style. B&W; 78m. **DIR:** Raoul Walsh. **CAST:** Jack Benny, Alexis Smith, Dolores Moran, John Alexander, Reginald Gardiner, Allyn Joslyn, Margaret Dumont, Guy Kibbee, Franklin Pangborn. 1945

HORNET'S NEST ★★ Commando Rock Hudson leads a group of orphaned Italian boys in a raid on a Nazi-held dam. Some fair action scenes but pretty farfetched. Rated PG. 110m. **DIR:** Phil Karlson. **CAST:** Rock Hudson, Sylva Koscina. 1970

•**HORRIBLE DOCTOR BONES, THE** 🖤 The title says it all. Dr. Bones looks to take over the world with zombies controlled by hip-hop music. Rated R for violence, profanity, and sexual situations. 72m. **DIR:** Art Carnage. **CAST:** Darrow Igus, Larry Bates, Sarah Scott. 2000 DVD

HORRIBLE DR. HICHCOCK, THE (TERROR OF DR. HICHCOCK, THE) ★★1/2 Robert Flemyng's naïve second wife is unaware of his plans to use her in a plot to revive her late predecessor. The U.S. version of this above-average Italian period-horror shocker is handicapped by its distributor's cutting of twelve minutes from the movie—mostly to eliminate details of the title character's obsession with necrophilia. The British release (also available as The Terror of Dr. Hichcock) is slightly longer. 76m. **DIR:** Robert Hampton (Riccardo Freda). **CAST:** Barbara Steele, Robert Flemyng. 1962

HORRIBLE HORROR ★★1/2 Beloved 1950s Shock Theater host Zacherley (aka John Zacherle) is in vintage form for this direct-to-video compilation of clips, outtakes, and trailers from mostly awful horror movies. The dumb framing device will have you fast-forwarding through Zacherley's routines after about twenty minutes and slowing down to savor vignettes from The Brainiac, Killers from Space, Devil Bat, She Demons, and dozens more. Not rated. 110m. **DIR:** David Bergman. **CAST:** Zacherley. 1987

HORROR EXPRESS ★★★★ Director Eugenio Martin creates a neat shocker about a prehistoric manlike creature terrorizing a trans-Siberian train when he is awakened from his centuries-old tomb. Lively cast includes a pre-Kojak Telly Savalas in the role of a crazed Russian Cossack intent on killing the thing. Rated R. 88m. **DIR:** Eugenio Martin. **CAST:** Peter Cushing, Christopher Lee, Telly Savalas. 1972 DVD

HORROR HOSPITAL ★★ A crazy doctor (Michael Gough) performing gruesome brain experiments at a remote English hospital runs into trouble when a nosy young couple begins snooping around. Slow-moving gorefest. Rated R for violence and blood. 84m. **DIR:** Anthony Balch. **CAST:** Michael Gough, Robin Askwith, Dennis Price. 1973 DVD

HORROR HOTEL ★★★ Christopher Lee is a sinister teacher who urges a female student to research a witchcraft thesis at a New England village that's the perfect embodiment of Lovecraftian isolation. A good cast, screenwriter George Baxt (Circus of Horrors), and some top technicians—including legendary cinematographer Desmond Dickinson (Olivier's Hamlet)—overcome a tiny budget and make this witchcraft saga a miniclassic of the British horror renaissance. B&W; 76m. **DIR:** John Llewellyn Moxey. **CAST:** Dennis Lotis, Betta St. John, Christopher Lee, Venetia Stevenson. 1960 DVD

HORROR ISLAND 🖤 Goofballs search for treasure in a haunted castle. B&W; 61m. **DIR:** George Wagner. **CAST:** Dick Foran, Leo Carrillo, Peggy Moran, Fuzzy Knight, Iris Adrian. 1941

HORROR OF DRACULA ★★★★1/2 This is the one that launched Hammer Films's popular Dracula series, featuring Christopher Lee in the first—and best—of his many appearances as the Count and Peter Cushing as his archnemesis Van Helsing. A stylish, exciting reworking of Bram Stoker's classic story of a bloodthirsty vampire on the prowl from Transylvania to London and back again. Genuinely scary film, with a hell of an ending, too. 82m. **DIR:** Terence Fisher. **CAST:** Christopher Lee, Peter Cushing, Michael Gough, Melissa Stribling, Miles Malleson. 1958

HORROR OF FRANKENSTEIN ★★★★ Young medical student, fed up with school, decides to drop out and continue his studies alone. So what if his name just happens to be Frankenstein and he just happens to be making a monster? Good entry in the series has many ghoulish sequences, along with some welcome touches of humor. Recommended. Rated R. 95m. **DIR:** Jimmy Sangster. **CAST:** Ralph Bates, Kate O'Mara, Veronica Carlson, Dennis Price. 1970

HORROR OF PARTY BEACH, THE 🖤 A really horrendous horror film about radioactive lizard-like monsters. 72m. **DIR:** Del Tenney. **CAST:** John Scott, Alice Lyon. 1964

HORROR OF THE BLOOD MONSTERS ❤ Astronauts land on mystery planet and find it inhabited by stock footage from Filipino monster movies. Rated R. 85m. **DIR:** Al Adamson. **CAST:** John Carradine, Robert Dix, Vicki Volante. 1970

HORROR OF THE ZOMBIES ❤ When Spain's ongoing series of Knights Templar zombie movies was issued as one of VidAmerica's "World's Worst Videos," someone took out what little gore there was. The original version is available on Super Video. Rated R. 90m. **DIR:** Amando de Ossorio. **CAST:** Maria Perschy, Jack Taylor. 1971

HORROR RISES FROM THE TOMB ★★ Five hundred years after an evil knight is beheaded, he returns to make trouble for his descendants when they visit the family castle. Tired shocks, though better than many of the slasher cheapies on the video racks. Not rated, with the usual violence and tepid gore. 80m. **DIR:** Carlos Aured. **CAST:** Paul Naschy, Emma Cohen. 1972

HORROR SHOW, THE ★★1/2 Executed killer Brion James haunts the family of the cop who captured him, turning their dreams into deadly nightmares. Standard horror yarn goes for shocks at the expense of logic. Rated R for strong violence. 95m. **DIR:** James Isaac. **CAST:** Lance Henriksen, Brion James, Rita Taggart, Alvy Moore. 1989

HORRORS OF BURKE AND HARE ❤ Witless rehash of the exploits of Edinburgh's famed body snatchers, with the emphasis on R-rated gore. 91m. **DIR:** Vernon Sewell. **CAST:** Harry Andrews, Derren Nesbitt. 1971

•**HORRORS OF THE BLACK MUSEUM** ★★ Twisted mystery writer transforms his assistant into a homicidal monster, sells the stories he has written about the gruesome crimes, and adds the implements of death to his "museum." This sadistic shocker used a gimmick called "HypnoVision" to validate its excesses and saturated drive-in screens with the blood and gore found in the crime comics of the early 1950s. The opening sequence is still a stunner and hallmark of bad taste. Not rated; contains violence and brutal murders. 95m. **DIR:** Arthur Crabtree. **CAST:** Michael Gough, June Cunningham, Graham Curnow, Shirley Anne Field, Geoffrey Keen. 1959

HORSE, THE ★★★ Grim tale of a father and son from a small village forced to travel to Istanbul to find work. Their struggles and the conditions in which the impoverished must live are realistically portrayed. Not rated, but far too bleak for kids. In Turkish with English subtitles. 116m. **DIR:** Ali Ozgenturk. **CAST:** Genco Erkal. 1982

HORSE FEATHERS ★★★★★ The funniest of the films starring the four Marx Brothers, this features Groucho as the president of Huxley College, which desperately needs a winning football team. So Groucho hires Chico and Harpo to help him fix the season. Meanwhile, Groucho is competing for the attentions of the sexy college widow, Thelma Todd. The team's most outrageous and hilarious gagfest. B&W; 69m.

DIR: Norman Z. McLeod. **CAST:** The Marx Brothers, Thelma Todd, David Landau. 1932 **DVD**

HORSE FOR DANNY, A ★★★ A perfect tale for children who love horses. An orphaned girl who lives with her horse trainer uncle finds a horse she believes can become a champion. Sure enough, the horse proves to be special, but there are those who want the horse stopped. Entertaining if somewhat bland family film has its heart in the right place. Rated PG. 92m. **DIR:** Dick Lowry. **CAST:** Robert Urich, Ron Brice, Gary Basaraba, Erik Jensen, LeeLee Sobieski. 1995

HORSE IN THE GRAY FLANNEL SUIT, THE ★★ This Disney film takes you back to America's early awareness of Madison Avenue and the many games and gimmicks it devises to get the almighty dollar. Dean Jones is an executive who develops an ad campaign around his daughter's devotion to horses. 113m. **DIR:** Norman Tokar. **CAST:** Dean Jones, Diane Baker, Lloyd Bochner, Fred Clark, Kurt Russell. 1968

HORSE OF PRIDE, THE ★★ Unconvincing study of peasant life set in Brittany at the turn of the century, as seen through the eyes of a young boy. In French with English subtitles. Not rated. 118m. **DIR:** Claude Chabrol. **CAST:** Jacques Dufilho, Bernadette Lesache, François Cluzet. 1980

HORSE SOLDIERS, THE ★★★★ Based on a true incident during the Civil War, this a minor, but enjoyable, John Ford cavalry outing. John Wayne and William Holden play well-matched adversaries. 119m. **DIR:** John Ford. **CAST:** John Wayne, William Holden, Constance Towers, Hoot Gibson. 1959

HORSE THIEF, THE ★★★★ The mysterious barren landscape of Tibet becomes the setting for a tribal drama of theft, ostracism, and horrible retribution. Beautifully photographed amidst a series of Buddhist rituals captured wordlessly. In Mandarin with English subtitles. Not rated. 88m. **DIR:** Tian Zhuangzhuang. **CAST:** Tseshang Rigzin. 1987

HORSE WHISPERER, THE ★★★★★ This isn't a film, it's a symphony: a magnificent project that perfectly suits Robert Redford's taste, style, and abilities. The story's focus is a 14-year-old New York teenager who suffers a horrible accident with her favorite horse and loses her spirit along with one leg. The girl's career-oriented mother, galvanized by this tragedy, drags both the girl and the horse across the country to Montana, where she hopes for a miracle at the hands of a talented horse trainer. The subsequent romantic overtures between these two adults from different worlds play out against the Herculean task of helping the tormented girl and her terrified animal. Redford once again proves himself the most generous of directors; all the best scenes and lines go to his costars. This is, without question, 1998's most elegant and meticulously crafted picture. Rated PG-13 for the brutally intense accident that opens the story. 164m. **DIR:** Robert Redford. **CAST:** Robert Redford, Kristin Scott Thomas, Sam Neill, Dianne Wiest, Scarlett Johansson, Chris Cooper. 1998 **DVD**

HORSE WITHOUT A HEAD, THE ★★★ Good old Disney fun as a group of boys give more trouble to a band of thieves than they can handle. An excellent cast headed by Leo McKern as a devious no-gooder. The whole family will enjoy this unrated film. 89m. **DIR:** Don Chaffey. **CAST:** Leo McKern, Jean-Pierre Aumont, Herbert Lom, Pamela Franklin, Vincent Winter. 1963

HORSEMAN ON THE ROOF, THE ★★★ Immensely silly French romantic epic, in which a chivalrous Italian rebel escorts a Gallic noblewoman through a region plagued by cholera. A not-so-subtle AIDS metaphor gets overworked here, much to the detriment of the heroic atmosphere the filmmaker clearly wished to establish. Set in the 1830s, against gorgeous landscapes that won't look so good on video. In French with English subtitles. Rated R. 119m. **DIR:** Jean-Paul Rappeneau. **CAST:** Juliette Binoche, Olivier Martinez. 1995

HORSEMASTERS ★★ Annette and Tommy team up once again in this average story about young Americans pursuing their careers in horse training among the great riding academies of Europe. 77m. **DIR:** William Fairchild. **CAST:** Annette Funicello, Janet Munro, Tommy Kirk, Donald Pleasence, Tony Britton. 1961

HORSEMEN, THE 🖤 In this dull action film, Omar Sharif, as an Afghan tribesman, attempts to outride his father. Rated PG. 109m. **DIR:** John Frankenheimer. **CAST:** Omar Sharif, Jack Palance, Leigh Taylor-Young, Peter Jeffrey, Eric Pohlmann. 1970

HORSEPLAYER ★★ Strange tale, unremarkably told, of two takers (M. K. Harris and Sammi Davis) who use a disturbed man (Brad Dourif) for their own ends. Rated R for violence and profanity. 89m. **DIR:** Kurt Voss. **CAST:** Brad Dourif, Sammi Davis, M. K. Harris, Vic Tayback. 1990

HORSE'S MOUTH, THE ★★★1/2 Star Alec Guinness, who also penned the script, romps in high comic style through this film version of Joyce Cary's mocking novel about an eccentric painter. 93m. **DIR:** Ronald Neame. **CAST:** Alec Guinness, Kay Walsh, Renee Houston, Michael Gough. 1958

HOSPITAL, THE ★★★★1/2 You definitely don't want to check in. But if you like to laugh, you'll want to check it out. This 1971 black comedy did for the medical profession what *... And Justice for All* did for our court system and *Network* did for television. Paddy Chayefsky's Oscar-winning screenplay casts George C. Scott as an embittered doctor battling against the outrageous goings-on at the institution of the title. Rated PG. 103m. **DIR:** Arthur Hiller. **CAST:** George C. Scott, Diana Rigg, Barnard Hughes. 1971

HOSPITAL MASSACRE 🖤 Another *Halloween* clone, this one is set in a hospital where a psycho killer murders everyone in an attempt to get revenge on the girl who laughed at his Valentine's Day card twenty years before. Rated R for nudity and gore. 88m. **DIR:** Boaz Davidson. **CAST:** Barbi Benton, Chip Lucia, Jon Van Ness. 1982

HOSTAGE (1987) 🖤 Idiotic story of a South African farmer who must rescue his wife and child from evil Arabs. Rated R for language and violence. 94m. **DIR:** Hanro Möhr. **CAST:** Wings Hauser, Karen Black, Kevin McCarthy, Nancy Locke. 1987

HOSTAGE (1992) ★★ Sam Neill stars as a James Bondish secret agent who finds retirement a rather harrowing option. Shooting and bombings pervade. Rated R for sex and violence. 100m. **DIR:** Robert Young. **CAST:** Sam Neill, Talisa Soto, James Fox. 1992

HOSTAGE FOR A DAY ★★1/2 John Candy directed this made-for-television comedy about a henpecked husband who plans to run off with his girlfriend. That is, until he finds out his scheming wife has cleaned out his secret bank account. In order to get the money back, he stages a hostage situation in his house with himself as the victim. Likable cast helps save this mildly entertaining comedy. Rated PG. 92m. **DIR:** John Candy. **CAST:** George Wendt, Robin Duke, John Vernon, John Candy, Christopher Templeton. 1994

HOSTAGE TOWER, THE ★★1/2 A successful international criminal sought by major police organizations puts together a special team of experts for his next spectacular crime, broadly hinted at in the title. Intrigue and private purposes abound in this action film, wherein the cast successfully outweighs the movie. Rated PG for violence. 97m. **DIR:** Claudio Guzman. **CAST:** Peter Fonda, Maud Adams, Billy Dee Williams, Rachel Roberts, Douglas Fairbanks Jr. 1980

HOSTAGE TRAIN ★★ Much ado about nothing as cop Judge Reinhold tries to save his girlfriend and a trainload of passengers being held hostage by terrorists in a collapsed tunnel. No big deal, especially Reinhold's turn as an action star. Rated R for language and violence. 98m. **DIR:** Robert Lee. **CAST:** Judge Reinhold, Carol Alt, Michael Sarrazin. 1996

HOSTAGES ★★1/2 Bernard MacLaverty's well-meaning made-for-cable account of the five-year hostage crisis in Lebanon suffers from simplified characters and events compressed past the point of conveying much drama. No doubt this superficial tone results from the lack of participation by those who were there. Director David Wheatley also elicits very little passion from his strong ensemble cast. The result is oddly uninvolving. 96m. **DIR:** David Wheatley. **CAST:** Colin Firth, Ciaran Hinds, Jay O. Sanders, Josef Sommer, Harry Dean Stanton, Kathy Bates, Natasha Richardson. 1993

HOSTILE GUNS ★★ Incredible cast of veteran B-movie Western actors is the main attraction in this routine drama of two peace officers who transport an unsavory group of criminals to prison. 91m. **DIR:** R. G. Springsteen. **CAST:** George Montgomery, Tab Hunter, Yvonne De Carlo, Brian Donlevy, John Russell, Leo Gordon, Richard Arlen, Don Barry, Emile Meyer. 1967

HOSTILE INTENT ★★ A group of computer hackers finds their weekend war game is the real thing after they tap into a secret government database, triggering the agency to hunt them down. They would have been better off downloading dirty pictures from the net. Rated R for language and violence. 90m. **DIR:** Jonathan Heap. **CAST:** Rob Lowe, Sofia Shinas, Saul Rubinek, John Savage. 1996

HOSTILE INTENTIONS ★★ Good intentions land three women in hot water when they travel to Tijuana for girls' night out. There, they are forced to defend themselves against corrupt police and locals, and must use their wits in order to make it back across the border. Rated R for violence, drug abuse, and adult language. 90m. **DIR:** Catherine Cyran. **CAST:** Tia Carrere, Tricia Leigh Fisher, Lisa Dean Ryan, Carlos Gomez. 1994

HOSTILE TAKE OVER ★★★1/2 Apt direction by George Mihalka elevates what would be another psycho-on-the-loose cheapie. David Warner plays a lonely employee who holds three colleagues hostage. A tense thriller rated R for nudity, profanity, and violence. 93m. **DIR:** George Mihalka. **CAST:** David Warner, Michael Ironside, Kate Vernon, Jayne Eastwood. 1988

HOSTILE WATERS ★★★1/2 An actual 1986 incident involving a Soviet nuclear sub is the jumping-off point for this tense little drama, which strongly suggests that a near reactor meltdown resulted from a collision between Soviet and American subs involved in standard cat-and-mouse games in the Atlantic. Rutger Hauer and his crew struggle to avoid a nuclear incident while saving their own lives in this engrossing film. Rated PG-13 for profanity and violent peril. 95m. **DIR:** David Drury. **CAST:** Rutger Hauer, Martin Sheen, Colm Feore, Rob Campbell, Harris Yulin, Regina Taylor, Max von Sydow. 1997

HOT BOX, THE ★★ Low-budget Filipino-shot women's-prison film was cowritten and produced by Jonathan Demme. Rated R; contains nudity, profanity, and violence. 85m. **DIR:** Joe Viola. **CAST:** Margaret Markov, Andrea Cagen, Charles Dierkop. 1972

HOT CHILD IN THE CITY 🐢 This small-cast whodunit has an insufficient number of suspects. Not rated, has violence, profanity, and nudity. 85m. **DIR:** John Florea. **CAST:** Leah Ayres, Shari Shattuck, Antony Alda, Ronn Moss. 1987

HOT CHOCOLATE ★★1/2 A French chocolate factory is going broke and a millionaire Texas cowgirl (Bo Derek) wants to buy it. Low-expectation fun. Rated PG-13 for violence. 93m. **DIR:** Josee Dayan. **CAST:** Robert Hays, Bo Derek, Francois Mathouret, Howard Hesseman. 1992

HOT DOG ... THE MOVIE ★★ David Naughton costars with onetime Playboy Playmate of the Year Shannon Tweed in this comedy about high jinks on the ski slopes. Rated R for nudity, profanity, and suggested sex. 96m. **DIR:** Peter Markle. **CAST:** David Naughton, Patrick Houser, Shannon Tweed. 1984

HOT HEAD ★★1/2 Patrick Dewaere stars in this so-so French comedy about a freewheeling soccer athlete who gets kicked off the team after an incident with a star player, finds himself drifting in the streets, and eventually is framed for a rape he didn't commit. Dubbed (poorly) in English. Rated R for nudity. 90m. **DIR:** Jean-Jacques Annaud. **CAST:** Patrick Dewaere, France Dougnac, Dorothee Jemma. 1978

HOT ICE 🐢 Extremely dull (and uncredited) Ed Wood script about jewel thieves at a ski lodge. Rated R for brief nudity. 85m. **DIR:** Stephen C. Apostolof. **CAST:** Harvey Shain, Patti Kelly. 1974

HOT LEAD ★★★ Tim Holt must team up with an ex-con in order to stop a murderous gang of train robbers. B&W; 60m. **DIR:** Stuart Gilmore. **CAST:** Tim Holt, Richard Martin, John Dehner, Joan Dixon, Ross Elliott. 1951

HOT LEAD AND COLD FEET ★★ This predictable, occasionally funny Western stars Jim Dale as twin brothers; one is a drunk who terrorizes the town and the other a missionary. Rated G. 89m. **DIR:** Robert Butler. **CAST:** Jim Dale, Karen Valentine, Don Knotts, Jack Elam, Darren McGavin. 1978

HOT MILLIONS ★★★★ A wry comedy with a skillful cast that pokes fun at the computer age. A con man poses as a computer genius and gets a job with a million dollar corporation. He then transfers the company's funds into his own account. When he gets caught, he uses his wits to stay one step ahead. Rated G. 106m. **DIR:** Eric Till. **CAST:** Peter Ustinov, Bob Newhart, Maggie Smith, Karl Malden, Robert Morley, Cesar Romero, Julie May, Melinda May. 1968

HOT MOVES 🐢 Here's another teen lust comedy. Rated R. 80m. **DIR:** Jim Sotos. **CAST:** Michael Zorek, Adam Silbar, Jeff Fishman, Johnny Timko. 1985

HOT PURSUIT ★★ In this comedy, a college student (John Cusack) misses the plane on which he was to join his girlfriend (Wendy Gazelle) and her wealthy parents on a vacation cruise. He then finds himself embarking on a series of wildly improbable misadventures as he attempts to catch up with them. Rated PG-13 for profanity and violence. 90m. **DIR:** Steven Lisberger. **CAST:** John Cusack, Robert Loggia, Wendy Gazelle, Jerry Stiller, Monte Markham. 1987

HOT RESORT 🐢 *Airplane*-style takeoff on the resort industry. Rated R for nudity, profanity, and simulated sex. 92m. **DIR:** John Robins. **CAST:** Tom Parsekian, Michael Berz, Bronson Pinchot, Marcy Walker, Frank Gorshin. 1984

HOT ROCK, THE ★★★★ A neatly planned jewelry heist goes awry and the fun begins. Peter Yates's direction is razor sharp. The cast is absolutely perfect. This movie is a crowd-pleasing blend of action, humor, and suspense. Rated PG. 105m. **DIR:** Peter Yates. **CAST:** Robert Redford, George Segal, Ron Leibman, Paul Sand, Zero Mostel, Moses Gunn, William Redfield, Charlotte Rae. 1972

HOT SHOT ★★★1/2 More than just a soccer version of *The Karate Kid*, this film of a young man's conquest of adversity stands on its own. Jim Youngs is a rich kid who runs away to Rio de Janeiro, where he pursues his idol, Pelé, the greatest soccer player of all time. An enjoyable family film and a must for soccer fans. Rated PG. 94m. **DIR:** Rick King. **CAST:** Jim Youngs, Pelé, Billy Warlock, Weyman Thompson, Mario Van Peebles. 1986 DVD

HOT SHOTS ★★★★ This hilarious parody of *Top Gun*–style films stars Charlie Sheen as a renegade navy pilot who must live with the stigma of his father's past. Look for scenes poking fun at movies as diverse as *The Fabulous Baker Boys*, *Gone With the Wind*, *Dances With Wolves*, and—in the film's funniest scene—*9 Weeks*. Rated PG-13 for brief profanity. 85m. **DIR:** Jim Abrahams. **CAST:** Charlie Sheen, Cary Elwes, Valeria Golino, Lloyd Bridges, Kevin Dunn, Jon Cryer, William O'Leary, Efrem Zimbalist Jr. 1991

HOT SHOTS PART DEUX ★★★1/2 *Airplane* codirector Jim Abrahams is at it again with this slapstick sequel that blasts *Rambo*esque action flicks. Charlie Sheen leads the assault with fellow *Hot Shot*-ers Valeria Golino and Lloyd Bridges. Rated PG-13 for profanity and violence. 90m. DIR: Jim Abrahams. CAST: Charlie Sheen, Lloyd Bridges, Valeria Golino, Richard Crenna, Brenda Bakke. 1993

HOT SPELL ★★★ Entertaining thoughts of leaving her for a younger woman, macho husband Anthony Quinn has anguishing housewife Shirley Booth sweating out this near remake of *Come Back, Little Sheba*. Booth invokes empathy, Quinn again proves his depth of talent, Shirley MacLaine shows why stardom soon was hers; but a soap opera is a soap opera. B&W; 86m. DIR: Daniel Mann. CAST: Shirley Booth, Anthony Quinn, Shirley MacLaine, Earl Holliman, Eileen Heckart. 1958

HOT SPOT ★★1/2 Director Dennis Hopper keeps the *Hot Spot* on simmer when it needs to boil over with tension and excitement. Don Johnson is semicomatose as a low-life who drifts into a small Texas town where he robs the local bank and gets involved with two women, one bad (Virginia Madsen) and one innocent (Jennifer Connelly). Rated R for simulated sex, nudity, profanity, and violence. 129m. DIR: Dennis Hopper. CAST: Don Johnson, Virginia Madsen, Jennifer Connelly, Charles Martin Smith, Bill Sadler, Jerry Hardin, Barry Corbin. 1990 DVD

HOT STUFF ★★★1/2 An entertaining, old-fashioned comedy that whips right along. Director-star Dom DeLuise makes the most of his dual role. The story concerns a government fencing operation for capturing crooks and the results are humorous. Rated PG. 87m. DIR: Dom DeLuise. CAST: Dom DeLuise, Jerry Reed, Suzanne Pleshette, Ossie Davis. 1979

HOT TARGET 💔 The bored wife of a British business tycoon finds herself being extorted. Explicit nudity. Rated R. 93m. DIR: Denis Lewiston. CAST: Simone Griffeth, Bryan Marshall, Steve Marachuk. 1984 DVD

HOT TO TROT ★★1/2 Cute update on the Francis the Talking Mule comedies of the Fifties. This time we have a witty horse. What gets tiresome is the horse's dumb friend Fred (Bob Goldthwait). The best lines go to John Candy as the horse's voice. Rated PG for profanity. 83m. DIR: Michael Dinner. CAST: Bob Goldthwait, Dabney Coleman, Virginia Madsen, Cindy Pickett, Mary Gross. 1988

HOT UNDER THE COLLAR ★★1/2 Poor Richard Gabai. He's so in love with Angela Visser that he'll follow her anywhere, even when she checks into the local convent. Desperate, Gabai disguises himself as a priest, and then a nun, and then must really go undercover when the convent is infiltrated by a gangster in search of hidden loot. Congenial comedy. Rated R. 87m. DIR: Richard Gabai. CAST: Angela Visser, Richard Gabai. 1991

HOTEL ★★1/2 This film is based on Arthur Hailey's bestseller, which eventually spawned a TV series. In its *Airport*-style story, a number of characters and events unfold against the main theme of Melvyn Douglas's attempt to keep from selling the hotel to a tycoon who would modernize and change the landmark. 125m. DIR: Richard Quine. CAST: Rod Taylor, Catherine Spaak, Melvyn Douglas, Karl Malden,

Richard Conte, Michael Rennie, Merle Oberon, Kevin McCarthy. 1967

HOTEL COLONIAL 💔 In this uncredited adaptation of Joseph Conrad's *Heart of Darkness*, John Savage searches the jungles of Colombia for his brother. Rated R for nudity and violence. 107m. DIR: Cinzia Torrini. CAST: John Savage, Robert Duvall, Rachel Ward, Massimo Troisi. 1987

HOTEL DE LOVE ★★1/2 Director-writer Craig Rosenberg's debut is a sweet and funny romantic comedy. Aden Young and Simon Bossell star as two brothers who fall in love with the same woman (a delicious Saffron Burrows), in high school. Ten years later they meet up at the Hotel de Love, where she has come to get married. Now it's up to the two brothers to stop her from walking down the aisle. Rated R for adult situations, language, and nudity. 93m. DIR: Craig Rosenberg. CAST: Aden Young, Simon Bossell, Saffron Burrows. 1996

HOTEL NEW HAMPSHIRE, THE ★★ Based on John Irving's novel, this muddled motion picture has its moments. Beau Bridges stars as the head of a family that weathers all sorts of disasters. Rated R for profanity. 110m. DIR: Tony Richardson. CAST: Beau Bridges, Jodie Foster, Rob Lowe, Nastassja Kinski, Amanda Plummer. 1984

HOTEL PARADISO ★★★ Mild sex farce. Alec Guinness attempts a tryst with his neighbor's wife, but everything and everyone blocks his way. 96m. DIR: Peter Glenville. CAST: Alec Guinness, Gina Lollobrigida, Robert Morley, Akim Tamiroff. 1966

HOTEL RESERVE ★★1/2 Intrigue and romance are the chief ingredients of this lightweight spy melodrama set just before the outbreak of World War II in a fancy resort hotel. B&W; 80m. DIR: Victor Hanbury. CAST: James Mason, Lucie Mannheim, Herbert Lom, Patricia Medina. 1944

HOTEL ROOM ★★★★ One hotel room, three weird stories. David Lynch directed the two most effective tales. In one, Harry Dean Stanton is a cantankerous drunk with an eerie past. In the other, Crispin Glover embarks on an unsettling psychological journey with his unstable wife. Chelsea Field is fighting mad at shallow boyfriend Griffin Dunne in a slighter, more comic story. Not rated; contains adult themes, sexual situations, and violence. 96m. DIR: David Lynch, James Signorelli. CAST: Harry Dean Stanton, Glenne Headly, Griffin Dunne, Chelsea Field, Crispin Glover. 1992

HOTEL TERMINUS: THE LIFE AND TIMES OF KLAUS BARBIE ★★★1/2 A fascinating film chronicle of the life of Nazi SS Captain Klaus Barbie, the "Butcher of Lyon," responsible for the deportation and death of thousands of Jews, and the brutal torture of French Resistance members. Oscar winner as best documentary. In English and French, German, and Spanish with English subtitles. Not rated, but with graphic discussion of torture, so parental discretion is advised. B&W/color; 267m. DIR: Marcel Ophuls. 1988

H.O.T.S. ★★ Drive-in special about two feuding sororities whose battles culminate in a topless football game. Cheerfully raunchy trash for those times when you're not quite up to Ingmar Bergman. Rated

R for plentiful nudity. 95m. DIR: Gerald Sindell. CAST: Susan Kiger, Lisa London, Danny Bonaduce. 1979

HOUDINI (1953) ★★★1/2 Tony Curtis is quite good in this colorful but sketchy account of the famed illusionist. Enjoyable fluff makes up for lack of substance with good period atmosphere and dandy reenactments of Houdini's most famous escapes. 106m. DIR: George Marshall. CAST: Tony Curtis, Janet Leigh, Ian Wolfe, Torin Thatcher. 1953

HOUDINI (1998) ★★★ Those hoping for a definitive portrait of the celebrated magician and illusionist will leave disappointed, because this superficial and melodramatic biography turns Houdini into a shrill narcissist. This TNT original film has "TV movie" written all over it: The production values look cheap, and the most talented actors turn up in only brief supporting roles. Rated PG for dramatic intensity. 95m. DIR: Pen Densham. CAST: Johnathon Schaech, Stacy Edwards, Paul Sorvino, George Segal, Rhea Perlman, David Warner. 1998

HOUND OF THE BASKERVILLES, THE (1939) ★★★★ The second best of the Basil Rathbone–Nigel Bruce Sherlock Holmes movies, this 1939 release marked the stars' debut in the roles for which they would forever be known. (*The Adventures of Sherlock Holmes*, which was made the same year, featured the on-screen detective team at its peak.) Holmes and Watson are called upon by Henry Baskerville to save him from a curse—in the form of a hound from hell—that has plagued his family for centuries. B&W; 84m. DIR: Sidney Lanfield. CAST: Basil Rathbone, Nigel Bruce, John Carradine, Lionel Atwill, Mary Gordon, E. E. Clive, Richard Greene. 1939

HOUND OF THE BASKERVILLES, THE (1959) ★★★★ One of the better adaptations of Conan Doyle's moody novel, and particularly enjoyable for its presentation of Peter Cushing (as Sherlock Holmes) and Christopher Lee together in nonhorror roles. This British entry (from the Hammer House of Horror) caught more of the murky atmosphere than any other version of any other Holmes tale. Intelligent scripting, compelling acting, and spooky cinematography. 84m. DIR: Terence Fisher. CAST: Peter Cushing, Christopher Lee, Andre Morell, Marla Landi, Miles Malleson. 1959

HOUND OF THE BASKERVILLES, THE (1977) 🎔 Truly abysmal send-up of the novel by Conan Doyle. 84m. DIR: Paul Morrissey. CAST: Dudley Moore, Peter Cook, Denholm Elliott, Joan Greenwood, Hugh Griffith, Terry-Thomas, Roy Kinnear. 1977

HOUND OF THE BASKERVILLES, THE (1983) ★★★1/2 Ian Richardson makes a fine Sherlock Holmes in this enjoyable version of Sir Arthur Conan Doyle's oft-filmed tale. While we prefer the Basil Rathbone and Peter Cushing vehicles, there's certainly nothing wrong with this suspenseful, well-mounted and atmospheric thriller. 101m. DIR: Douglas Hickox. CAST: Ian Richardson, Donald Churchill, Denholm Elliott, Martin Shaw, Brian Blessed, Ronald Lacey, Eleanor Bron, Edward Judd, Glynis Barber. 1983 DVD

HOUR OF THE ASSASSIN ★1/2 Action thriller set in the fictional South American country of San Pedro where Erik Estrada has been hired by the military forces to kill the president. Robert Vaughn plays the CIA agent who has to stop him. Although this film has its share of car crashes, gunfire, and explosions, it lacks any real suspense. Rated R. 96m. DIR: Luis Llosa. CAST: Erik Estrada, Robert Vaughn. 1986

HOUR OF THE GUN, THE ★★★★ This sequel to *Gunfight at the O.K. Corral* deserves to be counted as a minor classic. James Garner is superb as an embittered and obsessed Wyatt Earp, who, with the help of an increasingly ailing Doc Holliday, sets out to bring Ike Clanton to justice. 100m. DIR: John Sturges. CAST: James Garner, Jason Robards Jr., Robert Ryan, Steve Ihnat, Albert Salmi, Charles Aidman, Michael Tolan, Frank Converse, Larry Gates, Karl Swenson, Jon Voight, Monte Markham, William Windom. 1967

HOUR OF THE STAR ★★★ A homely, dull-witted girl from the Brazilian countryside comes to São Paulo. She gets a job as a typist (even though she can neither type nor spell) while dreaming of a better life such as she has seen in the movies. Relentlessly depressing. In Portuguese with English subtitles. Not rated. 96m. DIR: Suzana Amaral. CAST: Marcelia Cartaxo. 1977

HOUR OF THE WOLF ★★★★ Ingmar Bergman's surreal, claustrophobic look into the personality of a tormented artist. Bizarre hallucinations shape the artist's world, creating a disturbing vision that seems at times completely out of control. Probably the closest Bergman has ever come to creating a horror film. In Swedish with English subtitles. B&W; 89m. DIR: Ingmar Bergman. CAST: Max von Sydow, Liv Ullmann, Ingrid Thulin. 1968

HOURGLASS 🎔 A vanity piece for C. Thomas Howell, who struts through this muddled story of a powerful fashion designer who tosses away his life for a beautiful woman (Sofia Shinas). Howell's directorial debut. Rated R for profanity, nudity, violence, and sexual situations. 91m. DIR: C. Thomas Howell. CAST: C. Thomas Howell, Sofia Shinas, Ed Begley Jr., Terry Kiser, Timothy Bottoms, Anthony Clark, Kiefer Sutherland. 1995

HOURS AND TIMES ★★★★1/2 This short (60-minute) feature marks an auspicious debut for writer-director Christopher Munch. It's an impressive, wonderfully intimate drama that supposes what might have gone on between John Lennon and his manager, Brian Epstein, during a weekend in 1963, when they flee the insanity of Beatlemania for a little solitude in Barcelona. David Angus and Ian Hart are fabulous as the fabled rock star and his manager. B&W; 60m. DIR: Christopher Munch. CAST: David Angus, Ian Hart, Stephanie Pack. 1992

HOUSE ★★1/2 A comedy-thriller about an author who moves into an old mansion left to him by an aunt who committed suicide. The cast is good, but the shocks are predictable, crippling the suspense. Rated R for violence and profanity. 93m. DIR: Steve Miner. CAST: William Katt, George Wendt, Kay Lenz, Richard Moll. 1986

HOUSE II: THE SECOND STORY ★★ In this unwarranted sequel to *House*, a young man inherits a mansion and invites his best friend to move in with him. A series of humorous and mysterious events lead the wo to exhume the grave of the young man's great-randfather, who is magically still alive. Rated PG-13 or foul language and some violence. 88m. DIR: Ethan Wiley. CAST: Arye Gross, Jonathan Stark, Royal Dano, ill Maher, John Ratzenberger. 1987

HOUSE IV ★★1/2 A famous horror writer dies and eaves his wife and daughter the old family home, ut his half brother has other plans. Soon the whole amily is up to their necks in spooky goings on. Rated R for nudity and violence. 94m. DIR: Lewis Abernathy. CAST: Terri Treas, Scott Burkholder, William Katt. 1991

HOUSE ACROSS THE BAY, THE ★★1/2 An airplane designer (Walter Pidgeon) swipes the waiting wife Joan Bennett) of a gangster (George Raft) while Raft is paying his dues in the joint. Then he gets out . . . Classic Raft film. Tense, exciting, but familiar. Lloyd Nolan plays a shyster very well. B&W; 86m. DIR: Archie Mayo. CAST: George Raft, Joan Bennett, Lloyd Nolan, Gladys George, Walter Pidgeon. 1940

HOUSE ARREST ★★ There are very few laughs in this occasionally ugly and mean-spirited HBO comedy starring Jamie Lee Curtis and Kevin Pollak as a couple on the brink of divorce. Their kids decide the best way to keep the family together is to lock the parents in the basement and force-feed them a kind of marriage counseling. So silly you have to wonder for whom this was targeted. Rated PG for profanity. 109m. DIR: Harry Winer. CAST: Jamie Lee Curtis, Kevin Pollak, Jennifer Tilly, Ray Walston, Wallace Shawn, Christopher McDonald. 1995

HOUSE BY THE CEMETERY ★★ One of the better latter-day spaghetti horrors, this merging of *The Amityville Horror* and *The Innocents* actually has some suspense to go along with the explicit gore. But don't let the kids see it. Rated R. 86m. DIR: Lucio Fulci. CAST: Katherine MacColl. 1981

HOUSE BY THE RIVER ★★★ Fritz Lang explores one of his favorite themes: obsession. A moody chamber work about a man who kills his maid out of passionate rage, then implicates his own brother to relieve his guilt. Full of fascinating psychological touches that manage to create a disturbing atmosphere. B&W; 88m. DIR: Fritz Lang. CAST: Louis Hayward, Jane Wyatt, Lee Bowman, Ann Shoemaker, Kathleen Freeman. 1950

HOUSE CALLS ★★★★1/2 Here's a romantic comedy reminiscent of films Spencer Tracy and Katharine Hepburn made together mostly because of the teaming of Walter Matthau and Glenda Jackson. A recently widowed doctor (Matthau) finds his bachelor spree cut short by a romantic encounter with a nurse (Jackson) who refuses to be just another conquest. A delightful battle of the sexes with two equally matched opponents. Rated PG. 96m. DIR: Howard Zieff. CAST: Walter Matthau, Glenda Jackson, Richard Benjamin, Art Carney. 1978

HOUSE IN THE HILLS, A ★★1/2 While house-sitting, an aspiring actress is taken hostage and falls in love with her captor. Very bizarre love story with an even more bizarre ending. Rated R for nudity, simulated sex, and profanity. 89m. DIR: Ken Wiederhorn. CAST: Michael Madsen, Helen Slater, James Laurenson, Elyssa Davalos, Jeffrey Tambor. 1993

HOUSE OF ANGELS ★★★1/2 This offbeat comedy examines the culture clash that occurs when the leather-clad granddaughter of a recently deceased landowner roars into town on a motorcycle to claim her inheritance and shocks the stuffy locals with her openly decadent lifestyle. Not for all tastes. In Swedish with English subtitles. Rated R for profanity, nudity, and simulated sex. 119m. DIR: Colin Nutley. CAST: Helena Bergstrom, Rikard Wolff, Sven Wollter, Viveka Sidahl, Per Oscarsson. 1993

HOUSE OF CARDS ★★★★ Strange but gripping drama about a young girl who retreats into her mind after seeing her father fall to his death. Frantic, her mother, Kathleen Turner, calls in psychiatrist Tommy Lee Jones to help reach the girl, but everything they try seems to make the situation worse. Heartrending. Rated PG-13 for adult situations. 109m. DIR: Michael Lessac. CAST: Kathleen Turner, Tommy Lee Jones, Asha Menina, Shiloh Strong, Esther Rolle, Park Overall, Michael Horse. 1993 DVD

HOUSE OF DARK SHADOWS ★★★ Gore and murder run rampant throughout this film based on the TV soap *Dark Shadows*. Barnabas Collins (Jonathan Frid), a particularly violent vampire, will stop at nothing to be reunited with Josette, his fiancée 200 years ago. Rated PG for violence. 98m. DIR: Dan Curtis. CAST: Jonathan Frid, Kathryn Leigh Scott, Grayson Hall, Joan Bennett. 1970

HOUSE OF DRACULA ★★1/2 Scientist Onslow Stevens falls under the spell of Count Dracula while Larry Talbot, aka the Wolfman, seeks to end the horror once and for all. The movie's nostalgia value makes it fun to watch, but it is by no means a classic. B&W; 67m. DIR: Erle C. Kenton. CAST: Lon Chaney Jr., John Carradine, Martha O'Driscoll, Lionel Atwill, Onslow Stevens, Glenn Strange, Jane Adams, Ludwig Stossel. 1945

HOUSE OF EXORCISM, THE ♥ Incomprehensible. Rated R for profanity, nudity, gore, and violence. 93m. DIR: Mickey Lion, Mario Bava. CAST: Telly Savalas, Robert Alda, Elke Sommer. 1975 DVD

HOUSE OF FEAR ★★★ The last of the high-quality entries in the Universal Sherlock Holmes series has Holmes (Basil Rathbone) and Watson (Nigel Bruce) attempting to solve a series of murders among the guests at a Scottish mansion. It was based on Conan Doyle's "The Adventure of the Five Orange Pips" and combines atmosphere, pacing, fine acting, and sure direction. B&W; 69m. DIR: Roy William Neill. CAST: Basil Rathbone, Nigel Bruce, Aubrey Mather, Dennis Hoey. 1945

HOUSE OF FRANKENSTEIN ★★★1/2 Universal Pictures' first all-star monsterfest may have signaled the beginning of the end of the company's reign of horror, but it's nevertheless an enjoyable film for fans of old-time chillers. Boris Karloff is excellent as the mad scientist who escapes from an insane asylum and proceeds to wreak havoc on his enemies with the expert help of Dracula, the Wolfman and the Frankenstein monster. Good for a rainy night. B&W; 71m. DIR: Erle C. Kenton. CAST: Boris Karloff, J. Carrol Naish, Lon Chaney Jr., John Carradine, Lionel Atwill, George Zucco, Glenn Strange, Anne Gwynne, Elena Verdugo, Sig Ruman. 1944

HOUSE OF GAMES ★★★1/2 Pulitzer Prize–winning playwright David Mamet makes an impressive directorial debut with this suspense-thriller. Lindsay Crouse, the writer-director's wife, gives an effective performance as a psychiatrist who attempts to intercede with a con man (Joe Mantegna) on behalf of one of her patients, a compulsive gambler who owes him several thousand dollars. She is sucked into a world of mirrors where nothing is what it seems. Rated R for profanity and violence. 102m. DIR: David Mamet. CAST: Lindsay Crouse, Joe Mantegna, Lilia Skala. 1987

HOUSE OF HORRORS ★★ An untalented sculptor simply decides to kill off his critics in this lame tale of unrequited love and revenge. Only interesting for Rondo Hatton's appearance as The Creeper. Hatton, who suffered from a disease of the pituitary gland, needed no makeup to play the monstrous bad guy, but he could have used acting lessons. Not rated. B&W; 65m. DIR: Jean Yarbrough. CAST: Rondo Hatton, Martin Kosleck, Virginia Grey, Bill Goodwin, Robert Lowery. 1946

HOUSE OF 1,000 DOLLS ★★ Sexploitation potboiler, a British/Spanish coproduction starring Vincent Price as an illusionist who runs a white slavery racket on the side. Variously campy, sleazy, and boring. 83m. DIR: Jeremy Summers. CAST: Vincent Price, Martha Hyer, George Nader. 1967

HOUSE OF PSYCHOTIC WOMEN 🎬 The "World's Worst Videos" version of this already cut (for U.S. release) Spanish shocker about a sex murderer. Rated R. 90m. DIR: Carlos Aured. CAST: Paul Naschy, Diana Lorys. 1973

HOUSE OF SEVEN CORPSES, THE ★★1/2 Veteran cast almost saves this minor yarn about a film crew shooting a horror movie in a foreboding old mansion. Semi-entertaining nonsense. Rated PG. 90m. DIR: Paul Harrison. CAST: John Ireland, Faith Domergue, John Carradine. 1973

HOUSE OF STRANGERS ★★★1/2 Well-acted, engrossing tale of the fall of a wealthy banker's family. Edward G. Robinson plays the patriarch whose four sons are now at odds with him and each other for various reasons. B&W; 101m. DIR: Joseph L. Mankiewicz. CAST: Edward G. Robinson, Luther Adler, Richard Conte, Susan Hayward. 1949

HOUSE OF TERROR 🎬 A private nurse and her ex-con boyfriend try to bilk a millionaire out of his riches. Rated PG for violence. 90m. DIR: Sergei Goncharff. CAST: Jennifer Bishop, Arell Blanton, Mitchell Gregg. 1987

HOUSE OF THE LONG SHADOWS ★★★ This is the good old-fashioned–type horror film that doesn't rely on blood and gore to give the viewer a scare. This gothic thriller is a great choice for horror fans who still like to use their imaginations. Rated PG. 102m. DIR: Pete Walker. CAST: Vincent Price, John Carradine, Christopher Lee, Desi Arnaz Jr., Peter Cushing. 1984

HOUSE OF THE RISING SUN ★★ Technically sound but artistically soulless film that attempts to give an Eighties look to a Thirties murder mystery. Jamie Barrett is an aspiring reporter, willing to do anything to get the lowdown on pimp Frank Annese. Not rated; contains adult situations. 86m. DIR: Greg Gold. CAST: Frank Annese, Jamie Barrett, Tawny Moyer, Deborah Wakeham, James Daughton, John J. York. 1987

HOUSE OF THE SEVEN GABLES, THE ★★★1/2 The only rendition of the Nathaniel Hawthorne classic made during the talkie era thus far, and a good one. Vincent Price and George Sanders one-up each other with cynical dialogue and scenery chewing, and the script is faithful to the book. The story of a jealous man who sends an innocent man to prison is hauntingly photographed and uses replicas of the nineteenth-century New England house that inspired it. B&W; 90m. DIR: Joe May. CAST: Vincent Price, Margaret Lindsay, George Sanders, Nan Grey, Alan Napier, Dick Foran. 1940

HOUSE OF THE SPIRITS, THE ★★1/2 Even a high-powered cast cannot save this sketchy depiction of seventy years in the history of an unnamed country (reportedly Chile) as seen by three generations of aristocracy. Not quite an all-out embarrassment, but close. Rated R for violence, profanity, nudity, and simulated sex. 138m. DIR: Bille August. CAST: Jeremy Irons, Meryl Streep, Glenn Close, Winona Ryder, Antonio Banderas, Vanessa Redgrave, Armin Mueller-Stahl, Maria Conchita Alonso, Sarita Choudhury. 1994

HOUSE OF USHER, THE 🎬 Boring retelling of the Edgar Allan Poe classic. Rated R for violence and profanity. 92m. DIR: Alan Birkinshaw. CAST: Oliver Reed, Donald Pleasence, Romy Windsor. 1990

HOUSE OF WAX ★★★1/2 Vincent Price stars as a demented sculptor who, after losing the use of his hands in a fire, turns to murder in this above-average horror film. 88m. DIR: André de Toth. CAST: Vincent Price, Phyllis Kirk, Carolyn Jones. 1953

HOUSE OF WHIPCORD 🎬 A pair of elderly Brits kidnap voluptuous young singles and torture them. Rated R. 102m. DIR: Pete Walker. CAST: Barbara Markham, Patrick Barr, Ray Brooks. 1974 DVD

HOUSE OF YES, THE ★★★ College student Josh Hamilton brings fiancée Tori Spelling home to meet his grotesquely dysfunctional family. The whole thing is too clever for its own good, but it's smoothly directed, with shrewd and witty acting. Spelling, who gives the standout performance, plays the only normal person in sight. Rated R for profanity and incest-related humor. 90m. DIR: Mark Waters. CAST: Parker Posey, Josh Hamilton, Genevieve Bujold, Tori Spelling, Freddie Prinze Jr. 1997 DVD

HOUSE ON 92ND STREET, THE ★★★1/2 One of the first successful docudramas, the movie focuses on espionage activity in New York during World War II. As spies try to steal atomic secrets, the camera follows them every step of the way. B&W; 88m. DIR: Henry Hathaway. CAST: Signe Hasso, William Eythe, Lloyd Nolan, Gene Lockhart, Leo G. Carroll, Harry Bellaver. 1945

HOUSE ON CARROLL STREET, THE ★★★ Commendable suspense film about a young accused communist (Kelly McGillis) who becomes involved in a Nazi smuggling ring in 1951 Washington, D.C. Jeff Daniels is one of the investigating FBI men who falls for McGillis. A good costume piece, and McGillis and Daniels turn in solid performances, along with Jessica Tandy as McGillis's crusty employer. Rated PG r language, violence, and slight nudity. 111m. DIR: eter Yates. CAST: Kelly McGillis, Jeff Daniels, Jessica andy, Mandy Patinkin. 1988

OUSE ON GARIBALDI STREET ★★ Run-of-the-ill suspense tale chronicling the abduction of Nazi ar criminal Adolf Eichmann by Israelis in South merica. Effectively performed, though. 104m. DIR: eter Collinson. CAST: Martin Balsam, Topol, Janet uzman, Leo McKern. 1979

HOUSE ON HAUNTED HILL (1958) ★★★ Vincent rice is at his most relaxed and confident in this fun right flick about the wealthy owner of a creepy old ortress who offers a group a fortune if they can sur-ive a night there. Humorous at times, deadly serious t others. B&W; 75m. DIR: William Castle. CAST: Vin-ent Price, Carol Ohmart, Richard Long, Elisha Cook r., Carolyn Craig, Alan Marshal. 1958 DVD

HOUSE ON HAUNTED HILL (1999) ★★ Amuse-ment-park impresario Geoffrey Rush invites five guests to spend the night in a former insane asylum, with those who stay until dawn receiving a $1 million prize. Even with its high-tech special effects, this re-make of the 1958 William Castle film is tackier than the original. The supposedly sophisticated guests wander off by themselves despite the threatening at-nosphere of the "house," exhibiting behavior we found difficult to accept even by teenagers in low-budget slasher movies. Rated R for violence, gore, profanity, and nudity. 96m. DIR: William Malone. CAST: Geoffrey Rush, Taye Diggs, Famke Janssen, Pe-ter Gallagher, Chris Kattan, Bridgette Wilson, Max Per-ich, Jeffrey Coombs, Peter Graves. 1999 DVD

HOUSE ON SKULL MOUNTAIN 🎬 Relatives gath-ered in an old, dark house for the reading of a will are killed off one by one. Rated PG. 89m. DIR: Ron Hon-thaner. CAST: Victor French, Mike Evans. 1974

HOUSE ON SORORITY ROW A group of college girls takes over their sorority and kills the house mother. Rated R. 90m. DIR: Mark Rosman. CAST: Eileen Davidson. 1983

HOUSE ON TOMBSTONE HILL, THE ★★ College students take up residence in a cursed mansion, and become prey to the old lady who guards the attic. Un-known cast gives their all in this creaky thriller. Not rated; contains nudity and violence. 92m. DIR: J. Rif-fel. CAST: Mark Zobian. 1988

HOUSE PARTY ★★★★ This delightful rap musical was one of the sleeper hits of 1990. The plot is stan-dard   let's-have-a-party-while-my-folks-are-away stuff, but with a surprisingly fresh humor and some dynamite dance numbers. The R rating (for profan-ity) makes it unsuitable for small children, but for mature teens and adults it's a great good time. 105m. DIR: Reginald Hudlin. CAST: Kid'n'Play, Full Force, Robin Harris. 1990 DVD

HOUSE PARTY 2 ★★1/2 Inferior sequel. The film, which is dedicated to the late comedian Robin Har-ris (seen in flashback scenes) and features Whoopi Goldberg in a brief cameo, has some funny moments, most of which are provided by Martin Lawrence as Kid 'N' Play's out-of-control disc jockey. Otherwise, it's pretty standard fare. Rated R for profanity and vi-olence. 90m. DIR: Doug McHenry, George Jackson. CAST: Christopher Reid, Christopher Martin, Martin

Lawrence, Tisha Campbell, Georg Stanford Brown, William Schallert. 1991 DVD

HOUSE PARTY 3 ★★ Rappers Kid 'N' Play get lost in the cluttered shuffle of their own hip-hop comedy. Kid's bachelor party and the duo's management of an all-girl group hit a few snags. Rated R for profanity. 94m. DIR: Eric Meza. CAST: Christopher Reid, Christo-pher Martin, Bernie Mac, Angela Means, Khandi Alexander. 1994 DVD

HOUSE THAT BLED TO DEATH, THE ★★ Margin-ally scary horror film about a house that is pos-sessed. Possessed by what or who? Don't ask us—the film refuses to give up the reason for all the blood that keeps shooting out of the pipes, or the various bloody members that show up in the fridge now and then. Not rated, but would probably merit a PG for vi-olence and gore. 50m. DIR: Tom Clegg. CAST: Nicholas Ball. 1985

HOUSE THAT DRIPPED BLOOD, THE ★★★1/2 All-star horror-anthology high jinks adapted from the stories of Robert Bloch. It's not quite on a par with the pioneering British release *Dead of Night*, but it'll do. Best segment: a horror star (Jon Pertwee) dis-covers a vampire's cape and finds himself becoming a little too convincing in the role of a bloodsucker. Rated PG. 102m. DIR: Peter Duffell. CAST: Christopher Lee, Peter Cushing, Denholm Elliott, Jon Pertwee, In-grid Pitt. 1970

HOUSE THAT MARY BOUGHT, THE ★★★1/2 In this thriller, adapted from Tim Wynne-Jones's novel, *Odd's End*, a married couple settle into a gorgeous little home by the coast, only to discover that some-one keeps breaking into the place and engaging in all sorts of mischief. Or is it one of them, trying to drive the other into a nervous breakdown? The luxu-rious Brittany and Luxembourg settings are a poetic counterpoint to the creepy story. Rated PG for mild violence. 104m. DIR: Simon MacCorkindale. CAST: Susan George, Ben Cross, Maurice Thorogood, Vernon Dobtcheff, Jean-Paul Muel, Charlotte Valandrey. 1994

HOUSE THAT VANISHED, THE ★ Exploitative suspense tale about a woman who sees a murder but can't convince anyone that it happened. There's a lot of nudity and an underdeveloped plot in this British-made film, which was fifteen minutes longer when it was originally released as *Scream and Die*. Rated R. 84m. DIR: Joseph Larraz. CAST: Andrea Allan. 1973

HOUSE WHERE EVIL DWELLS, THE ★★ Depress-ing little horror romp with a Japanese background. In a savagely violent opening, a young samurai swordsman discovers the amorous activities of his less-than-faithful wife, and a gory fight ensues. This traps some really angry spirits in the house, which Edward Albert and Susan George move into cen-turies later. Rated R for nudity, violence, and lan-guage. 91m. DIR: Kevin O'Connor. CAST: Edward Al-bert, Susan George, Doug McClure. 1985

HOUSEBOAT ★★★ A minor entry in Cary Grant's *oeuvre* of romantic fluff, largely unremarkable be-cause of its ho-hum script. With this sort of insub-stantial material coming his way, it's little wonder Grant chose to retire eight years later. He lives on a houseboat *sans* wife; Sophia Loren is the house-keeper-maid with whom he falls in love. Not rated;

suitable for family viewing. 110m. DIR: Melville Shavelson. CAST: Cary Grant, Sophia Loren, Martha Hyer, Harry Guardino. 1958

HOUSEGUEST ★★ An editing disaster, this overlong series of sight gags and one-liners doesn't do Sinbad's multitalents justice. To avoid the mob, he poses as a distinguished dentist and stays with a troubled family that he attempts to help (à la *Uncle Buck*). Phil Hartman provides some chuckles as his totally unhip host. The ending attempts to bring it all together but, alas, it's just too little too late. Rated PG for cartoon-variety violence. 110m. DIR: Randall Miller. CAST: Sinbad, Phil Hartman, Jeffrey Jones, Kim Greist. 1994

HOUSEHOLD SAINTS ★★★1/2 Not as well etched as director Nancy Savoca's debut *True Love*, but a well-meaning pleasure nonetheless. The lives and loves of three generations of Italian-American women living in New York's Little Italy, come alive thanks to excellent performances by Tracey Ullman, Judith Malina, and, most notably, Lili Taylor as the current bearer of the torch. Nicely woven tale of the human spirit. Rated R for adult situations, language, and nudity. 124m. DIR: Nancy Savoca. CAST: Tracey Ullman, Judith Malina, Lili Taylor, Vincent D'Onofrio. 1993

HOUSEHOLDER, THE ★★★★ Engaging low-budget comedy about a naïve young man and woman learning to adjust to their arranged marriage. The first collaboration by the legendary team of producer Ismail Merchant, writer Ruth Prawer Jhabvala, and director James Ivory, aided by an uncredited Satyajit Ray as editor. In English. B&W; 100m. DIR: James Ivory. CAST: Shashi Kapoor. 1963

HOUSEKEEPER, THE ★★★ A slightly demented housekeeper is driven over the edge by a Bible-thumping ex-hooker and proceeds to kill the family she works for. A suspenseful atmosphere moves the film along. Rated R for violence. 97m. DIR: Ousama Rawi. CAST: Rita Tushingham, Rose Petty, Jackie Burroughs. 1987

HOUSEKEEPING ★★★ Director Bill Forsyth makes superbly quirky movies, and *Housekeeping*, based on Marilynne Robinson's novel, is a worthy addition to his body of work. Christine Lahti plays a contented transient who comes to the Pacific Northwest to care for her two orphaned nieces. Lahti makes the offbeat moments resound with weird humor. Rated PG. 112m. DIR: Bill Forsyth. CAST: Christine Lahti, Andrea Burchill, Sarah Walker. 1987

HOUSESITTER ★★★1/2 Architect Newton Davis (Steve Martin) is rebuffed in love, then finds a relative stranger (Goldie Hawn) posing as his wife. Hawn, Martin, and director Frank Oz manage to hit the funnybone consistently enough for this to be a fun romp. Rated PG. 102m. DIR: Frank Oz. CAST: Steve Martin, Goldie Hawn, Dana Delany, Julie Harris, Donald Moffat, Peter MacNicol. 1992 DVD

HOUSEWIFE ★★ When a would-be rapist and thief breaks into the house of a well-to-do Beverly Hills couple, he unleashes the tensions that exist beneath the surface of their well-ordered lives. Exploitative drama with a cast that deserves better. Rated R for violence and sexual situations. 95m. DIR: Larry Co-

hen. CAST: Yaphet Kotto, Andrew Duggan, Joyce Van Patten, Jeannie Berlin. 1972

HOUSEWIFE FROM HELL ♥ Silliness about a vindictive housewife who returns from the dead to get even with her unscrupulous husband. This was dead on arrival. Not rated; contains nudity, adult situations, strong language, and some violence. 82m. DIR: James Lane, Don Jones. CAST: Gregg Bullock, Lisa Comshaw, Marcia Gray, Ron Jeremy, Jacqueline St. Clair. 1993

HOW FUNNY CAN SEX BE? ★★1/2 Mediocre anthology featuring eight tales about love and sex. Giancarlo Giannini and Laura Antonelli liven up their segments, but you might want to fast-forward through some of the others. Rated R for nudity. 97m. DIR: Dino Risi. CAST: Giancarlo Giannini, Laura Antonelli. 1976

HOW GREEN WAS MY VALLEY ★★★★★ This 1941 best-picture Oscar winner is a tribute to the lasting value of a family's love. Director John Ford also won an Oscar for the way he brings out the soul of Richard Llewellyn's bestseller, which concerns a Welsh mining family, as seen through the eyes of its youngest member (Roddy McDowall, in one of his most famous child-star roles). 118m. DIR: John Ford. CAST: Walter Pidgeon, Maureen O'Hara, Roddy McDowall, Donald Crisp, John Loder, Barry Fitzgerald. 1941 DVD

HOW I GOT INTO COLLEGE ♥ Uninspired and dull adolescent comedy. Rated PG-13. 98m. DIR: Savage Steve Holland. CAST: Anthony Edwards, Corey Parker. 1989

HOW I WON THE WAR ★★★1/2 John Lennon had his only solo screen turn (away from the Beatles) in this often hilarious war spoof. Directed by Richard Lester, it features Michael Crawford as a military man who has a wacky way of distorting the truth as he reminisces about his adventures in battle. 109m. DIR: Richard Lester. CAST: Michael Crawford, John Lennon, Michael Hordern, Jack MacGowran. 1967

HOW STELLA GOT HER GROOVE BACK ★★1/2 Forty-year-old stockbroker and single mom has a love affair with a twenty-year-old Jamaican while vacationing in the tropics. This reversal of Hollywood's usual coupling of older man/younger woman begins as a brisk comedy and then sputters down the stretch as a rather shallow, sentimental romance. Rated R for language, nudity, and simulated sex. 124m. DIR: Kevin Sullivan. CAST: Angela Bassett, Taye Diggs, Whoopi Goldberg, Regina King, Suzzanne Douglas, Michael J. Pagan. 1998 DVD

HOW THE WEST WAS FUN ★★★ It's fun on the range as the adorable Olsen twins join their father in an attempt to save a dude ranch that their mother once attended as a child. Kids will enjoy this harmless, made-for-television romp. Not rated. 92m. DIR: Stuart Margolin. CAST: Mary-Kate Olsen, Ashley Olsen, Martin Mull, Patrick Cassidy, Ben Cardinal. 1994

HOW THE WEST WAS WON ★★★1/2 Any Western with this cast is worth a glimpse. Sadly, much of the grandeur of the original version is lost because it was released on the three-screen Cinerama process. For a taste of its original grandeur, check out the letterboxed Laserdisc version, where the clear, sharp pic-

re and excellent stereo sound do the film justice.
55m. **DIR:** Henry Hathaway, George Marshall, John
ord. **CAST:** Gregory Peck, Henry Fonda, James Stew-
t, John Wayne, Debbie Reynolds, Walter Brennan,
arl Malden, Richard Widmark, Robert Preston, George
eppard, Carolyn Jones, Carroll Baker. 1963 DVD

OW TO BEAT THE HIGH CO$T OF LIVING ★★ A
reat cast all dressed up with no place to go ... ex-
ept Jane Curtin, whose shopping-mall striptease is
 marginal high point in a caper comedy not even up
o the substandards of an average made-for-televi-
ion movie. Tiresome and taxing. Rated PG. 110m.
IR: Robert Scheerer. **CAST:** Jessica Lange, Susan
aint James, Jane Curtin, Richard Benjamin, Fred
Villard, Dabney Coleman. 1980

OW TO BREAK UP A HAPPY DIVORCE ★★★ Ex-
wife Barbara Eden wants ex-husband Hal Linden
ack. To make him jealous, she dates a well-known
layboy. Comic mayhem follows. Lots of sight gags.
his is an unrated TV movie. 78m. **DIR:** Jerry Paris.
AST: Hal Linden, Barbara Eden, Harold Gould. 1976

OW TO FRAME A FIGG ★★★★ Classic, slapstick
omedy starring Don Knotts as a naïve accountant
who is set up as the patsy for a city council that's
een stealing money from the city. A charming, very
unny outing with a hysterical performance by
Knotts. Rated G. 103m. **DIR:** Alan Rafkin. **CAST:** Don
Knotts, Yvonne Craig, Elaine Joyce, Joe Flynn, Edward
Andrews. 1971

OW TO GET AHEAD IN ADVERTISING ★★ During
an ad campaign for a new pimple cream, a British ad-
ertising executive goes completely berserk when a
oil erupts on his neck, grows into a human head,
and spews forth abrasive slogans ad nauseam. This
eavy-handed assault on the marketing of useless
and even harmful commodities is ultimately more
abrasive than fun. Rated PG-13. 94m. **DIR:** Bruce
Robinson. **CAST:** Richard E. Grant, Rachel Ward,
Jacqueline Tong, Susan Wooldridge. 1989

HOW TO IRRITATE PEOPLE ★★★★★ Even before
Monty Python, John Cleese's sense of aggressive humor was fully developed, as can be seen in this hilar-
ous collection of skits. As in all of his best work,
Cleese (who wrote this BBC special along with future *Python* mate Graham Chapman) mines humor
from the disparity between the surface politeness of
the English and the frustrated rage underneath. Not
rated. 65m. **DIR:** Ian Fordyce. **CAST:** John Cleese, Graham Chapman, Michael Palin, Connie Booth, Tim
Brooke-Taylor. 1968

HOW TO MAKE A MONSTER ♥ Hollywood makeup
artist goes off the deep end. B&W/color; 75m. **DIR:**
Herbert L. Strock. **CAST:** Robert H. Harris, Paul Brinegar, Gary Conway, Gary Clarke, Malcolm Atterbury.
1958

HOW TO MAKE AN AMERICAN QUILT ★★★1/2
Based on Whitney Otto's celebrated book, the film
has emotionally scarred women sharing their pain in
an effort to show marriage-shy Winona Ryder the
value of commitment. Some of the episodic tales succeed, while others seem trivial. It's a pleasure to see
so many Hollywood icons in one project. Rated PG-13
for profanity, sexual candor, and drug use. 116m.
DIR: Jocelyn Moorhouse. **CAST:** Winona Ryder, Maya

Angelou, Anne Bancroft, Ellen Burstyn, Kate Nelligan,
Jean Simmons, Lois Smith, Alfre Woodard, Dermot
Mulroney, Rip Torn, Kate Capshaw, Claire Danes,
Melinda Dillon, Samantha Mathis. 1995 DVD

HOW TO MARRY A MILLIONAIRE ★★★ The stars,
Marilyn Monroe, Lauren Bacall, and Betty Grable,
are fun to watch in this comedy. However, director
Jean Negulesco doesn't do much to keep our interest. The story in this slight romp is all in the title—
with William Powell giving the girls a run for his
money. 96m. **DIR:** Jean Negulesco. **CAST:** Lauren Bacall, Marilyn Monroe, Betty Grable, William Powell,
Cameron Mitchell, David Wayne, Rory Calhoun. 1953

HOW TO MURDER YOUR WIFE ★★1/2 Jack Lemmon plays a comic-strip artist whose well-structured
life is disrupted when he discovers he has married a
beautiful woman after a night of drunken partying.
Finding the situation intolerable, Lemmon contrives
to take out his frustration by murdering his new
bride in the comic strip. Some clever bits, but the
premise and attitudes are unbelievably sexist. 118m.
DIR: Richard Quine. **CAST:** Jack Lemmon, Virna Lisi,
Terry-Thomas, Eddie Mayehoff, Claire Trevor, Sidney
Blackmer, Jack Albertson, Mary Wickes. 1965

HOW TO STEAL A MILLION ★★★★1/2 A delightful romp with sophisticated dialogue, excellent acting, and colorful sets and costumes. The plot revolves around a museum heist that's done to save the
"honor" of a magnificent forger, by his daughter and
a noted burglar. 127m. **DIR:** William Wyler. **CAST:** Audrey Hepburn, Peter O'Toole, Charles Boyer, Eli Wallach, Hugh Griffith. 1966

HOW TO STUFF A WILD BIKINI ★★ It's no surprise
to see Frankie Avalon and Annette Funicello together in this beach-party film. Dwayne Hickman
tries his hand at romancing Annette in this one. Not
much plot, but lots of crazy (sometimes funny)
things are going on. 90m. **DIR:** William Asher. **CAST:**
Frankie Avalon, Annette Funicello, Dwayne Hickman,
Mickey Rooney, Buster Keaton. 1965 DVD

**HOW TO SUCCEED IN BUSINESS WITHOUT RE-
ALLY TRYING ★★★★** A near-perfect musical
based on the Pulitzer Prize–winning Broadway
show, with most of the original cast intact. Robert
Morse plays the window washer who plots his way to
the top of the Worldwide Wicket Company. The musical numbers are staged with inventiveness and performed with exuberance. Maureen Arthur is a standout as the buxom beauty all the managers want in
their secretarial pool. 121m. **DIR:** David Swift. **CAST:**
Robert Morse, Rudy Vallee, Michele Lee, Anthony
Teague, Maureen Arthur, Sammy Smith. 1967 DVD

HOW U LIKE ME NOW ★★★ Extremely low-budget
account of the struggles of a couple of African-American friends on Chicago's South Side. The acting is
uneven, but writer/director/producer Darryl Roberts
turned out a gritty, honest, and funny script with
enough warmth and humor to help you over the
rough patches. Rated R for profanity and sexual situations. 109m. **DIR:** Darryl Roberts. **CAST:** Darnell
Williams, Salli Richardson, Daniel Gardner, Raymond
Whitfield, Darryl Roberts. 1992

HOWARD THE DUCK ♥ An extremely rotten egg.
Unwisely rated PG, considering some smarmy sex

scenes and frightening monster makeup. 111m. DIR: Willard Huyck. CAST: Lea Thompson, Jeffrey Jones, Tim Robbins, Ed Gale. 1986

HOWARDS END ★★★★★ Two relatively liberated middle-class sisters become entangled with the members of an upper-crust British family. The creative team that adapted E. M. Forster's *Room with a View* and *Maurice* saved the best for this Forster adaptation, a gorgeous and engrossing story of the first decade of the twentieth century, propelled through distinctive characters, rich dialogue, delicious irony, and evocative locales. Rated PG. 140m. DIR: James Ivory. CAST: Emma Thompson, Anthony Hopkins, Vanessa Redgrave, Helena Bonham Carter, James Wilby, Samuel West. 1992 DVD

HOWARDS OF VIRGINIA, THE ★★ Tiring, too-long retelling of the Revolutionary War centering on an aristocratic Virginia family. In the Cary Grant filmography, it is just plain awful. B&W; 117m. DIR: Frank Lloyd. CAST: Cary Grant, Martha Scott, Cedric Hardwicke, Alan Marshal, Richard Carlson, Paul Kelly, Anne Revere, Irving Bacon. 1940

HOWLING, THE ★★★★ Every spooky scene you've ever seen, every horror movie cliché that's ever been overspoken, and every guaranteed-to-make-'em-jump, out-of-the-dark surprise that Hollywood ever came up with for its scary movies. It also has the best special effects since *Alien* and some really off-the-wall humor. Rated R for gruesome adult horror. 91m. DIR: Joe Dante. CAST: Dee Wallace, Christopher Stone, Patrick Macnee, Dennis Dugan, Slim Pickens, John Carradine. 1981

HOWLING II ... YOUR SISTER IS A WEREWOLF 🎦 Poor follow-up to *The Howling*. Rated R for nudity, blood, and gore. 91m. DIR: Philippe Mora. CAST: Christopher Lee, Reb Brown, Annie McEnroe, Sybil Danning. 1984

HOWLING III ★★1/2 Werewolves turn up in Australia, only these are marsupials. A sociologist falls in love with one of them and tries to save the whole tribe. The story focuses more on character than gore, and you find yourself strangely engrossed. Rated PG-13 for brief nudity and violence. 95m. DIR: Philippe Mora. CAST: Barry Otto. 1987

HOWLING IV 🎦 Werewolves are scarce in this third sequel about a woman haunted by the ghost of a nun who was killed by one of the lycanthropes. Rated R for violence and nudity. 94m. DIR: John Hough. CAST: Romy Windsor, Michael T. Weiss, Antony Hamilton. 1988

HOWLING V—THE REBIRTH ★★★1/2 A group of people gather at a castle that has been shut for 500 years—for a rather fun game of who's the werewolf. Only the title has any relation to the previous movies in the series. Enjoyable. Rated R for violence and nudity. 99m. DIR: Neal Sundstrom. CAST: Philip Davis. 1989

HOWLING VI: THE FREAKS ★★1/2 A carnival freak show is the scene of a battle between a vampire and the werewolf-drifter who pursues him. Special effects that leave a lot to be desired diminish this really strange entry in the long-running werewolf series. Rated R for violence and profanity. 102m. DIR: Hope Perello. CAST: Brendan Hughes, Michelle Mathe-

son, Sean Gregory Sullivan, Antonio Fargas, Carol Lynley. 1990

HOWLING, THE: NEW MOON RISING 🎦 Ridiculous follow-up to the popular werewolf film series. An undercover reporter investigates a series of bloody murders in an off-the-map town. Bad acting, nonexistent direction, and some really terrible country/western music performed by the cast. Rated R for profanity and werewolf violence. 90m. DIR: Cliff Turner. CAST: John Ramsden, Ernest Kester, Clive Turner, John Hoff, Elisabeth Shue. 1994

H. P. LOVECRAFT'S NECRONOMICON: BOOK OF THE DEAD ★★1/2 When horror author H. P. Lovecraft visits a mysterious library, the stories he read come to life in the form of these three horrific tales. Loaded with blood and guts, so-so horror film will entertain fans of the genre but won't win over anyone else. Rated R for horror violence. 96m. DIR: Brian Yuzna, Christopher Gans, Shusuke Kaneko. CAST: Jeffrey Combs, David Warner, Bruce Payne, Belinda Bauer. 1993

HUCK AND THE KING OF HEARTS ★★★ Credit scripter Christopher Sturgeon with an inventive idea: To redo *Huckleberry Finn* as a contemporary family adventure with clever echoes of Mark Twain. Thus, young Chauncey Leopardi flees a hard-hearted stepfather, joins forces with small-time grifter "Injun" Joe (Graham Greene), and heads for Las Vegas and a meeting with a long-estranged grandfather (John Astin). Rated PG for violence. 98m. DIR: Michael Keusch. CAST: Chauncey Leopardi, Joe Piscopo, Dee Wallace, Gretchen Becker, John Astin, Graham Greene. 1993

HUCKLEBERRY FINN (1974) ★★ The weakest version of the popular story, mainly because forgettable songs take the place of personality. The basic plot of a young boy learning about life from a runaway slave is there, but the players look and act bored. Rated G. 117m. DIR: J. Lee Thompson. CAST: Jeff East, Paul Winfield, David Wayne, Harvey Korman, Arthur O'Connell, Gary Merrill, Kim O'Brien. 1974

HUCKLEBERRY FINN (1975) ★★★★ Ron Howard does a fine job as Mark Twain's mischievous misfit. This made-for-TV film is well worth watching. The supporting actors are fun to watch, too. 74m. DIR: Robert Totten. CAST: Ron Howard, Donny Most, Antonio Fargas, Merle Haggard, Jack Elam, Royal Dano, Sarah Selby. 1975

HUCKSTERS, THE ★★ Exposé of the advertising business is as vapid as the products pushed by the advertisers in this overlong melodrama. A mature Clark Gable, recently returned from duty in World War II, heads a stunning but ultimately wasted cast that includes Deborah Kerr and Ava Gardner as the two gals who want him. B&W; 115m. DIR: Jack Conway. CAST: Clark Gable, Deborah Kerr, Sydney Greenstreet, Adolphe Menjou, Ava Gardner, Keenan Wynn, Edward Arnold, Frank Albertson, Douglas Fowley. 1947

HUD ★★★★★ In one of his most memorable performances, Paul Newman stars as the arrogant ne'er-do-well son of a Texas rancher (Melvyn Douglas) who has fallen on hard times. Instead of helping his father, Hud drunkenly pursues the family's housekeeper (Patricia Neal), who wants nothing to do with him. When asked, Newman dubbed this one "pretty good." An understatement. B&W; 112m. **DIR:** Martin Ritt. **CAST:** Paul Newman, Patricia Neal, Melvyn Douglas, Brandon de Wilde. **1963**

HUDSON HAWK ★★★ Fans of Bruce Willis's wise-cracking comedy style will enjoy this critically lambasted spoof of spy thrillers filled with slapstick comedy, unexpected musical numbers, and goofy supporting characters. Willis plays a cat burglar who is forced back into the biz. Rated R for profanity and violence. 95m. **DIR:** Michael Lehmann. **CAST:** Bruce Willis, Danny Aiello, Andie MacDowell, James Coburn, Richard E. Grant, Sandra Bernhard. **1991 DVD**

HUDSUCKER PROXY, THE ★★1/2 This film falls a little short with its twisted send-up of Frank Capra's populist dramas of the 1930s and 1940s. Tim Robbins is a schnook who is promoted from the mailroom to the presidency of a corporation after his predecessor leaps to his death (presumably out of boredom). Paul Newman steals the movie as the main manipulator, while Jennifer Jason Leigh goes a little overboard as a tough gal reporter. Rated PG. 111m. **DIR:** Joel Coen. **CAST:** Tim Robbins, Paul Newman, Jennifer Jason Leigh, Charles Durning, John Mahoney, Jim True, Bill Cobbs, Bruce Campbell. **1994 DVD**

HUGH HEFNER: ONCE UPON A TIME ★★★ An involving examination of the changing moral values of America in the past four decades as seen through the eyes of publisher-philosopher Hugh Hefner, creator of *Playboy* magazine. A surprisingly candid documentary that eschews nudity. 88m. **DIR:** Robert Heath. **1992**

HUGO POOL ★★★1/2 Forced to rely on her dysfunctional parents to help meet an impossible deadline in her pool-cleaning business, a young woman spends a wild day among the rich and strange in Los Angeles. Some truly odd vignettes and a sweet subplot highlight this independent film. There's a lot of heart as well as strong performances and surprise cameos in this riveting little gem. Rated R. 92m. **DIR:** Robert Downey. **CAST:** Alyssa Milano, Patrick Dempsey, Malcolm McDowell, Robert Downey Jr., Cathy Moriarty, Richard Lewis, Sean Penn, Bert Remsen, Chuck Barris. **1997 DVD**

HULA ★★1/2 Clara Bow chews up the palm fronds as Hula, wild daughter of an Irish planter in Hawaii who defies domesticity until she falls for a starched-shirt, married engineer. This liberated love story had a surefire audience eager for anything by Jazz-Age wildcat Bow. A piece of fluff, but entertaining. B&W; 64m. **DIR:** Victor Fleming. **CAST:** Clara Bow, Clive Brook, Arlette Marchal, Arnold Kent, Maude Truax, Albert Gran. **1927**

HULLABALOO OVER GEORGE AND BONNIE'S PICTURES ★★1/2 British and American art dealers compete to gain access to a valuable art collection belonging to an Indian prince. A lesser effort from the team behind *A Room with a View*; gently funny in spots, but it never really goes anywhere. Not rated, but nothing objectionable. 85m. **DIR:** James Ivory. **CAST:** Peggy Ashcroft, Victor Banerjee, Saeed Jaffrey. **1976**

HUMAN COMEDY, THE ★★★1/2 California author William Saroyan's tender and touching story of life in a small valley town during World War II is a winner all around in this compassionate, now-nostalgic film. Mickey Rooney shines as the Western Union messenger verging on manhood. A sentimental slice of life, comic and tragic. B&W; 118m. **DIR:** Clarence Brown. **CAST:** Mickey Rooney, Frank Morgan, "Butch" Jenkins, Ray Collins, Darryl Hickman, Marsha Hunt, Fay Bainter, Donna Reed, James Craig, Van Johnson. **1943**

HUMAN CONDITION, THE, PART ONE: NO GREATER LOVE ★★★★ Based on a Japanese bestseller, this is the story of a sensitive, compassionate man who tries to maintain his humanity through the spiraling horrors of World War II. Part One opens in 1943. The film is quite long, but never dull, with breathtaking wide-screen photography (also available in a letter box video format). The fractured-English subtitles are the only drawback. Not rated. B&W; 200m. **DIR:** Masaki Kobayashi. **CAST:** Tsuya Nakadai, Michiyo Aratama, Chikage Awashima. **1958**

HUMAN CONDITION, THE, PART TWO: THE ROAD TO ETERNITY ★★★1/2 Director Masaki Kobayashi's epic film trilogy continues, with hero Kaji entering the imperial army in the closing months of World War II. Despite his doubts about Japanese war aims, he proves a good soldier and acquits himself bravely. Unlike the first film in the trilogy, this one ends with a cliff-hanger. Not rated, but not for children or squeamish adults. B&W; 180m. **DIR:** Masaki Kobayashi. **CAST:** Tatsuya Nakadai. **1959**

HUMAN CONDITION, THE, PART THREE: A SOLDIER'S PRAYER ★★★★ Director Masaki Kobayashi's magnum opus comes to its shattering conclusion as Kaji, his unit wiped out in battle, leads a band of stragglers and refugees through the Manchurian wilderness. Acting, cinematography, and editing are all first-rate in this heartwrenching tale of Japan's darkest days. Not rated. B&W; 190m. **DIR:** Masaki Kobayashi. **CAST:** Tatsuya Nakadai. **1961**

HUMAN DESIRE ★★★1/2 Broderick Crawford turns in a compelling performance as a hot-tempered husband who kills an innocent man with whom he suspects his wife of having an affair. Fritz Lang's remake of Jean Renoir's *La Bête Humaine*. B&W; 90m. **DIR:** Fritz Lang. **CAST:** Glenn Ford, Broderick Crawford, Gloria Grahame, Edgar Buchanan. **1954**

HUMAN DESIRES ★★1/2 Soft-core porn flick masquerading as a murder mystery. Keep your finger on the fast-forward button. Rated R for language, violence, nudity, and sexual situations. 94m. **DIR:** Ellen Earnshaw. **CAST:** Shannon Tweed, Christian Noble, Dawn Ann Billings, Ashby Adams, Peggy Trentini, Duke Stroud. **1996**

HUMAN DUPLICATORS, THE ★★ Alien giant Richard Kiel comes to Earth to create identical duplicates of its populace but fails in love instead. Hokey, cheap, and badly acted. 82m. **DIR:** Hugo Grimaldi. **CAST:** George Nader, Barbara Nichols, Hugh Beaumont, George Macready, Richard Arlen, Richard Kiel. **1965**

HUMAN EXPERIMENTS ♥ Cheap, ugly, and viciously sexploitative prison potboiler. Rated R. 85m. **DIR:** Gregory Goodell. **CAST:** Linda Haynes, Geoffrey Lewis, Ellen Travolta. **1980**

HUMAN FACTOR, THE ★★★ Nicol Williamson is a lower-grade British agent who because of personal ties to South Africa releases minor secrets to a Soviet-front organization there. When superiors start to investigate he sets about to defect to Russia although it is his assistant who initially comes under suspicion. A strangely remote working of Graham Greene's novel that never catches the suspense intended. Robert Morley is great as an investigator who makes snap decisions and acts upon them. Inexplicably rated R for minor sexual content. 115m. **DIR:** Otto Preminger. **CAST:** Nicol Williamson, Richard Attenborough, John Gielgud, Derek Jacobi, Robert Morley, Ann Todd, Iman. **1979**

HUMAN HEARTS ★★1/2 Old-fashioned story of a criminally manipulated big-city woman who comes between a devoted father and son. Set in a peaceful village in Arkansas. Handkerchief material. Silent. B&W; 99m. **DIR:** King Baggott. **CAST:** House Peters, Russell Simpson, Mary Philbin. **1922**

HUMAN MONSTER, THE (DARK EYES OF LONDON) ★★★ Creaky but sometimes clever suspense thriller about a humanitarian (Bela Lugosi) who may not be as philanthropic as he seems. Strange murders have been occurring in the vicinity of his charitable facility. This preposterous Edgar Wallace story has its moments. B&W; 73m. **DIR:** Walter Summers. **CAST:** Bela Lugosi, Hugh Williams, Greta Gynt, Edmon Ryan. **1939 DVD**

HUMAN SHIELD, THE ♥ This boring, violent story revolves around an Iraqi general who tortures an American. Bad plot, bad acting. Rated R for violence. 92m. **DIR:** Ted Post. **CAST:** Michael Dudikoff, Tommy Hinkley, Steve Inwood. **1991**

•**HUMAN TRAFFIC** ★★ Five Welsh teens drink, drug, and dance through a weekend pub and rave scene before staring into another mundane Monday. This kaleidoscopic recruitment poster for the "chemical generation" is surprisingly flat for a story propelled by pounding techno rock and hyper, surrealistic camera work. Characters include a store clerk troubled by impotency and a party girl rebounding from soured relationships. Rated R for strong sexuality, language, and drug use. 99m. **DIR:** Justin Kerrigan. **CAST:** John Simm, Lorraine Pilkington, Shaun Parkes, Nicola Reynolds, Danny Dyer. **2000**

HUMAN VAPOR, THE ★★ Essentially reworking the premise of the more interesting Honda film, *The H-Man*, this tells of a scientist transformed by a misbegotten experiment into a hideous, gaseous killer. Film dispenses with the draggy subplots of its forerunner, but still manages to outlast its welcome. 79m. **DIR:** Inoshiro Honda. **CAST:** Yoshio Tsuchiya. **1964**

HUMANOID, THE ★★★ Japanese animation set on a far-off and idyllic planet. The title character is a "young" humanoid that is just beginning to understand and participate in human relationships. Unfortunately, "her" life is suddenly disturbed by a scheming villain. In Japanese with English subtitles. 45m. **DIR:** Shin-Ichi Masaki. **1986**

HUMANOID DEFENDER ♥ This movie is actually two episodes from a TV series that never made it, sort of a mix of *The Six Million Dollar Man* and *The*

Fugitive. 94m. **DIR:** Ron Satlof. **CAST:** Terence Knox, Gary Kasper, Aimee Eccles, Marie Windsor. **1985**

HUMANOIDS FROM THE DEEP (1996) ★★ One of producer Roger Corman's own remakes for cable TV, this bears little resemblance to the earlier *Humanoids*, and is actually less graphic. But it's also pretty contrived, with just about everything ineptly borrowed from some better monster movie. Rated R for violence, gore, nudity, and profanity. 86m. **DIR:** Jeff Yonis. **CAST:** Robert Carradine, Emma Samms, Justin Walker, Clint Howard. **1996**

HUMONGOUS ♥ Idiotic teenagers become shipwrecked on an island whose only inhabitant is a hairy, murderous mutant. Rated R for violence. 90m. **DIR:** Paul Lynch. **CAST:** Janet Julian, David Wallace. **1982**

HUMORESQUE ★★★★ Terrific dialogue highlights this wonderfully trashy story of a talented violinist (John Garfield) who sells his soul and body to a wealthy, older woman (Joan Crawford) who promises to further his career. Witty, sophisticated and lavish in its production values, this is a weepie par excellence. 125m. **DIR:** Jean Negulesco. **CAST:** Joan Crawford, John Garfield, Oscar Levant, J. Carrol Naish, Craig Stevens. **1946**

HUNCHBACK (1982) ★★★1/2 Handsome TV adaptation of Victor Hugo's novel *The Hunchback of Notre Dame*, with Anthony Hopkins in fine form as the tragic Quasimodo. Excellent supporting cast and stunning set design make this version of the classic one to cherish. 150m. **DIR:** Michael Tuchner. **CAST:** Anthony Hopkins, Derek Jacobi, Lesley-Anne Down, Robert Powell, John Gielgud, David Suchet, Tim Pigott-Smith. **1982**

HUNCHBACK, THE (1997) ★★★★ TNT hits pay dirt with Mandy Patinkin's excellent portrayal of Victor Hugo's Quasimodo. Patinkin's makeup and mannerisms hearken back to Charles Laughton's in the same role, allowing the character's pain to be fully revealed. Richard Harris is pathological as the sadistic priest, and Salma Hayek is luminescent as the beautiful gypsy who befriends Quasimodo. This is not made for children. Not rated; contains adult themes, cruelty, and sadism. **DIR:** Peter Medak. **CAST:** Mandy Patinkin, Richard Harris, Salma Hayek. **1997**

HUNCHBACK OF NOTRE DAME, THE (1923) ★★★★1/2 Although it has been remade, with varying degrees of success, in the sound era, no film has surpassed the Lon Chaney version in screen spectacle or in the athletic excellence of moviedom's "man of a thousand faces." A musical score has been added. B&W; 108m. **DIR:** Wallace Worsley. **CAST:** Lon Chaney Sr., Patsy Ruth Miller, Ernest Torrence. **1923 DVD**

HUNCHBACK OF NOTRE DAME, THE (1939) ★★★★ In this horror classic, Charles Laughton gives a tour-de-force performance as the deformed bell-ringer who comes to the aid of a pretty gypsy (Maureen O'Hara). Cedric Hardwicke and Edmond O'Brien also give strong performances in this remake of the silent film. B&W; 117m. **DIR:** William Dieterle. **CAST:** Charles Laughton, Thomas Mitchell, Maureen O'Hara, Edmond O'Brien, Cedric Hardwicke. **1939 DVD**

HUNCHBACK OF NOTRE DAME, THE (1997) ★★★★ Disney's animated musical version of Victor Hugo's classic is the studio's most mature cartoon to date. Issues of prejudice, sexual obsession, and religious hypocrisy are at the foreground, yet there's enough action and spectacle to keep kids enchanted. Quasimodo himself is a little more cuddly than in the book, but other than that and the obligatory happy ending, the Disney animators are faithful to Hugo's pessimistic worldview. Of course, they create an astounding fifteenth-century Paris. Rated G. 90m. DIR: Gary Trousdale, Kirk Wise. **1997 DVD**

HUNGARIAN FAIRY TALE, A ★★★★1/2 An imaginative and affecting tale from Hungary, blending myth, social satire, and a Dickensian story of a Budapest orphan. Filmed in stunning black and white, and employing little dialogue. In Hungarian with English subtitles. 97m. DIR: Gyula Gazdag. CAST: David Vermes. **1988**

HUNGER (1966) ★★★ Hauntingly funny portrait of a starving writer in Norway, circa 1890. The would-be writer explores his fantasies as he stumbles through the streets penniless. Per Oscarsson turns in a brilliant performance that netted him the best actor award at the Cannes Film Festival. A must-see! In Swedish with English subtitles. B&W; 100m. DIR: Henning Carlsen. CAST: Per Oscarsson, Gunnel Lindblom. **1966**

HUNGER, THE (1983) ★★ Arty and visually striking yet cold, this kinky sci-fi horror film features French actress Catherine Deneuve as a seductive vampire. Her centuries-old boyfriend (David Bowie) is about to disintegrate, so she picks a new lover (Susan Sarandon). Rated R for gore, profanity, and nudity. 94m. DIR: Tony Scott. CAST: Catherine Deneuve, David Bowie, Susan Sarandon, Cliff De Young. **1983**

HUNGRY HILL ★★ A heavy-handed interpretation of Daphne duMaurier's novel set in nineteenth-century Britain where two Irish families fight over rights to the land. B&W; 92m. DIR: Brian Desmond Hurst. CAST: Jean Simmons, Dennis Price, Margaret Lockwood, Siobhan McKenna, Eileen Herlie. **1947**

HUNK 💣 A social outcast makes a deal with the devil. Rated PG. 90m. DIR: Lawrence Bassoff. CAST: John Allen Nelson, Steve Levitt, Rebeccah Bush, Robert Morse, James Coco, Avery Schreiber, Deborah Shelton. **1987**

•**HUNLEY, THE** ★★ This TNT original chronicles the Confederate attempt to prevent the fall of Charleston to the Yankee navy in 1864. Their invention of a torpedo-wielding submarine puts the lives of its daring crew on the line. Flashbacks throughout and ghost-story overtones fail because we're never really grounded in the events that led to the sub's creation or the molding of the military leaders' characters. Not rated; contains violence. 90m. DIR: John Gray. CAST: Armand Assante, Donald Sutherland, Alex Jennings, Sebastian Roche. **1999**

HUNT, THE ★★★1/2 A powerful, uncompromising meditation on violence, about three veterans of the Spanish Civil War who hunt rabbits a generation later in the same hills across which they fought. In Spanish with English subtitles. Not rated; contains graphic violence. B&W; 92m. DIR: Carlos Saura. CAST: Ismael Merlo. **1954**

HUNT FOR RED OCTOBER, THE ★★★★1/2 In this edge-of-your-seat winner adapted from Tom Clancy's best-selling suspense novel, Sean Connery plays a Soviet submarine captain who uses Russia's ultimate underwater weapon as a means to defect to the West. A superb supporting cast enlivens this crackerjack thriller. Rated PG for brief violence. 132m. DIR: John McTiernan. CAST: Sean Connery, Alec Baldwin, Scott Glenn, James Earl Jones, Sam Neill, Richard Jordan, Tim Curry, Jeffrey Jones, Peter Firth, Joss Ackland. **1990 DVD**

HUNT FOR THE NIGHT STALKER ★★★ Involving made-for-television police drama that follows the exploits of the two detectives who diligently pursued serial killer Richard Ramirez, whose reign of terror put southern California in a panic. Good performances and painstaking detail. Also known as *Manhunt: Search for the Night Stalker*. 100m. DIR: Bruce Seth Green. CAST: Richard Jordan, A Martinez, Lisa Eilbacher. **1989**

HUNT THE MAN DOWN ★★1/2 A public defender has the difficult chore of defending a man who has been a fugitive from a murder charge for twelve years. In attempting to follow an ice-cold trail and prove his defendant innocent, Gig Young fights an uphill battle. B&W; 68m. DIR: George Archainbaud. CAST: Gig Young, Lynne Roberts (Mary Hart), Mary Anderson, Willard Parker, Carla Balenda, Gerald Mohr, James Anderson, Harry Shannon, Cleo Moore. **1950**

HUNTED, THE (1995) ★★ An American businessman becomes Ninja bait. Howlingly awful at times and drenched in carnage, this action-fu flick reaches a pinnacle of delirious excess during a massacre and showdown aboard a speeding train. Rated R for violence, sex, and language. 110m. DIR: J. F. Lawton. CAST: Christopher Lambert, John Lone, Joan Chen, Yoshio Harada, Yoko Shimada. **1995 DVD**

•**HUNTED (1997)** ★★1/2 An insurance investigator finds herself facing off with a madman when she journeys to a remote forest in search of missing millions. Run-of-the-mill chase-thriller with above-average performances. Rated R for violence. 96m. DIR: Stuart Cooper. CAST: Harry Hamlin, Madchen Amick. **1997**

HUNTER (1971) ★★1/2 A brainwashed agent is programmed to release a deadly virus. The scheme is discovered, and a good guy takes his place to catch the bad guys. Made for television. 73m. DIR: Leonard Horn. CAST: John Vernon, Steve Ihnat, Fritz Weaver, Edward Binns. **1971**

HUNTER, THE (1980) ★★ An uneven action film that focuses on a modern-day bounty hunter. Steve McQueen plays real-life troubleshooter Ralph "Papa" Thorson. Though old and a bit awkward, Thorson leads—at least on screen—a dangerous, action-filled life. Rated PG. 97m. DIR: Buzz Kulik. CAST: Steve McQueen, Eli Wallach, LeVar Burton, Ben Johnson, Kathryn Harrold. **1980**

HUNTER IN THE DARK ★★★ Japan circa 1750: dissatisfied with their corrupt government, Japanese warriors create underground groups that wield Mafia-type power. Some brilliant shots of Edo, the

perfect land acquisition. Letter-boxed, which makes reading subtitles easy. In Japanese with English subtitles. Not rated, contains nudity, violence, and profanity. 138m. **DIR:** Hideo Gosha. **CAST:** Tatsuya Nakadai. **1979**

HUNTER'S BLOOD 💔 *Deliverance*, but without any of that film's tension or acting. Rated R for language and violence. 101m. **DIR:** Robert C. Hughes. **CAST:** Sam Bottoms, Clu Gulager, Kim Delaney, Mayf Nutter, Ken Swofford, Joey Travolta. **1987**

•**HUNTER'S MOON** 💔 Painful tale of a backwoods Georgia father, played by Burt Reynolds, hunting down the man who loves his daughter. Possibly the worst film Reynolds has ever made. Rated R for adult situations, language, nudity, and violence. 104m. **DIR:** Richard Weinman. **CAST:** Burt Reynolds, Keith Carradine, Hayley DuMond, Pat Hingle, Brion James, Charles Napier. **1999 DVD**

HUNTING ★★★ Torrid drama finds rich, attractive John Savage playing with the emotions of both friends and business associates. When he lures young, married Kerry Armstrong into an affair, blackmail and murder ensue. Rated R for nudity and violence. 97m. **DIR:** Frank Howson. **CAST:** John Savage, Kerry Armstrong, Guy Pearce, Rebecca Rigg. **1991**

•**HUNTRESS, THE** ★★★ When a woman's bounty-hunter husband is killed, she and her daughter take up the family business to pay off their debts. The result is nonstop comedy and action, as the two women start to bring in the bad guys, as well as look for whoever killed their husband and father. This made-for-cable original is supposedly based on a true story. Not rated; contains violence. 95m. **DIR:** Jeffrey Reiner. **CAST:** Annette O'Toole, Aleksa Palladino, Alanna Ubach, Vicki Lewis, Matthew Glave, Craig T. Nelson. **2000**

HUNTRESS: SPIRIT OF THE NIGHT ★★ A young woman returns to her homeland to claim her ancestral castle—and the family curse. The scary parts aren't scary and the sexy parts aren't anything to write home about either. Rated R for profanity and simulated sex. 86m. **DIR:** Mark S. Manos. **CAST:** Jenna Bodner. **1996**

•**HURLYBURLY** ★★★1/2 David Mamet's acerbic play about Hollywood lowlifes finds its way to the big screen, and the results are just as unsavory. The problem isn't with the performers, who are at their best, but with the characters. There isn't a redeemable one in the bunch, and while it is interesting to watch them self-destruct, the outcome leaves a bad taste in your mouth. Sean Penn is exceptional as the casting director whose party days are getting the best of him. Rated R for adult situations, language, nudity, and violence. 123m. **DIR:** Anthony Drazan. **CAST:** Sean Penn, Kevin Spacey, Robin Wright, Chazz Palminteri, Garry Shandling, Anna Paquin, Meg Ryan. **1998 DVD**

HURRICANE, THE (1937) ★★★ One of early Hollywood's disaster films. The lives and loves of a group of stereotyped characters on a Pacific island are interrupted by the big wind of the title. The sequences involving people are labored, but the special effects of the hurricane make this picture worth watching. B&W; 102m. **DIR:** John Ford. **CAST:** Jon Hall, Dorothy Lamour, Raymond Massey, Mary Astor. **1937**

HURRICANE (1979) 💔 Another Dino de Laurentiis misfire, an awful remake of the John Ford classic. Rated PG. 119m. **DIR:** Jan Troell. **CAST:** Jason Robards Jr., Mia Farrow, Dayton Ka'ne, Max von Sydow, Trevor Howard. **1979**

•**HURRICANE, THE (1999)** ★★1/2 Real-life boxer Rubin "Hurricane" Carter was convicted for the 1966 murder of three white bar patrons in Patterson, New Jersey. This film dramatizes his arrest, railroading, and incarceration, and the racism that soiled his case. It features a riveting performance from Denzel Washington, but Carter's complex personality and past feel too sanitized, and the script reinvents and oversimplifies his path to exoneration. Rated R for language and violence. 125m. **DIR:** Norman Jewison. **CAST:** Denzel Washington, Vicellous Reon Shannon, Deborah Kara Unger, Liev Schreiber, John Hannah, Dan Hedaya. **1999**

HURRICANE EXPRESS ★★ Big John Wayne stars in his second serial for Mascot Pictures and plays an aviator on the trail of the mysterious "Wrecker." This feature, edited down from a twelve-chapter serial, displays a high level of energy and excitement, a great deal of it as a direct result of young Wayne's whole-hearted involvement in this basically simple chase film. B&W; 80m. **DIR:** Armand Schaefer, J. P. McGowan. **CAST:** John Wayne, Tully Marshall, Conway Tearle, Shirley Grey. **1932**

HURRICANE SMITH ★★1/2 Texas tough Carl Weathers blows into Australia like a hurricane when his sister is killed by drug lord Jurgen Prochnow. Watch Carl weather plenty of evil mates, teaching them a *Rocky* lesson in manners. Rated R for violence and nudity. 87m. **DIR:** Colin Budd. **CAST:** Carl Weathers, Jurgen Prochnow, Tony Bonner. **1991**

HURRICANE STREETS ★★ Brendan Sexton III is effective as a street punk desperate for a better life. He agrees to one more score to raise money to relocate to New Mexico, but things turn sour. Familiar tale gets points for Morgan J. Freeman's direction that attempts to make it all matter. Rated R for language, violence, and adult situations. 86m. **DIR:** Morgan J. Freeman. **CAST:** Brendan Sexton III, Shawn Elliott, L. M. "Kit" Carson, Edie Falco, Antoine McLean, Mtume Gant. **1997**

HURRY UP OR I'LL BE 30 ★★★ Aimless comedy-drama will appeal to those with a fondness for slice-of-life movies. Set in Brooklyn, the movie follows an almost-thirty single guy (John Lefkowitz) who is frustrated over his life. Danny DeVito has a supporting part as a fellow Brooklynite. Rated R for sexual situations and profanity. 88m. **DIR:** Joseph Jacoby. **CAST:** John Lefkowitz, Linda De Coff, Danny DeVito. **1973**

HUSBANDS AND LOVERS 💔 Seemingly endless and pointless film features Joanna Pacula as a selfish wife who demands weekends off to spend with her abusive lover. Comes in R and unrated versions, both containing violence and nudity. 94m. **DIR:** Mauro Bolognini. **CAST:** Julian Sands, Joanna Pacula, Tcheky Karyo. **1991**

HUSBANDS AND WIVES ★★★1/2 Off-camera events eclipsed this Woody Allen comedy-drama during its initial release, detracting from the power of an often brilliant study of marriages under stress. Judy Davis is simply magnificent as a fault-finding shrew. While the characters are uniformly excellent, the film is severely compromised by Carlo Di Palma's headache-inducing hand-held camera (intended to suggest a documentary approach). Rated R for profanity. 107m. **DIR:** Woody Allen. **CAST:** Woody Allen, Mia Farrow, Judy Davis, Sydney Pollack, Juliette Lewis, Liam Neeson. 1992

HUSH ... HUSH, SWEET CHARLOTTE ★★★ Originally planned as a sequel to *What Ever Happened to Baby Jane?*, reuniting stars of that movie Bette Davis and Joan Crawford, this effort was filmed with Bette opposite her old Warner Bros. cellmate—Olivia de Havilland. This time they're on opposite sides of the magnolia bush, with Olivia trying to drive poor Bette, who's not all there to begin with, mad. B&W; 133m. **DIR:** Robert Aldrich. **CAST:** Bette Davis, Olivia de Havilland, Joseph Cotten, Agnes Moorehead, Cecil Kellaway, Mary Astor, Bruce Dern. 1965

HUSH LITTLE BABY ★★1/2 In this made-for-cable movie, an adopted woman is located by her biological mother. They become friends, but she doesn't know that her mother tried to kill her when she was a child. This so-so film's story has been done much better before. Not rated; contains violence. 95m. **DIR:** Jorge Montesi. **CAST:** Diane Ladd, Wendel Meldrum, Geraint Wyn Davies, Illya Woloshyn, Ingrid Veninger. 1993 DVD

HUSSY ★★ Both the talented British actress Helen Mirren and director Matthew Chapman (his debut) usually do much better work than in this dreary melodrama about a nightclub hostess and part-time prostitute. Chapman succeeds at re-creating the oppressive atmosphere of a seedy British nightclub all too well. Rated R for nudity. 95m. **DIR:** Matthew Chapman. **CAST:** Helen Mirren, John Shea. 1980

HUSTLE ★★1/2 *Hustle* reteams director Robert Aldrich and actor Burt Reynolds after their box-office success with *The Longest Yard*. Fine character performances from Eddie Albert, Ernest Borgnine, and Jack Carter help to elevate the macho/action yarn, but it is Academy Award winner Ben Johnson who provides the real show. Rated R. 120m. **DIR:** Robert Aldrich. **CAST:** Burt Reynolds, Catherine Deneuve, Eddie Albert, Ernest Borgnine, Jack Carter, Ben Johnson. 1975

HUSTLER, THE ★★★★★ This film may well contain Paul Newman's best screen performance. As pool shark Eddie Felson, he's magnificent. A two-bit hustler who travels from pool room to pool room taking suckers—whom he allows to win until the stakes get high enough, then wipes them out—Felson decides to take a shot at the big time. He challenges Minnesota Fats (nicely played by Jackie Gleason) to a big money match. B&W; 135m. **DIR:** Robert Rossen. **CAST:** Paul Newman, Jackie Gleason, Piper Laurie, George C. Scott, Murray Hamilton, Myron McCormick. 1961

HUSTLING ★★★★ An investigative report delves into the world of big-city prostitution in this adult TV movie. Fine performances and a good script place this above the average TV film. 100m. **DIR:** Joseph Sargent. **CAST:** Lee Remick, Jill Clayburgh, Alex Rocco, Monte Markham. 1975

HYPE! ★★★ Sympathetic documentary about Seattle's so-called "grunge" music scene, whose explosion in popularity in the early 1990s was less than welcomed by many of the bands involved. Filmmaker Doug Pray captures the essence of rock 'n' roll irony, in which the music is rendered meaningless by success. Give it an extra star if you're a fan of Soundgarden, the Melvins, Pearl Jam, or other bands who appear. Not rated; contains profanity. 84m. **DIR:** Doug Pray. 1997

HYPER SAPIAN: PEOPLE FROM ANOTHER STAR ★★ Two youngsters from another star system escape their elders to visit Wyoming. Predictable, bland nonsense. Rated PG for violence. 95m. **DIR:** Peter R. Hunt. **CAST:** Ricky Paul Goldin, Sydney Penny, Keenan Wynn, Gail Strickland, Peter Jason. 1986

HYPNOTIC EYE, THE ★★1/2 Surprisingly sleazy (for its time) thriller in which beautiful women who volunteer to help out in a stage hypnotist's act later mysteriously mutilate themselves. B&W; 79m. **DIR:** George Blair. **CAST:** Jacques Bergerac, Allison Hayes, Marcia Henderson, Merry Anders, Ferdinand Demara. 1960

HYSTERIA ★★1/2 After their success in remaking old Universal horror movies, the folks at England's Hammer Films decided to try their luck with Hitchcockian suspense. This film is one of the results. Robert Webber plays an American amnesia victim in England. This unrated film contains some mild violence. B&W; 85m. **DIR:** Freddie Francis. **CAST:** Robert Webber, Lelia Goldoni, Maurice Denham, Jennifer Jayne. 1964

HYSTERICAL ★★ Zany horror spoof generates a sprinkling of laughs. This movie was supposed to make the Hudson Brothers the Marx Brothers of the 1980s. Rated PG. 87m. **DIR:** Chris Bearde. **CAST:** William Hudson, Mark Hudson, Brett Hudson, Cindy Pickett, Richard Kiel, Julie Newmar, Bud Cort, Robert Donner, Murray Hamilton, Clint Walker. 1983

I AM A CAMERA ★★★1/2 Julie Harris is perfect as the easy, good-time English bohemian Sally Bowles in this finely honed film clone of the play adapted by John Van Druten from novelist Christopher Isherwood's autobiographical stories about pre–World War II Berlin. The Broadway and screen versions ultimately became the musical *Cabaret*. 98m. **DIR:** Henry Cornelius. **CAST:** Julie Harris, Laurence Harvey, Shelley Winters, Ron Randell, Patrick McGoohan. 1955

I AM A FUGITIVE FROM A CHAIN GANG ★★★★ Dark, disturbing, and effective Paul Muni vehicle.

The star plays an innocent man who finds himself convicted of a crime and brutalized by a corrupt court system. An unforgettable film. B&W; 90m. DIR: Mervyn LeRoy. CAST: Paul Muni, Glenda Farrell, Helen Vinson, Preston Foster. 1932

I AM CUBA ★★★★★ It's the artistry—not the politics—that makes this dreamy, somber propaganda film so exhilarating. This Russian-Cuban "friendship project" was to glorify the isle's liberation from Batista's dictatorship and Ugly Americanism. It ended up emphasizing a visually poetic style rather than romanticizing Communism. In Spanish, Russian, and dubbed English with English subtitles. Not rated. 141m. DIR: Mikhail K. Kalatozov. CAST: Luz Maria Collazo, Jose Gallardo, Sergio Corrieri, Mario Gonzales Broche, Raul Garcia, Jean Bouise, Celia Rodriguez, Luisa Maria Jimenez. 1964 DVD

I AM CURIOUS BLUE ★★ Both I Am Curious Yellow and Blue were derived from the same footage, shot by director Vilgot Sjoman in the late Sixties. When the finished product turned out to be too long, he turned it into two movies instead. Ergo, Curious Blue is less a sequel than simply more of the same meandering inquiry into social issues, punctuated by an occasional naked body. In Swedish with English subtitles. Not rated; the movie features frank but unerotic sex. B&W; 103m. DIR: Vilgot Sjoman. CAST: Lena Nyman, Vilgot Sjoman, Borje Ahlstedt. 1968

I AM CURIOUS YELLOW ★ 1/2 This Swedish import caused quite an uproar when it was released in the mid-1960s, because of its frontal nudity and sexual content. It seems pretty dull today. There isn't much of a plot built around the escapades of a young Swedish sociologist whose goal in life appears to be having sex in as many weird places as she can. In Swedish with English subtitles. B&W; 121m. DIR: Vilgot Sjoman. CAST: Lena Nyman, Borje Ahlstedt. 1967

I AM THE CHEESE ★★1/2 A teenager who has witnessed the death of his parents is confined to a psychiatric hospital where doctors try to get him to deal with his tragedy. The dime-store psychology is the only drawback to this well-played movie. Rated PG. 95m. DIR: Robert Jiras. CAST: Robert MacNaughton, Hope Lange, Don Murray, Robert Wagner, Cynthia Nixon, Lee Richardson. 1983

I AM THE LAW ★★★ This slick but somewhat silly crime melodrama stars Edward G. Robinson as a crusading district attorney out to get a group of mobsters headed by a corrupt civic leader. B&W; 83m. DIR: Alexander Hall. CAST: Edward G. Robinson, Barbara O'Neil, John Beal, Wendy Barrie, Otto Kruger, Marc Lawrence. 1938

I BURY THE LIVING ★★1/2 Rash of sudden deaths among cemetery plot owners gives mortuary manager Richard Boone grave suspicions he has the power to "put the lid" on his clients. Murder mystery with supernatural overtones is complemented by imaginative design and cinematography. B&W; 76m. DIR: Albert Band. CAST: Richard Boone, Theodore Bikel, Peggy Maurer, Herbert Anderson. 1958

I, CLAUDIUS ★★★★★ This PBS series brilliantly recounts the history of the Roman Empire—the reign of Augustus, the infamous cruelty of Tiberius and his successor, Caligula, and the reign of the mild and amiable Claudius. One of the most popular Masterpiece Theater presentations. 780m. DIR: Herbert Wise. CAST: Derek Jacobi, Sian Phillips, Brian Blessed, John Hurt. 1976

I COME IN PEACE ★★ Ridiculous subplot involving a preppie gang mars the first half of this sci-fi adventure. Dolph Lundgren must stop an alien's murderous rampage. The alien's method of sucking the endorphins of his victims' brains is pretty disgusting. Rated R for violence and gore. 90m. DIR: Craig R. Baxley. CAST: Dolph Lundgren, Brian Benben, Betsy Brantley. 1990

I CONFESS ★★★ In spite of shortcomings, this is the film that best reflects many of Hitch's puritanical ethics. Montgomery Clift stars as a priest who takes confession from a man who—coincidentally—killed a blackmailer who knew of Clift's prevows relationship with Anne Baxter. (Whew!) Moody and atmospheric. B&W; 95m. DIR: Alfred Hitchcock. CAST: Montgomery Clift, Karl Malden, Anne Baxter, Brian Aherne. 1953

I COULD GO ON SINGING ★★★ In this, her last film, with a disturbing true-to-her-life plot, Judy Garland plays a successful concert singer beset by personal problems. When Judy sings, the film lives. When she doesn't, it's wistful, teary, and a bit sloppy. Strictly for Garland fanatics. 99m. DIR: Ronald Neame. CAST: Judy Garland, Dirk Bogarde, Jack Klugman, Aline MacMahon. 1963

I COVER THE WATERFRONT ★★★ One, and one of the better, of a spate of newspaper stories that vied with gangster films on 1930s screens. In this one, a ruthless fisherman who smuggles Chinese into the United States doesn't think twice about pushing them overboard when approached by the Coast Guard. Claudette Colbert is his innocent daughter. Ace reporter Ben Lyon courts her in an effort to get at the truth. B&W; 70m. DIR: James Cruze. CAST: Claudette Colbert, Ernest Torrence, Ben Lyon, Wilfred Lucas, George Humbert. 1933

I DIED A THOUSAND TIMES ★★1/2 Color remake of Raoul Walsh's High Sierra features Jack Palance as Mad Dog Earle, whose criminal tendencies are softened by a young woman (Lori Nelson) who needs surgery in order to lead a normal life. 110m. DIR: Stuart Heisler. CAST: Jack Palance, Shelley Winters, Lee Marvin, Lori Nelson, Earl Holliman, Lon Chaney Jr. 1955

I DISMEMBER MAMA 💔 Great title—horrible movie. Rated R for violence and nudity. 86m. DIR: Paul Leder. CAST: Zooey Hall, Greg Mullavey. 1972

I DO! I DO! ★★★ Lee Remick and Hal Linden step into the parts originally created on Broadway by Mary Martin and Robert Preston in this video of a performance taped before an audience. The play deals with the marriage of Michael to Agnes—from the night before their wedding to the day when they leave their home of forty years. Solid entertainment. 116m. DIR: Gower Champion. CAST: Lee Remick, Hal Linden. 1982

I DON'T BUY KISSES ANYMORE ★★★1/2 Sweetheart of a romantic comedy. Jason Alexander stars as an overweight shoe salesman who thinks he's hit pay dirt when a college student shows an interest in him. What blossoms is true love and a film that revels in that celebration. Rated PG. 112m. **DIR:** Robert Mascarelli. **CAST:** Jason Alexander, Nia Peeples, Eileen Brennan, Lainie Kazan, Lou Jacobi. **1991**

I DON'T WANT TO TALK ABOUT IT ★★ On her daughter's second birthday, a wealthy Latin American widow plunges into denial that her only child is a dwarf and pressures town locals to never discuss the girl's small stature. Enter a mysterious, melancholy stranger who disrupts her reluctance to face reality. This languid contemplation of the mysteries of love, set in the 1930s, attempts to build with a fablelike tone, but never plumbs the full passion or depth of its characters. In Spanish with English subtitles. Rated PG-13. 102m. **DIR:** Maria Luisa Bemberg. **CAST:** Alejandra Podesta, Luisina Brando, Marcello Mastroianni. **1994**

I DOOD IT ★★1/2 A musical based on an old Buster Keaton silent comedy about a tailor's assistant (Red Skelton) going gaga over dancer (Eleanor Powell). Powell's tap dancing is especially noteworthy. B&W; 102m. **DIR:** Vincente Minnelli. **CAST:** Red Skelton, Eleanor Powell, Lena Horne, Hazel Scott, Butterfly McQueen, Helen O'Connell, Bob Eberly, Sam Levene, John Hodiak, Morris Ankrum (Stepen Morris), Thurston Hall. **1943**

I DREAM TOO MUCH ★★1/2 This picture is more of a showcase for Lily Pons's vocal abilities in the operetta form. Henry Fonda and Pons are two performers who face career obstacles. The music is okay. B&W; 95m. **DIR:** John Cromwell. **CAST:** Henry Fonda, Lily Pons, Lucille Ball, Eric Blore. **1935**

•I DREAMED OF AFRICA ★★1/2 An Italian divorcée homesteads on a farm in Africa with her new husband and young son. Based on the memoirs of Kuki Gallmann, the film plods monotonously through two decades on the veldt without working up much dramatic momentum. The earnest acting and beautiful African scenery help somewhat. Rated PG-13 for mild profanity and brief violence. 112m. **DIR:** Hugh Hudson. **CAST:** Kim Basinger, Vincent Perez, Eva Marie Saint, Liam Aiken, Winston Ntshona. **2000**

I DRINK YOUR BLOOD ★★1/2 Devil worshipers go berserk after they are fed the blood of a rabid dog. Ferociously violent film with elements of social commentary was severely cut after being threatened with an X rating; the restored version is available on video. Not rated; contains extreme violence and nudity. 83m. **DIR:** David E. Durston. **CAST:** Bhaskar, Jadine Wong, Ronda Fultz. **1971**

I GOT THE HOOK UP 💙 Two low-life hustlers get into trouble when they sell off a carload of stolen cellular phones. Crude, racist, sexist, and abominably acted, this sorry mess is strictly for die-hard fans of hip-hop artist Master P, who starred and directed. Rated R for brief drug use, nudity, and incessant profanity. 94m. **DIR:** Michael Martin, Master P. **CAST:** Master P, A. J. Johnson, Gretchen Palmer, Tiny Lister Jr., John Witherspoon. **1998**

I HEARD THE OWL CALL MY NAME ★★★1/2 In this mystical tale of love and courage, Tom Courtenay beautifully portrays Father Mark Brian, a young Anglican priest whose bishop, played by Dean Jag-

ger, sends him to make his mark. He finds himself among the proud Indians of the Northwest. Rated G. 79m. **DIR:** Daryl Duke. **CAST:** Tom Courtenay, Dean Jagger, Paul Stanley. **1973**

I KILLED RASPUTIN 💙 It can't have been easy, but they actually managed to make a completely boring movie about Rasputin, the peasant monk who gained control over the czar of Russia in the period prior to the Russian Revolution. Actually, Rasputin isn't in it that much, and when he is they've cleaned up his act. Dubbed in English. 95m. **DIR:** Robert Hossein. **CAST:** Gert Fröbe, Peter McEnery, Geraldine Chaplin, Ivan Desny. **1967**

I KNOW WHAT YOU DID LAST SUMMER ★★ Two teen couples have late-night sex on a North Carolina beach and then crash their car into a pedestrian on the way home. They dump the body off a pier to avoid legal hassles (their vehicle reeks of spilled booze) and swear not to discuss the incident with anyone—or even among themselves. Their secret comes back to stalk them literally in a dumb, brutal slasher movie that has huge morality play ambitions. Rated R for violence, language, nudity, and sex. 96m. **DIR:** Jim Gillespie. **CAST:** Jennifer Love Hewitt, Sarah Michelle Gellar, Ryan Philippe, Freddie Prinze Jr., Anne Heche. **1997 DVD**

I KNOW WHY THE CAGED BIRD SINGS ★★★1/2 Based on writer Maya Angelou's memoirs of her early life in the Depression years in the South. Often very touching and effective, this made-for-TV film details the author's reaction to her parents' divorce and the struggle of her grandparents to raise her and her brother. 100m. **DIR:** Fielder Cook. **CAST:** Diahann Carroll, Ruby Dee, Esther Rolle, Roger E. Mosley. **1979**

I LIKE IT LIKE THAT ★★1/2 An independent-minded Bronx woman takes a job in a record company to support her family after her bike-messenger husband is jailed for looting during a blackout. She's got three rowdy kids, a transvestite brother, and an overbearing mother-in-law in this scrappy, randy take on ethnic neighborhood life where everyone is either sharing door stoops, lunging at each other's throats, or both. Gritty, comic, but uninvolving. Rated R for language, nudity, and simulated sex. 106m. **DIR:** Darnell Martin. **CAST:** Lauren Velez, Jon Seda, Lisa Vidal, Griffin Dunne, Rita Moreno. **1994**

I LIVE MY LIFE ★★★ A wealthy young woman falls in love with an archaeologist while on a cruise. Charming romantic drama. B&W; 97m. **DIR:** W. S. Van Dyke. **CAST:** Joan Crawford, Brian Aherne, Frank Morgan, Aline MacMahon. **1935**

I LIVE WITH ME DAD ★★★ Yes, the title is correct. That's what a poor Australian boy keeps repeating to the various child-welfare and police authorities who try to take him from his father. Not rated. 86m. **DIR:** Paul Moloney. **CAST:** Haydon Samuels, Rebecca Gibney. **1985**

I LOVE LUCY (TV SERIES) ★★★★★ The archetypical TV sitcom. Domestic squabbles have never been more entertaining. Ricky's accent and temper, Lucy's schemes and ambitions, Ethel's submissiveness, Fred's parsimoniousness, all added up to sure-fire hilarity. Classic moments include Lucy and Ethel toiling in a chocolate factory, Lucy stomping grapes,

Lucy meeting William Holden, Ricky getting the news that he's a father, and Lucy selling a health tonic. Each tape 48m. **DIR:** William Asher. **CAST:** Lucille Ball, Desi Arnaz Sr., Vivian Vance, William Frawley. **1951–1956**

I LOVE MELVIN ★★★ Entertaining little MGM musical has Donald O'Connor pretending to be a man with connections so he can have a chance with perky Debbie Reynolds. The story is slight, but the laughs and songs are good, and O'Connor and Reynolds work well together. Entertaining and amusing. 76m. **DIR:** Don Weis. **CAST:** Debbie Reynolds, Donald O'Connor, Una Merkel, Allyn Joslyn, Noreen Corcoran, Richard Anderson, Jim Backus, Barbara Ruick. **1953**

I LOVE MY WIFE 🎗 The problems of an upper-class couple and their ridiculous attempts to solve them. Rated PG. 95m. **DIR:** Mel Stuart. **CAST:** Elliott Gould, Brenda Vaccaro, Angel Tompkins, Dabney Coleman, Joan Tompkins. **1970**

I LOVE N.Y. 🎗 Scott Baio plays a hotheaded photographer who falls for a famous actor's daughter. Rated R for profanity. 100m. **DIR:** Alan Smithee. **CAST:** Scott Baio, Christopher Plummer, Jennifer O'Neill. **1988**

I LOVE TROUBLE ★★★ Uneven mix of suspensethriller and romantic comedy comes up short because of the lack of real chemistry between Julia Roberts and Nick Nolte, reporters from competing Chicago newspapers who solve the mystery of a derailed train. Still, there are enough effective moments to make it watchable. Rated PG for violence and profanity. 123m. **DIR:** Charles Shyer. **CAST:** Julia Roberts, Nick Nolte, Saul Rubinek, James Rebhorn, Robert Loggia, Kelly Rutherford, Olympia Dukakis, Marsha Mason, Eugene Levy, Charles Martin Smith. **1994 DVD**

I LOVE YOU (EU TE AMO) ★★★ This release, starring Brazilian sexpot Sonia Braga, is a high-class hard-core—though not close-up—sex film with pretensions of being a work of art. And if that turns you on, go for it. Not rated, the film has nudity and profanity. 104m. **DIR:** Arnaldo Jabor. **CAST:** Sonia Braga, Paulo Cesar Pereio. **1982**

I LOVE YOU AGAIN ★★★★ Master con artist William Powell awakes from a nine-year bout of amnesia and learns he has become a stuffy but successful small-town businessman about to be divorced by wife Myrna Loy. He recalls nothing of the nine years, yet wants to win back his wife and pull an oil scam on the town. Witty dialogue, hilarious situations, and just plain fun. B&W; 99m. **DIR:** W. S. Van Dyke. **CAST:** William Powell, Myrna Loy, Frank McHugh, Edmund Lowe, Carl "Alfalfa" Switzer. **1940**

I LOVE YOU ALICE B. TOKLAS! ★★★ Peter Sellers plays a lawyer-cum-hippie in this far-out comedy about middle-age crisis. Rated PG. 93m. **DIR:** Hy Averback. **CAST:** Peter Sellers, Leigh Taylor-Young, Jo Van Fleet. **1968**

I LOVE YOU, DON'T TOUCH ME! ★★★ A young woman looks for love in several wrong places, never having the good sense until the final babe-out to fall for the swell guy who adores her. An overfamiliar story is given a pleasant polish (and a welcome female perspective) by writer-director Julie Davis in her feature debut, aided immensely by the attractive performances of Marla Schaffel and Mitchell Whitfield in the two leads. Rated R for profanity and sexual scenes. 85m. **DIR:** Julie Davis. **CAST:** Marla Schaffel, Mitchell Whitfield, Meredith Scott Lynn, Michael Harris, Darryl Theirse. **1998**

I LOVE YOU TO DEATH ★★★★ Offbeat true-life murder comedy, in which loving wife Tracey Ullman decides to dispatch philandering husband Kevin Kline with the help of her mom (Joan Plowright), an admirer (River Phoenix), and two stoned-out hit men (William Hurt and Keanu Reeves). Funny, but not for all tastes. Rated R for profanity and violence. 96m. **DIR:** Lawrence Kasdan. **CAST:** Kevin Kline, Tracey Ullman, Joan Plowright, River Phoenix, William Hurt, Keanu Reeves, James Gammon, Victoria Jackson. **1990**

I, MADMAN ★★ A bookstore employee (Jenny Wright) becomes so engrossed in a horror novel that she begins living its terrors. This film provides the same kind of tacky entertainment found in such masterpieces of ineptitude as *Plan 9 from Outer Space* and *Robot Monster*. Rated R for violence, simulated sex, and profanity. 95m. **DIR:** Tibor Takacs. **CAST:** Jenny Wright, Clayton Rohner. **1989**

I MARRIED A CENTERFOLD ★★1/2 When a nerdish engineer bets $500 that he can meet Miss November, a centerfold, he not only finds her, but the two fall in love. Made for TV. 100m. **DIR:** Peter Werner. **CAST:** Teri Copley, Timothy Daly, Diane Ladd, Anson Williams. **1984**

•**I MARRIED A MONSTER** ★★ Campy sci-fi flick about an alien race that comes to Earth to impregnate women. Noteworthy for some fine, unintentionally hilarious moments. Rated PG-13 for violence. 90m. **DIR:** Nancy Malone. **CAST:** Richard Burgi, Susan Walters, Tim Ryan, Richard Herd, Barbara Niven. **1998**

I MARRIED A MONSTER FROM OUTER SPACE ★★★ This riveting story is about aliens who duplicate their bodies in the form of Earth men in hopes of repopulating their planet. One earthwoman who unknowingly marries one of the aliens discovers the secret, but can't get anyone to believe her. B&W; 78m. **DIR:** Gene Fowler Jr. **CAST:** Tom Tryon, Gloria Talbott, Ken Lynch, Maxie Rosenbloom. **1958**

•**I MARRIED A STRANGE PERSON** ★★★★ Bill Plympton wrote, directed, and animated this hilarious venture into the surreal that involves a man with a very mundane existence. While watching television, a peculiar boil grows on the back of his neck—one that gives the man the power to bring whatever he thinks of into reality. This turns his marriage upside down, and now, the evil Smiley Corporation wants this fantastic power for itself. Witty and original, this bizarre tale is full of laughs and classic Bill Plympton animation techniques. Rated R for animated sex, violence, and language. 73m. **DIR:** Bill Plympton. **1997 DVD**

I MARRIED A VAMPIRE 🎗 Boring nonsense, more about a country girl's adventures in the big city than a horror flick. 85m. **DIR:** Jay Raskin. **CAST:** Rachel Golden, Brendan Hickey. **1983**

I MARRIED A WITCH ★★★1/2 The whimsy of humorist Thorne Smith (the author of *Topper*) shows its age, but watching Veronica Lake and Fredric

March perform together is a treat in this very pre-*Bewitched* farce. Look for Susan Hayward in a small role. B&W; 76m. DIR: René Clair. CAST: Veronica Lake, Fredric March, Cecil Kellaway, Robert Benchley. 1942

I MARRIED A WOMAN ★★ George Gobel plays an advertising man who is having difficulty holding on to both his biggest account and his wife, who feels he's not paying her enough attention. Angie Dickinson and John Wayne have walk-on parts. B&W/color; 80m. DIR: Hal Kanter. CAST: George Gobel, Diana Dors, Adolphe Menjou, Jessie Royce Landis, Nita Talbot, William Redfield, John McGiver. 1958

I MARRIED AN ANGEL ★★ In this, their final film together, playboy Nelson Eddy dreams he courts and marries angel Jeanette MacDonald. *Leaden* and *bizarre* are but two of the words critics used. B&W; 84m. DIR: W. S. Van Dyke. CAST: Jeanette MacDonald, Nelson Eddy, Edward Everett Horton, Binnie Barnes, Reginald Owen. 1942

I MARRIED JOAN (TV SERIES) ★★★ Joan Davis, following the popularity of *I Love Lucy*, starred in this sitcom involving a goofy housewife and the judge she married. B&W; 80m. DIR: Philip Rapp, Marc Daniels. CAST: Joan Davis, Jim Backus. 1952–1953

I, MOBSTER ★★★1/2 Fast-moving gangster story recounted by mob boss Steve Cochran, looking back on his career while he testifies before the Senate Rackets Committee. Familiar stuff, but well-made. B&W; 81m. DIR: Roger Corman. CAST: Steve Cochran, Lita Milan, Robert Strauss, Celia Lovsky, Lili St. Cyr, Yvette Vickers, Robert Shayne. 1958

I NEVER PROMISED YOU A ROSE GARDEN ★★★1/2 Kathleen Quinlan plays a schizophrenic teenager seeking treatment from a dedicated psychiatrist in this well-acted but depressing drama. Rated R. 96m. DIR: Anthony Page. CAST: Bibi Andersson, Kathleen Quinlan, Diane Varsi. 1977

I NEVER SANG FOR MY FATHER ★★★1/2 A depressing but finely crafted film about a man (Gene Hackman) who must deal with the care of his elderly father (Melvyn Douglas). Everyone in this touching film does a superb job. Based on a play of the same name by Robert Anderson. Rated PG. 93m. DIR: Gilbert Cates. CAST: Melvyn Douglas, Gene Hackman, Estelle Parsons, Dorothy Stickney. 1970

I ONLY WANT YOU TO LOVE ME ★★★★ Fans of prolific but short-lived German filmmaker Rainer Werner Fassbinder shouldn't miss this rarely-seen film, made for German television. Like much of his work, it deals with the stress of modern life on someone who can't handle it, in this case a young lawyer who gets in over his head while trying to impress his unfeeling father. Not rated. In German with English subtitles. 104m. DIR: Rainer Werner Fassbinder. CAST: Vitus Zeplichal, Elke Aberle, Ernie Mangold. 1976

I OUGHT TO BE IN PICTURES ★★★★ Neil Simon's best work since *The Goodbye Girl*, this heartwarming story stars Walter Matthau as a father who deserts his Brooklyn family. Dinah Manoff is the daughter who wants to be a movie star, and Ann-Margret is the woman who brings the two together. Rated PG for mild profanity and brief nudity. 107m.

DIR: Herbert Ross. CAST: Walter Matthau, Ann-Margret, Dinah Manoff. 1982

I POSED FOR PLAYBOY 🐢 Three women pose nude and must live with the repercussions. Slow, bland, and listless melodrama. Rated R for nudity and profanity. 103m. DIR: Stephen Stafford. CAST: Lynda Carter, Michele Greene, Amanda Peterson. 1991

I REMEMBER MAMA ★★★1/2 Irene Dunne is Mama in this sentimental drama about an engaging Norwegian family in San Francisco. Definitely a feel-good film for the nostalgic-minded. Hearts of gold all the way! B&W; 148m. DIR: George Stevens. CAST: Irene Dunne, Barbara Bel Geddes, Oscar Homolka, Philip Dorn, Ellen Corby. 1948

I SEE A DARK STRANGER ★★★1/2 Known in Great Britain as *The Adventuress*, this delightful picture tells of a high-strung yet charming Irish girl who, hating the British, helps a Nazi spy during World War II. Wry humor serves as counterpoint to the suspense. A class act. B&W; 98m. DIR: Frank Launder. CAST: Deborah Kerr, Trevor Howard, Raymond Huntley, Liam Redmond. 1947

I SENT A LETTER TO MY LOVE ★★★ Simone Signoret and Jean Rochefort star as sister and brother in this absorbing study of love, devotion, loneliness, and frustration. After Signoret places a personal ad (requesting male companionship) in the local paper, Rochefort responds—and they begin a correspondence, via mail, that brings passion and hope to their otherwise empty lives. In French with English subtitles. 96m. DIR: Moshe Mizrahi. CAST: Simone Signoret, Jean Rochefort, Delphine Seyrig. 1981

I SHOT A MAN IN VEGAS ★★ Four young people try to reconstruct the events leading up to the shooting death of their friend as they drive across the Nevada desert with his corpse in the trunk. Talky film filled with clunky dialogue, implausible plot revelations, and characters you wouldn't want to be stuck with in a car. Rated R for violence, adult situations, and language. 80m. DIR: Keoni Waxman. CAST: John Stockwell, Janeane Garofalo, Brian Dillinger, David Cubitt. 1995

I SHOT ANDY WARHOL ★★★ More interested in re-creating the surface sheen of Warhol's 1960s art scene than in understanding his coterie of cronies, Mary Harron's movie is a pretty conventional period piece, considering its outrageous subject matter. Lili Taylor is ferocious as the mad, radical-feminist genius who did the title deed, but it's a performance that eventually wears on more than it illuminates. Not rated; contains foul language, drug use, and sex, with some minor violence and nudity. 106m. DIR: Mary Harron. CAST: Lili Taylor, Jared Harris, Stephen Dorff, Martha Plimpton. 1996

I SPIT ON MY CORPSE 🐢 A team of larcenous females goes on a killing spree across the country. Not rated; contains nudity and violence. 88m. DIR: Al Adamson. CAST: Georgina Spelvin. 1974

I SPIT ON YOUR GRAVE 🐢 After being brutally raped by a gang of thugs (one of whom is retarded), a young woman takes sadistic revenge. Most videotapes of this title contain the longer X-rated version. Rated R or X. 88m. DIR: Meir Zarchi. CAST: Camille Keaton. 1981 DVD

I SPY (TV SERIES) ★★★★ Remember Bill Cosby before terminal cuteness and a bank account the size of Guam overwhelmed him? This classic TV series will remind you of his charm and ability. It also focuses much-deserved attention on the colossally cool and clever Robert Culp. There's plenty of fun and suspense as spies Kelly Robinson and Alexander Scott, under the guise of tennis pro and trainer, do battle against the international forces of evil. Each episode: 60m. **DIR:** Richard C. Sarafian, Paul Wendkos. **CAST:** Robert Culp, Bill Cosby. 1965–1968 DVD

I STAND CONDEMNED ★★★ A jealous suitor frames a rival in order to have a clear field for the affections of the woman both love. Not much here, except a young and dashing Laurence Olivier in one of his first films. B&W; 75m. **DIR:** Anthony Asquith. **CAST:** Harry Baur, Laurence Olivier, Robert Cochran. 1935

I STILL KNOW WHAT YOU DID LAST SUMMER ★★ Although its predecessor contained a modicum of wit, genuine suspense, and restraint, this sequel is a bland, body-count endurance test which doesn't even try for logic or common sense as that guy with the baling hook is still after poor Jennifer Love Hewitt. Viewers can safely assume that any ancillary character is guaranteed to be impaled. Rated R for violence, gore, drug use, and profanity. 96m. **DIR:** Danny Cannon. **CAST:** Jennifer Love Hewitt, Freddie Prinze Jr., Brandy, Mekhi Phifer, Muse Watson, Bill Cobbs, Jeffrey Combs, Jennifer Esposito. 1998 DVD

I, THE JURY 💗 Armand Assante is a passable Mike Hammer in this sleazy hybrid of James Bond and *Death Wish II*. Rated R. 111m. **DIR:** Richard T. Heffron. **CAST:** Armand Assante, Barbara Carrera, Alan King. 1982

I THINK I DO 💗 College pals reunite several years after graduation as gay and straight romances blossom and crumble in awkward cliché-laden episodes. Rated R for sexuality, language, and drug use. 94m. **DIR:** Brian Sloan. **CAST:** Alexis Arquette, Christian Maelen, Tuc Watkins, Lauren Velez, Marianne Hagan. 1998

I VITELLONI ★★★★ Five men in a small town on the Adriatic become discontented and restless. Stunning cinematography highlights this consideration of rootlessness, a central theme that runs throughout Fellini's work. In Italian with English subtitles. B&W; 104m. **DIR:** Federico Fellini. **CAST:** Franco Interlenghi, Alberto Sordi, Franco Fabrizi. 1953

I WAKE UP SCREAMING ★★★ Laird Cregar's performance as a menacing and sinister detective bent on convicting an innocent Victor Mature for the murder of Carole Landis dominates this suspense-filled *film noir*. Betty Grable is surprisingly effective in her first nonmusical role as the victim's sister, who finds herself attracted to the chief suspect. A classy whodunit. B&W; 82m. **DIR:** H. Bruce Humberstone. **CAST:** Betty Grable, Victor Mature, Carole Landis, Laird Cregar, William Gargan. 1941

I WALKED WITH A ZOMBIE ★★★★1/2 Director Jacques Tourneur made this classic horror film, involving voodoo and black magic, on an island in the Pacific. One of the best of its kind, this is a great Val Lewton production. B&W; 69m. **DIR:** Jacques Tourneur. **CAST:** Frances Dee, Tom Conway, James Ellison. 1943

I WANNA HOLD YOUR HAND ★★★ A group of New Jersey teens try to get tickets to the Beatles' first appearance on the *Ed Sullivan Show*. This was one of the biggest money losers of 1978, but it's not that bad. Fast-paced and energetic, with a nice sense of period and some fine performances. Rated PG. 104m. **DIR:** Robert Zemeckis. **CAST:** Nancy Allen, Bobby DiCicco, Marc McClure, Theresa Saldana, Eddie Deezen, Will Jordan, Wendie Jo Sperber. 1978

I WANT TO LIVE! ★★★ Pulling all stops out, Susan Hayward won an Oscar playing antiheroine B-girl Barbara Graham in this shattering real-life drama. Stupidly involved in a robbery-murder, Graham was indicted, railroaded to conviction, and executed at California's infamous San Quentin State Prison in 1955. To sit through this one you have to be steel-nerved or supremely callous, or both. B&W; 120m. **DIR:** Robert Wise. **CAST:** Susan Hayward, Simon Oakland, Virginia Vincent, Theodore Bikel. 1958

I WANT WHAT I WANT ★★ The search for emotional and sexual identity is the focal point of this British production about a man who undergoes a sex-change operation and falls in love. Although the subject matter is still controversial today, this film is remarkably tame. 97m. **DIR:** John Dexter. **CAST:** Anne Heywood, Harry Andrews, Jill Bennett, Michael Coles, Nigel Flatley. 1972

●**I WANT YOU** ★★★1/2 Michael Winterbottom's psychological thriller delivers lots of sexual heat and tension, but is so muddled you want to throw your arms up in surrender. Rachel Weisz is stunning as Helen, a shy hairdresser who has become the obsession of a teenage mute boy. After sabotaging her previous relationships, the young man meets his match when one of Helen's former lovers returns. Winterbottom lines the film with dark, twisted secrets and revelations, delivered with a heavy hand and little flair. Rated R for adult situations, language, nudity, and violence. 87m. **DIR:** Michael Winterbottom. **CAST:** Rachel Weisz, Alessandro Nivola, Luka Petrusic, Labina Mitevska. 1998

I WAS A MALE WAR BRIDE ★★★★ Cary Grant plays Henri Rochard, a real-life French officer who married an American WAC in post–World War II Germany just as she was to return to the United States. A great farce from beginning to end, with Grant a riot in drag attempting to board a ship full of war brides bound for America. B&W; 105m. **DIR:** Howard Hawks. **CAST:** Cary Grant, Ann Sheridan, Marion Marshall, Kenneth Tobey. 1949

I WAS A TEENAGE FRANKENSTEIN ★★ A descendant of the infamous Dr. Frankenstein sets up shop in America and pieces together a new creature out of hotrod-driving teenagers. This follow-up to *I Was A Teenage Werewolf* is campy fun with mad scientist Whit Bissell uttering lines like "Answer me, you fool! I know you have a civil tongue in your head. I sewed it there myself!" B&W/color; 72m. **DIR:** Herbert L. Strock. **CAST:** Whit Bissell, Phyllis Coates, Robert Burton, Gary Conway. 1957

I WAS A TEENAGE WEREWOLF ★★1/2 All things considered (the low budget, the demands of the teen/drive-in genre), this is a pretty good exploitation monster movie. Buoyed by Michael Landon's passionate performance and Gene Fowler Jr.'s energetic direction (which opens the film with a fist thrown straight at the audience). B&W; 70m. **DIR:** Gene Fowler Jr. **CAST:** Michael Landon, Yvonne Lime, Whit Bissell. 1957

WAS A TEENAGE ZOMBIE 💔 A drug pusher is murdered and his body thrown into a river contaminated by a nuclear power plant. Not rated; contains violence, adult language, and brief nudity. 90m. **DIR:** John Elias Michalakis. **CAST:** Michael Rubin, Steve McCoy. 1986 DVD

WAS A ZOMBIE FOR THE FBI ★★ Intentionally (and sometimes winningly) campy satire about alien invaders who pollute the world's soft drink industry while seeking a top-secret cola formula. Contains a hokey, claymation monster and granite-jaw acting. B&W; 105m. **DIR:** Marius Penczner. **CAST:** James Raspberry, Larry Raspberry. 1982

WAS STALIN'S BODYGUARD ★★★1/2 Fascinating, controversial documentary about the last surviving personal bodyguard of Josef Stalin. Filmmaker Semeon Arranovitch brilliantly weaves together firsthand testimony with rare footage, including Stalin's home movies, creating a penetrating glimpse into a violent, repressive era of the Soviet Union. In Russian with English subtitles. Not rated. 73m. **DIR:** Semeon Arranovitch. 1990

WENT DOWN ★★★ This wry Irish crime-comedy is an entertaining road movie featuring two mismatched hoods, hard luck ex-con Gil and hardcore goon Bunny. This shaggy-dog tale is more talk than action and lightly peppered with impending retribution. Rated R for language, violence, nudity, and suggested sex. 107m. **DIR:** Paddy Breathnach. **CAST:** Peter McDonald, Tony Doyle, Brendan Gleeson, Peter Caffrey. 1998

WILL FIGHT NO MORE FOREVER ★★★1/2 Effective and affecting story of how the Nez Percé Indian tribe, under Chief Joseph, were driven to war with the U.S. government in 1877. The Nez Percé tied up five thousand troops for more than eight months, even though fighting with only a hundred able-bodied warriors. Ned Romero is superb as the proud but wise Chief Joseph, and James Whitmore turns in a fine performance as the craggy General Howard. Made for TV. 106m. **DIR:** Richard T. Heffron. **CAST:** Ned Romero, James Whitmore, Sam Elliott, Linda Redfern. 1975

WILL, I WILL ... FOR NOW 💔 A Santa Barbara sex clinic where "nothing is unnatural." Rated R. 96m. **DIR:** Norman Panama. **CAST:** Elliott Gould, Diane Keaton, Paul Sorvino, Victoria Principal, Robert Alda, Warren Berlinger. 1976

WORSHIP HIS SHADOW 💔 The first of a four-part film, *Tales from a Parallel Universe*, made for cable television, this overwrought space opera-parody gives every indication of having been made up as it was being filmed. The ensuing films in the series are even worse. Rated R for violence, profanity, and adult situations. 94m. **DIR:** Paul Donovan. **CAST:** Brian Downey, Eva Habermann, Michael McManus, Barry Bostwick. 1995

I, ZOMBIE ★★★ Surprisingly good take on zombies from British director Andrew Parkinson. A journalist on assignment finds himself attacked by a woman who appears to be mutilated. Slowly, the man finds himself decaying and the need for blood becomes an increasing urge to suppress. The first film from Fangoria Video is gory but is made enjoyable by the filmmakers' talent and enthusiasm. Not rated; contains gore and violence. 89m. **DIR:** Andrew Parkinson. **CAST:** Giles Aspen, Ellen Softley. 1999 DVD

ICE ★★ Jewel thief (Traci Lords) and her brother find themselves caught between two rival groups of gangsters after they steal a cache of diamonds from the head honcho of one of the gangs. Glitz and glitter can't hide the flaws in this one. Rated R for violence, nudity, and profanity. 90m. **DIR:** Brook Yeaton. **CAST:** Traci Lords, Zach Galligan, Phillip Troy. 1993

ICE CASTLES ★★1/2 Alexis Wintson (Lynn-Holly Johnson) is a girl from a small midwestern town who dreams of skating in the Olympics. No matter how fetching and believable Johnson may be, nothing can surmount the soggy sentimentality of this cliché-ridden work. Rated PG. 109m. **DIR:** Donald Wrye. **CAST:** Robby Benson, Lynn-Holly Johnson, Colleen Dewhurst, Tom Skerritt. 1979

ICE CREAM MAN 💔 The neighborhood ice cream man, recently released from an insane asylum, goes around town collecting unsuspecting youngsters to serve as ingredients in his gourmet ice cream. Ultra-low-budget gorefest for undiscriminating horror fans and celebrity watchers only. Not rated; contains many scenes of graphic horror. 87m. **DIR:** Norman Apstein. **CAST:** Clint Howard, Justin Isfeld, Anndi McAfee, JoJo Adams. 1995

ICE PALACE ★★★1/2 Film adaptation of Edna Ferber's soap-opera saga about Alaska's statehood. Zeb Kennedy (Richard Burton) fights against statehood while Thor Storm (Robert Ryan) devotes his life to it. Beautifully acted, particularly by Carolyn Jones as the woman both men love. 144m. **DIR:** Vincent Sherman. **CAST:** Richard Burton, Robert Ryan, Carolyn Jones, Martha Hyer, Jim Backus. 1960

ICE PIRATES ★★★1/2 This entertaining and often funny sci-fi film takes place countless years from now, when the universe has run out of water. Rated PG for violence, profanity, scatological humor, and suggested sex. 91m. **DIR:** Stewart Raffill. **CAST:** Robert Urich, Mary Crosby, John Matuszak, Anjelica Huston, John Carradine. 1984

ICE RUNNER ★★★ CIA agent (Edward Albert) is sentenced to a Russian gulag in Siberia for espionage. During transit by rail, he switches identities with a dead prisoner. When he runs afoul of the camp commandant, a war of wits and nerves begins. Strange mix of political intrigue and mysticism skates around the thin ice in the plot. Rated R for nudity, profanity, and violence. 114m. **DIR:** Barry Samson. **CAST:** Edward Albert, Victor Wong, Olga Kabo, Eugene Lazarev, Alexander Kurnitzov, Basil Hoffman. 1993

ICE STATION ZEBRA ★★★ This long cold war cliffhanger about a submarine skipper awaiting orders while cruising to the North Pole under the ice was eccentric billionaire Howard Hughes's favorite film.

The suspense comes with a British agent's hunt for the usual Russian spy. Rated G. 148m. DIR: John Sturges. CAST: Rock Hudson, Ernest Borgnine, Patrick McGoohan, Jim Brown, Tony Bill, Lloyd Nolan. 1968

ICE STORM, THE ★★★ This film is based on Rick Moody's novel about Thanksgiving 1973 in a middle-class New England family, with adolescent children fumbling with puberty while their parents flounder in the backwash of the sexual revolution. Though expertly made and well acted, the film's characters are uptight and repellent, and the story is bleak and oversymbolic. More to be admired than enjoyed. Rated R for profanity and sexual themes. 113m. DIR: Ang Lee. CAST: Kevin Kline, Joan Allen, Christina Ricci, Sigourney Weaver, Elijah Wood, Tobey Maguire, Adam Hann-Byrd. 1997

ICELAND ★★★1/2 A typical Sonja Henie musical with lots of music, romancing, and slapstick comedy. Henie plays an ice skater who falls in love with an American marine. She tells her parents she is going to marry him so her younger sister can marry the man of her dreams. (In their culture, the oldest daughter always marries first.) Now she has to make good on her promise. B&W; 79m. DIR: H. Bruce Humberstone. CAST: Sonja Henie, John Payne, Jack Oakie, Felix Bressart, Osa Massen, Fritz Feld, Joan Merrill, Adeline de Walt Reynolds, Sammy Kaye. 1942

ICEMAN ★★★1/2 Timothy Hutton stars in this often gripping and always watchable movie as an anthropologist who is part of an arctic exploration team that discovers the body of a prehistoric man (John Lone), who is still alive. Hutton finds himself defending the creature from those who want to poke, prod, and even dissect their terrified subject. Rated PG for violence and profanity. 99m. DIR: Fred Schepisi. CAST: Timothy Hutton, Lindsay Crouse, John Lone, Josef Sommer. 1984

ICICLE THIEF, THE ★★★★1/2 Writer-director-actor Maurizio Nichetti has been called the Woody Allen of Italy, so it's appropriate that he's now made a wonderful film combining some of the ideas of Purple Rose of Cairo with the technical virtuosity of Zelig. A delightfully inventive parody-satire, this explores the ability of movies to carry us into other worlds. In Italian with English subtitles. Not rated. 90m. DIR: Maurizio Nichetti. CAST: Maurizio Nichetti. 1990

ICY BREASTS ★★★ Detective Alain Delon discovers that his beautiful client has been killing the men in her life. Effective suspense-drama. In French with English subtitles. 105m. DIR: Georges Lautner. CAST: Alain Delon, Mireille Darc. 1975

IDAHO TRANSFER 🞰 Young scientists invent a time-travel machine. No rating. 90m. DIR: Peter Fonda. CAST: Keith Carradine, Kelly Bohannon. 1973

IDENTITY CRISIS ★★ A witch fuses the soul of a murdered fashion designer with a rapper's body in this fluffy comedy. Rated R for profanity and nudity. 98m. DIR: Melvin Van Peebles. CAST: Mario Van Peebles, Ilan Mitchell-Smith. 1990

IDIOT, THE ★★★★★ Early gem by Akira Kurosawa based on the novel by Dostoyevski about the confrontation between a demented ruffian and a holy fool prince. Akira Kurosawa transports this tale of

madness and jealousy to postwar Japan and places it among blizzards and claustrophobic, madly lit interiors. Highly recommended! In Japanese with English subtitles. B&W; 166m. DIR: Akira Kurosawa. CAST: Toshiro Mifune, Masayuki Mori, Setsuko Hara. 1951

IDIOT'S DELIGHT ★★★1/2 An all-star cast makes memorable movie history in this, the last antiwar film produced before World War II erupted. Norma Shearer is at her best as a Garbo-like fake-Russian-accented mistress companion of munitions tycoon Edward Arnold. Clark Gable is her ex, a wisecracking vaudeville hoofer. With other types, they are stranded in a European luxury hotel as war looms. B&W; 105m. DIR: Clarence Brown. CAST: Clark Gable, Norma Shearer, Edward Arnold, Charles Coburn, Burgess Meredith, Laura Hope Crews, Joseph Schildkraut, Virginia Grey. 1938

IDLE HANDS ♥ This comedy-horror flick is more repulsive than funny or frightening as a demonic spirit takes over the right hand of a teen stoner who murders his parents and attacks everyone within reach. Rated R for gore, violence, drug use, sexual content, and language. 92m. DIR: Rodman Flender. CAST: Devon Sawa, Jessica Alba, Seth Green, Elden Henson. 1999 DVD

IDOL DANCER, THE ★★1/2 A drunken Yankee beachcomber befriends a young native girl on an island in the South Seas. B&W; 76m. DIR: D. W. Griffith. CAST: Richard Barthelmess, Clarine Seymour, Creighton Hale. 1920

IDOLMAKER, THE ★★★★ This superior rock 'n' roll drama stands with a handful of pictures—The Buddy Holly Story and American Hot Wax among them—as one of the few to capture the excitement of rock music while still offering something in the way of a decent plot and characterization. Ray Sharkey is excellent as a songwriter-manager who pulls, pushes, punches, and plunders his way to the top of the music world. The score, by Jeff Barry, is top-notch. Rated PG. 119m. DIR: Taylor Hackford. CAST: Ray Sharkey, Tovah Feldshuh, Peter Gallagher, Maureen McCormick. 1980 DVD

IF ... ★★★★ This is British director Lindsay Anderson's black comedy about English private schools and the revolt against their strict code of behavior taken to the farthest limits of the imagination. Malcolm McDowell's movie debut. Rated R. 111m. DIR: Lindsay Anderson. CAST: Malcolm McDowell, David Wood, Richard Warwick. 1969

IF EVER I SEE YOU AGAIN ♥ Fresh from his success with You Light Up My Life, writer-director-composer Joe Brooks threw together this celluloid love poem to model Shelley Hack. Rated PG. 105m. DIR: Joseph Brooks. CAST: Joe Brooks, Shelley Hack, Jimmy Breslin, George Plimpton. 1978

IF I HAD A MILLION ★★★★1/2 Wonderful episodic tale where wealthy Richard Bennett picks names from the telephone book, giving each person one million dollars. The two funniest segments star Charles Laughton and W. C. Fields. Both comic masterpieces. B&W; 90m. DIR: Various. CAST: Gary Cooper, W. C. Fields, Charles Laughton, George Raft, Richard Bennett, Mary Boland, Frances Dee, Jack

Dakie, Gene Raymond, Charlie Ruggles, Alison Skip-worth. **1932**

F I WERE KING ★★★ Ronald Colman makes a great François Villon in this story of "The Vagabond King" who takes the place of France's Louis XI when he wins a bet. B&W; 101m. **DIR:** Frank Lloyd. **CAST:** Ronald Colman, Basil Rathbone, Frances Dee, Ellen Drew, Henry Wilcoxon. **1938**

F I WERE RICH ★★★ How to live and avoid paying bills while waiting for prosperity to return is the theme of this entertaining British comedy. Robert Donat fails just before Wendy Barrie when he arrives to shut off her once-rich-but-now-bankrupt father Edmund Gwenn's electricity. The debonair Donat is a delight in this early pairing with Barrie. B&W; 63m. **DIR:** Zoltán Korda. **CAST:** Robert Donat, Wendy Barrie, Edmund Gwenn. **1933**

F IT'S TUESDAY, THIS MUST BE BELGIUM ★★★1/2 Plenty of laughs with a group of Americans on a wild eighteen-day bus tour of Europe, running from one mishap to another. Added fun with lots of guest stars in surprise cameos. Rated G. 99m. **DIR:** Mel Stuart. **CAST:** Suzanne Pleshette, Ian McShane, Mildred Natwick, Murray Hamilton, Michael Constantine, Norman Fell, Peggy Cass, Marty Ingels, Pamela Britton, Sandy Baron. **1969**

F LOOKS COULD KILL (1986) ★★ A photographer is hired to videotape a woman's apartment to gather evidence against her. Suspense and duplicity follow. But the dialogue is poor and the direction is mediocre. Rated R for violence, profanity, nudity, and sex. 90m. **DIR:** Chuck Vincent. **CAST:** Kim Lambert, Tim Gail. **1986**

F LOOKS COULD KILL (1991) ★★★ Richard Grieco is a high school student mistaken for an undercover secret agent. As such, he enjoys all the frills (car, clothes, women) that go with the job. Unfortunately, he must also contend with bad guys. A wonderful, action-packed conclusion. Rated PG-13 for profanity and violence. 90m. **DIR:** William Dear. **CAST:** Richard Grieco, Linda Hunt, Roger Rees, Robin Bartlett, Roger Daltrey. **1991**

F LUCY FELL 💔 In this annoying, witless comedy, platonic roommates Sarah Jessica Parker and Eric Schaeffer vow to jump off the Brooklyn Bridge if they don't find true love within a month. Naturally, the characters end up together—but not at the bottom of the East River, where they belong. Rated R for profanity. 93m. **DIR:** Eric Schaeffer. **CAST:** Sarah Jessica Parker, Eric Schaeffer, Elle Macpherson, Ben Stiller. **1996**

F THESE WALLS COULD TALK ★★★1/2 The abortion movement fuels this advocacy cinema, which tells three pivotal stories occurring within the same large house. Demi Moore is first-rate as a widowed nurse in the early 1950s, who lives in abject terror of the pregnancy she feels will ruin her life. Cher (also making her directorial debut) turns up in the 1990s segment as a compassionate clinic physician, who crosses picket lines. Ironically, the best segment—set in the 1970s—focuses on happily married Sissy Spacek and her crisis over a surprise pregnancy. Lacking the shrill tone and one-sided approach of the other two tales, it reaches an honest conclusion.

Rated R for profanity, nudity, violence, and strong dramatic content. 95m. **DIR:** Cher, Nancy Savoca. **CAST:** Demi Moore, Sissy Spacek, Cher, Shirley Knight, C.C.H. Pounder, Xander Berkeley, Joanna Gleason, Anne Heche, Jada Pinkett. **1996 DVD**

IF YOU COULD SEE WHAT I HEAR ★★ The film is supposedly the biography of blind singer-composer Tom Sullivan. You'd have to be not only blind but deaf and, most of all, dumb to appreciate this one. Rated PG. 103m. **DIR:** Eric Till. **CAST:** Marc Singer, R. H. Thomson, Sarah Torgov, Shari Belafonte, Douglas Campbell. **1982**

IF YOU KNEW SUSIE ★★1/2 If you enjoy the comedy and musical stylings of Joan Davis and Eddie Cantor, you'll probably be pleased with this thin story of two entertainers who discover a will signed by George Washington. Dated and held together only by Cantor's sure touch and slick performance. B&W; 90m. **DIR:** Gordon Douglas. **CAST:** Eddie Cantor, Joan Davis, Allyn Joslyn. **1948**

IKE: THE WAR YEARS ★★ Robert Duvall is D-day commander General Dwight Eisenhower, and Lee Remick is his wartime romance Kay Summersby, in this tedious retelling of high-echelon soldiering and whitewashed hanky-panky during the European phase of World War II. Trimmed drastically from an original six-hour miniseries. 196m. **DIR:** Melville Shavelson, Boris Sagal. **CAST:** Robert Duvall, Lee Remick, J. D. Cannon, Darren McGavin. **1978**

IKIRU ★★★1/2 *Ikiru* is the Japanese infinitive *to live.* The film opens with a shot of an X ray; a narrator tells us the man—an Everyman—is dying of cancer. But a dream flickers to life, and his last years are fulfilled by a lasting accomplishment. It packs a genuine emotional wallop. In Japanese with English subtitles. B&W; 143m. **DIR:** Akira Kurosawa. **CAST:** Takashi Shimura. **1952**

IL BIDONE ★★★ Broderick Crawford gives a strong performance in this nearly forgotten film by Federico Fellini, about an aging con man who realizes his lifetime of selfishness has only made his existence meaningless. In Italian with English subtitles. B&W; 92m. **DIR:** Federico Fellini. **CAST:** Broderick Crawford, Richard Basehart, Giulietta Masina, Franco Fabrizi. **1955 DVD**

IL GRIDO (OUTCRY, THE) ★★1/2 Drab film about a worker and his child wandering around rural Italy. Also known as *The Outcry.* In Italian with English subtitles. 102m. **DIR:** Michelangelo Antonioni. **CAST:** Steve Cochran, Alida Valli, Betsy Blair. **1957**

IL LADRO DI BAMBINI (STOLEN CHILDREN) ★★★★★ An 11-year-old girl and her younger brother are taken away from their mother, who has been supporting the family from her daughter's earnings as a prostitute. It falls to a young, good-hearted military officer to escort the youngsters to a children's home, and he turns the trip into a rediscovery of love and happiness for both of them. Both hard-edged and heartwarming, this is a brilliant motion picture. In Italian with English subtitles. 116m. **DIR:** Gianni Amelio. **CAST:** Enrico Lo Verso, Valentina Scalici, Guiseppe Ieracitano. **1992**

I'LL BE HOME FOR CHRISTMAS 💔 Smug West Coast college student glued inside a Santa suit has several lame misadventures as he travels to join his family in New York for Christmas. Rated PG. 86m. DIR: Arlene Sanford. CAST: Jonathan Taylor Thomas, Jessica Biel, Adam LaVorgna, Gary Cole, Eve Gordon, Lauren Maltby. 1998 DVD

I'LL CRY TOMORROW ★★★1/2 In addition to giving one of the most professional performances of her career, Susan Hayward sang (and very well) the songs in this screen biography of Lillian Roth. Her masterful portrayal, supported by a solid cast, won her a Cannes Film Festival award. B&W; 117m. DIR: Daniel Mann. CAST: Susan Hayward, Eddie Albert, Richard Conte, Jo Van Fleet, Don Taylor, Ray Danton. 1955

I'LL DO ANYTHING ★★1/2 Writer-director James L. Brooks *badly* miscalculated in this saga of struggling Hollywood actor and single father Nick Nolte, whose stabs at cinematic fame are derailed by the need to care for his precocious daughter Whittni Wright. Although shooting for the vicious insider's humor of *The Player*, this overblown mess staggers beneath its own pretensions. Rated PG-13 for profanity and brief nudity. 115m. DIR: James L. Brooks. CAST: Nick Nolte, Albert Brooks, Julie Kavner, Joely Richardson, Tracey Ullman, Whittni Wright. 1994

ILL MET BY MOONLIGHT ★★★ In 1944 on the island of Crete, the British hatch a plot to kidnap a German general and smuggle him to Cairo. This sets off a manhunt with twenty thousand German troops and airplanes pursuing the partisans through Crete's mountainous terrain. B&W; 105m. DIR: Michael Powell. CAST: Dirk Bogarde, Marius Goring, David Oxley, Cyril Cusack. 1957

I'LL SEE YOU IN MY DREAMS ★★★1/2 This sugarcoated biography of lyricist Gus Kahn contains a truly warm performance by Danny Thomas, coupled with fine renditions of Kahn's songs ("Pretty Baby," "It Had To Be You," "Love Me Or Leave Me," etc.) B&W; 110m. DIR: Michael Curtiz. CAST: Danny Thomas, Doris Day, Frank Lovejoy, Patrice Wymore, James Gleason, Mary Wickes, Jim Backus. 1951

I'LL TAKE SWEDEN ★★ Bob Hope takes a job in Sweden to break up his daughter's love affair and finds romance himself. Misfires all the way. 96m. DIR: Frederick de Cordova. CAST: Bob Hope, Tuesday Weld, Frankie Avalon, Dina Merrill, John Qualen. 1965

ILLEGAL ENTRY ✰ Daughter of murdered scientists looks for their killers while guarding a secret formula. Not a formula for success. Rated R for violence, language, and nudity. 88m. DIR: Henri Charr. CAST: Barbara Lee Alexander, Gregory Vignolle, Arthur Roberts, Sabyn Genét. 1993

ILLEGAL IN BLUE ★★ Pedestrian sex thriller dishes up the one about the clean cop in love with a woman who may be a murder suspect. Plenty of steamy rendezvous in the not-rated version. Rated R. Unrated version available. 94m. DIR: Stuart Segall. CAST: Stacey Dash, Dan Gauthier, Louis Giambalvo, Trevor Goddard. 1995

ILLEGALLY YOURS ✰ A bumbling jury member falls for the plaintiff in a murder case. Rated PG. 102m. DIR: Peter Bogdanovich. CAST: Rob Lowe, Colleen Camp, Kenneth Mars, Kim Myers. 1988

ILLICIT ★★ A sexy title for a dull movie about a loose-living woman who tries to settle down until she gets bored with marriage. The same story is better presented in the Bette Davis remake called *Ex-Lady*. B&W; 81m. DIR: Archie Mayo. CAST: Barbara Stanwyck, Joan Blondell, Charles Butterworth, Ricardo Cortez, James Rennie. 1931

ILLICIT BEHAVIOR ★★ Mediocre film with a twisted plot involving good and bad cops. Jack Scalia spends most of the movie either roughing up or killing people he dislikes, only to find out that he has severely tangled himself up in a conspiracy. Rated R for violence, nudity, and language. 101m. DIR: Worth Keeter. CAST: Robert Davi, Joan Severance, Jack Scalia, James Russo, Kent McCord, Jenilee Harrison. 1992

ILLTOWN ★★ A Miami drug dealer becomes embroiled in a power struggle against a former friend just out of prison and nursing some long-held grudge. The film is so cryptic and pretentious, the characters so repellent, and the symbolism so smug and heavy-handed, that by the time writer-director Nick Gomez finally gets around to explaining what the grudge is, you probably won't care. Rated R for profanity, violence, scenes of drug use, and brief nudity. 103m. DIR: Nick Gomez. CAST: Michael Rapaport, Lili Taylor, Kevin Corrigan, Adam Trese, Tony Danza, Isaac Hayes. 1996

•**ILLUMINATA** 🎬 A playwright (John Turturro, who also directed, and badly) agonizes over his latest play while the members of his theater company fear he's about to abandon them. A good cast founders helplessly in a pretentious, bombastic script. Rated R for mature themes and brief nudity. 111m. DIR: John Turturro. CAST: John Turturro, Katherine Borowitz, Beverly D'Angelo, Susan Sarandon, Christopher Walken, Ben Gazzara, Rufus Sewell. 1998 DVD

ILLUSION TRAVELS BY STREETCAR ★★★ Two employees of a municipal public transport company in Mexico City are dissatisfied with their superiors, so they withdraw an old tram, get drunk at a local festival, and take one last trip through the town. Light comedy from director Luis Buñuel during his prolific Mexican cinema period. In Spanish with English subtitles. 90m. DIR: Luis Buñuel. CAST: Lilia Prado, Carlos Navarro, Agustin Isunza. 1953

ILLUSIONS ★★ Mediocre story in which a former mental patient (Heather Locklear) believes her sister-in-law is trying to drive her insane. Narration distracts the viewer and only exists to fill gaps in the plot. Not rated; contains nudity. 90m. DIR: Victor Kulle. CAST: Robert Carradine, Heather Locklear, Emma Samms, Ned Beatty, Paul Mantee, Susannah York. 1992

ILLUSTRATED MAN, THE 🎬 Ponderous, dull, and overly talkie adaptation of the work of Ray Bradbury. Rated PG for violence and partial nudity. 103m. DIR: Jack Smight. CAST: Rod Steiger, Claire Bloom, Robert Drivas. 1969

ILSA, THE WICKED WARDEN 🎬 Also titled: *Greta the Mad Butcher, Ilsa—Absolute Power*. Rated R. 90m. DIR: Jess (Jesus) Franco. CAST: Dyanne Thorne, Lina Romay, Jess Franco. 1977

I'M A FOOL ★★★ Ron Howard stars as a naïve young man who abandons his Ohio home for life on the road as a horse trainer. His desperate attempts to make himself worthy in the eyes of the opposite sex escalate until he's passing himself off as the son of a fabulously wealthy man. From a Sherwood Anderson story. Introduced by Henry Fonda; unrated and suitable for family viewing. 38m. **DIR:** Noel Black. **CAST:** Ron Howard, Amy Irving, John Light. **1976**

I'M ALL RIGHT JACK ★★★1/2 British comedies can be marvelously entertaining, especially when they star Peter Sellers, as in this witty spoof of the absurdities of the labor movement carried to its ultimate extreme. B&W; 101m. **DIR:** John Boulting. **CAST:** Peter Sellers, Terry-Thomas, Ian Carmichael. **1960**

I'M ALMOST NOT CRAZY: JOHN CASSAVETES—THE MAN AND HIS WORK ★★★★ Penetrating look at filmmaker-actor John Cassavetes, whose low-budget American movies earned the praise of film directors and critics internationally. His working methods are explored on the set of *Love Streams* (his final screen bid). Cassavetes's brutal, uncompromising approach to his craft is brilliantly captured by Michael Ventura. Not rated; contains some profanity. 60m. **DIR:** Michael Ventura. **1989**

I'M DANCING AS FAST AS I CAN 💣 Based on documentary filmmaker Barbara Gordon's bestselling autobiography, which dealt with her valiant—and sometimes horrifying—struggle with Valium addiction. Rated PG for profanity. 107m. **DIR:** Jack Hofsiss. **CAST:** Jill Clayburgh, Nicol Williamson, Geraldine Page. **1981**

I'M DANGEROUS TONIGHT 💣 An Aztec ceremonial cloak serves as a catalyst for murders in a small college town. Originally aired on cable TV. 92m. **DIR:** Tobe Hooper. **CAST:** Madchen Amick, R. Lee Ermey, Anthony Perkins, Dee Wallace. **1990**

I'M GONNA GIT YOU SUCKA! ★★★★ Keenen Ivory Wayans wrote and directed this uproariously funny parody of the blaxploitation flicks of the early Seventies. The gags run fast and loose, and the result is a satisfying laughfest. Rated R for language. 88m. **DIR:** Keenen Ivory Wayans. **CAST:** Keenen Ivory Wayans, Bernie Casey, Jim Brown, Isaac Hayes, Antonio Fargas, Steve James, John Vernon, Clu Gulager. **1989**

•I'M LOSING YOU ★★ Writer Bruce Wagner adapts his own novel and directs this pedestrian effort starring Frank Langella trying to balance a wife, a mistress, his health, and his public appearance. Lots of missed opportunities and a waste of talent. Rated R for language. 100m. **DIR:** Bruce Wagner. **CAST:** Frank Langella, Amanda Donohoe, Elizabeth Perkins, Rosanna Arquette, Andrew McCarthy, Salome Jens. **1998 DVD**

I'M NO ANGEL ★★★★ One of her funniest films, Mae West had complete creative control over script, camera angles, costars, and director. She plays a circus performer who cons gullible old men out of their money. The highlight of the show is the courtroom scene with West acting as her own attorney and compromising the judge, as well as everyone else. B&W; 87m. **DIR:** Wesley Ruggles. **CAST:** Mae West, Cary Grant, Kent Taylor, Edward Arnold, Gregory Ratoff, Gertrude Michael, Dennis O'Keefe, Ralf Harolde. **1933 DVD**

I'M NOT RAPPAPORT ★★1/2 Two feisty octogenarians—African American building superintendent Midge and Jewish left-wing radical Nate—spend time squabbling on a Central Park bench in this sometimes clunky rework of Herb Gardner's award-winning play. This meandering character study works best when Midge plays straight man to Nate's elaborate yarns. When they leave their bench to battle a park punk and a drug dealer, the film loses its wily comic realism. Rated PG-13 for brief violence and drug content. 131m. **DIR:** Herb Gardner. **CAST:** Walter Matthau, Ossie Davis, Amy Irving, Martha Plimpton, Craig T. Nelson. **1996**

I'M THE ONE YOU'RE LOOKING FOR ★★★★ A beautiful model is raped, then becomes curiously obsessed with her attacker, willing to endure anything and anyone to find him. Set in the seedy, seething atmosphere of Barcelona, this is a fascinating exploration of the macabre aspect of human sexual longing. In Spanish with English subtitles. Rated R for nudity. 85m. **DIR:** Jaime Chavarri. **CAST:** Patricia Adrian. **1988**

IMAGE, THE ★★★1/2 Ratings-hungry telejournalists turn a critical eye on themselves in this crackling topical drama—a study of a network news star who begins to believe his own reviews. This made-for-cable movie is unrated, but contains explicit language and brief nudity. 89m. **DIR:** Peter Werner. **CAST:** Albert Finney, John Mahoney, Kathy Baker, Swoosie Kurtz, Marsha Mason. **1990**

IMAGE OF PASSION 💣 In this unimpressive romance, a young advertising executive begins a passionate affair with a male stripper. 105m. **DIR:** Susan Orlikoff-Simon. **CAST:** James Horan, Susan D. Shaw. **1982**

IMAGEMAKER, THE ★★★1/2 Intriguing exposé on the selling of American politicians. Michael Nouri plays a deposed political power maker whose life is threatened when he plans to tell all. Anne Twomey plays the TV reporter who had ruined his previous career. Rated R for nudity, violence, and profanity. 93m. **DIR:** Hal Weiner. **CAST:** Michael Nouri, Anne Twomey, Jerry Orbach, Jessica Harper, Farley Granger. **1985**

IMAGINARY CRIMES ★★★★ Harvey Keitel once again delivers a stunning performance as a con-man father who has been playing the game so long he is now conning his family and himself. Rated PG for language. 106m. **DIR:** Anthony Drazan. **CAST:** Harvey Keitel, Fairuza Balk, Kelly Lynch, Vincent D'Onofrio, Christopher Penn, Seymour Cassel. **1994**

IMAGINE: JOHN LENNON ★★★★★ Superb documentary chronicles the life, times, and untimely death of rock 'n' roll icon John Lennon. Carefully selected footage from the career of the Beatles is combined with television interviews and never-before-seen film of Lennon's private life for a remarkably insightful and emotionally moving work. Rated R for nudity and profanity. 103m. **DIR:** Andrew Solt. **CAST:** John Lennon, Yoko Ono, George Harrison. **1988**

IMITATION OF LIFE ★★★1/2 Earnest performances and gifted direction make this soap-operaish, Fannie Hurst tearjerker tolerable viewing. Lana Turner is a fame-greedy actress who neglects her daughter for her career. Juanita Moore is her black friend whose daughter repudiates her heritage and breaks her mother's heart by passing for white. 124m. DIR: Douglas Sirk. CAST: Lana Turner, John Gavin, Sandra Dee, Dan O'Herlihy, Susan Kohner, Troy Donahue, Robert Alda, Juanita Moore. 1959

IMMEDIATE FAMILY ★★★1/2 Unable to have children, a wealthy couple decide to adopt a teenager's baby. Meeting the girl and her boyfriend proves to be both touching and humorous. Rated PG-13 for adult topic. 100m. DIR: Jonathan Kaplan. CAST: Glenn Close, James Woods, Mary Stuart Masterson, Kevin Dillon. 1989

IMMORTAL BACHELOR, THE ★★ A female juror hearing the case of a cleaning woman who killed her cheating husband fantasizes about the dead man. But for the well-known cast, this Italian comedy would never have been imported. Dubbed in English. Not rated, but a PG equivalent. 95m. DIR: Marcello Fondato. CAST: Giancarlo Giannini, Monica Vitti, Vittorio Gassman, Claudia Cardinale. 1979

IMMORTAL BATTALION, THE (THE WAY AHEAD) ★★★1/2 Based on an idea conceived by Lt. Col. David Niven, this highly effective wartime semidocumentary follows his attempts to turn a group of newly activated civilians into a combat team. This gem skillfully mixes training and combat footage with filmed sequences to create a powerful mood while delicately balancing great performances. 91m. DIR: Carol Reed. CAST: David Niven, Stanley Holloway, Raymond Huntley, Peter Ustinov, Trevor Howard, Leo Genn, James Donald. 1944

IMMORTAL BELOVED ★★1/2 After Ludwig van Beethoven's death, his assistant searches for the master composer's long-lost love who is to inherit Ludwig's music and estate. Through interviews with associates and possible lovers, the story speculates on the lady's identity and unearths a dark life of child abuse, womanizing, tormenting deafness, and bristling attitude. The film is gorgeously staged and photographed, but sluggishly paced. Rated R for language, violence, nudity, and simulated sex. 125m. DIR: Bernard Rose. CAST: Gary Oldman, Jeroen Krabbé, Valeria Golino, Isabella Rossellini, Johanna ter Steege. 1994 DVD

IMMORTAL COMBAT ★★ Unintentional humor and inane plot twists keep this routine martial arts expo from beating itself to death. Roddy Piper and Sonny Chiba play Los Angeles police detectives who sneak onto an island fortress to stop a madwoman planning to take over the world. Meg Foster swallows the screen whole in her over-the-top portrayal of the deadly dragon lady. Lots of punching and kicking, and little else. Rated R for violence, language, and adult situations. 109m. DIR: Daniel Neira. CAST: Roddy Piper, Sonny Chiba, Meg Foster, Tiny Lister Jr. 1994 DVD

IMMORTAL SERGEANT, THE ★★★1/2 Henry Fonda gives a solid performance as a corporal in the Canadian army, attached to the British Eighth Army in North Africa during World War II. During a battle with Nazi troops, his squad sergeant is killed and he is forced into command. From a novel by John Brophy. B&W; 91m. DIR: John M. Stahl. CAST: Henry Fonda, Maureen O'Hara, Thomas Mitchell, Allyn Joslyn, Reginald Gardiner, Melville Cooper. 1943

IMMORTAL SINS ★★ Heir to a Spanish castle is also the last male in his cursed line. This atmospheric thriller would be more effective if it were focused more on the antagonism between the heir's wife and a mysterious woman hoping to set their marriage asunder. Rated R for simulated sex. 80m. DIR: Herve Hachuel. CAST: Cliff De Young, Maryam D'Abo, Shari Shattuck. 1992

IMMORTAL STORY ★★★★ A powerful, cynical old man tries to turn a myth into reality by hiring people to enact it for his amusement. Made for French television, this adaptation of a short story by Isak Dinesen shows a subtler and more contemplative side of director Orson Welles, not the brash youth who made *Citizen Kane*. 63m. DIR: Orson Welles. CAST: Orson Welles, Jeanne Moreau, Roger Coggio, Fernando Rey. 1968

IMMORTALS, THE ★★★ Although ostensibly a gory heist caper, this little thriller is oddly appealing. Nightclub manager Eric Roberts assembles eight men and women to rob four cash-laden suitcases from crime lord Tony Curtis, only to see the plan backfire when the subordinates realize what they all have in common. A refreshing change from the usual genre entries. Rated R for violence, profanity, drug use, and nudity. 92m. DIR: Brian Grant. CAST: Eric Roberts, Tia Carrere, Tony Curtis, Joe Pantoliano, Clarence Williams III, William Forsythe. 1995 DVD

IMPACT ★★ Shades of *Double Indemnity*! Unfaithful wife and lover plot to kill rich husband, but lover gets bumped instead. Interesting, but don't believe the title. B&W; 111m. DIR: Arthur Lubin. CAST: Brian Donlevy, Helen Walker, Tony Barrett, Ella Raines, Charles Coburn, Anna May Wong. 1948 DVD

IMPLICATED ★★ Run-of-the-mill thriller about a supposedly nice guy named Tom who plans to kidnap his new girlfriend and his boss's daughter in a twisted game of revenge. It won't put you to sleep, or maybe it will. Rated R for language, violence, and adult situations. 95m. DIR: Irving Belateche. CAST: William McNamara, Amy Locane, Frederic Forrest, Priscilla Barnes, Philip Baker Hall. 1998

IMPORTANCE OF BEING EARNEST, THE ★★★★★ A peerless cast of stage professionals brings this version of Oscar Wilde's classic Victorian Era comedy of manners to vivid life in high style. Once again, the problem of Mr. Worthing's cloakroom origins delights with hilarious results. A very funny film. 95m. DIR: Anthony Asquith. CAST: Michael Redgrave, Edith Evans, Margaret Rutherford, Joan Greenwood, Michael Denison, Dorothy Tutin, Richard Wattis. 1952

IMPOSSIBLE SPY, THE ★★★★ This video is based on the true exploits of Elie Cohen, a spy for Israel's Mossad. Cohen, played by John Shea, is recruited by the Mossad in 1959 and sent to Argentina, where he works his way into the good graces of a group that is plotting to overthrow the Syrian government. He participates while sending information to Israel. The results of his work affect not only his family but the future of Israel. Made for British television, this is unrated. 96m. DIR: Jim Goddard. CAST: John Shea, Eli Wallach, Sasson Gabay. 1987 DVD

IMPOSSIBLE YEARS, THE 🎔 Kids using bad words at school and having premarital sex, all done in bad taste. Inexplicably rated G. 92m. DIR: Michael Gordon. CAST: David Niven, Lola Albright, Chad Everett, Ozzie Nelson, Cristina Ferrare, Jeff Cooper, Don Beddoe. 1968

IMPOSTER, THE 🎔 Con artist in a private war against juvenile drug dealers. Not rated. 95m. DIR: Michael Pressman. CAST: Anthony Geary, Billy Dee Williams, Lorna Patterson, Penny Johnson, Jordan Charney. 1984

IMPOSTORS, THE ★★★ Stanley Tucci and Oliver Platt play Depression-era actors desperately trying to stay alive between theater roles. Circumstance finds them stowaways onboard a ship of fools crawling with folks who aren't quite what they appear. Rated R for profanity and crude sexual candor. 102m. DIR: Stanley Tucci. CAST: Stanley Tucci, Oliver Platt, Alfred Molina, Lili Taylor, Tony Shalhoub, Steve Buscemi, Isabella Rossellini, Billy Connolly, Dana Ivey, Hope Davis. 1998 DVD

IMPROMPTU ★★★★ George Sand, the female novelist with the men's pants and stylish cigars, and Frederic Chopin, the Polish composer, pianist, and all-around sensitive soul, were the talk of Paris as they embarked on a most unusual and passionate affair. That's the subject of this extravagant and entertaining period romance spiced with unexpected comedy and lovely music. Rated PG-13. 109m. DIR: James Lapine. CAST: Judy Davis, Hugh Grant, Mandy Patinkin, Bernadette Peters, Julian Sands, Emma Thompson. 1991

IMPROPER CHANNELS ★★ Story of an overeager social worker who accuses a father (Alan Arkin) of child abuse. Rated PG for language. 92m. DIR: Eric Till. CAST: Alan Arkin, Mariette Hartley, Monica Parker. 1981

IMPULSE (1974) 🎔 William Shatner plays an emotionally disturbed ex–mental patient with a penchant for murder. Not rated, but with several unconvincing murders and lots of phony blood. 85m. DIR: William Grefe. CAST: William Shatner, Ruth Roman, Harold Sakata. 1974

IMPULSE (1984) ★★ This mildly interesting thriller takes place in a town where the inhabitants find they have increasing difficulties in controlling their urges. A hasty, unconvincing final ten minutes. Rated R for profanity and violence. 91m. DIR: Graham Baker. CAST: Tim Matheson, Meg Tilly, Hume Cronyn. 1984 DVD

IMPULSE (1990) ★★★ Honest cop Theresa Russell yields to temptation while working undercover as a hooker, then tries to extricate herself from the ensuing investigation. Director Sondra Locke keeps the action tense through some pretty implausible plot twists. Rated R for violence and language. 109m. DIR: Sondra Locke. CAST: Theresa Russell, Jeff Fahey, George Dzundza. 1990

IMPURE THOUGHTS ★★1/2 A group of friends who attended the same Catholic grammar school in the early Sixties meet after death and reminisce about their youths. Rated PG. 87m. DIR: Michael A. Simpson. CAST: Brad Dourif, Lane Davies, Terry Beaver, John Putch. 1986

IN & OUT ★★★1/2 Kevin Kline is a literature and drama teacher in a small town in the Midwest whose life is turned topsy-turvy when he is "outed" by a former student during an Oscars telecast. Soon to be married and unaware of his more feminine characteristics, Kline recoils from this disclosure and sets out to prove how macho he is. But gay reporter Tom Selleck and the townsfolk won't let him forget his new reputation. Kline brings many funny and touching moments to the screen. Rated PG-13 for profanity. 90m. DIR: Frank Oz. CAST: Kevin Kline, Tom Selleck, Joan Cusack, Matt Dillon, Debbie Reynolds, Wilford Brimley, Bob Newhart, Deborah Rush. 1997 DVD

IN A GLASS CAGE ★★ Horrifying film about an ex-Nazi doctor, now confined to an iron lung, who is tracked down by a young man who survived his sexual tortures. Made with great skill but overwrought—few will be able to stomach it. In Spanish with English subtitles. Not rated; definitely not for children. 112m. DIR: Agustin Villaronga. CAST: Gunter Meisner, David Sust. 1986

IN A LONELY PLACE ★★★★ Humphrey Bogart gives one of his finest performances in this taut psychological thriller. He plays a hard-drinking, fiercely opinionated screenwriter whose violent temper has more than once landed him in trouble. He has an affair with a sexy neighbor (Gloria Grahame) who begins to fear for her life when Bogart becomes the prime suspect in a murder case. B&W; 91m. DIR: Nicholas Ray. CAST: Humphrey Bogart, Gloria Grahame, Frank Lovejoy, Robert Warwick. 1950

IN A MOMENT OF PASSION 🎔 This laughably melodramatic clunker, with Chase Masterson simply awful as a Hollywood ingenue cuddling up to killer Maxwell Caulfield, plays like a student film given ill-advised mainstream distribution. Rated R for profanity, violence, and nudity. 100m. DIR: Zbigniew Kaminski. CAST: Maxwell Caulfield, Chase Masterson, Vivian Schilling. 1993

IN A SHALLOW GRAVE ★★ Michael Biehn stars as a disfigured World War II vet who returns to an empty home and life. Patrick Dempsey is a drifter who becomes a messenger between Biehn and his ex-fiancée (Maureen Mueller). The resulting love triangle, both heterosexual and homosexual, is too short on plot, and the movie ends without an ending. Rated R. 92m. DIR: Kenneth Bowser. CAST: Michael Biehn, Patrick Dempsey, Michael Beach, Maureen Mueller. 1988

IN A STRANGER'S HANDS ★★★ Robert Urich is the private investigator tracking down a missing girl. The deeper he digs, the more complex the case gets, until he comes face-to-face with the kidnapper. Tough, gritty, and socially relevant, this made-for-cable thriller works, although some of the subject matter is grim. 93m. DIR: David Greene. CAST: Robert

Urich, Megan Gallagher, Brett Cullen, Isabella Hoffmann. 1991

•IN A YEAR OF 13 MOONS ★★★1/2 A man undergoes a sex-change operation to please his male lover, only to be abandoned and forced to deal with the new life he has made for himself. Best appreciated by viewers already familiar with the work of the prolific German filmmaker Rainer Werner Fassbinder; others may find this bleak and visually off-putting film a chore to watch. In German with English subtitles. Not rated; not for kids. 129m. DIR: Rainer Werner Fassbinder. CAST: Volker Spengler, Ingrid Caven, Eva Mattes. 1978

IN COLD BLOOD ★★★★★ A chilling documentary-like re-creation of the senseless murder of a Kansas farm family. This stark black-and-white drama follows two ex-convicts (Robert Blake and Scott Wilson) from the point at which they hatch their plan until their eventual capture and execution. This is an emotionally powerful film that is not for the faint of heart. B&W; 134m. DIR: Richard Brooks. CAST: Robert Blake, Scott Wilson, John Forsythe, Jeff Corey. 1967

IN COUNTRY ★★★1/2 A Kentucky teenager (Emily Lloyd) tries to understand the Vietnam War and why her father had to die in this uneven but well-intentioned and ultimately powerful film. Bruce Willis gives an effective performance as Lloyd's uncle, a Vietnam vet who has never fully recovered from his combat experience. Rated R for brief violence and profanity. 106m. DIR: Norman Jewison. CAST: Bruce Willis, Emily Lloyd, Joan Allen, Kevin Anderson, Richard Hamilton, Judith Ivey, Peggy Rea. 1989 DVD

IN CUSTODY ★★ An idealistic schoolteacher in India learns that his idol, renowned as the greatest living poet of the Urdu language, is really a sloppy, dissolute old drunkard. Any film with long passages of poetry will suffer in translation, but even so, this one is a terrible bore, belaboring every little point. In Hindi and Urdu with English subtitles. Not rated; contains mild profanity. 150m. DIR: Ismail Merchant. CAST: Om Puri, Shashi Kapoor. 1994

IN DANGEROUS COMPANY 🐾 Unexciting, glitzy Sidney Sheldon-ish piece has Tracy Scoggins as a beautiful woman who uses her body to square one bad guy off against the other. Rated R for nudity, simulated sex, violence, and language. 92m. DIR: Reuben Preuss. CAST: Tracy Scoggins, Cliff De Young, Chris Mulkey, Henry Darrow, Richard Portnow, Steven Keats. 1988

IN DARK PLACES ★★ Joan Severance stars in this standard erotic thriller as an artist who moves in with the brother she never knew after their father dies, then screws up his life with more-than-sisterly interest. The sex scenes are relatively tame, and the plot is predictable. Rated R for nudity, sexual situations, and profanity. 96m. DIR: James Burke. CAST: Joan Severance, Bryan Kestner, John Vargas. 1997

IN DREAMS ★★1/2 A woman's dreams foretell the murder of her daughter, but the horror doesn't stop there—it seems the killer is actually stalking her through her psychic nightmares. Annette Bening is riveting as the dreamer, and director Neil Jordan gives everything an eerie, otherworld look, but the film suffers from a weak third act and the miscasting of Robert Downey Jr., unintentionally comical as the killer. Rated R for violence and profanity. 100m. DIR: Neil Jordan. CAST: Annette Bening, Robert Downey Jr., Aidan Quinn, Stephen Rea, Paul Guilfoyle. 1999 DVD

IN EARLY ARIZONA ★★★1/2 In this big-budget B, Wild Bill Elliott tames the town of Tombstone by getting rid of the evil Harry Woods. A fine example of this type of Western lore. Plenty of action and energy. B&W; 53m. DIR: Joseph Levering. CAST: William Elliott, Harry Woods, Charles King. 1938

IN GOLD WE TRUST 🐾 Renegade MIAs in Southeast Asia murder their own rescue party to steal the ransom money. Insipid. Not rated, contains profanity and violence. 89m. DIR: P. Chalong. CAST: Jan-Michael Vincent, Sam Jones, James Phillips, Michi McGee, Sherrie Rose. 1990

IN HARM'S WAY ★★ John Wayne leads the United States Navy into a monumental struggle against the Japanese. Kirk Douglas is the antihero who stirs up a fuss. The ships are models and the battles are conducted in a bathtub. It's too big and too long. B&W; 167m. DIR: Otto Preminger. CAST: John Wayne, Kirk Douglas, Patricia Neal, Tom Tryon, Paula Prentiss, Brandon de Wilde, Stanley Holloway, Jill Haworth, Burgess Meredith, Henry Fonda, Dana Andrews, Franchot Tone, Patrick O'Neal. 1965

IN HIS FATHER'S SHOES ★★★1/2 A young boy finds magical shoes and literally gets the opportunity to "walk in his father's footsteps." While shedding no new light on the battles between parent and child, the story demonstrates—without being shrill—just how much things have changed for black Americans. This one deserves to be watched by all members of the family, with its implications discussed later. Rated G; suitable for all ages. 105m. DIR: Vic Sarin. CAST: Lou Gossett Jr., Barbara Eve Harris, Rachel Crawford, Dejanet Sears, Robert Richard. 1997

IN-LAWS, THE ★★★★ This delightful caper comedy mixes mystery and action with the fun. Vince Ricardo (Peter Falk) is the mastermind behind a bold theft of engravings of U.S. currency from a Treasury Department armored car. Sheldon Kornpett (Alan Arkin) is a slightly neurotic dentist. Soon they're off on a perilous mission. Falk and Arkin make a great team, playing off each other brilliantly. Rated PG. 103m. DIR: Arthur Hiller. CAST: Peter Falk, Alan Arkin, Penny Peyser, Michael Lembeck. 1979

IN LIKE FLINT ★★★ James Coburn's smooth portrayal of super-secret agent Derek Flint is ample reason to catch this spy spoof, the sequel to *Our Man Flint*. An evil organization is substituting duplicates for all the world's leaders. Jerry Goldsmith contributes another droll jazz score. Not rated; suitable for family viewing. 114m. DIR: Gordon Douglas. CAST: James Coburn, Lee J. Cobb, Jean Hale, Andrew Duggan. 1967

IN LOVE AND WAR ★★★ James Woods portrays navy pilot Jim Stockdale who is shot down over enemy territory and suffers POW camp tortures for nearly eight years of war in Vietnam. This emotionally compelling story pays tribute to America's fighting men and the parts their resolute wives play in the politics of bringing their husbands home. Rated R for mature subject matter. 96m. **DIR:** Paul Aaron. **CAST:** James Woods, Jane Alexander, Haing S. Ngor. 1991

IN LOVE AND WAR (1996) ★★1/2 This wartime romance between cub reporter Ernest Hemingway and older nurse Agnes is strong on gauzy atmosphere and weak on passion. Stationed in WWI Italy, Ernie is shot while lugging an Italian infantryman to safety. Agnes saves his leg and wins his heart in a fictionalized affair that plunges the aspiring writer into terminal bitterness. Rated PG-13 for graphic battle injuries and suggested sex. 115m. **DIR:** Richard Attenborough. **CAST:** Sandra Bullock, Chris O'Donnell, Ingrid Lacey, Emilio Bonnucci, Mackenzie Astin. 1996 DVD

IN LOVE WITH AN OLDER WOMAN ★★1/2 San Francisco lawyer John Ritter falls in love with a woman fifteen years older than him. They move in together. Made-for-TV movie (can't you tell?), though not bad. 96m. **DIR:** Jack Bender. **CAST:** John Ritter, Karen Carlson, Jamie Rose, Jeff Altman. 1982

IN NAME ONLY ★★★1/2 This is a classic soap opera. Cary Grant is desperately in love with sweet and lovely Carole Lombard. Unfortunately, he's married to venomous Kay Francis. You can't help but get completely wrapped up in the skillfully executed story. B&W; 102m. **DIR:** John Cromwell. **CAST:** Carole Lombard, Cary Grant, Kay Francis, Charles Coburn, Helen Vinson, Peggy Ann Garner. 1939

IN NOME DEL PAPA RE (IN THE NAME OF THE POPE-KING) ★★★★ A compelling drama of intrigue, political conflict, and murder. In 1867, as Italian patriots fight to unify their country, an affluent public official's resignation is complicated when his son becomes a prime suspect in the bombing of a military barracks. Nino Manfredi's performance netted him a best actor award at the Paris Film Festival. In Italian with English subtitles. Not rated; contains profanity and violence. 115m. **DIR:** Luigi Magni. **CAST:** Nino Manfredi. 1987

IN OLD AMARILLO ★★★1/2 A severe range drought that threatens ranchers is compounded by a vicious ranch foreman who plans to profit from the disaster. Another in the ahead-of-their-time environmental Roy Rogers contemporary Westerns. B&W; 67m. **DIR:** William Witney. **CAST:** Roy Rogers, Estelita Rodriguez, Penny Edwards, Pinky Lee, Roy Barcroft. 1951

IN OLD ARIZONA ★★ The first Western talkie and the first sound film made outdoors is also the first movie to spawn a series. Warner Baxter (in his Oscarwinning role) plays O. Henry's Mexican bandido, the Cisco Kid, changing the concept to suit his personality. The Cisco Kid was originally a parody on Billy the Kid. Baxter gave him an accent, an eagerness to enjoy life, and a girlfriend. The movie is slow by today's standards, so it is mostly a curiosity piece. B&W; 63m. **DIR:** Raoul Walsh, Irving Cummings. **CAST:** Warner Baxter, Dorothy Burgess, Edmund Lowe, J. Farrell MacDonald. 1929

IN OLD CALIENTE ★★★★ The coming of the Americans to California provides the story to one of Roy Rogers's finest musical Westerns from the early years. Classic Rogers–Gabby Hayes duet, "We're

Not Comin' Out Tonight." B&W; 54m. **DIR:** Joseph Kane. **CAST:** Roy Rogers, Lynne Roberts (Mary Hart), George "Gabby" Hayes, Jack LaRue, Katherine DeMille. 1939

IN OLD CALIFORNIA ★★★ In one of his numerous B-plus pictures for Republic Studios, John Wayne plays a mild-mannered pharmacist who is forced to take up arms when he settles down in a Western town' run by the corrupt Albert Dekker. Director William McGann keeps things moving at a sprightly pace, which is more than one can say of the other films in the series. B&W; 88m. **DIR:** William McGann. **CAST:** John Wayne, Binnie Barnes, Albert Dekker, Helen Parrish, Patsy Kelly, Edgar Kennedy. 1942 DVD

IN OLD CHEYENNE ★★ Forgotten low-budget star Rex Lease takes a backseat to a smart stallion. Predictable old creaker. B&W; 60m. **DIR:** Stuart Paton. **CAST:** Rex Lease, Dorothy Gulliver, Harry Woods, Jay Hunt. 1931

IN OLD CHICAGO ★★★★ Tyrone Power attempts to control Chicago through corruption and vice while his brother, Don Ameche, heads a reform movement. Fast-moving story leading to a spectacular re-creation of the 1871 fire. Supporting Oscar for Alice Brady as their mother (Mrs. O'Leary), who owns the cow that kicks over the lantern that ... B&W; 95m. **DIR:** Henry King. **CAST:** Tyrone Power, Alice Faye, Don Ameche, Alice Brady, Andy Devine, Brian Donlevy, Phyllis Brooks, Tom Brown, Sidney Blackmer, Rondo Hatton. 1938

IN OLD COLORADO ★★1/2 Ma Woods and her fellow "nesters" are fenced in and cut off from water by a big rancher who thinks they've been rustling his cattle. Hopalong Cassidy and the Bar-20 to the rescue. B&W; 65m. **DIR:** Howard Bretherton. **CAST:** William Boyd, Russell Hayden, Andy Clyde, Margaret Hayes, Morris Ankrum (Stepen Morris), Stanley Andrews. 1941

IN OLD MEXICO ★★★ In this suspense-Western, a sequel to *Borderland*, Hopalong Cassidy solves a murder while working in Mexico. A good script plus fine direction and acting make this a sure-bet B Western. B&W; 62m. **DIR:** Edward Venturini. **CAST:** William Boyd, George "Gabby" Hayes, Russell Hayden, Jan Clayton, Glenn Strange. 1938

IN OLD SANTA FE ★★★ As this film proves, Gene Autry was not the first singing cowboy no matter what he claims. Ken Maynard sings here as he'd done a few times before. Introductory Autry film has Gene and Smiley Burnette performing at a dance while Maynard stops the villain. B&W; 64m. **DIR:** David Howard. **CAST:** Ken Maynard, George "Gabby" Hayes, Evalyn Knapp, Gene Autry, Smiley Burnette. 1934

IN PERSON ★★★ Vivacious, shrewish film star flees to a resort incognito and meets a handsome stranger who is totally unimpressed when he learns who she really is. Enjoyable. B&W; 85m. **DIR:** William A. Seiter. **CAST:** Ginger Rogers, George Brent, Alan Mowbray, Grant Mitchell, Samuel S. Hinds, Edgar Kennedy. 1935

IN PRAISE OF OLDER WOMEN ❤ A man's reflections on his various affairs. Rated R. 108m. **DIR:**

George Kaczender. **CAST:** Tom Berenger, Karen Black, Susan Strasberg, Alexandra Stewart. **1978**

IN PURSUIT OF HONOR ★★★★ This thoughtful Depression-era drama is adapted from events concerning the disbanding of the U.S. Cavalry forces. When ordered to oversee the slaughter of their extra horses, an insubordinate lieutenant and sergeant steal the animals in an effort to somehow save their lives. Rated PG-13 for profanity and one horrendous scene of animal extermination. 110m. **DIR:** Ken Olin. **CAST:** Don Johnson, Craig Sheffer, Gabrielle Anwar, Bob Gunton, James B. Sikking, John Dennis Johnston, Rod Steiger. **1995**

IN SEARCH OF ANNA 💙 Pseudo-art movie about an ex-con and a flaky model. 94m. **DIR:** Esben Storm. **CAST:** Richard Moir, Judy Morris, Chris Hayward, Bill Hunter. **1977**

IN SEARCH OF HISTORIC JESUS 💙 Low-budget reenactments of key events in Jesus' life. Rated G. 91m. **DIR:** Henning Schellerup. **CAST:** John Rubinstein, John Anderson, Morgan Brittany, Nehemiah Persoff, John Hoyt. **1979**

IN SEARCH OF THE CASTAWAYS ★★★★ Young Hayley Mills enlists the aid of financial backers Maurice Chevalier and Wilfrid Hyde-White in search for her missing father, a ship captain. Superb special effects depict the many obstacles and natural disasters the searchers must overcome. 100m. **DIR:** Robert Stevenson. **CAST:** Hayley Mills, Maurice Chevalier, George Sanders, Wilfrid Hyde-White, Michael Anderson Jr. **1962**

IN SEARCH OF THE SERPENT OF DEATH 💙 A *Raiders of the Lost Ark* rip-off. Rated R for violence. 97m. **DIR:** Anwar Kawadri. **CAST:** Jeff Fahey, Camilla More. **1989**

IN SELF DEFENSE 💙 Linda Purl testifies against a crazed murderer after the police promise her protection they can't provide in this unimaginative, overacted thriller. Rated PG for substance abuse and violence. 94m. **DIR:** Bruce Seth Green. **CAST:** Linda Purl, Yaphet Kotto, Billy Drago. **1987**

IN SOCIETY ★★1/2 Abbott and Costello are mistaken for pillars of upscale society. Imagine the possibilities. Slick, fast-paced comedy from their initial Universal period. B&W; 75m. **DIR:** Jean Yarbrough. **CAST:** Bud Abbott, Lou Costello, Arthur Treacher, Marion Hutton, Kirby Grant. **1944**

IN THE AFTERMATH: ANGELS NEVER SLEEP ★★ Uneasy mixture of animation and live-action in this sci-fi story concerning an angel sent to assist an Earthman after the nuclear holocaust. The animation and the live action are good, but the two don't gel. A decent attempt to add life to an overworked genre, though. Contains rough language and violence. 85m. **DIR:** Carl Colpaert. **CAST:** Tony Markes, Rainbow Dolan. **1987**

IN THE ARMY NOW ★★ A goofy electronics-store sales clerk joins the military reserves, makes a mess of basic training, and is sent to the desert front lines of a Libyan war where he is befriended by a timid dentist and harassed by a special-forces bully. There are some wild, hilarious moments, but the bombs dropped here are not only by American war planes. Rated PG. 91m. **DIR:** Daniel Petrie Jr. **CAST:** Pauly Shore, David Alan Grier, Lori Petty, Andy Dick, Esai Morales. **1994**

IN THE COLD OF THE NIGHT 💙 Jeff Lester is a man plagued by a nightmare in which he attempts to kill a mysterious woman. Rated R for nudity and violence. 112m. **DIR:** Nico Mastorakis. **CAST:** Jeff Lester, Adrienne Sachs, David Soul, Tippi Hedren. **1990**

IN THE COMPANY OF MEN ★★★★ Bloodied by relationships with women, emasculated by corporate cannibalism, and frustrated by injustices of the twentieth century, a duo of white-collar weasels is intoxicated with thoughts of revenge. Their whipping boy will be the first vulnerable woman they can romantically dupe and dump. This brutal look at misogyny, infected human dynamics, and the ugliness of life in today's business trenches makes no apologies for the evil that lurks in the hearts of men. Rated R for language. 93m. **DIR:** Neil LaBute. **CAST:** Aaron Eckart, Matt Malloy, Stacy Edwards. **1997 DVD**

●**IN THE COMPANY OF SPIES** ★★★★ When one of their agents is arrested in North Korea, the CIA assembles a team to determine what critical piece of information he was trying to deliver, and how to extract him from the country. This made-for-cable original is tense and gritty, and gives a wonderfully accurate portrayal of the inner workings of the CIA (at least, according to the CIA). As an action film, it is easily the equal to Tom Clancy fare, and is chock-full of excitement for the viewer. Not rated; contains profanity and violence. 104m. **DIR:** Tim Matheson. **CAST:** Tom Berenger, Ron Silver, Alice Krige, Arye Gross, Elizabeth Arlen, Clancy Brown. **1999**

IN THE DEEP WOODS ★★1/2 Red herrings abound in this made-for-TV whodunit about a children's-book illustrator who may hold the key to a series of unexplained murders. Despite its hackneyed plot twists, the film remains notable for Anthony Perkins's final role, as a shady private investigator. 93m. **DIR:** Charles Correll. **CAST:** Rosanna Arquette, Anthony Perkins, Will Patton, D. W. Moffett, Christopher Rydell, Amy Ryan, Beth Broderick. **1992**

IN THE GLOAMING ★★★1/2 Christopher Reeve's directorial debut is a moving document of an AIDS-afflicted young man who returns home to die. But this disappointingly brief adaptation of Alice Elliott Dark's story leaves too many dramatic stones unturned, most notably the sister who feels left out by parents who always preferred her brother. Glenn Close is radiant as the mother who tries to grasp as much as she can before her son leaves her forever. Rated PG for theme. 60m. **DIR:** Christopher Reeve. **CAST:** Glenn Close, Robert Sean Leonard, David Strathairn, Bridget Fonda, Whoopi Goldberg. **1997**

IN THE GOOD OLD SUMMERTIME ★★★ Despite its title, most of the action of this remake of the classic romantic comedy *The Shop Around the Corner* takes place in winter. Judy Garland and Van Johnson work in the same music store. They dislike each other, but are unknowingly secret pen pals who have much in common. Truth wins out, but by the time it does, love has struck. Buster Keaton is wasted as comic relief. 102m. **DIR:** Robert Z. Leonard. **CAST:** Judy Garland, Van Johnson, S. Z. Sakall, Buster Keaton, Spring Byington. **1949**

IN THE HEAT OF PASSION ★★1/2 In this case, the end doesn't justify the means as Sally Kirkland leads Nick Corri on a wild sleazefest. She appears to be a bored but fabulously wealthy wife out to have forbidden pleasure with a younger man. Comes in both R and an unrated version, both containing violence, nudity, and profanity. 93m. DIR: Rodman Flender. CAST: Sally Kirkland, Nick Corri, Jack Carter. 1991

IN THE HEAT OF THE NIGHT ★★★★ A rousing murder mystery elevated by the excellent acting of Rod Steiger and Sidney Poitier. Racial tension is created when a rural southern sheriff (Steiger) and a black northern detective reluctantly join forces to solve the crime. The picture received Oscars for best picture and Steiger's performance. 109m. DIR: Norman Jewison. CAST: Sidney Poitier, Rod Steiger, Warren Oates, Lee Grant. 1967

IN THE HEAT OF PASSION II: UNFAITHFUL 💔 When Barry Bostwick and his lover permanently dispose of his wife, they plan to take his inheritance money and live it up. A series of unexpected events, however, makes that plan somewhat impossible to execute and the tension builds to the point of explosion—and a surprise ending. Another erotic thriller that's much more predictable than it is sexy. Rated R for profanity, nudity, and sexual situations. 107m. DIR: Catherine Cyran. CAST: Barry Bostwick, Lesley-Anne Down, Teresa Hill. 1994

IN THE LAND OF THE DEAF ★★★★ The title aptly sums up this excursion into a place few of us have ever visited. Director Nicolas Philibert reveals an entire culture that is perhaps more emotional, communicative, and expressive than that experienced by the hearing. He brings his camera into schools, a wedding, even an apartment-hunting expedition as he dispels misconceptions about the 130 million deaf people worldwide. Quite touching, thanks to sensitivity and truthfulness in every frame. In French with English subtitles. Not rated. 99m. DIR: Nicolas Philibert. 1993

IN THE LINE OF DUTY: AMBUSH IN WACO ★★★1/2 Riveting, up-to-the-minute TV drama about self-proclaimed evangelical leader David Koresh, and his magnetic hold on his followers. Events depict Koresh's battle with the government, when he held the Bureau of Alcohol, Tobacco and Firearms at bay until a deadly showdown lit the skies of Waco, Texas. Powerful performances from Tim Daly as Koresh, and Dan Lauria as the bureau captain who takes control of the siege. Rated R for violence. 93m. DIR: Dick Lowry. CAST: Timothy Daly, Dan Lauria, William O'Leary. 1993

IN THE LINE OF FIRE ★★★1/2 This is the ultimate *Dirty Harry* movie. Even though Clint Eastwood plays Secret Service agent Frank Horrigan (instead of Harry Callahan), this film is to his cop movies what *Unforgiven* is to his Westerns. Fans of the detective series will recognize familiar plot elements as Eastwood attempts to prevent psycho John Malkovich from assassinating the president. Rated R for violence and profanity. 135m. DIR: Wolfgang Petersen. CAST: Clint Eastwood, John Malkovich, René Russo, Dylan McDermott, Gary Cole, Fred Dalton Thompson, John McHoney. 1993 DVD

IN THE MOOD ★★1/2 Patrick Dempsey plays a conniving teenager who becomes a media star by repeatedly marrying older women. Although this period (1940s) comedy has some funny bits and lines, the story is slapdash. Rated PG-13. 100m. DIR: Phil Alden Robinson. CAST: Patrick Dempsey, Talia Balsam, Beverly D'Angelo, Michael Constantine, Kathleen Freeman. 1987

IN THE MOUTH OF MADNESS ★★★1/2 John Carpenter's creepy take on a popular horror author who mysteriously disappears and the private investigator hired to locate him after his latest book causes readers to go insane. Paired with the author's editor, the P.I. seeks out the author and finds him in the fictional town featured in the book. Carpenter draws a thin line between reality and illusion and keeps the audience guessing. Rated R for violence and language. 95m. DIR: John Carpenter. CAST: Sam Neill, Julie Carmen, Jurgen Prochnow, Charlton Heston. 1995 DVD

•IN THE NAME OF JUSTICE 💔 Citizens pose as government agents to get revenge on the drug lord who killed their loved ones. No-budget action film that slips into incompetence. Rated R for violence, profanity, nudity, and sex. 95m. DIR: John R. Poague. CAST: Jerry Trimble, Paul R. Ellis. 1998

IN THE NAME OF THE FATHER ★★★★ This political thriller is based on the true story of Gerry Conlon, an Irish youth accused of a crime he didn't commit. Conlon is enjoying the freewheeling lifestyle of the swinging '60s in London and has an antiestablishment attitude, but he isn't guilty of the terrorist bombing for which he and his innocent father are arrested. Emma Thompson adds vitality to the courtroom scenes as she attempts to prove their innocence. Riveting and brilliantly acted. Rated R for violence and profanity. 125m. DIR: Jim Sheridan. CAST: Daniel Day-Lewis, Emma Thompson, Pete Postlethwaite. 1993

IN THE PRESENCE OF MINE ENEMIES ★★★ Rod Serling's 1960 *Playhouse 90* television script has lost some of its edge since its original appearance. Armin Mueller-Stahl stars as a rabbi trying to retain his hope and dignity amid the atrocities committed by the Nazis who control the Warsaw ghetto where he lives. His attempt to find God's greater meaning in all acts of casual cruelty eventually drives him mad. Interesting, but more of a period piece at this point. Rated PG-13 for violence and dramatic intensity. 100m. DIR: Joan Micklin Silver. CAST: Armin Mueller-Stahl, Charles Dance, Elina Lowensohn, Don McKellar, Chad Lowe. 1997

IN THE REALM OF PASSION ★★★ Nagisa Oshima, Japan's most controversial director, scores some high and low points with this erotic, metaphysical ghost story about a woman who, along with her lover, kills her husband only to suffer a haunting by his vengeful spirit. Excellent performances by both leads along with some impressive atmospheric cinematography. In Japanese with English subtitles. Not rated; contains nudity and violence. 108m. DIR: Nagisa Oshima. CAST: Kazuko Yoshiyuki, Tatsuya Fuji. 1980 DVD

IN THE REALM OF THE SENSES ★★ Uneasy blend of pornography and art in this tale of sexual obsession. Director Nagisa Oshima delves into the mystery of human sexuality, but comes away with a shallow pretentious result. In Japanese with English subtitles. Rated X for its depiction of sex. 104m. DIR: Nagisa Oshima. CAST: Tatsuya Fuji, Eiko Matsuda. 1976 DVD

IN THE SHADOW OF KILIMANJARO 🎬 The supposedly true story of what happened in Kenya when ninety thousand baboons went on a killing spree because of the 1984 drought. Rated R for violence. 97m. DIR: Raju Patel. CAST: John Rhys-Davies, Timothy Bottoms, Irene Miracle, Michele Carey. 1986

IN THE SHADOW OF THE SUN ★★1/2 Interesting but overlong experimental film by Derek Jarman. This multilayered, hypnotic, nonlinear film was shot in Super-8 at the cost of $200 and features a dizzying soundtrack with the music of Throbbing Gristle and Chris Carter. Not rated. 54m. DIR: Derek Jarman. 1974

•**IN THE SHADOWS** ★★1/2 Writer-director Meg Richman updates Henry James's *The Wings of the Dove*, and despite modern sensibilities, the translation fails to capture the heart of the story. A waitress agrees to take care of a terminally ill rich woman, played by Joely Richardson, and sees an opportunity to have her cake and eat it too. The film lacks the emotional impact of the 1997 version. Also released as *Under Heaven*. Rated R for adult situations and language. 112m. DIR: Meg Richman. CAST: Molly Parker, Joely Richardson, Aden Young. 1998 DVD

IN THE SOUP ★★ Very bizarre movie in which an aspiring film writer finds an extremely strange man to help him finance his script. Don't expect to laugh during this film, unless you like off-the-wall humor. Not rated; contains nudity and profanity. 96m. DIR: Alexandre Rockwell. CAST: Seymour Cassel, Steve Buscemi, Jennifer Beals, Will Patton, Stanley Tucci, Pat Moya, Jim Jarmusch, Carol Kane. 1992

IN THE SPIRIT ★★★1/2 Marlo Thomas stands out in a top-flight cast as a lovable New Age nut who involves a hapless married couple (Elaine May, Peter Falk) in murder and mayhem when her protégé, a prostitute (Jeannie Berlin), is found dead. Berlin, May's daughter, co-wrote the script. Rated R for profanity and violence. 95m. DIR: Sandra Seacat. CAST: Jeannie Berlin, Olympia Dukakis, Peter Falk, Melanie Griffith, Elaine May, Marlo Thomas. 1990

IN THE TIME OF BARBARIANS 🎬 Doran, the good barbarian king of Armana, faces danger as he pursues an evil marauder across his lands and into present-day Los Angeles. Rated R for violence and nudity. 96m. DIR: Joseph L. Barmettler. CAST: Deron Michael McBee, Jo Ann Ayres. 1990

IN THE TIME OF BARBARIANS II ★★ Wandering swordsman Galen finds service with the good guys as two sisters battle for the throne of a magical land. Falling in love with a beautiful princess, he soon finds that his employer is not as pure as he once thought. Rated R for violence and nudity. 85m. DIR: Ricardo Jacques Gale. CAST: Diana Frank, Lenore Andriel, Tom Schultz. 1992

IN THE WHITE CITY ★★★ A naval mechanic leaves his ship in Lisbon. He wanders the city, photographing it with his Super-8 camera, and sends the films back to his wife to explain why he won't come home. An elegantly photographed but slow-moving mood piece. In French with English subtitles. Not rated. 108m. DIR: Alain Tanner. CAST: Bruno Ganz, Teresa Madruga. 1983

IN THIS OUR LIFE ★★★1/2 The best Bette Davis movies are those in which she must work to keep the spotlight, such as when paired with skillful Olivia de Havilland. They play sisters in love with the same man (Dennis Morgan). Humphrey Bogart and the cast of *The Maltese Falcon* have walk-ons in a bar scene. B&W; 97m. DIR: John Huston. CAST: Bette Davis, Olivia de Havilland, Dennis Morgan, Charles Coburn, George Brent, Hattie McDaniel, Frank Craven, Billie Burke, Lee Patrick. 1942

•**IN TOO DEEP** ★★1/2 An undercover cop finds himself growing a little too close to the drug kingpin he's supposed to be working against. Smooth direction and first-rate acting almost—but not quite—overcome a dreary, cliché-ridden script. Rated R for violence and profanity. 104m. DIR: Michael Rymer. CAST: Omar Epps, Nia Long, LL Cool J, Veronica Webb, Pam Grier, Stanley Tucci. 1999 DVD

IN WHICH WE SERVE ★★★★★ Noel Coward wrote, produced, directed, and acted in this, one of the most moving wartime portrayals of men at sea. It is not the stirring battle sequences that make this film stand out but the intimate human story of the crew, their families, and the ship they love. A great film in all respects. B&W; 115m. DIR: Noel Coward, David Lean. CAST: Noel Coward, John Mills, Michael Wilding. 1942

INCIDENT, THE (1967) ★★★1/2 Gritty inner-city horror story takes place on a late-night subway ride as two young thugs (Martin Sheen and Tony Musante, in their first film) terrorize each of the passengers. Definitely worth a watch! Not rated; contains violence. B&W; 99m. DIR: Larry Peerce. CAST: Tony Musante, Martin Sheen, Beau Bridges, Donna Mills, Gary Merrill, Thelma Ritter, Ruby Dee. 1967

INCIDENT, THE (1989) ★★1/2 During World War II, a small-town lawyer (Walter Matthau) finds himself railroaded by a powerful judge (Harry Morgan) into defending an accused murderer (Peter Firth). The problem is that Matthau's client is a German soldier from a nearby POW camp, where he allegedly killed the town doctor (Barnard Hughes), who was also the lawyer's longtime friend. Well-done. Made for TV. 94m. DIR: Joseph Sargent. CAST: Walter Matthau, Harry Morgan, Robert Carradine, Susan Blakely, Peter Firth, Barnard Hughes. 1989

INCIDENT AT DARK RIVER ★★ Predictable environmental-pollution teledrama is nonetheless enjoyable, due largely to reliable Mike Farrell (who also wrote the story). A battery factory is dumping nasty things in the river out back—and denying everything. 94m. DIR: Michael Pressman. CAST: Mike Farrell, Tess Harper, Helen Hunt. 1989

INCIDENT AT DECEPTION RIDGE ★★★1/2 In this taut little thriller, newly released ex-con Michael O'Keefe gets involved with some nasty types trying to recover a suitcase filled with stolen cash, and the chase is on. Folks annoyed by this genre's frequent reliance on gore will be pleased by Randy Kornfield and Ken Hixon's script, which downplays needless violence in favor of genuine suspense. Rated PG-13 for profanity and mild violence. 94m. **DIR:** John McPherson. **CAST:** Michael O'Keefe, Ed Begley Jr., Miguel Ferrer, Linda Purl, Michelle Johnson, Colleen Flynn. 1994

INCIDENT AT OGLALA ★★★★ Director Michael Apted and the Native Americans interviewed in this documentary make a compelling case for a retrial of Leonard Peltier, a leader in the American Indian Movement who is now serving two consecutive life terms for his alleged murder of two FBI agents during a confrontation. Apted somewhat fictionalized the conflicts between traditionalist Indians and their "mixed-blood" tribal leaders in *Thunderheart*, which should be viewed before watching this heartrending documentary. Rated PG. 93m. **DIR:** Michael Apted. 1992 DVD

INCOGNITO ★★1/2 This romance-thriller undercuts its suspense by exposing its ending and then flashing back to a caper gone sour. A globetrotting art forger negotiates with an oily trio of art dealers to paint a fake Rembrandt. He also discusses life's nuances with his ailing mentor father and has sex with a European art expert he mistakes for a student. The details of the art forgery are fascinating, but the forger's extracurricular activities are boring. Rated R for language, nudity, and suggested sex. 109m. **DIR:** John Badham. **CAST:** Jason Patric, Irène Jacob, Rod Steiger, Ian Richardson. 1998 DVD

INCONVENIENT WOMAN, AN ★★ Dominick Dunne's celebrated novel arrives as a made-for-TV soap opera with murder, double crosses, and plenty of scenery chewing. Great cast makes the best of a mediocre situation. 126m. **DIR:** Larry Elikann. **CAST:** Rebecca DeMornay, Jason Robards Jr., Jill Eikenberry, Peter Gallagher. 1991

INCREDIBLE HULK, THE ★★1/2 Bill Bixby is sincere in the role of Dr. David Banner, a scientist whose experiments with gamma rays result in his being transformed into a huge green creature (Lou Ferrigno) whenever something angers him. Pilot for the series is a lot of fun, with better production values than most TV efforts. Based on the Marvel Comics character. 100m. **DIR:** Kenneth Johnson. **CAST:** Bill Bixby, Susan Sullivan, Lou Ferrigno, Jack Colvin, Charles Siebert. 1977

INCREDIBLE HULK RETURNS, THE ★★ First of three made-for-TV movies based on the series. The script dumbs down the muscle-bound Hulk and, in introducing fellow Marvel Comics hero Thor, creates an even dumber character. Not rated, but suitable for the kiddies. 96m. **DIR:** Nicholas Corea. **CAST:** Lou Ferrigno, Bill Bixby, Eric Allen Kramer, Charles Napier, Lee Purcell, Tim Thomerson. 1988

INCREDIBLE JOURNEY, THE ★★★★1/2 This live-action Walt Disney film is the story of two dogs and a cat that make a treacherous journey across Canada to find their home and family. It's impossible to dislike this heartwarming tale. 80m. **DIR:** Fletcher Markle. **CAST:** Emile Genest, John Drainie. 1963

INCREDIBLE JOURNEY OF DR. MEG LAUREL, THE ★★★1/2 In this made-for-television film, Lindsay Wagner stars as Meg Laurel. From humble beginnings as an orphan from the Appalachian Mountains, she becomes a doctor. After graduating from Harvard Medical School, she sets up practice in 1930s Boston. But Wagner decides to return to the mountain people and administer the latest in medical procedures. 150m. **DIR:** Guy Green. **CAST:** Lindsay Wagner, Jane Wyman, Dorothy McGuire, James Woods, Gary Lockwood, Charles Tyner, Andrew Duggan, Brock Peters, John C. Reilly. 1978

INCREDIBLE MELTING MAN, THE ★★ Superb makeup by Rick Baker highlights this story of an astronaut (Alex Rebar) who contracts a strange ailment that results in his turning into a gooey, melting mess upon his return to Earth. Wild stuff. Rated R for terminal grossness. 86m. **DIR:** William Sachs. **CAST:** Alex Rebar, Burr DeBenning, Myron Healey, Ann Sweeney. 1978

INCREDIBLE MR. LIMPET, THE ★★ What can you say about a film whose hero is a fishbowl fancier who wishes himself into a fish so he can help the U.S. Navy defeat enemy submarines during World War II? Don Knotts as Henry Limpet is guilty as charged. Although popular with children, this outré excursion into fantasy will leave most viewers scratching their scales and flapping their gills wondering why on earth it was ever made. 102m. **DIR:** Arthur Lubin. **CAST:** Don Knotts, Carole Cook, Jack Weston, Andrew Duggan, Larry Keating. 1964

INCREDIBLE PETRIFIED WORLD, THE 🖓 Stupefying concoction, set almost entirely in a diving bell. B&W; 78m. **DIR:** Jerry Warren. **CAST:** John Carradine, Phyllis Coates. 1958

INCREDIBLE ROCKY MOUNTAIN RACE, THE ★★★ This Western with a comic touch is about a race used by townspeople to get rid of two troublemakers. These troublemakers include Mark Twain (Christopher Connelly) and his archenemy, Mike Fink (Forrest Tucker). There is more comedy as the snags increase and the problems get out of hand. Rated G. 97m. **DIR:** James L. Conway. **CAST:** Christopher Connelly, Forrest Tucker, Larry Storch, Jack Kruschen, Mike Mazurki. 1985

INCREDIBLE SARAH, THE ★★ As the legendary French actress Sarah Bernhardt—in her time the toast of Paris, London, and New York—Glenda Jackson tears passions to tatters, to very rags. Theater history buffs may like this pseudobiography. 106m. **DIR:** Richard Fleischer. **CAST:** Glenda Jackson, Daniel Massey, Yvonne Mitchell. 1976

INCREDIBLE SHRINKING MAN, THE ★★★★ Good special effects as a man (Grant Williams), exposed to a strange radioactive mist, finds himself becoming smaller ... and smaller ... and smaller. Well-mounted thriller from Universal with many memorable scenes, including the classic showdown with an ordinary house spider. B&W; 81m. **DIR:** Jack Arnold. **CAST:** Grant Williams, Randy Stuart, Paul Langton, April Kent. 1957

INCREDIBLE SHRINKING WOMAN, THE ★★ This comedy, starring Lily Tomlin, falls prey to the law of diminishing returns. But to simply dismiss it as a failure would be inaccurate and unfair. This comic adaptation of Richard Matheson's classic science-fiction novel (*The Shrinking Man*) is not a bad movie. It's more like ... well ... the perfect old-fashioned Disney movie—a little corny and strained at times but not a total loss. Rated PG. 88m. **DIR:** Joel Schumacher. **CAST:** Lily Tomlin, Ned Beatty, Henry Gibson, Elizabeth Wilson, Charles Grodin, Pamela Bellwood, Mike Douglas, Mark Blankfield. 1981

INCREDIBLE TWO-HEADED TRANSPLANT, THE ❤ A sadistic killer's head is grafted to the body of a dimwitted giant. Rated PG. 88m. **DIR:** Anthony M. Lanza. **CAST:** Bruce Dern, Pat Priest, Casey Kasem. 1971

INCREDIBLY STRANGE CREATURES WHO STOPPED LIVING AND BECAME MIXED-UP ZOMBIES, THE ❤ This movie doesn't live up to its title; how could it? It was later released as *Teenage Psycho Meets Bloody Mary*. 81m. **DIR:** Ray Dennis Steckler. **CAST:** Cash Flagg, Brett O'Hara, Carolyn Brandt, Atlas King. 1965

INCREDIBLY TRUE ADVENTURE OF TWO GIRLS IN LOVE, THE ★★1/2 Two high-school students discover a flirtatious attraction that ripens into physical love. Writer-director Maria Maggenti tries for a lighthearted girl-meets-girl romance, but her writing is flat, her directing awkward, and the ending dissolves in chaos. Laurel Holloman and Nicole Parker are appealing in the title roles, but the supporting cast is largely inept. Rated R for profanity and nudity. 94m. **DIR:** Maria Maggenti. **CAST:** Laurel Holloman, Nicole Parker. 1995

INDECENCY ★★★ A suspenseful whodunit about the murder of an ad agency owner. Was it the soon-to-be ex-husband, the partner who was sleeping with the husband, or the drug dealer? Good plot and good acting make this an enjoyable film. Rated PG-13 for sensuality and profanity. 88m. **DIR:** Marisa Silver. **CAST:** Jennifer Beals, Sammi Davis, James Remar, Barbara Williams, Christopher John Fields. 1992

INDECENT OBSESSION, AN ★★★ A bleak, intense view of the results of war. Wendy Hughes is the compassionate nurse for shell-shocked British soldiers and other war-torn crazies. A sensitive adaptation of Colleen McCullough's bestseller. Not rated; contains violence, nudity, and profanity. 100m. **DIR:** Lex Marinos. **CAST:** Wendy Hughes, Gary Sweet, Richard Moir. 1985

INDECENT PROPOSAL ★★1/2 Good performances cannot save this brainless soap opera. Extremely wealthy Robert Redford offers $1 million to married Demi Moore if she'll spend the night with him. Naturally, Moore and her hubby, a whining, less-than-effective Woody Harrelson, are in deep financial trouble and the rest of the film is just as predictable. Rated R for profanity, nudity, and simulated sex. 113m. **DIR:** Adrian Lyne. **CAST:** Robert Redford, Demi Moore, Woody Harrelson, Oliver Platt, Seymour Cassel. 1993

INDEPENDENCE DAY ★★★★ Excellent little story about a young woman (Kathleen Quinlan) who wants to leave the stifling environment of her hometown. She's helped and hindered by a growing attachment to David Keith, a garage mechanic with his own problems. Rated R for violence and sex. 110m. **DIR:** Robert Mandel. **CAST:** David Keith, Kathleen Quinlan, Richard Farnsworth, Frances Sternhagen, Cliff De Young, Dianne Wiest. 1983

INDEPENDENCE DAY (1996) ★★★★1/2 The best retro science-fiction epic since George Lucas released *Star Wars* is also a distant cousin to the 1970s disaster flick: a slam-bang, thrill-a-minute effort that truly puts the motion in "motion picture." With a nod to H. G. Wells's *War of the Worlds*, this film is a star-studded tale of extraterrestrial invasion, human dignity, and good ol' American know-how. Bill Pullman makes a grand United States president; Jeff Goldblum is the absentminded scientist who ultimately saves the day. But the Oscar-winning special effects carry this high-octane actionfest. Rated PG-13 for profanity and violence. 145m. **DIR:** Roland Emmerich. **CAST:** Will Smith, Bill Pullman, Jeff Goldblum, Mary McDonnell, Judd Hirsch, Margaret Colin, Randy Quaid, Robert Loggia, Brent Spiner. 1996 DVD

INDESTRUCTIBLE MAN ★★ Lon Chaney looks uncomfortable in the title role of an electrocuted man brought back to life who seeks revenge on the old gang who betrayed him. Nothing new has been added to the worn-out story, unless you want to count the awful narration, which makes this passable thriller seem utterly ridiculous at times. B&W; 70m. **DIR:** Jack Pollexfen. **CAST:** Lon Chaney Jr., Marian Carr, Ross Elliott, Casey Adams. 1956 DVD

INDIAN IN THE CUPBOARD, THE ★★★1/2 Children familiar with Lynne Reid Banks's original story may be disappointed with this big-screen adaptation, which leaves out several important characters and events. Judged on its own merits, however, this is an entertaining, sometimes fascinating tale of a young boy who discovers a way to bring his toys alive. Even adults will find it worth watching. Rated PG. 96m. **DIR:** Frank Oz. **CAST:** Hal Scardino, Litefoot, Lindsay Crouse, Richard Jenkins, Rishi Bhat, David Keith, Steve Coogan. 1995

INDIAN RUNNER, THE ★★★1/2 As a first-time director, actor Sean Penn has fashioned a movie that's not unlike one of his better performances—edgy, rough-hewn, daring, passionate, and fascinating. His movie revolves around the conflicts arising from two brothers as unalike as Cain and Abel. Though a box-office failure, *The Indian Runner* offers hope for a substantial directorial career from Penn. Rated R, with profanity and violence. 125m. **DIR:** Sean Penn. **CAST:** David Morse, Viggo Mortensen, Valeria Golino, Patricia Arquette, Charles Bronson, Sandy Dennis. 1991

INDIAN SUMMER ★★★ This amiable, warmhearted comedy is best described as *The Big Chill* goes to summer camp. An Ontario camp director invites his favorite kids from the "golden years" of the early 1970s back for a twenty-year reunion. It's a movie full of big grins and tolerable, skin-deep goo. Rated PG-13 for language, drug use, and simulated sex. 98m. **DIR:** Mike Binder. **CAST:** Alan Arkin, Matt Craven, Diane Lane, Bill Paxton, Elizabeth Perkins, Kevin Pollak, Sam Raimi, Vincent Spano, Julie Warner, Kimberly Williams. 1993

INDIAN UPRISING ★★ The surrender of Apache Indian Chief, Geronimo—here, highly fictionalized to involve mercenary white men and heroic cavalry men. Although the cassette box lists 74 minutes, this is a severely edited print of an original color film. B&W; 60m. **DIR:** Ray Nazarro. **CAST:** George Montgomery, Audrey Long, Carl Benton Reid, Joe Sawyer. 1952

INDIANA JONES AND THE LAST CRUSADE ★★★1/2 In the last film of this entertaining cliffhanger series, Indiana Jones embarks on a quest for the Holy Grail when his father disappears while on the same mission. Father and son are soon slugging it out with some nasty Nazis in this all-ages delight. Rated PG-13 for violence and profanity. 127m. **DIR:** Steven Spielberg. **CAST:** Harrison Ford, Sean Connery, Denholm Elliott, John Rhys-Davies, River Phoenix. 1989

INDIANA JONES AND THE TEMPLE OF DOOM ★★★★ This sequel is almost as good as the original, *Raiders of the Lost Ark*. The story takes place before the events of *Raiders* with its two-fisted, whip-wielding hero, Dr. Indiana Jones (Harrison Ford) performing feats of derring-do in Singapore and India circa 1935. Parents may want to see this fast-paced and sometimes scary film before allowing their kids to watch it. Rated PG for profanity and violence. 118m. **DIR:** Steven Spielberg. **CAST:** Harrison Ford, Kate Capshaw. 1984

INDICTMENT: THE MCMARTIN TRIAL ★★★★1/2 Producer Oliver Stone and cowriter Abby Mann positively excoriate the Los Angeles–area preschool legal and media circus that lasted 2,489 days, destroyed the lives of defendants, and ultimately failed to find any of them guilty. Overzealous prosecutors and a child therapist with questionable credentials emerge as the villains, while defense attorney James Woods eventually becomes galvanic with righteous indignation. The entire cast in this HBO-made film is excellent. Rated R for profanity and brief nudity. 132m. **DIR:** Mick Jackson. **CAST:** James Woods, Mercedes Ruehl, Sada Thompson, Henry Thomas, Shirley Knight, Lolita Davidovich. 1995

INDIO ★★ Marvin Hagler stars as a half-breed Marine Corps officer who returns to his native land in the Amazon to find that developers have ravaged the countryside and his people. As a former U.S. army colonel, Brian Dennehy brings a little class to an otherwise routine *Rambo* rip-off. Rated R for violence and profanity. 94m. **DIR:** Anthony M. Dawson. **CAST:** Francesco Quinn, Brian Dennehy, Marvin Hagler. 1989

INDIO 2: THE REVOLT 🎦 Marvelous Marvin Hagler isn't so marvelous as Sergeant Iron, a U.S. Marine leading Amazonian tribes against greedy developers. Not rated; contains violence. 104m. **DIR:** Anthony M. Dawson. **CAST:** Marvin Hagler, Charles Napier, Frank Cuervo. 1990

INDISCREET (1931) 🎦 Gloria Swanson trying to conceal her questionable past. B&W; 92m. **DIR:** Leo McCarey. **CAST:** Gloria Swanson, Ben Lyon, Arthur Lake. 1931

INDISCREET (1958) ★★1/2 Dated comedy about an on-again, off-again affair between rich actress Ingrid Bergman and playboy bachelor Cary Grant. These stars could make anything watchable, but this isn't

one of their best. 100m. **DIR:** Stanley Donen. **CAST:** Cary Grant, Ingrid Bergman, Cecil Parker. 1958

INDISCREET (1998) 🎦 Another B-grade sex thriller with a Z-grade plot: A detective falls in love with the woman he's been hired to follow, the wife of a millionaire who ends up dead. Of course. No matter what they call it, it's the same direct-to-video movie you've seen before. Rated R for violence, language, and adult situations. 95m. **DIR:** Marc Beinstock. **CAST:** Luke Perry, Gloria Reuben, Adam Baldwin, Peter Coyote. 1998

INDISCRETION OF AN AMERICAN WIFE ★★1/2 One hour and three minutes of emotional turmoil played out against the background of Rome's railway station as adultress Jennifer Jones meets her lover, Montgomery Clift, for the last time. B&W; 63m. **DIR:** Vittorio De Sica. **CAST:** Jennifer Jones, Montgomery Clift, Gino Cervi, Richard Beymer. 1954 DVD

INDOCHINE ★★★★1/2 Set in French Indochina in 1930, this exquisite import chronicles the violent changes that led to the creation of Vietnam from the ruins of colonialism. Catherine Deneuve is superb in the pivotal role of an Asian-born, French-descended owner of a rubber plantation. In French with English subtitles. Rated PG-13 for violence, nudity, and profanity. 155m. **DIR:** Regis Wargnier. **CAST:** Catherine Deneuve, Vincent Perez, Dan Pham Linh, Jean Yanne. 1992 DVD

INDUSTRIAL SYMPHONY NO. 1 THE DREAM OF THE BROKEN HEARTED ★★★1/2 Bizarre glimpse into a broken love affair set against the backdrop of an industrial wasteland from the director of *Eraserhead*, *Twin Peaks*, and *Wild At Heart*. This surreal opera was performed at The Brooklyn Academy of Music opera house and features an impressive score by composer Angelo Badalamenti, with lyrics by David Lynch. Not rated; contains some nudity. 50m. **DIR:** David Lynch. **CAST:** Laura Dern, Nicolas Cage, Julee Cruise. 1989

INFAMOUS DOROTHY PARKER, THE ★★1/2 A quickie documentary put together for the release of *Mrs. Parker and the Vicious Circle*, this provides a decent background of Parker during her adult years. Entertaining and informative as this may be, the overly slick, intrusive graphics may cause you to scream. Ditto for host Wendy Lieberman. Made for A&E. Not rated. 49m. **DIR:** Robert Yuhas. **CAST:** Wendy Lieberman, Jennifer Jason Leigh, Alan Rudolph, Fran Lebowitz, Campbell Scott, Matthew Broderick, Gloria Steinem. 1994

INFERNO (1980) ★★ This Italian horror flick is heavy on suspense but weak on plot. Leigh McCloskey is the hero who comes to help his sister when she discovers that her apartment is inhabited by an ancient evil spirit. Voices are dubbed, even American actor McCloskey's, and something may have been lost in the translation. Rated R for gore. 83m. Original running time 102m. **DIR:** Dario Argento. **CAST:** Eleonora Giorgi, Leigh McCloskey, Gabriele Lavia. 1980 DVD

•**INFERNO (1998)** ★★★★ Well-made disaster flick tells the story of a burst of radioactive heat from the sun that turns up the Earth's temperature to 145 degrees for several days. The story focuses on the lives of several people and how the heat wave affects them. Rated PG-13 for violence. 90m. **DIR:** Ian Barry. **CAST:** James Remar, Stephanie Niznik, Daniel Von Bargen, Jonathan LaPaglia. 1998

INFERNAL TRIO ★★★1/2 Lurid, stylishly gruesome black comedy about a sociopathic lawyer (Michel Piccoli) who, after seducing two sisters, enlists them to marry and murder victims and defraud their insurance companies. Based on an actual police case. In French with English subtitles. Not rated; contains violence and nudity. 100m. **DIR:** Francis Girod. **CAST:** Romy Schneider, Michel Piccoli, Andrea Ferreol. 1974

INFESTED (TICKS) 🍂 Wood ticks pumped up on herbal steroids crawl under the skin of forest visitors in this low-budget horrorama. Rated R for violence, gore, and language. 85m. **DIR:** Tony Randel. **CAST:** Rosalind Allen, Ami Dolenz, Seth Green, Virginya Keehne, Ray Oriel, Alfonso Ribeiro, Peter Scolari, Dina Dayrit, Michale Medeiros, Barry Lynch, Clint Howard. 1993

INFILTRATOR, THE ★★★ Israeli-American journalist Yaron Svoray's covert penetration of the modern German neo-Nazi movement must have been incredibly perilous, but this screen adaptation makes the whole endeavor seem trite. Oliver Platt is properly dedicated in the central role, and the subject's deadly seriousness is ill-served by this simplistic adaptation of Svoray's book, *In Hitler's Shadow.* Rated R for profanity, violence, nudity, and rape. 102m. **DIR:** John Mackenzie. **CAST:** Oliver Platt, Arliss Howard, Tony Haygarth, Michael Byrne, Julian Glover, Peter Riegert, Alan King. 1995

INFINITY ★★1/2 Star Matthew Broderick makes his directorial debut with this bio-pic of physicist Richard Feynman during World War II, who works on the Manhattan Project in New Mexico while spending weekends with his wife who is dying of tuberculosis. Clearly a labor of love, the film has several fine moments but succumbs to its own earnestly plodding pace and too many disease-of-the-week clichés. Rated PG for profanity and mild sensuality. 119m. **DIR:** Matthew Broderick. **CAST:** Matthew Broderick, Patricia Arquette, Peter Riegert. 1996 DVD

INFORMANT, THE ★★★1/2 An IRA terrorist having unsuccessfully tried to "resign," is roped into a high-profile assassination and then gets caught. Faced with life in prison, he chooses instead to save his own hide by ratting out his former friends and associates. This adaptation of Gerald Seymour's *Field of Blood* becomes yet another intellectual analysis of the Irish "troubles," but this one wears its opinion on its sleeve, showing all IRA participants in a negative light. Rated R for profanity, nudity, rape, simulated sex, and violence. 105m. **DIR:** Jim McBride. **CAST:** Cary Elwes, Anthony Brophy, Timothy Dalton, Maria Lennon, Sean McGinley. 1997

INFORMER, THE ★★★★ John Ford's classic about a slow-witted Irish pug (Victor McLaglen), who turns his friend in for money to impress his ladylove and gets his comeuppance from the IRA, has lost none of its atmospheric punch over the years. McLaglen is superb, and the movie lingers in your memory long after the credits roll. B&W; 91m. **DIR:** John Ford.

CAST: Victor McLaglen, Heather Angel, Preston Foster. 1935

INFRA-MAN ★★1/2 Mainly for kids, this *Ultraman* rip-off, about a giant superhero protecting the Earth from a bunch of crazy-looking monsters, still manages to succeed, despite the lame acting and hokey special effects. Ridiculous but enjoyable. Rated PG. 92m. **DIR:** Hua-Shan. **CAST:** Wang Hsieh. 1976

INHERIT THE WIND (1960) ★★★★★ In this superb film based on the stage play of the notorious Scopes monkey trial, a biology teacher is put on trial for teaching the theory of evolution. The courtroom battle that actually took place between Clarence Darrow and Willian Jennings Bryan could not have been more powerful or stimulating than the acting battle put on by two of America's most respected actors—Spencer Tracy and Fredric March. 127m. **DIR:** Stanley Kramer. **CAST:** Spencer Tracy, Fredric March, Gene Kelly, Dick York, Claude Akins. 1960

•**INHERIT THE WIND** (1999) ★★★★ Time has not diminished the intensity of Jerome Lawrence and Robert E. Lee's grand play, and this film faithfully adapts the 1960 script for which Nedrick Young and Harold Jacob Smith received Oscar nominations. Jack Lemmon stands in for Spencer Tracy, and George C. Scott for Fredric March, in the slightly fictionalized but still-powerful Scopes monkey courtroom battle resulting from one schoolteacher's attempt to teach evolution in Hillsboro High School in 1925. (Indeed, it could be argued that this story became even more timely in the late 1990s.) Scott chews up the scenery grandly as the visiting prosecutor who preaches fire and brimstone, while Lemmon has the quieter—but far more piercing—role as the defender forced to challenge and even humiliate the man he once regarded as a good friend. Beau Bridges comments from the side as the cynical journalist (based on H. L. Mencken) who regarded the trial as the height of absurdity, and Piper Laurie is warm and dignified as Scott's wife. While not quite up to the original, this remake still packs quite a punch. Rated PG for dramatic content. 113m. **DIR:** Daniel Petrie. **CAST:** Jack Lemmon, George C. Scott, Lane Smith, Tom Everett Scott, Kathryn Morris, John Cullum, Piper Laurie, Beau Bridges. 1999

INHERITORS, THE ★★1/2 A mean-spirited Austrian farmer, recently murdered, has left his farm to the ten peasants who work there—not because he likes them, but because he thinks they'll kill each other fighting over it. Meanwhile, the local landowners scheme to get the farm away from the peasants. Gloomy, turgid, pessimistic—writer-director Ruzowitzky seems to share the dead farmer's contempt for humanity. In German with English subtitles. Rated R for mature themes. 90m. **DIR:** Stefan Ruzowitzky. **CAST:** Simon Schwartz, Sophie Rois, Lars Rudolph, Julia Gschnitzer. 1998 DVD

INHUMANOID 🍂 This blindingly inept sci-fi chiller opens with a ridiculously gratuitous sex scene, proceeds through the grotesque murder of a little girl, and then utilizes laughable cardboard sets during a protracted duel between a killer android and the world's dumbest female protagonist. Rated R for nudity, simulated sex, profanity, violence, and gore.

87m. **DIR:** Victoria Muspratt. **CAST:** Richard Grieco, Lara Harris, Corbin Bernsen. 1996

INITIATION OF SARAH, THE ★★ Adequate TV movie features Kay Lenz as a young college girl being victimized by other students during initiation, and her subsequent revenge upon acquiring supernatural powers. Hokey thriller should have been better, judging from the cast. 100m. **DIR:** Robert Day. **CAST:** Kay Lenz, Shelley Winters, Kathryn Crosby, Morgan Brittany, Tony Bill. 1978

INKWELL, THE ★★ This amateurish coming-of-age story has its heart in the right place, but it's a dramatic and comic mess. A decent but troubled African-American teen from New York City and his parents spend their 1976 summer vacation with affluent relatives on Martha's Vineyard. The fashions—especially the bell-bottomed, polyester jumpsuits—are a scream. But the film never draws a credible bead on its characters or their relationships. Rated R for language and suggested sex. 112m. **DIR:** Matty Rich. **CAST:** Larenz Tate, Suzzanne Douglas, Joe Morton, Glynn Turman, Jada Pinkett. 1994

INN OF THE SIXTH HAPPINESS, THE ★★★★ Superb acting marks this heartwarming biography of China missionary Gladys Aylward (Ingrid Bergman). The movie opens with her determined attempt to enter the missionary service and follows her to strife-torn China. The highlight is her cross-country adventure as she leads a group of orphans away from the war zone. 158m. **DIR:** Mark Robson. **CAST:** Ingrid Bergman, Curt Jurgens, Robert Donat. 1958

INNER CIRCLE, THE ★★★1/2 This drama, released within weeks of the dismantling of the Soviet Union, comes along to remind us of the coldly cruel totalitarianism of Josef Stalin. Tom Hulce stars as Ivan Sanshin, a young KGB projectionist who is shocked and thrilled to find himself selected as chief projectionist for the movie buff and dictator. The fact that it's based on a true story, and was filmed entirely in the Kremlin and other parts of Russia, lends authenticity and impact. Rated PG-13. 137m. **DIR:** Andrei Konchalovsky. **CAST:** Tom Hulce, Lolita Davidovich, Bob Hoskins. 1991

INNER SANCTUM ★★1/2 Wheelchair-bound wife Valerie Wildman suspects her husband and new nurse are plotting to drive her insane. The plot's not hot, but the sex in the unrated version is pretty steamy. Available in both a tamer R version and a soft-core unrated version. 90m. **DIR:** Fred Olen Ray. **CAST:** Joseph Bottoms, Margaux Hemingway, Tanya Roberts, Valerie Wildman, William Butler, Brett Clark. 1991

INNER SANCTUM 2 🐢 Another erotic thriller lacking eroticism and thrills. Available in R-rated and unrated versions; both contain profanity, nudity, and sexual situations. 93m. **DIR:** Fred Olen Ray. **CAST:** Michael Nouri, Tracy Brooks Swope, Sandahl Bergman. 1994

INNERSPACE ★★★★ Get this story line: Dennis Quaid is a real astronaut who is miniaturized in order to be injected into the body of a rabbit. By accident the syringe carrying Quaid ends up being injected into the body of hypochondriac Martin Short. Sound weird? It is. Sound funny? We thought so.

Rated PG for profanity and violence. 130m. **DIR:** Joe Dante. **CAST:** Dennis Quaid, Martin Short, Meg Ryan, Kevin McCarthy, Fiona Lewis, Henry Gibson. 1987

INNOCENCE UNPROTECTED ★★★★ Controversial Yugoslavian filmmaker Dusan Makavejev took a 1942 melodrama (the first feature film made in the Serb language), restored and recut it, and added new interviews with its director and cast. He then used it as the basis for a singular collage incorporating other elements of contemporary political importance. The result is alternately ironic, satirical, and serious, but always compelling. In Serb with English subtitles. Not rated. 78m. **DIR:** Dusan Makavejev. 1968

INNOCENT, THE (1976) ★★★★ Some rate this as the most beautiful of all Luchino Visconti's films. Set in a nineteenth-century baronial manor, it's the old tale of the real versus the ideal, but beautifully done. In Italian with English subtitles. Rated R due to some explicit scenes. 115m. **DIR:** Luchino Visconti. **CAST:** Laura Antonelli, Giancarlo Giannini, Jennifer O'Neill. 1976

INNOCENT, THE (1993) ★★★★1/2 Paranoia, fierce sexuality, and an unexpected murder merge in this unusual thriller set against the political backdrop of the cold war. Campbell Scott is the naïve Brit sent to Berlin to work on a top-secret engineering project but is tempted into deep waters by Isabella Rossellini. Anthony Hopkins joins them in an unholy alliance of secrecy and deceit. The little moments tell a lot in this story that heads in surprising directions. Rated R for profanity, nudity, violence, and sexual situations. 99m. **DIR:** John Schlesinger. **CAST:** Anthony Hopkins, Isabella Rossellini, Campbell Scott, Ronald Nitschke. 1993

INNOCENT BLOOD ★★★ Director John Landis returns to his roots with this mostly amusing spin on vampire lore, which finds sultry Anne Parillaud as a selective bloodsucker who feeds only on those deserving to die. Rated R for gore, profanity, explicit sex, and nudity. 112m. **DIR:** John Landis. **CAST:** Anne Parillaud, Robert Loggia, Anthony LaPaglia, Don Rickles. 1992 DVD

INNOCENT MAN, AN ★★★★ Jimmie Rainwood (Tom Selleck) is a decent guy; an airplane mechanic who likes his job and loves his wife. But a mistake by two overzealous undercover detectives changes his simple life into a nightmare. Well directed by Peter Yates, *An Innocent Man* has a solid dramatic story line, and fine performances. Rated R for violence and profanity. 113m. **DIR:** Peter Yates. **CAST:** Tom Selleck, F. Murray Abraham, Laila Robins, David Rasche. 1989

INNOCENT LIES ★★ Creepy thriller finds a detective investigating the death of his best friend. When he's drawn to the victim's sister, he learns that the family is hiding some dark secrets involving the girl and her overly protective brother. Incest theme is a bit touchy for such fare. Not rated; contains adult situations and language. 88m. **DIR:** Patrick DeWolf. **CAST:** Stephen Dorff, Gabrielle Anwar, Adrian Dunbar. 1995

INNOCENT VICTIM ★★★ Lauren Bacall stars as a woman recovering from a nervous breakdown visiting her daughter (Helen Shaver) in England. When Shaver's son dies suddenly, Bacall makes a fateful decision. Fine performances by Bacall and Shaver highlight this quirky little thriller, based on Ruth Rendell's *Tree of Hands*. Rated R for violence and profanity. 100m. DIR: Giles Foster. CAST: Lauren Bacall, Helen Shaver, Peter Firth. 1990

INNOCENTS, THE ★★★★1/2 Henry James's *The Turn of the Screw* becomes a marvelously atmospheric period thriller in director Jack Clayton's hands. Deborah Kerr sparkles as a governess hired to watch over the two motherless young children who inhabit one of those oppressively gloomy British mansions; after spending some time with her new charges, our heroine begins to suspect that they've been possessed by the spirits of former servants who died under unhappy circumstances. Or is she simply imagining things? The film will keep you guessing and proves once and for all that considerable terror can be generated by what is merely suggested, rather than what is shown. Great stuff, but perhaps too intense for young viewers. 100m. DIR: Jack Clayton. CAST: Deborah Kerr, Michael Redgrave, Peter Wyngarde, Megs Jenkins, Pamela Franklin, Martin Stephens. 1961

INQUIRY, THE ★★ Italian-made film about the investigation by a Roman official (Keith Carradine) into the resurrection of Christ. Carradine is fine but Harvey Keitel makes an uneasy Pontius Pilate because of his tough-guy accent. Not rated; contains some nudity and violence. 106m. DIR: Damiano Damiani. CAST: Keith Carradine, Harvey Keitel, Phyllis Logan. 1986

INSECT WOMAN ★★★★ Sachiko Hidari gives an emotionally supercharged performance that gained her a best actress award at the Berlin Film Festival. In this harrowing drama, she plays an impoverished country girl who escapes a brutal existence by fleeing to Tokyo where she finds success as a madam. Director Shohei Imamura weaves a dark and often humorous story with shocking overtones. Winner of Japanese film awards for best actress, director, and film. In Japanese with English subtitles. B&W; 123m. DIR: Shohei Imamura. CAST: Sachiko Hidari. 1963

INSERTS 🎬 Dreary film about a once-great 1930s film director now making porno movies. Rated R. 99m. DIR: John Byrum. CAST: Richard Dreyfuss, Jessica Harper, Bob Hoskins, Veronica Cartwright. 1976

INSIDE ★★★ Scripter Bima Stagg's prison drama opens well but runs out of steam before a highly unsatisfying conclusion. The setting is South Africa in 1988; the game, a round of intense psychological warfare, involving a sadistic police official, his liberal white prisoner, and a black fellow prisoner later given the authority to investigate the situation. Too bad the story can't match the intensity of all three performances. Rated R for violence, torture, profanity, nudity, and simulated sex. 94m. DIR: Arthur Penn. CAST: Nigel Hawthorne, Eric Stoltz, Lou Gossett Jr. 1996

INSIDE DAISY CLOVER ★★ Natalie Wood plays a teenager who wants to be a star. Robert Redford is the matinee idol she marries to get her name in the gossip columns. A grim story about Hollywood that has better performances than plot. 128m. DIR: Robert Mulligan. CAST: Natalie Wood, Robert Redford, Christopher Plummer, Roddy McDowall, Ruth Gordon. 1964

INSIDE MAN, THE ★★★1/2 Inspired by a 1981 incident in which a Soviet submarine ran aground in Sweden, this exciting adventure film really moves. A CIA agent (Dennis Hopper) sets up a young ex-Marine (Gosta Ekman) as the inside man who must investigate the theft of a laser-submarine search device. Check this one out. It's unrated, but contains some strong language. 90m. DIR: Tom Clegg. CAST: Dennis Hopper, Hardy Krüger, Gosta Ekman, Celia Gregory. 1984 DVD

INSIDE MONKEY ZETTERLAND ★★★ Monkey Zetterland is a former teen movie star turned scriptwriter. His extended family includes a mother who's a soap star, a hairdresser brother, a gay sister and her pregnant girlfriend, a pair of terrorists, and his wandering biker dad. The ensemble cast struggles gamely to rise above the erratic script. Rated R for adult situations, profanity, and brief violence. 93m. DIR: Jefery Levy. CAST: Steve Antin, Patricia Arquette, Sandra Bernhard, Sofia Coppola, Tate Donovan, Rupert Everett, Katherine Helmond, Bo Hopkins, Ricki Lake, Debi Mazar, Martha Plimpton. 1992

INSIDE MOVES ★★★★ This is a film that grows on you as the heartwarming story unfolds. With a unique blend of humor and insight, director Richard Donner and screenwriters Valerie Curtin and Barry Levinson provide a captivating look into a very special friendship. John Savage plays a man who, after failing at suicide, succeeds at life with the help of some disabled friends. Rated PG. 113m. DIR: Richard Donner. CAST: John Savage, David Morse, Amy Wright, Tony Burton. 1980

INSIDE OUT (1975) ★★★ An unlikely trio (Telly Savalas, Robert Culp, and James Mason) band together to recover $6 million in gold that Hitler had hidden. The action and suspense in this film should hold most viewers' attention. Rated PG. 98m. DIR: Peter Duffell. CAST: Telly Savalas, Robert Culp, James Mason, Aldo Ray. 1975

INSIDE OUT (1986) ★★1/2 Compelling drama that tackles agoraphobia, the fear of open spaces. Elliott Gould stars as a man who fears leaving his New York apartment; his only contact with the outside world are the phone and delivery services. Rated R for profanity. 87m. DIR: Robert Taicher. CAST: Elliott Gould, Howard Hesseman, Jennifer Tilly, Dana Elcar. 1986

INSIDE THE THIRD REICH ★★★1/2 This made-for-TV miniseries is based on the autobiography of Albert Speer, the German architect who became Hitler's chief builder. Rutger Hauer portrays Speer as a man obsessed with the opportunity to build extensively while being blissfully unaware of the horrors of war around him. 250m. DIR: Marvin J. Chomsky. CAST: Rutger Hauer, Derek Jacobi, Blythe Danner, John Gielgud, Ian Holm, Elke Sommer, Trevor Howard, Robert Vaughn. 1982

•INSIDER, THE ★★★★1/2 When the *60 Minutes* producer gets a tobacco-industry scientist to reveal the darkest secrets of his employers on camera, it seems CBS News has the story of the decade; however, executives at the network are not thrilled with this big scoop and attempt to use their power to influence the news department not to run the story, thus endangering the life of the scientist and his family. Russell Crowe, as the scientist, and Christopher Plummer, as Mike Wallace, give the standout performances, but everything about this drama is first class. Rated R for profanity and an atmosphere of danger. 157m. **DIR:** Michael Mann. **CAST:** Al Pacino, Russell Crowe, Christopher Plummer, Diane Venora, Gina Gershon, Lindsay Crouse. **1999 DVD**

INSIGNIFICANCE ★★ Michael Emil's absolutely wonderful impersonation of Albert Einstein makes this film worth seeing. In 1954 Marilyn Monroe comes to visit Einstein in his hotel room to explain the theory of relativity to him. Charming, but it eventually loses its uniqueness as it incorporates disjunctive symbolic flashbacks into the narrative. Rated R. 110m. **DIR:** Nicolas Roeg. **CAST:** Michael Emil, Theresa Russell, Gary Busey, Tony Curtis, Will Sampson. **1985**

●**INSOMNIA** ★★★★ A former Swedish detective finds himself in Norway on a murder investigation in this harrowing exploration of one man's fall from grace. Jonas Engström, once a highly successful detective, is looking for personal redemption, but instead encounters his personal demons. In his debut, director Erik Skjoldbjærg has created a film that is both suspenseful and unnerving. Once the film casts its spell, you won't be able to close your eyes. In Swedish with English subtitles. Not rated; contains adult situations, language, and violence. 97m. **DIR:** Erik Skjoldbjærg. **CAST:** Stellan Skarsgard, Sverre Anker Ousdal. **1997 DVD**

●**INSPECTOR GADGET** ★★★1/2 Thanks to leaping advancements in special effects and morphing technology, Disney's take on *Inspector Gadget* can be branded the very first wholly live-action cartoon, in every sense of the word (and we mean that as a compliment). Blessed with furious energy and impeccable comic timing, this is gobs o' fun, from the very first second—a spring-laden spoof of the familiar Disney logo—to the very last. The film is further blessed with suitably heroic protagonists, marvelously flamboyant villains, and a director who perfectly understands the nature of this project. Matthew Broderick, who has based his career on humanizing characters under odd or even extreme circumstances, makes a stalwart cyborg investigator, albeit one not taken seriously, and Rupert Everett is sublime as the nefarious Sanford Scolex. This one, to borrow one of its own phrases, is a wowser: lots of fun and wonderfully inventive. Rated PG for comic mayhem. 80m. **DIR:** David Kellogg. **CAST:** Matthew Broderick, Rupert Everett, Joely Fisher, Michelle Trachtenberg, Andy Dick, Cheri Oteri, Dabney Coleman. **1999 DVD**

INSPECTOR GENERAL, THE ★★★★ In this classic comedy set in Russia of the 1800s, Danny Kaye is the town fool who is mistaken for a confidant of Napoleon. The laughs come when Danny is caught up in court intrigue and really has no idea what is going on. Kaye's talents are showcased in this film. 102m. **DIR:** Henry Koster. **CAST:** Danny Kaye, Walter Slezak, Elsa Lanchester. **1949**

INSPECTOR MORSE (TV SERIES) ★★★★1/2 Colin Dexter's introspective and moody Chief Inspector Morse and his amiable assistant, Detective-Sergeant Lewis, are perfectly rendered in this British mystery series. Morse, an opera lover who enjoys his pints of bitter, is a lonely bachelor, but solves his murder cases with zeal and intelligence. Lewis, an affable family man, makes an excellent counterpart to his demanding boss. A well-paced set of stories set in Oxford. Each episode: 52m. **DIR:** Peter Hammond, Brian Parker, Alastair Reid. **CAST:** John Thaw, Kevin Whately, Peter Woodthorpe, Norman Jones. **1987–1988**

INSPECTORS, THE ★★★ This valentine to our dedicated, resourceful, hardworking U.S. postal inspectors turns them into crack investigators on a par with the most seasoned FBI agent. Bruce Zimmerman's script is pure contrivance, but stars Lou Gossett Jr. and Jonathan Silverman give events dignity and credibility. Rated R for profanity, violence, sexual candor, and a grim autopsy scene. 102m. **DIR:** Brad Turner. **CAST:** Lou Gossett Jr., Jonathan Silverman, Gregory Thirloway, Tobias Mehler. **1998 DVD**

INSPIRATION ★★★ Greta Garbo plays a Parisian model and courtesan with whom an aspiring politician becomes infatuated, even though aware of and troubled by her past. The high rating is for the legion of Garbo fans; others may find it dated and dull. B&W; 74m. **DIR:** Clarence Brown. **CAST:** Greta Garbo, Robert Montgomery, Lewis Stone, Marjorie Rambeau. **1931**

INSTANT JUSTICE 🎬 Michael Paré plays Marine Sergeant Youngblood, who has a penchant for headbutting. Rated R. 101m. **DIR:** Craig T. Rumar. **CAST:** Michael Paré, Tawny Kitaen, Charles Napier. **1986**

INSTANT KARMA 🎬 A young creative consultant for a television network looks for love. Not rated. 91m. **DIR:** Roderick Taylor. **CAST:** Craig Sheffer, David Cassidy, Chelsea Noble, Alan Blumenfeld. **1990**

INSTINCT ★★★ Suggested by Daniel Quinn's novel *Ishmael*, this film is woefully derivative of *Silence of the Lambs* and *One Flew Over the Cuckoo's Nest*, with bits of *Gorillas in the Mist* thrown in. That said, the interactions between characters are all well sculpted and portrayed. Once again Anthony Hopkins is behind bars, ostensibly deranged but actually far smarter and craftier than both his captors and the compassionate but naïve psychiatrist sent to evaluate him. The issue is why Hopkins, a brilliant primatologist, would have killed several park rangers in Rwanda, where he was studying gorillas. Trust us: You'll figure it out long before the psychiatrist does. Rated R for violence and dramatic intensity. 124m. **DIR:** Jon Turteltaub. **CAST:** Anthony Hopkins, Cuba Gooding Jr., Donald Sutherland, Maura Tierney, George Dzundza, John Ashton. **1999 DVD**

INTERCEPTOR ★★★1/2 High marks to this spiffy airborne thriller, which finds a pilot as the sole "wild card" able to prevent a terrorist hijacking. Crisp direction and a good, high-tech script from John Brancato and Michael Ferris. Rated PG-13 for profanity and violence. 88m. **DIR:** Michael Cohn. **CAST:** Andrew Divoff, Elizabeth Morehead, Jurgen Prochnow. **1992 DVD**

INTERIORS ★★★★ Woody Allen tips his hat to Swedish director Ingmar Bergman with this very downbeat drama about a family tearing itself apart. Extremely serious stuff, with fine performances by all. Allen shows he can direct more than comedy. Rated R for language. 99m. DIR: Woody Allen. CAST: Diane Keaton, E. G. Marshall, Geraldine Page, Richard Jordan, Sam Waterston. 1978 DVD

INTERLOCKED 🖤 Another ho-hum erotic thriller about two people who meet over the Internet, only to have their cyber affair turn into a real nightmare. Rated R for violence, language, and adult situations. 98m. DIR: Rick Jacobson. CAST: Sandra Ferguson, Schae Harrison, Jeff Trachta. 1998 DVD

INTERMEZZO (1936) ★★★★ Original version of the story about an affair between young pianist Ingrid Bergman and married violinist Gosta Ekman. Long unseen (David O. Selznick suppressed it when he remade it in Hollywood three years later), this rediscovery is a video treasure for Bergman fans. In Swedish with English subtitles. B&W; 88m. DIR: Gustav Molander. CAST: Gosta Ekman, Ingrid Bergman. 1936 DVD

INTERMEZZO (1939) ★★★★ A love affair between a married concert violinist and a young woman doesn't stray very far from the standard eternal love triangle. This classic weeper has more renown as the English-language debut of Ingrid Bergman. B&W; 70m. DIR: Gregory Ratoff. CAST: Leslie Howard, Ingrid Bergman, Cecil Kellaway. 1939

INTERNAL AFFAIRS ★★★ Brutal, sexually charged thriller about an Internal Affairs investigator (Andy Garcia) who is obsessed with busting a degenerate street cop (Richard Gere). The unrelenting tension mounts as the pursuit of justice becomes a very personal vendetta. Gere is at his best here as a creep you'll just love to hate. Rated R for sex, violence, and profanity. 115m. DIR: Mike Figgis. CAST: Richard Gere, Andy Garcia, Nancy Travis, Laurie Metcalf, William Baldwin. 1990 DVD

INTERNATIONAL HOUSE ★★★1/2 An offbeat, must-see film involving a melting pot of characters gathered at the luxurious International House Hotel to bid on the rights to the radioscope, an early version of television. As usual, a Russian muddies the waters with cunning and craft, while an American bumbles to the rescue. W. C. Fields and Burns and Allen are in rare form throughout. B&W; 70m. DIR: A. Edward Sutherland. CAST: W. C. Fields, Peggy Hopkins Joyce, Baby Rose Marie, Cab Calloway, Stu Erwin, George Burns, Gracie Allen, Bela Lugosi, Franklin Pangborn, Sterling Holloway, Jeanne Marie. 1933

INTERNATIONAL TOURNÉE OF ANIMATION VOL. I, THE ★★★1/2 Fine collection of animated shorts from the nineteenth International Tournée of Animation. This video package features some award-winning animation by filmmakers from around the world. Some of the best selections from this compilation are Marv Newland's *Anijam,* John Canemaker's *Bottom's Dream,* Osamu Tezuka's *Jumping,* and the Academy Award–winning *Anna & Bella,* by Dutch cartoonist Borge Ring. Amusing and inventive. 88m. DIR: Various. 1988

INTERNATIONAL TOURNÉE OF ANIMATION VOL. II, THE ★★★ Highly impressive collection of animated shorts from around the world featuring some of the best new animation around. Some of the compilations' best works are the Academy Award–winning short "A Greek Tragedy," from Belgium; "The Frog, The Dog and The Devil," from New Zealand; Bill Plympton's "Your Face"; and "Drawing on My Mind," by Bob Kurtz featuring dialogue and the voice of comic George Carlin. 86m. DIR: Various. 1989

INTERNATIONAL VELVET ★★ A disappointing sequel to *National Velvet* (1944), with Tatum O'Neal only passable as the young horsewoman who rides to victory. Rated PG. 127m. DIR: Bryan Forbes. CAST: Tatum O'Neal, Christopher Plummer, Anthony Hopkins. 1978

INTERNECINE PROJECT, THE ★★★ James Coburn plays an ambitious business tycoon who finds he has to kill four associates to meet a business agreement. The fashion in which he does this proves to be interesting. Worth a look for the trick ending. Rated PG. 89m. DIR: Ken Hughes. CAST: James Coburn, Lee Grant, Harry Andrews, Ian Hendry, Michael Jayston, Keenan Wynn. 1974

INTERNS, THE ★★★ This melodrama of the lives of interns in an American hospital has it all. The new doctors must deal with death, drugs, abortions, and personal problems. Competently acted and directed. B&W; 130m. DIR: David Swift. CAST: Cliff Robertson, Michael Callan, James MacArthur, Nick Adams, Suzy Parker, Buddy Ebsen, Telly Savalas. 1962

INTERNS CAN'T TAKE MONEY ★★★1/2 Gangsters, doctas, and dames in distress all figure into this genre-defying installment that launched the Dr. Kildare flicks. Joel McCrea is steady and handsome as the young doc, but this is Barbara Stanwyck's show as a wronged woman trying to salvage her life. Watch for Lloyd Nolan as a hoodlum with a sensitive streak. Not rated. B&W; 79m. DIR: Alfred Santell. CAST: Barbara Stanwyck, Joel McCrea, Lloyd Nolan, Stanley Ridges, Lee Bowman, Barry Macollum, Irving Bacon, Gaylord Pendelton. 1937

INTERROGATION ★★★★ A cabaret singer is imprisoned after sleeping with a military officer. This is a harrowing drama of one woman's struggle to survive unyielding cruelty and atrocious living conditions. Upon completion, the movie was banned by the Polish government, until the director managed to smuggle it out of the country. A gem. In Polish with English subtitles. Not rated; the film has nudity and violence. 118m. DIR: Richard Bugajski. CAST: Krystyna Janda, Adam Ferency, Agnieszka Holland. 1982

INTERRUPTED MELODY ★★★★1/2 An excellent movie biography of Australian opera singer Marjorie Lawrence. She was stricken with polio but continued her career in spite of her handicap. Eleanor Parker stars as Lawrence with vocals dubbed by opera star Eileen Farrell. 106m. DIR: Curtis Bernhardt. CAST: Eleanor Parker, Glenn Ford, Roger Moore, Cecil Kellaway, Stephen Bekassy. 1955

INTERSECTION Vancouver architect floundering in a midlife crisis watches chunks of his life pass before him during a nasty rural auto accident. Rated R for sex, nudity, and language. 105m. **DIR:** Mark Rydell. **CAST:** Richard Gere, Sharon Stone, Lolita Davidovich, Martin Landau, David Selby. **1994**

INTERVAL ★★ Merle Oberon's last feature film is a weepy story of a woman who tours the world trying to find her one true love while attempting to forget her past. Passable, but hardly a distinguished finale for Oberon's career. Rated PG. 84m. **DIR:** Daniel Mann. **CAST:** Merle Oberon, Robert Wolders, Claudio Brook, Russ Conway. **1973**

INTERVIEW WITH THE VAMPIRE ★★★★1/2 This adaptation of Anne Rice's bestseller features an unexpectedly dead-on performance by Tom Cruise as the decadent Lestat and a poignant one by Brad Pitt as his reluctant disciple. The story begins with reporter Christian Slater interviewing Pitt, who spins a tale of evil, corruption, and heartbreak, and ends in a pulse-pounding, high-speed pursuit. Fans of the genre will be well pleased; casual viewers will applaud the relative restraint used in the blood-and-gore category. Rated R for violence, gore, profanity, nudity, and sexual content. 122m. **DIR:** Neil Jordan. **CAST:** Tom Cruise, Brad Pitt, Antonio Banderas, Stephen Rea, Christian Slater, Kirsten Dunst. **1994** DVD

•**INTERZONE** ❤ In a futuristic society the remaining humans battle mutants but fail to do anything original. Rated R for violence. 97m. **DIR:** Deran Sarafian. **CAST:** Bruce Abbott. **1988**

INTIMATE BETRAYAL ★★ Former friends engage in a battle of wits over the woman who left one for the other. Pretentious and lurid drama about the nature of male bonding. Rated R for nudity, sexual situations, strong profanity, and violence. 90m. **DIR:** Andrew Behar. **CAST:** Dwier Brown, Jessica Hecht, Richard Edson, Annabelle Gurwitch. **1996**

INTIMATE CONTACT ★★★ Claire Bloom and Daniel Massey are wonderful as an affluent couple confronted with the specter of AIDS. A sobering account of a family's attempt to deal with this tragic disease. Rate PG. 159m. **DIR:** Waris Hussein. **CAST:** Claire Bloom, Daniel Massey, Sylvia Syms, Mark Kingston, Maggie Steed. **1987**

INTIMATE OBSESSION ❤ Bored wife meets dangerous stranger in this cheap "erotic mystery" that's as generic as its title. Rated R for nudity and sexual situations. 80m. **DIR:** Lawrence Unger. **CAST:** Jodie Fisher, James Quarter. **1992**

INTIMATE POWER ★★★ This is the true story of a French girl sold into slavery who becomes the sultan's favorite. She bears him a male heir and then proceeds to instill in her son the rights of the Turkish people hoping for reform when he becomes sultan. Rated R for violence and nudity. 104m. **DIR:** Jack Smight. **CAST:** F. Murray Abraham, Maud Adams. **1989**

INTIMATE RELATIONS ★★1/2 When an affair develops between a frumpy English housewife and her young lodger, the woman's teenage daughter jealously moves to interfere. Based on a real-life 1950s case that ended in a double murder, Philip Goodhew's film is, on the one hand, jokey and overdone, while on the other hand plodding and listless. Acting is a saving grace—especially Julie Walters as the frustrated older woman. Rated R for sexual themes,

some profanity, and climactic violence. 105m. **DIR:** Philip Goodhew. **CAST:** Julie Walters, Rupert Graves, Laura Sadler, Matthew Walker. **1996**

INTIMATE STRANGER ★★ Deborah Harry takes a part-time job on a sex phone line and meets up with the ultimate psycho. Now she must find him before he gets her. Rated R for profanity, nudity, and violence. 96m. **DIR:** Allan Holzman. **CAST:** Deborah Harry, James Russo, Tim Thomerson, Grace Zabriskie. **1991**

INTIMATE STRANGERS ★★ Dennis Weaver and Sally Struthers are husband and wife who permit a lack of self-esteem to drag them into the dark areas of psychological warfare and wife beating. Melvyn Douglas is outstanding and Tyne Daly was nominated for an Emmy Award for her work in this made-for-TV film. 120m. **DIR:** John Llewellyn Moxey. **CAST:** Dennis Weaver, Sally Struthers, Tyne Daly, Larry Hagman, Melvyn Douglas. **1977**

INTO THE BADLANDS ★★ This trio of weird made-for-cable Western tales ranges from tepid to terrible. Rod Serling might have penned the first, with Helen Hunt and Dylan McDermott sharing a damned romance, on a bad day; the other two make absolutely no sense. Only Dern's engaging narration saves this mess from turkeydom. 93m. **DIR:** Sam Pillsbury. **CAST:** Bruce Dern, Mariel Hemingway, Helen Hunt, Dylan McDermott, Lisa Pelikan, Andrew Robinson. **1991** DVD

INTO THE FIRE ❤ A young drifter finds himself in the middle of deceit and treachery when he stops at a roadside diner. Rated R for nudity and violence. 88m. **DIR:** Graeme Campbell. **CAST:** Art Hindle, Olivia D'Abo, Lee Montgomery, Susan Anspach. **1988**

INTO THE HOMELAND ★★★ This HBO release is a topical but predictable story starring Powers Boothe as an ex-cop who endeavors to rescue his kidnapped daughter from a white supremacist organization headed by Paul LeMat. The shockingly real portrayal of the supremacists' ethics make this movie worth viewing. Not rated; contains violence and strong language. 120m. **DIR:** Lesli Linka Glatter. **CAST:** Powers Boothe, C. Thomas Howell, Paul LeMat, Cindy Pickett. **1987**

INTO THE NIGHT ★★1/2 Packed with cinematic in-jokes and guest appearances by more than a dozen film directors, this is a film fan's dream. Unfortunately, it might also be a casual viewer's nightmare. Jeff Goldblum and Michelle Pfeiffer stumble into international intrigue and share a bizarre and deadly adventure in contemporary Los Angeles. Rated R for violence and profanity. 115m. **DIR:** John Landis. **CAST:** Jeff Goldblum, Michelle Pfeiffer, Paul Mazursky, Kathryn Harrold, Richard Farnsworth, Irene Papas, David Bowie, Dan Aykroyd. **1985**

INTO THE SUN ★★★★ To research a role, an obnoxious movie star rides shotgun with a crack pilot in the Middle East. Some movies, by sheer force of the talent involved, turn out to be much better than anyone had a right to expect. Director Fritz Kiersch and his cast (including a hilarious Terry Kiser) make this one seem fresh and even innovative. Rated R for profanity and violence. 100m. **DIR:** Fritz Kiersch. **CAST:** Anthony Michael Hall, Michael Paré, Terry Kiser. **1992**

INTO THE WEST ★★★★ Here's a wonderful family film that kids will adore and adults will find fascinating. Two Irish boys find themselves off on an exciting journey after they are "adopted" by a magical horse. The lads are part of a little-known Irish subculture: the Travelers, a gypsylike clan descended from an ancient Celtic tribe. Rated PG for very brief profanity. 91m. **DIR:** Mike Newell. **CAST:** Gabriel Byrne, Ellen Barkin, Colm Meaney, Ciaran Fitzgerald, Rory Conroy, David Kelly, Johnny Murphy. **1993**

INTOLERANCE ★★★★ This milestone silent epic tells and blends four stories of injustice, modern and ancient. The sets for the Babylonian sequence were the largest ever built for a film. One scene alone involved 15,000 people and 250 chariots. The acting is dated, but the picture presents a powerful viewing experience. B&W; 123m. **DIR:** D. W. Griffith. **CAST:** Lillian Gish, Bessie Love, Mae Marsh, Elmo Lincoln, Tully Marshall, Eugene Pallette, Tod Browning, Monte Blue, Robert Harron, Constance Talmadge, Erich Von Stroheim. **1916 DVD**

INTRIGUE ★★ Robert Loggia plays a former CIA agent who has defected to the KGB. Realizing that he's terminally ill, he wants to return to the United States. Slow start, decent middle, and just okay ending sum up the quality of this made-for-TV spy flick. Rated PG for violence. 96m. **DIR:** David Drury. **CAST:** Scott Glenn, Robert Loggia, William Atherton. **1988**

•**INTRODUCING DOROTHY DANDRIDGE** ★★★★ Star-producer Halle Berry shepherded this mesmerizing study of Dorothy Dandridge, the first black actress ever to garner an Academy Award nomination for Best Actress (in 1954's *Carmen Jones*) ... a milestone event not even acknowledged by most film references. Adapted from the unabashed valentine of a biography by Earl Mills (played here by Brent Spiner), this melancholy drama follows Dandridge's rise from dancer and chanteuse to the fiery actress who blossomed on the big screen, under the guidance of director Otto Preminger. Unfortunately Preminger also wielded far too much influence over his protégé, and what should have been a meteoric career rise stalled when Dandridge began refusing roles she deemed offensive or token. Director Martha Coolidge's film gracefully moves back and forth via flashback, and Berry displays the same fire and grit that must have made Dandridge herself such a sensation. Spiner also is fine, as the manager/friend who carried a torch from afar. The script, alas, stalls when considering the ill-advised husbands—one reduced to little more than a footnote—who must have hurt Dandridge's career. Rated R for profanity, nudity, rape, and simulated sex. 115m. **DIR:** Martha Coolidge. **CAST:** Halle Berry, Brent Spiner, Obba Babatundé, Loretta Devine, Cynda Williams, Klaus María Brandauer, William Atherton, D. B. Sweeney. **1999 DVD**

INTRUDER, THE (1961) ★★★1/2 Gripping film about a racist (William Shatner) who attempts to block court-ordered integration in a small-town school. Shatner's performance is very good, and the finale is especially intense. A.k.a. *Shame* and *I Hate Your Guts*. Not rated. B&W; 80m. **DIR:** Roger Corman.

CAST: William Shatner, Leo Gordon, Jeanne Cooper. 1961

INTRUDER (1988) ★★ A bloodthirsty killer is locked in a supermarket with employees preparing for a going-out-of-business sale. Slasher fans should find this amusing. Rated R for violence and profanity. 90m. **DIR:** Scott Spiegel. **CAST:** Elizabeth Cox, Danny Hicks, René Estevez. **1988**

INTRUDER IN THE DUST ★★★★ One of the best adaptations of a William Faulkner novel, this was one of the first movies to take a stand on racial issues. Basically, it's the story of the lynching of an African-American by rednecks in the South. It deals as much with the reaction of the white population as it does with that of the black community. B&W; 88m. **DIR:** Clarence Brown. **CAST:** David Brian, Juano Hernandez, Claude Jarman Jr., Will Geer, Elizabeth Patterson, Porter Hall, Charles Kemper. **1949**

INTRUDER WITHIN, THE ♥ Cheesy *Alien*. Action takes place on an ocean oil-drilling rig instead of commercial spacecraft. 100m. **DIR:** Peter Carter. **CAST:** Chad Everett, Joseph Bottoms, Jennifer Warren. **1981**

INTRUDERS ★★★★ Two sisters, through hypnotic regression, convince a psychologist that they've been repeatedly abducted, since childhood, by aliens. The story moves suspensefully, exploring government conspiracies and theories why extraterrestrials are kidnapping humans. Made for TV, yet still effectively creepy. 163m. **DIR:** Dan Curtis. **CAST:** Richard Crenna, Mare Winningham, Susan Blakely, Daphne Ashbrook. **1992**

INVADER ★★ A reporter for a trashy tabloid discovers government officials and scientists working on a new computerized weapons system from an abandoned UFO. But no one will believe him, until the megacomputer tries to take control of military bases and personnel. Rated R for violence and profanity. 95m. **DIR:** Philip Cook. **CAST:** Hans Bachmann, A. Thomas Smith, Rick Foucheux, John Cooke, Ally Sheedy. **1993**

INVADER, THE ★★1/2 A visitor from another planet impregnates a human female in order to save his dying race. However, the visitor's mortal enemy wants to stop him. Silly but entertaining science fiction. Not rated; contains violence and profanity. 97m. **DIR:** Mark Rosman. **CAST:** Sean Young, Ben Cross, Daniel Baldwin, Nick Mancuso. **1996**

INVADERS, THE ★★★★ Based on the popular television series from the 1960s, this made-for-TV miniseries is suspenseful, well-acted, and eerily effective. Scott Bakula stars as a man who uncovers the invasion of Earth by an alien species but can't convince his fellow Earthlings, who think he's crazy. Not rated; contains mild violence and profanity. 180m. **DIR:** Paul Shapiro. **CAST:** Scott Bakula, Elizabeth Peña, Richard Thomas, Roy Thinnes, Delane Matthews, Richard Belzer. **1995**

INVADERS FROM MARS (1953) ★★★★ Everybody remembers this one. Kid sees a flying saucer land in a nearby field, only nobody will believe him. Some really weird visuals throughout this minor sci-fi classic. 78m. **DIR:** William Cameron Menzies. **CAST:**

Helena Carter, Jimmy Hunt, Leif Erickson, Arthur Franz. 1953 DVD

INVADERS FROM MARS (1986) ★★★ Director Tobe Hooper maintains the tone of the original; this version feels like a 1950s movie made with 1980s production values. Rated PG-13 for rather intense situations and ugly beasties. 94m. DIR: Tobe Hooper. CAST: Karen Black, Hunter Carson, Timothy Bottoms, Laraine Newman, James Karen, Louise Fletcher, Bud Cort. 1986 DVD

INVASION EARTH: THE ALIENS ARE HERE ★★ Comedic aliens take over a cinema presenting a sci-fi film festival, subverting humans into blank-eyed underwear-clad zombies. But some kids get wise to the scheme and try to put a stop to it before it's too late. Unfunny as comedy, but with great clips of classic sci-fi and horror films from years past. Not rated, but suitable for most age-groups. 84m. DIR: George Maitland. CAST: Janis Fabian, Christian Lee. 1987

INVASION FOR FLESH AND BLOOD 🎬 Campy sci-fi film is a one-man show with Warren F. Disbrow doing writing, directing, producing, and special effects. Not rated; contains violence, gore, nudity, and profanity. 90m. DIR: Warren F. Disbrow. CAST: Kathy Monks, Warren Disbrow Sr., Lori Karz, Tim Ferrante. 1991

INVASION OF PRIVACY ★★ A worn-out story line about a psychotic ex-convict who goes to work for the journalist that he idolizes. Robby Benson still can't act, and Jennifer O'Neill doesn't do much better. Made for cable. 95m. DIR: Kevin Meyer. CAST: Robby Benson, Jennifer O'Neill, Ian Ogilvy. 1992

INVASION OF PRIVACY (1996) ★★1/2 Nice girl thinks she meets the guy of her dreams, only to learn he's a petulant psychopath. At this point, Larry Cohen's script veers into truly bewildering waters, as our now-pregnant heroine is kidnapped by the guy and held in a mountain cabin until she's past the point of obtaining a legal abortion. The final act is strident, annoying, and just plain stupid. Rated R for profanity, nudity, rape, and violence. 95m. DIR: Anthony Hickox. CAST: Johnathon Schaech, Mili Avital, Naomi Campbell, Tom Wright, R. G. Armstrong, David Keith, Charlotte Rampling. 1996

INVASION OF THE ANIMAL PEOPLE 🎬 Extraterrestrial visitors assume various forms. B&W; 73m. DIR: Virgil Vogel, Jerry Warren. CAST: Robert Burton, Barbara Wilson, John Carradine (narrator). 1962

INVASION OF THE BEE GIRLS ★★★ Enjoyable film about strange female invaders doing weird things to the male population of a small town in California. Plot is not too important in this wacky sci-fi spoof. Not for kids. Rated PG. 85m. DIR: Denis Sanders. CAST: Victoria Vetri, William Smith, Cliff Osmond, Anitra Ford. 1973

INVASION OF THE BODY SNATCHERS (1956) ★★★★ Quite possibly the most frightening film ever made, this stars Kevin McCarthy as a small-town doctor who discovers his patients, family, and friends are being taken over by cold, emotionless, human-duplicating pods from outer space. Not many films can be considered truly disturbing, but this one more than qualifies. Coming from the B-movie science-fiction boom of the 1950s, it has emerged as a cinema classic. B&W; 80m. DIR: Don Siegel. CAST: Kevin McCarthy, Dana Wynter, Carolyn Jones, King Donovan. 1956 DVD

INVASION OF THE BODY SNATCHERS (1978) ★★★★ Excellent semisequel to Don Siegel's 1956 classic of the same name, with Donald Sutherland fine in the role originally created by Kevin McCarthy (who has a cameo here). This time the story takes place in San Francisco, with mysterious "seeds" from outer space duplicating—then destroying—San Francisco Bay Area residents at an alarming rate. Rated PG. 115m. DIR: Phil Kaufman. CAST: Donald Sutherland, Brooke Adams, Leonard Nimoy, Jeff Goldblum, Veronica Cartwright. 1978 DVD

INVASION OF THE FLESH HUNTERS ★★★ A new twist on the zombie flick. This time these guys aren't dead. They just have a cannibalistic disease brought back from Southeast Asia. Good effects. Not rated. 90m. DIR: Anthony M. Dawson. CAST: John Saxon. 1982

INVASION OF THE GIRL SNATCHERS 🎬 An assistant detective and a cult leader in the service of aliens from outer space do battle. Not rated; the film contains nudity and sexual suggestiveness. 90m. DIR: Lee Jones. CAST: Elizabeth Rush. 1973

INVASION OF THE SAUCER MEN ★★★ Goofy-looking aliens with alcohol for blood battle hot-rodding teens. A minor camp classic that doesn't take itself seriously for a moment. B&W; 69m. DIR: Edward L. Cahn. CAST: Steve Terrell, Gloria Castillo, Frank Gorshin. 1957

INVASION OF THE SPACE PREACHERS ★★1/2 Nerds camping in West Virginia help a beautiful female alien track bad guys from her planet. No big laughs, but a genial time waster. Rated R for nudity and profanity. 100m. DIR: Daniel Boyd. CAST: Jim Wolfe, Guy Nelson. 1990

●**INVASION OF THE STAR CREATURES** ★★ Two bumbling soldiers foil the efforts of statuesque beauties in high heels and their pot-grown vegetable men to conquer Earth. Any film that opens with "R. I. Diculous Presents" and credits its music as "electronic noise" is worth a watch. As a send-up of the space and science-fiction films from the early 1960s, this cheapo's a match for the worst of Ed Wood's movies; but the cast and crew were in on the joke. Annoyingly enjoyable. B&W; 81m. DIR: Bruno De Sota. CAST: Bob Ball, Frankie Ray, Gloria Victor, Dolores Reed, Slick Slavin, Mark Ferris, Jim Almanzar. 1962

INVASION UFO ★★ Strictly for fans of the short-lived science-fiction TV series, whose title explains all. 97m. DIR: Gerry Anderson, David Lane, David Tomblin. CAST: Ed Bishop, George Sewell, Michael Billington. 1980

INVASION USA (1952) 🎬 Tacky "red scare" movie about a Communist invasion of the United States. B&W; 74m. DIR: Alfred E. Green. CAST: Gerald Mohr, Peggie Castle, Dan O'Herlihy, Phyllis Coates, Noel Neill. 1952

INVASION U.S.A. (1985) ★★★ Chuck Norris plays a one-man army (as always) who comes to the rescue of the good ol' U.S.A. and pummels the minions of psychotic spy Richard Lynch. Rated R for violence, gore, and profanity. 107m. DIR: Joseph Zito. CAST: Chuck Norris, Richard Lynch, Melissa Prophet. 1985

INVENTING THE ABBOTTS ★★★1/2 Two rival working-class brothers mix it up sexually and romantically with the three rich Abbott girls. Set in the late 1950s, the story finds its true soul in the relationship between Jacey and Doug Holt, who live with their widowed mother in an Illinois town. The two siblings unravel the circumstances of their father's death and their mother's social isolation, slither into adulthood, and develop very different relationships with each of the Abbott women. The acting is potent and the emotional payoff is satisfying. Rated R for language, sex, and nudity. 105m. DIR: Pat O'Connor. CAST: Joaquin Phoenix, Billy Crudup, Joanna Going, Jennifer Tilly, Liv Tyler, Will Patton, Kathy Baker, Jennifer Connelly. 1997

INVESTIGATION ★★★ When the village tannery owner (Victor Lanoux) kills his wife to marry his pregnant girlfriend (Valerie Mairesse), a meticulous inspector comes to investigate. His Columbo-ish tactics pick up the film's pace and turn a so-so melodrama into a delightful winner. In French with English subtitles. Rated R for violence. 116m. DIR: Etienne Perier. CAST: Victor Lanoux, Jean Carmet, Valerie Mairesse, Michel Robin. 1979

INVISIBLE ADVERSARIES ★★1/2 Controversial avant-garde film about a Viennese photographer who believes that extraterrestrial beings are taking over the minds of her fellow citizens while raising their level of human aggression. This dark satire is interesting but uneven. In German with English subtitles. Not rated; contains explicit nudity and graphic violence. 112m. DIR: Valie Export. CAST: Susanne Wild, Peter Weibel. 1977

INVISIBLE AGENT ★★★ Universal Pictures recycles H. G. Wells's *The Invisible Man* again, this time as a World War II spy thriller. The result is above-average—crisply plotted and atmospheric. Jon Hall plays the dashing title character, but John P. Fulton's special effects are the real star. B&W; 81m. DIR: Edwin L. Marin. CAST: Ilona Massey, Jon Hall, Cedric Hardwicke, Peter Lorre. 1942

INVISIBLE BOY, THE ★★ Sci-fi parable about a computer's scheme to rule the world. The special effects are okay, and Robby the Robot has a supporting role, but it was too dull even in the 1950s. B&W; 85m. DIR: Herman Hoffman. CAST: Richard Eyer, Diane Brewster, Philip Abbott. 1957

INVISIBLE DAD ★★ The production team behind *Invisible Mom* rehashes the same formula, this time with Dad becoming the invisible member of the family. Same film, different name, with a much inferior script. Rated PG. 90m. DIR: Fred Olen Ray. CAST: Saran Norris, Mary Elizabeth McGlynn, Karen Black, Charles Dierkop. 1996

INVISIBLE GHOST 🎬 Bela Lugosi is an unwitting murderer, used by his supposedly dead wife to further her schemes. B&W; 64m. DIR: Joseph H. Lewis. CAST: Bela Lugosi, Polly Ann Young, John McGuire, Betty Compson, Jack Mulhall. 1941

INVISIBLE INVADERS 🎬 Moon monsters possess dead bodies to attack Earth. Invisible thrills. B&W; 67m. DIR: Edward L. Cahn. CAST: John Agar, Jean Byron, John Carradine, Robert Hutton. 1959

INVISIBLE KID, THE ★★ Geared for preteens, this sci-fi comedy about a boy who accidentally discovers an invisibility potion might be a little too juvenile for all audiences. Rated PG for language and nudity. 96m. DIR: Avery Crounse. CAST: Jay Underwood, Wally Ward, Mike Genovese, Karen Black. 1988

INVISIBLE MAN, THE ★★★★1/2 Claude Rains goes unseen until the finish in his screen debut. He plays Jack Griffin, the title character in H. G. Wells's famous story of a scientist who creates an invisibility serum—with the side effect of driving a person slowly insane. Frightening film could initially be mistaken for a comedy, with large chunks of humor in the first half, turning deadly serious thereafter. B&W; 71m. DIR: James Whale. CAST: Claude Rains, Gloria Stuart, Una O'Connor, Henry Travers, E. E. Clive, Dwight Frye. 1933

INVISIBLE MAN RETURNS ★★★ Convicted of his brother's murder and condemned to die, Vincent Price is injected with a serum that renders him invisible and aids in his effort to catch the real killer. John Fulton's special effects and a top-notch cast make this, the second in Universal's series, another one of their winning chillers. B&W; 81m. DIR: Joe May. CAST: Cedric Hardwicke, Vincent Price, Nan Grey, John Sutton, Alan Napier, Cecil Kellaway. 1940

INVISIBLE MANIAC ★★ Tacky Fifties-style sci-fi pastiche has voyeuristic physics professor perfecting an invisibility potion for the purpose of ogling the high school cheerleading team. Titillating silliness has its camp moments. Rated R. 85m. DIR: Rif Coogan. CAST: Noel Peters. 1990

INVISIBLE MAN'S REVENGE, THE ★★ A sequel to a sequel that boasts a better cast than script. Jon Hall is injected with an invisibility drug by John Carradine, who then refuses to reverse the process. Lackluster script and direction. Not rated. B&W; 65m. DIR: Ford Beebe. CAST: Jon Hall, Alan Curtis, Evelyn Ankers, Leon Errol, John Carradine. 1944

INVISIBLE MOM ★★★ Dee Wallace is a delight both on and off the screen in this formulaic yet enjoyable romp. She's the harried wife of a science professor whose latest experiment has rendered her invisible. Lots of fun as Mom tries to run the household and Dad scrambles for a cure. Rated PG. 83m. DIR: Fred Olen Ray. CAST: Dee Wallace, Barry Livingston, Trent Knight, Russ Tamblyn, Christopher Stone, Stella Stevens. 1997

INVISIBLE RAY, THE ★★★ Boris Karloff and Bela Lugosi are teamed in this interesting story. A brilliant research scientist (Karloff), experimenting in Africa, is contaminated by a hunk of radioactive meteor landing nearby and soon discovers that his mere touch can kill. Neat Universal thriller features first-rate effects and good ensemble acting. B&W; 81m. DIR: Lambert Hillyer. CAST: Boris Karloff, Bela Lugosi, Frances Drake, Frank Lawton. 1936

INVISIBLE STRANGLER 🎬 A murderer on death row discovers he has a psychic power to make himself invisible. Not rated; contains graphic violence. 85m. DIR: John Florea. CAST: Robert Foxworth, Stefanie Powers, Elke Sommer. 1984 DVD

INVISIBLE: THE CHRONICLES OF BENJAMIN KNIGHT ♥ Dreadful foray into the *Invisible Man* genre presents nothing new, but borrows heavily from other films. Produced as a sequel to *Mandroid*. Rated R for violence, language, and nudity. 80m. DIR: Jack Ersgard. CAST: Brian Cousins, Jennifer Nash, Alan Oppenheimer, Aharon Ipale. 1994

INVISIBLE WOMAN, THE ★★★ Featherweight sci-fi comedy as a scientist turns a fashion model invisible, but it's got the best cast of any Universal programmer of the 1940s. B&W; 72m. DIR: A. Edward Sutherland. CAST: John Barrymore, Virginia Bruce, John Howard, Charlie Ruggles, Margaret Hamilton, Oscar Homolka. 1941

INVITATION AU VOYAGE ★★★1/2 Here is a strange but watchable French import with plenty of suspense and surprises for those willing to give it a chance to work its unusual magic. Peter Del Monte's film allows the viewer to make assumptions and then shatters those conceptions with a succession of inventive twists and revelations. In French with English subtitles. Rated R for adult content. 100m. DIR: Peter Del Monte. CAST: Laurent Malet, Aurore Clement, Mario Adorf. 1982

INVITATION TO A GUNFIGHTER ★★ Studio-slick Western is short on action and long on dialogue as a hired professional killer comes to town and changes the balance of power. Everybody gets a chance to emote in this gabfest. 92m. DIR: Richard Wilson. CAST: Yul Brynner, George Segal, Janice Rule, Pat Hingle. 1964

INVITATION TO HELL ♥ A family visits a posh vacation resort, only to be seduced by a beautiful Satan worshiper. Bland telefilm. 96m. DIR: Wes Craven. CAST: Robert Urich, Joanna Cassidy, Susan Lucci, Kevin McCarthy. 1984

INVITATION TO THE DANCE ★★★ Strictly for lovers of Terpsichore, this film tells three stories entirely through dance. It sort of drags until Gene Kelly appears in a live action-cartoon sequence about "Sinbad" of Arabian Nights fame. 93m. DIR: Gene Kelly. CAST: Gene Kelly. 1957

INVITATION TO THE WEDDING ★★ A feeble little British tale about a young American college student who falls in love with his best friend's sister, who just so happens to be engaged to an English war hero. John Gielgud offers the only comic relief as an Englishman-turned-Southern evangelist. 89m. DIR: Joseph Brooks. CAST: John Gielgud, Ralph Richardson, Paul Nicholas, Elizabeth Shepherd. 1973

IPCRESS FILE, THE ★★★★ First and by far the best of Michael Caine's three "Harry Palmer" films, this one introduces Len Deighton's reluctant thief-turned-secret agent. Caine, relentlessly serious behind owl-like spectacles, investigates the mystery of specialists kidnapped and relocated to parts unknown. John Barry's moody jazz score superbly counterpoints the action, and Sidney J. Furie's direction is taut and suspenseful. Not rated, suitable for family viewing. 108m. DIR: Sidney J. Furie. CAST: Michael Caine, Nigel Green, Guy Doleman, Gordon Jackson, Sue Lloyd. 1965 DVD

IP5: THE ISLAND OF PACHYDERMS ★★ This beautiful but confusing film is about two Parisian street kids, a teenage Hispanic graffiti artist and an 11-year-old black street rapper. They steal a car, only to discover an elderly man (Yves Montand in his last performance) asleep in the backseat. He teaches them mysterious lessons about nature and life. In French with English subtitles. 119m. DIR: Jean-Jacques Beineix. CAST: Yves Montand, Olivier Martinez, Sekkou Sail, Geraldine Pailhas. 1992

IPHIGENIA ★★★★★ A stunning film interpretation of the Greek classic *Iphigenia in Aulis*. Irene Papas is brilliant as Clytemnestra, the caring and outraged mother. Intense score by Mikos Theodorakis. In Greek with English subtitles. No MPAA rating. 127m. DIR: Michael Cacoyannis. CAST: Irene Papas. 1978

I.Q. ★★★★ Walter Matthau is an absolute delight as Albert Einstein, who plays cupid to his brainy niece, Meg Ryan, and good-hearted garage mechanic, Tim Robbins. Ryan is all set to marry stuffy college professor Stephen Fry because he's the proper kind of husband" for a member of the Einstein family, but Uncle Albert and his eccentric cronies have other ideas. Featuring top-notch performances in every role, this lighthearted romantic comedy recalls Hollywood's golden era. Rated PG for light profanity. 107m. DIR: Fred Schepisi. CAST: Meg Ryan, Tim Robbins, Walter Matthau, Stephen Fry, Lou Jacobi, Gene Saks, Joseph Maher, Charles Durning, Frank Whaley. 1994

IRAN DAYS OF CRISIS ★★★ Fact-based account of the Iranian takeover of the American embassy in Tehran and the subsequent hostage crisis. Engrossing, thought-provoking film boasts good performances and realistic locales. Made for cable. 183m. DIR: Kevin Connor. CAST: Jeff Fahey, George Grizzard, Arliss Howard, Alice Krige, Tony Goldwyn, Daniel Gélin, Valerie Kaprisky. 1991

IREZUMI (SPIRIT OF TATTOO) ★★★★1/2 An erotic tale of obsession that calls forth the rebirth of a near-dead art. A woman defies cultural taboos and gets her back elaborately tattooed to fulfill her mate's obsession. Rated R for nudity. 88m. DIR: Yoichi Takabayashi. CAST: Masayo Utsunomiya, Tomisaburo Wakayama. 1983

•**IRIS BLOND** ★★ Occasionally amusing tale of a middle-aged, washed-up pop singer whose lease on life is renewed when he visits a fortune-teller. Romeo dumps his girlfriend for a young muse who resembles the fortune-teller's prophecy. Sparked by his new love, Romeo learns that love and happiness don't always go hand in hand. The Italian-French co-production tries to be hip, but the characters aren't very likable, while the film's look and feel are trashy. In French and Italian with English subtitles. Rated R for adult situations and language. 113m. DIR: Carlo Verdone. CAST: Carlo Verdone, Claudia Gerini, Andrea Ferreol. 1996

IRISHMAN, THE ★★★1/2 Excellent Australian drama set in the 1920s. An immigrant Irish worker, who has made a living in rough territory with his team of horses, refuses to recognize progress in the form of a gas-driven truck that will put him out of business. His unwillingness to adapt tears apart his family, who wants to back him up but recognizes that he is wrong. 108m. DIR: Donald Crombie. CAST: Michael Craig, Simon Burke, Robyn Nevin, Lou Brown. 1978

IRMA LA DOUCE ★★★ Gendarme Jack Lemmon gets involved with prostitute Shirley MacLaine in what director Billy Wilder hoped would be another MacLaine/Lemmon hit like *The Apartment*. It isn't. It's raw humor in glorious color. Send the "Silver Spoons" set off to bed before you screen this one. 142m. DIR: Billy Wilder. CAST: Shirley MacLaine, Jack Lemmon, Lou Jacobi, Herschel Bernardi. 1963

IRMA VEP ★★★★ This playful swat at the egos, mechanics, and exasperations involved in filmmaking is shot in a breezy docudrama style. A Hong Kong action heroine is hired to star as a slinky cat burglar in a French remake of a silent black-and-white vampire serial. The production is in chaos, and the resilient actress is tossed into a sea of warring personalities. The title of the film is an anagram for vampire. In French with English subtitles. Not rated. 96m. DIR: Olivier Assayas. CAST: Maggie Cheung, Jean-Pierre Léaud, Nathalie Richard, Bulle Ogier, Lou Castel. 1996 DVD

IRON & SILK ★★★ Mark Salzman's experiences in China to master martial arts jump from book to the big screen in a film that's filled with visual splendor and compelling characters. Cultures clash in a winning way as Salzman forsakes his western ways to become more in tune with his surroundings. Rated PG. 94m. DIR: Shirley Sun. CAST: Mark Salzman. 1990

IRON DUKE, THE ★★★★ A thoroughly English stage actor, George Arliss did not make this, his first British film, until late in the decade he spent in the Hollywood studios. His Duke of Wellington, victor over Napoleon at Waterloo, is picture perfect. Buffs will particularly enjoy a younger Felix Aylmer, later Polonius in Laurence Olivier's 1948 *Hamlet*. B&W; 88m. DIR: Victor Saville. CAST: George Arliss, A. E. Matthews, Emlyn Williams, Felix Aylmer, Gladys Cooper. 1936

IRON EAGLE ★★ A better name for this modern war movie might have been *Ramboy*, so shamelessly does it attempt to be a *Rambo* for the teen-age set. Jason Gedrick stars as an 18-year-old would-be pilot who steals an F-16 fighter plane to rescue his father (Tim Thomerson), a prisoner of war in the Middle East. A terminally dull fantasy of blood lust. Rated PG-13 for violence and profanity. 115m. DIR: Sidney J. Furie. CAST: Lou Gossett Jr., Jason Gedrick, Tim Thomerson, David Suchet. 1986 DVD

IRON EAGLE II 💔 Ridiculous sequel to the preposterous original. Rated PG for violence and profanity. 105m. DIR: Sidney J. Furie. CAST: Lou Gossett Jr., Mark Humphrey, Stuart Margolin, Alan Scarfe. 1988

IRON EAGLE IV ★★ Yet another retread of tired material, this time with Lou Gossett's stalwart military hero trying to turn twentysome-thing delinquents into crack fighter pilots. Completely ludicrous, and a waste of the star's talents. Rated PG-13 for profanity and violence. 95m. DIR: Sidney J. Furie. CAST: Lou Gossett Jr., Jason Cadieux, Al Waxman, Joanne Vannicola. 1995

•IRON GIANT, THE ★★★★ Working from the celebrated short story by England's Ted Hughes, coadaptor-director Brad Bird and screenwriter Tim McCanlies have crafted a positively enchanting tale of friendship and honesty. But the film also serves as something of a time capsule. The setting is 1957; in the beeping Sputnik is silent observer to a large fireball that plunges from space into the ocean off the coast of bucolic Rockwell, Maine. The visitor turns out to be a massive robot, designed as a "living weapon" but disoriented enough to befriend a 9-year-old boy who, in turn, does everything possible to help this new comrade. All this unfolds via a somewhat "flat" animation style that owes far more to the late 1950s and early 1960s than the lush three-dimensionality of modern Disney features. This is not a bad thing; Bird's stylistic decision greatly adds to the story's quaint, Norman Rockwell qualities. It's also one of the most intelligent animated parables we've seen in a while: a carefully crafted tale with heart and a shrewd moral. Rated PG for occasional dramatic intensity. 86m. DIR: Brad Bird. 1999 DVD

IRON MAJOR, THE ★★1/2 Decent Hollywood biopic about disabled World War I hero Frank Cavanaugh, who became a trophy-winning college football coach. Loaded with sentiment, spunk, and humor. B&W; 90m. DIR: Ray Enright. CAST: Pat O'Brien, Ruth Warrick, Robert Ryan, Leon Ames. 1943

IRON MASK, THE ★★★1/2 The last of Douglas Fairbanks's truly memorable series of historical adventures is a rousing version of the Dumas story of the later adventures of D'Artagnan and his efforts to restore the rightful king to the throne of France. Well-budgeted and full of good stunts and deadly encounters, this film was released with sound effects and a synchronized score. B&W; 87m. DIR: Allan Dwan. CAST: Douglas Fairbanks Sr., Nigel de Brulier, Marguerite de la Motte. 1929

IRON MAZE ★★ Japanese tycoon buys a shut down steel plant in an economically depressed American town. Sparks fly when his impulsive American wife has an affair with a former employee of the plant. Meandering maze of cinematic clichés. Rated R for profanity, violence, and nudity. 102m. DIR: Hiroaki Yoshida. CAST: Jeff Fahey, Bridget Fonda, J. T. Walsh. 1991 DVD

IRON TRIANGLE, THE ★★★ The Vietnam War seen through the eyes of a hardboiled American captain (Beau Bridges, fine as always). Haing S. Ngor (Oscar winner for *The Killing Fields*) plays a small part as a Cong officer. Solid, blood-and-guts war drama bogs down in the middle but ends with a well-staged climactic battle. Rated R for graphic combat scenes and profanity. 94m. DIR: Eric Weston. CAST: Beau Bridges, Haing S. Ngor, Johnny Hallyday. 1988

IRON WARRIOR 💔 *Conan*-type action flick with plenty of sabers, smoke, and skin. Rated R for violence and nudity. 82m. DIR: Al Bradley. CAST: Miles O'Keeffe, Savina Gersak, Tim Lane. 1987

IRON WILL ★★★ Dakota teen enters the world's most grueling dogsled marathon to save the family farm and earn his college tuition in this gloriously old-fashioned adventure. Some events don't gel—the death of the kid's dad seems avoidable, the trek's final short cut isn't really *that* treacherous—but the action cracks along sharply, the bad guys are easy to hate, and a wry subtext about journalists working feverishly to define a race and man-child in legendary terms is entertaining. Rated PG. 97m. DIR: Charles Haid. CAST: Mackenzie Astin, Kevin Spacey, David Ogden Stiers, August Schellenberg, Brian Cox, Penelope Windust. 1993

IRONCLADS ★★1/2 This TV movie dramatizes the historic sea battle between the *Monitor* and the *Merrimack*. History lesson is almost ruined with silly subplots. 94m. DIR: Delbert Mann. CAST: Virginia Madsen, Alex Hyde-White, Reed Edward Diamond, Philip Casnoff, E. G. Marshall, Fritz Weaver. 1991

IRONHEART 💔 Tired vengeance scenario about a cop tracking the white slaver who killed his partner. Rated R for violence and sex. 83m. DIR: Robert Clouse. CAST: Britton Lee, Bolo Yeung, Richard Norton. 1993

IRONWEED ★★★★1/2 William Kennedy's adaptation of his Pulitzer Prize–winning novel turns into a showcase for Jack Nicholson and Meryl Streep, both playing skid-row alcoholics. Director Hector Babenco superbly captures the grinding, hand-to-mouth dreariness of this Depression era tale, which traces the relationship of opportunity and convenience between the two leads. This may be Streep's finest hour; her complete descent into the part is riveting. Rated R for language, violence, and brief nudity. 144m. DIR: Hector Babenco. CAST: Jack Nicholson, Meryl Streep, Carroll Baker, Michael O'Keefe, Tom Waits, Fred Gwynne. 1987

IRRECONCILABLE DIFFERENCES ★★1/2 Drew Barrymore plays a little girl who sues her self-centered, career-conscious parents—Ryan O'Neal and Shelley Long—for divorce. The laughs are few, but there are some effective scenes of character development. Rated PG for profanity and nudity. 101m. DIR: Charles Shyer. CAST: Drew Barrymore, Ryan O'Neal, Shelley Long. 1984

IS PARIS BURNING? ★★★ A spectacular war movie that plays like a newsreel with famous stars in bit parts. The story of the liberation of Paris, and the Nazi attempt to burn it to the ground is dramatic, moving, and educational. B&W; 175m. DIR: René Clement. CAST: Kirk Douglas, Glenn Ford, Orson Welles, Jean-Paul Belmondo, Charles Boyer, Leslie Caron, Yves Montand, Simone Signoret, Robert Stack, Jean-Pierre Cassel, Claude Dauphin, Gert Fröbe, Daniel Gélin, Alain Delon. 1966

ISADORA (1969) ★★★ A straightforward biography of American modern dance pioneer Isadora Duncan. Vanessa Redgrave ably carries the burden of bringing this eccentric, early flower child to life. Unfortunately she is often undone by a script that drags, becomes repetitious, and rambles. 138m. DIR: Karel Reisz. CAST: Vanessa Redgrave, James Fox, Jason Robards Jr. 1969

ISHTAR 💔 A bloated, disjointed, and ponderous megabuck vanity production. Rated PG-13 for language and brief nudity. 107m. DIR: Elaine May. CAST: Warren Beatty, Dustin Hoffman, Isabelle Adjani, Charles Grodin, Jack Weston, Tess Harper, Carol Kane. 1987

•ISLAND, THE (1962) ★★★★1/2 A family struggles to survive on an isolated island where they are the only inhabitants. Filmed with no dialogue, this is nevertheless an elegant and moving allegory of human life. B&W; 92m. DIR: Kaneto Shindo. CAST: Nobuko Otowa, Shinji Tanaka. 1962

ISLAND, THE (1980) 💔 Michael Caine as a reporter investigating the mysterious disappearances of pleasure craft and their owners in the Caribbean. Rated R. 113m. DIR: Michael Ritchie. CAST: Michael Caine, David Warner, Angela Punch McGregor. 1980

ISLAND AT THE TOP OF THE WORLD, THE ★★★ A rich man ventures into the Arctic in search of his son. Unbelievably, he finds a Viking kingdom. Rated G. 93m. DIR: Robert Stevenson. CAST: David Hartman, Mako, Donald Sinden. 1974 DVD

ISLAND CLAWS ★★ As science-fiction horror thrillers go, this one is about average. *Attack of the Killer Crabs* would have been a more appropriate title, though. Dr. McNeal (Barry Nelson) is a scientist who is experimenting to make larger crabs as a food source. Rated PG for violence. 91m. DIR: Hernan Cardenas. CAST: Robert Lansing, Barry Nelson, Steve Hanks, Nita Talbot. 1980

ISLAND FURY 💔 Hokey action film about two teenage girls who, as children, accidentally stumbled across a cache of mob money while vacationing on a small island. Now the mob wants them killed so the secret can be kept. Not rated; contains violence, language, and adult situations. 90m. DIR: Henri Charr. CAST: Monet Elizabeth, Tanya Louise, Michael Wayne, Ross Hamilton. 1994

ISLAND IN THE SKY ★★1/2 Pilot John Wayne is forced to land his C-47 on the frozen, uncharted tundra of Labrador. Talky, slow-moving drama. B&W; 109m. DIR: William Wellman. CAST: John Wayne, Lloyd Nolan, Walter Abel, James Arness, Andy Devine, Allyn Joslyn, Jimmy Lydon, Harry Carey Jr., Hal Baylor, Sean McClory, Regis Toomey, Paul Fix, George Chandler, Bob Steele, Darryl Hickman, Mike Connors, Carl "Alfalfa" Switzer. 1953

ISLAND OF DESIRE ★★ A trio become involved in a romantic triangle when they are marooned on an island during World War II. The whole thing is substandard, but Linda Darnell is still worth watching. 103m. DIR: Stuart Heisler. CAST: Linda Darnell, Tab Hunter, Donald Gray. 1952

ISLAND OF DR. MOREAU, THE (1977) ★★ Remake of 1933's *Island of Lost Souls* isn't nearly as good. Burt Lancaster develops process of turning animals into half-humans on a desolate tropical island. Watchable only for Burt's sturdy performance and Richard Basehart's portrayal of one of the beasts. Rated PG. 104m. DIR: William Witney. CAST: Burt Lancaster, Michael York, Barbara Carrera, Richard Basehart. 1977

ISLAND OF DR. MOREAU, THE (1996) 💔 H. G. Wells's creepy morality tale about genetic research and man's infatuation with godlike power is reduced to tiresome "mad scientist" rubbish. Rated PG-13 for violence, gore, and horror special effects. 96m. DIR: John Frankenheimer. CAST: Marlon Brando, Val Kilmer, David Thewlis, Fairuza Balk, Ron Perlman. 1996 DVD

ISLAND OF LOST SOULS ★★★★ This seminal horror melodrama of the 1930s still has the power to enthrall, thanks to its otherworldly atmosphere and sequences of unbridled, sadistic horror. H. G. Wells's *The Island of Dr. Moreau* is the basis for this tense chiller in which a shipwreck victim, the unwilling "guest" of the exiled doctor, discovers Moreau speeding up evolution to transform jungle beasts into humans ... sort of. A classic. B&W; 70m. DIR: Erle C. Kenton. CAST: Charles Laughton, Richard Arlen, Leila Hyams, Bela Lugosi, Kathleen Burke, Stanley Fields. 1933

ISLAND OF TERROR ★★★ On an island off the coast of Ireland, scientists battle lab-created, turtle-like mutants that live on human bone marrow. Fun thriller with some terrifically queasy sound effects. 87m. DIR: Terence Fisher. CAST: Peter Cushing, Edward Judd, Carole Gray. 1966

ISLAND OF THE BLUE DOLPHINS ★★★ Alone on an island, a girl and her brother struggle to survive. When attacked by wild dogs, the girl manages to befriend the fiercest one. This adventure will be especially interesting for 7- to 12-year-olds. 93m. DIR: James B. Clark. CAST: Celia Kaye, George Kennedy, Larry Domasin. 1964

ISLAND OF THE LOST ★★1/2 A scientist and his family become shipwrecked on an island inhabited by assorted beasts with genetic disorders. Not rated; contains mild violence. 92m. DIR: John Florea. CAST: Richard Greene, Luke Halpin, Mart Hulswit, Robin Mattson. 1968

ISLAND TRADER ★★ A young boy on an island finds a wrecked airplane laden with gold bullion. He is then pursued by a dangerous criminal and a tugboat skipper, both of whom want the treasure. This potentially exciting adventure film is marred by amateurish direction, a low budget, and uninspired acting. 95m. DIR: Howard Rubie. CAST: John Ewart, Ruth Cracknell, Eric Oldfield. 1970

ISLANDER, THE ★★★ A young girl grapples with sexism and diminished expectations in a quiet fishing village of Norwegian immigrants along the shores of Lake Michigan. Quaint coming-of-age film. Rated PG. 99m. DIR: Nany Thurow. CAST: Kit Wholihan, Jeff Weborg. 1988

ISLANDS IN THE STREAM ★★★ This is really two movies in one. The first part is an affecting look at a broken family. The second is a cheap action-adventure. Thomas Hudson, a famous painter and sculptor, lives the life of a recluse in the Bahamas. His only companions are his seagoing crew. One summer, his three sons arrive to see him for the first time in four years. Rated PG for violence and profanity. 105m. DIR: Franklin J. Schaffner. CAST: George C. Scott, Julius W. Harris, David Hemmings, Brad Savage, Hart Bochner, Claire Bloom. 1977

ISLE OF THE DEAD ★★★1/2 Atmospheric goings-on dominate this typically tasteful horror study from producer Val Lewton. A group of people are stranded on a Greek island during a quarantine. Star Boris Karloff is, as usual, outstanding. B&W; 72m. DIR: Mark Robson. CAST: Boris Karloff, Ellen Drew, Jason Robards Sr. 1945

•ISN'T SHE GREAT ★★ Soap-opera synopsis of Jacqueline Susann's life as a failed actress, disappointed mother, and outlandish, bestselling author fails on several levels. Bette Midler, as Susann, goes through an endless parade of flamboyant costumes which are supposed to define her character. Also, there is an uncomfortable blending of comedy and tragedy as she deals with her autistic son and breast cancer. Nathan Lane, as her manager and husband, and David Hyde Pierce, as her uptight editor, hint at what could have been a better film. Rated R for language and sexual innuendo. 95m. DIR: Andrew Bergman. CAST: Bette Midler, Nathan Lane, David Hyde Pierce. 2000 DVD

ISTANBUL (1956) ★★ Limpid remake of 1947's *Singapore*, with Errol Flynn as the smuggler who finds more than mere memories of a lost love when he returns to Istanbul. Unfortunately, this is a *film noir* that forgot the *noir* and plays out like a melodrama. Casting did not help, as Flynn was too old for the part. Not rated. 85m. DIR: Joseph Pevney. CAST: Errol Flynn, Cornell Borchers, John Bentley, Nat King Cole, Leif Erickson, Peggy Knudsen, Martin Benson, Werner Klemperer, Torin Thatcher. 1956

ISTANBUL 💗 A grungy American with a mysterious past meets a penniless student in Belgium and involves him in a kidnapping. This English-dubbed thriller from France is hampered by the hammy overacting of Brad Dourif. Rated R for nudity, profanity, and sexual situations. 90m. DIR: Marc Didden. CAST: Brad Dourif, Dominique Deruddere, Ingrid De Vos. 1985

ISTANBUL: KEEP YOUR EYES OPEN ★ A father searches for his daughter in this very odd drama. Director Mats Ahern leads his cast around and around, eventually leading them, and the audience, into confusion. Rated PG-13. 88m. DIR: Mats Ahern. CAST: Timothy Bottoms, Twiggy, Robert Morley. 1990

IT (1927) ★★★ Advance promotion about *It* (read: sex appeal) made this clever little comedy about shop girl Clara Bow chasing and catching her boss Antonio Moreno a solid hit. It also boosted red-haired Brooklyn bombshell Clara to superstardom. Rising star Gary Cooper appears only briefly. Silent. B&W; 71m. DIR: Clarence Badger. CAST: Clara Bow, Antonio Moreno, William Austin, Lloyd Corrigan, Jacqueline Gadsden, Gary Cooper. 1927

IT (1991) ★★★1/2 Although scripters Lawrence D. Cohen and Tommy Lee Wallace do a superb job setting up the events of Stephen King's lengthy bestseller, the ultimate payoff—when It is finally given a form—is quite disappointing. That's a shame, because this teleplay's first half is perhaps the best King adaptation ever lensed. Made for TV, but probably too intense for very young viewers. 192m. DIR: Tommy Lee Wallace. CAST: Harry Anderson, Dennis Christopher, Richard Masur, Annette O'Toole, Tim Reid, John Ritter, Richard Thomas, Tim Curry. 1991

IT CAME FROM BENEATH THE SEA ★★★★ Ray Harryhausen's powerhouse special effects light up the screen in this story of a giant octopus from the depths of the Pacific that causes massive destruction along the North American coast as it makes its way toward San Francisco. A little talky at times, but the brilliantly achieved effects make this a must-see movie even on the small screen. B&W; 80m. DIR: Robert Gordon. CAST: Kenneth Tobey, Faith Domergue, Donald Curtis, Ian Keith. 1955

IT CAME FROM OUTER SPACE ★★★★ Science-fiction author Ray Bradbury wrote the screenplay for this surprisingly effective 3-D chiller from the 1950s about creatures from outer space taking over the bodies of Earthlings. It was the first film to use this theme and still holds up today. B&W; 81m. DIR: Jack Arnold. CAST: Richard Carlson, Barbara Rush, Charles Drake. 1953

IT CAME UPON A MIDNIGHT CLEAR ★★ Cornball story about a New York cop (Mickey Rooney) who dies from a heart attack but arranges with heavenly higher-ups to spend one last Christmas with his grandson (Scott Grimes). *It's a Wonderful Life* this is not. Made for television. 99m. DIR: Peter H. Hunt. CAST: Mickey Rooney, Scott Grimes, Barrie Youngfellow, George Gaynes, Hamilton Camp. 1984

IT CONQUERED THE WORLD ★★ Paul Blaisdell's five-foot-high monster, which resembles an angry, upended cucumber that comes to a point at the top, looks better in the stills printed in monster magazines of the Sixties than in the movie itself—an above-average variation on *Invasion of the Body Snatchers*. A campy, frantic B movie. B&W; 68m. DIR: Roger Corman. CAST: Peter Graves, Beverly Garland, Lee Van Cleef. 1956

IT COULD HAPPEN TO YOU ★★★1/2 Good-hearted beat cop Nicolas Cage promises to split his potential winnings on a lottery ticket with waitress Bridget Fonda when he's short of change for a tip. Of course, he wins the big prize, which causes all sorts of complications. This is a winning, unassuming little movie with the stars doing an outstanding job. Rated PG for light profanity. 101m. DIR: Andrew Bergman. CAST: Nicolas Cage, Bridget Fonda, Rosie Perez, Wendell Pierce, Isaac Hayes, Victor Rojas, Seymour Cassel, Stanley Tucci, Red Buttons. 1994 DVD

IT COULDN'T HAPPEN HERE ♥ A flat and self-indulgent Pet Shop Boys vehicle consisting of loosely related scenes serving only to showcase the British music duo's all-time synth-drenched hits. Boring. Rated PG-13 for adult themes. 89m. DIR: Jack Bond. CAST: Neil Tennant, Chris Lowe, Gareth Hunt, Neil Dickson. 1992

IT HAPPENED AT THE WORLD'S FAIR ★★1/2 Adorable tyke plays matchmaker for Elvis Presley and Joan O'Brien at the Seattle World's Fair. It's a breezy romantic comedy with bouncy songs. Elvis hadn't yet reached the point where he was just going through the motions. He seems to be having fun and you will, too. 105m. DIR: Norman Taurog. CAST: Elvis Presley, Joan O'Brien, Gary Lockwood, Yvonne Craig. 1963

IT HAPPENED IN BROOKLYN ★★ A modest musical made to capitalize on the hit-parade popularity of Frank Sinatra. The story concerns several Brooklynites trying to make the big time in show business. The only energy of note is Jimmy Durante. Passable. B&W; 105m. DIR: Richard Whorf. CAST: Frank Sinatra, Kathryn Grayson, Jimmy Durante, Peter Lawford, Gloria Grahame. 1947

IT HAPPENED IN NEW ORLEANS ★★ Bobby Breen, the male Shirley Temple, stars as a Civil War orphan forced to leave his ex-slave mammy and go to New York. There, his Yankee relatives give him a

hard time until his renditions of Stephen Foster tunes and his overwhelming cuteness win them over. Also known as *Rainbow on the River*. B&W; 83m. DIR: Kurt Neumann. CAST: Bobby Breen, May Robson, Charles Butterworth, Louise Beavers, Alan Mowbray, Benita Hume, Henry O'Neill, Eddie "Rochester" Anderson. 1936

IT HAPPENED ONE NIGHT ★★★★★ Prior to *One Flew over the Cuckoo's Nest*, this 1934 comedy was the only film to capture all the major Academy Awards. Clark Gable stars as a cynical reporter on the trail of a runaway heiress, Claudette Colbert. They fall in love, of course, and the result is vintage movie magic. B&W; 105m. DIR: Frank Capra. CAST: Clark Gable, Claudette Colbert, Ward Bond. 1934 DVD

IT HAPPENS EVERY SPRING ★★★1/2 Great farce with chemistry professor Ray Milland accidentally developing a compound that, when applied, results in a baseball repulsing anything made of wood, including a bat. His major-league career as a pitcher is short-lived but lots of fun. B&W; 87m. DIR: Lloyd Bacon. CAST: Ray Milland, Jean Peters, Paul Douglas, Ed Begley Sr., Ted de Corsia, Ray Collins, Jessie Royce Landis, Alan Hale Jr. 1949

IT LIVES AGAIN ★★★ In an effort to outdo the original *It's Alive!*, this film has three mutated babies on the loose, and everybody in a panic. Doesn't quite measure up to its predecessor, but still successful due to another fine makeup job by Rick Baker. Rated R. 91m. DIR: Larry Cohen. CAST: Frederic Forrest, Kathleen Lloyd, John P. Ryan, John Marley, Andrew Duggan. 1978

IT RAINED ALL NIGHT THE DAY I LEFT ★★1/2 Tony Curtis and Lou Gossett Jr. play two small-time weapons salesmen who are ambushed in Africa. They go to work for a recently widowed woman (Sally Kellerman) who controls all the water in this extremely hot and dry region. Because she blames the natives for her husband's death, she rations their water. Rated R for sex and violence. 100m. DIR: Nicolas Gessner. CAST: Lou Gossett Jr., Sally Kellerman, Tony Curtis. 1978

IT SHOULD HAPPEN TO YOU ★★★1/2 Judy Holliday plays an actress who's desperate to garner publicity and hopes splashing her name across billboards all over New York City will ignite her career. The movie provides steady chuckles. Jack Lemmon makes an amusing screen debut. Holliday is hard to resist. B&W; 81m. DIR: George Cukor. CAST: Judy Holliday, Peter Lawford, Jack Lemmon, Michael O'Shea, Vaughn Taylor. 1954

IT STARTED IN NAPLES ★★ Clark Gable and Sophia Loren together sounds good on paper but doesn't work in this predictable comedy about an American man trying to get custody of his Italian nephew. 100m. DIR: Melville Shavelson. CAST: Clark Gable, Sophia Loren, Vittorio De Sica. 1960

IT STARTED WITH A KISS ★★★ A show girl looking for a rich husband marries an air force sergeant instead, then wants the marriage kept platonic until she is sure. Fred Clark, as a general, again steals the show. 104m. DIR: George Marshall. CAST: Glenn Ford, Debbie Reynolds, Eva Gabor, Fred Clark, Edgar Buchanan, Harry Morgan. 1959

•IT STARTED WITH EVE ★★★★ Most of Deanna Durbin's movies have dated badly, but this comedy still retains a lot of charm. She plays a hatcheck girl who agrees to pose as the fiancée of multimillionaire Bob Cummings in order to grant the dying wish of his father. Problems start when the old man turns out not to be dying after all. B&W; 90m. DIR: Henry Koster. CAST: Deanna Durbin, Charles Laughton, Robert Cummings, Guy Kibbee. 1941

IT TAKES A THIEF (TV SERIES) ★★★★ Suave and debonair Robert Wagner secured the television role of his career in this late-Sixties series, very loosely adapted from Alfred Hitchcock's *To Catch a Thief* (1955). Burglar Alexander Mundy put his talents to work for a supersecret government agency (the SIA). Actual European locales added to the show's luxurious tone, as did the occasional appearance of Fred Astaire (as Alexander's father, Alister, a retired thief). Delightful fun. 52m. DIR: Various. CAST: Robert Wagner, Malachi Throne, Fred Astaire. 1968–70

IT TAKES TWO (1988) ★★ This young boy's fantasy features George Newbern as a reluctant bridegroom who has an affair with a fast car and a hot blonde car dealer. Only teens may fully appreciate this trite sex comedy. Rated PG-13 for profanity and sexual situations. 79m. DIR: David Beaird. CAST: George Newbern, Kimberly Foster. 1988

IT TAKES TWO (1995) ★★1/2 A poor little rich girl and her orphan look-alike (identical twins Ashley and Mary-Kate Olsen) try to fix up the rich kid's widowed dad with the orphan's favorite social worker. *The Prince and the Pauper* meets *The Parent Trap* in a bland, inoffensive comedy for very small children. The Olsen twins perform dutifully but lack the experience to carry a whole film. Rated PG. 98m. DIR: Andy Tennant. CAST: Kirstie Alley, Steve Guttenberg, Mary-Kate Olsen, Ashley Olsen, Philip Bosco, Jane Sibbett. 1995

IT! THE TERROR FROM BEYOND SPACE 💙 Supposedly the inspiration for *Alien*, this is a dull tale of a spaceship returning from Mars in 1973, carrying a hitchhiking scaly being that disposes of the crew, one by one. B&W; 69m. DIR: Edward L. Cahn. CAST: Marshall Thompson, Ann Doran. 1958

ITALIAN JOB, THE ★★★ An ex-con creates the world's biggest traffic jam in an attempt to steal millions in gold. The only problem is the mob doesn't like the idea. A fairly funny caper comedy. 99m. DIR: Peter Collinson. CAST: Michael Caine, Noel Coward, Benny Hill, Rossano Brazzi. 1969

ITALIAN STRAW HAT, THE ★★★ The future happiness of newlyweds is threatened when the groom must find a replacement for a straw hat eaten by a horse. Failure means fighting a duel with the lover of the married woman who was wearing the hat. In a silent classic with English intertitles and musical score. B&W; 72m. DIR: René Clair. CAST: Albert Préjean, Olga Tschechowa. 1927

IT'S A BIG COUNTRY ★★★ This loving tribute to the United States is a grab bag of short stories glorifying the American way of life. The best has Ethel Barrymore set out to change our vital statistics because no one counted her in the last census. B&W;

89m. DIR: Clarence Brown, Don Hartman, John Sturges, Richard Thorpe, Charles Vidor, Don Weis, William Wellman. CAST: Ethel Barrymore, Keefe Brasselle, Gary Cooper, Nancy Davis, Van Johnson, Gene Kelly, Janet Leigh, Marjorie Main, Fredric March, George Murphy, William Powell, S. Z. Sakall, Lewis Stone, James Whitmore, Keenan Wynn. 1951

IT'S A COMPLEX WORLD ★★ Strange film involving a nightclub, politics, bad singing, terrorists, and bizarre characters. The narration doesn't help this plot that jumps all over the place. Rated R for violence and profanity. 81m. DIR: James Wolpaw. CAST: Stanley Mathis, Lou Albano. 1989

IT'S A DATE ★★★ A teenager competes with her widowed mother for a mature man. Corny plot, but it works because of the refreshing Deanna Durbin and her crystal-clear soprano voice. Remade with Jane Powell as *Nancy Goes to Rio* with different songs and didn't work nearly as well. B&W; 103m. DIR: William A. Seiter. CAST: Deanna Durbin, Walter Pidgeon, Kay Francis, Eugene Pallette, S. Z. Sakall, Fritz Feld, Samuel S. Hinds. 1940

IT'S A DOG'S LIFE ★★ A scrappy bull terrier from the waterfront becomes the Bowery's paws-down champ under Jeff Richards's patronage, but cleans up his act when he comes under the influence of kindly Edmund Gwenn and his loving daughter Sally Fraser. Should warm the hearts of dog lovers everywhere. 88m. DIR: Herman Hoffman. CAST: Jeff Richards, Jarma Lewis, Edmund Gwenn, Dean Jagger, Sally Fraser, Richard Anderson. 1955

IT'S A GIFT ★★★★★ In a class with the best of the comedies of the 1930s (including *Duck Soup*, *I'm No Angel*, *My Man Godfrey*), this classic was produced during the peak of Fields's association with Paramount and is his archetypal vehicle, peopled with characters whose sole purpose in life seems to be to annoy his long-suffering Harold Bissonette. A sidesplitting series of visual delights. B&W; 73m. DIR: Norman Z. McLeod. CAST: W. C. Fields, Kathleen Howard, Baby LeRoy. 1934

IT'S A GREAT FEELING ★★★ Doris Day's third movie is more of a comedy than a musical, but she still gets to sing a half-dozen sprightly songs. Jack Carson plays an obnoxious movie star. Cameo bits by Errol Flynn, Gary Cooper, Joan Crawford, Sydney Greenstreet, Jane Wyman, Edward G. Robinson, Ronald Reagan, Eleanor Parker, Patricia Neal, and Danny Kaye. 85m. DIR: David Butler. CAST: Doris Day, Dennis Morgan, Jack Carson, Bill Goodwin. 1949

IT'S A GREAT LIFE ★★★ Dagwood and Blondie Bumstead sure could get away with silly story lines, and this is one of the silliest. Dagwood buys a horse because he misunderstood his instructions—he was told to buy a house. The players make it work. B&W; 75m. DIR: Frank Strayer. CAST: Penny Singleton, Arthur Lake, Danny Mummert, Hugh Herbert, Marjorie Ann Mutchie, Irving Bacon, Alan Dinehart. 1943

IT'S A JOKE, SON! ★★ Radio's Senator Claghorn comes to life in the form of Kenny Delmar, whose bombastic talk and Old South attitude entertained millions on Fred Allen's popular network show. The blustering politician is hijacked by some underhanded rivals and only the strains of his beloved "Dixie" give him the strength to win the day. Cornball but fun. B&W; 63m. DIR: Ben Stoloff. CAST: Kenny Delmar, Una Merkel, June Lockhart, Kenneth Farrell, Douglass Dumbrille. 1947

IT'S A MAD MAD MAD MAD WORLD ★★★★ Spencer Tracy and a cast made up of "Who's Who of American Comedy" are combined in this wacky chase movie to end all chase movies. Tracy is the crafty police captain who is following the progress of various money-mad citizens out to beat one another in discovering the buried hiding place of 350,000 stolen dollars. 154m. DIR: Stanley Kramer. CAST: Spencer Tracy, Milton Berle, Jonathan Winters, Buddy Hackett, Sid Caesar, Phil Silvers, Mickey Rooney, Peter Falk, Dick Shawn, Ethel Merman, Buster Keaton, Jimmy Durante, Edie Adams, Dorothy Provine. 1963

IT'S A WONDERFUL LIFE ★★★★1/2 Have you ever wished you'd never been born? What if that wish were granted? That's the premise of Frank Capra's heartbreaking, humorous, and ultimately heartwarming *It's a Wonderful Life*. The story is about a good man who is so busy helping others that life seems to pass him by. B&W; 129m. DIR: Frank Capra. CAST: James Stewart, Donna Reed, Lionel Barrymore, Thomas Mitchell, Ward Bond, Henry Travers. 1946 DVD

IT'S ALIVE! ★★★1/2 Camp classic about a mutated baby with a thirst for human blood has to be seen to be believed. Convincing effects work by Rick Baker and a fantastic score by Bernard Herrmann make this film one to remember. Rated PG. 91m. DIR: Larry Cohen. CAST: John P. Ryan, Sharon Farrell, Andrew Duggan, Guy Stockwell, Michael Ansara. 1974

IT'S ALIVE III: ISLAND OF THE ALIVE ★★1/2 In this sequel, the mutant babies are sequestered on a desert island, where they reproduce and make their way back home to wreak havoc. Although this is a surprisingly strong entry in the *Alive* series, it suffers from some sloppy effects and mediocre acting. Rated R for violence. 95m. DIR: Larry Cohen. CAST: Michael Moriarty, Karen Black, Gerrit Graham, James Dixon. 1986

IT'S ALL TRUE ★★★★1/2 This fresh glimpse of Orson Welles's three aborted 1942 docudramas about Latin American culture—commissioned to promote President Roosevelt's Good Neighbor Policy—sadly reminds us of all the great films Welles never made. His unfinished shorts about a Mexican boy and his bull, the samba, and four Brazilian fishermen on a social protest voyage are mixed with interviews of the legendary filmmaker and his associates. The result is part travelogue, part historic treasure, and part passion play. Rated G. 89m. DIR: Richard Wilson, Myron Meisel, Bill Krohn. CAST: Orson Welles. 1993

IT'S ALWAYS FAIR WEATHER ★★★ World War II buddies Gene Kelly, Dan Dailey, and Michael Kidd meet a decade after discharge and find they actively dislike one another. Enter romance, reconciliation ploys, and attempted exploitation of their reunion

on televison. Don't be surprised to realize it recalls *On the Town*. 102m. DIR: Gene Kelly, Stanley Donen. CAST: Gene Kelly, Dan Dailey, Michael Kidd, Cyd Charisse, Dolores Gray, David Burns. 1955

IT'S GOOD TO BE ALIVE ★★★1/2 The tragedy of a great athlete being struck down in the prime of his career is dealt with in this story of Brooklyn Dodgers catcher Roy Campanella (Paul Winfield). Campanella had two spectacular seasons with the Dodgers before being permanently crippled from the waist down in a car accident in 1958. This film focuses on Campanella's struggle with self-respect after the wreck. A good companion piece to *Brian's Song*. 100m. DIR: Michael Landon. CAST: Paul Winfield, Lou Gossett Jr., Ruby Dee, Ramon Bieri, Lloyd Gough. 1974

IT'S IN THE BAG ★★★ The plot (if there ever was one) derives from the Russian fable about an impoverished nobleman on a treasure hunt. Continuity soon goes out the window, however, when the cast starts winging it in one hilarious episode after another. This is Fred Allen, acerbic and nasal as always, in his best screen comedy. B&W; 87m. DIR: Richard Wallace. CAST: Fred Allen, Jack Benny, Binnie Barnes, Robert Benchley, Victor Moore, Sidney Toler, Rudy Vallee, William Bendix, Don Ameche. 1945

IT'S IN THE WATER (1996) ★★ Homophobia rears its nasty head in small-town Texas when an AIDS hospice opens up; meanwhile a housewife finds herself attracted to one of the female nurses. Writer-director Kelli Herd's heart is in the right place, but her script is shrill and preachy and her direction stilted. Not rated; contains frank discussion of sexual orientation. 100m. DIR: Kelli Herd. CAST: Keri Jo Chapman, Teresa Garrett, Barbara Lasater. 1996 DVD

•IT'S IN THE WATER (1998) ★★★1/2 In this independent comedy, Keri Jo Chapman plays a woman trapped in a loveless marriage, who has a lesbian affair with an old friend. As word gets out, the gossip induces hysteria in the small-town citizens who fear that there's something in the water. While some performances are rough around the edges and some dialogue is clumsy, the overall effect is one of joy and celebration. Simple, refreshing message delivered in a simple, refreshing manner. Not rated; contains adult situations and language. 100m. DIR: Kelli Herd. CAST: Keri Jo Chapman, Teresa Garrett, John Hallum. 1998 DVD

IT'S MY PARTY ★★★1/2 Eric Roberts plays an architect with AIDS who, as death nears, gathers friends and family around him for a last farewell; unexpectedly, his ex-lover shows up as well. Much of the film tends toward predictable soap opera, but it avoids maudlin excess thanks to sensitive direction and fine acting. Rated R for profanity and mature themes. 110m. DIR: Randal Kleiser. CAST: Eric Roberts, Gregory Harrison, Margaret Cho, Bronson Pinchot, Lee Grant, Marlee Matlin, Olivia Newton-John, George Segal, Roddy McDowall, Paul Regina. 1996

IT'S MY TURN ★★ Jill Clayburgh is a college professor confused about her relationship with live-in lover Charles Grodin, a Chicago real estate salesman. Then she meets baseball player Michael Douglas. They fall in love. The viewer yawns. Rated R. 91m. DIR: Claudia Weill. CAST: Jill Clayburgh, Michael Douglas, Beverly Garland, Charles Grodin. 1980

IT'S PAT: THE MOVIE ★★ Another *Saturday Night Live* character limps to the big screen, and even though this film clocks in at a measly 78 minutes, it still seems 60 minutes too long. Some good laughs are derived from attempting to discover title character's gender, but Charles Rocket as an obsessed neighbor is way out there. Rated PG-13 for plenty of sexual innuendo. 78m. DIR: Adam Bernstein. CAST: Julia Sweeney, David Foley, Charles Rocket, Kathy Griffin, Julie Hayden. 1994

IVAN THE TERRIBLE—PART I & PART II ★★½ ★★★ Considered among the classics of world cinema, this epic biography of Russia's first czar was commissioned by Joseph Stalin to encourage acceptance of his harsh and historically similar policies. World-renowned director Sergei Eisenstein, instead, transformed what was designed as party propaganda into a panoramic saga of how power corrupts those seeking it. B&W; 188m. DIR: Sergei Eisenstein. CAST: Nikolai Cherkassov, Ludmila Tselikovskaya. 1945 DVD

IVANHOE (1952) ★★★★ Robert Taylor stars as Sir Walter Scott's dashing knight Ivanhoe. His mission is to secure the ransom for King Richard the Lionhearted, who has been captured while returning from the Crusades. Action and swordplay abound as Ivanhoe strives for Richard's release and protects two very fair maidens (Elizabeth Taylor and Joan Fontaine) from the lecherous grasp of archvillain George Sanders. 106m. DIR: Richard Thorpe. CAST: Robert Taylor, Elizabeth Taylor, Joan Fontaine, George Sanders, Sebastian Cabot. 1952

IVANHOE (1982) ★★★★ Lavish remake of the 1952 version of Sir Walter Scott's novel of chivalry and derring-do. This time, Anthony Andrews is the disinherited knight who joins ranks with Robin Hood to recapture King Richard's throne from the sniveling Prince John. Brilliant costuming and pageantry. Originally a TV mini-series. 180m. DIR: Douglas Camfield. CAST: Anthony Andrews, James Mason, Sam Neill, Olivia Hussey. 1982

●**IVANHOE (1997)** ★★★ Sir Walter Scott's classic about love and loyalty is remade, yet again, this time as a TV miniseries with an emphasis on the ill treatment afforded Jews in twelfth-century England. Remaining loyal to the displaced King Richard, Ivanhoe takes on Prince John and his minions. This forms the backdrop to his long-time romance with Rowena and new friendship with Rebecca as his heroism extends to protecting her and her father. Splendid pageantry and costuming. Not rated; contains violence and animal brutality. 180m. DIR: Stuart Orme. CAST: Steven Waddington, Susan Lynch, Victoria Smurfit, Ralph Brown. 1997

I'VE ALWAYS LOVED YOU ★★★ A lavish musical featuring Arthur Rubinstein on the soundtrack performing selections by Rachmaninoff, Tchaikovsky, Beethoven, Chopin, Liszt, Wagner, and Mendels-

sohn—to underscore the romance of an arrogant orchestra conductor and the lady pianist who upstages him. The UCLA archivally restored print restores the vibrant Technicolor and provides a clean soundtrack. 117m. DIR: Frank Borzage. CAST: Catherine McLeod, Philip Dorn, Maria Ouspenskaya, Felix Bressart, Elizabeth Patterson, Vanessa Brown, Adele Mara, Fritz Feld, Stephanie Bachelor, Cora Witherspoon. 1946

●**I'VE BEEN WAITING FOR YOU** ★★★ Effective adaptation of Lois Duncan's novel *Gallows Hill*, a reincarnation/witchcraft chiller set in a high school. Here, the descendants of those who participated in a witch trial are compelled to relive the event. Rated PG-13 for violence. 90m. DIR: Christopher Leitch. CAST: Sarah Chalke, Christian Campbell, Soleil Moon Frye, Markie Post. 1998 DVD

I'VE HEARD THE MERMAIDS SINGING ★★★ A slight but often engaging story about a naïve photographer (Sheila McCarthy) who longs to be a part of the elitist art world. The cloyingly whimsical ending is the only thunk in this nifty debut from director Patricia Rozema. Rated PG. 83m. DIR: Patricia Rozema. CAST: Sheila McCarthy, Paule Viallargeon, Anne-Marie Macdonald. 1987

IVORY HUNTERS ★★★½ Powerful made-for-cable drama reveals the horrors of elephants mutilated for their tusks. Manages to make its point without overt preaching. John Lithgow plays an author in Nairobi looking for his missing researcher. There he meets a dedicated field biologist (Isabella Rossellini) and a police inspector (James Earl Jones) waging their own wars against poachers. 94m. DIR: Joseph Sargent. CAST: John Lithgow, Isabella Rossellini, James Earl Jones, Tony Todd. 1990

IVORY-HANDLED GUN, THE ★★½ Buck Ward and the Wolverine Kid have a score to settle that goes back to their father's time and they each have one ivory-handled gun and want the other. Released with a serial chapter, cartoon, and newsreel. B&W; 59m. DIR: Ray Taylor. CAST: Buck Jones, Charlotte Wynters, Walter Miller, Carl Stockdale, Frank Rice, Bob Kortman, Stanley Blystone. 1935

IZZY & MOE ★★★½ Together for the last time, Jackie Gleason and Art Carney are near-perfect as ex-vaudevillians who become New York Prohibition agents in this made-for-TV movie based on actual characters. The two stars still worked beautifully together after all those years. 100m. DIR: Jackie Cooper. CAST: Jackie Gleason, Art Carney, Cynthia Harris, Zohra Lampert. 1985

JABBERWOCKY ★★1/2 Monty Python fans will be disappointed to see only one group member, Michael Palin, in this British film. Palin plays a dim-witted peasant during the Dark Ages. A monster called Jabberwocky is destroying villages all over the countryside, so Palin tries to destroy the monster. There are some funny moments but nothing in comparison with true Python films. No MPAA rating. 100m. DIR: Terry Gilliam. CAST: Michael Palin, Max Wall, Deborah Fallender. **1977**

J'ACCUSE ★★★★ Director Abel Gance's remake of this classic silent film shows the horrors of war as it affects two friends, soldiers in love with the same woman. Cinematically rich, with an unforgettable sequence showing war casualties rising from their graves. In French with English subtitles. B&W; 95m. DIR: Abel Gance. CAST: Victor Francen, Jean Max. **1938**

JACK ★★★ Robin Williams adds another misfit to his résumé in this mostly lighthearted fantasy–tragedy about a little boy with an unusual disease that causes premature aging. James DeMonaco and Gary Nadeau's script too often takes the easy way out, focusing on the comedic aspects of a boy trapped inside a man's body, rather than dwelling on the situation's truly tragic aspects. Rated PG-13 for profanity and blue humor. 113m. DIR: Francis Ford Coppola. CAST: Robin Williams, Diane Lane, Jennifer Lopez, Brian Kerwin, Fran Drescher, Bill Cosby. **1996**

JACK AND SARAH ★★★ A recently widowed London attorney (Richard E. Grant) impulsively hires an American waitress (Samantha Mathis) as nanny to his infant daughter. This affable romantic comedy-drama tends to wander from scene to scene and juggles a few more plot threads than it can handle; still, it never becomes predictable, and the surprising rapport between Grant and Mathis (along with the excellent supporting cast) carries the day. Rated R for profanity and brief nudity. 100m. DIR: Tim Sullivan. CAST: Richard E. Grant, Samantha Mathis, Judi Dench, Ian McKellen, David Swift, Eileen Atkins, Cherie Lunghi. **1996**

JACK BE NIMBLE ★★1/2 Some creepy moments aren't enough to distinguish this supernatural thriller from the rest of the pack. As babies, Jack and Dora were abandoned and split up by adoption. Dora uses her extrasensory powers to locate Jack and finds that he is in danger. Not rated; contains intense situations. 93m. DIR: Garth Maxwell. CAST: Alexis Arquette, Sarah Kennedy, Bruno Lawrence. **1994 DVD**

JACK BENNY PROGRAM, THE (TV SERIES) ★★★★ Following the formula that had made him a smash on radio, Jack Benny became a fixture on TV. Bolstered by the top-notch character actors who popped up on the show, Benny held the spotlight with a pregnant pause, a hand on the chin, or a shift of the eyes. Comic bits frequently revolved around Benny's stinginess and deadly violin playing. Video appearances include Ernie Kovacs, Jayne Mansfield, Johnny Carson, Connie Francis, The Smothers Brothers, George Burns, Humphrey Bogart, Kirk Douglas, Fred Allen, Ann-Margret, and Bob Hope. B&W; 30m. DIR: Frederick de Cordova. CAST: Jack Benny, Mary Livingstone, Eddie "Rochester" Anderson, Dennis Day, Don Wilson, Mel Blanc. **1950–1965**

•**JACK BULL, THE** ★★★★ This unusual Western focuses on one man's quest for justice. When two of Myrl Redding's (John Cusack) horses and one of his workers are abused by the richest man in the territory of Wyoming, Redding seeks justice, first through the law, then by his own means. Politics and loyalties work against Redding's quest, but in the end he triumphs ... at great cost. This made-for-cable original is based on a true story, and contains enough grit and moral dilemma to chew on for a week. Excellent performances by the entire cast enhance the offbeat story of one man's justice. Rated R for profanity and violence. 116m. DIR: John Badham. CAST: John Cusack, John Goodman, L. Q. Jones, Miranda Otto, John C. McGinley, John Savage. **1999 DVD**

JACK FROST ★★ When a serial killer is accidentally exposed to experimental genetic materials, he is transformed into a murderous snowman. Horror spoof is too gruesome to be funny and too goofy to be scary—and features some of the phoniest snow you've ever seen. Rated R for gruesome violence and profanity. 89m. DIR: Michael Cooney. CAST: Christopher Allport, Scott McDonald, F. William Parker. **1997 DVD**

JACK FROST (1998) 🎬 Decent special effects can't salvage this sappy disaster. Michael Keaton plays a blues singer who becomes a better dad to his son when he is reincarnated as a talking snowman who throws a mean snowball. Rated PG for a sexual situation. 100m. DIR: Troy Miller. CAST: Michael Keaton, Kelly Preston, Mark Addy, Joseph Cross. **1998 DVD**

JACK KNIFE MAN, THE ★★★★ A lonely old river rat finds his life changed for the better by an orphan boy left in his care. Better than the hokey plot sounds, with believable characterizations and impressively atmospheric direction by a young King Vidor. Silent with musical score. B&W; 86m. DIR: King Vidor. CAST: Fred Turner, Harry Todd, Bobby Kelso, Florence Vidor. **1920**

JACK LONDON ★★ Episodic, fictionalized account of one of America's most popular authors is entertaining, but one wishes for a more definitive biography. Heavily influenced by the anti-Japanese sentiment rampant at the time of its release, the tragic tale of the poor boy who gained and alienated the love of America and the world cries out to be remade in today's more permissive atmosphere. B&W; 94m. DIR: Alfred Santell. CAST: Michael O'Shea, Susan Hayward, Osa Massen, Harry Davenport, Frank Craven, Virginia Mayo. **1943**

JACK THE BEAR ★★★★ The joys and horrors of childhood are explored in this insightful film in which a local TV personality, who hosts monster movies, attempts to raise his two sons after the tragic death of his wife. The title character is his eldest son, a preteen whose adventures with first love and new friends are darkened by the specter of a psychotic neighbor. Rated PG for brief profanity and violence. 99m. DIR: Marshall Herskovitz. CAST: Danny DeVito, Robert J. Steinmiller, Miko Hughes, Gary Sinise, Art La Fleur, Stefan Gierasch, Erica Yohn, Julia Louis-Dreyfus, Reese Witherspoon, Bert Remsen. 1993

JACK THE GIANT KILLER ★★★1/2 A delightful reworking of "Jack and the Beanstalk," with many innovative special effects to give it adult appeal. Kerwin Mathews of Ray Harryhausen's *Sinbad* movies fights giants and monsters molded by Harryhausen's disciple, Jim Danforth. Lots of fun. 94m. DIR: Nathan Juran. CAST: Kerwin Mathews, Torin Thatcher, Judi Meredith. 1962

JACK THE RIPPER (1959) ★★ This thoroughly fictionalized rendering of the exploits of Whitechapel's mass murderer hasn't aged well. B&W; 84m. DIR: Robert S. Baker, Monty Berman. CAST: Lee Patterson, Eddie Byrne, George Rose. 1959

JACK THE RIPPER (1979) ★★ Klaus Kinski plays Jack the Ripper, and Josephine Chaplin is Cynthia, the Scotland Yard inspector's girlfriend. Jack the Ripper is terrorizing London by killing women and disposing of their bodies in the Thames River. Rated R for violence and nudity. 82m. DIR: Jess (Jesus) Franco. CAST: Klaus Kinski, Josephine Chaplin. 1979 DVD

JACK THE RIPPER (1988) ★★★★ For more than a century the enigma of Jack the Ripper and why he disemboweled five prostitutes in 1888 London has plagued criminologists and historians. In this fine teleplay, all who have been suspect are introduced and examined. Director David Wickes comes up with what is both a possible and probable solution as to why he has never been identified. Michael Caine is outstanding as Frederick Abberline, the alcoholic Scotland Yard inspector in charge of the investigation. Not rated; surprisingly little gore, but not for the kids. 200m. DIR: David Wickes. CAST: Michael Caine, Armand Assante, Ray McAnally, Susan George, Jane Seymour, Lewis Collins, Ken Bones, Harry Andrews. 1988

JACKAL, THE ★★★1/2 Events have been updated and key points have been modified in this absorbing remake of *The Day of the Jackal*. As before, this is a disturbing parable on a free society's vulnerability to terrorists and the shocking ease with which a methodical killer—in this case, Bruce Willis—could snuff any of our public figures. Sleek, intelligent, well cast, and always fun to watch. Rated R for violence and profanity. 124m. DIR: Michael Caton-Jones. CAST: Bruce Willis, Richard Gere, Sidney Poitier, Diane Venora, Mathilda May. 1997 DVD

•JACKER 2: DESCENT TO HELL ♥ This low-budget horror movie is nothing short of mind-numbing as an unkillable carjacker runs rampant on a spree of destruction and mayhem. Not rated; contains profanity, violence, nudity, and simulated sex. 89m. DIR: Barry Gaines. CAST: Philip Herman, Barry Gaines, Ben Stanski, Nancy Feliciano. 1999

JACKIE BROWN ★★★★ At long last, the immensely talented Pam Grier gets her due as the star of this crime caper, based on the novel *Rum Punch*

by Elmore Leonard. This tense thriller, full of surprises and outstanding performances, is no *Pulp Fiction*, but it'll do just fine for fans of the filmmaker's offbeat style. Rated R for violence, profanity, and nudity. 155m. DIR: Quentin Tarantino. CAST: Pam Grier, Samuel L. Jackson, Robert Forster, Bridget Fonda, Michael Keaton, Robert De Niro, Michael Bowen, Chris Tucker, Lisa Gay Hamilton, Tiny Lister Jr. 1997

JACKIE CHAN'S FIRST STRIKE ★★★ There are plenty of thrills, chills, and spills in this Jackie Chan movie, which also is known as *Police Story 4: First Strike*. But by editing it for American audiences, the distributors have taken all the sense out of the story and left our globe-trotting hero bouncing from one life-or-death encounter to another. *Rumble in the Bronx* was a better example of making a Hong Kong release into watchable U.S. fare. Rated PG-13 for violence. 88m. DIR: Stanley Tong. CAST: Jackie Chan, Jackson Lou. 1996

JACKIE CHAN'S POLICE FORCE ♥ A lame, comedic kung fu mixture. Rated PG-13 for violence. 101m. DIR: Jackie Chan. CAST: Jackie Chan, Brigitte Lin. 1986

JACKIE COLLINS' LUCKY CHANCES ★★1/2 This TV miniseries combines two of Jackie Collins's steamy novels. The first and better half traces crime boss Gino Santangelo's rise to power, while the remainder of the film is devoted to his headstrong and not very endearing daughter, Lucky (Nicollette Sheridan), and her quest to win Dad's approval. Predictable and melodramatic, but you'll get hooked anyway. Not rated; contains mild sex and violence. 285m. DIR: Buzz Kulik. CAST: Nicollette Sheridan, Vincent Irizarry, Michael Nader. 1990

JACKIE ROBINSON STORY, THE ★★★★ This is one of the best baseball films ever—the biography of Jackie Robinson, first black to play in the major leagues. The performances (including Mr. Robinson as himself) are very good, and the direction is sharp. B&W; 76m. DIR: Alfred E. Green. CAST: Jackie Robinson, Ruby Dee, Minor Watson, Louise Beavers. 1950 DVD

JACKKNIFE ★★★★ Ed Harris and Kathy Baker star as brother and sister in this drama about veterans who suffer from post-Vietnam stress syndrome. Robert De Niro plays another vet who comes into their lives, causing volatile changes. Rated R, with profanity and violence. 102m. DIR: David Jones. CAST: Robert De Niro, Ed Harris, Kathy Baker. 1989

JACK-O ♥ Land developers unearth an ancient demon, who continues his centuries-old quest for blood. *Pumpkinhead* did it first and much better. Rated R for violence and adult language. 90m. DIR: Steve Latshaw. CAST: Linnea Quigley, Rebecca Wicks, Gary Doles, John Carradine. 1995 DVD

JACKO AND LISE ♥ This film should have been called *Jacko and Freddie* because most of it concerns Jacko and his pal Freddie escaping responsibility and adulthood by doing juvenile things. In French. Rated PG. 92m. DIR: Walter Bal. CAST: Laurent Malet, Annie Girardot, Michel Montanary, Evelyne Bouix, Françoise Arnoul. 1975

JACKPOT, THE ★★★★ A satire on radio quiz programs that pokes fun at public reaction more than industry greed and has the cast to put it over. B&W; 87m. DIR: Walter Lang. CAST: James Stewart, Barbara Hale, James Gleason, Natalie Wood, Tommy Rettig, Patricia Medina. 1950

JACK'S BACK ★★★ Not a splatter film, but a fairly thoughtful suspense melodrama. James Spader portrays twin brothers in this tale of a Jack-the-Ripper copycat killer operating in modern-day Los Angeles. Rated R for gore. 90m. DIR: Rowdy Herrington. CAST: James Spader, Cynthia Gibb, Robert Picardo, Rod Loomis, Chris Mulkey. 1988

JACKSON COUNTY JAIL ★★★1/2 This chase film is pretty good. Yvette Mimieux escapes from jail with fellow inmate Tommy Lee Jones. Audiences can't help but sympathize with Mimieux, because she was unfairly arrested and then raped by her jailer. Rated R. 89m. DIR: Michael Miller. CAST: Yvette Mimieux, Tommy Lee Jones, Robert Carradine. 1976

JACKSONS, THE: AN AMERICAN DREAM ★★★1/2 Though slanted in favor of its title characters, this made-for-TV movie features excellent performances by a star-studded cast as they act out the saccharine history of one of America's most talented dysfunctional families. Main attraction Michael is played by fifteen different actors as he ages. Not rated. 225m. DIR: Karen Arthur. CAST: Holly Robinson, Angela Bassett, Billy Dee Williams, Margaret Avery, Lawrence Hilton-Jacobs, Vanessa L. Williams. 1992

JACOB 🐌 It would take a miracle to pull this flat biblical romance together. Matthew Modine, as the hardworking Jacob, spends fourteen years laboring in order to win Rachel's (Lara Flynn Boyle) hand. Hurt by wooden acting, slow pacing, and occasional time leaps that are neither explained nor believable. Not rated; contains sexual situations. 100m. DIR: Peter Hall. CAST: Matthew Modine, Lara Flynn Boyle, Sean Bean, Giancarlo Giannini. 1994

JACOB I HAVE LOVED ★★★ Fine adaptation of Katherine Paterson's Newbery Award–winning book. Bridget Fonda portrays a tomboy who plays second fiddle to her glamorous and talented twin sister. Resentment turns to hatred until Fonda befriends an old sea captain. Originally shown on PBS's *Wonderworks* series. 57m. DIR: Victoria Hochberg. CAST: Bridget Fonda, Jenny Robertson, John Kellogg. 1989

JACOB TWO-TWO MEETS THE HOODED FANG ★★★1/2 Delightful tale of a boy nicknamed Jacob Two-Two because he has to say everything twice when talking to grownups. (They never listen to him the first time.) Fed up with adults, he dreams that he is sentenced to Slimer's Island, a children's prison where his guard is the Hooded Fang (a funny performance by Alex Karras). The low budget shows, but most of the humor of Mordecai Richler's book is retained. Rated G. 80m. DIR: Theodore J. Flicker. CAST: Stephen Rosenberg, Alex Karras. 1979

JACOB'S LADDER ★★★ A spiritual tale about a Vietnam veteran who is plagued by strange nightmares and, after a while, daymares. Is it the aftereffects of a drug tested on soldiers? Is a parallel universe of demons invading our own? Does the film get a little carried away with all this "other-side" stuff? You decide for yourself. Rated R for violence, nudity, and profanity. 115m. DIR: Adrian Lyne. CAST: Tim Robbins, Elizabeth Peña, Danny Aiello, Matt Craven, Jason Alexander, Macaulay Culkin. 1990 DVD

JADE 🐌 Assistant district attorney David Caruso finds himself compromised when his investigation into the murder of a prominent figure seems to lead to the wife of a longtime friend. It's pure, unadulterated trash. Rated R for violence, profanity, nudity, sex, and rape. 90m. DIR: William Friedkin. CAST: David Caruso, Linda Fiorentino, Chazz Palminteri, Michael Biehn, Richard Crenna, Kevin Tighe. 1995 DVD

JADE MASK, THE ★★ *Charlie Chan* programmer from cheapie Monogram period. Charlie seeks an inventor's murderer. Routine. B&W; 66m. DIR: Phil Rosen. CAST: Sidney Toler, Mantan Moreland, Edwin Luke, Janet Warren, Frank Reicher. 1945

JAGGED EDGE ★★1/2 A publishing magnate (Jeff Bridges) is accused of the ritualistic slaying of his wife; an attorney (Glenn Close) is hired to defend him. They fall in love, conduct an affair during the trial(!), which is not noticed by the ambitious prosecutor (Peter Coyote) (!), and generally behave like total fools; during this, we and Close ponder the burning question: Did Bridges do the dirty deed? Too bad the story doesn't measure up. Rated R for violence. 108m. DIR: Richard Marquand. CAST: Glenn Close, Jeff Bridges, Peter Coyote, Robert Loggia, Leigh Taylor-Young. 1985 DVD

JAIL BAIT (1954) ★★ Delightfully awful crime melodrama from everyone's favorite bad auteur, Ed *(Plan 9 From Outer Space)* Wood. Hardboiled punk Tim Farrell involves the son of a famous plastic surgeon in a robbery, then forces the doctor to help him escape from the police. There's lots of ridiculous dialogue, cheap sets, a final plot twist you'll spot a mile away, and one of the most god awful droning musical scores you'll ever hear. A must-see for camp aficionados. B&W; 70m. DIR: Edward D. Wood Jr. CAST: Timothy Farrell, Dolores Fuller, Lyle Talbot, Herbert Rawlinson, Steve Reeves. 1954

JAILBAIT (1992) ★★ C. Thomas Howell is the burnt-out cop who gets involved with a teenage runaway who witnessed a murder. Pretty seedy affair corrals all of the clichés. Not rated and R-rated versions available. Rated R for nudity, violence, and language; unrated version has more nudity. 100m/103m. DIR: Rafal Zielinski. CAST: C. Thomas Howell, Renee Humphrey. 1992

JAILHOUSE ROCK ★★★★ Quite possibly Elvis Presley's best as far as musical sequences go, this 1957 film is still burdened by a sappy plot. Good-hearted Presley gets stuck in the slammer, only to hook up with a conniving manager (Mickey Shaughnessy). Forget the plot and enjoy the great rock 'n' roll songs. B&W; 96m. DIR: Richard Thorpe. CAST: Elvis Presley, Mickey Shaughnessy, Dean Jones, Judy Tyler. 1957 DVD

JAKE SPANNER PRIVATE EYE ★★ Robert Mitchum plays Jake Spanner, a retired private detective in this mediocre made-for-cable movie. A group of senior citizens decide to help Jake find the double-crossing Ernest Borgnine before an evil drug queen does. 95m. DIR: Lee H. Katzin. CAST: Robert Mitchum, Ernest Borgnine, John Mitchum, Richard Yniguez, Jim

Mitchum, Dick Van Patten, Stella Stevens, Kareem Abdul-Jabbar, Edie Adams. **1989**

JAKE SPEED ★★★1/2 Quirky little adventure thriller, from the folks involved with the equally deft *Night of the Comet.* When Karen Kopins's younger sister is kidnapped and threatened with white slavery by John Hurt's delightfully oily villain, Speed (Wayne Crawford) and his associate Remo (Dennis Christopher) materialize and offer to help. Rated PG for mild violence. 100m. **DIR:** Andrew Lane. **CAST:** Wayne Crawford, Dennis Christopher, Karen Kopins, John Hurt, Leon Ames, Donna Pescow, Barry Primus, Monte Markham. **1986**

•**JAKOB THE LIAR** ★★ Widowed, melancholy cafe owner hides a child from the Gestapo and brings hope to the inhabitants of a Jewish Ghetto in Nazi-occupied 1944 Poland by sharing news he allegedly hears on a secreted radio. The first-rate set designs, costumes, cinematography, and score of this serio-comic Holocaust fable establish a bleak Euroscape. The film nonetheless collapses in a heavy-breathing marriage of irony and unearned sentiment. Rated PG-13 for violence. 113m. **DIR:** Peter Kassovitz. **CAST:** Robin Williams, Alan Arkin, Bob Balaban, Liev Schreiber, Armin Mueller-Stahl, Hannah Taylor Gordon. **1999** DVD

JAMAICA INN ★★★ Not one of Alfred Hitchcock's best directorial efforts. But the cast makes it, just the same. Charles Laughton is Squire Pengallon, the evil chief of a band of cutthroats in Victorian England. Maureen O'Hara is a beautiful damsel in distress. B&W; 98m. **DIR:** Alfred Hitchcock. **CAST:** Charles Laughton, Maureen O'Hara, Leslie Banks, Emlyn Williams, Robert Newton, Mervyn Johns. **1939** DVD

JAMES AND THE GIANT PEACH ★★★★ Roald Dahl's classic children's story gets ambitious treatment from director Henry Selick. Young Paul Terry loses his parents and endures the contempt of two outrageously cruel aunts, until encountering an old beggar with magical, luminescent "crocodile tongues." They infect a dying peach tree, which produces a stadium-sized fruit; once James climbs inside, the live-action performers are replaced by huge, animated insects. James and his new friends experience all sorts of adventures while en route to New York City, none better than an ocean encounter with an impressively frightening mechanical shark. Rated PG for occasional intensity. 80m. **DIR:** Henry Selick. **CAST:** Paul Terry, Joanna Lumley, Miriam Margolyes, Pete Postlethwaite. **1996**

JAMES DEAN—A LEGEND IN HIS OWN TIME ★★1/2 Lackluster dramatization of actor James Dean's life as seen through the eyes of a friend. Stephen McHattie qualifies as a James Dean lookalike and gives a solid performance. This film features a fine supporting cast. 99m. **DIR:** Robert Butler. **CAST:** Michael Brandon, Stephen McHattie, Candy Clark, Amy Irving, Meg Foster, Jayne Meadows, Brooke Adams. **1976**

JAMES DEAN STORY, THE ★★1/2 Robert Altman's first feature film was this unexceptional documentary about the late actor that relies heavily on clips from his films and television appearances. Not rated.

79m. **DIR:** Robert Altman, George W. George. **1957** DVD

JAMES JOYCE'S WOMEN ★★★★1/2 A delicious, verbally erotic movie. With Joyce as the writer and Fionnula Flanagan (writer and producer) as interpreter, things are bound to be intense. The film is virtually a one-woman show, with Flanagan portraying seven different characters from Joyce's life and works. The humor and sensuality will thrill Joyce fans. Rated R for nudity and sexual situations. 89m. **DIR:** Michael Pearce. **CAST:** Fionnula Flanagan, Timothy E. O'Grady, Chris O'Neill. **1985**

JAMON, JAMON ★★1/2 A male model is hired to woo a young woman by her well-to-do mother, who disapproves of the girl's love for the son of the town prostitute. This film was named best picture at the Venice Film Festival, but we thought it was little more than a silly sex comedy with a soap-opera-style plot. In Spanish with English subtitles. Not rated, the film has nudity, simulated sex, profanity, and violence. 95m. **DIR:** Bigas Luna. **CAST:** Anna Galiena, Stefania Sandrelli, Javier Bardem, Penelope Cruz. **1993**

JANE AND THE LOST CITY ★★★1/2 World War II British comic-strip heroine, Jane, comes to life in the form of lovely Kristen Hughes. She must help England's war effort by finding the diamonds of Africa's Lost City before the Nazis get them. A treasure trove of chuckles. Rated PG for profanity. 94m. **DIR:** Terry Marcel. **CAST:** Kristen Hughes, Maud Adams, Sam Jones. **1987**

JANE AUSTEN IN MANHATTAN ★★ The team responsible for *A Room with a View* comes up empty with this satire about two off-Broadway producers battling for the rights to a little-known play written by Jane Austen when she was 12 years old. The infighting among the theatrical community is amusing, but the movie is predominantly cold and unmoving. Not rated. 108m. **DIR:** James Ivory. **CAST:** Anne Baxter, Robert Powell, Sean Young, Tim Choate. **1980**

JANE AUSTEN'S MAFIA ★★1/2 Director Jim Abrahams gives the *Airplane!* treatment to *The Godfather* (not to mention *Casino, Forrest Gump, The English Patient,* and *Showgirls*). There are a few good laughs, but not enough to overcome the duds and misfires. Alternate title: *Mafia!* Rated PG-13 for risqué humor. 84m. **DIR:** Jim Abrahams. **CAST:** Jay Mohr, Billy Burke, Christina Applegate, Pamela Gidley, Olympia Dukakis, Lloyd Bridges, Tony Lo Bianco. **1998**

JANE DOE ★★1/2 A passable suspense movie about a woman who is brutally attacked and left for dead in a shallow grave. She survives with amnesia, but she can't identify her attacker. Made for TV. 96m. **DIR:** Ivan Nagy. **CAST:** Karen Valentine, William Devane, Eva Marie Saint, David Huffman. **1983** DVD

JANE EYRE (1934) ★★ A willing second-tier cast and the passage of time make something of a curiosity of this classic story of a young orphan girl who grows up to become a governess. Tolerable. B&W; 70m. **DIR:** Christy Cabanne. **CAST:** Colin Clive, Virginia Bruce. **1934**

JANE EYRE (1944) ★★★★ Devotee's of Charlotte Brontë's romantic novel about a young woman leaving an orphans' home and being placed as a governess may be disappointed. But for others, the movie really starts with the appearance of Orson Welles and his interpretation of the moody and mysterious Edward Rochester. B&W; 96m. **DIR:** Robert Stevenson. **CAST:** Orson Welles, Joan Fontaine, Margaret O'Brien, Peggy Ann Garner, John Sutton, Sara Allgood, Henry Daniell, Agnes Moorehead, Elizabeth Taylor. **1944**

JANE EYRE (1983) ★★★★ This marvelous BBC production honors Charlotte Brontë's classic tale of courage and romance. A thrilling and thorough adaptation. Zelah Clarke plays the orphaned, mistreated, and unloved Jane who later falls for the darkly mysterious Mr. Rochester (Timothy Dalton). 239m. **DIR:** Julian Amyes. **CAST:** Timothy Dalton, Zelah Clarke. **1983**

JANE EYRE (1996) ★★★★ The only drawback in this adaptation of Charlotte Brontë's classic novel of unlikely romance is its brevity. Anna Paquin is properly spirited as the young orphan abandoned in a sepulchral girls' school by distant relatives; she matures into the equally vigorous Charlotte Gainsbourg, who accepts a position as governess for the ward of brooding Edward Rochester (William Hurt). Amid secrets involving an insolent maid and long-unglimpsed rooms, Jane unwisely falls in love with Rochester. Although faithfully capturing the massive book's middle section, this film concludes with dissatisfying abruptness. Rated PG. 112m. **DIR:** Franco Zeffirelli. **CAST:** William Hurt, Charlotte Gainsbourg, Joan Plowright, Anna Paquin, Geraldine Chaplin, Billie Whitelaw, Maria Schneider, Fiona Shaw, Elle Macpherson, John Wood. **1996**

JANIS ★★★ The most comprehensive documentary study of flower child Janis Joplin, this is filled with poignant memories and electrifying performances. Rated R for language. 96m. **DIR:** Howard Alk, Seaton Findlay. **1974**

JANUARY MAN, THE ★★ Whew! We've seen some weird movies in our time, but this one deserves a special place in some museum. John Patrick Shanley (*Moonstruck*) wrote this goofy mystery about a former police detective (Kevin Kline) who is drafted back into service when a serial killer begins to terrorize New York City. Rated R for profanity and violence. 110m. **DIR:** Pat O'Connor. **CAST:** Kevin Kline, Susan Sarandon, Mary Elizabeth Mastrantonio, Harvey Keitel, Danny Aiello, Alan Rickman, Rod Steiger. **1989**

JASON AND THE ARGONAUTS (1963) ★★★★ The captivating special effects by master Ray Harryhausen are the actual stars of this movie. This is the telling of the famous myth of Jason (Todd Armstrong), his crew of derring-doers, and their search for the Golden Fleece. 104m. **DIR:** Don Chaffey. **CAST:** Todd Armstrong, Gary Raymond, Honor Blackman. **1963 DVD**

•**JASON AND THE ARGONAUTS (2000)** ★★ Despite lavish costuming and special effects, this big-budget, TV miniseries disappoints viewers. Acting ranges from emotionless line reading to corny melodrama, while battles with assorted creatures will only dazzle preteens. Stick with Ray Harryhausen's 1963 version. Not rated; contains violence. 180m. **DIR:** Nick Willing. **CAST:** Jason London, Dennis Hopper, Natasha Henstridge. **2000 DVD**

JASON GOES TO HELL: THE FINAL FRIDAY ★★★ Fans of the *Friday the 13th* films will enjoy this ninth and final (?) trip to the infamous Crystal Lake. We wouldn't reveal anything by saying Jason is killed in this movie. He's been killed so often it is hard to keep track. But some loose ends are made tighter, and an intriguing explanation for Jason's evil is offered. Watch to the very end. Rated R for violence, profanity, and plenty of gore. 88m. **DIR:** Adam Marcus. **CAST:** John D. LeMay, Kari Keegan, Kane Hodder, Steven Williams, Steven Culp, Erin Gray, Allison Smith, Kipp Marcus. **1993**

JASON'S LYRIC ★★1/2 Jason is a store clerk who dates a waitress while attending to the emotional needs of his widowed mother and the welfare of his ex-con, gang-linked brother. This hard-edged African-American romance is punctuated with flashbacks to a fatal domestic altercation, resulting in a disturbing vision of life on the edge of a Texas ghetto. The acting and script that propel the film's courtship are weak. Rated R for violence, nudity, language, and simulated sex. 119m. **DIR:** Doug McHenry. **CAST:** Allen Payne, Bokeem Woodbine, Jada Pinkett, Forest Whitaker, Suzzanne Douglas. **1994 DVD**

•**JAWBREAKER** ★★★ When a birthday prank proves deadly for high-school power brokers, their ruthless leader devises the perfect cover-up. The plot thickens a bit when an awkward nerd discovers the murder. Dark comedy seeks redemption with the perfect comeuppance. Rated R for violence, language, sexual innuendo, and sexual situations. 87m. **DIR:** Darren Stein. **CAST:** Rebecca Gayheart, Rose McGowan, Julie Benz, Judy Greer. **1999 DVD**

JAWS ★★★★★ A young Steven Spielberg (27 at the time) directed this 1975 scare masterpiece based on the Peter Benchley novel. A large shark is terrorizing the tourists at the local beach. The eerie music by John Williams heightens the tension to underscore the shark's presence and scare the audience right out of their seats. Roy Scheider, Robert Shaw, and Richard Dreyfuss offer outstanding performances. Rated PG. 124m. **DIR:** Steven Spielberg. **CAST:** Roy Scheider, Robert Shaw, Richard Dreyfuss, Lorraine Gary, Murray Hamilton. **1975 DVD**

JAWS 2 ★★★ Even though it's a sequel, *Jaws 2* delivers. Police chief Martin Brody (Roy Scheider) believes there's a shark in the waters off Amity again, but his wife and employers think he's crazy. Rated PG. 120m. **DIR:** Jeannot Szwarc. **CAST:** Roy Scheider, Lorraine Gary, Murray Hamilton, Jeffrey Kramer. **1978**

JAWS 3 ★★ Among those marked for lunch in this soggy, unexciting sequel are Lou Gossett Jr., Dennis Quaid, and Bess Armstrong. They look bored. You'll be bored. Rated PG. 97m. **DIR:** Joe Alves. **CAST:** Lou Gossett Jr., Dennis Quaid, Bess Armstrong, Simon MacCorkindale. **1983**

JAWS: THE REVENGE 💗 This third sequel is lowest-common-denominator filmmaking, a by-the-numbers effort. Rated PG-13. 89m. **DIR:** Joseph Sargent. **CAST:** Lorraine Gary, Lance Guest, Michael Caine, Mario Van Peebles, Karen Young. **1987 DVD**

JAWS OF DEATH, THE ★★ Low-rent *Jaws* clone features Jaeckel as a shark breeder who rents his finny friends out to Florida aquariums. But when he finds out that the sharks are being exploited, he seeks revenge. Better than *Jaws: The Revenge*, but not by much. 93m. DIR: William Grefe. CAST: Richard Jaeckel, Jennifer Bishop, Harold Sakata. 1976

JAWS OF SATAN ★★ Satan merrily breezes into town in the form of a cobra seeking revenge on a priest whose ancestors persecuted the Druids. What the viewer gets is this movie from hell, disguised as a rough-hewn horror film. Rated R for gore. 92m. DIR: Bob Claver. CAST: Fritz Weaver, Gretchen Corbett, Jon Korkes. 1984

JAYHAWKERS, THE ★★★ A routine Western story line enhanced by strong personalities in leading roles. Jeff Chandler and Fess Parker come to blows in a power struggle, and French actress Nicole Maurey is caught in the middle. 100m. DIR: Melvin Frank. CAST: Jeff Chandler, Fess Parker, Nicole Maurey, Henry Silva, Herbert Rudley. 1959

JAYNE MANSFIELD STORY, THE ★★ Loni Anderson gives only an average performance as 1950s blonde sex bomb Mansfield. Made for television. 100m. DIR: Dick Lowry. CAST: Loni Anderson, Arnold Schwarzenegger, Kathleen Lloyd. 1980

JAZZ SINGER, THE (1927) ★★★1/2 Generally considered the first talking film, this milestone in motion-picture history is really a silent film with a musical score and a few spoken lines. Al Jolson plays the son of an orthodox cantor who wants his son to follow in his footsteps. Jolson, though touched by his father's wishes, feels he must be a jazz singer. B&W; 89m. DIR: Alan Crosland. CAST: Al Jolson, May McAvoy, Warner Oland, William Demarest, Roscoe Karns, Myrna Loy. 1927

JAZZ SINGER, THE (1953) ★★★1/2 Danny Thomas is a cantor's son who chooses a show-business career over a traditional life in a synagogue. Forget this is a remake of Al Jolson's historic first talkie and view it on its own musical merits. You will be surprised at Thomas's easy way with a song and wonder why he and Peggy Lee were never used to such good advantage again. 107m. DIR: Michael Curtiz. CAST: Danny Thomas, Peggy Lee, Mildred Dunnock, Eduard Franz, Tom Tully, Allyn Joslyn. 1953

JAZZ SINGER, THE (1980) 🦃 Mushy mishmash that only Diamond's most devoted fans will love. Rated PG. 115m. DIR: Richard Fleischer. CAST: Neil Diamond, Laurence Olivier, Lucie Arnaz. 1980 DVD

JAZZMAN ★★★1/2 Good-humored, accessible story about a classically trained Soviet musician who tries to start a jazz combo in the 1930s. In Russian with English subtitles. Not rated. 95m. DIR: Karen Chakhnazarov. CAST: Igor Skoliar, Alexandre Pankratov-Tchiorny. 1983

J.D.'S REVENGE ★★★1/2 A gangster, murdered in 1940s New Orleans, returns from the dead thirty-five years later, possessing the body of a law student in his quest for revenge. Surprisingly well-crafted low-budget thriller. Rated R for strong violence and profanity. 95m. DIR: Arthur Marks. CAST: Glynn Turman, Joan Pringle, Lou Gossett Jr. 1976

JE VOUS AIME (I LOVE YOU ALL) ★★ Some films are so complicated and convoluted you need a viewer's guide while watching them. So it is with this flashback-ridden French import. About a 35-year-old woman, Alice (Catherine Deneuve), who finds it impossible to keep a love relationship alive, it hops, skips, and jumps back and forth through her life. No MPAA rating; the film has sexual situations and nudity. 105m. DIR: Claude Berri. CAST: Catherine Deneuve, Jean-Louis Trintignant, Serge Gainsbourg, Gérard Depardieu. 1981

JEAN DE FLORETTE ★★★★ This is a sort of French *Days of Heaven*, an epic set close to the land, specifically the hilly farm country of Provence. Land is the central issue around which the action swirls. Yves Montand is spellbinding as an ambitious, immoral farmer who dupes his city-bred neighbor Jean de Florette (played by the equally impressive Gérard Depardieu). The rest of the story is told in *Manon of the Spring*. In French with English subtitles. Rated PG. 122m. DIR: Claude Berri. CAST: Yves Montand, Gérard Depardieu, Daniel Auteuil. 1987

JEEVES AND WOOSTER (TV SERIES) ★★★★ P. G. Wodehouse fans will love these faithful renditions of tales about bumbling Bertie Wooster and his all-knowing retainer, Jeeves, who always manages to pull his master's bacon out of the most improbable fires. Aside from Wodehouse's piquant verbal byplay, there's nothing more delightful than watching Jeeves puncture the balloons of his aristocratic, stuffed-shirt employer ... who never even perceives he's been humbled. 52m. each episode. DIR: Robert Young. CAST: Stephen Fry, Hugh Laurie. 1990

JEFFERSON IN PARIS ★★1/2 Sumptuous but plodding account of Thomas Jefferson's tenure as American minister to France (1784–1789). The film dawdles over decor and can't decide whether to focus on Jefferson's personal life or the social unrest in pre-Revolutionary France. Rated PG-13 for mature themes. 144m. DIR: James Ivory. CAST: Nick Nolte, Greta Scacchi, Thandie Newton, Gwyneth Paltrow, Simon Callow, James Earl Jones, Seth Gilliam, Michel Lonsdale, Lambert Wilson. 1995

JEFFREY ★★★1/2 A gay man gives up sex for fear of AIDS, then meets his HIV-positive Mr. Right. Paul Rudnick's brilliantly witty off-Broadway hit gets a faithful (though rather stage-bound) screening, with an excellent all-star cast and Rudnick's hilarious lines compensating for awkward direction and a preening performance by Steven Weber in the title role. Rated R for profanity and frank dialogue. 94m. DIR: Christopher Ashley. CAST: Steven Weber, Patrick Stewart, Michael T. Weiss, Bryan Batt, Sigourney Weaver, Olympia Dukakis, Kathy Najimy, Nathan Lane. 1995

JEKYLL & HYDE ★★★ Michael Caine dons two faces in this remake. Familiar tale gets few new plot twists in this made-for-television thriller. Rated R for horror, violence. 95m. DIR: David Wickes. CAST: Michael Caine, Cheryl Ladd, Joss Ackland, Lionel Jeffries. 1990

JEKYLL & HYDE—TOGETHER AGAIN ★★★ If you like offbeat, crude, and timely humor, you'll enjoy this 1980s-style version of Robert Louis Stevenson's horror classic. Though the film needs some editing, Mark Blankfield is a riot as the mad scientist. Rated R for heavy doses of vulgarity and sexual innuendo.

87m. **DIR:** Jerry Belson. **CAST:** Mark Blankfield, Bess Armstrong, Krista Erickson. 1982

JENNIFER ★★ A carbon copy of *Carrie*—but with snakes. Jennifer is a sweet, innocent child on a poor-kid's scholarship at an uppity school for rich girls. She is tormented until she is harassed into a frenzy. What's the catch? Jennifer was raised by a cult of religious fanatics who believe that God has given her the power to command reptiles. Rated PG. 90m. **DIR:** Brice Mack. **CAST:** Lisa Pelikan, Bert Convy, Nina Foch, John Gavin, Wesley Eure. 1978

JENNIFER 8 ★★★1/2 A solid, inventive ending and crisp dialogue help this sometimes contrived thriller, in which burned-out L.A. cop Andy Garcia joins former partner Lance Henriksen on a small-town police force only to find himself on the trail of a serial killer. Rated R for violence, profanity, and nudity. 127m. **DIR:** Bruce Robinson. **CAST:** Andy Garcia, Uma Thurman, John Malkovich, Lance Henriksen, Kathy Baker, Graham Beckel, Kevin Conway, Perry Lang, Lenny Von Dohlen. 1992 DVD

JENNY LAMOUR ★★★★ Without each other's knowledge, a venal cabaret singer and her doting husband try to cover up what they believe to be their involvement in a murder. But a dogged policeman (a wonderfully sardonic performance by Louis Jouvet) is determined to discover the truth. Witty, atmospheric, and professional. Dubbed. B&W; 105m. **DIR:** Henri-Georges Clouzot. **CAST:** Louis Jouvet, Suzy Delair, Bernard Blier. 1947

JENNY'S WAR ★★1/2 When her son, an RAF pilot, is shot down over Germany during World War II, Jenny Baines (Dyan Cannon) disguises herself as a man and heads to Germany to find him. It may have been based on a real story, but this lengthy made-for-TV movie is utterly preposterous. Not rated; contains no objectionable material. 192m. **DIR:** Steven Gethers. **CAST:** Dyan Cannon, Elke Sommer, Robert Hardy, Christopher Cazenove, Hugh Grant. 1985

JEREMIAH JOHNSON ★★★★ Robert Redford plays Johnson, a simple man who has no taste for cities. We see him as he grows from his first feeble attempts at survival to a hunter who has quickened his senses with wild meat and vegetation—a man who is a part of the wildlife of the mountains. Gives a sense of humanness to a genre that had, up until its release, spent time reworking the same myths. Rated PG. 107m. **DIR:** Sydney Pollack. **CAST:** Robert Redford, Will Geer, Charles Tyner, Stefan Gierasch, Allyn Ann McLerie. 1972 DVD

JERICHO ★★★1/2 Paul Robeson plays a black soldier who is convicted of manslaughter for the accidental murder of his sergeant. He takes advantage of the kindness of officer Henry Wilcoxon to escape across the African desert and begin a new life. Absorbing study of revenge and human dignity. B&W; 77m. **DIR:** Thornton Freeland. **CAST:** Paul Robeson, Henry Wilcoxon, Wallace Ford. 1937

JERICHO FEVER ★★★ In this made-for-cable original, two doctors must battle an unknown disease that was accidentally brought into the United States by terrorists. Now the terrorists must be captured to obtain the cure. A solid plot and good acting make this enjoyable. Not rated; contains violence. 95m.

DIR: Sandor Stern. **CAST:** Stephanie Zimbalist, Perry King, Branscombe Richmond, Alan Scarfe, Ari Barak, Elyssa Davalos, Kario Salem. 1993

JERICHO MILE, THE ★★★★ This tough, inspiring TV movie tells the story of a man, serving a life sentence at Folsom Prison, who dedicates himself to becoming an Olympic-caliber runner. Director Michael Mann makes sure the film is riveting and realistic at all times. 100m. **DIR:** Michael Mann. **CAST:** Peter Strauss, Roger E. Mosley, Brian Dennehy, Billy Green Bush, Ed Lauter, Beverly Todd. 1979

JERK, THE ★★★★ Steve Martin made a very funny starring debut in this wacky comedy. Nonfans probably won't like it, but for those who think he's hilarious, the laughs just keep on coming. Rated R. 94m. **DIR:** Carl Reiner. **CAST:** Steve Martin, Bernadette Peters, Bill Macy, Jackie Mason. 1979 DVD

JERKY BOYS, THE ★★ Two immature louts make prank phone calls out of boredom; even they couldn't be bored enough to sit through this stinker. Rated R for constant profanity. 85m. **DIR:** James Melkonian. **CAST:** Johnny Brennan, Kamal Ahmed, William Hickey, Alan Arkin. 1995

JERRY MAGUIRE ★★★★1/2 This frothy comedy-drama mixes perceptive social commentary, witty dialogue, and a touching love affair. Tom Cruise is an ultraslick sports agent who one night realizes that quality should be more important than quantity; Renee Zellweger is an agency secretary and single mother who comes along when he abandons the fast-lane lifestyle for his own firm. He has but one client: an Arizona Cardinals wide receiver—Cuba Gooding Jr., delivering an Academy Award–winning performance—with as much attitude as natural talent. At least three main storylines occupy this picture, but Cameron Crowe keeps a firm handle on each. Rated R for profanity, nudity, and strong sexual content. 138m. **DIR:** Cameron Crowe. **CAST:** Tom Cruise, Cuba Gooding Jr., Renee Zellweger, Kelly Preston, Jerry O'Connell, Jonathan Lipnicki. 1996 DVD

JERSEY GIRL ★★★1/2 Winning fairy tale about Jersey girl Jami Gertz looking for Mr. Right in Manhattan. She literally runs into him when she sideswipes Dylan McDermott's Mercedes. He's everything she's looking for, but she reminds him of everything he's worked so hard to leave behind. But you know what they say about .opposites. The fun is watching Gertz pursue her man against all odds. Funny, warm, and sweet. Rated PG-13 for language and adult situations. 95m. **DIR:** David Burton Morris. **CAST:** Jami Gertz, Dylan McDermott, Joseph Bologna, Star Jasper, Molly Price, Aida Turturro. 1993

JERUSALEM ★★★★ In turn-of-the-century Sweden, a rural village is torn apart by the preachings of a charismatic faith healer, who leads his followers to resettle in the Holy Land. Director Bille August (adapting a novel by Nobel Prize winner Selma Lagerlof) tells his story of alienation, suffering, and redemption through the lives of two young lovers. The film is slow-moving and overlong, but psychologically complex and superbly acted. In Swedish with English subtitles. Rated PG-13 for brief nudity and mature themes. 166m. **DIR:** Bille August. **CAST:** Maria Bonnevie, Ulf Friberg, Pernilla August, Lena Endre,

Sven-Bertil Taube, Max von Sydow, Olympia Dukakis. 1996

JESSE ★★ By-the-numbers TV movie based on a true story about a small-town nurse who provides medical care in place of the often-absent regional doctor. The contrived dramatic conflict renders much of the story unbelievable. 100m. **DIR:** Glenn Jordan. **CAST:** Lee Remick, Scott Wilson, Richard Marcus, Albert Salmi. 1988

JESSE JAMES ★★★1/2 Tyrone Power is Jesse, and Henry Fonda is Frank in this legend-gilding account of the life and misdeeds of Missouri's most famous outlaw. Bending history, the film paints Jesse as a peaceful man driven to a life of crime by heartless big business in the form of a railroad, and a loving husband and father murdered for profit by a coward. 105m. **DIR:** Henry King. **CAST:** Tyrone Power, Henry Fonda, Nancy Kelly, Randolph Scott, Henry Hull, Jane Darwell, Brian Donlevy, Donald Meek, John Carradine, Slim Summerville, J. Edward Bromberg. 1939

JESSE JAMES AT BAY ★★1/2 Roy Rogers is a fictionalized Jesse James who rides not against the railroads, but against one evil bunch misrepresenting the railroad and stealing the land of poor, honest farmers. A top contender for *the* most farfetched, fallacious frontier foolishness ever filmed. B&W; 56m. **DIR:** Joseph Kane. **CAST:** Roy Rogers, George "Gabby" Hayes, Sally Payne. 1941

JESSE JAMES MEETS FRANKENSTEIN'S DAUGHTER 🦃 The feeble plot pits hero Jesse James against the evil daughter of the infamous doctor of the title. 88m. **DIR:** William Beaudine. **CAST:** John Lupton, Estelita, Cal Bolder, Jim Davis. 1966

JESSE OWENS STORY, THE ★★★ This made-for-TV movie of the Olympic hero provides a provocative insight into the many behind-the-scenes events that plague people who are thrust into public admiration. Dorian Harewood is perfect in his performance of the not-always-admirable hero, a victim of his own inabilities and the uncontrollable events surrounding him. This film also holds up a mirror to our society's many embarrassing racial attitudes. 180m. **DIR:** Richard Irving. **CAST:** Dorian Harewood, Debbi Morgan, George Kennedy, Georg Stanford Brown, Tom Bosley, LeVar Burton. 1984

JESUS ★★ More a Bible study than entertainment; this film is narrated by Alexander Scourby and the words are taken from the Good News Bible, the Book of Luke. Filmed in the Holy Land. 117m. **DIR:** Peter Sykes, John Kirsh. **CAST:** Brian Deacon, Rivka Noiman. 1979

JESUS CHRIST, SUPERSTAR ★★★1/2 Believe it or not, this could be the ancestor of such rock videos as Michael Jackson's "Thriller." The movie illustrates segments of Jesus Christ's later life by staging sets and drama to go along with the soundtrack. This will not offer any religious experiences in the traditional sense, but is interesting nonetheless. Rated G. 103m. **DIR:** Norman Jewison. **CAST:** Ted Neeley, Carl Anderson, Yvonne Elliman. 1973 DVD

JESUS OF MONTREAL ★★★★1/2 Denys Arcand, the French-Canadian writer-director, finds original things to say with a not totally original idea—that the actor playing Jesus in a modern-day passion play

may, in fact, *be* Jesus. Lothaire Bluteau is superb in the title role. In French with English subtitles. Rated R for profanity. 119m. **DIR:** Denys Arcand. **CAST:** Lothaire Bluteau, Denys Arcand. 1990

JESUS OF NAZARETH ★★★★ This vivid TV movie of the life of Jesus is beautifully directed by the poetic genius Franco Zeffirelli. An outstanding cast gives warm and sensitive performances in what is the finest film to date of the familiar Bible story. It fills *three* cassettes but well worth the time. 371m. **DIR:** Franco Zeffirelli. **CAST:** Robert Powell, Anne Bancroft, James Mason, Rod Steiger, Olivia Hussey. 1976 DVD

JET ATTACK 🦃 John Agar tries to rescue an American scientist captured by the North Koreans. B&W; 68m. **DIR:** Edward L. Cahn. **CAST:** John Agar, Audrey Totter, Gregory Walcott. 1958

JET BENNY SHOW, THE ★★1/2 Peculiar spoof stars Jack Benny impersonator Steve Norman as a Buck Rogers–type hero accompanied on his adventures in outer space by a Rochester-like robot. The concept is as elusive as the humor, though fans of the old Jack Benny TV show may want to check it out. Not rated. 77m. **DIR:** Roger D. Evans. **CAST:** Steve Norman, Kevin Dees. 1975

●**JET LI'S THE ENFORCER** ★★1/2 The formula in this 1995 Hong Kong import still works. Jet Li plays an undercover Beijing cop whose public and private lives are about to clash on his latest assignment. The pedestrian plot deals with traditional themes like the loss of a loved one and loyalty, but it is Li who gives the film the punch it needs. Reedited from *My Father Is a Hero*. Rated R for violence. 100m. **DIR:** Corey Yuen. **CAST:** Jet Li, Anita Mui, Tse Miu. 1995 DVD

JETSONS: THE MOVIE ★★ Those futuristic Flintstones—George, Jane, Judy, and Elroy Jetson—get the big-screen treatment with a movie that suffers from too many commercial tie-ins and songs by Tiffany (who voices Judy Jetson). Still there are some funny moments in the story, which has Mr. Spacely (a last bow by the late Mel Blanc) transferring George and family to an outpost in outer space. Rated G. 87m. **DIR:** William Hanna, Joseph Barbera. 1990

JEWEL IN THE CROWN, THE ★★★★★ Based on Paul Scott's *Raj Quartet*, this Emmy Award–winning series first aired on British television in fourteen episodes. It is a wonderful epic that depicts Britain's last years of power in India (1942–1947). The story revolves around the love of an Indian man for a white woman, and the repercussions of their forbidden romance. The love-hate relationship of the English and the Indians is well depicted. 700m. **DIR:** Christopher Morahan, Jim O'Brien. **CAST:** Tim Pigott-Smith, Geraldine James, Peggy Ashcroft, Charles Dance, Susan Wooldridge, Art Malik, Judy Parfitt. 1984

JEWEL OF THE NILE, THE ★★★1/2 This generally enjoyable sequel to *Romancing the Stone* details the further adventures of novelist Joan Wilder (Kathleen Turner) and soldier of fortune Jack Colton (Michael Douglas) in the deserts of North Africa. Danny DeVito supplies the laughs. Rated PG. 106m.

DIR: Lewis Teague. **CAST:** Michael Douglas, Kathleen Turner, Danny DeVito, Avner Eisenberg. 1985 DVD

JEZEBEL ★★★★ Bette Davis gives one of her finest performances as a spoiled southern belle in this release. Directed by William Wyler, it brought Davis her second best-actress Oscar—and a well-deserved one at that. She's superb as the self-centered "Jezebel" who takes too long in deciding between a banker (Henry Fonda) and a dandy (George Brent) and loses all. B&W; 103m. **DIR:** William Wyler. **CAST:** Bette Davis, Henry Fonda, George Brent, Spring Byington. 1938 DVD

JEZEBEL'S KISS ★★ Steamy, sleazy thriller about a beautiful young woman who seeks revenge for the death of her grandfather. Inept. Rated R for nudity, violence, and profanity. 95m. **DIR:** Harvey Keith. **CAST:** Katherine Barrese, Malcolm McDowell, Everett McGill, Meredith Baxter-Birney, Meg Foster, Bert Remsen. 1990

JFK ★★★★ Director Oliver Stone's fascinating examination of the assassination of President John F. Kennedy attempts to disprove the contention that Lee Harvey Oswald was the lone killer. Kevin Costner stars as Jim Garrison, the New Orleans district attorney who attempted to prosecute a local businessman for conspiracy in the Nov. 22, 1963, murder. Stone, a master of overstatement, is on his best behavior, but there are moments of unnecessary sensationalism. Rated R for violence, profanity, and suggested sex. 190m. **DIR:** Oliver Stone. **CAST:** Kevin Costner, Sissy Spacek, Joe Pesci, Tommy Lee Jones, Gary Oldman, Jay O. Sanders, Michael Rooker, Laurie Metcalf, Gary Grubbs, John Candy, Jack Lemmon, Walter Matthau, Edward Asner, Donald Sutherland, Kevin Bacon, Brian Doyle-Murray, Sally Kirkland. 1991 DVD

JFK: RECKLESS YOUTH ★★★ Patrick Dempsey delivers an exceptional performance as the young Kennedy, long before the White House. The conflicts that permeated his life, from his decision to disobey his father's wishes to the women and illness that plagued his life, come to the forefront in this made-for-TV miniseries. The emotional impact and production values are better-than-average. Not rated. 182m. **DIR:** Harry Winer. **CAST:** Patrick Dempsey, Terry Kinney, Loren Dean, Diana Scarwid, Andrew Lowery. 1993

JIGSAW MAN, THE ★★★★ Michael Caine plays a British secret agent who has defected, under orders, to Russia. Before leaving, he discovered a list of Soviet spies operating in England and hid it. After forty years, he returns to England in order to get the list with spies from both countries hot on his trail. This is a wonderfully entertaining puzzle of a movie. Rated PG for violence and profanity. 90m. **DIR:** Freddie Francis. **CAST:** Michael Caine, Laurence Olivier, Susan George, Robert Powell, Charles Gray. 1984

JIGSAW MURDERS, THE 🎔 A psycho killer leaves body parts around L.A. 98m. **DIR:** Jag Mundhra. **CAST:** Chad Everett, Yaphet Kotto, Michelle Johnson, Michael Sabatino. 1988

JIM THORPE—ALL AMERICAN ★★★ This well-intentioned bio-pic stretches much of the truth in the sad story of American Indian athlete Jim Thorpe, Olympic medalist and professional baseball, football, and track star. Director Michael Curtiz places most of the sympathy with Burt Lancaster, sidestepping Thorpe's personal demons. Burt is in fine physical shape as he re-creates some of Thorpe's feats for the camera. B&W; 107m. **DIR:** Michael Curtiz. **CAST:** Burt Lancaster, Charles Bickford, Steve Cochran, Phyllis Thaxter, Dick Wesson. 1951

JIMI HENDRIX ★★★★ Jimi Hendrix, the undisputed master of psychedelia, is captured brilliantly through concert footage and candid film clips in this excellent all-around 1973 rockumentary. The film explores Hendrix's career through interviews and rare concert footage of his performances from London's Marquee Club in 1967, and the Monterey Pop, Woodstock, and Isle of Wight festivals. Director Gary Weis was responsible for some great film shorts on *Saturday Night Live.* 103m. **DIR:** Gary Weis. **CAST:** Jimi Hendrix, Billy Cox, Mitch Mitchell, Eric Clapton, Pete Townshend, Little Richard, Dick Cavett. 1984 DVD

JIMMY CLIFF—BONGO MAN ★★1/2 This little-known documentary is a tribute to reggae singer-songwriter Jimmy Cliff. The film attempts to, somewhat confusingly, to portray him as a man of the people, a champion of human rights during a period of racial and political turbulence in Jamaica. Cliff's other movie vehicle, *The Harder They Come,* a crudely shot musical-drama, remains stronger than *Bongo Man.* 89m. **DIR:** Stefan Paul. **CAST:** Jimmy Cliff. 1985

JIMMY HOLLYWOOD ★★ A struggling, manic actor, who goes ballistic when his car is burglarized, becomes America's first video vigilante by taping criminals at work and leaving the evidence and tied-up crooks for the cops. The self-obsessed thespian tries to parlay his new Bronson-with-a-camcorder fame into a career of sorts. This meandering, oddball comedy about the down side of Tinsel Town stardom never gels. Rated R for language and violence. 110m. **DIR:** Barry Levinson. **CAST:** Joe Pesci, Christian Slater, Victoria Abril. 1994

JIMMY THE KID ★★ Paul LeMat leads a band of bungling criminals in an attempt to kidnap the precocious son (Gary Coleman) of extremely wealthy singers (Cleavon Little and Fay Hauser). To everyone's surprise, Jimmy doesn't mind being kidnapped. Yawn. Rated PG. 85m. **DIR:** Gary Nelson. **CAST:** Paul LeMat, Gary Coleman, Cleavon Little, Fay Hauser, Dee Wallace. 1983

JINGLE ALL THE WAY ★★★ Arnold Schwarzenegger displays his comedic skills as a dad determined to fulfill his son's Christmas wish. Sinbad, as a mailman with plenty of time on his hands, becomes his archenemy as the two scour the city for the last Turbo Man toy available. Meanwhile, Schwarzenegger's wife is pursued by their sleazy neighbor. This film makes a fine satire of Christmas's commercialization. Rated PG for comic-book violence. 91m. **DIR:** Brian Levant. **CAST:** Arnold Schwarzenegger, Sinbad, Rita Wilson, Phil Hartman, Robert Conrad, James Belushi. 1996 DVD

JINXED ★★1/2 Bette Midler is in peak form as a would-be cabaret singer who enlists the aid of a blackjack dealer (Ken Wahl) in a plot to murder her gambler boyfriend (Rip Torn) in this often funny black comedy. If it weren't for Midler, you'd notice how silly and unbelievable it all is. Rated R for profanity and sexual situations. 103m. **DIR:** Don Siegel. **CAST:** Bette Midler, Ken Wahl, Rip Torn, Benson Fong. **1982**

JIT ★★★★ A young country boy tries to win the love of a sophisticated city girl in this charming and sometimes surprising African comedy. He tries to overcome his biggest hurdle, the exorbitant bride price demanded by her father, with the help of a "Jukwa," his guiding spirit who would rather he return to his village. The first major film produced in Zimbabwe. Not rated; contains no objectionable material. 98m. **DIR:** Michael Raeburn. **CAST:** Dominic Makuvachurna, Sibongile Nene. **1990**

JIVE JUNCTION ★★1/2 Weird World War II musical about high school music students who give up playing the classics and turn to jazz in order to help the war effort! How? By opening up a canteen where soliders can dance their troubles away. Written by future novelist Irving Wallace. B&W; 62m. **DIR:** Edgar G. Ulmer. **CAST:** Dickie Moore, Tina Thayer. **1943**

J. LYLE ★★★ Best known for his distinctive pencil-sketch animation, filmmaker Bill Plympton retains much of his bizarre humor in his first live-action film (which features some animated segments). But like his previous (all-animated) feature, *The Tune*, this tale of a greedy lawyer who has a change of heart while trying to evict the residents of an apartment complex has a few too many dull stretches mixed in with the flashes of wit. Not rated; contains nothing objectionable. 75m. **DIR:** Bill Plympton. **CAST:** Richard Kuranda, Jennifer Corby, John Bader. **1996**

JO JO DANCER, YOUR LIFE IS CALLING ★★★★1/2 In this show-biz biography, Richard Pryor plays Jo Jo Dancer, a well-known entertainer at the peak of his popularity and the depths of self-understanding and love. A drug-related accident puts Jo Jo in the hospital and forces him to reexamine his life. Rated R for profanity, nudity, suggested sex, drug use, and violence. 100m. **DIR:** Richard Pryor. **CAST:** Richard Pryor, Debbie Allen, Art Evans, Fay Hauser, Barbara Williams, Carmen McRae, Paula Kelly, Diahnne Abbott, Scoey Mitchell, Billy Eckstine, Wings Hauser, Michael Ironside. **1986**

JOAN OF ARC ★★★ Ingrid Bergman is touching and devout in this by-the-book rendering of Maxwell Anderson's noted play, but too much talk and too little action strain patience and buttocks. 100m. **DIR:** Victor Fleming. **CAST:** Ingrid Bergman, José Ferrer, Francis L. Sullivan, J. Carrol Naish, Ward Bond. **1948 DVD**

JOAN OF PARIS ★★ Allied fliers parachute into Nazi-held France and enlist a local barmaid to help them find their way to British Intelligence. It all made sense back in 1942, and this melodrama is strong on love, duty, and sacrifice, and thick with snarling Nazis and long-winded patriots. B&W; 93m. **DIR:** Robert Stevenson. **CAST:** Michele Morgan, Paul Henreid, Thomas Mitchell, Laird Cregar, May Robson, Alan Ladd. **1942**

JOCKS ✔ A tennis coach must make his goofy team champions. Rated R for nudity and obscenities. 90m. **DIR:** Steve Carver. **CAST:** Scott Strader, Perry Lang,

Mariska Hargitay, Richard Roundtree, Christopher Lee. **1986**

JOE ★★★ Peter Boyle stars in this violent film about a bigot who ends up associating much more closely with the people he hates. Falling short in the storytelling, *Joe* is nevertheless helped along by top-notch acting. Rated R. 107m. **DIR:** John G. Avildsen. **CAST:** Peter Boyle, Dennis Patrick, Susan Sarandon. **1970**

•**JOE GOULD'S SECRET** ★★★1/2 *New Yorker* writer Joseph Mitchell strikes up an odd friendship with an eccentric, exasperating street bohemian who claims to be working on a vast oral history of modern times. Based on two articles by the real Mitchell, "Professor Sea Gull" and "Joe Gould's Secret," the film is a loving eulogy to the friendlier Manhattan of the 1940s, with a bravura performance by Ian Holm and a more subdued but equally good one from Stanley Tucci. Rated R for profanity. 108m. **DIR:** Stanley Tucci. **CAST:** Ian Holm, Stanley Tucci, Patricia Clarkson, Hope Davis, Susan Sarandon, Steve Martin. **1999**

JOE KIDD ★★★1/2 While not exactly a thrill-a-minute movie, this Western has a number of memorable moments. Director John Sturges has been better, but Clint Eastwood and Robert Duvall are at the peak of their forms in this story of a gunman (Eastwood) hired by a cattle baron (Duvall) to track down some Mexican-Americans who are fighting back because they've been cheated out of their land. Rated PG. 88m. **DIR:** John Sturges. **CAST:** Clint Eastwood, Robert Duvall, John Saxon, Don Stroud. **1972 DVD**

JOE LOUIS STORY, THE ★★ Real-life boxer Coley Wallace brings some sense of authenticity to this all-too-familiar Hollywood sketch of an athlete's rise to fame. Newsreel footage elevates this otherwise routine low-budget bio-pic. B&W; 88m. **DIR:** Robert Gordon. **CAST:** Coley Wallace, Paul Stewart, Hilda Simms, James Edwards, John Marley. **1953 DVD**

JOE PISCOPO LIVE! ★★★ This HBO concert was taped on the UCLA campus. Joe Piscopo showcases some of his characterizations as Robert De Niro (*Taxi Driver, Raging Bull*) and as Phil Donahue (to George Wallace's Oprah Winfrey). It's an uneven show and Piscopo sometimes appears to be entertaining himself more than the fans. 60m. **DIR:** David Grossman. **CAST:** Joe Piscopo, George Wallace. **1987**

JOE TORRE: CURVEBALLS ALONG THE WAY ★★★ Lightweight reenactment of the events surrounding baseball manager Joe Torre's career-topping efforts to bring the New York Yankees to the World Series. Paul Sorvino displays aw-shucks charm and instinctive talent as Torre, a guy with baseball in the blood who nonetheless rates family above all else. And he gets a full plate, as one beloved brother dies mere months into this all-important season, and another (Robert Loggia) declines and winds up hospitalized. While not up to the quality or emotional punch of *Bang the Drum Slowly*, scripter Philip Rosenberg delivers a heartfelt little story. Rated PG for dramatic intensity. 85m. **DIR:** Sturla Gunnarsson. **CAST:** Paul Sorvino, Robert Loggia, Barbara Williams, Isaiah Washington, Kenneth Welsh. **1997**

JOE VERSUS THE VOLCANO ★★★1/2 You have to be in the right mood to enjoy this featherweight comedy from writer-director John Patrick Shanley. When a millionaire offers Tom Hanks an expense account and a leisurely trip to the South Seas, Hanks accepts—even though it means jumping into a volcano. Meg Ryan is superb in three hilarious supporting roles. Rated PG for brief profanity. 94m. DIR: John Patrick Shanley. CAST: Tom Hanks, Meg Ryan, Lloyd Bridges, Robert Stack, Abe Vigoda, Dan Hedaya, Ossie Davis. 1990

JOE'S APARTMENT ★★ An Iowa farm boy (Jerry O'Connell) moves to New York and makes acquaintances of the millions of singing, dancing cockroaches inhabiting his apartment. The five-minute MTV short is blown up to feature length and loses all its meager charm. The roach musical numbers are actually rather entertaining; it's all the stuff with the humans that stinks. O'Connell seems never to have washed his face during shooting. Rated PG-13 for crude humor. 80m. DIR: John Payson. CAST: Jerry O'Connell, Megan Ward, Robert Vaughn. 1996 DVD

JOEY ★★★ Delightful family tale about a young boy who finds a baby kangaroo and makes his way to Sydney to reunite the joey with his family. Unbeknown to the boy, the young kangaroo's family has been captured by poachers who plan on using them in an illegal kangaroo-boxing scheme. Rated PG. 97m. DIR: Ian Barry. CAST: Alex McKenna, Ed Begley Jr. 1997

JOEY BREAKER ★★★ An obnoxious, smooth-talking agent on the fast track to money and power falls in love with a waitress who is striving to complete her education as a nurse. Quirky, offbeat film benefits from the performances of its talented cast members. Rated R for nudity and profanity. 92m. DIR: Steven Starr. CAST: Richard Edson, Cedella Marley, Erik King, Gina Gershon. 1992

JOHN AND THE MISSUS ★★★ The beautiful coast of Newfoundland provides the backdrop for this otherwise depressing Canadian film. A town loses its source of income when the local mine is closed. Gordon Pinsent plays a stubborn, courageous man who refuses the meager resettlement money the government offers. Rated PG for mature themes. 98m. DIR: Gordon Pinsent. CAST: Gordon Pinsent, Jackie Burroughs, Timothy Webber. 1987

JOHN & YOKO: A LOVE STORY ★★ Episodic account of the John Lennon–Yoko Ono relationship—from the famous "Christ" remark in 1966 to his assassination in 1980—is marred by unbelievable characters and a condensed mix of fact and fabrication. The technical adviser was Lennon's friend, Elliot Mintz (played briefly by David Baxt). Not rated. 180m. DIR: Sandor Stern. CAST: Mark McGann, Kim Miyori, Peter Capaldi, Richard Morant. 1989

JOHN CARPENTER PRESENTS: BODY BAGS ★★1/2 Although this *Tales from the Crypt* wannabe is laced with the appropriate gore, two of the three stories are strictly dullsville. The third, blessed with a grand performance by Stacy Keach as a fellow horrified by encroaching baldness, brings new meaning to a full-bodied head of hair. Rated R for profanity, nudity, simulated sex, and gobs o' gore. 95m. DIR: John Carpenter. CAST: Robert Carradine, Stacy Keach,

David Warner, Sheena Easton, Deborah Harry, Mark Hamill, Twiggy. 1993 DVD

JOHN CARPENTER'S ESCAPE FROM L.A. ★★1/2 Bigger doesn't exactly mean better, as proved by this fifteen-years-later sequel. Featuring essentially the same plot as Carpenter's lower-budgeted but superior *Escape from New York*, it once again puts laconic Snake Plissken in a do-or-die situation involving the president and national security. Rated R for violence and profanity. 101m. DIR: John Carpenter. CAST: Kurt Russell, Stacy Keach, Steve Buscemi, Valeria Golino, Peter Fonda, Pam Grier, Cliff Robertson, Michelle Forbes, George Corraface, Bruce Campbell. 1996 DVD

JOHN CARPENTER'S VAMPIRES ★★★1/2 Although James Woods is brilliantly cast as a foul-mouthed, Vatican-backed vampire slayer who heads an enthusiastic team of mercenaries, the film turns sour when our "hero" abandons his common sense while seeking vengeance against a 600-year-old vampire master. The storyline becomes ludicrously arbitrary is *not* scary. Rated R for gore, violence, profanity, and nudity. 107m. DIR: John Carpenter. CAST: James Woods, Daniel Baldwin, Sheryl Lee, Thomas Ian Griffith, Tim Guinee, Maximilian Schell. 1998 DVD

JOHN HUSTON—THE MAN, THE MOVIES, THE MAVERICK ★★★★★ A wonderful, robust, and entertaining documentary biography of the great director, compiled from rare home movies, film clips, and interviews, narrated by Robert Mitchum (who speaks from a fantasy attic of engrossing Huston memorabilia). John Huston was an utterly fascinating eccentric and adventurer. This TV biography is a superb tribute. 129m. DIR: Frank Martin. 1989

JOHN PAUL JONES ★★1/2 John Farrow's direction is as wooden as Robert Stack's performance in this lackluster attempt to chronicle the life of America's first naval hero. Lots of familiar faces in cameo appearances, e.g., Bette Davis as Catherine the Great. 127m. DIR: John Farrow. CAST: Robert Stack, Marisa Pavan, Charles Coburn, Macdonald Carey, Jean-Pierre Aumont, Peter Cushing, Bruce Cabot, David Farrar, Bette Davis. 1959

JOHN WOO'S ONCE A THIEF ★★★ Action director John Woo helms an American remake of his own earlier hit with mixed results; while the players are engaging and the plot suitably fast-paced, the stunts are subdued in deference to this film's made-for-television origins. Ex-thieves turned undercover form an unlikely romantic triangle, while participating in a caper involving a former friend-turned-rival. Wholly preposterous but fun to watch. Rated PG for violence. 95m. DIR: John Woo. CAST: Sandrine Holt, Ivan Sergei, Nicholas Lea, Robert Ito, Michael Wong, Jennifer Dale. 1996

◆**JOHNNY 2.0** ★★★ In a future where everything is run by a faceless but sinister corporation, a scientist wakes up after fifteen years in a coma to find that his memory has been removed and transplanted. This made-for-cable production has enough interesting concepts to keep sci-fi buffs happy despite the so-so special effects. Rated PG-13 for violence and sexuality. 95m. DIR: Neill L. Fearnley. CAST: Jeff Fahey, Tahnee Welch, Michael Ironside, John Neville. 1998 DVD

JOHNNY & CLYDE ★★★ Johnny's a kid left in charge of the house one day, while Clyde is a cute but slobbering bloodhound who prompts all sorts of havoc. Undemanding children will have a lot of fun with this silly little tale. Suitable for all ages. 84m. **DIR:** William Bindley. **CAST:** Michael Rooker, Johnny White, Sam Malkin, David B. Nichols. **1995**

JOHNNY ANGEL ★★★ Above-average gangster film provides some nice moments. George Raft seeks the killer of his father while busting up the mob. Nothing special, but fun to watch. B&W; 79m. **DIR:** Edwin L. Marin. **CAST:** George Raft, Claire Trevor, Signe Hasso, Hoagy Carmichael. **1945**

JOHNNY APOLLO ★★★★ Tyrone Power's father is exposed as a white-collar criminal; bitter Tyrone turns to crime himself and winds up in the same cell block as Dad. Tough, engrossing crime melodrama is solid entertainment all the way. B&W; 93m. **DIR:** Henry Hathaway. **CAST:** Tyrone Power, Dorothy Lamour, Edward Arnold, Lloyd Nolan, Charley Grapewin, Lionel Atwill. **1940**

JOHNNY BE GOOD ❤ Anthony Michael Hall is a high school football player who is heavily recruited by every major college in the United States. Rated R for language, partial nudity, and sexual situations. 86m. **DIR:** Bud Smith. **CAST:** Anthony Michael Hall, Robert Downey Jr., Paul Gleason, Uma Thurman, Steve James, Seymour Cassel, Michael Greene, Robert Downey Sr. **1988**

JOHNNY BELINDA ★★★★ Jane Wyman won an Oscar for her remarkable performance as a deaf-mute farm girl. Her multidimensional characterization lifts this movie over mere melodrama. The many disasters that befall its put-upon heroine, including rape and trying to raise the resulting offspring in the face of community pressure, would be scoffed at in a lesser actress. B&W; 103m. **DIR:** Jean Negulesco. **CAST:** Jane Wyman, Lew Ayres, Charles Bickford, Agnes Moorehead. **1948**

JOHNNY CARSON: HIS FAVORITE MOMENTS ★★★★★ Four-tape collection chronicles the best and sometimes the worst of the King of Late Night. Carefully selected highlights from almost thirty years of *The Tonight Show* capture the very essence of Carson and his trademark reactions as he weathers classic comedians, wrangles out-of-control animals, and introduces a stellar line-up of guests. The first three tapes are broken down by decade, while the last tape is a complete copy of the last episode. Not rated. Each tape 50m. **DIR:** Not credited. **CAST:** Johnny Carson, Ed McMahon. **1962–1992**

JOHNNY COME LATELY ★★★ A good showcase for James Cagney's feisty personality with a wholesome touch not often seen in today's movies. He plays a vagrant who happens onto a job on a small-town newspaper, and winds up playing cupid to the publisher's daughter and her boyfriend. B&W; 97m. **DIR:** William K. Howard. **CAST:** James Cagney, Grace George, Hattie McDaniel, Marjorie Lord, Marjorie Main. **1943**

JOHNNY DANGEROUSLY ❤ In this fitfully funny spoof of 1930s gangster movies, Michael Keaton and Joe Piscopo play rival crime lords. Directed by Amy Heckerling, it leaves the viewer with genuinely mixed feelings. Rated PG-13 for violence and profanity. 90m. **DIR:** Amy Heckerling. **CAST:** Michael Keaton, Joe Piscopo, Marilu Henner, Maureen Stapleton. **1984**

JOHNNY EAGER ★★★1/2 When the DA's daughter falls for a good-looking mobster, sparks fly. Few cops-and-robbers movies are as well cast as this one. Robert Taylor was no longer known as a pretty boy after playing the role of the gangster, and Lana Turner established her image as a sizzling sex symbol. Van Heflin earned a best-supporting-actor's Oscar for his role of the gangster with a conscience. B&W; 107m. **DIR:** Mervyn LeRoy. **CAST:** Lana Turner, Robert Taylor, Robert Sterling, Edward Arnold, Glenda Farrell, Patricia Dane, Barry Nelson, Van Heflin. **1941**

JOHNNY GOT HIS GUN ★★1/2 Featuring Timothy Bottoms as an American World War I soldier who loses his legs, eyes, ears, mouth, and nose after a German artillery shell explodes, this is a morbid, depressing antiwar film with flashes of brilliance. Rated PG. 111m. **DIR:** Dalton Trumbo. **CAST:** Timothy Bottoms, Marsha Hunt, Jason Robards Jr., Donald Sutherland, Diane Varsi, David Soul, Anthony Geary. **1971**

JOHNNY GUITAR ★★★1/2 A positively weird Western, this Nicholas Ray film features the ultimate role reversal. Bar owner Joan Crawford and landowner Mercedes McCambridge shoot it out while their gun-toting boyfriends (Sterling Hayden and Scott Brady) look on. 110m. **DIR:** Nicholas Ray. **CAST:** Joan Crawford, Mercedes McCambridge, Sterling Hayden, Scott Brady, Ward Bond, Ernest Borgnine, John Carradine. **1954**

JOHNNY HANDSOME ★★★1/2 Mickey Rourke plays a badly disfigured criminal double-crossed during a robbery and sent to prison, where plastic surgery is performed on his face as part of a new rehabilitation program. Once released, he plots revenge on those responsible for his capture. Be warned: the violence is extreme. Rated R for violence, language, and nudity. 93m. **DIR:** Walter Hill. **CAST:** Mickey Rourke, Elizabeth McGovern, Ellen Barkin, Lance Henriksen, Morgan Freeman, Forest Whitaker. **1989**

JOHNNY MNEMONIC ★★★1/2 Few motion pictures have captured the storytelling style of comic books as well as this futuristic adventure about a human computer in a race against time. Keanu Reeves is appropriately downbeat as the title character, whose childhood memories have been replaced with a computer chip that allows him to smuggle highly classified information. Rated R for violence, profanity, and nudity. 98m. **DIR:** Robert Longo. **CAST:** Keanu Reeves, Dolph Lundgren, Takeshi Kitano, Ice T, Dina Meyer, Denis Akiyama, Henry Rollins. **1995 DVD**

JOHNNY MYSTO ★★ Silliness abounds in this tale of a young aspiring magician who accidentally makes his sister disappear. His attempt to find her involves an old magician, time travel, and a stint in King Arthur's court to defeat an evil wizard. Rated PG. 87m. **DIR:** Jeff Burr. **CAST:** Toran Caudell, Patrick Renna, Amber Tamblyn, Michael Ansara, Ian Abercrombie, Russ Tamblyn. **1996**

JOHNNY RENO ★★ Another in producer A. C. Lyles's anachronistic, mid-Sixties Paramount Westerns featuring old-time sagebrush stars in an old-fashioned oater. Relentlessly corny, but watchable. 88m. **DIR:** Dana Andrews, Jane Russell, Lon Chaney Jr., John Agar, Lyle Bettger, Tom Drake, Richard Arlen, Robert Lowery. **1966**

JOHNNY SHILOH ★★1/2 After his parents are killed during the Civil War, young Johnny Shiloh joins up with a group of soldiers led by the crusty Brian Keith. The performances are good and it's pure Walt Disney adventure. 90m. **DIR:** James Neilson. **CAST:** Brian Keith, Kevin Corcoran, Darryl Hickman, Skip Homeier. **1963**

JOHNNY STECCHINO ★★ This is a silly slapstick farce of mistaken identity that was the most popular film at the Italian box office up till that time. Roberto Benigni directs and plays the dual roles of a tough mafioso and a timid look-alike bus driver. When the shy driver is mistaken for a mob boss, his life is changed dramatically. The overlong film offers wacky, simplistic humor, not unlike a Jerry Lewis movie with an Italian accent. In Italian with English subtitles. 122m. **DIR:** Roberto Benigni. **CAST:** Roberto Benigni, Nicoletta Braschi, Paolo Bonacelli. **1992**

JOHNNY SUEDE ★★1/2 Brad Pitt plays a lackluster, aimless adolescent who discovers a purpose in life when he's literally hit on the head with a pair of suede shoes. The low-budget comedy is from the surreal, off-the-wall school, and owes much to the early work of Jim Jarmusch (for whom Tom DiCillo was once a cinematographer). Only fans of cult films and the preciously weird need apply. 97m. **DIR:** Tom DiCillo. **CAST:** Brad Pitt, Catherine Keener, Calvin Levels, Alison Moir, Nick Cave, Tina Louise. **1992**

JOHNNY TIGER ★★1/2 Chad Everett is a half-breed Seminole, Robert Taylor is a sympathetic teacher, and Geraldine Brooks is a sympathetic doctor, all trying to reach some valid conclusion about the American Indians' role in the modern world. It's nothing to get excited about. 102m. **DIR:** Paul Wendkos. **CAST:** Robert Taylor, Geraldine Brooks, Chad Everett. **1966**

JOHNNY TREMAIN ★★★1/2 Colorful Walt Disney Revolutionary War entry is a perfect blend of schoolboy heroics and Hollywood history, with young Johnny Tremain an apprentice silversmith caught up in the brewing American Revolution. Heavy on the patriotism, with picture-book tableaus of the Boston Tea Party, Paul Revere's ride, and the battles at Concord. Infectious score throughout. 80m. **DIR:** Robert Stevenson. **CAST:** Hal Stalmaster, Luana Patten, Sebastian Cabot, Richard Beymer. **1957**

JOHNNY'S GIRL ★★1/2 After her mother dies, a teenage girl moves in with and tries to reform her father, a small-time Alaskan con artist. Decent, even heartfelt performances can't overcome an uneven script and muddled direction in this made-for-TV flick. Not rated; contains profanity. 120m. **DIR:** John Kent Harrison. **CAST:** Treat Williams, Mia Kirshner. **1995**

JOHNS ★★ A day in the life of two male hustlers plying the sun-bleached wastes of Santa Monica Boulevard. The day, with arch symbolism, happens to be Christmas Eve, and that should give you an idea of how things will end up. Writer-director Scott Silver's first film is shallow and self-conscious—supposedly based on the stories of real hustlers, but crammed with familiar clichés. Rated R for mature themes, profanity, and simulated sex. 96m. **DIR:** Scott Silver. **CAST:** Lukas Haas, David Arquette, Arliss Howard, Keith David, Elliott Gould, John C. McGinley. **1996 DVD**

•**JOHNSONS, THE** ★★★ Bizarre Danish film in which a young girl is haunted by the titular brothers. The Johnsons worship a fertility god named Xangadix and require the pubescent girl for a ceremony. Director Rudolf Van Den Berg fills the film with atmosphere, but some scenes may be too much for the fainthearted. In Danish with English subtitles. Not rated; contains violence, gore, and sexual situations. 103m. **DIR:** Rudolf Van Den Berg. **CAST:** Monique van De Ven, Esmee De La Bretonere. **1992 DVD**

JOKE OF DESTINY ★★ Italian audiences may have laughed uproariously at this new film by director Lina Wertmuller. However, American viewers are unlikely to get the joke. In Italian with English subtitles. Rated PG for profanity. 105m. **DIR:** Lina Wertmuller. **CAST:** Ugo Tognazzi, Piera Degli Esposti, Gastone Moschin. **1984**

JOLLY CORNER, THE ★★★ The uncertainties of diverging career paths lie at the heart of this TV adaptation of the moody Henry James short story. Fritz Weaver returns to turn-of-the-century America after having lived abroad for thirty-five years, and he becomes obsessed by the memories contained within his ancestral home. Introduced by Henry Fonda; unrated and suitable for family viewing. 43m. **DIR:** Arthur Barron. **CAST:** Fritz Weaver, Salome Jens. **1975**

JOLSON SINGS AGAIN ★★1/2 Larry Parks again does the great and incomparable Al Jolson to a turn; Jolson himself again sings his unforgettable standards. But the film, trumped up to cash in, hasn't the class, charm, or swagger of the original. 96m. **DIR:** Henry Levin. **CAST:** Larry Parks, Barbara Hale, William Demarest, Bill Goodwin, Ludwig Donath, Myron McCormick. **1949**

JOLSON STORY, THE ★★★★ The show-business life story of vaudeville and Broadway stage great Al Jolson gets all-stops-out treatment in this fast-paced, tune-full film. Larry Parks acts and lip-synchs the hard-driving entertainer to a T. Jolson himself dubbed the singing. 128m. **DIR:** Alfred E. Green. **CAST:** Larry Parks, William Demarest, Evelyn Keyes, Bill Goodwin, Ludwig Donath. **1946**

JON JOST'S FRAMEUP ★★ This tale of two losers on the road has been done before and done better. Writer-director Jon Jost filmed this low-rent morality play in just ten days, and it looks it. Jost may capture the tragicomic aspects of the relationship between a dim waitress and her ex-con lover, but the style is more student film than cutting edge. Not rated; contains profanity, violence, sexual situations, nudity, and adult themes. B&W; 91m. **DIR:** Jon Jost. **CAST:** Howard Swain, Nancy Carlin. **1993**

JONAH WHO WILL BE 25 IN THE YEAR 2000 ★★★1/2 A provocative, Swiss-French character study, centering on eight people thrust together by the social and political events of the late 1960s. The title obliquely refers to the unborn child carried by the pregnant Myriam Boyer. Mature, playful, and entertaining, it is bookended by the same director's *No*

Man's Land. In French with English subtitles. Rated PG. 115m. **DIR:** Alain Tanner. **CAST:** Jean-Luc Bideau, Rufus, Miou-Miou, Jacques Denis, Dominique Labourier, Myriam Boyer, Roger Jendly. 1976

JONATHAN LIVINGSTON SEAGULL 💔 Overblown and laughable. Rated G. 120m. **DIR:** Hall Bartlett. 1973

JORY ★★★ A surprisingly sensitive film for the genre finds Robby Benson, in his first film role, as a 15-year-old boy who must learn to go it alone in the Wild West after his father is senselessly murdered. While remaining exciting and suspenseful, the film takes time to make commentary about manhood and machismo in an adult, thoughtful manner. Rated PG. 97m. **DIR:** Jorge Fons. **CAST:** Robby Benson, John Marley, B. J. Thomas, Linda Purl. 1972

JOSEPH ★★1/2 The talents and larger than life presence of Ben Kingsley and Martin Landau put this biblical epic a notch above other Turner Pictures endeavors. Landau plays Joseph's doting father while Kingsley becomes his Egyptian slave owner after his jealous brothers sell him. Not rated; contains violence and sexual situations. 180m. **DIR:** Roger Young. **CAST:** Paul Mercurio, Ben Kingsley, Martin Landau, Lesley Ann Warren. 1995

JOSEPH ANDREWS ★★ The adventures of Joseph Andrews (Peter Firth) as he rises from lowly servant to personal footman. This is director Tony Richardson's second attempt to transform a Henry Fielding novel to film. Unfortunately, the first-rate cast cannot save this ill-fated attempt to restage *Tom Jones.* Rated R for sex and profanity. 99m. **DIR:** Tony Richardson. **CAST:** Ann-Margret, Peter Firth, Beryl Reid, Michael Hordern, Jim Dale, John Gielgud, Hugh Griffith, Wendy Craig, Peggy Ashcroft. 1977

JOSEPHA ★★ Infidelity ruins the professional and personal lives of a married pair of actors. Writer Christopher Frank adapted his own novel but can't get this self-serious drama to work on screen. French, dubbed in English. Not rated; sexual situations. 100m. **DIR:** Christopher Frank. **CAST:** Claude Brasseur, Miou-Miou, Bruno Cremer. 1983

JOSEPHINE BAKER STORY, THE ★★★★ Lynn Whitfield *owns* this ambitious, unblushingly sexy HBO biography of singer and dancer Josephine Baker, who scandalized the States with her uninhibited personality and erotic choreography. Rubén Blades and David Dukes are fine as two of the significant men in her life. Craig T. Nelson's riveting cameo as Walter Winchell reveals the newscaster in far less than his usual flattering light. Rated R for nudity. 134m. **DIR:** Brian Gibson. **CAST:** Lynn Whitfield, Rubén Blades, David Dukes, Kene Holiday, Craig T. Nelson, Lou Gossett Jr. 1991

JOSH AND S.A.M. ★★1/2 Teenager Josh convinces his younger brother, Sam, that he is "S.A.M.," a Strategically Altered Mutant who has been sold to the government by their estranged parents and turned into a robotic child warrior. During one shuffle between Mom and Dad, the troubled youths run away to Canada on an adventure of self-discovery. Part road movie and part domestic drama, this uneven story of adolescent angst has an engaging, offbeat charm. Rated PG-13 for language and violence.

97m. **DIR:** Billy Weber. **CAST:** Jacob Tierney, Noah Fleiss, Martha Plimpton, Stephen Tobolowsky, Joan Allen, Christopher Penn. 1993

JOSH KIRBY, TIME WARRIOR (SERIES) ★★1/2 In this direct-to-video serial, young Josh Kirby is caught up in a race to save the universe from ultimate destruction. While some episodes make it, others may bore the youngsters at whom the series is aimed. Episode titles include *Planet of the Dino-Knights, The Human Pets, Trapped on Toy World, Eggs from 70 Million B.C., Journey to the Magic Cavern,* and *Last Battle for the Universe.* Rated PG for violence. Times vary from 88–93m. **DIR:** Ernest Farino, Frank Arnold. **CAST:** Corbin Allred, Derek Webster, Jennifer Burns, Barrie Ingham. 1995

JOSH KIRBY ... TIME WARRIOR: TRAPPED ON TOY WORLD ★★ Teenager Josh Kirby continues his efforts to save the universe in this third edition of the direct-to-video serial. Here, Kirby finds himself on a planet inhabited by human-size toys. Star Corbin Allred is an engaging hero for the grammar-school set, as are the story and special effects. Rated PG. 90m. **DIR:** Frank Arnold. **CAST:** Corbin Allred, Jennifer Burns, Derek Webster, Sharon Lee Jones, Buck Kartalian, J. P. Hubell, Barrie Ingham. 1995

JOSH KIRBY ... TIME WARRIOR: JOURNEY TO THE MAGIC CAVERN ★★ The fifth in the direct-to-video series. This time, Kirby and his cohorts join forces with a colony of Mushroom People in their fight to save the universe from the forces of evil. One of the best of the series, the film will keep the young 'uns entertained for its duration. Rated PG. 93m. **DIR:** Ernest Farino. **CAST:** Corbin Allred, Jennifer Burns, Derek Webster, Matt Winston, Nick DeGruccio, Cindy L. Sorensen, Barrie Ingham. 1995

JOSHUA THEN AND NOW ★★★★1/2 Based by screenwriter Mordecai Richler (*The Apprenticeship of Duddy Kravitz*) on his autobiographical novel of the same name, this little-known gem is blessed with humor, poignancy, and insight. Jewish writer Joshua Shapiro's life seems to be in shambles. Surviving an embarrassing upbringing by a gangster father, Joshua nearly meets his match in the snobbish high society of his WASP wife. Rated R for profanity, nudity, suggested sex. 118m. **DIR:** Ted Kotcheff. **CAST:** James Woods, Alan Arkin, Gabrielle Lazure, Michael Sarrazin, Linda Sorenson. 1985

JOUR DE FÊTE ★★1/2 Jacques Tati is the focal point of this light comedy loosely tied to the arrival of a carnival in a small village. As François, the bumbling postman, Tati sees a film on the heroism of the American postal service and tries to emulate it on his small rural route. In French with subtitles. B&W; 81m. **DIR:** Jacques Tati. **CAST:** Jacques Tati, Guy Decomble, Paul Frankeur. 1949

JOURNEY ★★★1/2 This *Hallmark Hall of Fame* TV special focuses on a boy who struggles to come to terms with his restless mother and her abandonment of him and his sister. His grandparents take on the parental responsibilities and attempt to create their own family and history. Strong message about the fragile nature of the family unit and the inner strength that must be tapped in a crisis. Strong performances delivered by all. Not rated; contains mature themes. 100m. **DIR:** Tom McLoughlin. **CAST:** Jason Robards Jr., Brenda Fricker, Max Pomeranc, Meg Tilly, Eliza Dushku. **1995**

JOURNEY BACK TO OZ ★★1/2 This cartoon version sequel to *The Wizard of Oz* leaves the Wizard out. The voices of famous stars help maintain adult interest. Rated G. 90m. **DIR:** Hal Sutherland. **1974**

JOURNEY FOR MARGARET ★★★ A childless journalist in war-ravaged England falls for two little orphans, and he and his wife become involved with their future. Margaret O'Brien pushes all the emotional buttons in a phenomenal film debut. This is solid MGM wartime filmmaking at its propagandistic best. B&W; 81m. **DIR:** W. S. Van Dyke. **CAST:** Robert Young, Laraine Day, Fay Bainter, Nigel Bruce, Margaret O'Brien. **1942**

JOURNEY INTO FEAR (1942) ★★★★ A sometimes confusing but always suspenseful World War II tale of an American ordnance expert (Joseph Cotten) targeted for assassination in Istanbul. Like *The Magnificent Ambersons*, this faulted classic was started by Orson Welles but was taken over by RKO. Uncredited Welles partly directed and, with Cotten, adapted this Eric Ambler mystery for the screen. Remade in 1975. B&W; 69m. **DIR:** Norman Foster, Orson Welles. **CAST:** Joseph Cotten, Orson Welles, Dolores Del Rio, Ruth Warrick, Agnes Moorehead, Everett Sloane, Edgar Barrier, Hans Conried. **1942**

JOURNEY INTO FEAR (1975) ★★ Canadian remake of Orson Welles's 1942 spy drama is occasionally intriguing but ultimately ambiguous and lacking in dramatic punch. Sam Waterston's portrayal of a research geologist, and wide-ranging European locations, help sustain interest. Rated PG. 103m. **DIR:** Daniel Mann. **CAST:** Sam Waterston, Zero Mostel, Yvette Mimieux, Scott Marlowe, Ian McShane, Joseph Wiseman, Shelley Winters, Stanley Holloway, Donald Pleasence, Vincent Price. **1975**

JOURNEY OF AUGUST KING, THE ★★★ Jason Patric is the widowed, nineteenth-century farmer who crosses paths with an exotic runaway slave, played with delicate sensibility by Thandie Newton. As much about her trek north as the emotional journey both undertake, this is surprising in its realism. The visuals are impressive, but this needed more intensity from Patric and a less-relaxed pace to keep from slowly fading. Rated PG-13 for off-screen violence and implied sexual situations. 92m. **DIR:** John Duigan. **CAST:** Jason Patric, Thandie Newton, Larry Drake, Sam Waterston. **1995**

JOURNEY OF HONOR ★★ Historic tale of feuding Japanese warlords in 1602 has epic written all over it, but comes across trite and clichéd. Visuals are the only saving grace. Rated PG-13 for violence. 107m. **DIR:** Gordon Hessler. **CAST:** Sho Kosugi, Christopher Lee, Norman Lloyd, John Rhys-Davies, Toshiro Mifune. **1991**

JOURNEY OF HOPE ★★★★ Swiss director Xavier Koller's Oscar-winning film chronicles the harrowing journey of a family of Kurds who attempt to leave the abject poverty of their Turkish village for the "promised land" of Switzerland. Based in part on fact and in part on Koller's imaginings, this is nevertheless a gripping motion picture. In Kurdish, Turkish, German, and Italian. Not rated; contains subject matter too harsh for children. 110m. **DIR:** Xavier Koller. **CAST:** Necmettin Cobanoglu. **1990**

JOURNEY OF NATTY GANN, THE ★★★★ With this superb film, the Disney Studios returned triumphantly to the genre of family films. Meredith Salenger stars as Natty, a 14-year-old street urchin who must ride the rails from Chicago to Seattle during the Depression to find her father (Ray Wise). Rated PG for light violence. 101m. **DIR:** Jeremy Paul Kagan. **CAST:** Meredith Salenger, Ray Wise, John Cusack, Lainie Kazan, Scatman Crothers. **1985**

JOURNEY TO SPIRIT ISLAND ★★★1/2 A teenage Native American girl takes up her grandmother's quest to save a sacred island, used to bury their ancestors, from unscrupulous developers. Above-average family adventure, beautifully photographed in the Pacific Northwest by Vilmos Zsigmond. Rated PG. 93m. **DIR:** Laszlo Pal. **CAST:** Bettina, Maria Antoinette Rodgers, Brandon Douglas. **1988**

JOURNEY TO THE CENTER OF THE EARTH (1959) ★★★ Jules Verne story was impressive when first released, but it looks pretty silly these days. However, James Mason is always fascinating to watch, production values are high, and kids should enjoy its innocent fun. 132m. **DIR:** Henry Levin. **CAST:** James Mason, Pat Boone, Arlene Dahl, Diane Baker. **1959**

JOURNEY TO THE CENTER OF THE EARTH (1987) ❤ There's little Jules Verne in this hopelessly muddled adventure, notable only for some impressive sets. Rated PG. 79m. **DIR:** Rusty Lemorande. **CAST:** Nicola Cowper, Ilan Mitchell-Smith, Paul Carafotes, Kathy Ireland, Emo Philips. **1987**

JOURNEY TO THE CENTER OF TIME (TIME WARP) ★★1/2 A group of scientists working on a time-travel device are accidentally propelled five thousand years into the future following an equipment malfunction. Once there, they discover an alien civilization (headed by a young Lyle Waggoner) attempting to take over the world. Low-budget film features passable special effects, but the dialogue and acting are subpar. 82m. **DIR:** David L. Hewitt. **CAST:** Scott Brady, Gigi Perreau, Anthony Eisley, Abraham Sofaer, Lyle Waggoner. **1967 DVD**

JOURNEY TO THE FAR SIDE OF THE SUN ★★★1/2 Extremely clever sci-fi thriller concerns the discovery of a planet rotating in Earth's orbit, but always hidden from view on the other side of the Sun. Thoughtful, literate, and fascinating, this effort is marred only by a needlessly oblique and frustrating conclusion. Not rated; suitable for family viewing. 99m. **DIR:** Robert Parrish. **CAST:** Roy Thinnes, Lynn Loring, Herbert Lom, Patrick Wymark, Ian Hendry. **1969 DVD**

JOURNEY'S END: THE SAGA OF STAR TREK: THE NEXT GENERATION ★★★ Only fans of this *Star Trek* spin-off series will appreciate the behind-the-scenes segments. In addition, host Jonathan Frakes makes an appearance at a *Star Trek* convention and Marina Sirtis conducts the series' score. Clips from the final episode and the feature film *Generations* hint that the voyages of the *Enterprise 1701-D* will continue, at least through theatrical releases. Not rated. 46m. **DIR:** Donald R. Beck. **CAST:** Jonathan

Frakes, Marina Sirtis, Patrick Stewart, John de Lancie. 1994

JOY HOUSE ★★1/2 Spooky and interesting, but ultimately only mildly rewarding, this film features Jane Fonda in one of her sexy French roles as a free-spirited waif attempting to seduce her cousin's chauffeur (Alain Delon). 98m. DIR: René Clement. CAST: Jane Fonda, Alain Delon, Lola Albright, Sorrell Booke. 1964

JOY LUCK CLUB, THE ★★★★★ Employing multiple flashbacks that never become confusing, this film, based on Amy Tan's best-selling novel, explores the turbulent lives of four Chinese women, each of whom emerges from mainland China's male-dominated society to face the challenge of coping with a now-grown daughter raised in the United States. Each vignette manages to be more poignant and compelling than its predecessor. Rated R for violence, profanity, and strong sexual themes. 138m. DIR: Wayne Wang. CAST: Kieu Chinh, Ming-Na Wen, Tamlyn Tomita, Tsai Chin, France Nuyen, Lauren Tom, Lisa Lu, Rosalind Chao. 1993

JOY OF LIVING ★★★ Engaging screwball musical-comedy about a playboy who will stop at nothing to win the affection of a bright singing star. Great songs by Jerome Kern. B&W; 90m. DIR: Tay Garnett. CAST: Irene Dunne, Douglas Fairbanks Jr., Lucille Ball. 1938

JOY OF SEX, THE ★★ This comedy, about the plight of two virgins, male and female, in a sex-crazy age, has few offensive elements. But there is one problem: it isn't funny. Rated R for profanity, suggested sex, and scatological humor. 93m. DIR: Martha Coolidge. CAST: Michelle Meyrink, Cameron Dye, Lisa Langlois. 1984

JOY STICKS 💔 A wealthy businessman wants to shut down the local video game room. Rated R. 88m. DIR: Greydon Clark. CAST: Joe Don Baker, Leif Green, Logan Ramsey. 1983

JOYLESS STREET ★★★ Greta Garbo has her first starring role as a young woman who succumbs to hard times in the decadent Vienna of World War I. Look for Marlene Dietrich in a cameo. B&W; 65m. DIR: G. W. Pabst. CAST: Greta Garbo, Asta Nielsen. 1925

JOYRIDE (1977) ★★1/2 Four second-generation actors acquit themselves fairly well in this loosely directed drama about a quartet of youngsters who start off in search of adventure and find themselves turning to crime. Rated R. 92m. DIR: Joseph Ruben. CAST: Desi Arnaz Jr., Robert Carradine, Melanie Griffith, Anne Lockhart, Tom Ligon. 1977

JOYRIDE (1997) ★★ Trying to escape her pimp, a hooker and her innocent boyfriend make the mistake of stealing the car of a hit woman whose most recent victim is still in the trunk. Flashy direction doesn't compensate for a tired script that asks more of a second-rate cast than it can deliver. Rated R for profanity, violence, and sexual situations. 92m. DIR: Quinton Peeples. CAST: Tobey Maguire, Wilson Cruz, Adam West, Benicio Del Toro. 1997

JU DOU ★★★★★ This Oscar-nominated Chinese film is a lovely, sensual, ultimately tragic tale of illicit love in the strict, male-dominated feudal society of rural China, circa 1920. On visual imagery alone, the film would be worthy of attention. In Chinese with English subtitles. Not rated. 93m. DIR: Yimou Zhang. CAST: Gong Li, Li Baotian. 1990 DVD

JUAREZ ★★★★ Warner Bros. in the 1930s and '40s seemed to trot out veteran actor Paul Muni every time they attempted to film a screen biography. This re-creation of the life of Mexico's famous peasant leader was no exception. Surrounded by an all-star cast, including Bette Davis and Brian Aherne, this big budget bio is well mounted and well intentioned. B&W; 132m. DIR: William Dieterle. CAST: Paul Muni, Bette Davis, Brian Aherne, Claude Rains, John Garfield. 1939

JUBAL ★★★1/2 Adult Western finds drifter Jubal Troop (Glenn Ford) enmeshed in just about everybody's problems when he signs on with rancher Ernest Borgnine. Beautifully photographed and well acted, this tale of jealousy and revenge is standout entertainment. 101m. DIR: Delmer Daves. CAST: Glenn Ford, Ernest Borgnine, Valerie French, Rod Steiger, Charles Bronson, Noah Beery Jr., Felicia Farr. 1956

JUBILEE ★★ Avant-garde filmmaker Derek Jarman's surreal fantasy about a futuristic England, a postpunk-Thatcherian wasteland where civilization is in anarchaic terrorism. Highly uneven. Not rated; contains nudity and graphic violence. 105m. DIR: Derek Jarman. CAST: Jenny Runacre, Jordan, Little Nell, Richard O'Brien, Adam Ant. 1978

JUBILEE TRAIL ★★ Tired romantic triangle in old California is short on action and long on melodrama as a young woman has to choose among the roughhewn men who court her. This fine cast can't drag the film out of the syrupy mire it settles into. Director Joseph Kane had a lot more luck with Gene Autry and Roy Rogers programmers. 103m. DIR: Joseph Kane. CAST: Forrest Tucker, Vera Hruba Ralston, Joan Leslie, John Russell, Jim Davis, Pat O'Brien, Barton MacLane, Ray Middleton, Buddy Baer, Jack Elam. 1953

JUD SUSS ★★ This film, *The Jew, Suss*, is infamous as the most rabid of the anti-Semitic films made by the Nazis under personal supervision of propaganda minister Joseph Goebbels. It depicts "the Jewish menace" in both symbolic and overt terms in a story about a wandering Jew who enters a small European country and nearly brings it to ruin. Any serious student of cinema should see it as an example of the medium's enormous power to proselytize. In German with English subtitles. B&W; 97m. DIR: Veidt Harlan. CAST: Ferdinand Marian, Werner Krauss. 1940

•JUDAS KISS ★★★ A few small-time criminals decide to try something bigger than they're used to—a four million dollar kidnapping scheme. With federal agents on their trail, each player must decide who he can trust, and who he can betray. The pacing and acting is good, but the occasionally forced homage to *film noir* is completely unnecessary. Rated R for nudity, violence, and language. 108m. DIR: Sebastian Gutierrez. CAST: Emma Thompson, Gil Bellows, Hal Holbrook, Alan Rickman, Carla Gugino, Til Schweiger. 1998

JUDAS PROJECT, THE ★★ Well-meaning but preachy film about the last three years of Jesus Christ's life, presented in a modern-day setting. Director-writer James H. Barden has struck upon a novel idea, but his execution is too heavy-handed and the untalented cast doesn't help. Rated PG-13 for violence. 97m. DIR: James H. Barden. CAST: John O'Banion, Ramy Zada, Richard Herd, Gerald Gordon, Jeff Corey. 1992

JUDE ★★★1/2 This adaptation of Thomas Hardy's classic tragedy is as haunting as it is beautiful. Christopher Eccleston is the title character trapped by the convents and social hierarchy of the late nineteenth century. Spirited, intellectual Kate Winslet is the soul mate who aids his downfall. The novel's sensibilities are captured equally by visuals and faultless performances, but the supporting roles are weak. Rated R for nudity, sexual situations, and a graphic childbirth scene. 122m. DIR: Michael Winterbottom. CAST: Chris Eccleston, Kate Winslet. 1996

JUDEX ★★★1/2 This remake of a serial from the early days of cinema will make you laugh out loud one moment and become misty-eyed with nostalgia the next. Based on an old potboiler by Feuillade and Bernede, *Judex* ("the judge") is an enjoyable adventure of a superhero who is lovable, human, and fallible. In French with English subtitles. B&W; 103m. DIR: Georges Franju. CAST: Channing Pollock, Jacques Jouanneau, Edith Scob, Michel Vitold, Francine Berge. 1963

JUDGE AND JURY ★★1/2 An executed criminal returns from the dead to get revenge on the innocent man be blames for the death of his wife. Action-packed thriller benefits from a fun performance by David Keith as the unstoppable maniac. Rated R for violence and profanity. 90m. DIR: John Eyres. CAST: David Keith, Martin Kove, Laura Johnson. 1997 DVD

JUDGE AND THE ASSASSIN, THE ★★★ In nineteenth-century France, a rural judge tries to ascertain whether a serial killer is insane or merely faking to escape execution. Interesting but ultimately vague (at least to American eyes) historical drama. In French with English subtitles. Not rated; brief nudity. 130m. DIR: Bertrand Tavernier. CAST: Philippe Noiret, Michel Galabru, Jean-Claude Brialy, Isabelle Huppert. 1976

JUDGE DREDD ★★★1/2 Sylvester Stallone stars as British-created superhero, Judge Dredd, a judge, jury, and executioner in the twenty-second century. Big, loud, and jam-packed with special effects, the movie took a critical lambasting in its theatrical release, but it's not as bad as its reputation would suggest. Rated R for violence and profanity. DIR: Danny Cannon. CAST: Sylvester Stallone, Armand Assante, Diane Lane, Rob Schneider, Joan Chen, Jurgen Prochnow, Max von Sydow, Joanna Miles, Balthazar Getty. 1995 DVD

JUDGE PRIEST ★★★1/2 A slice of Americana, and a good one. Life and drama in an old southern town, with all the clichés painted brilliantly. Will Rogers is fine. Stepin Fetchit is properly Uncle Tom. John Ford's sensitive direction makes this film one for the books. A touching, poignant portrait of community life lost and gone forever. B&W; 71m. DIR: John Ford. CAST: Will Rogers, Anita Louise, Stepin Fetchit, Henry B. Walthall, Tom Brown, Hattie McDaniel. 1934

JUDGE STEPS OUT, THE ★★★1/2 A Boston judge (Alexander Knox) runs away from his increasingly empty life to find happiness as a short-order cook in California. He falls in love and must choose between responsibility and pleasure. B&W; 91m. DIR: Boris Ingster. CAST: Alexander Knox, Ann Sothern, George Tobias, Florence Bates, Frieda Inescort. 1949

JUDGMENT ★★★★ The Catholic church takes a beating in this gripping teledrama, loosely lifted from an actual court case. The setting is a small-town Louisiana parish filled with staunch Catholics who idolize local priest David Strathairn (superb in a chilling role). Alas, the good father regards his altar boys with decidedly unhealthy affection. Rated PG-13 for frank sexual themes. 90m. DIR: Tom Topor. CAST: Keith Carradine, Blythe Danner, David Strathairn, Michael Faustino, Mitchell Ryan, Robert Joy, Jack Warden. 1990

JUDGMENT AT NUREMBERG ★★★★ An all-star cast shines in this thoughtful social drama. During the late stages of the Nazi war crimes trial, an American judge (Spencer Tracy) must ponder the issue of how extensive is the responsibility of citizens for carrying out the criminal orders of their governments. B&W; 178m. DIR: Stanley Kramer. CAST: Spencer Tracy, Burt Lancaster, Maximilian Schell, Richard Widmark, Marlene Dietrich, Montgomery Clift, Judy Garland. 1961

●**JUDGMENT DAY** ❤ Fragments of a splintered meteor threaten the Earth, and only a spiritual rebel in South America can save the world from oblivion. This movie is abhorrently worse than a dozen or so films with the same plot. Rated R for violence and language. 90m. DIR: John Terlesky. CAST: Ice T, Suzy Amis, Tiny Lister Jr., Coolio, Mario Van Peebles. 1999 DVD

JUDGMENT IN BERLIN ★★★ Intelligent courtroom drama in the *Inherit the Wind* and *Judgment at Nuremberg* vein. An East German hijacks a Polish airliner and has it fly to West Berlin, where he seeks political asylum. Instead of offering safety, the U.S. government puts him on trial for terrorism. Martin Sheen as the no-nonsense judge carries the film. Rated PG for language. 110m. DIR: Leo Penn. CAST: Martin Sheen, Sam Wanamaker, Max Gail, Sean Penn. 1988

JUDGMENT NIGHT ★★★ Four buddies get lost in Chicago on the way to a boxing match and end up being chased by a vicious gang in this above-average urban thriller, with high-voltage villain Denis Leary as the main attraction. Rated R for profanity and violence. 109m. DIR: Stephen Hopkins. CAST: Emilio Estevez, Cuba Gooding Jr., Denis Leary, Stephen Dorff, Jeremy Piven, Peter Greene, Michael DeLorenzo, Michael Wiseman. 1993 DVD

JUDICIAL CONSENT ★★★ In this courtroom thriller, hard-line judge Bonnie Bedelia tries a case involving the murder of an associate, and gradually realizes that *she* is being framed for the crime. The strong cast provides more credibility than this film deserves, considering the idiotic behavior in the climax. Rated R for nudity, simulated sex, profanity, and violence. 100m. DIR: William Bindley. CAST: Bonnie Bedelia, Billy Wirth, Will Patton, Lisa Blount, Dabney Coleman, Kevin McCarthy. **1995**

JUDITH OF BETHULIA ★★★ The first American four-reel film designed for feature-length exhibition, this lavish biblical spectacle of deep emotional conflict and deception brings together two stories: (1) the forty-day siege of the great Judean walled city of Bethulia and (2) the innocent lovers the siege engulfs and threatens. A brilliant example of early film drama presaging Cecil B. DeMille. Silent with musical score. B&W; 65m. **DIR:** D. W. Griffith. **CAST:** Blanche Sweet, Henry B. Walthall, Mae Marsh, Robert Harron, Lillian Gish, Dorothy Gish. **1914**

•**JUDY BERLIN** ★★★1/2 A solar eclipse in a Long Island town catches a number of the local inhabitants with their quirks showing, and the film follows them as they wander around town—a lonely schoolteacher (Barbara Barrie), her starstruck daughter Judy (Edie Falco, in an exquisite performance), a former classmate of Judy's (Aaron Harnick, representing writer-director Eric Mendelsohn), and his flighty mother (the late Madeline Kahn, wistful and touching in her last film). All but plotless, the film is nevertheless a minor gem, affectionate and observant. Rated R for mature themes and mild profanity. B&W; 93m. **DIR:** Eric Mendelsohn. **CAST:** Edie Falco, Aaron Harnick, Madeline Kahn, Bob Dishy, Barbara Barrie. **1999**

JUDY GARLAND AND FRIENDS ★★★★ Back in 1963, a then 21-year-old pre-*Funny Girl* singer named Barbra Streisand got her first television exposure on this classic *Judy Garland Show*. Besides her young daughter Liza Minnelli, Garland also welcomes the grande dame of Broadway, Ethel Merman. The singing (including an eight-song medley with Streisand) is superb, and is a tribute to the talent and personality of Garland. B&W; 55m. **DIR:** Bill Hobin. **1992**

JUGGERNAUT (1936) ★★1/2 In this low-budget mystery-drama filmed in England, Boris Karloff plays Dr. Sartorius, a brilliant (but cracked) specialist on the verge of perfecting a cure for paralysis. He makes a deal with a patient to murder her husband. B&W; 64m. **DIR:** Henry Edwards. **CAST:** Boris Karloff. **1936**

JUGGERNAUT (1974) ★★★★1/2 Here's a first-rate, suspenseful thriller about demolitions expert Richard Harris attempting to deactivate a bomb aboard a luxury liner. Richard Lester elevates the familiar plot line with inspired direction, and Lester regular Roy Kinnear is on hand to add some deft bits of comedy. Rated PG. 109m. **DIR:** Richard Lester. **CAST:** Richard Harris, Omar Sharif, David Hemmings, Anthony Hopkins, Shirley Knight, Ian Holm, Roy Kinnear. **1974**

JUGULAR WINE ★★★ After being seduced and bitten by a beautiful vampire, an anthropologist becomes obsessed with death. Obviously a low-budget production, this film succeeds due to its impressive cast of illustrious celebrities, as well as first-time writer and director Blair Murphy's panache. Rated R for violence, nudity, and profanity. 95m. **DIR:** Blair Murphy. **CAST:** Shaun Irons, Stan Lee, Frank Miller,

Henry Rollins, Lisa Malkiewicz, Vladimir Kehkaial, Michael Colyar. **1994**

JUICE ★★★1/2 Spike Lee's cinematographer, Ernest R. Dickerson, makes his directorial debut with this gritty, downbeat chronicle of life on the streets of Harlem. Four friends edge around the outside of the law until the fateful moment when they finally step over the line and find themselves on the run. It's not unlike an inner-city version of *The Wild Bunch*. Rated R for profanity, violence, and suggested sex. 96m. **DIR:** Ernest R. Dickerson. **CAST:** Omar Epps, Jermaine Hopkins, Khalil Kain, Tupac Shakur. **1992**

JULES AND JIM ★★★★★ Superb character study, which revolves around a bizarre ménage à trois. It is really a film about wanting what you can't have and not wanting what you think you desire once you have it. In French with English subtitles. B&W; 104m. **DIR:** François Truffaut. **CAST:** Oskar Werner, Jeanne Moreau, Henri Serre. **1961 DVD**

JULIA ★★★★1/2 Alvin Sargent won an Oscar for his taut screen adaptation of the late Lillian Hellman's bestselling memoir *Pentimento*. It's a harrowing tale of Hellman's journey into Germany to locate her childhood friend who has joined in the resistance against the Nazis. Great performances by all cast members. Rated PG. 118m. **DIR:** Fred Zinnemann. **CAST:** Jane Fonda, Vanessa Redgrave, Jason Robards Jr., Maximillian Schell, Meryl Streep. **1977**

JULIA AND JULIA ❤ Dreary Italian-made, English-language movie is an uninspired rehash of the parallel-worlds plot from the old science-fiction pulp magazines. Rated R for profanity, nudity, and violence. 95m. **DIR:** Peter Del Monte. **CAST:** Kathleen Turner, Gabriel Byrne, Sting, Gabriele Ferzetti. **1988**

JULIA HAS TWO LOVERS ❤ Daphna Kastner was unknown as a writer and actress before this horrid film, whose title is self-explanatory, and hopefully she will never be heard from again. Rated R for nudity and simulated sex. 87m. **DIR:** Bashar Shbib. **CAST:** Daphna Kastner, David Duchovny, David Charles. **1990**

JULIA MISBEHAVES ★★★★ Delightful farce with Greer Garson as a London chorine, long separated from stuffy husband Walter Pidgeon and their refined daughter, Elizabeth Taylor, coming back into their lives for the marriage of the latter. Garson is wonderful in her only comic role, even allowing herself to become foil to a group of acrobats. B&W; 99m. **DIR:** Jack Conway. **CAST:** Greer Garson, Walter Pidgeon, Peter Lawford, Elizabeth Taylor, Cesar Romero, Lucile Watson, Nigel Bruce, Mary Boland, Henry Stephenson, Ian Wolfe, Veda Ann Borg. **1948**

JULIAN PO ★★ A nondescript young man (Christian Slater) wanders into a small mountain town, and the locals are suspicious. But when they learn he's come to kill himself, they become suddenly respectful and solicitous. First-time filmmaker Alan Wade transplants a Serbo-Croatian story to rural Appalachia, and the result is like a weird mixture of Franz Kafka, Samuel Beckett, and Mark Twain. Slater is earnest, but like the rest of the cast he's hampered by the heavy-handed allegory of the script. Rated PG-13 for mild profanity. 78m. **DIR:** Alan

Wade. **CAST:** Christian Slater, Robin Tunney, Michael Parks, Harve Presnell, Dina Spybey, Zeljko Ivanek. 1997

•**JULIE** ★★ Campy melodrama with Doris Day as an airline stewardess who realizes that her second husband—is a psychopath who killed her first husband—and may do the same to her. You'll find it hard to keep a straight face during the ridiculous finale in which Doris has to land a jumbo jet by herself. B&W; 99m. **DIR:** Andrew L. Stone. **CAST:** Doris Day, Louis Jourdan, Barry Sullivan, Frank Lovejoy, Jack Kruschen. 1956

JULIET OF THE SPIRITS ★★★★★ The convoluted plot in this classic centers around a wealthy wife suspicious of her cheating husband. Giulietta Masina (in real life, Mrs. Fellini) has never been so tantalizingly innocent with her Bambi eyes. This is Fellini's first attempt with color. 148m. **DIR:** Federico Fellini. **CAST:** Giulietta Masina, Sandra Milo, Valentina Cortese, Sylva Koscina. 1965 DVD

JULIUS CAESAR (1953) ★★★★ Cool, confident, star-bright performances mark this stirring, memorable mounting of Shakespeare's great classic of honor and the struggle for power in ancient Rome. A superb blend of eloquent language and judicious camera art. Standouts: John Gielgud as the cunning Cassius and Marlon Brando, whose fire-hot/ice-cold portrayal of Mark Antony alone makes the film worthwhile. B&W; 120m. **DIR:** Joseph L. Mankiewicz. **CAST:** Louis Calhern, Marlon Brando, James Mason, John Gielgud, Edmond O'Brien, Greer Garson, Deborah Kerr. 1953

JULIUS CAESAR (1970) ★★ A good cast, but Shakespeare loses in this so-so rendering of ambition, greed, jealousy, and politics in toga Rome. 117m. **DIR:** Stuart Burge. **CAST:** Charlton Heston, Jason Robards Jr., John Gielgud, Robert Vaughn, Richard Chamberlain, Diana Rigg, Christopher Lee. 1970

JUMANJI ★★★1/2 Terrific computer-generated effects highlight this fantasy about youngsters who find their lives taken over by a bizarre and all-powerful board game. Robin Williams is fine in a *Hook*-style role as an adult involved in the games, but it is David Allen Grier, as a hapless policeman, who provides the laughs. Heartwarming and fun. Rated PG. 104m. **DIR:** Joe Johnston. **CAST:** Robin Williams, Bonnie Hunt, Kirsten Dunst, Bradley Pierce, Bebe Neuwirth, Jonathan Hyde, David Alan Grier, Patricia Clarkson. 1995 DVD

JUMBO ★★ A big-budget circus-locale musical that flopped, despite Rodgers and Hart songs, William Daniels photography, a Sidney Sheldon script from a Hecht and MacArthur story, and a cast that should have known better. 125m. **DIR:** Charles Walters. **CAST:** Doris Day, Stephen Boyd, Jimmy Durante, Martha Raye, Dean Jagger. 1962

JUMPIN' AT THE BONEYARD ★★1/2 Two brothers accidentally meet for the first time in years and try to connect again. One is divorced and unemployed, the other a drug-addicted thief, and their visit to the Bronx slum where they grew up mirrors their bleak lives. Sometimes compelling but ultimately pointless and downbeat. Rated R for profanity and drug use. 107m. **DIR:** Jeff Stanzler. **CAST:** Tim Roth, Alexis Arquette, Danitra Vance, Samuel L. Jackson, Luis Guzman. 1992

JUMPIN' JACK FLASH ★★1/2 Whoopi Goldberg's inspired clowning is the only worthwhile element in her first big-screen comedy. She plays a computer operator who finds herself involved in international intrigue. Rated R for profanity and violence. 100m. **DIR:** Penny Marshall. **CAST:** Whoopi Goldberg, Stephen Collins, John Wood, Carol Kane, James Belushi, Annie Potts, Peter Michael Goetz, Roscoe Lee Browne, Jeroen Krabbé, Jonathan Pryce. 1986

JUMPING JACKS ★★★ It's all Jerry Lewis antics as two nightclub entertainers join the parachute corps. Not on a par with *At War With The Army*. B&W; 96m. **DIR:** Norman Taurog. **CAST:** Dean Martin, Jerry Lewis, Mona Freeman, Don DeFore, Robert Strauss, Ray Teal. 1952

JUNE BRIDE ★★★1/2 A noted correspondent is forced to work for his ex-flame, now an editor of a woman's magazine. His cynicism causes complications with the bride and her family. Robert Montgomery, as the reporter, steals the show. B&W; 97m. **DIR:** Bretaigne Windust. **CAST:** Bette Davis, Robert Montgomery, Fay Bainter, Tom Tully, Mary Wickes, Jerome Cowan. 1948

JUNE NIGHT ★★★1/2 Ingrid Bergman gives a harrowing performance in this well-crafted melodrama about a young woman who changes her identity in order to escape the scars of a violent incident at the hands of a former lover. This poignant film gives viewers a chance to experience a young Bergman before her success in Hollywood. In Swedish with English subtitles. B&W; 90m. **DIR:** Per Lindberg. **CAST:** Ingrid Bergman. 1940 DVD

JUNGLE BOOK (1942) ★★★★ This one's for fantasy fans of all ages. Sabu stars in Rudyard Kipling's tale of a boy raised by wolves in the jungle of India. Beautiful color presentation holds the viewer from start to finish. Rated G. 109m. **DIR:** Zoltán Korda. **CAST:** Sabu, Joseph Calleia, John Qualen. 1942 DVD

JUNGLE BOOK, THE (1967) ★★★★ Phil Harris's Baloo the Bear steals the show in this rendition of Rudyard Kipling's *Mowgli* stories, the last full-length animated film that reflected Walt Disney's personal participation. Although not as lavishly illustrated as earlier Disney efforts, *The Jungle Book* benefits from its clever songs ("The Bare Necessities," among others) and inspired vocal casting. 78m. **DIR:** Wolfgang Reitherman. 1967 DVD

JUNGLE CAPTIVE ★★ Acquanetta's missing from this second and last sequel to *Captive Wild Woman*, replaced by Vicky Lane as the ape-turned-woman who kills when upset. B&W; 63m. **DIR:** Harold Young. **CAST:** Otto Kruger, Amelita Ward, Phil Brown, Vicky Lane. 1945

JUNGLE FEVER ★★★ Writer-director Spike Lee's story of an interracial romance between a married black architect (Wesley Snipes) and his single Italian-American secretary (Annabella Sciorra) has some terrific performances and unforgettable moments. Sad to say, you have to wade through quite a bit of tedium to get to them. Rated R for profanity, violence, and nudity. 135m. DIR: Spike Lee. CAST: Wesley Snipes, Annabella Sciorra, Spike Lee, Anthony Quinn, Ossie Davis, Ruby Dee, Lonette McKee, John Turturro, Tim Robbins, Brad Dourif. 1991 DVD

JUNGLE HEAT ★★ Dr. Evelyn Howard (Deborah Raffin), an anthropologist from L.A., hires an alcoholic ex–Vietnam vet (Peter Fonda) to fly her into the jungles of South America. There she looks for an ancient tribe of pygmies but finds instead monsters that greatly resemble the Creature from the Black Lagoon. Rated PG for language and gore. 93m. DIR: Gus Trikonis. CAST: Peter Fonda, Deborah Raffin, John Amos. 1984

JUNGLE JIM ★★★ The first entry in Columbia's long-running series starring Johnny Weissmuller finds Alex Raymond's comic-strip hero helping a female scientist search for a rare drug that can help cure polio. Future Superman George Reeves plays the heavy. B&W; 73m. DIR: William Berke. CAST: Johnny Weissmuller, Virginia Grey, George Reeves, Lita Baron, Rick Vallin. 1948

JUNGLE PATROL ★★ This is a routine World War II story about a squadron of fliers commanded by a young officer who has been ordered to hold an airfield against the Japanese. The subplot is a silly romance between the officer and a USO performer. Best ingredient: the music score by Emil Newman and Arthur Lange. B&W; 72m. DIR: Joseph M. Newman. CAST: Kristine Miller, Arthur Franz, Ross Ford, Tommy Noonan, Gene Reynolds, Richard Jaeckel, Harry Lauter. 1948

JUNGLE RAIDERS ★★ Christopher Connelly plays an adventurer–con man hired to find the Ruby of Gloom in Malaysia. This *Raiders of the Lost Ark* rip-off is too plodding for most viewers. It includes a few fun, action-filled moments but stick to the Lucas-Spielberg classic. Rated PG for violence and profanity. 102m. DIR: Anthony M. Dawson. CAST: Christopher Connelly, Marina Costa, Lee Van Cleef. 1985

JUNGLE 2 JUNGLE ★★1/2 Tim Allen plays a New York stockbroker who discovers he's a father while seeking a divorce in a Venezuelan jungle. Returning to the big city with his son, he gains a better perception of what is important in life. Mildly humorous with some gorgeous rain-forest shots. Otherwise, predictable Disney fare reminiscent of the *Love Bug* series era. Rated PG for sexual innuendo. 95m. DIR: John Pasquin. CAST: Tim Allen, Sam Huntington, JoBeth Williams, Bob Dishy, Martin Short, Lolita Davidovich, David Ogden Stiers. 1997

JUNGLE WARRIORS ★★1/2 The idea of a group of female models in Peru for a shoot in the jungle is quite absurd. If you can overlook the premise, though, this action film is modestly satisfying. It's rather like an episode of *Miami Vice* but with scantily dressed women packing machine guns. Rated R for violence, profanity, and nudity. 96m. DIR: Ernst R. von Theumer. CAST: Sybil Danning, Marjoe Gortner, Nina Van Pallandt, Paul Smith, John Vernon, Alex Cord, Woody Strode, Kai Wulfe, Dana Elcar. 1983

JUNGLE WOMAN ★★ Lots of footage from *Captive Wild Woman* is used to pad out this sequel that, beginning with scientist J. Carrol Naish reviving apewoman Acquanetta, has essentially the same plot.

B&W; 60m. DIR: Reginald LeBorg. CAST: Acquanetta, Evelyn Ankers, J. Carrol Naish, Samuel S. Hinds, Milburn Stone. 1944

JUNGLEGROUND ★★ Roddy Piper plays a police lieutenant who gets trapped inside "Jungleground," the worst crime-ridden area of the city. Apprehended by the local gang's vicious leader, Piper is set loose for a nasty game of cat and mouse. Rated R for violence and language. 90m. DIR: Don Allan. CAST: Roddy Piper, Tori Higginson, Peter Williams. 1994 DVD

JUNIOR (1984) 💣 Despicable sadomasochism. Not rated; contains violence, nudity, and profanity. 80m. DIR: Jim Henley. CAST: Linda Singer. 1984

JUNIOR (1994) ★★1/2 Arnold Schwarzenegger follows in the footsteps of Billy Crystal (*Rabbit Test*) as "the world's first pregnant man." The big guy pokes fun at his macho image by playing an absent-minded scientist coerced into embryo implantation by not-so-ethical colleague Danny DeVito, complicating a budding romance with accident-prone scientist Emma Thompson. The film never quite achieves the heights of hilarity trod by *Twins*, but it does have its moments. Rated PG-13 for mature situations. 109m. DIR: Ivan Reitman. CAST: Arnold Schwarzenegger, Danny DeVito, Emma Thompson, Frank Langella, Pamela Reed, Judy Collins, James Eckhouse, Aida Turturro. 1994 DVD

JUNIOR BONNER ★★★ A rodeo has-been, Steve McQueen, returns home for one last rousing performance in front of the home folks. McQueen is quite good as the soft-spoken cowboy who tries to make peace with his family. Robert Preston is a real scene stealer as his hard-drinking carouser of a father. Rated PG. 103m. DIR: Sam Peckinpah. CAST: Steve McQueen, Robert Preston, Ida Lupino, Ben Johnson, Joe Don Baker. 1972 DVD

JUNIOR'S GROOVE ★★★ Engaging tale of a piano prodigy who escapes his urban world through elaborate fantasy. When his home life becomes desperate, he's forced to team up with a kid from the streets in order to survive both what is real and imaginary. Lynn Whitfield is excellent as the prodigy's mother. Rated R for language, violence, and adult situations. 91m. DIR: Clement Virgo. CAST: Lynn Whitfield, Margot Kidder, Martin Villafana, Clark Johnson, Rainbow Sun Francks. 1997 DVD

JUNIPER TREE, THE ★★★ Adaptation of a story by the Brothers Grimm about two sisters who use magical powers to battle for the affections of a widower. Probably only released in America because of the presence of alternative music star Bjork (here using her full name), this is a bleakly filmed tale that may appeal to art-house buffs, but which certainly will bore children to tears. Not rated; contains nothing objectionable. 78m. DIR: Nietzchka Keene. CAST: Bjork Gudmundsdottir, Byrndla Petra Bragadottir, Vladimir Orn Flygenring. 1987

JUNKMAN, THE 💣 From the makers of *Gone in 60 Seconds*, this sequel is tagged as the "chase film for the '80s." Rated PG. 99m. DIR: H. B. Halicki. CAST: Christopher Stone, Susan Shaw, Lang Jeffries, Lynda Day George. 1982

JUNO AND THE PAYCOCK ★★1/2 Sean O'Casey's famous play gets the Hitchcock treatment, and the result is an intriguing blend of Irish melodrama and sinister moods. The setting is the Dublin uprising, the characters members of a poor family with more than its share of grief. A young unwed mother, an anticipated inheritance, and an unwise young man are the focus for various sorts of tragedy. B&W; 85m. DIR: Alfred Hitchcock. CAST: Sara Allgood, Edward Chapman, Sidney Morgan. 1929

JUPITER'S DARLING ★★★ If you are in a lighthearted mood, this spoof of Hannibal's siege of Rome is a perfect way to pass time. Witty songs and situations coupled with a likable cast. 96m. DIR: George Sidney. CAST: Esther Williams, Howard Keel, George Sanders, Marge Champion, Gower Champion, Richard Haydn. 1955

JUPITER'S THIGH ★★★1/2 The delightful *Dear Inspector* duo is back in this delicious sequel directed by Philippe de Broca (*King of Hearts*). This time, the lady detective (Annie Girardot) and her Greek archaeologist lover (Philippe Noiret) get married and honeymoon—where else?—in Greece. But they aren't there long before they find themselves caught up in mayhem. It's great fun, served up with sophistication. In French with English subtitles. 90m. DIR: Philippe de Broca. CAST: Annie Girardot, Philippe Noiret. 1983

JUPITER'S WIFE ★★★★★ When filmmaker Michel Negroponte met Maggie, a fortysomething homeless woman who lived in Manhattan's Central Park with her dogs, he was struck by her good cheer and the complexity of her seemingly incoherent ramblings. So he spent two years meeting with and filming her, gradually uncovering the history that led to her situation. After watching this utterly compelling documentary, you'll never again view "those people" as faceless nuisances. Not rated. 78m. DIR: Michel Negroponte. 1995

JURASSIC PARK ★★★★ In this adaptation from the novel by Michael Crichton, dinosaurs are genetically re-created to populate the ultimate theme park, and a special few are allowed a sneak preview. Awe and wonder soon turns to terror as the creatures break out of their confines and go on a rampage. Rated PG-13 for violence. 120m. DIR: Steven Spielberg. CAST: Sam Neill, Laura Dern, Jeff Goldblum, Richard Attenborough, Bob Peck, Martin Ferrero, B. D. Wong, Samuel L. Jackson, Wayne Knight, Joseph Mazzello, Ariana Richards. 1993

JUROR, THE ★★1/2 A juror on a high-profile Mafia trial is terrorized by a hoodlum (Alec Baldwin) who wants her to hang the jury. The film is hokey and contrived, and its resemblance to *Trial by Jury* (1994) may be more than coincidental, but this version of the story is a marginal improvement, sparked by Baldwin's succulently hammy performance. Rated R for violence, profanity, and brief nudity. 107m. DIR: Brian Gibson. CAST: Demi Moore, Alec Baldwin, James Gandolfini, Joseph Gordon-Levitt, Anne Heche, Lindsay Crouse. 1996 DVD

JURY DUTY ★★ Cashing in on America's obsession with the O. J. Simpson murder trial, this spoofs the jury system in general and the sequestering of jurors in particular. Pauly Shore portrays a goofy loser who parlays his position as juror number six into a luxury vacation. Rated PG-13 for profanity. 88m. DIR: John Fortenberry. CAST: Pauly Shore, Tia Carrere, Stanley Tucci, Brian Doyle-Murray, Abe Vigoda, Charles Napier. 1995

JUST A GIGOLO 🎭 Prussian aristocrat ends up as a disillusioned male prostitute. 96m. DIR: David Hemmings. CAST: David Bowie, Sydne Rome, Kim Novak, David Hemmings, Marlene Dietrich, Maria Schell, Curt Jurgens. 1978

JUST ANOTHER GIRL ON THE I.R.T. ★★★1/2 Powerful debut from director Leslie Harris, who draws a memorable performance out of Ariyan Johnson as a determined Brooklyn high-school student attempting to make a better life for herself. Her dreams of higher education take a backseat to reality when she finds herself pregnant. Excellent slice-of-life drama is sometimes funny, sometimes sad, but always interesting and well directed. Rated R for language and adult situations. 96m. DIR: Leslie Harris. CAST: Ariyan Johnson, Kevin Thigpen. 1993

JUST AROUND THE CORNER ★★★ This bucket of sap has nearly too-sweet Shirley Temple ending the Depression by charming a crusty sourpussed millionaire into providing new jobs. The ridiculous becomes sublime when Shirley dances with the incomparable Bill Robinson. B&W; 70m. DIR: Irving Cummings. CAST: Shirley Temple, Joan Davis, Charles Farrell, Bill Robinson, Bert Lahr. 1938

JUST BEFORE DAWN ★★ Same old, same old as characters head into the wilderness—after being warned not to—where they are besieged by mountain men. Deborah Benson delivers a performance that is far better than this film deserves. Rated R for violence and profanity. 90m. DIR: Jeff Lieberman. CAST: Deborah Benson, George Kennedy, Chris Lemmon. 1982

JUST BETWEEN FRIENDS ★★★1/2 Mary Tyler Moore stars in this big-screen soap opera as a homemaker happily married to Ted Danson. She meets TV news reporter Christine Lahti and they become friends. They have a lot in common—including being in love with the same man. Rated PG-13 for profanity and suggested sex. 115m. DIR: Allan Burns. CAST: Mary Tyler Moore, Christine Lahti, Sam Waterston, Ted Danson, Mark Blum. 1986

JUST CAUSE ★★★1/2 Law professor Sean Connery is coaxed into action when a condemned killer appeals to his sense of justice. Part *Silence of the Lambs* and part *Cape Fear*, this is an effective suspense thriller. High-voltage performances by a strong cast and sleight-of-hand direction by Arne Glimcher keep the viewer involved despite the familiarity of some of the story elements and a couple of contrived plot twists (taken directly from John Katzenbach's original novel). Rated R for violence and profanity. 102m. DIR: Arne Glimcher. CAST: Sean Connery, Laurence Fishburne, Kate Capshaw, Blair Underwood, Ed Harris, Christopher Murray, Ruby Dee, Scarlett Johansson, Daniel J. Travanti, Ned Beatty, Liz Torres, Kevin McCarthy, Hope Lange, Chris Sarandon, George Plimpton. 1995 DVD

JUST FOR THE HELL OF IT ★★ Teen vandals terrorize a Florida town. Not rated, but unsuitable for young children. 88m. DIR: Herschell Gordon Lewis.

CAST: Rodney Bedell, Ray Sager, Nancy Lee Noble. 1967

•JUST IMAGINE ★★ Cornball character from 1930 is suspended for fifty years and wakes up in New York of 1980. Trifling plot takes a backseat to the special effects created in part by some of the team from *King Kong* and later used in the *Flash Gordon* serials. Incredibly silly, this science-fiction musical has one plus: a beautiful Maureen O'Sullivan in one of her first roles. They don't make 'em like this anymore, and it's amazing that they ever did. B&W; 108m. DIR: David Butler. CAST: El Brendel, Maureen O'Sullivan, John Garrick, Kenneth Thompson, Mischa Auer, Ivan Lino, Marjorie White, Hobart Bosworth. 1930

JUST LIKE A WOMAN ★★★ Breezy performances punctuate this offbeat comedy about cross-dressing. An American businessman in London falls for his landlady who finds her new tenant quite an eyeful. When they finally get together, she learns of his desire to wear women's clothing. How they come to grips with his desire while maintaining a normal relationship provides plenty of insight and laughter. Rated R for language. 102m. DIR: Christopher Monger. CAST: Julie Walters, Adrian Pasdar, Paul Freeman. 1992

JUST ONE OF THE GIRLS ♥ Lowbrow teen fantasy has Corey Haim cross-dressing on campus to avoid the school bully and get closer to the bully's sister. Exactly what you'd expect, but worse. Rated R for nudity and language. 94m. DIR: Michael Keusch. CAST: Corey Haim, Nicole Eggert, Cameron Bancroft, Gabe Khouth. 1993

JUST ONE OF THE GUYS ★★★ A sort of reverse *Tootsie*, this surprisingly restrained teen-lust comedy stars Joyce Hyser as an attractive young woman who switches high schools and sexes. The premise is flimsy and forced, but director Lisa Gottlieb and her cast keep the viewer entertained. Rated PG-13 for nudity, violence, and profanity. 88m. DIR: Lisa Gottlieb. CAST: Joyce Hyser, Clayton Rohner, Billy Jacoby, Toni Hudson. 1985

JUST TELL ME WHAT YOU WANT ★★ Alan King gives a fine performance in this otherwise forgettable film as an executive who attempts to get his mistress (Ali MacGraw) back. She's in love with a younger man (Peter Weller). Rated R. 112m. DIR: Sidney Lumet. CAST: Alan King, Ali MacGraw, Peter Weller, Myrna Loy, Keenan Wynn, Tony Roberts, Dina Merrill. 1980

•JUST THE TICKET ★★ Dull comedy-romance is sabotaged by a complete lack of chemistry between stars Andy Garcia and Andie MacDowell. Rated R for profanity. 112m. DIR: Richard Wenk. CAST: Andy Garcia, Andie MacDowell, Elizabeth Ashley, Ron Leibman, Chris Lemmon, Don Novello, Abe Vigoda. 1998 DVD

JUST THE WAY YOU ARE ★★1/2 Kristy McNichol gives a fine performance as a pretty flautist who cleverly overcomes the need to wear a leg brace. But this deception brings an unexpected moment of truth. Even the plodding direction of Edouard Molinaro can't prevent this well-written work from occasionally being witty, and touching. Rated PG. 95m. DIR:

Edouard Molinaro. CAST: Kristy McNichol, Michael Ontkean, Kaki Hunter. 1984

JUST WILLIAM'S LUCK ★★ Based on a series of children's books that were popular in Great Britain, this isn't likely to do as well with American kids. William and his pals are mischief-makers who spend most of the film getting into various sorts of trouble. 87m. DIR: Val Guest. CAST: William Graham, Garry Marsh. 1947

•JUST WRITE ★★★1/2 Beverly Hills tour-bus driver finds a new focus to his life when he meets the actress he adores and she mistakes him for a screenwriter. Feel-good romantic comedy is a movie lover's delight filled with interesting characters and the usual setbacks before the final fade-out. This one is really like "the kind they used to make." Rated PG-13 for mild profanity and adult situations. 95m. DIR: Andrew Gallerani. CAST: Jeremy Piven, Sherilyn Fenn, JoBeth Williams, Jeffrey Sams, Alex Rocco, Wallace Shawn, Costas Mandylor, Yeardley Smith. 1997 DVD

JUST YOU AND ME, KID ★★ The delights of George Burns as an ex-vaudeville performer do not mask the worthless plot in this tale of Burns's attempt to hide a young runaway (Brooke Shields) fleeing a drug dealer. Shields's inability to move with Burns's rhythm rapidly becomes annoying. Rated PG for mild language and brief nudity. 93m. DIR: Leonard Stern. CAST: George Burns, Brooke Shields, Ray Bolger, Lorraine Gary, Burl Ives. 1979

JUST YOUR LUCK ★★1/2 In this Quentin Tarantino wannabe, patrons of an all-night diner try to decide what to do with a $6 million lottery ticket after its owner has a heart attack. A good ensemble cast can't do much with the weak dialogue and weaker plot. Rated R for violence and profanity. 88m. DIR: Gary Auerbach. CAST: Virginia Madsen, Sean Patrick Flanery, Ernie Hudson, Alanna Ubach, Vince Vaughn, Jon Favreau, Jon Polito, Mike Starr, Carroll Baker, John Lurie, Flea, Bill Erwin. 1996

JUSTIN MORGAN HAD A HORSE ★★★ Agreeable Disney film focuses on the ingenuity and foresight of a poor Vermont schoolteacher following the Revolutionary War. He trained and bred the first Morgan horse, which was noted for its speed, strength, and stamina. 91m. DIR: Hollingsworth Morse. CAST: Don Murray, Lana Wood, Gary Crosby. 1972

JUSTINE ★★ This compression of four volumes of Laurence Durrell's *Alexandria Quartet* into one film tells the story of a Middle Eastern prostitute who rises to a position of power in her country. Fans of the novels will be disappointed; those unfamiliar with the story will be confused. Rated R for nudity and sexual situations. 117m. DIR: George Cukor. CAST: Anouk Aimée, Dirk Bogarde, Robert Forster, Anna Karina, Philippe Noiret, Michael York, John Vernon, Jack Albertson, Cliff Gorman, Michael Constantine, Severn Darden. 1969

KAFKA ★★★1/2 This odd, tongue-in-cheek thriller will delight some viewers and annoy others. About an insurance claims clerk in Prague, circa 1919, it's a study in paranoia, with the title character being thrust into a world of plots and counterplots. It has little to do with the life and writings of Franz Kafka. Rated PG-13 for violence. 98m. **DIR:** Steven Soderbergh. **CAST:** Jeremy Irons, Theresa Russell, Joel Grey, Ian Holm, Jeroen Krabbé, Armin Mueller-Stahl, Alec Guinness, Brian Glover, Keith Allen, Robert Flemyng. 1992

KAGEMUSHA ★★★★★ A 70-year-old Akira Kurosawa outdoes himself in this epic masterpiece about honor and illusion. Kurosawa popularized the samurai genre—which has been described as the Japanese equivalent of the Western—in America with his breathtaking, action-packed films. This is yet another feast for the eyes, heart, and mind. Rated PG. 159m. **DIR:** Akira Kurosawa. **CAST:** Tatsuya Nakadai. 1980

KALIFORNIA ★★★1/2 This *Bad Lands* for the 1990s is a tense, chilling psychodrama and darkly comic road movie. While visiting America's most infamous murder sites to develop material for a book, a liberal journalist and his photographer lover share a convertible and traveling expenses with a white-trash sociopath and his incredibly dumb girlfriend. The characters are brilliantly developed and interconnected during the trek. Rated R for sex, violence, and profanity. 117m. **DIR:** Dominic Sena. **CAST:** Brad Pitt, Juliette Lewis, David Duchovny, Michelle Forbes. 1993

KAMA SUTRA: A TALE OF LOVE ★★1/2 This exotic adult fable is rich in mythic sixteenth-century Indian atmosphere, but plays like a harem soap opera. Tara is a spoiled princess who marries into royalty. Maya is her sensuous servant who seduces Tara's husband on their wedding night and reenters her court as chief courtesan for Tara's decadent spouse. The film's attempt to connect with the spiritual embodiment of *The Kama Sutra of Vatsayana* only partly succeeds. Not rated; contains strong language, nudity, sex, and violence. 114m. **DIR:** Mira Nair. **CAST:** Indira Varma, Sarita Choudhury, Naveen Andrews, Ramon Tikaram. 1996 DVD

KAMERADSCHAFT ★★★1/2 The story development is slow, but the concept is so strong and the sense of cross-cultural camaraderie so stirring that the film remains impressive. The story concerns French miners getting trapped by a mine disaster, with German miners attempting a daring rescue. In German and French with English subtitles. B&W; 87m. **DIR:** G. W. Pabst. **CAST:** George Chalia, David Mendaille, Ernest Busch. 1931

KAMIKAZE 89 ★★★ The late Rainer Werner Fassbinder stars in this bizarre fantasy-thriller set in a decadent German city in 1989. A bomb has been planted in the headquarters of a giant conglomerate and a police lieutenant (Fassbinder) has very little time to locate it. In German with English subtitles. 90m. **DIR:** Wolf Gremm. **CAST:** Rainer Werner Fassbinder, Gunther Kaufmann, Brigitte Mira, Franco Nero. 1983

KANAL ★★★★ Andrzej Wajda's compelling war drama about the Polish resistance fighters during World War II brought international acclaim to the Polish cinema. This film explores the dreams, the despair, and the struggle of a generation who refused to be held captive in their own land by the Nazi war machine in 1944. In Polish with English subtitles. B&W; 96m. **DIR:** Andrzej Wajda. **CAST:** Teresa Izewska. 1957

KANDYLAND ★★★ Fairly interesting story centers around a girl's desire to make a living at exotic dancing. The nice thing about this film is that it concentrates on the people involved, not the dances. Rated R for nudity, profanity, and violence. 94m. **DIR:** Robert Schnitzer. **CAST:** Sandahl Bergman, Kim Evenson. 1987

KANGAROO ★★★★ Real-life husband and wife Colin Friels and Judy Davis give superb performances in this Australian film adaptation of the semiautobiographical novel by D. H. Lawrence. Writer Richard Somers (Friels), a thinly veiled version of Lawrence, finds himself vilified by critics in his native England for writing sexually suggestive novels and, with his German-born wife Harriet (Davis), journeys down under in search of a better life. Rated R for violence, nudity, and profanity. 100m. **DIR:** Tim Burstall. **CAST:** Colin Friels, Judy Davis, John Walton, Hugh Keays-Byrne. 1986

KANSAN, THE ★★★ Tough, two-fisted Richard Dix sets his jaw and routs the baddies in a wide-open prairie town but must then contend with a corrupt official in this enjoyable Western, the third to pair him with Jane Wyatt and heavies Victor Jory and Albert Dekker. B&W; 79m. **DIR:** George Archainbaud. **CAST:** Richard Dix, Jane Wyatt, Victor Jory, Albert Dekker, Eugene Pallette, Robert Armstrong. 1943

KANSAS ★★ Lethargic melodrama has fresh-faced Andrew McCarthy teaming up with sleazy Matt Dillon, who cons him into robbing a bank. Rated R for profanity and violence. 105m. **DIR:** David Stevens. **CAST:** Matt Dillon, Andrew McCarthy, Leslie Hope, Kyra Sedgwick. 1988

KANSAS CITY ★★ Robert Altman's ode to his jazz roots is an absolute mess, a film that wastes a good cast and comes alive only during its musical interludes. The ridiculous plot involves a working-class girl who hopes to leverage her lover from a crime lord by kidnapping a stoned socialite. Any potential drama is lost during interminable speeches—all deadly dull. Rated R for violence, profanity, and drug use. 115m. **DIR:** Robert Altman. **CAST:** Jennifer Jason Leigh, Miranda Richardson, Harry Belafonte, Michael Murphy, Dermot Mulroney, Steve Buscemi. 1996

KANSAS CITY CONFIDENTIAL ★★★ Four masked men pull a split-second-timed bank heist and get away while innocent ex-con John Payne gets the third degree. After the police lose interest in him, Payne follows the robbers to Guatemala. Good photography and atmosphere, but overlong. B&W; 98m.

DIR: Phil Karlson. **CAST:** John Payne, Coleen Gray, Preston Foster, Lee Van Cleef, Neville Brand, Jack Elam. **1952**

KANSAS CITY MASSACRE, THE ★★★ Dale Robertson reprises his role of the outlandish Melvin Purvis that he originated in 1974s *Melvin Purvis, G-Man.* Practically every notorious gangster who ever lived meets the unstoppable G-Man in this made-for-TV film. Watch for the acting debut of the notorious ex-governor of Georgia, Lester Maddox. Here he's governor of Oklahoma. 120m. **DIR:** Dan Curtis. **CAST:** Dale Robertson, Bo Hopkins, Robert Walden, Mills Watson, Scott Brady, Harris Yulin. **1975**

KANSAS CYCLONE ★★ A crooked mine owner is holding up gold ore shipments from other mines and running the ore back through his dummy mine. Don Barry, an undercover marshal, poses as a geologist to catch the bandits. The action, under the capable hands of Yakima Canutt, and a couple of interesting subplots from screenwriter Oliver Drake lift this one above the average. B&W; 58m. **DIR:** George Sherman. **CAST:** Don Barry, Lynn Merrick. **1941**

KANSAS PACIFIC ★★1/2 Railroad drama set in pre–Civil War days has rangy Sterling Hayden romancing Eve Miller and battling pro-Confederate saboteurs. 73m. **DIR:** Ray Nazarro. **CAST:** Sterling Hayden, Eve Miller, Barton MacLane, Douglas Fowley, Myron Healey, Clayton Moore, Reed Hadley. **1953**

KANSAS TERRORS ★★★ The Three Mesquiteers must recover gold paid them for selling a herd of horses. They encounter a tyrant who rules an island in the Caribbean. B&W; 57m. **DIR:** George Sherman. **CAST:** Robert Livingston, Duncan Renaldo, Raymond Hatton, Jacqueline Wells, Howard Hickman. **1939**

KAOS ★★★1/2 Italian writer-directors Paolo and Vittorio Taviani adapted four short stories by Luigi Pirandello for this sumptuously photographed film about peasant life in Sicily. For all its beauty and style, this is a disappointing, uneven work. The first two stories are wonderful, but the final pair leave a lot to be desired. In Italian with English subtitles. Rated R for nudity and violence. 188m. **DIR:** Paolo Taviani, Vittorio Taviani. **CAST:** Margarita Lozano, Enrica Maria Mudugno, Omero Antonutti. **1986**

KARATE COP ♥ Futuristic chop-socky about the last cop on Earth and a beautiful scientist who team up to find a precious stone. Rated R for violence and language. 91m. **DIR:** Alan Roberts. **CAST:** Ron Marchini, Carrie Chambers, David Carradine, Michael Bristow. **1992**

KARATE KID, THE ★★★1/2 A heartwarming, surefire crowd pleaser, this believable and touching work about the hazards of high school days and adolescence will have you cheering during its climax and leave you with a smile on your face. You'll find yourself rooting for the put-upon hero, Daniel (Ralph Macchio), and booing the bad guys. Rated PG for violence and profanity. 126m. **DIR:** John G. Avildsen. **CAST:** Ralph Macchio, Noriyuki "Pat" Morita, Elisabeth Shue. **1984 DVD**

KARATE KID PART II, THE ★★★1/2 This second in the *Karate Kid* series begins moments after the conclusion of the first film. Mr. Miyagi (Noriyuki "Pat" Morita) receives word that his father, residing in Ok-

inawa, is dying, so he drops everything and heads for home, with young Daniel (Ralph Macchio) along for the ride. Once in Okinawa, Miyagi encounters an old rival and an old love, while Daniel makes a new enemy and a new love. Rated PG for mild violence. 113m. **DIR:** John G. Avildsen. **CAST:** Ralph Macchio, Noriyuki "Pat" Morita, Nobu McCarthy, Martin Kove, William Zabka. **1986**

KARATE KID PART III, THE ★★ Back for the third time as Daniel "The Karate Kid" LaRusso, Ralph Macchio prepares to defend his championship. Even the watchable Pat Morita can't make this one a winner. Rated PG. 111m. **DIR:** John G. Avildsen. **CAST:** Ralph Macchio, Noriyuki "Pat" Morita, Martin Kove. **1989**

KATHERINE ★★★ This television movie follows Sissy Spacek from a middle-class young student to a social activist and finally to an underground terrorist. Spacek is very convincing in this demanding role. The movie tends to remind one of the Patty Hearst case and features good, solid storytelling. 100m. **DIR:** Jeremy Paul Kagan. **CAST:** Sissy Spacek, Art Carney, Henry Winkler, Jane Wyatt, Julie Kavner. **1975**

KATIE'S PASSION ★★ The story of a poor country girl's struggle to survive in Holland during the economic crisis of the 1880s. Director Paul Verhoeven misses the mark with this saga. Rutger Hauer delivers a rather lackluster performance as a vain banker. Not much passion, or anything else here. In Dutch with English subtitles. 107m. **DIR:** Paul Verhoeven. **CAST:** Rutger Hauer, Monique van de Ven. **1988**

KAVIK THE WOLF DOG ★★ This average made-for-TV movie is the story of Kavik, a brave sled dog who journeys back to the boy he loves when a ruthless, wealthy man transports him from Alaska to Seattle. 104m. **DIR:** Peter Carter. **CAST:** Ronny Cox, John Ireland, Linda Sorenson, Andrew Ian McMillan, Chris Wiggins. **1980**

KAZAAM ★★ Basketball superstar Shaquille O'Neal is a likable genie prepared to deliver three wishes to a troubled boy. The plot is overly involved with the boy's estranged father's illegal dealings, his mother's desire to remarry, and a gang of hoodlums making his life miserable. There are as many tense scenes as comic ones, which gives the film a split personality unlikely to satisfy either the fluff or action seeker. Uneven performances by many of the key players don't help either. Rated PG for violence. 90m. **DIR:** Paul Michael Glaser. **CAST:** Shaquille O'Neal, Francis Capra, Ally Walker, James Acheson. **1996**

KEATON RIDES AGAIN/RAILROADER ★★★★ Coupled delightfully in this Buster Keaton program are a biographical profile with interviews, and a solo opus of Buster in trouble on a handcar rolling along the seemingly endless tracks of the Canadian National Railway. Both were lovingly produced by the National Film Board of Canada less than a year before the great comic's life ended. B&W; 81m. **DIR:** John Spotton, Gerald Potterton. **CAST:** Buster Keaton. **1965**

KEATON'S COP ★★ Former mobster Abe Vigoda is on a hit list and requires police protection. Lee Majors becomes his macho bodyguard in this shoot-'em-up that can't decide whether it's a comedy or actioner. Rated R for profanity and violence. 95m. DIR: Robert Burge. CAST: Lee Majors, Abe Vigoda, Don Rickles. 1998

KEEP, THE ★★ A centuries-old presence awakens in an old castle. Rated R for nudity and violence. 96m. DIR: Michael Mann. CAST: Ian McKellen, Alberta Watson, Scott Glenn, Jurgen Prochnow. 1983

KEEP THE CHANGE ★★★1/2 An uninspired artist (William L. Petersen) realizes he needs to return to his family's ranch in Montana to get back to his roots. Not rated; contains implied sex. 95m. DIR: Andy Tennant. CAST: William L. Petersen, Lolita Davidovich, Rachel Ticotin, Jack Palance, Buck Henry, Jeff Kober, Lois Smith. 1992

KEEPER, THE ★★ The owner of an insane asylum preys on the wealthy families of his charges. Rated R. 96m. DIR: T. Y. Drake. CAST: Christopher Lee, Sally Gray. 1984

KEEPER OF THE CITY ★★1/2 Anthony LaPaglia flips out—too much abuse as a child—and embarks on a one-man crusade to rid Chicago of its aging crime lords. Lou Gossett's hardened and weary cop lifts this routine made-for-cable thriller slightly above other genre entries, no thanks to Gerald De-Pego's pedestrian adaptation of his own novel. 95m. DIR: Bobby Roth. CAST: Lou Gossett Jr., Anthony La-Paglia, Peter Coyote, Renee Soutendijk. 1992

KEEPER OF THE FLAME ★★★★ In this second teaming of Spencer Tracy and Katharine Hepburn, he is a noted journalist who plans to write a tribute to a respected and admired patriot killed in a vehicle accident; she is the patriot's widow. Fine adult drama. B&W; 100m. DIR: George Cukor. CAST: Spencer Tracy, Katharine Hepburn, Richard Whorf, Margaret Wycherly, Forrest Tucker, Percy Kilbride, Darryl Hickman, Donald Meek, Howard DaSilva. 1942

•KEEPING THE FAITH ★★★★ First-time director Edward Norton's scrumptious romantic triangle begins stiffly but soon settles into a consistent groove: The broad gestures mellow out, and the character interaction becomes more important than attempts to milk laughs from Stuart Blumberg's improbable tale, which involves a Roman Catholic priest, a rabbi, and the vivacious, corporate executive who has reentered their lives after a two-decade absence. As children, these three had been inseparable; the question now is whether the new element of romantic tension will strengthen or shatter their close rapport. What eventually occurs proves amusing, poignant, and surprisingly believable. Rated PG-13 for sexual candor. 129m. DIR: Edward Norton. CAST: Ben Stiller, Edward Norton, Jenna Elfman, Anne Bancroft, Eli Wallach, Ron Rifkin, Milos Forman, Holland Taylor. 2000

KEEPING TRACK ★★1/2 Superior action thriller follows Michael Sarrazin and Margot Kidder as two innocent bystanders who witness a murder and a robbery. Once they find the $5 million, they must learn to trust one another because everyone is after them, including the CIA and Russian spies. This one will keep you guessing. Rated R. 102m. DIR: Robin Spry. CAST: Michael Sarrazin, Margot Kidder, Alan Scarfe, Ken Pogue. 1985

KELLY'S HEROES ★★★ An amiable rip-off of The Dirty Dozen, this 1970 war comedy was funnier at the time of its original release. Stoic Clint Eastwood is stuck with a bunch of goof-offs (Telly Savalas, Donald Sutherland, Don Rickles, and Gavin McLeod) as he searches for Nazi treasure. Sutherland's World War II hippie ("Give me those positive waves, man") is a little tough to take these days, but this caper picture still has its moments. Rated PG. 145m. DIR: Brian G. Hutton. CAST: Clint Eastwood, Telly Savalas, Donald Sutherland, Don Rickles, Gavin MacLeod, Carroll O'Connor. 1970 DVD

KENNEDY (TV MINISERIES) ★★★★ This outstanding made-for-TV miniseries is even more enjoyable when viewed in one sitting. This upfront portrait of John F. Kennedy from presidential campaign to assassination shows the warts as well as the charm and mystique of the entire Kennedy clan. The cast is excellent. An easy-to-swallow history lesson on Camelot. 278m. DIR: Jim Goddard. CAST: Martin Sheen, John Shea, Blair Brown, E. G. Marshall, Geraldine Fitzgerald, Vincent Gardenia. 1983

KENNEL MURDER CASE, THE ★★★★ A classic detective thriller, this features William Powell as the dapper Philo Vance solving a locked-door murder. The supporting players complement his suave characterization perfectly. Dated, but good. B&W; 73m. DIR: Michael Curtiz. CAST: William Powell, Mary Astor, Eugene Pallette, Ralph Morgan, Jack LaRue. 1933 DVD

KENT STATE ★★★★ Disturbing docudrama traces the events leading up to the killing of four students by National Guardsmen during a 1970 antiwar protest. Objectively filmed, this TV movie is a memorable and effective history lesson. 180m. DIR: James Goldstone. CAST: Jane Fleiss, Charley Lang, Talia Balsam, Keith Gordon, John Getz, Jeff McCracken. 1981

KENTUCKIAN, THE ★★★ Pushing west in the 1820s, Burt Lancaster bucks all odds to reach Texas and begin a new life. A good mix of history, adventure, romance, and comedy makes this one worth a family watching. 104m. DIR: Burt Lancaster. CAST: Burt Lancaster, Diana Lynn, Dianne Foster, Walter Matthau, John Carradine, Una Merkel. 1955

KENTUCKY FRIED MOVIE ★★★ The first film outing of the creators of Airplane! is an on-again, off-again collection of comedy skits. Directed by John Landis, the best bits involve a Bruce Lee takeoff and a surprise appearance by Wally and the Beaver. Rated R. 78m. DIR: John Landis. CAST: Evan Kim, Master Bong SooHan, Bill Bixby, Donald Sutherland. 1977

KENTUCKY KERNELS ★★1/2 Wheeler and Woolsey (a now-forgotten early Thirties comedy team) and Our Gang/Little Rascals star Spanky McFarland travel to the heart of Dixie to claim an inheritance. Breezy, slapstick comedy has aged surprisingly well. One of the first features directed by George Stevens. B&W; 75m. DIR: George Stevens. CAST: Bert Wheeler, Robert Woolsey, Mary Carlisle, Spanky McFarland. 1934

KENTUCKY RIFLE ★★1/2 Pioneers going west are stranded in Comanche country. They must barter the Kentucky long rifles in their wagons for safe passage. Passable oater. 80m. DIR: Carl K. Hittleman. CAST:

Chill Wills, Jeanne Cagney, Cathy Downes, Lance Fuller, Sterling Holloway. 1955

KEROUAC ★★★ Reenactments, interviews, and early television clips are used to probe the mental illness and alcoholism of Beat writer Jack Kerouac. The old TV clips are more intriguing and revealing than the cheesy scenes filmed with an actor. This touches all the bases but doesn't provide much insight, even if it did garner awards when first released. Narrated by Peter Coyote. Not rated; contains profanity. B&W/color; 73m. **DIR:** John Antonelli. **CAST:** Jack Kerouac, William S. Burroughs, Allen Ginsberg, Jack Coulter. 1984

KEY, THE ★★1/2 A strange, moody curio, directed in somber tones by British filmmaker Carol Reed, and noteworthy as the first British film to star Sophia Loren. She plays a kept woman who comes with the London flat belonging to a succession of tugboat captains during World War II. B&W; 125m. **DIR:** Carol Reed. **CAST:** William Holden, Sophia Loren, Trevor Howard, Oscar Homolka, Bernard Lee. 1958

KEY EXCHANGE ★★★ This movie is a good study of modern-day relationships. Brooke Adams and Ben Masters play a couple making a firm commitment in their relationship. Daniel Stern is hilarious as a friend of the couple who is going through his own domestic crisis. Rated R for language, sex, and nudity. 96m. **DIR:** Barnet Kellman. **CAST:** Brooke Adams, Ben Masters, Daniel Stern, Danny Aiello, Tony Roberts. 1985

KEY LARGO ★★★★ Humphrey Bogart is one of a group of dissimilar individuals held in a run-down Florida Keys hotel by a band of hoodlums on the lam. Lauren Bacall looks to him as her white knight, but as a disillusioned war vet he has had enough violence. That is, until a crime kingpin (Edward G. Robinson) pushes things a little too far. B&W; 101m. **DIR:** John Huston. **CAST:** Humphrey Bogart, Lauren Bacall, Edward G. Robinson, Claire Trevor, Lionel Barrymore. 1948 DVD

KEY TO REBECCA, THE ★★1/2 Ken Follett's best-selling World War II–set novel becomes a rather stodgy TV movie, with David Soul as a Nazi spy involved in a battle of wits with British officer Cliff Robertson. It all looks pretty fake, though at least Follett's story holds your attention. 192m. **DIR:** David Hemmings. **CAST:** Cliff Robertson, David Soul, Season Hubley, Anthony Quayle, David Hemmings, Robert Culp. 1985

KEY TO THE CITY ★★★1/2 Prim Loretta Young and roughneck Clark Gable meet at a mayor's convention in San Francisco, and a wacky and rocky romance follows. A much underrated movie with hilarious situations handled expertly by pros. Marilyn Maxwell's striptease is a hoot. B&W; 101m. **DIR:** George Sidney. **CAST:** Clark Gable, Loretta Young, Marilyn Maxwell, Frank Morgan, Lewis Stone, Raymond Burr, James Gleason, Raymond Walburn, Pamela Britton, Clinton Sundberg. 1950

KEYS TO THE KINGDOM, THE ★★★1/2 Gregory Peck is a Scottish priest in this bleak tale of poverty and despotism in 1930s war-torn China. As the missionary who bests the odds, Peck is fine. B&W; 137m.

DIR: John M. Stahl. **CAST:** Gregory Peck, Vincent Price, Thomas Mitchell, Roddy McDowall. 1944

KEYS TO TULSA ★★1/2 This pulp crime-drama is also a dark multiple character study. The black sheep son of an oil tycoon returns to Tulsa after an unexplained absence; gets involved with a blackmail scheme; resurrects his relationship with an old flame, her gun-crazy brother, and druggie husband; and falls in lust with a zonked-out stripper. The film, like its characters, is all attitude with no real soul. Rated R for violence, nudity, sex, language, and drug use. 113m. **DIR:** Leslie Greif. **CAST:** Eric Stoltz, James Spader, Deborah Unger, Joanna Going, Michael Rooker, Mary Tyler Moore, James Coburn. 1996

KEYSTONE COMEDIES: VOL. 1–5 ★★★ The Mack Sennett Studios produced some of the most celebrated slapstick of the silent screen. In these volumes great comic performers display some of their finest talents for some marvelous movie mayhem and magic. Silent. B&W; 42–58m. **DIR:** Roscoe Arbuckle. **CAST:** Roscoe "Fatty" Arbuckle, Mabel Normand, Edgar Kennedy, Minta Durfee, Al St. John, Louise Fazenda, Joe Bordeaux, Alice Davenport, Dora Rogers, Owen Moore, Glen Cavender, Ford Sterling, Mae Busch. 1915

KHARTOUM ★★★★ Underrated historical adventure-drama recalls the British defeat in northern Africa by Arab tribesmen circa 1833. Location filming, exciting battle scenes, and fine acting raise this spectacle to the level of superior entertainment. 134m. **DIR:** Basil Dearden. **CAST:** Laurence Olivier, Charlton Heston, Ralph Richardson, Richard Johnson, Alexander Knox. 1966

KICK FIGHTER ♥ A martial arts expert kicks his way out of the gutters of Bangkok, only to be held back by crime lords who want him to throw his shot at the championship. Gobble-gobble. 92m. **DIR:** Anthony Maharaj. **CAST:** Richard Norton, Benny Urquidez. 1991

KICK OR DIE ★★ Predictable campus psycho film has coeds on the run from a sadistic rapist. Enter Kevin Bernhardt as a former kick-boxing champ. Rated R for profanity, violence, and nudity. 87m. **DIR:** Charles Norton. **CAST:** Kevin Bernhardt. 1987

KICKBOXER ★★1/2 This flick looks a little like *Rocky* and a lot like *The Karate Kid*, but it is a step up for Jean-Claude Van Damme in the acting department. Good action scenes and a fun plot. Rated R for violence and language. 97m. **DIR:** Mark DiSalle, David Worth. **CAST:** Jean-Claude Van Damme, Dennis Alexio, Dennis Chan. 1989 DVD

KICKBOXER 2: THE ROAD BACK ♥ With more kick-you-in-the-face action, this sequel, sans original star Jean-Claude Van Damme, is weak in the joints. Rated R for violence. 90m. **DIR:** Albert Pyun. **CAST:** Sasha Mitchell, Peter Boyle, Dennis Chan, John Diehl. 1990

KICKBOXER 3: ART OF WAR ★★ While in Rio de Janeiro for a kick-boxing exhibition, America's champion Sasha Mitchell rescues a kidnapped girl. Standard martial arts flick. Rated R for strong violence and profanity. 92m. **DIR:** Rick King. **CAST:** Sasha Mitchell, Dennis Chan. 1992

KICKBOXER 4: AGGRESSOR, THE ★★ By-the-book martial arts showcase, with handsome Sasha Mitchell as the high-kicking David Sloan. This outing, Sloan is in prison after being framed for murder but makes a deal with the DEA: To win his freedom he must track down his longtime nemesis, Tong Po. It doesn't take much persuasion when Sloan finds out that his wife has been abducted by Po. Sloan enters a martial arts tournament at the evil master's guarded fortress in order to rescue her. Rated R for violence and language. 90m. **DIR:** Albert Pyun. **CAST:** Sasha Mitchell, Kamel Krifia, Brad Thornton. 1993

●**KICKBOXER 5: REDEMPTION** ★★1/2 Another sequel, another star. This one features Mark Dacascos as a martial artist out to avenge the murder of a friend. Although kick boxing is all that this film has in common with its predecessors, it's better than the first three in the series. Rated R for violence. 87m. **DIR:** Kristine Peterson. **CAST:** Mark Dacascos, James Ryan, Geoff Meed, Tony Caprari. 1994

KICKED IN THE HEAD 💣 A slacker airhead (Kevin Corrigan, who cowrote the atrocious script) alternates adventures in his "voyage of self-discovery" with shady errands for his disreputable uncle (James Woods). Woods (who could energize a funeral even when playing the corpse) is the only asset in this aimless, pointless, and brainless film. Rated R for profanity, drug use, and mild violence. 87m. **DIR:** Matthew Harrison. **CAST:** Kevin Corrigan, Linda Fiorentino, Michael Rapaport, James Woods, Lili Taylor, Burt Young. 1997

KICKING AND SCREAMING ★★★ Four college roommates, terrified of "real life," continue frittering their lives away after graduation—sulking and pouting. A little kicking and screaming might have made these selfish crybabies more interesting. Still, the wickedly clever dialogue and the talented cast help keep the lead-balloon premise afloat. Rated R for profanity. 96m. **DIR:** Noah Baumbach. **CAST:** Josh Hamilton, Olivia D'Abo, Carlos Jacott, Eric Stoltz, Parker Posey, Jason Wiles, Christopher Eigeman. 1995

KID ★★★1/2 Exciting thriller about a mysterious stranger (C. Thomas Howell) who wants revenge for his parents' deaths. Great editing and terrific sound effects help make this film quite entertaining. Rated R for violence and profanity. 94m. **DIR:** John Mark Robinson. **CAST:** C. Thomas Howell, Sarah Trigger, Brian Austin Green, R. Lee Ermey. 1990 DVD

KID, THE/THE IDLE CLASS ★★★★ A skillful blend of comedy and pathos, The Kid, the first of Charles Chaplin's silent feature films, has his famous tramp alter ego adopting an abandoned baby boy whose mother, years later, suddenly appears to claim him. Chaplin is magnificent. Coogan's performance in the title role made him the first child superstar. Also on the bill: The Idle Class, a satire on the leisure of the rich involving mistaken identity. Silent. B&W; 86m. **DIR:** Charles Chaplin. **CAST:** Charlie Chaplin, Edna Purviance, Jackie Coogan. 1921

●**KID CALLED DANGER, A** ★★★ Looking to follow in the steps of his police-officer father, a young teen and his friends try to capture a jewel thief they have spotted in the neighborhood. Suspenseful, made-for-video adventure aimed at young teens.

Rated PG for mild violence. 90m. **DIR:** Eric Hendershot. **CAST:** Clayton Taylor, Mac Melonas, Devin Gardner. 1999 DVD

●**KID FOR TWO FARTHINGS, A** ★★★★ A young London boy buys a goat with only one horn and believes it is a unicorn that has the power to work magic. It's a magical movie, directed by Carol Reed with the same zest he later brought to Oliver. 91m. **DIR:** Carol Reed. **CAST:** Jonathan Ashmore, Celia Johnson, Diana Dors, David Kossoff. 1956

KID FROM BROOKLYN, THE ★★★ Danny Kaye is fine as the comedy lead in this remake of Harold Lloyd's The Milky Way: He plays the milkman who becomes a prizefighter. Good family entertainment. 104m. **DIR:** Norman Z. McLeod. **CAST:** Danny Kaye, Virginia Mayo, Vera-Ellen, Steve Cochran, Eve Arden. 1946

KID FROM LEFT FIELD, THE ★★★ Gary Coleman plays a batboy who leads the San Diego Padres to victory through the advice of his father (a former baseball great). Ed McMahon costars in this remake of the 1953 Dan Dailey version. Made for TV. 100m. **DIR:** Adell Aldrich. **CAST:** Gary Coleman, Tab Hunter, Gary Collins, Ed McMahon. 1979

KID GALAHAD (1937) ★★★1/2 Solid gangster tale has fight promoter Edward G. Robinson discovering a boxer in bellhop Wayne Morris. It's prime Warner Bros. melodrama, deliciously played. Because of the Elvis Presley remake, this was retitled The Battling Bellhop for television. B&W; 101m. **DIR:** Michael Curtiz. **CAST:** Edward G. Robinson, Bette Davis, Humphrey Bogart, Wayne Morris, Harry Carey, Jane Bryan, William Haade, Ben Welden, Veda Ann Borg, Frank Faylen. 1937

KID GALAHAD (1962) ★★1/2 Remake of a film of the same title made in 1937 starring Edward G. Robinson, Bette Davis, and Humphrey Bogart. In this version, Elvis Presley is a boxer who prefers life as a garage mechanic. Presley fans will enjoy this one, of course. 95m. **DIR:** Phil Karlson. **CAST:** Elvis Presley, Gig Young, Lola Albright, Joan Blackman, Ned Glass. 1962

KID IN KING ARTHUR'S COURT, A ★★★ Kids will get a kick out of this lightweight adaptation of Mark Twain's A Connecticut Yankee in King Arthur's Court in which our young hero thwarts the villains with the help of Rollerblades and a CD player. However, adults may not be so charmed. Rated PG. 89m. **DIR:** Michael Gottlieb. **CAST:** Thomas Ian Nicholas, Joss Ackland, Art Malik, Paloma Baeza, Kate Winslet, Ron Moody. 1995

KID MILLIONS ★★ The fifth of six elaborate musicals produced with Eddie Cantor by Samuel Goldwyn. Banjo Eyes inherits a fortune and becomes the mark for a parade of con artists. Lavish Busby Berkeley musical numbers help to salvage an otherwise inane plot. B&W; 90m. **DIR:** Roy Del Ruth. **CAST:** Eddie Cantor, Ethel Merman, Ann Sothern, George Murphy, Warren Hymer. 1934

KID RANGER ★★★ Trouble begins when a ranger shoots a man he wrongly believes to be part of an outlaw gang. Two-fisted hero Bob Steele must track down the real gang. B&W; 56m. **DIR:** Robert N. Bradbury. **CAST:** Bob Steele, Joan Barclay, William Farnum, Charles King. **1936**

KID VENGEANCE 🎬 A boy witnesses the death of his parents at the hands of an outlaw gang. He goes in pursuit with the aid of another victim of the gang, and eliminates the band one by one until only he and the bandit leader remain. This vehicle for teen-idol Leif Garrett wastes the talents of Jim Brown and Lee Van Cleef. Filmed in Israel. Rated R for violence and brief nudity. 90m. **DIR:** Joseph Manduke. **CAST:** Leif Garrett, Jim Brown, Lee Van Cleef, Glynnis O'Connor, Matt Clark, Timothy Scott, John Marley. **1976**

KID WHO LOVED CHRISTMAS, THE ★★★★ Heartwarming Christmas tale about an orphan who will do anything to be with his adopted father for the holidays. With an all-star cast and a wonderful message, this made-for-TV drama is pure magic. 100m. **DIR:** Arthur Allan Seidelman. **CAST:** Trent Cameron, Cicely Tyson, Mike Warren, Sammy Davis Jr., Gilbert Lewis, Della Reese. **1990**

KID WITH THE BROKEN HALO, THE ★★ Sort of a *Different Strokes* meets *It's A Wonderful Life*, this television movie tells of a little angel forced to earn his wings by making things right for people in three vignettes. The film was actually an unsold pilot, and the fare is sweet and gentle enough. 100m. **DIR:** Leslie Martinson. **CAST:** Gary Coleman, Robert Guillaume, June Allyson, Ray Walston, Mason Adams, Telma Hopkins, Georg Stanford Brown, John Pleshette. **1982**

KID WITH THE 200 I.Q., THE ★★ In this predictable TV movie, Gary Coleman plays a 13-year-old genius who enters college. Mildly amusing at best. 96m. **DIR:** Leslie Martinson. **CAST:** Gary Coleman, Robert Guillaume, Dean Butler, Kari Michaelson, Harriet Nelson. **1983**

KIDNAP SYNDICATE, THE ★★ James Mason plays a millionaire whose child has been kidnapped. Luc Merenda is the poor father of a child who has been taken along with Mason's. Director Fernando Di Leo tries to juxtapose the irony of the two fathers, but it comes off like a trite melodrama with lots of blood spilling and profanity. 105m. **DIR:** Fernando Di Leo. **CAST:** James Mason, Luc Merenda, Valentina Cortese. **1976**

KIDNAPPED ★★★ Walt Disney takes a shot at this Robert Louis Stevenson eighteenth-century adventure. A young man (James MacArthur) is spirited away to sea just as he is about to inherit his family's estate. Plenty of swashbuckling for children of all ages. 94m. **DIR:** Robert Stevenson. **CAST:** James MacArthur, Peter Finch. **1960**

•**KIDNAPPED IN PARADISE** ★★1/2 Pirates kidnap a woman's sister, and she sets off to save her only sibling. This made-for-cable original falls victim to predictability and the only surprise here is how little action there is in this "action" film. Not rated; contains violence. 95m. **DIR:** Rob Hedden. **CAST:** Joely Fisher, Charlotte Ross, Rob Knepper, David Beecroft. **1999**

KIDNAPPING OF THE PRESIDENT, THE ★★★★ As the title implies, terrorists kidnap the president and hold him hostage in this excellent action-thriller. The acting is excellent, the suspense taut, and the direction tightly paced. 120m. **DIR:** George

Mendeluk. **CAST:** William Shatner, Hal Holbrook, Van Johnson, Ava Gardner. **1979**

KIDS ★★★1/2 Scripter Harmony Korine follows a pack of inner-city kids through an average day of sex, drugs, and rock 'n' roll, focusing on a young man who "lives to seduce virgins" and doesn't realize that he's infected with AIDS. The dialogue is brutal, the contempt for humanity is appalling, and the sexual content is rough. This frightening wake-up call should be required viewing for every parent and politician in the land. Not rated, but equivalent to an NC-17 for profanity, nudity, drug use, and simulated sex. 90m. **DIR:** Larry Clark. **CAST:** Leo Fitzpatrick, Justin Pierce, Chloe Sevigny, Sarah Henderson. **1995**

KIDS ARE ALRIGHT, THE ★★★1/2 More a documentary detailing the career of British rock group the Who than an entertainment, this film by Jeff Stein still manages to capture the spirit of rock 'n' roll. Rated PG. 108m. **DIR:** Jeff Stein. **CAST:** The Who, Ringo Starr, Steve Martin, Tom Smothers. **1979**

KIDS IN THE HALL: BRAIN CANDY ★★ Canadian TV-comedy players Kids in the Hall make their theatrical film debut in this satirical story of a miracle feel-good drug unleashed on the public before its full effects are known. A halfway-decent idea for a brief sketch is dragged out far beyond its merits, with few laughs. The Kids' modest talents may play better on video than on the big screen. Rated R for profanity. 97m. **DIR:** Kelly Makin. **CAST:** David Foley, Bruce McCulloch, Kevin McDonald, Mark McKinney, Carrot Top (Scott Thompson). **1996**

KIKA ★★★★ Nominally about a none-too-bright woman who loves both a photographer and his American stepfather, who may be a murderer, the story is just an excuse to poke fun at our morbid, media-fed fascination with serial criminals. The film includes what can only be called the silliest rape scene ever staged, though it's likely to outrage many viewers. In English and Spanish with English subtitles. Not rated, with lots of slapstick sex, nudity, and some violence. 95m. **DIR:** Pedro Almodóvar. **CAST:** Veronica Forque, Peter Coyote, Victoria Abril, Alex Casanovas, Rossy De Palma. **1993 DVD**

KILL, THE ★★ Richard Jaeckel plays a world-weary, womanizing private eye in this overly familiar story of a hunt for stolen money in the byways of the Orient. The locale is Macao, famed gambling haven across the bay from Hong Kong. No rating, but contains violence and nudity. 81m. **DIR:** Rolf Bamer. **CAST:** Richard Jaeckel. **1973**

KILL AND KILL AGAIN ★★ Kung fu champ James Ryan repeats his starring role from *Kill or Be Killed*. This time, martial arts master Steve Chase (Ryan) has been hired to rescue a Nobel Prize–winning chemist from the clutches of a demented billionaire. Rated R. 100m. **DIR:** Ivan Hall. **CAST:** James Ryan, Anneline Kriel. **1981 DVD**

KILL CASTRO (CUBA CROSSING, MERCENARIES (1978), SWEET VIOLENT TONY) 🎬 Implausible adventure yarn. Rated R. 90m. **DIR:** Peter Barton. **CAST:** Stuart Whitman, Caren Kaye, Robert Vaughn, Woody Strode, Albert Salmi, Michael Gazzo, Sybil Danning, Raymond St. Jacques. **1978**

KILL CRUISE ★★ Spur of the moment decision by an alcoholic yachtsman to sail to Barbados with two young British women leads to the predictable clash of passions. Listless voyage propelled only by capable performances and a twist ending. Rated R for violence, profanity, and nudity. 99m. DIR: Peter Keglevic. CAST: Jurgen Prochnow, Patsy Kensit, Elizabeth Hurley. 1990 DVD

KILL ME AGAIN ★★ A fairly suspenseful thriller about a private eye who gets caught up in plot twist after plot twist after a woman asks him to fake her death. Predictable, but there are worse ways to spend an hour and a half. Rated R for violence. 94m. DIR: John Dahl. CAST: Val Kilmer, Joanne Whalley, Michael Madsen, Jonathan Gries, Michael Greene, Bibi Besch. 1990

KILL OR BE KILLED ★★ A former Nazi pits himself against the Japanese master who defeated him in an important tournament during World War II. Run-of-the-mill martial arts nonsense. James Ryan shows a glimmer of personality to go with his physical prowess. Rated PG. 90m. DIR: Ivan Hall. CAST: James Ryan, Norman Combes, Charlotte Michelle. 1980

KILL ZONE ★ Totally derivative war film has wigged-out Colonel Wiggins, played by David Carradine, pushing his platoon one mission too far. Director Cirio Santiago pushed this genre one film too far. Rated R for language and violence. 95m. DIR: Cirio H. Santiago. CAST: David Carradine, Tony Dorsett, Rob Youngblood, Vic Trevino. 1993

KILLER, THE ★★★★★ John Woo's best film features Chow Yun-Fat as an honorable assassin trying to get out of the business. Impeccable pacing and incredible action choreography create an operatic intensity that leaves you feeling giddy. Available both dubbed and in Cantonese with English subtitles. Not rated; very strong violence. 102m. DIR: John Woo. CAST: Chow Yun-Fat, Sally Yeh, Danny Lee. 1989

KILLER: A JOURNAL OF MURDER ★★★ In the 1920s, a hardened criminal (James Woods) tells the story of his life to an idealistic young prison guard (Robert Sean Leonard). Based on the diaries of a psychopathic killer, this is an excellent vehicle for Woods, though the story isn't as interesting as the character. Rated R for graphic violence and profanity. B&W/color; 91m. DIR: Tim Metcalfe. CAST: James Woods, Robert Sean Leonard, Ellen Greene, Steve Forrest. 1996

KILLER ELITE, THE ★★1/2 Secret service agent James Caan is double-crossed by his partner (Robert Duvall) while guarding a witness. Disabled by a bullet wound, he has to begin a long process of recovery. He wants revenge. There are some good action scenes. However, considering all the top-flight talent involved, it is a major disappointment. Rated PG. 120m. DIR: Sam Peckinpah. CAST: James Caan, Robert Duvall, Arthur Hill, Bo Hopkins, Mako, Burt Young, Gig Young. 1975 DVD

KILLER FISH ★ Bad acting and lousy Spanish accents help to make this a total bust. Rated PG, but contains violence and some nudity. 101m. DIR: Anthony M. Dawson. CAST: Lee Majors, Karen Black, Margaux Hemingway, Marisa Berenson, James Franciscus. 1978

KILLER FORCE ★★ Diamond security officer fakes a theft to secure the confidence of a ruthless smuggling ring. Predictable heist film. 100m. DIR: Val Guest. CAST: Telly Savalas, Peter Fonda, Hugh O'Brian, O. J. Simpson, Maud Adams, Christopher Lee. 1983

KILLER IMAGE ✇ Confusing film with a complete lack of continuity starts with the murder of a photographer who just happens to capture a murderer on film. Now his brother is pursued by the psycho. Rated R for violence and profanity. 97m. DIR: David Winning. CAST: Michael Ironside, M. Emmet Walsh, John Pyper-Ferguson, Krista Erickson. 1992

KILLER INSIDE ME, THE ★★★ Stacy Keach plays a schizophrenic sheriff in a small town. A tightly woven plot offers the viewer plenty of surprises. Rated R for violence and profanity. 99m. DIR: Burt Kennedy. CAST: Stacy Keach, Susan Tyrrell, Tisha Sterling, Keenan Wynn, Charles McGraw, John Dehner, Pepe Serna, Royal Dano, John Carradine, Don Stroud. 1975 DVD

KILLER INSTINCT ★★★ Two brothers toughing it out during the 1920s Prohibition become gangsters and take on the mob. Handsome production values and some close-to-the-cuff performances, but this story has been told before, and better. Rated R for violence, language, and nudity. 101m. DIR: Greydon Clark, Ken Stein. CAST: Ken Stein, Chris Bradley, Rachel York, Bruce Nozick. 1992

KILLER KLOWNS FROM OUTER SPACE ★★★1/2 Lon Chaney once opined that "there is nothing more frightening than a clown after midnight." This sci-fi—horror thriller proves that claim with a mixture of camp, comedy, and chills. The title says it all, but the results are more entertaining than one might expect. Rated PG-13 for profanity and violence. 90m. DIR: Stephen Chiodo. CAST: Grant Cramer, Suzanne Snyder, John Allen Nelson, Royal Dano, John Vernon. 1988

KILLER LOOKS ✇ Another erotic thriller that's neither erotic nor thrilling. Available in R and unrated versions, both featuring nudity and violence. 97m. DIR: Toby Phillips. CAST: Sara Suzanne Brown, Michael Artura, Len Donato. 1994

KILLER PARTY ✇ The only original thing in this lame slasher flick is the addition of a supernatural presence. Rated R for violence, nudity, profanity, and simulated sex. 91m. DIR: William Fruet. CAST: Martin Hewitt, Elaine Wilkes, Paul Bartel. 1986

KILLER SHREWS, THE ✇ Crackpot scientist on an isolated island breeds shrews the size and shape of large, bewigged dogs that eat everything (and everyone) in their path. B&W; 69m. DIR: Ray Kellogg. CAST: James Best, Ingrid Goude, Ken Curtis, Baruch Lumet. 1959

KILLER TOMATOES EAT FRANCE ★★★ Part four of the killer tomato trilogy is a cute spoof on just about everything. Dr. Mortimer Gangreen, played wonderfully by John Astin, breaks out of prison and tries to put a fake King Louie on the throne of France. Not rated; contains humorous violence. 90m. DIR: John DeBello. CAST: Marc Price, Angela Visser, Steve Lundquist, John Astin. 1991

KILLER TOMATOES STRIKE BACK ✇ Third installment of the killer tomato saga features John Astin as

Professor Gangreen attempting—once again—to dominate the world. Beyond corny, this reduces the original to an all-time low. Not rated. 88m. DIR: John DeBello. CAST: John Astin. 1990

•KILLER TONGUE ★★ If it weren't for the film's over-the-top premise and execution, this affair would deserve a tongue-lashing. Melinda Clarke gets more than she bargained for when she swallows an alien life-form in her soup. Instead of getting a stomachache, she develops a ten-foot killer tongue with an insatiable taste for blood. Totally silly, this low-budget film gets points for effort. Not rated; contains adult situations, language, nudity, and violence. 97m. DIR: Alberto Sciamma. CAST: Melinda Clarke, Robert Englund, Jason Durr, Mapi Galan. 1996

KILLERS, THE ★★★ Two hit men piece together a story on the man they've just killed. A tense thriller loosely based on a short story by Ernest Hemingway. This remake of the 1946 classic emphasizes violence rather than storytelling. Ronald Reagan is excellent as an unscrupulous business tycoon. Rated PG; contains graphic violence. 95m. DIR: Don Siegel. CAST: Lee Marvin, John Cassavetes, Angie Dickinson, Ronald Reagan. 1964 DVD

KILLERS FROM SPACE ♥ Bug-eyed men from outer space. B&W; 68m. DIR: W. Lee Wilder. CAST: Peter Graves, James Seay. 1954

KILLERS IN THE HOUSE ★★ When a family visits a house they just inherited, they are taken hostage by a group of bank robbers who thought the house was empty. This made-for-cable original has mostly dumb dialogue and flat acting. Rated R for violence. 95m. DIR: Michael Schultz. CAST: Mario Van Peebles, Holly Robinson, Andrew Divoff, Hal Linden. 1998

KILLER'S KISS ★★ A boxer rescues a singer from the lecherous clutches of her boss. This ultra-low-budget melodrama is a curiosity piece primarily because Stanley Kubrick wrote, photographed, directed, and edited it. 67m. DIR: Stanley Kubrick. CAST: Jamie Smith, Irene Kane, Frank Silvera. 1955 DVD

KILLING, THE ★★★★ Strong noir thriller from Stanley Kubrick has Sterling Hayden leading a group of criminals in an intricately timed heist at a racetrack. Excellent performances and atmospheric handling of the subject matter mark Kubrick, even at this early stage of his career, as a filmmaker to watch. B&W; 83m. DIR: Stanley Kubrick. CAST: Sterling Hayden, Coleen Gray, Jay C. Flippen, Marie Windsor, Timothy Carey, Vince Edwards, Elisha Cook Jr. 1956 DVD

KILLING AFFAIR, A ★★★ Exceptional psychological drama about a young woman (Kathy Baker) who befriends a stranger (Peter Weller). As it turns out, he killed her husband to avenge the death of his own wife and family. The relationship between the two intensifies to an unexpected, terrifying conclusion. Rated R for nudity and violence. 100m. DIR: David Saperstein. CAST: Peter Weller, Kathy Baker, John Glover, Bill Smitrovich. 1988

KILLING AT HELL'S GATE ★★★ Made-for-TV action film about a group of people, including a controversial U.S. senator, who take a raft trip only to find that the bullets are harder to dodge than the jagged rocks. This ain't no Deliverance, but it's watchable. 96m. DIR: Jerry Jameson. CAST: Robert Urich, Deborah Raffin, Lee Purcell, Joel Higgins, George DiCenzo, Paul Burke, Brion James, John Randolph. 1981

KILLING CARS ★★ A car designer finds that the Berlin company he works for is going to shelve his environmentally safe automobile, so he sets out to sell the plans to someone who will manufacture the machine. Rated R for violence, nudity, and profanity. 104m. DIR: Michael Verhoeven. CAST: Jurgen Prochnow, Senta Berger, Bernhard Wicki, William Conrad, Daniel Gélin. 1986

KILLING EDGE, THE ★★ Fairly decent low-budget account of one man's search through a nuclear wasteland for his wife and son. The acting is good and the writing is solid, but the film occasionally gets bogged down in repetition. Not rated, contains violence and language. 90m. DIR: Lindsay Shonteff. CAST: Bill French, Marv Spencer. 1986

KILLING 'EM SOFTLY ★★ George Segal is a down-and-out musician who kills the friend of a young singer (Irene Cara) in an argument over the death of his dog. While attempting to prove that Segal is not the killer, Cara falls in love with him. An interesting and well-acted story bogs down in the attempt to turn this film into a music video. The music is good, but it overpowers the story. Filmed in Canada. 90m. DIR: Max Fischer. CAST: George Segal, Irene Cara, Joyce Gordon, Barbara Cook. 1985

KILLING FIELDS, THE ★★★★★ Here's an unforgettable motion picture. Based on the experiences of New York Times correspondent Sidney Schanberg during the war in Cambodia and his friendship with Cambodian guide and self-proclaimed journalist Dith Pran (whom Schanberg fights to save from imprisonment), it is a tale of love, loyalty, political intrigue, and horror. The viewer cannot help but be jarred and emotionally moved by it. Rated R for violence. 142m. DIR: Roland Joffe. CAST: Sam Waterston, Haing S. Ngor, John Malkovich, Julian Sands, Craig T. Nelson. 1984 DVD

KILLING FLOOR, THE ★★★ Honest and forthright depiction of union squabbles in the Chicago stockyards during World War II. Credible performances and a well-honed script add to a realistic picture of working life in the sticky goo of a slaughterhouse operating under Dickensian stringency. Not rated. 117m. DIR: Bill Duke. CAST: Damien Leake, Moses Gunn, Alfre Woodard, Clarence Felder. 1984

KILLING GAME, THE ♥ Made-for-video film tries to evoke a cynical, hardboiled style but lacks the talent behind (and in front of) the camera. Not rated, but featuring nudity and substantial violence. 83m. DIR: Joseph Merhi. CAST: Chad Hayward, Cynthia Killion. 1988

KILLING HEAT ★★1/2 Uneven acting and a general lack of atmosphere hinder the screen adaptation of Doris Lessing's novel The Grass is Singing. Karen Black plays a city woman who marries a small-time farmer and slowly goes insane while trying to adapt herself to the rural life-style. Set in South Africa in the early 1960s. Not rated; contains nudity and violence. 104m. DIR: Michael Raeburn. CAST: Karen Black, John Thaw, John Kani. 1984

KILLING HOUR, THE ★★ Elizabeth Kemp plays a clairvoyant art student who, through her drawings, becomes involved in a series of murders. The story is a rip-off of *The Eyes of Laura Mars*. With that said, suspense is achieved during the last fifteen minutes of the film. Rated R for violence, nudity, and profanity. 97m. DIR: Armand Mastroianni. CAST: Perry King, Elizabeth Kemp, Norman Parker, Kenneth McMillan. **1984 DVD**

KILLING IN A SMALL TOWN ★★ Based on a true case, this just passable TV murder-of-the-week entry falls flat with Barbara Hershey internalizing the drab exterior of her character—ignoring the fact that she is also a passionate ax murderess. 95m. DIR: Stephen Gyllenhaal. CAST: Barbara Hershey, Brian Dennehy, John Terry, Richard Gilliland. **1990**

KILLING JAR, THE ★★★ When Michael Sanford drives by the scene of a brutal murder, images of the slaying converge with dreams from a repressed childhood trauma, causing him to doubt his sanity. Things heat up when Michael becomes the main suspect in a series of murders, keeping us in suspense until the shocking finale. Rated R for violence, language, and nudity. 101m. DIR: Evan Crooke. CAST: Brett Cullen, Tamlyn Tomita, Brion James, Wes Studi, M. Emmet Walsh. **1996 DVD**

KILLING MAN, THE ★★ Yawner about a professional killer (Jeff Wincott) who is double-crossed by the mob and becomes a government operative. Rated R for violence and adult language. 100m. DIR: David Mitchell. CAST: Jeff Wincott, Terri Hawkes, David Bolt, Michael Ironside. **1994 DVD**

KILLING MIND, THE 💘 A young girl witnesses a murder and grows up to become a homicide investigator so that she can reopen the case. This murder-mystery plot is so old and tired it would be a bigger mystery why anyone would have trouble figuring it out in this made-for-cable film. 96m. DIR: Michael Ray Rhodes. CAST: Stephanie Zimbalist, Daniel Roebuck, Tony Bill. **1991**

KILLING OF A CHINESE BOOKIE ★★★1/2 Downbeat character study stars Ben Gazzara as a small-time nightclub owner who finds himself in big-time trouble when he's coerced into murdering a Chinese crime lord to pay off a debt. Director John Cassavetes's most accessible film is nevertheless a meandering character study with shaky cinematography and a bit too much improvisation. At least it goes somewhere. Rated R for violence and profanity. 113m. DIR: John Cassavetes. CAST: Ben Gazzara, Timothy Carey, Seymour Cassel. **1976 DVD**

KILLING OF ANGEL STREET, THE ★★ The misleading title and packaging of *The Killing of Angel Street* makes it look like a teenage slasher flick, but the title refers to an actual street in a neighborhood in Australia. The plot involves the citizens' struggle to keep their homes from demolition by corrupt businessmen. 100m. DIR: Donald Crombie. CAST: Liz Alexander, John Hargreaves, Reg Lye. **1981**

KILLING OF RANDY WEBSTER, THE ★★ Hal Holbrook and Dixie Carter, his real-life wife, portray parents searching desperately for meaning in the death of their troubled teenage son. The boy steals a van, then leads Houston police on a wild chase. They fire as the boy pulls a gun. Or did he? Made for television. 90m. DIR: Sam Wanamaker. CAST: Hal Holbrook, Dixie Carter, Jennifer Jason Leigh, Sean Penn. **1985**

KILLING OF SISTER GEORGE, THE ★★1/2 Now that the initial controversy that swirled around this film's honest depiction of a lesbian relationship has died away, a retrospective viewing shows a passable yet uninspired story and wooden acting in its central performances. This stage play of an aging actress whose career and relationships are crumbling around her was not brought to the screen with much spirit. Rated R for nudity. 140m. DIR: Robert Aldrich. CAST: Beryl Reid, Susannah York, Coral Browne. **1968 DVD**

KILLING SPREE ★★ This low-budget bloodfest about a jealous husband who kills the imagined suitors of his wife does contain some unique death scenes. But the lighting is often overbearing, and it's hard to hear what the actors (who aren't very good anyway) are saying. Not rated; contains violence. 88m. DIR: Tim Ritter. CAST: Asbestos Felt. **1987**

KILLING STREETS ★★ Michael Paré takes on the dual roles of a government operative kidnapped in Lebanon and his twin brother who leads an attempt to rescue him in this sometimes exciting, but ultimately mediocre, shoot-'em-up. Not rated; contains violence and profanity. 106m. DIR: Stephen Cornwell. CAST: Michael Paré, Lorenzo Lamas, Jennifer Runyon. **1991**

KILLING TIME (1996) ★★★1/2 Crafty thriller stars Bruce Fairbrass as a cop who hires a professional hit woman to kill the scum who killed his partner. When he realizes he can't afford to pay off the assassin, he hires a cheaper hit man to kill her. Then the real fun begins. Nice, tidy stab at *film noir*. Rated R for language and violence. 91m. DIR: Bharat Nalluri. CAST: Bruce Fairbrass, Kendra Torgan, Peter Harding, Neil Armstrong. **1996**

KILLING TIME, THE (1987) ★★★★ Kiefer Sutherland is a killer posing as a new deputy sheriff in a small resort town. Beau Bridges is to be the new sheriff upon the retirement of Joe Don Baker. But there is much more to be discovered in this tense drama of murder, deception, and suspicion. Rated R for violence and profanity. 94m. DIR: Rick King. CAST: Beau Bridges, Kiefer Sutherland, Wayne Rogers, Joe Don Baker. **1987**

KILLING ZOE ★★ When a Paris bank robbery goes sour, the robbers begin killing indiscriminately. No plot twists, no character revelations, just a slow buildup to a long parade of violence and gore. Rated R for extreme violence. 96m. DIR: Roger Avary. CAST: Eric Stoltz, Jean-Hugues Anglade, Julie Delpy. **1994 DVD**

KILLING ZONE, THE ★★ Daron McBee of television's *American Gladiators* stars in this actioner as the convict nephew of an ex–DEA agent. Not rated; contains violence and profanity. 90m. DIR: Addison Randall. CAST: Deron Michael McBee. **1990**

KILL-OFF, THE ★★★★ Despite being bedridden, smalltown gossip Luanne (Loretta Gross) is able to wield an evil influence, making more than a few enemies who wouldn't mind seeing her dead. One of the best adaptations of the work of pulp novelist Jim

Thompson (*After Dark, My Sweet; The Grifters*), this is a film whose low budget works in its favor, evoking the oppressively fatalistic atmosphere at which Thompson excelled. Rated R for profanity, violence, and brief nudity. 100m. DIR: Maggie Greenwald. CAST: Loretta Gross, Jackson Sims, Cathy Haase, Steve Monroe. 1990

KIM ★★★1/2 Rudyard Kipling's India comes to life in this colorful story of the young son of a soldier and his adventures with a dashing secret operative in defense of queen and country. Dean Stockwell is one of the finest and most believable of child stars, and the great Errol Flynn is still capable of personifying the spirit of adventure and romance in this one-dimensional but entertaining story. 113m. DIR: Victor Saville. CAST: Errol Flynn, Dean Stockwell, Paul Lukas, Thomas Gomez, Cecil Kellaway. 1951

KIMAGURE ORANGE ROAD, VOLS. 1—4 ★★★ Japanese animation. It is difficult to categorize this engrossing series as there are so many different elements involved in the stories. Essentially, this is a drama centering around a young man's relationship with two different girls. In Japanese with English subtitles. Not rated; contains nudity. 50m. DIR: Morikawa Shigeru. 1988

KIMAGURE ORANGE ROAD: THE MOVIE ★★★1/2 Japanese animation. Two of the young characters from the Orange Road series have gone on to college where they confront their feelings for one another, much to the dismay of the third corner of their love triangle. Absorbing drama series. In Japanese with English subtitles. Not rated; contains nudity. 70m. DIR: Mochizuki Tomomichi. 1988

KIND HEARTS AND CORONETS ★★★★ A young man (Dennis Price) thinks up a novel way to speed up his inheritance—by killing off the other heirs. This is the central premise of this arresting black comedy, which manages to poke fun at mass murder and get away with it. Alec Guinness plays all eight victims. 104m. DIR: Robert Hamer. CAST: Dennis Price, Alec Guinness, Valerie Hobson. 1949

KIND OF LOVING, A ★★ This British romance features Alan Bates as a young man infatuated with a cute blonde at work. When she gets pregnant, he marries her and realizes how ill-prepared he was for this commitment. Not rated; this contains nudity and adult themes equivalent to an R. B&W; 107m. DIR: John Schlesinger. CAST: Alan Bates, Thora Hird, June Ritchie. 1962

KINDERGARTEN ★★★1/2 Poet Yevgenii Yevtushenko wrote and directed this film based on his own childhood memories of life in Moscow during World War II, especially the evacuation of the city as the Nazis approached. The chaos as seen through childlike eyes is compelling, even strangely beautiful. In Russian with English subtitles. Not rated. 159m. DIR: Yevgenii Yevtushenko. 1983

KINDERGARTEN COP ★★★1/2 High-concept comedy has big Arnold Schwarzenegger playing an undercover narcotics detective who has to pose as a kindergarten teacher to get the goods on a nasty drug lord (Richard Tyson). If it weren't for all the violence, this could have been a fun film for the whole family. As it is, Schwarzenegger is often funny, and

Pamela Reed does a bang-up job as his unpredictable partner. Rated PG-13 for violence. 111m. DIR: Ivan Reitman. CAST: Arnold Schwarzenegger, Penelope Ann Miller, Pamela Reed, Linda Hunt, Richard Tyson, Carroll Baker, Cathy Moriarty. 1990 DVD

KINDRED, THE 🖤 Derivative horror film, which steals its creature from *Alien* and its plot from any one of a hundred run-of-the-razor slasher flicks. Rated R for profanity, violence, and gore. 95m. DIR: Jeffrey Obrow, Stephen Carpenter. CAST: David Allen Brooks, Amanda Pays, Rod Steiger, Kim Hunter. 1987

KING ★★★★ Paul Winfield and Cicely Tyson star as the Rev. Martin Luther King Jr. and Coretta Scott King in this outstanding docudrama of the martyred civil rights leader's murder-capped battle against segregation and for black human dignity. Director Abby Mann, who also scripted, interpolated actual newsreel footage with restaged confrontation incidents for maximum dramatic impact. 272m. DIR: Abby Mann. CAST: Paul Winfield, Cicely Tyson, Ossie Davis, Roscoe Lee Browne, Howard Rollins Jr., Cliff De Young, Dolph Sweet, Lonny Chapman. 1978

KING AND FOUR QUEENS, THE ★★★1/2 This blend of mystery, comedy, and romance takes place in a western ghost town where stagecoach robbery gold is hidden. Desperado Clark Gable plays up to four women in hopes of finding the money. B&W; 86m. DIR: Raoul Walsh. CAST: Clark Gable, Eleanor Parker, Jo Van Fleet, Jean Willes, Barbara Nichols, Sara Shane, Roy Roberts, Jay C. Flippen, Arthur Shields. 1956

KING AND I, THE (1956) ★★★★1/2 Yul Brynner and Deborah Kerr star in this superb 1956 Rodgers and Hammerstein musicalization of *Anna and the King of Siam*. Kerr is the widowed teacher who first clashes, then falls in love, with the King (Brynner). 133m. DIR: Walter Lang. CAST: Yul Brynner, Deborah Kerr, Rita Moreno. 1956 DVD

KING AND I, THE (1999) 🖤 Taken on its own, this animated version of the Rodgers and Hammerstein classic is merely third-rate, but the way it trashes a masterpiece of American musical theater makes it one of the most despicable acts of artistic vandalism in movie history. Rent the 1956 movie instead; even your kids will like it better. Rated G. 88m. DIR: Richard Rich. CAST: Miranda Richardson, Martin Vidnovic, Ian Richardson. 1999 DVD

KING ARTHUR, THE YOUNG WARLORD ★★ *King Arthur, the Young Warlord* follows the English legend in his early years through subplots that lead nowhere. It must be noted that the violence displayed may not be some people's idea of good ol' G-rated fun despite the MPAA approval. 96m. DIR: Sidney Hayers, Pat Jackson, Peter Sasdy. CAST: Oliver Tobias, Michael Gothard, Jack Watson, Brian Blessed, Peter Firth. 1975

•KING COBRA 🖤 This rip-off of *Jaws* and everything that came after features a giant rubber snake and a lot of bad acting. The scariest thing about the film is that it got made. Rated PG-13 for language and violence. 93m. DIR: David Hillenbrand, Scott Hillenbrand. CAST: Noriyuki "Pat" Morita, Hoyt Axton, Scott Hillenbrand, Courtney Gains. 1999 DVD

KING CREOLE ★★★★ A surprisingly strong Elvis Presley vehicle, this musical, set in New Orleans, benefits from solid direction from Michael Curtiz and a first-rate cast. 116m. DIR: Michael Curtiz. CAST: Elvis Presley, Carolyn Jones, Dolores Hart, Dean Jagger, Walter Matthau. 1958 DVD

KING DAVID ★★★ Only biblical scholars will be able to say whether the makers of *King David* remained faithful to the Old Testament. As a big-screen production, however, it is impressive. Directed by Australian filmmaker Bruce Beresford, it is one of the few responsible attempts at filming the Bible. Rated PG-13 for nudity and violence. 115m. DIR: Bruce Beresford. CAST: Richard Gere, Edward Woodward, Alice Krige, Denis Quilley. 1985

KING IN NEW YORK, A ★★1/2 Supposedly anti-American, this 1957 film by Charles Chaplin, not seen in the United States until 1973, was a big letdown to his fans, who had built their worship on *Easy Street*, *City Lights*, *Modern Times*, and *The Great Dictator*. It pokes fun at the 1950s, with its witch-hunts and burgeoning post-war technology. It is not the Chaplin of old, but just old Chaplin, and too much of him. B&W; 105m. DIR: Charles Chaplin. CAST: Charlie Chaplin, Dawn Addams, Michael Chaplin. 1957 DVD

KING KONG (1933) ★★★★★ This classic was one of early sound film's most spectacular successes. The movie, about the giant ape who is captured on a prehistoric island and proceeds to tear New York City apart until his final stand on the Empire State Building, is the stuff of which legends are made. Its marriage of sound, music, image, energy, pace, and excitement made *King Kong* stand as a landmark film. B&W; 100m. DIR: Merian C. Cooper, Ernest B. Schoedsack. CAST: Robert Armstrong, Fay Wray, Bruce Cabot, Frank Reicher, Noble Johnson. 1933

KING KONG (1976) ★★ This remake, starring Jeff Bridges and Jessica Lange, is a pale imitation of the 1933 classic. For kids only. Rated PG for violence. 135m. DIR: John Guillermin. CAST: Jeff Bridges, Jessica Lange, Charles Grodin. 1976 DVD

KING KONG LIVES 🎬 Romance of the resuscitated Kong and his new love, Lady Kong. Rated PG-13 for violence. 105m. DIR: John Guillermin. CAST: Brian Kerwin, Linda Hamilton, John Ashton, Peter Michael Goetz. 1986

KING KONG VS. GODZILLA ★★ King Kong and Godzilla duke it out atop Mount Fuji in this East meets West supermonster movie. Here, though, Kong is a junkie hooked on some wild jungle juice. The bouts are quite humorous. Not rated. 91m. DIR: Inoshiro Honda. CAST: Michael Keith, Tadao Takashima, Kenji Sahara. 1963 DVD

KING LEAR (1971) ★★★1/2 Sturdy but truncated film adaptation of Shakespeare's play about a mad king and his cruel, power-hungry children. The Danish set location lends a disturbing air to this production, which features a powerful portrayal from Paul Scofield. 137m. DIR: Peter Brook. CAST: Paul Scofield, Irene Worth, Jack MacGowran, Alan Webb, Cyril Cusack, Patrick Magee. 1971

KING LEAR (1982) ★★★ A good stage production of what is possibly Shakespeare's most tragic of tales. Mike Kellen is very good as the aging Lear, betrayed by his daughters, but acting honors go to Charles Aidman as the tortured Gloucester. David Groh is interesting as his plotting bastard son, Edmund. A Bard Productions Ltd. release. 182m. DIR: Alan Cooke. CAST: Mike Kellen, Darryl Hickman, Charles Aidman, David Groh, Joel Baily. 1982

KING LEAR (1984) ★★★ Produced for television, this version of Shakespeare's great tragedy of greed and lust for power became an instant classic, and promptly won an Emmy. A career-crowning achievement for Laurence Olivier. 158m. DIR: Michael Elliot. CAST: Laurence Olivier, Diana Rigg, Anna Calder-Marshall, Dorothy Tutin, Leo McKern, John Hurt, Robert Lindsay. 1984

KING LEAR (1988) ★★★1/2 Patrick Magee stars in this Shakespearean tragedy about a foolish king who surrounds himself with treacherous flatterers while banishing those who remain true to him. Fine acting and glorious costumes and sets make this British television production most watchable. 110m. CAST: Patrick Magee, Ray Smith, Ronald Radd. 1988

KING OF COMEDY, THE ★★★★ This is certainly one of the most unusual movies of all time; a sort of black-comedy variation on creator Martin Scorsese's *Taxi Driver*. The star of that film, Robert De Niro, stars as aspiring comic Rupert Pupkin. In order to get his big break on television, Pupkin kidnaps a talk-show host (Jerry Lewis). Rated PG. 109m. DIR: Martin Scorsese. CAST: Robert De Niro, Jerry Lewis, Sandra Bernhard. 1983

KING OF HEARTS ★★★1/2 Philippe de Broca's wartime fantasy provides delightful insights into human behavior. A World War I Scottish infantryman (Alan Bates) searching for a hidden enemy bunker enters a small town that, after being deserted by its citizens, has been taken over by inmates of an insane asylum. In French with English subtitles. No MPAA rating. 102m. DIR: Philippe de Broca. CAST: Alan Bates, Genevieve Bujold. 1966

KING OF JAZZ, THE ★★★ Lavish big-budget musical revue chock-full of big production numbers and great songs. Shot in early two-color Technicolor. Imaginative settings and photography make this last of the all-star extravaganzas most impressive. 93m. DIR: John Murray Anderson. CAST: Paul Whiteman, John Boles, Bing Crosby. 1930

KING OF KINGS, THE (1927) ★★★ Cecil B. DeMille was more than ready when he made this one. It's silent, but Hollywood's greatest showman displays his gift for telling a story with required reverence. Naturally, since it's by DeMille, the production is a lavish one. B&W; 115m. DIR: Cecil B. DeMille. CAST: H. B. Warner, Ernest Torrence, Jacqueline Logan, William Boyd, Joseph Schildkraut. 1927

KING OF KINGS (1961) ★★★ Well-told tale of the life of Christ, performed with understanding and compassion, though flawed by too much attention to the spectacular, rather than the spiritual. Has its moving moments, nonetheless. Narrated by Orson Welles. 168m. DIR: Nicholas Ray. CAST: Jeffrey Hunter, Siobhan McKenna, Robert Ryan, Hurd Hatfield, Viveca Lindfors, Rita Gam, Rip Torn, Royal Dano, George Coulouris. 1961

KING OF MARVIN GARDENS, THE ★★★ Jack Nicholson and Bruce Dern, at the peak of their young careers, play brothers involved in an Atlantic City swindle. Some entertaining theatrics, but once the novelty wears off, the film is overpoweringly depressing. Rated R for profanity, and brief nudity. 104m. DIR: Bob Rafelson. CAST: Jack Nicholson, Bruce Dern, Ellen Burstyn, Scatman Crothers. 1972

•**KING OF MASKS, THE** ★★★1/2 This fascinating, gorgeously photographed melodrama about sexism in 1930s China is both blatantly manipulative and deeply moving. Old street performer Wang is befriended by a female impersonator from the Sichuan opera who urges him to pass along his artistic secrets before he dies. Wang buys a child at a slave market to live aboard his small houseboat and become the heir of his illusions involving silk face masks. Their relationship becomes a hotbed of complications and shredded emotions. In Mandarin with English subtitles. Not rated. 101m. DIR: Wu Tianming. CAST: Zhu Xu, Zhou Renying, Zhao Zhigang. 1999 DVD

KING OF NEW YORK ★★★1/2 Overlooked gangster film follows a New York drug kingpin's attempts to reclaim territory lost during his stay in prison. Cult director Abel Ferrara pulls out all the stops in this violent, fast-paced crime-drama. Rated R for violence, language, drug use, and nudity. 103m. DIR: Abel Ferrara. CAST: Christopher Walken, Laurence Fishburne, David Caruso, Victor Argo, Wesley Snipes, Janet Julian. 1990

KING OF THE BULLWHIP ★★1/2 Looking every bit like Humphrey Bogart's twin brother in a black hat, Lash LaRue was the whip-wielding westerner in a series of low-budget shoot-'em-ups in the 1950s. This, his first for a major distributor, sees one of his better efforts. Lash and his sidekick Al St. John must go undercover when a bandit pretends to be our hero while robbing a bank. 60m. DIR: Ron Ormond. CAST: Lash LaRue, Al St. John, Jack Holt, Dennis Moore, Tom Neal, Anne Gwynne. 1951

KING OF THE CARNIVAL ❤ The serial in America was settling into rigor mortis when this stock-footage-fest about circus aerialists battling counterfeiters limped into a television-saturated theater market and died. B&W; 12 chapters. DIR: Franklin Adreon. CAST: Harry Lauter, Fran Bennett, Keith Richards, Robert Shayne, Gregory Gay, Rick Vallin. 1955

KING OF THE COWBOYS ★★★★ Roy Rogers at his best as a government agent working undercover as a rodeo performer infiltrating a ring of WWII saboteurs. B&W; 54m. DIR: Joseph Kane. CAST: Roy Rogers, Smiley Burnette, Peggy Moran, Sons of the Pioneers, Gerald More. 1943

KING OF THE GRIZZLIES ★★1/2 Wahb, a grizzly cub, loses his mother and sister to cattlemen protecting their herd. He quickly gets into trouble but is rescued by John Yesno, a Cree Indian. Average animal adventure film in the Disney mold. Rated G. 93m. DIR: Ron Kelly. CAST: John Yesno, Chris Wiggins, Hugh Webster. 1969

KING OF THE GYPSIES ★★★ Dave Stepanowicz (Eric Roberts) is the grandson of King Zharko Stepanowicz (Sterling Hayden), the patriarch of a gypsy tribe who is both intelligent and violent. Though Dave renounces his gypsy heritage, he is unable to escape it. The performances are uniformly excellent. Director Frank Pierson is the only one who can be held responsible for the film's lack of power. Rated R. 112m. DIR: Frank Pierson. CAST: Eric Roberts, Sterling Hayden, Susan Sarandon, Annette O'Toole, Brooke Shields, Shelley Winters. 1978

KING OF THE HILL ★★★★★ A. E. Hotchner's Depression-era memoirs are the basis for this poignant study of childhood strength in the face of escalating tragedy. Young Jesse Bradford watches as his family is scattered, and then—when his father accepts a distant job—becomes the sole occupant of their seedy hotel rooms. This enthralling tale is populated with eclectic characters, all rendered splendidly by a masterful ensemble cast. Rated PG-13 for mild profanity and dramatic intensity. 103m. DIR: Steven Soderbergh. CAST: Jesse Bradford, Jeroen Krabbé, Lisa Eichhorn, Spalding Gray, Elizabeth McGovern, Karen Allen. 1993

KING OF THE KICKBOXERS, THE ❤ A kung fu cop travels to Thailand to break up a snuff film ring and avenge his brother's murder. An embarrassment. Rated R for violence, nudity, and profanity. 97m. DIR: Lucas Lowe. CAST: Loren A. Verdon, Richard Jaeckel, Don Stroud. 1991

KING OF THE MOUNTAIN ★★ The quest for success by a trio of buddies leads mostly to unexciting night races on Hollywood's winding Mulholland Drive and clichéd back-stabbing in the music business. Rated PG. 90m. DIR: Noel Nosseck. CAST: Harry Hamlin, Richard Cox, Joseph Bottoms, Dennis Hopper. 1981

KING OF THE PECOS ★★★ John Wayne uses his law school training and a proficiency with firearms to exact revenge on the land robber who killed our hero's father. Standard B Western plot is enhanced by plenty of action, and Wayne's increasing skill in front of the camera. B&W; 54m. DIR: Joseph Kane. CAST: John Wayne, Muriel Evans, Cy Kendall, Jack Clifford, Yakima Canutt. 1936

KING OF THE ROARING TWENTIES ★★ The career (supposedly) of the notorious bookie who, among other things, fixed the 1919 World Series. No excitement or conviction; David Janssen is miscast. Not rated, but with the usual gangster gunplay. B&W; 106m. DIR: Joseph M. Newman. CAST: David Janssen, Dianne Foster, Jack Carson, Diana Dors, Mickey Rooney. 1961

KING OF THE ROCKETMEN ★★★ This chapterplay precursor to the *Commando Cody* television series has longtime baddie Tristram Coffin joining the good guys for a change. Strapping on his flying suit, he does battle with evil conspirators. Good fun for serial fans, with highly implausible last-minute escapes. B&W; 12 chapters. DIR: Fred Brannon. CAST: Tristram Coffin, Mae Clarke, Dale Van Sickel, Tom Steele. 1949

KING OF THE WIND ★★★1/2 Rousing family entertainment based on the popular novel by Marguerite Henry. Teenager Navin Chowdhry tames a wild Arabian horse. The horse is sent from Northern Africa to the King of France, and Chowdhry follows. When he discovers that the magnificent creature will be sent to war, he attempts to steal it. The youth lands in jail, and his only way out is to ride the horse in a special race. Exciting and enthralling every hoof step of the way. Not rated. 101m. DIR: Peter Duffell. CAST: Richard Harris, Glenda Jackson, Jenny Agutter, Navin Chowdhry. 1993

KING OF THE ZOMBIES ♥ Typical mad scientist-zombie movie with evil genius attempting to create an invulnerable army of mindless slaves. B&W; 67m. DIR: Jean Yarbrough. CAST: Dick Purcell, Joan Woodbury, Mantan Moreland, John Archer. 1941 DVD

KING, QUEEN AND KNAVE ♥ Even with the wonderful grace and charm of David Niven, this story anchored by Vladimir Nabokov is a dud. Not rated. 92m. DIR: Jerzy Skolimowski. CAST: David Niven, Gina Lollobrigida, John Moulder-Brown, Mario Adorf. 1972

KING RALPH ★★★ When a freak accident wipes out the entire royal family, Las Vegas entertainer John Goodman is the sole heir to the English crown. With the help of Peter O'Toole and Richard Griffiths (in fine performances), Goodman's good-natured, lovable slob attempts to rise to the occasion. Amiably entertaining comedy. Rated PG for brief profanity. 97m. DIR: David S. Ward. CAST: John Goodman, Peter O'Toole, John Hurt, Camille Courdi, Richard Griffiths. 1991 DVD

KING RAT ★★★★ A Japanese prison camp in World War II is the setting for this stark drama of survival of the fittest, the fittest in this case being "King Rat" (George Segal), the opportunistic head of black-market operations within the compound. B&W; 133m. DIR: Bryan Forbes. CAST: George Segal, Tom Courtenay, James Fox, John Mills. 1965

KING RICHARD AND THE CRUSADERS ♥ George Sanders is far from kingly in this rip-off of Sir Walter Scott's The Talisman. The uninspired cast drags the show down. 114m. DIR: David Butler. CAST: George Sanders, Rex Harrison, Virginia Mayo, Laurence Harvey. 1954

KING RICHARD II ★★★1/2 David Birney is quite effective as Shakespeare's scheming, then remorseful Richard, in this well-made, filmed stage production. Acting honors are shared by Paul Shenar as his cousin, the betrayed and vengeful Bolingbroke (later Henry IV), and Peter MacLean as their uncle, the Duke of York. A Bard Productions Ltd. release. 172m. DIR: William Woodman. CAST: David Birney, Paul Shenar, Peter MacLean, Mary Joan Negro, Logan Ramsey, Nan Martin, Jay Robinson, Nicholas Hammond. 1982

KING SOLOMON'S MINES (1937) ★★★1/2 H. Rider Haggard's splendid adventure story received its first sound-film treatment here. This version is superior in many respects to the more famous 1950 color remake. The action and battle sequences (many shot on location with real tribesmen) rival the best early MGM Tarzan films for costumes and feel. B&W; 79m. DIR: Robert Stevenson. CAST: Cedric Hardwicke, Paul Robeson, Roland Young, John Loder, Anna Lee. 1937

KING SOLOMON'S MINES (1950) ★★★★★ The "great white hunter" genre of adventure films has been a movie staple for ages, yet only this one rates

as a cinema classic. Stewart Granger guides a party through darkest Africa in search of a lady's husband. On the way, the hunter and the lady (Deborah Kerr) become fast friends. 102m. DIR: Compton Bennett, Andrew Marton. CAST: Stewart Granger, Deborah Kerr, Hugo Haas. 1950

KING SOLOMON'S MINES (1985) ♥ A crime against H. Rider Haggard's classic adventure novel—a compendium of cornball clichés and stupid slapstick. Rated PG-13 for violence and profanity. 100m. DIR: J. Lee Thompson. CAST: Richard Chamberlain, Sharon Stone, John Rhys-Davies, Herbert Lom, Ken Gampu. 1985

KING SOLOMON'S TREASURE ♥ This mindless adventure features a stuttering David McCallum pursuing treasure in Africa's Forbidden City. 90m. DIR: Alvin Rakoff. CAST: David McCallum, Britt Ekland, Patrick Macnee, John Colicos. 1976

KING TUT: THE FACE OF TUTANKHAMUN ★★★1/2 The four 50-minute segments of this documentary produced for A&E are hosted by series writer and historian Christopher Frayling. The length stretches somewhat beyond the material, but some dazzling artifacts are showcased as the historical and apocryphal aspects of the boy king are unraveled. Not rated. 200m. DIR: Derek Towers, David Wallace. 1992

KINGDOM, THE ★★★ Creepy tale about a busy Danish hospital and the ghost that haunts it, searching for redemption. Eerie, well-acted, and visually stunning film runs way too long. In Danish with English subtitles (but imagery is so rich that viewers won't want to read at the same time). Not rated, but features horrific images and gory pieces of medical footage. 265m. DIR: Lars von Trier. CAST: Ernst-Hugo Jaregard, Kirsten Rolffes, Holger Juul Ransen, Soren Pilmark, Ghita Norby, Jens Okking, Otto Brandenburg, Udo Kier. 1994

KINGDOM OF THE SPIDERS ★★★ William Shatner stars in this unsuspenseful thriller with lurid special effects. The title tells it all. Rated PG. 94m. DIR: John "Bud" Cardos. CAST: William Shatner, Tiffany Bolling, Woody Strode. 1977

KINGDOM OF THE VAMPIRE ★★ Made for less money than a used car, this film follows a vampire who works in a liquor store. The acting ranges from bad to mediocre, but at least the production tries. Not rated; contains violence and profanity. 75m. DIR: J. R. Bookwalter. CAST: Matthew Jason Walsh, Cherie Patry, Shannon Doyle. 1991

KINGFISH: A STORY OF HUEY P. LONG ★★★1/2 John Goodman delivers a full-bodied performance as Democratic Louisiana Sen. Huey P. Long, whose days of drinking and loving are captured here as entertainment. Evenhanded script and Goodman's strong presence make this made-for-cable movie more about the man than the madness. 97m. DIR: Thomas Schlamme. CAST: John Goodman, Matt Craven, Anne Heche, Ann Dowd, Jeff Perry. 1995

KINGPIN ★★ Washed-up pro bowler Woody Harrelson grooms Amish farmboy Randy Quaid for the "big time" in Reno. Directing brothers Peter and Bobby Farrelly recycle the story from their own Dumb and Dumber, with the earlier film's greatest assets—

stars Jim Carrey and Jeff Daniels—conspicuously missing. This time there are only a few scattered laughs and more than a few repulsive moments. Rated PG-13 for mild profanity and sexual humor. 113m. DIR: Peter Farrelly, Bobby Farrelly. CAST: Woody Harrelson, Randy Quaid, Vanessa Angel, Bill Murray, Chris Elliott. 1996 DVD

KINGS AND DESPERATE MEN: A HOSTAGE INCIDENT ★★★ Improbable but engrossing account of terrorists taking over a radio talk show to present their case to the public. Patrick McGoohan lends his commanding presence as the abrasive, cynical talk-show host. A strange, almost cinema vérité portrayal, the title comes from a John Donne poem that's quoted by McGoohan. Rated PG-13 for language and violence. 117m. DIR: Alexis Kanner. CAST: Patrick McGoohan, Alexis Kanner, Andrea Marcovicci, Margaret Trudeau. 1989

KINGS GO FORTH ★★★★ A World War II melodrama with social consciousness. Frank Sinatra and Tony Curtis play two skirt chasers in the army who fall for the same girl (Natalie Wood). When they find out one of her parents is black, the true colors of the soldiers are revealed. B&W; 110m. DIR: Delmer Daves. CAST: Tony Curtis, Frank Sinatra, Natalie Wood, Leora Dana. 1958

KINGS OF THE ROAD ★★★★ This is the film that put the new-wave German cinema on the map. Wim Wenders's classic road tale of wanderlust in Deutschland centers on a traveling movie projectionist-repairman who encounters a hitchhiker who is depressed following the collapse of his marriage. The men form an unusual relationship while en route from West to East Germany. A truly astonishing film with a great rock 'n' roll score. In German with English subtitles. B&W; 176m. DIR: Wim Wenders. CAST: Rudiger Vogler, Hanns Zischler, Lisa Kreuzer. 1976

KING'S ROW ★★★★★ A small American town at the turn of the century is the setting where two men (Ronald Reagan and Robert Cummings) grow up to experience the corruption and moral decay behind the facade of a peaceful, serene community. This brilliantly photographed drama is close to being a masterpiece, thanks to exceptional performances by many of Hollywood's best character actors. B&W; 127m. DIR: Sam Wood. CAST: Ann Sheridan, Robert Cummings, Ronald Reagan, Claude Rains, Charles Coburn, Betty Field, Judith Anderson. 1941

KING'S WHORE, THE ★★★ A European king is obsessed with a happily married woman who wants nothing to do with him. Good acting, but the story drags on too long. Rated R for profanity, nudity, and violence. 111m. DIR: Axel Corti. CAST: Timothy Dalton, Valeria Golino, Stephane Freiss, Margaret Tyzack, Feodor Chaliapin, Eleanor David, Paul Crauchet, Robin Renucci. 1990

KINJITE (FORBIDDEN SUBJECTS) 💗 Again Charles Bronson plays a vigilante who deals out his own brand of justice. Rated R for nudity, profanity, and violence. 96m. DIR: J. Lee Thompson. CAST: Charles Bronson, Perry Lopez, Peggy Lipton. 1989

KIPPERBANG ★★1/2 This is another World War II coming-of-age saga, in the same category as Hope and Glory, Empire of the Sun, and Au Revoir les Enfants. Charming and wistful at times, it doesn't quite reach the heights. Rated PG. 80m. DIR: Michael Apted. CAST: John Albasiny, Alison Steadman. 1982

KISMET (1944) ★★ Ronald Colman plays the beggar-of-beggars who cons his way into the Caliph's palace and romances Marlene Dietrich. The musical version has the same story line and the advantage of Borodin's music to make it more romantic. 100m. DIR: William Dieterle. CAST: Ronald Colman, Marlene Dietrich, Edward Arnold, James Craig, Joy Page, Hugh Herbert, Florence Bates, Harry Davenport, Robert Warwick, Hobart Cavanaugh. 1944

KISMET (1955) ★★1/2 The Borodin-based Arabian Nights fantasy, a hit on Broadway, is stylishly staged and ripe with "Baubles, Bangles, and Beads" and Dolores Gray's show-stopping "Bagdad." Sadly, however, the title of film loses the snap and crackle despite great singing by Howard Keel, Vic Damone, and Ann Blyth. The earlier Ronald Colman version (1944) is more fun and half a star better. 113m. DIR: Vincente Minnelli. CAST: Howard Keel, Ann Blyth, Monty Woolley, Vic Damone, Dolores Gray. 1955

KISS, THE (1929) ★★★★ The kind of smooth, stylish, and sophisticated production that best represents the apex of the silent-film period. Irene (Greta Garbo) gets caught up in a messy domestic tangle of infidelity and murder. The highly stylized courtroom scenes (redolent of German Expressionism) and flashback sequences give the film a flamboyant, visually arresting look. B&W; 70m. DIR: Jacques Feyder. CAST: Greta Garbo, Conrad Nagel. 1929

KISS, THE (1988) ★★ An African voodoo priestess (Joanna Pacula) is looking for an heir. So she invades the lives of her dead sister's family. That old black magic just ain't there. Rated R for nudity and violence. 105m. DIR: Pen Densham. CAST: Joanna Pacula, Meredith Salenger. 1988

KISS BEFORE DYING, A ★★1/2 Psychotic Matt Dillon stalks Sean Young in this all-too-familiar tale—derived from Ira Levin's novel. Still, the leads are fine, especially Young in a dual role as sisters. The 1956 adaptation is better. Rated R for violence, nudity, and profanity. 93m. DIR: James Dearden. CAST: Matt Dillon, Sean Young, Max von Sydow, Diane Ladd, James Russo. 1991

KISS DADDY GOODBYE 💗 Two psychic kids reanimate their father's corpse for some revenge in this tepid entry. Not rated; contains violence and profanity. 81m. DIR: Patrick Regan. CAST: Fabian Forte, Marilyn Burns. 1981

KISS DADDY GOOD NIGHT ★★ Uma Thurman stars as a struggling model who survives by picking up wealthy men in bars, then drugging and robbing them. She finds the situation reversed when an obsessive suitor decides that he wants her all to himself. Moody, ultimately incomprehensible thriller. Rated R for nudity and violence. 89m. DIR: Peter Ily Huemer. CAST: Uma Thurman, Paul Dillon, Paul Richards. 1988

KISS ME A KILLER 💗 A young wife and a drifter plot to eliminate her older husband. This is the Hispanic version of The Postman Always Rings Twice. The final irony this time out isn't nearly as satisfying.

Rated R for nudity and profanity. 91m. DIR: Marcus De Leon. CAST: Julie Carmen, Robert Beltran, Guy Boyd, Ramon Franco, Charles Boswell. 1991

KISS ME DEADLY ★★★1/2 Robert Aldrich's adaptation of Mickey Spillane's Mike Hammer novel was hailed by French new wave film critics in the 1960s as a masterpiece. Brutal and surrealistic, it has Hammer attempting to protect a woman (Cloris Leachman) from the men who want to kill her. B&W; 105m. DIR: Robert Aldrich. CAST: Ralph Meeker, Albert Dekker, Cloris Leachman, Paul Stewart. 1955

KISS ME GOODBYE ★★★ Sally Field plays a widow of three years who has just fallen in love again. Her first husband was an electrifying Broadway choreographer named Jolly (James Caan). Her husband-to-be is a slightly stuffy Egyptologist (Jeff Bridges). Before her wedding day, she receives a visit from Jolly's ghost, who is apparently upset about the approaching wedding. Rated PG for profanity and sexual situations. 101m. DIR: Robert Mulligan. CAST: Sally Field, James Caan, Jeff Bridges, Claire Trevor. 1982

KISS ME GUIDO ★★★★ Frankie Zito is an aspiring actor who lives with his family and works in their pizza joint. When he catches his brother fooling around with his fiancée, he decides to move out. Naïve Frankie answers a classified ad for a GWM roommate, not realizing that it stands for Gay White Male. When Frankie realizes that his roommate is gay, a lack of funds forces him to stay leading to a hilarious series of events. Rated R for adult situations and language. 90m. DIR: Tony Vitale. CAST: Nick Scotti, Anthony Barrile, Anthony De Sando. 1997

KISS ME KATE ★★★ That which is Shakespeare's *Taming of the Shrew* in the original is deftly rendered by Cole Porter, scripter Dorothy Kingsley, and George Sidney's graceful direction, by way of some fine performances by Howard Keel and Kathryn Grayson as a married pair whose onstage and offstage lives mingle. 109m. DIR: George Sidney. CAST: Howard Keel, Kathryn Grayson, Keenan Wynn, James Whitmore, Ann Miller, Tommy Rall, Bobby Van, Bob Fosse. 1953

KISS ME, STUPID ★★★1/2 A skirt-chasing boozing singer (Dean Martin) stops in the town of Climax, Nevada, and is waylaid by a would-be songwriter. This sex farce is on its way to cult status. When released it was condemned by the Legion of Decency and panned by critics and the general public; but it's worth a second look. Scripted by I. A. L. Diamond and director Billy Wilder. B&W; 126m. DIR: Billy Wilder. CAST: Dean Martin, Kim Novak, Ray Walston, Felicia Farr, Cliff Osmond, Alice Pearce. 1964

KISS MEETS THE PHANTOM OF THE PARK ❤ Flaccid made-for-TV movie about the heavy-metal group and a loony amusement park handyman. 100m. DIR: Gordon Hessler. CAST: Peter Criss, Ace Frehley, Gene Simmons, Paul Stanley. 1978

KISS OF DEATH (1947) ★★★★1/2 Finely crafted gangster film deals with convict Victor Mature infiltrating a gang run by psychopath Richard Widmark (in his film debut) so that Mature can obtain evidence on Widmark. Contains the now-famous scene of Widmark gleefully pushing a wheelchair-bound woman to her death down a flight of stairs. B&W;

98m. DIR: Henry Hathaway. CAST: Victor Mature, Richard Widmark, Brian Donlevy, Karl Malden, Coleen Gray. 1947

KISS OF DEATH (1995) ★★★1/2 David Caruso is excellent as the tortured Jimmy Kilmartin, a small-time car thief whose attempts to go straight are thwarted by a psychopath. Despite the impending clash between these two, scripter Richard Price gets far more mileage out of the complicated, strange and wonderful relationship between Caruso and Samuel L. Jackson's police investigator. Rated R for violence, profanity, and nudity. 101m. DIR: Barbet Schroeder. CAST: David Caruso, Samuel L. Jackson, Nicolas Cage, Helen Hunt, Kathryn Erbe, Stanley Tucci, Michael Rapaport, Ving Rhames. 1995

KISS OF THE SPIDER WOMAN ★★★★ This first English-language film by Hector Babenco is a somber, brilliantly acted tale about a gay window dresser, Molina (William Hurt), and a revolutionary, Valentin (Raul Julia), who slowly begin to care for each other and understand each other's viewpoint while imprisoned together in a South American prison. It is stark, violent, and daring. Rated R for profanity, violence, and suggested sex. 119m. DIR: Hector Babenco. CAST: William Hurt, Raul Julia, Sonia Braga. 1985

KISS OF THE TARANTULA ❤ Unhinged girl obliterates her enemies with the help of some eight-legged friends. Rated PG for mild gore. 85m. DIR: Chris Munger. CAST: Suzanne Ling, Eric Mason. 1972

KISS OF THE VAMPIRE ★★★1/2 A solidly creepy British vampire flick from Hammer Studios that really has some bite to it, even if Noel Willman is a Christopher Lee clone. A period piece set around the turn of the century, this has a few tricks up its bloody sleeve. Also released in a heavily edited U.S. version, *Kiss of Evil*. Not rated; contains implied violence. 88m. DIR: Don Sharp. CAST: Clifford Evans, Edward DeSouza, Noel Willman, Jennifer Daniel. 1963 DVD

KISS OR KILL ★★1/2 Australian lovers lure businessmen into motel rooms for sex and then drug and rob them in this edgy but pointless slice of outback *noir*. They become the target of a sprawling manhunt when one of their tricks dies and they flee the scene with a videotape that incriminates a local soccer legend as an active pedophile. The outlaw sweethearts are pursued as the body count grows. An irritating exercise in jump-cut editing. Rated R for nudity, sex, language, and violence. 96m. DIR: Bill Bennett. CAST: Frances O'Connor, Matt Day, Chris Haywood, Barry Langrishe, Barry Otto, Andrew S. Gilbert. 1997

KISS SHOT ★★★ Single mom struggles after being laid off. In desperation she hustles pool while being wooed by both her manager and a playboy. Solid performances and well-paced plot development maintain viewer interest. Rated PG for violence. 88m. DIR: Jerry London. CAST: Whoopi Goldberg, Dennis Franz, Dorian Harewood. 1989 DVD

KISS THE GIRLS ★★★1/2 Morgan Freeman, a forensic psychologist on the Washington, D.C., police force, is drawn to Durham, North Carolina, when his niece becomes the latest victim of a serial killer. But is she dead? According to the only victim to escape, our villain kills only those women who won't follow the rules of his fantasy game. Although there is a lack of mystery to the identity of the villain, there's still plenty of suspense. Rated R for violence, profanity, nudity, and suggested sex. 120m. DIR: Gary Fleder. CAST: Morgan Freeman, Ashley Judd, Cary Elwes, Tony Goldwyn, Jay O. Sanders, Bill Nunn, Brian Cox, Alex McArthur, Richard T. Jones, Jeremy Piven, William Converse-Roberts. 1997 DVD

KISS THE GIRLS GOODBYE 🖤 Repulsive exploitation about a man who kidnaps a young woman and bends her to his will. Not rated; contains strong violence, profanity, sexual situations, and substance abuse. 92m. DIR: Lee Karaim. CAST: Frankie Ray, Stephanie Smith, Ann O'Leary. 1997

•KISS THE SKY ★★1/2 On a business trip to the Philippines, Jeff and Marty decide to dump their humdrum jobs and families for a chance to rediscover the irresponsibility of their youth, but paradise turns ugly when their previous lives and a beautiful woman surface. Gorgeous cinematography and a sense of wonderment go a long way. Rated R for adult situations, language, nudity, and violence. 105m. DIR: Roger Young. CAST: William Petersen, Gary Cole, Sheryl Lee, Patricia Charbonneau, Terence Stamp. 1998 DVD

KISS TOMORROW GOODBYE ★★★ Violent, fast-paced gangster film brings back the days of the B movie. James Cagney is cast once again as a ruthless gangster who knows no limits. A rogue's gallery of character actors lends good support to this overlooked entry into the genre. 102m. DIR: Gordon Douglas. CAST: James Cagney, Luther Adler, Ward Bond, Barbara Payton, Barton MacLane, Neville Brand, Kenneth Tobey, Steve Brodie. 1950

KISSED ★★1/2 A young girl shows a morbid fascination with dead animals; as an adult she becomes an apprentice embalmer, and her fascination grows into a sexual obsession with her "patients." Writer-director Lynne Stopkewich's first feature film (adapted from a story by Canadian writer Barbara Gowdy) avoids sensationalizing its grim subject, but it's so resolutely tactful that the heroine's obsession never seems deeply felt. Not rated; contains frontal nudity and graphic scenes of necrophiliac sex. 72m. DIR: Lynne Stopkewich. CAST: Molly Parker, Peter Outerbridge, Jay Brazeau, Natasha Morley, James Timmons. 1996

KISSES FOR MY PRESIDENT ★★★ With a little more care, this could have been a great comedy. As it is, there is some fun when Fred MacMurray, the husband of the first woman president of the United States (Polly Bergen), falls heir to many of the tasks and functions handled by our first ladies. B&W; 113m. DIR: Curtis Bernhardt. CAST: Fred MacMurray, Polly Bergen, Arlene Dahl, Edward Andrews. 1964

KISSIN' COUSINS ★★ Would Elvis in dual roles double the fun? Divide it by two is closer to the truth. This time he is both an air force lieutenant and a *blond* hillbilly. He manages to fall in love while belting a few country tunes such as "Smokey Mountain Boy" and "Barefoot Ballad." 96m. DIR: Gene Nelson. CAST: Elvis Presley, Arthur O'Connell, Jack Albertson. 1964

KISSING A FOOL ★★ An egotistical TV personality (David Schwimmer) tests the fidelity of his fiancée (Mili Avital) by asking his best friend (Jason Lee) to try to seduce her. The clichéd premise has some mild possibilities, but none is developed in this dumb, unfunny comedy. Schwimmer's character is obnoxious, Lee's is a whiner, and Avital's seems too good for either of them. In a stunning misjudgment, director Doug Ellin gives away the "surprise" ending in the very first shot. Rated R for profanity. 105m. DIR: Doug Ellin. CAST: David Schwimmer, Jason Lee, Mili Avital, Bonnie Hunt, Kari Wuhrer. 1998 DVD

KISSING BANDIT, THE ★★★ A shy eastern-bred nerd tries to carry on the legend of his bandit father, a Casanova of the West. Made at the low point of Frank Sinatra's first career and recommended only as a curiosity piece for his fans. Ricardo Montalban, Ann Miller, and Cyd Charisse are teamed for one dance number. 102m. DIR: Laslo Benedek. CAST: Frank Sinatra, Kathryn Grayson, Mildred Natwick, J. Carrol Naish, Billy Gilbert, Ricardo Montalban, Ann Miller, Cyd Charisse. 1948

KISSING PLACE, THE ★★★★ An absolutely chilling performance by Meredith Baxter-Birney sparks this made-for-TV thriller. She's a woman who has kidnapped a boy to replace her dead child. All goes well for nearly eight years until unsettling dreams force the boy to question his identity. 88m. DIR: Tony Wharmby. CAST: Meredith Baxter-Birney, David Ogden Stiers, Nathaniel Moreau, Victoria Snow. 1989

KISSINGER AND NIXON ★★ Need a nap? Ten minutes of this talkfest and REM will have a whole new meaning. Strong performances by Beau Bridges as Richard Nixon and Ron Silver as Henry Kissinger cannot save this behind-the-scenes look at the negotiations to end the war in Vietnam. They talk in conference, they negotiate in Paris, they chat in the Oval Office, and they'll put you to sleep. Made for cable. Not rated; contains profanity. 90m. DIR: Daniel Petrie. CAST: Beau Bridges, Ron Silver, Matt Frewer, George Takei, Ron White. 1995

KIT CARSON ★★★1/2 This lively Western about the two-fisted frontiersman gave Jon Hall one of his best roles. Good action scenes. B&W; 97m. DIR: George B. Seitz. CAST: Jon Hall, Dana Andrews, Lynn Bari. 1940

KITCHEN TOTO, THE ★★★★ Powerful, uncompromising drama about a 10-year-old black boy who becomes hopelessly caught in the middle of racial violence between East African tribesmen and white British colonists in 1952 Kenya. Brilliantly performed and directed. Rated PG. Contains violence and nudity. 90m. DIR: Harry Hook. CAST: Bob Peck, Phyllis Logan. 1988

KITTY AND THE BAGMAN ★★1/2 Overambitious period piece about two Australian crime queens battling for control. The Roaring Twenties sets and the constant shifts back and forth from broad comedy to drama to shoot-'em-up action should entertain some viewers. Not rated. 95m. DIR: Donald Crombie. CAST: John Stanton, Liddy Clark. 1982

KITTY FOYLE ★★★★ Ginger Rogers, who became a star in comedies and musicals, went dramatic (and won an Oscar) in this three-hanky tearjerker about the troubled love life of an attractive secretary. Pure soap opera, but splendidly presented. B&W; 107m. DIR: Sam Wood. CAST: Ginger Rogers, Dennis Morgan, James Craig, Eduardo Ciannelli, Gladys Cooper, Ernest Cossart. 1940

KLANSMAN, THE ♥ Lee Marvin and Richard Burton fight the Klan in a southern town. Rated R. 112m. DIR: Terence Young. CAST: Lee Marvin, Richard Burton, Cameron Mitchell, O. J. Simpson, Lola Falana, Linda Evans. 1974

KLEPTOMANIA ★★★ This intriguing—albeit flawed—character study pairs a street hustler with a bored, bulimic society wife. They become each other's lifeline, share a fetish for stealing, and could use some strong counseling. Although it's interesting to speculate where the script is heading, the film's conclusion is both disappointing and unlikely. Rated R for profanity, rape, nudity, and violence. 90m. DIR: Don Boyd. CAST: Amy Irving, Patsy Kensit, Victor Garber, Gregg Baker, Delbert McClinton. 1993

KLONDIKE ANNIE ★★★1/2 Mae West stars in this comedy as a shady lady who leaves the Barbary Coast for Alaska, where she takes on the identity of a zealous nun and finds out religion isn't as much of a sham as she thought. It's unusual for West, but she keeps it respectable—and so did the overzealous censors, who cut out all of her double-entendres. B&W; 78m. DIR: Raoul Walsh. CAST: Mae West, Victor McLaglen, Helen Jerome Eddy, Phillip Reed, Harold Huber. 1936 DVD

KLUTE ★★★★ Jane Fonda dominates every frame in this study of a worldly call girl. Her Oscar-winning performance looks into the hidden sides of a prostitute's lifestyle; the dreams, fear, shame, and loneliness of her world are graphically illustrated. Donald Sutherland costars as an out-of-town cop looking for a missing friend. He feels Fonda holds the key to his whereabouts. Rated R. 114m. DIR: Alan J. Pakula. CAST: Jane Fonda, Donald Sutherland, Roy Scheider. 1971

KNACK ... AND HOW TO GET IT, THE ★★★★ Ray Brooks plays the lad with a knack for handling the ladies. Michael Crawford is the novice who wants to learn. Rita Tushingham is the lass caught in the middle. A British sex comedy produced before sex comedies were fashionable, meaning there's more talk than action. But the talk is witty, the direction zesty and the acting close to perfection. B&W; 85m. DIR: Richard Lester. CAST: Michael Crawford, Ray Brooks, Donal Donnelly, Rita Tushingham, Charlotte Rampling, Peter Copley. 1965

KNICKERBOCKER HOLIDAY ★★ A plodding, lackluster rendition of the Kurt Weill/Maxwell Anderson musical about Peter Stuyvesant and Dutch New York. The best song, "September Song," was originally sung by Walter Huston. Unfortunately, he's not in the film. B&W; 85m. DIR: Harry Brown. CAST: Nelson Eddy, Charles Coburn, Shelley Winters, Chester Conklin, Constance Dowling, Percy Kilbride. 1944

•KNIFE IN THE HEAD ★★★ When an innocent man is shot in the head during a police attack on a political rally, he loses his memory and physical coordination. His difficult recovery is slowed when the police, who need to justify their actions, accuse him of being a terrorist. Bruno Ganz is excellent in the lead role,

but the ambitious film may be difficult to follow for American viewers unfamiliar with German politics. In German with English subtitles. 112m. DIR: Reinhard Hauff. CAST: Bruno Ganz, Angela Winkler, Hans Brenner. 1978

KNIFE IN THE WATER ★★★★ Absolutely fascinating feature-film debut for director Roman Polanski. A couple off for a sailing holiday encounter a young hitchhiker and invite him along. The resulting sexual tension is riveting, the outcome impossible to anticipate. In many ways, this remains one of Polanski's finest pictures. In Polish with English subtitles. Not rated; the film has sexual situations. B&W; 94m. DIR: Roman Polanski. CAST: Leon Niemczyk, Jolanta Umecka, Zygmunt Malanowicz. 1962

KNIGHT MOVES ★★ At an international chess tournament in the Pacific Northwest one of the top touring masters becomes the prime suspect in a macabre, ritual murder. This atmospheric thriller makes less sense the more one thinks about it, but it certainly isn't dull. Rated R for violence and language. 110m. DIR: Carl Schenkel. CAST: Christopher Lambert, Diane Lane, Tom Skerritt, Daniel Baldwin. 1993

KNIGHT WITHOUT ARMOUR ★★★ This melodrama, about a British national caught up in the Russian Revolution and his attempts to save aristocrat Marlene Dietrich, is filled with beautiful photography but remains basically a curiosity, one of the few American films to depict communism in the 1930s. Robert Donat is an unassuming, gentle hero. B&W; 107m. DIR: Jacques Feyder. CAST: Robert Donat, Marlene Dietrich, Miles Malleson, David Tree. 1937

KNIGHTRIDERS ★★★ What was supposed to be a modern-day look at the lost Code of Honor comes across on screen as a bunch of weirdos dressed in armor riding motorcycles in a traveling circus. At a length of almost two-and-a-half hours, there isn't enough to hold the viewer's interest. Rated PG. 145m. DIR: George A. Romero. CAST: Ed Harris, Tom Savini, Amy Ingersoll. 1981

KNIGHTS ★★★ Vampiric cyborgs in futuristic Taos see people as a handy source of fuel. Hoping to save humankind, robot Kris Kristofferson teaches kickboxing champ Kathy Long all the right moves. Aside from the weak ending and a laughable battle scene (featuring a dismembered Kristofferson), this sword-and-sorcery cheapo isn't bad. Rated R for violence and profanity. 89m. DIR: Albert Pyun. CAST: Kris Kristofferson, Lance Henriksen, Kathy Long. 1992

KNIGHTS AND ARMOR ★★★ A seamless blend of interviews with well-versed historians, this provides a couple of intriguing biographies of famous knights, as well as a rundown of the Middle Ages. There is even a quick lesson concerning the complications of armor and heraldry. Easily digestible and informative, but with little crossover appeal if you aren't interested in this subject. Made for A&E. Not rated. 100m. DIR: Andy Stevenson. 1994

KNIGHTS AND EMERALDS ★★★1/2 A young drummer in a marching band in working-class Birmingham defies the racism of his family and friends when he takes up with a competing band of black youths. Original and endearing, sidestepping countless clichés into which it could easily have fallen. A good family item. Rated PG. 94m. DIR: Ian Emes. 1986 CAST: Christopher Wild, Beverly Hills, Warren Mitchell.

KNIGHTS OF THE CITY ✔ A New York street gang is also a pop musical group. Rated R. 89m. DIR: Dominic Orlando. CAST: Leon Isaac Kennedy, Nicholas Campbell, John Mengatti, Wendy Barry, Stoney Jackson, The Fat Boys, Michael Ansara. 1987

KNIGHTS OF THE ROUND TABLE ★★1/2 Colorful wide-screen epic of King Arthur's court is long on pageantry but lacks the spirit required to make this type of film work well. 115m. DIR: Richard Thorpe. CAST: Robert Taylor, Ava Gardner, Mel Ferrer, Stanley Baker, Felix Aylmer, Robert Urquhart. 1953

K-9 ★★★ James Belushi is terrific as a maverick cop whose single-minded pursuit of a drug dealer (Kevin Tighe) makes him a less-than-desirable partner. Enter Jerry Lee, a feisty police dog who proves to be more than a match for Belushi. Rated PG-13 for profanity and violence. 95m. DIR: Rod Daniel. CAST: James Belushi, Mel Harris, Kevin Tighe. 1989 DVD

KNOCK OFF ★★★ Watchable action-adventure film plays a bit like a cheap kung fu movie but, thanks to a screenplay by actionmeister Steven E. De Souza and sharp direction by Tsui Hark, it's entertaining. Rated R for violence and language. 91m. DIR: Tsui Hark. CAST: Jean-Claude Van Damme, Rob Schneider, Lela Rochon, Michael Fitzgerald, Paul Sorvino. 1998 DVD

KNOCK ON ANY DOOR ★★★1/2 Before John Derek became a Svengali for Ursula Andress, Linda Evans, and Bo Derek, he was an actor—and a pretty good one, too, as he proves in this courtroom drama directed by Nicholas Ray. He's a kid who can't help having gotten into trouble, and Humphrey Bogart is the attorney who attempts to explain his plight to the jury. B&W; 100m. DIR: Nicholas Ray. CAST: John Derek, Humphrey Bogart, Susan Perry, Allene Roberts. 1949

●**KNOCKING ON DEATH'S DOOR** ★★1/2 Newly wed paranormal investigators spend their honeymoon at a haunted house in Maine, where the resident ghosts take a particular interest in the young bride. Filmed in Ireland, this Roger Corman production at least looks good, and has a few shocks mixed into a largely predictable plot. Rated R for nudity, sexual situations, and violence. 92m. DIR: Mitch Marcus. CAST: Brian Bloom, Kimberly Rowe, David Carradine, John Doe. 1997 DVD

●**KNOCKOUT** ★★★ Good intentions abound in this female Hispanic *Rocky*, starring Sophia Adella Hernandez as Belle, who wants to follow in her father's boxing footsteps. She's good in the ring, but is she good-enough to beat the rival who put her best friend in the hospital? While the pedestrian script fails to reach a KO, the cast adds punch. Rated PG-13 for language and violence. 100m. DIR: Lorenzo Doumani. CAST: Sophia Adella Hernandez, Maria Conchita Alonso, Paul Winfield, Tony Plana, William McNamara. 2000 DVD

KNUTE ROCKNE—ALL AMERICAN ★★★ This is an overly sentimental biography of the famous Notre Dame football coach. But if you like football or you want to see Ronald Reagan show off his moves, it

could hold your interest. Pat O'Brien has the central role, and he plays it with real gusto. B&W; 84m. DIR: Lloyd Bacon. CAST: Ronald Reagan, Pat O'Brien, Donald Crisp. 1940

KOJIRO ★★★★ This first-rate semisequel to director Hiroshi Inagaki's *Samurai Trilogy* casts Tatsuya Nakadai as the fabled master swordsman, Musashi Miyamoto, whose exploits made up the three previous films. But he is not the main character here. Instead, the focus is on Kojiro (Kikunosuke Onoe), whose goal is to become the greatest swordsman in all Japan and thus follow the trail blazed by Miyamoto. In Japanese with English subtitles. Not rated; the film contains violence. 152m. DIR: Hiroshi Inagaki. CAST: Kikunosuke Onoe, Yuriko Hoshi, Tatsuya Nakadai. 1967

KOKO: A TALKING GORILLA ★★★ Does a gorilla that has been taught a three-hundred-plus-word vocabulary have civil rights? That's one of the arguments raised as this film looks at the efforts of a psychology researcher to keep the ape, borrowed from the San Francisco Zoo, which she has taught to "speak" (via sign language). 82m. DIR: Barbet Schroeder. 1978

●**KOLOBOS** ★★ Offered the chance to appear on a "reality" TV show, a group of teens heads for a remote location where they are stalked and slaughtered by a monster. This gruesome tale is a slight notch above average low-budget horror, but the unsatisfying ending is annoying. Not rated; contains violence, gore, and profanity. 87m. DIR: Daniel Liatowitsch, David Todd Ocvirk. CAST: Amy Weber, Promise LeMarco, Linnea Quigley. 1999 DVD

KOLYA ★★★★★ The 1996 Academy Award winner for best foreign film is an enchanting tale of a lonely man brought out of his shell by a wholly unexpected housemate. A down-on-his-luck Czech cellist, reduced to performing for funerals, accepts some quick cash via an arranged marriage with a young Russian woman who desires Czech citizenship. Scarcely days after this illegal transaction is completed, she flees into the arms of her German lover (a trip made possible by her new papers), leaving behind a confused 6-year-old son. Although the man and boy don't even speak each other's language, they eventually bond under droll circumstances. Rated PG-13 for mild sensuality. 105m. DIR: Jan Sverak. CAST: Zdenek Sverak, Andrej Chalimon, Ondrez Vetchy, Stella Zazvorkova. 1996

KONGA ★★ Botanist Michael Gough develops a serum that causes his chimpanzee, Konga, to grow into a monstrous ape who kills at Gough's bidding. This sleazy British monster movie isn't too bad until the climax, which is ruined by laughable special effects. B&W; 90m. DIR: John Lemont. CAST: Michael Gough, Margo Johns, Jess Conrad, Claire Gordon. 1960

KOROSHI ★★1/2 Patrick McGoohan's popular *Secret Agent* television series is poorly represented by this attempt to string two episodes into a full-length feature. The color photography—the series was B&W—is the only legitimate appeal; the episodes themselves are rather weak. For serious fans only. Not rated; suitable for family viewing. 100m. DIR:

Michael Truman, Peter Yates. **CAST:** Patrick Mc-Goohan, Kenneth Griffith, Amanda Barrie, Ronald Howard. 1966

KOSTAS ★★1/2 A tormented Greek-Cypriot tries to find love with an Australian girl in England. Director Paul Cox has created a character study with little depth and too much tedium. Not for the easily bored. Rated R for suggested sex. 110m. **DIR:** Paul Cox. **CAST:** Takis Emmanuel, Wendy Hughes. 1979

KOTCH ★★ Walter Matthau is in top form as a feisty senior citizen who takes to the road when his family tries to put him in a retirement home. First-time director Jack Lemmon does himself proud with this alternately witty and warmly human comedy. Rated PG. 113m. **DIR:** Jack Lemmon. **CAST:** Walter Matthau, Deborah Winters, Felicia Farr, Charles Aidman. 1971

KOUNTERFEIT ★★ Mildly diverting tale of two low-life hoods who try to hit the big time by cashing in $3 million of counterfeit money for a million of the real thing. Their simple transaction attracts the attention of cops, hit men, and a woman with a vendetta. Rated R for language and violence. 87m. **DIR:** John Mallory Asher. **CAST:** Bruce Payne, Corbin Bernsen, Hilary Swank, Michael Gross, Mark Paul Gosselaar. 1996

KOVACS ★★★★ Ernie Kovacs was one of the most innovative forces in the early days of television. His ingenious approach to comedy revolutionized the medium, and its impact can still be felt today. This definitive anthology contains some of his best moments, including his famous "Mack the Knife" blackout segments. His career on television lasted from 1950 to 1962, when his life was cut short by a fatal car accident. B&W; 85m. **DIR:** Ernie Kovacs. **CAST:** Ernie Kovacs. 1971

KOYAANISQATSI ★★★★ The title is a Hopi Indian word meaning "crazy life, life in turmoil, life disintegrating, life out of balance, a state of life that calls for another way of living." In keeping with this, director Godfrey Reggio contrasts scenes of nature to the hectic life of the city. There is no plot or dialogue. Instead, the accent is on the artistic cinematography, by Ron Fricke, and the score, by Philip Glass. It is a feast for the eyes and ears. No MPAA rating. 87m. **DIR:** Godfrey Reggio. 1983

KRAMER VS. KRAMER ★★★★ Dustin Hoffman and Meryl Streep star in the Academy Award–winning drama about a couple who separate, leaving their only son in the custody of the father, who is a stranger to his child. Just when the father and son have learned to live with each other, the mother fights for custody of the child. *Kramer vs. Kramer* jerks you from tears to laughs and back again—and all the while you're begging for more. Rated PG. 104m. **DIR:** Robert Benton. **CAST:** Dustin Hoffman, Meryl Streep, Jane Alexander, Howard Duff, JoBeth Williams. 1979

KRAYS, THE ★★★★ From British filmmaker Peter Medak comes this compelling, chilling portrait of Ronald and Reginald Kray, psychotic twins who ruled the London underworld in the 1960s. Features first-rate performances. Rated R for profanity and violence. 119m. **DIR:** Peter Medak. **CAST:** Billie

Whitelaw, Gary Kemp, Martin Kemp, Susan Fleetwood. 1990

KRIEMHILDE'S REVENGE ★★★★ This is a perfect sequel to the splendid *Siegfried*. Watch them both in one sitting if you get the chance. Siegfried's vengeful lover Kriemhilde raises an army to atone for his death. Beautifully photographed and edited, this international success placed German cinema in the vanguard of filmmaking. Silent. B&W; 95m. **DIR:** Fritz Lang. **CAST:** Margarete Schon, Rudolf Klein-Rogge, Paul Richter, Bernhard Goetzke. 1925

KRIPPENDORF'S TRIBE ★★ This wincingly awkward misfire further emphasizes the notion that Richard Dreyfuss—here playing an anthropologist forced to "fabricate" an undiscovered tribe in New Guinea—remains one of our most inconsistent actors. The premise is moronic and the characters too far removed from reality. Rated PG-13 for mild profanity and sexuality. 94m. **DIR:** Todd Holland. **CAST:** Richard Dreyfuss, Jenna Elfman, Natasha Lyonne, Gregory Edward Smith, Carl Michael Lindner, Lily Tomlin. 1998

KRONOS ★★★ In this alien invasion film, a giant, featureless robot is sent to Earth. The robot absorbs all forms of energy and grows as it feeds. The scientists must find a way to destroy the giant before it reaches the high-population areas of southern California. Although the special effects are nothing by today's filmmaking standards, this picture is one of the best from a decade dominated by giant monsters and alien invaders. B&W; 78m. **DIR:** Kurt Neumann. **CAST:** Jeff Morrow, Barbara Lawrence. 1957

KRULL ♥ In this poor sci-fi–sword-and-sorcery film, a young man is called upon to do battle with a master of evil to save a beautiful princess. Rated PG for violence. 117m. **DIR:** Peter Yates. **CAST:** Ken Marshall, Freddie Jones, Lysette Anthony. 1983

KRUSH GROOVE ♥ Lame rap musical. Rated R. 95m. **DIR:** Michael Schultz. **CAST:** Blair Underwood, Sheila E., Kurtis Blow, The Fat Boys, Run DMC. 1985

K2 ★★ This disappointing adventure, adapted from Patrick Meyers's successful stage play, rehashes every mountain-climbing movie cliché. An obnoxious attorney (Michael Biehn) and his physicist pal (Matt Craven) join a team that climbs the second highest and most treacherous mountain in the world. Rated R for violence and profanity. 104m. **DIR:** Franc Roddam. **CAST:** Michael Biehn, Matt Craven, Raymond J. Barry, Patricia Charbonneau, Hiroshi Fujioka, Luca Bercovici. 1992

KUFFS ★★1/2 When police officer Bruce Boxleitner is killed, his ne'er-do-well brother, Christian Slater, takes over the family-owned, patrol-special business in hopes of finding the killer. Director Bruce A. Evans uses a crisp, tongue-in-cheek storytelling style, mixing action, romance, and comedy. Rated PG-13 for profanity and violence. 106m. **DIR:** Bruce A. Evans. **CAST:** Christian Slater, Tony Goldwyn, Milla Jovovich, Bruce Boxleitner. 1992

KULL THE CONQUEROR ★★ Kull, a muscular slave-warrior turned king, discovers his sensual young bride is a 3,000-year-old witch who has been reincarnated to kill him. He then journeys to the Isle of Ice to save the world. This moronic, sanitized version of Conan author Robert E. Howard's pulp fiction superhero of the 1930s also features an irritating heavy-metal rock score. Rated PG-13 for violence and sensuality. 95m. DIR: John Nicolella. CAST: Kevin Sorbo, Tia Carrere, Karina Lombard, Joe Shaw, Roy Brocksmith, Harvey Fierstein, Litefoot, Edward Tudor Pole. 1997 DVD

KUNDUN ★★ This visually gorgeous film, complemented by equally opulent costumes, is about as interesting as waiting for paint to dry. No matter how limited your knowledge of China, Tibet, and the fourteenth Dalai Lama, the film will not shed additional insight. For all the depth of Melissa Mathison's script, this endurance test could have been compressed into a fifteen-minute newsreel short. Rated PG-13 for violence. 135m. DIR: Martin Scorsese. CAST: Tenzin Thuthob Tsarong, Sonam Phuntsok, Lobsang Samten, Gyatso Lukhang, Gyurme Tethong. 1997 DVD

KUNG FU (1971) ★★★ The pilot of the 1970s television series starring David Carradine has its moments for those who fondly remember the show. Carradine plays a Buddhist monk roaming the Old West. When his wisdom fails to mollify the bad guys, he is forced to use martial arts to see justice done. 75m. DIR: Jerry Thorpe. CAST: David Carradine, Keye Luke, Philip Ahn, Keith Carradine, Barry Sullivan. 1971

KUNG FU—THE MOVIE (1986) ★★ David Carradine returns to his decade-old hit TV series, as Kwai Chang Caine, a fugitive Buddhist monk. Caine is still on the run from Chinese assassins. Brandon Lee also stars as his son under the spell of an evil sorcerer to kill his father. (Carradine's role as Caine in the TV series was originally offered to Bruce Lee, Brandon Lee's father.) 92m. DIR: Richard Lang. CAST: David Carradine, Brandon Lee, Kerrie Keane, Mako, Bill Lucking, Luke Askew, Keye Luke, Benson Fong. 1986

KURT VONNEGUT'S MONKEY HOUSE ★★★ This made-for-cable production features three Kurt Vonnegut short stories. Sociological debate and brutal danger make "All the King's Men" the strongest tale: A U.S. ambassador must use his family and military advisers in a human chess game against a communist rebel leader. Other tales: "Next Door" and "The Euphio Question." Mild violence, but otherwise suitable for family viewing. 90m. DIR: Allan Winton King, Paul Shapiro, Gilbert Shilton. CAST: Len Cariou, Miguel Fernandes, Gordon Clapp, Donnelly Rhodes. 1991

KWAIDAN ★★★★ An anthology of ghost stories adapted from books by Lafcadio Hearn, an American writer who lived in Japan in the late nineteenth century. Colorful, eerie, and quite unique, it's one of the most visually stunning horror films ever produced. The movie isn't for children, though—it could induce nightmares. In Japanese with English subtitles. 164m. DIR: Masaki Kobayashi. CAST: Michiyo Aratama, Keiko Kishi, Tatsuya Nakadai. 1963

L.A. BOUNTY ★★ Wings Hauser was born to play wigged-out pyschos, and he's a standout in this otherwise pedestrian cop thriller. Rated R for violence and profanity. 85m. DIR: Worth Keller. CAST: Wings Hauser, Sybil Danning, Henry Darrow. 1989

L.A. CONFIDENTIAL ★★★★1/2 The seamy side of Hollywood in the 1950s is explored in this multilayered film based on James Ellroy's novel, which centers around the activities of the L.A. police force and a muckraking magazine publisher (Danny DeVito). Kevin Spacey is a high-profile cop who benefits from DeVito's busts of movie stars and political figures, while Russell Crowe steals the film as the straight-arrow detective who finds himself caught up in the corruption of the city's underbelly because, in part, of his love affair with a high-priced hooker (Oscar-winning Kim Basinger). Rated R for violence, profanity, and suggested sex. 136m. DIR: Curtis Hanson. CAST: Kevin Spacey, Russell Crowe, Guy Pearce, Danny DeVito, James Cromwell, David Strathairn, Kim Basinger, Graham Beckel, Paul Guilfoyle. 1997 DVD

L.A. CRACKDOWN ★★ An undercover cop (Pamela Dixon) battles crack dealers and blows away bad guys by the dozen. Made-for-video cheapie that is more concerned with showing sexy women than their problems. The sequel followed so fast, it was probably made at the same time. Not rated; nudity, violence. 84m. DIR: Joseph Merhi. CAST: Pamela Dixon, Tricia Parks. 1988

L.A. CRACKDOWN II ★★ More of the same, with Pamela Dixon and her new partner stalking a serial killer with a penchant for bar girls. Not rated; nudity, strong violence. 87m. DIR: Joseph Merhi. CAST: Pamela Dixon, Anthony Gates. 1988

L.A. GODDESS ★★ Lust on a movie set as a studio executive falls for a star's stunt double. The comedic tone seems an afterthought to shore up the soft-core erotica. Available in R and unrated versions; contains sex and profanity. 92m./93m. DIR: Jag Mundhra. CAST: David Heavener, Kathy Shower, Jeff Conaway, Joe Estevez. 1993

L.A. LAW ★★★1/2 Above-average television movie introduced the cast of characters of the successful series. Set in a high-powered Los Angeles law firm, this is both compelling and humorous. A must for fans of the series. 97m. DIR: Gregory Hoblit. CAST: Harry Hamlin, Susan Dey, Jimmy Smits, Michael Tucker, Jill Eikenberry, Richard Dysart, Corbin Bernsen, Alan Rachins, Susan Ruttan. 1987

L.A. STORY ★★★★ In writer Steve Martin's *Manhattan*-style comedy about Los Angeles, a wacky weatherman (Martin) becomes disillusioned with his television job, his status-crazy girlfriend (Marilu Henner), and life in general until a British journalist (Martin's wife Victoria Tennant) brings romance back into his world. Great fun for Martin's fans, with a hilarious supporting performance by Sarah Jessica Parker as a gum-popping Valley Girl. Rated PG-13 for profanity. 95m. **DIR:** Mick Jackson. **CAST:** Steve Martin, Victoria Tennant, Richard E. Grant, Marilu Henner, Sarah Jessica Parker. **1991 DVD**

L.A. VICE ★★ Detective Jon Chance quits the L.A.P.D. when an old friend is killed, but comes back to solve the case. Sequel to *L.A. Heat* is an improvement, but still not particularly memorable. Not rated, but an R equivalent for violence, profanity, and sexual situations. 88m. **DIR:** Joseph Merhi. **CAST:** Lawrence Hilton-Jacobs, William Smith, Jean Levine, Jastereo Covaire, R. W. Munchkin. **1989**

●**L'AGE D'OR** ★★★★ Banned for years in many countries, this satire remains a shocking but funny film. A couple trying to make love (in a most unromantic way) are thwarted by every possible repressive social institution—although in the mocking eyes of director Luis Buñuel, *every* social institution is repressive. The film's surreal nature makes it a fresh viewing experience despite its age. Though he is credited as codirector, Salvador Dali (who earlier collaborated with Buñuel on the short *Un Chien Andalou*) had nothing to do with this film. 60m. **DIR:** Luis Buñuel. **CAST:** Gaston Modot, Lya Lys. **1930**

L'ANGE (THE ANGEL) ★★★ Strange concoction of the bizarre and grotesque make up this metaphysical animation feature depicting murderous phantasms stuck in a parallel universe. This film contains some dazzling images; too bad they found their way into an incoherent movie. In French with English subtitles. Not rated; contains nudity and violence. 70m. **DIR:** Patrick Bokanowski. **1982**

L'ARGENT ★★★★★ Robert Bresson's last film, almost a fable, charts the inexorable moral degradation of a man condemned for a crime he didn't commit. Like all of this great director's work, it demands close attention, but rewards it with unforgettable images of overpowering emotional resonance. In French with English subtitles. Not rated. 90m. **DIR:** Robert Bresson. **CAST:** Christian Patey, Sylvie van den Elsen. **1983**

L'ATALANTE ★★★ The ocean and the elements form a backdrop for director Jean Vigo's surrealistic exercise. A disjointed but intriguing journey into the mind of an artist. Vigo died before his thirtieth birthday, shortly after completing *L'Atalante*, robbing the world of a promising filmmaker. In French with English subtitles. B&W; 82m. **DIR:** Jean Vigo. **CAST:** Michel Simon, Jean Dasté, Dita Parlo. **1934**

L'AVENTURA ★★★★ A girl disappears on a yachting trip, and while her lover and best friend search for her, they begin a wild romantic affair. Antonioni's penetrating study of Italy's bored and idle bourgeoisie contains some staggering observations on spiritual isolation and love. Winner of the Special Jury Award at Cannes. Italian with English subtitles. B&W; 145m. **DIR:** Michelangelo Antonioni. **CAST:** Monica Vitti, Gabriele Ferzetti, Lea Massari. **1960**

LA BALANCE ★★★★ This is an homage of sorts to the American cop thriller. It turns the genre inside out, however, by focusing on the plight of two unfortunates—a prostitute (Nathalie Baye) and a petty criminal (Philippe Léotard)—who get caught in a vise between the cops and a gangland chief. The result is a first-rate crime story. In French with English subtitles. Rated R for nudity, profanity, and violence. 102m. **DIR:** Bob Swaim. **CAST:** Nathalie Baye, Philippe Léotard, Richard Berry, Maurice Ronet. **1982**

LA BAMBA ★★★★ At the age of 17, with three huge hits under his belt, Ritchie Valens joined Buddy Holly and the Big Bopper on an ill-fated airplane ride that killed all three and left rock 'n' roll bereft of some giant talent. In this biography, *Zoot Suit* writer-director Luis Valdez achieves a fine blend of rock 'n' roll and soap opera. Rated PG-13 for language. 108m. **DIR:** Luis Valdez. **CAST:** Lou Diamond Phillips, Rosana De Soto, Esai Morales, Danielle von Zerneck, Elizabeth Peña. **1987 DVD**

LA BELLE NOISEUSE ★★★★ As one wag put it, this art film is *really* about watching paint dry. Yet, it's also a fascinating examination of the creative process. Its subject is the relationship between a gorgeous woman and the retired painter she inspires to return to painting. The scenes in which he nervously contemplates reentering the painful world of creation make the four-hour running time a small price to pay. In French with English subtitles. 240m. **DIR:** Jacques Rivette. **CAST:** Michel Piccoli, Jane Birkin, Emmanuelle Beart, Marianne Denicourt, David Bursztein. **1991**

LA BÊTE HUMAINE ★★★★1/2 Remarkable performances by Jean Gabin, Fernand Ledoux, and Simone Simon, along with Jean Renoir's masterful editing and perfectly simple visuals, elevate a middling and grim Emile Zola novel to fine cinema. The artistry of this film about duplicity and murder transcends what could have been a seedy little tale. In French with English subtitles. B&W; 99m. **DIR:** Jean Renoir. **CAST:** Jean Gabin, Julien Carette, Fernand Ledoux, Jean Renoir, Simone Simon. **1938**

LA BOUM ★★★ A teenager (Sophie Marceau) discovers a whole new world open to her when her parents move to Paris. Her new set of friends delight in giving "boums"—French slang for big parties. Although this film seems overly long, many scenes are nevertheless tender and lovingly directed by Claude Pinoteau. In French with English subtitles. No MPAA rating. 100m. **DIR:** Claude Pinoteau. **CAST:** Sophie Marceau, Brigitte Fossey, Claude Brasseur. **1980**

LA CAGE AUX FOLLES ★★★★ A screamingly funny French comedy and the biggest-grossing foreign-language film ever released in America, this stars Ugo Tognazzi and Michel Serrault as lovers who must masquerade as husband and wife so as not to obstruct the marriage of Tognazzi's son to the daughter of a stuffy bureaucrat. In French with English subtitles. Rated PG for mature situations. 110m. **DIR:** Edouard Molinaro. **CAST:** Ugo Tognazzi, Michel Serrault. **1978**

LA CAGE AUX FOLLES II ★★ This follow-up to the superb French comedy is just more proof "sequels aren't equals." In French with English subtitles. Rated PG for mature situations. 101m. **DIR:** Edouard Molinaro. **CAST:** Ugo Tognazzi, Michel Serrault. **1981**

LA CAGE AUX FOLLES III, THE WEDDING ●Pathetic and dreadful second sequel to *La Cage Aux Folles*. In French with English subtitles. Rated PG-13. 88m. **DIR:** Georges Lautner. **CAST:** Michel Serrault, Ugo Tognazzi, Stéphane Audran. **1986**

LA CÉRÉMONIE ★★★★ Antagonism between social classes escalates from verbal sparring and malicious surveillance to bloodshed in this sinfully clever suspense yarn. The female owner of a chic gallery on France's northern coast hires an oddly passive maid to care for her home and family. The maid is befriended by the local psycho postmistress and a sinister conspiracy evolves as they share dark secrets. Wait for the final credits or you'll miss the punch line. In French with English subtitles. Not rated; contains profanity and violence. 111m. **DIR:** Claude Chabrol. **CAST:** Sandrine Bonnaire, Isabelle Huppert, Jacqueline Bisset, Virginie Ledoyen, Valentin Merlet, Jean-Pierre Cassel. **1995**

LA CHIENNE ★★★★ Jean Renoir's first sound feature stars Michel Simon as a married man who finds himself involved with a prostitute after rescuing her from a beating by her pimp. Remade by Fritz Lang in 1945 as *Scarlet Street*. In French with English subtitles. B&W; 95m. **DIR:** Jean Renoir. **CAST:** Michel Simon, Janie Mareze. **1931**

•**LA CHUTE DE LA MAISON USHER** ★★★1/2 Avant-garde artist Jean Epstein turned to filmmaking for this memorable adaptation of the famous Edgar Allan Poe story, in which a man is haunted by the sister he caused to be buried alive. The stylized images and photographic techniques were unusual at the time, and if they no longer seem so fresh, this short, silent film is still compelling. B&W; 48m. **DIR:** Jean Epstein. **CAST:** Marguerite Gance, Jean Debucourt. **1928**

LA DOLCE VITA ★★★★ Federico Fellini's surreal journey through Rome follows a society journalist (Marcello Mastroianni) as he navigates a bizarre world in which emotions have been destroyed by surface realities, moral conventions, and unresolved guilts. This film is considered a landmark in cinematic achievement. In Italian with English subtitles. Not rated. B&W; 175m. **DIR:** Federico Fellini. **CAST:** Marcello Mastroianni, Anouk Aimée, Anita Ekberg, Barbara Steele, Nadia Gray. **1960**

LA FEMME NIKITA ★★★★ Luc Besson's stylishly inventive, ultraviolent, high-energy thriller about the recruitment of a convicted drug addict to be a secret service assassin. This visceral thriller isn't for the squeamish, but action fans who also like to think and who have a sense of style ought to love it. In French with English subtitles. Rated R. 117m. **DIR:** Luc Besson. **CAST:** Anne Parillaud, Jean-Hugues Anglade, Tcheky Karyo. **1991**

LA GRANDE BOURGEOISE ★★ This should be a suspenseful film about a brother who murders his sister's lackluster husband. However, the movie's primary concern is with costume and soft-focus lenses so that even the lukewarm emotions are overshadowed. In Italian with English subtitles. 115m. **DIR:** Mauro Bolognini. **CAST:** Catherine Deneuve, Giancarlo Giannini, Fernando Rey. **1974**

LA GRANDE VADROUILLE ★★★ Three Royal Air Force members are shot down over occupied France in this humorous film. Unfortunately, half of the French and German spoken is not translated into English. In English, French, and German with English subtitles. Not rated. 122m. **DIR:** Gerard Oury.

CAST: Courvil, Bourvil, Louis de Funes, Claudio Brook, Andrea Parisy, Collette Brosset, Mike Marshall. **1964**

LA LECTRICE (THE READER) ★★★ Clever comedy for ultraliterary types, with Miou-Miou at her charming best as a woman who hires herself out as a professional reader. She becomes a confidante, booster, adviser, and friend to a collection of loners, loonies, and emotionally unstable individuals. In French with English subtitles. 98m. **DIR:** Michel Deville. **CAST:** Miou-Miou, Maria Casares, Patrick Chesnais. **1989**

LA MACHINE ★★ Psychiatrist Gérard Depardieu invents a machine that allows him to exchange personalities with other people and tests it on a criminal psychopath. Subtitles are the only difference between this and dozens of other hokey mad-scientist movies. Not rated; contains graphic violence, nudity, sexual situations, adult situations, and profanity. In French with English subtitles. 96m. **DIR:** Francois Dupeyron. **CAST:** Gérard Depardieu, Nathalie Baye, Didier Bourdon. **1994**

LA MARSEILLAISE ★★★★ Though its plot is somewhat uneven, this film contains many beautiful sequences. The documentary-like story (and Jean Renoir's call to his countrymen to stand fast against the growing threat of Hitler) parallels the rise of the French Revolution with the spread of the new rallying song as 150 revolutionary volunteers from Marseilles march to Paris and join with others to storm the Bastille. In French with English subtitles. B&W; 130m. **DIR:** Jean Renoir. **CAST:** Pierre Renoir, Louis Jouvet, Julien Carette. **1937**

LA NUIT DE VARENNES ★★1/2 An ambitious and imaginative, but ultimately disappointing, film of King Louis XVI's flight from revolutionary Paris in 1791 as seen through the sensibilities of Casanova (Marcello Mastroianni), Restif de la Bretonne (Jean-Louis Barrault), and Tom Paine (Harvey Keitel). All these folks do is talk, talk, talk. In French with English subtitles. Rated R for nudity, sex, and profanity. 133m. **DIR:** Ettore Scola. **CAST:** Marcello Mastroianni, Jean-Louis Barrault, Harvey Keitel. **1983**

LA PASSANTE ★★1/2 Romy Schneider is featured in a dual role as Elsa, a German refugee, and as Lina, the wife of a contemporary world leader. The story centers on the relationship of two lovers caught up in a drama of political intrigue in France. Both Schneider and Michel Piccoli give excellent performances in this otherwise slow-moving thriller. In French with English subtitles. Contains nudity and violence; recommended for adult viewing. 106m. **DIR:** Jaques Rouffio. **CAST:** Romy Schneider, Michel Piccoli, Maria Schell. **1983**

LA PETITE BANDE ★★★ A group of bored London schoolchildren stow away across the English Channel and wreak havoc in France. Like a Steven Spielberg adventure (grownup villains eventually threaten the kids) without the special effects. There is no dialogue, just a persistent musical score. Not rated, but okay for children. 91m. **DIR:** Michel Deville. **CAST:** Andrew Chandler, Helene Dassule. **1983**

LA PROMESSE ★★★ The son of a Belgian slumlord gets the first stirrings of a conscience when one of the illegal aliens his father is exploiting dies in an accident and the boy feels responsible for the man's widow and child. This film has the air of tough street realism and the feel of actual behavior caught on camera almost by accident. Despite a weak and inconclusive ending, it's well acted. In French with English subtitles. Not rated; suitable for mature audiences. 90m. DIR: Jean-Pierre Dardenne, Luc Dardenne. CAST: Jeremie Renier, Olivier Gourmet, Assita Ouedraogo, Rasmane Ouedraogo. 1996

LA PURITAINE ★★★★ Penetrating drama played out in an empty theater where the artistic manager prepares for the homecoming of the daughter who ran away a year earlier. He ensembles a group of young actresses of his troupe in order to have them impersonate behavioral aspects of his daughter. Brilliant cinematography by William Lubtchansky. In French with English subtitles. Not rated, but is recommended for adult viewers. 90m. DIR: Jacques Doillon. CAST: Michel Piccoli, Sandrine Bonnaire. 1986

LA RONDE ★★★ It would be hard to imagine any film more like a French farce than *La Ronde*, in spite of its Austrian origins. This fast-paced, witty look at amours and indiscretions begins with the soldier (Serge Reggiani) and lady of easy virtue (Simone Signoret). Their assignation starts a chain of events that is charmingly risqué. In French with English subtitles. B&W; 97m. DIR: Max Ophüls. CAST: Anton Walbrook, Serge Reggiani, Simone Simon, Simone Signoret, Daniel Gélin, Danielle Darrieux. 1950

LA SCORTA ★★★ Four state policemen are assigned to protect a prosecuting magistrate from the violent wrath of Sicilian hoods in this intimate, compelling tale about determined idealism and male bonding under duress. The film paints an ugly picture of how coalitions between the Mafia and greedy government factions have corrupted rural and urban Italian life. In Italian with English subtitles. Not rated. 92m. DIR: Ricky Tognazzi. CAST: Carlo Checchi, Claudio Amendola, Enrico Lo Verso, Tony Sperandeo, Ricky Memphis. 1994

•LA SEPARATION ★★1/2 Pierre and Anne seem to have it all, including an infant son, yet passion has disappeared from their marriage. When Anne takes on a lover, the revelation takes its toll on Pierre. While it's not definitive, the film manages to explore the fragile landscape traveled by a couple in trouble. In French with English subtitles. Not rated; contains adult situations and language. 85m. DIR: Christian Vincent. CAST: Isabelle Huppert, Daniel Auteuil. 1994 DVD

LA SIGNORA DI TUTTI ★★ A famous actress attempts suicide, and we are taken on a retrospective journey through her life. Her beauty enchants and intoxicates men, who go as far as committing suicide to prove their love. Tacky, dated, and laughable at times, but with a hint of naïve historical charm that just barely saves it from the dreaded poultry symbol. In Italian with English subtitles. B&W; 89m. DIR: Max Ophüls. CAST: Isa Miranda. 1934

LA STRADA ★★★★★ This is Fellini's first internationally acclaimed film. Gelsomina (Giulietta Masina), a simpleminded peasant girl, is sold to a circus strongman (Anthony Quinn), and as she follows him on his tour through the countryside, she falls desperately in love with him. She becomes the victim of his constant abuse and brutality until their meeting with an acrobat (Richard Basehart) dramatically changes the course of their lives. B&W; 94m. DIR: Federico Fellini. CAST: Giulietta Masina, Anthony Quinn, Richard Basehart. 1954

LA TRAVIATA ★★★★ Franco Zeffirelli set out to make a film of Verdi's opera that would appeal to a general audience as well as opera buffs, and he has handsomely succeeded. He has found the right visual terms for the pathetic romance of a courtesan compelled to give up her aristocratic lover. The score is beautifully sung by Teresa Stratas, as Violetta, and Placido Domingo, as Alfredo. In Italian with English subtitles. Rated G. 112m. DIR: Franco Zeffirelli. CAST: Teresa Stratas, Placido Domingo. 1982 DVD

LA TRUITE (THE TROUT) ★★★ Sometimes disjointed story of a young girl who leaves her rural background and arranged marriage to climb the rocky path to success in both love and business. Although director Joseph Losey generally has the right idea, in the end, it lacks warmth and a sense of cohesion. In French with English subtitles. Rated R. 100m. DIR: Joseph Losey. CAST: Lissette Malidor, Isabelle Huppert, Jacques Spiesser. 1982

LA VIE CONTINUE ★★ Soap-operaish story about a woman trying to build a new life for herself and her children after her husband dies suddenly. The American remake, *Men Don't Leave*, was actually much better. French, dubbed in English. Not rated. 93m. DIR: Moshe Mizrahi. CAST: Annie Girardot, Jean-Pierre Cassel, Pierre Dux, Michel Aumont. 1981

•LABOR PAINS ★★ Cutesy romantic comedy suffers from sitcom dialogue and situations. Kyra Sedgwick stars as a columnist desperate to hide her pregnancy from her family and ex-boyfriend. Everything is played for a joke in this flat, uninteresting direct-to-video effort. Rated R for adult themes and language. 89m. DIR: Tracey Alexson. CAST: Kyra Sedgwick, Rob Morrow, Mary Tyler Moore, Robert Klein, Lela Rochon. 2000

LABYRINTH ★★★ A charming fantasy that combines live actors with another impressive collection of Jim Henson's Muppets. Jennifer Connelly wishes for the Goblin King (David Bowie) to kidnap her baby brother; when that idle desire is granted, she must journey to an enchanted land and solve a giant maze in order to rescue her little brother. Rated PG for mild violence. 101m. DIR: Jim Henson. CAST: David Bowie, Jennifer Connelly, Toby Froud. 1986 DVD

LABYRINTH OF PASSION ★★ Unengaging screwball comedy about the misadventures of a nympho punk rockette, an incestuous gynecologist, and a desperate empress in search of sperm from a member of the imperial family of Iran. In Spanish with English subtitles. Rated R for nudity and profanity. 100m. DIR: Pedro Almodóvar. CAST: Celia Roth, Imanol Arias, Antonio Banderas. 1983

LACEMAKER, THE ★★★1/2 Isabelle Huppert had her first major role here as a shy young Parisian beautician who falls in love with a university student while on vacation. But when they try to keep the affair going back in Paris, class differences drive them apart. Huppert's sympathetic performance pulls the film through occasional patches of pathos. In French with English subtitles. Not rated; the film features sexual situations. 107m. DIR: Claude Goretta. CAST: Isabelle Huppert, Yves Beneyton. 1977

LADIES CLUB ★★ A policewoman and a female doctor organize a support group to help rape victims deal with their feelings of rage and disgust. The club of the title soon turns into a vigilante group with the women punishing repeat offenders. Rated R for violence and gore. 86m. DIR: A. K. Allen. CAST: Karen Austin, Diana Scarwid, Christine Belford, Beverly Todd. 1987

LADIES' MAN, THE ★★ Jerry Lewis plays a houseboy for an all-female boardinghouse in Hollywood. Lewis wrote, directed, and stars in this silly slapstick farce. Watch for an amusing cameo by George Raft. 106m. DIR: Jerry Lewis. CAST: Jerry Lewis, Helen Traubel, Kathleen Freeman, Hope Holiday, Pat Stanley. 1961

LADIES OF LEISURE ★★★ Gold-digger Barbara Stanwyck snares a rich fiancé, but her past reputation gets in the way. Dated melodrama, but worth seeing for the young Stanwyck. B&W; 98m. DIR: Frank Capra. CAST: Barbara Stanwyck, Ralph Graves, Lowell Sherman, Marie Prevost. 1930

LADIES OF THE CHORUS ★★ The story of a chorus girl who tries to keep her young daughter from making romantic mistakes is pure detergent drama. A minor Marilyn Monroe musical, but her first major role so it's a curiosity piece. Adele Jergens is fine as the mother. B&W; 61m. DIR: Phil Karlson. CAST: Marilyn Monroe, Adele Jergens, Rand Brooks. 1949

LADIES ON THE ROCKS ★★★ Had Thelma and Louise taken to the stage instead of a life of crime, their adventures might have resembled this amusing low-key comedy. Two women tour rural Denmark with their male-bashing cabaret show. In Danish with English subtitles. Not rated; contains adult themes and sexual situations. 100m. DIR: Christian Braad Thomsen. CAST: Helle Ryslinge, Annemarie Helger. 1983

LADIES SING THE BLUES, THE ★★★★ Some of the finest ladies of blues are beautifully represented here in great archival footage. Even though the narration is weak, the music is powerful and sweet. Standout Billie Holiday is backed by brilliant sidemen Coleman Hawkins, Lester Young, and Ben Webster as they groove together on "Fine and Mellow." 60m. DIR: Tom Jenz. CAST: Billie Holiday, Dinah Washington, Bessie Smith, Lena Horne, Peggy Lee, Sarah Vaughan. 1989

LADIES THEY TALK ABOUT ★★★ Bank robber Barbara Stanwyck is rehabilitated in prison by goodhearted Preston Foster. Pre-Production Code movie, adapted from the play *Women in Prison*, raised some eyebrows with its frank dialogue. B&W; 69m. DIR: Howard Bretherton, William Keighley. CAST: Barbara Stanwyck, Lyle Talbot, Preston Foster, Lillian Roth. 1933

LADY AND THE DOG, THE ★★★ Anton Chekhov's short story is transformed into a Victorian melodrama about two wealthy people with too much time on their hands. In Russian with English subtitles. B&W; 89m. DIR: Josef Heifitz. CAST: Iya Savvina, Alexei Batalov. 1960

LADY AND THE TRAMP ★★★★ One of the sweetest animated tales from the Disney canon, this fantasy concerns a high-bred cocker spaniel (Lady) and the adventures she has with a raffish mongrel stray (The Tramp). Since Disney originally had the film released in CinemaScope, more attention has been given to the lush backgrounds. Not rated; suitable for family viewing. 75m. DIR: Hamilton Luske, Clyde Geronimi, Wilfred Jackson. 1955 DVD

LADY AVENGER ★★ Tough Peggie Sanders busts out of prison to get even with her brother's murderers. Forgettable made-for-video cheap thrills. Rated R for sexual situations, profanity, and violence. 82m. DIR: David DeCoteau. CAST: Peggie Sanders, Tony Josephs, Jacolyn Leeman, Michelle Bauer, Daniel Hirsch. 1989

LADY BE GOOD ★★★1/2 A lively musical version of a George Gershwin Broadway show using a different plot and only part of the original score. Some Gershwin classics are presented with originality. But the best tune, "The Last Time I Saw Paris," was written by Gershwin's competitor, Jerome Kern who won an Oscar for it; it has been associated with this musical ever since. B&W; 112m. DIR: Norman Z. McLeod. CAST: Ann Sothern, Robert Young, Dan Dailey, Virginia O'Brien, Red Skelton, Lionel Barrymore, Eleanor Powell, Phil Silvers. 1941

LADY BEWARE ★★ Decent but unriveting film along the lines of *Fatal Attraction*, with a psychotic pursuing pretty window dresser Diane Lane. The rest of the cast and situations are stereotypical and fairly mundane. Rated R for nudity and violence. 108m. DIR: Karen Arthur. CAST: Diane Lane, Michael Woods, Cotter Smith. 1987

LADY BY CHOICE ★★★ The sequel to *Lady for a Day*, remade as *Pocketful of Miracles*, with Carole Lombard as a do-gooder who turns May Robson into a proper lady. Witty Depression comedy. B&W; 80m. DIR: David Burton. CAST: Carole Lombard, May Robson, Roger Pryor, Walter Connolly, Arthur Hohl. 1934

LADY CAROLINE LAMB ★★ Without shame, this banal film victimizes the wife of an English politician who openly carried on with poet and womanizer Lord Byron. Writer-director Robert Bolt created this fiasco. 118m. DIR: Robert Bolt. CAST: Sarah Miles, Richard Chamberlain, John Mills, Laurence Olivier, Ralph Richardson, Margaret Leighton, Jon Finch. 1972

LADY CHATTERLEY'S LOVER (1959) ★★ Cinematic telling of D. H. Lawrence's risqué novel. It concerns the wife of a crippled and impotent mine owner who has an affair with a handsome gamekeeper. It's not very good in any respect. A British-French coproduction. B&W; 101m. DIR: Marc Allegret. CAST: Danielle Darrieux, Leo Genn, Erno Crisa. 1959

LADY CHATTERLEY'S LOVER (1981) ★★ A beautifully staged, but banal, version of the D. H. Lawrence classic. Rated R. 100m. DIR: Just Jaeckin. CAST: Sylvia Kristel, Nicholas Clay. 1981

LADY DRAGON ★★ Weak kickboxing effort succeeds only due to presence of star Cynthia Rothrock. She's a bundle of dynamite playing a former government agent, who is ambushed and left for dead while trying to avenge her husband's death. She's saved by a martial-arts expert who nurses her back to health and then retrains her to finish the job. Rated R for violence, nudity, and strong language. 90m. DIR: David Worth. CAST: Cynthia Rothrock, Richard Norton. 1992 DVD

LADY DRAGON 2 ★★ The stakes are higher, but it's still pretty much the same old thing. This time kickboxing champ Cynthia Rothrock sets out to recover $25 million in diamonds from bad guy Billy Drago. Fans will get a kick out of this workable sequel. Rated R for violence, strong language, and adult situations. 95m. DIR: David Worth. CAST: Cynthia Rothrock, Billy Drago, Sam Jones. 1993

LADY EVE, THE ★★★★ Barbara Stanwyck, Henry Fonda, and Charles Coburn are first-rate in this romantic comedy, which was brilliantly written and directed by Preston Sturges. Fonda is a rather simpleminded millionaire, and Stanwyck is the conniving woman who seeks to snare him. The results are hilarious. B&W; 94m. DIR: Preston Sturges. CAST: Barbara Stanwyck, Henry Fonda, Charles Coburn, William Demarest. 1941

LADY FOR A DAY ★★★★ An elderly beggar woman elicits the aid of a petty mobster and an oddball assortment of New York down-and-outers. She needs to palm herself off as a society matron in order to convince a Spanish noble family to accept her daughter as a suitable mate for their son. Remade by Frank Capra as Pocketful of Miracles. B&W; 95m. DIR: Frank Capra. CAST: May Robson, Warren William, Guy Kibbee, Glenda Farrell, Walter Connolly. 1933

LADY FOR A NIGHT 💀 John Wayne plays second fiddle to Joan Blondell. He's a saloon singer fighting for a measure of respectability. B&W; 87m. DIR: Leigh Jason. CAST: John Wayne, Joan Blondell, Ray Middleton. 1941

LADY FRANKENSTEIN 💀 Joseph Cotten ill-used as Baron Frankenstein attempting once again to create life in yet another silly-looking assemblage of spare parts. Rated R for violence. 84m. DIR: Mel Welles. CAST: Joseph Cotten, Mickey Hargitay. 1971

LADY FROM LOUISIANA ★★ John Wayne is a crusading lawyer in this middling Republic period piece. B&W; 82m. DIR: Bernard Vorhaus. CAST: John Wayne, Ray Middleton, Ona Munson. 1941

LADY FROM SHANGHAI ★★★1/2 Orson Welles and Rita Hayworth were husband and wife when they made this taut, surprising thriller about a beautiful, amoral woman, her crippled, repulsive lawyer husband, his partner, and a somewhat naïve Irish sailor made cat's-paw in a murder scheme. Under Welles's inventive direction, Everett Sloane and the camera steal the show with a climactic scene in the hall of mirrors at San Francisco's old oceanfront Playland. B&W; 87m. DIR: Orson Welles. CAST: Rita Hayworth, Orson Welles, Everett Sloane, Glenn Anders, Erskine Sanford, Ted de Corsia. 1948

LADY FROM YESTERDAY, THE ★★ Made-for-TV movie with a less-than-original plot: an ex-soldier, now a happily married businessman, is shocked when the Vietnamese woman he had an affair with shows up on his doorstep, complete with the child he never knew they had. Viewers will be somewhat less surprised. 98m. DIR: Robert Day. CAST: Wayne Rogers, Bonnie Bedelia, Pat Hingle, Tina Chen. 1985

LADY GODIVA 💀 Tiresome historical spectacle with Maureen O'Hara as history's most famous nudist—and no, you don't see anything. 89m. DIR: Arthur Lubin. CAST: Maureen O'Hara, George Nader, Victor McLaglen. 1955

LADY GREY 💀 A woman makes the long, hard climb to the top of the show-biz ladder, only to lose her soul along the way. Not rated, but an R equivalent for sexual situations. 100m. DIR: Worth Keeter. CAST: Ginger Alden. 1980

LADY ICE ★★ Donald Sutherland is an investigator for an insurance firm and Jennifer O'Neill is his romantic interest. The catch is that her father is a crook who sells stolen gems. Rated PG. 93m. DIR: Tom Gries. CAST: Donald Sutherland, Robert Duvall, Jennifer O'Neill, Patrick Magee. 1973

LADY IN A CAGE ★★★★ Superb shocker may finally get the recognition it deserves, thanks to home video. Olivia de Havilland is terrorized by a gang of punks when she becomes trapped in an elevator in her home. Good acting, especially by a young James Caan, and excellent photography help make this film really something special. Very violent at times. B&W; 93m. DIR: Walter Grauman. CAST: Olivia de Havilland, James Caan, Ann Sothern. 1964

LADY IN CEMENT ★★ Sequel to Tony Rome misses the mark. Once again private eye Frank Sinatra is immersed under the underbelly of Miami, this time with rather undistinguished results. 93m. DIR: Gordon Douglas. CAST: Frank Sinatra, Raquel Welch, Richard Conte, Dan Blocker, Lainie Kazan, Martin Gabel. 1968

LADY IN QUESTION ★★ Brian Aherne plays a French merchant who acts as a juror on a murder trial where young Rita Hayworth is the defendant. After her eventual release, Aherne takes pity on her and brings her to his home to work and live while keeping her identity a secret from his family. Remake of the French film Gribouille. B&W; 78m. DIR: Charles Vidor. CAST: Brian Aherne, Rita Hayworth, Glenn Ford, Irene Rich, George Coulouris, Lloyd Corrigan, Evelyn Keyes. 1940

LADY IN RED ★★★1/2 A splendid screenplay by John Sayles energizes this telling of the Dillinger story from the distaff side, with Pamela Sue Martin as the gangster's moll enduring the results of a life of crime. Director Lewis Teague keeps things moving right along. Rated R for profanity, nudity, and violence. 93m. DIR: Lewis Teague. CAST: Pamela Sue Martin, Robert Conrad, Robert Forster, Louise Fletcher, Robert Hogan. 1979

LADY IN THE LAKE ★★★ Director-star Robert Montgomery's adaptation of Raymond Chandler's mystery is a failed attempt at screen innovation. Montgomery uses a subjective camera to substitute for detective Philip Marlowe's first-person narrative of his efforts to find a missing wife. A clever but ineffectual whodunit. B&W; 103m. DIR: Robert Montgomery. CAST: Robert Montgomery, Audrey Totter, Lloyd Nolan, Jayne Meadows, Tom Tully, Leon Ames. 1946

LADY IN WHITE ★★★★ A high-grade suspenser. A grade-school boy (Lukas Haas) is locked in his classroom closet. While there, he sees the ghost of one of ten children who've been molested and killed in the past ten years. He also sees (but not clearly) the murderer, who then begins pursuing him. Now the question: Who did it? Well worth a watch! Rated PG-13 for violence and obscenities. 112m. DIR: Frank LaLoggia. CAST: Lukas Haas, Len Cariou, Alex Rocco, Katherine Helmond. **1988 DVD**

LADY IS WILLING, THE ★★★1/2 Marlene Dietrich wants to adopt an abandoned baby she found but needs a husband of convenience. She decides on Fred MacMurray, a handy pediatrician. Lightweight comedy but the stars shine. B&W; 92m. DIR: Mitchell Leisen. CAST: Marlene Dietrich, Fred MacMurray, Aline MacMahon, Stanley Ridges, Arline Judge. **1942**

LADY JANE ★★★1/2 Excellent costume political soap opera about Lady Jane Grey, accidental successor to the English throne. Helena Bonham Carter glows as Lady Jane, the strong-willed suffragist who engages in a power struggle with Mary I for the throne of England. Rated PG-13 for adult situations and violence. 140m. DIR: Trevor Nunn. CAST: Helena Bonham Carter, Cary Elwes, John Wood, Michael Hordern, Jill Bennett, Jane Lapotaire, Sara Kestleman, Patrick Stewart. **1985**

LADY KILLER ★★★1/2 The stars of the smash-hit *Public Enemy*, James Cagney and Mae Clarke, were reunited for this less-popular gangster film. Watching Cagney go from theater usher to hotshot hood to movie star is a real hoot. B&W; 74m. DIR: Roy Del Ruth. CAST: James Cagney, Mae Clarke, Margaret Lindsay, Henry O'Neill, Raymond Hatton, Russell Hopton, Douglass Dumbrille. **1933**

LADY KILLERS ✦ Lady Killers, a male strip joint, attracts police attention when one of the performers is murdered. A good-looking officer goes undercover as a stripper to solve the crime. Unbelievably bad! Not rated, contains nudity and violence. 93m. DIR: Robert Lewis. CAST: Marilu Henner, Susan Blakely, Lesley-Anne Down, Thomas Calabro. **1988**

LADY L ★★ Too much style and not enough substance, with the preposterous premise that Sophia Loren would enter an in-name-only marriage with David Niven while dallying with anarchist Paul Newman. The movie is all posturing and posing and leads absolutely nowhere. 124m. DIR: Peter Ustinov. CAST: Sophia Loren, Paul Newman, Peter Ustinov, David Niven, Marcel Dalio, Claude Dauphin, Michel Piccoli. **1965**

LADY MOBSTER ✦ Susan Lucci wallows in excess as a woman hell bent on revenge when her parents are murdered by the mob, in this made-for-cable film. 94m. DIR: John Llewellyn Moxey. CAST: Susan Lucci, Michael Nader, Roscoe Born, Thomas Bray. **1988**

LADY OF BURLESQUE ★★★ Slick and amusing adaptation of Gypsy Rose Lee's clever mystery novel of top bananas, blackouts, and strippers, *The G-String Murder*. Interesting look into an aspect of show business that now exists only in fading memories. B&W; 91m. DIR: William Wellman. CAST: Barbara Stanwyck, Michael O'Shea, J. Edward Bromberg, Iris Adrian, Pinky Lee. **1943**

LADY OF THE HOUSE ★★ Dyan Cannon stars in this TV dramatization of the life of Sally Stanford, Mayor of Sausalito, California. Cannon gives a better performance than usual, and Armand Assante is even better. 90m. DIR: Ralph Nelson, Vincent Sherman. CAST: Dyan Cannon, Armand Assante, Zohra Lampert, Susan Tyrrell. **1978**

•LADY OF THE LAKE ★★★★ Beautifully shot, sensuous fantasy from Canadian filmmaker Maurice Devereaux took five years to film, but the end result is well worth it. The lady here is a medieval gypsy witch named Viviane, who was murdered by a spiteful knight. Upon the death of his uncle, a man inherits a house by the lady's lake and discovers the secrets within. Second Fangoria video release. Rated R for violence, profanity, and simulated sex. 85m. DIR: Maurice Devereaux. CAST: Tennyson Loeh, Erik Rutherford, Chris Piggins. **1999 DVD**

LADY ON A TRAIN ★★★★ A delightful mystery-comedy with Deanna Durbin as the heroine who sees a murder committed through a train window. The police ignore her so she decides to solve the murder herself. The upshot, when her snooping leads her to an especially nutty family, is both suspenseful and witty. B&W; 95m. DIR: Charles David. CAST: Deanna Durbin, Ralph Bellamy, David Bruce, Edward Everett Horton, Patricia Morison, Dan Duryea, William Frawley, George Coulouris. **1945**

LADY ON THE BUS ★★ Story of a shy bride who is frigid on her wedding night. She first turns to her husband's friends and then strangers she meets on buses. Marginal comedy. In Portuguese with English subtitles. Rated R for sex. 102m. DIR: Neville D'Almeida. CAST: Sonia Braga. **1978**

LADY SCARFACE ★★1/2 Role reversal is the order of the day for this story of a hardened dame who spits lead and asks questions later, ruling her gang with a velvet glove and leading the police and authorities on a grim chase. Atmospheric but pretentious, this isn't as good as it could have been despite the presence of classy Judith Anderson. B&W; 66m. DIR: Frank Woodruff. CAST: Judith Anderson, Dennis O'Keefe, Frances Neal, Eric Blore, Marc Lawrence. **1941**

LADY SINGS THE BLUES ★★★1/2 Diana Ross made a dynamic screen debut in this screen biography of another singing great, Billie Holiday, whose career was thwarted by drug addiction. Rated R. 144m. DIR: Sidney J. Furie. CAST: Diana Ross, Billy Dee Williams, Richard Pryor. **1972**

LADY TAKES A CHANCE, A ★★★ John Wayne is a rough-'n'-ready, not-the-marrying kind, rodeo star. Jean Arthur is an innocent girl from New York City out west. He falls off a horse into her lap, she falls for him, and the chase is on. *It Happened One Night* with spurs. B&W; 86m. DIR: William A. Seiter. CAST: Jean Arthur, John Wayne, Phil Silvers, Charles Winninger, Grady Sutton, Hans Conried, Grant Withers, Mary Field. **1943**

LADY TERMINATOR ★★ Enjoyably bad blood 'n' sex saga. An American anthropology student in the South Seas is possessed by the vengeful spirit of a long-dead queen. Rated R for strong violence and nudity. 83m. **DIR:** Jalil Jackson. **CAST:** Barbara Anne Constable, Christopher J. Hart. 1989

LADY VANISHES, THE (1938) ★★★★★ Along with *The Thirty-nine Steps*, this is the most admired film from Alfred Hitchcock's early directorial career. The comedy-suspense-thriller centers around a group of British types on a train trip from central Europe to England. A young woman (Margaret Lockwood) seeks the aid of a fellow passenger (Michael Redgrave) in an attempt to locate a charming old lady (Dame May Whitty) she had met earlier on the train and who now is apparently missing. B&W; 97m. **DIR:** Alfred Hitchcock. **CAST:** Margaret Lockwood, Michael Redgrave, May Whitty. 1938 DVD

LADY VANISHES, THE (1979) ★ A better title for this remake might be *The Plot Vanishes*. Rated PG. 95m. **DIR:** Anthony Page. **CAST:** Elliott Gould, Cybill Shepherd, Angela Lansbury, Herbert Lom, Arthur Lowe, Ian Carmichael. 1979

LADY WINDERMERE'S FAN ★★★★1/2 This is a dynamite version of Oscar Wilde's play. The very enigmatic Mrs. Erlynne comes close to scandalizing all of London society. This is one of Ernst Lubitsch's best silent films. B&W; 80m. **DIR:** Ernst Lubitsch. **CAST:** Ronald Colman, May McAvoy, Irene Rich. 1925

LADYBIRD, LADYBIRD ★★★1/2 A single mother (Crissy Rock, in an electrifying acting debut) battles with social services for custody of her four kids, and for two others she has with a gentle Paraguayan expatriate (Vladimir Vega). The film gives a 1990s update to the working-class anger of British plays and films of forty years ago. The mother's anger is uncontrollable and self-destructive, and the film is powerful and, ultimately, frustrating. Not rated; contains brief violence and extensive profanity. 102m. **DIR:** Kenneth Loach. **CAST:** Crissy Rock, Vladimir Vega, Ray Winstone, Sandie Lavelle. 1994

LADYBUGS ★★ Dangerfield is an inept girls' soccer coach who convinces his fiancée's son to dress up like a girl and help run the team. Dangerfield's trademark one-liners are the best things about the film. Rated PG-13 for brief profanity and sexual innuendo. 91m. **DIR:** Sidney J. Furie. **CAST:** Rodney Dangerfield, Jackée, Jonathan Brandis, Ilene Graff, Vinessa Shaw, Tom Parks. 1992

LADYHAWKE ★★★1/2 In this 700-year-old legend of love and honor, Rutger Hauer and Michelle Pfeiffer are lovers separated by an evil curse. Hauer, a valiant knight, is aided by a wisecracking thief, Matthew Broderick, in his quest to break the spell by destroying its creator. This is a lush and lavish fantasy that will please the young and the young at heart. Rated PG-13 for violence. 124m. **DIR:** Richard Donner. **CAST:** Matthew Broderick, Rutger Hauer, Michelle Pfeiffer, Leo McKern, John Wood. 1985 DVD

LADYKILLER ★★★1/2 An ex-police detective turned evidence photographer (Mimi Rogers) becomes obsessed with a murder case. She joins a computer dating service, only to be matched with the prime murder suspect. Good acting all around. Made for cable. 91m. **DIR:** Michael Scott. **CAST:** Mimi Rogers, John Shea, Tom Irwin, Alice Krige, Bob Gunton, Bert Remsen. 1992

LADYKILLER (1996) ★★ Ben Gazzara's world-weary detective is the only good thing about this otherwise routine police thriller, which involves a serial maniac who kills his nubile victims by stuffing them with absurd amounts of loose change. As befits producer Roger Corman, there's plenty of gratuitous nudity. Rated R for violence, profanity, nudity, and simulated sex. 90m. **DIR:** Terence H. Winkless. **CAST:** Ben Gazzara, Alex McArthur, Stephen Davies, Terri Treas. 1996

LADYKILLERS, THE ★★★★1/2 England had a golden decade of great comedies during the 1950s. *The Ladykillers* is one of the best. Alec Guinness and Peter Sellers are teamed as a couple of small-time criminals who have devised what they believe to be the perfect crime. Unfortunately, their plans are thwarted by the sweetest, most innocent little old landlady you'd ever want to meet. Great fun! 87m. **DIR:** Alexander Mackendrick. **CAST:** Alec Guinness, Peter Sellers, Cecil Parker. 1955

LAGUNA HEAT ★★★1/2 This well-written script was made for HBO cable. Harry Hamlin is an ex–L.A. cop who lives with his father in Laguna Beach. He soon gets involved in a murder investigation. Director Simon Langton keeps the action moving and the plot twisting. 110m. **DIR:** Simon Langton. **CAST:** Harry Hamlin, Jason Robards Jr., Rip Torn, Catherine Hicks, Anne Francis, James Gammon. 1987

LAIR OF THE WHITE WORM ★ Ken Russell writhes again, disgustingly perverse and snidely campy. Rated R. 99m. **DIR:** Ken Russell. **CAST:** Amanda Donohoe, Hugh Grant, Sammi Davis, Catherine Oxenberg, Peter Capaldi. 1988 DVD

LAKE CONSEQUENCE ★★1/2 Arty smut-maven Zalman King turns producer for this melodramatic tale of a suburban housewife (Joan Severance) who slips into debauched sex with the tightly wired stud (Billy Zane) pruning the trees in her neighborhood. Lots of bare skin. Rated R for nudity and profanity. 85m. **DIR:** Rafael Eisenman. **CAST:** Billy Zane, Joan Severance, May Karasun. 1993

•**LAKE PLACID** ★★★1/2 This mainstream monster movie opens with a supremely gory moment, just to show that it means business, and then introduces its heroes and settles back for the acerbic, eccentric character banter that we'd expect of writer-producer David E. Kelley, best known for TV creations *The Practice* and *Ally McBeal*. The monster in question resides in tranquil Black Lake, in the backwoods of Maine, where it routinely chomps on anybody foolish enough to fall into the water. But, deft script and engaging characters aside, something must have gone wrong during production, because the film concludes—*very* abruptly—just as it has kicked into gear. Matters are resolved so quickly that you're likely to feel cheated. Let's therefore call this one suspenseful, skillfully scripted, well-performed, and quite entertaining … for two-thirds of a movie. Rated R for violence, profanity, and dollops of gore. 80m. **DIR:** Steve Miner. **CAST:** Bill Pullman, Bridget Fonda, Oliver Platt, Brendan Gleeson, Betty White, Meredith Salenger. 1999 DVD

LAKOTA WOMAN: SIEGE AT WOUNDED KNEE ★★★ Good but preachy account of how one Lakota woman took a stand at Wounded Knee, South

Dakota, in 1973 in order to regain her dignity. Irene Bedard makes a fine debut as Mary Crow Dog, a woman ignorant of her heritage until she took part in the bloody siege that proved a turning point for American Indians. Made-for-cable film tries too hard to be politically correct. Not rated; contains violence. 113m. DIR: Frank Pierson. CAST: Irene Bedard, August Schellenberg, Joseph Running Fox, Floyd Red Crow Westerman, Tantoo Cardinal. 1994

LAMBADA ★★ This attempt to exploit the sensuous dance from Brazil (do you know anyone who's actually "done" this dance?) is slightly better than *The Forbidden Dance*, which was released simultaneously—but that's not saying much. There is some nice choreography by Shabba-Doo. Rated PG. 97m. DIR: Joel Silberg. CAST: J. Eddie Peck, Melora Hardin, Dennis Burkley. 1990

L'AMERICA ★★★★ Two Italian scam artists have hopes of securing government grants for their phony shoe factory in desperately poor post-communist Albania. They pluck a feeble-minded old man from a prison camp to act as the company's puppet chairman only to have him disappear into the flood of refugees escaping to Italy. This haunting story about the realities of mass immigration is told with documentary-like sweep. In Italian with English subtitles. Not rated. 116m. DIR: Gianni Amelio. CAST: Enrico Lo Verso, Michele Placido, Carmelo Di Mazzarelli, Piro Mikani. 1996

LANCELOT OF THE LAKE ★★★★★ With characteristic austerity, Robert Bresson recounts the breakup of King Arthur's fabled Round Table as the ideals of chivalry give way to petty squabbles and sexual philandering. In French with English subtitles. Not rated. 85m. DIR: Robert Bresson. CAST: Luc Simon, Laura Duke Condominas. 1974

LAND AND FREEDOM ★★★ An interesting approach to the Spanish Civil War—from the point of view of a naïve English Marxist who sees the Stalinists undercutting their anti-Fascist allies—that gets bogged down in political rhetoric and clichéd characterizations. A beautifully filmed tale of wartime disillusionment that could have been more intellectually and emotionally captivating. Not rated; contains military violence, language, and a sex scene. 110m. DIR: Kenneth Loach. CAST: Ian Hart. 1995

LAND BEFORE TIME, THE ★★★★ This terrific animated film from director Don Bluth follows the journey of five young dinosaurs as they struggle to reach the Great Valley, the only place on Earth as yet untouched by a plague that has ravaged the world. On the way, they have several funny, suspenseful, and life-threatening adventures. The result is a wonderful film for the younger set. Rated G. 66m. DIR: Don Bluth. 1988 DVD

LAND BEFORE TIME II, THE ★★ Some rather awful songs litter an otherwise bland direct-to-video sequel that likely will bore all but the very youngest of viewers. In this one, Littlefoot the dinosaur and his mischievous friends find unexpected perils in their happy valley home. Rated G. 72m. DIR: Roy Allen Smith. 1994

LAND BEFORE TIME III, THE ★★★ Littlefoot and pals face new danger in this third entry in the animated movie series. In this direct-to-video release, their water supply is cut off, forcing the dinosaurs to ration, with conflicts and greed resulting. Bullying adolescents and bickering parents contrast sharply with the caring, sharing little ones. Animation, though passable, doesn't measure up to the original theatrical release. Rated G. 71m. DIR: Roy Allen Smith. 1995

LAND GIRLS, THE ★★1/2 In this silly soap opera–sex farce, three lovely London lasses head to rural Dorset to pitch in while the men are off fighting World War II. They all illogically have affairs with the farmer's sullen son, who doesn't deserve any of them. This romantic piffle truly has no clue as to what it's really about. Rated R for sex, language, and mild violence. 112m. DIR: David Leland. CAST: Catherine McCormack, Rachel Weisz, Anna Friel, Steven Mackintosh. 1997

LAND OF FARAWAY, THE ★★ An orphaned 11-year-old boy is rescued from his dreary, dismal existence and spirited away to *The Land of Faraway.* The boy's father turns out to be the king of Faraway, and he finds the joy in life that he's been missing. But he has to earn his new inheritance by destroying the evil knight, Kato. Poor production values and sloppy direction spoil an otherwise good fairy tale. Rated PG. 95m. DIR: Vladimir Grammatikor. CAST: Timothy Bottoms, Susannah York, Christopher Lee. 1987

LAND OF THE MINOTAUR ★★ Peter Cushing, in one of his few truly villainous roles, plays the leader of a bloodthirsty devil cult that preys on tourists in modern Greece. Already slow-paced, this low-budget creature feature is gravely handicapped by its American distributor's decision to cut six minutes of nudity and violence, thereby ensuring a PG rating. What remains is picturesque but tame. Brian Eno composed and performs the eerie electronic score. 88m. DIR: Costa Carayiannis. CAST: Peter Cushing, Donald Pleasence. 1976

LAND OF THE OPEN RANGE ★★1/2 Sheriff Tim Holt has his hands full of ex-cons when a local no-good dies and leaves his ranch open to a land rush. However, to qualify for a homestead, each man must have served two years or more in prison. A different twist on the standard B land grab plot, and one of Holt's better prewar efforts. B&W; 60m. DIR: Edward Killy. CAST: Tim Holt, Ray Whitley, Roy Barcroft. 1942

LAND OF THE PHARAOHS ★★1/2 Joan Collins plays the cunning villainess in a story about ancient Egypt. Talky but colorful historical drama with a visual tour of Egypt in all its splendor. 106m. DIR: Howard Hawks. CAST: Jack Hawkins, Joan Collins, Sydney Chaplin, James Robertson Justice, Dewey Martin. 1955

LAND RAIDERS ♥ Spanish-made violent oater with Telly Savalas as the Indian-hating town boss. 101m. DIR: Nathan Juran. CAST: Telly Savalas, George Maharis, Arlene Dahl. 1970

LAND THAT TIME FORGOT, THE ★★ Poor Edgar Rice Burroughs, his wonderful adventure books for kids rarely got the right screen treatment. This British production tries hard, but the cheesy special effects eventually do it in. A sequel, *The People That*

Time Forgot, fared no better. Rated PG. 90m. **DIR:** Kevin Connor. **CAST:** Doug McClure, Susan Penhaligon, John McEnery. **1975**

LAND UNKNOWN, THE ★★ A navy helicopter forced down in the Antarctic lands in a warm-water region where prehistoric animals still live. The production is better than the average B movie, but the dinosaurs are cheesy. B&W; 79m. **DIR:** Virgil Vogel. **CAST:** Jock Mahoney, Shawn Smith, William Reynolds. **1957**

LAND WITHOUT BREAD ★★★ A powerful documentary from director Luis Buñuel about the impoverished people living in the Las Hurdes region of Spain. In Spanish with English subtitles. B&W; 45m. **DIR:** Luis Buñuel. **1932**

LANDLADY, THE ★★ Talia Shire stars as Melanie Leroy, a desperate woman whose pursuit of a perfect life is shattered when she catches her husband cheating. After dispatching him, Melanie becomes the landlady of an apartment building, a position she uses to find the ideal husband. Instead, she's forced to dispatch those who get in the way of her happiness. And all 3-C wanted to do was borrow some butter. Pedestrian thrills fail to rise above that level. Rated R for violence and language. 98m. **DIR:** Robert Malenfant. **CAST:** Talia Shire, Jack Coleman, Melissa Behr, Susie Singer, Bette Ford, Bruce Weitz. **1997 DVD**

LANDSLIDE ★★★ Intriguing mystery follows young geologist Anthony Edwards's trek back to a small town he left years ago. Several of the locals try to figure out if he's the mysterious stranger who disappeared after a fatal car crash that killed the town leader and his family. Director Jean-Claude Lord guides his attractive cast through their paces with a tight reign. Rated PG-13 for violence. 95m. **DIR:** Jean-Claude Lord. **CAST:** Anthony Edwards, Tom Burlinson, Joanna Cassidy, Melody Anderson, Lloyd Bochner. **1992**

LANGOLIERS, THE ★★★1/2 A planeload of familiar faces find themselves trapped in a time vortex that is quickly collapsing. When ten passengers on a red-eye flight from Los Angeles to Boston awaken, they find that everyone else has disappeared. When they land, they discover a world where time stands still, and ferocious little critters eat everything in sight. This television miniseries, based on a Stephen King novella, is a little long in the tooth, but fascinating nonetheless. 180m. **DIR:** Tom Holland. **CAST:** Patricia Wettig, Dean Stockwell, Bronson Pinchot, David Morse, Mark Lindsay Chapman, Christopher Collet, Kate Maberly. **1995 DVD**

L'ANNÉE DES MEDUSES 💔 If Jackie Collins were French, she'd probably be churning out stuff like this. On the Riviera, a young girl competes with her mother for the pick of the season's hunk crop. In French with English subtitles. Not rated, but loaded with nudity and soft-core sex. 110m. **DIR:** Christopher Frank. **CAST:** Valerie Kaprisky, Bernard Giraudeau, Caroline Cellier. **1986**

•**LANSKY** ★★ This low-key made-for-cable original about Mafia financial whiz Meyer Lansky suffers from a staggering cast of characters and confusion over what is happening in each scene (rapid dialogue and obscure references account for this). Pepper this mess with trite and clichéd dialogue, and the film simply falls flat. Rated R for profanity, violence, and nudity. 116m. **DIR:** John McNaughton. **CAST:** Richard Dreyfuss, Eric Roberts, Max Perlich, Matthew Settle, Beverly D'Angelo, Anthony LaPaglia. **1999 DVD**

LANTERN HILL ★★★★ A brilliant new *Wonderworks* production partially filmed on Prince Edward Island in Canada. Marion Bennett is Jane Stewart, a young girl whose powers are revealed in uniting her estranged parents in the mysterious Maritime Islands. A classic tale of family love. Made for television. 120m. **DIR:** Kevin Sullivan. **CAST:** Zoe Caldwell, Sam Waterston, Colleen Dewhurst, Marion Bennett, Sarah Polley. **1991**

LAP DANCING 💔 Bright-eyed country girl heads to Hollywood with stars in her eyes but ends up lap dancing at a sleazy club. Rated R for nudity, adult situations, and language. Unrated version also available. 93m. **DIR:** Mike Sedan. **CAST:** Lorissa McComass, Tane McClure, C. T. Miller. **1995 DVD**

LARGER THAN LIFE ★★ Slick motivational speaker inherits a female circus elephant from his deceased clown father. He takes the huge orphan across America by train, truck, and foot and plans to sell her on the West Coast either to a kind animal researcher or a mean-spirited circus boss. The film is sometimes amusing, but the elephant is given nothing special to do other than trumpet and raise a leg. This road comedy adds up to just peanuts for audiences expecting big and frequent laughs. Rated PG. 93m. **DIR:** Howard Franklin. **CAST:** Bill Murray, Linda Fiorentino, Matthew McConaughey, Janeane Garofalo, Pat Hingle. **1996**

LARKS ON A STRING ★★★1/2 Love blooms for a young couple in a reeducation camp, and their fellow detainees decide to give them a wedding and honeymoon under the noses of the camp authorities. This high-spirited comedy was banned by Soviet authorities until Glasnost. In Czech with English subtitles. Not rated. B&W; 96m. **DIR:** Jiri Menzel. **CAST:** Vera Kresadlova, Vaclav Neckar. **1969**

LAS VEGAS HILLBILLYS 💔 Hillbilly Ferlin Husky inherits a failing Las Vegas bar and makes it a success by turning it into Vegas's only country-and-western nightclub. The 1967 sequel *Hillbillys in a Haunted House*, is equally dismal. 90m. **DIR:** Arthur C. Pierce. **CAST:** Ferlin Husky, Jayne Mansfield, Mamie Van Doren, Sonny James, Richard Kiel. **1966 DVD**

LAS VEGAS LADY 💔 Lame plot about a big money heist. 87m. **DIR:** Noel Nosseck. **CAST:** Stella Stevens, Stuart Whitman, George DiCenzo, Lynne Moody, Linda Scruggs. **1976**

LAS VEGAS STORY, THE 💔 Las Vegas loser. B&W; 88m. **DIR:** Robert Stevenson. **CAST:** Jane Russell, Victor Mature, Vincent Price, Hoagy Carmichael, Jay C. Flippen, Brad Dexter. **1952**

LAS VEGAS WEEKEND ★★ After getting kicked out of college, a nerdy computer whiz decides to take his foolproof blackjack system to Las Vegas. Mild comedy could have been funnier. Rated R for brief nudity.

82m. **DIR:** Dale Trevillion. **CAST:** Barry Hickey, Ray Dennis Steckler. **1985**

LASER MAN, THE ★★★ A funny and inventive melting-pot comedy about a Chinese-American laser researcher living in Manhattan. However, the comedy is tempered by an incongruously serious subplot about arms dealers and the morality of scientific research. Not a total success, but worth seeing. 93m. **DIR:** Peter Wang. **CAST:** Marc Hayashi, Maryann Urbano, Tony Leung Chiu-Wai, Peter Wang, Sally Yeh. **1988**

LASER MISSION ★★ The largest and most precious diamond in the world has been stolen. Ernest Borgnine is a professor with the know-how to turn that power into a destructive laser. Enter Bruce Lee's son Brandon, who saves the world from total destruction without once breaking into sweat. Rated R for violence. 90m. **DIR:** Beau Davis. **CAST:** Brandon Lee, Ernest Borgnine. **1990 DVD**

LASER MOON ★★ Former porn star Traci Lords gets down and dirty again as an undercover policewoman using herself as bait to trap a killer. Of note, the killer uses a laser on his victims, and then indulges his fantasies. Not rated, contains nudity, violence, and adult language. 90m. **DIR:** Douglas K. Grimm. **CAST:** Traci Lords, Crystal Shaw, Harrison Leduke, Bruce Carter. **1992 DVD**

LASERBLAST ★★ Dreadful low-budget film with some excellent special effects by David Allen. Story concerns a young man who accidentally lays his hands on an alien ray gun. Rated PG. 90m. **DIR:** Michael Raye. **CAST:** Kim Milford, Cheryl Smith, Roddy McDowall, Keenan Wynn. **1978 DVD**

LASSIE ★★★1/2 Solid family entertainment has the cuddly collie coming to the aid of a disaffected teen dismayed by his family's move from the city to the country. Soon, our young hero learns something about old-fashioned values as he helps his folks stand up to an unscrupulous rival in the sheepranching business. It's just what you'd expect from a Lassie movie—no more, no less. Rated PG for light violence. 92m. **DIR:** Daniel Petrie. **CAST:** Tom Guiry, Helen Slater, Jon Tenney, Brittany Boyd, Frederic Forrest, Richard Farnsworth, Michelle Williams. **1994**

LASSIE COME HOME ★★★★ Heart-tugging story of a boy forced to give up the pet he loves is family drama at its best. An impeccable cast, beautiful photography, and intelligent scripting of Eric Knight's timeless novel highlight this wonderful tale of unsurmountable obstacles overcome by kindness and fidelity. 88m. **DIR:** Fred M. Wilcox. **CAST:** Roddy McDowall, Donald Crisp, Elizabeth Taylor, Nigel Bruce, Elsa Lanchester, May Whitty, Edmund Gwenn. **1943**

LASSITER ★★★ Tom Selleck stars as yet another jewel thief in the 1930s who attempts to steal a cache of uncut diamonds from the Nazis. Good-but-not-great entertainment. Rated R for nudity, suggested sex, violence, and profanity. 100m. **DIR:** Roger Young. **CAST:** Tom Selleck, Jane Seymour, Lauren Hutton, Bob Hoskins. **1984**

LAST ACTION HERO, THE ★★1/2 An 11-year-old movie buff gets a magic ticket and finds himself thrust into the big-screen adventures of his hero, Jack Slater. Although not a total turkey, this bloated movie-within-a-movie has some serious flaws. The last half is plagued by lapses in logic and sappy sentimentality. Rated PG-13 for violence and brief profanity. 130m. **DIR:** John McTiernan. **CAST:** Arnold Schwarzenegger, F. Murray Abraham, Art Carney, Charles Dance, Frank McRae, Tom Noonan, Robert Prosky, Anthony Quinn, Mercedes Ruehl, Joan Plowright, Austin O'Brien. **1993 DVD**

LAST AMERICAN HERO, THE ★★★★ An entertaining action film about the famous whiskey runner from North Carolina who becomes a legend when he proves himself a great stock-car driver. Jeff Bridges's portrait of the rebel Junior Jackson is engaging, but Art Lund steals the show as Johnson's bootlegger father. Rated PG for profanity and sex. 95m. **DIR:** Lamont Johnson. **CAST:** Jeff Bridges, Valerie Perrine, Geraldine Fitzgerald, Ned Beatty, Gary Busey, Art Lund, Ed Lauter, William Smith. **1973**

LAST ANGRY MAN, THE ★★★1/2 Paul Muni, one of Hollywood's most respected actors, gave his final screen performance in this well-made version of Gerald Greene's novel about an aging family doctor in Brooklyn. The sentiment gets a little thick occasionally, but Muni's performance keeps it all watchable. Look for Godfrey Cambridge in a small role. Not rated, but suitable for the whole family. B&W; 100m. **DIR:** Daniel Mann. **CAST:** Paul Muni, David Wayne, Betsy Palmer, Luther Adler, Joby Baker. **1959**

LAST ASSASSINS ★★ How many times are they going to make this movie? Nancy Allen stars as an ex-CIA agent who is lured back into the business for one more mission with her old commander. Of course, he's a bad guy who is blackmailing her, so she steals his top-secret plans. Then he kidnaps her daughter, and . . . . The plot elements might be tweaked a little, but it's all too familiar. Rated R for violence and language. 90m. **DIR:** William H. Molina. **CAST:** Nancy Allen, Lance Henriksen, Scott Lincoln, Dean Scofield, Floyd Red Crow Westerman. **1996 DVD**

LAST BEST YEAR, THE ★★★★ Mary Tyler Moore and Bernadette Peters are excellent in this heartbreaking story. Peters plays Jane Murray, a woman who only has six months left to live. Mary Tyler Moore plays Wendy Haller, a psychologist who reaches out to Jane. Together they find strength in each other, and a reason to live. This made-for-television weeper is a cut above the rest. Rated PG for adult content. 88m. **DIR:** John Erman. **CAST:** Mary Tyler Moore, Bernadette Peters, Carmen Mathews, Kate Reid, Kenneth Welsh, Dorothy McGuire. **1990**

LAST BOY SCOUT, THE ★★★★ A private detective must team up with an ex-football star to catch the killer of a topless dancer. Bruce Willis bounced back nicely from the *Hudson Hawk* debacle with this rip-roaring action movie in the style of the *Die Hard* films. Rated R for violence, profanity, nudity, and suggested sex. 105m. **DIR:** Tony Scott. **CAST:** Bruce Willis, Damon Wayans, Chelsea Field, Noble Willingham, Taylor Negron, Bruce McGill. **1991 DVD**

LAST BREATH ★★★ Creepy thriller about a devoted husband who will do anything to save the life of his wife. When his wife is struck down by a debilitating lung disease, Martin Devoe (Luke Perry) does what every conscientious husband would do: he begins dating. The only hitch is he plans to use his new girlfriend as a donor for his wife. And they say secondhand smoke kills. Rated R for adult situations, language, and violence. 90m. DIR: P.J. Posner. CAST: Luke Perry, Gia Carides, David Margulies, Francie Swift. 1996 DVD

•LAST BROADCAST, THE ★★★ Four men travel into the New Jersey Pine Barrens in an attempt to video the fabled Jersey Devil. Everything goes wrong, and only one of them escapes with his life. A year later, a documentary filmmaker tries to piece together the events of that fateful night to decide once and for all whether the lone survivor or something else was behind the vicious slayings. It is rumored that this movie inspired *The Blair Witch Project.* Rated R for violence and language. 87m. DIR: Stefan Avalos, Lance Weiler. CAST: David Beard, Jim Seward, Rein Clabbers, Michele Pulaski. 1997 DVD

LAST BUTTERFLY, THE ★★★★ Haunting drama is about an actor and mime forced by the Germans to perform in Terezin, a model city, as a facade to show the world how well the Nazis are treating the imprisoned Jews. When he finds out that the children in his show are destined for the gas chambers, he decides to give the Nazis a show they won't forget. Not rated; contains violence. 106m. DIR: Karel Kachyna. CAST: Tom Courtenay, Brigitte Fossey, Freddie Jones, Linda Jablonska. 1994

LAST CALL ★★ William Katt has a business deal go sour, so he and Shannon Tweed pair up for a little sex and vengeance in this confusing drama about greed. Too much sex and not enough plot. Not rated; contains violence and profanity. 90m. DIR: Jag Mundhra. CAST: William Katt, Shannon Tweed, Joseph Campanella, Stella Stevens. 1990

LAST CALL AT MAUD'S ★★★ Informative, sentimental documentary covering the closing of the famous San Francisco lesbian bar is actually a funny, sad history of lesbianism over the last fifty years. Utilizing nostalgic newsreels, newspaper clippings, and documentary footage, this fond farewell remains a positive statement despite its sad subject. Not rated; contains mature themes. 77m. DIR: Paris Poirer. 1993

LAST CHASE, THE ★★1/2 Made at the end of the OPEC oil crisis, this film assumes the crisis only got worse until there was a civil war in America and the eastern states banned all cars and planes. Lee Majors plays an aged race-car driver who flees New York to California with a runaway (Chris Makepeace). Confusing at times, and the Orwellian touches have been done so often that all the scare has left them. Not rated. 106m. DIR: Martyn Burke. CAST: Lee Majors, Chris Makepeace, Burgess Meredith. 1980

LAST COMMAND, THE (1928) ★★★★ German star Emil Jannings's second U.S. film has him portraying a czarist army commander who flees the Russian Revolution to America. Here, he sinks into poverty and winds up as a Hollywood extra. Art imitates life when he is cast to play a Russian general in a film directed by a former revolutionary (and former rival in love). William Powell plays the director, a stiff, unbending sadist bent upon humiliating Jannings. Silent. B&W; 80m. DIR: Josef von Sternberg.

CAST: Emil Jannings, William Powell, Evelyn Brent. 1928

LAST COMMAND, THE (1955) ★★1/2 This is a watchable Western about the famed last stand at the Alamo during Texas's fight for independence from Mexico. Jim Bowie (Sterling Hayden), Davy Crockett (Arthur Hunnicutt), and Colonel Travis (Richard Carlson) are portrayed in a more realistic manner than they were in John Wayne's *The Alamo*, but the story is still mostly hokum. 110m. DIR: Frank Lloyd. CAST: Sterling Hayden, Richard Carlson, Anna Maria Alberghetti, Ernest Borgnine, Arthur Hunnicutt, Jim Davis, J. Carrol Naish. 1955

LAST CONTRACT, THE ★★ In this violent film, Jack Palance stars as an artist and a hit man who is hired to kill his best friend. Unable to do it, he is ordered to assassinate a rival crime lord. When he kills the wrong man, the deadly game of hit and counterhit gets out of hand. Rated R. 85m. DIR: Allan A. Buckhantz. CAST: Jack Palance, Rod Steiger, Bo Svenson, Richard Roundtree, Ann Turkel. 1986

LAST DANCE (1991) 💔 Silly slasher film features sexy dancers being murdered one by one. Insipid. Not rated, contains nudity, violence, and profanity. 86m. DIR: Anthony Markes. CAST: Cynthia Bassinet, Elaine Hendrix, Kurt T. Williams. 1991

LAST DANCE (1996) ★★1/2 Sharon Stone plays a death-row inmate awaiting execution; Rob Morrow is the attorney who tries to get her sentence commuted to life in prison. Stone tears into her showy role with hardboiled relish, but the script plays more like a catalogue of prison-movie clichés than a genuine statement on capital punishment. Well-directed by Bruce Beresford, but Morrow's bland, pedestrian performance is, like the script, a major liability. Rated R for profanity and brief violence. 107m. DIR: Bruce Beresford. CAST: Sharon Stone, Rob Morrow, Peter Gallagher, Randy Quaid, Jack Thompson. 1996

LAST DAYS, THE ★★★★1/2 Five survivors of the Holocaust—a grandmother, teacher, businessman, artist, and congressman from California—vividly recount and reflect on the roundup and massacre of Hungarian Jews in 1944. This powerful, Oscar-winning documentary ties individual human faces, intimate testimony, and archival footage to the horrors of genocide and makes a lucid case that pure evil does exist on Earth. Not rated. 88m. DIR: James Moll. 1998 DVD

LAST DAYS OF CHEZ NOUS, THE ★★★★ Quirky, European-style comedy-drama from Australian director Gillian Armstrong focuses on a writer and her relationships with a French-born husband, troubled sister, and crochety father. Armstrong's low-key, believable and touching handling of the subject matter is what makes *The Last Days of Chez Nous* such a treasure. Not rated, the film has profanity and brief nudity. 96m. DIR: Gillian Armstrong. CAST: Lisa Harrow, Bruno Ganz, Kerry Fox, Miranda Otto, Kiri Paramore, Bill Hunter. 1993

LAST DAYS OF DISCO, THE ★★★1/2 It's the early 1980s. Shy Alice and bitchy Charlotte are editorial assistants who frequent Manhattan's disco scene. In this nostalgic comedy, they and several friends discuss feelings, philosophies, sex, and relationships with polished, deadpan sincerity. A subplot misfires, but this invasion of yesteryear's tribal stomping grounds is mostly fun. Rated R for sexual content, nudity, and drug use. 113m. **DIR:** Whit Stillman. **CAST:** Chloe Sevigny, Kate Beckinsale, Christopher Eigeman, Matt Keeslar, Matt Keeslar, Robert Sean Leonard, Matthew Ross, Mackenzie Astin, Tara Subkoff. 1998 DVD

LAST DAYS OF FRANK AND JESSE JAMES ★★★ Once you get past the country-western motif, this is an honorable biography of the notorious Wild West hoodlums. Kris Kristofferson and Johnny Cash are convincingly brotherly, and director William A. Graham adds just enough grittiness to make them a little less than heroic. 97m. **DIR:** William A. Graham. **CAST:** Kris Kristofferson, Johnny Cash, Willie Nelson. 1988

LAST DAYS OF FRANKIE THE FLY, THE ★★1/2 Yet another Quentin Tarantino clone, this violent gangster-comedy-thriller is worth seeing mostly for Dennis Hopper as a non-too-smart mob underling who embezzles his boss's money to finance a porn film. Rated R for profanity and violence. 96m. **DIR:** Peter Markle. **CAST:** Dennis Hopper, Kiefer Sutherland, Michael Madsen, Daryl Hannah, Dayton Callie. 1997

LAST DAYS OF MAN ON EARTH, THE ★★1/2 Kinetic adaptation of Michael Moorcock's weird little novel, *The Final Programme*, the first of his adventures featuring Jerry Cornelius. Jon Finch plays Jerry as a smart-assed James Bond, and the prize he fights for is a microfilm containing the secret to self-replicating beings ... highly useful in case of nuclear war. Finch encounters a variety of oddball characters, none stranger than Jenny Runacre, an enigmatic adversary who absorbs her lovers. Rated R for violence and sex. 73m. **DIR:** Robert Fuest. **CAST:** Jon Finch, Sterling Hayden, Patrick Magee, Jenny Runacre, Hugh Griffith. 1973

LAST DAYS OF PATTON, THE ★★★ A three-star adaptation of Ladislas Farago's book, which follows four-star General George S. Patton's 1945 peacetime career as commander of the Third Army, military governor of Bavaria, and finally as head of the Fifteenth Army. This made-for-TV sequel to George C. Scott's Oscar-winner lacks much of its predecessor's blood and guts. 146m. **DIR:** Delbert Mann. **CAST:** George C. Scott, Erika Hoffman, Eva Marie Saint, Richard Dysart, Murray Hamilton, Ed Lauter. 1985

LAST DAYS OF POMPEII, THE (1935) ★★★ Roman blacksmith Preston Foster becomes a gladiator after tragedy takes his wife and baby. En route to fortune, he adopts the young son of one of his victims. In Judea, he sees but refuses to help Christ, who cures the boy following serious injury. Touched by Jesus, the boy grows up to help runaway slaves. Tremendous special effects. B&W; 96m. **DIR:** Ernest B. Schoedsack. **CAST:** Preston Foster, Basil Rathbone, Alan Hale Sr., Louis Calhern. 1935

LAST DAYS OF POMPEII (1960) ★★ A different scenario than the 1935 original. Steve Reeves plays a hero in the Roman army stationed in Greece who tries to save a group of Christians that has been jailed and condemned to death. The story is interesting, but the action scenes are rather dumb. 93m. **DIR:** Mario Bonnard. **CAST:** Steve Reeves, Fernando Rey, Christine Kaufmann, Barbara Carroll, Angel Aranda. 1960

LAST DETAIL, THE ★★★★ Two veteran navy men (Jack Nicholson and Otis Young) are assigned to transport a young sailor to the brig for theft. They take pity on the naïve loser (Randy Quaid) and decide to show him one last good time. By opening the youngster's eyes to the previously unknown world around him, their kindness is in danger of backfiring in this drama. Rated R. 105m. **DIR:** Hal Ashby. **CAST:** Jack Nicholson, Otis Young, Randy Quaid, Michael Moriarty, Nancy Allen. 1973 DVD

LAST DON, THE ★★★1/2 Danny Aiello is excellent as the mob boss whose daughter ends up marrying the son of his rival, igniting a long-simmering vendetta. Video version of the miniseries, based on the Mario Puzo novel, is a leaner and meaner effort. Rated R for adult situations, language, nudity, and violence. 148m. **DIR:** Graeme Clifford. **CAST:** Danny Aiello, Joe Mantegna, Jason Gedrick, Daryl Hannah, Kirstie Alley, Penelope Ann Miller. 1997 DVD

LAST DRAGON, THE ★★1/2 Produced by Motown Records man Berry Gordy, this is lively, unpretentious nonsense about a shy karate champ (Taimak) fending off villains threatening a disc jockey (Vanity). Good, silly fun. Rated PG-13 for violence. 109m. **DIR:** Michael Schultz. **CAST:** Taimak, Vanity, Christopher Murney. 1985

LAST EMBRACE, THE ★★★1/2 A CIA agent must track down an obsessed, methodical killer. A complex, intelligent thriller in the Hitchcock style with skilled performances, a lush music score, and a cliff-hanging climax at Niagara Falls. Rated R for nudity and violence. 102m. **DIR:** Jonathan Demme. **CAST:** Roy Scheider, Janet Margolin, Sam Levene, Marcia Rodd, Christopher Walken, John Glover, Charles Napier. 1979

LAST EMPEROR, THE ★★★★★ An awe-inspiring epic that tells a heartrending, intimate story against a backdrop of spectacle and history. The screenplay by Mark Peploe and director Bernardo Bertolucci dramatizes the life of Pu Yi (John Lone), China's last emperor. When he was taken from his home at the age of 3 to become the all-powerful Qing Emperor, the youngster was ironically condemned to a lifetime of imprisonment. Rated PG-13 for violence, brief nudity, and frank sexuality. 160m. **DIR:** Bernardo Bertolucci. **CAST:** John Lone, Peter O'Toole, Joan Chen, Ying Ruocheng, Victor Wong, Dennis Dun. 1987 DVD

LAST EXIT TO BROOKLYN ★★★★ Uli Edel's film is a dark, unflinching drama about mislaid dreams, unfulfilled expectations, and gritty survival, set in the midst of waterfront labor unrest in the Brooklyn of the early Fifties. Adapted from the cult 1964 novel by Hubert Selby Jr. Rated R, with strong violence and profanity. 102m. **DIR:** Uli Edel. **CAST:** Stephen Lang, Jennifer Jason Leigh, Peter Dobson, Ricki Lake, Jerry Orbach. 1990

LAST EXIT TO EARTH ★★ The "Great Feminist Revolution" eventually leads to male sterility in this sci-fi cheapie from producer Roger Corman, which concerns a quartet of women from the year 2500 who travel back in time to abduct some male breeding stock. Plot and dialogue are trite, predictable, and poorly realized by a disinterested cast. Rated R for nudity, violence, and profanity. 90m. DIR: Katt Shea Ruben. CAST: Kim Greist, Costas Mandylor, Amy Hathaway, David Groh, Hilary Shephard. 1996

LAST FIVE DAYS, THE ★★★1/2 During the Nazi reign, a brother and sister are placed in jail to be questioned. The sister encounters Else, a prison clerk, who is awaiting her own trial. The viewer experiences the despair of the sister's last five days and her emotional encounter with Else and other anti-Hitler sympathizers. In German with English subtitles. Not rated, suitable for all audiences. 115m. DIR: Percy Adlon. CAST: Irm Hermann, Lena Stolze, Will Spindler, Hans Hirschmuller, Philip Arp, Joachim Bernhard. 1982

LAST FLIGHT OF NOAH'S ARK ★★★ This is the story of an unemployed pilot (Elliott Gould) who, against his better judgment, agrees to fly a plane full of farm animals to a Pacific island for a young missionary (Genevieve Bujold). This film, while not one of Disney's best, does offer clean, wholesome fun for the younger (and young-at-heart) audience. Rated G. 97m. DIR: Charles Jarrott. CAST: Elliott Gould, Genevieve Bujold, Rick Schroder, Vincent Gardenia. 1980 DVD

LAST FLIGHT TO HELL 💘 Mundane chase flick has hunky Reb Brown tracking down a group of terrorists who have kidnapped a South American drug lord. Why? 84m. DIR: Paul D. Robinson. CAST: Reb Brown, Chuck Connors. 1991

LAST FLING, THE ★★★ Cute made-for-TV movie about a philanderer (John Ritter) who finally finds his perfect match (Connie Sellecca) only to have her disappear. His attempts to find her are usually funny and often hilarious. 95m. DIR: Corey Allen. CAST: John Ritter, Connie Sellecca, Scott Bakula, Paul Sand, John Bennett Perry. 1986

LAST GAME, THE ★★ Maudlin tale of an attractive and responsible clean-cut college kid who works two jobs, goes to school, and takes care of his blind father while his father dreams that one day his boy will play pro football. This movie is just too banal for recommendation. No MPAA rating, but equal to a PG for sex and profanity. 107m. DIR: Martin Beck. CAST: Howard Segal, Ed L. Grady, Terry Alden, Joan Hotchkis. 1980 DVD

LAST GASP ★★ Deceitful contractor Robert Patrick murders a Mexican Indian interfering with a project, and is "rewarded" by a curse which turns him into a feral killer forced to slice up a new victim every twenty days. Only playa Joanna Pacula stands in his way, in this trite and predictable thriller. Rated R for violence, gore, nudity, simulated sex, and profanity. 90m. DIR: Scott McGinnis. CAST: Robert Patrick, Joanna Pacula, Vyto Ruginis, Mimi Craven. 1995

LAST GOOD TIME, THE ★★1/2 An elderly violinist (Armin Mueller-Stahl) strikes up an unusual friendship with a young woman (Olivia d'Abo) on the run from her abusive boyfriend. Low-key and muted, the film is reminiscent of Louis Malle's *Atlantic City* but

not nearly as good. Rated R for profanity and brief nudity. 89m. DIR: Bob Balaban. CAST: Armin Mueller-Stahl, Olivia D'Abo, Maureen Stapleton, Lionel Stander, Adrian Pasdar. 1995

LAST GUN, THE ★★ In this Italian Western dubbed into English, a gunfighter tired of killing hangs up his pistols and settles down in a small town. The story is classic. The acting and directing are not. 98m. DIR: Serge Bergone. CAST: Cameron Mitchell, Frank Wolff, Carl Mohner. 1964

LAST HIT, THE ★★★ A government assassin wants to retire, but is told he must first kill one more person. He falls in love with the woman he purchased his house from, and then realizes his target is her father. A few good twists and good acting will keep you watching. Not rated, made for cable, but contains violence. 95m. DIR: Jan Egleson. CAST: Bryan Brown, Brooke Adams, Daniel Von Bargen, Sally Kemp, Rider Strong, Harris Yulin. 1993

LAST HOLIDAY ★★★★ Alec Guinness is magnificent as a failed salesman told he has only months to live. He plans to quietly live out his time at a resort hotel, but becomes an important influence on the guests and staff. Bittersweet, witty story by J. B. Priestley. B&W; 88m. DIR: Henry Cass. CAST: Alec Guinness, Beatrice Campbell, Kay Walsh, Bernard Lee, Wilfrid Hyde-White. 1950

LAST HORROR FILM, THE 💘 Mama's boy obsessed with a horror-movie actress goes on a killing spree at the Cannes Film Festival. Rated R for violence. 87m. DIR: David Winters. CAST: Caroline Munro, Joe Spinell. 1984

LAST HOUR, THE ★★ A cop tries to rescue his ex-wife from mobsters. Low-budget rip-off of *Die Hard.* Rated R for violence, profanity, nudity, and simulated sex. 85m. DIR: William Sachs. CAST: Michael Paré, Shannon Tweed, Bobby DiCicco. 1991

LAST HOUSE ON THE LEFT 💘 Two teenage girls are tortured and killed by a sadistic trio. Graphic torture and humiliation scenes rate this one an R at best. 91m. DIR: Wes Craven. CAST: David Hess, Lucy Grantham, Sandra Cassel. 1973

LAST HUNT, THE ★★1/2 A downer disguised as an upper. This outdoor drama has more talk than action, as buffalo try to escape from crafty white men. Stewart Granger makes a weak hero, but Robert Taylor is pretty good as the villain. 108m. DIR: Richard Brooks. CAST: Robert Taylor, Stewart Granger, Constance Ford, Debra Paget, Lloyd Nolan, Joe De Santis, Russ Tamblyn. 1955

LAST HURRAH, THE ★★★★ Spencer Tracy gives a memorable performance as an Irish-Catholic mayor running for office one last time. Jeffrey Hunter is Tracy's nephew, a cynical reporter who comes to respect the old man's values and integrity. B&W; 111m. DIR: John Ford. CAST: Spencer Tracy, Jeffrey Hunter, Dianne Foster, Pat O'Brien, Basil Rathbone, Donald Crisp, James Gleason, Edward Brophy, John Carradine, Wallace Ford, Frank McHugh, Jane Darwell. 1958 DVD

LAST INNOCENT MAN, THE ★★★★ When a talented young district attorney meets a mysterious and beautiful woman in a bar, their ensuing affair entangles him in a web of deceit. This suspenseful courtroom drama provides a number of intriguing plot twists and makes for a delicious combination of action and suspense. Produced by Home Box Office; has brief nudity and sexual situations. 114m. **DIR:** Roger Spottiswoode. **CAST:** Ed Harris, Roxanne Hart, David Suchet, Bruce McGill. 1982

LAST LAUGH, THE ★★★★ Historically recognized as the first film to exploit the moving camera, this silent classic tells the story of a lordly luxury hotel doorman who is abruptly and callously demoted to the menial status of a washroom attendant. Deprived of his job and uniform, his life slowly disintegrates. Emil Jannings gives a brilliant performance. B&W; 74m. **DIR:** F. W. Murnau. **CAST:** Emil Jannings. 1924

LAST LIGHT ★★★★★ A masterful character study from first-time director Kiefer Sutherland, who also stars as an unrepentant killer. While waiting on death row, he finds an unlikely friend in prison guard Forest Whitaker. Robert Eisele's script offers no apologies for the murderer's brutality but makes a case for treating even the most heinous individual with dignity. You'll be riveted from the first few shocking frames. Rated R for violence and profanity. 104m. **DIR:** Kiefer Sutherland. **CAST:** Forest Whitaker, Kiefer Sutherland, Amanda Plummer, Kathleen Quinlan, Lynne Moody, Clancy Brown. 1993

LAST MAN ON EARTH, THE ★★★1/2 In this nightmarish tale, a scientist (Vincent Price) is a bit late in developing a serum to stem the tide of a plague epidemic. He becomes the last man on Earth and lives in fear of the walking dead, who crave his blood. This paranoid horror film (based on Richard Matheson's *I Am Legend*) is more chilling than its higher-budget remake, *The Omega Man.* B&W; 86m. **DIR:** Sidney Salkow. **CAST:** Vincent Price, Franca Bettoia, Emma Danieli, Giacomo Rossi-Stuart. 1964

LAST MAN STANDING (1988) ★★★★ Surprisingly good prizefight film in which Vernon Wells plays a down-and-out boxer who attempts to find work outside the ring. The brutality of the fight game is well captured. Rated R for profanity and violence. 92m. **DIR:** Damien Lee. **CAST:** Vernon Wells, William Sanderson, Franco Columbu. 1988

LAST MAN STANDING (1994) ★★★ Smartly-directed action picture stars Jeff Wincott as a cop who risks it all to stop a group of dirty policemen who have worked out a look-the-other-way deal with a drug czar. Great action sequences and stunts are enhanced by a better-than-average screenplay and performances. Rated R for violence, profanity, nudity, and sexual situations. 95m. **DIR:** Joseph Merhi. **CAST:** Jeff Wincott, Jillian McWhirter, Steve Eastin, Jonathan Fuller, Jonathan Banks. 1994

LAST MAN STANDING (1996) ★★★★ Dashiell Hammett's *Red Harvest* comes full circle, from feudal Japan (in Akira Kurosawa's *Yojimbo*) and the Old West (in Sergo Leone's *A Fistful of Dollars*) back to America in the 1920s. Bruce Willis pits two rival gangs against each other to break their reign of terror in a small town. Walter Hill's fans will love it, but the impartial will not be impressed. Rated R for violence, profanity, and suggested sex. 100m. **DIR:** Walter Hill. **CAST:** Bruce Willis, Christopher Walken, Bruce Dern, Alexandra Powers, David Patrick Kelly, William Sanderson, Karina Lombard, R. D. Call. 1996 DVD

LAST MARRIED COUPLE IN AMERICA, THE ❤ Lamebrained little sex farce about one perfect couple's struggle to hold their own marriage together. Rated R for profanity and nudity. 103m. **DIR:** Gilbert Cates. **CAST:** Natalie Wood, George Segal, Arlene Golonka, Bob Dishy, Priscilla Barnes, Dom DeLuise, Valerie Harper. 1980

LAST METRO, THE ★★★1/2 Catherine Deneuve and Gérard Depardieu star in this drama about a Parisian theatrical company that believes "the show must go on" despite the restrictions and terrors of the Nazis during their World War II occupation of France. This film has several nice moments and surprises that make up for its occasional dull spots and extended running time. Rated PG. 133m. **DIR:** François Truffaut. **CAST:** Catherine Deneuve, Gérard Depardieu, Jean Poiret. 1980 DVD

LAST MILE, THE ★★★ No-win prison film (based on a stage play) is a claustrophobic foray into death row. This archetypal prison-break melodrama has a quiet dignity that elevates the dialogue between the inmates. Preston Foster as Killer Miles plays the toughest con in the block and the leader of the break attempt. B&W; 70m. **DIR:** Sam Bischoff. **CAST:** Preston Foster, Howard Phillips, George E. Stone, Paul Fix. 1932

LAST MOVIE, THE (CHINCHERO) ❤ Dennis Hopper's abysmal follow-up to *Easy Rider* wastes a talented cast in this incoherent story about a film crew after they pull out of a small Peruvian village. Rated R for nudity and profanity. 108m. **DIR:** Dennis Hopper. **CAST:** Dennis Hopper, Julie Adams, Peter Fonda, Kris Kristofferson, Sylvia Miles, John Phillip Law, Samuel Fuller, Dean Stockwell. 1971

●**LAST NIGHT** ★★★ At midnight the world will end and everyone seems to know it. What people decide to do with their last hours on Earth is up to them—some stories are funny, and others poignant. Rated R for sex, violence, and language. 96m. **DIR:** Don McKellar. **CAST:** Don McKellar, Sandra Oh, Callum Keith Rennie, Sarah Polley, David Cronenberg, Geneviève Bujold. 1998 DVD

LAST NIGHT AT THE ALAMO ★★★★ On the night before the demolition of a run-down Houston bar, the regulars gather to mourn its passing. The satire of Kim Henkel's script, which targets machismo, is balanced by a real affection for these losers who depend on beer and bull to face the world. Recommended. Not rated, the film features plentiful profanity. 82m. **DIR:** Eagle Pennell. **CAST:** Sonny Davis. 1983

LAST OF ENGLAND, THE ★★★★★ Painter-poet-filmmaker Derek Jarman has created a stunning visionary work that is a mysterious, well-crafted montage of image and sound, evoking a world of apocalyptic fury—filmed in Belfast and London. With a British strain of convulsive romanticism Jarman uses Super-8 lyricism, gay erotica, and old home movies to illustrate the fall of England. Not rated; contains nudity and violence. B&W/color; 87m. **DIR:** Derek Jarman. **CAST:** Tilda Swinton, Spencer Leigh. 1987

LAST OF HIS TRIBE, THE ★★★ Graham Greene contributes a moving and dignified interpretation of Ishi, the last free-living Yahi Indian who in 1911 was taken to San Francisco and placed under the care of Professor Albert Kroeber. Made for cable, with graphic surgical footage. Rated PG-13 for sexual frankness and explicit medical procedures. 90m. **DIR:** Harry Hook. **CAST:** Jon Voight, Graham Greene, David Ogden Stiers, Jack Blessing, Anne Archer. 1992

LAST OF MRS. CHENEY, THE ★★★ Jewel thieves in high society. This star-studded remake of Norma Shearer's 1929 hit version of Frederick Lonsdale's evergreen comedy falls a mite short, but is nonetheless worth watching. As always, Robert Montgomery and William Powell are urbanity in spades. Good show. B&W; 98m. **DIR:** Richard Boleslawski. **CAST:** Robert Montgomery, Joan Crawford, William Powell, Frank Morgan, Jessie Ralph, Benita Hume, Nigel Bruce. 1937

LAST OF MRS. LINCOLN, THE ★★★★ Julie Harris shines in her portrayal of Mary Todd Lincoln during the last seventeen years of her life. Bearing enormous debts accumulated during her stay in the White House and denied a pension by the Senate because of her Southern heritage, she eventually falls into penury and insanity. Michael Cristofer and Robby Benson play the two surviving Lincoln sons. Made for television. 117m. **DIR:** George Schaefer. **CAST:** Julie Harris, Michael Cristofer, Robby Benson, Patrick Duffy, Denver Pyle, Priscilla Morrill. 1984

LAST OF PHILIP BANTER, THE ★★1/2 Scott Paulin gives a stunning performance in this lurid psychodrama. He's a self-destructive alcoholic whose life degenerates into madness after the discovery of some mysterious manuscripts. Rated R; contains profanity and violence. 100m. **DIR:** Herve Hachuel. **CAST:** Scott Paulin, Irene Miracle, Gregg Henry, Kate Vernon, Tony Curtis. 1986

LAST OF SHEILA, THE ★★★★ A cleverly planned, very watchable whodunit. Because of some unusual camera angles and subtle dialogue, the audience is drawn into active participation in the mystery. A sundry collection of Hollywood types are invited on a yachting cruise by James Coburn. It seems one of them has been involved in the death of Coburn's wife. Rated PG. 120m. **DIR:** Herbert Ross. **CAST:** James Coburn, Dyan Cannon, James Mason, Raquel Welch, Richard Benjamin. 1973

LAST OF THE COMANCHES ★★ Tough cavalry sergeant has to lead a stagecoach load of passengers to safety across the desert following an Indian raid. Broderick Crawford was woefully miscast in the handful of Westerns he did. B&W; 85m. **DIR:** André de Toth. **CAST:** Broderick Crawford, Barbara Hale, Lloyd Bridges. 1953

LAST OF THE DOGMEN ★★★1/2 Modern-day outlaw tracker Tom Berenger goes after three fugitives in the wilds of Montana only to find himself confronting ghostly warriors from the past. Director Tab Murphy builds suspense nicely in the first third of the film; so much so that the eventual revelation is something of a disappointment. But things pick up again, and the result is an old-fashioned piece of entertainment that will please those who worry that "they don't make 'em like they used to." Rated PG. 117m. **DIR:** Tab Murphy. **CAST:** Tom Berenger, Barbara Hershey, Kurtwood Smith, Steve Reevis, Andrew Miller. 1995 DVD

LAST OF THE FINEST, THE ★★ Four Los Angeles undercover cops (led by burly Brian Dennehy) are temporarily suspended. When one member of this elite squad gets murdered, the other three seek revenge. This standard shoot-'em-up is rated R for language and violence. 106m. **DIR:** John Mackenzie. **CAST:** Brian Dennehy, Joe Pantoliano, Jeff Fahey, Bill Paxton, Michael C. Gwynne, Henry Darrow. 1990

LAST OF THE MOHICANS, THE (1920) ★★★1/2 The most faithful version of James Fenimore Cooper's story with some surprisingly strong dramatic moments. Almost none of this was shot in a studio, and the location filming is still impressive, now that the film has been restored by the Eastman House. Silent. B&W; 72m. **DIR:** Clarence Brown, Maurice Tourneur. **CAST:** Wallace Beery, Barbara Bedford, Albert Roscoe. 1920

LAST OF THE MOHICANS, THE (1936) ★★★★ Blood, thunder, and interracial romance during the French and Indian War are brought to life from James Fenimore Cooper's novel. Randolph Scott is the intrepid Hawkeye; Robert Barrat is the noble Chingachgook; Binnie Barnes is Alice Monroe. The star-crossed lovers are Phillip Reed, as Uncas, the title character, and Heather Angel, as Cora Monroe. B&W; 100m. **DIR:** George B. Seitz. **CAST:** Randolph Scott, Binnie Barnes, Heather Angel, Robert Barrat, Phillip Reed, Henry Wilcoxon, Bruce Cabot. 1936

LAST OF THE MOHICANS (1985) ★★1/2 In this TV film based on James Fenimore Cooper's classic, a small party headed for a fort is deserted by their guide and must turn to Hawkeye and Chingachgook to bring them to safety. When two of the party are captured, our heroes must rescue them and battle the leader of the Indians. 97m. **DIR:** James L. Conway. **CAST:** Steve Forrest, Ned Romero, Andrew Prine, Robert Tessier. 1985

LAST OF THE MOHICANS, THE (1992) ★★★★★ A classy romance angle and director Michael Mann's sweeping vision highlight this retelling of James Fenimore Cooper's novel of colonial America. A first-class production all the way, this historic tale never feels dated, and the action scenes are state-of-the-art. Rated R for violence. 120m. **DIR:** Michael Mann. **CAST:** Daniel Day-Lewis, Madeleine Stowe, Russell Means, Eric Schweig, Jodhi May, Steven Waddington, Maurice Roeves, Wes Studi, Patrice Chereau. 1992 DVD

LAST OF THE PONY RIDERS ★★★1/2 Gene Autry's last feature film concerns the old West transition period from pony express to stagecoach and telegraph. Action-packed ending to Autry's twenty years of B-Western films. B&W; 59m. **DIR:** George Archainbaud. **CAST:** Gene Autry, Smiley Burnette, Dick Jones, Kathleen Case. 1953

LAST OF THE RED HOT LOVERS 🐢 A married man uses his mother's apartment for amorous dalliances. Rated PG. 98m. **DIR:** Gene Saks. **CAST:** Alan Arkin, Paula Prentiss, Sally Kellerman. 1972

LAST OF THE REDMEN ★★★ Low-budget remake of James Fenimore Cooper's immortal *Last of the Mohicans* story with Michael O'Shea sorely miscast as an Irish Hawkeye. The French-Indian wars rage in gorgeous Cinecolor as Hawkeye and Rick Vallin as Uncas, the last of the Mohicans, brave danger to rescue two sisters from warring Iroquois Indians. 79m. **DIR:** George Sherman. **CAST:** Jon Hall, Michael O'Shea, Buster Crabbe, Evelyn Ankers, Julie Bishop, Rick Vallin. 1947

LAST OF THE WARRIORS 💙 Ridiculous futuristic dud is a mishmash of leather-clad bad guys, cult religious leaders, and near-normal rebels. A real time waster. Not rated; contains violence, nudity, and profanity. 98m. **DIR:** Lloyd A. Simandl, Michael Mazo. **CAST:** Melanie Kilgour, William Smith, Ken Farmer. 1989

LAST OUTLAW, THE (1936) ★★★½ Possibly Harry Carey's best film as a star, this is a delightful remake of a John Ford story of the silent era. Carey is a former outlaw released from prison, only to find that the West he knew is gone. Hoot Gibson is Carey's old saddle pal, and they soon take on a group of modern-day outlaws. B&W; 62m. **DIR:** Christy Cabanne. **CAST:** Harry Carey, Hoot Gibson, Henry B. Walthall, Tom Tyler. 1936

LAST OUTLAW, THE (1993) ★★½ After a prologue stolen from *The Wild Bunch*, this laughably macho revenge saga becomes an exercise in sadistic gore ... no surprise, considering the involvement of scripter Eric Red (*The Hitcher*). Betrayed by his own gang, outlaw Mickey Rourke joins the posse hunting his former associates ... just so he can kill them, one by one. Rated R for profanity and extreme violence. 90m. **DIR:** Geoff Murphy. **CAST:** Mickey Rourke, Dermot Mulroney, Ted Levine, John C. McGinley. 1993

LAST PARTY, THE ★★★½ Robert Downey Jr. is the host of this satiric, in-your-face documentary chronicling the 1992 presidential race. Downey finds plenty to poke fun at and recruits some famous names and faces to help him try to find meaning at the Democratic and Republican National Conventions. You know the participants in this celluloid mirror are politicians because they keep making donkeys out of themselves. Not rated; contains strong language. 96m. **DIR:** Martin Benjamin, Marc Levin. 1993

LAST PICTURE SHOW, THE ★★★★★ Outstanding adaptation of Larry McMurtry's novel about a boy's rites of passage in a small Texas town during the 1950s. Virtually all the performances are excellent due to the deft direction of Peter Bogdanovich, who assured his fame with this picture. Ben Johnson, as a pool-hall owner, and Cloris Leachman, as a lonely wife, deservedly won Oscars for their supporting performances. Rated R for brief nudity and adult situations. B&W; 118m. **DIR:** Peter Bogdanovich. **CAST:** Timothy Bottoms, Ben Johnson, Jeff Bridges, Cloris Leachman, Cybill Shepherd, Randy Quaid, Eileen Brennan. 1971 DVD

LAST PLANE OUT 💙 Poor rip-off of *Under Fire*. 98m. **DIR:** David Nelson. **CAST:** Jan-Michael Vincent, Lloyd Batista, Julie Carmen. 1983

LAST POLKA, THE ★★★★ This made-for-HBO special features the unique Second City comedy of Yosh (John Candy) and Stan (Eugene Levy) Schmenge, a delightful pair of polka bandleaders, as they reminisce about their checkered musical careers. Fellow *SCTV* troupe members Catherine O'Hara and Rick Moranis add to this adept send-up of *The Last Waltz*, Martin Scorsese's documentary chronicling the final concert of real-life rock legends The Band. 60m. **DIR:** John Blanchard. **CAST:** John Candy, Eugene Levy, Catherine O'Hara, Rick Moranis. 1984

LAST PROSTITUTE, THE ★★★★ This heartwarming made-for-cable coming-of-age drama features two teenage boys seeking the services of an infamous prostitute. They're disappointed to find her retired from the business. Fine acting and directing make this an unforgettable gem. 93m. **DIR:** Lou Antonio. **CAST:** Sonia Braga, Wil Wheaton, Cotter Smith, David Kaufman. 1991

LAST REMAKE OF BEAU GESTE, THE 💙 Vapid foreign legion comedy. Rated PG—sexual situations. 84m. **DIR:** Marty Feldman. **CAST:** Marty Feldman, Michael York, Ann-Margret, Trevor Howard. 1977

LAST RESORT ★★½ Charles Grodin and family are off on vacation to Club Sand. Amid slapstick jokes and Grodin's exasperated yelling is an intermittently entertaining movie. Rated R for sex and language. 80m. **DIR:** Zane Buzby. **CAST:** Charles Grodin, Jon Lovitz, Robin Pearson Rose, Megan Mullally, John Ashton. 1985

LAST RIDE, THE (1991) ★★½ Recently paroled ex-convict innocently accepts a ride from a psychotic truck driver, only to have it turn into the ride of his life. Doesn't put the pedal to the metal, but grabs your interest. 84m. **DIR:** Karl Krogstad. **CAST:** Dan Ranger. 1991

LAST RIDE, THE (1994) ★★ Mickey Rourke is Frank T. Wells, outlaw rodeo rider, always living on the edge. Lori Singer is an unstable woman on the run from the law. When their worlds collide, there's an explosion of passion and bullets. Good cast is wasted in this weak action film. Rated R for violence, nudity, and language. 102m. **DIR:** Michael Karbelnikoff. **CAST:** Mickey Rourke, Lori Singer, Brion James, Rodney A. Grant, Peter Berg. 1994

LAST RIDE OF THE DALTON GANG, THE ★★½ When two former Dalton Gang train robbers are reunited in Hollywood in 1934, they relive the early days as they share a bottle of whiskey. 146m. **DIR:** Dan Curtis. **CAST:** Jack Palance, Larry Wilcox, Dale Robertson, Bo Hopkins, Cliff Potts. 1979

LAST RITES (1988) ★★ A young Italian priest (Tom Berenger) runs afoul of the Mafia when he grants sanctuary to a woman (Daphne Zuniga) who has witnessed a murder. Interesting but the story turns silly when priest and witness fall in love. Rated R for violence, nudity, and profanity. 103m. **DIR:** Donald P. Bellisario. **CAST:** Tom Berenger, Daphne Zuniga, Paul Dooley. 1988

•LAST RITES (1998) ★★ Randy Quaid is electrifying as a death-row prisoner whose electric chair experience leaves him a changed man. Once a mean-spirited killer, Jeremy Dillon undergoes a transformation when a power outage interrupts his execution, sending only a partial charge through his body. Now it's up to a psychiatrist to prove he's telling the truth. Interesting idea gets bogged down by flat script and supporting cast. Rated R for language and violence. 88m. DIR: Kevin Dowling. CAST: Randy Quaid, Embeth Davidtz, A Martinez. 1998

LAST ROUND-UP ★★★ Gene Autry's first for his own production company at Columbia Pictures is his personal favorite. Set in the modern West, Gene must relocate a tribe of Indians when their homeland is marked for an aqueduct project. B&W; 77m. DIR: John English. CAST: Gene Autry, Bobby Blake, Jean Heather, Ralph Morgan. 1947

LAST SAFARI ★★ Director Henry Hathaway's trademark machismo got the better of him in this dreary drama about an aging big-game hunter who escorts a young couple to Africa. 110m. DIR: Henry Hathaway. CAST: Stewart Granger, Kaz Garas. 1967

LAST SEASON, THE 🖤 A bunch of redneck hunters invades a peaceful forest. Not rated; contains nudity and violence. 90m. DIR: Raja Zahr. CAST: Christopher Gosch, Louise Dorsey, David Cox. 1987

LAST SEDUCTION, THE ★★★1/2 Though amoral and bereft of sympathetic characters, *The Last Seduction* is absorbing; credit the energetic performances, stylish direction, and mellow jazz soundtrack. Bored city gal Linda Fiorentino cons husband Bill Pullman a onetime drug sale, after which she flees (with the cash) into upstate New York … where she intrigues good ol' boy Peter Berg. Her hubbie, of course, follows her. Rated R for profanity, nudity, violence, and simulated sex. 110m. DIR: John Dahl. CAST: Linda Fiorentino, Peter Berg, Bill Pullman, J. T. Walsh, Bill Nunn. 1993

LAST STAND AT SABER RIVER ★★★★ Returning from the Civil War as a Confederate hero, Tom Selleck reunites with wife Suzy Amis, only to find that his youngest child is dead and that she wants to go home to Arizona, where Confederate soldiers are not considered heroes. But return they do—to fight for their land and their way of life. Adapted from the Elmore Leonard novel. Made for TV. 96m. DIR: Dick Lowry. CAST: Tom Selleck, Suzy Amis, David Carradine, Keith Carradine, Harry Carey Jr., Rex Linn, Patrick Kilpatrick. 1997

LAST STARFIGHTER, THE ★★★★ In this enjoyable comedy–science-fiction film, a young man (Lance Guest) beats a video game called the Starfighter and soon finds himself recruited by an alien (Robert Preston) to do battle in outer space. Thanks to its witty dialogue and hilarious situations, this hybrid is a viewing delight. Rated PG for violence and profanity. 100m. DIR: Nick Castle. CAST: Lance Guest, Robert Preston, Dan O'Herlihy, Catherine Mary Stewart, Barbara Bosson. 1984 DVD

•**LAST STOP** ★★★ Fairly entertaining thriller about a group of strangers, snowed in at a small greasy spoon, who discover there are bank robbers/murderers in their midst. But who is who? Rated R for profanity, violence, and sexuality. 94m. DIR: Mark Malone. CAST: Adam Beach, Jurgen Prochnow, Rose McGowan, Amy Adamson. 2000 DVD

LAST SUMMER ★★1/2 Engrossing tale of teen desires, frustrations, and fears, played out in disturbingly dark fashion. Bruce Davison and Cathy Burns are especially memorable in unusual roles. Rated R. 97m. DIR: Frank Perry. CAST: Richard Thomas, Barbara Hershey, Bruce Davison, Cathy Burns, Ralph Waite, Conrad Bain. 1969

LAST SUMMER IN THE HAMPTONS ★★★★ As an extended family of theater professionals prepare a stage performance for an invitation-only audience, their own lives become kindred spirits to the work of playwright Anton Chekhov and filmmaker Jean Renoir. This ensemble piece bites rapturously into the dynamics of blood relations as well as art. Not rated. 105m. DIR: Henry Jaglom. CAST: Victoria Foyt, Viveca Lindfors, Jon Robin Baitz, Melissa Leo, Martha Plimpton, Nick Gregory, Andre Gregory, Holland Taylor. 1995

LAST SUPPER, THE (1976) ★★★ Uncompromising drama based on an incident from eighteenth-century Cuban history about a petit-bourgeois slaveholder who decides to improve his soul by instructing his slaves in the glories of Christianity. He invites twelve of them to participate in a reenactment of the Last Supper in hopes of instilling Christian ideals. In Spanish with English subtitles. Not rated; contains violence and nudity. 110m. DIR: Tomas Gutierrez Alea. CAST: Nelson Villagra. 1976

LAST SUPPER, THE (1996) ★★★ Marginally successful political satire in which a houseful of Iowa graduate students invites repulsive right-wing ideologues to dinner and poisons them. Inevitably, our politically-correct avengers succumb to infighting and paranoia. Director Stacy Title doesn't seem certain whether Dan Rosen's stagey scenario is a comedy, an ironic morality play, or an important social statement. Rated R. 94m. DIR: Stacy Title. CAST: Cameron Diaz, Annabeth Gish, Ron Eldard, Jonathan Penner, Courtney B. Vance, Ron Perlman. 1996

LAST TANGO IN PARIS ★★★ A middle-aged man (Marlon Brando) and a young French girl (Maria Schneider) have a doomed love affair. This pretentious sex melodrama is mainly notable for being banned when it first came out. Rated NC-17 for sex. 129m. DIR: Bernardo Bertolucci. CAST: Marlon Brando, Maria Schneider, Jean-Pierre Léaud. 1972 DVD

LAST TEMPTATION OF CHRIST, THE ★★★ This adaptation of Nikos Kazantzakis's controversial novel contains some unnecessary scenes of nudity and simulated sex. Nevertheless, what emerges is a heartfelt work that has some moments of true power—especially when the story's reluctant savior accepts his divine nature and performs miracles. Rated R for nudity and violence. 164m. DIR: Martin Scorsese. CAST: Willem Dafoe, Harvey Keitel, Barbara Hershey, Harry Dean Stanton, David Bowie, Verna Bloom, Andre Gregory. 1988 DVD

LAST TIME I COMMITTED SUICIDE, THE ★★★★ Life story of Beat-movement pioneer Neal Cassady is stylish and entertaining and features a standout performance by Keanu Reeves as one of Cassady's friends. Rated R for language. 93m. DIR: Stephen Kay. CAST: Thomas Jane, Keanu Reeves, Adrien Brody, Claire Forlani, Marg Helgenberger. 1996

LAST TIME I SAW PARIS, THE ★★★ The Metro-Goldwyn-Mayer glitter shows clearly in this dramatic account of post–World War II Paris. This Paris, though, is filled with divorce, domestic quarrels, and jaded lives. Donna Reed gives the best performance. 116m. **DIR:** Richard Brooks. **CAST:** Van Johnson, Elizabeth Taylor, Donna Reed, Walter Pidgeon, Eva Gabor. **1954 DVD**

LAST TRAIN FROM GUN HILL ★★★1/2 In this hybrid suspense-Western, a marshal (Kirk Douglas) is searching for the man who raped and murdered his wife. When the culprit (Earl Holliman) turns out to be the son of a wealthy rancher (Anthony Quinn), our hero holes up in a hotel room and takes on all comers until the next train arrives. A minor classic. 94m. **DIR:** John Sturges. **CAST:** Kirk Douglas, Anthony Quinn, Carolyn Jones, Earl Holliman, Brad Dexter. **1959**

LAST TRAIN HOME ★★★ When a Canadian family is broken up by its father's participation in a barroom brawl, the teenage son treks cross-country seeking his fleeing dad. The family dog, an adorable Benji look-alike, steals every scene. Made for the Family Channel. 92m. **DIR:** Randy Bradshaw. **CAST:** Noam Zylberman, Ron White, Nick Mancuso, Ned Beatty. **1990**

LAST TYCOON, THE ★★★ Tantalizing yet frustrating, this slow-moving attempt to film F. Scott Fitzgerald's last (and unfinished) book is a conglomeration of talent at all levels, but appears as a confusing collection of scenes and confrontations. Robert De Niro plays Monroe Starr, the sickly motion picture magnate and the "last tycoon." 125m. **DIR:** Elia Kazan. **CAST:** Robert De Niro, Robert Mitchum, Tony Curtis, Jeanne Moreau, Jack Nicholson, Donald Pleasence, Peter Strauss, Ray Milland, Ingrid Boulting, Dana Andrews, John Carradine. **1976**

LAST UNICORN, THE ★★★1/2 Well-written and nicely animated feature about a magical unicorn who goes on a quest to find the rest of her kind. Strong characters and a sprightly pace make this a gem, which features the voices of Alan Arkin, Jeff Bridges, Mia Farrow, Tammy Grimes, Robert Klein, Angela Lansbury, Christopher Lee, and Keenan Wynn. It's a class act. Rated G. 85m. **DIR:** Arthur Rankin Jr., Jules Bass. **1982**

LAST VALLEY, THE ★★★ Impressive and thought-provoking adventure epic about a warrior (Michael Caine) who brings his soldiers to a peaceful valley that, in the seventeenth century, has remained untouched by the Thirty Years War. Rated R. 128m. **DIR:** James Clavell. **CAST:** Michael Caine, Omar Sharif. **1971 DVD**

LAST VOYAGE, THE ★★★★ Director Andrew L. Stone has taken a fairly suspenseful disaster-at-sea tale, making it a completely absorbing and fascinating movie. Filmed aboard the famous luxury liner, *Ile de France*, before it was scrapped. 91m. **DIR:** Andrew L. Stone. **CAST:** Robert Stack, Dorothy Malone, George Sanders, Edmond O'Brien, Woody Strode. **1960**

LAST WALTZ, THE ★★★★ Director Martin Scorsese's (*Taxi Driver*) superb film of The Band's final concert appearance is an unforgettable celebration of American music. Rated PG. 117m. **DIR:** Martin Scorsese. **CAST:** The Band, Bob Dylan, Neil Young, Joni Mitchell, Van Morrison, Eric Clapton, Neil Diamond, Muddy Waters. **1978**

•**LAST WARNING, THE** ★★★1/2 A mysterious caped and masked murderer terrorizes a Broadway theater's cast and crew in this stylish thriller, which employs all sorts of gimmickry to good effect. Originally released with sound, this visually stimulating whodunit exists now only in its silent version and is considered must-see viewing among film historians and aficionados. Silent, with musical accompaniment. B&W; 78m. **DIR:** Paul Leni. **CAST:** Laura LaPlante, Montagu Love, John Boles, Roy D'Arcy, Bert Roach, Margaret Livingston, Mack Swain. **1929**

LAST WARRIOR, THE ★★★★ Two Marines, one American, the other Japanese, are left on an island in the closing days of World War II. What ensues is a tightly directed, action-packed fight to the death. Rated R for violence and brief nudity. 94m. **DIR:** Martin Wragge. **CAST:** Gary Graham. **1989**

LAST WAVE, THE ★★★1/2 In this suspenseful, fascinating film, Richard Chamberlain plays a lawyer defending a group of aborigines on trial for murder. His investigation into the incident leads to a frightening series of apocalyptic visions. Rated PG. 106m. **DIR:** Peter Weir. **CAST:** Richard Chamberlain, Olivia Hamnett. **1977**

LAST WAY OUT, THE ★★★★ Low-budget *film noir* hits the mark, because it's packed with all the necessary elements. Kurt Johnson is the former career criminal forced back into business by his old partners. Not rated; contains adult situations, language, and violence. B&W; 88m. **DIR:** Mark Steensland. **CAST:** Kurt Johnson, Kevin Reed, Katie Brown, John Lamb, David Pierini. **1996**

LAST WINTER, THE ❤ Kathleen Quinlan and Yona Elian are wives of Israeli soldiers missing in action during the Yom Kippur War of 1973. 92m. **DIR:** Riki Shelach. **CAST:** Kathleen Quinlan, Yona Elian, Stephen Macht. **1984**

LAST WORD, THE (1979) ★★★ When police try to evict him and his family from a run-down apartment building, inventor Danny Travis (Richard Harris) takes a police officer hostage. His goal is to get the attention of the newspapers so that he can expose the governor's crooked real estate racket and save his home. Likable comedy-drama in the Frank Capra mold. Rated PG. 105m. **DIR:** Roy Boulting. **CAST:** Richard Harris, Karen Black, Martin Landau, Dennis Christopher, Biff McGuire, Christopher Guest, Penelope Milford, Michael Pataki. **1979**

LAST WORD, THE (1995) ★★★ An investigative journalist falls in love with a stripper/hooker and then finds that the relationship impairs his ability to transform his underworld exposés into a coherent film script. Although acceptable, the film would have benefited by concentrating on central characters. Rated R for profanity, nudity, and simulated sex. 95m. **DIR:** Tony Spiridakis. **CAST:** Timothy Hutton, Joe Pantoliano, Michelle Burke, Richard Dreyfuss, Tony Goldwyn, Chazz Palminteri, Cybill Shepherd, Jimmy Smits. **1995 DVD**

LAST YEAR AT MARIENBAD ★★★ This film provides no middle ground—you either love it or you hate it. The confusing story is about a young man

(Giorgio Albertazzi) finding himself in a monstrous, baroque hotel trying to renew his love affair with a woman who seems to have forgotten that there is an affair to renew. The past, present, and future all seem to run parallel, cross over, and converge. In French with English subtitles. B&W; 93m. DIR: Alain Resnais. CAST: Delphine Seyrig, Giorgio Albertazzi, Sacha Pitoeff. 1962 DVD

LATCHO DROM ★★★★★ Generically referred to as "gypsies," the Rom people of Europe have been wanderers through their long history, often in reaction to efforts of different countries to destroy them. In this documentary, various members tell the history of their people in song. The music itself is richly satisfying, but the lyrics, which are subtitled in English, are what make the film so compelling. Not rated. 88m. DIR: Tony Gatlif. 1996

LATE CHRYSANTHEMUMS ★★★★★ With limited options available to them, four aging geisha try to plan for their futures. Beautifully acted, realistic but never melodramatic; a wonderful film from Mikio Naruse, an overlooked (outside of his own country) master of the Japanese cinema. In Japanese with English subtitles. B&W; 101m. DIR: Mikio Naruse. CAST: Haruko Sugimura. 1954

LATE FOR DINNER ★★★★ In what is sort of a cross between Back to the Future and Of Mice and Men, Brian Wimmer and Peter Berg drive from Santa Fe, New Mexico, to Pomona, California, in 1962 only to wake up twenty-nine years later in 1991 with no idea what happened. What begins as a wacky, offbeat romp becomes a profoundly moving story about loss and reconciliation. Rated PG for violence. 106m. DIR: W. D. Richter. CAST: Brian Wimmer, Peter Berg, Marcia Gay Harden, Colleen Flynn, Kyle Secor, Michael Beach, Peter Gallagher. 1991

LATE SHIFT, THE ★★★ This HBO "docu-comedy," based on Bill Carter's book, details the network war that erupted when NBC-TV finally replaced Johnny Carson as host of The Tonight Show. David Letterman wanted the job; Jay Leno wound up with it. This adaptation demonstrates the industry's callous venality and absence of loyalty, and captures Rich Little's dead-on Johnny Carson imitation. Rated R for profanity. 96m. DIR: Betty Thomas. CAST: Kathy Bates, John Michael Higgins, Daniel Roebuck, Bob Balaban, Ed Begley Jr., Peter Jurasik, Reni Santoni, Treat Williams, Rich Little. 1995

LATE SHOW, THE ★★★★1/2 Just prior to directing Kramer vs. Kramer, Robert Benton created this little gem. It stars Art Carney as an aging private eye out to avenge the death of his partner (Howard Duff) with the unwanted help of wacky Lily Tomlin. Loosely lifted from Sam Peckinpah's Ride the High Country and John Huston's The Maltese Falcon, this detective story is a bittersweet, sometimes tragic, takeoff on the genre. That it works so well is a credit to all involved. Rated PG. 94m. DIR: Robert Benton. CAST: Art Carney, Howard Duff, Lily Tomlin, Bill Macy, John Considine. 1977

LATE SPRING ★★★★★ Afraid that his grown daughter will become an old maid, a widower pretends that he wishes to remarry to persuade her to leave home. Yasujiro Ozu made a number of films

with a similar theme, but this is the best. In Japanese with English subtitles. 107m. DIR: Yasujiro Ozu. CAST: Setsuko Hara, Chishu Ryu. 1949

LATE SUMMER BLUES 🐾 Trite, contrived sentimentality, and the acting ability of dried flattened roadkill. In Hebrew with English subtitles. Not rated. 101m. DIR: Renen Schorr. CAST: Dor Zweigen Bom. 1987

LATIN LOVERS ★★ A movie with a few musical numbers, but not enough to make it move, this is one of Lana Turner's self-indulgent romances. She plays a woman looking for true love while touring South America and not able to find it anywhere. Not until she matches wits with Ricardo Montalban. Colorful settings, but colorless acting. 104m. DIR: Mervyn LeRoy. CAST: Lana Turner, Ricardo Montalban, John Lund, Louis Calhern, Rita Moreno, Jean Hagen, Beulah Bondi, Eduard Franz. 1953

LATINO ★★ Master cinematographer Haskell Wexler tries his hand at writing and directing in this story of a Chicago Green Beret who questions the activities required of him in the Nicaraguan war. This is a fairly routine war story, with the exception of the protagonist being a Latin American. 108m. DIR: Haskell Wexler. CAST: Robert Beltran, Annette Cardona, Tony Plana. 1985

LATITUDE ZERO ★★1/2 Jules Verne-style fantasy about a scientist (Joseph Cotten) who has built a research city on the bottom of the ocean. This Japanese movie would be better if only the special effects (bat-men, giant rats, and flying lion with a human brain) weren't so cheesy, though Cesar Romero makes a nicely hissable villain. Rated G. 99m. DIR: Inoshiro Honda. CAST: Joseph Cotten, Cesar Romero, Richard Jaeckel, Patricia Medina, Linda Haynes, Akira Takarada. 1969

LAUGH FOR JOY (PASSIONATE THIEF (1954)) ★★★ Delightful comedy of errors set on New Year's Eve. Anna Magnani plays a film extra who complicates things for a pickpocket (Ben Gazzara). Also released on videocassette under the title Passionate Thief, which is dubbed in English. In Italian with English subtitles. B&W; 106m. DIR: Mario Monicelli. CAST: Anna Magnani, Ben Gazzara, Toto, Fred Clark. 1954

LAUGHING HORSE 🐾 A stranded traveler in the desert becomes a driver for a strange couple. 60m. DIR: Michael Blake. CAST: John Coinman, Irene Miracle. 1986

LAUGHING POLICEMAN, THE ★★★1/2 Little-known police thriller that deserved far better than it got at the box office. Walter Matthau and Bruce Dern are a pair of cops seeking a mass murderer who preys on bus passengers. Taut drama, taken from the superb thriller by Maj Sjowall and Per Wahloo. Rated R for violence. 111m. DIR: Stuart Rosenberg. CAST: Walter Matthau, Bruce Dern, Lou Gossett Jr., Albert Paulsen, Cathy Lee Crosby, Anthony Zerbe. 1974

LAUGHING SINNERS ★★1/2 In the first of their eight screen teamings, Clark Gable is a Salvation Army officer who "saves" Joan Crawford after she has been seduced and abandoned by a fast-talking traveling salesman. B&W; 72m. DIR: Harry Beaumont. CAST: Joan Crawford, Clark Gable, Neil Hamilton, Marjorie Rambeau, Roscoe Karns, Guy Kibbee, Cliff Edwards. 1931

LAURA ★★★★★ A lovely socialite (Gene Tierney) is apparently murdered, and the police detective (Dana Andrews) assigned to the case is up to his neck in likely suspects. To compound matters, he has developed a strange attraction for the deceased woman through her portrait. So starts one of the most original mysteries ever to come from Hollywood. B&W; 88m. DIR: Otto Preminger. CAST: Gene Tierney, Dana Andrews, Vincent Price, Judith Anderson, Clifton Webb. 1944

LAUREL AND HARDY CLASSICS: VOL. 1–9 ★★★ Stan Laurel and Oliver Hardy demonstrate why most consider them one of the funniest comedy teams of the silver screen. This standout compilation of their shorts contains *Another Fine Mess*, *The Music Box*, *Hog Wild*, *The Fixer-Uppers*, *Night Owls*, *Any Old Port*, *Oliver the Eighth*. Silent. B&W; 70–108m. DIR: James Parrott, Charles R. Rogers, George Marshall, Lloyd French, James W. Horne, Lewis R. Foster. CAST: Stan Laurel, Oliver Hardy, Billy Gilbert, Charlie Hall, Stanley Sanford, Mae Busch, James Finlayson, Walter Long, Edgar Kennedy, Anita Garvin, Jean Harlow. 1930–1938

LAUREL AVENUE ★★★★ Compelling saga focuses on a close-knit family's struggle with changing values and increasing inner-city crime. Spanning three generations and an emotionally charged weekend, we're given a vivid—at times painful—glimpse into the struggles of each member. An HBO miniseries, with violence, profanity, drug use, and sexual situations. 160m. DIR: Carl Franklin. CAST: Mary Alice, Jay Brooks, Juanita Jennings, Scott Lawrence, Dan Martin. 1993

LAVENDER HILL MOB, THE ★★★★★ Fun, fun, and more fun from this celebrated British comedy. Alec Guinness is a mousy bank clerk. He has a plan for intercepting the bank's armored-car shipment. With the aid of a few friends he forms an amateur robbery squad. Lo and behold, they escape with the loot. After all, the plan was foolproof. Or was it? B&W; 82m. DIR: Charles Crichton. CAST: Alec Guinness, Stanley Holloway, Sidney James, Alfie Bass. 1951

LAW AND JAKE WADE, THE ★★1/2 A robust Western with Richard Widmark chewing the scenery as the bad guy looking for buried treasure and conning good guy Robert Taylor into helping him. *Star Trek's* DeForest Kelley has an important supporting role. 86m. DIR: John Sturges. CAST: Robert Taylor, Richard Widmark, Patricia Owens, Robert Middleton, DeForest Kelley, Henry Silva. 1958

LAW AND ORDER ★★★★ In a story coscripted by John Huston, Walter Huston gets one of the best roles of his career as a Wyatt Earp–style lawman. Harry Carey and Raymond Hatton are superb as his ready-for-anything sidekicks in an excellent Western that still seems fresh and innovative today. B&W; 70m. DIR: Edward L. Cahn. CAST: Walter Huston, Harry Carey, Raymond Hatton, Andy Devine. 1932

LAW FOR TOMBSTONE ★★1/2 Buck and his fellow Texas Rangers head to Tombstone to get the draw on Twin-Gun Jack, but they have to do it cautious-like 'cause Jack's got plenty of crooks on his side. Released with a serial chapter, cartoon, and newsreel. B&W; 59m. DIR: Buck Jones, B. Reeves "Breezy" Eason. CAST: Buck Jones, Muriel Evans, Harvey Clark, Carl Stockdale, Earle Hodgins, Alexander Cross. 1937

LAW OF DESIRE ★★★ Spain's Pedro Almodóvar likes to play with the clichés of movie melodrama in a manner that endears him to movie buffs. This film, which first gained him wide attention in the U.S., deals with a gay movie director who wants to live as passionately as his transsexual brother (now his sister). He gets his wish in this topsy-turvy farce. In Spanish with English subtitles. Not rated, but an R equivalent. 100m. DIR: Pedro Almodóvar. CAST: Eusebio Poncela, Carmen Maura, Antonio Banderas, Miguel Molina. 1986

LAW OF THE PAMPAS ★★★ South-of-the-border action. This is a good Hopalong Cassidy with all the right elements and an exotic locale to boot. B&W; 74m. DIR: Nate Watt. CAST: William Boyd, Russell Hayden, Sidney Blackmer, Sidney Toler, Pedro De Cordoba, Glenn Strange. 1939

LAW OF THE SEA ★★★ Wreck survivors are rescued by a sadistic sea captain, whose lust drives a woman to suicide. Creaky curiosity. B&W; 60m. DIR: Otto Brower. CAST: William Farnum. 1932

LAW WEST OF TOMBSTONE ★★★1/2 Enjoyable, folksy Western has the marvelous Harry Carey starring as a con artist who becomes the law in Tombstone. Tim Holt, in a strong film debut, is the young hothead he befriends and reforms. Look for Allan "Rocky" Lane in a brief bit at the beginning as Holt's saddle pal. B&W; 72m. DIR: Glenn Tryon. CAST: Harry Carey, Tim Holt, Evelyn Brent, Ward Bond, Allan "Rocky" Lane. 1938

LAWLESS FRONTIER ★★1/2 A Mexican bandit (Earl Dwire) manages to evade the blame for a series of crimes he's committed because the sheriff is sure that John Wayne is the culprit. The Duke, of course, traps the bad guy and clears his good name in this predictable B Western. B&W; 59m. DIR: Robert N. Bradbury. CAST: John Wayne, Sheila Terry, George "Gabby" Hayes, Earl Dwire. 1935 DVD

LAWLESS NINETIES, THE ★★★ When outlaws use underhanded tactics to keep the citizens of Wyoming from voting for statehood, it's up to government agent John Wayne and his men to put a stop to it. Gabby Hayes has an uncharacteristic role as a Southern gentleman. It's predictable, but a notch above many oaters. B&W; 55m. DIR: Joseph Kane. CAST: John Wayne, Ann Rutherford, Lane Chandler, Harry Woods, George "Gabby" Hayes, Snowflake, Charles King. 1936

LAWLESS STREET, A ★★★ Randolph Scott portrays a no-nonsense marshal in Medicine Bend until the arrival of an old flame (Angela Lansbury) and the evil plottings of a power-hungry citizen (Warner Anderson) threaten to cost him his job—and maybe his life. Some amusing quips from Scott and the involving climax make this one worth watching. 78m. DIR: Joseph H. Lewis. CAST: Randolph Scott, Angela Lansbury, Warner Anderson, Jean Parker, Wallace Ford, John Emery, Michael Pate, Don Megowan. 1955

LAWLESS VALLEY ★★★★ Prison parolee George O'Brien returns home to clear his name and put the true guilty parties behind bars in this solid series Western. In a nice touch, Fred Kohler Sr. and Fred Kohler Jr. play father-and-son heavies. B&W; 59m. DIR: Bert Gilroy. CAST: George O'Brien, Kay Sutton, Walter Miller, Fred Kohler Sr., Fred Kohler Jr., Chill Wills. 1938

LAWMAN ★★ There's no fire in Burt Lancaster this time around. He plays a marshal who is determined to bring in the bad guys, despite the protestations of an entire town. The story has promise, but doesn't deliver. Robert Ryan is worth watching, cast against type as a meek sheriff. Rated PG. 98m. DIR: Michael Winner. CAST: Burt Lancaster, Robert Ryan, Lee J. Cobb, Robert Duvall, Sheree North, Richard Jordan, Ralph Waite, John Hillerman, J. D. Cannon, Albert Salmi. 1971

LAWMAN IS BORN, A ★★1/2 Former football star Johnny Mack Brown is a two-fisted good guy who foils the nefarious plans of an outlaw gang. This time, the baddies are after land (as opposed to the alternate formulas of cattle, money, gold, or horses). It's fun for fans. B&W; 58m. DIR: Sam Newfield. CAST: Johnny Mack Brown, Iris Meredith, Al St. John. 1937

LAWN DOGS ★★★ Sexual tensions rise in this steamy tale of a small gated community. While their husbands pursue professional status, the lonely wives have affairs. The comfortable facade is destroyed when a young stud named Trent enters: Trent does more than just mow their lawns; he forces the residents into an emotional showdown. Rated R for nudity, language, and adult situations. 101m. DIR: John Duigan. CAST: Sam Rockwell, Christopher McDonald, Kathleen Quinlan, Mischa Barton. 1997 DVD

LAWNMOWER MAN, THE ★★★1/2 The mind-blowing special effects of this film lose a little in the translation to the small screen. But they still are the highlight of this story about a scientist (Pierce Brosnan) who uses computer "virtual reality" to turn a simpleminded gardener (Jeff Fahey) into a psychopathic genius. Some of the most outstanding computer animation since Disney's *Tron*. Rated R for violence, profanity, and nudity. 148m. DIR: Brett Leonard. CAST: Jeff Fahey, Pierce Brosnan, Jenny Wright, Geoffrey Lewis. 1992 DVD

LAWNMOWER MAN 2: JOBE'S WAR (LAWN-MOWER MAN: BEYOND CYBERSPACE) 🐨 Not only is the title character different from that in the original *Lawnmower Man*, as Matt Frewer has stepped into Jeff Fahey's shoes, but we are now magically transferred to a future where nothing makes sense—not the plot, the costumes, the lousy sets, or the point of this supposed sequel. Rated PG-13 for profanity and violence. 93m. DIR: Farhad Mann. CAST: Patrick Bergin, Matt Frewer, Ely Pouget, Austin O'Brien, Kevin Conway. 1995

LAWRENCE OF ARABIA ★★★★★ Director David Lean brings us an expansive screen biography of T. E. Lawrence, the complex English leader of the Arab revolt against Turkey in World War I. This is a tremendous accomplishment in every respect. Peter O'Toole is stunning in his first major film role as T. E. Lawrence. A definite thinking person's spectacle. 222m. DIR: David Lean. CAST: Peter O'Toole, Alec Guinness, Anthony Quinn, Arthur Kennedy, Omar Sharif. 1962

LAWRENCEVILLE STORIES, THE ★★★1/2 Award-winning miniseries takes a humorous look at a turn-of-the-century boarding school. Owen Johnson's delightful short story collection sets the stage for endless pranks perpetuated by teenage boys. 180m. DIR: Allan A. Goldstein, Robert Iscove. CAST: Zach Galligan, Edward Herrmann, Robert Joy, Nicholas Rowe. 1988

LAWS OF GRAVITY 🐨 With no redeeming social value, this silly, violence-packed film focuses on two ruthless thieves and their low-life friends. Belongs in filmdom's hall of shame. Rated R for violence and profanity. 93m. DIR: Nick Gomez. CAST: Adam Trese, Peter Greene, Edie Falco, Arabella Field. 1992

LAZARUS SYNDROME, THE ★★ When the illicit practices of a hospital administrator drive another practitioner to distraction, he joins forces with a patient who just happens to be a journalist in order to expose the bad guy and his lackeys. Made for television. 90m. DIR: Jerry Thorpe. CAST: Lou Gossett Jr., Ronald Hunter, E. G. Marshall, Sheila Frazier. 1976

LBJ: THE EARLY YEARS ★★★★ This superlative made-for-TV movie is the story of Lyndon Johnson from 1934, when he was first entering politics as a congressman's aide, to his swearing in as president aboard *Air Force One*. Randy Quaid and Patti LuPone are outstanding. 144m. DIR: Peter Werner. CAST: Randy Quaid, Patti LuPone, Morgan Brittany, Pat Hingle, Kevin McCarthy, Charles Frank. 1986

LE BAL ★★★★ European history of the last half century is reduced to some fifty popular dance tunes—and a variety of very human dancers—in this innovative and entertaining film. The unusual import eschews dialogue for tangos, fox trots, and jazz to make its points. Ettore Scola chronicles the dramatic changes in political power, social behavior, and fashion trends from the 1930s to the present without ever moving his cameras out of an art deco ballroom. No MPAA rating; the film has brief violence. 109m. DIR: Ettore Scola. 1983

LE BEAU MARIAGE ★★★★ A young woman decides it is high time she got married. She chooses the man she wants, a busy lawyer, and tells her friends of their coming wedding. He knows nothing of this, but she is confident. By French director Eric Rohmer. In French with English subtitles. Rated R. 100m. DIR: Eric Rohmer. CAST: Beatrice Romand, Arielle Dombasle, André Dussolier. 1982

LE BEAU SERGE ★★ An ailing theology student, home for a rest cure, is reunited with his boyhood friend, who is now an alcoholic stuck in an unhappy marriage. Vague drama is of interest only as an early example of the French new wave. In French with English subtitles. Not rated. 97m. DIR: Claude Chabrol. CAST: Gerard Blain, Jean-Claude Brialy, Bernadette Lafont. 1958

LE BONHEUR ★★ Extremely boring story about happiness. A husband is happy with his wife, but becomes even happier when he takes a mistress. In French with English subtitles. Not rated; contains nudity and graphic sex. 77m. **DIR:** Agnes Varda. **CAST:** Jean-Claude Druou, Claire Druou, Marie-France Boyer. **1976**

LE BOUCHER (THE BUTCHER) ★★★★ French director Claude Chabrol's mini-masterwork about a hunt for a serial killer in provincial France. Jean Yanne is the ex–army butcher who may or may not be the murderer. Prim schoolmistress Stéphane Audran (director Chabrol's wife) is irresistibly drawn to him. There are a few affectionate Hitchcock touches, but mostly, this ball-of-twine thriller is Chabrol's own, and that is its considerable strength. English subtitles (beware of the dubbed version). Rated R for violence. 94m. **DIR:** Claude Chabrol. **CAST:** Stéphane Audran, Jean Yanne, Antonio Passalia, Mario Beccaria. **1969**

LE BOURGEOIS GENTILHOMME ★★ This adaptation of Molière's satire about a social climber is a recording of the stage performance, and will seem static and overacted to most viewers. Worth checking out for Molière enthusiasts and French language classes, but not recommended for general audiences. In French with English subtitles. 97m. **DIR:** Jean Meyer. **CAST:** Jean Meyer, Louis Seigner, Jacques Charon. **1958**

LE CAS DU DR. LAURENT ★★1/2 Dated tale about a kindly old doctor who tries to introduce modern methods of medicine and sanitation to the residents of a small farming village. In particular, he tries to ease the suffering of women as they endure childbirth. Noteworthy for the performance of Gabin as the doctor and for footage of an actual childbirth. In French. B&W; 88m. **DIR:** Jean-Paul Le Chanois. **CAST:** Jean Gabin, Nicole Courcel, Sylvia Monfort. **1957**

LE CAVALEUR ★★★★ A poignantly philosophical, yet witty and often hilarious farce about the perils of a middle-aged heartbreak kid. Our cad about town is unerringly portrayed by Jean Rochefort as a classical pianist trying to juggle his art and the many past, present, and possible future women in his life. Nudity but generally innocent adult situations. 106m. **DIR:** Philippe de Broca. **CAST:** Jean Rochefort, Annie Girardot. **1980**

LE CHÈVRE (THE GOAT) ★★1/2 The stars of *Les Compères*, Pierre Richard and Gérard Depardieu, romp again in this French comedy as two investigators searching for a missing girl in Mexico. While this import may please staunch fans of the stars, it is far from being a laugh riot. In French with English subtitles. Not rated; the film has profanity and violence. 91m. **DIR:** Francis Veber. **CAST:** Pierre Richard, Gérard Depardieu, Michel Robin, Pedro Armendariz Jr. **1981**

LE COMPLOT (THE CONSPIRACY) ★★★1/2 Complex political thriller, based on true events, about an explosive game of espionage between leftist rebels, the police, and Gaullist patriots. Quite suspenseful. In French with English subtitles. Rated R for profanity and violence. 120m. **DIR:** René Gainville. **CAST:** Jean Rochefort, Michel Bouquet, Marina Vlady. **1973**

LE CORBEAU (THE RAVEN) (1943) ★★★★ Citizens of a French provincial town are upset to find that someone is on to all their guilty secrets and is revealing them in a series of poison pen letters. An intelligent, involving thriller, remade in the United States as *The Thirteenth Letter*. In French with English subtitles. 91m. **DIR:** Henri-Georges Clouzot. **CAST:** Pierre Fresnay, Pierre Larquey. **1943**

LE CRABE TAMBOUR ★★1/2 Hard-to-follow story of the exploits of a French naval officer over a span of two decades. The beautiful wide-screen photography is diminished on video, and even French historians will have difficulty navigating the complexities of the plot. In French with English subtitles. Not rated. 120m. **DIR:** Pierre Schoendoerffer. **CAST:** Jean Rochefort, Claude Rich, Jacques Perrin. **1977**

LE DÉPART ★★★ Jean-Pierre Léaud, best known from François Truffaut's semiautobiographical films *The 400 Blows* and *Love on the Run*, stars as another disaffected youth. He's desperately trying to borrow or rent a Porsche so that he can enter a race. Zany comedy is noteworthy for Léaud's performance and as an early effort by Polish director Jerzy Skolimowski. In French with English subtitles. Not rated. B&W; 89m. **DIR:** Jerzy Skolimowski. **CAST:** Jean-Pierre Léaud, Catherine Isabelle Duport. **1967**

LE DOULOS ★★★★ Outstanding, complex crime-drama about a police informer who attempts to expose a violent underworld crime ring. An excellent homage to American gangster films of the 1940s. Brilliant cinematography and sizzling performances by a great cast make this suspenseful thriller a film classic. In French with English subtitles. B&W; 105m. **DIR:** Jean-Pierre Melville. **CAST:** Jean-Paul Belmondo, Serge Reggiani, Michel Piccoli. **1961**

LE GAI SAVOIR (THE JOY OF KNOWLEDGE) ★★ Incomprehensible film about two aliens. The poor extraterrestrials may have had better luck if they hadn't landed in this movie. In French with English subtitles. 96m. **DIR:** Jean-Luc Godard. **CAST:** Jean-Pierre Léaud, Juliet Berto. **1965**

LE GENTLEMAN D'ESPOM (DUKE OF THE DERBY) ★★★ This lighthearted look at the sport of kings gives veteran French film star Jean Gabin ample chance to shine as the title character, an aged, suave snob living by his wits and luck handicapping and soliciting bets from the rich. Everything is fine until, eager to impress an old flame, he passes a bad check. B&W; 83m. **DIR:** Jacques Juranville. **CAST:** Jean Gabin, Madeleine Robinson, Paul Frankeur. **1962**

LE GRAND CHEMIN (THE GRAND HIGHWAY) ★★★★ A delightful film about an 8-year-old Parisian boy's summer in the country. Along with his friend Martine (Vanessa Guedj), Louis (played by director Jean-Loup Hubert's son Antoine) learns about the simple pleasures and terrors of life and love. This is great cinema for old and young alike, despite some nudity. In French with English subtitles. 104m. **DIR:** Jean-Loup Hubert. **CAST:** Vanessa Guedj, Antoine Hubert, Richard Bohringer, Anemone. **1988**

LE JOUR SE LÈVE (DAYBREAK) (1939) ★★★ An affecting, atmospheric French melodrama by the director of the classic *Children of Paradise*. Jean Gabin plays a man provoked to murder his lover's seducer. There is some brilliant, sensuous moviemaking here. The existing print lacks sufficient subtitling but is still worth viewing. B&W; 85m. **DIR:** Marcel Carné. **CAST:** Jean Gabin, Jules Berry, Arletty, Jacqueline Laurent. **1939**

LE MAGNIFIQUE ★★★ A writer of spy novels imagines himself as his own character, a James Bond type, with the girl next door as his trusty sidekick. Though it never builds up a full head of steam, this French comedy holds your interest through the dull stretches. Written by Francis Verber (*La Cage Aux Folles, Three Fugitives*). In French with English subtitles. 93m. DIR: Philippe de Broca. CAST: Jean-Paul Belmondo, Jacqueline Bisset. 1974

LE MILLION ★★★★ Made more than fifty years ago, this delightful comedy about the efforts of a group of people to retrieve an elusive lottery ticket is more applicable to American audiences of today than it was when originally released. René Clair's classic fantasy-adventure is freewheeling and fun. French, subtitled in English. B&W; 85m. DIR: René Clair. CAST: Annabella, René Lefèvre. 1931 DVD

LE PETIT AMOUR ★★1/2 Romantic comedy based on a short story by Jane Birkin about a 40-year-old divorcée who falls for a 15-year-old schoolboy. Mediocre, but with good performances. In French with English subtitles. Rated R for nudity. 80m. DIR: Agnes Varda. CAST: Jane Birkin, Mathieu Demy, Charlotte Gainsbourg. 1987

LE PLAISIR ★★1/2 Max Ophüls (*La Ronde*) adapts three ironic stories by Guy de Maupassant with his customary style, most evident in his extremely mobile camera work. However, the stories themselves are mediocre and not really up to the elaborate treatment. In French with English subtitles. B&W; 97m. DIR: Max Ophüls. CAST: Jean Gabin, Danielle Darrieux, Simone Simon. 1952

LE REPOS DU GUERRIER (WARRIOR'S REST) ★★★★ Brigitte Bardot plays a proper French girl who rescues a sociopathic drifter from a suicide attempt. The drifter immediately takes over Bardot's life, ruining her reputation and abusing her verbally and emotionally, yet denying her attempts to form a real relationship. This is a precursor of *The Servant, 9 Weeks*, and other frank observations of sexual obsession. In French. 98m. DIR: Roger Vadim. CAST: Brigitte Bardot, Robert Hossein, James Robertson Justice, Jean-Marc Bory. 1962

•**LE ROUGE ET LE NOIR** ★★★ The great French novel fails to come to life in this lavish but vacant adaptation, which follows the career of Julien Sorel, a social climber who enters the priesthood in order to rise above his family's social status. Also known as *The Red and the Black*. In French with English subtitles. 170m. DIR: Claude Autant-Lara. CAST: Gérard Philipe, Danielle Darrieux. 1954

LE SAMOURAI ★★★★★ John Woo's *The Killer* was largely inspired by this classic that can be enjoyed both as a gripping thriller and as a muted but wholly intoxicating exercise in cinematic style. Alain Delon is the quintessence of cool as the hired killer who lets himself be weakened by emotion. In French with English subtitles. Not rated; contains violence. 95m. DIR: Jean-Pierre Melville. CAST: Alain Delon, François Perier, Nathalie Delon. 1967

LE SCHPOUNTZ ★★★1/2 Country doofus Fernandel, convinced that he's the next Charles Boyer, tries to break into the movies in this consistently funny satire of the film world. In French with English sub-titles. B&W; 140m. DIR: Marcel Pagnol. CAST: Fernandel, Orane Demazis, Charpin, Robert Vattier, Pierre Brasseur. 1938

LE SECRET ★★★ Jean-Louis Trintignant plays an escapee from a psychiatric prison who finds shelter with a reclusive writer and his wife by persuading them that he has been tortured for information. Fine performances, a tense atmosphere, and music by Ennio Morricone make this worth your while. In French with English subtitles. Not rated. 100m. DIR: Robert Enrico. CAST: Jean-Louis Trintignant, Marlene Jobert, Philippe Noiret. 1974

LE SEX SHOP ★★★★ Wry, satirical film about an owner of a failing little bookstore, who converts his business into a sex shop, where he peddles pornographic books and sexual devices in order to make ends meet. Excellent social-sexual satire. In French with English subtitles. Not rated; contains nudity and profanity. 90m. DIR: Claude Berri. CAST: Claude Berri, Juliet Berto. 1973

LE VOYAGE IMAGINAIRE ★★1/2 A daydreaming clerk imagines a fantasy where he vies for the love of his coworker against the office Romeos. His dream takes them to a land of abandoned fairies where magic changes the young lovers into animals; when the dream ends the spell doesn't. Surreal French comedy. B&W; 66m. DIR: René Clair. CAST: Jean Borlin, Dolly Davys, Albert Préjean, Jim Geralds. 1925

LEADER OF THE BAND ★★★ In this charming comedy Steve Landesberg plays an unemployed musician who becomes the band instructor for a group of misfits. Too much footage is devoted to marching-band performances, but all in all this film has general appeal. Rated PG for profanity. 90m. DIR: Nessa Hyams. CAST: Steve Landesberg, Gailard Sartain, Mercedes Ruehl. 1987

LEADING MAN, THE ★★★★ American action-film hero Robin Grange is cast as an assassin torn between love and duty in a London play written by Felix Webb. When Grange discovers that the writer wants to leave his spouse for a young actress, he offers to seduce Webb's wife to expedite the situation. Webb agrees and soon finds his life being rewritten by his ruthless coconspirator. Rated R for language and sexuality. 96m. DIR: John Duigan. CAST: Jon Bon Jovi, Lambert Wilson, Thandie Newton, Anna Galiena, David Warner, Barry Humphries. 1998 DVD

LEAGUE OF GENTLEMEN, THE ★★★ A British army officer assembles a group of other military retirees and plots a perfect robbery. One of those light-hearted thrillers where the joy comes from watching professionals pull off an incredibly detailed crime. B&W; 114m. DIR: Basil Dearden. CAST: Jack Hawkins, Nigel Patrick, Roger Livesey, Richard Attenborough, Bryan Forbes, Kieron Moore. 1961

LEAGUE OF THEIR OWN, A ★★★1/2 Director Penny Marshall's tribute to the first women's baseball league is a nice little movie that runs out of steam a bit in the last 45 minutes. Geena Davis is superb as "the natural" who finds herself caught in a battle of wills with sister/pitcher Lori Petty and the team's cranky coach, Tom Hanks, a one-time baseball great. The comedy bits by Madonna, Rosie O'Donnell, Megan Cavanaugh, and (seen all too briefly) Jon Lovitz help to buoy the film's melodramatic plotline. Rated PG. 118m. **DIR:** Penny Marshall. **CAST:** Tom Hanks, Geena Davis, Madonna, Lori Petty, Jon Lovitz, David Strathairn, Garry Marshall, Megan Cavanaugh, Rosie O'Donnell, Tracy Reiner, Bill Pullman. **1992 DVD**

LEAN ON ME ★★★★ Morgan Freeman gives a superb performance as real-life high school principal Joe Clark, who almost single-handedly converted Eastside High in Paterson, New Jersey, from a den of drugs, gangs, and corruption into an effective place of learning. Director John Avildsen has created a feel-good movie that conveys a timely message. Rated PG-13 for profanity and violence. 104m. **DIR:** John G. Avildsen. **CAST:** Morgan Freeman, Robert Guillaume, Beverly Todd. **1989 DVD**

LEAP OF FAITH ★★★1/2 The glorious gospel music is the main reason to catch Steve Martin's act as a dancin' preacher who decides to con the residents of a small town. Debra Winger plays the cynical righthand man to Martin's phony faith healer. *Leap of Faith* pours on the sentimentality a bit thick, but the music—hallelujah! Rated PG-13 for profanity. 108m. **DIR:** Richard Pearce. **CAST:** Steve Martin, Debra Winger, Liam Neeson, Lolita Davidovich, Lukas Haas, Meat Loaf, Philip Seymour Hoffman, M. C. Gainey, Delores Hall, John Toles-Bey, Albertina Walker. **1992**

LEAPIN' LEPRECHAUNS ★★★ Kids will enjoy this fun, magical romp that takes its cue from vintage Walt Disney efforts like *Darby O'Gill and the Little People* and *The Gnome-Mobile.* Four leprechauns are forced into action when an ambitious American plans to turn their homeland into an amusement park called "Ireland-Land." They do whatever it takes, including befriending the developer's young daughter. Rated PG. 84m. **DIR:** Ted Nicolaou. **CAST:** John Bluthal, Grant Cramer, Sharon Lee Jones, Sylvester McCoy, James Ellis, Gregory Edward Smith. **1994**

LEARNING TREE, THE ★★★★ In adapting his own novel about the coming-of-age of a young black man in Kansas circa 1920, photographer-turned-filmmaker Gordon Parks not only wrote and directed, but also produced the project and composed its musical score. The result is a uniquely personal vision. Rated PG for violence, profanity, and racial epithets. 107m. **DIR:** Gordon Parks Jr. **CAST:** Kyle Johnson, Alex Clarke, Estelle Evans, Dana Elcar. **1969**

LEATHER BOYS, THE ★★ Considered adult and controversial when first released in England, this slice-of-life drama about teenagers who marry for sex and settle into drab existences doesn't carry the weight it once did. Rather depressing, this film is an interesting look at life in London in the early 1960s, but it has dated badly. B&W; 108m. **DIR:** Sidney J. Furie. **CAST:** Rita Tushingham, Dudley Sutton, Colin Campbell. **1963**

LEATHER BURNERS, THE ★★1/2 In this oddball series Western, Hopalong Cassidy (William Boyd) and his sidekick, California (Andy Clyde), are framed for murder by a calculating cattle rustler (Victor Jory). It's up to a junior detective (Bobby Larson) to prove our heroes' innocence in time to allow them to participate in the final showdown. B&W;

58m. **DIR:** Joseph E. Henabery. **CAST:** William Boyd, Andy Clyde, Victor Jory, Bobby Larson, Robert Mitchum. **1943**

•LEATHER JACKET LOVE STORY ★★ David DeCoteau's attempt at a romantic comedy aimed at the gay market falls shy of the mark. While the film has likable characters and a solid story, the actors bring down the rest of the film with their poor work. Not rated; contains nudity and profanity. B&W; 85m. **DIR:** David DeCoteau. **CAST:** Sean Tataryn, Chris Bradley, Mink Stole, Nicholas Worth. **1997**

LEATHER JACKETS ★★ A one-dimensional bluecollar vehicle for leading man Cary Elwes. Rated R for violence, profanity, nudity, and some strongly suggestive sex scenes involving former porn queen Ginger Lynn Allen. 90m. **DIR:** Lee Drysdale. **CAST:** Bridget Fonda, Cary Elwes, D. B. Sweeney, Ginger Lynn Allen. **1992**

LEATHERFACE—THE TEXAS CHAINSAW MASSACRE III ★★1/2 Some light comedy helps break up the terror in this story of two travelers who make the mistake of stopping in Texas for directions. Not as scary as the first film in the series and not as bloody as the second. Rated R for violence. 87m. **DIR:** Jeff Burr. **CAST:** Viggo Mortensen, William Butler, Ken Foree. **1989**

LEAVE 'EM LAUGHING ★★★★1/2 Mickey Rooney is outstanding portraying real-life Chicago clown Jack Thum. Thum and his wife (played by Anne Jackson) cared for dozens of unwanted children. When Thum realizes he has terminal cancer, he falls apart and his wife must help him regain his inner strength and deal with reality. A real tearjerker! Made for TV, this is unrated. 104m. **DIR:** Jackie Cooper. **CAST:** Mickey Rooney, Anne Jackson, Red Buttons, William Windom, Elisha Cook Jr. **1981**

LEAVE HER TO HEAVEN ★★★★ A fine translation of the Ben Ames Williams novel about a jealous woman who causes more torment to those she loves than to those she doesn't care about—going so far as to destroy herself if it causes her husband to suffer. Very stylish and beautifully acted. 110m. **DIR:** John M. Stahl. **CAST:** Gene Tierney, Cornel Wilde, Jeanne Crain, Vincent Price, Darryl Hickman, Mary Philips. **1945**

LEAVE IT TO BEAVER ★★★1/2 This successful update of the popular 1957–1963 television series retains the family love and moral integrity that hallmarked the show. Christopher McDonald projects genuine warmth as the world's most perfect dad, but Janine Turner is less successful as Mom, the sole character to exhibit just-plain-dumb throwback behavior (vacuuming the house while dressed for the opera). Modern kids may find this too wholesome, but it'll be good for 'em. Rated PG for mild profanity. 88m. **DIR:** Andy Cadiff. **CAST:** Christopher McDonald, Janine Turner, Cameron Finley, Erik von Detten, Adam Zolotin. **1997 DVD**

LEAVES FROM SATAN'S BOOK ★★ Carl Dreyer's second film is a surprising mixture of leering and posturing clichés. The story tells of Satan's appearance in four different disguises to perform his unholy temptations. Beautiful sets and effective character types, but hopelessly melodramatic stereotypes.

Silent. B&W; 165m. DIR: Carl Dreyer. CAST: Heige Nissen, Jacob Texiere. 1919

LEAVING LAS VEGAS ★★★1/2 Nicolas Cage took home an Oscar for his all-stops-out performance as a failed Hollywood player determined to drink himself to death. After cashing out his entire life and relocating to Las Vegas, he encounters soft-hearted hooker Elisabeth Shue, who falls in love with him. The powerhouse performances are complemented by director Mike Figgis's quasi-surreal blend of Vegas flash-trash and *film noir* smokiness. Rated R for violence, profanity, nudity, and rape. 112m. DIR: Mike Figgis. CAST: Nicolas Cage, Elisabeth Shue, Julian Sands. 1995 DVD

LEAVING NORMAL ★★★ In what could unkindly be called *Thelma and Louise II*, a tough, no-nonsense waitress (Christine Lahti) and a naïve young woman (Meg Tilly) fleeing an abusive husband go on a road trip from Normal, Wyoming, to the wilds of Alaska. The performances and a few surprises on the way help mitigate a now-too-familiar story. Rated R for profanity, violence, and nudity. 110m. DIR: Edward Zwick. CAST: Christine Lahti, Meg Tilly, Lenny Von Dohlen, James Gammon. 1992

L'ECOLE BUISSONNIERE ★★★1/2 A teacher with modern ideas goes to work for a small village, and now the once bored students are excited about going to school. A few elders in the village decide that the new teacher is a bad influence on the children; they make a bet with him, the stakes being his job. You'll be rooting for the teacher in this nicely portrayed, neo-realist film. In French with English subtitles. B&W; 84m. DIR: Jean-Paul Le Chanois. CAST: Bernard Blier, Juliette Faber, Pierre Coste. 1951

LEECH WOMAN, THE ★★ The neglected wife of a cosmetics researcher discovers an African potion that can restore her faded youth, but she has to kill young men to obtain the "secret ingredient." Coleen Gray gives an all-out performance, but there's too much setup and too little payoff. B&W; 77m. DIR: Edward Dein. CAST: Coleen Gray, Grant Williams, Gloria Talbott. 1959

LEFT FOR DEAD ♥ Contrived murder drama, staged in a series of flashbacks. Not rated; contains violence, profanity, and nudity. 88m. DIR: Murray Markowitz. CAST: Elke Sommer, Donald Pilon, Chuck Shamata, George Touliatos. 1978

LEFT HAND OF GOD, THE ★★★1/2 Humphrey Bogart is an American forced to pose as a priest while on the run from a renegade Chinese warlord (Lee J. Cobb). It's not the fastest-moving adventure story, but Bogart and Cobb are quite good, and Gene Tierney is an effective heroine. The result is worthy entertainment. 87m. DIR: Edward Dmytryk. CAST: Humphrey Bogart, Lee J. Cobb, Gene Tierney, Agnes Moorehead. 1955

LEFT HANDED GUN, THE ★★★1/2 Effective Western follows the exploits of Billy the Kid from the Lincoln County cattle wars until his death at the hands of Pat Garrett. One of the best of several Westerns to deal with the legend of Billy the Kid. B&W; 102m. DIR: Arthur Penn. CAST: Paul Newman, John Dehner, James Best, Hurd Hatfield, Lita Milan. 1958

LEGACY, THE ★★ A young American couple (Katharine Ross and Sam Elliott) staying at a mysterious English mansion discover that the woman has been chosen as the mate for some sort of ugly, demonic creature upstairs. Rated R for violence and language. 100m. DIR: Richard Marquand. CAST: Katharine Ross, Sam Elliott, John Standing, Roger Daltrey. 1979

LEGACY FOR LEONETTE ★★ Romance Theatre tries a murder mystery but devotes too much time to the love angle. A young woman goes to England to investigate her father's mysterious death but is distracted by her handsome lawyer. Episodic and mildly entertaining. Not rated; contains no objectionable material. 99m. DIR: Jim Drake. CAST: Loyita Chapel, Michael Anderson Jr., Dinah Anne Rogers, Shane McCamey. 1982

LEGACY OF HORROR ♥ Another of Andy Milligan's lethally dull and thoroughly amateurish shockers, a remake of his own *The Ghastly Ones*. Rated R. 90m. DIR: Andy Milligan. CAST: Elaine Bois, Chris Broderick. 1978

LEGACY OF LIES ★★ Michael Ontkean portrays a good Chicago cop who is caught up in a politically motivated murder. Martin Landau plays his father, a crooked Chicago police officer who's willing to take the fall to prevent his son from becoming corrupt. Weak story line undermines this made-for-cable drama. 91m. DIR: Bradford May. CAST: Michael Ontkean, Martin Landau, Joe Morton, Patricia Clarkson, Chelcie Ross, Eli Wallach. 1992

LEGAL DECEIT ★★1/2 A lawyer agrees to join a coworker's plan to boost their careers by blackmail only to regret it when she finds he is willing to extend his criminal actions to murder. Second-rate thriller is notable only as a starring vehicle for Lela Rochon before she made *Waiting to Exhale*. Not rated. 93m. DIR: Monika Harris. CAST: Lela Rochon, Phil Morris, John Stockwell. 1995

LEGAL EAGLES ★★★1/2 This comedy-mystery features Robert Redford as an assistant district attorney and Debra Winger as a defense attorney. The two partner in a complex case involving art theft and a loopy performance artist, played by Daryl Hannah. Redford and Winger keep things moving with energy and charisma. Rated PG for mild adult situations. 114m. DIR: Ivan Reitman. CAST: Robert Redford, Debra Winger, Daryl Hannah, Brian Dennehy, Terence Stamp, Steven Hill, Jennie Dundas, Roscoe Lee Browne. 1986 DVD

LEGALESE ★★★★ High-profile courtroom high jinks get lambasted in this cynical drama about modern celebrity trials. James Garner has a reputation for being able to get *anybody* off, maybe even a flamboyant celebrity accused of killing her sister's husband. This film doesn't say much for the current state of justice in American courts, but that's the point. Rated PG-13 for violence and sexual content. 95m. DIR: Glenn Jordan. CAST: James Garner, Gina Gershon, Mary-Louise Parker, Edward Kerr, Kathleen Turner. 1998

LEGEND ♥ Tom Cruise simply looks embarrassed as a forest-living lad who joins a quest to save a unicorn, keeper of his world's Light. Rated PG for mild violence. 89m. **DIR:** Ridley Scott. **CAST:** Tom Cruise, Tim Curry, Mia Sara, David Bennent, Billy Barty. 1986

LEGEND OF BILLIE JEAN, THE ❤ A girl from Texas (Helen Slater) becomes an outlaw. Rated PG-13 for language and violence. 92m. **DIR:** Matthew Robbins. **CAST:** Helen Slater, Keith Gordon, Christian Slater, Peter Coyote. 1985

LEGEND OF BOGGY CREEK ★★ One of the better "mystery of" docudramas, which were the rage of the early 1970s, this supposedly true story focuses on a monster that lurks in the swamps of Arkansas. Rated PG. 95m. **DIR:** Charles B. Pierce. **CAST:** Willie E. Smith, John P. Nixon. 1972

LEGEND OF FRENCHIE KING, THE ❤ Muddled Western about a gang of female outlaws falls flat. Rated R for profanity, violence, and adult situations. 97m. **DIR:** Christian-Jaque. **CAST:** Brigitte Bardot, Claudia Cardinale, Guy Casaril, Michael J. Pollard. 1971

LEGEND OF GATOR FACE, THE ★★★ Move the suburban setting to swamp country, and replace an alien visitor with a friendly alligator/human hybrid, and you've got this odd little spin on *E.T.* The story moves along reasonably well while the two young stars attempt to inject some life into their sleepy small town, but things go downhill after we finally get a glimpse of the badly conceived title creature. Suitable for all ages. 100m. **DIR:** Vic Sarin. **CAST:** John White, Dan Warry-Smith, Charlotte Sullivan, C. David Johnson, Paul Winfield. 1996

LEGEND OF HELL HOUSE, THE ★★★1/2 Richard Matheson's riveting suspense tale of a group of researchers attempting to survive a week in a haunted house in order to try to solve the mystery of the many deaths that have occurred there. Jarring at times, with very inventive camera shots and a great cast headed by Roddy McDowall as the only survivor of a previous investigation. Rated PG for violence. 95m. **DIR:** John Hough. **CAST:** Roddy McDowall, Pamela Franklin, Gayle Hunnicutt, Clive Revill. 1973

LEGEND OF HILLBILLY JOHN, THE ★★ When a young man's grandfather challenges the devil and loses, he decides to take on the master of Hell himself, armed with only his guitar. Flawed low-budget production with intermittent charms. 86m. **DIR:** John Newland. **CAST:** Hedge Capers, Severn Darden, Denver Pyle. 1973

•**LEGEND OF 1900, THE** ★★★1/2 Baby boy abandoned on a transatlantic ocean liner is named for the year of his birth. He matures into a famous pianist without venturing onto dry land, is challenged to a keyboard duel by an arrogant Jelly Roll Morton, and is tempted to jump ship in pursuit of a young muse. The tale is narrated by a trumpet player who tries to help 1900 find his true niche in life. This overly long fable is full of magical moments that do not quite gel into a wondrous whole. Rated R for language. 119m. **DIR:** Giuseppe Tornatore. **CAST:** Tim Roth, Pruitt Taylor Vince, Clarence Williams III, Bill Nunn, Melanie Thierry. 1999

LEGEND OF SLEEPY HOLLOW, THE (1949) ★★★★ One of the finest of the Disney "novelette" cartoons, this adaptation is given a properly sepulchral tone by narrator Bing Crosby. Reasonably scary, particularly for small fry, who might get pretty nervous during poor Ichabod Crane's final, fateful ride. 49m. **DIR:** Jack Kinney, Clyde Geronimi, James Algar. 1949

LEGEND OF SURAM FORTRESS, THE ★★★★ Idiosyncratic retelling of a medieval Georgian legend about the attempt to build a fortress to repel invaders. Difficult to comprehend (unless you know a lot about Georgian folklore), the film's many striking images make for a memorable viewing experience. In Georgian with English subtitles. 87m. **DIR:** Sergi Parajanov, Dodo Abashidze. **CAST:** Levan Uchaneishvili. 1984

LEGEND OF THE EIGHT SAMURAI ★★ Shizu is the princess who leads her warriors into battle against a giant centipede, ghosts, and a nearly immortal witch. An interesting story line, but derivative, slow in spots, badly dubbed, and disappointing. Not rated; contains moderate violence. 130m. **DIR:** Haruki Kadokawa. **CAST:** Hiroku Yokoshimaru, Sonny Chiba. 1984

LEGEND OF THE FOREST ★★ The story is inconsequential in this awkward tribute to Disney's *Fantasia* that strives for experimental depth but doesn't deliver. Using a typically Western animation setting (the forest), the evolution of animation style from the last sixty years unfolds to music from Tchaikovsky's Fourth Symphony. High concept with only limited results. In Japanese with English subtitles. Not rated. 26m. **DIR:** Osamu Tezuka. 1987

LEGEND OF THE LONE RANGER, THE ❤ While kids may slightly enjoy this often corny, slow-paced Western—adults will probably be falling asleep. Rated PG. 98m. **DIR:** William Fraker. **CAST:** Klinton Spilsbury, Michael Horse, Jason Robards Jr. 1981 DVD

LEGEND OF THE LOST ★★ Cornball adventure-romance borrows several themes from *Treasure of the Sierra Madre* and doesn't improve upon them. John Wayne is a cynical soldier of fortune who escorts idealist Rossano Brazzi and prostitute Sophia Loren through the desert in search of ancient treasure. 107m. **DIR:** Henry Hathaway. **CAST:** John Wayne, Sophia Loren, Rossano Brazzi, Kurt Kasznar. 1957

LEGEND OF THE LOST TOMB ★★★ Amiable family-style adventure, smartly adapted from Walter Dean Myers's *Tales of a Dead King*, about two teenagers searching for the mysterious treasure promised by a lost scroll, while battling the evil minions of antiquities thief Stacy Keach. Broadly played and mostly good-natured fun, allowing for a few genuinely frightening scenes involving scorpions. Rated PG for mild violence. 93m. **DIR:** Jonathan Winfrey. **CAST:** Brock Pierce, Kimberlee Peterson, Rick Rossovich, Stacy Keach, Khaled El Sawy. 1997

LEGEND OF THE NORTH WIND, THE ★★1/2 In seventeenth-century Newfoundland, three children try to prevent an unscrupulous explorer from unleashing an evil spirit as part of his plan to capture whales. This well-intentioned but corny animated film is for young children only. Rated G. 74m. 1995

LEGEND OF THE SPIRIT DOG ★★★ A mysterious wolf-dog is rescued in the Alaska wilderness by a female environmentalist and her young son. When a company begins illegal dumping on a sacred mountain, Spirit helps his new family save the day. Panoramic location photography, a rousing plot, and family and earth values add to this spiritual adventure. Rated PG for violence. 90m. **DIR:** Michael Spence, Martin Goldman. **CAST:** Morgan Brittany, Martin Balsam, Martin Landau, David Richards. **1994**

LEGEND OF THE WEREWOLF ★★ Peter Cushing's ever-professional performance is the only noteworthy element. British werewolf movie. Not rated, but the equivalent of PG-13. 90m. **DIR:** Freddie Francis. **CAST:** Peter Cushing, Ron Moody, Hugh Griffith. **1974**

LEGEND OF THE WHITE HORSE ❤ The two directors make it obvious: there seems to be two separate films on one tape. Part focuses on a witch and a transforming horse while the rest makes an environmental statement about an exploitative company. Not rated Polish film contains violence. 91m. **DIR:** Jerzy Domaradzki, Janusz Morgenstern. **CAST:** Dee Wallace, Christopher Lloyd, Christopher Stone, Soon-Teck Oh, Luke Askew. **1985**

LEGEND OF VALENTINO ★★ TV movie released close to the fiftieth anniversary of the fabled actor's death adheres to some facts concerning the archetypal Latin lover, but still presents an unsatisfying and incomplete portrait. But this film still leaves too many questions either unanswered or glossed over. Not too bad for a TV movie. 100m. **DIR:** Melville Shavelson. **CAST:** Franco Nero, Suzanne Pleshette, Judd Hirsch, Lesley Ann Warren, Milton Berle, Yvette Mimieux, Harold J. Stone. **1975**

LEGEND OF WALKS FAR WOMAN, THE ❤ Badly miscast Raquel Welch portrays an Indian heroine facing the perils of the Indian versus white man's culture clash. 150m. **DIR:** Mel Damski. **CAST:** Raquel Welch, Bradford Dillman, George Clutesi, Nick Mancuso, Nick Ramos. **1982**

LEGENDS OF THE AMERICAN WEST (SERIES) ★★★1/2 Rare photos, diaries, interviews with relatives of the legends, movie clips, and reenactments are used to give a factual account of the American West and the famous characters we have known through myth and legend. *Jesse James, Billy The Kid,* and *Wyatt Earp and the Gunfighters* are the best with fine use of memorabilia, photos, and new facts. The uneven *Cowboys and Indians* emphasizes truth over movie distortion, and the Indians get a fair shake for once. *The West Remembered* is disappointing. Not rated. each. 30m. **DIR:** Marina Amoruso. **1992**

LEGENDS OF THE FALL ★★★★ Sprawling, old-fashioned melodrama about disillusioned U.S. Cavalry officer raising three sons near the remote Montana Rockies. War, politics, Prohibition, and the love of a fickle woman turn brother against brother, and father against son. Director Edward Zwick handles the Shakespearean tragedy without descending into bathos, and John Toll's cinematography is exquisite. Rated R for profanity, violence, and simulated sex. 134m. **DIR:** Edward Zwick. **CAST:** Brad Pitt, Anthony Hopkins, Aidan Quinn, Julia Ormond, Henry Thomas. **1994 DVD**

LEGENDS OF THE NORTH ★★ A hidden cache of gold buried in a Canadian lake sparks a race for ownership. Randy Quaid plays the fortune hunter, who

seeks advice from the son of the man who hid the gold. Gorgeous scenery fills the screen, but the action and acting are pretty mundane. Rated PG. 98m. **DIR:** Rene Manzor. **CAST:** George Corraface, Randy Quaid, Macha Grenon, Bill Merasty. **1994**

●**LEGION OF THE NIGHT** ★★1/2 Grim, disturbing film has soldier Tim Lovelace learning of a government experiment with cybernetic zombie assassins and running afoul of drug-running gangsters. Not rated; contains gore, violence, and profanity. 85m. **DIR:** Matt Jaissle. **CAST:** Tim Lovelace, Ron Asheton, Heather Fine, Bill Hinzman. **1995**

LEGIONNAIRE ★★ Standard-issue French Foreign Legion dust drama jumps from one worn-out cliché to the next, with Jean-Claude Van Damme playing a boxer who is forced to join the Legion when he refuses to throw a fight and is hunted down by a mob boss. Even at ninety-nine minutes the film feels long and drawn out. Rated R for violence, language, and adult situations. 99m. **DIR:** Peter MacDonald. **CAST:** Jean-Claude Van Damme, Steven Berkoff, Adewale Akinnuoye-Agbaje, Daniel Caltagirone, Nicolas Farrell. **1998 DVD**

LEMON DROP KID, THE ★★★ Great group of character actors makes this Damon Runyon story of an incompetent bookie work like a charm. Fast-talking Bob Hope has the tailor-made leading role. Deadly Lloyd Nolan plays the guy putting the screws to Hope, and Marilyn Maxwell plays the girl caught in the middle. B&W; 91m. **DIR:** Sidney Lanfield. **CAST:** Bob Hope, Marilyn Maxwell, Lloyd Nolan, Jane Darwell, Andrea King, Fred Clark, Jay C. Flippen, William Frawley. **1951**

LEMON SISTERS, THE ★★ Engaging characters are in desperate need of a coherent story as three middle-aged, part-time lounge singers find their show-biz dreams slipping away in 1982 Atlantic City. Hollow comedy-cum-drama. Rated PG-13. 100m. **DIR:** Joyce Chopra. **CAST:** Diane Keaton, Carol Kane, Kathryn Grody, Rubén Blades, Aidan Quinn, Elliott Gould. **1990**

LEMORA—LADY DRACULA ★★★1/2 Shot in black-and-white, this atmospheric vampire film is an oddity in that it is a period piece made on a fraction of the budget of much larger films. Future exploitation star Cheryl "Rainbeaux" Smith appears as the Singing Angel, on whom just about everyone wants to get their hands. Rated PG for violence. 80m. **DIR:** Richard Blackburn. **CAST:** Lesley Glib, Cheryl Smith. **1973**

LENA'S HOLIDAY ★★1/2 Decent romantic thriller. A newly freed East German on vacation in Los Angeles becomes inadvertently involved with diamond thieves and must run for her life. Rated PG-13. 97m. **DIR:** Michael Keusch. **CAST:** Felicity Waterman, Chris Lemmon, Michael Sarrazin, Nick Mancuso. **1990**

L'ENFER ★★★★ One man's descent into madness is explored in this harrowing film, whose production history was equally harrowing. Shot and reshot over a period of thirty years, the final product is a testament to endurance. Paul and Nelly have a wonderful life. Paul works at a resort hotel, a job he has held for the past fifteen years. When Paul makes the bold step to buy the hotel, the couple's life begins to crumble as Paul slips into madness and extreme jealousy. In French with English subtitles. 105m. DIR: Claude Chabrol. CAST: François Cluzet, Emmanuelle Beart, Natalie Cardone. **1994 DVD**

LENINGRAD COWBOYS GO AMERICA ❤ Don't waste 80 minutes of your life watching this horrible Finnish farce about an eccentric Finnish polka band that tours the United States. In Finnish with English subtitles. Rated PG-13 for language. 80m. DIR: Aki Kaurismaki. CAST: Matti Pellonpaa. **1989**

LENNY ★★★★★ Bob Fosse brilliantly directed this stark biography of self-destructive, controversial persecuted comic talent Lenny Bruce. Dustin Hoffman captures all those contrary emotions in his portrayal of the late 1950s and '60s stand-up comedian. Valerie Perrine is a treasure in her low-key role as Bruce's stripper wife. Rated R. B&W; 112m. DIR: Bob Fosse. CAST: Dustin Hoffman, Valerie Perrine, Jan Miner. **1974**

LENNY BRUCE PERFORMANCE FILM, THE ★★★★ This simple, straightforward solo showcases Lenny Bruce, the master of bitter satire, in all his gritty brilliance. Bruce was an original, a pioneer who paved the way for George Carlin, Richard Pryor, and all the rest. Also included is Bruce's color-cartoon parody of the Lone Ranger, "Thank You Masked Man." Otherwise, black and white. Rated R for language. 70m. DIR: John Magnuson. CAST: Lenny Bruce. **1968**

LEO TOLSTOY'S ANNA KARENINA (1997) ★★ The novel of upper-class adultery in czarist Russia takes its worst beating yet in this turgid, disjointed shambles. Alfred Molina hogs the action as Levin, spouting dense passages of Tolstoyan philosophy. Meanwhile, Sophie Marceau plays the tragic Anna as a selfish neurotic; James Fox, as her husband, is far more sympathetic. Rated PG-13 for mature themes and brief simulated sex. 110m. DIR: Bernard Rose. CAST: Sophie Marceau, Sean Bean, Alfred Molina, Mia Kirshner, James Fox, Danny Huston, Saskia Wickham, Fiona Shaw. **1997**

LEOLO ★★★★ This surreal memoir of growing up poor in Montreal's ghetto alternates between images of great beauty and great coarseness. The boy at the center of the story is fed up with a bizarre family life. He creates a fantasy background, concluding that he was accidentally fathered by an Italian peasant in a wacky accident that has to be seen to be believed. Though original and audacious, this film is not for the easily offended. In French with English subtitles. Rated R, with profanity, scatological humor, and sexual situations. 107m. DIR: Jean-Claude Lauzon. CAST: Maxime Collin, Ginetta Reno, Julien Guiomar. **1993**

LEON THE PIG FARMER ★★★1/2 Good intentions and goofy humor ease this little film past its duller moments. Mark Frankel is a London Jew who discovers his real father raises pigs. Already at odds with his career, sex life, and identity, this news nearly pushes poor Leon over the edge. Not as funny as it wants to be, but it's consistently amusing and infectiously bubbly. Some scenes could have been lifted right out of a Monty Python skit. Not rated; contains mild profanity. 98m. DIR: Vadim Jean, Gary Sinyor.

CAST: Mark Frankel, Janet Suzman, Brian Glover, Connie Booth, David De Keyser, Maryam D'Abo. **1992**

LEONARD PART 6 ❤ Bill Cosby, forced into saving the world, does so, but he can't save the picture. Rated PG. 83m. DIR: Paul Weiland. CAST: Bill Cosby, Tom Courtenay, Joe Don Baker, Moses Gunn. **1987**

LEOPARD, THE ★★★★ Luchino Visconti's multigenerational spectacle of nineteenth-century Sicily has been restored on video, replacing the dubbed version that was cut by 40 minutes and presented to confused American audiences in the mid-1960s. Burt Lancaster is surprisingly effective as the formidable head of an Italian (!) dynasty. 205m. DIR: Luchino Visconti. CAST: Burt Lancaster, Alain Delon, Claudia Cardinale. **1963**

LEOPARD IN THE SNOW ★★ Silly romance between a spoiled rich girl and a maimed former racecar driver. The dialogue is slow and some scenes lead nowhere. The pluses include the driver's pet leopard and his butler Bolt (Jeremy Kemp). Rated PG for one scene in which our lovebirds *almost* become passionate. 89m. DIR: Gerry O'Hara. CAST: Keir Dullea, Susan Penhaligon, Kenneth More, Billie Whitelaw, Jeremy Kemp. **1977**

LEOPARD MAN, THE ★★★1/2 This Val Lewton-produced thriller depicts the havoc and killing that begin when a leopard escapes and terrorizes a New Mexico village. B&W; 59m. DIR: Jacques Tourneur. CAST: Dennis O'Keefe, Isabel Jewell. **1943**

LEOPARD SON, THE ★★★ The Discovery Channel's first theatrically released film is a combination of documentary and storyline narrated by John Gielgud. Naturalist Hugo van Lawick captured two years in the life of a Serengeti leopard cub. Although viewers are not spared the harsh realities of surviving in the animal kingdom, they are also made privy to all its joy and wonderment as the male cub learns to be self-sufficient. Fabulous footage of a multitude of species with appropriate soundtrack for each. Not rated. 85m. DIR: Hugo van Lawick. **1996**

LEPKE ★★★ Tony Curtis gives an effective performance in the lead role of this gangster drama. He's the head of Murder Inc. The story sticks close to the facts. It's no classic, but watchable. Rated R. 110m. DIR: Menahem Golan. CAST: Tony Curtis, Anjanette Comer, Michael Callan, Warren Berlinger, Milton Berle, Vic Tayback. **1975**

LEPRECHAUN ❤ No luck of the Irish for writer-director Mark Jones, whose abysmal little fright flick concerns a nasty Lucky Charms refugee. Nothing but blarney. Rated R for violence and profanity. 92m. DIR: Mark Jones. CAST: Warwick Davis, Jennifer Aniston, Ken Olandt, Mark Holton. **1993 DVD**

LEPRECHAUN 2 ★★ In search of a bride, the wily leprechaun goes to America where he causes the usual mayhem (including killing an irritating waiter with his own espresso machine). Some cleverness manages to struggle through briefly before being bludgeoned to death by the dead-end story. Rated R for violence, nudity, and profanity. 84m. DIR: Rodman Flender. CAST: Warwick Davis, Charlie Heath, Shevonne Durkin, Clint Howard. **1994 DVD**

LEPRECHAUN 3 ❤ Unless you loved *Leprechaun* and *Leprechaun 2*, you won't want to watch this version in which the leprechaun terrorizes Las Vegas. Rated R for profanity, violence, nudity, and simulated sex. 93m. **DIR:** Brian Trenchard-Smith. **CAST:** Warwick Davis, John Gatins, Lee Armstrong. 1995

LEPRECHAUN 4 IN SPACE ★★★ The vicious little leprechaun's third outing takes place in a distant galaxy, where the leprechaun is holding an alien princess hostage until he can marry her. Headed from Earth is a spaceship filled with space marines intent on saving the princess. The leprechaun sneaks aboard and starts killing them one by one. New setting and gory special effects breathe new life into the franchise. Rated R for violence and language. 98m. **DIR:** Brian Trenchard-Smith. **CAST:** Warwick Davis, Rebekah Carlton, Debbe Dunning. 1996

•**LEPRECHAUN IN THE HOOD** ♥ The dastardly, diminutive demon finally runs out of steam in a film that wants to be funny and scary, but winds up neither. Setting the film in the hood fails to generate anything new or exciting. Time to make a wish and send this guy packing. Rated R for adult situations, language, and violence. 90m. **DIR:** Robert Spera. **CAST:** Warwick Davis, Ice T, Coolio, Postmaster P, Stray Bullet. 1999 DVD

LES ABYSSES ★★★ Straightforward adaptation of the notorious murder case that inspired Jean Genet's *The Maids*. Two sisters try to stop the sale of a vineyard that is their only means of support; when they fail, they kill the owner for whom they have worked all their lives. In French with English subtitles. B&W; 90m. **DIR:** Nico Papatakis. **CAST:** Francine Berge, Colette Berge. 1963

LES BICHES ★★★ This story revolves around Frederique and Why, two lesbian lovers in love with the same man. Good music, but the acting could be better. In French with English subtitles. Not rated; contains profanity. 104m. **DIR:** Claude Chabrol. **CAST:** Jean-Louis Trintignant, Jacqueline Sassard, Stéphane Audran. 1968

LES CARABINIERS ★★★1/2 One of Jean-Luc Godard's strangest films, an extreme attack on the absurdity of war seen through the eyes of two morons who enlist as mercenaries. Not rated. In French with English subtitles. B&W; 80m. **DIR:** Jean-Luc Godard. **CAST:** Marino Masé, Albert Juross. 1962

LES CHOSES DE LA VIE (THINGS IN LIFE, THE) ★★★1/2 A hospitalized businessman, injured in an automobile accident, reflects on his relationship with his wife and mistress. Mediocre drama gets a lift from a strong cast. In French with English subtitles. 90m. **DIR:** Claude Sautet. **CAST:** Romy Schneider, Michel Piccoli, Lea Massari. 1970

LES COMPERES ★★★★ Pierre Richard and Gérard Depardieu star in this madcap French comedy as two strangers who find themselves on the trail of a runaway teenager. Both think they're the father—it was the only way the boy's mother could think of to enlist their aid. In French with English subtitles. Rated PG for profanity and brief violence. 90m. **DIR:** Francis Veber. **CAST:** Pierre Richard, Gérard Depardieu. 1984

LES COUSINS ★★★1/2 Innocent country lad, in Paris for the first time to attend university, moves in with his unscrupulous cousin. Melancholy study of big-city decadence directed with a cold, clear eye by Claude Chabrol. In French with English subtitles. Not rated. 110m. **DIR:** Claude Chabrol. **CAST:** Gerard Blain, Jean-Claude Brialy, Juliette Mayniel. 1958

•**LES ENFANTS TERRIBLES** ★★★1/2 Jean Cocteau wrote (but did not direct) this drama as a companion piece to his earlier *Les Parents Terribles*. In a similarly claustrophobic story, the nearly incestuous relationship between a teenage brother and sister destroys them when it is shattered by other people of their same age. Director Jean-Pierre Melville, then at the beginning of his career, turns the low budget to his stylistic advantage. Also known as *The Strange Ones*. In French with English subtitles. B&W; 100m. **DIR:** Jean-Pierre Melville. **CAST:** Nicole Stephane, Edouard Dermithe. 1949

LES GIRLS ★★★★ Gene Kelly is charming, Mitzi Gaynor is funny, Taina Elg is funnier, Kay Kendall is funniest in this tale of a libel suit over a published memoir. Three conflicting accounts of what was and wasn't emerge from the courtroom. A witty film with Cole Porter music and stylish direction by George Cukor. 114m. **DIR:** George Cukor. **CAST:** Gene Kelly, Kay Kendall, Taina Elg, Mitzi Gaynor, Jacques Bergerac. 1957

LES GRANDES GUEULES (JAILBIRDS' VACATION) ★★1/2 This comedy-drama about parolees working on a backwoods sawmill would be better if it were shorter and the extended fistfight scenes were cut measurably. Otherwise, the "jailbirds" are a lively, entertaining bunch. In French with English subtitles. 125m. **DIR:** Robert Enrico. **CAST:** Lino Ventura, Bourvil, Marie Dubois. 1965

LES LIAISONS DANGEREUSES ★★★ Complex, amoral tale of a diplomat and his wife whose open marriage and numerous affairs eventually lead to tragedy. Well photographed and acted (especially by Jeanne Moreau), this adult and downbeat film fluctuates at times between satire and comedy and depression, but overall the experience is pretty grim. In French with English subtitles. B&W; 108m. **DIR:** Roger Vadim. **CAST:** Gérard Philipe, Jeanne Moreau, Jeanne Valerie, Annette Vadim, Simone Renant, Jean-Louis Trintignant. 1959

LES MISERABLES (1935) ★★★★ The most watchable and best acted of the many versions of Victor Hugo's story of good and evil. Fredric March steals a loaf of bread to survive, only to undergo a lifetime of torment. Charles Laughton is absolutely frightening as the personification of an uncaring legal system. B&W; 108m. **DIR:** Richard Boleslawski. **CAST:** Fredric March, Charles Laughton, Cedric Hardwicke, Florence Eldridge. 1935

LES MISERABLES (1957) ★★★★ The length weakens the story, but this is probably the most complete film version of Victor Hugo's novel. The story of a detective's relentless pursuit of a man for stealing bread inspired many modern chase films. In French with English subtitles. B&W; 210m. **DIR:** Jean-Paul Le Chanois. **CAST:** Jean Gabin, Daniele Delorme, Bourvil, Bernard Bljer, Gianni Esposito. 1957

LES MISERABLES (1978) ★★★1/2 Lavish television version of Victor Hugo's classic tale of a petty thief's attempt to forget his past only to be hounded through the years by a relentless police inspector. Richard Jordan as the thief turned mayor and Anthony Perkins as his tormentor are extremely good. 150m. DIR: Glenn Jordan. CAST: Richard Jordan, Anthony Perkins, John Gielgud, Cyril Cusack, Flora Robson, Claude Dauphin. 1978

LES MISÉRABLES (1995) ★★★ This loose weaving of Victor Hugo's 1862 novel into the twentieth century unfolds as two parallel epics. When an illiterate Frenchman helps a wealthy Jewish family flee Nazi persecution, he discovers that his life mirrors that of Jean Valjean, and that he shares Valjean's desperate struggle to assert the dignity of man. The film is saturated with soap-opera sensibilities and seductive historical resonance. In French with English subtitles. Rated R for violence, language, and sex. 174m. DIR: Claude Lelouch. CAST: Jean-Paul Belmondo, Michel Boujenah, Alessandra Martines, Annie Girardot, Philippe Léotard. 1995

LES MISÉRABLES (1998) ★★★★ Until the third act, this opulent adaptation of Victor Hugo's classic superbly re-creates Javert's maniacal pursuit of Jean Valjean, the ex-convict who wishes only to forge a new life of compassion and dignity. The lead players are excellent: Liam Neeson is believably powerful as Valjean; hawk-nosed Geoffrey Rush is positively chilling as the implacable Javert. Details are meticulous, but the long-awaited conclusion lacks closure and is irritatingly abrupt. Getting there, however, is the stuff of great melodrama. Rated PG-13 for violence and dramatic intensity. 129m. DIR: Bille August. CAST: Liam Neeson, Geoffrey Rush, Uma Thurman, Claire Danes, Hans Matheson, Reine Brynolfsson, Peter Vaughan. 1998 DVD

•LES PARENTS TERRIBLES ★★★★ Unwilling to let her son escape her clutches, a domineering middle-class woman tries to interfere with his upcoming marriage, not knowing that her son's fiancée is also her henpecked husband's mistress. In adapting his own stage play, director Jean Cocteau maintains the stage setting (which consists of only two scenes) in order to emphasize the claustrophobic lives these people live. A subtle but effective drama. Also known as The Storm Within. In French with English subtitles. B&W; 98m. DIR: Jean Cocteau. CAST: Jean Marais, Yvonne de Bray, Gabrielle Dorziat. 1948

LES PATTERSON SAVES THE WORLD ★★★ Barry Humphries, the immensely popular Australian comic best known here for his character Dame Edna Everage, plays both the good dame and Sir Les Patterson, a fat, flatulent, drunken ambassador from down under. The plot, a spy-movie spoof, holds together a string of outrageous slapstick gags involving bodily functions, ethnic humor, and sexual etiquette. Not rated; it's not for kids. 105m. DIR: George Miller. CAST: Barry Humphries, Pamela Stephenson. 1987

LES RENDEZ-VOUS D'ANNA ★★★★ Anna is a film director who lives a life of desultory detachment while traveling through Europe. She indulges in anonymous sex and is plagued by people talking relentlessly about themselves, to whom she listens with comically placid disinterest. A fascinating movie, shot with flawless fluidity. In French with English subtitles. Rated R for nudity. 120m. DIR: Chantal Akerman. CAST: Aurore Clement, Helmut Griem, Magali Noel, Lea Massari, Jean-Pierre Cassel. 1978

LES TRICHEURS ★★1/2 A roulette addict tries to break his habit with the help of a woman he meets at the tables. Lackluster gambling drama, set in the casinos of Europe. In French with English subtitles. Not rated. 93m. DIR: Barbet Schroeder. CAST: Jacques Dutronc, Bulle Ogier, Kurt Raab. 1984

LES VIOLONS DU BAL ★★★ Clever movie combines the story of director-star Michel Drach's childhood (in France under the Nazi occupation) and his attempts as an adult to film the story. Engaging coming-of-age story. In French with English subtitles. 108m. DIR: Michel Drach. CAST: Michel Drach, Jean-Louis Trintignant, Marie-Jose Nat. 1974

LES VISITEURS DU SOIR ★★★ In medieval France, the devil sends two of his servants to disrupt the engagement party of a baron's daughter. A handsome but lightweight morality play. In French with English subtitles. B&W; 110m. DIR: Marcel Carné. CAST: Arletty, Jules Berry, Marie Dea, Alain Cuny. 1942

LES VOLEURS ★★★ French filmmaker Andre Techine recycles the old brothers-on-opposite-sides-of-the-law plot, dressing it up with Pulp Fiction–style flashing back and forth in time. The result is well acted (especially by Laurence Cote) but overlong with Cote, is wasted in a glorified cameo. In French with English subtitles. Rated R for violence, profanity (in subtitles), nudity, and simulated sex. 113m. DIR: André Téchiné. CAST: Daniel Auteuil, Catherine Deneuve, Laurence Cote, Benoit Magimel. 1996

LESS THAN ZERO 🦃 A movie meant to illuminate the meaninglessness of Los Angeles's post-college-crowd cool. Rated R for violence and profanity. 100m. DIR: Marek Kanievska. CAST: Andrew McCarthy, Jami Gertz, Robert Downey Jr., James Spader, Tony Bill, Nicholas Pryor, Michael Bowen. 1987

•LESSER EVIL, THE ★★★ A quartet of men are reunited when the police begin to reinvestigate a crime in which they were involved as teenagers. The cast is the best reason to see this suspense drama, though too much of the film consists of flashbacks to their teenage years. Rated R for profanity, violence, and brief nudity. 96m. DIR: David Mackay. CAST: David Paymer, Arliss Howard, Tony Goldwyn, Colm Feore. 1998

LESSON IN LOVE, A ★★★ Gunnar Björnstrand plays a philandering gynecologist who realizes that his long-suffering wife is the woman he loves the most, and he sets out to win her back. This is a little ponderous for a true romantic comedy, but good writing and good acting move the film along and provide some funny yet realistic situations. In Swedish with subtitles. B&W; 97m. DIR: Ingmar Bergman. CAST: Gunnar Björnstrand, Eva Dahlbeck, Harriet Andersson. 1954

LET FREEDOM RING ★★★ In the West of the 1880s, Nelson Eddy leads homesteaders against the selfish interests of a group of tycoons. Unadorned flag-waving written by Ben Hecht, but it works as Eddy sings many familiar American standards. B&W;

100m. **DIR:** Jack Conway. **CAST:** Nelson Eddy, Virginia Bruce, Victor McLaglen, Lionel Barrymore, Edward Arnold, Guy Kibbee, Charles Butterworth, H. B. Warner, Raymond Walburn. **1939**

LET HIM HAVE IT ★★★★★ One of the best films of 1991—a powerful tale of a miscarriage of justice in the London of 1952, based on the true story of two teens convicted of murdering a policeman. Peter Medak's film details how one of the kids, a sweet-natured, simpleminded adolescent, ended up on death row, when he shouldn't even have been tried. Rated R, with profanity and violence. 110m. **DIR:** Peter Medak. **CAST:** Chris Eccleston, Paul Reynolds, Tom Courtenay. **1991**

LET IT BE ★★★1/2 The last days of the Beatles are chronicled in this cinema verité production, which was originally meant to be just a documentary on the recording of an album. What emerges, however, is a portrait of four men who have outgrown their images and, sadly, one another. There are moments of abandon, in which they recapture the old magic, but overall, the movie makes it obvious that the Beatles would never get back to where they once belonged. Rated G. 80m. **DIR:** Michael Lindsay-Hogg. **CAST:** The Beatles. **1970**

LET IT RIDE ★★★1/2 One last binge at the racetrack by a chronic gambler (Richard Dreyfuss), who can't resist a hot tip on the horses, turns into a riotous fiasco in this breezy, modest comedy. Rated PG-13. 91m. **DIR:** Joe Pytka. **CAST:** Richard Dreyfuss, Teri Garr, David Johansen, Allen Garfield, Jennifer Tilly. **1989**

LET IT ROCK ★★ This ludicrous behind-the-scenes view of the music business features Dennis Hopper as a manic rock-music promoter. Rated R for nudity, profanity, and violence. 75m. **DIR:** Roland Klick. **CAST:** Dennis Hopper, Terrance Robay, David Hess. **1988**

LET'S DANCE ★★ A listless, disappointing musical. A miscast Betty Hutton and Fred Astaire stumble through the tired story of a song-and-dance team that splits up and reunites. 112m. **DIR:** Norman Z. McLeod. **CAST:** Betty Hutton, Fred Astaire, Roland Young, Ruth Warrick. **1950**

LET'S DO IT AGAIN ★★★1/2 After scoring with *Uptown Saturday Night*, Sidney Poitier and Bill Cosby decided to reteam for this tale of a couple of lodge brothers taking on the gangsters. Rated PG. 112m. **DIR:** Sidney Poitier. **CAST:** Sidney Poitier, Bill Cosby, Jimmie Walker, Calvin Lockhart, John Amos. **1975**

LET'S GET HARRY ★★1/2 When an American (Mark Harmon) is kidnapped during a South American revolution, a group of his friends decide to bring him home. They hire a soldier of fortune (Robert Duvall) to lead them into the jungles of Colombia where, against all odds, they fight to bring Harry home. Rated R for violence and language. 98m. **DIR:** Alan Smithee. **CAST:** Robert Duvall, Gary Busey, Mark Harmon, Glenn Frey, Michael Schoeffling. **1986**

LET'S MAKE IT LEGAL ★★★ Claudette Colbert and Zachary Scott are the best players in this sophisticated comedy about marriage, divorce, and friendship. Marilyn Monroe shines in a supporting role. B&W; 74m. **DIR:** Richard Sale. **CAST:** Claudette Colbert, Marilyn Monroe, Macdonald Carey, Zachary Scott, Robert Wagner. **1951**

LET'S MAKE LOVE ★★★ A tasty soufflé filled with engaging performances. Yves Montand plays a millionaire who wants to stop a musical show because it lampoons him. When he meets cast member Marilyn Monroe, he changes his mind. He hires Milton Berle to teach him comedy, Gene Kelly to teach him dance, and Bing Crosby as a vocal coach. Monroe's "My Heart Belongs to Daddy" number is a highlight. 118m. **DIR:** George Cukor. **CAST:** Marilyn Monroe, Yves Montand, Tony Randall, Wilfrid Hyde-White. **1960**

LET'S SCARE JESSICA TO DEATH ★★ A young woman staying with some odd people out in the country witnesses all sorts of strange things, like ghosts and blood-stained corpses. Is it real, or some kind of elaborate hoax? The title tells it all in this disjointed terror tale, though it does contain a few spooky scenes. Rated PG. 89m. **DIR:** John Hancock. **CAST:** Zohra Lampert, Barton Heyman. **1971**

LET'S SPEND THE NIGHT TOGETHER ★★★1/2 In this concert film, directed by Hal Ashby, the Rolling Stones are seen rockin' and rollin' in footage shot during the band's 1981 American tour. It's a little too long—but Stones fans and hard-core rockers should love it. Rated PG for suggestive lyrics and behavior. 94m. **DIR:** Hal Ashby. **CAST:** The Rolling Stones. **1982**

L'ETAT SAUVAGE (THE SAVAGE STATE) ★★★ Engrossing political thriller set in 1960s Africa after independence from colonial rule. A government official returns looking for his wife, who is living with a powerful black minister in the new government. A genuine sexual potboiler. In French with English subtitles. Not rated; contains nudity and violence. 111m. **DIR:** Francis Girod. **CAST:** Jacques Dutronc, Marie-Christine Barrault, Michel Piccoli. **1978**

LETHAL CHARM ★★ Familiar tale has White House correspondent Barbara Eden playing mentor to novice Heather Locklear, only to have Locklear take over Eden's life, her son, and eventually her job. When Locklear becomes volatile, Eden uses her investigative skills to get to the bottom of things. Hohum made-for-TV affair. Not rated. 92m. **DIR:** Richard Michaels. **CAST:** Barbara Eden, Heather Locklear. **1990**

LETHAL GAMES 🎬 Citizens of a small town band together to fight off the mob. They turn to ex-Vietnam vet Frank Stallone for assistance. Yeah, right! 83m. **DIR:** John Bowen. **CAST:** Frank Stallone, Brenda Vaccaro. **1991**

LETHAL LOLITA—AMY FISHER: MY STORY 🎬 Trashy sensationalized made-for-TV movie about an immature 16-year-old girl and her scandalous affair with a married man. 93m. **DIR:** Bradford May. **CAST:** Ed Marinaro, Noelle Parker, Boyd Kestner, Pierrette Lynch, Kathleen Laskey. **1992**

LETHAL NINJA ★★ Ex-CIA agent journeys to Africa to rescue his wife from evil Ninjas in the employ of a Nostradamus-inspired fanatic out to poison the world's water supply. (Yes, *that* old story again!) For kick-boxing fans only. Rated R for strong violence. 83m. **DIR:** Yossi Wein. **CAST:** Ross Kettle, Karyn Hill, Frank Notaro. **1993**

LETHAL OBSESSION 🎬 Contrived suspense yarn about drugs and murder. Rated R; contains nudity, profanity, and violence. 100m. DIR: Peter Patzack. CAST: Tahnee Welch, Elliott Gould, Michael York, Peter Maffay. 1987

LETHAL TENDER ★★ Dreary and familiar tale of terrorists holding the department of water hostage as a diversionary tactic to steal millions in bonds. Jeff Fahey looks tired as the cop jumping through bad guy Gary Busey's hoops in order to save the day. Rated R for language and violence. 93m. DIR: John Bradshaw. CAST: Jeff Fahey, Kim Coates, Gary Busey. 1996

LETHAL WEAPON ★★★★ This fast, frantic, and wholly improbable police thriller owes its success to the chemistry between the two leads. Mel Gibson is fine as the cop on the edge (the weapon of the title). Danny Glover is equally good as his laid-back, methodical partner. Rated R for violence. 105m. DIR: Richard Donner. CAST: Mel Gibson, Danny Glover, Gary Busey, Mitchell Ryan, Tom Atkins, Darlene Love. 1987 DVD

LETHAL WEAPON 2 ★★★1/2 Mel Gibson and Danny Glover return as odd-couple police officers Riggs and Murtaugh in this enjoyable action sequel. This time, our mismatched heroes are up against some bad guys from South Africa. Predictable but fun. Rated R for violence, profanity, nudity, and simulated sex. 110m. DIR: Richard Donner. CAST: Mel Gibson, Danny Glover, Joe Pesci, Joss Ackland, Patsy Kensit. 1989 DVD

LETHAL WEAPON 3 ★★★1/2 More madness and mayhem from the lethal team of Mel Gibson and Danny Glover as they, with the help of comic relief Joe Pesci, go after a renegade cop who is selling formerly confiscated weapons to L.A. street gangs. It's almost too much of a good thing, as director Richard Donner and his collaborators pack the movie with every gag, shoot-out, and chase they can come up with. Rated R for violence and profanity. 117m. DIR: Richard Donner. CAST: Mel Gibson, Danny Glover, Joe Pesci, René Russo, Stuart Wilson, Darlene Love. 1992 DVD

LETHAL WEAPON 4 ★★1/2 Maverick cops Mel Gibson and Danny Glover are back again, this time battling an Asian gangster (Hong Kong action star Jet Li) who is smuggling immigrants and counterfeit Chinese currency. The series has become a bloated, bizarre mix of slapstick and high explosives, but Gibson and Glover are as appealing as ever, and director Richard Donner somehow keeps things moving along. Rated R for violence and profanity. 125m. DIR: Richard Donner. CAST: Mel Gibson, Danny Glover, René Russo, Joe Pesci, Chris Rock, Jet Li. 1998 DVD

LETHAL WOMAN ★★ A rape victim takes revenge by luring all involved to her island and killing them. Not rated but contains nudity, violence, and gore. 96m. DIR: Christian Marnham. CAST: Robert Lipton, Merete VanKamp, Shannon Tweed. 1989

LET'S TALK ABOUT SEX 💘 Watch for a sharp rise in voluntary celibacy if sex ever becomes as unsatisfying as this amateurish melodrama about Miami roommates who videotape a pilot TV show in which females talk bluntly and crudely about men, dating, and mating. Rated R for language and sexual con-

tent. 82m. DIR: Troy Beyer. CAST: Troy Beyer, Randi Ingerman, Paget Brewster. 1998

LETTER, THE ★★★★ Bette Davis stars in this screen adaptation of Somerset Maugham's play as the coldly calculating wife of a rubber plantation owner (Herbert Marshall) in Malaya. In a fit of pique, she shoots her lover and concocts elaborate lies to protect herself. With tension mounting all the way, we wonder if her evil ways will eventually lead to her downfall. B&W; 95m. DIR: William Wyler. CAST: Bette .Davis, Herbert Marshall, James Stephenson. 1940

LETTER FROM AN UNKNOWN WOMAN ★★★ Disregarding the fact that concert pianist Louis Jourdan uses her without pity, beautiful Joan Fontaine stupidly continues to love him through the years. Romantic direction and smooth performances make the clichés work. B&W; 90m. DIR: Max Ophüls. CAST: Joan Fontaine, Louis Jourdan, Mady Christians, Art Smith, Erskine Sanford. 1948

LETTER OF INTRODUCTION ★★★★ An enjoyable melodrama, this is the story of a young actress (Andrea Leeds) who seeks out the advice of an old actor (Adolphe Menjou). The aging star encourages her in her various endeavors. The relationship between the two lead characters is so real, so warm that it carries the film. B&W; 100m. DIR: John M. Stahl. CAST: Adolphe Menjou, Andrea Leeds, Edgar Bergen, George Murphy, Eve Arden, Rita Johnson, Ernest Cossart, Ann Sheridan. 1938

LETTER TO BREZHNEV ★★★1/2 This wistful, spunky little movie presents two young women from Liverpool who befriend a couple of Russian sailors. Teresa (played by Liverpool comedienne Margi Clarke) is just after some fun, but Elaine (Alexandra Pigg) falls in love with her sailor. Peter Firth plays Elaine's love and he's the quintessence of sweetness. Alexandra Pigg gives the film some street-talking sass, and Firth imbues it with adorable innocence. 95m. DIR: Chris Bernard. CAST: Alexandra Pigg, Alfred Molina, Peter Firth, Margi Clarke. 1985

LETTER TO MY KILLER ★★1/2 An average couple try their hand at simple blackmail in this made-for-cable original, only to find themselves in a nightmare of consequences. Starts out slow and never picks up speed. Rated PG-13 for violence. 92m. DIR: Janet Mayers. CAST: Mare Winningham, Nick Chinlund, Rip Torn. 1995

LETTER TO THREE WIVES, A ★★★1/2 Three wives receive a letter from a friend saying that she has run off with one of their husbands. The viewer is then shown three stories that tell why each of the women's husbands might have left them. Very interesting screenplay and superb acting make this an enjoyable film. B&W; 103m. DIR: Joseph L. Mankiewicz. CAST: Jeanne Crain, Linda Darnell, Ann Sothern, Kirk Douglas, Paul Douglas, Barbara Lawrence, Jeffrey Lynn. 1949

LETTERS FROM THE PARK ★★★★ Charming love story à la *Cyrano de Bergerac* features Victor La Place as a sensitive man who writes letters professionally in Cuba in 1913. Hired by an awkward young man who prefers hot air balloons to poetry, he begins a romantic correspondence which becomes real for him. Originally made for Spanish television, this contains mature themes. In Spanish with English subtitles. 85m. DIR: Tomas Gutierrez Alea. CAST: Victor La Place, Ivonne Lopez, Miguel Paneque. 1988

LETTERS TO AN UNKNOWN LOVER ★★★ A soldier who has been carrying on a romance through the mail with a Frenchwoman he has never met dies. When his friend escapes from a Nazi prison camp, he pretends to be the dead man in order to get the woman and her sister to hide him. This engrossing tale, a French and British coproduction, is unrated; it contains some nudity and sexual situations. 100m. DIR: Peter Duffell. CAST: Cherie Lunghi, Yves Beneyton, Mathilda May. 1985

LETTING THE BIRDS GO FREE ★★ Slow-moving and passionless Romance Theatre production features a homely woman who shares the endless duties of her family's small farm. Amid her daily drudgery, a mysterious stranger comes to work on their machinery. Her attraction to him is a desperate attempt to escape her boring life. Never romantic. Not rated; contains no objectionable material. 60m. DIR: Moira Armstrong. CAST: Carolyn Pickles, Tom Wilkinson, Martin Stone, Lionel Jeffries. 1987

LEVIATHAN ★★ The crew of an undersea mining platform comes across a sunken Soviet ship that has been scuttled in an effort to keep some genetic experiment gone awry away from the world. What the miners encounter is part *Alien*, part *20,000 Leagues Under the Sea*, part *The Thing*. Since these other films are so much better, it's best to leave this one alone. Rated R for violence. 98m. DIR: George Pan Cosmatos. CAST: Peter Weller, Richard Crenna, Amanda Pays, Daniel Stern, Ernie Hudson, Meg Foster, Lisa Eilbacher, Hector Elizondo. 1989 DVD

L'HOMME BLESSÉ (THE WOUNDED MAN) ★★★1/2 Lurid sexual psychodrama about a withdrawn young man's obsession for a street hustler he meets by chance. His frustrated lust builds until it finds its shocking release. A powerful and disturbing piece of cinema for adults only. In French with English subtitles. Not rated; contains profanity, nudity, and violence. 90m. DIR: Patrice Chereau. CAST: Jean-Hugues Anglade, Vittorio Mezzogiorno, Roland Bertin, Lisa Kreuzer. 1988

LIANNA ★★★★ The problem with most motion pictures about gays is they always seem to be more concerned with sex than love. In comparison, this film, written and directed by John Sayles stands as a remarkable achievement. About a married housewife named Lianna (Linda Griffiths) who decides to have an affair with, and eventually move in with, another woman (Jane Halloren), it is a sensitive study of one woman's life and loves. Rated R for nudity, sex, and profanity. 110m. DIR: John Sayles. CAST: Linda Griffiths, Jane Halloren, Jon De Vries, Jo Henderson. 1983

LIAR, LIAR ★★★★ This comedy with heart provides the perfect showcase for star Jim Carrey. He's a successful lawyer who finds himself magically committed to speaking only the truth, the result of a son's birthday wish. Carrey's rubber-man gyrations make the film move, but the on-target screenplay holds it all together. Rated PG-13. 87m. DIR: Tom Shadyac. CAST: Jim Carrey, Maura Tierney, Jennifer Tilly, Swoosie Kurtz, Amanda Donohoe, Jason Bernard, Cary Elwes, Mitchell Ryan, Anne Haney, Justin Cooper, Randall "Tex" Cobb. 1997 DVD

LIARS, THE ★★ A woman and her lover pose as mother and son to gain the confidence of a rich man and then murder him for his money. Dreary melodrama. In French with English subtitles. B&W; 92m. DIR: Edmond Gréville. CAST: Dawn Addams, Jean Servais, Claude Brasseur. 1964

LIARS' CLUB, THE ★★1/2 Somewhat interesting tale about a group of high-school friends who try to cover up a rape and end up involved in a murder. The more they try to conceal their crimes, the deeper they sink. Rated R for nudity and language. 91m. DIR: Jeffrey Porter. CAST: Wil Wheaton, Brian Krause, Michael Cudutz, Bruce Weitz. 1993

LIAR'S MOON ★★★1/2 Two young lovers encounter unusually hostile resistance from their parents. Their elopement produces many of the expected problems faced by youths just starting out: limited finances, inexperience, and incompatibility. Rated PG for language. 106m. DIR: David Fisher. CAST: Matt Dillon, Cindy Fisher, Christopher Connelly, Hoyt Axton, Yvonne De Carlo, Susan Tyrrell. 1983 DVD

LIBELED LADY ★★★★★ Their fame as Nick and Nora Charles in the *Thin Man* series notwithstanding, this is the finest film to have paired William Powell and Myrna Loy. They take part in a deliciously funny tale of a newspaper that, when faced with a libel suit from an angered woman, attempts to turn the libel into irrefutable fact. Spencer Tracy and Jean Harlow lend their considerable support, and the result is a delight from start to finish. B&W; 98m. DIR: Jack Conway. CAST: William Powell, Myrna Loy, Spencer Tracy, Jean Harlow. 1936

LIBERATION OF L. B. JONES, THE 🖤 A wealthy black man is deluded into divorcing his wife because of her believed infidelity with a white cop. Rated R. 102m. DIR: William Wyler. CAST: Lola Falana, Roscoe Lee Browne, Lee J. Cobb, Lee Majors, Barbara Hershey. 1970

LIBERTY AND BASH ★★ *Tarzan*-star Miles O'Keeffe and *Hercules/Hulk* Lou Ferrigno are featured in this typically on-par action flick about two war buddies out to stop murderous Miami drug runners. Rated R for language. 92m. DIR: Myrl A. Schreibman. CAST: Miles O'Keeffe, Lou Ferrigno. 1989

●LIBERTY HEIGHTS ★★★★ Baltimore in 1954 is the setting of this intimate, bittersweet trip down memory lane. A Jewish teen makes friends with an upper-class black girl and has his loyalty tested. His college-age brother learns that dream girl and worst nightmare can describe the same date. Their father runs a numbers racket and a burlesque club, and their mother tries to keep ethnic tradition alive in the family. This lush, warmly detailed story about issues and distinctions of race, religion, and social class gives us plenty to feel, think, and grin about. Rated R for language and sexual content. 122m. DIR: Barry Levinson. CAST: Ben Foster, Adrien Brody, Joe Mantegna, Rebekah Johnson, Carolyn Murphy, Bebe Neuwirth. 1999 DVD

LICENSE TO DRIVE ★★★ Wildly improbable yet frenetically funny account of how young Les (Corey Haim) flunks his driver's license exam yet steals his grandfather's Cadillac for a hot date. Richard Masur is perfect as the quiet, sane father trying to deal with insanity. Rated PG-13 for profanity. 88m. DIR: Greg Beeman. CAST: Corey Haim, Corey Feldman, Carol Kane, Richard Masur, Heather Graham. 1988

LICENSE TO KILL ★★★★ Timothy Dalton, in his second outing as James Bond, seeks revenge when his pal, former CIA-agent-turned-DEA-man Felix Leiter, is maimed and Leiter's bride is murdered. Uncommonly serious tone is a boost to the once-formulaic series, and Dalton comes into his own as the modern 007. Rated PG-13. 135m. DIR: John Glen. CAST: Timothy Dalton, Robert Davi, Carey Lowell. 1989 DVD

LIE DOWN WITH DOGS ★★★1/2 Film-school graduate Wally White wrote, directed, and stars in this hilarious exposé of one man's outrageous summer in Provincetown. White plays a reserved gay man whose job passing out handbills is going nowhere. He joins some friends for the summer, trying to get a job as a houseboy to pay his bills. Although not to everyone's taste, this film is funny and fresh. Rated R for adult situations and language. 84m. DIR: Wally White. CAST: Wally White, Kevin Mayes, Darren Dryden, Bash Halow. 1995

LIEBELEI ★★★★ A young lieutenant's love for a Viennese girl is disrupted when he is provoked to a duel by a baron (who mistakenly believes the young man in love with his wife). One of the first masterworks by Max Ophüls, a touching evocation of imperial Vienna. A minor masterpiece. In German with English subtitles. B&W; 88m. DIR: Max Ophüls. CAST: Magda Schneider, Wolfgang Liebeneiner. 1933

LIEBESTRAUM ★★★ A strange tale comparable to the stylings of director David Lynch. Here a young architect is enmeshed in an ill-fated love triangle when he becomes obsessed with an old office building. Rated R for sexual situations and violence. 105m. DIR: Mike Figgis. CAST: Kevin Anderson, Pamela Gidley, Kim Novak, Bill Pullman. 1991

LIES ★★★★ Ann Dusenberry plays a starving actress who gets sucked into a complicated and treacherous plan to gain the inheritance of a rich patient in a mental hospital. The plot is complicated and the good acting balances the intensity. The best part: a great performance by Gail Strickland, who plays a character you'll love to hate. Rated R for violence, sex, nudity, and profanity. 93m. DIR: Ken Wheat, Jim Wheat. CAST: Ann Dusenberry, Gail Strickland, Bruce Davison, Clu Gulager, Terence Knox, Bert Remsen. 1986

LIES & WHISPERS ★★★★ Gripping drama that deals with the pain and embarrassment that a couple faces when the woman discovers that her grandfather was a Nazi war criminal. Dr. Lauren Graham, a child psychologist, meets and falls in love with a Czech author who is a candidate for minister of culture. Their romance is threatened when Graham uncovers her grandfather's secret past. This film deals with the consequences with intelligence and humanity. Rated R for language and violence. 95m. DIR: Roger L. Simon. CAST: Gina Gershon, Rade Serbedzija, Patricia Hodge, Otakar Brousek, Gordon Lovitt. 1998 DVD

LIES BEFORE KISSES ★★★ Above-average made-for-TV vengefest features Ben Gazzara being framed for the murder of a beautiful blackmailer. The setup is obvious, but who hates him enough to do this must be revealed. Satisfying ending. 93m. DIR: Lou Antonio. CAST: Jaclyn Smith, Ben Gazzara, Nick Mancuso, Greg Evigan. 1991

●**LIES MY FATHER TOLD ME** ★★★1/2 Sympathetic tale of a Jewish boy growing up in a Montreal ghetto during the 1920s. Young David sees through the eyes of wonderment as his simple grandfather passes on his stories, a rich tapestry of tradition and family. Rated PG. 102m. DIR: Ján Kadár. CAST: Yossi Yadin, Jeffrey Lynas, Len Birman, Marilyn Lightstone. 1975

LIES OF THE TWINS ★★1/2 Aidan Quinn has a field day playing identical twin psychiatrists (or *are* they actually two different people?), the gentler of whom falls in love with fashion model Isabella Rossellini. Things keep us guessing; alas, concluding events are just plain silly. Made for cable. 93m. DIR: Tim Hunter. CAST: Aidan Quinn, Isabella Rossellini, Iman, Hurd Hatfield. 1991

LT. ROBIN CRUSOE, U.S.N. ♥ Modern-day story of Robinson Crusoe, poorly done and with few laughs. Rated G. 113m. DIR: Byron Paul. CAST: Dick Van Dyke, Nancy Kwan, Akim Tamiroff. 1966

LIFE ★★ Small-time hustler Eddie Murphy and innocent bystander Martin Lawrence get railroaded for a murder in 1932 Mississippi, and wind up in a hard-time prison that looks an awful lot like a country club, given how much our two stars *don't* suffer. It's all nonsense, and utterly lacking in humor: yet another Eddie Murphy vehicle that shoots for the lowest common denominator … and scores. Rated R for profanity and violence. DIR: Ted Demme. CAST: Eddie Murphy, Martin Lawrence, Obba Babatundé, Nick Cassavetes, Anthony Anderson. 1999 DVD

LIFE AND ASSASSINATION OF THE KINGFISH, THE ★★★ A docudrama chronicling the life of flamboyant Louisiana politician Huey Long (Edward Asner). Told as a flashback, during the time Long lay dying from an assassin's bullet, this is an insightful look at an unforgettable time in U.S. history. 96m. DIR: Robert Collins. CAST: Edward Asner, Nicholas Pryor. 1976

LIFE AND DEATH OF COLONEL BLIMP, THE ★★★★ A truly superb film chronicling the life and times of a staunch for-king-and-country British soldier. Sentimentally celebrating the human spirit, it opens during World War II and unfolds through a series of flashbacks that reach as far back as the Boer War. Roger Livesey is excellent in the title role. Deborah Kerr portrays the four women in his life across four decades with charm and insight. Definitely a keeper. 163m. DIR: Michael Powell, Emeric Pressburger. CAST: Roger Livesey, Deborah Kerr, Anton Walbrook. 1943

LIFE AND NOTHING BUT ★★★★★ This antiwar film, which focuses on a group of people attempting to find the bodies of dead soldiers—husbands, fathers, and other loved ones—after World War I, has all the elements of a true classic: unforgettable characters, romance, suspense, and magnificent visuals. Philippe Noiret adds a great characterization to his list of credits. In French with English subtitles. Rated PG. 135m. **DIR:** Bertrand Tavernier. **CAST:** Philippe Noiret, Sabine Azema. **1989**

LIFE AND NOTHING MORE ... ★★★★ Blurring the line between fiction and reality, this exquisite Iranian film is set shortly after an earthquake that killed 50,000 people. As a filmmaker and his son search for two boys who had appeared in one of the man's films, they see how people are coping with this devastation. American viewers may initially find this rather slow, but the lyrical quality keeps building. In Iranian with English subtitles. Not rated. 91m. **DIR:** Abbas Kiarostami. **CAST:** Farhad Kheradmad, Puya Payvar. **1992**

LIFE AND TIMES OF GRIZZLY ADAMS, THE ★★ Fur trapper Dan Haggerty heads for the hills when he's unjustly accused of a crime. There he befriends an oversized bear and they live happily ever after. Rated G. 93m. **DIR:** Dick Friedenberg. **CAST:** Dan Haggerty, Don Shanks, Lisa Jones, Marjory Harper, Bozo. **1976**

LIFE AND TIMES OF JUDGE ROY BEAN, THE ★★★ Weird Western with Paul Newman as the fabled hanging judge. It has some interesting set pieces among the strangeness. Stacy Keach is outstanding as Bad Bob. Rated PG. 120m. **DIR:** John Huston. **CAST:** Paul Newman, Stacy Keach, Victoria Principal, Jacqueline Bisset, Ava Gardner. **1972**

LIFE BEGINS FOR ANDY HARDY ★★★ Andy Hardy, fresh out of high school, tries on New York City for size, comes to grips with a mature woman, and learns a few big-city lessons before deciding college near home and hearth is best. The eleventh and one of the best in the series. B&W; 100m. **DIR:** George B. Seitz. **CAST:** Mickey Rooney, Judy Garland, Lewis Stone, Fay Holden, Ann Rutherford, Sara Haden. **1941**

LIFE IN THE THEATER, A ★★★1/2 Wonderful acting by Jack Lemmon and Matthew Broderick and a witty script by David Mamet highlight this look at theatrical actors. Lemmon and Broderick deliver all the dialogue as the old pro and the promising newcomer. A real treat to watch. Made for TV. 94m. **DIR:** Gregory Mosher. **CAST:** Jack Lemmon, Matthew Broderick. **1993**

LIFE IS BEAUTIFUL ★★★★★ This film begins as a delightful romantic comedy before taking a startling detour. The setting is WWII-era Italy, with star-director-cowriter Roberto Benigni cast as a Jewish waiter named Guido, who marries a beautiful young schoolteacher. After several years, with Italy now overrun by German soldiers, the couple and their young son are hurled into a concentration camp. Determined to shield the boy, Guido employs his quick wit to persuade the impressionable child that it is an elaborate escapade, one filled with countless traps to "trick" and "fool" lesser players into losing. Benigni's audaciousness is damn near unparalleled, because he has done the impossible by setting a film in a Jewish concentration camp and retaining both a sense of humor and the triumph of human spirit. Rated PG-13 for dramatic intensity. 115m. **DIR:** Roberto Benigni. **CAST:** Roberto Benigni, Nicoletta Braschi, Gior-

gio Cantarini, Giustino Durano, Sergio Bustric, Horst Buchholz. **1998 DVD**

LIFE IS SWEET ★★★1/2 Writer-director Mike Leigh is a social visionary, who prior to his first movie *High Hopes*, enthralled and captivated Britain with his made-for-television plays. This, his second movie, is a superlative portrait of a British family: a nurturing mother, a lovably blundering father, and two daughters. The complete spectrum of human emotion is covered and evoked as we observe the family members interact. Rated R for profanity, nudity, and simulated sex. 103m. **DIR:** Mike Leigh. **CAST:** Timothy Spall, Jane Horrocks, Alison Steadman, Jim Broadbent. **1991**

LIFE LESS ORDINARY, A ★★★1/2 This manic contemporary screwball comedy will either delight or utterly baffle viewers. Put-upon janitor Ewan McGregor, seeking revenge after being fired, "kidnaps" his boss's daughter with more than a little assistance from the lady in question. It's all orchestrated by a pair of "celestial cops" who've been ordered by God to make these two young people fall in love. What follows is part musical, part comedy, part pathos, and all madness. Rated R for profanity and violence. 103m. **DIR:** Danny Boyle. **CAST:** Ewan McGregor, Cameron Diaz, Holly Hunter, Delroy Lindo, Ian Holm, Ian McNeice, Stanley Tucci, Dan Hedaya, Tony Shalhoub. **1997 DVD**

LIFE OF BRIAN ★★★★ Religious fanaticism gets a real drubbing in this irreverent and often sidesplitting comedy, which features and was created by those Monty Python crazies. Graham Chapman plays the title role of a reluctant "savior" born in a manger just down the street from Jesus Christ's. Rated R for nudity and profanity. 93m. **DIR:** Terry Jones. **CAST:** Terry Jones, John Cleese, Eric Idle, Michael Palin, Terry Gilliam, Graham Chapman. **1979 DVD**

LIFE OF EMILE ZOLA, THE ★★★★ Paul Muni is excellent in the title role of the nineteenth-century novelist who championed the cause of the wrongly accused Captain Dreyfus (Joseph Schildkraut). A lavish production! B&W; 93m. **DIR:** William Dieterle. **CAST:** Paul Muni, Joseph Schildkraut, Gale Sondergaard, Gloria Holden, Donald Crisp, Louis Calhern. **1937**

LIFE OF HER OWN, A ★★ Can a career woman find love and still have a life of her own? If she looks like Lana Turner, she obviously can in this tearjerker about two models who want careers and husbands in that order. Sluggish pacing and pretentious dialogue make this movie look like a TV soap opera. B&W; 108m. **DIR:** George Cukor. **CAST:** Lana Turner, Ray Milland, Ann Dvorak, Barry Sullivan, Louis Calhern, Tom Ewell, Jean Hagen, Sara Haden, Phyllis Kirk. **1950**

LIFE OF OHARU ★★★★1/2 All but unknown in the U.S., Japanese director Kenji Mizoguchi was one of the great artists of the cinema. This story, of a woman in feudal Japan who, after disgracing the honor of her samurai father, is sold into prostitution, may seem somewhat melodramatic to Western audiences. But Mizoguchi's art rested in his formalistic visual style, consisting of carefully composed shots, long takes, and minimal editing. In Japanese with English subtitles. B&W; 136m. **DIR:** Kenji Mizoguchi. **CAST:** Kinuyo Tanaka, Toshiro Mifune. **1952**

LIFE ON A STRING ★★1/2 A blind musician can regain his sight only by so devoting his life to music that he breaks one thousand strings while playing his banjo. While the plot of this Chinese fable is occasionally obscure, director Chen Kaige (*Farewell My Concubine*) provides breathtaking scenery and an unforgettable battle scene. Not rated; contains no objectionable material. 110m. **DIR:** Chen Kaige. **CAST:** Liu Zhong Yuan, Huang Lei. **1990**

LIFE ON THE MISSISSIPPI ★★★ A veteran riverboat pilot takes on a young apprentice. Good ensemble acting and beautiful location photography enhance this TV movie based on Mark Twain's novel about his own experiences during the glorious days of riverboats. 115m. **DIR:** Peter H. Hunt. **CAST:** Robert Lansing, David Knell, James Keane, Donald Madden. **1980**

LIFE 101 ★★★ Though predictable, you should still find yourself caught up in this sweetly goofy look at the life of a college frosh (Corey Haim) in the 1960s. There is nothing new to the life lessons here, but both Haim and Keith Coogan charm their way through this romantic comedy. Not rated; contains profanity and sexual situations. 95m. **DIR:** Redge Mahaffey. **CAST:** Corey Haim, Keith Coogan, Ami Dolenz, Louis Mandylor, Kyle Cody, Traci Adell. **1995**

LIFE STINKS ★★1/2 A kinder, gentler Mel Brooks directed, cowrote, and stars in this message movie about a rich land developer who bets he can spend a month on the streets of Los Angeles. Even though the film is quite funny, he unfortunately tends to be a tad preachy. Rated PG-13 for profanity and suggested sex. 91m. **DIR:** Mel Brooks. **CAST:** Mel Brooks, Lesley Ann Warren, Jeffrey Tambor, Stuart Pankin, Howard Morris. **1991**

LIFE WITH FATHER ★★★★ A warm, witty, charming, nostalgic memoir of life and the coming of age of author Clarence Day in turn-of-the-century New York City. Centering on his staid, eccentric father (William Powell), the film is a 100 percent delight. Based on the long-running Broadway play. 118m. **DIR:** Michael Curtiz. **CAST:** William Powell, Irene Dunne, Edmund Gwenn, ZaSu Pitts, Jimmy Lydon, Elizabeth Taylor, Martin Milner. **1947 DVD**

LIFE WITH MIKEY ★★★1/2 The story of a former child star who runs a talent agency has built-in laugh spots. Especially with Michael J. Fox as the agent who needs a child star for a commercial or his agency will go under. Fox has a handle on comic reactions and gets to use them. Rated PG. 106m. **DIR:** James Lapine. **CAST:** Michael J. Fox, Nathan Lane, Cyndi Lauper, Christina Vidal. **1993**

LIFEBOAT ★★★1/2 A microcosm of American society, survivors of a World War II torpedoing, adrift in a lifeboat, nearly come a cropper when they take a Nazi aboard. Dumbly dismissed as an artistic failure by most critics, it has some ridiculous flaws, but is nonetheless an interesting and engrossing film. Tunnel-voiced Tallulah Bankhead is tops in this seagoing *Grand Hotel.* Look for Hitchcock's pictorial trademark in a newspaper. B&W; 96m. **DIR:** Alfred Hitchcock. **CAST:** Tallulah Bankhead, John Hodiak, William Bendix, Walter Slezak, Henry Hull, Canada Lee, Hume Cronyn, Heather Angel. **1944**

LIFEFORCE ★★ In this disappointing and disjointed science-fiction–horror film by director Tobe Hooper (*Poltergeist*), ancient vampires from outer space return to Earth via Halley's Comet to feed on human souls. Rated R for violence, gore, nudity, profanity, and suggested sex. 96m. **DIR:** Tobe Hooper. **CAST:** Steve Railsback, Peter Firth, Mathilda May, Frank Finlay, Michael Gothard. **1985 DVD**

LIFEFORCE EXPERIMENT, THE ★★★1/2 Scientist Donald Sutherland is working on a top-secret project, and the CIA sends agent Mimi Kuzyk to investigate. Appalled by what she discovers, Kuzyk wants her bosses to stop the experiment, but they have other plans. Good, but not great made-for-cable adaptation of the Daphne du Maurier story. 96m. **DIR:** Piers Haggard. **CAST:** Donald Sutherland, Mimi Kuzyk, Vlasta Vrana, Corin Nemec, Hayley Reynolds, Miguel Fernandes, Michael Rudder, Michael J. Reynolds. **1994**

LIFEFORM ★★★ Okay *Alien* knockoff begins when a lost Mars probe returns to Earth with an alien egg attached. Before you can say "space-pod," the little dickens has hatched and a tiny monster with an attitude becomes a big monster with a body count. Slow at times but otherwise engaging film. Rated R for violence, profanity, and gore. 90m. **DIR:** Mark H. Baker. **CAST:** Cotter Smith, Deirdre O'Connell, Robert Wisdom, Ryan Philippe. **1995**

LIFEGUARD ★★1/2 After his fifteen-year high school reunion, Sam Elliott begins to feel twinges of fear and guilt. How long can he go on being a lifeguard? Shouldn't he be making the move into a career with a future? The film is likable and easygoing, like its star. If your interest starts to drift, Elliott's charisma will pull you back. Rated PG. 96m. **DIR:** Daniel Petrie. **CAST:** Sam Elliott, Anne Archer, Kathleen Quinlan, Parker Stevenson, Stephen Young. **1976**

LIFELINE ★★ This mildly interesting, but wholly unrealistic, made-for-cable original is about a woman's quest to find her daughter, who has been kidnapped by a white-slave cartel. Not rated; contains violence. 95m. **DIR:** Fred Gerber. **CAST:** Lorraine Bracco, Lisa Jakub, Jean-Marc Barr, Stephen Shellen, Victor Lanoux. **1995 DVD**

LIFEPOD ★★★ It's Alfred Hitchcock's *Lifeboat* in outer space as eight people are trapped in a crippled escape pod after an intergalactic passenger ship is blown up en route. Supplies are short and communications down, plus one of the survivors seems intent on killing off the others. Good special effects and performances help make this film involving, though unexceptional. Made for TV. 90m. **DIR:** Ron Silver. **CAST:** Robert Loggia, Ron Silver, Jessica Tuck, Stan Shaw, Adam Storke, Kelli Williams, Ed Gale, C.C.H. Pounder. **1993**

LIFESPAN 🎦 A young scientist tries to discover the secret of a long-life formula that belonged to a dead colleague. Not rated; it does have nudity and simulated sex. 96m. **DIR:** Alexander Whitelaw. **CAST:** Klaus Kinski, Hiram Keller, Tina Aumont, Fons Rademakers. **1974**

LIFETAKER, THE 🎦 A boring sex thriller about a housewife who entices a young man into her home.

Not rated; contains violence and sexual scenes. 97m. DIR: Michael Papas. CAST: Terence Morgan. 1989

LIFT, THE ★★★ Grizzly supernatural thriller about a demonic elevator that mysteriously claims the lives of innocent riders. The film mixes dark humor with the macabre. This Dutch-made horror film was a major box-office hit in Europe. Rated R for nudity and graphic violence. In Dutch with English subtitles. Also available in a dubbed version. 95m. DIR: Dick Maas. CAST: Huub Stapel. 1985

LIGHT AT THE END OF THE WORLD, THE 💔 Kirk Douglas is a lighthouse keeper whose isolated island is invaded by ruthless pirates. Tedious. Not rated, contains violence and sexual suggestions. 126m. DIR: Kevin Billington. CAST: Kirk Douglas, Yul Brynner, Samantha Eggar, Jean-Claude Drouu, Fernando Rey. 1971

LIGHT IN THE FOREST, THE ★★1/2 James MacArthur stars as a young man who had been captured and raised by the Delaware Indians and is later returned to his white family. Generally a good story with adequate acting, the ending is much too contrived and trite. 92m. DIR: Herschel Daugherty. CAST: James MacArthur, Fess Parker, Wendell Corey, Joanne Dru, Carol Lynley. 1958

LIGHT IN THE JUNGLE 💔 Malcolm McDowell plays Dr. Albert Schweitzer as he brings medicine and music to Africa. Schweitzer, who won the Nobel Peace Prize in 1953, deserves a better bio than this static, sentimental, and unfulfilling bit of window dressing. Rated PG. 91m. DIR: Gary Hofmeyr. CAST: Malcolm McDowell, Susan Strasberg. 1990

•LIGHT IT UP ★★1/2 Decorated New York cop brings a troubled past to his new job as security guard. He becomes a hostage when an altercation fueled by unbearable conditions at a Queens high school escalates into a standoff between students and police. It's a cautionary tale about tolerance, bureaucratic neglect, and emotional baggage and plays better than it sometimes deserves due to its highly talented cast. Rated R for violence and language. 100m. DIR: Craig Bolotin. CAST: Forest Whitaker, Usher Raymond, Robert Ri'chard, Clifton Collins Jr., Rosario Dawson, Sara Gilbert, Judd Nelson. 1999 DVD

LIGHT OF DAY ★★1/2 The dead-end lives of a Cleveland bar band. There's Michael J. Fox as the guitarist willing to compromise in life for some stability. And there's his nihilistic sister (Joan Jett), the leader of the group who says that the beat of the music is all-important. Rated PG-13. 107m. DIR: Paul Schrader. CAST: Michael J. Fox, Gena Rowlands, Joan Jett, Jason Miller, Michael McKean. 1987

LIGHT SLEEPER ★★★ 40-year-old drug delivery boy (Willem Dafoe) must come to terms with his future when his boss (Susan Sarandon) decides to shut down her upscale drug service. A very moody piece, with fine performances by Dafoe and Sarandon. Rated R for profanity and violence. 103m. DIR: Paul Schrader. CAST: Willem Dafoe, Susan Sarandon, Dana Delany, David Clennon, Mary Beth Hurt, Victor Garber, Jane Adams. 1992 DVD

LIGHTHORSEMEN, THE ★★★1/2 Vivid dramatization of the encounter between the Australian and Turkish forces at Beersheba in the North African desert during World War I. Film's main focus is on a young recruit who cannot bring himself to kill in battle. Beautiful cinematography and fine performances by the entire cast make this one a winner. Rated PG. 110m. DIR: Simon Wincer. CAST: Jon Blake, Peter Phelps, Tony Bonner, Bill Kerr, John Walton, Sigrid Thornton. 1988

LIGHTNIN' CRANDALL ★★★★ Bob Steele buys a ranch that is sandwiched between two feuding cattle ranches. Terrific action and stunt work make this one a cavalcade of fast thrills, and one of Steele's best. B&W; 60m. DIR: Sam Newfield. CAST: Bob Steele, Lois January, Dave O'Brien, Charles King. 1937

LIGHTNING INCIDENT, THE 💔 Absolutely laughable saga of a psychic woman (Nancy McKeon) whose newborn son is kidnapped by voodoo cultists. Moderately violent; made for cable. Rated R for language and violence. 90m. DIR: Michael Switzer. CAST: Nancy McKeon, Tantoo Cardinal, Elpidia Carrillo, Polly Bergen, Tim Ryan. 1991

LIGHTNING JACK ★★★ Easygoing outlaw Paul Hogan justs wants to be wanted—by the law—but his attempts at infamy are continually thwarted. It's the mild, mild West, with Cuba Gooding Jr. supplying most of the laughs as Hogan's mute sidekick in a pleasant movie that should please the star's fans. Rated PG-13 for suggested sex and light violence. 98m. DIR: Simon Wincer. CAST: Paul Hogan, Cuba Gooding Jr., Beverly D'Angelo, Kamala Dawson, Pat Hingle, Richard Riehle, L. Q. Jones, Frank McRae. 1994

LIGHTNING OVER WATER ★★★1/2 This haunting film chronicles the final days in the life of American film director Nicholas Ray, whose movies include *Rebel Without a Cause*, *Johnny Guitar*, and *In a Lonely Place*. Wim Wenders presents a warm and gentle portrait of the director as he slowly dies from cancer. Filmed on location in Ray's loft in New York City. Poignant and unforgettable. 91m. DIR: Wim Wenders. CAST: Nicholas Ray, Wim Wenders. 1980

LIGHTNING, THE WHITE STALLION 💔 In this disappointing family film, Mickey Rooney plays a down-on-his-luck gambler who owns a champion jumper. Rated PG. 93m. DIR: William A. Levey. CAST: Mickey Rooney, Susan George. 1986

LIGHTS, CAMERA, ACTION, LOVE ★★ This Romance Theatre production about an actress who must choose between a cameraman and her director could easily be dismissed for its poor acting, inane dialogue; and contrived plot. Its soap-opera style, however, may appeal to those hooked on either soaps or Harlequin romances. Introduced by Louis Jourdan. Not rated; contains no objectionable material. 97m. DIR: Jim Balden. CAST: Laura Johnson, Gary Hudson, Kathleen Nolan, Elissa Leeds, Robert Phelps. 1972

LIGHTS OF OLD SANTA FE ★★★ A sneaky rival rodeo owner has his eyes on Dale Evans's show, and her, too! Roy Rogers and sidekick Gabby Hayes to the rescue. No dramatic climax, just a big rodeo finale weakens this one. B&W; 78m. DIR: Frank McDonald. CAST: Roy Rogers, George "Gabby" Hayes, Dale Evans, Tom Keene, Lloyd Corrigan. 1944

LIGHTSHIP, THE ★★ The chief interest in this allegorical suspense drama is in seeing Robert Duvall play an over-the-top villain. But the story itself—a trio of sadistic bank robbers hijack a floating, anchored lighthouse and the ship's pacifist captain (Klaus Maria Brandauer) tries to stop his crew from fighting back—is short on suspense. Rated R. 90m. **DIR:** Jerzy Skolimowski. **CAST:** Robert Duvall, Klaus Maria Brandauer, Michael Lyndon. **1986**

LIKE FATHER, LIKE SON ★★ Father and son (Dudley Moore and Kirk Cameron) accidentally transfer brains. The film too often sinks to tasteless and juvenile stunts to spice up the lone idea. Rated PG-13. 99m. **DIR:** Rod Daniel. **CAST:** Dudley Moore, Kirk Cameron, Margaret Colin, Catherine Hicks, Sean Astin, Patrick O'Neal. **1987**

LIKE WATER FOR CHOCOLATE ★★★★ Romance, fantasy, comedy, and drama blend in delicious fashion. Based on the celebrated novel by Laura Esquivel, the movie depicts a young woman whose engagement is thwarted by her selfish mother. The frustrated woman transfers her passion into her cooking, which takes on a supernatural quality. There is a magical aura to the film, which is also extremely sensual. In Spanish with English subtitles. Rated R for nudity and suggested sex. 113m. **DIR:** Alfonso Arau. **CAST:** Lumi Cavazos, Marco Leonardi, Regina Torne, Mario Ivan Martinez. **1993 DVD**

LI'L ABNER (1940) ★★ The first of two filmed versions of Al Capp's popular comic strip boasts a great cast of silent film's best clowns. B&W; 78m. **DIR:** Albert S. Rogell. **CAST:** Granville Owen, Martha Driscoll, Buster Keaton, Kay Sutton, Edgar Kennedy, Chester Conklin, Billy Bevan, Al St. John. **1940**

LI'L ABNER (1959) ★★★★ A perfectly delightful combination of satire, music, and cartoonish fun based on the popular Broadway musical with most of the original cast. The highlight is the Sadie Hawkins Day race in which the women in Dogpatch get to marry the man they catch. With such songs as "Bring Them Back the Way They Was," "The Country's in the Very Best of Hands," and "I'm Past My Prime." 112m. **DIR:** Melvin Frank. **CAST:** Peter Palmer, Leslie Parrish, Julie Newmar, Stubby Kaye, Stella Stevens, Howard St. John, Billie Hayes, Robert Strauss. **1959**

LILACS IN THE SPRING (LET'S MAKE UP) 💔 Errol Flynn is much too braggadocio-like in this English-made musical about a highborn lady trying to decide which suitor to marry. Flynn looks embarrassed and well he should be with this script. 94m. **DIR:** Herbert Wilcox. **CAST:** Errol Flynn, Anna Neagle, David Farrar. **1954**

LILI ★★★★ "Hi Lili, Hi Lili, Hi Low," the famous song by composer Bronislau Kaper, is just one of the delights in this musical fantasy about a French orphan who tags along with a carnival and a self-centered puppeteer. A certified pleasure to keep your spirits up. 81m. **DIR:** Charles Walters. **CAST:** Leslie Caron, Mel Ferrer, Zsa Zsa Gabor, Jean-Pierre Aumont. **1953**

LILI MARLEEN ★★1/2 The popular song of the Forties and the wartime adventures of the singer of the song, who became known as Lili to the German troops, are the basis for this engrossing film. In German with English subtitles. Rated R because of nudity and implied sex. 120m. **DIR:** Rainer Werner Fass-

binder. **CAST:** Hanna Schygulla, Giancarlo Giannini, Mel Ferrer. **1981**

LILIES ★★ A Catholic bishop, lured to a prison to hear a dying inmate's confession, is treated instead to a reenactment of scenes from his own past, when he and the inmate were students together. Pretentious, contrived, and amateurishly acted, with nearly incoherent dialogue, this affected film inexplicably won several awards. Not rated; contains mature themes, sexual content, and brief nudity. 95m. **DIR:** John Greyson. **CAST:** Ian D. Clark, Marcel Sabourin, Jason Cadieux, Danny Gilmore, Brent Carver, Matthew Ferguson. **1996 DVD**

LILIES OF THE FIELD (1930) ★★ Corinne Griffith loses custody of her child and finds a new life as a show girl. A real weeper in the most mawkish tarnished-woman tradition. Stolid and overwrought. B&W; 65m. **DIR:** Alexander Korda. **CAST:** Corinne Griffith, Ralph Forbes. **1930**

LILIES OF THE FIELD (1963) ★★★★ Sidney Poitier won an Academy Award for his portrayal of a handyman who happens upon a group of nuns who have fled from East Germany and finds himself building a chapel for them. With little or no buildup, the movie went on to become a big hit. B&W; 93m. **DIR:** Ralph Nelson. **CAST:** Sidney Poitier, Lilia Skala. **1963**

LILITH ★★ This is an intriguing, somber, frequently indecipherable journey into the darker depths of the human psyche. Warren Beatty is a young psychiatric therapist at a mental institute who falls in love with a beautiful schizophrenic patient (Jean Seberg), with tragic results. Visually impressive, it remains dramatically frustrating due to its ambiguous blending of sanity and madness. B&W; 114m. **DIR:** Robert Rossen. **CAST:** Warren Beatty, Jean Seberg, Peter Fonda, Kim Hunter, Anne Meacham, Jessica Walter, Gene Hackman. **1964**

LILLIE ★★★★ The fascinating, fashionable, passionate, scandal-marked life of Edwardian beauty Lillie Langtry, international stage star and mistress of Edward, Prince of Wales, heir to Queen Victoria, is colorfully told in this excellent PBS series of manners and mannerisms. 690m. **DIR:** Tony Wharmby. **CAST:** Francesca Annis, Peter Egan, Anton Rodgers. **1977**

LILY DALE ★★1/2 Horton Foote's claustrophobic stageplay makes an unwieldy transition to the screen. The result is an awkward series of confrontations between people who explain neither themselves nor their motives during an estranged son's visit with his mother and high-strung sister. Rated PG. 95m. **DIR:** Peter Masterson. **CAST:** Mary Stuart Masterson, Sam Shepard, Stockard Channing, Tim Guinee, John Slattery, Jean Stapleton. **1996**

LILY IN LOVE ★★★★ Christopher Plummer is superb as an aging, egocentric actor who disguises himself as a younger man in an attempt to snag a plum role in a film written by his wife (Maggie Smith), and succeeds all too well. *Lily in Love* is a marvelously warm and witty adult comedy. Not rated, the film has some profanity. 105m. **DIR:** Karoly Makk. **CAST:** Christopher Plummer, Maggie Smith, Elke Sommer, Adolph Green. **1985**

LILY WAS HERE ★★1/2 Dutch film about a decent girl who plans to move to America with a wholesome soldier. When he is murdered, she leaves her cold-hearted mother and decides to have the baby she's carrying. Melodramatic but watchable. Rated R for violence. 110m. **DIR:** Ben Verbong. **CAST:** Marion Van Thijn, Thom Hoffman, Monique van de Ven. **1989**

LIMBIC REGION, THE ★★1/2 Dedicated cop Edward James Olmos alienates family and friends while obsessing over a serial murderer clearly patterned on San Francisco's Zodiac killer, in this mildly intriguing but ultimately boring drama. Scripters Todd Johnson and Patrick Ranahan spend too much time with the reenacted murders and not enough with Olmos; the flashback narration is also intrusive. Rated R for violence, profanity, nudity, and simulated sex. 95m. **DIR:** Michael Pattinson. **CAST:** Edward James Olmos, George Dzundza, Roger R. Cross, Gwynyth Walsh. **1996**

LIMBO ★★★ The point here scarcely does the fascinating characters justice, and the unexpectedly abrupt fade-out is infuriatingly oblique. The story, set in modern-day Alaska, concerns a fisherman turned land-based handyman after a decades-old tragedy from which he still hasn't recovered. He catches the eye of a perky lounge singer who's got problems of her own when it comes to handling her clearly troubled teenage daughter. Unexpected circumstances isolate this trio, and what begins as an interesting ensemble character drama transforms into a fight for survival. Rated R for profanity, earthy dialogue, and brief violence. 126m. **DIR:** John Sayles. **CAST:** David Strathairn, Mary Elizabeth Mastrantonio, Vanessa Martinez, Kris Kristofferson, Casey Siemaszko. **1999 DVD**

LIMELIGHT ★★★1/2 Too long and too much Charlie Chaplin (who trimmed Buster Keaton's part when it became obvious he was stealing the film), this is nevertheless a poignant excursion. Chaplin is an aging music hall comic on the skids who saves a ballerina (Claire Bloom) from suicide and, while bolstering her hopes, regains his confidence. The score, by Chaplin, is haunting. B&W; 145m. **DIR:** Charles Chaplin. **CAST:** Charlie Chaplin, Claire Bloom, Buster Keaton, Sydney Chaplin, Nigel Bruce. **1952 DVD**

•LIMEY, THE ★★★★ Upon his release from a British prison, a professional thief (Terence Stamp) journeys to Southern California, where he hopes to learn the truth about his daughter's mysterious death. The trail leads him to a high-rolling record producer (Peter Fonda) involved with underworld figures. Stylishly directed by Steven Soderbergh and filled with outstanding performances. Rated R for violence, profanity, and brief nudity. 90m. **DIR:** Steven Soderbergh. **CAST:** Terence Stamp, Peter Fonda, Lesley Ann Warren, Luis Guzman, Barry Newman, Joe Dallesandro, Nicky Katt, Bill Duke, Amelia Heinle, Melissa George. **1999 DVD**

LIMIT UP ★★ Nancy Allen stars as a woman who wants to be a trader on Chicago's Mercantile Exchange. She's enticed by one of Satan's disciples into a contract for her soul. Harmless, predictable. Watch for cameos by Sally Kellerman and Ray Charles. Rated PG-13 for profanity. 88m. **DIR:** Richard Martini.

CAST: Nancy Allen, Dean Stockwell, Brad Hall, Danitra Vance. **1989**

LINCOLN ASSASSINATION, THE ★★★★ A two-part History Channel production that is as addictive as any fictional drama. Everyone knows the basics, but this painstakingly outlines the events up to and after the assassination, including far-reaching effects. Narrated by Tom Berenger and featuring historical photographs, combined with interviews of both historians and descendants of some of the participants. Not rated. 100m. **DIR:** Lazar Verklan. **1995**

LINDA ★★★★ In this made-for-cable movie based on a John D. MacDonald novella, two neighboring couples become good friends and go on vacation together. Tensions build and one wife shoots the other couple. Thus starts one very twisted plot. Good acting and a suspenseful plot keep the viewer watching. Rated PG-13 for violence. 88m. **DIR:** Nathaniel Gutman. **CAST:** Virginia Madsen, Richard Thomas, Ted McGinley, Laura Harrington, T. E. Russell. **1993**

LINDBERGH KIDNAPPING CASE, THE ★★★ Still another look at one of this century's most famous and fascinating tragedies, this made-for-television version is above average. Anthony Hopkins rates four stars as Bruno Hauptmann, the man convicted and executed for the crime. 150m. **DIR:** Buzz Kulik. **CAST:** Cliff De Young, Anthony Hopkins, Joseph Cotten, Denise Alexander, Sian Barbara Allen, Martin Balsam, Peter Donat, Dean Jagger, Walter Pidgeon. **1976**

LINE KING, THE ★★★★ Al Hirschfeld, the cartoonist whose distinctive ink caricatures have graced *The New York Times* and other publications for seventy years, is the subject of this appealing documentary. While Hirschfeld's rich and varied life makes this an appealing film for most audiences, it is especially recommended to theater buffs, as many Broadway luminaries can be seen paying tribute to the artist. Not rated. 87m. **DIR:** Susan W. Dryfoos. **1996**

LINGUINI INCIDENT, THE ★★ David Bowie's even performance as a man desperate to get married can't compensate for Rosanna Arquette's annoyingly brittle portrayal of a would-be escape artist. The two join with hilarious Eszter Balint to rob an ultra-trendy restaurant. Rated R for profanity. 93m. **DIR:** Richard Shepard. **CAST:** Rosanna Arquette, David Bowie, Eszter Balint, Andre Gregory, Buck Henry, Marlee Matlin. **1992**

LINK ★★1/2 A student (Elisabeth Shue) takes a job with an eccentric anthropology professor (Terence Stamp) and finds herself menaced by a powerful, intelligent ape named Link. The story leaves a number of questions unanswered, but the film can be praised for taking the old cliché of an ape being on the loose and making it surprisingly effective. Rated R for profanity, brief nudity, and violence. 103m. **DIR:** Richard Franklin. **CAST:** Terence Stamp, Elisabeth Shue. **1986**

LION AND THE HAWK, THE ★★★ Turkey in 1923 is the backdrop for this film about a young rebel (Simon Dutton) who runs off with a woman betrothed to a powerful regional governor's nephew. Not rated; has sex, nudity, and violence. 105m. **DIR:** Peter Ustinov. **CAST:** Peter Ustinov, Herbert Lom, Simon Dutton, Leonie Mellinger, Denis Quilley, Michael Elphick. **1983**

LION IN WINTER, THE ★★★★1/2 Acerbic retelling of the clash of wits between England's King Henry II (Peter O'Toole) and Eleanor of Aquitaine (Katharine Hepburn), adapted by James Goldman from his Broadway play. Hepburn won an Oscar for her part, and it's quite well played. The story's extended power struggle rages back and forth, with Henry and Eleanor striking sparks throughout. Rated PG. 135m. DIR: Anthony Harvey. CAST: Katharine Hepburn, Peter O'Toole, Anthony Hopkins, John Castle, Timothy Dalton, Nigel Terry. 1968

LION IS IN THE STREETS, A ★★★1/2 An overlooked, and neglected, movie with James Cagney as a southern hustler and con artist, making it big in politics, stepping on anyone and everyone he meets. In lesser hands than Cagney's, and his favorite director Raoul Walsh, this would be only so-so, but with them it packs a wallop. 88m. DIR: Raoul Walsh. CAST: James Cagney, Barbara Hale, Anne Francis, Jeanne Cagney, Lon Chaney Jr. 1953

LION KING, THE ★★★★1/2 Yet another winner from the modern-day Disney animation masters focuses on a young cub sent into exile when his father is betrayed and killed by a power-hungry sibling. Combining some surprisingly hard-edged moments with plenty of comedy and music, *The Lion King* sets another high-water mark for animated storytelling. Jeremy Irons is outstanding as the voice of the treacherous and scheming Uncle Scar. Rated G. 87m. DIR: Roger Allers, Rob Minkoff. 1994

LION OF AFRICA, THE ★★ This HBO action film is long-winded and a tad too derivative of *Romancing the Stone*. Odd couple Brian Dennehy and Brooke Adams race across Africa with a hot rock that attracts a host of bad guys. Not rated, has violence and profanity. 110m. DIR: Kevin Connor. CAST: Brian Dennehy, Brooke Adams, Don Warrington, Carl Andrews, Katharine Schofield. 1987

LION OF THE DESERT ★★★1/2 This epic motion picture gives an absorbing portrait of the 1929–31 war in the North African deserts of Libya when Bedouin troops on horseback faced the tanks and mechanized armies of Mussolini. Anthony Quinn is Omar Mukhtar, the desert lion who became a nationalist and a warrior at the age of 52 and fought the Italians until they captured and hanged him twenty years later. Rated PG. 162m. DIR: Moustapha Akkad. CAST: Anthony Quinn, Oliver Reed, Rod Steiger. 1981 DVD

LION, THE WITCH AND THE WARDROBE, THE ★★★1/2 Four children pass through a wardrobe into a wondrous land of mythical creatures where an evil Ice Queen has been terrorizing her subjects. This enjoyable made-for-television cartoon was based on C. S. Lewis's *Chronicles of Narnia*. 95m. DIR: Bill Melendez. 1979

LIONHEART (1986) ★★★ On his way to join King Richard's crusade in France, a young knight is joined by a ragtag band of kids on the run from the evil Black Prince. It's enjoyable and suitable for children. It's also captioned for the hearing impaired. Rated PG. 105m. DIR: Franklin J. Schaffner. CAST: Eric Stoltz, Gabriel Byrne, Nicola Cowper, Dexter Fletcher. 1986

LIONHEART (1991) ★★ In this lackluster Jean-Claude Van Damme vehicle, he plays a foreign legionnaire who comes to the U.S. after his brother is killed—all just an excuse for the usual string of martial arts battles. Rated R for violence, profanity, and nudity. 105m. DIR: Sheldon Lettich. CAST: Jean-Claude Van Damme, Harrison Page, Deborah Rennard, Lisa Pelikan, Ashley Johnson. 1991 DVD

LIP SERVICE (1988) ★★★1/2 This HBO film exposes the decline of TV news shows in an offbeat, at times hilarious, style. Old-timer Paul Dooley is forced to share his early morning show with a brash, brainless youngster (Griffin Dunne) who specializes in cheap theatrics. Contains profanity. 77m. DIR: W. H. Macy. CAST: Griffin Dunne, Paul Dooley. 1988

•L.I.P. SERVICE (1999) 💗 Soft-core romp has three private eyes following a porn star for a client in this poor excuse for coupling. Available in two editions, R-rated and not rated; both feature nudity and simulated sex. 90m. DIR: Art Carnage. CAST: Zoe Paul, Venessa Blair, Elina Madison. 1999

LIPSTICK 💗 Model is sexually molested by a composer. Rated R. 89m. DIR: Lamont Johnson. CAST: Margaux Hemingway, Mariel Hemingway, Anne Bancroft, Perry King, Chris Sarandon. 1976

LIPSTICK CAMERA ★★ An aspiring television newscaster uses a miniature camera to get a scoop and impress her idol. But after novice reporter Ele Keats has the film developed, someone makes every attempt to silence her and retrieve the film. Pedestrian and underexposed. Rated R for nudity, adult situations, and violence. 93m. DIR: Mike Bonifer. CAST: Brian Wimmer, Ele Keats, Terry O'Quinn, Sandahl Bergman, Charlotte Lewis, Corey Feldman. 1993 DVD

LIQUID SKY ★★★1/2 An alien spaceship lands on Earth in search of chemicals produced in the body during sex. One of the aliens enters the life of a new wave fashion model and feeds off her lovers, most of whom she's more than happy to see dead. *Liquid Sky* alternately shocks and amuses us with this unusual, stark, and ugly—but somehow fitting—look at an American subculture. Rated R for profanity, violence, rape, and suggested sex. 112m. DIR: Slava Tsukerman. CAST: Anne Carlisle, Paula E. Sheppard. 1983 DVD

LISA ★★ A teenage girl plays flirtatious sex games on the telephone, unaware that her latest "partner" is a vicious serial killer. Implausible plot, cheap thrills. Rated PG-13. 95m. DIR: Gary A. Sherman. CAST: Cheryl Ladd, D. W. Moffett, Staci Keanan. 1990

LISBON ★★ Maureen O'Hara's husband is in a communist prison. International gentleman thief Claude Rains hires Ray Milland to rescue him. Not James Bond caliber. Not *To Catch a Thief* classy. Not really worth much. 90m. DIR: Ray Milland. CAST: Ray Milland, Claude Rains, Maureen O'Hara, Francis Lederer, Percy Marmont. 1956

LISBON STORY ★★★1/2 Commissioned to make a film portrait of Lisbon, German director Wim Wenders turned the occasion into an excuse to make a diverting comedy about his usual preoccupations, the nature and history of cinema. The story, about a sound engineer who comes to Portugal to work on a film only to find that the director has disappeared, is little more than a frame for a lot of talk mixed with lovely cityscapes. Quite diverting for Wenders buffs. Not rated; contains mild profanity. 103m. **DIR:** Wim Wenders. **CAST:** Rudiger Vogler, Patrick Bauchau, Teresa Salgueiro. **1994**

LIST OF ADRIAN MESSENGER, THE ★★★1/2 Excellent suspenser has a mysterious stranger visiting an English estate and the puzzling series of murders that coincide with his arrival. Crisp acting, coupled with John Huston's taut direction, make this crackerjack entertainment. With cameo appearances by Kirk Douglas, Tony Curtis, Burt Lancaster, Robert Mitchum, Frank Sinatra. B&W; 98m. **DIR:** John Huston. **CAST:** George C. Scott, Dana Wynter, Clive Brook, Herbert Marshall. **1963**

LISTEN ★★ Two girls eavesdropping on callers to a phone-sex line discover that one of them is a serial killer. Well-made but uninvolving (and overlong) erotic thriller. Rated R for nudity and violence. 104m. **DIR:** Gavin Wilding. **CAST:** Brooke Langton, Sarah Buxton, Gordon Currie. **1997**

LISTEN, DARLING ★★★ A clever family comedy with Judy Garland introducing "Zing Went the Strings of My Heart," one of her trademark tunes. She also sings "Nobody's Baby" while she and her teenaged brother (Freddie Bartholomew) search for the right mate for their widowed mother. An enjoyable musical. B&W; 70m. **DIR:** Edwin L. Marin. **CAST:** Judy Garland, Freddie Bartholomew, Mary Astor, Walter Pidgeon, Charley Grapewin, Scotty Beckett, Gene Lockhart. **1938**

LISTEN TO ME ♥ Members of a college debating team take time out to find romance. Rated PG-13. 107m. **DIR:** Douglas Day Stewart. **CAST:** Kirk Cameron, Jami Gertz, Roy Scheider, Anthony Zerbe. **1989**

LISTEN TO YOUR HEART ★★★ This cute but predictable romantic comedy features a book editor (Tim Matheson) falling in love with his art director (Kate Jackson). Made for TV, this is unrated. 104m. **DIR:** Don Taylor. **CAST:** Kate Jackson, Tim Matheson, Cassie Yates, George Coe, Tony Plana. **1983**

LISZTOMANIA ♥ Hokey screen biography of composer Franz Liszt. Rated R. 105m. **DIR:** Ken Russell. **CAST:** Roger Daltrey, Sara Kestleman, Paul Nicholas, Fiona Lewis, Ringo Starr. **1975**

LITTLE ANNIE ROONEY ★★★ The title character is a teenaged street kid in braids, but America's Sweetheart, Mary Pickford, who played her, was 32 at the time. Pickford gets away with it—as she did in many of her films. As the daughter of a widowed New York cop, Annie keeps house, runs a street gang, and anguishes when her father is killed and her boyfriend is wrongly accused of the crime. Silent. B&W; 60m. **DIR:** William Beaudine. **CAST:** Mary Pickford, Spec O'Donnell, Hugh Fay. **1925**

LITTLE BIG HORN ★★★★ A small patrol of cavalry men attempt to get through hostile Indian Territory to warn Custer's Seventh Cavalry of the impending Sioux-Cheyenne ambush. Highly suspenseful. B&W; 86m. **DIR:** Charles Marquis Warren. **CAST:** Lloyd Bridges, John Ireland, Marie Windsor, Reed Hadley, Hugh O'Brian, Jim Davis. **1951**

LITTLE BIG MAN ★★★★ Dustin Hoffman gives a bravura performance as Jack Crabbe, a 121-year-old survivor of Custer's last stand. An offbeat Westerncomedy, this film chronicles, in flashback, Crabbe's numerous adventures in the Old West. It's a remarkable film in more ways than one. Rated PG. 150m. **DIR:** Arthur Penn. **CAST:** Dustin Hoffman, Chief Dan George, Faye Dunaway, Martin Balsam, Jeff Corey, Richard Mulligan. **1970**

LITTLE BIGFOOT ★★★ Kids will enjoy this outdoor adventure about a family on vacation that discovers a baby Bigfoot. Young Payton Shoemaker (Ross Malinger) is looking for a little excitement while spending his summer vacation with his family in the wilderness. He gets his wish when he stumbles across the title creature. It's up to Payton and his family to save the infant from a ruthless logging company owner and his band of thugs. Rated PG for violence and language. 99m. **DIR:** Art Camacho. **CAST:** Ross Malinger, P. J. Soles, Kenneth Tigar, Kelly Packard, Don Stroud, Matt McCoy. **1995**

LITTLE BOY LOST ★★★ Newspaperman Bing Crosby can't tell which kid is his as he searches for his son in a French orphanage following World War II. Get out the Kleenex. 95m. **DIR:** George Seaton. **CAST:** Bing Crosby, Claude Dauphin, Nicole Maurey. **1953**

LITTLE BUDDHA ★★1/2 This reverent epic is really two different films rather clumsily patched together. One half, about the ancient Prince Siddhärtha (Keanu Reeves) and his spiritual transformation into Buddha, the Enlightened One, is interesting and enjoyable. The other half, about the modern-day search for the reincarnation of a venerated Buddhist monk, is dull and lifeless. Rated PG. 123m. **DIR:** Bernardo Bertolucci. **CAST:** Keanu Reeves, Chris Isaak, Bridget Fonda, Alex Wiesendanger, Ying Ruocheng, Jigme, Kunsang, Raju Lai, Greishma Makar Singh. **1994 DVD**

LITTLE CAESAR ★★★ Historically, this is an important film. Made in 1930, it started the whole genre of gangster films. As entertainment, this veiled biography of Al Capone is terribly dated. Edward G. Robinson's performance is like a Warner Bros. cartoon in places, but one has to remember this is the original. B&W; 80m. **DIR:** Mervyn LeRoy. **CAST:** Edward G. Robinson, Douglas Fairbanks Jr. **1930**

LITTLE CITY ★★★ Amusing, complicated romantic drama about six people who leave more than their hearts in San Francisco. An exciting cast fleshes out this tale of friends, roommates, and lovers who wind up sharing each other's company and beds before the end of the film. Filled with sparkling dialogue and engaging performances, *Little City* proves that New York isn't the only city that never sleeps. Rated R for language and adult situations. 90m. **DIR:** Roberto Benabib. **CAST:** Jon Bon Jovi, Josh Charles, Joanna Going, Penelope Ann Miller, Annabella Sciorra, JoBeth Williams. **1998**

LITTLE COLONEL, THE ★★★1/2 Grandpa Lionel Barrymore is on the outs with daughter Evelyn Venable as the South recovers from the Civil War. Adorable Shirley Temple smoothes it all over. Film's high point is her step dance with Mr. Bojangles, Bill Robinson. B&W; 80m. DIR: David Butler. CAST: Shirley Temple, Lionel Barrymore, Evelyn Venable, Bill Robinson, Sidney Blackmer. 1935

LITTLE DARLINGS ★★ A story of the trials and tribulations of teen-age virginity, this film too often lapses into chronic cuteness. *Little Darlings* follows the antics of two 15-year-old outcasts—rich, sophisticated Ferris Whitney (Tatum O'Neal) and poor, belligerent Angel Bright (Kristy McNichol)—as they compete to "score" with a boy first. Rated R. 95m. DIR: Ronald F. Maxwell. CAST: Tatum O'Neal, Kristy McNichol, Matt Dillon, Armand Assante. 1980

LITTLE DEATH, THE ★★★ A young musician finds himself falling in love with his stepmother after his father is suddenly murdered. However, the affair uncovers more than lust—there seems to be a conspiracy at hand as well. Almost completely predictable thriller is still watchable thanks to performances by Pamela Gidley and Brent Fraser. Rated R for profanity, violence, and nudity. 90m. DIR: Jan Verheyen. CAST: Pamela Gidley, J. T. Walsh, Dwight Yoakam, Brent Fraser, D. W. Moffett, Richard Beymer. 1995

LITTLE DORRIT ★★★★★ Told in two parts, "Nobody's Fault" and "Little Dorrit's Story," this is a splendid six-hour production of Charles Dickens's most popular novel of his time. Derek Jacobi plays Arthur Clennam, a businessman whose life is forever changed when he meets the good-hearted heroine of the title (newcomer Sarah Pickering). An epic of human suffering, compassion, and triumph. Rated G. 356m. DIR: Christine Edzard. CAST: Alec Guinness, Derek Jacobi, Sarah Pickering, Joan Greenwood, Roshan Seth. 1988

LITTLE DRUMMER GIRL, THE ★★1/2 Director George Roy Hill did everything he could to make this adaptation of John Le Carré's best-seller a fast-paced, involving political thriller. However, his work is thwarted by an unconvincing lead performance by Diane Keaton, who plays an actress recruited by an Israeli general (Klaus Kinski) to help trap a terrorist. Rated R for violence, profanity, suggested sex, and nudity. 130m. DIR: George Roy Hill. CAST: Diane Keaton, Yorgo Voyagis, Klaus Kinski. 1984

LITTLE FOXES, THE ★★★★ The ever-fascinating, ever-unique Bette Davis dominates this outstanding rendering of controversial playwright Lillian Hellman's drama of amoral family greed and corruption down South. Davis's ruthless matriarch, Regina, is the ultimate Edwardian bitch, for whom murder by inaction is not beyond the pale when it comes to achieving her desires. B&W; 116m. DIR: William Wyler. CAST: Bette Davis, Herbert Marshall, Teresa Wright, Richard Carlson, Dan Duryea. 1941 DVD

LITTLE GHOST ★★ Mildly diverting tale of a 12-year-old boy who teams with a girl ghost to save her castle from becoming an exclusive resort. Rated G. 88m. DIR: Linda Shayne. CAST: Kristine Wayborn, James Fitzpatrick, Sally Kirkland, Linda Bruneau, Trishalee Hardy. 1997

LITTLE GIANT ★★ Title refers to a vacuum cleaner that Lou Costello sells door to door. Bud Abbott's in the movie, too, but they don't have any scenes together. Were they feuding? Whatever the reason, the

gimmick doesn't work. B&W; 91m. DIR: William A. Seiter. CAST: Bud Abbott, Lou Costello, Brenda Joyce. 1946

LITTLE GIANTS ★★★1/2 The *Bad News Bears* formula gets a first-class, kid-pleasing shift to the football field. Put-upon younger brother Rick Moranis decides to challenge the supremacy of sports hero, older brother Ed O'Neill by putting together a ragtag team of rejects to compete for a local championship. There are few surprises here, but there is something to be said for a movie that delivers exactly what it promises. Rated PG for kiddie-style toilet humor. 105m. DIR: Duwayne Dunham. CAST: Rick Moranis, Ed O'Neill, John Madden, Shawna Waldron, Mary Ellen Trainor, Brian Haley. 1994

LITTLE GIRL WHO LIVES DOWN THE LANE, THE ★★★1/2 A remarkably subdued film from a genre that has existed primarily on gore, violence, and audience manipulation. Jodie Foster gives an absorbingly realistic performance in the title role. Martin Sheen is the child molester who menaces her. It's a well-acted chiller. Rated PG. 94m. DIR: Nicolas Gessner. CAST: Jodie Foster, Martin Sheen, Alexis Smith. 1976

LITTLE GLORIA, HAPPY AT LAST ★★★★ This TV miniseries focuses on the unhappy childhood of Gloria Vanderbilt and the tug-of-war surrounding her custody trial in 1934. It's hard not to pity the poor little rich girl as portrayed in William Haney's bestseller and adapted in this teleplay. Definitely worth a watch! 208m. DIR: Waris Hussein. CAST: Martin Balsam, Bette Davis, Michael Gross, Lucy Gutteridge, Glynis Johns, Angela Lansbury, Maureen Stapleton. 1982

LITTLE HEROES ★★1/2 Adorable tale of a little girl and her trusty mutt, who prove to a small town that miracles can still come true. There's a lot of heart and some great messages in this family film. 78m. DIR: Craig Clyde. CAST: Raeanin Simpson. 1991

LITTLE HOUSE ON THE PRAIRIE (TV SERIES) ★★★ The long-running series was based on Laura Ingalls Wilder's novels about her family's adventures on the Kansas frontier. Michael Landon portrayed Charles Ingalls, the idealistic, sensitive husband and father. Episodes tend to be genuinely heartwarming. Each episode 60m. (Special TV-movies are 100 minutes.) DIR: Michael Landon. CAST: Michael Landon, Karen Grassle, Melissa Gilbert, Melissa Sue Anderson, Lindsay and Sidney Greenbush, Victor French, Dean Butler, Matthew Laborteaux. 1974–1984

LITTLE INDIAN, BIG CITY ★★1/2 Disney's English-dubbed version of the 1994 French hit features a Parisian businessman off in the jungles of Venezuela to get his long-departed wife to sign their divorce papers. He brings back a tribal 13-year-old son he didn't know he had sired and is soon up to his eyeballs in adventure. The film is a little rough for the kiddies and only marginally funny. Rated PG. 90m. DIR: Herve Palud. CAST: Ludwig Briand, Thierry Lhermitte, Miou-Miou, Arielle Dombasle, Patrick Timsit. 1996

LITTLE KIDNAPPERS ★★★1/2 Remake of 1954 British film about two orphans living with their grandfather in turn-of-the-century Canada. Feeling ignored and desperate for family, the two boys kidnap a baby so they can raise it themselves. Heartfelt and honest portrayal of family values. Not rated. 93m. **DIR:** Donald Shebib. **CAST:** Patricia Gage, Bruce Greenwood, Charlton Heston, Charles Miller, Leo Wheatley. 1990

LITTLE LADIES OF THE NIGHT ★★ Linda Purl plays a teenage runaway who is forced into prostitution. TV-movie sexploitation. 100m. **DIR:** Marvin J. Chomsky. **CAST:** Linda Purl, David Soul, Lou Gossett Jr., Carolyn Jones, Paul Burke, Dorothy Malone. 1977

LITTLE LORD FAUNTLEROY (1936) ★★★★ Far from a syrupy-sweet child movie, this is the affecting tale of a long-lost American heir (Freddie Bartholomew) brought to live with a hard-hearted British lord (C. Aubrey Smith) whose icy manner is warmed by the cheerful child. B&W; 98m. **DIR:** John Cromwell. **CAST:** Freddie Bartholomew, C. Aubrey Smith, Dolores Costello, Jessie Ralph, Mickey Rooney, Guy Kibbee. 1936

LITTLE LORD FAUNTLEROY (1980) ★★★★ This is the made-for-television version of the heartwarming classic about a poor young boy (Rick Schroder) whose life is dramatically changed when his wealthy grandfather (Alec Guinness) takes him in. Well-done. 120m. **DIR:** Jack Gold. **CAST:** Rick Schroder, Alec Guinness, Eric Porter, Colin Blakely, Connie Booth. 1980

LITTLE MAN TATE ★★★★ For her directorial debut, actress Jodie Foster joins forces with screenwriter Scott Frank to dramatize the struggle between a working-class mother and a wealthy educator for custody of a gifted child. It isn't often that a family film is both heartwarming and thought-provoking, but this little gem is one of the exceptions. Rated PG for brief profanity. 106m. **DIR:** Jodie Foster. **CAST:** Jodie Foster, Dianne Wiest, Adam Hann-Byrd, Harry Connick Jr., David Pierce, Josh Mostel. 1991

LITTLE MEN (1998) ★★★★ Surprisingly rich tale of a home for boys and the trials and tribulations therein. Based on the book by Louisa May Alcott, who also penned *Little Women*. Rated PG. 98m. **DIR:** Rodney Gibbons. **CAST:** Mariel Hemingway, Michael Caloz, Ben Cook, Chris Sarandon. 1998

LITTLE MEN (1935) ★★ A sentimental tale about a boys' school, and the wayward youths who live there is told with honesty and sincerity but not much personality. This is a poor man's *Boys Town* and needs the likes of a Mickey Rooney or Spencer Tracy to make it come alive. B&W; 56m. **DIR:** Phil Rosen. **CAST:** Frankie Darro, Erin O'Brien-Moore, Ralph Morgan, Junior Durkin, Dickie Moore, Richard Quine. 1935

LITTLE MEN (1940) 🤎 Louisa May Alcott's classic of childhood turned into a travesty. B&W; 84m. **DIR:** Norman Z. McLeod. **CAST:** Jack Oakie, Kay Francis, George Bancroft, Jimmy Lydon, Ann Gillis, William Demarest, Sterling Holloway, Isabel Jewell. 1940

LITTLE MERMAID, THE (1978) ★★ Not to be confused with the Disney classic, this is a passably animated version of the Hans Christian Andersen story, and it hews closer to the original tale. Children may be disappointed by the downbeat ending. Rated G. 71m. **DIR:** Tim Reid. 1979

LITTLE MERMAID, THE (1989) ★★★★★ This adaptation of the Hans Christian Andersen story is, in our opinion, even better than the celebrated

movies produced during Walt Disney's heyday. Writer-directors John Musker and Ron Clements, with invaluable assistance from producer Howard Ashman and his songwriting partner Alan Menken, have created the best screen fairy tale of them all. Even the songs are integral to the story, which has some of the most memorable characters to grace an animated film. Rated G. 76m. **DIR:** John Musker, Ron Clements. 1989 DVD

LITTLE MINISTER, THE ★★★1/2 An early effort in the career of Katharine Hepburn. This charming story, of a proper Scottish minister who falls in love with what he believes is a gypsy girl, is not just for Hepburn fans. B&W; 110m. **DIR:** Richard Wallace. **CAST:** Katharine Hepburn, Donald Crisp, John Beal, Andy Clyde. 1934

LITTLE MISS BROADWAY ★★★ Orphan Shirley Temple is placed with the manager of a theatrical hotel whose owner, crusty Edna May Oliver, dislikes show people. When she threatens to ship Shirley back to the orphanage, nephew George Murphy sides with the actors. Along the way, Shirley dances with Murphy and clowns with hotel guest Jimmy Durante. B&W; 70m. **DIR:** Irving Cummings. **CAST:** Shirley Temple, George Murphy, Jane Darwell, Edna May Oliver, Jimmy Durante, El Brendel, Donald Meek. 1938

LITTLE MISS MARKER (1934) ★★★★ Delightful Shirley Temple vehicle has our heroine left as an I.O.U. on a gambling debt and charming hardhearted racetrack denizens into becoming better people. The best of the screen adaptations of Damon Runyon's story. B&W; 88m. **DIR:** Alexander Hall. **CAST:** Adolphe Menjou, Shirley Temple, Dorothy Dell, Charles Bickford, Lynne Overman. 1934

LITTLE MISS MARKER (1980) 🤎 Turgid remake. Rated PG. 103m. **DIR:** Walter Bernstein. **CAST:** Walter Matthau, Julie Andrews, Tony Curtis, Bob Newhart, Sara Stimson, Lee Grant. 1980

LITTLE MISS MILLIONS ★★ Winsome comedy finds poor-little-rich-girl Jennifer Love Hewitt looking for her real mother, while greedy stepmother Anita Morris hires private eye Howard Hesseman to find her. He does, but then Morris claims he kidnapped the girl. The two hit the road to clear their names and find Hewitt's real mom. Congenial fun. Rated PG. 90m. **DIR:** Jim Wynorski. **CAST:** Howard Hesseman, Jennifer Love Hewitt, Anita Morris, Steve Landesberg. 1993

LITTLE MONSTERS 🤎 Irritating, ugly monsters living in a dark, chaotic netherworld pop out from under unsuspecting children's beds at night. Rated PG, but it's definitely not Disney fare. 103m. **DIR:** Richard Alan Greenburg. **CAST:** Fred Savage, Howie Mandel, Daniel Stern, Frank Whaley, Margaret Whitton, Ben Savage. 1989

LITTLE MOON & JUD McGRAW 🤎 Comedy-Western that has James Caan as a falsely accused man hunting for the real crook. Rated R, contains nudity and violence. 92m. **DIR:** Bernard Girard. **CAST:** James Caan, Stefanie Powers, Sammy Davis Jr., Aldo Ray, Barbara Werle, Robert Walker Jr. 1978

LITTLE MURDERS ★★★★ Jules Feiffer's savagely black comedy details the nightmarish adventures of a mild-mannered New Yorker (Elliott Gould) who finds the world becoming increasingly insane and violent. What seemed like bizarre fantasy when *Little Murders* was originally released is today all too close to reality. Strangely, this makes the film easier to watch while taking away none of its bite. Rated PG for violence and profanity. 107m. DIR: Alan Arkin. CAST: Elliott Gould, Marcia Rodd, Vincent Gardenia, Elizabeth Wilson, Donald Sutherland, Lou Jacobi, Alan Arkin. 1971

LITTLE NELLIE KELLY ★★★ Charles Winninger is a stubborn Irishman who refuses to recognize the marriage of his daughter Judy Garland to George Murphy. Based on George M. Cohan's Broadway musical-comedy. Fine renditions of many old standards. B&W; 100m. DIR: Norman Taurog. CAST: Judy Garland, George Murphy, Charles Winninger, Arthur Shields. 1940

LITTLE NEMO: ADVENTURES IN SLUMBERLAND ★★★ In this fairly entertaining animated movie, Little Nemo is a youngster whose dreams lead him into Slumberland, where the Dream King has plans for the boy to be his successor. Meanwhile, the mischievous Flip (voiced by Mickey Rooney) leads our hero to unintentionally unleash the Nightmare King. Rated G. 83m. DIR: Masanori Hata, William Hurtz. 1992

LITTLE NIGHT MUSIC, A ★★1/2 Based on Ingmar Bergman's comedy about sexual liaisons at a country mansion, this musical version doesn't quite come to life. Rated PG. 124m. DIR: Harold Prince. CAST: Elizabeth Taylor, Diana Rigg, Lesley-Anne Down. 1978

LITTLE NIKITA ★★★1/2 Well-crafted, old-fashioned espionage story about the awakening of "sleeper" agents (planted by the Soviets twenty years earlier in San Diego). Sidney Poitier is the FBI agent tracking the situation, and River Phoenix plays a teenager caught in the middle. Richard Bradford is great as a manipulative but likable KGB agent. Rated PG for language and violence. 98m. DIR: Richard Benjamin. CAST: Sidney Poitier, River Phoenix, Richard Jenkins, Caroline Kava, Richard Bradford, Richard Lynch, Loretta Devine, Lucy Deakins. 1988

LITTLE NINJAS ★★1/2 Slight, derivative kiddy romp about three karate-chopping youngsters who come into possession of a treasure map while on vacation. When they return home to Los Angeles, they must join forces to fight off the bad guys who have come for the map. Kids will enjoy this mindless exercise. Rated PG. 85m. DIR: Emmett Alston. CAST: Jon Anzaldo, Steven Nelson. 1993

LITTLE NOISES ★★ Low-budget, seemingly pointless film. A talentless writer sells the poems of a mute man as his own. Now he must deal with his conscience. Not rated. 80m. DIR: Jane Spencer. CAST: Crispin Glover, Tatum O'Neal, Rik Mayall, Tate Donovan. 1991

LITTLE ODESSA ★★★1/2 Although bleak to the point of total despair, writer-director James Gray's feature debut is a contemporary, Russian-Jewish spin on *The Godfather*: a mesmerizing study of a small-time gangster trying to reconcile estranged family ties. Tim Roth is chilling as the wholly amoral killer, whose return to New York's Brighton Beach proves disastrous for the parents and younger brother he left behind. Gray's matter-of-fact approach to this violent tale is positively haunting. Rated R for violence, profanity, and nudity. 111m. DIR: James Gray. CAST: Tim Roth, Maximilian Schell, Vanessa Redgrave, Edward Furlong, Moira Kelly. 1995 DVD

LITTLE ORPHAN ANNIE ★★1/2 The first sound version featuring the adventures of Harold Gray's pupilless, precocious adolescent. A good cast and engaging score by Max Steiner add to the charm of this undeservedly neglected comic-strip adaptation. B&W; 60m. DIR: John S. Robertson. CAST: Mitzi Green, Edgar Kennedy, Buster Phelps, May Robson. 1932

LITTLE PATRIOT, THE ★★ Colonial minipic tells the story of a young boy and his family and their trials and tribulations in the new land that would become New York City. Rated PG. 88m. DIR: J. Christian Ingvordsen. CAST: Dan Haggerty, John Christian, Rick Washburne, Jacqueline Knox. 1992

LITTLE PRINCE, THE ★★ Aviator Richard Kiley teaches an alien boy about life and love. This picture has a great cast, beautiful photography, and is based on the children's classic by Antoine de Saint-Exupéry. Unfortunately, it also has a poor musical score by Alan J. Lerner and Frederick Loewe. Rated G. 88m. DIR: Stanley Donen. CAST: Richard Kiley, Steven Warner, Bob Fosse, Gene Wilder. 1974

LITTLE PRINCESS, THE (1939) ★★★1/2 The 1930s supertyke shined in one of her very best vehicles in this Victorian-era tearjerker. In it, she's a sweet-natured child who is mistreated at a strict boarding school when her father disappears during the Boer War. Get out your handkerchiefs. B&W; 93m. DIR: Walter Lang. CAST: Shirley Temple, Richard Greene, Anita Louise, Ian Hunter, Cesar Romero, Arthur Treacher. 1939 DVD

LITTLE PRINCESS, A (1986) ★★1/2 Melodramatic tale of an indulged girl who, having lived in India with her lively, free-spending father, is enrolled in a prissy English boarding school. The girl's constant sermonizing about her plight is most annoying. A lesser WonderWorks production. 174m. DIR: Carol Wiseman. CAST: Amelia Shankley, Nigel Havers, Maureen Lipman. 1986

LITTLE PRINCESS, A (1995) ★★★★★ This magical, visually intoxicating drama and hankie twister has about a young girl who is uprooted from India to a grim New York City boarding school. The story focuses on the power of imagination and inner spirit, and the film's critical relationship between Dad and daughter has a powerful beauty not often found in movies today. Rated G. 98m. DIR: Alfonso Cuaron. CAST: Liesel Matthews, Eleanor Bron, Liam Cunningham, Vanessa Lee Chester, Rusty Schwimmer. 1995 DVD

LITTLE RASCALS, THE (1994) ★★1/2 This re-creation of yesteryear's *Our Gang* comedies substitutes gross humor for charm. Example: When members of the He-Man Woman Haters' Club decide to dissuade Alfalfa from courting Darla, one of their tricks is to put used kitty litter in his peanut-butter sandwiches. This is a kids' movie? That said, youngsters will probably love it, and there is some nostalgic fun in seeing the most memorable characters from the series join forces in a big-screen romp. Rated PG for toilet humor. 82m. **DIR:** Penelope Spheeris. **CAST:** Travis Tedford, Bug Hall, Brittany Ashton Holmes, Kevin Jamal Woods, Zachary Mabry, Ross Elliot Bagley, Mel Brooks, Whoopi Goldberg, Daryl Hannah, Reba McEntire. **1994 DVD**

LITTLE RIDERS, THE ★★★★ This made-for-cable production, based on Margareth Shemin's novel, concerns a little girl's efforts to save a Dutch town's soul from the Nazis. Half-American Noley Thornton lives with her grandparents, and helps care for the horseriding figurines that signal each hour from the clocktower. When an occupational Nazi leader decides to melt down the figurines as a means to destroy local spirit, she and her grandparents concoct a desperate scheme. Rated PG for violence. 108m. **DIR:** Kevin Connor. **CAST:** Paul Scofield, Rosemary Harris, Noley Thornton, Benedick Blythe, Luke Edwards, Malcolm McDowell, Derek de Lint. **1996**

LITTLE ROMANCE, A ★★★★1/2 Everyone needs *A Little Romance* in their life. This absolutely enchanting film by director George Roy Hill has something for everyone. Its story of two appealing youngsters (Thelonious Bernard and Diane Lane) who fall in love in Paris is full of surprises, laughs, and uplifting moments. Rated PG. 108m. **DIR:** George Roy Hill. **CAST:** Thelonious Bernard, Diane Lane, Laurence Olivier, Sally Kellerman, Broderick Crawford, David Dukes. **1979**

LITTLE SEX, A ★★ A New York director of television commercials can't keep his hands off his actresses, even though he's married to a beautiful, intelligent woman. This is a tepid romantic comedy. Rated R. 95m. **DIR:** Bruce Paltrow. **CAST:** Tim Matheson, Kate Capshaw, Edward Herrmann. **1982**

LITTLE SHOP OF HORRORS, THE (1960) ★★★★ Dynamite Roger Corman superquickie about a meek florist shop employee (Jonathan Haze) who inadvertently creates a ferocious man-eating plant. This horror-comedy was filmed in two days and is one of the funniest ever made. B&W; 72m. **DIR:** Roger Corman. **CAST:** Jonathan Haze, Mel Welles, Jackie Joseph, Jack Nicholson, Dick Miller. **1960 DVD**

LITTLE SHOP OF HORRORS (1986) ★★★★1/2 This totally bent musical–horror–comedy was based on director Roger Corman's bizarre horror cheapie from 1960. Rick Moranis is wonderful as the schnook who finds and cares for a man-eating plant set on conquering the world. Uproariously funny, marvelously acted, spectacularly staged, and tuneful. Rated PG-13 for violence. 94m. **DIR:** Frank Oz. **CAST:** Rick Moranis, Ellen Greene, Vincent Gardenia, Steve Martin, James Belushi, John Candy, Bill Murray, Christopher Guest. **1986 DVD**

LITTLE SISTER ★★1/2 Likable comedy with Jonathan Silverman as a love-struck student who dons women's clothing in order to sneak into a sorority. Been-there, done-that comedy still manages to be quite entertaining. Rated PG-13 for sexual content. 94m. **DIR:** Jimmy Zeilinger. **CAST:** Jonathan Silverman, Alyssa Milano, George Newbern. **1991**

LITTLE SWEETHEART ★★★ Not since *The Bad Seed* have we seen a little girl as deadly as 9-year-old

Thelma (played by newcomer Cassie Barasch). She delves in blackmail of a couple on the run from a bank embezzlement job. Rated R for violence. 93m. **DIR:** Anthony Simmons. **CAST:** John Hurt, Karen Young, Cassie Barasch, Barbara Bosson. **1990**

LITTLE THEATRE OF JEAN RENOIR, THE ★★★ The great director's last film (actually made for television) is better seen as a postscript to his long career. The three segments (plus a musical interlude from Jeanne Moreau) remind the viewer of his best work rather than recapitulating it. In French with English subtitles. 100m. **DIR:** Jean Renoir. **CAST:** Jeanne Moreau, Jean Carmet, Fernand Sardou, Pierre Olaf, Françoise Arnoul. **1969**

LITTLE THIEF, THE ★★★★ François Truffaut was working on this script, sort of a female version of *The 400 Blows*, at the time of his death; it was completed and filmed by his friend Claude Miller. Charlotte Gainsbourg gives a strong performance as a rebellious adolescent girl, struggling to raise herself after she is abandoned by her mother. In French with English subtitles. Not rated; features adult themes. 104m. **DIR:** Claude Miller. **CAST:** Charlotte Gainsbourg, Didier Bezace. **1989**

LITTLE TREASURE ★★★ While the synopsis on the back of the box may give one the impression this release is a rip-off of *Romancing the Stone*, only the rough outline of the story is lifted from the 1984 hit. The Margot Kidder/Ted Danson team is not a copy of the Kathleen Turner/Michael Douglas couple; these characters are more down-home. And the concentration on domestic drama almost fills the gap left by the absence of action. Rated R for nudity and language. 95m. **DIR:** Alan Sharp. **CAST:** Margot Kidder, Ted Danson, Burt Lancaster. **1985**

LITTLE VEGAS ★★★★ A fantastic movie about a man (Anthony Denison) trying to escape from the mob-like life of his family. After the death of a matronly woman who was taking care of him, he must contend with the other residents of a small desert town who see him as a gigolo. Rated R for nudity and profanity. 91m. **DIR:** Perry Lang. **CAST:** Anthony Denison, Catherine O'Hara, Anne Francis, Michael Nouri, Perry Lang, John Sayles, Bruce McGill, Jerry Stiller. **1990**

LITTLE VERA ★★★ Glasnost takes a front-row-center seat in this angst-ridden drama about the thoroughly modern Moscovite Vera. Her alcoholic father and ineffectual mother constantly worry about Vera's untraditional ways. She falls in love and moves her fiancé into the family's tight quarters. This is the first widely released Soviet film to show present-day teenage culture—plus—simulated sex. In Russian with English subtitles. Not rated. 130m. **DIR:** Vasily Pichul. **CAST:** Natalya Negoda. **1989**

LITTLE WHITE LIES ★★★ While on vacation in Rome, surgeon Tim Matheson and detective Ann Jillian meet and fall in love. Harmless fluff, pleasant diversion for a made-for-television feature. 95m. **DIR:** Anson Williams. **CAST:** Tim Matheson, Ann Jillian. **1989**

LITTLE WITCHES ★★ Catholic schoolgirls discover the uses and abuses of black magic in this rip-off of *The Craft.* If you liked that, you'll probably like this—just not as much. Rated R for violence and nudity. 91m. **DIR:** Jane Simpson. **CAST:** Jennifer Rubin, Jack Nance, Zelda Rubinstein, Sheeri Rappaport. **1996 DVD**

LITTLE WOMEN (1933) ★★★1/2 George Cukor's *Little Women* is far and away the best of the four film versions of Louisa May Alcott's timeless story of the March family. Katharine Hepburn is excellent as the tomboyish Jo. B&W; 115m. **DIR:** George Cukor. **CAST:** Katharine Hepburn, Spring Byington, Joan Bennett, Frances Dee, Jean Parker. **1933**

LITTLE WOMEN (1949) ★★1/2 Textbook casting and intelligent performances make this a safe second rendering of Louisa May Alcott's famous story of maturing young women finding romance in the nineteenth century. Technicolor is an enhancement, but the 1933 original is vastly superior. 121m. **DIR:** Mervyn LeRoy. **CAST:** June Allyson, Peter Lawford, Elizabeth Taylor, Mary Astor, Janet Leigh, Margaret O'Brien. **1949**

LITTLE WOMEN (1994) ★★★★ This adaptation of Louisa May Alcott's American classic is a triumph of casting and period authenticity, if perhaps possessed of too much feminism for its era. Jo is once again the cinematic focus, as she defies the passive female stereotypes of the 1860s to pursue a writing career. The production design is perfect, and you can almost feel the cozy family's love jumping out from the screen. Rated PG for dramatic intensity. 119m. **DIR:** Gillian Armstrong. **CAST:** Winona Ryder, Susan Sarandon, Trini Alvarado, Eric Stoltz, Christian Bale, Gabriel Byrne, Claire Danes, Kirsten Dunst. **1994 DVD**

LITTLE WORLD OF DON CAMILLO, THE ★★★ The emotional and often grim struggle between Church and State has never been more humanely or lovingly presented than in the novels of Giovanni Guareschi, expertly brought to life in this gentle, amusing film. The great French comedian Fernandel captures the essence of the feisty priest who is a perpetual thorn in the side of the communist mayor of his village and parish. B&W; 96m. **DIR:** Julien Duvivier. **CAST:** Fernandel, Gino Cervi, Sylvie, Franco Interlenghi. **1953**

LITTLEST ANGEL, THE ★★ This made-for-TV musical fantasy loses something in its video translation. A young shepherd finds his transition into heaven difficult to accept. 77m. **DIR:** Joe Layton. **CAST:** Johnny Whitaker, Fred Gwynne, Connie Stevens, James Coco, E. G. Marshall, Tony Randall. **1969**

LITTLEST HORSE THIEVES, THE ★★★ At the turn of the century, some children become alarmed that the ponies working in the coal mines are to be destroyed. The children decide to steal the ponies. Rather predictable but with good characterizations and a solid period atmosphere. Rated G. 104m. **DIR:** Charles Jarrott. **CAST:** Alastair Sim, Peter Barkworth, Maurice Colbourne, Susan Tebbs, Andrew Harrison, Chloe Franks. **1976 DVD**

LITTLEST OUTLAW, THE ★★★ This Walt Disney import from Mexico tells a familiar but pleasant story of a young boy who befriends a renegade horse and saves him from destruction. The kids should like it, and this one will appeal to the adults as well. 73m. **DIR:** Roberto Gavaldon. **CAST:** Pedro Armendariz,

Joseph Calleia, Rodolfo Acosta, Andres Velasquez. **1954**

LITTLEST REBEL, THE ★★★1/2 Prime Shirley Temple, in which, as the daughter of a Confederate officer during the Civil War, she thwarts a double execution by charming President Lincoln. The plot stops, of course, while she and Bojangles dance. B&W; 70m. **DIR:** David Butler. **CAST:** Shirley Temple, John Boles, Jack Holt, Bill Robinson, Karen Morley, Guinn Williams, Willie Best. **1935**

LITTLEST VIKING, THE ★★ Very slow-moving tale about a young boy and his family's violent feud with the neighbors in the fjord next door. Quite a few moral lessons are given in the film, but you'll have to stay awake. Rated PG. 85m. **DIR:** Knut W. Jorfald, Lars Rasmussen, Paul Trevor Bale. **CAST:** Kristian Tonby, Per Jansen, Terje Stromdahl, Rulle Smit. **1989**

LIVE A LITTLE, LOVE A LITTLE 🎬 The interesting thing about this Elvis vehicle is that the sexual innuendos are more blatant than in his other romantic comedies. Rated PG for mild profanity. 89m. **DIR:** Norman Taurog. **CAST:** Elvis Presley, Michele Carey, Don Porter, Dick Sargent. **1968**

LIVE AND LET DIE ★★ The first Roger Moore (as James Bond) adventure is a hodgepodge of the surrealistic and the slick that doesn't quite live up to its Connery-powered predecessors. The chase-and-suspense formula wears thin. Rated PG. 121m. **DIR:** Guy Hamilton. **CAST:** Roger Moore, Jane Seymour, Yaphet Kotto, Geoffrey Holder. **1973 DVD**

LIVE BY THE FIST 🎬 Boring choreography and an annoying, trite script drop-kick this martial-arts fistfest right into the turkey pile. Rated R for violence. 77m. **DIR:** Cirio H. Santiago. **CAST:** Jerry Trimble, George Takei. **1993**

LIVE FLESH ★★★★ When a young man finishes his prison sentence for shooting and crippling a cop, he hovers uncomfortably close to the cop and his wife. Is it just coincidence, or does he have some subtle plan in mind? Loosely adapted from a novel by English mystery writer Ruth Rendell the basic idea veers in a completely different direction, and the result is erotic, psychologically complex, and entirely unpredictable. In Spanish with English subtitles. Rated R for profanity (in subtitles) and sexual situations. 101m. **DIR:** Pedro Almodóvar. **CAST:** Javier Bardem, Francesca Neri, Liberto Rabal, Angela Molina. **1997**

LIVE! FROM DEATH ROW ★★★ In this skillfully directed made-for-TV nail biter, Bruce Davison gives a high-powered performance as a condemned murderer who takes a tabloid reporter and her crew hostage just before his scheduled execution. Not rated; contains adult situations. 94m. **DIR:** Patrick Duncan. **CAST:** Bruce Davison, Joanna Cassidy, Jason Tomlins, Kathleen Wilhoite, Art La Fleur. **1992**

LIVE NUDE GIRLS ★★★1/2 Engaging ensemble film about a group of women who throw their friend a party in honor of her third trip down the aisle. The fun and games spill over into a slumber party, where each of the women unveils her deepest and darkest desires, fears, and fantasies. It's *The Big Chill* on estrogen, a funny and enlightening comedy-drama where women bare their souls more than their bodies. Rated R for profanity and nudity. 100m. **DIR:** Ju-

Iianna Lavin. **CAST:** Cynthia Stevenson, Kim Cattrall, Olivia D'Abo, Laila Robins. **1995**

LIVE WIRE ★★★ A bomb kills a senator, but no traces of an explosive can be found. An FBI agent (Pierce Brosnan) must find the cause of the explosion while fighting his own inner battles. Very good acting by Brosnan and Ron Silver, who plays a corrupt senator, but the plot is predictable. Rated R for violence, profanity, and nudity. 85m. **DIR:** Christian Duguay. **CAST:** Pierce Brosnan, Ron Silver, Ben Cross, Lisa Eilbacher, Brent Jennings, Tony Plana, Al Waxman. **1992**

LIVE WIRE: HUMAN TIMEBOMB ★★ Mediocre sequel finds special agent Jim Parker being abducted by the Cuban government, whose ruthless general installs a microchip in the agent's neck. Now under the command of the general, Parker becomes his country's most feared enemy. Ho hum. Rated R for violence and adult language. 98m. **DIR:** Mark Roper. **CAST:** Bryan Genesse, Joe Lara, J. Cynthia Brooks. **1995**

LIVES OF A BENGAL LANCER, THE ★★★★1/2 One of the great adventure films, this action-packed epic stars Gary Cooper and Franchot Tone as fearless friends in the famed British regiment. Their lives become complicated when they take the commander's son (Richard Cromwell) under their wings and he turns out to be less than a model soldier. B&W; 109m. **DIR:** Henry Hathaway. **CAST:** Gary Cooper, Franchot Tone, Richard Cromwell, Guy Standing, C. Aubrey Smith, Monte Blue, Kathleen Burke. **1935**

LIVIN' LARGE ★★1/2 In this hit-and-miss comedy, Terrence "T. C." Carson plays a young man devoted to getting into television. When his big break comes, his devotion to his career threatens to alienate his longtime friends. Rated R for profanity and violence. 96m. **DIR:** Michael Schultz. **CAST:** Terrence "T. C." Carson, Lisa Arrindell, Nathaniel Hall, Blanche Baker, Julia Campbell. **1991**

LIVING DAYLIGHTS, THE ★★★1/2 Timothy Dalton adds a dimension of humanity to James Bond in his screen bow as the ultimate spy hero. The silly set pieces and gimmicks that marred even the later Roger Moore entries in the series are gone. Instead, the filmmakers have opted for a strong plot about a phony KGB defector (Jeroen Krabbé) and a renegade arms dealer (Joe Don Baker). Rated PG. 130m. **DIR:** John Glen. **CAST:** Timothy Dalton, Maryam D'Abo, Jeroen Krabbé, Joe Don Baker, John Rhys-Davies, Art Malik, Desmond Llewellyn. **1987**

LIVING END, THE ★★★★ This hard-core, unsentimental road movie/romance between two HIV-positive gay men manages to be bizarre, bitter, *and* intriguing. Figuring they have nothing to lose, Craig Gilmore and Mike Dytri hit the road and act out their bad-boy fantasies amid provocative conversations. Tough to watch, but nihilism rarely looks this good. Not rated, but includes profanity, violence, nudity, and sexual situations. 85m. **DIR:** Gregg Araki. **CAST:** Craig Gilmore, Mike Dytri, Darcy Marta, Scot Goetz, Johanna Went, Mary Woronov. **1992**

LIVING FREE ★★ Disappointing sequel to *Born Free*, with Elsa the lioness now in the wilderness and raising three cubs. The chemistry just isn't here in this film. 91m. **DIR:** Jack Couffer. **CAST:** Susan Hampshire, Nigel Davenport, Geoffrey Keen. **1972**

LIVING IN A BIG WAY ★★ A comedy-drama about a wartime marriage that goes sour, this movie uses music for all the wrong reasons. It works up to a point, mainly because Gene Kelly is such an exuberant dancer. His costar, Marie McDonald, looks a lot better than she acts. B&W; 102m. **DIR:** Gregory La Cava. **CAST:** Gene Kelly, Marie McDonald, Charles Winninger, Spring Byington, Phyllis Thaxter, Clinton Sundberg. **1947**

LIVING IN OBLIVION ★★★1/2 Low-budget gem focuses on the endless mishaps likely to occur on a low-budget film set. The harried director vainly attempts to ease tensions between his female lead and the male "prima donna" hired simply for his name. Slow start makes a dramatic recovery with numerous gut-splitting scenes of hilarious absurdity. Satisfying on a multitude of levels. Rated R for sex, nudity, and profanity. B&W/color; 90m. **DIR:** Tom DiCillo. **CAST:** Dermot Mulroney, Catherine Keener, James LeGros, Steve Buscemi. **1995**

LIVING IN PERIL ★★★ Familiar faces help elevate this pedestrian whodunit about an architect who finds himself framed for murder. Rob Lowe stars as Walter, the architect hired by millionaire James Belushi to build his new home. When a woman ends up dead in his apartment, Walter suspects that someone is trying to ruin him. Moderately entertaining with the prerequisite plot elements. Rated R for language and violence. 95m. **DIR:** Jack Ersgard. **CAST:** Rob Lowe, James Belushi, Dean Stockwell, Dana Wheeler-Nicholson. **1998**

LIVING ON TOKYO TIME ★★★★ Explores an Asian-American culture clash from the Japanese point of view. Kyoko (Minako Ohashi), a young woman, comes from Japan to San Francisco. She agrees to a marriage of convenience with a junkfood-eating Japanese-American who wants to be a rock star. The result is a warmhearted character study blessed with insight and humor. In English and Japanese with subtitles. Not rated. 83m. **DIR:** Steven Okazaki. **CAST:** Minako Ohashi, Ken Nakagawa. **1987**

LIVING OUT LOUD ★★★1/2 A recently divorced New Yorker's path crosses that of the doorman in her apartment building just as both are trying to rebuild their lives. Loosely adapted from two Chekhov short stories, the film never overcomes the fact that it's telling two unrelated tales. Still, there are many pleasures and fine moments. Rated R for profanity and sexual themes. 93m. **DIR:** Richard LaGravanese. **CAST:** Holly Hunter, Danny DeVito, Queen Latifah, Martin Donovan, Elias Koteas. **1998 DVD**

LIVING PROOF: THE HANK WILLIAMS, JR., STORY 🎭 A miscast made-for-television stink bomb. 100m. **DIR:** Dick Lowry. **CAST:** Richard Thomas, Clu Gulager, Allyn Ann McLerie. **1983**

LIVING THE BLUES ★★ White suburban boy who wants to be a blues guitarist pesters the uncle of his inner-city girlfriend for a spot in his band. Well-intended but amateurish. Not rated; contains mild sexual situations. 78m. **DIR:** Alan Gorg. **CAST:** Michael

Kerr, Galyn Gorg, Sam Taylor, Gwyn Gorg, Martin Raymond. 1986

LIVING TO DIE ★★ Private eye Nick Carpenter is called upon to stop an embezzling scheme that involves a Las Vegas luminary. The Vegas backdrop enlivens what is essentially a dreary story. Rated R for nudity and violence. 92m. DIR: Wings Hauser. CAST: Wings Hauser, Darcy Demiss. 1990

LIVING VENUS ★★ Harvey Korman probably would like to forget that he made his debut in this melodrama loosely based on the story of Hugh Hefner and *Playboy* magazine. Not rated; contains adult situations. B&W; 71m. DIR: Herschell Gordon Lewis. CAST: William Kerwin, Danica D'Hondt, Harvey Korman. 1961

•LIZARD IN A WOMAN'S SKIN, A ★★1/2 In this thriller from Italian goremeister Lucio Fulci, a woman may or may not be part of a gruesome murder. Did she really do it? Is this real or a hallucination? At times the film can be slow, but Fulci makes up for it with wild camera work. Rated R for violence and gore. 105m. DIR: Lucio Fulci. CAST: Florinda Balkan. 1971

LLOYD'S OF LONDON ★★★★ An old-fashioned look at how the big business developed. Freddie Bartholomew is top-billed as the lad who grows up to be the hero of England's insurance industry. Highly entertaining. B&W; 115m. DIR: Henry King. CAST: Tyrone Power, George Sanders, Madeleine Carroll, Freddie Bartholomew, C. Aubrey Smith, Virginia Field. 1936

L'ODEUR DES FAUVES (SCANDAL MAN) ♥ A hack photographer-reporter earns his living digging up *National Enquirer*-type stories. 86m. DIR: Richard Balducci. CAST: Maurice Ronet, Josephine Chaplin, Vittorio De Sica. 1966

LOADED ★★ Murky murder mystery takes place on the set of a low-budget horror movie being shot in rural England. It's the directorial debut of Jane Campion's sister Anna, who seems more interested in letting her characters yak about their personal feelings than in telling a story. Rated R for profanity, nudity, and sexual situations. 96m. DIR: Anna Campion. CAST: Catherine McCormack, Thandie Newton, Matthew Eggleton. 1996

LOADED PISTOLS ★★★★ Well-handled, typical B-Western plot finds Gene Autry safeguarding young cowpoke Russell Arms (of TV's "Your Hit Parade") wrongly accused of murder. B&W; 77m. DIR: John English. CAST: Gene Autry, Barbara Britton, Jack Holt, Russell Arms, Chill Wills, Robert Shayne. 1948

LOBSTER FOR BREAKFAST ★★1/2 Screwball comedy Italian style about the loves and misadventures of a toilet salesman. In Italian with English subtitles. Not rated; contains profanity and nudity. 93m. DIR: Giorgio Capitani. CAST: Janet Agren, Claudine Auger. 1982

LOBSTER MAN FROM MARS ★★ A sometimes funny comedy about a movie producer who, in need of a tax-sheltering flop, calls upon an amateur filmmaker and his sci-fi flick to save him. Old and overused jokes and sight gags cause this parody to flop more often than fly. Rated PG. 84m. DIR: Stanley Sheff. CAST: Tony Curtis, Deborah Foreman, Patrick Macnee, Billy Barty. 1990

LOCAL HERO ★★★★1/2 A wonderfully offbeat comedy by Bill Forsyth. Burt Lancaster plays a Houston oil baron who sends Peter Riegert to the west coast of Scotland to negotiate with the natives for North Sea oil rights. As with *Gregory's Girl*, which was about a gangly, good-natured boy's first crush, this film is blessed with sparkling little moments of humor, unforgettable characters, and a warmly human story. Rated PG for language. 111m. DIR: Bill Forsyth. CAST: Burt Lancaster, Peter Riegert, Fulton MacKay. 1983 DVD

LOCH NESS ★★★ So-so drama sends yet another scientist (Ted Danson) to Scotland to investigate the Loch Ness creature's possible existence. This is overshadowed by Danson's romance with a pretty innkeeper. Gorgeous location shots are really a plus, but the limited screen time allotted to the creatures is quite a disappointment. Rod Stewart's tribute to his homeland, "Rhythm of My Heart," provides a fitting finale. Rated PG for violence. 160m. DIR: John Henderson. CAST: Ted Danson, Joely Richardson, Kirsty Graham, Ian Holm, James Frain. 1996

LOCH NESS HORROR, THE ♥ Japan isn't the only country that has monsters that look like muppets. Rated PG. Has some violence. 93m. DIR: Larry Buchanan. CAST: Barry Buchanan, Sandy Kenyon. 1982

LOCK AND LOAD ★★ Members of the 82nd Airborne Special Forces group are stealing large sums of cash and jewels and killing themselves. One such member, haunted by dreams, wants to know why. Interesting premise. Rated R for violence. 89m. DIR: David A. Prior. CAST: Jack Vogel. 1990

LOCK, STOCK AND TWO SMOKING BARRELS ★★1/2 This darkly cheeky crime caper hops from bloody shoot-outs to torture scenes with quick winks and nudges to all that is Tarantino. The plot nearly ties itself in knots as four London lads lose a high-stakes poker game to a porn king and then rob other crooks to repay the underworld loan. Rated R for language, violence, drug content, and brief nudity. 103m. DIR: Guy Ritchie. CAST: Nick Moran, Jason Statham, Dexter Fletcher, Jason Flemyng, P. H. Moriarty, Vinnie Jones, Lenny McLean. 1999 DVD

LOCK UP ★★★1/2 Sylvester Stallone gives one of his best performances in this melodramatic prison drama, which is reminiscent of similarly themed Warner Bros. movies of the Thirties and Forties. Stallone is a model prisoner who, just before he is about to be released, finds himself transferred to a high-security facility run by an old enemy (Donald Sutherland) who wants to see him dead. Rated R for profanity, violence, and suggested sex. 106m. DIR: John Flynn. CAST: Sylvester Stallone, Donald Sutherland, John Amos, Darlanne Fluegel. 1989 DVD

•LOCKED IN SILENCE ★★★ Two brothers are forced to share a terrible secret in this somewhat unconvincing drama; the younger boy retreats behind a wall of hysterical muteness, a condition that proves vexing to parents who grow desperate. Bruce Davison has the difficult role, as the father who means well but is quick to anger. But the basic premise in David A. Simons and Dalene Young's script never quite gels; it's difficult to imagine, for example, that the boy would maintain his self-imposed silence even when his mother's life is at stake ... and the resolution—the reason behind it all—is dissatisfying and anticlimactic. Rated PG for dramatic intensity. 94m. DIR: Bruce Pittman. CAST: Bonnie Bedelia, Bruce Davison, Marc Donato, Bill Switzer, Steven McCarthy, Helen Hughes, Dan Hedaya. **1999**

LOCUSTS, THE ★★★ John Steinbeckesque tale of a drifter and his war of grit against a disturbed female beef farmer. Excellent performances buoy this ultimately depressing flick. Rated R for sexual situations and profanity. 125m. DIR: John Patrick Kelley. CAST: Kate Capshaw, Jeremy Davies, Vince Vaughn, Paul Rudd, Daniel Meyer, Ashley Judd. **1997**

LODGER, THE ★★★★ Alfred Hitchcock's first signature thriller remains a timeless piece of wonder, showcasing the unique visual and stylistic tricks that would mark his work for years to come. Ivor Novello stars as a man who checks into a boardinghouse and becomes the object of scrutiny when a series of murders plague the area. Silent. B&W; 75m. DIR: Alfred Hitchcock. CAST: Ivor Novello, Malcolm Keen, Marie Ault. **1926 DVD**

LOGAN'S RUN ★★★ Popular but overlong sci-fi film concerning a futuristic society where people are only allowed to live to the age of 30, and a policeman nearing the limit who searches desperately for a way to avoid mandatory extermination. Nice production is enhanced immeasurably by outlandish sets and beautiful, imaginative miniatures. Rated PG. 120m. DIR: Michael Anderson. CAST: Michael York, Jenny Agutter, Peter Ustinov, Richard Jordan. **1976 DVD**

LOIS GIBBS AND THE LOVE CANAL ★★1/2 Marsha Mason is good as the housewife-turned-activist who fought for justice for residents of Niagara Falls after it was discovered that their homes were built over a toxic waste dump. But this made-for-TV movie tends to trivialize that real-life tragedy. 95m. DIR: Glenn Jordan. CAST: Marsha Mason, Bob Gunton, Penny Fuller. **1982**

LOLA (1960) ★★★★ Jacques Demy adapts the intoxicating camera pyrotechnics and style of Max Ophüls (to whom the film is dedicated) in this unjustly forgotten new wave classic starring Anouk Aimée as a cabaret singer romantically involved with three men. A delight. In French with English subtitles. Not rated. 91m. DIR: Jacques Demy. CAST: Anouk Aimée, Marc Michel. **1960**

LOLA (1982) ★★★ Viewers can't help but be dazzled and delighted with the late Rainer Werner Fassbinder's offbeat remake of *The Blue Angel.* Centering his story on a singer-prostitute named Lola (Barbara Sukowa), Fassbinder reveals a cynical view of humanity. Rated R. In German with English subtitles. 114m. DIR: Rainer Werner Fassbinder. CAST: Barbara Sukowa, Armin Mueller-Stähl, Mario Adorf. **1982**

LOLA MONTES ★★★★ A dazzlingly beautiful film. Mirroring the fragmented flashbacks in which the heroine, now reduced to a circus act, recounts her love affairs through nineteenth-century Europe, Max Ophüls's camera swoops and spins through the entire span of the expanded screen, retained in the video's letter box format. In French with English subtitles. Not rated. 110m. DIR: Max Ophüls. CAST:

Martine Carol, Peter Ustinov, Anton Walbrook, Oskar Werner. **1955 DVD**

LOLA'S GAME 🖤 Shoddily made, poorly plotted thriller of a cop searching for the killer of his girlfriend. The pits. Rated R for nudity, sexual situations, profanity, and violence. 75m. DIR: Tim Andrew. CAST: Doug Jeffrey, Elise Miller, Antonio Guma, Joe Estevez. **1998**

LOLITA (1962) ★★★ A man's unconventional obsession for a "nymphet" is the basis for this bizarre satire. James Mason and Sue Lyon are the naughty pair in this film, which caused quite a stir in the 1960s but seems fairly tame today. B&W; 152m. DIR: Stanley Kubrick. CAST: James Mason, Sue Lyon, Shelley Winters, Peter Sellers. **1962 DVD**

LOLITA (1997) ★★★★ In this absorbing adaptation of Vladimir Nabokov's controversial novel, Jeremy Irons portrays the doomed and tragic Humbert Humbert. Employing a somber and self-critical voice-over, Irons introduces himself as damaged goods: a man who never fully left adolescence, thanks to the unexpected death of a childhood sweetheart. He therefore finds redemption of the damned upon meeting teenaged Lolita while seeking lodging in a 1947 New England town; from that point onward, the atmosphere of impending doom intensifies with the slow-motion horror of a train wreck. Despite her sexpot tendencies, inherited from a man-hungry mother, it's obvious that Lolita is anything but happy. Make no mistake: This is not a happy story. Rated R for profanity, nudity, violence, and extremely strong sexual content. 137m. DIR: Adrian Lyne. CAST: Jeremy Irons, Dominique Swain, Melanie Griffith, Frank Langella. **1997 DVD**

LOLITA 2000 🖤 A minimal plot about a censor of the future is a thin excuse for linking soft-core sex scenes (presented as the stories she is viewing). Not rated, but a hard R equivalent for sex and nudity. 90m. DIR: Cybil Richards. CAST: Jacqueline Lovell, Gabriella Hall, Eric Acsell. **1997**

LONDON KILLS ME ★★★ True-to-life portrayal of a London drug dealer who wants to get a real job, but must first buy decent shoes. If you can sit through the gritty first half, you'll actually start rooting for the main character. Rated R for violence and nudity. 107m. DIR: Hanif Kureishi. CAST: Justin Chadwick, Steven Mackintosh, Emer McCourt, Roshan Seth, Fiona Shaw, Brad Dourif. **1992**

LONDON MELODY ★★★ Intrigued by her beauty and spunk, a kindhearted diplomat secretly helps a struggling cockney street singer realize her ambitions by financing her musical training. Charming slice of London nightlife before World War II. B&W; 71m. DIR: Herbert Wilcox. CAST: Anna Neagle, Tullio Carminati. **1937**

LONE DEFENDER, THE ★★ Two prospectors are ambushed and one of them, Rin Tin Tin's master, is murdered. For the next twelve installments of this early sound serial, Rinty chases and is chased by the Cactus Kid and his low-down thievin' gang. B&W; 12 chapters. DIR: Richard Thorpe. CAST: Rin Tin Tin, Walter Miller. **1930**

LONE JUSTICE ★★ So much for truth in packaging. This is only the first portion of the *Ned Blessing* television miniseries. Soon after star Daniel Baldwin arrives on screen to play the Western gunfighter as an adult, the tape screeches to a halt without resolving any plot elements. Don't be suckered by this one. Rated PG-13 for violence and profanity. 94m. **DIR:** Peter Werner. **CAST:** Daniel Baldwin, Luis Avalos, Chris Cooper, Julia Campbell, René Auberjonois, Jeff Kober. 1993

LONE JUSTICE 2 ★★★ Stalwart gunfighter Ned Blessing is back, although his sidekick (Crecencio) is the only continuity between this and the previous installment. Even Blessing is played by somebody else! The good news is that Brad Johnson is far more believable in the role, but Bill Wittliff's screenplay provides no more closure than we found in part one. Rated PG for violence and mild profanity. 93m. **DIR:** Jack Bender. **CAST:** Brad Johnson, Luis Avalos, Brenda Bakke, Rob Campbell, Wes Studi. 1993

LONE RANGER, THE (1938) ★★★1/2 One of America's most popular heroes rode out of the radio and onto the screen in one of the best and most fondly remembered serials of all time. The ballyhoo that accompanied the release of this exciting chapterplay made it an overwhelming hit at the box office. Thought to be lost until recently, most versions of this serial feature two chapters in French, the only copy available. B&W; 15 chapters. **DIR:** William Witney, John English. **CAST:** Lee Powell, Chief Thundercloud, Bruce Bennett, Lynne Roberts (Mary Hart), William Farnum, Lane Chandler, George Montgomery, Hal Taliaferro, George Cleveland. 1938

LONE RANGER, THE (1956) ★★★1/2 The first color feature film based on the legend of the Lone Ranger is a treat for the kids and not too tough for the adults to sit through. Clayton Moore and Jay Silverheels reprise their television roles and find themselves battling white settlers, led by an evil Lyle Bettger, and the much put-upon Indians, riled up by a surly Michael Ansara. 86m. **DIR:** Stuart Heisler. **CAST:** Clayton Moore, Jay Silverheels, Lyle Bettger, Bonita Granville. 1956

LONE RANGER, THE (TV SERIES) ★★★1/2 Emerging from a cloud of dust, with a hearty "Hi-yo Silver!" the Lone Ranger, with his faithful Indian companion, Tonto, leads the fight for law and order in the Old West. Wearing a black mask fashioned from the vest of his murdered brother, the former Texas Ranger uses silver bullets to remind him of the value of human life. He sought justice, not vengeance, and became a hero to millions of youngsters. Now, these two-episode videocassettes enable you to return to those thrilling days of yesteryear. Each tape 55m. **DIR:** Various. **CAST:** Clayton Moore, Jay Silverheels. 1949–1965

LONE RANGER AND THE LOST CITY OF GOLD, THE ★★1/2 The Lone Ranger and Tonto, as immortalized by Clayton Moore and Jay Silverheels, expose the murderers who hold a clue to a fabulously wealthy lost city's location. B&W. **DIR:** Lesley Selander. **CAST:** Clayton Moore, Jay Silverheels, Douglas Kennedy, Noreen Nash, John Miljan. 1958

LONE RUNNER 🎦 Our hero runs around a desert with a Rambo crossbow (complete with exploding arrows). Rated PG for violence and profanity. 84m.

DIR: Ruggero Deodato. **CAST:** Miles O'Keeffe, Savina Gersak, Donal Hodson, Ronald Lacey. 1986

LONE STAR (1952) ★★★ This rip-roaring Western disguised as a historical document works as both. Lionel Barrymore steals every scene he's in as the aging Andrew Jackson. He sends no-nonsense cattleman (Clark Gable) to keep Sam Houston from establishing Texas as a republic. Good action and lots of glamour from the stars. B&W; 94m. **DIR:** Vincent Sherman. **CAST:** Clark Gable, Ava Gardner, Broderick Crawford, Lionel Barrymore, Beulah Bondi, Ed Begley Sr. 1952

LONE STAR (1996) ★★★1/2 An ambitious drama that combines a mystery story with social commentary, set amid three cultures—anglo, Mexican, black—in a Texas border town. Chris Cooper stars as a sheriff whose investigation into a decades-old murder may involve his father, the late, legendary former sheriff in town. Director John Sayles is also a novelist, and this is his most novel-like screenplay; in fact, it may be too broad based; the storyline sometimes meanders. 130m. **DIR:** John Sayles. **CAST:** Chris Cooper, Kris Kristofferson, Elizabeth Peña, Matthew McConaughey, Joe Morton, Clifton James. 1996 DVD

LONE STAR RAIDERS ★★ The Three Mesquiteers try to save an old lady's ranch from bankruptcy by selling a herd of wild horses. Weak Mesquiteers entry burdened by too much stock footage. B&W; 54m. **DIR:** George Sherman. **CAST:** Robert Livingston, Bob Steele, Rufe Davis, Sarah Padden. 1940

LONE STAR TRAIL ★★★1/2 In this entertaining oater, Johnny Mack Brown is framed in a robbery case. Obviously upset, he hits the trail to find the real perpetrators. In the process, he meets up with outlaw Robert Mitchum, and one of the great fistfights in movie history is the result. Certainly worth a view. B&W; 77m. **DIR:** Ray Taylor. **CAST:** Johnny Mack Brown, Tex Ritter, Fuzzy Knight, Robert Mitchum. 1943

LONE WOLF ★★ Small-town students investigate a series of gory murders and discover a werewolf. Better than many such low-budget efforts, but barely worth seeing unless you're an avid lycanthrophile. Not rated, the film has some violence and gore. 96m. **DIR:** John Callas. **CAST:** Dyann Brown, Kevin Hart, Jamie Newcomb, Ann Douglas, Tom Henry. 1989

LONE WOLF AND CUB: SWORD OF VENGEANCE ★★★★ The first entry in the Japanese series, previously seen in America only as *Shogun Assassin*, which reedited scenes from several of the films. The films are known to fans as the "Baby Cart" series because the hero, a former shogun executioner, pulls his infant son along in a baby cart while he wanders, searching for his wife's murderers. Newly subtitled and letterboxed, these films are all classics of Japanese cinema, though the squeamish can't be warned too strongly about the intense violence. Not rated; contains graphic violence and nudity. 83m. **DIR:** Kenji Misumi. **CAST:** Tomisaburo Wakayama, Fumio Watanabe. 1973

LONE WOLF MCQUADE ★★★1/2 Chuck Norris plays a Texas Ranger who forgets the rules in his zeal to punish the bad guys. Norris meets his match in David Carradine, the leader of a gun-smuggling ring. The worth-waiting-for climax is a martial arts battle between the two. Rated PG for violence and profanity. 107m. **DIR:** Steve Carver. **CAST:** Chuck Norris, L. Q. Jones, R. G. Armstrong, David Carradine, Barbara Carrera. 1983

LONELINESS OF THE LONG DISTANCE RUNNER, THE ★★★★★ Powerful British drama about a youth in a reform school who runs in order to escape his dreary surroundings. Tom Courtenay is superb as Colin, a troubled youth who finds freedom of the mind with every step he runs. Michael Redgrave plays the governor of the reform school who sees opportunity in the boy's ability. Colin agrees to run in a race against another reform school in exchange for more freedom and how that decision affects his beliefs brings the film to a natural yet frustrating conclusion. 104m. **DIR:** Tony Richardson. **CAST:** Tom Courtenay, Michael Redgrave, Avis Bunnage, Peter Madden, James Fox, Alec McCowen. 1962

LONELY ARE THE BRAVE ★★★★ A "little" Hollywood Western set in modern times has a lot to offer those who can endure its heavy-handed message. Kirk Douglas is just right as the cowboy out of step with his times. His attempts to escape from jail on horseback in contrast to the mechanized attempts to catch him by a modern police force are handled well. B&W; 107m. **DIR:** David Miller. **CAST:** Kirk Douglas, Walter Matthau, Gena Rowlands. 1962

LONELY GUY, THE ★★★ Steve Martin stars in this okay comedy as a struggling young writer. One day he comes to find his live-in mate (Robyn Douglass) in bed with another man and becomes the "Lonely Guy" of the title. Only recommended for Steve Martin fans. Rated R for brief nudity and profanity. 90m. **DIR:** Arthur Hiller. **CAST:** Steve Martin, Robyn Douglass, Charles Grodin, Merv Griffin, Dr. Joyce Brothers. 1984 DVD

LONELY HEARTS (1981) ★★★½ A funny, touching Australian romantic comedy about two offbeat characters who fall in love. Peter (Norman Kaye) is a 50-year-old mama's boy who doesn't know what to do with his life when his mother dies. Then he meets Patricia (Wendy Hughes), a woman who has never had a life of her own. It's a warmly human delight. Rated R. 95m. **DIR:** Paul Cox. **CAST:** Norman Kaye, Wendy Hughes, Julia Blake. 1981

LONELY HEARTS (1991) ★★★½ Eric Roberts plays an unscrupulous swindler who wines and dines lonely women before taking all their assets for bogus investments. Beverly D'Angelo cramps his style by clinging desperately to him. Suspenseful made-for-cable thriller. 109m. **DIR:** Andrew Lane. **CAST:** Eric Roberts, Beverly D'Angelo, Joanna Cassidy, Herta Ware. 1991

LONELY IN AMERICA ★★★½ Bittersweet comedy concerns an East Indian man's rude awakening to the less inviting aspects of immigrating to the United States. Some of his experiences are more painful than hilarious and, as such, send home a message about compassion and tolerance. Rated PG-13 for sexual situations. 96m. **DIR:** Barry Alexander Brown. **CAST:** Ranjit Chowdhry, Adelaide Miller, Robert Kessler. 1990

LONELY LADY, THE 🦃 Pia Zadora as an aspiring writer who is used and abused by every man she

meets. Rated R for violence, nudity, and profanity. 92m. **DIR:** Peter Sasdy. **CAST:** Pia Zadora, Lloyd Bochner, Bibi Besch. 1983

LONELY MAN, THE ★★★ Interesting, but not exciting, this tautly directed oater is about a gunfighter, bent on reforming, who returns to his family after a seventeen-year hiatus. A brooding Jack Palance is the gunfighter. He is not warmly welcomed home by his deserted son, brooding Anthony Perkins. B&W; 87m. **DIR:** Henry Levin. **CAST:** Jack Palance, Anthony Perkins, Neville Brand, Robert Middleton, Elisha Cook Jr., Lee Van Cleef. 1957

LONELY PASSION OF JUDITH HEARNE, THE ★★★★ Maggie Smith gives a superb, seamless performance as Judith Hearne, an Irish spinster in the 1950s sequestered from the carnal world by plainness and Catholicism. When she meets an Americanized Irishman (brilliantly portrayed by Bob Hoskins, New York accent and all), parts of her character's dormant personality spring to life. Rated R. 115m. **DIR:** Jack Clayton. **CAST:** Maggie Smith, Bob Hoskins, Marie Kean, Wendy Hiller. 1987

LONELY TRAIL, THE ★★★ When former Yankee soldier John Wayne returns to his Texas ranch after the Civil War, he is greeted with suspicion and open hostility by his neighbors, whose sympathies were on the side of the Confederacy. Solid sagebrush saga. B&W; 58m. **DIR:** Joseph Kane. **CAST:** John Wayne, Ann Rutherford, Cy Kendall, Snowflake, Bob Kortman, Dennis Moore, Yakima Canutt. 1936

LONELYHEARTS ★★ A perfect example of how Hollywood can ruin great material. Montgomery Clift is tortured, Robert Ryan is cynical, and Maureen Stapleton is pitifully sex-starved in this disappointing adaptation of Nathaniel West's brilliant novel about an agony columnist who gets too caught up in a correspondent's life. Baloney! B&W; 101m. **DIR:** Vincent J. Donehue. **CAST:** Montgomery Clift, Robert Ryan, Myrna Loy, Maureen Stapleton, Dolores Hart, Jackie Coogan, Mike Kellin, Frank Overton, Onslow Stevens. 1958

LONESOME DOVE ★★★★★ Superb miniseries adapted from the sprawling novel by Larry McMurtry and originally written as a screenplay for John Wayne, Jimmy Stewart, and Henry Fonda. This is truly one of the great Westerns. Robert Duvall and Tommy Lee Jones give what are arguably the finest performances of their careers as a pair of aging Texas Rangers who go on one last adventure: a treacherous cattle drive to Montana. 384m. **DIR:** Simon Wincer. **CAST:** Robert Duvall, Tommy Lee Jones, Danny Glover, Diane Lane, Robert Urich, Frederic Forrest, D. B. Sweeney, Rick Schroder, Anjelica Huston, Chris Cooper, Timothy Scott, Glenne Headly, Barry Corbin, William Sanderson. 1989 DVD

LONG AGO TOMORROW ★★★ Malcolm McDowell stars in this in-depth story about an arrogant soccer player who is paralyzed by a mysterious disease. A pretty young woman who shares the same disability is able to help him adapt. McDowell keeps the plot alive with a very believable performance. Rated PG. 116m. **DIR:** Bryan Forbes. **CAST:** Malcolm McDowell, Nanette Newman, Georgia Brown, Gerald Sim, Bernard Lee, Michael Flanders. 1970

LONG DAY CLOSES, THE ★★★1/2 This is another masterful and affecting stream-of-consciousness movie memoir from the creator of *Distant Voices/Still Lives*. Once again, he explores his rough-and-tumble, working-class English childhood. This later film spotlights his much warmer and loving feelings about his mother. Once again, colorful family members come and go, and the world is spiced with lovingly re-created songs of memory. Davies's movies are an acquired taste, but one well worth acquiring. 84m. **DIR:** Terence Davies. **CAST:** Marjorie Yates, Leigh McCormack, Anthony Watson. **1993**

LONG DAY'S JOURNEY INTO NIGHT (1962) ★★★★★ This superb film was based on Eugene O'Neill's play about a troubled turn-of-the-century New England family. Katharine Hepburn is brilliant as the drug-addict wife. Ralph Richardson is equally good as her husband, a self-centered actor. One of their sons is an alcoholic, while the other is dying of tuberculosis. Although depressing, it is an unforgettable viewing experience. B&W; 136m. **DIR:** Sidney Lumet. **CAST:** Katharine Hepburn, Ralph Richardson, Jason Robards Jr., Dean Stockwell. **1962**

LONG DAY'S JOURNEY INTO NIGHT (1987) ★★★★ Excellent television adaptation of Eugene O'Neill's harrowing drama about a New England family in deep crisis. The stunning direction by Jonathan Miller makes this almost the equal of the 1962 film. Jack Lemmon turns in another powerful performance. Recommended for mature audiences. 169m. **DIR:** Jonathan Miller. **CAST:** Jack Lemmon, Bethel Leslie, Peter Gallagher, Kevin Spacey. **1987**

LONG GONE ★★★★ This very likable film follows the exploits of a minor-league baseball team and their manager (William Petersen) during one magical season in Florida during the early Fifties. Insightful HBO-produced movie is not unlike *Bull Durham* in that both take a loving look at America's favorite pastime while dissecting other societal concerns. 110m. **DIR:** Martin Davidson. **CAST:** William L. Petersen, Virginia Madsen, Henry Gibson. **1987**

LONG GOOD FRIDAY, THE ★★★★★ This superb British film depicts the struggle of an underworld boss (Bob Hoskins, in a brilliant performance) to hold on to his territory. It's a classic in the genre on a par with *The Godfather*, *The Public Enemy*, and *High Sierra*. Rated R for nudity, profanity, and violence. 114m. **DIR:** John Mackenzie. **CAST:** Bob Hoskins, Helen Mirren, Pierce Brosnan. **1980 DVD**

LONG GOODBYE, THE ★★★★ In this revisionist, haunting telling of the Raymond Chandler detective novel, "It's okay with me" is the easygoing credo of private eye Philip Marlowe as he drifts among the rich and nasty. This multilayered movie adapted by Leigh Brackett is not for all tastes, but a must-see in our book. Rated R for violence and profanity. 112m. **DIR:** Robert Altman. **CAST:** Elliott Gould, Nina Van Pallandt, Sterling Hayden, Henry Gibson, Mark Rydell, Jim Bouton, David Carradine, David Arkin, Warren Berlinger. **1973**

LONG GRAY LINE, THE ★★★ John Ford stock company regulars Maureen O'Hara and Ward Bond join heartthrob Tyrone Power in this sentimental tale of a celebrated West Point athletic trainer, and his years of devoted service to the academy and its plebes before cheating scandals and racial bigotry. 138m. **DIR:** John Ford. **CAST:** Tyrone Power, Maureen O'Hara, Robert Francis, Ward Bond, Donald Crisp, Betsy Palmer. **1955**

LONG HAUL ★★ Blond bombshell Diana Dors entices unhappily married trucker Victor Mature into nefarious schemes. Limp British drama. B&W; 100m. **DIR:** Ken Hughes. **CAST:** Victor Mature, Patrick Allen, Diana Dors. **1957**

LONG HOT SUMMER, THE (1958) ★★★★ Paul Newman drifts into a Mississippi town and sets hearts aflutterin' and tongues awaggin' as he fascinates the womenfolk, alienates the menfolk, and aggravates Big Daddy Varner, the town's monied redneck. Based on parts of two short stories and one novel by William Faulkner, this hodgepodge of sex, scandal, and suspicion is great fun. 115m. **DIR:** Martin Ritt. **CAST:** Paul Newman, Joanne Woodward, Orson Welles, Anthony Franciosa, Lee Remick, Angela Lansbury. **1958**

LONG HOT SUMMER, THE (1985) ★★★1/2 Don Johnson is a drifter who comes to a small southern town and upsets the routine of a family clan headed by patriarch Jason Robards. As well as being a moving, steamy tale of lust and greed, it also shows that director Stuart Cooper can get above-average performances from the likes of Johnson and Cybill Shepherd. This telemovie was originally shown in two parts. 208m. **DIR:** Stuart Cooper. **CAST:** Don Johnson, Jason Robards Jr., Cybill Shepherd, Judith Ivey, Ava Gardner, Wings Hauser. **1985**

LONG JOHN SILVER ★★★ Avast me hearties, Robert Newton is at his scene-chewing best in this otherwise unexceptional (and unofficial) sequel to Disney's *Treasure Island*. 109m. **DIR:** Byron Haskin. **CAST:** Robert Newton, Connie Gilchrist, Kit Taylor, Grant Taylor. **1954**

LONG KISS GOODNIGHT, THE ★★★★ OK, so this story, about a suburban mom with amnesia who discovers she's a highly trained, remorseless assassin, is pure hokum. If you can forget the implausibility of the premise, it's great fun for action fans, as star Geena Davis and her reluctant companion, Samuel L. Jackson, get out of one tight scrape after another. Director Renny Harlin keeps his tongue planted firmly in cheek throughout. Rated R for violence and profanity. 120m. **DIR:** Renny Harlin. **CAST:** Geena Davis, Samuel L. Jackson, Patrick Malahide, Craig Bierko, Brian Cox, David Morse, G. D. Spradlin. **1996 DVD**

LONG LIVE YOUR DEATH ★★ A fake prince, a fake Mexican revolutionary hero, and a journalist try to locate a hidden treasure. A comedy-spaghetti Western set in Mexico with some good sight gags and dialogue. Eli Wallach is at his best. Not rated; contains violence. 98m. **DIR:** Duccio Tessari. **CAST:** Franco Nero, Eli Wallach, Lynn Redgrave, Marilu Tolo, Eduardo Fajardo. **1974**

LONG LONG TRAIL ★★★ Hooter is the Ramblin' Kid in a typical, but above-average, lighthearted Gibson Western. This one's a racehorse story. Love interest Sally Eilers became the real Mrs. Gibson a few months later. B&W; 60m. **DIR:** Arthur Rosson. **CAST:** Hoot Gibson, Sally Eilers, Walter Brennan. **1929**

LONG, LONG TRAILER, THE ★★★ You might not love Lucy in this one, but you'll sure like her a lot. Ball and Desi Arnaz portray a couple not unlike the Ricardos. Their honeymoon trip is complicated by an impossibly long trailer. Once their dream vehicle, this trailer becomes a nightmare. 103m. **DIR:** Vincente Minnelli. **CAST:** Lucille Ball, Desi Arnaz Sr., Marjorie Main, Keenan Wynn. **1954**

LONG RIDERS, THE ★★★1/2 Film about the James-Younger Gang has a few deficiencies. Character development and plot complexity are ignored in favor of lots of action. This is partially offset by the casting of real-life brothers. While it sounds like a gimmick, it actually adds a much-needed dimension of character to the picture. Rated R for violence. 100m. **DIR:** Walter Hill. **CAST:** David Carradine, Keith Carradine, Robert Carradine, Stacy Keach, James Keach, Nicholas Guest, Christopher Guest, Dennis Quaid, Randy Quaid. **1980**

LONG ROAD HOME, THE ★★1/2 A family of Texas migrant workers, led by a former rodeo star, longs to escape their existence and move into their own house. There are some good performances in this heartfelt made-for-cable drama, but it's no *Grapes of Wrath.* Not rated; contains mild violence. 88m. **DIR:** John Korty. **CAST:** Mark Harmon, Lee Purcell, Morgan Weisser, Leon Russom. **1991**

LONG VOYAGE HOME, THE ★★★★1/2 Life in the merchant marines as experienced and recalled by Nobel Prize–winning playwright Eugene O'Neill. The hopes and dreams and comradeship of a group of seamen beautifully blended in a gripping, moving account of men, a ship, and the ever-enigmatic sea. The major characters are superbly drawn by those playing them. Definitely a must-see, and see-again, film. Classic. B&W; 105m. **DIR:** John Ford. **CAST:** John Wayne, Barry Fitzgerald, Thomas Mitchell, Mildred Natwick. **1940**

LONG WALK HOME, THE ★★★★ Superb performances by Sissy Spacek and Whoopi Goldberg highlight this absorbing drama about the first civil rights action: the Montgomery, Alabama, bus boycott of 1956. Rated PG for racial epithets and brief violence. 97m. **DIR:** Richard Pearce. **CAST:** Sissy Spacek, Whoopi Goldberg, Dwight Schultz, Ving Rhames, Dylan Baker. **1990**

LONG WAY HOME, THE ★★★ Director Michael Apted turns his cameras on Russian rock 'n' roller Boris Grebenshikov, whose musical odyssey is both tune-filled and inspirational. From Leningrad to New York to Los Angeles, the cameras document Russia's equivalent of Bruce Springsteen. Musical cameos by Dave Stewart, Annie Lennox, and Chrissie Hynde. Not rated. 82m. **DIR:** Michael Apted. **1989**

LONG WEEKEND ★★★1/2 This Australian film is a must-see for environmentalists. We are introduced to a couple who carelessly start a forest fire, run over a kangaroo, senselessly destroy a tree, shoot animals for the sport of it, and break an eagle's egg. Then nature avenges itself. Not rated, this contains obscenities, nudity, and gore. 95m. **DIR:** Colin Eggleston. **CAST:** John Hargreaves, Briony Behets. **1986**

LONGEST DAY, THE ★★★★★ A magnificent re-creation of the Allied invasion of Normandy in June of 1944 with an all-star cast, this epic war film succeeds where others may fail—*Midway* and *Tora! Tora! Tora!,* for example. A big-budget film that shows you where the money was spent, it's first-rate in all respects. B&W; 180m. **DIR:** Ken Annakin, Andrew Marton, Bernhard Wicki. **CAST:** John Wayne, Robert Mitchum, Henry Fonda, Richard Burton, Rod Steiger, Sean Connery, Robert Wagner. **1963** DVD

LONGEST DRIVE, THE ★★1/2 Culled from the 1976 television series, *The Quest,* this passable Western features Kurt Russell and Tim Matheson as two young brothers who help save an Irish rancher's herd, land, and fiery reputation. 92m. **DIR:** Bernard McEveety. **CAST:** Kurt Russell, Tim Matheson, Dan O'Herlihy, Keenan Wynn, Woody Strode, Erik Estrada. **1976**

LONGEST HUNT, THE ★★ A legendary gunfighter named Stark is hired by a wealthy Mexican landowner to bring back his rebellious son who has joined a gang of American bandits. Stark succeeds but a surprise awaits when he finds out the boy is not the landowner's son. A good story twist makes this an enjoyable film. Not rated; contains violence. 89m. **DIR:** Frank B. Corlish. **CAST:** Brian Kelly, Keenan Wynn, Erica Blanc, Fred Munroe, Virginia Field, Duane Rowland. **1968**

LONGEST YARD, THE ★★★★ An ex–professional football quarterback (Burt Reynolds) is sent to a Florida prison for stealing his girlfriend's car. The warden (Eddie Albert) forces Reynolds to put together a prisoner team to play his semipro team made up of guards. Great audience participation film with the last third dedicated to the game. Rated R for language and violence. 123m. **DIR:** Robert Aldrich. **CAST:** Burt Reynolds, Eddie Albert, Michael Conrad, Bernadette Peters, Ed Lauter. **1974**

LONGHORN ★★★★ Rancher Bill Elliott tries to drive Herefords backward on the Oregon Trail to mate with Texas longhorns and form a tough new breed of cattle. Along the way he battles Indians, discontent cowhands, and a treacherous partner. The first, and possibly best, of Elliott's later Allied Artists films after leaving Republic where he'd starred in 34 Westerns over an eight-year period. B&W; 70m. **DIR:** Lewis D. Collins. **CAST:** William Elliott, Phyllis Coates, Myron Healey, John Hart. **1951**

LONGSHOT (1981) 🚫 A soccer star turns down a scholarship at a prestigious university in order to attend the football championships in Europe. 100m. **DIR:** E. W. Swackhamer. **CAST:** Leif Garrett, Ralph Seymour, Zoe Chaveau, Linda Manz. **1981**

LONGSHOT, THE (1985) 🚫 Dreck about small-time horse players. Rated PG. 110m. **DIR:** Paul Bartel. **CAST:** Tim Conway, Harvey Korman, Jack Weston, Ted Wass, Anne Meara, Stella Stevens, Jonathan Winters. **1985**

LONGTIME COMPANION ★★★★ An accessible and affecting film that puts a much-needed human face on the tragedy of AIDS. An ensemble piece following the lives and relationships among nine gay New Yorkers and one woman friend over nine years.

The cast is superb, with Bruce Davison especially memorable. The perceptive script is by playwright Craig Lucas. Rated R for profanity. 96m. DIR: Norman René. CAST: Bruce Davison, Campbell Scott, Dermot Mulroney, Mark Lamos, Patrick Cassidy, John Dossett, Mary-Louise Parker. 1990

LOOK BACK IN ANGER (1958) ★★★1/2 This riveting look into one of the "angry young men" of the 1950s has Richard Burton and Claire Bloom at their best. Burton exposes the torment and frustration these men felt toward their country and private life with more vividness than you may want to deal with, but if you're looking for a realistic recreation of the period, look no further. B&W; 99m. DIR: Tony Richardson. CAST: Richard Burton, Claire Bloom. 1958

LOOK BACK IN ANGER (1980) ★★ Jimmy Porter is a failed trumpet player and lower-class intellectual who turns his dashed hopes into a symphony of verbal abuse played upon his wife and best friend. McDowell serves up a Porter who is smug and easy to despise, but his portrayal lacks the powerful rage of Richard Burton in the 1958 film version of this mid-Fifties stage smash. 101m. DIR: Lindsay Anderson. CAST: Malcolm McDowell, Lisa Banes, Fran Brill, Robert Brill, Raymond Hardie. 1980

LOOK BACK IN ANGER (1989) ★★★★ Kenneth Branagh is brilliant as a detestable young man who constantly lashes out at his wife and business partner. This spellbinding adaptation of John Osborne's play was produced for British television. Not rated; contains profanity. 114m. DIR: David Jones. CAST: Kenneth Branagh, Emma Thompson, Gerard Horan, Siobhan Redmond. 1989

LOOK FOR THE SILVER LINING ★★★ This supposed biography of Marilyn Miller is a familiar vaudeville-to-Broadway story. Take it as such and enjoy the songs from that era. Ray Bolger, as Miller's mentor, has some very good numbers. 100m. DIR: David Butler. CAST: June Haver, Ray Bolger, Gordon MacRae, Charlie Ruggles, Rosemary DeCamp, S. Z. Sakall, Walter Catlett, Will Rogers Jr. 1949

LOOK WHO'S LAUGHING ★★ Pretty weak comedy featuring radio favorites Edgar Bergen and Fibber McGee and Molly. Rather lean on laughs, except when Charlie McCarthy takes the spotlight. B&W; 78m. DIR: Allan Dwan. CAST: Edgar Bergen, Jim Jordan, Marion Jordan, Lucille Ball, Harold Peary. 1941

LOOK WHO'S TALKING ★★★★ Hilarious adventure of an unmarried woman (Kirstie Alley) seeking the perfect father for her baby. John Travolta becomes the baby's unconventional sitter. Baby Mikey's humorous impressions from conception to age one are relayed through the offscreen voice of Bruce Willis. PG-13 for an opening sex-ed sequence of Mikey's conception. 100m. DIR: Amy Heckerling. CAST: Kirstie Alley, John Travolta, Olympia Dukakis, George Segal. 1989 DVD

LOOK WHO'S TALKING TOO ❤ A totally unfunny sequel that reunites the original cast but can't come up with the spark that made the first so enjoyable. Also featuring the voices of Bruce Willis, Roseanne Barr, and Damon Wayans. 81m. DIR: Amy Heckerling.

CAST: John Travolta, Kirstie Alley, Olympia Dukakis, Elias Koteas. 1990

LOOK WHO'S TALKING NOW ❤ Precocious family dogs spar with voices supplied by Danny DeVito and Diane Keaton in this tired, insulting sequel. Rated PG. 97m. DIR: Tom Ropelewski. CAST: John Travolta, Kirstie Alley. 1993

LOOKALIKE, THE ★★★1/2 Kate Wilhelm's thoughtful story becomes an absorbing made-for-cable thriller. Melissa Gilbert stars as a young woman not entirely convinced of her sanity, following the death of her young daughter. It all builds to a stylish climax, with a few well-hidden surprises. Brief violence. Rated PG-13. 88m. DIR: Gary Nelson. CAST: Melissa Gilbert, Diane Ladd, Thaao Penghlis, Frances Lee McCain. 1990

LOOKER ★★ Writer-director Michael Crichton describes this movie as "a thriller about television commercials," but it's really a fairly simpleminded suspense film. Plastic surgeon Albert Finney discovers a plot by evil mastermind James Coburn to clone models for television commercials. This is fiction? Rated PG because of nudity and violence. 94m. DIR: Michael Crichton. CAST: Albert Finney, James Coburn, Susan Dey, Leigh Taylor-Young. 1981

LOOKIN' TO GET OUT ★★★ This offbeat comedy stars Jon Voight and Burt Young as a couple of compulsive gamblers out to hit the fabled "big score" in Las Vegas. It does drag a bit in the middle. However, the first hour zips by before you know it, and the ending is a humdinger. Rated R for violence and profanity. 104m. DIR: Hal Ashby. CAST: Jon Voight, Burt Young, Ann-Margret, Bert Remsen. 1982

LOOKING FOR MIRACLES ★★★1/2 The summer of 1935 marks the reunion of two brothers separated by poverty. Heartwarming family entertainment originally made for the Disney Channel. 104m. DIR: Kevin Sullivan. CAST: Greg Spottiswood, Zachary Bennett, Joe Flaherty. 1990

LOOKING FOR MR. GOODBAR ★★ A strong performance by star Diane Keaton almost saves this dismal character study about a woman drawn to sleazy sex and low-lifes. Rated R. 135m. DIR: Richard Brooks. CAST: Diane Keaton, Tuesday Weld, Richard Gere, Richard Kiley, Tom Berenger. 1977

LOOKING FOR RICHARD ★★1/2 Al Pacino's attempt to bring Shakespeare to the masses is a vanity production that sags beneath the star-director's incessant mugging. Intended as a primer to *Richard III*, this opus instead becomes an exercise in frustration; every time we get involved in the play's drama and intrigue, Pacino drags us right back out. Not rated, but equivalent to a PG for profanity. 109m. DIR: Al Pacino. CAST: Al Pacino, Harris Yulin, Penelope Allen, Alec Baldwin, Kevin Spacey, Estelle Parsons, Winona Ryder, Aidan Quinn. 1996

LOOKING FOR TROUBLE ★★ A girl who longs for a pet tries to save an abused elephant from a circus. Third-rate kids' fare whose only virtue is inoffensiveness. Rated PG. 73m. DIR: Jay Aubrey. CAST: Holly Butler, Shawn McAllister, Susan Gallagher. 1996

LOOKING GLASS WAR, THE ★★ This plodding adaptation of John Le Carré's espionage novel about a Pole sent to get the scam on a rocket in East Berlin never gets off the ground. Most of the acting is as wooden as bleacher seating. Where's Smiley when we need him? Rated PG. 106m. **DIR:** Frank Pierson. **CAST:** Christopher Jones, Pia Degermark, Ralph Richardson, Anthony Hopkins. 1970

LOONEY, LOONEY, LOONEY BUGS BUNNY MOVIE ★★★1/2 This follow-up to the *Bugs Bunny/Road Runner Movie* lacks the earlier film's inventiveness, but then Chuck Jones was always the most cerebral of the Warner Bros. cartoon directors. Friz Freleng, on the other hand, only tried to make people laugh. This collection of his cartoons—which feature Daffy Duck, Porky Pig, Tweety Pie, and Yosemite Sam, among others, in addition to Bugs—does just that with general efficiency. Rated G. 79m. **DIR:** Friz Freleng. 1981

LOOPHOLE ★★1/2 In yet another heist film, unemployed architect Albert Finney concocts an ambitious plan to break into a highly guarded and impenetrable London bank. There is a bit of snap in the scenario and dialogue, but ultimately the film loses its freshness. Susannah York gives a fine performance. Not rated. 105m. **DIR:** John Quested. **CAST:** Albert Finney, Martin Sheen, Susannah York, Colin Blakely. 1980

LOOSE CANNONS ★★ Gene Hackman stars as a hard-nosed career policeman who gets stuck with the deranged Dan Aykroyd as a partner. Only a few funny scenes provided by Aykroyd, including one in which he imitates the Road Runner, save this uneven cop comedy. Rated R for profanity and violence. 90m. **DIR:** Bob Clark. **CAST:** Gene Hackman, Dan Aykroyd, Dom DeLuise, Ronny Cox, Nancy Travis, Robert Prosky, Paul Koslo. 1990

LOOSE CONNECTIONS ★★★1/2 In this cult comedy, an Englishwoman (Lindsay Duncan) builds a car with two female friends so that they can attend a feminist convention in Germany. At the last minute, her friends back out, and she is forced to accept a goofy substitute (Stephen Rea) as her traveling companion. Offbeat entertainment. Rated PG for profanity. 90m. **DIR:** Richard Eyre. **CAST:** Stephen Rea, Lindsay Duncan. 1984

LOOSE SHOES 💔 Failed attempt to spoof B movies. Rated R. 73m. **DIR:** Ira Miller. **CAST:** Buddy Hackett, Howard Hesseman, Bill Murray, Susan Tyrrell, Avery Schreiber. 1977

LOOT ★★ A hearse driver and his friend rob a bank and store the loot inside a coffin, setting off a slapstick, cliché-ridden comedy complete with a runaway funeral procession—and every graveyard quip in the book. Dated now, this was probably racy in its day. Not rated. 102m. **DIR:** Silvio Narizzano. **CAST:** Lee Remick, Richard Attenborough, Milo O'Shea, Hywel Bennett. 1972

LORD JIM ★★★★ Joseph Conrad's complex novel of human weakness has been simplified for easier appreciation and brought to the screen in a lavish visual style. Peter O'Toole is Jim, a sailor in Southeast Asia who is adopted by a suppressed village as its leader in spite of a past clouded by allegations of cowardice. The belief shown in him by the native villagers is put to the test by a group of European thugs.

154m. **DIR:** Richard Brooks. **CAST:** Peter O'Toole, James Mason, Eli Wallach. 1965

LORD LOVE A DUCK ★★★1/2 A cynic's delight that makes a big joke out of greed, lust, and egomania. Roddy McDowall plays a high school senior who helps classmate Tuesday Weld con her father, marry a hunk, become a movie star and—when she gets bored with everything else—become a widow. A lot of laughs, but not for every taste. B&W; 105m. **DIR:** George Axelrod. **CAST:** Roddy McDowall, Tuesday Weld, Lola Albright, Ruth Gordon, Max Showalter, Martin Gabel, Harvey Korman, Donald Murphy, Sarah Marshall. 1966

LORD OF ILLUSIONS 💔 Horror impresario Clive Barker's nasty little shocker, intended to be a suspenseful marriage of Lovecraft and detective *film noir*, emerges instead as an incoherent mess with a hero who behaves like a daft fool at all times. Rated R for violence, profanity, and gore. 108m. **DIR:** Clive Barker. **CAST:** Scott Bakula, Kevin J. O'Connor, Famke Janssen, Vincent Schiavelli. 1995 DVD

LORD OF THE FLIES (1963) ★★★★ William Golding's grim allegory comes to the screen in a near-perfect adaptation helmed by British stage director Peter Brook. English schoolboys, stranded on an island and left to their own devices, gradually revert to the savage cruelty of wild animals. Visually hypnotic and powerful, something you just can't tear your eyes away from. The cast is outstanding, and what the film fails to take from Golding's symbolism, it compensates for with raw energy. B&W; 91m. **DIR:** Peter Brook. **CAST:** James Aubrey, Hugh Edwards, Tom Chapin. 1963 DVD

LORD OF THE FLIES (1989) ★★ This 1989 Americanization of Sir William Golding's apocalyptic novel has the external trappings of a good film—lush scenery, and a fine cast of unknowns. But the depth and sensitivity of the 1963 Peter Brook version are blatantly missing. Rated R for profanity and violence. 120m. **DIR:** Harry Hook. **CAST:** Balthazar Getty. 1989

LORD OF THE RINGS, THE 💔 J.R.R. Tolkien's beloved epic fantasy is trashed in this animated film. Rated PG. 133m. **DIR:** Ralph Bakshi. 1978

LORDS OF DISCIPLINE, THE ★★★1/2 A thought-provoking film, *Lords* contains many emotionally charged and well-played scenes. David Keith stars as a student at a military academy who puts his life in danger by helping a black cadet being hazed. Rated R for profanity, nudity, and violence. 102m. **DIR:** Franc Roddam. **CAST:** David Keith, Robert Prosky, G. D. Spradlin, Rick Rossovich. 1983

LORDS OF FLATBUSH, THE ★★1/2 Of all the leads, only Paul Mace didn't go on to bigger things. The film provides a fairly satisfying blend of toughness and sentimentality, humor and pathos, as it tells a story of coming-of-age in 1950s New York. Rated PG. 88m. **DIR:** Stephen F. Verona, Martin Davidson. **CAST:** Perry King, Sylvester Stallone, Henry Winkler, Paul Mace, Susan Blakely. 1974 DVD

LORDS OF THE DEEP 💔 Poverty-row quickie, designed solely to cash in on the underwater menace subgenre spearheaded by *The Abyss*. Inexplicably rated PG-13. 79m. **DIR:** Mary Ann Fisher. **CAST:** Bradford Dillman, Priscilla Barnes. **1989**

LORENZO'S OIL ★★★★★ In a switch from his *Mad Max* films, doctor-turned-director George Miller uses the full force of his knowledge and skills to make gripping this emotionally powerful tale about a couple fighting for the life of their seriously ill son. In refusing to accept the verdict of a stodgy, entrenched medical establishment, the parents use every means possible to find a cure. Based on a true story. Rated PG-13 for profanity. 135m. **DIR:** George Miller. **CAST:** Nick Nolte, Susan Sarandon, Peter Ustinov, Kathleen Wilhoite. **1992**

LORNA DOONE ★★★1/2 Beautiful, made-for-British-television adaptation of R. D. Blackmore's romantic novel stars Sean Bean and Polly Walker as star-crossed lovers whose union adds some kinks to a family feud. After his parents are killed, John Ridd vows to kill the Doone family, but unexpectedly falls for their daughter Lorna. Wonderfully romantic and steeped in period detail. Rated PG. 90m. **DIR:** Andrew Grieve. **CAST:** Sean Bean, Polly Walker, Clive Owen, Billie Whitelaw. **1990**

LOS OLVIDADOS ★★★★★ Luis Buñuel marks the beginning of his mature style with this film. Hyperpersonal, shocking, erotic, hallucinogenic, and surrealistic images are integrated into naturalistic action: two youths of the Mexican slums venture deeper and deeper into the criminal world until they are beyond redemption. In Spanish with English subtitles. B&W; 88m. **DIR:** Luis Buñuel. **CAST:** Alfonso Mejía, Roberto Cobo. **1950**

LOSERS, THE 🎦 Imagine *Rambo* made as a biker film and you'll have *The Losers*. Rated R for violence and nudity. 95m. **DIR:** Jack Starrett. **CAST:** William Smith, Bernie Hamilton, Adam Roarke. **1970**

LOSIN' IT ★★★ Better-than-average teen exploitation flick, this one has four boys off to Tijuana for a good time. Shelley Long ("Cheers") adds interest as a runaway wife who joins them on their journey. Rated R. 104m. **DIR:** Curtis Hanson. **CAST:** Tom Cruise, Shelley Long, Jackie Earle Haley, John Stockwell. **1982**

LOSING CHASE ★★★1/2 Helen Mirren dominates this character study, as a depressed wife trying to regain her stability following a public nervous breakdown. Her attentive husband hires a "mother's helper" to keep the two young children in line, but the newcomer proves more beneficial to Mirren. Anne Meredith's thoughtful script builds to an unexpected twist but then stops too soon; it would be nice to see what happens next. Rated PG-13 for profanity and dramatic content. 95m. **DIR:** Kevin Bacon. **CAST:** Helen Mirren, Kyra Sedgwick, Beau Bridges, Michael Yarmush, Lucas Denton. **1996**

LOSING ISAIAH ★★1/2 Adoptive Caucasian parents of an abandoned African American crack baby land in court when the kid's rehabbed, biological mom tries to get him back. The performances are first-rate, but the film feels just as manipulative as its dueling attorneys. Rated R for language and drug use. 108m. **DIR:** Stephen Gyllenhaal. **CAST:** Jessica Lange, Halle Berry, David Strathairn, Samuel L. Jackson, Cuba Gooding Jr. **1995**

•**LOSS OF SEXUAL INNOCENCE, THE** ★★1/2 This plot-free film plays like a stream of dreams. The downside is that it also feels like a film-school experiment driven by Calvin Klein ad aesthetics. The core story is about a filmmaker who has lost much more than the film's provocative title suggests. Scenes in which a curious child evolves to a jaded adult are also intercut with a modern version of Adam and Eve in which a black man and white woman emerge from a small lake. There's enough philosophical and cinematic doodling here for several films. Rated R for nudity, sexuality, language, and violence. 101m. **DIR:** Mike Figgis. **CAST:** Julian Sands, Jonathan Rhys-Meyers, Saffron Burrows, Femi Ogumbanjo, Hanne Klintoe. **1999 DVD**

LOST! ★★★1/2 Even though it contains no nudity or violence, this is a movie that you should be careful about letting children see. Based on a true incident, it tells of three people adrift in the Pacific Ocean on an overturned boat. One, a religious zealot, feels that their plight is a test of God, and that they should do nothing to try to help themselves. Not rated. 94m. **DIR:** Peter Rowe. **CAST:** Kenneth Walsh, Helen Shaver, Michael Hogan. **1986**

LOST AND FOUND (1979) ★★ After teaming up successfully for *A Touch of Class*, writer-director Melvin Frank and his stars, Glenda Jackson and George Segal, tried again. But the result was an unfunny comedy about two bickering, cardboard characters. Rated PG. 112m. **DIR:** Melvin Frank. **CAST:** Glenda Jackson, George Segal, Maureen Stapleton. **1979**

LOST & FOUND (1999) 🎦 David Spade plays a loser who kidnaps the dog of a beautiful French woman in order to win her heart. Go figure. One highlight: Spade doing his Neil Diamond impression. Rated PG-13 for language, sexual innuendo, and partial nudity. 97m. **DIR:** Jeff Pollack. **CAST:** David Spade, Sophie Marceau, Artie Lange, Patrick Bruel. **1999**

LOST ANGELS ★★★★ Adam Horovitz ("King Ad Rock" of the Beastie Boys) makes an impressive dramatic debut as Tim Doolan, a misguided teenager who winds up in a Los Angeles psychiatric counseling center, where one of the staff psychiatrists wants to see the troubled youngsters properly treated. Rated R for language and violence. 121m. **DIR:** Hugh Hudson. **CAST:** Adam Horovitz, Donald Sutherland, Amy Locane, Don Bloomfield, Celin Weston, Graham Beckel. **1989**

LOST BOYS, THE ★★ In this vampire variation on *Peter Pan*, director Joel Schumacher seems more interested in pretty shots and fancy costumes than atmosphere and plot. The story has Jason Patric falling in with a group of hip bloodsuckers led by Kiefer Sutherland. Rated R for violence, suggested sex, and profanity. 98m. **DIR:** Joel Schumacher. **CAST:** Jason Patric, Dianne Wiest, Corey Haim, Barnard Hughes, Edward Herrmann, Kiefer Sutherland, Jami Gertz, Corey Feldman. **1987 DVD**

LOST CAPONE, THE 🎦 Al Capone and his little-known brother, who became a lawman in Nebraska and fought the bootleggers sent by Brother Al. Dull television movie. 93m. **DIR:** John Gray. **CAST:** Adrian

Pasdar, Ally Sheedy, Eric Roberts, Jimmie F. Skaggs. **1990**

LOST CITY, THE ★★ Incredibly bad serial becomes an incredible feature as crazy Zolok, maniacal ruler of a lost African city, uses a kidnapped scientist to wreak havoc on the rest of the world. Laughable thriller. B&W; 74m. **DIR:** Harry Revier. **CAST:** William "Stage" Boyd, Kane Richmond, George "Gabby" Hayes. **1935**

LOST COMMAND ★★★ A good international cast and fine direction bring to vivid life this story of French-Algerian guerrilla warfare in North Africa following World War II. Anthony Quinn is especially effective. Great action scenes. 130m. **DIR:** Mark Robson. **CAST:** Anthony Quinn, Alain Delon, George Segal, Michele Morgan, Claudia Cardinale. **1966**

LOST CONTINENT, THE (1951) ★★ Air Force pilot Cesar Romero teams up with scientist John Hoyt to find a rocket ship that crash-landed on an uncharted island. They discover death and dinosaurs instead. Mild adventure-fantasy. 83m. **DIR:** Sam Newfield. **CAST:** Cesar Romero, Hillary Brooke, Chick Chandler, John Hoyt, Acquanetta, Sid Melton, Whit Bissell, Hugh Beaumont. **1951**

●**LOST CONTINENT, THE (1968)** ★★1/2 Hammer adaptation of Dennis Wheatley's novel *Uncharted Seas* is a film that should have played more with adventure. Not up to the standards set by other Hammer productions. Rated G. 89m. **DIR:** Michael Carreras. **CAST:** Eric Porter, Suzanna Leigh. **1968 DVD**

LOST EMPIRE, THE 🦃 Inept, hokey film about the island stronghold of a mysterious ruler. Rated R for some nudity and violence. 86m. **DIR:** Jim Wynorski. **CAST:** Melanie Vincz, Raven De La Croix, Angela Aames, Paul Coufos, Robert Tessier. **1983**

LOST HIGHWAY ★★★ This weird, disturbing creep show is part nightmare, part surreal mystery. Fred Madison is a jazz saxophonist with a paranoia problem. The film's unofficial first act ends as Fred is arrested for his wife's murder. In act two, Fred morphs into a young car mechanic while on death row. He is released and begins a different life that intersects with his own past, a volatile crime boss, and a powder-faced sorcerer. Rated R for language, nudity, sex, and violence. 135m. **DIR:** David Lynch. **CAST:** Bill Pullman, Patricia Arquette, Balthazar Getty, Robert Loggia, Robert Blake. **1996**

LOST HONOR OF KATHARINA BLUM, THE ★★★ Angela Winkler's performance as Katharina Blum is the central force behind Schlondorff's interpretation of Heinrich Böll's novel. Katharina Blum is a poor, young housekeeper who spends one night with a suspected political terrorist. Her life is thereby ruined by the police and the media. In German with English subtitles. Rated R. 97m. **DIR:** Volker Schlöndorff. **CAST:** Angela Winkler. **1977**

LOST HORIZON ★★★★ Novelist James Hilton's intriguing story of a group of disparate people who survive an air crash and stumble onto a strange and haunting Tibetan land. One of the great classic films of the late 1930s. Long-missing footage has recently been restored, along with so-called lost scenes. B&W; 132m. **DIR:** Frank Capra. **CAST:** Ronald Colman, Jane Wyatt, John Howard, Edward Everett Horton,

Margo, Sam Jaffe, Thomas Mitchell, Isabel Jewell, H. B. Warner. **1937 DVD**

LOST IN A HAREM ★★★ Abbott and Costello as traveling magicians attempt to save a singer from the clutches of a sheikh. Best bit is Costello locked up with a murderer who explains: "S-l-o-w-l-y, I turned." 89m. **DIR:** Charles F. Riesner. **CAST:** Bud Abbott, Lou Costello, Marilyn Maxwell, Douglass Dumbrille. **1944**

LOST IN ALASKA ★★ Gambling, mining, the Alaska gold rush, and anything else the writers could think of is tossed into this mess of a comedy, one of Abbott and Costello's weakest. B&W; 76m. **DIR:** Jean Yarbrough. **CAST:** Bud Abbott, Lou Costello, Tom Ewell, Mitzi Green. **1952**

LOST IN AMERICA ★★★★1/2 *Lost in America* is Albert Brooks' funniest film to date. Some viewers may be driven to distraction by Brooks's all-too-true study of what happens when a "successful" and "responsible" married couple chucks it all and goes out on an *Easy Rider*–style trip across the country. Brooks makes movies about the things most adults would consider their worst nightmare. If you can stand the pain, the pleasure is well worth it. Rated R for profanity and adult situations. 92m. **DIR:** Albert Brooks. **CAST:** Albert Brooks, Julie Hagerty, Garry Marshall. **1985**

LOST IN SPACE (TV SERIES) ★★★ The Robinson family volunteers to help Earth solve its overpopulation problem by exploring space. That incessantly fussy saboteur, Colonel Zachary Smith, thwarts their mission. Terrifically tacky special effects and loads of campy humor earned the show a cult following. The robot proved to be the most endearing personality on board. 60m. **DIR:** Leo Penn, Alexander Singer, Tony Leader. **CAST:** Guy Williams, June Lockhart, Mark Goddard, Jonathan Harris, Marta Kristen, Angela Cartwright, Billy Mumy. **1965–1968**

LOST IN SPACE (1998) ★★★ The special effects in this big-screen re-creation of the tacky TV series are admittedly impressive, as is costar Matt LeBlanc's turn as the no-nonsense pilot. Otherwise, this version of *Swiss Family Robinson* in space is a convoluted affair, with a time-travel subplot that gets weirder and less convincing as it goes along. It's nice to see the quickie appearances by the original TV cast, but youngsters are sure to love it whether they know the old series or not. Rated PG-13 for violence. 131m. **DIR:** Stephen Hopkins. **CAST:** William Hurt, Mimi Rogers, Gary Oldman, Heather Graham, Lacey Chabert, Jack Johnson, Matt LeBlanc, Mark Goddard, June Lockhart, Edward Fox, Marta Kristen, Angela Cartwright. **1998 DVD**

LOST IN YONKERS ★★★★ Playwright Neil Simon wrote the screenplay for this adaptation of his Pulitzer and Tony Award–winning play about two brothers left with their crotchety old grandmother in the 1930s. Mercedes Ruehl is fabulous as the boys' aunt, a slightly dim-witted woman living with her mother (Irene Worth). Richard Dreyfuss also makes a fine impression as the boys' gangster uncle. Rated PG for adult themes. 110m. **DIR:** Martha Coolidge. **CAST:** Richard Dreyfuss, Mercedes Ruehl, Irene Worth, David Strathairn, Brad Stoll. **1993**

LOST LANGUAGE OF CRANES, THE ★★★ Set in England, this film deals with a homosexual who decides to tell his parents the truth, only to find out that his father has suppressed his own homosexuality for years. Eileen Atkins wonderfully portrays the mother who cannot accept her son's lifestyle and then loses her husband. Not rated; contains homosexual activity. 85m. **DIR:** Nigel Finch. **CAST:** Brian Cox, Eileen Atkins, Angus MacFadyen, Corey Parker, René Auberjonois, John Schlesinger, Cathy Tyson, Richard Warwick. 1992

LOST MISSILE, THE ★★★ Scientists race to destroy an unmanned alien missile that, at a temperature of one million degrees, is melting everything in its path—and is heading for Manhattan. Reasonably tense low-budget sci-fi thriller with a good performance from its star, a very young Robert Loggia. B&W; 65m. **DIR:** Lester Berke. **CAST:** Robert Loggia, Ellen Parker, Philip Pine, Larry Kerr. 1958

LOST MOMENT, THE ★★1/2 A low-key, dark, offbeat drama based on Henry James's novel *The Aspern Papers*, which was based on a true story. A publisher (Robert Cummings), seeking love letters written by a long-dead great poet, goes to Italy to interview a very old lady and her niece. The old lady is spooky, the niece neurotic, the film fascinating. Those who know Cummings only from his TV series will be pleasantly surprised with his serious acting. B&W; 88m. **DIR:** Martin Gabel. **CAST:** Robert Cummings, Susan Hayward, Agnes Moorehead, Eduardo Ciannelli. 1947

LOST PATROL, THE ★★★★ An intrepid band of British cavalrymen lost in the Mesopotamian desert are picked off by the Arabs, one by one. Brisk direction and top-notch characterizations make this a winner—though it is grim. B&W; 65m. **DIR:** John Ford. **CAST:** Victor McLaglen, Boris Karloff, Wallace Ford, Reginald Denny, Alan Hale Sr., J. M. Kerrigan, Billy Bevan. 1934

LOST PLANET, THE ★★ Interplanetary nonsense for the grammar-school set is the order of the day as reporters Judd Holdren and Vivian Mason lock electrons with an evil scientist and his allies from the planet Ergro. Suitably silly serial. B&W; 15 chapters. **DIR:** Spencer Gordon Bennet. **CAST:** Judd Heldren, Vivian Mason. 1953

LOST PLATOON 🎬 World War II vet begins to suspect that The Lost Platoon are actually vampires, fighting their way through two centuries of war. Pretty anemic for an action-horror film. Not rated; contains violence. 91m. **DIR:** David A. Prior. **CAST:** David Parry, Ted Prior. 1989

LOST SQUADRON ★★★ Mystery-adventure about the "accidental" deaths of former World War I pilots engaged as stunt fliers for the movies. Full of industry "in-jokes," breezy dialogue, and good stunts, this is a fun film—especially for anyone with an interest in stunt flying or aviation in general. B&W; 79m. **DIR:** George Archainbaud. **CAST:** Richard Dix, Mary Astor, Erich Von Stroheim, Joel McCrea, Dorothy Jordan, Robert Armstrong. 1932

LOST STOOGES, THE ★★★ Leonard Maltin narrates this compilation of early film appearances by Ted Healy and the Three Stooges in MGM musicals and two-reel fillers—before Moe Howard, Larry Fine, and Curly Howard broke off to make their successful series of shorts for Columbia. These excerpts are primarily of interest for their historical value. Not rated, this direct-to-video release has Stooges-type violence. B&W; 68m. **DIR:** Mark Lamberti. **CAST:** Moe Howard, Larry Fine, Curly Howard, Ted Healy. 1990

LOST TRIBE, THE 🎬 A story about twin brothers involved in smuggling, adultery, and murder. Not rated; contains violence. 96m. **DIR:** John Laing. **CAST:** John Bach, Darien Takle, Emma Takle. 1983

LOST WEEKEND, THE ★★★★★ Gripping, powerful study of alcoholism and its destructive effect on one man's life. Arguably Ray Milland's best performance (he won an Oscar) and undeniably one of the most potent films of all time. Forty years after its release, the movie has lost none of its importance or effectiveness. Additional Oscars for best picture, director, and screenplay. B&W; 101m. **DIR:** Billy Wilder. **CAST:** Ray Milland, Jane Wyman, Philip Terry, Howard DaSilva, Frank Faylen. 1945

LOST WORLD, THE (1925) ★★★★ Silent version of Arthur Conan Doyle's classic story of Professor Challenger and his expedition to a desolate plateau roaming with prehistoric beasts. The movie climaxes with a brontosaurus running amok in London. An ambitious production, interesting as film history and quite entertaining, considering its age. B&W; 60m. Also available in a restored 102m. version. **DIR:** Harry Hoyt. **CAST:** Bessie Love, Lewis Stone, Wallace Beery. 1925 DVD

LOST WORLD, THE (1992) ★★ Lackluster adaptation of Sir Arthur Conan Doyle's fanciful tale of a lost land where dinosaurs still roam. The film's low budget betrays its aspirations, making this period piece seem cheap and undermined. A group led by Professor Challenger (John Rhys-Davies) and zoological expert David Warner encounters cave men, the elements, and unconvincing dinosaurs. Not rated; contains some violence. 99m. **DIR:** Timothy Bond. **CAST:** David Warner, John Rhys-Davies, Eric McCormack, Tamara Gorski. 1992

LOST WORLD, THE: JURASSIC PARK ★★★ In this weak sequel to *Jurassic Park*, Jeff Goldblum returns as the wisecracking, chaos-theory scientist, who this time leads a small team to investigate the doings at "Site B," the "nursery" where the dinosaurs were bred and later shipped to the first film's ill-fated park. The script bears little resemblance to Michael Crichton's novel, and matters really go to hell when our heroes are joined by a team of mercenaries bent on capturing dinosaurs and hauling them off to the San Diego Zoo. Rated PG-13 for profanity, violence, and gore. 134m. **DIR:** Steven Spielberg. **CAST:** Jeff Goldblum, Julianne Moore, Pete Postlethwaite, Arliss Howard, Richard Attenborough, Vince Vaughn, Vanessa Lee Chester. 1997

LOTS OF LUCK ★★ Made for Disney's cable channel, this mildly funny family film exposes the darker side of striking it rich. A family (Martin Mull and Annette Funicello play dad and mom) suddenly wins the lottery. Unfortunately they lose their friends and privacy. 88m. **DIR:** Peter Baldwin. **CAST:** Martin Mull,

Annette Funicello, Fred Willard, Polly Holliday, Mia Dillon, Tracey Gold. **1985**

LOTTO LAND ★★★★ Enjoyable, upbeat drama about how a missing New York lottery ticket worth $27 million sets a small Brooklyn neighborhood on its ear. Director-writer John Rubino has created a modern-day fable about hope and opportunity that's contagious. Larry Gilliard Jr. shines as a confused teenager trying to make sense of his life. The film has the most engaging characters and situations. Not rated; contains profanity and adult situations. 90m. **DIR:** John Rubino. **CAST:** Lawrence Gilliard Jr., Wendell Holmes, Suzanne Costallos, Barbara Gonzales. **1994 DVD**

LOTUS EATERS, THE ★★★1/2 Bittersweet comedy chronicles the loss of innocence of a family on a British Columbian island. While the husband falls under the spell of a sexy new teacher, the teenage daughter experiments with sex. These changes affect the 10-year-old daughter, through whose eyes much is revealed. Both compelling and shocking to see the family's rapid, negative metamorphosis. Winner of multiple Genie and Atlantic Film Festival awards. Rated PG-13 for nudity and profanity. 101m. **DIR:** Paul Shapiro. **CAST:** Sheila McCarthy, Aloka McLean, R. H. Thomson, Tara Frederick, Michele-Barbara Pelletier. **1993**

LOUISIANA ❤ Southern belle manages to destroy the lives of all around her. Made for television. 206m. **DIR:** Philippe de Broca. **CAST:** Margot Kidder, Ian Charleson, Victor Lanoux, Andrea Ferreol. **1984**

LOUISIANA PURCHASE ★★★1/2 Attempts are made to frame an honest purdy-duddy senator (Victor Moore). Moore is a joy, but it is Bob Hope's classic filibuster that is the highlight of the movie. Based on an Irving Berlin musical; a few good songs were retained. 98m. **DIR:** Irving Cummings. **CAST:** Bob Hope, Vera Zorina, Victor Moore, Dona Drake, Raymond Walburn, Maxie Rosenbloom, Frank Albertson. **1941**

LOUISIANA STORY, THE ★★★ This last film by noted documentarian Robert Flaherty dramatizes the effect of oil development on the lives of a young boy, his family, and his pet raccoon in Louisiana. Score by Virgil Thomson, played by the Philadelphia Symphony Orchestra. B&W; 79m. **DIR:** Robert Flaherty. **1948**

LOULOU ★★★1/2 In this mixture of unabashed eroticism and deeply felt romanticism Isabelle Huppert and Gérard Depardieu play lovers who embark on a freewheeling relationship. Lustful, explosive sexual psychodrama. In French with English subtitles. Rated R for nudity and profanity. 110m. **DIR:** Maurice Pialat. **CAST:** Isabelle Huppert, Gérard Depardieu, Guy Marchand. **1980**

LOVE ★★★★ Rich character study of two long-suffering women thrown together to enact the final chapter of the older woman's life. Lili Darvas is excellent as the fragile but feisty elder. In Hungarian with English subtitles. B&W; 92m. **DIR:** Karoly Makk. **CAST:** Lili Darvas, Mari Torocsik. **1971**

LOVE AFFAIR (1939) ★★★★ Romantic drama is at once sensitive, poignant, heartbreaking, and heartening. It tells the story of two jaded people who meet on shipboard, fall in love, part, agree to get together six months later, and are thwarted and tested by fate in the form of an accident. The plot is corn syrup, but the charm, grace, and razor-sharp timing of the stars raise it to minor classic status. Remade in 1957 as *An Affair to Remember*. 88m. **DIR:** Leo McCarey. **CAST:** Irene Dunne, Charles Boyer, Maria Ouspenskaya, Lee Bowman. **1939 DVD**

LOVE AFFAIR (1994) ★★★ A remake of Cary Grant and Deborah Kerr's 1957 *An Affair to Remember*, this film fails to temper the melodrama down for today's more cynical audiences. This time, Warren Beatty is a philandering fiancé (to Kate Capshaw) who's suddenly compelled to change his life in order to woo Annette Bening. Both Beatty and Bening are appealing but the sappy plot isn't to be believed. Rated PG-13 for adult themes and sexual situations. 95m. **DIR:** Glenn Gordon Caron. **CAST:** Warren Beatty, Annette Bening, Pierce Brosnan, Katharine Hepburn, Kate Capshaw, Garry Shandling. **1994**

LOVE AMONG THE RUINS ★★★★ In this made-for-TV comedy-romance, Katharine Hepburn plays opposite Laurence Olivier. The delightful story focuses on the plight of an aging actress who is being sued by a young gigolo for breach of promise. Her situation is further complicated when the prominent barrister handling her defense turns out to be a lovestruck former suitor. 100m. **DIR:** George Cukor. **CAST:** Katharine Hepburn, Laurence Olivier, Leigh Lawson, Joan Sims. **1975**

LOVE & A .45 ★★★★ A hot musical soundtrack and hot young stars make this modern-day Bonnie and Clyde tale a fast-and-furious treat. Gil Bellows and Renee Zellweger are sensational as the young lovers who tire of their small Texas town and turn to a life of crime. When a young girl is murdered during a robbery, the outlaw couple makes a run for the border, followed in hot pursuit by the law. Similar in theme to *Natural Born Killers* minus the acid trip. Rated R for violence, adult situations, and language. 120m. **DIR:** Darin Scott. **CAST:** Gil Bellows, Renee Zellweger, Rory Cochrane. **1994**

LOVE AND ANARCHY ★★★★ Giancarlo Giannini gets to eat up the screen with this role. Comic, tragic, and intellectually stimulating, this is Wertmuller's best film. Giannini is bent on assassinating Mussolini right after the rise of fascism but somehow gets waylaid. A classic. Rated R for sexual situations, language, and some nudity. 117m. **DIR:** Lina Wertmuller. **CAST:** Giancarlo Giannini, Mariangela Melato. **1973 DVD**

●**LOVE AND BASKETBALL** ★★★ Childhood sweethearts enter into an extended rocky romance while chasing dreams of becoming professional hoop stars. Though well-acted, this romantic drama's many conflicts are too slickly developed and resolved to be deeply moving. The film was a huge hit at the Sundance Film Festival. Rated PG-13 for sexuality and language. 118m. **DIR:** Gina Prince-Bythewood. **CAST:** Sanaa Lathan, Omar Epps, Alfre Woodard, Dennis Haysbert, Debbi Morgan. **2000**

LOVE AND BULLETS ❤ Charles Bronson is hired to snatch Jill Ireland from crime lord Rod Steiger. Rated PG for violence. 103m. **DIR:** Stuart Rosenberg.

CAST: Charles Bronson, Rod Steiger, Strother Martin, Bradford Dillman, Henry Silva, Jill Ireland. **1979**

LOVE AND DEATH ★★★★ This comedy set in 1812 Russia is one of Woody Allen's funniest films. Diane Keaton is the high-minded Russian with assassination (of Napoleon) in mind. Allen is her cowardly accomplice with sex on the brain. The movie satirizes not only love and death, but politics, classic Russian literature (Tolstoy's *War and Peace*), and foreign films, as well. Use of Prokofiev music enhances the piece. Rated R. 82m. **DIR:** Woody Allen. **CAST:** Woody Allen, Diane Keaton, Harold Gould, Alfred Lutter, Zvee Scooler. **1975 DVD**

LOVE AND DEATH ON LONG ISLAND ★★★★ John Hurt plays an esoteric English writer—so out of tune with modern times that he doesn't even know a VCR needs a television to work—who becomes unexpectedly obsessed with a small-time American film actor (Jason Priestley). He even moves to New York to be near the object of his affection. Odd and offbeat, with many sensitive touches, this quiet little film sneaks up on you. Rated PG-13 for brief profanity. 103m. **DIR:** Richard Kwietniowski. **CAST:** John Hurt, Jason Priestley, Fiona Loewi, Sheila Hancock, Maury Chaykin. **1997 DVD**

LOVE AND HATE ★★★ Based on *A Canadian Tragedy* by Maggie Siggins, this powerful film looks at the life of a prominent Saskatchewan family. Kate Nelligan plays the battered wife who finally leaves, only to be terrorized by her husband (Kenneth Welsh). Not rated. 176m. **DIR:** Francis Mankiewicz. **CAST:** Kate Nelligan, Kenneth Welsh, Leon Pownall, Brent Carver. **1989**

LOVE AND HUMAN REMAINS ★★ Quebec filmmaker Denys Arcand's first English-language film loses something in the translation. Sporadically funny dark comedy follows a bunch of young urban adults in pursuit of their kaleidoscopic sexual preferences, fears, and fetishes. Rated R for sex, violence, nudity, language, and drug use. 99m. **DIR:** Denys Arcand. **CAST:** Thomas Gibson, Ruth Marshall, Cameron Bancroft, Mia Kirshner, Rick Roberts, Joanne Vannicola. **1994**

LOVE AND MURDER ★★1/2 Decent low-budget thriller features a struggling photographer suddenly involved in a girl's questionable suicide. Rated R for violence and profanity. 87m. **DIR:** Steven H. Stern. **CAST:** Todd Waring. **1988**

LOVE AND OTHER CATASTROPHES ★★★★ This contemporary screwball comedy follows a quintet of Australian university students during an average day of love, lust, and library fines. One woman enters a Kafkaesque bureaucratic maze while attempting to switch departments; another tries to spark romantic flames with a philosophical gigolo, while remaining blind to the puppy love of a second fellow. This $37,000 wonder is loads more entertaining than most million-dollar Hollywood misfires. Rated R for profanity, drug use, and strong sexual content. 79m. **DIR:** Emma-Kate Croghan. **CAST:** Matt Day, Matthew Dyktynski, Alice Garner, Frances O'Connor, Radha Mitchell. **1996**

LOVE AND THE FRENCHWOMAN ★★★ Seven short films about women at different stages of life.

Lightweight stuff, but not without some charming and comical moments. Dubbed. B&W; 135m. **DIR:** Henri Decoin, Jean Delannoy, Michel Boisrond, René Clair, Henri Verneuil, Christian-Jaque. **CAST:** Annie Girardot, Martine Lambert, Michel Serrault, Jean-Paul Belmondo. **1960**

LOVE AND WAR ★★★ An account of navy pilot Jim Stockdale's eight-year imprisonment in a North Vietnamese prison camp. James Woods is excellent as Stockdale, conveying uncertainty behind his undying patriotic loyalty. Painful but enlightening made-for-TV movie. 96m. **DIR:** Paul Aaron. **CAST:** James Woods, Jane Alexander, Haing S. Ngor. **1987**

LOVE AT FIRST BITE ★★★★ The Dracula legend is given the comedy treatment in this amusing parody of horror films. George Hamilton plays the campy Count, who has an unorthodox way with the ladies. (In this case, it's Susan Saint James, much to the chagrin of her boyfriend, Richard Benjamin.) Even though the humor is heavy-handed in parts, you find yourself chuckling continually in spite of yourself. Rated PG. 96m. **DIR:** Stan Dragoti. **CAST:** George Hamilton, Susan Saint James, Richard Benjamin, Dick Shawn, Arte Johnson. **1979**

LOVE AT FIRST SIGHT 🎬 Dan Aykroyd tries for laughs as a blind man in love with a girl whose family won't have him for a son-in-law. Rated PG. 85m. **DIR:** Rex Bromfield. **CAST:** Mary Ann McDonald, Dan Aykroyd, Barry Morse. **1977**

LOVE AT LARGE ★★★★ Writer-director Alan Rudolph serves up a deliciously offbeat spoof of the mystery movie with his tale of a private eye (Tom Berenger) hired by a mysterious woman (Anne Archer). It's funny and intriguing; a movie buff's delight. Rated R for profanity and violence. 97m. **DIR:** Alan Rudolph. **CAST:** Tom Berenger, Elizabeth Perkins, Anne Archer, Kate Capshaw, Annette O'Toole, Ted Levine, Ann Magnuson, Neil Young. **1990**

LOVE AT STAKE 🎬 Attempted spoof of witchcraft and black-magic films is a dismal failure. Rated R for nudity and profanity. 88m. **DIR:** John Moffitt. **CAST:** Barbara Carrera, Bud Cort, Dave Thomas, Patrick Cassidy, Stuart Pankin. **1988**

LOVE AT THE TOP ★★★★ In this delightful film, Glynnis (Janis Paige) is at the top of her career as a lingerie designer. While being considered for promotion, she finds herself pitted against the son-in-law of the boss, a very romantic young man. Excellent. 105m. **DIR:** John Bowab. **CAST:** Janis Paige, Richard Young, Jim McKrell. **1982**

LOVE BUG, THE ★★★1/2 This is a delightful Disney comedy. A family film about a Volkswagen with a mind of its own and some special talents as well, it was the first of the fun "Herbie" films. Rated G. 107m. **DIR:** Robert Stevenson. **CAST:** Michele Lee, Dean Jones, Buddy Hackett, Joe Flynn. **1969**

LOVE BUTCHER 🎬 A series of grisly murders of young women are committed by a deranged psycho. Rated R. 84m. **DIR:** Mikel Angel, Don Jones. **CAST:** Erik Stern. **1983**

LOVE, CHEAT & STEAL ★★★1/2 Financial wizard John Lithgow returns to his roots to help save his father's bank and uncovers a drug-tinged money-laundering scheme. As if that weren't bad enough, he gets a visit from the "brother" of his attractive new wife ... whom we know is actually her dangerously vengeful first husband. This complex yarn of double and triple crosses is quite fun. Rated R for profanity, violence, and nudity. 96m. DIR: William Curran. CAST: John Lithgow, Eric Roberts, Madchen Amick, Richard Edson, Donald Moffat, David Ackroyd. 1993

LOVE CHILD ★★★★ Although its ads gave *Love Child* the appearance of a cheapo exploitation flick, this superb prison drama is anything but. Directed by Larry Peerce, it is the gripping story of a young woman, Terry Jean Moore (Amy Madigan), who became pregnant by a guard in a women's prison in Florida and fought for the right to keep her baby. Rated R for profanity, nudity, sex, and violence. 96m. DIR: Larry Peerce. CAST: Amy Madigan, Beau Bridges, Mackenzie Phillips. 1982

LOVE CRAZY ★★★★ Crazy is right, in this screwball comedy where innocent William Powell is found by his wife (Myrna Loy) in a compromising situation with an old flame. She sues for divorce; he feigns insanity to keep her, carrying the act all the way to a lunacy hearing. B&W; 99m. DIR: Jack Conway. CAST: William Powell, Myrna Loy, Gail Patrick, Jack Carson, Florence Bates, Sidney Blackmer, Sig Ruman. 1941

LOVE CRIMES ★★ For most of its brief running time, this movie, about the capture of a clever con man–rapist, is a gripping thriller with erotic overtones—then it ends abruptly, leaving the viewer wondering exactly what happened. This is because the studio nixed director Lizzie Borden's original ending and a quick fix was substituted. Rated R for nudity, violence, and profanity. 85m. DIR: Lizzie Borden. CAST: Sean Young, Patrick Bergin, Arnetia Walker, James Read, Ron Orbach. 1992

LOVE FEAST, THE 🖤 Ed Wood was at the bottom of the barrel when he starred in this sex comedy his fans would best avoid. Not rated; contains nudity and sexual situations. 63m. DIR: Joseph F. Robertson. CAST: Edward D. Wood Jr., Linda Coplin. 1969

LOVE FIELD ★★★★ Michelle Pfeiffer is a 1960s Dallas housewife who models herself after Jacqueline Kennedy. When President John F. Kennedy is assassinated, Pfeiffer decides she has to attend the funeral. On the way, she encounters Dennis Haysbert, a black man traveling with his daughter. Pfeiffer and Haysbert (in a role originally given to Denzel Washington, who left the picture) are superb. Rated PG-13 for profanity and violence. 104m. DIR: Jonathan Kaplan. CAST: Michelle Pfeiffer, Dennis Haysbert, Stephanie McFadden, Brian Kerwin, Louise Latham, Peggy Rea. 1992

LOVE FINDS ANDY HARDY ★★★ In this fourth film of the series, the love that finds Mickey Rooney as Andy Hardy is then-teenager Lana Turner. As usual, it's an all-innocent slice of small-town American family life. B&W; 90m. DIR: George B. Seitz. CAST: Mickey Rooney, Lewis Stone, Fay Holden, Judy Garland, Cecilia Parker, Lana Turner, Ann Rutherford. 1938

•LOVE FROM A STRANGER (1937) ★★1/2 A suave killer who woos wealthy women and does away with them after the nuptials raises the suspicions of a lottery winner he chooses as his next victim. Whether one views this film as a first-class, melodramatic thriller or hilarious camp, it's an entertaining gem from the "forgotten horrors" catalogue. B&W; 90m. DIR: Rowland V. Lee. CAST: Ann Harding, Basil Rathbone, Binnie Hale, Bruce Seton, Jean Cadell, Bryan Powley. 1937

LOVE FROM A STRANGER (1947) ★★★ Just-married woman suspects her new husband is a murderer and that she will be his next victim in this suspense-thriller in the vein of *Suspicion*. B&W; 81m. DIR: Richard Whorf. CAST: Sylvia Sidney, John Hodiak, John Howard, Isobel Elsom, Ernest Cossart. 1947

LOVE GOD?, THE ★★ Meek Don Knotts is turned into a Hugh Hefner-ish "swinger" by shady Edmond O'Brien, who wants to turn Knotts's bird-lovers' magazine into a porno mag. This feeble comedy was dated even when it first came out. Rated PG for suggestive situations. 101m. DIR: Nat Hiken. CAST: Don Knotts, Anne Francis, Edmond O'Brien, James Gregory, Maureen Arthur. 1969

LOVE HAPPY ★★ The last Marx Brothers movie, this 1949 production was originally set to star only Harpo, but Chico and, later, Groucho were brought in to beef up its box-office potential. They should've known better. Only Groucho's ogling of then-screen-newcomer Marilyn Monroe makes it interesting for movie buffs. B&W; 91m. DIR: David Miller. CAST: The Marx Brothers, Marilyn Monroe, Raymond Burr. 1949

LOVE HAS MANY FACES 🖤 Anachronistic, tame sex opera—filmed in Acapulco—with Lana Turner, Cliff Robertson and Hugh O'Brian. Unwatchable. 105m. DIR: Alexander Singer. CAST: Lana Turner, Cliff Robertson, Hugh O'Brian, Ruth Roman, Stefanie Powers, Virginia Grey. 1965

LOVE HURTS ★★ Womanizer is forced into dealing with his irresponsible past when he finds his ex-wife and kids have moved in with his parents. Rated R for profanity and suggested sex. 110m. DIR: Bud Yorkin. CAST: Jeff Daniels, Judith Ivey, John Mahoney, Cynthia Sikes, Amy Wright, Cloris Leachman. 1989

LOVE IN GERMANY, A ★★ During World War II, the Germans bring in Polish POWs to do menial labor. Frau Kopp (Hanna Schygulla) hires a young Polish POW. The first half of the film is effective, but the second half receives an excessively sensational treatment, ultimately diminishing the flavor and appeal. In French with English subtitles. Rated R for violence and nudity. 107m. DIR: Andrzej Wajda. CAST: Hanna Schygulla, Marie-Christine Barrault, Bernhard Wicki. 1984

LOVE IN THE AFTERNOON ★★★★ Audrey Hepburn shares fantastic chemistry with both Maurice Chevalier and Gary Cooper in this film classic, which explores the love interests of an American entrepreneur and his lopsided involvement with a young French ingenue. When her doting father (a detective) is asked to investigate the American's love life, it makes for a touching, charming bit of entertainment that never loses its appeal. 130m. DIR: Billy Wilder. CAST: Gary Cooper, Audrey Hepburn, Maurice Chevalier, John McGiver. 1957

LOVE IN THE PRESENT TENSE ★★1/2 Millie Perkins adds style and class to this Romance Theatre soap. A former model returns to New York to promote her daughter's career and falls for an irresistible photographer. Made for TV. 97m. **DIR:** Tony Mordente. **CAST:** Millie Perkins, Thomas MacGreevy, Deborah Foreman, Doris Roberts. 1982

LOVE IS A GUN ★★★ Eric Roberts plays a police photographer whose involvement with a mystery woman turns his simple life upside down. When Roberts finds a photo of model Kelly Preston in his locker, he's instantly smitten. His dream lover becomes his nightmare when she ends up dead, and he's the only suspect. Atmospheric thriller is served well by star Roberts, who delivers a riveting performance. Rated R for violence, adult situations, and language. 92m. **DIR:** David Hartwell. **CAST:** Eric Roberts, Kelly Preston, Eliza Roberts, R. Lee Ermey, Joseph Sirola. 1994

LOVE IS A MANY-SPLENDORED THING ★★★ Clichéd story of ill-starred lovers from two different worlds who don't make it. Jennifer Jones is a Eurasian doctor who falls in love with war correspondent William Holden during the Korean conflict. 102m. **DIR:** Henry King. **CAST:** Jennifer Jones, William Holden, Isobel Elsom, Richard Loo. 1955 DVD

LOVE IS ALL THERE IS 🖤 Two competing catering companies play out a comedic modern-day version of *Romeo and Juliet* that is buffoonish, stereotypical, frantic, and loud. Rated R for profanity and implied sexuality. 105m. **DIR:** Renee Taylor, Joseph Bologna. **CAST:** Lainie Kazan, Joseph Bologna, Barbara Carrera, Paul Sorvino, Renee Taylor, Abe Vigoda, Connie Stevens, Dick Van Patten. 1996

LOVE IS BETTER THAN EVER ★★1/2 Elizabeth Taylor is a children's dancing-school teacher out to hook a hard-boiled talent agent, Larry Parks. The songs are completely forgettable. Tom Tully, as Taylor's father, saves the movie. B&W; 81m. **DIR:** Stanley Donen. **CAST:** Elizabeth Taylor, Larry Parks, Josephine Hutchinson, Tom Tully, Ann Doran, Kathleen Freeman. 1952

LOVE IS THE DEVIL ★★★ British painter Francis Bacon and the decadent art scene of 1960s London are the subjects of this unsettling movie. Bacon, the film tells us, was a tortured genius who vented his anger on those around him. John Maybury was denied the use of Bacon's vivid, misshapen paintings, so he makes the whole film look like one of the artist's canvases, shooting through mirrors and distorting glass. Not rated; contains profanity, mature themes, and scenes of sadomasochism. 91m. **DIR:** John Maybury. **CAST:** Derek Jacobi, Daniel Craig, Tilda Swinton, Anne Lambton. 1998 DVD

LOVE JONES ★★★1/2 Boy meets girl, and they almost lose each other because neither one wants to be the first to utter the dreaded "L word." This romantic "dramedy" compensates for a slender plot with good writing, appealing performances, and the refreshing novelty of seeing the courtship ritual played out by middle-class African Americans. Rated R for profanity. 108m. **DIR:** Theodore Witcher. **CAST:** Larenz Tate, Nia Long, Isaiah Washington, Lisas Nicole Carson, Khalil Kain, Leonard Roberts, Bernadette L. Clarke, Bill Bellamy. 1997 DVD

LOVE KILLS (1991) ★★ Increasingly chaotic plot twists muddy this otherwise tedious made-for-cable thriller, which features Virginia Madsen as a professional photographer led to believe that her criminal psychologist husband has hired a maniac to kill her. Madsen sighs and pouts a lot, but she really doesn't make us care. Rated PG-13 for mild profanity and sexual themes. 92m. **DIR:** Brian Grant. **CAST:** Virginia Madsen, Lenny Von Dohlen, Erich Anderson, Jim Metzler. 1991

●LOVE KILLS (1999) ★★ Mario Van Peebles is a con man who dupes rich widows out of their inheritances. When he tries to pull a scam on Lesley Ann Warren, he starts to have second thoughts. In the meantime, family members, friends, and brief acquaintances try to outwit each other in the attempt to find a cache of gems somewhere on her estate. When Daniel Baldwin shows up, anarchy reigns supreme. Rated R for sex, violence, and language. 95m. **DIR:** Mario Van Peebles. **CAST:** Mario Van Peebles, Lesley Ann Warren, Daniel Baldwin, Louise Fletcher. 1999 DVD

LOVE LAUGHS AT ANDY HARDY ★★ America's all-American, lovable, irritating, well-meaning wimp comes home from World War II and plunges back into the same adolescent rut of agonizing young love. The change of times has made this cookie-cutter film very predictable, but it's fun anyway. B&W; 93m. **DIR:** Willis Goldbeck. **CAST:** Mickey Rooney, Lewis Stone, Fay Holden, Sara Haden, Bonita Granville. 1946

LOVE LEADS THE WAY ★★★★ This Disney TV movie features Timothy Bottoms in the true story of Morris Frank, the first American to train with a Seeing-Eye dog. Blinded while boxing, Frank at first refuses to accept his handicap and later resents the dog who offers to be his eyes. Fortunately, he adapts and later lobbies for acceptance of Seeing-Eye dogs throughout the United States. Bottoms turns in an exceptional performance as the struggling Frank. 99m. **DIR:** Delbert Mann. **CAST:** Timothy Bottoms, Eva Marie Saint, Arthur Hill, Susan Dey. 1984

LOVE LETTER, THE (1998) ★★ Disappointing *Hallmark Hall of Fame* drama about love that crosses the time barrier is both sappy and unbelievable. A modern man obsessed with the Civil War era buys an antique desk that contains the romantic longings of a nineteenth-century woman. He responds with a letter of his own, thus igniting their literary love affair. Naturally, this wreaks havoc with his current relationship to his fiancée. Unfortunately, there is little chemistry between any of the three leads. Not rated; contains adult situations. 90m. **DIR:** Dan Curtis. **CAST:** Campbell Scott, Jennifer Jason Leigh, Daphne Ashbrook, David Dukes, Estelle Parsons. 1998

LOVE LETTER, THE (1999) ★★★ Kooky little romance includes surreal moments as a small Massachusetts town is transformed by an anonymous love letter. The heart-stopping note makes its way into many people's hands and each believes it was intended for him or her. Amusing and slow paced, this is not for action fans. Rated PG-13 for language and sexual situations. 89m. **DIR:** Peter Ho-Sun Chan. **CAST:** Kate Capshaw, Tom Everett Scott, Tom Selleck, Ellen DeGeneres. 1999 DVD

LOVE LETTERS ★★★★ In this impressive character study, the heroine, played by Jamie Lee Curtis, wonders aloud to her friend (Amy Madigan): "Sometimes it's right to do the wrong thing, isn't it?" Probing the emotions that lead to infidelity, this is a true adult motion picture. This concept is intelligently explored by writer-director Amy Jones. Rated R for graphic sex. 98m. **DIR:** Amy Jones. **CAST:** Jamie Lee Curtis, Amy Madigan, Bud Cort, James Keach. 1983

LOVE, LIES AND MURDER ★★★ Made as a TV miniseries, this violent thriller is based on a 1985 murder. It appears at first to be clear-cut. However, there were actually two murderers and one Manson-like manipulator behind the ugly scenes. Talk about dysfunctional families! 200m. **DIR:** Robert Markowitz. **CAST:** Clancy Brown, Sheryl Lee, Moira Kelly, John Ashton. 1991

LOVE MACHINE, THE ★★ A lust for power drives a television newscaster into the willing arms of the network president's wife. Pessimistic tale of the motivations that move the wheels of television news. Sexy, soapy adaptation of the Jacqueline Susann novel. Rated R. 108m. **DIR:** Jack Haley Jr. **CAST:** Dyan Cannon, John Phillip Law, Robert Ryan, Jackie Cooper, David Hemmings, Shecky Greene, William Roerick. 1971

LOVE MATTERS ★★★ In spite of some preachiness, this little melodrama makes a few perceptive points on the hard work and dedication required for a successful marriage. Unfortunately, we don't see enough of distanced lovers Griffin Dunne and Annette O'Toole; too much time is wasted on the selfish antics of a shallow friend (Tony Goldwyn) and his latest sexual conquest. Rated R for profanity, nudity, and simulated sex. 97m. **DIR:** Eb Lottimer. **CAST:** Griffin Dunne, Tony Goldwyn, Annette O'Toole, Gina Gershon, Kate Burton, Gerrit Graham. 1993

LOVE ME OR LEAVE ME ★★★★ This musical biopic about ambitious singer Ruth Etting and her crude and domineering racketeer husband found usually cute Doris Day and old pro James Cagney scorching the screen with strong performances. Along with biting drama, a record-setting thirteen Doris Day solos, including the title song and "Ten Cents a Dance," are served. The story won an Oscar. 122m. **DIR:** Charles Vidor. **CAST:** James Cagney, Doris Day, Cameron Mitchell, Robert Keith, Tom Tully. 1955

LOVE ME TENDER ★★★ Western drama takes place in Texas after the Civil War, with Elvis and his brother fighting over Debra Paget. The most distinguishing characteristic of this movie is the fact that it was Elvis's first film. Elvis fans will, of course, enjoy his singing the ballad "Love Me Tender." B&W; 89m. **DIR:** Robert D. Webb. **CAST:** Elvis Presley, Debra Paget, Richard Egan. 1956

LOVE ME TONIGHT ★★★★★ A romantic musical that set a pattern for many that followed. Rodgers and Hart wrote the music, and most are still being played. This is the film that introduced "Lover," "Mimi," and "Isn't It Romantic?" all sung by Maurice Chevalier with verve and style. Pure charm. B&W; 104m. **DIR:** Rouben Mamoulian. **CAST:** Jeanette MacDonald, Maurice Chevalier, Myrna Loy, Charlie Ruggles, Charles Butterworth, C. Aubrey Smith, Elizabeth Patterson. 1932

LOVE MEETINGS ★★ Messy, unorganized documentary that explores the sexual attitudes of Italians in the early 1960s. Featuring interviews with philosophers, poets, students, clergymen, farmers, factory workers, and children. Dated material with completely unreadable English subtitles. B&W; 90m. **DIR:** Pier Paolo Pasolini. 1964

LOVE NEST ★★1/2 An ex-GI returns home to find that his wife has purchased a run-down apartment building whose tenants come to dominate their lives. Mild comedy, mostly of interest to Marilyn Monroe completists. B&W; 84m. **DIR:** Joseph M. Newman. **CAST:** William Lundigan, June Haver, Frank Fay, Marilyn Monroe, Jack Paar. 1951

LOVE OF JEANNE NEY ★★★ A romance between a French girl and a Russian Communist is thwarted at every turn. Lots of action in this Russian Revolution–set tale. Silent. B&W; 102m. **DIR:** G. W. Pabst. **CAST:** Brigitte Helm. 1926

LOVE ON THE DOLE ★★★1/2 Based on Walter Greenwoods's novel, this film is about a London family trying to subsist during the Depression. A classy cast gives top-notch performances. 89m. **DIR:** John Baxter. **CAST:** Deborah Kerr, Clifford Evans, Mary Merrall. 1941

LOVE ON THE RUN (1936) ★★★ When a foreign correspondent helps a publicity-shy heiress flee from her own wedding ceremony (sound familiar?), they become involved with spies and intrigue. Good escapism. B&W; 80m. **DIR:** W. S. Van Dyke. **CAST:** Joan Crawford, Clark Gable, Franchot Tone, Reginald Owen, William Demarest, Donald Meek, Billy Gilbert. 1936

LOVE ON THE RUN (1979) ★★★1/2 François Truffaut's tribute to himself. *Love on the Run* is the fifth film (*400 Blows*; *Love at Twenty*; *Stolen Kisses*; *Bed & Board*) in the series for character Antoine Doinel (Jean-Pierre Léaud). Now in his thirties and on the eve of divorce, Doinel rediscovers women. Light romantic work filled with humor and compassion. In French with English subtitles. Rated PG. 93m. **DIR:** François Truffaut. **CAST:** Jean-Pierre Léaud, Claude Jade, Marie-France Pisier. 1979 DVD

LOVE OR MONEY? ★★ A rising young real estate turk wrestles with his conscience. Should he nail the big deal or follow his heart down the path of love with his client's daughter? Trite comedy. Rated PG-13. 90m. **DIR:** Todd Hallowell. **CAST:** Timothy Daly, Haviland Morris, Kevin McCarthy, Shelley Fabares, David Doyle. 1988

LOVE POTION #9 ★★★★ Dweeb, zero-charisma scientists Tate Donovan and Sandra Bullock trade in their beakers for romance when they down that famous love potion from gypsy Anne Bancroft. Funny, charming comedy finds new avenues for laughter. The complications are pretty typical, but the script and direction by Dale Launer are sharp and on the money. Rated PG-13 for sexual situations and language. 99m. **DIR:** Dale Launer. **CAST:** Tate Donovan, Sandra Bullock, Dale Midkiff, Anne Bancroft. 1992

LOVE SERENADE ★★★ When a famous Australian disc jockey moves to a tiny outback town in the middle of nowhere, he disrupts the quietly desperate lives of the sisters who live next door. Another quirky, oddball Australian comedy, but this time the quirkiness runs out of steam and the characters become distasteful before the contrived ending. Still, there are compensating pleasures, chief among them Rebecca Frith's performance as the more outgoing (and more desperate) older sister. Rated R for sexual themes. 100m. DIR: Shirley Barrett. CAST: Miranda Otto, Rebecca Frith, George Shevtsov, John Alansu. 1995

LOVE SONGS (PAROLES ET MUSIQUE) ★★ Christopher Lambert plays a bisexual rock singer having an affair with a woman (Catherine Deneuve). Pointless and frequently incomprehensible. Dubbed (execrably) into English. 107m. DIR: Elie Chouraqui. CAST: Catherine Deneuve, Christopher Lambert, Nick Mancuso, Richard Anconina, Jacques Perrin. 1985

LOVE SPELL 🐢 A dud based on the legend of Tristan and Isolde and their doomed love. 90m. DIR: Tom Donavan. CAST: Richard Burton, Kate Mulgrew, Nicholas Clay, Cyril Cusack. 1979

•**LOVE STINKS** ★★ This lumbering sex farce blends the worst elements of a TV sitcom with enough tiresome profanity to keep it off the networks for a while. It's mostly a starring vehicle for television actor French Stewart, admittedly funny as a writer-producer unlucky enough to get stuck with The Shrew from Hell. Mostly, though, this is a weary retread of *The War of the Roses*. Rated R for profanity and strong sexual candor. 94m. DIR: Jeff Franklin. CAST: French Stewart, Bridgette Wilson, Bill Bellamy, Tyra Banks, Jason Bateman, Tiffani-Amber Thiessen, Colleen Camp. 1999 DVD

LOVE STORY ★★★★ Unabashedly sentimental and manipulative, this film was a box-office smash. Directed by Arthur Hiller and adapted by Erich Segal from his bestselling novel, it features Ryan O'Neal and Ali MacGraw as star-crossed lovers who meet, marry, make it, and then discover she is dying. Rated PG. 99m. DIR: Arthur Hiller. CAST: Ryan O'Neal, Ali MacGraw, Ray Milland, John Marley. 1970

LOVE STREAMS ★★ A depressing story of a writer who involves himself in the lives of lonely women for inspiration, and his emotionally unstable sister, whom he takes in after a difficult divorce has left her without possession of her child. There are some funny moments and some heartfelt scenes, as well, but John Cassavetes's direction is awkward. Rated PG-13 for language and adult situations. 122m. DIR: John Cassavetes. CAST: John Cassavetes, Gena Rowlands, Diahnne Abbott, Seymour Cassel. 1984

LOVE STREET 🐢 Direct-to-video sleaze exists only so the female leads can disrobe in three short tales. Rated R for nudity, simulated sex, and profanity. 90m. DIR: Various. CAST: Christina Whitaker, Lisa Verlo, David Frailey. 1993

LOVE TO KILL ★★★ Mob hit men Moe (Tony Danza) and Franco (Michael Madsen) are ready to retire. Moe wants to settle down with his new girlfriend, Monica, but a gun deal gone wrong and an old mob vendetta keep him busy. When Monica discovers her sister's dead body at Moe's, she comes after him, too. Quirky, offbeat story of love and vengeance.

Rated R for adult situations, language, and violence. 102m. DIR: James Bruce. CAST: Tony Danza, Michael Madsen, Elizabeth Barondes, James Russo, Louise Fletcher. 1997 DVD

LOVE! VALOUR! COMPASSION! ★★★ A group of gay men spend three country weekends together over the course of a summer. The film moves from Memorial Day to Labor Day, tracing the ups and downs of everyone's lives. Essentially plotless, but has a witty script and first-rate acting. Especially good are Jason Alexander as a lonely HIV-positive man, and John Glover, who gives a tour de force as identical twin brothers—one a saint, the other a scoundrel. Rated R for profanity, nudity, and sexual situations. 115m. DIR: Joe Mantello. CAST: Jason Alexander, Randy Becker, Stephen Bogardus, John Glover, John Benjamin Hickey, Justin Kirk, Stephen Spinella. 1997

LOVE WITH A PERFECT STRANGER ★★ Chance encounters on a train, exotic international locations, carriage rides, curiously abandoned fine restaurants, and luxury hotels all create an atmosphere for romance. This Harlequin Romance has dialogue and interplay patterned after the popular books. Not rated British television production is suitable for any age. 98m. DIR: Desmond Davis. CAST: Marilu Henner, Daniel Massey. 1988

LOVE WITH THE PROPER STRANGER ★★★★ This neatly crafted tale of a pregnant young woman (Natalie Wood) and a restless trumpet player (Steve McQueen) offers generous portions of comedy, drama, and romance. Wood is at her most captivating. McQueen, veering a bit from his trademark cool, gives a highly engaging performance. Their relationship creates ample sparks. 100m. DIR: Robert Mulligan. CAST: Natalie Wood, Steve McQueen, Edie Adams, Herschel Bernardi, Tom Bosley. 1963

LOVE WITHOUT PITY 🐢 Extremely dull film involving an arrogant man who treats women like trash until he falls in love with a woman who treats him the same. In French with English subtitles. Rated R for language. 88m. DIR: Adeline Lecallier. CAST: Hippolyte Girardot, Mireille Perrier. 1989

LOVE YOUR MAMA ★★ If good intentions and a conscientious heart were all it took, *Love Your Mama* would be a classic. *Love Your Mama* is a rough-hewn, amateurish-looking drama about a black family in the Chicago ghetto, held together through the love and hard work of the mother. It's too bad it wasn't more polished. Rated PG-13, with profanity. 92m. DIR: Ruby L. Oliver. CAST: Carol E. Hall, Audrey Morgan. 1993

LOVED ONE, THE ★★★★1/2 A naïve British poet finds himself in the California funeral industry, which includes human and animal customers. The all-star cast includes Jonathan Winters in a dual role as an unscrupulous clergyman and the director of a pet cemetery. Brilliantly written by Christopher Isherwood and Terry Southern. B&W; 116m. DIR: Tony Richardson. CAST: Robert Morse, Rod Steiger, Robert Morley, Jonathan Winters, Tab Hunter, Milton Berle, Lionel Stander, Anjanette Comer, Liberace, James Coburn, John Gielgud. 1965

LOVELESS, THE ★★ This could have been called *The Senseless* thanks to its lack of plot and emphasis on violence. It's a biker picture set in the 1950s and stars Willem Dafoe, who gives a good performance with the scant dialogue he's given. Though a poor tribute to *The Wild One*, this film does have a cult following. Rated R for violence, nudity, and sex scenes. 85m. **DIR:** Kathryn Bigelow, Monty Montgomery. **CAST:** Willem Dafoe, Robert Gordon, Marin Kanter. **1984**

LOVELIFE ★★★1/2 Director Jon Harmon Feldman's intricate and insightful screenplay guides a splendid cast through this tale of love and life. The campus of a graduate school is the breeding ground for romance and betrayal as student Saffron Burrows cheats on her boyfriend with a professor. The relationship causes a chain reaction that forces everyone involved to examine their priorities. Sharply written and executed. Rated R for adult situations and language. 96m. **DIR:** Jon Harmon Feldman. **CAST:** Sherilyn Fenn, Saffron Burrows, Jon Tenney, Bruce Davison, Matthew Letscher. **1997**

LOVELINES 🎬 Dreadful teen comedy. Rated R for nudity, suggested sex, violence, and profanity. 93m. **DIR:** Rod Amateau. **CAST:** Michael Winslow, Greg Bradford, Mary Beth Evans. **1984**

LOVELY BUT DEADLY 🎬 A teenage boy dies by drowning while under the influence of illegal drugs. Rated PG. 88m. **DIR:** David Sheldon. **CAST:** Lucinda Dooling, John Randolph, Marie Windsor, Mark Holden. **1981**

LOVELY TO LOOK AT ★★★★ Jerome Kern's Broadway and movie hit *Roberta* gets a face-lift with a charismatic cast, Technicolor, and inventive staging. Marge and Gower Champion dance "I Won't Dance" as a ballet. All in all, a musical treat, although the story about a trio of men inheriting a dress shop strains credibility. 105m. **DIR:** Mervyn LeRoy. **CAST:** Kathryn Grayson, Howard Keel, Red Skelton, Marge Champion, Gower Champion, Ann Miller, Zsa Zsa Gabor, Kurt Kasznar. **1952**

LOVER, THE ★★★ Although director-coscenarist Jean-Jacques Annaud gives Marguerite Duras's infamous bestseller the serious treatment it deserves, the aggravatingly sparse story line seems mere window-dressing. French schoolgirl Jane March enters a relationship with twentysomething Chinese gentleman Tony Leung. Considerable arty coupling. Rated R for nudity and simulated sex. 110m. **DIR:** Jean-Jacques Annaud. **CAST:** Jane March, Tony Leung Chiu-Wai, Frederique Meininger. **1992**

LOVER COME BACK ★★★★ Rock Hudson and Doris Day are rival advertising executives battling professionally, psychologically, and sexually. A bright comedy that builds nicely. One of their best. Silly, innocent fun with a great supporting cast. 107m. **DIR:** Delbert Mann. **CAST:** Rock Hudson, Doris Day, Tony Randall, Edie Adams, Jack Oakie, Jack Kruschen, Ann B. Davis, Joe Flynn, Jack Albertson. **1961**

LOVERBOY 🎬 Lame sex farce. Rated PG-13 for profanity and sexual situations. 98m. **DIR:** Joan Micklin Silver. **CAST:** Patrick Dempsey, Kate Jackson, Carrie Fisher, Barbara Carrera, Kirstie Alley, Robert Ginty. **1989**

LOVERS, THE (1958) ★★ Notorious in the early Sixties, when it was prosecuted in the U.S. for obscenity, this French drama looks mighty tame now. All the fuss was over an extended lovemaking scene between rich wife Jeanne Moreau and a young man she has just met. What little interest the film retains is in its wide-screen photography, which is lost in the transfer to home video, anyway. In French with English subtitles. B&W; 90m. **DIR:** Louis Malle. **CAST:** Jeanne Moreau, Alain Cuny, Jean-Marc Bory. **1958**

LOVERS (1992) ★★★★ Just out of General Franco's army, a young soldier makes wedding plans with his virginal fiancée—when he's not involved in steamy sex and shady scams with his new landlady. In Spanish with English subtitles. Not rated; contains profanity, nudity, and violence. 103m. **DIR:** Vicente Aranda. **CAST:** Victoria Abril, Jorge Sanz, Maribel Verdu. **1992**

LOVERS AND LIARS ★★1/2 The first thing that occurs to you while watching this film is a question: What's Goldie Hawn doing in a dubbed Italian sex comedy? Costarring Giancarlo Giannini it is a modestly entertaining piece of fluff tailored primarily for European tastes and, therefore, will probably disappoint most of Hawn's fans. Rated R. 96m. **DIR:** Mario Monicelli. **CAST:** Goldie Hawn, Giancarlo Giannini, Laura Betti. **1979 DVD**

LOVERS AND OTHER STRANGERS ★★★1/2 A funny film about young love, marriage, and their many side effects on others. Marks Diane Keaton's debut in pictures. The late Gig Young is a delight. 106m. **DIR:** Cy Howard. **CAST:** Gig Young, Diane Keaton, Bea Arthur, Bonnie Bedelia, Anne Jackson, Harry Guardino, Richard Castellano, Michael Brandon, Cloris Leachman, Anne Meara. **1970**

LOVER'S KNOT ★★★ Cupid sends a caseworker (Tim Curry) to Earth to help a couple who are fated to be together but just can't seem to get going. Average romantic comedy benefits from many whimsical touches à la *Annie Hall*. Rated R for brief nudity, sexual situations, adult situations, and profanity. 85m. **DIR:** Pete Shaner. **CAST:** Bill Campbell, Jennifer Grey, Tim Curry, Adam Baldwin. **1995**

LOVERS' LOVERS ★★ Limp sex fantasy finds a couple trying to spice up their relationship by bringing another couple into their bedroom. They should have tried counseling. Rated R for nudity and language. 90m. **DIR:** Serge Rodnunsky. **CAST:** Serge Rodnunsky, Jennifer Ciesar, Cindy Parker, Ray Bennett. **1993**

•LOVERS OF THE ARCTIC CIRCLE ★★★★ Saga of two people with intertwining destinies, where random happenings can turn into life-changing events. While chasing a lost ball, a young boy happens upon a girl hiding in the woods. This unexpected encounter is just the beginning of a life of chance meetings and coincidental occurrences between the two of them. A movie about near misses, this is one film that always stays on target. In Spanish with English subtitles. Rated R for sex and some violence. 108m. **DIR:** Julio Medem. **CAST:** Najwa Nimri, Fele Martinez. **1998**

LOVERS OF THEIR TIME ★★ In this passable film, a married man (Edward Petherbridge) leads a boring life until he meets his dream love. 60m. **DIR:**

Robert Knights. **CAST:** Edward Petherbridge, Cheryl Prime. 1986

LOVERS ON THE BRIDGE ★★★★ This audacious film elevates the story of two homeless lovers to an artful exploration of love, need, and values. Beautifully crafted, the film follows the on-again, off-again relationship of two people who live on Paris's Pont-Neuf Bridge, when they're not trying to find food or emotional sustenance in the cold world. In French with English subtitles. 126m. **DIR:** Léos Carax. **CAST:** Denis Lavant, Juliette Binoche. 1992

LOVES AND TIMES OF SCARAMOUCHE, THE ❤ Michael Sarrazin, as Scaramouche, stumbles through this ridiculous swashbuckler. 92m. **DIR:** Enzo G. Castellari. **CAST:** Michael Sarrazin, Ursula Andress, Aldo Maccioni, Gian Carlo Prete. 1976

LOVES OF A BLONDE ★★★1/2 This dark comedy from Milos Forman centers on a young girl working in a small-town factory who pursues a musician. Often hilarious. In Czech with English subtitles. B&W; 88m. **DIR:** Milos Forman. **CAST:** Hana Brejchova, Josef Sebanek. 1965

LOVES OF CARMEN, THE ★★ Rita Hayworth plays an immoral gypsy hussy who ruins the life of a young Spanish officer (Glenn Ford). It's melodramatic and corny at times but still fun to see sparks fly between Hayworth as the beautiful vixen and an ever-so-handsome Ford. 98m. **DIR:** Charles Vidor. **CAST:** Rita Hayworth, Glenn Ford, Ron Randell, Victor Jory, Luther Adler, Arnold Moss. 1948 DVD

LOVES OF THREE QUEENS ★★ A three-hour Italian epic starring Hedy Lamarr as three of history's most memorable women—Guinevere, Empress Josephine, Helen of Troy—was chopped down to less than half its original length for American release, so don't expect it to make a lot of sense. Dubbed. 80m. **DIR:** Marc Allegret. **CAST:** Hedy Lamarr. 1953

LOVE'S SAVAGE FURY ❤ TV-movie attempt to recreate the passion of *Gone with the Wind.* 100m. **DIR:** Joseph Hardy. **CAST:** Jennifer O'Neill, Perry King, Raymond Burr, Connie Stevens. 1979

LOVESICK ★★★ You won't fall out of your seat laughing or grab a tissue to dab away the tears. But this movie, about a psychiatrist's (Dudley Moore) obsession with his patient (Elizabeth McGovern) does have its moments. Rated PG. 95m. **DIR:** Marshall Brickman. **CAST:** Dudley Moore, Elizabeth McGovern, Alec Guinness, John Huston. 1983 DVD

LOVING COUPLES ★★ The plot is that old and tired one, about two couples who swap partners for a temporary fling only to reunite by film's end happier and wiser for the experience. It's a premise that's been worn thin and is badly in need of retirement. Rated PG. 97m. **DIR:** Jack Smight. **CAST:** Shirley MacLaine, James Coburn, Susan Sarandon, Stephen Collins. 1980

LOVING YOU ★★★ This better-than-average Elvis Presley vehicle features him as a small-town country boy who makes good when his singing ability is discovered. It has a bit of romance but the main attraction is Elvis singing his rock 'n' roll songs, including the title tune. 101m. **DIR:** Hal Kanter. **CAST:** Elvis Presley, Lizabeth Scott, Wendell Corey, Dolores Hart. 1957

LOW BLOW ❤ A private investigator tries to rescue a millionaire's daughter from a religious cult. Rated R for violence and profanity. 85m. **DIR:** Frank Harris. **CAST:** Leo Fong, Cameron Mitchell, Troy Donahue, Akosua Busia, Stack Pierce. 1986

LOW DOWN DIRTY SHAME, A ★★1/2 Shame, a former L.A. cop who was unfairly discredited, struggles to make it as a private detective only to find himself right back in the middle of the case that ruined his law-enforcement career. Jada Pinkett's animated performance as Shame's fast-talking girl Friday is one of the few outstanding elements in this otherwise so-so spoof of blaxploitation pictures. Rated R for violence, profanity, nudity, and simulated sex. 100m. **DIR:** Keenen Ivory Wayans. **CAST:** Keenen Ivory Wayans, Charles Dutton, Jada Pinkett, Salli Richardson, Andrew Divoff, Corwin Hawkins, Gary Cervantes, Gregory Sierra. 1994

LOW LIFE, THE ★★1/2 Mopey college grad Rory Cochrane drifts around the fringes of L.A., working dead-end jobs and hoping to become a screenwriter. Director George Hickenlooper has a nice feel for the seedy atmosphere, and the ensemble cast is strong, but the script is as aimless and off-putting as the characters it describes. Sean Astin, as Cochrane's earnest, lonely roommate, gives the film's most interesting and sympathetic performance. Rated R for profanity. 99m. **DIR:** George Hickenlooper. **CAST:** Rory Cochrane, Kyra Sedgwick, Sean Astin, Christian Meoli, Sara Melson. 1996

LOWER DEPTHS (1936) ★★★★ Another poignant observation by Jean Renoir about social classes. This time the director adapts Maxim Gorky's play about an impoverished thief (brilliantly performed by Jean Gabin) who meets a baron and instructs him in the joys of living without material wealth. In French with English subtitles. 92m. **DIR:** Jean Renoir. **CAST:** Jean Gabin, Louis Jouvet. 1936

LOWER DEPTHS, THE (1957) ★★★★ Brilliant adaptation of Maxim Gorky's play about a group of destitute people surviving on their tenuous self-esteem, while living in a ghetto. Akira Kurosawa explores this crippled society with tolerance, biting humor, and compassion. In Japanese with English subtitles. B&W; 125m. **DIR:** Akira Kurosawa. **CAST:** Toshiro Mifune. 1957

LOWER LEVEL ★★★ A psychotic security guard manipulates elevators, doors, and alarms to set up the perfect date with his object of obsession. Surprisingly watchable. Rated R for nudity, violence, and gore. 85m. **DIR:** Kristine Peterson. **CAST:** David Bradley, Elizabeth Gracen, Jeff Yagher. 1990 DVD

LOYALTIES ★★ In this Canadian-made drama, an upper-class Englishwoman reluctantly moves to a small town in one of the northwest territories, where she becomes friends with her housekeeper, a hell-raising half-Indian woman. The story of the two women is well-handled, but the movie turns into an unbelievable melodrama about the wife having to suffer for her husband's indiscretions. Rated R for violence and sexual situations. 98m. **DIR:** Anne Wheeler. **CAST:** Susan Wooldridge, Tantoo Cardinal, Kenneth Welsh. 1987

LUCAS ★★★★ Charming tale of young love, leagues above the usual teen-oriented fare due to an intelligent and compassionate script by writer-director David Seltzer. Corey Haim stars as a 14-year-old whiz kid "accelerated" into high school who falls in love, during the summer between terms, with 16-year-old Kerri Green. Rated PG-13 for language. 100m. **DIR:** David Seltzer. **CAST:** Corey Haim, Kerri Green, Charlie Sheen, Courtney Thorne-Smith, Winona Ryder. **1986**

LUCKY JIM ★★★ High jinks and antics at a small British university as a young lecturer tries to improve his lot by sucking up to his superior, but continually goofs. Acceptable adaptation of the Kingsley Amis novel. 95m. **DIR:** John Boulting. **CAST:** Ian Carmichael, Terry-Thomas, Hugh Griffith. **1957**

LUCKY LUCIANO ★★ The last years of one of crime land's most "influential" bosses. The film started out to be an important one for Francesco Rosi, but the distributors of the English edition went in for the sensationalism with too graphic subtitles and/or dubbing, depending on the version. Not a bad film if you know Italian. If you don't, stick with *The Godfather*. Rated R for profanity and violence. 110m. **DIR:** Francesco Rosi. **CAST:** Gian Maria Volonté, Rod Steiger, Edmond O'Brien, Vincent Gardenia, Charles Cioffi. **1974**

LUCKY LUKE ★★ Don't expect to laugh while watching this mediocre comedy-Western about a sheriff who's "faster than his shadow." Roger Miller lends his voice to the narrating horse. Not rated; contains mild violence. 91m. **DIR:** Terence Hill. **CAST:** Terence Hill, Nancy Morgan, Roger Miller, Fritz Sperberg. **1994 DVD**

LUCKY LUKE: THE BALLAD OF THE DALTONS ★★ Overlong yarn of the Old West starring an all-American cowboy (complete with immovable cigarette on the lower lip): Lucky Luke. References to killing are taken in stride, but for the most part this is harmless cartoon fare. Not rated. 82m. **DIR:** René Goscinny. **1978**

LUCKY ME ★★ The title does not mean the viewer. Love finds an unemployed Florida chorus girl seeking work. Only the caliber of the cast keeps this matte-finished song-and-dancer from being a complete bomb. Angie Dickinson's film debut. 100m. **DIR:** Jack Donohue. **CAST:** Doris Day, Robert Cummings, Phil Silvers, Eddie Foy Jr., Nancy Walker, Martha Hyer, Angie Dickinson. **1954**

LUCKY PARTNERS ★★★ Artist Ronald Colman wishes passing errand girl Ginger Rogers good luck, thereby touching off a chain of events ending in romance. Lightweight comedy with, for the time, raw touches. Ginger's naïve charm and Ronald's urbanity make for interesting interplay. B&W; 99m. **DIR:** Lewis Milestone. **CAST:** Ginger Rogers, Ronald Colman, Spring Byington, Jack Carson, Harry Davenport. **1940**

LUCKY STIFF ★★★ Lovelorn Joe Alaskey can't believe his luck when he's picked up by gorgeous Donna Dixon and invited to her family's home for Christmas dinner. What he doesn't know is that he's the entree-to-be for this cannibal clan. Writer Pat Proffit provides plenty of hilariously demented characters and funny one-liners. Rated PG. 82m. **DIR:** Anthony Perkins. **CAST:** Joe Alaskey, Donna Dixon, Jeff Kober. **1988**

LUCKY TEXAN ★★★ Gold miners John Wayne and Gabby Hayes strike it rich. But before they can cash in their claim, Hayes is falsely accused of robbery and murder. Of course, the Duke rides to his aid. Creaky, but fun for fans. B&W; 56m. **DIR:** Robert N. Bradbury. **CAST:** John Wayne, Barbara Sheldon, George "Gabby" Hayes. **1934 DVD**

LUCY AND DESI: A HOME MOVIE ★★★★1/2 This revealing film about Lucille Ball and Desi Arnaz—which won an Emmy after airing on NBC in 1993 and is now extended by thirteen minutes—delves into their once-happy marriage and the dissolution caused by the pressures of Hollywood. Upbeat footage of the successful Desilu production company helps to balance the pain of watching two people drift apart in this documentary of surprising depth. Not rated; contains mild profanity. B&W/Color. 111m. **DIR:** Lucie Arnaz. **CAST:** Lucille Ball, Desi Arnaz Sr., Lucie Arnaz, Desi Arnaz Jr. **1994**

LUCY AND DESI: BEFORE THE LAUGHTER ★★★ A warts-and-all portrayal of America's favorite couple of the 1960s, particularly distinguished by Frances Fisher's passionate turn as the redheaded queen of comedy. Not recommended for those who maintain the *I Love Lucy* image. Not rated. 96m. **DIR:** Charles Janot. **CAST:** Frances Fisher, Maurice Bernard. **1991**

LUGGAGE OF THE GODS 🦃 A primitive tribe, unaware of the advances of man, is both delighted and frightened by an airplane emptying its cargo pit over their territory. Rated G. 78m. **DIR:** David Kendall. **CAST:** Mark Stolzenberg, Gabriel Barr, Gwen Ellison. **1983**

LUGOSI, THE FORGOTTEN KING ★★★★ Forrest J. Ackerman hosts this comprehensive look at the life and career of Bela Lugosi, featuring outtakes, trailers, and interviews with some of his costars (including John Carradine and Ralph Bellamy). Not rated. B&W/color. 55m. **DIR:** Mark S. Gilman Jr., Dave Stuckey. **1983**

LULLABY OF BROADWAY ★★1/2 Musical-comedy with show girl Doris Day returning from England, believing her mother to be a Broadway star, learning she is over-the-hill, singing and boozing in a bar. Many old standards by George Gershwin, Cole Porter, Harry Warren, etc. 92m. **DIR:** David Butler. **CAST:** Doris Day, Gene Nelson, Gladys George, Billy DeWolfe, S. Z. Sakall, Florence Bates. **1951**

•**LULU ON THE BRIDGE** ★★★1/2 Writer Paul Auster (*Blue in the Face*) makes an auspicious debut as director with a stylish slice of *film noir*. Harvey Keitel is excellent as jazz saxophonist Izzy Maurer, whose near-death experience leads him down a rabbit hole filled with dark and sinister characters. Mira Sorvino is luminous as a film actress whose life inadvertently becomes entangled with Izzy's. Moody and unexpected. Rated PG-13 for language and violence. 103m. **DIR:** Paul Auster. **CAST:** Harvey Keitel, Mira Sorvino, Willem Dafoe, Gina Gershon, Mandy Patinkin, Vanessa Redgrave. **1998 DVD**

LUMIERE 🦃 The only thing this film illuminates is Jeanne Moreau's pretentiousness. In French. 95m. **DIR:** Jeanne Moreau. **CAST:** Jeanne Moreau, Francine

Racette, Bruno Ganz, François Simon, Lucia Bose, Keith Carradine. 1976

LUNA PARK ★★★ Riveting, at times harrowing portrait of Russian skinheads. Interesting plot twist comes when one of the gang discovers that his father was a Jewish composer. In Russian with English subtitles. Not rated; contains strong images of violence. 105m. DIR: Pavel Lounguine. CAST: Oleg Borisou, Andrei Goutine, Natalie Egorova. 1991

LUNATIC, THE ★★★ Delicious comedy stars Paul Campbell as the title character, a freewheeling, free-loving reggae man who talks to trees and is generally considered an annoyance. Excellent musical soundtrack enhances the lush, natural beauty of the film and characters. Rated R for sexual situations. 93m. DIR: Lol Creme. CAST: Julie T. Wallace, Paul Campbell. 1992

LUNATICS: A LOVE STORY ★★★ Lunatic Theodore Raimi (brother of writer-director Sam) hides out in his apartment, afraid of the real world. When he accidentally connects on the phone with on-the-run Deborah Foreman, he sees his chance to escape his mental cell. Pretty wacky stuff, including some outrageous special effects. Rated PG-13 for language and surreal violence. 87m. DIR: Josh Becker. CAST: Theodore Raimi, Deborah Foreman, Bruce Campbell. 1992

LUNATICS & LOVERS ★★ Tepid morality play stars Marcello Mastroianni as a wealthy aristocrat whose delusions upset the locals. When a musician attempts to replace his imaginary wife with the real thing, chaos ensues. In Italian with English subtitles. Rated PG. 92m. DIR: Flavio Mogherini. CAST: Marcello Mastroianni, Lino Toffalo, Claudia Mori, Lino Morelli. 1975

LUNCH WAGON ★★1/2 The vehicle of the title belongs to three enterprising young women who set up near a construction site. Spirited drive-in comedy offers more laughs than most of its ilk along with the requisite jiggle. Rated R for nudity and profanity. 88m. DIR: Ernest Pintoff. CAST: Pamela Bryant, Rose Marie. 1980

LUPIN III: TALES OF THE WOLF (TV SERIES) ★★★ Taken from the popular Japanese series, these episodes feature the animated adventures of cunning cat-burglar Wolf and his crafty comrades. With plenty of action and lighthearted fun, *Lupin* will be enjoyed by animation fans who value cleverness over graphic violence. Dubbed in English. Not rated, but suitable for most audiences (some brief illustrated nudity). 30m. each DIR: Hayao Miyazaki. 1977

LUPO ★★★ In this warmhearted comedy from Israel, Yuda Barkan is charming as Lupo, a cart driver. Like a modern Fiddler on the Roof, he's caught in the currents of change. His horse is killed by a car, his daughter is wooed by a rich banker's son, and the city plans to demolish the old shack he calls home. Rated G. 100m. DIR: Menahem Golan. CAST: Yuda Barkan, Gabi Amrani, Esther Greenberg. 1970

LURKERS ✔ Hopelessly meandering tale about an abused young girl haunted by the forces of evil. Rated R for violence and nudity. 95m. DIR: Roberta Findlay. CAST: Christine Moore, Gary Warner. 1988

LURKING FEAR ★★ Evil creatures are eating the inhabitants of a small town in this movie adapted from a story by H. P. Lovecraft. Bad acting, directing, and dialogue, and lots of gore. Not rated; contains violence and profanity. 76m. DIR: C. Courtney Joyner. CAST: Jon Finch, Blake Bailey, Ashley Lauren, Jeffrey Combs, Allison Mackie, Vincent Schiavelli. 1994

LUSH LIFE ★★★★ Best friends Jeff Goldblum and Forest Whitaker are hardworking jazz "session men" (the anonymous fellows lending background support for better-known stars). After providing a fascinating glimpse of this taxing profession, the story kicks into gear when Whitaker is diagnosed with a brain tumor; he decides to go out in style by throwing the world's biggest jazz party. Watch for actual jazz greats such as Jack Sheldon, Ernie Andrews, and Charlie Heath. Rated R for profanity, simulated sex, and drug use. 96m. DIR: Michael Elias. CAST: Jeff Goldblum, Forest Whitaker, Kathy Baker, Tracey Needham, Lois Chiles. 1994

LUST FOR A VAMPIRE ★★★ All-girls school turns out to be a haven for vampires, with a visiting writer (Michael Johnson) falling in love with one of the undead students (Yutte Stensgaard). Atmospheric blending of chills and fleshy eroticism combined with a terrific ending. Rated R. 95m. DIR: Jimmy Sangster. CAST: Suzanna Leigh, Michael Johnson, Ralph Bates, Barbara Jefford, Yutte Stensgaard. 1970

LUST FOR FREEDOM ✔ Woman unjustly sentenced for a crime she didn't commit finds herself fighting for her life and loins in a brutal prison. Not rated; contains graphic violence and nudity. 92m. DIR: Eric Louzil. CAST: Melanie Coll. 1991

LUST FOR GOLD ★★★1/2 Based on the true story of the Lost Dutchman mine, told in flashbacks and recounting the double dealings of Glenn Ford, Ida Lupino, and husband Gig Young as they plot against one another. B&W; 90m. DIR: S. Sylvan Simon. CAST: Glenn Ford, Ida Lupino, Edgar Buchanan, Will Geer, Gig Young. 1949

LUST FOR LIFE ★★★1/2 A standout performance by Kirk Douglas, in the role of artist Vincent van Gogh, creates a rare, affecting portrait of a tormented man driven by the frenzied energy of passion. Unfortunately this overblown Hollywood production fails to exploit the beauty of some of the locations that inspired the paintings. 123m. DIR: Vincente Minnelli. CAST: Kirk Douglas, Anthony Quinn, James Donald, Pamela Brown. 1956

LUST IN THE DUST ★★ Tab Hunter and female impersonator Divine (who's anything but), who first teamed in *Polyester*, star in this so-so spoof of spaghetti Westerns, directed by Paul Bartel. The ad blurb tells all: "He rode the West. The girls rode the rest. Together they ravaged the land." Rated R for nudity, suggested sex, and violence. 86m. DIR: Paul Bartel. CAST: Tab Hunter, Divine, Lainie Kazan, Geoffrey Lewis, Henry Silva, Cesar Romero. 1985

LUSTY MEN, THE ★★★★ The world of rodeo cowboys is explored in this well-made film directed by cult favorite Nicholas Ray. Robert Mitchum has one of his best roles as a broken-down ex–rodeo star who gets a second chance at the big money by tutoring an egotistical newcomer on the circuit, well played by

Arthur Kennedy. B&W; 113m. **DIR:** Nicholas Ray. **CAST:** Robert Mitchum, Susan Hayward, Arthur Kennedy, Arthur Hunnicutt. **1952**

LUTHER ★★★ Stacy Keach's gripping performance as Martin Luther is more than enough reason to see this otherwise turgid version of John Osborne's play (minimally adapted for this American Film Theater presentation) about the founder of Protestantism. Rated G. 108m. **DIR:** Guy Green. **CAST:** Stacy Keach, Patrick Magee, Hugh Griffith, Leonard Rossiter, Judi Dench, Maurice Denham. **1974**

LUTHER, THE GEEK 🐄 A chicken-clucking killer terrorizes a Midwestern family. For geeks only. Rated R for violence, nudity, and profanity. 92m. **DIR:** Carlton J. Albright. **CAST:** Edward Terry, Joan Roth, J. Jerome Clarke, Tom Mills. **1994**

LUV ★★ When talent the caliber of Jack Lemmon, Peter Falk, and Elaine May cannot breathe life into a film, then nothing can. The plot concerns three New York intellectuals and their tribulations. Who cares? 95m. **DIR:** Clive Donner. **CAST:** Jack Lemmon, Elaine May, Peter Falk, Severn Darden. **1967**

LUXURY LINER ★★1/2 Jane Powell plays Cupid for her widowed sea-captain father. Forget the plot. Enjoy the music. 98m. **DIR:** Richard Whorf. **CAST:** George Brent, Jane Powell, Lauritz Melchior, Frances Gifford, Xavier Cugat, Connie Gilchrist, Richard Derr. **1948**

LUZIA ★★1/2 Modern Western features a young woman seeking revenge for her parents' murder. She begins working as a cowhand at the ranch of the powerful men responsible for making her an orphan. Slow moving and a bit too melodramatic. Not rated, contains nudity, violence, and profanity. In Portuguese with English subtitles. 112m. **DIR:** Fabio Barreto. **CAST:** Claudia Ohana, Thales Pan Chacon, Luzia Falcao. **1988**

LYDIA ★★★1/2 This sentimental treatment of the highly regarded French film *Carnet du Bal* is well acted and directed. It's the story of an elderly woman who has a reunion with four of her former loves. Merle Oberon's performance is one of her best. B&W; 104m. **DIR:** Julien Duvivier. **CAST:** Merle Oberon, Joseph Cotten, Edna May Oliver, Alan Marshal. **1941**

M ★★★★★ A child-killer is chased by police, and by other criminals who would prefer to mete out their own justice. Peter Lorre, in his first film role, gives a striking portrayal of a man driven by uncontrollable forces. A classic German film, understated, yet filled with haunting images. Beware of videocassettes containing badly translated, illegible subtitles. In German with English subtitles. Not rated. B&W; 99m. **DIR:** Fritz Lang. **CAST:** Peter Lorre, Gustav Grundgens. **1931 DVD**

MA AND PA KETTLE (THE FURTHER ADVENTURES OF MA AND PA KETTLE) ★★★ *The Egg and I* scene stealers Marjorie Main and Percy Kilbride were such a hit as the displaced Washington-state "hillbillies," Ma and Pa Kettle, their own series was inevitable. In the opener Pa wins a futuristic home in a slogan contest. An obvious but well-used tool to introduce many good sight gags. Corny, but fun. B&W; 76m. **DIR:** Charles Lamont. **CAST:** Marjorie Main, Percy Kilbride, Richard Long, Meg Randall, Patricia Alphin, Esther Dale, Barry Kelley, O. Z. Whitehead. **1949**

MA AND PA KETTLE AT HOME ★★1/2 Ma and Pa tidy up the farm to impress the college official checking out their request for a scholarship for their son. A rainstorm ruins their home so Ma and Pa use their wits to get that scholarship in one of the funnier titles in the series. B&W; 81m. **DIR:** Charles Lamont. **CAST:** Marjorie Main, Percy Kilbride, Brett Halsey, Mary Wickes, Alan Mowbray. **1954**

MA AND PA KETTLE AT THE FAIR ★★★ This fourth series entry has Ma intending to enter the jam-making contest at the state fair but in error registering Pa's plow horse in the harness race. The gags and situations are still lowbrow, but you'll laugh in spite of yourself. B&W; 79m. **DIR:** Charles Barton. **CAST:** Marjorie Main, Percy Kilbride, Lori Nelson, James Best, Esther Dale, Russell Simpson, Emory Parnell. **1951**

MA AND PA KETTLE AT WAIKIKI ★★ Notable primarily because it marks Percy Kilbride's last appearance as Pa Kettle. B&W; 79m. **DIR:** Lee Sholem. **CAST:** Percy Kilbride, Marjorie Main, Byron Palmer, Lori Nelson, Hilo Hattie. **1955**

MA AND PA KETTLE BACK ON THE FARM ★★★ In this third entry in the series the Kettles become grandparents, meet their stuffy Boston in-laws, and when Pa seemingly discovers uranium on the old farm he becomes radioactive. The gags include an arithmetic lesson "borrowed" from Universal Studio coworkers, Abbott and Costello. Still corny, still funny. B&W; 81m. **DIR:** Edward Sedgwick. **CAST:** Marjorie Main, Percy Kilbride, Richard Long, Meg Randall, Ray Collins, Esther Dale, Barbara Brown, Emory Parnell, Peter Leeds. **1951**

MA AND PA KETTLE GO TO TOWN ★★★1/2 A typical fish-out-of-water story with Ma and Pa at their countrified best. They get involved with a gangster, lose the gangster's money, and meddle in their children's lives in between chase scenes in the Big Apple. B&W; 79m. **DIR:** Charles Lamont. **CAST:** Marjorie Main, Percy Kilbride, Richard Long, Meg Randall, Jim Backus, Charles McGraw, Elliott Lewis. **1950**

MA AND PA KETTLE ON VACATION ★★ Corn-pone humor and Paris society don't mix, but the Kettles manage to keep the film afloat with predictable gags and grimaces. B&W; 75m. **DIR:** Charles Lamont. **CAST:** Marjorie Main, Percy Kilbride, Sig Ruman, Teddy Hart, Ray Collins, Rita Moreno. **1953**

MA BARKER'S KILLER BROOD ★★ Sweet, grandmotherly Lurene Tuttle, delivering an absolutely ferocious, chop-licking portrayal of Ma Barker, lends fleeting interest to this otherwise overlong gangster cheapie. B&W; 82m. **DIR:** Bill Karn. **CAST:** Lurene Tuttle, Tristram Coffin, Paul Dubov. **1960**

MA SAISON PREFERÉE ★★★ A doctor (Daniel Auteuil) and his lawyer sister (Catherine Deneuve) grapple with their precarious relationship as their mother's health begins to fail. The plot smacks of soap opera, but Auteuil and Deneuve have extraordinary rapport. An extraneous subplot slows the action. In French with English subtitles. Not rated; contains brief nudity and mature themes. 125m. DIR: André Téchiné. CAST: Daniel Auteuil, Catherine Deneuve, Marthe Villalonga, Anthony Prada, Chiara Mastroianni, Carmen Chaplin. 1993

MA VIE EN ROSE ★★★1/2 A French boy is convinced that when he grows up he will be a girl and marry the son of his father's boss; in the meantime, his innocent certainty causes confusion and perplexity among his family and their suburban middle-class neighbors. The film's whimsical charm and fine acting compensate for occasional slips into broad sitcom exaggeration. In French with English subtitles. Rated R for some profanity and mature themes of sexual identity. 88m. DIR: Alain Berliner. CAST: Georges Du Fresne, Michele Laroque, Jean-Philippe Ecoffey, Hélène Vincent, Julien Riviere. 1997 DVD

MAC ★★★★ Writer-director-star John Turturro's tribute to the life and work ethic of his father, is a collection of real-life vignettes superbly acted and visualized. While not for all tastes, *Mac* is obviously a labor of love. Set in Queens in 1954 and focusing on three brothers who make the heartbreaking mistake of going into business together, it is an offbeat yet sometimes intensely moving film. Rated R for profanity, violence, and simulated sex. 118m. DIR: John Turturro. CAST: John Turturro, Michael Badalucco, Carl Capotoro, Katherine Borowitz, Ellen Barkin, John Amos, Olek Krupa. 1993

MAC AND ME 💔 Imagine the most product-friendly film ever made and you have (Big) *Mac and Me*. To be fair, the film stars the courageous Jade Calegory, a paraplegic wheelchair-bound since birth, and a share of the producer's net profits will be donated to Ronald McDonald's Children's Charities. But the plot rips off everything in sight. Rated PG. 101m. DIR: Stewart Raffill. CAST: Jade Calegory, Christine Ebersole, Jonathan Ward. 1988

MACABRE SERENADE ★★ One of the four Mexican films featuring footage of Boris Karloff but assembled after his death (see *Sinister Invasion*), this is the best of a bad lot. He plays a toy maker whose creations seek revenge on his evil relatives after his death. There's a sloppily cut version also on video called *Dance of Death*; it originally played theatres as *House of Evil*. 75m. DIR: Juan Ibanez, Jack Hill. CAST: Boris Karloff. 1968

MACAO ★★ Jane Russell is a singer in the fabled Oriental port and gambling heaven of Macao, across the bay from Hong Kong. She's in love with Robert Mitchum, a good guy caught in a web of circumstance. Russell is the only thing about this film that isn't flat. B&W; 80m. DIR: Josef von Sternberg. CAST: Jane Russell, Robert Mitchum, William Bendix, Gloria Grahame, Thomas Gomez. 1952

MACARIO ★★★★ Excellent poetic fable based on a story by the mysterious author B. Traven (*The Trea-sure of the Sierra Madre*). Tarso Ignacio Lopez gives a deeply felt performance as an impoverished woodcutter. One of the most honored Mexican films, and the first to earn an Oscar nomination. In Spanish with English subtitles. B&W; 91m. DIR: Roberto Gavaldon. CAST: Tarso Ignacio Lopez, Pina Pellicer. 1960

MACARONI ★★★1/2 Wonderful Italian comedy-drama from the director of *A Special Day* and *Le Bal*. This one concerns an American executive (Jack Lemmon) who returns to Naples for a business meeting forty years after his stay there with the army. He is visited by an old friend (Marcello Mastroianni). Both Lemmon and Mastroianni deliver brilliant performances. Rated PG for profanity. 104m. DIR: Ettore Scola. CAST: Jack Lemmon, Marcello Mastroianni, Daria Nicolodi. 1985

MACARTHUR ★★★ Gregory Peck is cast as the famous general during the latter years of his long military career. It begins with his assumption of command of the Philippine garrison in World War II and continues through his sacking by President Truman during the Korean conflict. The film takes a middle ground in its depiction of this complex man and the controversy that surrounded him. Peck's performance is credible, but the film remains uneven. Rated PG. 130m. DIR: Joseph Sargent. CAST: Gregory Peck, Dan O'Herlihy, Ed Flanders. 1977

MACARTHUR'S CHILDREN ★★ This import deals with effects of Japan's occupation by America, on a group of youngsters and adults living on a tiny Japanese island. Rated PG for profanity and suggested sex. In Japanese with English subtitles. 120m. DIR: Masahiro Shinoda. CAST: Takaya Yamauchi, Yoshiyuki Omori. 1984

MACBETH (1948) ★★★ Shakespeare's noted tragedy, filmed according to a script by Orson Welles. Interesting movie—made on a budget of $700,000 in three weeks. Welles is an intriguing Macbeth, but Jeanette Nolan as his lady is out of her element. Edgar Barrier and Dan O'Herlihy are fine as Banquo and Macduff. B&W; 105m. DIR: Orson Welles. CAST: Orson Welles, Roddy McDowall, Jeanette Nolan, Edgar Barrier, Dan O'Herlihy. 1948

MACBETH (1961) ★★★1/2 As the crown-hungry Scottish thane Macbeth, Maurice Evans is superb and superbly abetted by Dame Judith Anderson, as the grasping, conniving Lady Macbeth. Another in the developing series of made-for-television *Hallmark Hall of Fame* programs being released on videocassette. B&W; 103m. DIR: George Schaefer. CAST: Maurice Evans, Judith Anderson. 1961

MACBETH (1971) ★★★1/2 The violent retelling of this classic story was commissioned and underwritten by publisher Hugh Hefner. Shakespeare's tragedy about a man driven to self-destruction by the forces of evil is vividly brought to life by director Roman Polanski. Grim yet compelling, this version of one of our great plays is not for everyone and contains scenes that make it objectionable for children (or squeamish adults). 140m. DIR: Roman Polanski. CAST: Jon Finch, Francesca Annis, Martin Shaw, Nicholas Selby, John Stride. 1971

MACBETH (1981) ★★1/2 Allowing for this being a film of a stage production, it is a disappointing and somewhat slow-moving telling of Shakespeare's tale. Interesting and offbeat casting. A Bard Productions std. release. 150m. DIR: Arthur Allan Seidelman. CAST: Jeremy Brett, Piper Laurie, Simon MacCorkindale, Barry Primus, Millie Perkins, Alan Oppenheimer, Fay Robinson, Johnny Crawford. 1981

MACHINE-GUN KELLY ★★1/2 Grade-B bio-pic about the famed Depression-era hoodlum, with an excellent performance by Charles Bronson in the title role and an intelligent script by R. Wright Campbell. One of Roger Corman's best early features. B&W; 84m. DIR: Roger Corman. CAST: Charles Bronson, Susan Cabot, Morey Amsterdam. 1958

MACHINE GUN KILLERS ★★ A falsely accused Union officer is given thirty days to prove that he was not the thief of a machine gun that ended up in Confederate hands. Tight direction and acting place this spaghetti Western a cut above. Rated PG. 98m. DIR: Paolo Bianchini. CAST: Robert Woods, John Ireland, Evelyn Stewart, Claudie Lange, Gerard Herter, Roberto Camardiel. 1968

MACHO CALLAHAN ★★★ David Janssen convincingly portrays Macho Callahan, a man hardened by his confinement in a horrid Confederate prison camp. When he kills a man (David Carradine) over a bottle of champagne, the man's bride (Jean Seberg) seeks revenge. Rated R for violence and gore. 99m. DIR: Bernard Kowalski. CAST: David Janssen, Jean Seberg, Lee J. Cobb, James Booth, David Carradine, Bo Hopkins. 1970

MACISTE IN HELL ★★ Italian muscle-hero Maciste (Kirk Morris), the *real* hero of dozens of sword-and-sorcery epics with bogus Hercules titles appended for U.S. release, anachronistically pops up in medieval Scotland(!), where he combats a vengeful witch. 78m. DIR: Riccardo Freda. CAST: Kirk Morris, Helene Chanel. 1962

MACK, THE ★★ Typical of the blaxploitation films of the early 1970s, a broadly overacted story about a southern California pimp. It gets two stars only because it's a fair example of the genre. Rated R for violence and language. 110m. DIR: Michael Campus. CAST: Richard Pryor, Max Julien, Roger E. Mosley, Don Gordon. 1973

MACK THE KNIFE ❤ The subtle refinements of Bertolt Brecht and Kurt Weill's *Threepenny Opera* have been unceremoniously trashed in this dull-edged bore of a musical. Rated PG-13, with moderate violence and adult situations. 122m. DIR: Menahem Golan. CAST: Raul Julia, Julia Migenes-Johnson, Richard Harris, Julie Walters, Roger Daltrey. 1990

MACKENNA'S GOLD ★★ Disappointing "big" Western follows search for gold. Impressive cast cannot overcome a poor script and uninspired direction. 128m. DIR: J. Lee Thompson. CAST: Gregory Peck, Omar Sharif, Telly Savalas, Julie Newmar, Lee J. Cobb. 1969

MACKINTOSH MAN, THE ★★★ A cold war spy thriller with all the edge-of-seat trimmings: car chases, beatings, escapes, and captures. Trouble is, it has been done before, before, and before. Paul Newman is the agent; wily and wonderful James Ma-

son is the communist spy he must catch. Rated PG. 98m. DIR: John Huston. CAST: Paul Newman, James Mason, Dominique Sanda, Ian Bannen, Nigel Patrick. 1973

MACON COUNTY JAIL ❤ Star power isn't enough to salvage this derivative made-for-cable collision of *Jackson County Jail* and *Macon County Line*. Rated R for violence, language, and nudity. 88m. DIR: Victoria Muspratt. CAST: Ally Sheedy, David Carradine, Charles Napier. 1997

MACON COUNTY LINE ★★★ A very effective little thriller based on a true incident. Set in Georgia in the 1950s, the story concerns three youths hunted by the law for a murder they did not commit. Producer Max Baer Jr. has a good eye for detail and the flavor of the times. Rated R. 89m. DIR: Richard Compton. CAST: Alan Vint, Max Baer, Jr., Geoffrey Lewis. 1974 DVD

MACROSS PLUS ★★ Technically brilliant animation scenes are wasted on a trite story wherein a hot-shot pilot becomes a hotshot test pilot. If you thought *Top Gun* was the greatest movie ever made, you might enjoy this as well. In Japanese with English subtitles. Not rated; contains profanity. Each 40m. DIR: Shoji Kawamori, Shinichiro Watanabe. 1994

MAD ABOUT MUSIC ★★★1/2 An early Deanna Durbin vehicle that uses her youthful appearance and mature voice to advantage. She plays the daughter of a socialite who doesn't want people to know about her teenage offspring. Daughter loses herself in a fantasy world to impress her schoolmates and winds up playing cupid for her mother. B&W; 96m. DIR: Norman Taurog. CAST: Deanna Durbin, Gail Patrick, Herbert Marshall, Marcia Mae Jones, Arthur Treacher, William Frawley. 1938

MAD ABOUT YOU ★★ Barely watchable heiress-on-the-move flick, features a millionaire's daughter dating three men simultaneously. Rated PG. 92m. DIR: Lorenzo Doumani. CAST: Claudia Christian, Joe Gian, Adam West, Shari Shattuck. 1988

MAD AT THE MOON ★★ Bizarre, confused horror-Western stars Mary Stuart Masterson as a young woman forced by her mother into marriage with a well-to-do rancher. When her husband turns out to be a werewolf, it's up to the man she loves to save her life. An arty misfire. Rated R for violence, simulated sex, and nudity. 98m. DIR: Martin Donovan. CAST: Mary Stuart Masterson, Hart Bochner, Fionnula Flanagan, Cec Verrell, Stephen Blake. 1992

MAD BOMBER, THE ❤ Bert I. Gordon wrote, produced, and directed this mess. It's not even up to his usual low standards. Rated R for violence. 91m. DIR: Bert I. Gordon. CAST: Vince Edwards, Chuck Connors, Neville Brand. 1973

MAD BULL ★★1/2 A wrestler struggles to escape the sensationalism of his profession. Alex Karras is believable as a man haunted by the assassination of his tag-team brother. Schmaltzy at times, but enjoyable nonetheless. 100m. DIR: Walter Doniger, Len Steckler. CAST: Alex Karras, Susan Anspach, Nicholas Colasanto, Elisha Cook Jr., Danny Dayton. 1977

MAD CITY ★★★1/2 Dustin Hoffman is a nearly washed-up television news reporter who stumbles onto the story of a lifetime: a disgruntled ex-employee (John Travolta) takes over a city museum at gunpoint. All Travolta wants is his job back or, at least, someone to listen to his side of the story, while Hoffman parlays the working stiff's plight into a comeback to national prominence. The film's message—about the power of the media and the egos that manipulate it—is pounded home so mercilessly that what might have been an insightful drama becomes a one-dimensional political statement. Rated R for violence and profanity. 114m. DIR: Constantin Costa-Gavras. CAST: John Travolta, Dustin Hoffman, Mia Kirshner, Alan Alda, Robert Prosky, Blythe Danner, William Atherton, Ted Levine. 1997 DVD

MAD DOCTOR OF MARKET STREET, THE ★★ Lionel Atwill hams enjoyably as a doctor who persuades the natives of a tropical island that he can revive the dead. Director Joseph H. Lewis became a cult following for some of his later B movies, but this one is pretty uninspired. B&W; 60m. DIR: Joseph H. Lewis. CAST: Lionel Atwill, Una Merkel, Nat Pendleton, Claire Dodd, Anne Nagel, Noble Johnson. 1942

MAD DOG AND GLORY ★★★★ Police photographer-detective Robert De Niro inadvertently saves the life of gangster Bill Murray and finds himself the recipient of a special favor: one week of the live-in charms of Uma Thurman. At first, De Niro wants no part of it, then he begins falling in love with Thurman—much to the chagrin of Murray. De Niro, Thurman, and Murray are excellent. Rated R for violence, profanity, and nudity. 97m. DIR: John McNaughton. CAST: Robert De Niro, Uma Thurman, Bill Murray, Kathy Baker, David Caruso, Mike Starr, Tom Towles. 1993 DVD

MAD DOG MORGAN ★★1/2 Dennis Hopper plays an Australian bush ranger in this familiar tale of a man forced into a life of crime. Good support from aborigine David Gulpilil and Australian actor Jack Thompson help this visually stimulating film, but Hopper's excesses and a muddled ending weigh against it. Early prison sequences and scattered scenes are brutal. Rated R. 102m. DIR: Philippe Mora. CAST: Dennis Hopper, Jack Thompson, David Gulpilil, Michael Pate. 1976

MAD DOGS AND ENGLISHMEN ★★★1/2 Joe Cocker and friends, including Rita Coolidge and Leon Russell, put together one of the zaniest rock tours ever in the early 1970s, leaving a legendary trail of drugs and groupies in their wake. Fortunately, the superstar group was also able to function on stage, and this movie effectively captures the spirit of the 1970 tour. Performances of "With a Little Help from My Friends," "Superstar," and "Feeling Alright" can be considered rock classics. 118m. DIR: Pierre Adidge. CAST: Joe Cocker, Leon Russell, Rita Coolidge. 1972

MAD EXECUTIONERS, THE ★★1/2 After Dark Eyes of London, this is probably the quintessential Edgar Wallace–style chiller from West Germany (albeit based on a story by his son, Bryan). A vigilante court is executing elusive criminals, while in an unrelated subplot, a mad scientist is beheading women! Ignore the dubbing and concentrate on the pulpy thrills and creepy set design. B&W; 94m. DIR:

Edward Willeg. CAST: Wolfgang Preiss, Harry Riebauer, Chris Howland. 1963

MAD GHOUL, THE ♥ A cast of unknown (over)actors and offscreen special effects rule in this silliness about a "poisonous vapor" that turns men into monsters and puts them under a scientist's power. Not rated. B&W; 65m. DIR: James Hogan. CAST: David Bruce, George Zucco, Evelyn Ankers, Turhan Bey, Charles McGraw. 1943

MAD LOVE (1935) ★★★1/2 Colin Clive plays a gifted pianist who loses his hands in a rail accident and finds that the hands miraculously grafted to his wrists by Peter Lorre belonged to a murderer and follow the impulses of the former owner. This complex story of obsession is a murder mystery with an odd twist. A compelling study of depravity. B&W; 67m. DIR: Karl Freund. CAST: Peter Lorre, Colin Clive, Frances Drake, Ted Healy, Sara Haden, Edward Brophy, Keye Luke. 1935

MAD LOVE (1995) ♥ Great title but a pathetic tale of a high-school senior drawn like a moth to a flame to manic-depressive Drew Barrymore, whose performance is little more than an annoying twitch. Rated PG-13 for profanity and sexual situations. 99m. DIR: Antonia Bird. CAST: Chris O'Donnell, Drew Barrymore. 1995 DVD

MAD, MAD MONSTERS, THE ♥ A gruesome glomeration of ghoulies gathers for the wedding celebration of Frankenstein's monster. 60m. DIR: Arthur Rankin Jr., Jules Bass. 1972

MAD MAX ★★★1/2 Exciting sci-fi adventure features Mel Gibson as a fast-driving cop who has to take on a gang of crazies in the dangerous world of the future. Rated R. 93m. DIR: George Miller. CAST: Mel Gibson, Joanne Samuel, Hugh Keays-Byrne, Tim Burns, Roger Ward. 1979 DVD

MAD MAX BEYOND THUNDERDOME ★★★1/2 Mad Max is back—and he's angrier than ever. Those who enjoyed Road Warrior will find more of the same in director George Miller's third post-apocalypse, action-packed adventure film. This time the resourceful futuristic warrior (Mel Gibson) confronts evil ruler Tina Turner. Rated PG-13 for violence and profanity. 109m. DIR: George Miller, George Ogilvie. CAST: Mel Gibson, Tina Turner, Helen Buday, Frank Thring, Bruce Spence. 1985 DVD

MAD MISS MANTON ★★★ A group of high-society ladies led by Miss Manton (Barbara Stanwyck) help solve a murder mystery with comic results—sometimes. The humor is pretty outdated, and the brand of romanticism, while being in step with the 1930s, comes off rather silly in the latter part of the twentieth century. Henry Fonda plays a newspaper editor who falls in love with the mad Miss Manton. B&W; 80m. DIR: Leigh Jason. CAST: Barbara Stanwyck, Henry Fonda, Sam Levene, Frances Mercer, Stanley Ridges. 1938

MAD MONSTER ♥ Scientist George Zucco is mad and Glenn Strange is the monster he creates in order to get even with disbelievers. B&W; 77m. DIR: Sam Newfield. CAST: Johnny Downs, George Zucco, Anne Nagel, Glenn Strange. 1942

MAD MONSTER PARTY ★★1/2 An amusing little puppet film; a lot more fun for genre buffs who will understand all the references made to classic horror films. Worth seeing once, as a novelty. 94m. **DIR:** Jules Bass. **CAST:** Boris Karloff, Phyllis Diller, Ethel Ennis, Gale Garnett. **1967**

MAD WEDNESDAY (SEE ALSO SIN OF HAROLD DIDDLEBOCK) ★★1/2 The great silent comedian Harold Lloyd stars in an update of his famous brash, go-getting 1920s straw-hatted, black-rimmed-glasses character. A good, but not well executed, idea. Originally issued in 1947 as *The Sin of Harold Diddlebrock* in the director's version. This was producer Howard Hughes's "improved" version. B&W; 90m. **DIR:** Preston Sturges. **CAST:** Harold Lloyd, Frances Ramsden, Jimmy Conlin, Raymond Walburn, Arline Judge, Lionel Stander, Rudy Vallee, Edgar Kennedy. **1950**

●**MADAME BEHAVE** ★★1/2 A struggling young architect can't seem to stay out of women's clothes as he goes from one wild situation to another in an attempt to get his girl an engagement ring and win her away from a foppish suitor. Lots of clever captions and cross-dressing in this fast-paced farce by the only actor to make a film (and stage) career as a female impersonator in America, Julian Eltinge. B&W; 54m. **DIR:** Scott Sidney. **CAST:** Julian Eltinge, Ann Pennington, Lionel Belmore, David James, Jack Duffy, Tom Wilson. **1925**

MADAME BOVARY (1934) ★★★ Valentine Tessier is superb in the role of a woman who is half swan and half goose in director Jean Renoir's charming offbeat version of Flaubert's great novel. In French with English subtitles. B&W; 96m. **DIR:** Jean Renoir. **CAST:** Pierre Renoir, Valentine Tessier. **1934**

MADAME BOVARY (1949) ★★★ Emma Bovary is an inexorable romantic whose affairs of the heart ultimately lead to her destruction. Jennifer Jones is superb as Emma. Louis Jourdan plays her most engaging lover. Van Heflin portrays her betrayed husband. James Mason portrays Gustave Flaubert, on whose classic French novel the film is based. B&W; 115m. **DIR:** Vincente Minnelli. **CAST:** Jennifer Jones, Louis Jourdan, Van Heflin, James Mason. **1949**

MADAME BOVARY (1991) ★★★★ This gorgeously filmed, spectacularly designed adaptation of Gustave Flaubert's once-controversial novel features a stunning performance by Isabelle Huppert as Emma Bovary, who uses marriage to escape the boredom of a provincial life and then turns into an adultress when seeking escape from her unimaginative spouse. A soap opera to be sure, but on a grand, impressive scale. In French with English subtitles. Not rated; this import has suggested sex. 131m. **DIR:** Claude Chabrol. **CAST:** Isabelle Huppert, Jean-François Balmer, Christophe Malavoy. **1991**

MADAME BUTTERFLY ★★★1/2 Puccini's classic opera, of the Japanese geisha seduced and abandoned by an American naval officer in turn-of-the-century Nagasaki, makes a graceful, and surprisingly stirring film. Sumptuous cinematography and a lush rendition of Puccini's beautiful music are two of the many pleasures in this lovely, melodic film. A French production, sung in Italian with English subtitles. Not rated; suitable for general audiences. 129m. **DIR:** Frederic Mitterrand. **CAST:** Ying Huang, Richard Troxell,

Ning Liang, Richard Cowan, Jing-Ma Fan, Christopheren Nomura, Constance Hauman, Yo Kuskabe. **1996**

MADAME CURIE ★★★1/2 An excellent biography of the woman who discovered radium, balanced by a romantic retelling of her private life with her husband. The show belongs to Greer Garson and Walter Pidgeon in the third film to costar them and make the most of their remarkable chemistry. B&W; 124m. **DIR:** Mervyn LeRoy. **CAST:** Greer Garson, Walter Pidgeon, May Whitty, Henry Travers, Albert Basserman, Robert Walker, C. Aubrey Smith, Victor Francen, Reginald Owen, Van Johnson, Margaret O'Brien. **1943**

MADAME ROSA ★★★★★ This superbly moving motion picture features Simone Signoret in one of her greatest roles. It is a simple, human story that takes place six flights up in a dilapidated building where a once-beautiful prostitute and survivor of Nazi concentration camps cares for the children of hookers. No MPAA rating. 105m. **DIR:** Moshe Mizrahi. **CAST:** Simone Signoret, Sammy Den Youb, Claude Dauphin. **1977**

MADAME SATAN ★★★ A wealthy socialite tries to win her husband back from the arms of a chorus girl. Bizarre extravaganza in which the story only gets in the way of a lot of DeMille spectacularizing. B&W; 115m. **DIR:** Cecil B. DeMille. **CAST:** Kay Johnson, Reginald Denny, Lillian Roth, Roland Young. **1930**

MADAME SIN ★★★ Undistinguished film in which Bette Davis plays a female Fu Manchu opposite Robert Wagner's sophisticated hero. Written expressly for the actress, it was the most expensive made-for-TV movie of its time and won high ratings. 73m. **DIR:** David Greene. **CAST:** Robert Wagner, Bette Davis, Roy Kinnear, Paul Maxwell, Denholm Elliott, Gordon Jackson. **1971**

MADAME SOUSATZKA ★★★ A flamboyant star turn from Shirley MacLaine fuels this gentle story about an eccentric piano teacher and the gifted prodigy who comes to her for lessons in both music and life. The adaptation of Bernice Rubens's novel devotes equal time to richly drawn supporting characters: Peggy Ashcroft's wistful landlady and Twiggy's aspiring singer, among others. Rated PG-13 for language. 122m. **DIR:** John Schlesinger. **CAST:** Shirley MacLaine, Navin Chowdhry, Peggy Ashcroft, Twiggy. **1988**

MADAME X (1937) ★★★ One of the few versions of the famous stage play that relies on acting and characterization more than glamour and pretense. Character actress Gladys George adds heart, soul, and a lot of acting technique to the story of a diplomat's daughter who has a brief affair and is forced into prostitution because of it. B&W; 75m. **DIR:** Sam Wood. **CAST:** Gladys George, Warren William, John Beal, Reginald Owen, Henry Daniell, Phillip Reed, Ruth Hussey, Emma Dunn, Lynne Carver, Luis Alberni, George Zucco, Cora Witherspoon. **1937**

MADAME X (1966) ★★★ In this sentimental old chestnut, filmed six times since 1909, a woman is defended against murder charges by an attorney who is not aware he is her son. Lana Turner is good and is backed by a fine cast, but Technicolor and a big budget make this one of producer Ross Hunter's mistakes. Constance Bennett's last film. 100m. DIR: David Lowell Rich. CAST: Lana Turner, John Forsythe, Constance Bennett, Ricardo Montalban, Burgess Meredith. 1966

M.A.D.D.: MOTHERS AGAINST DRUNK DRIVING
★★1/2 True story of Candy Lightner and her struggle to establish M.A.D.D., the national anti-drunk-driving organization. A convincing performance by Mariette Hartley as the California housewife whose life is thrown into turmoil and tragic heartbreak when her daughter is killed by a drunk driver. Above-average TV movie. 100m. DIR: William A. Graham. CAST: Mariette Hartley, Paula Prentiss, Bert Remsen, John Rubinstein, Cliff Potts, David Huddleston, Grace Zabriskie, Nicolas Coster. 1983

MADDENING, THE 🎗 A scenery-chewing, vindictive-spewing Burt Reynolds kidnaps Mia Sara so that his wacko wife, played by a mummified Angie Dickinson, will have company in their swamp-front home. Rated R for profanity and violence. 97m. DIR: Danny Huston. CAST: Burt Reynolds, Angie Dickinson, Mia Sara, Brian Wimmer, Josh Mostel, William Hickey. 1995

MADE FOR EACH OTHER ★★★★ This is a highly appealing comedy-drama centering on the rocky first years of a marriage. The young couple (Carole Lombard and James Stewart) must do battle with interfering in-laws, inept servants, and the consequences of childbirth. The real strength of this film lies in the screenplay, by Jo Swerling. It gives viewers a thoughtful and tasteful picture of events that we can all relate to. B&W; 100m. DIR: John Cromwell. CAST: Carole Lombard, James Stewart, Charles Coburn, Lucile Watson, Harry Davenport. 1939 DVD

MADE IN AMERICA ★★★ Some of the funniest slapstick scenes ever filmed are in this movie, but they are used to cover up its serious themes rather than clarify them. The story of a black teenager who wants a father so badly she seeks out his identity against her mother's wishes. When the teen finds out her father was a sperm bank donor and is white, to boot, sparks fly in every direction. Rated PG. 118m. DIR: Richard Benjamin. CAST: Whoopi Goldberg, Ted Danson, Will Smith, Nia Long, Paul Rodriguez, Jennifer Tilly, Peggy Rea. 1993 DVD

MADE IN HEAVEN (1948) ★★ This silly English comedy stars a very young Petula Clark. Following a tradition started by Henry VI, a local village holds an annual contest to determine if a couple can survive one year of unmarried married bliss. The hiring of a flirtatious, Hungarian maid complicates the matter. 90m. DIR: John Paddy Carstairs. CAST: David Tomlinson, Petula Clark, Sonja Ziemann, A. E. Matthews. 1948

MADE IN HEAVEN (1987) 🎗 Timothy Hutton stars as a lad who dies heroically, winds up in Heaven, and falls in love with unborn spirit Kelly McGillis. Rated PG for brief nudity. 103m. DIR: Alan Rudolph. CAST: Timothy Hutton, Kelly McGillis, Maureen Stapleton, Mare Winningham, Ellen Barkin, Debra Winger. 1987

MADE IN USA ★★1/2 Bonnie and Clyde–style drama about a couple of drifters who leave their brutal job as coal miners in Pennsylvania for the sunny horizon of California. While en route west they en-

counter sexy hitchhiker Lori Singer and embark on a crime spree. Good cast fails to lift this overdone crime-drama above mediocrity. Pretty disappointing. Rated R. 82m. DIR: Ken Friedman. CAST: Adrian Pasdar, Christopher Penn, Lori Singer. 1988

MADELINE (1998) ★★★ The title character is an outspoken British orphan who is the littlest and bravest of twelve girls living in a Paris boarding school under supervision of a nun. This update of Ludwig Bemelman's stories shapes disparate elements of the series that began in 1939 into a whimsical outing. Rated PG. 89m. DIR: Daisy von Scherler Mayer. CAST: Hatty Jones, Frances McDormand, Nigel Hawthorne. 1998 DVD

MADEMOISELLE ★★★1/2 A lusty melodrama tailor-made for international sex-goddess Jeanne Moreau. She makes the most of her role as a sexually repressed schoolteacher who works out her frustration by committing a variety of crimes. She then seduces a woodcutter and claims he raped her and is the real crime doer in the community. *Then* she goes after the woodcutter's teenaged son. Outlandish but fascinating. B&W; 103m. DIR: Tony Richardson. CAST: Jeanne Moreau, Ettore Manni, Umberto Orsini, Keith Skinner, Mony Rey. 1966

MADEMOISELLE FIFI ★★1/2 An allegory about Nazis inspired by two different Guy de Maupassant short stories. A bullish Prussian gets his comeuppance from a French laundress during the Franco-Prussian War. Alluring performances, but very predictable. B&W; 69m. DIR: Robert Wise. CAST: Kurt Kreuger, Simone Simon, John Emery, Alan Napier, Jason Robards Sr., Norma Varden. 1944

MADEMOISELLE STRIPTEASE ★★1/2 Lightweight comedy made just before Brigitte Bardot became an international sensation. She plays a free spirit sent to Paris, where romance and trouble lurk. Brief nudity scenes were trimmed for American release (and this video). French, dubbed in English. B&W; 100m. DIR: Marc Allegret. CAST: Brigitte Bardot, Daniel Gélin, Robert Hirsch. 1956

MADHOUSE (1972) ★★★ Vincent Price and Peter Cushing share more screen time in their third film together (following *Scream and Scream Again* and *Dr. Phibes Rises Again*), thus lifting it above most horror movies of its decade. In a story slightly reminiscent of the superior *Theatre of Blood*, Price plays an actor who is released from a hospital after suffering a nervous breakdown, only to discover that his TV-series alter ego, Dr. Death, is living up to his name. Rated PG for violence. 92m. DIR: Jim Clark. CAST: Vincent Price, Peter Cushing, Robert Quarry, Adrienne Corri, Linda Hayden. 1972

MADHOUSE (1987) ★★1/2 When a woman's deranged twin escapes from the loony bin and crashes her sibling's party, you can imagine the bloodfest that results. Although the story sounds simple, there are some surprises. Stylishly filmed and well acted, with a bigger budget this might have been a classic. As it is, it's worth a look. Not rated; contains violence. 93m. DIR: Ovidio Assonitis (Oliver Hellman). CAST: Trish Everly, Michael MacRae. 1987

MADHOUSE (1990) ★★ Yuppie couple Kirstie Alley and John Larroquette find their dream house invaded and destroyed by unwanted houseguests. Only the game performances of Larroquette and Alley save this painful-to-watch comedy. Rated PG-13 for profanity and simulated sex. 100m. DIR: Tom Ropelewski. CAST: John Larroquette, Kirstie Alley, Alison La Placa, John Diehl, Jessica Lundy, Dennis Miller, Robert Ginty. 1990

MADIGAN ★★★1/2 Well-acted, atmospheric police adventure-drama pits tough Brooklyn cop Richard Widmark and New York's finest against a crazed escaped murderer. Realistic and exciting, this is still one of the best of the "behind-the-scenes" police films. 101m. DIR: Don Siegel. CAST: Richard Widmark, Henry Fonda, Harry Guardino, James Whitmore, Inger Stevens, Michael Dunn, Steve Ihnat, Sheree North. 1968 DVD

MADIGAN'S MILLIONS ❤ Only the most fanatical Dustin Hoffman fans need bother with this tedious spy farce. 86m. DIR: Stanley Prager. CAST: Dustin Hoffman, Elsa Martinelli, Cesar Romero. 1967

MADNESS OF KING GEORGE, THE ★★★1/2 Alan Bennett's play about the periodic dementia that afflicted Britain's George III comes to the screen in an elegant, well-acted production. The film focuses on the petty political maneuvers to fill the vacuum left by the king's illness, with the royal health taking a backseat to parliamentary self-preservation. Not rated; contains mild profanity and suggested sexual situations. 107m. DIR: Nicholas Hytner. CAST: Nigel Hawthorne, Helen Mirren, Ian Holm, Amanda Donohoe, Rupert Graves, Rupert Everett. 1994

MADO ★★★1/2 The midlife crisis of a French businessman sparks this complex, intelligent look at social unrest in modern France. In French with English subtitles. Not rated; contains sexual situations. 130m. DIR: Claude Sautet. CAST: Michel Piccoli, Romy Schneider, Charles Denner, Ottavia Piccolo. 1976

MADONNA ❤ Not the singer, but an unimaginative twist on *Fatal Attraction*. Rated R for nudity. 92m. DIR: Alain Zaloum. CAST: Deborah Mansy. 1990

MADONNA: INNOCENCE LOST ★★ So-so telling of the phenomenally successful pop star's life features a dead-on performance by Terumi Matthews as Madonna but is sabotaged by a hokey script and clichéd dialogue. Made for TV and based upon the book *Madonna Unauthorized* by Christopher Andersen. Not rated, but features mild profanity and adult situations. 90m. DIR: Bradford May. CAST: Terumi Matthews, Wendie Malick, Jeff Yagher, Diana LeBlanc, Dean Stockwell. 1994

MADOX-01 ★★★ Japanese animation. Havoc ensues when a university student trapped in a high-tech military attack unit (Madox-01) runs afoul of a psychotic tank commander. Superior animation. In Japanese with English subtitles. Not rated, with violence and mild profanity. 48m. DIR: Aramaki Nobuyuki. 1989

MADRON ★★1/2 You've heard of the spaghetti Western. Well here's an Israeli Western. The story involves a nun and a gunslinger who, after a typical wagon-train massacre, are chased by a band of Apaches. The actors are good, but the story is pedestrian. Rated PG. 93m. DIR: Jerry Hopper. CAST: Richard Boone, Leslie Caron, Paul Smith, Gabi Amrani. 1970

MADWOMAN OF CHAILLOT, THE ★★ Self-conscious story about an eccentric who feels the world is better off without the greed of mercenary interests. Everyone looks embarrassed. Rated G because it is completely innocuous. 132m. DIR: Bryan Forbes. CAST: Katharine Hepburn, Charles Boyer, Yul Brynner, Danny Kaye, John Gavin, Nanette Newman, Giulietta Masina, Richard Chamberlain, Edith Evans, Paul Henreid, Donald Pleasence, Margaret Leighton, Oscar Homolka. 1969

MAE WEST ★★★1/2 This TV biography features a very convincing Ann Jillian as siren Mae West. (Some poetic license has been taken in order to make this complimentary to West.) Roddy McDowall, as a female impersonator, trains West to be sultry, alluring, and ultradesirable while James Brolin plays the longtime love who offers her stability. 100m. DIR: Lee Philips. CAST: Ann Jillian, James Brolin, Roddy McDowall, Piper Laurie. 1982

MAEDCHEN IN UNIFORM ★★★★ At once a fascinating and emotionally disturbing film, this German classic turns mainly on the love of a sexually repressed young girl for a compassionate female teacher in a state-run school. Remade in 1958 with Romy Schneider and Lili Palmer. In German with English subtitles. B&W; 90m. DIR: Leontine Sagan. CAST: Emilia Unda, Dorothea Wieck. 1931

MAFIA PRINCESS ❤ Susan Lucci plays the spoiled daughter of a Mafia crime lord. Made for TV. 100m. DIR: Robert Collins. CAST: Tony Curtis, Susan Lucci, Kathleen Widdoes, Chuck Shamata. 1986

MAFIA: THE HISTORY OF THE MOB IN AMERICA ★★ Only an occasionally interesting segment makes this rather repetitive tracing of mob growth watchable. Sections of note include the early days of the Kennedy clan, the failure of Prohibition, and the rise of labor unions. Some graphic images taken from photographs may not be suitable for younger viewers. 200m. DIR: David Royle, Edward Gray, David Meyer. 1993

MAGDALENE ★★ This film plays like a Barbara Cartland romance novel with Nastassja Kinski as a beautiful woman who spurns the love of a powerful baron. Corny. Rated R for nudity. 89m. DIR: Monica Teuber. CAST: Nastassja Kinski, David Warner, Steve Bond, Franco Nero. 1990

MAGIC ★★★1/2 Will make your skin crawl. The slow descent into madness of the main character, Corky (Anthony Hopkins), a ventriloquist-magician, is the most disturbing study in terror to hit the screens since *Psycho*. Rated R. 106m. DIR: Richard Attenborough. CAST: Anthony Hopkins, Burgess Meredith, Ed Lauter, Ann-Margret. 1978 DVD

MAGIC BOW, THE ★★ A superficial film biography of nineteenth-century composer and violinist Niccolo Paganini. The story goes into more detail than necessary about the composer's romance with a wealthy woman. Too many lulls between musical numbers, but the music is gorgeous. B&W; 106m. DIR: Bernard Knowles. CAST: Stewart Granger, Phyllis Calvert, Jean Kent, Cecil Parker, Dennis Price, Yehudi Menuhin. 1946

MAGIC CHRISTIAN, THE ★★★ A now-dated comedy about the world's wealthiest man (Peter Sellers) and his adopted son (Ringo Starr) testing the depths of degradation to which people will plunge themselves for money still has some funny scenes and outrageous cameos by Christopher Lee (as Dracula), Raquel Welch, and Richard Attenborough. Rated PG. 93m. DIR: Joseph McGrath. CAST: Peter Sellers, Ringo Starr, Christopher Lee, Raquel Welch, Richard Attenborough, Yul Brynner. 1970

MAGIC CHRISTMAS TREE, THE 🎬 A laughable effort, with only the most tenuous connection to Christmas. Not rated. 70m. DIR: Richard C. Parish. CAST: Chris Kroegen, Valerie Hobbs, Robert Maffei, Dick Parish, Terry Bradshaw. 1966

MAGIC FLUTE, THE ★★★ Ingmar Bergman's highly imaginative and richly stylized presentation of Mozart's last opera. The camera starts from a position within the audience at an opera house, but after the curtain rises, it moves freely within and around the stage. The adaptation remains highly theatrical, and quite magical, and the music, of course, is glorious. Sung in Swedish with English subtitles. Not rated. 150m. DIR: Ingmar Bergman. 1974 DVD

MAGIC GARDEN, THE ★★★ Charming South African comedy featuring an amateur cast. A sum of money stolen from a church keeps finding its way into the hands of people who need it! A good family movie. Also known as *Pennywhistle Blues*. B&W; 63m. DIR: Donald Swanson. CAST: Tommy Ramokgopa. 1952

MAGIC HUNTER ★★1/2 The director of the arthouse hit *My 20th Century* lets his ambition get the better of him in this inventive but frustrating exercise. At the center is a folk story of a hunter who sells his soul in exchange for seven bullets guaranteed to hit their targets. But the continual jumps between different times and places in this vague political allegory simply wear out the viewer. In Hungarian with English subtitles. Not rated. 106m. DIR: Ildiko Enyedi. CAST: Gary Kemp, Sadie Frost, Alexander Kaidanovsky, Peter Vallai. 1996

MAGIC IN THE MIRROR ★★1/2 This version of *Alice Through the Looking Glass* features colorful characters and enough magical mayhem to entertain kids, but adults will see right through this looking-glass adventure. When young Mary Margaret steps through the antique mirror once owned by her grandmother, she's transported to a magical world. Now Mary Margaret has to find a way back. Rated G. 86m. DIR: Ted Nicolaou. CAST: Jamie Renée Smith, Kevin Wixted, Saxon Trainor, David Brooks. 1996

MAGIC IN THE WATER, THE ★★★1/2 Enjoyable family film about a work-obsessed psychiatrist who doesn't realize what a mess he's making of his life, to say nothing of his relationship with his children, until a magical creature intervenes. Rated PG. 98m. DIR: Rick Stevenson. CAST: Mark Harmon, Harley Jane Kozak, Joshua Jackson, Sarah Wayne. 1995

MAGIC KID ★★★ As the kick-boxing title character, young Ted Jan Roberts does little but frown and fight goons in this pleasant, cartoonish fantasy (which, at times, seems little more than a plug for Universal Studios theme park). The film is rescued from oblivion by jittery Stephen Furst, simply wonderful as the boy's uncle, a washed-up Hollywood agent in debt to mob boss Joseph Campanella. Rated PG for violence. 87m. DIR: Joseph Merhi. CAST: Stephen Furst, Billy Hufsey, Ted Jan Roberts, Shonda Whipple, Joseph Campanella, Don "The Dragon" Wilson. 1993

MAGIC KID 2 ★★1/2 This sequel isn't helped by the clearly inexperienced direction of star Stephen Furst (who also cowrote the simplistic script). Kickboxing youngster and his hapless uncle are now stuck in the Hollywood star-making system. Rated PG for mild violence. 86m. DIR: Stephen Furst. CAST: Stephen Furst, Ted Jan Roberts, Jennifer Savidge, Dana Barron, Donald Gibb. 1994

MAGIC OF LASSIE, THE ★★1/2 Like the Disney live-action films of yore, *The Magic of Lassie* tries to incorporate a little of everything: heartwarming drama, suspense, comedy, and even music. But here the formula is bland. The story is okay, but it is all too long. Rated G. 100m. DIR: Don Chaffey. CAST: James Stewart, Mickey Rooney, Pernell Roberts, Stephanie Zimbalist, Michael Sharrett, Alice Faye, Gene Evans, Lane Davies, Mike Mazurki, Lassie. 1978

MAGIC STONE, THE ★★1/2 Not one of writer-director Pamela Berger's best. She could not overcome a low budget in this telling of an Irish slave brought to North America in the late tenth century by Vikings. Based on historical research and actual archaeological findings, this sweet film has much to say about cultural acceptance. Too many directorial glitches undermine the script's romance and adventure. Rated PD-M for violence. 95m. DIR: Pamela Berger. CAST: Christopher Johnson, Robert McDonough, Eva Kim, Jonah Ming Lee, Gino Montesinos, Robert Mason Ham. 1994

MAGIC SWORD, THE ★★ Young Gary Lockwood is on a quest to free an imprisoned princess and fights his way through an ogre, dragon, and other uninspired monsters with the help of the witch in the family, Estelle Winwood. Basil Rathbone makes a fine old evil sorcerer, relishing his foul deeds and eagerly planning new transgressions. The kids might like it, but it's laughable. 80m. DIR: Bert I. Gordon. CAST: Gary Lockwood, Anne Helm, Basil Rathbone, Estelle Winwood, Liam Sullivan. 1962

MAGIC TOWN ★★ After successfully collaborating with Frank Capra on some of his finest films, writer Robert Riskin teamed with director William Wellman for this mildly entertaining but preachy tale. An advertising executive (James Stewart) finds the perfect American community, which is turned topsyturvy when the secret gets out. B&W; 103m. DIR: William Wellman. CAST: James Stewart, Jane Wyman, Ned Sparks. 1947

MAGIC VOYAGE, THE ★★ This mediocre animated film is meant to be a history lesson about Christopher Columbus's voyage to America, but it's actually just a love story between a wood worm and a firefly. Rated G. 80m. DIR: Michael Schoemann. 1994 DVD

MAGICAL MYSTERY TOUR ★★ This is a tour by bus and by mind. Unfortunately, the minds involved must have been distorted at the time that the film was made. Occasional bursts of wit and imagination come through, but sometimes this chunk of psychedelic pretension is a crashing bore. Good songs, though. 60m. **DIR:** The Beatles. **CAST:** The Beatles, Bonzo Dog Band. **1967 DVD**

MAGICAL TWILIGHT ★★ A pair of good student witches are sent to Earth as part of their final exam while, unknown to them, a third witch (this one evil) also has been sent for the same purpose, but with an opposing goal in mind. In Japanese with English subtitles. Not rated; contains nudity and sexual situations. 25m. **DIR:** Toshiaki Kobayashi. **1994**

MAGICIAN, THE ★★★ Dark and somber parable deals with the quest for an afterlife by focusing on confrontation between a mesmerist and a magician. This shadowy allegory may not be everyone's idea of entertainment, but the richness of ideas and the excellent acting of director Ingmar Bergman's fine stable of actors make this a compelling film. Swedish, subtitled in English. B&W; 102m. **DIR:** Ingmar Bergman. **CAST:** Max von Sydow, Ingrid Thulin, Gunnar Björnstrand, Bibi Andersson. **1959**

MAGICIAN OF LUBLIN, THE 💗 Superficial adaptation of Isaac Bashevis Singer's novel about a Jewish traveling magician in nineteenth-century Europe. Rated R for nudity. 105m. **DIR:** Menahem Golan. **CAST:** Alan Arkin, Louise Fletcher, Valerie Perrine, Shelley Winters, Lou Jacobi, Warren Berlinger, Lisa Whelchel. **1979**

MAGNETIC MONSTER, THE ★★★ Intelligent sci-fi thriller with a unique monster—an energy-consuming isotope (created by research scientists, of course) that turns energy into matter and doubles in size every twelve hours. B&W; 76m. **DIR:** Curt Siodmak. **CAST:** Richard Carlson, King Donovan, Jean Byron, Harry Ellerbe, Strother Martin. **1953**

MAGNIFICENT AMBERSONS, THE ★★★★★ Orson Welles's legendary depiction of the decline of a wealthy midwestern family and the comeuppance of its youngest member is a definite must-see motion picture. Much has been made about the callous editing of the final print by studio henchmen, but that doesn't change the total impact. It's still a classic. Special notice must be given to Welles and cameraman Stanley Cortez for the artistic, almost portrait-like, look of the film. B&W; 88m. **DIR:** Orson Welles. **CAST:** Joseph Cotten, Tim Holt, Agnes Moorehead. **1942**

MAGNIFICENT OBSESSION ★★★ Rock Hudson, a drunken playboy, blinds Jane Wyman in an auto accident. Stricken, he reforms and becomes a doctor in order to restore her sight in this melodramatic tearjerker. First filmed in 1935, with Irene Dunne and Robert Taylor. 108m. **DIR:** Douglas Sirk. **CAST:** Jane Wyman, Rock Hudson, Agnes Moorehead, Otto Kruger. **1954**

•**MAGNIFICENT SEVEN, THE (TV SERIES)** ★★★1/2 After the Civil War, a band of renegade Confederate soldiers terrorize a community consisting of Seminole Indians and runaway slaves, and it's up to the title characters to ride to the rescue. Because this pilot for the television series bears the burden of introducing its main characters, the first half is slow. But once the seven heroes charge into

action, the plot picks up. Ron Perlman, as a "spiritual man," stands out in a surprisingly solid cast. Made for TV. 90m. **DIR:** Geoff Murphy. **CAST:** Michael Biehn, Eric Close, Ron Perlman, Dale Midkiff, Andrew Ravovit, Anthony Starke, Rick Worthy, Kurtwood Smith, Laurie Holden, Tony Burton, Rick Greyeyes, Ned Romero. **1999**

MAGNIFICENT SEVEN, THE ★★★★ Japanese director Akira Kurosawa's *The Seven Samurai* served as the inspiration for this enjoyable Western, directed by John Sturges (*The Great Escape*). It's the rousing tale of how a group of American gunfighters come to the aid of a village of Mexican farmers plagued by bandits. 126m. **DIR:** John Sturges. **CAST:** Yul Brynner, Steve McQueen, Charles Bronson, James Coburn, Eli Wallach, Robert Vaughn. **1960**

MAGNIFICENT YANKEE, THE ★★★1/2 Moving film biography of the Washington years of Oliver Wendell Holmes. The movie opens with his appointment to the Supreme Court in 1902 (at age 61) and closes just before his retirement in 1933. This also happens to be a charming love story. Louis Calhern was Oscar nominated for his portrayal. B&W; 80m. **DIR:** John Sturges. **CAST:** Louis Calhern, Ann Harding, Eduard Franz, Philip Ober, Ian Wolfe, Richard Anderson, Jimmy Lydon. **1950**

•**MAGNOLIA** ★★★ This brilliant mess interweaves the lives of a dozen characters during a random twenty-four-hour period in the San Fernando Valley. By turns fascinating and compelling, tiresome and repulsive, audacious and self-indulgent, the film is too long, and enduring the final act will be more than many viewers can stand. The plot explores the notion that we're all interconnected by random events, spontaneous friendships, and undisclosed blood ties. Interesting thought, but the film is a series of one-acts in search of a binding thread that ultimately isn't present. Rated R for profanity and drug use. 180m. **DIR:** P. T. Anderson. **CAST:** Jeremy Blackman, Tom Cruise, Philip Baker Hall, Philip Seymour Hoffman, William H. Macy, Julianne Moore, John C. Reilly, Jason Robards Jr., Melora Walters. **1999**

MAGNUM FORCE ★★★ This is the second and least enjoyable of the five Dirty Harry films. Harry (Clint Eastwood) must deal with vigilante cops as well as the usual big-city scum. Clint is iron-jawed and athletic, but the film still lacks something. Rated R for language, violence, nudity, and gore. 124m. **DIR:** Ted Post. **CAST:** Clint Eastwood, Hal Holbrook, David Soul, Tim Matheson, Robert Urich, Suzanne Somers. **1973**

MAHABHARATA, THE ★★★★ An exquisite six-part Shakespearean-style production made in Paris for public television of the eighteen book Sanskrit epic of mankind's search for Dharma (truth). Dealing with the fortunes of rival ruling families, the Kauravas and Pandavas, this tale weaves historical elements and myth to expose man's ultimate choice between destiny and freedom. 222m. **DIR:** Peter Brook. **CAST:** Robert Langton-Lloyd. **1989**

MAHLER ★★1/2 Ken Russell's fantasy film about the biography of composer Gustav Mahler. Robert Powell's portrayal of Mahler as a man consumed with passion and ambition is a brilliant one.

Georgina Hale as Alma, Mahler's wife, is also well played. Unfortunately, the cast cannot give coherence to the script. 115m. **DIR:** Ken Russell. **CAST:** Robert Powell, Georgina Hale, Richard Morant. **1974** DVD

MAHOGANY ★★ The highlight of this unimpressive melodrama is Diana Ross's lovely wardrobe. She plays a poor girl who makes it big as a famous model and, later, dress designer after Anthony Perkins discovers her. This one jerks more yawns than tears. Rated PG. 109m. **DIR:** Berry Gordy. **CAST:** Diana Ross, Anthony Perkins, Billy Dee Williams. **1975**

MAID, THE ★★ Businessman Martin Sheen falls for businesswoman Jacqueline Bisset and becomes her maid to get closer to her in this sometimes predictable, but always entertaining, romantic comedy. Rated PG for mild profanity. 91m. **DIR:** Ian Toynton. **CAST:** Martin Sheen, Jacqueline Bisset, Jean-Pierre Cassel, James Faulkner. **1991**

MAID TO ORDER ★★1/2 This modern retelling of the Cinderella fable isn't much of a star vehicle for Ally Sheedy, who's constantly upstaged by the supporting players. She's a spoiled little rich girl whose hip fairy godmother (Beverly D'Angelo) turns her into a nonentity, forced to work for an honest dollar. Rated PG for language and brief nudity. 96m. **DIR:** Amy Jones. **CAST:** Ally Sheedy, Beverly D'Angelo, Michael Ontkean, Valerie Perrine, Dick Shawn, Tom Skerritt. **1987**

MAID'S NIGHT OUT, THE ★★ This energetic comedy tells of a millionaire's son (Allan Lane) who becomes a milkman for a month to win a bet with his self-made millionaire father (George Irving). Along the way, he meets Joan Fontaine. Lowbrow but fun. B&W; 64m. **DIR:** Ben Holmes. **CAST:** Joan Fontaine, Hedda Hopper, Allan "Rocky" Lane, Cecil Kellaway. **1938**

MAIN EVENT, THE 🎬 A limp boxing comedy that tried unsuccessfully to reunite the stars of *What's Up Doc?* Rated PG. 112m. **DIR:** Howard Zieff. **CAST:** Barbra Streisand, Ryan O'Neal, Paul Sand. **1979**

MAIN STREET TO BROADWAY ★★ The story of a young playwright's rise to success on Broadway is nothing you haven't seen before. The only attraction here is an endless array of cameo appearances by Ethel and Lionel Barrymore, Shirley Booth, Rex Harrison, Rodgers and Hammerstein, Mary Martin, Lilli Palmer, Cornel Wilde, and other notables of the theater world. B&W; 102m. **DIR:** Tay Garnett. **CAST:** Tom Murton, Mary Murphy, Agnes Moorehead, Rosemary DeCamp, Tallulah Bankhead. **1953**

MAITRESSE ★★★ A normal young man becomes involved with a professional dominatrix. Odd film is neither exploitative nor pornographic, but it sure is peculiar. In French with English subtitles. Not rated, but the subject matter marks it as adults-only territory. 110m. **DIR:** Barbet Schroeder. **CAST:** Gérard Depardieu, Bulle Ogier, Andre Rouyer. **1975**

MAJOR BARBARA ★★★1/2 In the title role as a Salvation Army officer, Wendy Hiller heads a matchless cast in this thoughtful film of George Bernard Shaw's comedy about the power of money and the evils of poverty. Rex Harrison, as her fiancé, and Robert Newton, as a hard case with doubts about the

honesty and motives of do-gooders, are excellent. B&W; 136m. **DIR:** Gabriel Pascal. **CAST:** Wendy Hiller, Rex Harrison, Robert Morley, Robert Newton, Emlyn Williams, Sybil Thorndike, Deborah Kerr. **1941**

MAJOR DUNDEE ★★★ This is a flawed but watchable Western directed with typical verve by Sam Peckinpah. The plot follows a group of Confederate prisoners who volunteer to go into Mexico and track down a band of rampaging Apache Indians. 124m. **DIR:** Sam Peckinpah. **CAST:** Charlton Heston, Richard Harris, James Coburn, Jim Hutton, Warren Oates, Ben Johnson. **1965**

MAJOR LEAGUE ★★★1/2 In this often funny but clichéd baseball comedy, the Cleveland Indians find themselves headed for oblivion when the new owner, former show girl Margaret Whitton, decides to put together the worst possible team. Tom Berenger, Charlie Sheen, and Corbin Bernsen are fine as three inept players, and character actor James Gammon shines as their coach. Rated R for profanity and violence. 95m. **DIR:** David S. Ward. **CAST:** Tom Berenger, Charlie Sheen, Corbin Bernsen, Margaret Whitton, James Gammon. **1989**

MAJOR LEAGUE II ★★ The sequel to the 1989 baseball hit is more of the same, with an almost identical plot and nearly the entire cast reprising their original roles (Omar Epps replaces Wesley Snipes). This time, though, the zest is gone—everyone looks tired and just a little embarrassed. Rated PG, but with profanity some may find offensive. 105m. **DIR:** David S. Ward. **CAST:** Charlie Sheen, Tom Berenger, Corbin Bernsen, James Gammon, David Keith, Omar Epps. **1994** DVD

MAJOR PAYNE ★★ Gung ho Marine is discharged by the military—"there's no one left to kill, he's killed them all"—and takes a job training junior ROTC at a private academy in this predictable band-of-misfits comedy. Rated PG-13 for language. 97m. **DIR:** Nick Castle. **CAST:** Damon Wayans, Karyn Parsons, William Hickey, Michael Ironside, Albert Hall. **1995** DVD

•**MAJOR ROCK** ★★ The plot about a rescue team sent to save five centerfolds and the president's daughter from South American terrorists is a thin excuse for plentiful sex and nudity (even more in the unrated version, which is 12 minutes longer). Rated R for nudity, sexual situations, and profanity. 78m. **DIR:** Charles Allen. **CAST:** Tabitha Stevens, Don Fisher, Buck Adams. **1999**

MAJORETTES, THE ★★ Written before *Halloween* but not produced until well after that film, this slasher film has an edge on the competition in that it has a plot that involves more than just the killings of the titular cheerleaders. Scripted by John Russo. Rated R for violence, profanity, and nudity. 92m. **DIR:** Bill Hinzman. **CAST:** Kevin Kindlon, Terrie Godfrey, Sueanne Seamens. **1987**

MAJORITY OF ONE, A ★★★★ In spite of miscasting, the charm and wit of Leonard Spiegelgass's Broadway play shine through. Rosalind Russell tries to play a typical Jewish mother and this just calls attention to her WASPishness. Sir Alec Guinness drops his "l's" and rolls his "r's" as a Japanese gentleman and gets laughs in the wrong places. Very predictable but fun. 156m. **DIR:** Mervyn LeRoy. **CAST:** Rosalind Russell, Alec Guinness, Madlyn Rhue, Ray Danton, Mae Questel, Alan Hugeny, Alan Mowbray, Gary Vinson, Marc Mamo. **1961**

MAKE A WISH ❤ Basil Rathbone is a jolly good composer. Henry Armetta, Leon Errol, and Donald Meek want to steal Basil's latest operetta. B&W; 80m. **DIR:** Kurt Neumann. **CAST:** Bobby Breen, Basil Rathbone, Marion Claire, Henry Armetta, Leon Errol, Donald Meek. **1937**

MAKE HASTE TO LIVE ★★★ A mobster, framed for killing his wife, is finally released. Now he wants revenge from the one woman who escaped his grasp by outsmarting him. Compact, chilling thriller. B&W; 90m. **DIR:** William A. Seiter. **CAST:** Dorothy McGuire, Stephen McNally, Edgar Buchanan. **1954**

MAKE ME AN OFFER ❤ A young woman makes her way to the top by becoming a quick study in the California real estate business. Made for television. 100m. **DIR:** Jerry Paris. **CAST:** Susan Blakely, Patrick O'Neal, Stella Stevens, John Rubinstein. **1980**

MAKE MINE MINK ★★★★ Bright dialogue and clever situations make this crazy comedy from Britain highly enjoyable. An ex-officer, a dowager, and a motley crew of fur thieves team to commit larceny for charity. Gap-toothed Terry-Thomas is in top form in this one. 100m. **DIR:** Robert Asher. **CAST:** Terry-Thomas, Athene Seyler, Billie Whitelaw. **1960**

MAKE ROOM FOR TOMORROW ★★★ More a collection of mildly humorous events than an out-and-out comedy. Victor Lanoux plays a father going through a midlife crisis. Rated R for language and nudity. 104m. **DIR:** Peter Kassovitz. **CAST:** Victor Lanoux, Jane Birkin, Georges Wilson. **1982**

MAKE THEM DIE SLOWLY ❤ South American cannibals. Not rated; contains nudity, profanity, and extreme violence. 92m. **DIR:** Umberto Lenzi. **CAST:** John Morghen, Lorainne DeSelle. **1980 DVD**

MAKING CONTACT ★★ After his father dies, a little boy begins to exhibit telekinetic powers and begins giving life to his favorite toys. Obviously aimed at children, this film is quite imaginative. 82m. **DIR:** Roland Emmerich. **CAST:** Joshua Morell, Eve Kryll. **1985**

MAKING LOVE ★★ Kate Jackson discovers that her husband (Michael Ontkean) is in love with another … man (Harry Hamlin). Rated R because of adult subject matter, profanity, and implicit sexual activity. 113m. **DIR:** Arthur Hiller. **CAST:** Kate Jackson, Michael Ontkean, Harry Hamlin. **1982**

MAKING MR. RIGHT ★★1/2 This mild satire, about a female image consultant who falls for the android she's supposed to be promoting, doesn't come close to the energy level of director Susan Seidelman's *Desperately Seeking Susan*. Rated PG-13. 98m. **DIR:** Susan Seidelman. **CAST:** John Malkovich, Ann Magnuson, Ben Masters, Glenne Headly, Laurie Metcalf, Polly Bergen, Hart Bochner. **1987**

MAKING THE GRADE ★★1/2 A rich kid pays a surrogate to attend prep school for him. Typical teen-exploitation fare. Rated R. 105m. **DIR:** Dorian Walker. **CAST:** Judd Nelson, Jonna Lee, Carey Scott. **1984**

MALAREK ★★★ Victor Malarek's biographical novel (*Hey, Malarek*) exposes the abuse of teens in the Montreal Detention Center. As a rookie reporter, Malarek witnessed the cold-blooded shooting of an escaped teen. His investigation inspired his book and this film. Rated R for violence and profanity. 105m. **DIR:** Roger Cardinal. **CAST:** Elias Koteas, Kerrie Keane, Al Waxman, Michael Sarrazin. **1988**

MALCOLM ★★★1/2 An absolutely charming Australian entry that swept that country's Oscars the year it was released. Colin Friels has the title role as an emotionally immature young man who, after he loses his job with a local rapid-transit company (for building his own tram with company parts), finds himself among thieves and loves it. 90m. **DIR:** Nadia Tess. **CAST:** Colin Friels, John Hargreaves, Lindy Davies, Chris Haywood. **1986**

MALCOLM X ★★★★★ Writer-director Spike Lee's most passionate film may also be his greatest. In chronicling the life of the black activist from his Harlem gangster years to his 1965 assassination at the age of 39 by followers of Elijah Muhammad, Lee pays scrupulous attention to detail and avoids the rambling, self-indulgent qualities that hampered his previous projects. At the heart of the film is a superb performance in the title role by Denzel Washington. Brilliant! Rated PG-13 for violence, suggested sex, and profanity. 193m. **DIR:** Spike Lee. **CAST:** Denzel Washington, Spike Lee, Angela Bassett, Albert Hall, Al Freeman Jr., Delroy Lindo, Kate Vernon, Lonette McKee. **1992 DVD**

MALE AND FEMALE ★★★ Cecil B. DeMille yarn from his best period of exotic, erotic fables. Loosely derived from James M. Barrie's play, *The Admirable Crichton*. For DeMille fans, it's quintessential fun. Silent. B&W; 100m. **DIR:** Cecil B. DeMille. **CAST:** Gloria Swanson, Thomas Meighan, Lila Lee. **1919 DVD**

•MALEVOLENCE ★★ Unpleasant film about a racist convict who is used as a pawn in the assassination of a black politician. Rated R for profanity, violence, and sexuality. 95m. **DIR:** Belle Avery. **CAST:** Joe Cortese, Michael McGrady, Brion James, Lou Rawls, Michael Stone. **1996**

MALIBU BIKINI SHOP, THE ❤ An exploitative romp about two brothers who inherit a bikini shop. Rated R for nudity and profanity. 90m. **DIR:** David Wechter. **CAST:** Michael David Wright, Bruce Greenwood, Barbara Horan, Debra Blee, Jay Robinson. **1985**

MALIBU EXPRESS ❤ The amazing thing about this film is how it managed to get an R rating when it is clearly soft porn. 101m. **DIR:** Andy Sidaris. **CAST:** Darby Hinton, Sybil Danning, Shelley Taylor Morgan, Brett Clark, Art Metrano. **1984**

MALICE ★★★ When a serial killer begins murdering female students in a New England college town, the institution's mild-mannered dean becomes involved in the investigation while simultaneously wondering about the cocky surgeon who has taken a room in his house. And when the dean's wife unexpectedly winds up in the hospital, things *really* get interesting. This thriller starts off extremely well, but then settles into television-style drama. Even so, it never gets boring. Rated R for profanity, violence, and simulated sex. 106m. **DIR:** Harold Becker. **CAST:** Alec Baldwin, Nicole Kidman, Bill Pullman, Bebe

Neuwirth, George C. Scott, Anne Bancroft, Peter Gallagher, Josef Sommer. **1993 DVD**

MALICIOUS (1974) ★★★1/2 Italian beauty Laura Antonelli is hired as a housekeeper for a widower and his three sons. Not surprisingly, she becomes the object of affection for all four men—particularly 14-year-old Nino. Rated R. 98m. **DIR:** Salvatore Samperi. **CAST:** Laura Antonelli, Turi Ferro, Alessandro Momo, Tina Aumont. **1974**

MALICIOUS (1995) ★★ Only for people who want to see Molly Ringwald naked. She plays a complete psycho trying to land a college-baseball player with whom she shared a one-night stand. An unimaginative *Fatal Attraction* rip-off that is hardly enhanced by Ringwald's mouth-breathing, out-of-control harpy. Rated R for profanity, sexual situations, nudity, and violence. 92m. **DIR:** Ian Corson. **CAST:** Molly Ringwald, John Vernon, Patrick McGaw, Sarah Lassez. **1995**

MALL RATS 🖤 In this crude, dull misadventure, two guys spend a day at a shopping mall trying to reconcile with the girlfriends who dumped them. Rated R for profanity, nudity, and sex. 97m. **DIR:** Kevin Smith. **CAST:** Jason Lee, Jeremy London, Shannen Doherty, Claire Forlani, Michael Rooker. **1995 DVD**

MALONE ★★★1/2 In this modern-day Western, Burt Reynolds is in top form as Malone, an ex-CIA hit man on the run. Underneath all the car chases, big-bang explosions, and the blitz fire of automatic weapons is the simplest of all B-Western plots—in which a former gunfighter is forced out of retirement by the plight of settlers forced off their land by black-hatted villains. Rated R for profanity, violence, and suggested sex. 92m. **DIR:** Harley Cokliss. **CAST:** Burt Reynolds, Cliff Robertson, Kenneth McMillan, Scott Wilson, Lauren Hutton, Cynthia Gibb. **1987**

MALOU ★★★ Moving drama of a woman's search for the truth about the marriage between her French mother and a German Jew during Hitler's terrifying reign. The story unfolds through a rich tapestry of flashbacks. In German with English subtitles. Not rated. 94m. **DIR:** Jeanine Meerapfel. **CAST:** Ingrid Caven, Helmut Griem. **1983**

MALTA STORY, THE ★★★ Set in 1942, this is about British pluck on the island of Malta while the British were under siege from the Axis forces and the effect the war has on private lives. Flight Lieutenant Ross's (Alec Guinness) love for a native girl (Muriel Pavlow) goes unrequited when his commanding officer (Anthony Steel) sends him on a dangerous mission. B&W; 103m. **DIR:** Brian Desmond Hurst. **CAST:** Alec Guinness, Jack Hawkins, Anthony Steel, Muriel Pavlow. **1953**

MALTESE FALCON, THE ★★★★★ One of the all-time great movies, John Huston's first effort as a director is the definitive screen version of Dashiell Hammett's crime story. In a maze of double crosses and back stabbing, Humphrey Bogart, as Sam Spade, fights to get hold of a black bird, "the stuff that dreams are made of." B&W; 100m. **DIR:** John Huston. **CAST:** Humphrey Bogart, Mary Astor, Sydney Greenstreet, Peter Lorre, Elisha Cook Jr., Ward Bond. **1941 DVD**

MAMA, THERE'S A MAN IN YOUR BED ★★★★ This is a somewhat unlikely but sweet and funny romantic tale of a white Parisian executive and his unexpected love for the black cleaning woman at his office. Daniel Auteuil (the slow-witted nephew Ugolin in *Jean de Florette*) stars. In French with English subtitles. Not rated but of a PG-13 quality, with adult situations. 108m. **DIR:** Coline Serreau. **CAST:** Daniel Auteuil, Fir-mine Richard. **1990**

MAMA TURNS 100 ★★★ A comparatively light-hearted attack on Franco's Spain from Carlos Saura. He reunites the cast of his 1972 *Anna and the Wolves* for this similar story of a greedy family battling among themselves. The humor is hit-and-miss, and the social analysis may be lost on American audiences. In Spanish with English subtitles. Not rated. 115m. **DIR:** Carlos Saura. **CAST:** Geraldine Chaplin. **1979**

MAMBO ★★ Dated B movie features Silvano Mangano as an impoverished Venetian who seeks wealth and fame, first as a dancer and then as a count's wife. She has an annoying habit of thinking aloud rather than showing her emotions. B&W; 94m. **DIR:** Robert Rossen. **CAST:** Silvana Mangano, Michael Rennie, Shelley Winters, Vittorio Gassman. **1954**

MAMBO KINGS, THE ★★★★ Oscar Hijuelos's Pulitzer Prize–winning novel of Cuban immigrants, has been brought to the screen with great passion, energy and style. An engrossing story of brotherhood and cultural pride, and a vibrant showcase for magnificent Cuban music, it spotlights Armand Assante and Antonio Banderas, who charms in his first English-language role. Rated R, with profanity, violence, and nudity. 125m. **DIR:** Arne Glimcher. **CAST:** Armand Assante, Antonio Banderas, Cathy Moriarty, Maruschka Detmers, Desi Arnaz Jr., Tito Puente. **1992**

MAME 🖤 You won't love Lucy in this one. Rated PG. 131m. **DIR:** Gene Saks. **CAST:** Lucille Ball, Robert Preston, Jane Connell, Bea Arthur. **1974**

MAMA DRACULA 🖤 A horror–black comedy that fails on both counts. Not rated; contains nudity and adult situations. 93m. **DIR:** Boris Szulzinger. **CAST:** Louise Fletcher, Maria Schneider, Marc-Henri Wajnberg, Alexander Wanberg, Jess Hahn. **1988**

•**MAMMA ROMA** ★★★ Anna Magnani's larger-than-life performance is the best reason to see this somewhat dated melodrama. She plays a prostitute in Rome who tries to get out of the business and raise her son to be a respectable middle-class citizen. Filmmaker Pier Paolo Pasolini has a great eye for location filming. In Italian with English subtitles. B&W; 110m. **DIR:** Pier Paolo Pasolini. **CAST:** Anna Magnani, Franco Citti, Ettore Garofolo. **1962**

MAN, A WOMAN AND A BANK, A ★★ An odd little caper flick that never quite gets off the ground. A couple of guys decide to rob a bank via computer, and—of course—things don't work out as planned. Rated PG. 100m. **DIR:** Noel Black. **CAST:** Donald Sutherland, Brooke Adams, Paul Mazursky. **1979**

MAN ALONE, A ★★★ Ray Milland's first directorial effort finds him hiding from a lynch mob in a small Western town. And who is he hiding with? The sheriff's daughter! Not too bad, as Westerns go. 96m. **DIR:**

Ray Milland. **CAST:** Ray Milland, Mary Murphy, Ward Bond, Raymond Burr, Lee Van Cleef. **1955**

MAN AND A WOMAN, A ★★★★ This is a superbly written, directed, and acted story of a young widow and widower who fall in love. Anouk Aimée and race-car driver Jean-Louis Trintignant set this film on fire. A hit in 1966 and still a fine picture. French, dubbed into English. 102m. **DIR:** Claude Lelouch. **CAST:** Anouk Aimée, Jean-Louis Trintignant, Pierre Barouh, Valerie Lagrange. **1966**

MAN AND A WOMAN, A: 20 YEARS LATER 🎬 The director of this movie took his 1966 *A Man and a Woman* and, after twenty years, assembled the origi-nal lead actors and created a monster. In French. Rated PG. 112m. **DIR:** Claude Lelouch. **CAST:** Anouk Aimée, Jean-Louis Trintignant, Richard Berry. **1986**

MAN AND BOY ★★1/2 Bill Cosby and his family try to make a go of it by homesteading on the prairie. The story provides ample opportunity for some Cos-byesque explanations about the black experience of that period. Rated G. 98m. **DIR:** E. W. Swackhamer. **CAST:** Bill Cosby, Gloria Foster, George Spell, Leif Er-ickson, Yaphet Kotto, Douglas Turner Ward, John An-derson, Henry Silva, Dub Taylor. **1971**

MAN AND THE MONSTER, THE ★★ The Mexican monster movies that were made in the late 1950s at the Churubusco-Azteca Studios are an acquired taste. Their crisp, black-and-white photography is richly atmospheric, but production values are mea-ger and acting is mediocre. This one, a Jekyll-Hyde potboiler involving a musician who changes into a hairy beast at inconvenient times, is directed by the man who made this odd subgenre's best films. B&W; 74m. **DIR:** Rafael Baledon. **CAST:** Enrique Rabal, Abel Salazar. **1958**

MAN BEAST 🎬 A search for the Abominable Snow-man. B&W; 72m. **DIR:** Jerry Warren. **CAST:** Rock Madi-son, Virginia Maynor. **1955**

MAN BITES DOG ★★ Several brilliant cinematic shots cannot justify this sick spoof of the documen-tary. A camera crew follows a cold-blooded killer on his brutal daily routine. Unsettling and difficult to watch. Rated NC-17, it contains countless acts of vio-lence as well as profanity, sex, and gore. In French with English subtitles. B&W; 96m. **DIR:** Rémy Bel-vaux. **CAST:** Benoit Poelvoorde, Rémy Belvaux, Jenny Drye, Malou Madou. **1992**

MAN CALLED ADAM, A 🎬 A world-class jazz trum-pet player can't live with the guilt of accidentally killing his wife and child. B&W; 103m. **DIR:** Leo Penn. **CAST:** Sammy Davis Jr., Louis Armstrong, Peter Law-ford, Mel Torme, Frank Sinatra Jr., Lola Falana, Ossie Davis, Cicely Tyson. **1966**

MAN CALLED FLINTSTONE, A ★★★1/2 The Ralph Kramden and Ed Norton of the kiddie-set, Fred Flintstone and Barney Rubble are featured in this full-length animated cartoon. Fred takes over for lookalike secret agent, Rack Slag, and goes after the "Green Goose" and his henchmen, SMIRK agents. Great fun for the kids. 87m. **DIR:** William Hanna, Joseph Barbera. **1966**

MAN CALLED HORSE, A ★★★ Richard Harris (in one of his best roles) portrays an English aristocrat who's enslaved and treated like a pack animal by

Sioux Indians in the Dakotas. He loses his veneer of sophistication and finds the core of his manhood. This strong film offers an unusually realistic depic-tion of American Indian life. Rated PG. 114m. **DIR:** Elliot Silverstein. **CAST:** Richard Harris, Judith Ander-son, Jean Gascon, Corinna Tsopei, Dub Taylor. **1970**

MAN CALLED NOON, THE ★★★★ The Louis L'Amour classic remains faithful to the book. A bounty hunter and a female rancher help Jubal Noon, a gunfighter with amnesia, unravel his iden-tity while seeking vengeance for the deaths of his wife and child. Great photography, direction, and score make this one of the best. Rated R for violence. 90m. **DIR:** Peter Collinson. **CAST:** Richard Crenna, Stephen Boyd, Farley Granger, Rosanna Schiaffino, Patty Shepard. **1974**

MAN CALLED PETER, A ★★★1/2 This warm, win-ning film biography tells the story of Scottish clergy-man Peter Marshall, who was appointed chaplain of the U.S. Senate. Beautifully played by Richard Todd and Jean Peters. 117m. **DIR:** Henry Koster. **CAST:** Richard Todd, Jean Peters, Marjorie Rambeau, Les Tremayne. **1955**

MAN CALLED RAGE, A 🎬 Rage, a Mad Max–type of character, leads a team to find uranium deposits that are vital to the survival of the human race. Rated PG for violence. 90m. **DIR:** Anthony Richmond. **CAST:** Conrad Nichols. **1987**

MAN CALLED SARGE, A 🎬 World War II misfits against Rommel's desert forces. Rated PG-13. 88m. **DIR:** Stuart Gillard. **CAST:** Gary Kroeger, Gretchen Ger-man, Jennifer Runyon, Marc Singer. **1990**

MAN CALLED TIGER, A 🎬 Fist-and-foot nonsense about the Chinese Mafia. Rated R for violence and nudity. 70m. **DIR:** Lo Wei. **CAST:** Wang Yu. **1973**

●MAN ESCAPED, A ★★★★ Engrossing drama based on the true story of a French resistance offi-cer's escape from a Nazi prison. Director Robert Bresson heightens our participation with attention to the most minute details, including a detailed re-construction of the actual prison cell. In French with English subtitles. Not rated; contains no objection-able material. B&W; 102m. **DIR:** Robert Bresson. **CAST:** Francois Leterrier, Charles Le Clainche, Roland Monot. **1956**

MAN FACING SOUTHEAST ★★★1/2 A haunting, eerie mystery in which an unknown man—possibly an alien—inexplicably appears in the midst of a Buenos Aires psychiatric hospital. Rich with Christ-ian symbolism, this film leaves one wondering who is really sick—society or those society finds insane. Some nudity and sexual situations. In Spanish with English subtitles. 105m. **DIR:** Eliseo Subiela. **CAST:** Lorenzo Quinteros, Hugo Soto. **1987**

MAN FOR ALL SEASONS, A ★★★★★ This splen-did film, about Sir Thomas More's heartfelt refusal to help King Henry VIII break with the Catholic church and form the Church of England, won the best-pic-ture Oscar in 1966. Paul Scofield, who is magnificent in the title role, also won best actor. Directed by Fred Zinnemann and written by Robert Bolt, the picture also benefits from memorable supporting perfor-mances by an all-star cast. 120m. **DIR:** Fred Zinnemann. **CAST:** Paul Scofield, Wendy Hiller, Robert Shaw, Orson Welles, Susannah York. 1966 DVD

MAN FROM ATLANTIS, THE ★★1/2 The pilot for the 1977 TV sci-fi series. Patrick Duffy plays the man from beneath the waves, recruited by the navy to retrieve a top-secret submarine. Belinda Montgomery is the marine biologist who holds Duffy's reins. 60m. **DIR:** Lee H. Katzin. **CAST:** Patrick Duffy, Belinda Montgomery, Victor Buono, Art Lund, Lawrence Pressman. 1977

MAN FROM BEYOND, THE ★★★ Legendary escape artist Harry Houdini wrote and starred in this timeless story of a man encased in a block of ice for one hundred years who is discovered, thawed out, and thrust into twentieth-century life. While the special effects lack sophistication and the acting seems pretty broad, this is one of the few existing examples of Houdini's film work. Silent. B&W; 50m. **DIR:** Burton King. **CAST:** Harry Houdini. 1921

MAN FROM COLORADO, THE ★★★ A great cast and solid performances elevate this post–Civil War psychological Western about a former northern colonel (Glenn Ford) who becomes a federal judge in Colorado. William Holden plays his friend. 99m. **DIR:** Henry Levin. **CAST:** Glenn Ford, William Holden, Ellen Drew, Ray Collins, Edgar Buchanan, Jerome Courtland, Denver Pyle. 1948

MAN FROM LARAMIE, THE ★★★1/2 Magnificent Western has James Stewart as a stranger who finds himself at odds with a powerful ranching family. The patriarch (Donald Crisp) is going blind, so the running of the ranch is left to his psychotic son (Alex Nicol) and longtime ranch foreman (Arthur Kennedy). Possibly the summit of director Anthony Mann's career; certainly Stewart's finest Western performance. 101m. **DIR:** Anthony Mann. **CAST:** James Stewart, Arthur Kennedy, Donald Crisp, Alex Nicol, Cathy O'Donnell, Jack Elam. 1955 DVD

MAN FROM LEFT FIELD, THE ★★★ Burt Reynolds directed and stars in this heartfelt made-for-TV drama about a homeless man who ends up coaching a ragtag kids' baseball team. Although a mystery to the locals and even himself, he begins to unlock his past and learns how he lost everything. Reba McEntire has some nice moments as a mom who helps him. Not too sweet, but inspiring. 96m. **DIR:** Burt Reynolds. **CAST:** Burt Reynolds, Reba McEntire. 1993

MAN FROM MONTEREY, THE ★★★ Swashbuckling action mixes with gunplay in this enjoyable Warner Bros. B Western set in Old California. American army officer John Wayne rides to the rescue of a Spanish aristocrat, while silent-screen veteran Francis Ford (brother of director John) adds class as the chief heavy. Luis Alberni provides a few chuckles in comic support. B&W; 57m. **DIR:** Mack V. Wright. **CAST:** John Wayne, Ruth Hall, Francis Ford, Donald Reed, Lafe McKee, Luis Alberni, Slim Whitaker. 1933

MAN FROM MUSIC MOUNTAIN ★★★ Gene Autry thwarts unscrupulous land developers attempting to sell worthless mining stock. Routine. B&W; 54m. **DIR:** Joseph Kane. **CAST:** Gene Autry, Smiley Burnette, Carol Hughes, Sally Payne, Earl Dwire. 1938

MAN FROM NOWHERE, THE ★★★1/2 A henpecked small-town man seizes the opportunity to

move to Rome and start a new life when he is mistakenly reported dead. Stylish, ironic comedy, based on a Luigi Pirandello novel and (unusual, for the time) filmed on location in Italy. In French with English subtitles. B&W; 98m. **DIR:** Pierre Chenal. **CAST:** Pierre Blanchar, Isa Miranda, Ginette Leclerc. 1937

MAN FROM PAINTED POST, THE ★★★1/2 Early Fairbanks actioner about a good bad man. Great stunts on horseback and with the lasso. Silent. 55m. **DIR:** Joseph E. Henabery. **CAST:** Douglas Fairbanks Sr., Eileen Percy, Frank Campeau. 1917

MAN FROM PLANET X, THE ★★★ Creepy sets and a strong, offbeat story set this low-budget film apart. When a space traveler lands in the foggy moors of the Scottish highlands, his intentions are anything but evil—until he gets a lesson in just how venal some members of the human race can be. B&W; 70m. **DIR:** Edgar G. Ulmer. **CAST:** Robert Clarke, Margaret Field, Raymond Bond, William Schallert. 1951

MAN FROM SNOWY RIVER, THE ★★★★ If you've been looking for an adventure film for the whole family, this Australian Western about the coming-of-age of a mountain man (Tom Burlinson) is it. Rated PG, the film has no objectionable material. 115m. **DIR:** George Miller. **CAST:** Tom Burlinson, Kirk Douglas, Jack Thompson, Bruce Kerr. 1982

MAN FROM THE ALAMO, THE ★★★1/2 An exciting, well-acted story of a soldier (Glenn Ford) who escapes from the doomed Alamo in an effort to warn others about Santa Ana's invasion of Texas. After the Alamo falls, he is branded a traitor and deserter and must prove his mettle to the Texicans. Historically inaccurate, but exciting and fun. 79m. **DIR:** Budd Boetticher. **CAST:** Glenn Ford, Julie Adams, Victor Jory, Chill Wills, Hugh O'Brian, Neville Brand. 1953

MAN FROM U.N.C.L.E., THE (TV SERIES) ★★★1/2 This tongue-in-cheek spy series was one of the mid-Sixties' hottest cult phenomena. The central character, Napoleon Solo, was suavely rendered by Robert Vaughn. Solo was assisted by Illya Kuryakin (David McCallum), and both answered to Leo G. Carroll's paternalistic Alexander Waverly, who dispatched his agents on their global peacekeeping missions. The episodes taken from the show's debut season are by far the best. *Star Trek* fans should take note of "The Project Strigas Affair," which includes William Shatner and Leonard Nimoy. Each tape contains two hour-length episodes. Each episode 104m. **DIR:** John Brahm, Alf Kjellin, Joseph Sargent. **CAST:** Robert Vaughn, David McCallum, Leo G. Carroll. 1964–68

MAN FROM UTAH, THE ★★ Low, low-budget Western with a very young John Wayne as a lawman going undercover to catch some crooks using a rodeo to bilk unsuspecting cowboys. The rodeo footage was used over and over again by the film company, Monogram Pictures, in similar films. B&W; 57m. **DIR:** Robert N. Bradbury. **CAST:** John Wayne, Polly Ann Young, George "Gabby" Hayes, Yakima Canutt, George Cleveland. 1934 DVD

MAN HUNT (1941) ★★★★ Based on *Rogue Male*, Geoffrey Household's crackerjack suspense novel about a British big-game hunter who wants to see if it's possible to assassinate Hitler, this is one of Fritz

Lang's tensest American films. Dudley Nichols's script and Walter Pidgeon's performance lend authority and conviction, and the only shortcoming is a sentimental subplot with Joan Bennett. B&W; 105m. **DIR:** Fritz Lang. **CAST:** Walter Pidgeon, George Sanders, Joan Bennett. **1941**

MAN I LOVE, THE ★★★1/2 A moody melodramatic movie that benefits from sexy stars and sensational music by George Gershwin, Jerome Kern, and Johnny Green. Ida Lupino is sensuous as a streetwise cabaret singer who keeps mobsters at arm's length in order to protect her family. Not much story, but plenty of sophistication. B&W; 96m. **DIR:** Raoul Walsh. **CAST:** Ida Lupino, Robert Alda, Andrea King, Bruce Bennett, Dolores Moran, John Ridgely, Martha Vickers, Alan Hale Sr., Craig Stevens. **1946**

MAN IN GREY, THE ★★★ A tale of attempted husband-stealing that worked well to make the prey, James Mason, a star. Margaret Lockwood is the love thief who proves to intended victim Phyllis Calvert that with her for a friend she needs no enemies. Mason is a stand-out as the coveted husband. B&W; 116m. **DIR:** Leslie Arliss. **CAST:** Margaret Lockwood, James Mason, Phyllis Calvert, Stewart Granger, Martita Hunt. **1943**

MAN IN LOVE, A 💜 European actress finds herself involved in an affair with an egotistical American film star. Rated R for nudity, profanity, and simulated sex. 108m. **DIR:** Diane Kurys. **CAST:** Peter Coyote, Greta Scacchi, Peter Riegert, Jamie Lee Curtis, Claudia Cardinale, John Berry. **1987**

MAN IN THE ATTIC, THE ★★★ In this fascinating tale of obsessive love, Neil Patrick Harris plays Edward, the young man caught up in a love affair with married woman Anne Archer. Lover by day, Edward retreats to a secret attic hideaway at night when hubby is home. This goes on for several years until Edward finally cracks. Good performances make it all seem plausible in this made-for-cable drama. Rated PG-13 for adult situations and language. 104m. **DIR:** Graeme Campbell. **CAST:** Anne Archer, Neil Patrick Harris, Len Cariou, Alex Carter. **1994**

MAN IN THE EIFFEL TOWER, THE ★★★★ A rarely seen little gem of suspense: an intriguing plot, a crafty police inspector (Charles Laughton), an equally crafty murderer (Franchot Tone), and an exciting conclusion. Well acted. 97m. **DIR:** Burgess Meredith. **CAST:** Charles Laughton, Franchot Tone, Burgess Meredith, Robert Hutton, Jean Wallace. **1949**

•MAN IN THE GLASS BOOTH ★★★★ Robert Shaw's electrifying play was brought to the screen as part of the experimental American Film Theater series, and even though the video is hard to find, the experience is well worth it. Maximilian Schell is outstanding as Arthur Goldman, whose life becomes a living nightmare when he's kidnapped by Israeli soldiers and deported to face charges of being an ex-Nazi. Placed in a glass booth for the duration of his trial, Goldman's story slowly unfolds as the truth comes out. Director Arthur Hiller deftly sidesteps the theatrical flourishes to tell the story of one man's frightening odyssey. Not rated. 117m. **DIR:** Arthur Hiller. **CAST:** Maximilian Schell, Lois Nettleton, Luther Adler, Lawrence Pressman, Lloyd Bochner. **1975**

MAN IN THE GRAY FLANNEL SUIT, THE ★★★1/2 The title of Sloan Wilson's novel became a catchphrase to describe the mind-set of corporate America in the 1950s. Considering that, it's a pleasant surprise to find that Nunnally Johnson's film has hardly dated at all. 153m. **DIR:** Nunnally Johnson. **CAST:** Gregory Peck, Jennifer Jones, Fredric March, Marisa Pavan, Lee J. Cobb, Keenan Wynn, Gene Lockhart. **1956**

MAN IN THE IRON MASK, THE (1939) ★★★ Louis Hayward plays twin brothers—a fop and a swashbuckler—in this first sound version of Dumas's classic novel of malice, mayhem, intrigue, and ironic revenge in eighteenth-century France. Separated at birth, one brother becomes the king of France, the other a sword-wielding cohort of the Three Musketeers. Their clash makes for great romantic adventure. B&W; 110m. **DIR:** James Whale. **CAST:** Louis Hayward, Joan Bennett, Warren William, Alan Hale Sr., Joseph Schildkraut. **1939**

MAN IN THE IRON MASK, THE (1977) ★★★ This is the Alexandre Dumas tale of twin brothers, separated at birth. One becomes the wicked king of France, the other, a heroic peasant. The story receives a top-drawer treatment in this classy TV movie. Richard Chamberlain proves he's the most appealing swashbuckler since Errol Flynn retired his sword. 100m. **DIR:** Mike Newell. **CAST:** Richard Chamberlain, Patrick McGoohan, Louis Jourdan, Jenny Agutter, Ralph Richardson. **1977**

MAN IN THE IRON MASK, THE (1998) ★★★1/2 D'Artagnan and the legendary musketeers once more come to life in this sumptuous adaptation, played here by veteran actors who acquit themselves far better than Leonardo DiCaprio, somewhat miscast as the young, villainous King of France. This marks the directorial debut of Randall Wallace, and while all the elements are properly in place and Wallace works with a cast that most directors would kill for, the results are rather slow. Rated PG-13 for violence, discreet nudity, and suggested sex. 117m. **DIR:** Randall Wallace. **CAST:** Leonardo DiCaprio, Jeremy Irons, John Malkovich, Gérard Depardieu, Anne Parillaud, Judith Godreche. **1998 DVD**

MAN IN THE MOON, THE ★★★★ About two sisters who fall in love with the same boy, this coming-of-age movie skillfully captures all the angst, joy, and heartbreak of adolescence and first love. It might have been a simple tearjerker if not for its remarkable sense of realism and honesty. Rated PG-13 for suggested sex and mature themes. 103m. **DIR:** Robert Mulligan. **CAST:** Sam Waterston, Tess Harper, Gail Strickland, Reese Witherspoon, Jason London, Emily Warfield. **1991**

MAN IN THE SADDLE ★★★★ Insanely jealous Alexander Knox tries to run Randolph Scott off the range after Scott's former girl, Joan Leslie, decides to marry Knox. One of director André de Toth's best Westerns. Memorable for its prolonged well-staged fight between Scott and John Russell. 87m. **DIR:** André de Toth. **CAST:** Randolph Scott, Joan Leslie, John Russell, Alexander Knox, Ellen Drew, Cameron Mitchell. **1951**

MAN IN THE SANTA CLAUS SUIT, THE ★★★ In one of his last performances, Fred Astaire plays seven characters who enrich the lives of everybody in a small community. This made-for-TV production is a delightful Christmastime picture. 100m. **DIR:** Corey Allen. **CAST:** Fred Astaire, John Byner, Nanette Fabray, Gary Burghoff, Bert Convy, Harold Gould. **1978**

MAN IN THE WHITE SUIT, THE ★★★★★ In *The Man in the White Suit*, Alec Guinness is the perfect choice to play an unassuming scientist who invents a fabric that can't be torn, frayed, or stained! Can you imagine the furor this causes in the textile industry? This uniquely original script pokes fun at big business and big labor as they try to suppress his discovery. Joan Greenwood is a treasure in a supporting role. B&W; 84m. **DIR:** Alexander Mackendrick. **CAST:** Alec Guinness, Joan Greenwood, Cecil Parker. **1952**

MAN IN THE WILDERNESS ★★★1/2 Exciting outdoor adventure film follows the exploits of a trapper left for dead by his fellow hunters after a bear attack. Gritty film is beautifully filmed and acted. Rated R for violence. 105m. **DIR:** Richard C. Sarafian. **CAST:** Richard Harris, John Huston, John Bindon, Prunella Ransome, Henry Wilcoxon. **1971**

MAN IN UNIFORM, A ★★★★ Eerie, compelling, and startling drama about an actor (Tom McCamus) who can't stop playing the cop he portrays on TV, even after the cameras have stopped rolling. In his off-hours, he haunts the streets, slowly but surely immersing himself in a world that eventually will swallow him. Creepy but effective performances and a shockingly realistic atmosphere make this riveting. Rated R for violence and profanity. 102m. **DIR:** David Wellington. **CAST:** Tom McCamus, Brigitte Bako, David Hemblen, Kevin Tighe. **1993 DVD**

MAN INSIDE, THE (1984) ★★1/2 In this so-so film, James Franciscus is a Canadian vice squad agent who works his way into the organization of a major heroin dealer. In the course of his assignment he has the opportunity to split with $2 million, and is tempted to do so. This Canadian film is unrated. 96m. **DIR:** Gerald Mayer. **CAST:** James Franciscus, Stefanie Powers, Jacques Godin, Len Birman, Donald Davis, Allan Royale. **1984**

MAN INSIDE, THE (1990) ★★ Well-intentioned drama about a crusader (Jurgen Prochnow) who goes undercover to expose a corrupt, muckraking West German newspaper that goes over the top a bit too often. Rated R for violence and profanity. 93m. **DIR:** Bobby Roth. **CAST:** Jurgen Prochnow, Peter Coyote, Dieter Laser, Nathalie Baye. **1990**

•**MAN IS NOT A BIRD** ★★★★ In his first feature, Yugoslav director Dusan Makavejev (*Montenegro*) mixes documentary footage of a grimy copper factory with a fictional story of an engineer who works there and his relationship with a woman. Makavejev's "guerrilla" mixture of stylistic techniques makes the film continually engrossing. In Serbian with English subtitles. B&W; 80m. **DIR:** Dusan Makavejev. **CAST:** Milena Dravic, Janez Vrhovec. **1965**

MAN LIKE EVA, A ★★ Curious but unsatisfying film is a thinly disguised biography of German filmmaker Rainer Werner Fassbinder, here played by a woman. A poorly written movie. In German with English subtitles. Not rated. 92m. **DIR:** Radu Gabrea. **CAST:** Eva Mattes, Lisa Kreuzer. **1984**

MAN MADE MONSTER (THE ATOMIC MONSTER) ★★★ Scientist Lionel Atwill, who envisions a race of superhuman killers fueled by electricity, chooses hapless Lon Chaney Jr. as his glowing guinea pig. Chaney brings class to this unusual, and intriguing, little B flick. Not rated. B&W; 59m. **DIR:** George Wagner. **CAST:** Lon Chaney Jr., Lionel Atwill, Frank Albertson, Anne Nagel, Ben Taggart, Samuel S. Hinds. **1941**

MAN OF A THOUSAND FACES ★★1/2 Sentimentalized, soap-opera bio-pic of Lon Chaney Sr., the screen's greatest horror star, dwells too much on his troubled private life and too little on films. James Cagney turns in a moving performance in the title role. Chaney's films, currently available on video, speak more eloquently without dialogue. 122m. **DIR:** Joseph Pevney. **CAST:** James Cagney, Dorothy Malone, Jane Greer, Marjorie Rambeau, Jim Backus, Robert Evans, Jeanne Cagney, Snub Pollard. **1957 DVD**

MAN OF FLOWERS ★★★★★ Kinky, humorous, and touching, this winner from Australia affirms Paul Cox (of *Lonely Hearts* fame) as one of the wittiest and most sensitive directors from Down Under. Norman Kaye is terrific as an eccentric old man who collects art and flowers and watches pretty women undress. To him these are things of beauty that he can observe but can't touch. Rated R for nudity. 90m. **DIR:** Paul Cox. **CAST:** Norman Kaye, Alyson Best, Chris Haywood, Werner Herzog. **1984**

MAN OF IRON ★★★★ This work of fiction set against the backdrop of stark truth in Communist Poland shows the dramatic events that bridged the Gdansk student rebellions of the 1960s and the Solidarity strikes of 1980. The story is told through the eyes of a journalism student looking for evidence of political skulduggery. In Polish with English subtitles. Rated PG. 140m. **DIR:** Andrzej Wajda. **CAST:** Jerzy Radziwilowicz, Krystyna Janda, Marian Opiana, Irene Byrska. **1981**

MAN OF LA MANCHA 🐢 For those who loved the hit Broadway musical and those who heard about how wonderful it was, this adaptation is a shameful and outrageous letdown. Rated G. 130m. **DIR:** Arthur Hiller. **CAST:** Peter O'Toole, Sophia Loren, James Coco, Harry Andrews. **1972**

MAN OF MARBLE ★★★★ Epic film that reconstructs the life of a Polish laborer, a forgotten heroic figure, through his political efforts against the Stalinist power structure of the 1950s. Engrossing. In Polish with English subtitles. Not rated. B&W/color; 160m. **DIR:** Andrzej Wajda. **CAST:** Jerzy Radziwilowicz, Krystyna Janda. **1977**

MAN OF NO IMPORTANCE, A ★★★ In 1963 Dublin, a repressed homosexual busman (Albert Finney) with a fixation on Oscar Wilde, meets persecution from a former friend when he attempts to mount a production of Wilde's banned *Salomé* with the cast taken from the passengers on his bus. Finney's bravura performance dominates this well-acted but slight, rather meandering film. Rated R for mature themes and a brief scene of simulated sex. 98m. **DIR:** Suri Krishnamma. **CAST:** Albert Finney, Brenda Fricker, Michael Gambon, Tara Fitzgerald, Rufus Sewell. **1994**

MAN OF PASSION, A ★★ Typical story of a young boy's coming-of-age. The young boy is left with his grandfather, a famous painter. There he learns about life and sex. Not rated; contains nudity and simulated sex. 95m. **DIR:** J. Anthony Loma. **CAST:** Anthony Quinn, Maud Adams, Ramon Sheen, Ray Walston, Elizabeth Ashley. **1989**

MAN OF THE FOREST ★★★★ This is one of two very good Westerns made by Randolph Scott in a year that produced many fine films. Based on Zane Grey's novel, Scott plays a cowboy who kidnaps a young woman to keep her from the clutches of a bad guy. Zesty and action-packed. B&W; 62m. **DIR:** Henry Hathaway. **CAST:** Randolph Scott, Harry Carey, Buster Crabbe, Noah Beery Sr., Guinn Williams. **1933**

MAN OF THE FRONTIER (RED RIVER VALLEY) ★★1/2 This early entry in the Gene Autry series features Gene as an undercover agent out to stop a gang bent on sabotaging construction of a much-needed dam. Very enjoyable, and a nice example of the kind of film Autry could make but didn't have to after a while. B&W; 60m. **DIR:** B. Reeves "Breezy" Eason. **CAST:** Gene Autry, Smiley Burnette, Frances Grant. **1936**

MAN OF THE HOUSE ★★1/2 When his divorced mom (Farrah Fawcett) considers marriage to a lawyer (Chevy Chase), a young boy (Jonathan Taylor Thomas of TV's *Home Improvement*) sulks and schemes to get rid of the newcomer. Rated PG. 98m. **DIR:** James Orr. **CAST:** Jonathan Taylor Thomas, Chevy Chase, Farrah Fawcett, George Wendt. **1995**

MAN OF THE WEST ★★★★ Reformed outlaw Gary Cooper reluctantly falls in with former boss Lee J. Cobb to save innocent hostages from Cobb's gang. This tense, claustrophobic Western takes place almost entirely indoors. A minor classic. 100m. **DIR:** Anthony Mann. **CAST:** Gary Cooper, Lee J. Cobb, Julie London, Arthur O'Connell, Jack Lord, John Dehner. **1958**

MAN OF THE YEAR ★★★1/2 When a model is chosen *Playgirl* magazine's "Man of the Year," he gets to spend a year as the fantasy of every woman—as long as no one finds out he's gay. Beneath the humor of this clever "mockumentary" is a lot of provocative commentary about sexual stereotyping and role-playing in American life. Not rated. 85m. **DIR:** Dirk Shafer. **CAST:** Dirk Shafer. **1995 DVD**

MAN ON A STRING ★★1/2 An undercover government agent tries to break up two mob factions by setting them against each other. Predictable made-for-TV movie. Not rated; contains no objectionable material. 74m. **DIR:** Joseph Sargent. **CAST:** Christopher George, William Schallert, Joel Grey, Keith Carradine, Kitty Winn, Jack Warden, James B. Sikking. **1972**

MAN ON FIRE 💔 Scott Glenn plays an ex-CIA agent hired to protect the daughter of a wealthy American couple. Glenn is the film's only redemption. Rated R for language and graphic violence. 92m. **DIR:** Elie Chouraqui. **CAST:** Scott Glenn, Brooke Adams, Danny Aiello, Joe Pesci, Jonathan Pryce. **1987**

•MAN ON THE MOON ★★★1/2 Jim Carrey stars in the life of Andy Kaufman, the oddball comic who amused millions as Latka Gravas on *Taxi*, then irritated many of those same people with his other rou- tines and his abrasive alter ego, lounge singer Tony Clifton. People never knew quite what to make of Kaufman, and in a way the film doesn't either. Still, Carrey's performance is uncanny, and because Carrey is so naturally funny, Kaufman's other antics come off as funnier and less annoying than we remember them. Rated R for profanity. 118m. **DIR:** Milos Forman. **CAST:** Jim Carrey, Danny DeVito, Courtney Love, Paul Giamatti. **1999 DVD**

MAN ON THE ROOF ★★★★ Gripping adaptation of the novel by Mal Sjöwall and Per Wahloo starring Carl-Gustav Linstedt as veteran detective Martin Beck, who is called upon to find a killer with a grudge against cops. While many of the naturalistic techniques pioneered in this thriller have become commonplace, it doesn't dilute this film's power. In Swedish with English subtitles. 109m. **DIR:** Bo Widerberg. **CAST:** Carl-Gustav Linstedt, Halan Serner, Sven Wollter. **1976**

MAN RAY CLASSIC SHORTS ★★1/2 Abstract photographer-artist Man Ray uses animation, superimposition, and lens distortions in these early silent experimental films shot in and around 1920s Paris. Interesting cinematography gets redundant at times. With French subtitles. Silent. B&W; 45m. **DIR:** Man Ray. **1924–1926**

MAN THAT CORRUPTED HADLEYBURG, THE ★★★★★ Robert Preston shows up in Hadleyburg with a sack of gold. Would-be saints and holier-than-thou guardians of public decency are exposed as ordinary people with quite human failings in this delightfully sly adaptation of Mark Twain's acerbic story. Henry Fonda's introduction includes rare film footage of Twain. Not rated and suitable for family viewing. 40m. **DIR:** Ralph Rosenblum. **CAST:** Robert Preston, Fred Gwynne, Frances Sternhagen, Tom Aldredge. **1980**

MAN THEY COULD NOT HANG, THE ★★★ Boris Karloff's fine performance carries this fast-paced tale of a scientist executed for murder and brought back to life and his bizarre plan of revenge on the judge and jury who convicted him. B&W; 72m. **DIR:** Nick Grindé. **CAST:** Boris Karloff, Lorna Gray, Robert Wilcox. **1939**

MAN TROUBLE ★★ A terrific cast is wasted in this inept comedy about a down-on-his-luck security expert. Jack Nicholson mugs shamelessly, while Beverly D'Angelo gives this supposed comedy's only funny performance. Rated PG-13 for profanity, simulated sex, and violence. 100m. **DIR:** Bob Rafelson. **CAST:** Jack Nicholson, Ellen Barkin, Harry Dean Stanton, Beverly D'Angelo, Michael McKean, Saul Rubinek, Viveka Davis, Veronica Cartwright, David Clennon, Paul Mazursky. **1992**

MAN UPSTAIRS, THE ★★ An awkward performance by Ryan O'Neal doesn't help this stagy made-for-TV comedy about a prison escapee who hides in the home of an elderly woman (Katharine Hepburn). It's not an inspired teaming; their timing is off and the frequent attempts at humor fall flat. 95m. **DIR:** George Schaefer. **CAST:** Katharine Hepburn, Ryan O'Neal, Henry Beckman, Helena Carroll, Brenda Forbes. **1992**

MAN WHO BROKE 1000 CHAINS, THE ★★★★1/2
An excellent retelling of *I am a Fugitive from a Chain Gang* with Val Kilmer in the Paul Muni role. Kilmer's performance is as sharp as Muni's, and the supporting players, notably Charles Durning, are superb. Not rated, has violence and profanity. 113m. **DIR:** Daniel Mann. **CAST:** Val Kilmer, Sonia Braga, Charles Durning, Kyra Sedgwick, James Keach. **1987**

MAN WHO CAME TO DINNER, THE ★★★★★ The classic George Kaufman and Moss Hart farce features Monty Woolley in his original Broadway role. High camp and high comedy result when a cynical newspaper columnist falls and supposedly breaks his leg. Bette Davis has a straight role as the secretary. Wacky and lots and lots of fun. 112m. **DIR:** William Keighley. **CAST:** Monty Woolley, Bette Davis, Ann Sheridan, Jimmy Durante, Mary Wickes, Reginald Gardiner, Grant Mitchell, Richard Travis, Billie Burke. **1941**

MAN WHO CAPTURED EICHMANN, THE ★★★★ Robert Duvall gives a chilling performance as Nazi war criminal Eichmann in this story about an Israeli team and its efforts to bring him to justice. Not rated; contains adult language. 95m. **DIR:** William A. Graham. **CAST:** Robert Duvall, Arliss Howard, Jeffrey Tambor, Joel Brooks, Jack Laufer, Nicolas Surovy, Sam Robards. **1997**

MAN WHO CHEATED HIMSELF, THE ★★★1/2 The man of the title is the police lieutenant who falls in love with a woman who accidentally shot her husband. He helps her get rid of the body in an atmospheric murder mystery that capitalizes on suspense more than violence. Good acting and clever writing. B&W; 81m. **DIR:** Felix Feist. **CAST:** Jane Wyatt, Lee J. Cobb, John Dall, Lisa Howard, Terry Frost. **1950**

MAN WHO COULD WORK MIRACLES, THE ★★★1/2 A timid department store clerk suddenly finds he possesses the power to do whatever he desires. Roland Young is matchless as the clerk, and is supported by a first-rate cast in this captivating fantasy. B&W; 82m. **DIR:** Lothar Mendes. **CAST:** Roland Young, Ralph Richardson, Joan Gardner, George Zucco. **1937**

MAN WHO FELL TO EARTH, THE ★★★★ A moody, cerebral science-fiction thriller about an alien (David Bowie) who becomes trapped on our planet. Its occasional ambiguities are overpowered by sheer mind-tugging bizarreness and directorial brilliance. Rated R. 140m. **DIR:** Nicolas Roeg. **CAST:** David Bowie, Rip Torn, Candy Clark, Buck Henry. **1976 DVD**

MAN WHO HAD POWER OVER WOMEN, THE ★★ This British picture, adapted from Gordon Williams's novel, takes a semiserious look at a talent agency. A passable time filler, with some unexpected touches. Rated R. 89m. **DIR:** John Krish. **CAST:** Rod Taylor, James Booth, Carol White. **1970**

MAN WHO HAUNTED HIMSELF, THE ★★★1/2 Freaky melodrama about a car crash with unexpected side effects. Recovering from the wreck, a man (Roger Moore) begins to question his sanity when it appears that his exact double has assumed his position in the world. Imaginative film keeps the viewer involved from start to finish. Rated PG. 94m. **DIR:** Basil Dearden. **CAST:** Roger Moore, Hildegard Neil. **1970**

MAN WHO KNEW TOO LITTLE, THE ★★★★ Bill Murray, a naïve American visitor to England whose vulgar ways almost upset a crucial business deal being set up by his brother, is cleverly sent off on a "Theater of Life" spy adventure. The only problem is, Murray ends up in the middle of a real life-or-death situation while thwarting his assailants through sheer nonchalance and ineptitude. Fans of the star will love it, and some classic sequences should win over the skeptical. Rated PG-13 for violence and profanity. 94m. **DIR:** Jon Amiel. **CAST:** Bill Murray, Peter Gallagher, Joanne Whalley, Alfred Molina, John Standing. **1997 DVD**

MAN WHO KNEW TOO MUCH, THE (1934) ★★★★★ The remake with James Stewart can't hold a candle to this superb suspense film about a man (Leslie Banks) who stumbles onto a conspiracy and then is forced into action when his child is kidnapped to ensure his silence. This is Hitchcock at his best, with Peter Lorre in fine fettle as the sneering villain. B&W; 83m. **DIR:** Alfred Hitchcock. **CAST:** Leslie Banks, Peter Lorre, Edna Best, Nova Pilbeam. **1934 DVD**

MAN WHO KNEW TOO MUCH, THE (1955) ★★★ James Stewart and Doris Day star in this fairly entertaining Hitchcock thriller as a married couple who take a vacation trip to Africa and become involved in international intrigue when they happen on the scene of a murder. It's no match for the original, but the director's fans no doubt will enjoy it. 120m. **DIR:** Alfred Hitchcock. **CAST:** James Stewart, Doris Day, Carolyn Jones. **1955**

●**MAN WHO LAUGHS, THE** ★★★ In this adaptation of a Victor Hugo novel, the king orders that a rebellious nobleman's infant son be surgically mutilated to wear an external grin. Given to gypsies, who cast him adrift a few years later, he saves an infant girl he finds in the arms of her dead mother. A traveling carnival performer takes them in and turns the boy into a comedy star. This long-winded story of intrigue and perversion in the court of England plays against the tender love story of the tragic actor and the young, blind girl he rescued. Action, melodrama, and sweeping spectacle make this one of the more interesting films from the end of the silent era. Silent, with musical score. B&W; 110m. **DIR:** Paul Leni. **CAST:** Conrad Veidt, Mary Philbin, Olga Baclanova, Brandon Hurst, Cesare Gravine, Stuart Holms, Sam de Grasse. **1928**

MAN WHO LIVED AGAIN, THE ★★★ One of Karloff's rare British films of the 1930s, this is an initially slow-moving, mad scientist melodrama about mind transference, which gradually builds to a potent second half. B&W; 61m. **DIR:** Robert Stevenson. **CAST:** Boris Karloff, Anna Lee, John Loder. **1936**

MAN WHO LOVED CAT DANCING, THE 🐝 Burt Reynolds is wasted in this tale of a train robber. Rated PG. 114m. **DIR:** Richard C. Sarafian. **CAST:** Burt Reynolds, Sarah Miles, George Hamilton, Lee J. Cobb, Jack Warden. **1973**

MAN WHO LOVED WOMEN, THE (1977) ★★★★ The basis for a 1983 Blake Edwards film starring

Burt Reynolds, this comedy-drama from François Truffaut has more irony and bite than the remake. Beginning with the protagonist's funeral, the movie examines why he wants and needs women so much, and why they respond to him as well. Like most Truffaut films, it has a deceptively light tone. In French with English subtitles. 119m. DIR: François Truffaut. CAST: Charles Denner, Brigitte Fossey, Leslie Caron, Nathalie Baye. 1977

MAN WHO LOVED WOMEN, THE (1983) ★★★ The first collaboration of Burt Reynolds, Julie Andrews, and her director hubby, Blake Edwards, didn't sound like the kind of thing that would make screen history. And it isn't. But it is a pleasantly entertaining—and sometimes uproariously funny—adult sex comedy. The always likable Reynolds plays a guy who just can't say no to the opposite sex. Rated R for nudity and profanity. 110m. DIR: Blake Edwards. CAST: Burt Reynolds, Julie Andrews, Marilu Henner, Kim Basinger, Barry Corbin. 1983

MAN WHO NEVER WAS, THE ★★★1/2 British intelligence pulls the wool over Nazi eyes in this intriguing true tale of World War II espionage involving fake invasion plans planted on a corpse dressed as a British officer. 102m. DIR: Ronald Neame. CAST: Clifton Webb, Gloria Grahame, Robert Flemyng, Stephen Boyd, Laurence Naismith, Michael Hordern. 1955

MAN WHO SAW TOMORROW, THE ★★★1/2 Orson Welles narrates and appears in this fascinating dramatization of the prophecies of sixteenth-century poet, physician, and psychic Michel de Nostradamus. Nostradamus was astonishingly accurate and, in some cases, actually cited names and dates. His prediction for the future is equally amazing—and, sometimes, terrifying. Rated PG. 90m. DIR: Robert Guenette. 1981

MAN WHO SHOT LIBERTY VALANCE, THE ★★★★★ This release was director John Ford's bittersweet farewell to the western. John Wayne reprises his role of the western man of action, this time with a twist. James Stewart's part could well be called *Mr. Smith Goes to Shinbone*, it draws so much on his most famous image. Combined with Ford's visual sense and belief in sparse dialogue, as well as fine ensemble playing in supporting roles, it adds up to a highly satisfying film. B&W; 119m. DIR: John Ford. CAST: John Wayne, James Stewart, Vera Miles, Lee Marvin, Edmond O'Brien, Woody Strode, Andy Devine, Strother Martin, Lee Van Cleef. 1962

MAN WHO WASN'T THERE, THE 🎦 Espionage and invisibility. This was originally released in 3-D. Rated R for nudity and language. 111m. DIR: Bruce Malmuth. CAST: Steve Guttenberg, Jeffrey Tambor, Lisa Langlois, Art Hindle, Vincent Baggetta. 1983

MAN WHO WOULD BE KING, THE ★★★1/2 A superb screen adventure, this is loosely based on Rudyard Kipling's story and was made at the same time Sean Connery and John Huston starred in the other sand-and-camel flick, the excellent *The Wind and the Lion*. Both are classics in the adventure genre. Rated PG. 129m. DIR: John Huston. CAST: Sean Connery, Michael Caine, Christopher Plummer. 1975 DVD

MAN WITH A GUN ★★★ Appealing cast fleshes out this predictable tale of a hit man (Michael Madsen) asked to kill his boss's scheming wife Rena (Jennifer Tilly). Unfortunately, the hit man is in love with Rena and struggles with the assignment. Then Rena suggests he kill her twin sister instead, a decision that sends John down a road of self-discovery, where his conscience is tested to the limit. Rated R for violence, profanity, and nudity. 96m. DIR: David Wyles. CAST: Michael Madsen, Jennifer Tilly, Gary Busey, Robert Loggia. 1994

MAN WITH BOGART'S FACE, THE ★★1/2 A modern-day Humphrey Bogart–type mystery. Film has fun with the genre while avoiding outright parody. A warmhearted homage. Enjoyable, but of no great importance. Rated PG. 106m. DIR: Robert Day. CAST: Robert Sacchi, Michelle Phillips, Olivia Hussey, Franco Nero, Misty Rowe, Victor Buono, Herbert Lom, Sybil Danning, George Raft, Mike Mazurki. 1980

MAN WITH ONE RED SHOE, THE ★★★1/2 An American remake of the French comedy *The Tall Blond Man with One Black Shoe*, this casts Tom Hanks as a concert violinist who is pursued by a group of spies. Hanks is nearly the whole show. Jim Belushi (as his practical-joke-loving buddy) and Carrie Fisher (as an overly amorous flute player) also provide some hearty laughs. Rated PG for profanity and violence. 96m. DIR: Stan Dragoti. CAST: Tom Hanks, Dabney Coleman, Charles Durning, Lori Singer, James Belushi, Carrie Fisher, Edward Herrmann. 1985

MAN WITH THE GOLDEN ARM, THE ★★★ This dated film attempts to be *The Lost Weekend* of drug-addiction movies. Frank Sinatra is the loser on the needle and the nod in sleazy Chicago surroundings. Eleanor Parker is his crippled wife. Kim Novak, in an early role, is the girl who saves him. As a study of those who say yes, it carries a small jolt. B&W; 119m. DIR: Otto Preminger. CAST: Frank Sinatra, Eleanor Parker, Kim Novak, Arnold Stang, Darren McGavin, Robert Strauss. 1955

MAN WITH THE GOLDEN GUN, THE ★★ In spite of the potentially sinister presence of Christopher Lee as the head baddie, this is the most poorly constructed of all the Bond films. Roger Moore sleepwalks through the entire picture, and the plot tosses in every cliché. Rated PG—some violence. 125m. DIR: Guy Hamilton. CAST: Roger Moore, Christopher Lee, Britt Ekland, Maud Adams, Herve Villechaize, Bernard Lee, Lois Maxwell. 1974 DVD

MAN WITH THE PERFECT SWING, THE ★★1/2 Lighthearted and low-budget comedy-drama about a middle-aged man who sees his life as a failure, until he comes up with a new golf swing that can make anyone a golf pro. The hard part comes in trying to convince everyone that the one-time loser is now a winner. Rated PG-13 for profanity. 93m. DIR: Michael Hovis. CAST: James Black, Suzanne Savoy, Marco Perella, James Belcher. 1995

MAN WITH THE STEEL WHIP, THE 🎦 The last of the Zorro/Lone Ranger–style chapterplays from Republic Studios is a sad blend of tired formula and stock footage from better days pitting reservation Indians against greedy whites with all the thrills of a 30-minute TV show dripped into a four-hour format.

B&W; 12 chapters. **DIR:** Franklin Adreon. **CAST:** Richard Simmons, Barbara Bestar, Dale Van Sickel, Mauritz Hugo, Lane Bradford, Roy Barcroft. 1954

MAN WITH TWO BRAINS, THE ★★★★ Steve Martin stars in this generally amusing takeoff of 1950s horror-sci-fi flicks as a scientist with a nasty wife (Kathleen Turner) and a sweet patient (the voice of Sissy Spacek). There's only one problem with the latter: all that's left of her is her brain. Rated R for nudity, profanity, and violence. 93m. **DIR:** Carl Reiner. **CAST:** Steve Martin, Kathleen Turner, David Warner, Paul Benedict. 1983 DVD

MAN WITH TWO HEADS 🖤 This semiremake of *Dr. Jekyll & Mr. Hyde* is loaded with gore and guts. Rated R. 80m. **DIR:** Scott Williams. 1982

MAN WITHOUT A FACE, THE ★★★★ Touching drama about a 12-year-old boy who dreams of attending a prestigious military academy. When he fails to pass the entrance exam, the lad turns to a reclusive former teacher, whose scarred face and tragic past have caused him to be viewed as a monster by the other kids living in their coastal village. Rated PG-13 for brief profanity and sexual undertones. 114m. **DIR:** Mel Gibson. **CAST:** Mel Gibson, Margaret Whitton, Fay Masterson, Gaby Hoffman, Geoffrey Lewis, Richard Masur, Nick Stahl, Michael DeLuise. 1993

MAN WITHOUT A STAR ★★★ With charm, fists, and guns, foreman Kirk Douglas swaggers through this stock story of rival ranchers. Jeanne Crain is his beautiful boss; Claire Trevor is, as usual, a big-hearted saloon hostess. 89m. **DIR:** King Vidor. **CAST:** Kirk Douglas, Jeanne Crain, Claire Trevor, Richard Boone, Jack Elam, Mara Corday. 1955

MAN, WOMAN AND CHILD ★★★1/2 Here's a surprisingly tasteful and well-acted tearjerker written by Erich Segal. Martin Sheen stars as a married college professor who finds out he has a son in France, the result of an affair ten years before. Sheen decides to bring his son to America, which causes complications. Rated PG for language and adult situations. 99m. **DIR:** Dick Richards. **CAST:** Martin Sheen, Blythe Danner, Sebastian Dungan. 1983

MANAGUA 🖤 A good cast is wasted in this confusing, sex-soaked thriller about American agents infiltrating Latin American drug cartels. Rated R for nudity, violence, profanity, substance abuse, and sexual situations. 108m. **DIR:** Michele Taverna. **CAST:** Lou Gossett Jr., Assumpta Serna, John Savage, John Diehl, Robert Beltran, Michael Moriarty. 1997

MANCE LIPSCOMB: A WELL-SPENT LIFE ★★★★ Les Blank's stirring portrait of Texas songster Mance Lipscomb is a moving tribute to a legendary bluesman. Lipscomb's crafty, bottleneck-slide guitar style is reminiscent of country-blues giant Furry Lewis and contemporary Texas-blues great Lightnin' Hopkins. 44m. **DIR:** Les Blank. 1981

MANCHURIAN CANDIDATE, THE ★★★★1/2 This cold-war black comedy is still topical, chilling, and hilarious. Frank Sinatra gives a superbly controlled performance as a Korean War veteran who begins to believe that the honored heroics of a former member of his squad (Laurence Harvey) may be the product of brainwashing by an enemy with even more sinister designs. A delicate balance between hilarity and

horror. Not rated, the film has violence. B&W; 126m. **DIR:** John Frankenheimer. **CAST:** Frank Sinatra, Laurence Harvey, Janet Leigh, Angela Lansbury, James Gregory, Leslie Parrish. 1962 DVD

MANDELA ★★★ Although Danny Glover and Alfre Woodard put heart and soul into their interpretations of South African activists Nelson and Winnie Mandela, Ronald Harwood's poorly balanced script sets events in a one-sided vacuum. A less involving drama than Richard Attenborough's *Cry Freedom*. Not rated; suitable for family viewing. 135m. **DIR:** Philip Saville. **CAST:** Danny Glover, Alfre Woodard, Warren Clarke, Julian Glover. 1987

MANDELA AND DE KLERK ★★★★ This made-for-cable original portrays Nelson Mandela's struggle to attain freedom for the blacks in South Africa. Sydney Poitier is a natural as Mandela, exuding the force of character and strength of conviction that sustained the title character during his twenty-seven years in prison. And while the story may not be entertaining, it is a fascinating study of history and how one man can make a difference. Not rated; contains violence. 113m. **DIR:** Joseph Sargent. **CAST:** Sidney Poitier, Michael Caine, Tina Lifford. 1997

MANDINGO 🖤 Sick film concerning Southern plantations before the Civil War and the treatment of the black slaves. Rated R. 127m. **DIR:** Richard Fleischer. **CAST:** James Mason, Susan George, Perry King, Richard Ward, Brenda Sikes. 1975

MANDROID ★★★ Scientists and the CIA struggle for control of a powerful, man-made element with both curative and destructive powers—depending on who has it. Covers every sci-fi detail from invisibility to a mad doctor in an iron mask! Just don't ponder the details. Rated R for violence, profanity, and brief nudity. 81m. **DIR:** Jack Ersgard. **CAST:** Brian Cousins, Janette Allyson Caldwell, Michael DellaFemina, Curt Lowens, Patrick Ersgard. 1993

MANFISH 🖤 Probably the only low-budget attempt to cash in on calypso music using Edgar Allan Poe, boats, and fish. 76m. **DIR:** W. Lee Wilder. **CAST:** John Bromfield, Lon Chaney Jr., Victor Jory, Barbara Nichols. 1956

MANGLER, THE 🖤 Massive industrial laundry-pressing device is possessed by evil spirits and begins folding people into lumps of grisly pulp. Rated R for violence, gore, and language. 106m. **DIR:** Tobe Hooper. **CAST:** Robert Englund, Ted Levine, Daniel Matmore, Jeremy Crutchley. 1995

MANHANDLED ★★1/2 Disappointing vehicle for Gloria Swanson. Believe it or not, she's a department store salesclerk—but never fear, Swanson gets ample opportunities to model exotic gowns as she impersonates a Russian countess. Slick but routine. Silent. B&W; 70m. **DIR:** Allan Dwan. **CAST:** Gloria Swanson, Tom Moore. 1924

MANHATTAN ★★★★★ Reworking the same themes he explored in *Play It Again, Sam* and *Annie Hall*, Woody Allen again comes up with perhaps his greatest masterpiece. Diane Keaton returns as the object of his awkward but well-meaning affections. It's heartwarming, insightful, screamingly funny, and a feast for the eyes. The black-and-white cinematography of long-time Allen collaborator Gordon Willis recalls the great visuals of *Citizen Kane* and *The Third Man*. Rated R. B&W; 96m. **DIR:** Woody Allen. **CAST:** Diane Keaton, Woody Allen, Michael Murphy, Mariel Hemingway, Meryl Streep. **1979**

MANHATTAN BABY 💖 An archaeologist's daughter is possessed by an Egyptian demon. This film lacks the style and substance of some other Italian horror features. Not rated, but with lots of fake blood. 90m. **DIR:** Lucio Fulci. **CAST:** George Hacker, Christopher Connelly, Martha Taylor. **1983**

MANHATTAN MELODRAMA ★★★★ In MGM's best version of an oft-told story, two boyhood pals (Clark Gable, William Powell) end up on opposite sides of the law as adults but maintain their friendship and friendly competition for the affections of Myrna Loy. The wonderful cast makes it delicious, old-fashioned movie fun. Historical note: this is the movie John Dillinger was watching before he was shot down by the FBI outside the Biograph Theatre in Chicago. B&W; 93m. **DIR:** W. S. Van Dyke. **CAST:** Clark Gable, William Powell, Myrna Loy, Mickey Rooney, Leo Carrillo, Isabel Jewell, Nat Pendleton. **1934**

MANHATTAN MERENGUE ★★ Tired tale of an illegal immigrant who dreams of dancing on Broadway and comes close when he becomes a janitor at a dance school. When Miguel attracts the attention of the head instructor, she wants to see all of his moves, on the floor and in bed. Their affair creates havoc for the dancer, who now must contend with immigration authorities and a jealous instructor. Rated PG-13 for adult situations and language. 94m. **DIR:** Joseph B. Vasquez. **CAST:** George Perez, Lumi Cavazos, Marco Leonardi, Alyson Reed. **1994 DVD**

MANHATTAN MERRY-GO-ROUND ★★1/2 Incredible lineup of popular performers is the main attraction of this catchall production about a gangster who takes over a recording company. This oddity runs the gamut from Gene Autry's country crooning to the jivin' gyrations of legendary Cab Calloway. B&W; 80m. **DIR:** Charles F. Riesner. **CAST:** Gene Autry, Phil Regan, Leo Carrillo, Ann Dvorak, Tamara Geva, Ted Lewis, Cab Calloway, Joe DiMaggio, Louis Prima, Henry Armetta, Max Terhune, Smiley Burnette, James Gleason. **1938**

MANHATTAN MURDER MYSTERY ★★★★ Joyous reunion for Woody Allen and Diane Keaton presents them as a married couple at odds over whether a neighbor has committed murder. She's sure of it, he thinks she's gone off the deep end, and the audience is almost too busy laughing to care. A cleverly constructed howdunit from Allen and Marshall Brickman, who previously collaborated on *Annie Hall* and *Manhattan*. Rated PG for brief violence. 108m. **DIR:** Woody Allen. **CAST:** Woody Allen, Diane Keaton, Alan Alda, Anjelica Huston, Jerry Adler, Joy Behar, Ron Rifkin. **1993 DVD**

MANHATTAN PROJECT, THE ★★★ Contemporary comedy-adventure-thriller concerns a high-school youth (Christopher Collet) who, with the aid of his idealistic girlfriend (Cynthia Nixon), steals some plutonium and makes his own nuclear bomb. There's a pleasing balance of humor and suspense. Rated PG for violence. 115m. **DIR:** Marshall Brickman. **CAST:**

John Lithgow, Christopher Collet, Cynthia Nixon, Jill Eikenberry. **1986**

MANHUNT (1973) (THE ITALIAN CONNECTION) ★★ Unbeknownst to him, a small-time Milano crook is framed as a big-time drug dealer, which results in the murder of his wife. He sets out in search of an explanation and revenge. Mediocre action picture was retitled *The Italian Connection* to cash in on the success of *The French Connection*. Dubbed in English. Rated R. 93m. **DIR:** Fernando Di Leo. **CAST:** Mario Adorf, Henry Silva, Woody Strode, Adolfo Celi, Luciana Paluzzi, Sylva Koscina, Cyril Cusack. **1973**

MANHUNT FOR CLAUDE DALLAS ★★1/2 True-life made-for-television adventure traces the exploits of mountain man Claude Dallas, whose murder spree and eventual capture made headlines. Fascinating look at law enforcement. 100m. **DIR:** Jerry London. **CAST:** Matt Salinger, Claude Akins, Lois Nettleton, Rip Torn. **1986**

MANHUNTER ★★★★1/2 Thoroughly engrossing tale of an FBI man (William Petersen) following a trail of blood through the southeast left by a ruthless, calculating psychopath known only as "The Tooth Fairy," for reasons made shockingly clear. Rated R for violence and various adult contents. 118m. **DIR:** Michael Mann. **CAST:** William L. Petersen, Kim Greist, Brian Cox, Dennis Farina, Joan Allen. **1986**

MANIA ★★★1/2 After *The Body Snatcher* (1945), this powerful British melodrama is the best fictional reworking of the scandalous saga of Edinburgh's Dr. Robert Knox and his clandestine pact with grave robbers Burke and Hare. Cushing, as Knox, is dagger-sharp as always, and the direction of John Gilling evenly balances the requisite sensationalism with a mature script. B&W; 87m. **DIR:** John Gilling. **CAST:** Peter Cushing, June Laverick, Donald Pleasence. **1959**

MANIAC (1934) ★★ Legendary film about a mad doctor and his even madder assistant knocked 'em dead at the men's clubs and exploitation houses in the 1930s and 1940s, but it seems pretty mild compared to today's color gorefests. Not rated. B&W; 52m. **DIR:** Dwain Esper. **CAST:** Bill Woods, Horace Carpenter. **1934 DVD**

MANIAC (1962) ★★★ Spooky mystery film about a madman on the loose in France, with Kerwin Mathews perfect as an American artist whose vacation there turns out to be anything but. Chilling atmosphere. B&W; 86m. **DIR:** Michael Carreras. **CAST:** Kerwin Mathews, Nadia Gray, Donald Houston. **1962**

MANIAC (1980) 💖 A plethora of shootings, stabbings, decapitations, and scalpings. Rated R for every excess imaginable. 87m. **DIR:** William Lustig. **CAST:** Joe Spinell, Caroline Munro, Gail Lawrence, Kelly Piper, Tom Savini. **1980 DVD**

MANIAC COP 💖 A deranged killer cop is stalking the streets of New York. Rated R for violence, nudity, and adult situations. 92m. **DIR:** William Lustig. **CAST:** Tom Atkins, Bruce Campbell, Richard Roundtree, William Smith, Sheree North. **1988 DVD**

MANIAC COP 2 ★★★ This sequel resurrects the homicidal cop out to avenge his unwarranted incarceration in Sing-Sing. Viciously maimed in prison, he sets out to dispatch any responsible party (and a few just for the hell of it). Rated R for violence, profanity, and gore. 90m. **DIR:** William Lustig. **CAST:** Robert Davi, Claudia Christian, Michael Lerner, Bruce Campbell, Clarence Williams III, Leo Rossi. 1990

MANIAC COP 3: BADGE OF SILENCE ★★★ When a fellow police officer is wounded in action and then framed, the undead Maniac Cop sets out to clear her name, systematically eliminating all those who stand in the way. He seems to be rather inexact in his methods (to be expected from a moldering corpse, we suppose). Rated R for violence. 85m. **DIR:** William Lustig. **CAST:** Robert Davi, Robert Z'dar, Caitlin Dulany, Gretchen Becker, Jackie Earle Haley. 1993

MANIFESTO ★★★1/2 A colorful, eccentric comedy from the director of *Montenegro* and *The Coca-Cola Kid.* It's a wacky tale of revolutionaries trying to alter the political system in a picturesque European country, circa 1920. Romance, misguided idealism, and ineptitude get in the way of all their efforts, but viewers have a lot of fun along the way. 96m. **DIR:** Dusan Makavejev. **CAST:** Camilla Soeberg, Alfred Molina, Eric Stoltz, Simon Callow, Lindsay Duncan. 1988

MANIONS OF AMERICA, THE ★★★★ A bit sudsy at times, this was originally televised as a miniseries. It is an absolutely absorbing saga of a rebellious Irish lad's life as an immigrant in the United States. His hotheadedness can only be matched by the willfulness and determination of his British wife. 360m. **DIR:** Joseph Sargent. **CAST:** Pierce Brosnan, Kate Mulgrew, David Soul, Linda Purl. 1981

MANIPULATOR, THE ★★ Schizophrenic movie makeup man abducts an actress. Rated R for violence, profanity, and nudity. 91m. **DIR:** Yabo Yablonsky. **CAST:** Mickey Rooney, Luana Anders, Keenan Wynn. 1971

MANITOU, THE ★ Hilariously hokey film about a woman who by some strange trick of chance is growing an ancient Indian out of her neck! Rated PG. 104m. **DIR:** William Girdler. **CAST:** Tony Curtis, Susan Strasberg, Michael Ansara, Ann Sothern, Burgess Meredith, Stella Stevens. 1978

MANKILLERS 🐝 The FBI hires a band of twelve ruthless female prisoners to dispose of an ex-agent turned renegade. Not rated. 90m. **DIR:** David A. Prior. **CAST:** Edd Byrnes, Gail Fisher, Edy Williams. 1987

MANNEQUIN (1937) ★★★ Poor working girl sees only the riches of a self-made millionaire as a way to happiness, yet lets herself be manipulated by a cad. Pros at work. The song "Always And Always" was Oscar-nominated. B&W; 95m. **DIR:** Frank Borzage. **CAST:** Joan Crawford, Spencer Tracy, Alan Curtis, Ralph Morgan. 1937

MANNEQUIN (1987) 🐝 MTV glitz and worn-out comedy bits. Rated PG. 90m. **DIR:** Michael Gottlieb. **CAST:** Andrew McCarthy, Kim Cattrall, Estelle Getty, G. W. Bailey, Meshach Taylor. 1987

MANNEQUIN TWO: ON THE MOVE ★★ William Ragsdale is a modern-day descendant of royalty who discovers that a department-store mannequin is really alive. Good comic turns by Terry Kiser as a dastardly count and Meshach Taylor, who reprises his role as an effeminate art director. Rated PG. 98m. **DIR:** Stewart Raffill. **CAST:** Kristy Swanson, William Ragsdale, Terry Kiser, Stuart Pankin, Meshach Taylor. 1991

MANNY & LO ★★1/2 Two young sisters on the run kidnap a maternity-store clerk to help with the older sister's impending childbirth. Writer-director Lisa Krueger's film is sweet and gentle-hearted but also contrived and rather cloying. It benefits greatly from the warm, no-nonsense performance of Mary Kay Place as the kidnap victim. Rated R for profanity. 90m. **DIR:** Lisa Krueger. **CAST:** Scarlett Johansson, Aleksa Palladino, Mary Kay Place, Glenn Fitzgerald, Angie Phillips. 1996

MANNY'S ORPHANS (COME THE TIGERS) 🐝 Another *Bad News Bears* movie, but of course not within striking distance of the original. 90m. **DIR:** Sean S. Cunningham. **CAST:** Richard Lincoln. 1978

MANON ★★1/2 Disappointing update of a classic love story takes place during the German occupation of France. The two stars are rather wan, leaving the gritty depiction of war-torn Paris as the film's sole saving grace. In French with English subtitles. Not rated. 90m. **DIR:** Henri-Georges Clouzot. **CAST:** Cecile Aubrey, Michel Auclair. 1951

MANON OF THE SPRING ★★★★★ For its visual beauty alone, this sequel to *Jean de Florette* is a motion picture to savor. But it has a great deal more to offer. Chief among its pleasures are superb performances by Yves Montand and Daniel Auteuil. A fascinating tale of revenge and unrequited love. In French with English subtitles. Rated PG-13 for nudity. 113m. **DIR:** Claude Berri. **CAST:** Yves Montand, Daniel Auteuil, Emmanuelle Beart, Elisabeth Depardieu. 1987

MAN'S BEST FRIEND (1993) ★★ A genetically engineered guard dog runs amok when a crusading TV reporter, thinking she is rescuing him from vivisection, smuggles him home. Plenty of nasty shocks, with dumb characters doing the usual dumb things and getting their throats ripped out. Rated R for violence. 87m. **DIR:** John Lafia. **CAST:** Ally Sheedy, Lance Henriksen. 1993

MAN'S FAVORITE SPORT? ★★★ Comedy about a nonfishing outdoor-sports columnist who finds himself entered in an anglers' contest is fast and funny and provides Rock Hudson with one of his best roles. Screwball Paula Prentiss spends most of her time gumming up the works for poor Rock. The situations and dialogue are clever and breezy, employing director Howard Hawks's famous overlapping dialogue to maximum advantage. 120m. **DIR:** Howard Hawks. **CAST:** Rock Hudson, Paula Prentiss, John McGiver, Roscoe Karns, Maria Perschy, Charlene Holt. 1964

•**MANSFIELD PARK** ★★★ Fanny Price, perhaps the meekest and least admirable of Jane Austen's various heroines, has been given something of a makeover in filmmaker Patricia Rozema's adaptation of *Mansfield Park*; the results are mixed. Now more a late twentieth-century feminist than an early nineteenth-century rebel, this change completely mutates the story's dynamics. Fanny gets the opportunity to blossom when removed from her poor childhood environment to be raised by wealthy, condescending relatives, and she has more decency and good breeding than most. But the film itself is slow—even for this genre of gentility—and rather dreary, and the script a poor condensation of

Austen's novel. Rated PG-13 for the brutal contents of a sketchbook. 110m. **DIR:** Patricia Rozema. **CAST:** Embeth Davidtz, Jonny Lee Miller, Alessandro Nivola, Frances O'Connor, Harold Pinter. **1999 DVD**

MANSION OF THE DOOMED ♥ Uncredited remake of *Eyes without a Face* that is notable only as the first film for producer Charles Band, actor Lance Henriksen, special effects man Stan Winston, and future action director Andrew Davis. Not rated; contains violence and gore. 89m. **DIR:** Michael Pataki. **CAST:** Richard Basehart, Gloria Grahame, Lance Henriksen. 1975

MANSTER, THE ★★1/2 Peter Dyneley plays a skirt-chasing, alcoholic reporter who falls victim to a Japanese mad scientist's experiments, eventually becoming a two-headed monster. A trash film must-see, with a welcome bonus: it's genuinely creepy in addition to being lurid. It's also got a unique *technical* hook: it's not a dubbed import, but one of the first international coproductions. B&W; 72m. **DIR:** George Breakston, Kenneth Crane. **CAST:** Peter Dyneley, Jane Hylton. 1962

MANXMAN, THE ♥ Afternoon soap operas are nothing compared to this howler, the last of director Alfred Hitchcock's silent films. B&W; 70m. **DIR:** Alfred Hitchcock. **CAST:** Carl Brisson, Malcolm Keen, Anny Ondra. **1929 DVD**

MAP OF THE HUMAN HEART ★★★★ With great cinematic panache, director Vincent Ward tells the epic story of a young Eskimo who falls in love with a woman of mixed race. Through decades, they encounter obstacles to their romance. Anne Parillaud is particularly compelling as the object of the naïve Eskimo lad's desire. The WWII flying sequences are dazzling. The film reminds us of the value of primitive cultures. Rated R for nudity and suggested sex. 95m. **DIR:** Vincent Ward. **CAST:** Anne Parillaud, Patrick Bergin, Jason Scott Lee, John Cusack, Jeanne Moreau. 1993

•**MAP OF THE WORLD, A** ★★★1/2 A Wisconsin farm wife sees her life unravel when, first, a friend's daughter drowns in her pond and, next, she is accused of sexually abusing a local boy. Adapted from Jane Hamilton's novel, the film relies too much on voice-over narration, especially in the last third. But the acting is strong throughout, and the central role is a real showcase for Sigourney Weaver. Rated R for profanity, nudity, and brief sexual scenes. 127m. **DIR:** Scott Elliott. **CAST:** Sigourney Weaver, Julianne Moore, David Strathairn, Arliss Howard, Chloe Sevigny, Louise Fletcher. 1999

MAPP & LUCIA ★★★ Filmed in the mid-1980s and set in the late 1920s, this frothy Channel Four British import has long been a cult favorite of Anglophiles and satirists. Lucia is played by Geraldine McEwan, an affected village doyenne in constant battle with the equally formidable Mapp (Prunella Scales). All five parts in the series deftly exhibit the brio and bull twaddle of E. F. Benson's widely read novel. Not rated. 260m. **DIR:** Donald McWhinnie. **CAST:** Geraldine McEwan, Prunella Scales, Nigel Hawthorne. 1984

MARAT/SADE ★★★★ Glenda Jackson made her film debut in this terrifying adaptation of Peter Weiss's play about a performance staged by some in-

mates of a French insane asylum, under the direction of the Marquis de Sade. Peter Brook's direction is superb, as he creates a dark, claustrophobic atmosphere. Great ensemble acting. Not for the squeamish. 115m. **DIR:** Peter Brook. **CAST:** Patrick Magee, Glenda Jackson, Ian Richardson. **1966 DVD**

MARATHON ★★1/2 In this comic examination of mid-life crisis, Bob Newhart becomes enamored of a woman he sees at a local running event, only to discover his true feelings. The uninspired direction and screenplay weaken the efforts of a veteran cast. Rated PG for mild language. 97m. **DIR:** Jackie Cooper. **CAST:** Bob Newhart, Herb Edelman, Dick Gautier, Anita Gillette, Leigh Taylor-Young, John Hillerman. 1985

MARATHON MAN ★★★★ A young student (Dustin Hoffman) unwittingly becomes involved in the pursuit of an ex-Nazi war criminal (Laurence Olivier) in this chase thriller. The action holds your interest throughout. Rated R. 125m. **DIR:** John Schlesinger. **CAST:** Dustin Hoffman, Laurence Olivier, Roy Scheider, William Devane, Marthe Keller. 1976

MARCH OF THE WOODEN SOLDIERS (BABES IN TOYLAND (1934)) ★★★★ This film features Stan Laurel and Oliver Hardy as the toy maker's assistants in the land of Old King Cole. Utterly forgettable songs slow down an otherwise enjoyable fantasy film. Stan and Ollie are integrated well into the storyline, finally saving the town from the attack of the boogeymen. B&W; 73m. **DIR:** Gus Meins. **CAST:** Stan Laurel, Oliver Hardy, Charlotte Henry. **1934 DVD**

MARCH OR DIE ★★1/2 Old-fashioned epic adventure that reminds us of *Beau Geste* and *The Charge of the Light Brigade*, but lacks credibility and style. Gene Hackman stars as an iron-willed major in the French foreign legion, who defends a desert outpost in Africa from marauding Arabs. Catherine Deneuve provides the romance. Not rated, but equivalent to an R for violence and mature situations. 104m. **DIR:** Dick Richards. **CAST:** Gene Hackman, Terence Hill, Max von Sydow, Catherine Deneuve. 1977

MARCIANO ★★ This made-for-TV bio-film concentrates far too much on the private life of the only boxer ever to retire from the pugilistic sport world undefeated—Rocky Marciano. More footage should have been devoted to his professional fighting career. There's nothing special here. 100m. **DIR:** Bernard Kowalski. **CAST:** Tony Lo Bianco, Belinda Montgomery, Vincent Gardenia, Richard Herd. 1979

MARCO POLO JR. ★★ An ancient prophecy sends a young man on a musical mission to the fabled kingdom of Xanadu. The soundtrack is reminiscent of those moldy Bobby Vinton albums hidden away in your attic. 82m. **DIR:** Eric Porter. 1972

MARDI GRAS FOR THE DEVIL ★★1/2 Twenty years after his father was killed, a cop finds that the murderer, who rips his victims' hearts out, is after him. Unfortunately, the killer is the devil, who just may be unstoppable. Don't even try to find a plot. Not rated; contains nudity and graphic sex. 95m. **DIR:** David A. Prior. **CAST:** Robert Davi, Michael Ironside, Lesley-Anne Down, Lydie Denier, Mike Starr, Lillian Lehman, Margaret Avery, John Amos. 1993

MARGARET'S MUSEUM ★★★★ The treacherous, tough life of a coal miner takes center stage in this haunting tale of lost love. Helena Bonham Carter is captivating as Margaret MacNeil, whose love for coal miner Clive Russell upsets her mother, who lost her own husband in a mining accident. Eternal love takes on new meaning when Russell is killed in an accident and Margaret is left to sort out her life. Set in Canada during the 1940s, this exquisite period piece deals with emotional issues in a most unusual way. Rated R for language and nudity. 118m. DIR: Mort Ransen. CAST: Helena Bonham Carter, Kate Nelligan, Clive Russell, Kenneth Welsh. 1995

MARIANNE & JULIANE ★★★ Tie between two estranged sisters develops when one is imprisoned for revolutionary anarchy. The more conservative sister can't resist rebuilding their childhood camaraderie. Strange but engrossing with flashbacks indicating that the two had swapped personalities at some point in their lives. Stark, artful, and sometimes painful to watch. In German with English subtitles. Not rated; contains nudity and gore. 103m. DIR: Margarethe von Trotta. CAST: Barbara Sukowa, Jutta Lampe, Rudiger Vogler, Doris Schade. 1981

MARIA'S LOVERS ❤ A former World War II prisoner of war and his loving wife. Rated R for profanity, nudity, suggested sex, and violence. 105m. DIR: Andrei Konchalovsky. CAST: Nastassja Kinski, John Savage, Keith Carradine, Robert Mitchum, Vincent Spano, Bud Cort. 1985

MARIE ★★★ Sissy Spacek plays real-life heroine Marie Ragghianti, whose courage and honesty brought about the fall of a corrupt administration in Tennessee. Marie is a battered housewife who leaves her cruel husband. Struggling to raise her three children, she eventually works her way up to becoming the state's first female parole board head. Rated PG-13 for violence and profanity. 100m. DIR: Roger Donaldson. CAST: Sissy Spacek, Jeff Daniels, Keith Szarabajka. 1986

MARIE ANTOINETTE ★★★ A regal rendition of the queen who lost her head, but not her stature in history. The film traces the life of the Austrian princess who became queen of France, and covers the period when she had a romantic attachment for the Swedish Count Axel de Fersen (Tyrone Power). B&W; 149m. DIR: W. S. Van Dyke. CAST: Norma Shearer, Tyrone Power, Robert Morley, John Barrymore, Joseph Schildkraut, Gladys George, Anita Louise, Reginald Gardiner. 1938

MARIE BAIE DES ANGES ★★ A sexually adventurous 15-year-old turns an American navy outpost on the French Riviera into her own personal playground when she meets and mates with a young sociopath. This swirl of colorful nonlinear narrative and ominous moral decay is seductively crafted but glorifies juvenile angst while failing to get under the skin of its characters. In French with English subtitles. Rated R for violence, nudity, profanity, sexual assault, and sexual situations. 90m. DIR: Manuel Pradal. CAST: Vahina Giocante, Frederic Malgras. 1998

MARILYN & BOBBY: HER FINAL AFFAIR ❤ This made-for-cable original is just another boring, poorly acted account of the last days of Marilyn Monroe. Not rated. 95m. DIR: Bradford May. CAST: Melody Anderson, James F. Kelly, Jonathan Banks, Kristoffer Tabori,

Geoffrey Blake, Thomas Wagner, Ian Buchanan, Tomas Millan, Richard Dysart. 1993

MARINE RAIDERS ★★1/2 Tough but fair-minded Marine commanding officer tries to steer his favorite captain away from the rocky reefs of romance but finally relents and lets love lead the lucky couple to the altar. B&W; 90m. DIR: Harold Schuster. CAST: Pat O'Brien, Robert Ryan, Ruth Hussey, Frank McHugh, Barton MacLane, Richard Martin. 1944

MARIUS ★★★ This French movie is a marvelous view of the working class in Marseilles between the wars. The story revolves around Marius (Pierre Fresnay) and his love for Fanny (Orane Demazis), the daughter of a fish store proprietess. The poetic essence of the film is captured with style as Marius ships out to sea, unknowingly leaving Fanny with child. In French with English subtitles. B&W; 125m. DIR: Alexander Korda. CAST: Raimu, Pierre Fresnay, Orane Demazis, Alida Rouffe. 1931

MARJOE ★★★1/2 The life of evangelist-turned-actor Marjoe Gortner is traced in this entertaining documentary. Film offers the viewer a peek into the world of the traveling evangelist. When Marjoe gets his act going, the movie is at its best. At times a little stagy, but always interesting. Rated PG for language. 88m. DIR: Howard Smith, Sarah Kernochan. CAST: Marjoe Gortner. 1972

MARJORIE MORNINGSTAR ★★★ Natalie Wood and Gene Kelly give fine performances in this adaptation of the novel by Herman Wouk. Wood falls for show biz and for carefree theatrical producer Kelly. As Wood's eccentric uncle, Ed Wynn almost steals the show. A fine score by Max Steiner. 123m. DIR: Irving Rapper. CAST: Gene Kelly, Natalie Wood, Ed Wynn, Claire Trevor, Everett Sloane, Martin Milner, Carolyn Jones. 1958

MARK OF CAIN ★★★ Though this film overdoes the eerie music and protracted conversations, it is a compelling tale about twin brothers. A graphic murder sets the plot in motion. A lovely old home surrounded by breathtaking winter scenery is the principal setting. 90m. DIR: Bruce Pittman. CAST: Robin Crew, Wendy Crewson, August Schellenberg. 1984

MARK OF THE BEAST, THE ❤ An anthropologist avenges her twin sister's ritual murder. Ineptly written and acted. Not rated; contains nudity, profanity, violence, and simulated sex. 88m. DIR: Jeff Hathcock. CAST: Bo Hopkins, Richard Hill, Sheila Cann. 1990

MARK OF THE DEVIL ❤ A sadistic German-British film about an impotent, overachieving witch finder. Notorious as the only movie in history to offer free stomach-distress bags to every patron. Rated R. 96m. DIR: Michael Armstrong. CAST: Herbert Lom, Udo Kier, Reggie Nalder. 1970 DVD

MARK OF THE DEVIL, PART 2 ❤ After the frolic of the original *Mark of the Devil*, what's left for this sequel to the notorious, medieval witch-hunting saga? Not much. Rated R. 88m. DIR: Adrian Hoven. CAST: Anton Diffring, Jean-Pierre Zola, Reggie Nalder, Erica Blanc. 1972

MARK OF THE HAWK, THE ❤ African man struggles to integrate his people into the societal mainstream. A snooze. 84m. DIR: Michael Audley. CAST:

Sidney Poitier, Juano Hernandez, Eartha Kitt, John McIntire. **1958**

MARK OF THE VAMPIRE ★★★1/2 MGM's atmospheric version of *Dracula*, utilizing the same director and star. This time, though, it's Count Mora (Bela Lugosi) terrorizing the residents of an old estate along with his ghoulish daughter (Carol Borland). Lionel Barrymore is the believer who tries to put an end to their nocturnal activities. B&W; 61m. **DIR:** Tod Browning. **CAST:** Lionel Barrymore, Elizabeth Allan, Bela Lugosi, Lionel Atwill, Carol Borland. **1935**

MARK OF ZORRO, THE (1920) ★★★1/2 Douglas Fairbanks took a chance in 1920 and jumped from comedy-adventures to *costumed* comedy-adventures; with this classic film, he never turned back. Fairbanks made the character of Zorro his own and quickly established himself as an American legend. Silent. B&W; 90m. **DIR:** Fred Niblo. **CAST:** Douglas Fairbanks Sr., Marguerite de la Motte, Noah Beery Sr., Robert McKim. **1920 DVD**

MARK OF ZORRO, THE (1940) ★★★★1/2 Glossy MGM swashbuckler is stylishly directed by Rouben Mamoulian, with Tyrone Power well cast as the foppish aristocrat who lives a secret life as the masked avenger, Zorro, in old California. The inspired casting of Basil Rathbone, Eugene Pallette, and Montagu Love in supporting roles recalls the Errol Flynn classic, *The Adventures of Robin Hood*, while Power's duel with Rathbone almost outdoes it. B&W; 93m. **DIR:** Rouben Mamoulian. **CAST:** Tyrone Power, Basil Rathbone, J. Edward Bromberg, Linda Darnell, Gale Sondergaard, Eugene Pallette, Montagu Love, Robert Lowery. **1940**

MARKED FOR DEATH ★★1/2 Suburbia is infested with Jamaican drug pushers led by the fearsome, dreadlocked Screwface (Basil Wallace) until a nononsense, retired DEA agent (Steve Seagal) decides to clean up the neighborhood. Bone-cruncher Seagal makes a great action-fu star. But this isn't one of his best. Rated R for language and violence. 93m. **DIR:** Dwight H. Little. **CAST:** Steven Seagal, Keith David, Basil Wallace, Joanna Pacula. **1990 DVD**

MARKED MAN ★★1/2 So-so action film is the story of a convict who witnesses the murder of a mob boss in prison by a pair of guards. From that point on, he fits the description of the title character, with the law, the Mafia, and a whole slew of unsavory characters trying to track him down and put a bullet through his memory. Lots of action, some decent performances, and a quick pace make this watchable. Rated R for profanity and violence. 94m. **DIR:** Marc Voizard. **CAST:** Roddy Piper, Jane Wheeler, Alina Thompson, Miles O'Keeffe. **1996**

MARKED WOMAN ★★★ Iron-hided district attorney Humphrey Bogart, in one of his early good-guy roles, convinces Bette Davis and other ladies of the evening to squeal on their boss, crime kingpin Eduardo Ciannelli. B&W; 99m. **DIR:** Lloyd Bacon. **CAST:** Bette Davis, Humphrey Bogart, Eduardo Ciannelli, Lola Lane, Isabel Jewell, Allen Jenkins. **1937**

MARLENE ★★★★ In this documentary, director Maximilian Schell puHs off something close to a miracle: he creates an absorbing and entertaining study of Marlene Dietrich without ever having her on camera during the interviews. (She refused to be photographed.) Instead, we hear her famous husky voice talking about her life, loves, and movies as scenes from the latter—as well as newsreels and TV clips—play onscreen. 95m. **DIR:** Maximilian Schell. **CAST:** Marlene Dietrich, Maximilian Schell. **1985 DVD**

MARLOWE ★★★1/2 In this adaptation of Raymond Chandler's *The Little Sister*, James Garner makes a spiffy Philip Marlowe. This time, the noble detective is hired to find a missing man, and Bruce Lee, in an early but sparkling film appearance, is one of several interested parties who wants our hero to drop the case. 95m. **DIR:** Paul Bogart. **CAST:** James Garner, Gayle Hunnicutt, Carroll O'Connor, Rita Moreno, Sharon Farrell, William Daniels, Jackie Coogan, Bruce Lee. **1969**

MARNIE ★★★1/2 Unsung Alfred Hitchcock film about a strange young woman (Tippi Hedren) who isn't at all what she appears to be, and Sean Connery as the man determined to find out what makes her tick. Compelling, if overlong, but in the best Hitchcock tradition. 129m. **DIR:** Alfred Hitchcock. **CAST:** Sean Connery, Tippi Hedren, Diane Baker, Martin Gabel, Bruce Dern. **1964 DVD**

MAROC 7 ★★1/2 Generic, British-made robbery tale with Gene Barry as a secret agent hot on the trail of a shrewd thief. Efficient, but routine. 91m. **DIR:** Gerry O'Hara. **CAST:** Gene Barry, Elsa Martinelli, Cyd Charisse. **1967**

MAROONED 🍅 Tale of three astronauts unable to return to Earth and the ensuing rescue attempt. Rated PG. 134m. **DIR:** John Sturges. **CAST:** Gregory Peck, Richard Crenna, David Janssen, Gene Hackman, James Franciscus, Lee Grant. **1969**

MARQUIS ★★★ Weird, weird, weird French satire based on the writings of de Sade, in which the marquis and his jailers are played by actors in animal masks and his stories are enacted (quite graphically in some instances) with Claymation figures. In French with English subtitles. Not rated, but definitely not for kids. 88m. **DIR:** Henri Xhonneux. **CAST:** Philippe Bizot, Gabrielle van Damme. **1989**

MARQUIS DE SADE ★★ Frilly costumes and shadow-enshrouded dungeons are a flimsy excuse for exploitative nudity and sadomasochistic sex in this ludicrously trivial "account" of the infamous Marquis de Sade. It's a wonder the actors can speak their florid dialogue without bursting into laughter. Rated R for rape, violence, profanity, nudity, torture, and simulated sex. 92m. **DIR:** Gwyneth Gibby. **CAST:** Nick Mancuso, Janet Gunn, Charlotte Nielsen, John Rhys-Davies. **1996**

MARRIAGE CIRCLE, THE ★★★★★ Arguably Ernst Lubitsch's best American silent. A comedy of erotic manners ensues when a professor tries to divorce his wife after seeing her flirt with the husband of her best friend. Silent. B&W; 104m. **DIR:** Ernst Lubitsch. **CAST:** Florence Vidor, Monte Blue, Marie Prevost, Adolphe Menjou. **1924**

•**MARRIAGE ITALIAN STYLE** ★★★1/2 Sophia Loren and Marcello Mastroianni are perfectly cast in this bawdy farce about the efforts of a longtime mistress to get her lover to marry her. It's openly sexual in a way that American films of the time were not, which shows off Loren to best advantage. Dubbed in English. 102m. **DIR:** Vittorio De Sica. **CAST:** Sophia Loren, Marcello Mastroianni, Marilu Tolo. **1964**

MARRIAGE OF MARIA BRAUN, THE ★★1/2 Probably Rainer Werner Fassbinder's easiest film to take because it's basically straightforward and stars the sensual and comedic Hanna Schygulla. She plays Maria Braun, a tough cookie who marries a Wehrmacht officer whom she loses to the war and then prison. The film is full of Fassbinder's overly dramatic, sordid sexual atmosphere. It can be both funny and perverse. In German. Rated R. 120m. **DIR:** Rainer Werner Fassbinder. **CAST:** Hanna Schygulla, Klaus Lowitsch, Ivan Desny. **1979**

MARRIED MAN, A ★★ A love triangle leads to murder in this oh-so-British boudoir-and-drawing-room tale. Expect to yawn frequently during this made-for-TV feature. 200m. **DIR:** John Davies. **CAST:** Anthony Hopkins, Ciaran Madden, Lise Hilboldt, John Le Mesurier. **1984**

MARRIED PEOPLE, SINGLE SEX ★★★ Three couples find themselves struggling with their love lives. One couple wants to end their marriage. One wife turns outside her marriage for thrills, while another husband finds pleasure on the phone. It's *thirtysomething* with plenty of nudity and sex as everyone tries to come to terms with their impending midlife crisis. Literate and sexy. Available in rated R and unrated version; both contain plenty of adult language, situations, and nudity. 110m. **DIR:** Mike Sedan. **CAST:** Chase Masterson, Joseph Pilato, Bob Rudd, Darla Slavens, Teri Thompson. **1993**

MARRIED TO IT ★★1/2 Three New York City couples become friends while planning a school play for their children. Some funny and poignant bits, but ultimately doesn't live up to the sum of its parts. Rated R for profanity and nudity. 105m. **DIR:** Arthur Hiller. **CAST:** Beau Bridges, Stockard Channing, Robert Sean Leonard, Mary Stuart Masterson, Cybill Shepherd, Ron Silver. **1991**

MARRIED TO THE MOB ★★★★1/2 This concoction includes humor, oddball set design, eccentric characters galore, and music that sets the scene and the audience in motion. Michelle Pfeiffer plays a beautiful, innocent-yet-fatal femme, here doing her darnedest to extricate herself from the Long Island mob scene after her mobster husband is "iced"; Dean Stockwell is the threatening Don Juan don; Matthew Modine is the savior-nerd. Rated R for language and adult situations. 106m. **DIR:** Jonathan Demme. **CAST:** Michelle Pfeiffer, Matthew Modine, Dean Stockwell, Mercedes Ruehl. **1988 DVD**

MARRIED TOO YOUNG ★★ An uncredited Ed Wood contributed to the script of this drab potboiler about a teen couple whose life together goes downhill after they quit high school to get married. B&W; 76m. **DIR:** George Moskov. **CAST:** Harold Lloyd Jr., Trudy Marshall, Anthony Dexter. **1962**

MARRIED WOMAN, A ★★★ One of Jean-Luc Godard's most conventional films, a study of a Parisian woman who doesn't know if the father of her unborn child is her husband or her lover. In French with English subtitles. 94m. **DIR:** Jean-Luc Godard. **CAST:** Macha Meril, Philippe Leroy, Bernard Noel. **1964**

MARRYING MAN, THE ★★1/2 Neil Simon's screenplay sprinkles laughs into the romance between a toothpaste heir and a torch singer. Stand-up comedian Paul Reiser does a fine job of delivering the best zingers as he narrates their on-again, off-again love story. Rated R for profanity, violence, and simulated sex. 115m. **DIR:** Jerry Rees. **CAST:** Kim Basinger, Alec Baldwin, Robert Loggia, Elisabeth Shue, Armand Assante, Paul Reiser, Fisher Stevens, Peter Dobson. **1991**

MARS ATTACKS! ★★ Iconoclastic director Tim Burton finally bites off more than he can chew with this mean-spirited freak show of a film. Based loosely on an infamous series of early 1960s trading cards, the plot concerns Earth's invasion by bubbleheaded Martians who apparently grew up gleefully ripping the wings off Martian flies. There's no plot to speak of, just a series of depraved sight gags involving big-name stars getting tortured or killed by the giggling little invaders. Rated PG-13 for profanity and quite graphic violence. 103m. **DIR:** Tim Burton. **CAST:** Jack Nicholson, Glenn Close, Annette Bening, Pierce Brosnan, Danny DeVito, Martin Short, Sarah Jessica Parker, Lukas Haas, Natalie Portman. **1996 DVD**

MARS NEEDS WOMEN ♥ Laughable science-fiction yarn featuring Tommy Kirk as a Martian who invades Earth in search of female mates. Ridiculous costumes and special effects only add to the campy effect. Not rated. 80m. **DIR:** Larry Buchanan. **CAST:** Tommy Kirk. **1966**

MARSHAL LAW ★★ Jimmy Smits's engaging debut as an action hero is overshadowed by director Stephen Cornwell's extremely annoying "video verité" camera work, in this otherwise-routine kill-or-be-killed saga. Cornwell clearly watched Oliver Stone's *Natural Born Killers* too many times. Rated R for violence, profanity, drug use, and simulated sex. 95m. **DIR:** Stephen Cornwell. **CAST:** Jimmy Smits, James LeGros, Vonte Sweet, Scott Plank, Kristy Swanson. **1996**

MARSHAL OF CEDAR ROCK ★★★ Marshal Rocky Lane lets a young man escape from prison in order to lead him to money the man apparently stole in a bank robbery. Instead, the trail leads him straight into a railroad land-grab swindle. B&W; 54m. **DIR:** Harry Keller. **CAST:** Allan "Rocky" Lane, Phyllis Coates, Roy Barcroft, William Henry, Robert Shayne, Eddy Waller. **1953**

MARSHAL OF CRIPPLE CREEK ★★★★ Last of the Republic Red Ryder series is one of the fastest-paced, most action-packed of the twenty-three they produced. The discovery of gold in Cripple Creek causes the boomtown to be overrun by a lawless element. B&W; 54m. **DIR:** R. G. Springsteen. **CAST:** Allan "Rocky" Lane, Robert Blake, Gene Roth, Trevor Bardette. **1947**

MARSHAL OF MESA CITY ★★★★ Outstanding series Western features George O'Brien as a retired lawman who rides into a town ruled by a corrupt sheriff (Leon Ames) and stays on to end his reign of terror. Excellent character development and plot twists. B&W; 62m. **DIR:** David Howard. **CAST:** George O'Brien, Virginia Vale, Leon Ames, Henry Brandon. **1939**

MARTIAL LAW ★★ Two policemen use hands and feet to fight crime. A film geared entirely to the martial arts viewing public. Rated R for violence. 90m. **DIR:** S. E. Cohen. **CAST:** Chad McQueen, Cynthia Rothrock, David Carradine. **1990**

MARTIAL LAW TWO—UNDERCOVER 💔 Martial arts expert Cynthia Rothrock goes undercover to catch a cop killer. Nothing revealing here. Rated R for nudity, violence, and profanity. 92m. **DIR:** Kurt Anderson. **CAST:** Jeff Wincott, Cynthia Rothrock, Billy Drago. **1991**

MARTIAL OUTLAW ★★ Brothers Jeff Wincott and Gary Hudson find themselves on opposite sides of the law. Wincott's a DEA agent assigned to infiltrate a $20 million drug deal; Hudson is a crooked cop with a piece of the action. The two stars show off their martial-arts skills, but the story stinks. Rated R for violence. 89m. **DIR:** Kurt Anderson. **CAST:** Jeff Wincott, Gary Hudson, Richard Jaeckel. **1993**

MARTIAN CHRONICLES, PARTS I-III, THE ★★★ Mankind colonizes Mars in this adaptation of the Ray Bradbury classic. As this was originally a TV miniseries, the budget was low and it shows in the cheap sets and poor special effects. The acting is very good, however. 314m. **DIR:** Michael Anderson. **CAST:** Rock Hudson, Darren McGavin, Gayle Hunnicutt, Bernadette Peters, Nicholas Hammond, Roddy McDowall. **1979**

MARTIANS GO HOME 💔 Some wisecracking aliens come to Earth. Rated PG-13 for adult language. 89m. **DIR:** David Odell. **CAST:** Randy Quaid, Margaret Colin, John Philbin, Anita Harris. **1990**

MARTIN ★★★ Director George Romero creates a good chiller with a lot of bloodcurdling power about a young man who thinks he's a vampire. This is very well-done. Rated R. 95m. **DIR:** George A. Romero. **CAST:** John Amplas, Lincoln Maazel. **1978**

MARTIN CHUZZLEWIT ★★★★★ Charles Dickens's stinging and hilarious satire is exquisitely presented in this lush three-part BBC import. Paul Scofield heads an extended, self-involved family panting after, and plotting for, his vast fortune. From the actors' intriguing faces to the elaborately detailed costumes, this is an impeccable production much enhanced by a brilliant cast. So cunningly adapted and performed it can be watched easily in one sitting, regardless of the length. Not rated; contains implied violence. 288m. **DIR:** Pedr James. **CAST:** Paul Scofield, John Mills, Pete Postlethwaite, Julia Sawalha. **1994**

MARTIN LUTHER ★★1/2 This biography of the cleric who broke with the Catholic Church and founded Protestantism is handsomely photographed but overly respectful—Luther seems too saintly, wasting the talents of Old Vic veteran Niall MacGinnis. B&W; 104m. **DIR:** Irving Pichel. **CAST:** Niall MacGinnis, John Ruddock. **1953**

MARTIN'S DAY ★★1/2 Richard Harris plays an escaped convict who kidnaps young Justin Henry but ends up being his friend in this Canadian production. A good idea with a pedestrian resolution. Rated PG. 98m. **DIR:** Alan Gibson. **CAST:** Richard Harris, Lindsay Wagner, John Ireland, James Coburn, Justin Henry, Karen Black. **1984**

MARTY (1955) ★★★★★ This heartwarming movie about a New York butcher captured the Academy Award for best picture and another for Ernest Borgnine's poignant portrayal. Two lonely people manage to stumble into romance in spite of their own insecurities and the pressures of others. B&W; 91m. **DIR:** Delbert Mann. **CAST:** Ernest Borgnine, Betsy Blair. **1955**

MARTY (1953) (TELEVISION) ★★★★ The original *Marty*, written for the *Goodyear Playhouse* by Paddy Chayefsky in 1953. Rod Steiger is tremendously sincere in his first starring role as the lonely butcher who meets a plain schoolteacher (Nancy Marchand) one night at the Waverly ballroom. Powerful, low-key drama, hardly hurt by the poor technical standards of the time. Hosted by Eva Marie Saint; interviews with the stars and the director thrown in for good measure. B&W; 60m. **DIR:** Delbert Mann. **CAST:** Rod Steiger, Nancy Marchand, Esther Minciotti, Joe Mantell, Betsy Palmer, Nehemiah Persoff. **1953**

MARVELOUS LAND OF OZ, THE ★★★ This teleplay, based on the works of L. Frank Baum, is an excellent means of introducing children to the experience of live theater. It boasts marvelous costuming and presentation by the Minneapolis Children's Theatre Company and School. 101m. **DIR:** John Driver, John Clark Donohue. **CAST:** Wendy Lehr, Christopher Passi. **1981**

MARVIN AND TIGE ★★★★ Touching story of a runaway (Gibran Brown) who finds a friend in a poor and lonely man (John Cassavetes). Cassavetes's beautiful loser character works so well with Brown's streetwise pomp that the tension created by the clash of personalities makes their eventual deep relationship that much more rewarding. Rated PG for a few profane words. 104m. **DIR:** Eric Weston. **CAST:** John Cassavetes, Gibran Brown, Billy Dee Williams, Denise Nicholas, Fay Hauser. **1982**

MARVIN'S ROOM ★★ Scott McPherson's intimate little play becomes a treacly, disease-of-the-week sudser helped not at all by Meryl Streep or Diane Keaton. The latter is a saintly woman who has spent twenty years caring for family members, only to discover she has leukemia. This forces a reunion with estranged sister Streep and wayward nephew Leonardo DiCaprio. What follows is the sort of smarmy nonsense that wouldn't be believed by *Love Story* fans. Rated PG-13 for profanity and medical candor. 98m. **DIR:** Jerry Zaks. **CAST:** Meryl Streep, Diane Keaton, Leonardo DiCaprio, Robert De Niro, Hume Cronyn, Gwen Verdon. **1996 DVD**

MARY AND JOSEPH: A STORY OF FAITH 💔 One can wish for a good telling of the story of Mary, she of the Immaculate Conception, and the devout Joseph, chosen "parents" of Christ, but this TV movie is not it. Dull, badly acted, and sustains no interest either historically or religiously. 146m. **DIR:** Eric Till. **CAST:** Blanche Baker, Jeff East, Lloyd Bochner, Colleen Dewhurst. **1979**

MARY HARTMAN, MARY HARTMAN (TV SERIES) ★★★★ Full of whimsy and satire, this off-the-wall show plunged into subjects considered taboo by normal sitcoms, such as impotence and marijuana. Louise Lasser, as Mary, fashioned a unique character with which a wide audience empathized. This series is worth another look. 70m. DIR: Joan Darling, Jim Drake. CAST: Louise Lasser, Greg Mullavey, Mary Kay Place, Graham Jarvis, Victor Kilian, Debralee Scott, Martin Mull. 1976

MARY, MARY, BLOODY MARY ★★ A bloody and grisly film depicting the horror of vampirism and mass murder. A beautiful vampire and artist, Mary (Cristina Ferrare), goes to Mexico to fulfill her need for blood. This film is rated R for nudity, violence, and gore. 95m. DIR: Juan Lopez Moctezuma. CAST: Cristina Ferrare, David Young, Helena Rojo, John Carradine. 1987

MARY MY DEAREST ★★ A magician converts a thief, marries him, and has him join her in a traveling show. She inadvertently hitches a ride with people being transported to an insane asylum where she becomes trapped. Poorly acted and very depressing. In Spanish with English subtitles. Not rated; contains nudity and suggested sex. 100m. DIR: Jaime Humberto Hermosillo. CAST: Maria Rojo, Hector Bonilla, Ana Ofelia Morguia. 1983

MARY OF SCOTLAND ★★★★ Katharine Hepburn plays one of history's tragic figures in director John Ford's biography of the sixteenth-century queen of Scotland. Fredric March is Bothwell, her supporter (and eventual lover) in her battle for power. The last scene, where Mary confronts her English accusers in court, is so well acted and photographed, it alone is worth the price of the rental. B&W; 123m. DIR: John Ford. CAST: Katharine Hepburn, Fredric March, John Carradine. 1936

MARY POPPINS ★★★★★ Here's Julie Andrews in her screen debut. She plays a nanny who believes that "a spoonful of sugar makes the medicine go down." Andrews is great in the role and sings ever so sweetly. The song and dance numbers are attractively laid on, with Dick Van Dyke, as Mary's Cockney beau, giving an amusing performance. Rated G. 140m. DIR: Robert Stevenson. CAST: Julie Andrews, Dick Van Dyke, David Tomlinson, Glynis Johns, Karen Dotrice, Matthew Garber, Jane Darwell, Ed Wynn, Arthur Treacher, Hermione Baddeley. 1964 DVD

MARY REILLY ★★ The oft-told tale of Dr. Jekyll and Mr. Hyde (John Malkovich), seen through the eyes of Jekyll's adoring housemaid (Julia Roberts). Murky, mushy, glacially slow, and devoid of suspense, with one-note performances from the stars. Roberts, unable to deploy her trademark smile, cowers like a scared rabbit, while Malkovich inexplicably plays Jekyll and Hyde as looking and sounding almost exactly alike. Rated R for brief but intense violence. 118m. DIR: Stephen Frears. CAST: Julia Roberts, John Malkovich, Glenn Close, Michael Gambon, George Cole, Kathy Staff. 1996

MARY SHELLEY'S FRANKENSTEIN ★★1/2 Kenneth Branagh's retelling of Mary Shelley's story is a major disappointment. The emphasis seems to be more on the lavish sets than the characters, despite the efforts of cast and director. Like the monster Victor Frankenstein creates, this movie is an often awkward patchwork. Give us *Bride of Frankenstein* any day. Rated R for violence, gore, simulated sex, and nudity. 123m. DIR: Kenneth Branagh. CAST: Robert De Niro, Kenneth Branagh, Tom Hulce, Helena Bonham Carter, Aidan Quinn, Ian Holm, John Cleese. 1994 DVD

MARZIPAN PIG, THE ★★★ Tim Curry narrates this animated food chain fable about the effect of a candy pig on the mouse who ate him and the owl who ate the mouse. Seems a harsh metaphor for the 5- to 8-year-olds it's aimed at, but ends on a light, upbeat note. 30m. DIR: Michael Sporn. 1990

MASADA ★★★★ A spectacular TV movie based on the famous battle of Masada during the Roman domination of the known world. Fine acting, especially by Peter O'Toole, and excellent production values elevate this one far above the average small-screen movie. Not rated. 131m. DIR: Boris Sagal. CAST: Peter O'Toole, Peter Strauss, Barbara Carrera. 1984

MASALA ★★★★ Silliness abounds in this delightfully funny domestic comedy. A distraught Indian woman living in Canada summons a Hindu god to help her dysfunctional family. Before the day is done, various family members will confront terrorists, marital woes, government agents, and a son who arrives with some interesting news. Multicultural effort is in English. Not rated; contains adult situations, nudity, and strong language. 105m. DIR: Srinivas Krishna. CAST: Saeed Jaffrey, Srinivas Krishna, Zohra Segal. 1992

MASCARA ♥ Luridly exploitative film about a sister and brother with a very kinky relationship. Rated R for nudity, profanity, and violence. 99m. DIR: Patrick Conrad. CAST: Charlotte Rampling, Michael Sarrazin, Derek de Lint. 1987

MASCULINE FEMININE ★★★ Jean-Luc Godard's eleventh film is an uneven attempt at exploring the relationship between a young Parisian radical, effectively portrayed by Jean-Pierre Leaud, and a slightly promiscuous woman (Chantal Goya) in fifteen discontinuous, contrapuntal vignettes. Good camera work and interesting screenplay lose strength in a muddled and disjointed story. In French with English subtitles. B&W; 103m. DIR: Jean-Luc Godard. CAST: Jean-Pierre Léaud, Chantal Goya, Catherine Isabelle Duport, Marlene Jobert. 1966

M*A*S*H ★★★★1/2 Fans of the television series of the same name and *Trapper John, M.D.* may have a bit of trouble recognizing their favorite characters, but this is the original. One of eccentric film director Robert Altman's few true artistic successes, this release is outrageous good fun. Rated PG. 116m. DIR: Robert Altman. CAST: Elliott Gould, Donald Sutherland, Sally Kellerman, Tom Skerritt, Robert Duvall, Jo Ann Pflug, Bud Cort, Gary Burghoff. 1970

M*A*S*H (TV SERIES) ★★★★ Nobody expected director Robert Altman's wry 1970 war comedy to translate well on the small screen, but a decade's worth of episodes and an impressive string of Emmy Awards proved the folly of that particular prediction. Alan Alda and Wayne Rogers became perfectly acceptable substitutes for Elliott Gould and Donald Sutherland, and the series also introduced many supporting players—notably McLean Stevenson as Lieutenant Colonel Henry Blake—who eventually went on to successes of their own. (Gary Burghoff's anticipatory Corporal Radar O'Reilly was the only carryover from film to series.) This television classic owes most of its success to Larry Gelbart's thoughtful scripts. Each tape includes two half-hour episodes. 52m. **DIR:** Hy Averback, Jackie Cooper, Gene Reynolds. **CAST:** Alan Alda, Wayne Rogers, McLean Stevenson, Loretta Swit, Larry Linville, Gary Burghoff. 1972–1983

MASK, THE (1961) 💖 Low-budget chiller, shot in 3-D, about a psychiatrist who discovers an ancient ritual mask that causes violent hallucinations. B&W; 85m. **DIR:** Julian Roffman. **CAST:** Paul Stevens, Claudette Nevins. 1961

MASK (1985) ★★★★★ They used to call them moving pictures, and few films fit this phrase as well as this one, starring Cher, Sam Elliott, and Eric Stoltz. The story of a teenage boy coping with a disfiguring disease, it touches the viewer's heart as few movies have ever done. *Mask* rises above simple entertainment with its uplifting true-life tale. Rated PG-13. 120m. **DIR:** Peter Bogdanovich. **CAST:** Cher, Sam Elliott, Eric Stoltz, Laura Dern. 1985 DVD

MASK, THE (1994) ★★★★ A good-hearted, put-upon bank employee discovers a mask that frees his inhibitions and gives him eye-popping magical powers. Star Jim Carrey is marvelous in this cartoon-style film that salutes the groundbreaking animated shorts made at Warner Bros. and MGM by Tex Avery and Bob Clampett. Cameron Diaz is a real knockout, even keeping pace with the rubber-legged Carrey in a dance sequence that has to be seen to be believed. Rated PG-13 for violence and profanity. 101m. **DIR:** Charles Russell. **CAST:** Jim Carrey, Cameron Diaz, Peter Riegert, Peter Greene, Amy Yasbeck, Richard Jeni. 1994 DVD

MASK OF DEATH ★★★ Better-than-average Lorenzo Lamas vehicle has the macho action star doing double duty, portraying a ruthless murderer plus the undercover detective who undergoes plastic surgery to replace the killer after he's murdered. Lamas actually emotes as detective Dan McKenna, who becomes two-faced in order to avenge the murder of his wife. Decent action and cast keep this one on its toes. Rated R for language, nudity, and violence. 89m. **DIR:** David Mitchell. **CAST:** Lorenzo Lamas, Rae Dawn Chong, Billy Dee Williams, Conrad Dunn. 1997

MASK OF FU MANCHU, THE ★★★1/2 The best of all the movies adapted from Sax Rohmer's novels about an evil mastermind intent on taking over the world features Boris Karloff as the title character and Lewis Stone as his Sherlock Holmes–style nemesis, Nayland Smith. If one can overlook the unfortunate racial stereotypes (Rohmer often referred to Fu Manchu as "The Yellow Peril"), this film makes for fun viewing. B&W; 72m. **DIR:** Charles Babin. **CAST:** Boris Karloff, Lewis Stone, Karen Morley, Myrna Loy, Charles Starrett, Jean Hersholt. 1932

MASK OF ZORRO, THE ★★★★★ Expertly crafted action entertainment. Anthony Hopkins plays the aged California folk hero who trains Antonio Banderas to take up the sword against corrupt Spanish officials. Fantastic fencing, spectacular stunts, a good dose of comedy, and even some moving acting make this the best filmed incarnation yet of the Mexican masked man. Executive produced by Steven Spielberg, who obviously had a lot of say in the film's shaping. Rated PG-13 for violence. 137m. **DIR:** Martin Campbell. **CAST:** Antonio Banderas, Anthony Hopkins, Catherine Zeta-Jones, Stuart Wilson, Matthew Letscher. 1998 DVD

MASKED MARVEL, THE ★★1/2 The mysterious Masked Marvel comes to the aid of the World-Wide Insurance Company to battle the evil Sakima, a former Japanese envoy, and his gang of saboteurs, who are threatening the security of America. Practically nonstop action and top stunt work highlight this wartime Republic serial, which is about as patriotic as a serial can be. B&W; 12 chapters. **DIR:** Spencer Gordon Bennet. **CAST:** William Forrest, Louise Currie, Johnny Arthur. 1943

MASKS OF DEATH ★★★ Twenty-seven years after playing Sherlock Holmes in the Hammer Films version of *The Hound of the Baskervilles*, Peter Cushing returned to the role for this enjoyable thriller. This time, the Great Detective and Dr. Watson (John Mills) investigate a series of bizarre murders, which leave their victims' faces frozen in expressions of terror. 80m. **DIR:** Roy Ward Baker. **CAST:** Peter Cushing, John Mills, Anne Baxter, Ray Milland. 1986

MASQUE OF THE RED DEATH, THE (1964) ★★★ The combination of Roger Corman, Edgar Allan Poe, and Vincent Price meant first-rate (though low-budget) horror films in the early 1960s. This was one of the best. Price is deliciously villainous. 86m. **DIR:** Roger Corman. **CAST:** Vincent Price, Hazel Court, Jane Asher, David Weston, Patrick Magee. 1964

MASQUE OF THE RED DEATH (1989) ★★★ A fine rendition of the classic Edgar Allan Poe story of paranoia and death. Producer Roger Corman adds a smattering of sex and violence, but what elevates this film are the sumptuous sets and costumes. Rated R. 83m. **DIR:** Larry Brand. **CAST:** Patrick Macnee, Jeff Osterhage. 1989

MASQUERADE (1986) ★★★1/2 Bizarre psychodrama about a famous young actor who, disillusioned by his popularity, escapes into a world where reality and fantasy become obscured. Unconventional, stylistic approach by director Janusz Kijowski (one of Poland's new-wave filmmakers). In Polish with English subtitles. 102m. **DIR:** Janusz Kijowski. **CAST:** Boguslaw Linda. 1986

MASQUERADE (1988) ★★1/2 Overblown variation on Hitchcock's *Suspicion* with Rob Lowe playing the devious but attractive husband who may be after heiress Meg Tilly's money. Some new plot twists are introduced, but unfortunately these don't save *Masquerade* from playing a lot like *Dallas*. Rated R for language, nudity, simulated sex, and violence. 98m. **DIR:** Bob Swaim. **CAST:** Rob Lowe, Meg Tilly, Kim Cattrall, Doug Savant, John Glover, Dana Delany. 1988

MASS APPEAL ★★★★1/2 A first-rate discussion of the dichotomy between private conscience and mass appeal, this film finds a mediocre and worldly priest, Father Tim Farley (Jack Lemmon), walking a political tightrope between the young seminarian (Zeljko Ivanek) he has befriended and his superior, Monsignor Burke (Charles Durning). At times both comic and tragic, it is not only a fine memorial but also a splendid motion picture. Rated PG. 99m. **DIR:**

Glenn Jordan. **CAST:** Jack Lemmon, Zeljko Ivanek, Charles Durning, Louise Latham, James Ray. **1984**

MASSACRE AT CENTRAL HIGH ★★★ Low-budget production has a teenager exacting his own brand of revenge on tough gang members who are making things hard for the students at a local high school. This violent drama has a lot going for it, except for some goofy dialogue. Otherwise, nicely done. Rated R. 85m. **DIR:** Renee Daalder. **CAST:** Andrew Stevens, Kimberly Beck, Derrel Maury, Robert Carradine. **1976**

MASSACRE AT FORT HOLMAN (REASON TO LIVE ... A REASON TO DIE, A) ★1/2 Spaghetti Western of marginal interest. Eight condemned men led by James Coburn get a chance to redeem themselves by overtaking a rebel fort. Plenty of action can't help the worn-out plot or Western clichés. Rated PG for violence and profanity. 90m. **DIR:** Tonino Valerii. **CAST:** James Coburn, Telly Savalas, Bud Spencer. **1984**

MASSACRE IN ROME ★★★1/2 Chilling drama about a priest (Marcello Mastroianni) opposing a Nazi colonel (Richard Burton) who must execute hundreds of Roman citizens in retaliation for the death by partisans of some Nazi troops. Rated PG for violence. 103m. **DIR:** George Pan Cosmatos. **CAST:** Richard Burton, Marcello Mastroianni, Leo McKern, John Steiner. **1973**

MASSIVE RETALIATION 💙 A group of friends gathers at their own civil-defense fort during a national emergency. Not rated; has profanity and violence. 90m. **DIR:** Thomas A. Cohen. **CAST:** Tom Boyer, Karlene Crockett, Peter Donat, Marilyn Hassett, Jason Gedrick. **1984**

MASTER BLASTER 💙 A survival-game competition gets out of hand. Rated R for violence, profanity, and nudity. 94m. **DIR:** Glenn Wilder. **CAST:** Jeff Moldovan, Donna Rosae, Joe Hess, Peter Lunblad. **1985**

MASTER HAROLD AND THE BOYS ★★★★ An intense movie filmed in a single setting with a cast of three. Matthew Broderick gives a moving performance as a white English boy in 1950s South Africa. Zakes Mokae, in a brilliant portrayal as a black servant, tries to lead the boy gently toward manhood. Not rated; contains profanity. 90m. **DIR:** Michael Lindsay-Hogg. **CAST:** Matthew Broderick, Zakes Mokae, John Kani. **1984**

MASTER OF BALLANTRAE, THE ★★ Errol Flynn's disappointing swan song as a swashbuckler is about two brothers who take different sides in squabbles over the British throne. 89m. **DIR:** William Keighley. **CAST:** Errol Flynn, Anthony Steel, Roger Livesey, Beatrice Campbell, Yvonne Furneaux. **1953**

MASTER OF THE HOUSE (DU SKAL AERE DIN HUSTRU) ★★★★ In this funny satire of middle-class life, a wife runs away from her husband, a chauvinist pig who treats her brutally. Later, the wife is reunited with her husband after an old nurse has taught him a lesson. Silent. B&W; 81m. **DIR:** Carl Dreyer. **CAST:** Johannes Meyer, Astrid Holm. **1925**

MASTER OF THE WORLD ★★★ Jules Verne's tale brought excitingly to the screen. Vincent Price plays a self-proclaimed god trying to end all war by flying around the world in a giant airship, blowing ships from the water, etc. Lots of fun. 104m. **DIR:** William

Witney. **CAST:** Vincent Price, Charles Bronson, Henry Hull. **1961**

MASTER RACE, THE ★★★ Hitler's Third Reich collapses. A dedicated Nazi officer escapes. His refusal to accept defeat becomes an engrossing study of blind obedience to immorality. B&W; 96m. **DIR:** Herbert J. Biberman. **CAST:** George Coulouris, Stanley Ridges, Osa Massen, Lloyd Bridges. **1944**

MASTERMIND ★★★ Zero Mostel spoofs Charlie Chan in this 1969 comedy that wasn't released until 1976. It's better than it sounds, with in-jokes for old-movie buffs and lots of slapstick for the whole family. It's even rated G! 84m. **DIR:** Alex March. **CAST:** Zero Mostel, Bradford Dillman, Jules Munshin. **1976**

MASTERMINDS ★★1/2 When the students at an upper-crust private school are held hostage by their new security consultant, only one student, a recently expelled computer-hacking troublemaker, stands between the villain and a $650 million ransom. Silly, farfetched, and way over-the-top, it's sort of a children's production of *Die Hard* crossed with *The Rock*, with plenty of violence but no blood or death—which isn't very convincing, but at least it protects the PG-13 rating. Patrick Stewart's lip-smacking gusto as the chief bad guy is the film's main asset. Rated PG-13 for violent action. 106m. **DIR:** Roger Christian. **CAST:** Patrick Stewart, Vincent Kartheiser, Brenda Fricker, Bradley Whitford, Matt Craven. **1997**

MASTERS OF MENACE ★★★ Cameos by Jim Belushi, John Candy, George Wendt, and Dan Aykroyd help this story of a young lawyer who must follow a motorcycle gang around and make sure they don't get into any trouble. He doesn't have any luck. Rated PG-13 for violence and profanity. 97m. **DIR:** Daniel Raskov. **CAST:** David Rasche, Catherine Bach, David L. Lander, Teri Copley, Ray Baker. **1990**

MASTERS OF THE UNIVERSE ★★1/2 Those toy and cartoon characters come to life on the silver screen, and all things considered, the translation is fairly successful. He-Man and friends are exiled to Earth, where they befriend a teenage couple and battle Skeletor's evil minions. A small amount of foul language and one scene of graphic violence may be deemed unsuitable for young children by some parents. Rated PG. 106m. **DIR:** Gary Goddard. **CAST:** Dolph Lundgren, Frank Langella, Courteney Cox, James Tolkan, Meg Foster. **1987**

MATA HARI (1931) ★★★ Casting Greta Garbo as history's most alluring spy proved to be big box office. She captivated Ramon Novarro—*and* the audience! The legend's throaty voice is hypnotic. B&W; 90m. **DIR:** George Fitzmaurice. **CAST:** Greta Garbo, Ramon Novarro, Karen Morley, Lionel Barrymore, Lewis Stone. **1931**

MATA HARI (1985) ★★ Liberally sprinkled with action, erotica, and existentialism, *Mata Hari* is one of Sylvia (*Emmanuelle*) Kristel's better works. This story traces the erotic dancer from Indonesia as she unwittingly becomes the tool of the German government during World War II. Rated R for sex and nudity. 103m. **DIR:** Curtis Harrington. **CAST:** Sylvia Kristel, Christopher Cazenove, Oliver Tobias. **1985**

MATADOR ★★★★ Mind-boggling psychosexual melodrama carried to hilarious extremes by director Pedro Almodóvar. The story centers around a lame ex-bullfighter who derives sexual gratification from murder. In Spanish with English subtitles. Rated R for nudity and violence. 107m. **DIR:** Pedro Almodóvar. **CAST:** Assumpta Serna, Antonio Banderas, Carmen Maura. **1988**

MATCHMAKER, THE (1958) ★★★★ Gabby Shirley Booth takes it upon herself to find a wife for rich merchant Paul Ford, but finds herself attracted to the stuffy old crank, and they end up an item. Young Anthony Perkins and Shirley MacLaine fall in love along the way, and everything ends up swell. This pleasant little comedy was written for the stage by Thornton Wilder, and it found its way to the stage and the screen again as *Hello Dolly.* B&W; 101m. **DIR:** Joseph Anthony. **CAST:** Shirley Booth, Paul Ford, Anthony Perkins, Shirley MacLaine, Robert Morse, Wallace Ford, Rex Evans, Russell Collins, Gavin Gordon. **1958**

MATCHMAKER, THE (1997) ★★★★ Comedian-turned-actress Janeane Garofalo is totally delightful as a Boston congressional aide who is sent to Ireland to dig up some history on her boss. Instead, she stumbles into a small village's matchmaker festival, where she learns about love and herself. David O'Hara shines as one of the locals who steals her heart, while Denis Leary checks in as an ungrateful political assistant. A feel-goody comedy with lots of heart and laughs. Rated R for language. 97m. **DIR:** Mark Joffe. **CAST:** Janeane Garofalo, David O'Hara, Milo O'Shea, Denis Leary, Jay O. Sanders. **1997 DVD**

MATERNAL INSTINCTS ★★1/2 A woman who desperately wants to have a baby becomes obsessed with ruining her doctor's life after undergoing an emergency hysterectomy. The acting in this made-for-cable original is stiff and unconvincing. Rated PG-13 for violence. 92m. **DIR:** George Kaczender. **CAST:** Delta Burke, Beth Broderick, Garwin Sanford. **1996**

MATEWAN ★★★★1/2 Writer-director John Sayles's masterpiece about the massacre of striking West Virginia coal miners in 1920 has both heart and humor. Chris Cooper is the soft-spoken union organizer who tries to avoid violence. James Earl Jones is the leader of a group of black workers who were shocked to find, too late, that they were brought in as scabs. And David Strathairn is memorable as the town sheriff who attempts to keep the peace. Rated PG-13 for violence and profanity. 132m. **DIR:** John Sayles. **CAST:** Chris Cooper, Will Oldham, Mary McDonnell, James Earl Jones, David Strathairn, Josh Mostel. **1987 DVD**

MATILDA ★★★1/2 A cute comedy about a boxing kangaroo who becomes a legend in the sport. Elliott Gould plays a small-time booking agent who becomes the manager of the heavyweight marsupial. Sentimental at times and a bit corny, too, but worth the time. Recommended for family viewing. Rated G. 105m. **DIR:** Daniel Mann. **CAST:** Elliott Gould, Robert Mitchum, Clive Revill, Harry Guardino, Roy Clark, Lionel Stander, Art Metrano. **1978**

MATILDA (1996) ★★★★ In this dark comedy and modern-day fable, resourceful Matilda develops her telekinetic powers to even the odds between herself and a sadistic school principal, while distancing herself from her ill-mannered, uneducated, and unethical parents by immersing herself in the world of books. Powerful messages delivered without obvious preaching. Rated PG for simulated child abuse. 93m. **DIR:** Danny DeVito. **CAST:** Mara Wilson, Danny DeVito, Rhea Perlman, Pam Ferris, Embeth Davidtz. **1996 DVD**

MATINEE ★★★★ Charlie Haas's screenplay is set during the Cuban Missile Crisis in Key West, where John Goodman is staging a premiere of his latest masterwork: *Mant*—"Half Man, Half Ant, All Terror!" while the populace deals with the fear of impending nuclear war. Goodman's deft performance is complemented by a well-played, coming-of-age story. Rated PG for profanity. 97m. **DIR:** Joe Dante. **CAST:** John Goodman, Cathy Moriarty, Simon Fenton, Omri Katz, Kellie Martin, Lisa Jakub, Jesse White, Dick Miller, John Sayles, William Schallert, Robert Cornthwaite. **1993 DVD**

MATING GAME, THE ★★★★ A straight-as-an-arrow tax collector finds himself being wooed by both the farmer and his daughter, who have never seen any good reason to pay taxes. Great comedy, exceptional cast, with special mention for Fred Clark as the evil head of the Internal Revenue Service. 101m. **DIR:** George Marshall. **CAST:** Debbie Reynolds, Tony Randall, Paul Douglas, Fred Clark, Una Merkel, Philip Ober. **1951**

●**MATING HABITS OF THE EARTHBOUND HUMAN, THE** ★★★1/2 David Hyde Pierce narrates this take on nature documentaries, where we follow the sex lives of two humans in their natural habitats, including a typical human-meeting facility—the nightclub. This hilarious farce parodies all of those animal shows seen on PBS in a new, creative way. Rated R for sexual situations. 90m. **DIR:** Jeff Abugov. **CAST:** Mackenzie Astin, Carmen Electra, David Hyde Pierce. **1999**

MATING SEASON, THE ★★★ An enjoyable romantic comedy set among the flora and fauna commonly inhabited by bird-watchers. When an emotional lady attorney resorts to bird-watching for relaxation, she meets a charming businessman. Affable little TV movie. 96m. **DIR:** John Llewellyn Moxey. **CAST:** Lucie Arnaz, Laurence Luckinbill, Swoosie Kurtz, Diane Stilwell, Joel Brooks. **1986**

MATRIX, THE ★★★★ This slick cyberpunk tale, which boasts an ingenious plot and bravura filmmaking, is a first-class head trip that's both fun to watch and intellectually stimulating. The story's focus is a conservative, buttoned-down software programmer (Keanu Reeves) with an after-hours fixation on a hacker's legend—somebody named Morpheus—reputed to know "great things" about cyberspace. That proves to be the understatement of the century, when our hero finds himself the target of powerful and sinister "agents" of some oblique government entity. The mesmerizing blend of hyperspeed imagery and slow-motion flourish will keep you dazzled for days. And yet, however wild things get, it all makes sense. Rated R for violence, profanity, and special effects. 138m. DIR: Larry Wachowski, Andy Wachowski. CAST: Keanu Reeves, Laurence Fishburne, Carrie Anne Moss, Hugo Weaving, Joe Pantoliano. 1999 DVD

MATT THE GOOSEBOY ★★★1/2 Beautifully detailed animation garnishes this presentation of a classic Hungarian folktale, wherein a young peasant boy must act to end the oppression of his people and country. 77m. DIR: Attila Durgay, Luis Elman. 1978

MATTER OF DEGREES, A ★★★ When a college threatens to change its progressive campus radio station to a more laid-back listening format, staff members and students revolt. Rated R for sexual situations. 90m. DIR: W. T. Morgan. CAST: Arye Gross, Judith Hoag, Tom Sizemore. 1990

MATTER OF PRINCIPLE, A ★★★★ Delightful tale about a selfish tyrant (Alan Arkin) who is suddenly overthrown by his much-put-upon wife (Barbara Dana, Arkin's real-life wife). She takes their eleven children after he destroys their first Christmas tree. Finally, he must wake up and think about someone besides himself. Not rated, but fine family entertainment. 60m. DIR: Gwen Arner. CAST: Alan Arkin, Barbara Dana, Tony Arkin. 1983

MATTER OF TIME, A 🐺 A penniless countess takes a country-bumpkin-come-to-the-big-city hotel chambermaid in hand. Rated PG. 99m. DIR: Vincente Minnelli. CAST: Liza Minnelli, Ingrid Bergman, Charles Boyer, Spiro Andros, Isabella Rossellini. 1976

MATTERS OF THE HEART ★★ Made-for-cable melodrama concerning a talented college musician (Christopher Gartin) who falls in love with a world-famous pianist (Jane Seymour at her bitchiest) . . . who, naturally, has cancer! Brief nudity. 94m. DIR: Michael Ray Rhodes. CAST: Jane Seymour, Christopher Gartin, James Stacy, Geoffrey Lewis. 1990

MAURICE ★★★ Based on E. M. Forster's long-suppressed, semiautobiographical novel, this film details the love of a middle-class college student (James Wilby) for his aristocratic classmate (Hugh Grant). A minor, but handsome film. Rated R for nudity and implied sex. 140m. DIR: James Ivory. CAST: James Wilby, Hugh Grant, Rupert Graves, Denholm Elliott. 1987

MAUSOLEUM 🐺 Housewife wreaks devastation on assorted victims because of a demonic possession. Rated R. 96m. DIR: Jerry Zimmerman, Michael Franzese. CAST: Bobbie Bresee, Marjoe Gortner. 1983

MAUVAISE GRAINE (BAD SEED) ★★★1/2 Fans of Billy Wilder (and what film buff isn't?) will give thanks that this early feature by the director has been unearthed. Made in France while the young Wilder was in the process of emigrating to the United States from his native Germany, this is a surprisingly racy look at criminal life in Paris during the Jazz Age. In French with English subtitles. B&W; 76m. DIR: Billy Wilder, Alexander Esway. CAST: Pierre Mingand, Raymond Galle, Danielle Darrieux. 1933

MAVERICK ★★★★1/2 This big-screen adaptation of the TV series features Mel Gibson as gambler and reluctant hero Bret Maverick. James Garner, the first actor to play the title character, costars as a lawman who anticipates Maverick's every move. Sexy grifter Jodie Foster keeps our hero preoccupied in

other ways, as this unlikely trio heads for a high-stakes poker competition. It's great fun for Western fans, since a number of TV and movie cowboys make cameo appearances. Rated PG for violence. 129m. DIR: Richard Donner. CAST: Mel Gibson, Jodie Foster, James Garner, James Coburn, Graham Greene, Alfred Molina, Max Perlich, Leo Gordon, Danny Glover, Margot Kidder, Robert Fuller, Denver Pyle, Dennis Fimple, Bert Ramson, Doug McClure, Will Hutchins, Waylon Jennings. 1994 DVD

MAVERICK (TV SERIES) ★★★★ One of the best TV Western series, this tongue-in-cheek show starred James Garner and Jack Kelly as the Maverick brothers, Bret and Bart, and after Garner left, Roger Moore as British cousin Beau. The first two episodes to be released on video are classics. "Shady Deal at Sunny Acres" has Bret and Bart outwitting corrupt banker John Dehner with the help of the series' semiregular shady characters. "Duel at Sundown" features a young Clint Eastwood as a trigger-happy character. B&W; each. 49m. DIR: Leslie Martinson, Arthur Lubin. CAST: James Garner, Jack Kelly, Roger Moore, Clint Eastwood, Efrem Zimbalist Jr., Richard Long, Diane Brewster, John Dehner, Leo Gordon, Edgar Buchanan, Abby Dalton. 1958–1962

MAVERICK QUEEN, THE ★★★ Sparks erupt when a Pinkerton detective works undercover at a Wyoming gambling hotel that is a hangout for an outlaw gang. Barbara Stanwyck is cast astely as the beauty who owns the hotel and is caught between her jealous lover and the lawman. 90m. DIR: Joseph Kane. CAST: Barbara Stanwyck, Barry Sullivan, Scott Brady, Mary Murphy, Wallace Ford. 1955

MAX AND HELEN ★★★1/2 Thoughtful, often heartbreaking story looks at two victims of the Holocaust. Max (Treat Williams) tells his story to famed Nazi hunter Simon Wiesenthal (Martin Landau), who has located the camp commandant where Max and his fiancée Helen (Alice Krige) were held. Made for cable TV. No rating, but contains scenes of torture and rape. 79m. DIR: Philip Saville. CAST: Martin Landau, Treat Williams, Alice Krige. 1990

MAX DUGAN RETURNS ★★★1/2 After spending many years in jail and gambling to big winnings, Max Dugan (Jason Robards) seeks his daughter (Marsha Mason) to bestow gifts upon her and her son. Though grateful, she finds it difficult to explain to her policeman-boyfriend, Donald Sutherland. The charm of this Neil Simon fable wears thin. Rated PG. 98m. DIR: Herbert Ross. CAST: Jason Robards Jr., Marsha Mason, Donald Sutherland. 1983

MAX HEADROOM ★★★1/2 The original British production, later remade as a short-lived American TV series. Post-apocalypse newsman discovers an insidious form of advertising that causes viewers to explode. After being murdered by network executives, he's reborn as a computer-generated figure named Max Headroom. A sly parody of ratings-hungry television, the film is visually superb. 96m. DIR: Rocky Morton, Annabel Jankel. CAST: Matt Frewer, Nickolas Grace, Hilary Tindall, Morgan Sherpard, Amanda Pays. 1986

MAX IS MISSING ★★★1/2 You'll enjoy this kid-oriented adventure saga, which stars Toran Caudell as a

12-year-old American boy who clashes with artifact thieves while visiting Peru's Machu Picchu ruins. After befriending a local boy (Victor Rojas), our resourceful hero struggles to deliver a priceless Inca amulet to its rightful heirs. Great fun, intelligently executed, and highlighted by credible performances from both boys. Rated PG for mild violence. 95m. DIR: Mark Griffiths. CAST: Toran Caudell, Victor Rojas, Matthew Sullivan, Alexandra Hedison, Rick Dean, Charles Napier. 1995

MAX MON AMOUR ★★★1/2 A proper Frenchwoman falls in love with a chimpanzee in this unusually civilized comedy about the limits of civilization. Not rated; contains adult themes. 94m. DIR: Nagisa Oshima. CAST: Charlotte Rampling, Anthony Higgins, Victoria Abril. 1986

MAXIE ★★ Cute but not particularly impressive fantasy about a conservative secretary (Glenn Close) who becomes possessed by the spirit of a flamboyant flapper (Close, too). The star is wonderful, but the predictable plot and the uninspired direction let her—and the viewer—down. Rated PG for suggested sex. 98m. DIR: Paul Aaron. CAST: Glenn Close, Mandy Patinkin, Ruth Gordon, Barnard Hughes, Valerie Curtin. 1985

MAXIMUM BREAKOUT 💔 Ridiculous flick about a baby farm features muscle-bound misfits seeking to rescue their leader's girlfriend. Not rated, contains profanity, violence, and sexual situations. 93m. DIR: Tracy Lynch Britton. CAST: Bobby Johnston. 1991

MAXIMUM FORCE ★★ Three crackerjack cops go undercover to infiltrate a crime lord and destroy him. The only thing maximum about this action-adventure is the title. Rated R for profanity, nudity, and violence. 90m. DIR: Joseph Merhi. CAST: John Saxon, Mickey Rooney, Sam Jones, Jason Lively, Richard Lynch, Sherrie Rose. 1992

•MAXIMUM IMPACT ★★ Upon witnessing the brutalizing of a teen prostitute, a man steals her and takes her to safety, thus bringing the wrath of a gang down on his family. After his family is killed he becomes a loose cannon. Full of brutal violence but little style or excitement. Not rated; contains violence. 70m. DIR: Lance Randas. CAST: Ken Jarosz, James Black, Jo Norcia, Bill Morrison. 1992

MAXIMUM OVERDRIVE 💔 Chaotic mess, loosely based on Stephen King's short story "Trucks." 97m. DIR: Stephen King. CAST: Emilio Estevez, Pat Hingle, Laura Harrington, Yeardley Smith, Ellen McElduff, J. C. Quinn. 1986

MAXIMUM RISK ★★★ Action star Jean-Claude Van Damme investigates the murder of the twin brother he never knew he had, and his search takes him to New York's Little Odessa and the Russian mafia. A better-than-average script, along with the usual outlandish violence, makes this slugfest one of Van Damme's best efforts. Rated R for profanity and violence. 126m. DIR: Ringo Lam. CAST: Jean-Claude Van Damme, Natasha Henstridge, Jean-Hugues Anglade, Stéphane Audran. 1996 DVD

MAXIMUM SECURITY 💔 An unjustly imprisoned cop battles nuclear-armed terrorists in a high-tech prison in this made-for-video thriller that is almost dumb enough to be entertaining—but not quite.

Rated R for violence, profanity, nudity, and sexual situations. 80m. DIR: Fred Olen Ray. CAST: Paul Michael Robinson, Landon Hall, George Franklin. 1996

MAY FOOLS ★★★★ An upper-class French family (and a few hangers-on) gather for their mother's funeral at a country estate, just as the 1968 Paris student riots seem to be setting off another French Revolution. A leisurely comedy-drama from director Louis Malle (cowriting with Jean-Claude Carrière). Rated R for profanity, nudity, and simulated sex. 105m. DIR: Louis Malle. CAST: Michel Piccoli, Miou-Miou, Michel Duchaussoy, Harriet Walter, Bruno Carette, Paulette Dubost. 1989

MAY WINE ★★★ Pleasant bedroom romp features a Parisian gynecologist (Guy Marchand) being shamelessly pursued by two Americans. The twist is that the two women are mother (Joanna Cassidy) and daughter (Lara Flynn Boyle). Contrived, but guaranteed to elicit a giggle or two. Rated R for nudity and language. 88m. DIR: Carol Wiseman. CAST: Joanna Cassidy, Guy Marchand, Lara Flynn Boyle, Paul Freeman. 1990

MAYA ★★★ A boy living with his hunter father in India feels neglected and takes off with a native boy to deliver a sacred white elephant to a remote holy city. Preteens will enjoy this; location filming is a plus. 91m. DIR: John Berry. CAST: Clint Walker, Jay North, I. S. Johar. 1966

MAYBE, MAYBE NOT ★★1/2 A philandering young rake, thrown out by his long-suffering girlfriend, is taken in by a gay friend. Predictable and presumably hilarious complications ensue. The film is stylish and handsomely mounted, but the characters remain two-dimensional and the premise hackneyed. In German with English subtitles. Rated R for mature themes, profanity, and brief nudity. 96m. DIR: Sonke Wortmann. CAST: Til Schweiger, Katja Riemann, Joachim Krol, Rufus Beck. 1995

MAYERLING ★★★ Fine-tuned, convincing performances mark this French-made romantic tragedy based upon Austrian Crown Prince Rudolph's ill-starred clandestine love for court lady-in-waiting Countess Marie Vetsera, in 1889. A 1969 British remake stinks by comparison. In French with English subtitles. B&W; 91m. DIR: Anatole Litvak. CAST: Charles Boyer, Danielle Darrieux, Suzy Prim. 1936

MAYFLOWER MADAM ★★ TV-movie bio of Mayflower descendant and debutante Sydney Biddle Barrows. Though allegedly based on fact, the events depicted here seem strictly soap-operaish. 96m. DIR: Lou Antonio. CAST: Candice Bergen, Chris Sarandon, Chita Rivera. 1987

MAYTIME ★★★1/2 A curio of the past. A penniless tenor meets and falls in love with an opera star suffering in a loveless marriage to her adoring and jealous teacher and mentor. The hands Fate deals are not pat. See if you can tell that John Barrymore is reading his lines from idiot boards off-camera. This film is one of the Eddy/MacDonald duo's best. B&W; 132m. DIR: Robert Z. Leonard. CAST: Jeanette MacDonald, Nelson Eddy, John Barrymore, Sig Ruman. 1937

MAZES AND MONSTERS ★★ TV movie portrays the lives of several college students whose interest in a Dungeons and Dragons type of role-playing game becomes hazardous. If you're into this sword-and-sorcery stuff, rent *Ladyhawke* instead. 103m. DIR: Steven H. Stern. CAST: Tom Hanks, Chris Makepeace, Wendy Crewson, David Wallace, Lloyd Bochner, Peter Donat, Louise Sorel, Susan Strasberg. 1982

M. BUTTERFLY ★★ Playwright David Henry Hwang's 1988 Tony-winning play, *M. Butterfly*, was based on the true story of a French diplomat tried and convicted of espionage in 1986 after having a twenty-year affair with a Chinese opera singer who turned out to be a spy—and a man. It's a fascinating tale, but one that is more suited to the illusions of the stage than the harsh reality of the camera. Rated R for profanity, simulated sex, and violence. 101m. DIR: David Cronenberg. CAST: Jeremy Irons, John Lone, Barbara Sukowa, Ian Richardson. 1993

MCBAIN 🖤 It's hard to keep track of what's going on in this lamebrained action-adventure flick involving a mercenary team out to dethrone a Central American dictator. Rated R for profanity and violence. 104m. DIR: James Glickenhaus. CAST: Christopher Walken, Maria Conchita Alonso, Michael Ironside. 1991

MCCABE AND MRS. MILLER ★★★★ Life in the turn-of-the-century Northwest is given a first-class treatment in director Robert Altman's visually perfect comedy-drama. Sparkling performances by Warren Beatty, as a small-town wheeler-dealer, and Julie Christie, as a whore with a heart that beats to the jingle of gold. Rated R. 121m. DIR: Robert Altman. CAST: Warren Beatty, Julie Christie, Shelley Duvall, Keith Carradine. 1971

•**MCCINSEY'S ISLAND** ★★ Former secret agent Hulk Hogan and cult leader Grace Jones battle to find a hidden treasure buried on a tropical island. This tame thriller is intended primarily for young viewers, who won't appreciate the sheer weirdness of its casting. Rated PG for mild violence. 94m. DIR: Sam Firstenberg. CAST: Hulk Hogan, Grace Jones, Todd Sheeler, Robert Vaughn. 1998

MCCONNELL STORY, THE ★★1/2 Run-of-the-mill romanticized bio-pic of real-life jet-test pilot has Alan Ladd acting like a stick, June Allyson as his devoted wife tearfully waiting on the tarmac. 107m. DIR: Gordon Douglas. CAST: Alan Ladd, June Allyson, James Whitmore, Frank Faylen. 1955

MCGUFFIN, THE ★★★ British suspense-drama begins like Alfred Hitchcock's *Rear Window*, which is well and good, considering its title is taken from a phrase coined by Hitchcock himself! Charles Dance offers an excellent portrayal of a movie critic who becomes embroiled in a government cover-up. Brief nudity and sexual situations. 104m. DIR: Colin Bucksey. CAST: Charles Dance, Brian Glover, Ritza Brown, Francis Matthews, Phyllis Logan, Jerry Stiller. 1985

MCHALE'S NAVY 🖤 This mirthless action-comedy is an insult to its silly 1960s TV sitcom namesake, as retired naval officer McHale protects a sleepy Caribbean island and the world's leaders from an East German terrorist. Rated PG. 105m. DIR: Bryan Spicer. CAST: Tom Arnold, Debra Messing, Bruce Campbell, Dean Stockwell, David Alan Grier, Tim Curry. 1997

MCLINTOCK! ★★★1/2 Broad Western-comedy stars John Wayne as a prosperous rancher who attempts to keep the peace between settlers and landowners while fighting a war of his own with headstrong Maureen O'Hara. A bit overlong, the film still features some priceless scenes. 127m. DIR: Andrew V. McLaglen. CAST: John Wayne, Maureen O'Hara, Yvonne De Carlo, Patrick Wayne, Stefanie Powers, Robert Lowery, Hank Worden. 1963 DVD

MCQ ★★★1/2 The success of *Dirty Harry* and the slow death of the Western prompted John Wayne to shed his Stetson and six-guns for cop clothes. While this John Sturges film doesn't quite match the Clint Eastwood–Don Siegel production that inspired it, there are some good scenes and suspense. Rated PG. 116m. DIR: John Sturges. CAST: John Wayne, Al Lettieri, Eddie Albert, Diana Muldaur, Clu Gulager, Colleen Dewhurst. 1974

MCVICAR ★★★ In this interesting British film, Roger Daltrey (lead singer for the Who) portrays John McVicar, whose real-life escape from the high-security wing of a British prison led to him being named "public enemy No. 1." Rated R. 111m. DIR: Tom Clegg. CAST: Roger Daltrey, Adam Faith, Jeremy Blake. 1980

MD GEIST ★★ In this animated story, Geist, a bio-engineered superman exiled because of his particularly dangerous nature, engages in a little private warfare after he manages to return to "civilization." Not rated; contains violence, nudity, and profanity. 41m. DIR: Ikeda Hayato. 1986

ME AND HIM ★★ You'd think a comedy about a staid businessman who gets life lessons from his newly loquacious penis would offer a few laughs, and this does. *Very* few. There are songs, too, though not from *him*. Rated R for nudity and sexual situations. 94m. DIR: Doris Dörrie. CAST: Griffin Dunne, Ellen Greene, Carey Lowell, Craig T. Nelson, Mark Linn-Baker. 1987

ME AND THE KID ★★ Two burglars attempt to rob a mansion, but all they find is an empty safe and a neglected rich kid, whom they decide to kidnap. When one of the burglars attempts to return the victim, the boy doesn't want to go home. Unfortunately, the story drags a bit. Not rated; contains violence and profanity. 95m. DIR: Dan Curtis. CAST: Danny Aiello, Joe Pantoliano, Cathy Moriarty, Alex Zuckerman, David Dukes, Anita Morris, Rick Aiello. 1993

ME AND THE MOB ★★★ Sometimes too silly but often just-funny-enough spoof of life in the mob. Rated R for language and violence. 86m. DIR: Frank Rainone. CAST: Sandra Bullock, John Castelloe, Tony Darrow, James Lorinz. 1994

ME & VERONICA 🖤 False sentiment as hard-living Patricia Wettig dumps her kids with sister Elizabeth McGovern just before she heads off to jail. Slow and uninteresting. Rated R for adult situations and language. 97m. DIR: Don Scardino. CAST: Elizabeth McGovern, Patricia Wettig, Michael O'Keefe. 1992

ME, MYSELF & I 🖤 Irritating comedy finds writer George Segal trying to make sense of neighbor Jo-Beth Williams's twin personalities. Dull and uninteresting. Rated R for language and adult situations.

97m. **DIR:** Pablo Ferro. **CAST:** George Segal, JoBeth Williams, Shelley Hack, Don Calfa. **1992**

•**ME, MYSELF & IRENE** ★★1/2 A too-nice Rhode Island State Trooper (Jim Carrey) reacts to years of mistreatment by developing an alternate personality named Hank, who doesn't take any guff from anyone. The premise gives Carrey plenty of opportunity for the kind of rubber-faced comedy only he does so well. But the plot—Carrey escorting a woman (Renee Zellweger) back to New York to face charges, with both of his personalities falling for her on the way—is distended and uninvolving. Laughs are only scattered. Rated R for profanity and raunchy humor. 116m. **DIR:** Bobby Farrelly, Peter Farrelly. **CAST:** Jim Carrey, Renee Zellweger, Robert Forster, Chris Cooper, Richard Jenkins. **2000**

MEAN GUNS ★★★ In this bizarre but undeniably lively futuristic thriller, a hundred violent felons are taken to an abandoned prison, armed with baseball bats and guns, and told that $10 million will be divided up among three of them—the last three survivors. Rated R for violence and profanity. **DIR:** Albert Pyun. **CAST:** Christopher Lambert, Ice T, Kimberly Warren. **1997 DVD**

MEAN JOHNNY BARROWS ❤ Fred Williamson plays a Vietnam war hero, dishonorably discharged for striking an officer. Rated R. 80m. **DIR:** Fred Williamson. **CAST:** Fred Williamson, Roddy McDowall, Stuart Whitman, Elliott Gould. **1976**

MEAN SEASON, THE ★★★1/2 Miami crime reporter Kurt Russell finds himself the unwilling confidant of a maniacal killer in this exciting thriller. The film occasionally relies on stock shocks. Still, it is fast-paced and inventive enough to overcome the clichés. Rated R for violence. 109m. **DIR:** Phillip Borsos. **CAST:** Kurt Russell, Richard Jordan, Mariel Hemingway, Richard Masur. **1985**

•**MEAN STREAK** ★★ A thoroughly predictable and completely lackluster cop drama is given some extra juice by making its central character (Scott Bakula) something of a racist, and then forcing him to team up with a black partner; the resulting interaction isn't nearly as provocative as writers David F. Ryan and John Fasano intended. Television police shows tell better stories, and they're also better directed. Rated R for violence, profanity, nudity, and simulated sex. 97m. **DIR:** Tim Hunter. **CAST:** Scott Bakula, Leon, Bridgid Coulter, Ron McLarty, Howard Dell. **1999**

MEAN STREETS ★★★1/2 This impressive film by director Martin Scorsese has criminal realism and explosive violence. Robert De Niro gives a high-energy performance as a ghetto psycho in New York's Little Italy who insults a Mafia loan shark by avoiding payment. He then rips off the friend who tries to save him. This study of street life at its most savage is a cult favorite. Rated R. 110m. **DIR:** Martin Scorsese. **CAST:** Robert De Niro, Harvey Keitel, Amy Robinson, Robert Carradine, David Carradine. **1973 DVD**

MEANEST MAN IN THE WORLD, THE ★★★1/2 Jack Benny's best picture. He plays a lawyer who can't win a case, and decides the only way to get ahead in the world is to be rotten to people. The film is good satire that still holds true, and Benny plays the role to the hilt. B&W; 57m. **DIR:** Sidney Lanfield.

CAST: Jack Benny, Priscilla Lane, Eddie "Rochester" Anderson, Edmund Gwenn, Anne Revere, Tor Johnson. **1943**

MEANEST MEN IN THE WEST, THE ❤ Two episodes of the 1960s television series *The Virginian* edited together. 92m. **DIR:** Samuel Fuller, Charles S. Dubin. **CAST:** Charles Bronson, Lee Marvin, Lee J. Cobb, James Drury, Albert Salmi, Charles Grodin. **1962 DVD**

MEANTIME ★★★★ British filmmaker Mike Leigh's drama about life under Thatcherism may be a bit vague to American audiences who aren't familiar with the issues involved. But it is typically well acted, especially Tim Roth as a slow-witted unemployed youth and Gary Oldman as his skinhead friend (it was the film debut of both). Made for British television. Not rated; contains mature themes and profanity. 103m. **DIR:** Mike Leigh. **CAST:** Marion Bailey, Phil Daniels, Tim Roth, Gary Oldman, Pam Ferris, Alfred Molina. **1983 DVD**

MEATBALLS ★★★1/2 Somehow, this *Animal House*-style comedy's disjointedness is easier to swallow than it should be. Elmer Bernstein's music gets sentimental in the right places, and star Bill Murray is fun to watch. Rated PG. 92m. **DIR:** Ivan Reitman. **CAST:** Bill Murray, Harvey Atkin, Kate Lynch, Chris Makepeace. **1979 DVD**

MEATBALLS PART II ❤ Pitifully unfunny high jinks at summer camp. Rated PG for sexual references. 87m. **DIR:** Ken Wiederhorn. **CAST:** Richard Mulligan, Kim Richards, John Mengatti, Misty Rowe. **1984**

MEATBALLS III ❤ Lousy. Rated R for nudity, profanity, and suggested sex. 94m. **DIR:** George Mendeluk. **CAST:** Sally Kellerman, Patrick Dempsey, Al Waxman, Shannon Tweed. **1987**

MEATBALLS 4 ❤ Hey kids, it's the old let's-save-the-summer-camp scenario one more time. Boring. Rated R for nudity and language. 84m. **DIR:** Bob Logan. **CAST:** Corey Feldman, Jack Nance, Sarah Douglas. **1992**

MEATEATER, THE ❤ An abandoned movie house is haunted by a mad killer. Not rated; the film contains violence and gore. 85m. **DIR:** Derek Savage. **CAST:** Peter M. Spitzer. **1979**

MECHANIC, THE ★★1/2 A professional hit man (Charles Bronson) teaches his craft to a young student (Jan-Michael Vincent). Slow-moving for the most part, with a few good action scenes. Rated R for violence and language. 100m. **DIR:** Michael Winner. **CAST:** Charles Bronson, Jan-Michael Vincent, Jill Ireland, Keenan Wynn. **1972**

MEDEA ★★★★ Maria Callas enacts the title role in this film adaptation of Euripides' tragedy. The diva is an exciting screen presence. In Italian with English subtitles. Rated R for nudity and violence. 100m. **DIR:** Pier Paolo Pasolini. **CAST:** Maria Callas. **1970**

MEDICINE HAT STALLION, THE ★★ Decent TV movie about a young lad (Leif Garrett) who, with the help of Indian Chief Red Cloud (Ned Romero), runs off to join the Pony Express. Well acted, but overlong, and the commercial breaks are jarring and obvious. 85m. **DIR:** Michael O'Herlihy. **CAST:** Leif Garrett, Mitchell Ryan, Bibi Besch, John Anderson, Charles Tyner, John Quade, Milo O'Shea, Ned Romero. **1977**

MEDICINE MAN ★★★ For those of us who could derive enjoyment in watching Sean Connery in a dogfood commercial, this muddled adventure-drama will do just fine. While one would expect better from director John McTiernan, there's not much even Howard Hawks could do with this "politically correct" story about a crotchety scientist who finds and then loses a cure for cancer in the threatened rain forests of Brazil. Rated PG-13 for violence and profanity. 104m. DIR: John McTiernan. CAST: Sean Connery, Lorraine Bracco, José Wilker. 1992 DVD

MEDICINE RIVER ★★1/2 Amiable comedy about a photojournalist named Will, a Blackfeet Indian who returns home to Medicine River after a twenty-year absence to attend his mother's funeral. Set in his ways, Will becomes involved with a rascal named Harlen Greene, who helps him regain his lost identity. Good cast, interesting situations, and sense of self-discovery make this Canadian import worth a look. Rated PG. 96m. DIR: Stuart Margolin. CAST: Graham Greene, Tom Jackson, Sheila Tousey, Jimmy Herman, Raul Trujillo. 1992

MEDITERRANEO ★★★★ In 1941, several misfit soldiers arrive on a Greek isle. The men, none very gung ho about their mission, are to hold and protect the island for Mussolini and the cause of fascism. A pleasant, bittersweet fable. In Italian with English subtitles. Not rated; the film has profanity and nudity. 90m. DIR: Gabriele Salvatores. CAST: Diego Abatantuono, Claudio Biagli, Giuseppi Cederna, Claudio Bisio. 1991

MEDIUM COOL ★★★★1/2 Robert Forster stars as a television news cameraman in Chicago during the 1968 Democratic convention. All the political themes of the 1960s are here—many scenes were filmed during the riots. Cinematographer Haskell Wexler's first try at directing is a winner. Highly recommended. Rated R for nudity and language. 110m. DIR: Haskell Wexler. CAST: Robert Forster, Verna Bloom, Peter Bonerz. 1969

MEDUSA TOUCH, THE ★★★ Born with the power to kill by will, Richard Burton goes completely out of control after someone almost beats him to death. This is a strange, disturbing film. Burton is effective, but Lee Remick is out of place as his psychiatrist. Rated R. 110m. DIR: Jack Gold. CAST: Richard Burton, Lee Remick, Gordon Jackson, Lino Ventura, Harry Andrews. 1978

MEET DANNY WILSON ★★1/2 A low-grade Frank Sinatra vehicle with old standards instead of new songs. The story is old hat as well. Sinatra is the singer who falls in love with his mobster boss's girlfriend. B&W; 86m. DIR: Joseph Pevney. CAST: Frank Sinatra, Raymond Burr, Shelley Winters, Alex Nicol. 1952

MEET DR. CHRISTIAN ★★ Folksy Jean Hersholt enacts the title role, meeting and besting medical crisis after medical crisis, in this first of six films translated from the popular 1930s radio series. B&W; 63m. DIR: Bernard Vorhaus. CAST: Jean Hersholt, Dorothy Lovett, Robert Baldwin, Paul Harvey, Marcia Mae Jones, Jackie Moran. 1939

MEET JOE BLACK ★★1/2 This provocative remake of 1934's *Death Takes a Holiday* is nearly undone by its absurd length. That said, viewers cannot help being intrigued by the premise: Death Incarnate, en route to collecting another mortal whose time on Earth has come to an end, allows himself to be distracted by fleshly concerns. Wanting to better understand earthly motivations, Death takes human form and, thus concealed, walks among us. Complications ensue when Death falls in love with his host's daughter but great human truths are at the heart of what follows. Rated PG-13 for profanity and sensuality. 180m. DIR: Martin Brest. CAST: Brad Pitt, Anthony Hopkins, Claire Forlani, Jake Webber, Marcia Gay Harden, Jeffrey Tambor. 1998 DVD

MEET JOHN DOE ★★★★ A penniless drifter (Gary Cooper) gets caught up in a newspaper publicity stunt. He is groomed and presented as the spokesman of the common man by powerful men who manipulate his every action for their own purposes. When he finally resists, he is exposed as a fraud. His fellow common men turn against him, or do they? Barbara Stanwyck is the newspaperwoman who first uses him and with whom he predictably falls in love. B&W; 132m. DIR: Frank Capra. CAST: Gary Cooper, Barbara Stanwyck, Walter Brennan, Spring Byington. 1941 DVD

MEET ME IN LAS VEGAS ★★1/2 Dan Dailey romances ballerina Cyd Charisse in this inoffensive time killer. A number of star cameos (Paul Henreid, Lena Horne, Frankie Laine, Jerry Colonna) add some fun, but the film is more belly flop than big splash. 112m. DIR: Roy Rowland. CAST: Dan Dailey, Cyd Charisse, Agnes Moorehead, Lili Darvas, Jim Backus. 1956

MEET ME IN ST. LOUIS ★★★★ Here's a fun-filled entertainment package made at the MGM studios during the heyday of their musicals. This nostalgic look at a family in St. Louis before the 1903 World's Fair dwells on the tension when the father announces an impending transfer to New York. Judy Garland's songs remain fresh and enjoyable today. 112m. DIR: Vincente Minnelli. CAST: Judy Garland, Margaret O'Brien, Tom Drake. 1944

MEET THE APPLEGATES 🎦 A family of insects disguised as humans. Rated R for profanity and sexual themes. 90m. DIR: Michael Lehmann. CAST: Ed Begley, Jr., Stockard Channing, Bobby Jacoby, Dabney Coleman. 1989

MEET THE DEEDLES ★★ Twin surfer dudes with saltwater for brains are sent to a Wyoming summer boot camp by their filthy-rich father for a taste of discipline. They escape from the camp commander's pickup truck and are mistaken for rookie female park rangers who are en route to save Yellowstone Park from a prairie dog infestation. They then uncover a plot by a deranged former ranger to harness Old Faithful as his own theme park. Rated PG-13 for language. 96m. DIR: Steve Boyum. CAST: Paul Walker, Steve Van Wormer, A. J. Langer, Dennis Hopper, John Ashton, Eric Braeden. 1998

MEET THE FEEBLES ★★★ Like his early gore epics *Bad Taste* and *Dead Alive*, this Peter Jackson film is bound to offend at least someone. Essentially this is a raunchy version of the Muppets. Onstage they are cute and fuzzy. Offstage they are anything but.

Highly over the top. Not rated; contains violence, profanity, gore, and simulated sex. 96m. **DIR:** Peter Jackson. 1989

MEET THE HOLLOWHEADS ★★ Five minutes of introduction would have saved viewers the first twenty minutes of confusion as we enter the lives of a family living in an unknown place and at an undisclosed time. Things don't really pick up until Mr. Hollowhead brings his villainous boss home to dinner. Rated PG-13 for sexual innuendo and gore. 87m. **DIR:** Tom Burman. **CAST:** John Glover, Nancy Mette, Richard Portnow, Anne Ramsey. 1988

MEET THE NAVY ★★★ This British musical fell into obscurity because the cast contains no star names. That's because they're all from the Royal Canadian Navy revue, a troupe of drafted performers. However, there are enough talented singers, dancers, and funnymen here to make you wonder why none went on to greater success. B&W; 81m. **DIR:** Alfred Travers. **CAST:** Lionel Murton, Margaret Hurst. 1946

MEET WALLY SPARKS ★★ In this spoof of talk TV, Rodney Dangerfield plays an outrageous show host who ends up staying with the governor who wants him off TV. Parade of talk-show hosts makes cameo appearances. There's also a parade of situation-comedy stars. Sexual wisecracks are tiresome, but other genuinely funny scenes make the film bearable. Rated R for language and sexual situations. 102m. **DIR:** Peter Baldwin. **CAST:** Rodney Dangerfield, David Ogden Stiers, Debi Mazar, Cindy Williams, Burt Reynolds, Alan Rachins. 1996 **DVD**

MEETING AT MIDNIGHT 🎬 Flat, dark, dreary *Charlie Chan* programmer from the Monogram Pictures period. Charlie investigates fortune tellers and mediums. A bore. B&W; 67m. **DIR:** Phil Rosen. **CAST:** Sidney Toler, Mantan Moreland, Frances Chan. 1944

MEETING VENUS ★★1/2 Glenn Close enters the rarefied air of opera for a romantic film in the tradition of Ingrid Bergman's high-class romance, *Intermezzo*. She plays a world-class diva who falls hard for her conductor during the hectic rehearsals for a Parisian production of *Tannhauser*. The film, however, frequently has more in common with soap opera than grand opera. Rated PG-13. 120m. **DIR:** Istvan Szabo. **CAST:** Glenn Close, Neils Arestrup. 1991

MEETINGS WITH REMARKABLE MEN ★★★★ The quest for spiritual truth and self-realization by Russian philosopher G. I. Gurdjieff (Dragan Maksimovic) is the subject of this intriguing work. Director Peter Brook concentrates on Gurdjieff's early days. Not rated. 102m. **DIR:** Peter Brook. **CAST:** Dragan Maksimovic, Mikica Dimitrijevic, Terence Stamp, Athol Fugard, Gerry Sundquist, Warren Mitchell. 1979

MEGAFORCE 🎬 Dull sci-fi adventure about a rapid-deployment defense unit that galvanizes into action whenever freedom is threatened. PG for no discernible reason. 99m. **DIR:** Hal Needham. **CAST:** Barry Bostwick, Michael Beck, Persis Khambatta, Henry Silva. 1982

MEGAVILLE ★★ In the world of the future, intimacy is reviled, openness is frowned upon, and commercial TV is a capital offense. Enter Megaville, a television-free zone that the government must send an ex-

perimental supersoldier to eliminate. An overblown plot. Rated R for violence, profanity, and nudity. 96m. **DIR:** Peter Lehner. **CAST:** Billy Zane, J. C. Quinn, Grace Zabriskie, Daniel J. Travanti. 1991

MELANIE ★★★ This drama about an illiterate Arkansas woman trying to regain custody of her son from her ex-husband in California is full of cliches but works anyway thanks to sincere direction and performances. Singer Burton Cummings plays a washed-up rock star who helps Melanie and is redeemed in the process; he also contributed the musical score. Not rated, but the equivalent of a PG-13. 109m. **DIR:** Rex Bromfield. **CAST:** Glynnis O'Connor, Burton Cummings, Paul Sorvino, Don Johnson. 1982

MELO ★★★ An offering of quiet, subtle charms, one of those typically French chamber romances in which small gestures or glances speak volumes. It's a straightforward exploration of a romantic triangle, set in the world of contemporary classical music, and features a memorable, César-winning performance by Sabine Azema. In French with English subtitles. 112m. **DIR:** Alain Resnais. **CAST:** Sabine Azema, Pierre Arditi, Fanny Ardant, André Dussolier. 1988

MELODIE EN SOUS-SOL (THE BIG GRAB) (ANY NUMBER CAN WIN) ★★★ Fresh from prison, aging gangster Jean Gabin makes intricate and elaborate plans to score big by robbing a major Riviera gambling casino. Alain Delon joins him in conniving their way to the casino vault by seducing a showgirl to gain vital backstage access. Gabin, as the cool, experienced ex-convict, and Delon, as his young, upstart, eager partner, are part-perfect. In French with English subtitles. B&W; 118m. **DIR:** Henri Verneuil. **CAST:** Jean Gabin, Alain Delon, Viviane Romance, Carla Marlier. 1963

MELODY ★★ A cute story, completely destroyed by montage after montage set to a musical score by the Bee Gees. Not enough dialogue here to carry this innocent tale about two 10-year-olds who fall in love and decide to get married. Slow. 130m. **DIR:** Waris Hussein. **CAST:** Jack Wild, Mark Lester, Tracy Hyde, Roy Kinnear, Kate Williams, Ken Jones. 1972

MELODY CRUISE ★★1/2 Two millionaires enjoy cruising with a bevy of willing babes. All goes well until the bachelor (Charlie Ruggles) falls hard for a sweet little schoolmarm. This dated romp has its moments. B&W; 75m. **DIR:** Mark Sandrich. **CAST:** Charlie Ruggles, Phil Harris, Helen Mack. 1933

MELODY FOR THREE ★★ In the last (and weakest) of the Dr. Christian movies, the compassionate MD branches out into psychology by restoring a family torn apart by divorce. Gratuitous musical numbers only make this short feature seem longer than it is. 67m. **DIR:** Erle C. Kenton. **CAST:** Jean Hersholt, Fay Wray, Irene Ryan. 1941

MELODY MASTER (THE GREAT AWAKENING) (NEW WINE) ★★ This film is another one in a long line of tortured-composer melodramas. Alan Curtis gives a bland portrayal of Franz Schubert. There are some good comedy spots supplied by Binnie Barnes and Billy Gilbert. B&W; 84m. **DIR:** Reinhold Schunzel. **CAST:** Alan Curtis, Ilona Massey, Albert Basserman,

Binnie Barnes, Billy Gilbert, Sterling Holloway, John Qualen, Sig Arno, Forrest Tucker. **1941**

MELODY RANCH ★★1/2 The creative forces at Republic Studios decided to team Gene Autry with Jimmy Durante and Ann Miller, replace Smiley Burnette with Gabby Hayes, and pretend nothing was different. Venerable heavy Barton MacLane provides the menace as a local gangster intent on running honorary sheriff Gene Autry out of town, but there isn't enough action. B&W; 80m. **DIR:** Joseph Santley. **CAST:** Gene Autry, Jimmy Durante, Ann Miller, Barton MacLane, George "Gabby" Hayes. **1940**

MELODY TRAIL ★★1/2 The fifth Gene Autry–Smiley Burnette film is a pleasant story about a rodeo rider who loses his winnings and is forced to work for a rancher with a romantic daughter. B&W; 60m. **DIR:** Joseph Kane. **CAST:** Gene Autry, Smiley Burnette, Ann Rutherford. **1935**

MELVIN AND HOWARD ★★★★★ This brilliantly directed slice-of-life film works marvelously well on two levels. On the surface, it's the entertaining tale of how Melvin Dummar (Paul LeMat) met Howard Hughes (Jason Robards)—or did he? Underneath, it's a hilarious spoof of our society. Mary Steenburgen costars in this triumph of American filmmaking, a rare gem that deserves to be seen and talked about. Rated R. 95m. **DIR:** Jonathan Demme. **CAST:** Paul LeMat, Jason Robards Jr., Mary Steenburgen, Pamela Reed. **1980 DVD**

MELVIN PURVIS: G-MAN ★★★ In the tradition of the Warner Bros. gangster films of the Thirties, Melvin Purvis (Dale Robertson) holds nothing back in this fictionalized account of the all-consuming search for Machine Gun Kelly. Wild and fast-paced, this made-for-TV film is exciting and entertaining. 78m. **DIR:** Dan Curtis. **CAST:** Dale Robertson, Harris Yulin, Margaret Blye, Dick Sargent. **1974**

MEMBER OF THE WEDDING, THE (1953) ★★★★ Julie Harris plays an awkward 12-year-old who is caught between being a child and growing up. She yearns to belong and decides to join her brother and his bride on their honeymoon. Her total introversion allows her to ignore the needs of her motherly nanny (brilliantly played by Ethel Waters) and her loyal cousin (Brandon de Wilde). Depressing but riveting. B&W; 91m. **DIR:** Fred Zinnemann. **CAST:** Julie Harris, Ethel Waters, Brandon de Wilde, Arthur Franz. **1953**

MEMBER OF THE WEDDING, THE (1996) ★★★ Carson McCullers's novel emerges as a peculiar film, rendered almost boring by its heavy reliance on dialogue, and our inability to empathize with the self-centered adolescent girl who draws her excitement vicariously. Anna Paquin establishes a presence as this precocious lass, but her performance is too mannered to seem genuine. Rated PG for mild profanity. 95m. **DIR:** Fielder Cook. **CAST:** Alfre Woodard, Anna Paquin, Corey Dunn, Enrico Colantoni, Anne Tremko, Pat Hingle. **1996**

MEMOIRS OF AN INVISIBLE MAN ★★★★ Terrific special effects and inventive comedy combine to make this adaptation of the book by H. F. Saint much more than just another Chevy Chase vehicle. Chase plays an executive who turns invisible as the result of a freak accident, and finds himself pursued by a

ruthless spy (Sam Neill). Thanks to top-notch direction by John Carpenter, plenty of suspense and excitement. Rated PG-13, for violence and nudity. 99m. **DIR:** John Carpenter. **CAST:** Chevy Chase, Daryl Hannah, Sam Neill, Michael McKean, Stephen Tobolowsky. **1992**

MEMORIAL DAY ★★★ Made-for-TV movie with stirring, sensitive performances by Mike Farrell, Robert Walden, and Edward Hermann. Farrell portrays a successful attorney who has a reunion with his former Vietnam combat buddies. The reunion awakens painful memories and a dark secret. Shelley Fabares plays Farrell's psychologist wife. Rated PG. 95m. **DIR:** Joseph Sargent. **CAST:** Mike Farrell, Shelley Fabares, Robert Walden, Edward Herrmann, Danny Glover, Bonnie Bedelia. **1988**

MEMORIES OF A MARRIAGE ★★★★ Sensitive film allows a mild-mannered husband to reflect on his married life through a series of revealing flashbacks. In each scene, his wife is passionate, stubborn, or charitable—but never lukewarm. In Danish with English subtitles. Not rated, contains mature themes. 90m. **DIR:** Kaspar Rostrup. **CAST:** Ghita Norby, Frits Helmuth, Rikke Bendsen, Henning Moritzen. **1989**

MEMORIES OF ME ★★ A New York doctor (Billy Crystal) has a heart attack and decides to reevaluate his priorities as well as his stormy relationship with his father (Alan King). Rated PG-13 for profanity and adult situations. 104m. **DIR:** Henry Winkler. **CAST:** Billy Crystal, Alan King, JoBeth Williams. **1988**

MEMORIES OF MURDER ★★ A wealthy Seattle socialite wakes up one morning to find she has been leading an alternate life for two years. 94m. **DIR:** Robert Lewis. **CAST:** Nancy Allen, Vanity, Robin Thomas, Olivia Brown, Donald Davis. **1990**

MEMORIES OF UNDERDEVELOPMENT ★★★ In the early 1960s, a Europeanized Cuban intellectual too lazy to leave Miami and too eccentric to fit into Cuban society engages in a passionate sexual affair with a beautiful young woman. A scathing satire on sex and politics. In Spanish with English subtitles. B&W; 97m. **DIR:** Tomas Gutierrez Alea. **CAST:** Sergio Corrieri. **1968**

MEMPHIS ★★★ Engrossing thriller follows the kidnapping of the son of a black banker by three whites in the 1950s. Film boasts strong performances and a real eye for period detail. Made for cable. 93m. **DIR:** Yves Simoneau. **CAST:** Cybill Shepherd, J. E. Freeman, Richard Brooks, Moses Gunn. **1992**

MEMPHIS BELLE ★★★★ This spectacular British-American production about U.S. pilots in World War II was based on the 1943 documentary made during the war by Hollywood director William Wyler. The story concerns the twenty-fifth and final mission of the crew of the Memphis Belle, a giant B17 bomber that was known as a flying fortress in its day. Topflight. Rated PG-13 for brief profanity and violence. 101m. **DIR:** Michael Caton-Jones. **CAST:** Matthew Modine, Eric Stoltz, Tate Donovan, D. B. Sweeney, Billy Zane, Sean Astin, Harry Connick Jr., Courtney Gains, John Lithgow, David Strathairn. **1990 DVD**

MEN ★★1/2 Sean Young turns in a strong, sexy performance as a woman bored with her dreary New

York existence and alcoholic, impotent boyfriend. As Stella, Young gets her groove back when she jets to Los Angeles and encounters numerous eccentric characters, both givers and takers. Director Zoe Clarke-Williams is obviously trying for something more serious than the usual straight-to-video sex drama, and she almost always succeeds. Rated R for language, nudity, and adult situations. 93m. DIR: Zoe Clarke-Williams. CAST: Sean Young, Dylan Walsh, Richard Hillman, Karen Black, John Heard. 1997 DVD

MEN, THE (1950) ★★★★ Marlon Brando's first film, this is about a paralyzed World War II vet trying to deal with his injury. A sensitive script and good acting make this film a classic. Better than *Coming Home* in depicting vets' feelings and attitudes about readjusting to society. B&W; 85m. DIR: Fred Zinnemann. CAST: Marlon Brando, Jack Webb, Teresa Wright. 1950

MEN ... (1985) ★★★★ In this tongue-in-cheek anthropological study by German writer-director Doris Dörrie, a hotshot advertising executive, who has been having a fling with his secretary, is outraged to discover that his wife has a lover. Devastated at first, he finally decides to get even, and his revenge is one of the most inventive and hilarious ever to grace the screen. In German with English subtitles. Not rated; the film has profanity. 99m. DIR: Doris Dörrie. CAST: Uwe Ochenknecht, Ulrike Kriener, Heiner Lauterbach. 1985

MEN AT WORK ★★ Cool garbagemen discover a nefarious plot to pollute the environment in what is best described as *Police Academy Meets Big Green*. Better luck next time, boys! Rated PG-13 for violence and profanity. 98m. DIR: Emilio Estevez. CAST: Charlie Sheen, Emilio Estevez, Leslie Hope, Keith David, Dean Cameron, John Getz. 1990

MEN DON'T LEAVE ★★★★ Jessica Lange struggles to raise two precocious sons after their father dies in a freak accident. The death of a loved one is no laughing matter—unless we're referring to this remarkable movie from Paul Brickman, who waited six years after hitting it big with *Risky Business* to make his second film. Rated PG-13 for adult themes. 120m. DIR: Paul Brickman. CAST: Jessica Lange, Arliss Howard, Joan Cusack, Tom Mason, Kathy Bates. 1990

MEN IN BLACK ★★★★1/2 This science-fiction-comedy, about an unofficial government agency that regulates and polices the secret immigration of outer-space aliens living on Earth, is an enticing romp based on a little-known comic-book series. Tommy Lee Jones is the ultimate straight man, playing against Will Smith, a darling of contemporary cinema. One of the most flat-out entertaining films of the decade. The only reason it doesn't deserve five stars is because, well, it isn't quite on the level of *Citizen Kane*. Rated PG-13 for language and violence. 98m. DIR: Barry Sonnenfeld. CAST: Tommy Lee Jones, Will Smith, Linda Fiorentino, Vincent D'Onofrio, Rip Torn, Tony Shalhoub. 1997

MEN IN LOVE ★★★1/2 Shot on video, this film presents a human, honest approach to the subject of AIDS. Sensitive, inspiring tale of a gay man who returns his lover's ashes to Hawaii for dispersal. There he meets his lover's friends, who console him. 87m. DIR: Marc Huestis. CAST: Doug Self, Joe Tolbe, Emerald Starr. 1990

MEN IN WAR ★★★★ This outstanding Korean War action film with Robert Ryan and Aldo Ray fighting the Chinese and each other is one of the very best "war is hell" films. B&W; 104m. DIR: Anthony Mann. CAST: Robert Ryan, Aldo Ray, Vic Morrow. 1957 DVD

MEN OF BOYS TOWN ★★★ Spencer Tracy and Mickey Rooney are back again as Father Flanagan and Whitey Marsh in this sentimental sequel to MGM's *Boys Town*. Here a completely reformed Rooney is involved in rehabilitating kids and raising the money to keep the institution operating. Good family entertainment. B&W; 107m. DIR: Norman Taurog. CAST: Spencer Tracy, Mickey Rooney, Bobs Watson, Larry Nunn, Darryl Hickman, Lee J. Cobb, Mary Nash. 1941

MEN OF RESPECT ★★ With Francis Ford Coppola making *The Godfather Part III* into a gangster version of Shakespeare's *King Lear*, it probably made sense to writer-director William Reilly to adapt *Macbeth* for a similarly styled film. Unlike Coppola's majestic movie, however, *Men of Respect* is dreary, overacted, and overwrought. Rated R for violence, profanity, and nudity. 122m. DIR: William Reilly. CAST: John Turturro, Katherine Borowitz, Dennis Farina, Peter Boyle, Rod Steiger, Lilia Skala, Steven Wright, Stanley Tucci. 1991

MEN OF SHERWOOD FOREST ★★ The inspirational saga of nobleman-turned-outlaw receives scant embellishment in this ho-hum addition to the Robin Hood canon. Produced by fledgling Hammer Studios hard on the heels of the popular Walt Disney feature and the syndicated Richard Greene television show. 77m. DIR: Val Guest. CAST: Don Taylor, Reginald Beckwith. 1954

MEN OF THE FIGHTING LADY ★★★1/2 Based on two separate factual articles for the *Saturday Evening Post* by James Michener and Navy Commander Harry A. Burns, this story of a jet fighter squadron off the coast of Korea was fashioned to fit Van Johnson. Exciting battle scenes. Not rated. 80m. DIR: Andrew Marton. CAST: Van Johnson, Walter Pidgeon, Louis Calhern, Dewey Martin, Keenan Wynn, Frank Lovejoy, Robert Horton. 1954

MEN OF WAR ★★★ OK action film stars musclebound Dolph Lundgren as a mercenary assigned to "convince" a group of islanders it's time to move to the mainland (so greedy developers can exploit the island's abundance of guano). Lundgren, however, winds up befriending the islanders and coming to their defense. Lots of action and machismo make up for lack of story. Rated R for violence and profanity. 102m. DIR: Perry Lang. CAST: Dolph Lundgren, Charlotte Lewis, B. D. Wong, Anthony Denison, Tiny Lister Jr., Kevin Tighe, Perry Lang. 1994

MEN WITH GUNS ★★1/2 A widowed, wealthy physician in a nameless Latin-American country sets off to visit his old students in rural villages and finds the countryside awash in persecution and murder. An abandoned boy, an army deserter, and a defrocked priest join him on the journey. This laborious, slow-paced drama about the sociopolitical toll of ignorance, denial, and government-supported brutality is haunting but repetitious. In Spanish, English, and Indian dialects with English subtitles. Rated R for language and violence. 128m. DIR: John Sayles. CAST: Federico Luppi, Damian Delgado, Dan Rivera Gonzales, Tania Cruz, Damian Alcazar. 1998

MENACE ON THE MOUNTAIN ★★1/2 This lesser Disney coming-of-age film features Mitch Vogel as a spunky 14-year-old forced to become the man of the house. While his Confederate dad fights the Yankees during the Civil War, Vogel must face thieving deserters who threaten his family. The plot is weak, the dialogue insipid. Not rated; contains violence. 89m. DIR: Vincent McEveety. CAST: Mitch Vogel, Pat Crowley, Albert Salmi, Charles Aidman. 1970

MENACE II SOCIETY ★★★★ Sobering, insightful film about the horrors of inner-city life focuses on the moral crisis confronting a teenage gang member who attempts to turn his life around with the help of a no-nonsense teacher and a straitlaced young woman. The filmmakers and actors do an excellent job of showing the audience the predicaments, pressure, and prejudices that can turn a basically decent kid into a cold-blooded killer. Powerful stuff. Rated R for violence, profanity, and simulated sex. 104m. DIR: Allen Hughes, Albert Hughes. CAST: Tyrin Turner, Jada Pinkett, Larenz Tate, Bill Duke, Charles Dutton, Samuel L. Jackson, Glenn Plummer. 1993 DVD

MÉNAGE ★★★ Two down-and-outers (Michel Blanc and Miou-Miou) are taken in by a flamboyant thief (Gérard Depardieu), who introduces them to a life of crime and kinky sex in this alternately hilarious and mean-spirited comedy. The first half of this bizarre work is enjoyable, but the acceptance of the last part will depend on the taste—and tolerance—of the viewer. In French with English subtitles. Not rated; the film has profanity, violence, nudity, and simulated sex. 84m. DIR: Bertrand Blier. CAST: Gérard Depardieu, Michel Blanc, Miou-Miou, Bruno Cremer. 1986

MEN'S CLUB, THE ★★★ Fine performances by an all-star cast in this offbeat and disturbing film about a boy's night out that is turned into an exploration of men's attitudes toward women. The changes remain hidden inside the characters, although we can guess what has happened by their actions. Rated R for nudity, profanity, suggested sex, and violence. 93m. DIR: Peter Medak. CAST: Roy Scheider, Frank Langella, Harvey Keitel, Treat Williams, Richard Jordan, David Dukes, Craig Wasson, Stockard Channing, Ann Wedgeworth, Jennifer Jason Leigh, Cindy Pickett. 1986

MEPHISTO ★★★★★ Winner of the 1981 Academy Award for best foreign-language film, this brilliant movie, by Hungarian writer-director Istvan Szabo, examines the conceits of artists with devastating honesty and insight. Klaus Maria Brandauer, in a stunning performance, plays an actor whose overwhelming desire for artistic success leads to his becoming a puppet of the Nazi government. The film has nudity and violence. In German with English subtitles. 135m. DIR: Istvan Szabo. CAST: Klaus Maria Brandauer, Krystyna Janda. 1981

MEPHISTO WALTZ, THE ★★ Satanism and the transfer of souls are at the heart of this needlessly wordy and laughably atmospheric chiller. The thin material—and the viewer's patience—are stretched about twenty minutes too long. Rated R for violence. 108m. DIR: Paul Wendkos. CAST: Alan Alda, Jacqueline Bisset, Curt Jurgens. 1971

MERCENARY 🎈 The muddled script and direction don't help an overacting John Ritter as a billionaire who wages war against a Middle East terrorist (Martin Kove in thick pancake makeup and thicker phony accent). Rated R for profanity, violence, and nudity. 97m. DIR: Avi Nesher. CAST: John Ritter, Olivier Gruner, Robert Culp, Ed Lauter, Martin Kove. 1996

•MERCENARY 2: THICK AND THIN 🎈 Some movies beg for a sequel. Mercenary wasn't one of them. Rated R for adult situations, language, and violence. 100m. DIR: Philippe Mora. CAST: Olivier Gruner, Robert Townsend, Claudia Christian, Nicholas Turturro. 1997

MERCENARY FIGHTERS ★★ U.S. mercenaries (Peter Fonda and company) are hired to get rid of tribesmen who are blocking the building of a new dam. When they discover the dam would force the tribe off its homeland, the mercenaries begin to fight among themselves. The actors took some heat for participating in this film, which was made in South Africa and the results are certainly nothing you'd want to put your career on the line for. 91m. DIR: Riki Shelach. CAST: Peter Fonda, Reb Brown, Ron O'Neal, Jim Mitchum, Robert DoQui. 1986

MERCHANT OF FOUR SEASONS, THE ★★ Melodramatic character study about a fruit peddler who drinks himself to death. This slice-of-life soap opera gone amok lacks emotional power. In German with English subtitles. Not rated; contains nudity and profanity. 88m. DIR: Rainer Werner Fassbinder. CAST: Irm Hermann, Hanna Schygulla. 1972

MERCI LA VIE ★★ Even one of France's greatest filmmakers, Bertrand Blier, is entitled to an occasional miscue. This saga of two young women on an odyssey of self-discovery is often aimless, frequently enigmatic, and surreal in its use of time shifts. It romps through a confusing world of the mind. In French with English subtitles. Not rated. 117m. DIR: Bertrand Blier. CAST: Charlotte Gainsbourg, Anouk Grinberg, Gérard Depardieu, Michel Blanc, Jean-Louis Trintignant. 1991

MERCURY RISING ★★★1/2 In this thriller, Bruce Willis plays another world-weary lone wolf. The central character is an autistic 9-year-old boy unable to comprehend the danger he's in after he accidentally decodes a government communications cipher. Rather than invest in a new cipher, NSA bad guy Alec Baldwin elects to eliminate the kid. Young Miko Hughes is almost uncanny in his ability to play a kid who's there-but-not-quite-there. Rated R for violence, profanity, and peril directed at a helpless child. 110m. DIR: Harold Becker. CAST: Bruce Willis, Alec Baldwin, Miko Hughes, Chi McBride, Kim Dickens. 1998 DVD

MERCY (1996) ★★1/2 A powerful millionaire finds out that he has less control over the world than he thought when his daughter is kidnapped. The script has a bit more depth than Mel Gibson's *Ransom* (which came out at the same time), but it soon becomes predictable as the rich man is humiliated by his tormentors. Rated R. 85m. DIR: Richard Shepard. CAST: John Rubinstein, Amber Kain, Sam Rockwell, Jane Lanier, Maura Tierney. 1996

•**MERCY (1999)** ★★ *Mercy* is what the filmmakers should have had on the viewers instead of subjecting them to this tiresome effort about a homicide detective investigating a nasty serial killer who preys on members of an elite lesbian club. Her search leads her into a kinky, sexual underworld where trust is in short supply. Julian Sands costars as a transvestite. Oh mercy! Rated R for adult situations, language, nudity, and violence. 94m. DIR: Damian Harris. CAST: Ellen Barkin, Julian Sands, Wendy Crewson, Peta Wilson, Karen Young. 1999 DVD

MERCY MISSION (THE RESCUE OF FLIGHT 711) ★★★ Excellent performances salvage this tale of courage and heroism. Scott Bakula plays the pilot of a small Cessna who gets lost over the Pacific Ocean when his compass malfunctions. Robert Loggia shines as the pilot of a commercial airliner who comes to his rescue, risking his and his passengers' lives. The stars make this made-for-television melodrama fly. Rated PG for intensity. 92m. DIR: Roger Young. CAST: Robert Loggia, Scott Bakula. 1993

MERIDIAN (KISS OF THE BEAST) ★★1/2 This Italian throwback to their horror flicks of the Sixties comes complete with haunted castle and the group of wandering sideshow performers who focus on the beautiful castle mistress (Sherilyn Fenn). The added twist is a Beauty and the Beast theme with British actor Malcolm Jamieson playing twins—one evil, one good. Rated R for nudity, violence, and gore. 90m. DIR: Charles Band. CAST: Sherilyn Fenn, Malcolm Jamieson, Hilary Mason, Alex Daniels. 1990

MERLIN ★★ Reporter Christy Lake (Nadia Cameron) learns that she's the reincarnated daughter of legendary magician Merlin, and she must guard a powerful sword from an evil wizard who is chasing her through time. This confusing film relies too heavily on gimmicks and mediocre special effects. Rated PG-13 for violence and adult situations. 112m. DIR: Paul Hunt. CAST: Nadia Cameron, Richard Lynch, Peter Phelps, James Hong. 1992 DVD

MERLIN & THE SWORD 🐢 Retelling of the King Arthur legend. Not rated, contains mild sex and violence. 94m. DIR: Clive Donner. CAST: Malcolm McDowell, Candice Bergen, Edward Woodward, Dyan Cannon, Rupert Everett. 1982

MERLIN OF THE CRYSTAL CAVE ★★★ Although slow at times, this film redeems itself through fabulous hillside photography and decent special effects. Adapted from Mary Stewart's book, this BBC production chronicles Merlin's life before young Arthur became his protégé. As a child, Merlin suffered the fate of being the royal "bastard" and turned to a wise hermit for guidance and an introduction to mysterious powers. Not rated; contains violence. 159m. DIR: Michael Darlow. CAST: George Winter, Thomas Lambert, Jody David, Robert Powell, Trevor Peacock. 1992

MERLIN'S SHOP OF MYSTICAL WONDERS ★★1/2 In this film set in the present day, Merlin, his wife, and some magical creatures open up a shop with the hope of bringing magic and wonder to all who enter. Complications ensue when a snoopy reporter sets out to prove the proprietor isn't really Merlin. Kids will enjoy this little romp. FAB Rating: PD (Parental discretion). 92m. DIR: Kenneth J. Burton. CAST: George Milan, Bunny Summers, John Terrence, Patricia Sansone, Ernest Borgnine. 1996

MERMAIDS ★★★1/2 Terrific performances by Cher, Bob Hoskins, and Winona Ryder highlight this uneven but generally entertaining and decidedly offbeat comedy. Ryder is the confused 15-year-old daughter of the unpredictable Cher. A sort of *Harold and Maude* of the mother-daughter set, this one is not for all tastes. Rated PG-13 for profanity. 115m. DIR: Richard Benjamin. CAST: Cher, Bob Hoskins, Winona Ryder, Michael Schoeffling, Christina Ricci. 1990

MERRY CHRISTMAS, MR. LAWRENCE ★★★1/2 Set in a prisoner-of-war camp in Java in 1942, this film, by Nagisa Oshima, focuses on a clash of cultures—and wills. Oshima's camera looks on relentlessly as a British officer (David Bowie), who refuses to cooperate or knuckle under, is beaten and tortured by camp commander Ryuichi Sakomoto. Rated R for violence, strong language, and adult situations. 122m. DIR: Nagisa Oshima. CAST: David Bowie, Ryuichi Sakamoto, Tom Conti. 1983

MERRY-GO-ROUND, THE ★★ A mismatched love affair between a count and a hurdy-gurdy operator with the backdrop of World War I. Silent. B&W; 115m. DIR: Rupert Julian. CAST: Norman Kerry, Mary Philbin. 1923

MERRY WAR, A ★★★★ Delightful romp about a copywriter at an advertising firm in London during the 1930s. Dissatisfied with his situation, Gordon Comstock quits his job to become a poet. His decision plays havoc with his girlfriend's desire to get married. How Gordon comes to realize his self-worth is just part of the joy of this film based on the best-selling novel *Keep the Aspidistra Flying* by George Orwell. Rated R for adult situations. 101m. DIR: Robert Bierman. CAST: Richard E. Grant, Helena Bonham Carter, Harriet Walter. 1998 DVD

•**MERRY WIDOW, THE (1925)** ★★★1/2 If ever a film deserved to be called "quirky," this adaptation of a once-popular operetta is it. Director Erich Von Stroheim undercuts his story about two European princes fighting for the love of an American showgirl with so much odd slapstick that you never know when you should be taking anything seriously. B&W; 111m. DIR: Erich Von Stroheim. CAST: Mae Murray, John Gilbert, Roy D'Arcy. 1925

MERRY WIDOW, THE (1934) ★★★ A carefully chosen cast, a witty script, an infectious score, lavish sets, and the fabled Lubitsch touch at the helm make this musical-comedy sparkle. Maurice Chevalier and Jeanette MacDonald are perfect. B&W; 99m. DIR: Ernst Lubitsch. CAST: Maurice Chevalier, Jeanette MacDonald, Una Merkel, Edward Everett Horton. 1934

MERRY WIVES OF WINDSOR, THE ★★ A slow-moving stage production of Shakespeare's comedy of morals with the colorful Sir John Falstaff (Leon Charles) out to seduce two married women and have them support his habits. Interesting casting of Gloria Grahame as Mistress Page, but, overall, disappointing. A Bard Productions Ltd. release. 160m. DIR: Jack Manning. CAST: Leon Charles, Gloria Grahame, Valerie Sedle Snyder, Dixie Neyland, Joel Asher, John Houseman. 1970

MERTON OF THE MOVIES ★★★★ Red Skelton enlivens a very dated script with the help of comedy genius Buster Keaton. Both of them devised the slapstick routines that freshen the story of a movie-theater usher who climbs Hollywood's ladder of success with a gentle push from his friends. The show-business atmosphere is amiable and authentic, and the comedic timing is terrific. B&W; 83m. DIR: Robert Alton. CAST: Red Skelton, Virginia O'Brien, Gloria Grahame, Leon Ames, Alan Mowbray, Hugo Haas. 1947

MESMERIZED (SHOCKED) ★★1/2 In this modern takeoff on *Svengali*, Jodie Foster plays a young orphan whose marriage to an older man (John Lithgow) proves stifling. Her imagination turns to murder, with the lovely New Zealand landscape in perfect contrast to her dreary thoughts. Not rated, contains mild profanity and sexual innuendo. 90m. DIR: Michael Laughlin. CAST: Jodie Foster, John Lithgow, Michael Murphy, Dan Shor. 1984 DVD

MESSAGE, THE (MOHAMMAD, MESSENGER OF GOD) ★★1/2 Viewers expecting to see Mohammad in this three-hour epic will be disappointed.... He never appears on the screen. Instead, we see Anthony Quinn, as Mohammad's uncle, struggling to win religious freedom for Mohammad. The film tends to drag a bit and is definitely overlong. Rated PG. 180m. DIR: Moustapha Akkad. CAST: Anthony Quinn, Irene Papas, Michael Ansara, Johnny Sekka. 1977

MESSAGE IN A BOTTLE ★★★ This mawkish tale, adapted from Nicholas Sparks's equally dissatisfying novel puts audiences through the wringer and concludes in a way intended to be "spiritually uplifting" ... a buzz phrase for "sadder than all get-out." This is just sudsy melodrama: very well performed and beautifully filmed on North Carolina's Outer Banks, but wholly dissatisfying and damn near pointless. The final scenes are discordantly jarring enough to feel as though they've been yanked from some other story. Robin Wright Penn's a *Chicago Tribune* researcher who finds a bottle on the beach, and becomes obsessed by locating the man who wrote the exquisitely romantic note inside; when she does find him, they begin a tentative relationship ... two wounded birds attempting to find happiness together. But it will not, alas, be that easy. Rated PG-13 for profanity and dramatic content. 132m. DIR: Luis Mandoki. CAST: Kevin Costner, Robin Wright, Paul Newman, John Savage, Illeana Douglas, Robbie Coltrane. 1998 DVD

MESSENGER, THE ★★★1/2 Director Norman Loftis has infused this independent, urban remake of Vittorio De Sica's *The Bicycle Thief* with a realism and urgency seldom found in Hollywood films. A minuscule budget and some scenery chewing by lead actor Richard Barboza are detractions, but this is just stylish and gritty enough to hold your attention. Not rated; contains profanity and violence. 80m. DIR: Norman Loftis. CAST: Richard Barboza, Carolyn Kinebrew, Scott Ferguson. 1994

•**MESSENGER: THE STORY OF JOAN OF ARC, THE** ★★ Director Luc Besson takes a roaring blood-and-thunder crack at the career of the Maid of Orleans. Joan anguishes over the horrors of war, but that doesn't keep Besson from wallowing in several endless battle scenes and the rape and murder of a fictitious sister of Joan's. Performances are arch and overstated, except for Timothy West as Joan's chief inquisitor, who is restrained and oddly sympathetic. Rated R for violence. 141m. DIR: Luc Besson. CAST: Milla Jovovich, John Malkovich, Faye Dunaway, Dustin Hoffman, Timothy West. 1999 DVD

MESSENGER OF DEATH ★★1/2 Middling Charles Bronson vehicle features the star in a convincing portrayal of a newspaper reporter investigating the bizarre murder of a Mormon family. A strong, suspenseful opening degenerates into a routine thriller. However, J. Lee Thompson does elicit believable performances from the cast. Rated R for violence and profanity. 98m. DIR: J. Lee Thompson. CAST: Charles Bronson, Trish Van Devere, John Ireland, Jeff Corey, Laurence Luckinbill, Marilyn Hassett. 1988

MESSIN' WITH THE BLUES ★★★★ Recorded live on June 28, 1974, at the Montreux Jazz Festival in Switzerland, this fine documentary records master bluesman Muddy Waters leading his disciples (Junior Wells, Buddy Guy, Pinetop Perkins, and Bill Wyman) through a fine set of Chicago boogie. A set by Wells and Guy kicks off the tape. 54m. DIR: Jean Bovon. 1974

METALSTORM: THE DESTRUCTION OF JARED-SYN 🎬 An outer-space ranger takes on the powerful villain of the title. Rated PG for violence. 84m. DIR: Charles Band. CAST: Jeffrey Byron, Mike Preston, Tim Thomerson, Kelly Preston. 1983

METAMORPHOSIS 🎬 Scientist performs DNA tests on himself—with predictably disastrous results. Rated R for gratuitous blood, violence, and shadowed nudity. 93m. DIR: G. L. Eastman. CAST: Gene Le Brock. 1989

METAMORPHOSIS: THE ALIEN FACTOR ★★ Splashy special effects highlight this pedestrian science-fiction entry about a lab scientist who begins to mutate after being bitten by a frog injected with a mysterious serum from outer space. Will his co-workers cure him before they become lunch? Rated R for gore, nudity, language, and violence. 92m. DIR: Glen Takakijan. CAST: George Gerard, Tony Gigante, Katherine Romaine. 1993

METEOR 🎬 A comet strikes an asteroid, and sends a huge chunk of rock hurtling on a collision course with Earth. Rated PG. 103m. DIR: Ronald Neame. CAST: Sean Connery, Natalie Wood, Karl Malden, Brian Keith, Henry Fonda. 1979 DVD

METEOR MAN ★★★ A timid schoolteacher in a crime-ridden inner-city neighborhood acquires superpowers. There are some very funny moments in this uneven, family-oriented comedy, especially as our hero learns about his new abilities. Good stuff, too. Rated PG for light violence. 100m. DIR: Robert

Townsend. **CAST:** Robert Townsend, Marla Gibbs, Robert Guillaume, James Earl Jones, Bill Cosby, Eddie Griffin, Sinbad, Frank Gorshin, Nancy Wilson. **1993**

METEOR MONSTER (TEENAGE MONSTER) 🎬 Former Universal horror siren Anne Gwynne shielding her idiot son—who has been changed into a hairy monster by a meteor shower. B&W; 65m. **DIR:** Jacques Marquette. **CAST:** Anne Gwynne, Stuart Wade, Gloria Castillo. **1958**

METEORITES! ★★ This made-for-cable original is a pale knockoff of the bigger hit of the year, *Armageddon*. A stream of meteorites bombards a small town, and everyone must put aside his problems and try to survive. Much of the story is unbelievable and has little to no impact. Rated PG-13 for violence. 95m. **DIR:** Chris Thomson. **CAST:** Roxanne Hart, Tom Wopat, Pato Hoffman. **1998**

METRO ★★ A hostage negotiator on the San Francisco police force (Eddie Murphy) tangles with a psychotic jewel thief. After a good opening scene, the hostage negotiation angle goes out the window, and the film becomes *Beverly Hills Cop* with cable cars, with Murphy once again playing the kind of unappealing loudmouth he parodied as Buddy Love in *The Nutty Professor*. Rated R for violence and profanity. 117m. **DIR:** Thomas Carter. **CAST:** Eddie Murphy, Michael Rapaport, Michael Wincott, Carmen Ejogo. **1996 DVD**

METROLAND ★★★ A London suburbanite begins to question his middle-class contentment when an old chum sneers at him for selling out. Based on a novel by Julian Barnes, the film is forthright and sincere, aided greatly by the performances of Emily Watson and Elsa Zylberstein. Rated R for profanity, nudity, and sexual scenes. 101m. **DIR:** Philip Saville. **CAST:** Christian Bale, Emily Watson, Lee Ross, Elsa Zylberstein. **1997 DVD**

METROPOLIS (1926) ★★★★★ Fritz Lang's 1926 creation embodies the fine difference between classic and masterpiece. Using some of the most innovative camera work in film of any time, it's also an uncannily accurate projection of futuristic society. It is a silent-screen triumph. B&W; 120m. **DIR:** Fritz Lang. **CAST:** Brigitte Helm, Alfred Abel. **1926 DVD**

METROPOLIS (1984 MUSICAL VERSION) ★★★★★ Fritz Lang's 1926 silent science-fiction classic has been enhanced with special individual coloring and tints, recently recovered scenes, storyboards, and stills. The rock score, supervised by Giorgio Moroder, features Pat Benatar, Bonnie Tyler, Loverboy, Billy Squier, Adam Ant, Freddie Mercury, Jon Anderson, and Cycle V. 87m. **DIR:** Fritz Lang, Giorgio Moroder. **CAST:** Brigitte Helm, Alfred Abel. **1984**

METROPOLITAN ★★★★1/2 This deliciously different, independently made movie allows viewers a glimpse at the fading preppie-debutante social scene of New York by introducing a middle-class outsider into this rarefied world. An accidental meeting brings him into the "Sally Fowler Rat Pack" where a nice girl develops a crush on him. Rated PG-13 for profanity. 107m. **DIR:** Whit Stillman. **CAST:** Carolyn Farina, Edward Clements, Christopher Eigeman, Taylor Nichols. **1990**

MEXICALI ROSE ★★★★ Radio singer Gene Autry discovers the oil company sponsoring his radio show is involved in a stock promotion fraud. Among their victims is an orphanage run by a girl. One of Autry's best. B&W; 60m. **DIR:** George Sherman. **CAST:** Gene Autry, Smiley Burnette, Noah Beery Sr., William Farnum, Luana Walters. **1939**

MEXICAN HAYRIDE ★★ Lou Costello chases swindler Bud Abbott to Mexico and dim-wittedly aids him. Substandard entry in the series. B&W; 77m. **DIR:** Charles Barton. **CAST:** Bud Abbott, Lou Costello, Virginia Grey, John Hubbard, Pedro De Cordoba, Fritz Feld. **1948**

MEXICAN SPITFIRE ★★★1/2 This is one of a series of second-feature comedies about a youngish businessman and his temperamental Mexican wife. Though the stars are Lupe Velez and Donald Woods, the simplistic plot shifts early on to the young man's accident-prone uncle Matt and his rich and proper boss Lord Epping, both of whom were played by the spaghetti-legged Ziegfeld comic Leon Errol. He's in top form here. B&W; 75m. **DIR:** Leslie Goodwins. **CAST:** Lupe Velez, Donald Woods, Leon Errol. **1939**

MGM'S THE BIG PARADE OF COMEDY ★★ Disappointing and disjointed; an incoherent grab bag of short scenes from comic silent and sound films, compiled by the usually dependable Robert Youngson. B&W; 100m. **DIR:** Robert Youngson. **CAST:** Stan Laurel, Oliver Hardy, Bud Abbott, Lou Costello, Marion Davies. **1963**

MI VIDA LOCA ★★★ Three interrelated stories set among female gang members living in the Echo Park barrio of Los Angeles. The first and third stories are more dramatically compelling than the second, which causes the film's pace to slacken. Still, it's a vivid, well-acted group portrait of young women trying to live decent lives amid violence and despair. Rated R for profanity. 92m. **DIR:** Allison Anders. **CAST:** Angel Aviles, Seidy Lopez, Jacob Vargas, Panchito Gomez, Jesse Borrego. **1994**

MIAMI BLUES ★★1/2 A sociopath (Alec Baldwin) goes on a crime spree in Miami, hooks up with a trusting hooker (Jennifer Jason Leigh) and eludes a slow-witted cop (Fred Ward). Director George Armitage was trying for something stylishly offbeat and ended up with something that was mostly off. Rated R for violence, nudity, and profanity. 96m. **DIR:** George Armitage. **CAST:** Fred Ward, Alec Baldwin, Jennifer Jason Leigh, Nora Dunn, Charles Napier. **1990**

MIAMI COPS 🎬 This boring Italian film features a seasoned cop attempting to break up an international drug-smuggling ring. B&W; 103m. **DIR:** Al Bradley. **CAST:** Richard Roundtree. **1989**

MIAMI HORROR 🎬 Poorly dubbed Italian thriller about scientists who believe that Earth life originated from bacteria on meteorites from outer space. 88m. **DIR:** Martin Herbert. **CAST:** David Warbeck, Laura Trotter, John Ireland. **1985**

MIAMI HOT TALK ★★1/2 The on-air sex fantasies of a Miami radio host cause problems for both her and her listeners. Slightly better than average soft-core sexploitation. Rated R for nudity, sexual situations, and profanity. 80m. **DIR:** Andrew Blake. **CAST:** Seana Ryan, Frank Rodriguez, Tiffany Berlingame. **1996**

MIAMI HUSTLE ★★ Supermodel Kathy Ireland makes her starring debut in this failed caper thriller as a supposedly shrewd con artist who uses her body to help separate marks from their assets. Alas, Ireland can't act a lick. Philip Collins and Daniel Miller's script begins reasonably well, but the final act is ridiculous. *The Sting* it ain't. Rated PG-13 for nudity and mild profanity. 81m. **DIR:** Lawrence Lanoff. **CAST:** Kathy Ireland, John Enos, Audie England, Richard Sarafian, Eduardo Yanez, Allan Rich. 1995

MIAMI RHAPSODY ★★★ Writer-director David Frankel's big-screen debut is so strongly reminiscent of Woody Allen and Neil Simon that he should pay royalties. Perky Sarah Jessica Parker, nervous about tying the knot with her fiancé, confers with family members ... only to find each one involved in an extramarital affair. Clever dialogue and amusing one-liners abound, but the whole is somewhat less than the sum of its talented parts. Rated PG-13 for profanity and sexual candor. 95m. **DIR:** David Frankel. **CAST:** Sarah Jessica Parker, Gil Bellows, Antonio Banderas, Mia Farrow, Paul Mazursky, Kevin Pollak, Carla Gugino. 1995 DVD

MIAMI SUPERCOPS 🎦 The stars of *They Call Me Trinity* ditch the Old West for Miami in this Italian import that's so bad, it's unbearable. Rated PG. 97m. **DIR:** Bruno Corbucci. **CAST:** Terence Hill, Bud Spencer. 1985

MIAMI VICE ★★★★ This pilot for the popular NBC series is slam-bang entertainment. A New York City cop (Philip Michael Thomas) on the trail of the powerful drug kingpin who killed his brother traces him to Miami, running into a vice cop (Don Johnson) who's after the same guy. All the trademarks of the series are here: great music, rapid-fire editing, gritty low-key performances, and bursts of sporadic violence. The only real flaw in this tape is the sound quality, which, even in hi-fi stereo, is muffled. 97m. **DIR:** Thomas Carter. **CAST:** Don Johnson, Philip Michael Thomas, Saundra Santiago, Michael Talbott, John Diehl, Gregory Sierra, Bill Smitrovich, Belinda Montgomery, Martin Ferrero, Mykelti Williamson, Olivia Brown, Miguel Pinero. 1984

MIAMI VICE: "THE PRODIGAL SON" ★★★ The pastel duo, Crockett (Don Johnson) and Tubbs (Philip Michael Thomas), trek up to New York in search of the bad guys in this watchable second-season opener. 99m. **DIR:** Paul Michael Glaser. **CAST:** Don Johnson, Philip Michael Thomas, Edward James Olmos, Olivia Brown, Penn Jillette, Pam Grier. 1985

MICHAEL ★★★1/2 John Travolta is the title character, an angel come to Earth for one last visit to set straight a pair of cynical journalists, Andie MacDowell and William Hurt. With Bob Hoskins on hand to add hilarity as their ethically challenged publisher, *Michael* is fun to watch, just not very memorable. Rated PG. 105m. **DIR:** Nora Ephron. **CAST:** John Travolta, Andie MacDowell, William Hurt, Bob Hoskins, Robert Pastorelli, Jean Stapleton, Teri Garr. 1996 DVD

MICHAEL COLLINS ★★★★ Director Neil Jordan creates a magnificent epic glorifying IRA militant Michael Collins. His only filmmaking weakness appears in a lack of background to support the extreme violence that consumes much of the film. Liam Neeson brilliantly brings the title character to a larger-than-life existence. Aidan Quinn plays his closest friend, with Julia Roberts as their mutual love interest. Rated R for violence and profanity. 135m. **DIR:** Neil Jordan. **CAST:** Liam Neeson, Aidan Quinn, Julia Roberts, Alan Rickman, Ian Hart, Stephen Rea. 1996 DVD

MICHAEL JACKSON MOONWALKER ★★★★1/2 Spectacle is what we expect of Michael Jackson, and he delivers in a stunning twenty-first-century Saturday-morning special that runs the course from Disney to Claymation to sizzling sci-fi effects. But what makes it such a treat is the sensational show of humor as Jackson parodies his own treatment by the tabloids, his kooky fetishes, even his own success. 84m. **DIR:** Jerry Kramer, Collin Chivers. **CAST:** Michael Jackson, Sean Lennon. 1988

•MICKEY BLUE EYES ★★★★ A proper English auctioneer falls in love with a New York schoolteacher only to find out that she's the daughter of a Mafia kingpin. It's as much a comedy of mistaken identity as it is a send-up of mob pictures, with Hugh Grant in top form as the clumsy, embarrassed hero who is out of his depth. The highlight is Grant's marbles-in-the-mouth attempt to master mobster jargon. Reminiscent of *The Freshman*, it features James Caan, an alumnus of *The Godfather*, as "the bad guy," and an amiable, winking-of-the-eye quality. Rated PG-13 for profanity, violence, and suggested sex. 101m. **DIR:** Kelly Makin. **CAST:** Hugh Grant, James Caan, Jeanne Tripplehorn, Burt Young, James Fox, Joe Viterelli, Gerry Becker, Maddie Corman, Tony Darrow, Paul Lazar, Vincent Pastore, Frank Pelligrino. 1999 DVD

MICKI & MAUDE ★★★1/2 In this hysterically funny comedy Dudley Moore stars as a television personality who tries to juggle marriages to two women, Amy Irving and Ann Reinking. Directed by Blake Edwards, it's a triumph for filmmaker and cast alike. Rated PG-13 for profanity and suggested sex. 96m. **DIR:** Blake Edwards. **CAST:** Dudley Moore, Amy Irving, Ann Reinking, George Gaynes, Wallace Shawn. 1984

MICROCOSMOS ★★★1/2 This amazing, intimate venture into the insect kingdom includes birth, death, survival, romance, decapitations, comedy, high drama, and stunning beauty. High-tech close-ups of the French countryside unveil an amazing bugscape. Caterpillars parade like seasoned Shriners. Raindrops fall like bombs. Snails entwine to rapturous music. And a lush soundtrack plays second fiddle to the munching, buzzing, and scratching of daily insect activity. The nonchalant squishing of bugs will never be the same. Rated G. 77m. **DIR:** Claude Nuridsnay, Marie Perennou. 1996

MICROWAVE MASSACRE 🎦 The title says it all. Rated R for violence, nudity, and profanity. 75m. **DIR:** Wayne Betwick. **CAST:** Jackie Vernon. 1979

MIDAS TOUCH, THE ★★ Lighthearted kiddie tale about a young boy who strikes a deal with a witch so that everything he touches literally turns to gold. Then young Billy turns his grandmother into a golden statue, and thieves steal her. Young children will appreciate the ample antics as Billy and his friends save the day. Rated PG. 92m. DIR: Peter Manoogian. CAST: Trevor O'Brien, Ashley Cafagna, Joey Simmrin, David Jeremiah. 1997

MIDDLE-AGE CRAZY ★★★ Bruce Dern lives the lyrics of this pop song—turned-film, playing a fellow who shorts out upon reaching the mid-life crisis of his fortieth birthday. Wife Ann-Margret is abandoned for a football cheerleader, and the family car is pushed aside by a Porsche. Director John Trent resists the easy opportunity for cheap comedy, however, and treats the material with surprising compassion. Rated PG. 95m. DIR: John Trent. CAST: Bruce Dern, Ann-Margret, Graham Jarvis. 1980

MIDDLE OF THE NIGHT ★★★ A melodrama about marriage that symbolized a moral awakening for middle-aged America in the late 1950s. Fine-tuned film treatment of Paddy Chayefski's stage play. B&W; 119m. DIR: Delbert Mann. CAST: Fredric March, Kim Novak, Glenda Farrell, Martin Balsam, Lee Grant, Joan Copeland. 1959

MIDDLEMARCH ★★★1/2 In spite of fine acting and impeccable production values, the didactic tone of George Eliot's 1871–72 novel never lets you forget you are in BBC land. Still, this three-cassette, PBS miniseries is richly detailed, lushly photographed, and contemporary in spirit. The letter-box strip across the bottom broadens the ratio without reducing the players to puppets on the screen. Not rated. 357m. DIR: Anthony Page. CAST: Juliet Aubrey, Robert Hardy, Douglas Hodge, Michael Hordern, Peter Jeffrey, Patrick Malahide, Trevyn McDowell, Rufus Sewell. 1994

MIDNIGHT (1934) ★★ Based on a well-received stage play, this rather implausible melodrama concerns a jury foreman who insists on a death verdict in the case of a young woman who killed a cruel lover. The juror then has to turn his own daughter over to the authorities for the same crime. Its main appeal now is Humphrey Bogart in a supporting role as a slick gangster. B&W; 74m. DIR: Chester Erskine. CAST: O. P. Heggie, Sidney Fox, Henry Hull, Lynne Overman, Margaret Wycherly, Humphrey Bogart, Richard Whorf. 1934 DVD

MIDNIGHT (1939) ★★★1/2 One of the movies that made 1939 Hollywood's best year, this comic romp is about a con woman who's hired to pose as a rich countess to come between a playboy and her employer's wife. And what a job she does! The movie proves that graphic sex isn't necessary to make a sexy movie. B&W; 94m. DIR: Mitchell Leisen. CAST: Claudette Colbert, Don Ameche, John Barrymore, Mary Astor, Francis Lederer, Monty Woolley, Hedda Hopper. 1939

MIDNIGHT (1980) 🎔 Two college guys and a female hitchhiker end up in a town plagued by a family of Satan worshipers. Rated R for violence and profanity. 91m. DIR: John Russo. CAST: Lawrence Tierney, Melanie Verlin, John Amplas. 1980

MIDNIGHT 2 ★★ Writer-director John Russo's sequel to his 1980 film is better than the first in a variety of ways, but still falls way short of the standard of excellence set by the groundbreaking Night of the Living Dead. Here, Russo uses his low budget to the benefit of the tale of college kids getting knocked off

in a small town. Not rated; contains violence, profanity, nudity, and simulated sex. 72m. DIR: John Russo. CAST: Matthew Jason Walsh. 1993

MIDNIGHT (1989) ★★1/2 A sultry hostess who introduces horror movies is pursued by a struggling actor and fan. On the soundtrack: some listenable original songs and a nice version of "Low Spark of High-Heeled Boys," sung by Jim Capaldi. Rated R for language. 90m. DIR: Norman Thaddeus Vane. CAST: Lynn Redgrave, Tony Curtis, Frank Gorshin, Wolfman Jack. 1989

MIDNIGHT CABARET 🎔 Satanic time waster. Rated R for nudity and violence. 93m. DIR: Pece Dingo. CAST: Lisa Hart Carroll, Michael Des Barres, Paul Drake, Laura Harrington. 1988

MIDNIGHT CLEAR, A ★★★★ Based on William Wharton's autobiographical novel, this compelling antiwar drama is about a group of young American soldiers sent on a reconnaissance mission into enemy territory during World War II. This impressive film recalls the impact and filmmaking technique of Stanley Kubrick's Paths of Glory. Rated R for profanity and violence. 107m. DIR: Keith Gordon. CAST: Ethan Hawke, Kevin Dillon, Peter Berg, Arye Gross, Frank Whaley, Gary Sinise, John C. McGinley. 1992

MIDNIGHT CONFESSIONS 🎔 Tawdry thriller about a radio sex therapist who's stalked by one of her regular callers. Rated R for adult situations and profanity. 85m. DIR: Allan Shustak. CAST: Carol Hoyt, David Willbern, Richard Lynch, Julie Strain, Christina Rich, Monique Parent. 1995

MIDNIGHT COWBOY ★★★★★ In this tremendous film, about the struggle for existence in the urban nightmare of New York's Forty-second Street area, Jon Voight and Dustin Hoffman deliver brilliant performances. The film won Oscars for best picture, best director, and best screenplay. Voight plays handsome Joe Buck, who arrives from Texas to make his mark as a hustler, only to be outhustled by everyone else, including the crafty, sleazy "Ratso," superbly played by Hoffman. Rated R. 113m. DIR: John Schlesinger. CAST: Jon Voight, Dustin Hoffman, Sylvia Miles, Barnard Hughes, Brenda Vaccaro. 1969 DVD

MIDNIGHT CROSSING 🎔 Poorly written and realized film about four people on a treasure hunt into Cuba. Rated R for language, violence, and nudity. 104m. DIR: Roger Holzberg. CAST: Faye Dunaway, Daniel J. Travanti, Kim Cattrall, John Laughlin, Ned Beatty. 1988

MIDNIGHT DANCER ★★★ A young ballerina balances her artistic yearning with a night job in the chorus line of Club Paradise. Hints of gangsters, drugs, and seedy sex give this Australian film an honest coating of grit—rare among dance movies. Rated R. 97m. DIR: Pamela Gibbons. CAST: Deanne Jeffs, Mary Regan. 1987

MIDNIGHT DANCER (1994) ★★★ Three brothers work as go-go boys in a sleazy Manila sex club to help keep their family together. This world of dirty dancing and prostitution is seen through the eyes of the youngest brother, who dances by night, and tries to keep his mother from worrying about her sons the rest of the time. The brothers consider themselves heterosexual, but often engage in homosexual activity. Tough viewing. In Filipino with English subtitles. Not rated; contains nudity, profanity, and violence. 118m. DIR: Mel Chionglo. CAST: Alex Del Rosario, Gandong Cervantes, Lawrence David, Perla Bautista. 1994

MIDNIGHT EDITION 🖤 A real snoozer of a movie about a reporter who becomes obsessed with a death-row inmate. Rated R for nudity, violence, and profanity. 98m. DIR: Howard Libov. CAST: Will Patton, Michael DeLuise, Clare Wren, Nancy Moore Atchison. 1993

MIDNIGHT EXPRESS ★★★1/2 This is the true story of Billy Hayes, who was busted for trying to smuggle hashish out of Turkey and spent five years in the squalor and terror of a Turkish prison. *Midnight Express* is not an experience easily shaken. Yet it is a film for our times that teaches a powerful and important lesson. Rated R. 121m. DIR: Alan Parker. CAST: Brad Davis, John Hurt, Randy Quaid. 1978 DVD

MIDNIGHT HEAT ★★ Tim Matheson fails to score as Tyler Grey, a football player who is having an affair with the team owner's wife. When the team owner ends up dead, Grey finds himself framed for the murder. Watch him do the quarterback shuffle as he tries to prove his innocence. Rated R for violence, nudity, and adult language. 97m. DIR: Harvey Frost. CAST: Tim Matheson, Mimi Craven, Stephen Mendel. 1994

MIDNIGHT HOUR ★★★ High school students recite an ancient curse as a Halloween prank and unintentionally release demons from hell and the dead from their graves. Enjoyable cross between *Night of the Living Dead* and *An American Werewolf in London*, helped along by humor and a lively cast. Rated R for gore, violence, and profanity. 87m. DIR: Jack Bender. CAST: Shari Belafonte, LeVar Burton, Lee Montgomery, Dick Van Patten, Kevin McCarthy. 1986

MIDNIGHT IN THE GARDEN OF GOOD AND EVIL ★★★ Clint Eastwood's fascination with southern Gothic surfaces in service of this enigmatic, captivating, and frustrating adaptation of John Berendt's equally puzzling novel. Based on actual events, this is a study of a young New York–based writer who becomes the journalist of choice when a wealthy Savannah, Georgia, aristocrat is charged with homicide. Alas, the film's eccentric characters eventually overwhelm it. Rated R for violence, profanity, and sexual candor. 135m. DIR: Clint Eastwood. CAST: Kevin Spacey, John Cusack, Jude Law, Jack Thompson, Paul Hipp, Alison Eastwood, Irma P. Hall, The Lady Chablis. 1997 DVD

MIDNIGHT KISS ★★ A murderer who removes the blood from his victims is running loose, so a female detective is used as bait and is attacked. She cannot believe that vampires exist, until she becomes one herself. Extremely bad dialogue and horrible acting really take a bite out of this picture. In R-rated and unrated versions; contains profanity, violence, and nudity. 85m. DIR: Joel Bender. CAST: Michelle Owens, Gregory A. Greer, Michael McMillin, Robert Milano, B. J. Gates, Michael Shawn. 1992

MIDNIGHT LACE ★★★ A fine mystery with a cast that makes the most of it. Doris Day is an American living in London and married to successful business-man Rex Harrison. She soon finds her life in danger. Some viewers may find it less sophisticated than present-day thrillers, but there's plenty of suspense and plot twists to recommend it. 100m. DIR: David Miller. CAST: Doris Day, Rex Harrison, John Gavin, Myrna Loy, Roddy McDowall, Herbert Marshall, Natasha Perry. 1960

MIDNIGHT MADNESS 🖤 A midnight scavenger hunt. Rated PG. 110m. DIR: David Wechter, Michael Nankin. CAST: David Naughton, Debra Clinger, Eddie Deezen, Stephen Furst. 1980

MIDNIGHT MAN ★★1/2 So-so action-adventure, based on the novel by Jack Higgins. A former terrorist is enlisted by the British government to help stop a terrorist's attack on the royal family. Rated R for violence and profanity. 104m. DIR: Lawrence Gordon Clark. CAST: Rob Lowe, Kenneth Cranham, Deborah Moore. 1998

MIDNIGHT MOVIE MASSACRE ★★★ This is definitely a candidate for the midnight-movie cult crowd—set in 1956 while an audience of outrageous characters are watching a sci-fi movie. A real flying saucer lands outside, and the monster invades the theater. Gross fun, a crowd pleaser with surprisingly good photography and production. Not rated, with graphic violence and simulated sex. 86m. DIR: Mark Stock. CAST: Robert Clarke, Ann Robinson. 1986

MIDNIGHT MURDERS ★★★ Rod Steiger stars as a David Koresh–like religious fanatic who is arrested for tax evasion. He begins gathering weapons to protect his "people" from the government and the feds respond in kind. Fast-paced and controversial action-thriller. Rated R for violence. 95m. DIR: Dick Lowry. CAST: Rod Steiger, Michael Gross, Gary Basaraba. 1991

MIDNIGHT RIDE ★★ Michael Dudikoff stars as a cop whose estranged wife is kidnapped by madman Mark Hamill and taken on the wildest ride of her life. So-so chase film is hampered by Dudikoff's lifeless performance but buoyed by Hamill's over-the-top insanity, a cameo by Robert Mitchum, and some exciting action sequences. Rated R for profanity and violence. 93m. DIR: Bob Bralver. CAST: Michael Dudikoff, Mark Hamill, Robert Mitchum, Savina Gersak. 1992

MIDNIGHT RUN ★★★★ Robert De Niro is wonderfully funny as a bounty hunter charged with bringing in fugitive Charles Grodin. The latter is hiding out after stealing $15 million from a crime boss and giving it to charity. Mixing laughs, surprises, and oodles of action, Martin Brest has come up with the perfect follow-up to his megahit, *Beverly Hills Cop*. Rated R for profanity and violence. 125m. DIR: Martin Brest. CAST: Robert De Niro, Charles Grodin, Yaphet Kotto, John Ashton, Dennis Farina. 1988 DVD

MIDNIGHT TEASE 🖤 The dancers at a local strip club are being killed one by one. Ridiculous excuse to show naked women parade past the camera at regular intervals. No story, no suspense. Dreadful. Available in R-rated and unrated versions; both contain profanity, nudity, and violence. 87m. DIR: Scott Levy. CAST: Cassandra Leigh, Rachel Reed, Edmund Halley. 1994 DVD

MIDNIGHT WITNESS ★★ After a fight with his live-in girlfriend, Paul can't sleep, so he decides to play with his new video camera. Shooting out his window, he videotapes the police beating up a suspect. Now he and his girlfriend must run for their lives. Try not to fall asleep due to the bad plot and poor acting. Not rated; contains violence, nudity, and simulated sex. 90m. DIR: Peter Foldy. CAST: Paul Johansson, Maxwell Caulfield, Karen Moncrieff, Jan-Michael Vincent, Mick Murray, Mark Pellegrino, Virginia Mayo. 1992

MIDNIGHT'S CHILD ★★ Run-of-the-mill made-for-TV thriller with cult member Olivia D'Abo taking a job as a nanny in order to abduct her charge to be the bride of Satan. She doesn't rock the cradle but manages to stir up the household a bit. Not rated. 89m. DIR: Colin Bucksey. CAST: Marcy Walker, Cotter Smith, Olivia D'Abo, Elizabeth Moss. 1992

MIDSUMMER NIGHT'S DREAM, A (1935) ★★★★ Warner Bros. rolled out many of its big-name contract stars during the studio's heyday for this engrossing rendition of Shakespeare's classic comedy. Enchantment is the key element in this fairy-tale story of the misadventures of a group of mythical mischief makers. B&W; 117m. DIR: Max Reinhardt. CAST: James Cagney, Olivia de Havilland, Dick Powell, Mickey Rooney. 1935

MIDSUMMER NIGHT'S DREAM, A (1968) ★★1/2 Special effects and countryside locales strangely distract from the overall hilarity of Shakespeare's spoof on love. Some of the most pun-filled lines are lost as some of the cast members confuse talking fast for authentic articulation. Diana Rigg is rather pathetic as the lovelorn Helena while Ian Holm's Puck provides laughs. Not rated; features Judi Dench as the Fairy Queen in very scanty attire. 124m. DIR: Peter Hall. CAST: Diana Rigg, David Warner, Ian Holm, Judi Dench, Ian Richardson. 1968

MIDSUMMER NIGHT'S SEX COMEDY, A ★★1/2 Woody Allen's sometimes dull cinematic treatise—albeit sweet-natured, and beautifully photographed by Gordon Willis—on the star-writer-director's favorite subjects: sex and death. That's not to say *A Midsummer Night's Sex Comedy* doesn't have its humorous moments. Allen's fans will undoubtedly enjoy it. Rated PG for adult themes. 88m. DIR: Woody Allen. CAST: Woody Allen, Mia Farrow, José Ferrer, Julie Hagerty, Tony Roberts, Mary Steenburgen. 1982

MIDWAY ★★★ An all-star cast was assembled to bring to the screen this famous sea battle of World War II. Midway became famous as the site of the overwhelming victory of American carrier forces, which shifted the balance of power in the Pacific. As a historical drama, this film is accurate and maintains interest. However, a romance subplot is totally out of place. Rated PG. 132m. DIR: Jack Smight. CAST: Henry Fonda, Charlton Heston, Robert Mitchum, Hal Holbrook, Edward Albert, Cliff Robertson. 1976 DVD

MIDWINTER'S TALE, A ★★1/2 A group of theatrical misfits tries to stage a production of *Hamlet* in a deserted country church. Director Kenneth Branagh's breakneck pace can't quite conceal the hey-kids-let's-put-on-a-show clichés of his own script, and much of the dialogue is unintelligible to American ears. The talented cast, however, is a major asset. Rated R for profanity. B&W; 98m. DIR: Ken-

neth Branagh. CAST: Michael Maloney, Jennifer Saunders, Joan Collins, Richard Briers, Nicolas Farrell, Ann Davies. 1996

•MIFUNE ★★★★ In this beguiling drama-romance about hidden pasts and family ties, a married Copenhagen yuppie returns alone to his family's farm to bury his father and care for his mentally challenged brother. He hires a housekeeper who has a troubled brother of her own. The film embraces the Danish Dogma 95 film collective's "vow of chastity," which dictates the use of handheld cameras, and natural lighting and sound. In Danish with English subtitles. Rated R for sexuality, language, and violence. 99m. DIR: Soeren Kragh-Jacobsen. CAST: Anders W. Berthelsen, Jesper Asholt, Iben Hjejle, Emil Tarding, Sofie Grabol. 2000

MIGHTY, THE ★★★★ Great "small" film in which two young boys, both considered outcasts, find new strength in their friendship. Exceptional cast is terrific in this heartwarming tearjerker. Rated PG-13. 100m. DIR: Peter Chelsom. CAST: Sharon Stone, Harry Dean Stanton, Gillian Anderson, Kieran Culkin, Gena Rowlands, Meat Loaf. 1998 DVD

MIGHTY APHRODITE ★★★1/2 A deliciously comic performance by Mira Sorvino as a naïve prostitute is the main attraction in this middleweight comedy from actor-writer-director Woody Allen, whose screen character becomes obsessed with discovering the identity of his adopted son's mother. A bizarre Greek chorus periodically comments on events. Rated R for profanity and sexual situations. DIR: Woody Allen. CAST: Woody Allen, Helena Bonham Carter, Mira Sorvino, Michael Rapaport, F. Murray Abraham, Claire Bloom, Olympia Dukakis, David Ogden Stiers, Jack Warden, James Woods, Dan Moran. 1995 DVD

MIGHTY DUCKS, THE ★★★1/2 Fast-living lawyer Emilio Estevez is assigned 500 hours of community service after being convicted on a drunk-driving arrest, and he finds himself coaching a hockey team made up of league misfits. *The Bad News Bears* on ice. Rated PG for brief vulgarity. 93m. DIR: Stephen Herek. CAST: Emilio Estevez, Joss Ackland, Lane Smith, Heidi Kling. 1992 DVD

MIGHTY JOE YOUNG (1949) ★★★1/2 In this timeless fantasy from the creator of *King Kong* (Willis O'Brien with his young apprentice, Ray Harryhausen), the story follows the discovery of a twelve-foot gorilla in Africa by a fast-talking, money-hungry nightclub owner (Robert Armstrong), who schemes to bring the animal back to Hollywood. B&W; 94m. DIR: Ernest B. Schoedsack. CAST: Terry Moore, Ben Johnson, Robert Armstrong, Frank McHugh. 1949

MIGHTY JOE YOUNG (1998) ★★★★ Faithful remake of the 1949 classic has a few 1990s updates including a wild-animal sanctuary meant to protect the lovable giant gorilla. Bill Paxton plays a zoologist who's gaga over both the beast and the girl. Ruthless poachers create strong, clear-cut villains at which to hiss. There is a seamless blend of stop-motion, computer-generated images, blue screen, full-size animatronics, and the man in a gorilla suit thrown in for good measure. This film socks home a strong "save the wildlife" message. Rated PG-13 for violence.

114m. **DIR:** Ron Underwood. **CAST:** Charlize Theron, Bill Paxton, Rade Serbedzija, Naveen Andrews, David Paymer. 1998 DVD

MIGHTY MORPHIN POWER RANGERS: THE MOVIE ★★ Cheesy, big-screen version of the kiddie TV series is nothing but a feature-length commercial for the tie-in toys. Special effects are cheap, and the Power Rangers are played by blandly pretty faces. With broad acting and infantile comic relief, it's strictly for undemanding toddlers—except that their parents may well object to the film's nonstop (though cartoonish) violence. Rated PG. 96m. **DIR:** Bryan Spicer. **CAST:** Karan Ashley, Johnny Yong Bosch, Steve Cardenas, Jason David Frank, Amy Jo Johnson, David Yost, Paul Freeman. 1995

•**MIGHTY PEKING MAN** ★★★ Some movies are so bad they're funny. This is one of them. After an earthquake destroys a small village, an expedition is formed to track down a legendary ape man in the Himalayan jungles. The giant ape man has nothing to do with the earthquake. It's just a device to bring him down off his mountaintop home. When the expedition arrives, they not only discover the ape man, but his female friend, a buxom blonde who was orphaned and grew up in the jungle. This 1977 Hong Kong effort apes the *King Kong* legend for all it's worth, inducing laughter with shameful special effects, dreadful dialogue, and even worse dubbing. Rated PG-13 for adult situations and violence. 90m. **DIR:** Ho Meng-Hua. **CAST:** Danny Lee, Evelyne Kraft, Hsiao Yao, Ku Feng. 1977 DVD

MIGHTY QUINN, THE ★★★ A quirky, entertaining mystery story, set in the reggae world of a Caribbean island. Denzel Washington plays the local police chief—"The Mighty Quinn"—who is on the trail of a murderer. Director Carl Schenkel contributes an inventive visual style and makes ample use of a wonderful reggae score. Rated R, with profanity, violence, and mild sexual situations. 95m. **DIR:** Carl Schenkel. **CAST:** Denzel Washington, Robert Townsend, James Fox, Sheryl Lee Ralph, Mimi Rogers. 1989

MIGRANTS, THE ★★★★ Nominated for six Emmy Awards, this moving adaptation of Tennessee Williams's story accurately depicts the trials and tribulations of migrant farm workers. Cloris Leachman brilliantly portrays Viola, who has seen too much suffering but maintains a glimmer of hope for her children. Despite major setbacks, Ron Howard, as her oldest son, tries to fulfill her dreams. Not rated; contains adult themes. 83m. **DIR:** Tom Gries. **CAST:** Cloris Leachman, Ron Howard, Sissy Spacek, Cindy Williams, Lisa Lucas. 1973

MIKADO, THE (1939) ★★★1/2 Members of the D'Oyly Carte Opera Company perform in this colorful British-made movie of the Gilbert and Sullivan operetta. Kenny Baker furnishes the American influence, but the real stars are the music, fanciful sets, and gorgeous Technicolor cinematography. As enjoyable as a professional staging. 90m. **DIR:** Victor Schertzinger. **CAST:** Kenny Baker, Martyn Green, Jean Colin. 1939 DVD

MIKADO, THE (1987) ★★★1/2 Gilbert and Sullivan's delightfully amusing light opera is majestically performed at the London Coliseum by the English National Opera. Eric Idle dominates as Lord High Executioner of the town of Titipu. Special optical effects and camera angles add to the fun. 131m. **DIR:** John Michael Phillips. **CAST:** Eric Idle, Bonaventura Bottone, Lesley Garrett. 1987

MIKE'S MURDER ★★★ This could have been an interesting tale of a small-time Los Angeles drug dealer and part-time tennis pro involved in a drug rip-off. But a string of confusing plot devices doesn't work. Rated R for violence, language, and nudity. 97m. **DIR:** James Bridges. **CAST:** Debra Winger, Mark Keyloun, Darrell Larson. 1984

MIKEY ★★★1/2 Talk about problem children. Young Mikey, played by Brian Bonsall, has a real attitude problem. When he feels unloved, he murders his parents, and then moves on to the next foster home. This bad seed continues his reign of terror until he falls for the girl next door. Rated R for violence, nudity, and language. 92m. **DIR:** Dennis Dimster-Denk. **CAST:** John Diehl, Lyman Ward, Brian Bonsall, Josie Bissett. 1992 DVD

MIKEY AND NICKY ★★★ The story of a fateful day and the relationship of two small-time crooks who have been best friends since childhood. This hauntingly funny film slowly builds to its climax in the Elaine May tradition. Great acting from Peter Falk and John Cassavetes. Rated R for profanity. 119m. **DIR:** Elaine May. **CAST:** Peter Falk, John Cassavetes, Ned Beatty, Joyce Van Patten. 1976

MILAGRO BEANFIELD WAR, THE ★★★ There are fine perfomances in this slight, but enjoyable comedy-drama in which a group of citizens from a small town attempt to save their way of life by fighting big-money interests. The story is simplistic but a real spirit lifter. Rated R for violence and profanity. 117m. **DIR:** Robert Redford. **CAST:** Rubén Blades, Richard Bradford, Sonia Braga, Julie Carmen, James Gammon, Melanie Griffith, John Heard, Daniel Stern, Christopher Walken, Chick Vennera. 1988

MILDRED PIERCE ★★★★ Bored housewife Joan Crawford parlays waiting tables into a restaurant chain and an infatuation with Zachary Scott. Her spoiled daughter, Ann Blyth, hits on him. Emotions run high and taut as everything unravels in this A-one adaptation of James M. Cain's novel of murder and cheap love. Her performance in the title role won Joan Crawford an Oscar for best actress. B&W; 109m. **DIR:** Michael Curtiz. **CAST:** Joan Crawford, Jack Carson, Zachary Scott, Eve Arden, Ann Blyth, Bruce Bennett, George Tobias, Lee Patrick. 1945

MILES FROM HOME ★★ Richard Gere and Kevin Anderson star as brothers in this uneven drama about tragic rural figures. The brothers' farm is lost to foreclosure. They respond by torching the place and heading off on a confused odyssey of crime and misadventure. Rated R for profanity and violence. 103m. **DIR:** Gary Sinise. **CAST:** Richard Gere, Kevin Anderson. 1988

MILES TO GO ★★★ When she learns she is dying of cancer, a woman lays plans for the future of her family by seeking her own "replacement." Unusual premise is handled tastefully in this TV movie. 98m.

DIR: David Greene. **CAST:** Jill Clayburgh, Tom Skerritt, Mimi Kuzyk. 1986

MILK MONEY ★★★1/2 An adolescent boy heads into the big bad city with some friends, intending to trade lunch money for a glimpse of a hooker's breasts, and winds up bringing perky Melanie Griffith home to meet his single father. R. J. Stewart's screenplay gets renewed mileage from the hooker-with-a-heart-of-gold stereotype, thanks mostly to clever dialogue and Griffith's warmhearted performance. Rated PG-13 for profanity, brief nudity, and violence. 108m. **DIR:** Richard Benjamin. **CAST:** Melanie Griffith, Ed Harris, Michael Patrick Carter, Malcolm McDowell. 1994

MILKY WAY, THE (1936) ★★★★ In this superb compendium of gags flowing from his character of a milkman who innocently decks the champion during a brawl, the great Harold Lloyd amply proves why he was such a success. Lloyd was a master comic craftsman. This is the finest of his few talking films. B&W; 83m. **DIR:** Leo McCarey. **CAST:** Harold Lloyd, Adolphe Menjou, Helen Mack. 1936

MILKY WAY, THE (1970) ★★★★ Haunting comedy about two men making a religious pilgrimage through France. Excellent supporting cast and outstanding direction by Luis Buñuel. French dialogue with English subtitles. Not rated. 102m. **DIR:** Luis Buñuel. **CAST:** Paul Frankeur, Laurent Terzieff, Alain Cuny, Bernard Verley, Michel Piccoli, Delphine Seyrig. 1970

MILL OF THE STONE WOMEN ★★★ A fascinating one-shot, made in Holland by French and Italian filmmakers, about a mad professor who turns women into statues. Visually innovative, scary, and original. 63m. **DIR:** Giorgio Ferroni. **CAST:** Pierre Brice, Wolfgang Preiss, Scilla Gabel. 1960

MILL ON THE FLOSS, THE ★★★1/2 Geraldine Fitzgerald is Maggie and James Mason is Tom Tolliver in this careful and faithful adaptation of novelist George Eliot's story of ill-starred romance. B&W; 77m. **DIR:** Tim Whelan. **CAST:** Geraldine Fitzgerald, James Mason. 1939

MILLE BOLLE BLU ★★★★ One day in the life of the residents of an Italian apartment building in 1961, as they wait for a total eclipse of the sun. Like an Italian *Slacker*, the film's invisible star is the endlessly gliding camera that moves us effortlessly from person to person. A memorable debut from director Leone Pompucci, who gets an astonishing range of life into a brief film. Not rated; contains profanity. In Italian with English subtitles. 83m. **DIR:** Leone Pompucci. **CAST:** Paolo Bonacelli, Stefania Montorsi, Stefano Dionisi, Nicoletta Boris. 1993

MILLENNIUM (1989) 💔 Terrible time-travel story has Kris Kristofferson as an air-disaster troubleshooter, who meets a mysterious woman from the future. Rated PG-13 for violence and suggested sex. 110m. **DIR:** Michael Anderson. **CAST:** Kris Kristofferson, Cheryl Ladd, Daniel J. Travanti, Robert Joy. 1989 DVD

MILLENNIUM (1996) ★★★1/2 Chris Carter, the producer of the cult hit *The X-Files*, attacked an unsuspecting populace with this second TV outing, a dark thriller about the approaching turn of the century and the corresponding rise in crime. What ensued was a somewhat depressing but always fascinating look at the human condition. The tape includes the pilot and the second episode, "Gehenna." Not rated; contains graphic and disturbing content. 88m. **DIR:** David Nutter. **CAST:** Lance Henriksen, Megan Gallagher, Terry O'Quinn, Bill Smitrovich, Brittany Tiplady. 1996

MILLER'S CROSSING ★★★★ Corrupt political boss (Albert Finney) of an eastern city severs ties with his best friend and confidant (Gabriel Byrne) in 1929 when they both fall for the same woman and find themselves on opposing sides of a violent gang war. An underworld code of ethics, protocol, and loyalty provides the ground rules for this very entertaining, slightly bent homage to past mobster films. Rated R for language and violence. 115m. **DIR:** Joel Coen. **CAST:** Gabriel Byrne, Marcia Gay Harden, John Turturro, Albert Finney, Jon Polito. 1990

MILLION DOLLAR DUCK, THE ★★ A duck is accidentally given a dose of radiation that makes it produce eggs with solid gold yolks. Dean Jones and Sandy Duncan, as the owners of the duck, use the yolks to pay off bills until the Treasury Department gets wise. Mildly entertaining comedy in the Disney tradition. Rated G. 92m. **DIR:** Vincent McEveety. **CAST:** Dean Jones, Sandy Duncan, Joe Flynn, Tony Roberts. 1971

MILLION DOLLAR MERMAID ★★ Esther Williams swims through her role as famous early distaff aquatic star Annette Kellerman, who pioneered one-piece suits and vaudeville tank acts. Victor Mature woos her in this highly fictionalized film biography. The Busby Berkeley production numbers are a highlight. 115m. **DIR:** Mervyn LeRoy. **CAST:** Esther Williams, Victor Mature, Walter Pidgeon, David Brian, Jesse White. 1952

MILLION DOLLAR MYSTERY 💔 A gimmick film that originally offered $1 million to the first audience member who could put the movie's clues together. Rated PG. 95m. **DIR:** Richard Fleischer. **CAST:** Jamie Alcroft, Royce D. Applegate, Tom Bosley, Eddie Deezen, Rich Hall, Mack Dryden. 1987

MILLION TO JUAN, A ★★ Comedian Paul Rodriguez plays a Hispanic father in L.A. working for his green card who receives a million-dollar check. The catch: he can only "use" it, not cash it. The film is well-intentioned, but the script (loosely adapted from a Mark Twain story) tries to be too many things—romantic comedy, social satire, rags-to-riches fantasy—and winds up a mess. Rated PG. 93m. **DIR:** Paul Rodriguez. **CAST:** Paul Rodriguez, Edward James Olmos, Richard "Cheech" Marin, Rubén Blades, Polly Draper. 1994

MILLIONAIRE'S EXPRESS (SHANGHAI EXPRESS) ★★★★1/2 Deliriously entertaining action comedy featuring Sammo Hung. He plays a rogue who tries to hijack a train filled with rich people to his hometown, hoping they'll spend money there. But he has to do battle with bandits who want all that money for themselves. Something of a tribute to the Westerns of Sergio Leone, this is hurt only by a sloppy story. Not rated; contains comic violence. 107m. **DIR:** Sammo Hung. **CAST:** Sammo Hung, Rosamund Kwan,

Yuen Biao, Cynthia Rothrock, Yukari Oshima. 1986 DVD

MILLIONS ★★ Spoiled young man whose ambitions outstrip his brainpower decides to make his fortune. Lots of sex cheapens the plot. Rated R for nudity and profanity. 90m. DIR: Carlo Vanzina. CAST: Billy Zane, Lauren Hutton, Carol Ait, Donald Pleasence, Alexandra Paul. 1991

MILO 🎬 If this movie were any more of a dog it would have fleas. You'll still wind up scratching your head wondering why the filmmakers thought we needed another *Halloween* rip-off about a woman who believes that her childhood attacker has come back to finish the job. Rated R for violence and language. 91m. DIR: Pascal Franchot. CAST: Paula Cale, Vincent Schiavelli, Antonio Fargas, Jennifer Jostyn. 1998 DVD

MIMIC ★★★1/2 Mexican director Guillermo del Toro has made his American film debut an exciting, old-fashioned monster movie that unapologetically harkens back to the "giant bug" epics of the 1950s. Genetic engineers concoct a "designer predator" to combat a virulent disease carried by New York City cockroaches; unfortunately, after three years the cure proves much worse than the affliction. The film's first half is intriguing science and character development, leading to a slam-bang suspense finale in the bowels of the city subway system. Rated R for violence, gore, and profanity. 105m. DIR: Guillermo del Toro. CAST: Mira Sorvino, Jeremy Northam, Josh Brolin, Charles Dutton, Giancarlo Giannini, F. Murray Abraham. 1997 DVD

MIN AND BILL ★★★ Their first picture together as a team puts Marie Dressler and Wallace Beery to the test when the future of the waif (Dorothy Jordan) she has reared on the rough-and-tumble waterfront is threatened by the girl's disreputable mother, Marjorie Rambeau. Her emotional portrayal won Marie Dressler an Oscar for best actress and helped make the film the box-office hit of its year. B&W; 70m. DIR: George Hill. CAST: Marie Dressler, Wallace Beery, Dorothy Jordan, Marjorie Rambeau. 1931

MINA TANNENBAUM ★★★1/2 À la *Entre Nous* or *Beaches*, this French drama chronicles the relationship between two young girls and how it changes as they face the challenges of adulthood. Well acted and engrossingly written, it suffers only from some overreacting on the part of first-time writer-director Martine Dugowson. In French with English subtitles. 124m. DIR: Martine Dugowson. CAST: Romane Bohringer, Elsa Zylberstein, Florence Thomassin. 1994

MINBO, OR THE GENTLE ART OF JAPANESE EXTORTION ★★★ A hotel owner tries to escape the *yakuza*—Japanese mobsters—who have infiltrated his building and are driving away his customers. Filmmaker Juzo Itami had his own trouble with *yakuza*, and this film is an act of revenge, though it's a subpar effort. Still, there are enough amusing tangents to keep viewers entertained. In Japanese with English subtitles. Not rated; contains violence, nudity, and profanity. 123m. DIR: Juzo Itami. CAST: Nobuko Miyamoto, Akira Takarada, Takehiro Murata, Yasuo Daichi. 1992

MIND FIELD ★★1/2 When cop Michael Ironside starts hallucinating, he traces the cause of his delusions to a secret CIA experiment involving LSD. Rated R for violence. 92m. DIR: Jean-Claude Lord. CAST: Michael Ironside, Sean McCann, Christopher Plummer, Lisa Langlois. 1990

MIND KILLER ★★ A nerdy library worker uncovers a manuscript about the power of positive thinking. Soon he has the power to control minds and to lift objects mentally. But the power has its drawbacks, turning him into a monster. The movie is low-budget, but the filmmakers try hard. Not rated; contains adult language and situations. 84m. DIR: Michael Krueger. CAST: Joe McDonald. 1987

MIND RIPPER ★★ Low-budget thriller about a government experiment gone awry and the former supervisor who is called back into action to kill the manmade creature. Even though most of the action takes place in an underground laboratory, this film isn't nearly claustrophobic enough. Rated R for violence and adult language. 90m. DIR: Joe Gayton. CAST: Lance Henriksen, John Diehl, Natasha Gregson Wagner, Dan Blom, Claire Stansfield. 1995

MIND SNATCHERS, THE ★★★ Christopher Walken plays a nihilistic U.S. soldier in West Germany who is admitted to a mental institution. He finds out later the hospital is actually a laboratory where a German scientist is testing a new form of psychological control. Walken's performance is excellent and the idea is an interesting one, but the film moves slowly. Rated PG for violence and profanity. 94m. DIR: Bernard Girard. CAST: Christopher Walken, Ronny Cox, Joss Ackland, Ralph Meeker. 1972

MINDGAMES ★★★ Taut thriller features Maxwell Caulfield as a psychotic hitchhiker who attaches himself to an unhappy couple and their son. What follows is a series of violent and unnerving mind games. Rated R for violence. 93m. DIR: Bob Yari. CAST: Maxwell Caulfield, Edward Albert, Shawn Weatherly. 1989

MINDTWISTER 🎬 Schlockmeister Fred Olen Ray refurbishes one of his soft-core quickies by adding disparate scenes with Telly Savalas, who undoubtedly had no control over how his footage was used. Beware this cut-and-paste rubbish. Rated R for nudity, simulated sex, violence, and profanity. 95m. DIR: Fred Olen Ray. CAST: Telly Savalas, Suzanne Slater, Gary Hudson, Erika Nann, Richard Roundtree. 1993

MINDWALK ★★★ A trio of archetypes—a scientist (Liv Ullmann), a politician (Sam Waterston), and a poet (John Heard)—discuss the current "crisis in perspective," which comes from the discovery, in physics, that the old, "mechanistic" way of looking at life (thinking about living things in terms of their components) should be replaced by a more holistic view. More of a lecture than a movie, *Mindwalk* will fascinate those who appreciate novelist-turned-screenwriter Fritjof Capra's theories. Rated PG. 111m. DIR: Berndt Capra. CAST: Liv Ullmann, Sam Waterston, John Heard, Ione Skye. 1991

MINDWARP ★★1/2 After a nuclear war, randomly chosen individuals dwell in underground bunkers, living their lives out in computer-generated fantasies. But when one girl rebels, she is exiled to the surface. Low-budget, but fun gross-out action-thriller. Rated R for nudity, profanity, and violence. 91m. DIR: Steve Barnett. CAST: Bruce Campbell, Angus Scrimm, Elizabeth Kent. 1991

MINE OWN EXECUTIONER ★★★ Noted psychiatrist Burgess Meredith accepts ex–fighter pilot and Japanese prisoner of war Kieron Moore as a patient. He finds himself in the thick of a schizophrenic's hell, resulting in murder and suicide. Top-notch suspense. B&W; 105m. DIR: Anthony Kimmins. CAST: Burgess Meredith, Kieron Moore, Dulcie Gray. 1948

MINES OF KILIMANJARO ★★ *Raiders of the Lost Ark* imitation with an American college student in Africa searching for the lost diamond mines of Kilimanjaro. Trying to stop him are the Nazis, Chinese gangsters, and native tribesmen. The action footage is badly choreographed, the music is strident, and the historical accuracy is a laugh. Not rated; contains violence. 88m. DIR: Mino Guerrini. CAST: Tobias Hoesl, Elena Pompei, Christopher Connelly. 1987

MINGUS ★★★ Revealing portrait of Charles Mingus, the great bassist, considered to be one of the most influential figures in jazz. Most of this film was shot in his cluttered New York loft as he awaited eviction in the wake of a legal tangle with the city. B&W; 58m. DIR: Thomas Reichmann. 1968

MINISTRY OF VENGEANCE 🎥 Loathsome in every respect—a minister reverts to his military training to seek revenge on terrorists. Rated R for violence. 93m. DIR: Peter Maris. CAST: John Schneider, Ned Beatty, James Tolkan, Apollonia Kotero, Robert Miano, Yaphet Kotto, George Kennedy. 1989

MINIVER STORY, THE ★★1/2 Post–World War II sequel to the popular *Mrs. Miniver* has Greer Garson putting her family's affairs in order while hiding the fact that she is dying. Good performances by the stars, but it is really just pure soap opera. B&W; 104m. DIR: H. C. Potter. CAST: Greer Garson, Walter Pidgeon, John Hodiak, Leo Genn, Cathy O'Donnell, Reginald Owen, Peter Finch, Henry Wilcoxon. 1950

MINOR MIRACLE, A ★★1/2 A heartwarming story about a group of orphaned children and their devoted guardian (John Huston), who band together to save the St. Francis School for Boys. If you liked *Going My Way* and *Oh God!* you'll like this G-rated movie. 100m. DIR: Raoul Lomas. CAST: John Huston, Pelé, Peter Fox. 1983

•**MINUS MAN, THE** ★★★ An amiable drifter befriends strangers, soothes them with drawling small talk, then kills them with a painless, fast-acting poison. The film hints at deep waters under the killer's placid surface, but never plumbs them. It's disconnected and a little frustrating to watch, but the film's elusiveness seems to embody that of the central character. Rated R for mature themes. 112m. DIR: Hampton Fancher. CAST: Owen C. Wilson, Brian Cox, Janeane Garofalo, Dwight Yoakam, Mercedes Ruehl, Dennis Haysbert, Sheryl Crow. 1999 DVD

MINUTE TO PRAY, A SECOND TO DIE, A ★★ This is a routine Western with Alex Cord as an outlaw trying to turn himself in when amnesty is declared by the governor of New Mexico (played by Robert Ryan). Arthur Kennedy, as the marshal, has other

plans. Rated R for violence. 99m. DIR: Franco Giraldi. CAST: Alex Cord, Arthur Kennedy, Robert Ryan, Nicoletta Machiavelli. 1967

MIRACLE, THE (1959) ★★★ In Spain in the early 1800s, a postulant nun deserts her order to search for a soldier she loves and becomes a noted gypsy, singer, and courtesan. Tries for deep religious meaning but misses the mark. 120m. DIR: Irving Rapper. CAST: Carroll Baker, Roger Moore, Walter Slezak, Vittorio Gassman, Katina Paxinou, Dennis King. 1959

MIRACLE, THE (1990) ★★★ Two Irish teenagers (Niall Byrne and Lorraine Pilkington) while away their days fantasizing about people they encounter. When a mysterious woman (Beverly D'Angelo) arrives, Byrne takes it a step further only to find out that she's the mother he never knew. A pleasant surprise. Rated PG for profanity. 100m. DIR: Neil Jordan. CAST: Beverly D'Angelo, Niall Byrne, Donal McCann, Lorraine Pilkington. 1990

MIRACLE BEACH ★★★ Delightful fantasy unfolds when an all-around loser finds a genie who can grant all his wishes. Rated R for nudity and simulated sex. 88m. DIR: Skott Snider. CAST: Dean Cameron, Ami Dolenz, Felicity Waterman, Noriyuki "Pat" Morita. 1991

MIRACLE DOWN UNDER ★★★1/2 This moving drama is actually *A Christmas Carol* Australian style. Only a small boy's kindness can rekindle an evil miser's Christmas spirit. This fine family film contains no objectionable material. 106m. DIR: George Miller. CAST: Dee Wallace, John Waters, Charles Tingwell, Bill Kerr, Andrew Ferguson. 1987

MIRACLE IN MILAN ★★★1/2 A baby found in a cabbage patch grows up to be Toto the Good, who organizes a shantytown into the perfect commune. Or so he had hoped, but it is not to be—even with the help of the old lady who found him, now an angel of mercy. This fantasy by Vittorio De Sica also delivers a message of social satire and innocence. Winner of the Cannes Grand Prix and the New York Film Critics' Circle best foreign film awards. In Italian with English subtitles. B&W; 96m. DIR: Vittorio De Sica. CAST: Francesco Golisano, Paolo Stoppa. 1951

MIRACLE IN ROME ★★★ Spanish TV film adaptation of Gabriel Garcia Marquez's intriguing tale of one man's struggle with sainthood. Frank Ramirez plays the bereaved father who's lost his vivacious 7-year-old daughter. Heartwarming, though morbid, insight into a man's undying love and devotion for his innocent child. In Spanish with English subtitles. 76m. DIR: Lisandro Duque Naranjo. CAST: Frank Ramirez. 1988

MIRACLE IN THE WILDERNESS ★★ Heavy-handed message film spreads the "give peace a chance" motto. When settlers (Kris Kristofferson and Kim Cattrall) are kidnapped by vengeful Blackfeet Indians, Kristofferson's violent attempts to save his wife and child are in vain. Only Cattrall's gentle ways can free them. Preachy and unbelievable made-for-cable drama. 88m. DIR: Kevin James Dobson. CAST: Kris Kristofferson, Kim Cattrall, John Dennis Johnston. 1991

MIRACLE MILE ★★★★ A fascinatingly frightful study of mass hysteria centered on a spreading rumor that a nuclear holocaust is imminent. Anthony

Edwards accidentally overhears a phone conversation that "the button has been pushed." He learns that Los Angeles is seventy minutes from destruction and must scramble about, trying to discover the truth and possibly save himself and others. Superb. Rated R. 87m. **DIR:** Steve DeJarnett. **CAST:** Anthony Edwards, Mare Winningham, John Agar. 1989

MIRACLE OF MORGAN'S CREEK, THE ★★★★1/2 All comic hell breaks loose when Betty Hutton finds herself pregnant following an all-night party, can't recall who the father is, and eventually gives birth to sextuplets. An audacious, daring Bronx cheer at American morals and ideals, this rollicking farce, cram-jammed with comic lines, is a real winner. B&W; 99m. **DIR:** Preston Sturges. **CAST:** Betty Hutton, Eddie Bracken, William Demarest, Diana Lynn, Brian Donlevy, Akim Tamiroff, Jimmy Conlin, Porter Hall. 1944

MIRACLE OF OUR LADY OF FATIMA, THE ★★★1/2 Remarkably well-told story of the famous appearance of the Virgin Mary in the small town of Fatima, Portugal. The Virgin appears to some farm children and they try to spread her word to a skeptical world. Not rated, but equivalent to a G. 102m. **DIR:** John Brahm. **CAST:** Gilbert Roland, Frank Silvera, Sherry Jackson. 1952

MIRACLE OF THE BELLS, THE ★★★ A miracle takes place when a movie star is buried in her coal-mining hometown. Hard-bitten press agent Fred MacMurray comes mushy to see "the kid" gets the right send-off. The story is trite and its telling too long, but the cast is earnest and the film has a way of clicking. B&W; 120m. **DIR:** Irving Pichel. **CAST:** Fred MacMurray, Alida Valli, Frank Sinatra, Lee J. Cobb. 1948

MIRACLE OF THE HEART ★★★ Made-for-TV sequel to the 1938 *Boys Town*, which featured Spencer Tracy as Father Flanagan. This time, Art Carney plays one of Flanagan's boys, who is now an older priest. Touching and heartwarming. 96m. **DIR:** Georg Stanford Brown. **CAST:** Art Carney, Casey Siemaszko, Jack Bannon, Darrell Larson. 1986

MIRACLE OF THE WHITE STALLIONS ★★ True story of the evacuation of the famed Lipizzan stallions from war-torn Vienna doesn't pack much of a wallop, but kids and horse fans should enjoy it. 92m. **DIR:** Arthur Hiller. **CAST:** Robert Taylor, Lilli Palmer, Curt Jurgens, Eddie Albert, James Franciscus, John Larch. 1963

MIRACLE ON ICE ★★1/2 This made-for-TV movie reenacts the American hockey victory at the 1980 Lake Placid Olympic Games. Karl Malden plays his usual tough-but-fair persona to the hilt as character-building coach Herb Brooks. 140m. **DIR:** Steven H. Stern. **CAST:** Karl Malden, Andrew Stevens, Steve Guttenberg, Jessica Walter. 1981

MIRACLE ON 34TH STREET (1947) ★★★★★ In this, one of Hollywood's most delightful fantasies, the spirit of Christmas is rekindled in a young girl (Natalie Wood) by a department store Santa. Edmund Gwenn is perfect as the endearing Macy's employee who causes a furor when he claims to be the real Kris Kringle. Is he or isn't he? That is for you to decide in this heartwarming family classic. B&W;

96m. **DIR:** George Seaton. **CAST:** Natalie Wood, Edmund Gwenn, Maureen O'Hara. 1947 DVD

MIRACLE ON 34TH STREET (1994) ★★★★ Young Mara Wilson *owns* this heartfelt remake of George Seaton's holiday classic, as a precocious little girl who'd like to believe in Santa Claus ... if only her overly practical mother would permit it. Richard Attenborough is the angelic Kris Kringle, whose tenure as a department-store Santa prompts all sorts of holiday magic. Rated PG. 114m. **DIR:** Les Mayfield. **CAST:** Richard Attenborough, Elizabeth Perkins, Dylan McDermott, Mara Wilson, J. T. Walsh, James Remar, Jane Leeves, Simon Jones, William Windom, Robert Prosky. 1994

MIRACLE WORKER, THE (1962) ★★★★1/2 Anne Bancroft and Patty Duke are superb when re-creating their acclaimed Broadway performances in this production. Patty Duke is the untamed and blind deaf-mute Helen Keller and Bancroft is her equally strong-willed, but compassionate, teacher. Their harrowing fight for power and the ultimately touching first communication make up one of the screen's great sequences. B&W; 107m. **DIR:** Arthur Penn. **CAST:** Anne Bancroft, Patty Duke, Andrew Prine. 1962

MIRACLE WORKER, THE (1979) ★★★1/2 This made-for-TV biography features Patty Duke as Anne Sullivan, teacher and friend of a disturbed deaf and blind girl. Melissa Gilbert takes the role of Helen Keller, which garnered an Oscar for Duke in 1962. This version is not quite as moving as the earlier one, but it's still worth watching. 100m. **DIR:** Paul Aaron. **CAST:** Patty Duke, Melissa Gilbert, Charles Siebert. 1979

MIRACLES ★★1/2 This film involves a sick little girl in a remote Mexican jungle, a doctor and his recently divorced wife in L.A., and a bungling burglar. The story revolves around the sometimes funny circumstances that bring all these characters together. Rated PG for language and mild violence. 90m. **DIR:** Jim Kouf. **CAST:** Tom Conti, Teri Garr, Paul Rodriguez, Christopher Lloyd. 1986 DVD

MIRAGE (1965) ★★★ Some really fine scenes and top-notch actors enliven this slow but ultimately satisfying mystery thriller. Gregory Peck is David Stillwell, a man who has lost his memory. Occasionally snappy dialogue, with an interesting but overdone use of flashbacks. B&W; 108m. **DIR:** Edward Dmytryk. **CAST:** Gregory Peck, Diane Baker, Walter Matthau, Kevin McCarthy, Jack Weston, George Kennedy, Leif Erickson, Walter Abel. 1965

MIRAGE (1995) ★★★ An ex-cop is hired to protect a mysterious, beautiful woman and they find themselves drawn to each other. Amid their passion, however, a hidden, sinister plot exposes itself. Entertaining mystery-thriller offers a gritty performance from Edward James Olmos and an intriguing turn by Sean Young. Rated R for profanity, violence, and nudity. 92m. **DIR:** Paul Williams. **CAST:** Edward James Olmos, Sean Young, James Andronica. 1995

MIRROR, THE ★★★★ A young boy is hypnotized in an attempt to cure a chronic stutter in this poetic mixture of dream and reality in the Soviet Union's most visionary film director, Andrei Tarkovsky. Brilliant use of color and black-and-white cinematograhy. Mesmerizing. In Russian with English subtitles. 0m. DIR: Andrei Tarkovsky. CAST: Margarita Terekova. 1976 DVD

MIRROR CRACK'D, THE ★★ Elizabeth Taylor, Kim Novak, and Tony Curtis seem to be vying to see who can turn in the worst performance in this tepid adaptation of the Agatha Christie murder mystery. Angela Lansbury makes an excellent Miss Marple, and Edward Fox is top-notch as her Scotland Yard inspector nephew. Rated PG. 105m. DIR: Guy Hamilton. CAST: Elizabeth Taylor, Kim Novak, Tony Curtis, Angela Lansbury, Edward Fox, Rock Hudson. 1980

MIRROR CRACK'D FROM SIDE TO SIDE, THE ★★★1/2 This Agatha Christie mystery is an enjoyable puzzle filled with red herrings. Miss Marple must help her nephew, Inspector Craddock, find the murderer. Not rated; suitable for family viewing. 100m. DIR: Norman Stone. CAST: Joan Hickson, Claire Bloom, Barry Newman, Glynis Barber, John Castle, Judy Cornwell, David Horovitch. 1992

MIRROR HAS TWO FACES, THE ★★★ Typical Barbra Streisand "Am I pretty?" neurosis is pleasantly showcased in this romantic comedy. A good date film, this features Streisand as a prof pursued by a sexy math whiz (Jeff Bridges) who seeks a platonic marital relationship. Frustrated by their lack of intimacy, Streisand sells out by transforming herself into a hot looker. Rated PG-13 for language and sexual situations. 125m. DIR: Barbra Streisand. CAST: Barbra Streisand, Jeff Bridges, Pierce Brosnan, George Segal, Mimi Rogers, Lauren Bacall, Brenda Vaccaro. 1996 DVD

MIRROR IMAGES ♥ Penthouse pet Delia Sheppard plays twin sisters, one a stripper, the other a bored housewife. When the housewife steps into her sister's stiletto shoes, they take her face-to-face with a psychotic madman. Not rated; contains enough nudity to make it equivalent to soft porn. 92m. DIR: Alexander Gregory Hippolyte. CAST: Delia Sheppard, Jeff Conaway, John O'Hurley, Nels Van Patten. 1991

MIRROR IMAGES II ♥ In spite of its pretensions as an erotic thriller, the only element separating this pathetic, would-be drama from hard-core sex films is the absence of gynecological close-ups. Available in R-rated and unrated versions, both with incessant nudity, profanity, and simulated sex. 92m. DIR: Alexander Gregory Hippolyte. CAST: Shannon Whirry, Luca Bercovici, Tom Reilly. 1993

MIRROR MIRROR ★★1/2 An awkward teenage girl uses black magic, gained from an arcane mirror, to avenge herself on her cruel classmates. The film tries hard, but there's no payoff. Rated R for violence and profanity. 105m. DIR: Marina Sargenti. CAST: Karen Black, Rainbow Harvest, Yvonne De Carlo, William Sanderson. 1990

•MIRROR, MIRROR 2: RAVEN DANCE ★★ Ballerina Tracy Wells, recovering from a bad fall at a nunnery, comes across the haunted mirror and unleashes the terrors within. The actors chew the scenery, while everything else just trudges along at a ho-hum pace. Rated R for violence. 91m. DIR: Jimmy Lifton. CAST: Tracy Wells, Sally Kellerman, Roddy Mc-

Dowall, Sarah Douglas, Veronica Cartwright, William Sanderson. 1993

MIRROR OF DEATH ♥ An abused woman takes up voodoo as therapy. Not rated, but has violence, gore, and profanity. 85m. DIR: Deryn Warren. CAST: Julie Merrill. 1987

MIRRORS ★★1/2 An aspiring ballerina must choose between the love of her straitlaced boyfriend and her struggle to become a dancer in New York. Her small-town values are challenged by the free-spirited theatrical gypsies with whom she works. The idea is riveting, but plot twists seem contrived. Not rated; contains nudity. 99m. DIR: Harry Winer. CAST: Marguerite Hickey, Timothy Daly, Shanna Reed, Antony Hamilton, Keenan Wynn. 1985

MISADVENTURES OF BUSTER KEATON, THE ★★ The world-famous "Great Stone Face" has his moments in this sound version of one of his classic silent comedies but falls short of what he did in his prime. Still, Keaton running a small theater, bumbling and fumbling at every turn, is a delight to behold. B&W; 65m. DIR: Arthur Hilton. CAST: Buster Keaton, Marcia Mae Jones. 1950

MISADVENTURES OF MERLIN JONES, THE ★★1/2 Tommy Kirk stars as a boy genius whose talents for mind reading and hypnotism land him in all sorts of trouble. Entertaining for the young or indiscriminate; pretty bland for everybody else. 88m. DIR: Robert Stevenson. CAST: Tommy Kirk, Annette Funicello, Leon Ames, Stu Erwin, Alan Hewitt. 1964

MISADVENTURES OF MR. WILT, THE ★★★1/2 Screwball British comedy about a man trying to explain to the police that he didn't kill his wife, but a life-size blow-up doll. Told in flashback, this is an effective little film that is hampered only by a disappointing ending. Rated R for profanity. 84m. DIR: Michael Tuchner. CAST: Griff Rhys Jones, Mel Smith, Alison Steadman, Diana Quick. 1989

MISCHIEF ★★★ In this disarming coming-of-age comedy, Doug McKeon (On Golden Pond) plays Jonathan, whose hopes of romance are thwarted until Gene (Chris Nash), a kid from the big city, shows him how. Rated R for violence, profanity, nudity, and simulated sex. 93m. DIR: Mel Damski. CAST: Doug McKeon, Catherine Mary Stewart, Chris Nash, Kelly Preston, D. W. Brown. 1985

MISERY ★★★★ In this black-comedy thriller, James Caan stars as a popular novelist, who is kept captive by his most ardent fan (Kathy Bates, who scored a best-actress Oscar)—who just happens to be a psychopath. As written by Academy Award–winner William Goldman, it's the best Stephen King adaptation since Rob Reiner's Stand by Me. Rated R for profanity and violence. 104m. DIR: Rob Reiner. CAST: James Caan, Kathy Bates, Richard Farnsworth, Frances Sternhagen, Lauren Bacall. 1990

MISFIT BRIGADE, THE ★★★ Oliver Reed and David Carradine have cameo roles in this takeoff on The Dirty Dozen. Bruce Davison, David Patrick Kelly, and their buddies are assorted criminals from a Nazi penal brigade. The cast has a lot of fun with the tongue-in-cheek action. Rated R. 99m. DIR: Gordon Hessler. CAST: Bruce Davison, David Patrick Kelly,

D. W. Moffett, Oliver Reed, David Carradine, Jay O. Sanders. 1987

MISFITS, THE ★★★ Arthur Miller's parable of a hope-stripped divorcée and a gaggle of her boot-shod cowpoke boyfriends shagging wild horses in the Nevada desert, this film was the last hurrah for Marilyn Monroe and Clark Gable. The acting is good, but the story line is lean. B&W; 124m. DIR: John Huston. CAST: Marilyn Monroe, Clark Gable, Montgomery Clift, Thelma Ritter, Eli Wallach, Estelle Winwood. 1961

MISFITS OF SCIENCE ★★1/2 Dean Paul Martin stars as the ringleader of a group of individuals possessing unique abilities. He rallies them together to combine their powers. No rating. This was the first installment in the failed television series. 96m. DIR: James D. Parriott. CAST: Dean Paul Martin, Kevin Peter Hall, Mark Thomas Miller, Courteney Cox. 1986

MISHIMA: A LIFE IN FOUR CHAPTERS ★★★★ By depicting this enigmatic writer's life through his art, filmmaker Paul Schrader has come close to illustrating the true heart of an artist. This is not a standard narrative biography but a bold attempt to meld an artist's life with his life's work. The movie is, as suggested in the title, divided into four parts: "Beauty," "Art," "Action," and the climactic "A Harmony of Pen and Sword." Rated R for sex, nudity, violence, and adult situations. 121m. DIR: Paul Schrader. CAST: Ken Ogata, Ken Swada, Yasusuka Brando. 1985

MISPLACED ★★★ A modest but appealing independent film about the hurdles facing a teenage immigrant, newly arrived in America. Set in 1981, *Misplaced* is part coming-of-age tale and part cross-cultural drama. Not rated. 98m. DIR: Louis Yansen. CAST: John Cameron Mitchell, Elzbieta Czyzewska, Viveca Lindfors. 1991

MISS ANNIE ROONEY ★★ The highlight of this film comes when Dickie Moore gives Shirley Temple her first screen kiss. The rest of this average picture involves a poor girl who falls in love with a rich dandy. No sparks here. 84m. DIR: Edwin L. Marin. CAST: Shirley Temple, William Gargan, Guy Kibbee, Dickie Moore, Peggy Ryan, Gloria Holden. 1942

MISS EVERS' BOYS ★★★★ Recent American history is filled with atrocities, and this remains one of the worst: the 1932 "Tuskegee Study" that took place in Macon County, Alabama, and traced the development of untreated syphilis in the African American male. Alfre Woodard plays the title character in this HBO production, a nurse who fully understands the consequences of what she condones by her silence, but rationalizes that the "study" somehow contributes to a greater good. Your heart will ache for the trusting men who naïvely believed they were being cured. Rated PG-13 for profanity and sexual candor. 120m. DIR: Joseph Sargent. CAST: Alfre Woodard, Laurence Fishburne, Craig Sheffer, Joe Morton, Obba Babatundé, E. G. Marshall, Ossie Davis. 1996

MISS FIRECRACKER ★★★★ A wacky, colorful, feel-good movie about a young Mississippi woman whose hunger for self-respect takes her through the rigors of her hometown Yazoo City Miss Firecracker Contest. Holly Hunter is marvelous as the misguided woman, while Mary Steenburgen shines as her cousin. From the off-Broadway play by Beth (*Crimes of the Heart*) Henley. Rated PG. 102m. DIR: Thomas Schlamme. CAST: Holly Hunter, Mary Steenburgen, Tim Robbins, Alfre Woodard, Scott Glenn. 1989

MISS GRANT TAKES RICHMOND ★★★ Lucille Ball plays a dizzy secretary who outwits a band of thieves and wins handsome William Holden (who looks just as baffled as he did years later guest-starring on *I Love Lucy*). Agreeable star vehicle has a stalwart supporting cast. B&W; 87m. DIR: Lloyd Bacon. CAST: Lucille Ball, William Holden, Janis Carter, James Gleason, Frank McHugh. 1949

MISS JULIE (1950) ★★ An impetuous young Swedish countess rejected by her fiancé flirts with and then seduces a handsome servant. Brooding melodrama based on a Strindberg play becomes a very tedious experience. In Swedish with English subtitles. Not rated; contains nudity. B&W; 90m. DIR: Alf Sjoberg. CAST: Anita Bjork, Ulf Palme, Max von Sydow. 1950

•**MISS JULIE (1999)** ★★ A haughty young Swedish countess is irresistibly drawn to her father's valet. August Strindberg's play, a groundbreaker for its sexual frankness one hundred years ago, has not retained its cutting edge and it's frankly an excruciating bore. Rated R for sexual content and some profanity. 100m. DIR: Mike Figgis. CAST: Saffron Burrows, Peter Mullan, Maria Doyle Kennedy. 1999 DVD

MISS LULU BETT ★★★ Miss Lulu is the family drone who is tricked into marriage and seemingly loses her chance at happiness with the man she loves. How she liberates herself from a life of servitude is a surprisingly frank look at an unmarried woman's role in the first decades of the twentieth century and is one of the best-remembered vehicles of pioneer women's rights activist Lois Wilson. B&W; 65m. DIR: William C. de Mille. CAST: Lois Wilson, Theodore Roberts, Milton Sills, Helen Ferguson, Mary Girachi, Mabel Van Buren, Taylor Graves. 1921

MISS MARY ★★★1/2 A good knowledge of the history of Argentina—specifically between the years 1930 and 1945—will help viewers appreciate this biting black comedy. Julie Christie gives a marvelous performance as a British governess brought to South America country to work for a wealthy family. Through her eyes, in a series of flashbacks, we see how the corrupt aristocracy slowly falls apart. In both English and Spanish. Rated R for profanity, nudity, and suggested and simulated sex. 100m. DIR: Maria Luisa Bemberg. CAST: Julie Christie, Nacha Guevara, Tato Pavlovsky. 1987

MISS RIGHT ★★ This vignettish, uneven sex comedy strongly resembles TV's *Love American Style*. A UPI correspondent in Rome (William Tepper) becomes involved with several beautiful women. Rated R for profanity and nudity. 98m. DIR: Paul Williams. CAST: William Tepper, Karen Black, Margot Kidder, Virna Lisi, Marie-France Pisier, Clio Goldsmith. 1988

MISS ROSE WHITE ★★★ *Hallmark Hall of Fame* movie starring Kyra Sedgwick as a young Jewish career woman forced to confront her family's heritage and tragic past. Heartwarming with captivating performances by the entire cast. 95m. DIR: Joseph Sargent. CAST: Kyra Sedgwick, Maximilian

Schell, Amanda Plummer, D. B. Sweeney, Penny Fuller, Milton Selzer. 1992

MISS SADIE THOMPSON ★★1/2 A remake of *Rain*, the 1932 adaptation of Somerset Maugham's novel with Joan Crawford and Walter Huston, this production (with music) is notable only for the outstanding performance by Rita Hayworth in the title role. 91m. DIR: Curtis Bernhardt. CAST: Rita Hayworth, José Ferrer, Aldo Ray. 1953

MISSILE TO THE MOON 💔 Silly story of renegade expedition to the Moon. B&W; 78m. DIR: Richard Cunha. CAST: Richard Travis, Cathy Downes, K. T. Stevens, Michael Whalen, Tommy Cook, Gary Clarke. 1958 DVD

MISSILES OF OCTOBER, THE ★★★★1/2 This is a superbly cast, well-written, excitingly directed made-for-TV drama dealing with the crucial decisions that were made during the Cuban missile crisis of October 1962. It follows the hour-by-hour situations that occurred when the U.S. government discovered that the Soviet Union was installing offensive missiles in Cuba. Gripping and realistic. 175m. DIR: Anthony Page. CAST: William Devane, Ralph Bellamy, Martin Sheen, Howard DaSilva. 1974

MISSING ★★★★★ A superb political thriller directed by Costa-Gavras, this stars Jack Lemmon and Sissy Spacek as the father and wife of a journalist who disappears during a bloody South American coup. Rated R for nudity, and profanity. 122m. DIR: Constantin Costa-Gavras. CAST: Jack Lemmon, Sissy Spacek, John Shea, Melanie Mayron, Janice Rule, David Clennon. 1982

MISSING IN ACTION ★★★1/2 Chuck Norris is a one-man army in this Vietnam-based action film. Anyone else might be laughable in such a role. But the former karate star makes it work. The story focuses on an attempt by Col. James Braddock (Norris), a former Vietnam prisoner of war, to free the other Americans he believes are still there. Rated R for profanity, violence, and brief nudity. 101m. DIR: Joseph Zito. CAST: Chuck Norris, M. Emmet Walsh, Lenore Kasdorf, James Hong. 1984 DVD

MISSING IN ACTION 2: THE BEGINNING ★★1/2 Following on the heels of the previous year's surprise hit, this "prequel" is really the same movie, only it tells the story of how Colonel Braddock (Chuck Norris) and his men escaped their Vietnam prison camp after ten years of torture. The acting is nonexistent, the action predictable and violent. Rated R for violence. 95m. DIR: Lance Hool. CAST: Chuck Norris, Cosie Costa, Soon-Teck Oh, Steven Williams. 1985

MISSING LINK ★★★1/2 A beautifully photographed story of a man-ape's journey across the desolate African plain after his people are killed by the encroachment of man. A pseudo-documentary style offers a breathtaking view of some of Earth's strangest creatures. First-rate man-ape makeup by Academy Award–winner Rick Baker. Rated PG. 92m. DIR: David Hughes, Carol Hughes. CAST: Peter Elliott, Michael Gambon. 1988

MISSING PIECES (1994) ★★1/2 An ancient riddle sends two friends on a quest for fame and fortune in this so-so comedy. Eric Idle plays Wendell, a greeting-card writer whose life is in a slump—then he in-

herits an ancient riddle from a Chinese relative. It sets the scene for a madcap chase across the United States, ending up in San Francisco. Rated PG. 93m. DIR: Leonard Stern. CAST: Eric Idle, Robert Wuhl, Lauren Hutton, Richard Belzer. 1994

●**MISSING PIECES (2000)** ★★★1/2 Based on Ron Hansen's novel *Atticus*, this suspenseful *Hallmark Hall of Fame* film focuses on a parent's inability to accept his estranged son's apparent suicide. Determined to find out what really happened to his son in Mexico, he begins his own investigation. Despite a slow start, the plot's many twists reel viewers in for a surprising, satisfying conclusion. Not rated; contains mature themes. 99m. DIR: Carl Schenkel. CAST: James Coburn, Paul Kersey, Lisa Zane. 2000

MISSION, THE ★★★1/2 Jeremy Irons plays a Spanish Jesuit who goes into the South American wilderness to build a mission in the hope of converting the Indians of the region. Robert De Niro plays a slave hunter who is converted and joins Irons in his mission. When Spain sells the colony to Portugal, they are forced to defend all they have built against the Portuguese aggressors. Rated PG for violence and sex. 125m. DIR: Roland Joffe. CAST: Jeremy Irons, Robert De Niro, Liam Neeson, Ray McAnally, Aidan Quinn. 1986

MISSION GALACTICA: THE CYLON ATTACK ★★1/2 Feature-length reediting of episodes from TV's *Battlestar Galactica* finds crew of this extremely simplistic, juvenile space opera under attack from their mortal enemy, the Cylons. 108m. DIR: Vince Edwards. CAST: Lorne Greene, Dirk Benedict. 1979

MISSION: IMPOSSIBLE ★★★★ A crack team of American undercover agents is assigned to set up operations in Prague to catch a double agent in the act. Based on the 1960s television series, this film keeps viewers wondering what's going to happen next, right up to the spectacular, climactic train sequence. Rated PG-13 for violence and profanity. 110m. DIR: Brian De Palma. CAST: Tom Cruise, Jon Voight, Emmanuelle Beart, Emilio Estevez, Vanessa Redgrave, Harry Czerny, Jean Reno, Ving Rhames, Kristin Scott Thomas. 1996 DVD

●**MISSION: IMPOSSIBLE 2** ★★★★ Trust legendary action director John Woo to revitalize this big-screen franchise, which got off to a rocky start with the morose and overly complicated events of its predecessor. This time out, covert operative Ethan Hunt (Tom Cruise) reprises a story line lifted from Alfred Hitchcock's *Notorious* by recruiting a civilian (Thandie Newton), falling for her, and then reluctantly ordering her to patch things up with—and spy on—a former lover who's threatening the world with a super-virus. The twisty love triangle carries more depth than you'd expect, and pleasantly occupies us until Woo's all-stops-out climax. Cruise fits superbly with the director's signature flourishes; the result is a high-octane action epic that doesn't have much to do with the original TV series, but is nonetheless exciting and entertaining. Rated PG-13 for violence and sensuality. 126m. DIR: John Woo. CAST: Tom Cruise, Dougray Scott, Thandie Newton, Richard Roxburgh, Ving Rhames, John Polson, Brendan Gleeson, Rade Sherbedgia. **2000**

MISSION IN MOROCCO ★★ Lex Barker stars as an American oil executive whose murdered partner possessed a microfilm that shows the location of oil in Morocco. Tired adventure yawner shot on location in Morocco. B&W; 79m. **DIR:** Anthony Squire. **CAST:** Lex Barker, Juli Redding. **1959**

MISSION MARS 🎬 Danger-in-outer-space adventure has a trio of astronauts coping with mysterious forces while on the way to Mars. 95m. **DIR:** Nicholas Webster. **CAST:** Darren McGavin, Nick Adams. **1968**

MISSION OF JUSTICE ★★★ A large city is plagued with crime, but the woman who is running for mayor has a new solution: the Peacemakers—a group of disadvantaged youths who roam the streets and prevent crime. At first glance, this film looks pretty bad, but you'll keep watching. Rated R for violence and profanity. 95m. **DIR:** Steve Barnett. **CAST:** Jeff Wincott, Brigitte Nielsen, Luca Bercovici, Matthias Hues. **1992**

MISSION OF THE SHARK ★★★ Though compelling, this film doesn't develop the characters of the Americans aboard the USS *Indianapolis* before they're struck by Japanese torpedoes in July 1945. Stacy Keach plays Captain Charles McVay, who ultimately is blamed for the deaths of over 800 men. Terrifying scenes of the men's struggle to survive for five days without food or water in the shark-infested ocean. Not rated; contains violence. 92m. **DIR:** Robert Iscove. **CAST:** Stacy Keach, Richard Thomas, Carrie Snodgress. **1991**

MISSION STARDUST ★★ Only die-hard fans of Italian space operas are likely to seek out this adaptation of one of the Perry Rhodan pulp novels. And that's a shame, because, given its meager budget and indifferent dubbing, this is still one of the more imaginative European sci-fi adventures. 90m. **DIR:** Primo Zeglio. **CAST:** Essy Persson, Gianni Rizzo. **1965**

MISSION TO GLORY 🎬 The true story of Father Francisco Kin, the Spanish padre who helped develop California in the late seventeenth century. Rated PG for violence. 97m. **DIR:** Ken Kennedy. **CAST:** Ricardo Montalban, Cesar Romero, Rory Calhoun, Michael Ansara, Keenan Wynn, Richard Egan. **1979**

•**MISSION TO MARS** ★★1/2 If a half century of science-fiction films could evaporate overnight, this might be an impressive little picture. But we cannot pretend that far superior efforts like *Close Encounters of the Third Kind* and *Contact* never happened. Director Brian De Palma paces this routine mysterious-red-planet saga with the slow, self-important deliberation of 1950s efforts such as *Destination Moon*, in a style that today seems lethargic, dreary, and old-fashioned. Rated PG for brief violence. 113m. **DIR:** Brian De Palma. **CAST:** Gary Sinise, Tim Robbins, Don Cheadle, Connie Nielsen, Jerry O'Connell. **2000**

MISSIONARY, THE ★★★1/2 Monty Python's Michael Palin, who also wrote the script, plays a well-meaning American minister assigned the task of saving the souls of London's fallen women. Not a nonstop, gag-filled descent into absurdity like the Monty Python movies. It is, instead, a warmhearted spoof with the accent on character and very sparing

but effective in its humor. Rated R. 90m. **DIR:** Richard Loncraine. **CAST:** Michael Palin, Maggie Smith, Denholm Elliott, Trevor Howard, Michael Hordern. **1982**

MISSISSIPPI ★★★1/2 A delightful mixture of music and personality with Bing Crosby at his best singing Rodgers and Hart's "It's Easy to Remember But So Hard to Forget." He boards a showboat run by rascally W. C. Fields. The plot comes from Booth Tarkington's novel *Magnolia*, but the personalities are pure Hollywood. B&W; 73m. **DIR:** A. Edward Sutherland. **CAST:** Bing Crosby, W. C. Fields, Joan Bennett, Gail Patrick, Queenie Smith, John Miljan, Ann Sheridan. **1935**

MISSISSIPPI BLUES ★★★★★ French film director Bertrand Tavernier joins American author Robert Parrish on a spellbinding odyssey through the deep South. Tavernier and his French camera crew beautifully capture the true spirit of the South through the religious fervor of the black evangelical movement. Some great location photography laced with a rich blues soundtrack. In English and French with English subtitles. 92m. **DIR:** Bertrand Tavernier, Robert Parrish. **CAST:** Roosevelt Barnes, Joe Cooper, Hayword Mills. **1987**

MISSISSIPPI BURNING ★★★★ As the master of dramatic propaganda, Alan Parker presents this hair-raising account of what *might* have happened back in 1964 when three civil rights activists turned up missing in Mississippi. Laid-back Gene Hackman and by-the-book Willem Dafoe are the FBI agents in charge of the investigation. If good intentions excuse execution, then this is worthy fiction; at the very least, it allows Hackman to demonstrate his considerable range. Definitely not for the squeamish. Rated R for language and brutal violence. 125m. **DIR:** Alan Parker. **CAST:** Gene Hackman, Willem Dafoe, Frances McDormand, Brad Dourif, R. Lee Ermey. **1988** DVD

MISSISSIPPI MASALA ★★★★ Director Mira Nair manages to achieve something of a miracle with this story of love between a black businessman (Denzel Washington) and an Indian immigrant (Sarita Choudhury) who become outcasts in the Deep South. A serious, insightful examination of racial prejudice wedded with heartwarming and sexy romance. Washington is particularly impressive. Rated R for profanity, nudity, and violence. 117m. **DIR:** Mira Nair. **CAST:** Denzel Washington, Roshan Seth, Sarita Choudhury, Charles Dutton, Tico Wells, Joe Seneca. **1991**

MISSISSIPPI MERMAID ★★★ Interesting drama about a wealthy industrialist living on an island who orders a bride by mail. All this eventually leads to deception and murder. Solid performances by Jean-Paul Belmondo and Catherine Deneuve. In French with English subtitles. Not rated. 123m. **DIR:** François Truffaut. **CAST:** Jean-Paul Belmondo, Catherine Deneuve, Michel Bouquet. **1969**

MISSOURI BREAKS, THE ★★ For all its potential, this Western really lets you down. Jack Nicholson is acceptable as the outlaw trying to ply his trade. Marlon Brando, on the other hand, is inconsistent as a relentless bounty hunter. Rated PG. 126m. **DIR:**

Arthur Penn. **CAST:** Marlon Brando, Jack Nicholson, Kathleen Lloyd, Harry Dean Stanton. **1976**

MISSOURIANS, THE ★★★★ A band of vicious killers, known as the Missourians, attempt to hide out in a town where the leader's Polish immigrant mother and brother live; only complicating matters for them as the town already holds malice against foreigners. Strong story line and good action make this one of Monte Hale's best. B&W; 60m. **DIR:** George Blair. **CAST:** Monte Hale, Paul Hurst, Roy Barcroft. **1950**

MR. ACE ★★ Potboiler about a spoiled society woman (Sylvia Sidney) who uses a gangster (George Raft) to win a congressional seat. George goes through the motions but very little else. B&W; 84m. **DIR:** Edwin L. Marin. **CAST:** George Raft, Sylvia Sidney, Stanley Ridges, Sara Haden, Jerome Cowan. **1946 DVD**

MR. AND MRS. BRIDGE ★★★★ Adapted from the novels *Mr. Bridge* and *Mrs. Bridge* by Evan S. Connell, this slice of Americana presents an affecting chronicle of the lives of an upper-class WASP family. Composed of vignettes in the characters' lives, some of which are more compelling than others, it nonetheless adds up to a satisfying motion picture. Rated PG-13 for profanity. 127m. **DIR:** James Ivory. **CAST:** Paul Newman, Joanne Woodward, Blythe Danner, Simon Callow, Kyra Sedgwick, Robert Sean Leonard, Austin Pendleton. **1990**

MR. AND MRS. LOVING ★★★1/2 Timothy Hutton and Lela Rochon generate sympathy as the working-class title characters whose pursuit for dignity changed the very fabric of the United States. After being thrown out of their native state of Virginia because their mixed-race marriage violated racist antimiscegenation laws—and this in the early 1960s!—the Supreme Court ruled on the issue and forever abolished such heinous restrictions. Sadly, we learn absolutely nothing about how the Lovings survived the arduous process needed to *reach* the Supreme Court. Rated PG-13 for simulated sex and mild profanity. 95m. **DIR:** Dick Friedenberg. **CAST:** Timothy Hutton, Lela Rochon, Ruby Dee, Bill Nunn, Corey Parker, Isaiah Washington. **1996**

MR. AND MRS. SMITH ★★★★ This film deals with the love-hate-love relationship of Carole Lombard and Robert Montgomery, who play a couple who discover their marriage isn't legal. The bouncy dialogue by Norman Krasna is justly famous and includes some of the most classic comedy scenes ever. Directing this enjoyable farce, in his only pure comedy, is Alfred Hitchcock. B&W; 95m. **DIR:** Alfred Hitchcock. **CAST:** Carole Lombard, Robert Montgomery, Gene Raymond, Jack Carson. **1941**

MR. ARKADIN (CONFIDENTIAL REPORT) ★★1/2 Actor-writer-director Orson Welles confuses the audience more than he entertains them in this odd story of an amnesiac millionaire financier who hires an investigator to find his past. The intriguing story fails to translate effectively to the screen; even the efforts of a fine cast couldn't help Welles turn this into a critical or commerical success. B&W; 99m. **DIR:** Orson Welles. **CAST:** Orson Welles, Michael Redgrave, Akim Tamiroff, Patricia Medina, Mischa Auer. **1955**

MR. BASEBALL ★★★ Tom Selleck mugs his way through this fish-out-of-water comedy about an American major league baseball player who is sent to play in Japan. Rated PG-13 for profanity. 110m. **DIR:** Fred Schepisi. **CAST:** Tom Selleck, Ken Takakura, Dennis Haysbert. **1992 DVD**

MR. BEAN ★★★★ Rowan Atkinson's Mr. Bean is a hapless little nebbish who contrives outlandish solutions to everyday problems. Some episodes are lengthy dramas; others feature several short blackout sketches. Many are poignant and some are cruel, but they're always hysterical;·be on the lookout for wayward swimming trunks in a public pool, and Mr. Bean's adventures in a fancy hotel. Not rated, but suitable for all ages. Each 60m. **DIR:** John Birkin, John Howard Davies. **CAST:** Rowan Atkinson, Robin Driscoll, Matilda Ziegler. **1989–1995**

MR. BILLION ★★1/2 Sappy but seductive story about a humble Italian mechanic (Terence Hill) who will inherit a financial empire if he can get to the signing over of his uncle's will before a gang of kidnappers or the corporation's chairman (Jackie Gleason) gets to him first. Rated PG for violence and sex. 89m. **DIR:** Jonathan Kaplan. **CAST:** Terence Hill, Valerie Perrine, Jackie Gleason, Slim Pickens, William Redfield, Chill Wills, Dick Miller. **1977**

MR. BLANDINGS BUILDS HIS DREAM HOUSE ★★★★ In this screwball comedy, Cary Grant plays a man tired of the hustle and bustle of city life. He decides to move to the country, construct his private Shangri-La, and settle back into a serene rural lifestyle. His fantasy and reality come into comic conflict. Myrna Loy is cast as his ever-patient wife in this very fine film. B&W; 94m. **DIR:** H. C. Potter. **CAST:** Cary Grant, Myrna Loy, Melvyn Douglas. **1948**

MR. CORBETT'S GHOST ★★★ New Year's Eve, 1767, somewhere in England and young Ben Partridge has a choice to make: desire or duty. His decision on which road to pursue forms the basis of this fine atmospheric ghost story, produced for TV. 75m. **DIR:** Danny Huston. **CAST:** John Huston, Paul Scofield, Burgess Meredith, Mark Farmer. **1986**

•**MR. DEATH: THE RISE AND FALL OF FRED A. LEUCHTER JR.** ★★★★1/2 This documentary is a complex yet lucid character study that evolves into a meditation on the roots of evil. Fred Leuchter Jr. is a self-taught execution expert who worked on gas chambers, lethal injection systems, and a gallows until he was hired by a Holocaust revisionist to refute the existence of gas chambers at Auschwitz. The film strings Leuchter's deadpan monologues, archival photos, reenactments, and grainy home movies into a riveting story about corrupted ideals, flawed scientific logic, and the fragility of truth. Rated PG-13 for mature themes. 96m. **DIR:** Errol Morris. **2000 DVD**

MR. DEEDS GOES TO TOWN ★★★★★ The quiet unassuming world of a contented New Englander (Gary Cooper) is severely tested when he inherits a fortune in this classic Frank Capra comedy. An amusing series of misadventures results when our hero's straightforward values are caught in a tug-of-war with the corruption of big city money and snobbishness. B&W; 120m. **DIR:** Frank Capra. **CAST:** Gary

Cooper, Jean Arthur, Douglass Dumbrille, Lionel Stander, George Bancroft. **1936 DVD**

MR. DESTINY ★★1/2 James Belushi plays a pencil pusher who believes he is a failure. Michael Caine, who can shape people's lives, shows him the difference in this passable comedy that reminds one of *It's a Wonderful Life*. Rated PG-13 for profanity. 117m. **DIR:** James Orr. **CAST:** James Belushi, Linda Hamilton, Jon Lovitz, Hart Bochner, Michael Caine. **1990**

MR. FROST ★★★1/2 After being arrested for twenty-four murders by an English detective (Alan Bates), the mysterious Mr. Frost (Jeff Goldblum) refuses to speak for three years until a psychiatrist (Kathy Baker) attempts to reach him. That's when Frost begins claiming he is Satan. Intriguing blend of suspense and black comedy. Rated R for violence and profanity. 92m. **DIR:** Philip Setbon. **CAST:** Jeff Goldblum, Alan Bates, Kathy Baker. **1990**

MR. HALPERN AND MR. JOHNSON ★★★ Laurence Olivier plays a recently widowed Jewish manufacturer who, to his surprise, is asked to join a stranger named Johnson (Jackie Gleason) for a drink after the funeral. It seems that Johnson was once in love with the late Mrs. Halpern. What's more, they carried on a friendship for a number of years right up to just before her death. And therein lies the drama of this slight tale. 57m. **DIR:** Alvin Rakoff. **CAST:** Laurence Olivier, Jackie Gleason. **1983**

MR. HOBBS TAKES A VACATION ★★★ Somewhat against his better judgment, ever-patient James Stewart takes his wife Maureen O'Hara and their children and grandchildren on vacation. They wind up in a ramshackle old house on the Pacific Coast, and he winds up more hassled than when home or at work. Good acting and a clever script make this thin-plotted comedy amusing. 116m. **DIR:** Henry Koster. **CAST:** James Stewart, Maureen O'Hara, Marie Wilson, Fabian, John Saxon. **1962**

MR. HOLLAND'S OPUS ★★★★ In this wonderful family film, Richard Dreyfuss gives an outstanding performance as a music teacher who struggles to have a positive effect on the lives of his students despite complications at home. We don't want to give away any more of the story than this. Suffice it to say, this is a feel-good movie in the best sense, with accolades deserved by all involved. Rated PG-13 for profanity and adult themes. 142m. **DIR:** Stephen Herek. **CAST:** Richard Dreyfuss, Glenne Headly, Alicia Witt, Jay Thomas, Olympia Dukakis, William H. Macy, Jean Louisa Kelly. **1995 DVD**

MR. HORN ★★★ A bittersweet, near-melancholy chronicle of the exploits of Horn (David Carradine), who is shown first as an idealistic young man helping an old-timer (Richard Widmark) track down Geronimo and later as a cynical gunman hired to eliminate some rustlers. 200m. **DIR:** Jack Starrett. **CAST:** David Carradine, Richard Widmark, Karen Black, Richard Masur, Jeremy Slate, Pat McCormick, Jack Starrett. **1979**

MR. HULOT'S HOLIDAY ★★★1/2 A delightfully lighthearted film about the natural comedy to be found in vacationing. Jacques Tati plays the famous Monsieur Hulot, who has some silly adventures at a seaside resort. Although partially dubbed in English, this film has a mime quality that is magical. B&W;

86m. **DIR:** Jacques Tati. **CAST:** Jacques Tati, Nathalie Pascaud. **1953**

MR. IMPERIUM ★★ A musical that misses because there's no chemistry whatsoever between the leads. Ezio Pinza's Broadway charm isn't photogenic so it's difficult to relate to Lana Turner's attraction to him. They sing such songs as "My Love and My Mule" in a willy-nilly attempt to tug the audience's heart strings. 87m. **DIR:** Don Hartman. **CAST:** Lana Turner, Ezio Pinza, Marjorie Main, Debbie Reynolds, Barry Sullivan, Keenan Wynn. **1951**

MR. INSIDE/MR. OUTSIDE ★★ Hal Linden and Tony LoBianco are fine in this made-for-television cop thriller as two New York City detectives attempting to foil a smuggling ring. Director William Graham's pacing makes you forget how much this movie is like so many other works created for TV. 74m. **DIR:** William A. Graham. **CAST:** Hal Linden, Tony Lo Bianco, Phil Bruns, Paul Benjamin, Stefan Schnabel. **1973**

MR. JEALOUSY ★★1/2 Cute but claustrophobic romantic comedy about a jealous boyfriend who can't stand the fact that his latest girlfriend had a life before him. When his jealousy consumes their relationship, he joins the therapy group of his girlfriend's ex-boyfriend, unwittingly bringing the couple back together again. Witty dialogue and a decent cast help make this exercise in yuppie angst bearable. Rated R for language and adult situations. 100m. **DIR:** Noah Baumbach. **CAST:** Eric Stoltz, Annabella Sciorra, Christopher Eigeman, Bridget Fonda, Marianne Jean-Baptiste. **1998 DVD**

MISTER JOHNSON ★★★★ A poignant drama about the clash of cultures in the colonial western Africa of the 1920s. Adapted from Joyce Cary's 1939 novel, it follows the tragicomic exploits of a black African clerk named Johnson as he attempts to ingratiate himself into the lives and society of the ruling white colonialists. Rated PG-13. 102m. **DIR:** Bruce Beresford. **CAST:** Maynard Eziashi, Pierce Brosnan, Edward Woodward. **1991 DVD**

MR. JONES ★★ Doctor-patient romances don't get much more unconvincing than this. A wild-eyed, mysterious manic-depressive so infatuates a hospital shrink that she sacrifices her professional ethics for offscreen sex with her emotionally kinetic charge. The film's two stars keep the film promising, but the sterile love story doesn't do justice to its serious themes of emotional alienation and mental care. It's a tantalizing puzzle that has several missing pieces. Rated R for profanity. 110m. **DIR:** Mike Figgis. **CAST:** Richard Gere, Lena Olin. **1993 DVD**

MR. KLEIN ★★★1/2 Dark-sided character study of a Parisian antique dealer who buys artwork and personal treasures from Jews trying to escape Paris in 1942. He (Alain Delon) finds himself mistaken for a missing Jew of the same name. Rated PG. Available in French version. 123m. **DIR:** Joseph Losey. **CAST:** Alain Delon, Jeanne Moreau, Juliet Berto, Michel Lonsdale, Jean Bouise, Francine Berge. **1976**

MR. LOVE ★★1/2 Slow-moving yet interesting study of a middle-aged man who wins the love of women by being caring and encouraging. Barry Jackson is the soft-spoken British gardener who, stuck in a loveless marriage, seeks to befriend the lonesome women he encounters. Rated PG-13. 91m. DIR: Roy Battersby. CAST: Barry Jackson, Maurice Denham, Margaret Tyzack. 1985

MR. LUCKY ★★★ Cary Grant is a gambler attempting to bilk money from a charity relief program. He changes his tune when he falls for a wealthy society girl, Laraine Day. This is a slick piece of wartime fluff. The plot has nothing you haven't seen before, but the charm of Grant makes it watchable. B&W; 100m. DIR: H. C. Potter. CAST: Cary Grant, Laraine Day. 1943

MR. MAGOO ❤ Give director Stanley Tong, of Jackie Chan's *Super Cop* and *Rumble in the Bronx*, a wacky comedy and what do you get? A series of kung fu fights and a lack of Magoo-like madness. The limited plot has Magoo (Leslie Nielsen) being drawn into an international plot to steal a world-renowned gem. Within thirty minutes, you'll be wishing that you were as nearsighted as Magoo and didn't have to witness this celluloid disaster. Rated PG for violence. 86m. DIR: Stanley Tong. CAST: Leslie Nielsen, Kelly Lynch, Ernie Hudson, Stephen Tobolowsky, Nick Chinlund. 1997 DVD

MR. MAGOO'S CHRISTMAS CAROL ★★★★★ Mr. Magoo is Ebenezer Scrooge in this first-rate animated musical of Charles Dickens's holiday classic, which remains the best animated adaptation to date. The songs by Jule Styne and Bob Merrill are magnificent. 53m. DIR: Abe Levitow. 1962

MR. MAJESTYK ★★★1/2 In this better-than-average Charles Bronson vehicle, he's a watermelon grower (!) coming up against gangster Al Lettieri (in a first-rate performance). Rated R. 103m. DIR: Richard Fleischer. CAST: Charles Bronson, Al Lettieri, Linda Cristal, Lee Purcell, Paul Koslo. 1974

MR. MOM ★★★★ Michael Keaton is hilarious as an engineer who loses his job at an automobile manufacturing plant and, when wife Teri Garr gets a high-paying job at an advertising agency, becomes a hopelessly inept househusband. The story is familiar and predictable, but Keaton's off-the-wall antics and boyish charm make it all seem fresh and lively. Rated PG for light profanity. 91m. DIR: Stan Dragoti. CAST: Michael Keaton, Teri Garr, Ann Jillian, Martin Mull. 1983 DVD

MR. MOTO IN DANGER ISLAND ★★1/2 The globe-trotting detective goes to Puerto Rico to crack a diamond-smuggling ring. This was the last of the eight Mr. Moto movies, and it shows: Peter Lorre, tired of the character, often seems to be just going through the paces. B&W; 64m. DIR: Herbert Leeds. CAST: Peter Lorre, Jean Hersholt, Amanda Duff, Richard Lane, Leon Ames. 1939

MR. MOTO TAKES A CHANCE ★★1/2 Mr. Moto gets to exercise his mastery of disguise as he investigates a potentially murderous cult in Indochina. The fourth Mr. Moto movie, this suffers from an over-stuffed plot. B&W; 63m. DIR: Norman Foster. CAST: Peter Lorre, Rochelle Hudson, Robert Kent, J. Edward Bromberg. 1938

MR. MOTO TAKES A VACATION ★★1/2 Too busy fighting international criminals to take a real vacation, Mr. Moto is actually posing as a tourist in order to trap a thief who's after the jewels of the Queen of Sheba. One of the lesser Mr. Moto movies. B&W; 65m. DIR: Norman Foster. CAST: Peter Lorre, Joseph Schildkraut, Lionel Atwill, Virginia Field, Willie Best. 1939

MR. MOTO'S GAMBLE ★★★ Aided by students from a detective class he is teaching, Mr. Moto investigates the murder of a boxer. An unusual entry in the series in that it was supposed to be a Charlie Chan movie until Warner Oland died in the middle of filming! B&W; 71m. DIR: James Tinling. CAST: Peter Lorre, Keye Luke, Dick Baldwin, Maxie Rosenbloom, Ward Bond, Lon Chaney Jr. 1938

MR. MOTO'S LAST WARNING ★★★ One of the last in the low-budget series that produced eight films in less than three years. This time out, the detective gets involved with terrorist spies intent on blowing up the French fleet in the Suez Canal. Enjoyable, quaint entertainment with a good supporting cast. B&W; 71m. DIR: Norman Foster. CAST: Peter Lorre, Ricardo Cortez, Virginia Field, John Carradine, George Sanders. 1939

•MR. MURDER ★★★1/2 Solid TV miniseries adaptation of Dean Koontz's bestseller. Stephen Baldwin plays a successful author of murder mysteries whose life is thrown upside down when a man who looks just like him shows up and claims to be him. While some events have been added or expanded upon from the novel, the general feel of the book comes through on the small screen. Not rated; contains violence. 193m. DIR: Dick Lowry. CAST: Stephen Baldwin, Julie Warner, Thomas Haden Church, James Coburn. 1999 DVD

MR. MUSIC ★★ Bing Crosby is an easygoing songwriter living beyond his means. Nancy Olson is hired to handle his finances. Slow-moving, completely forgettable songs, and wasted guest stars. B&W; 113m. DIR: Richard Haydn. CAST: Bing Crosby, Nancy Olson, Charles Coburn, Ruth Hussey, Robert Stack, Tom Ewell, Peggy Lee, Groucho Marx, Richard Haydn. 1950

MR. NANNY ★★ A retired professional wrestler (Hulk Hogan) wants work as a bodyguard but winds up baby-sitting two neglected kids. Hogan is no Anthony Hopkins, but he is likable on screen; too bad the film, with a labored plot and unfunny gags, doesn't give him the support he needs. Rated PG. 83m. DIR: Michael Gottlieb. CAST: Hulk Hogan, Austin Pendleton, Sherman Hemsley, David Johansen. 1993

MR. NICE GUY ★★★ A celebrity TV chef/martial arts expert is chased through Melbourne by Australian gangsters seeking an incriminating videotape made by a local reporter. The plot is thin, but the film's exhilarating chases and acrobatics include brawls aboard a horse-drawn carriage and inside a delivery van and a battle at a construction site. In English and Cantonese with English subtitles. Rated PG-13 for violence. 83m. DIR: Sammo Hung. CAST: Jackie Chan, Richard Norton, Gabrielle Fitzpatrick, Miki Lee, Karen McLynont. 1998 DVD

MR. NORTH ★★★1/2 In this fantasy a young Yale graduate arrives in elite Newport, Rhode Island as a tutor and ends up touching the citizens in seemingly magical ways. Based on Thornton Wilder's novel, *Theophilus North*, and directed by the late John Huston's son, Danny, this small-scale piece of whimsy is a winner. Rated PG. 92m. DIR: Danny Huston. CAST: Anthony Edwards, Robert Mitchum, Lauren Bacall, Harry Dean Stanton, Anjelica Huston. 1988

MR. PEABODY AND THE MERMAID ★★ This is Splash, 1940s-style. A married New Englander (William Powell) snags an amorous mermaid while fishing and transfers her to his swimming pool, with the expected results. B&W; 89m. DIR: Irving Pichel. CAST: William Powell, Ann Blyth, Irene Hervey. 1948

MR. RELIABLE ★★★1/2 True stories are always the strangest, as proven by this depiction of Australia's first hostage crisis in the summer of 1968. An unwed mom moves in with a petty criminal, but an addled police force thinks she and the baby are captives. Sparkling, offbeat humor is deftly woven into more serious scenes, maintaining a consistent level of weirdness. Rated PG-13 for profanity and sexual situations. 109m. DIR: Nadia Tass. CAST: Colin Friels, Jacqueline McKenzie, Paul Sonkkila. 1996

MISTER ROBERTS ★★★★1/2 A navy cargo ship well outside the World War II battle zone is the setting for this hit comedy-drama. Henry Fonda is Lieutenant Roberts, the first officer who helps the crew battle their ceaseless boredom and tyrannical captain (James Cagney). Jack Lemmon began his road to stardom with his sparkling performance as the irrepressible con-man Ensign Pulver. 123m. DIR: John Ford, Mervyn LeRoy. CAST: Henry Fonda, James Cagney, Jack Lemmon, William Powell, Ward Bond. 1955 DVD

MR. ROBINSON CRUSOE ★★★ Dashing Douglas Fairbanks Sr. bets he can survive like Crusoe on a South Sea island. Just how he does it makes for great fun. Fairbanks was just short of 50 when he made this film, but he was still the agile, athletic swashbuckler whose wholesome charm made him the idol of millions. B&W; 76m. DIR: A. Edward Sutherland. CAST: Douglas Fairbanks Sr., William Farnum, Maria Alba. 1932

MR. SATURDAY NIGHT ★★★★ Billy Crystal gives a smashing performance in this poignant comedy chronicling fifty years in the life of a stand-up comedian. Costar David Paymer almost steals Crystal's show as his brother-manager who must put up with the increasingly irritating comic. Rated R for profanity. 119m. DIR: Billy Crystal. CAST: Billy Crystal, David Paymer, Julie Warner, Helen Hunt, Ron Silver, Jerry Orbach. 1992 DVD

MR. SKEFFINGTON ★★★ Selfish and self-centered Bette Davis goes from reigning society beauty to hag in this typical soap opera of the upper crust—ranging across decades through feast and famine, indulgence and deceit. Time takes its toll on her. Then comes her one chance to do the right thing. Davis's performance is splendid. B&W; 147m. DIR: Vincent Sherman. CAST: Bette Davis, Claude Rains, Walter Abel, George Coulouris, Jerome Cowan, Gigi Perreau. 1944

MR. SKITCH ★★★ Will Rogers, broke after a bank failure, heads West hoping to recoup at a gambling casino. A dollar wins him a bundle—that wife ZaSu Pitts promptly loses. Typical Rogers comedy fare sprinkled with quick quips and homespun philosophy. B&W; 70m. DIR: James Cruze. CAST: Will Rogers, ZaSu Pitts, Rochelle Hudson, Eugene Pallette. 1933

MR. SMITH GOES TO WASHINGTON ★★★★★ This Frank Capra classic is the story of a naïve senator's fight against political corruption. James Stewart stars as Jefferson Smith, the idealistic scoutmaster who is appointed to fill out the term of a dead senator. Upon arriving in the capitol, he begins to get a hint of the corruption in his home state. His passionate filibuster against this corruption remains one of the most emotionally powerful scenes in film history. B&W; 129m. DIR: Frank Capra. CAST: James Stewart, Jean Arthur, Claude Rains. 1939 DVD

MR. STITCH ★★★ Surrealistic film about a mad doctor who creates his own creature using the body parts of eighty-eight men and women. The result is a patchwork quilt of a human who is supposed to be completely controllable. Instead, the creature has flashbacks into the lives of some of the people who made up his being and begins to question the experiment. Final third of the movie takes an unbelievable turn. Interesting comment on scientific research. Rated R for violence. 80m. DIR: Roger Avary. CAST: Rutger Hauer, Wil Wheaton, Nia Peeples. 1995

MR. SUPERINVISIBLE ★★ Disney-like comedy with Dean Jones as the scientist who stumbles upon a virus that causes invisibility. Cute in spots; kids should like it. 90m. DIR: Anthony M. Dawson. CAST: Dean Jones, Gastone Moschin, Ingeborg Schoener, Rafael Alonso, Peter Carsten. 1973

MR. SYCAMORE 💔 A mailman decides to turn into a tree. Peculiar and pointless. Not rated. 87m. DIR: Pancho Kohner. CAST: Jason Robards Jr., Sandy Dennis, Jean Simmons, Mark Miller. 1975

MR. VAMPIRE (VOL. 1–4) ★★★1/2 This Chinese vampire movie is a surreal and hilarious romp filled with remarkable martial arts and bizarre special effects laced with great slapstick and vampire erotica. Director Lau Koon Wai has created a bloodsucker who sports long purple fingernails and yellow fangs and, when not levitating, hops like a bunny. In Chinese with English subtitles. Not rated; contains violence and nudity. 375m. DIR: Wong Kee Hung, Law Lit, Sung Kam Shing. CAST: Ricky Hui, Yuen Biao, Richard Ng, Lam Ching Ying. 1986–1988

MR. WINKLE GOES TO WAR ★★★ Edward G. Robinson is a henpecked bookkeeper who gets drafted into the army during World War II. As the saying goes, the army makes a man out of him. Like so many films of its time, Mr. Winkle Goes to War was part of the war effort, and as such, hasn't worn very well; what was considered heartfelt or patriotic back in the 1940s is now rendered maudlin or just corny. Still, the acting is excellent. B&W; 80m. DIR: Alfred E. Green. CAST: Edward G. Robinson, Ruth Warrick, Richard Lane, Robert Armstrong. 1944

MR. WONDERFUL ★★★★ Fine acting highlights this insightful study of relationships. Matt Dillon plays a Con Edison electrical worker who is being strapped by alimony payments; fiancée Mary-Louise Parker suspects he's still in love with ex-wife Annabella Sciorra. Rated PG-13 for brief profanity and simulated sex. 101m. DIR: Anthony Minghella. CAST: Matt Dillon, Annabella Sciorra, Mary-Louise Parker, William Hurt, Vincent D'Onofrio, David Barry

Gray, Bruce Kirby, Dan Hedaya, Luis Guzman, Joanna Merlin, Jessica Harper, Adam LeFevre. **1993 DVD**

MR. WONG, DETECTIVE ★★★ First of five Mr. Wong films starring Boris Karloff as Hugh Wiley's black-suited sleuth is a notch above most of Monogram Pictures programmers. Mr. Wong attempts to solve the deaths of three industrialists, which have baffled the authorities and have the government and media in an uproar. Fun for mystery and detective fans. B&W; 69m. **DIR:** William Nigh. **CAST:** Boris Karloff, Grant Withers, Evelyn Brent, Maxine Jennings, Lucien Prival. **1938 DVD**

MR. WONG IN CHINATOWN ★★ A Chinese princess and her bodyguards are killed while she is trying to buy defense planes for her homeland, and Mr. Wong steps in to find the culprits. Tepid entry to a tolerable series. B&W; 70m. **DIR:** William Nigh. **CAST:** Boris Karloff, Grant Withers, Marjorie Reynolds. **1939 DVD**

MR. WRITE ★★ Likable Paul Reiser is ill served by this forced comedy, adapted by Howard J. Morris from what must have been an excruciating play. Reiser's would-be playwright toils amid the horrors of television commercials, while concocting a stage epic just as shrill and bizarre as this whole film. Rated PG-13 for profanity and suggested sex. 89m. **DIR:** Charlie Loventhal. **CAST:** Paul Reiser, Jessica Tuck, Doug Davidson, Wendie Jo Sperber, Martin Mull. **1994**

MR. WRONG ★★★ Lonely and single Ellen De-Generes meets a sexy guy (Bill Pullman) who seems too good to be true; by the time she realizes what a loser he is, she can't get rid of him. The script is predictable and Nick Castle's direction is only adequate, but DeGeneres's personal charm and a few inspired gags make it all worthwhile. Rated PG-13 for mild profanity and comic violence. 92m. **DIR:** Nick Castle. **CAST:** Ellen DeGeneres, Bill Pullman, Joan Cusack, Dean Stockwell, Joan Plowright. **1996**

MISTRAL'S DAUGHTER ★★ This sudsy adaptation of Judith Krantz's novel features Stefanie Powers as the model and then mistress of a cynical artist (Stacy Keach). Made for television, this miniseries is unrated but contains partial nudity and simulated sex. 300m. **DIR:** Douglas Hickox. **CAST:** Stefanie Powers, Stacy Keach, Lee Remick, Timothy Dalton, Robert Urich, Stéphane Audran. **1984**

MISTRESS, THE (1953) ★★★1/2 Tragic tale of a Japanese woman trapped in a life as mistress to a greedy Shylock. When she falls in love with a medical student, her reputation causes nothing but heartache and sorrow. In Japanese with English subtitles. B&W; 106m. **DIR:** Shiro Toyoda. **CAST:** Hideko Takamine, Hiroshi Akutagawa. **1953**

MISTRESS (1987) ★★ Sudsy coming-of-age melodrama about a mistress who must support herself after her wealthy lover dies. Made for TV, this contains adult themes. 96m. **DIR:** Michael Tuchner. **CAST:** Victoria Principal, Don Murray, Joanna Kerns, Kerrie Keane. **1987**

MISTRESS (1992) ★★★ A writer (Robert Wuhl) tries to get his long forgotten script made into a movie, while a trio of wealthy men attempt to get their mistresses shoehorned into acting roles. Barry

Primus directs from his own story and deftly captures the games Hollywood wannabes play; similar to Robert Altman's *The Player*. Look for comic shenanigans from Robert De Niro. Rated PG. 109m. **DIR:** Barry Primus. **CAST:** Robert Wuhl, Robert De Niro, Martin Landau, Danny Aiello, Eli Wallach, Laurie Metcalf, Sheryl Lee Ralph, Jean Smart, Ernest Borgnine, Christopher Walken. **1992 DVD**

MRS. BROWN ★★1/2 The true story of the bond between the widowed Queen Victoria (Judi Dench) and her Scottish stableman John Brown (Billy Connolly) is given a stately *Masterpiece Theater* treatment, but the result is unconvincing, primarily because of the lack of chemistry between Dench and Connolly. Dench's Victoria is dour and haughty, Connolly's Brown is coarse and loutish; both are decades too old for their roles. Rated PG. 103m. **DIR:** John Madden. **CAST:** Judi Dench, Billy Connolly, Antony Sher, Geoffrey Palmer, Richard Pasco, David Westhead. **1997 DVD**

MRS. BROWN YOU'VE GOT A LOVELY DAUGHTER ★★ England's Herman's Hermits star in this film, named after one of their hit songs. The limited plot revolves around the group acquiring a greyhound and deciding to race it. Caution: Only for hard-core Hermits fans! Rated G. 110m. **DIR:** Saul Swimmer. **CAST:** Herman's Hermits, Stanley Holloway. **1968**

MRS. DALLOWAY ★★★1/2 This marvelous adaptation of Virginia Woolf's classic novel portrays a day in the life of a wealthy Englishwoman, with flashbacks to the days when she had her whole life before her. This lyrical film miraculously draws the two worlds of Clarissa Dalloway, the gulf of years that separates them, and the poignant memories that unite them. Rated PG-13 for brief nudity and mature themes. 97m. **DIR:** Marleen Gorris. **CAST:** Vanessa Redgrave, Natascha McElhone, Rupert Graves, Michael Kitchen, John Standing, Lena Headey. **1997 DVD**

MRS. DOUBTFIRE ★★★★ Robin Williams is a howl as a father so desperate to be near his kids after separating from his wife that he masquerades as their elderly Irish nanny. Sally Field proves to be a terrific "straight man" for her costar. Rated PG-13 for brief profanity and scatological humor. 125m. **DIR:** Chris Columbus. **CAST:** Robin Williams, Sally Field, Pierce Brosnan, Harvey Fierstein, Polly Holliday, Lisa Jakub, Matthew Lawrence, Mara Wilson, Robert Prosky, Anne Haney, Sydney Walker, Martin Mull. **1993 DVD**

MRS. MINIVER ★★★★ This highly sentimental story of the English home front during the early years of World War II is one of the best examples of cinematic propaganda ever produced. It follows the lives of the Miniver family, especially Mrs. Miniver (Greer Garson), as they become enmeshed in a series of attempts to protect what will always be an England. It won seven Academy Awards, including best picture. B&W; 134m. **DIR:** William Wyler. **CAST:** Greer Garson, Walter Pidgeon, Teresa Wright, May Whitty, Richard Ney, Henry Travers, Henry Wilcoxon, Reginald Owen. **1942**

MRS. MUNCK ★★1/2 Diane Ladd directed and scripted this vanity project, which teams her with former offscreen husband Bruce Dern. He's an embittered, crippled, and unloved old man; she's his betrayed ex-lover who takes him in, for possibly vengeful purposes that are never clearly explained. Rated PG-13 for profanity, brief nudity, and simulated sex. 99m. **DIR:** Diane Ladd. **CAST:** Diane Ladd, Bruce Dern, Kelly Preston, Shelley Winters. **1995**

MRS. PARKER AND THE VICIOUS CIRCLE ★★★1/2 It may be clever and sentient, but this biopic of Dorothy Parker and her witty companions plays like a Who's Who of the literati. Jennifer Jason Leigh gets under your skin emotionally in a performance that is at once brilliant and arch. Rated R for profanity, nudity, and sexual situations. 124m. **DIR:** Alan Rudolph. **CAST:** Jennifer Jason Leigh, Matthew Broderick, Campbell Scott, Andrew McCarthy, Stephen Gallagher, Stephen Baldwin, Gwyneth Paltrow, Lili Taylor. **1994**

MRS. PARKINGTON ★★★1/2 Over a sixty-year period a poor girl from a Nevada mining town becomes the matriarch of a powerful New York family. Fine performances from an outstanding cast, witty dialogue, and interesting subplots. Oscar nominations for Greer Garson and, in support, Agnes Moorehead. B&W; 124m. **DIR:** Tay Garnett. **CAST:** Greer Garson, Walter Pidgeon, Agnes Moorehead, Edward Arnold, Cecil Kellaway, Gladys Cooper, Frances Rafferty, Dan Duryea, Hugh Marlowe, Lee Patrick, Tom Drake, Rod Cameron, Selena Royle, Peter Lawford. **1944**

MRS. SANTA CLAUS ★★★ Irrepressible Angela Lansbury stars in the title role of this musical. Feeling unappreciated by her famous spouse (Charles Durning), she takes off with the reindeer! Landing in New York in 1910, she becomes involved with the suffrage rights movement and child labor reform. Frothy fun is capped by a customary happy holiday ending. Rated G. 91m. **DIR:** Terry Hughes. **CAST:** Angela Lansbury, Charles Durning, Michael Jeter, David Norona, Lynsey Bartilson, Debra Wiseman. **1996**

MRS. SOFFEL ★★1/2 We assume Australian director Gillian Armstrong's intent was to make more than a simple entertainment about a warden's wife (Diane Keaton) who helps two prisoners (Mel Gibson and Matthew Modine) escape. But she creates a shapeless "statement" about the plight of women at the turn of the century. Even the stars' excellent performances can't save it. Rated PG-13 for violence, suggested sex, and profanity. 112m. **DIR:** Gillian Armstrong. **CAST:** Diane Keaton, Mel Gibson, Matthew Modine, Edward Herrmann, Trini Alvarado. **1984**

MRS. WIGGS OF THE CABBAGE PATCH ★★ This sentimental twaddle about a poor but optimistic family from the wrong side of the tracks is a throwback to nineteenth-century stage melodrama, saved only by the presence of the great W. C. Fields, ZaSu Pitts, and a fine cast of character actors. If you are a Fields fan, beware—the much-put-upon comedian only appears in the last part of the film. Creaky. B&W; 80m. **DIR:** Norman Taurog. **CAST:** Pauline Lord, W. C. Fields, ZaSu Pitts, Evelyn Venable, Kent Taylor, Charles Middleton, Donald Meek. **1934**

MRS. WINTERBOURNE ★★1/2 Pregnant, unmarried Ricki Lake is mistaken for the new wife of a recently deceased millionaire and welcomed into the bosom of his aristocratic family. The Cornell Woolrich mystery novel *I Married a Dead Man* is rather grotesquely mutated into a rehash with a talented cast struggling against the strained, predictable script. Rated PG-13 for mild profanity. 104m. **DIR:** Richard Benjamin. **CAST:** Shirley MacLaine, Ricki Lake, Brendan Fraser, Loren Dean, Miguel Sandoval. **1996**

MS. BEAR ★★★ A lost bear cub looking for its mother escapes the clutches of a hunter and is adopted by a young girl. Against the wishes of her father, the girl keeps the bear cub, who eventually becomes a member of the family. When the hunter shows up, she helps the bear escape once again. Lots of fun for the family, this is a comedy with heart. Rated G. 95m. **DIR:** Paul Ziller. **CAST:** Ed Begley Jr., Shaun Johnston, Kaitlyn Burke, Kimberly Warnat. **1997**

MS. .45 ★★★★ An attractive mute woman is raped and beaten twice in the same evening. She slips into madness and seeks revenge with a .45 pistol. A female version of *Death Wish* with an ending at a Halloween costume party that will knock your socks off. Not for all tastes. Rated R for violence, nudity, rape, language, and gore. 90m. **DIR:** Abel Ferrara. **CAST:** Zoe Tamerlis. **1981 DVD**

MS. SCROOGE ★★ This modernized, made-for-cable retelling of Charles Dickens's classic is one of the most lackluster and watered-down versions out there. Cicely Tyson's Ebonita Scrooge is so tightlipped that she's barely understandable, and much of the original tale simply doesn't translate well into the present day. Rated G. 95m. **DIR:** John Korty. **CAST:** Cicely Tyson, Michael Beach, John Bourgeois, Katherine Helmond. **1997**

MISTRIAL ★★1/2 Writer-director Heywood Gould's positively ludicrous script finds veteran cop Bill Pullman dissatisfied with a controversial courtroom verdict ... so he holds judge, jury, and defendant at gunpoint and forces all concerned to reenact the trial. And they do! Sincere concerns about flaws in the U.S. justice system are wholly overshadowed by the ridiculous premise. Rated R for violence and profanity. 89m. **DIR:** Heywood Gould. **CAST:** Bill Pullman, Robert Loggia, Blair Underwood, Leo Burmester, Roma Maffia, James Rebhorn, Josef Sommer. **1996**

MISTY ★★★ A thoroughly enjoyable family film about two youngsters who teach a young horse new tricks. Film version of Marguerite Henry's bestseller *Misty of Chincoteague*. Filmed on an island off the Virginia coast, so the scenery is a selling point. 92m. **DIR:** James B. Clark. **CAST:** David Ladd, Arthur O'Connell, Anne Seymour, Pam Smith. **1961**

MISUNDERSTOOD (1984) 💔 A rich businessman raises two young sons who are traumatized by the sudden death of their mother. Rated PG for profanity. 91m. **DIR:** Jerry Schatzberg. **CAST:** Gene Hackman, Henry Thomas, Huckleberry Fox. **1984**

MISUNDERSTOOD (1988) ★★ This is an Italian production of the U.S. film release that starred Gene Hackman. The slow, depressing story did not need to be done twice. In this version, Anthony Quayle is a British consul in Italy. He is trying to raise his two sons following the death of his wife. The focus is on the father's relationship with the older son, which lacks understanding and compassion. The director,

Luigi Comencini, takes far too long to reach the too late conclusion. Rated PG for adult themes. 101m. **DIR:** Luigi Comencini. **CAST:** Anthony Quayle, Stefano Colagrande, Georgia Moll. 1988

MIXED BLOOD ★★1/2 Paul Morrissey, the man who brought you Andy Warhol's versions of *Frankenstein* and *Dracula*, has made a serious film about the Alphabet City drug subculture and its inherent violent nature. Here the surroundings are brutal and unforgiving, and the cheap film stock gives the movie a newsreel feeling. Not rated; contains violence and profanity. 98m. **DIR:** Paul Morrissey. **CAST:** Marilia Pera, Richard Ulacia, Linda Kerridge, Geraldine Smith, Angel David, Rodney Harvey. 1985

MIXED NUTS 🦃 No one dies laughing in this strained comedy about Christmas Eve day at a Venice Beach suicide-prevention center staffed by misfits who are about to be evicted. Rated PG-13 for language. 97m. **DIR:** Nora Ephron. **CAST:** Steve Martin, Madeline Kahn, Juliette Lewis, Robert Klein, Adam Sandler, Rita Wilson, Rob Reiner, Garry Shandling. 1994

MO' BETTER BLUES ★★1/2 Writer-director Spike Lee was trying to make a movie about a jazz musician that was free of the usual clichés—primarily in response to Clint Eastwood's *Bird*—but only Wesley Snipes's volatile performance as a sax-playing rival energizes this lackadaisical affair about a successful, slick, and attractive trumpeter (Denzel Washington). Rated R for profanity, nudity, and violence. 120m. **DIR:** Spike Lee. **CAST:** Denzel Washington, Spike Lee, Wesley Snipes, Giancarlo Esposito, Robin Harris, Joie Lee, Cynda Williams, Bill Nunn, John Turturro, Rubén Blades, Dick Anthony Williams. 1990

MO' MONEY ★★★1/2 Damon Wayans wrote and stars in this comedy about a small-time street hustler who falls in love and tries to go straight. There are some terrific moments of hilarity in this fast-paced, fun flick, which also features an impressive feature-film acting debut by Marlon Wayans. Rated R for profanity, nudity, and violence. 97m. **DIR:** Peter MacDonald. **CAST:** Damon Wayans, Marlon Wayans, Stacey Dash, Joe Santos, John Diehl. 1992

MOB BOSS ★★1/2 Sometimes funny gangster story about an aging don (William Hickey) who calls upon his absolutely useless son (Eddie Deezen) to take over the family business. Deezen's training as a mobster is hilarious. Rated R for nudity and profanity. 93m. **DIR:** Fred Olen Ray. **CAST:** Morgan Fairchild, Eddie Deezen, William Hickey, Don Stroud, Jack O'Halloran, Mike Mazurki, Stuart Whitman. 1990

MOB JUSTICE ★★1/2 Unspoken peace agreement between the mob and law enforcement agencies is broken when a small-time hood kills an undercover federal agent. Tony Danza is convincing as the killer who must hide out from both the law and his employers. Rated R for violence and profanity. 95m. **DIR:** Peter Markle. **CAST:** Tony Danza, Ted Levine, Dan Lauria, Nicholas Turturro, Samuel L. Jackson. 1991

MOB STORY ★★1/2 A moderately funny comedy-drama. A mob kingpin escapes to Winnipeg to stay with relatives. His attempts to train his nephew in the fine art of crime run afoul as his enemies track him down. Rated PG-13. 98m. **DIR:** Jancarlo Markiw,

Gabriel Markiw. **CAST:** Margot Kidder, John Vernon, Kate Vernon, Al Waxman. 1989 DVD

MOB WAR 🦃 Bargain-basement flick about a young mob turk. Rated R for violence and profanity. 96m. **DIR:** J. Christian Ingvordsen. **CAST:** Johnny Stumper, Jake La Motta. 1988 DVD

MOBSTERS ★★ In what might be called *Young Guns in the Roaring Twenties*, Christian Slater plays Lucky Luciano and Patrick Dempsey is Meyer Lansky in yet another gangster movie. It's no *Good-Fellas*, but there's plenty of action, with F. Murray Abraham and Anthony Quinn adding class. Rated R for violence and profanity. 110m. **DIR:** Michael Karbelnikoff. **CAST:** Christian Slater, Patrick Dempsey, Richard Grieco, F. Murray Abraham, Anthony Quinn. 1991

MOBY DICK (1956) ★★★1/2 Director John Huston's brilliant adaptation of Herman Melville's classic novel features Gregory Peck in one of his best performances as the driven Captain Ahab. 116m. **DIR:** John Huston. **CAST:** Gregory Peck, Richard Basehart, Leo Genn, Orson Welles. 1956

MOBY DICK (1998) ★★★★ Rich, extremely well acted adaptation of the classic Herman Melville novel offers breathtaking sets and scenery, impressive special effects, and a complex cast of fascinating characters. Rated PG. 145m. **DIR:** Franc Roddam. **CAST:** Patrick Stewart, Henry Thomas, Ted Levine, Gregory Peck. 1998 DVD

MOCKERY ★★1/2 Silent-screen master of menace Lon Chaney Sr. stars in this MGM melodrama set during the Russian Revolution. Modern viewers may find it slow-going. Worth seeing for Chaney in a straight role, however, and for the stylish direction of Benjamin Christensen, which includes a chilling opening shot. B&W; 90m. **DIR:** Benjamin Christensen. **CAST:** Lon Chaney Sr., Barbara Bedford, Ricardo Cortez, Mack Swain. 1927

MOD SQUAD, THE ★★ This update of the 1960s TV series is a mess from the outset, stranding the talented young stars and a strong supporting cast in a half-baked story that makes absolutely no sense—beginning with the fact that it's set in the 1990s, when nobody uses words like *mod* anymore. Rated R for violence and profanity. 94m. **DIR:** Scott Silver. **CAST:** Claire Danes, Giovanni Ribisi, Omar Epps, Dennis Farina, Josh Brolin, Michael Lerner. 1999 DVD

MOD SQUAD, THE (TV SERIES) ★★★1/2 Three youths are busted for minor crimes and then recruited to go undercover. Pete is a poor little rich boy who's rebelling against his Beverly Hills parents. Linc is a ghetto black who seethes beneath a stoic exterior. Julie, the sensitive blonde, is the daughter of a prostitute. The series effectively combined action, positive messages, and a mildly antiestablishment bent. 60m. **DIR:** Various. **CAST:** Michael Cole, Clarence Williams III, Peggy Lipton, Tige Andrews. 1968–1973

MODEL BY DAY ★★1/2 After her roommate is attacked, a model decides to do her part to rid the city of crime. The film has some good comedic moments, but the plot is unbelievable. Rated R for nudity and violence. 89m. **DIR:** Christian Duguay. **CAST:** Famke

Janssen, Stephen Shellen, Shannon Tweed, Sean Young, Clark Johnson, Traci Lind, Kim Coates. **1993**

MODERN AFFAIR, A ★★★ Businesswoman Lisa Eichhorn decides to have a baby via artificial insemination. But after she's pregnant, she becomes consumed with curiosity about her unborn child's anonymous father and decides to find him. Likable romantic comedy. Rated R for sexual situations and profanity. 91m. **DIR:** Vern Oakley. **CAST:** Lisa Eichhorn, Stanley Tucci, Caroline Aaron, Mary Jo Salerno, Robert Joy, Tammy Grimes. **1994**

MODERN GIRLS ★★★ Cynthia Gibb, Virginia Madsen, and Daphne Zuniga turn in fine individual performances as the *Modern Girls*, but this well-edited and visually striking film has some slow scenes among the funny. However, younger viewers should find it enjoyable overall. Rated PG-13 for profanity and sexual situations. 82m. **DIR:** Jerry Kramer. **CAST:** Cynthia Gibb, Virginia Madsen, Daphne Zuniga, Clayton Rohner, Stephen Shellen, Chris Nash. **1987**

MODERN LOVE ★★ Robby Benson's ideal concept of marital bliss is marred by the realities of daily life. Some funny bits, but Benson's fantasies get unbelievably out of hand. (His real wife, Karla DeVito, is great as his harried film wife and a new mother.) Rated R for nudity. 110m. **DIR:** Robby Benson. **CAST:** Robby Benson, Karla DeVito, Burt Reynolds, Rue McClanahan. **1990 DVD**

MODERN PROBLEMS ★★ In this passable comedy, directed by Ken (*The Groove Tube*) Shapiro, Chevy Chase plays an air traffic controller who may be permanently out to lunch. Rated PG because of its brief nudity and sexual theme. 91m. **DIR:** Ken Shapiro. **CAST:** Chevy Chase, Patti D'Arbanville, Mary Kay Place. **1981**

MODERN ROMANCE ★★★★ Love may be a many-splendored thing for some people, but it's sheer torture for Robert Cole (Albert Brooks) in this contemporary comedy. Brooks wrote, directed, and starred in this very entertaining, often hilarious story about a self-indulgent, narcissistic Hollywood film editor whose love life has the stability of Mount St. Helens. Rated R. 93m. **DIR:** Albert Brooks. **CAST:** Albert Brooks, Kathryn Harrold, Bruno Kirby. **1981**

MODERN TIMES ★★★★ Charlie Chaplin must have had a crystal ball when he created *Modern Times*. His satire of life in an industrial society has more relevance today than when it was made. Primarily it is still pure Chaplin, with his perfectly timed and edited sight gags. The story finds the Little Tramp confronting all the dehumanizing inventions of a futuristic manufacturing plant. B&W; 89m. **DIR:** Charles Chaplin. **CAST:** Charlie Chaplin, Paulette Goddard. **1936 DVD**

MODERNS, THE ★★ This ironic look at the Paris art scene of the Twenties just isn't funny *enough*. Director Alan Rudolph is always poised at the crossroads of humorous seriousness, but in *The Moderns* he's got his vision in limbo too much of the time. Keith Carradine is good as an expatriate painter, and Wallace Shawn has the best lines as a gossip columnist. Not rated. 126m. **DIR:** Alan Rudolph. **CAST:** Keith Carradine, Linda Fiorentino, John Lone, Wallace Shawn, Genevieve Bujold, Geraldine Chaplin, Kevin J. O'Connor. **1988**

MOGAMBO ★★★ This remake of the film classic *Red Dust* stars Clark Gable as the great white hunter who dallies with a sophisticated married woman (Grace Kelly), only to return to the arms of a jaded lady (Ava Gardner, who is quite good in the role of the woman with a past). It's not great John Ford, but it'll do. 115m. **DIR:** John Ford. **CAST:** Clark Gable, Grace Kelly, Ava Gardner. **1953**

MOHAWK ★1/2 Cornball story about love between settler Scott Brady and Indian Rita Gam must have been inspired by access to footage from John Ford's classic *Drums Along the Mohawk*. 79m. **DIR:** Kurt Neumann. **CAST:** Scott Brady, Rita Gam, Neville Brand, Lori Nelson, Allison Hayes, Ted de Corsia. **1956 DVD**

MOJAVE FIREBRAND ★★★ Wild Bill Elliott helps old pal Gabby Hayes protect his silver mine from a lawless element. B&W; 56m. **DIR:** Spencer Gordon Bennet. **CAST:** William Elliott, George "Gabby" Hayes, Anne Jeffreys, LeRoy Mason. **1944**

MOJAVE MOON ★★★ Decent cast struggles to overcome oddball script and weak direction in this misguided character study. Danny Aiello stars as a Los Angeles car salesman so desperate for love that he agrees to drive a young woman to her home in the Mojave Desert. Once there, he becomes involved with the girl's mom and her wacky boyfriend, who recruits Aiello into his paranoid world. Rated R for adult situations, language, nudity, and violence. 95m. **DIR:** Kevin Dowling. **CAST:** Danny Aiello, Anne Archer, Angelina Jolie, Michael Biehn. **1996**

MOLE PEOPLE, THE ★★ Explorers discover a lost civilization of albino Sumerians living under a mountain. For fright-night nostalgists only. B&W; 78m. **DIR:** Virgil Vogel. **CAST:** John Agar, Hugh Beaumont, Alan Napier. **1956**

MOLL FLANDERS ★★★★ Sumptuous, triumphant feminist adaptation of Daniel Defoe's eighteenth-century novel. Robin Wright's Moll is a plucky lass whose spirit is never broken, though class prejudice, prostitution, and melodramatic tragedy all conspire to do the poor woman in. Even better, American Wright keeps her cockney accent consistent. Essentially a costume soap opera, but a stirring one. Rated PG-13. 123m. **DIR:** Pen Densham. **CAST:** Robin Wright, Morgan Freeman, Stockard Channing, John Lynch. **1996**

MOLL FLANDERS (1996) ★★★1/2 Comely Alex Kingston climbs into the role of Daniel Defoe's adventures with such sexual force and strength of personality that one is instantly caught up in Flanders's rich life story. A very spirited and surprisingly erotic Masterpiece Theater production that communicates the novel's sentiment while convincingly re-creating the early 1700s. Released as a two-tape set. Not rated; contains profanity, nudity, and sexual situations. 220m. **DIR:** David Attwood. **CAST:** Alex Kingston, Daniel Craig, Diana Rigg, Ronald Fraser. **1996 DVD**

•MOLLY ★★1/2 An institutionalized young woman gets an operation that frees her from her mental illness—but only temporarily. Director John Duigan's film was delayed for nearly a year and shows the signs of editing-room tinkering; even so, it's hard to see how it could ever have been anything but a derivative retread of films like *Charly* and *Awakenings*. Rated PG-13 for brief nudity. 89m. DIR: John Duigan. CAST: Elisabeth Shue, Aaron Eckhart, Jill Hennesy, Thomas Jane, D. W. Moffett. **1999 DVD**

MOLLY & GINA ★★ Female bonding films are all the rage since *Thelma & Louise*, but you wouldn't want to drive off a cliff with Molly and Gina. Frances Fisher and Natasha Gregson Wagner play the girlfriends of two dead Los Angeles punks. When they attempt to investigate, they are met with the usual parade of bullets, bad guys, and close calls on the mean streets of L.A. Familiar faces can't save this routine thriller. Rated R for violence and nudity. 93m. DIR: Paul Leder. CAST: Frances Fisher, Natasha Gregson Wagner, Peter Fonda, Bruce Weitz, Stella Stevens. **1993**

MOLLY MAGUIRES, THE ★★★ The Molly Maguires were a group of terrorists in the 1870s who fought for better conditions for the Pennsylvania coal miners. In this dramatization, Sean Connery is their leader and Richard Harris is a Pinkerton detective who infiltrates the group. The film gives a vivid portrayal of the miners' dreadful existence. Performances are first-rate. A little long, but worth checking out. 123m. DIR: Martin Ritt. CAST: Sean Connery, Richard Harris, Samantha Eggar, Frank Finlay, Art Lund. **1970**

MOM 💛 A television reporter tries to protect his family and the community from his mother, a flesh-eating ghoul. Rated R for violence and profanity. 95m. DIR: Patrick Rand. CAST: Mark Thomas Miller, Art Evans, Mary McDonough, Jeanne Bates. **1990**

MOM AND DAD ★★ Don't know nuthin' 'bout birthin' no babies? Then see this once-banned roadshow classic that toured the country for decades. Not rated. B&W; 83m. DIR: William Beaudine. CAST: Hardie Albright, Lois Austin, June Carlson. **1947**

MOM AND DAD SAVE THE WORLD ★★★1/2 Kids will get plenty of howls out of this goofy comedy, in which an American family is whisked away to the planet Spéngo—in the station wagon. The result is a latter-day version of those so-bad-they're-funny sci-fi flicks of the 1950s. Rated PG for silly violence. 87m. DIR: Greg Beeman. CAST: Teri Garr, Jeffrey Jones, Jon Lovitz, Eric Idle, Wallace Shawn, Thalmus Rasulala. **1992**

MOMMIE DEAREST ★★★1/2 At times this trashy screen version of Christine Crawford's controversial autobiography—which stars Faye Dunaway in an astounding performance as Joan Crawford—is so harrowing and grotesque you're tempted to stop the tape. But it's so morbidly fascinating you can't take your eyes off the screen. Rated PG. 129m. DIR: Frank Perry. CAST: Faye Dunaway, Diana Scarwid, Steve Forrest. **1981**

MOMMY ★★ *Bad Seed* Patty McCormack grows up to become the *Mommy*, a woman so possessive of her daughter that she will do anything to protect her. Good chance for the actors to chew scenery and not much more. Rated PG for language and violence. 89m. DIR: Max Allan Collins. CAST: Patty McCormack, Jason Miller, Brinke Stevens, Majel Barrett. **1994 DVD**

MOMMY 2: MOMMY'S DAY 💛 Unjustifiable sequel to the already poor *Mommy* is nearly impossible to

watch. Psycho mother Patty McCormack, upon her release from prison, goes after everyone who tries to keep her away from the daughter she nearly murdered in the first film. Low-budget disaster. Not rated; contains violence. 89m. DIR: Max Allan Collins. CAST: Patty McCormack, Paul Petersen, Gary Sandy, Brinke Stevens. **1996**

MON HOMME (MY MAN) ★★★★ The failure of the sexes to understand each other, as well as men's fear of female sexuality, are explored in this occasionally surreal comedy about a happy hooker who fashions a homeless bum into a successful pimp. In French with English subtitles. Not rated; the film features strong sexual content. 95m. DIR: Bertrand Blier. CAST: Anouk Grinberg, Gerard Lanvin, Valeria Bruni-Tedeschi, Olivier Martinez, Mathieu Kassovitz. **1997**

MON ONCLE ANTOINE ★★★1/2 Above-average coming-of-age story about a boy in rural Canada during the 1940s. In French with English subtitles. Not rated, but fine for the entire family. 110m. DIR: Claude Jutra. CAST: Jacques Gagnon, Claude Jutra. **1971**

MON ONCLE D'AMERIQUE ★★★★ In this bizarre French comedy, director Alain Resnais works something close to a miracle: he combines intelligence with entertainment. On one level, a delectable farce with the requisite ironies, surprise complications, and bittersweet truths. Underneath, it is a thought-provoking scientific treatise—by biologist Henri Laborit—on the human condition. In French with English subtitles. Rated PG. 123m. DIR: Alain Resnais. CAST: Gérard Depardieu, Nicole Garcia, Roger Pierre. **1980**

MONA LISA ★★★★1/2 Bob Hoskins is Britain's answer to Humphrey Bogart and James Cagney. In this crime-thriller, Hoskins plays a simple but moral man whose less than honest endeavors have landed him in prison. Upon his release, he goes to his former boss (Michael Caine) in search of a job. Not rated; the film has profanity, suggested sex, and violence. 100m. DIR: Neil Jordan. CAST: Bob Hoskins, Cathy Tyson, Michael Caine, Clark Peters. **1986**

MONDO ★★★ A homeless boy with no memory of his past becomes the center of a loose-knit community of outsiders in the French seaport town of Nice. Filmmaker Tony Gatlif (*Latcho Drom, Gadjo Dilo*) used mostly nonactors to create this visually pleasing but rather naïve fable. In French with English subtitles. Not rated; contains nudity. 80m. DIR: Tony Gatlif. CAST: Ovidiu Balan, Philippe Petit. **1995**

MONDO CANE II ★★ Disappointing sequel to the controversial and bizarre cult documentary released in 1963. Again the strange and fascinating world of human ritual is explored but without the intensity or the humor that the first film managed to create. Not rated; contains violence and nudity. 90m. DIR: Gualtiero Jacopetti. **1964**

MONDO NEW YORK 💛 A young girl observes the depravity and senselessness of New York City. Not rated, contains vile language and nudity. 83m. DIR: Harvey Keith. CAST: Joey Arias, Rick Aviles, Charlie Barnett. **1987**

MONDO TRASHO 💛 This is not a sync-sound movie, and the 1950s rock 'n' roll, along with the occasional wild dubbed-over dialogue, gets tiresome after twenty minutes. Not rated, but this is equivalent to an X for violence, gore, and sex. 130m. DIR: John Waters. CAST: Divine, Mary Vivian Pearce, Mink Stole, David Lochary. 1971

•MONEY ★★ Pedestrian thriller about a man willing to do whatever it takes to retrieve his father's stolen money. Eric Stoltz is oddly cast in this Italian-French effort as the son who teams up with some eccentric characters to track down the culprits. The plot is all over the map. The scenery is nice, but who wants to sit through a financial thriller travelogue? Not rated; contains adult situations and violence. 117m. DIR: Steven H. Stern. CAST: F. Murray Abraham, Eric Stoltz, Maryam D'Abo, Christopher Plummer. 1990

MONEY FOR NOTHING ★★★★ The fact-based story of Joey Coyle, an unemployed Philadelphia dock worker who finds $1.2 million when it falls out of an armored car on its way to an Atlantic City casino. The film bends the facts somewhat—it has the satiric feel of a 1940s Preston Sturges farce—but it makes fine entertainment, fast-paced and well acted by an excellent cast. Rated R for profanity. 100m. DIR: Ramon Menendez. CAST: John Cusack, Debi Mazar, Michael Madsen, Maury Chaykin. 1993

MONEY KINGS ★★★1/2 High-profile cast elevates this pedestrian thriller about a bar owner and one of his customers who decide to take on the Boston mob. Peter Falk is Vinnie, the owner of the pub who runs an illegal gambling den in the back. When the mob wants a piece of his action, they send a young, ambitious collector to oversee his operation and things get out of hand. Rated R for language, violence, and adult situations. 96m. DIR: Graham Theakston. CAST: Peter Falk, Timothy Hutton, Freddie Prinze Jr., Lauren Holly, Tyne Daly, Colm Meaney. 1999 DVD

MONEY PIT, THE ★★ In this gimmicky, contrived Steven Spielberg production, Tom Hanks plays a rock 'n' roll lawyer who falls in love with musician Shelley Long. When these lovebirds buy a fixer-upper, they encounter all sorts of problems. Rated PG for profanity and suggested sex. 90m. DIR: Richard Benjamin. CAST: Tom Hanks, Shelley Long, Alexander Godunov, Maureen Stapleton, Joe Mantegna, Philip Bosco, Josh Mostel. 1986

MONEY TALKS ★★1/2 When fast-talking street hustler Chris Tucker is unwittingly involved in a jailbreak that leaves several cops dead, he turns to maverick TV newsman Charlie Sheen to help him clear his name and find the real killers. Although it is a hopeless mess, with a jumbled plot ending with everyone practically demolishing the L.A. Coliseum, Tucker manages to inject the film with some energy, and he and Sheen have a few good scenes. Rated R for violence and nonstop profanity. 95m. DIR: Brett Ratner. CAST: Chris Tucker, Charlie Sheen, David Warner, Heather Locklear, Paul Sorvino. 1997

MONEY TO BURN ★★ Plodding action-thriller stars McQueen and Swayze (not Steve and Patrick but Chad and Don), who seem right at home in this predictable combination of sex and violence. The guys go on a spending spree with $5 million a friend has given them—do they ever stop and wonder

where the money came from? Of course, it belongs to the mob, who have sent one of their best hit men to retrieve it. No-brainer from the first frame. Rated R for nudity, language, and violence. 96m. DIR: John Sjorgen. CAST: Chad McQueen, Don Swayze, Joe Estevez. 1993

MONEY TRAIN ★★1/2 Two foster brothers (Wesley Snipes, Woody Harrelson) work as transit cops in New York City and continually run afoul of their sadistic supervisor (Robert Blake). Enjoyable in its funny, fast-paced first half, this film takes a turn for the worse halfway through, causing us to lose sympathy for the main characters and doubt the sanity of the filmmakers. Blake is terrific, however. Rated R for violence, profanity, and simulated sex. 110m. DIR: Joseph Ruben. CAST: Wesley Snipes, Woody Harrelson, Jennifer Lopez, Robert Blake, Chris Cooper, Joe Grifasi. 1995 DVD

MONEYTREE, THE ★★ A marijuana grower attempts to ply his trade despite a materialistic, disapproving girlfriend, cops, and rip-off artists. There are some bright moments among the predictable, poorly improvised, and preachy pro-drug ones. Not rated; the film has profanity, violence, and nudity. 94m. DIR: Alan Dienstag. CAST: Christopher Dienstag. 1991

MONGREL ♥ Young Jerry has dreams in which he turns into a weredog and mutilates innocent people. Not rated, with lots of fake gore. 90m. DIR: Robert A. Burns. CAST: Terry Evans, Aldo Ray. 1982

MONIKA ★★ Young Harriet Andersson is Monika, a sultry, precocious teenager who escapes her poverty with the help of a young man. Pretty dull stuff. Also known by the title Summer With Monika. In Swedish with English subtitles. B&W; 82m. DIR: Ingmar Bergman. CAST: Harriet Andersson. 1952

MONKEY BUSINESS (1931) ★★★★1/2 The Marx Brothers are stowaways on a cruise ship, deflating pomposity and confusing authority. This movie dispenses with needless subplots and stagy musical numbers. It's undiluted Marx zaniness, and one of the team's best films. B&W; 77m. DIR: Norman Z. McLeod. CAST: The Marx Brothers, Thelma Todd, Ruth Hall. 1931 DVD

MONKEY BUSINESS (1952) ★★★★ A romping screwball comedy about a genius chemist (Cary Grant) who invents a formula that delays the aging process. A chimpanzee in the lab pours the formula in the public water fountain, causing all concerned to revert to adolescence. A minor classic. B&W; 97m. DIR: Howard Hawks. CAST: Cary Grant, Marilyn Monroe, Ginger Rogers, Charles Coburn, Hugh Marlowe, Larry Keating. 1952

MONKEY GRIP ★★★1/2 One year in the life of a divorced mother as she struggles to keep some sense of herself while trying to support herself and her child and maintain a relationship with a drug-addicted musician. Possibly too slow for some tastes, but overall this Australian film offers a probing look at contemporary life-styles. Not rated; the film contains frank discussions of sex. 100m. DIR: Ken Cameron. CAST: Noni Hazlehurst, Colin Friels, Christina Amphlett. 1982

ONKEY SHINES: AN EXPERIMENT IN FEAR ★★ A virile young man doesn't take too readily to becoming a paralytic overnight, immobilized and wheelchair-bound. Enter Ella, a superintelligent (through the miracle of modern science) monkey who is brought in to help with absolutely everything, including revenge. Genuine amusement—and some recent chills—for aficionados of the genre. Rated R for violence, sex, and terror. 115m. DIR: George A. Romero. CAST: Jason Beghe, Kate McNeil, John Pankow, Joyce Van Patten. 1988 DVD

ONKEY TROUBLE ★★★★ Delightful film about a youngster (Thora Birch) who finds a capuchin monkey, whom she calls Dodger. Soon both of them are dodging cops, criminals, and befuddled parents because the cute little monkey is actually a well-trained jewel thief. His original master (Harvey Keitel) needs him back to make good on a promise to a powerful and ruthless mobster. Rated PG for brief profanity and light violence. 95m. DIR: Franco Amurri. CAST: Thora Birch, Harvey Keitel, Mimi Rogers, Christopher McDonald, Kevin Scannell, Alison Elliott, Robert Miranda, Victor Argo. 1994

MONKEYS GO HOME ♥ Stupid monkeyshines. Rated G. 89m. DIR: Andrew V. McLaglen. CAST: Maurice Chevalier, Dean Jones, Yvette Mimieux. 1966

MONKEY'S UNCLE, THE ★★ This sequel to *The Misadventures of Merlin Jones* finds whiz kid Tommy Kirk up to no good with a flying machine and a sleep-learning technique employed on a monkey. More of the same from Disney, really: mild slapstick, and G-rated romance with Annette Funicello. For young minds only. 87m. DIR: Robert Stevenson. CAST: Tommy Kirk, Annette Funicello, Leon Ames, Arthur O'Connell, Frank Faylen. 1965

MONOLITH ★★ Two cops who dislike each other discover a government secret—an alien being that grows more powerful every day. Extremely bad acting and not much of a plot. Rated R for profanity and violence. 96m. DIR: John Eyres. CAST: Bill Paxton, Lindsay Frost, John Hurt, Lou Gossett Jr. 1993

MONOLITH MONSTERS, THE ★★★ Fragments of a meteor grow to enormous proportions when exposed to moisture in the Arizona desert. The good script has a novel premise, but B production values hold it back. B&W; 78m. DIR: John Sherwood. CAST: Grant Williams, Lola Albright, Les Tremayne. 1957

MONSIEUR BEAUCAIRE ★★★1/2 Bob Hope is King Louie XV's barber, tricked into impersonating a court dandy, not knowing an assassination is planned. Joan Caulfield is a beautiful chambermaid. Lots of laughs. Very loosely based on Booth Tarkington's novel. B&W; 93m. DIR: George Marshall. CAST: Bob Hope, Joan Caulfield, Patric Knowles, Marjorie Reynolds, Cecil Kellaway, Joseph Schildkraut, Reginald Owen, Constance Collier, Hillary Brooke. 1946

MONSIEUR HIRE ★★★★ A grouchy recluse, already suspected of murder, spies on his lovely neighbor; is he working up to kill again? Slow-moving but suspenseful, beautifully photographed and acted. In French with English subtitles. Rated PG-13 for subtle eroticism. 88m. DIR: Patrice Leconte. CAST: Michel Blanc, Sandrine Bonnaire, Luc Thuillier, Eric Berenger. 1990

MONSIEUR VERDOUX ★★★★ A trend-setting black comedy in which a dandified, Parisian Bluebeard murders wives for their money. Wry humor abounds. Charlie Chaplin is superb in the title role. But it's Martha Raye who steals the film—most decidedly in the rowboat scene. The genius that made Chaplin famous the world over shows throughout. B&W; 123m. DIR: Charles Chaplin. CAST: Charlie Chaplin, Martha Raye, Isobel Elsom, Marilyn Nash, William Frawley. 1947 DVD

MONSIEUR VINCENT ★★★★ Winner of a special Academy Award, this is a moving, beautifully photographed biography of St. Vincent de Paul, patron saint of social workers. Even if you don't think you'd be interested in the subject matter, it's worth seeing for the performance of Pierre Fresnay, one of France's greatest actors. In French with English subtitles. 73m. DIR: Maurice Cloche. CAST: Pierre Fresnay, Aimée Clairiond, Jean Debucourt. 1949

MONSIGNOR ♥ A Vatican priest seduces a student nun and makes deals with the Mafia to help the Church's finances. Rated R for profanity, nudity, and violence. 122m. DIR: Frank Perry. CAST: Christopher Reeve, Genevieve Bujold, Fernando Rey, Jason Miller. 1982

MONSIGNOR QUIXOTE ★★★1/2 When a newly appointed monsignor (Alec Guinness) sets out on a holiday with a confirmed Communist (Leo McKern), the two form a strong friendship. Together they challenge corruption within the church. Guinness, playing Don Quixote's grandson, is an innocent idealist while McKern plays the crusty cynic. Made for HBO. 123m. DIR: Rodney Bennett. CAST: Alec Guinness, Leo McKern, Ian Richardson. 1985

MONSOON ♥ An American finds love in the arms of his fiancée's mysterious, jungle-wandering sister. 79m. DIR: Rod Amateau. CAST: Ursula Thiess, George Nader, Myron Healey, Diana Douglas, Ellen Corby. 1953 DVD

MONSTER, THE (1925) ★★★ Horror buffs who grew up seeing tantalizing stills from this Lon Chaney Sr. vehicle in monster magazines may be disappointed initially to find that it's a comedy. But there is atmosphere to spare, and Chaney—as a mad scientist and the title fiend—is a bonus. B&W; 86m. DIR: Roland West. CAST: Lon Chaney Sr., Gertrude Olmstead. 1925

MONSTER, THE (1996) ★★ A small-time nobody is mistaken for a sex-crazed serial killer and unwittingly stumbles deeper in trouble with the police. The jokes keep coming, but most haven't been funny since the long-ago heyday of burlesque. If sheer physical effort could make someone funny, the frenetic Benigni would be Buster Keaton—but it can't, and he isn't. In Italian with English subtitles. Not rated; contains brief nudity, suggested violence, and much sexual humor. 110m. DIR: Roberto Benigni. CAST: Roberto Benigni, Michel Blanc, Nicoletta Braschi, Dominique Lavanant, Jean-Claude Brialy. 1996 DVD

MONSTER AND THE GIRL, THE ★★1/2 White slavery is an intriguing, *noir*ish theme before the sci-fi element spins the story out of control when a criminal's brain is transplanted into an ape's skull. Not rated. B&W; 65m. DIR: Stuart Heisler. CAST: George Zucco, Ellen Drew, Robert Paige, Paul Lukas. **1941**

MONSTER CLUB, THE ★★1/2 Better-than-average series of horror tales by Ronald Chetwynd-Hayes, linked by a sinister nightclub where the guys 'n' ghouls can hang out. All the stories keep tongue firmly in cheek and involve imaginary creatures of mixed parentage, such as a "shadmonk," born of a vampire and werewolf. Rated PG for violence. **1981**. DIR: Roy Ward Baker. CAST: Vincent Price, John Carradine, Donald Pleasence, Stuart Whitman, Britt Ekland, Simon Ward. **1981**

MONSTER DOG 💣 Alice Cooper's music video, shown in the first five minutes of the film, is the only part of this release worth watching. Not rated; the film has violence. 88m. DIR: Clyde Anderson. CAST: Alice Cooper, Victoria Vera. **1986**

MONSTER FROM A PREHISTORIC PLANET ★ A bit of added humanity makes this more than just another Japanese big-rubber-monster movie. Parents of a captive baby monster smash across the countryside trying to find him. Plenty of smashed models and bad dialogue make this a must for fans of this genre. Rated PG. 90m. DIR: Haruyasu Noguchi. CAST: Tarrin. **1967**

MONSTER FROM GREEN HELL ★★ Giant rubber wasps on the rampage in Africa. Our heroes battle a lethargic script to the death. In an attempt to revive the audience, the last reel of the movie was filmed in color. Big deal. B&W/color; 71m. DIR: Kenneth Crane. CAST: Jim Davis, Barbara Turner, Eduardo Ciannelli. **1957**

MONSTER FROM THE OCEAN FLOOR, THE 💣 A legendary sea monster is discovered off the coast of Mexico. B&W; 64m. DIR: Wyott Ordung. CAST: Anne Kimball, Stuart Wade, Wyott Ordung. **1954**

MONSTER HIGH 💣 Inept, dull, and tasteless attempt to spoof the alien invader, end of the world, and monster genres—all of it taking place at a high school. Rated R for gore, language, and nudity. 84m. DIR: Rudiger Poe. CAST: Dean Iandoli. **1989**

MONSTER IN A BOX ★★★★ Nobody can sit and talk to the camera like Spalding Gray. In this, the monologist's second filmed stage performance, Gray discusses his brushes with life and death as he wrote his pseudoautobiographical novel *Impossible Vacation*. Rated PG-13 for profanity. 90m. DIR: Nick Broomfield. CAST: Spalding Gray. **1991**

MONSTER IN THE CLOSET ★★1/2 Horror spoof about a music-loving, bloodthirsty mutant that inhabits people's closets. Some jokes bomb, but most hit home. John Carradine is priceless in his short role. Rated PG for profanity and brief nudity. 100m. DIR: Bob Dahlin. CAST: Donald Grant, Denise Dubarry, Claude Akins, Henry Gibson, John Carradine, Stella Stevens. **1987** DVD

MONSTER MAKER, THE ★★ A scientist conducting experiments in glandular research injects a pianist with a serum that causes his body to grow abnormally large, especially his hands. Low-budget thriller does very little. B&W; 64m. DIR: Sam Newfield. CAST: J. Carrol Naish, Ralph Morgan, Wanda McKay, Sam Flint, Glenn Strange. **1944** DVD

MONSTER OF PIEDRAS BLANCAS, THE 💣 This monstrosity features a human-shaped sea creature with a penchant for separating humans from their heads. B&W; 71m. DIR: Irvin Berwick. CAST: Le Tremayne, Forrest Lewis. **1958**

MONSTER OF THE ISLAND, THE 💣 The "Monster" in this cheap, misleadingly titled Italian crime drama is the ruthless head of a drug-smuggling ring. B&W; 87m. DIR: Roberto Montero, Alberto Vecchietti. CAST: Boris Karloff. **1953**

MONSTER ON THE CAMPUS ★★ The blood of a prehistoric fish turns a university professor into a murderous ape-beast. Below-average effort from sci-fi specialist Jack Arnold. B&W; 77m. DIR: Jack Arnold. CAST: Arthur Franz, Joanna Moore, Judson Pratt, Troy Donahue. **1959**

MONSTER SQUAD, THE ★★★ A group of kids form a club to help combat an infiltration of monsters in their town. What unfolds is a clever mixture of Hollywood sci-fi monster effects and a well-conceived spoof of horror movies, past and present. Rated PG-13 for violence. 82m. DIR: Fred Dekker. CAST: Andre Gower, Duncan Regehr, Stan Shaw, Tommy Noonan. **1987**

MONSTER THAT CHALLENGED THE WORLD, THE ★★ This late-1950s sci-fi programmer is set apart by only one thing: the giant monster, which is life-size (not a miniature) and given plenty of screen time. Hero Tim Holt is ludicrous as a navy commander battling huge, caterpillar-like creatures and romancing a young widow. B&W; 83m. DIR: Arnold Laven. CAST: Tim Holt, Audrey Dalton, Hans Conried. **1957**

MONSTER WALKS, THE ★★1/2 This independently produced creaker contains most of the elements popular in old-house horror shows of the late 1920s and early 1930s, including deadly apes, secret passages, gloomy storms, and thoroughly petrified ethnic types. Tolerably funny if you overlook the racist portrayal by Sleep 'n' Eat (Willie Best): B&W; 57m. DIR: Frank Strayer. CAST: Rex Lease, Vera Reynolds, Mischa Auer, Sheldon Lewis, Willie Best. **1932**

MONTANA (1990) ★★1/2 Very slow-paced story of a Montana cattle-ranching family torn between the old values of the land and selling out to coal developers. Film loses its focus early on. Hit-and-miss script by Larry McMurtry doesn't help. Made for cable. 73m. DIR: William A. Graham. CAST: Richard Crenna, Gena Rowlands, Lea Thompson, Justin Deas, Elizabeth Berridge, Scott Coffey, Darren Calton, Peter Fonda. **1990**

MONTANA (1997) ★★1/2 Kyra Sedgwick and Robin Tunney are the main reasons to sit through this formulaic thriller about a professional female assassin named Claire (Sedgwick) and her boss's runaway girlfriend, whom she's assigned to bring back. It's a low-level job, one that Claire resents, but when Kitty (Tunney) ends up killing someone while in her custody, the two find themselves on the run from both sides of the law. Some spirited moments don't add up to a whole. Rated R for violence, language, and adult situations. 96m. DIR: Jennifer Leitzes. CAST: Kyra Sedgwick, Stanley Tucci, Robin Tunney, Robbie Coltrane, John Ritter, Philip Seymour Hoffman. **1997**

MONTANA BELLE ★★1/2 Jane Russell plays notorious Belle Starr, the female bandit who rode with the

Dalton Gang. As Western programmers go, this is not bad, but Jane in a blonde wig just doesn't cut it! Originally filmed in color, but video copies are in black and white. B&W; 81m. DIR: Allan Dwan. CAST: Jane Russell, George Brent, Scott Brady, Forrest Tucker. **1951**

MONTE CARLO ★★ Tacky TV miniseries features Joan Collins as a singing spy during World War II. If you enjoy soap operas, you won't mind. Scenery is a plus. 205m. DIR: Anthony Page. CAST: Joan Collins, George Hamilton, Lauren Hutton, Malcolm McDowell. **1986**

MONTE WALSH ★★★1/2 Sad but satisfying Western about a couple of saddle pals (Lee Marvin, Jack Palance) attempting to make the transition to a new age and century. Cinematographer William Fraker made an impressive directorial debut with this fine film. Rated R for violence. 106m. DIR: William Fraker. CAST: Lee Marvin, Jack Palance, Jeanne Moreau, Mitchell Ryan, Jim Davis. **1970**

MONTENEGRO ★★★★ Susan Anspach stars as a discontented housewife who wanders into a Yugoslavian nightclub, finds herself surrounded by sex and violence, and discovers she rather likes it, in this outlandish, outrageous, and sometimes shocking black comedy. The laughs come with the realization that this movie is totally bonkers. Rated R because of profanity, nudity, sex, and violence. 98m. DIR: Dusan Makavejev. CAST: Susan Anspach, John Zacharias. **1981 DVD**

MONTEREY POP ★★★★ Despite its ragged sound by today's digital standards, *Monterey Pop* is a historical masterpiece. A chance to see legendary Sixties soloists and groups in their prime far outweighs any technical drawbacks. This was the concert that kicked off 1967's Summer of Love, and with it, a generation of mega-performer shows that culminated in Woodstock. 72m. DIR: D. A. Pennebaker. CAST: Jimi Hendrix, Otis Redding, The Who, The Animals, Jefferson Airplane, Janis Joplin, Country Joe and the Fish, The Mamas and the Papas, Booker T. and the MGs, Ravi Shankar. **1969**

MONTH BY THE LAKE, A ★★★ At an Italian resort before World War II, a middle-aged spinster vies with a pretty American governess for the attention of a stuffy retired soldier. Details of the story and period don't always ring true, and director John Irvin maintains a too-hectic pace, but the acting is good and the film's warmth is real. Rated PG. 97m. DIR: John Irvin. CAST: Vanessa Redgrave, Edward Fox, Uma Thurman, Alessandro Gassman, Carlo Cartier, Alida Valli. **1995**

MONTH IN THE COUNTRY, A ★★★ Two emotionally scarred World War I veterans find themselves working for a month in a small Yorkshire village. The acting is flawless, but a gripping plot never quite materializes. Rated PG. 96m. DIR: Pat O'Connor. CAST: Colin Firth, Kenneth Branagh, Natasha Richardson. **1987**

MONTY PYTHON AND THE HOLY GRAIL ★★★1/2 The Monty Python gang assault the legend of King Arthur and his knights in this often uproariously funny, sometimes tedious, movie. Rated PG. 90m. DIR: Terry Gilliam. CAST: Terry Jones, Graham Chapman, John Cleese, Terry Gilliam, Michael Palin. **1974 DVD**

MONTY PYTHON LIVE AT THE HOLLYWOOD BOWL ★★★★ Hold on to your sides! Those Monty Python crazies are back with more unbridled hilarity. Rated R for profanity, nudity, and the best in bad taste. 73m. DIR: Terry Hughes. CAST: John Cleese, Eric Idle, Graham Chapman, Terry Jones, Michael Palin, Terry Gilliam. **1982**

MONTY PYTHON'S FLYING CIRCUS (TV SERIES) ★★★★ This is a series of videos featuring highlights from the popular English TV show of the early 1970s. All the madcap characters remain intact along with the innovative and trendsetting animation by Terry Gilliam. You don't have to be British to enjoy the various political asides and lampoons. You do have to like fast-paced, off-the-wall craziness. The talented cast also conceived and wrote all of the material. Each tape 60m. DIR: Ian McNaughton. CAST: Graham Chapman, John Cleese, Terry Gilliam, Eric Idle, Terry Jones, Michael Palin. **1970–1972 DVD**

MONTY PYTHON'S THE MEANING OF LIFE ★★★★ Those Monty Python goons perform a series of sketches on the important issues of life. According to Michael Palin, the film "ranges from philosophy to history to medicine to halibut—especially halibut." This heady mixture of satiric and surreal bits about the life cycle from birth to death may prove offensive to some and a sheer delight to others. Rated R for offensive goings-on. 103m. DIR: Terry Jones. CAST: John Cleese, Eric Idle, Graham Chapman, Terry Jones, Terry Gilliam. **1983 DVD**

MONUMENT AVE. ★★★ A small-time hoodlum begins to question the worth of his aimless life among the Irish gangs of South Boston. The film has a documentary feel and some of the muttered dialogue is almost unintelligible; but the story is believably low-key and the acting excellent. Not rated; contains drug use, violence, and extensive profanity. 93m. DIR: Ted Demme. CAST: Denis Leary, Colm Meaney, Martin Sheen, Billy Crudup, Ian Hart. **1998 DVD**

MOON AND SIXPENCE, THE ★★★1/2 One of the better movies based on a Somerset Maugham novel. George Sanders is appropriately disillusioned as artist Charles Strickland, a character loosely based on real-life painter Paul Gauguin. He moves to Tahiti to fulfill his ambitions when the constrictions of European society get him down. B&W; 89m. DIR: Albert Lewin. CAST: George Sanders, Herbert Marshall, Florence Bates, Doris Dudley, Elena Verdugo, Albert Basserman, Eric Blore. **1942**

MOON 44 ★★1/2 Michael Paré is an internal affairs cop for a large corporation investigating the theft of giant outer-space mining rigs in this passable sci-fi adventure. Good flying effects. Rated R for violence and profanity. 102m. DIR: Roland Emmerich. CAST: Michael Paré, Lisa Eichhorn, Malcolm McDowell, Stephen Geoffreys, Roscoe Lee Browne. **1990**

MOON IN SCORPIO 🖤 Three Vietnam War vets and their girlfriends go on a sailing trip that turns to horror. Not rated; has violence, profanity, and nudity. 90m. DIR: Gary Graver. CAST: Britt Ekland, John Phillip Law, William Smith. **1987**

MOON IN THE GUTTER, THE 🖤 A pretentious, self-consciously artistic bore that seems to defy any viewer to sit through it. Rated R for profanity, nudity, and violence. In French with subtitles. 126m. **DIR:** Jean-Jacques Beineix. **CAST:** Gérard Depardieu, Nastassja Kinski, Victoria Abril. 1983

MOON IS BLUE, THE ★★ It's hard to believe this comedy, based on a stage hit, was once considered highly controversial. We doubt that even your grandmother would be offended by this very moral film. The thin plot concerns a young woman who fends off two slightly aging playboys by repeatedly vowing to remain a virgin until married. B&W; 95m. **DIR:** Otto Preminger. **CAST:** William Holden, David Niven, Maggie McNamara, Tom Tully, Dawn Addams. 1953

MOON OF THE WOLF ★★ Another ABC Movie of the Week makes it to video. Disappointing yarn of the search for a werewolf on the loose in Louisiana. Good acting by the leads, but there's not enough action or excitement to sustain interest. 73m. **DIR:** Daniel Petrie. **CAST:** David Janssen, Barbara Rush, Bradford Dillman, John Beradino. 1972

MOON OVER BROADWAY ★★★1/2 Documentarians D. A. Pennebaker and Chris Hegedus follow the development of a Broadway play (Ken Ludwig's *Moon over Buffalo*, starring Carol Burnett and Philip Bosco) from first rehearsals to opening night. It's a rare glimpse behind the curtain of big-time theater, with all its pleasures, squabbles, and insecurities. All are to be commended for allowing such a generous look at the often awkward creative process. Not rated; suitable for all audiences. 97m. **DIR:** Chris Hegedus, D. A. Pennebaker. **CAST:** Carol Burnett, Philip Bosco, Ken Ludwig, Tom Moore. 1997 DVD

MOON OVER HARLEM ★★1/2 Uneven melodrama featuring an all-black cast. The unlikely director is German émigré Edgar G. Ulmer, the visionary film poet who worked with F. W. Murnau and other German Expressionists. Ulmer has a considerable reputation among French critics. B&W; 77m. **DIR:** Edgar G. Ulmer. **CAST:** Bud Harris. 1939 DVD

MOON OVER MIAMI ★★★ Texas sisters Betty Grable and Carole Landis arrive in Miami to hunt for rich husbands. After a suitable round of romantic adventures, they snare penniless Don Ameche and millionaire Robert Cummings. A fun film that helped establish Grable. 91m. **DIR:** Walter Lang. **CAST:** Don Ameche, Robert Cummings, Betty Grable, Carole Landis, Charlotte Greenwood, Jack Haley. 1941

MOON OVER PARADOR ★★1/2 This misfired comedy thrusts Richard Dreyfuss, who plays a modestly successful actor, into the role of his career: impersonating the recently deceased dictator of an anonymous Caribbean country. Political strongman Raul Julia wants the charade to continue until he can take over smoothly. Everything rattles to a most unconvincing conclusion. Rated PG-13 for language and mild sexual themes. 105m. **DIR:** Paul Mazursky. **CAST:** Richard Dreyfuss, Raul Julia, Sonia Braga, Jonathan Winters, Fernando Rey, Polly Holliday. 1988

MOON PILOT ★★★1/2 Tom Tryon gets volunteered to become the first astronaut to circle the moon. Good script, with satire and laughs in ample quantities. Rated G. 98m. **DIR:** James Neilson. **CAST:** Tom

Tryon, Brian Keith, Edmond O'Brien, Dany Saval. 1962

MOON TRAP ♥ Two astronauts find a race of resourceful mechanical aliens on the lunar surface. Rated R for language and nudity. 92m. **DIR:** Robert Dyke. **CAST:** Walter Koenig, Bruce Campbell. 1989

MOONBASE ★★ In the year 2045, inhabitants of Earth have resorted to using the moon as a dump. That's the good news. The bad news is that some vicious criminals have escaped from an orbiting prison and have landed on the moon. They plan to use the nuclear weapons buried there as their ticket back to Earth. OK effects, but no big deal. Rated R for language and violence. 89m. **DIR:** Paolo Mazzucato. **CAST:** Scott Plank, Jocelyn Seagrave, Kurt Fuller, Robert O'Reilly. 1997

MOONCHILD ★★1/2 Arguably Todd Sheets's best film, this tale of genetically created werewolves could have been an intriguing sci-fi shocker. Instead, what we get is a gore flick with little plot interest. Not rated; contains violence, gore, and profanity. 102m. **DIR:** Todd Sheets. **CAST:** Auggi Alvarez, Kathleen McSweeney. 1994

MOONCUSSERS ★★1/2 Kevin Corcoran stars as a boy who discovers the secrets of the Mooncussers—pirates who work on moonless nights to draw ships to their doom by means of false signal lamps on shore. 85m. **DIR:** James Neilson. **CAST:** Oscar Homolka, Kevin Corcoran, Robert Emhardt, Joan Freeman. 1962

MOONDANCE ★★★ The bond between two brothers is stretched to the breaking point when they fall in love with the same beautiful young girl. Well-acted film features songs by Van Morrison. Rated R for nudity, sexual situations, and profanity. 96m. **DIR:** Dagmar Hirtz. **CAST:** Ruaidhri Conroy, Ian Shaw, Julie Brendler, Marianne Faithfull. 1994

MOONLIGHT AND VALENTINO ★★ Recent widow receives solace from her sister, best friend, and ex-stepmother. The film should be a powerhouse of female bonding, but the script is aimless and dithering, and no one—least of all director David Anspaugh—knows what to do with it. Rated R for profanity and brief nudity. 104m. **DIR:** David Anspaugh. **CAST:** Elizabeth Perkins, Gwyneth Paltrow, Kathleen Turner, Whoopi Goldberg, Jon Bon Jovi, Josef Sommer, Peter Coyote. 1995

MOONLIGHTING (1983) ★★★★1/2 This film, a political parable criticizing the Soviet Union's suppression of Solidarity in Poland, may sound rather heavy, gloomy, and dull. It isn't. Written and directed by Jerzy Skolimowski, it focuses on four Polish construction workers remodeling a flat in London. Give it a look. In Polish with English subtitles. Rated PG for very brief nudity. 97m. **DIR:** Jerzy Skolimowski. **CAST:** Jeremy Irons, Eugene Lipinski. 1983

MOONLIGHTING (1985) (TV PILOT) ★★★★ This is the pilot film for the delightfully offbeat ABC series. Maddie, a supersuccessful model, suddenly finds herself facing poverty, thanks to an embezzler. She decides to sell off all her assets, including a money-losing detective agency. David, a fast-talking, irresistible eccentric, tries to talk her into making a career of sleuthing instead. Bruce Willis is dazzling as David. And the chemistry beween Willis and Cybill Shepherd heats up to just the right temperature. 97m. DIR: Robert Butler. CAST: Cybill Shepherd, Bruce Willis, Allyce Beasley. 1985 DVD

MOONRAKER 🎬 The James Bond series hit absolute rock bottom in 1979 with this outer-space adventure. Rated PG. 126m. DIR: Lewis Gilbert. CAST: Roger Moore, Lois Chiles, Michel Lonsdale. 1979 DVD

MOONRISE ★★ Being the son of a man hanged for murder isn't easy, and Danny (Dane Clark) has grown up with quite a chip on his shoulder. Very melodramatic. B&W; 90m. DIR: Frank Borzage. CAST: Dane Clark, Gail Russell, Lloyd Bridges, Ethel Barrymore. 1948

MOONSHINE COUNTY EXPRESS ★★ In this bogus action flick, William Conrad has his hands full with the three vengeful daughters of a man he just murdered. Rated PG for mild language and violence. 95m. DIR: Gus Trikonis. CAST: John Saxon, Susan Howard, William Conrad, Dub Taylor. 1977

MOONSHINE HIGHWAY ★★1/2 This tale of illicit love and illegal alcohol is set in Tennessee in 1957, during the days when dry states still offered outlets to those who manufactured black-market moonshine. Restless Kyle MacLachlan divides his time between playing highway tag with the Feds and romancing the local sheriff's wife. Eventually, he's forced to make choices. Rated PG-13 for profanity and violence. 96m. DIR: Andy Armstrong. CAST: Kyle MacLachlan, Randy Quaid, Maria Del Mar, Alex Carter, Jeremy Ratchford, Gary Farmer. 1995

MOONSPINNERS, THE ★★★ A young girl (Hayley Mills) becomes involved in a jewel theft in Crete. The best features of this film are the appearance of a "grownup" Hayley Mills and the return to the screen of Pola Negri. The film is essentially a lightweight melodrama in the Hitchcock mold. 118m. DIR: James Neilson. CAST: Hayley Mills, Eli Wallach, Pola Negri, Peter McEnery, Joan Greenwood, Irene Papas. 1964

MOONSTRUCK ★★★★1/2 Cher, Nicolas Cage, and a superb supporting cast enliven this delightful comedy about a group of Italian-Americans who find amore when the moon shines bright. Director Norman Jewison and screenwriter John Patrick Shanley make one hilarious complication follow another. Rated PG for profanity and suggested sex. 102m. DIR: Norman Jewison. CAST: Cher, Nicolas Cage, Vincent Gardenia, Olympia Dukakis, Danny Aiello, Julie Bovasso, John Mahoney, Feodor Chaliapin. 1987 DVD

MORAN OF THE LADY LETTY ★★★ A shanghaied socialite meets and falls in love with a tough seafarer, who turns out to be a woman in disguise. Dandy location photography around Catalina. A change of pace for Valentino purists. Silent. B&W; 70m. DIR: George Melford. CAST: Rudolph Valentino. 1922

MORE ★★★1/2 A German youth, on the road after finishing college, becomes enamored of a free-spirited American girl in Paris. Barbet Schroeder's first film as a director, this grim portrait of directionless young people is ironically best remembered for its Pink Floyd score. In English. Not rated, contains nudity. 110m. DIR: Barbet Schroeder. CAST: Mimsy Farmer, Klaus Grunberg. 1969

MORE AMERICAN GRAFFITI ★★ Sequel to George Lucas's high-spirited, nostalgic *American Graffiti* lacks the charm of the original as it follows up on the lives of the various characters. There are a few bright moments, but a split-screen technique that didn't work when the film was initially released is even more annoying on video. Rated PG. 111m. DIR: B.W.L. Norton. CAST: Ron Howard, Paul LeMat, Candy Clark, Bo Hopkins, Cindy Williams, Charles Martin Smith, Mackenzie Phillips, Harrison Ford, Scott Glenn, Mary Kay Place, Rosanna Arquette. 1979

MORE THE MERRIER, THE ★★★★ This delightful comedy is set in Washington, D.C., during the hotel and housing shortage of the hectic World War II years. Charles Coburn earned a supporting Oscar as the old curmudgeon trying to cope with the housing problem while advising Joel McCrea and Jean Arthur on how to handle their love life. (Cary Grant played Coburn's character when this was remade as *Walk, Don't Run*.) B&W; 104m. DIR: George Stevens. CAST: Joel McCrea, Jean Arthur, Charles Coburn. 1943

MORE WILD WILD WEST ★★1/2 TV movie is a pale reminder of the irresistible original series. The Old West's most invincible secret service agents, James West and Artemus Gordon, again come out of retirement, this time to rescue the world from an invisibility plot. Jonathan Winters hams it up as the villainous Albert Paradine II. There's too much silly comedy, not enough excitement. 94m. DIR: Burt Kennedy. CAST: Robert Conrad, Ross Martin, Jonathan Winters, Harry Morgan, René Auberjonois, Liz Torres, Victor Buono, Dr. Joyce Brothers, Emma Samms. 1980

MORGAN ★★★★ In this cult favorite, Vanessa Redgrave decides to leave her wacky husband (David Warner). He's a wild man who has a thing for gorillas (this brings scenes from *King Kong*). Nevertheless, he tries to win her back in an increasingly unorthodox manner. Deeply imbedded in the 1960s, this film still brings quite a few laughs. B&W; 97m. DIR: Karel Reisz. CAST: Vanessa Redgrave, David Warner, Robert Stephens, Irene Handl. 1966

MORGAN STEWART'S COMING HOME ★★ Made before *Pretty in Pink* but released after it to take advantage of the impression Jon Cryer made in that John Hughes teen comedy. The young actor stars in this tepid comedy as a preppie who tries to reorder his family's priorities. Cryer has some good moments, and Lynn Redgrave is top-notch as his mom, but the laughs just aren't there. Rated PG-13. 92m. DIR: Alan Smithee. CAST: Jon Cryer, Lynn Redgrave, Viveka Davis, Paul Gleason, Nicholas Pryor. 1987

MORGAN THE PIRATE ★★★ This fictionalized account of the adventures of the historical Henry Morgan (with muscle man Steve Reeves in the title role) is perhaps the most entertaining of that actor's many Italian-made features. Even by current standards, there is plenty of action and romance. 93m. DIR: André de Toth; Primo Zeglio. CAST: Steve Reeves, Valerie Lagrange, Ivo Garbani. 1961

MORITURI ★★1/2 Marlon Brando portrays a spy working for the British who, through a series of moral equations involving anti-Nazism versus Nazism, convinces the captain of a German freighter on a voyage from Japan to Germany to side with the

Allies. The concept is good, but the script gets weaker and weaker as the film progresses. B&W; 128m. DIR: Bernhard Wicki. CAST: Marlon Brando, Yul Brynner, Janet Margolin, Trevor Howard, Wally Cox, William Redfield. 1965

MORK & MINDY (TV SERIES) ★★★1/2 Sitcom that launched stand-up comic Robin Williams to superstardom. Playing Mork from the planet Ork, he makes zany observations and assessments of Earth life and customs. Some of his funniest bits were unscripted ad-lib. Pam Dawber plays it straight as his kindly and informative roommate. Four volumes, each containing two episodes and lasting approximately 50m. DIR: Howard Storm, Jeff Chambers. CAST: Robin Williams, Pam Dawber, Conrad Janis, Elizabeth Kerr, Tom Poston, Jay Thomas. 1978–1982

MORNING AFTER, THE ★★★1/2 An alcoholic ex–movie star (Jane Fonda) wakes up one morning in bed next to a dead man and is unable to remember what happened the night before. Fonda is terrific as the heroine-victim, and Jeff Bridges gives a solid performance as the ex-cop who comes to her aid. The result is an enjoyable thriller in the style of Jagged Edge. Rated R for profanity. 103m. DIR: Sidney Lumet. CAST: Jane Fonda, Jeff Bridges, Raul Julia, Diane Salinger, Richard Foronjy. 1986

MORNING GLORY (1933) ★★1/2 A naïve young actress comes to New York to find fame and romance. Based on the Zoe Akins play, the stagy film version hasn't aged well. But Katharine Hepburn is charismatic as the actress. She won her first Academy Award for this showy performance. B&W; 74m. DIR: Lowell Sherman. CAST: Katharine Hepburn, Adolphe Menjou, Douglas Fairbanks Jr., C. Aubrey Smith. 1933

MORNING GLORY (1992) ★★1/2 Based on a book by LaVyrle Spencer, an ex-con applies for a job as the husband of a reclusive woman. Just when they fall in love, he's charged with killing a floozy. Unfortunately the story is very slow and boring. Rated PG-13 for profanity. 96m. DIR: Steven H. Stern. CAST: Christopher Reeve, Deborah Raffin, Lloyd Bochner, Nina Foch, Helen Shaver, J. T. Walsh. 1992

MOROCCO ★★★ The fabulous and fabled Marlene Dietrich in her first Hollywood film. She's a cabaret singer stranded in exotic, sinister Morocco, who must choose between suave, rich Adolphe Menjou, or dashing French Legionnaire Gary Cooper. The scene at the oasis is classic 1930s cinematography. B&W; 92m. DIR: Josef von Sternberg. CAST: Gary Cooper, Adolphe Menjou, Marlene Dietrich. 1930

MORONS FROM OUTER SPACE ★★1/2 Four aliens from a distant planet crash-land on Earth, but their arrival is not a secret and they soon become international celebrities. The comedy comes from the fact that they're idiots and act accordingly. Unfortunately, the morons are not as funny as the viewer would hope. Rated PG for language. 78m. DIR: Mike Hodges. CAST: Griff Rhys Jones, Mel Smith, James B. Sikking, Dinsdale Landen. 1985

MORRISON MURDERS, THE ★★★1/2 This made-for-cable original, based on a true story, focuses on two brothers who try to cope with the savage murders of their parents and younger brother. Hard times await both of them, as grief is soon followed by

accusations that one of them is the killer. Good acting by John Corbett and company in this engaging story. Not rated; contains violence. 95m. DIR: Chris Thomson. CAST: John Corbett, Jonathon Scarfe, Maya McLaughlin, Gordon Clapp. 1996

MORTAL KOMBAT ★★1/2 Yet another tiresome video-game-turned-film, this one highlighted mostly by its shrill shock-rock soundtrack. The plot is stolen shamelessly from Enter the Dragon, with three stalwart heroes battling extraterrestrial champions over the fate of Earth. Christopher Lambert looks particularly silly as a wise sage who speaks in fortune-cookie riddles. Rated PG-13 for surprisingly savage violence. 101m. DIR: Paul Anderson. CAST: Robin Shou, Linden Ashby, Bridgette Wilson, Cary-Hiroyuki Tagawa, Talisa Soto, Christopher Lambert. 1995 DVD

MORTAL KOMBAT: ANNIHILATION ★★ The song lyric "Everybody was kung fu fighting" summarizes the plot, character, and theme of this video game spinoff. The chosen defenders of Earth must defeat the evil minions of an alternate dimension. Elaborate special effects can't compensate for the mediocre acting and near plotless premise. This loud music/video arcade combo is just an excuse for nonstop violence. Rated PG-13 for violence. 95m. DIR: John R. Leonetti. CAST: Robin Shou, Talisa Soto, Brian Thompson, Sandra Hess, Lynn Red Williams. 1997 DVD

MORTAL KOMBAT: THE ANIMATED MOVIE ★★1/2 The Mortal Kombat franchise becomes an animated, direct-to-video movie that's sure to please fans of the video game. Using computer-generated animation, this film depicts the origins of the series' characters and engages them in plenty of action and mayhem. Rated PG for animated violence. 60m. DIR: Joe Franck. 1995

MORTAL PASSIONS 🎗 A slut plots to murder her wealthy husband with the help of her sheepish boyfriend. Rated R for violence, nudity, and profanity. 96m. DIR: Andrew Lane. CAST: Zach Galligan, Krista Erickson, Luca Bercovici, Michael Bowen. 1990

MORTAL SINS (1990) (DANGEROUS OBSESSION) ★★1/2 Private eye Brian Benben becomes embroiled in a series of murders that lead to television ministries and the mysterious daughter of a powerful television evangelist. Rated R for violence and nudity. 85m. DIR: Yuri Sivo. CAST: Debrah Farentino, Brian Benben, Anthony LaPaglia, James Harper. 1990

MORTAL SINS (1992) ★★★ It appears that a priest is murdering young women, then giving them last rites. Father Thomas (Christopher Reeve) hears the confession of the murderer and starts to play detective. A few good twists keep the viewer guessing. Not rated, made for cable, but contains violence. 95m. DIR: Bradford May. CAST: Christopher Reeve, Roxann Biggs, Francis Guinan, Weston McMillan, Phillip R. Allen, Lisa Vultaggio, George Touliatos, Mavor Moore, Karen Kondazian. 1992

MORTAL STORM, THE ★★★★ Phyllis Bottome's famous novel about the rise of Nazism makes good screen fare in spite of the screenwriter's apparent reluctance to call a spade a spade. Germany is never identified even though it is quite obvious in this story about a schoolteacher's family in the early days of

VIDEO MOVIE GUIDE 2001

739

World War II. Very well acted. B&W; 100m. DIR: Frank Borzage. CAST: James Stewart, Margaret Sullavan, Robert Young, Bonita Granville, Frank Morgan, Irene Rich, Dan Dailey, Tom Drake, Robert Stack, Maria Ouspenskaya, Gene Reynolds, Ward Bond. **1940**

MORTAL THOUGHTS ★★★ Demi Moore and Glenne Headly give strong performances in this relentlessly downbeat and disturbing drama. Director Alan Rudolph and screenwriters William Reilly and Claude Kerven explore the possible murder of an abusive, foulmouthed, drug-addicted husband (Bruce Willis) by his wife (Headly) and her best friend (Moore). Rated R for violence and profanity. 104m. DIR: Alan Rudolph. CAST: Demi Moore, Glenne Headly, Bruce Willis, John Pankow, Harvey Keitel, Billie Neal, Frank Vincent. **1991 DVD**

MORTUARY ACADEMY ★★ Academic comedy fails to advance to the head of the class. The brothers Grimm (yes, that's their last name) must make it through the dreaded academy in order to inherit big bucks. Typical. Rated R for nudity, language, and some violence. 86m. DIR: Michael Schroeder. CAST: Christopher Atkins, Tracey Walter, Lynn Danielson, Mary Woronov, Perry Lang. **1992**

MOSAIC PROJECT, THE 🎭 Nonsensical spy saga about two small-town men who are mistakenly implanted with computer chips that transform them into superintelligent, superathletic government agents. Rated R for violence. 89m. DIR: John Sjorgen. CAST: Jon Tabler, Ben Marley, Colleen Coffey, Julie Strain, Joe Estevez, Robert Z'dar, Lea Osborn. **1995**

MOSCOW DOES NOT BELIEVE IN TEARS ★★★★ For all its rewards, this film requires a bit of patience on the part of the viewer. The first hour of the tragic comedy is almost excruciatingly slow. But once it gets deeper into the story, you're very glad you toughed it out. MPAA unrated, but contains brief nudity and brief violence. 152m. DIR: Vladimir Menshov. CAST: Vera Alentova, Irina Muravyova. **1980**

MOSCOW ON THE HUDSON ★★★★1/2 Robin Williams stars in this sweet, funny, sad, and sexy comedy as a Russian circus performer who, while on tour in the United States, decides to defect after experiencing the wonders of Bloomingdale's department store in New York. Paul Mazursky cowrote and directed this touching character study. Rated R for profanity, nudity, suggested sex, and violence. 115m. DIR: Paul Mazursky. CAST: Robin Williams, Maria Conchita Alonso, Cleavant Derricks. **1984**

MOSES (1975) ★★★ This biblical screen story of the Hebrew lawgiver is fairly standard as such films go. Burt Lancaster is well suited to play the stoic Moses. However, in trimming down this six-hour TV miniseries for video release, its makers lost most of the character development in the supporting roles. 141m. DIR: Gianfranco De Bosio. CAST: Burt Lancaster, Anthony Quayle, Irene Papas, Ingrid Thulin, William Lancaster. **1975**

MOSES (1996) ★★★ In this TNT original miniseries, Ben Kingsley shines as a stuttering, self-effacing, reluctant leader to the Hebrews. He leads his people out of Egypt and slavery and then his real problems begin. His people whine and grumble incessantly during their forty years in the desert. Spe-

cial effects are OK but not spectacular and the dialogue is often insipid. Not rated; contains violence. 170m. DIR: Roger Young. CAST: Ben Kingsley, Frank Langella, David Suchet, Maurice Roeves, Philip Stone, Christopher Lee, Enrico Lo Verso, Geraldine McEwan. **1996**

MOSQUITO ★★ Dopey mutant-bug movie saved by hokey special effects and a fondness for the genre. They're big, they're bad, and they suck human blood. Rated R for violence and language. 92m. DIR: Gary Jones. CAST: Gunnar Hansen, Ron Asheton, Steve Dixon, Rachel Loiselle, Tim Lovelace. **1994 DVD**

MOSQUITO COAST, THE ★★★ In spite of the top-notch talent involved, this remains a flawed endeavor. Allie Fox (Harrison Ford) is a monomaniacal genius who can't bear what he perceives to be the rape of the United States, so he drags his wife and four children to the untamed wilderness of the Mosquito Coast in a self-indulgent attempt to mimic the Swiss Family Robinson. Rated PG. 117m. DIR: Peter Weir. CAST: Harrison Ford, Helen Mirren, River Phoenix, Conrad Roberts, Andre Gregory, Martha Plimpton. **1986 DVD**

MOST DANGEROUS GAME, THE ★★★1/2 This sister production to *King Kong* utilizes the same sets, same technical staff, and most of the same cast to tell the story of Count Zaroff, the insane ruler of a secret island where he spends his time hunting the victims of the ships that he wrecks. Filmed many times since and used as a theme for countless television plots, this original is still the standard to measure all the others by. Nonstop action for sixty-three tight minutes. B&W; 63m. DIR: Ernest B. Schoedsack, Irving Pichel. CAST: Joel McCrea, Fay Wray, Leslie Banks, Robert Armstrong. **1932 DVD**

MOST WANTED (1976) ★★1/2 So-so pilot for Robert Stack's TV series. As the head of a special police unit, he works with a computer whiz, psychologist, and undercover detective to crack the most difficult cases. Here, they find a psychopath who has been raping and murdering nuns. Aside from Stack, many of the costars (including Tom Selleck) did not stay with the show. Made-for-TV, this is unrated but contains violence. 78m. DIR: Walter Grauman. CAST: Robert Stack, Tom Selleck, Leslie Charleson, Shelly Novack. **1976**

MOTEL HELL ★★1/2 "It takes all kinds of critters to make Farmer Vincent Fritters!" Ahem! This above-average horror-comedy stars Rory Calhoun (who overplays grandly) as a nice ol' farmer who has struck gold with his dried pork treats. His secret ingredient happens to be human flesh. Rated R for violence. 102m. DIR: Kevin Connor. CAST: Rory Calhoun, Nancy Parsons, Paul Linke, Nina Axelrod, Elaine Joyce. **1980**

MOTHER (1952) ★★★★ This is a beautifully shot black-and-white movie about a working-class mother who must raise her family after her husband's death in post–World War II. While the story appears to be simple, there is great depth in each character. This was voted Japan's best film in 1952. In Japanese with English subtitles. B&W; 98m. DIR: Mikio Naruse. CAST: Kinuyo Tanaka. **1952**

MOTHER (1994) ★★★ Tension builds when an obsessive mom (Diane Ladd) believes she's losing her son to a girlfriend, college, etc. She'll do anything to keep him. Not surprisingly there's more to this little family than meets the eye, making Mom more wacko than originally assumed. Olympia Dukakis plays the lecherous neighbor who has the hots for the son. Rated R for profanity, violence, and gore. 95m. DIR: Frank LaLoggia. CAST: Diane Ladd, Olympia Dukakis, Morgan Weisser, Ele Keats, Matt Clark, Scott Wilson. 1994

MOTHER (1996) ★★★★ Hilarious twist to the traditional coming-of-age film features Albert Brooks as a forty-something writer who returns to his childhood home seeking answers to his personal failures from his mom (Debbie Reynolds). Her penny-pinching ways and sly remarks are meant as constructive criticism but inevitably lead to future psychosis. Brooks reverts to his troubled youth, challenging his mother's every move while avoiding her attempts to send him packing. Unlikely scenario is the film's running joke, and it's a surprisingly good one! Rated PG-13 for language. 97m. DIR: Albert Brooks. CAST: Debbie Reynolds, Albert Brooks, Rob Morrow. 1996

MOTHER AND THE LAW, THE ★★★★★ One of the undisputed masterpieces of the silent cinema. This is the rarely seen complete version of the so-called modern episode of D. W. Griffith's *Intolerance*. A young husband (Bobby Harron) is unjustly indicted for murder and is saved only at the last minute in one of Griffith's most sensational last-minute-rescue climaxes. Silent. B&W; 93m. DIR: D. W. Griffith. CAST: Mae Marsh, Robert Harron. 1914

•**MOTHER AND THE WHORE, THE** ★★★1/2 Considered a masterpiece by those on its wavelength, this long, talky film is not for all viewers. Not unlike *Last Tango in Paris*, it dissects modern soullessness through the sexual yearnings of a male character and the women involved with him. It's a grim challenge, recommended for serious film enthusiasts. In French with English subtitles. Not rated; contains sexual situations and nudity. B&W; 215m. DIR: Jean Eustache. CAST: Jean-Pierre Léaud, Bernadette Lafont, Francoise Lebrun. 1973

MOTHER, JUGS, AND SPEED ★★★ Hang on tight! This is a fast and furious black comedy about a run-down ambulance service that puts body count ahead of patient welfare in the race to the hospital. Bill Cosby and Raquel Welch make an odd combination that clicks. There's also some scene-stealing hilarity from Larry Hagman as an oversexed driver. Rated R. 95m. DIR: Peter Yates. CAST: Bill Cosby, Raquel Welch, Larry Hagman, Harvey Keitel. 1976

MOTHER KUSTERS GOES TO HEAVEN ★★★ When a German factory worker kills his boss and then commits suicide, his widow must deal with the convoluted aftermath. Emotionally and politically charged, this potent, pro-communist tract was banned by the Berlin Film Festival. In German with English subtitles. Rated R for adult themes. 108m. DIR: Rainer Werner Fassbinder. CAST: Brigitte Mira, Ingrid Caven, Margit Carstensen. 1975

MOTHER LODE ★★ Although this modern-day adventure yarn about a search for gold boasts a feasible plot and fine acting by Charlton Heston (who also directed) and John Marley, its liabilities far outweigh its assets. Rated PG, the film contains occasional obscenities and violence. 101m. DIR: Charlton Heston. CAST: Charlton Heston, John Marley, Nick Mancuso, Kim Basinger. 1982

MOTHER NIGHT ★★ This creaky psychological thriller, based on Kurt Vonnegut's novel, is about an American spy (Nick Nolte) who poses as a successful German propaganda minister during World War II, only to worry he may have become his own creation. Alan Arkin livens up the mood as a sympathetic and personable painter. Another plus is John Goodman's dangerous but cuddly military man. Rated R for profanity, nudity, and sexual situations. 113m. DIR: Keith Gordon. CAST: Nick Nolte, Sheryl Lee, Alan Arkin, John Goodman, Kirsten Dunst. 1996 DVD

MOTHER TERESA ★★★★★ Many consider her to be a living saint and her selfless dedication to the world's sick of heart, body, mind, and soul seems to justify that claim. Mother Teresa is, at the very least, a heroic figure who simply believes that "we must all be holy in what we do." Five years in the making, this documentary lets an extraordinary life speak for itself. Not rated, this film has shocking scenes of poverty and starvation. 83m. DIR: Ann Petrie, Jeanette Petrie. 1987

MOTHER WORE TIGHTS ★★★★ This landmark musical is the story of two vaudeville performers who meet, marry, have a family, and continue with their careers. The musical score won an Oscar, and stars Betty Grable and Dan Dailey became a popular movie team. 107m. DIR: Walter Lang. CAST: Betty Grable, Dan Dailey, Mona Freeman, Connie Marshall, William Frawley, Kathleen Lockhart, Robert Arthur, Señor Wences. 1947

MOTHER'S BOYS ★★1/2 A mentally unbalanced woman is willing to go to terrible lengths to get back the husband and three sons she abandoned years before. Everything-but-the-kitchen-sink thriller is stylish and effective, but has a nasty edge that keeps the suspense from being pleasurable. Rated R for violence. 96m. DIR: Yves Simoneau. CAST: Jamie Lee Curtis, Peter Gallagher, Joanne Whalley, Vanessa Redgrave, Joss Ackland. 1994 DVD

MOTHER'S DAY 🎬 This slasher has a twist: a "loving" mother has trained her sons to kidnap and torture innocent victims. Rated R for nudity, profanity, and violence. 98m. DIR: Charles Kaufman. CAST: Nancy Hendrickson, Deborah Luce. 1980

MOTHER'S PRAYER, A ★★1/2 A mediocre, drawnout, made-for-cable original about a widow who is looking to find a family for her son before she dies of AIDS. Not rated; contains profanity. 94m. DIR: Larry Elikann. CAST: Linda Hamilton, Noah Fleiss, Bruce Dern, Kate Nelligan, RuPaul. 1995

MOTHRA ★★★ Two six-inch-tall princesses are taken from their island home to perform in a Tokyo nightclub. A native tribe prays for the return of the princesses, and their prayers hatch a giant egg, releasing a giant caterpillar. The caterpillar goes to Tokyo searching for the princesses and turns into a giant moth while wrecking the city. Although the story may sound corny, this is one of the best of the giant-monster movies to come out of Japan. 100m. **DIR:** Inoshiro Honda. **CAST:** Lee Kresel, Franky Sakai, Hiroshi Koizumi. **1962**

MOTORAMA ★★★★ Ten-year-old Jordan Christopher Michael takes off in a stolen car, questing for Motorama game cards and instant wealth. This darkly funny, extremely bizarre road movie features a strange supporting cast and gallons of imagination. For unusual tastes only. Rated R for profanity and brief nudity. 90m. **DIR:** Barry Shils. **CAST:** Jordan Christopher Michael, Flea, Meat Loaf, Drew Barrymore, Garrett Morris, Michael J. Pollard, Mary Woronov, Martha Quinn. **1991**

MOTORCYCLE GANG ★★ Cut-rate variation on *The Wild One* (and every other teen-J.D. movie cliché they could cram in) runs on too long, but is still lurid fun. Yes, Carl Switzer is indeed "Alfalfa," captured here shortly before his violent offscreen death. B&W; 78m. **DIR:** Edward L. Cahn. **CAST:** Anne Neyland, Steve Terrell, John Ashley, Carl "Alfalfa" Switzer. **1957**

MOUCHETTE ★★★★ Director Robert Bresson's unique cinematic style has never been more evident than in this heartfelt drama. The story depicts the hardships of a young peasant girl who desperately attempts to transcend a brutal household where she lives with her alcoholic, bootlegger father and brothers. In French with English subtitles. Not rated. 90m. **DIR:** Robert Bresson. **CAST:** Nadine Nortier. **1966**

MOULIN ROUGE ★★★★ Overlooked gem by director John Huston, with José Ferrer memorable as Henri de Toulouse-Lautrec, the famous nineteenth-century Parisian artist whose growth was stunted by a childhood accident. Lavish photography and Oscar-winning art direction and costumes make this a feast for the eyes. 123m. **DIR:** John Huston. **CAST:** José Ferrer, Zsa Zsa Gabor, Suzanne Flon, Christopher Lee, Peter Cushing. **1952**

MOUNTAIN, THE ★★★ Though this moralistic drama lacks punch, the fine performances of Spencer Tracy and Robert Wagner make it worth watching. They play mountaineering brothers risking a treacherous climb to find the wreckage of a passenger plane. 105m. **DIR:** Edward Dmytryk. **CAST:** Spencer Tracy, Robert Wagner, Claire Trevor, William Demarest, Richard Arlen, E. G. Marshall. **1956**

MOUNTAIN FAMILY ROBINSON ★★1/2 *Mountain Family Robinson* delivers exactly what it sets out to achieve. Predictable and a bit corny. The cast displays an affability that should charm the children and make this film a relaxing, easy time passer for parents as well. Rated G. 100m. **DIR:** John Cotter. **CAST:** Robert Logan, Susan D. Shaw, Heather Rattray, Ham Larsen. **1979**

MOUNTAIN MEN, THE ♥ A buddy movie about two bickering fur trappers who get involved in Indian uprisings. Rated R. 102m. **DIR:** Richard Lang. **CAST:** Charlton Heston, Brian Keith, Victoria Racimo, Stephen Macht. **1980**

MOUNTAINS OF THE MOON ★★★1/2 Bob Rafelson's robust African adventure about the search for the source of the Nile is also an engrossing and intelligent portrait of the charismatic explorer Sir Richard Burton. A film of epic scope and exotic textures, a superbly entertaining re-creation of the Victorian Age of exploration, and the story of a most complex and colorful explorer. Rated R, with violence, as well as a brief reminder that Burton was also obsessed with erotica. 130m. **DIR:** Bob Rafelson. **CAST:** Patrick Bergin, Iain Glen, Roger Rees, Fiona Shaw. **1990 DVD**

MOUNTAINTOP MOTEL MASSACRE ♥ A deranged widow accidentally kills her daughter, and she takes her guilt out on the guests who stay at her hotel. Rated R for violence and brief nudity. 95m. **DIR:** Jim McCullough. **CAST:** Bill Thurman, Anna Chappell. **1983**

MOUSE AND HIS CHILD, THE ★★ Muddled cartoon feature about a pair of windup toys who attempt to escape from the tyranny of an evil rat. It's an uneasy combination of a simple children's story with a heavy-handed metaphor. The voices are provided by Peter Ustinov, Cloris Leachman, Andy Devine, and Sally Kellerman. Rated G. 82m. **DIR:** Fred Wolf, Charles Swenson. **1977**

MOUSE HUNT ★★★1/2 Dreamworks pulled out all the stops to tickle our funny bones in this delightful farce. Nathan Lane and Lee Evans play Laurel-and-Hardy-ish brothers determined to rid their recently inherited house of a pesky little rodent. Their insane attempts at extermination are constantly outwitted by the clever mouse. Endless sight gags come fast and furious, allowing those that fail to be quickly replaced by ones that don't. Rated PG for scary situations and comic-book violence. 100m. **DIR:** Gore Verbinski. **CAST:** Nathan Lane, Lee Evans, Christopher Walken. **1997 DVD**

MOUSE THAT ROARED, THE ★★★★ Any film that features Peter Sellers at his peak can't help but be funny. In this British movie, a tiny European nation devises a foolproof method of filling its depleted treasury. It declares war on the United States with the intention of losing and collecting war reparations from the generous Americans. Even foolproof plans don't always go as expected ... in this case with hilarious results. 83m. **DIR:** Jack Arnold. **CAST:** Peter Sellers, Jean Seberg, Leo McKern. **1958**

MOVERS AND SHAKERS ★★ This star-studded film starts off well but quickly falls apart. Walter Matthau plays a Hollywood producer who begins work on a movie project with only the title, *Love in Sex*, to start with. Charles Grodin plays the screenwriter who is commissioned to write the script, which is intended as a tribute to love. But with serious marital problems, Grodin is hardly the proper candidate. Rated PG for profanity. 80m. **DIR:** William Asher. **CAST:** Walter Matthau, Charles Grodin, Vincent Gardenia, Tyne Daly, Bill Macy, Gilda Radner, Steve Martin, Penny Marshall. **1985**

MOVIE, IN YOUR FACE! ♥ Bad Chinese farce is voiced over to create an even sillier film. Rated R for profanity and violence. 85m. **DIR:** David Merwin, Joseph Butcher. **CAST:** Tommy Sledge, Tom Sparks, Stan Evans. **1990**

MOVIE MOVIE ★★★1/2 Clever, affectionate spoof of 1930s pictures presents a double feature: *Dynamite Hands* is a black-and-white boxing story; *Baxter's Beauties of 1933* is a lavish, Busby Berkeley–type extravaganza. This nostalgic package even includes a preview of coming attractions. Rated

PG. 107m. **DIR:** Stanley Donen. **CAST:** George C. Scott, Trish Van Devere, Eli Wallach, Red Buttons, Barry Bostwick, Harry Hamlin, Barbara Harris, Art Carney, Ann Reinking, Kathleen Beller. **1978**

MOVIE STRUCK (PICK A STAR) ★★ Typical story about a young girl trying to break into pictures is brightened by a brief appearance by Stan Laurel and Oliver Hardy, who demonstrate the effectiveness of breakaway glass during a barroom confrontation with a tough. Strange musical numbers and some witty dialogue buoy this thin story a little, but Stan and Ollie are still the main reasons to catch this one—and there just isn't that much of them. B&W; 70m. **DIR:** Edward Sedgwick. **CAST:** Stan Laurel, Oliver Hardy, Jack Haley, Patsy Kelly. **1937**

MOVING ★★ Chalk this up as another disappointment from Richard Pryor. Pryor plays an out-of-work mass-transit engineer who finds a job in Idaho and must move his family from their home in New Jersey. Rated R for profanity and violence. 90m. **DIR:** Alan Metter. **CAST:** Richard Pryor, Beverly Todd, Dave Thomas, Dana Carvey, Randy Quaid, Rodney Dangerfield. **1988**

MOVING FINGER, THE ★★★1/2 The sleepy village of Lymston loses its serenity when residents begin receiving nasty anonymous letters; the situation is upsets the vicar's wife that she summons her good friend Miss Marple (Joan Hickson). This tale is highlighted by its engaging characters. Not rated; suitable for family viewing. 102m. **DIR:** Roy Boulting. **CAST:** Joan Hickson, Michael Culver, Sandra Payne, Richard Pearson, Andrew Bicknell. **1984**

MOVING TARGET (1990) 🎬 Linda Blair plays a woman on the run who has witnessed the murder of her boyfriend. Pathetic. Rated R for violence and language. 85m. **DIR:** Marius Mattei. **CAST:** Ernest Borgnine, Linda Blair. **1990**

MOVING TARGET (1996) ★★ Typical action flick brings nothing new to the genre. The only real fun comes from watching Billy Dee Williams and fondly remembering his days as Lando Calrissian. Rated R for violence, profanity, and sexuality. 106m. **DIR:** Damien Lee. **CAST:** Michael Dudikoff, Billy Dee Williams. **1996 DVD**

MOVING THE MOUNTAIN ★★★★★ If you thought it was electrifying to watch a lone man face a line of tanks in Tiananmen Square in 1989, wait until you hear the rest of the story. Director Michael Apted fashioned together newsreel footage, dramatic reenactments, and heart-wrenching interviews with many of the student leaders. He not only brings this historic episode to life, but infuses it with a current edge. Apted captures our hearts by wisely depending on simple talking heads to reveal the pain and guilt of the now-exiled student leaders. Not rated. 83m. **DIR:** Michael Apted. **1994**

MOVING VIOLATION ★★1/2 Another southern carchase movie from the Roger Corman factory, this one features some pretty good high-speed pyrotechnics. (Those scenes were done by second-unit director Barbara Peeters.) The plot, which is merely an excuse for the chases, has an innocent couple being pursued by a corrupt sheriff. Rated PG. 91m. **DIR:** Charles S. Dubin. **CAST:** Stephen McHattie, Kay Lenz,

Eddie Albert, Lonny Chapman, Will Geer, Dick Miller. **1976**

MOVING VIOLATIONS ★★ Neal Israel and Pat Proft, who brought us *Police Academy* and *Bachelor Party*, writhe again with another "subject" comedy—this time about traffic school. Star John Murray does a reasonable job of imitating his older brother, Bill. Rated PG-13 for profanity and suggested sex. 90m. **DIR:** Neal Israel. **CAST:** John Murray, Jennifer Tilly, James Keach, Wendie Jo Sperber, Sally Kellerman, Fred Willard. **1985**

MOZART BROTHERS, THE ★★1/2 This surrealistic film about a zany director's insane production of *Don Giovanni* owes far more to the Marx Brothers than the music of Mozart. Étienne Glaser is splendid as the spacy director. However refreshing, the plot is not developed beyond the initial sniggers. In Swedish with English subtitles. Not rated. 111m. **DIR:** Suzanne Osten. **CAST:** Étienne Glaser, Philip Zanden. **1988**

MOZART STORY, THE ★★1/2 Though produced in Austria, this Mozart biography plays as loose with the facts as any Hollywood bio-pic. You'll only want to see it for the music, played by the Vienna Philharmonic Orchestra and Vienna State Opera. Includes excerpts from all of Mozart's best-known works. Curt Jurgens (billed as Curd Juergens) plays Emperor Joseph II. Dialogue dubbed in English. B&W; 95m. **DIR:** Carl Hartl. **CAST:** Hans Holt, Winnie Markus, Curt Jurgens. **1937**

MUCH ADO ABOUT NOTHING ★★★★ Kenneth Branagh again brings energy, accessibility, and cinematic style to one of William Shakespeare's classic stories. Confirmed bachelor Benedick trades barbs with the caustic Beatrice, and young Claudio suspects duplicity on the part of the innocent Hero. Great fun! Rated PG-13 for brief nudity and suggested sex. 110m. **DIR:** Kenneth Branagh. **CAST:** Kenneth Branagh, Michael Keaton, Robert Sean Leonard, Keanu Reeves, Emma Thompson, Denzel Washington, Kate Beckinsale, Brian Blessed, Imelda Staunton, Phyllida Law. **1993 DVD**

MUDHONEY ★★★★ A cult favorite from Russ Meyer about the exploits of some rural folks involved in the pursuit of cheap thrills and the meaning of life. Considered an adults-only film when released, it now seems quite tame. Plot has a local scum terrorizing Antoinette Cristiani, a deaf-and-dumb beautiful blonde until her rescue by Hal Hopper. Not rated, but an R rating would be in order because of some nudity and adult themes. B&W; 92m. **DIR:** Russ Meyer. **CAST:** Hal Hopper, Antoinette Cristiani. **1965**

MUGSY'S GIRLS 🎬 A predictable bit of fluff about a sorority out to earn rent money through mud wrestling. Rated R for nudity and profanity. 87m. **DIR:** Kevin Brodie. **CAST:** Ruth Gordon, Laura Branigan, Eddie Deezen. **1985**

MULAN ★★★★1/2 Chinese design elements and storytelling simplicity make this one of the better latter-day Disney animated features. Humor, action, romance, social commentary, and musical interludes are balanced perfectly in this medieval tale of an awkward young woman who disguises herself as a man to take her aged warrior father's place in battle.

More than any previous Disney cartoon, this plays like a well-crafted adventure film that just happens to be animated. Rated G. 87m. **DIR:** Barry Cook, Tony Bancroft. **1998 DVD**

MULE TRAIN ★★1/2 Gene Autry helps a pal keep a valuable cement claim from crooked businessman, Bob Livingston. Classic song incorporated into a so-so plot with an actionless windup. Sidekick Pat Buttram and Shelia Ryan were real-life man and wife. B&W; 70m. **DIR:** John English. **CAST:** Gene Autry, Pat Buttram, Sheila Ryan, Robert Livingston, Gregg Barton. **1950**

MULHOLLAND FALLS ★★★1/2 Gritty period detective movie stars Nick Nolte as the leader of The Hat Squad, an elite quartet of Los Angeles police detectives who answer to no one as they rid the city of mobsters. When Nolte's former mistress is found murdered, the trail leads to a possible government cover-up. Strong performances and suspense throughout. Rated R for violence, profanity, nudity, and simulated sex. 107m. **DIR:** Lee Tamahori. **CAST:** Nick Nolte, Melanie Griffith, Chazz Palminteri, Michael Madsen, Christopher Penn, Ed Lauter. **1996**

MULTIPLE MANIACS 🖤 A homage to gore king Herschell Gordon Lewis's *Two Thousand Maniacs*. Not rated, but the equivalent of an X. B&W; 70m. **DIR:** John Waters. **CAST:** Divine, Mink Stole, Paul Swift, Cookie Mueller, David Lochary, Mary Vivian Pearce, Edith Massey. **1971**

MULTIPLICITY ★★★1/2 Michael Keaton revives his *Mr. Mom* persona with a twist; unable to keep up with a job and a home life, he has himself cloned. Then the executive Keaton decides he needs a clone and it begins. Keaton is a master clown, and he gets terrific support from Andie MacDowell, Harris Yulin, Richard Masur, and the rest of the cast. While not a comedy classic, it does provide plenty of chuckles and complications. Rated PG-13 for suggested sex. 117m. **DIR:** Harold Ramis. **CAST:** Michael Keaton, Harris Yulin, Andie MacDowell, Richard Masur, Eugene Levy, Anne Cusack, John de Lancie, Brian Doyle-Murray, Julie Bowen. **1996 DVD**

•**MUMFORD ★★★★** A small-town psychologist (Loren Dean) dispenses common-sense advice to his patients, inspiring unexpected results. Meanwhile, there's something odd about the good doctor, who just happens to have the same name as the town and operates in a highly unorthodox fashion. In this quirky comedy-drama, writer-director Lawrence Kasdan creates characters and situations that offer insight into the human condition while keeping the viewer well entertained. Rated R for profanity and sexual situations. 96m. **DIR:** Lawrence Kasdan. **CAST:** Loren Dean, Sofie Crisp, Jason Lee, Alfre Woodard, Mary McDonnell, Pruitt Taylor Vance, Zooey Deschanel, Martin Short, David Paymer, Jane Adams, Dana Ivey, Kevin Tighe, Ted Danson, Jason Ritter. **1999 DVD**

MUMMY, THE (1932) ★★★★ First-rate horror-thriller about an Egyptian mummy returning to life after 3,700 years. Boris Karloff plays the title role in one of his very best performances. Superb makeup, dialogue, atmosphere, and direction make this one an all-time classic. B&W; 73m. **DIR:** Karl Freund. **CAST:** Boris Karloff, Zita Johann, David Manners, Edward Van Sloan. **1932 DVD**

MUMMY, THE (1959) ★★★1/2 Excellent updating of the mummy legend. Christopher Lee is terrifying as the ancient Egyptian awakened from his centuries-old sleep to take revenge on those who desecrated the tomb of his beloved princess. Well-photographed, atmospheric production is high-quality entertainment. 88m. **DIR:** Terence Fisher. **CAST:** Peter Cushing, Christopher Lee, Yvonne Furneaux. **1959**

MUMMY, THE (1999) ★★★1/2 Few films successfully walk the line when trying to be all things to all people, but this reboot of the venerable Universal monster franchise manages that difficult task: It's definitely scary, unquestionably funny, and a rousing good adventure yarn. The forces of virtue are led by a dashing foreign legionnaire who returns to the ruined city of Hamunaptra with a curvaceous but clumsy Egyptologist and her ne'er-do-well brother. Events get out of hand and an "ancient evil" is unleashed upon the world ... until and unless our heroes can bottle it up again. It's all handled with impressive panache and grand pacing by a director who's equally comfortable with hair's-breadth-escape action, pratfallish belly laughs, and creepy moments of suspense. Rated PG-13 for violence and cursed evil doings. 127m. **DIR:** Stephen Sommers. **CAST:** Brendan Fraser, Rachel Weisz, John Hannah, Arnold Vosloo, Kevin J. O'Connor. **1999 DVD**

MUMMY AND THE CURSE OF THE JACKALS, THE 🖤 This Las Vegas–based monster mess was unfinished and theatrically unreleased, and remains unwatchable. Not rated. 86m. **DIR:** Oliver Drake. **CAST:** Anthony Eisley, Martina Pons, John Carradine. **1969**

MUMMY'S CURSE, THE ★★1/2 In Universal's final *Mummy* movie, the monster turns up in the Louisiana bayou, where high priests Peter Coe and Martin Kosleck send him on a rampage. Unoriginal but creepy and fast-paced. B&W; 62m. **DIR:** Leslie Goodwins. **CAST:** Lon Chaney Jr., Peter Coe, Virginia Christine, Martin Kosleck. **1944**

MUMMY'S GHOST, THE ★★1/2 Universal Pictures' screenwriters used one new wrinkle in each of their otherwise routine *Mummy* chillers. In this one, the gimmick is the climactic fate of the heroine. Also, check out John Carradine as the mad high priest. B&W; 60m. **DIR:** Reginald LeBorg. **CAST:** Lon Chaney Jr., John Carradine, Ramsay Ames, Robert Lowery. **1944**

MUMMY'S HAND, THE ★★★ A pair of carnival barker archaeologists team up with a magician's daughter and go into the grave-robbing business. Their efforts bring them within a bandage width of the shambling mummy and the evil priest who brings the dead back to life. Tom Tyler makes a good mummy and the film has chills. B&W; 67m. **DIR:** Christy Cabanne. **CAST:** Dick Foran, Peggy Moran, Wallace Ford, Eduardo Ciannelli, Tom Tyler, George Zucco. **1940**

•**MUMMY'S SHROUD, THE ★★**1/2 After a slow and overly long opening, this film picks up as an archaeological expedition removes the mummy from its tomb and unleashes the beast by accident. The plot is clichéd and full of enough holes to nearly sink it, but the acting saves it. 90m. **DIR:** John Gilling. **CAST:** Andre Morell, John Phillips, David Buck, Elizabeth Sellars, Maggie Kimberley. **1967**

MUMMY'S TOMB, THE ★★1/2 This sequel to *The Mummy's Hand* was Lon Chaney Jr.'s first *Mummy* movie for Universal. Egyptian high priest Turhan Bey revives the Mummy at a New England museum and sends him on a rampage. Note: This 1993 video release is missing the scene in which Mary Gordon is murdered. B&W; 61m. **DIR:** Harold Young. **CAST:** Lon Chaney Jr., Elyse Knox, John Hubbard, Turhan Bey. **1942**

MUNCHIE ❤ In this silly sequel, a magical imp (the voice of Dom DeLuise) helps an unpopular youngster through some difficult childhood traumas. Although adults may find little substance here, children may be mildly entertained. Rated PG for violence. 85m. **DIR:** Jim Wynorski. **CAST:** Loni Anderson, Andrew Stevens, Arte Johnson. **1991**

MUNCHIES ❤ Harvey Korman has dual parts as an archaeologist who discovers a junk-food-eating creature, and as a con artist who kidnaps the little critters. Rated PG for sexual innuendo. 83m. **DIR:** Bettina Hirsch. **CAST:** Harvey Korman, Charles Stratton, Alix Elias. **1987**

MUNCHIE STRIKES BACK ❤ Why? Even the target audience, young children, will find this low-budget effort derivative and boring. Rated PG. 80m. **DIR:** Jim Wynorski. **CAST:** Lesley-Anne Down, Andrew Stevens. **1994**

MUNSTERS' REVENGE, THE ★★★ More schlock than shock and chock full of predictable puns, this munster mash is super Saturday-morning fun. Most of the original players from the TV series are back, with outstanding guests like Sid Caesar as the curator of a wax museum. **DIR:** Don Weis. **CAST:** Fred Gwynne, Yvonne De Carlo, Al Lewis, Sid Caesar. **1981 DVD**

MUPPET CHRISTMAS CAROL, THE ★★★1/2 Kermit the Frog as Bob Crachit? Director Brian Henson somehow makes it work in this family-oriented telling of the classic Charles Dickens tale. It's no match for the acclaimed 1951 version starring Alastair Sim, but Michael Caine makes a fine Scrooge. Rated G. 86m. **DIR:** Brian Henson. **CAST:** Michael Caine. **1992**

MUPPET MOVIE, THE ★★★1/2 Though there is a huge all-star guest cast, the Muppets are the real stars of this superior family film in which the characters trek to Hollywood in search of stardom. Rated G. 94m. **DIR:** James Frawley. **CAST:** Muppets, Edgar Bergen, Milton Berle, Mel Brooks, James Coburn, Dom DeLuise, Elliott Gould, Bob Hope, Madeline Kahn, Carol Kane, Cloris Leachman, Steve Martin, Richard Pryor, Telly Savalas, Orson Welles, Paul Williams. **1979**

MUPPET TREASURE ISLAND ★★★ Robert Louis Stevenson's classic story about loyalty and pirate loot has become an entertaining mix of adventure, music, and Muppet madness. The film closely follows the book's journey from a grungy English seaside inn to a tropical paradise with the brisk clip of a blustery trade wind. Rated G. 99m. **DIR:** Brian Henson. **CAST:** Tim Curry, Kevin Bishop, Billy Connolly, Jennifer Saunders. **1996**

•**MUPPETS FROM SPACE** ★★★★ This, like all Muppet endeavors, is that most perfect of family pleasures: a film silly enough and flamboyantly colorful enough to delight the small fry, and funny enough—without ever turning crass—to keep adults captivated. The story centers on Gonzo, one of the few Muppet regulars not based on a recognizable Terran life-form, and that's the crux of the matter. Obsessed by a search for his roots, Gonzo is excited when his breakfast cereal starts spelling out messages, but such contact from afar does not sit well with a paranoid government operative (Jeffrey Tambor), who is convinced that life out there means us harm. Subsequent adventures tweak everything from *Hitchhiker's Guide to the Galaxy* to *The X-Files*: all in all, a lot of fun. Rated G; suitable for all ages. 82m. **DIR:** Tim Hill. **CAST:** Jeffrey Tambor, F. Murray Abraham, Ray Liotta, Andie MacDowell, Rob Schneider. **1999 DVD**

MUPPETS TAKE MANHATTAN, THE ★★★ Jim Henson's popular puppets take a bite of the Big Apple in their third and least effective screen romp. Playwright Kermit and his pals try to get their musical on the Broadway stage. Rated G. 94m. **DIR:** Frank Oz. **CAST:** Muppets, Art Carney, Dabney Coleman, Joan Rivers, Elliott Gould, Liza Minnelli, Brooke Shields. **1984**

MURDER ★★★ An early Alfred Hitchcock thriller, and a good one, although it shows its age. Herbert Marshall, a producer-director, is selected to serve on a murder-trial jury. He believes the accused, an aspiring actress, is innocent of the crime and takes it upon himself to apprehend the real killer. B&W; 92m. **DIR:** Alfred Hitchcock. **CAST:** Herbert Marshall, Norah Baring. **1930 DVD**

MURDER AHOY ★★1/2 Threadbare mystery has Miss Marple (Margaret Rutherford) investigating murder aboard ship. This was the last film in the British series, although it was released in America before the superior *Murder Most Foul.* Despite her considerable talents, Rutherford could not raise this sinking ship above the level of mediocrity. B&W; 74m. **DIR:** George Pollock. **CAST:** Margaret Rutherford, Lionel Jeffries, Stringer Davis, Charles Tingwell. **1964**

MURDER AT 1600 ★★1/2 After a bloody female corpse is found in a White House restroom, a civil-war buff/homicide cop smells a cover-up, and teams up with a sharpshooter secret-service agent to sift through the case. The action ends with a ludicrous romp through tunnels that Lincoln had built under the White House. Rated R for violence, language, nudity, and sexuality. 106m. **DIR:** Dwight H. Little. **CAST:** Wesley Snipes, Daniel Benzali, Diane Lane, Alan Alda, Ronny Cox, Dennis Miller. **1997 DVD**

MURDER AT THE GALLOP ★★★★ Margaret Rutherford has her best Miss Marple outing in this adaptation of Agatha Christie's Hercule Poirot mystery, *After the Funeral.* She and Robert Morley play off each other beautifully in this comedy-laced tale, which has Marple insinuating herself into a murder investigation. Her assistant, Mr. Stringer, is played by Rutherford's real-life husband, Stringer Davis. B&W; 81m. **DIR:** George Pollock. **CAST:** Margaret

Rutherford, Robert Morley, Flora Robson, Stringer Davis, Charles Tingwell. 1963

MURDER AT THE VANITIES ★★★1/2 A musical whodunit, this blend of comedy and mystery finds tenacious Victor McLaglen embroiled in a murder investigation at Earl Carroll's Vanities, a popular and long-running variety show of the 1930s and 1940s. Musical numbers and novelty acts pop up between clues in this stylish oddity. Lots of fun. B&W; 89m. **DIR:** Mitchell Leisen. **CAST:** Jack Oakie, Kitty Carlisle, Victor McLaglen, Carl Brisson, Donald Meek, Gail Patrick, Jessie Ralph, Duke Ellington, Ann Sheridan. 1934

MURDER AT THE VICARAGE ★★★★ Originally published in 1930, this Agatha Christie story introduced the elderly, spinster detective Miss Marple. This BBC production perfectly captures the cozy English village of St. Mary Mead, where Miss Marple resides. Commenting on a missing pound note in the collection box, and a well-planned murder, our white-haired heroine says, "There is a great deal of wickedness in village life." A must-see for any mystery buff. Rated G. 102m. **DIR:** Julian Amyes. **CAST:** Joan Hickson, Paul Eddington, Cheryl Campbell, David Horovitch. 1986

MURDER BY DEATH ★★★★ Mystery buffs will get a big kick out of this spoof of the genre, penned by Neil Simon. Peter Sellers, Peter Falk, David Niven, Maggie Smith, and James Coco play thinly disguised send-ups of famed fictional detectives who are invited to the home of Truman Capote to solve a baffling murder. Rated PG. 94m. **DIR:** Robert Moore. **CAST:** Peter Sellers, Peter Falk, David Niven, Maggie Smith, James Coco, Alec Guinness. 1976

MURDER BY DECREE ★★★1/2 Excellent cast stylishly serves up this Sherlock Holmes mystery. Christopher Plummer and James Mason are well suited to the roles of Holmes and Dr. Watson. The murky story deals with Jack the Ripper. Rated R for violence and gore. 121m. **DIR:** Bob Clark. **CAST:** Christopher Plummer, James Mason, Donald Sutherland, Genevieve Bujold, Susan Clark, David Hemmings, John Gielgud, Anthony Quayle. 1979

MURDER BY MOONLIGHT 🖤 Detective thriller set in a colony on the Moon, circa 2105. NASA agent Brigitte Nielsen joins Russian counterpart Julian Sands to solve a murder in this low-budget effort. Rated PG-13 for violence. 100m. **DIR:** Michael Lindsay-Hogg. **CAST:** Julian Sands, Brigitte Nielsen, Brian Cox, Gerald McRaney. 1989

MURDER BY NUMBERS 🖤 A dud. Rated PG-13. 91m. **DIR:** Paul Leder. **CAST:** Sam Behrens, Shari Belafonte, Dick Sargent, Cleavon Little, Jayne Meadows, Ronee Blakley. 1989

MURDER BY PHONE ★★★ In this okay shocker, Richard Chamberlain is cast as an environmentalist whose lecture engagement in New York City turns out to be an opportunity to investigate the gruesome death of one of his students. Rated R. 79m. **DIR:** Michael Anderson. **CAST:** Richard Chamberlain, John Houseman. 1980

MURDER BY TELEVISION ★★ Bela Lugosi plays an inventor in this low-budget murder mystery. Television was still something out of *Science and Inven-tion* back in 1935, so it was fair game as a contrivance used to commit the crime. B&W; 60m. **DIR:** Clifford Sanforth. **CAST:** Bela Lugosi, June Collyer, George Meeker, Hattie McDaniel. 1935

MURDER ELITE ★★ Ali MacGraw plays a woman who, after losing all her money in America, comes back to her native England to start fresh. Meanwhile, there is a killer on the loose. The two stories ultimately collide, but MacGraw's uninspired acting and the poor direction make the film rather plodding. Not rated. 104m. **DIR:** Claude Whatham. **CAST:** Ali MacGraw, Billie Whitelaw, Hywel Bennett, Ray Lonnen. 1985

MURDER IN COWETA COUNTY ★★★1/2 Andy Griffith is outstanding as a Georgia businessman who thinks he can get away with murder. Johnny Cash plays the determined sheriff who's willing to go to any lengths to prove Griffith's guilt. This made-for-TV suspense-drama was based on an actual Georgia murder that took place in 1948. 104m. **DIR:** Gary Nelson. **CAST:** Andy Griffith, Johnny Cash, Earl Hindman. 1983

MURDER IN MIND ★★★ An amnesiac is the chief suspect in her husband's murder, and the police recruit a noted therapist to hypnotize her and unlock her memory. They get more than they bargain for when her recollection of the event differs from the facts. The fun comes in trying to separate the fact from the fiction. Rated R for adult situations, language, and violence. 89m. **DIR:** Andy Morahan. **CAST:** Nigel Hawthorne, Mary-Louise Parker, Jimmy Smits, Jason Scott Lee, Gailard Sartain. 1997

MURDER IN NEW HAMPSHIRE ★★1/2 Passable TV killer-of-the-week saga focuses on a video production teacher's plot to use her student as her husband's assassin. At times unbelievable, although this is based on fact. 93m. **DIR:** Joyce Chopra. **CAST:** Helen Hunt, Chad Allen, Larry Drake, Ken Howard, Howard Hesseman. 1992 DVD

MURDER IN SPACE ★★ As you watch this made-for-TV whodunit, you must immediately look for clues. If not, you'll get bored and the long-awaited solution won't make sense to you. Wilford Brimley as the head of Mission Control tries to put the pieces together. 95m. **DIR:** Steven H. Stern. **CAST:** Wilford Brimley, Michael Ironside, Martin Balsam, Arthur Hill. 1985

MURDER IN TEXAS ★★★★ Absorbing TV docudrama based on a true story. Sam Elliott is Dr. John Hill, a prominent plastic surgeon accused of murdering his socialite wife. A gripping study of psychopathic behavior. Good performances all around, including Farrah Fawcett and Andy Griffith, who reaped an Emmy nomination. 200m. **DIR:** William Hale. **CAST:** Farrah Fawcett, Sam Elliott, Katharine Ross, Andy Griffith, Bill Dana. 1983

MURDER IN THE FIRST ★★★1/2 Dan Gordon's gritty and memorable script concerns the actual Alcatraz convict whose three straight years in solitary confinement paved the way for prison reform. Kevin Bacon plays the Depression-era youth who wound up among hardened killers after stealing five dollars to feed his younger sister. The entire U.S. penal system is put on trial after Bacon murders a prison snitch.

Rated R for profanity, violence, torture, and explicit sexual content. 120m. **DIR:** Marc Rocco. **CAST:** Christian Slater, Kevin Bacon, Gary Oldman, Embeth Davidtz, Brad Dourif, William H. Macy, R. Lee Ermey. **1995 DVD**

MURDER IS ANNOUNCED, A ★★★1/2 The sedate personals column of Chipping Cleghorn's *North Benham Gazette*, usually filled with pleas regarding lost dogs and bicycles for sale, is enlivened by a classified announcing a murder, which then takes place, as scheduled. Miss Marple (Joan Hickson) is summoned by the village constabulary. This is one of Agatha Christie's more convoluted stories. Not rated; suitable for family viewing. 153m. **DIR:** David Giles. **CAST:** Joan Hickson, Ursula Howells, Renée Asherson, John Castle, Sylvia Syms, Joan Sims. **1984**

MURDER MOST FOUL ★★★1/2 Like *Murder at the Gallop*, this is another Miss Marple adventure fashioned out of a Hercule Poirot mystery (*Mrs. McGinty's Dead*). The plot is only a framework for Margaret Rutherford's delightful antics. This time, she is the only dissenting member of a jury in a murder case. B&W; 91m. **DIR:** George Pollock. **CAST:** Margaret Rutherford, Ron Moody, Charles Tingwell, Stringer Davis, Francesca Annis, Dennis Price. **1964**

MURDER MY SWEET ★★★★ In the mid-1940s, Dick Powell decided to change his clean-cut crooner image by playing Raymond Chandler's hardboiled detective, Philip Marlowe. It worked marvelously, with Powell making a fine white knight in tarnished armor on the trail of killers and blackmailers. B&W; 95m. **DIR:** Edward Dmytryk. **CAST:** Dick Powell, Claire Trevor, Anne Shirley. **1944**

•MURDER OF CROWS, A ★★★★ A lawyer, wrongfully disbarred, writes a novel about his experiences and opens a floodgate of trouble when the horrific incidents in his novel mimic those of a bloodthirsty serial killer. Requires a solid suspension of disbelief but is entertaining and peppered with fantastic performances. Rated R for violence, profanity, nudity, and sexual situations. 101m. **DIR:** Rowdy Herrington. **CAST:** Cuba Gooding Jr., Tom Berenger, Marianne Jean-Baptiste, Eric Stoltz. **1999 DVD**

MURDER OF MARY PHAGAN, THE ★★★★ True story of 1913 Georgia governor John Slaton's fight to free a factory manager accused of killing a young girl. He has to fight a lynch mob determined to hang the factory manager because he was Jewish. This TV movie is long, but well worth seeing. 250m. **DIR:** William Hale. **CAST:** Jack Lemmon, Peter Gallagher, Richard Jordan, Robert Prosky, Kevin Spacey, Kathryn Walker, Paul Dooley, Rebecca Miller. **1988**

MURDER OF THE CENTURY ★★★★ In this era of media overkill, it is surprising to learn that one week after the murder of architect Stanford White by millionaire Harry K. Thaw over the affections of Thaw's wife, Evelyn Nesbit, there was a silent-film version in the theaters. Narrated by David Ogden Stiers with Blair Brown providing the voice of Nesbit, and illustrated by scores of photos and early film clips, this provides a fascinating glimpse at turn-of-the-century America. Made for PBS. Not rated. B&W/color; 60m. **DIR:** Carl Charlson. **1995**

MURDER ON FLIGHT 502 ★★ A mad bomber threatens to blow an international airliner to pieces. He is thwarted by Robert Stack and other reluctant heroes. Reminiscent of *Airport* and a half-dozen sequels. The cast alone keeps this made-for-TV potboiler from falling flat on its baggage carousel. 120m. **DIR:** George McCowan. **CAST:** Ralph Bellamy, Polly Bergen, Robert Stack, Theodore Bikel, Sonny Bono, Dane Clark, Laraine Day, Fernando Lamas, George Maharis, Farrah Fawcett, Hugh O'Brian, Brooke Adams, Walter Pidgeon, Molly Picon. **1975**

MURDER ON LINE ONE ★★ Standard horror flick set in London. This time, the murderer films the killings and gets his kicks rewatching his work—transgressor of the VCR age. Rated R for violence and bloodshed. 103m. **DIR:** Anders Palm. **CAST:** Emma Jacobs, Peter Blake. **1990**

MURDER ON THE BAYOU ★★★1/2 German director Volker Schlondörff examines the American South, specifically the Bayou country of Louisiana, where an elderly black man (Lou Gossett Jr.) is suspected of killing a white racist. Marvelously well-acted TV movie, rich in character moments, and surprisingly upbeat given its subject matter. 91m. **DIR:** Volker Schlöndorff. **CAST:** Lou Gossett Jr., Richard Widmark, Holly Hunter, Joe Seneca, Will Patton, Woody Strode. **1987**

MURDER ON THE ORIENT EXPRESS ★★★★1/2 Belgian detective Hercule Poirot solves a murder on a train in this stylish prestige picture based on the Agatha Christie mystery. Albert Finney is terrific as the detective and is supported by an all-star cast. Rated PG. 127m. **DIR:** Sidney Lumet. **CAST:** Albert Finney, Ingrid Bergman, Lauren Bacall, Sean Connery, Vanessa Redgrave, Michael York, Jacqueline Bisset. **1974**

MURDER ONE ♥ An odyssey of madness, mayhem, and murder. Rated R for nudity, profanity, and violence. 82m. **DIR:** Graeme Campbell. **CAST:** Henry Thomas, James Wilder, Stephen Shellen. **1988**

MURDER 101 ★★★★ Pierce Brosnan's considerable charm works perfectly in this cable-TV mystery by writer-director Bill Condon. Brosnan stars as a college writing instructor teaching his students the fundamentals of suspense fiction; naturally, somebody adopts his lesson plan and makes the poor professor Suspect Number One in a deft murder. Rated PG-13. 93m. **DIR:** Bill Condon. **CAST:** Pierce Brosnan, Dey Young, Raphael Sbarge, Kim Thomson. **1991 DVD**

MURDER OVER NEW YORK ★★ The world's most famous Asian detective, Charlie Chan (Sidney Toler), goes after a gang of saboteurs plaguing the airways after a Scotland Yard inspector is felled by poisonous gas. Although cast with plenty of top-flight character actors, this one falls a little flat. The formula was wearing pretty thin after twenty-four films. B&W; 64m. **DIR:** Harry Lachman. **CAST:** Sidney Toler, Marjorie Weaver, Robert Lowery, Ricardo Cortez, Donald MacBride, Melville Cooper, Kane Richmond, Clarence Muse, John Sutton. **1940**

MURDER SHE SAID ★★★★ Now that Joan Hickson has brought Agatha Christie's Miss Marple to life in the superb BBC series, it has become common for mystery buffs to denigrate the four films starring

Margaret Rutherford as Marple. We beg to differ. Rutherford makes a delightful screen sleuth, and this adaptation of *4:50 to Paddington* is quite enjoyable. The first entry in the series, it has Marple witnessing a murder on a train. B&W; 87m. DIR: George Pollock. CAST: Margaret Rutherford, Arthur Kennedy, Charles Tingwell, Muriel Pavlow, James Robertson Justice, Thorley Walters, Joan Hickson. 1961

MURDER SO SWEET ★★★ Better-than-average network telefilic "based on actual events," with dependable Harry Hamlin starring as hunkish good ol' boy Steve Catlin, an unrepentant ladies' man who loved 'em and left 'em ... dead. Plucky Helen Shaver decides to take him down. Lurid boxart suggests otherwise, but this is pretty tame stuff. Rated PG for mild profanity. 94m. DIR: Larry Peerce. CAST: Harry Hamlin, Helen Shaver, Terence Knox, Ed Lauter, Faith Ford, Eileen Brennan. 1993

MURDER STORY ★★★1/2 In this little-known gem, an aspiring mystery writer (Bruce Boa) involves his mentor-hero (Christopher Lee) in a real-life killing. The story is a trifle contrived but generally enjoyable. Lee gets a rare chance to play a heroic character and makes the most of it. A must-see for fans of the genre. Rated PG. 90m. DIR: Eddie Arno, Markus Innocenti. CAST: Christopher Lee, Bruce Boa. 1989

MURDER WEAPON 🎬 In this film, which came at the end of the slasher craze, the killer spends more time killing teenage boys than girls, but still can't come up with a reason why. Not rated; contains violence, profanity, and nudity. 81m. DIR: Ellen Cabot. CAST: Linnea Quigley, Karen Russell, Lyle Waggoner. 1989

MURDER WITH MIRRORS ★★★ Inspired casting saves an otherwise pedestrian TV adaptation of Agatha Christie. Helen Hayes (never the best Miss Marple) comes to the aid of an old friend (Bette Davis), whose ancestral home is threatened. Although noteworthy as the only time Hayes and Davis appeared in the same project, George Eckstein's script is pretty ho-hum. 100m. DIR: Dick Lowry. CAST: Helen Hayes, Bette Davis, John Mills, Leo McKern. 1985

MURDER WITHOUT MOTIVE ★★★ Subtitled *The Edmund Perry Story* and based on Robert Sam Anson's book *Best Intentions*, this is the tragic account of a Harlem honor student's loneliness and frustration at an exclusive private high school. Curtis McClarin is convincing in the lead. Not rated; contains violence and drug use. 93m. DIR: Kevin Hooks. CAST: Curtis McClarin, Anna Maria Horsford, Carla Gugino, Christopher Daniel Barnes. 1991

•MURDERCYCLE ★★1/2 Some films have a great concept but a weak plot to back it up. This is the dilemma of *Murdercycle*: the tale of an evil alien entity that takes the form of a motorcycle armed to the extreme with high-tech weaponry. Everything about the film seems to run on cruise control from there on out. Rated PG-13 for violence and profanity. 90m. DIR: Thomas L. Callaway. CAST: Charles Wesley. 1999

MURDERED INNOCENCE ★★ An escaped con and an ex-con come toe-to-toe to finish what they began twenty years ago when one of their mothers was murdered. Comically clichéd thriller is way overdone in the style department and is further marred by an unnecessarily convoluted screenplay. Rated R for violence and sexual situations. 77m. DIR: Frank Coraci. CAST: Jason Miller, Fred Carpenter, Jacqueline Macario, Gary Aumiller. 1994

MURDERERS AMONG US: THE SIMON WIESENTHAL STORY ★★★1/2 Powerful HBO reenactment of real-life Nazi concentration camp victim Simon Wiesenthal's postwar search for Nazi leaders. Among those he brings to justice are the notorious Adolf Eichmann and Franz Murer. Ben Kingsley is unforgettable as Wiesenthal. 155m. DIR: Brian Gibson. CAST: Ben Kingsley, Renee Soutendijk, Craig T. Nelson. 1989

MURDERERS' ROW ★★1/2 This entry into the Matt Helm secret agent series is pretty dismal. Dean Martin has been much better in other films. The Matt Helm series was an attempt to grab the Bond and Flint audience, but Martin just couldn't cut it as a superspy. 108m. DIR: Henry Levin. CAST: Dean Martin, Ann-Margret, Karl Malden, James Gregory. 1966

MURDEROUS VISION ★★1/2 A missing-persons investigator (Bruce Boxleitner) teams with a reluctant psychic (Laura Johnson) to track down a psychotic killer with a penchant for severed heads. Writer Paul Joseph Gulino borrows pretty heavily from Thomas Harris's *Silence of the Lambs* for this chaotic made-for-cable thriller. Rated R for violence and language. 93m. DIR: Gary A. Sherman. CAST: Bruce Boxleitner, Laura Johnson, Robert Culp. 1991

MURDERS IN THE RUE MORGUE (1932) ★★1/2 Very little of Edgar Allan Poe's original story is evident in this muddled and perverse story of Dr. Mirakle and his efforts to mate his companion (an ape) with the leading lady of the film. Bela Lugosi as the evil doctor grimaces often and wears a black cape. B&W; 62m. DIR: Robert Florey. CAST: Bela Lugosi, Sidney Fox, Leon Ames, Arlene Francis, Noble Johnson. 1932

MURDERS IN THE RUE MORGUE (1971) ★★ Members of a horror theatre troupe in nineteenth-century Paris are dispatched systematically by a mysterious fiend. Good cast, nice atmosphere, but confusing and altogether too artsy for its own good. Rated PG. 87m. DIR: Gordon Hessler. CAST: Jason Robards Jr., Herbert Lom, Michael Dunn, Lilli Palmer, Christine Kaufmann, Adolfo Celi. 1971

MURDERS IN THE RUE MORGUE (1986) ★★★ Here again: the Poe tale of a grisly double murder in nineteenth-century Paris. Solid performances by a top-notch cast, along with fine atmospheric cinematography give this made-for-television production a lift. Rated PG. 100m. DIR: Jeannot Szwarc. CAST: George C. Scott, Rebecca DeMornay, Ian McShane, Neil Dickson. 1986

MURDERS IN THE ZOO ★★★ Wild, pre-Code horror from Paramount. Lionel Atwill is a zookeeper who's also a jealous husband. In the first scene, set in the Asian jungle, he sews his wife's lover's mouth shut, leaving him to die in the jungle. Back home, he dumps one victim into a crocodile pool, and kills another with snake venom. Lurid fun—not for the kiddies, even now. B&W; 64m. DIR: A. Edward Sutherland. **CAST:** Lionel Atwill, Charlie Ruggles, Randolph Scott, Gail Patrick, John Lodge, Kathleen Burke. **1933**

MURIEL ★★★★ Like *Last Year at Marienbad*, this stylized Alain Resnais film is largely about the burden of memory, as experienced by four interlinked characters. Difficult and demanding, it is composed of many short, overlapping scenes. But for those who accept its challenge, the emotional payoff can be extraordinary. In French with English subtitles. 116m. **DIR:** Alain Resnais. **CAST:** Delphine Seyrig, Jean-Pierre Kérien, Nita Klein. **1963**

MURIEL'S WEDDING ★★★★ Fans of *Strictly Ballroom* and *The Adventures of Priscilla Queen of the Desert* will adore this equally flamboyant Australian comedy that stars Toni Collette as a socially inept ugly duckling desperate to become a swan. She's a melancholy fixture in the small town of Porpoise Spit and a young woman so out of touch that she worships the tunes of 1970s pop group Abba. Rated R for profanity and brief nudity. 105m. **DIR:** P. J. Hogan. **CAST:** Toni Collette, Bill Hunter, Rachel Griffiths, Jeanie Drynan, Gennie Nevinson, Matt Day. **1994 DVD**

MURMUR OF THE HEART ★★★ Director Louis Malle's story of a sickly French teenager and his youthful, free-spirited mother in the 1950s gets off to a wonderful start, then runs out of steam in its second half as the two check into a health resort. Still, it has charm, wit, and style to spare. Not rated, but Malle's treatment of a single act of incest may raise American eyebrows, although the subject is very tastefully handled. In French with English subtitles. 118m. **DIR:** Louis Malle. **CAST:** Lea Massari, Benoit Ferreux, Daniel Gélin, Michel Lonsdale. **1971**

MURPH THE SURF ★★1/2 In this based-on-real-life thriller, two Florida beachniks connive to do the impossible: steal the fabled 564-carat Star of India sapphire out of New York's American Museum of Natural History. Re-creation of the 1964 crime induces sweat, along with a good speedboat chase, but the picture never really catches a wave. 101m. **DIR:** Marvin J. Chomsky. **CAST:** Robert Conrad, Don Stroud, Donna Mills, Luther Adler. **1975**

MURPHY'S LAW ♥ Charles Bronson is a cop framed for the murder of his ex-wife. Rated R. 101m. **DIR:** J. Lee Thompson. **CAST:** Charles Bronson, Carrie Snodgress, Kathleen Wilhoite. **1986**

MURPHY'S ROMANCE ★★★★ This sweet little love story marks the finest performance by James Garner. He's a crusty small-town pharmacist, a widower with no shortage of home-cooked meals but little interest in anything more permanent. Garner and Sally Field are great together, and the result is a complete charmer. Rated PG-13. 107m. **DIR:** Martin Ritt. **CAST:** Sally Field, James Garner, Brian Kerwin, Corey Haim. **1985 DVD**

MURPHY'S WAR ★★★ World War II sea drama follows a British seaman, sole survivor of a brutal massacre of his ship's crew by a German U-boat, as he seeks revenge. Peter O'Toole gives a hard-hitting, no-holds-barred performance as the outraged, bloodthirsty Murphy. Rated PG. 108m. **DIR:** Peter Yates. **CAST:** Peter O'Toole, Sian Phillips, Horst Janson, Philippe Noiret, John Hallam. **1971**

MURROW ★★★★ Compassionate HBO film about the famous radio and television journalist Edward R. Murrow, played brilliantly by Daniel Travanti. The film devotes most of its running time to the journalist's struggle against McCarthyism. 114m. **DIR:** Jack Gold. **CAST:** Daniel J. Travanti, Dabney Coleman, Edward Herrmann, John McMartin, David Suchet, Kathryn Leigh Scott. **1985**

MUSCLE BEACH PARTY ★★ Everyone's favorite surfing couple, Frankie and Annette, and their beach buddies return for more fluff in the sun. This features the first screen appearance of Little Stevie Wonder. 94m. **DIR:** William Asher. **CAST:** Frankie Avalon, Annette Funicello, Buddy Hackett, Luciana Paluzzi, Don Rickles, John Ashley, Jody McCrea, Morey Amsterdam. **1964**

•**MUSE, THE** ★★★★ When a screenwriter (Albert Brooks) is told that he's "lost his edge," he takes the advice of another scripter and gets himself a muse (Sharon Stone). Allegedly descended from the goddesses of ancient Greece, this unusually demanding woman makes his life in the Hollywood jungle even more frantic and bewildering than it already was, bringing welcome laughs and an inside peek into the fickle world of Hollywood. Writer-director Brooks's fans will love this smart, knowing movie, as he continues to chronicle the lives and changing perspectives of baby boomers. The uninitiated may need to watch some of his earlier films to get in the groove. Rated PG-13 for profanity. 97m. **DIR:** Albert Brooks. **CAST:** Albert Brooks, Sharon Stone, Andie MacDowell, Jeff Bridges, Mark Fuerstein, Steven Wright, Bradley Whitford, Mario Opinato, Cybill Shepherd, Lorenzo Lamas, Jennifer Tilly, Rob Reiner, James Cameron, Martin Scorsese. **1999 DVD**

MUSIC BOX, THE ★★★1/2 An American lawyer is called upon to defend her Hungarian immigrant father when he is accused of having committed heinous war crimes during World War II in Nazi-occupied Hungary. Jessica Lange is excellent in this mystery with a message. Rated PG-13 for profanity. 123m. **DIR:** Constantin Costa-Gavras. **CAST:** Jessica Lange, Armin Mueller-Stahl, Frederic Forrest, Lukas Haas. **1989**

MUSIC FROM ANOTHER ROOM ★★1/2 A high-profile cast can't salvage this whimsical romantic drama. Danny, as a boy, helped his father deliver a little girl named Anna and then announced he would marry her one day. Years later, Danny bumps into Anna, now a grown-up beauty. Unfortunately, she is saddled with a dying mother and a dysfunctional family that demands her time. Will Danny be able to sway Anna to leave her responsibilities and get a life of her own? Rated PG-13 for language and adult situations. 104m. **DIR:** Charlie Peters. **CAST:** Jude Law, Gretchen Mol, Jennifer Tilly, Martha Plimpton, Brenda Blethyn, Jon Tenney, Jeremy Piven. **1997**

MUSIC LOVERS, THE ★★ A tasteless movie biography of Tchaikovsky, that gets two stars for the way the music is presented, not story or acting. Director Ken Russell overdoes it with phallic symbols and homoerotic references that are embarrassing to watch. 124m. **DIR:** Ken Russell. **CAST:** Glenda Jackson,

Richard Chamberlain, Christopher Gable, Max Adrian, Kenneth Colley. 1971

MUSIC MAN, THE ★★★1/2 They sure don't make musicals like this anymore, a smashing adaptation of Meredith Willson's Broadway hit. Robert Preston reprises the role of his life as a smooth-talkin' salesman who cajoles the parents of River City, Iowa, into purchasing band instruments and uniforms for their children. 151m. DIR: Morton Da Costa. CAST: Robert Preston, Shirley Jones, Buddy Hackett, Ron Howard, Paul Ford, Hermione Gingold. 1962 DVD

MUSIC OF CHANCE, THE ★★★ Dreamers Mandy Patinkin and James Spader enter a high-stakes poker game with two eccentric gamblers. When they lose, they are forced to build a wall to pay off their debt—once construction begins, all rhyme and reason end. Interesting cast makes this gambler's bluff pay off. Rated R for strong language. 98m. DIR: Philip Haas. CAST: James Spader, Mandy Patinkin, M. Emmet Walsh, Joel Grey, Charles Durning, Samantha Mathis. 1993

•**MUSIC OF THE HEART ★★★** This drama, based on the 1995 Oscar-nominated documentary *Small Wonders*, is more reverent than compelling or exhilarating. It chronicles the efforts of teacher-musician Roberta Guaspari-Tzvaras to establish a violin program in the public schools of East Harlem. The tenacious teacher/mentor brings a sense of pride and accomplishment to her students while battling racism and a budget crunch that threatens to terminate her classes. Rated PG. 123m. DIR: Wes Craven. CAST: Meryl Streep, Aidan Quinn, Gloria Estefan, Cloris Leachman, Angela Bassett. 1999 DVD

MUSIC SCHOOL, THE ★★★ The mathematical precision of music as a metaphor for the ideal life unattainable by mere mortals is the driving force behind this John Updike story. Ron Weyand stars as a typically angst-ridden Updike hero. The story unfolds through Updike's off-camera commentary. Introduced by Henry Fonda; aside from fleeting nudity, suitable for family viewing. 30m. DIR: John Korty. CAST: Ron Weyand, Dana Larsson, Cathleen Bauer. 1974

MUSIC TEACHER, THE ★★★★★ Belgian director and co-scenarist Gerard Corbiau weave an incredibly sensual story of the love of a gifted singer (Anne Roussel) for her music teacher (José Van Dam). Superb acting, exquisite cinematography, and great music. In French with English subtitles. Rated PG for suggested sex. 100m. DIR: Gerard Corbiau. CAST: José Van Dam, Anne Roussel, Philippe Volter. 1989

MUSSOLINI AND I ★★★ A weak and confusing narrative hinders this HBO film about the Fascist leader and his family's struggle with power. Bob Hoskins plays the Italian premier with a British accent; ditto for Anthony Hopkins who portrays Galeazzo Ciano, Italy's minister of foreign affairs and the dictator's brother-in-law. Still, the story is kept interesting despite its length. Not rated, but the equivalent of a PG for violence. 130m. DIR: Alberto Negrin. CAST: Anthony Hopkins, Susan Sarandon, Bob Hoskins, Annie Girardot, Barbara de Rossi, Vittorio Mezzogiorno, Fabio Testi, Kurt Raab. 1985

MUTANT ❤ Idiocy. Rated R for violence. 100m. DIR: John "Bud" Cardos. CAST: Bo Hopkins, Wings Hauser,

Jennifer Warren, Cary Guffey, Lee Montgomery. 1983

MUTANT HUNT ❤ The mutants are actually cyborgs run amok in this terrible sci-fi effort. Not rated; contains violence, profanity, gore, and nudity. 77m. DIR: Tim Kincaid. CAST: Rick Gianasi, Mary Fahey, Stormy Spill. 1987

MUTANT ON THE BOUNTY ★★ Silly yet sometimes amusing sci-fi spoof about a research team on a spaceship. Not rated. 93m. DIR: Robert Torrance. CAST: John Roarke, Deborah Benson, John Furey. 1989

MUTANT SPECIES ★★ A team of mercenaries enters a forest in search of an alien symbiont/weapon. When the weapon combines itself with one of the soldiers, creating an unfeeling killing machine, soldiers begin to die at a very rapid pace. Ludicrous and overplayed feature offers a thrill or two. Rated R for violence and profanity. 100m. DIR: David A. Prior. CAST: Leo Rossi, Powers Boothe, Wilford Brimley, Denise Crosby, Grant Gelt. 1995

MUTANTS IN PARADISE ★★1/2 Campus loser, roped into an experiment to create a "nuke-proof" man, becomes a local celebrity. Rambling student-made film has cute ideas but lacks the budget to flesh them out. For one thing, there aren't any mutants. Not rated; contains no objectionable material. 77m. DIR: Scott Apostolou. CAST: Brad Greenquist, Anna Nicholas, Edith Massey, Ray "Boom Boom" Mancini. 1985

•**MUTATOR ★★** Mediocre nature-run-amok/genetic-experiment thriller with only so-so hairy monster effects. Here, the lab must be sealed off to keep the monsters from getting out. The sole point of interest is Brion James in a rare hero role. Rated R for violence. 91m. DIR: John R. Bowey. CAST: Brion James, Carolyn Ann Clark. 1991

MUTE WITNESS ★★★★ Being scared is rarely this much fun. Russian actress Marina Sudina is fab in the title role as a speechless special-effects woman working a low-budget American-movie gig in Russia. Sudina, who would have made a great silent-screen actress, so articulates her terror upon witnessing a crime that you'll soon shift to the edge of your seat. The overall effect is furiously suspenseful. Watch for Alec Guinness in an unbilled cameo. Rated R for profanity, violence, and nudity. 98m. DIR: Anthony Waller. CAST: Marina Sudina, Fay Ripley, Evan Richards, Oleg Jankovskii, Alec Guinness. 1994

MUTILATOR, THE ❤ More gore galore as a psycho kills off his sons' friends when they visit the family island. Rated R. 86m. DIR: Buddy Cooper. CAST: Matt Mitler. 1984

MUTINY IN OUTER SPACE ★★ After exploring caves on the moon, astronauts become infected with an alien fungus. Overplotted sci-fi potboiler bears some similarity to *Alien*, though not enough to make it interesting. B&W; 80m. DIR: Hugo Grimaldi. CAST: William Leslie, Dolores Faith, Pamela Curran, Richard Garland, Harold Lloyd Jr., Glenn Langan. 1965

MUTINY ON THE BOUNTY (1935) ★★★★ The first and best known of three versions of the now-classic account of mutiny against the tyranny of Captain William Bligh during a worldwide British naval expedition in 1789. Charles Laughton is superb as the merciless Bligh, Clark Gable unquestionably fine as the leader of the mutiny, Fletcher Christian. The film won an Oscar for best picture and still entertains today. B&W; 132m. **DIR:** Frank Lloyd. **CAST:** Charles Laughton, Clark Gable, Franchot Tone, Dudley Digges, Eddie Quillan, Donald Crisp, Henry Stephenson. **1935**

MUTINY ON THE BOUNTY (1962) ★★ This years-later remake hits the South Seas with a gigantic belly flop. Trevor Howard is commanding as the tyrannical Captain Bligh, but Marlon Brando as mutiny leader Fletcher Christian? Yucko! 179m. **DIR:** Lewis Milestone. **CAST:** Marlon Brando, Trevor Howard, Richard Harris, Hugh Griffith, Richard Haydn, Gordon Jackson. **1962**

•MUTUAL NEEDS ★★ An ambitious junior executive rises in the ranks after the hooker he hired to pose as his wife impresses his boss. But his luck turns when she decides she deserves a piece of his good fortune. An erotic thriller whose plot mostly just fills time between heavy-breathing scenes with Rochelle Swanson. Rated R for profanity, nudity, sex, and violence. 88m. **DIR:** Robert Angelo. **CAST:** Eric Woods, Richard Grieco, Rochelle Swanson, Charlotte Lewis. **1997**

MY AMERICAN COUSIN ★★★★ This delightful Canadian comedy-drama focuses on what happens when the dull life of 12-year-old Sandra (played by feisty newcomer Margaret Langrick) is invaded by her high-spirited 17-year-old relative, Butch (John Wildman), from California. A warm character study with a number of funny moments, this is a refreshing antidote to the mindless teen flicks so common today. Rated PG for mild sexuality. 110m. **DIR:** Sandy Wilson. **CAST:** Margaret Langrick, John Wildman, Richard Donat. **1986**

MY ANTONIA ★★★ Willa Cather's novels about frontier life tend to translate smoothly to video; and this is no exception. Neil Patrick Harris is the orphaned teenager who falls for a poor immigrant girl. The land is as much a character as the people in this enjoyable family picture. Rated PG for adult themes. 92m. **DIR:** Joseph Sargent. **CAST:** Neil Patrick Harris, Jan Triska, Jason Robards Jr., Eva Marie Saint, Norbert Weisser. **1994**

MY BEAUTIFUL LAUNDRETTE ★★★1/2 In modern-day England, a young Pakistani immigrant is given a laundrette by his rich uncle and, with the help of his punk-rocker boyfriend turns it into a showplace. A racist gang decides to close them down. British director Stephen Frears keeps things from becoming too heavy by adding deft touches of comedy. Rated R for profanity, suggested and simulated sex, and violence. 103m. **DIR:** Stephen Frears. **CAST:** Saeed Jaffrey, Roshan Seth, Daniel Day-Lewis, Gordon Warnecke, Shirley Anne Field. **1985**

MY BEST FRIEND IS A VAMPIRE ★★ Teen romance with a twist: Our hero has just become a vampire. Abundant car-chase scenes should intrigue teen viewers. Rated PG for Jeremy's seduction by the sexy vampire. 90m. **DIR:** Jimmy Huston. **CAST:** Robert Sean Leonard, Cheryl Pollak, René Auberjonois, Fannie Flagg. **1986**

MY BEST FRIEND'S GIRL ★★★ A philosophical comedy about two best but very different friends who find themselves in love with the same girl. Isabelle Huppert marvelously plays the sultry object of both men's desire, but the real gem of this film is the performance of Coluche, who falls in love with his best friend's girl. In French with English subtitles. Nudity and simulated sex. 99m. **DIR:** Bertrand Blier. **CAST:** Isabelle Huppert, Thierry Lhermitte, Coluche. **1984**

MY BEST FRIEND'S WEDDING ★★★ Julia Roberts realizes she's in love with her best friend of ten years (Dermot Mulroney), when he announces his engagement to wonderful rich girl Cameron Diaz. Roberts' attempts to sabotage the wedding lack comic energy, while the film explores emotional issues only superficially. Rupert Everett almost saves the show as Roberts's gay boss, reluctantly posing as her lover. Rated PG-13. 105m. **DIR:** P. J. Hogan. **CAST:** Julia Roberts, Dermot Mulroney, Cameron Diaz, Rupert Everett. **1997 DVD**

MY BLOODY VALENTINE ★★ Candy boxes stuffed with bloody human hearts signal the return of a legendary murderous coal miner to Valentine Bluffs. This film provides a few doses of excitement and a tidal wave of killings. Rated R. 91m. **DIR:** George Mihalka. **CAST:** Paul Kelman, Lori Hallier, Neil Affleck. **1981**

MY BLUE HEAVEN ★★★ Steve Martin and Rick Moranis are fun to watch in this gangster comedy, which has Martin as a mob informer in the witness protection program and Moranis as the FBI agent assigned to watch over him. Don't expect to laugh uproariously. Rated PG-13 for profanity and violence. 95m. **DIR:** Herbert Ross. **CAST:** Steve Martin, Rick Moranis, Joan Cusack, Melanie Mayron, Carol Kane, Bill Irwin, Deborah Rush. **1990 DVD**

MY BODYGUARD ★★★★ This is a wonderfully funny and touching movie. Fifteen-year-old Clifford Peache (Chris Makepeace) must face the challenges of public high school after nine years of private education. His classes are easy. It's his schoolmates who cause problems. Specifically, there's Moody (Matt Dillon), a nasty young thug who extorts money from the other students. Rated PG. 96m. **DIR:** Tony Bill. **CAST:** Chris Makepeace, Matt Dillon, Martin Mull, Ruth Gordon, Adam Baldwin. **1980**

MY BOYFRIEND'S BACK ★★★1/2 When love-struck nerd Andrew Lowery is shot saving Traci Lind's life, his dying wish is that she will accompany him to the prom. She agrees; he dies. Lowery keeps his date by returning from the dead, setting off some hilarious complications. Humor is derived mainly from his home life, and the interaction of his goofy parents. Rated PG-13 for comic gore and adult language. 85m. **DIR:** Bob Balaban. **CAST:** Andrew Lowery, Traci Lind, Mary Beth Hurt, Edward Herrmann, Paul Dooley, Cloris Leachman. **1993**

MY BOYS ARE GOOD BOYS ★★ It's good to see veteran actors Ralph Meeker and Ida Lupino again, but it's too bad the occasion is this low-budget effort. They play parents of juvenile delinquents who rob an armored car. Pretty mediocre. Rated PG. 90m. **DIR:**

Bethel Buckalew. **CAST:** Ralph Meeker, Ida Lupino, Lloyd Nolan, David Doyle. **1978**

MY BRILLIANT CAREER ★★★1/2 A superb Australian import, *My Brilliant Career*, is about a young woman clearly born before her time. It is the waning years of the nineteenth century, when the only respectable status for a woman is to be married. Sybylla Melvyn (Judy Davis), who lives with her family in the Australian bush, does not want to marry. She has "immortal longings." Rated G. 101m. **DIR:** Gillian Armstrong. **CAST:** Judy Davis, Sam Neill, Wendy Hughes. **1979**

MY BROTHER'S WIFE ★★ John Ritter lends some heart to this tired tale of a man who spends two decades pursuing his sister-in-law. Ritter helps save this made-for-television comedy, based on A. R. Gurney's play *The Middle Ages*. 100m. **DIR:** Jack Bender. **CAST:** John Ritter, Mel Harris, Polly Bergen. **1989**

MY CHAUFFEUR ★★1/2 In this better-than-average (for the genre) soft-core sex comedy, an aggressive, slightly kooky young woman upsets things at an all-male limousine company. Rated R for oodles of nudity, leering dirty old men by the truckload, suggested sex, and profanity. Don't let the kids rent this while you're out playing poker. 97m. **DIR:** David Beaird. **CAST:** Deborah Foreman, Sam Jones, Howard Hesseman, E. G. Marshall, Sean McClory. **1986 DVD**

MY COUSIN VINNY ★★★★ A fledgling Brooklyn lawyer attempts to free his cousin, who has been arrested on a murder charge in backward Wahzoo City, Alabama. It's a movie you won't want to miss. Joe Pesci is terrific, and so is Marisa Tomei as his gum popping fiancée. Rated R for profanity and brief violence. 116m. **DIR:** Jonathan Lynn. **CAST:** Joe Pesci, Ralph Macchio, Marisa Tomei, Mitchell Whitfield, Fred Gwynne, Lane Smith, Austin Pendleton, Bruce McGill, Maury Chaykin. **1991**

MY DARLING CLEMENTINE ★★★1/2 The epic struggle between good and evil is wrapped up in this classic retelling of the shoot-out at the O.K. Corral, between the Earps and the lawless Clanton family. Henry Fonda gives his Wyatt Earp a feeling of believability, perfectly matched by Walter Brennan's riveting portrayal of villainy as the head of the Clanton gang. B&W; 97m. **DIR:** John Ford. **CAST:** Henry Fonda, Victor Mature, Walter Brennan, Linda Darnell, Ward Bond, Tim Holt. **1946**

MY DAUGHTER'S KEEPER ★★1/2 British entry into *The Hand That Rocks the Cradle* subgenre features (surprise) a psychotic nanny who takes over the household, her charge, and finally the husband. Some chilling moments, but it all seems derivative at this point in the game. Not rated; contains violence, nudity, and adult language. 109m. **DIR:** Heinrich Dahms. **CAST:** Nicholas Guest, Ana Padrao, Jocelyn Broderick, Kelly Westhof. **1993**

MY DEAR SECRETARY ★★1/2 A comedy battle of quips and wits between writer Kirk Douglas and bestselling author Laraine Day. Both lose the picture to Keenan Wynn, who is a droll delight. B&W; 94m. **DIR:** Charles Martin. **CAST:** Laraine Day, Kirk Douglas, Helen Walker, Keenan Wynn, Alan Mowbray. **1948**

MY DEMON LOVER ★★★1/2 Scott Valentine is delightful as a lovable bum who is possessed by the

devil. His infatuation with a very gullible Denny (Michelle Little) becomes complicated when he is transformed into a demon every time he gets amorous. Rated PG for simulated sex and mild gore. 87m. **DIR:** Charlie Loventhal. **CAST:** Scott Valentine, Michelle Little, Robert Trebor, Gina Gallego, Alan Fudge. **1987**

MY DINNER WITH ANDRE ★★★★★ One of the most daring films ever made, this fascinating work consists almost entirely of a dinner conversation between two men. It's a terrific little movie. You'll be surprised how entertaining it is. No MPAA rating. The film has no objectionable material. 110m. **DIR:** Louis Malle. **CAST:** Andre Gregory, Wallace Shawn. **1981 DVD**

•MY DOG SKIP ★★★★ This sentimental tale of a boy and his dog, based on Willie Morris's bestselling memoir, is adapted with sparkle and a rich tapestry of memorable characters. Everything is perfect, from Gail Gilchriest's poignant script to narrator Harry Connick Jr.'s honeyed southern drawl, which whisks us back to 1942, to the small town of Yazoo, Mississippi. The story concerns Willie, an undersized 8-year-old only child (Frankie Muniz), who has been badly sheltered from life's possible traumas by a gruff father. Only after an enthusiastic canine is introduced into the house does this pattern begin and Willie finds himself able to make those connections into solid boyhood that had, until now, eluded him. The result is a slice of cinema heaven: a film with the narrative depth of *To Kill a Mockingbird* and the sentimental intensity of that killer-of-all-killer family films, *Old Yeller*. Rated PG for dramatic intensity. 93m. **DIR:** Jay Russell. **CAST:** Frankie Muniz, Diane Lane, Kevin Bacon, Luke Wilson. **2000 DVD**

MY DREAM IS YOURS ★★★ Doris Day becomes a radio star in a snappy musical-comedy based on Dick Powell's 1934 hit, *Twenty Million Sweethearts*. Day plays the role Powell played in the original, a would-be singer who makes the big time in radio. A dream sequence with Bugs Bunny is a highlight. 101m. **DIR:** Michael Curtiz. **CAST:** Doris Day, Jack Carson, Lee Bowman, Adolphe Menjou, Eve Arden, S. Z. Sakall, Edgar Kennedy, Sheldon Leonard, Franklin Pangborn. **1949**

MY FAIR LADY ★★★★1/2 *Pygmalion*, the timeless George Bernard Shaw play, has been a success in every form in which it has been presented. This Oscar-winning 1964 movie musical adaptation is no exception. Rex Harrison, as Professor Henry Higgins, is the perfect example of British class snobbishness. Audrey Hepburn gives a fine performance as Eliza Doolittle (with Marni Nixon supplying the singing). 170m. **DIR:** George Cukor. **CAST:** Rex Harrison, Audrey Hepburn, Stanley Holloway. **1964 DVD**

MY FAMILY ★★★ An intimate epic covering sixty years of a Mexican-American family's struggles, triumphs, and absurdities. The narrative is, unfortunately, spread too thin, and only the all-Latino ensemble's best actors (Jimmy Smits, Edward James Olmos) manage to make their characters rise above symbolic status. Rated R for language, violence, sex, nudity, and drugs. 130m. **DIR:** Gregory Nava. **CAST:** Jimmy Smits, Esai Morales, Eduardo Lopez Rojas,

Jenny Gago, Elpidia Carrillo, Edward James Olmos, Constance Marie. 1995

MY FATHER IS COMING ★★★ A young German woman living in Manhattan pretends to be married when her father pays a visit, then watches in amazement as the supposedly stuffy old man has an affair with a sex therapist. Amusing exploration of modern sexuality. Not rated; contains nudity and frank sexual discussions. B&W; 82m. DIR: Monika Treut. CAST: Shelley Kastner, Alfred Edel, Annie Sprinkle. 1991

MY FATHER, THE HERO ★★★1/2 Genial, goofy Disney comedy is obviously intended to increase French superstar Gérard Depardieu's popularity in America. Though at first seemingly miscast, Depardieu is fine as the father of a feisty teenage girl. She tries to pass him off as her older lover while they're on vacation in order to appear sexy and sophisticated to a young suitor. It's charming, corny, and humorous all at the same time. Rated PG. DIR: Steve Miner. CAST: Gérard Depardieu, Katherine Heigl, Dalton James, Faith Prince, Stephen Tobolowsky, Emma Thompson. 1994

MY FATHER'S GLORY ★★★★★ French filmmaker Yves Robert's remarkable film is the unforgettable chronicle of author and filmmaker Marcel Pagnol's idyllic remembrances of his childhood. The most commonplace events are made to seem magical in this import and its sequel, *My Mother's Castle*. Not since *Jean de Florette* and *Manon of the Spring* has a French filmmaker so artfully mined a literary source. Bravo! In French with English subtitles. Rated G. 110m. DIR: Yves Robert. CAST: Philippe Caubère, Nathalie Roussel, Thérèse Liotard, Didier Pain. 1991

MY FAVORITE BLONDE ★★★★ Funny outing with cowardly vaudeville star Bob Hope on his way to Hollywood. (His trained penguin just won a contract.) He becomes involved with a British secret agent and assassinations. B&W; 78m. DIR: Sidney Lanfield. CAST: Bob Hope, Madeleine Carroll, Gale Sondergaard, George Zucco. 1942

MY FAVORITE BRUNETTE ★★★1/2 Classic Bob Hope comedy with Bob as a photographer who, thanks to a case of mistaken identity, makes No. 1 on the death list of a gang of thugs, played beautifully by Peter Lorre, Lon Chaney Jr., John Hoyt, and Elisha Cook Jr. Bob tries every trick in the book to save his neck, as well as Dorothy Lamour's. A scream! B&W; 87m. DIR: Elliott Nugent. CAST: Bob Hope, Dorothy Lamour, Peter Lorre, Lon Chaney Jr., John Hoyt. 1947 DVD

MY FAVORITE MARTIAN ★★★ Remaining faithful to the TV series, this plays out as more of a sequel than a remake. Jeff Daniels stumbles on the ship after being dumped by the boss's spoiled brat and plunges into an endless series of problems after the martian moves in with him. Physical humor and sight gags get a bit tiresome. Rated PG for comic-book violence and sexual innuendo. 91m. DIR: Donald Petrie. CAST: Jeff Daniels, Christopher Lloyd, Daryl Hannah, Elizabeth Hurley, Ray Walston. 1999 DVD

MY FAVORITE WIFE ★★★★★ Cary Grant and Irene Dunne teamed up for many hilarious films, but the best is this often-copied comedy. Grant is a widower about to be remarried when his long-lost and presumed-dead wife (Dunne) is rescued after years on an island with a handsome young scientist (Randolph Scott). The delightful complications that result make this one of the 1940s' best comedies. B&W; 88m. DIR: Garson Kanin. CAST: Cary Grant, Irene Dunne, Randolph Scott. 1940

MY FAVORITE YEAR ★★★★1/2 This warmhearted, hilarious comedy is an affectionate tribute to the frenzied Golden Age of television, that period when uninhibited comics like Sid Caesar faced the added pressure of performing live. With superb performances all around and on-the-money direction by Richard Benjamin, it's a real treasure. Rated PG for slight profanity and sexual situations. 92m. DIR: Richard Benjamin. CAST: Peter O'Toole, Mark Linn-Baker, Joseph Bologna, Lainie Kazan, Bill Macy. 1982

MY FELLOW AMERICANS ★★★★ In James Garner, Jack Lemmon finds as worthy a comic partner as Walter Matthau in what could just as easily have been called *Grumpy Old Presidents*. Longtime rivals Lemmon, a Republican, and Garner, a Democrat, find themselves thrown together in a life-or-death situation when the current president decides he wants them dead. There have been some dirty dealings at the White House, and the new prez wants to pin it on someone else. Rated PG-13 for suggested sex, profanity, and violence. 101m. DIR: Peter Segal. CAST: Jack Lemmon, James Garner, Dan Aykroyd, John Heard, Sela Ward, Wilford Brimley, Everett McGill, Lauren Bacall, Bradley Whitford, James Rebhorn, Esther Rolle, Conchata Ferrell. 1996 DVD

MY FIRST WIFE ★★★1/2 In the tradition of *Ordinary People*, *Kramer vs. Kramer*, and *Smash Palace* comes another film about the dissolution of a marriage. The story deals with a classical music programmer/composer who finds that his wife doesn't love him anymore. Rated PG for adult situations and language. 95m. DIR: Paul Cox. CAST: John Hargreaves, Wendy Hughes. 1985

MY FOOLISH HEART ★★★★ One of the most popular romances from WW II years, this movie inspired a popular song and helped establish the romantic image that made Susan Hayward famous. A woman falls in love with a soldier about to be shipped out and carries his child in this romantic melodrama. B&W; 98m. DIR: Mark Robson. CAST: Susan Hayward, Dana Andrews, Robert Keith, Gigi Perreau, Kent Smith, Lois Wheeler. 1949

MY FORBIDDEN PAST ★★ Set in steamy New Orleans in 1890, this one's about Ava Gardner's cold-blooded attempts to buy married-man Robert Mitchum's affections with the help of an unexpected inheritance. His wife is killed. He's accused of her murder. Gardner, revealing her unsavory past in order to save him, wins his love. B&W; 81m. DIR: Robert Stevenson. CAST: Robert Mitchum, Ava Gardner, Janis Carter, Melvyn Douglas, Lucile Watson. 1951

MY FRIEND FLICKA ★★★1/2 A young boy raises and nourishes a sickly colt despite his father's warning that the horse came from wild stock and could be unstable. Fine rendition of Mary O'Hara's timeless novel and one of the last of a genre that flourished in the 1940s before Disney cornered the market a few years later. 89m. DIR: Harold Schuster. CAST: Roddy McDowall, Preston Foster, Rita Johnson, James Bell, Jeff Corey, Diana Hale, Arthur Loft. 1943

MY FRIEND IRMA ★★1/2 The plan to transpose a popular radio show about the "dumbest" of all "dumb blondes" to the screen went astray when it became the vehicle to introduce the team of Dean Martin and Jerry Lewis. The creator of the radio show, Cy Howard, coscripted, but he and his star, the lovely Marie Wilson, were all but lost in the shuffle. B&W; 113m. DIR: George Marshall. CAST: John Lund, Diana Lynn, Don DeFore, Marie Wilson, Dean Martin, Jerry Lewis, Hans Conried. 1949

MY GEISHA ★★★ A Hollywood actress disguises herself as a geisha to convince her producer-husband to cast her in his Japan-based production of *Madame Butterfly.* Shirley MacLaine is delightful in an *I Love Lucy* sort of plot. 120m. DIR: Jack Cardiff. CAST: Shirley MacLaine, Yves Montand, Edward G. Robinson, Robert Cummings. 1962

MY GIANT ★★ Small-time agent Billy Crystal discovers what he thinks is his ticket to the big time in a towering Romanian peasant (NBA star Gheorghe Muresan). Gradually the gentle giant brings out the human side of the cynical agent. The only laughs come in the first few minutes. The film gradually dissolves into mushy sentiment. Rated PG. 103m. DIR: Michael Lehmann. CAST: Billy Crystal, Gheorghe Muresan, Kathleen Quinlan, Joanna Pacula, Zane Carney, Harold Gould, Doris Roberts, Steven Seagal. 1998 DVD

MY GIRL ★★★★ A genuinely touching, frequently hilarious and heartfelt film about the difficult adjustments forced on an 11-year-old girl who secretly fears that she was responsible for her mother's death. Lovable characters and the essence of truth make this a good film for families to watch and discuss afterward. Rated PG for brief vulgarity. 90m. DIR: Howard Zieff. CAST: Dan Aykroyd, Jamie Lee Curtis, Macaulay Culkin, Anna Chlumsky, Richard Masur, Griffin Dunne. 1991 DVD

MY GIRL 2 💣 Vada Sultenfuss, the hypochondriac daughter of a widowed mortician, hits her teens in this terminally dull sequel as she researches the life of the mother she never knew. Rated PG. 99m. DIR: Howard Zieff. CAST: Anna Chlumsky, Austin O'Brien, Dan Aykroyd, Jamie Lee Curtis, Richard Masur. 1994

MY GIRL TISA ★★1/2 Tired story of a pretty, diligent immigrant girl's efforts to bring her father to New York from the old country. B&W; 95m. DIR: Elliott Nugent. CAST: Lilli Palmer, Sam Wanamaker, Akim Tamiroff, Alan Hale Sr., Stella Adler. 1948

MY GRANDPA IS A VAMPIRE 💣 Grandpa (Al Lewis) does not meet vampire criteria. He's able to survive in sunlight, doesn't suck blood, and performs a number of magic tricks. This film, made in New Zealand, takes the bite out of the would-be vampire thus reducing him to an ET-ish ghoul. Not rated, contains violence. 92m. DIR: David Blyth. CAST: Al Lewis. 1991

MY HEROES HAVE ALWAYS BEEN COWBOYS ★★★★ The themes explored in Sam Peckinpah's *Junior Bonner* get a reworking in this surprisingly effective film about a rodeo bull rider (Scott Glenn) who comes home to heal his injuries and ends up rescuing his father (Ben Johnson) from a retirement home. Wonderful performances and strong character development even make up for the expected *Rocky*-style ending. Rated PG for brief profanity and violence. 106m. DIR: Stuart Rosenberg. CAST: Scott Glenn, Kate Capshaw, Ben Johnson, Tess Harper, Gary Busey, Mickey Rooney, Balthazar Getty, Clarence Williams III, Dub Taylor, Clu Gulager. 1991

MY HUSBAND'S SECRET LIFE ★★★ A woman investigates the on-the-job life of her recently deceased husband—a police detective—in the hopes of releasing money due her family from the government. Diverting if not inspiring. Rated PG-13. 93m. DIR: Graeme Clifford. CAST: Anne Archer, James Russo, Maria Conchita Alonso. 1998

MY LEFT FOOT ★★★★★ Everything is right in the screen biography of handicapped Irish writer-artist Christy Brown who was afflicted with cerebral palsy from birth. Writer-director Jim Sheridan and co-scripter Shane Connaughton tell Brown's story without succumbing to cliché or audience manipulation. Oscar-winner Daniel Day-Lewis gives what may be the performance of his career. Rated R for profanity and violence. 119m. DIR: Jim Sheridan. CAST: Daniel Day-Lewis, Ray McAnally, Brenda Fricker, Fiona Shaw, Hugh O'Connor, Cyril Cusack. 1989 DVD

MY LIFE ★★★ A career-obsessed public relations executive, dying of cancer, spends his last months making peace with his parents and videotaping himself for his unborn child. Solid, surefire performances from stars Michael Keaton and Nicole Kidman redeem this predictable disease-of-the-week tearjerker. Rated PG-13 for mild profanity and mature themes. 114m. DIR: Bruce Joel Rubin. CAST: Michael Keaton, Nicole Kidman, Michael Constantine, Haing S. Ngor. 1993

MY LIFE AND TIMES WITH ANTONIN ARTAUD ★★★★ Exquisitely photographed and performed tale of poet Antonin Artaud, who founded the infamous "Theater of Cruelty." When Artaud is released from a Parisian mental institution in 1946, he is befriended by young poet Jacques Prevel. This haunting tale, which details their tumultuous relationship is uncomfortable at times, but always watchable. In French with English subtitles. Not rated; contains profanity and mature themes. 93m. DIR: Gérard Mordillat. CAST: Sami Frey, Marc Barbé, Julie Jézéquel, Valerie Jeannet. 1993

MY LIFE AS A DOG ★★★★ This charming, offbeat, and downright lovable import from Sweden is a big surprise. It tells of a young boy in 1950s Sweden who's shipped off to a country village when his mother becomes seriously ill. There, as he tries to come to terms with his new life, he encounters a town filled with colorful eccentrics and a young tomboy who becomes his first love. In Swedish with

English subtitles. 101m. DIR: Lasse Hallstrom. CAST: Anton Glanzelius. **1987 DVD**

•**MY LIFE SO FAR** ★★★1/2 Rich, privileged clan and their servants gather at an idyllic country estate in 1920 Scotland. The central character is a 10-year-old boy who is introduced to the mysteries of the flesh when he raids a secret attic library. His relationship with his inventor father and both their lives are complicated when an uncle brings his young French fiancée for a visit. This both dark and whimsical family portrait is based on the memoirs of Royal Opera House director Denis Forman. Rated PG-13 for sexual content. 93m. DIR: Hugh Hudson. CAST: Robert Norman, Colin Firth, Malcolm McDowell, Irène Jacob. **1999 DVD**

MY LIFE TO LIVE ★★★ Early piece of groundbreaking cinema by Jean-Luc Godard features Anna Karina as a young woman who leaves her husband to become an actress but eventually turns to prostitution. As with any Jean-Luc Godard film, the point is not so much the plot as the director's relentless experimentation with film technique and probing of social issues. In French with English subtitles. B&W; 85m. DIR: Jean-Luc Godard. CAST: Anna Karina, Saddy Rebbot. **1963 DVD**

MY LIFE'S IN TURNAROUND 💔 If you like profanity and plotless stories, you'll love this film about two guys trying to make a movie about their lives. Rated R for profanity and nudity. 84m. DIR: Eric Schaeffer, Donald Lardnerward. CAST: Eric Schaeffer, Donald Lardnerward, Lisa Gerstein. **1994**

MY LITTLE CHICKADEE ★★★★★ W. C. Fields and Mae West enter a marriage of convenience in the Old West. It seems the card sharp (Fields) and the tainted lady (West) need to create an aura of respectability before they descend upon an unsuspecting town. That indicates trouble ahead for the town, and lots of fun for viewers. B&W; 83m. DIR: Eddie Cline. CAST: W. C. Fields, Mae West, Dick Foran, Joseph Calleia. **1940**

MY LITTLE GIRL ★★ Familiar tale of a do-good rich kid's introduction to the real world. Mary Stuart Masterson stars as a 16-year-old high school student who volunteers to spend a summer working at a state-run shelter. The performances raise this (just barely) to the tolerable level. Rated R for violence and profanity. 118m. DIR: Connie Kaiserman. CAST: James Earl Jones, Geraldine Page, Mary Stuart Masterson, Anne Meara. **1986**

MY LITTLE PONY: THE MOVIE ★★★ Darling ponies are threatened by the evil witch family. Children under 7 should enjoy this, but older children and adults may feel it's too long. Danny DeVito, Madeline Kahn, Cloris Leachman, Rhea Perlman, Tony Randall (voices). Rated G. 85m. DIR: Michael Joens. **1986**

MY LOVE FOR YOURS (HONEYMOON IN BALI) ★★★ An eager cast and a witty script make a passable entertainment of this otherwise trite story of a cool, self-assured career girl thawed by love. B&W; 99m. DIR: Edward H. Griffith. CAST: Madeleine Carroll, Fred MacMurray, Allan Jones, Helen Broderick, Akim Tamiroff, Osa Massen, John Qualen. **1939**

MY LUCKY STAR ★★★★ Sonja Henie skates like a dream as a student working at a department store to pay for college. She falls for teacher Richard Greene, flirts with department-store heir Cesar Romero and performs in an "Alice in Wonderland" ice ballet to help the department store out of a jam. B&W; 81m. DIR: Roy Del Ruth. CAST: Sonja Henie, Richard Greene, Cesar Romero, Gypsy Rose Lee, Buddy Ebsen, Billy Gilbert, Arthur Treacher. **1938**

MY MAGIC DOG ★★ An invisible dog that only an 8-year-old boy can see saves the day when he thwarts bullies and an evil aunt out to make off with the kid's inheritance. Only the youngest of children will appreciate the predictable format. Not rated. 98m. DIR: John Putch. CAST: Leo Millbrook, Russ Tamblyn, John Phillip Law. **1997**

MY MAN ADAM ★★ Daydreaming teenager Raphael Sbarge gets a chance to live out his fantasies when he uncovers a sinister plot at school. Disappointing comedy has some clever moments but the plot seems slapped together. Rated R, though there's nothing really offensive. 84m. DIR: Roger L. Simon. CAST: Raphael Sbarge, Page Hannah, Dave Thomas, Veronica Cartwright. **1985**

MY MAN GODFREY (1936) ★★★★★ *My Man Godfrey* is one of the great screwball comedies of the 1930s. Carole Lombard plays the most eccentric member of an eccentric family. William Powell is the relatively sane portion of the formula. Carole finds him when she is sent to find a "lost man." Powell seems to fit the bill, since he's living a hobo's life on the wrong side of the tracks. B&W; 95m. DIR: Gregory La Cava. CAST: Carole Lombard, William Powell, Gail Patrick, Alice Brady, Eugene Pallette. **1936 DVD**

MY MAN GODFREY (1957) ★★1/2 Passable but otherwise doomed update of the 1936 classic screwball comedy will play better for those not familiar with the original. The stars try. 92m. DIR: Henry Koster. CAST: June Allyson, David Niven, Jessie Royce Landis, Robert Keith, Eva Gabor, Jay Robinson, Jeff Donnell, Martha Hyer. **1957**

MY MAN (MON HOMME) ★★★★ The perennial bad boy of French cinema, Bertrand Blier shows he hasn't mellowed much since his Oscar-winning *Get Out Your Handkerchiefs*. The failure of the sexes to understand each other, as well as men's fear of female sexuality, remain his favorite subjects in this occasionally surreal comedy about a happy hooker who fashions a homeless bum into a successful pimp. In French with English subtitles. Not rated; the film features strong sexual content. 95m. DIR: Bertrand Blier. CAST: Anouk Grinberg, Gerard Lanvin, Valeria Bruni Tedeschi, Olivier Martinez, Mathieu Kassovitz. **1997**

MY MOM'S A WEREWOLF ★★ When a bored housewife (Susan Blakely) succumbs to a charming stranger (John Saxon), she is horrified to find herself transforming into a werewolf. Now her daughter and her ghoulish pal must figure out how to transform Blakely back into dear old mom. PG for profanity and violence. 90m. DIR: Michael Fischa. CAST: Susan Blakely, John Saxon, Katrina Caspary, Ruth Buzzi. **1988 DVD**

MY MOTHER'S CASTLE ★★★★ More glorious adventures for young Marcel Pagnol in the exquisite sequel to *My Father's Glory*. Once again, filmmaker Yves Robert brings out all of the suspense, humor, and heartbreak in this autobiographical tale. In French with English subtitles. Rated PG. 98m. DIR: Yves Robert. CAST: Philippe Caubère, Nathalie Roussel, Thérèse Liotard, Didier Pain, Jean Rochefort. 1991

MY MOTHER'S SECRET LIFE ★★ Long-lost daughter turns up on Mom's doorstep. To her horror, Mom (Loni Anderson) turns out to be an expensive call girl. Hard to believe and just barely watchable. 94m. DIR: Robert Markowitz. CAST: Loni Anderson, Paul Sorvino, Amanda Wyss. 1984

MY NAME IS BARBRA ★★★★ Barbra Streisand fans have a real treasure awaiting them in *My Name Is Barbra*. Shown in 1965, shot in black and white, and featuring no guests, it was Streisand's first television special. It's a wonderful opportunity to see this exceptional performer early in her career. Viewers will also be treated to knockout versions of "When the Sun Comes Out" and "My Man." 60m. DIR: Dwight Hemion. CAST: Barbra Streisand. 1965

MY NAME IS BILL W ★★★1/2 Impressive made-for-TV drama depicts the personal tragedies of Bill Wilson (James Woods) that led to the founding of Alcoholics Anonymous. It is difficult to watch at times, specifically in the scenes where Wilson's life and career turn sour because of excessive drinking. But this, of course, is the point of the film. Outstanding performances by a fine cast. Made for TV. 100m. DIR: Daniel Petrie. CAST: James Woods, James Garner, Jo-Beth Williams, Gary Sinise, Fritz Weaver, Robert Harper, George Coe. 1989

MY NAME IS IVAN ★★★★ The title character is a 12-year-old boy who works as a scout for the Soviet army during World War II. An affecting study of the horrors of war. Young Kolya Burlaiev is remarkable as Ivan. In Russian with English subtitles. Not rated. 84m. DIR: Andrei Tarkovsky. CAST: Kolya Burlaiev, Valentin Zubkov. 1963

MY NAME IS JOE ★★★★ Recovering Glasgow alcoholic coaches a ragtag soccer team and falls in love. His sober life is jeopardized when he tries to free one of his players from debts to a local crime lord. This realistic drama escorts us into a social rat's nest in which unemployment and domestic violence run rampant, and people rely on street savvy for survival. In thick Scottish accents with English subtitles. Rated R for language, violence, nudity, and sex. 105m. DIR: Kenneth Loach. CAST: Peter Mullan, Louise Goodall, David McKay, David Hayman, Anne-Marie Kennedy. 1999

MY NAME IS NOBODY ★★★1/2 This is a delightful spoof of the Clint Eastwood spaghetti Westerns. Terence Hill is a gunfighter who worships old-timer Henry Fonda, who merely wishes to go away and retire. Rated PG. 115m. DIR: Tonino Valerii. CAST: Henry Fonda, Terence Hill, Leo Gordon, Geoffrey Lewis. 1974

MY NEIGHBOR TOTORO ★★★1/2 Pleasant animated diversion from Japan will appeal to younger children, who will find its colorful animation and adorable title character enchanting. Totoro is a funny little blue forest spirit, who takes two small sisters on a magical journey. Better-than-average dubbing and a universal story make this film better than most. Rated G. 86m. DIR: Hayao Miyazaki. 1988

MY NEIGHBORHOOD ★★★ An offbeat comedy with a dark tone featuring director-actor Michell Kriegman as neurotic pub owner who invites strangers off the street to view bizarre, homemade videos. Original and recommended. 28m. DIR: Michael Kriegman. CAST: Michael Kriegman. 1982

MY NEW GUN ★★1/2 This droll comedy doesn't quite deliver on its entertaining premise, but it satisfies modestly, thanks to the principal players. Diane Lane stars as a yuppie housewife who doesn't quite know how to react when her husband (Stephen Collins) gives her a gun for protection. 100m. DIR: Stacy Cochran. CAST: Diane Lane, Stephen Collins, James LeGros, Tess Harper. 1992

MY NEW PARTNER ★★★★ Walrus-faced Philippe Noiret is hilarious in this French comedy that swept the César Awards (the French Oscars). He plays a corrupt but effective police detective who is saddled with a new partner, an idealistic young police-academy graduate. Hollywood would never make a comedy this cynical about police work; they've seldom made one as funny either. In French with English subtitles. Rated R for nudity and sexual situations. 106m. DIR: Claude Zidi. CAST: Philippe Noiret, Thierry Lhermitte, Regine. 1984

MY NIGHT AT MAUD'S ★★★★ The first feature by Eric Rohmer to be shown in the United States. It is the third film of the cycle he called *Six Moral Tales*. A man is in love with a woman, but his eyes wander to another. However, the transgression is only brief, for, according to Rohmer, the only true love is the love ordained by God. Beautifully photographed in black and white, the camera looks the actors straight in the eye and captures every nuance. In French with English subtitles. B&W; 105m. DIR: Eric Rohmer. CAST: Jean-Louis Trintignant, Françoise Fabian, Marie-Christine Barrault. 1970 DVD

MY OLD MAN ★★★★ Excellent made-for-television adaptation of a short story by Ernest Hemingway about a down-on-his-luck horse trainer (Warren Oates) and the daughter (Kristy McNichol) who loves him even more than horses. Oates gives a fabulous performance; certainly one of the best of his too-brief career. Eileen Brennan lends support as a sympathetic waitress. Not rated; suitable for family viewing. 104m. DIR: John Erman. CAST: Warren Oates, Kristy McNichol, Eileen Brennan. 1979

MY OLD MAN'S PLACE ★★ Outdated cliché-ridden melodrama about a soldier's return home from Vietnam bringing two army friends with him. The inevitable clash of wills and personalities leads to the film's deadly conclusion. Rated R for nudity, profanity, and violence. 92m. DIR: Edwin Sherin. CAST: Arthur Kennedy, Mitchell Ryan, William Devane, Michael Moriarty. 1973

MY OTHER HUSBAND ★★★★ At first, this French import starring the marvelous Miou-Miou seems rather like a scatterbrained, faintly funny retread of the old person-with-two-spouses comedy plot. But it goes on to become an affecting, sweetly sad little treasure. In French with English subtitles. Rated

PG-13 for profanity. 110m. **DIR:** Georges Lautner. **CAST:** Miou-Miou, Roger Hanin, Eddy Mitchell. **1981**

MY OWN COUNTRY ★★★1/2 The story, told with perhaps too much brevity, follows Dr. Abraham Verghese as he becomes one of the first AIDS experts while tending patients in Johnson City, Tennessee. The episodic screenplay focuses on several cases, how they affect the lives of loved ones, and how Verghese finds himself consumed by trying to understand the implacable disease. Rated PG-13 for profanity and strong dramatic content. 106m. **DIR:** Mira Nair. **CAST:** Naveen Andrews, Glenne Headly, Hal Holbrook, Swoosie Kurtz, Marisa Tomei, Adam Tomei. **1998**

MY OWN PRIVATE IDAHO ★★★★ Stylishly photographed road movie about two young male street hustlers on their own personal vision quest. River Phoenix gives a heartfelt performance as a street prostitute who suffers from narcolepsy. Keanu Reeves plays a troubled bisexual youth from an affluent family. Moving, bittersweet movie. Rated R for nudity, profanity, and violence. 110m. **DIR:** Gus Van Sant. **CAST:** Keanu Reeves, River Phoenix, William Richert. **1991**

MY PAL, THE KING ★★★ Cowboy Tom Mix befriends boy king Mickey Rooney and teaches him the ways of the West. Mix's Wild West Show takes center stage for some entertaining passages, and cliffhanger action keeps the story moving along. B&W; 74m. **DIR:** Kurt Neumann. **CAST:** Tom Mix, Mickey Rooney. **1932**

MY PAL TRIGGER ★★★1/2 One of the most fondly remembered and perhaps the best of all the Roy Rogers movies, this gentle story centers on Roy's attempts to mate his mare with a superb golden stallion. Villain Jack Holt is responsible for the death of the mare, and Roy is blamed and incarcerated. B&W; 79m. **DIR:** Frank McDonald. **CAST:** Roy Rogers, George "Gabby" Hayes, Dale Evans, Jack Holt. **1946**

MY SAMURAI ★★ A reluctant martial arts student learns the value of his lessons when his master takes on gang members. As martial arts flicks go, this is watchable with some very impressive fight scenes. Not rated; contains plenty of violence. 87m. **DIR:** Fred Dresch. **CAST:** Julian Lee, Mako, Bubba Smith, Terry O'Quinn, Jim Turner, John Kallo. **1992**

MY SCIENCE PROJECT ★★ John Stockwell finds some UFO debris abandoned (!) by the military in 1959. The doohickey quickly rages out of control sending Stockwell and chums to battle dinosaurs and futuristic soldiers. Rated PG for profanity. 94m. **DIR:** Jonathan Betuel. **CAST:** John Stockwell, Danielle von Zerneck, Fisher Stevens, Dennis Hopper, Richard Masur. **1985 DVD**

MY SIDE OF THE MOUNTAIN ★★★★ File this in that all-too-small category of films that both you and your kids can enjoy. A 13-year-old Toronto boy decides to prove his self-worth by living in a Quebec forest for one year with no resources other than his own wits. Gus the Raccoon steals the show, but you'll be charmed and entertained by the rest of the movie as well. Rated G. 100m. **DIR:** James B. Clark. **CAST:** Teddy Eccles, Theodore Bikel. **1969**

MY SISTER EILEEN ★★★ Fast-moving musical remake of the 1940 stage play about two small-town sisters overwhelmed by New York's Greenwich Village and its inhabitants. Jack Lemmon joins Betty Garrett in a knockout rendition of "It's Bigger Than You or Me." 108m. **DIR:** Richard Quine. **CAST:** Janet Leigh, Betty Garrett, Jack Lemmon, Bob Fosse, Kurt Kasznar, Dick York, Hal March, Queenie Smith, Richard Deacon, Tommy Rall. **1955**

MY SISTER, MY LOVE (THE MAFU CAGE) ★★★ Offbeat story concerns two loving, but unbalanced, sisters who eliminate anyone who tries to come between them. Good acting all around and a perverse sense of style are just two elements that make this movie click. Rated R. 99m. **DIR:** Karen Arthur. **CAST:** Carol Kane, Lee Grant, Will Geer, James Olson. **1979**

•**MY SON THE FANATIC** ★★★ Pakistani taxi driver in northern England self-destructs after being goaded into leading a more hedonistic lifestyle by a kinky German businessman. He has an affair with a prostitute and his life is further destabilized as his son embraces Islamic fundamentalism and invites a religious leader into their home. Hanif Kureishi adapted this dark and sometimes funny tale of displacement, racism, and culture clashes from his own 1994 short story. Rated R for language and sexual content. 86m. **DIR:** Udayan Prasad. **CAST:** Om Puri, Stellan Skarsgard, Rachel Griffiths, Akbar Kurtha. **1999 DVD**

MY STEPMOTHER IS AN ALIEN ★★1/2 A beautiful alien (Kim Basinger) comes to Earth to reverse the effects of a ray that has changed the gravity of her planet. Unfortunately, the creator of the ray (Dan Aykroyd) doesn't know how to re-create it. Thinking he is lying, she marries him to get the secret. A so-so farce with a predictably sweet ending. Rated PG-13. 108m. **DIR:** Richard Benjamin. **CAST:** Dan Aykroyd, Kim Basinger, Jon Lovitz, Alyson Hannigan. **1988 DVD**

MY STEPSON, MY LOVER ★★ A nurse marries an older, wealthy businessman, and a few months later she starts eyeing her husband's twentysomething hunk of a son. Poor acting and a wishy-washy plot line kill this made-for-cable original before it can get off the ground. Not rated. 95m. **DIR:** Mary Lambert. **CAST:** Rachel Ward, Joshua Morrow, Al Wiggins, Terry O'Quinn. **1997**

MY SUMMER STORY ★★★1/2 Eleven years separated this droll little comedy from its predecessor, *A Christmas Story*, but humorist-essayist Jean Shepherd's childhood reminiscences are every bit as pungent and wacky. She has the gift of making viewers nostalgic for a childhood they never personally experienced. Rated PG for mild profanity. 86m. **DIR:** Bob Clark. **CAST:** Charles Grodin, Kieran Culkin, Mary Steenburgen, Christian Culkin, Al Mancini, Glenn Shadix. **1994**

MY SWEET CHARLIE ★★★★ The fine performances of Patty Duke and Al Freeman Jr. make this made-for-TV drama especially watchable. Duke plays a disowned, unwed mom-to-be who meets a black lawyer being pursued by the police. They hit it off and manage to help each other. A must-see for viewers interested in drama with a social comment.

97m. **DIR:** Lamont Johnson. **CAST:** Patty Duke, Al Freeman Jr., Ford Rainey. **1969**

•**MY SWEET SUICIDE** ★★★ When a depressed man is unable to kill himself, he enlists the aid of a sympathetic girl in committing the perfect suicide. This black comedy has its technical drawbacks, but may interest fans of indie movies. Not rated; contains mature themes and profanity. 79m. **DIR:** David Michael Flanagan. **CAST:** Matthew Aldrich, Michelle Thompson. **1998**

MY TEACHER'S WIFE 🎭 Every generation deserves its own "Hey, I'm having sex with my teacher's wife" comedy. Here's to the class of 1999. A.k.a. *Learning Curves*. Rated R for language and adult situations. 90m. **DIR:** Bruce Leddy. **CAST:** Jason London, Tia Carrere, Christopher McDonald, Jeffrey Tambor. **1995 DVD**

MY TUTOR 🎭 A young man gets an education in more than just reading, writing, and 'rithmetic. Rated R for nudity and implied sex. 97m. **DIR:** George Bowers. **CAST:** Matt Lattanzi, Caren Kaye, Kevin McCarthy. **1983 DVD**

MY 20TH CENTURY ★★★★ Two long-separated twins are reunited on the Orient Express on New Year's Eve, 1899. Though completely different—one is a vain young woman, the other a fiery revolutionary—both are lovers of the same man. A witty look at the genesis of our era, with two wonderful performances by Dorotha Segda as both sisters. In Hungarian with English subtitles. Not rated. B&W; 104m. **DIR:** Ildiko Enyedi. **CAST:** Dorotha Segda, Oleg Jankovskij. **1988**

MY UNCLE (MON ONCLE) ★★★★ The second of Jacques Tati's cinematic romps as Mr. Hulot (the first was the famous *Mr. Hulot's Holiday*), this delightful comedy continues Tati's recurrent theme of the common man confronted with an increasingly mechanized and depersonalized society. (It's also the only Tati film to win the Academy Award for best foreign film.) 116m. **DIR:** Jacques Tati. **CAST:** Jacques Tati, Jean-Pierre Zola. **1958**

MY WICKED, WICKED WAYS ★★ Errol Flynn's fast-paced life is slowed down a bit for this TV movie. It seems to have lost its zest in the translation. But choosing Duncan Regehr to play Flynn was an inspiration. 142m. **DIR:** Don Taylor. **CAST:** Duncan Regehr, Barbara Hershey, Darren McGavin, Hal Linden. **1984**

MY WONDERFUL LIFE 🎭 Italian fantasy features Carol Alt in a series of abusive relationships, more nauseating than erotic. Rated R for nudity, profanity, and violence. 107m. **DIR:** Carlo Vanzina. **CAST:** Carol Alt, Elliott Gould, Jean Rochefort, Pierre Cosso. **1989**

MYRA BRECKENRIDGE ★★ Infamous film version of Gore Vidal's satiric novel about a gay movie buff who has a sex-change operation (turning him into Raquel Welch!). Not very good, but the prententious psychedelic style and parade of old movie stars in cameo roles make it a must-see for camp enthusiasts and Sixties nostalgists. Originally rated X, the brief nudity and sexual concerns would barely earn this an R today. 94m. **DIR:** Michael Sarne. **CAST:** Raquel Welch, Mae West, John Huston, Rex Reed, John Carradine, Farrah Fawcett, Tom Selleck. **1970**

MYSTERIANS, THE ★★1/2 An alien civilization attempts takeover of Earth after its home planet is destroyed. Massive destruction from the director of *Godzilla*. Quaint Japanese-style special effects look pretty silly these days, but the film can be fun if seen in the right spirit. 85m. **DIR:** Inoshiro Honda. **CAST:** Kenji Sahara. **1959**

MYSTERIES ★★★ Rutger Hauer plays an affluent foreigner in a seaside village who becomes obsessed by a local beauty. This intriguing drama is hampered by poorly dubbed dialogue. Not rated, but has sex and nudity. 93m. **DIR:** Paul de Lussanet. **CAST:** Sylvia Kristel, Rutger Hauer, David Rappaport, Rita Tushingham, Andrea Ferreol. **1984**

MYSTERIOUS DESPERADO ★★★ Tim Holt's sidekick is heir to a large estate. Ruthless land grabbers have other plans for the property and frame Chito's cousin on a murder charge. B&W; 60m. **DIR:** Lesley Selander. **CAST:** Tim Holt, Richard Martin, Edward Norris, Robert Livingston. **1949**

MYSTERIOUS DR. FU MANCHU ★★1/2 Former humanitarian Dr. Fu Manchu vows vengeance on the "white devils" who killed his wife and son during the Boxer Rebellion. Using the child of a dead missionary as his hypnotized agent, Fu tracks down those he holds responsible and murders them by devious means until he comes to a reckoning with nemesis Nayland-Smith. First talking Fu Manchu film is a bit long but fluid, action-packed, and sprinkled with lines like, "I assure you that your body, if it is found, will be quite unrecognizable." B&W; 85m. **DIR:** Rowland V. Lee. **CAST:** Warner Oland, Jean Arthur, Neil Hamilton, O. P. Heggie, William Austin, Noble Johnson. **1929**

MYSTERIOUS DR. SATAN ★★★ Eduardo Cianelli unleashes his death-dealing robot upon a helpless public. Chockful of great stunts, last-minute escapes, and logic that defies description, this prime chapterplay from Republic's thrill factory had just about everything a juvenile audience could ask for and then some. B&W; 15 chapters. **DIR:** William Witney, John English. **CAST:** Eduardo Ciannelli, Robert Wilcox, William Newell, C. Montague Shaw, Dorothy Herbert, Ella Neal, Jack Mulhall, Edwin Stanley. **1940**

MYSTERIOUS ISLAND ★★★★ Fantasy-adventure based on Jules Verne's novel about a group of Civil War prisoners who escape by balloon and land on an uncharted island in the Pacific, where they must fight to stay alive against incredible odds. With fantastic effects work by Ray Harryhausen and a breathtaking Bernard Herrmann score. 101m. **DIR:** Cy Endfield. **CAST:** Michael Craig, Joan Greenwood, Michael Callan, Gary Merrill, Herbert Lom. **1961**

MYSTERIOUS LADY, THE ★★★1/2 Greta Garbo plays Tania, a Russian spy who falls in love with an Austrian soldier, calling into question her political loyalties. Early Garbo vehicle whose preposterous love story and willfully arbitrary plot machinations nonetheless make for great fun. Silent. B&W; 84m. **DIR:** Fred Niblo. **CAST:** Greta Garbo, Conrad Nagel, Gustav von Seyffertitz. **1928**

MYSTERIOUS MR. MOTO ★★1/2 Mr. Moto comes to the aid of Scotland Yard by infiltrating the League of Assassins before they can murder an industralist needed in the war effort. B&W; 62m. **DIR:** Norman Foster. **CAST:** Peter Forre, Mary Maguire, Henry Wilcoxon, Leon Ames. **1938**

MYSTERIOUS MR. WONG, THE ★★ Not to be confused with the Mr. Wong detective series that starred Boris Karloff, this low-budget mystery has Bela Lugosi in the title role, portraying a fiendish criminal bent on possessing twelve coins connected with Confucius. B&W; 68m. **DIR:** William Nigh. **CAST:** Bela Lugosi, Wallace Ford, Arline Judge. **1935**

MYSTERIOUS STRANGER, THE ★★★★ A wonderful adaptation of a Mark Twain story about a printer's apprentice who daydreams he's back in the sixteenth century. Add to this a magical stranger and a not so magical alchemist, and you have fun for the whole family. Not rated. 89m. **DIR:** Peter H. Hunt. **CAST:** Chris Makepeace, Lance Kerwin, Fred Gwynne, Bernhard Wicki. **1982**

•MYSTERY, ALASKA ★★★1/2 In an out-of-the-way town in Alaska obsessed with hockey, a former resident sets up a nationally televised game pitting the locals against professional pucksters, the New York Rangers, as part of what he hopes to be a triumphant homecoming. Of course, he causes more consternation than jubilation among the locals. What starts as a typical sports movie about underdogs getting their big chance is enriched by fine performances and an above-average script by David E. Kelley. Rated R for profanity, brief nudity, and sexual references. 118m. **DIR:** Jay Roach. **CAST:** Russell Crowe, Hank Azaria, Mary McCormack, Burt Reynolds, Colm Meaney, Lolita Davidovich, Maury Chaykin, Ron Eldard, Judith Ivey, Mike Meyers, Ryan Northcott, Michael Buie, Kevin Durand, Scott Grimes. **1999 DVD**

MYSTERY DATE ★★1/2 This teenage version of Martin Scorsese's *After Hours* is only moderately funny and is saved from total video-shelf hell by young star Ethan Hawke. Rated PG-13 for violence and profanity. 90m. **DIR:** Jonathan Wacks. **CAST:** Ethan Hawke, Teri Polo, Brian McNamara, Fisher Stevens, B. D. Wong. **1991**

MYSTERY ISLAND ★★★ When four children whose boat has run out of gas discover what appears to be a deserted island, they promptly name it Mystery Island. The children find a case of counterfeit money which belongs to villains, who later return to the island for it. The best part about this children's film is the beautiful underwater photography. 75m. **DIR:** Gene Scott. **CAST:** Jayson Duncan, Niklas Juhlin. **1981**

MYSTERY MAN ★★★ Hopalong Cassidy and his pals foil an outlaw gang's attempt to rob a bank. For revenge, the gang steals Hoppy's cattle and turns him over to the sheriff as the real outlaw leader. The most action-packed of all the Cassidy series. B&W; 60m. **DIR:** George Archainbaud. **CAST:** William Boyd, Andy Clyde, Jimmy Rogers, Eleanor Stewart. **1944**

MYSTERY MANSION ❤ A girl with strange but true dreams, two escaped convicts, and hidden treasure—all involved with an old Victorian mystery house. Rated G. 95m. **DIR:** David F. Jackson. **CAST:** Dallas McKennon, Greg Wynne, Jane Ferguson. **1986**

•MYSTERY MEN ★★★ When Champion City's greatest superhero, Captain Amazing (Greg Kinn-

ear), is captured by his arch rival, Cassanova Frankenstein (Geoffrey Rush), a group of second-rate, wannabe crime fighters—Blue Raja (Hank Azaria), Bowler (Janeane Garofalo), Shoveler (William H. Macy), Invisible Boy (Kel Mitchell), Spleen (Paul Reubens), Mr. Furious (Ben Stiller), and Sphinx (Wes Studi)—attempt to save the day. Adapted from the Dark Horse comic book, there are some very funny moments in this movie, which tries too hard to be hip and is encumbered by an overlong running time. Still, it's better than *Howard the Duck*. Rated PG-13 for profanity, scatological humor, and light violence. 120m. **DIR:** Kinka Usher. **CAST:** Hank Azaria, Janeane Garofalo, William H. Macy, Kel Mitchell, Paul Reubens, Ben Stiller, Wes Studi, Greg Kinnear, Geoffrey Rush, Lena Olin, Tom Waits, Eddie Izzard, Louise Lasser. **1999 DVD**

MYSTERY, MR. RA ★★ Filmmaker Frank Cassenti captures Sun Ra and his band during rehearsals and rare concert footage from Sun Ra's remarkable Afro-psychedelic music circus. Disappointing look at the thirty-five-year-career of this remarkable musician, bandleader, philosopher, and shaman. 51m. **DIR:** Frank Cassenti. **CAST:** Sun Ra. **1983**

MYSTERY MONSTERS ★★ Low-budget affair tries to make up in imagination what it lacks in production values, but there's not much here to recommend. When they're not being held captive by television host Cap'n Mike, three magical monsters pose as puppets on a daytime kiddie show. When an evil witch arrives to steal the monsters, it's up to the show's kid stars to save them. Rated PG for violence. 81m. **DIR:** Robert Talbot. **CAST:** Ashley Cafagna, Ted Redwine, Daniel Hartley, Michael Dennis. **1997**

MYSTERY OF ALEXINA, THE ★★★★ True story of a sexually ambiguous young man, raised in the nineteenth century as a woman, who becomes aware of his true identity only when he falls in love with a young woman. The script doesn't answer all the questions it raises, but there's more than enough to compel your interest. In French with English subtitles. 84m. **DIR:** René Feret. **CAST:** Philippe Vullemin, Valerie Stroh. **1985**

MYSTERY OF EDWIN DROOD, THE ★★★ An unfinished Charles Dickens story is the basis for this moody suspense drama about a drug-addicted choirmaster who is accused of killing his nephew. Claude Rains is fine as suspect John Jasper, whose infatuation with his nephew's fiancée helps seal his fate. Nothing is what it seems in this Victorian thriller. Not rated. 86m. **DIR:** Stuart Walker. **CAST:** Claude Rains, Douglass Montgomery, Heather Angel, David Manners. **1935**

MYSTERY OF PICASSO, THE ★★★★★ Pablo Picasso conceives, prepares, sketches, and paints fifteen canvasses—all of which were destroyed after the film was completed. A one-of-a-kind look at the artistic process, sensitively directed with exquisite music and photography (by Claude Renoir). In French with English subtitles. 85m. **DIR:** Henri-Georges Clouzot. **1956**

MYSTERY OF RAMPO, THE ★★★ Surreal, sometimes confusing tale of a mystery writer who suspects that his latest novel has taken on a life all its own. When he reads an account of a woman who murdered her husband, the writer notices startling similarities to his latest manuscript. When his curiosity gets the best of him, he's swept into a world where reality collides with fantasy. In Japanese with English subtitles. Not rated; contains violence, nudity, and adult situations. **DIR:** Kazuyoshi Okuyama. **CAST:** Naoto Takenaka, Michiko Hada, Masahiro Motoki. **1994**

MYSTERY OF THE HOODED HORSEMEN ★★1/2 One of Tex Ritter's most popular oaters. A group of night riders in dark hoods and cloaks add just a touch of the supernatural to an otherwise standard story of land greed and cattle conniving. B&W; 60m. **DIR:** Ray Taylor. **CAST:** Tex Ritter, Iris Meredith, Charles King, Forrest Taylor, Earl Dwire, Lafe McKee, Hank Worden, Joe Girard. **1937**

MYSTERY OF THE MARIE CELESTE, THE (THE PHANTOM SHIP) ★★★ On December 4, 1872, the brigantine *Marie Celeste*, said to have been jinxed by death, fire, and collision since its launching in 1861, was found moving smoothly under half-sail, completely deserted, east of the Azores. No trace of the crew was ever found. To this day, what happened remains a true mystery of the sea. This account offers one explanation. B&W; 64m. **DIR:** Dension Clift. **CAST:** Bela Lugosi, Shirley Grey. **1937**

MYSTERY OF THE WAX MUSEUM ★★★ Dated but interesting tale of a crippled, crazed sculptor (the ever-dependable Lionel Atwill) who murders people and displays them in his museum as his own wax creations. Humorous subplot really curbs the attention, but stick with it. One of the earliest color films, it is often shown on television in black and white. 77m. **DIR:** Michael Curtiz. **CAST:** Lionel Atwill, Fay Wray, Glenda Farrell, Frank McHugh. **1933**

•**MYSTERY RANCH** ★★★1/2 Crazed rancher holds his dead partner's daughter against her will in order to marry her, but a stalwart lawman takes it upon himself to save her and break the grip of fear the madman and his henchmen have on the territory. Spooky Western with mystery overtones is one of the finest of its kind. B&W; 65m. **DIR:** David Howard. **CAST:** George O'Brien, Cecilia Parker, Charles Middleton, Roy Stewart, Noble Johnson, Charles Stevens, Forrester Harvey. **1932**

MYSTERY SCIENCE THEATRE 3000: THE MOVIE ★★★ The popular series from cable-TV's Comedy Central (known as *MST3K* to fans) comes to the big screen with its premise intact (a human and two whimsical robots make fun of a cheesy sci-fi film). The object of their derision, 1955's *This Island Earth* (see our listing for details), is better than most of the cable series' targets, but there are still ample opportunities for the impudent wisecracks that made the series such irresistible fun. Rated PG-13 for some sexual humor. 87m. **DIR:** James Mallon. **CAST:** Michael J. Nelson, Trace Beaulieu. **1996 DVD**

MYSTERY SQUADRON ★★1/2 Mascot Studios continued its effort to be the best producer of serials with this fast-moving story of the sinister Mystery Squadron and its fanatical leader, the Black Ace. Bob Steele and "Big Boy" Williams trade in their chaps and horses for parachutes and planes as they

do their utmost to apprehend the Black Ace, a deadly saboteur. B&W; 12 chapters. **DIR:** Colbert Clark, David Howard. **CAST:** Bob Steele, Guinn Williams, Lucille Brown, Jack Mulhall, Purnell Pratt. **1933**

MYSTERY TRAIN ★★★1/2 Offbeat character study that takes place in Memphis. The film centers around a couple of Japanese tourists with a penchant for Elvis nostalgia, an Italian woman who arrives to bury her murdered husband, and an unemployed Englishman who is breaking up with his American girlfriend. Some hilarious moments. Rated R for nudity and profanity. 110m. **DIR:** Jim Jarmusch. **CAST:** Youki Kaudoh, Masatochi Nagase, Joe Strummer, Screamin' Jay Hawkins. **1990 DVD**

MYSTIC PIZZA ★★★1/2 This coming-of-age picture has all of the right ingredients of a main-course favorite. The antics involve three women—two sisters and a friend—who work at a pizza parlor in the resort town of Mystic, Connecticut. The superb young players and the dazzling New England scenery are a slice of heaven. Rated R for language. 102m. **DIR:** Donald Petrie. **CAST:** Annabeth Gish, Julia Roberts, Lili Taylor, Vincent D'Onofrio, William R. Moses, Adam Storke, Matt Damon. **1988**

MYTH OF FINGERPRINTS, THE ★★★ Thanksgiving reunion ticks like a time bomb as one of New England's covertly dysfunctional families works its way through a hellish gathering of the tribe. This frosty drama explores the cracks in blood and flesh relationships amid a patriarchal repression that allows old resentments to gnaw away the soul of a family. Rated R for sex, nudity, and language. 93m. **DIR:** Bart Freundlich. **CAST:** Roy Scheider, Blythe Danner, Noah Wyle, Julianne Moore, Michael Vartan, Laurel Holloman, Arija Bareikis, Hope Davis, James LeGros, Brian Kerwin. **1997 DVD**

NADINE ★★★ A cute caper comedy. Kim Basinger is a not-so-bright hairdresser who finds herself involved in murder and mayhem. She enlists the aid of her estranged husband (Jeff Bridges). Rip Torn gives a fine performance as the chief villain. Rated PG for light violence and profanity. 95m. **DIR:** Robert Benton. **CAST:** Jeff Bridges, Kim Basinger, Rip Torn, Gwen Verdon, Glenne Headly, Jerry Stiller. **1987**

NADJA ★★ The female offspring of a famous vampire stalks New York looking for fresh blood. Uncredited semiremake of *Dracula's Daughter* (1936) is amateurish, and its low budget is all too apparent. Scenes in "Pixelvision" (actually shot with a cheap toy camera) are more annoying than arresting. Rated R for violence. B&W; 92m. **DIR:** Michael Almereyda. **CAST:** Elina Lowensohn, Peter Fonda, Martin Donovan, Suzy Amis, Galaxy Craze. **1995**

NAILS ★★ Bad boy Dennis Hopper's *way*-over-the-top performance as a brutal cop barely saves Larry Ferguson's humdrum script from turkeydom. Rated R for nudity, profanity, and considerable violence. 96m. DIR: John Flynn. CAST: Dennis Hopper, Anne Archer, Tomas Milian, Keith David, Cliff De Young. 1992

NAIROBI AFFAIR ★★ Charlton Heston plays a safari photographer who is having an affair with his son's ex-wife (Maud Adams). Rated PG for violence. 95m. DIR: Marvin J. Chomsky. CAST: John Savage, Maud Adams, Charlton Heston. 1986

NAIS ★★★ A hunchbacked laborer helps the girl he loves in her romance with the son of a rich landowner. Though he only wrote the screenplay (adapted from an Émile Zola story), this touching film bears the unmistakable stamp of Marcel Pagnol. In French with English subtitles. B&W; 95m. DIR: Raymond Leboursier. CAST: Fernandel, Jacqueline Pagnol. 1945

NAKED ★★★★ A bleak, stark drama about Johnny, a homeless young man who roams the streets of London in search of sex and shelter, both of which he gets often. Numerous characters come and go, and most of them are emotionally manipulated or machinated by our young antihero. Disturbing and dazzling. Rated R for nudity and violence. 126m. DIR: Mike Leigh. CAST: David Thewlis, Lesley Sharp, Katrin Cartlidge, Greg Cruttwell. 1994

NAKED AND THE DEAD, THE ★★★ This action-packed World War II film is based on Norman Mailer's famous book. Not nearly as good as the book, nevertheless the film is still quite powerful and exciting. Worth a watch. 131m. DIR: Raoul Walsh. CAST: Aldo Ray, Joey Bishop, Cliff Robertson, Raymond Massey. 1958

NAKED CITY, THE ★★★1/2 Detailed story of a police investigation into the murder of a model takes the backseat to the star of this movie—New York City. Pace-setting location filming helps this interesting crime-drama that was the basis for the superior and long-running TV series. Producer-narrator Mark Hellinger died shortly before the premier showing. B&W; 96m. DIR: Jules Dassin. CAST: Barry Fitzgerald, Howard Duff, Dorothy Hart, Don Taylor, Ted de Corsia, House Jameson, James Gregory, Paul Ford. 1948 DVD

NAKED CIVIL SERVANT, THE ★★★1/2 Exceptional film based on the biography of the famous English homosexual Quentin Crisp. John Hurt's remarkable performance earned him a British Academy Award for his sensitive portrayal. Not rated, but recommended for mature audiences. 80m. DIR: Jack Gold. CAST: John Hurt, Patricia Hodge. 1975

NAKED COUNTRY, THE ★★★ A rancher, his lonely wife, and an alcoholic policeman form a deadly triangle in Australia's outback. Set in 1955, this beautifully filmed story is rooted in soap opera, but becomes a violent struggle with the aborigines that resonates with remorse. Rated R for nudity, profanity, and violence. 90m. DIR: Tim Burstall. CAST: John Stanton, Rebecca Gilling. 1984

NAKED DETECTIVE, THE 💔 Sex-soaked private-eye comedy that makes Benny Hill look sophisticated. Rated R for nudity, sex, and profanity. 90m. DIR:

Ernest G. Sauer. CAST: Julia Parton, Jim Gardiner, Greg Tracy, Taylore St. Claire. 1997

NAKED EDGE, THE ★★★ Familiar, slow-moving story of a wife who suspects her husband is a murderer. Lots of red herrings. Gary Cooper's last film. B&W; 97m. DIR: Michael Anderson. CAST: Gary Cooper, Deborah Kerr, Eric Portman, Diane Cilento, Hermione Gingold, Peter Cushing, Michael Wilding. 1961

NAKED FACE, THE ★★★ A psychiatrist (Roger Moore) finds himself the target of murder in this enjoyable suspense film. The police think he's the killer, as the first attempt on his life results in the death of a patient who had borrowed his raincoat. Rated R for violence and profanity. 98m. DIR: Bryan Forbes. CAST: Roger Moore, Rod Steiger, Elliott Gould, Art Carney, Anne Archer. 1984

NAKED GUN, THE ★★★★ Fans of the short-lived television series *Police Squad!* will love this full-length adventure featuring Leslie Nielsen's stiff-lipped Frank Drebin, the toughest—and clumsiest—cop in the universe. This parody of 1960s television cop shows is riddled with countless sight gags, outrageous puns, and over-the-top characterizations. Rated PG-13 for language and mild sexual coarseness. 85m. DIR: David Zucker. CAST: Leslie Nielsen, George Kennedy, Priscilla Presley, Ricardo Montalban, O. J. Simpson, Nancy Marchand. 1988

NAKED GUN 2 1/2, THE ★★★1/2 The loony *Police Squad* gang is back in this wacky sequel to the smash-hit police parody. In this saga, the amazingly brain-dead Lt. Frank Drebin (Leslie Nielsen) gets involved in efforts to bust a criminal hatching a nefarious antiecology crime. The film lacks the zip of the original, but it's still a nutty romp. Rated PG-13 for profanity and adult humor. 88m. DIR: David Zucker. CAST: Leslie Nielsen, Priscilla Presley, Robert Goulet, George Kennedy, O. J. Simpson. 1991

NAKED GUN 33 1/3, THE—THE FINAL INSULT ★★1/2 TV's *Police Squad!* originators make their third regurgitation of comic chaos as klutzy cop Lt. Frank Drebin comes out of brief retirement to nab a mad bomber. This film climaxes with Drebin being mistaken for Phil Donahue as he brings an Oscars telecast to its knees. Cameo surprises abound, but this romp is not as funny as its predecessors. Rated PG-13 for suggested sex and language. 83m. DIR: Peter Segal. CAST: Leslie Nielsen, Priscilla Presley, Fred Ward, George Kennedy, O. J. Simpson. 1994

NAKED HEART, THE ★★ After five years in a convent, a young woman returns to her home in the frozen Canadian north and tries to decide which of her three suitors to marry. Filmed in Europe, this slow, somewhat depressing tale has little going for it. B&W; 96m. DIR: Marc Allegret. CAST: Michele Morgan, Kieron Moore, Françoise Rosay. 1950

NAKED IN NEW YORK ★★★1/2 An eclectic supporting cast and a breezy screenplay lend support to this romantic comedy about a pair of college sweethearts attempting to make the best of a long-distance relationship. Rated R for adult situations and language. 89m. DIR: Dan Algrant. CAST: Eric Stoltz, Mary-Louise Parker, Ralph Macchio, Jill Clayburgh, Kathleen Turner, Whoopi Goldberg. 1994

NAKED IN THE SUN ★★1/2 Osceola (James Craig), war chief of the Seminole Indians, must battle unscrupulous whites, the United States government, and his own tribe to live in dignity. This is well-acted and effective in evoking audience sympathy. 79m. **DIR:** R. John Hugh. **CAST:** James Craig, Barton MacLane, Lita Milan, Tony Hunter. **1957**

NAKED JUNGLE, THE ★★ In this studio soap opera made from the short story *Leninnen Versus the Ants*, Charlton Heston is slightly out of place but still powerful as the South American plantation owner. Eleanor Parker is ridiculous as his new wife, and a young, thin William Conrad is along for the ride. Not rated, contains slight violence. 95m. **DIR:** Byron Haskin. **CAST:** Charlton Heston, Eleanor Parker, Abraham Sofaer, William Conrad, Romo Vincent, Douglas Fowley. **1953**

NAKED KISS, THE ★★★1/2 An ex-hooker makes a break and winds up in a small town only to discover more evil and trouble. Constance Towers as the girl who begins to find herself is a standout; the cast includes former veteran star Patsy Kelly and the silent screen's *Peter Pan*, Betty Bronson. Gritty *film noir* mystery. B&W; 90m. **DIR:** Samuel Fuller. **CAST:** Constance Towers, Anthony Eisley, Michael Dante, Virginia Grey, Patsy Kelly, Betty Bronson. **1965 DVD**

NAKED LIES ★★ Laughably awful action picture about a disgraced female cop who must go undercover to sniff out a drug dealer. Not even the expected "erotic sequences" can save this one. Rated R for violence, nudity, sexual situations, and profanity. 93m. **DIR:** Ralph Portillo. **CAST:** Shannon Tweed, Fernando Allende, Jay Baker, Michael Rose, Steven Bauer. **1997**

NAKED LUNCH ★★★ A nightmare brought to life with sometimes nauseating intensity, director David Cronenberg's adaptation of William S. Burroughs's novel weds incidents from the author's life into the fantastical, drug-induced hallucinations that comprised the book. Peter Weller is the exterminator who, through the encouragement of wife Judy Davis, becomes addicted to bug powder and ends up in Interzone. Utterly bizarre and not for all tastes. Rated R for profanity, violence, and nudity. 115m. **DIR:** David Cronenberg. **CAST:** Peter Weller, Judy Davis, Ian Holm, Julian Sands, Roy Scheider. **1992**

NAKED MAJA, THE ★★ Dull telling of the eighteenth-century romance between artist Francisco Goya and the duchess of Alba which led to their fall from grace with the Spanish court and the Catholic Church. 111m. **DIR:** Henry Koster. **CAST:** Ava Gardner, Anthony Franciosa, Amadeo Nazzari, Gino Cervi. **1958**

•**NAKED MAN, THE** ★★★ Director J. Todd Anderson throws everything but the kitchen sink into this madcap collection of bizarre characters and even more bizarre circumstances. Michael Rapaport is hysterically funny as a young chiropractor who moonlights as a professional wrestler. Cowriter Ethan Coen helps blend outrageous comedy with unforgettable characters into a frenzied farce. Direct-to-video. Rated R for language, violence, and adult situations. 98m. **DIR:** J. Todd Anderson. **CAST:** Michael Rapaport, Michael Jeter, Rachael Leigh Cook, Joe Grifasi. **1998**

NAKED OBSESSION ★★ When a councilman samples his city's red-light district, he's framed for murder. This sexually explicit film plays faintly as a dark comic buddy picture. Not rated, but with considerable nudity and profanity. 85m. **DIR:** Dan Golden. **CAST:** William Katt, Maria Ford, Rick Dean, Roger Craig, Elena Sahagun. **1990**

NAKED PREY, THE ★★★ An African safari takes a disastrous turn and Cornel Wilde winds up running naked and unarmed through the searing jungle as a large band of native warriors keeps on his heels, determined to finish him off. This is an amazingly intense adventure of man versus man and man versus nature. Wilde does a remarkable job, both as star and director. 94m. **DIR:** Cornel Wilde. **CAST:** Cornel Wilde, Gert Van Den Bergh, Ken Gampu. **1966**

NAKED SOULS ★★1/2 Memory researcher Brian Krause would rather perfect a means to transfer consciousness than pay attention to sexy girlfriend Pamela Anderson Lee—silly boy!—and winds up working with sinister millionaire David Warner. Frank Dietz's script covers familiar genre territory, and not all that well. Rated R for nudity, violence, profanity, and simulated sex. 85m. **DIR:** Lyndon Chubbuck. **CAST:** Brian Krause, Pamela Anderson Lee, David Warner, Clayton Rohner, Dean Stockwell. **1995**

NAKED SPUR, THE ★★★1/2 Superb Western finds bounty hunter James Stewart chasing bad guy Robert Ryan through the Rockies. Once captured, Ryan attempts to cause trouble between Stewart and his sidekicks. 91m. **DIR:** Anthony Mann. **CAST:** James Stewart, Janet Leigh, Robert Ryan, Ralph Meeker, Millard Mitchell. **1953**

NAKED TANGO ★★★ In the 1920s, a young woman comes to Buenos Aires as a mail-order bride, only to find that she has been sold into white slavery by her intended husband. The film is an overheated melodrama of male-domination fantasies but, dark, moody photography and strong acting make it engrossing and hard to dismiss. Rated R for violence and sexual situations. 90m. **DIR:** Leonard Schrader. **CAST:** Vincent D'Onofrio, Mathilda May, Esai Morales, Fernando Rey, Josh Mostel. **1991**

NAKED TRUTH (YOUR PAST IS SHOWING) ★★1/2 This oddball British comedy involves a group of loonies who are brought together to get rid of the editor of a smutty magazine. Peter Sellers is good as a disgusting television celebrity and Terry-Thomas is very effective as a politician. 92m. **DIR:** Mario Zampi. **CAST:** Terry-Thomas, Dennis Price, Peter Sellers, Shirley Eaton. **1957**

NAKED VENGEANCE 🎦 Unpleasant exploitation flick about a woman who seeks vengeance after she is raped and her parents murdered. Available in both R and unrated versions; we'd suggest that you avoid both. 97m. **DIR:** Cirio H. Santiago. **CAST:** Deborah Tranelli, Kaz Garas, Bill McLaughlin, Nick Nicholson. **1986**

NAKED VENUS ★★ Famed cult director Edgar G. Ulmer's last film is a slow-moving drama about an American artist whose marriage to a nudist-model is torn apart by his wealthy mother. The film explores the barriers of prejudice concerning nudist colonies.

Not rated; contains nudity. B&W; 80m. DIR: Edgar G. Ulmer. CAST: Patricia Conelle. 1958

NAKED YOUTH ★★ A good kid gets involved with a bad apple and together they wind up in prison—and then break out. It's hardly the camp classic the distributors would have you believe. B&W; 80m. DIR: John Schreyer. CAST: Robert Hutton, John Goddard, Carol Ohmart. 1961

NAME OF THE ROSE, THE ★★★ In this passable screen adaptation of Umberto Eco's bestseller, Sean Connery stars as a monkish Sherlock Holmes trying to solve a series of murders in a fourteenth-century monastery. Connery is fun to watch, but the plot is rather feeble. Rated R for nudity, simulated sex, and violence. 118m. DIR: Jean-Jacques Annaud. CAST: Sean Connery, F. Murray Abraham, Christian Slater, Elya Baskin, Feodor Chaliapin, William Hickey, Michel Lonsdale, Ron Perlman. 1986

NAMU, THE KILLER WHALE ★★★1/2 A well-made family film that isn't as sinister as its title. It's based on the true story of a whale in a public aquarium. Namu was so friendly and intelligent it was set free. The 1993 movie, *Free Willy*, was inspired by this film. 86m. DIR: Laslo Benedek. CAST: Robert Lansing, Lee Meriwether, John Anderson, Richard Erdman, Robin Mattson. 1966

NANA ★★1/2 Adaptation of Émile Zola's oft-filmed story about the girl who will do anything to get out of the slums. This handsomely produced vehicle for Martine Carol (wife of director Christian-Jacque) is otherwise undistinguished. In French with English subtitles. 120m. DIR: Christian-Jaque. CAST: Martine Carol, Charles Boyer. 1955

NANCY GOES TO RIO ★★★ Nancy (Jane Powell) wins the leading role in a musical play that her mother (Ann Sothern) has her eye on. Both old standards and original songs fill in the slight plot. 99m. DIR: Robert Z. Leonard. CAST: Ann Sothern, Jane Powell, Louis Calhern, Barry Sullivan, Carmen Miranda. 1950

NANNY, THE ★★★ A strong performance in the title role by Bette Davis marks this story of a jealous, guilt-ridden nursemaid pitted against a mentally disturbed 10-year-old in a classic battle of wills ending in attempted murder. 93m. DIR: Seth Holt. CAST: Bette Davis, Wendy Craig, Jill Bennett, William Dix, Maurice Denham. 1965

NANOOK OF THE NORTH ★★★★ Crude and primitive as the conditions under which it was made, this direct study of Eskimo life set the standard for and has remained the most famous of the early documentary films. A milestone in stark realism; the walrus hunt sequence is especially effective. B&W; 55m. DIR: Robert Flaherty. 1922 DVD

NAPOLEON (1927) ★★★★★ Over a half century after its debut this film remains a visual wonder, encompassing a number of filmmaking techniques, some of which still seem revolutionary. The complete film—as pieced together by British film historian Kevin Brownlow over a period of twenty years—is one motion picture event no lover of the art form will want to miss even on the small screen without the full effect of its spectacular three-screen climax.

B&W; 235m. DIR: Abel Gance. CAST: Albert Dieudonné, Antonin Artaud. 1927

NAPOLEON (1955) 🖤 Boring. 115m. DIR: Sacha Guitry. CAST: Orson Welles, Maria Schell, Yves Montand, Erich Von Stroheim. 1955

NAPOLEON (1995) ★★★ Family film starring an adorable golden retriever puppy that gets into all sorts of predicaments. When Muffin accidentally falls into a hot air ballon, he is whisked off to the forest, where he must make his way back home. All ages will enjoy this all-animal adventure. Rated G. 81m. DIR: Mario Andreacchio. 1995

NAPOLEON AND JOSEPHINE: A LOVE STORY 🖤 TV miniseries. Armand Assante plays Napoleon from his pregeneral days until his exile. Jacqueline Bisset is his loving Josephine. 300m. DIR: Richard T. Heffron. CAST: Jacqueline Bisset, Armand Assante, Anthony Perkins, Stephanie Beacham. 1987

NAPOLEON AND SAMANTHA ★★★1/2 This Disney film features Johnny Whitaker as Napoleon, an orphan who decides to hide his grandpa's body when the old man dies and care for their pet lion, Major. When a college student/goat herder named Danny (Michael Douglas) helps bury Grandpa, Napoleon decides to follow him to his flock. Samantha (Jodie Foster) joins him and the lion as they face the dangers of a fierce mountain lion and a bear. Rated G. 91m. DIR: Bernard McEveety. CAST: Johnny Whitaker, Jodie Foster, Michael Douglas, Will Geer, Arch Johnson, Henry Jones. 1972 DVD

NARROW MARGIN, THE (1952) ★★★1/2 Tight crime entry has tough cop Charles McGraw assigned to transport the widow of a gangster to trial despite threats of hit men. Action takes place on a speeding train as McGraw and the hit men play a deadly cat-and-mouse game. Unrelenting suspense makes this one of the better films made in the Fifties. B&W; 70m. DIR: Richard Fleischer. CAST: Charles McGraw, Marie Windsor, Jacqueline White, Queenie Leonard. 1952

NARROW MARGIN (1990) ★★★ An update of the 1952 thriller, this absorbing drama's lapses in logic are compensated for by two gripping performances by Gene Hackman and Anne Archer. She's a frightened murder witness hiding out in the wilderness; he's the Los Angeles deputy district attorney determined to bring her back. Great fun, until its rather abrupt conclusion. Rated R for language and violence. 97m. DIR: Peter Hyams. CAST: Gene Hackman, Anne Archer, James B. Sikking, M. Emmet Walsh. 1990 DVD

NARROW TRAIL, THE ★★★ "Better a painted pony than a painted woman" was the slogan selling this above-average Western about a cowboy's love for his horse. One of early-Western star William S. Hart's many pictures, this one was something of a paean to his great horse, Fritz. Like all Hart films, this one is marked by his scrupulous attention to authenticity of setting, scenery, and costume. Silent. B&W; 56m. DIR: Lambert Hillyer. CAST: William S. Hart. 1917

NASHVILLE ★★★★★ Robert Altman's classic study of American culture is, on the surface, a look into the country-western music business. But underneath, Altman has many things to say about all of us.

Great ensemble acting by Keith Carradine, Lily Tomlin, Ned Beatty, and Henry Gibson, to name just a few, makes this one of the great films of the 1970s. Rated R for language and violence. 159m. DIR: Robert Altman. CAST: Keith Carradine, Lily Tomlin, Ned Beatty, Henry Gibson, Karen Black, Ronee Blakley. 1975

NASTY GIRL, THE ★★★★★ This Oscar-nominated film is the most highly original movie to come out of Germany since the glory days of Fassbinder and Herzog. And the key to its freshness is its unique blend of charming, upbeat comedy with a serious topic: the scars and guilt from the Nazi era that still run deep in modern German life. In German with English subtitles. Not rated. 96m. DIR: Michael Verhoeven. CAST: Lena Stolze. 1990

NASTY HABITS *Nasty Habits* promises much more than it delivers. As a satire of the Watergate conspiracy, placed in a convent, it relies too heavily on the true incident for its punch. Rated PG, with some profanity. 96m. DIR: Michael Lindsay-Hogg. CAST: Glenda Jackson, Sandy Dennis, Susan Penhaligon, Edith Evans, Melina Mercouri. 1977

NASTY HERO ★★ An ex-con comes to Miami to get revenge on the hoods who sent him to prison. Car chases substitute for solid storytelling, but some of the actors are quite good. Rated PG-13. 79m. DIR: Nick Barwood. CAST: Scott Feraco, Robert Sedgwick, Raymond Serra. 1987

NASTY RABBIT ★★ Stilted *Blazing Saddles*–type parody is a curiosity piece, featuring Mexican bandits, Japanese soldiers, Nazi troopers, Indians, cowboys, and circus freaks, all rolled into one long-winded mess. 85m. DIR: James Landis. CAST: Arch Hall Jr., Richard Kiel. 1964

NATE AND HAYES ★★★ Tommy Lee Jones as a good pirate, Michael O'Keefe as his missionary accomplice, and Max Phipps as their cutthroat nemesis make this a jolly movie. Set in the South Seas of the late nineteenth century, it's unpretentious, old-fashioned movie fun. Rated PG for violence. 100m. DIR: Ferdinand Fairfax. CAST: Tommy Lee Jones, Michael O'Keefe, Max Phipps. 1983

NATIONAL LAMPOON'S ATTACK OF THE 5′ 2″ WOMEN ★★ A made-for-cable double feature starring comic Julie Brown in parodies of Tonya Harding and Lorena Bobbitt. Despite an impressive supporting cast, both minifeatures are crude, mean-spirited, and only rarely funny. Brown is often annoying enough to make you reach for the stop button on the nearest remote control. Rated R for profanity and sexual situations. 83m. DIR: Richard Wenk. CAST: Julie Brown, Sam McMurray, Adam Storke, Priscilla Barnes. 1994

NATIONAL LAMPOON'S CHRISTMAS VACATION ★★★ Chevy Chase glides charmingly through this frantic farce. This sequel to the two Lampoon *Vacation* flicks has the Griswold family staying home for the holidays and being invaded by bickering relatives. Randy Quaid excels as the ultimate slob. Rated PG-13 for scatological humor and profanity. 97m. DIR: Jeremiah S. Chechik. CAST: Chevy Chase, Beverly D'Angelo, Randy Quaid, Diane Ladd, John Randolph, E. G. Marshall, Juliette Lewis. 1989 DVD

NATIONAL LAMPOON'S CLASS OF '86 ★★★ You've got to be in a *National Lampoon* frame of mind to enjoy this comedy revue, which means embracing the off-the-wall humor for which the magazine is noted. Though unrated, it's strictly adult fare. 86m. DIR: Jerry Adler. CAST: Rodger Bumpass, Veanne Cox, Annie Golden, Tommy Koenig, John Michael Higgins, Brian O'Connor. 1986

NATIONAL LAMPOON'S CLASS REUNION 🦃 The graduating class of 1972 returns to wreak havoc on its alma mater. Rated R for nudity. 84m. DIR: Michael Miller. CAST: Gerrit Graham, Stephen Furst, Zane Buzby, Michael Lerner. 1982 DVD

NATIONAL LAMPOON'S EUROPEAN VACATION 🦃 The sappy sequel to *Vacation*. Rated PG-13 for profanity. 95m. DIR: Amy Heckerling. CAST: Chevy Chase, Beverly D'Angelo, Dana Hill, Jason Lively, Eric Idle, Victor Lanoux, John Astin. 1985

NATIONAL LAMPOON'S FAVORITE DEADLY SINS ★★★ Lust, greed, and anger are the focus of this compilation film's three vignettes. Denis Leary's fixation on a gorgeous neighbor quickly becomes tiresome, while Andrew Clay's rendition of chronic rage is little more than a blackout sketch. But Joe Mantegna scores as a venal TV miniseries producer. Rated R for profanity, nudity, violence, and simulated sex. 100m. DIR: David Jablin, Denis Leary. CAST: Denis Leary, Annabella Sciorra, Andrew Clay, Joe Mantegna, Cassidy Rae, Brian Keith, William Ragsdale, Gerrit Graham. 1995

•**NATIONAL LAMPOON'S GOLF PUNKS** ★★ Well-intentioned slob comedy stars Tom Arnold as a former golf pro leading a group of ragtag young players in a tournament against the snobs. Some laughs, but film suffers from a serious case of déjà vu. Rated PG for language. 92m. DIR: F. Harvey Frost. CAST: Tom Arnold, James Kirk, Rene Tardif, Gregory Thirloway. 1998 DVD

NATIONAL LAMPOON'S LAST RESORT 🦃 Made-for-video lame duck take on the old, "Hey gang, let's save the summer camp" premise. Teen has-beens Corey Haim and Corey Feldman save the day. Who will save us? Rated PG-13 for language and sexual situations. 91m. DIR: Rafal Zielinski. CAST: Corey Feldman, Corey Haim, Geoffrey Lewis, Robert Mandan. 1994 DVD

NATIONAL LAMPOON'S LOADED WEAPON 1 🦃 It's amazing that an action-comedy parody under the *National Lampoon* banner could be so lame and deadly dull, but this cop-action satire is a misfired groanfest. Rated PG-13 for violence and language. 97m. DIR: Gene Quintano. CAST: Emilio Estevez, Samuel L. Jackson, Jon Lovitz, Tim Curry, William Shatner, Whoopi Goldberg, Bruce Willis, Charlie Sheen, Kathy Ireland. 1993

NATIONAL LAMPOON'S SENIOR TRIP 🦃 High school's senior slackers write a letter to the U.S. president about public education and are manipulated to become reform-bill poster kids in this offensive tripe. Rated R for language, suggested sex, and nudity. 93m. DIR: Kelly Makin. CAST: Rob Moore, Jeremy Renner, Valerie Mahaffey, Fiona Loewi, Matt Frewer, Tommy Chong. 1995

NATIONAL LAMPOON'S VACATION ★★★ Clark Griswold (Chevy Chase) goes on a disastrous vacation with his wife, Ellen (Beverly D'Angelo), and kids, Rusty (Anthony Michael Hall) and Audrey (Dana Barron). Rated R for nudity and profanity. 98m. DIR: Harold Ramis. CAST: Chevy Chase, Beverly D'Angelo, Anthony Michael Hall, Dana Barron, Christie Brinkley, John Candy. 1983 DVD

NATIONAL VELVET ★★★★ This heartwarming tale of two youngsters determined to train a beloved horse to win the famed Grand National Race is good for the whole family, especially little girls who love horses and sentimentalists who fondly recall Elizabeth Taylor when she was young, innocent, and adorable. Have Kleenex on hand. 125m. DIR: Clarence Brown. CAST: Mickey Rooney, Elizabeth Taylor, Donald Crisp, Anne Revere, Angela Lansbury, Reginald Owen. 1944 DVD

NATIVE AMERICANS, THE ★★★★★ Informative and entertaining, this fast-moving, TBS production is told exclusively from the viewpoint of American Indians. It is kept lively and relevant by the exploration of oral histories, myths, art, and the spirituality of the past. Rich in detail and emotions, it delves into painful memories and makes intriguing, intelligent analogies. Each of the six episodes rates an A+ for high production values and disarming honesty. Not rated. Each tape 52m. DIR: John Borden, Phil Lucas, George Burdeau. 1994

NATIVE SON (1950) ★★1/2 Seeing author Richard Wright playing his fictional character, Bigger Thomas, is the chief interest of this low-budget adaptation of his groundbreaking novel. B&W; 91m. DIR: Pierre Chenal. CAST: Richard Wright, Jean Wallace, Gloria Madison. 1950

NATIVE SON (1986) ★★1/2 In this screen adaptation of Richard Wright's 1940 novel, a 19-year-old black youth takes a job as a chauffeur to a wealthy white couple. His hopes for a brighter future are shattered when a tragic accident leads to the death of their daughter and he is accused of murder. Rated R for nudity, suggested sex, violence, and gore. 101m. DIR: Jerrold Freedman. CAST: Victor Love, Geraldine Page, Elizabeth McGovern, Matt Dillon, Oprah Winfrey, Akosua Busia, Carroll Baker, Art Evans, David Rasche, Lane Smith, John McMartin. 1986

NATIVITY, THE ★★ Nicely filmed but dramatically unimpressive TV movie about Joseph's (John Shea) wooing of Mary (Madeline Stowe). Leo McKern is the mad King Herod. Not one of the top Biblical epics by a long shot. 97m. DIR: Bernard Kowalski. CAST: John Shea, Madeleine Stowe, Jane Wyatt, Paul Stewart, Leo McKern, John Rhys-Davies, Kate O'Mara. 1978

NATURAL, THE ★★★★ A thoroughly rewarding, old-fashioned screen entertainment, this adaptation of Bernard Malamud's novel about an unusually-gifted baseball player is a must-see. With its brilliant all-star cast, superb story, unforgettable characters, sumptuous cinematography, and sure-handed direction, this film recalls the Golden Age of Hollywood at its best. Rated PG for brief violence. 134m. DIR: Barry Levinson. CAST: Robert Redford, Robert Duvall, Glenn Close, Kim Basinger, Wilford Brimley, Richard Farnsworth, Robert Prosky, Joe Don Baker. 1984

NATURAL BORN KILLERS 🖤 Writer-director Oliver Stone's bombastic study of mass murder is a self-indulgent, migraine-inducing mess that shrilly indicts the incestuous, bread-and-circus relationship between violence and media celebrity as if it were something new. Less a coherent film and more a masturbatory, MTV-style assault on the senses. Rated R for graphic violence, gore, profanity, gruesome images, and deviant sexuality. 120m. DIR: Oliver Stone. CAST: Woody Harrelson, Juliette Lewis, Robert Downey Jr., Tommy Lee Jones, Rodney Dangerfield. 1994 DVD

NATURAL CAUSES ★★ When a woman journeys to Thailand to visit her mother, she finds herself in the midst of a violent political conspiracy that only she has the power to stop. Dull thriller offers just enough story to keep dedicated viewers awake but will put most everyone else fast asleep. Rated PG-13 for violence and profanity. 90m. DIR: James Becket. CAST: Linda Purl, Cary-Hiroyuki Tagawa, Will Patton, Tim Thomerson, Ali MacGraw. 1993

NATURAL ENEMIES ★★★★ Excellent study of domestic murder. Hal Holbrook plays a successful magazine editor who murders his wife and three children. Louise Fletcher is great as Holbrook's emotionally unstable wife. Depressing, to be certain, but worth watching. Rated R for violence, profanity, sex, nudity, and adult subject matter. 100m. DIR: Jeff Kanew. CAST: Hal Holbrook, Louise Fletcher, Viveca Lindfors, José Ferrer, Patricia Elliott. 1979

NATURAL ENEMY ★★1/2 Donald Sutherland and William McNamara are fine as the stockbroker and the student intent on ruining his business in this made-for-cable effort. Even though the film travels down a well-worn path, the stars keep you interested, especially McNamara once again playing a psycho. Not rated; contains violence. 88m. DIR: Douglas Jackson. CAST: Donald Sutherland, William McNamara, Lesley Ann Warren, Joe Pantoliano, Tia Carrere. 1997

NATURE OF THE BEAST ★★ Two men, a businessman and a drifter, hook up for one psychotic road trip. One is probably the thief who lifted a cool mil from the mob, the other is probably a serial killer who favors hatchets. But which man is the killer? Who cares? Rated R for profanity, violence, sexual situations, brief nudity, drug use, and dismemberment. 91m. DIR: Victor Salva. CAST: Eric Roberts, Lance Henriksen, Brion James. 1995

NAUGHTY MARIETTA ★★★ This warm, vibrant rehash of Victor Herbert's tuneful 1910 operetta established leads Jeanette MacDonald and Nelson Eddy as the screen's peerless singing duo. The plot's next to nothing—a French princess flees to America and falls in love with an Indian scout—but the music is stirring, charming, and corny. B&W; 106m. DIR: W. S. Van Dyke. CAST: Jeanette MacDonald, Nelson Eddy, Frank Morgan, Douglass Dumbrille, Elsa Lanchester, Akim Tamiroff. 1935

NAUGHTY NINETIES, THE ★★ Suitably attired for the period, the always eager Bud and Lou find themselves hip-deep in Mississippi riverboat gamblers.

The pair's usual ripostes, including "Who's on First," prevail. The finale is tried-and-true slapstick. B&W; 76m. DIR: Jean Yarbrough. CAST: Bud Abbott, Lou Costello, Joe Sawyer, Alan Curtis, Rita Johnson, Lois Collier. 1945

NAVAJO BLUES 💗 Everyone looks bored in this listless thriller about a Las Vegas cop hiding from the mob on a Navajo reservation. Rated R for violence, sexual situations, and profanity. 87m. DIR: Joey Travolta. CAST: Steven Bauer, Charlotte Lewis, Irene Bedard. 1997

•NAVIGATOR, THE (1924) ★★★1/2 Buster Keaton used a condemned ocean liner as the set for this feature where he plays a millionaire stuck on an abandoned ship with only one other person: the woman who just rejected his proposal of marriage. There are many memorable gags, but our favorite features Buster taking a walk on the ocean floor. This tape also contains two Keaton shorts, *The Boat* and *The Love Nest*. B&W; 110m. DIR: Donald Crisp, Buster Keaton. CAST: Buster Keaton, Kathryn McGuire. 1924

NAVIGATOR: A MEDIEVAL ODYSSEY, THE ★★★★1/2 A visionary film from New Zealand that involves a medieval quest through time. The film opens in Cumbria in 1348, in the midst of the terrifying Black Plague. A village of miners tries to appease what they view as a vengeful God by vowing to travel a great distance to fulfill a child's vision. The adventurers travel through the center of the Earth—and surface in a modern-day New Zealand town. Astonishingly original. In B&W and color. 91m. DIR: Vincent Ward. CAST: Bruce Lyons, Chris Haywood. 1989

NAVY BLUE AND GOLD ★★★ Familiar but entertaining story of three Annapolis middies learning (by way of the annual Army-Navy football game) the meaning of esprit de corps. Billie Burke is a particular delight. B&W; 94m. DIR: Sam Wood. CAST: Robert Young, James Stewart, Lionel Barrymore, Florence Rice, Billie Burke, Tom Brown, Samuel S. Hinds, Paul Kelly, Frank Albertson, Minor Watson. 1937

NAVY SEALS ★★ When Middle Eastern terrorists acquire some American stinger missiles, it's up to the rough-and-ready Navy SEALS (Sea, Air and Land) to blow them up. Director Lewis Teague cannot overcome the tedium of the predictable screenplay, although the action scenes are robust. Rated R for violence and profanity. 118m. DIR: Lewis Teague. CAST: Charlie Sheen, Michael Biehn, Joanne Whalley, Rick Rossovich. 1990 DVD

NAVY VS. THE NIGHT MONSTERS, THE 💗 Homicidal plants scheme to take over the world. 90m. DIR: Michael Hoey. CAST: Mamie Van Doren, Anthony Eisley, Pamela Mason, Bobby Van. 1966

NAZARIN ★★★★★ A priest is cast out of his church for giving shelter to a prostitute. A remarkable film by Luis Buñuel that presents a clever variation of the Don Quixote theme, applied to religion and hypocrisy. This surrealistic comedy won the Grand Prize at the Cannes Film Festival. In Spanish with English subtitles. B&W; 92m. DIR: Luis Buñuel. CAST: Francisco Rabal. 1958

NEA (A YOUNG EMMANUELLE) ★★★ In this French sex comedy, a young girl, Sybille Ashby (Ann Zacharias), stifled by the wealth of her parents, turns to anonymously writing erotic literature via firsthand experience. A relatively successful and entertaining film of its kind, it has sex and adult themes. In French with English subtitles. Rated R. 103m. DIR: Nelly Kaplan. CAST: Sami Frey, Ann Zacharias, Micheline Presle. 1978

NEANDERTHAL MAN, THE 💗 Serum from a prehistoric fish turns a scientist into the titular beastie. B&W; 77m. DIR: E. A. Dupont. CAST: Robert Shayne, Richard Crane, Doris Merrick, Robert Long. 1953

NEAR DARK ★★★1/2 A stylish story of nomadic vampires. A girl takes a fancy to a young stud and turns him into a vampire, forcing him to join the macabre family. His problem is that he can't bring himself to make his first kill. It's the character development and acting that make this movie worthwhile. Rated R for violence and language. 95m. DIR: Kathryn Bigelow. CAST: Adrian Pasdar, Jenny Wright, Tim Thomerson, Jenette Goldstein, Lance Henriksen, Bill Paxton. 1987

NEAR MISSES ★★1/2 Executive Judge Reinhold balances two wives and a secretary-girlfriend on the side, but his troubles really begin when he asks fellow coworker Casey Siemaszko to impersonate him when his yearly army reserve duty comes up. Rated PG-13 for profanity. 92m. DIR: Baz Taylor. CAST: Judge Reinhold, Casey Siemaszko, Rebecca Pauley, Cecile Paoli. 1990

'NEATH ARIZONA SKIES ★★1/2 Formula B Western has John Wayne as the protector of the heir to rich oil lands, a little Indian girl. Of course, the baddies try to kidnap her and the Duke rides to the rescue. Low-budget and predictable. B&W; 57m. DIR: Henry Frazer. CAST: John Wayne, Sheila Terry, Yakima Canutt, George "Gabby" Hayes. 1934

NECESSARY PARTIES ★★★★ Clever film about a teenager who refuses to accept his parents' divorce. With the help of an idealistic part-time lawyer/full-time auto mechanic, the boy sues his folks as an affected third party. This sensitive presentation from TV's *Wonderworks* offers occasional chuckles. 109m. DIR: Gwen Arner. CAST: Alan Arkin, Mark Paul Gosselaar, Barbara Dana, Donald Moffat, Adam Arkin, Julie Hagerty. 1988

NECESSARY ROUGHNESS ★★★★ While the premise of this football comedy is familiar—a group of losers banding together against almost impossible odds—the execution seems fresh. Not only is this a very funny comedy, it has something to say about the state of college athletics. Rated PG-13 for profanity. 104m. DIR: Stan Dragoti. CAST: Scott Bakula, Robert Loggia, Harley Jane Kozak, Sinbad, Hector Elizondo, Jason Bateman, Kathy Ireland, Larry Miller. 1991

NECROMANCER ★★ A sorceress possesses a young woman, using her to kill men and steal their life forces. Violence and bloodshed abound unfortunately, but not much suspense. Rated R for graphic violence and nudity. 88m. DIR: Dusty Nelson. CAST: Elizabeth Cayton, Russ Tamblyn. 1988

NECROPOLIS 💗 A 300-year-old witch, looking pretty good for her age, is resurrected in New York City. Rated R. 96m. DIR: Bruce Hickey. CAST: Lee Anne Baker. 1987

NEEDFUL THINGS ★★★ In Castle Rock, Maine, a mysterious stranger opens a curio shop that seems to have something for everyone. Just one problem: The owner is actually the devil, and he only trades for souls. He turns the locals against each other, setting off a chain reaction of murder and mayhem that culminates in an explosive finale between evil and the law. Viciously tongue-in-cheek. Rated R for strong violence and adult language. 113m. **DIR:** Fraser Heston. **CAST:** Max von Sydow, Ed Harris, Bonnie Bedelia, J. T. Walsh, Amanda Plummer. **1993 DVD**

NEGATIVES ★★★ Quirky satire of a married couple (Glenda Jackson and Peter McEnery) whose fantasy world of playacting and charades is interrupted by the intrusive overtures of a third person. Peter Medak's direction is sharp, and the fantasy sequences are pungently imaginative. 99m. **DIR:** Peter Medak. **CAST:** Glenda Jackson, Peter McEnery. 1968

NEGOTIATOR, THE ★★★★ Gripping thriller about a police hostage negotiator who takes a few hostages himself after being framed for killing his partner. The script, though taut, has its logic lapses. But Samuel L. Jackson, as the distraught but cagey suspect, and Kevin Spacey, as the second negotiator brought in to finesse the crisis, play it for all it's worth, and because of them there's never a down moment. Rated R for violence and language. 135m. **DIR:** F. Gary Gray. **CAST:** Samuel L. Jackson, Kevin Spacey, Ron Rifkin, John Spencer, J. T. Walsh. **1998 DVD**

NEIGHBOR, THE ★★★ Earnest performances give Kurt Wimmer's predictable script far more power than it deserves. Linda Kozlowski is properly sympathetic as a pregnant woman who fears next-door neighbor Rod Steiger might be more than a beloved, small-town obstetrician. Naturally, hubby Ron Lea dismisses her concerns as second-trimester hysteria. Steiger, for once subdued, delivers his best work in years. Rated PG for intensity and mild violence. 93m. **DIR:** Rodney Gibbons. **CAST:** Linda Kozlowski, Ron Lea, Rod Steiger. 1993

NEIGHBORS ★★★1/2 This is a strange movie. John Belushi plays a suburban homeowner whose peaceful existence is threatened when his new neighbors (played by Dan Aykroyd and Cathy Moriarty) turn out to be complete wackos. It isn't a laugh-a-minute farce, but there are numerous chuckles and a few guffaws along the way. Rated R because of profanity and sexual content. 94m. **DIR:** John G. Avildsen. **CAST:** John Belushi, Dan Aykroyd, Cathy Moriarty, Kathryn Walker, Tim Kazurinsky. 1981

NEKROMANTIK 🎬 A disgusting ode to necrophilia. In German with English subtitles. Not rated; contains violence, profanity, nudity, simulated sex, and gore. 74m. **DIR:** Jorg Buttgereit. **CAST:** Daktari Lorenz. **1987 DVD**

NEKROMANTIK 2 🎬 Nympho finds the decapitated head of the first film's necrolover and begins her own descent into depravity. In German with English subtitles. Not rated; contains violence, profanity, nudity, simulated sex, and gore. 100m. **DIR:** Jorg Buttgereit. **CAST:** Monika M, Mark Reeder. 1991

NELL ★★★★ Jodie Foster shines as a young woman raised apart from civilization in the backwoods of North Carolina. Nell is left to fend for her-self when the woman who raised her dies, and it's up to the sympathetic town doctor to help her adjust to the increasingly intruding outside world. Gripping and emotionally rewarding, this offbeat story never compromises its clear-eyed point of view. Rated PG-13 for nudity and profanity. 113m. **DIR:** Michael Apted. **CAST:** Jodie Foster, Liam Neeson, Natasha Richardson, Richard Libertini, Nick Searcy, Robin Mullins. 1994

NELLY AND MONSIEUR ARNAUD ★★★★★ A wealthy, aging judge hires a beautiful young divorcée to type up his memoirs; they stir complex feelings in each other that neither can quite fathom or bear. Director Claude Sautet's understanding of the vagaries of the human heart has never been more acute, and the lead actors are marvels of poise, originality, and honesty. In French with English subtitles. Not rated, but addresses thoroughly adult issues and has a brief sex scene. 106m. **DIR:** Claude Sautet. **CAST:** Emmanuelle Beart, Michel Serrault, Jean-Hugues Anglade. 1995

NEMESIS (1986) ★★★1/2 Joan Hickson's Miss Marple beomes the "unbeatable rival no man may escape" in this adaptation of Agatha Christie's last novel. The English countryside forms the backdrop for this clever story. Not rated; suitable for family viewing. 102m. **DIR:** David Tucker. **CAST:** Joan Hickson, Margaret Tyzack, Anna Cropper, Valerie Lush, Peter Tilbury, Bruce Payne, Helen Cherry. 1986

NEMESIS (1992) ★★ In the year 2027, an ex-L.A.P.D. detective must determine whether the humans or the cyborgs are his enemy. He has three days to complete his mission or else the bomb in his heart will explode. Rated R for violence and profanity. 92m. **DIR:** Albert Pyun. **CAST:** Olivier Gruner, Tim Thomerson, Cary-Hiroyuki Tagawa, Merle Kennedy, Yuji Okumoto, Marjorie Monaghan, Brion James, Deborah Shelton. **1993 DVD**

NEMESIS 2 🎬 Strictly low-rent affair about a cyborg sent to kill a woman who holds the secret to save humanity. If this is our future, then humanity doesn't need saving. Rated R for violence. 83m. **DIR:** Albert Pyun. **CAST:** Sue Price, Tina Cote, Earl White, Chad Stahelski. 1995

NEMESIS 3: TIME LAPSE ★★ Nothing new in this continuing tale about evil cyborgs intent on wiping out mankind. A woman with superhuman DNA holds the key to the world's salvation. Rated R for violence, profanity, and nudity. 91m. **DIR:** Albert Pyun. **CAST:** Sue Price, Tim Thomerson, Norbert Weisser, Xavier Declie. 1995

•**NEMESIS 4** 🎬 Fourth and final(?) chapter in this tale of cyborgs with heart is short on acting talent, budget, and running time. Rated R for violence, nudity, gore, and profanity. 65m. **DIR:** Albert Pyun. **CAST:** Andrew Divoff, Sue Price, Norbert Weisser. 1995

NEON BIBLE, THE ★★★★1/2 Charismatic Gena Rowlands struts her stuff as a radio singer who shores up a sad nephew desperate for both affection and a connection to a different life. This film, which captures the insulation and poverty of the American South, is so visually arresting you can't shake it free. Not rated; contains violence and profanity. 92m. **DIR:**

Terence Davies. **CAST:** Gena Rowlands, Denis Leary, Diana Scarwid, Jacob Tierney. **1994 DVD**

NEON CITY ★★1/2 In order to get to the fabled Neon City, a group of travelers must cross a barren wasteland where they are in constant danger of solar flares and attacks by mutant bandits. Some great stunt work helps this futuristic adventure. Rated R for violence and profanity. 107m. **DIR:** Monte Markham. **CAST:** Michael Ironside, Vanity, Lyle Alzado, Richard Sanders. **1991**

NEON EMPIRE, THE ★★ This tedious, cut-down version of a four-hour made-for-cable gangster flick merely wastes the talents of performers who sleepwalk through their parts. Pete Hamill's pedestrian screenplay should have been the stuff of intrigue and crackling suspense. Not rated but contains profanity and considerable violence. 120m. **DIR:** Larry Peerce. **CAST:** Ray Sharkey, Gary Busey, Linda Fiorentino, Martin Landau, Dylan McDermott, Julie Carmen, Harry Guardino. **1989**

NEON MANIACS ★★1/2 Ancient evil beings are released into present-day San Francisco, killing everyone in their path. Three teenagers learn the demons' weakness and go on a crusade to destroy them. With good special effects, original creatures, and lots of scares, this film is worth a look. Rated R for violence. 90m. **DIR:** Joseph Mangine. **CAST:** Allan Hayes, Leilani Sarelle. **1985**

NEO-TOKYO ★★ This collection of short animated stories is a rather uneven showcase for three of Japan's premiere animation directors. Two of the features are merely exercises in self-indulgence, but the last, "An Order to Stop Construction" from *Akira* director Katsuhiro Otomo, is definitely worth seeing. In Japanese with English subtitles. Not rated; contains some graphic violence. 50m. **DIR:** Rin Taro, Yoshiaki Kawajiri, Katsuhiro Otomo. **1986**

NEPTUNE FACTOR, THE ★★ Ben Gazzara stars as the commander of an experimental deep-sea submarine. He is called in to rescue an aquatic research team trapped in the remains of their lab on the ocean floor. Why they built it in the middle of a quake zone is the first in a series of dumb plot ideas. Rated G. 94m. **DIR:** Daniel Petrie. **CAST:** Ben Gazzara, Yvette Mimieux, Walter Pidgeon, Ernest Borgnine. **1973**

NEPTUNE'S DAUGHTER ★★1/2 Big-budgeted aquatic musical from MGM studios has Esther Williams playing a (what else?) swimsuit designer on holiday in South America floating in and out of danger with Red Skelton. The plot isn't important as long as you can keep time with Xavier Cugat's mambo beat. Harmless, enjoyable nonsense. 93m. **DIR:** Edward Buzzell. **CAST:** Esther Williams, Red Skelton, Keenan Wynn, Ricardo Montalban, Betty Garrett, Mel Blanc, Mike Mazurki, Ted de Corsia, Xavier Cugat. **1949**

NERVOUS TICKS ★★★ Airline employee Bill Pullman tries to run off to Rio with married Julie Brown. Interesting for having been shot in "real time," but the plot is just too wacky. Rated R for violence, profanity, and nudity. 95m. **DIR:** Rocky Lang. **CAST:** Bill Pullman, Peter Boyle, Julie Brown, Brent Jennings, James LeGros. **1991**

NEST, THE (1981) ★★1/2 *The Nest* is the story of a tragic relationship between a 60-year-old widower and a 12-year-old girl. The movie takes a far too romantic view of the widower's sacrifices to the friendship. Hector Alterio as the older man has a warm and inviting face and voice. He is the one who enlists our sympathies. In Spanish with English subtitles. 109m. **DIR:** Jaime De Arminan. **CAST:** Hector Alterio, Ana Torrent. **1981**

NEST, THE (1988) ★★★1/2 A skin-rippling tale of a genetic experiment gone awry. Flesh-eating cockroaches are on the verge of overrunning a small island and they are not about to let anything stand in their way. What's worse, they're mutating into the form of whatever they consume. Special effects are above par and definitely not for the squeamish. Rated R. 88m. **DIR:** Terence H. Winkless. **CAST:** Robert Lansing, Lisa Langlois, Franc Luz, Stephen Davies, Nancy Morgan. **1988**

NESTING, THE ★★ Tolerable haunted-house film about a writer (Robin Groves) who rents a house in the country so as to get some peace and quiet. But guess what? You got it—the house is plagued with undead spirits. Rated R for nudity and violence. 104m. **DIR:** Armand Weston. **CAST:** Robin Groves, Christopher Loomis, John Carradine, Gloria Grahame. **1980**

NET, THE ★★★ Sandra Bullock, once again cast as the most personable lonely woman in the world, brings more credibility to this film than Michael Ferris and John Brancato's often-silly script really deserves. She's a genius computer hacker who stumbles upon some dangerous software, and then finds herself targeted by a suave assassin who quite sadistically toys with her. The plot is illogical enough to stretch credibility. Rated PG-13 for profanity and violence. 112m. **DIR:** Irwin Winkler. **CAST:** Sandra Bullock, Jeremy Northam, Dennis Miller, Diane Baker. **1995 DVD**

NETHERWORLD ★★★ The heir to a Louisiana mansion is asked to bring his father back from the dead as a condition of the deed. The film creates a sort of ornithological voodooist mythology. Not rated, but has profanity and brief nudity. 87m. **DIR:** David Schmoeller. **CAST:** Michael Bendetti, Denise Gentile, Anjanette Comer. **1991 DVD**

NETWORK ★★★★★ "I'm mad as hell and I'm not going to take it anymore!" Peter Finch (who won a posthumous Academy Award for best actor), William Holden, Faye Dunaway, Robert Duvall, and Ned Beatty give superb performances in this black comedy about the world of television as penned by Paddy Chayefsky. It's a biting satire on the inner workings of this century's most powerful medium. Rated R. 121m. **DIR:** Sidney Lumet. **CAST:** Peter Finch, William Holden, Faye Dunaway, Robert Duvall, Ned Beatty, Beatrice Straight. **1976 DVD**

NEUROTIC CABARET ★★★ A strange and entertaining movie. The plot revolves around two people's attempts to get their movie made. Tammy Stones, who also penned the script, stars as a strip-joint dancer. An amusing vehicle played tongue in cheek. Rated R for nudity. 97m. **DIR:** John Woodward. **CAST:** Tammy Stones, Dennis Worthington. **1990**

NEVADA ★★★ When a mysterious woman stumbles into a tiny town, some of the local women there embrace her—while others are suspicious. Excellent performances and crisp writing and direction make this an involving, riveting film. Rated R for profanity. 109m. **DIR:** Gary Teche. **CAST:** Amy Brenneman, Kirstie Alley, Gabrielle Anwar, Saffron Burrows, Angus MacFadyen, Kathy Najimy, Dee Wallace, James Wilder, Bridgette Wilson. 1997

NEVADA SMITH ★★★ Steve McQueen, in the title role, is butcher's-freezer–cold, calculating, and merciless in this hard-hitting, gripping Western. The focus is on a senseless, vicious double murder and the revenge taken by the son of the innocent victims. Story and characters are excerpted from a section of Harold Robbins's sensational novel *The Carpetbaggers* not used in the 1964 film. 135m. **DIR:** Henry Hathaway. **CAST:** Steve McQueen, Karl Malden, Brian Keith, Arthur Kennedy, Suzanne Pleshette, Raf Vallone, Pat Hingle, Howard DaSilva, Martin Landau. 1966

NEVADAN, THE ★★1/2 Government agent Randolph Scott works undercover with outlaw Forrest Tucker to retrieve stolen gold. Originally filmed in color, only B&W prints seem to exist today. B&W; 81m. **DIR:** Gordon Douglas. **CAST:** Randolph Scott, Dorothy Malone, Forrest Tucker, George Macready, Jock Mahoney. 1950

NEVER A DULL MOMENT 💣 Dick Van Dyke doing his sophisticated version of Jerry Lewis at his worst. Rated G. 100m. **DIR:** Jerry Paris. **CAST:** Dick Van Dyke, Edward G. Robinson, Dorothy Provine, Henry Silva. 1968

NEVER BEEN KISSED ★★1/2 Drew Barrymore stars as a shy *Chicago Sun Times* copy editor, whose passion to become a "real" reporter bears fruit when she's sent undercover to a local high school and ordered to find a sizzling story on today's teenagers. For Barrymore, this is like returning to the Seventh Level of Hell; her original high-school experiences were an unrelenting series of base and humiliating traumas. Unfortunately, this film can't quite decide what it wants to be when it grows up: romantic comedy or exaggerated farce. Rated PG-13 for mild profanity and sexual content. 107m. **DIR:** Raja Gosnell. **CAST:** Drew Barrymore, David Arquette, Molly Shannon, John C. Reilly, LeeLee Sobieski, Jeremy Jordan, Garry Marshall. 1999 DVD

NEVER CRY WOLF ★★★★★ Carroll Ballard made this breathtakingly beautiful, richly rewarding Disney feature about a lone biologist (Charles Martin Smith) learning firsthand about the white wolves of the Yukon by living with them. It's an extraordinary motion picture in every sense of the word. Rated PG for brief nudity. 105m. **DIR:** Carroll Ballard. **CAST:** Charles Martin Smith; Brian Dennehy. 1983 DVD

NEVER FORGET ★★★1/2 Fact-based TV account of Jewish concentration camp survivor Mel Mermelstein's fight against the Institute for Historical Review, an organization that refused to accept the fact that the Holocaust ever took place. Leonard Nimoy has never been better. 94m. **DIR:** Joseph Sargent. **CAST:** Leonard Nimoy, Blythe Danner, Dabney Coleman, Paul Hampton. 1991

NEVER GIVE A SUCKER AN EVEN BREAK ★★★★ This is a wild and woolly pastiche of hilarious gags and bizarre comedy routines revolving around W. C. Fields's attempt to sell an outlandish script to a movie studio. Some of the jokes misfire, but the absurdity of the situations makes up for the weak spots. B&W; 71m. **DIR:** Eddie Cline. **CAST:** W. C. Fields, Gloria Jean, Leon Errol. 1941

NEVER LET GO ★★ Peter Sellers bombs out in his first dramatic role as a ruthless criminal in this thin story about car stealing. The sure acting of Mervyn Johns, longtime dependable supporting player, helps things but cannot begin to save the film. Nor can Richard Todd's efforts. B&W; 90m. **DIR:** John Guillermin. **CAST:** Peter Sellers, Richard Todd, Elizabeth Sellars, Carol White, Mervyn Johns. 1960

NEVER LET ME GO ★★★ Clark Gable, a correspondent in post–World War II Russia, marries ballerina Gene Tierney just before he is expelled from the country. When authorities detain her, he sets about to help her escape. B&W; 94m. **DIR:** Delmer Daves. **CAST:** Clark Gable, Gene Tierney, Bernard Miles, Richard Haydn, Belita, Kenneth More, Theodore Bikel. 1953

NEVER LOVE A STRANGER 💣 John Drew Barrymore as a young hustler whose success puts him on a collision course with his old boss and an eager district attorney. 91m. **DIR:** Robert Stevens. **CAST:** John Drew Barrymore, Lita Milan, Steve McQueen. 1958

NEVER ON SUNDAY ★★★★ A wimpy egghead tries to make a lady out of an earthy, fun-loving prostitute. The setting is Greece; the dialogue and situations are delightful. Melina Mercouri is terrific. 91m. **DIR:** Jules Dassin. **CAST:** Melina Mercouri, Jules Dassin. 1960

NEVER ON TUESDAY ★★★ Two best friends, leaving their boring hometown for sunny L.A., are stranded for two days in the desert with a beautiful girl. Unexpected cameo appearances by Charlie Sheen and Emilio Estevez. Rated R for nudity and simulated sex. 90m. **DIR:** Adam Rifkin. **CAST:** Claudia Christian, Andrew Lauer, Peter Berg. 1988

NEVER SAY DIE 💣 Tired action film about a special-forces agent who has to square off against his former mentor. Ho hum. Rated R for violence and language. 99m. **DIR:** Yossi Wein. **CAST:** Frank Zagarino, Billy Drago, Jennifer Miller, Todd Jensen. 1994

NEVER SAY GOODBYE ★★ An outdated comedy about marriage and morals, this movie takes advantage of Errol Flynn's reputation as a womanizer to get laughs. He plays a divorced man courting his wife again. A few laughs and lots of clichéd comments. B&W; 96m. **DIR:** James V. Kern. **CAST:** Errol Flynn, Eleanor Parker, Donald Woods, Peggy Knudsen, Forrest Tucker, S. Z. Sakall, Hattie McDaniel. 1946

NEVER SAY NEVER AGAIN ★★★★1/2 Sean Connery returns to the role of James Bond in this high-style, tongue-in-cheek remake of *Thunderball*. Once again, agent 007 goes up against the evil Largo, the sexy and deadly Fatima, and the ever-present head of SPECTRE, Blofeld. Action-packed and peppered with laughs. Rated PG for violence and nudity. 137m. **DIR:** Irvin Kershner. **CAST:** Sean Connery, Klaus Maria Brandauer, Max von Sydow, Barbara Carrera, Kim

Basinger, Edward Fox, Bernie Casey, Alec McCowen. 1983

NEVER SO FEW ★★★ Adroitly led by a group of American officers, a band of Burmese guerrillas fight a series of vicious battles against invading Japanese troops in this World War II action picture. The battle scenes are quite good, but the film is marred at times by the philosophizing of U.S. Army officer Frank Sinatra. It's good, but talky. 124m. DIR: John Sturges. CAST: Frank Sinatra, Gina Lollobrigida, Peter Lawford, Steve McQueen, Paul Henreid, Charles Bronson, Richard Johnson, Brian Donlevy, Dean Jones. 1959

NEVER STEAL ANYTHING SMALL ★★1/2 Unbelievable musical-comedy-drama about a goodhearted union labor leader is saved by the dynamic James Cagney, who was always enough to make even the most hackneyed story worth watching. 94m. DIR: Charles Lederer. CAST: James Cagney, Shirley Jones, Roger Smith, Cara Williams, Nehemiah Persoff, Royal Dano, Horace McMahon. 1959

NEVER TALK TO STRANGERS ★★ A criminal psychologist gets picked up in a grocery market by a charming yet dangerous Latino. When creepy things start happening, she hires a private detective to trail her new lover and sift through his murky identity. The psychologist's tormented past leads to a daring but unconvincing finale. Rated R for language, nudity, sex, and violence. 102m. DIR: Peter Hall. CAST: Rebecca DeMornay, Antonio Banderas, Dennis Miller, Len Cariou, Harry Dean Stanton. 1995 DVD

NEVER TOO LATE ★★★1/2 The villain, a conniving jail official, cleverly frames the handsome young hero in order to steal his girl in this classic melodrama. Originally, on the stage, the play resulted in sweeping reforms in the British penal system in the mid–nineteenth century. B&W; 67m. DIR: David MacDonald. CAST: Tod Slaughter. 1937 DVD

NEVER TOO YOUNG TO DIE 💔 A really rotten film that steals everything it can from the James Bond and *Road Warrior* series. Rated R for violence. 90m. DIR: Gil Bettman. CAST: John Stamos, Vanity, Gene Simmons, George Lazenby. 1986

●**NEVER 2 BIG** ★★★ A man, accused of killing his superstar sister, must uncover the conniving record producer who's really behind the murder. Not bad but often contrived and over-the-top thriller. Rated R for violence, profanity, and nudity. 100m. DIR: Peter Gathings Bunche. CAST: Ernie Hudson, Nia Long, Donnie Wahlberg, Shermar Moore. 1998

NEVER WAVE AT A WAC (PRIVATE WORE SKIRTS, THE) ★★★ Ancestor of *Private Benjamin*, with Rosalind Russell as a spoiled socialite who joins the Women's Army Corps. Russell may be a bit old for the part, but she and dumb-blonde sidekick Marie Wilson provide some laughs. B&W; 87m. DIR: Norman Z. McLeod. CAST: Rosalind Russell, Marie Wilson, Paul Douglas, Louise Beavers. 1952

NEVERENDING STORY III, THE: ESCAPE TO FANTASIA ★★★1/2 Bastian, a teenager who can't stand his new stepsister or his new school, seeks refuge in the school library, where he escapes into his favorite book, *The Neverending Story*. Swept away to the magical city of Fantasia, he meets a cast of unusual

characters brought to life by the Jim Henson Creature Shop. Kids will enjoy this live-action adventure-filled comedy. Rated G. 95m. DIR: Peter MacDonald. CAST: Jason James Richter, Melody Kay, Jack Black, Freddie Jones, Tony Robinson, Moya Brandy. 1994

NEVERENDING STORY, THE ★★★★1/2 This is a superb fantasy about a sensitive 10-year-old boy named Bastian (Barrett Oliver) who takes refuge in a fairy tale. In reading it, he's swept off to a land of startlingly strange creatures and heroic adventures where a young warrior, Atreyu (Noah Hathaway), does battle with the Nothing, a force that threatens to obliterate the land of mankind's hopes and dreams—and only Bastian has the power to save the day. Rated PG for slight profanity. 92m. DIR: Wolfgang Petersen. CAST: Barret Oliver, Noah Hathaway. 1984

NEVERENDING STORY II, THE ★★1/2 Disappointing sequel to director Wolfgang Petersen's original has a new actor (Jonathan Brandis) as Bastion, the young reader/hero who is once again called upon to save the magical world of Fantasia. Rated PG for scary stuff. 90m. DIR: George Miller. CAST: Jonathan Brandis, Kenny Morrison, Clarissa Burt, John Wesley Shipp. 1991

NEW ADVENTURES OF CHARLIE CHAN, THE (TV SERIES) ★★★ What do you get when you have an Irish actor (J. Carrol Naish) playing a retired Chinese detective? Unintentional but nonetheless delightful camp. Each of the three volumes released thus far contain three episodes of this British TV mystery series. B&W; 90m. DIR: Charles Haas. CAST: J. Carrol Naish, James Hong. 1957

NEW ADVENTURES OF PIPPI LONGSTOCKING, THE ★★ Something has been lost in the film adaptation of Astrid Lindgren's tale. This time spunky but lovable Pippi is a brat who manages to give adult viewers a headache and children ideas about driving adults over the edge. A few catchy tunes but nothing else to recommend this. Rated G. 100m. DIR: Ken Annakin. CAST: Tami Erin, Eileen Brennan, Dennis Dugan, Dianne Hull. 1988

NEW ADVENTURES OF TARZAN ★★1/2 For the first time on film, Edgar Rice Burroughs's immortal jungle lord spoke and behaved the way he had been created. This sometimes slow, but basically enjoyable twelve-episode chapterplay wove a complex story about a search for Tarzan's missing friend and a treacherous agent intent on stealing an ancient Mayan stone. B&W; 12 chapters. DIR: Edward Kull, W. F. McGaugh. CAST: Bruce Bennett, Ula Holt, Frank Baker, Dale Walsh, Harry Ernest. 1935

NEW AGE, THE ★★1/2 Film is supposed to be a scathing dark comedy about commercialism and consumerism, but emerges as a dry, overlong whining contest between stars Peter Weller and Judy Davis. A successful married couple gets a dose of reality when he quits his job and she loses her designing firm. Instead of coping rationally, they open a boutique in the trendy Melrose section of Hollywood. Much ado about nothing. Rated R for nudity, adult situations, and language. 106m. DIR: Michael Tolkin. CAST: Peter Weller, Judy Davis, Adam West, John Diehl. 1994

•NEW BLOOD ★★★★ Writer-director Michael Hurst breathes new life into an old formula, creating a hybrid that manages to rise above the rest. Danny is a gangster wannabe who uses his own crew for a kidnapping that goes wrong. Wounded and on the run from the local mob, Danny seeks shelter at the home of his estranged father, who sees opportunity in Danny's condition. Unexpected twists, compelling dialogue, and strong direction create fireworks. Rated R for adult situations, language, and violence. 92m. DIR: Michael Hurst. CAST: John Hurt, Nick Moran, Carrie Anne Moss, Joe Pantoliano, Shawn Wayans. 1999 DVD

NEW CENTURIONS, THE ★★★★ A blend of harsh reality and soap opera. The moral seems to be "It is no fun being a cop." Watching George C. Scott and Stacy Keach get their lumps, we have to agree. Rated R. 103m. DIR: Richard Fleischer. CAST: George C. Scott, Stacy Keach, Jane Alexander, Erik Estrada. 1972

NEW CRIME CITY: LOS ANGELES 2020 ★★★ In the future, when crime has run rampant, a cop is assigned the duty of tracking down and destroying a vial containing a dangerous virus. Violent, gritty, and intriguing sci-fi trash. Rated R for violence and nudity. 95m. DIR: Jonathan Winfrey. CAST: Rick Rossovich, Stacy Keach, Sherrie Rose, Rick Dean. 1994

NEW CUTEY HONEY, THE ★★1/2 Veteran comic creator Go Nagai's animated, ever-changing female superhero is weakly updated. Pitted against a shadowy arch villain in a battle for the control of her city, Honey-chan must defeat creatures and cutthroats with the aid of her motley sidekicks. Too much formula action does nothing to set it apart from the low end of the genre. In Japanese with English subtitles. Not rated; contains nudity, sexual situations, and violence. 65m. each DIR: Yasuchika Nagaoka. 1994

NEW DOMINION TANK POLICE ★★★ With first-rate animation and action, the "Tank Police" from Dominion are back and under fire from both slick crooks and irate citizens. This time, our heroine and her beloved minitank "Bonaparte" must battle a villain with an uncanny knowledge of the police force's strengths and weaknesses. Not rated; contains some profanity. 60m. DIR: Furuse Noboru. 1995

NEW EDEN ★★★ This science-fiction spin on The Road Warrior has all the earmarks of a failed television pilot, from squeaky-clean action scenes to slow blackouts every twenty minutes. Catch it for an early look at Stephen Baldwin, cast as Adams, the first "civilized man" to utilize technology in the desert wastelands of some nameless prison planet. Lisa Bonet makes a pretty vacuous Eve. Needlessly rated R for minimal violence and suggested sex. 89m. DIR: Alan Metzger. CAST: Stephen Baldwin, Lisa Bonet, Tobin Bell, Michael Bowen. 1994

NEW FACES ★★1/2 This is a filmed version of the 1952 smash Broadway revue with a thin story line added. Ronny Graham is very good in a parody of Death of a Salesman. Eartha Kitt became a star through this vehicle and Robert Clary, Paul Lynde, and Alice Ghostley are used to good advantage. 99m. DIR: Harry Horner. CAST: Ronny Graham, Eartha Kitt, Paul Lynde, Robert Clary, Alice Ghostley, Carol Lawrence. 1954

NEW FRONTIER ★★1/2 In a familiar plot, John Wayne is the son of a murdered sheriff out to find the baddies who did the dirty deed. Creaky but fun for fans. B&W; 59m. DIR: Carl Pierson. CAST: John Wayne, Muriel Evans, Mary McLaren, Murdock McQuarrie, Warner Richmond, Sam Flint, Earl Dwire. 1935

NEW JACK CITY ★★★★ Wesley Snipes gives an explosive performance as a powerful Harlem drug lord who is targeted to be brought down by two undercover cops (rap singer Ice T and Judd Nelson). Director Mario Van Peebles delivers all the thrills, chills, and suspense the action crowd craves while still creating an effective anti-drug movie. Rated R for profanity, violence, and nudity. 97m. DIR: Mario Van Peebles. CAST: Wesley Snipes, Ice T, Chris Rock, Mario Van Peebles, Judd Nelson. 1991 DVD

NEW JERSEY DRIVE ★★★ This study of ghetto youth whose main thrill in life is joyriding in stolen cars finds itself going in circles rather early. Though gritty and authentic-seeming, the cycle of thoughtless self-destructiveness and vindictive police brutality gets tedious. Rated R for violence, language, and drug use. 97m. DIR: Nick Gomez. CAST: Sharron Corley, Gabriel Casseus, Saul Stein. 1995 DVD

NEW KIDS, THE 🖤 Two easygoing kids try to make friends at a new high school. Their attempt is thwarted by the town bully. Rated R for profanity, nudity, and violence. 96m. DIR: Sean S. Cunningham. CAST: Shannon Presby, Lori Loughlin, James Spader. 1985

NEW KIND OF LOVE, A ★★ A minor romantic comedy that gets one star for showcasing the real-life vibes between Paul Newman and Joanne Woodward. It gets another star for having Maurice Chevalier sing "Mimi" and "Louise." The rest of it gets zilch. 110m. DIR: Melville Shavelson. CAST: Paul Newman, Joanne Woodward, Maurice Chevalier, Thelma Ritter, Eva Gabor, George Tobias, Marvin Kaplan. 1963

NEW LAND, THE ★★★★1/2 The displaced Swedish farmers introduced in The Emigrants return in this outstanding sequel. It is 1850 Minnesota and they are ready to "work the ground" where they settle. The two films, as a whole, are a true epic of faith and determination. Oscar-nominated for best foreign-language film. Swedish, dubbed in English. Rated PG. 161m. DIR: Jan Troell. CAST: Max von Sydow, Liv Ullmann. 1972

NEW LEAF, A ★★★★ A rare (and wonderful) triple play from an American female talent: writer-director-star Elaine May makes an impressive mark with this latter-day screwball comedy, about a bankrupt rogue (Walter Matthau) who must find a rich woman to marry—within six weeks. His target turns out to be a clumsy botanist (May) seeking immortality by finding a new specimen of plant life (hence one element of the title). Rated PG for adult situations. 102m. DIR: Elaine May. CAST: Walter Matthau, Elaine May, Jack Weston, James Coco, William Redfield. 1971

NEW LIFE, A ★★★ This amusing examination of life after divorce features a couple who stumbles into other relationships after an agreeable separation. Rated PG-13 for language and sexual themes.

104m. **DIR:** Alan Alda. **CAST:** Alan Alda, Ann-Margret, Hal Linden, Veronica Hamel, John Shea, Mary Kay Place, Beatrice Alda. **1988**

NEW MOON ★★★ This melodramatic romance, which takes place during the French Revolution, features Jeanette MacDonald as a spoiled aristocrat who falls for an extraordinary bondsman (Nelson Eddy). Some comic moments, and Eddy comes off looking much better than MacDonald in this one, one of eight love stories they brought to the screen. B&W; 106m. **DIR:** Robert Z. Leonard. **CAST:** Jeanette MacDonald, Nelson Eddy, Mary Boland, George Zucco. **1940**

•**NEW ROSE HOTEL** ★★ Scattershot telling of the William Gibson tale in which two men train a woman to seduce their competition and steal his industrial secrets. Rated R for profanity, violence, and nudity. 92m. **DIR:** Abel Ferrara. **CAST:** Christopher Walken, Willem Dafoe, Annabella Sciorra, Gretchen Mol. **1998 DVD**

NEW YEAR'S DAY ★★★1/2 This gentle movie is a fairly intimate, if familiar, character study about three women who aren't quite ready to move out of the New York apartment that Henry Jaglom has recently leased. The film explores younger women's attachments to older men, and vice versa. May be too slow paced for some people. Rated R for nudity and profanity. 90m. **DIR:** Henry Jaglom. **CAST:** Henry Jaglom, Maggie Jakobson, Gwen Welles, Irene Moore, Milos Forman. **1990**

NEW YEAR'S EVIL 🖤 A crazy killer stalks victims at a televised New Year's Eve party. Rated R for all the usual reasons. 90m. **DIR:** Emmett Alston. **CAST:** Roz Kelly, Kip Niven, Chris Wallace. **1980**

NEW YORK COP ★★ An NYPD detective bonds with the street gang he's assigned to infiltrate. Serviceable crime opus, with a high body count and appropriately hammy acting. Rated R for violence, strong language, and adult situations. 88m. **DIR:** Toru Murakawa. **CAST:** Toru Nakamura, Chad McQueen, Andreas Katsulas, Mira Sorvino, Conan Lee, Tony Sirico. **1995**

NEW YORK, NEW YORK ★★★1/2 This is a difficult film to warm to, but worth it. Robert De Niro gives a splendid performance as an egomaniacal saxophonist who woos sweet-natured singer Liza Minnelli. The songs (especially the title tune) are great, and those with a taste for something different in musicals will find it rewarding. Rated PG. 163m. **DIR:** Martin Scorsese. **CAST:** Robert De Niro, Liza Minnelli, Lionel Stander, Georgie Auld, Mary Kay Place. **1977**

NEW YORK RIPPER, THE 🖤 Explicitly gory—yet dull—Italian horror about a sex murderer. R rating (four minutes were cut to avoid an X). 88m. **DIR:** Lucio Fulci. **CAST:** Jack Hedley. **1982 DVD**

NEW YORK STORIES ★★★★1/2 Here's a wonderful creation that provides three terrific movies for the price of one. Woody Allen's *Oedipus Wrecks* marks his return to comedy. Starring Allen as a lawyer who cannot escape his mother's overbearing influence, it's a hilarious vignette. Francis Coppola's *Life Without Zoe* is a light but charming fantasy about a sophisticated youngster named Zoe and her adventures in New York City. The best of this splen-

did trio is Martin Scorsese's *Life Lessons*, about the obsessive love of a celebrated painter for his protégée. Rated PG for profanity. 119m. **DIR:** Woody Allen, Francis Ford Coppola, Martin Scorsese. **CAST:** Woody Allen, Rosanna Arquette, Mia Farrow, Giancarlo Giannini, Julie Kavner, Heather McComb, Nick Nolte, Don Novello, Patrick O'Neal, Talia Shire. **1989**

NEW YORK THE WAY IT WAS ★★★★ The use of vintage footage and interviews with Alan King, Joe Franklin, and Mario Cuomo makes you feel as if you grew up in the Big Apple. This sentimental nostalgia trip won a much deserved Emmy when it aired on PBS, but it's packaged into a boxed set with two other easily missed, 58-minute documentaries, *The Old Neighborhood* and *Wish You Were Here!*. Not rated. 58m. **DIR:** Fred Fischer. **1993**

NEWMAN'S LAW 🖤 George Peppard plays a good cop accused of corruption and suspended from the force. Rated PG for violence. 98m. **DIR:** Richard T. Heffron. **CAST:** George Peppard, Roger Robinson, Abe Vigoda, Eugene Roche. **1974**

NEWS AT ELEVEN ★★★★ Martin Sheen plays a news anchorman whose integrity is threatened by the demands of his ratings-crazed news director. This is a jolting reminder of the enormous power of the press, with Sheen delivering a superior performance. 95m. **DIR:** Mike Robe. **CAST:** Martin Sheen, Barbara Babcock, Sheree Wilson, Peter Riegert. **1985**

NEWS FROM HOME 🖤 Sandwiched between the spectacular and seedy elements of New York, there is the mundane, to which we are treated in huge elongated slices. If you want something exciting to happen while watching this, look out the window. In French with English subtitles. Not rated. 85m. **DIR:** Chantal Akerman. **1991**

NEWSFRONT ★★★★ A story of a newsreel company from 1948 until technology brought its existence to an end, this is a warm and wonderful film about real people. It's an insightful glimpse at the early days of the news business, with good character development. Rated PG. 110m. **DIR:** Phillip Noyce. **CAST:** Bill Hunter, Wendy Hughes, Gerald Kennedy. **1978**

NEWSIES ★★★ While this Disney production may not fulfill its promise to resurrect the movie musical, it is an entertaining picture for the whole family. The songs of Academy Award–winning composer Alan Menken propel the story of the 1899 newspaper boys strike. Rated PG for violence. 120m. **DIR:** Kenny Ortega. **CAST:** Christian Bale, David Moscow, Bill Pullman, Luke Edwards, Max Casella, Michael Lerner, Ann-Margret, Robert Duvall. **1992**

NEWTON BOYS, THE ★★1/2 Between 1919 and 1924, Willis Newton and his three brothers robbed more than eighty banks from Texas to Canada, then capped their career with America's largest train robbery. Unfortunately these four actors aren't given more than a shred of depth between them. Fast-forward to the closing credits footage of actual Newtons who are much more captivating than the fictitious younger selves portrayed here. Rated PG for mild violence and profanity. 113m. **DIR:** Richard Linklater. **CAST:** Matthew McConaughey, Ethan Hawke, Skeet Ulrich, Dwight Yoakam, Vincent D'Onofrio, Julianna Margulies. **1998 DVD**

•**NEXT BEST THING, THE** ★★ When a woman (Madonna) gets pregnant after a one-night stand with her gay best friend (Rupert Everett), the two decide to raise the kid together as platonic housemates. This self-deluded fantasy is smarmy and false every inch of the way, from the unbelievable premise to the ludicrous happily-ever-after ending. Rated PG-13 for mature themes and mild profanity. 107m. **DIR:** John Schlesinger. **CAST:** Madonna, Rupert Everett, Benjamin Bratt, Josef Sommer, Lynn Redgrave. **2000**

NEXT DOOR ★★★ College professor James Woods unleashes the wrath of neighbor Randy Quaid, a butcher with no fondness for educators, and matters quickly get out of control. Scripter Barney Cohen's study of neighborhood warfare begins well, but suffers from an identity crisis. The darkly satirical mood is sabotaged by a far-too-serious climax that also escalates events past the point of credibility. Even so, the opening act is guaranteed to generate discomfort. Rated R for profanity and violence. 95m. **DIR:** Tony Bill. **CAST:** James Woods, Randy Quaid, Kate Capshaw, Lucinda Jenney. **1994**

•**NEXT FRIDAY** ★★ In this sequel to and retread of the 1995 comedy *Friday*, a pot-smoking South Central Los Angeles slacker flees to the suburban home of his uncle when the neighborhood thug he helped send to prison escapes and seeks revenge. Some scattered, funny moments amid the film's raunchy misadventures. The soundtrack features the first song in nearly a decade from N.W.A. (with Snoop Dogg replacing the late Eazy-E). Rated R for drug use, language, nudity, and sexual content. 98m. **DIR:** Steve Carr. **CAST:** Ice Cube, John Witherspoon, Mike Epps, Don (DC) Curry, Tiny Lister Jr. **2000 DVD**

NEXT KARATE KID, THE ★★ The fourth film in the series is an improvement over the third, but that's not saying much. Noriyuki "Pat" Morita is back, but the original "kid," Ralph Macchio, has grown up and moved on. This time, the old master teaches martial arts and self-respect to (gasp!) a girl—and that's about the only new twist on the old formula. Rated PG. 97m. **DIR:** Christopher Cain. **CAST:** Noriyuki "Pat" Morita, Hilary Swank, Michael Ironside, Constance Towers, Chris Conrad. **1994**

NEXT OF KIN (1984) ★★★1/2 A young man suffering from boredom and dissatisfaction with his upper-middle-class family undergoes video therapy with his parents. He becomes fascinated by a videotape of an Armenian family who feel guilty about surrendering their infant son to a foster home. Poignant look at a young WASP's displacement and response to his upper-middle-class role in Canadian society. Highly original filmmaking. Not rated. 74m. **DIR:** Atom Egoyan. **CAST:** Patrick Tierney. **1984**

NEXT OF KIN (1987) 🎬 Boring Australian suspense film has a young heiress inheriting her mother's mansion. Not rated; contains nudity, simulated sex, and violence. 90m. **DIR:** Tony Williams. **CAST:** Jackie Kerin, John Jarratt. **1987**

NEXT OF KIN (1989) ★★ When his younger brother (Bill Paxton) is killed by a local mobster (Adam Baldwin), Patrick Swayze, as a Chicago cop from the "hollers" of Kentucky, takes justice in his own hands. Formula flick with a preposterous ending. Rated R for profanity and violence. 111m. **DIR:** John Irvin. **CAST:** Patrick Swayze, Liam Neeson, Adam Baldwin, Helen Hunt, Bill Paxton. **1989 DVD**

NEXT ONE, THE 🎬 A prophet from the future suddenly appears on the beach of a Greek island. Not rated. 105m. **DIR:** Nico Mastorakis. **CAST:** Keir Dullea, Adrienne Barbeau, Jeremy Licht, Peter Hobbs. **1981**

NEXT STOP, GREENWICH VILLAGE ★★★★ One of writer-director Paul Mazursky's first attempts to dramatize his youth, this film is a seriocomic study of the eccentricities of Greenwich Villagers. Unique as well as entertaining. 109m. **DIR:** Paul Mazursky. **CAST:** Lenny Baker, Shelley Winters, Ellen Greene, Christopher Walken, Jeff Goldblum, Lou Jacobi, Lois Smith. **1976**

NEXT STOP WONDERLAND ★★★1/2 Independent film focuses on a Boston night-shift nurse who, having just been dumped by her boyfriend, has decided that Fate is overrated and defiantly defends her now-single lifestyle. Her mother, not buying this nonsense, places a newspaper personal ad for her daughter … which garners sixty-four responses. The subsequent adventures in the dating scene prove a fertile ground for some zesty dialogue. All told, this is a genuinely delightful romantic comedy. Rated R for profanity. 96m. **DIR:** Brad Anderson. **CAST:** Hope Davis, Alan Gelfant, Philip Seymour Hoffman, Callie Thorne, Holland Taylor, Robert Klein. **1998 DVD**

NEXT SUMMER ★★★1/2 This romantic comedy features some of France's top stars in a story about a family in which personal frustrations conflict with passions in the quest for power and beauty. Excellent performances by a top-notch cast. In French with English subtitles. Not rated. 100m. **DIR:** Nadine Trintignant. **CAST:** Claudia Cardinale, Fanny Ardant, Philippe Noiret, Marie Trintignant, Jean-Louis Trintignant. **1986**

NEXT TIME I MARRY ★★★ A madcap comedy about marriage with Lucille Ball as an heiress who marries the first man she sees in order to get her inheritance. Ball has a ball, and it's contagious. B&W; 80m. **DIR:** Garson Kanin. **CAST:** Lucille Ball, Lee Bowman, James Ellison, Mantan Moreland. **1938**

NEXT VOICE YOU HEAR, THE ★★1/2 Man's-man director William Wellman was an odd choice to direct this preachy tract—typical of Dore Schary's well-meaning but ponderous message pictures of the Fifties—in which the voice of God speaks to mankind via a radio broadcast. The solid performances by James Whitmore and Jeff Corey lend the film what strength it has. B&W; 83m. **DIR:** William Wellman. **CAST:** James Whitmore, Nancy Davis, Jeff Corey. **1950**

NEXT YEAR IF ALL GOES WELL ★★ Innocuous comedy about a pair of cohabitating lovers trying to decide whether to take the leap into marriage. Likable performances by Isabelle Adjani and Thierry Lhermitte. Dubbed. Rated R for brief nudity. 95m. **DIR:** Jean-Loup Hubert. **CAST:** Isabelle Adjani, Thierry Lhermitte. **1981**

NIAGARA ★★★1/2 A sexy, slightly sleazy, and sinister Marilyn Monroe plots the murder of husband Joseph Cotten in this twisted tale of infidelity and greed, shot against the pulsing scenic grandeur of Niagara Falls. But plans go awry and the falls redeem a killer. Excellent location camera work adds to the thrills. 89m. **DIR:** Henry Hathaway. **CAST:** Marilyn Monroe, Joseph Cotten, Jean Peters. **1953**

NIAGARA NIAGARA ★★ Robin Tunney and Henry Thomas play two misfit teenagers who take off for Canada on a feckless search for a particular kind of doll, falling into petty crime on the way. The acting is excellent, but it's not enough to redeem what is yet another young-outlaw-lovers-on-the-run film. Rated R for profanity, violence, and sexual scenes. 93m. **DIR:** Bob Gosse. **CAST:** Henry Thomas, Robin Tunney, Michael Parks, Stephen Lang, John McKay. **1997**

NICE DREAMS ★★★ Cheech and Chong are the counterculture kings of drug-oriented comedy. Their third feature film doesn't have quite as many classic comic gems as its predecessors, but it's more consistently entertaining. Rated R for nudity and profanity. 87m. **DIR:** Thomas Chong. **CAST:** Cheech and Chong, Evelyn Guerrero, Pee-wee Herman, Stacy Keach. **1981**

NICE GIRL LIKE ME, A ♥ Dated Sixties comedy that was considered risqué for its time, but now seems silly and contrived. Rated PG. 91m. **DIR:** Desmond Davis. **CAST:** Barbara Ferris, Harry Andrews, Gladys Cooper. **1969**

NICE GIRLS DON'T EXPLODE ★★ Droll, slow-moving comedy about a girl (Michelle Meyrink) who causes spontaneous combustion of objects. William O'Leary as her current boyfriend is exceptional. Rated PG, the film contains some strong language and mild nudity. 92m. **DIR:** Chuck Martinez. **CAST:** Barbara Harris, Michelle Meyrink, William O'Leary, Wallace Shawn. **1987**

NICHOLAS AND ALEXANDRA ★★ This is an overlong, overdetailed depiction of the events preceding the Russian Revolution until the deaths of Czar Nicholas (Michael Jayston), his wife (Janet Suzman) and family. Some of the performances are outstanding, and the sets and costumes are top-notch. However, the film gets mired in trying to encompass too much historical detail. Rated PG. 183m. **DIR:** Franklin J. Schaffner. **CAST:** Michael Jayston, Janet Suzman, Tom Baker, Laurence Olivier, Michael Redgrave. **1971 DVD**

NICHOLAS NICKLEBY ★★★1/2 Proud but penniless young Nicholas Nickleby struggles to forge a life for himself and his family while contending with a money-mad scheming uncle and lesser villains. Good acting and authentic Victorian settings bring this classic Dickens novel to vivid screen life. Not quite in the mold of *Great Expectations*, but well above average. B&W; 108m. **DIR:** Alberto Cavalcanti. **CAST:** Derek Bond, Cedric Hardwicke, Sally Ann Howes, Cathleen Nesbitt. **1947**

NICK KNIGHT ★★★ Pilot movie for the TV series stars Rick Springfield as a vampire turned detective for the Los Angeles Police Department. 94m. **DIR:** Farhad Mann. **CAST:** Rick Springfield, John Kapelos, Robert Harper, Richard Fancy, Laura Johnson, Michael Nader. **1991**

NICK OF TIME ★★★1/2 This clever thriller plays itself out in "real time"; that is, the entire action takes place during the time required to watch it. Devoted father Johnny Depp is forced to become an unwilling assassin when his daughter is kidnapped after their arrival at Los Angeles's Union train station; either he kills the governor of California during a speech-making appearance, or the little girl dies. Although the premise is wholly improbable, you'll be too absorbed to care. Rated R for violence and profanity. 104m. **DIR:** John Badham. **CAST:** Johnny Depp, Christopher Walken, Charles Dutton, Peter Strauss, Roma Maffia, Gloria Reuben, Courtney Chase, Marsha Mason. **1995 DVD**

NICKEL & DIME ★★ C. Thomas Howell, a con artist who tries to match "long lost" heirs with unclaimed estates, is saddled with obnoxious accountant Wallace Shawn. A jumble, but Shawn and Howell forge a strangely endearing odd-couple relationship. Rated PG for profanity. 96m. **DIR:** Ben Moses. **CAST:** C. Thomas Howell, Wallace Shawn. **1992**

NICO ICON ★★★1/2 Documentary chronicles the life of Nico from her teen glory days as lovely French *Vogue* fashion model to her final years as ravaged drug addict. In between she became a Warhol Factory "superstar" and sang with the 1960s rock group the Velvet Underground. Through home movies, interviews, performance clips, and photographs, her self-destructive path as irresponsible mother and casual lover is spread before us in lurid detail without grandstanding or moralizing. In English, German, and French with English subtitles. Not rated; contains drug-related material. 75m. **DIR:** Suzanne Ofteringer. **1995 DVD**

NIGHT AFTER NIGHT ★★★★ Mae West's first movie is one of her funniest, and she only has a brief supporting role. The real star is George Raft as a rich hoodlum who tries to break into New York society during the Depression. West plays one of the hoodlum's former girlfriends, and she flounces in to turn society on its ear in this delightfully witty farce. B&W; 70m. **DIR:** Archie Mayo. **CAST:** George Raft, Constance Cummings, Alison Skipworth, Mae West, Wynne Gibson, Louis Calhern. **1932**

NIGHT AMBUSH ★★★1/2 Suspenseful World War II drama set in Crete, about a group of British soldiers who kidnap a German general right under the noses of his fellow officers. Solid performances. B&W; 93m. **DIR:** Michael Powell. **CAST:** Dirk Bogarde, Marius Goring, David Oxley, Cyril Cusack. **1957**

NIGHT AND DAY (1946) ★★★★ There was no way Hollywood could make an accurate biography of Cole Porter in those days—it had to play footsie with his ruthless social lionizing and sexual proclivities—but the film stands out as a remarkable document of the performers and performances available to the cameras at the time. Where else can you see Mary Martin doing "My Heart Belongs to Daddy" and Monte Woolley declaiming "Miss Otis Regrets"? 132m. **DIR:** Michael Curtiz. **CAST:** Cary Grant, Alexis Smith, Alan Hale Sr., Mary Martin, Monty Woolley. **1946**

NIGHT AND DAY (1991) ★★★1/2 The meter's constantly running during this sharp-edged comedy about a woman who keeps two lovers. They're both cab drivers—one works the night shift, the other the day shift. She alternates between them and finds that she actually loves both men and her situation. Erotic and unconventional. In French with English subtitles. Not rated; contains sexual situations. 90m. **DIR:** Chantal Akerman. **CAST:** Guilaine Londez, Thomas Langmann, Francois Negret. **1991**

NIGHT AND THE CITY (1950) ★★★★ Director Jules Dassin's drama is *film noir* at its best. Richard Widmark is the fight promoter, hustling up some action in London's East End, trying to make the score of a lifetime while keeping ahead of his debtors. Gene Tierney is splendid as the loyal girlfriend being taken for a ride. Plenty of mood and atmosphere permeate this entry. B&W; 95m. **DIR:** Jules Dassin. **CAST:** Richard Widmark, Gene Tierney, Googie Withers, Herbert Lom, Hugh Marlowe, Mike Mazurki. **1950**

NIGHT AND THE CITY (1992) ★★★1/2 Director Irwin Winkler's remake of Jules Dassin's 1950 *film noir* benefits from strong performances by Robert De Niro, Jessica Lange, and a distinguished cast of supporting players. The downbeat story has lawyer De Niro romancing the wife (Lange) of bar owner and longtime buddy Cliff Gorman while attempting to scam his way into the big time. Not a classic, but worth watching. Rated R for profanity and violence. 104m. **DIR:** Irwin Winkler. **CAST:** Robert De Niro, Jessica Lange, Cliff Gorman, Alan King, Jack Warden, Eli Wallach, Barry Primus, Gene Kirkwood. **1992**

NIGHT AND THE MOMENT, THE ★★ Lush production values and European settings do little to enhance this weary romantic drama. Willem Dafoe stars as a writer out to seduce Lena Olin, and uses tales of his previous liaisons as foreplay. It all looks pretty, but the actors and director never ignite a flame of passion. Rated R for adult situations, language, and nudity. 90m. **DIR:** Anna Maria Tato. **CAST:** Willem Dafoe, Lena Olin, Miranda Richardson. **1994**

NIGHT ANGEL ★★ Predictable horror fare about a soul-searching seductress raising some hell when she poses as a fashion model. She violently dispatches plenty of weak-willed men. Rated R for nudity. 90m. **DIR:** Dominique Othenin-Girard. **CAST:** Isa Andersen, Linden Ashby, Debra Feuer, Karen Black. **1990**

NIGHT AT THE OPERA, A ★★★★★ Despite the songs and sappy love story, the Marx Brothers (minus Zeppo) are in peak form in this classic musical comedy, which costars the legendary Margaret Dumont. B&W; 92m. **DIR:** Sam Wood. **CAST:** The Marx Brothers, Margaret Dumont, Kitty Carlisle, Allan Jones, Sig Ruman. **1935**

NIGHT AT THE ROXBURY, A ★★ Like numerous other attempts to bring *Saturday Night Live* characters to the big screen, this fails to maintain consistent humor and viewer interest. The head-bobbing Butabi brothers (Will Ferrell and Chris Kattan) try to make their mark on the nightclub scene despite their father's best efforts to turn them into responsible adults. Rated PG-13 for sexual situations. 82m. **DIR:** John Fortenberry. **CAST:** Will Ferrell, Chris Kattan, Dan Hedaya, Molly Shannon, Loni Anderson. **1998 DVD**

NIGHT BEFORE, THE ★★★ A senior prom date turns into a hilarious nightmare in this riveting, offbeat comedy. After waking up in an alley, a young man (Keanu Reeves) finds his date and wallet missing along with his father's sports car. And then things get surreal—in the style of *After Hours.* Rated R for language and violence. 85m. **DIR:** Thom Eberhardt. **CAST:** Keanu Reeves, Lori Loughlin, Theresa Saldana, Trinidad Silva. **1988**

NIGHT BREED ★★ Great monsters, fantastic makeup effects, exploding action—and very little plot. Horror writer Clive Barker's second turn as director lacks cohesion as the plot runs through the Canadian wilderness in search of a serial killer and an ancient tribe of monsters called the Night Breed. Rated R for violence. 97m. **DIR:** Clive Barker. **CAST:** Craig Sheffer, David Cronenberg, Charles Haid. **1989**

NIGHT CALLER FROM OUTER SPACE ★★1/2 Here's another one of those perennial sci-fi plots: outer space alien from a dying world comes to Earth looking for human women to serve as breeding stock. (With a planet named Ganymede, it's no wonder they're dying out!) A little British reserve keeps this in check; not bad of its type. B&W; 84m. **DIR:** John Gilling. **CAST:** John Saxon, Maurice Denham, Patricia Haines, Alfred Burke. **1965 DVD**

NIGHT CREATURE ★ Grade-Z film has Donald Pleasence playing a half-crazed adventurer who captures a killer leopard and brings the creature to his private island. Rated PG. 83m. **DIR:** Lee Madden. **CAST:** Donald Pleasence, Nancy Kwan, Ross Hagen. **1978**

NIGHT CROSSING ★★★1/2 This Disney film is about a real-life escape from East Germany by two families in a gas-filled balloon. Unfortunately, minor flaws, such as mismatched accents and Americanized situations, prevent it from being a total success. Rated PG for violence. 106m. **DIR:** Delbert Mann. **CAST:** John Hurt, Jane Alexander, Beau Bridges, Ian Bannen. **1981**

NIGHT FALLS ON MANHATTAN ★★★ While exploring the gray areas that shape personal and professional lives, this film unleashes several fine performances. When police try to arrest a Harlem drug lord, the ensuing shoot-out leaves three cops dead. A young New York assistant district attorney then sifts through police dirty laundry while trying the case in court. Rated R for language and violence. 114m. **DIR:** Sidney Lumet. **CAST:** Andy Garcia, Lena Olin, Richard Dreyfuss, Ian Holm, Ron Leibman, James Gandolfini, Colm Feore, Shiek Mahmud-Bey. **1997 DVD**

NIGHT FIRE ★★ Video vixen Shannon Tweed stars as a wealthy businesswoman whose plans for a romantic weekend alone with her husband are shattered when a strange couple arrives at her country home. Amidst much sex and double crossing, a murderous plot is uncovered. Mildly entertaining trash isn't one of Tweed's best and her supporting cast hams its way through in a most embarrassing manner. Surprise ending is more of an anticlimax than a revelation. Rated R for nudity, sexual situations, and violence. 97m. **DIR:** Mike Sedan. **CAST:** Shannon Tweed, John Laughlin, Martin Hewitt. **1994 DVD**

NIGHT FLIER, THE ★★★ In adapting Stephen King's short story, the filmmakers added new characters and plot points while maintaining the feel of the original tale. Miguel Ferrer plays a tabloid reporter who is hot on the trail of a mysterious Cessna that lands at small airports then vanishes after everyone is murdered. While the vampire monster is a little bit cheesy looking, the film has a creepy feel that gets to you. Rated R for gore, profanity, and violence. 97m. **DIR:** Mark Pavia. **CAST:** Miguel Ferrer, Julie Entwisle. **1997 DVD**

NIGHT FLIGHT FROM MOSCOW ★★★ A decent, if overly talky, espionage film with a strong cast. Yul Brynner is a Russian diplomat who engages in a complicated plan to defect to the West. Rated PG. 113m. **DIR:** Henri Verneuil, **CAST:** Henry Fonda, Yul Brynner, Farley Granger, Dirk Bogarde, Virna Lisi, Philippe Noiret. **1973**

NIGHT FRIEND 💘 A crusading priest becomes involved in organized crime. Rated R for profanity, nudity, and violence. 94m. **DIR:** Peter Gerretsen. **CAST:** Art Carney, Chuck Shamata. **1987**

NIGHT FULL OF RAIN, A ★★★ After a series of stunning successes in the early Seventies, Italian director Lina Wertmuller began a downward slide with this film, her first attempt at an English-language movie. It details the ins and outs of the relationship between an independent woman (Candice Bergen) and her old-fashioned husband (Giancarlo Giannini). 104m. **DIR:** Lina Wertmuller. **CAST:** Giancarlo Giannini, Candice Bergen, Jill Eikenberry. **1978**

NIGHT GALLERY ★★★ Pilot for the TV series. Three tales of terror by Rod Serling told with style and flair. Segment one is the best, with Roddy McDowall eager to get his hands on an inheritance. Segment two features Joan Crawford as a blind woman with a yearning to see. Segment three, involving a paranoid war fugitive, is the least of the three. 98m. **DIR:** Boris Sagal, Steven Spielberg, Barry Shear. **CAST:** Roddy McDowall, Joan Crawford, Richard Kiley. **1969**

NIGHT GAME ★★1/2 Familiar story of a police officer (Roy Scheider) attempting to track down a serial killer before he can claim another female victim. The predictable ending is a bummer. Good performances, though. Rated R for violence and profanity. 95m. **DIR:** Peter Masterson. **CAST:** Roy Scheider, Karen Young, Richard Bradford, Paul Gleason, Carlin Glynn. **1989**

NIGHT GAMES ★★★ This film, which was originally made for television, led to the *Petrocelli* TV series for Barry Newman. He plays a lawyer who defends Stefanie Powers when she's accused of her husband's murder. There's enough intrigue and suspense in this film to capture most viewers' attention. Rated R. 78m. **DIR:** Don Taylor. **CAST:** Barry Newman, Susan Howard, Albert Salmi, Luke Askew, Ralph Meeker, Stefanie Powers. **1974**

NIGHT HAS EYES, THE ★★★1/2 This suspense film from war-weary Great Britain focuses on a schoolmarm who searches for a colleague who is missing on a mist-shrouded moor. Joyce Howard is excellent as the teacher-sleuth and the young James Mason does a credible job as a disturbed composer.

B&W; 79m. **DIR:** Leslie Arliss. **CAST:** James Mason, Joyce Howard, Wilfrid Lawson. **1942**

NIGHT HUNTER ★★ Chop-socky star Don "The Dragon" Wilson adds guns and silver bullets to his arsenal of martial arts moves to battle vampires. A few good action scenes amid a lot of tedium. Rated R for violence and brief nudity. 86m. **DIR:** Rick Jacobson. **CAST:** Don "The Dragon" Wilson, Nicholas Guest, Maria Ford, Melanie Smith. **1996**

NIGHT IN CASABLANCA, A ★★★ Although the formula was wearing thin by 1946, Groucho's wisecracks and the incomparable antics of Chico and Harpo still carry the film. Joining forces in post-WWII Casablanca, the brothers wreak havoc in the staid Hotel Casablanca. B&W; 85m. **DIR:** Archie Mayo. **CAST:** The Marx Brothers, Charles Drake, Lisette Verea, Lois Collier. **1946**

NIGHT IN HEAVEN, A 💘 College teacher falls in lust with student-male stripper. Rated R for nudity, slight profanity, and simulated sex. 80m. **DIR:** John G. Avildsen. **CAST:** Lesley Ann Warren, Christopher Atkins, Robert Logan, Carrie Snodgress. **1983**

NIGHT IN THE LIFE OF JIMMY REARDON, A 💘 Jimmy Reardon is a teenage sex fiend in 1962 Evanston, Illinois. Rated R for profanity and leering sexual content. 92m. **DIR:** William Richert. **CAST:** River Phoenix, Meredith Salenger, Ione Skye, Louanne, Ann Magnuson. **1988**

NIGHT IS MY FUTURE ★★★1/2 In this early Ingmar Bergman film, a film that at the same time is dark in mood but bright with promise of things to come, we meet a blinded military veteran (Birger Malmsten) who is at war with the world and with himself due to his handicap. Through the selfless efforts of a maid, he learns to accept his problems and make a new life for himself. In Swedish with English subtitles. B&W; 87m. **DIR:** Ingmar Bergman. **CAST:** Mai Zetterling, Birger Malmsten. **1947**

NIGHT LIFE ★★★1/2 Four teenage corpses come back to life to haunt a young mortuary employee in this funny zombie picture. The corpses just want to party, and that they do until Scott Grimes can do away with them in grisly fashion. Rated R for violence, profanity, and gore. 92m. **DIR:** David Acomba. **CAST:** Scott Grimes, Cheryl Pollak, Anthony Geary, Alan Blumenfeld, John Astin. **1990**

NIGHT MONSTER ★★★ Bela Lugosi has a small but effective role as a butler in this thriller about the mysterious murders of doctors treating bedridden patient Ralph Morgan. Old-fashioned thriller will please fans of Universal monster movies. B&W; 80m. **DIR:** Ford Beebe. **CAST:** Bela Lugosi, Lionel Atwill, Ralph Morgan, Irene Hervey, Don Porter, Nils Asther, Leif Erickson. **1942**

'NIGHT, MOTHER ★★ Playwright Marsha Norman's argument in favor of suicide is incredibly depressing material. Sissy Spacek plays a woman who has chosen to end her life. She decides to commit the act in her mother's house, with her mother there. We are only shown Spacek's unhappiness, and this limited manipulative view leaves us with nothing to do but wait uncomfortably for the outcome. Rated PG-13. 97m. **DIR:** Tom Moore. **CAST:** Sissy Spacek, Anne Bancroft. **1986**

NIGHT MOVES ★★★★ A dark and disturbing detective study with Gene Hackman superb as the private eye trying to solve a baffling mystery. This release was unfairly overlooked when in theaters—but you don't have to miss it now. Rated R. 95m. **DIR:** Arthur Penn. **CAST:** Gene Hackman, Susan Clark, Melanie Griffith. 1975

NIGHT MUST FALL ★★★★ A suspenseful stage play makes a superbly suspenseful movie by letting the audience use its imagination. Robert Montgomery neatly underplays the role of the mad killer who totes his victim's head in a hatbox. Rosalind Russell is the girl who believes in him, but slowly learns the truth. B&W; 117m. **DIR:** Richard Thorpe. **CAST:** Robert Montgomery, Rosalind Russell, May Whitty, Alan Marshal, E. E. Clive, Kathleen Harrison. 1937

NIGHT NURSE ★★★ No-nonsense Barbara Stanwyck plays the title role, using underworld contacts to safeguard two small children. A tough, taut melodrama that still works, thanks to its intriguing personalities. B&W; 73m. **DIR:** William Wellman. **CAST:** Barbara Stanwyck, Clark Gable, Ben Lyon, Joan Blondell, Charles Winninger. 1931

NIGHT OF BLOODY HORROR 💊 When a young man is released from a mental institution, a series of gory murders begins. Not rated. 89m. **DIR:** Joy N. Houck Jr. **CAST:** Gerald McRaney. 1969

NIGHT OF DARK SHADOWS ★★ The new owner of a spooky mansion is haunted by his ancestors. Barnabas Collins is nowhere to be found in this second film based on the original *Dark Shadows* TV series. Given that the series itself is on video, there's no reason to bother with this tired leftover. Rated PG. 97m. **DIR:** Dan Curtis. **CAST:** David Selby, Lara Parker, Kate Jackson, Grayson Hall. 1971

NIGHT OF TERROR 💊 Forgettable murder mystery with Bela Lugosi cast, as he was all too often, in a supporting role as a red herring. B&W; 65m. **DIR:** Ben Stoloff. **CAST:** Bela Lugosi, George Meeker, Tully Marshall, Bryant Washburn. 1933

NIGHT OF THE BLOODY TRANSPLANT 💊 Not to be confused with *Night of the Bloody Apes*—although both films resort to open-heart surgery footage to wake up the audience—this is an amateurish soap opera about a renegade surgeon. Rated R. 90m. **DIR:** David W. Hanson. **CAST:** Dick Grimm. 1986

NIGHT OF THE COBRA WOMAN ★★ Former underground filmmaker Andrew Meyer (not to be confused with the utterly untalented Andy Milligan) coauthored and directed this sleazy, often boring, but nonetheless watchable drive-in horror flick, shot in the Philippines for Roger Corman. Rated R. 85m. **DIR:** Andrew Meyer. **CAST:** Marlene Clark, Joy Bang. 1972

NIGHT OF THE COMET ★★★1/2 The passage of the comet wipes out all but a few people on our planet. The survivors, mostly young adults, are hunted by a pair of baddies, played by Geoffrey Lewis and Mary Woronov. It all adds up to a zesty low-budget spoof of science-fiction movies. Rated PG-13. 94m. **DIR:** Thom Eberhardt. **CAST:** Geoffrey Lewis, Mary Woronov, Catherine Mary Stewart, Kelli Maroney. 1984

NIGHT OF THE CREEPS ★★★1/2 A film derived from virtually every horror movie ever made, this does a wonderful job paying homage to the genre. The story involves an alien organism that lands on Earth and immediately infects someone. Some thirty years later, when this contaminated individual is accidentally released, he wanders into a college town spreading these organisms in some rather disgusting ways. Not rated; contains violence. 89m. **DIR:** Fred Dekker. **CAST:** Jason Lively, Steve Marchall, Jill Whitlow, Tom Atkins, Dick Miller. 1986

NIGHT OF THE CYCLONE 💊 Chicago detective stumbles onto a murder when he travels to the Caribbean. Rated R for profanity, nudity, and violence. 90m. **DIR:** David Irving. **CAST:** Kris Kristofferson, Jeff Meek, Marisa Berenson. 1989

NIGHT OF THE DEATH CULT ★★1/2 This is one of a popular series of Spanish horror movies concerning the Templars, blind medieval priests who rise from the dead when their tombs are violated. The film contains nudity, violence, and gore, though as a whole it is more subdued than American zombie movies. 85m. **DIR:** Amando de Ossorio. **CAST:** Victor Petit, Maria Kosti. 1975

NIGHT OF THE DEMON 💊 This is a boring little bomb of a movie with an intriguing title and nothing else. 97m. **DIR:** James C. Wasson. **CAST:** Michael Cutt, Jay Allen. 1983

NIGHT OF THE DEMONS ★★★ A great creaky-house movie about a group of teenagers who hold a séance in an abandoned mortuary. What they conjure up from the dead is more than they bargained for. Rated R for violence and nudity. 90m. **DIR:** Kevin S. Tenney. **CAST:** William Gallo. 1989

NIGHT OF THE DEMONS 2 ★★1/2 Inventive special effects and occasional flashes of wit elevate this haunted-house sequel above most gorefests, but the rigid formula has got pretty tiresome: good girls and boys survive the demonic carnage, while bad things happen to all their promiscuous friends. Rated R for violence, nudity, suggested sex, and profanity. 96m. **DIR:** Brian Trenchard-Smith. **CAST:** Bobby Jacoby, Amelia Kinkade, Zoe Trilling, Christi Harris. 1994

NIGHT OF THE DEMONS 3 ★★ Another group of stereotypical teens meets the demon Angela and gets turned into zombies. If you've seen the first two, then don't bother with this one. Not rated; contains violence, profanity, nudity, and simulated sex. 86m. **DIR:** James Kaufman. **CAST:** Amelia Kinkade. 1997

NIGHT OF THE DEVILS 💊 Tepid modern-vampire melodrama. It's based on the same Tolstoy story that inspired the Boris Karloff sequence in *Black Sabbath*. No rating, but contains moderate violence and sex. English dubbed. 82m. **DIR:** Giorgio Ferroni. **CAST:** Gianni Garko, Agostina Belli, Mark Roberts. 1972

NIGHT OF THE FOLLOWING DAY, THE ★★★ Three men and a woman abduct an heiress as she returns home to France. Marlon Brando plays the compassionate Bud, who is tired of being a criminal. His coconspirators include a drug addict, an old washed-up criminal, and a sadist. The story line moves slowly but becomes very suspenseful near the end. Rated R for violence and nudity. 93m. **DIR:** Hubert Cornfield.

AST: Marlon Brando, Richard Boone, Rita Moreno, amela Franklin, Jess Hahn. **1968**

NIGHT OF THE FOX ★★ Preposterous adaptation of ack Higgins's WWII-set thriller about an under-over mission to rescue an American officer from erman-occupied territory. Choppily edited from a ix-hour miniseries, leaving nothing but the clichés. 5m. **DIR:** Charles Jarrott. **CAST:** George Peppard, eborah Raffin, Michael York, David Birney, John Mills. **990**

NIGHT OF THE GENERALS ❤ Lurid WWII murder nystery, revolving around a group of Nazi generals. 48m. **DIR:** Anatole Litvak. **CAST:** Peter O'Toole, Omar harif, Tom Courtenay, Donald Pleasence, Joanna Pet-et, Christopher Plummer. **1967**

NIGHT OF THE GHOULS ★★ From the director of *Plan 9 from Outer Space* and *Glen or Glenda* comes a film so bad it was never released. Not nearly as en-oyably bad as Edward Wood's other work, but defi-iitely worth a look for movie buffs. For the record, wo young innocents stumble upon a haunted house filled with some very tiresome bad actors). B&W; 5m. **DIR:** Edward D. Wood Jr. **CAST:** Kenne Duncan, Criswell. **1958**

NIGHT OF THE GRIZZLY, THE ★★★★ In order to maintain a peaceful standing in the rugged Old West, oig Clint Walker must fight all the local bad guys who should have known better) as well as a giant grizzly bear who moves in and out of camera range on a wheeled dolly. Nice outdoor sets and some good characterization help this no-frills family story. 102m. **DIR:** Joseph Pevney. **CAST:** Clint Walker, Martha Hyer, Ron Ely, Jack Elam. **1966**

NIGHT OF THE HOWLING BEAST ★★ The Wolfman meets the Abominable Snowman. Paul Naschy is the horror king of Spain, but after his movies have been chopped up and dubbed for American release, it's pretty hard to see why. Not rated, but the equivalent of a light R. 87m. **DIR:** Miguel Iglesias Bonns. **CAST:** Paul Naschy. **1975**

NIGHT OF THE HUNTER ★★★★1/2 Absolutely the finest film from star Robert Mitchum, who is cast as a suave, smooth-talking—and absolutely evil—preacher determined to catch and kill his stepchil-dren. The entire film is eerie, exquisitely beautiful, and occasionally surreal; watch for the graceful, haunting shot of the children's freshly killed mother. B&W; 93m. **DIR:** Charles Laughton. **CAST:** Robert Mitchum, Shelley Winters, Lillian Gish, James Glea-son. **1955 DVD**

NIGHT OF THE IGUANA, THE ★★★ In this film, based on Tennessee Williams's play, Richard Burton is a former minister trying to be reinstated in his church. Meanwhile, he takes a menial job as a tour guide, from which he gets fired. His attempted sui-cide is foiled and confusing. Finally, he finds other reasons to continue living. Sound dull? If not for the cast, it would be. B&W; 118m. **DIR:** John Huston. **CAST:** Richard Burton, Ava Gardner, Deborah Kerr, Sue Lyon. **1964**

NIGHT OF THE JUGGLER ★★ Psychopath kidnaps little girl for ransom. It's the wrong little girl. Her daddy's an ex-cop with no money and lots of rage. The movie, buoyed by James Brolin's potent perfor-

mance, initially grabs viewers' attention. Eventually, it wheezes to a predictable conclusion. Rated R. 101m. **DIR:** Robert Butler. **CAST:** James Brolin, Cliff Gorman, Richard Castellano, Abby Bluestone, Linda G. Miller, Mandy Patinkin. **1980**

NIGHT OF THE KICKFIGHTERS ❤ Half of this ac-tioner is wasted on picking a team of good guys to de-stroy terrorists willing to sell global destructors to the highest bidder. Confrontation between the two groups is saved for the final moments and is not worth the wait. Not rated; contains violence. 87m. **DIR:** Buddy Reyes. **CAST:** Andy Bauman, Marcia Karr, Adam West. **1990**

NIGHT OF THE LIVING DEAD (1968) ★★★★ This gruesome low-budget horror film still packs a punch for those who like to be frightened out of their wits. It is an unrelenting shockfest laced with touches of black humor that deserves its cult status. B&W; 96m. **DIR:** George A. Romero. **CAST:** Duane Jones, Judith O'Dea, Keith Wayne. **1968 DVD**

NIGHT OF THE LIVING DEAD (1990) ★★★1/2 This remake, directed by makeup master Tom Savini and produced by George Romero, combines all the terror of the 1968 original with 1990 special effects. Sur-prisingly, Savini, known for his realistic effects in *Dawn of the Dead* and *Friday the 13th*, doesn't pile the blood on. Rated R for violence, profanity, and gore. 96m. **DIR:** Tom Savini. **CAST:** Tony Todd. **1990 DVD**

NIGHT OF THE RUNNING MAN ★★★ While not long on logic, this compelling little thriller is fueled by Scott Glenn's stylish performance as an implaca-ble professional killer. Cabby Andrew McCarthy stu-pidly flees with ill-gotten mob money, only to find Glenn at every port of call. John Glover also shines as Glenn's cheerfully sadistic partner. Rated R for pro-fanity, violence, torture, nudity, and simulated sex. 93m. **DIR:** Mark L. Lester. **CAST:** Scott Glenn, Andrew McCarthy, Janet Gunn, Wayne Newton, John Glover. **1994**

NIGHT OF THE SCARECROW ★★★ Creative plot twists elevate this a notch above the average slasher film. This time the small town is being terrorized by a harmless-looking scarecrow that has an odd assort-ment of weapons and magic at his disposal. Actually, he's a warlock imprisoned generations ago now seek-ing revenge and restoration of his powers from his captors' ancestors. Rated R for nudity, sex, profanity, violence, and gore. 88m. **DIR:** Jeff Burr. **CAST:** Eliza-beth Barondes, John Mese, Stephen Root, Bruce Glover, Gary Lockwood, Dirk Blocker, John Lazar, Howard Swain. **1995**

NIGHT OF THE SHARKS ★★1/2 Blackmail and in-trigue, washed prettily in the lustrous clear water of Cancun, Mexico, compensate somewhat for the pre-dictable post-*Jaws* approach, in which a one-eyed monster shark makes tropical snorkeling sticky. Rated R. 87m. **DIR:** Anthony Richmond. **CAST:** Treat Williams, Antonio Fargas, Christopher Connelly. **1989**

NIGHT OF THE SHOOTING STARS ★★1/2 Made by Paolo and Vittorio Taviani, this Italian import is about the flight of peasants from their mined village in pastoral Tuscany during the waning days of World War II. Despite its subject matter, the horrors of war, it is a strangely unaffecting—and ineffective—motion picture. In Italian with English subtitles. Not rated; the film has violence. 116m. DIR: Paolo Taviani, Vittorio Taviani. CAST: Omero Antonutti, Margarita Lozano. 1982

NIGHT OF THE WARRIOR ★★ Lorenzo Lamas plays the photographer-nightclub proprietor-kick boxer extraordinaire who's been making a fortune for fight promoter Anthony Geary. When Lamas wants to quit fighting, Geary frames him for murder. Rated R for nudity, profanity, and violence. 96m. DIR: Rafal Zielinski. CAST: Lorenzo Lamas, Anthony Geary, Kathleen Kinmont, Arlene Dahl. 1990 DVD

NIGHT OF THE ZOMBIES (1981) 💔 More socially conscious gore from the director of *Bloodsucking Freaks*. Not rated; contains violence, language, and gore. 88m. DIR: Joel M. Reed. CAST: Jamie Gillis, Ryan Hilliard, Samantha Grey. 1981

NIGHT OF THE ZOMBIES (1983) 💔 It's just one long cannibal feast. Rated R for violence and gore. 101m. DIR: Bruno Mattei. CAST: Frank Garfield, Margie Newton. 1983

NIGHT ON EARTH ★★★ Episodic film about four cabdrivers and their oddball encounters with an array of passengers on the same night in different countries. As with most of director Jim Jarmusch's films, the determinedly low-key and offbeat *Night on Earth* is a cinematic non sequitur, and only his fans will find it completely satisfying. Rated R for profanity. 128m. DIR: Jim Jarmusch. CAST: Gena Rowlands, Winona Ryder, Armin Mueller-Stahl, Giancarlo Esposito, Rosie Perez, Roberto Benigni. 1992

•NIGHT OWL ★★ The first offense of this film is false advertising as neither Caroline Munro nor John Leguizamo are major characters despite top billing. Second offense is that the movie is dull. Not rated; contains gore and profanity. B&W; 77m. DIR: Jeffrey Arsenault. CAST: James Raftery, John Leguizamo, Caroline Munro. 1994

NIGHT PATROL 💔 A bumbling rookie policeman doubles as "The Unknown Comic," cracking jokes in Los Angeles comedy clubs while wearing a paper bag over his head. Rated R. 84m. DIR: Jackie Kong. CAST: Linda Blair, Pat Paulsen, Jaye P. Morgan, Jack Riley, Billy Barty, Murray Langston. 1985

NIGHT PORTER, THE 💔 Sordid outing about an ex-Nazi and the woman he used to abuse sexually in a concentration camp. Lots of kinky scenes, including lovemaking on broken glass. Rated R for violence, nudity, and profanity. 115m. DIR: Lilliana Cavani. CAST: Dirk Bogarde, Charlotte Rampling, Philippe Leroy, Gabriele Ferzetti, Isa Miranda. 1974 DVD

NIGHT RHYTHMS 💔 Radio talk-show host Martin Hewitt awakes from one of his little after-hours liaisons, and finds his companion dead and himself framed for murder. Dull soft-core porn. Rated R for nudity, language, and violence; unrated version contains more of the same. 99m. DIR: Alexander Gregory Hippolyte. CAST: Martin Hewitt, Sam Jones, Deborah Driggs, Tracy Reed, David Carradine. 1992

NIGHT RIDE HOME ★★★ This *Hallmark Hall of Fame* film features a family torn apart after the only son dies while horseback riding. Rebecca DeMornay plays the despicably self-centered mother who cares

little for her grief-stricken husband or daughter. Acting is good but topic may make some uncomfortable. Not rated; contains mature topics. 98m. DIR: Glenn Jordan. CAST: Rebecca DeMornay, Keith Carradine, Thora Birch, Ellen Burstyn. 1999

NIGHT RIDERS, THE ★★1/2 The Three Mesquiteers (John Wayne, Ray Corrigan, and Max Terhune) make like Zorro by donning capes and masks to foil a villain's attempt to enforce a phony Spanish land grant. Good formula Western fun. B&W; 58m. DIR: George Sherman. CAST: John Wayne, Ray "Crash" Corrigan, Max Terhune, Doreen McKay, Ruth Rogers, Tom Tyler, Kermit Maynard. 1939

NIGHT SCHOOL 💔 Students are (literally) losing their heads with worry over their grades. Rated R for graphic, but sloppy, violence. 88m. DIR: Ken Hughes. CAST: Leonard Mann, Rachel Ward, Drew Snyder, Joseph R. Sicari. 1981

NIGHT SCREAMS 💔 Three escaped convicts crash a teenage party. Not rated; contains graphic violence and nudity. 85m. DIR: Allen Plone. CAST: Janette Allyson Caldwell, Joe Manno, Ron Thomas. 1986 DVD

NIGHT SHIFT ★★★★ When a nerdish morgue attendant (Henry Winkler) gets talked into becoming a pimp by a sweet hooker (Shelley Long) and his crazed coworker (Michael Keaton), the result is uproarious comedy. While the concept is a little weird, director Ron Howard packs it with so many laughs and such appealing characters that you can't help but like it. Rated R for nudity, profanity, sex, and violence. 105m. DIR: Ron Howard. CAST: Henry Winkler, Shelley Long, Michael Keaton. 1982 DVD

NIGHT STALKER, THE (1971) ★★★★ A superb made-for-television chiller about a modern-day vampire stalking the streets of Las Vegas. Richard Matheson's teleplay is tight and suspenseful, with Darren McGavin fine as the intrepid reporter on the bloodsucker's trail. 73m. DIR: John Llewellyn Moxey. CAST: Darren McGavin, Carol Lynley, Claude Akins. 1971 DVD

NIGHT STALKER, THE (1986) ★★★ A Vietnam veteran hits the street, brutally murdering prostitutes. An over-the-hill, alcoholic police detective pursues him. The acting is uneven, but the suspense is solid. Worth a look. Rated R for nudity, profanity, and graphic violence. 91m. DIR: Max Kleven. CAST: Charles Napier, Michelle Reese, Joe Gian, Leka Carlin. 1986

NIGHT STALKER, THE: TWO TALES OF TERROR (TV SERIES) ★★★★ Two episodes ("The Ripper" and "The Vampire") from the fascinating but gruesome series feature Darren McGavin as a reporter who is forever abandoning his assigned stories in favor of the latest offbeat police report. This time he tracks down Jack the Ripper in Chicago and a female vampire in L.A. Not rated; contains violence and gore. 98m. DIR: Allen Baron, Don Weis. CAST: Darren McGavin, Simon Oakland, Beatrice Colen, William Daniels, Suzanne Charney, Jan Murray, Kathleen Nolan. 1974

NIGHT STRANGLER, THE ★★★ Newsman with a nose for the macabre unearths a centenarian killer in Seattle's underground city. Second *Kolchak* feature made for television is as fun and lively as its predecessor and led to a network series featuring the

eedy monster hunter. Not rated. 74m. **DIR:** Dan Cur-
s. **CAST:** Darren McGavin, Simon Oakland, Wally Cox,
ichard Anderson, Jo Ann Pflug, John Carradine, Mar-
aret Hamilton, Al Lewis. **1972 DVD**

NIGHT TERROR ★★ Tepid made-for-TV suspense
with Valerie Harper as terrified motorist pursued by
madman Richard Romanus. Strictly by-the-num-
ers. 78m. **DIR:** E. W. Swackhamer. **CAST:** Valerie
Harper, Richard Romanus, Nicholas Pryor. **1977 /**

NIGHT THAT NEVER HAPPENED, THE ♥ Thin sex
antasy from the Playboy Channel about three guys
reating their best friend to a night on the town be-
ore his wedding. Not rated; contains adult situa-
ions, language, and nudity. 95m. **DIR:** James Winner.
CAST: Colleen McDermott, Lissa Boyle, Joshua D.
Comen, Scott Coppola, Judd Dunning. **1997 DVD**

NIGHT THE CITY SCREAMED, THE ★★ Made-for-
TV movie shows how different urban characters react to a power blackout on a hot summer night. The
best subplot follows rookie cops David Cassidy and
Clifton Davis as they try to contain an outbreak of
ooting. Rated PG for mild violence. 96m. **DIR:** Harry
Falk. **CAST:** Georg Stanford Brown, Raymond Burr,
David Cassidy, Robert Culp, Clifton Davis, Don Mered-
th, Linda Purl. **1980**

NIGHT THE LIGHTS WENT OUT IN GEORGIA, THE
★★★1/2 Gutsy, lusty, and satisfying film about a
country singer (Dennis Quaid) with wayward ap-
petites and his levelheaded sister-manager (Kristy
McNichol) who run into big trouble while working
their way to Nashville. The gritty Deep South settings, fine action, a cast of credible extras, some
memorable musical moments, and a dramatic script
with comic overtones add up to above-average entertainment. Rated PG. 120m. **DIR:** Ronald F. Maxwell.
CAST: Kristy McNichol, Mark Hamill, Dennis Quaid,
Don Stroud. **1981**

NIGHT THEY RAIDED MINSKY'S, THE ★★★1/2
Director William Friedkin's tale of a religious girl's
(Britt Ekland) involvement, much to her father's dis-
may, with a burlesque comic (Jason Robards). It's a
nice look at what early burlesque was like, with good
performances by all. Rated PG. 99m. **DIR:** William
Friedkin. **CAST:** Britt Ekland, Jason Robards Jr., Elliott
Gould. **1968**

NIGHT THEY SAVED CHRISTMAS, THE ★★★ In
this excellent made-for-television film, three kids
strive to protect Santa's toy factory from being destroyed by an oil company. Art Carney is delightful as
Saint Nick. 100m. **DIR:** Jackie Cooper. **CAST:** Jaclyn
Smith, Art Carney, Paul LeMat, Mason Adams, June
Lockhart, Paul Williams. **1984**

NIGHT TIDE ★★★ Dennis Hopper stars in this surreal fantasy about a young sailor on leave who falls in
love with a mysterious woman posing as a mermaid
in a seafront carnival. Avant-garde filmmaker Curtis
Harrington, in his first feature, manages to create a
mystical and nightmarish world in which his characters' true motivations are often obscured. Recommended for connoisseurs of the offbeat. B&W; 84m.
DIR: Curtis Harrington. **CAST:** Dennis Hopper, Linda
Lawson, Gavin Muir. **1961 DVD**

NIGHT TO DISMEMBER, A ★★ A must for bad-
movie buffs, this insanely disjointed slasher movie

features almost no dialogue, actors whose hairstyles
and clothes change in mid-scene, and a tacked-on
narration desperately trying to make sense of it all.
Not rated, but with nudity and hilariously bad gore
effects. 70m. **DIR:** Doris Wishman. **CAST:** Samantha
Fox. **1983**

NIGHT TO REMEMBER, A (1943) ★★★★ This is a
very interesting comedy-whodunit about a Greenwich Village mystery author and his wife who try to
solve a real murder. Performances are wonderful
and the direction is taut. B&W; 91m. **DIR:** Richard
Wallace. **CAST:** Loretta Young, Brian Aherne, Jeff Donnell, William Wright, Sidney Toler, Gale Sondergaard.
1943

NIGHT TO REMEMBER, A (1958) ★★★★ Authen-
ticity and credibility mark this documentarylike en-
actment of the sinking of the luxury passenger liner
H.M.S. *Titanic* in deep icy Atlantic waters in April,
1912. Novelist Eric Ambler scripted from historian
Walter Lord's meticulously detailed account of the
tragedy. B&W; 123m. **DIR:** Roy Ward Baker. **CAST:**
Kenneth More, Jill Dixon, David McCallum, Laurence
Naismith, Honor Blackman, Frank Lawton, Alec Mc-
Cowen, George Rose. **1958 DVD**

NIGHT TRAIN TO KATMANDU ★★ Standard family
fare about two youngsters who are uprooted from
their comfortable suburban home in the United
States to live with their anthropologist parents in
Nepal. There they get involved in the quest for the
legendary City That Never Was. Nothing special. Not
rated. 102m. **DIR:** Robert Wiemer. **CAST:** Pernell
Roberts, Eddie Castrodad. **1988**

NIGHT TRAIN TO MUNICH (NIGHT TRAIN)
★★★★1/2 Based on Gordon Wellesley's novel *Re-
port on a Fugitive*, this taut thriller concerns a
British agent (Rex Harrison) trying to rescue a
Czech scientist who has escaped from the Gestapo.
Along with a fine cast and superb script and direc-
tion, this film is blessed with the moody and wonder-
ful photography of Otto Kanturek. B&W; 93m. **DIR:**
Carol Reed. **CAST:** Rex Harrison, Margaret Lockwood,
Paul Henreid, Basil Radford, Naunton Wayne. **1940**

NIGHT TRAIN TO TERROR ★★ Segments from
three bad horror movies are condensed (which improves them considerably) and introduced by actors
playing God and Satan. It's still pretty bad, but the
edited stories are fast-moving and sleazily entertaining. See if you can recognize Richard "Bull" Moll (in
two segments) with his hair. Rated R for nudity,
graphic violence, and gore. 93m. **DIR:** John Carr, Jay
Schlossberg-Cohen. **CAST:** Cameron Mitchell, John
Phillip Law, Marc Lawrence, Richard Moll. **1985 DVD**

NIGHT TRAIN TO VENICE ♥ Hugh Grant is a journalist dogged by neo-Nazis as he travels to Venice in
this mindless and melodramatic oddity. Rated R for
violence, profanity, sexual situations, and nudity.
98m. **DIR:** Carlo U. Quinterio. **CAST:** Hugh Grant, Malcolm McDowell, Tahnee Welch. **1993**

NIGHT VISITOR, THE (1970) ★★★ Revenge is the
name of the game in this English-language Danish
production. Max von Sydow plays an inmate in an insane asylum who comes up with a plan to escape for
a single night and take revenge on the various people
he believes are responsible for his current predica-

ment. Performances are fine. Rated PG. 106m. **DIR:** Laslo Benedek. **CAST:** Max von Sydow, Liv Ullmann, Trevor Howard, Per Oscarsson, Rupert Davies. 1970 DVD

NIGHT VISITOR (1989) ★★ When a compulsive liar (Derek Rydall) witnesses a Satanic murder committed by his history teacher, no one believes him. Rydall's childish whining is inconsistent with his role. Rated R for nudity, violence, and profanity. 93m. **DIR:** Rupert Hitzig. **CAST:** Derek Rydall, Allen Garfield, Michael J. Pollard, Shannon Tweed, Elliott Gould, Richard Roundtree. 1989

NIGHT WALKER, THE ★★★1/2 Robert Bloch's intriguing script is the chief attraction of this moody little thriller, definitely among the best of director-producer William Castle's gimmick horror films. Wealthy Barbara Stanwyck can't stop dreaming about her dead husband, and the recurring nightmares prove to have an unusual cause. 86m. **DIR:** William Castle. **CAST:** Barbara Stanwyck, Robert Taylor, Lloyd Bochner. 1964

NIGHT WARNING ★★ As in many gory movies, the victims and near victims have a convenient and unbelievable way of hanging around despite clear indications they are about to get it. Consequently, in spite of good performances, this is an unremarkable splatter film. Rated R for violence. 96m. **DIR:** William Asher. **CAST:** Jimmy McNichol, Bo Svenson, Susan Tyrrell. 1982

NIGHT WATCH ★★ In this so-so suspense–thriller, Elizabeth Taylor stars as a wealthy widow recovering from a nervous breakdown. From her window, she seems to witness a number of ghoulish goings-on. But does she? The operative phrase here after a while is "Who cares?" Rated PG. 98m. **DIR:** Brian G. Hutton. **CAST:** Elizabeth Taylor, Laurence Harvey, Billie Whitelaw, Robert Lang, Tony Britton. 1973

NIGHT WE NEVER MET, THE ★★★1/2 A sophisticated comedy with strong players who understand the meaning of teamwork. Kevin Anderson timeshares his New York apartment to help pay the rent. Would-be lothario Matthew Broderick and unhappily married Annabella Sciorra rent on alternate days. You know in advance that they will find each other, but the fun is finding out how. Delightful dialogue. 99m. **DIR:** Warren Light. **CAST:** Matthew Broderick, Annabella Sciorra, Kevin Anderson, Jeanne Tripplehorn, Justine Bateman, Garry Shandling, Louise Lasser, Katharine Houghton. 1993

NIGHT ZOO ★★★ An impressive, quirky French-Canadian film that brings together the unlikely combination of a tough, visceral, urban thriller and a sensitive, bittersweet story about the renewed love between a dying father and his grown son. The film moves from the dark streets of nighttime Montreal to a strange encounter with an elephant during a nocturnal visit to the zoo. Rated R, with strong violence and profanity. 107m. **DIR:** Jean-Claude Lauzon. **CAST:** Gilles Maheu, Roger Le Bel. 1987

NIGHTBREAKER ★★★★ Effective message film takes us behind the scenes of nuclear tests on military personnel in Nevada, 1956. The atomic bomb horrors are both realistic and terrifying. Made for TV.

99m. **DIR:** Peter Markle. **CAST:** Emilio Estevez, Martin Sheen, Lea Thompson. 1989

NIGHTCOMERS, THE ★★1/2 Strange prequel to *The Turn of the Screw*, this uneven effort contains some fine acting and boasts some truly eerie scenes, but is hampered by Michael Winner's loose direction and a nebulous story line. Marlon Brando is in good form as the mysterious catalyst, but this murky melodrama still lacks the solid story and cohesiveness that could have made it a true chiller. Rated R. 96m. **DIR:** Michael Winner. **CAST:** Marlon Brando, Stephanie Beacham, Thora Hird, Harry Andrews. 1971

NIGHTFALL 🖤 David Birney is the ruler of a land that has never known night. Rated PG-13, but contains abundant nudity and violence. 83m. **DIR:** Paul Mayersberg. **CAST:** David Birney, Sarah Douglas. 1988

NIGHTFLYERS ★★★ A motley crew of space explorers search for an ancient and mysterious entity. Their ship is controlled by a computer, programmed from the brain patterns of an abused, jealous, and telepathic woman. This film's only weaknesses are inconsistent special effects and an ending that leaves you hanging. Sci-fi fans should find this entertaining. Rated R for violence and language. 90m. **DIR:** T. C. Blake. **CAST:** Catherine Mary Stewart, Michael Praed, John Standing, Lisa Blount, Michael Des Barres. 1987

NIGHTFORCE ★★ Linda Blair as a commando. A group of kids venture to Central America to free the kidnapped daughter of a prominent American politician. Rated R for violence. 82m. **DIR:** Lawrence D. Foldes. **CAST:** Linda Blair, Claudia Udy, James Van Patten, Richard Lynch, Chad McQueen, Cameron Mitchell. 1987

NIGHTHAWKS ★★★★1/2 From its explosive first scene to the breathtakingly suspenseful denouement, *Nighthawks*, about a police detective hunting a wily terrorist, is a thoroughly enjoyable, supercharged action film. Rated R for violence, nudity, and profanity. 99m. **DIR:** Bruce Malmuth. **CAST:** Sylvester Stallone, Billy Dee Williams, Rutger Hauer, Lindsay Wagner. 1981 DVD

NIGHTJOHN ★★★★1/2 Inspirational tale of a young slave girl named Sarny, whose prayer for knowledge is answered when her master brings home a new slave named Nightjohn. When Nightjohn defies tradition by teaching Sarny to read, her new skill opens up a whole new world to her, teaching her important lessons about life and the human spirit. Outstanding performances and period detail make this made-for-cable production a moving experience. Rated PG-13 for violence. 96m. **DIR:** Charles Burnett. **CAST:** Beau Bridges, Carl Lumbly, Allison Jones, Lorraine Toussaint, Bill Cobbs. 1996

NIGHTKILL ★★★ Largely unreleased in theaters, this is a tidy little cat-and-mouse thriller with former Charlie's Angel Jaclyn Smith as a conniving widow and Robert Mitchum as the world-weary investigator who gets caught up in her scheme. Despite some inept direction, the last half hour is a nail biter, particularly scenes in a bathroom shower. Rated R for violence, nudity, and profanity. 97m. **DIR:** Ted Post. **CAST:** Jaclyn Smith, Robert Mitchum, James Franciscus. 1983

NIGHTLIFE ★★★1/2 A doctor finds a beautiful patient with a strange taste for blood in this funny and scary horror show, made for cable. Keith Szarabajka, as a doctor, steals the show by being both spooky and comically warped. Great fun. 90m. **DIR:** Daniel Taplitz. **CAST:** Maryam D'Abo, Ben Cross, Keith Szarabajka. 1989

NIGHTMAN, THE ★★★ Steamy southern romantic thriller. A woman suspects she's being stalked by a former lover who spent eighteen years in prison for the murder of her mother. In flashbacks, she recalls the events and the passion that led to a bitter love triangle and the killing. Rated R for simulated sex, nudity, violence, and profanity. 96m. **DIR:** Charles Haid. **CAST:** Joanna Kerns, Jenny Robertson, Latanya Richardson, Lou Walker. 1993

NIGHTMARE (1964) ★★★ Dreams and visions haunt a teenager who begins to think she is losing her mind. Or is it all a plot to drive her crazy? Intriguing Hammer Studios thriller with enough red herrings and devious characters to keep you guessing. Not rated; contains implied violence. B&W; 83m. **DIR:** Freddie Francis. **CAST:** David Knight, Moira Redmond, Brenda Bruce, John Welsh. 1964

NIGHTMARE (1991) ★★ Average made-for-television thriller about a girl who is abducted by a serial killer, escapes, and then has to face the nightmare all over again when the killer is caught and released on a technicality. No surprises here. Rated PG-13 for intense situations. 95m. **DIR:** John Pasquin. **CAST:** Victoria Principal, Paul Sorvino, Jonathan Banks, Danielle Harris, Gregg Henry. 1991

NIGHTMARE AT BITTERCREEK ★★ Nazi survivalists stalk a group of women camping in the mountains. The mediocre script offers a few chills and a modicum of suspense, but overall leaves one feeling unsatisfied. Made for TV. 92m. **DIR:** Tim Burstall. **CAST:** Lindsay Wagner, Tom Skerritt, Constance McCashin, Joanna Cassidy. 1990

NIGHTMARE AT NOON ♥ A group of renegade scientists testing a germ-warfare virus. Rated R for violence. 96m. **DIR:** Nico Mastorakis. **CAST:** Wings Hauser, Bo Hopkins, George Kennedy, Brion James. 1987 DVD

NIGHTMARE BEFORE CHRISTMAS, THE ★★★★ Literally years in the making, 92m Tim Burton's warped holiday fantasy is a true stunner. Employing a blend of conventional stop-motion and replacement animation (the latter rarely seen beyond George Pal's efforts), Burton and scripter Caroline Thompson spin a wonderfully weird tale about Halloweentown-hero Jack Skellington's efforts to redefine Christmas. While not for average tastes, this is one of those rare films with "sense of wonder" to spare. Rated G. 75m. **DIR:** Henry Selick. 1993 DVD

NIGHTMARE CASTLE ★★ Barbara Steele plays two roles in this lurid Italian shocker about a faithless wife and the gory revenge exacted by her jealous husband. Routine theatrics, atmospherically photographed—and cut by fifteen minutes for its U.S. release. B&W; 90m. **DIR:** Mario Caiano. **CAST:** Barbara Steele, Paul Muller, Helga Line. 1965

NIGHTMARE CIRCUS (BARN OF THE LIVING DEAD) (TERROR CIRCUS) ★★ A young man who was abused as a child abducts women and chains them in the family barn. This graphically violent low-budget R-rater was the first theatrical feature by the now highly respected director Alan Rudolph. 86m. **DIR:** Alan Rudolph. **CAST:** Andrew Prine, Sherry Alberoni. 1973

NIGHTMARE HOUSE ♥ Previously available on video under its original title *Scream, Baby, Scream,* the movie is rated R for violence and brief nudity. 83m. **DIR:** Joseph Adler. **CAST:** Ross Harris. 1969

NIGHTMARE IN BLOOD ★★ A film that's fun for genre fans only. A horror-movie star appears at a horror convention that people are dying to get into. The twist is he isn't just playing a vampire in his films; he *is* one. The cassette box says "filmed in and around picturesque San Francisco," and most viewers will think that's the best thing about it. Not rated; contains mild bloodletting. 92m. **DIR:** John Stanley. **CAST:** Jerry Walter, Barrie Youngfellow, Kerwin Mathews. 1975

NIGHTMARE IN WAX (CRIMES IN THE WAX MUSEUM) ♥ Cameron Mitchell plays a disfigured ex–makeup man running a wax museum in Hollywood. Rated PG. 91m. **DIR:** Bud Townsend. **CAST:** Cameron Mitchell, Anne Helm, Scott Brady. 1969

NIGHTMARE ON ELM STREET, A ★★★★ Wes Craven directed this clever shocker about a group of teenagers afflicted with the same bad dreams. Horror movie buffs, take note. Rated R for nudity, violence, and profanity. 91m. **DIR:** Wes Craven. **CAST:** John Saxon, Ronee Blakley, Heather Langenkamp, Robert Englund. 1985 DVD

NIGHTMARE ON ELM STREET 2, A: FREDDY'S REVENGE ♥ Another teen exploitation film. Rated R for nudity, language, and gore. 83m. **DIR:** Jack Sholder. **CAST:** Mark Patton, Kim Myers, Clu Gulager, Hope Lange. 1985 DVD

NIGHTMARE ON ELM STREET 3, A: THE DREAM WARRIORS ♥ Freddy is at it again. Rated R. 97m. **DIR:** Charles Russell. **CAST:** Robert Englund, Heather Langenkamp, Patricia Arquette, Craig Wasson. 1987 DVD

NIGHTMARE ON ELM STREET 4, A: THE DREAM MASTER ★★ America's favorite child-molesting burn victim Freddy Krueger (Robert Englund) is back in this fourth installment of the hit series. Freddy's favorite pastime, killing teenagers in their dreams, is played to the hilt with fantastic special effects. Rated R for violence and gore. 97m. **DIR:** Renny Harlin. **CAST:** Robert Englund, Lisa Wilcox. 1988 DVD

NIGHTMARE ON ELM STREET 5, A: THE DREAM CHILD ★★★ This fifth installment in the series is a wild ride filled with gruesome makeup effects and mind-blowing visuals. Never mind that Freddy's return is not explained. (He was supposedly killed in part 4.) This time he enters the dreams of the heroine's unborn child, attempting to place the souls of those he kills into the fetus. Rated R for violence, profanity, and plenty o' gore. 91m. **DIR:** Stephen Hopkins. **CAST:** Robert Englund, Lisa Wilcox. 1989 DVD

NIGHTMARE ON THE 13TH FLOOR ♥ Haunted hotel chiller. This made-for-cable movie has minimal violence. Rated PG-13. 85m. **DIR:** Walter Grauman. **CAST:** Michele Greene, Louise Fletcher, James Brolin, John Karlen. **1990**

NIGHTMARE SISTERS 💔 The spirit of a succubus possesses three straitlaced sorority girls. Rated R for nudity and simulated sex. 83m. **DIR:** David DeCoteau. **CAST:** Linnea Quigley. **1988**

NIGHTMARE WEEKEND 💔 An incomprehensible film about a scientist who invents a computer system that can transform solid inorganic objects into deadly weapons. Rated R for graphic violence and nudity. 88m. **DIR:** H. Sala. **CAST:** Debbie Laster, Debra Hunter, Lori Lewis. **1985**

NIGHTMARE YEARS, THE ★★★★ William L. Shirer's first-person account of the rise of Hitler comes to life in this made-for-cable bio. Sam Waterston plays the daring American reporter in Berlin, Vienna, and France from 1934 to 1940. 474m. **DIR:** Anthony Page. **CAST:** Sam Waterston, Marthe Keller, Kurtwood Smith. **1989**

NIGHTMARES ★★ Four everyday situations are twisted into tales of terror in this mostly mediocre horror film in the style of *Twilight Zone—the Movie* and *Creepshow*. Rated R for violence and profanity. 99m. **DIR:** Joseph Sargent. **CAST:** Cristina Raines, Emilio Estevez, Lance Henriksen. **1983 DVD**

NIGHTS IN WHITE SATIN ★★1/2 Hokey Cinderella story has Prince Charming as an ace fashion photographer. The glass slippers are snapshots of a ragsdressed beauty who lives among the poor just a motorcycle ride from the photographer's elegant loft. Rated R for nudity. 99m. **DIR:** Michael Bernard. **CAST:** Kenneth Gilman, Priscilla Harris. **1987**

NIGHTS OF CABIRIA ★★★★ Federico Fellini's seventh film can be hailed as a tragicomic masterpiece. The story focuses on an impoverished prostitute (Giulietta Masina) living on the outskirts of Rome, who is continuously betrayed by her faith in human nature. Masina gives an unforgettable performance. In Italian with English subtitles. B&W; 110m. **DIR:** Federico Fellini. **CAST:** Giulietta Masina, Amadeo Nazzari, François Perier. **1957 DVD**

NIGHTSCARE ★★★ When a vicious serial killer is administered an experimental drug, it releases him from the prison of his earthly body so he can renew his bloodshed through the dreams of his victims. Sometimes atmospheric, sometimes overly bloody, horror film features plenty of jolts and a surprisingly good performance from model Elizabeth Hurley who stars as the inventor of the treatment serum. Rated R for violence, profanity, and sexual situations. 89m. **DIR:** Vadim Jean. **CAST:** Elizabeth Hurley, Craig Fairbrass, Keith Allen, Anita Hobson, Craig Kelly. **1993**

NIGHTSIEGE-PROJECT: SHADOWCHASER 2 ★★ Plenty of sci-fi action and some decent special effects aren't enough to breathe life into this tired premise. Three unlikely heroes are brought together in order to stop an android that has the capability of turning the planet into toast. Utter nonsense dressed up with no place to go. R-rated and unrated versions; both contain extreme violence and adult language. 97/98m. **DIR:** John Eyres. **CAST:** Bryan Genesse, Beth Toussaint, Frank Zagarino. **1994**

NIGHTSTICK ★★★ A fast-paced thriller with Bruce Fairbairn as an unorthodox cop who is hunting down two ex-convict brothers. The deadly duo are placing bombs in banks and threatening to blow them up unless a ransom is met. A good cast and above-average script make this one worth renting. Equivalent to an R, violent! 94m. **DIR:** Joseph L. Scanlan. **CAST:** Bruce Fairbairn, Robert Vaughn, Kerrie Keane, John Vernon, Leslie Nielsen. **1987**

NIGHTTIME IN NEVADA ★★★ Remorse-ridden killer Grant Withers, to cover up a murder he committed sixteen years ago, plans to steal Roy Rogers's cattle to pay off and make amends to the dead man's daughter. B Western bad-man logic. B&W; 67m. **DIR:** William Witney. **CAST:** Roy Rogers, Gabby Hayes, Adele Mara, Grant Withers, Bob Nolan and the Sons of the Pioneers. **1948**

NIGHTWATCH ★★1/2 A young law student (Ewan McGregor), while working as a night watchman at the city morgue, finds himself the prime suspect in a series of grisly murders. The actors are good (though McGregor's American accent comes and goes), and there are some genuinely creepy scenes, but the story is full of holes and the plot twists are telegraphed a mile in advance. Rated R for nudity, profanity, and gore. 105m. **DIR:** Ole Bornedal. **CAST:** Ewan McGregor, Nick Nolte, Josh Brolin, Patricia Arquette, Brad Dourif. **1998**

NIGHTWING 💔 Absolutely laughable tale, derived from an abysmal Martin Cruz Smith novel, about a flock (herd? pack?) of vampire bats. Rated PG. 105m. **DIR:** Arthur Hiller. **CAST:** David Warner, Kathryn Harrold, Nick Mancuso, Strother Martin. **1979**

NIGHTWISH ★★ A team of graduate student dream researchers explores supernatural phenomena in a house haunted by a sinister alien presence. There are some good effects, and a fairly imaginative ending given the confused story line. Not rated, but with partial nudity and profanity. 96m. **DIR:** Bruce R. Cook. **CAST:** Clayton Rohner, Jack Starrett, Robert Tessier, Brian Thompson. **1990**

NIJINSKY ★★★ George de la Pena stars as the legendary dancer and Alan Bates is his lover, a Ballet Russe impresario. Herbert Ross (*The Turning Point*) is no stranger to ballet films. Here, he has assembled an outstanding cast and filmed them beautifully. Rated R. 125m. **DIR:** Herbert Ross. **CAST:** Alan Bates, George de la Pena, Leslie Browne, Jeremy Irons. **1980**

NIKKI, WILD DOG OF THE NORTH ★★★ The rugged wilderness of northern Canada provides the backdrop to this story of a dog that is separated from his owner. 73m. **DIR:** Jack Couffer. **CAST:** Don Haldane, Jean Coutu, Emile Genest. **1961 DVD**

NIL BY MOUTH ★★★★ This gritty skid through squalid working-class South London is a ferocious slice of social realism that slithers into dark, dysfunctional family relationships. Raymond is a human time bomb fueled by alcohol. His abuse of his wife and drug-addicted brother-in-law leads to several harrowing moments in a life bloodied by ugly machismo, self-loathing, and self-pity. Rated R for language, domestic violence, nudity, and graphic drug use. 128m. **DIR:** Gary Oldman. **CAST:** Ray Winstone, Kathy Burke, Charlie Creed-Miles, Laila Morse, Edna Dore. **1998**

NINA TAKES A LOVER ★★★★ Funny, enlightening, and involving romance stars Laura San Giacomo as a young woman wondering what to do with her spare time since her husband is on the road so often. She opts for an unusual affair. Well acted, written, and directed, film hits the bull's-eye more often than not. Rated R for profanity and sexuality. 100m. DIR: Alan Jacobs. CAST: Laura San Giacomo, Paul Rhys, Michael O'Keefe, Cristi Conaway, Fisher Stevens. **1995**

9 NINJAS ★★★ A slapstick spoof of ninja movies and *9 Weeks*. A nonexistent plot, but solid hilarity. Michael Phenice is terrific. Rated R for nudity. 82m. DIR: Aaron Worth. CAST: Michael Phenice. **1990**

9 1/2 WEEKS ★★ Somewhere between toning down the bondage and liberating the heroine, this movie's story definitely loses out to the imagery. Mickey Rourke is quite believable in the lead role of the masochistic seducer, but Kim Basinger does little more than look pretty. This couple makes steamy work of simple things like dressing and eating. Rated R for sex and violence. 113m. DIR: Adrian Lyne. CAST: Mickey Rourke, Kim Basinger, Margaret Whitton, David Branski, Karen Young. **1986 DVD**

NINE DAYS A QUEEN ★★★ This well-acted historical drama picks up after the death of Henry VIII and follows the frenzied and often lethal scramble for power that went on in the court of England. Lovely Nova Pilbeam plays Lady Jane Grey, the heroine of the title who is taken to the headsman's block by Mary Tudor's armies after a pathetic reign of only nine days. Tragic and moving, this British film was well received by critics when it premiered but is practically forgotten today. B&W; 80m. DIR: Robert Stevenson. CAST: Cedric Hardwicke, Nova Pilbeam, John Mills, Sybil Thorndike, Leslie Perrins, Felix Aylmer, Miles Malleson. **1936**

NINE DEATHS OF THE NINJA 🎦 Another grunt-and-groan, low-budget martial arts mess. Rated R. 94m. DIR: Emmett Alston. CAST: Sho Kosugi, Brent Huff, Emilia Lesniak, Blackie Dammett. **1985**

NINE LIVES OF ELFEGO BACA, THE ★★★ Robert Loggia, as the long-lived hero of the Old West, faces one of his most harrowing perils as he confronts scores of gunmen. Lots of action and fun for the whole family. Rated G. 78m. DIR: Norman Foster. CAST: Robert Loggia, Robert F. Simon, Lisa Montell, Nestor Paiva. **1958**

NINE LIVES OF FRITZ THE CAT ★★1/2 A streetwise alley cat tries to escape his mundane existence in the sequel to the 1972 cult favorite, *Fritz the Cat*. Fritz is his usual witty, horny self. The animation is excellent and the film is written with a hip sense of humor. This is not Saturday-morning material, however, as there is a distinctly erotic tone to virtually every scene. Rated R for adult theme and language. 77m. DIR: Robert Taylor. **1974**

NINE MONTHS ★★1/2 So-so comedy about a young couple, Hugh Grant and Julianne Moore, nervously on the verge of parenthood. More to the point, she's looking forward to being a mother, but he is panic-stricken at the thought of becoming a father. It's watchable enough, although annoying "friendly"

parents played by Tom Arnold and Joan Cusack sabotage some of the film's potentially best scenes. Rated PG-13 for light profanity. 103m. DIR: Chris Columbus. CAST: Hugh Grant, Julianne Moore, Tom Arnold, Joan Cusack, Jeff Goldblum, Robin Williams. **1995**

NINE TO FIVE ★★★★ In this delightful comedy, Jane Fonda almost ends up playing third fiddle to two marvelous comediennes, Lily Tomlin and Dolly Parton. (That's right, Dolly Parton!) The gifted singer-songwriter makes one of the brightest acting debuts ever in this hilarious farce about three secretaries who decide to get revenge on their sexist, ego-maniacal boss (Dabney Coleman). Rated PG. 110m. DIR: Colin Higgins. CAST: Jane Fonda, Lily Tomlin, Dolly Parton, Dabney Coleman. **1980**

90 DAYS ★★★ A fine little comedy shot in documentary style. The narrator has sent for a Korean pen pal to come to be his wife in Canada. The resultant cultural differences are humorously explored. Not rated. 100m. DIR: Giles Walker. CAST: Stefas Wodoslavsky, Sam Grana. **1986**

●NINETY DEGREES IN THE SHADE ★★ Strange combination of sex drama and morality tale about a grocery-store clerk whose loyalty to her boss leads to tragic consequences. The Anglo-Czech coproduction attempts to be daring in its mid-1960s depiction of forbidden lust, yet it seems tame and tiresome by today's standards. Not rated; contains adult situations. B&W; 90m. DIR: Jiri Weiss. CAST: Anne Heywood, James Booth, Rudolf Hrusínsky, Jirina Jiraskova. **1965**

92 IN THE SHADE ★★★ This wild and hilarious adaptation of first-time director Thomas McGuane's prize-winning novel concerns rival fishing-boat captains in Florida. Entire cast is first-rate in this sleeper. Rated R. 93m. DIR: Thomas McGuane. CAST: Peter Fonda, Warren Oates, Margot Kidder, Harry Dean Stanton, Burgess Meredith, Elizabeth Ashley, Sylvia Miles. **1975**

99 AND 44/100 PERCENT DEAD 🎦 A hit man is hired to rub out a gangland boss. Rated PG for violence. 98m. DIR: John Frankenheimer. CAST: Richard Harris, Chuck Connors, Edmond O'Brien, Bradford Dillman, Ann Turkel. **1974**

99 WOMEN 🎦 Eurojunk set in a women's prison with all the usual stereotypes. Rated R. 90m. DIR: Jess (Jesus) Franco. CAST: Maria Schell, Mercedes McCambridge, Herbert Lom, Luciana Paluzzi. **1969**

976-EVIL ★★★1/2 Actor Robert Englund makes his directorial debut with this tale of a wimpish teenager who slowly becomes possessed by a 976 "Horrorscope" number. Englund gives his film a genuinely eerie feel without missing his chance to throw in a little comedy. Rated R for violence. 92m. DIR: Robert Englund. CAST: Jim Metzler, Stephen Geoffreys, Sandy Dennis, Robert Picardo. **1989**

976-EVIL II: THE ASTRAL FACTOR ★★ An occult-oriented telephone service assists a murderer in astrally projecting himself from jail so that he may continue his killing spree. A fair sequel. Rated R for graphic violence, profanity, and nudity. 93m. DIR: Jim Wynorski. CAST: Rene Assa, Brigitte Nielsen, Patrick O'Bryan. **1991**

1900 ★★ This sprawling, self-conscious, exhausting film seems to revel in violence for its own sake. An insincere mishmash of scenes, *1900* chronicles the adventures of two young men set against the backdrop of the rise of fascism and socialism in Italy. The performances of Gérard Depardieu, Robert De Niro, and Dominique Sanda are lost in all the flashiness and bravado of Bernardo Bertolucci's direction. Rated R. 240m. **DIR:** Bernardo Bertolucci. **CAST:** Robert De Niro, Gérard Depardieu, Dominique Sanda, Burt Lancaster. 1976

1918 ★★★ Minor-key slice-of-life film focuses on the denizens of a small Texas town in 1918. After introducing the main characters (including some based on members of his own family), screenwriter Horton Foote details the effects of a devastating epidemic of influenza that ravaged the town that year. The result is an almost academic but well-acted look at a bygone era. Rated PG. 94m. **DIR:** Ken Harrison. **CAST:** William Converse-Roberts, Hallie Foote, Matthew Broderick, Rochelle Oliver, Michael Higgins. 1984

1941 ★ Steven Spielberg laid his first multimillion-dollar egg with this unfunny what-if comedy about the Japanese attacking Los Angeles during World War II. Rated PG. 118m. **DIR:** Steven Spielberg. **CAST:** John Belushi, Dan Aykroyd, Toshiro Mifune, Christopher Lee, Slim Pickens, Ned Beatty, John Candy, Nancy Allen, Tim Matheson, Murray Hamilton, Treat Williams. 1979 DVD

1969 ★★★ Writer-director Ernest Thompson's reminiscences of the flower-power era feature Kiefer Sutherland and Robert Downey Jr. as high school buddies who face the challenges of college and the abyss of military service in Vietnam. Thompson goes for too many larger-than-life moments in his directorial debut. But Sutherland and Bruce Dern create sparks as son and father, and the other actors are fine, too. Rated R for profanity, nudity, and violence. 105m. **DIR:** Ernest Thompson. **CAST:** Kiefer Sutherland, Robert Downey Jr., Bruce Dern, Mariette Hartley, Winona Ryder, Joanna Cassidy. 1988

1984 (1955) ★★ Workmanlike adaptation of George Orwell's famous novel that, in spite of a good stab at Winston Smith by Edmond O'Brien, just doesn't capture the misery and desolation of the book. Frankly, this plays more like a postwar polemic than a drama, and great liberties have been taken with the story line. B&W; 91m. **DIR:** Michael Anderson. **CAST:** Edmond O'Brien, Jan Sterling, Michael Redgrave, Donald Pleasence. 1955

1984 (1984) ★★★★1/2 A stunning adaptation of George Orwell's novel, which captures every mote of bleak despair found within those pages. John Hurt looks positively emaciated as the forlorn Winston Smith, the tragic figure who dares to fall in love in a totalitarian society where emotions are outlawed. Richard Burton, in his last film role, makes a grand interrogator. Rated R for nudity and adult themes. 123m. **DIR:** Michael Radford. **CAST:** John Hurt, Richard Burton, Suzanna Hamilton, Cyril Cusack. 1984

1990: THE BRONX WARRIORS 🖤 Near the end of the 1980s, the Bronx becomes a kind of no-man's-land ruled by motorcycle gangs. Rated R for violence and language. 89m. **DIR:** Enzo G. Castellari. **CAST:** Vic Morrow, Christopher Connelly, Mark Gregory. 1983

NINJA III: THE DOMINATION 🖤 *The Exorcist* meets *Enter the Dragon.* Rated R for violence and profan-

ity. 95m. **DIR:** Sam Firstenberg. **CAST:** Lucinda Dickey, Sho Kosugi. 1984

NINOTCHKA ★★★★ "Garbo laughs," proclaimed the ads of its day; and so will you in this classic screen comedy. Greta Garbo is a Soviet commissar sent to Paris to check on the lack of progress of three bumbling trade envoys who have been seduced by the decadent trappings of capitalism. Melvyn Douglas, as a Parisian playboy, meets Garbo at the Eiffel Tower and plans a seduction of his own, in this most joyous of Hollywood comedies. B&W; 110m. **DIR:** Ernst Lubitsch. **CAST:** Greta Garbo, Melvyn Douglas, Bela Lugosi. 1939

NINTH CONFIGURATION, THE ★★★1/2 This terse, intense film is not for everyone, but the plot, screenplay, and acting are top-notch. Stacy Keach plays a psychiatrist caring for Vietnam War veterans who suffer from acute emotional disorders. Rated R for profanity and violence. 115m. **DIR:** William Peter Blatty. **CAST:** Stacy Keach, Scott Wilson, Jason Miller, Ed Flanders, Neville Brand, George DiCenzo, Moses Gunn, Robert Loggia, Joe Spinell, Alejandro Rey, Tom Atkins. 1979

•**NINTH GATE, THE** ★★★ Despite an intriguing premise and a solid first act, this supernatural tale eventually sinks beneath its own arty pretensions; director Roman Polanski works this film far beyond what most viewers will endure. That's a shame; Johnny Depp's lead performance and the production design are superb. Depp plays a cheerfully mercenary New York "book broker" who agrees to authenticate a seventeenth-century satanic text rumored to give its owner the ability to summon the devil himself. Judging by its surface gloss, this film should have been mesmerizing from start to finish ... but, then, you can't always judge a book by its cover. Rated R for violence, profanity, nudity, and sexual content. 133m. **DIR:** Roman Polanski. **CAST:** Johnny Depp, Frank Langella, Lena Olin, Emmanuelle Seigner, Barbara Jefford. 2000 DVD

NITTI: THE ENFORCER ★★1/2 Made-for-TV portrait of Frank Nitti (played with conviction by Anthony LaPaglia), who became Al Capone's right-hand man and enforcer in Chicago. Stunning period piece looks great, and supporting cast all do their best. 100m. **DIR:** Michael Switzer. **CAST:** Anthony LaPaglia, Trini Alvarado, Bruno Kirby, Michael Moriarty, Michael Russo. 1988

NIXON ★★1/2 Many of Richard Nixon's family and associates criticized this portrayal of his life, but you don't have to be a Nixon admirer to be put off by this turgid, melodramatic film. Nixon becomes here a sweaty, glowering gnome, skulking drunkenly around the White House, obsessed with the assassination of JFK. Stone's picture is long, uninvolving, and largely fanciful. Rated R for profanity. 190m. **DIR:** Oliver Stone. **CAST:** Anthony Hopkins, Joan Allen, Powers Boothe, Ed Harris, Bob Hoskins, E. G. Marshall, David Paymer, David Hyde Pierce, Paul Sorvino, Mary Steenburgen, J. T. Walsh, James Woods. 1995 DVD

NO BIG DEAL ★★ Kevin Dillon plays an underprivileged punk who makes a lot of nice friends during trips to juvenile hall. Low production values and limited acting don't help matters. 90m. **DIR:** Robert

Charlton. **CAST:** Kevin Dillon, Christopher Gartin, Mary Joan Negro, Sylvia Miles, Tammy Grimes. **1984**

NO CONTEST ★★1/2 Although Shannon Tweed is a wholly unbelievable substitute for Bruce Willis, this *Die Hard* rip-off remains reasonably entertaining due to sheer momentum. Tweed, on the loose in a barricaded skyscraper, is the only one capable of stopping terrorists holed up with hostage beauty contestants. Although her fights are badly doubled, the wonderfully reprehensible villains give the story some additional juice. Rated R for violence and profanity. 98m. **DIR:** Paul Lynch. **CAST:** Shannon Tweed, Robert Davi, Andrew Clay, Roddy Piper, Nicholas Campbell, John Colicos. **1994**

NO DEAD HEROES 🐝 Another post–Vietnam War film where our heroes go in and kick some commie tail. Not rated. 86m. **DIR:** J. C. Miller. **CAST:** John Dresden, Max Thayer, Dave Anderson, Nick Nicholson, Mike Monte, Toni Nero. **1986**

NO DEPOSIT, NO RETURN ★★ Two kids decide to escape from their multimillionaire grandfather (David Niven) and visit their mother in Hong Kong. On their way to the airport, they end up in a getaway car with two incompetent safecrackers. It is unrealistic and not very believable, with occasional bits of real entertainment. Rated G. 115m. **DIR:** Norman Tokar. **CAST:** David Niven, Don Knotts, Darren McGavin, Herschel Bernardi, Barbara Feldon. **1976**

NO DESSERT DAD UNTIL YOU MOW THE LAWN ★★★ When parents Robert Hays and Joanna Kerns attempt to kick the smoking habit by way of self-hypnosis tapes their neglected kids alter the tapes, giving their parents a more youthful outlook on life. Watching their transformation from strung-out chain-smokers to vibrant, healthy parents is both funny and poignant. Rated PG. 93m. **DIR:** Howard McCain. **CAST:** Robert Hays, Joanna Kerns, Larry Linville, Joshua Schaefer, Allison Mack, Jimmy Marsden, Richard Moll. **1994**

NO DRUMS, NO BUGLES ★★★ Because he refuses to kill, a West Virginian farmer (Martin Sheen) spends three years during the Civil War hiding in the Blue Ridge Mountains. Generally the movie is excellent; Sheen commands your interest in what is essentially a one-man show, and the nature photography is striking. It's ruined for the home viewer, though, by a terrible film-to-video transfer in which much of the wide-screen dimension has been compressed into the square television ratio. What a waste! Rated PG. 85m. **DIR:** Clyde Ware. **CAST:** Martin Sheen. **1971**

NO ESCAPE ★★★ In the year 2022, decorated soldier Ray Liotta is sent to prison for shooting his commanding officer. When he fails to follow the rules, Liotta is dropped on a prison island where a tribe of grungy killers called the "Outsiders" do battle with the more civilized "Insiders." It's diverting and action-packed, but little more. Rated R for violence and gore. 118m. **DIR:** Martin Campbell. **CAST:** Ray Liotta, Lance Henriksen, Stuart Wilson, Kevin Dillon, Ernie Hudson, Michael Lerner, Kevin J. O'Connor. **1994** DVD

NO ESCAPE, NO RETURN ★★ Recognizable faces flesh out this typical actioner. Three rogue cops are

sent undercover to bring down a vicious drug lord. Pedestrian effort adds nothing new to the genre. Rated R for violence, language, and sexual situations. 96m. **DIR:** Charles Kanganis. **CAST:** Michael Nouri, John Saxon, Maxwell Caulfield, Denise Loveday, Kevin Benton. **1993**

NO HIGHWAY IN THE SKY ★★★ An adventure about flying safety instead of airplane crashes, this movie benefits more from the chemistry between its players than the development of the plot. B&W; 98m. **DIR:** Henry Koster. **CAST:** James Stewart, Marlene Dietrich, Glynis Johns, Dora Bryan, Jack Hawkins. **1951**

NO HOLDS BARRED ★★ Muscle-bound rip-off of *Rocky III*. Rated PG-13 for violence and profanity. 92m. **DIR:** Thomas Wright. **CAST:** Hulk Hogan, Joan Severance, Tiny Lester. **1989**

NO JUSTICE ★★ Rival factions battle for power in a small Southern town. Everything you'd expect from a movie apparently made for the drive-in market. Rated R for violence. 91m. **DIR:** Richard Wayne Martin. **CAST:** Bob Orwig, Cameron Mitchell, Steve Murphy, Philip Newman, Donald Farmer. **1990**

NO LAUGHING MATTER ★★1/2 A teenage boy forces his mother to quit drinking after her addiction has ruined both of their lives. Credible performances from both Suzanne Somers and Chad Christ, but this made-for-cable original just doesn't inspire like it should. Rated PG-13. 95m. **DIR:** Michael Elias. **CAST:** Suzanne Somers, Chad Christ, Selma Blair, Robert Desiderio. **1997**

NO LOOKING BACK ★★★★ Drifting mechanic returns home and tries to resurrect the glory days of a failed romance with a bitter diner waitress who is living with one of his childhood buddies. The emotional texture and working-class roots of this melancholy drama are strengthened by a moody sound track featuring songs by Bruce Springsteen and his wife, Patti Scialfa. Rated R for profanity and sexual situations. 96m. **DIR:** Edward Burns. **CAST:** Edward Burns, Lauren Holly, Jon Bon Jovi, Blythe Danner, Ben Affleck. **1998**

NO LOVE FOR JOHNNIE ★★★ This oddly titled drama is about a member of the British Parliament beset by problems in his personal and professional lives. Enjoyable for the performances by the outstanding character actors. B&W; 111m. **DIR:** Ralph Thomas. **CAST:** Peter Finch, Stanley Holloway, Mary Peach, Donald Pleasence, Billie Whitelaw, Dennis Price. **1961**

NO MAN OF HER OWN ★★★★ A big-time gambler marries a local girl on a bet and tries to keep her innocent of his activities. This vintage film has everything the average film fan looks for—drama, romance, and comedy. B&W; 85m. **DIR:** Wesley Ruggles. **CAST:** Clark Gable, Carole Lombard. **1932**

NO MAN'S LAND ★★1/2 Predictable police melodrama, with D. B. Sweeney as a young undercover cop tracking a Porsche theft ring in Los Angeles, headed by smoothie Charlie Sheen. The dialogue is sometimes childish, but the film has pace and economy. Rated R for language and violence. 107m. **DIR:** Peter Werner. **CAST:** Charlie Sheen, D. B. Sweeney, Randy Quaid, Lara Harris, Bill Duke, Arlen Dean Snyder. **1987**

NO MERCY ★★ A rapid-paced thriller about a Chicago cop (Richard Gere) who travels to New Orleans to avenge the murder of his partner. Kim Basinger is the Cajun woman who is Gere's link to the villain. Rated R for violence, language, and sexual situations. 107m. **DIR:** Richard Pearce. **CAST:** Richard Gere, Kim Basinger, Jeroen Krabbé, George Dzundza, William Atherton, Terry Kinney, Bruce McGill, Ray Sharkey, Gary Basaraba. **1986 DVD**

NO, NO NANETTE ★★1/2 A cute and clever version of the 1925 stage hit about a financially troubled old man and his doting niece. The story takes a backseat to Vincent Youmans's songs, chiefly "Tea for Two" and "I Want to Be Happy." Good cast, including some of Hollywood's veteran comics. B&W; 96m. **DIR:** Herbert Wilcox. **CAST:** Anna Neagle, Victor Mature, Richard Carlson, ZaSu Pitts, Roland Young, Eve Arden, Tamara, Billy Gilbert, Helen Broderick, Keye Luke. **1940**

NO ONE CRIES FOREVER ★★★ Don't let the confusing start discourage you—this one gets better! An innocent South African girl is forced into prostitution. When she falls in love with a charming conservationist, her madam has her face disfigured and her boyfriend sets out in search of her. Contains violence and gore. 96m. **DIR:** Jans Rautenbach. **CAST:** Elke Sommer, Howard Carpendale, James Ryan. **1985**

NO PLACE TO HIDE ★★★ Taut thriller finds hard-edged cop Kris Kristofferson attempting to protect Drew Barrymore, who has been targeted for death by the man who killed her sister. The unlikely pair find themselves on the run, trying to stay alive while Kristofferson tracks down the killer. Good performances including Martin Landau as a police chief with an attitude, and fine writing and direction distinguish this entry. Rated R for violence, language, and adult situations. 95m. **DIR:** Richard Danus. **CAST:** Kris Kristofferson, Drew Barrymore, Martin Landau, O. J. Simpson, Dey Young, Bruce Weitz. **1993**

NO REGRETS FOR OUR YOUTH ★★★★ Poignant drama of feminist self-discovery set against the backdrop of a militarist Japanese society. Setsuko Hara gives a harrowing performance as a spoiled housewife who becomes enlightened to the hypocrisy of politics when her lover, a disaffected leftist, is arrested and executed for espionage. In Japanese with English subtitles. B&W; 110m. **DIR:** Akira Kurosawa. **CAST:** Setsuko Hara, Takashi Shimura. **1946**

NO RETREAT, NO SURRENDER 💣 An uninspired cross between *The Karate Kid* and *Rocky IV*. 85m. **DIR:** Corey Yuen. **CAST:** Kurt McKinney, J. W. Fails, Ron Pohnel, Jean-Claude Van Damme. **1985**

NO RETREAT, NO SURRENDER II ★★1/2 An American attempts to rescue his abducted Thai fiancée, who is being held by Russian and Vietnamese troops in the jungles of Southeast Asia. This is a cross between the *Rambo* movies and *Star Wars*, with the addition of whirling legs, kicking feet, and fists flying fast and furious. Rated R for violence. 92m. **DIR:** Corey Yuen. **CAST:** Loreen Avedon, Max Thayer. **1987**

NO RETREAT, NO SURRENDER 3: BLOOD BROTHERS ★★★ In this largely enjoyable martial arts action film, two rival siblings must avenge their father's murder. Well-choreographed fight scenes,

which are a thrill a minute. Rated R for profanity and violence. 97m. **DIR:** Lucas Lo. **CAST:** Loreen Avedon, Keith Vitali, Joseph Campanella. **1990**

NO SAFE HAVEN 💣 Wings Hauser plays a CIA agent whose family is killed by Bolivian drug smugglers. Rated R for violence, nudity, and suggested sex. 92m. **DIR:** Ronnie Rondell. **CAST:** Wings Hauser, Robert Tessier. **1987**

NO SECRETS 💣 Silly teen fantasy features three wealthy girls vacationing at a remote ranch. When a psychotic drifter joins them, each girl finds his antisocial behavior irresistible. Senseless time waster. Rated R for profanity, violence, and sexual situations. 92m. **DIR:** Dezso Magyar. **CAST:** Adam Coleman Howard, Amy Locane. **1990**

NO SMALL AFFAIR ★★1/2 A 16-year-old amateur photographer named Charles Cummings (Jon Cryer) falls in love with an up-and-coming 23-year-old rock singer, Laura Victor (Demi Moore). A mixture of delightfully clever and unabashedly stupid elements. Rated R for nudity, violence, and profanity. 102m. **DIR:** Jerry Schatzberg. **CAST:** Jon Cryer, Demi Moore. **1984**

NO SURRENDER ★★ Eccentric British film about a New Year's Eve party at a run-down nightclub in Liverpool. There is a moral subtext here, but little else that is engaging. Rated R. Contains violence and profanity. 100m. **DIR:** Peter Smith. **CAST:** Michael Angelis, Avis Bunnage, James Ellis, Tom Georgeson, Bernard Hill, Ray McAnally, Joanne Whalley, Elvis Costello. **1986**

•**NO TELLING** ★★1/2 Somber independent film about a husband and wife spending the summer in the country: she tries to do some painting, but he (a medical researcher) locks himself in the barn and conducts experiments on wild animals he's captured. His final masterpiece is probably the most pitiful thing you've ever seen. Not rated; contains profanity and simulated sex. 93m. **DIR:** Larry Fessenden. **CAST:** Miriam Healy-Louie, Stephen Ramsey, David Van Tieghem. **1991**

NO TIME FOR SERGEANTS ★★★★ In this hilarious film version of the Broadway play by Ira Levin, young Andy Griffith is superb as a country boy drafted into the service. You'll scream with laughter as good-natured Will Stockdale (as portrayed by Andy on stage as well as here) proceeds to make a complete shambles of the U.S. Air Force through nothing more than sheer ignorance. B&W; 119m. **DIR:** Mervyn LeRoy. **CAST:** Andy Griffith, Nick Adams, Myron McCormick, Murray Hamilton, Don Knotts. **1957**

NO TIME FOR SERGEANTS (TELEVISION) ★★1/2 Andy Griffith turns in a good performance as a Georgia hick drafted into the army in this 1955 comedy written especially for television. Unfortunately, this type of physical comedy needs lots of rehearsal, something to which live television did not lend itself. Also, the innocent-turning-the-establishment-on-its-ear storyline dates the play. In this case, the theatrical movie is better. B&W; 60m. **DIR:** Alex Segal. **CAST:** Andy Griffith, Harry Clark, Robert Emhardt, Eddie Le Roy, Alexander Clark. **1955**

NO WAY BACK ★★ A cop goes up against a group of white supremacists and their cohorts in this loud, overdone action-adventure film. Rated R for violence and profanity. 92m. **DIR:** Frank Cappello. **CAST:** Russell Crowe, Helen Slater, Michael Lerner, Etsushi Toyokawa. 1996

NO WAY HOME ★★★1/2 Tim Roth delivers a powerful performance as Joey, just out of prison for murder. His attempt to stay straight is complicated when he moves in with his criminal brother and his stripper wife. It doesn't take long before Joey's brother tries to entice him back into a life of crime. Better than one would expect from a straight-to-video effort. Rated R for adult situations, language, nudity, and violence. 101m. **DIR:** Buddy Giovinazzo. **CAST:** Tim Roth, James Russo, Deborah Unger, Saul Stein. 1996

NO WAY OUT ★★★1/2 In this gripping, sexy, and surprising suspense thriller, Kevin Costner stars as a morally upright naval hero who accepts a position with the secretary of defense (Gene Hackman) and his somewhat overzealous assistant (Will Patton, who walks away with the film). Things become a bit sticky when the secretary becomes involved in murder. Rated R for nudity, sexual situations, language, and violence. 116m. **DIR:** Roger Donaldson. **CAST:** Kevin Costner, Gene Hackman, Sean Young, Will Patton, Howard Duff, Iman. 1987 DVD

NO WAY TO TREAT A LADY ★★★★ Excellent thriller with a tour-de-force performance by Rod Steiger, who dons various disguises and personas to strangle women and imprint them with red lipstick lips. Superb script, adapted from William Goldman's novel, and a skilled supporting cast: George Segal as a mothered cop, Eileen Heckart as his delightfully pick-pick-picking mother, and Lee Remick as the attractive love interest. Rated PG for violence. 108m. **DIR:** Jack Smight. **CAST:** Rod Steiger, George Segal, Lee Remick, Eileen Heckart, Michael Dunn, Murray Hamilton. 1968

•**NOAH** ★★★★ Tony Danza scores in this update of the biblical story, playing a crooked construction company owner who is approached by a stranger to build an ark. The film handles all three stages of disbelief with aplomb: First, he's skeptical, then his children, then the townsfolk. With a little bit of faith and the love of his three sons, can a sinner change his ways and create a miracle? Excellent family values and a sense of adventure flood every frame of this made-for-television film. Not rated. 92m. **DIR:** Ken Kwapis. **CAST:** Tony Danza, Jane Sibbett, Wallace Shawn, Chris Marquette, Jesse Moss, Michal Suchanek. 1998

NOAH'S ARK ★★★ A silent epic that uses the Old Testament story of Noah as a simile for World War I. Several animals and bit players actually drowned during the spectacular flood sequence so the torment shown is authentic. The story is corny, but the special effects are excellent. B&W; 127m. **DIR:** Michael Curtiz. **CAST:** George O'Brien, Dolores Costello, Myrna Loy, Noah Beery Sr., Guinn Williams, Louise Fazenda. 1929 DVD

NOBODY LOVES ME ★★★1/2 Being single and pushing age thirty is eating Fanny Fink alive. The attractive airport-security agent is both alone and lonely. Then she meets a gay black psychic and torch singer who looks into her future and changes her life. This exasperating search for a soul mate comically chomps at late-life relationships and a social climate starved for true romance. In German with English subtitles. Not rated; contains adult fare. 104m. **DIR:** Doris Dörrie. **CAST:** Maria Schrader, Pierre Sanoussi-Bliss, Michael Von Au, Elisabeth Trissenaar. 1996

NOBODY'S BOY ★★ Blandly animated run-of-the-mill video fare about an orphan's search for his mother. Along the way he's befriended by a St. Bernard, a chimp, and a parrot. Featuring the voice of Jim Backus. 80m. **DIR:** Jim Flocker. 1985

NOBODY'S CHILDREN ★★★ This made-for-cable movie is based on the true story of an American couple who go to Romania to adopt a child. They must struggle with corrupt politicians, the black market, and the Romanian government bureaucracy. The story is all right, but too long. Not rated; contains graphic news footage. 95m. **DIR:** David Wheatley. **CAST:** Ann-Margret, Jay O. Sanders, Dominique Sanda, Reiner Schoene, Clive Owen. 1994

NOBODY'S FOOL (1986) 🎗 Despite its pedigree—a screenplay by playwright Beth Henley (*Crimes of the Heart*)—this film is a real disappointment. Rated PG-13 for mild violence. 107m. **DIR:** Evelyn Purcell. **CAST:** Rosanna Arquette, Eric Roberts, Mare Winningham, Jim Youngs, Louise Fletcher. 1986

NOBODY'S FOOL (1994) ★★★★ As a 60-year-old construction worker at odds with his family, his boss, and the world in general, Paul Newman is at the peak of his form. This insightful character study, based on Richard Russo's novel, also features topflight support from Jessica Tandy, Bruce Willis, and Melanie Griffith, but make no mistake—it's Newman's own. Rated R for profanity, nudity, and brief violence. 124m. **DIR:** Robert Benton. **CAST:** Paul Newman, Jessica Tandy, Bruce Willis, Melanie Griffith, Dylan Walsh, Pruitt Taylor Vince, Gene Saks, Josef Sommer, Philip Bosco. 1994

NOBODY'S GIRLS ★★★★ Filmmaker Mirra Bank dramatizes the actual lives of five adventurous women who helped settle our last frontier with archival photos, rare film footage, journal entries, and reenactments shot on location in New Mexico and Montana. Cloris Leachman steals the show as a mother-turned-madam, but all involved bring their portrayals to life. Made for PBS, this film boasts high production values. Not rated; contains brief nudity and adult themes. 90m. **DIR:** Mirra Bank. **CAST:** Cloris Leachman, Esther Rolle, Tantoo Cardinal, Angela Alvarado, Bai Ling. 1995

NOBODY'S PERFECT ★★1/2 *Some Like it Hot* redux. This time, the boy behind the skirt (Chad Lowe) is posing as the new girl on the tennis team. Rated PG-13 for language. 90m. **DIR:** Robert Kaylor. **CAST:** Chad Lowe, Gail O'Grady, Robert Vaughn. 1989

NOBODY'S PERFEKT ★★ Three friends all undergoing psychoanalysis (Gabe Kaplan, Robert Klein, and Alex Karras) decide to extort $650.00 from the city of Miami to pay for their car, which was totaled because they ran into a large pothole. Along the way, they become heroes by capturing armored-car robbers. 96m. DIR: Peter Bonerz. CAST: Gabe Kaplan, Alex Karras, Robert Klein, Susan Clark, Paul Stewart, Alex Rocco. 1981

NOCTURNA 💙 This fourth-rate imitation of *Old Dracula* and *Love at First Bite* has Dracula's granddaughter moving to Manhattan. Rated R for nudity. 85m. DIR: Harry Tampa. CAST: Nai Bonet, John Carradine, Yvonne De Carlo, Sy Richardson. 1979

NOCTURNE ★★★ Somewhat deliberate but involving mystery yarn has police detective George Raft risking his career to prove that a composer's apparent suicide was actually murder. Colorful characters and good dialogue. B&W; 88m. DIR: Edwin L. Marin. CAST: George Raft, Lynn Bari, Virginia Huston, Joseph Pevney. 1946

NOISES OFF ★★★★ Hilarious adaptation of the play by Michael Frayn presents Michael Caine as a director struggling to get a saucy comedy and its sometimes sauced performers ready. Director Peter Bogdanovich and his all-star cast capture the total mania of a classic Marx Brothers movie. Rated PG-13 for humorous violence, brief profanity, and suggestive double entendres. 104m. DIR: Peter Bogdanovich. CAST: Carol Burnett, Michael Caine, Denholm Elliott, Julie Hagerty, Marilu Henner, Mark Linn-Baker, Christopher Reeve, John Ritter, Nicollette Sheridan. 1992

NOMADS ★★★ In this thought-provoking and chilling shocker, Pierce Brosnan is a French anthropologist who discovers a secret society of malevolent ghosts living in modern-day Los Angeles. In doing so, he incurs their wrath and endangers the life of a doctor (Lesley-Anne Down). Rated R for profanity, nudity, and violence. 95m. DIR: John McTiernan. CAST: Lesley-Anne Down, Pierce Brosnan, Adam Ant, Mary Woronov. 1986

NOMADS OF THE NORTH ★★1/2 A trapper and his beloved flee to the farthest reaches of the wilderness to escape imprisonment for an accidental murder. But it's the moral struggle of a Canadian Mountie that's at the heart of this picture. This was Lon Chaney's first starring role. B&W; 78m. DIR: David M. Hartford. CAST: Lon Chaney Sr., Betty Blythe, Lewis Stone, Francis McDonald. 1920

NONE BUT THE BRAVE ★★1/2 Story about American and Japanese soldiers stranded on an island during World War II is an interesting premise, but does not make compelling film fare. Frank Sinatra, fine in a small role as a doctor, made his directing debut in this film, the first joint American-Japanese production. 105m. DIR: Frank Sinatra. CAST: Frank Sinatra, Clint Walker, Tommy Sands, Brad Dexter, Tony Bill. 1965

NONE BUT THE LONELY HEART ★★★ Old pro Ethel Barrymore won an Oscar for her sympathetic portrayal of a moody, whining cockney as Cary Grant's mother Ma Mott in this murky drama of broken dreams, thwarted hopes, and petty crime in the slums of London in the late 1930s. Nothing else like it in the Grant filmography. B&W; 113m. DIR: Clifford Odets. CAST: Cary Grant, Ethel Barrymore, Barry Fitzgerald, Jane Wyatt, June Duprez, Dan Duryea. 1944

NOON WINE ★★★★1/2 The fickle nature of human opinion and its ability to savage a victim already down on his luck are the bitter lessons in this adaptation of Katharine Anne Porter's perceptive tale. Porter establishes a stable protagonist (Fred Ward) whose life eventually collapses after he generously provides work on his turn-of-the-century Texas farm for a taciturn loner (Stellan Skarsgard). Suitable for family viewing. 81m. DIR: Michael Fields. CAST: Fred Ward, Lise Hilboldt, Stellan Skarsgard, Pat Hingle, Jon Cryer. 1985

NOOSE HANGS HIGH, THE ★★ One of the comedy team's lesser efforts, and they take a backseat to veteran laugh-getters in the supporting cast. The plot is about $50,000 of stolen money, with Abbott and Costello trying to get it back. B&W; 77m. DIR: Charles Barton. CAST: Bud Abbott, Lou Costello, Leon Errol, Cathy Downes, Mike Mazurki, Joseph Calleia, Fritz Feld. 1948

NORMA JEAN AND MARILYN ★★★1/2 This study of Marilyn Monroe's rise from obscurity to stardom concerns the duality between hardscrabble Norma Jean (Ashley Judd), who'd do anything to succeed, and insecure Marilyn (Mira Sorvino), who just wants people to love her. Even after Norma Jean "becomes" Marilyn, the former hangs around as a nagging conscience; thus, both actresses give their own spin to events in the latter half of this woman's life, but watching her become famous is more intriguing. Rated R for nudity, rape, simulated sex, drug use, profanity, and violence. 133m. DIR: Tim Fywell. CAST: Ashley Judd, Mira Sorvino, Josh Charles, Ron Rifkin, David Dukes, Peter Dobson, Lindsay Crouse. 1996

NORMA RAE ★★★★ Sally Field won her first Oscar for her outstanding performance as a southern textile worker attempting to unionize the mill with the aid of organizer Ron Leibman. Film is based on a true story and has good eyes and ears for authenticity. Entire cast is first-rate. Rated PG, some language, minor violence. 113m. DIR: Martin Ritt. CAST: Sally Field, Ron Leibman, Pat Hingle, Beau Bridges. 1979

NORMAL LIFE ★★★1/2 This fascinating made-for-cable original, based on a true story, chronicles the descent of an ex-cop (Luke Perry) and his drug-dependent wife (Ashley Judd) into debt and crime. Perry and Judd deliver fine performances, and you can't help but pity their characters. The movie would have been better without the numerous and pointless nude scenes. Rated R for violence and nudity. 102m. DIR: John McNaughton. CAST: Ashley Judd, Luke Perry, Jim True. 1996

NORMAN CONQUESTS, THE, EPISODE 1: TABLE MANNERS ★★★1/2 Alan Ayckbourn's clever trilogy is set in a family home in a small English town. Each segment takes place in a different part of the house but encompasses the same span of time. Furthermore, each part is complete in itself, but blends with the others. In the dining room, Norman tries to seduce his two sisters-in-law and draws the rest of the family into the tangle with surprising results. Sara is a treat as she tries to organize meals and control the others. 108m. DIR: Herbert Wise. CAST:

Richard Briers, Penelope Keith, Tom Conti, David Troughton, Fiona Walker, Penelope Wilton. **1980**

NORMAN CONQUESTS, THE, EPISODE 2: LIVING TOGETHER ★★1/2 The parlor is the setting as the family gathers for the weekend. Norman (Tom Conti) keeps everyone on the run as he drinks, manipulates, and seduces. 93m. **DIR:** Herbert Wise. **CAST:** Richard Briers, Penelope Keith, Tom Conti, David Troughton, Fiona Walker, Penelope Wilton. **1980**

NORMAN CONQUESTS, THE, EPISODE 3: ROUND AND ROUND THE GARDEN ★★★1/2 A garden setting rounds out a zany weekend at an English house. As Norman (Tom Conti) pursues his wife's sister, Tom (David Troughton), the visiting vet, misinterprets the goings-on and embarrasses himself in the bargain. 106m. **DIR:** Herbert Wise. **CAST:** Richard Briers, Penelope Keith, Tom Conti, David Troughton, Fiona Walker, Penelope Wilton. **1980**

NORMAN … IS THAT YOU? ★★ This embarrassing look at homophobia has a skillful cast that deserved better. Redd Foxx tries too hard to be funny as a father who finds out his son is gay. The Motown soundtrack is much better than the plot. Rated PG for its discreet handling of an R-rated topic. 91m. **DIR:** George Schlatter. **CAST:** Redd Foxx, Pearl Bailey, Michael Warren, Jayne Meadows, Dennis Dugan. **1976**

NORMAN LOVES ROSE ★★★1/2 In this Australian-made comedy, Tony Owen plays a love-struck teenager who is enamored of his sister-in-law, Carol Kane. When she gets pregnant, the question of paternity arises. Lots of laughs in this one! Rated R. 98m. **DIR:** Henri Safran. **CAST:** Carol Kane, Tony Owen, Warren Mitchell. **1982**

NORMAN'S AWESOME EXPERIENCE 🎬 Boneheaded saga of a nuclear technician, a magazine-cover model, and an Italian photographer accidentally transported back to the Roman Empire. Not rated. 95m. **DIR:** Paul Donovan. **CAST:** Tom McCamus, Laurie Paton, Jacques Lussier. **1989**

NORSEMAN, THE 🎬 This low-budget story of the Vikings is full of stupid historical errors. Rated PG. 90m. **DIR:** Charles B. Pierce. **CAST:** Lee Majors, Charles B. Pierce Jr., Cornel Wilde, Mel Ferrer. **1978**

NORTH ★★1/2 Neglected "perfect son" Elijah Wood decides to become a free agent and trade in his parents for a more attentive couple, in this unsatisfying adaptation of Alan Zweibel's fanciful novel. Despite several dozen weighty cameo appearances, the parental "trial runs" generate no emotion, and a subplot involving a scheming young friend is quite irritating. Only Bruce Willis lends charm, as an unusual guardian angel. Rated PG for mild violence and profanity. 88m. **DIR:** Rob Reiner. **CAST:** Elijah Wood, Bruce Willis, Jon Lovitz, Matthew McCurley. **1994**

NORTH AND SOUTH ★★★1/2 Epic, all-star TV miniseries detailing the events leading up to the Civil War springs vividly to life from the pages of John Jakes's bestselling historical novel. The human drama unfolds on both sides of the conflict, inside the war rooms and bedrooms, and tears apart two friends, played by Patrick Swayze and James Read. Not rated. 561m. **DIR:** Richard T. Heffron. **CAST:** Patrick Swayze, James Read, Kirstie Alley, David Carra-

dine, Lesley-Anne Down, Robert Guillaume, Hal Holbrook, Gene Kelly. **1985**

NORTH AVENUE IRREGULARS, THE ★★1/2 Average Disney film about a young priest (Edward Herrmann) who wants to do something about crime. He enlists a group of churchgoing, do-good women to work with him. Quality cast is wasted on marginal script. Rated G. 100m. **DIR:** Bruce Bilson. **CAST:** Edward Herrmann, Barbara Harris, Cloris Leachman, Susan Clark, Karen Valentine, Michael Constantine, Patsy Kelly, Virginia Capers. **1979 DVD**

NORTH BY NORTHWEST ★★★★ Cary Grant and Eva Marie Saint star in this classic thriller by the master himself, Alfred Hitchcock, who plays (or preys) on the senses and keeps the action at a feverish pitch. The story is typical Hitchcock fare—a matter of mistaken identity embroils a man in espionage and murder. 136m. **DIR:** Alfred Hitchcock. **CAST:** Cary Grant, Eva Marie Saint, James Mason, Martin Landau. **1959 DVD**

NORTH DALLAS FORTY ★★★1/2 Remarkably enough, *North Dallas Forty* isn't just another numbingly predictable sports film. It's an offbeat, sometimes brutal, examination of the business of football. A first-rate Nick Nolte stars. Rated R. 119m. **DIR:** Ted Kotcheff. **CAST:** Nick Nolte, Bo Svenson, G. D. Spradlin, Dayle Haddon, Mac Davis. **1979**

NORTH OF THE RIO GRANDE ★★★ When Hopalong Cassidy's brother is murdered, he, Lucky, and Windy travel to Cottonwood Gulch to find the killers. There's a full-blown Irish musical number tucked into this winner and a saloon girl with a heart for Hoppy who exclaims "It's funny … all my life men like Cassidy have been saying good-bye to me!" as the three friends ride off into the distance. B&W; 67m. **DIR:** Nate Watt. **CAST:** William Boyd, George "Gabby" Hayes, Russell Hayden, Stepen Morris (Morris Ankrum), Lee J. Cobb. **1937**

NORTH SHORE ★★1/2 Matt Adler plays an Arizona teen who desperately wants to make it in Hawaii's North Shore surfing pipeline. The pipeline shots are terrific. Rated PG for mild violence. 92m. **DIR:** William Phelps. **CAST:** Matt Adler, Nia Peeples, John Philbin, Gregory Harrison. **1987**

NORTH SHORE FISH ★★★ This film adaptation of Israel Horovitz's stage play concerns the last day of a struggling Gloucester fish-packing plant and its impact on the already downsized staff. It's a slight piece that may have played well in front of a live audience but seems quaint and somewhat forced in this format; the half-dozen female employees are characterized by little beyond their curses, delivered in impeccable Massachusetts accents, and their contempt for lady-killing manager Tony Danza. Rated R for profanity. 93m. **DIR:** Steve Zuckerman. **CAST:** Mercedes Ruehl, Peter Riegert, Tony Danza, Carroll Baker, Wendie Malick. **1997**

NORTH STAR, THE (1943) ★★★★ This is a well-done World War II film about Russian peasants battling Nazi invaders during the early days of the German invasion of Russia in 1941. It's a bit corny and sentimental in places, but the battle scenes have the usual Milestone high-quality excitement. B&W;

105m. **DIR:** Lewis Milestone. **CAST:** Ruth Gordon, Walter Huston, Anne Baxter, Dana Andrews. **1943**

NORTH STAR (1996) ★★ The production values are surprisingly decent and the scenery quite pleasing, but a weak script and lousy casting pull this apart at the plot seams. James Caan plays the corrupt miner pitted against a half-Indian trapper (Christopher Lambert) in this revisionist thriller set in Alaska. Rated R for violence, profanity, nudity, and sexual situations. 89m. **DIR:** Nils Gaup. **CAST:** James Caan, Christopher Lambert, Catherine McCormack, Burt Young, Jacques François. **1996**

NORTH TO ALASKA ★★★★ Rather than a typical John Wayne Western, this is a John Wayne Northern. It's a rough-and-tumble romantic comedy. Delightfully tongue-in-cheek, it presents the Duke at his two-fisted best. 122m. **DIR:** Henry Hathaway. **CAST:** John Wayne, Stewart Granger, Capucine, Fabian, Ernie Kovacs. **1960**

NORTHEAST OF SEOUL ★★ Three unlikely down-and-outers join forces and end up double-crossing each other in their pursuit of an ancient mystical sword. Very routine. Rated PG for violence. 84m. **DIR:** David Lowell Rich. **CAST:** Anita Ekberg, John Ireland, Victor Buono. **1972**

NORTHERN EXPOSURE (TV SERIES) ★★★★ This little drama began as a routine fish-out-of-water tale and matured into a densely layered, delightful account of the history and ongoing vitality of fictitious Cicely, Alaska (pop. 813). Rob Morrow is a droll bundle of neuroses forced into temporary servitude to repay the state of Alaska for medical school. To catch this program's rhythm, you'll do better to rent or buy all of the episodes. 52m. **CAST:** Rob Morrow, Janine Turner, Barry Corbin, John Corbett, Darren E. Burrows, John Cullum, Cynthia Geary, Elaine Miles, Peg Phillips. **1990–93**

NORTHERN EXTREMES ★★★ A tiny island secedes from Canada after losing its fishing rights and uses a deserted Soviet submarine to underscore the situation. Sharp satire of government and some quirky characterizations, but the tiny budget gets in the way. A good-hearted little comedy, even if the technical quality is extremely uneven. Rated PG for violence and sexual situations. 90m. **DIR:** Paul Donovan. **CAST:** Paul Gross, Denise Virieux. **1993**

NORTHERN LIGHTS ★★★★ Produced, directed, and edited by Rob Nilsson and John Hanson, this independently made feature presents the rich chronicle of a group of Swedish farmers in North Dakota during the winter of 1915–16. Though the budget was a slight $330,000, the film is a triumph of craft and vision. No MPAA rating. B&W; 98m. **DIR:** John Hanson, Rob Nilsson. **CAST:** Robert Behling, Joe Spano. **1979**

NORTHERN PASSAGE ★★ Animals and wildlife are gorgeously photographed, but when people enter they're merely talking heads. A woman with roots in both the white and native worlds tries to find her place in this tale of life in the Canadian frontier. Jeff Fahey, who is given top billing, merely rides through a couple of times. Rated PG-13 for profanity and violence. 97m. **DIR:** Arnaud Selignac. **CAST:** Jeff Fahey,

Neve Campbell, Lorne Brass, Jacques Weber, Genevieve Rochette. **1994**

NORTHERN PURSUIT ★★★ Despite Raoul Walsh's capable direction, this film, about a German heritage Canadian Mountie (Errol Flynn) who feigns defection and guides a party of Nazi saboteurs is pure claptrap. It marked the beginning of Flynn's slow descent into obscurity and, eventually, illness. B&W; 94m. **DIR:** Raoul Walsh. **CAST:** Errol Flynn, Julie Bishop, Tom Tully. **1943**

NORTHWEST MOUNTED POLICE ★★★★ Predictable but loads of fun, the story is set in the Canadian Rockies. The hero is a Texas Ranger. One of the heroines is a half-breed, another a frontier woman with an English accent. 125m. **DIR:** Cecil B. DeMille. **CAST:** Gary Cooper, Paulette Goddard, Madeleine Carroll, Robert Preston, Akim Tamiroff, Robert Ryan, Preston Foster, Lon Chaney Jr., Lynne Overman. **1940**

NORTHWEST OUTPOST ★★ Nelson Eddy's last movie is not up to snuff. The setting of a Russian village in nineteenth-century California is colorful, and the prospect of an Indian attack on the Russian fort is suspenseful. But the story is downright dull. So is the music, even though it was composed by Rudolf Friml. B&W; 91m. **DIR:** Allan Dwan. **CAST:** Nelson Eddy, Ilona Massey, Joseph Schildkraut, Elsa Lanchester, Hugo Haas, Lenore Ulric. **1947**

NORTHWEST PASSAGE ★★★1/2 Spencer Tracy is the hard-driving, intrepid leader of Roger's Rangers, slogging through swamps and over mountains to open new territory in colonial America. Greenhorns Robert Young and Walter Brennan endure his wrath along the way. Adventure abounds. 125m. **DIR:** King Vidor. **CAST:** Spencer Tracy, Robert Young, Walter Brennan, Ruth Hussey, Nat Pendleton. **1940**

NORTHWEST TRAIL ★★ Mountie Bob Steele uncovers a plot to rob the Canadian government by taking gold from an old mine and flying it across the border. 62m. **DIR:** Derwin Abrahams. **CAST:** Bob Steele, Joan Woodbury, John Litel. **1945**

NOSFERATU ★★★★ A product of the German Expressionist era, this is a milestone in the history of world cinema. Director F. W. Murnau seems to make the characters jump out at you. With his skeletal frame, rodent face, long nails, and long, pointed ears, Max Schreck is the most terrifying of all screen vampires. Silent. B&W; 63m. **DIR:** F. W. Murnau. **CAST:** Max Schreck, Gustav von Waggenheim. **1922 DVD**

NOSTALGHIA ★★★★ Andrei Tarkovsky's first film made outside his native Russia is this highly personal work about a Russian poet on a research project in Italy who attempts to turn his longing for his home and family into a positive experience. Tarkovsky's seemingly unblinking stare (you've never seen a camera move so slowly) can yield moments of intense beauty, but you have to be in the mood for it. In Russian and Italian with English subtitles. Not rated. B&W/color; 120m. **DIR:** Andrei Tarkovsky. **CAST:** Oleg Yankovsky, Erland Josephson. **1983 DVD**

NOSTRADAMUS 💔 The life of the fabled medieval physician and seer is turned into a ridiculous, unbelievable bore. If Nostradamus was such a great prophet, why didn't he warn us about films like this? Rated R for nudity. 118m. DIR: Roger Christian. CAST: Tcheky Karyo, Amanda Plummer, Rutger Hauer, F. Murray Abraham. 1994

NOSTRADAMUS KID, THE ★★★ Amusing Australian period piece about a religious youth who believes his preacher's word that the world is coming to an end. Afraid that he will die a virgin, young Ken Elkin breaks free of his conservative background and sets out to experience life and love, and love, and love. Then he meets the right girl, who happens to have the wrong father, who just might end Elkin's world for real. Funny and touching. Rated R for nudity, adult situations, and language. 120m. DIR: Bob Ellis. CAST: Noah Taylor, Miranda Otto, Arthur Dingham, Peter Gwynn. 1992

NOT A PENNY MORE, NOT A PENNY LESS ★★★1/2 A merciless business tycoon fleeces four investors residing in England, one of whom is a transplanted American college instructor. Refusing to remain a victim, the professor gathers the other three and proposes they regain all their losses—not a penny more, nor a penny less—by whatever means necessary. Solid TV adaptation of the Jeffrey Archer novel. 180m. DIR: Clive Donner. CAST: Ed Begley Jr., Edward Asner, François-Eric Gendron, Brian Protheroe, Nicholas Jones, Maryam D'Abo, Jenny Agutter. 1990

NOT AS A STRANGER ★★★★ A testament to the medical profession that doesn't skirt on those with lack of ethics. Olivia de Havilland is somewhat self-conscious in a blond wig and Swedish accent. But she tries hard as the nurse willing to put medical student Robert Mitchum through school by marrying him and caring for him. B&W; 135m. DIR: Stanley Kramer. CAST: Olivia de Havilland, Robert Mitchum, Charles Bickford, Frank Sinatra, Gloria Grahame, Lee Marvin, Broderick Crawford, Lon Chaney Jr., Harry Morgan, Virginia Christine. 1955

NOT FOR PUBLICATION ★★1/2 A writer and a photographer attempt to break out of sleazy tabloid journalism by doing an investigative piece about high-level corruption. Playful, but not as distinctive as Paul Bartel's other works, such as *Eating Raoul* and *Lust in the Dust*. Rated PG for profanity. 87m. DIR: Paul Bartel. CAST: Nancy Allen, David Naughton, Laurence Luckinbill. 1984

NOT IN THIS TOWN ★★★1/2 This made-for-cable drama, based on a true story, is a gripping examination of hate crimes and how one town stood together against the perpetrators. Fine performances from both Kathy Baker and Adam Arkin and an inspiring solution to the problem make this a powerful statement and good entertainment. Rated PG-13 for violence. 95m. DIR: Donald Wrye. CAST: Kathy Baker, Adam Arkin, Ed Begley Jr. 1997

NOT LIKE US 🎥 Producer Roger Corman is releasing some pretty dreadful stuff these days, and this extremely wet little comedy—concerning aliens who skin human beings in order to walk among us unseen—really scrapes the bottom of the barrel. Rated R for gore, violence, nudity, simulated sex, and profanity. 90m. DIR: David Payne. CAST: Joanna Pac-

ula, Peter Onorati, Rainer Grant, Morgan Englund. 1995

NOT MY KID ★★★ Not just another disease-of-the-week vehicle. This telefilm is a well-written look at teenage drug abuse and the havoc it wreaks in a family. 100m. DIR: Michael Tuchner. CAST: George Segal, Stockard Channing, Andrew Robinson, Tate Donovan. 1985

NOT OF THIS EARTH ★★★ Purposely trashy remake of a Roger Corman sci-fi classic from the Fifties. Plenty of action, campy comedy, and sex to hold your interest. Traci Lords is a private nurse assigned to administer blood transfusions to a mysterious, wealthy patient. Once she starts nosing around, the fun starts. Rated R for nudity, simulated sex, and violence. 82m. DIR: Jim Wynorski. CAST: Traci Lords, Arthur Roberts. 1988

NOT OF THIS EARTH (1995) ★★★ Intentionally low-budget remake enjoys healthy special effects, a fun script, and decent performances. Michael York plays an alien who has come to Earth in search of blood. At first he just helps himself, but when he starts meeting resistance, he resorts to all sorts of fiendish ways to extract the crimson gold. Then he meets Amanda, and his whole world is turned upside down. Rated R for nudity, violence, profanity, and adult situations. 92m. DIR: Terence H. Winkless. CAST: Michael York, Parker Stevenson, Richard Belzer, Elizabeth Barondes. 1995

●**NOT ONE LESS** ★★★★ A 13-year-old substitute teacher in a rural Chinese school goes in search of one of her students who has run away to find work in the city. Master director Zhang Yimou offers a change of pace in this surprisingly nimble and sweet-tempered comedy, with charming, natural performances from the children in the school (all of whom use their real names as the names of their characters). In Mandarin with English subtitles. Rated G. 106m. DIR: Zhang Yimou. CAST: Wei Minzhi, Zhang Huike, Tian Zhenda, Gao Enman, Sun Zhimei, Feng Yuying, Li Fanfan. 1999

NOT QUITE HUMAN ★★★ Made for the Disney Channel, this is the first of a trilogy of films about a likable android (Jay Underwood) and his eccentric creator (Alan Thicke). After completing his "project," Thicke flees with his daughter and new "son" to escape toy-company leaders who want to transform the android into the ultimate war toy. Underwood is terrific as the amiable robot. Fun family viewing. 95m. DIR: Steven H. Stern. CAST: Alan Thicke, Jay Underwood, Robyn Lively, Joseph Bologna, Robert Harper. 1987

NOT QUITE HUMAN 2 ★★★1/2 This second film in the Disney trilogy about Chip the android (Jay Underwood) is the most hilarious and heartwarming. Chip goes to college and falls in love with a beautiful android. He must also contend with a computer virus that threatens to destroy him. The gentle romance upgrades an otherwise zany family film. 92m. DIR: Eric Luke. CAST: Jay Underwood, Alan Thicke, Robyn Lively, Katie Barberi, Dey Young. 1989

NOT QUITE PARADISE ★★ A disparate group of people from around the world volunteer to work on an Israeli kibbutz. Surprisingly mean-spirited movie resembles a teens-at-camp comedy, though it offers some laughs in spite of itself. Rated R for sexual humor. 105m. DIR: Lewis Gilbert. CAST: Sam Robards, Joanna Pacula. 1986

NOT WANTED ★★★1/2 Former actress Ida Lupino made her uncredited start as the director of this intelligent melodrama (which she also cowrote and coproduced), replacing Elmer Clifton when he had a heart attack three days into production. Sally Forrest plays a waitress who finds herself an outcast when she bears a child out of wedlock. B&W; 94m. DIR: Elmer Clifton, Ida Lupino. CAST: Sally Forrest, Keefe Brasselle, Leo Penn. 1949

NOT WITHOUT MY DAUGHTER ★★★1/2 The true story of Betty Mahmoody, a Michigan housewife who accompanied her Iranian doctor-husband to his home country for a visit and found herself a prisoner. A terrific performance by Sally Field in the lead role makes it worth the watch. Rated PG-13 for violence and profanity. 115m. DIR: Brian Gilbert. CAST: Sally Field, Alfred Molina, Sheila Rosenthal, Roshan Seth. 1991

NOTHING BUT A MAN ★★★★1/2 Originally released in 1964, this stark tale of class problems within the black community, as compounded by racial pressures, was far ahead of its time. Ivan Dixon is a laborer who falls for Abbey Lincoln, the educated daughter of a preacher. Their social standings, along with the corrosive and wearisome effects of discrimination, put undue strain on their relationship. Not only a superb drama, but an astonishingly astute social history. Not rated. B&W; 92m. DIR: Michael Roemer. CAST: Ivan Dixon, Abbey Lincoln, Gloria Foster, Yaphet Kotto. 1964

NOTHING BUT TROUBLE (1944) ★★1/2 Stan Laurel and Oliver Hardy are the chef and the table server, bringing havoc to a society partygiver. Some good sight gags, but not enough. B&W; 69m. DIR: Sam Taylor. CAST: Stan Laurel, Oliver Hardy, Mary Boland. 1944

NOTHING BUT TROUBLE (1991) ★★ Disappointing, gross comedy—aimed by writer-director Dan Aykroyd at the Police Academy/Porky's crowd—about New Yorkers Chevy Chase and Demi Moore setting off for Atlantic City and being arrested. Rated PG-13 for profanity and gore. 90m. DIR: Dan Aykroyd. CAST: Chevy Chase, Dan Aykroyd, John Candy, Demi Moore. 1991 DVD

NOTHING IN COMMON ★★★1/2 Tom Hanks plays a hotshot advertising executive who must deal with his increasingly demanding parents, who are divorcing after thirty-four years of marriage. Jackie Gleason gives a subtle, touching portrayal of the father. The film succeeds at making the difficult shift from zany humor to pathos. Rated PG for profanity and suggested sex. 120m. DIR: Garry Marshall. CAST: Tom Hanks, Jackie Gleason, Eva Marie Saint, Hector Elizondo, Barry Corbin, Bess Armstrong, Sela Ward. 1986

NOTHING PERSONAL (1980) 💌 A romantic comedy about the fight to stop the slaughter of baby seals? Rated PG. 97m. DIR: George Bloomfield. CAST: Donald Sutherland, Suzanne Somers, Lawrence Dane, Roscoe Lee Browne, Dabney Coleman, Saul Rubinek, John Dehner. 1980

NOTHING PERSONAL (1997) ★★★ In 1975 Belfast, a bombing escalates the state of violence between terrorist factions. This tale of the dehumanizing effects of "the troubles" is well acted but doesn't add much to other films on the subject. Rated R for violence and profanity. 85m. DIR: Thaddeus O'Sullivan. CAST: James Frain, Ian Hart, Michael Gambon, John Lynch. 1997

NOTHING SACRED ★★★★ Ace scriptwriter Ben Hecht's cynical mixture of slapstick and bitterness, perfectly performed by Fredric March and Carole Lombard, makes this satirical comedy a real winner. Vermont innocent, Lombard, is mistakenly thought to be dying of a rare disease. A crack New York reporter (March) pulls out all the stops in exploiting her to near-national sainthood. The boy-bites-man scene is priceless. 75m. DIR: William Wellman. CAST: Carole Lombard, Fredric March, Walter Connolly, Charles Winninger. 1937 DVD

NOTHING TO LOSE ★★1/2 This misfired buddy "road comedy" apparently didn't grow much beyond its inspired teaming of Martin Lawrence and Tim Robbins, who are undeniably funny together. Robbins is a totally square advertising exec who returns home unexpectedly one afternoon only to hear the sounds of betrayal coming from the bedroom; his subsequent near-catatonia behind the wheel is interrupted by high-strung carjacker Lawrence, actually a "decent family man" trying to put food on the table (right). Writer-director Steve Oedekerk winds up with wasted supporting characters and thumpingly unfunny distractions. Rated R for profanity and violence. 97m. DIR: Steve Oedekerk. CAST: Martin Lawrence, Tim Robbins, John C. McGinley, Giancarlo Esposito, Kelly Preston, Michael McKean. 1997 DVD

NOTHING UNDERNEATH 💌 A ranger from Yellowstone goes to Italy, to investigate the disappearance of his kid sister. Not rated; contains violence and nudity. 96m. DIR: Carlo Vanzina. CAST: Tom Schanley, Renée Simonson, Donald Pleasence. 1987

NOTORIOUS ★★★★1/2 Notorious is among the finest Alfred Hitchcock romantic thrillers. Cary Grant, as an American agent, and Ingrid Bergman, as the "notorious" daughter of a convicted traitor, join forces to seek out Nazis in postwar Rio. Claude Rains gives one of his greatest performances. B&W; 101m. DIR: Alfred Hitchcock. CAST: Cary Grant, Ingrid Bergman, Claude Rains, Louis Calhern. 1946 DVD

NOTORIOUS NOBODIES ★★★1/2 Eight vignettes based on true events take place on the same day in different countries and show the range of human-rights violations that occur every day. The film's power comes from its widespread canvas. While individual scenes may be dramatically weak, the cumulative effect is much more than the sum of its parts. Subtitled. Not rated; contains violence. 102m. DIR: Stanislav Stanojevic. 1985

NOTTING HILL ★★★★1/2 You just can't do much better than this extraordinarily charming and entertaining romantic comedy. Circumstances bring together the owner of a barely successful travel bookstore with an elegant American film star who has grown weary of the pretense and insincerity of everybody in her own social circle. But even if such opposites attract, can they stay together? What follows is a winning mixture of sly wit and touching romantic *frisson*. Rated PG-13 for sexual candor and earthy content. 123m. DIR: Roger Michell. CAST: Julia Roberts, Hugh Grant, Hugh Bonneville, Emma Chambers, James Dreyfuss, Rhys Ifans. 1999 DVD

NOUS N'IRONS PLUS AU BOIS ★★ A group of young French Resistance fighters harass German troops in a forest held by the Germans. They capture a young German soldier who falls in love with a French girl. Aside from the presence of Marie-France Pisier, there's little here likely to interest an American audience. In French with English subtitles. 90m. DIR: Georges Dumoulin. CAST: Marie-France Pisier, Siegfried Rauch, Richard Leduc. 1969

NOVEMBER CONSPIRACY, THE ★★★ Political intrigue highlights this familiar tale of a woman reporter assigned to cover a presidential candidate. What should have been a simple assignment turns into a deadly cat-and-mouse chase as the reporter dodges political assassins and deals with the murder of her boyfriend. This direct-to-video effort features a high-profile cast of B-list actors and C-grade plotting. Rated R for language and violence. 103m. DIR: Conrad Janis. CAST: Paige Turco, Dirk Benedict, George Segal, Elliott Gould, Bo Hopkins. 1995

NOVEMBER MEN, THE ★★★ When a Hollywood director goes to work on a film when an assassin planning to kill George Bush during the 1992 presidential campaign, his girlfriend starts to suspect that the movie is only a blueprint for the real thing. A true independent movie from filmmaker Paul Williams (*Dealing*); what this lacks in polish it makes up for in ideas. Rated PG for profanity and violence. 98m. DIR: Paul Williams. CAST: Paul Williams, Leslie Bevis, James Andronica, Robert Davi. 1994

NOW AND FOREVER 🎬 A boutique owner comes back from a clothes-buying trip to find that her husband has been accused of rape. Rated R for violence. 93m. DIR: Adrian Carr. CAST: Cheryl Ladd, Robert Coleby, Carmen Duncan. 1983

NOW AND THEN ★★1/2 Four female childhood friends reunite in Indiana to witness the birth of one chum's baby and yak about the summer of 1970 when they all turned 12 years old. Most of the film is a nostalgia-sweetened flashback, a sort of female *Stand by Me* with *Big Chill* bookends. Rated PG-13 for language and partial nudity. 98m. DIR: Lesli Linka Glatter. CAST: Christina Ricci, Thora Birch, Gaby Hoffman, Ashleigh Aston Moore, Rosie O'Donnell, Melanie Griffith, Demi Moore, Rita Wilson. 1995 DVD

NOW, VOYAGER ★★★1/2 Bette Davis plays a neurotic, unattractive spinster named Charlotte Vale; an ugly duckling, who, of course, blossoms into a beautiful swan. And it's all thanks to the expert counsel of her psychiatrist (Claude Rains) and a shipboard romance with a married man (Paul Henreid). Directed by Irving Rapper, it features the famous cigarette-lighting ritual that set a trend in the 1940s. B&W; 117m. DIR: Irving Rapper. CAST: Bette Davis, Claude Rains, Paul Henreid. 1942

NOW YOU SEE HIM, NOW YOU DON'T ★★ Kurt Russell discovers a formula that will make a person or item invisible. Bad guy Cesar Romero attempts to hijack the discovery for nefarious purposes, which leads to disastrous results. Rated G. 85m. DIR: Robert Butler. CAST: Kurt Russell, Joe Flynn, Jim Backus, Cesar Romero, William Windom. 1972

NOWHERE ★★ The final part of a loose trilogy about whacked-out, culture-obsessed modern teens (following *Totally F***ked Up* and *The Doom Generation*), *Nowhere* is a plotless film about obnoxious L.A. kids. Though intended at least partly as a parody/satire, it is all but unwatchable for any viewers other than the under-25s to whom it panders. Rated R for profanity, drug usage, violence, and sexual situations. 85m. DIR: Gregg Araki. CAST: James Duval, Christina Applegate, Rachel True, Debi Mazar, Chiara Mastroianni, Heather Graham, Traci Lords, Shannen Doherty, John Ritter. 1997

NOWHERE TO HIDE ★★★★ Amy Madigan stars in this exciting adventure of relentless pursuit. Her husband, a marine officer, has uncovered a defective part that is causing accidents in his helicopter squadron. Before he can go public, he is killed. The assassins believe Madigan has the damaging evidence, and the chase is on. An exhilarating climax. Not rated. 100m. DIR: Mario Azzopardi. CAST: Amy Madigan, Michael Ironside, John Colicos, Daniel Hugh-Kelly. 1987

NOWHERE TO RUN (1989) ★★ This coming-of-age film is based on an actual series of murders in Caddo, Texas, during 1960. When paroled con (David Carradine) goes on a killing spree for revenge, six high school seniors find themselves swept into a world of corrupt politicians, crooked cops, and their own hormones. Rated R for violence and profanity. 87m. DIR: Carl Franklin. CAST: David Carradine, Jason Priestley, Henry Jones. 1989

NOWHERE TO RUN (1993) ★★1/2 Jean-Claude Van Damme flexes his biceps and slowly progressing acting ability as an escaped convict who helps a widow save her ranch. Some witty dialogue here and there. Rated R for violence, profanity, and nudity. 90m. DIR: Robert Harmon. CAST: Jean-Claude Van Damme, Rosanna Arquette, Kieran Culkin, Ted Levine, Joss Ackland. 1993 DVD

NUDE BOMB, THE (RETURN OF MAXWELL SMART, THE) ★★ Maxwell Smart (Don Adams), of the *Get Smart!* television series, gets the big-screen treatment in this barely watchable spy spoof about a crazed villain's attempt at world domination—by vaporizing all clothing. This film endured some editing-room "touching up" by *Robot Monster* director Phil Tucker. Rated PG. 94m. DIR: Clive Donner. CAST: Don Adams, Andrea Howard, Vittorio Gassman, Dana Elcar, Rhonda Fleming, Sylvia Kristel, Joey Forman, Norman Lloyd. 1980

NUDES ON THE MOON 🎬 Laughable, cheapo production about a couple of airhead scientists who blast off for the moon. Not rated; contains nudity. 76m. DIR: Anthony Brooks. CAST: Marietta, William Mayer. 1963

•NUDIST COLONY OF THE DEAD ★★1/2 They sing, they dance, they're dead. Nudists commit mass suicide when a church shuts down their colony. When teens show up later at the site, now a religious camp, the nudists rise from the dead and the fun begins.

Some hilarious songs enliven this groaner. Not rated; contains nudity and violence. 90m. DIR: Mark Pirro. CAST: Deborah Stern, Rachel Latt, Braddon Mendelson, Forrest J. Ackerman. 1992

NUDITY REQUIRED 🖤 Two low-lifes pose as producers. Not rated; contains nudity and profanity. 90m. DIR: John Bowman. CAST: Julie Newmar, Troy Donahue. 1990

NUDO DI DONNA (PORTRAIT OF A WOMAN, NUDE) ★★★ Nino Manfredi stars in this Italian comedy as a husband shocked to discover his wife (Eleonora Giorgi) may have posed nude for a painting. Told the model was a hooker, the skeptical Manfredi attempts to discover the truth in this madcap import. In Italian with English subtitles. Not rated. 112m. DIR: Nino Manfredi. CAST: Nino Manfredi, Eleonora Giorgi. 1982

NUEBA YOL ★★★★ An immigrant's fragile dreams have seldom been better illustrated than in this story of a man from Santo Domingo who takes a chance to emigrate to the United States. Life in New York City turns out to be rougher than he had imagined, but he works as best he can to fit in. A charming film filled with gentle humor that makes for excellent family viewing. Not rated; contains no offensive material. In Spanish with English subtitles. 105m. DIR: Angel Muniz. CAST: Luisito Marti, Raul Carbonell. 1995

NUKIE 🖤 Even children will be bored by this tale of two alien brothers who get lost on Earth and must find each other. Rated G. 99m. DIR: Sias Odendal. CAST: Glynis Johns, Steve Railsback. 1993

NUMBER ONE FAN ★★ More *Fatal Attraction*-lite as a sexy actor sleeps with a fan, believing it to be a one-night stand. Then the fan becomes obsessed and people start disappearing. Formula thriller has become a genre unto itself. Rated R for language, nudity, and violence. 93m. DIR: Jane Simpson. CAST: Chad McQueen, Catherine Mary Stewart, Renee Ammann, Hoyt Axton, Nina Blackwood. 1994

NUMBER ONE OF THE SECRET SERVICE ★★★ In this enjoyable spoof of James Bond films, secret agent Charles Blind attempts to stop evil Arthur Loveday from killing prominent international financiers. Rated PG. 87m. DIR: Lindsay Shonteff. CAST: Nicky Henson, Richard Todd, Aimi MacDonald, Geoffrey Keen, Sue Lloyd, Dudley Sutton, Jon Pertwee. 1970

NUMBER ONE WITH A BULLET ★★ Uninspired police thriller-buddy movie suffers from a contrived script. Rated R for violence, profanity, and nudity. 103m. DIR: Jack Smight. CAST: Robert Carradine, Billy Dee Williams, Valerie Bertinelli, Peter Graves, Doris Roberts. 1987

NUMBER 17 ★★1/2 Seldom-seen thriller from Alfred Hitchcock is a humorous departure from his later more obsessive films, but it still maintains his wry touches and unusual characters. Once again an unsuspecting innocent (in this case, a hobo) comes across something that places him in jeopardy (a gang of jewel thieves). B&W; 83m. DIR: Alfred Hitchcock. CAST: Leon M. Lion, Anne Grey, Donald Calthrop, Barry Jones. 1932 DVD

NUN, THE (LA RELIGIEUSE) ★★ Forced into a nunnery by her family's poverty, a young woman tries to maintain her personal dignity despite physical and sexual abuse. While this is new-wave director Jacques Rivette's most accessible film, it still isn't easygoing. A serious film that is a chore to watch. In French with English subtitles. B&W; 140m. DIR: Jacques Rivette. CAST: Anna Karina, Lilo Pulver, Francisco Rabal. 1965

NUNS ON THE RUN ★★★★ In this hilarious farce, Eric Idle and Robbie Coltrane play lower-echelon English crooks who decide to rip off their boss and fly to Brazil. When their plan goes awry, they are forced to hide in a convent and disguise themselves as nuns. What writer-director Jonathan Lynn and his actors do with the premise will have you gasping for breath after fits of uproarious laughter. Rated PG-13 for profanity and sexual humor. 90m. DIR: Jonathan Lynn. CAST: Eric Idle, Robbie Coltrane, Janet Suzman. 1990

NUN'S STORY, THE ★★★ A record of a devoted nun's ultimate rebellion against vows of chastity, obedience, silence, and poverty, this Audrey Hepburn starrer was one of the big box-office hits of the 1950s. The wistful and winning Miss Hepburn shines. The supporting cast is excellent. 152m. DIR: Fred Zinnemann. CAST: Audrey Hepburn, Edith Evans, Peter Finch, Dean Jagger, Beatrice Straight, Colleen Dewhurst, Peggy Ashcroft, Mildred Dunnock. 1959

NURSE, THE ★★★ Wicked genre thriller about a woman seeking revenge on the man who pushed her father into killing himself and his family. Laura has waited for the right moment to get even with Bob Martin. That moment arrives when he has a sudden stroke, and Laura signs on as his personal nurse. Poor Bob. Rated R for adult situations, language, nudity, and violence. 94m. DIR: Robert Malenfant. CAST: Lisa Zane, John Stockwell, Janet Gunn, William R. Moses, Nancy Dussault, Jay Underwood. 1996

NURSE EDITH CAVELL ★★★ The story of England's second most famous nurse, who helped transport refugee soldiers out of German-held Belgium during World War I. The film delivered a dramatically satisfying antiwar message just as World War II got under way. B&W; 95m. DIR: Herbert Wilcox. CAST: Anna Neagle, Edna May Oliver, George Sanders, ZaSu Pitts, H. B. Warner, May Robson, Robert Coote, Martin Kosleck, Mary Howard. 1939

•**NUT, THE** ★★1/2 Eccentric socialite tries to win the girl of his dreams by helping her in her scheme to rehabilitate underprivileged children. Douglas Fairbanks spoofs social work in an uneven mix of gangsters, gags, innovative filming, and pedestrian humor. Silent. B&W; 87m. DIR: Ted Reed. CAST: Douglas Fairbanks Sr., Marguerite de la Motte, William Lowery, Barbara La Marr. 1921

NUTCRACKER PRINCE, THE ★★1/2 Animated version of E.T.A. Hoffman's book *The Nutcracker and the Mouse King* benefits greatly from the voice talents of Kiefer Sutherland, Megan Follows, Peter O'Toole, Mike McDonald, and Phyllis Diller, who bring life to this fanciful tale of a young girl who joins the Nutcracker in his battle against the evil Mouse King. Rated G. 75m. DIR: Paul Schibli. 1990

NUTS ★★★★ Star-producer Barbra Streisand chaperoned Tom Topor's deft play to the big screen and gave herself a meaty starring role in the process. She's a high-toned prostitute facing a murder charge who may not get her day in court, because her mother and stepfather would rather bury her in an insane asylum. Rated R for language and sexual themes. 116m. DIR: Martin Ritt. CAST: Barbra Streisand, Richard Dreyfuss, Maureen Stapleton, Eli Wallach, Robert Webber, James Whitmore, Karl Malden. 1987

NUTT HOUSE, THE ♥ Unfunny bit of juvenilia about twin brothers, one an institutionalized nutcase and the other a politician. Rated PG-13 for implied sexual activity, brief nudity, and cartoonish violence. 90m. DIR: Adam Rifkin. CAST: Stephen Kearney, Traci Lords, Amy Yasbeck. 1992 DVD

NUTTY PROFESSOR, THE ★★★★ Jerry Lewis's funniest self-directed comedy, this release—a take-off on Robert Louis Stevenson's *Dr. Jekyll and Mr. Hyde*—is about a klutz who becomes a smoothie when he drinks a magic formula. Reportedly, this was Lewis's put-down of former partner Dean Martin. 107m. DIR: Jerry Lewis. CAST: Jerry Lewis, Stella Stevens, Kathleen Freeman. 1963

NUTTY PROFESSOR, THE (1996) ★★★★ Eddie Murphy comes back with a vengeance in this remake of the 1963 Jerry Lewis comedy. As shy, overweight professor Sherman Klump, Murphy discovers a formula that allows him to shed pounds and inhibitions. It comes just in time, as Sherman has fallen in love with beautiful grad student Jada Pinkett, whom he can now romance—without revealing his true identity—as a slender man-about-town. Unfortunately, Sherman's chemical concoction proves to be anything but stable, bringing plenty of laughs to this surprisingly heartwarming tale. Rated PG-13 for profanity and scatological humor. 95m. DIR: Tom Shadyac. CAST: Eddie Murphy, Jada Pinkett, James Coburn, Larry Miller, Dave Chappelle, John Ales. 1996 DVD

NYMPHOID BARBARIAN IN DINOSAUR HELL, A ♥ The best thing about this film is its title. Not rated; contains violence and nudity. 84m. DIR: Brett Piper. CAST: Linda Corwin. 1990 DVD

O LUCKY MAN! ★★★★ Offbeat, often stunning story of a young salesman (Malcolm McDowell) and his efforts and obstacles in reaching the top rung of the success ladder. Allegorical and surrealistic at times, this film takes its own course like a fine piece of music. Great acting by a great cast (many of the principals play multiple roles) makes this a real viewing pleasure. Some adult situations and language. Rated R. 173m. DIR: Lindsay Anderson. CAST: Malcolm McDowell, Rachel Roberts, Ralph Richardson, Alan Price, Lindsay Anderson. 1973

O PIONEERS! ★★1/2 Eons distant from her film debut in Kong's palm, a self-assured, strong Jessica Lange bests male sibling opposition and competition and the rigors of Nebraska farm life to win and prevail. The gait is slow, the mood a mite somber, but the aim is true. 100m. DIR: Glenn Jordan. CAST: Jessica Lange, David Strathairn, Tom Aldredge, Anne Heche, Heather Graham. 1992

OASIS OF THE ZOMBIES ♥ Awful chopped-up version of a European movie. Zombies guard a Nazi treasure buried in the desert. Dubbed. Not rated; contains violence. 94m. DIR: Jess (Jesus) Franco. CAST: Manuel Gelin, Eduardo Fajardo, Lina Romay, Antonio Mayans. 1982

OBJECT OF BEAUTY, THE ★★ The best things in life may be free, but you can't prove it to the Gold Card–flashing Jake and Tina, a jet-setting duo who've been living a life of incredible luxury. Played by John Malkovich and Andie MacDowell, they're the central characters in this inconsistent and somewhat flat comedy from writer-director Michael Lindsay-Hogg. Rated R. 110m. DIR: Michael Lindsay-Hogg. CAST: John Malkovich, Andie MacDowell, Rudi Davies. 1991 DVD

OBJECT OF MY AFFECTION, THE ★★★ A young social worker (Jennifer Aniston) finds herself falling in love with her gay roommate (Paul Rudd) just as she becomes pregnant by her insensitive boyfriend (John Pankow). This glossy, unusual romantic comedy has an intelligent script by Pulitzer Prize–winning playwright Wendy Wasserstein, deft direction by Nicholas Hytner, and an appealing cast. Rated R for profanity and mature themes. 111m. DIR: Nicholas Hytner. CAST: Jennifer Aniston, Paul Rudd, John Pankow, Alan Alda, Allison Janney, Nigel Hawthorne. 1998

OBJECT OF OBSESSION ♥ Run-of-the-mill sex thriller about two strangers who ignite each other's passions, driving them to extremes. Simple and silly. Rated R for nudity, violence, and adult language. 91m. DIR: Alexander Gregory Hippolyte. CAST: Scott Valentine, Erika Anderson, Liza Whitcraft, Robert Keith. 1994 DVD

OBJECTIVE, BURMA! ★★1/2 During World War II a tough bunch of paratroopers are dropped into Burma to destroy a radar station and kill Japanese—but even with Errol Flynn in charge, they run into trouble. Overlong action film. B&W; 142m. DIR: Raoul Walsh. CAST: Errol Flynn, William Prince, James Brown, George Tobias, Henry Hull, Warner Anderson, Richard Erdman, Anthony Caruso, Hugh Beaumont. 1945

OBLIVION ★★ Briefly glimpsed stop-motion monsters cannot save this inept science-fiction Western that exists only to give paychecks to B-actors trading on their old television roles. It's pretty embarrassing to watch George Takei cradle a bottle of whiskey and slur, "Jim … beam me up!" Rated PG-13 for violence and profanity. 94m. DIR: Sam Irvin. CAST: Richard Joseph Paul, Jackie Swanson, Meg Foster, Isaac Hayes, Julie Newmar, George Takei. 1994

OBLIVION 2: BACKLASH ★★ Low-budget nonsense set in Badlands, a real wild West located in another galaxy. There, in the small rustic town of Oblivion, a bounty hunter named Sweeney is trying to keep his prisoner safe from an evil warlord. Lots of dusty, tumbleweed performances and so-so makeup effects do little to inspire the weak story. Rated PG-13 for violence. 82m. DIR: Sam Irvin. CAST: Richard Joseph Paul, Jackie Swanson, Andrew Divoff, Meg Foster, Isaac Hayes, Julie Newmar, George Takei. 1995

OBLOMOV ★★★★ This thoroughly delightful film has as its main character Oblomov, a man who has chosen to sleep his life away. Then along comes a childhood friend who helps him explore a new meaning of life. A beautifully crafted triumph for director Nikita Mikhalkov (*A Slave of Love*). In Russian with English subtitles. MPAA not rated. 146m. DIR: Nikita Mikhalkov. CAST: Oleg Tabakov, Elena Soloyei. 1980

OBLONG BOX, THE ★★ This little gothic horror, taken from an Edgar Allan Poe short story, can't escape the clichés of its genre: grave robbers, screaming women, lots of cleavage, and the hero's bride to be, who is unaware of her betrothed's wrongdoings. Sound familiar? Rated R (but more like a PG by today's standards) for violence. 91m. DIR: Gordon Hessler. CAST: Vincent Price, Christopher Lee, Rupert Davies, Sally Geeson. 1969

OBSESSED ★★★1/2 After her son is accidentally struck and killed by the car of an American businessman, a Montreal woman feels improperly served by the legal system and plots revenge. Intelligently written drama about grief and responsibility. Rated PG-13. 103m. DIR: Robin Spry. CAST: Kerrie Keane, Daniel Pilon, Saul Rubinek, Colleen Dewhurst, Alan Thicke. 1988

OBSESSION ★★★★ This is director Brian De Palma's tour de force. Bernard Hermann scores again, his music as effective as that in *Taxi Driver*. The script, about a widower who meets his former wife's exact double, was written by Paul Schrader (in collaboration with De Palma). Critics enthusiastically compare this with prime Hitchcock, and it more than qualifies. Rated PG. 98m. DIR: Brian De Palma. CAST: Cliff Robertson, Genevieve Bujold, John Lithgow. 1976

OBSESSION: A TASTE FOR FEAR 🖤 Tacky, tasteless, disgusting Italian film about the brutal murders of women starring in bondage-type porno films. 90m. DIR: Piccio Raffanini. CAST: Virginia Hey, Gerard Darmon. 1989

OBSESSIVE LOVE ★★1/2 *Fatal Attraction*–like made-for-TV thriller has soap-opera star Simon Mac-Corkindale fending off fan Yvette Mimieux. Handsome leads and topical story make up for an overly familiar plot. Not rated; contains adult language and situations. 97m. DIR: Steven H. Stern. CAST: Yvette Mimieux, Simon MacCorkindale, Constance McCashin, Lainie Kazan, Kin Shriner. 1984

O.C. & STIGGS ★★★ Inspired by characters from *National Lampoon*, this offbeat film has two teenagers whose goal is to make life completely miserable for the local bigot (Paul Dooley), an obnoxious insurance magnate. Another energetic iconoclastic comedy from Robert Altman. Not rated.

109m. DIR: Robert Altman. CAST: Daniel H. Jenkins, Neill Barry, Paul Dooley, Jane Curtin, Martin Mull, Dennis Hopper, Ray Walston, Jon Cryer, Melvin Van Peebles. 1987

OCCASIONAL HELL, AN ★★1/2 Not-bad thriller with Tom Berenger as a college professor who reverts to his former career as a cop when a colleague's widow (Valeria Golino) is accused of murder. The storyline is overly crowded, but it does hold your attention. Rated R for nudity, profanity, substance abuse, and sexual situations. 93m. DIR: Salome Breziner. CAST: Tom Berenger, Valeria Golino, Kari Wuhrer, Robert Davi, Stephen Lang. 1997 DVD

OCCULTIST, THE 🖤 Pseudocampy adventure about a private eye hired to protect a visiting Caribbean leader from voodoo and assassins. Not rated, it has mild violence and suggestiveness. 80m. DIR: Tim Kincaid. CAST: Rick Gianasi, Joe Derrig, Jennifer Kanter, Matt Mitler. 1987

OCCURRENCE AT OWL CREEK BRIDGE, AN ★★★1/2 This fascinating French film looks at the last fleeting moments of the life of a man being hanged from the bridge of the title during the American Civil War. This memorable short film works on all levels. B&W; 22m. DIR: Robert Enrico. CAST: Roger Jacquet, Anne Cornaly. 1962

OCEAN'S ELEVEN ★★★ A twist ending, several stars, and good production values save this tale of an attempted robbery in Las Vegas. Frank Sinatra is the leader of the gang, and his now-famous "rat pack" are the gang members. Lightweight but pleasant. 127m. DIR: Lewis Milestone. CAST: Frank Sinatra, Dean Martin, Sammy Davis Jr., Peter Lawford, Angie Dickinson, Cesar Romero. 1960

OCEANS OF FIRE ★★ Predictable formula adventure-saga about five ex-cons and head honcho, Gregory Harrison, putting up an oil rig off the South American coast. Only a star-studded cast saves this one from the depths of mediocrity. Rated PG. 90m. DIR: Steve Carver. CAST: Gregory Harrison, Billy Dee Williams, Lyle Alzado, Tony Burton, Ray "Boom Boom" Mancini, Ken Norton, Lee Ving, Cynthia Sikes, David Carradine. 1987

OCTAGON, THE ★★ This "kung fu" flick stars Chuck Norris as a bodyguard for Karen Carlson. Norris naturally takes on multiple opponents and beats them easily. Rated R. 103m. DIR: Eric Karson. CAST: Chuck Norris, Karen Carlson, Lee Van Cleef, Jack Carter. 1980

OCTAMAN ★★ Dull low-budget effort with a group of vacationers under attack by a funny-looking walking octopus-man created by a very young Rick Baker, who has since gone on to much bigger and better things. Rated PG for mild violence. 90m. DIR: Harry Essex. CAST: Kerwin Mathews, Pier Angeli, Jeff Morrow. 1971

OCTAVIA 🖤 A ridiculously sappy fairy tale that quickly falls into an exploitation mode. Rated R. 93m. DIR: David Beaird. CAST: Susan Curtis, Neil Kinsella, Jake Foley. 1982

OCTOBER (TEN DAYS THAT SHOOK THE WORLD) ★★★★ This contribution to the tenth anniversary of the Russian Revolution of 1917 is as dazzling in its imagery as it is obscure in its storyline. The events leading up to the Cossacks' storming of the Winter Palace are refracted through a sensibility more interested in "Intellectual Cinema" than in routine plot formulas—making it perhaps more interesting to film history buffs than casual viewers. Silent. B&W; 85m. **DIR:** Sergei Eisenstein. **CAST:** V. Nikandrov, N. Popov. **1928**

OCTOBER SKY ★★★★ Heroes sometimes come in deceptive packages, and that's the case with this uplifting and fact-based story of Homer H. Hickam Jr., a West Virginia coal miner's son who stared up into the sky during that fateful day when the Soviet satellite Sputnik first passed overhead, and decided to become something other than an early candidate for death by black lung. Encouraged by a high-school teacher, Homer and several friends develop an interest in rocketry. Scripter Lewis Colick, working from Hickam's biography, *Rocket Boys*, fashions a tale that initially, makes us sympathetic disbelievers, just like Homer's classmates. But we're slowly won over with small and credible triumphs of Homer and his friends. This one's a winner: a film about real people who overcame unimaginable obstacles. Rated PG for mild profanity. 108m. **DIR:** Joe Johnston. **CAST:** Jake Gyllenhaal, Chris Cooper, William Lee Scott, Chris Owen, Chad Lindberg, Natalie Canerday, Laura Dern. **1999 DVD**

OCTOPUSSY ★★★1/2 Roger Moore returns as James Bond in the thirteenth screen adventure of Ian Fleming's superspy. It's like an adult-oriented *Raiders of the Lost Ark*: light, fast-paced, funny, and almost over before you know it—almost, because the film tends to overstay its welcome just a bit. Rated PG for violence and suggested sex. 130m. **DIR:** John Glen. **CAST:** Roger Moore, Maud Adams, Louis Jourdan. **1983**

ODD ANGRY SHOT, THE ★★★ This low-key film about Australian soldiers stationed in Vietnam during the undeclared war is a good attempt to make sense out of a senseless situation as Bryan Brown and his comrades attempt to come to grips with the morality of their involvement in a fight they have no heart for. Odd, sometimes highly effective blend of comedy and drama characterize this offbeat war entry. Some violence; adult situations and language. 89m. **DIR:** Tom Jeffrey. **CAST:** Bryan Brown, John Hargreaves, Graham Kennedy. **1979**

ODD COUPLE, THE ★★★★ Walter Matthau as Oscar Madison and Jack Lemmon as Felix Unger bring Neil Simon's delightful stage play to life in this comedy. They play two divorced men who try living together. The biggest laughs come from the fact that Felix is "Mr. Clean" and Oscar is a total slob—they're constantly getting on each other's nerves. Rated G. 105m. **DIR:** Gene Saks. **CAST:** Walter Matthau, Jack Lemmon, John Fiedler, Herb Edelman. **1968**

ODD COUPLE II, THE ★★★ In the wake of both *Grumpy Old Men* films and *Out to Sea*, the old dogs (Jack Lemmon and Walter Matthau) don't have any tricks that we haven't already seen repeatedly. Felix Ungar and Oscar Madison reunite, after seventeen years, for the wedding of the former's daughter to the latter's son (stolen without so much as a by-your-leave from the aforementioned *Grumpy Old Men*

sagas). Rated PG-13 for profanity and mild vulgarity. 97m. **DIR:** Howard Deutch. **CAST:** Jack Lemmon, Walter Matthau, Christine Baranski, Barnard Hughes, Jonathan Silverman, Jean Smart. **1998 DVD**

ODD JOB, THE ★★1/2 Monty Python's Graham Chapman wrote and starred in this comedy about a depressed businessman who hires a hitman to kill him. When he decides that life is worth living after all, he finds that he can't cancel his contract. Full of oddball characters and silly situations, but somehow it never builds up a full head of steam. Not rated. 86m. **DIR:** Peter Medak. **CAST:** Graham Chapman, David Jason, Diana Quick, Bill Paterson, Simon Williams. **1978**

ODD MAN OUT ★★★★ Carol Reed directed this suspenseful drama about a wounded IRA gunman (James Mason) on the run in Belfast and the people who help and hinder his escape. One of the hallmarks of postwar British cinema. B&W; 113m. **DIR:** Carol Reed. **CAST:** James Mason, Robert Newton, Kathleen Ryan, Dan O'Herlihy. **1946 DVD**

ODD OBSESSION ★★ An aging man hopes to revive his waning potency. In Japanese with often incomplete or confusing English subtitles. Not rated, it contains off-camera sex. 107m. **DIR:** Kon Ichikawa. **CAST:** Machiko Kyo, Tatsuya Nakadai. **1960**

ODDBALL HALL ✓ Jewel thieves masquerade as members of a fraternal order of do-gooders in this flat comedy of mistaken identities. Rated PG. 87m. **DIR:** Jackson Hunsicker. **CAST:** Don Ameche, Burgess Meredith, Bill Maynard. **1990**

ODDBALLS ✓ Confusing comedy. Rated PG for obscenities and sexual situations. 92m. **DIR:** Miklos Lente. **CAST:** Foster Brooks, Michael Macdonald. **1984**

ODE TO BILLY JOE ★★★ For those who listened to Bobbie Gentry's hit song and wondered why Billy Joe jumped off the Talahatchie Bridge, this movie tries to provide one hypothesis. Robby Benson plays Billy Joe with just the right amount of innocence and confusion to be convincing as a youth who doubts his sexual orientation. Rated PG. 108m. **DIR:** Max Baer. **CAST:** Robby Benson, Glynnis O'Connor, Joan Hotchkis. **1976**

ODESSA FILE, THE ★★ Frederick Forsyth wrote the bestselling novel, but little of the zip remains in this weary film adaptation. German journalist Jon Voight learns of a secret file that may expose some former Nazis. Rated PG for violence. 128m. **DIR:** Ronald Neame. **CAST:** Jon Voight, Maximilian Schell, Derek Jacobi, Maria Schell. **1974 DVD**

ODYSSEY, THE ★★★ Armand Assante, properly Homeric in the central role, evolves from arrogant warrior to mature leader over a twenty-year period. Faithful wife Penelope never wavers in her devotion, while he is seduced by a witch and a beautiful goddess, and fights strange creatures on his long voyage home. Great location shots, fine costumes, and decent special effects make this very watchable. The only flaw is a lack of character development, due to the ambitious desire to cram Homer's twenty-four books into a two-night extravaganza. Not rated; contains violence and sexual situations. 180m. **DIR:** Andrei Konchalovsky. **CAST:** Armand Assante, Greta

Scacchi, Isabella Rossellini, Eric Roberts, Bernadette Peters, Vanessa L. Williams. **1997**

OEDIPUS REX (1957) ★★1/2 Good adaptation of Sophocles's tragedy. Douglas Rain plays Oedipus, the doomed hero, who kills his father and marries his mother in fulfillment of the prophecy. 87m. **DIR:** Tyrone Guthrie. **CAST:** Douglas Rain, Douglas Campbell. **1957**

OEDIPUS REX (1967) ★★ Disappointing adaptation of Sophocles' tragedy, offered in both contemporary and historical settings. Visually satisfying, but too excessive and unengaging. In Italian with English subtitles. Not rated; contains nudity and violence. 110m. **DIR:** Pier Paolo Pasolini. **CAST:** Franco Citti, Silvana Mangano, Alida Valli, Julian Beck. **1967**

OF HUMAN BONDAGE (1934) ★★★1/2 A young doctor (Leslie Howard) becomes obsessed with a sluttish waitress (Bette Davis), almost causing his downfall. Fine acting by all, with Davis an absolute knockout. No rating, but still a little adult for the kiddies. B&W; 83m. **DIR:** John Cromwell. **CAST:** Bette Davis, Leslie Howard, Alan Hale Sr., Frances Dee. **1934**

OF HUMAN BONDAGE (1964) ★★★★1/2 Excellent remake of the 1934 film with Bette Davis. This time Kim Novak plays Mildred Rogers, the promiscuous free spirit who becomes the obsession of Philip Carey (Laurence Harvey). Harvey's performance is wonderfully understated, and Novak plays the slut to the hilt without overdoing it. B&W; 100m. **DIR:** Ken Hughes. **CAST:** Kim Novak, Laurence Harvey, Robert Morley, Siobhan McKenna, Roger Livesey, Nanette Newman, Ronald Lacey. **1964**

OF HUMAN HEARTS ★★★1/2 A fine piece of Americana features Walter Huston as a backwoods traveling preacher whose son doesn't understand his faith and dedication to others. You'll even forgive the hokey ending with Abraham Lincoln (John Carradine) chiding selfish James Stewart for neglecting his mother. B&W; 100m. **DIR:** Clarence Brown. **CAST:** Walter Huston, James Stewart, Beulah Bondi, Guy Kibbee, Charles Coburn, John Carradine, Ann Rutherford, Charley Grapewin, Gene Lockhart, Clem Bevans, Gene Reynolds. **1938**

OF LOVE AND SHADOWS ❤ Like *The House of the Spirits,* this is a potboiler based on a novel by Isabel Allende that tried to mix sociopolitical analysis of Chile with trashy soap opera. Rated R for violence, profanity, and sexual situations. 109m. **DIR:** Betty Kaplan. **CAST:** Antonio Banderas, Jennifer Connelly, Camille Gallardo, Stefania Sandrelli. **1994**

OF MICE AND MEN (1981) ★★★1/2 Robert Blake is George, Randy Quaid is big, dim-witted Lenny in this Blake-produced TV remake of the classic 1939 Burgess Meredith/Lon Chaney Jr. rendition of John Steinbeck's morality tale. While not as sensitive as the original, this version merits attention and appreciation. 125m. **DIR:** Reza S. Badiyi. **CAST:** Robert Blake, Randy Quaid, Lew Ayres, Pat Hingle, Cassie Yates. **1981**

OF MICE AND MEN (1992) ★★★★★ Actor-director Gary Sinise, working with a superb script from Horton Foote, delivers a hauntingly poignant adaptation of John Steinbeck's melancholy study of Depression-era California migrant workers. John Malkovich steals the film as the hulking Lenny, an inarticulate simpleton equally fascinated by puppies and pretty girls. Rated PG-13 for profanity and violence. 110m. **DIR:** Gary Sinise. **CAST:** Gary Sinise, John Malkovich, Casey Siemaszko, Ray Walston, Sherilyn Fenn. **1992**

OF PURE BLOOD ★★ A hoot of a made-for-television movie that wastes the talents of star Lee Remick who plays the distraught mother of a man killed in Germany. When she investigates her son's death, she immediately is thrown into a conspiracy involving Nazis and a genetic-breeding program. One-dimensional characters, corny dialogue, and laughable situations. 100m. **DIR:** Joseph Sargent. **CAST:** Lee Remick, Patrick McGoohan, Gottfried John, Richard Munch, Edith Schneider. **1986**

OF UNKNOWN ORIGIN ★★1/2 Flashes of unintentional humor enliven this shocker, about a suburban family terrorized in their home by a monstrous rat. Contains some inventive photography and effects, but mediocre acting and forgettable music. Bring on the exterminator! Rated R. 88m. **DIR:** George Pan Cosmatos. **CAST:** Peter Weller, Jennifer Dale, Lawrence Dane. **1983**

OFF AND RUNNING ★★ This witless romantic comedy sat on the shelf for five years before winning pay-cable release, and it's easy to see why. Mitch Glazer's ridiculous script doesn't even begin to make sense, and leads Cyndi Lauper and David Keith have zero chemistry. They become involved with the death of a champion racehorse, a kidnapped kid, and a standard-issue assassin. Rated PG-13 for profanity and violence. 91m. **DIR:** Edward Bianchi. **CAST:** Cyndi Lauper, David Keith, Johnny Pinto, Jose Perez, David Thornton, Richard Belzer. **1990**

OFF BEAT ★★ This attempt at an old-fashioned romantic comedy succeeds as a romance, but as a comedy, it elicits only an occasional chuckle. One gains instant sympathy for captivating Meg Tilly's vulnerable big-city police officer. Rated PG. 100m. **DIR:** Michael Dinner. **CAST:** Meg Tilly, Judge Reinhold, Cleavant Derricks, Harvey Keitel. **1986**

OFF LIMITS (1953) ★★ Marilyn Maxwell adds a little "oomph" to this otherwise silly story of two army buddies and their antics. B&W; 89m. **DIR:** George Marshall. **CAST:** Bob Hope, Mickey Rooney, Marilyn Maxwell, Marvin Miller. **1953**

OFF LIMITS (1988) ★★★ Saigon, 1968, makes a noisy and violent background for this murder mystery. Willem Dafoe and Gregory Hines are a pair of military investigators assigned to find the high-ranking killer of local prostitutes. The two leads have good chemistry, Amanda Pays is credible as a sympathetic nun, and Scott Glenn is superb as a warped, messianic infantry colonel. Don't expect the plot to make much sense. Rated R for extreme language, violence, and brief nudity. 102m. **DIR:** Christopher Crowe. **CAST:** Willem Dafoe, Gregory Hines, Fred Ward, Amanda Pays, Scott Glenn. **1988**

OFF THE MARK ★★ This off-the-wall comedy centers around Mark Neely, who once hosted a Russian boy (Terry Farrell) in his home for a year. Now they're both grown up and competing in a triathlon. The two leads are a delight. 81m. **DIR:** Bill Berry.

CAST: Mark Neely, Terry Farrell, Virginia Capers, Jon Cypher, Barry Corbin. 1986

OFF THE WALL 🎬 A Tennessee speed demon (Rosanna Arquette) picks up two handsome hitchhikers. Rated R. 86m. DIR: Rick Friedberg. CAST: Paul Sorvino, Patrick Cassidy, Rosanna Arquette, Billy Hufsey, Mickey Gilley, Monte Markham. 1982

OFFENCE, THE ★★★1/2 A series of child molestations causes London detective Sean Connery to go over the edge. Director Sidney Lumet tells the story in what is essentially a three-act play of Connery's confrontations with superior officer Trevor Howard, disillusioned wife Vivien Merchant, and suspect Ian Bannen. It's a superbly played, disturbing character study. Rated R for violence and profanity. 122m. DIR: Sidney Lumet. CAST: Sean Connery, Trevor Howard, Vivien Merchant, Ian Bannen, Derek Newark. 1973

OFFERINGS 🎬 *Halloween* clone about a psychotic teen who escapes from a mental hospital and pursues cannibalistic activities. Rated R for gore. 92m. DIR: Christopher Reynolds. CAST: Loretta Leigh Bowman, Elizabeth Greene, G. Michael Smith, Jerry Brewer. 1989

OFFICE KILLER ★★★ A meek and mild-mannered office employee, Dorine, uses her job as a copy editor for a consumer magazine to escape her horrid home life with her mother. When word filters down that employee downsizing is needed, Dorine, fearing for her job, begins a little housecleaning of her own, killing her coworkers. Dastardly funny, *Office Killer* is just the ticket for someone who has either been abused or ignored at his job. Rated R for violence, language, and adult situations. 83m. DIR: Cindy Sherman. CAST: Carol Kane, Jeanne Tripplehorn, Molly Ringwald. 1997

OFFICE ROMANCES ★★ Slow-moving British soap. A plain, lonely country girl comes to work in London and is seduced by a selfish, married coworker. Ironically, she feels lucky to have been chosen by him. Not rated. 48m. DIR: Mary McMurray. CAST: Judy Parfitt, Ray Brooks. 1981

OFFICE SPACE ★★★ This crude but funny whack at life in the white-collar trenches is about a computer programmer who begins dropping out of the rat race when his hypnotherapist drops dead during their first session. His sudden professional nonchalance and candid conversations with company consultants lead to promotions as he dates a waitress and stages a computer swindle. Rated R for language and sexual situations. 90m. DIR: Mike Judge. CAST: Ron Livingston, Jennifer Aniston, Stephen Root, Gary Cole. 1999 DVD

OFFICER AND A DUCK, AN (LIMITED GOLD EDITION 2) ★★★★1/2 Six exceptional animated treats. Donald Duck turns unwilling soldier in these rarely seen entries, from his first days of "Donald Gets Drafted" to his ambitious scheme to go AWOL in "The Old Army Game," a plan that backfires with hilarious results. 50m. DIR: Walt Disney. 1942–1943

OFFICER AND A GENTLEMAN, AN ★★★★1/2 Soap opera has never been art. However, this funny, touching, corny, and predictable movie, starring Richard Gere and Debra Winger, takes the genre as close to it as any of the old three-handkerchief clas-sics. Director Taylor Hackford keeps just the right balance between the ridiculous and the sublime, making *An Officer and a Gentleman* one of the best of its kind. Rated R for nudity, profanity, and simulated sex. 125m. DIR: Taylor Hackford. CAST: Richard Gere, Debra Winger, Lou Gossett Jr., David Keith, Harold Sylvester. 1982

OFFICIAL DENIAL ★★★1/2 Parker Stevenson believes he's been abducted and examined by extraterrestrials, but no one will believe him, including wife Erin Gray. Then a spacecraft crashes near his home, leaving an alien stranded, and the military decides to let Stevenson attempt to communicate with it. A well-acted and thought-provoking science-fiction thriller. Made for cable. 96m. DIR: Brian Trenchard-Smith. CAST: Parker Stevenson, Erin Gray, Dirk Benedict, Chad Everett. 1993

OFFICIAL STORY, THE ★★★★★ This winner of the Oscar for best foreign-language film unforgettably details the destruction of a middle-class Argentinian family. The beginning of the end comes when the wife (brilliantly played by Norma Aleandro) suspects that her adopted baby daughter may be the orphan of parents murdered during the "dirty war" of the 1970s. In Spanish with English subtitles. Not rated, the film has violence. 110m. DIR: Luis Puenzo. CAST: Norma Aleandro, Hector Alterio, Analia Castro. 1985 DVD

OFFSPRING, THE ★★★★ Four scary and original short stories are tied together by the narration of an old man (Vincent Price) who lives in a small town that seems to make people kill. Well written and acted, with decent special effects. Horror fans will love this. Rated R for violence and brief nudity. 99m. DIR: Jeff Burr. CAST: Vincent Price, Clu Gulager, Terry Kiser. 1986

OH, ALFIE 🎬 Alan Price is an uncaring ladies' man. Rated R for nudity. 99m. DIR: Ken Hughes. CAST: Alan Price, Jill Townsend, Joan Collins, Rula Lenska, Hannah Gordon. 1975

OH! CALCUTTA! ★★ Only historians of the 1960s will have any reason to watch this, a videotaped performance of the musical revue that became infamous because it dealt with sex and featured onstage nudity. None of the sketches retain any humor or bite, a disappointment considering that the writers included Sam Shepard, John Lennon, Jules Feiffer, and Dan Greenberg. Not rated. 108m. DIR: Guillaume Martin Aucion. CAST: Raina Barrett, Mark Dempsey, Samantha Harper, Bill Macy. 1972

OH DAD, POOR DAD—MAMA'S HUNG YOU IN THE CLOSET AND I'M FEELING SO SAD ★★★1/2 A cult favorite, and deservedly so. The plot has something to do with an odd young man (Robert Morse) whose mother (Rosalind Russell) drags him off on a vacation in the tropics with the boy's dead father. Morse excels in this unique, well-written, often hilarious film. 86m. DIR: Richard Quine. CAST: Rosalind Russell, Robert Morse, Barbara Harris, Jonathan Winters, Lionel Jeffries. 1967

OH, GOD! ★★★★ God is made visible to a supermarket manager in this modern-day fantasy. The complications that result make for some predictable humor, but the story is kept flowing by some inspired casting. Ageless George Burns is a perfect vision of a God for Everyman in his tennis shoes and golf hat. John Denver exudes the right degree of naïveté as the put-upon grocer. Rated PG. 104m. **DIR:** Carl Reiner. **CAST:** George Burns, John Denver, Teri Garr, Ralph Bellamy. 1977

OH, GOD! BOOK II ★★ George Burns, as God, returns in this fair sequel and enters a little girl's life, assigning her the task of coming up with a slogan that will revive interest in him. So she comes up with "Think God" and begins her campaign. It's passable family fare. Rated PG. 94m. **DIR:** Gilbert Cates. **CAST:** George Burns, Suzanne Pleshette, David Birney, Louanne, Howard Duff. 1980

OH, GOD, YOU DEVIL! ★★★1/2 George Burns is back as the wisecracking, cigar-smoking deity. Only this time he plays a dual role—appearing as the devil. Ted Wass is the songwriter who strikes a Faustian bargain with Burns's bad side. This delightful comedy-with-a-moral is guaranteed to lift your spirits. Rated PG for suggested sex and profanity. 96m. **DIR:** Paul Bogart. **CAST:** George Burns, Ted Wass, Roxanne Hart, Ron Silver, Eugene Roche. 1984

OH, HEAVENLY DOG! ★★ Chevy Chase should have known better. This movie is an overly silly cutesy about a private eye (Chase) who is murdered and then comes back as a dog (Benji) to trap his killers. Kids, however, should enjoy it. Rated PG. 103m. **DIR:** Joe Camp. **CAST:** Benji, Chevy Chase, Jane Seymour, Omar Sharif, Robert Morley. 1980

OH! SUSANNA ★★★ Gene Autry is mistaken for a bad man and must clear his name. B&W; 59m. **DIR:** Joseph Kane. **CAST:** Gene Autry, Smiley Burnette, Frances Grant. 1936

OH, WHAT A NIGHT ★★★ Nostalgic soundtrack and innocent teen pranks highlight this better-than-average period piece about some 1950s teens trying to sow their wild oats. Young Corey Haim gets more than he bargained for when he falls for older woman Barbara Williams. Unexpectedly warm and sensitive. Made in Canada. Not rated; contains adult situations. 93m. **DIR:** Eric Till. **CAST:** Corey Haim, Barbara Williams, Keir Dullea, Robbie Coltrane, Genevieve Bujold. 1992

O'HARA'S WIFE ★★ Trite little tale about a businessman whose dead wife returns from the grave to help him along in life. Made for television. 87m. **DIR:** William Bartman. **CAST:** Edward Asner, Mariette Hartley, Jodie Foster, Tom Bosley. 1982

O. J. SIMPSON STORY, THE ★★1/2 Tabloid-TV addicts can delight in the cheap thrills contained in this quickly produced made-for-television movie. Not rated; contains violence. 90m. **DIR:** Alan Smithee. **CAST:** Bobby Hosea, Jessica Tuck, David Roberson, Bruce Weitz, James Handy, Kimberly Russell. 1995

OKEFENOKEE ★★ The Florida swamplands are the setting for this forgettable story about smugglers who use the Seminole Indians to help bring drugs into the country. When the Indians are pushed too far, they strike back. What swamp did they dig this one out of? 78m. **DIR:** Roul Haig. **CAST:** Peter Coe, Henry Brandon. 1960

OKLAHOMA! ★★★★ This movie adaptation of Rodgers and Hammerstein's Broadway musical stars Shirley Jones as a country girl (Laurie) who is courted by Curly, a cowboy (Gordon MacRae). Rod Steiger plays a villainous Jud, who also pursues Laurie. A very entertaining musical. 140m. **DIR:** Fred Zinnemann. **CAST:** Shirley Jones, Gordon MacRae, Rod Steiger, Eddie Albert, Gloria Grahame. 1956 DVD

OKLAHOMA ANNIE ❤ Judy Canova chases varmints out of town and brings decency to her community. 90m. **DIR:** R. G. Springsteen. **CAST:** Judy Canova, John Russell, Grant Withers, Allen Jenkins, Almira Sessions, Minerva Urecal. 1952

OKLAHOMA KID, THE ★★★ Definitely one of the oddest of all major sagebrush sagas, this film, about a feared gunman (James Cagney) taking revenge on the men who hanged his innocent father, boasts a great cast of familiar characters as well as a musical interlude with Cagney singing "I Don't Want to Play in Your Yard" to the accompaniment of a honky-tonk piano and pair of six-shooters. A competent curio. B&W; 85m. **DIR:** Lloyd Bacon. **CAST:** James Cagney, Humphrey Bogart, Rosemary Lane, Donald Crisp, Charles Middleton, Ward Bond, Harvey Stephens. 1939

OKLAHOMAN, THE ★★ Run-of-the-trail Western with Joel McCrea riding point to protect the rights of an outcast Indian against white-eyed crooks. 80m. **DIR:** Francis D. Lyon. **CAST:** Joel McCrea, Barbara Hale, Brad Dexter, Douglas Dick, Verna Felton. 1957

OLD BOYFRIENDS ❤ A woman decides to exact revenge on those men who made her past miserable. Rated R for profanity and violence. 103m. **DIR:** Joan Tewkesbury. **CAST:** Talia Shire, Richard Jordan, Keith Carradine, John Belushi, John Houseman, Buck Henry. 1979

OLD CORRAL ★★★ Sheriff Gene Autry pursues a group of singing bandits, the Sons of the Pioneers, and battles tommy gun–wielding gangsters in order to save a runaway lounge singer who witnessed a murder. Noteworthy as the B Western where Autry fights Roy Rogers and forces Rogers to yodel. B&W; 54m. **DIR:** Joseph Kane. **CAST:** Gene Autry, Smiley Burnette, Roy Rogers, Bob Nolan and the Sons of the Pioneers, Hope Manning, Lon Chaney Jr. 1936

OLD CURIOSITY SHOP, THE (1975) ★★★ This enjoyable British-made follow-up to Scrooge, the successful musical adaptation of Charles Dickens's A Christmas Carol, adds tunes to the author's The Old Curiosity Shop and casts songwriter-singer Anthony Newley as the villain. Rated PG. 118m. **DIR:** Michael Tuchner. **CAST:** Anthony Newley, David Hemmings, David Warner, Michael Hordern, Jill Bennett. 1975

OLD CURIOSITY SHOP, THE (1994) ★★★★ Handsome production of Charles Dickens's popular tale of Nell Trent, a precocious girl who's on the run with her grandfather from their sinister landlord, Quilp. Outstanding production design, a literate script, and an excellent cast headed by Sir Peter Ustinov as the grandfather and Tom Courtenay as Quilp make this Hallmark TV presentation a must-see. Rated G. 190m. **DIR:** Kevin Connor. **CAST:** Peter Ustinov, Tom Courtenay, James Fox, Sally Walsh. 1994

OLD DARK HOUSE, THE (1932) ★★★★ A superb cast of famous faces enlivens this deliciously dark, comic tale of travelers stranded in a spooky mansion during a storm. On a par with director James Whale's very best—*Frankenstein, The Invisible Man,* and *Bride of Frankenstein*—this was long thought to be a lost film; its rediscovery is cause for celebration among film fans everywhere. B&W; 75m. DIR: James Whale. CAST: Boris Karloff, Melvyn Douglas, Charles Laughton, Gloria Stuart, Lilian Bond, Ernest Thesiger, Raymond Massey. 1932

OLD DARK HOUSE, THE (1963) ★★ This messy, comedy-cum-chills rehash of the 1932 James Whale horror classic (which is still unavailable except in bootleg video versions) demonstrates mainly that William Castle, who directed the film, and Hammer Films, which coproduced it, were unsuited to collaboration. 86m. DIR: William Castle. CAST: Tom Poston, Robert Morley, Janette Scott, Joyce Grenfell, Mervyn Johns. 1963

OLD ENOUGH 💘 A prepubescent "coming-of-age" movie. Rated PG. 91m. DIR: Marisa Silver. CAST: Sarah Boyd, Rainbow Harvest, Neill Barry, Danny Aiello. 1984

OLD EXPLORERS ★★1/2 Family adventure about two senior citizens who refuse to let old age stand in their way of having a full, exciting life. Using their imaginations, they span the globe, taking in such sights as the Sahara and the jungles of South America. Rated PG. 91m. DIR: William Pohlad. CAST: José Ferrer, James Whitmore. 1990

OLD GRINGO, THE ★★★ Based on the novel by Carlos Fuentes, Jane Fonda hesitantly portrays an American schoolteacher on a quest for adventure with Pancho Villa's army during the 1910 Mexican revolution. Gregory Peck is an aging expatriate journalist traveling along for the last ride of his life. This project shows more aesthetic sensitivity during battle scenes than in dialogue sequences. Rated R for adult language. 120m. DIR: Luis Puenzo. CAST: Jane Fonda, Gregory Peck, Jimmy Smits. 1989

OLD IRONSIDES ★★ This big-budget, action-packed yarn of wooden ships and iron men besting pirates in the Mediterranean has a big director, big stars, big scenes, and was ballyhooed at its premiere, but it was scuttled by a lackluster script. Silent. B&W; 88m. DIR: James Cruze. CAST: Charles Farrell, Esther Ralston, Wallace Beery, George Bancroft, Fred Kohler Sr., Boris Karloff. 1926

OLD LADY WHO WALKED IN THE SEA, THE ★★★★ An aging con artist defies her partner in crime when she brings in a young man. Lady M., anxious to pass along her tricks of the trade to the new student, hopes to make him her last, great love. Her passion clouds her judgment and jeopardizes the team's final con game. In French with English subtitles. Not rated; contains profanity and adult situations. 94m. DIR: Laurent Heynemann. CAST: Jeanne Moreau, Michel Serrault, Luc Thuillier. 1994

OLD MAID, THE ★★★1/2 Tearjerking film version of the Zoe Akins play based on the Edith Wharton novel about an unwed mother (Bette Davis) who gives up her daughter to be raised by a married cousin (Miriam Hopkins), and suffers the consequences. Hopkins works hard to upstage Davis. A solid box-office winner. B&W; 95m. DIR: Edmund

Goulding. CAST: Bette Davis, Miriam Hopkins, George Brent, Donald Crisp. 1939

OLD MAN ★★★1/2 In this *Hallmark Hall of Fame* adaptation of a William Faulkner short story, a convict gets a second chance at life when he becomes an unlikely hero during the great Mississippi flood of 1927. Well-told study of poor southerners whose normally difficult lives suddenly seem impossible. Not rated, but will appeal primarily to mature audiences. 90m. DIR: John Kent Harrison. CAST: Arliss Howard, Jeanne Tripplehorn, Leo Burmester. 1997

OLD MAN AND THE SEA, THE (1958) ★★ Direction and script faithfully follow Ernest Hemingway's classic about a tired old fisherman who fights the unforgiving sea and giant prey only to win by losing. Spencer Tracy, in the title role, is overwhelmingly disappointing. The score won an Oscar, so buy the CD. 86m. DIR: John Sturges. CAST: Spencer Tracy, Felipe Pazos, Harry Bellaver. 1958

OLD MAN AND THE SEA, THE (1990) ★★★1/2 Ernest Hemingway's saga is revitalized by Anthony Quinn's stirring performance as the old fisherman. Catching a fish is a symbol of his usefulness in the world but when sharks destroy his catch, he has to come to terms with his philosophy of life. Made for TV. 95m. DIR: Jud Taylor. CAST: Anthony Quinn, Patricia Clarkson, Alexis Cruz. 1990

OLD SPANISH CUSTOM, AN ★★1/2 Set in Spain and filmed in England, this Buster Keaton sound comedy feature is best appreciated by diehard Keaton fans. Keaton is a bumbling yachtsman pursuing a scheming senorita. B&W; 56m. DIR: Adrian Brunel. CAST: Buster Keaton. 1935

OLD SWIMMIN' HOLE, THE ★★ Easygoing homage to small-town America focuses on young Jackie Moran's plans to become a doctor, and his and his mother's life in simpler times. Modest and pleasant enough. B&W; 78m. DIR: Robert McGowan. CAST: Marcia Mae Jones, Jackie Moran, Leatrice Joy, Charles Brown. 1940

OLD YELLER ★★★★ Here's a live-action Walt Disney favorite. A big yellow mongrel is taken in by a southwestern family. The warm attachment and numerous adventures of the dog and the two boys of the family are sure to endear this old mutt to your heart. A few tears are guaranteed to fall at the conclusion, so you'd best have a hankie. 83m. DIR: Robert Stevenson. CAST: Dorothy McGuire, Fess Parker, Tommy Kirk, Chuck Connors. 1957

OLDEST CONFEDERATE WIDOW TELLS ALL ★★★★ A lonely young girl (Diane Lane) marries a deranged Confederate vet (Donald Sutherland), who is at least three times her age, and spends much of their married years mothering him. Lane is a standout in this fine miniseries that was nominated for nine Emmy Awards. Anne Bancroft takes over the title role as she recounts her youth from the confines of her rest home. Cicely Tyson plays Lane's friend and confidante to perfection. Not rated; contains violence and sexual situations. 183m. DIR: Ken Cameron. CAST: Diane Lane, Donald Sutherland, Cicely Tyson, Anne Bancroft. 1994

OLDEST LIVING GRADUATE, THE ★★★★ *The Oldest Living Graduate* features a memorable performance by Henry Fonda as the oldest living member of a prestigious Texas military academy. Cloris Leachman shines in her role of the colonel's daughter-in-law. The final moments of this teleplay are poignantly realistic. 90m. **DIR:** Jack Hofsiss. **CAST:** Henry Fonda, George Grizzard, Harry Dean Stanton, Penelope Milford, Cloris Leachman, David Ogden Stiers, Timothy Hutton. **1983**

OLDEST PROFESSION, THE ★★1/2 Jean-Luc Godard's contribution, the final of six segments in this omnibus comedy about prostitution through the ages, is worth seeing. But the rest resembles a Gallic version of *Love, American Style*. In French with English subtitles. Not rated. 97m. **DIR:** Franco Indovina, Mauro Bolognini, Philippe de Broca, Michel Pfleghar, Claude Autant-Lara, Jean-Luc Godard. **CAST:** Elsa Martinelli, Gastone Moschin, Raquel Welch, Anna Karina, Jean-Pierre Léaud. **1967**

OLEANNA ★★★★ David Mamet directed his powerful stage production for the big screen, and the results are equally powerful. William H. Macy plays a professor whose life is falling apart. He seeks redemption through a female student who desperately needs his help. Things heat up when the student accuses the professor of sexual harassment. Mamet carefully explores both sides of the coin before coming up with a conclusion. Rated R for language. 89m. **DIR:** David Mamet. **CAST:** William H. Macy, Debra Eisenstadt. **1994**

OLIVER ★★★★ Charles Dickens never was such fun. *Oliver Twist* has become a luxurious musical and multiple Oscar-winner (including best picture). Mark Lester is the angelic Oliver, whose adventures begin one mealtime when he pleads, "Please, sir, I want some more." Jack Wild is an impish Artful Dodger, and Ron Moody steals the show as Fagin. Oliver Reed prevents the tale from becoming *too* sugarcoated. Rated G. 153m. **DIR:** Carol Reed. **CAST:** Ron Moody, Oliver Reed, Hugh Griffith, Shani Wallis, Mark Lester, Jack Wild. **1968 DVD**

OLIVER & COMPANY ★★★1/2 Disney's feature animation renaissance of the 1990s actually began with this charming reworking of Charles Dickens's *Oliver Twist*, which concerns a precocious kitten "adopted" by a gang of mischievous mutts. Superstar lyricist Howard Ashman, who later collected Oscars, makes an early mark with the tune—"Once Upon a Time in New York City"—which opens this film. Excellent voice "performances" turned in by Billy Joel, Richard Mulligan, and Bette Midler. Rated G. 73m. **DIR:** George Scribner. **1988**

OLIVER TWIST (1922) ★★★ Young Jackie Coogan, teamed with the legendary "Man of a Thousand Faces" Lon Chaney to portray, respectively, abused orphan Oliver Twist and literature's great manipulator of thieving children, Fagin, in this loose adaptation of Charles Dickens's enduring classic. Something of an oddity, this is one of at least eight film versions of the world-famous novel. Silent. B&W; 77m. **DIR:** Frank Lloyd. **CAST:** Jackie Coogan, Lon Chaney Sr., Gladys Brockwell, Esther Ralston. **1922**

OLIVER TWIST (1933) ★★ Low-budget version of the popular Charles Dickens story features some interesting performances and a few effective mo-

ments. This is a curiosity for students of literature or early sound film. Print quality is marginal. B&W; 77m. **DIR:** William Cowen. **CAST:** Dickie Moore, Irving Pichel, William "Stage" Boyd, Barbara Kent. **1933**

OLIVER TWIST (1948) ★★★★ Alec Guinness and Robert Newton give superb performances as the villains in this David Lean adaptation of the Charles Dickens story about a young boy who is forced into a life of thievery until he's rescued by a kindly old gentleman. B&W; 105m. **DIR:** David Lean. **CAST:** Alec Guinness, Robert Newton, John Howard Davies. **1948 DVD**

OLIVER TWIST (1982) ★★★★ A well-cast version of the Charles Dickens classic made for TV. The young hero symbolizes the state of English society in the nineteenth century when poverty, crime, and government neglect cried out for social reform. George C. Scott makes an effective Fagin. 100m. **DIR:** Clive Donner. **CAST:** George C. Scott, Tim Curry, Lysette Anthony, Michael Hordern, Timothy West, Eileen Atkins. **1982**

OLIVER TWIST (1997) ★★★1/2 Originally aired on the *Wonderful World of Disney*, this rendition of Charles Dickens's classic novel is surprisingly frank about the horrors faced by kids on the street. Oliver is befriended by the Artful Dodger after being thrown out of an orphanage. He is turned over to the tutelage of the seemingly benevolent, but highly manipulative, Fagin. Fagin's deadly associate, Bill Sikes, may give the wee ones nightmares. Not rated; contains violence and mental cruelty. 88m. **DIR:** Tony Bill. **CAST:** Richard Dreyfuss, Alex Trench, Elijah Wood, David O'Hara. **1997**

OLIVER'S STORY ♥ Even if you loved *Love Story*, you'll find it difficult to like this lame sequel. Rated PG. 92m. **DIR:** John Korty. **CAST:** Ryan O'Neal, Candice Bergen, Nicola Pagett, Edward Binns, Ray Milland. **1978**

OLIVIER, OLIVIER ★★★★ An unusual French mystery of loss and identity, exploring themes similar to those in *The Return of Martin Guerre* and *Sommersby*. Once again, a person returns to a family after an absence of several years, and questions arise about his identity. Is he who we desperately want to believe he is? The contemporary story incorporates elements of fable and parapsychology. Rated R, with profanity, violence, and sexual material, including incest. 110m. **DIR:** Agnieszka Holland. **CAST:** Gregoire Colin, Marina Golovine. **1992**

OLLIE HOPNOODLE'S HAVEN OF BLISS ★★★★ Fans of Jean Shepherd's autobiographical *A Christmas Story* will be equally delighted by this sequel, in which the author's childhood alter ego has grown (but not matured) into a teenager. Various events conspire against the family's annual cabin outing. As always, Shepherd's witty narration evokes both whimsy and nostalgia. Made-for-cable; family fare. 90m. **DIR:** Richard Bartlett. **CAST:** Jerry O'Connell, James B. Sikking, Dorothy Lyman, Jason Adams, Jean Shepherd. **1988**

OMAHA (THE MOVIE) ★★1/2 First-time writer-director Dan Mirvish shows promise by relying on his savvy imagination to overcome a zero budget. Hughston Walkinshaw is the young Omahan who hits the road every time technology overwhelms him. Several elements, however, block his path to spiritual fulfillment, from a band of Colombian jewel thieves to a family hooked on factoid TV programs. Uneven, but clever, this valentine is energetic and endearing. Not rated; contains profanity. 85m. **DIR:** Dan Mirvish. **CAST:** Hughston Walkinshaw, Jill Anderson, Dick Mueller. **1994**

OMAR KHAYYAM ★★ Big-budget costume epic with Cornel Wilde as the Persian hero. Unfortunately, the producers skimped on the Saturday-matinee script, which is very weak. 100m. **DIR:** William Dieterle. **CAST:** Cornel Wilde, Debra Paget, John Derek, Raymond Massey, Yma Sumac, Michael Rennie, Sebastian Cabot. **1957**

OMEGA COP 💔 Futuristic story of a cop struggling to get three women back to the safety of police headquarters. Rated R for violence. 89m. **DIR:** Paul Kyriazi. **CAST:** Ron Marchini, Adam West, Meg Thayer, Stuart Whitman, Troy Donahue. **1990**

OMEGA DOOM 💔 Yet another apocalyptic movie about a cyborg warrior who gains cyberreligion and helps Earth fight against ultimate doom. Rated PG-13 for language and violence. 84m. **DIR:** Albert Pyun. **CAST:** Rutger Hauer, Shannon Whirry, Tina Cote, Norbert Weisser. **1996 DVD**

OMEGA MAN, THE ★★★ Charlton Heston does a last-man-on-Earth number in this free adaptation of Richard Matheson's *I Am Legend*. The novel's vampirism has been toned down, but Chuck still is holed up in his high-rise mansion by night, and killing robed (and sleeping) zombies by day. Although this is no more faithful to Matheson's work than 1964s *The Last Man on Earth*, it has enough throat-grabbing suspense to keep it moving. Rated PG—considerable violence. 98m. **DIR:** Boris Sagal. **CAST:** Charlton Heston, Anthony Zerbe, Rosalind Cash. **1971 DVD**

OMEGA SYNDROME ★★ Ken Wahl is a single parent who teams up with his old Vietnam war buddy (George DiCenzo) to track down his daughter's abductors. A very manipulative screenplay makes the film hard to take seriously. Rated R for violence and profanity. 90m. **DIR:** Joseph Manduke. **CAST:** Ken Wahl, George DiCenzo, Doug McClure, Ron Kuhlman, Patti Tippo. **1986**

OMEN, THE ★★★★ This, first of a series of movies about the return to Earth of the devil, is a real chiller. In the form of a young boy, Damien, Satan sets about reestablishing his rule over man. A series of bizarre deaths points to the boy. Rated R. 111m. **DIR:** Richard Donner. **CAST:** Gregory Peck, Lee Remick, Billie Whitelaw, David Warner. **1976**

OMEN IV: THE AWAKENING 💔 Made-for-TV continuation finds the devil continuing his reign of terror. 97m. **DIR:** Jorge Montesi, Dominique Othenin-Girard. **CAST:** Michael Lerner, Faye Grant, Michael Woods. **1992**

ON A CLEAR DAY, YOU CAN SEE FOREVER 💔 A psychiatrist discovers that one of his patients has lived a former life and can recall it under hypnosis. Rated G. 129m. **DIR:** Vincente Minnelli. **CAST:** Barbra Streisand, Yves Montand, Bob Newhart, Larry Blyden, Jack Nicholson. **1970**

ON AN ISLAND WITH YOU ★★ Lightweight story of navy flyer Peter Lawford pursuing actress Esther Williams while on location in the South Seas. Jimmy Durante's comedy and Cyd Charisse's dancing are the highlights. 117m. **DIR:** Richard Thorpe. **CAST:** Esther Williams, Peter Lawford, Ricardo Montalban, Jimmy Durante, Cyd Charisse. **1948**

ON APPROVAL ★★★ Former Sherlock Holmes Clive Brook displays a confident hand at directing in this enjoyable farce about women who exchange boyfriends. Fun and breezy with terrific performances by some of England's best talents, this film gave beloved Beatrice Lillie one of her best screen roles. B&W; 80m. **DIR:** Clive Brook. **CAST:** Beatrice Lillie, Clive Brook, Googie Withers, Roland Culver. **1943 DVD**

ON BORROWED TIME ★★★1/2 Lionel Barrymore is concerned about the future of his orphaned grandson. When death (Mr. Brink) calls, he tricks him up a tree and delays the inevitable. A rewarding fantasy. B&W; 98m. **DIR:** Harold S. Bucquet. **CAST:** Lionel Barrymore, Cedric Hardwicke, Beulah Bondi, Una Merkel, Bobs Watson, Henry Travers. **1939**

ON DANGEROUS GROUND (1951) ★★1/2 Robert Ryan does a credible job as a crime-weary patrol cop who takes out his frustrations on the men he arrests and winds up transferred after bloodying one too many suspects. B&W; 82m. **DIR:** Nicholas Ray. **CAST:** Robert Ryan, Ida Lupino, Ward Bond, Ed Begley Sr., Cleo Moore, Olive Carey. **1951**

ON DANGEROUS GROUND (1995) ★★ Jack Higgins's bestselling thriller is ill served by this low-rent adaptation, which compounds its problems by miscasting Rob Lowe as a rogue IRA-terrorist-turned-good-guy. He and the remaining protagonists seem clueless about the labyrinthine plot, which involves the Mafia, assassination attempts, and a priceless document that might keep Hong Kong out of Chinese hands for another century. A total snooze. Rated PG-13 for violence and profanity. 166m. **DIR:** Lawrence Gordon Clark. **CAST:** Rob Lowe, Kenneth Cranham, Deborah Moore, Ingeborga Dapkounaite, Daphne Cheung, Jurgen Prochnow. **1995**

ON DEADLY GROUND ★★1/2 Director-star Steven Seagal has come up with a martial arts movie with an environmental message. As you might guess, it's an uneasy combination, although action fans will find Seagal in top form as a one-man army out to stop oil tycoon Michael Caine (in a delightfully over-the-top role) from turning Alaska into one big ecological disaster. Rated R for violence and profanity. 98m. **DIR:** Steven Seagal. **CAST:** Steven Seagal, Michael Caine, Joan Chen, John C. McGinley, R. Lee Ermey, Irvin Brink, Richard Hamilton. **1994 DVD**

ON GOLDEN POND ★★★★★ Henry Fonda, Katharine Hepburn, and Jane Fonda are terrific in this warm, funny, and often quite moving film, written by Ernest Thompson, about the conflicts and reconciliations among the members of a family that take place during a fateful summer. Rated PG because of brief profanity. 109m. **DIR:** Mark Rydell. **CAST:** Henry Fonda, Katharine Hepburn, Jane Fonda, Doug McKeon. **1981 DVD**

ON HER MAJESTY'S SECRET SERVICE ★★★★ With Sean Connery temporarily out of the James Bond series, Australian actor George Lazenby stepped into the 007 part for this entry—and did remarkably well. Director Peter Hunt keeps this moving at an incredibly fast pace, and this story about everyone's favorite superspy falling in love with an heiress (Diana Rigg) is one of author Ian Fleming's best. Rated PG. 140m. **DIR:** Peter R. Hunt. **CAST:** George Lazenby, Diana Rigg, Telly Savalas. **1969 DVD**

•**ON HOSTILE GROUND** ★★★ Decent disaster film focuses on an underground sinkhole big enough to devour New Orleans. By the way, it's Mardi Gras and the geologist who wants to stop the festivities is at odds with his girlfriend who works for the mayor. Riveting, with plenty of close calls and body bags. Not rated; contains violence. 91m. **DIR:** Mario Azzopardi. **CAST:** John Corbett, Jessica Steen, Brittany Daniel. **2000**

ON MOONLIGHT BAY ★★★ Small-town setting, circa World War I, with tomboyish Doris Day falling for a college hero who is concerned about upcoming army service. Booth Tarkington's *Penrod* series set to music. Many fine songs of the era. 95m. **DIR:** Roy Del Ruth. **CAST:** Doris Day, Gordon MacRae, Leon Ames, Rosemary DeCamp, Billy Gray, Jack Smith, Mary Wickes, Ellen Corby. **1951**

ON THE AVENUE ★★★1/2 Dick Powell spoofs a noted spoiled heiress in his musical play. She buys out the backers and tries to sabotage the show and his reputation. Ah, but love steps in. Wonderful songs by Irving Berlin. Some cassettes open with an "added feature," a comedy sketch with Alice Faye and the Ritz Brothers. B&W; 88m. **DIR:** Roy Del Ruth. **CAST:** Dick Powell, Madeleine Carroll, Alice Faye, The Ritz Brothers, George Barbier, Cora Witherspoon, Alan Mowbray, Walter Catlett, Joan Davis, Stepin Fetchit, Sig Ruman, Billy Gilbert. **1937**

ON THE BEACH ★★★★ The effect of a nuclear holocaust on a group of people in Australia makes for engrossing drama in this film. Gregory Peck is a submarine commander who ups anchor and goes looking for survivors as a radioactive cloud slowly descends upon this apparently last human enclave. Director Stanley Kramer is a bit heavy-handed in his moralizing and the romance between Peck and Ava Gardner is distracting, yet the film remains a powerful antiwar statement. B&W; 133m. **DIR:** Stanley Kramer. **CAST:** Gregory Peck, Ava Gardner, Fred Astaire, Anthony Perkins. **1959 DVD**

ON THE BLOCK ★★1/2 Baltimore strip joints threatened by a greedy land developer. This low-budget film would have been better if they had cut back on the dance acts. Rated R for nudity, profanity, and violence. 96m. **DIR:** Steve Yeager. **CAST:** Marilyn Jones, Michael Gabel, Howard Rollins Jr. **1991**

ON THE BOWERY ★★★ Gritty, uncompromising docudrama, dealing with life among the tragic street people of the Lower East Side in New York City. An extraordinary, agonizing glimpse into the world of the depraved alcoholic nomads whose lives become a constant daily struggle. Excellent black-and-white cinematography. B&W; 65m. **DIR:** Lionel Rogosin.

CAST: Ray Sayler, Gorman Hendricks, Frank Mathews. **1956**

ON THE EDGE ★★★1/2 Bruce Dern gives a solid performance as a middle-aged runner hoping to regain the glory that escaped him twenty years earlier when he was disqualified from the 1964 Olympic trials. The race to test his ability is the grueling 14.2-mile annual Cielo Sea Race over California's Mount Tamalpais. The mobile camera action in the training and race sequences is very effective. Rated PG. 95m. **DIR:** Rob Nilsson. **CAST:** Bruce Dern, Bill Bailey, Jim Haynie, John Marley, Pam Grier. **1985**

ON THE LINE ★★1/2 David Carradine smuggles aliens across the Mexican border. Scott Wilson pledges to nail Carradine and his operation. This mediocre adventure is not rated. 103m. **DIR:** José Luis Borau. **CAST:** David Carradine, Scott Wilson, Victoria Abril, Jeff Delger, Paul Richardson, Jesse Vint, Sam Jaffe. **1987**

ON THE MAKE ★★1/2 Well-intended but preachy movie about dating in the AIDS era. Teens obsessed with scoring at the local disco are heedless of such consequences as disease, pregnancy, and emotional numbness. Rated R for sexual situations and brief nudity. 74m. **DIR:** Samuel Herwitz. **CAST:** Steve Irlen, Mark McKelvey, Teresina, Kirk Baltz, Tara Leigh. **1989**

ON THE NICKEL ★★1/2 Ralph Waite, of TV's *The Waltons*, wrote, produced, and directed this drama about derelicts on L.A.'s skid row. It's a well-intentioned effort that is too unfocused and sentimental to work, though Donald Moffat's performance as a cleaned-up drunk is worth seeing. Rated R for rough language. 96m. **DIR:** Ralph Waite. **CAST:** Donald Moffat, Ralph Waite, Hal Williams, Jack Kehoe, Ellen Geer. **1980**

ON THE RIGHT TRACK ★★ Gary Coleman (of television's "Diff'rent Strokes") plays a tyke with a talent for picking the winners in horse races. Without Coleman, this would be an awful movie. Even with him, it is nothing to shout about. Rated PG. 98m. **DIR:** Lee Philips. **CAST:** Gary Coleman, Maureen Stapleton, Michael Lembeck, Norman Fell. **1981**

ON THE TOWN ★★★★ This is a classic boy-meets-girl, boy-loses-girl fable set to music. Three sailors are on a twenty-four-hour leave and find themselves (for the first time) in the big city of New York. They seek romance and adventure—and find it. 98m. **DIR:** Gene Kelly, Stanley Donen. **CAST:** Gene Kelly, Frank Sinatra, Ann Miller, Vera-Ellen, Jules Munshin, Betty Garrett. **1949 DVD**

ON THE WATERFRONT ★★★★★ Tough, uncompromising look at corruption on the New York waterfront. Marlon Brando is brilliant as Terry Malloy, a one-time fight contender who is now a longshoreman. Led into crime by his older brother (Rod Steiger), Terry is disgusted by the violent tactics of boss Lee J. Cobb. Yet if he should turn against the crooks, it could mean his life. A classic film with uniformly superb performances. B&W; 108m. **DIR:** Elia Kazan. **CAST:** Marlon Brando, Eva Marie Saint, Karl Malden, Lee J. Cobb, Rod Steiger. **1954**

ON THE YARD ★★ Subpar prison melodrama pits John Heard against a prison-yard boss. Some good performances help, but this never gets going, nor does it ring true. Rated R. 102m. DIR: Raphael D. Silver. CAST: John Heard, Mike Kellin, Richard Bright, Thomas Waites, Joe Grifasi. 1979

ON TOP OF THE WHALE ★★1/2 Confusing, nonlinear metaphysical drama about an anthropologist who attempts to unravel the mystery concerning two Indians who speak a strange language made up of only a few phrases. Shot in five languages that only add to the film's confusion. In Dutch with English subtitles. Not rated; contains profanity and violence. 93m. DIR: Raúl Ruiz. CAST: Willeke Van Ammelrooy. 1982

ON VALENTINE'S DAY ★★1/2 Horton Foote created this small-town love story about his own parents. A young couple (William Converse and Hallie Foote) tries to make ends meet after eloping. Her parents haven't spoken to her since they ran away, but all that is about to change. Rated PG. 106m. DIR: Ken Harrison. CAST: William Converse-Roberts, Hallie Foote, Michael Higgins, Steven Hill, Rochelle Oliver, Matthew Broderick. 1986

ON WINGS OF EAGLES ★★★ Well-acted, long-form TV production about what happens when two business executives are imprisoned in Tehran just before the fall of the shah of Iran. Burt Lancaster is top-notch as the grizzled ex-military man who trains the company's other executives for a raid on the prison. Richard Crenna's take-charge tycoon in this fact-based film was modeled on Ross Perot. 221m. DIR: Andrew V. McLaglen. CAST: Burt Lancaster, Richard Crenna, Paul LeMat, Jim Metzler, Esai Morales, Constance Towers. 1986

ONASSIS: THE RICHEST MAN IN THE WORLD ★★1/2 Mediocre made-for-TV biography of Aristotle Onassis's life focusing on his rise to wealth and power and unhappy marriages. Raul Julia stands out in the lead but has little support from his female counterpart. 120m. DIR: Waris Hussein. CAST: Raul Julia, Jane Seymour, Anthony Quinn, Francesca Annis, Anthony Zerbe. 1990

ONCE A HERO ★★ Yesteryear's comic-book superhero, Captain Justice, is slowly fading away. His fans are deserting him, so he decides to cross from his world of fantasy to our world of today with predictable but occasionally amusing results. Not rated. 74m. DIR: Claudia Weill. CAST: Jeff Lester, Robert Forster, Milo O'Shea. 1988

ONCE A THIEF ★★★1/2 Raised from childhood to be master art thieves, three friends are double-crossed by their former mentor. John Woo's equivalent to Hitchcock's To Catch a Thief is a genial, relatively lighthearted film compared to The Killer, aided by the boundless charms of his regular star, Chow Yun-Fat. And there are enough action and stunt scenes to keep regular Woo fans happy. Not rated; contains violence. 108m. DIR: John Woo. CAST: Chow Yun-Fat, Leslie Cheung, Cherie Chung. 1991 DVD

ONCE AROUND ★★★1/2 If it weren't for off-putting, vulgar language and some skimpy character development, this offbeat comedy in the style of Moonstruck would be a real winner. As it is, there are some truly delightful and hilarious moments in its tale of a Boston woman (Holly Hunter) who finds

romance in the arms of an oddball, middle-aged millionaire (Richard Dreyfuss). Rated R for profanity. 115m. DIR: Lasse Hallstrom. CAST: Richard Dreyfuss, Holly Hunter, Danny Aiello, Laura San Giacomo, Gena Rowlands. 1991

ONCE BITTEN ★★★ Sly little vampire film about an ancient bloodsucker (Lauren Hutton) who can remain young and beautiful only by periodically supping on youthful male virgins. Likable Jim Carrey is her latest target, and their first few encounters (three's the magic number) leave him with an appetite for raw hamburgers and a tendency to sleep during the day so as to avoid sunlight. Rated PG-13 for sexual situations. 92m. DIR: Howard Storm. CAST: Lauren Hutton, Jim Carrey, Karen Kopins, Cleavon Little. 1985

ONCE IN PARIS ★★★ Effervescent romantic comedy about a script doctor (Wayne Rogers) called to Paris to repair a screenplay. Once there, he falls in love and ends up ignoring his work. Sparkling writing perks up an old story. Rated PG for adult situations. 100m. DIR: Frank D. Gilroy. CAST: Wayne Rogers, Gayle Hunnicutt, Jack Lenoir, Tanya Lopert, Doris Roberts. 1978

ONCE IS NOT ENOUGH 🎃 Trash based on Jacqueline Susann's novel of jet-set sex. Rated R. 121m. DIR: Guy Green. CAST: Kirk Douglas, Alexis Smith, David Janssen, Deborah Raffin, George Hamilton, Melina Mercouri, Brenda Vaccaro. 1975

ONCE UPON A CRIME ★★ Obnoxious, all-star comedy about murder and mayhem in Monte Carlo. The few moments of funny were by the cast members make it tolerable, but why did director Eugene Levy have the actors scream nearly every line at the top of their lungs? Rated PG for profanity and goofy violence. 94m. DIR: Eugene Levy. CAST: John Candy, James Belushi, Cybill Shepherd, Sean Young, Richard Lewis, Ornella Muti, Giancarlo Giannini, George Hamilton. 1992

ONCE UPON A FOREST ★★1/2 Only Robin Williams's humorous antics as the voice of klutzy Batty make this animated environmental fable worth watching. An idealistic fairy discovers to her horror that humankind is ravaging her rain-forest home. It's a bit too preachy for adults, but kids will enjoy it. Rated G. 71m. DIR: Charles Grosvenor. 1993

ONCE UPON A HONEYMOON ★★1/2 In this travesty, one Cary Grant preferred to forget, he plays a newspaperman trying to get innocent stripteaser Ginger Rogers out of Europe as the German army advances. This amusing adventure-comedy is a bit dated, but Grant fans won't mind. B&W; 117m. DIR: Leo McCarey. CAST: Ginger Rogers, Cary Grant, Walter Slezak, Albert Dekker, Albert Basserman, Harry Shannon, John Banner. 1942

ONCE UPON A TIME ... WHEN WE WERE COLORED ★★★★ A loving, honorable film based on African American writer Clifton L. Taulbert's memoir of his rural Mississippi childhood in the years between World War II and the Civil Rights Movement of the 1960s. Director Tim Reid struggles with the script's uneventful, episodic structure, which makes the film seem longer than it is, but the acting is excellent and the essential decency of the story shines through. Rated PG. 112m. DIR: Tim Reid. CAST: Al Freeman Jr., Phylicia Rashad, Leon, Paula Kelly, Willie Norwood Jr., Damon Hines, Polly Bergen, Richard Roundtree. 1996

ONCE UPON A TIME AND THE EARTH WAS CREATED ... ★★1/2 A basic trek through the evolution theory, reminiscent of those physical science films you may remember from fifth grade. There's a disquieting air of indifference when it comes to the elimination of characters through "natural selection," as well as some violent confrontations between neighboring tribes and hungry dinosaurs. Otherwise pretty harmless. 77m. DIR: Albert Barillé. 1985

ONCE UPON A TIME IN AMERICA (LONG VERSION) ★★★★ Italian director Sergio Leone's richly rewarding gangster epic; a $30 million production starring Robert De Niro in a forty-five-year saga of Jewish gangsters in New York City. Leone is best-known for his spaghetti westerns. This release culminates ten years of planning and false starts by the filmmaker. It was well worth the wait. Rated R for profanity, nudity, suggested sex, and violence. 225m. DIR: Sergio Leone. CAST: Robert De Niro, James Woods, Elizabeth McGovern, Tuesday Weld, Treat Williams, Burt Young. 1984

ONCE UPON A TIME IN THE WEST ★★★★★ This superb film is the only spaghetti Western that can be called a classic. A mythic tale about the coming of the railroad and the exacting of revenge with larger-than-life characters, it is a work on a par with the best by great American Western film directors. Like The Wild Bunch, it has a fervent—and well-deserved—cult following in America. Rated PG. 165m. DIR: Sergio Leone. CAST: Claudia Cardinale, Henry Fonda, Charles Bronson, Jason Robards Jr., Jack Elam, Woody Strode, Lionel Stander. 1969

ONCE WERE WARRIORS ★★★★1/2 Maori mother of five reevaluates her eighteen-year marriage to her alcoholic, volcanically tempered husband when his barroom vice and violence slop tragically into their home life. It's a raw, passionate story that has the electricity and visual wallop usually reserved for straight action pictures. Rated R for violence, sex, and language. 92m. DIR: Lee Tamahori. CAST: Rena Owen, Temuera Morrison, Julian Arahanga, Taungaroa Emile, Mamaengaroa Kerr-Bell. 1995

ONE AGAINST THE WIND ★★★★ A British socialité (Judy Davis) risks her life to guide Allied soldiers through Nazi-occupied France in this Hallmark Hall of Fame drama. Based on an actual person, Davis is captivating as the complex woman whose life disintegrates as she saves lives, using only her wits and impeccable manners. Made for TV. 96m. DIR: Larry Elikann. CAST: Judy Davis, Sam Neill. 1991

ONE AND ONLY, THE ★★★ Writer Steve Gordon got started with this tale of an obnoxious college show-off who eventually finds fame as a wrestling showboater. Henry Winkler was still struggling to find a big-screen personality, but his occasional character flaws often are overshadowed by Gordon's deft little script. Rated PG. 98m. DIR: Carl Reiner. CAST: Henry Winkler, Kim Darby, Herve Villechaize, Harold Gould, Gene Saks, William Daniels. 1978

ONE AND ONLY, GENUINE, ORIGINAL FAMILY BAND, THE ★★1/2 This period comedy, set in the Dakota territories, features Walter Brennan—who struggles to keep his family's band together in order to get invited to the Democratic convention in St. Louis. This is a lightweight movie but is, nonetheless, moderately enjoyable for the whole family. Rated G. 110m. DIR: Michael O'Herlihy. CAST: Walter Brennan, Buddy Ebsen, Lesley Ann Warren, John Davidson, Goldie Hawn. 1967

ONE ARABIAN NIGHT ★★ Heavy-handed screen version of the stage pantomime, Sumurun, by Max Reinhardt. The title character is the mistress of a sheikh who prefers romance with his son. Silent. B&W; 85m. DIR: Ernst Lubitsch. CAST: Pola Negri. 1920

ONE BODY TOO MANY ★★1/2 Snappy dialogue and a memorable cast make this fast-paced whodunit worth a watch. Wisecracking Jack Haley is mistaken for a private investigator and finds himself in the thick of murder and intrigue. Bela Lugosi is again typecast as a menace. Nothing special, but not too bad for a low-budget programmer. B&W; 75m. DIR: Frank McDonald. CAST: Bela Lugosi, Jack Haley, Jean Parker, Blanche Yurka, Lyle Talbot, Douglas Fowley. 1944

ONE COOKS, THE OTHER DOESN'T ★★ Suzanne Pleshette is the driving force behind this TV movie about a woman who finds herself having to share quarters with her ex-husband and his youthful bride-to-be when he is unable to make ends meet in the realty business. Though high in dimple quotient, it's engaging enough. 100m. DIR: Richard Michaels. CAST: Suzanne Pleshette, Rosanna Arquette, Joseph Bologna, Oliver Clark. 1983

ONE CRAZY NIGHT ★★★★ Five Australian teens are trapped in the basement of a Melbourne hotel housing the Beatles in 1964. During the course of the night, these very different people swap their ideas on hero worship, sexual fantasies, fears, and expectations. It has that Breakfast Club feel, but bittersweet humor and a fresh cast make for an appealing diversion. Rated PG-13 for profanity. 92m. DIR: Michael Pattinson. CAST: Beth Champion, Malcolm Kennard, Dannii Minogue, Willa O'Neill, Noah Taylor. 1991

ONE CRAZY SUMMER ★★1/2 Star John Cusack and writer-director Savage Steve Holland of Better Off Dead are reunited in this weird, slightly sick, and sometimes stupidly funny comedy about a college hopeful (Cusack) who must learn about love to gain entrance to an institute of higher learning. If you accept that silly premise, then you may get a few laughs. Rated PG. 94m. DIR: Savage Steve Holland. CAST: John Cusack, Demi Moore, Curtis Armstrong, Bob Goldthwait, Joe Flaherty, Tom Villard. 1986

ONE DARK NIGHT ★★1/2 Meg Tilly and Adam "Batman" West star in this story of a young woman (Tilly) who is menaced by an energy-draining ghost. Rated R. 89m. DIR: Tom McLoughlin. CAST: Meg Tilly, Adam West, Robin Evans, Elizabeth Daily. 1983

ONE DAY IN THE LIFE OF IVAN DENISOVICH ★★★ Tom Courtenay does a fine job as the title character, a prisoner in a Siberian labor camp. The famed novel by Alexander Solzhenitsyn is beautifully and bleakly photographed. Not an uplifting story, but a significant one. 100m. **DIR:** Caspar Wrede. **CAST:** Tom Courtenay, Espen Skjønberg, James Maxwell, Alfred Burke. **1971**

ONE DEADLY SUMMER ★★★ Isabelle Adjani stars as a promiscuous young woman who returns to a small village to seek revenge on three men who beat and raped her mother many years before. Exceptionally well acted, especially by Alain Souchon as her sympathetic boyfriend, and veteran European actress Suzanne Flon as his slightly crazy aunt. In French with English subtitles. Rated R for nudity and violence. 133m. **DIR:** Jean Becker. **CAST:** Isabelle Adjani, Alain Souchon, François Cluzet, Suzanne Flon, Manuel Gelin. **1983**

ONE DOWN, TWO TO GO ★★ Kung fu fighter (Jim Kelly) suspects a tournament is fixed and calls on his buddies (Jim Brown and director Fred Williamson) for help in this low-budget, theatrically unreleased sequel to *Three the Hard Way*. Some actors are hopelessly amateurish, and the story is a mere sketch. Not rated, the film has violence. 84m. **DIR:** Fred Williamson. **CAST:** Fred Williamson, Jim Brown, Jim Kelly, Richard Roundtree. **1983**

ONE-EYED JACKS ★★★★ Star Marlon Brando took over the reins of directing this Western from Stanley Kubrick midway through production, and the result is a terrific entry in the genre. Superb supporting performances help this beautifully photographed film about an outlaw seeking revenge on a double-dealing former partner. 141m. **DIR:** Marlon Brando. **CAST:** Marlon Brando, Karl Malden, Katy Jurado, Ben Johnson, Slim Pickens, Elisha Cook Jr. **1961** DVD

ONE FALSE MOVE ★★★1/2 Terrific crime drama chronicles the exploits of three criminals, two men and a woman, from their initial cocaine rip-off in Los Angeles to a slam bang finale in a small Arkansas town. Entire cast is excellent under first-time director Carl Franklin's sure hand. Rated R for violence and language. 104m. **DIR:** Carl Franklin. **CAST:** Bill Paxton, Cynda Williams, Michael Beach, Jim Metzler. **1992** DVD

ONE FINE DAY ★★★ George Clooney and Michelle Pfeiffer are a couple of single parents thrown together during a particularly hectic working day; of necessity, each watches the other's respective child when required. Clooney's daughter is a perfectly reasonable individual, but Pfeiffer's monster of a son brings this otherwise sweet-tempered story to a thudding halt. Rated PG for mild sensuality. 108m. **DIR:** Michael Hoffman. **CAST:** Michelle Pfeiffer, George Clooney, Mae Whitman, Alex D. Linz, Charles Durning. **1996** DVD

ONE FLEW OVER THE CUCKOO'S NEST ★★★★★ Not since Capra's *It Happened One Night* had a motion picture swept all the major Academy Awards. Jack Nicholson sparkles as Randall P. McMurphy, a convict who is committed to a northwestern mental institution for examination. While there, he stimulates in each of his ward inmates an awakening spirit of self-worth and frees them from their passive acceptance of the hospital authorities' domination.

Louise Fletcher is brilliant as the insensitive head nurse. Rated R. 133m. **DIR:** Milos Forman. **CAST:** Jack Nicholson, Louise Fletcher, Will Sampson, Danny DeVito, Christopher Lloyd, Scatman Crothers, Brad Dourif. **1975** DVD

ONE FRIGHTENED NIGHT ★★ A stormy night, a spooky mansion, an eccentric millionaire, and a group of people stranded together was about all it used to take to make a scary movie. A good cast and some witty dialogue help, but there's only so much that can be done with this kind of mystery. B&W; 69m. **DIR:** Christy Cabanne. **CAST:** Wallace Ford, Mary Carlisle, Hedda Hopper, Charley Grapewin. **1935**

ONE FROM THE HEART ★★ This Francis Coppola film is a ballet of graceful and complex camera movements occupying magnificent sets—but the characters get lost in the process. Teri Garr and Frederic Forrest play a couple flirting with two strangers (Raul Julia and Nastassja Kinski), but they fade away in the flash and fizz. Rated R. 100m. **DIR:** Francis Ford Coppola. **CAST:** Teri Garr, Frederic Forrest, Raul Julia, Nastassja Kinski, Harry Dean Stanton, Allen Garfield, Luana Anders. **1982**

ONE GOOD COP ★★★ When his partner is killed in a shoot-out with a drug-crazed criminal, detective Michael Keaton and his wife take in the partner's three daughters. Familiar material is handled well by a committed cast. Rated R for violence and profanity. 106m. **DIR:** Heywood Gould. **CAST:** Michael Keaton, René Russo, Anthony LaPaglia, Kevin Conway, Rachel Ticotin, Tony Plana. **1991**

ONE GOOD TURN ★★★ Better-than-average revenge thriller about a couple who invites a stranger into their house with deadly results. Matt agrees to let the man who saved his life twelve years ago stay in his home. Little does he realize that the stranger has a grudge he's been harboring all those years. Decent cast and taut direction elevate the mundane into suspense. Rated R for violence, profanity, and adult situations. 90m. **DIR:** Tony Randel. **CAST:** Lenny Von Dohlen, James Remar, Suzy Amis, John Savage. **1995** DVD

ONE IN A MILLION ★★★ Sonja Henie's film debut is only slightly dated. The center of the movie is her skating ability, and no one has ever topped her. She plays an unknown skater recruited to save a traveling show and winds up at Madison Square Garden with a proud papa, a handsome boyfriend, and an adoring public. B&W; 95m. **DIR:** Sidney Lanfield. **CAST:** Sonja Henie, Don Ameche, Adolphe Menjou, The Ritz Brothers, Jean Hersholt, Arline Judge, Ned Sparks, Dixie Dunbar, Borrah Minevich, Bess Flowers, Leah Ray. **1936**

ONE LAST RUN ★★ Male bonding theme is just an excuse for endless ski stunts. Not rated, contains profanity. 80m. **DIR:** Glenn Gebhard, Peter Winograd. **CAST:** Russell Todd, Craig Branham, Nels Van Patten, Ashley Laurence, Chuck Connors, Tracy Scoggins. **1990**

ONE MAGIC CHRISTMAS ★★★★1/2 Mary Steenburgen stars in this touching, feel-good movie as a young mother who has lost the spirit of Christmas. She regains it with the help of a Christmas angel (played by that terrific character actor Harry Dean

Stanton). Rated G. 95m. **DIR:** Phillip Borsos. **CAST:** Mary Steenburgen, Harry Dean Stanton, Gary Basaraba, Arthur Hill, Ken Pogue. **1985 DVD**

ONE MAN ARMY 💔 Low-rent kick-boxing effort pits champ Jerry Trimble against the crooked small-town officials who killed his grandfather, but doesn't bring anything new to the arena. Rated R for violence and strong language. 90m. **DIR:** Cirio H. Santiago. **CAST:** Jerry Trimble, Melissa Moore, Dennis Hayden, Yvonne Michelle, Rick Dean. **1994**

ONE-MAN FORCE ★★★ John Matuszak plays an L.A. cop seeking to avenge his partner's murder. Good action drama. Rated R for violence and profanity. 90m. **DIR:** Dale Trevillion. **CAST:** John Matuszak, Ronny Cox, Charles Napier. **1989**

•**ONE MAN'S HERO** ★★1/2 Set in the 1840s during the Mexican-American War, this tale of prejudice, freedom, romance, and tragedy chronicles the formation of St. Patrick's Battalion, a group of mostly Irish Catholics who desert the bigoted American army and fight with the Mexicans. This neglected, compelling slice of history is dramatized with uneven results. The dialogue is stiff and battles are awkwardly staged. Rated R for violence. 122m. **DIR:** Lance Hool. **CAST:** Tom Berenger, Daniela Romo, Joaquim de Almeida. **1999 DVD**

ONE MAN'S JUSTICE ★★1/2 A routine vengeance saga that concerns a military man's search for the maniac who killed his wife and young daughter. Enlivened slightly by Brian Bosworth's charm and DeJuan Guy, who stands out as a streetwise kid. Rated R for violence, profanity, and drug use. 101m. **DIR:** Kurt Wimmer. **CAST:** Brian Bosworth, Bruce Payne, Jeff Kober, DeJuan Guy, Hammer. **1995 DVD**

ONE MAN'S WAR ★★★ A superb ensemble cast does not compensate for the bewildering lack of punch to Mike Carter and Sergio Toledo's fact-based account of a family's battle with the corrupt government of 1976 Paraguay. Anthony Hopkins is mesmerizing as the proud and stubborn Dr. Joel Filartiga, who believes political "connections" will protect his family. Made for cable TV. 91m. **DIR:** Sergio Toledo. **CAST:** Anthony Hopkins, Norma Aleandro, Fernanda Torres, Rubén Blades. **1991**

ONE MAN'S WAY ★★★ More a tribute than an in-depth biography of clergyman Norman Vincent Peale and his early ministry. Don Murray is fine in the title role and there is passion when he delivers some of Peale's actual sermons. Good insight into the questions raised by other clerics over his book, *The Power of Positive Thinking.* B&W; 105m. **DIR:** Denis Sanders. **CAST:** Don Murray, Diana Hyland, William Windom, Virginia Christine, Veronica Cartwright, Ian Wolfe. **1964**

ONE MINUTE TO ZERO ★★ Sluggish film about the Korean War benefits from some good acting by the male leads. The romantic subplot doesn't help much, but then not much could help this barely serviceable story about servicemen. B&W; 105m. **DIR:** Tay Garnett. **CAST:** Robert Mitchum, Ann Blyth, William Talman, Charles McGraw, Richard Egan. **1952**

ONE MORE SATURDAY NIGHT ★★★1/2 Al Franken and Tom Davis, who were writers and semiregulars on the original *Saturday Night Live* TV show, star in this enjoyable comedy, which they also wrote, about the problems encountered by adults and teenagers when trying to get a date on the most important night of the week. In its humane and decidedly offbeat way, *One More Saturday Night* is about the human condition in all its funny/sad complexity. Rated R for profanity and simulated sex. 95m. **DIR:** Dennis Klein. **CAST:** Al Franken, Tom Davis, Moira Harris. **1986**

ONE NIGHT IN THE TROPICS ★★1/2 Comics Abbott and Costello were brought in to enliven this revue-style romance with a few of their routines. They stole the movie, and it launched their screen careers. The nominal story line centers on a love triangle and Oscar Hammerstein, Jerome Kern, and Dorothy Fields wrote the songs. B&W; 82m. **DIR:** A. Edward Sutherland. **CAST:** Allan Jones, Nancy Kelly, Robert Cummings, Bud Abbott, Lou Costello, Leo Carrillo. **1940**

ONE NIGHT OF LOVE ★★★ The prototype of the operatic film cycle of the 1930s, it bolstered the flagging fortunes of opera star Grace Moore, who had been making movies since 1930, and successfully blended classical numbers with more "popular" song stylings. Film composer Louis Silvers won an Oscar for his score. B&W; 95m. **DIR:** Victor Schertzinger. **CAST:** Grace Moore, Lyle Talbot. **1934**

ONE NIGHT STAND (1995) ★★ Talia Shire made her director's debut with this pedestrian erotic thriller about a bored Ally Sheedy looking for Mr. Perfect. Instead, she settles for Mr. One Night Stand, played by A Martinez. He's great in bed and he's got killer looks, but there's something about him that disturbs Sheedy. Ho-hum sexual game of cat and mouse. Not rated; contains nudity, adult language, and strong sexuality. 92m. **DIR:** Talia Shire. **CAST:** Ally Sheedy, A Martinez, Frederic Forrest, Gina Hecht, Diane Salinger, Jodi Thelen. **1995**

ONE NIGHT STAND (1997) ★★ Affluent Los Angeles commercial director returns to his wife after having a torrid fling with a New York woman and slides into a midlife funk. A year later he crosses paths with his lover and reignites their relationship. A rather bogus rationalization of the main characters' actions takes the bite out of a seductively photographed story about infidelity, friendship, and terminal illness. Rated R for nudity, sex, drug use, violence, and language. 103m. **DIR:** Mike Figgis. **CAST:** Wesley Snipes, Nastassja Kinski, Robert Downey Jr., Ming-Na Wen, Kyle MacLachlan. **1997 DVD**

ONE OF OUR AIRCRAFT IS MISSING ★★★★ This British production is similar to *Desperate Journey* (1942) with Errol Flynn and Ronald Reagan. The story concerns an RAF crew who are shot down over Holland during World War II and who try to escape to England. High-caliber suspense. B&W; 106m. **DIR:** Michael Powell, Emeric Pressburger. **CAST:** Godfrey Tearle, Eric Portman, Pamela Brown, Hugh Williams, Googie Withers, Peter Ustinov. **1941**

ONE OF OUR DINOSAURS IS MISSING ★★1/2 In this moderately entertaining comedy-spy film, Peter Ustinov plays a Chinese intelligence agent attempting to recover some stolen microfilm. Helen Hayes plays a nanny who becomes involved in trying to get the film to the British authorities. Rated G. 101m. **DIR:** Robert Stevenson. **CAST:** Peter Ustinov, Helen Hayes, Derek Nimmo, Clive Revill. **1975**

ONE ON ONE ★★★★ The harsh world of big-time college athletics is brought into clearer focus by this unheralded "little film." Robby Benson is a naïve small-town basketball star who has his eyes opened when he wins a scholarship at a large western university. He doesn't play up to his coach's expectations, and the pressure is put on to take away his scholarship. Rated R. 98m. **DIR:** Lamont Johnson. **CAST:** Robby Benson, Annette O'Toole, G. D. Spradlin. **1980**

ONE RAINY AFTERNOON ★★ Silly movie about a young man who causes a furor when he kisses the wrong girl during a performance in the theater. It's a pretty slight premise, but under the skillful hands of director Rowland V. Lee (*The Count of Monte Cristo, Son of Frankenstein*), it becomes entertaining fare. A fine supporting cast helps flesh out the thin story, and a young Ida Lupino makes for a lovely leading lady. B&W; 79m. **DIR:** Rowland V. Lee. **CAST:** Francis Lederer, Ida Lupino, Roland Young, Hugh Herbert, Erik Rhodes, Mischa Auer. **1936**

ONE RIOT, ONE RANGER ★★★ Decent pilot for Chuck Norris's TV series *Walker, Texas Ranger* features the martial artist taking on a ruthless gang of bank robbers. His new partner (Clarence Gilyard Jr.) steals a number of scenes, but fights between lesser characters are poorly staged. Rated PG-13 for violence. 95m. **DIR:** Virgil Vogel. **CAST:** Chuck Norris, Clarence Gilyard Jr., Sheree Wilson, Gailard Sartain, Floyd Red Crow Westerman. **1993**

ONE RUSSIAN SUMMER 🎬 In czarist Russia of the eighteenth century, an anarchist peasant arrives at the estate of a brutish landowner to seek revenge. Rated R. 112m. **DIR:** Antonio Calenda. **CAST:** Oliver Reed, John McEnery, Claudia Cardinale, Carole André, Raymond Lovelock. **1973**

ONE SHOE MAKES IT MURDER ★★1/2 In this made-for-television movie, reminiscent in plot of *Out of the Past*, Robert Mitchum plays a world-weary detective who is hired by a crime boss (Mel Ferrer) to find his wayward wife (Angie Dickinson). Mitchum is watchable, but the story and direction never achieve a level of intensity. 97m. **DIR:** William Hale. **CAST:** Robert Mitchum, Angie Dickinson, Mel Ferrer, Jose Perez, John Harkins, Howard Hesseman. **1982**

ONE SINGS, THE OTHER DOESN'T ★★1/2 Labeled early on as a feminist film, this story is about a friendship between two different types of women spanning 1962 to 1976. When they meet again at a women's rally after ten years, they renew their • friendship. 105m. **DIR:** Agnes Varda. **CAST:** Valerie Mairesse, Thérèse Liotard. **1977**

ONE STEP TO HELL ★★ On their way to a South African jail, a trio of killers escape and head for the jungle in search of a hidden gold mine, with police officer Ty Hardin hot on their trail. Not bad, but you wouldn't want to expend a lot of effort looking for it. 94m. **DIR:** Sandy Howard. **CAST:** Ty Hardin, Pier Angeli, Rossano Brazzi, George Sanders. **1968**

ONE THAT GOT AWAY, THE ★★★★ Excellent adaptation of the book by Kendal Burt and James Leasor about a captured German aviator who keeps escaping from a multitude of British prisoner-of-war camps. Based on a true story and especially well directed and performed, this adventure is highly recommended. B&W; 106m. **DIR:** Roy Ward Baker. **CAST:** Hardy Krüger, Colin Gordon, Michael Goodliffe. **1958**

ONE TOUCH OF VENUS ★★ The Pygmalion myth gets the Hollywood treatment, long before *My Fair Lady*, although this is a wee bit diluted. Robert Walker plays a window decorator who becomes smitten, predictably, when a display statue of Venus comes to life in the form of Ava Gardner. The potentially entertaining premise is left flat by a script that lacks originality and wit. B&W; 90m. **DIR:** William A. Seiter. **CAST:** Robert Walker, Ava Gardner. **1948**

ONE TOUGH COP ★★★★ Excellent, gritty cop film tells a familiar story in an exceptional way. The title cop finds himself wedged between a lifelong friendship to the town mobster and a pair of overzealous FBI agents who want to use him as a tool to get to his buddy. Fine performances, taut direction, and razor-sharp writing throughout. Rated R for violence, profanity, and nudity. 90m. **DIR:** Bruno Barreto. **CAST:** Stephen Baldwin, Christopher Penn, Gina Gershon, Mike McGlone, Paul Guilfoyle. **1998 DVD**

ONE TRICK PONY ★★★1/2 This good little movie looks at life on the road with a has-been rock star. Paul Simon is surprisingly effective as the rock star who finds both his popularity slipping and his marriage falling apart. Rated R for nudity. 98m. **DIR:** Robert M. Young. **CAST:** Paul Simon, Lou Reed, Rip Torn, Blair Brown, Joan Hackett. **1980**

ONE TRUE THING ★★★1/2 This adaptation of Anna Quindlen's autobiographical novel of white upper-middle-class angst is about a grown child who makes a great show of wanting not to become like her parents, only to discover that she has fallen into familiar patterns—a solemn and familiar topic. There's no question that the heavyweight cast worked hard to produce something more powerful than the disease-of-the-month clichés of *Love Story*, and yet that very level of triteness occasionally overcomes the goodwill generated by the brilliant actors. Rated R for brief profanity and dramatic content. 120m. **DIR:** Carl Franklin. **CAST:** Meryl Streep, Renee Zellweger, William Hurt, Tom Everett Scott, Lauren Graham, Nicky Katt. **1998 DVD**

ONE, TWO, THREE ★★★1/2 James Cagney's "retirement" film (and his only movie with famed director Billy Wilder) is a nonstop, madcap assault on the audience. Wilder's questionable humor and odd plot about the clash between capitalism and communism could have spelled catastrophe for any other leading man, but veteran Cagney pulls it off with style. B&W; 108m. **DIR:** Billy Wilder. **CAST:** James Cagney, Arlene Francis, Horst Buchholz, Pamela Tiffin, Lilo Pulver, Red Buttons. **1961**

ONE WILD MOMENT ★★★★ In French director Claude Berri's warm and very sensitive film, a middle-aged man (Jean-Pierre Marielle) is told by his best friend's daughter that she's in love with him. Enjoy the story (which was adapted by director Stanley Donen for *Blame it on Rio*) as it should be told, as delicately and thoughtfully handled by Berri. In French with English subtitles. Not rated; the film has nudity, and profanity. 90m. **DIR:** Claude Berri. **CAST:** Jean-Pierre Marielle, Victor Lanoux. **1980**

ONE WOMAN OR TWO ★★★1/2 Gérard Depardieu plays an anthropologist digging for "the missing link." Dr. Ruth debuts as a philanthropist whose money will continue the search. And Sigourney Weaver is the advertising executive who almost ruins the entire project. Wonderful acting and superb dialogue are the highlights of this French turn on *Bringing Up Baby*. In French with English subtitles. 95m. **DIR:** Daniel Vigne. **CAST:** Sigourney Weaver, Gérard Depardieu, Dr. Ruth Westheimer. **1987**

187 ★★1/2 Dedicated Brooklyn high-school science teacher moves to California after he is nearly stabbed to death by a student. He finds the West Coast public school system is also under a state of siege and adopts a warped interpretation of the Serenity Prayer to validate vigilante justice. This feverish thriller begins with a jolt but becomes progressively muddled. The film's title refers to the penal code for homicide. Rated R for language, violence, drug use, suggested sex, and nudity. 121m. **DIR:** Kevin Reynolds. **CAST:** Samuel L. Jackson, John Heard, Kelly Rowan, Clifton Gonzalez, Lobo Sebastian, Karina Arroyave. **1997 DVD**

1-900 ★★★ Director Theo van Gogh's sexually frank comedy about two lonely professionals who meet through a sex line. What begins as a one-time fantasy escalates into a weekly habit. Ariane Schluter and Ad van Kempen are honest and sincere as the two strangers who never meet, yet share every detail of their lives over the phone. In Dutch with English subtitles. Not rated; contains adult situations and profanity. 80m. **DIR:** Theo van Gogh. **CAST:** Ariane Schulter, Ad Van Kempen. **1995 DVD**

ONE HUNDRED MEN AND A GIRL ★★★★1/2 Story of go-getting Deanna Durbin arranging a sponsor and a guest conductor for her unemployed symphony musician father (Adolphe Menjou) and his friends is a joyful musical feast. Oscar for the music department of Charles Previn and a nomination for the original story by William A. Wellman and Robert Carson. B&W; 84m. **DIR:** Henry Koster. **CAST:** Deanna Durbin, Leopold Stokowski, Adolphe Menjou, Alice Brady, Eugene Pallette, Mischa Auer, Billy Gilbert, Frank Jenks. **1937**

100 RIFLES ★★ The picture stirred controversy over Raquel Welch's interracial love scene with Jim Brown. But at this point, who cares? We're left with a so-so Western yarn. Rated R. 110m. **DIR:** Tom Gries. **CAST:** Burt Reynolds, Raquel Welch, Jim Brown, Fernando Lamas, Dan O'Herlihy. **1969**

ONE HUNDRED AND ONE DALMATIANS ★★★★ Walt Disney animated charmer, concerning a family of Dalmations—far fewer than 101, at least initially—which runs afoul of the deliciously evil Cruella de Vil. In keeping with the jazzier soundtrack, the animation has rougher edges and more vibrant colors, rather than the pastels that marked the studio's earlier efforts. 79m. **DIR:** Wolfgang Reitherman, Hamilton Luske, Clyde Geronimi. **1961 DVD**

101 DALMATIANS (1996) ★★★ Although this is a delightful time passer, it is not the equal of the original Disney classic since here the animals are restricted to meaningful glances, head nods, and tail wags rather than the zesty dialogue allowed in the animated format. The pups play second fiddle to a sexy, though deranged Cruella De Vil. In this update, De Vil is the ruthless owner of a fashion house with Anita playing employee rather than former classmate. Roger now designs video games instead of writing songs. Still, young viewers can relax and enjoy! Rated G. 90m. **DIR:** Stephen Herek. **CAST:** Glenn Close, Jeff Daniels, Joely Richardson, Joan Plowright. **1996 DVD**

1001 RABBIT TALES ★★★★ Fourteen classic cartoons are interwoven with new footage to make another feature-length film out of the well-known Warner Bros. characters. This time the theme is fairy tales. Bugs and the gang spoof "Goldilocks and the Three Bears," "Jack and the Bean Stalk," and "Little Red Riding Hood," among others. This one also contains Chuck Jones's "One Froggy Evening," one of the greatest cartoons ever! Rated G. 76m. **DIR:** Friz Freleng, Chuck Jones. **1982**

ONE MILLION B.C. ★★ D. W. Griffith reportedly directed parts of this prehistoric-age picture before producer Hal Roach and his son took over. Victor Mature, Carole Landis, and Lon Chaney Jr. try hard—and there are some good moments—but the result is a pretty dumb fantasy film. B&W; 80m. **DIR:** Hal Roach, Hal Roach Jr. **CAST:** Victor Mature, Carole Landis, Lon Chaney Jr. **1940**

ONIBABA ★★★★1/2 Director Kaneto Shindo's brilliantly photographed, savage tale of lust and survival in war-ravaged medieval Japan. A mother and daughter are drawn into deep conflict over a cunning warrior, who seduces the younger one, causing the mother to seek violent revenge. In Japanese with English subtitles. Not rated; contains nudity and is recommended for adults. B&W; 103m. **DIR:** Kaneto Shindo. **CAST:** Nobuko Otowa. **1964**

ONION FIELD, THE ★★★★ Solid screen version of Joseph Wambaugh's book about a cop (John Savage) who cracks up after his partner is murdered. James Woods and Franklyn Seales are memorable as the criminals. While not for all tastes, this film has a kind of subtle power and an almost documentary-like quality that will please those fascinated by true-crime stories. Rated R. 124m. **DIR:** Harold Becker. **CAST:** John Savage, James Woods, Franklyn Seales, Ted Danson, Ronny Cox, Dianne Hull. **1979**

ONIONHEAD ★★ One of the few Andy Griffith comedies that doesn't work, but it's not his fault. He plays a country boy in the coast guard who is sent to the galley to learn how to cook. Walter Matthau is his teacher, and their scenes together are fine. It's the silly slapstick scenes involving love-starved girls that turn the movie topsy-turvy. B&W; 110m. **DIR:** Norman Taurog. **CAST:** Andy Griffith, Walter Matthau, Erin O'Brien, Ray Danton, Felicia Farr, Joey Bishop, Joe Mantell, James Gregory, Claude Akins, Roscoe Karns. **1958**

ONLY ANGELS HAVE WINGS ★★★★ Director Howard Hawks at his best tells yet another tale of professionals: pilots who fly the mail through treacherous weather and terrain in South America. Snappy dialogue and no-nonsense characters are handled deftly by the entire cast. It's great stuff, with Rita Hayworth getting a career-starting, glamorous role. B&W; 121m. **DIR:** Howard Hawks. **CAST:** Cary Grant, Jean Arthur, Richard Barthelmess, Rita Hayworth, Thomas Mitchell, John Carroll, Sig Ruman, Allyn Joslyn, Noah Beery Jr. **1939 DVD**

ONLY LOVE ★★1/2 Another *Love Story* from author Erich Segal, this one starring Rob Morrow and Mathilda May as doctors who fall in love, but when she's torn from his side, he marries the lovely Marisa Tomei. Then May returns with a debilitating illness that only Morrow can cure. If it sounds like the substance of a made-for-television soap opera, it is. Not rated. 130m. **DIR:** John Erman. **CAST:** Rob Morrow, Mathilda May, Marisa Tomei, Jeroen Krabbé, Paul Freeman. **1998**

ONLY ONE NIGHT ★★★1/2 Ingrid Bergman plays a woman courted by a circus performer who feels he is really beneath her station. She thinks so, too, and makes sure he doesn't forget it. One of her last Swedish films, and one of the films her new Hollywood bosses didn't dare remake because of the suggestive material. B&W; 89m. **DIR:** Gustav Molander. **CAST:** Ingrid Bergman, Edvin Adolphson. **1939**

ONLY THE BRAVE ★★★ For those who like particularly brutal coming-of-age stories. Two teenage girls live bleak lives in the shadow of an Australian oil refinery and forge a turbulent friendship that soon crosses all boundaries as they find themselves trapped in a nihilistic vortex. This may be startling for its realism, but it's just too dark for its own good. Letter-boxed. Not rated; contains profanity and violence. 62m. **DIR:** Ana Kokkinos. **CAST:** Elena Mandalis, Dora Kaskanis, Maude Davy. **1994**

ONLY THE LONELY ★★★1/2 Those *Home Alone* guys, writer John Hughes and director Chris Columbus, cooked up this follow-up to their surprise box-office smash. John Candy stars as a 38-year-old local cop who falls in love with a mortician's daughter (Ally Sheedy), much to the disapproval of his feisty, opinionated Irish mother (a delightful performance by scene-stealer Maureen O'Hara). Rated PG-13 for profanity. 110m. **DIR:** Chris Columbus. **CAST:** John Candy, Maureen O'Hara, Ally Sheedy, Anthony Quinn, James Belushi, Kevin Dunn, Milo O'Shea, Bert Remsen, Macaulay Culkin. **1991**

ONLY THE STRONG ★★★ A world-class, martial-arts champion pits his strength and know-how against juvenile gangs and teaches them self-respect. The martial-arts sequences using the Brazilian Capoeira techniques are exciting to watch, and the story, though predictable, is well staged and well acted. Rated R for violence and profanity. 112m. **DIR:** Sheldon Lettich. **CAST:** Mark Dacascos, Stacey Travis, Paco Christian Prieto, Tod Susman, Richard Coca, Geoffrey Lewis. **1993**

ONLY THE VALIANT ★★1/2 Cavalry captain Gregory Peck is saddled not only with problems with Native Americans but irritability among his own troops. Produced by Cagney Productions, this Western is predictable but entertaining. B&W; 105m. **DIR:** Gordon Douglas. **CAST:** Gregory Peck, Ward Bond, Barbara Payton; Gig Young. **1951**

ONLY THRILL, THE ★★ True love never runs smooth, but this romantic drama is like riding an inner tube over Niagara Falls. Diane Keaton and Sam Shepard are wasted in this plain-Jane romance about two neighbors afraid of commitment who spend twenty-five years flirting with each other. When their children fall in love, they must reconcile their feelings. Robert Patrick and Diane Lane are miscast as the lovelorn children; the film lacks chemistry between the leads. Rated R for language. 103m. **DIR:** Peter Masterson. **CAST:** Diane Keaton, Sam Shepard, Diane Lane, Robert Patrick. **1997**

ONLY TWO CAN PLAY ★★★1/2 Peter Sellers is fabulous as a frustrated but determined Don Juan with aspirations of wooing society woman Mai Zetterling. As in so many of his roles, Sellers is funny and appealing in every move and mood. And Zetterling is the perfect choice for the haughty object of his attentions. 106m. **DIR:** Sidney Gilliat. **CAST:** Peter Sellers, Mai Zetterling, Richard Attenborough, Virginia Maskell. **1962**

ONLY WHEN I LAUGH ★★★ A brilliant but self-destructive actress (Marsha Mason) and her daughter (Kristy McNichol) reach toward understanding in this sometimes funny, sometimes tearful, but always entertaining adaptation by Neil Simon of his play *The Gingerbread Lady*. Rated R for profanity. 121m. **DIR:** Glenn Jordan. **CAST:** Marsha Mason, Kristy McNichol, James Coco, Joan Hackett. **1981**

ONLY WITH MARRIED MEN ★★ This TV movie is a pleasant yet thoroughly predictable light sex comedy about a woman (Michele Lee) who decides she will only date married men. She mistakes a bachelor (David Birney) for his married partner. 74m. **DIR:** Jerry Paris. **CAST:** David Birney, Michele Lee, Dom DeLuise, Judy Carne, Gavin MacLeod. **1974**

ONLY YOU (1991) ★★★ Enjoyable romantic romp features an adorable cast and some witty dialogue. Andrew McCarthy takes time off from his busy schedule to be with gorgeous Kelly Preston at a scenic seaside resort, where he meets cute Helen Hunt. Director Betty Thomas keeps everything light and charming. Rated PG-13 for language. 85m. **DIR:** Betty Thomas. **CAST:** Andrew McCarthy, Kelly Preston, Helen Hunt. **1991**

ONLY YOU (1994) ★★★★ Marisa Tomei makes an adorable Audrey Hepburn-type heroine for the 1990s in this hilarious love hunt with some ties to Hepburn's *Roman Holiday*. Tomei plays a soon-to-be-wed schoolteacher who flies to Rome hoping to find her fated lover before she weds a reserved podiatrist. Once there, she finds Robert Downey Jr., who appears to be her missing half. Don't miss the fun! Rated PG for sexual situations. 99m. **DIR:** Norman Jewison. **CAST:** Marisa Tomei, Robert Downey Jr., Bonnie Hunt, Joaquim de Almeida, Fisher Stevens, Billy Zane, John Benjamin Hickey. **1994 DVD**

OPEN CITY ★★★★1/2 Stunning study of resistance and survival in World War II Italy was the first important film to come out of postwar Europe and has been considered a classic in realism. Co-scripted by a young Federico Fellini, this powerful story traces the threads of people's lives as they interact and eventually entangle themselves in the shadow of their Gestapo-controlled "open city." In Italian with English subtitles. B&W; 105m. **DIR:** Roberto Rossellini. **CAST:** Aldo Fabrizi, Anna Magnani. **1946 DVD**

OPEN DOORS ★★★★ A sturdy and slow-moving but engrossing Italian drama about a stubbornly determined judge attempting to establish justice in a courtroom dominated by Fascist dictates. It earned an Oscar nomination as best foreign-language film. In Italian with English subtitles. 109m. **DIR:** Gianni Amelio. **CAST:** Gian Maria Volonté. **1991**

OPEN HOUSE 🎬 This slasher movie features some particularly repellent and sadistic murders, along with nudity and sexual situations. A definite R. 95m. **DIR:** Jag Mundhra. **CAST:** Joseph Bottoms, Adrienne Barbeau, Rudy Ramos, Tiffany Bolling. **1987**

OPEN SEASON ★★★★ Very funny, biting film about what happens when the television-ratings system gets screwed up, and—for a short while—it appears TV audiences have learned to appreciate class and culture. Written and directed by Robert Wuhl. Rated R for profanity and nudity. 105m. **DIR:** Robert Wuhl. **CAST:** Robert Wuhl, Rod Taylor, Gailard Sartain, Helen Shaver. **1996**

OPEN YOUR EYES ★★★★★ A handsome young playboy is horribly disfigured when a spurned lover commits suicide by driving her car into a wall with him in the passenger seat. But is he going crazy, or is she not really dead? This stylish, wildly original psychological thriller, fiendishly clever and intricately plotted, will keep you guessing right up to the end. In Spanish with English subtitles. Rated R for nudity, sexual scenes, brief violence, and profanity (in subtitles). 117m. **DIR:** Alejandro Amenabar. **CAST:** Eduardo Noriega, Penelope Cruz, Fele Martinez, Najwa Nimri. **1997**

OPENING NIGHT ★★★ Gena Rowlands delivers a potent performance as an actress coming to grips with her life on the opening night of her new play. Director John Cassavetes guides Rowlands through this emotional roller coaster with his usual improvisational style, giving Rowlands every opportunity to shine. The events leading up to and following the actual production provide the fine cast with plenty of room to strut their stuff. Rated PG-13 for language. 144m. **DIR:** John Cassavetes. **CAST:** Gena Rowlands, Ben Gazzara, Joan Blondell, Paul Stewart, Zohra Lampert. **1977 DVD**

OPERA DO MALANDRO ★★★ A homage to the Hollywood musicals of the Forties, this vibrant, stylish film is set in Rio's seedy backstreets on the eve of the Pearl Harbor invasion. The story is about a gangster whose search for the American dream is disrupted by his love for a beautiful Brazilian girl. In Portuguese with English subtitles. 108m. **DIR:** Ruy Guerra. **CAST:** Edson Celulari, Claudia Ohana. **1987**

OPERATION AMSTERDAM ★★★ It's 1940 and Allied spies penetrate Holland to prevent the invading Nazis from getting their hands on Amsterdam's rich cache of diamonds. Filmed in a semidocumentary style, this movie is standard but well acted and pro-

duced. B&W; 105m. **DIR:** Michael McCarthy. **CAST:** Peter Finch, Eva Bartok, Tony Britton, Alexander Knox. **1960**

OPERATION C.I.A. ★★1/2 Political intrigue in Vietnam before the United States's full involvement finds a youthful Burt Reynolds as an agent assigned to derail an assassination attempt. Good location photography and Reynolds's enthusiasm and believability mark this film as one of the best chase films of the mid-1960s. B&W; 90m. **DIR:** Christian Nyby. **CAST:** Burt Reynolds, Kieu Chinh, Danielle Aubry, John Hoyt. **1965**

OPERATION CONDOR (JACKIE CHAN) ★★★ International soldier of fortune Jackie Chan accepts an assignment to locate a huge cache of gold supposedly buried by Nazis beneath the Sahara during the closing days of World War II. Our hero's adventures involve the usual clumsy villains and decorative women, and everything climaxes in an impressive subterranean Nazi stronghold that provides Chan with opportunities for his trademarked fight sequences with "convenient" objects. Rated PG-13 for violence and brief nudity. 90m. **DIR:** Jackie Chan. **CAST:** Jackie Chan, Carol Cheng, Eva Cobo De Garcia, Shoko Ikeda. **1997 DVD**

OPERATION CONDOR (DON "THE DRAGON" WILSON) 🎬 Don "The Dragon" Wilson heads up yet another mindless exercise in violence, playing a cop hot on the trail of his partner's killer in India. Wilson has played this role so many times he could do it in his sleep, which is the case here. Rated R for adult situations, language, and violence. 88m. **DIR:** Fred Olen Ray. **CAST:** Don "The Dragon" Wilson. **1997**

OPERATION CROSSBOW ★★★★ A trio of specially trained commandos are sent to head off Hitler's rapidly developing rocket program. Suspenseful and exciting, with a top-notch international cast, fine special effects. 116m. **DIR:** Michael Anderson. **CAST:** George Peppard, Sophia Loren, Trevor Howard, John Mills, Richard Johnson, Tom Courtenay, Lilli Palmer, Jeremy Kemp, Paul Henreid, Helmut Dantine, Richard Todd, Sylvia Syms. **1965**

OPERATION DELTA FORCE 🎬 Awful action film about a group of terrorists planning to release an Armageddon disease to the world. Talented cast deserves better. Rated R for violence and profanity. 93m. **DIR:** Sam Firstenberg. **CAST:** Ernie Hudson, Jeff Fahey, Frank Zagarino, Hal Holbrook, Reb Stewart. **1996**

OPERATION DELTA FORCE 2 🎬 The original *Delta Force* franchise with Chuck Norris wasn't that good to begin with. Do we really need another rip-off sequel? Rated R for violence and language. 98m. **DIR:** Yossi Wein. **CAST:** Michael McGrady, Simon Jones, K. Kenneth Campbell, Dale Dye. **1997 DVD**

OPERATION DUMBO DROP ★★★ Danny Glover and Ray Liotta play American officers in Vietnam who set out to obtain an elephant for a friendly native village. The Vietnam War makes an unorthodox background for a lightweight family comedy, but the film is pleasant entertainment. Slapstick is efficiently mixed with sentiment. Rated PG for war action and mild profanity. 102m. **DIR:** Simon Wincer.

CAST: Danny Glover, Ray Liotta, Denis Leary, Corin Nemec, Doug E. Doug. **1995**

OPERATION GOLDEN PHOENIX 🐢 Laughable codswallop involving two medallions and a hidden treasure fuels this low-rent Canadian-Lebanese martial arts opus. Director-star Jalal Merhi wears two hats too many; he may kick with style, but he couldn't emote to save his life ... and doesn't know the first thing about helming a film. Rated R for violence and profanity. 95m. **DIR:** Jalal Merhi. **CAST:** Jalal Merhi, Loreen Avedon, James Hong. **1994**

OPERATION INTERCEPT ★★ A pair of American fighter pilots attempt to stop a Russian scientist out for revenge. An interesting characterization by Natasha Andreichenko as the mad Russian is all that keeps this cheapo thriller from being completely forgettable. Rated R for profanity and violence. 94m. **DIR:** Paul Levine. **CAST:** Bruce Payne, Natasha Andreichenko, John Stockwell, Lance Henriksen, Corinne Bohrer. **1995**

OPERATION 'NAM ★★ Run-of-the-mill tale about a group of bored Vietnam vets going back to Vietnam to rescue their leader, still held in a POW camp. Notable only for the appearance of Ethan Wayne, one of John's sons. Not rated; contains violence, language, and nudity. 85m. **DIR:** Larry Ludman. **CAST:** Oliver Tobias, Christopher Connelly, Manfred Lehman, John Steiner, Ethan Wayne, Donald Pleasence. **1985**

OPERATION PACIFIC ★★★1/2 Action, suspense, comedy, and romance are nicely mixed in this fact-based film about the rush to perfect American torpedoes during World War II. John Wayne and Ward Bond are the navy men frustrated by the nonexploding, submerged missiles, and Patricia Neal is the nurse who can't quite decide whether or not she loves Wayne. B&W; 111m. **DIR:** George Waggner. **CAST:** John Wayne, Patricia Neal, Ward Bond, Scott Forbes, Philip Carey, Paul Picerni, Martin Milner, Jack Pennick, William Campbell. **1951**

OPERATION PETTICOAT ★★★★ The ageless Cary Grant stars with Tony Curtis in this wacky service comedy. They are captain and first officer of a submarine that undergoes a madcap series of misadventures during World War II. Their voyage across the Pacific is further complicated when a group of navy women is forced to join the crew. 124m. **DIR:** Blake Edwards. **CAST:** Cary Grant, Tony Curtis, Dina Merrill, Gene Evans, Arthur O'Connell, Dick Sargent. **1959**

OPERATION THUNDERBOLT ★★ Another film, like *The Raid on Entebbe*, dealing with the Israeli commando raid in Uganda in 1976 to free 104 hijacked airline passengers. Overly sentimental, with routine action sequences. No MPAA rating. 125m. **DIR:** Menahem Golan. **CAST:** Yehoram Gaon, Klaus Kinski, Assaf Dayan. **1977**

OPERATION WAR ZONE 🐢 Courier lost in Vietnam possesses a document that could affect the outcome of the war. Too bad it wasn't the script for this film. 89m. **DIR:** David A. Prior. **CAST:** David Marriott, Joe Spinell. **1989**

OPERATOR 13 ★★★ Two of Hollywood's most glamorous players get in a romantic clinch similar to Scarlett O'Hara and Rhett Butler's five years before *Gone with the Wind*. Marion Davies plays a Yankee spy during the Civil War. Gary Cooper is a southern sympathizer. They square off against each other and love blooms. Very romantic, very flashy, and slightly dated. B&W; 86m. **DIR:** Richard Boleslawski. **CAST:** Marion Davies, Gary Cooper, Jean Parker, Katharine Alexander, Ted Healy, Hattie McDaniel, Russell Hardie, Fuzzy Knight, Douglass Dumbrille. **1934**

OPPONENT, THE ★★1/2 A boxer rescues a mob boss's daughter, only to be swept up in her father's corrupt world. Now he's fighting for his life in a film that plays like a low-budget *Rocky*. Rated R for violence. 102m. **DIR:** Sergio Martino. **CAST:** Daniel Greene, Ernest Borgnine, Mary Stavin. **1990**

OPPORTUNITY KNOCKS ★★★ Mixing elements from *Trading Places* and *The Sting*, this is a big-screen sitcom designed to show off the talents of *Saturday Night Live* regular Dana Carvey. It does its job well. Carvey is a hoot as a con-man who lucks into a big score while hiding from a revenge-minded gangster. Rated PG-13 for profanity and adult humor. 95m. **DIR:** Donald Petrie. **CAST:** Dana Carvey, Robert Loggia, Todd Graff, Julia Campbell, Milo O'Shea, James Tolkan. **1990**

OPPOSING FORCE ★★1/2 In this average action-adventure movie, a group of soldiers undergo simulated prisoner-of-war training. When the commanding officer (Anthony Zerbe) goes insane, he rapes the sole female soldier (Lisa Eichhorn) and sets into motion a chain of violent events. Rated R for profanity and violence. 97m. **DIR:** Eric Karson. **CAST:** Tom Skerritt, Lisa Eichhorn, Anthony Zerbe, Richard Roundtree, John Considine. **1986**

●**OPPOSITE CORNERS** ★★★ Gritty drama about a mafioso and the son he relentlessly pushes toward the dream he himself could never achieve: that of a championship boxer. That relentlessness, and a dark secret, may eventually push the two forever apart. Rated R for profanity, violence, and sexual situations. 106m. **DIR:** Louis D'Esposito. **CAST:** Cathy Moriarty, Anthony Dennison, Billy Warlock, Frankie Valli, Ray "Boom Boom" Mancini, Jay Acovone. **1996**

OPPOSITE OF SEX, THE ★★1/2 This audacious skewering of straight and gay relationships, dysfunctional families, and manipulative movie conventions is wickedly funny for half its run and then gradually withers. A trailer-park Lolita is the catalyst of an outrageous soap opera in which she runs away from home, seduces and marries her gay half-brother's lover, becomes pregnant, and cheats on her new spouse. Rated R for language and sexuality. 105m. **DIR:** Don Roos. **CAST:** Christina Ricci, Martin Donovan, Lisa Kudrow, Lyle Lovett, Ivan Sergei. **1998 DVD**

OPPOSITE SEX, THE (1956) ★★1/2 An uninspired remake of Clare Boothe's *The Women*, a good satire about woman's inhumanity to woman. They diluted it by adding macho male stereotypes instead of just talking about them like the first version did. 117m. **DIR:** David Miller. **CAST:** June Allyson, Ann Sheridan, Joan Blondell, Joan Collins, Ann Miller, Charlotte Greenwood, Jim Backus, Dolores Gray, Agnes Moorehead, Leslie Nielsen, Jeff Richards. **1956**

OPPOSITE SEX (AND HOW TO LIVE WITH THEM), THE (1993) 🐢 A waste of time and talent. The sexcapades of young singles are exploited more than they are explained in a laughless comedy about people who can't keep their hormones under control. The big scene is a "Strip Twister" dance scene followed by group wine tasting. Rated R for obvious reasons. 86m. DIR: Matthew Meshekoff. CAST: Arye Gross, Courteney Cox, Kevin Pollak, Julie Brown, Mitchell Ryan, Jack Carter, Phil Bruns, Mitzi McCall, B. J. Ward. 1993

OPTIONS ★★ Modest little comedy features a nerdish contract man for TV movies treading the wilds of Africa—in complete suit and tie, plus briefcase!—to get the option on another life story. Rated PG for violence. 105m. DIR: Camilo Vila. CAST: Matt Salinger, Joanna Pacula, John Kani. 1988

ORACLE, THE ★★ A woman discovers that the last occupant of her new apartment was a murder victim. Reaching out from beyond the grave, he tries to force her to avenge his death. Better than average for this sort of low-budget chiller, with some effective shocks and a few interesting plot twists. Rated R for gore. 94m. DIR: Roberta Findlay. CAST: Caroline Capers Powers, Roger Neil. 1985

•ORANGES ARE NOT THE ONLY FRUIT ★★★★ Made for British television, this adaptation of Jeanette Winterson's novel follows the growing pains of Jess, a teenager in a Northern England mill town where everyone belongs to a strict fundamentalist church. Jess's discovery that she is a lesbian will cause her banishment from the flock (and her zealous mother's house) if it is divulged. Richly drawn characters and splashes of rueful humor makes this an intelligent film with which any viewer can sympathize. Not rated; contains sexual situations. 165m. DIR: Beeban Kidron. CAST: Charlotte Coleman, Geraldine McEwan, Kenneth Cranham, Celia Imrie. 1990

ORCA ★★★ Where *Jaws* was an exaggerated horror story, *Orca* is based on the tragic truth. Motivated by profit, Richard Harris and his crew go out with a huge net and find a family of whales. He misses the male and harpoons the female, who dies and aborts, leaving her huge mate to wreak havoc on the tiny seaport. Rated PG. 92m. DIR: Michael Anderson. CAST: Richard Harris, Keenan Wynn, Will Sampson, Bo Derek, Robert Carradine, Charlotte Rampling. 1977

ORCHESTRA REHEARSAL ★★1/2 Subpar Fellini film, made for Italian television, has squabbling members of an orchestra rebel against their dictatorial conductor. This political allegory is at best vague and at worst incomprehensible to those unschooled in Italian current events. Not rated; contains some profanity. In Italian with English subtitles 72m. DIR: Federico Fellini. CAST: Balduin Bass, Clara Colosimo. 1979

ORCHESTRA WIVES ★★★ Taking second place to the wonderful music of Glenn Miller and his orchestra is a story about the problems of the wives of the band members, both on and off the road. Academy Award nomination for Harry Warren and Mack Gordon's "I've Got A Gal In Kalamazoo." B&W; 98m. DIR: Archie Mayo. CAST: Glenn Miller, Lynn Bari, Carole Landis, George Montgomery, Cesar Romero, Ann Rutherford. 1942

ORDEAL BY INNOCENCE ★★ In this production of yet another Agatha Christie novel, the cast may be stellar, but the performances are almost all phoned in. Donald Sutherland plays a man who is certain that justice has been ill served in a small British community. Rated PG-13 for language and nudity. 91m. DIR: Desmond Davis. CAST: Donald Sutherland, Sarah Miles, Christopher Plummer, Ian McShane, Diana Quick, Faye Dunaway. 1984

ORDEAL IN THE ARCTIC ★★★ Made-for-cable adventure stars Richard Chamberlain as the pilot of a military transport plane that crashes in the outer regions of the Arctic. A rescue attempt is aborted when a severe storm moves into the area. Human drama involves the survivors and their quest to stay alive. Exciting action sequences and a decent cast hold this familiar tale together. Rated PG. 93m. DIR: Mark Sobel. CAST: Richard Chamberlain, Melanie Mayron, Catherine Mary Stewart. 1997

ORDEAL OF DR. MUDD, THE ★★★1/2 The true story of Dr. Samuel Mudd, who innocently aided the injured, fleeing John Wilkes Booth following Lincoln's assassination and was sent to prison for alleged participation in the conspiracy. Dennis Weaver's fine portrayal of the ill-fated doctor makes this film well worthwhile. More than a century passed before Mudd was cleared, thanks to the efforts of a descendant, newscaster Roger Mudd. Rated PG. 143m. DIR: Paul Wendkos. CAST: Dennis Weaver, Susan Sullivan, Richard Dysart, Arthur Hill. 1980

ORDER OF THE BLACK EAGLE ★★ Ian Hunter is the James Bondish main character, Duncan Jax, abetted in destroying a neo-Nazi group by his sidekick, a baboon, and a band of misfits. Rated R for violence and language. 93m. DIR: Worth Keeter. CAST: Ian Hunter, Charles K. Bibby, William T. Hicks, Jill Donnellan, Anna Rappagna, Flo Hyman. 1987

ORDER OF THE EAGLE ★★★ On a camping trip in the woods, a boy scout discovers computer discs in a plane wreck. They contain secret military plans that bad guy Frank Stallone wants back. Well-written thriller. Not rated; contains mild violence. 82m. DIR: Thomas Baldwin. CAST: Frank Stallone, William Zipp, Casey Hirsch. 1989

ORDET ★★★★1/2 Possibly the greatest work of Carl Dreyer, the Danish director whose films (*The Passion of Joan of Arc, Day of Wrath*) demonstrate an intellectual obsession with the nature of religious faith in the modern world. In this drama, based on a play written by a priest who was murdered by the Nazis, characters in a small, God-fearing town wrestle between two varieties of faith, one puritanical, the other life affirming. In Danish with English subtitles. B&W; 125m. DIR: Carl Dreyer. CAST: Henrik Malberg. 1955

ORDINARY HEROES ★★★ A moving love story about a young couple torn apart when the man (Richard Dean Anderson) is drafted into the army and sent to Vietnam. He returns from combat blinded and attempts to piece his broken life back together with his former girlfriend (Valerie Bertinelli). This absorbing drama gets its strength from strong performances by both leads. Rated PG.

90m. **DIR:** Peter H. Cooper. **CAST:** Richard Dean Anderson, Valerie Bertinelli, Doris Roberts. **1986**

ORDINARY MAGIC ★★★ Inspiring family film stars Ryan Reynolds as an orphan who must leave India and live with his aunt in Canada. His interest in Indian culture and his practice of yoga make him a prime target for ridicule. When his aunt's house is scheduled for demolition, he wages a personal battle to save his new home. Glenne Headly lends nice support as the withdrawn aunt who comes alive. Not rated. 96m. **DIR:** Giles Walker. **CAST:** Glenne Headly, David Fox, Paul Anka, Ryan Reynolds. **1993**

ORDINARY PEOPLE ★★★★1/2 This moving human drama, which won the Academy Award for best picture of 1980, marked the directorial debut of Robert Redford … and an auspicious one it is, too. Redford elicits memorable performances from Mary Tyler Moore, Donald Sutherland, Timothy Hutton, and Judd Hirsch and makes the intelligent, powerful script by Alvin Sargent seem even better. Rated R for adult situations. 123m. **DIR:** Robert Redford. **CAST:** Mary Tyler Moore, Donald Sutherland, Timothy Hutton, Judd Hirsch, Elizabeth McGovern, Dinah Manoff, James B. Sikking. **1980**

ORGANIZATION, THE ★★★ This is the third and last installment of the Virgil Tibbs series based on the character Sidney Poitier originated in *In the Heat of the Night*. Tibbs is out to break up a ring of dope smugglers. A pretty good cop film, with some exciting action scenes. Rated PG; some strong stuff for the kids. 107m. **DIR:** Don Medford. **CAST:** Sidney Poitier, Barbara McNair, Raul Julia, Sheree North. **1971**

ORGANIZER, THE ★★★★ An Oscar nominee for best original screenplay, this is an effective period drama from director Mario Monicelli, better known for comedies like *Big Deal on Madonna Street*. Marcello Mastroianni stars as an unemployed teacher who helps organize a labor union at a factory in turn-of-the-century Turin. Not rated. In Italian with English subtitles. 127m. **DIR:** Mario Monicelli. **CAST:** Marcello Mastroianni, Renato Salvatori, Annie Giradot, Bernard Blier. **1964**

ORGAZMO 🐾 A nice Mormon boy stumbles into the porno business, where he becomes a star playing Orgazmo, a well-endowed superhero. This incompetent, humor-free comedy drew protests and pickets from the Mormon Church, but despite the free publicity it deservedly sank at the box office. Rated NC-17 for profanity, nudity, and raunchy jokes. 95m. **DIR:** Trey Parker. **CAST:** Trey Parker, Dian Bachar, Robyn Lynne Raab, Michael Dean Jacobs. **1998**

ORGUSS, VOLS. 1–4 ★★ Japanese animation. Mediocre series involving a young soldier who is transplanted suddenly from his own world into a parallel dimension. Standard television-series entry. Not rated, with brief nudity. 55m.–80m. **DIR:** Noboru Ishiguro, Yasuyoshi Mikamoto. **1983**

ORGY OF THE DEAD 🐾 There's no plot to speak of, as the "Emperor of the Dead" (Criswell) holds court in a graveyard. Not rated. 82m. **DIR:** A. C. Stephen. **CAST:** Criswell, Pat Barringer, William Bates. **1965**

ORIANE ★★★ A taut gothic romance about a young woman who returns to a hacienda inherited from her aunt only to find herself caught up in a mystery concerning past events. Fina Torres scores some high marks in her first feature film that won the coveted Camera d'Or at Cannes in 1985. In Spanish and French with English subtitles. Not rated; contains nudity. 88m. **DIR:** Fina Torres. **CAST:** Doris Wells. **1985**

ORIGINAL GANGSTAS ★★ Retired football hero returns to his economically struggling hometown when his father is assaulted after witnessing a drive-by killing. The gridiron great and his former "Buds in the Hood" reband to wipe out a vicious, heavily armed mob that has evolved from their old neighborhood clique. The movie tries both to transcend and exploit its action roots with uneven, predictable results. Rated R for language and violence. 99m. **DIR:** Larry Cohen. **CAST:** Fred Williamson, Pam Grier, Jim Brown, Ron O'Neal, Richard Roundtree, Wings Hauser, Oscar Brown Jr. **1996 DVD**

ORIGINAL INTENT ★★ Preachy, heavy-handed film about a yuppie lawyer becoming aware of the homeless problem and trying to save a shelter from a greedy developer. Rated PG for profanity. 97m. **DIR:** Robert Marcarelli. **CAST:** Jay Richardson, Candy Clark, Martin Sheen, Kris Kristofferson, Vince Edwards, Robert DoQui. **1991**

•**ORIGINAL SINS** ★★★ Bound to tick off at least someone—especially Catholics—this little indie flick is a satirical look at faith as three devout teenagers meet a mysterious salesman (who may be the savior) and proceed to faint. They wake up to find they've been taken advantage of. Nothing is sacred as the directors take a shot at just about every institution possible and prove that the indie scene is very much alive. Not rated; contains nudity, violence, and profanity. 108m. **DIR:** Matthew Howe, Howard Berger. **CAST:** Cheryl Clifford, Angelique de Rochambeau, Faustina, Scooter McCrae. **1994**

ORLANDO ★★ The plight of women throughout the ages is examined in director Sally Potter's smug, off-putting screen adaptation of the novella by Virginia Woolf. It's visually stunning, but woe to anyone who expects to be entertained. Worst of all, Potter misuses gifted actress Tilda Swinton, who is expected to portray both a man and a woman. Balderdash. Rated PG-13 for violence, nudity, and suggested sex. 93m. **DIR:** Sally Potter. **CAST:** Tilda Swinton, Billy Zane, John Wood, Charlotte Valandrey, Heathcote Williams, Quentin Crisp, Peter Eyre, Thom Hoffman, Dudley Sutton. **1993 DVD**

ORPHAN BOY OF VIENNA, AN ★★ The only reason to see this hokey tearjerker about a boy who struggles to adjust to life in a German orphanage is the presence of the famous Vienna Boys' Choir, accompanied in several performances by the Vienna Philharmonic. In German with English subtitles. B&W; 90m. **DIR:** Max Neufeld. **CAST:** Ferdinand Materhofer. **1937**

ORPHAN TRAIN ★★★1/2 Inspirational tale of a young woman's desire to help thousands of orphans who were roaming the streets of New York in the 1850s. Realizing that her soup kitchen can't keep the kids out of trouble, she takes a group out west in hopes of finding farming families willing to adopt them. Originally shown on TV. 150m. **DIR:** William A.

Graham. **CAST:** Jill Eikenberry, Kevin Dobson, Linda Manz, Glenn Close. **1979**

ORPHANS ★★★★ Based on the play by Lyle Kessler, this compact drama is a psychological thriller with a poignant twist. Albert Finney effectively portrays an affluent American gangster who does more than merely befriend two homeless young men—Treat, an angry delinquent (Matthew Modine), and Phillips (Kevin Anderson), his helpless younger brother. In a short time, he changes their lives. Rated R. 115m. **DIR:** Alan J. Pakula. **CAST:** Albert Finney, Matthew Modine, Kevin Anderson. **1987**

ORPHANS OF THE STORM ★★★1/2 Film's first master director blends fact and fiction, mixing the French Revolution with the trials and tribulations of two sisters—one blind and raised by thieves, the other betrayed by self-saving aristocrats. The plot creaks with age, but the settings and action spell good entertainment. Silent. B&W; 125m. **DIR:** D. W. Griffith. **CAST:** Lillian Gish, Dorothy Gish, Sidney Herbert, Sheldon Lewis, Monte Blue, Joseph Schildkraut, Creighton Hale, Morgan Wallace. **1922 DVD**

ORPHEUS ★★★1/2 Jean Cocteau's surreal account of the Greek myth with Jean Marais as Orpheus, the successful, envied, and despised poet who thrusts himself beyond mortality. Maria Casares costars as the lonely, troubled, passionate Death. Cocteau's poetic imagery will pull you deep into the fantasy. In French with English subtitles. B&W; 86m. **DIR:** Jean Cocteau. **CAST:** Jean Marais, Maria Casares. **1949 DVD**

ORPHEUS DESCENDING ★★★1/2 Fascinatingly horrifying made-for-cable adaptation of Tennessee Williams's slice-of-southern-Gothic stage play. Vanessa Redgrave fails at an Italian accent, but when she abandons an overused hysterical laugh, she delivers her usual fine performance. Not rated, contains nudity, profanity, and violence. 117m. **DIR:** Peter Hall. **CAST:** Vanessa Redgrave, Kevin Anderson, Brad Sullivan. **1990**

OSAKA ELEGY ★★★★ Excellent dramatic comedy that realistically shows the exploitation of women in Japanese society. Isuzu Yamada plays a tough, sassy working girl who is continuously taken advantage of by men notorious for their greed and spinelessness. In Japanese with English subtitles. B&W; 75m. **DIR:** Kenji Mizoguchi. **CAST:** Isuzu Yamada. **1936**

OSCAR, THE (1966) 💘 An unscrupulous actor advances his career at the expense of others. 119m. **DIR:** Russell Rouse. **CAST:** Stephen Boyd, Elke Sommer, Tony Bennett, Eleanor Parker, Ernest Borgnine, Joseph Cotten. **1966**

OSCAR (1991) ★★★ This farce features a perfectly capable comic performance from Sylvester Stallone as a gangster who promises his dying father (Kirk Douglas in a hilarious cameo) that he'll go straight. But complications make keeping his vow difficult. An all-star supporting cast help buoy the story, which often drags under John Landis's laid-back direction. Rated PG for brief profanity. 110m. **DIR:** John Landis. **CAST:** Sylvester Stallone, Ornella Muti, Peter Riegert, Vincent Spano, Tim Curry, Chazz Palminteri, Marisa Tomei, Elizabeth Barondes, Kirk Douglas, Don Ameche, Yvonne De Carlo, Eddie

Bracken, Martin Ferrero, Harry Shearer, Linda Gray, William Atherton. **1991**

OSSESSIONE ★★★★ James M. Cain's *The Postman Always Rings Twice* as adapted to Italian locations. The fatal triangle here is a dissatisfied wife, a vulgar husband, and the inevitable charming stranger. A landmark in the development of both *film noir* and Italian neorealism. In Italian with English subtitles. B&W; 135m. **DIR:** Luchino Visconti. **CAST:** Clara Calamai, Massimo Girotti. **1942**

OSTERMAN WEEKEND, THE ★★ Sam Peckinpah's last is a confusing action movie with scarce viewing rewards for the filmmaker's fans. Based on Robert Ludlum's novel, it tells a complicated and convoluted story of espionage, revenge, and duplicity. Rated R for profanity, nudity, sex, and violence. 102m. **DIR:** Sam Peckinpah. **CAST:** Rutger Hauer, John Hurt, Burt Lancaster, Dennis Hopper, Chris Sarandon, Meg Foster. **1983**

OTAKU NO VIDEO ★★★ Incredibly dense with inside jokes and industry references, this tongue-in-cheek animated entry may be too esoteric for the casual viewer but any rabid animation fan (or *otaku*) will find it funny. The Japanese subculture of animation enthusiasts (somewhat comparable to *Star Trek* fans in the U.S.) is examined through an animated story interspersed with live, mock interviews of fans and statistical charts. In Japanese with English subtitles. Not rated; contains nudity. 100m. **DIR:** Mori Takeshi. **1991**

OTELLO ★★★★★ As with his screen version of *La Traviata*, Franco Zeffirelli's *Otello* is a masterpiece of filmed opera. In fact, it may well be the best such motion picture ever made. Placido Domingo is brilliant in the title role, both as an actor and a singer. And he gets able support from Katia Ricciarelli as Desdemona and Justino Diaz as Iago. Rated PG for stylized violence. 122m. **DIR:** Franco Zeffirelli. **CAST:** Placido Domingo, Katia Ricciarelli, Justino Diaz, Urbano Barberini. **1987**

OTHELLO (1922) ★★★★ Despite the silence of this early version of the Shakespeare tragedy, the essence of the drama is effectively conveyed by memorable quotes on title cards, elaborate sets and costuming, and fine performances. Silent. B&W; 81m. **DIR:** Dimitri Buchowetzki. **CAST:** Emil Jannings, Werner Krauss, Lya de Putti. **1922**

OTHELLO (1952) ★★★★1/2 Months of high-tech restoration have done much to reverse the damage done by years of neglect to Orson Welles's cockeyed masterpiece. Shot entirely out of sequence over four years and under the most inhospitable circumstances, *Othello*, nevertheless, bears the unmistakable mark of the American genius. The sparest cinematography, the monumental sets, the stark choral and instrumental music, and the reduced essence of Shakespeare are melded by the alchemist Welles into an unforgettable film experience. Best feature film, 1952 Cannes Film Festival. B&W; 91m. **DIR:** Orson Welles. **CAST:** Orson Welles, Suzanne Cloutier, Micheal MacLiammoir, Robert Coote, Fay Compton. **1952 DVD**

•**OTHELLO (1965)** ★★★★ Laurence Olivier offers the most humanized portrayal of Shakespeare's vengeful Moor in this film, adapted from a stage production that Olivier had just appeared in. Its stage-to-film origins are obvious but forgotten thanks to superb performances by Olivier, Maggie Smith as Desdemona, and Frank Finlay as Iago. Not rated, 166m. **DIR:** Stuart Burge. **CAST:** Laurence Olivier, Frank Finlay, Maggie Smith, Derek Jacobi. **1965**

OTHELLO (1982) ★★★1/2 A fine stage production with William Marshall impressive as the valiant, but tragic Moor of Venice, Othello, tricked into madness and murder by his jealous aide, Iago (Ron Moody). Moody is magnificent as Shakespeare's greatest villain. Released by Bard Productions Ltd. 195m. **DIR:** Frank Melton. **CAST:** William Marshall, Ron Moody, Jenny Agutter, DeVeren Bookwalter, Peter MacLean, Jay Robinson. **1982**

OTHELLO (1995) ★★★ The fifth major film version of Shakespeare's tragedy (heavily edited by director Oliver Parker) is the first to feature an African American actor (Laurence Fishburne) in the title role. Fishburne is a fine actor, but he seems uncomfortable, both with Shakespeare's poetry and with Othello's volatile jealousy. Kenneth Branagh, as Iago, is more at ease with the Bard, and easily dominates the film. Rated R for violence, nudity, and simulated sex. 125m. **DIR:** Oliver Parker. **CAST:** Laurence Fishburne, Kenneth Branagh, Irène Jacob, Nathaniel Parker, Michael Maloney. **1996 DVD**

OTHER, THE ★★★1/2 Screenwriter Thomas Tryon, adapting his bestselling novel, raises plenty of goose bumps. This supernatural tale of good and evil, as personified by twin brothers, creates a genuinely eerie mood. Legendary acting coach Uta Hagen contributes a compelling performance. Director Robert Mulligan, keeping the emphasis on characterizations, never allows the suspense to lag. 100m. **DIR:** Robert Mulligan. **CAST:** Uta Hagen, Diana Muldaur, Chris Udvarnoky, Martin Udvarnoky, John Ritter. **1972**

OTHER HELL, THE 🌠 An Italian film about a convent inhabited by the devil. Rated R for graphic violence and nudity. 88m. **DIR:** Stephan Oblowsky. **CAST:** Franca Stoppi, Carlo De Meio. **1980**

OTHER PEOPLE'S MONEY ★★★1/2 Danny DeVito has a field day as a ruthless corporate raider conniving to take over upstanding Gregory Peck's business while romancing Peck's daughter. It's a modern-day version of a Capra film, but in the Nineties it is not a foregone conclusion that the good guys will win. Adapted by screenwriter Alvin Sargent from the play by Jerry Sterner. Rated R for profanity. 103m. **DIR:** Norman Jewison. **CAST:** Danny DeVito, Gregory Peck, Penelope Ann Miller, Piper Laurie, Dean Jones. **1991**

OTHER SIDE OF MIDNIGHT, THE 🌠 Glossy soap opera derived from schlockmaster Sidney Sheldon's bestselling novel. Rated R. 165m. **DIR:** Charles Jarrott. **CAST:** Marie-France Pisier, John Beck, Susan Sarandon, Raf Vallone, Clu Gulager. **1977**

OTHER SIDE OF THE MOUNTAIN, THE ★★★ Absolutely heart-wrenching account of Jill Kinmont, an Olympic-bound skier whose career was cut short by a fall that left her paralyzed. Marilyn Hassett, in her film debut, makes Kinmont a fighter whose determination initially backfires and prompts some to have unreasonable expectations of her limited recovery.

Rated PG. 103m. **DIR:** Larry Peerce. **CAST:** Marilyn Hassett, Beau Bridges. **1975**

OTHER SIDE OF THE MOUNTAIN, PART II, THE ★★ A sequel to the modest 1975 hit, the film continues the story of Jill Kinmont, a promising young skier who was paralyzed from the shoulders down in an accident. The tender romance, well played by Hassett and Bottoms, provides some fine moments. Rated PG. 100m. **DIR:** Larry Peerce. **CAST:** Marilyn Hassett, Timothy Bottoms, Nan Martin, Belinda Montgomery. **1978**

OTHER WOMAN, THE ★★ In this silly story about political corruption, an investigative reporter thinks her husband is having an affair with a hooker and later finds herself sexually attracted to the woman. Sam Jones is a corrupt politician with a punk hairdo. Rated R for nudity. 92m. **DIR:** Jag Mundhra. **CAST:** Sam Jones, Adrian Zmed, Lee Anne Beaman. **1992**

OUR DAILY BREAD ★★1/2 This vintage Depression social drama about an idealistic man organizing community farms and socialistic society is pretty creaky despite director King Vidor. Lead actor Tom Keene did better in cowboy films. B&W; 74m. **DIR:** King Vidor. **CAST:** Tom Keene, Karen Morley, John Qualen, Addison Richards. **1934 DVD**

OUR DANCING DAUGHTERS ★★★ One of the most famous flaming-youth movies of the late 1920s, and the one that really got Joan Crawford on her way as a top star for MGM. She plays Diana, a vivacious flapper who jiggles a lot and takes frequent belts from her hip flask. Silent. B&W; 86m. **DIR:** Harry Beaumont. **CAST:** Joan Crawford, Johnny Mack Brown, Nils Asther. **1928**

OUR FAMILY BUSINESS ★★ Two sons take different tacks in surviving within a Mafia family. Sam Wanamaker and Ray Milland give strong performances in this generally slow, uninspired twist on the *Godfather* theme. Made for television. 74m. **DIR:** Robert Collins. **CAST:** Ted Danson, Sam Wanamaker, Vera Miles, Ray Milland. **1981**

OUR FRIEND, MARTIN ★★★ Fascinating all-star feature that combines lively animation with the life story of Dr. Martin Luther King Jr. Rated G. 60m. **DIR:** Vincenzo Trippetti, Rob Smiley. **CAST:** Ed Asner, Angela Bassett, Lucas Black, LeVar Burton, Danny Glover, Whoopi Goldberg, Samuel L. Jackson, James Earl Jones, Ashley Judd, Dexter King, Yolanda King, Robert Ri-Chard, Susan Sarandon, John Travolta. **1998**

OUR HOSPITALITY ★★★★ Based on the legendary Hatfield-McCoy feud, this period comedy has Buster Keaton as innocent and unsuspecting Willie McKay journeying south to claim his inheritance. Keaton's comic and daredevil antics are brilliant. Silent. B&W; 74m. **DIR:** Buster Keaton, John G. Blystone. **CAST:** Buster Keaton, Natalie Talmadge, Ralph Bushman, Michael Keaton, Buster Keaton Jr. **1923 DVD**

OUR LITTLE GIRL ★★★ Curly-top Shirley's physician father (Joel McCrea) is away so much that his lovely wife (Rosemary Ames) seeks solace from neighbor Lyle Talbot. Shirley is so distressed by this turn of events that she runs away, forcing her parents to reunite in their search for her. Fine melodrama. B&W; 63m. **DIR:** John S. Robertson. **CAST:**

Shirley Temple, Rosemary Ames, Joel McCrea, Lyle Talbot. **1935**

OUR MAN FLINT ★★★1/2 Of the numerous imitators who followed James Bond's footsteps in the spy-crazed 1960s, Derek Flint of ZOWIE was by far the best. Ultracool and suavely sophisticated, James Coburn puts his earsplitting grin to good use as a renegade secret agent. One sequel followed: *In Like Flint*. Not rated; suitable for family viewing. 107m. **DIR:** Daniel Mann. **CAST:** James Coburn, Lee J. Cobb, Gila Golan, Edward Mulhare. **1966**

OUR MISS BROOKS (TV SERIES) ★★★ Desilu, basking in the success of *I Love Lucy*, adapted this likable vehicle for comedienne Eve Arden. The show, previously a hit on radio, stars Arden as Connie Brooks, a well-meaning English teacher at Madison High. Miss Brooks goes to extremes to earn the affection—or even the attention—of biology instructor Philip Boynton (Robert Rockwell). Each episode 30m. **DIR:** Al Lewis. **CAST:** Eve Arden, Gale Gordon, Robert Rockwell, Richard Crenna, Gloria McMillan, Jane Morgan. **1952–1957**

OUR MODERN MAIDENS ★★★ Jazz-age drama of love and infidelity bears more than a passing resemblance to *Our Dancing Daughters*, with Joan Crawford once again a flapper who makes a bad marriage. Ignore the story and enjoy the art deco sets and elaborate Adrian costumes. B&W; 75m. **DIR:** Jack Conway. **CAST:** Joan Crawford, Douglas Fairbanks Jr., Rod La Rocque, Anita Page. **1929**

OUR MOTHER'S MURDER ★★ A divorced woman with two teenage daughters marries an abusive alcoholic. Unfortunately, they have a child together, so she sticks with him, despite the worsening situation. This made-for-cable drama is based on a true story, but sophomoric narration and an overbearing message squash whatever entertainment value it had. Rated PG-13 for violence. 97m. **DIR:** Bill L. Norton. **CAST:** Holly Marie Combs, Roxanne Hart, Sarah Chalke, James Wilder. **1997**

OUR RELATIONS ★★★1/2 Stan Laurel and Oliver Hardy play two sets of twins. One set are sailors; the other are happily married civilians. When the boys' ship docks in the same city, a hilarious case of mistaken identity occurs. Highly enjoyable, the film doesn't lag at all. It features excellent performances by James Finlayson, Alan Hale, and Sidney Toler. B&W; 74m. **DIR:** Harry Lachman. **CAST:** Stan Laurel, Oliver Hardy, James Finlayson, Alan Hale Sr., Sidney Toler. **1936**

OUR SONS ★★★1/2 Touching portrait of a mother's attempt to cope when she learns her son is homosexual. Julie Andrews is splendid as the San Diego businesswoman who discovers her son is gay. When she learns that his lover is HIV positive, she visits the man's mother, a cocktail waitress in Arkansas, played by Ann-Margret. The cast in this made-for-television movie shines, while the writers make every attempt to steer clear of clichés. 96m. **DIR:** John Erman. **CAST:** Julie Andrews, Ann-Margret, Hugh Grant, Zeljko Ivanek, Tony Roberts. **1991**

OUR TOWN (1940) ★★★★ Superb performances from a top-flight cast add zest to this well-done adaptation of Thornton Wilder's play about life in a small

town. B&W; 90m. **DIR:** Sam Wood. **CAST:** Frank Craven, William Holden, Martha Scott, Thomas Mitchell, Fay Bainter. **1940**

OUR TOWN (1980) ★★★1/2 Not as good as the 1940s theatrical version, this TV version of the award-winning play by Thornton Wilder is notable for the fine performance of Hal Holbrook. The simple telling of the day-to-day life of Grover's Corners is done with remarkable restraint. 100m. **DIR:** Franklin J. Schaffner. **CAST:** Ned Beatty, Sada Thompson, Ronny Cox, Glynnis O'Connor, Robby Benson, Hal Holbrook, John Houseman. **1980**

OUR VINES HAVE TENDER GRAPES ★★★★★ A shining example of a sentimental movie that doesn't go overboard, this film is set in Wisconsin among Scandinavian immigrants. The focus is on the relationship between two youngsters and their very wise father with lots of witty dialogue and plenty of humorous situations. B&W; 105m. **DIR:** Roy Rowland. **CAST:** Edward G. Robinson, Margaret O'Brien, "Butch" Jenkins, Agnes Moorehead, James Craig, Frances Gifford, Sara Haden. **1945**

OUT ★★ You may want out before the final countdown of this offbeat, surrealistic action film. Peter Coyote is an urban guerrilla who starts out in Greenwich Village and goes cross-country on assignments from a mysterious commander. This comedy-action pastiche tries very hard to be artsy. Rated PG. 88m. **DIR:** Eli Hollander. **CAST:** Peter Coyote, Danny Glover, O-Lan Shephard, Gail Dartez, Jim Haynie, Scott Beach. **1983**

OUT CALIFORNIA WAY ★★1/2 Monte Hale, a cowboy looking for work in Hollywood, comes to the attention of a movie producer. Hale's debut film. Guest Stars: Allan "Rocky" Lane, Roy Rogers, Dale Evans, Don Barry. 67m. **DIR:** Lesley Selander. **CAST:** Monte Hale, Adrian Booth, Robert Blake, John Dehner. **1946**

OUT COLD ★★★ Dark comedy featuring Teri Garr as a sultry housewife who enlists the aid of John Lithgow after she puts her philandering husband on ice. Some hilarious moments in an otherwise uneven movie. Rated R for sexual situations and violence. 92m. **DIR:** Malcolm Mowbray. **CAST:** John Lithgow, Teri Garr, Randy Quaid. **1989**

OUT FOR BLOOD ★★★ Martial arts revenge saga, with Don "The Dragon" Wilson typically charming as a lawyer determined to punish the drug dealers who murdered his wife and son. Although the story is an extended cliché—down to the wise old-timer—events occur rapidly enough to avoid becoming boring. Closing dialogue hints at a sequel. Rated R for violence and profanity. 86m. **DIR:** Richard W. Munchkin. **CAST:** Don "The Dragon" Wilson, Shari Shattuck, Michael De Lano, Ron Steelman, Aki Aleong, Todd Curtis. **1993**

OUT FOR JUSTICE ★★★★1/2 Steven Seagal is top-notch as a maverick police detective out to avenge the death of his partner. The best fist-and-foot-style action film to date, this release has pure adrenaline-pumping, jaw-dropping thrills and chills from beginning to end. Rated R for violence, drug use, profanity, and nudity. 90m. **DIR:** John Flynn. **CAST:** Steven Seagal, William Forsythe, Jerry Orbach. **1991 DVD**

OUT OF AFRICA ★★★1/2 Robert Redford and Meryl Streep are at the peaks of their considerable talents in this 1985 Oscar winner for best picture, a grand-scale motion picture also blessed with inspired direction, gorgeous cinematography, and a haunting score. This epic romance, based on the life and works of Isak Dinesen, concerns the love of two staunch individualists for each other and the land in which they live. Rated PG for a discreet sex scene. 160m. DIR: Sydney Pollack. CAST: Robert Redford, Meryl Streep, Klaus Maria Brandauer, Michael Kitchen, Malick Bowens, Michael Gough, Suzanna Hamilton. 1985 DVD

OUT OF ANNIE'S PAST ❤ Try to stay awake while watching this made-for-cable original about a woman whose past comes back to haunt her. Rated R for violence. 95m. DIR: Stuart Cooper. CAST: Catherine Mary Stewart, Scott Valentine, Dennis Farina. 1994

OUT OF BOUNDS ❤ A naïve Iowa boy journeys to Los Angeles and accidentally switches luggage with a nasty heroin smuggler. Rated R for extreme violence. 93m. DIR: Richard Tuggle. CAST: Anthony Michael Hall, Jenny Wright, Jeff Kober, Glynn Turman, Raymond J. Barry. 1986

OUT OF CONTROL ❤ A group of teenagers take off for an exciting weekend on a private island. Rated R for obscenities, nudity, and violence. 78m. DIR: Allan Holzman. CAST: Martin Hewitt, Betsy Russell, Jim Youngs. 1984

OUT OF SEASON ★★ This British mood piece is full of atmosphere, but its strange love story, about a man who returns to England to find the woman with whom he had an affair twenty years before, is nothing more than average. Rated R. 90m. DIR: Alan Bridges. CAST: Vanessa Redgrave, Cliff Robertson, Susan George. 1975

OUT OF SIGHT ★★★★ During an escape an imprisoned hunk of a bank robber encounters a female federal marshal who is torn between tracking down and getting down with the felon. Once out, the criminal plans a jewel heist with a number of unsavory characters and his hopeful paramour close behind. A character-driven caper film, this is a surprisingly funny movie, a cross between *Pulp Fiction* and *Get Shorty*. It features what is probably the funniest fatal-head-wound scene ever filmed. Rated R for violence. 110m. DIR: Steven Soderbergh. CAST: George Clooney, Jennifer Lopez, Ving Rhames, Don Cheadle, Dennis Farina, Albert Brooks. 1998 DVD

OUT OF SIGHT OUT OF MIND ❤ Confusing tale involving a serial killer. A real waste of time. Rated R for violence. 94m. DIR: Greydon Clark. CAST: Susan Blakely, Edward Albert, Lynn-Holly Johnson, Wings Hauser. 1991

OUT OF SYNC ★★ As if he isn't in enough trouble for failing to pay his bookie, an L.A. nightclub deejay falls for the girlfriend of a vicious drug dealer. Slow-moving and stiffly acted film takes too long to go nowhere. Rated R for profanity, sexual situations, and nudity. 105m. DIR: Debbie Allen. CAST: LL Cool J, Victoria Dillard, Yaphet Kotto, Howard Hesseman, Aries Spears. 1995

OUT OF THE BLUE ★★★ A not-very-innocent young woman passes out in a naïve married man's apartment, making all sorts of trouble in this entertaining romantic comedy of errors and such. B&W; 84m. DIR: Leigh Jason. CAST: George Brent, Virginia Mayo, Ann Dvorak, Turhan Bey, Carole Landis. 1947

OUT OF THE DARK ❤ Contrived thriller about a psychotic killer who systematically eliminates beautiful women who work at an erotic phone service. Rated R for profanity, nudity, and violence. 89m. DIR: Michael Schroeder. CAST: Cameron Dye, Karen Black, Bud Cort, Divine, Paul Bartel. 1989

OUT OF THE DARKNESS ★★★ Fine reenactment of the New York police chase of the serial killer known as Son of Sam. Martin Sheen plays the man responsible for his capture. Made for TV. 96m. DIR: Jud Taylor. CAST: Martin Sheen, Hector Elizondo, Matt Clark. 1985

OUT OF THE PAST ★★★★1/2 This film, which stars Robert Mitchum, is perhaps the quintessential example of *film noir*. A private eye (Mitchum, in a role intended for Bogart) allows himself to be duped by the beautiful but two-faced mistress (Jane Greer) of a big-time gangster (Kirk Douglas). It's a forgotten masterwork. B&W; 97m. DIR: Jacques Tourneur. CAST: Robert Mitchum, Jane Greer, Kirk Douglas, Richard Webb, Rhonda Fleming, Dickie Moore, Steve Brodie. 1947

OUT OF THE RAIN ★★ A drifter returns home to find his brother murdered and too many questions regarding his death. Although the movie offers a few surprises, it tries too hard to be a taut suspense-thriller, rarely delivering. Not rated; contains violence, profanity, and brief nudity. 91m. DIR: Gary Winick. CAST: Bridget Fonda, Michael O'Keefe, John E. O'Keefe, John Seitz. 1990

OUT OF TOWNERS, THE (1970) ★★★ Jack Lemmon and Sandy Dennis star in this Neil Simon comedy of a New York City vacation gone awry. It's a good idea that doesn't come off as well as one would have hoped. Rated PG for language. 97m. DIR: Arthur Hiller. CAST: Jack Lemmon, Sandy Dennis, Sandy Baron, Anne Meara, Billy Dee Williams. 1970

OUT-OF-TOWNERS, THE (1999) ★★1/2 This is an amnesia movie: By the following morning, you won't even remember having seen it. Remade from a 1970 Neil Simon script that frankly wasn't too good to begin with, this update is bland, occasionally amusing, and utterly lacking in outstanding features. It does have the good sense to make its central characters likable and sympathetic but absent the talented Steve Martin and Goldie Hawn, this tale of midwesterners out of their depth in big, bad New York City wouldn't have much going for it. The film's best moments revolve around Martin's attempts to control his near-apoplectic fury. Rated PG-13 for mild profanity, mild sexual content, and comedic drug use. 92m. DIR: Sam Weisman. CAST: Steve Martin, Goldie Hawn, John Cleese. 1999 DVD

OUT ON A LIMB (1986) ★★1/2 This TV film recounts Shirley MacLaine's move into metaphysics, discovering who she is and where she came from. Much too long, but if you like MacLaine, you might be amused. 159m. DIR: Robert Butler. CAST: Shirley MacLaine, Charles Dance, John Heard, Anne Jackson, Jerry Orbach. 1986

OUT ON A LIMB (1992) ★★ There are few laughs in this comedy about a corporate executive (Matthew Broderick) who has a disaster-fraught journey from the big city to his rural hometown. The rest of the cast seems to be struggling to ignore how ridiculous the whole thing is. Rated PG for profanity, nudity, and violence. 83m. **DIR:** Francis Veber. **CAST:** Matthew Broderick, Jeffrey Jones, Heidi Kling, John C. Reilly, Marian Mercer, Larry Hankin, David Margulies. 1992

OUT ON BAIL ★★1/2 Sort of a redneck version of *A Fistful of Dollars.* Drifter Robert Ginty turns the tables on small-town bad guys who try to force him to do their dirty work. Too bad it doesn't go all the way into spaghetti territory. Rated R for sexual situations and violence. 102m. **DIR:** Gordon Hessler. **CAST:** Robert Ginty, Kathy Shower, Tom Badal, Sidney Lassick, Leo Sparrowhawk. 1989

OUT THERE ★★ Bill Campbell and a host of cameo players are grievously wasted in this inept tale of extraterrestrials who slowly take over Earth, by pervasively dulling our senses with Muzak. Too stupid to be taken seriously, but not clever enough to succeed as satire. Rated PG for profanity. 97m. **DIR:** Sam Irvin. **CAST:** Bill Campbell, Wendy Schaal, Rod Steiger, Jill St. John, June Lockhart, Bill Cobbs, Paul Dooley, David Rasche. 1995

OUT TO SEA ★★1/2 Two battling brothers-in-law pose as dance hosts on a Caribbean cruise ship to meet—and hopefully fleece—the wealthy women on board. No comedy milestones but if you're a fan of Lemmon and Matthau, you will find both actors in fine form. The supporting cast is first-rate. Rated PG-13 for language. 106m. **DIR:** Martha Coolidge. **CAST:** Jack Lemmon, Walter Matthau, Dyan Cannon, Gloria De Haven, Brent Spiner, Elaine Stritch, Hal Linden, Donald O'Connor, Edward Mulhare. 1997

OUTBREAK ★★★★1/2 Top-notch thriller stars Dustin Hoffman as an army doctor battling a devastating virus and government cover-up, each of which threatens to wipe out the population of a small town. Featuring a first-rate supporting cast, it's edge-of-your-seat entertainment of the first order. Rated R for violence, profanity, and gore. 127m. **DIR:** Wolfgang Petersen. **CAST:** Dustin Hoffman, René Russo, Morgan Freeman, Kevin Spacey, Cuba Gooding Jr., Donald Sutherland, Patrick Dempsey. 1995 DVD

OUTCAST, THE ★★ Before he became disenchanted with acting and turned to still photography, John Derek made a number of mostly mediocre films, this one among them. In this standard Western, he fights to win his rightful inheritance. Justice prevails, of course, but you know that going in. B&W; 90m. **DIR:** William Witney. **CAST:** John Derek, Joan Evans, Jim Davis. 1954

OUTER LIMITS: SANDKINGS ★★★ George R. R. Martin's science-fiction shocker makes an uneasy transition to the screen, as the opening installment of cable's updated *Outer Limits* franchise. Obsessed scientist Beau Bridges smuggles home dangerous extraterrestrial eggs but quickly learns the folly of his actions when the ant-sized critters multiply rapidly ... and start growing. Viewers may be intrigued by the novelty casting, which features three generations of the Bridges family. Rated PG for violence.

93m. **DIR:** Stuart Gordon. **CAST:** Beau Bridges, Lloyd Bridges, Helen Shaver, Dylan Bridges. 1995

OUTER LIMITS, THE (TV SERIES) ★★★1/2 This television classic of science fiction produced some fine morality plays. Assisted by the control voice that promised "there is nothing wrong with your television set," viewers experienced compelling *film noir* science fiction. With literate and absorbing scripts, the episodes hold up quite well today. The best is "Demon with a Glass Hand." Other noteworthy episodes include "The Sixth Finger," in which Welsh coal miner takes a trip into his own biologic future, and "The Man Who Was Never Born." Suitable for family viewing, although a bit intense for small fry. B&W; 52m. per tape. **DIR:** Laslo Benedek, John Erman, James Goldstone, Charles Haas, Byron Haskin, Leonard Horn, Gerd Oswald. **CAST:** Robert Culp, Bruce Dern, Robert Duvall, Cedric Hardwicke, Shirley Knight, Martin Landau, David McCallum, Vera Miles, Edward Mulhare, Donald Pleasence, Cliff Robertson, Martin Sheen, Robert Webber. 1964

OUTFIT, THE 💗 Boring mishmash about Dutch Schultz, Legs Diamond, and Lucky Luciano creaks under the weight of macho posturing and a script shot full of holes. Rated R for violence, nudity, and profanity. 92m. **DIR:** J. Christian Ingvordsen. **CAST:** Lance Henriksen, Billy Drago, Martin Kove. 1993

OUTING, THE 💗 A teenage girl is possessed by a demon and convinces her friends to spend the night in her father's museum. Not rated but contains brief nudity and graphic violence. 87m. **DIR:** Tom Daley. **CAST:** Deborah Winters, James Huston, Danny D. Daniels. 1986

OUTLAND ★★★★ Sean Connery stars as the two-fisted marshal in this thoroughly enjoyable outer-space remake of *High Noon* directed by Peter Hyams. Much of the credit for that goes to Connery. As he has proved in many pictures, he is one of the few actors today who can play a fully credible adventure hero. Rated R. 109m. **DIR:** Peter Hyams. **CAST:** Sean Connery, Peter Boyle, Frances Sternhagen. 1981 DVD

OUTLAW, THE ★★ This once-notorious Western now seems almost laughable. Jane Russell keeps her best attributes forward, but one wonders what Walter Huston and Thomas Mitchell are doing in this film. Only for those who want to know what all the fuss was about. 103m. **DIR:** Howard Hughes, Howard Hawks. **CAST:** Jane Russell, Walter Huston, Thomas Mitchell, Jack Buetel. 1943 DVD

OUTLAW AND HIS WIFE, THE ★★★ In nineteenth-century Iceland a farmer is accused of stealing sheep and must retreat to the hills to escape capture. An amazing work for its time, this silent movie from Sweden was restored in 1986 and dons a full orchestral score. Not rated. B&W; 73m. **DIR:** Victor Sjöström. **CAST:** Victor Sjöström. 1917

OUTLAW BLUES ★★1/2 Yet another of Peter Fonda's harmless but rather bland light comedies. He's an ex-con with a talent for songwriting but little in the way of industry smarts; he naïvely allows established country-western star James Callahan to make off with a few hits. Aided by backup singer Susan Saint James, in a charming little part, Fonda figures out how to succeed on his own. Rated PG for light violence and brief nudity. 100m. DIR: Richard T. Heffron. CAST: Peter Fonda, Susan Saint James, James Callahan, Michael Lerner. 1977

OUTLAW FORCE ★★ It had to happen. Somebody crossed *Rambo* with *Urban Cowboy*. A gang run out of town by a handsome country singer (David Heavener) gets revenge when they rape and kill his wife, then kidnap his daughter and return to (where else?) Hollywood. Heavener, a Vietnam vet, takes justice into his own hands. Rated R for violence. 95m. DIR: David Heavener. CAST: David Heavener, Paul Smith, Frank Stallone, Warren Berlinger. 1987

OUTLAW JOSEY WALES, THE ★★★1/2 This Western is a masterpiece of characterization and action. Josey Wales is a farmer whose family is murdered by Red Legs, a band of cutthroats allied with the Union Army. Wales joins the Confederacy to avenge their deaths. After the war, everyone in his troop surrenders to the victorious Union except Wales. Rated PG. 135m. DIR: Clint Eastwood. CAST: Clint Eastwood, Sondra Locke, Chief Dan George, Bill McKinney, John Vernon, John Mitchum, John Russell. 1976 DVD

OUTLAW OF GOR 🌀 Boring follow-up to the Conan-style original, *Gor*. Rated PG-13 for nudity. 90m. DIR: John "Bud" Cardos. CAST: Urbano Barberini, Rebecca Ferratti, Jack Palance. 1987

OUTLAWS OF SONORA ★★1/2 A vicious outlaw captures his exact double: Bob Livingston of the Three Mesquiteers. When the outlaw leader then robs a bank and murders the banker, the other Mesquiteers believe their pal has turned killer. B&W; 56m. DIR: George Sherman. CAST: Robert Livingston, Ray "Crash" Corrigan, Max Terhune, Jack Mulhall. 1938

OUTLAWS OF THE DESERT ★★ Hopalong Cassidy and his pals travel to Arabia (Hoppy in a burnoose is a sight!) to buy horses for the government and encounter warring tribes and kidnappers. Doesn't measure up to the usual quality of the series. The print material on this title is dark and most of the scenes at night are barely discernible. B&W; 53m. DIR: Howard Bretherton. CAST: William Boyd, Andy Clyde, Brad King, Duncan Renaldo, Jean Phillips, Forrest Stanley. 1941

OUTPOST IN MOROCCO ★★ George Raft is out of his element as a French legionnaire assigned to stop the activities of desert rebels only to find himself falling in love with the daughter (Marie Windsor) of their leader (Akim Tamiroff). Pure hokum and slow moving, too. B&W; 92m. DIR: Robert Florey. CAST: George Raft, Marie Windsor, Akim Tamiroff. 1949

OUTRAGE! ★★★1/2 Compelling courtroom drama that takes on the judicial system with a vengeance. Robert Preston is superb as a man who readily admits to killing his daughter's murderer. Beau Bridges shines as his attorney. This made-for-television film tackles important issues without flinching. 100m. DIR: Walter Grauman. CAST: Robert Preston, Beau Bridges, Anthony Newley, Burgess Meredith, Linda Purl. 1986

OUTRAGE (1994) ★★1/2 After taking murderous revenge on three men who raped her, a circus per-

former is forced to live as a fugitive. Subpar effort from veteran Spanish filmmaker Carlos Saura. Not rated; contains violence, nudity, and sexual situations. In Spanish with English subtitles. 108m. DIR: Carlos Saura. CAST: Antonio Banderas, Francesca Neri, Walter Vidarte. 1994

OUTRAGEOUS ★★★★ A very offbeat and original comedy-drama concerning a gay nightclub performer's relationship with a pregnant mental patient. A different kind of love story, told with taste and compassion. Female impersonator Craig Russell steals the show. Take a chance on this one. Rated R. 100m. DIR: Richard Benner. CAST: Craig Russell, Hollis McLaren, Richert Easley. 1977

OUTRAGEOUS FORTUNE ★★★★ Yet another delightfully inventive adult comedy from Disney's Touchstone arm, highlighted by a show-stealing performance by the Mae West of the 1980s: Bette Midler. Her strutting, strident would-be actress is a scream, a word that also describes the level at which she delivers her rapid-fire dialogue. Rated R for profanity. 100m. DIR: Arthur Hiller. CAST: Bette Midler, Shelley Long, Peter Coyote, Robert Prosky, John Schuck, George Carlin. 1987 DVD

OUTSIDE CHANCE OF MAXIMILIAN GLICK, THE ★★★★ Delightfully engaging character study of a young Jewish boy's introduction to real life. He wants to enter a dual piano competition with a pretty gentile girl. But his parents disapprove of this relationship, and try to keep him from seeing her. Rated G. 95m. DIR: Allan A. Goldstein. CAST: Saul Rubinek, Jan Rubes, Fairuza Balk. 1989

●**OUTSIDE OZONA** ★★★ An eclectic collection of characters finds itself slowly drawn together during a serial killer's spree. Rated R for profanity and violence. 99m. DIR: J. S. Cardone. CAST: Robert Forster, Kevin Pollak, Sherilyn Fenn, David Paymer, Penelope Ann Miller, Swoosie Kurtz, Taj Mahal, Meat Loaf, Lucy Webb. 1998

●**OUTSIDE PROVIDENCE** ★★★1/2 A blue-collar misfit attempts to redeem himself in this amiable coming-of-age saga, adapted from an earthy, semiautobiographical novel by filmmaker Peter Farrelly. Set in Rhode Island during the 1970s, where high-school senior Timothy Dunphy is rapidly trashing his life with loser friends, our hero winds up at preppy Cornwall Academy, where he decides to teach the anal-retentive administrators a thing or three. And, oh yes, he also falls in love. This is not a story for prudes; marijuana is as plentiful here as the incessant profanity. But the tale has a solid heart, and those with open minds are apt to be surprised by its poignance. Rated R for profanity and drug use. 102m. DIR: Michael Corrente. CAST: Shawn Hatosy, Alec Baldwin, Amy Smart, George Wendt, Gabriel Mann, Jonathan Brandis, Tommy Bone. 1999 DVD

OUTSIDE THE LAW (1921) ★★★ Director Tod Browning's long association with the greatest of all character actors and one of the biggest stars of the silent screen began in 1921 when Lon Chaney supported female star Priscilla Dean in this crimedrama. The incomparable Chaney plays Black Mike, the meanest and smarmiest of hoodlums, as well as an old Chinese man, the faithful retainer to Miss

Dean. Silent. B&W; 77m. **DIR:** Tod Browning. **CAST:** Priscilla Dean, Lon Chaney Sr., Ralph Lewis, Wheeler Oakman. **1921**

OUTSIDE THE LAW (1994) ★★ David Bradley plays a cop on the edge who is falling for the prime suspect in a murder investigation. Decent production values help save this direct-to-video crime-thriller, but lackluster writing and direction make the clichés hard to swallow. Rated R for violence, nudity, and language. 95m. **DIR:** Boaz Davidson. **CAST:** David Bradley, Anna Thomson. **1994**

OUTSIDERS, THE 💜 Based on S. E. Hinton's popular novel, this is a simplistic movie about kids from the wrong side of the tracks. Rated PG for profanity and violence. 91m. **DIR:** Francis Ford Coppola. **CAST:** C. Thomas Howell, Matt Dillon, Ralph Macchio, Emilio Estevez, Tom Cruise, Leif Garrett, Patrick Swayze. **1983** DVD

OVER HER DEAD BODY ★★ Black comedy features Elizabeth Perkins and Judge Reinhold as adulterers who kill in self-defense when they're caught in the act. The whole film centers around Perkins's attempts to dump the body and make it look like an accident. Rated R for profanity and violence. 105m. **DIR:** Maurice Phillips. **CAST:** Elizabeth Perkins, Judge Reinhold, Maureen Mueller, Jeffrey Jones, Rhea Perlman. **1989**

OVER THE BROOKLYN BRIDGE ★★1/2 Elliott Gould stars in this occasionally interesting but mostly uneven slice-of-life story about a slovenly, diabetic Jewish luncheonette owner who dreams of getting out by buying a restaurant in downtown Manhattan. Rated R for nudity and profanity. 108m. **DIR:** Menahem Golan. **CAST:** Elliott Gould, Shelley Winters, Sid Caesar, Carol Kane, Burt Young, Margaux Hemingway. **1983**

OVER THE EDGE ★★★★ An explosive commentary on the restlessness of today's youth, this film also serves as an indictment against America's hypocritically permissive society. The violence that was supposedly caused by the release of gang films like *The Warriors, Boulevard Nights,* and *The Wanderers* caused the movie's makers to shelve it. However, Matt Dillon, who made his film debut herein, is now a hot property, and that's why this deserving movie is out on video. Rated R. 95m. **DIR:** Jonathan Kaplan. **CAST:** Matt Dillon, Michael Kramer, Pamela Ludwig. **1979**

OVER THE HILL ★★1/2 Unwanted widow Olympia Dukakis takes a road trip in the Australian outback. Its very oddness works in its favor, but the action drags and the ending is melodramatic. Rated PG for brief nudity. 102m. **DIR:** George Miller. **CAST:** Olympia Dukakis, Sigrid Thornton, Derek Fowlds, Aden Young. **1992**

•**OVER THE LINE** 💜 A college professor's life is turned upside down when she enters into a sexual relationship with a student. Rated R for adult situations, language, nudity, and violence. 108m. **DIR:** Oliver Hellman. **CAST:** Lesley-Anne Down, John Enos, Lady B. Pearl. **1993**

OVER THE TOP ★★ Thoroughly silly effort. Sylvester Stallone stars as a compassionate trucker who only wants to spend time with the son (David Mendenhall) whom he left, years before, in the custody of his wife (Susan Blakely, in a thankless role)

and her rich, iron-willed father (Robert Loggia, as a one-note villain). This clichéd story has little of interest. Rated PG for mild violence. 94m. **DIR:** Menahem Golan. **CAST:** Sylvester Stallone, Robert Loggia, Susan Blakely, David Mendenhall. **1987**

OVERBOARD 💜 A haughty heiress falls off her yacht and loses her memory. Rated PG. 106m. **DIR:** Garry Marshall. **CAST:** Goldie Hawn, Kurt Russell, Edward Herrmann, Katherine Helmond. **1988** DVD

OVERCOAT, THE ★★★ Based on a story by Gogol, this Russian film tells the story of an office clerk who is content with his modest life and ambitions until he buys a new overcoat and enters on an upward track. Entertaining satire. In Russian with English subtitles. B&W; 78m. **DIR:** Alexi Batalov. **CAST:** Rolan Bykov. **1960**

OVEREXPOSED ★★ Gorefest surrounds a beautiful soap opera star (Catherine Oxenberg) when the people closest to her are killed one after another. Rated R for nudity, violence, and gore. 80m. **DIR:** Larry Brand. **CAST:** Catherine Oxenberg, David Naughton, Jennifer Edwards, Karen Black. **1990**

OVERINDULGENCE ★★ Tame rendition of the scandalous 1940s South African murder trial that shocked the world. A sordid tale of adultery, drugs, and child abuse is told by Juanita Carberry, one of the daughters of the decadent British settlers. Sir Jock Broughton is the accused murderer, and only Juanita knows the truth. This dramatic story is done in by a lightweight script, amateurish direction, and mediocre acting. For substance, sophistication, and style on the subject, check out *White Mischief.* Rated PG-13. 95m. **DIR:** Ross Devenish. **CAST:** Denholm Elliott, Holly Aird, Michael Bryne, Kathryn Pogson. **1987**

OVERKILL (1986) 💜 Racist, violent *Miami Vice*–type of crime story. Rated R for extreme violence and nudity. 81m. **DIR:** Ulli Lommel. **CAST:** Steve Rally, John Nishio, Laura Burkett, Allen Wisch, Roy Summersett, Antonio Caprio. **1986**

OVERKILL (1996) 💜 How many more inept remakes of Richard Connell's "The Most Dangerous Game" must we endure? Aaron Norris slouches through the jungle here, while avoiding the laughably demented Michael Nouri and his minions. Rated R for profanity and violence. 88m. **DIR:** Dean Ferrandini. **CAST:** Aaron Norris, Michael Nouri, Pamela Dickerson, David Rowe, Kenny Moskow. **1996**

OVERLAND STAGE RAIDERS ★★1/2 Louise Brooks made her last big-screen appearance in this series Western, which has the Three Mesquiteers investing in an airport used by gold miners to ship ore. Of course, our heroes must battle a group of crooks attempting to rob the shipments. B&W; 55m. **DIR:** George Sherman. **CAST:** John Wayne, Louise Brooks, Ray "Crash" Corrigan, Max Terhune. **1938**

OVERNIGHT DELIVERY ★★★ Chaos ensues when a college student suspects that his hometown girlfriend is cheating on him. To retaliate, he sends her a letter through an overnight delivery service. When he learns he's wrong, he makes a valiant attempt to retrieve the letter with the help of a friendly stripper. Lots of fun. Rated PG-13 for adult situations and language. 87m. **DIR:** Jason Bloom. **CAST:** Reese Witherspoon, Paul Rudd, Christine Taylor. **1997**

OVERSEAS ★★★1/2 Three French sisters share their joys and tragedies over an eighteen-year period (1946–1964) in Algeria. The native uprising forces each to say good-bye to her innocence. Lively musical score and touching moments are marred by confusing time jumps. Not rated; contains nudity, violence, and profanity. In French with English subtitles. 96m. **DIR:** Brigitte Rouan. **CAST:** Nicole Garcia, Marianne Basler, Brigitte Rouan, Philippe Galland. **1992**

OWL AND THE PUSSYCAT, THE ★★★★ Barbra Streisand plays a street-smart but undereducated prostitute who teams up with intellectual snob and bookstore clerk George Segal. The laughs abound as the two express themselves, through numerous debates. Rated R. 95m. **DIR:** Herbert Ross. **CAST:** Barbra Streisand, George Segal, Robert Klein. **1970**

OX-BOW INCIDENT, THE ★★★★1/2 One of the finest Westerns ever made, this thought-provoking drama stars Henry Fonda and Harry Morgan as a pair of drifters who try to stop the lynching of three men (Dana Andrews, Anthony Quinn, and Francis Ford) who may be innocent. Seldom has the terror of mob rule been so effectively portrayed. B&W; 75m. **DIR:** William Wellman. **CAST:** Henry Fonda, Dana Andrews, Mary Beth Hughes, Anthony Quinn, William Eythe, Harry Morgan, Jane Darwell, Frank Conroy, Harry Davenport. **1943**

OXFORD BLUES ★★ Rob Lowe plays a brash American attending England's Oxford University. Writer-director Robert Boris has even worked in the sports angle, by making Lowe a rowing champ who has to prove himself. A formula picture. Rated PG-13. 93m. **DIR:** Robert Boris. **CAST:** Rob Lowe, Amanda Pays. **1984**

•**OXYGEN** ★★★ A rich woman is kidnapped and buried alive with approximately twenty-four hours worth of air. Her husband must get the ransom money in the kidnapper's hands, and then the location of the interred woman will be revealed. But the husband panics and contacts the authorities. This thriller is full of twists—some expected and others unpredictable. Rated R for violence and language. 92m. **DIR:** Richard Shepard. **CAST:** Adrien Brody, Maura Tierney, Dylan Baker, Terry Kinney. **1998 DVD**

OZONE ★★1/2 Perhaps given a larger budget, this could have been a great movie. As it is, the low budget definitely hinders this ambitious film. Even gunshots are dubbed. Not rated; contains violence and profanity. 83m. **DIR:** J. R. Bookwalter. **CAST:** James Black, Tom Hoover, Bill Morrison, James L. Edwards. **1993**

PACIFIC CONNECTION, THE 🦃 Move over *Plan 9 from Outer Space*—this may just be the worst film ever made. Martial arts champ Roland Dantes saves his impressive skills for the final scene in this hodge-podge of inconsistencies, poor acting, and inane plot. Dantes must avenge the deaths of his parents by a corrupt Spanish governor and his foppish sons (one of whom is Dean Stockwell in a best forgotten role). Not rated; contains nudity, violence, and sex. 87m. **DIR:** Luis Nepomuceno. **CAST:** Roland Dantes, Nancy Kwan, Guy Madison, Alejandro Rey, Dean Stockwell, Gilbert Roland. **1960**

PACIFIC HEIGHTS ★★★★ When a yuppie couple purchases a Victorian apartment house in San Francisco, they figure they've found the home of their dreams. Then a secretive tenant moves in without permission and begins slowly destroying their property. An intelligent and gripping thriller that holds you right up to the climax. Rated R for profanity and violence. 107m. **DIR:** John Schlesinger. **CAST:** Melanie Griffith, Matthew Modine, Michael Keaton, Beverly D'Angelo, Nobu McCarthy, Laurie Metcalf, Carl Lumbly, Dorian Harewood, Luca Bercovici, Tippi Hedren. **1990 DVD**

PACIFIC INFERNO ★★1/2 This war adventure film is set in the Philippines during the final fall and capture of U.S. and Filipino sailors. Jim Brown and Richard Jaeckel are American navy prisoners. Good, steady action follows. Not rated. 90m. **DIR:** Rolf Bayer. **CAST:** Jim Brown, Richard Jaeckel, Tim Brown, Tad Horino, Wilma Redding, Vic Diaz. **1985 DVD**

PACK, THE ★★ Slightly above-average horror film about a pack of dogs that goes wild and tries to kill two families. Rated R. 99m. **DIR:** Robert Clouse. **CAST:** Joe Don Baker, Hope Alexander Willis, Richard B. Shull, R. G. Armstrong. **1977**

PACK UP YOUR TROUBLES ★★★ Stan Laurel and Oliver Hardy join the army in World War I, with the usual disastrous results. After being discharged, they assume responsibility for a fallen comrade's young daughter and search for her grandparents. The plot line and scripting aren't as solid as in other films, but the boys squeeze out every laugh possible. B&W; 68m. **DIR:** George Marshall. **CAST:** Stan Laurel, Oliver Hardy. **1932**

PACKAGE, THE ★★★★ In this taut thriller, skillfully directed by Andrew Davis, Gene Hackman gives one of his best performances as a soldier assigned to take a prisoner (Tommy Lee Jones) from Berlin to Washington, D.C. When his prisoner escapes, Hackman finds himself in the middle of a conspiracy whose masterminds want him out of the way. Rated R for violence and profanity. 109m. **DIR:** Andrew Davis. **CAST:** Gene Hackman, Tommy Lee Jones, Joanna Cassidy, John Heard, Dennis Franz, Pam Grier. **1989 DVD**

PACKIN' IT IN ★★★1/2 When Gary and Dianna Webber (Richard Benjamin and Paula Prentiss) flee from the pollution and crime of Los Angeles, they find themselves living among survivalists in Woodcrest, Oregon. The laughs begin as these city folks, including their punked-out daughter (played by Molly Ringwald), try to adjust to life in the wilderness. 92m. **DIR:** Jud Taylor. **CAST:** Richard Benjamin, Paula Prentiss, Molly Ringwald, Tony Roberts, Andrea Marcovicci. **1982**

PADDY ★★1/2 Excellent performances by all the actors, especially Des Cave in the title role, cannot save this rather confused coming-of-age comedy. Despite moments of true hilarity, the film remains at best mildly amusing. 97m. **DIR:** Daniel Haller. **CAST:** Des Cave, Milo O'Shea, Peggy Cass. **1969**

PADRE PADRONE ★★★1/2 Although slow-moving, this low-budget film is a riveting account of a young Sardinian's traumatizing relationship with his overbearing father in a patriarchal society. The son bears the brutality, but eventually breaks the emotional bonds. This quietly powerful film depends on the actors for its punch. In Sardinian (Italian dialect) with English subtitles. 114m. **DIR:** Vittorio Taviani, Paolo Taviani. **CAST:** Omero Antonutti, Saverio Marioni. **1977** DVD

PAGAN LOVE SONG ★★ Watered-down love story about American schoolteacher Howard Keel who falls for native girl Esther Williams is just another excuse for singing, swimming, and a tired old plot line. 76m. **DIR:** Robert Alton. **CAST:** Esther Williams, Howard Keel, Minna Gombell, Rita Moreno. **1950**

PAGEMASTER, THE ★★ Seeking sanctuary from a storm, a neurotic kid scurries into a huge library where paintings on the ceiling splash down and turn the precocious lad and his surroundings into a cartoon. He teams up with caricatures of a pirate, a fairy godmother, and a fraidy-cat goblin and dives into the pages of several classics. But the adventure lacks vitality. Rated G. 75m. **DIR:** Joe Johnston, Maurice Hunt. **CAST:** Macaulay Culkin, Christopher Lloyd, Whoopi Goldberg, Patrick Stewart, Leonard Nimoy, Frank Welker, Phil Hartman. **1994**

PAIN IN THE A—, A ★★ A professional hit man (Lino Ventura) arrives in Montpellier to kill a government witness who is set to testify against the mob. This unfunny slapstick comedy was adapted by director Billy Wilder for the equally disappointing *Buddy, Buddy* with Jack Lemmon and Walter Matthau. In French with English subtitles. Rated PG for light violence. 90m. **DIR:** Edouard Molinaro. **CAST:** Lino Ventura, Jacques Brel. **1973**

PAINT IT BLACK ★★★1/2 Talented young sculptor (Rick Rossovich) is under bondage to an unscrupulous gallery owner (Sally Kirkland). He meets a slightly off-center art collector (Doug Savant) who complicates his life with favors. Impressive little thriller. Rated R for violence, nudity, and adult situations. 101m. **DIR:** Tim Hunter. **CAST:** Rick Rossovich, Sally Kirkland, Martin Landau, Julie Carmen, Doug Savant. **1989**

PAINT JOB, THE ★★1/2 Margaret has a problem. She's in love with two men. One is her husband. One is a painter who also happens to be her neighbor. Her husband also happens to be the neighbor's boss. Torn between two lovers, she could be torn apart when she finds out that one of them is a serial killer. Interesting cast makes this confusing thriller click. Rated R for violence, language, and adult situations. 90m. **DIR:** Michael Taav. **CAST:** Will Patton, Bebe Neuwirth, Robert Pastorelli. **1992**

PAINT YOUR WAGON ★★★1/2 Clint Eastwood and Lee Marvin play partners during the California gold rush era. They share everything, including a bride (Jean Seberg) bought from a Mormon traveler (John Mitchum), in this silly, but fun musical. Rated PG. 166m. **DIR:** Joshua Logan. **CAST:** Clint Eastwood, Lee Marvin, Jean Seberg, Harve Presnell, John Mitchum. **1969**

PAINTED DESERT, THE ★★1/2 The future Hopalong Cassidy, William Boyd, plays a foundling who grows up on the other side of the range from his ladylove and must decide between the family feud and the cattle or Helen Twelvetrees and the cattle. A young Clark Gable plays the dark cloud that is menacing the future of these two nice kids. B&W; 75m. **DIR:** Howard Higgin. **CAST:** William Boyd, Helen Twelvetrees, William Farnum, J. Farrell MacDonald, Clark Gable. **1931**

PAINTED FACES ★★★★ Many of Hong Kong's top stars trained at the Peking Opera School. This docudrama tribute to the now-closed school, set in the 1960s, shows the rigorous training and strict discipline students received there, as well as the amazing results. In Cantonese with English subtitles. Not rated. 100m. **DIR:** Alex Law. **CAST:** Sammo Hung, Kam-bo, Chang Pei-pei. **1987**

PAINTED HERO ★★★1/2 Country singer Dwight Yoakam gives a laconic but convincing performance in this decidedly offbeat character study as a rodeo clown/bullfighter whose reluctant reentry into the big time brings him face-to-face with the past and the people he's tried to leave behind. It's a real sleeper. Rated R for profanity, simulated sex, nudity, and violence. 105m. **DIR:** Terry Benedict. **CAST:** Dwight Yoakam, Bo Hopkins, Michelle Joyner, Keirsten Warren, Cindy Pickett, John Getz. **1995**

PAINTED HILLS, THE ★★★1/2 A sentimental tale with Lassie starring as an intelligent canine who doesn't let human beings get away with anything. Set in the 1870s with greedy gold miners killing partners and rivals. But Lassie knows who the real good guys are! Well-photographed and nicely choreographed with a beautifully edited performance by Lassie that will make an animal lover out of just about anybody. 65m. **DIR:** Harold F. Kress. **CAST:** Gary Gray, Paul Kelly, Bruce Cowling, Ann Doran, Chief Yowlachie, Andrea Virginia Lester. **1951**

PAINTED STALLION, THE ★★ History-bending serial finds Kit Carson, Davy Crockett, and Jim Bowie coming to the aid of Hoot Gibson as he leads a wagon train to Santa Fe. Lots of action and plot reversals. B&W; 12 chapters. **DIR:** William Witney, Ray Taylor. **CAST:** Ray "Crash" Corrigan, Hoot Gibson, Sammy McKim, Jack Perrin, Hal Taliaferro, Duncan Renaldo, LeRoy Mason, Yakima Canutt. **1937**

PAINTED VEIL, THE ★★★ A better-than-average Garbo melodrama because it has a better-than-average source. Somerset Maugham wrote the novel that inspired this sophisticated love story about a woman who cheats on her husband, then tries to make amends. B&W; 85m. **DIR:** Richard Boleslawski. **CAST:** Greta Garbo, George Brent, Herbert Marshall, Warner Oland, Jean Hersholt, Keye Luke, Cecilia Parker, Beulah Bondi. **1934**

PAIR OF ACES ★★ Kris Kristofferson and Willie Nelson star in this made-for-television modern-day Western. Kristofferson plays a Texas Ranger tracking down a serial killer while trying to keep tabs on a safecracker in his custody, played by Nelson. Not rated. 100m. **DIR:** Aaron Lipstadt. **CAST:** Willie Nelson, Kris Kristofferson, Rip Torn, Helen Shaver, Jane Cameron. **1990**

PAISAN ★★★1/2 Six separate stories of survival are hauntingly presented by writer Federico Fellini and director Roberto Rossellini in this early postwar Italian film. Shot on the streets and often improvised, the strong drama exposes the raw nerves brought on by living in a battlegound. B&W; 90m. **DIR:** Roberto Rossellini. **CAST:** Carmela Sazio, Robert Van Loon, Gar Moore. **1946**

PAJAMA GAME, THE ★★★★ This, one of the best film versions yet made of a Broadway musical, features John Raitt (his only big-screen appearance) in his stage role as the workshop superintendent who must deal with a union demand for a 7 -cent-per-hour raise. Doris Day plays the leader of the grievance committee, who fights and then falls for him. Broadway dancer Carol Haney also repeats her supporting role. 101m. **DIR:** George Abbott, Stanley Donen. **CAST:** Doris Day, John Raitt, Eddie Foy Jr., Carol Haney, Barbara Nichols, Reta Shaw. **1957 DVD**

PAL JOEY ★★★★ Frank Sinatra plays the antihero of this Rodgers and Hart classic about a hip guy who hopes to open a slick nightclub in San Francisco. With love interests Rita Hayworth and Kim Novak vying for Ol' Blue Eyes, and George Sidney's fast-paced direction, the picture is an enjoyable romp. The Rodgers and Hart score is perhaps their finest. 111m. **DIR:** George Sidney. **CAST:** Frank Sinatra, Rita Hayworth, Kim Novak, Barbara Nichols. **1957 DVD**

PALAIS ROYALE ★★ The Hollywood gangster is viewed through a peculiarly Canadian prism in this Toronto-made *film noir*. Matt Craven plays an ambitious advertising executive, circa 1959, who stumbles into a world of gangsters and goons. Slovenly. 100m. **DIR:** Martin Lavut. **CAST:** Dean Stockwell, Kim Cattrall, Matt Craven. **1988**

PALE BLOOD ★ A suave vampire tries to catch the psycho giving his breed a bad name. Usual vampire exploitation flick, this bloodsucker begins on a creepy note but falters under a lousy script and a lopsided amount of violence against women. Rated R for profanity, violence, and nudity. 93m. **DIR:** Dachin Hsu. **CAST:** George Chakiris, Wings Hauser, Pamela Ludwig. **1990**

PALE RIDER ★★★1/2 Star-producer-director Clint Eastwood donned six-guns and a Stetson for the first time since the classic *The Outlaw Josey Wales* (1976) for this enjoyable Western. The star is a mysterious avenger who comes to the aid of embattled gold prospectors in the Old West. Rated R for violence and profanity. 113m. **DIR:** Clint Eastwood. **CAST:** Clint Eastwood, Michael Moriarty, Carrie Snodgress, Christopher Penn, Richard Dysart, Richard Kiel, John Russell. **1985 DVD**

PALEFACE, THE ★★★★ Hope stars as a cowardly dentist who marries Calamity Jane (Jane Russell in rare form) and becomes, thanks to her quick draw, a celebrated gunslinger. It inspired a sequel, *Son of Paleface*, and a remake, *The Shakiest Gun in the West*, with Don Knotts, but the original is still tops. 91m. **DIR:** Norman Z. McLeod. **CAST:** Bob Hope, Jane Russell, Robert Armstrong. **1948**

PALERMO CONNECTION, THE ★★★ Political intrigue surrounds New York's mayoral candidate after he proposes drug legalization. On his honeymoon, he's framed by the mob. Now he must choose between accepting the status quo and challenging the Sicilian Mafia. Not rated, contains violence, profanity, and nudity. 100m. **DIR:** Francesco Rosi. **CAST:** James Belushi, Mimi Rogers, Joss Ackland, Vittorio Gassman. **1989**

PALLBEARER, THE ★★★★ David Schwimmer stars in this offbeat comedy as a college graduate who can't get started on his career in architecture, but this is nothing compared with the pickle he gets himself into when he agrees to attend the funeral of "the best friend" he doesn't remember. This character study boasts fine performances and some moments of sheer hilarity. Rated PG-13 for profanity and suggested sex. 97m. **DIR:** Matt Reeves. **CAST:** David Schwimmer, Gwyneth Paltrow, Michael Rapaport, Barbara Hershey, Toni Collette, Carol Kane. **1996 DVD**

PALM BEACH ★★★ Four different stories concerning troubled Australian teens converge at the title location, a popular Aussie beach. Fans of the new Australian cinema will want to take a look, though the accents may be a bit thick for others. Not rated. 88m. **DIR:** Albie Thomas. **CAST:** Nat Young, Ken Brown, Amanda Berry, Bryan Brown. **1979**

PALM BEACH STORY, THE ★★★★ Preston Sturges was perhaps the greatest of all American writer-directors. This light story of an engineer's wife (Claudette Colbert) who takes a vacation from marriage in sunny Florida and encounters one of the oddest groupings of talented characters ever assembled may well be his best film. B&W; 90m. **DIR:** Preston Sturges. **CAST:** Claudette Colbert, Joel McCrea, Rudy Vallee, Mary Astor, Sig Arno, William Demarest, Franklin Pangborn, Jimmy Conlin. **1942**

PALM SPRINGS WEEKEND ★★ It's sun, fun, and romance as some wild guys and cool chicks take a break from higher education and Watusi themselves silly during spring break. Harmless fun. 100m. **DIR:** Norman Taurog. **CAST:** Troy Donahue, Connie Stevens, Stefanie Powers, Robert Conrad, Ty Hardin, Jack Weston, Andrew Duggan. **1963**

PALMETTO 🖤 Hollywood has perpetrated a crime against novelist James Hadley Chase's work. Chase's unflinching violence has been replaced with laughable sex scenes between characters clearly unable to articulate their mock-sultry dialogue without looking as though they're about to burst into laughter. The story concerns a newspaper reporter who gets in over his head with a larcenous femme fatale. Try not to fall asleep. Rated R for profanity, violence, and strong sexual content. 112m. **DIR:** Volker Schlöndorff. **CAST:** Woody Harrelson, Elisabeth Shue, Gina Gershon, Rolf Hoppe, Michael Rapaport, Chloe Sevigny. **1998 DVD**

PALOMBELLA ROSSA ★★★1/2 A Fellini-inspired water-polo game becomes the waiting room for a politician's life after he has an auto accident. Michele (Nanni Moretti) finds himself searching for life's answers, while desperately trying to stay afloat during the game of his life. Truly inspired moments set against a surreal backdrop make this comedy a winner. In Italian with English subtitles. Not rated. 87m. DIR: Nanni Moretti. CAST: Nanni Moretti, Alfonso Santagata, Claudio Morganti, Asia Argento. 1989

PALOOKA ★★1/2 First filmed version of Ham Fisher's popular *Joe Palooka* is an okay little film about country bumpkin Stu Erwin's rise to the top in the fight game. This film shares a niche with the other seldom-seen comic-strip film adaptations of the 1930s, and its availability on video is a pleasant gift to the fan who loves those tough and slightly goofy movies of the early 1930s. B&W; 86m. DIR: Ben Stoloff. CAST: Jimmy Durante, Stu Erwin, Lupe Velez, Marjorie Rambeau, Robert Armstrong, William Cagney, Thelma Todd, Mary Carlisle. 1934

PALOOKAVILLE ★★★★ Most crooks get the basics right. You set up a jewelry store; you rob a jewelry store; but not the three likable Jersey City losers, the soul of this gentle caper comedy, who mistakenly rob the bakery next door and then plan to hold up an armored car. These sad-sack schemers hold court in seedy coffee shops and struggle with romance in a stubbornly nonviolent update of Italo Calvino's folksy 1940s short stories about economic survival in postwar Italy. Rated R for language. 92m. DIR: Alan Taylor. CAST: William Forsythe, Adam Trese, Vincent Gallo, Gareth Williams, Kim Dickens, Lisa Gay Hamilton, Frances McDormand, Bridgit Ryan. 1996

PALS ★★★ George C. Scott and Don Ameche are delightful as two senior citizens who stumble across a cache of drug money. Made-for-television. 100m. DIR: Lou Antonio. CAST: George C. Scott, Don Ameche, Sylvia Sidney. 1986

PALS OF THE SADDLE ★★1/2 The Three Mesquiteers (John Wayne, Ray Corrigan, and Max Terhune) help a woman government agent (Doreen McKay) trap a munitions ring in this enjoyable B Western series entry. B&W; 60m. DIR: George Sherman. CAST: John Wayne, Ray "Crash" Corrigan, Max Terhune, Doreen McKay, Frank Milan, Jack Kirk. 1938

PANAMA DECEPTION, THE ★★★★ This blistering, Oscar-winning documentary chronicles the events leading to the U.S. invasion of Panama, actually a crusade designed to renegotiate the treaty that would have given Panama control of the strategically critical Panama Canal by the year 2000. Although these often grim images are laced with explicit footage of burned children and civilians crushed by tanks, the most chilling fact to emerge is that the U.S. mainstream media were duped into reporting only what the Reagan and Bush administrations wanted them to see. Not rated; contains graphic violence. 91m. DIR: Barbara Trent. 1992

PANAMA HATTIE ★★ Take one hit musical play about a Panama nightclub owner, throw out all but a couple of Cole Porter tunes, refashion it for Red Skelton, then subdue him, and you have this lackluster movie that sat on the shelf for over a year before being released. Saved only by the debut of Lena Horne. B&W; 79m. DIR: Norman Z. McLeod. CAST: Red Skelton, Ann Sothern, Marsha Hunt, Virginia O'Brien, Lena Horne. 1942

PANAMA LADY ★★ Lucille Ball does her best to liven up this tired story about a saloon dancer stuck in the tropics with her pick of the local sweat-soaked swains. Future Saturday-matinee cowboy favorite Allan "Rocky" Lane plays the two-fisted hombre who whisks everybody's favorite redhead off to the romantic oil fields in the jungle that he calls home. This is a remake of *Panama Flo* (1932). B&W; 65m. DIR: Jack B. Hively. CAST: Lucille Ball, Allan "Rocky" Lane, Donald Briggs, Evelyn Brent, Abner Biberman. 1939

PANCHO BARNES ★★★1/2 The incredible true-life story of little-known Florence Pancho Barnes, portrayed fabulously by Valerie Bertinelli. This remarkable woman raced against Amelia Earhart, became a stunt pilot, and trained some of the most famous army boys to fly. Made for TV. 180m. DIR: Richard T. Heffron. CAST: Valerie Bertinelli, Ted Wass, James Stephens, Cynthia Harris, Geoffrey Lewis, Sam Robards. 1988

PANCHO VILLA ★★ Telly Savalas plays the famous bandit to the hilt and beyond. Clint Walker runs guns for him. Chuck Connors postures as a stiff and stuffy military type. You'll soon see why the title role forever belongs to Wallace Beery. It all builds to a rousing head-on train wreck. Rated R. 92m. DIR: Eugenio Martin. CAST: Telly Savalas, Clint Walker, Chuck Connors, Anne Francis. 1972

PANDEMONIUM ★★★ After attacks on cheerleading camps across the nation, there is only one place left to learn—Bambi's Cheerleading School. In this parody of slasher movies, Carol Kane steals the show as Candy, a girl with supernatural powers who just wants to have fun. Tom Smothers is a displaced Canadian Mountie; Paul Reubens (Pee-Wee Herman) plays his assistant. Rated PG for obscenities. 82m. DIR: Alfred Sole. CAST: Carol Kane, Tom Smothers, Debralee Scott, Candy Azzara, Miles Chapin, Tab Hunter, Paul Reubens. 1980

PANDORA AND THE FLYING DUTCHMAN ★★★1/2 Lush photography gives this legendary love story an edge. Ava Gardner is exotically beautiful as a self-centered woman romantically involved with a race-car driver, a matador, and the ghost of a man doomed to sail the oceans until he meets a woman who loves him enough to die for him. The pace is slow, but the romantic appeal is exceptional. 122m. DIR: Albert Lewin. CAST: Ava Gardner, James Mason, Nigel Patrick, Harry Warrender. 1951 DVD

PANDORA PROJECT, THE ✺ It took two directors, including infamous low-budget impresario Jim Wynorsky, to churn out this awful mess about a renegade commando who has stolen a top-secret weapon. It's one of those movies where even if you didn't pay to see it, you'd still want your money back. Not rated; contains violence. 92m. DIR: Jim Wynorsky, John Terlesky. CAST: Daniel Baldwin, Erika Eleniak, Richard Tyson, Tony Todd. 1998 DVD

PANDORA'S BOX ★★★★1/2 Here is a gem from the heyday of German silent screen Expressionism. The film follows a winning yet amoral temptress, Lulu (a sparkling performance by Louise Brooks). Without concerns or inhibitions, Lulu blissfully ensnares a variety of weak men, only to contribute to their eventual downfall. B&W; 131m. DIR: G. W. Pabst. CAST: Louise Brooks, Fritz Kortner. 1929

PANIC BUTTON ★★ Looking for a tax loss, a gangster bankrolls a film sure to be so bad that he'll lose money on it. Did Mel Brooks see this obscure comedy before he made *The Producers* (which is much funnier)? B&W; 90m. **DIR:** George Sherman. **CAST:** Maurice Chevalier, Eleanor Parker, Jayne Mansfield, Mike Connors, Akim Tamiroff. 1964

PANIC IN NEEDLE PARK ★★★★ Still one of the best films ever made about drug abuse, as a likable young couple destroy their lives when they become hooked on heroin. Al Pacino is excellent in his first starring role, in a film that is almost queasily realistic in its depiction of urban drug culture. Rated R for drug use. 110m. **DIR:** Jerry Schatzberg. **CAST:** Al Pacino, Kitty Winn, Alan Vint, Richard Bright, Raul Julia, Paul Sorvino. 1971

PANIC IN THE STREETS ★★★★ Oscar-winning story focuses on a New Orleans criminal who is unknowingly the carrier of a deadly virus. The police attempt to capture him before he can infect others. Taut thriller. B&W; 93m. **DIR:** Elia Kazan. **CAST:** Richard Widmark, Jack Palance, Paul Douglas, Barbara Bel Geddes, Zero Mostel. 1950

PANIC IN THE YEAR ZERO ★★★1/2 Low-budget yet extremely effective tale of paranoia from producer Roger Corman. Ray Milland, who also directed, stars as the head of a family attempting to leave Los Angeles when the bombs drop. Outside the city limits, the family runs into massive chaos when panicking citizens take the law into their own hands. Their biggest fear isn't the bombs, but man himself. 95m. **DIR:** Ray Milland. **CAST:** Ray Milland, Joan Freeman, Frankie Avalon, Jean Hagen, Richard Garland. 1962

PANIQUE ★★★1/2 Based on a thriller by Georges Simenon, this gripping story features Michel Simon as a stranger who is framed for murder. A taut film comparable to the best of the chase *noir* genre so prevalent in French and American cinema of the mid-1940s. In French with English subtitles. B&W; 87m. **DIR:** Julien Duvivier. **CAST:** Michel Simon, Viviane Romance. 1946

PANTALOONS ★★★ In this period comedy, horse-faced Fernandel gets a chance to fill in for his master, Don Juan. Unfortunately, the circumstances are so hectic that he can't take advantage of any of the women who so want to be conquered by the great lover, even if he looks somewhat less dashing than they'd imagined. Dubbed. 93m. **DIR:** John Berry. **CAST:** Fernandel, Carmen Seville, Fernando Rey. 1957

PANTHER ★★ Whitewashed urban action-movie approach to the Sixties black-power party's story. The Black Panthers are portrayed as less complex, and less violent, than they really were, and the film's thesis that the FBI and the mob teamed up to destroy them with cheap drugs is, well, cheap propaganda. Rated R for violence, language, and drug use. 93m. **DIR:** Mario Van Peebles. **CAST:** Kadeem Hardison, Bokeem Woodbine, Courtney B. Vance, Marcus Chong, Joe Don Baker, M. Emmet Walsh. 1995 DVD

PANTHER GIRL OF THE CONGO ♥ Republic Studio's penultimate cliffhanger about a chemist who creates giant crayfish to guard his diamond hoard was a definite contributor to the genre's demise. B&W; 12 chapters. **DIR:** Franklin Adreon. **CAST:** Phyllis Coates, Myron Healey, Arthur Space. 1955

PAPA'S DELICATE CONDITION ★★1/2 Somewhat stolid but pleasant enough story of family life in a small Texas town and the sometimes unpleasant notoriety brought to a family by their alcoholic patriarch, Jackie Gleason. Not as good a film as it was considered when released, this is still an enjoyable movie. 98m. **DIR:** George Marshall. **CAST:** Jackie Gleason, Glynis Johns, Charlie Ruggles, Laurel Goodwin, Charles Lane, Elisha Cook Jr., Juanita Moore, Murray Hamilton. 1963

PAPER, THE ★★★★ Michael Keaton stars as an editor in this ensemble comedy-drama about a New York daily tabloid newspaper. He has only a few hours to get the scoop on a murder and stop cost-conscious managing editor Glenn Close from printing a sensationalistic cover that implies two innocent youngsters are guilty. Rated R for profanity and violence. 110m. **DIR:** Ron Howard. **CAST:** Michael Keaton, Glenn Close, Marisa Tomei, Randy Quaid, Robert Duvall, Jason Robards Jr., Jason Alexander, Spalding Gray, Catherine O'Hara, Jack Kehoe, Clint Howard. 1994 DVD

PAPER BRIGADE, THE ★★★ When his family moves to the suburbs, a big city teen takes a paper route to make some money and finds out that the 'burbs aren't always as peaceful as everyone says. Enjoyable kids' comedy. Rated PG for mild violence. 89m. **DIR:** Blair Treu. **CAST:** Kyle Howard, Travis Wester, Robert Englund. 1996

PAPER CHASE, THE ★★★★ John Houseman won the Oscar for best actor in a supporting role in 1973 with his first-rate performance in this excellent film. Timothy Bottoms stars as a law student attempting to earn his law degree in spite of a stuffy professor (Houseman). Rated PG. 111m. **DIR:** James Bridges. **CAST:** Timothy Bottoms, John Houseman, Lindsay Wagner. 1973

PAPER LION ★★★1/2 Based on George Plimpton's book, this film tells the story of the author's exploits when he becomes an honorary team member of the Detroit Lions pro football team. Alan Alda is fine as Plimpton and Alex Karras is a standout in his support. 107m. **DIR:** Alex March. **CAST:** Alan Alda, Lauren Hutton, Alex Karras, David Doyle, Ann Turkel, Roger Brown. 1968

PAPER MARRIAGE (1988) ★★1/2 Martial arts star Sammo Hung plays an out-of-work Chinese boxer in Canada who reluctantly accepts a promise to marry a Hong Kong girl. Though highly uneven, the film has some funny moments. In Cantonese with English subtitles. Not rated; contains violence. 102m. **DIR:** Sammo Hung. **CAST:** Sammo Hung, Maggie Cheung. 1988

PAPER MARRIAGE (1992) ★★ Silly tale of a Polish girl arriving in London to marry her fiancé. When his mom disapproves of the union, she marries an unemployed man. Problems naturally result in their bizarre marriage, but these are nothing compared to the effect that the emotionless actors have on the film. Not rated, contains sex, violence, and profanity. 90m. **DIR:** Krzysztof Lang. **CAST:** Gary Kemp, Joanna Trepechinska, Rita Tushingham. 1992

PAPER MASK ★★★ Intriguing British thriller features Paul McGann as an ambitious young man who poses as an emergency room doctor. His lack of training has a deadly effect on a female patient (Barbara Leigh-Hunt). The nurse on duty (Amanda Donohoe) may cover up for or expose him. Rated R for nudity and violence. 105m. DIR: Christopher Morahan. CAST: Paul McGann, Amanda Donohoe, Frederick Treves, Tom Wilkinson, Barbara Leigh-Hunt. 1989

PAPER MOON ★★★★★ Critic-turned-director Peter Bogdanovich ended his four-film winning streak—which included *Targets*, *The Last Picture Show*, and *What's Up Doc?*—with this comedy, starring Ryan O'Neal and Tatum O'Neal as a con man and a kid in the 1930s who get involved in some pretty wild predicaments and meet up with a variety of wacky characters. It's delightful entertainment from beginning to end. Rated PG. B&W; 102m. DIR: Peter Bogdanovich. CAST: Ryan O'Neal, Tatum O'Neal, Madeline Kahn, John Hillerman. 1973

PAPER TIGER ★★ Stiffly British David Niven is tutor to the son (Ando) of a Japanese ambassador (Toshiro Mifune). He and his young charge are kidnapped by terrorists for political reasons. Derring-do follows, but it's all lukewarm and paplike. Rated PG. 99m. DIR: Ken Annakin. CAST: David Niven, Toshiro Mifune, Ando, Hardy Krüger. 1976

PAPER WEDDING ★★★1/2 In order to save a political refugee from being deported, a single woman agrees to marry him. But the name-only marriage becomes real when the couple is forced to live together. This strong comedy was made before the similar *Green Card*, and the acting is excellent. Not rated, the film has suggested sex. 95m. DIR: Michel Brault. CAST: Geneviève Bujold, Manuel Aranguiz, Dorothee Berryman. 1989 DVD

PAPERBACK ROMANCE ★★★ A young romance writer (Gia Carides) meets a handsome man (Anthony LaPaglia) at the library, but with her leg in a brace from childhood polio, she's too self-conscious to encourage him. When she breaks the afflicted leg, she uses the cast as "cover," never thinking what she'll do when the break heals. Similarly, writer-director Ben Lewin doesn't seem to have thought about how to develop his offbeat premise. On the plus side is the sexy rapport of the two stars (married in real life) and several unexpectedly funny scenes. Originally released in Australia at 94 minutes, with the wittier title *Lucky Break*. Not rated; suitable for mature audiences. 87m. DIR: Ben Lewin. CAST: Gia Carides, Anthony LaPaglia, Rebecca Gibney, Jacek Koman. 1994

PAPERBOY, THE ★★1/2 A deranged teenager turns his crush on a neighbor into a murderous rampage. Typical thriller is slightly better if you turn off the sound—Marc Marut (as the paperboy) has a voice that is as caustic as battery acid. Rated R for violence and profanity. 93m. DIR: Douglas Jackson. CAST: Alexandra Paul, Marc Marut, William Katt, Frances Bay. 1994

PAPERHOUSE ★★★★ In this original film from England, a lonely, misunderstood 11-year-old girl (Charlotte Burke) begins retreating into a fantasy world. Her world turns nightmarish when it starts to take over her dreams and a flu-like disease keeps making her faint. Visually impressive, well-acted, and intelligent fare. Rated PG-13 for violence. 94m. DIR: Bernard Rose. CAST: Charlotte Burke, Glenne Headly, Ben Cross. 1989

PAPILLON ★★★★1/2 Unfairly criticized, this is a truly exceptional film biography of the man who escaped from Devil's Island. Steve McQueen gives an excellent performance, and Dustin Hoffman is once again a chameleon. Director Franklin Schaffner invests the same gusto here that he did in *Patton*. Rated PG. 150m. DIR: Franklin J. Schaffner. CAST: Steve McQueen, Dustin Hoffman, Victor Jory, Don Gordon. 1973 DVD

PARADE ★★1/2 Sadly, the great comedian Jacques Tati's last film is his least distinguished work. He plays host to a group of circus performers in this semidocumentary that is little more than a footnote in his filmography. In French with English subtitles. 85m. DIR: Jacques Tati. CAST: Jacques Tati. 1974

PARADINE CASE, THE ★★ Even the Master of Suspense can't win 'em all. Obviously chafing under the rein of mentor David O. Selznick, Alfred Hitchcock produced one of his few failures—a boring, talky courtroom drama that stalls long before its conclusion. Not rated; suitable for family viewing. B&W; 112m. DIR: Alfred Hitchcock. CAST: Gregory Peck, Ann Todd, Charles Laughton, Ethel Barrymore, Charles Coburn, Louis Jourdan, Alida Valli, Leo G. Carroll, John Williams. 1947 DVD

PARADISE (1982) ★★ Willie Aames and Phoebe Cates star as two teenagers who, as members of a caravan traveling from Baghdad to Damascus in the nineteenth century, escape a surprise attack by a sheikh intent on adding Cates to his harem. Rated R for frontal male and female nudity. 100m. DIR: Stuart Gillard. CAST: Willie Aames, Phoebe Cates, Tuvia Tavi. 1982

PARADISE (1991) ★★★1/2 When a 10-year-old boy spends the summer with an emotionally estranged couple, they all help each other overcome personal tragedies. This film, adapted from the French *Le Grand Chemin* (*The Grand Highway*), has some very touching and funny moments. Rated PG-13 for profanity and nudity. 104m. DIR: Mary Agnes Donoghue. CAST: Don Johnson, Melanie Griffith, Elijah Wood, Thora Birch, Sheila McCarthy, Eve Gordon, Louise Latham. 1991

PARADISE ALLEY 🖤 Turgid mess about three brothers hoping for a quick ride out of the slums. Rated PG for violence. 107m. DIR: Sylvester Stallone. CAST: Sylvester Stallone, Armand Assante, Lee Canalito. 1978

PARADISE HAWAIIAN STYLE ★★1/2 Elvis Presley returns to Hawaii after his 1962 film, *Blue Hawaii*. This time he plays a pilot who makes time for romance while setting up a charter service. Some laughs and lots of songs. 91m. DIR: Michael Moore. CAST: Elvis Presley, Suzanna Leigh. 1966

PARADISE LOST: THE CHILD MURDERS AT ROBIN HOOD HILLS ★★★★ First shown on HBO, this is one of the most important documentaries of the 1990s. When three young boys are horribly murdered in a small Tennessee town, the residents immediately suspect three teens who are the local oddballs. Although filmmakers Joe Berlinger and Bruce Sinofsky remain nonjudgmental, their record of the trial offers a devastating indictment of the justice system. Not rated, but not recommended for young children. 150m. DIR: Joe Berlinger, Bruce Sinofsky. 1997

PARADISE MOTEL ★★★ Another teen romp, but with a surprise: the appealing cast can act. Gary Hershberger is a student whose father keeps moving the family around in pursuit of his get-rich schemes. The latest venture is the Paradise Motel. To gain acceptance, Hershberger loans out one of the rooms to the class stud. Rated R for language and nudity. 87m. DIR: Cary Medoway. CAST: Gary Herschberger, Robert Krantz, Joanna Leigh Stack. 1985

PARADISE ROAD ★★★1/2 Bruce Beresford's heartfelt account of a little-known chapter in World War II ultimately suffers from being *too* tragic; his film doesn't maintain the dignity—or conclude with the triumph—of Spielberg's *Schindler's List*. His portrayal of British and ANZAC women imprisoned in a Japanese concentration camp does not address the subject with the proper depth. The top-lined stars portray compelling characters, but many of the supporting players and their eventual fates fail to generate the appropriate passion. Rated R for violence, torture, and nudity. 115m. DIR: Bruce Beresford. CAST: Glenn Close, Pauline Collins, Cate Blanchett, Frances McDormand, Julianna Margulies, Jennifer Ehle. 1997

PARALLAX VIEW, THE ★★★★ This fine film offers a fascinating study of a reporter, played by Warren Beatty, trying to penetrate the cover-up of an assassination in which the hunter becomes the hunted. Rated R. 102m. DIR: Alan J. Pakula. CAST: Warren Beatty, Paula Prentiss, William Daniels. 1974 DVD

PARALLEL LIVES ★★★1/2 An impressive ensemble cast is the best reason to watch director Linda Yellin's follow-up to *Chantilly Lace*, which employs the same technique of actor improvisation on a sketchy plot. The setting is a multigenerational sorority/fraternity reunion that allows old friends and foes the opportunity for one last encounter. It's great fun until the third act, which is marred by the needless intrusion of a murder investigation. Rated R for profanity and simulated sex. 105m. DIR: Linda Yellen. CAST: James Belushi, Liza Minnelli, JoBeth Williams, Jill Eikenberry, Gena Rowlands, Ben Gazzara, Ally Sheedy, Helen Slater, LeVar Burton, Treat Williams, Patricia Wettig, Jack Klugman, Paul Sorvino, Lindsay Crouse. 1994

PARAMEDICS ★★1/2 A good guys–bad guys flick disguised as a sex comedy. Two paramedics are transferred to a nasty part of the city where a vicious gang is killing people to sell their organs. The comedy comes in the form of a mysterious beauty with a rather fatal sex drive. Rated PG-13 for sexual references. 91m. DIR: Stuart Margolin. CAST: George Newbern, Christopher McDonald, Lawrence Hilton-Jacobs, John Pleshette, James Noble, John P. Ryan. 1987

PARANOIA (1969) 💘 American widow makes the mistake of taking an evil young couple into her isolated villa. Originally rated X for nudity and sexual situations, but a tame R equivalent now. 91m. DIR:

Umberto Lenzi. CAST: Carroll Baker, Lou Castel, Colette Descombes. 1969

PARANOIA (1998) ★★ In this by-the-numbers thriller, Larry Drake plays Calvin Hawks, incarcerated for sadistically killing a woman's family. Since then she has been a recluse, using her home computer to communicate with the outside world. Then Calvin starts sending threatening E-mails that he's getting out soon. Rated R for violence, language, and adult situations. 86m. DIR: Larry Brand. CAST: Larry Drake, Brigitte Bako, Sally Kirkland, Scott Valentine, Stephen Gevedon. 1998 DVD

PARANOIAC ★★1/2 An overwrought Oliver Reed is surprised to see his long-dead brother return to the family mansion. Too much Sturm and Drang weighs down this unwieldly thriller from Hammer Studios. Not rated; contains implied violence. B&W; 80m. DIR: Freddie Francis. CAST: Oliver Reed, Janette Scott, Alexander Davion, Liliane Brousse, Sheila Burrell, Maurice Denham. 1963

PARASITE ★★1/2 If director Charles Band intended a film that would sicken its audience, he succeeded. Memorable scenes include parasites bursting through the stomach of one victim and the face of another. Rated R. 85m. DIR: Charles Band. CAST: Robert Glaudini, Demi Moore, Luca Bercovici, Vivian Blaine, Tom Villard. 1982 DVD

PARATROOP COMMAND ★★1/2 World War II drama set in North Africa, where a paratrooper tries to make amends after he accidentally shoots a member of his own squadron. Effective action direction lifts this above the pedestrian. B&W; 71m. DIR: William Witney. CAST: Dick Bakalyan. 1959

PARDON MON AFFAIRE ★★★★ Enjoyable romantic comedy about a middle-class, happily married man (Jean Rochefort) who pursues his fantasy of meeting a beautiful model (Anny Duperey) and having an affair. Later remade in America as *The Woman in Red*. In French with English subtitles. Rated PG. 105m. DIR: Yves Robert. CAST: Jean Rochefort, Claude Brasseur, Anny Duperey, Guy Bedos, Victor Lanoux. 1976

PARDON MON AFFAIRE, TOO! ★★ Lukewarm comedy of infidelity and friendship. The focus is on four middle-aged men who share their troubles and feelings about their marriages and sex lives. No real laughs. In French with English subtitles. 110m. DIR: Yves Robert. CAST: Jean Rochefort, Claude Brasseur, Guy Bedos, Victor Lanoux, Daniele Delorme. 1977

PARDON MY SARONG ★★★ Two Chicago bus drivers are hired by a playboy to drive him to California, and somehow they end up on his yacht sailing the seas. Good musical interludes (including the Ink Spots) contribute to the success of this early A&C outing. B&W; 83m. DIR: Erle C. Kenton. CAST: Bud Abbott, Lou Costello, Robert Paige, Virginia Bruce, Lionel Atwill, William Demarest, Samuel S. Hinds. 1942

PARDON MY TRUNK (HELLO ELEPHANT!) ★★1/2 An Italian schoolteacher (Vittorio De Sica), struggling against poverty does a good deed for a visiting Hindu prince. In gratitude, the Indian sends him a gift: a baby elephant. De Sica's performance elevates what otherwise would have been merely a silly slapstick exercise. Dubbed in English. B&W; 85m. DIR:

Gianni Franciolini. **CAST:** Vittorio De Sica, Maria Mereader, Sabu, Nando Bruno. **1952**

PARDON US ★★★★ Stan Laurel and Oliver Hardy are sent to prison for selling home-brewed beer. They encounter all the usual prison stereotypical characters and play off them to delightful comedy effect. During an escape, they put on black faces and pick cotton along with blacks and Ollie sings "Lazy Moon." B&W; 55m. **DIR:** James Parrott. **CAST:** Stan Laurel, Oliver Hardy, Wilfred Lucas. **1931**

PARENT TRAP, THE (1961) ★★★★ Walt Disney doubled the fun in this comedy when he had Hayley Mills play twins. Mills plays sisters who meet for the first time at camp and decide to reunite their divorced parents (Brian Keith and Maureen O'Hara). 124m. **DIR:** David Swift. **CAST:** Hayley Mills, Brian Keith, Maureen O'Hara, Joanna Barnes. **1961**

PARENT TRAP, THE (1998) ★★★1/2 Although formulaic, at times uneven, and needlessly slapstick during the introductory scenes, this update of Disney's 1961 film grows on you. Like its new young star, Lindsay Lohan, this film wins over its audience through charm and personality. Lohan plays twins separated shortly after birth, and raised by divorced parents who never really fell out of love with each other. Once reunited at a summer camp, the girls scheme to bring their folks back together, a plan given extra urgency because Dad has been targeted by a money-hungry shark in Cute Young Thing's clothing. Nothing new here, but the result is certain to please all ages. Rated PG for no particular reason. 124m. **DIR:** Nancy Meyers. **CAST:** Dennis Quaid, Natasha Richardson, Lindsay Lohan, Elaine Hendrix, Lisa Ann Walter, Simon Kunz. **1998 DVD**

PARENTHOOD ★★★★★ In this heartwarming comedy, Steve Martin and Mary Steenburgen are superb as model parents coping with career and kids. There's fine support from Rick Moranis as a yuppie who pushes his 3-year-old daughter to learn Kafka and karate, Dianne Wiest as a Woodstock-goer coping with three troubled teens, and Jason Robards as the granddad who discovers that parenthood is a job for life. Rated PG-13 for profanity and sexual themes. 110m. **DIR:** Ron Howard. **CAST:** Steve Martin, Mary Steenburgen, Tom Hulce, Jason Robards Jr., Dianne Wiest, Rick Moranis, Martha Plimpton, Keanu Reeves. **1989 DVD**

PARENTS ♥ Black comedy about a cannibalistic couple and their relationship with their suspicious young son. Rated R. 90m. **DIR:** Bob Balaban. **CAST:** Randy Quaid, Mary Beth Hurt, Sandy Dennis, Bryan Madorsky. **1989 DVD**

PARIAH ★★ When his African-American girlfriend is raped and driven to suicide by skinheads, a young man infiltrates the gang that did it; soon he finds himself adopting their twisted outlook on life. At least that seems to be writer-director Randolph Kret's intention, but the script lacks definition, the pacing is sluggish, and acting is amateurish. Not rated; contains profanity (including racial slurs), violence, nudity, and sexual scenes. 105m. **DIR:** Randolph Kret. **CAST:** Damon Jones, Dave Oren Ward, David Lee Wilson, Aimee Chaffin. **1998**

PARIS BELONGS TO US ★★ The first film directed by Jácques Rivette and the first feature-length release in the French new wave. Quite a *cause célèbre* in 1957, it stands as a testament to the initial, highly self-conscious experimentations of the generation. The incomprehensible plot seems to be the story of a young actress who becomes involved in a murderous intrigue hatched by an American novelist. In French with English subtitles. B&W; 135m. **DIR:** Jacques Rivette. **CAST:** Betty Schneider, Daniel Crohem, Jean-Claude Brialy. **1957**

PARIS BLUES ★★★1/2 Duke Ellington's superb jazz score enhances this drama. The action takes place in Paris where two jazz musicians (Paul Newman and Sidney Poitier) fall for two lovely tourists (Joanne Woodward and Diahann Carroll). What the plot lacks in originality is amply made up for by the fine music and outstanding cast. 98m. **DIR:** Martin Ritt. **CAST:** Paul Newman, Joanne Woodward, Diahann Carroll, Sidney Poitier, Louis Armstrong, Serge Reggiani. **1961**

PARIS EXPRESS, THE ★★1/2 Based on acclaimed mystery writer Georges Simenon's novel, this film details the exploits of a finance clerk (Claude Rains) who turns embezzler. Hoping to travel the world with his ill-gotten gains, he runs into more trouble and adventure than he can handle. 80m. **DIR:** Harold French. **CAST:** Claude Rains, Marta Toren, Anouk Aimée, Marius Goring, Herbert Lom. **1953**

PARIS FRANCE ★★★1/2 Unadulterated kink is the highlight of this nonflinching dark comedy about one woman's quest for sexual fulfillment. When her husband fails to satisfy her, Lucy, played by the alluring Leslie Hope, turns to a young stranger to punch her buttons. Their sexual escapades escalate until they explode in a very unconventional finale. Rated NC-17 for nudity, sexual situations, and adult language. 96m. **DIR:** Gerard Ciccoritti. **CAST:** Leslie Hope, Victor Ertmanis. **1993**

PARIS HOLIDAY ★★ Film-within-a-film show business story featuring Bob Hope and French comic Fernandel never gets off the ground. Statuesque Anita Ekberg succeeds in diverting attention from the two uncomfortable comedians. 101m. **DIR:** Gerd Oswald. **CAST:** Bob Hope, Fernandel, Anita Ekberg, Martha Hyer, Preston Sturges. **1957**

PARIS IS BURNING ★★★★ This superb documentary takes us through the public and private domain of poor black and Hispanic gays in New York City who vamp at lavish balls. At these events, participants imitate fashion models, Marines, Wall Street brokers, and other figures culled from magazine advertisements. Rated R for some nudity. 78m. **DIR:** Jennie Livingston. **1990**

PARIS, TEXAS ★★★★1/2 *Paris, Texas* is a haunting vision of personal pain and universal suffering, with Harry Dean Stanton impeccable as the weary wanderer who returns after four years to reclaim his son (Hunter Carson) and search for his wife (Nastassja Kinski). It is the kind of motion picture we rarely see, one that attempts to say something about our country and its people—and succeeds. Rated R for profanity and adult content. 144m. **DIR:** Wim

Wenders. **CAST:** Harry Dean Stanton, Nastassja Kinski, Dean Stockwell, Aurore Clement, Hunter Carson. **1984**

PARIS TROUT ★★1/2 Pete Dexter's bleak take on 1949 Georgia gets first-cabin treatment but remains as inexplicably pointless as his novel. Dennis Hopper stars as the titular character, a venal and paranoid storekeeper who shoots and kills a young black girl and then dismisses the act as "nothing scandalous." Made-for-cable drama includes shocking violence and coarse language. 100m. **DIR:** Stephen Gyllenhaal. **CAST:** Dennis Hopper, Barbara Hershey, Ed Harris. **1991**

PARIS WAS A WOMAN ★★★ The community of women artists, writers, and intellectuals who took up residence in Paris's Left Bank in the 1920s is a fascinating subject. Unfortunately, this documentary is hampered by a lack of film footage of its subjects, resulting in too many talking heads and too much attention paid to lesser lights simply because there was footage of them available. You'd be better off reading a book on the subject. Not rated. 75m. **DIR:** Greta Schiller. **1996**

PARIS WHEN IT SIZZLES ★★★ Uneven story-within-a-story about a screenwriter (William Holden) who "creates" a Parisian fantasyland for himself and the assistant (Audrey Hepburn) with whom he's fallen in love. As the story progresses, they—and the viewer—have an increasingly difficult time distinguishing fact from scripted fiction. 110m. **DIR:** Richard Quine. **CAST:** William Holden, Audrey Hepburn, Noel Coward, Gregoire Aslan, Marlene Dietrich. **1954**

PARK IS MINE, THE ★★1/2 After his friend is killed, unstable Vietnam vet (Tommy Lee Jones) invades New York's Central Park and proclaims it to be his. Predictable ending. Pretty farfetched stuff. An HBO Film. 102m. **DIR:** Steven H. Stern. **CAST:** Tommy Lee Jones, Helen Shaver, Yaphet Kotto. **1985**

PARKER ADDERSON, PHILOSOPHER ★★★★ Man's ability to inflict torment even on those with nothing left to lose is the theme of this deft adaptation of the Ambrose Bierce short story. Harris Yulin stars as a Yankee spy caught red-handed by the ragtag troops of Douglas Watson's Confederate general. Introduced by Henry Fonda; suitable for family viewing. 39m. **DIR:** Arthur Barron. **CAST:** Harris Yulin, Douglas Watson, Darren O'Connor. **1974**

PARLOR, BEDROOM AND BATH ★★★ Some genuine belly laughs buoy this slight comedy about a bewildered bumpkin (Buster Keaton) at the mercy of some society wackos. Charlotte Greenwood works well with the Great Stone Face. B&W; 75m. **DIR:** Edward Sedgwick. **CAST:** Buster Keaton, Charlotte Greenwood, Reginald Denny, Cliff Edwards, Dorothy Christy, Joan Peers, Sally Eilers, Natalie Moorhead, Edward Brophy. **1932**

PARRISH ★★ Lust among the young and greed among the old in the tobacco fields of Connecticut. Karl Malden saves this. 140m. **DIR:** Delmer Daves. **CAST:** Troy Donahue, Claudette Colbert, Karl Malden, Dean Jagger, Connie Stevens, Diane McBain, Dub Taylor. **1961**

PARTING GLANCES ★★★★ Nick (Steve Buscemi), a rock singer, discovers he is dying of AIDS. Writer-

director Bill Sherwood charts the effect this discovery has on Nick and his estranged lover, Michael (Richard Ganoung), who now lives with Robert (John Bolger). Subject matter aside, *Parting Glances* has a number of funny moments and is a life-affirming look at the gay lifestyle. 90m. **DIR:** Bill Sherwood. **CAST:** Richard Ganoung, John Bolger, Steve Buscemi, Adam Nathan, Kathy Kinney, Patrick Tull. **1986**

PARTNER ★★★ Bernardo Bertolucci apes Godard with less than optimal results in this story of a shy youth who creates an alternative self that possesses the qualities he lacks. Occasionally incoherent. In Italian and French with English subtitles. Not rated. 112m. **DIR:** Bernardo Bertolucci. **CAST:** Pierre Clementi, Tina Aumont, Stefania Sandrelli. **1968**

PARTNERS ★★★ Ryan O'Neal and John Hurt are two undercover detectives assigned to pose as lovers in order to track down the murderer of a gay man in this warm, funny, and suspenseful comedy-drama written by Francis Veber (*La Cage aux Folles*). Rated R for nudity, profanity, violence, and adult themes. 98m. **DIR:** James Burrows. **CAST:** Ryan O'Neal, John Hurt. **1982**

•PARTNERS IN CRIME 🦃 A disgraced ex-policeman turned private detective must turn to his ex-wife, a beautiful FBI agent, to help exonerate him from a kidnapping and murder rap. If you can believe former model Paulina Porizkova as the FBI agent, you might buy the rest of this claptrap. Rated R for adult situations, language, and violence. 90m. **DIR:** Jennifer Warren. **CAST:** Rutger Hauer, Paulina Porizkova, Andrew Dolan, Frank Gerrish. **2000 DVD**

PARTNERS IN CRIME (SECRET ADVERSARY) (TV SERIES) ★★★1/2 Agatha Christie's high-society private detectives, Tommy and Tuppence, are introduced in the feature-length WWI-era tale, *The Secret Adversary*; lacking personal finances or steady jobs after having left war service, they advertise their services as amateur sleuths. Series highlights include "Finessing the King," where sharp-eyed viewers will find all the clues necessary to match wits with the detectives; "The Affair of the Pink Pearl," in which their "guaranteed twenty-four-hour-service" is put to the test; and "The Case of the Missing Lady," where Tuppence's attempts to work undercover become particularly amusing. 51m. **DIR:** Paul Annett, Christopher Hodson, Tony Wharmby. **CAST:** Francesca Annis, James Warwick, Reece Dinsdale. **1982–1983 DVD**

PARTY, THE ★★★ The closest Peter Sellers ever came to doing a one-man show on film. He plays an actor from India who mistakenly gets invited to a plush Hollywood party, where he falls all over himself and causes more mishaps and pratfalls than the Three Stooges. 99m. **DIR:** Blake Edwards. **CAST:** Peter Sellers, Claudine Longet, Denny Miller, Marge Champion, Gavin MacLeod. **1968**

PARTY CAMP ★★ Andrew Ross takes a job as a camp counselor with the object of turning the militarylike operation into party time for all. Just another teen romp with the usual caricatures, obligatory nudity, and titillation. Rated R. 96m. **DIR:** Gary Graver. **CAST:** Andrew Ross, Kerry Brennan, Peter Jason. **1986**

PARTY GIRL (1958) ★★★1/2 Crime-drama with lawyer Robert Taylor as a cunning mouthpiece for the mob in 1930s Chicago. All hell breaks loose when he decides to go 'legit. Familiar, but well-produced. 99m. DIR: Nicholas Ray. CAST: Robert Taylor, Cyd Charisse, Lee J. Cobb, John Ireland, Kent Smith. 1958

PARTY GIRL (1995) ★★★ A painfully hip New York scenester discovers that her real purpose in life is to become a librarian. Sassy star Parker Posey's irrepressible sardonic charm triumphs over the precious concept and sometimes amateurish staging. Rated R for language, drug use, sex, and brief nudity. 98m. DIR: Daisy von Scherler Mayer. CAST: Parker Posey, Omar Townsend, Sasha von Scherler, Guillermo Diaz. 1995

PARTY GIRLS (PARTY INC.) 🎦 Overdone film-within-a-film. Rated R for nudity, profanity, and sexual situations. 90m. DIR: Chuck Vincent. CAST: Marilyn Chambers. 1989

PARTY LINE 🎦 Disconnected nonsense about telephone party-line callers who turn up dead. Rated R for violence, profanity, and nudity. 91m. DIR: William Webb. CAST: Richard Hatch, Leif Garrett, Richard Roundtree. 1988

PARTY PLANE 🎦 Naughty stewardesses save their failing company by entertaining male passengers with a striptease. Lame adolescent fantasy flick. Not rated, but with considerable nudity and profanity. 81m. DIR: Ed Hansen. CAST: Kent Stoddard. 1987

PASCALI'S ISLAND ★★★★ A quietly enigmatic film about town loyalties, hypocrisy, and broader philosophical issues of art and romanticism, as represented by three characters on a Greek island in 1908. Ben Kingsley is brilliant as a low-level bureaucrat and semispy who will never challenge what he does or why, even when it threatens to destroy everything he cares about. Rated PG-13. 101m. DIR: James Dearden. CAST: Ben Kingsley, Helen Mirren, Charles Dance. 1988

PASS THE AMMO ★★★1/2 Tim Curry's deliciously scheming evangelist is merely one of the delights in this inventive satire of television sermonizing. Bill Paxton and Linda Kozlowski play a couple of good ol' folks who plot to "steal back" some inheritance money the televangelist bilked from her family. Rated PG-13 for language and violence. 93m. DIR: David Beaird. CAST: Tim Curry, Bill Paxton, Linda Kozlowski, Annie Potts, Glenn Withrow, Dennis Burkley. 1987

PASSAGE TO INDIA, A ★★★★★ After an absence from the screen of fourteen years, British director David Lean returned triumphantly, with the brilliant *A Passage to India*. Based on the 1924 novel by E. M. Forster, this brilliant screen adaptation compares favorably with David Lean's finest films. Ostensibly about the romantic adventures of a young Englishwoman in "the mysterious East" that culminate in a court trial (for attempted rape), it is also a multilayered, symbolic work about "the difficulty of living in the universe." Rated PG. 163m. DIR: David Lean. CAST: Judy Davis, Victor Banerjee, Alec Guinness, Peggy Ashcroft. 1984

PASSAGE TO MARSEILLES ★★★ The performances of Humphrey Bogart, Claude Rains, Sydney Greenstreet, and Peter Lorre are all that's good about this muddled film about an escape from Devil's Island during World War II. Directed by Michael Curtiz, its flashback-within-flashback scenes all but totally confuse the viewer. B&W; 110m. DIR: Michael Curtiz. CAST: Humphrey Bogart, Claude Rains, Sydney Greenstreet, Peter Lorre. 1944

PASSED AWAY ★★★ In this black comedy written and directed by Charlie Peters, members of an Irish family must set aside differences when the 70-year-old patriarch (Jack Warden) dies unexpectedly. The performances by a terrific cast of character actors make this movie worth seeing. Rated PG-13 for profanity. 96m. DIR: Charlie Peters. CAST: Bob Hoskins, Blair Brown, Tim Curry, Frances McDormand, William L. Petersen, Pamela Reed, Peter Riegert, Maureen Stapleton, Nancy Travis, Jack Warden. 1992

PASSENGER, THE (1975) ★★ Billed as a suspense-drama, this is a very slow-moving tale about a disillusioned TV reporter (Jack Nicholson) working in Africa. He becomes involved with arms smugglers. Rated R. 119m. DIR: Michelangelo Antonioni. CAST: Jack Nicholson, Maria Schneider, Jenny Runacre, Ian Hendry. 1975

PASSENGER 57 ★★★1/2 Slam-bang action film is an airborne retread on *Die Hard*. This time, the hero is an airline security expert who is caught on a plane skyjacked by terrorists. Featuring a strong lead performance by Wesley Snipes, this little gem is so exciting, funny, suspenseful, and packed with great bits that you don't dare take your eyes off the screen for a second. Rated R for violence and profanity. 85m. DIR: Kevin Hooks. CAST: Wesley Snipes, Bruce Payne, Tom Sizemore, Bruce Greenwood, Robert Hooks, Michael Horse. 1992 DVD

PASSENGER, THE (1963) ★★★1/2 A chance meeting between two women—one a former guard at Auschwitz, the other one of her prisoners—triggers painful, unresolved memories of the Holocaust. Director Andrej Munk was killed in an auto accident before he could finish this film; the footage was assembled by a colleague who used still photos to approximate the rest of it. Had it been completed, it likely would have been a masterpiece. What is here is a mesmerizing (albeit frustrating) work. In Polish with English subtitles. Not rated; contains violence, adult situations, and nudity. B&W; 63m. DIR: Andrej Munk. CAST: Aleksandra Slaska, Anna Ciepielewska, Marek Walczewski. 1963

PASSING GLORY ★★★★ Andre Braugher shines as an activist priest in this uplifting tale, set in Louisiana circa 1965, which concerns efforts to integrate the local high-school basketball league. Our central character—who teaches history but is pressed to become a basketball coach—shares the frustration of his players, who believe that white teams don't deserve "bragging rights" until they've played *all* local challengers. The ensemble cast delivers the goods in this exciting underdog tale. Rated PG for mild profanity. 95m. DIR: Steve James. CAST: Andre Braugher, Rip Torn, Ruby Dee, Sean Squire, Bill Nunn. 1999

PASSION (1919) ★★★ Combining realism with spectacle, this account of famous eighteenth-century French courtesan Madame Du Barry was the first German film to earn international acclaim after World War I. As a result, the director and the stars received Hollywood contracts. The film is still recognized as the best of seven made about the subject between 1915 and 1954. Silent. B&W; 134m. **DIR:** Ernst Lubitsch. **CAST:** Pola Negri, Emil Jannings. **1919**

PASSION (1954) ★★ Colorful hokum about a hot-blooded adventurer (Cornel Wilde) and his quest for vengeance in old California. Directed by veteran filmmaker Allan Dwan, this okay adventure boasts a nice cast of character actors. 84m. **DIR:** Allan Dwan. **CAST:** Cornel Wilde, Yvonne De Carlo, Raymond Burr, Lon Chaney Jr., John Qualen. **1954**

PASSION FISH ★★★★★ This superb character study focuses on a soap-opera actress who is left paralyzed after being hit by a cab in New York City. Embittered, she returns to her childhood home in the Louisiana swamplands where a succession of live-in nurses leads to friendship between two emotionally scarred and scared women. David Strathairn adds heart to this touching, but unsentimental story. Rated R for profanity. 134m. **DIR:** John Sayles. **CAST:** Mary McDonnell, Alfre Woodard, David Strathairn, Vondie Curtis-Hall, Angela Bassett, Maggie Renzi. **1992 DVD**

PASSION FLOWER ★★1/2 In Singapore, a young playboy banker gets tangled up with the married daughter of a prominent financial figure in the British and American business community. Nicol Williamson is dandy as a sadistic and manipulative father who has his daughter's lover right where he wants him. This made-for-television movie contains mild profanity. 95m. **DIR:** Joseph Sargent. **CAST:** Bruce Boxleitner, Barbara Hershey, Nicol Williamson. **1985**

PASSION FOR LIFE ★★★ An enthusiastic young teacher in a provincial school fights resistance from parents and his fellow teachers to introduce more effective new methods. Unsurprising but effective drama. In French with English subtitles. B&W; 89m. **DIR:** Jean-Paul Le Chanois. **CAST:** Bernard Blier, Juliette Faber. **1949**

PASSION IN THE DESERT ★★★ Earnest, somewhat insane study of a Napoleonic soldier who, lost in the Egyptian desert, has a meaningful relationship with a leopard. Something about that man's capacity for animalistic behavior is being explored here, and the big cat is a magnficent beast. But for all its heartfelt love of nature, this movie offers too many scenes that dare you not to laugh at them. Based on a Balzac short story. Rated PG-13 for nudity and violence. 93m. **DIR:** Lavinia Currier. **CAST:** Ben Daniels, Michel Piccoli. **1998**

PASSION OF ANNA, THE ★★★★1/2 One of Ingmar Bergman's greatest works is also one of his bleakest; an unflinching look into man's capacity for self-destruction. Four people are thrown together on an isolated island. Their interactions reveal their needs and insecurities, as well as the defenses they have developed. Bergman distances viewers from the film just as the characters try to distance themselves from others. In Swedish with English subtitles. Not rated. 101m. **DIR:** Ingmar Bergman. **CAST:** Liv Ull-

mann, Bibi Andersson, Max von Sydow, Erland Josephson. **1969**

●**PASSION OF AYN RAND, THE** ★★1/2 This pretentious claptrap, clearly a view of Ayn Rand as seen by fatuous admirers, does little but dishonor the memory and career of a progressive social thinker who may well have been the manipulative shrew Helen Mirren makes her here, but who nonetheless deserves better. Scripters Howard Korder and Mary Gallagher, working from Barbara Branden's book, have fashioned a tedious, talky drama in which condescending characters play at being holier-than-thou while justifying their own selfishness and lust. The result is tiresome, boring, and intellectually dishonest. Rated R for profanity, nudity, and simulated sex. 104m. **DIR:** Chris Menaul. **CAST:** Helen Mirren, Eric Stoltz, Julie Delpy, Peter Fonda, Sybil Temchen, Tom McCamus. **1998**

PASSION OF DARKLY NOON, THE ★★★ Darkly Noon, the only survivor of a religious community, is taken in by a free-spirited woman who lives in a secluded forest house. Unable to deal with his repressed sexuality, he approaches madness when his hostess's absent lover returns. Rated R for graphic violence, nudity, and sexual situations. 106m. **DIR:** Philip Ridley. **CAST:** Brendan Fraser, Ashley Judd, Viggo Mortensen, Loren Dean, Grace Zabriskie. **1995**

PASSION OF JOAN OF ARC, THE ★★★★★ This is simply one of the greatest films ever made. Its emotional intensity is unsurpassed. Faces tell the tale of this movie. Maria Falconetti's Joan is unforgettable. Silent. B&W; 114m. **DIR:** Carl Dreyer. **CAST:** Maria Falconetti, Eugene Silvain, Antonin Artaud. **1928 DVD**

PASSION OF LOVE ★★★★ In 1862 Italy just after the war, a decorated captain (Bernard Giraudeau) is transferred to a faraway outpost, where he becomes the love object of his commander's cousin (Valeria D'Obici). What follows is a fascinating study of torment. Dubbed in English. Not rated. 117m. **DIR:** Ettore Scola. **CAST:** Valeria D'Obici, Bernard Giraudeau, Laura Antonelli, Bernard Blier, Jean-Louis Trintignant, Massimo Girotti. **1982**

PASSION TO KILL, A ★★★ Erotic thriller about a psychiatrist (Scott Bakula) who succumbs to the temptations of his best friend's wife. They keep the tryst a secret, which works to their advantage when the husband ends up dead. Now Bakula must discern whether he's making love to a murderer or not. Nice plot twist at the end. Rated R for nudity, violence, adult situations, and language. 93m. **DIR:** Rick King. **CAST:** Scott Bakula, Chelsea Field, Sheila Kelly, John Getz, Rex Smith. **1993**

PASSIONATE THIEF, THE (1961) ★★ This less-than-hilarious Italian comedy is poorly dubbed. Ben Gazzara plays a thief at a New Year's Eve party. His suave attempts at removing the jewels are thwarted when Anna Magnani shows up and decides that he's interested in her. Monotonous. B&W; 100m. **DIR:** Mario Monicelli. **CAST:** Ben Gazzara, Anna Magnani, Toto, Fred Clark, Edy Vessel. **1961**

PASSPORT TO PIMLICO ★★★1/2 One of a number of first-rate comedies turned out by Britain in the wake of World War II. A salty group of characters form their own self-governing enclave smack in the middle of London. Sly Margaret Rutherford and Stanley Holloway divide comedy chores with cricket-crazy Basil Radford and Naunton Wayne. B&W; 85m. **DIR:** Henry Cornelius. **CAST:** Margaret Rutherford, Stanley Holloway, Hermione Baddeley, Basil Radford, Naunton Wayne. **1948**

PAST MIDNIGHT ★★★ Rutger Hauer stars as a parolee trying to get a new start after serving fifteen years in prison. Natasha Richardson is the social worker assigned to ease him back into society. But someone doesn't want Hauer free and starts terrorizing Richardson. Fine performances by Hauer and Richardson keep your attention away from the overworked plot. Rated R for nudity, violence, and profanity. 100m. **DIR:** Jan Eliasberg. **CAST:** Rutger Hauer, Natasha Richardson, Clancy Brown, Guy Boyd. **1991**

PAST PERFECT ★★1/2 Intriguing philosophical questions get lost amid the sloppy scripting and truly ludicrous violence of this science-fiction thriller, which concerns agents from the future who return to our present, assigned to kill young thugs before they blossom into multiple murderers. Even undiscriminating viewers will be bothered by the countless time-travel paradoxes. Rated R for violence, profanity, and drug use. 92m. **DIR:** Jonathan Heap. **CAST:** Eric Roberts, Nick Mancuso, Saul Rubinek, Laurie Holden, Mark Hildreth. **1996**

PAST TENSE ★★★★ High marks to this inventive thriller, where nothing is quite what it seems. During evenings, a would-be novelist hatches complicated plots over his typewriter; by day, he's a methodical police detective. His intriguing fantasies mimic his own experiences, but with endless twists . . . and always involving his enigmatic neighbor. Rated R for violence, nudity, profanity, and simulated sex. 91m. **DIR:** Graeme Clifford. **CAST:** Scott Glenn, Anthony LaPaglia, Lara Flynn Boyle, David Ogden Stiers. **1994**

PAST THE BLEACHERS ★★★1/2 Moving story of a father who has just lost his son. Richard Dean Anderson stars as Bill Parish, who coaches a Little League baseball team to help ease his pain. When Parish meets a boy with natural talent, he takes him under his wing. Eventually Parish finds it in himself to open up again. This made-for-television drama punches the right buttons. Rated PG. 120m. **DIR:** Michael Switzer. **CAST:** Richard Dean Anderson, Barnard Hughes, Grayson Fricke, Glynnis O'Connor. **1995**

PASTIME ★★★★ Wonderfully entertaining film deals with a minor-league relief pitcher in the twilight of his career and his relationship with a shy rookie pitcher who appears to have the stuff to make the big leagues. William Russ gives a beautiful performance as the aging pitcher. Rated PG. 91m. **DIR:** Robin B. Armstrong. **CAST:** William Russ, Glenn Plummer, Noble Willingham, Jeffrey Tambor, Scott Plank, Deirdre O'Connell. **1991**

PAT AND MIKE ★★★ Cameo appearances by a host of tennis and golf greats, including Babe Didrikson and Don Budge, stud this five-iron tale of athlete Katharine Hepburn and promoter-manager Spencer Tracy at odds with each other on a barnstorming golf and tennis tour. As always, the Tracy and Hepburn chemistry assures good comedy. B&W; 95m. **DIR:**

George Cukor. **CAST:** Spencer Tracy, Katharine Hepburn, Aldo Ray, William Ching. **1952**

PAT GARRETT AND BILLY THE KID ★★★★1/2 Sam Peckinpah's last masterpiece—in this "Restored Director's Cut"—begins with a stunning, never-before-seen ten-minute credit sequence that finally puts the film in focus. Other restored sequences make sense of what happens later between the main characters, Pat Garrett and Billy, and feature a who's who of character actors doing what they do best. Rated R for violence, nudity, and profanity. 122m. **DIR:** Sam Peckinpah. **CAST:** James Coburn, Kris Kristofferson, Bob Dylan, Jason Robards Jr., Barry Sullivan, Matt Clark, Elisha Cook Jr., Dub Taylor. **1973**

PATCH ADAMS ★★★ Although amiable and competent, this fact-based drama also is two-dimensional and predictable. Hunter "Patch" Adams is a doctor and audacious rebel with a clown's gift for raising smiles who routinely challenges the conventional wisdom of the established medical hierarchy. The choice of Robin Williams in the title role is indicative of the film's greater problems: Everything is superficial and simplistic, up to and including a performance that Williams has . . . um . . . patched together from pictures such as *Good Morning, Vietnam* and *Dead Poets Society*. You'll laugh a little and shed a tear or two, but not for a moment will you believe that this is anything but a fairy tale. Rated PG-13 for profanity. 120m. **DIR:** Tom Shadyac. **CAST:** Robin Williams, Monica Potter, Daniel London, Philip Seymour Hoffman, Bob Gunton. **1998 DVD**

PATCH OF BLUE, A ★★★1/2 A blind white girl who does not know her compassionate boyfriend is black, and her overprotective mother, are deftly brought together in this corn-filled but touching story. Shelley Winters as the mother won her second Oscar. B&W; 105m. **DIR:** Guy Green. **CAST:** Sidney Poitier, Elizabeth Hartman, Shelley Winters, Wallace Ford, Ivan Dixon. **1965**

PATCHWORK GIRL OF OZ, THE ★★★ One of the many sequels to L. Frank Baum's now-classic fantasy story, this film version tells the story of a poor Munchkin boy's adventures en route to Oz's Emerald City. The Patchwork Girl is just one of many strange and wonderful characters encountered. Silent, with musical score. B&W; 81m. **DIR:** J. Farrell McDonald. **1914**

PATERNITY ★★1/2 Buddy Evans (Burt Reynolds) decides to have a son—without the commitment of marriage—and recruits a music student working as a waitress (Beverly D'Angelo) to bear his child in this adult comedy. The first two-thirds provide belly laughs and chuckles. The problem comes with the unoriginal and predictable romantic ending. Rated PG because of dialogue involving sex and childbirth. 94m. **DIR:** David Steinberg. **CAST:** Burt Reynolds, Beverly D'Angelo, Norman Fell, Elizabeth Ashley, Lauren Hutton. **1981**

PATH TO PARADISE ★★★ The events leading to the World Trade Center bombing are detailed in this docudrama, which purports to demonstrate just how naïve Americans are and how easy it is to invade the United States. Arty camerawork and cinema verité stylings distract from the fascinating story. The final message is that we got off lucky that time and shouldn't expect the next terrorists to be so stupid. Rated R for violence and profanity. 91m. **DIR:** Leslie Libman, Larry Williams. **CAST:** Peter Gallagher, Art Malik, Ned Eisenberg, Marcia Gay Harden, Andreas Katsulas, Jeffrey DeMunn. **1997**

PATHER PANCHALI ★★★★ The first part of Satyajit Ray's *Apu* trilogy shows Apu's boyhood in an impoverished Bengal village after his father is forced to leave the family in order to seek work. Ray, who had no experience in filmmaking when he began, commands your attention with a lack of cinematic trickery, telling a universal story with a pure and unaffected style. The trilogy also includes *Aparajito* and *The World of Apu*. In Bengali with English subtitles. 112m. **DIR:** Satyajit Ray. **CAST:** Subir Banerji, Karuna Banerji. **1954**

PATHFINDER ★★★1/2 Brutal film about peaceful tribesmen being ruthlessly slaughtered by a savage group of scavengers. Action takes place in icy Norway with a treacherous chase through snow-covered mountains. In Lapp with English subtitles. Not rated, contains violence and nudity. 88m. **DIR:** Nils Gaup. **CAST:** Mikkel Gaup. **1987**

PATHFINDER, THE ★★ A gorgeously lensed, but spiritually empty, adaptation of James Fenimore Cooper's classic. The restored ships and forts give the production a sanitized luster wholly at odds with the gritty adventure yarn. Add phony-French accents and "Native Americans" apparently recruited from Venice Beach, and the result is often unintentionally funny. Rated PG for mild violence. 105m. **DIR:** Donald Shebib. **CAST:** Kevin Dillon, Graham Greene, Laurie Holden, Jaimz Woolvett, Michael Hogan, Russell Means, Stacy Keach. **1996**

PATHS OF GLORY ★★★★★ A great antiwar movie! Kirk Douglas plays the compassionate French officer in World War I who must lead his men against insurmountable enemy positions, and then must defend three of them against charges of cowardice when the battle is lost. Adolphe Menjou and George Macready perfectly portray Douglas's monstrous senior officers. B&W; 86m. **DIR:** Stanley Kubrick. **CAST:** Kirk Douglas, Adolphe Menjou, George Macready, Timothy Carey, Ralph Meeker. **1957** DVD

PATLABOR: THE MOBILE POLICE ★★★1/2 In a future metropolis where "labors" are giant robots designed for heavy construction use, the police have their hands full investigating a seemingly random plague of malfunctions that send the normally compliant machines into destructive rampages. Tasty animation combined with a nice science-fiction mystery. In Japanese with English subtitles. Not rated; contains profanity. 98m. **DIR:** Mamoru Oshii. **1989**

PATRICK ★★1/2 This film revolves around Patrick, who has been in a coma for four years. He is confined to a hospital, but after a new nurse comes to work on his floor he begins to exhibit psychic powers. Some violence, but nothing extremely bloody. Rated PG. 96m. **DIR:** Richard Franklin. **CAST:** Susan Penhaligon, Robert Helpmann. **1979**

PATRIOT (1986) ♥ Underwater commandos fight terrorists. Rated R for nudity and violence. 90m. **DIR:** Frank Harris. **CAST:** Gregg Henry, Simone Griffeth,

Michael J. Pollard, Jeff Conaway, Stack Pierce, Leslie Nielsen. **1986**

•**PATRIOT, THE (2000)** ★★1/2 A South Carolina planter (Mel Gibson) joins the American Revolution to avenge the murder of his son at the hands of a British officer. Robert Rodat's script falsifies everything about the period, from the behavior of the British to the status of slaves, and is shamelessly manipulative—there's no one the film won't kill to get us worked up. Director Roland Emmerich plays the melodrama for all it's worth, but he leans too heavily on Caleb Deschanel's beautiful cinematography and John Williams's bombastic music to sustain our interest throughout the lengthy film. Rated R for violence. 137m. **DIR:** Roland Emmerich. **CAST:** Mel Gibson, Heath Ledger, Chris Cooper, Jason Isaacs, Joely Richardson. **2000**

PATRIOT GAMES ★★★1/2 First-rate suspense-thriller has Harrison Ford taking over the role of novelist Tom Clancy's CIA analyst Jack Ryan from Alec Baldwin, who played the character in *The Hunt for Red October*. This time Ryan must save his wife and daughter from renegade Irish terrorists. Taut and exciting, especially during the nail-biting climax. Rated R for profanity and violence. 118m. **DIR:** Phillip Noyce. **CAST:** Harrison Ford, Anne Archer, Patrick Bergin, Sean Bean, James Earl Jones, Richard Harris, James Fox. **1992** DVD

PATSY, THE ★★1/2 A very minor Jerry Lewis comedy, though the stellar supporting cast is fun to watch. This one is for Lewis fans only; new viewers to Jerry's type of comedy should take in *The Errand Boy* or *The Nutty Professor* first. 101m. **DIR:** Jerry Lewis. **CAST:** Jerry Lewis, Everett Sloane, Ina Balin, Keenan Wynn, Peter Lorre, John Carradine. **1964**

PATTERNS ★★★1/2 Ed Begley dominates this Rod Serling drama of manipulation and machinations in the executive suite. The classic corporate-power-struggle story has changed in recent years, dating this film somewhat, but the game people play to climb to the top is still fascinating. B&W; 83m. **DIR:** Fielder Cook. **CAST:** Van Heflin, Everett Sloane, Ed Begley Sr., Beatrice Straight. **1956**

PATTES BLANCHES (WHITE PAWS) ★★★★ Engrossing melodrama about a reclusive aristocrat ridiculed in a small fishing community over a pair of white shoes he is fond of wearing. A well-crafted film by Jean Gremillon. In French with English subtitles. 92m. **DIR:** Jean Gremillon. **CAST:** Paul Bernard, Suzy Delair. **1948**

PATTI ROCKS ★★★★ Controversial sequel to 1975s *Loose Ends* picks up twelve years later. Bill (Chris Mulkey) has been having an affair with Patti Rocks (Karen Landry), who has informed him that she is pregnant. A very human story with a genuine twist. Rated R for profanity, nudity, and simulated sex. 86m. **DIR:** David Morris. **CAST:** Chris Mulkey, John Jenkins, Karen Landry. **1987**

PATTON ★★★★★ Flamboyant, controversial General George S. Patton is the subject of this Oscar-winning picture. George C. Scott is spellbinding in the title role. Scott's brilliant performance manages to bring alive this military hero, who strode a fine line between effective battlefield commander and demigod. Rated PG. 169m. **DIR:** Franklin J. Schaffner. **CAST:** George C. Scott, Karl Malden, Stephen Young, Tim Considine. **1970 DVD**

PATTY HEARST ★★★ Paul Schrader provides a restless, relentless, and often moving story of revolutionary idealism gone amok in this documentary-style drama of the kidnapping and subversion of Patty Hearst (Natasha Richardson). Performances are top notch, yet the film leaves a lot of questions unanswered. Rated R for profanity, nudity, and violence. 108m. **DIR:** Paul Schrader. **CAST:** Natasha Richardson, William Forsythe, Ving Rhames, Frances Fisher. **1988**

PAULIE ★★ Talking parrot is exiled to the basement of a research lab after embarrassing a scientist in front of his colleagues. Befriended by a Russian janitor, Paulie (via the voice of Jay Mohr) tells his life story. The janitor is touched by the bird's history and helps him find his original owner. The film's flashbacks want to be poignant, but Paulie just wants to wisecrack. Rated PG. 87m. **DIR:** John Roberts. **CAST:** Tony Shalhoub, Bruce Davison, Gena Rowlands, Richard "Cheech" Marin, Buddy Hackett. **1998 DVD**

PAULINE AT THE BEACH ★★★★ The screen works of French writer-director Eric Rohmer are decidedly unconventional. In this, one of his "Comedies and Proverbs," the 14-year-old title character (Amanda Langlet) shows herself to have a better sense of self and reality than the adults around her. In French with English subtitles. Rated R for nudity. 94m. **DIR:** Eric Rohmer. **CAST:** Amanda Langlet, Arielle Dombasle, Pascal Greggory, Feodor Atkine. **1983**

PAUL'S CASE ★★ Eric Roberts's impassioned portrayal of the working-class youth from turn-of-the-century Pittsburgh is the only draw. The outcome will leave viewers wondering. Introduced by Henry Fonda; suitable for family viewing. 52m. **DIR:** Lamont Johnson. **CAST:** Eric Roberts, Michael Higgins, Lindsay Crouse. **1980**

PAWNBROKER, THE ★★★★★ This is a somber and powerfully acted portrayal of a Jewish man who survived the Nazi Holocaust, only to find his spirit still as bleak as the Harlem ghetto in which he operates a pawnshop. Rod Steiger gives a tour-de-force performance as a man with dead emotions who is shocked out of his zombielike existence by confronting the realities of modern urban life. B&W; 116m. **DIR:** Sidney Lumet. **CAST:** Rod Steiger, Geraldine Fitzgerald, Brock Peters. **1965**

PAY OR DIE ★★★1/2 Ernest Borgnine plays the fabled leader of the Italian Squad, New York's crack police detectives who dealt with the turn-of-the-century Black Hand. Borgnine and his fellow Italian-Americans use force and intimidation to combat the savage Mafia-connected hoodlums who extort and murder their own people in Little Italy. An underrated crime film. B&W; 110m. **DIR:** Richard Wilson. **CAST:** Ernest Borgnine, Zohra Lampert, Al Austin. **1960**

PAYBACK (1990) ★★★1/2 Prison detail escapee falls in love with a small-town sheriff's daughter. Rated R for language and delicate seduction scenes. 94m. **DIR:** Russell Solberg. **CAST:** Corey Michael Eubanks, Michael Ironside, Don Swayze, Teresa Blake, Bert Remsen. **1990**

PAYBACK (1994) ★★★ Complicated plot twists keep the suspense turned up high in this tale of lust and revenge. C. Thomas Howell plays a prisoner who promises a dying old-timer that he will take care of the guard who beat him in exchange for the location of some buried loot. Years later, all of the pieces begin to fall into place for the final showdown. Rated R for violence, nudity, adult situations, and language. 93m. **DIR:** Anthony Hickox. **CAST:** C. Thomas Howell, Joan Severance, R. G. Armstrong, Marshall Bell. **1994**

PAYBACK (1999) ★★★1/2 One of Donald E. Westlake's early novels gets a second workout in this updated remake of *Point Blank*. Mel Gibson makes an unstoppable force in this nasty tale of a burglar whose chutzpah is larger than his common sense, and who stubbornly takes on the entire big-city criminal empire in order to retrieve what he perceives is his share of a recent heist. The story is wholly improbable and violent as hell, but Gibson's irresistible … even as a bad guy. Rated R for violence, profanity, torture, nudity, and drug use. 104m. **DIR:** Brian Helgeland. **CAST:** Mel Gibson, Gregg Henry, Maria Bello, David Paymer, Deborah Unger, William Devane. **1999 DVD**

PAYDAY ★★★★ Bravura performance by Rip Torn as a hard-drinking, ruthless country singer who's bent on destroying himself and everyone around him. Gripping, emotionally draining drama. Rarely seen in theaters, this one is definitely worth viewing on tape. Rated R for language, nudity, sexual situations. 103m. **DIR:** Daryl Duke. **CAST:** Rip Torn, Ahna Capri, Elayne Heilveil, Michael C. Gwynne. **1973**

PAYOFF ★★★1/2 Keith Carradine is sympathetic as an affable fellow forever haunted by the memory of—while a child—having unknowingly delivered a bomb that killed his parents. Earnest performances and slick pacing hide the plot flaws in this engaging little thriller. Made for cable, with violence and brief nudity. 111m. **DIR:** Stuart Cooper. **CAST:** Keith Carradine, Kim Greist, Harry Dean Stanton, John Saxon, Robert Harper. **1991**

PCU ★★ At small Port Charles University (PCU, get it?), every special-interest group has its pet cause, and the ultrasensitive president (Jessica Walter) is persecuting the only fraternity that wants to have fun. It's a 1990s *Animal House*—only without John Belushi, and with too few laughs. Rated PG-13. 81m. **DIR:** Hart Bochner. **CAST:** Jeremy Piven, Chris Young, David Spade, Megan Ward, Sarah Trigger, Jessica Walter. **1994**

PEACEMAKER (1990) ★★1/2 An interplanetary serial killer is hunted down on Earth by a policeman from back home—but which one is which? Limp effects and dull direction may weaken your concern. Rated R. 90m. **DIR:** Kevin S. Tenney. **CAST:** Robert Forster, Lance Edwards, Robert Davi. **1990 DVD**

PEACEMAKER, THE (1997) ★★★★ It's a fine suspense thriller. Reviewers couldn't resist taking a swipe at Steven Spielberg and his partners for this relatively low-key first Dreamworks production, ignoring the strong pacing of director Mimi Leder and writing of Michael Schiffer. George Clooney and Nicole Kidman are first-rate as the lone duo aware of a world-threatening conspiracy involving nuclear weapons. Rated R for violence and profanity. 123m. DIR: Mimi Leder. CAST: George Clooney, Nicole Kidman, Michael lures, Armin Mueller-Stahl, Jim Haynie. 1997

PEANUT BUTTER SOLUTION, THE ★★1/2 Remember sitting around a campfire when you were a kid and creating a story that just went on and on? This is a campfire movie. Part of the *Tales for All* series, it combines old houses, ghosts, an evil madman, enforced child labor, and a main character with a real hairy problem, all mixed together in sort of a story. 96m. DIR: Michael Rubbo. CAST: Mathew Mackay, Siluk Saysanasy, Helen Hughes. 1985

PEARL, THE ★★ John Steinbeck's heavy-handed parable about the value of wealth when compared with natural treasures is beautifully photographed and effectively presented, but the film suffers from the same shortcoming inherent in the book. The plight of the loving couple and their desperately ill son is relentlessly hammered home. 77m. DIR: Emilio Fernandez. CAST: Pedro Armendariz, Maria Elena Marques. 1948

PEARL OF DEATH, THE ★★★★ Director Roy William Neill fashions Arthur Conan Doyle's "The Six Napoleons" into a rip-snorting screen adventure for Holmes (Basil Rathbone) and Watson (Nigel Bruce). They're tracking a trio of criminals: Giles Conover (Miles Mander), Naomi (Evelyn Ankers), and the Creeper (Rondo Hatton). Good stuff. B&W; 69m. DIR: Roy William Neill. CAST: Basil Rathbone, Nigel Bruce, Evelyn Ankers, Miles Mander, Dennis Hoey, Mary Gordon, Ian Wolfe, Rondo Hatton. 1944

PEARL OF THE SOUTH PACIFIC 🎗 A dull film about murder in the tropics. 86m. DIR: Allan Dwan. CAST: Virginia Mayo, Dennis Morgan, David Farrar, Murvyn Vye. 1955

PEARLS OF THE CROWN, THE ★★★1/2 This featherweight historical extravaganza was presented as a celebration of the coronation of England's George VI, but it was clearly an excuse for writer-codirector Sacha Guitry to concoct choice scenes for some of the best theatrical actors in France. Some of the bits are delightful, but some drag on. In English, and in French and Italian with English subtitles. B&W; 120m. DIR: Sacha Guitry, Christian-Jaque. CAST: Sacha Guitry, Renée Saint-Cyr, Arletty, Raimu. 1937

PEBBLE AND THE PENGUIN, THE ★★★ So-so musical score and uneven plot jumps mar this Don Bluth production. Martin Short gives voice to the likable but lovelorn Hubie, yet it is Jim Belushi's savvy Rocko who manages to steal the show. Rated G. 74m. DIR: Appel Gyorgy. 1995 DVD

PECKER ★★1/2 A cheerful teenage amateur photographer (Edward Furlong) is discovered by the trendy Manhattan art scene, and the resulting celebrity all but ruins his life. Writer-director John Waters makes a none-too-subtle comment on his own career, but he flatters himself. Despite an appealing cast, the predictable story and amateurish production soon wear out their welcome. Rated R for brief but graphic nudity. 87m. DIR: John Waters. CAST: Edward Furlong, Christina Ricci, Lili Taylor, Mary Kay Place, Martha Plimpton. 1998 DVD

PECK'S BAD BOY ★★★ Jackie Coogan shines as the mischievous scamp who commits all manner of mayhem, yet miraculously escapes the lethal designs his victims must harbor. Silent. B&W; 54m. DIR: Sam Wood. CAST: Jackie Coogan, Wheeler Oakman, Doris May, Raymond Hatton, Lillian Leighton. 1921

PECK'S BAD BOY WITH THE CIRCUS ★★ Tommy Kelly, the mischievous Peck's Bad Boy, and his ragamuffin gang of troublemakers (including an aging Spanky MacFarland) wreak havoc around the circus. Comedy greats Edgar Kennedy and Billy Gilbert are the best part of this kids' film. B&W; 78m. DIR: Eddie Cline. CAST: Tommy Kelly, Ann Gillis, Edgar Kennedy, Billy Gilbert, Benita Hume, Spanky McFarland, Grant Mitchell. 1938

PEDESTRIAN, THE ★★★1/2 The directorial debut for Maximilian Schell, this is a disturbing near masterpiece of drama exploring the realm of guilt and self-doubt that surrounds ex–World War II Nazis. Gustav Rudolph Sellner's haunting and quiet performance as an aging industrialist who is exposed as an ex-Nazi is a little tedious but thought-provoking in the outcome—much like the film itself. 97m. DIR: Maximilian Schell. CAST: Gustav Rudolph Sellner, Peter Hall, Maximilian Schell. 1974

PEEPING TOM ★★★1/2 Carl Boehm gives a chilling performance as a lethal psychopath who photographs his victims as they are dying. This film outraged both critics and viewers alike when it was first released, and rarely has been revived since. Not for all tastes, to be sure, but if you're adventurous, give this one a try. Rated R. 109m. DIR: Michael Powell. CAST: Carl Boehm, Moira Shearer, Anna Massey. 1960 DVD

PEE-WEE HERMAN SHOW, THE ★★1/2 Adult fans of Pee-Wee Herman will fit right into his childish but risquÇ playhouse. Others will no doubt wonder what planet he's from. Not rated, but some of the humor is sexual in nature. 58m. DIR: Marty Callner. CAST: Pee-wee Herman, Phil Hartman, Brian Seff. 1981

PEE-WEE'S BIG ADVENTURE ★★★1/2 You want weird? Here it is. Pee-Wee Herman made the jump from television to feature films with this totally bizarre movie about a man-size, petulant, 12-year-old goofball (Herman) going on a big adventure after his most prized possession—a bicycle—is stolen by some nasties. Rated PG for a scary scene and some daffy violence. 90m. DIR: Tim Burton. CAST: Pee-wee Herman, Elizabeth Daily, Mark Holton, Diane Salinger. 1985 DVD

PEGGY SUE GOT MARRIED ★★★★1/2 Wistful, and often joyously funny, this delightful film features Kathleen Turner as Peggy, a 43-year-old mother of two who is facing divorce. When she attends her twenty-fifth annual high school reunion, she is thrust back in time and gets a chance to change the course of her life. Rated PG-13 for profanity and suggested sex. 103m. DIR: Francis Ford Coppola. CAST: Kathleen Turner, Nicolas Cage, Barry Miller, Catherine Hicks, Joan Allen, Kevin J. O'Connor, Lisa Jane Persky, Barbara Harris, Don Murray, Maureen O'Sullivan, Leon Ames, John Carradine. 1986 DVD

PEKING OPERA BLUES ★★★★1/2 The circuslike Peking Opera provides an appropriately colorful backdrop for this period adventure that brings three dissimilar young women together to battle an evil general. High-spirited fun. In Cantonese with English subtitles. Not rated; contains violence. 98m. DIR: Tsui Hark. CAST: Lin Ching Hsia, Sally Yeh, Cherie Chung. 1986 DVD

PELICAN BRIEF, THE ★★★1/2 Overlong but suspenseful adaptation of the bestselling novel by John Grisham casts Julia Roberts as a student who accidentally stumbles onto the truth behind the killings of two Supreme Court justices, a discovery that puts her life in danger. Charismatic Denzel Washington plays the investigative reporter who comes to her aid. Rated R for violence and profanity. 141m. DIR: Alan J. Pakula. CAST: Julia Roberts, Denzel Washington, Sam Shepard, John Heard, John Lithgow, Hume Cronyn, Tony Goldwyn, James B. Sikking, William Atherton, Robert Culp, Stanley Tucci. 1993 DVD

PELLE THE CONQUEROR ★★★★★ Bille August's superb drama casts Max von Sydow as a Swedish widower who takes his young son to Denmark in the hope of finding a better life. Once there, they must endure even harder times. In Danish and Swedish with English subtitles. Not rated, the film has nudity, violence, and profanity. 138m. DIR: Bille August. CAST: Max von Sydow, Pelle Hvenegaard. 1988

PENDULUM ★★ In this rather confusing mystery, police captain George Peppard must acquit himself of a murder charge and catch the real culprit. A good cast perks things up some, but the story is too full of holes to be taken seriously. Some violence and adult situations. Rated PG. 106m. DIR: George Schaefer. CAST: George Peppard, Richard Kiley, Jean Seberg, Charles McGraw. 1969

PENITENT, THE ★★ Raul Julia is a member of the Penitents, a religious cult that remembers the suffering of Christ by affixing one of its members to a cross and leaving him in the desert sun for an entire day—often to die as "God's will." Exploration of this intriguing milieu is set aside in favor of a silly soap opera about Julia's problem with his young wife and lusty pal. Rated PG for suggested sex. 90m. DIR: Cliff Osmond. CAST: Raul Julia, Armand Assante, Julie Carmen. 1988

PENITENTIARY ★★ Leon Isaac Kennedy dons boxing gloves as the black Rocky to triumph over pure evil in this lurid, but entertaining, movie. 94m. DIR: Jamaa Fanaka. CAST: Leon Isaac Kennedy, Thommy Pollard. 1979 DVD

PENITENTIARY II 🛇 A retread. Rated R for violence and profanity. 108m. DIR: Jamaa Fanaka. CAST: Leon Isaac Kennedy, Glynn Turman, Ernie Hudson, Mr. T. 1982 DVD

PENITENTIARY III 🛇 Lock this one up in solitary confinement. 91m. DIR: Jamaa Fanaka. CAST: Leon Isaac Kennedy, Anthony Geary, Steve Antin, Ric Mancini, Jim Bailey. 1987

PENN & TELLER GET KILLED ★★★ Your appreciation for this bizarre comedy will depend upon your reaction to Penn & Teller, an abrasive comedy-magic team who specialize in fake gory magic tricks. While engaging in sick humor and magician debunking, our heroes discover that someone is trying to kill them. Like it or hate it, you have to admit that it's different.

Rated R for violence and profanity. 90m. DIR: Arthur Penn. CAST: Penn Jillette, Teller, Caitlin Clarke, David Patrick Kelly. 1989

PENNIES FROM HEAVEN ★★★1/2 Steve Martin and Bernadette Peters star in this downbeat musical. The production numbers are fabulous, but the dreary storyline—with Martin as a down-and-out song-plugger in Depression-era Chicago—may disappoint fans of the genre. Rated R for profanity and sexual situations. 107m. DIR: Herbert Ross. CAST: Steve Martin, Bernadette Peters, Jessica Harper. 1981

PENNY SERENADE ★★★★ Cary Grant and Irene Dunne are one of the most fondly remembered comedy teams in films such as *The Awful Truth* and *My Favorite Wife*. This 1941 film is a radical change of pace, for it is a ten-hankie tearjerker about a couple's attempt to have children. They are excellent in this drama far removed from their standard comic fare. B&W; 125m. DIR: George Stevens. CAST: Cary Grant, Irene Dunne, Edgar Buchanan. 1941 DVD

PENPAL MURDERS 🛇 A man's pen pal comes for a visit and unfortunately waits until the end of this stinker to kill the cast. Not rated. 118m. DIR: Steve Postal. CAST: Jay Brockman, Jennifer Tuck, Angela Shepard. 1991

PENTAGON WARS, THE ★★★★ A wonderful adaptation of Col. James G. Burton's book, which described the U.S. military's invention of a scout tank that neither fulfilled its function nor protected the soldiers inside. Kelsey Grammer is deliciously stubborn and egomaniacal as the driving force behind the Bradley Fighting Vehicle, while Cary Elwes is the White House–authorized "analyst" who refuses to approve it until satisfied by tests ... every one continually sabotaged by those in charge, who want only to get the thing into production. Made-for-cable-film is a fascinating story. Rated R for profanity. 103m. DIR: Richard Benjamin. CAST: Kelsey Grammer, Cary Elwes, Viola Davis, John C. McGinley, Clifton Powell, Olympia Dukakis, Richard Benjamin. 1998

PENTATHLON ★★ Silly Cold War thriller with Dolph Lundgren as an East German athlete who defects to the United States. Years later, his spiteful ex-coach, a neo-Nazi, takes drastic measures to ruin his big comeback. Rated R for violence and language. 101m. DIR: Bruce Malmuth. CAST: Dolph Lundgren, David Soul, Roger E. Mosley, Renee Colman. 1994

PENTHOUSE, THE 🛇 Oh, boy, another woman-in-jeopardy thriller. This one has Robin Givens trapped in her high-rise with a fanatical ex-boyfriend. 93m. DIR: David Greene. CAST: Robin Givens, David Hewlett, Robert Guillaume, Cedric Smith. 1993

PEOPLE, THE ★★ This TV movie is a fair interpretation of the science-fiction stories of Zenna Henderson about psychically talented aliens whose home world has been destroyed and who must survive on Earth. The script gives Henderson's subtle themes a heavy-handed and unbalanced treatment. 74m. DIR: John Korty. CAST: William Shatner, Dan O'Herlihy, Diane Varsi, Kim Darby. 1971

PEOPLE ARE FUNNY ★★1/2 From the Pine-Thomas B unit at Paramount comes this agreeable little comedy. Jack Haley is a small-town radio announcer who has aspirations to be a big-time radio personality. Inspired by the radio program that later became a successful television series with Art Linkletter as the host. B&W; 94m. **DIR:** Sam White. **CAST:** Jack Haley, Rudy Vallee, Ozzie Nelson, Art Linkletter, Helen Walker, Frances Langford. **1946**

PEOPLE THAT TIME FORGOT, THE ★★ Edgar Rice Burroughs probably would have been outraged by this and its companion piece, *The Land That Time Forgot*. Doug McClure gets rescued by friend Patrick Wayne from a fate worse than death on a strange island circa 1919. Laughable rubber-suited monsters mix it up with ludicrous wire-controlled beasties. Rated PG. 90m. **DIR:** Kevin Connor. **CAST:** Doug McClure, Patrick Wayne, Sarah Douglas, Thorley Walters. **1977**

PEOPLE UNDER THE STAIRS, THE ★★★ A young boy from the ghetto gets more than he bargained for when he breaks into a house looking for money to help his cancer-stricken mother. It seems the home owners are a couple, with more than a few screws loose, who keep a group of boys locked in their basement. Hybrid of *Dawn of the Dead* and *Die Hard*. Rated R for violence and profanity. 102m. **DIR:** Wes Craven. **CAST:** Brandon Adams, Everett McGill, Wendy Robie, Ving Rhames, Kelly Jo Minter. **1991**

PEOPLE VS. JEAN HARRIS ★★ A sedate reenactment of a lengthy trial transcript, shot entirely inside a courtroom. A long, long, boring trial. Made for TV. 147m. **DIR:** George Schaefer. **CAST:** Ellen Burstyn, Martin Balsam, Richard Dysart, Peter Coyote. **1981**

PEOPLE VS. LARRY FLYNT, THE ★★ This serio-comic, bio-pic pits Flynt—the flamboyant pope of pornography—against the religious right and state censorship. But this film makes a feeble case for Flynt. It soft pedals *Hustler* as a blue-collar *Playboy* by calling it more honest—something this film needs to be. Rated R for language, nudity, sexual content, and drug use. 103m. **DIR:** Milos Forman. **CAST:** Woody Harrelson, Courtney Love, Edward Norton, Brett Harrelson, James Cromwell. **1996 DVD**

PEOPLE WILL TALK ★★★1/2 Wonderful witty story of a doctor whose mysterious background is being investigated by jealous peers at his university. Meanwhile, he marries a young girl who is about to have another man's child. Yes, it is a comedy, and a great one. B&W; 110m. **DIR:** Joseph L. Mankiewicz. **CAST:** Cary Grant, Jeanne Crain, Finlay Currie, Hume Cronyn, Walter Slezak, Sidney Blackmer, Will Wright, Margaret Hamilton, Billy House. **1951**

PEOPLE'S HERO ★★★ Taken as a hostage during someone else's botched bank holdup, a cunning gangster turns the situation to his advantage. Hong Kong thriller downplays the usual firepower for plot, though the ending is explosive. In Cantonese with English subtitles. Not rated; contains strong violence. 82m. **DIR:** Yee Tung-shing. **CAST:** Ti Lung, Tony Leung Chiu-Wai, Ronald Wong. **1987**

PEPE LE MOKO ★★★1/2 Algiers criminal Pepe Le Moko (Jean Gabin) is safe just as long as he remains in the city's picturesque, squalid native quarter. His passionate infatuation with a beautiful visitor from his beloved Paris, however, spells his doom. In French with English subtitles. B&W; 93m. **DIR:** Julien Duvivier. **CAST:** Jean Gabin, Mireille Balin, Gabriel Gario, Marcel Dalio. **1937**

PEPI, LUCI, BOM AND OTHER GIRLS ★★★ The plot, a satirical pastiche of melodramatic clichés, is less important than the nonstop swipes at bourgeois society in Pedro Almodóvar's first film. Crudely made on an amateur budget, this will be of interest mainly to fans of his later films. In Spanish with English subtitles. Not rated; contains sexual situations. 80m. **DIR:** Pedro Almodóvar. **CAST:** Carmen Maura, Felix Rotaeta. **1980**

•**PEPPERMINT SODA** ★★★1/2 The first of French director Diane Kurys's semiautobiographical films (the best known of which is *Entre Nous*) depicts the growing pains of two teenage sisters. The setting is Paris, 1963, when society seems to be going through as many upheavals as the two girls. Meandering but generally delightful. In French with English subtitles. Rated PG. 100m. **DIR:** Diane Kurys. **CAST:** Eleonore Klarwein, Odile Michel. **1977**

PERCY & THUNDER ★★★★ The underbelly of professional boxing is exposed in this riveting drama. Courtney B. Vance stars as a middleweight boxer who has what it takes to go all the way. James Earl Jones costars as his trainer, a former boxer who knows what it takes to win the title. Billy Dee Williams plays the stumbling block, a seedy character who controls the boxing game, and is willing to let anyone in for a price. Fine performances distinguish this exciting made-for-cable drama. Not rated. 90m. **DIR:** Ivan Dixon. **CAST:** Courtney B. Vance, James Earl Jones, Billy Dee Williams, Zakes Mokae, Robert Wuhl. **1992**

PEREZ FAMILY, THE ★★★★ A romantic fable set against the backdrop of the 1980 Mariel boatlift of Cuban refugees. A twenty-year resident of Castro's prisons comes to Miami in hopes of finding his long-gone wife and daughter. Circumstances team him up with a fiery young woman while his wife—who thinks he didn't make the last boat—finally lets herself fall in love with a new man. Rated R for sex, language, and mild violence. 112m. **DIR:** Mira Nair. **CAST:** Marisa Tomei, Alfred Molina, Anjelica Huston, Chazz Palminteri. **1995**

PERFECT ★★ In this irritatingly uneven and unfocused film, John Travolta stars as a *Rolling Stone* reporter out to do an exposé on the health-club boom. Jamie Lee Curtis is the aerobics instructor he attempts to spotlight in his story. Just another moralizing mess about journalistic ethics. Rated R for profanity, suggested sex, and violence. 120m. **DIR:** James Bridges. **CAST:** John Travolta, Jamie Lee Curtis, Jann Wenner, Marilu Henner, Laraine Newman. **1985**

PERFECT ALIBI ★★★ What starts off as a standard-issue thriller builds up steam thanks to a talented cast and director Kevin Meyer's crafted screenplay. Kathleen Quinlan plays a woman who wants to get back to work, and hires a nanny for the children. It doesn't take long before everyone suspects hubby and the new nanny of doing more than watching the kids. Those who get too nosy end up dead in this made-for-cable thriller. Not rated; contains violence. 100m. **DIR:** Kevin Meyer. **CAST:** Kathleen Quinlan, Teri Garr, Hector Elizondo, Alex McArthur. **1994**

PERFECT BRIDE, THE ★★ Nut-cake Sammi Davis, reacting violently to a childhood trauma (finally revealed after three ponderous flashbacks), repeatedly becomes engaged to nice young fellows, only to murder them on the eve of the wedding day. Plucky Kelly Preston senses something amiss. Made-for-cable chiller. 90m. **DIR:** Terrence O'Hara. **CAST:** Sammi Davis, Kelly Preston, Linden Ashby, John Agar. **1991**

PERFECT CRIME ★★★1/2 After a long weekend, a woman Marine turns up missing, and her soon-to-be ex-husband is suspected of killing her. But military investigators have a difficult time collecting any evidence to convict the guy. This made-for-cable mystery is based on a true story and does a fine job following the investigation. Good acting and a good story, but something's still lacking. Rated PG-13 for violence. 95m. **DIR:** Robert Lewis. **CAST:** Mitzi Kapture, Nick Searcy, Scott Lawrence, Jasmine Guy. **1996**

PERFECT DAUGHTER, THE ★★★ Two years after she left her parents' house and disappeared from their lives, a young woman turns up in a hospital with a head injury. She returns home, but the past she can't remember returns to haunt her. This made-for-cable original has an engaging plot and pretty good acting. Not rated; contains violence. 95m. **DIR:** Harry S. Longstreet. **CAST:** Tracey Gold, Bess Armstrong, Mark Joy, Kerrie Keane. **1996**

PERFECT FAMILY ★★ A young, widowed mother hires a housekeeper who moves in along with her brother; incidentally, his family died in a mysterious accident. The story is ruined in the middle, and there's really no reason to finish watching. Not rated, made for cable, but contains violence. 95m. **DIR:** E. W. Swackhamer. **CAST:** Bruce Boxleitner, Jennifer O'Neill, Juliana Hansen, Shiri Appleby, Joanna Cassidy. **1992**

PERFECT FURLOUGH ★★ Perfectly forgettable fluff about soldier Tony Curtis (who is taking the leave for his entire unit, which is stationed in the Arctic). At least he gets to meet and eventually win Janet Leigh (Mrs. Tony Curtis at that time). 93m. **DIR:** Blake Edwards. **CAST:** Tony Curtis, Janet Leigh, Keenan Wynn, Linda Cristal, Elaine Stritch, Troy Donahue. **1958**

PERFECT HARMONY ★★★★ Heartwarming film about enlightenment in a sleepy South Carolina town and its exclusive boys' prep school in 1959. A Yankee schoolteacher exposes the boys to non-Southern views of the Civil War, equality, etc. Amidst this awakening, a friendship blossoms between the caretaker's grandson and one of the privileged students. Not rated, this Disney-channel film uses a minimum of violence and racial slurs to prove its point. 93m. **DIR:** Will Mackenzie. **CAST:** Peter Scolari, Darren McGavin, Moses Gunn, Justin Whalin, David Faustino. **1990**

PERFECT LITTLE MURDER, A ★★ Amiable made-for-cable comedy stars Teri Garr as a housewife who overhears a murder plot in her small town and then must go undercover to prove it. Pleasant diversion as Garr and husband Robert Urich deal with her harebrained schemes. Rated PG for sexual innuendo. 94m. **DIR:** Anson Williams. **CAST:** Teri Garr, Robert Urich. **1990**

PERFECT MARRIAGE ★★ On their tenth wedding anniversary Loretta Young and David Niven suddenly decide they can't stand each other and go their separate, flirtatious ways. Dull. B&W; 87m. **DIR:** Lewis Allen. **CAST:** Loretta Young, David Niven, Eddie Albert, Charlie Ruggles, Virginia Field, Rita Johnson, ZaSu Pitts, Jerome Cowan, Ann Doran. **1947**

PERFECT MATCH, THE ★★ Although Marc McClure and Jennifer Edwards create some funny moments, the pacing and the dialogue are iffy in this romantic hodgepodge. The couple meets through a misleading personal ad—with both parties claiming to be something they're not. Rated PG for no apparent reason. 93m. **DIR:** Mark Deimel. **CAST:** Marc McClure, Jennifer Edwards, Diane Stilwell, Rob Paulsen, Karen Witter. **1987**

PERFECT MURDER, A ★★★ This contemporary riff on Hitchcock's 1954 *Dial M for Murder* is a string of wicked conspiracy twists that lead to a rather weak finale. Money and infidelity, the top two contributing elements to spousal murder, drive a rich Manhattan industrialist to plot the demise of his unfaithful heiress wife. Pure evil also surfaces as the slighted husband dangles a carrot of his own in front of his wife's lover. Rated R for simulated sex, nudity, language, and violence. 107m. **DIR:** Andrew Davis. **CAST:** Michael Douglas, Gwyneth Paltrow, Viggo Mortensen. **1998 DVD**

•**PERFECT STORM, THE** ★★★★ Sebastian Junger's nonfiction bestseller about the killer storm of October 1991 comes to the screen as a harrowing, white-knuckle thriller, centering on an ill-fated fishing boat skippered by George Clooney with Mark Wahlberg and John C. Reilly among the crew. Director Wolfgang Petersen and a throng of special effects artists make the storm—the worst of the century, by all accounts—a horrifying experience. The sheer scale of the film may suffer on home video, but the tension and suspense will still come through. Rated PG-13 for profanity and intense action. 129m. **DIR:** Wolfgang Petersen. **CAST:** George Clooney, Mark Wahlberg, Diane Lane, John C. Reilly, William Fichtner, Karen Allen, Bob Gunton, Mary Elizabeth Mastrantonio. **2000**

PERFECT STRANGERS ★★1/2 A hired assassin loses his cool when he discovers that an infant boy witnessed his last contract. An uneven but gritty suspense film with many nice touches and effective use of grungy Manhattan locations. Rated R for violence. 90m. **DIR:** Larry Cohen. **CAST:** Anne Carlisle, Brad Rijn, Stephen Lack. **1984**

PERFECT WEAPON ★★1/2 Standard martial arts action, as our strong, silent hero (Jeff Speakman) goes after the killers of an old family friend. Fans of the genre will like this one; the fight scenes are quite well staged. Rated R for violence. 90m. **DIR:** Mark DiSalle. **CAST:** Jeff Speakman, Mako. **1991**

PERFECT WITNESS ★★★★1/2 This crackling suspenser, first aired on HBO, puts family man Aidan Quinn into a crime-infested nightmare. After witnessing a mob-style execution and telling the police what he knows, Quinn receives threats; but when he backs down, special attorney Brian Dennehy tosses him into jail for perjury. Terry Curtis Fox and Ron

Hutchinson have scripted the ultimate horror—personal vs. social responsibility—and Quinn plays the part to frustrated perfection. 104m. **DIR:** Robert Mandel. **CAST:** Brian Dennehy, Aidan Quinn, Stockard Channing, Laura Harrington. **1989**

PERFECT WORLD, A ★★★★ Escaped convict Kevin Costner takes a young boy hostage and flees with Texas Ranger Clint Eastwood hot on his trail. That this serious-sounding film contains moments of comedy is one of the many pleasant surprises in an essentially downbeat morality play. Costner plays against type, and Eastwood successfully tries a John Wayne turn as an aged-in-the-saddle professional. Rated R for violence, profanity, and lewdness. 136m. **DIR:** Clint Eastwood. **CAST:** Kevin Costner, Clint Eastwood, Laura Dern, T. J. Lowther, Keith Szarabajka. **1993**

PERFECTLY NORMAL ★★★1/2 This is a relaxed, off-kilter Canadian comedy showcasing the entertaining English comic actor, Robbie Coltrane. He plays Alonzo Turner, a mysterious, eccentric stranger who enlivens the life of a dull brewery worker. Original and offbeat. Rated R for profanity. 101m. **DIR:** Yves Simoneau. **CAST:** Robbie Coltrane, Michael Riley. **1990**

PERFORMANCE ★★★★ Mick Jagger, the leader of the Rolling Stones rock group, stars in this bizarre film as Turner, a rock singer who decides to switch identities with a hunted hit man (James Fox). Codirected by Nicolas Roeg and Donald Cammell, the film is a chilling, profoundly disturbing cinematic nightmare about the dark side of man's consciousness. Rated R for profanity, nudity, and violence. 105m. **DIR:** Nicolas Roeg, Donald-Cammell. **CAST:** Mick Jagger, James Fox, Anita Pallenberg. **1970**

PERFUMED NIGHTMARE ★★★★ Hilarious, poignant view of the impact of American cultural colonialism through the eyes of a young Philippines man. Brilliant meditation on the American dream shot on super 8mm for less than $10,000. Winner of the International Critics Award at the Berlin Film Festival. In Tagalog with English dialogue and subtitles. 91m. **DIR:** Kidlat Tahimik. **1983**

PERIL ★★ Nicole Garcia plays the wife of a wealthy businessman who is having an affair with their daughter's guitar instructor (Christophe Malavoy). Filmmaker Michel Deville aims too high in his direction with French new wave–like scene cuts. In French with English subtitles. Rated R for nudity, violence, profanity, and adult subject matter. 100m. **DIR:** Michel Deville. **CAST:** Christophe Malavoy, Nicole Garcia, Richard Bohringer, Anemone, Michel Piccoli. **1985**

PERILS OF PAULINE, THE (1933) ★★ Sound serial version of the famous Pearl White cliff-hanger retains only the original title. The daughter of a prominent scientist and her companion struggle to keep the formula for a deadly gas out of the hands of evil Dr. Bashan and his slimy assistant Fang. This serial lacks the charisma of later efforts from Universal Studios. B&W; 12 chapters. **DIR:** Ray Taylor. **CAST:** Evalyn Knapp, Robert Allen, James Durkin, John Davidson, Sonny Ray. **1933**

PERILS OF PAULINE, THE (1947) ★★★ Betty Hutton plays Pearl White, the queen of the silent serials, in this agreeable little movie. The old-style chase scenes and cliff-hanger situations make up for the overdose of sentimentality. 96m. **DIR:** George Marshall. **CAST:** Betty Hutton, John Lund, Billy DeWolfe, William Demarest, Constance Collier, Frank Faylen. **1947 DVD**

PERIOD OF ADJUSTMENT ★★★1/2 Newlyweds Jane Fonda and Jim Hutton start marriage on the wrong foot. Friend Anthony Franciosa, whose own marriage is on the rocks, attempts to straighten them out. Fine performances in a rare light comedy from Tennessee Williams. B&W; 111m. **DIR:** George Roy Hill. **CAST:** Anthony Franciosa, Jane Fonda, Jim Hutton, Lois Nettleton, John McGiver, Jack Albertson. **1962**

PERMANENT MIDNIGHT ★★★ Writer-director David Veloz's film is based on fact (TV writer Jerry Stahl's memoir about his own drug addiction), but it hits every monkey-on-my-back cliché with clockwork precision. Ben Stiller's tour-de-force performance as Stahl—frantic, mercurial, reckless, harrowing—makes the familiar tale worth watching. Rated R for profanity, drug use, and sexual scenes. 85m. **DIR:** David Veloz. **CAST:** Ben Stiller, Elizabeth Hurley, Maria Bello, Owen C. Wilson. **1998 DVD**

PERMANENT RECORD ★★1/2 This drama stars Keanu Reeves as Chris, whose best friend, a popular, talented, seemingly well-adjusted high school senior, commits suicide. The film focuses on the effects the suicide has on his closest friends and how they come to accept it. Rated PG-13. 92m. **DIR:** Marisa Silver. **CAST:** Keanu Reeves, Alan Boyce, Richard Bradford. **1988**

PERMISSION TO KILL ★★ An exiled politician (Bekim Fehmiu) from an Eastern bloc nation living in Austria decides to return to his native country. A Western intelligence agent (Dirk Bogarde) must stop him. Rated PG for violence, profanity, and nudity. 96m. **DIR:** Cyril Frankel. **CAST:** Dirk Bogarde, Ava Gardner, Bekim Fehmiu, Timothy Dalton, Nicole Calfan, Frederic Forrest. **1975**

PERSECUTION 💔 This tale of murder and deception never shows minimal signs of life. Rated R. 92m. **DIR:** Don Chaffey. **CAST:** Lana Turner, Trevor Howard, Ralph Bates. **1974**

PERSONA ★★★ Liv Ullmann gives a haunting performance as an actress who suddenly becomes mute and is put in the charge of a nurse (Bibi Andersson). The two women become so close that they change personalities. Ingmar Bergman's use of subtle split-screen effects dramatizes the metaphorical quality of this quiet film. In Swedish with English subtitles. B&W; 81m. **DIR:** Ingmar Bergman. **CAST:** Liv Ullmann, Bibi Andersson, Gunnar Björnstrand. **1966**

PERSONAL BEST ★★★★ Oscar-winning screenwriter Robert Towne wrote, directed, and produced this tough, honest, and nonexploitive story about two women who are friends, teammates, and sometimes lovers (Mariel Hemingway, Patrice Donnelly) preparing for the 1980 Olympics. Hemingway's and Donnelly's stunning performances make the film an impressive achievement. Rated R for nudity, strong language, and drug use. 124m. **DIR:** Robert Towne. **CAST:** Mariel Hemingway, Patrice Donnelly, Scott Glenn. 1982

PERSONAL PROPERTY ★★★1/2 A clever comedy designed to make the most of two fiery sex symbols of their time, this comedy-drama marks the only teaming of Robert Taylor and Jean Harlow. The story is a silly setup of contrivances to get the two together. It works as a personality piece. B&W; 85m. **DIR:** W. S. Van Dyke. **CAST:** Jean Harlow, Robert Taylor, Reginald Owen, Una O'Connor, E. E. Clive, Cora Witherspoon. 1937

PERSONAL SERVICES ★★★ The true-life story of Christine Painter, a British waitress who happened into a very successful career as a brothel madam. Julie Walters gives an all-out performance that's fascinating, but the movie's bluntness may be off-putting to most American viewers. It's rated R for language. 105m. **DIR:** Terry Jones. **CAST:** Julie Walters, Alec McCowen, Shirley Stelfox. 1987

PERSONALS, THE ★★★1/2 Entertaining light comedy about a recently divorced Minneapolis man (Bill Schoppert) trying to get back in the dating game. Schoppert has the characteristics of Woody Allen, showing both pathos and a knack for one-liners. Rated PG for profanity. 90m. **DIR:** Peter Markle. **CAST:** Bill Schoppert, Karen Landry, Paul Eiding, Michael Laskin. 1983

•**PERSONS UNKNOWN** ★★★1/2 A beautiful blonde uses Joe Mantegna, the owner of a security agency, to get at money belonging to one of his clients. At least that's how it first appears, in this twisty, low-key thriller where you can never be sure who's zooming whom. Rated R for violence, drug use, profanity, and sex. 99m. **DIR:** George Hickenlooper. **CAST:** Joe Mantegna, Kelly Lynch, Jon Favreau, J. T. Walsh, Xander Berkeley, Naomi Watts. 1996

PERSUADERS, THE (TV SERIES) ★★★ This tongue-in-cheek adventure series lasted just one season on ABC, but it offers a fair bit of action, humor, and style. Set in the glamour spots of Europe, the show follows two dashing playboys: Brett Sinclair (Roger Moore), a British lord, and Daniel Wilde (Tony Curtis), a self-made millionaire from the Bronx. Moore and Curtis are fun to watch in these tailor-made roles, smoothly handling the roughhousing, rivalry, and romance. 60m. **DIR:** Basil Dearden, Val Guest. **CAST:** Roger Moore, Tony Curtis, Laurence Naismith. 1972

PERSUASION (1971) ★★ A BBC production so subtle you might just mistake it for dry and dull. This lacks effective sound quality and camera work; one can spot displaced shadows and hear an occasional flubbed line. This is very confined, even when the action moves outdoors, and none of the performances will inspire you to endure its length. Not rated. 225m. **DIR:** Howard Baker. **CAST:** Ann Firbank, Bryan Marshall. 1971

PERSUASION (1995) ★★★1/2 A young woman (Amanda Root) still loves the suitor she foolishly rejected years before (Ciaran Hinds); now she watches in agony as he courts her brother-in-law's younger sister. Jane Austen's last novel is given a first-class filming, Root's character blossom from an amiable wallflower to a confident beauty. Rated PG. 102m. **DIR:** Roger Michell. **CAST:** Amanda Root, Ciaran Hinds, Susan Fleetwood, Corin Redgrave, Fiona Shaw. 1995 DVD

PEST, THE 🖤 Imagine a manic Jim Carrey or Jerry Lewis at warp speed and you have John Leguizamo as the most appropriately named title character. The anorexic plot, which is just an excuse for his lightning-speed barrage of costume and character changes, features Leguizamo agreeing to become the human prey for wealthy hunters. Enough ethnic and sexual-orientation jokes to offend just about everyone. Rated PG-13 for language and bad taste. 84m. **DIR:** Paul Miller. **CAST:** John Leguizamo, Jeffrey Jones, Edoardo Ballerini, Freddy Rodriguez, Charles Hallahan. 1997 DVD

PET SEMATARY ★★★1/2 This scarefest is the most faithful film adaptation of a Stephen King novel yet. A young doctor moves his family to an idyllic setting in the Maine woods. The calm is shattered when first the family's cat and then their son are killed on the nearby highway. If you can bear this, you'll love the all-out terror that follows. Rated R for violence. 102m. **DIR:** Mary Lambert. **CAST:** Dale Midkiff, Fred Gwynne, Denise Crosby. 1989

PET SEMATARY TWO ★★ This disappointing gorefest returns to that cryptic Maine burial ground. Young Edward Furlong hopes to return his mother to life … in spite of having seen his best friend's dog and stepfather revived as savage killers. So much for common sense. Rated R for violence and profanity. 102m. **DIR:** Mary Lambert. **CAST:** Edward Furlong, Anthony Edwards, Clancy Brown, Jared Rushton, Jason McGuire. 1992

PET SHOP ★★★ Anyone who ever wanted a pet as a child will enjoy this lighthearted comedy about a Brooklyn family who must move to Arizona after the father testifies against a mobster. The children are delightful, but the story falls a bit short. Not rated, but suitable for all audiences. 88m. **DIR:** Hope Perello. **CAST:** Leigh Ann Orsi, Spencer Vrooman, Joanne Baron, David Wagner, Jane Morris, Jeff Michalski, Shashawnee Hall, Terry Kiser. 1994

PETE KELLY'S BLUES ★★1/2 Guys, gals, gangsters, gin, and Dixieland jazz are done to a turn in this ultrarealistic re-creation of the Roaring Twenties. 95m. **DIR:** Jack Webb. **CAST:** Jack Webb, Janet Leigh, Edmond O'Brien, Jayne Mansfield, Lee Marvin, Peggy Lee, Ella Fitzgerald, Martin Milner, Andy Devine. 1955

PETE 'N' TILLIE ★★ Bloated, morose mess features a chronically depressed Carol Burnett married to skirt chaser Walter Matthau. Matthau and Burnett never click, and fans of the duo are warned to steer clear. Rated PG for profanity. 100m. **DIR:** Martin Ritt. **CAST:** Walter Matthau, Carol Burnett, Geraldine Page, Barry Nelson. 1972

PETER AND THE WOLF ★★★★★ Originally intended as the centerpiece for Walt Disney's planned sequel to *Fantasia*, this luxuriously animated rendition of Prokofiev's musical fable was instead repackaged as part of 1946s *Make Mine Music*. Sterling Holloway's narration adds a bit of contemporary humor to the gentle fable of a small Russian boy who goes wolf hunting. 30m. **DIR:** Walt Disney. 1946

PETER GUNN (TV SERIES) ★★★1/2 Blake Edwards earned his Hollywood reputation with this stylish television detective series. Star Craig Stevens established an image that was endlessly imitated: suave, urbane, and self-mocking in the face of certain peril. Despite temptations, Gunn always remained true to his steady girl, Edie (Lola Albright), who worked as a singer in a waterfront nightclub dubbed Mother's. The most fun resulted from Gunn's contacts: an outrageous assortment of snitches, all willing to sing for a discreetly tendered sawbuck. Composer Henry Mancini began a trend with his jazzy themes. Each volume includes two episodes; the best are "Death House Testament" and "The Comic" (which earned Edwards an award from the Mystery Writers of America). B&W; each 55m. **DIR:** Blake Edwards, Boris Sagal. **CAST:** Craig Stevens, Lola Albright, Herschel Bernardi, Hope Emerson. **1958–1961**

•**PETER PAN (1924)** ★★★★ First and perhaps best of the three versions of this fantasy classic contains all the elements familiar to modern audiences while retaining the charm of an era long gone. Author James Barrie personally chose young Betty Bronson for the lead and kept a watchful eye on his best-known property, insuring just the right tone and mood for what was to become one of the great film hits of the 1920s. Skillful mix of theater (actors in costumes for all animal roles) and the best film effects available at the time blend beautifully in this beloved children's favorite. Silent, with tinted sequences and orchestral score. B&W; 101m. **DIR:** Herbert Brenon. **CAST:** Betty Bronson, Ernest Torrence, Mary Brian, Esther Ralston, Virginia Brown Faire, Philippe deLacey, Jack Murphy, Anna May Wong. **1924**

PETER PAN (1953) ★★★1/2 While this 1953 Disney release doesn't qualify as one of the studio's animated classics, it is nonetheless an entertaining version of James M. Barrie's children's play about Never-Never-Land, and the three Darling children taken there by Peter Pan and his fairy companion, Tinker Bell. Rated G. 77m. **DIR:** Hamilton Luske, Clyde Geronimi, Wilfred Jackson. **1953 DVD**

PETER PAN (1960) ★★★★ The magic is still there, remarkably, in this 1960 NBC Television production of the musical based on the book by James M. Barrie. Mary Martin stars in her most beloved role. Unusually high-quality release from GoodTimes Video, which has added four minutes of footage not seen in twenty years. 100m. **DIR:** Vincent J. Donehue. **CAST:** Mary Martin, Cyril Ritchard, Sondra Lee, Margalo Gilmore. **1960 DVD**

PETER'S FRIENDS ★★★1/2 A *Big Chill*–style reunion of English theatrical types in this humorous and touching soufflé from Kenneth Branagh. Costar-screenwriter Rita Rudner's script doesn't always hit the mark, but the cast does. Rated R for profanity and nudity. 102m. **DIR:** Kenneth Branagh. **CAST:** Kenneth Branagh, Emma Thompson, Rita Rudner, Stephen Fry, Hugh Laurie, Imelda Staunton, Alphonsia Emmanuel, Tony Slattery, Phyllida Law, Alex Lowe. **1993**

PETE'S DRAGON ★★1/2 Only the kiddies will get a kick out of this Disney feature, which combines live action with animation. In Maine, circa 1908, a 9-year-old boy (Sean Marshall) escapes his overbearing foster parents with the aid of the pet dragon that only he can see. Sort of a children's version of *Harvey*, it's generally lackluster and uninspired. Rated G. 134m. **DIR:** Don Chaffey. **CAST:** Mickey Rooney, Jim Dale, Helen Reddy, Red Buttons, Jim Backus, Sean Marshall. **1977**

PETIT CON ★★ France's equivalent of our American teenage-boy-in-heat flicks, with a few differences. The film tries for a serious side involving the trauma that Michel (Bernard Brieux) is causing his family. In French with English subtitles. Rated R. 90m. **DIR:** Gerard Lauzier. **CAST:** Guy Marchand, Caroline Cellier, Bernard Brieux, Souad Amidou. **1986**

PETRIFIED FOREST, THE ★★★1/2 This adaptation of the Robert Sherwood play seems a bit dated at first. It's about a gangster (Humphrey Bogart, in one of his first important screen roles) who holds a writer (Leslie Howard), a waitress (Bette Davis), and others hostage in a diner. The first-rate story, exquisite ensemble acting and taut direction by Archie Mayo soon mesmerize the viewer. B&W; 83m. **DIR:** Archie Mayo. **CAST:** Humphrey Bogart, Leslie Howard, Bette Davis, Dick Foran. **1936**

PETTICOAT PLANET ★★ A bunch of men crashland on a planet full of women who live in a Wild West–like environment. The usual soft-core couplings occur. For fans of this type of film only. Rated R for nudity and simulated sex. 78m. **DIR:** David De-Coteau. **CAST:** Troy Vincent, Betsy Lyn George, Elizabeth Kaitan. **1996 DVD**

PETULIA ★★★★ A story of complex relationships that centers around a prominent doctor (George C. Scott) who gets involved with a kooky young socialite (Julie Christie). A brilliant tragicomedy, one of Richard Lester's major achievements. Rated R. 105m. **DIR:** Richard Lester. **CAST:** George C. Scott, Julie Christie, Richard Chamberlain, Shirley Knight, Joseph Cotten, Arthur Hill. **1968**

PEYTON PLACE ★★★★ A landmark movie from a landmark novel with Lana Turner in her Oscar-nominated role of unwed mother Constance MacKenzie. She lives a lie so that her daughter, Alison, will never know the facts of her life. But Alison discovers facts of her own as the movie explores the morals of small-town life. 160m. **DIR:** Mark Robson. **CAST:** Lana Turner, Diane Varsi, Lloyd Nolan, Betty Field, Hope Lange, Arthur Kennedy, David Nelson, Terry Moore, Lee Philips, Russ Tamblyn, Leon Ames, Mildred Dunnock, Barry Coe, Lorne Greene. **1957**

PHANTASM ★★1/2 This strange mixture of horror and science fiction, while not an outstanding film by any account, does provide viewers with several thrills and unexpected twists. If you like to jump out of your seat, watch this alone with all the lights out. R-rated after scenes were cut from the original X-rated version. 87m. **DIR:** Don Coscarelli. **CAST:** Michael Baldwin, Bill Thornbury, Reggie Bannister. **1979 DVD**

PHANTASM II ★★ After ten years, the Tall Man (Angus Scrimm) is back, and he's nastier than ever. No longer is he merely looting cemeteries to enslave the dead for his fiendish purposes. He's also going after the living. But the heroes from the first film are hot on his trail. Lacks the wit, style, and originality of its predecessor. Rated R for nudity, profanity, and graphic violence. 90m. DIR: Don Coscarelli. CAST: James LeGros, Reggie Bannister, Angus Scrimm. 1988

PHANTASM III: LORD OF THE DEAD ★★1/2 As is true of its predecessors, sheer momentum keeps this weird horror film going in spite of the ridiculous story. Our heroes are still after the wonderfully malevolent Tall Man. Young Kevin Conners brings enthusiasm to his performance as an orphaned boy determined to avenge his whole community's disappearance. Rated R for gore, profanity, nudity, and simulated sex. 91m. DIR: Don Coscarelli. CAST: Reggie Bannister, Michael Baldwin, Angus Scrimm, Gloria Lynn Henry, Kevin Conners. 1994

PHANTASM IV: OBLIVION ★★★ The Tall Man returns to transform more corpses into his zombie slaves. More campy horror fun from the creators of the first three *Phantasm* movies. Doesn't make a lick of sense but has more style and humor than one might expect. Rated R for profanity, horror, and violence. 90m. DIR: Don Coscarelli. CAST: Michael Baldwin, Reggie Bannister, Bill Thornbury, Heidi Marnhout, Bob Ivy, Angus Scrimm. 1998

PHANTOM, THE (1931) ★★ Creaky thriller about a mysterious prison escapee with scores to settle and the rookie reporter who cracks the case boasts one of the silliest villains on film. B&W; 62m. DIR: Alvin J. Neitz. CAST: Guinn Williams, Allene Ray, Niles Welch, Tom O'Brien, Wilfred Lucas, Sheldon Lewis. 1931

PHANTOM, THE (1996) ★★★ Leisurely screen adaptation of Lee Falk's comic strip about "The Ghost Who Walks" and his alter ego, Kit Walker, in a story that pits the masked, purple-clad avenger against a power-crazed villain. Set in the 1930s, the movie has a fine period flavor and pokes fun at itself without becoming campy. Rated PG for violence. 100m. DIR: Simon Wincer. CAST: Billy Zane, Kristy Swanson, Treat Williams, Catherine Zeta Jones, Samantha Eggar, Patrick McGoohan, James Remar, Cary-Hiroyuki Tagawa. 1996 DVD

PHANTOM BROADCAST, THE ★★★ The murder of a popular radio crooner reveals he was little more than the handsome lip-synching front for the real offstage singer, a twisted hunchback with a velvet voice. Cleverly plotted drama. B&W; 68m. DIR: Phil Rosen. CAST: Ralph Forbes, Gail Patrick, Guinn Williams, George "Gabby" Hayes. 1933

PHANTOM CHARIOT ★★ The legend of the Coachman of Death being replaced each year by the last man to die on December 31 is used here to drive home a sermon on the evils of drink. In its day the use of multiple-layered flashbacks and double-exposure techniques made this Swedish silent a great success; today, alas, it only seems tedious and unendurably slow-paced. Silent. B&W; 83m. DIR: Victor Sjöström. CAST: Victor Sjöström. 1920

PHANTOM CREEPS, THE ★★1/2 This Saturday-afternoon crowd pleaser features a crazed scientist, a giant robot, an invisibility belt, and a meteorite fragment that can render an entire army immobile—just about anything a kid can ask for in a serial. Good fun. B&W; 12 chapters. DIR: Ford Beebe, Saul Goodkind. CAST: Bela Lugosi, Regis Toomey. 1939

PHANTOM EMPIRE (1935) ★★★ Gene Autry, with the aid of Frankie Darro, champion rider Betsy King Ross, and the Junior Thunder Riders, overcomes threats from greedy crooks and the deadly threat of Murania, the futuristic city twenty thousand feet beneath the ground. Plenty of action, the wonders of the "city of the future," and good special effects (including a death ray) make this one of Mascot Films's best serials. B&W; 12 chapters. DIR: Otto Brewer, B. Reeves "Breezy" Eason. CAST: Gene Autry, Frankie Darro, Betsy King Ross, Smiley Burnette. 1935

PHANTOM EMPIRE, THE (1986) ★★★ Fans of old serials and Fifties sci-fi adventures will want to check out this good-natured parody. The plot, about a group of adventurers trying to salvage a cache of diamonds from a mutant-infested cavern, is a thin frame for lots of tongue-in-cheek dialogue and injokes. Rated R for nudity. 83m. DIR: Fred Olen Ray. CAST: Ross Hagen, Jeffrey Combs, Russ Tamblyn, Sybil Danning. 1986

PHANTOM OF DEATH ★★ A concert pianist, dying of a rare disease that causes rapid aging, takes out his frustration on women from his past by hacking them to pieces. Donald Pleasence and Michael York are old pros, but the direction is flat and any suspense is worn quickly into the ground. Not rated; contains nudity and violence. 95m. DIR: Ruggero Deodato. CAST: Michael York, Edwige Fenech, Donald Pleasence. 1987

PHANTOM OF LIBERTY, THE ★★ A kaleidoscope of satirical vignettes composed of outrageous riddles, jokes, and associations all mocking mankind's inexplicable willingness to enslave itself in order to be "free." A big disappointment from Luis Buñuel whose use of tricks from his other films make this one seem cliched. In French with English subtitles. 104m. DIR: Luis Buñuel. CAST: Jean-Claude Brialy, Adolfo Celi, Michel Piccoli, Monica Vitti. 1974

PHANTOM OF THE MALL—ERIC'S REVENGE ★★ A killer seeks revenge on the developers who burned down his house and accidentally disfigured him while clearing the way for a new shopping mall. Good characters make this slasher flick marginally entertaining. Rated R for nudity. 91m. DIR: Richard Friedman. CAST: Derek Rydall, Jonathan Goldsmith, Rob Estes, Morgan Fairchild. 1988

PHANTOM OF THE OPERA (1925) ★★★★★ Classic silent horror with Lon Chaney Sr. in his most poignant and gruesome role. This 1925 sample of Chaney's brilliance—he was truly the "man of a thousand faces"—still has enough power to send chills up your spine. Enjoy. B&W; 79m. DIR: Rupert Julian. CAST: Lon Chaney Sr., Mary Philbin, Norman Kerry. 1925 DVD

PHANTOM OF THE OPERA (1943) ★★★ Overabundance of singing hurts this otherwise good remake of the 1925 silent. The well-known story concerns a Paris opera house being terrorized by a disfigured composer (Claude Rains) whose best works have been stolen. Acting is great, production values are high, but that singing has got to go! 92m. DIR: Arthur Lubin. CAST: Claude Rains, Susanna Foster, Nelson Eddy, Edgar Barrier, Miles Mander, Hume Cronyn. 1943

PHANTOM OF THE OPERA (1962) ★★1/2 Herbert Lom plays the title role as much for sympathy as scares in this low-key remake from England's Hammer Studios. Otherwise, the plot doesn't vary much from the preceding versions. 84m. **DIR:** Terence Fisher. **CAST:** Herbert Lom, Heather Sears, Thorley Walters, Michael Gough. 1962

PHANTOM OF THE OPERA (1989) ★★ This muddled retread owes more to the slasher genre than to Gaston Leroux. Although Jill Schoelen makes an appealing heroine, she seems far too intelligent to so casually accept the attention of the heard-but-not-seen guardian angel who lurks beneath the Opera House. He, of course, is none other than serial killer Robert Englund—hiding behind a suitably gory facial-skin mask. Rated R for violence and brief nudity. 93m. **DIR:** Dwight H. Little. **CAST:** Robert Englund, Jill Schoelen, Alex Hyde-White. 1989

•PHANTOM OF THE OPERA (1998) ❤ In this, Dario Argento's version of the classic story, Julian Sands plays the mysterious half man, half monster, who is lurking around underneath the opera house, lusting after a talented singer played by Asia Argento. Nepotism aside, this ghastly take on *Phantom* fails to capture any of the drama and romance of the original tale. Rated R for gore and violence. 100m. **DIR:** Dario Argento. **CAST:** Julian Sands, Asia Argento. 1998 DVD

PHANTOM OF THE PARADISE ★★1/2 Before he became obsessed with Hitchcock *hommages* and ultraviolent bloodbaths, director Brian De Palma did this odd little blend of Faust and *Phantom of the Opera*. William Finley sells his soul to Paul Williams and learns the dangers of achieving fame too quickly. Wildly erratic, with tedious dialogue alternating with droll visual bits. Rated PG—mild violence. 92m. **DIR:** Brian De Palma. **CAST:** Paul Williams, William Finley, Jessica Harper. 1974

PHANTOM OF THE PLAINS ★★★ A pompous, polished crook whose specialty is marrying wealthy women is about to dupe the duchess until Red Ryder steps in to expose his con game. B&W; 56m. **DIR:** Lesley Selander. **CAST:** William Elliott, Robert Blake, Alice Fleming, Ian Keith, Virginia Christine. 1945

PHANTOM OF THE RITZ ★★1/2 Taking its cue from *Phantom of the Opera* and *Phantom of the Paradise*, this campy little comedy kicks off in 1952 with a drag race that ends in tragedy. Then it's off to 1992, with entrepreneur Peter Bergman reopening the infamous Ritz theater. His plans for a gala opening are jeopardized when he realizes that an evil presence is making the rounds. Fun in a cheap sort of way, with the legendary Coasters lending musical support. Rated R for violence. 89m. **DIR:** Allen Plone. **CAST:** Peter Bergman, Deborah Van Valkenburgh. 1988

PHANTOM THUNDERBOLT ★★1/2 The Thunderbolt Kid is hired by a town's citizens to round up a lawless gang. B&W; 63m. **DIR:** Alan James. **CAST:** Ken Maynard, Frances Dade, Bob Kortman. 1933

PHANTOM 2040 (TV SERIES) ★★★1/2 The Phantom, guardian of his jungle domain, carries his ecological concerns into the future as descendants of the original comic-book hero take on the mantle of "The Ghost That Walks." Nontraditional character design and thoughtful stories boost this animated series a step above most Saturday-morning programming. Each 50m. **DIR:** Vincent Bassol, Michel Lyman, Mike Kaweski, Bertrand Tager Kagan. 1994

PHANTOMS ★★ Dr. Jenny Pailey returns to her Colorado mountain village with her sister. The ladies notice that all the townsfolk are dead or missing and cross paths with a sheriff and his lecherous deputy. The quartet is then terrorized by a supernatural power responsible for mass human disappearances throughout history. Rated R for language, gore, and violence. 91m. **DIR:** Joe Chappelle. **CAST:** Joanna Going, Rose McGowan, Ben Affleck, Peter O'Toole, Liev Schreiber. 1997 DVD

PHAR LAP ★★★1/2 Absolutely chilling (and true) account of the superb Australian racehorse that chewed up the track in the 1920s and early 1930s. Tom Burlinson stars as the stable boy who first believed in, and then followed to fame, the indefatigable Phar Lap. This film's indictment of early horse-racing practices will make you shudder. Rated PG—very intense for younger children. 106m. **DIR:** Simon Wincer. **CAST:** Tom Burlinson, Ron Leibman, Martin Vaughn. 1984

PHARAOH'S ARMY ★★★★ A quiet antiwar film that explores the far-reaching effects of the Civil War on a stoical Kentucky woman trying to protect her teenage son and their hardscrabble farm from the Yanks. An understanding slowly builds between her and a Yankee invader that is touching not only for what they have in common, but because they can never find common ground. Rated PG-13 for violence and mild profanity. 90m. **DIR:** Robby Henson. **CAST:** Chris Cooper, Patricia Clarkson, Will Lucas, Richard Tyson, Robert Joy, Kris Kristofferson, Huckleberry Fox. 1995

PHASE IV ★★★1/2 An interesting sci-fi mood piece from 1973 about scientists (Nigel Davenport, Michael Murphy) attempting to outwit superintelligent mutant ants. Good effects and fine acting. Rated PG. 86m. **DIR:** Saul Bass. **CAST:** Nigel Davenport, Michael Murphy, Lynne Frederick. 1974

PHAT BEACH ★★★ Entertaining if loopy comedy about a pair of friends who head out to the beach for their summer vacation. Problem is, they've got no money, they "borrowed" Dad's Mercedes, and only one of them is responsible enough to realize this could mean trouble. Rated R for profanity and nudity. 88m. **DIR:** Doug Ellin. **CAST:** Jermaine "Huggy" Hopkins, Coolio, Brian Hooks, Tiny Lister Jr. 1996

PHEDRE ★★1/2 The performance of Marie Bell, the great French tragedienne, is the only reason to dig out this abbreviated adaptation of the Greek myth about the queen who fell in love with her stepson and caused her husband's death. The production is stagy. Poorly served by the subtitles. In French with English subtitles. 93m. **DIR:** Pierre Jourdan. **CAST:** Marie Bell, Jacques Dacqumine, Claude Giraud. 1968

PHENOMENON ★★★★ Sweet-natured, small-town resident George Malley gets quite a shock on his thirty-seventh birthday, when a blinding light leaves him with heightened awareness and an insatiable appetite for knowledge. John Travolta is wonderful as the amiable fellow wholly unable to cope with his rapidly escalating intellect. Mostly, he'd just like to get closer to Kyra Sedgwick, a quiet single mom with an aversion to new love interests. Rated PG for mild sensuality. 117m. **DIR:** Jon Turteltaub. **CAST:** John Travolta, Kyra Sedgwick, Forest Whitaker, Robert Duvall, David Gallagher, Brent Spiner. **1996 DVD**

PHILADELPHIA ★★★★ Tom Hanks's Oscar-winning portrayal of an AIDS-infected attorney battling for his rights is the main draw in this heartfelt drama. Denzel Washington is equally good as the homophobic attorney who must confront his own prejudice and ignorance after he agrees to take on the case, in which Hanks alleges that he lost his job at a prestigious law firm because of discrimination. Rated PG-13 for profanity and mature subject matter. 119m. **DIR:** Jonathan Demme. **CAST:** Tom Hanks, Denzel Washington, Jason Robards Jr., Mary Steenburgen, Antonio Banderas, Ron Vawter, Robert Ridgely, Charles Napier, Lisa Summerour. **1993 DVD**

PHILADELPHIA EXPERIMENT, THE ★★★1/2 Reportedly based on a true incident during World War II involving an antiradar experiment that caused a naval battleship to disappear in Virginia, this entertaining science-fiction film stars Michael Paré as a sailor on that ship. But instead of ending up in Virginia, he finds himself in the modern world of 1984. Rated PG for violence and profanity. 102m. **DIR:** Stewart Raffill. **CAST:** Michael Paré, Nancy Allen, Bobby DiCicco, Eric Christmas. **1984**

PHILADELPHIA EXPERIMENT 2, THE ★★★ Although it bears little relation to its predecessor, Kevin Rock and Nick Paine have scripted an engaging time-travel thriller that explores the consequences of a stealth bomber unexpectedly landing in Nazi hands during World War II. Brad Johnson makes a suitably wholesome hero, and Gerrit Graham is amusing as a reckless scientist. Rated PG-13 for violence. 98m. **DIR:** Stephen Cornwell. **CAST:** Brad Johnson, Marjean Holden, Gerrit Graham, John Christian Graas. **1993**

PHILADELPHIA STORY, THE ★★★★★ This is one of the best comedies to come out of Hollywood. From the first scene, where Tracy Lord (Katharine Hepburn) deposits her ex-husband's (Cary Grant) golf clubs in a heap at her front door and in return, Grant deposits Hepburn in a heap right next to the clubs, the 1940s version of *The Taming of the Shrew* proceeds at a blistering pace. Grand entertainment. B&W; 112m. **DIR:** George Cukor. **CAST:** Katharine Hepburn, Cary Grant, James Stewart, Ruth Hussey, John Howard. **1940 DVD**

PHILBY, BURGESS AND MACLEAN: SPY SCANDAL OF THE CENTURY ★★★★ Yes, you can have an exciting spy story without James Bond chases and gimmicks. This riveting film spins the quiet, chilling tale of three of Britain's most notorious spies. They attended college together, were recruited by the Russians, and held high government security posts for thirty years before their discovery. Not rated. 83m. **DIR:** Gordon Flemyng. **CAST:** Anthony Bate, Derek Jacobi, Michael Culver, Ingrid Hafner, Elizabeth Seal. **1986**

PHOBIA 🦃 An almost-unwatchable nonthrilling thriller that combines psychobabble with murder.

Rated R. 90m. **DIR:** John Huston. **CAST:** Paul Michael Glaser, Susan Hogan, John Colicos, Patricia Collins. **1980**

PHOENIX ★★★★ In this *film noir* of crooked cops in Phoenix, tensions rise as detective Harry Collins tries to get his gambling addiction under control. When a local loan shark sets out to collect his debt, Harry and his cop friends are forced into pulling off a dangerous heist that could end all of their problems. Filled with dark, interesting characters and escalating tension, Danny Cannon's film punches all the right buttons. Rated R for violence, language, and adult situations. 107m. **DIR:** Danny Cannon. **CAST:** Ray Liotta, Anthony LaPaglia, Anjelica Huston, Daniel Baldwin, Jeremy Piven, Kari Wuhrer. **1997 DVD**

PHOENIX THE WARRIOR 🦃 In the distant future germ warfare has killed all the men, and women have become warriors. Not rated; contains violence. 90m. **DIR:** Robert Hayes. **CAST:** Persis Khambatta. **1987**

PHONE CALL FROM A STRANGER ★★★ Fine acting by a stellar cast lifts this soap opera above the bubbles. Gary Merrill plays confessor to various fellow passengers on an ill-fated airline flight, and brings comfort and understanding to their families when most are killed in the crash. B&W; 96m. **DIR:** Jean Negulesco. **CAST:** Shelley Winters, Gary Merrill, Michael Rennie, Keenan Wynn, Bette Davis, Craig Stevens, Hugh Beaumont. **1952**

PHOTOGRAPHING FAIRIES ★★★1/2 Toby Stephens delivers a haunting performance as photographer Charles Castle who is presented with a photograph of supposedly real fairies that a woman says her two daughters took. His subsequent intervention with the woman, her two daughters, and her skeptical husband set into motion a tragic series of events. Based on the novel of the same name by Steve Szilagyi. Rated R for nudity, adult situations, and language. 107m. **DIR:** Nick Willing. **CAST:** Toby Stephens, Emily Woof, Ben Kingsley, Frances Barber, Philip Davis, Edward Hardwicke. **1997**

PHYSICAL EVIDENCE ★★1/2 Polished performances by Theresa Russell and Burt Reynolds are wasted in this convoluted police thriller. Russell is a public defender assigned to defend Reynolds, a cop accused of murder. A threadbare, erratic plot and haphazard direction by Michael Crichton ruin what could have been a first-rate film. Rated R for adult situations, violence, and profanity. 100m. **DIR:** Michael Crichton. **CAST:** Burt Reynolds, Theresa Russell, Ned Beatty, Kay Lenz. **1989**

PI ★★★★★ Max Cohen is a math genius who is going nuts. He lives in a squalid Manhattan apartment crammed with high-tech electronics and is obsessed with harnessing the chaos of the universe. Between bouts of paranoia and crippling migraines he is stalked by a shady brokerage firm and a Hasidic cabal. This microbudget study in madness uses bleached out black-and-white imagery as a Kafkaesque search for absolute truth blends reality with cyberpunk myth. Rated R for language and disturbing images. 85m. **DIR:** Darren Aronofsky. **CAST:** Sean Gullette, Mark Margolis, Samia Shoaib, Pam Hart, Ben Shenkman, Stephen Pearlman. **1998 DVD**

PIANO, THE ★★★★ Jane Campion's mesmerizing film is about a mute-by-choice Scotswoman (Oscar-winner Holly Hunter) who journeys to the jungles of nineteenth-century New Zealand to marry Sam Neill, a man she's never met. Once there, she is horrified to find her beloved piano left on the beach until a neighbor (Harvey Keitel) offers to let her play it in exchange for romantic favors. Electrifying and offbeat, this is for lovers of original cinema. Rated R for nudity, simulated sex, and brief violence. 121m. DIR: Jane Campion. CAST: Holly Hunter, Harvey Keitel, Sam Neill, Anna Paquin. 1993 DVD

PIANO FOR MRS. CIMINO, A ★★★★ Blessed with great humor and a terrific performance by Bette Davis, this made-for-television film about growing old with dignity is manipulative at times. In light of all the wonderful moments, however, the contrivances don't seem so bad. Davis plays a widow who is institutionalized for senility. The film follows her through her recovery and her rebirth as a single, self-sufficient woman. 96m. DIR: George Schaefer. CAST: Bette Davis, Keenan Wynn, Alexa Kenin, Penny Fuller, Christopher Guest, George Hearn. 1982

PIANO LESSON, THE ★★★★ Powerful Pulitzer Prize–winning play by August Wilson is expertly adapted to film in this *Hallmark Hall of Fame* production. Controversy centers around an ornate piano, carved with ancestral images, that has been in the central family for eighty years. It may be too strong for young viewers. 95m. DIR: Lloyd Richards. CAST: Charles Dutton, Alfre Woodard, Carl Gordon, Courtney B. Vance, Tommy Hollis. 1995

PICKLE, THE ♥ This film is just as bad as the film-within-a-film that has been director Danny Aiello makes in an attempt to revive his career. Extremely dreadful considering its pedigree. Rated R for language and nudity. 103m. DIR: Paul Mazursky. CAST: Danny Aiello, Dyan Cannon, Shelley Winters, Christopher Penn. 1993

PICKPOCKET ★★★★1/2 Inspired by *Crime and Punishment*, this is one of the best films from the French master Robert Bresson, whose work is marked by an unblinking austerity that requires a little getting used to for American audiences. An intelligent young man decides to make a career of petty crime, despite his knowledge of the immorality of his actions. In French with English subtitles. Not rated; contains no offensive material. B&W; 75m. DIR: Robert Bresson. CAST: Martin LaSalle, Marika Green. 1959

PICK-UP ARTIST, THE ♥ An absolute mess. Rated PG-13 for language and sexual content. 81m. DIR: James Toback. CAST: Molly Ringwald, Robert Downey Jr., Dennis Hopper, Harvey Keitel. 1987

PICKUP ON SOUTH STREET ★★★★ Samuel Fuller's lean and mean thriller about a pickpocket (Richard Widmark) who accidentally lifts a roll of top-secret microfilm and becomes a target for espionage agents. It's prime Fuller: suspenseful, tough, and violent. B&W; 80m. DIR: Samuel Fuller. CAST: Richard Widmark, Jean Peters, Thelma Ritter. 1953

PICKWICK PAPERS, THE ★★★ Arguably the best cinema condensation of Charles Dickens. Here recorded are the clever antics of Samuel Pickwick, Alfred Jingle, and Sam Weller as they move through their corner of mid-nineteenth-century England. 109m. DIR: Noel Langley. CAST: James Hayter, James Donald, Joyce Grenfell, Nigel Patrick, Hermione Baddeley. 1954

PICNIC ★★★★ This is one of the best films about small-town life ever lensed, blessed with a cast that makes it even more credible. William Holden plays a drifter who, while visiting old school chum Cliff Robertson, falls for his friend's fiancée (Kim Novak). Derived from the William Inge stage play. 115m. DIR: Joshua Logan. CAST: William Holden, Kim Novak, Rosalind Russell, Susan Strasberg, Arthur O'Connell, Cliff Robertson, Nick Adams. 1956 DVD

PICNIC AT HANGING ROCK ★★★★1/2 Surreal, hypnotic suspense story revolves around the mysterious disappearance of a group of students from an all-girls' school at the turn of the century in Australia. Director Peter Weir fashions a truly unsettling motion picture. His fans will rank it among his best. 110m. DIR: Peter Weir. CAST: Rachel Roberts, Dominic Guard, Helen Morse, Jacki Weaver. 1975 DVD

PICNIC ON THE GRASS ★★★ Director Jean Renoir's tribute to French Impressionism takes place in the beautiful countryside as a scientific outing turns into a drunken reverie. In French with English subtitles. 92m. DIR: Jean Renoir. CAST: Paul Meurisse, Catherine Rouvel, Jacqueline Morane. 1959

PICTURE BRIDE ★★1/2 After the death of her parents in 1916, a young Japanese woman emigrates to Hawaii as the mail-order bride of a sugarcane worker. Thoroughly researched, interesting—but uninvolving. Partially in English, mostly in Japanese with English subtitles. Rated PG-13 for mature themes. 94m. DIR: Kayo Hatta. CAST: Youki Kudoh, Akira Takayama, Tamlyn Tomita, Cary-Hiroyuki Tagawa, Toshiro Mifune. 1995

PICTURE MOMMY DEAD ★★ The tragic death of her mother causes a young girl to lose her memory. Afterward, she is possessed by the spirit of her late mommy. Ooh! Meanwhile the father, Don Ameche, marries again. Thus a rather silly battle ensues between stepmom and stepdaughter. Good acting; too bad the script isn't better. 88m. DIR: Bert I. Gordon. CAST: Don Ameche, Martha Hyer, Zsa Zsa Gabor, Signe Hasso, Susan Gordon. 1966

PICTURE OF DORIAN GRAY, THE ★★★★ The classic adaptation of Oscar Wilde's famous novel, this features Hurd Hatfield giving a restrained performance in the title role of a young man whose portrait ages while he remains eternally youthful. Though talky and slow-moving, this film nevertheless keeps you glued to the screen. A few key scenes shot in Technicolor for effect. B&W/color; 110m. DIR: Albert Lewin. CAST: George Sanders, Hurd Hatfield, Donna Reed, Angela Lansbury, Peter Lawford. 1945

PICTURE PERFECT ★★ Single working woman tries to snag a promotion at an advertising agency by faking she has a fiancé. Complications arise when the guy she pretends to be marrying turns out to be a much nicer guy than the corporate alley cat she sleeps with on the sly. Rated PG-13 for language and suggested sex. 101m. DIR: Glenn Gordon Caron. CAST: Jennifer Aniston, Jay Mohr, Illeana Douglas, Kevin Bacon, Olympia Dukakis, Kevin Dunn. 1997 DVD

PICTURE WINDOWS ★★1/2 A talented cast and several experienced directors manage to add up to almost no surprises in this made-for-cable trilogy. All three stories represent a reflection on romance, but only the third, directed by Jonathan Kaplan, evokes much emotion. Rated R for violence, nudity, and profanity. 95m. DIR: Norman Jewison, Peter Bogdanovich, Jonathan Kaplan. CAST: Alan Arkin, Rosana De Soto, Dan Hedaya, George Segal, Sally Kirkland, Brooke Adams, Michael Lerner, Tamara Gorski, Joel Bissonnette. 1995 DVD

PIE IN THE SKY ★★★ Harmless little romantic comedy in which a young man obsessed with traffic woos the girl of his dreams over a number of years, thousands of cars, and a brief encounter with his idol—the king of traffic reporters. Outrageous performance by Christine Lahti is a highlight. Rated R for profanity and sexual situations. 94m. DIR: Bryan Gordon. CAST: Josh Charles, Anne Heche, Peter Riegert, Christine Ebersole, Christine Lahti, John Goodman, Brent Spiner. 1995

PIECE OF THE ACTION, A ★★★ Third entry in the Bill Cosby–Sidney Poitier partnership (after *Uptown Saturday Night* and *Let's Do It Again*), this one showing Poitier's greater comfort on both sides of the camera. The story concerns a pair of rascals given one of Life's Awful Choices: prison, or a team-up with some social workers to help a group of ghetto kids. Rated PG. 135m. DIR: Sidney Poitier. CAST: Sidney Poitier, Bill Cosby, Denise Nicholas, James Earl Jones. 1977

PIECES ♥ This movie promises, "You don't have to go to Texas for a chain-saw massacre!" While not rated by the MPAA, the picture would probably qualify for an X. 85m. DIR: Juan Piquer Simon. CAST: Christopher George, Lynda Day George, Edmund Purdom. 1983

PIERROT LE FOU ★★★1/2 Complex drama about a man who leaves his rich wife and runs off with a beautiful young woman who is fleeing some gangsters. Shot on location throughout the south of France, this existential character drama will fascinate some viewers while boring others. In French with English subtitles. 110m. DIR: Jean-Luc Godard. CAST: Jean-Paul Belmondo, Anna Karina, Samuel Fuller, Jean-Pierre Léaud. 1965 DVD

PIGS (DADDY'S DEADLY DARLING) ♥ Mental patient meets human-scarfing swine. Not rated, film contains violence. 79m. DIR: Marc Lawrence. CAST: Jesse Vint, Jim Antonio, Marc Lawrence. 1973

PIG'S TALE, A ★★ Low-budget *Meatballs* rip-off has a group of social rejects engaging in a battle of pranks, relay races, and bathroom humor against a group of spoiled rich brats. You've seen it done better before. Rated PG for mild profanity and crude humor. 94m. DIR: Paul Tassie. CAST: Joe Flaherty, Sean Babb, Mike Damus, Jonathan Hilario, Lisa Jakub, Andrew Harrison Leeds. 1994

PIGSTY ★★★ This dark fable of bourgeois repression links the stories of two extremely unconventional people—a medieval soldier forced into cannibalism and a modern young man whose alienation from society leads him to bestiality. Skillfully made, though obscure. In Italian with English subtitles.

Not rated; contains strong material and is not for children. 90m. DIR: Pier Paolo Pasolini. CAST: Pierre Clementi, Franco Citti, Jean-Pierre Léaud, Ugo Tognazzi. 1969

PILLOW BOOK, THE ★★★★ Another exquisitely composed, artsy outrage from England's Peter Greenaway (*The Cook, the Thief, His Wife & Her Lover*), though more accessible than many of his recent works. A young Japanese woman is sexually excited by having calligraphy drawn on her nude body. When she finds an Englishman who lets her write on him, she likes it even more. Then, as is typical of Greenaway, things go from sensual to gruesome. Not rated; contains sex, nudity, violence, drug use, and you name it. 126m. DIR: Peter Greenaway. CAST: Vivian Wu, Ewan McGregor, Yoshi Oida. 1996 DVD

PILLOW OF DEATH ★★ In the last *Inner Sanctum* mystery, Lon Chaney Jr. is a lawyer in love with his secretary and suspected of having smothered his wife to death. It's the only entry in the series in which Chaney turns out to be guilty—sort of. B&W; 65m. DIR: Wallace Fox. CAST: Lon Chaney Jr., Brenda Joyce, J. Edward Bromberg. 1945

PILLOW TALK ★★★★ If you like the fluffy light comedy of Doris Day and Rock Hudson, this is their best effort. The ever-virginal Miss Day is keeping the wolves at bay. Tony Randall is excellent as the suitor who never wins the girl. 105m. DIR: Michael Gordon. CAST: Doris Day, Rock Hudson, Tony Randall, Thelma Ritter. 1959 DVD

PILOT, THE ★★1/2 Cliff Robertson directed and starred in this film about an airline pilot's struggle with alcohol. Robertson's directing is not as convincing as his acting. Rated PG for profanity. 98m. DIR: Cliff Robertson. CAST: Cliff Robertson, Frank Converse, Diane Baker, Gordon MacRae, Dana Andrews, Milo O'Shea, Edward Binns. 1979

PIMPERNEL SMITH ★★★ Star Leslie Howard, who also produced, brought his 1934 role in *The Scarlet Pimpernel* up to modern times in this anti-Nazi thriller involving a daring rescue of important scientists from prison. B&W; 122m. DIR: Leslie Howard. CAST: Leslie Howard, David Tomlinson, Philip Friend, Hugh McDermott, Mary Morris. 1942

PIN ★★★1/2 Superb psychological thriller from the screenwriter of *The Amityville Horror* about a schizophrenic youth who develops a mad fixation with a medical dummy called Pin. David Hewlett is excellent as the manic youth torn between fantasy and reality. Rated R for nudity and violence. 103m. DIR: Sandor Stern. CAST: David Hewlett, Terry O'Quinn. 1989

PIN-UP GIRL ★★★ Another in the series of happy musical comedies Betty Grable starred in during World War II, *Pin-Up Girl* logically took its title from her status with GIs. This time, a secretary falls for a sailor. To be near him, she pretends to be a Broadway star. 83m. DIR: H. Bruce Humberstone. CAST: Betty Grable, John Harvey, Martha Raye, Joe E. Brown, Eugene Pallette. 1944

PING PONG ★★ A young lawyer must gather the feuding members of a large family in order to administer a dead man's will. The plot is merely an excuse to guide us around the Chinese section of London.

Modestly appealing. Rated PG. 100m. DIR: Po-Chih Leong. CAST: Lucy Sheen, David Yip. 1988

PINK ANGELS ★★1/2 *Easy Rider* meets *The Adventures of Priscilla, Queen of the Desert.* Rated R for profanity and violence. 81m. DIR: Larry Brown. CAST: John Alderman, Tom Basham, Bruce Kimball, Michael Pataki, Dan Haggerty. 1971

PINK CADILLAC ★★ Clint Eastwood returns to the *Every Which Way But Loose*–style action-comedy with this mediocre effort, in which he plays a skip tracer out to nab the bail-jumping Bernadette Peters. There are some good lines in this formula film, but it is predictable, overdone, and ultimately boring. Rated PG-13 for violence, profanity, and suggested sex. 122m. DIR: Buddy Van Horn. CAST: Clint Eastwood, Bernadette Peters, John Dennis Johnston, William Hickey, Geoffrey Lewis, Bill McKinney. 1989

PINK CHIQUITAS, THE 🎦 An army of women turned sex-starved by a pink meteor. Rated PG-13 for language and sexual situations. 85m. DIR: Anthony Currie. CAST: Frank Stallone, Bruce Pirrie, Elizabeth Edwards, Eartha Kitt. 1987

PINK FLAMINGOS ★★ The story of Babs Johnson (Divine), the "filthiest person alive," and Connie and Raymond Marble (Mink Stole and David Lochary), two challengers who are jealous of Babs's notoriety. As in all of Waters's films, the point here is to shock. If this doesn't, nothing will. Rated NC-17 for violence, nudity, and very poor taste. 95m. DIR: John Waters. CAST: Divine, Mink Stole, David Lochary, Mary Vivian Pearce, Edith Massey. 1972

PINK FLOYD: THE WALL ★★ For all its apparent intent, this visually impressive film, which has very little dialogue but, rather, uses garish visual images to the accompaniment of the British rock band's music, ends up being more of a celebration of insanity and inhumanity than an indictment of it as intended. Rated R for violence. 99m. DIR: Alan Parker. CAST: Bob Geldof, Christine Hargreaves, Bob Hoskins. 1982 DVD

PINK MOTEL 🎦 Phyllis Diller and Slim Pickens as owners of a less than prosperous motel. Not rated, this contains sexual situations. 90m. DIR: Mike MacFarland. CAST: Phyllis Diller, Slim Pickens, Terri Berland, Squire Fridell. 1982

PINK NIGHTS 🎦 Yet another teen sex comedy. Rated PG for profanity. 87m. DIR: Phillip Koch. CAST: Shaun Allen, Kevin Anderson. 1985

PINK PANTHER, THE ★★1/2 Peter Sellers is featured in his first bow as Inspector Jacques Clouseau, the inept French detective, on the trail of a jewel thief known as the Phantom in this, the original *Pink Panther.* This release has some good—and even hilarious—moments. But the sequel, *A Shot in the Dark*, is better. 113m. DIR: Blake Edwards. CAST: Peter Sellers, David Niven, Capucine, Claudia Cardinale, Robert Wagner. 1964 DVD

PINK PANTHER STRIKES AGAIN, THE ★★★1/2 Peter Sellers's fourth time out as the clumsy Inspector Clouseau. Clouseau's former supervisor, Herbert Lom, cracks up and tries to destroy the world with a superlaser. Meanwhile, he's hired a team of international killers to do away with Clouseau. One turns out to be Lesley-Anne Down, who falls in love with

the diminutive Frenchman. Rated PG. 103m. DIR: Blake Edwards. CAST: Peter Sellers, Herbert Lom, Lesley-Anne Down, Burt Kwouk, Colin Blakely. 1976 DVD

PINKY ★★★1/2 Still powerful story of a light-skinned black girl. She has been passing for white, but her status becomes known when she returns home to a small Mississippi town. Straightforward handling and presentation of what was then rather explosive material. Outstanding performances. B&W; 102m. DIR: Elia Kazan. CAST: Jeanne Crain, Ethel Barrymore, Ethel Waters, William Lundigan, Arthur Hunnicutt. 1949

PINOCCHIO (1940) ★★★★ In this timeless Walt Disney animated classic, a puppet made by a lonely old man gets the chance to become a real boy. *Pinocchio* is one of those rare motion pictures that can be enjoyed over and over again by adults as well as children. If you remember it as a "kid's show," watch it again. You'll be surprised at how wonderfully entertaining it is. Rated G. 87m. DIR: Walt Disney. 1940 DVD

PINOCCHIO (1983) ★★★★ An excellent adaptation of the classic tale about a wooden puppet who turns into a real boy. This *Faerie Tale Theatre* production, as with most of the others, will be best appreciated—and understood—by adults. It's blessed with just the right touch of humor, and Lainie Kazan is wonderful as the "Italian" fairy godmother. 51m. DIR: Peter Medak. CAST: James Coburn, Carl Reiner, Pee-wee Herman, James Belushi, Lainie Kazan, Don Novello. 1983

PINOCCHIO AND THE EMPEROR OF THE NIGHT ★★ This scary continuation of the classic tale features an incorrigible Pinocchio who manages to lose his father's prized jewel box as well as his own right to be a real boy. Animation is okay, but somehow you feel as though you're watching an overlong Saturday-morning cartoon. Edward Asner, Tom Bosley, James Earl Jones, Don Knotts, William Windom (voices). Rated G. 91m. DIR: Hal Sutherland. 1987

PINOCCHIO'S REVENGE ★★★1/2 This ain't no fairy tale. When a possessed wooden Pinocchio doll falls into the hands of an impressionable 8-year-old girl, he begins a vicious reign of terror. Rated R for violence and language. 96m. DIR: Kevin S. Tenney. CAST: Rosalind Allen, Lewis Van Bergen, Janet MacLachlan, Thomas Wagner, Brittany Alyse-Smith. 1996

PIONEER WOMAN ★★1/2 In this passable made-for-television movie, the trials and tribulations of homesteading in Wyoming during the 1860s are told through the point of view of a wife and mother. After her husband is killed, she must make the difficult decision about staying on or going back east. 78m. DIR: Buzz Kulik. CAST: Joanna Pettet, William Shatner, David Janssen, Lance LeGault, Helen Hunt. 1973

PIPE DREAMS 🎦 A wife moves to Alaska to win back her estranged man who is working on the pipeline. Rated PG for violence, profanity, and adult subject matter. 89m. DIR: Stephen F. Verona. CAST: Gladys Knight, Barry L. Hankerson, Bruce French, Wayne Tippitt. 1976

PIPPI LONGSTOCKING ★★ The adventures of the spunky, irrepressible heroine of Astrid Lindgren's popular children's books are turned into an inoffensive but inert animated feature, produced in Sweden and revamped in Canada for English-speaking audiences. The animation is colorful but flat, and the soundtrack is threadbare, with sparse sound effects and dinky orchestrations that fail to pump life into the forgettable musical score. Rated G. 75m. **DIR:** Bill Giggie, Michael Schaack, Clive Smith. **1997**

PIRANHA (1978) ★★★ Director Joe Dante and writer John Sayles sent up *Jaws* in this nifty, gag-filled horror film. Full of scares and chuckles. Rated R. 92m. **DIR:** Joe Dante. **CAST:** Bradford Dillman, Kevin McCarthy, Heather Menzies, Keenan Wynn. **1978 DVD**

PIRANHA (1995) ★★ The 1978 original had the intelligence to emerge as a parody, but this inept remake tries to play it straight … with lamentable results. Alexandra Paul and William Katt try to stop mutant killer fish from devouring campers. Rated R for gore, nudity, and profanity. 81m. **DIR:** Scott Levy. **CAST:** Alexandra Paul, William Katt, Darleen Carr, Soleil Moon Frye, James Karen, Monte Markham. **1995**

PIRANHA PART TWO: THE SPAWNING ★★ Sequel to *Piranha* by the man who would later give us with *The Terminator*. A mutated strain of piranha (with the ability to fly, no less) launches an air and sea tirade of violence against a group of vacationers at a tropical resort. Rated R for mild gore. 88m. **DIR:** James Cameron. **CAST:** Tricia O'Neil, Steve Marachuk, Lance Henriksen, Leslie Graves. **1981**

PIRATE, THE ★★★★ This splashy, though at times narratively weak, musical features Judy Garland and Gene Kelly singing and dancing their way through a Cole Porter score. It features a terrific dance sequence titled "Be a Clown" featuring clown-pirate-acrobat Kelly and the marvelous Nicholas Brothers. Watch it for the songs and the dances. 102m. **DIR:** Vincente Minnelli. **CAST:** Judy Garland, Gene Kelly, Gladys Cooper, Reginald Owen, Walter Slezak. **1948**

PIRATE MOVIE, THE ★★ This rock 'n' roll adaptation of Gilbert and Sullivan's *The Pirates of Penzance* is passable entertainment. Expect a lot of music, a lot of swashbuckling, and a little sappy romance. This film is rated PG for slight profanity and sexual innuendo. 99m. **DIR:** Ken Annakin. **CAST:** Christopher Atkins, Kristy McNichol, Ted Hamilton, Bill Kerr. **1982**

PIRATES 🎭 A turgid, overblown mess. Rated PG-13 for vulgarity. 117m. **DIR:** Roman Polanski. **CAST:** Walter Matthau, Cris Campion, Charlotte Lewis, Roy Kinnear. **1986**

PIRATES OF DARK WATERS, THE: THE SAGA BEGINS ★★★ Animated high seas adventure about a young prince who must restore his kingdom by discovering the secrets of thirteen hidden treasures. Voices by Dick Gautier, Hector Elizondo, Brock Peters, Tim Curry, Darleen Carr, and Roscoe Lee Browne. Not rated; contains violence. 90m. **DIR:** Don Lusk. **1991**

PIRATES OF PENZANCE, THE ★★★★ Stylized sets and takeoffs of Busby Berkeley camera setups give *Pirates* a true cinematic quality. Add to that outstanding work by the principals, some nice bits of slapstick comedy, and you have an enjoyable film for the entire family. Rated G. 112m. **DIR:** Wilford Leach.

CAST: Angela Lansbury, Kevin Kline, Linda Ronstadt, Rex Smith, George Rose. **1983 DVD**

•**PIRATES OF SILICON VALLEY** ★★★1/2 This TNT original paints an unflattering picture of the meteoric rise of Steve Jobs (Noah Wyle) at Apple Computers and the equally astounding expansion of Bill Gates (Anthony Michael Hall) and Microsoft Computers. Though the two men have different lifestyles, neither's image is unscathed as they "pirate" from any and all to get ahead. Good acting by the principals and a fourth-wall technique which allows the actors to step outside the story to reflect make this very watchable. Humor, sprinkled throughout, doesn't hurt either. Not rated; contains drug use and sexual situations. 90m. **DIR:** Martyn Burke. **CAST:** Noah Wyle, Anthony Michael Hall, John DiMaggio, Joey Slotnick. **1999**

PIRATES OF THE HIGH SEAS ★★ Buster Crabbe plays a rugged adventurer who sails to the aid of an old friend whose freight line is being sabotaged. This serial is pretty long in the tooth and if it weren't for the welcome presence of the heroic Crabbe, it would barely be worth watching. B&W; 15 chapters. **DIR:** Spencer Gordon Bennet, Thomas Carr. **CAST:** Buster Crabbe, Lois Hall, Tommy Farrell, Gene Roth, Tristram Coffin. **1950**

PIRATES OF THE PRAIRIE ★★★ Deputy marshal Tim Holt is assigned to go undercover as a gunsmith and find out why vigilantes have been terrorizing the citizens of East Spencerville. Solid effort from director Howard Bretherton in a series that managed to maintain an impressive standard of quality for its entire run. B&W; 57m. **DIR:** Howard Bretherton. **CAST:** Tim Holt, Cliff Edwards, Roy Barcroft. **1942**

PIRATES ON HORSEBACK ★★1/2 A gang murders a prospector before it finds where his diggings are. Hopalong Cassidy, Lucky, and California Carlson (a distant relative of the prospector) start their own search and take on the crime boss and his gang. B&W; 69m. **DIR:** Lesley Selander. **CAST:** William Boyd, Russell Hayden, Andy Clyde, Evelyn Stewart, Morris Ankrum (Stepen Morris). **1941**

PISTOL, THE: THE BIRTH OF A LEGEND ★★★★ Writer Darrel Campbell did a fantastic job of transforming the life of basketball great Pistol Pete Maravich into a delightful film. Adam Guier does a great job as the young Pistol and has the viewer rooting for him the entire time. Rated G. 104m. **DIR:** Frank C. Schroeder. **CAST:** Millie Perkins, Nick Benedict, Adam Guier. **1990**

PIT AND THE PENDULUM, THE (1961) ★★★ More stylish, low-budget Edgar Allan Poe–inspired terror with star Vincent Price and director Roger Corman reteaming for this release. This is for fans of the series only. 80m. **DIR:** Roger Corman. **CAST:** Vincent Price, John Kerr, Barbara Steele, Luana Anders, Anthony Carbone. **1961**

PIT AND THE PENDULUM, THE (1991) ★★ Gorefest claims to be based on Edgar Allan Poe's short story, but actually bears little resemblance to it. When a sympathetic woman tries to stop the beating of a small boy by Spanish Inquisition guards, she's imprisoned for witchcraft. Rated R for nudity, profanity, torture, and gore. 97m. **DIR:** Stuart Gordon.

CAST: Lance Henriksen, Rona De Ricci, Jonathan Fuller, Jeffrey Combs. **1991 DVD**

PITCH BLACK ★★1/2 A starship crash-lands on a desert planet with three suns. The planet is also inhabited by carnivorous creatures that thrive on darkness—and a rare solar eclipse is on the way. Director David Twohy has an excellent visual flair (the film really does seem to be on another planet) and performances are strong. Unfortunately, all are defeated by the script, a banal and predictable rehash of *Alien*. Rated R for violence. 107m. DIR: David N. Twohy. CAST: Vin Diesel, Radha Mitchell, Cole Hauser, Keith David, Lewis Fitz-Gerald, Claudia Black, Rhiana Griffith. **2000**

PITFALL ★★★ A tightly directed melodrama about a married man who strays and gets involved in a murder. Dick Powell made this one as a follow-up to *Murder, My Sweet*. This is the last movie Byron Barr made under that name; he changed it to Gig Young for future films. B&W; 84m. DIR: André de Toth. CAST: Dick Powell, Jane Wyatt, Lizabeth Scott, John Litel, Gig Young, Ann Doran, Raymond Burr, Dick Wessel. **1948**

PITTSBURGH ★★★ John Wayne dominates the screen as Pittsburgh Markham, an ambitious coal miner who risks it all to make his dreams come true. Interestingly, Pittsburgh is more of an opportunist than a hero. Somewhat slow and awkward, this is still a step up from most of Wayne's would-be Republic A-pictures from the same era. B&W; 90m. DIR: Lewis Seiler. CAST: Marlene Dietrich, Randolph Scott, John Wayne, Frank Craven, Louise Allbritton, Thomas Gomez, Shemp Howard, Ludwig Stossel, Paul Fix. **1942**

PIXOTE ★★★★ In Rio, half the population is younger than 18. Kids, only 10 or 12 years old, become thieves, beggars, and prostitutes. This is the story of one of these unfortunates. For some viewers it may be too powerful and disturbing, yet it is not the least bit exploitative or exaggerated. Rated R for violence, explicit sex, and nudity. 127m. DIR: Hector Babenco. CAST: Fernando Ramos Da Silva, Marilia Pera. **1981**

PIZZA MAN ★★★ Pizza delivery guy Elmo Bunn is caught in the middle of a campy worldwide conspiracy. Occasionally clever political satire. Not rated, but with some violence. 90m. DIR: J. D. Athens. CAST: Bill Maher, Annabelle Gurwitch. **1992**

P.K. & THE KID ★★★ Molly Ringwald, in one of her earliest films, is running away from her abusive father, Alex Rocco. She hitches up with Paul LeMat, who is driving to California for the annual armwrestling championships. The characters are well developed, and you can see a star in the making. 90m. DIR: Lou Lombardo. CAST: Paul LeMat, Molly Ringwald, Alex Rocco, Esther Rolle, John Madden. **1985**

PLACE CALLED TODAY, A 💔 Political drama laid in a city beset by racial strife. Also on video as *City in Fear*. Rated R for nudity and violence. 103m. DIR: Don Schain. CAST: J. Herbert Kerr Jr., Lana Wood, Cheri Caffaro. **1972**

PLACE CALLED TRINITY, A 💔 A gunfighting gambler and his brother, a Mormon preacher, have different ideas on how to spend their sizable inheritance,

but first they have to find the bandits who stole it. This idiotic comedy-Western filmed in Spain shows why spaghetti Westerns got their undeserved reputation. Only for the easily entertained. Not rated. 97m. DIR: James London. CAST: Richard Harrison, Donal O'Brien, Anna Zinneman, Rick Boyd. **1972**

PLACE FOR ANNIE, A ★★★★ This *Hallmark Hall of Fame* feature will restore your faith in mankind as Sissy Spacek brilliantly portrays a nurse whose heart is big enough not only for an HIV-positive infant but for the baby's rather unsavory mother as well. Top rate, not to be missed. Not rated; contains mature themes. 95m. DIR: John Gray. CAST: Sissy Spacek, Mary-Louise Parker, Joan Plowright, S. Epatha Merkerson, Jack Noseworthy. **1994**

PLACE IN THE SUN, A ★★★★ Elizabeth Taylor, Montgomery Clift, and Shelley Winters are caught in a tragic love triangle, based on Theodore Dreiser's *An American Tragedy*. All three artists give first-rate performances. The story of a working-class man who falls for a wealthy girl is a traditional one, yet the eroticism conveyed in the scenes between Taylor and Clift keeps this production well above the standard. B&W; 122m. DIR: George Stevens. CAST: Elizabeth Taylor, Montgomery Clift, Shelley Winters, Keefe Brasselle, Raymond Burr, Anne Revere. **1951**

PLACE OF WEEPING ★★★1/2 The first film about the South African struggle made by South Africans, this drama follows the battle of one woman who, with the help of a white reporter, stands against the system of apartheid. Although this film is a bit slow-moving and obviously made on a low budget, its political importance cannot be denied. Rated PG. 88m. DIR: Darrell Roodt. CAST: James Whylie, Geina Mhlope, Charles Comyn. **1986**

PLACES IN THE HEART ★★★★ Based on Robert Benton's childhood memories in Waxahachie, Texas, this film stars Sally Field, who plays Edna Spalding, a mother of two who is suddenly widowed. Almost immediately, she is pressured by the bank to sell her home and the surrounding property. Rated PG for suggested sex, violence, and profanity. 110m. DIR: Robert Benton. CAST: Sally Field, Ed Harris, Lindsay Crouse, John Malkovich, Danny Glover. **1984**

PLAGUE, THE ★★★★ The bubonic plague strikes a city in South America. A doctor (William Hurt), with the help of a French reporter and her videographer, battles both the disease and the local government. Raul Julia brilliantly portrays a local cab driver who isn't quite what he seems. A gripping story, well acted and directed. Rated R for nudity and violence. 105m. DIR: Luis Puenzo. CAST: William Hurt, Robert Duvall, Raul Julia, Sandrine Bonnaire, Jean-Marc Barr. **1993**

PLAGUE DOGS, THE ★★★★1/2 This animated film is definitely *not* for children. It is a powerfully disturbing film that makes an unforgettable statement about animal rights. In it, two dogs escape from an experimental veterinary lab in which they had both been subjected to cruel and senseless operations and tests. Once free, they are hunted by both the "white coats" (lab doctors) and the nearby sheep owners. Rated PG. 99m. DIR: Martin Rosen. **1984**

•PLAGUE OF THE ZOMBIES ★★★1/2 A couple of years before George Romero awoke the dead, Hammer produced this nifty little chiller. Here the zombies are resurrected by voodoo in order to work as slaves on a plantation mine in a Cornish village. The dead are stylishly presented, sets are high quality, and the direction captures the gloom and atmosphere of the surroundings. Recommended for fans of Hammer *and* zombie movies. 90m. **DIR:** John Gilling. **CAST:** Andre Morell, Diane Clare, Brook Williams, Jacqueline Pearce. **1966 DVD**

PLAIN CLOTHES ★★★1/2 A 24-year-old police detective (Arliss Howard) goes undercover as a high school student. From this not-very-promising plot, director Martha Coolidge and screenwriter A. Scott Frank have fashioned a marvelously tongue-in-cheek hybrid of mystery, teen comedy, and suspense thriller. Rated PG for profanity and violence. 100m. **DIR:** Martha Coolidge. **CAST:** Arliss Howard, Suzy Amis, George Wendt, Seymour Cassel, Abe Vigoda, Robert Stack, Harry Shearer. **1988**

PLAINSMAN, THE ★★★ If you can imagine a scenario uniting George Custer, Wild Bill Hickok, Calamity Jane, and Abraham Lincoln and you're willing to suspend historical disbelief, you should enjoy this stylish Cecil B. DeMille shoot-'em-up. Gary Cooper as Wild Bill Hickok does his best to keep Charles Bickford from selling guns to the Indians. B&W; 113m. **DIR:** Cecil B. DeMille. **CAST:** Gary Cooper, Jean Arthur, Charles Bickford, George "Gabby" Hayes. **1936**

PLAN B ★★★ Generation Xers realize their lives are going nowhere and consider moving on to Plan B. Jon Cryer is the novelist who is at a stalemate. He tags up with four of his friends on holiday and they sit around and wonder what went wrong. Angst-driven vehicles have been driven down this road before, but this one manages to make it to the end. Rated R for language. 102m. **DIR:** Gary Leva. **CAST:** Jon Cryer, Lance Guest, Lisa Darr, Mark Mathieson, Sara Mornell. **1997**

PLAN 9 FROM OUTER SPACE ★★★ Ever see a movie that was so bad it was funny? Well, this low-budget 1950s program is considered to be the very worst picture ever made, and it's hilarious. Written and directed by Edward D. Wood, it's a ponderous science-fiction cheapie that attempts to deliver an antiwar message as well as thrills and chills. It does neither. Even worse than the atrocious acting, cardboard sets, and moronic dialogue, Bela Lugosi is top-billed even though he had died months before. Undaunted, Wood used silent home-movie footage of the once-great horror film star. B&W; 79m. **DIR:** Edward D. Wood Jr. **CAST:** Bela Lugosi, Gregory Walcott, Tom Keene, Duke Moore, Mona McKinnon. **1959 DVD**

PLAN 10 FROM OUTER SPACE ♥ Despite the title, this would-be cult movie about alien Mormons has nothing to do with Ed Wood's anticlassic *Plan 9*—or anything else, as far as we could tell. Not rated; contains brief nudity and profanity. 85m. **DIR:** Trent Harris. **CAST:** Karen Black, Stefene Russell. **1996**

PLANES, TRAINS AND AUTOMOBILES ★★★ Although it tends to lose momentum in the last half, this screamingly funny film features Steve Martin

and John Candy at the peak of their comedic powers. Martin is an uptight marketing executive en route from New York to Chicago to celebrate Thanksgiving with his family, only to end up on a bizarre cross-country odyssey with an obnoxious bozo played by Candy. Rated R for profanity. 100m. **DIR:** John Hughes. **CAST:** Steve Martin, John Candy, Michael McKean, Laila Robins, Martin Ferrero, Charles Tyner. **1987**

PLANET EARTH ★★ After the original *Star Trek* went off the air but before it was revived on the big screen, creator Gene Roddenberry experimented with several failed television series pilots. *Planet Earth*, essentially Woody Allen's *Sleeper* as straight drama, was one of the silliest. Lead hunk John Saxon goes under in 1979 and awakens in 2133, only to discover that a "great catastrophe" has reshaped people into a series of iconoclastic colonies. 74m. **DIR:** Marc Daniels. **CAST:** John Saxon, Janet Margolin, Ted Cassidy, Diana Muldaur. **1974**

PLANET OF BLOOD (QUEEN OF BLOOD) ★★ Curtis Harrington's two-week wonder is the best of a handful of space operas cobbled together using footage from the late Fifties Soviet sci-fi epic, *Planet of Storms*. An expedition rescues a strange, mute alien, not realizing she's the vampire who wiped out a previous ship from Earth! Slow-paced but oddly fascinating. 81m. **DIR:** Curtis Harrington. **CAST:** John Saxon, Basil Rathbone, Judi Meredith, Dennis Hopper, Florence Marly. **1966**

PLANET OF THE APES ★★★★ Here is the first and best of the *Planet of the Ape* sci-fi series. Four American astronauts crash on a far-off planet and discover a culture where evolution has gone awry. The dominant form of primates are apes and gorillas. Man is reduced to a beast of burden. Much of the social comment is cutesy and forced, but this remains an enjoyable fantasy. Rated PG for violence. 112m. **DIR:** Franklin J. Schaffner. **CAST:** Charlton Heston, Kim Hunter, Roddy McDowall, Maurice Evans. **1968**

PLANET OF THE DINOSAURS ★★ A spacecraft crash-lands on a planet inhabited by dinosaurs. Juvenile time killer with decent animation effects. Rated PG. 85m. **DIR:** James K. Shea. **CAST:** James Whitworth. **1978**

PLANET OF THE VAMPIRES ★★ After landing on a mysterious planet, astronauts are possessed by formless alien vampires trying to reach Earth. An Italian-Spanish production, also known as *Demon Planet*. The film is plodding and poorly dubbed. Watch director Mario Bava's *Black Sunday* instead. 86m. **DIR:** Mario Bava. **CAST:** Barry Sullivan, Norma Bengell, Angel Aranda. **1965**

PLANTS ARE WATCHING, THE ★★1/2 Originally titled *The Kirlian Witness*, this low-budget melodrama is a well-intentioned fantasy about a clairvoyant woman who taps into the "minds" of plants. She uses the gift to learn the identity of the murderer of her sister. Clever and original, if unexciting. Not rated. 100m. **DIR:** Jonathan Sarno. **CAST:** Nancy Snyder, Joel Colodner, Nancy Boykin. **1978**

PLATINUM BLONDE ★★★★ Jean Harlow's namesake film shows her self-mocking style to advantage. She plays a rich girl who marries a poor newspaper reporter and drags herself up to his level of humanity. The story is similar to *It Happened One Night* but predated it by three years. B&W; 89m. DIR: Frank Capra. CAST: Jean Harlow, Loretta Young, Robert Williams. 1931

PLATINUM HIGH SCHOOL ★★ Overheated nonsense, good for a few laughs. Mickey Rooney as a grieving father trying to uncover the conspiracy of silence behind his son's "accidental" death at an exclusive school. B&W; 93m. DIR: Charles Haas. CAST: Mickey Rooney, Terry Moore, Dan Duryea, Yvette Mimieux, Conway Twitty. 1960

PLATOON ★★★★★ Writer-director Oliver Stone's Oscar-winning work is not just the best film made on the subject of Vietnam; it is a great cinematic work that stands high among the finest films ever made. Charlie Sheen is the well-meaning youth who volunteers for military service to become a real person instead of, in his words, "a fake human being." Not only does every step and noise bring the threat of death, but there is an intercompany war going on. Rated R for profanity, gore, and violence. 120m. DIR: Oliver Stone. CAST: Tom Berenger, Willem Dafoe, Charlie Sheen, Forest Whitaker, Francesco Quinn, John C. McGinley, Richard Edson. 1986

PLATOON LEADER ★ Leaden bore. Rated R for violence. 93m. DIR: Aaron Norris. CAST: Michael Dudikoff, Robert F. Lyons, Rick Fitts, William Smith. 1988

PLAY IT AGAIN, CHARLIE BROWN ★★★1/2 Lucy and Schroeder are featured in this animated Peanuts special that combines strong animation with some classic gags on unrequited love. Beethoven-loving Schroeder refuses to even notice Lucy, until she gets him a performing gig for a PTA benefit show. One major problem: he's been told to play rock music! Not rated. 25m. DIR: Bill Melendez. 1971

PLAY IT AGAIN, SAM ★★★★1/2 Woody Allen plays a movie columnist and feature writer who lives his life watching movies. Humphrey Bogart is his idol, and the film commences with the final scenes from *Casablanca.* Allen's wife leaves him, and the film revolves around some unsuccessful attempts by his friends (Diane Keaton and Tony Roberts) to set him up with a girl. In an age when funny movies may make you smile at best, this is an oasis of sidesplitting humor. Rated PG. 87m. DIR: Herbert Ross. CAST: Woody Allen, Diane Keaton, Tony Roberts, Jerry Lacy, Susan Anspach. 1972

●**PLAY IT TO THE BONE** 💔 In this stale road comedy, two middleweight boxing buddies hitch a ride from Los Angeles to Las Vegas with a woman who has dated them and then fight each other on the opening card for a Mike Tyson bout. Rated R for language, violence, and simulated sex. 125m. DIR: Ron Shelton. CAST: Woody Harrelson, Antonio Banderas, Lolita Davidovich, Tom Sizemore. 2000 DVD

PLAY MISTY FOR ME ★★★★ A suspenseful shocker in which director-star Clint Eastwood, playing a disc jockey, is stalked by a crazed fan (Jessica Walter). It puts goose bumps on your goose bumps and marked an auspicious directorial debut for the squinty-eyed star. Rated R. 102m. DIR: Clint Eastwood. CAST: Clint Eastwood, Jessica Walter, Donna Mills, John Larch, Irene Hervey. 1971

PLAY NICE ★★ A game of cat and mouse is played by an angry cop and a brutal serial killer. Predictable thriller. Rated R for violence and language. 89m. DIR: Terri Treas. CAST: Ed O'Ross. 1992

PLAYBACK ★★ Erotic video star Shannon Whirry plays a conniving businesswoman who will stop at nothing to rise to the top. With the help of a private detective, she begins her smear campaign on a rising executive whose position she wants. Predictable payoff. Rated R for nudity, adult situations, and language. 91m. DIR: Oley Sassone. CAST: Charles Grant, Shannon Whirry, George Hamilton, Tawny Kitaen, Harry Dean Stanton. 1995

PLAYBOY OF THE WESTERN WORLD ★★★★ Everything about this story is fresh and inspiring, especially the dialogue and accents. A wonderful adaptation of the classic Irish play about a young woman and her fellow villagers falling in love with a handsome roguish stranger. 100m. DIR: Brian Desmond Hurst. CAST: Siobhan McKenna, Gary Raymond, Michael O'Brian. 1962

PLAYBOYS, THE ★★★★ A sense of foreboding runs through this period piece based on coscreenwriter Shane Connaughton's childhood reminiscences of traveling troupes who performed at Irish villages in the 1950s. Robin Wright is splendid as the freethinking single mother who comes into conflict with the locals—until she's rescued from her situation by a flamboyant actor (Aidan Quinn). Rated PG-13 for profanity and violence. 113m. DIR: Gillies MacKinnon. CAST: Albert Finney, Aidan Quinn, Robin Wright, Milo O'Shea, Alan Devlin. 1992

PLAYER, THE ★★★★★ Robert Altman uses Michael Tolkin's screenplay to savage the motion-picture industry in a deft dark comedy about a sleazy studio executive who fears for his life when a screenwriter starts sending a series of threatening postcards. A must-see for movie buffs. Rated R for profanity, violence, and nudity. 123m. DIR: Robert Altman. CAST: Tim Robbins, Greta Scacchi, Fred Ward, Whoopi Goldberg, Peter Gallagher, Brion James, Cynthia Stevenson, Vincent D'Onofrio, Dean Stockwell, Richard E. Grant, Sydney Pollack, Lyle Lovett, Dina Merrill. 1992 DVD

PLAYERS 💔 Ali MacGraw is the bored mistress of Maximilian Schell; she falls for tennis pro Dean Paul Martin. Rated PG—sexual situations. 120m. DIR: Anthony Harvey. CAST: Ali MacGraw, Dean Paul Martin, Maximilian Schell. 1979

PLAYERS CLUB, THE ★★ A single parent works her way through college as a stripper in the South. She is dubbed Diamond by a greedy boss who spends the entire film dodging a loan shark. Diamond tries to keep her cousin out of trouble when she also starts gyrating at the club. The film has a sassy, gritty realism that is burdened with stereotypical characters and a jaded message: "Make the money. Don't let the money make you." Rated R for language, sexual content, and violence. 103m. DIR: Ice Cube . CAST: Lisa Raye, Chrystale Wilson, Bernie Mac, Jamie Foxx, Monica Calhoun, Ice Cube. 1998 DVD

PLAYGIRL KILLER, THE 💔 An insane painter kills his models and stores them in deep freeze. This Canadian film is not rated. 90m. DIR: Enrick Santamaran. **CAST:** William Kirwin, Jean Christopher, Neil Sedaka. **1969**

●**PLAYING BY HEART** ★★★★ Terrific romantic comedy about a family and their lives with excellent performances throughout, especially by Gillian Anderson, Jon Stewart, and Sean Connery in a decidedly different role. Rated R for profanity. 121m. **DIR:** Willard Carroll. **CAST:** Sean Connery, Gena Rowlands, Gillian Anderson, Jon Stewart, Ryan Phillippe. **1998 DVD**

PLAYING FOR KEEPS 🎬 Teenagers inherit a dilapidated hotel and turn it into a rock 'n' roll resort for kids. Rated PG-13 for profanity, violence, nudity, and suggested sex. 103m. **DIR:** Bob Weinstein, Harvey Weinstein. **CAST:** Daniel Jordano, Matthew Penn, Leon W. Grant, Harold Gould, Jimmy Baio. **1986**

PLAYING FOR TIME ★★★★ This outstanding TV drama won numerous Emmy Awards. It's the true story of Fania Fenelon (Vanessa Redgrave) and a group of women prisoners in Auschwitz who survived by forming a small orchestra and performing for the Nazi officers. 148m. **DIR:** Daniel Mann. **CAST:** Vanessa Redgrave, Jane Alexander, Maud Adams, Viveca Lindfors, Shirley Knight. **1980**

PLAYING GOD ★★ Unlicensed L.A. surgeon performs surgery on a shooting victim in a bar. He then becomes the personal physician for a sleazy smuggler, falls in love with the hoodlum's girlfriend, and is dogged by federal investigators before stumbling into redemption. The premise is smart and spooky, but this overly bloody thriller is more worried about being cool than convincing. Rated R for violence, language, and drug use. 94m. **DIR:** Andy Wilson. **CAST:** David Duchovny, Timothy Hutton, Angelina Jolie. **1997 DVD**

PLAYING THE FIELD 🎬 Moronic Italian comedy about an ambitious soccer referee. Poorly dubbed. Contains profanity and sexual situations. 90m. **DIR:** Louis D'Amico. **CAST:** Lando Buzzanca, Joan Collins. **1974**

PLAYMAKER ★★ Would-be starlet Jennifer Rubin seeks cinematic glory in this turgid erotic thriller, whose climactic plot twists cannot compensate for a first hour laden with pretentious pop psychology and unfocused execution. By the time the story smartens up, you'll be long past caring. Rated R for nudity, profanity, and violence. 91m. **DIR:** Yuri Zeltser. **CAST:** Colin Firth, Jennifer Rubin, John Getz, Jeff Perry. **1994**

PLAYMATES ★★★★ This is a very good romantic comedy about two divorced men who become friends and then secretly begin to date each other's ex-wife, with crazy results. Good cast, fine direction, and an energized screenplay by Richard Baer make this TV movie sparkle. 73m. **DIR:** Theodore J. Flicker. **CAST:** Alan Alda, Connie Stevens, Barbara Feldon, Doug McClure, Severn Darden, Roger Bowen, Eileen Brennan. **1972**

PLAYROOM ★★ Bizarre plot unfolds when an immortal prince draws a young archaeologist back to the site of his parents' murder. Adequate. Rated R for nudity, profanity, violence, and gore. 87m. **DIR:** Manny Coto. **CAST:** Lisa Aliff, Aron Eisenberg, Christopher McDonald, Vincent Schiavelli. **1989**

PLAYTIME ★★★1/2 Mr. Hulot is back again in this slapstick comedy as he attempts to keep an appointment in the big city. Paris and all of its buildings, automobiles, and population seem to conspire to thwart Mr. Hulot at every turn, and there are plenty of visual gags. The subtitled American release version is over thirty minutes shorter than the original French release. 108m. **DIR:** Jacques Tati. **CAST:** Jacques Tati. **1967 DVD**

PLAZA SUITE ★★★1/2 Walter Matthau is at his comic best as he re-creates three separate roles from Neil Simon's stage comedy. The movie is actually three tales of what goes on in a particular suite. Rated PG. 115m. **DIR:** Arthur Hiller. **CAST:** Walter Matthau, Maureen Stapleton, Barbara Harris, Lee Grant. **1971**

PLEASANTVILLE ★★★★ This sly, provocative allegory reveals the shortcomings of 1950s-style sitcom "utopias" in a manner that is as subversive as the ingenious storyline. During the film's first half, you'll giggle and gasp at the execution of the witty premise: two modern-day teens get zapped back into the black-and-white universe of a vintage television situation comedy, where they're unable to resist "meddling" with the quaintly idealistic values found within the picture-perfect setting. The film initially exaggerates these old-fashioned conventions, and it's hard not to laugh ... until we see what happens when *any* establishment grows uneasy about change. It's astonishing to consider that 1998 brought us this film and *The Truman Show*, two similarly creative and enlightening allegories, with each disclosing the limitations of artificially ideal environments. Rated PG for profanity and sexual candor. 124m. **DIR:** Gary Ross. **CAST:** Tobey Maguire, Jeff Daniels, Reese Witherspoon, Joan Allen, William H. Macy, J. T. Walsh. **1998 DVD**

PLEASE DON'T EAT MY MOTHER! ★★ Uncredited remake of *Little Shop of Horrors* is even worse—and almost as funny. Middle-aged Henry Fudd (Buck Kartalian, who also directed under a pseudonym) takes time out from being a peeping Tom to feed murder victims to his man- (and woman-) eating plant. Cheesy but fun. Also known as *Hungry Pets*. Not rated; plentiful nudity. 98m. **DIR:** Jack Beckett. **CAST:** Buck Kartalian. **1972**

PLEASE DON'T EAT THE DAISIES ★★★ Witty David Niven meets his match when he crosses Doris Day's path and questions her ambitions. A clever comedy about a drama critic who copes with his wife's remodeling plans and a conniving actress friend at the same time. Based on Jean Kerr's bestseller and the basis for a TV series during the 1960s. 111m. **DIR:** Charles Walters. **CAST:** Doris Day, David Niven, Janis Paige, Spring Byington, Margaret Lindsay, Richard Haydn, Patsy Kelly, Jack Weston. **1960**

PLEASURE PALACE ★★ No, this is not a porno flick—the characters in this made-for-TV movie are more like old-fashioned melodrama icons. Hope Lange plays an honest widowed casino owner (yea!) who is afraid she will lose her casino to an influential oil baron (boo!). Despite the lack of subtlety in characters, some of the gambling scenes have real tension in them. Not rated, but the equivalent of a PG for violence. 92m. DIR: Walter Grauman. CAST: Omar Sharif, Victoria Principal, Walter Grauman, J. D. Cannon, Gerald S. O'Loughlin, José Ferrer, Hope Lange. 1980

PLEASURE UNLIMITED 💔 A woman leaves her husband and tries to deal with the sexual revolution in this potboiler written by Ed Wood. Not rated; contains nudity and strong sexual situations. 72m. DIR: A. C. Stephen. CAST: Angela Carnon, Terry Johnson, Lynn Harris. 1973

PLEDGE NIGHT ★★★1/2 A nicely original horror movie about a group of fraternity guys who are menaced by the ghost of a pledge killed in their house twenty years ago. Inspired special effects keep this from being just another meat-dead-slasher movie. Not rated; contains violence, nudity, and profanity. 90m. DIR: Paul Ziller. CAST: Todd Eastland, Shannon McMahon, Joey Belladonna, Will Kempe. 1988

PLENTY ★★★★ In this difficult but rewarding film, Meryl Streep is superb as a former member of the French Resistance who finds life in her native England increasingly maddening during the postwar reconstruction period. Rated R for profanity, suggested sex, and violence. 120m. DIR: Fred Schepisi. CAST: Meryl Streep, Charles Dance, Sam Neill, Tracey Ullman, John Gielgud, Sting, Ian McKellen. 1985 DVD

PLOT AGAINST FATHER, THE ★★★★ Shot in a casual black-and-white style that matches the material, this is a tale of the misadventures of an amiable Jewish racketeer, freshly released from prison. Witty satire on middle-class Jewish immigrant life. Not rated, but of PG-13 tone. B&W; 81m. DIR: Michael Roemer. CAST: Martin Priest. 1969

PLOT TO KILL HITLER, THE ★★★1/2 Moderately entertaining thriller documents the attempted coup to overthrow Adolf Hitler. Not rated. 93m. DIR: Lawrence Schiller. CAST: Brad Davis, Madolyn Smith, Ian Richardson, Kenneth Colley, Jonathan Hyde, Rupert Everett. 1990

PLOUGHMAN'S LUNCH, THE ★★ A morality piece about opportunism and exploitation portrayed through the world of journalism. The problem is that almost everyone in the film is a weasel. The point is to call attention to this fact, but it doesn't make for very enjoyable movie watching. Rated R. 107m. DIR: Richard Eyre. CAST: Jonathan Pryce, Tim Curry, Rosemary Harris, Frank Finlay, Charlie Dore. 1984

PLOW THAT BROKE THE PLAINS, THE ★★★★ Written, directed, and produced by master documentarian Pare Lorentz, with a musical score by Virgil Thomson, this cornerstone film is a moving and dramatic account of man's abuse of America's Great Plains: Grass is its heroine, sun and wind its villain, its players nameless farmers whose farming practices produced the Dust Bowl and the Oklahoma-Kansas-Nebraska exodus. Coupled with it is "Night Mail," the John Grierson film tribute to the British postal and railway systems. B&W; 49m. DIR: Pare Lorentz. 1934–1936

PLUMBER, THE ★★★1/2 A slightly unhinged plumber completely destroys a young couple's bathroom and begins to terrorize the woman of the house during his visits to make the repairs. A very black comedy-horror-film from the director of Witness.

Originally made for Australian television. No rating; contains some strong language. 76m. DIR: Peter Weir. CAST: Ivar Kants, Judy Morris, Robert Coleby. 1980

PLUNDER ROAD ★★ This ingenious update to The Great Train Robbery leaves five men on the run with $10 million in gold. The crime-does-not-pay theme prevails. The acting is not the greatest. B&W; 76m. DIR: Hubert Cornfield. CAST: Gene Raymond, Wayne Morris, Jeanne Cooper. 1957

PLUNKETT & MACLEANE ★★1/2 Two rogues become known in 1748 London as the Gentlemen Highwaymen. Their story relies heavily on predictable Western contours as the scoundrels slowly bond while robbing filthy rich aristocrats. They soon attain mythic reputations and are pursued by a sadistic lawman who likes to gouge out the eyes of his captives. This sometimes rousing crime-adventure is thick with atmosphere and cinematic flash but thin on character development and credible romance. Rated R for violence, language, and sex. 95m. DIR: Jake Scott. CAST: Robert Carlyle, Jonny Lee Miller, Ted Stott, Liv Tyler. 1999 DVD

PLUTONIUM BABY 💔 A heroic, shape-changing mutant squares off with his evil counterpart in New York City. Not rated; contains violence and nudity. 85m. DIR: Ray Hirschman. CAST: Patrick Molloy, Danny Guerra. 1987

POCAHONTAS (1994) ★★★ One of several recent releases about a peace-loving Indian girl, this is an Enchanted Tale presented by Golden Films. Despite a lack of big bucks found in the Disney production, this manages to have decent animation and pleasant original tunes. Pocahontas, here, has a talking canoe, an eagle, and a hawk as advisers. Her adventures in England are also covered, along with her romance with John Smith. 48m. DIR: Kamoon Song. 1994

POCAHONTAS (1995) ★★★★ While not an instant classic on a par with other contemporary animated musicals from the Disney Studios, Pocahontas is still a genuine pleasure, with fine songs (by Alan Menken and Stephen Schwartz), superb animation, and a story that will entertain young and old alike. Enjoy another triumph from the studio that makes the world's finest feature-length cartoons. Rated G. 87m. DIR: Mike Gabriel, Eric Goldberg. 1995 DVD

POCKET MONEY ★★1/2 Cowpoke Paul Newman and con man Lee Marvin fall in with a calculating cattleman and spend the rest of the film getting themselves out of it. Likable enough but really doesn't go anywhere. 102m. DIR: Stuart Rosenberg. CAST: Paul Newman, Lee Marvin, Christine Belford, Strother Martin, Kelly Jean Peters, Wayne Rogers. 1972

POCKETFUL OF MIRACLES ★★★ The term Capracorn could have been coined in response to this overly sentimental picture, basically a remake of the director's 1933 Lady for a Day. But Bette Davis is a delight as Apple Annie and Glenn Ford is winningly earnest as the producer who tries to turn her into a lady. Ann-Margret's film debut. 136m. DIR: Frank Capra. CAST: Bette Davis, Glenn Ford, Hope Lange, Thomas Mitchell, Peter Falk, Edward Everett Horton, Jack Elam, Ann-Margret. 1961

POCKETFUL OF RYE, A ★★1/2 Agatha Christie's Miss Marple (Joan Hickson) arrives late in this mystery, which concerns a murder that is somehow connected with a nursery rhyme. Not rated, suitable for family viewing. 102m. **DIR:** Guy Slater. **CAST:** Joan Hickson, Peter Davison, Fabia Drake, Timothy West, Tom Wilkinson, Clive Merrison. **1984**

POETIC JUSTICE ★★ Director John Singleton's follow-up to *Boyz N the Hood* is essentially a self-indulgent mess about the offbeat love affair between a self-styled poet (Janet Jackson, in her film debut) and a troubled young man (Tupac Shakur). Jackson's inexpressive performance is further hampered by her inappropriate, overdubbed readings of Maya Angelou's poetry. Rated R for profanity, simulated sex, and violence. 108m. **DIR:** John Singleton. **CAST:** Janet Jackson, Tupac Shakur, Regina King, Joe Torry, Tyra Ferrell, Maya Angelou. **1993 DVD**

POINT, THE ★★★★1/2 The cartoon adventures of Oblio, a little boy who is banished from his homeland because (unlike everyone else there) his head doesn't come to a point. Completely irresistible for kids and grownups, with narration by Ringo Starr and songs by Harry Nilsson (including "Me and My Arrow"). Made for TV. 74m. **DIR:** Fred Wolf. **1971**

POINT BLANK (1967) ★★★★ This brutal crime-drama is one of the finest films of its type. Gangster Lee Marvin is double-crossed by his wife and crime partner, who shoot him and leave him for dead on Alcatraz Island—only to have him turn up a few years later, bent on revenge. Entire cast pulls out all of the stops; it's one of Lee Marvin's strongest performances. Rated R. 92m. **DIR:** John Boorman. **CAST:** Lee Marvin, Angie Dickinson, Lloyd Bochner, Keenan Wynn, Carroll O'Connor, John Vernon. **1967**

POINT BLANK (1998) ★★ When a busload of death-row inmates is ambushed and taken over by the prisoners, the jail break catches the attention of former cop turned mercenary Rudy Ray who has a brother on board the bus. Things heat up when the inmates take a mall hostage, leaving Ray and his former partner the only two people who can get inside and save the day. Been there, done that. Rated R for violence, language, and adult situations. 90m. **DIR:** Matt Earl Beesley. **CAST:** Mickey Rourke, Frederic Forrest, Kevin Gage, Michael Wright, Danny Trejo, James Gammon. **1998 DVD**

POINT BREAK ★★★1/2 For most of its running time, this release, about two FBI agents (Keanu Reeves, Gary Busey) attempting to catch the perpetrators (who may be led by surfer/guru Patrick Swayze) behind a series of bank robberies, is a terrific action movie. But *Point Break* tends to overstay its welcome with more false endings than we've ever seen. Rated R for violence and profanity. 125m. **DIR:** Kathryn Bigelow. **CAST:** Patrick Swayze, Keanu Reeves, Gary Busey, Lori Petty, John C. McGinley, James LeGros. **1991**

POINT OF IMPACT ★★1/2 A talented cast is wasted in this humdrum cop thriller where plot exists only to fill the spaces between the energetic coupling by Michael Paré and Barbara Carrera. He's a former U.S. Customs agent, she's a crime lord's wife needing protection from parties never adequately specified.

Available in both R and unrated versions, each with considerable profanity, violence, nudity, and simulated sex. 96m. **DIR:** Bob Misiorowski. **CAST:** Michael Paré, Barbara Carrera, Michael Ironside, Lehua Reid. **1993**

POINT OF NO RETURN ★★★ American, scene-for-scene remake of French director Luc Besson's *La Femme Nikita* lacks the subtlety and poignance of the original. Instead, director John Badham puts the emphasis on violence, with street punk Bridget Fonda drafted as an assassin by a supersecret government organization. Fonda's committed performance is the only high-quality element in this no-excuses action romp. Rated R for violence, profanity, nudity, and simulated sex. 108m. **DIR:** John Badham. **CAST:** Bridget Fonda, Gabriel Byrne, Dermot Mulroney, Anne Bancroft, Harvey Keitel, Miguel Ferrer, Olivia D'Abo, Richard Romanus, Geoffrey Lewis. **1993 DVD**

POINTSMAN, THE ★★★ A lady from Holland mysteriously disembarks from a train in the Scottish Highlands. The only person at the depot is the point man who resides at this isolated outpost. This most unusual film requires patience, but it has a strangely compelling attraction. The interesting characters, the fine photography, and the sensual development between the two leads keep you rapt until the end. Rated R for nudity and adult situations. 95m. **DIR:** Jos Stelling. **CAST:** Stephane Excoffier. **1988**

POIROT (SERIES) ★★★★★ Agatha Christie's endearing and eccentric private detective, Hercule Poirot—a Belgian policeman who fled to England in 1914 as a refugee—is perfectly portrayed by David Suchet in this engaging series of mysteries faithfully dramatized by Clive Exton. Poirot—joined by his faithful companion Captain Hastings and loyal and efficient secretary Miss Lemon—solves a variety of murder mysteries with panache. Highlights include "Murder in the Mews," in which Poirot and his friend, Inspector Japp of Scotland Yard, work together to solve a murder; "Triangle at Rhodes," filmed on location in the beautiful Greek islands, with a wonderfully tricky plot and an intriguing cast of characters; and "Problem at Sea," where Poirot and Hastings's Mediterranean cruise soon turns into a busman's holiday. each tape. 52m. **DIR:** Edward Bennett, Renny Rye. **CAST:** David Suchet, Hugh Fraser, Philip Jackson, Pauline Moran. **1989 DVD**

POISON ★★ Disturbing, at times disgusting, trilogy of stories spliced together jumping back and forth from one horror to the next. In one, a seven-year-old murders his father; another features a mad scientist whose experiment transforms him into a leper; and finally there's a cruel glimpse into a sadistic homosexual relationship behind prison bars. Not rated, contains nudity, violence, and profanity. 85m. **DIR:** Todd Haynes. **CAST:** Edith Meeks, Larry Maxwell, Susan Norman, Scott Renderer, James Lyons. **1990 DVD**

POISON IVY (1985) ★★ Top talents save this banal TV movie about life at a summer camp. Michael J. Fox is the hip counselor; Nancy McKeon is an assistant nurse and Fox's love interest; and Robert Klein is the bombastic camp director. All right for idle watching. 97m. **DIR:** Larry Elikann. **CAST:** Michael J.

Fox, Nancy McKeon, Robert Klein, Caren Kaye, Jason Bateman, Adam Baldwin. **1985**

POISON IVY (1992) ★★★1/2 Drew Barrymore makes a heck of an impact in a very adult role as Ivy, a sleazy teen who is taken in by a wealthy family. Ivy likes what she sees, especially dad (Tom Skerritt), whom she slowly seduces as she works to make the family her own. Rated R for profanity and suggested sex. 92m. **DIR:** Katt Shea Ruben. **CAST:** Drew Barrymore, Sara Gilbert, Tom Skerritt, Cheryl Ladd. **1992**

POISON IVY 2: LILY ★★ Former child actress Alyssa Milano takes another step to erase her goody-goody image. Here she plays an art student who stumbles across the diary of Ivy from the first film. Ivy's words inspire her to explore her own sexual desires. Rated R for nudity and adult language. Unrated version also available. 112m. **DIR:** Anne Goursand. **CAST:** Alyssa Milano, Xander Berkeley, Jonathan Scaech. **1995 DVD**

POISON IVY: THE NEW SEDUCTION ★★ Pointless sequel covers pretty much the same territory as the previous two entries in this sagging franchise. Newcomer Jaime Pressly stars as Violet, the evil sister of the original Ivy, who returns to her hometown to wreak havoc on the family she believes betrayed her sister. Violet systematically seduces her best friend's father and fiancé as retribution. Just another excuse to rehash a once-popular formula. R-rated and unrated versions; both contain nudity, violence, and language. 93/95m. **DIR:** Kurt Voss. **CAST:** Jaime Pressly, Michael Des Barres, Megan Edwards, Greg Vaughan, Susan Tyrrell. **1997**

POISONOUS PLANTS ★★ A disillusioned journalist gets caught up in the lives of a teenage prostitute, a man falsely imprisoned for murder, and a botanist who raises poisonous plants. Unengaging drama set in contemporary Poland. In Polish with English subtitles. Not rated. 70m. **DIR:** Robert Glinsky. **CAST:** Boguslaw Linda. **1975**

•POKÉMON THE FIRST MOVIE: MEWTWO STRIKES BACK ★★ Japan's animated pocket monsters and human trainers leap from TV into feature films with this preachy adventure about fighting being the wrong way to settle issues. The mysterious Mew, a powerful Pokémon, is cloned by scientists into the even more powerful Mewtwo. When Mewtwo realizes he is a man-made freak and decides humans are evil, he raises havoc with an army of clones. Rated G. 69m. **DIR:** Kunihiko Yuyama. **1999 DVD**

POKER ALICE ★★1/2 A nifty supporting cast outclasses Elizabeth Taylor in this poky TV movie. Liz seems bored playing a New Orleans gambler who travels to the Old West and wins a bordello in a poker game. 109m. **DIR:** Arthur Allan Seidelman. **CAST:** Elizabeth Taylor, Tom Skerritt, George Hamilton, Susan Tyrrell, Richard Mulligan, David Wayne. **1987**

POLAR BEAR KING, THE ★★★ In this slow-moving fairy tale, a prince is turned into a polar bear by a wicked witch. He travels north and encounters a young woman. They fall in love and battle the evil crone together. Rated PG. 87m. **DIR:** Ola Solum. **CAST:** Maria Bonnevie, Jack Fieldstad, Tobias Hoesl, Anna-Lotta Larsson, Jon Laxdal, Monica Nordquist. **1992**

POLICE ★★1/2 Dull crime-drama about a tough French cop (Gérard Depardieu), who becomes emotionally involved with a beautiful drug dealer (Sophie Marceau). Not much chemistry between the central characters. In French with English subtitles. Not rated; contains nudity and profanity. 113m. **DIR:** Maurice Pialat. **CAST:** Gérard Depardieu, Sophie Marceau, Richard Anconina, Sandrine Bonnaire. **1985**

POLICE ACADEMY ★★ Here's another *Animal House*–style comedy that tries very hard to be funny. Sometimes it is, and sometimes it isn't. Rated R for nudity, violence, and profanity. 95m. **DIR:** Hugh Wilson. **CAST:** Steve Guttenberg, George Gaynes, Kim Cattrall, Bubba Smith, Michael Winslow, Andrew Rubin. **1984 DVD**

POLICE ACADEMY II: THEIR FIRST ASSIGNMENT ★★ Those inept would-be officers from Hugh Wilson's *Police Academy* return in this less funny but still box-office–potent production. Episodic and silly. Rated PG-13 for profanity. 90m. **DIR:** Jerry Paris. **CAST:** Steve Guttenberg, Bubba Smith, David Graf, Michael Winslow, Bruce Mahler, Colleen Camp, Marion Ramsey, Howard Hesseman, George Gaynes. **1985**

POLICE ACADEMY III: BACK IN TRAINING 💔 Moronic. Rated PG for silly violence and references to body parts. 90m. **DIR:** Jerry Paris. **CAST:** Steve Guttenberg, Bubba Smith, Michael Winslow, Marion Ramsey, Leslie Easterbrook, Art Metrano, Tim Kazurinsky, Bob Goldthwait, George Gaynes. **1986**

POLICE ACADEMY 4: CITIZENS ON PATROL 💔 Let's just say that if you liked the first three, there's no reason you shouldn't like the fourth. Rated PG for mild profanity. 87m. **DIR:** Jim Drake. **CAST:** Steve Guttenberg, Bubba Smith, Michael Winslow, David Graf, Tim Kazurinsky, Sharon Stone, G. W. Bailey, Bob Goldthwait. **1987**

POLICE ACADEMY 5: ASSIGNMENT: MIAMI BEACH 💔 Silly fifth entry in the series. Rated PG for language and ribald humor. 90m. **DIR:** Alan Myerson. **CAST:** Bubba Smith, David Graf, Michael Winslow, Leslie Easterbrook, Marion Ramsey, Janet Jones, René Auberjonois. **1988**

POLICE ACADEMY 6: CITY UNDER SIEGE 💔 Rated PG for violence and profanity. 87m. **DIR:** Peter Bonerz. **CAST:** Bubba Smith, Kenneth Mars, George Gaynes, David Graf, Michael Winslow, G. W. Bailey. **1989**

POLICE ACADEMY: MISSION TO MOSCOW 💔 Totally unfunny sequel finds the remaining inept recruits helping Moscow solve its problems. The only laugh is that they shot this turkey on location. Did someone say Cold War? Rated PG for slapstick violence. 83m. **DIR:** Alan Metter. **CAST:** George Gaynes, Michael Winslow, David Graf, Leslie Esterbrook, Charlie Schlatter. **1994**

POLICE SQUAD! ★★★★ Originally a 1982 summer TV show, with only six episodes aired, this is now a minor cult classic. The folks who made *Airplane!* went all out on this. Each one of the episodes is hilarious, much funnier than the popular film *Police Academy*. 75m. **DIR:** Jim Abrahams, David Zucker, Jerry Zucker, Joe Dante, Reza S. Badiyi. **CAST:** Leslie Nielsen, Alan North. **1982**

POLICE STORY III—SUPER COP ★★★★ With fantastic stunts, snappy touches of comedy, international locales, and a likable lead actor, this Hong Kong import comes extremely close to matching action films such as *Lethal Weapon*. Jackie Chan is a Hong Kong cop who goes undercover in Communist China in an effort to flush out a nasty drug lord. Chan—who does all his own stunts—really makes this a winner. In Cantonese with English subtitles. Not rated; contains violence and brief profanity. 100m. DIR: Stanley Tong. CAST: Jackie Chan, Michelle Yeoh, Maggie Cheung, Ken Tsang, Yuen Wah, Bill Tung, Josephine Koo. 1992

POLISH VAMPIRE IN BURBANK, A ★★1/2 Low-budget, sophomoric horror-comedy that, nonetheless, provides a few laughs. Mark Pirro plays a "virgin" vampire. His sultry sister, another vampire, takes him out one night for a bite. One of those films that you giggle at, then feel very sheepish. Not rated; contains sexual suggestion and some ghoulish violence. 84m. DIR: Mark Pirro. CAST: Mark Pirro, Lori Sutton, Eddie Deezen. 1985

POLISH WEDDING ★★1/2 In Chicago, the sexual maturity of a teenage girl causes consternation for her Polish-American family, headed by Lena Olin (who is Swedish) and Gabriel Byrne (Irish). *Polish Wedding* wants to be to Polish Americans what *Moonstruck* was to Italian Americans but wholly lacks that film's sense of whimsy and romance. Rated PG-13 for profanity and sexual situations. 101m. DIR: Theresa Connelly. CAST: Claire Danes, Lena Olin, Gabriel Byrne, Rade Serbedzija. 1998 DVD

POLLYANNA (1920) ★★★1/2 Mary Pickford (at age 27 in 1920) portrays 12-year-old Pollyanna as she melts the hearts of everyone. If you admire silent films or Pickford, or both, you should see this one. B&W; 78m. DIR: Paul Powell. CAST: Mary Pickford, Katharine Griffith, Howard Ralston. 1920

POLLYANNA (1960) ★★★1/2 Walt Disney's version of this classic childhood book is good entertainment for the whole family. Hayley Mills is the energetic and optimistic young girl who improves the lives of everyone she meets. Jane Wyman, Agnes Moorehead, and Adolphe Menjou head an exceptional supporting cast for this film. 134m. DIR: David Swift. CAST: Hayley Mills, Jane Wyman, Agnes Moorehead, Adolphe Menjou, Karl Malden, Nancy Olson. 1960

POLTERGEIST ★★★★★ The ultimate screen ghost story, this is guaranteed to raise goose pimples while keeping viewers marvelously entertained. A sort of *Close Encounters* of the supernatural, it's a scary story about the plight of a suburban family whose home suddenly becomes a house of horrors. Rated PG for tense situations. 114m. DIR: Tobe Hooper. CAST: Craig T. Nelson, JoBeth Williams, Beatrice Straight, Dominique Dunne. 1982 DVD

POLTERGEIST II: THE OTHER SIDE ★★ Mere months (screen time) after their last film adventure, the stalwart Freeling family is up to its eyeballs in spooks again—although the ghosts stay backstage while another collection of effects parades before the audience. The whole project collapses under its own weight. Rated PG-13 for violence. 92m. DIR: Brian-Gibson. CAST: JoBeth Williams, Craig T. Nelson,

Heather O'Rourke, Oliver Robins, Zelda Rubinstein, Will Sampson, Geraldine Fitzgerald. 1986

POLTERGEIST III 🎬 Little Carol Ann (Heather O'Rourke) moves to Chicago to attend a school for gifted children with mental disorders. Rated PG-13 for violence. 90m. DIR: Gary A. Sherman. CAST: Tom Skerritt, Nancy Allen, Heather O'Rourke, Zelda Rubinstein. 1988

POLTERGEIST: THE LEGACY ★★★ This moderately entertaining cable-series pilot has nothing to do with the *Poltergeist* series. Dedicated good guy Derek de Lint assembles a crew of resourceful demon chasers to track an evil entity that has impregnated an unsuspecting woman; the delivery of that infant must be seen to be believed. Rated R for nudity, rape, violence, gore, and profanity. 90m. DIR: Stuart Gillard. CAST: Derek de Lint, Martin Cummins, Robbi Chong, Patrick Fitzgerald, Alexandra Purvis, Helen Shaver, Bill Sadler. 1996

POLYESTER ★★ Anyone for bad taste? Female impersonator Divine and 1950s heartthrob Tab Hunter play lovers in this film by writer-producer-director John Waters (*Pink Flamingos*). A special gimmick called "Odorama" allowed viewers to experience the story's various smells via a scratch-and-sniff card. Rated R. 86m. DIR: John Waters. CAST: Divine, Tab Hunter, Edith Massey, Mary Garlington. 1981

POLYMORPH ★★★1/2 Exciting action-based sci-fi film that has a meteor crashing on Earth and bringing with it an organism that can emulate its victims. Into the woods comes a group of people who run into a drug runner infected with the organism. What follows is a clever tale of paranoia that has everyone questioning who is still himself. Not rated; contains violence, profanity, and gore. 86m. DIR: J. R. Bookwalter. CAST: James L. Edwards, Ariauna Albright, Sasha Graham, Joseph Daw, Jennifer Huss. 1996

POMPATUS OF LOVE, THE ★★★ Four New York twentysomething men confront their feelings about love and commitment in this talky but engaging comedy-drama that benefits from a likable cast. Rated R for nudity, profanity, and adult situations. 99m. DIR: Richard Schenkman. CAST: Jon Cryer, Arabella Field, Tim Guinee, Adrian Pasdar, Adam Oliensis, Mia Sara, Jennifer Tilly, Kristin Scott Thomas, Michael McKean. 1996 DVD

PONETTE ★★★★1/2 Brilliant, is the only way to describe the powerful performance of Victoire Thivisol, a 4-year-old actress at the heart of Jacques Doillon's haunting film about the loss of a parent. Except for an ending that seems to lose track of the film's message, *Ponette* is filled with heart and heartbreak. Little Ponette doesn't understand why her mother has been taken away from her, and spends most of the film looking for her, or at least the spirit of the woman who loved her so much. An exceptional, rare experience. In French with English subtitles. Not rated. 97m. DIR: Jacques Doillon. CAST: Victoire Thivisol, Delphine Schiltz, Matiaz Bureau Caton, Marie Trintignant. 1996 DVD

PONTIAC MOON ★★ It's a painful sight when the most animated thing on the screen is Ted Danson's hairpiece. Inspired by the Apollo XI astronauts, eccentric Danson takes his sheltered son on a road trip. Mary Steenburgen deserves respect for making the most of her awkwardly scripted role as an agoraphobic mother. Rated PG-13 for a fistfight and profanity. 108m. **DIR:** Peter Medak. **CAST:** Ted Danson, Mary Steenburgen, Cathy Moriarty, Eric Schweig. **1994**

PONY EXPRESS ★★★ Bigger than they were in life, Western legends Buffalo Bill Cody and Wild Bill Hickok battle stagecoach station owners and Cheyenne Indians to establish the short-lived but glamorous pony express mail route in the early 1860s. Rousing good action for the historical Western fan who doesn't check every fact. 101m. **DIR:** Jerry Hopper. **CAST:** Charlton Heston, Rhonda Fleming, Jan Sterling, Forrest Tucker. **1953**

PONY EXPRESS RIDER ★★★★ A young man joins the pony express to find those responsible for the murder of his father. Solid performances from a host of veteran Western character actors. 100m. **DIR:** Hal Harrison Jr. **CAST:** Stewart Peterson, Henry Wilcoxon, Buck Taylor, Joan Caulfield, Maureen McCormick, Ken Curtis, Slim Pickens, Dub Taylor, Jack Elam. **1976**

PONY SOLDIER ★★ An obvious effort to regenerate Tyrone Power's lagging career, this Western relies on old cowboy-and-Indian ideas instead of an original story. It's set in the Canadian mountains to give it a different look, but the stories and characters are straight out of old-time Saturday-afternoon Westerns. 82m. **DIR:** Joseph M. Newman. **CAST:** Tyrone Power, Penny Edwards, Thomas Gomez, Robert Horton, Cameron Mitchell. **1952**

POODLE SPRINGS ★★★1/2 Novelist Robert Parker did a superb job of completing Raymond Chandler's last unfinished Philip Marlowe novel, which screenwriter Tom Stoppard efficiently brings to the screen. James Caan is rumpled and tired as the aging Marlowe, a man out of time in 1963, with modern technology soon to render his brand of sleuthing obsolete. But he's still got the juice, and this little thriller delivers plenty of twists while showcasing a new side of the P.I. as he adjusts to marriage with a wealthy lawyer half his age. Rated PG-13 for violence and brief nudity. 100m. **DIR:** Bob Rafelson. **CAST:** James Caan, Dina Meyer, David Keith, Tom Bower, Julia Campbell, Brian Cox, Joe Don Baker. **1998**

POOL HUSTLERS, THE ★★★ Comedy-drama about an amateur pool player out to take the title away from the national champion. In Italian with English subtitles. Not rated, the film has sexual situations. 101m. **DIR:** Maurizio Ponzi. **CAST:** Francesco Nuti. **1983**

POOR LITTLE RICH GIRL, THE (1917) ★★★ Mary Pickford's main claim to fame was her uncanny ability to convincingly portray females many years her junior. She stunted her range by doing so again and again, but the public loved it and willingly paid for it. She earned high critical acclaim demonstrating her range in this sentimental comedy-drama. One critic said that she was 8 years old, then a haughty 16, with no warning or motivation for the mercurial change. Silent, with organ music. B&W; 64m. **DIR:** Maurice Tourneur. **CAST:** Mary Pickford. **1917**

POOR LITTLE RICH GIRL (1936) ★★★★ A strong supporting cast makes this Shirley Temple vehicle one of her finest. She plays a motherless child who gets lost. Befriended by vaudevillians Alice Faye and Jack Haley, she joins the act, wows 'em, and wins 'em. As movie musicals go this one is tops. B&W; 72m. **DIR:** Irving Cummings. **CAST:** Shirley Temple, Alice Faye, Jack Haley, Michael Whalen, Gloria Stuart, Henry Armetta, Sara Haden, Jane Darwell. **1936**

POOR LITTLE RICH GIRL: THE BARBARA HUTTON STORY 💔 Farrah Fawcett plays the title role in this shallow but well-dressed biography of the unhappy American heiress. Edited down from a 250-minute TV miniseries, this is extremely choppy and superficial. Not rated; contains profanity. 98m. **DIR:** Charles Jarrott. **CAST:** Farrah Fawcett, Bruce Davison, Kevin McCarthy, James Read. **1987**

POOR WHITE TRASH 💔 Yankee architect clashes with the business (and moral) ethics of Louisiana developers. Not rated, but with nudity and violence. B&W; 90m. **DIR:** Harold Daniels. **CAST:** Peter Graves, Lita Milan, Douglas Fowley, Timothy Carey, Jonathan Haze. **1961**

POOR WHITE TRASH II 💔 Not really a sequel to *Poor White Trash*, just another lousy thriller about an insane Vietnam veteran who starts slaughtering people. Rated R for violence. 83m. **DIR:** S. F. Brownrigg. **CAST:** Gene Ross. **1976**

POPCORN ★★★1/2 A film student discovers her weird dreams are rooted in an old horror flick. Wonderfully entertaining chiller set during a festival of scare movies. Tom Villard is both humorous and frightening as a classmate who tries to kill the entire class. Rated R for violence and profanity. 93m. **DIR:** Mark Herrier. **CAST:** Jill Schoelen, Tom Villard, Dee Wallace, Kelly Jo Minter, Tony Roberts, Ray Walston. **1991**

POPE JOHN PAUL II ★★★★ Albert Finney is superb as the charismatic pontiff in this enactment of the Polish priest's adult life—from battles with Nazis and communism to his ascension to the throne of the Catholic church. Made for TV but with big-screen production values, the film represented Finney's American TV debut. 150m. **DIR:** Herbert Wise. **CAST:** Albert Finney, Nigel Hawthorne, Brian Cox, John McEnery, Ronald Pickup. **1984**

POPE MUST DIET, THE 💔 As a comedy, *The Pope Must Die* (retitled *The Pope Must Diet*) is about as unfunny as you can get. Director Peter Richardson delivers a pastiche of gags that will have you hitting the fast-forward button to find the good parts. There aren't any. Rated R for violence, profanity, and nudity. 90m. **DIR:** Peter Richardson. **CAST:** Robbie Coltrane, Beverly D'Angelo, Alex Rocco, Paul Bartel, Herbert Lom, Balthazar Getty, Peter Richardson. **1991**

POPE OF GREENWICH VILLAGE, THE ★★★1/2 This watchable film focuses on the hard-edged misadventures of two Italian cousins, Paulie (Eric Roberts) and Charlie (Mickey Rourke). Paulie is a not-so-bright dreamer who's obviously headed for trouble, and Charlie, who is smart enough to know better, always seems to get caught up in the middle of his cousin's half-baked and dangerous rip-off schemes. Rated R for profanity and violence. 120m. **DIR:** Stuart Rosenberg. **CAST:** Eric Roberts, Mickey Rourke, Daryl Hannah, Geraldine Page. **1984**

POPEYE ★★★ This adaptation of the famous comic strip by director Robert Altman is the cinematic equivalent of the old "good news, bad news" routine. The good news is that Robin Williams makes a terrific Popeye, and Shelley Duvall was born to play Olive Oyl. The bad news is that it's often boring. Still, it's hard to really dislike *Popeye*—it's so wonderfully weird to look at and so much fun at times. Rated PG. 114m. **DIR:** Robert Altman. **CAST:** Robin Williams, Shelley Duvall, Ray Walston, Paul Smith, Paul Dooley, Richard Libertini, Wesley Ivan Hurt, Bill Irwin. **1980**

POPI ★★1/2 Alan Arkin is Popi (Pappa), a hardworking if somewhat irresponsible Puerto Rican immigrant who comes up with a plan to provide his two young boys with new lives as Cuban refugees. Offbeat dramatic comedy, recommended only for families with older children. Rated G, although there is some violence and partial nudity. 115m. **DIR:** Arthur Hiller. **CAST:** Alan Arkin, Rita Moreno. **1969**

POPPY IS ALSO A FLOWER, THE ★★ Ian Fleming wrote the original story for this movie about efforts to destroy an international drug ring. Many in the huge cast worked for scale as a protest against drug abuse, but it backfired. So many stars pop up in small roles that they overwhelm the plot. Originally made for television, later released theatrically with added footage. Not rated; contains violence. 105m. **DIR:** Terence Young. **CAST:** E. G. Marshall, Trevor Howard, Gilbert Roland, Rita Hayworth, Anthony Quayle, Angie Dickinson, Yul Brynner, Eli Wallach, Marcello Mastroianni, Omar Sharif, Grace Kelly. **1966**

PORK CHOP HILL ★★★★ This no-win look at the Korean conflict features tough yet vulnerable Gregory Peck as the man forced to hold an insignificant mound of earth against overwhelming hordes of communist Chinese. A great cast and master director Lewis Milestone elevate this story to epic status. B&W; 97m. **DIR:** Lewis Milestone. **CAST:** Gregory Peck, Harry Guardino, Rip Torn, Woody Strode, George Peppard, Bob Steele, James Edwards. **1959 DVD**

PORKY'S 🎬 Teenagers in a fateful trip to a redneck dive called Porky's. Rated R for vulgarity, nudity, and adult themes. 94m. **DIR:** Bob Clark. **CAST:** Dan Monahan, Mark Herrier, Wyatt Knight, Roger Wilson, Kim Cattrall, Scott Colomby. **1981 DVD**

PORKY'S II: THE NEXT DAY 🎬 This time, the lustful kids of Angel Beach High battle with the Ku Klux Klan. Rated R for the usual garbage. 95m. **DIR:** Bob Clark. **CAST:** Dan Monahan, Wyatt Knight, Mark Herrier, Roger Wilson, Kaki Hunter, Scott Colomby, Nancy Parsons, Edward Winter. **1983**

PORKY'S REVENGE 🎬 It's just more of the same stupidity. Rated R for profanity, suggested sex, and nudity. 90m. **DIR:** James Komack. **CAST:** Dan Monahan, Wyatt Knight, Tony Ganios, Mark Herrier, Kaki Hunter, Scott Colomby. **1985**

PORNOGRAPHERS, THE ★★★★ A small-time porno filmmaker struggles to cope with the corrupt sexual ways of his family, the world outside, and himself. A brilliant black comedy that explores contemporary Japanese society with a kinky, perverse, irrational vision. In Japanese with English subtitles. B&W; 128m. **DIR:** Shohei Imamura. **CAST:** Shoichi Ozawa. **1966**

PORT OF CALL ★★★ When a seaman begins working on the docks, he falls in love with a suicidal young woman. The woman has had an unhappy childhood and a wild past, which has given her a bad reputation. This drama seems dated today. In Swedish with English subtitles. B&W; 100m. **DIR:** Ingmar Bergman. **CAST:** Nine-Christine Jonsson, Bengt Eklund. **1948**

PORT OF NEW YORK ★★1/2 A female narcotics smuggler decides to play ball with the police and deliver her former colleagues to them. Yul Brynner is the head smuggler who wants to stop the squealing—fast. Gritty and engrossing. B&W; 82m. **DIR:** Laslo Benedek. **CAST:** Scott Brady, Richard Rober, K. T. Stevens, Yul Brynner. **1949**

PORTFOLIO 🎬 This has no plot—just a series of interviews endeavoring to make modeling look appealing. Rated R for profanity. 83m. **DIR:** Robert Guralnick. **CAST:** Carol Alt, Julie Wolfe, Patty Owen, Kelly Emberg, Paulina Porizkova. **1983**

PORTNOY'S COMPLAINT ★★ Amazing that anyone had the nerve to attempt to translate Philip Roth's infamous novel to the screen. The neurotic Jewish boy, who has a strange relationship with his mother and an obsession with sex, should be neutered. It's worth viewing only as a curiosity. Rated R for profanity and sex. 101m. **DIR:** Ernest Lehman. **CAST:** Richard Benjamin, Karen Black, Lee Grant, Jack Somack, Jeannie Berlin, Jill Clayburgh. **1972**

PORTRAIT, THE ★★★ Sentimental story focuses on the twilight years of an elderly couple, while their daughter attempts to finish a portrait of the two. It's nice to see two great stars at work. Considering the wealth of talent involved, this film is a disappointment. 108m. **DIR:** Arthur Penn. **CAST:** Gregory Peck, Lauren Bacall, Cecilia Peck, Paul McCrane. **1993**

PORTRAIT OF A SHOWGIRL ★★ This made-for-television film is another attempt to chronicle the life of Las Vegas show girls. They meet men, they lose men. They lose jobs, they get jobs. 100m. **DIR:** Steven H. Stern. **CAST:** Lesley Ann Warren, Rita Moreno, Dianne Kay, Tony Curtis, Barry Primus, Howard Morris. **1982**

PORTRAIT OF A STRIPPER ★★ A dancer is forced to strip to label her fatherless son, causing the authorities to label her an unfit mother. Originally made for TV, timid presentation will, no doubt, disappoint many drooling video renters. 100m. **DIR:** John A. Alonzo. **CAST:** Lesley Ann Warren, Edward Herrmann, Vic Tayback, Sheree North. **1979**

PORTRAIT OF A LADY, THE ★★★ This adaptation of Henry James's novel is about a headstrong Victorian woman (Nicole Kidman) who meets her match in duplicitous Barbara Hershey (nominated for best supporting actress for this role). In an attempt to marry for love, Kidman is paired with a controlling monster (John Malkovich). Sounds fascinating, but the slow pace and plot development make this a seemingly endless film. Rated PG-13 for brief nudity and sexual fantasies. 144m. **DIR:** Jane Campion. **CAST:** Nicole Kidman, John Malkovich, Barbara Hershey, John Gielgud, Shelley Winters, Shelley Duvall. **1996 DVD**

PORTRAIT OF JENNIE ★★★★ A talented, unsung artist achieves fame and success after meeting a mysterious young girl who just might not be real in this charming, somewhat supernatural love story based on Robert Nathan's novel. A first-rate cast and high production values. B&W; 86m. DIR: William Dieterle. CAST: Jennifer Jones, Joseph Cotten, Ethel Barrymore, Lillian Gish, David Wayne, Henry Hull. 1948

PORTRAIT OF TERESA ★★1/2 Controversial emotionally charged drama about a disenchanted housewife who becomes involved with political and cultural groups in a postrevolutionary Cuban society. In Spanish with English subtitles. Not rated; contains profanity and violence. 115m. DIR: Pastor Vega. CAST: Daisy Granados. 1979

PORTRAIT OF THE ARTIST AS A YOUNG MAN, A ★★★ Fair adaptation of James Joyce's autobiographical novel about the coming-of-age of a young man while attending a Dublin university. The character intensely questions the morals of his day, which include the Catholic Church and the tyranny of family and state. Excellent ensemble acting by a superb cast. Not rated. 93m. DIR: Joseph Strick. CAST: Bosco Hogan, T. P. McKenna, John Gielgud. 1977

POSEIDON ADVENTURE, THE ★★★ It's New Year's Eve on the passenger liner *Poseidon*. A tidal wave overturns the ship, and from here on out the all-star cast, special effects, and imaginative sets take over. It's a fairly watchable disaster flick, nothing more. Rated PG. 117m. DIR: Ronald Neame. CAST: Gene Hackman, Ernest Borgnine, Shelley Winters, Roddy McDowall, Red Buttons, Stella Stevens. 1972 DVD

POSITIVE I.D. ★★1/2 Slow-developing story about a suburban housewife (Stephanie Rascoe) who, after being raped, assumes another identity to escape her past life. Rascoe makes a remarkable transformation from plain housewife to knockout, and the twist ending is ample reward for those patient enough to sit through the first hour of the film. Rated R for language and nudity. 93m. DIR: Andy Anderson. CAST: Stephanie Rascoe, John Davies, Steve Fromholz. 1988

POSITIVELY TRUE ADVENTURES OF THE ALLEGED TEXAS CHEERLEADER-MURDERING MOM, THE ★★★1/2 Trashy tabloid docudramas, and the media feeding-frenzy that creates them, are indicted in this often hilarious made-for-cable account of the Texas housewife (superbly played by Holly Hunter) who placed a contract on her daughter's cheerleading rival. Director Michael Ritchie maintains the darkly farcical tone against which his stars chew up the scenery. Rated R for profanity. 99m. DIR: Michael Ritchie. CAST: Holly Hunter, Beau Bridges, Swoosie Kurtz, Gregg Henry, Matt Frewer. 1993

POSSE (1975) ★★ Sheriff Kirk Douglas uses his pursuit of bandit Burce Dern to boost his career. This disappointing message Western juxtaposes the evil of political ambition against the basic honesty of traditional law-breaking. 94m. DIR: Kirk Douglas. CAST: Kirk Douglas, Bruce Dern, James Stacy, Bo Hopkins,

Luke Askew, David Canary, Alfonso Arau, Katherine Woodville, Mark Roberts. 1975

POSSE (1993) ★★★★ A rip-snortin' Western with a twist. Black infantrymen desert their unit after the Spanish-American War, and their sadistic commanding officer goes after them. Fine acting by an unusual cast and plenty of action (including a love scene that caused rating problems) add up to a highly charged adventure. Rated R for violence, profanity, nudity, and simulated sex. 107m. DIR: Mario Van Peebles. CAST: Mario Van Peebles, Stephen Baldwin, Charles Lane, Tiny Lister Jr., Tone Loc, Reginald Vel Johnson, Woody Strode. 1993 DVD

POSSESSED (1931) ★★★1/2 Wonderful melodrama featuring Joan Crawford as a beautiful gold digger who becomes Clark Gable's mistress. When he has a chance to run for governor, she must choose between her luxurious lifestyle and his chance for a political career. Don't confuse this with Crawford's efforts as a schizophrenic in the 1947 *Possessed*. This gem was released to celebrate MGM's Diamond Jubilee. B&W; 77m. DIR: Clarence Brown. CAST: Joan Crawford, Clark Gable, Wallace Ford. 1931

POSSESSED (1947) ★★★ A cold and clinical account of loveless marriage, mysterious suicide, frustrated love for a scoundrel, murder, and schizophrenia. The much-maligned Joan Crawford heads a fine, mature cast and gives one of her finer performances as a mentally troubled nurse. Extremely watchable. The opening scene is a real grabber. B&W; 108m. DIR: Curtis Bernhardt. CAST: Van Heflin, Joan Crawford, Raymond Massey, Geraldine Brooks, Stanley Ridges. 1947

POSSESSED, THE (1977) ★★ A not-too-scary *Exorcist* clone. James Farentino is a defrocked priest who travels around in search of evil and is drawn to a girls' school. Made-for-TV demonic possession flick. 75m. DIR: Jerry Thorpe. CAST: James Farentino, Claudette Nevins, Eugene Roche, Harrison Ford, Ann Dusenberry, Diana Scarwid, Joan Hackett. 1977

POSSESSED BY THE NIGHT ★★1/2 A sizzling thriller about a strange talisman that unleashes a writer's most erotic and dangerous desires. While in a tender relationship with wife Sandahl Bergman, Ted Prior tests the limits of his control by bedding sensual Shannon Tweed. When he becomes uncontrollable, the fireworks really begin to explode. Rated R for nudity, language, and violence; unrated version contains more sex. 87m. DIR: Fred Olen Ray. CAST: Ted Prior, Shannon Tweed, Sandahl Bergman, Chad McQueen, Henry Silva. 1993

●**POSSUMS** ★★★ Mac Davis plays a small-town radio announcer who, like many of his neighbors, is upset when the mayor disbands the high-school team (even if they have gone thirteen years without scoring a point). So he continues to broadcast imaginary games, in which the team starts to win. Likable entertainment for the whole family. Rated PG. 97m. DIR: J. Max Burnett. CAST: Mac Davis, Cynthia Sikes, Andrew Prine, Jay Underwood. 1999

POST COITUM ★★1/2 A comfortably married French publisher (director and cowriter Brigitte Rouan) has an affair with the handsome young friend of one of her writers. When he dumps her, her life falls apart. This romantic comedy–drama has some good scenes, but Rouan's incessant wailing and blubbering over her lost love is monotonous and exasperating. Get over it, already! In French with English subtitles. Not rated; contains nudity, profanity (in subtitles), and sexual situations. 97m. **DIR:** Brigitte Rouan. **CAST:** Brigitte Rouan, Patrick Chesnais, Boris Terral, Nils Tavernier. **1997**

POSTAL INSPECTOR ★★ Story of a bankrupt nightclub owner and the fearless agent who brings him to justice is a paean to the post office and its fraud investigators. Highlight of this slow-moving programmer is a speedboat chase through a flooded city. B&W; 58m. **DIR:** Otto Brewer. **CAST:** Ricardo Cortez, Bela Lugosi, Patricia Ellis, Michael Loring. **1936**

POSTCARDS FROM THE EDGE ★★★★ Meryl Streep lets it all hang out in this outrageous adaptation of Carrie Fisher's bestselling autobiographical book. A superb supporting cast contributes to this tale of an actress whose drug dependence is getting out of hand, and so is her relationship with her show-biz mom. The result is a movie that sparkles with wit, energy, and surprises. Rated R for profanity, drug use, and suggested sex. 106m. **DIR:** Mike Nichols. **CAST:** Meryl Streep, Shirley MacLaine, Dennis Quaid, Gene Hackman, Richard Dreyfuss, Rob Reiner, Mary Wickes, Conrad Bain, Annette Bening, Gary Morton, C.C.H. Pounder. **1990**

POSTMAN, THE ★★★1/2 Kevin Costner positions himself as no less than the one man who might restore civilization to a badly fragmented, near-future (year 2013) United States decimated by war, ecological disaster, and the Messianic fervor of a disenfranchised lunatic who rallies like-minded white men in a campaign against all things technological. In such a world, with good citizens literally starving for hope and rationality, it would be easy for a symbol—a U.S. mail carrier—to take root and grow into a near-unstoppable force for good. The premise is so clever, so ennobling, that even an egomaniac such as Costner can't really blunt its power. We still need our heroes, and this film is a nice statement in a cynical age that could use a few beacons of hope. Rated R for violence, nudity, and simulated sex. 180m. **DIR:** Kevin Costner. **CAST:** Kevin Costner, Will Patton, Larenz Tate, Olivia Williams, James Russo, Tom Petty. **1997 DVD**

POSTMAN, THE (IL POSTINO) ★★★★1/2 A sweetly dim-witted Italian mailman (Massimo Troisi) makes friends with the exiled Chilean poet Pablo Neruda; in the process he discovers unexpected poetic depths in himself. This tender, sun-drenched Mediterranean tragicomedy is just about irresistible, with sensitive, first-rate performances. It was the first international success for Troisi, a popular star in Italy who, sadly, died the day after filming was complete. In Italian with English subtitles. Rated PG. 115m. **DIR:** Michael Radford. **CAST:** Massimo Troisi, Philippe Noiret, Maria Grazia Cucinotta, Linda Moretti. **1994 DVD**

POSTMAN ALWAYS RINGS TWICE, THE (1946) ★★★★ If you wondered what went wrong in the sometimes steamily sexy and all too often soggy 1981 screen version of James M. Cain's celebrated novel, you need only watch this 1946 adaptation. John Garfield and Lana Turner play the lovers who murder the husband who stands in the way of their lust and suffer the consequences. B&W; 113m. **DIR:** Tay Garnett. **CAST:** John Garfield, Lana Turner, Cecil Kellaway, Hume Cronyn. **1946**

POSTMAN ALWAYS RINGS TWICE, THE (1981) ★★★ Jack Nicholson plays the drifter whose lust for a married woman (Jessica Lange) leads to murder in this disappointing remake based on James M. Cain's hardboiled novel of sex and violence. After an electric first hour, it begins to ramble and ends abruptly, leaving the viewer dissatisfied. Rated R for graphic sex and violence. 123m. **DIR:** Bob Rafelson. **CAST:** Jessica Lange, Jack Nicholson, John Colicos, Michael Lerner, John P. Ryan, Anjelica Huston. **1981 DVD**

POT O' GOLD ★★ An amusing time passer based on a one-time popular radio show. The plot concerns an enthusiastic young man's effort to get Horace Heidt and his orchestra on his uncle's radio program. Gee! B&W; 86m. **DIR:** George Marshall. **CAST:** James Stewart, Paulette Goddard, Horace Heidt, Charles Winninger, Mary Gordon. **1941 DVD**

P.O.W.: THE ESCAPE ★★1/2 David Carradine's considerable acting talents are wasted once again in this *Rambo* rip-off that is missing everything but action. Rated R for profanity and violence. 90m. **DIR:** Gideon Amir. **CAST:** David Carradine, Mako, Charles R. Floyd, Steve James. **1986**

POWAQQATSI ★★★★ Director Godfrey Reggio's follow-up to *Koyaanisqatsi* is a sumptuous treat for the eyes and the ears. Subtitled *Life in Transformation*, it combines gorgeous cinematography with exquisite music by Philip Glass. Like its predecessor, it's an engaging but sobering look at the cost of what some call progress. 99m. **DIR:** Godfrey Reggio. **1988**

POWDER ★★★ A child born of lightning and forced to live in darkness is discovered after his caretaker dies. When Powder, an enigmatic white-skinned albino, emerges from the shadows, his strange looks and eagerness to be accepted put him at odds with the locals. It doesn't help his cause when they learn that he has advanced intelligence and the ability to transfer thoughts. This tale of understanding and friendship is occasionally heartwarming. Rated PG-13 for adult situations, language, nudity, and violence. 111m. **DIR:** Victor Salva. **CAST:** Mary Steenburgen, Sean Patrick Flanery, Lance Henriksen, Jeff Goldblum, Susan Tyrrell, Missy Crider. **1995 DVD**

POWDERKEG ★★ Mildly entertaining Western about two barnstorming adventurers (Rod Taylor and Dennis Cole) hired by a railroad owner to liberate a train taken hostage by a Mexican bandit. This was the pilot for the mid-Seventies TV series *The Bearcats*. 88m. **DIR:** Douglas Heyes. **CAST:** Rod Taylor, Dennis Cole, Fernando Lamas, Michael Ansara, Tisha Sterling, Luciana Paluzzi. **1976**

POWDERSMOKE RANGE ★★1/2 Despite its impressive all-star cast of Western players, this is just an average B Western. Its significance lies in it being the first film to feature William Colt MacDonald's Three Mesquiteers. 71m. **DIR:** Wallace Fox. **CAST:**

Harry Carey, Hoot Gibson, Bob Steele, Tom Tyler, Guinn Williams, William Farnum, William Desmond. **1935**

POWER, THE (1980) 🎦 Aztec idol is unearthed by some youngsters, who must face the consequences. Rated R for profanity, violence, and gore. 87m. **DIR:** Jeffrey Obrow, Stephen Carpenter. **CAST:** Susan Stokey, Warren Lincoln, Lisa Erickson. **1980**

POWER (1986) ★★★★ Sidney Lumet, who directed *Network*, once again takes viewers into the bowels of an American institution with this hard-edged study of the manipulation of the political process by market research and advertising. Richard Gere gives one of his better performances as a ruthless hustler who is given pause when the one politician he believes in (E. G. Marshall) becomes a pawn in the political power trade. Rated R for profanity, violence, and suggested sex. 111m. **DIR:** Sidney Lumet. **CAST:** Richard Gere, Julie Christie, Gene Hackman, Kate Capshaw, Denzel Washington, E. G. Marshall, Beatrice Straight. **1986**

POWER 98 🎦 Shock-jock Eric Roberts and young partner Jason Gedrick are suspected by the police when a listener confesses to a murder on their show. Avoid at all costs. Rated R for profanity, sexual situations, and brief nudity. **DIR:** Jaime Hellman. **CAST:** Eric Roberts, Jason Gedrick, Jennie Garth, Larry Drake, Stephen Tobolowsky. **1997**

POWER OF ATTORNEY ★★ Routine crime-thriller about a mob boss on trial for murder. A handpicked idealistic young defense attorney is seduced by power and money until his conscience finally catches up with him. By then, it may be too late. Rated R for violence and language. 96m. **DIR:** Howard Himelstein. **CAST:** Danny Aiello, Elias Koteas, Rae Dawn Chong, Nina Siemaszko, Roger Wilson. **1995**

POWER OF ONE, THE ★★★1/2 Remarkably effective epic about a young man's fight against prejudice in South Africa. Set in the Thirties and Forties, the film details the adventures of an English boy who survives being tormented by youthful Afrikaners with the help of two mentors, one white and one black. Director John Avildsen uses the same combination of sports excitement and characterization that made *Rocky* so satisfying, and the result is stunning. Rated PG-13 for violence and profanity. 127m. **DIR:** John G. Avildsen. **CAST:** Stephen Dorff, Armin Mueller-Stahl, Morgan Freeman, John Gielgud, Fay Masterson, Daniel Craig, Dominic Walker, Alois Moyo, Ian Roberts, Marius Weyers. **1992 DVD**

POWER, PASSION, AND MURDER ★★ Hollywood of the late Thirties is the setting for a rising star's tragic affair with a married man. This telefilm is marred by daydreams of wannabes and has-beens. 104m. **DIR:** Paul Bogart. **CAST:** Michelle Pfeiffer, Brian Kerwin, Hector Elizondo. **1987 DVD**

POWER WITHIN, THE ★★1/2 A high-school martial artist comes into possession of a ring with mystical powers. Well-intentioned but slow-moving *Karate Kid* clone. Rated PG-13 for violence. 99m. **DIR:** Art Camacho. **CAST:** Ted Jan Roberts, Karen Valentine, Keith Coogan, John O'Hurley, William Zabka, Gerald Okamura, P. J. Soles, Ed O'Ross, Don "The Dragon" Wilson. **1995**

POWWOW HIGHWAY ★★★1/2 Taking a lighthearted look at a serious subject isn't easy, but this film does an excellent job. The subject is mistreatment of Indians on American reservations, from poor housing and bad job conditions to deprivation of tribal cultures and history. Though not rated, this is geared to an adult audience. 91m. **DIR:** Jonathan Wacks. **CAST:** A Martinez, Gary Farmer, Amanda Wyss. **1988**

PRACTICAL MAGIC ★★ Nothing could be less interesting than a story that makes stuff up as it goes along, fails to establish any parameters for reasonable behavior, and then wraps everything up with some thumpingly anticlimactic, *deus ex machina* intervention. All charges apply to this dim-bulb fantasy-comedy, which fritters away the talents of its four stars and does no justice at all to Alice Hoffman's source novel. Sandra Bullock and Nicole Kidman star as a pair of witches whose "white magic" proves incapable of properly dispatching a nasty fellow with a tendency to rise from the dead. Forget this misfire; it's practically incomprehensible. Rated PG-13 for violence and sensuality. 103m. **DIR:** Griffin Dunne. **CAST:** Sandra Bullock, Nicole Kidman, Dianne Wiest, Stockard Channing, Aidan Quinn. **1998 DVD**

PRAIRIE RUSTLERS ★★★ Buster Crabbe is accused of his outlaw cousin's crimes because of their dead-ringer resemblance. B&W; 56m. **DIR:** Sam Newfield. **CAST:** Buster Crabbe, Al St. John, Evelyn Finley, Karl Hackett. **1945**

PRANCER ★★★ With some movies you have to hang in there. So it is with this film about a troubled girl who finds an injured reindeer just before Christmas. It takes nearly an hour for the story to engage the viewer fully, but from then on *Prancer* is very satisfying. Rated G. 100m. **DIR:** John Hancock. **CAST:** Sam Elliott, Cloris Leachman, Abe Vigoda, Michael Constantine. **1989**

PRAY FOR DEATH ★★★ A Ninja movie with a plot? What a concept! Kick master Sho Kosugi plays a loving husband and father who moves from Japan to the United States. Here he encounters gangsters who must be dealt with. Rated R for violence. 93m. **DIR:** Gordon Hessler. **CAST:** Sho Kosugi, James Booth, Donna Kei Benz, Normann Burton, Kane Kosugi, Shane Kosugi. **1985**

PRAY FOR THE WILDCATS 🎦 Three businessmen on a macho motorcycle trip in the desert. Made for TV. 100m. **DIR:** Robert Michael Lewis. **CAST:** Andy Griffith, William Shatner, Angie Dickinson, Janet Margolin, Robert Reed, Marjoe Gortner, Lorraine Gary. **1974**

PRAY TV (1980) ★★1/2 Dabney Coleman plays Marvin Fleece, penny-ante con man, who takes faltering TV station KRUD and turns it into K-GOD. A really funny satire on religion and television, betrayed only by a weak ending. Rated PG for language and general tastelessness. 92m. **DIR:** Rick Friedberg. **CAST:** Dabney Coleman, Archie Hahn, Joyce Jameson, Nancy Morgan, Roger E. Mosley, Marcia Wallace. **1980**

PRAY TV (1982) ★★1/2 Interesting TV movie about a young minister (John Ritter) who comes under the spell of a charismatic televangelist (Ned Beatty). Beatty is superb, but Ritter's performance is lackluster. 96m. **DIR:** Robert Markowitz. **CAST:** John Ritter,

Ned Beatty, Richard Kiley, Madolyn Smith, Louise Latham. **1982**

PRAYER FOR THE DYING, A ★★ An overwrought adaptation of Jack Higgins's exciting thriller which sounds preachy even when trying to be suspenseful. Mickey Rourke is an IRA assassin who finds his conscience after unintentionally killing some schoolchildren; he flees to London and engages natty Alan Bates to help him out of the country. Rated R for language and violence. 107m. **DIR:** Mike Hodges. **CAST:** Mickey Rourke, Bob Hoskins, Alan Bates, Sammi Davis. **1987**

PRAYER IN THE DARK, A ★★★ Two escaped convicts take a family of Quakers hostage and demand that the mother take $4 million from the bank where she works, or her family will die. This made-for-cable original is a taut thriller with some interesting nonviolent solutions to the situation, but the acting is a little stilted, and the story not credible at parts. Rated PG-13 for violence. 95m. **DIR:** Gerard Ciccoritti. **CAST:** Lynda Carter, Teri Polo, Colin Ferguson. **1997**

PRAYER OF THE ROLLERBOYS ★★1/2 The Rollerboys are a gang of fascistic, drug-running teens who terrorize Los Angeles of the near future, zipping around on roller blades. Good stunt work and a *Blade Runner*–like look at the future make up for a too-familiar plot. Rated R for violence. 94m. **DIR:** Rick King. **CAST:** Corey Haim, Patricia Arquette, Christopher Collet, J. C. Quinn. **1991**

PRAYING MANTIS ★★★ In this made-for-cable original, a woman (Jane Seymour) who was abused as a child by her father kills her husbands on their wedding nights. Now she has fallen in love with a bookstore owner (Barry Bostwick), whose son and sister-in-law (Frances Fisher) don't trust her. Very good acting by Bostwick and Fisher, but the plot is on the predictable side. Rated PG-13 for violence. 90m. **DIR:** James Keach. **CAST:** Jane Seymour, Barry Bostwick, Chad Allen, Frances Fisher. **1993**

PREACHER'S WIFE, THE ★★★★ Director Penny Marshall has come up with what deserves to be a holiday perennial. The story is about Dudley, an angel sent from heaven to save the marriage of a pastor and the wife he seems to have shut out of his life. Dudley can't convince the reverend that he's the real article, but the title character certainly notices his gentle ways and healing touch. It's a love triangle straight from heaven. Rated PG. 124m. **DIR:** Penny Marshall. **CAST:** Denzel Washington, Whitney Houston, Courtney B. Vance, Gregory Hines, Jenifer Lewis, Lionel Ritchie. **1996**

PRECIOUS FIND ★★1/2 The California Gold Rush takes to the heavens in this futuristic action-thriller. In 2049 a whole new gold rush is taking place in outer space. A young miner, who has the ability to sniff it out, travels to a nearby planet with a card shark and space pilot, where they battle a claim jumper and her gang of bandits. Some thrills. Rated R for language and violence. 90m. **DIR:** Philippe Mora. **CAST:** Rutger Hauer, Harold Pruett, Joan Chen, Brion James. **1996**

PREDATOR ★★★★1/2 Sort of an earthbound *Alien*, *Predator* stars Arnold Schwarzenegger as a commando out to terminate a kill-crazy creature in a Latin American jungle. Although it sounds derivative, this film delivers a pulse-pounding tale. Rated R for profanity and violence. 107m. **DIR:** John McTiernan. **CAST:** Arnold Schwarzenegger, Carl Weathers, Elpidia Carrillo, Bill Duke, Sonny Landham, Richard Chaves, R. G. Armstrong, Kevin Peter Hall, Jesse Ventura. **1987 DVD**

PREDATOR 2 🖤 This sequel lacks the creativity. Rated R for violence, profanity, nudity, and gore. 108m. **DIR:** Stephen Hopkins. **CAST:** Danny Glover, Gary Busey, Rubén Blades, Maria Conchita Alonso, Bill Paxton, Robert Davi, Adam Baldwin, Kent McCord, Morton Downey Jr. **1990**

PREFONTAINE ★★★ Biography of Olympic runner Steve Prefontaine combines live action, interviews, and news footage for a decent docudrama. The focus throughout is on Pre's (Jared Leto) obsession with being the best while rebelling against the press and track association. Standout performances by Ed O'Neill and R. Lee Ermey as university coaches elevate the film a notch. Rated PG-13 for profanity and violence. 107m. **DIR:** Steve James. **CAST:** Jared Leto, R. Lee Ermey, Ed O'Neill, Amy Locane. **1997**

PREHISTORIC BIMBOS IN ARMAGEDDON CITY 🖤 After World War III, the world is reduced to a wasteland full of cyborgs and warrior bimbos in this dopey sci-fi comedy. Not rated; contains violence, nudity, and profanity. 75m. **DIR:** Todd Sheets. **CAST:** Holly Star, Jenny Admire, Veronica Orr, Robert Vollrath, Tonia Monahan. **1993**

PREHISTORIC WOMEN (1950) 🖤 A tribe of female bimbos runs into a tribe of male bimbos. 74m. **DIR:** Gregg Tallas. **CAST:** Laurette Luez, Allan Nixon, Joan Shawlee. **1950**

PREHISTORIC WOMEN (1967) 🖤 A dreadful film about a tribe of phallus-worshipping women. 91m. **DIR:** Michael Carreras. **CAST:** Martine Beswick. **1967 DVD**

PREHYSTERIA ★★★★ The plot may be derivative, but this solid slice of kiddie entertainment has surprisingly imaginative dialogue. A comic-book bad guy tries to strong-arm a farming family into handing over five dino eggs they accidentally acquired. A lot of fun for the kids, especially the pygmy dinos. Rated PG for mild profanity. 86m. **DIR:** Charles Band, Albert Band. **CAST:** Austin O'Brien, Brett Cullen, Samantha Mills. **1993**

PREHYSTERIA 2 ★★1/2 Fans of the first outing will enjoy this sequel that dishes up more of the same. The five miniature dinosaurs are back for more fun, this time helping a young boy thwart the plans of his evil governess to send him to military school, while helping the boy and his friend restore his father's prized train set. The critters are playful creations, providing plenty of adventure and mayhem. Rated PG. 81m. **DIR:** Albert Band. **CAST:** Kevin R. Connors, Jennifer Harte, Dean Scofield, Owen Bush, Larry Hankin. **1994**

PREHYSTERIA! 3 ★★ The kids might get a kick out of this third entry for the tiny dinosaurs, but adults may want to take the time to read a book. This time they help a girl save a mini-putt from a rival country club. Rated PG for humorous pranks. 85m. **DIR:** Julian Breen. **CAST:** Fred Willard, Whitney Anderson. 1995

PRELUDE TO A KISS ★★★★ It's a dream marriage for both Alec Baldwin and Meg Ryan when they finally tie the knot, which begins to unravel in seminightmarish fashion when the bride is kissed by an old man with whom she swaps souls. A charming, low-key romance with nice performances from Baldwin and Ryan. Rated PG-13. 105m. **DIR:** Norman René. **CAST:** Alec Baldwin, Meg Ryan, Kathy Bates, Ned Beatty, Patty Duke, Sydney Walker. 1992

PRE-MADONNAS (SOCIAL SUICIDE) ★★ A rebellious debutante chooses a blue-collar boy as her escort to a haughty deb ball. Routine teenage farce intended for nondiscriminating fans of *Clueless* and *Beverly Hills 90210*. Shot in 1987. Rated PG-13 for sexual situations and strong language. 98m. **DIR:** Lawrence D. Foldes. **CAST:** Shannon Sturges, Peter Anthony Elliott, Bobbie Bresee, Kenn Cooper, Dan Cashman. 1995

PREMATURE BURIAL, THE ★★ A medical student's paranoia about being buried alive causes his worst fears to come true. Roger Corman's only Poe-derived film without Vincent Price. Lacking Price's playful and hammy acting style, it all seems too serious. 81m. **DIR:** Roger Corman. **CAST:** Ray Milland, Hazel Court, Richard Ney, Heather Angel. 1962

PREMONITION, THE ★★1/2 Well-written but turgidly directed terror film about a young adopted girl kidnapped by her natural mother. The girl's adoptive parents turn to ESP to locate her, and fall into a strange world. Not rated, but has intense situations and some violence. 94m. **DIR:** Robert Schnitzer. **CAST:** Sharon Farrell, Richard Lynch, Jeff Corey, Danielle Brisebois. 1975

PREP SCHOOL ★★1/2 This comedy-drama about a coed prep school in New England has the usual cast of characters. Familiar, but nicely performed. Rated PG-13 for profanity. 97m. **DIR:** Paul Almond. **CAST:** Leslie Hope, Andrew Sabiston. 1981

PREPPIE MURDER, THE ★★★ William Baldwin is convincingly creepy as convicted killer Robert Chambers in this chilling made-for-TV crime-drama. After he strangles his girlfriend, played by Lara Flynn Boyle, in Central Park, his perfect life begins to unravel, and a portrait of a monster begins to surface. Danny Aiello is the detective who pieces it all together. Not rated; contains adult situations. 94m. **DIR:** John Herzfeld. **CAST:** Danny Aiello, William Baldwin, Lara Flynn Boyle, Joanna Kerns. 1990

PREPPIES ♥ R-rated sexploitation. Rated R for nudity, simulated sex, and profanity. 90m. **DIR:** Chuck Vincent. **CAST:** Nitchie Barrett, Dennis Drake, Steven Holt, Katt Shea. 1984

PRESENCE, THE ★★ After narrowly escaping a plane crash on a small desert island, a group of castaways discovers a mysterious, abandoned laboratory, and begins to mutate and die one by one. Silly sci-fi/horror flick is made watchable only by its above-average performances and bizarre but definitely unique music score. Rated PG-13 for violence and profanity. 90m. **DIR:** Tommy Lee Wallace. **CAST:** Lisa Banes, Richard Beymer, Gary Graham, Kathy Ireland. 1992

PRESENTING LILY MARS ★★ Stagestruck girl plugs her way to stardom. High points are when Judy Garland sings and The Tommy Dorsey and Bob Crosby bands. B&W; 104m. **DIR:** Norman Taurog. **CAST:** Judy Garland, Van Heflin, Richard Carlson, Marta Eggerth, Connie Gilchrist, Fay Bainter, Spring Byington, Marilyn Maxwell, Tommy Dorsey, Bob Crosby. 1943

PRESIDENT'S ANALYST, THE ★★★★ Vastly underappreciated satire from writer-director Theodore J. Flicker, who concocts a wild tale concerning a psychiatrist (James Coburn) selected to be our president's "secret shrink." Coburn walks away with the picture, his wicked smile and piercing eyes becoming more and more suspicious as he falls prey to the paranoia of his elite assignment. Not rated; adult themes. 104m. **DIR:** Theodore J. Flicker. **CAST:** James Coburn, Godfrey Cambridge, Pat Harrington, Will Geer. 1967

PRESIDENT'S PLANE IS MISSING, THE ★★★ Crisis after crisis occurs when *Air Force One* disappears with the president on board. This story of indecision and desire for control against a background of international crisis is an engaging suspense yarn. A very good story is helped by a veteran cast. 100m. **DIR:** Daryl Duke. **CAST:** Buddy Ebsen, Peter Graves, Arthur Kennedy, Raymond Massey, Mercedes McCambridge, Rip Torn, Dabney Coleman. 1971

PRESIDIO, THE ★★★ An old-fashioned star vehicle, this murder mystery features Sean Connery as a military provost marshal at San Francisco's Presidio. Police detective Mark Harmon, who once served under Connery and still bears a grudge, is assigned to work with his former commanding officer. Forget the plot and enjoy seeing Connery excel in a tailor-made role. Rated R for violence and profanity. 97m. **DIR:** Peter Hyams. **CAST:** Sean Connery, Mark Harmon, Meg Ryan, Jack Warden, Dana Gladstone, Mark Blum. 1988 DVD

PRESSURE POINT ★★★1/2 During World War II, a black psychiatrist is assigned to evaluate a bigoted prisoner, jailed for sedition as a member of the American Nazi party. Interesting drama, fine performances, with a special nod to the underrated Bobby Darin. B&W; 91m. **DIR:** Hubert Cornfield. **CAST:** Sidney Poitier, Bobby Darin, Peter Falk, Carl Benton Reid. 1962

PRESUMED GUILTY ♥ A James Dean look-alike is paroled from prison for a crime he didn't commit only to return home to a number of disappointments. Not rated; the film includes violence and profanity. 91m. **DIR:** Lawrence Simone. **CAST:** Jack Vogel. 1991

PRESUMED INNOCENT ★★★★1/2 Director Alan J. Pakula's superb version of Scott Turow's critically acclaimed best-seller features Harrison Ford as a prosecuting attorney who finds himself under suspicion when his mistress is murdered. Even if you've read the novel, you'll want to watch this gripping thriller. Rated R for violence, profanity, and nudity. 124m. **DIR:** Alan J. Pakula. **CAST:** Harrison Ford, Brian Dennehy, Bonnie Bedelia, Greta Scacchi, Raul Julia, Paul Winfield, John Spencer. 1990 DVD

PRETTY BABY ★★★★ Forcing the audience to re-examine accepted concepts is just one of the effects of this brilliant work by Louis Malle. He is fascinated by Violet (Brooke Shields), the girl we see growing up in a whorehouse in New Orleans. For Violet, all that goes on around her is normal. Rated R. 109m. DIR: Louis Malle. CAST: Brooke Shields, Susan Sarandon, Keith Carradine, Frances Faye, Antonio Fargas. 1978

PRETTY IN PINK ★★★★ Molly Ringwald is wonderful as a young woman "from the poor side of town" who falls in love with rich kid Andrew McCarthy. The feeling is mutual, but their peers do everything they can to keep them apart. It is that rare teenage-oriented release that can be enjoyed by adults. Rated PG-13 for profanity and violence. 96m. DIR: Howard Deutch. CAST: Molly Ringwald, Harry Dean Stanton, Jon Cryer, Andrew McCarthy, Annie Potts, James Spader. 1986

PRETTY KILL 🎗 A madam involved with a police detective hires a hooker who just happens to have a multiple-personality disorder. Rated R for violence and nudity. 95m. DIR: George Kaczender. CAST: David Birney, Season Hubley, Yaphet Kotto. 1987

PRETTY POISON ★★★★ Anthony Perkins gives one of his finest performances in this bizarre drama about a troubled arsonist who enlists a sexy high school girl (Tuesday Weld) in a wild scheme. This surreal black comedy is sparked by Weld's vivid performance and a highly original screenplay by Lorenzo Semple Jr. Not rated. 89m. DIR: Noel Black. CAST: Anthony Perkins, Tuesday Weld, Beverly Garland. 1968

PRETTY SMART 🎗 Claptrap about a rebellious new student at an exclusive girls' school. Rated R. 84m. DIR: Dimitri Logothetis. CAST: Tricia Leigh Fisher, Lisa Lorient, Dennis Cole, Patricia Arquette. 1986

PRETTY WOMAN ★★★★ Imagine Cinderella as a young Hollywood hooker. Now put Prince Charming in a fancy sports car driving down the strip. Welcome to this fluffy, funny comedy about the unlikeliest of love mates: a runaway (Julia Roberts) and a corporate raider (Richard Gere). Rated R for profanity and sex. 119m. DIR: Garry Marshall. CAST: Richard Gere, Julia Roberts, Ralph Bellamy, Laura San Giacomo. 1990 DVD

PREY, THE 🎗 Six young hikers go up into the woods, where they run into a ghoul. Yum. Rated R for nudity and violence. 80m. DIR: Edwin Scott Brown. CAST: Debbie Thurseon, Steve Bond, Lori Lethin, Jackie Coogan. 1980

PREY FOR THE HUNTER 🎗 A lame reworking of *The Most Dangerous Game*, as businessmen hunt down a photographer deep in the African jungle. Dull presentation of an overused plot. Rated R for violence and profanity. 90m. DIR: John H. Parr. CAST: Todd Jensen, André Jacobs. 1992

PREY OF THE CHAMELEON ★★★ Escaped mental patient Daphne Zuniga adopts the identity and personality of each woman she meets and kills, much to the frustration of pursuing FBI agents. Good ol' boy James Wilder, making a mess of his reconciliation with girlfriend Alexandra Paul (nicely credible as a small-town deputy sheriff), unwittingly gives a ride to the wrong hitchhiker. Made-for-cable mystery.

91m. DIR: Fleming B. Fuller. CAST: Daphne Zuniga, James Wilder, Alexandra Paul, Don Harvey. 1992

PRICE ABOVE RUBIES, A ★★★★1/2 Renee Zellweger plays an Orthodox Jewish wife who, stifled by the traditions of her tight-knit community, risks ostracism by building a career for herself as a jewelry buyer. An unusual, provocative story is sensitively told, with touches of magic realism that enhance the emotional texture of this haunting and compassionate film. Rated R for sexual scenes and brief nudity. 117m. DIR: Boaz Yakin. CAST: Renee Zellweger, Chris Eccleston, Glenn Fitzgerald, Allen Payne, Julianna Margulies. 1998 DVD

•**PRICE OF GLORY** ★★1/2 A failed boxer (Jimmy Smits) tries to attain the fame and fortune that eluded him by making prizefighters of his three sons. Smits gives a good performance, supported by a strong cast. But his character is a selfish, detestable bully and—worse yet—the script is a parade of groan-inducing clichés. Rated PG-13 for mild profanity. 118m. DIR: Carlos Avila. CAST: Jimmy Smits, Maria Del Mar, Jon Seda, Clifton Collins Jr., Ernesto Hernandez, Ron Perlman, Louis Mandylor, Sal Lopez. 2000

PRICELESS BEAUTY 🎗 Italian-style *I Dream of Jeannie*. Rated R for nudity and profanity. 94m. DIR: Charles Finch. CAST: Christopher Lambert, Diane Lane, Francesco Quinn, J. C. Quinn. 1989

PRICK UP YOUR EARS ★★★★ The poignant love story at the center will be touching to some and shocking to others. But this film about the rise to prominence of British playwright Joe Orton (Gary Oldman) and his relationship with Kenneth Halliwell (Alfred Molina) never fails to fascinate. Rated R for profanity and scenes of graphic sex. 110m. DIR: Stephen Frears. CAST: Gary Oldman, Alfred Molina, Vanessa Redgrave, Julie Walters, Wallace Shawn. 1987

PRIDE AND PREJUDICE (1940) ★★★★ This film is an adaptation of Jane Austen's famous novel. The story takes place in nineteenth-century England with five sisters looking for suitable husbands. B&W; 116m. DIR: Robert Z. Leonard. CAST: Greer Garson, Laurence Olivier, Maureen O'Sullivan, Marsha Hunt. 1940

PRIDE AND PREJUDICE (1985) ★★★★ Marvelous BBC adaptation of Jane Austen's classic romance. Comic moments abound as a silly mother desperately tries to marry off her five daughters. Period costumes and English countryside and manor houses are authentic. 226m. DIR: Cyril Coke. CAST: Elizabeth Garvie, David Rintoul, Moray Watson, Priscilla Morgan. 1985

PRIDE AND PREJUDICE (1996) ★★★★★ Positively addictive. The cast and crew capture Jane Austen's timeless wit and cutting observations of the class system and human foibles. The costumes and settings are delicious and Colin Firth and Jennifer Ehle dominate this comedy of manners in which a wedding band is the ultimate goal. Originally shown on cable. Not rated. 300m. DIR: Simon Langton. CAST: Colin Firth, Jennifer Ehle, Alison Steadman, Benjamin Whitrow, Susannah Harker, Crispin Bonham Carter, Anna Chancellor, Julia Sawalha, David Bamber, David Bark-Jones. 1995 DVD

PRIDE AND THE PASSION, THE ★★ Here is a supreme example of how miscasting can ruin a movie's potential. Frank Sinatra is horrible as the Spanish peasant leader of a guerrilla army during the Napoleonic era. He secures the services of a gigantic cannon and a British navy officer (Cary Grant) to fire it. Sophia Loren is also in the cast, primarily as window dressing. 132m. **DIR:** Stanley Kramer. **CAST:** Frank Sinatra, Cary Grant, Sophia Loren, Theodore Bikel. **1957**

PRIDE OF JESSE HALLMAN, THE ★★ This is a well-meant but sluggish account of the quest for literacy by the title character, who is played by country singer-songwriter Johnny Cash. Made for television. 99m. **DIR:** Gary Nelson. **CAST:** Johnny Cash, Brenda Vaccaro, Eli Wallach, Ben Marley, Guy Boyd. **1981**

PRIDE OF ST. LOUIS, THE ★★1/2 The ups and downs of popular St. Louis Cardinals baseball player Dizzy Dean are affectionately chronicled in this warm and humorous sandlot-to-big-league bio. Dan Dailey is amusing and believable as the word-fracturing Dean. B&W; 92m. **DIR:** Harmon Jones. **CAST:** Dan Dailey, Joanne Dru, Richard Crenna, Hugh Sanders. **1952**

PRIDE OF THE BOWERY ★★ This offshoot of the famous Dead End Kids features Leo Gorcey and Bobby Jordan, two of the original "kids," along with Gorcey's brother David, who continued on and off for the rest of the series. Not quite as bad as their later efforts, this film still needs a dyed-in-the-wool East Side Kids fan to really enjoy it. B&W; 63m. **DIR:** Joseph H. Lewis. **CAST:** Leo Gorcey, Bobby Jordan, Donald Haines, Carleton Young, Kenneth Howell, David Gorcey. **1940**

PRIDE OF THE CLAN, THE ★★★★ Picturesque, crisply photographed saga of the Scottish Highlands. To those viewers who know Mary Pickford's later costume pictures in the 1920s, the spunky character and the action pacing will be a welcome surprise. Silent. B&W; 70m. **DIR:** Maurice Tourneur. **CAST:** Mary Pickford, Matt Moore. **1917**

PRIDE OF THE YANKEES, THE ★★★★★ Gary Cooper gives one of his finest performances as he captures the courageous spirit of New York Yankee immortal Lou Gehrig. This 1942 drama is a perfect blend of an exciting sports biography and a touching melodrama as we follow Gehrig's baseball career from its earliest playground beginnings until an illness strikes him down in his prime. Teresa Wright is just right in the difficult role of his loving wife. B&W; 127m. **DIR:** Sam Wood. **CAST:** Gary Cooper, Teresa Wright, Babe Ruth, Walter Brennan, Dan Duryea, Ludwig Stossel. **1942 DVD**

PRIEST ★★★ A conservative young priest in working-class Liverpool tries to control his own carnal nature while ministering to the spiritual needs of his parish. It's a genuinely entertaining melodrama about a crisis of faith. Rated R for mature themes, profanity, and homosexual love scenes. 105m. **DIR:** Antonia Bird. **CAST:** Linus Roache, Tom Wilkinson, Cathy Tyson, Robert Carlyle, Robert Pugh. **1994 DVD**

PRIEST OF LOVE ★★★★ The culmination of a decade-long quest to film the life of D. H. Lawrence results in a film that is absorbing, brilliantly acted,

and stunningly photographed. It deals with Lawrence's exile from his native England, where his books were generally reviled; his relationship with wife Frieda; and their final time together in Italy. Rated R for profanity and sex. 125m. **DIR:** Christopher Miles. **CAST:** Ian McKellen, Janet Suzman, Ava Gardner, John Gielgud, Penelope Keith, Jorge Rivero, Maurizio Merli. **1981**

PRIMAL FEAR ★★★★1/2 A high-caliber thriller, this keeps you guessing right up to the shocking ending. Red herrings and duplicitous plot twists are woven tightly into this intelligent script about a hotshot attorney who goes looking for the limelight and finds it filled with shadows. A compelling performance by newcomer Edward Norton really makes this film believable, though Richard Gere does a masterful job of underplaying an arrogant but brilliant criminal lawyer. Rated R for violence, profanity, nudity, and sexual situations. 131m. **DIR:** Gregory Hoblit. **CAST:** Richard Gere, Laura Linney, Edward Norton, John Mahoney, Alfre Woodard, Frances McDormand. **1996 DVD**

PRIMAL RAGE 🐌 An experiment on a college campus goes awry. Rated R for violence and profanity. 91m. **DIR:** Vittorio Rambaldi. **CAST:** Patrick Lowe, Bo Svenson. **1988**

PRIMAL SCREAM ★★ A futuristic psychological thriller that's heavy on psychology and weak on script and acting, but with some pretty neat special effects. Rated R for profanity, violence, and some nudity. 95m. **DIR:** William Murray. **CAST:** Kenneth McGregor. **1987**

PRIMAL SECRETS ★★1/2 Dark family secrets come to the surface in this made-for-cable suspense drama about an artist who's hired by a wealthy socialite. It's a dream job until the artist learns that she resembles her employer's daughter, who died under mysterious circumstances. What follows is a sometimes-interesting psychological drama with a disappointing finale. Rated PG-13. 93m. **DIR:** Ed Kaplan. **CAST:** Ellen Burstyn, Meg Tilly, Paxton Whitehead, Barnard Hughes. **1994**

PRIMARY COLORS ★★★★ Not since 1976s *All the President's Men* has a mainstream political drama demanded so much of its audience. Yet this film is fascinating: a full-throttle, all-stops-pulled-out analysis of the compromise-laden political scene. Its story turns on the moral question: To what degree can we forgive the failings of a politician whose intentions seem noble? This fictionalized account of President Clinton's primary race is galvanized by John Travolta's dead-on impersonation of the Prez; he and the picture itself are compelling from start to finish. Rated R for profanity and sexual content. 135m. **DIR:** Mike Nichols. **CAST:** John Travolta, Emma Thompson, Billy Bob Thornton, Kathy Bates, Adrian Lester, Maura Tierney, Larry Hagman. **1998 DVD**

PRIMARY MOTIVE ★★★ Judd Nelson comes on strong as a young press secretary who uncovers some dirt about his candidate's opposition. Business as usual in the political arena: double crosses, lies, intrigue. Rated R for language. 98m. **DIR:** Daniel Adams. **CAST:** Judd Nelson, Richard Jordan, Sally Kirkland, Justine Bateman, John Savage. **1992**

PRIMARY TARGET ★★ Vietnam 1977: a wealthy American's wife is kidnapped. Anyone watching for inconsistencies will have a field day, but writer-director Clark Henderson plays it soft with likable heroes and equally nefarious villains. Rated R for violence. 85m. DIR: Clark Henderson. CAST: John Calvin, Miki Kim, Joey Aresco. 1990

PRIME CUT ★★ Sissy Spacek made her film debut in this sleazy but energetic crime thriller about bigtime gangsters and the slaughterhouse they use to convert their enemies into sausage. The talents of Lee Marvin and Gene Hackman elevate this essentially tasteless offering. Rated R for nudity, gore, and violence. 86m. DIR: Michael Ritchie. CAST: Lee Marvin, Gene Hackman, Angel Tompkins, Gregory Walcott, Sissy Spacek. 1972

PRIME EVIL ★★1/2 A band of priests in New York City are actually disciples of Satan. A bloody sacrifice every thirteen years grants them immortality. Passable horror film has decent suspense and contains violent acts without being awash in gore. Rated R. 87m. DIR: Roberta Findlay. CAST: William Beckwith, Christine Moore. 1989 DVD

PRIME OF MISS JEAN BRODIE, THE ★★★★★ Maggie Smith's first Oscar-winning performance fuels this character study of a late 1930s Edinburgh schoolteacher who steers her young charges past the rocky shoals of life, interlacing their studies with priceless descriptions of her affairs. Jay Presson Allen's deft script is drawn from Muriel Spark's novel, and rarely has the spirit of a book been so well captured on screen. Rated PG for frank dialogue. 166m. DIR: Ronald Neame. CAST: Maggie Smith, Robert Stephens, Celia Johnson, Pamela Franklin, Gordon Jackson. 1969

PRIME RISK ★★★1/2 Two frustrated young people (Lee Montgomery and Samuel Bottoms) devise a scheme to rip off automatic teller machines. Trouble arises when they stumble on to a greater conspiracy involving foreign agents. Nonstop action with Keenan Wynn as a suitable villain. Rated PG-13 for mature situations and language. 98m. DIR: Michael Frakas. CAST: Lee Montgomery, Sam Bottoms, Toni Hudson, Keenan Wynn, Clu Gulager. 1984

PRIME SUSPECT (1982) (FEATURE) 🎬 A young girl is murdered. A decent, honest, hardworking citizen becomes the prime suspect in the case. 100m. DIR: Noel Black. CAST: Mike Farrell, Teri Garr, Veronica Cartwright, Lane Smith, Barry Corbin, James Sloyan, Charles Aidman. 1982 DVD

PRIME SUSPECT 1 ★★★★★ Author Lynda La Plante's outspoken Detective Chief Inspector Jane Tennison is determined to make her mark in the mostly all-boys club of the British police force. Tennison inherits a baffling murder case and then comes across a connected second murder. The story ranks among the best police procedurals, and Tennison always fascinates. 240m. DIR: Chris Menaul. CAST: Helen Mirren, Tom Bell, John Benfield, John Bowe, Zoe Wanamaker. 1990 DVD

PRIME SUSPECT 2 ★★★★ Detective Chief Inspector Jane Tennison, tries to integrate her squad with the team's first black inspector. The remains of a young girl are found beneath an apartment patio in a primarily Afro-Caribbean neighborhood, and race relations are strained past the breaking point by an opportunistic politician. While at times overly melodramatic, this miniseries, by most standards, is a corker. 240m. DIR: John Strickland. CAST: Helen Mirren, Colin Salmon, John Benfield, Jack Ellis, Claire Benedict, George Harris. 1992 DVD

PRIME SUSPECT 3 ★★★★ Detective Chief Inspector Jane Tennison, having been demoted from homicide to Soho's Vice Squad, must again endure the sexist derision of a colleague she thought she had left behind (back in *Prime Suspect 1*). Personal antagonisms are shuttled aside, however, when the burned body of a 15-year-old male prostitute is found in the apartment of a cross-dressing cabaret entertainer. Creator Lynda La Plante weaves a complex mystery involving cover-ups, departmental spying, and homophobia. 240m. DIR: David Drury. CAST: Helen Mirren, Tom Bell, Peter Capaldi, David Thewlis, Michael J. Shannon, Mark Strong. 1993

PRIME SUSPECT: SCENT OF DARKNESS ★★★★ Investigating a series of murders that strongly resembles an earlier case she had solved, detective Jane Tennison (Helen Mirren) begins to wonder if the first killer she arrested was the right man. Another intelligently plotted entry in the popular British series. Not rated; contains adult situations. 102m. DIR: Paul Marcus. CAST: Helen Mirren, Tim Woodward, Stephen Boxer. 1996

PRIME TARGET 🎬 While a courier for the FBI, a hick lawman discovers that he and the handcuffed crime boss he's transporting are moving targets. A third-rate version of *Midnight Run*. Rated R for nudity, violence, and profanity. 87m. DIR: David Heavener. CAST: David Heavener, Isaac Hayes, Robert Reed, Andrew Robinson, Jenilee Harrison, Don Stroud, Tony Curtis. 1991

PRIME TIME MURDER ★★1/2 Sleazy TV reporter hooks up with homeless ex-cop to stalk a slasher who only attacks defenseless street people. Tim Thomerson is intriguing as the eccentric former cop, but the script is much too typical. Rated R for violence and profanity. 95m. DIR: Gary Skeen Hall. CAST: Tim Thomerson, Anthony Finetti, Laura Reed, Sally Kirkland. 1992

PRIMO BABY ★★★1/2 A ward of the state is forced to live with a widowed rancher who has a mean-spirited, wheelchair-bound son. Though a rip-off of *The Secret Garden*, this film is still fun to watch. Not rated. 97m. DIR: Eda Lever Lishman. CAST: Duncan Regehr, Janet Laine Green. 1988

PRIMROSE PATH ★★★★ In one of her best dramatic roles, Ginger Rogers stars as a young woman from the wrong side of the tracks who cons Joel McCrea into marriage. A fine film with a literate script, deftly crafted characters, fine production values—and heart. B&W; 93m. DIR: Gregory La Cava. CAST: Ginger Rogers, Joel McCrea, Marjorie Rambeau, Henry Travers. 1940

PRINCE AND THE PAUPER, THE (1937) ★★★1/2 Enjoyable story of the young Prince of England trading places with his identical look-alike, a street beggar. One of Errol Flynn's lesser-known films. Erich Wolfgang Korngold wrote the music. B&W; 120m.

R: William Keighley. **CAST:** Errol Flynn, Claude Rains, ...arton MacLane, Alan Hale Sr., Billy Mauch, Bobby ...auch. **1937**

RINCE AND THE PAUPER, THE (1978) ★★★1/2 ...Mark Twain's novel of mistaken identity in not-so-...lly old England, Edward, the only son of King Henry ...III, trades places with his double, a child from the ...ondon slums. The young prince has trouble ever ...ith the aid of a swashbuckling soldier-of-fortune. ...he costumed adventure should satisfy young and ...d. Rated PG. 113m. **DIR:** Richard Fleischer. **CAST:** ...harlton Heston, Oliver Reed, George C. Scott, Rex ...arrison, Mark Lester. **1978**

RINCE AND THE SHOWGIRL, THE ★★1/2 Ro-...antic comedy about the attraction of a nobleman ...or an American show girl. Marilyn Monroe and Lau-...ence Olivier's acting talents are in full flower, and ...hey are fun to watch; however, they are so dissimilar ...hat they never click. 117m. **DIR:** Laurence Olivier. ...**AST:** Laurence Olivier, Marilyn Monroe, Sybil ...horndike, Jeremy Spencer. **1957**

PRINCE BRAT AND THE WHIPPING BOY ★★★★ ...veryone fears Prince Horace, a tiny terror next in ...ine to the throne. Jemmy, an orphan, is recruited as ...he prince's whipping boy. The adventure begins ...when both boys are kidnapped. The kidnappers ...hink Jemmy is the prince, so it's up to the real ...rince to rise above himself to help save the day. ...ine family entertainment. Rated G. 96m. **DIR:** Syd ...Macartney. **CAST:** Truan Monro, Nic Knight, Karen Salt, ...George C. Scott, Kevin Conway, Vincent Schiavelli. ...994

PRINCE OF BEL AIR ★★★ Ever-watchable Mark ...Harmon plays a pool cleaner who has his way with ...ountless wealthy and beautiful women. Silly TV ...movie—but Kirstie Alley shines as Harmon's true ...ove. 95m. **DIR:** Charles Braverman. **CAST:** Mark Har-...non, Kirstie Alley, Robert Vaughn. **1985**

PRINCE OF CENTRAL PARK, THE ★★ Ruth Gordon ...s, as usual, a bright spot in this made-for-TV chil-...iren's film about an orphaned brother and sister ...who flee their foster home for a tree house in Central ...Park. The script is a bit cynical for a story aimed at ...children, but Gordon's charm serves to turn that ...around to her benefit. 76m. **DIR:** Harvey Hart. **CAST:** ...T. J. Hargrave, Lisa Richards, Ruth Gordon, Marc Va-...nanian. **1976**

PRINCE OF DARKNESS ♥ Priest learns about a ...canister hidden below an unused church and sus-...pects he's found Satan's resting place. Rated R for vi-...olence and language. 110m. **DIR:** John Carpenter. ...**CAST:** Donald Pleasence, Jameson Parker, Victor ...Wong, Lisa Blount, Dennis Dun, Alice Cooper. **1987** ...DVD

PRINCE OF EGYPT ★★★★ This rendering of the ...biblical Exodus saga hits all the proper dramatic ...notes and tells its story without the artificially ...adorable frills one expects from a full-length ani-...mated feature. This is an ambitious film: There are ...moments of humor, even amid such great tragedy; ...more opera than musical, with nine primary songs ...superbly integrated into its script. The "money ef-...fects"—God's speaking to Moses from the burning ...bush, the parting of the Red Sea—are vivid and

breathtaking. Further assisted by some splendid vo-cal talents (Patrick Stewart, Val Kilmer, and Ralph Fiennes), this emerges as the best *Classics Illus-trated* Bible adaptation ever created. Rated PG for dramatic intensity. 99m. **DIR:** Brenda Chapman, Steve Hickner, Simon Wells. **1998 DVD**

PRINCE OF PENNSYLVANIA ♥ Keanu Reeves por-trays a morbid, morose teenager in a small Pennsyl-vania mining town. Rated R for nudity, violence, and profanity. 93m. **DIR:** Ron Nyswander. **CAST:** Fred Ward, Bonnie Bedelia, Keanu Reeves, Amy Madigan. **1988**

PRINCE OF THE CITY ★★★★ Director Sidney Lumet has created one of the screen's most intense character studies out of the true story of a corrupt New York narcotics cop, played wonderfully by Treat Williams. In becoming a government agent, the cop destroys the lives of his closest friends. Rated R be-cause of violence and strong profanity. 167m. **DIR:** Sidney Lumet. **CAST:** Treat Williams, Jerry Orbach, Richard Foronjy. **1981**

PRINCE OF TIDES, THE ★★★1/2 Strong themes are explored in Barbra Streisand's adaptation of Pat Conroy's novel. Streisand plays a psychiatrist at-tempting to delve into the deep psychological prob-lems of the suicidal Melinda Dillon with the help of brother Nick Nolte. Rated R for profanity, violence, and simulated sex. 132m. **DIR:** Barbra Streisand. **CAST:** Barbra Streisand, Nick Nolte, Blythe Danner, Kate Nelligan, Jeroen Krabbé, Melinda Dillon, Jason Gould, George Carlin, Brad Sullivan. **1991**

PRINCE VALIANT (1954) ★★★1/2 Harold Foster's splendid saga of a young Scandinavian prince who enters the court of King Arthur and returns his fam-ily to their throne and restores his birthright. High adventure and great to look at. Fun for the whole family. 100m. **DIR:** Henry Hathaway. **CAST:** Robert Wagner, James Mason, Janet Leigh, Debra Paget, Ster-ling Hayden, Victor McLaglen, Donald Crisp, Brian Ah-erne, Tom Conway, Neville Brand. **1954**

PRINCE VALIANT (1997) ★★ This German–United Kingdom coproduction does a decent job of bringing the comic strip to life, but the film as a whole is rather lackluster. Director Anthony Hickox also does a decent job of evoking the time and the place, yet budget constraints and sloppy editing sabotage the film at every turn. Hickox even has the audacity to link the action together with cartoon panels as a tribute to the strip. Rated PG for violence. 92m. **DIR:** Anthony Hickox. **CAST:** Stephen Moyer, Katherine Heigl, Edward Fox, Ron Perlman. **1997**

PRINCES IN EXILE ★★★ A tough subject, teenagers with life-threatening diseases, is handled adroitly by a cast of unknowns and director Giles Walker. The plot has vestiges of teen movies but the film never slips over the edge and loses its humor or intelligence. Rated PG-13. 103m. **DIR:** Giles Walker. **CAST:** Zachary Ansley, Nicholas Shields, Stacy Mistysyn. **1990**

PRINCESS ACADEMY, THE ♥ Another girls' school movie, in which the entire point is to cram in as many extraneous shower and bedroom scenes as possible. Rated R. 90m. **DIR:** Bruce Block. **CAST:** Eva Gabor, Lar Park Lincoln. **1987**

PRINCESS AND THE GOBLIN, THE ★★1/2 The title pretty much tells all in this passable piece of children's fare. There are a few high points in the storytelling, but these are hampered by crude, uninspired animation. That said, youngsters—especially girls under the age of eight—are likely to enjoy it. Rated G. 76m. DIR: Jozsef Gemes. 1994

PRINCESS AND THE PIRATE, THE ★★★ A happy, hilarious Bob Hope howler. He and the beautiful Virginia Mayo are pursued by pirates and trapped by potentate Walter Slezak. Victor McLaglen is menacing as a buccaneer bent on their destruction. Walter Brennan is something else—a pirate? This one's lots of fun for all! 94m. DIR: David Butler. CAST: Bob Hope, Virginia Mayo, Victor McLaglen, Walter Brennan, Walter Slezak. 1944 DVD

PRINCESS BRIDE, THE ★★★★1/2 In this grand adaptation of William Goldman's cult novel, Cary Elwes battles horrible monsters and makes unusual friends while fighting to save his beloved Buttercup from the clutches of the smarmy Prince Humperdinck. The cast is uniformly excellent, with Mandy Patinkin a standout. A wonderful fantasy for all ages. Rated PG for modest violence and language. 98m. DIR: Rob Reiner. CAST: Cary Elwes, Robin Wright, Mandy Patinkin, Andre the Giant, Chris Sarandon, Wallace Shawn, Billy Crystal, Carol Kane, Peter Falk, Fred Savage. 1987 DVD

PRINCESS CARABOO ★★★ Based on a true story, this mellow, romantic mystery plays like an adult fairy tale. A young woman traveling through the bandit-plagued countryside of nineteenth-century England is arrested as a vagrant. When she begins talking in an unidentifiable language, a socialite declares the stranger to be foreign royalty and takes her into her home while a sympathetic but determined journalist tries to verify her identity. Rated PG. 94m. DIR: Michael Austin. CAST: Phoebe Cates, Kevin Kline, John Lithgow, Jim Broadbent, Stephen Rea, Wendy Hughes. 1994

PRINCESS COMES ACROSS, THE ★★★1/2 Fred MacMurray sings, Carole Lombard vamps, and together they solve a mystery on a transatlantic ocean liner while falling for one another. Not rated. B&W; 77m. DIR: William K. Howard. CAST: Carole Lombard, Fred MacMurray, Douglass Dumbrille, Alison Skipworth, William Frawley, Porter Hall. 1936

PRINCESS DAISY ★★1/2 If you enjoy sleaze and glitter, then you should be tickled by this made-for-TV rendition of Judith Krantz's novel of a poor little rich girl. Stacy Keach and Claudia Cardinale give the best performances. 188m. DIR: Waris Hussein. CAST: Lindsay Wagner, Paul Michael Glaser, Robert Urich, Claudia Cardinale, Ringo Starr, Merete Van Kamp, Sada Thompson, Stacy Keach, Barbara Bach, Rupert Everett. 1983

•**PRINCESS MONONOKE** ★★★1/2 A medieval Japanese prince slays a monster, but not before it passes on a fatal infection to him; the prince spends his remaining time questing for the monster's origin. It's no wonder this animated epic was a huge hit in Japan, with its striking visuals, complex characters, and dense, evocative story. For American release, a first-rate voice cast was added, including Billy Crudup, Claire Danes, Billy Bob Thornton, and Minnie Driver. Rated PG-13 for images of violence and gore. 133m. DIR: Hayao Miyazaki. 1997 DVD

PRINCESS TAM TAM ★★★1/2 The best of several movies featuring the legendary Josephine Baker. She plays an African girl brought to Paris by a writer who passes her off as an Indian princess. In French with English subtitles. B&W; 77m. DIR: Edmond Gréville. CAST: Josephine Baker, Albert Préjean. 1935

PRINCESS WARRIOR 🛇 Fleeing to Earth from her home planet (where men are the weaker sex), the good Princess Ovule is pursued by her evil sister and her minions. Rated R for violence and nudity. 84m. DIR: Lindsay Norgard. CAST: Sharon Lee Jones, Mark Pacific. 1990 DVD

PRINCESS WHO HAD NEVER LAUGHED, THE ★★★★ In this funny Grimm's fairy tale, laughter does prove to be the best medicine for the forlorn princess (Ellen Barkin). When she locks herself in her room, her father decrees a Royal Laugh-off to make his daughter happy. 51m. DIR: Mark Cullingham. CAST: Howie Mandel, Ellen Barkin, Howard Hesseman. 1984

PRINCESS YANG KWEI FEI ★★★1/2 Color is used with great effect in this big-budget epic of eighth-century China. When the current empress dies, the emperor falls in love with and marries a servant girl. But her life is ruined by jealous members of the royal court. In Japanese with English subtitles. 91m. DIR: Kenji Mizoguchi. CAST: Masayuki Mori, Machiko Kyo. 1955

PRINCIPAL, THE ★★ Unrealistic treatment and poor writing sabotage this story of a renegade teacher (James Belushi) who, as punishment, is made principal of a high school where all the hardship cases from the other schools are relegated. Belushi doesn't do justice to his role, but Louis Gossett Jr. is good as the school's security chief. Rated R for language and violence. 110m. DIR: Christopher Cain. CAST: James Belushi, Lou Gossett Jr., Rae Dawn Chong, Michael Wright, Esai Morales. 1987

PRISON 🛇 An old prison is haunted by the vengeful ghost of a man executed in 1964. Rated R for language and violence. 102m. DIR: Renny Harlin. CAST: Lane Smith, Chelsea Field, Andre de Shields, Lincoln Kilpatrick. 1988

PRISON FOR CHILDREN ★★★ Depressing, fact-based story of young offenders beaten down by a brutal system that tosses abandonded kids in with delinquents. This made-for-TV story is told with sensitivity but is on the sappy side. Especially touching is Raphael Sbarge as a countrified teen warehoused in a vicious juvenile prison. Not rated; contains adult themes. 96m. DIR: Larry Peerce. CAST: Raphael Sbarge, Kenny Ransom, John Ritter, Betty Thomas, Jonathan Chapin, Josh Brolin. 1986

PRISON ON FIRE ★★★★ Sent to prison for killing a man in self-defense, a white-collar worker learns how to survive with the aid of a more hardened prisoner (Asian superstar Chow Yun-Fat). Ringo Lam, one of Hong Kong's top directors, keeps everything moving in this entertaining thriller. In Cantonese with English subtitles. Not rated; contains strong vi-lence. 98m. **DIR:** Ringo Lam. **CAST:** Chow Yun-Fat, eung Ka Fai. **1987 DVD**

PRISON PLANET 🎬 More *Mad Max*-inspired silliness about futuristic warriors beating each other senseless for an hour and a half. Rated R for violence. 90m. **DIR:** Armand Gazarian. **CAST:** James Phillips, Michael M. Foley, Deborah Thompson. **1992**

PRISON STORIES: WOMEN ON THE INSIDE ★★★ This three-segment made-for-cable anthology directed by and starring women attempts to draw attention to problems facing prison mothers. Because of its TV production values, a lot of the grit is missing. As a result, real-life drama has been downplayed as the main characters turn into disposable stereotypes. Partial nudity, profanity, and violence. 94m. **DIR:** Penelope Spheeris, Donna Deitch, Joan Micklin Silver. **CAST:** Lolita Davidovich, Rachel Ticotin, Rae Dawn Chong, Annabella Sciorra. **1991**

PRISONER, THE (1955) ★★★★ Gripping political drama with outstanding performances by Alec Guinness and Jack Hawkins. Guinness portrays a cardinal being held as a political prisoner in a communist country. Jack Hawkins is the head of the secret police in charge of breaking down and brainwashing Guinness. Not rated. 91m. **DIR:** Peter Glenville. **CAST:** Alec Guinness, Jack Hawkins. **1955**

PRISONER, THE (1968) (TV SERIES) ★★★★ This sci-fi series was the brainchild of star Patrick McGoohan, who intended it to be an oblique follow-up to his successful *Danger Man* and *Secret Agent* series. The main character (McGoohan), whose name never is given—although he is believed to be *Secret Agent*'s John Drake—abruptly resigns from a sensitive intelligence position without explanation. He is abducted and awakens one morning in a mysterious community known only as The Village where every resident is known only by a number. Superior episodes are "The Arrival," "The Chimes of Big Ben," "Schizoid Man," "Many Happy Returns," "Living in Harmony," an episode never shown on American television, and "Once upon a Time" and "Fallout," the two-parter that brings the story to a close. Each 52m. **DIR:** Patrick McGoohan, David Tomblin, Don Chaffey, Pat Jackson. **CAST:** Patrick McGoohan, Angelo Muscat, Leo McKern, Peter Bowles, Nigel Stock, Peter Wyngarde. **1968**

PRISONER OF HONOR ★★★★ Scripter Ron Hutchinson's fascinating account of 1895s Dreyfus Affair, which became a national scandal and an international embarrassment. Richard Dreyfuss, superbly proud and defiant as Colonel George Picquart, grows convinced that Captain Alfred Dreyfus was convicted of espionage simply because of being a Jew; the resulting investigation makes a public mockery of French justice. Compelling made-for-cable drama. 88m. **DIR:** Ken Russell. **CAST:** Richard Dreyfuss, Oliver Reed, Peter Firth, Jeremy Kemp, Brian Blessed, Lindsay Anderson. **1991**

•PRISONER OF LOVE 🎬 Model Naomi Campbell stars as a woman who witnesses a mob hit and finds herself targeted by the killer. Billed as an erotic thriller, it is neither erotic nor thrilling. Rated R for violence, language, and adult situations. 94m. **DIR:**

Steve DiMarco. **CAST:** Naomi Campbell, Eric Thal, Beau Starr, James Gallander. **1999 DVD**

PRISONER OF SECOND AVENUE, THE ★★★★ Neil Simon blends laughter with tears in this film about an executive (Jack Lemmon) who loses his job and has a nervous breakdown. Anne Bancroft plays Lemmon's wife. Rated PG. 105m. **DIR:** Melvin Frank. **CAST:** Jack Lemmon, Anne Bancroft, Gene Saks, Elizabeth Wilson, Florence Stanley. **1975**

PRISONER OF THE MOUNTAINS ★★★1/2 Two Russian soldiers are taken hostage in the ethnic strife that has accompanied the breakup of the Soviet Union; gradually they develop an awkward rapport with their captors, and with each other. This lyrical Russian film, loosely based on a children's story by Tolstoy, seems constantly on the verge of becoming predictable, then strikes off in new and surprising directions. It's a confident mix of comedy, tragedy, and magical realism, with excellent performances. In Russian with English subtitles. Rated R for violence. 99m. **DIR:** Sergei Bodrov. **CAST:** Oleg Menshikov, Sergei Bodrov Jr., Jemal Sikharulidze, Susanna Mekhralieva. **1996**

PRISONER OF ZENDA, THE (1937) ★★★1/2 An outstanding cast, lavish costuming and sets, and a wholesome derring-do plot combine to make this a highly entertaining film. Commoner Ronald Colman is forced to stand in for a "twin" cousin in a political plot to gain control of a small European kingdom. Of the five screen versions of Anthony Hope's famous 1894 novel, this is absolutely the best. B&W; 101m. **DIR:** John Cromwell. **CAST:** Ronald Colman, Madeleine Carroll, Mary Astor, Douglas Fairbanks Jr., C. Aubrey Smith, Raymond Massey, David Niven. **1937**

PRISONER OF ZENDA, THE (1952) ★★★ An innocent traveler in a small European country is the exact double of its king and gets involved in a murder plot. This is a flashy Technicolor remake of the famous 1937 Ronald Colman version. 101m. **DIR:** Richard Thorpe. **CAST:** Stewart Granger, Deborah Kerr, Jane Greer, Louis Calhern, James Mason, Lewis Stone. **1952**

PRISONER OF ZENDA, THE (1979) ★★★1/2 Zany rendition of the classic tale of a look-alike commoner who stands in for the endangered king of Ruritania. A warm and hilarious film despite the lack of critical acclaim. Rated PG for language. 108m. **DIR:** Richard Quine. **CAST:** Peter Sellers, Lionel Jeffries, Elke Sommer, Lynne Frederick. **1979**

PRISONER OF ZENDA, INC. ★★★1/2 William Shatner makes a delightfully hammy villain in this kid-oriented update of Anthony Hope's swashbuckling classic. Teenager Jonathan Jackson plays dual roles, as an introverted software genius whose company is coveted by the dastardly Shatner and as the baseball-loving "ordinary kid" who stands in when the computer nerd is abducted. Great fun for the entire family and suitable for all ages. Rated PG for mild mayhem. 100m. **DIR:** Stefan Scaini. **CAST:** Jonathan Jackson, William Shatner, Jay Brazeau, Richard Lee Jackson. **1996**

PRISONERS OF INERTIA ★★ Slow-paced comedy features newlyweds (Amanda Plummer and Christopher Rich) attempting to enjoy a Manhattan Sunday.

Inertia describes the film's tempo. Rated R for nudity. 92m. DIR: J. Noyes Scher. CAST: Amanda Plummer, Christopher Rich, John C. McGinley. 1989

PRISONERS OF THE LOST UNIVERSE ★★ A low-budget science-fantasy adventure about three people transported to a parallel universe. Once there, they must use modern technology and archaic weaponry to battle an evil warlord. Although riddled with poor special effects, the film is actually a lot of good-natured fun. Made for Showtime cable network; contains some profanity and mild violence. 94m. DIR: Terry Marcel. CAST: Richard Hatch, Kay Lenz, John Saxon. 1983

PRISONERS OF THE SUN ★★★ This Australian drama offers a complex look at justice in the West versus the East, especially when it's clouded by political corruption. Bryan Brown plays an Australian military lawyer pressing war-crimes charges against Japanese officers and soldiers who killed hundreds of Australian POWs in a death camp during World War II. Rated R. 109m. DIR: Stephen Wallace. CAST: Bryan Brown, George Takei, Terry O'Quinn. 1991

PRIVATE AFFAIRS 🎔 This is one affair they ought to keep private! The rich and elite mingle among the Rome fashion circles, spinning their wheels and little else in this tiresome mess. Rated R. 104m. DIR: Francesco Massaro. CAST: Kate Capshaw, David Naughton, Michele Placido. 1988

PRIVATE AFFAIRS OF BEL AMI, THE ★★★★ Nobody ever played a cad better than George Sanders, and this is his crowning achievement. He is the antihero in Guy de Maupassant's famous story of a charmer who loves the ladies and leaves them until it finally catches up with him. The ending is pure Hollywood. UCLA's Film Archive restored the original print for the video release. B&W; 112m. DIR: Albert Lewin. CAST: George Sanders, Angela Lansbury, Frances Dee, Ann Dvorak, Albert Basserman, John Carradine, Hugo Haas, Warren William, Marie Wilson. 1947

PRIVATE BENJAMIN ★★★★ This comedy is at its best in the first half, when Goldie Hawn, as a spoiled Jewish princess, joins the army. The last part of the movie gets a little heavy on the message end, but Hawn's buoyant personality makes it easy to take. Rated R for profanity, nudity, and implicit sex. 110m. DIR: Howard Zieff. CAST: Goldie Hawn, Eileen Brennan, Armand Assante, Robert Webber, Sam Wanamaker. 1980 DVD

PRIVATE BUCKAROO ★★ Showcase vehicle for Patty, LaVerne, and Maxene, the Andrews Sisters, who decide to put on a show for soldiers. The Donald O'Connor/Peggy Ryan duo stands out. B&W; 68m. DIR: Eddie Cline. CAST: The Andrews Sisters, Joe E. Lewis, Dick Foran, Jennifer Holt, Donald O'Connor, Peggy Ryan, Harry James. 1942

PRIVATE EYES, THE 🎔 Holmes and Watson sendup. Rated PG. 91m. DIR: Lang Elliott. CAST: Tim Conway, Don Knotts, Trisha Noble, Bernard Fox. 1980

PRIVATE FILES OF J. EDGAR HOOVER, THE ★★1/2 A soap-opera-style account of the life and times of J. Edgar Hoover, concentrating on the seamier side of the FBI man's investigations. James Wainwright plays the young protagonist with low-key (some would say boring) intensity, while Broderick Crawford growls his way through Hoover's elder years. Rated PG for language and gangster violence. 111m. DIR: Larry Cohen. CAST: Broderick Crawford, Michael Parks, José Ferrer, Celeste Holm, Rip Torn, Ronee Blakley, James Wainwright, Dan Dailey, Lloyd Nolan. 1977

PRIVATE FUNCTION, A ★★★★ The Michael Palin/Maggie Smith team repeat the success of *The Missionary* with this hilarious film about a meek foot doctor and his socially aspiring wife who become involved with the black market during the food rationing days of post–World War II England when they acquire an unlicensed pig. The humor is open to those who like Monty Python, but is also accessible to audiences who do not find that brand of humor funny. Rated R. 96m. DIR: Malcolm Mowbray. CAST: Michael Palin, Maggie Smith, Denholm Elliott, Richard Griffiths. 1985

PRIVATE HELL 36 ★★1/2 Tight, well-constructed story of two cops who skim money from a haul they have intercepted and have trouble living with it, is nicely acted by veteran performers. Ida Lupino, equally adept on either side of the camera, cowrote and produced this grim drama. B&W; 81m. DIR: Don Siegel. CAST: Ida Lupino, Steve Cochran, Howard Duff, Dean Jagger, Dorothy Malone. 1954

PRIVATE INVESTIGATIONS 🎔 Los Angeles architect is chased around town by bad guys who think he knows something that could expose their schemes. Rated R for language and violence. 91m. DIR: Nigel Dick. CAST: Clayton Rohner, Ray Sharkey, Paul LeMat, Talia Balsam, Anthony Zerbe. 1987

PRIVATE LESSONS 🎔 Soft-porn comedy, about a wealthy, virginal teenage boy. Rated R because of nudity. 87m. DIR: Alan Myerson. CAST: Sylvia Kristel, Howard Hesseman, Eric Brown, Pamela Bryant. 1981

PRIVATE LESSONS—ANOTHER STORY ★★ Like its predecessor, this film is nothing more than an excuse to get some good-looking, plastic performers naked. This one involves a female fashion photographer who has the hots for a mystery woman and a chauffeur. Nothing much develops. Rated R for nudity and adult situations. 86m. DIR: Dominique Othenin-Girard. CAST: Mariana Morgan, Ray Garaza, Theresa Morris. 1994

PRIVATE LIFE OF DON JUAN, THE ★★ A vehicle for the aging Douglas Fairbanks, his last picture is set in seventeenth-century Spain. A famous lover (Fairbanks) fakes a suicide in order to make a comeback in disguise. It is somewhat tragic that the first great hero of the screen should have ended up in this disappointment. B&W; 90m. DIR: Alexander Korda. CAST: Douglas Fairbanks Sr., Merle Oberon, Binnie Barnes, Benita Hume, Joan Gardner, Melville Cooper. 1934

PRIVATE LIFE OF HENRY THE EIGHTH, THE ★★★★ This well-paced historical chronicle of England's bluebeard monarch and his six wives stars Charles Laughton as the notorious king. Laughton's real-life spouse, Elsa Lanchester, plays Anne, the fourth wife. She manages to keep her head off the chopping block by humoring the volatile king during a memorable game of cards. B&W; 97m. DIR: Alexander Korda. **CAST:** Charles Laughton, Robert Donat, Merle Oberon, Elsa Lanchester, Binnie Barnes. **1933**

PRIVATE LIFE OF SHERLOCK HOLMES, THE ★★★1/2 Director Billy Wilder's affectionately satirical pastiche of the Conan Doyle stories reveals the "secrets" allegedly shared by Sherlock Holmes (Robert Stephens) and Dr. John H. Watson (Colin Blakely). It does so with wit, humor, taste, and even suspense. Rated PG. 125m. **DIR:** Billy Wilder. **CAST:** Robert Stephens, Colin Blakely, Genevieve Page, Christopher Lee, Irene Handl, Clive Revill, Stanley Holloway. **1970**

PRIVATE LIVES ★★★1/2 A divorced couple meet by accident on their second honeymoons; soon they've abandoned their new spouses and run off, endlessly bickering and making up. Noel Coward's sparkling play stylishly filmed; laughs multiply by the minute. B&W; 84m. **DIR:** Sidney Franklin. **CAST:** Norma Shearer, Robert Montgomery, Reginald Denny, Una Merkel. **1931**

PRIVATE LIVES OF ELIZABETH AND ESSEX, THE ★★★1/2 Bette Davis is Queen Elizabeth and Errol Flynn is her dashing suitor in this enjoyable costume drama. 106m. **DIR:** Michael Curtiz. **CAST:** Bette Davis, Errol Flynn, Olivia de Havilland, Vincent Price, Donald Crisp, Nanette Fabray, Henry Daniell, Alan Hale Sr., Robert Warwick, Henry Stephenson. **1939**

PRIVATE MATTER, A ★★★★★ The abortion movement's roots are traced in this unflinchingly forceful (and true) account. Sherri Finkbine, a host of the children's television show *Romper Room*, learns that her use of thalidomide-based tranquilizers has almost certainly harmed the baby she is carrying. Attempts to handle the situation go awry when a strong sense of moral outrage prompts her to spread the news, in the hopes of warning other women. Made for cable. 89m. **DIR:** Joan Micklin Silver. **CAST:** Sissy Spacek, Aidan Quinn, Estelle Parsons, Sheila McCarthy. **1992**

PRIVATE NAVY OF SGT. O'FARRELL, THE ★★ A tasteless comedy about a sergeant who recruits a group of nurses to improve the morale of the troops. Instead of beautiful women, he gets Phyllis Diller, the most unglamorous female of all. 92m. **DIR:** Frank Tashlin. **CAST:** Bob Hope, Phyllis Diller, Gina Lollobrigida, Mylene Demongeot, Jeffrey Hunter. **1968**

PRIVATE OBSESSION ★★ Erotic-thriller videovixen Shannon Whirry stars as a fashion model who is abducted by an obsessed fan. Pedestrian plot just an excuse to get Whirry out of her clothes again. Rated R for nudity, strong language, and adult situations. 90m. **DIR:** Lee Frost. **CAST:** Shannon Whirry, Michael Christian, Bo Svenson, Rip Taylor. **1994 DVD**

PRIVATE PARTS ★★ When a teenage runaway seeks refuge at her aunt's San Francisco hotel, she finds that the residents can get downright deadly, as well as kinky. Mildly entertaining for fans of hack-and-slash erotic thrillers. Rated R for violence and nudity. 86m. **DIR:** Paul Bartel. **CAST:** Ann Ruymen, Lucille Benson, John Ventantonio. **1972**

PRIVATE PARTS (1997) ★★★ The story of Howard Stern, radio's notorious "shock jock," is carefully crafted to make him a movie star, and Stern does have a genial, breezy screen presence. Director

Betty Thomas keeps the rags-to-riches story clipping along with zest. The pace flags, however, whenever Stern plops down in front of his microphone, and the film glosses over his more offensive on-air excesses. Rated R for profanity, nudity, and sexual humor. 108m. **DIR:** Betty Thomas. **CAST:** Howard Stern, Robin Quivers, Mary McCormack, Fred Norris. **1997 DVD**

PRIVATE RESORT ★★ This teen comedy features two young men (Rob Morrow and Johnny Depp) seeking romance and excitement at a luxurious resort. Few funny moments. Rated R for nudity, obscenities, and sexual situations. 82m. **DIR:** George Bowers. **CAST:** Rob Morrow, Johnny Depp, Tony Azito, Dody Goodman, Hector Elizondo. **1985**

PRIVATE SCHOOL ♥ Enroll at your own risk. Rated R for nudity and profanity. 97m. **DIR:** Noel Black. **CAST:** Phoebe Cates, Martin Mull, Sylvia Kristel, Ray Walston, Julie Payne, Michael Zorek, Matthew Modine. **1983**

PRIVATE SNUFFY SMITH ★★ Cloned from the comic strip "Barney Google and Snuffy Smith," this grade B time passer has cantankerous hillbilly Snuffy being allowed to join up after saving the life of an army sergeant. Supporting player Jimmie Dodd went on to shepherd Disney's Mouseketeers. B&W; 67m. **DIR:** Eddie Cline. **CAST:** Bud Duncan, Edgar Kennedy, Doris Linden, Jimmie Dodd. **1942**

PRIVATE WAR ★★ Former war hero goes to Vietnam as a DI for an elite military unit. Members of his squad meet with mysterious accidents before one member figures out the psychotic DI is responsible. Familiar territory. Rated R for violence and profanity. 95m. **DIR:** Frank DePalma. **CAST:** Martin Hewitt, Joe Dallesandro, Kimberly Beck. **1988**

PRIVATE WARS ★★★ An alcoholic ex-cop helps intimidated inner-city residents to eradicate a violent street gang. In the villain's corner: a rapacious businessman who wants to raze the neighborhood for a new high rise. The only major flaw is an abrupt, dissatisfying conclusion. Rated R for profanity, violence, and suggested sex. 94m. **DIR:** John Weidner. **CAST:** Steve Railsback, Michael Champion, Dan Tullis Jr., Holly Floria, Stuart Whitman. **1993**

PRIVATES ON PARADE ★★★1/2 While this story of a gay USO-type unit in the British army is a comedy, it has its serious moments. These come when the unit accidentally runs into a gang of gunrunners. John Cleese is hilarious as the pathetic army major who's ignorant of the foul play that goes on under his nose. Rated PG-13 for adult situations and profanity. 107m. **DIR:** Michael Blakemore. **CAST:** John Cleese, Denis Quilley, Michael Elphick, Simon Jones, Joe Melia, John Standing, Nicola Pagett. **1983**

PRIX DE BEAUTE (BEAUTY PRIZE) ★★★★ Directly after making *Pandora's Box* and *Diary of a Lost Girl*, Louise Brooks made one other memorable movie, this early French sound film. She plays an ambitious young beauty contestant who aspires to a movie career. Her actions, however, infuriate her jealous husband. In French with English subtitles. B&W; 97m. **DIR:** Augusto Genina. **CAST:** Louise Brooks. **1930**

PRIZE, THE ★★★★ A fast-moving thriller based on Irving Wallace's popular novel. Paul Newman plays a

Nobel Prize winner in Stockholm who gets involved in espionage, a passionate affair, and politics. 136m. DIR: Mark Robson. CAST: Paul Newman, Edward G. Robinson, Elke Sommer, Anna Lee, Kevin McCarthy, Micheline Presle, Don Dubbins, Sergio Fantoni, Leo G. Carroll, Diane Baker, Virginia Christine, John Qualen. 1963

PRIZE PULITZER, THE: THE ROXANNE PULITZER STORY ★★★ Uneven, but surprisingly sturdy telling of the divorce scandal of the 1980s. Made-for-TV bio-shocker. 95m. DIR: Richard A. Colla. CAST: Perry King, Courteney Cox, Chynna Phillips. 1989

PRIZEFIGHTER, THE ★★1/2 In addition to starring in this goofy comedy, Tim Conway wrote the story. In it, we get a glimpse of 1930s boxing, with Conway playing a stupid boxer who has Don Knotts for his manager. Children may find the corny gags amusing, but most adults will be disappointed. Rated PG. 99m. DIR: Michael Preece. CAST: Tim Conway, Don Knotts, David Wayne. 1979

PRIZZI'S HONOR ★★★★ This totally bent comedy is perhaps best described as The Godfather gone stark, raving mad. Jack Nicholson plays a Mafia hit man who falls in love with a mystery woman (Kathleen Turner), who turns out to be full of surprises. Perhaps the blackest black comedy ever made. It's a real find for fans of the genre. Rated R for nudity, suggested sex, profanity, and violence. 130m. DIR: John Huston. CAST: Jack Nicholson, Kathleen Turner, Robert Loggia, John Randolph, William Hickey, Anjelica Huston. 1985 DVD

PROBABLE CAUSE ★★ Silly but strangely involving tale of a cop accused of sexism and his new female partner. Someone is killing cops one by one and it seems as though both partners know more than they're telling. The "surprise" ending is anything but. Rated R for profanity, violence, and sexuality. 90m. DIR: Paul Ziller. CAST: Michael Ironside, Kate Vernon, Craig T. Nelson, M. Emmet Walsh, Kirk Baltz. 1994

PROBE ★★1/2 Pilot film for the TV series Probe. Hugh O'Brian stars as an agent with an electronic transmitter implanted in him, which allows him to relay and receive information from headquarters. 97m. DIR: Russ Mayberry. CAST: Hugh O'Brian, Elke Sommer, Lilia Skala, Burgess Meredith. 1972

PROBLEM CHILD ★★ A bickering yuppie couple (John Ritter, Amy Yasbeck) decide to adopt a child so they can get invited to all the upscale kiddie birthday parties. They end up with a foul-mouthed, destructive youngster (Michael Oliver). Moronic combination of Police Academy and The Exorcist. Rated PG for vulgar language and violence. 81m. DIR: Dennis Dugan. CAST: John Ritter, Jack Warden, Michael Oliver, Gilbert Gottfried, Amy Yasbeck, Michael Richards. 1990 DVD

PROBLEM CHILD 2 ★★ John Ritter and Michael Oliver return as Ben Healy and his devilish adopted son Junior in this sequel. Too bad the writers had to heap projectile vomiting and dog feces on the audience. Rated PG-13 for mild profanity and scatological humor. 91m. DIR: Brian Levant. CAST: John Ritter, Michael Oliver, Laraine Newman, Amy Yasbeck, Ivyann Schwan, Jack Warden. 1991

PRODIGAL, THE ★★★ Sexy stuff with Lana as a high priestess in biblical days who seduces Edmund Purdom and makes him wish he never left home. Somewhat silly and contrived but highly enjoyable thanks to a good cast. 114m. DIR: Richard Thorpe. CAST: Lana Turner, Edmund Purdom, Taina Elg, Neville Brand, Louis Calhern, Joseph Wiseman, Cecil Kellaway, James Mitchell. 1955

PRODUCERS, THE ★★★★ Mel Brooks's first film as a director remains a laugh-filled winner. Zero Mostel stars as a sleazy Broadway promoter who, with the help of a neurotic accountant (Gene Wilder), comes up with a scheme to produce an intentional flop titled Springtime for Hitler and bilk its backers. The plan backfires, and the disappointed duo ends up with a hit and more troubles than before. Rated PG. 88m. DIR: Mel Brooks. CAST: Zero Mostel, Gene Wilder, Kenneth Mars, Dick Shawn, Lee Meredith, Christopher Hewett. 1968

PROFESSIONAL, THE ★★★★ A fusion of the character-driven drama of French cinema and the conventions of the American action film, this film is a true oddity in which a simple-minded Italian hit man becomes the only friend of an abused 12-year-old girl. While not for all tastes, it's strangely compelling. You'll either love it or hate it. Rated R for violence and profanity. DIR: Luc Besson. CAST: Jean Reno, Gary Oldman, Natalie Portman, Danny Aiello, Peter Appel, Michael Badalucco, Ellen Greene. 1994 DVD

PROFESSIONALS, THE ★★★1/2 A rip-snorting adventure film with Lee Marvin, Burt Lancaster, Robert Ryan, and Woody Strode as the slick characters out to rescue the wife (Claudia Cardinale) of a wealthy industrialist (Ralph Bellamy) from the clutches of a Mexican bandit (Jack Palance) who allegedly kidnapped her. Directed with a fine eye for character and action by Richard Brooks. 117m. DIR: Richard Brooks. CAST: Lee Marvin, Burt Lancaster, Robert Ryan, Woody Strode, Claudia Cardinale, Ralph Bellamy. 1966 DVD

PROFILE FOR MURDER ★★1/2 Typical thriller stars Joan Severance as a criminal psychologist who finds herself under the influence of a man suspected of being a serial killer. Lance Henriksen opens up his usual bag of tricks as the enigmatic suspect while Severance still finds time to take off her clothes when she's not playing games with her subject. Rated R for adult situations, language, nudity, and violence. 95m. DIR: David Winning. CAST: Joan Severance, Lance Henriksen, Jeff Wincott. 1997

PROGENY 🖤 Even though the talent behind the camera comes with a horror pedigree, what they deliver on the screen in this direct-to-video effort is a dog. A husband suspects that his wife has been impregnated by aliens. So what else is new? Lame special effects. Rated R for violence, language, and adult situations. 96m. DIR: Brian Yuzna. CAST: Arnold Vosloo, Jillian McWhirter, Wilford Brimley, Brad Dourif. 1998 DVD

PROGRAM, THE ★★★★ Director David S. Ward's best-written work since The Sting. This ensemble piece features Craig Sheffer as the troubled quarterback for Eastern State University who believes he has to engage in life-threatening stunts to cement his position of leadership. About the enormous pressure on participants in college sports, *The Program* has many richly drawn characters and situations. Rated R for profanity, violence, and drug use. 114m. **DIR:** David S. Ward. **CAST:** James Caan, Halle Berry, Omar Epps, Craig Sheffer, Kristy Swanson, Abraham Benrubi, Duane Davis. **1993 DVD**

PROGRAMMED TO KILL ★ Sandahl Bergman plays a terrorist who is killed only to be brought back to life as a computer-controlled antiterrorist weapon for the United States. The plan backfires. Acting is poor and so is the script. Rated R for violence, profanity, and nudity. 91m. **DIR:** Allan Holzman. **CAST:** Robert Ginty, Sandahl Bergman, James Booth. **1987**

PROJECT A (PART I) ★★★ Vintage Jackie Chan period comedy full of Buster Keaton–style slapstick and martial arts action. Chan plays a Marine cadet in turn-of-the-century Hong Kong, who battles smugglers and pirates operating on the South China Sea. Remarkable stunts, brilliantly choreographed. In Cantonese with English subtitles. Not rated. 95m. **DIR:** Jackie Chan. **CAST:** Jackie Chan, Sammo Hung. **1983**

PROJECT A (PART II) ★★½ Jackie Chan returns as Dragon Ma, the only uncorrupt cop in turn-of-century Hong Kong, where he finds himself at odds with the Chinese syndicate. As usual, the brilliantly staged martial arts battles are laced with comedy. In Cantonese with English subtitles. Not rated. 101m. **DIR:** Jackie Chan. **CAST:** Jackie Chan, Maggie Cheung. **1987 DVD**

PROJECT A-KO ★★★ Another of the more lighthearted entries in the Japanese animation wave, the story here revolves around a simple rivalry for the friendship of a dopey kid named C-Ko as disputed by the two heroines, A-Ko and B-Ko, who both happen to possess superhuman powers. In Japanese with English subtitles. Not rated, with violence and illustrated nudity. 86m. **DIR:** Katsuhiko Nishijima. **1986 DVD**

PROJECT: ALIEN ♥ Confusing sci-fi dud surrounds an explosion and shower of flaming objects over Norway. Rated R for language. 92m. **DIR:** Frank Shields. **CAST:** Michael Nouri, Darlanne Fluegel, Maxwell Caulfield, Charles Durning. **1992**

PROJECT: ELIMINATOR ♥ Government agents track down terrorists who have kidnapped a special weapons specialist. A trying and tired film. Even David Carradine is powerless to add a little kick to the proceedings. Rated R for violence. 89m. **DIR:** H. Kaye Dyal. **CAST:** David Carradine, Frank Zagarino, Drew Snyder. **1989 DVD**

PROJECT: GENESIS ♥ Cheap, incoherent sci-fi nonsense set in a future world where an outlawed drug made from cosmic dust holds the key to a higher mode of being. Not rated; contains profanity and brief nudity. 79m. **DIR:** Philip Jackson. **CAST:** David Ferry, Olga Prokhorova, Ken LeMaire, Kyra Harper. **1995**

PROJECT: METALBEAST ♥ Another sorry tale of a government project to build the perfect living weapon gone awry, with Barry Bostwick simply awful as the leader of the project. Rated R for gore. 92m.

DIR: Alessandro de Gaetano. **CAST:** Kim Delaney, Barry Bostwick. **1994**

PROJECT MOON BASE ★★ Futuristic story (set in far-off 1970!) chronicles the fate of an expedition that leaves a space station orbiting Earth and heads for the Moon. Made by independent producer Robert Lippert, this dull space story was co-authored by the esteemed Robert E. Heinlein, but it doesn't reflect his touch. B&W; 53m. **DIR:** Richard Talmadge. **CAST:** Ross Ford, Donna Martell, James Craven. **1953**

PROJECT SHADOWCHASER 3000 ★★ *Alien* meets *The Terminator* in this so-so sequel. Frank Zagarino returns as the dead android purposely lost in space for the safety of all mankind. When a seemingly deserted mining vessel crashes into a space station, occupants have little time to plan before the android is up and running, wreaking havoc on the station. Rated R for violence and adult language. 99m. **DIR:** John Eyres. **CAST:** Frank Zagarino, Sam Bottoms, Musetta Vander, Christopher Atkins. **1995**

PROJECT X ★★ A misguided attempt to turn a serious issue—the abuse of research animals—into a mainstream comedy-drama. Matthew Broderick is an air force misfit who winds up assigned to a secret project involving chimpanzees and air-flight simulators. Rated PG for intensity of theme. 108m. **DIR:** Jonathan Kaplan. **CAST:** Matthew Broderick, Helen Hunt, Bill Sadler, Jonathan Stark, Robin Gammell, Stephen Lang. **1987**

PROJECTIONIST, THE ★★ A projectionist in a New York movie palace escapes his drab life by creating fantasies, casting himself as the hero in various films. The movie intercuts new footage into old classics, a technique used later by Steve Martin in *Dead Men Don't Wear Plaid*. The film has surprisingly little entertainment value. Rated R for profanity and partial nudity. 85m. **DIR:** Harry Hurwitz. **CAST:** Chuck McCann, Ina Balin, Rodney Dangerfield. **1970**

PROM NIGHT ★★ This okay slasher flick has a group of high school students being systematically slaughtered as payment for the accidental death of one of their friends when they were all children. Rated R. 92m. **DIR:** Paul Lynch. **CAST:** Jamie Lee Curtis, Leslie Nielsen, Casey Stevens. **1980 DVD**

PROM NIGHT III—LAST KISS ★★½ Prom queen from hell Mary Lou Maloney returns to her old high school to knock 'em dead. Done with some style and humor. Watch for the jukebox from hell. Rated R for nudity, violence, and profanity. 97m. **DIR:** Ron Oliver, Peter Simpson. **CAST:** Tom Conlon, Cyndy Preston. **1989**

PROM NIGHT IV—DELIVER US FROM EVIL ★★½ A religious fanatic stalks four teens he feels have transgressed the law of God. Really no different from a zillion other recent horror movies, but it's moderately well-done of its type. (It has, however, nothing to do with the other three *Prom Night* entries.) Rated R for violence. 95m. **DIR:** Clay Borris. **CAST:** Nikki De Boer, Alden Kane. **1991**

PROMISE, THE (1978) ★★½ After a car accident, Kathleen Quinlan accepts money from her fiancé's mother to have extensive reconstructive surgery and never see him again. Destiny and true love override all obstacles in this obvious romance. Rated PG for mild profanity. 97m. **DIR:** Gilbert Cates. **CAST:** Kathleen Quinlan, Stephen Collins, Beatrice Straight. **1978**

PROMISE, THE (1995) ★★★★ Director and cowriter Margarethe von Trotta puts a face on politics by depicting a romance splintered by the Berlin Wall. Beautifully shot, this intelligently made love story is a touching study of the human spirit. Von Trotta wisely used two sets of actors for the maturing lovers and propelled the story through time without pandering to her audience. In German with English subtitles. Rated R for sexual situations, nudity, and profanity. 115m. **DIR:** Margarethe von Trotta. **CAST:** Meret Becker, Corinna Harfouch, Anian Zollner, August Zirner. **1995**

PROMISE HER ANYTHING ★★1/2 Single mom Leslie Caron must find a father for her precocious son. Dated romp is a direct precursor to *Look Who's Talking*. 97m. **DIR:** Arthur Hiller. **CAST:** Warren Beatty, Leslie Caron, Robert Cummings, Keenan Wynn. **1965**

PROMISED A MIRACLE ★★★ Although greater depth should have been brought to this TV movie, it remains a thought-provoking account of two Christian parents seeking a miracle from God—the faith healing of their diabetic son. Based on the book *We Let Our Son Die* by Larry Parker. 94m. **DIR:** Stephen Gyllenhaal. **CAST:** Rosanna Arquette, Judge Reinhold, Maria O'Brien. **1988**

PROMISED LAND ★★ A segment from the lives of four young people, three of whom have just graduated from high school. And the film is all exposition and not much insight. Kiefer Sutherland is convincing as an insecure, misguided wanderer. Rated R for profanity. 101m. **DIR:** Michael Hoffman. **CAST:** Kiefer Sutherland, Meg Ryan, Jason Gedrick. **1988**

PROMISES IN THE DARK ★★★1/2 This film is about a young girl dying of cancer. Marsha Mason costars as her sympathetic doctor. Good movie, but very depressing! Rated PG. 115m. **DIR:** Jerome Hellman. **CAST:** Marsha Mason, Ned Beatty, Susan Clark, Michael Brandon, Kathleen Beller, Paul Clemens, Donald Moffat. **1979**

PROMISES, PROMISES 🐶 The only thing going for this film is the scenes of a next-to-totally-naked Jayne Mansfield. Silly and crude. 75m. **DIR:** King Donovan. **CAST:** Jayne Mansfield, Marie McDonald, Tommy Noonan, Mickey Hargitay, Fritz Feld. **1963**

PROMOTER, THE ★★★ Alec Guinness is clever, conniving, and all innocence in this comedy centering on a penniless young man who exploits every opportunity to get ahead in the world. Glynis Johns is delightful as the girl who believes in him. B&W; 88m. **DIR:** Ronald Neame. **CAST:** Alec Guinness, Glynis Johns, Valerie Hobson, Petula Clark. **1952**

PRONTO ★★★ Based on an Elmore Leonard novel, this strange crime comedy–drama can't decide what to be when it grows up. Career grifter Peter Falk gets set up for some action he didn't orchestrate, and wisely flees to remote parts ... but his tendency to share the same stories with anybody who'll listen brings the bad guys hot on his heels. Rated R for violence, profanity, nudity, and simulated sex. 100m. **DIR:** Jim McBride. **CAST:** Peter Falk, Glenne Headly, James LeGros, Sergio Castellitto, Walter Olkewicz, Glenn Plummer. **1997**

PROOF ★★★★ Blind since birth, Martin is convinced that his mother hated him for being blind and deceived him with her descriptions of what she saw. Now Martin wants to trust someone to describe to him the countless photographs he takes—thereby giving him the proof of a long-dead mother's love. Add a psychosexual love triangle, intriguing cinematography, and original music, and we have the film that swept the 1991 Australian Film Institute Awards. Rated R for profanity and nudity. 90m. **DIR:** Jocelyn Moorhouse. **CAST:** Hugo Weaving, Genevieve Picot, Russell Crowe. **1991**

PROPHECY (1979) 🐶 Dull ecological horror film about a mutated beast that inhabits a northeastern American forest. Rated PG. 95m. **DIR:** John Frankenheimer. **CAST:** Talia Shire, Robert Foxworth, Armand Assante, Richard Dysart, Victoria Racimo. **1979**

PROPHECY, THE (1995) ★★★ Instead of the usual unexplained gorefest, this horror flick makes a real statement about good and evil, both of which are of biblical proportions. The story of angels battling over the future of heaven is too convoluted, and probably too introspective to appeal to mainstream tastes. Rated R for violence and profanity. 97m. **DIR:** Gregory Widen. **CAST:** Christopher Walken, Eric Stoltz, Virginia Madsen, Viggo Mortensen, Amanda Plummer, Elias Koteas, Adam Goldberg, Maria Snyder. **1995 DVD**

PROPHECY II, THE ★★★ This second in the horror series is a taut thriller with all of the trimmings. Christopher Walken returns as the fallen angel Gabriel, sent to Earth to make sure that pregnant Jennifer Beals doesn't give birth to the spirit that will destroy men. This direct-to-video sequel is an impressive collection of special effects, engaging characters, and sharp dialogue. Rated R for adult situations, language, nudity, and violence. 83m. **DIR:** Greg Spence. **CAST:** Christopher Walken, Jennifer Beals, Russell Wong, Brittany Murphy, Eric Roberts. **1997 DVD**

●**PROPHECY 3: THE ASCENT** ★★ Christopher Walken reprises his role as the fallen angel Gabriel, now looking to return to seraphim status once again after having been made mortal at the end of the last movie. This series is going downhill fast, losing the story and intrigue established in the first movie—and Walken's hair is actually getting worse. Rated R for violence and language. 107m. **DIR:** Patrick Lussier. **CAST:** Christopher Walken, Vincent Spano, Brad Dourif. **1999 DVD**

PROPOSITION, THE ★★★1/2 Rather than be forced into marriage with a local lord, a widow decides to save her farm by driving her livestock to market herself. It sounds like a Western, but this drama is actually set in nineteenth-century Wales, and it's surprisingly good. Rated R for nudity and violence. 99m. **DIR:** Strathford Hamilton. **CAST:** Theresa Russell, Patrick Bergen, Richard Lynch. **1997**

PROPRIETOR, THE 🐶 Confusing and convoluted film follows a famous French novelist as she returns home in an attempt to attain closure with her long-dead mother. Even Jeanne Moreau—appropriately cast as the novelist—can't save this film. Rated R for brief sexuality. 103m. **DIR:** Ismail Merchant. **CAST:** Jeanne Moreau, Sean Young, Sam Waterston, Christopher Cazenove, Nell Carter, Jean-Pierre Aumont, Austin Pendleton. **1996**

PROSPERO'S BOOKS ★★★ In this dense, ornate, relentlessly lush version of *The Tempest*, director Peter Greenaway shocks with graphic exactness, yet charms with lavish sets and Renaissance costumes designed by someone seemingly on LSD. Sir John Gielgud speaking Shakespeare's magnificent lines makes the film occasionally soar. Rated R for nudity and violence. 126m. **DIR:** Peter Greenaway. **CAST:** John Gielgud, Michael Clark, Isabelle Pasco, Michel Blanc. **1991**

PROTECTOR, THE ★★1/2 Standard kung fu film distinguished by nicely photographed action sequences and a sense of humor. Story has Jackie Chan as an undercover New York cop traveling to Hong Kong to break up a big heroin ring. Rated R for violence, nudity, and language. 94m. **DIR:** James Glickenhaus. **CAST:** Jackie Chan, Danny Aiello, Roy Chiao. **1985**

PROTECTOR ★★ Mario Van Peebles heads up a strong cast in this mediocre crime-drama about an undercover cop given ten days to bring in the killers of a mob witness. His search is hindered when he is also saddled with keeping the slain witness's girlfriend alive. Utter nonsense delivered with a modicum of conviction and believability. Rated R for violence, language, nudity, and adult situations. 94m. **DIR:** B. D. Clark. **CAST:** Mario Van Peebles, Randy Quaid, Zerha Leverman, Ben Gazzara, Rae Dawn Chong. **1998 DVD**

PROTEUS ★★1/2 Aren't people ever going to learn? When their boat goes down, six survivors are forced to take refuge on an abandoned oil rig. Or at least they think it's abandoned. Actually, it's the home of a nasty scientific experiment that's hungry for company. This direct-to-video effort has decent special effects, an eerie setting, and an OK cast. Rated R for violence and profanity. 97m. **DIR:** Bob Keen. **CAST:** Craig Fairbrass, William Marsh, Doug Bradley, Ricco Ross. **1996**

PROTOCOL ★★★1/2 In this film, directed by Herbert Ross, Goldie Hawn is a lovable airhead who goes through a startling metamorphosis to become a true individual. Sound a little like *Private Benjamin?* You bet your blond movie actress. It's no classic. However, viewers could do a lot worse. Rated PG for violence, partial nudity, and adult situations. 96m. **DIR:** Herbert Ross. **CAST:** Goldie Hawn, Chris Sarandon, Richard Romanus, Cliff De Young, Gail Strickland. **1984 DVD**

PROTOTYPE ★★★ Christopher Plummer heads a government research team that has perfected an android. Contrary to his wishes, the Pentagon reprograms the android for its own sinister reasons. Nothing original, but entertaining nonetheless. Made for TV. 97m. **DIR:** David Greene. **CAST:** Christopher Plummer, David Morse, Stephen Elliott, Frances Sternhagen, Arthur Hill. **1983**

PROTOTYPE X29A ★★1/2 In a postnuclear-war future, cyborg hunter killers seek out mutants. This is basically a cross between *Robocop* and *Terminator*, with none of the originality that made those two films smash hits. Rated R for violence, profanity, and

nudity. 98m. **DIR:** Phillip Roth. **CAST:** Lane Lenhart. **1992**

PROUD AND THE DAMNED, THE ★★ Standard Western plot with a Latin accent results in a below-par account. The cast does a poor job, but the South American locales save this film from a lower rating. 94m. **DIR:** Ferde Grofe Jr. **CAST:** Chuck Connors, Jose Greco, Cesar Romero, Aron Kincaid. **1973 DVD**

PROUD MEN ★★1/2 Routine father-and-son conflicts are given conviction by a strong cast, led by Charlton Heston and Peter Strauss in this made-for-cable Western. 94m. **DIR:** William A. Graham. **CAST:** Charlton Heston, Peter Strauss, Belinda Balaski. **1987**

PROUD REBEL, THE ★★★1/2 A post–Civil War sentimental drama about a Confederate veteran searching for a doctor who can cure his mute son. The principals in this one are excellent, the chemistry great. Well worth the watching, this was the ill-fated Alan Ladd's last "class" film. 103m. **DIR:** Michael Curtiz. **CAST:** Alan Ladd, Olivia de Havilland, David Ladd, Dean Jagger, Henry Hull. **1958 DVD**

PROVIDENCE ★★★★ Director Alain Resnais's first English-language film includes the great cast of Dirk Bogarde, John Gielgud, Ellen Burstyn, and David Warner. An old and dying writer (Gielgud) completing his last novel invites his family up for the weekend. The fast cutting between the writer's imagined thoughts and real life makes this film difficult to follow for some. Rated R. 104m. **DIR:** Alain Resnais. **CAST:** Dirk Bogarde, John Gielgud, Ellen Burstyn, David Warner, Elaine Stritch. **1977**

PROVOCATEUR ★★★ A North Korean agent infiltrates a U. S. base masquerading as a nanny. Once there, however, she falls in love with her new "family" and her objectives become blurred. Rated R for nudity and profanity. 104m. **DIR:** Jim Donovan. **CAST:** Jane March, Nick Mancuso, Cary-Hiroyuki Tagawa, Stephen Mendel, Lillo Brancato. **1997**

PROWLER, THE ★★ Early slasher film features special effects by Tom Savini. They are the sole redeeming value to this nihilistic film. Rated R for violence, profanity, gore, and nudity. 88m. **DIR:** Joseph Zito. **CAST:** Farley Granger, Vicki Dawson, Lawrence Tierney. **1981**

PSYCHIC ★★ A serial killer is on the loose with a deadly belt buckle. A psychic (Zach Galligan) dreams the deaths of various females, including the professor (Catherine Mary Stewart) that he has fallen in love with. Poor writing and acting strangle this film. Made for cable. 91m. **DIR:** George Mihalka. **CAST:** Zach Galligan, Catherine Mary Stewart, Michael Nouri. **1992**

PSYCHIC KILLER ★★ This is a completely ordinary thriller about a man who acquires psychic powers. *Psychic Killer* doesn't take itself seriously and that's a plus, but it's not sufficiently engrossing. Rated PG. 89m. **DIR:** Ray Danton. **CAST:** Jim Hutton, Paul Burke, Julie Adams, Nehemiah Persoff, Neville Brand, Aldo Ray, Della Reese. **1975 DVD**

PSYCHIC, THE ★★ Jennifer O'Neill gives a wonderful performance in this otherwise mundane Italian shocker. Some psychic visions are worth a look, but overall Lucio Fulci's mad camera movements distract the viewer instead of adding suspense.

Rated R for violence, profanity, and gore. 89m. DIR: Lucio Fulci. CAST: Jennifer O'Neill, Gabriele Ferzetti, Marc Porel. 1977

PSYCHO (1960) ★★★★★ The quintessential shocker, which started a whole genre of films about psychotic killers enacting mayhem on innocent victims, still holds up well today. Anthony Perkins's performance and the ease with which Hitchcock maneuvers your emotions make *Psycho* far superior to the numerous films that tried to duplicate it. B&W; 109m. DIR: Alfred Hitchcock. CAST: Anthony Perkins, Janet Leigh, Vera Miles, John Gavin, John McIntire, Simon Oakland, John Anderson, Frank Albertson, Patricia Hitchcock, Martin Balsam. 1960 DVD

PSYCHO II ★★★1/2 Picking up where Alfred Hitchcock's original left off, this sequel begins with Norman Bates (Anthony Perkins) being declared sane after twenty-two years in an asylum. Old Normie goes right back to the Bates Motel, and strange things begin to happen. Directed with exquisite taste and respect for the old master by Richard Franklin. It's suspenseful, scary, and funny. Rated R for profanity and violence. 113m. DIR: Richard Franklin. CAST: Anthony Perkins, Vera Miles, Meg Tilly, Robert Loggia, Dennis Franz, Hugh Gillin. 1983 DVD

PSYCHO III ★★ Second follow-up to *Psycho* works mainly because actor-director Anthony Perkins understands poor Norman Bates inside and out. Although lensed beautifully by Bruce Surtees, the film fails in the most critical area: creating suspense. Rated R for gory violence. 93m. DIR: Anthony Perkins. CAST: Anthony Perkins, Diana Scarwid, Jeff Fahey, Hugh Gillin. 1986 DVD

PSYCHO 4: THE BEGINNING ★★★ Once more into the Bates Motel, dear friends … Scripter Joseph Stefano, who adapted Robert Bloch's novel for Hitchcock's original *Psycho*, returns with this made-for-cable tale purporting to explain why poor Norman Bates (Anthony Perkins) became such a monster. Rated R for sex, nudity, and violence. 95m. DIR: Mick Garris. CAST: Anthony Perkins, Henry Thomas, Olivia Hussey, C.C.H. Pounder. 1990

PSYCHO (1998) ★★1/2 What you've heard is true: It's a remake of Hitchcock's 1960 classic in every sense of the word, and it's fair to say that Hitchcock himself directed this film, nearly 20 years removed from the grave. At best, Gus Van Sant might be termed a conductor of somebody else's symphony. Van Sant's biggest contribution is to make everything more vulgar. This is no more than a novelty: a bit of celluloid trickery that will blissfully fade from memory. Rated R for violence, nudity, and sexual candor. 106m. DIR: Gus Van Sant. CAST: Vince Vaughn, Julianne Moore, Anne Heche, Viggo Mortensen, William H. Macy. 1998 DVD

PSYCHO COP 2 ❤ Wacko cop decides to break up an illicit bachelor party by killing those who participate in illegal activity. But who's going to stop the filmmakers from making *Psycho Cop 3*? Rated R for extreme violence, nudity, and strong language. 80m. DIR: Rif Coogan. CAST: Bobby Ray Shafer, Barbara Lee Alexander. 1993

PSYCHO GIRLS ★★★ Over-the-top horror parody will appeal most to avid horror fans, who will appreciate the black humor. A writer of mystery novels holds a dinner party that is disrupted by a psychotic woman. Rated R for violence and nudity. 90m. DIR: Gerard Ciccoritti. CAST: John Haslett Cuff, Darlene Wignacci. 1986

PSYCHO SISTERS (1972) ★★★★ After her husband is killed, a woman goes to stay with her sister—her sister who has only recently emerged from an insane asylum and is still hearing their dead mother's voice. This film is a classic of the early 1970s horror/gore/exploitation cycle. Rated PG for mild violence. 76m. DIR: Reginald LeBorg. CAST: Susan Strasberg, Faith Domergue, Charles Knox Robinson. 1972

•PSYCHO SISTERS (1998) ❤ Following the success of his previous version, director Pete Jacelone was given a bigger budget and some name stars and came up with this boring, watered-down version of the same film. Not rated; contains violence and gore. 96m. DIR: Pete Jacelone. CAST: J. J. North, Theresa Lynn, Nancy Sirianni. 1998

PSYCHOMANIA ★★ This British-made film is about a motorcycle gang. They call themselves the Living Dead because they committed a group suicide and only came back to life through a pact with the devil. The film moves slowly and includes lots of violence. Rated R. 95m. DIR: Don Sharp. CAST: George Sanders, Nicky Henson, Mary Larkin, Patrick Holt, Beryl Reid. 1971

PSYCHOPATH, THE ❤ The host of a children's television show spends his spare time killing parents who abuse their kids. Rated PG. 84m. DIR: Larry Brown. CAST: Tom Basham, John Ashton. 1973

PSYCHOS IN LOVE ★★1/2 This film is an *Eating Raoul*–style horror comedy. Joe is a bar owner who has no trouble meeting women and getting dates. The problem is that he is a psychopath who ends up killing them—generally when he finds out they like grapes! This made-for-video movie has lots of gore and nudity. 88m. DIR: Gorman Bechard. CAST: Carmine Capobianco, Debi Thibeault, Frank Stewart. 1985

PSYCH-OUT ★★1/2 The psychedelic Sixties couldn't have been more outrageous. A pretty, deaf runaway ends up in Haight-Ashbury while searching for her missing brother. She encounters a rock musician (Jack Nicholson) with whom she falls in love. Too self-important to be taken seriously. Rated PG. 82m. DIR: Richard Rush. CAST: Susan Strasberg, Jack Nicholson, Adam Roarke, Dean Stockwell, Bruce Dern. 1968

PT 109 ★★1/2 Cliff Robertson is John F. Kennedy in this monument to the former president's war adventures on a World War II PT boat. Robertson is credible, but the story is only interesting because of the famous people and events it represents. 140m. DIR: Leslie Martinson. CAST: Cliff Robertson, Robert Culp, Ty Hardin, James Gregory, Robert Blake, Grant Williams. 1963

PUBERTY BLUES ★★★1/2 This film takes a frank look at the coming-of-age of two teenagers as they grow up on the beaches of Australia. The two girls become temporary victims of peer group pressure that involves drugs, alcohol, and sex. Unlike many other teenage films, *Puberty Blues* offers interesting insights into the rite of passage as seen from a female point of view. Rated R. 86m. DIR: Bruce Beresford. CAST: Nell Schofield, Jad Capelja. 1981

PUBLIC ACCESS ★★★1/2 A stranger stirs up the citizenry of a small town in this tense and incisive low-budget effort. Whiley Pritcher is a newcomer to the town of Brewster who starts up a local call-in program to discuss "what's wrong" with the community. Director Bryan Singer infuses the proceedings with a subtle menace that draws the viewer in; unfortunately, the movie's finale fizzles. Not rated; contains strong language, adult situations, and violence. 86m. DIR: Bryan Singer. CAST: Ron Marquette, Dina Brooks, Burt Williams, Larry Maxwell, Charles Kavanaugh, Brandon Boyle. 1995 DVD

PUBLIC COWBOY #1 ★★1/2 Singing cowboy Gene Autry battles modern-day rustlers who utilize airplanes. B&W; 59m. DIR: Joseph Kane. CAST: Gene Autry, Smiley Burnette, Ann Rutherford, William Farnum. 1937

PUBLIC ENEMY ★★★★1/2 Public Enemy, with a snarling, unredeemable James Cagney in the title role, is still a highly watchable gangster film. William Wellman expertly directed this fast-paced and unpretentious portrait of the rise and fall of a vicious hoodlum. B&W; 84m. DIR: William Wellman. CAST: James Cagney, Jean Harlow, Mae Clarke, Edward Woods, Beryl Mercer. 1931

PUBLIC ENEMY #1 ★★★ Theresa Russell brings considerable sass to her energized portrayal of the infamous Ma Barker, whose devotion to "her boys" now includes more than a faint whiff of incest, thanks to C. Courtney Joyner's revisionist script. The action is lively enough to overcome the often corny dialogue. Rated R for violence, profanity, nudity, simulated sex, and drug use. 91m. DIR: Mark L. Lester. CAST: Theresa Russell, Dan Cortese, Gavin Harrison, Joseph Lindsey, Joseph Dain, James Marsden, Frank Stallone, Eric Roberts. 1995

PUBLIC EYE, THE ★★★1/2 Writer-director Howard Franklin's fascinating film noir homage concerns a scrappy 1940s tabloid photographer (Joe Pesci) whose reputation for quality makes him the shutterbug of choice when major criminals get booked. Our hero gets involved in a twisty case involving a nightclub owner. Rated R for violence and profanity. 98m. DIR: Howard Franklin. CAST: Joe Pesci, Barbara Hershey, Jared Harris, Stanley Tucci. 1992

PUCKER UP AND BARK LIKE A DOG ★★★1/2 Cute romantic comedy about a reclusive and shy painter who searches for the girl of his dreams while trying to display his paintings in public. Wendy O. Williams gives the title its kinkiness as a biker who shows him how to live a little. Rated R for violence and nudity. 74m. DIR: Paul Salvatore Parco. CAST: Jonathan Gries, Lisa Zane, Barney Martin, Robert Culp, Wendy O. Williams, Paul Bartel, Phyllis Diller, Isabel Sanford. 1989

PUDD'NHEAD WILSON ★★★1/2 Mark Twain's sometimes humorous but always entertaining tale of deceit is faithfully re-created in this American Playhouse production. When a rash of crimes are committed in a Midwest town, only Pudd'nhead Wilson and his newfangled fingerprinting theory can un-

earth the culprit. Fine slice of Americana! 90m. DIR: Alan Bridges. CAST: Ken Howard, Lise Hilboldt. 1984

PULP ★★1/2 Sometimes funny, sometimes lame black comedy casts Michael Caine as a pulp mystery writer hired to pen the biography of retired film star and reputed mobster Mickey Rooney. Caine carries the film well enough, with his voice-over narration a nice Chandleresque touch, and Rooney is excellent in his few scenes, but the film never really catches fire. Rated PG for profanity and violence. 95m. DIR: Mike Hodges. CAST: Michael Caine, Mickey Rooney, Lionel Stander, Lizabeth Scott, Al Lettieri. 1972

PULP FICTION ★★★★ Writer-director Quentin Tarantino spares the viewer little in this tale of the underbelly of Los Angeles, where philosophizing hit men and techno-druggies live on the thrill-packed edge. If nothing else, Pulp Fiction will be remembered as the movie that shot John Travolta's career full of adrenaline. It's quite a wild ride. Rated R for violence, profanity, nudity, and sex. 153m. DIR: Quentin Tarantino. CAST: John Travolta, Samuel L. Jackson, Uma Thurman, Harvey Keitel, Tim Roth, Amanda Plummer, Maria de Medeiros, Ving Rhames, Eric Stoltz, Rosanna Arquette, Christopher Walken, Bruce Willis. 1994 DVD

PULSE ♥ Cliff De Young against some incredibly vicious electrical pulses. Rated PG-13. 90m. DIR: Paul Golding. CAST: Cliff De Young, Roxanne Hart, Joey Lawrence, Matthew Lawrence, Charles Tyner, Dennis Redfield. 1988

PUMA MAN, THE ♥ Humorless Italian junk about a man given extraordinary powers to fight evil. 80m. DIR: Alberto De Martino. CAST: Donald Pleasence, Sydne Rome. 1980

PUMP UP THE VOLUME ★★★ Unable to make friends at his new high school, teenager Christian Slater creates a charismatic alter ego with a pirate radio station set up in his bedroom. Director Alan Moyle's script is a little sketchy, but the film has a hip, youthful energy and the cast is uniformly strong. Rated R for language and nudity. 100m. DIR: Alan Moyle. CAST: Christian Slater, Scott Paulin, Samantha Mathis, Ellen Greene, James Hampton. 1990 DVD

PUMPING IRON ★★★★ Very good documentary concerning professional bodybuilding. Arnold Schwarzenegger and Lou Ferrigno ("The Incredible Hulk") are at the forefront as they prepare for the Mr. Universe contest. Always interesting and at times fascinating. Rated PG for language. 85m. DIR: George Butler, Robert Fiore. CAST: Arnold Schwarzenegger, Lou Ferrigno, Matty and Victoria Ferrigno, Mike Katz. 1977

PUMPING IRON II: THE WOMEN ★★★★1/2 This documentary on the 1983 Women's World Cup held at Caesar's Palace is more than just beauty and brawn. While it does seem to side with one contestant (and when you see Bev Francis's massive body, you'll know why), the film has all the passion and wit of a first-rate narrative. Not rated, but an equivalent of a PG. 107m. DIR: George Butler. CAST: Lori Bowen, Carla Dunlap, Bev Francis, Rachel McLish. 1985

PUMPKINHEAD ♥ A backwoods witch. Rated R for violence. 87m. DIR: Stan Winston. CAST: Lance Henriksen, Jeff East. 1989

PUMPKINHEAD II: BLOODWINGS ★★1/2 Sequel lacks the raw edge of its predecessor, but provides enough creepy moments to satisfy. The creature is resurrected and immediately goes on a killing spree. Attempts to delve deeper into the legend, showing how the cruel hazing of a retarded boy led to his death, and the birth of the creature. Rated R for violence, language, and nudity. 88m. **DIR:** Jeff Burr. **CAST:** Ami Dolenz, Andrew Robinson, Steve Kanaly, Caren Kaye, Linnea Quigley, Soleil Moon Frye. 1994

PUNCH THE CLOCK ❤ A professional car thief and the law school grad who has the hots for her. A movie this bad is a crime. Rated R for violence. 88m. **DIR:** Eric L. Schlagman. **CAST:** Mike Rogen. 1990

PUNCHLINE ★★★ An energetic performance from Tom Hanks can't quite compensate for the bewildering miscasting of Sally Field in this tribute to Tom Hanks. Although hellishly difficult life of stand-up comics. Although Hanks superbly conveys the anguish of a failed medschool student with comedy in his blood, Field never convincingly captures the conservative housewife who yearns for more. Inexplicably rated R for language. 128m. **DIR:** David Seltzer. **CAST:** Tom Hanks, Sally Field, John Goodman, Mark Rydell. 1988

PUNISHER, THE ★★★ Lean and mean adaptation of the Marvel Comics publication has Dolph Lundgren (looking like a cross between Elvis Presley and Clint Walker in his *Cheyenne* days) as the Punisher, a police-officer-turned-vigilante. Solid entertainment in a comic-book vein. Rated R for violence and profanity. 92m. **DIR:** Mark Goldblatt. **CAST:** Dolph Lundgren, Lou Gossett Jr., Jeroen Krabbé, Kim Miyori. 1990 DVD

P.U.N.K.S. ★★1/2 Kids will enjoy this engaging romp about a preteen named Drew who decides he's had enough of school bullies. Drew and his friends turn the table on their tormentors and an evil scientist (Henry Winkler) when they steal his invention that turns ninety-pound weaklings into the sort of guys who kick sand in the faces of ninety-pound weaklings. Rated PG. 99m. **DIR:** Sean McNamara. **CAST:** Henry Winkler, Randy Quaid, Cathy Moriarty, Patrick Renna, Ted Redwine. 1997

PUPPET MASTER, THE ★★★1/2 Highly effective chiller about a puppet maker (William Hickey) who uses an ancient Egyptian power to breed life into his demonic dolls. After his untimely death by suicide, a group of psychics tries to locate these terrifying toys. Excellent animation and special effects by David Allen (*Willow, Batteries Not Included*). Rated R for nudity and graphic violence. 90m. **DIR:** David Schmoeller. **CAST:** Paul LeMat, Irene Miracle, William Hickey. 1989

PUPPET MASTER II ★★1/2 The diabolically deadly dolls from the first film resurrect their dead creator and go on another rampage. Moderately scary. Rated R for violence, profanity, and mild gore. 90m. **DIR:** David Allen. **CAST:** Elizabeth MacLellan, Collin Bernsen, Gregory Webb, Charlie Spradling, Steve Welles, Nita Talbot. 1990

PUPPET MASTER III: TOULON'S REVENGE ★★1/2 In this second sequel, we go back and watch how Toulon and his killer puppets murder Nazis and escape from World War II Germany. Rated R for violence and profanity. 95m. **DIR:** David DeCoteau. **CAST:** Guy Rolfe, Ian Abercrombie, Sarah Douglas, Richard Lynch. 1991

PUPPET MASTER FOUR ★★ Excellent special effects and creative animation remain the highlights in this continuing series. In this chapter, a genius whiz kid and friends conduct experiments in the abandoned hotel where viewers were first introduced to the lifelike puppets. This one will remind viewers of the old Saturday afternoon matinee serial chapterplays, à la Flash Gordon and Commando Cody. Rated R for violence, nudity, and profanity. 80m. **DIR:** Jeff Burr. **CAST:** Gordon Currie, Chandra West, Jason Adams, Teresa Hill, Guy Rolfe. 1993

PUPPET MASTER 5: THE FINAL CHAPTER ★★ It's hard to keep a good puppet down, as this direct-to-video series seems to suggest with each new entry. The deadly puppets must battle two foes: an evil doctor obsessed with learning the secret to their animation, and a demon from another dimension who plans to kill the Puppetmaster and steal the puppets' magic. Rated R for violence. 81m. **DIR:** Jeff Burr. **CAST:** Guy Rolfe, Gordon Currie, Chandra West, Nicholas Guest, Willard E. Pugh. 1994

PUPPET MASTERS, THE ★★1/2 Aliens invade Earth by taking over the bodies of American citizens, with only Donald Sutherland and his crew of agents standing between them and ultimate conquest. Half-hearted adaptation of Robert Heinlein's 1951 novel wastes the potential of its cast and source material. Rated R for violence and profanity. 109m. **DIR:** Stuart Orme. **CAST:** Donald Sutherland, Eric Thal, Julie Warner, Keith David, Will Patton, Richard Belzer, Yaphet Kotto. 1994

PUPPET ON A CHAIN ★★1/2 American agent battles a Dutch heroin ring in this lackluster Alistair MacLean thriller. There's an exciting speedboat chase through the canals of Amsterdam, but the rest of the film is a snoozer. Rated PG. 97m. **DIR:** Geoffrey Reeve. **CAST:** Sven-Bertil Taube, Barbara Parkins, Alexander Knox. 1972

PUPPETOON MOVIE, THE ★★★★ Pioneering fantasy director-producer George Pal established his initial Hollywood credentials with a series of so-called "Puppetoon" shorts, all made with a rarely used technique known as replacement animation. Pal and staff constructed up to five *thousand* wooden figures for each cartoon; minor distinctions from one figure to the next, when filmed one frame at a time, thus conveyed the illusion of movement. This collection of shorts gathers the best of Pal's work. 80m. **DIR:** Arnold Leibovit. 1987

PURCHASE PRICE, THE ★★★1/2 A good cast and skillful direction turn a predictable script into good entertainment. A torch singer trying to get away from her gangster boyfriend marries a perfect stranger. The stars make it believable. B&W; 74m. **DIR:** William Wellman. **CAST:** Barbara Stanwyck, George Brent, Lyle Talbot, David Landau. 1932

PURE COUNTRY ★★★ Featuring nearly a dozen George Strait songs destined for extended jukebox play, this warmhearted story about a personable country singer is predictable but entertaining. Too bad Strait's down-home charm is buried under a pile of clichés. Rated PG for language. 112m. **DIR:** Christopher Cain. **CAST:** George Strait, Lesley Ann Warren, John Doe, Isabel Glasser, Rory Calhoun. **1992 DVD**

PURE DANGER ★★ A short-order cook and his waitress girlfriend find a bag of diamonds and think they've hit pay dirt. Then they meet the mobsters who will do anything to get the gems back. Rated R for violence, profanity, and nudity. 99m. **DIR:** C. Thomas Howell. **CAST:** C. Thomas Howell, Teri Ann Linn, Leon, Michael Russo. **1995**

PURE FORMALITY, A ★★ A famous writer, under arrest in an isolated police station, is interrogated by a sinister official who professes to admire the writer, but pressures him to confess to some terrible unnamed crime. The two stars are excellent, but the film is sluggish; you'll probably guess the "surprise" ending long before it arrives. In French with English subtitles. Not rated; contains mature themes and brief nudity. 108m. **DIR:** Giuseppe Tornatore. **CAST:** Gérard Depardieu, Roman Polanski. **1994**

PURE LUCK ★★ In this Americanized version of Francis Veber's *Le Chevre*, Danny Glover plays a hapless detective assigned to work with a bumbling accountant in order to locate the world's most accident-prone heiress. The actors try hard, but it just ain't that funny, folks. Rated PG. 96m. **DIR:** Nadia Tass. **CAST:** Martin Short, Danny Glover, Sheila Kelley, Scott Wilson, Harry Shearer, Sam Wanamaker, Jorge Luke. **1991**

PURGATORY ★★★★ High marks to writer Gordon Dawson's marvelously clever Western allegory, which concerns a violent band of outlaws that stumbles into a strange little town—dubbed Refuge—where the sheriff doesn't carry a gun, and the oddly familiar citizens seem resigned to whatever Fate provides. Sam Shepard is perfect as the dignified yet powerful sheriff, while Eric Roberts is appropriately evil as the gang leader who unwisely decides to shear all these apparently sheeplike civilians. The results should please even those who don't normally care for conventional Westerns. Rated PG-13 for violence and profanity. 95m. **DIR:** Uli Edel. **CAST:** Sam Shepard, Eric Roberts, Peter Stormare, Brad Rowe, Donnie Wahlberg, Randy Quaid. **1999**

PURLIE VICTORIOUS ★★★1/2 Alan Alda made his film debut as a southern liberal in this good-humored comedy written by Ossie Davis. Davis and his wife, Ruby Dee, play an evangelist couple who try to convert an old barn into an integrated church. Their chief opposition comes from the bigot (Sorrel Booke) who owns the barn. Also known as *Gone Are the Days*. B&W; 93m. **DIR:** Nicholas Webster. **CAST:** Ossie Davis, Ruby Dee, Sorrell Booke, Alan Alda, Godfrey Cambridge, Beah Richards. **1963**

PURPLE HEART, THE ★★★★ Dana Andrews and Richard Conte are leaders of a group of American fliers who are captured by the Japanese after they bomb Tokyo and put on trial for war crimes. This fascinating film is a minor classic. B&W; 99m. **DIR:** Lewis Milestone. **CAST:** Dana Andrews, Richard Conte, Farley Granger, Sam Levene, Tala Birell, Nestor Paiva. **1944**

PURPLE HEARTS ★★ Anyone who can sit all the way through this Vietnam War–film romance deserves a medal. Ken Wahl stars as a surgeon in the United States Navy Medical Corps who falls in love with a nurse (Cheryl Ladd). There's an additional forty minutes of unnecessary and unoriginal story tacked on. Rated R for nudity, profanity, violence, and gore. 115m. **DIR:** Sidney J. Furie. **CAST:** Ken Wahl, Cheryl Ladd. **1984**

PURPLE MONSTER STRIKES, THE ★★★ The Purple Monster lands near Dr. Cyrus Layton's observatory and tricks him into revealing the plans for a new spaceship. Although the science is ridiculous and the effects unsophisticated by today's standards, this is one of Republic Studios' best-remembered serials of the mid-1940s and features master heavy Roy Barcroft in one of his finest roles. B&W; 15 chapters. **DIR:** Spencer Gordon Bennet, Fred Brannon. **CAST:** Dennis Moore, Linda Stirling, Roy Barcroft. **1945**

PURPLE NOON ★★★ An amoral wastrel (Alain Delon) is sent to the Mediterranean to bring an American playboy home but decides instead to murder him and assume his identity. Director René Clement builds an atmosphere of languid, decadent menace and draws a fascinating, reptilian performance from Delon, but the film is overlong and ambles through some false climaxes before the final, ironic twist. In French with English subtitles. Rated PG-13 for mature themes. 118m. **DIR:** René Clement. **CAST:** Alain Delon, Maurice Ronet, Marie Laforet. **1961**

PURPLE PEOPLE EATER ★★1/2 A sappy family flick about an alien (the title character) who comes to Earth to join a rock 'n' roll band. The fine cast, headed by Ned Beatty, is overshadowed by a sickeningly sweet alien puppet. Rated PG. 91m. **DIR:** Linda Shayne. **CAST:** Ned Beatty, Shelley Winters, Neil Patrick Harris, Peggy Lipton. **1988**

PURPLE RAIN ★★1/2 In his first movie, pop star Prince plays a struggling young musician searching for self-awareness and love while trying to break into the rock charts. The film unsuccessfully straddles the line between a concert release and a storytelling production. As it is, the music is great, but the plot leaves a lot to be desired. Rated R for nudity, suggested sex, and profanity. 113m. **DIR:** Albert Magnoli. **CAST:** Prince, Apollonia Kotero, Morris Day, Olga Karlatos. **1984 DVD**

PURPLE ROSE OF CAIRO, THE ★★★★ Mia Farrow is a Depression-era housewife who finds her dreary day-to-day existence enlivened when a dashing, romantic hero walks off the screen and sweeps her off her feet. Like Woody Allen's *Zelig* and *Broadway Danny Rose*, this mixes humor with very human situations. The result is a very satisfying work. Rated PG for violence. 85m. **DIR:** Woody Allen. **CAST:** Mia Farrow, Jeff Daniels, Danny Aiello, Edward Herrmann, John Wood. **1985**

PURPLE TAXI, THE ★★★ Fred Astaire, Edward Albert, and Philippe Noiret star in this exploration of angst, love, and friendship in Ireland, where a collection of expatriate characters impaled on memories and self-destructive compulsions work out their kinks before returning to various homelands. Fine backdrops in Ireland's "curtain of rain" and impressive acting. Rated R. 107m. **DIR:** Yves Boisset. **CAST:** Fred Astaire, Edward Albert, Philippe Noiret, Peter Ustinov, Charlotte Rampling, Agostina Belli. **1977**

PURSUED ★★★ A cowboy, Robert Mitchum, searches for the murderer of his father in this taut, atmospheric Western. The entire cast is very good, and famed action director Raoul Walsh keeps things moving along at a brisk pace. B&W; 101m. **DIR:** Raoul Walsh. **CAST:** Robert Mitchum, Teresa Wright, Judith Anderson, Dean Jagger, Harry Carey Jr., Alan Hale Sr. **1947**

PURSUIT ★★ So-so mercenary flick pits a purist against greedy cohorts in an attempt to recover the gold meant to stabilize an African nation's economy. Rated R for nudity, violence, and profanity. 94m. **DIR:** John H. Parr. **CAST:** James Ryan. **1990**

PURSUIT OF D. B. COOPER ★★1/2 The famous skyjacker is turned into a fun-loving good old boy in this hit-and-miss comedy starring Treat Williams, Robert Duvall, and Kathryn Harrold. If you liked *Smokey and the Bandit*, you'll probably enjoy this. Rated PG because of minimal violence and sexuality. 100m. **DIR:** Roger Spottiswoode. **CAST:** Treat Williams, Robert Duvall, Kathryn Harrold, Ed Flanders, Paul Gleason, R. G. Armstrong. **1981**

PURSUIT OF HAPPINESS, THE ★★★1/2 Although it will seem dated to many, this heartfelt drama about a young man standing up for his ideals is still worth a look. Robert Mulligan's direction is excellent, and the cast features many now-familiar faces in small roles. Rated PG. 85m. **DIR:** Robert Mulligan. **CAST:** Michael Sarrazin, Barbara Hershey, Robert Klein, Arthur Hill, E. G. Marshall, David Doyle, Barnard Hughes, Sada Thompson, Rue McClanahan, William Devane, Charles Durning. **1971**

PURSUIT OF THE GRAF SPEE ★★★1/2 Highly enjoyable account of the World War II sea chase and eventual battle involving British naval forces and the German's super warship, the *Graf Spee*. Featuring a solid cast, the film benefits from attention to detail and a realistic building of tension. 106m. **DIR:** Michael Powell, Emeric Pressburger. **CAST:** John Gregson, Anthony Quayle, Peter Finch, Bernard Lee, Ian Hunter, Patrick Macnee, Christopher Lee. **1957**

PURSUIT TO ALGIERS ★★★ Basil Rathbone's Holmes and Nigel Bruce's Watson become bodyguards accompanying the young heir to a royal throne on a hazardous sea voyage. Their client disguises himself as Watson's nephew, which makes for some droll dialogue. One of the few Rathbone/Bruce films that borrows nothing from the canon. Not rated—suitable for family viewing. B&W; 65m. **DIR:** Roy William Neill. **CAST:** Basil Rathbone, Nigel Bruce, John Abbott, Marjorie Riordan, Martin Kosleck, Rosalind Ivan. **1945**

PUSHED TO THE LIMIT ★★ Vengefest features a young woman taking on a ruthless Asian drug dealer who has killed her brother. Not rated; contains seemingly endless violence. 96m. **DIR:** Michael Mileham. **CAST:** Mimi Lesseos, Henry Hayshi. **1992**

PUSHING HANDS ★★★1/2 Seriocomic account of the culture clash that occurs when an elderly T'ai chi master from mainland China comes to live with his son's suburban New York family. Director Ang Lee's understated first feature is slow going at first but then exhibits a charm that's infectious. The unfamiliar cast prove completely at home in their roles—including Lee's son Haan as the American grandson living between two cultures. In English and Man-

darin with subtitles. Not rated. 108m. **DIR:** Ang Lee. **CAST:** Sihung Lung, Lai Wang, Bo Z. Wang, Deb Snyder, Haan Lee, Emily Liu. **1992 DVD**

PUSHING TIN ★★★ Two air traffic controllers develop an intense rivalry while their marriages fray in this *M*A*S*H* of the skyways. The acting, characters, and workplace details are engaging, but the story's underlying threat of professional and domestic mass hysteria is dulled by soap opera plotting and an unconvincing ending. Based on the article "Something's Got to Give" by Darcy Frey. Rated R for language, nudity, and sexual content. 110m. **DIR:** Mike Newell. **CAST:** John Cusack, Billy Bob Thornton, Cate Blanchett, Angelina Jolie. **1999 DVD**

PUTNEY SWOPE ★★★★ This wildly funny film concerns a black man who takes over a Madison Avenue advertising firm. Alan Abel, Mel Brooks, and Allen Garfield appear in this zany parody of American life-styles. Rated R. 88m. **DIR:** Robert Downey. **CAST:** Alan Abel, Mel Brooks, Allen Garfield, Pepi Hermine, Ruth Hermine, Antonio Fargas. **1969**

PYGMALION ★★★★1/2 This is an impeccable adaptation of George Bernard Shaw's classic play. The comedy is deliciously sophisticated. The performances are exquisite, particularly that of Leslie Howard, who'll make you forget Rex Harrison's Henry Higgins in an instant. As the professor's feisty Cockney pupil, Wendy Hiller is a delight. B&W; 95m. **DIR:** Anthony Asquith, Leslie Howard. **CAST:** Leslie Howard, Wendy Hiller, Wilfrid Lawson, Marie Lohr, David Tree. **1938**

PYRATES 🎬 Real-life husband-and-wife Kevin Bacon and Kyra Sedgwick play a couple who ignite sparks whenever they have sex, setting fires. Too bad they couldn't turn up the heat in this one-joke effort. Rated R for nudity. 98m. **DIR:** Noah Stern. **CAST:** Kevin Bacon, Kyra Sedgwick. **1991**

PYROMANIAC'S LOVE STORY, A ★★1/2 A bakery burns to the ground, igniting passionate fires in everyone connected to it, but the romantic entanglements are complicated and overdone. A few impressive performances, especially John Leguizamo as a well-meaning but muddled baker, but this romantic fable is too precious for its own good. Rated PG for profanity. 94m. **DIR:** Joshua Brand. **CAST:** William Baldwin, John Leguizamo, Sadie Frost, Erika Eleniak, Michael Lerner, Joan Plowright. **1995**

PYX, THE 🎬 A dead prostitute and the police investigation mounted to uncover her killer. Rated R for violence. 111m. **DIR:** Harvey Hart. **CAST:** Karen Black, Christopher Plummer, Donald Pilon. **1973**

Q ★★★★ This is an old-fashioned giant monster film. The stop-motion animation is excellent, the acting (done tongue-in-cheek) is perfect. The story revolves around the arrival of a giant flying lizard in New York City. A series of ritualistic murders follow and point to the monster being Quetzelcoatl (the flying serpent-god of the Aztecs). Rated R. 93m. DIR: Larry Cohen. CAST: Michael Moriarty, David Carradine, Candy Clark, Richard Roundtree, James Dixon. 1982

Q & A ★★★★ Nick Nolte gives a compelling performance as a much-decorated police detective whose brutal killing of a Puerto Rican drug dealer brings about an investigation, which novice assistant district attorney Timothy Hutton is drafted into conducting. Rated R for brutal violence, profanity, and nudity. 134m. DIR: Sidney Lumet. CAST: Nick Nolte, Timothy Hutton, Armand Assante, Patrick O'Neal. 1990 DVD

QB VII ★★★★ Leon Uris's hefty bestseller is vividly brought to life in this five-hours-plus made-for-television drama about a Polish expatriate doctor living in England who sues an American writer for libel when the writer accuses him of carrying out criminal medical activities for the Nazis during World War II. Anthony Hopkins is brilliant as the physician, Ben Gazzara is outraged and tenacious as the writer. Expect a powerful, engrossing ending. 312m. DIR: Tom Gries. CAST: Anthony Hopkins, Ben Gazzara, Leslie Caron, Lee Remick, Anthony Quayle. 1974

QUACKSER FORTUNE HAS A COUSIN IN THE BRONX ★★★★ This comedy-drama falls into the category of sleeper. Gene Wilder is delightful as an Irishman who marches to the beat of a different drummer. Margot Kidder is a rich American going to university in Dublin who meets and falls in love with him. Filmed in Ireland and rated R for nudity and language. 88m. DIR: Waris Hussein. CAST: Gene Wilder, Margot Kidder, Eileen Colgan. 1970 DVD

QUADROPHENIA ★★★1/2 Based on The Who's rock opera, this is the story of a teenager growing up in the early 1960s and the decisions he is forced to make on the path to adulthood. Rated R because the language is rough and the violence graphic. 115m. DIR: Franc Roddam. CAST: Phil Daniels, Mark Wingett, Philip Davis, Sting. 1979

QUAKE ★★ The good news is that lovely Erika Anderson has survived a ravaging San Francisco earthquake. The bad news is that Steve Railsback, obsessed with Anderson, kidnaps her amidst all the confusion. The psychological aftershocks between the two barely keep this slight effort from slipping into the cracks. Rated R for language and violence. 89m. DIR: Louis Morneau. CAST: Steve Railsback, Erika Anderson, Eb Lottimer, Burton Gilliam, Dick Miller. 1992

QUALITY STREET ★★1/2 In early nineteenth-century England, a schoolteacher (Katharine Hepburn) worries about whether her youthful flame (Eric Blore) will return from war. A familiar story, but a fine cast elevates the proceedings. B&W; 84m. DIR: George Stevens. CAST: Katharine Hepburn, Joan Fontaine, Eric Blore, Franchot Tone. 1937

QUANTUM LEAP (TV SERIES) ★★★★ When scientist Dr. Sam Beckett gets lost during a time-travel experiment, he's bounced from time to time, leaping into troubled individuals and helping them overcome their problems. His only companion is a holographic image of another scientist. Television series tackles important issues in a sensitive yet entertaining way. Available episodes include "The Pilot Episode," "The Color of Truth," "Camikazi Kid," "What Price Gloria?" and "Catch a Falling Star." Pilot episode 93m; other episodes 48m. DIR: David Hemmings, Mike Vejar, Alan J. Levi, Donald P. Bellisario. CAST: Scott Bakula, Dean Stockwell, Jennifer Runyon, Jason Priestley, John Cullum, Janine Turner. 1989 DVD

QUARANTINE ★★ A sense that this film has no real conclusion hurts what could have been a top-notch sci-fi film. A Gestapo-like police force herds carriers of a disease into a quarantined area. Interesting commentary on the AIDS epidemic. Rated PG-13 for violence and profanity. 92m. DIR: Charles Wilkinson. CAST: Garwin Sanford, Jerry Wasserman, Tom McBeath. 1989

QUARREL, THE ★★★1/2 Saul Rubinek and R. H. Thomson shine in this two-person exchange of ideas and faith. The men play Holocaust survivors who have lost their families to the death camps. Relocated in Montreal, the men meet in 1948. One has turned to his religion for strength; the other has turned his back on religion. As they discuss the past twenty years, their differences and similarities come to the surface. Not rated. 90m. DIR: Eli Cohen. CAST: Saul Rubinek, R. H. Thomson. 1990 DVD

QUARTERBACK PRINCESS ★★1/2 True story of Tami Maida, the girl who came to a small Oregon town and managed to become a star on the football team as well as the homecoming queen. Helen Hunt is adequate as Tami; Don Murray is better as her supportive dad. Made for television. 96m. DIR: Noel Black. CAST: Helen Hunt, Don Murray, Barbara Babcock, Dana Elcar, John Stockwell. 1983

QUARTET (1948) ★★★★ A dramatization of W. Somerset Maugham's favorite stories: "The Facts of Life," "The Alien Corn," "The Kite," and "The Colonel's Lady." All four are immensely watchable. B&W; 120m. DIR: Ken Annakin, Arthur Crabtree, Harold French, Ralph Smart. CAST: Dirk Bogarde, Hermione Baddeley, Mervyn Johns, Cecil Parker, Basil Radford, Françoise Rosay, Susan Shaw, Naunton Wayne, Mai Zetterling. 1948

QUARTET (1981) ★★ In terms of acting, this is a first-rate film. Unfortunately, the pathetic characters that mope around in this period piece drag down any positive points. Isabelle Adjani plays the wife of a convicted criminal who ends up in a ménage à trois with a married couple, played by Alan Bates and Maggie Smith. Rated R for nudity. 101m. DIR: James Ivory. CAST: Isabelle Adjani, Alan Bates, Anthony Higgins, Maggie Smith. 1981

QUATERMASS AND THE PIT ★★★ Nigel Kneale's inscrutable, indefatigable Prof. Quatermass—who launched rockets from Britain to deep space, locked horns with authority figures and became one of the most popular British TV heroes of the Fifties—is played here by Andre Morell in a full-length BBC telecast. It's technically primitive and rather talky, but as the talk is by top fantasy scripter Kneale, who's complaining? B&W; 180m. DIR: Rudolph Cartier. CAST: Andre Morell, Cec Linder, Anthony Bushell, Michael Ripper. 1958 DVD

QUATERMASS CONCLUSION, THE ★★ It's sad to see a great premise destroyed by bad editing and sloppy script continuity. Of course, the fact that this film is an edited-down version of a British miniseries may be the cause. In the strange future world of the story, society seems to be suffering a terrible case of inertia. The world's teen population is committing mass suicide, and only Dr. Quatermass (John Mills), genius scientist, can save them. 105m. **DIR:** Piers Haggard. **CAST:** John Mills, Simon MacCorkindale, Barbara Kellerman, Margaret Tyzack. **1979**

QUATERMASS EXPERIMENT, THE ★★★ The first Hammer Films horror film is a splendid, low-budget exercise in British suspense, science fiction, and futuristic horror. When an experimental spacecraft returns to Britain, its crew has mysteriously vanished—all save one member, who is comatose and covered in a thin layer of slime, which subtly begins to change him. This film launched the world horror and sci-fi revival that otherwise was dominated by dreadful teen horror flicks. Also titled (in U.S. only): *The Creeping Unknown.* B&W; 78m. **DIR:** Val Guest. **CAST:** Brian Donlevy, Jack Warner, Richard Wordsworth. **1956**

QUATORZE JUILET ★★★★ Paris had no better publicist than René Clair, whose early films were delightfully simple musical fantasies of living in that city. *Quatorze Juliet* follows two young lovers—a taxi driver and a flower peddler—as they come into contact with different citizens and neighborhoods of Paris. In French with English subtitles. B&W; 85m. **DIR:** René Clair. **CAST:** Annabella, George Rigaud. **1932**

QUEEN CHRISTINA ★★★★ This haunting romance might be laughable if anyone but Greta Garbo were in it. She plays the controversial Swedish queen who gave up her throne for the sake of love (according to the movie). The last scene—of Garbo looking wistfully into the camera—has become her trademark. B&W; 97m. **DIR:** Rouben Mamoulian. **CAST:** Greta Garbo, John Gilbert, Lewis Stone, C. Aubrey Smith, Reginald Owen. **1933**

QUEEN ELIZABETH ★★ Sarah Bernhardt stars as Queen Elizabeth I in this heavy-handed silent melodrama. The plot revolves around a love triangle involving the queen, the earl of Essex, and the countess of Nottingham. Silent. B&W; 46m. **DIR:** Henri Desfontanes. **CAST:** Sarah Bernhardt. **1927**

QUEEN KELLY ★★★ Gloria Swanson used her clout to keep Erich Von Stroheim's *Queen Kelly* buried for nearly sixty years. This reconstructed version is but a shadow of the five-hour epic Von Stroheim had intended to make. The sumptuously mounted melodrama is fascinating—and often hilarious—for its indulgences, decadence, and outright perversity. Swanson plays a rebellious schoolgirl who is kidnapped from a convent and introduced to the pleasures of life by a debauched prince. Silent. B&W; 95m. **DIR:** Erich Von Stroheim. **CAST:** Gloria Swanson. **1928**

QUEEN MARGOT ★★★★ The bloody Saint Bartholomew's Day Massacre of 1572, when thousands of French Protestants were slaughtered at the command of King Charles IX, provides the background for this sumptuous film of Alexandre Dumas's novel. The plot revolves around the marriage of Charles's sister Marguerite to the Protestant Henri Navarre and the intrigues of the French court. Florid, passionate, and enthralling. In French with English subtitles. Rated R for nudity, sex, and violence. 143m. **DIR:** Patrice Chereau. **CAST:** Isabelle Adjani, Daniel Auteuil, Jean-Hugues Anglade, Virna Lisi, Vincent Perez, Pascal Greggory. **1994**

QUEEN OF HEARTS ★★★★ A comedy-drama with dialogue primarily in English but a sensibility that is very Italian. By running away from her marriage to a wealthy Sicilian, the beautiful Rosa (Anita Zagaria) sets in motion a tragic and funny tale of revenge. Not rated, the film has profanity and violence. 112m. **DIR:** Jon Amiel. **CAST:** Anita Zagaria, Joseph Long, Eileen Way. **1989**

QUEEN OF OUTER SPACE ★★★ Earthmen venture to Venus to find an all-female civilization led by Zsa Zsa Gabor. So bad, it's hysterical. A must for all B-film fanatics. 80m. **DIR:** Edward L. Bernds. **CAST:** Zsa Zsa Gabor, Eric Fleming, Paul Birch. **1958**

QUEEN OF THE STARDUST BALLROOM ★★★★ Touching love story about a lonely widow (Maureen Stapleton) who finally finds Mr. Right (Charles Durning). Stapleton is outstanding. 100m. **DIR:** Sam O'Steen. **CAST:** Maureen Stapleton, Charles Durning, Michael Brandon, Michael Strong. **1975 DVD**

QUEEN VICTORIA AND THE ZOMBIES ♥ Queen Victoria and Prince Albert come from outer space to spend some time in a vacation cabin in this awful horror-comedy. Not rated. 118m. **DIR:** Steve Postal. **CAST:** Charlotte Leslie, Kendrick Kaufman, Eddie Crew, Jennifer Tuck, Angela Shepard, Melanie Lee, Maurice Postal. **1990**

QUEENIE ★★★ Lavish television production based on Michael Korda's novel, a fictionalized story of the youth and early movie career of his real-life aunt, Merle Oberon. The opening scenes, set in early 1930s India, are more interesting than her adult years. 235m. **DIR:** Larry Peerce. **CAST:** Mia Sara, Kirk Douglas, Claire Bloom, Joel Grey, Martin Balsam, Sarah Miles, Topol, Kate Emma Davies. **1987**

QUEENS LOGIC ★★★ Maturity and contentment can arrive at any age, assuming, of course, they arrive at all. That's the theme of this rambling, uneven, but amiable coming-of-age comedy-drama. It's *thirtysomething* crossed with *Diner.* Rated R for profanity. 116m. **DIR:** Steve Rash. **CAST:** Joe Mantegna, Kevin Bacon, John Malkovich, Ken Olin, Linda Fiorentino, Jamie Lee Curtis. **1991 DVD**

QUERELLE ★★1/2 In this depressing rendering of Jean Genet's story, Brad Davis stars in the title role as a young sailor whose good looks set off a chain reaction. This is a disturbing and depressing portrait of terminally unhappy people. In German with English subtitles. Rated R for nudity and obscenity. 120m. **DIR:** Rainer Werner Fassbinder. **CAST:** Rainer Werner Fassbinder, Brad Davis, Franco Nero, Jeanne Moreau. **1982**

QUEST, THE (1985) ★★ Henry Thomas plays a young boy living in Australia who has reason to believe that a monster lives in a small lake not far from his home. He sets out to prove the creature's existence—or to expose it as a fraud. Though slow, this film has decent acting. Rated PG. 94m. **DIR:** Brian Trenchard-Smith. **CAST:** Henry Thomas, Tony Barry, John Ewart. 1985

QUEST, THE (1996) ★★ The plot of Jean-Claude Van Damme's directorial debut (he is also credited with the original story) defies synopsis. Set in the 1920s, it has something to do with a gang of New York street urchins (led by Van Damme), South Sea pirates (who kidnap Van Damme), and a sort of international martial arts championship deep in the Himalayas (in which Van Damme competes). Not much sense or drama, but plenty of bone-crunching action for the director-star's fans. Rated PG-13 for martial arts violence. 95m. **DIR:** Jean-Claude Van Damme. **CAST:** Jean-Claude Van Damme, Roger Moore, James Remar. 1996 DVD

QUEST FOR CAMELOT 🎬 A young girl and a blind hermit thwart an evil knight's uprising against King Arthur. A weak story, shoddy animation, poor voice work, (despite the talented cast), and atrocious songs make this one of the worst cartoon features ever made. Featuring the voices of Jessalyn Gilsig, Cary Elwes, Eric Idle, Don Rickles, Gary Oldman, Jane Seymour, and Pierce Brosnan. Rated G. 85m. **DIR:** Frederik Du Chau. 1998 DVD

QUEST FOR FIRE ★★★1/2 In this movie, about the attempt to learn the secret of making fire by a tribe of primitive men, director Jean-Jacques Annaud (*Black and White in Color*) and screenwriter Gerard Brach (*Tess*) have achieved what once seemed to be impossible: a first-rate, compelling film about the dawn of man. Rated R for violence, gore, nudity, and semi-explicit sex. 97m. **DIR:** Jean-Jacques Annaud. **CAST:** Everett McGill, Rae Dawn Chong, Ron Perlman. 1981

QUEST FOR THE LOST CITY 🎬 No-budget adventure about a man searching out a lost city so he can track down and kill the tribal leader who murdered his father. Club Med this is not! Not rated; contains violence. 92m. **DIR:** T. Jardus Griedanus. **CAST:** Christian Malcom, Bruce Mitchell, Shane Marceau. 1993

QUEST FOR THE MIGHTY SWORD 🎬 Latest, and hopefully last, of the *Ator* sword-'n'-sorcery sagas. None of these films were any good, but this one's the pits. Rated PG-13 for violence. 94m. **DIR:** David Hills. **CAST:** Eric Allen Kramer, Margaret Lenzey, Donal O'Brian, Laura Gemser. 1989

QUEST OF THE DELTA KNIGHTS ★★★ In this enchanting, funny medieval story about good and evil, a young slave finds he's the key to the treasures of Archimedes and ventures on a dangerous journey. Good fight scenes. Rated PG. 97m. **DIR:** James Dodson. **CAST:** David Warner, Olivia Hussey, Corbin Allred, Brigid Conley Walsh, David Kind, Sarah Douglas. 1993

QUESTION OF FAITH ★★★1/2 Made-for-TV tearjerker, originally aired under the title *Leap of Faith*. Superior cast, led by Anne Archer and Sam Neill, and literate script help this incurable disease movie to transcend the boundaries usually associated with such fare. 90m. **DIR:** Stephen Gyllenhaal. **CAST:** Anne Archer, Sam Neill, Frances Lee McCain, Louis Giambalvo, James Tolkan, Michael Constantine. 1993

QUESTION OF HONOR, A ★★★★ Superior made-for-TV movie tells the true story of an honest New York narcotics officer who got caught in the middle of a federal drug scam and found himself accused of corruption. Based on a book by Sonny Grosso, the cop portrayed by Roy Scheider in *The French Connection*. Not rated. 134m. **DIR:** Jud Taylor. **CAST:** Ben Gazzara, Robert Vaughn, Paul Sorvino, Tony Roberts, Danny Aiello. 1982

QUESTION OF SILENCE, A ★★★★1/2 After an unusual murder is committed, three women, all strangers to one another, stand trial for the same crime. A woman psychiatrist is appointed to the case after the three openly display their hostilities toward male-dominated society. Rated R for profanity. Available in original Dutch or dubbed. 92m. **DIR:** Marleen Gorris. **CAST:** Cox Habbema, Nelly Frijda. 1983

QUICK ★★★1/2 Scripter Frederick Bailey's apparently routine crime thriller takes an intriguing turn when hit lady Teri Polo spares her latest target—a nerdish accountant, superbly played by Martin Donovan—and employs him as a bargaining chip to save her own skin. Their blossoming relationship sparkles in this low-budget saga. Rated R for nudity, simulated sex, profanity, and violence. 99m. **DIR:** Rick King. **CAST:** Jeff Fahey, Teri Polo, Robert Davi, Martin Donovan, Tia Carrere. 1993

QUICK AND THE DEAD, THE (1987) ★★★★ Made-for-HBO Western is the third in a trilogy of high-class shoot-'em-ups adapted from the stories by Louis L'Amour for star Sam Elliott. He is marvelous as a grizzled frontiersman who comes to the aid of a family (headed by Tom Conti and Kate Capshaw) making its way across the American wilderness. 90m. **DIR:** Robert Day. **CAST:** Sam Elliott, Kate Capshaw, Tom Conti, Matt Clark, Kenny Morrison. 1987

QUICK AND THE DEAD, THE (1995) ★★★1/2 Tribute to the spaghetti Western is a mixture of the good, the bad, and the sluggish. Sharon Stone convincingly plays a "lady" gunslinger on the revenge trail. Problem is, she has to wait her turn in a protracted quick-draw competition to get at villain Gene Hackman, and, as a result, the story moves in fits and starts. That said, it's generally enjoyable, especially for fans of this subgenre. Rated R for violence, gore, profanity, and nudity. 105m. **DIR:** Sam Raimi. **CAST:** Sharon Stone, Gene Hackman, Russell Crowe, Leonardo DiCaprio, Lance Henriksen, Keith David, Pat Hingle, Kevin Conway, Woody Strode. 1995 DVD

QUICK CHANGE ★★★1/2 Robbing a bank is easy for Bill Murray (who co-directed), Geena Davis, and Randy Quaid—three New Yorkers driven to desperate measures. It's the getaway that they find nearly impossible. Adapted from the 1981 novel by Jay Cronley, this fast-and-funny caper film benefits from Murray's off-the-cuff comedy style. Rated R. 98m. **DIR:** Bill Murray, Howard Franklin. **CAST:** Bill Murray, Geena Davis, Randy Quaid, Jason Robards Jr. 1990

QUICK, LET'S GET MARRIED 🎬 Made in 1964 but not released for seven years, this feeble farce has Ginger Rogers as the madam of a bordello conspiring to pull off a hoax on a supposedly innocent prostitute. 96m. **DIR:** William Dieterle. **CAST:** Ginger Rogers,

Ray Milland, Barbara Eden, Walter Abel, Michael Ansara, Elliott Gould. 1971

QUICKER THAN THE EYE ★★ Magic is the gimmick in this story of a group of terrorists who plan to assassinate a foreign diplomat. Poorly dubbed Swiss-produced film. Rated PG for language and violence. 94m. DIR: Nicolas Gessner. CAST: Ben Gazzara, Mary Crosby. 1989

QUICKSAND: NO ESCAPE ★★1/2 An honest family man (Tim Matheson) gets mixed up in deceit, bribery, and murder. Donald Sutherland is great at portraying the nemesis: a slimy private detective. The twists in this made-for-cable chiller seem interesting at first, but then they just become unbelievable. 96m. DIR: Michael Pressman. CAST: Donald Sutherland, Tim Matheson, Jay Acovone, Timothy Carhart. 1991

QUICKSILVER ★★ Wretched mess of a film. Kevin Bacon stars as a Wall Street wizard who blows it all one day and then puts his natural talents to work by becoming … a bicycle messenger! Rated PG for mild violence. 101m. DIR: Tom Donnelly. CAST: Kevin Bacon, Jami Gertz, Paul Rodriguez, Rudy Ramos, Laurence Fishburne. 1986

•**QUICKSILVER HIGHWAY** ★★★ Faithful but not particularly frightening adaptations of stories by Stephen King ("Chattery Teeth") and Clive Barker ("The Body Politic"). Fine score by Mark Mothersbaugh. Not rated; contains scenes of mild horror violence. 100m. DIR: Mick Garris. CAST: Christopher Lloyd, Matt Frewer, Raphael Sbarge, Missy Crider, Veronica Cartwright. 1998

QUIET COOL 🎬 New York cop journeys to the Pacific Northwest to take on maniacal marijuana growers. Rated R. 80m. DIR: Clay Borris. CAST: James Remar, Adam Coleman Howard, Daphne Ashbrook, Jared Martin, Nick Cassavetes. 1986

QUIET DAY IN BELFAST, A ★★★1/2 This fine Canadian message film reveals the hopelessness and insanity of Ireland's civil war. Margot Kidder plays Catholic twins, one in love with a British soldier. Not rated; contains profanity, nudity, and violence. 92m. DIR: Milad Bessada. CAST: Margot Kidder, Barry Foster. 1978

QUIET EARTH, THE ★★★★ First-rate science-fiction thriller from New Zealand. A scientific researcher (Bruno Lawrence) wakes one morning and discovers that all living beings—people and animals—have vanished. Fearful that the world-encircling energy grid on which he'd been working may have been responsible, he sets out to find other people. Intelligent and absorbing adaptation of the book by Craig Harrison. Rated R for nudity and sexual situations. 91m. DIR: Geoff Murphy. CAST: Bruno Lawrence, Alison Routledge. 1985

QUIET FIRE ★★ Passable low-budget shoot-'em-up features Lawrence-Hilton Jacobs running for his life when a corrupt Senate candidate decides to eliminate anyone capable of exposing his past. Rated R for nudity, profanity, and violence. 90m. DIR: Lawrence Hilton-Jacobs. CAST: Lawrence Hilton-Jacobs, Robert Z'dar, Karen Black. 1991

QUIET MAN, THE ★★★★ John Ford's easygoing and marvelously entertaining tribute to the people and the land of Ireland. The story centers around an American ex-boxer (John Wayne) who returns to his native land, his efforts to understand the culture and people of a rural village, and especially his interest in taming a spirited colleen (Maureen O'Hara) in spite of the disapproval of her brother (Victor McLaglen). 129m. DIR: John Ford. CAST: John Wayne, Maureen O'Hara, Victor McLaglen, Barry Fitzgerald, Mildred Natwick, Arthur Shields, Ward Bond, Jack MacGowran. 1952 DVD

QUIET ROOM, THE ★★1/2 A young girl reacts to her parents' fighting by punishing them with silence, causing her to become lost in her own fantasies. This admirable effort to look into the mind of a troubled child eventually demands too much patience from viewers, who won't find anything or anyone here to sympathize with. Rated PG. 91m. DIR: Rolf De Heer. CAST: Celine O'Leary, Paul Blackwell, Chloe Ferguson, Phoebe Ferguson. 1996

QUIET THUNDER 🎬 Inane cross between *Raiders of the Lost Ark* and *Crocodile Dundee*. No rating, but contains violence and brief nudity. 94m. DIR: David Rice. CAST: Wayne Crawford, June Chadwick. 1988

QUIGLEY DOWN UNDER ★★★★ In this rip-snorting adventure movie, Tom Selleck plays a sharpshooting American cowboy who travels to Australia in the 1860s to work for British rancher Alan Rickman. Old-fashioned Western that just as easily might have starred John Wayne or, in one of his mellower moods, Clint Eastwood. Fans of the genre should love it. Rated PG for light violence and nudity. 106m. DIR: Simon Wincer. CAST: Tom Selleck, Laura San Giacomo, Alan Rickman. 1990

QUILLER MEMORANDUM, THE ★★★1/2 First-rate espionage film abandons the gadgets and gimmickry that marked most of the spy movies of the 1960s and concentrates on Harold Pinter's intelligent script. An American secret agent (George Segal) goes undercover to shatter a neo-Nazi hate organization that is gaining strength in Berlin. 105m. DIR: Michael Anderson. CAST: George Segal, Alec Guinness, Max von Sydow, George Sanders, Senta Berger, Robert Helpmann. 1966

QUINTET ★★ This is about as pessimistic a view of the future as one is likely to see. Director Robert Altman has fashioned a murky, hard-to-follow film, concerning the ultimate game of death, set against the background of a frozen postnuclear wasteland. An intriguing idea, but Altman doesn't pull this one off. Rated R. 110m. DIR: Robert Altman. CAST: Paul Newman, Fernando Rey, Bibi Andersson. 1979

QUIZ SHOW ★★★★★ This thoughtful examination of the TV scandal of the 1950s boasts a compelling tale of what can happen when decent people allow themselves to be corrupted. John Turturro is unforgettable as the quiz-show champ whose middle-class, Jewish background is considered to be a ratings threat to the show's producers. They force him out in order to install clean-cut, Ivy League college professor Ralph Fiennes as their new champion—thus setting in motion a chain of events that leads to exposure of this and other questionable practices. Rated PG-13 for profanity. 130m. DIR: Robert Redford. CAST: John Turturro, Rob Morrow,

Ralph Fiennes, Paul Scofield, David Paymer, Hank Azaria, Christopher McDonald, Johann Carlo, Elizabeth Wilson, Martin Scorsese, Barry Levinson. **1994 DVD**

QUO VADIS (1951) ★★★ Colossal! Roman soldier Robert Taylor loves and pursues Christian maiden Deborah Kerr. It's Christians versus Nero and the lions in the eternal fight between good and evil. 171m. **DIR:** Mervyn LeRoy. **CAST:** Robert Taylor, Deborah Kerr, Peter Ustinov, Leo Genn, Finlay Currie, Patricia Laffan, Abraham Sofaer, Felix Aylmer, Buddy Baer. **1951**

QUO VADIS? (1985) ★★★ Lavish adaptation of Henryk Sienkiewicz's novel set during the reign of Nero. Klaus Maria Brandauer gives a brilliant performance as Nero in this made-for-Italian-television production. 200m. **DIR:** Franco Rossi. **CAST:** Klaus Maria Brandauer, Frederic Forrest, Cristina Raines, Francesco Quinn. **1985**

RABBIT RUN ★★ John Updike's novel concerning an ex–high school athlete's trouble adjusting to life off the field is brought to the screen in a very dull fashion. James Caan has the title role as the lost exjock. Supporting cast is good, but the script sinks everyone involved. 74m. **DIR:** Jack Smight. **CAST:** James Caan, Carrie Snodgress, Jack Albertson, Henry Jones, Anjanette Comer. **1970**

RABBIT TEST ❤ The world's first pregnant man. Rated R—profanity. 84m. **DIR:** Joan Rivers. **CAST:** Billy Crystal, Roddy McDowall, Joan Prather. **1978**

RABID ★★ This horror flick has become a cult favorite despite many repulsive scenes. In it, porn queen Marilyn Chambers on human blood after a motorcycle accident operation. For fans of director David Cronenberg only. Rated R. 90m. **DIR:** David Cronenberg. **CAST:** Marilyn Chambers, Joe Silver, Patricia Gage. **1977**

RABID GRANNIES ★★★ A birthday party for two old ladies turns into a zombiefest thanks to a present sent by the family Satanist. Gruesome special effects are the name of the game in this over-the-top horror movie. Not rated, but not for kids or the squeamish. 83m. **DIR:** Emmanuel Kervyn. **CAST:** Catherine Aymerie, Caroline Braekman. **1989 DVD**

•**RACE** ★★★ A Latino housepainter challenges a black ex-radical for a seat on the Los Angeles city council in a race that heats up as voters line up along ethnic lines. This low-budget film has excellent performances, though its simple-minded view of politics is irksome. Also released as *Melting Pot.* Rated R for profanity. 100m. **DIR:** Tom Musca. **CAST:** Paul Rodriguez, C.C.H. Pounder, Cliff Robertson, Una Damon. **1997 DVD**

RACE FOR GLORY ★★ In his quest to be a "legend in my own time," a talented, young motorcyclist

(Alex McArthur) abandons his friends for a chance to compete on the international racing circuit. This unrated mediocrity mixes profanity and violence. 105m. **DIR:** Rocky Lang. **CAST:** Alex McArthur, Peter Berg, Lane Smith. **1989**

RACE FOR YOUR LIFE, CHARLIE BROWN ★★★ Third entry in the "Peanuts" film series has moved further away from the poignant sophistication of *A Boy Named Charlie Brown* and closer to the mindless pap of Saturday-morning cartoon fare. Rated G. 75m. **DIR:** Bill Melendez. **1977**

RACE THE SUN ★★ Underdog Hawaiian highschool students design and race a solar-powered car inspired by the aerodynamics of a cockroach. This film has its heart in the right place but is just another mediocre teen-misfits-make-good movie. A real-life story of determination and courage turned into formulaic mush. Rated PG. 105m. **DIR:** Charles Kanganis. **CAST:** Halle Berry, James Belushi, Casey Affleck, Anthony Ruivivar, Bill Hunter, Eliza Dushku, Kevin Tighe, Steve Zahn, J. Moki Cho, Dion Basco. **1996**

RACE WITH THE DEVIL ★★ Good cast and exciting chase sequences can't save this muddled yarn. It's about two couples who accidentally intrude on a witches' sacrificial ceremony. Rated PG for violence. 88m. **DIR:** Jack Starrett. **CAST:** Warren Oates, Peter Fonda, Loretta Swit, Lara Parker. **1975**

RACERS, THE ★★★ A reworking of *Champion* set in the world of car racers, with Kirk Douglas as the idealist who becomes a racing champion and then an unethical competitor. The photography at the racetrack is unusually effective. 112m. **DIR:** Henry Hathaway. **CAST:** Kirk Douglas, Gilbert Roland, Bella Darvi, Cesar Romero, Katy Jurado, Lee J. Cobb. **1955**

RACHEL AND THE STRANGER ★★★1/2 This leisurely paced Western is made easier to watch by a fine cast. William Holden's love for his wife Loretta Young finally comes to full blossom only after she is wooed by stranger Robert Mitchum. A nice story done with charm and class. B&W; 93m. **DIR:** Norman Foster. **CAST:** William Holden, Loretta Young, Robert Mitchum. **1948**

RACHEL PAPERS ★★★1/2 Dexter Fletcher (who looks like a young Mick Jagger) plays an infatuated young man persistently pursuing the girl of his dreams (Ione Skye). When she finally acknowledges him, the film takes a decidedly serious and downhill turn. Rated R for profanity and nudity. 95m. **DIR:** Damian Harris. **CAST:** Dexter Fletcher, Ione Skye, Jonathan Pryce. **1989**

RACHEL, RACHEL ★★★1/2 Paul Newman's directorial debut focuses on a spinsterish schoolteacher (Joanne Woodward) and her awakening to a world beyond her job and her elderly mother's influence. This bittersweet story is perfectly acted by Woodward, with strong support by James Olson as her short-term lover and Estelle Parsons as her friend. Rewarding on all levels. Rated R. 101m. **DIR:** Paul Newman. **CAST:** Joanne Woodward, James Olson, Kate Harrington, Estelle Parsons. **1968**

RACHEL RIVER ★★★ *American Playhouse* presentation boasts a screenplay by *Ordinary People* author Judith Guest and an excellent cast in this tale of a lonely small-town woman who falls for the one guy in town who makes her happy. Watching these two opposites attract is magnetic. 97m. DIR: Sandy Smolan. CAST: Pamela Reed, Craig T. Nelson, Viveca Lindfors, James Olson. 1988

RACING WITH THE MOON ★★★1/2 Sean Penn and Elizabeth McGovern star in this thoroughly entertaining and touching comedy-romance set during World War II. He's just a regular town boy who discovers he's fallen in love with one of the area's rich girls. But that doesn't stop him from trying to win her heart. Rated PG for nudity, profanity, suggested sex, and brief violence. 108m. DIR: Richard Benjamin. CAST: Sean Penn, Elizabeth McGovern, Nicolas Cage, John Karlen, Rutanya Alda, Carol Kane. 1984

RACKET, THE ★★★ This pessimistic look at political corruption focuses on the steps honest police captain Robert Mitchum takes in order to bring underworld figure Robert Ryan to justice. Mitchum is a man alone as he confronts seemingly insurmountable opposition from both police and political higher-ups who want to keep things just as crooked as they are. B&W; 88m. DIR: John Cromwell. CAST: Robert Mitchum, Robert Ryan, Lizabeth Scott, William Talman, Ray Collins, Robert Hutton. 1951

RACKETEER ★★1/2 This early sound gangster film finds gang leader Robert Armstrong involved in the familiar eternal triangle as he falls for Carole Lombard. She, in turn, pines for an ailing concert violinist. This primitive talkie has some snappy dialogue and features lively performances. B&W; 68m. DIR: Howard Higgin. CAST: Robert Armstrong, Carole Lombard, John Loder, Paul Hurst, Hedda Hopper. 1930

RAD ★★1/2 Staunch character players Talia Shire, Ray Walston, and Jack Weston support this film about a daredevil bicyclist (Bill Allen) who competes to win a thousand dollars. Fairly entertaining, thanks to the exciting race sequences. Rated PG. 95m. DIR: Hal Needham. CAST: Bill Allen, Lori Loughlin, Talia Shire, Ray Walston, Jack Weston. 1986

RADAR MEN FROM THE MOON ★★ Commando Cody, Sky Marshal of the Universe and inventor of a flying suit and a rocket ship, uses all the means at his disposal to aid America in combating Retik, the ruler of the moon, who is bent on (what else?) invading the Earth. The bullet-headed hero chases villains on land, in the air, and all the way to the moon and back and gets his fair share of abuse along the way. Lots of fisticuffs and stock footage. B&W; 12 chapters. DIR: Fred Brannon. CAST: George Wallace, Aline Towne, Roy Barcroft. 1952

RADIO DAYS ★★★ One of writer-director Woody Allen's gentler fables, a pleasant little fantasy about people whose lives revolved around the radio during the days prior to World War II. This affectionate overview does for radio what The Purple Rose of Cairo did for the movies; unfortunately, many of the characters in the large ensemble cast get lost, and too much time is spent with others. Rated PG. 85m. DIR: Woody Allen. CAST: Mia Farrow, Seth Green, Julie Kavner, Josh Mostel, Michael Tucker, Dianne Wiest. 1987

RADIO FLYER ★★ Two youngsters attempt to escape the terrors inflicted on them by their violent stepfather by turning their Radio Flyer wagon into a flying machine. The horrors of child abuse are ineffectively wed with innocent childhood fantasies in this disturbing film. A misfire. Rated PG-13 for violence and profanity. 114m. DIR: Richard Donner. CAST: Lorraine Bracco, John Heard, Elijah Wood, Joseph Mazzello, Adam Baldwin, Tom Hanks, Ben Johnson. 1992

RADIO INSIDE ★★★ A lackluster cast and unfocused plotting sabotage what might have been a nice little spin on Truffaut's Jules and Jim. Two brothers vie for the romantic affections of a pouty young woman, while the younger sibling struggles to overcome guilt feelings relating to their father's accidental death. Occasional witty touches do not compensate for long, empty scenes. Rated PG-13 for profanity and brief nudity. 95m. DIR: Jeffrey Bell. CAST: William McNamara, Elisabeth Shue, Dylan Walsh. 1994

RADIO RANCH (MEN WITH STEEL FACES, PHANTOM EMPIRE) ★★1/2 Condensed version of popular science-fiction serial Phantom Empire, this sketchily tells the story of Gene Autry and his fight against scientists who want his Radio Ranch for the precious ore it contains, and his strange adventures in the underground city of Murania. The 12-chapter serial makes more sense. B&W; 80m. DIR: Otto Brewer, B. Reeves "Breezy" Eason. CAST: Gene Autry, Frankie Darro, Betsy King Ross, Dorothy Christy, Smiley Burnette. 1940

RADIOACTIVE DREAMS ★★★ This one has a little bit of everything: action, adventure, science fiction, fantasy, and an excellent score. Essentially a spoof, the story begins in a post-apocalypse fallout shelter where two boys have lived most of their lives. They end up in the middle of a gang war with a mutant surfer, hippie cannibals, and biker women. Rated R for nudity and violence. 94m. DIR: Albert Pyun. CAST: John Stockwell, Michael Dudikoff, George Kennedy, Don Murray, Michelle Little, Norbert Weisser, Lisa Blount. 1984

RADIOLAND MURDERS ★★ The behind-the-scenes happenings come so fast and furious in this confusing whodunit that most viewers are left scratching their heads. The only comprehensible plot line, the failed romance between Mary Stuart Masterson and Brian Benben, gets a much-needed shot in the arm when he becomes the prime suspect in a series of murders. Musical score is the only plus. Rated PG for violence and adult situations. 108m. DIR: Mel Smith. CAST: Mary Stuart Masterson, Brian Benben, Christopher Lloyd, Ned Beatty. 1994 DVD

RAFFERTY AND THE GOLD DUST TWINS ★★1/2 Amusing and entertaining little film with Sally Kellerman and Mackenzie Phillips kidnapping a hapless Alan Arkin and forcing him to drive them to New Orleans from California. Good cast and pacing make up for simple plot. Rated PG for profanity. 92m. DIR: Dick Richards. CAST: Sally Kellerman, Mackenzie Phillips, Alan Arkin, Alex Rocco, Charles Martin Smith, Harry Dean Stanton. 1975

RAFFLE, THE ★★1/2 Harmless fluff about two men who run an international raffle in which the winner gets a date with the most beautiful woman in the world. Now they have to come up with the prize, and their search takes them on a global quest. If film didn't have its heart in the right place, it might seem sexist. Rated R for adult situations. 100m. **DIR:** Gavin Wilding. **CAST:** Nicholas Lea, Bobby Dawson, Jennifer Clement, Jay Underwood, Mark Hamill, Teri-Lynn Rutherford. **1994**

●**RAGDOLL** ★★ After an extremely slow first hour, this revenge thriller set in an urban setting finally picks up. The problem is that you'll probably fall asleep way before then. The titular creature doesn't even show up to reek its mayhem until the hour mark and even then it is barely seen. Perhaps that is for the better since the effects are quite poor. Rated R for excessive profanity and violence. 90m. **DIR:** Ted Nicolaou. **CAST:** Russell Richardson, Jennia Watson. **1999**

RAGE (1972) ★★★ This pits a lone man against the impersonal Establishment (in this instance the U.S. Army). Not a happy film by any means, but an interesting one. Making his directorial debut, George C. Scott plays a peaceful sheep rancher whose son is the victim of military chemical testing. Seeking revenge, he sets out to nail those responsible. Rated PG. 104m. **DIR:** George C. Scott. **CAST:** George C. Scott, Martin Sheen, Richard Basehart, Barnard Hughes. **1972**

RAGE (1980) ★★★ David Soul travels through the agonies of intense therapy as a convicted rapist in this above-par TV-movie drama. Loaded with fine performances from an incredible cast. 100m. **DIR:** William A. Graham. **CAST:** David Soul, James Whitmore, Craig T. Nelson, Yaphet Kotto, Caroline McWilliams, Leo Gordon, Sharon Farrell, Vic Tayback. **1980**

RAGE (1995) ★★ Although this badly edited thriller makes no sense whatsoever, it boasts a few incredible action sequences. Nice guy Gary Daniels gets involved in some weird plot to make supersoldiers and winds up battling half the United States to win back his freedom. Rated R for violence, profanity, and deviant sexuality. 91m. **DIR:** Joseph Merhi. **CAST:** Gary Daniels, Kenneth Tigar, Fiona Hutchison. **1995**

RAGE, THE: CARRIE 2 ★★1/2 This predictable little chiller, unimaginatively follows the sequence of events from Stephen King's career-making first novel, and the landmark 1976 film adapted from it. A tormented high-school girl, mostly unaware of her telekinetic abilities, attracts the attention of a sports jock with a bit more compassion than his grunting-pig friends, and thus sets into motion a nasty plot hatched by the local "power crowd" that climaxes when our heroine, tragically embarrassed and betrayed, orchestrates fearsome vengeance during a huge party. The only real change relates to the escalated level of acceptable carnage, climaxing in a "money shot" that represents a new low, even for this genre. Rated R for violence, profanity, nudity, gore, and sexual content. 104m. **DIR:** Katt Shea. **CAST:** Emily Bergl, Jason London, Dylan Bruno, J. Smith-Cameron, Zachery Ty Bryan, Amy Irving, Gordon Clapp. **1999 DVD**

RAGE AND HONOR ★★ Martial-arts greats Cynthia Rothrock and Richard Norton team up to expose drug-dealing cops. She tries to protect her video

camera–wielding student while Norton attempts to clear his name after being framed for murder. If the gratuitous sleaze had been left out, this could have been an above-average kickfest. Rated R for profanity and violence. 93m. **DIR:** Terence H. Winkless. **CAST:** Cynthia Rothrock, Richard Norton, Terri Treas, Brian Thompson, Catherine Bach. **1992**

RAGE AND HONOR II: HOSTILE TAKEOVER ★★ Predictable martial-arts sequel finds CIA operative Cynthia Rothrock battling bad guys in Jakarta. Richard Norton, her former partner, helps her resolve a dispute between her employer and his greedy son. High kicks and little else. Rated R for violence and language. 98m. **DIR:** Guy Norris. **CAST:** Cynthia Rothrock, Richard Norton, Patrick Muldoon, Frans Tumbuan. **1992**

RAGE AT DAWN ★★★★ Solid Western has granite-jawed Randolph Scott as an undercover agent out to trap the infamous Reno brothers (played with zest by Forrest Tucker, J. Carrol Naish, and Myron Healey). Scott takes time out to romance their pretty sister (Mala Powers) before bringing the boys to justice. 87m. **DIR:** Tim Whelan. **CAST:** Randolph Scott, Forrest Tucker, Mala Powers, J. Carrol Naish, Myron Healey, Edgar Buchanan. **1955 DVD**

RAGE IN HARLEM, A ★★★ Adapted from the novel by Chester Himes, this movie can't make up its mind whether to be a comedy à la *The Sting* or a violent action film like *New York City*. Still, it's quite a roller-coaster ride as southern con-woman Robin Givens makes her way to Harlem with a load of stolen gold, seduces sweet-natured accountant Forest Whitaker, and tries to deal with gangster Danny Glover. Rated R for violence, nudity, and profanity. 115m. **DIR:** Bill Duke. **CAST:** Forest Whitaker, Gregory Hines, Danny Glover, Zakes Mokae, John Toles-Bey, Robin Givens. **1991**

RAGE OF ANGELS 🦃 Trashy TV movie. Not rated. 200m. **DIR:** Buzz Kulik. **CAST:** Jaclyn Smith, Ken Howard, Armand Assante, Ron Hunter, Kevin Conway. **1986**

RAGE OF HONOR 🦃 Sho Kosugi is an able martial artist, but he speaks English with such a thick accent that he's completely incomprehensible. Rated R for strong violence. 91m. **DIR:** Gordon Hessler. **CAST:** Sho Kosugi, Robin Evans. **1987**

RAGE OF PARIS, THE ★★★ Famed French star Danielle Darrieux made her U.S. film debut in this airy romantic comedy about mistaken identity and artful conniving. Deft direction steered the excellent cast through an engaging script. Good, clean fun all around. B&W; 78m. **DIR:** Henry Koster. **CAST:** Danielle Darrieux, Douglas Fairbanks Jr., Mischa Auer, Helen Broderick, Glenda Farrell, Louis Hayward, Harry Davenport, Samuel S. Hinds. **1938**

RAGGEDY MAN ★★★1/2 Sissy Spacek gives another outstanding performance as a World War II divorcée trying to raise two sons and improve their lives in a small Texas Gulf Coast town. The film is a curious mixture of styles. It begins as a character study and ends like a horror film. But it works. Rated PG for violence. 94m. **DIR:** Jack Fisk. **CAST:** Sissy Spacek, Eric Roberts, William Sanderson, Tracey Walter, Sam Shepard, Henry Thomas. **1981**

RAGGEDY RAWNEY, THE ★★1/2 A quaint, modest effort most notable because its first-time writer-director is the superb Cockney actor, Bob Hoskins. He created this folk fable about Gypsies and a myth about a speechless madwoman with magical powers who follows the caravans about. 102m. **DIR:** Bob Hoskins. **CAST:** Bob Hoskins, Dexter Fletcher. **1988**

RAGING ANGELS ★★ The one decent performance in this lame supernatural adventure is a wildly exuberant turn by Diane Ladd as a spiritualist with the knack to see demons and angels. A bloated Michael Pare phones in his performance as an evangelistic singer whose positive appearance belies an evil intent. Rated R for violence, profanity, and sexual situations. 97m. **DIR:** Alan Smithee. **CAST:** Sean Patrick Flanery, Diane Ladd, Michael Paré, Monet Mazur, Shelley Winters. **1994**

RAGING BULL ★★★★1/2 This tough, compelling film is one movie you won't want to miss. In playing prizefighter Jake La Motta from his twenties through to middle age, Robert De Niro undergoes a transformation that takes him from his normal weight of 150 to 212 pounds. Startling, yes, but the performance he gives is even more so—see it. Rated R. B&W; 128m. **DIR:** Martin Scorsese. **CAST:** Robert De Niro, Cathy Moriarty, Joe Pesci, Frank Vincent, Nicholas Colasanto, Theresa Saldana. **1980 DVD**

RAGS TO RICHES ★★ Joseph Bologna plays millionaire Nick Foley, who tries to soften his ruthless-businessman image by adopting six girls. This was a pilot for the TV series of the same name. 96m. **DIR:** Bruce Seth Green. **CAST:** Joseph Bologna, Tisha Campbell. **1986**

RAGTIME ★★★★1/2 James Cagney returned to the screen after an absence of twenty years in this brilliant screen adaptation of E. L. Doctorow's best-selling novel about New York City at the turn of the century. It's a bountifully rewarding motion picture. Rated PG for violence and nudity. 155m. **DIR:** Milos Forman. **CAST:** James Cagney, Brad Dourif, Pat O'Brien, Donald O'Connor, Elizabeth McGovern, Mary Steenburgen. **1981**

RAID ON ENTEBBE ★★★ Second of three dramas filmed in 1976–1977 about the daring Israeli commando assault on the Entebbe airport in Uganda, this TV movie avoids the soap-opera tone of the earlier *Victory at Entebbe* (also made for TV) and focuses on the action and power struggle between the Israelis and Idi Amin. More effective when it was initially shown, but it's still worth a watch. 150m. **DIR:** Irvin Kershner. **CAST:** Peter Finch, Charles Bronson, Horst Buchholz, Martin Balsam, John Saxon, Jack Warden, Yaphet Kotto. **1977**

RAID ON ROMMEL 💔 Substandard war film. Rated PG for violence. 98m. **DIR:** Henry Hathaway. **CAST:** Richard Burton, John Colicos, Clinton Greyn, Wolfgang Preiss. **1971 DVD**

RAIDERS OF THE LOST ARK ★★★★★ For sheer spirit-lifting entertainment, you can't do better than this film, by director Steven Spielberg and writer-producer George Lucas. Harrison Ford stars as Indiana Jones, the roughest, toughest, and most unpredictable hero to grace the silver screen, who risks life and limb against a set of the nastiest villains you've ever seen. It's all to save the world—what else? Rated PG for violence and gore. 115m. **DIR:** Steven Spielberg. **CAST:** Harrison Ford, Karen Allen, Wolf Kahler, Paul Freeman, Ronald Lacey, John Rhys-Davies, Denholm Elliott. **1981**

RAIDERS OF THE SUN ★★ Roger Corman produced this trite postnuclear-holocaust shoot-'em-up. Rated R for nudity, violence, and profanity. 80m. **DIR:** Cirio H. Santiago. **CAST:** Richard Norton. **1991**

RAILROADED ★★★ Future TV father Hugh Beaumont has his hands full as a police detective trying to run interference between gangster John Ireland and his intended victim Sheila Ryan. Tough, tight, and deadly, this early effort from director Anthony Mann oozes suspense and remains a fine example of American *film noir*, modestly budgeted and effectively conveyed. B&W; 71m. **DIR:** Anthony Mann. **CAST:** John Ireland, Sheila Ryan, Hugh Beaumont, Jane Randolph, Keefe Brasselle. **1947 DVD**

RAILWAY CHILDREN, THE ★★★★1/2 Wonderful family fare from Great Britain. Set in 1905, this tale focuses on a family whose idyllic life is shattered. Director Lionel Jeffries, a popular British comic actor, also wrote the screenplay based on the novel by E. Nesbit. Warmth, comedy, and adventure—a must-see. 104m. **DIR:** Lionel Jeffries. **CAST:** Dinah Sheridan, Bernard Cribbins, William Mervyn, Ian Cuthbertson, Jenny Agutter, Sally Thomsett, Gary Warren. **1972**

RAILWAY STATION MAN, THE ★★1/2 An offbeat love story set in Ireland involves painter Julie Christie with a red-haired, one-handed Donald Sutherland, who plays the title character. The two stars, working together twenty years after making *Don't Look Now*, make this TV movie watchable but cannot overcome a confusing subplot involving terrorists. 93m. **DIR:** Michael Whyte. **CAST:** Julie Christie, Donald Sutherland, John Lynch, Frank McCusker, Mark Tandy. **1993**

RAIN ★★★★ Joan Crawford plays island hussy Sadie Thompson in this depressing drama. Walter Huston is the preacher who wants to "save" her—for himself. B&W; 93m. **DIR:** Lewis Milestone. **CAST:** Joan Crawford, Walter Huston, William Gargan, Guy Kibbee, Walter Catlett, Beulah Bondi. **1932 DVD**

RAIN KILLER, THE ★★★ Good suspense film, in which the police try to track down a homicidal maniac, who only kills women during rainstorms. Many impressive plot twists, as well as interesting sets and lighting. Rated R for violence, nudity, and profanity. 94m. **DIR:** Ken Stein. **CAST:** Ray Sharkey, David Beecroft, Michael Chiklis, Tania Coleridge, Woody Brown. **1990**

RAIN MAN ★★★★ Dustin Hoffman gives the performance of his career as the autistic older brother of Tom Cruise, who plays a thoughtless, self-centered hustler with room in his life only for money. Greed propels him to take a cross-country road trip with Hoffman, who inherited the bulk of Dad's vast estate. The blend of pathos with gentle humor allows us to laugh with, but never at, Hoffman's autistic savant. Inexplicably rated R for occasional profanity. 140m. **DIR:** Barry Levinson. **CAST:** Dustin Hoffman, Tom Cruise, Valeria Golino. **1988 DVD**

RAIN PEOPLE, THE ★★★★ James Caan plays a retired football star who is picked up by a bored pregnant woman (played by Shirley Knight). She felt trapped as a housewife and ran away from her husband to be free. Directed by Francis Ford Coppola, this is an interesting, well-acted character study. Rated R. 102m. **DIR:** Francis Ford Coppola. **CAST:** James Caan, Shirley Knight, Robert Duvall, Tom Aldredge. **1969**

RAIN WITHOUT THUNDER ★★★1/2 This often-intriguing abortion rights drama with a decided pro-choice agenda is set in a not-so-distant future when abortion is again illegal. It assumes a mock documentary style to tell the story of a mother and daughter charged with traveling to Sweden to obtain an abortion. Rated PG-13, with profanity and adult issues. 87m. **DIR:** Gary Bennett. **CAST:** Jeff Daniels, Betty Buckley, Linda Hunt, Frederic Forrest, Graham Greene, Austin Pendleton. **1993**

RAINBOW, THE ★★★★ Director Ken Russell returns to D. H. Lawrence, the source of his great success, *Women in Love*. This time, he focuses on the companion novel, a prequel. Sammi Davis is wonderful as an adolescent English girl exposed to the ways of love at the hands of both a soldier and her teacher, and makes a decision to seek a more satisfying life for herself. Rated R. 102m. **DIR:** Ken Russell. **CAST:** Sammi Davis, Paul McGann, Glenda Jackson, Amanda Donohoe, David Hemmings, Christopher Gable. **1989**

RAINBOW DRIVE ★★1/2 Roderick Thorpe's suspense novel is not well served by this turgid made-for-cable police melodrama, which features Peter Weller as an honest cop embroiled in a cover-up. The cast tries to rise above the material. Not rated, but with violence and brief nudity. 96m. **DIR:** Bobby Roth. **CAST:** Peter Weller, Sela Ward, David Caruso, Bruce Weitz, Kathryn Harrold. **1990**

RAINBOW THIEF, THE ★★★1/2 Lunacy prevails when a rich, eccentric uncle succumbs to the pleasures of life, and his family fights over his estate. The good news is that Uncle Rudolph's dirt-poor nephew is the sole heir. The bad news is that he's totally nuts. When the family schemes to have him written out of the will, the crazy nephew and his best friend decide to take matters into their own hands. Peter O'Toole and Omar Sharif are delightful as the wacky nephew and his friend. Not rated. 88m. **DIR:** Alejandro Jodorowsky. **CAST:** Peter O'Toole, Omar Sharif, Christopher Lee. **1990**

RAINBOW VALLEY ★★★ A young John Wayne goes undercover to round up the outlaws who have been blocking the building of a road into the mining town of Rainbow Valley. In this breezy outing, Wayne works especially well with Gabby Hayes. B&W; 52m. **DIR:** Robert N. Bradbury. **CAST:** John Wayne, Lucille Brown, LeRoy Mason, George "Gabby" Hayes, Buffalo Bill Jr. **1935**

RAINBOW WARRIOR ★★1/2 Direct-to-video mystery is based on the real-life bombing of the Greenpeace vessel *Rainbow Warrior*, which resulted in the death of a crew member. Sam Neill and Jon Voight play men on opposite sides of the law who team up to solve the crime. Less preachy than one might expect, it makes a statement while remaining entertaining. Rated PG for violence. 93m. **DIR:** Michael Tuchner. **CAST:** Sam Neill, Jon Voight, Bruno Lawrence, Kerry Fox, John Callen. **1994**

RAINING STONES ★★★★ Director Ken Loach again cuts to the heart of human essence in this raw and quirky flick. Bruce Jones is an unemployed laborer determined to get his daughter an expensive outfit for her First Communion ceremony. As he scrambles through a series of jobs on both sides of the law, Jones depicts a comedy of errors that much of humanity enacts while searching for a better life. Not rated; contains profanity and nudity. 90m. **DIR:** Kenneth Loach. **CAST:** Bruce Jones, Julie Brown, Ricky Tomlinson, Tom Hickey, Gemma Phoenix. **1993 DVD**

RAINMAKER, THE (1956) ★★★1/2 Based on N. Richard Nash's play, the movie adaptation could easily have seemed confined, but the boundless intensity and energy of Burt Lancaster's performance as the smooth-talking con man gives the whole film an electric crackle. Katharine Hepburn has the magnetism to hold her own in the role of the spinster. 121m. **DIR:** Joseph Anthony. **CAST:** Burt Lancaster, Katharine Hepburn, Wendell Corey, Lloyd Bridges, Earl Holliman, Wallace Ford, Cameron Prud'homme. **1956**

RAINMAKER, THE (1997) ★★★★ Ah, what a fairy tale. This adaptation of John Grisham's bestseller is a tale ripped straight from modern headlines and our worst fears: on one side, represented by a team of one-grand-per-hour legal sharpies, a recalcitrant insurance company that refuses to honor what seems a legitimate claim for desperately needed medical technology; on the other side, the young Tennessee victim and his needy parents, represented by a kid fresh out of law school and one assistant who hasn't been able to pass the bar in six consecutive attempts. It's all wholly preposterous wish-fulfillment … and a delight, from start to finish. Rated PG-13 for violence, profanity, and dramatic intensity. 137m. **DIR:** Francis Ford Coppola. **CAST:** Matt Damon, Claire Danes, Jon Voight, Danny DeVito, Mary Kay Place, Mickey Rourke. **1997 DVD**

RAINS CAME, THE ★★★ Louis Bromfield's epic novel of India has been turned into a so-so drama of forbidden romance between a white woman and an Indian doctor. A spectacular earthquake and tidal wave, but little more. Remade in 1955 as *The Rains of Ranchipur*. B&W; 104m. **DIR:** Clarence Brown. **CAST:** Myrna Loy, Tyrone Power, George Brent, Brenda Joyce, Nigel Bruce, Maria Ouspenskaya, Joseph Schildkraut, Jane Darwell, Marjorie Rambeau, Henry Travers, H. B. Warner. **1939**

RAINTREE COUNTY ★★★ Civil War melodrama with Elizabeth Taylor as a southern belle is two and one-half hours of showy tedium that wastes a fine cast and miles of film. Bestselling novel comes to the screen as an extended soap opera with little promise and fewer results. 168m. **DIR:** Edward Dmytryk. **CAST:** Elizabeth Taylor, Montgomery Clift, Eva Marie Saint, Nigel Patrick, Lee Marvin, Rod Taylor, Agnes Moorehead, Walter Abel, Rhys Williams. **1957**

RAISE THE RED LANTERN ★★★★1/2 Chinese director Zhang Yimou's magnificent film chronicles the life of a 1920s maiden who, at her mother's urgings, agrees to marry a wealthy man. She becomes

"Fourth Mistress" in a house where being the master's favorite means all. Based on a novel by Su Tong. In Mandarin with English subtitles. Not rated; the film has suggested sex and violence. 125m. **DIR:** Yimou Zhang. **CAST:** Gong Li. 1991

RAISE THE TITANIC ❤ Disastrously dull disaster flick. Rated PG. 112m. **DIR:** Jerry Jameson. **CAST:** Jason Robards Jr., David Selby, Richard Jordan, Anne Archer, Alec Guinness, J. D. Cannon. 1980

RAISIN IN THE SUN, A (1961) ★★★★ A black family tries to escape from their crowded apartment life by moving to a house in an all-white neighborhood. Sidney Poitier delivers his usual outstanding performance in this film with a message about the limited opportunities open to blacks in the 1950s. B&W; 128m. **DIR:** Daniel Petrie. **CAST:** Sidney Poitier, Claudia McNeil, Ruby Dee, Diana Sands, Ivan Dixon, John Fiedler, Lou Gossett Jr. 1961 DVD

RAISIN IN THE SUN, A (1988) ★★★★ Gripping TV remake of the 1961 classic, with Danny Glover replacing Sidney Poitier as the angry young man who's ready to explode. Esther Rolle superbly struggles to reunite her family by buying a home that just happens to be in an all-white neighborhood. 171m. **DIR:** Bill Duke. **CAST:** Danny Glover, Esther Rolle, Starletta Dupois. 1988

RAISING ARIZONA ★★★★ An almost indescribable lunatic comedy from the makers of *Blood Simple*. Nicolas Cage plays an ex-convict married to policewoman Holly Hunter. Both want children but cannot have any. So they decide to help themselves to one. What follows is a delightful, offbeat comedy that is extremely fast-paced, with eye-popping cinematography and decidedly different characters. Rated PG-13. 94m. **DIR:** Joel Coen. **CAST:** Nicolas Cage, Holly Hunter, Randall "Tex" Cobb, Trey Wilson, John Goodman, William Forsythe. 1987 DVD

RAISING CAIN ❤ Psychological thrillers don't come much sillier than this hopelessly muddled study of a demented child psychologist (John Lithgow, *way* over the top) who kidnaps small children. A real low for director Brian De Palma. Rated R for violence and profanity. 95m. **DIR:** Brian De Palma. **CAST:** John Lithgow, Lolita Davidovich, Steven Bauer, Frances Sternhagen. 1992 DVD

RAISING HEROES ★★★ Unconventional action film stars Troy Sistillio and Henry White as a gay couple ready to adopt the baby of a late friend. Then White witnesses a mob hit, and their lives and the chances of adopting the child are in jeopardy. When the mob decides to silence them, the couple must rise to the occasion to clean up the mess. Low-budget affair tweaks conventional action films into a new hybrid. Not rated; contains adult situations, language, nudity, and violence. 85m. **DIR:** Douglas Langway. **CAST:** Troy Sistillio, Henry White, Edmond Sorel, Stewart Groves. 1996

•**RAISING THE HEIGHTS** ★★ Well-intended but incompetently made urban drama about a Brooklyn student trying to expose teachers who sell drugs to students. Rated R for profanity and violence. 86m. **DIR:** Max Gottlieb. **CAST:** Gilbert Brown Jr., Fia Perera. 1998

RAMBLING ROSE ★★★★ Everything is just right in this film about a 13-year-old boy who falls in love with his 19-year-old nanny, a sexy ball of fire called Rose. Rose scorches everyone in her path in this uproariously funny, heart-tugging, and sexy release adapted from the semiautobiographical book by Calder Willingham. Rated R for profanity, nudity, and suggested sex. 112m. **DIR:** Martha Coolidge. **CAST:** Laura Dern, Robert Duvall, Diane Ladd, Lukas Haas, John Heard, Kevin Conway. 1991 DVD

RAMBO: FIRST BLOOD II ★★★ This sequel to *First Blood* is an old-fashioned war movie. Its hero is larger than life, and the villains are pure mule-mean. In other words, it's an action fan's delight. Sylvester Stallone goes back to Vietnam to rescue American prisoners of war. Rated R. 94m. **DIR:** George Pan Cosmatos. **CAST:** Sylvester Stallone, Richard Crenna, Charles Napier, Steven Berkoff, Julia Nickson, Martin Kove. 1985 DVD

RAMBO III ★★ Sylvester Stallone's hammer-handed tendencies operate at overdrive in this second sequel to *First Blood*. As cowriter, Stallone is responsible for the jingoistic story that makes child-killing sadists of the Russians (led by Marc de Jonge's near-hysterical Soviet colonel) who control a particular sector of Afghanistan. This is button-pushing, lowest-common-denominator filmmaking all the way. Rated R for extreme violence. 101m. **DIR:** Peter MacDonald. **CAST:** Sylvester Stallone, Richard Crenna, Marc de Jonge, Kurtwood Smith. 1988 DVD

RAMPAGE ★★ Based on the "vampire killings" committed by Richard Trenton Chase in Sacramento, California, in the late 1970s, writer-director William Friedkin's film sat on the shelf for more than five years—and probably should have stayed there. Rated R for violence and profanity. 97m. **DIR:** William Friedkin. **CAST:** Michael Biehn, Alex McArthur, Nicholas Campbell, Deborah Van Valkenburgh, John Harkins, Art La Fleur. 1992

RAMPARTS OF CLAY ★★★★ Terse but hauntingly beautiful documentary-style film set against the harsh background of a poor North African village. A young woman (Leila Schenna) struggles to free herself from the second-class role imposed on her by the village culture, much as the village tries to liberate itself from subservience to the corporate powers that control its salt mines. In Arabic with English subtitles. Rated PG. 87m. **DIR:** Jean-Louis Bertucelli. **CAST:** Leila Schenna and the villagers of Tehouda, Algeria. 1970

RAMROD ★★1/2 It's sheep versus cattle again in the Old West. Joel McCrea fights off Preston Foster's murderous cowhands and the increasingly amorous Veronica Lake. B&W; 94m. **DIR:** André de Toth. **CAST:** Veronica Lake, Joel McCrea, Ian McDonald, Charlie Ruggles, Preston Foster, Arleen Whelan, Lloyd Bridges, Donald Crisp. 1947

RAN ★★★★★ This superb Japanese historical epic tells the story of a sixteenth-century warlord's time of tragedy. Based on Shakespeare's *King Lear*, this is yet another masterwork from Akira Kurosawa. It is stunningly photographed and acted, and blessed with touches of glorious humor and hair-raising battle sequences. In Japanese with English subtitles.

Rated R for violence and suggested sex. 160m. **DIR:** Akira Kurosawa. **CAST:** Tatsuya Nakadai, Akira Terao. 1985 DVD

RANCHO DELUXE ★★★ Two small-time cattle rustlers (Jeff Bridges, Sam Waterston) run afoul of lawmen almost as incompetent as they are. Raunchy but good-natured Western-comedy with slow stretches; look for country singer Jimmy Buffett in a small role. Rated R for nudity and profanity. 93m. **DIR:** Frank Perry. **CAST:** Jeff Bridges, Sam Waterston, Elizabeth Ashley, Clifton James, Slim Pickens, Harry Dean Stanton, Patti D'Arbanville. 1975

RANCHO NOTORIOUS ★★★1/2 Brooding revenge Western is a curio of the 1950s, one of those films that appears to mean something more than what the action implies. This film, while not a great Western, is fun to watch and a treat for Marlene Dietrich fans. 89m. **DIR:** Fritz Lang. **CAST:** Marlene Dietrich, Arthur Kennedy, Mel Ferrer, Lloyd Gough, William Frawley, Gloria Henry, Jack Elam, George Reeves. 1952

RANDOM HARVEST ★★★ Ronald Colman and Greer Garson are at their best in this touching, tearful story. A shell-shocked World War I veteran is saved from oblivion by the compassion of a music-hall entertainer. A stellar cast supports. B&W; 124m. **DIR:** Mervyn LeRoy. **CAST:** Ronald Colman, Greer Garson, Philip Dorn, Henry Travers, Reginald Owen. 1942

•RANDOM HEARTS ★★★ This one moves like molasses, despite director Sydney Pollack's intention to make another glossy, theatrical, star-driven, romantic melodrama in the mold of his *Out of Africa*. All the elements are in place: an environment of entitlement; Philippe Rousselot's gorgeous cinematography, which makes Washington, D.C., look much prettier than it deserves; and Dave Grusin's melancholy, languidly jazzy soundtrack. Yes, it's all nice to look at—as are Harrison Ford and Kristin Scott Thomas—but the pregnant pauses and tortured dialogue wear thin. Similarly, the notion that an Internal Affairs cop and a congresswoman would become an item, after being thrown together following the tragic deaths of their respective spouses (who were, themselves, having an affair), is too contrived for words. Needlessly rated R for violence, tasteful sensuality, and brief, completely gratuitous profanity. 132m. **DIR:** Sydney Pollack. **CAST:** Harrison Ford, Kristin Scott Thomas, Charles Dutton, Bonnie Hunt, Dennis Haysbert, Richard Jenkins, Paul Guilfoyle. 1999

RANDY RIDES ALONE ★★★ John Wayne stars in this enjoyable B Western as a lawman who goes undercover to catch a gang that has been robbing an express office. The opening is particularly good. B&W; 60m. **DIR:** Henry Frazer. **CAST:** John Wayne, Alberta Vaughan, George "Gabby" Hayes, Earl Dwire, Yakima Canutt. 1934 DVD

RANGE DEFENDERS ★★★ Cattlemen try to rid the range of sheep at all costs. The Three Mesquiteers settle the feud. Certainly nothing new, but well-done. B&W; 54m. **DIR:** Mack V. Wright. **CAST:** Robert Livingston, Ray "Crash" Corrigan, Max Terhune, Eleanor Stewart, Harry Woods. 1937

RANGE FEUD ★★★ It's *Romeo and Juliet* on the range as lawman Buck Jones tries to keep the peace between two feuding ranchers whose offspring have

fallen in love. A gangly John Wayne does just fine as the youthful hero in another better-than-B Western from the great Buck Jones. B&W; 64m. **DIR:** D. Ross Lederman. **CAST:** Buck Jones, John Wayne, Susan Fleming, Harry Woods, Glenn Strange. 1931

RANGE WAR ★★1/2 Hopalong Cassidy (William Boyd) rounds up a gang that is trying to stop construction on the railroad. Lesser entry in the Cassidy series. Britt Wood is no replacement for George "Gabby" Hayes or Andy Clyde, who was yet to come. B&W; 64m. **DIR:** Lesley Selander. **CAST:** William Boyd, Russell Hayden, Britt Wood. 1939

RANGER AND THE LADY, THE ★★1/2 Buckskin-clad Roy Rogers is a Texas Ranger trying to clear up some trouble on the old Santa Fe Trail in the days before the Civil War. Fetching Jacqueline Wells plays the lady leading a wagon train to Texas. B&W; 59m. **DIR:** Joseph Kane. **CAST:** Roy Rogers, George "Gabby" Hayes, Jacqueline Wells, Harry Woods, Henry Brandon, Noble Johnson, Yakima Canutt, Art Dillard. 1940

RANMA (TV SERIES) ★★★1/2 Despite a dubbed English soundtrack, the episodes are still quite entertaining. Ranma and his father, Genma, both avid martial-arts students, have fallen afoul of ancient curses that periodically change one into a young girl and the other into a giant panda. Another quirky series from Rumiko Takahashi (*Rumik World, Urusei Yatsura*). Dubbed in English. Not rated; contains some brief nudity. Each 50m. **DIR:** Tsutomu Shibayama. 1985–1987

RANSOM (1977) ★★1/2 When a psycho begins killing people in a small town and refuses to stop until he receives a $4 million ransom, Stuart Whitman (the richest man in town) hires a mercenary (Oliver Reed) to kill the extortionist. There are some slow moments, but worse than these are the unanswered questions about why the murderer dresses like an American Indian and what his motive really is. Rated PG for violence. 90m. **DIR:** Richard Compton. **CAST:** Oliver Reed, Stuart Whitman, Deborah Raffin, John Ireland, Jim Mitchum, Paul Koslo. 1977

RANSOM (1996) ★★★★ Gripping thriller casts Mel Gibson as a millionaire businessman whose son is kidnapped. Rather than leave it to the police, Gibson takes matters into his own hands. Plot twists abound as our hero finds he must match wits with the bad guys and the authorities. Although it invites some comparisons to *Death Wish*, this remake of the 1956 Glenn Ford film has a high gloss and believability. René Russo is top-notch as Gibson's concerned wife, and Gary Sinise is brilliant as a detective involved in the case. Rated R for profanity and violence. 120m. **DIR:** Ron Howard. **CAST:** Mel Gibson, René Russo, Gary Sinise, Delroy Lindo, Lili Taylor, Liev Schreiber, Evan Handler, Brawley Nolte, Dan Hedaya, Paul Guilfoyle. 1996 DVD

RAPA NUI ★★ This primitive, loincloth film is set in seventeenth-century Easter Island. Two young bucks from rival clans compete for the hand of a maiden and the blessing of their gods by swimming to a nearby isle and fetching a bird egg. The film's *National Geographic* splendor and provocative historical speculation is crippled by laughable accents and dialogue and limp pacing. But love those crazy statues. Rated R for violence, nudity, and suggested sex. 107m. **DIR:** Kevin Reynolds. **CAST:** Jason Scott Lee, Sandrine Holt, Esai Morales. **1994**

RAPE AND MARRIAGE: THE RIDEOUT CASE ★★ Despite the dramatic potential of its story line and a strong cast, this fact-based TV drama—about the infamous 1978 husband-wife rape case in Oregon—falls far short of answering any questions about the issues. 96m. **DIR:** Peter Levin. **CAST:** Mickey Rourke, Rip Torn, Linda Hamilton, Eugene Roche, Gail Strickland, Conchata Ferrell. **1980**

RAPE OF LOVE (L'AMOUR VIOLÉ) ★★★★ A graphic rape scene may scare some viewers away from this French export, but that would be unfortunate. It is a telling account of one woman's quest to come to terms with her tragic experience. In French with English subtitles. Not rated, but has graphic violence, nudity, and profanity. 111m. **DIR:** Yannick Bellon. **CAST:** Nathalie Nell, Alain Foures. **1979**

RAPE OF THE SABINES ♥ Roger Moore plays Romulus, founder of Rome, in this cheesy Italian-French coproduction. 100m. **DIR:** Richard Pottier. **CAST:** Mylene Demongeot, Roger Moore. **1961**

RAPID FIRE ★★★1/2 Compact action film casts Brandon Lee as a college student who runs afoul of the mob. Lee shows his father Bruce's talent for incorporating comedy into the fist-and-foot action. This is definitely better than the average kung fu flick. Rated R for violence, simulated sex, and profanity. 95m. **DIR:** Dwight H. Little. **CAST:** Brandon Lee, Powers Boothe, Nick Mancuso, Raymond J. Barry. **1992**

RAPPACCINI'S DAUGHTER ★★★1/2 This Nathaniel Hawthorne tale concerns a university student who accepts new lodgings overlooking a beautiful and mysterious garden. What follows is a particularly spellbinding tale of love and tragedy. Introduced by Henry Fonda; unrated and suitable for family viewing. 57m. **DIR:** Dezso Magyar. **CAST:** Kristoffer Tabori, Kathleen Beller, Michael Egan, Leonardo Cimino. **1980**

RAPPIN' ★★ Rap songs get the *Breakin'* treatment in this uninspired formula musical. Once again, a street performer (Mario Van Peebles) takes on the baddies and still has time to make it in show biz. Rated PG for profanity. 92m. **DIR:** Joel Silberg. **CAST:** Mario Van Peebles, Tasia Valenza, Charles Flohe. **1985**

RAPTURE, THE ★★★★ Mimi Rogers is riveting as a Los Angeles telephone operator who tires of mate-swapping and turns to a religious sect for spiritual guidance. Writer-director Michael Tolkin's bold approach to religious themes makes this tragic drama both a demanding and unforgettable experience. It's an amazing, disturbing story of squandered life, rebirth, and tested faith. Rated R for nudity and language. 102m. **DIR:** Michael Tolkin. **CAST:** Mimi Rogers, Kimberly Cullum, Patrick Bauchau. **1991**

RARE BREED, THE (1966) ★★★ This is a generally rewarding Western. Jimmy Stewart is a Texas cattle rancher who grudgingly assists an Englishwoman's (Maureen O'Hara) attempts to introduce a new line of short-horned cattle to the Texan range. The story is quite original and holds one's interest throughout. 108m. **DIR:** Andrew V. McLaglen. **CAST:** James Stew-

art, Maureen O'Hara, Brian Keith, Juliet Mills, Jack Elam, Ben Johnson. **1966**

RASCALS, THE ★★★ Two kids (Bernard Brieux and Thomas Chabrol) go through school together trying to beat the system. Taking place in the German-occupied France of 1942, the film deals with the coming-of-age themes we have seen many times. But the film's nationalistic subtext, which results in a triumphant ending, is, perhaps, a new one. In French with English subtitles. Rated R for sex and nudity. 93m. **DIR:** Bernard Revon. **CAST:** Bernard Brieux, Thomas Chabrol, Pascale Rocard. **1979**

RASHOMON ★★★★★ After a violent murder and rape is committed by a bandit, four people tell their own different versions of what happened. Set in medieval Japan, this examination of truth and guilt is charged with action. The combination of brilliant photography, stellar acting, direction, and script won this Japanese classic the Oscar for best foreign film. B&W; 89m. **DIR:** Akira Kurosawa. **CAST:** Toshiro Mifune, Machiko Kyo, Masayuki Mori. **1951**

RASPUTIN (1985) ★★★★ Controversial film that was suppressed by the Soviet Union for nearly a decade. Director Elem Klimov brilliantly captures the rise of the illiterate "prophet" who sparked the Russian Revolution. In Russian with English subtitles. Not rated but contains nudity and violence. 107m. **DIR:** Elem Klimov. **CAST:** Alexei Petrenko. **1985**

RASPUTIN (1996) ★★★ Despite its lavish production and strong cast, this is a routine, superficial study of the mad Russian monk who brought down a dynasty. Alan Rickman is well cast as the title character, but he's given little to do; Peter Pruce's script scarcely examines the supposed mystic. Instead, we're left with yet another chronicle of Nicholas and Alexandra's final days. It's a gripping story, but better told elsewhere. Rated R for violence and simulated sex. 105m. **DIR:** Uli Edel. **CAST:** Alan Rickman, Greta Scacchi, Ian McKellen, David Warner, John Wood, James Frain. **1996**

●**RASPUTIN: THE MAD MONK** ★★★ Hammer brought the famous Russian pseudopriest to life with Christopher Lee in the starring role in this effective if highly inaccurate telling of the story. Historical changes aside, the film presents Rasputin as a hypnotic and darkly sexy man who manages to insinuate himself into the last of the Russian monarchy, thereby increasing his stature. 92m. **DIR:** Don Sharp. **CAST:** Christopher Lee, Barbara Shelley. **1966 DVD**

RASPUTIN AND THE EMPRESS ★★1/2 Lionel Barrymore portrays the mad monk Rasputin (he's badly miscast), and siblings Ethel (in her sound-film debut) and John costar in this overlong historical melodrama of court intrigue during the troubled reign of Nicholas and Alexandra in czarist Russia. B&W; 123m. **DIR:** Richard Boleslawski. **CAST:** John Barrymore, Ethel Barrymore, Lionel Barrymore, Ralph Morgan. **1932**

RAT PACK, THE ★★★ Although you'll get a strong sense of late 1950s bedroom and back-room politics, this fantasy-laced "biography" of Frank Sinatra and his entertainer cronies plays fast and loose with known facts. Don Cheadle has one magnificent scene, playing Sammy Davis Jr. "striking back" at the racist boors who objected to his marriage to a Swedish actress, and Joe Mantegna makes a wonderfully dour Dean Martin ... but the rest aren't even close. Rated R for profanity, nudity, and simulated sex. 120m. DIR: Rob Cohen. CAST: Ray Liotta, Joe Mantegna, Don Cheadle, Angus MacFadyen, Zeljko Ivanek, William L. Petersen, Dan O'Herlihy, Veronica Cartwright, Bobby Slayton. 1998 DVD

RAT PFINK A BOO BOO 🎬 A loose parody of *Batman*, it has everything a bad-movie lover could ever want. 72m. DIR: Ray Dennis Steckler. CAST: Vin Saxon, Carolyn Brandt. 1965

RATBOY ★★ Not a horror film but a satirical allegory directed by and starring Sondra Locke. Eugene, a boy with the face of a rat, is torn out of his peaceful existence in a dump by an unemployed window dresser (Locke). With her two brothers, she sets out to market the "ratboy" as a media star. Rated PG-13 for profanity and some violence. 104m. DIR: Sondra Locke. CAST: Sondra Locke, Robert Townsend, Louie Anderson, Gerrit Graham, Christopher Hewett. 1986

RATINGS GAME, THE ★★★★ Danny DeVito directs and leads an amiable cast in this comedy about a millionaire trying to break into the Hollywood scene with his rotten screenplays. When he falls in love with an employee from the Computron company (Rhea Perlman), they fix the TV ratings. Not rated, has profanity. 102m. DIR: Danny DeVito. CAST: Danny DeVito, Rhea Perlman, Gerrit Graham, Louis Giambalvo, Ronny Graham, Huntz Hall, Kevin McCarthy, John Megna, Michael Richards, Mark L. Taylor. 1984

RATS 🎬 Italian-made gore-a-thon set in the future after The Bomb has destroyed civilization. Dubbed in English. Not rated, but loaded with violence. 97m. DIR: Vincent Dawn. CAST: Richard Raymond, Alex McBride. 1983

RATS ARE COMING! THE WEREWOLVES ARE HERE!, THE 🎬 England is besieged by a pack of werewolves in the 1800s. Rated R. 92m. DIR: Andy Milligan. CAST: Hope Stansbury, Jackie Skarvellis. 1972

RATTLE OF A SIMPLE MAN ★★★ One of the realistic, kitchen-sink dramas that were in vogue in England at the time, this resembles a British version of *Marty*. Middle-aged Percy, a virgin who lives with his mother, is goaded by his friends into a bet that he can't pick up and spend the night with an attractive waitress. In his attempt to do so, he finds love for the first time. B&W; 96m. DIR: Muriel Box. CAST: Harry H. Corbett, Diane Cilento, Michael Medwin. 1964

RATTLED ★★1/2 Not for the ophiophobic, this made-for-cable original features rattlesnakes running amok in a small town, mediocre acting (on the humans' part, that is), dull dialogue, and laughable scenes in snake-o-vision. Rated PG-13 for violence. 90m. DIR: Tony Randel. CAST: William Katt, Shanna Reed, Ed Lauter, Bibi Besch. 1996

RATTLER KID 🎬 An unjustly accused army officer escapes prison and turns to a life of crime. Believing his own press clippings, he thinks of himself as a legendary outlaw. An unbelievable story line makes this one of the worst of the spaghetti Westerns. Not rated; contains violence. 87m. DIR: Leon Klimovsky. CAST:

Richard Wyler, Brad Harris, Femi Benussi, William Spolt. 1968

RAVAGE ★★1/2 There is more excitement and action per square inch in this ultralow-budget flick than in any ten recent big-budget blockbusters. Director Ronnie Sortor's tale of a criminal psychologist who witnesses the murder of his family and then goes on a violent rampage is a tight, white-knuckle suspenser that will leave the viewer addicted right up to the end. Not rated; contains violence, gore, and profanity. 85m. DIR: Ronnie Sortor. CAST: Mark Brazaele, Dan Rowland, Dina Harris. 1996

RAVAGER ★★ Cheesy special effects and bargain-basement sets get a workout in this familiar tale of a spaceship crew who unleash a biological weapon that infects them one at a time. Ho hum. Rated R for language and violence. 92m. DIR: James D. Deck. CAST: Bruce Payne, Yancy Butler, Salvator Xuereb, Juliet Landau. 1997

RAVE REVIEW ★★★1/2 Outrageous antics ensue as a headstrong theatrical director bullies an influential critic to give him a good review. Instead, the director goes too far, and the critic ends up dead. Insightful humor and madcap lunacy make this little independent comedy a big winner in the laughs department. Rated PG-13 for adult language. 91m. DIR: Jeff Seymour. CAST: Ed Begley Jr., Leo Rossi, Joe Spano, James Handy. 1994

RAVEN 🎬 An ex-mercenary is hunted down by his former team leader, played by Burt Reynolds in a film so bad that he looks embarrassed to be in it. Rated R for violence, sexual situations, and profanity. 93m. DIR: Russell Solberg. CAST: Burt Reynolds, Matt Battaglia, Krista Allen. 1997 DVD

RAVEN, THE (1935) ★★★★ Solid Universal Pictures horror-thriller casts Bela Lugosi as a mad scientist who is obsessed with the writings of Edgar Allan Poe. Boris Karloff is the hapless fugitive Lugosi deforms in order to carry out his evil schemes. Unlike many of the 1930s horror classics, this one has retained its suspense and drama. Available on a double-feature videocassette with *Black Cat*. B&W; 62m. DIR: Louis Friedlander. CAST: Boris Karloff, Bela Lugosi, Irene Ware, Lester Matthews, Samuel S. Hinds. 1935

RAVEN, THE (1963) ★★★★ The best of the Roger Corman–directed Edgar Allan Poe adaptations, this release benefits from a humorous screenplay by Richard Matheson and tongue-in-cheek portrayals by Boris Karloff, Vincent Price, and Peter Lorre. Look for Jack Nicholson in an early role as Lorre's son. 86m. DIR: Roger Corman. CAST: Boris Karloff, Vincent Price, Peter Lorre, Jack Nicholson, Hazel Court. 1963

RAVEN HAWK ★★★ Here's a switch: a reasonably intelligent action-thriller blessed with a strong and credible female protagonist. If star Rachel McLish were a better actress, we'd be all set. She plays an American Indian, falsely accused of having killed her parents, who escapes from prison and pursues the men actually responsible for the heinous deed. While hardly in Tony Hillerman's league, scripter Kevin Elders successfully mixes this unfamiliar culture with standard heroics. Rated R for nudity, profanity, rape, and violence. 87m. **DIR:** Albert Pyun. **CAST:** Rachel McLish, John Enos, Ed Lauter, Matt Clark, William Atherton, John de Lancie. 1995

RAVEN TENGU KABUTO ★★★1/2 High-tech gadgetry meets samurai sword in this animated video entry as Japanese mythology is blended skillfully with dark science fiction. Kabuto, the wandering swordsman, matches his sword and mystic arts against an evil sorceress. In Japanese with English subtitles. Not rated, with violence and nudity. 45m. **DIR:** Buichi Terasawa. 1992

RAVENOUS ★★1/2 United States soldiers at a remote outpost in 1840s California are menaced by a madman who subsists on human flesh. Despite some pretentious speechifying about history and Manifest Destiny (about which writer Ted Griffin seems to know very little), this is really just a supernatural slasher movie dressed up with high-caliber actors who deserve better. Rated R for violence and gore. 100m. **DIR:** Antonia Bird. **CAST:** Guy Pearce, Robert Carlyle, Jeffrey Jones, Jeremy Davies, David Arquette. 1999 DVD

RAVISHING IDIOT, THE 💘 Thin plot concerns a spy out to steal NATO plans of ship movements. B&W; 110m. **DIR:** Edouard Molinaro. **CAST:** Anthony Perkins, Brigitte Bardot. 1965

RAW COURAGE ★★★★ Three cross-country runners must fend for themselves when they run into a group of weekend warriors in the Colorado desert lands. Ronny Cox is excellent as one of the runners. However, Cox, who wrote the screenplay, has taken a few too many pages from James Dickey's *Deliverance*. Still, *Raw Courage* has enough white-knuckle moments to make you forget about the lack of originality. Rated R for violence and profanity. 90m. **DIR:** Robert L. Rosen. **CAST:** Ronny Cox, Tim Maier, Art Hindle, M. Emmet Walsh, William Russ, Lisa Sutton, Lois Chiles. 1983

RAW DEAL ★★★1/2 Big Arnold Schwarzenegger stars in this fast-paced action film as a former FBI agent who is recruited by his former boss (Darren McGavin) to infiltrate the Chicago mob as an act of revenge. It's predictable, even formula. But the formula works. Rated R for profanity and violence. 107m. **DIR:** John Irvin. **CAST:** Arnold Schwarzenegger, Kathryn Harrold, Darren McGavin, Sam Wanamaker, Paul Shenar, Steven Hill, Joe Regalbuto, Ed Lauter, Robert Davi. 1986 DVD

RAW JUSTICE ★★ Caught in the crossfire of a conspiracy, dogged bounty hunter David Keith teams up with a wrongfully accused man and a hapless prostitute. While entertaining, this one can't quite decide whether it's a spoof or just a tremendous waste of talent. Rated R for violence and nudity. 92m. **DIR:** David A. Prior. **CAST:** David Keith, Robert Hays, Pamela Anderson. 1993

RAW MEAT ★★★ Stylish British horror film about a race of cannibals living under the subway system. An atmosphere of dread is maintained throughout as the underground dwellers make occasional trips to the surface for food and mates. Rated R for violence, profanity, and gore. 87m. **DIR:** Gary A. Sherman. **CAST:** Donald Pleasence, Christopher Lee, Clive Swift. 1973

RAW NERVE ★★1/2 A race car driver suddenly finds himself psychically connected with a killer. Better-than-average thriller utilizes best elements of the exploitation genre to its advantage. Rated R for violence and nudity. 91m. **DIR:** David A. Prior. **CAST:** Glenn Ford, Traci Lords, Ted Prior, Sandahl Bergman, Jan-Michael Vincent. 1991

RAW TARGET 💘 Kick-boxing champion goes undercover for the police as a gang member and learns the leader was responsible for his brother's death. Obviously the filmmakers have never seen another kick-boxing movie before. Rated R for language and violence. 92m. **DIR:** Tim Spring. **CAST:** Dale "Apollo" Cook, Ron Hall, Mychelle Charters, Nicholas Hill. 1996

RAWHEAD REX ★★1/2 A satanic demon is accidentally unearthed and begins to wreak havoc on a small village in Ireland. The acting and script are both low caliber, but worth watching if you like raunch. Rated R for profanity, nudity, and plenty-o'-gore. 89m. **DIR:** George Pavlou. **CAST:** David Dukes, Kelly Piper, Niall Toibin. 1986 DVD

RAWHIDE (1938) ★★ Lou Gehrig in a Western? Yes, the Pride of the Yankees made one sagebrush adventure in support of former bandleader Smith Ballew. Gehrig plays a rancher at constant odds with the badmen and Ballew plays the two-fisted young lawyer who helps to organize the honest folk. Ballew is a rather bland lead, but the presence of Gehrig makes this one worth a watch. B&W; 58m. **DIR:** Ray Taylor. **CAST:** Smith Ballew, Lou Gehrig, Lafe McKee, Evalyn Knapp. 1938

RAWHIDE (1951) ★★★ Sturdy Western concerns an outlaw gang holding hostages at a remote stagecoach station. Veteran director Henry Hathaway knows how to keep things clicking right along; the final shoot-out is electrifying. A good cast keeps this one on target. 86m. **DIR:** Henry Hathaway. **CAST:** Tyrone Power, Susan Hayward, Dean Jagger, Hugh Marlowe, Jack Elam, Edgar Buchanan, Jeff Corey, George Tobias. 1951

RAWHIDE (TV SERIES) ★★★★ One of TV's best written and directed Western series. The theme of the show was the long cattle drive from Texas to Kansas, but it was the wide variety of people that trail boss Gil Favor and his drovers encountered along the way that gave the series its momentum. B&W; Several volumes; two one-hour episodes **DIR:** Charles Marquis Warren. **CAST:** Eric Fleming, Clint Eastwood, Sheb Wooley, Paul Brinegar. 1959–1966

RAY BRADBURY'S CHRONICLES: THE MARTIAN EPISODES ★★★1/2 Although produced with minimal budgets, these five installments of TV's *Ray Bradbury Theater* are infinitely superior to the network-television's miniseries versions. Credit Bradbury himself, whose adaptations retain the pathos and poetic impact that have made his tales classics. "Mars Is Heaven" remains the best known, but "The Martian" is by far the best piece, featuring an alien willing to kill itself to please the strangers who've settled its native planet. The tape also includes "The Concrete Mixer," "And the Moon Be Still as Bright," and "The Earthmen." 112m. **DIR:** Various. **CAST:** Hal Linden, Ben Cross, John Vernon, Sheila Moore, David Carradine, David Birney. 1989–1990

RAY CHARLES: THE GENIUS OF SOUL ★★★★★ Superb made-for-TV documentary about Ray Charles's personal life and his music—which weds gospel, jazz, and blues to create soul music. Through narration and interviews writer-director Yvonne Smith gives viewers an uncompromising, in-depth and well-rounded look at a complex, brilliant man. David "Fathead" Newman, Dr John, Hank Crawford, Billy Joel, Willie Nelson, and Billy Preston are among those interviewed. 60m. DIR: Yvonne Smith. 1991

•**RAZOR BLADE SMILE** ★★ Director-writer Jake West seems more concerned with style over substance in this anemic tale of a female vampire who works as a contract killer. The visual flourishes are exciting, but not enough to keep the story from drying up. Rated R for violence, language, and nudity. 101m. DIR: Jake West. CAST: Eileen Daly, Christopher Adamson, Jonathon Coote, Kevin Howarth. 1998 DVD

RAZOR, THE: SWORD OF JUSTICE ★★1/2 If you liked the Japanese *Lone Wolf and Cub* movies, be sure to check out this, the first film in a similar series. *The Razor* is a nineteenth-century Tokyo policeman who battles injustice on both sides of the law. Sort of a Samurai Dirty Harry but much meaner (and sexier, too). Not rated; the film contains strong violence, nudity, and sexual situations. In Japanese with English subtitles. 90m. DIR: Misumi Kenji. CAST: Katsu Shintaro, Asaoka Yukiji. 1972

RAZORBACK ★★★1/2 This Australian film, concerning a giant pig that is terrorizing a small Aussie village, surprises the viewer by turning into a great little film. The special effects, photography, editing, and acting are great. Rated R. 95m. DIR: Russell Mulcahy. CAST: Gregory Harrison. 1983

RAZOR'S EDGE, THE (1946) ★★★★1/2 A long but engrossing presentation of Somerset Maugham's philosophical novel about a young man seeking the goodness in life. Full of memorable characterizations and scenes. Herbert Marshall steers the plot, playing the author. B&W; 146m. DIR: Edmund Goulding. CAST: Tyrone Power, Gene Tierney, Clifton Webb, Herbert Marshall, Anne Baxter, John Payne, Elsa Lanchester. 1946

RAZOR'S EDGE, THE (1984) ★★★1/2 Bill Murray gives a finely balanced comic and dramatic portrayal as a man searching for meaning after World War I in this adaptation of W. Somerset Maugham's novel. The result is a richly rewarding film, which survives the unevenness of John Byrum's direction. Rated PG-13 for suggested sex, violence, and profanity. 128m. DIR: John Byrum. CAST: Bill Murray, Theresa Russell, Catherine Hicks, James Keach, Brian Doyle-Murray. 1984

RE-ANIMATOR ★★★★ Stylishly grotesque and gory filming of H. P. Lovecraft's "Herbert West, Reanimator" hits the mark. This is Grand Guignol in the classic sense as we follow brilliant young medical student Herbert West in his deranged efforts to bring the dead back to life. Some outrageous scenes highlight this terror entry and, although very well-done, it's not for the squeamish. 86m. DIR: Stuart Gordon. CAST: Bruce Abbott, Barbara Crampton, David Gale, Robert Sampson, Jeffrey Combs. 1985 DVD

•**REACH THE ROCK** ★★ The preposterous script by John Hughes is filled with clichéd characters and outrageous plot development in this tale of a tough kid squaring off against an equally tough cop. Rated R for language and violence. 100m. DIR: William Ryan. CAST: Bill Sadler, Alessandro Nivola, Bruce Norris, Karen Sillas, Norman Reedus. 1998

REACHING FOR THE MOON (1917) ★★★ One of several products of the Douglas Fairbanks/Anita Loos/John Emerson triumvirate. Lots of brash, physical comedy and stunts in the early Fairbanks manner. Silent. B&W; 91m. DIR: John Emerson. CAST: Douglas Fairbanks Sr., Eileen Percy. 1917

REACHING FOR THE MOON (1931) ★★★ Robust and energetic Douglas Fairbanks plays a financier on whom liquor has an interesting effect. Edward Everett Horton is his valet and Bebe Daniels is the girl. B&W; 62m. DIR: Edmund Goulding. CAST: Douglas Fairbanks Sr., Bebe Daniels, Edward Everett Horton. 1931

•**READY TO RUMBLE** ★★ Two dimwit fans of professional wrestling set out to save the career of their favorite wrestler. There is a smattering of cheap laughs here and there, but generally the film is just as doltish and dull as the two heroes. The best moments belong to a gleeful Martin Landau as a famous old wrestling coach. Rated PG-13 for mild profanity and wrestling violence. 100m. DIR: Brian Robbins. CAST: David Arquette, Oliver Platt, Scott Caan, Rose McGowan, Diamond Dallas Page, Joe Pantoliano, Martin Landau. 2000

READY TO WEAR ★★★1/2 A murder-mystery plot loosely ties together the various goings-on in this irreverent and episodic study of the fashion scene. The results are not for all tastes. Indeed, the superficiality of the on-screen events seems to be a sort of commentary on the inflated self-importance of the players in the fashion world. Rated R for profanity, nudity, and scatological humor. 132m. DIR: Robert Altman. CAST: Sophia Loren, Marcello Mastroianni, Julia Roberts, Tim Robbins, Kim Basinger, Stephen Rea, Anouk Aimée, Lauren Bacall, Lili Taylor, Sally Kellerman, Linda Hunt, Tracey Ullman, Rupert Everett, Forest Whittaker. 1994 DVD

REAL AMERICAN HERO, THE ★★ Below-average TV movie does not do justice to slain sheriff Buford Pusser. Brian Dennehy plays Pusser, a frustrated law enforcer who will do anything—even risk his own life—to get the bad guys. Ken Howard plays a ruthless bar owner. *Walking Tall* says it all better. Not rated; contains profanity and violence. 94m. DIR: Lou Antonio. CAST: Brian Dennehy, Forrest Tucker, Brian Kerwin, Ken Howard, Sheree North. 1978

REAL BLONDE, THE ★★★1/2 Image and appearance make the world go 'round in this lively satire of 1990s relationships and America's fixation with glamour. This clever adult comedy tracks the overlapping personal and professional lives of several stubbornly foolish characters who try to survive their own obsessions and mistakes in trendy Manhattan. Rated R for sexual content and language. 105m. DIR: Tom DiCillo. CAST: Matthew Modine, Catherine Keener, Maxwell Caulfield, Daryl Hannah, Elizabeth Berkeley, Marlo Thomas. 1998 DVD

REAL GENIUS ★★★ This is a mildly amusing comedy about a group of science prodigies (led by Val Kilmer) who decide to thwart the plans of their egomaniacal mentor (William Atherton). Director Martha Coolidge does her best to keep things interesting, but she can't overcome the predictability of the climax. Rated PG for profanity. 105m. **DIR:** Martha Coolidge. **CAST:** Val Kilmer, Gabe Jarret, Michelle Meyrink, William Atherton, Ed Lauter. 1985

REAL GLORY, THE ★★★★ After the American army pulls out of the Philippines in 1910, it's left to a small band of professional soldiers to equip and train the natives to fight off a pirate-like tribe of cutthroats. This lesser-known adventure film ranks alongside *Beau Geste* and *The Lives of a Bengal Lancer* as one of Gary Cooper's best in the genre. B&W; 109m. **DIR:** Henry Hathaway. **CAST:** Gary Cooper, Andrea Leeds, David Niven, Reginald Owen, Broderick Crawford. 1939

●**REAL HOWARD SPRITZ, THE** ★★★★ Delightful family tale about a detective novelist who can't find a publisher for his latest hard-boiled epic. With the help of a little girl, he develops a series of books for children that becomes the cat's meow. Quaint, charming picture with a delightful performance by Kelsey Grammer. Rated PG. 93m. **DIR:** Vadim Jean. **CAST:** Kelsey Grammer, Amanda Donaho, Genevieve Tessier. 1998

REAL LIFE ★★★ Albert Brooks's fans will eat up this tasty satire parodying an unrelenting PBS series that put the day-to-day life of an American family under the microscope. In Brooks's film the typical family comes hilariously unglued under the omnipresent eye of the camera. The script (written by Brooks) eventually falters, but not before a healthy number of intelligent laughs are produced. Rated PG. 99m. **DIR:** Albert Brooks. **CAST:** Albert Brooks, Charles Grodin, Frances Lee McCain, J. A. Preston. 1979

REAL MCCOY, THE ★★ Kim Basinger plays an ace safecracker, trying to go straight, who is blackmailed into one last heist by her former boss. Except for the gender switch on the protagonist, the premise is old hat. Still, with the actors on hand, it could have been better if there had been a few surprises in the script or any suspense in the direction. Rated PG-13 for violence and profanity. 104m. **DIR:** Russell Mulcahy. **CAST:** Kim Basinger, Val Kilmer, Terence Stamp, Gailard Sartain. 1993 DVD

REAL MEN ★★★ This action-filled comedy features James Belushi as an infallible Bond-like CIA agent. His latest mission is to protect his wimpish new partner (John Ritter) and make contact with powerful aliens. Rated PG-13 for profanity, violence, and brief nudity. 86m. **DIR:** Dennis Feldman. **CAST:** James Belushi, John Ritter, Bill Morey, Gail Barl, Barbara Barrie. 1987

REAL THING, THE ★★★1/2 Riveting crime-drama about an ex-con who agrees to carry out his brother's plans to rob a popular nightclub in New York on New Year's Eve. He faces a big problem when another gang decides to hit the nightclub at the same time. Better-than-average results for this direct-to-video effort that features memorable characters and vicious violence. Rated R for language and violence.

89m. **DIR:** James Merendino. **CAST:** James Russo, Emily Lloyd, Gary Busey, Rod Steiger, Jeremy Piven, Max Perlich. 1996

REALITY BITES ★★★1/2 This mordantly amusing, often tragic drama is the first to speak for the Generation X'ers. College valedictorian Winona Ryder vacillates between financially successful dropout Ben Stiller and philosophical Ethan Hawke, who coasts through life. The film's video verité cinematography is the perfect statement for the MTV generation. Rated PG-13 for profanity, drug use, and sexual frankness. 99m. **DIR:** Ben Stiller. **CAST:** Winona Ryder, Ethan Hawke, Ben Stiller, Janeane Garofalo, Steve Zahn. 1994 DVD

REALLY WEIRD TALES ★★★ These three short stories produced for HBO have their moments. Martin Short plays a hack lounge singer at a playboy's swank party in "All's Well That Ends Strange." "Cursed with Charisma" features John Candy as a successful hustler. The last story, featuring Catherine O'Hara, is the best. "I'll Die Loving" is about a woman who is cursed with the odd power of loving people to death. Not rated, has profanity. 85m. **DIR:** Paul Lynch, Don McBrearty, John Blanchard. **CAST:** Joe Flaherty, John Candy, Catherine O'Hara, Martin Short, Dan Harron, Olivia D'Abo, Sheila McCarthy. 1986

REAP THE WILD WIND ★★★1/2 Bawdy tale of the shipping and salvage business off the coast of Georgia during the early nineteenth century. John Wayne is a robust sea captain and Ray Milland is a well-to-do owner of a shipping company. Plenty of old-fashioned action and humor with the typical Cecil B. DeMille touches. Entire cast is first-rate, especially the villainous Raymond Massey. The final underwater action scenes are classics. 124m. **DIR:** Cecil B. DeMille. **CAST:** John Wayne, Ray Milland, Raymond Massey, Paulette Goddard, Robert Preston, Charles Bickford, Susan Hayward. 1942 DVD

REAR WINDOW (1954) ★★★★★ James Stewart plays a magazine photographer who, confined to a wheelchair because of a broken leg, seeks diversion in watching his neighbors, often with a telephoto lens. He soon becomes convinced that one neighbor (Raymond Burr) has murdered his spouse and dismembered the body. One of the director's best. 112m. **DIR:** Alfred Hitchcock. **CAST:** James Stewart, Raymond Burr, Grace Kelly, Wendell Corey, Thelma Ritter, Judith Evelyn. 1954

●**REAR WINDOW** (1998) ★★★ A man confined to a wheelchair spies on his neighbors and thinks he overhears a murder. This two-dimensional remake of Alfred Hitchcock's classic acts more as a showcase of Christopher Reeve's new life as a disabled person than as a character study. Reeve can still act reasonably well, and the story is suspenseful in its updated version, but it lacks the multitude of stories that made the original so compelling. Rated PG for mild violence. 89m. **DIR:** Jeff Bleckner. **CAST:** Christopher Reeve, Daryl Hannah, Ruben Santiago Hudson, Anne Twomey, Robert Forster. 1998

REASON TO BELIEVE, A ★★★ Though somewhat simplistic, this unflinching tale of date rape paints a sadly accurate portrayal of college life. The assault of a popular young woman during a frat party brings out the worst in everyone around her. Friends don't believe her, strangers scream at her, and media-hungry feminists claim her as their poster child. Rated R for violence, sexual situations, and profanity. 108m. DIR: Douglas Tirola. CAST: Jay Underwood, Allison Smith, Daniel Quinn, Georgia Emelin, Kim Walker, Keith Coogan, Christopher Birt, Holly Marie Combs, Obba Babatundé. 1995

REASON TO DIE ★★ A razor fiend is tracked by a bounty hunter, after a series of erotic slicings. Typical slasher, though at least high-voltage actor Wings Hauser is the protagonist. Not rated. 96m. DIR: Tim Spring. CAST: Wings Hauser. 1989

REASONS OF THE HEART ★★★1/2 This sometimes predictable, sometimes surprising made-for-cable original is about a woman who visits a small town to woo a reclusive writer back into publishing, and to search for the secret of her own past. Solid, but not spectacular, performances by Terry Farrell and Jim Davidson; the story is what really keeps you watching. Not rated. 95m. DIR: Rick Jacobson. CAST: Terry Farrell, Jim Davidson. 1996

REBECCA ★★★★★ *Rebecca* won an Oscar for best picture and nominations for its stars, Laurence Olivier and Joan Fontaine. The popular Daphne du Maurier novel was transferred to the screen without losing any of its gothic blend of romance and mystery. Judith Anderson as the sinister housekeeper is one of the most compelling figures in film history. B&W; 130m. DIR: Alfred Hitchcock. CAST: Laurence Olivier, Joan Fontaine, George Sanders, Nigel Bruce, Reginald Denny, Judith Anderson. 1940 DVD

REBECCA OF SUNNYBROOK FARM (1917) ★★1/2 Once again, the adult Mary Pickford successfully portrays a saucy teenager who wins love, respect, and prosperity in this rags-to-riches tearjerker based on the famous Kate Douglas Wiggin bestseller. Shirley Temple starred in a talkie version in 1938. Silent. B&W; 77m. DIR: Marshall Neilan. CAST: Mary Pickford, Eugene O'Brien, Helen Jerome Eddy. 1917

REBECCA OF SUNNYBROOK FARM (1938) ★★★1/2 Lightweight but engaging Shirley Temple vehicle has the 1930s superstar playing a child performer who wants to be on radio. While Temple hoofs with the likes of Jack Haley and Bill "Bojangles" Robinson, Randolph Scott, in one of his few screen appearances out of the saddle, romances Gloria Stuart. B&W; 80m. DIR: Allan Dwan. CAST: Shirley Temple, Randolph Scott, Jack Haley, Gloria Stuart, Phyllis Brooks, Helen Westley, Slim Summerville, Bill Robinson. 1938

REBECCA'S SECRET 🐌 Awful rip-off of *Diabolique* in which the filmmakers were apparently so busy auditioning naked women they didn't take time to make sense of the plot. Rated R for nudity and sex. 84m. DIR: Ellyn Michaels. CAST: Amy Rochelle, Lauren Hays, Michael Baci. 1997 DVD

REBEL (1973) ★★ This early Sylvester Stallone movie casts him as a student radical who begins to ponder his future. This low-budget production only proves that Stallone started out mumbling. It is un-

rated. 80m. DIR: Robert Schnitzer. CAST: Sylvester Stallone, Anthony Page, Henry G. Sanders. 1973

REBEL (1985) 🐌 During World War II, a Marine sergeant in Australia goes AWOL and falls in love with a nightclub singer. Rated R for profanity. 93m. DIR: Michael Jenkins. CAST: Matt Dillon, Debbie Byrne, Bryan Brown, Bill Hunter, Ray Barrett. 1985

REBEL LOVE 🐌 Yankee widow falls in love with a Confederate spy. Not rated; there is some mild sexual content. 84m. DIR: Milton Bagby Jr. CAST: Jamie Rose, Terence Knox, Fran Ryan, Charles Hill. 1986

REBEL ROUSERS ★★ This drive-in biker film from the late 1960s would barely rate a second look if it weren't for a crop of future big-name stars and character performers who inhabit it. The ill-mannered-youth-on-motorcycles-versus-uptight-establishment-straights story takes a backseat to flamboyant characterizations in this one. 78m. DIR: Martin B. Cohen. CAST: Cameron Mitchell, Jack Nicholson, Bruce Dern, Diane Ladd, Harry Dean Stanton. 1967 DVD

REBEL STORM ★★1/2 Mildly diverting futuristic thriller about a group of freedom fighters attempting to overthrow a suppressive government. 99m. DIR: Franky Schaeffer. CAST: Zach Galligan, Wayne Crawford, June Chadwick, John Rhys-Davies. 1990

REBEL WITHOUT A CAUSE ★★★★★ This is the film that made James Dean a legend. Directed by Nicholas Ray, it is undoubtedly the classic film about juvenile delinquency. Featuring fine performances by Dean, Natalie Wood, and Sal Mineo as the teens in trouble, it has stood up surprisingly well over the years. 111m. DIR: Nicholas Ray. CAST: James Dean, Natalie Wood, Sal Mineo, Jim Backus, Ann Doran, Corey Allen, Edward Platt, Dennis Hopper, Nick Adams. 1955 DVD

REBELS, THE ★★★ The second of John Jakes's bicentennial bestsellers to be converted into a TV miniseries, this is a step up from *The Bastard*. Much of the sleaze has been replaced with swashbuckling adventure thanks to Don Johnson and Doug McClure's contributions. Using America's history from 1775 to 1781 as a background, this allows us to experience the eventual triumph of our Continental army. 190m. DIR: Russ Mayberry. CAST: Andrew Stevens, Don Johnson, Doug McClure, Joan Blondell, Tanya Tucker. 1979

REBOUND ★★★★ This is the true story of Earl "The Goat" Manigault, who was, according to such greats as Wilt Chamberlain and Kareem Abdul-Jabbar, the best basketball player who never made it to the NBA. A series of misfortunes, then a rapid descent into drug abuse, left "The Goat" without a future. This made-for-cable original is well acted and poignant. Not rated; contains profanity and violence. 111m. DIR: Eriq La Salle. CAST: Don Cheadle, James Earl Jones, Clarence Williams III, Eriq La Salle, Forest Whitaker. 1996

RECKLESS (1935) ★★ Jean Harlow, terribly miscast as a Broadway musical star, marries troubled alcoholic playboy Franchot Tone, who feels she entrapped him and heads downhill toward suicide. William Powell stands by until needed. B&W; 97m. DIR: Victor Fleming. CAST: Jean Harlow, William Powell, Franchot Tone, May Robson, Rosalind Russell, Mickey Rooney. **1935**

RECKLESS (1984) ★★ A 1980s version of the standard 1950s "angry young man" movie, this features Aidan Quinn as a motorcycle-riding, mumbling (à la James Dean and Marlon Brando) outcast and Daryl Hannah as the "good girl." That should give you an idea of how original this movie is. Rated R for nudity, profanity, violence, and suggested sex. 90m. **DIR:** James Foley. **CAST:** Aidan Quinn, Daryl Hannah, Kenneth McMillan, Cliff De Young, Lois Smith, Adam Baldwin, Dan Hedaya. **1984**

RECKLESS (1995) ★★★1/2 A happily married housewife discovers on Christmas Eve that her husband has plotted her murder and the film chronicles her picaresque adventures as she flees from the hired killer. Offbeat and unpredictable, this has its own weird charm and plenty of surprises; the biggest surprise of all, ultimately, is how genuinely touching it is by the time it's over. Rated PG-13 for mild profanity and seriocomic violence. 92m. **DIR:** Norman René. **CAST:** Mia Farrow, Scott Glenn, Mary-Louise Parker, Tony Goldwyn, Eileen Brennan, Stephen Dorff. **1995**

RECKLESS KELLY ★★1/2 Australian comic Yahoo Serious returns in a spoof of the career of outlaw Ned Kelly, Australia's answer to Jesse James. Serious is an engaging performer, and the film is fast-paced, with bright, carnival-colored wide-screen photography (which will suffer on video). High-spirited and likable, it's just not funny. Rated PG. 80m. **DIR:** Yahoo Serious. **CAST:** Yahoo Serious, Melora Hardin, Alexei Sayle, Hugo Weaving, Kathleen Freeman. **1994**

RECRUITS ❤ A sheriff hires hookers, thieves, and bums as deputies. Rated R. 90m. **DIR:** Rafal Zielinski. **CAST:** Alan Deveau, Annie McAuley. **1987**

RECTOR'S WIFE, THE ★★★★★ A subtle tale of duty and domination, this four-episode British production is based on the novel by Joanna Trollope. A vicar's wife in a small English parish finds she is disappearing under her title. As she slowly steps out of the rector's shadow, this mousy facilitator finds herself on a path of liberation, romance, and intrigue. Not rated. Each tape 52m. **DIR:** Giles Foster. **CAST:** Lindsay Duncan, Ronald Pickup, Jonathan Coy, Prunella Scales, Stephen Dillane. **1993**

RED ★★★1/2 Polish filmmaker Krzysztof Kieslowski concludes his *Three Colors* trilogy by examining the wary friendship that develops between a young fashion model and a retired judge who has become a voyeur in his old age. The film is slow-moving but fascinating, and its beautiful images linger in the mind. In French with English subtitles. Rated R for nudity and simulated sex. 99m. **DIR:** Krzysztof Kieslowski. **CAST:** Irène Jacob, Jean-Louis Trintignant, Frederique Feder, Jean-Pierre Lorit. **1994**

RED ALERT ★★★1/2 This 1977 made-for-TV film about a nuclear power plant is just as timely today as when it first aired. An incident at the plant has killed fourteen workers. Was it an accident, sabotage, or computer fault? A fine cast lends an air of reality and immediacy to this gripping mystery. 95m. **DIR:** William Hale. **CAST:** William Devane, Michael Brandon,

Ralph Waite, Adrienne Barbeau, David Hayward, M. Emmet Walsh, Don Wiseman. **1977**

RED AND THE WHITE, THE ★★★★ Hungarian director Miklos Jancso creates a bleak and startling film of the senseless slaughter and sheer absurdity of war. The film depicts the bloody encounters between Russia's Bolshevik Red Army and the counterrevolutionary forces in central Russia during the Civil War of 1918. In Russian with English subtitles. 92m. **DIR:** Miklos Jancso. **CAST:** Tibor Molnar, Andreas Kozak, Josef Madaras. **1968**

RED BADGE OF COURAGE, THE ★★★1/2 Natural performances mark this realistic treatment of Stephen Crane's famous Civil War novel of a young soldier's initiation to battle. A John Huston classic, and a major film achievement by any standard. B&W. 69m. **DIR:** John Huston. **CAST:** Audie Murphy, Bill Mauldin, Royal Dano, Arthur Hunnicutt, Douglas Dick. **1951**

RED BALLOON, THE ★★★★★ This fanciful, endearing tale of a giant balloon that befriends a small boy in Paris is a delight for children and adults alike. Outside of a catchable word or two here and there, the film is without dialogue. The story is crystal clear in the visual telling, punctuated by an engaging musical score. 34m. **DIR:** Albert Lamorisse. **CAST:** Pascal Lamorisse, Georges Sellier. **1956**

RED BARRY ★★1/2 Serial superstar Buster Crabbe plays comic-strip sleuth Red Barry in this decent chapterplay. It seems some scurrilous spies have stolen $2 million in negotiable bonds from a friendly ally, and the fate of the world hangs in the balance. B&W; 13 chapters. **DIR:** Ford Beebe, Alan James. **CAST:** Buster Crabbe, Frances Robinson, Edna Sedgewick. **1938**

RED BEARD ★★★★1/2 In the early nineteenth century, a newly graduated doctor hopes to become a society doctor. Instead, he is posted at an impoverished clinic run by Dr. Niide (Toshiro Mifune), whose destitute patients affectionately call him "Red Beard." Akira Kurosawa, at one of his directorial pinnacles, describes his film as a "monument to the goodness in man." In Japanese with English subtitles. B&W; 185m. **DIR:** Akira Kurosawa. **CAST:** Toshiro Mifune. **1965**

RED-BLOODED AMERICAN GIRL ★★1/2 A quirky story about a scientist (Andrew Stevens) who is called upon to reverse the effects of a new drug that causes vampirism. Rated R for language, violence, and nudity. 90m. **DIR:** David Blyth. **CAST:** Heather Thomas, Andrew Stevens, Lydie Denier, Christopher Plummer, Kim Coates. **1990**

RED CORNER ★★★ In this generally gripping drama, Richard Gere is an American businessman who becomes caught up in the Chinese legal system after being accused of a crime. Guilty until proven innocent, he must convince his defense advocate (Bai Ling) to use what are to her unorthodox methods in securing his freedom while he endures dehumanizing treatment on an almost daily basis. Gere successfully engages our sympathies as the innocent man caught up in almost impossible-to-overcome circumstances while Ling is even more impressive as the functionary who must rise to the occasion. Rated

R for violence, profanity, and partial nudity. 119m. **DIR:** Jon Avnet. **CAST:** Richard Gere, Bai Ling, Bradley Whitford, Byron Mann, Peter Donat, James Hong. 1997 DVD

RED DAWN ★★★1/2 Some viewers undoubtedly will feel that right-wing writer-director John Milius (*The Wind and the Lion* and *Conan the Barbarian*) has gone too far with this tale of the Russians invading a small American town. But we took this film as a simple "what if?" entertainment and really enjoyed it. Rated PG-13 for violence and profanity. 114m. **DIR:** John Milius. **CAST:** Patrick Swayze, C. Thomas Howell, Ron O'Neal, Lea Thompson, Ben Johnson, Harry Dean Stanton, William Smith, Powers Boothe, Charlie Sheen. 1984 DVD

RED DESERT ★★★★ An acutely depressed married woman (Monica Vitti) finds her life with an industrial-engineer husband to be demanding. Photographed in the industrial wasteland of northern Italy by Carlo Di Palma, this film remains one of the most beautiful of director Michelangelo Antonioni's works. Italian with English subtitles. 116m. **DIR:** Michelangelo Antonioni. **CAST:** Monica Vitti, Richard Harris. 1964 DVD

RED DUST ★★★★ *Red Dust* is one of those remarkable films where the performances of its stars propel a movie to classic status despite a rather uninspired story. A hackneyed story of a rubber plantation boss (Gable) who dallies with another man's wife only to return to the arms of a shady lady (Harlow) with the proverbial heart of gold. B&W; 83m. **DIR:** Victor Fleming. **CAST:** Clark Gable, Jean Harlow, Mary Astor, Donald Crisp, Gene Raymond, Tully Marshall. 1932

•**RED DWARF, THE** ★★★1/2 Jean-Yves Thual is excellent as Lucien in this fascinating, offbeat tale of a diminutive figure who composes incriminating letters for a law firm while dreaming of a better life. When an affair leads to tragedy, Lucien joins the circus to find redemption. Moody black-and-white images recall early David Lynch and Jean Cocteau. In French with English subtitles. Rated R for adult situations, language, nudity, and violence. 101m. **DIR:** Yvonne Le Moine. **CAST:** Jean-Yves Thual, Anita Kberg, Dyna Gauzy, Arno Chevrier. 1998 DVD

RED DWARF (TV SERIES) ★★★1/2 This wonderfully inventive British TV series is pure lunacy as the remnant crew of the *Red Dwarf*, a gigantic spaceship, hurtles through the universe millions of years in the future. Absolutely perfect casting, with Craig Charles as likable slob/hero Dave Lister and Chris Barrie as his obnoxious, repressed roommate. Each tape 84–90m. **DIR:** Ed Bye. **CAST:** Chris Barrie, Craig Charles, Danny John-Jules, Robert Llewellyn. 1988–1993 DVD

RED FIRECRACKER, GREEN FIRECRACKER ★★ A forbidden romance blossoms between a young fireworks manufacturer and her new hired hand, while the factory foreman looks on with sour jealousy. Turgid and sluggish, soap opera's pace is leaden even when the skyrockets and firecrackers are going full blast. In Mandarin with English subtitles. Not rated; suitable for general audiences. 117m. **DIR:** He Ping.

CAST: Ning Jing, Wu Gang, Zhao Xiao Rui, Gao Yang. 1994 DVD

RED FLAG: THE ULTIMATE GAME ★★1/2 The air force has a jet-fighter combat course located near Las Vegas that over the years has fine-tuned thousands of the best pilots in the air force. The combat game is called Red Flag. It's an older and weaker version of *Top Gun* and suffers by comparison. 90m. **DIR:** Don Taylor. **CAST:** Barry Bostwick, Joan Van Ark, Fred McCarren, George Coe. 1981

RED GARTERS ★★★1/2 A delightful and inventive spoof of Westerns with everything offbeat, from the casting to the stage-stylized sets and the original songs of Jay Livingston and Ray Evans. Oscar nomination for the truly surrealistic set decoration. 91m. **DIR:** George Marshall. **CAST:** Rosemary Clooney, Jack Carson, Guy Mitchell, Pat Crowley, Gene Barry, Cass Daley, Frank Faylen, Reginald Owen, Buddy Ebsen. 1954

RED-HEADED STRANGER, THE ★★★ Willie Nelson's country "opera" served as the basis for this little-seen Western, which most fans of the genre will enjoy. Nelson plays a right-thinking preacher who takes on an evil family (headed by Royal Dano) that is terrorizing the townspeople of this new parish. Rated R for violence and profanity. 105m. **DIR:** William Witliff. **CAST:** Willie Nelson, R. G. Armstrong, Morgan Fairchild, Royal Dano, Katharine Ross. 1986

RED-HEADED WOMAN ★★★1/2 Every female star on every major motion-picture lot wanted the plum role of the gal who followed her heart and her instincts to gain social prominence and a swell guy. Young Jean Harlow took the prize and made it her own in this pre-Code gem. B&W; 79m. **DIR:** Jack Conway. **CAST:** Jean Harlow, Chester Morris, Leila Hyams, Lewis Stone, Una Merkel, Henry Stephenson, May Robson. 1932

RED HEAT (1985) ★★ Linda Blair is mistakenly arrested as a spy and sentenced to prison. Lurid and excessively violent. 104m. **DIR:** Robert Collector. **CAST:** Linda Blair, Sylvia Kristel, William Ostrander, Sue Kiel. 1985

RED HEAT (1988) ★★★★ Director Walter Hill has taken his biggest hit, *48 Hrs.*, and reworked it as a vehicle for Arnold Schwarzenegger and James Belushi. Big Arnold plays a Soviet police officer forced to team up with a wisecracking Chicago cop (Belushi) to track down a Russian drug dealer (Ed O'Ross). It's fast and exciting; a best bet for action buffs. Rated R for violence, profanity, and nudity. 107m. **DIR:** Walter Hill. **CAST:** Arnold Schwarzenegger, James Belushi, Peter Boyle, Ed O'Ross, Laurence Fishburne, Gina Gershon, Richard Bright. 1988

RED HOT ★★★ Rock 'n' roll is called American propaganda and banned in the Soviet Union in 1959. One youth, Alexei, gets a taste of the music, refuses to give it up, and puts himself in jeopardy. Alexei risks everything to stay one step ahead of the KGB and satisfy his passion for rock 'n' roll. Interesting cast and a real sense of time and place make this enjoyable. Rated PG. 95m. **DIR:** Paul Haggis. **CAST:** Balthazar Getty, Carla Gugino, Jan Niklas, Hugh O'Connor, Donald Sutherland, Armin Mueller-Stahl. 1993

RED HOUSE, THE ★★★1/2 A gripping suspense melodrama enhanced by a musical score by Miklos Rozsa. Edward G. Robinson employs Rory Calhoun to keep the curious away from a decaying old house deep in the woods. But his niece and a young hired hand *must* learn the secret. B&W; 100m. **DIR:** Delmer Daves. **CAST:** Edward G. Robinson, Lon McCallister, Allene Roberts, Julie London, Judith Anderson, Rory Calhoun, Ona Munson. 1947 DVD

RED KIMONO, THE 🐾 A young lady is abandoned by her philandering husband and forced to become a scarlet woman. Silent. B&W; 95m. **DIR:** Walter Lang. **CAST:** Priscilla Bonner, Nellie Bly Baker, Mary Carr, Tyrone Power Sr. 1925

RED KING, WHITE KNIGHT ★★1/2 Tom Skerritt's impeccable rendering of a retired and weary CIA agent brought back into the fold (initially as a dupe) enlivens Ron Hutchinson's dreary story about a rogue Soviet KGB official who plots against Gorbachev to retain the cold war status quo. Things also improve considerably when the brilliant Max von Sydow appears. Made for HBO; considerable violence and frank dialogue. 107m. **DIR:** Geoff Murphy. **CAST:** Tom Skerritt, Max von Sydow, Helen Mirren, Tom Bell, Barry Corbin. 1989

RED KISS (ROUGE BAISER) ★★★1/2 In 1952 France, a teenage girl raised by leftist parents is caught between her upbringing and a romance with an apolitical news photographer. This autobiographical tale is reminiscent of the films of Diane Kurys, with an added political dimension. In French with English subtitles. Not rated; brief sexual situations. 110m. **DIR:** Vera Belmont. **CAST:** Charlotte Valandrey, Lambert Wilson, Marthe Keller, Gunter Lamprecht. 1985

RED LIGHT STING, THE ★★ Pale TV film about a young district attorney (Beau Bridges) who is assigned to buy a whorehouse to bring out an elusive big-time crook (Harold Gould). Not rated, but the equivalent of a PG for adult subject matter. 96m. **DIR:** Rod Holcomb. **CAST:** Farrah Fawcett, Beau Bridges, Harold Gould, Paul Burke, Alex Henteloff, Conrad Janis, James Luisi, Philip Charles MacKenzie. 1984

RED LINE ★★1/2 Spectacular car stunts and chase scenes highlight this otherwise unexceptional tale of a former professional race-car driver who finds himself enmeshed with a crime kingpin who wants him to steal cars. Rated R for profanity. 90m. **DIR:** John Sjorgen. **CAST:** Chad McQueen, Michael Madsen, Roxana Zal, Jan-Michael Vincent, Dom DeLuise, Corey Feldman, Chuck Zito. 1995 DVD

RED LINE 7000 ★★1/2 Car-race melodrama about three drivers and the women in their lives bogs down when the story leaves the track. Veteran director Howard Hawks would make only two more films after this tired actioner. 110m. **DIR:** Howard Hawks. **CAST:** James Caan, Laura Devon, Charlene Holt, Marianna Hill, James Ward, Norman Alden, George Takei. 1965

RED LION ★★★ Toshiro Mifune is well cast as a man who impersonates a military officer in order to return to his village in grand style. Once there, he must liberate his followers from an oppressive government. In Japanese with English subtitles. 115m.

DIR: Kihachi Okamoto. **CAST:** Toshiro Mifune, Shima Iwashita. 1969

RED MENACE, THE 🐾 A sloppily written movie made to capitalize on the McCarthy menace with onetime *Our Miss Brooks* hero Robert Rockwell menaced by Communist sympathizers in a very unconvincing way. B&W; 87m. **DIR:** R. G. Springsteen. **CAST:** Robert Rockwell, Betty Lou Gerson, Barbara Fuller, Hanne Axman. 1949

RED NIGHTS 🐾 A New England youth with stars in his eyes heads out to Hollywood. Rated R. 89m. **DIR:** Izhak Hanooka. **CAST:** Christopher Parker, Brian Matthews, Jack Carter, William Smith. 1988

RED PLANET MARS 🐾 Anti-commie sci-fi from the 1950s, as mysterious coded transmissions from Mars turn out to be God telling Earth that communists can't be trusted! Talky, uneventful, and visually flat. B&W; 87m. **DIR:** Harry Horner. **CAST:** Peter Graves, Andrea King, Marvin Miller. 1952

RED PONY, THE ★★ It is very hard to make a dull movie from a John Steinbeck novel. This rendition manages to. Myrna Loy and Robert Mitchum are wasted in this story of a young northern California boy who is given a colt, which runs away. 89m. **DIR:** Lewis Milestone. **CAST:** Myrna Loy, Robert Mitchum, Peter Miles, Louis Calhern, Shepperd Strudwick, Margaret Hamilton. 1948

RED RIVER ★★★★★ After seeing this Western, John Ford remarked, "I didn't know the big lug could act." The "big lug" he was referring to was the star, John Wayne, whom Ford had brought to stardom in 1939s *Stagecoach*. This shoot-'em-up adaptation of *Mutiny on the Bounty* features Wayne at his best in the role of a tough rancher making a historic cattle drive. B&W; 133m. **DIR:** Howard Hawks. **CAST:** John Wayne, Montgomery Clift, Walter Brennan, Joanne Dru, John Ireland, Noah Beery Jr., Paul Fix, Coleen Gray, Harry Carey, Harry Carey Jr. 1948 DVD

RED RIVER RANGE ★★1/2 When entire herds of cattle begin disappearing from the Red River range, the Three Mesquiteers are called in to solve the mystery. John Wayne's presence makes it worth watching for fans. B&W; 59m. **DIR:** George Sherman. **CAST:** John Wayne, Ray "Crash" Corrigan, Max Terhune, Polly Moran, Kirby Grant. 1938

RED RIVER RENEGADES ★★★1/2 Postal inspector Sunset Carson sets out to stop a series of mail robberies on the Red River stage line. He is helped and hindered by a female Pinkerton agent. B&W; 55m. **DIR:** Thomas Carr. **CAST:** Sunset Carson, Peggy Stewart, Tom London. 1946

RED RIVER SHORE ★★★1/2 Marshall Rex Allen is forced to kill a crooked businessman but vows to keep the man's guilt a secret. When the man's son arrives, trouble develops over the dead man's bogus oil-drilling operation. B&W; 54m. **DIR:** Harry Keller. **CAST:** Rex Allen, Slim Pickens, Douglas Fowley, Bill Phipps. 1953

RED ROCK WEST ★★★1/2 Try as he might, mostly honest drifter Nicolas Cage can't leave the small town of Red Rock West ... and he gets in more trouble each time he returns. The plot involves a corrupt sheriff arranging the murder of his scheming wife, and the impertinent killer hired for the job. The seri-comic tone properly emphasizes Cage's plight in a story that will keep you guessing. Rated R for profanity and violence. 98m. DIR: John Dahl. CAST: Nicolas Cage, Dennis Hopper, Lara Flynn Boyle, Timothy Carhart, J. T. Walsh. 1993 DVD

RED SCORPION 💗 A Soviet agent is sent to infiltrate and kill the leader of a band of African rebels. Rated R for violence. 100m. DIR: Joseph Zito. CAST: Dolph Lundgren, M. Emmet Walsh. 1989 DVD

RED SCORPION 2 ★★★ This sequel-in-name-only, a compact retread of *The Dirty Dozen*, is far better than its predecessor. Commando expert Matt Mc-Colm and plucky Jennifer Rubin lead a team of highly specialized assassins and technicians on a raid of a covert American hate group; the resulting action scenes are well-handled. Rated R for violence, torture, nudity, and simulated sex. 89m. DIR: Michael Kennedy. CAST: Matt McColm, John Savage, Jennifer Rubin, Paul Ben-Victor, Michael Ironside. 1994

RED SHOE DIARIES 💗 Chic smut purveyor Zalman King hits rock bottom. A flightly young woman tests her boyfriend by sleeping with a kinky, hunky shoe salesman. An interminable bore. Nudity, graphic sex, and profanity spice this made-for-cable porn parade. 105m. DIR: Zalman King. CAST: David Duchovny, Brigitte Bako, Billy Wirth, Kai Wulfe, Brenda Vaccaro. 1992

RED SHOE DIARIES II: DOUBLE DARE ★★ Three mediocre short subjects: two strangers meet every week for sexual intercourse; two people try to outdo each other in sex; a man and woman dare each other, via the fax machine, to perform sexual acts. Contains nudity, graphic sex, and profanity. 95m. DIR: Zalman King, Tibor Takacs. CAST: Steven Bauer, Joan Severance, Denise Crosby, Rob Knepper, Laura Johnson, Michael Woods, David Duchovny. 1992

RED SHOE DIARIES 3: ANOTHER WOMAN'S LIPSTICK ★ What started off as a hot and steamy series has been reduced to a peekaboo event thanks to lackluster stories. Here, three episodes explore different female fantasies, from making out with a delivery boy to laying rubber on a deserted highway. Ho-hum. Not rated; contains adult situations and language. 90m. DIR: Zalman King, Ted Kotcheff, Rafael Eisenman. CAST: Maryam D'Abo, Nina Siemaszko, Christina Fulton, Richard Tyson. 1993

RED SHOE DIARIES 4: AUTO EROTICA 💗 Three more vapid examples of the nonerotic erotica that has flooded the cable market in recent years. Available in R and unrated formats, both with nudity and sexual situations. 83m. DIR: Michael Karbelnikoff, Alan Smithee, Zalman King. CAST: Ally Sheedy, David Duchovny, Sheryl Lee. 1994

RED SHOE DIARIES 5: WEEKEND PASS ★★ Three more would-be scintillating tales from the Showtime cable-network series, one featuring Paula Barbieri. David Duchovny of television's *The X-Files* is featured as Jake, the mystery man who ties together the various vignettes. Rated R for nudity and language. 86m. DIR: Dominique Othenin-Girard, Peter Care, Ted Kotcheff. CAST: Francesco Quinn, Paula Barbieri, Ron Marquette, David Duchovny, Ely Pouget. 1993

RED SHOES, THE (1948) ★★★★ Fascinating backstage look at the world of ballet manages to overcome its unoriginal, often trite, plot. A ballerina (Moira Shearer) is urged by her forceful and single-minded impresario (Anton Walbrook) to give up a romantic involvement in favor of her career, with tragic consequences. Good acting and fine camera work save this British film. 136m. DIR: Michael Powell, Emeric Pressburger. CAST: Moira Shearer, Anton Walbrook, Marius Goring. 1948 DVD

RED SONJA ★★ Dreadful sword-and-sorcery film. Rated PG-13 for violence. 80m. DIR: Richard Fleischer. CAST: Arnold Schwarzenegger, Brigitte Nielsen, Sandahl Bergman, Paul Smith, Ernie Reyes Jr. 1985

RED SORGHUM ★★★★★ A superb pastoral epic from the People's Republic of China and the winner of the Golden Bear at the 1988 Berlin Film Festival. The story relates a passionate folk tale about village wine makers who fight against interloping Japanese invaders. Lyrical and affecting drama. In Chinese with English subtitles. 91m. DIR: Yimou Zhang. CAST: Gong Li, Jian Weng, Liu Ji. 1988

•RED SQUIRREL, THE ★★★ Style overcomes story in this Spanish drama about a rock singer who becomes involved with a woman who loses her memory after they are in an accident. At least she seems to have lost her memory—or is she just trying to escape her loony husband? In Spanish with English subtitles. Not rated; contains nudity, violence, profanity, and sexual situations. 104m. DIR: Julio Medem. CAST: Emma Suarez, Nacho Novo, Maria Barranco. 1993

RED SUN ★★1/2 All-star, fitfully entertaining Western has an interesting premise—samurai vs. cowboys—but ultimately wastes the considerable talents of the great Japanese actor Toshiro Mifune. Charles Bronson has another of those offbeat-character parts that he underplays into a leading role. Rated PG. 112m. DIR: Terence Young. CAST: Charles Bronson, Alain Delon, Toshiro Mifune, Ursula Andress, Capucine. 1972 DVD

RED SUN RISING ★★★ Entertaining players rise above pedestrian material in this modest martial arts saga, starring the always appealing Don "The Dragon" Wilson as a Japanese cop sent to the United States to extradite a criminal don and the hulking henchman who kills opponents with the legendary "death touch." Mystical elements are played too broadly, but the formula still works. Rated R for violence and profanity. 99m. DIR: Francis Megahy. CAST: Don "The Dragon" Wilson, Terry Farrell, Mako, Michael Ironside, Soon-Teck Oh, Edward Albert. 1993

RED SURF ★★1/2 Two drug-dealing surf bums try for one last big score. Things begin falling apart when one of their friends turns informer. Rated R for violence, profanity, and nudity. 104m. DIR: H. Gordon Boos. CAST: George Clooney, Doug Savant, Dedee Pfeiffer, Gene Simmons, Philip McKeon. 1990 DVD

RED TENT, THE ★★1/2 Sean Connery heads an international cast in this slow-moving reconstruction of a polar expedition that ended in tragedy in 1928. The scope of the film and the trials faced by the party in their struggles for survival are enthralling, but too much reliance on flashbacks works against this one. 121m. DIR: Mikhail K. Kalatozov. CAST: Sean Connery,

Claudia Cardinale, Hardy Krüger, Peter Finch, Massimo Girotti. **1970**

●**RED VIOLIN, THE ★★★★**1/2 While a rare old violin is being auctioned off in Paris, flashbacks tell the instrument's story through the centuries: its creation in Renaissance Italy, its travels from country to country over the years, and its final discovery in modern-day China. The stories are a bit uneven, but never less than engrossing, and sometimes quite moving. In English, French, German, Italian, and Mandarin, with subtitles where appropriate. Rated R for sexual scenes. 131m. **DIR:** Francois Girard. **CAST:** Samuel L. Jackson, Greta Scacchi, Jason Flemyng, Colm Feore, Don McKellar. **1998 DVD**

REDHEAD FROM WYOMING, THE ★★1/2 The title says it all in a Western about a colorful redhead who takes the rap for a scheming politician, then turns against him when she meets a more likable lawman. Very predictable but sprightly because of the personalities. 80m. **DIR:** Lee Sholem. **CAST:** Maureen O'Hara, Dennis Weaver, Alex Nicol, Alexander Scourby, William Bishop, Robert Strauss. **1952**

REDLINE 🖤 Poor Rutger Hauer. Once a major star, now relegated to direct-to-video trash such as this tale of a smuggler who is killed by his partner and brought back to life, exploiting every possible B-movie cliché known to man. Just dreadful. A.k.a. *Deathline* and *Armageddon.* Not rated; contains violence and language. 113m. **DIR:** Tibor Takacs. **CAST:** Rutger Hauer, Mark Dacascos, Yvonne Scio. **1997 DVD**

REDNECK 🖤 Vile crime story about two criminals who take a young boy hostage. Not rated. 89m. **DIR:** Silvio Narizzano. **CAST:** Telly Savalas, Franco Nero, Mark Lester. **1972**

REDNECK ZOMBIES 🖤 Rednecks consume a nasty beer that turns them into mindless creatures. And the difference is? Rated R for violence, profanity, and gore. 83m. **DIR:** Pericles Lewnes. **CAST:** Lisa De-Haven, William C. Benson, P. Floyd Piranha, Zoofoot. **1988 DVD**

REDS ★★★★★ Warren Beatty produced, directed, cowrote, and starred in this $33 million American film masterpiece. This three-hour-plus film biography of left-wing American journalist John Reed (Beatty) and Louise Bryant (Diane Keaton) also features brilliant bits from Jack Nicholson, Gene Hackman, and Maureen Stapleton. Rated PG because of profanity, silhouetted sex scenes, and war scenes. 200m. **DIR:** Warren Beatty. **CAST:** Warren Beatty, Diane Keaton, Jack Nicholson, Gene Hackman, Edward Herrmann, Maureen Stapleton, Jerzy Kosinski. **1981**

REDWOOD CURTAIN ★★★1/2 Rather convoluted plot for a *Hallmark Hall of Fame*, this focuses on the search of an Amerasian adoptee for her biological father. Her search takes her to the Redwoods and a homeless man who hides there. Startling ending is a satisfying reward for keeping up with multiple twists and turns. 95m. **DIR:** John Korty. **CAST:** Lea Salonga, John Lithgow, Jeff Daniels, Debra Monk, Catherine Hicks. **1995**

REEFER MADNESS ★★1/2 This 1930s anti-marijuana film is very silly, and sometimes funny. It's a cult film that really isn't as good as its reputation suggests. B&W; 67m. **DIR:** Louis J. Gasnier. **CAST:**

Dave O'Brien, Dorothy Short, Warren McCollum, Lillian Miles, Carleton Young. **1936 DVD**

REET, PETITE AND GONE ★★★1/2 Louis Jordan, the overlooked hero of prerock days, is well captured (along with his hot backup band, the Tympany Five) in this farcical all-black musical. Jordan's sound is a blues-pop fusion known as jumpin' jive, and it gets slick film treatment in this little-known movie treasure. 67m. **DIR:** William Forest Crouch. **CAST:** Louis Jordan. **1946**

REF, THE ★★★ Jewel thief Denis Leary soon regrets taking perennially bickering married couple Judy Davis and Kevin Spacey hostage in a ritzy neighborhood. It's supposed to be a black comedy, but it's just bleak at times, and lacks appealing characters. There are some very funny moments, though. Rated R for profanity and frank sexual discussions. 92m. **DIR:** Ted Demme. **CAST:** Denis Leary, Judy Davis, Kevin Spacey, Robert J. Steinmiller, Glynis Johns, Christine Baranski, Richard Bright, Adam LeFevre, Raymond J. Barry. **1994**

REFLECTING SKIN, THE ★★★★ The innocence of a small boy is stripped away as he observes the strange and macabre characters that surround him. Life in a small town is magnified beyond reality into a surreal quasi-fantasy that brilliantly fuses the mind of the child and that of the adult, directly challenging our idealized notions of the innocence of childhood. A must for those who appreciate the work of David Lynch, and enjoy challenging alternative cinema. Rated R for violence and suggested sex. 98m. **DIR:** Philip Ridley. **CAST:** Viggo Mortensen, Lindsay Duncan, Jeremy Cooper. **1991**

REFLECTION OF FEAR ★★1/2 Confusing, uninspired story of a beautiful young girl who becomes the central figure in a cobweb of crime and murder. Should have been better, considering the cast. Rated R. 102m. **DIR:** William Fraker. **CAST:** Robert Shaw, Mary Ure, Sally Kellerman, Signe Hasso, Sondra Locke. **1973**

REFLECTIONS IN A GOLDEN EYE ★★1/2 Very bizarre film concerning a homosexual army officer (Marlon Brando) stationed in the South. This very strange film very rarely works—despite a high-powered cast. 108m. **DIR:** John Huston. **CAST:** Marlon Brando, Elizabeth Taylor, Brian Keith, Julie Harris, Robert Forster. **1967**

REFLECTIONS IN THE DARK ★★ Pampered housewife, stifled by a sensitive, perfect husband who dotes on her every move, relieves her anguish by killing the poor slob. She justifies this bewildering act during a tedious monologue prior to her execution. Boring. Rated R for profanity, violence, and nudity. 84m. **DIR:** Jon Purdy. **CAST:** Mimi Rogers, Billy Zane. **1995**

REFLECTIONS OF MURDER ★★★ A wife and a mistress set out to kill their abusive mate. They set up a foolproof trap to lure him to his death. The "accident" that kills him leads to more terror and horror than either woman expected. A TV-movie version of the French classic *Diabolique.* 98m. **DIR:** John Badham. **CAST:** Tuesday Weld, Joan Hackett, Sam Waterston. **1987**

REFORM SCHOOL GIRL ★★ Gloria Castillo, a long way from her supporting role in *Night of the Hunter*, is the innocent teen packed off to reform school. Standard late-Fifties American-International programmer. B&W; 71m. **DIR:** Edward L. Bernds. **CAST:** Gloria Castillo, Ross Ford, Edd Byrnes, Ralph Reed, Sally Kellerman. 1957

REFORM SCHOOL GIRLS ★★ "So young. So bad. So what?" That was the promo line for this spoof of the women-in-prison genre. Writer-director Tom DeSimone manages to get in the usual exploitative ingredients—women taking showers, etc.—while simultaneously making fun of them. Rated R for violence, profanity, nudity, and simulated sex. 94m. **DIR:** Tom DeSimone. **CAST:** Wendy O. Williams, Sybil Danning, Pat Ast, Linda Carol. 1986

REGARDING HENRY ★★★★ Harrison Ford gives one of his finest performances as Henry Turner, a successful, self-centered attorney who loses all memory of his past when a robber shoots him in the head with a small-caliber weapon. Annette Bening is equally fine as the wife who finds herself falling in love with the gentle, childlike man who emerges in her husband's body. Rated PG-13 for violence and profanity. 107m. **DIR:** Mike Nichols. **CAST:** Harrison Ford, Annette Bening, Bill Nunn, Donald Moffat, Nancy Marchand, Elizabeth Wilson. 1991

REGENERATED MAN, THE 🎟 When a scientist is forced to drink the flesh-regenerating fluid he's invented, he becomes a horrible monster. Rated R for horror, violence, and language. 90m. **DIR:** Ted A. Bohus. **CAST:** Arthur Lindquist, Cheryl Hendricks, Chris Kidd. 1994

REGENERATION ★★★1/2 One of the first full-length gangster films ever made, this morality play follows the life of a street kid who is turned around by a well-meaning social worker. Age has taken its toll, as a few scenes are so worn you can barely make out what is happening. Packaged with a 10-minute Thomas Edison production *The Police Force of New York City* that records the daily activities of Gotham's finest in 1910. Silent. Not rated; contains violence. B&W; 72m. **DIR:** Raoul Walsh. **CAST:** Rockcliffe Fellowes, Anna Q. Nilsson, William Sheer, H. McCoy. 1915

REGGIE'S PRAYER 🎟 Well-intended but poorly made film starring football star Reggie White as a high-school coach trying to keep his players away from violent drug dealers. Not rated; contains mild violence. 94m. **DIR:** Paul McKellips. **CAST:** Reggie White, Noriyuki "Pat" Morita, Rosey Grier. 1997

REGINA ★★★ This strange psychological drama features Ava Gardner as a nagging wife and mother who is obsessed with keeping her 36-year-old son at home with her. Anthony Quinn is the much-put-upon husband. An Italian film, it is not rated but contains mature themes. 86m. **DIR:** Jean-Yves Prate. **CAST:** Anthony Quinn, Ava Gardner, Ray Sharkey, Anna Karina. 1983 DVD

REHEARSAL FOR MURDER ★★★1/2 Richard Levinson and William Link, those clever fellows behind the creation of *Columbo*, occasionally stray into the realm of made-for-television movies; this is one of the best. Robert Preston leads his stage

friends through the reading of a play designed to ferret out the killer of star Lynn Redgrave. Levinson and Link deliver another of their surprise conclusions. 100m. **DIR:** David Greene. **CAST:** Robert Preston, Lynn Redgrave, Jeff Goldblum, Patrick Macnee, William Daniels, Lawrence Pressman. 1982 DVD

REILLY: THE ACE OF SPIES ★★ Sam Neill is wasted in this slow-moving, so-called thriller about the first James Bond–type spy employed by the British. In 1901 Russia he manages not only to smuggle secret maps out of the country but also to lure a surly minister's young wife into his bed. Not rated, this made-for-TV production contains violence and nudity. 80m. **DIR:** Jim Goddard. **CAST:** Sam Neill, Leo McKern, Norman Rodway, Peter Egan. 1984

REINCARNATE, THE 🎟 A lawyer will live forever, as long as he can find a new body to inhabit when his present one dies. Rated PG. 89m. **DIR:** Don Haldane. **CAST:** Jack Creley, Jay Reynolds. 1971

REINCARNATION OF GOLDEN LOTUS, THE ★★🎟 ★★★ In this compelling and tastefully erotic Hong Kong production, a woman (Joey Wang) murdered by a powerful lord in ancient times uses reincarnation as a way of exacting revenge. In Chinese with English subtitles. Not rated, the film has violence and nudity. 99m. **DIR:** Clara Law. **CAST:** Joey Wang. 1989

REINCARNATION OF PETER PROUD, THE 🎟 Turgid direction, contrived plot. Rated R for considerable nudity. 104m. **DIR:** J. Lee Thompson. **CAST:** Michael Sarrazin, Jennifer O'Neill, Margot Kidder, Cornelia Sharpe. 1975

•**REINDEER GAMES** ★★★ Ehren Kruger's screenplay is sabotaged by an opening flash-forward that completely ruins any suspense. Ben Affleck stars as a minor felon whose prison buddy is killed mere days before his release; when Ben subsequently gets his own walking papers, he poses as his former friend to score with his voluptuous pen pal. Unfortunately, the gal has a crazy brother who wants assistance on a heist from the guy Ben *supposed* to be. When we reach the caper itself, with its telegraphed outcome, it's little more than wham, bam, thank you, ma'am. Rated R for profanity, nudity, sexual content, and considerable violence. 105m. **DIR:** John Frankenheimer. **CAST:** Ben Affleck, Gary Sinise, Charlize Theron, Dennis Farina, James Frain, Donal Logue, Clarence Williams III. 2000

REI-REI ★★ Very sexually oriented, this is the animated tale of a goddess of love who comes down to Earth to help solve problems of the romantic variety. Some story cleverness nearly saves this one. In Japanese with English subtitles. Not rated; contains nudity, sexual situations, and violence. 60m. **DIR:** Yoshikio Yamamoto. 1993

REIVERS, THE ★★★★ Grand adaptation of the William Faulkner tale concerning a young boy (Mitch Vogel) who, with the help of his mischievous older friends (Steve McQueen and Rupert Crosse), "borrows" an automobile and heads for fun and excitement in 1905 Mississippi. The charming vignettes include a stopover in a brothel and a climactic horse race that could spell doom for the adventurers. Rated PG. 107m. **DIR:** Mark Rydell. **CAST:**

Steve McQueen, Rupert Crosse, Will Geer, Sharon Farrell, Mitch Vogel, Michael Constantine. **1969**

REJUVENATOR, THE ★★★ This flick begins by resembling *Re-Animator* in more than just name, but it soon takes on a life of its own. A rich woman funds a doctor's research into reversing the aging process in hopes he will discover a way to make her young again. Some very nasty side effects occur. Above-average special effects make this a must for horror-film fans. Rated R for extreme violence. 90m. **DIR:** Brian Thomas Jones. **CAST:** Vivian Lanko, John MacKay. **1988**

RELATIVE FEAR ★★ What happens when the baby of a psychotic couple is switched at birth with the baby of a perfectly sane couple? The fun comes from watching the normal parents respond when their son starts showing his true colors. Some suspense in this made-for-cable thriller. Rated R for violence. 94m. **DIR:** George Mihalka. **CAST:** Darlanne Fluegel, Martin Neufeld, James Brolin, Denise Crosby, M. Emmet Walsh. **1995**

RELAX … IT'S JUST SEX ★★★ Writer/director P.J. Castellaneta follows the romantic ups and downs of a circle of friends (mostly gays and lesbians) in this awkward, occasionally preachy, but well-acted film. Castellaneta has a good hand with witty dialogue and the film's shifts from comedy to drama and back, but let the title be a warning—his frank treatment of sexual intercourse will not be to all tastes. Rated R for nudity, sexual scenes, and discussions of sexual themes. 110m. **DIR:** P.J. Castellaneta. **CAST:** Jennifer Tilly, Mitchell Anderson, Cynda Williams, Serena Scott-Thomas, Lori Petty. **1998 DVD**

RELENTLESS ★★★ Catch this modest police procedural as the vehicle to boost minor player Leo Rossi's career. He's cast as a transplanted New York cop itching, in the wake of a string of murders committed by a so-called Sunset Killer, to show new Los Angeles partner Robert Loggia a thing or two. The deft and sympathetic screenplay, although credited to one Jack T. D. Robinson, is actually the work of Phil Alden Robinson. Rated R for violence and brief nudity. 92m. **DIR:** William Lustig. **CAST:** Judd Nelson, Robert Loggia, Leo Rossi, Meg Foster. **1989**

RELENTLESS II: DEAD ON ★★ Meg Foster and Leo Rossi reprise their roles from *Relentless*. A woman and her child were menaced by a serial killer at the end of that film. This one shows what effect it had on that child. Very bloody and violent, but also exciting and suspenseful. Rated R for violence, nudity, and tension. 93m. **DIR:** Michael Schroeder. **CAST:** Ray Sharkey, Meg Foster, Leo Rossi, Marc Poppel, Dale Dye, Miles O'Keeffe. **1991**

RELENTLESS 3 ★★ Ex–New York cop Sam Dietz, played by series-star Leo Rossi, finds himself drawn into the case of a Los Angeles serial killer who carves up his victims and mails the evidence to the police. His interest in the case is heightened when he learns that his past connection to the killer could endanger his girlfriend. Familiar territory for Rossi, but William Forsythe has some good, creepy moments as the killer. Rated R for nudity, violence, and language. 84m. **DIR:** James Lemmo. **CAST:** Leo Rossi, William Forsythe, Signy Coleman, Robert Costanzo. **1992**

RELIC, THE ★★1/2 A ghastly monster imported from the South American jungle stalks the halls of Chicago's Field Museum; only tough cop Tom Sizemore and leggy scientist Penelope Ann Miller stand between the human race and annihilation. Director Peter Hyams relies on loud noises for thrills, and darkness to build suspense (no light bulb seems to burn more than ten watts). The monster is startling but not really scary, and the film is comfortably predictable. Rated R for violence and profanity. 110m. **DIR:** Peter Hyams. **CAST:** Tom Sizemore, Penelope Ann Miller, James Whitmore. **1996 DVD**

RELUCTANT ASTRONAUT, THE ★★ In this typical Don Knotts vehicle, he plays a nervous sort who wants to be an astronaut but is afraid of heights. Rated G. 101m. **DIR:** Edward Montagne. **CAST:** Don Knotts, Arthur O'Connell, Leslie Nielsen, Joan Freeman, Jesse White. **1967**

RELUCTANT DEBUTANTE, THE ★★★ Kay Kendall steals the show as the new stepmother of Rex Harrison's American-bred daughter. Angela Lansbury is deliciously vicious, as always, as Kendall's snooty cousin. 94m. **DIR:** Vincente Minnelli. **CAST:** Rex Harrison, Kay Kendall, Angela Lansbury, Sandra Dee, John Saxon. **1958**

RELUCTANT DRAGON, THE ★★★★1/2 This delightful, though somewhat unorthodox, medieval dragon tale is a must-see for anyone! Director Charles Nichols orchestrates a fast-paced, hilarious romp—a droll encounter between a bard and a dragon. This is truly a Disney gem. Not rated. Suitable for the entire family. 28m. **DIR:** Hamilton Luske. **1957**

REMAINS OF THE DAY ★★★★★ Anthony Hopkins and Emma Thompson give remarkable performances in this heart-wrenching exploration of English reserve and unrequited love. Hopkins is a gentleman's gentleman whose private life and longings are subjugated to his professional responsibilities; this very dedication leads to personal tragedy in a seamless blend of period detail and drama. Exquisite. Rated PG-13 for brief profanity. 134m. **DIR:** James Ivory. **CAST:** Anthony Hopkins, Emma Thompson, James Fox, Christopher Reeve, Peter Vaughan, Hugh Grant, Michel Lonsdale, Tim Pigott-Smith. **1993**

REMBRANDT ★★★★ This is one of the few satisfying movie biographies of an artist. The depiction of the famous Dutch painter and his struggle to maintain his artistic integrity is related with respectful restraint and attention to factual detail. Charles Laughton, as Rembrandt, is brilliant in what was for him an atypically low-key performance. B&W; 90m. **DIR:** Alexander Korda. **CAST:** Charles Laughton, Gertrude Lawrence, Elsa Lanchester. **1936**

REMBRANDT—1669 ★★★ From his start at painting dead bodies for a surgeon, to his ultimate bankruptcy and death, this film portrays Rembrandt's life in a dark and almost voiceless story. Although the characters are well portrayed by all the actors, the plot moves along too slowly. In Dutch with English subtitles. Not rated; contains nudity. 114m. **DIR:** Jos Stelling. **CAST:** Frans Stelling, Ton de Koff, Aye Fil. **1977**

REMEDY FOR RICHES ★★1/2 When not dispensing country medicine to his patients, kindly Dr. Christian keeps an eye out for their financial well-being by alerting them to a con man's phony oil scheme. Modest series entry with a parade of eccentric characters. 67m. **DIR:** Erle C. Kenton. **CAST:** Jean Hersholt, Dorothy Lovett, Edgar Kennedy. **1941**

•**REMEMBER THE NIGHT** ★★★★1/2 Preston Sturges wrote this excellent comedy-drama that deftly balances humor with sentimentality. A shoplifter awaiting trial (Barbara Stanwyck) sees the error of her ways when she spends Christmas with the family of the assistant D.A. (Fred MacMurray) whose job it is to prosecute her. 86m. **DIR:** Mitchell Leisen. **CAST:** Barbara Stanwyck, Fred MacMurray, Beulah Bondi, Sterling Holloway. **1940**

REMINGTON STEELE (TV SERIES) ★★★ Early episodes feature dashing Pierce Brosnan as a front man for Laura Holt's (Stephanie Zimbalist) savvy detective. Steele provides comic relief as he and another partner (played by James Read) vie for Holt's attentions. Very watchable, the first two volumes are entitled "Steele Crazy After All These Years" and "In the Steele of the Night." Each volume 50m. **DIR:** Don Weis, Burt Brinckerhoff. **CAST:** Stephanie Zimbalist, Pierce Brosnan, James Read. **1982–83**

REMO WILLIAMS: THE ADVENTURE BEGINS ★★★ This adaptation of the *Destroyer* novels is like a second-rate James Bond adventure. Fred Ward is fine as the hero of the title and Joel Grey is a kick as his Asian martial arts mentor, but the film takes too much time establishing the characters and too little giving us the adventure promised in the title. Rated PG-13 for violence and profanity. 121m. **DIR:** Guy Hamilton. **CAST:** Fred Ward, Joel Grey, Wilford Brimley, J. A. Preston, George Coe, Charles Cioffi, Kate Mulgrew. **1985**

REMOTE ★★★ This *Home Alone* wannabe stars Chris Carrara as a 13-year-old whiz kid trapped in a model home with three bungling burglars. Draggy in parts but kids may find it diverting. Rated PG for cartoonish violence. 80m. **DIR:** Ted Nicolaou. **CAST:** Chris Carrara, Jessica Bowman, John Diehl, Derya Ruggles, Tony Longo, Stuart Fratkin. **1993**

REMOTE CONTROL (1987) ★★1/2 The manager of a video-rental outlet learns that many of his customers are being brutally murdered after watching a certain cassette. Rated R for violence and profanity. 88m. **DIR:** Jeff Lieberman. **CAST:** Kevin Dillon, Jennifer Tilly, Deborah Goodrich. **1987**

REMOTE CONTROL (1992) ★★★ Craziness from Iceland follows a timid auto mechanic as his life is turned upside down when he attempts to save a kidnapped woman. In Icelandic with English subtitles. Not rated. 85m. **DIR:** Oskar Jonasson. **CAST:** Bjorn Jorundur Fridbjornsson, Eggert Thorliefsson, Helgi Bjornsson, Soley Eliasdottir. **1992**

RENAISSANCE MAN ★★★1/2 After losing a cushy advertising job, Danny DeVito winds up teaching remedial studies to an octet of goof-ups at a nearby army post. When all else fails, he finally grabs their attention with Shakespeare. (Right.) Jim Burnstein's script too often feels like an English professor's underdeveloped dream come true. Rated PG-13

for mild profanity. 130m. **DIR:** Penny Marshall. **CAST:** Danny DeVito, Gregory Hines, James Remar, Cliff Robertson, Kadeem Hardison, Richard T. Jones, Mark Wahlberg, Stacey Dash. **1994**

RENDEZ-VOUS ★★★ Provocative French import paints a rather unsettling portrait of alienated youth. Juliette Binoche is captivating as a promiscuous young woman wandering the Paris nightlife scene. In French with English subtitles. Not rated; contains nudity, profanity, and violence. 82m. **DIR:** André Téchiné. **CAST:** Juliette Binoche, Lambert Wilson, Wadeck Stanczak, Jean-Louis Trintignant. **1985**

RENDEZVOUS IN PARIS ★★1/2 Veteran French filmmaker Eric Rohmer gives us three stories of romantic mishaps between lovers and would-be lovers. Unfortunately, Rohmer's penchant for uneventful conversation makes this one tough going. It doesn't help that the first story is easily the best; it's all downhill from there. In French with English subtitles. Not rated; suitable for adults and mature teenagers. 95m. **DIR:** Eric Rohmer. **CAST:** Clara Bellar, Antoine Basler, Aurore Rauscher, Serge Renko. **1996**

RENEGADE ★★ Pilot film for the syndicated television series stars Lorenzo Lamas as a street cop named Reno, who is framed for murder. He hops on his motorcycle and leaves town, becoming a bounty hunter along the way. Not rated; contains violence. 95m. **DIR:** Ralph Hemecker, R. Marvin. **CAST:** Lorenzo Lamas, Kathleen Kinmont, Branscombe Richmond, Martin Kove, Charles Napier. **1993**

RENEGADE GIRL ★★1/2 Ann Savage plays a freethinking, vixen leader of a band of Confederate raiders. She tragically falls in love with the Union soldier stalking her. B&W; 65m. **DIR:** William Berke. **CAST:** Ann Savage, Alan Curtis, Russell Wade, Jack Holt, Ray "Crash" Corrigan, John King. **1946**

RENEGADE RANGER ★★★★ Star George O'Brien and director David Howard made some of the finest series Westerns in the Thirties and Forties. O'Brien, a member of director John Ford's stock company since starring in the classic *Iron Horse*, is in top form as a Texas Ranger who is assigned to bring in a female bandit (Rita Hayworth) accused of murder. B&W; 60m. **DIR:** David Howard. **CAST:** George O'Brien, Rita Hayworth, Tim Holt, Ray Whitley. **1938**

RENEGADE TRAIL ★★★ Hopalong Cassidy helps a woman and her son save the day when their cattle are the target of the woman's outlaw ex-husband and the boy's father whom he thinks died a hero. Bit slower than most of the Hoppy series. B&W; 61m. **DIR:** Lesley Selander. **CAST:** William Boyd, George "Gabby" Hayes, Russell Hayden, Roy Barcroft, Sonny Bupp. **1939**

RENEGADES ♥ Disappointing, lackluster thriller from the director of *The Hidden*. Rated R for profanity and violence. 110m. **DIR:** Jack Sholder. **CAST:** Kiefer Sutherland, Lou Diamond Phillips, Jami Gertz. **1989 DVD**

RENO AND THE DOC ★★1/2 Though it has a slow start, this tale of two middle-aged men brought together by mental telepathy soon gains momentum. Ken Walsh plays Reno, a solitary mountain man who is induced by Doc (Henry Ramer) to enter the pro-ski tour. Mild nudity and obscenities. 88m. **DIR:**

Charles Dennis. **CAST:** Kenneth Walsh, Henry Ramer, Linda Griffiths. 1984

RENT-A-COP ❤ When a drug bust goes awry and both cops and crooks are killed, a police detective is accused of masterminding the hit. Rated R for violence and profanity. 95m. **DIR:** Jerry London. **CAST:** Burt Reynolds, Liza Minnelli, James Remar, Richard Masur, Bernie Casey, Robby Benson, John P. Ryan. 1988 DVD

RENT-A-KID ★★★ Kids will enjoy this comedy about the joys and pains of parenthood. Leslie Nielsen plays Harry, a slick salesman who agrees to run his son's orphanage while he's away on vacation. Harry puts his marketing skills to good use when he rents out three of the kids to a couple who want a test-drive before they decide to have children. There's plenty of heart and havoc as the three kids give their new parents a run for their money. Rated G. 89m. **DIR:** Fred Gerber. **CAST:** Leslie Nielsen, Christopher Lloyd, Matt McCoy, Sherry Miller. 1992

RENTED LIPS ❤ Martin Mull and Dick Shawn play inept documentary filmmakers (*Aluminum, Our Friend,* etc.) who agree to complete a porno film called *Halloween in the Bunker.* Rated R for profanity, nudity, and violence. 85m. **DIR:** Robert Downey. **CAST:** Martin Mull, Dick Shawn, Jennifer Tilly, Robert Downey Jr., June Lockhart, Pat McCormick, Eileen Brennan. 1988

REPENTANCE ★★★ Set in Georgia in the Soviet Union, this richly varied film presents a central character who personifies all European villains—a cross, most obviously, between Stalin and Hitler. The film is not only a brutally direct comment on evil in politics, but a marvelous study of Georgian life. No rating but there are violent scenes. In Russian with English subtitles. 151m. **DIR:** Tenghiz Abuladze. **CAST:** Avtandil Makharadze. 1987

REPLACEMENT KILLERS, THE ★★★1/2 Hong Kong action star Chow Yun-Fat reprises his hit-man-with-a-conscience character in this American-made thriller. When he refuses to carry out an assignment—which would leave the son of a police officer fatherless—his contract is passed on to others, who are to eliminate him in the process. Mira Sorvino gets caught up in Yun-Fat's predicament and must shoot her way out of many a tight situation. It's fast-paced fun. Rated R for strong violence and language. 88m. **DIR:** Antoine Fuqua. **CAST:** Chow Yun-Fat, Mira Sorvino. 1998 DVD

REPLIKATOR: CLONED TO KILL ★★ Hodgepodge sci-fi film tries to create a chaotic world of the future and instead only confuses its viewers. Ned Beatty stars as a cop whose job it is to stop the supercriminal Replikator and his mechanical human beings. Above-average special effects and another great performance by Beatty don't overcome confusing atmosphere and pace. Rated R for violence. 96m. **DIR:** G. Philip Jackson. **CAST:** Michael St. Gerard, Brigitte Bako, Ned Beatty. 1994

REPO MAN ★★★★ Wild, weird, and unpredictable, this film stars Emilio Estevez as a young man who gets into the repossession racket. Under the tutelage of Harry Dean Stanton (in a typically terrific performance), Estevez learns how to steal cars from people who haven't kept up their payments. Meanwhile, bizarre events lead them to an encounter with what may be beings from space. Those who occasionally like to watch something different will enjoy it. Rated R. 92m. **DIR:** Alex Cox. **CAST:** Emilio Estevez, Harry Dean Stanton, Vonetta McGee, Sy Richardson, Tracey Walter. 1984

REPORT ON THE PARTY AND THE GUESTS, A ★★★★ Kafkaesque parable about a group of party guests who suffer a mean practical joke at the hands of their host. The cast is composed of prominent Prague artists and intellectuals, and many of the references will be lost on American viewers, but the overall allegory is clear. In Czech with English subtitles. Not rated. B&W; 71m. **DIR:** Jan Nemec. **CAST:** Ivan Vyskocil, Jan Klusak, Josef Skvorecky. 1966

REPORT TO THE COMMISSIONER ★★★★ One of the best of the urban crime films to come out in the early Seventies. Michael Moriarty plays an innocent rookie in the New York Police Department. Not understanding the politics of the cop on the beat, he commits a series of errors that leads to his downfall. Look for Richard Gere in a small part as a pimp. Rated PG for violence, profanity, and nudity. 113m. **DIR:** Milton Katselas. **CAST:** Michael Moriarty, Yaphet Kotto, Susan Blakely, Hector Elizondo, Tony King, William Devane, Richard Gere. 1974

REPOSSESSED ★★★1/2 Linda Blair gets to make fun of the genre she is most associated with in this uproarious parody of *Exorcist*-style flicks. Nielsen is great as a priest who relates the story of a possessed housewife (Blair) and his attempts to exorcise the devil from within her. Rated PG-13 for language. 89m. **DIR:** Bob Logan. **CAST:** Linda Blair, Ned Beatty, Leslie Nielsen. 1990

REPTILE, THE ★★1/2 A young couple moves to a Cornish village where people die of a strange malady known as "the black death" caused by two puncture wounds on the victim's neck. Stylish, atmospheric but uneven Hammer Studios film. 90m. **DIR:** John Gilling. **CAST:** Noel Willman, Jennifer Daniels, Ray Barrett, Jacqueline Pearce. 1966 DVD

REPTILICUS ❤ Simply dreadful action-adventure about scientists growing a prehistoric beast from its recently discovered tail. Welcome to Jurassic Bark. 90m. **DIR:** Sidney Pink. **CAST:** Carl Ottoson, Marla Behrens, Mimi Heinrich. 1962

REPULSION ★★★★1/2 This brilliant British production, the first English-language film directed by Roman Polanski, is a classic chiller. Catherine Deneuve plays a sexually repressed, mentally ill young girl who is terrified of men. Left alone at her sister's home for a weekend, she suffers a series of severe hallucinations that finally lead her to commit murder. B&W; 105m. **DIR:** Roman Polanski. **CAST:** Catherine Deneuve, Ian Hendry, Yvonne Furneaux, John Fraser, Patrick Wymark. 1965

REQUIEM FOR A HEAVYWEIGHT (1956) (TELEVISION) ★★★★ Superb drama written for *Playhouse 90* by Rod Serling, about a washed-up heavyweight boxer (Jack Palance) who is forced to find a life outside the ring. Keenan Wynn is magnificent as his gruff, self-centered manager, and Ed Wynn is perfect as the trainer. One of the best live dramas to come out of the Golden Age of Television. Hosted by Jack Klugman, with interviews with the stars and background information on the show. B&W; 89m. DIR: Ralph Nelson. CAST: Jack Palance, Keenan Wynn, Kim Hunter, Ed Wynn, Ned Glass. 1956

REQUIEM FOR A HEAVYWEIGHT (1962) ★★★1/2 Anthony Quinn, Julie Harris, Jackie Gleason, Mickey Rooney, and Muhammad Ali (at that time Cassius Clay) give fine performances in this watchable film about boxing corruption. An over-the-hill boxer (Quinn) receives career counseling from a social worker (Harris). B&W; 100m. DIR: Ralph Nelson. CAST: Anthony Quinn, Julie Harris, Jackie Gleason, Mickey Rooney. 1962

REQUIEM FOR DOMINIC ★★★ Torn from the headlines, a powerful and riveting true story of revolution and the inhumane treatment of prisoners. When a Romanian political exile looks into the disappearance of his childhood friend, he discovers that he is being held prisoner for the murder of eighty innocent workers. In German with English subtitles. Rated R for violence. 88m. DIR: Robert Dornhelm. CAST: Felix Mitterer. 1991

RESCUE, THE ★★ Another dopey movie about a group of teens who set out to rescue their dads from a prisoner-of-war camp. Ferdinand Fairfax achieves some genuine excitement and suspense along the way, but the basic premise is preposterous. Rated PG for profanity and violence. 99m. DIR: Ferdinand Fairfax. CAST: Kevin Dillon, Kristina Harnos, Marc Price, Charles Haid, Edward Albert. 1988

RESCUE FORCE ★★ The female CIA agents in this rescue force have names like Candy and Angel and run around half-dressed. You get the picture. Rated R for violence and nudity. 92m. DIR: Charles Nizet. CAST: Richard Harrison. 1980

RESCUE ME ♥ High-school loser bribes a Vietnam-vet drifter to rescue a cheerleader after she is kidnapped by two dim-witted hoods. Rated PG. 90m. DIR: Arthur Allan Seidelman. CAST: Stephen Dorff, Ami Dolenz, Michael Dudikoff, Peter DeLuise. 1993

RESCUERS, THE ★★★★ The first adventure of Mouse Rescue Aid Society operatives Bernard (voiced by Bob Newhart) and Bianca (Eva Gabor) is a little gem that signaled the awakening of the Disney animation giant after a long slumber of mediocrity. Don Bluth was partly responsible for the studio's return to quality in this story, based on the writings of Margery Sharp. Rated G. 77m. DIR: Wolfgang Reitherman, John Lounsbery, Art Stevens. 1977

RESCUERS DOWN UNDER ★★★ Disney's first sequel to an animated film doesn't match the charm of the original. Nevertheless, children will enjoy this feature about an Australian boy who takes on a ruthless trapper with the help of mouse heroes. Fine voice work by Bob Newhart, Eva Gabor, George C. Scott, and John Candy. Rated G. 74m. DIR: Hendel Butoy, Mike Gabriel. 1990 DVD

RESCUERS, STORIES OF COURAGE, "TWO WOMEN" ★★★ Two stories about courageous women who stood up to the Nazis during World War II. Inspiring. Barbra Streisand was executive producer. Rated PG-13 for adult situations and violence. 107m. DIR: Peter Bogdanovich. CAST: Elizabeth

Perkins, Sela Ward, Anne Jackson, Fritz Weaver, Al Waxman. 1997

RESERVOIR DOGS ★★★★1/2 Writer-director Quentin Tarantino debuts with this story of a diamond heist gone awry. Strong ensemble acting and a brain-twisting array of unexpected plot turns make this one of the best crime-thrillers ever made. The brutal violence may be too much for some, but it is never glorified. Rated R for violence and profanity. 99m. DIR: Quentin Tarantino. CAST: Harvey Keitel, Tim Roth, Michael Madsen, Christopher Penn, Steve Buscemi, Lawrence Tierney, Randy Brooks, Quentin Tarantino. 1992 DVD

REST IN PIECES ♥ A young couple inherit an old Spanish estate occupied by murderous Satanists. Not rated; contains graphic violence and nudity. 90m. DIR: Joseph Braunsteen. CAST: Carrot Top (Scott Thompson), Lorin Jean, Dorothy Malone, Patty Shepard. 1987

•RESTAURANT ★★★ Employees of an upscale Hoboken bar and grill struggle to maintain peace in the workplace and find happiness as their multiethnic friendships, artistic pursuits, and love lives fray. This provocative drama focuses on an anguished, alcoholic bartender who tries to exorcise emotional wounds left by a bigoted father and broken interracial romance just as a semiautobiographical play he wrote is cast and opens. Rated R for language and violence. 108m. DIR: Eric Bross. CAST: Adrien Brody, Elsie Neal, Malcolm-Jamal Warner, Lauryan Hill. 2000

RESTLESS ★★ This Greek movie with Raquel Welch, originally titled *The Beloved*, was unknown until it appeared on video, and if you watch it, you'll know why. There's a lot of pretty island scenery, but the plot about housewife Raquel having an affair with a childhood friend is a guaranteed sleep inducer. Not rated; the film contains sexual situations and violence. 75m. DIR: George Pan Cosmatos. CAST: Raquel Welch, Richard Johnson, Flora Robson. 1972

RESTLESS BREED, THE ★★ B Western murdered-father/son-takes-revenge plot. 86m. DIR: Allan Dwan. CAST: Scott Brady, Anne Bancroft, Jay C. Flippen, Jim Davis. 1957

RESTLESS NATIVES ★★★1/2 Okay, so it's not perfect—the humor and the characterizations are broad and the thick, Scottish accents sometimes make the dialogue difficult to decipher. But that doesn't stop this film from being thoroughly entertaining. Two young Scots, disguised as a clown and a wolf-man, rob tourist buses and become national heroes in the process. Rated PG. 90m. DIR: Michael Hoffman. CAST: Vincent Friell, Joe Mulloney, Teri Lolly, Ned Beatty. 1986

RESTORATION ★★★1/2 This bawdy, garish period piece is set in 1660s England, when years of somber Puritanical rule were replaced by a monarchy hot on exploring the arts and sciences. In this court climate, a disheveled, hedonistic, and latently heroic young physician squanders and then rekindles his own restorative talents, personifying both the lightness and darkness of an era engulfed in enlightenment, debauchery, natural disaster, and plagues. Rated PG. 113m. DIR: Michael Hoffman. CAST: Robert

Downey Jr., Sam Neill, David Thewlis, Meg Ryan. **1996 DVD**

RESURRECTED, THE ★★★ An enjoyable tongue-in-cheek production of H. P. Lovecraft's *The Case of Charles Dexter Ward*. The wife of a reclusive doctor asks a detective to find out what her husband has been doing in the lab late at night. Planted firmly in the dark comic tradition of the other Lovecraft-based films: *The Re-animator* and *From Beyond*. Rated R for gore and profanity. 108m. **DIR:** Dan O'Bannon. **CAST:** Chris Sarandon, John Terry, Jane Sibbett. **1991**

RESURRECTION (1980) ★★★★1/2 After Ellen Burstyn loses her husband and the use of her legs in a freak automobile accident, she discovers she has the power to heal not only herself but anyone who is sick or crippled. Pulitzer Prize–winning playwright Sam Shepard is memorable as the young hell-raiser who begins to believe she is Jesus reborn. Rated PG. 103m. **DIR:** Daniel Petrie. **CAST:** Ellen Burstyn, Sam Shepard, Richard Farnsworth, Roberts Blossom, Clifford David, Pamela Payton-Wright, Eva LeGallienne. **1980**

•RESURRECTION (1998) ★★ Fifteen minutes into the film, you get the idea that the filmmakers saw *Seven* and decided to rip it off. Christopher Lambert is a big city detective tracking down a serial killer who kills his victims with the precision of a doctor. You'll figure the plot out before the halfway mark in this made-for-cable thriller. Rated R for violence, language, and adult situations. 108m. **DIR:** Russell Mulcahy. **CAST:** Christopher Lambert, Robert Joy, Leland Orser, Barbara Tyson. **1998 DVD**

•RESURRECTION MAN ★★★1/2 Chilling Irish thriller about a thug who makes his living collecting debts on soccer bets. Stuart Townsend is absolutely menacing as Victor, a man who prides himself on a job well done, even if it means breaking kneecaps. When Victor and his gang use local politics to spread their terror, their newfound fame attracts all sorts of attention, including a local journalist whose life becomes entwined with the killers. Tough and brutal at every turn, the film never flinches. Rated R for adult situations, language, and violence. 100m. **DIR:** Marc Evans. **CAST:** Stuart Townsend, Brenda Fricker, David Williamson, George Shane, Lee Mulrooney. **1998**

RESURRECTION OF ZACHARY WHEELER, THE ★★ Disappointing science-fiction–mystery has a well-known senator (Bradford Dillman) taken to a bizarre out-of-the-way treatment center in New Mexico after a serious car accident. Confusing movie. Rated G. 100m. **DIR:** Bob Wynn. **CAST:** Bradford Dillman, Angie Dickinson, Leslie Nielsen. **1971**

RETREAT HELL ★★1/2 In this predictable war film, an untested Marine Corps combat unit battles it out behind enemy lines near the Chosin Reservoir in North Korea. All the tried-and-true ingredients are here, including a wet-behind-the-ears private and a tough-talking platoon sergeant. B&W; 95m. **DIR:** Joseph H. Lewis. **CAST:** Frank Lovejoy, Richard Carlson, Russ Tamblyn. **1954**

RETRIBUTION ★★ In this supernatural thriller, a mild-mannered, down-and-out artist attempts suicide at the same moment a small-time hood is tortured to death. The artist becomes possessed by the soul of the hood and then proceeds to avenge his murder. Low-budget shocker with an inadequate script. Rated R for violence and profanity. 109m. **DIR:** Guy Magar. **CAST:** Dennis Lipscomb, Leslie Wing, Hoyt Axton. **1988**

RETURN, THE (1980) 🦃 Terminally boring flick about a close encounter. Rated PG. 91m. **DIR:** Greydon Clark. **CAST:** Jan-Michael Vincent, Cybill Shepherd, Martin Landau, Raymond Burr, Neville Brand. **1980**

RETURN (1984) ★★ Right before her father's bid for the Arkansas governorship, Diana (Karlene Crockett) decides to find out about her grandfather's mysterious death. She meets a young man who relives her grandfather's life through hypnosis. Below-par mystery. Rated R for profanity, violence, and partial nudity. 78m. **DIR:** Andrew Silver. **CAST:** Karlene Crockett, John Walcutt, Anne Francis, Frederic Forrest. **1984 DVD**

RETURN FROM WITCH MOUNTAIN ★★ Christopher Lee and Bette Davis capture Ike Eisenmann to use his supernatural powers to accomplish their own purposes. Sequel to *Escape to Witch Mountain*, in which Eisenmann and Kim Richards discover their powers and the effect they can have on humans. A good children's film, but weak Disney. Rated G. 93m. **DIR:** John Hough. **CAST:** Bette Davis, Christopher Lee, Kim Richards, Ike Eisenmann. **1978**

RETURN OF A MAN CALLED HORSE, THE ★★★ Every bit as good as its predecessor, *A Man Called Horse*. Both films present an honest, and sometimes shocking, glimpse at the culture of the American Indian. The new film picks up with a bored and unhappy Morgan deciding to return to America. Rated PG for violence. 129m. **DIR:** Irvin Kershner. **CAST:** Richard Harris, Gale Sondergaard, Geoffrey Lewis, Bill Lucking, Jorge Luke, Enrique Lucero. **1976**

RETURN OF CAPTAIN INVINCIBLE, THE ★★1/2 Camp send-up of old comic-book-hero serials of the Thirties and Forties. Arkin is Captain Invincible, fighting crime and Nazis and preserving the American way of life. During the communist witch-hunt of the Fifties, though, the captain is accused of being a Red and quickly becomes a national disgrace. Alan Arkin flies high as Captain Invincible. Songs, special effects, and corny melodrama all combine to get you through the occasional dull bits. Rated PG for profanity and violence. 101m. **DIR:** Philippe Mora. **CAST:** Alan Arkin, Christopher Lee. **1984**

RETURN OF CHANDU (MAGICIAN, THE) ★★1/2 Crackerjack fantasy-adventure serial has enough action, trickery, and plot twists for two chapterplays as Bela Lugosi plays Chandu, Master of White Magic, hot on the trail of evil Lemurians who have stolen his beloved Princess Nadji. Hokey but fun family fare. B&W; 12 chapters. **DIR:** Ray Taylor. **CAST:** Bela Lugosi, Maria Alba, Clara Kimball Young, Lucien Prival, Bryant Washburn. **1934**

RETURN OF DR. FU MANCHU ★★1/2 Evil genius Dr. Fu Manchu returns to England to fulfill his vow to kill John Petrie, last of the descendants of those responsible for the death of Fu's family. Aerial kidnappings, mind-sapping potions, and action-filled fights form the backdrop as the well-fed fiend chews up the scenery, leering, and gloatingly uttering things like, "The thought of inflicting two deaths on a victim delights my peculiar sense of humor." B&W; 73m. DIR: Rowland V. Lee. CAST: Warner Oland, O. P. Heggie, Neil Hamilton, Jean Arthur, William Austin. 1930

RETURN OF DR. X ★★ Director Vincent Sherman's first motion picture is not, as one might assume, a sequel to *Dr. X*. Instead, it borrows from Boris Karloff's *The Walking Dead* in a tale of an executed man brought back to life. Worth watching for Humphrey Bogart's only appearance in a horror movie. B&W; 62m. DIR: Vincent Sherman. CAST: Dennis Morgan, Humphrey Bogart, Wayne Morris, Rosemary Lane, John Litel. 1939

RETURN OF DRACULA ★★1/2 Until Hammer Films revived him, Count Dracula wasn't seen much in the 1950s, but this above-average outing is one of the exceptions. Francis Lederer takes the title role, assuming a European painter's identity in order to bleed modern California dry. Video release includes a color climax. B&W; 77m. DIR: Paul Landres. CAST: Francis Lederer, Norma Eberhardt, Ray Stricklyn. 1958

RETURN OF ELIOT NESS, THE ★★1/2 Robert Stack suits up again as legendary crime fighter Eliot Ness in this made-for-television crime-drama. Now that Al Capone is out of the picture, the streets of Chicago are up for grabs. With every thug in town trying to make a name for himself, Ness comes out of retirement to clean up the streets. Stack is good as the resurrected Ness, but telefilm is more nostalgic than anything else. 94m. DIR: James A. Contner. CAST: Robert Stack, Jack Coleman, Philip Bosco, Charles Durning, Lisa Hartman. 1991

RETURN OF FRANK CANNON, THE ★★1/2 When an ex-CIA agent is murdered, portly detective Frank Cannon (William Conrad) comes out of retirement. Made for television. 96m. DIR: Corey Allen. CAST: William Conrad, Arthur Hill, Diana Muldaur, Ed Nelson. 1980

RETURN OF FRANK JAMES, THE ★★★ Gene Tierney made her film debut in this inevitable sequel to *Jesse James* (1939). Henry Fonda reprises his role as brother Frank and attempts to avenge Jesse's death at the hands of "dirty little coward" Bob Ford, played by John Carradine. Thanks to Fonda's fine acting and Fritz Lang's sensitive direction, what could have been a pale rip-off is an enjoyable Western. 92m. DIR: Fritz Lang. CAST: Henry Fonda, Gene Tierney, Donald Meek, John Carradine, Jackie Cooper, J. Edward Bromberg, Henry Hull. 1940

RETURN OF JAFAR, THE ★★★ Somewhere between Saturday-morning cartoons and Disney theatrical releases lies this direct-to-video sequel of *Aladdin*. The kids will still enjoy it, but parents will probably snooze. The same characters (Aladdin, Jasmine, Genie, Iago, and Abu) are confronted by the dastardly Jafar when a bandit releases the evil genie. Aladdin's friends must work together to set him free from Jafar's deadly lava pit. Not rated; contains plenty of comic-book violence. 66m. DIR: Toby Shelton, Tad Stones, Alan Zaslove. 1994

RETURN OF JESSE JAMES, THE ★★1/2 In this low-budget oater, John Ireland portrays a small-time outlaw who bears a striking resemblance to Jesse James. Taking advantage of this rumor, he sets out to prove to everyone that Jesse James, shot and killed by fellow gang member Bob Ford, did not die and is still in business. Plodding, but fairly well acted. B&W; 75m. DIR: Arthur Hilton. CAST: John Ireland, Ann Dvorak, Hugh O'Brian, Henry Hull. 1950

RETURN OF JOSEY WALES ★★ The name is the only similarity between Clint Eastwood's *The Outlaw Josey Wales* and this mediocre Western. Wanted man Wales stands up to a crooked Mexican sheriff. Rated R for a rape scene and violence. 90m. DIR: Michael Parks. CAST: Michael Parks. 1986

RETURN OF MARTIN GUERRE, THE ★★★1/2 Brilliantly absorbing account of an actual sixteenth-century court case in which a man returns to his family and village after years away at the wars, only to have his identity questioned. Gérard Depardieu and Nathalie Baye give outstanding, carefully restrained performances. In French with English subtitles. No MPAA rating. 111m. DIR: Daniel Vigne. CAST: Gérard Depardieu, Nathalie Baye, Roger Planchon. 1982 DVD

RETURN OF OCTOBER, THE ★★★ A girl thinks her uncle is reincarnated as the horse, October. This fun movie set the stage, tone, and sense of humor for body-switch movies that came along a generation later. 87m. DIR: Joseph H. Lewis. CAST: Glenn Ford, Terry Moore, James Gleason, May Whitty, Albert Sharpe, Henry O'Neill, Samuel S. Hinds, Nana Bryant, Jackie Gleason. 1948

RETURN OF PETER GRIMM, THE ★★★1/2 Enjoyable blend of *It's a Wonderful Life* and *A Christmas Carol* with the incomparable Lionel Barrymore as Peter Grimm, who dies and is given a second chance to return to Earth and reconcile his family and affairs. B&W; 82m. DIR: George Nicholls Jr. CAST: Lionel Barrymore, Helen Mack, Edward Ellis, Donald Meek. 1935

RETURN OF SPINAL TAP, THE ★★★★ The world's most lovable heavy-metal band is back in this wonderful follow-up to Rob Reiner's cult 1984 "rockumentary," *This Is Spinal Tap*. This time the boys are in their native England where they blend excellent live-concert footage (including some new songs), interviews with old friends, and recollections of their formative years. Great music and great fun. Not rated. 110m. DIR: Jim DiBergi. CAST: Christopher Guest, Michael McKean, Harry Shearer. 1993

RETURN OF SUPERFLY, THE ★★ Priest (Nathan Purdee) returns to the United States, only to be hunted by both the law and drug lords. The shaky plot and acting are marginally redeemed by the anti-drug message. Rated R for nudity, profanity, and violence. 94m. DIR: Sig Shore. CAST: Nathan Purdee, Margaret Avery, Christopher Curry, David Groh. 1990

RETURN OF THE ALIEN'S DEADLY SPAWN, THE ★★ Blood-filled horror film about alien creatures from outer space who kill and destroy anyone and everything that gets in their way. Lots of gore, ripped flesh, and off-the-wall humor. For people who like sick movies. Rated R for profanity and gore. 90m. DIR: Douglas McKeown. CAST: Charles George Hildebrandt. 1984

RETURN OF THE APE MAN ★★★ Scientists Bela Lugosi and John Carradine revive a Neanderthal man, who soon goes on a rampage. Above-average monogram poverty-row programmer, just fast-paced (and poker-faced) enough to be diverting. B&W; 68m. **DIR:** Phil Rosen. **CAST:** Bela Lugosi, John Carradine. 1944

RETURN OF THE BAD MEN ★★★ Randolph Scott has his hands full in this routine Western. No sooner does he settle down in Oklahoma than he must slap leather with Billy the Kid, the Dalton gang, the Younger brothers, and the Sundance Kid. As the latter, Robert Ryan shows aint't he appealing gun hand who rode with Butch Cassidy. B&W; 90m. **DIR:** Ray Enright. **CAST:** Randolph Scott, Anne Jeffreys, Robert Ryan, George "Gabby" Hayes, Lex Barker. 1948

RETURN OF THE DRAGON ★★★1/2 After seeing *Return of the Dragon*, we have no doubt that Bruce Lee, not Robert Clouse, directed *Enter the Dragon*. Lee was credited with staging the fight scenes, but our guess is that he was well aware of the latter film's possible impact and exercised control over the creative nonacting facets of the film whenever he could. *Return of the Dragon* was made before *Enter*, and it shows Lee's considerable directorial talent. A delightful film, brimful of comedy, action, and acrobatics. Rated R. 91m. **DIR:** Bruce Lee. **CAST:** Bruce Lee, Chuck Norris, Nora Miao. 1973 **DVD**

RETURN OF THE EVIL DEAD ★★ This Spanish zombie shocker has nothing to do with Sam Raimi's *Evil Dead* films. It's one of the entries in de Ossorio's intermittently scary Blind Dead cycle (see also *Return of the Zombies*), retitled for U.S. release. A few scenes of the rotting undead stalking their victims have a claustrophobic quality that foreshadows John Carpenter's *The Fog.* Rated R. 85m. **DIR:** Amando de Ossorio. **CAST:** Victor Petit. 1975

●**RETURN OF THE FAMILY MAN** 🐾 Low-budget ripoff of the far superior *The Stepfather* will leave you wondering why Hollywood can't come up with more than one or two ideas. Not rated; contains violence. 90m. **DIR:** John Murlowski. **CAST:** Ron Smerczak. 1990

RETURN OF THE FLY, THE ★★★ In this fine sequel to *The Fly*, the son of the original insect makes the same mistake as his father ... with identical results. Effective film benefits from stark black-and-white photography and solid effects. Watch out for the guinea-pig scene! B&W; 80m. **DIR:** Edward L. Bernds. **CAST:** Vincent Price, Brett Halsey, David Frankham. 1959

RETURN OF THE JEDI ★★★★★ Third film in the *Star Wars* series centers on the all-out attempt by the Rebel forces—led by Luke Skywalker, Han Solo, Princess Leia, and Lando Calrissian—to turn back the tidal wave of interplanetary domination by the evil Galactic Empire and its forces, led by Darth Vader. Rated PG. 133m. **DIR:** Richard Marquand. **CAST:** Mark Hamill, Harrison Ford, Carrie Fisher, Billy Dee Williams, Dave Prowse, Peter Mayhew, Anthony Daniels, James Earl Jones. 1983

RETURN OF THE KILLER TOMATOES ★★1/2 The mad scientist, whose experiments caused the first tomato war, perfects his process that creates intelligent vegetable life. Although it lacks the spontaneous humor the original exhibited, this *Return* has its moments. Language may not be suitable for younger audience. Rated PG. 99m. **DIR:** John DeBello. **CAST:** Anthony Starke, George Clooney, John Astin. 1988

RETURN OF THE LIVING DEAD, THE ★★★★ Extremely gory horror film produced with a great deal of style and ample amounts of comedy as well. The residents of a small Virginia cemetery are brought back to life after accidental exposure to a strange chemical, and they're hungry ... for human brains. Rated R for violence, nudity, and language. 91m. **DIR:** Dan O'Bannon. **CAST:** Clu Gulager, James Karen, Don Calfa, Thom Mathews. 1985

RETURN OF THE LIVING DEAD PART II ★★ The dead have once again risen from their long slumber and are hungry for human brains. A drum of special gas that seems to reanimate the dead has been discovered by a trio of children. They unwittingly loose the gas on the unsuspecting town. Definitely an R rating for the violence and language. 90m. **DIR:** Ken Wiederhorn. **CAST:** James Karen, Thom Mathews, Dana Ashbrook. 1988

RETURN OF THE LIVING DEAD 3 ★★★ Love never dies, at least not in this sequel. When Curt's girlfriend Mindy dies, he drags her body to a top-secret government lab where his father works on reanimating the dead. Curt revives Mindy, but when she starts craving human flesh, their relationship becomes strained. Goofy humor, outrageous special effects, and a likable cast make this series worth reviving. Rated R for nudity, language, and extreme violence. 96m. **DIR:** Brian Yuzna. **CAST:** J. Trevor Edmond, Mindy Clarke, Sarah Douglas, Kent McCord. 1993

RETURN OF THE MAN FROM U.N.C.L.E., THE ★★★ Secret agents Napoleon Solo (Robert Vaughn) and Illya Kuryakin (David McCallum) are called out of a fifteen-year retirement. Fans of the original series will find this lighthearted spy adventure especially entertaining. 109m. **DIR:** Ray Austin. **CAST:** Robert Vaughn, David McCallum, Patrick Macnee, Tom Mason, Gayle Hunnicutt, Geoffrey Lewis, Anthony Zerbe, Keenan Wynn, George Lazenby. 1983

RETURN OF THE MUSKETEERS ★★★★ Filled with humor and swashbuckling high adventure, this adaptation of Alexandre Dumas's *Twenty Years After* finds D'Artagnan and Porthos pitted against Athos and Aramis when they mistakenly ally themselves with the queen and her power-crazed lover/cardinal. Dedicated to the memory of the marvelous Roy Kinnear, who died as the result of an accident during the filming. 100m. **DIR:** Richard Lester. **CAST:** Michael York, Oliver Reed, Richard Chamberlain, Frank Finlay, C. Thomas Howell, Kim Cattrall, Geraldine Chaplin, Christopher Lee, Philippe Noiret, Roy Kinnear, Jean-Pierre Cassel, Alan Howard, Bill Paterson. 1989

RETURN OF THE NATIVE, THE ★★★★ Enchanting Catherine Zeta Jones plays Thomas Hardy's ill-fated heroine in this fine *Hallmark Hall of Fame* presentation. When Jones, as bewitching Eustacia Vye, joins her grandfather in a small, superstitious town, she has several of the young men falling in love with her. Her reckless actions stir gossip and tragedy. Costumes and fabulous English countryside are further complemented by the perfect score played by the Royal Philharmonic Orchestra. Not rated; contains mature themes. 98m. DIR: Jack Gold. CAST: Catherine Zeta Jones, Ray Stevenson, Clive Owen, Joan Plowright, Steven Mackintosh. 1994

RETURN OF THE PINK PANTHER, THE ★★★★ Writer-director Blake Edwards and star Peter Sellers revived their Inspector Clouseau character for a new series of comic adventures beginning with this slapstick classic. There are many funny scenes as Sellers attempts to track down the Phantom (Christopher Plummer) while making life intolerable for the chief inspector (Herbert Lom). Rated PG. 113m. DIR: Blake Edwards. CAST: Peter Sellers, Christopher Plummer, Herbert Lom, Catherine Schell, Burt Kwouk, Peter Arne. 1975 DVD

RETURN OF THE SAND FAIRY, THE ★★★1/2 Very cute, very British fairy tale set in the English countryside around 1910. Based on the story by children's writer Edith Nesbit, this revolves around the old adage, "careful for what you wish, it may come true." Four children, forced to visit a cranky great-aunt, discover a sand fairy who grants all their desires. This film has a witty intelligence and humor. Not rated. 139m. DIR: Marilyn Fox. CAST: Toby Uffindell-Phillips, Ellie Laura Clarke, Leonard Kirby, Vicci Avery. 1992

RETURN OF THE SECAUCUS 7 ★★★★1/2 Here's a gem of a movie about the reunion of seven friends ten years after they were wrongfully busted in Secaucus, New Jersey, while on their way to the last demonstration against the Vietnam war in Washington, D.C. It is a delicious blend of characterization, humor, and insight. No MPAA rating, but *Secaucus 7* has nudity, profanity, and implicit sex. 100m. DIR: John Sayles. CAST: Mark Arnott, Gordon Clapp, Maggie Cousineau, Adam LeFevre, Bruce MacDonald, Jean Passanante, Maggie Renzi. 1980

RETURN OF THE SEVEN ★★1/2 Drab, inferior sequel to *The Magnificent Seven* follows Yul Brynner doing what he does best, getting six Yankee gunfighters fool enough to take on scores of Mexican bandits for no pay at all. 96m. DIR: Burt Kennedy. CAST: Yul Brynner, Robert Fuller, Warren Oates, Claude Akins, Emilio Fernandez, Jordan Christopher. 1966

RETURN OF THE SOLDIER, THE ★★★★ During World War I, a soldier (Alan Bates) suffers shell shock and forgets the last twenty years of his life. His doctors must decide whether he should be allowed to enjoy what has resulted in a carefree second youth, or be brought back to real life and the responsibilities that go with it. Everyone in the cast is superb. Not rated; contains adult situations. 105m. DIR: Alan Bridges. CAST: Glenda Jackson, Julie Christie, Ann-Margret, Alan Bates, Ian Holm, Frank Finlay, Jeremy Kemp. 1985

RETURN OF THE SWAMP THING ★★★ The big, green monster-hero comes out of the swamp to do battle once again with evil scientist Louis Jourdan, while Heather Locklear is the object of his affections. Unlike the first film, which was also based on the DC Comics character, you're not supposed to take this sequel seriously. Rated PG-13. 87m. DIR:

Jim Wynorski. CAST: Louis Jourdan, Heather Locklear, Dick Durock. 1989

RETURN OF THE TALL BLOND MAN WITH ONE BLACK SHOE, THE ★★1/2 This sequel to the original *Tall Blond Man . . .* is, unfortunately, inferior. But it's still a delight to watch Pierre Richard go through his comic paces. Once again his reactions to what he's faced with are the reason to see this. In French with English subtitles. No MPAA rating. 84m. DIR: Yves Robert. CAST: Pierre Richard, Mireille Darc, Jean Rochefort. 1974

RETURN OF THE VAMPIRE, THE ★★★ Set during World War II, this surprisingly good vampire tale has the supposedly destroyed fiend, Armand Tesla (Bela Lugosi), unearthed by a German bombing raid on London. B&W; 69m. DIR: Lew Landers, Kurt Neumann. CAST: Bela Lugosi, Frieda Inescort, Nina Foch, Miles Mander, Matt Willis. 1943

RETURN TO BOGGY CREEK 🖤 A cheap and boring sequel about a mysterious creature that stalks the swamps of a small fishing community. Rated PG. 87m. DIR: Tom Moore. CAST: Dawn Wells. 1978

RETURN TO EDEN ★★★ This four-and-one-half-hour miniseries, originally made for Australian television, is a bit much to watch at one sitting. Fans of soaps, however, will find it holds their interest. A wealthy woman discovers that her handsome husband only married her for her money when he feeds her to the crocodiles. Miraculously surviving, she alters her appearance and sets about gaining revenge. Not rated, but with brief nudity. 259m. DIR: Karen Arthur. CAST: Rebecca Gilling, James Reyne, Wendy Hughes. 1983

RETURN TO FANTASY ISLAND ★★ If you liked the television series *Fantasy Island*, you'll like this made-for-TV movie. Ricardo Montalban is the suave operator of a wish-fulfillment island, assisted by his tiny friend Tattoo (Herve Villechaize). It's pure hokum, but it does offer a chance to watch some fine actors. 100m. DIR: George McCowan. CAST: Ricardo Montalban, Joseph Campanella, Joseph Cotten, Adrienne Barbeau, Laraine Day, Herve Villechaize, Cameron Mitchell, Karen Valentine, France Nuyen, George Chakiris, Horst Buchholz, George Maharis. 1977

RETURN TO FROGTOWN 🖤 Unbelievably bad sequel to *Hell Comes to Frogtown*. When a flying Texas ranger (Lou Ferrigno) is captured by a crazed amphibian, a sexy doctor and her reluctant partner try to rescue him. Grade-Z sets, story, and dialogue. Rated PG-13 for violence. 90m. DIR: Donald G. Jackson. CAST: Lou Ferrigno, Charles Napier, Robert Z'dar, Denice Duff, Don Stroud. 1992

RETURN TO LONESOME DOVE ★★★★ Sequel to the milestone miniseries lacks the quirky, bawdy qualities of its predecessor, but there is much for Western fans to enjoy in this sprawling epic. Captain Call and his son Newt become involved in a range war. Unrelated to author Larry McMurtry's continuation of the story, *Streets of Laredo.* 330m. DIR: Mike Robe. CAST: Jon Voight, Barbara Hershey, Rick Schroder, Lou Gossett Jr., William L. Petersen, Oliver Reed, Dennis Haysbert, Reese Witherspoon, Timothy

Scott, Chris Cooper, C.C.H. Pounder, Nia Peeples, William Sanderson. **1993**

RETURN TO MACON COUNTY 💜 Two fun-loving boneheads run afoul of the law in the rural South. Rated PG. 104m. **DIR:** Richard Compton. **CAST:** Don Johnson, Nick Nolte, Robin Mattson. **1975**

RETURN TO MAYBERRY ★★1/2 Nostalgia time. Andy, Barney, and most of the gang are reunited in this TV-movie valentine to *The Andy Griffith Show.* The many plot lines include Opie's impending fatherhood, Barney's campaign for sheriff, and the appearance of a monster in the lake. 95m. **DIR:** Bob Sweeney. **CAST:** Andy Griffith, Don Knotts, Ron Howard, Jim Nabors, George Lindsey, Aneta Corseaut, Betty Lynn. **1986**

•**RETURN TO ME** ★★★★ This captivating tale of love lost and found again concerns an architect (David Duchovny) who loses his wife unexpectedly; elsewhere, long-suffering Minnie Driver gets her life back with a heart transplant … taken from Duchovny's wife. Driver and Duchovny eventually meet and fall in love, neither aware of the medical miracle that bonds them; the point of the story is what will happen after they *do* find out. The result is a charming example of the kinder, gentler filmmaking that our parents often complain we "don't see enough of anymore." Rated PG for the mildest of expletives. 115m. **DIR:** Bonnie Hunt. **CAST:** David Duchovny, Minnie Driver, Carroll O'Connor, Robert Loggia, Bonnie Hunt, David Alan Grier, Joely Richardson, James Belushi. **2000**

RETURN TO OZ ★★★★ In this semisequel to *The Wizard of Oz,* viewers will hear no songs nor see any Munchkins. It is a very different, but equally enjoyable, trip down the Yellow Brick Road, with young star Fairuza Balk outstanding as Dorothy. It gets pretty scary at times and isn't all fluff and wonder like the Oz of yore. This is nevertheless a magical film for the child in everyone. Rated PG for scary stuff. 110m. **DIR:** Walter Murch. **CAST:** Fairuza Balk, Nicol Williamson, Jean Marsh, Piper Laurie, Matt Clark. **1985 DVD**

RETURN TO PARADISE (1953) ★★1/2 An American arrives on a remote South Seas island and locks horns with a religious fanatic who dominates the natives. *Very* loosely based on part of James Michener's *Tales of the South Pacific.* 88m. **DIR:** Mark Robson. **CAST:** Gary Cooper, Barry Jones, Roberta Haynes. **1953**

RETURN TO PARADISE (1998) ★★★1/2 A fascinating moral dilemma is at the heart of this captivating drama, which builds to an unexpectedly powerful climax. After a prologue showing that three vacationing guys in Malaysia just want to have fun, we flash-forward two years and discover that two of these young men have built lives for themselves. Enter passionate attorney Anne Heche, who explains that their friend has been in jail on a drug charge ever since they left him … and that he's soon to be executed, unless these two New Yorkers return to Malaysia and "share" a jail term. The performances are uniformly strong, and the script is surprisingly pungent and heartfelt. Nothing here should be taken for granted. Rated R for profanity, drug use, and sex-

ual content. 109m. **DIR:** Joseph Ruben. **CAST:** Vince Vaughn, Anne Heche, Joaquin Phoenix, David Conrad, Jada Pinkett Smith. **1998 DVD**

RETURN TO PEYTON PLACE ★★ A misfire that should have scored. The sequel to one of the most popular films of all time suffers from a bad case of miscasting. No one from the first film reappears in the sequel, and none of the players look or act at ease with their characters. 122m. **DIR:** José Ferrer. **CAST:** Eleanor Parker, Carol Lynley, Jeff Chandler, Robert Sterling, Tuesday Weld, Mary Astor, Bob Crane, Luciana Paluzzi, Brett Halsey, Gunnar Hellstrom. **1961**

RETURN TO SALEM'S LOT, A 💜 A divorced father, recently reunited with his teenage son, goes back to the town of his birth to find that its inhabitants are vampires. Rated R for nudity and violence. 101m. **DIR:** Larry Cohen. **CAST:** Michael Moriarty, Samuel Fuller, Andrew Duggan, Evelyn Keyes. **1987**

RETURN TO SAVAGE BEACH 💜 Filmmaker Andy Sidaris rehashes his triple-B formula (babes, bosoms, and bullets) in this tale of female agents after a stolen computer disk. Rated R for adult situations, language, nudity,` and violence. 98m. **DIR:** Andy Sidaris. **CAST:** Julie Strain, Julie K. Smith, Shae Marks, Cristian Letelier. **1998**

RETURN TO SNOWY RIVER, PART II ★★★1/2 In this spectacular sequel to *The Man from Snowy River,* Tom Burlinson returns to right wrongs and romance Sigrid Thornton in rugged, Old West–style Australia. Director Geoff Burrowes, who produced the first film, outdoes the original at every turn. A movie the whole family can love. Rated PG for some violence. 100m. **DIR:** Geoff Burrowes. **CAST:** Tom Burlinson, Sigrid Thornton, Brian Dennehy, Nicholas Eadie, Bryan Marshall. **1988**

RETURN TO THE BLUE LAGOON 💜 The beautifully photographed scenes of a lush tropical island cannot salvage this lame sequel which basically rehashes the story of its 1980 predecessor. Rated PG-13 for nudity and brief violence. 101m. **DIR:** William A. Graham. **CAST:** Milla Jovovich, Brian Krause, Lisa Pelikan, Courtney Phillips, Garette Patrick Ratliff. **1991**

RETURN TO THE LOST WORLD ★★1/2 Continuation of British remake is actually more exciting than the first try, although the dinosaurs are still laughable. A group of scientists and tagalongs returns to the mysterious plateau, now threatened by a greedy oil prospector and a volcano. Modest but engaging. Rated PG for violence. 99m. **DIR:** Timothy Bond. **CAST:** John Rhys-Davies, David Warner, Eric McCormack, Tamara Gorski, Nathania Stanford. **1992**

RETURN TO TREASURE ISLAND ★★★1/2 This five-tape series was produced for the Disney Channel. It is a sequel to Disney's 1950 film *Treasure Island,* based on Robert Louis Stevenson's classic novel. The action here takes place ten years later with young Jim Hawkins (Christopher Guard) now an educated young man being reunited with the scheming Long John (Brian Blessed). 101m. **DIR:** Piers Haggard. **CAST:** Brian Blessed, Christopher Guard, Kenneth Colley. **1985**

RETURN TO TWO-MOON JUNCTION ★★★ This languid girl-meets-boy erotic· drama fulfills the genre's requirements—attractive performers, idyllic setting, and playfully sensual lovemaking—and is quite superior to its predecessor. Rated R for nudity, simulated sex, and profanity. 96m. **DIR:** Farhad Mann. **CAST:** Melinda Clarke, John Clayton Schafer, Louise Fletcher. **1994**

RETURNING, THE ♥ A woman copes with the death of her son and the apparent madness of her husband. 86m. **DIR:** Joel Bender. **CAST:** Gabriel Walsh, Susan Strasberg. **1990**

REUBEN, REUBEN ★★★★1/2 A funny, touching, and memorable character study about an irascible Scottish poet, this film, directed by Robert Ellis Miller (*The Heart Is a Lonely Hunter*) and written by Julius J. Epstein (*Casablanca*), ranges from romantic to ribald, and from low-key believability to blistering black comedy. In short, it's a rare cinematic treat. First and foremost among the picture's assets is a superb leading performance by Tom Conti. Rated R for profanity and suggested sex. 101m. **DIR:** Robert Ellis Miller. **CAST:** Tom Conti, Kelly McGillis, Roberts Blossom, Cynthia Harris, E. Katherine Kerr, Joel Fabiani, Lois Smith. **1983**

REUNION ★★★★ Jason Robards portrays an elderly Jew who returns to Germany fifty-five years after escaping the rise of Hitler in this touching film about letting go of the past by grasping the present. But Robards's scenes are just bookends to the central story of his character as a boy and the friendship that develops between him and a German aristocrat's son. Rated PG-13 for brief nudity. 110m. **DIR:** Jerry Schatzberg. **CAST:** Jason Robards Jr. **1991**

REUNION IN FRANCE ★★ A romantic melodrama that is badly dated, especially considering the fact that it top lines John Wayne and he doesn't get the girl in the last reel. Joan Crawford is a sophisticated Parisian who finds out her lover (Philip Dorn) is apparently collaborating with the Nazis. She switches her affections to an American flier (John Wayne) running from the Gestapo. B&W; 102m. **DIR:** Jules Dassin. **CAST:** Joan Crawford, John Wayne, Philip Dorn, Reginald Owen, John Carradine. **1942**

REVENGE (1971) (JOAN COLLINS) ★★ When a little girl is abducted and murdered, her family kidnaps the man they believe responsible, torturing and finally killing him. Interesting suspense film, but it lacks the intensity it should have. Not rated. 85m. **DIR:** Sidney Hayers. **CAST:** Joan Collins, James Booth, Sinead Cusack. **1971**

REVENGE (1971) (SHELLEY WINTERS) ★★ Made for television, this has Shelley Winters out for—you guessed it—revenge for her daughter's rape. Not as bad as it could have been. 78m. **DIR:** Jud Taylor. **CAST:** Shelley Winters, Stuart Whitman, Bradford Dillman, Roger Perry. **1971**

REVENGE (1990) ★★ Pilot Kevin Costner falls in love with the beautiful young wife (Madeleine Stowe) of a powerful Mexican gangster (Anthony Quinn), whose life Costner once saved. Poorly paced melodrama, rated R for nudity, profanity, simulated sex, and violence. 120m. **DIR:** Tony Scott. **CAST:** Kevin Costner, Anthony Quinn, Madeleine Stowe, Sally Kirkland. **1990 DVD**

REVENGE OF DR. X, THE ★★ Worth hunting down for bad-movie buffs. Not rated, but unobjectionable

despite a brief skinny-dipping scene. 88m. **DIR:** Not credited. **CAST:** James Craig. **1970**

REVENGE OF FRANKENSTEIN ★★★★ The best of the Hammer Studios Frankenstein movies, this sequel to *The Curse of Frankenstein* sets the pace for all the entries that followed, focusing on the continuing exploits of Dr. Victor Frankenstein (Peter Cushing) rather than the amblings of his first creation. Once again, the doctor's essentially well-meant experiments create havoc, and Cushing is in top form. 91m. **DIR:** Terence Fisher. **CAST:** Peter Cushing, Francis Matthews, Eunice Gayson, Michael Gwynn, Lionel Jeffries. **1958**

REVENGE OF THE CHEERLEADERS ♥ There were never any good *Cheerleaders* movies, but this one is about the worst of a bad bunch. Rated R for nudity and profanity. 88m. **DIR:** Richard Lerner. **CAST:** Jeril Woods, Rainbeaux Smith, Carl Ballantine, David Hasselhoff. **1976**

REVENGE OF THE CREATURE ★★ Even as sequels go, this follow-up to *Creature from the Black Lagoon* is disappointing. Scientists capture him and take him to Florida, he gets loose, and they kill him. Only the ferocity of some of the murders and Clint Eastwood's screen debut as a dim-witted lab assistant break the monotony. B&W; 82m. **DIR:** Jack Arnold. **CAST:** John Agar, Lori Nelson, John Bromfield, Clint Eastwood. **1955**

REVENGE OF THE DEAD ♥ Talky Italian film with misleading title. Rated R for violence and profanity. 98m. **DIR:** Pupi Avati. **CAST:** Gabriele Lavia, Anne Canovas. **1984**

REVENGE OF THE KICKFIGHTER ♥ Marines discover gold in a Vietnamese village and plan to return for it after the war. Unfortunately they're being systematically bumped off. Thin, unbelievable plot and inferior acting mar otherwise average actioner. Not rated; contains profanity, simulated sex, and violence. 89m. **DIR:** Anthony Maharaj. **CAST:** Richard Norton. **1991**

•REVENGE OF THE MUSKETEERS ★★★ Sophie Marceau shines in this sexy version of the Dumas classic, playing the feisty daughter of D'Artagnan. When she learns of a plot against France, her father summons the musketeers for one last mission. There is much to relish in director Bertrand Tavernier's French production, including exquisite period detail and a wild sense of abandon. In French with English subtitles. Rated R for adult situations, language, nudity, and violence. 130m. **DIR:** Bertrand Tavernier. **CAST:** Sophie Marceau, Philippe Noiret, Claude Rich, Sami Frey, Jean-Luc Bideau, Raoul Billerey. **1994**

REVENGE OF THE NERDS ★★★ The title characters, Lewis (Robert Carradine) and Gilbert (Anthony Edwards), strike back at the jocks who tormented them in this watchable, fitfully funny comedy. Rated R. 90m. **DIR:** Jeff Kanew. **CAST:** Robert Carradine, Anthony Edwards, Julie Montgomery, Curtis Armstrong, Ted McGinley, Michelle Meyrink, James Cromwell, Bernie Casey, Timothy Busfield, John Goodman. **1984**

REVENGE OF THE NERDS II: NERDS IN PARADISE ♥ With this sequel, one assumes that the filmmakers were out for revenge against their audience.

Rated PG-13 for profanity and tasteless humor. 95m. DIR: Joe Roth. CAST: Robert Carradine, Timothy Busfield, Curtis Armstrong, Larry B. Scott, Courtney Thorne-Smith, Anthony Edwards, Ed Lauter. 1987

REVENGE OF THE NERDS III: THE NEXT GENERATION ✔ The nerds take their act to television, giving new meaning to the term "boob tube." 93m. DIR: Roland Mesa. CAST: Robert Carradine, Ted McGinley, Curtis Armstrong, Morton Downey Jr. 1992

REVENGE OF THE NERDS IV: NERDS IN LOVE ★★★ They're still lovable, but in this made-for-television comedy, the nerds have lost their edge. Most of the original cast returns, but their antics have been watered down for the small screen. Not rated. 90m. DIR: Steve Zacharias. CAST: Robert Carradine, Curtis Armstrong, Joseph Bologna, Ted McGinley, Larry B. Scott, Donald Gibb. 1994

REVENGE OF THE NINJA ✔ Japanese karate experts take on the mob in this kung fu flick. Rated R for violence and nudity. 88m. DIR: Sam Firstenberg. CAST: Sho Kosugi, Keith Vitali, Arthur Roberts, Mario Gallo. 1983

REVENGE OF THE PINK PANTHER, THE ★★★1/2 It is arguably the best of the slapstick series. It contains inspired bits penned by director Blake Edwards and played to perfection by Peter Sellers. Rated PG. 99m. DIR: Blake Edwards. CAST: Peter Sellers, Dyan Cannon, Robert Webber, Marc Lawrence, Herbert Lom, Burt Kwouk, Robert Loggia, Paul Stewart. 1978 DVD

REVENGE OF THE RED BARON ★★ A modicum of suspense saves this hokey thriller about a veteran flying ace (Mickey Rooney) who shot down the infamous Red Baron. Now in a wheelchair, Rooney must fight to save his family from a model biplane possessed by the spirit of the dead pilot. The plane creates havoc, but the film mostly creates laughs. Rated PG-13 for violence. 90m. DIR: Robert Gordon. CAST: Mickey Rooney, Toby Maguire, Cliff De Young, Laraine Newman, Ronnie Schell. 1994

REVENGE OF THE STEPFORD WIVES ✔ A TV sequel to the suspense classic. 95m. DIR: Robert Fuest. CAST: Arthur Hill, Don Johnson, Sharon Gless, Mason Adams, Audra Lindley. 1980

REVENGE OF THE TEENAGE VIXENS FROM OUTER SPACE ✔ This attempt to re-create the corny invader films of the 1950s nearly succeeds, but why bother? This time four hot chicks from outer space start hitting on high-school boys, so the boys' girlfriends decide to take the vixens on. Not rated. 83m. DIR: Jeff Ferrell. CAST: Lisa Schwedop, Howard Scott, Amy Crumpacker, Sterling Ramberg. 1985

REVENGE OF THE ZOMBIES ★★1/2 As soon as the Hollywood back-lot native walks across the foggy bog in baggy underwear and begins to wail "Whoooooo," you know this is going to be one of those films. And it sure is, with mad scientist John Carradine, his zombie wife Veda Ann Borg (in her best role), do-gooders Gale Storm and Robert Lowery, and "feets do yo' stuff" Mantan Moreland aiding escaping zombies and Nazis in this low-budget howler. B&W; 61m. DIR: Steve Sekely. CAST: John Carradine, Robert Lowery, Gale Storm, Veda Ann Borg, Mantan Moreland, Bob Steele. 1943

REVERSAL OF FORTUNE ★★★★ This absorbing drama is fueled by Ron Silver's portrayal of Alan Dershowitz, the fiercely driven Harvard law professor who accepted the challenge of defending the unloved and icily aristocratic Claus Von Bulow (rendered here with aloof arrogance by Oscar-winner Jeremy Irons). Glenn Close, as Sunny Von Bulow, contributes acerbic voice-over narration from her comatose state in a hospital bed. Rated R for language. 111m. DIR: Barbet Schroeder. CAST: Glenn Close, Jeremy Irons, Ron Silver, Annabella Sciorra, Uta Hagen. 1990

REVOLT OF JOB, THE ★★★★ In this moving account of the Holocaust in rural Hungary, an old Jewish couple awaiting the inevitable Nazi takeover adopt a gentile orphan boy to survive them. Nominated for best foreign-language film in 1983s Academy Awards. In Hungarian with English subtitles. No rating. 97m. DIR: Imre Gyongyossy. CAST: Fereno Zenthe, Hedi Tenessy. 1983

REVOLT OF THE ZOMBIES ★★ Following the unexpected success of their independently produced *White Zombie* in 1932, brothers Edward and Victor Halperin found themselves making another zombie movie in 1936. Lacking the style and imagination of their earlier effort, this quasi-supernatural story involves the use of a stupor-inducing potion that turns Cambodian troops into dull-eyed slaves. For curiosity seekers only. B&W; 65m. DIR: Victor Halperin. CAST: Dean Jagger, Roy D'Arcy, Dorothy Stone, George Cleveland. 1936 DVD

REVOLUTION ★★ Director Hugh Hudson must have had good intentions going into this project, examining what it might have been like to be involved in the American Revolution. Unfortunately, his actors are so miscast and the script so ragged that Hudson's project stalls almost before it gets started. Rated R. 125m. DIR: Hugh Hudson. CAST: Al Pacino, Nastassja Kinski, Donald Sutherland. 1986

REVOLVER ★★1/2 Robert Urich is fine as a secret service agent who's felled by a bullet, paralyzed and must come to accept his new life in a wheelchair if he is to track down the gangster who put him there. Made-for-TV action entry is most involving during Urich's struggles to adapt. 93m. DIR: Gary Nelson. CAST: Robert Urich, Dakin Matthews, Steven Williams. 1992

RHAPSODY ★★★ A soap opera with classical music background. Elizabeth Taylor plays a woman involved with a violinist and a pianist. They take out their frustration with flamboyant concerts. 115m. DIR: Charles Vidor. CAST: Elizabeth Taylor, Vittorio Gassman, John Ericson, Louis Calhern, Michael Chekhov. 1954

RHAPSODY IN AUGUST ★★★ In another screen poem not unlike his *Dreams*, Japanese director Akira Kurosawa looks back on the bombing of Nagasaki during World War II through the eyes of four Japanese youngsters. Richard Gere has a brief but effective role. In Japanese with English subtitles. 98m. DIR: Akira Kurosawa. CAST: Sachiko Murase, Hisashi Igawa, Richard Gere. 1992

RHAPSODY IN BLUE ★★★★ Don't for a minute think this is an accurate biography of George Gershwin (played by Robert Alda), but it's a lavish, colorful, and affectionate musical film. Of special interest are the appearances by Paul Whiteman (as himself) and the dubbed-in piano work of Gershwin's friend, Oscar Levant. The "Rhapsody in Blue" and "American in Paris" numbers are standouts. 139m. DIR: Irving Rapper. CAST: Robert Alda, Alexis Smith, Joan Leslie. 1945

RHINESTONE ♥ A country singer and a New York cabbie. Rated PG for profanity, sexual innuendo, and violence. 111m. DIR: Bob Clark. CAST: Sylvester Stallone, Dolly Parton, Richard Farnsworth, Ron Leibman. 1984

RHODES ★★★1/2 Exquisite period detail and a fine performance from Martin Shaw elevate this historical saga mired in controversy. Shaw plays Cecil Rhodes, the nineteenth-century businessman who used his wealth and success from the African silver mines to help colonize South Africa. Film deftly explores Rhodes's achievements without endorsing them. Made for BBC Television. Not rated; contains violence. 336m. DIR: David Drury. CAST: Martin Shaw, Frances Barber, Joe Shaw, Patrick Shai. 1996

RHODES OF AFRICA (RHODES) ★★★ The annexation and assimilation of a culture and people for material gain is not a plot that could sell a film today, but flagrant exploitation of the wealth of South Africa is still timely. Location photography, a good cast, and a standout performance by Walter Huston as the visionary opportunist whose dreams of empire are barely blunted by his philanthropic efforts make this film palatable to modern audiences. B&W; 89m. DIR: Berthold Viertel. CAST: Walter Huston, Oscar Homolka, Basil Sydney, Peggy Ashcroft, Bernard Lee. 1936

RHYTHM ON THE RANGE ★★★1/2 Der Bingle's rendition of "I'm an Old Cowhand" and "Empty Saddles" are enough to make this musical Western work. Bing Crosby plays a dude-ranch owner who helps an heiress dodge the wedding her father engineered for her. B&W; 85m. DIR: Norman Taurog. CAST: Bing Crosby, Frances Farmer, Martha Raye, Bob Burns, Lucille Gleason. 1936

RHYTHM ON THE RIVER ★★★1/2 Bing Crosby writes music, Mary Martin writes lyrics. Both are secret "ghost" partners of Basil Rathbone, who joins their works and reaps the profit and glory. Lots of fun in this easygoing musical comedy. The song "Only Forever" was Oscar nominated. B&W; 94m. DIR: Victor Schertzinger. CAST: Bing Crosby, Mary Martin, Basil Rathbone, Oscar Levant, Charley Grapewin, William Frawley, Jeanne Cagney. 1940

RICH AND FAMOUS ★★★★ Jacqueline Bisset and Candice Bergen star in this warm, witty, and involving chronicle of the ups, downs, joys, and heartbreak experienced by two friends during a twenty-year relationship. Hollywood great George Cukor directed in his inimitable style. Rated R because of profanity and sex. 117m. DIR: George Cukor. CAST: Jacqueline Bisset, Candice Bergen, David Selby, Hart Bochner, Steven Hill, Meg Ryan, Matt Lattanzi, Michael Brandon. 1981

RICH AND STRANGE ★★1/2 This quirky little drama from Alfred Hitchcock concerns a bickering couple (Henry Kendall and Joan Barry) who come into money, take a world cruise, and suffer through a few minor adventures. The domestic squabbling, which forms the story's only true conflict, is far from Hitchcock's forte; this probably will be of interest only to the director's devotees. Not rated; suitable for family viewing. B&W; 83m. DIR: Alfred Hitchcock. CAST: Henry Kendall, Joan Barry, Percy Marmont. 1932 DVD

RICH GIRL ★★★ Jill Schoelen is the title character who strikes out on her own as a waitress in a nightclub. The best rich-girl-falls-in-love-with-a-guy-from-the-wrong-side-of-the-tracks film since Dirty Dancing. Rated R for profanity and mild violence. 96m. DIR: Joel Bender. CAST: Jill Schoelen, Don Michael Paul, Sean Kanan, Ron Karabatsos, Paul Gleason, Willie Dixon. 1991

RICH IN LOVE ★★★★ Kathryn Erbe comes home from high school one day to find a note from her mother (Jill Clayburgh) to her father (Albert Finney) that says she has gone off "to start a second life." Skillful portrait of an American family crumbling from its core. Thought-provoking and insightful, it's a real gem. Rated PG-13 for profanity and nudity. 105m. DIR: Bruce Beresford. CAST: Albert Finney, Jill Clayburgh, Kathryn Erbe, Kyle MacLachlan, Piper Laurie, Ethan Hawke, Suzy Amis, Alfre Woodard. 1993

RICH KIDS ★★ A poor screenplay plagues this movie about two kids going through puberty. A great cast helps. Also, there is an unforgettable heartfelt moment between mother and daughter (Kathryn Walker and Trini Alvarado). Rated PG for language. 97m. DIR: Robert M. Young. CAST: Trini Alvarado, Jeremy Levy, John Lithgow, Kathryn Walker, Terry Kiser, Paul Dooley. 1979

RICH LITTLE—ONE'S A CROWD ★★1/2 Rich Little is both host and entire cast in a sort of "Greatest Hits" video album. Little is, of course, very good at his craft, but his self-written material is not always the best, and his unique talent wears a little thin after an hour or so. Not rated, but with mild profanity. 86m. DIR: Thomas E. Engel. CAST: Rich Little. 1988

RICH LITTLE'S LITTLE SCAMS ON GOLF ★★ Rich Little's talents are wasted in this compendium of ways to cheat at golf. Extremely boring. Not rated. 44m. DIR: Kimberlie Chambers. CAST: Rich Little. 1991

RICH MAN'S WIFE, THE ♥ This trashy, cruel-humored thriller is about an unhappy woman who spills her guts to a squabbling detective duo after becoming the primary suspect in the murder of her unfaithful, alcoholic husband. Rated R for violence, language, and sex. 94m. DIR: Amy Holden Jones. CAST: Halle Berry, Christopher McDonald, Peter Greene, Clive Owen, Clea Lewis. 1996 DVD

RICH, YOUNG AND PRETTY ★★ A slim excuse for a movie without glossy production numbers to back up the casting of Jane Powell and Vic Damone in the leading roles. Powell plays an American-raised daughter of French Danielle Darrieux. She goes to Paris to meet her mother and gets involved in romantic dalliances. 95m. DIR: Norman Taurog. CAST: Jane Powell, Vic Damone, Danielle Darrieux, Fernando

Lamas, Wendell Corey, Una Merkel, Hans Conried, Richard Anderson. 1951

RICHARD III (1955) ★★★★ Once again, as in *Henry V* and *Hamlet*, England's foremost player displays his near-matchless acting and directing skills in bringing Shakespeare to life on film. His royal crookback usurper is beautifully malevolent, a completely intriguing, smiling villain. The film fascinates from first to last. 161m. **DIR:** Laurence Olivier. **CAST:** Laurence Olivier, Ralph Richardson, John Gielgud, Claire Bloom. 1955

RICHARD III (1995) ★★★ Shakespeare's melodrama of treachery and murder during the War of the Roses is transplanted to the 1930s, with evil King Richard portrayed as a jackbooted fascist. The concept is intriguing, but it takes over the production and shoves Shakespeare into the background. Acting is generally good. Rated R for violence. 107m. **DIR:** Richard Loncraine. **CAST:** Ian McKellen, Annette Bening, Kristin Scott Thomas, Maggie Smith, Robert Downey Jr., Jim Broadbent. 1995 DVD

RICHARD'S THINGS ★★ Gloomy drama about a widow who gets seduced by her late husband's girlfriend. Liv Ullmann plays the patsy as if she were on depressants. 104m. **DIR:** Anthony Harvey. **CAST:** Liv Ullmann, Amanda Redman, David Markham. 1980

RICHIE RICH ★★★ Surprisingly entertaining bigscreen adaptation of the comic-book character dubbed "the richest boy in the world," who just wants to be like other kids. British actor Jonathan Hyde steals the film as the faithful and highly resourceful gentleman's gentleman. Rated PG. 94m. **DIR:** Donald Petrie. **CAST:** Macaulay Culkin, John Larroquette, Edward Herrmann, Jonathan Hyde, Christine Ebersole. 1994

RICOCHET ★★★1/2 A rookie cop rises to the position of deputy district attorney after capturing a heartless killer. This is a taut, action-packed crime-drama that is elevated above others in its genre by the acting. Rated R for violence, profanity, and nudity. 105m. **DIR:** Russell Mulcahy. **CAST:** Denzel Washington, John Lithgow, Ice T, Kevin Pollak, Lindsay Wagner, Josh Evans. 1991

RIDDLE OF THE SANDS ★★★★ Based on the spy novel by Erskine Childers, this is the story of two young Englishmen (Michael York, Simon Mac-Corkindale) who set sail on a holiday just prior to World War I and stumble upon political intrigue and adventure in the North Sea. The result is an absorbing adventure film. Rated PG for slight violence and profanity. 102m. **DIR:** Tony Maylam. **CAST:** Michael York, Jenny Agutter, Simon MacCorkindale. 1984

RIDE 🎬 A motley bunch of Harlem youths takes off in a decrepit bus for Florida, to appear in a rap star's music video. Sloppy, amateurish, and teeming with offensive racial stereotypes, the film is hopeless—even the beat of the hip-hop soundtrack is boring. Rated R for nonstop profanity. 90m. **DIR:** Millicent Shelton. **CAST:** Malik Yoba, Melissa DeSousa, Fredro Starr, John Witherspoon, Sticky Fingaz. 1998

RIDE A WILD PONY ★★★ This entertaining Disney film is the tale of a horse and the two children who want to own him, a poor boy and a rich girl with polio.

The setting is Australia. Rated G. 86m. **DIR:** Don Chaffey. **CAST:** Michael Craig, John Meillon. 1976

RIDE BEYOND VENGEANCE ★★ A buffalo hunter, branded by three badmen, sets out for revenge. A great cast, savage brutality, and sexual innuendo aren't able to save this adult Western from being a waste of time. 100m. **DIR:** Bernard McEveety. **CAST:** Chuck Connors, Michael Rennie, Kathryn Hays, Gary Merrill, Claude Akins, Gloria Grahame, Bill Bixby, Joan Blondell, James MacArthur, Ruth Warrick, Arthur O'-Connell. 1966

RIDE 'EM COWBOY ★★★ Two hot-dog vendors find themselves in the wild West working on a dude ranch. Some funny bits, a good cast, and top musical numbers and talent (including Ella Fitzgerald) make this Abbott and Costello comedy one of the best in the series. B&W; 84m. **DIR:** Arthur Lubin. **CAST:** Bud Abbott, Lou Costello, Anne Gwynne, Dick Foran, Johnny Mack Brown, Samuel S. Hinds, Douglass Dumbrille. 1942

RIDE 'EM COWGIRL ★★ Singing cowgirl Dorothy Page and her horse Snowy battle the bad guys who bilked her father out of $5,000. The concept seems designed to prove that a woman can rope, ride, and yodel as well as any cowboy. Well, in this case, they were wrong. 52m. **DIR:** Samuel Diege. **CAST:** Dorothy Page, Milton Frome, Vince Barnett. 1939

RIDE HIM COWBOY ★★1/2 Thanks to the unfunny antics of would-be comic relief Harry Gribbon and the belief-stretching feats of Duke, the miracle horse, John Wayne's first B Western for Warner Bros. has much less to recommend it than his later outings. Even the plot, in which a town is terrorized by a masked rider and his gang, is more melodramatic and simplistic than usual. B&W; 56m. **DIR:** Fred Allen. **CAST:** John Wayne, Ruth Hall, Henry B. Walthall, Otis Harlan, Harry Gribbon, Frank Hagney, Lafe McKee. 1932

RIDE IN THE WHIRLWIND 🎬 Throwaway Western with good cast goes nowhere in the muddled story of three riders wrongfully pursued by an unrelenting posse. 83m. **DIR:** Monte Hellman. **CAST:** Jack Nicholson, Cameron Mitchell, Millie Perkins, Harry Dean Stanton, Rupert Crosse. 1965

RIDE LONESOME ★★★★1/2 Lawman Randolph Scott competes with two bounty hunters for possession of outlaw James Best. Well written by Burt Kennedy; superbly acted under the able direction of Budd Boetticher, who directed Scott in some of the best Westerns made in the 1950s. 73m. **DIR:** Budd Boetticher. **CAST:** Randolph Scott, Pernell Roberts, Karen Steele, Lee Van Cleef, James Coburn, James Best. 1959

RIDE, RANGER, RIDE ★★1/2 Texas Ranger Gene Autry works undercover to stop Comanches from looting ammunition-laden wagon trains. Film debut of Max Terhune, who soon starred in Three Mesquiteer Westerns. B&W; 54m. **DIR:** Joseph Kane. **CAST:** Gene Autry, Smiley Burnette, Kay Hughes, Monte Blue, Max Terhune. 1936

RIDE THE HIGH COUNTRY ★★★★1/2 Joel McCrea and Randolph Scott play two old-time gunslingers who team up to guard a gold shipment. McCrea just wants to do a good job, but Scott cares nothing for noble purpose and tries to steal the gold. From that point on, they are friends no longer. The result is a picture so good that McCrea and Scott decided to retire after making it—both wanted to go out with a winner. 94m. **DIR:** Sam Peckinpah. **CAST:** Joel McCrea, Randolph Scott, Warren Oates, R. G. Armstrong, Mariette Hartley, John Anderson, James Drury, L. Q. Jones, Edgar Buchanan. **1962**

RIDE THE MAN DOWN ★★ A Western shot in the traditional manner. A ranch manager fights to keep the property out of the greedy hands of land grabbers. 90m. **DIR:** Joseph Kane. **CAST:** Brian Donlevy, Rod Cameron, Ella Raines, Chill Wills, Jack LaRue. **1952**

RIDE THE WILD SURF ★★ Though shot in Hawaii, this teens-on-the-beach musical contains innumerable shots of Fabian and Tab Hunter perched in front of back-projection screens of surfing footage, while someone off-camera sprays a hose at them. Jan and Dean sing the title tune. Overall, pretty feeble. 101m. **DIR:** Don Taylor. **CAST:** Fabian, Tab Hunter, Barbara Eden, Shelley Fabares. **1964**

RIDER FROM TUCSON ★★★ Tim Holt is a rodeo star who aids an old friend whose gold strike is the target of claim jumpers. B&W; 60m. **DIR:** Lesley Selander. **CAST:** Tim Holt, Richard Martin, Elaine Riley, Douglas Fowley, Veda Ann Borg, Robert Shayne. **1950**

RIDER ON THE RAIN ★★★★ Charles Bronson gives one of his finest screen performances in this gripping, Hitchcock-style thriller made in France. The story deals with the plight of a woman (Marlene Jobert) who kills an unhinged rapist and dumps his body into the sea. She is soon pursued by a mysterious American (Bronson). Thus begins a fascinating game of cat and mouse. Rated R for violence. 115m. **DIR:** René Clement. **CAST:** Charles Bronson, Marlene Jobert, Jill Ireland. **1970**

RIDERS FOR JUSTICE ★★★ Late-in-the-run Three Mesquiteers entry benefits from no-nonsense direction from John English, a relatively straightforward story, and the charisma of Western-film veterans Tom Tyler and Bob Steele. This time, our heroes are out to foil a gang of bank robbers who are implicating innocent men. Retitled from *Westward Ho* for release to television so as not to conflict with the John Wayne Western of the same name. B&W; 56m. **DIR:** John English. **CAST:** Tom Tyler, Bob Steele, Rufe Davis, Evelyn Brent, Donald Curtis, Kenne Duncan. **1942**

RIDERS OF DEATH VALLEY ★★★1/2 Dick Foran and his pals Buck Jones and Leo Carrillo head a group of men organized to police the mining districts and to fight it out with the thieves and murderers that flocked to the gold claims. A fine serial. B&W; 15 chapters. **DIR:** Ford Beebe, Ray Taylor. **CAST:** Dick Foran, Buck Jones, Leo Carrillo, Charles Bickford, Lon Chaney Jr., Noah Beery Jr., Guinn Williams, Monte Blue, Glenn Strange. **1941**

RIDERS OF DESTINY ★★★ The earliest low, low-budget John Wayne B Western available on tape, this casts an extremely young-looking Duke as Singin' Sandy, an undercover agent out to help ranchers regain their water rights. Fun for fans of the star. B&W; 50m. **DIR:** Robert N. Bradbury. **CAST:** John Wayne, Ce-

cilia Parker, George "Gabby" Hayes, Forrest Taylor, Al St. John, Heinie Conklin, Earl Dwire. **1933 DVD**

RIDERS OF THE BLACK HILLS ★★★ Just before the richest horse race of the year, an illustrious Thoroughbred is kidnapped in a daring train robbery. The Three Mesquiteers ride to the rescue. B&W; 54m. **DIR:** George Sherman. **CAST:** Robert Livingston, Ray "Crash" Corrigan, Max Terhune. **1938**

RIDERS OF THE PURPLE SAGE ★★★1/2 When a female rancher and her two ranch hands are threatened by the man who intends to marry her, a mysterious stranger rides to the rescue. Unlike previous adaptations of Zane Grey's story, this TNT production is dark and brooding, with excellent performances by Ed Harris and Amy Madigan in a sometimes confusing story of justice, revenge, and dark secrets. Made for TV. 96m. **DIR:** Charles Haid. **CAST:** Ed Harris, Amy Madigan, Henry Thomas, G. D. Spradlin, Tom Bower, Robin Tunney, Norbert Weisser. **1996**

RIDERS OF THE RIO GRANDE ★★★★ The last in an eight-year string of Three Mesquiteers Westerns is one of the best. Involved plot line has the Mesquiteers mistaken for the Cherokee Boys, a trio of outlaws. Plenty of action and a tongue-in-cheek story that often spoofs the genre without belittling it. B&W; 55m. **DIR:** Howard Bretherton. **CAST:** Bob Steele, Tom Tyler, Jimmie Dodd, Edward Van Sloan, Rick Vallin, Roy Barcroft, Charles King. **1943**

RIDERS OF THE ROCKIES ★★1/2 Entertaining Tex Ritter Western finds the two-fisted singer joining a gang of rustlers in order to get the goods on them. Silent comedian Snub Pollard plays his comic sidekick. One of Ritter's best Westerns. B&W; 56m. **DIR:** Robert N. Bradbury. **CAST:** Tex Ritter, Louise Stanley, Charles King, Snub Pollard, Yakima Canutt. **1937**

RIDERS OF THE STORM ♥ Dennis Hopper as the captain of an ancient B-29 that has been circling the country for fifteen years to broadcast an illegal television network. Rated R for nudity. 92m. **DIR:** Maurice Phillips. **CAST:** Dennis Hopper, Michael J. Pollard, Eugene Lipinski. **1987**

RIDERS OF THE TIMBERLINE ★★1/2 Hopalong Cassidy and company head for the hills to help an old friend whose timber business is being sabotaged. Ropin' and ridin', fightin' and shootin'. B&W; 54m. **DIR:** Lesley Selander. **CAST:** William Boyd, Brad King, Andy Clyde, J. Farrell MacDonald, Eleanor Stewart, Tom Tyler, Victor Jory. **1941**

RIDERS OF THE WHISTLING PINES ★★★1/2 Framed as a timberland killer and cattle poisoner, Gene Autry fights to prove his innocence and save the woodlands for the Forestry Department. B&W; 70m. **DIR:** John English. **CAST:** Gene Autry, Patricia White, Jimmy Lloyd, Clayton Moore. **1949**

RIDERS OF THE WHISTLING SKULL ★★★ The Three Mesquiteers gallop into one of their best adventures. They brave Indians and ghostly goings-on to find a fabled lost city and its fabulous treasure. An eerie story, and the easy camaraderie of the three saddle pals makes this outdoor adventure one of the most popular in the series. B&W; 58m. **DIR:** Mack V. Wright. **CAST:** Robert Livingston, Ray "Crash" Corrigan, Max Terhune, Mary Russell, Yakima Canutt, C. Montague Shaw, Chief Thundercloud. **1937**

RIDICULE ★★★ A man in seventeenth-century France learns that a sharp wit and a quick tongue are perhaps his most important tools of survival in this daringly original (sometimes too much so) film. Rated R for nudity, sexual situations, and violence. 102m. **DIR:** Patrice Leconte. **CAST:** Fanny Ardant, Charles Berling, Bernard Guirardeau, Jean Rochefort. **1996**

RIDING BEAN ★★★★ Japanese animation. Highly amusing tale set in (of all places) Chicago and involving a special courier named Bean, who, with the aid of a supercar and female assistant, takes on bad guys and a bumbling police force. In Japanese with English subtitles. Not rated with violence, profanity, and illustrated nudity. 46m. **DIR:** Tanaka Masahiro, Kamijoo Osamu, Oohira Hiroya, Okuda Tadashi. **1989**

RIDING HIGH ★★1/2 A Bing Crosby musical with a plot, this film revolves around a racehorse whose owner risks his marriage on the horse and loses both. Pleasant Crosby tunes. A human-interest musical remake of the Depression-era classic, *Broadway Bill.* B&W; 112m. **DIR:** Frank Capra. **CAST:** Bing Crosby, Coleen Gray, Charles Bickford, Frances Gifford, Oliver Hardy, Ward Bond, Joe Frisco, Percy Kilbride, William Demarest. **1950**

RIDING ON AIR ★★★ Lots of thrills and laughs in this topically dated comedy adventure about two small-town newspaper correspondents vying for the same girl and the scoop on a story. Joe E. Brown is, as always, warm, winning, and wholesome. B&W; 58m. **DIR:** Edward Sedgwick. **CAST:** Joe E. Brown, Florence Rice, Vinton Haworth, Guy Kibbee. **1937**

RIDING THE EDGE ★★ Formulaic adventure flick set in the Middle East—a ground attempt at *Iron Eagle.* A man has been captured by terrorists, so what do you send in? A trained professional? Nonsense. Send in his teenage son. Rated PG-13. 100m. **DIR:** James Fargo. **CAST:** Peter Haskell, Raphael Sbarge, Catherine Mary Stewart. **1990**

RIDING TORNADO, THE ★★★ A strong series entry for Tim McCoy. He's a wandering cowboy hired by rancher Shirley Grey, whose cattle are being systematically stolen. Of course, our hero sets things right. B&W; 64m. **DIR:** D. Ross Lederman. **CAST:** Tim McCoy, Shirley Grey. **1932**

RIDING WITH DEATH ★★ Compilation of two hourlong shows from *The Gemini Man* television series, edited together by some mysterious and unconvincing process. Ben Murphy plays a man who, through a scientific accident, can render himself invisible for short bursts of time. Real comic-book stuff. 97m. **DIR:** Alan J. Levi, Don McDougall. **CAST:** Ben Murphy, Katherine Crawford, Richard Dysart, William Sylvester, Andrew Prine, Alan Oppenheimer, Don Galloway. **1976**

RIFFRAFF (1936) ★★ The give-and-take banter between Spencer Tracy and Jean Harlow is all that holds together this muddled melodrama about the relationship of two tough-as-nails waterfront workers. A confusing script and an over-abundance of characters who are never knit into the central story. B&W; 89m. **DIR:** J. Walter Ruben. **CAST:** Spencer Tracy, Jean Harlow, Una Merkel, Joseph Calleia. **1936**

RIFFRAFF (1947) ★★1/2 Two-fisted private eye Pat O'Brien is hired as a bodyguard by a man with a chart to some rich South American oil fields, but when O'Brien signs on, he doesn't know that his employer is a killer and some heavy competition is gunning for them. This race-for-riches programmer quickly bogs down and runs out of pep. B&W; 80m. **DIR:** Ted Tetzlaff. **CAST:** Pat O'Brien, Walter Slezak, Anne Jeffreys, Percy Kilbride, Jerome Cowan. **1947**

RIFF-RAFF (1992) ★★★★ The fringes of British society are explored in this documentary-like drama about homeless men doing laborer work at a construction site. *Riff-Raff* is an excellent example of independent filmmaking. Naturalistic humor offsets the inherent social commentary as director Ken Loach helps his cast create unforgettable characters. Not rated, the film has profanity, nudity, suggested sex, and violence. 96m. **DIR:** Kenneth Loach. **CAST:** Robert Carlyle, Emer McCourt, Richard Belgrave, Jimmy Coleman, George Moss, Ricky Tomlinson. **1993**

RIFIFI ★★★★ A milestone that begat a continuing breed of films hinging on the big, carefully planned robbery that falls apart—usually just as the criminals and the audience are convinced of success. This one is sure to have you pumping adrenaline from start to finish, especially during the brilliant twenty-minute silent robbery sequence that is its selling point, and the falling out of thieves that follows. B&W; 115m. **DIR:** Jules Dassin. **CAST:** Jean Servais, Carl Mohner, Perlo Vita, Robert Manuel, Magali Noel. **1955**

RIFLEMAN, THE (TV SERIES) ★★★1/2 Created by Sam Peckinpah, this sometimes brutal, sometimes touching Western series starred brawny Chuck Connors as the rifle-toting rancher, Lucas McCain. A widower, McCain raises his young son, Mark (Johnny Crawford), as best he can, while frequently being called upon by Marshal Micah Torrance (Paul Fix) to help keep the peace in the town of Northfork, New Mexico. The early episodes are the best. B&W; 30m. **DIR:** Various. **CAST:** Chuck Connors, Johnny Crawford, Paul Fix, Joan Taylor, Patricia Blair. **1958–1963**

RIGHT HAND MAN, THE ❤ A dying, disabled, nobleman's repressed love for his doctor's daughter. Rated R for nudity and suggested sex. 101m. **DIR:** Di Drew. **CAST:** Rupert Everett, Hugo Weaving, Arthur Dignam, Jennifer Claire. **1987**

RIGHT OF WAY ★★★★ This made-for-cable work deals with a rather unusual decision made by an old married couple, (Bette Davis and James Stewart) who have decided to commit suicide. Thus begins a battle between daughter (Melinda Dillon) and parents. The result is a surprisingly gripping character study. 106m. **DIR:** George Schaefer. **CAST:** James Stewart, Bette Davis, Melinda Dillon, Priscilla Morrill, John Harkins. **1983**

RIGHT STUFF, THE ★★★★★ From Tom Wolfe's bestseller about the early years of the American space program, this epic screen tribute examines the men (both test pilots and astronauts) who "pushed the outside of the envelope," and the women who watched and waited while the world watched them. Rated PG for profanity. 193m. **DIR:**

Phil Kaufman. **CAST:** Sam Shepard, Scott Glenn, Ed Harris, Dennis Quaid, Barbara Hershey, Fred Ward, Kim Stanley, Veronica Cartwright, Pamela Reed, Donald Moffat, Levon Helm, Scott Wilson, Jeff Goldblum, Harry Shearer. **1983 DVD**

RIGHT TO REMAIN SILENT, THE ★★★1/2 Mark Fauser and Brent Briscoe's clever stage play turns into an equally intriguing drama, focusing on a new police recruit surviving her first graveyard-shift encounters with a half-dozen villains and victims. Their compelling stories are related via flashback and some work better than others, but each tale is well told by the impressive ensemble cast. Rated R for profanity, violence, and rape. 96m. **DIR:** Hubert de la Bouillerie. **CAST:** Lea Thompson, Robert Loggia, LL Cool J, Patrick Dempsey, Amanda Plummer, Carl Reiner, Judge Reinhold, Colleen Camp, Fisher Stevens, Christopher Lloyd, Laura San Giacomo. **1995**

RIKISHA-MAN ★★★★ In turn-of-the-century Japan, an uneducated rickshaw puller looks out for a boy whose father has died. Rewarding human story with a typically strong performance by Toshiro Mifune. In Japanese with English subtitles. 105m. **DIR:** Hiroshi Inagaki. **CAST:** Toshiro Mifune. **1958**

RIKKI AND PETE ★★★ An offbeat comedy from Australia. A geologist and her crazy brother abandon the city for the Australian outback. This film is a great crash course in living your own life. Highly engaging! Rated R for nudity and language. 101m. **DIR:** Nadia Tass. **CAST:** Nina Landis, Stephen Kearny, Bruce Spence, Bruno Lawrence. **1988**

RIKYU ★★★★ This poignant film, which won a special jury award at the Cannes Film Festival, explores the struggle between art and power in sixteenth-century Japan. The central character, Sen-no Rikyu, refined the art of the tea ceremony, lifting it to aesthetic, spiritual heights. A beautifully crafted character study with fine ensemble acting. In Japanese with English subtitles. Not rated. 116m. **DIR:** Hiroshi Teshigahara. **CAST:** Rentaro Mikuni, Tsutomu Yamazaki. **1990 DVD**

RIM OF THE CANYON ★★★1/2 Gene Autry in a dual role as a marshal who corrals a gang of stagecoach bandits and as his son who faces the same gang twenty years later in a ghost town showdown. Supernatural overtones give this one a different twist. B&W; 70m. **DIR:** John English. **CAST:** Gene Autry, Nan Leslie, Jock Mahoney, Alan Hale Jr., Thurston Hall. **1949**

RIMFIRE ★★★ Better-than-average B Western has federal agent James Millican looking for stolen gold. He's aided in his search by the ghost of a gambler who was unjustly hanged for cheating! 64m. **DIR:** B. Reeves "Breezy" Eason. **CAST:** James Millican, Mary Beth Hughes, Reed Hadley, Henry Hull, Fuzzy Knight, Jason Robards Sr., Glenn Strange. **1949**

RING, THE ★★ Long before Sylvester Stallone turned boxing into a filmic event, Alfred Hitchcock toyed with the sports medium in this unremarkable melodrama. The story is little more than a love triangle between two boxing champions (Carl Brisson and Ian Hunter) and the woman loved by both (Lillian Hall-Davies). Not rated; suitable for family viewing. B&W; 73m. **DIR:** Alfred Hitchcock. **CAST:** Carl Brisson, Lillian Hall-Davies, Ian Hunter. **1927 DVD**

RING OF BRIGHT WATER ★★★★ The stars of *Born Free* return for this delightful story of a secluded writer and his pet otter. The story has some odd quirks that adults will appreciate, but this underrated film also has terrific production values and an utterly irresistible animal star. Not rated. 107m. **DIR:** Jack Couffer. **CAST:** Bill Travers, Virginia McKenna. **1969**

RING OF FIRE 3: LION STRIKE ★★★ Kick-boxing physician Johnny Wu (Don Wilson) is forced back into action when he comes into possession of a computer disk belonging to international gangsters. Rated R for violence and profanity. 90m. **DIR:** Rick Jacobson. **CAST:** Don "The Dragon" Wilson, Bobbie Phillips. **1995**

RING OF SCORPIO ★★1/2 Three women seek revenge on the drug smugglers who used them as pawns during their college days. The women's story is exciting, but the flashbacks are ineffective. Made for cable. 120m. **DIR:** Ian Barry. **CAST:** Catherine Oxenberg, Jack Scalia, Caroline Goodall. **1991**

RING OF STEEL ★★★ An Olympic fencer accidently kills a man during a regional tournament. Expelled from the sport, he is hired by an illicit nightclub that stages duels for money. He soon learns that he either fights to the death or he and his girlfriend will be killed. Good swashbuckling action, fast-paced direction, humor, and style make for an entertaining film. Rated R for simulated sex, nudity, violence, and profanity. 94m. **DIR:** David Frost. **CAST:** Joe Don Baker, Carol Alt, Richard Chapin, Gary Kasper, Darlene Vogel. **1994**

RING OF THE MUSKETEER ★★1/2 In one of those "what must they have been thinking?" scenarios, David Hasselhoff, Alison Doody, Thomas Gottschalk, and Cheech Marin play great-great-great descendants of the original Musketeers, now fighting for decency in modern times. Their latest assignment: rescuing a boy from a mob figure. It may be more than they can handle, but they'll have fun trying. Rated PG-13 for language. 86m. **DIR:** John Paragon. **CAST:** David Hasselhoff, Richard "Cheech" Marin, Corbin Bernsen, Alison Doody, Thomas Gottschalk, John Rhys-Davies. **1993**

RINGMASTER 💔 This fictional valentine to Jerry Springer's sleazy TV show creeps backstage to uncover—*la duh*—more sleaze. Rated R for sexual content, profanity, and nudity. 90m. **DIR:** Neil Abramson. **CAST:** Jerry Springer, Jaimie Pressly, Molly Hagan, William McNamara, Wendy Raquel Robinson, Michael Jai Wite, Michael Dudikoff, Dawn Maxey, Ashely Holbrook. **1998 DVD**

RIO BRAVO ★★★★1/2 A super-Western, with John Wayne, Walter Brennan, Ward Bond, Ricky Nelson (aping Montgomery Clift's performance in *Red River*), and the scene-stealing Dean Martin taking on cattle baron John Russell, who's out to get his kill-crazy brother (Claude Akins) out of jail. 141m. **DIR:** Howard Hawks. **CAST:** John Wayne, Walter Brennan, Ward Bond, Ricky Nelson, Dean Martin, John Russell, Claude Akins, Angie Dickinson, Bob Steele. **1959**

RIO CONCHOS ★★★ Rip-roaring Western action ignites this briskly paced yarn set in post–Civil War Texas. Richard Boone and his pals go undercover to get the goods on outlaws responsible for stealing a shipment of rifles. Boone gives a wry performance. 107m. DIR: Gordon Douglas. CAST: Richard Boone, Stuart Whitman, Anthony Franciosa, Edmond O'Brien, Jim Brown. 1964

RIO DIABLO ★★1/2 Country singers ride the TV-movie West again in this middling tale of a hard-boiled bounty hunter reluctantly helping a young man track down the outlaws who kidnapped his bride. 97m. DIR: Rod Hardy. CAST: Kenny Rogers, Travis Tritt, Naomi Judd, Stacy Keach, Brion James, Bruce Greenwood, Laura Harring, Michael G. Hagerty. 1993

RIO GRANDE ★★★ The last entry in director John Ford's celebrated cavalry trilogy (which also includes *Fort Apache* and *She Wore a Yellow Ribbon*), this stars John Wayne as a company commander coping with renegade Indians and a willful wife (Maureen O'Hara), who wants to take their soldier son (Claude Jarman Jr.) home. B&W; 105m. DIR: John Ford. CAST: John Wayne, Maureen O'Hara, Claude Jarman Jr., Ben Johnson, Harry Carey Jr., Victor McLaglen, Chill Wills, J. Carrol Naish. 1950 DVD

RIO LOBO ★★★ Neither star John Wayne nor director Howard Hawks was exactly at the peak of his powers when this second reworking of *Rio Bravo* (the first being *El Dorado*) was released. If one adjusts the normally high expectations he or she would have for a Western made by these two giants, *Rio Lobo* is a fun show. Jack Elam is terrific in a delightful supporting role. Rated G. 114m. DIR: Howard Hawks. CAST: John Wayne, Jack Elam, Jorge Rivero, Jennifer O'Neill, Chris Mitchum, Mike Henry. 1970

RIO RITA ★★★ Vintage Bud Abbott and Lou Costello, with routines that somehow seem fresh and familiar at the same time. They stowaway in the trunk of a car thinking it is going to New York and end up at a Texas ranch infested with Nazi spies. B&W; 91m. DIR: S. Sylvan Simon. CAST: Bud Abbott, Lou Costello, Kathryn Grayson, John Carroll, Tom Conway, Barry Nelson. 1942

RIOT (1996) (TV MOVIE) ★★★1/2 Basically an arty examination of the 1991 L.A. riots, this made-for-cable original is composed of four separate but interlocking stories about everyday people. Good performances all around, but a sense of closure for any of these stories is lacking. Rated R for profanity and violence. 120m. DIR: David C. Johnson, Richard Dilello, Galen Yuen, Alex Muñoz. CAST: Mario Van Peebles, Cicely Tyson, Luke Perry, Dante Basco, Mako, Alexis Cruz, Yelba Osorio. 1996

RIOT (1969) ★★1/2 Familiar story of tough cons turning the tables on tough guards, taking over part of a prison in an escape attempt. Violence for violence sake. Filmed at the Arizona State Prison. Rated R. 97m. DIR: Buzz Kulik. CAST: Jim Brown, Gene Hackman, Mike Kellin, Gerald S. O'Loughlin. 1969

RIOT (1996) ★★★ When a British SAS officer (Gary Daniels) tries to rescue an ambassador's daughter taken hostage during a Florida race riot, he learns there's more to the explosive tensions than meets the eye. Solid vehicle for action star Daniels is aided by an odd but intriguing plot. Rated R for violence and profanity. 98m. DIR: Joseph Merhi. CAST: Gary Daniels, Sugar Ray Leonard, Paige Rowland, Charles Napier. 1996

RIOT IN CELL BLOCK ELEVEN ★★★1/2 This taut prison drama with a message depicts an aborted prison escape that ends with the convicts barricaded and demanding to be heard. Made at the height of the "exposé" and true-crime wave in the mid-Fifties, this film avoids the sensational and documentary style of its contemporaries and focuses on the action and the characterizations of the convicts, the prison staff, and the media. B&W; 80m. DIR: Don Siegel. CAST: Neville Brand, Leo Gordon, Emile Meyer, Frank Faylen. 1954

RIPE ★★★ It's hard to tell whether this drama about 14-year-old twin girls who take up with a pair of army workers after their parents are killed is an honest attempt to explore adolescent trauma or merely exploitative. Either way, the film's sexual content is both surprising and shocking. Rated R for profanity and sexual situations. 93m. DIR: Mo Ogrodnik. CAST: Monica Keena, Daisy Eagan, Ron Brice. 1997

RIPPER, THE (1985) 💔 In this poorly filmed modernization of the Jack the Ripper legend, a college professor finds a ring, originally belonging to the nineteenth-century killer. 104m. DIR: Christopher Lewis. CAST: Tom Schreier, Wade Tower. 1985

RIPPER, THE (1997) ★★★ Unremarkable telling of the Jack the Ripper story buoyed by excellent performances by its cast. Rated R for violence. 100m. DIR: Janet Meyers. CAST: Patrick Bergin, Gabrielle Anwar, Michael York. 1997

RIPPER MAN 💔 Ex-cop works in a nightclub as a hypnotist and when the bodies start piling up you know you've seen this all before. Rated R for violence, gore, nudity, and language. 89m. DIR: Phil Sears. CAST: Mike Norris, Timothy Bottoms. 1997

RIPPING YARNS ★★★1/2 Wildly funny series featuring Michael Palin in different roles as he romps through six vignettes that comically parody the social structure and history of the British empire. Originally produced for British TV, this double cassette features "Tomkin's Schooldays," "Escape from Stalag Luft 112B," "Golden Gordon," "The Testing of Eric Olthwaite," "Whinfrey's Last Case," and "The Curse of the Claw." Not rated. 180m. DIR: Jim Franklin, Alan Bell, Terry Hughes. CAST: Michael Palin. 1978

RIPTIDE ★★★ A soap opera about the failings of the rich that was obviously made to help a Depression-era audience feel superior to those who still had money. It holds up because of good acting and directing, not good writing. The bored rich heroine dallies with a former lover while her husband is away. B&W; 90m. DIR: Edmund Goulding. CAST: Norma Shearer, Robert Montgomery, Herbert Marshall, Mrs. Patrick Campbell, Lilyan Tashman, Skeets Gallagher, Arthur Treacher, Ralph Forbes. 1934

RISE AND FALL OF LEGS DIAMOND, THE ★★★1/2 One of the best gangster films, punchily directed and heartily acted by Ray Danton as the self-centered, manipulative low-life who became a Prohibition-era bigshot. Dyan Cannon's debut. 101m. DIR: Budd Boetticher. CAST: Ray Danton, Karen Steele, Elaine Stewart, Jesse White, Warren Oates, Dyan Cannon. 1960

RISE OF LOUIS XIV, THE ★★ Slow-paced docudrama chronicles King Louis XIV's acquisition of power over corrupt French noblemen. He is portrayed as a wise ruler despite his reputation. Lack of action, however, makes this import nearly impossible to sit through. In French with English subtitles. 100m. DIR: Roberto Rossellini. CAST: Jean-Marie Patte, Raymond Jourdan. 1966

RISING SON ★★★1/2 Superb TV drama focuses on an auto-parts plant-manager's life after he is laid off. With a son not wanting to finish college and a wife going back to work against his will to help support the family, Brian Dennehy's character is forced to reevaluate his own life and beliefs. 96m. DIR: John David Coles. CAST: Brian Dennehy, Graham Beckel, Matt Damon, Ving Rhames, Piper Laurie. 1990

RISING SUN ★★★1/2 In attempting to tone down the alleged Japan-bashing in Michael Crichton's novel, director Phil Kaufman delivers a somewhat confusing thriller that succeeds primarily because of the performances. Sean Connery and Wesley Snipes are terrific in what is best viewed as another in the long line of cop/buddy flicks. As such it's a cut above the competition. Rated R for violence, nudity, simulated sex, and profanity. 130m. DIR: Phil Kaufman. CAST: Sean Connery, Wesley Snipes, Harvey Keitel, Cary-Hiroyuki Tagawa, Kevin Anderson, Mako, Ray Wise, Stan Egi, Stan Shaw, Tia Carrere, Steve Buscemi. 1993 DVD

RISKY BUSINESS ★★★★ An ordinarily well-behaved boy (Tom Cruise) goes wild when his parents are on vacation. His troubles begin when a gorgeous hooker (Rebecca DeMornay) who doesn't exactly have a heart of gold makes a house call. It's stylish, funny, and sexy—everything, in fact, that most movies of this kind generally are not. Rated R for nudity, profanity, and suggested sex. 99m. DIR: Paul Brickman. CAST: Tom Cruise, Rebecca DeMornay, Curtis Armstrong, Bronson Pinchot, Raphael Sbarge, Joe Pantoliano, Nicholas Pryor, Richard Masur. 1983 DVD

RITA HAYWORTH: THE LOVE GODDESS ★★1/2 This lifeless attempt to re-create pinup queen Rita Hayworth's exciting life falls short of its goal. Beautiful Lynda Carter as Hayworth, however, keeps the viewer's attention. Made for television. 100m. DIR: James Goldstone. CAST: Lynda Carter, Michael Lerner, John Considine, Alejandro Rey. 1983

RITA, SUE AND BOB TOO ♥ This British flick follows a pair of best friends who lose their virginity to a man whose children they both baby-sit. Rated R for language. 90m. DIR: Alan Clarke. CAST: George Costigan, Siobhan Finneran, Michelle Holmes. 1986

•**RITES OF PASSAGE** ★★★ An aging father and his two sons meet up at the family's cabin in the woods. So do two escaped convicts. So-so storyline is rescued by sharp direction and sharper performances. Rated R for violence and profanity. 94m. DIR: Victor Salva. CAST: Dean Stockwell, Jason Behr, Robert Keith, Jaimz Woolvett, James Remar. 1999 DVD

RITUALS ★★ Several middle-aged men head up to the wilds on a camping trip, only to be stalked by a relentless killer. This cheap rip-off of *Deliverance* offers little in the way of entertainment. Rated R for violence and profanity. 100m. DIR: Peter Carter. CAST: Hal Holbrook, Lawrence Dane, Robin Gammell. 1981

RITZ, THE ★★★★ This film is brimful of belly laughs that will leave you exhausted. After the death of his father-in-law, Jack Weston (as Gaetano Proclo) flees Cleveland. His brother-in-law has put out a contract on him to prevent his inheriting any part of the family garbage business. His escape takes him to New York City and, by accident, a gay hotel called The Ritz. Rated R for profanity. 91m. DIR: Richard Lester. CAST: Jack Weston, Rita Moreno, Jerry Stiller, Kaye Ballard, F. Murray Abraham, Treat Williams. 1976

RIVER, THE (1951) ★★★1/2 Beautiful locations enhance this lyrical drama about English children growing up in Bengal. This well-orchestrated character study is brilliantly directed by cinema master Jean Renoir and is equally blessed with rich color photography by his brother Claude. 99m. DIR: Jean Renoir. CAST: Nora Swinburne, Arthur Shields. 1951

RIVER, THE (1984) ★★★1/2 Following as it does on the heels of two other first-rate farmer films, this work by director Mark Rydell often seems hopelessly unoriginal and, as a result, boring. As with *Country*, it deals with a farming family who must battle a severe storm and foreclosure proceedings. It simply has little new to say. Rated PG for nudity, violence, and profanity. 122m. DIR: Mark Rydell. CAST: Mel Gibson, Sissy Spacek, Scott Glenn. 1984 DVD

RIVER OF DEATH ♥ An adventurer wades his way through hostile Indians, cannibals, river pirates, and Nazis to rescue an archaeologist's daughter. Rated R for violence and profanity. 103m. DIR: Steve Carver. CAST: Michael Dudikoff, Robert Vaughn, Donald Pleasence, Herbert Lom, L. Q. Jones. 1990

RIVER OF DIAMONDS ♥ An adventurer braves villains to seek his fortune on a mysterious island. Rated PG-13 for violence and profanity. 88m. DIR: Robert J. Smawley. CAST: Dack Rambo, Angela O'Neill, Ferdinand Mayne. 1990

RIVER OF NO RETURN ★★★ Rory Calhoun has deserted Marilyn Monroe, believe it or not. She hires Robert Mitchum to track him down. The story line is predictable and sometimes plodding, under Otto Preminger's heavy directorial hand. Nevertheless, Mitchum's quirky strength and the gorgeous color shots of Monroe and western vistas make the film sufficiently entertaining. 91m. DIR: Otto Preminger. CAST: Robert Mitchum, Marilyn Monroe, Rory Calhoun, Tommy Rettig. 1954 DVD

RIVER OF UNREST ★★ Melodrama about the Sinn Fein rebellion in Ireland bears a strong resemblance to John Ford's classic *The Informer*, but there's more emphasis on the love story between Antoinette Cellier and the two men in her life. Good performances by a capable cast help this slow-moving story, which was based on a stage play. B&W; 69m. DIR: Brian Desmond, Walter Summers. CAST: John Lodge, John Loder, Antoinette Cellier, Niall MacGinnis, Clifford Evans. 1937

RIVER PIRATES, THE ★★★ Young Ryan Francis stars as a 12-year-old whose summer vacation in Mississippi during World War II provides the backdrop for a number of adventures. Familiar faces dot the landscape, but the focus is on Francis and his friends as they tackle everything from racial injustice to river pirates. Excellent production values and a genuine sense of adventure make this family film watchable. Rated PG. 108m. **DIR:** Tom G. Robertson. **CAST:** Ryan Francis, Richard Farnsworth, Gennie James, Doug Emerson, Anne Ramsey, Maureen O'Sullivan. 1988

RIVER RAT, THE ★★★1/2 Although essentially the story of the growing love between a long-separated father (Tommy Lee Jones), who has been in prison for thirteen years, and daughter (newcomer Martha Plimpton), this release is much more than a simple tearjerker. Writer-director Tom Rickman has invested his story with a grit and realism that set it apart from similar works. As a result, he's created a powerful, thought-provoking motion picture. Rated R for profanity and violence. 109m. **DIR:** Tom Rickman. **CAST:** Tommy Lee Jones, Martha Plimpton, Brian Dennehy. 1984

RIVER RUNS THROUGH IT, A ★★★★ Robert Redford's elegiac coming-of-age story is based on the memoir by Norman Maclean. Brad Pitt is the young man who finds peace and comradeship in fly-fishing. Redford narrates the film, which compares favorably with his first directorial triumph, *Ordinary People*, in every way. Rated PG for profanity and nudity. 123m. **DIR:** Robert Redford. **CAST:** Brad Pitt, Craig Sheffer, Tom Skerritt, Brenda Blethyn, Emily Lloyd, Edie McClurg, Stephen Shellen. 1992 **DVD**

RIVER WILD, THE ★★★1/2 Meryl Streep successfully invades Schwarzenegger and Stallone territory when her family is terrorized by a psychotic killer while on a white-water rafting vacation. Strong character development, top-flight performances, and effective commentary on the effect of modern-day stress on family relationships help make this more than just another by-the-numbers suspense thriller. Rated PG-13 for violence, nudity, and profanity. 111m. **DIR:** Curtis Hanson. **CAST:** Meryl Streep, Kevin Bacon, David Strathairn, Joseph Mazzello, John C. Reilly, Benjamin Bratt. 1994 **DVD**

RIVER'S EDGE ★★★1/2 This is a deeply disturbing film based on a real-life 1980 murder case. The teenage murderer in *River's Edge* takes his friends to see the corpse of his classmate-victim. The death becomes a secret bond among them until two decent kids (Keanu Reeves, Ione Skye) decide to do something about it. Rated R for violence, profanity, nudity, and simulated sex. 99m. **DIR:** Tim Hunter. **CAST:** Dennis Hopper, Crispin Glover, Keanu Reeves, Ione Skye, Roxana Zal, Daniel Roebuck, Tom Bower, Leo Rossi. 1987

•**RKO 281** ★★★★1/2 Any fan of *Citizen Kane* or Orson Welles has to see this award-winning made-for-cable movie, which dramatizes the events surrounding Welles's most famous film. The look of the film is lush and jazzy, perfect for setting the prewar mood, and Liev Schreiber puts in a superb performance as the "boy genius," who remains above all

else obsessed with his art. While you can't claim it's a straight documentary, the film is certainly entertaining. Not rated; contains profanity and nudity. 83m. **DIR:** Benjamin Ross. **CAST:** Liev Schreiber, James Cromwell, Melanie Griffith, John Malkovich, Brenda Blethyn, Roy Scheider. 1999 **DVD**

ROAD AGENT ★★★1/2 Tim Holt and his sidekick Chito pose as masked riders to overcome a tyrannical land boss. B&W; 60m. **DIR:** Lesley Selander. **CAST:** Tim Holt, Richard Martin, Dorothy Patrick, Tom Tyler. 1952

ROAD ENDS ★★★★ Stylish thriller about a mysterious stranger who comes to a small town and seems to bring nothing but trouble with him—until the townfolk discover he may be just another innocent victim in the bigger scheme of things. Excellent performances, a taut script, and fresh, stylish direction make this film much more than one might expect. Rated R for violence and profanity. 98m. **DIR:** Rick King. **CAST:** Dennis Hopper, Peter Coyote, Chris Sarandon, Joanna Gleason, Mariel Hemingway, Bert Remsen. 1997 **DVD**

ROAD GAMES ★★ An elusive latter-day Jack the Ripper is loose in Australia. Even though director Richard Franklin (*Psycho II*) actually studied under Alfred Hitchcock, he doesn't show any of his mentor's ability here. Rated PG. 100m. **DIR:** Richard Franklin. **CAST:** Stacy Keach, Jamie Lee Curtis, Marion Howard, Grant Page. 1981

ROAD HOME, THE ★★1/2 A sickly sweet continuation, of sorts, of *Boys' Town* with plot holes so huge even young kids won't miss them. Two orphaned brothers make their way across the country, with the help of some adorable hobos, to the famed Nebraska orphanage, now run by Mickey Rooney. Rated PG for a fiery explosion. 90m. **DIR:** Dean Hamilton. **CAST:** Charles Martin Smith, Kris Kristofferson, Danny Aiello, Dee Wallace, Mickey Rooney, Will Estes, Keegan MacIntosh. 1995

ROAD HOUSE (1948) ★★★1/2 Nifty little *film noir* about nightclub singer Ida Lupino and the two men competing for her. Gritty and well acted. B&W; 95m. **DIR:** Jean Negulesco. **CAST:** Ida Lupino, Cornel Wilde, Richard Widmark, Celeste Holm. 1948

ROAD HOUSE (1989) ★★ Hot on the heels of *Dirty Dancing*, Patrick Swayze turns to a rowdy, roughhouse movie about a bar bouncer who cleans out a Missouri saloon. A male action film with lots of fistfights, a high body count, and a disappointing level of sexist humor. Rated R. 108m. **DIR:** Rowdy Herrington. **CAST:** Patrick Swayze, Ben Gazzara, Sam Elliott. 1989

ROAD KILLERS, THE ★★ Where have you seen this one before? Vacationing family is terrorized on a rural highway by a gang of crazy joyriders. They may be on the highway to hell, but they have a devil of a time coming up with anything original. Rated R for language and violence. 89m. **DIR:** Deran Sarafian. **CAST:** Christopher Lambert, Craig Sheffer. 1993

ROAD LAWYERS AND OTHER BRIEFS ★★1/2 Three student-made films: "Road Lawyers," a *Mad Max* parody set in a future world where lawyers battle for clients; "Escape from Heaven," featuring an insufferable nun; and "Hairline," in which a man can't cope with losing his hair. Rounding out the package is a segment of the Fifties serial *Radar Men From the Moon* with new overdubbed (not very funny) dialogue. Not rated. 79m. **DIR:** Tim Doyle, James Desmarais, David Lipman, Robert Rhine. **1989**

ROAD TO BALI ★★1/2 Excellent entry in the Bob Hope/Bing Crosby *Road* series. In this one the boys play a pair of vaudeville performers in competition for Dorothy Lamour, pursuing her to the South Seas island of Bali, where they must contend with all sorts of jungle dangers, from cannibalistic natives to various Hollywood stars who appear in hilarious (though very brief) cameos. The Humphrey Bogart scene is a classic. 90m. **DIR:** Hal Walker. **CAST:** Bob Hope, Bing Crosby, Dorothy Lamour, Murvyn Vye. **1952**

•**ROAD TO EL DORADO, THE** ★★1/2 Lasting friendship and colonial conquest clash in this colorful, comic, animated adventure film, an uninspired recycling of Rudyard Kipling's *The Man Who Would Be King*. After two sixteenth-century con men win a treasure map to the legendary City of Gold in a crooked craps game, they travel to the New World and plot with a curvaceous native to steal a fortune in gold. Kevin Kline, Kenneth Branagh, Rosie Perez, Armand Assante, and Edward James Olmos supply the voices. Rated PG. 83m. **DIR:** Eric "Bibo" Bergeron, Don Paul. **2000**

ROAD TO FREEDOM: THE VERNON JOHNS STORY ★★★★ James Earl Jones delivers a stellar performance as the controversial reverend who incited his congregation to fight against injustice wherever they found it. His views weren't very popular back in Alabama in the early 1950s, even among his congregation, who replaced Rev. Johns with another young idealist, Martin Luther King Jr. This made-for-television drama is rich in period detail and excellent performances. Rated PG. 91m. **DIR:** Kenneth Fink. **CAST:** James Earl Jones, Mary Alice, Cissy Huston, Joe Seneca. **1994**

ROAD TO GALVESTON, THE ★★★ Cicely Tyson plays a recent widow who takes in Alzheimer's patients to pay the mortgage on her farm in this made-for-cable original. Not a very strong plot, but still viewable. Not rated, but suitable for all audiences. 95m. **DIR:** Michael Toshiyuki Uno. **CAST:** Cicely Tyson, Piper Laurie, Tess Harper, James McDaniel. **1996**

ROAD TO HONG KONG, THE ★★ Bob Hope and Bing Crosby play con men in this listless effort that involves international intrigue and space exploration. This was the last of the *Road* pictures, which means that Hope and Crosby made one *Road* picture too many. B&W; 91m. **DIR:** Norman Panama. **CAST:** Bing Crosby, Bob Hope, Joan Collins, Dorothy Lamour, Robert Morley, Peter Sellers. **1962**

ROAD TO MECCA, THE ★★★★ An eccentric widow living in a small South African town has a spiritual revelation to build a large sculpture garden in her yard, made to resemble Mecca. This unusual film is adapted by Athol Fugard from his play. Not rated. 106m. **DIR:** Athol Fugard, Peter Goldsmid. **CAST:** Kathy Bates, Yvonne Bryceland, Athol Fugard. **1991**

ROAD TO MOROCCO ★★★1/2 Fun in the sun as Bob Hope and Bing Crosby end up in sandy Morocco where Crosby sells Hope as a slave to princess Dorothy Lamour. The real fun begins when both men

attempt to win the heart of the princess. Enjoyable romp with pleasant songs and lots of laughs. 83m. **DIR:** David Butler. **CAST:** Bob Hope, Bing Crosby, Dorothy Lamour, Yvonne De Carlo, Anthony Quinn, Monte Blue. **1942 DVD**

ROAD TO RIO ★★★ More a straight comedy than madcap mayhem, this fifth *Road* show has Bob Hope and Bing Crosby hopping a boat to Rio de Janeiro. On board they meet and fall for Dorothy Lamour, who runs hot and cold because her wicked aunt (Gale Sondergaard) is hypnotizing her so she will accept an arranged marriage. Lots of laughs. B&W; 100m. **DIR:** Norman Z. McLeod. **CAST:** Bob Hope, Bing Crosby, Dorothy Lamour, Gale Sondergaard, Frank Faylen, Jerry Colonna, The Andrews Sisters. **1947**

ROAD TO RUIN, THE (1928) 🎬 A classic exploitation feature, this silent quickie is creaky and heavily moralistic. Silent. B&W; 45m. **DIR:** Norton S. Parker. **CAST:** Helen Foster, Grant Withers, Charles Miller. **1928**

ROAD TO RUIN (1991) ★★1/2 Decent romance features a playboy millionaire signing away his money in order to see if a beautiful model really loves him. Predictable time passer. Rated PG-13 for sexual situations. 94m. **DIR:** Charlotte Brandstrom. **CAST:** Peter Weller, Carey Lowell, Michel Duchaussoy. **1991**

ROAD TO SINGAPORE ★★★1/2 Two happy-go-lucky adventurers on the lam from responsibility end up in the tropics where they sing and perform with local lovely Dorothy Lamour, the object of their affection and rivalry. This breezy film was the first of seven pictures that cemented Bob Hope and Bing Crosby as a top comedy team and provided some of the easiest laughs of the 1940s. B&W; 85m. **DIR:** Victor Schertzinger. **CAST:** Bing Crosby, Bob Hope, Dorothy Lamour, Charles Coburn, Anthony Quinn, Jerry Colonna, Johnny Arthur, Miles Mander. **1940**

ROAD TO UTOPIA ★★★ The Klondike and a hunt for an Alaskan gold mine provide the background for this fourth of the seven *Roads* Bob Hope, Bing Crosby, and Dorothy Lamour traveled between 1940 and 1962. Rated the best of the bunch by fans, it's a mix of songs, sight gags, wisecracks, inside jokes, hoke, and the usual love triangle. B&W; 90m. **DIR:** Hal Walker. **CAST:** Bob Hope, Bing Crosby, Dorothy Lamour, Hillary Brooke, Douglass Dumbrille, Jack LaRue, Robert Benchley. **1945 DVD**

ROAD TO WELLVILLE, THE 🎬 Writer-director Alan Parker's treatment of the eccentric Dr. Kellogg's turn-of-the-century health sanatorium is moronic, embarrassing, and absolutely humorless. Rarely is such a talented cast so ill used. Rated R for nudity, simulated sex, and profanity. 120m. **DIR:** Alan Parker. **CAST:** Anthony Hopkins, Bridget Fonda, Matthew Broderick, John Cusack, Dana Carvey, Michael Lerner, Colm Meaney, Lara Flynn Boyle. **1994**

ROAD TO YESTERDAY, THE ★★★ This is Cecil B. DeMille's first independent film. The plot involves reincarnation and modern characters who flash back historically to seventeenth-century England and explain their actions and feelings years later. The action sequences make this a compelling mix of melodrama and spectacle. Silent with musical score. B&W; 136m. **DIR:** Cecil B. DeMille. **CAST:** Joseph

Schildkraut, William Boyd, Vera Reynolds, Sally Rand. 1925

ROAD TO ZANZIBAR ★★★★ Bob Hope and Bing Crosby play two fast-talking con men always just ahead of the authorities and ready to chuck everything for a sob story from a female. The story takes the adventurers to Africa in search of a diamond mine (and Dorothy Lamour!), but the funniest moments come as Fearless Frazier (Hope) is talked into one outlandishly dangerous stunt after another. B&W; 90m. **DIR:** Victor Schertzinger. **CAST:** Bing Crosby, Bob Hope, Dorothy Lamour, Una Merkel, Eric Blore, Iris Adrian, Douglass Dumbrille, Joan Marsh, Luis Alberni, Leo Gorcey. 1941

•**ROAD TRIP** ★★ New York college student Josh discovers in this raunchy, gross-out sex comedy that a videotape of his drunken infidelity has been mailed to his girlfriend in Texas. He and his buddies—a manic party animal, a virginal nerd, and a group intellectual—try to intercept the incriminating package amid misadventures involving a sperm bank deposit, a snake feeding, a desecrated order of French toast, and lots of gratuitous female nudity. Rated R for nudity, crude humor, sex, profanity, and drug use. 93m. **DIR:** Todd Phillips. **CAST:** Breckin Meyer, Rachel Blanchard, Amy Stuart, Seann William Scott, DJ Qualls, Paulo Costanzo, Tom Green. 2000

ROAD WARRIOR, THE ★★★★ A sequel to *Mad Max*, this exciting adventure features Mel Gibson as a fast-driving, cynical Robin Hood in the desolate post-apocalypse world of the future. Good fun! Rated R for violence, nudity, and profanity. 94m. **DIR:** George Miller. **CAST:** Mel Gibson, Bruce Spence, Vernon Wells, Mike Preston. 1981 DVD

ROADHOUSE 66 ★★★1/2 As teen exploitation films go, this one is pretty good. Judge Reinhold plays a yuppie stuck in a small New Mexico town with car trouble. Willem Dafoe is an ex-rock-and-roller and all-around tough guy. The film drags a bit and Dafoe overplays his role, but there are some good moments to be had. Rated R for sex, nudity, violence, and profanity. 94m. **DIR:** John Mark Robinson. **CAST:** Willem Dafoe, Judge Reinhold, Kaaren Lee, Kate Vernon, Stephen Elliott, Alan Autry. 1984

ROADRACERS ★★ Ultrastylish but not quite whole film from *El Mariachi* director Robert Rodriguez stars David Arquette as a rebel named Dude who just wants to play guitar—but the bad guys in his life (read overbearing authorities) just won't let him. Violence ensues. Rated R for language and violence. 93m. **DIR:** Robert Rodriguez. **CAST:** David Arquette, John Hawkes, Salma Hayek, Jason Wiles, Bill Sadler. 1994

ROADS TO THE SOUTH ★★★1/2 Sequel to *La Guerre Est Finie* reteams screenwriter Jorge Semprun and actor Yves Montand to give us an update on the antifascist exile (played to perfection by Montand) after he's joined the establishment enough to become a wealthy writer. In French with English subtitles. Not rated; contains profanity and violence. 100m. **DIR:** Joseph Losey. **CAST:** Yves Montand, Laurent Malet, Miou-Miou, Jose Luis Gomez. 1978

ROADSIDE PROPHETS ★★★★ Entrusted with the cremated remains of a man he barely knows, John Doe (of the rock group X) searches for the mythical Nevada town the man had once spoke of. Along the way he hooks up with a strange kid. A road movie with a difference. Rated R for profanity and nudity. 96m. **DIR:** Abbe Wool. **CAST:** John Doe, Adam Horovitz, John Cusack, David Carradine, Arlo Guthrie, Timothy Leary. 1992

ROAMIN' WILD ★★★ Undercover marshal (Tom Tyler) goes after a gang of outlaws operating in the goldfields trying to take over a woman's stage line. Fast-moving, with plenty of excitement. B&W; 56m. **DIR:** Bernard B. Ray. **CAST:** Tom Tyler, Carol Wyndham, Al Ferguson, George Chesebro. 1936

ROARING GUNS ★★★ A ruthless cattle baron attempts to drive out the independent ranchers. It's up to steely-eyed Tim McCoy to set things aright in this low-budget but enjoyable series Western. B&W; 66m. **DIR:** Sam Newfield. **CAST:** Tim McCoy, Rosalinda Price, Wheeler Oakman. 1936

ROARING ROAD, THE ★★★ Car salesman Wallace Reid represents his company in a famous auto race. Lots of real racing footage. Silent. B&W; 57m. **DIR:** James Cruze. **CAST:** Wallace Reid. 1919

ROARING TWENTIES, THE ★★★★1/2 James Cagney and Humphrey Bogart star in this superb Warner Bros. gangster entry. Produced by Mark Hellinger and directed by Raoul Walsh (*White Heat*), it's one of the best of its kind, with Cagney featured as a World War I veteran who comes back to no job and no future after fighting for his country. Embittered by all this, he turns to crime. B&W; 104m. **DIR:** Raoul Walsh. **CAST:** James Cagney, Humphrey Bogart, Priscilla Lane, Gladys George, Jeffrey Lynn, Frank McHugh, Joe Sawyer. 1939

ROB ROY ★★★★ Stately but lusty tale of the Scottish hero's fight for justice and honor in the Highlands of 1713. Neeson and Lange are glorious together, but it is Roth, as the embodiment of pure evil, who most enlivens this uncommonly serious-minded swashbuckler. Rated R for violence and simulated sex. 139m. **DIR:** Michael Caton-Jones. **CAST:** Liam Neeson, Jessica Lange, John Hurt, Tim Roth, Eric Stoltz, Andrew Keir, Brian Cox. 1995 DVD

ROB ROY, THE HIGHLAND ROGUE ★★ Slow-moving historical saga is not up to the usual Walt Disney adventure film and is perhaps the weakest of the three films made in England with sturdy Richard Todd as the heroic lead. The few battle scenes are enjoyable enough and the scenery is lovely, but the pace is erratic and there is just too much dead time. 85m. **DIR:** Harold French. **CAST:** Richard Todd, Glynis Johns, James Robertson Justice, Michael Gough, Finlay Currie. 1954

ROBBERS OF THE SACRED MOUNTAIN ★★ This action-adventure film could have been another *Raiders of the Lost Ark*. Unfortunately, poor acting and choppy editing leave it in the mediocre range. Rated R for sex, nudity, and violence. 90m. **DIR:** Bob Schulz. **CAST:** John Marley, Simon MacCorkindale, Louise Vallance, George Touliatos. 1982

ROBBERY ★★★1/2 Suspenseful crime-drama about the complex heist of the British Royal Mail. Solid direction and excellent performances surpass the predictable script. 114m. **DIR:** Peter Yates. **CAST:** Stanley Baker, Joanna Pettet, James Booth. 1967

ROBE, THE ★★★★ Richard Burton is the Roman tribune charged with overseeing the execution of Christ in this story of his involvement with the followers of Christ and the effect the robe of Jesus has on all involved. It is a well-made film, and not heavy-handed in its approach. 135m. **DIR:** Henry Koster. **CAST:** Richard Burton, Victor Mature, Jean Simmons, Michael Rennie, Richard Boone, Dean Jagger, Dawn Addams, Jay Robinson. 1953

ROBERT ET ROBERT ★★★1/2 A brilliant French film about two lonely but very different men (Charles Denner and Jacques Villeret) who strike up a tenuous friendship while waiting for their respective computer dates. It is a bittersweet tale of loneliness and compassion. No MPAA rating. 105m. **DIR:** Claude Lelouch. **CAST:** Charles Denner, Jacques Villeret, Jean-Claude Brialy, Macha Meril, Regine. 1978

ROBERTA ★★★1/2 This lighthearted story of a group of entertainers who find themselves operating a dress shop in Paris belongs to the second and third-billed Fred Astaire and Ginger Rogers. With the music of Jerome Kern and Otto Harbach, including those gems "Smoke Gets in Your Eyes" and "I Won't Dance," this carefree film is very enjoyable. Later remade as *Lovely to Look At*. B&W; 85m. **DIR:** William A. Seiter. **CAST:** Irene Dunne, Fred Astaire, Ginger Rogers, Randolph Scott, Helen Westley. 1935

ROBIN AND MARIAN ★★★1/2 Take the best director of swashbucklers, Richard Lester; add the foremost adventure film actor, Sean Connery; mix well with a fine actress with haunting presence, Audrey Hepburn; and finish off with some of the choicest character actors. You get *Robin and Marian*, a triumph for everyone involved. Rated PG. 112m. **DIR:** Richard Lester. **CAST:** Sean Connery, Audrey Hepburn, Richard Harris, Ian Holm, Robert Shaw, Nicol Williamson, Denholm Elliott, Kenneth Haigh. 1976

ROBIN & THE SEVEN HOODS ★★★ Musical reworking of the Robin Hood legend set in Jazz Age, gangster-ruled Chicago. Frank Sinatra and Dean Martin, et al. are the Merry Men, with Bing Crosby the silver-tongued spokesman Alan A. Dale. Sometimes stretches a point to be too Runyonesque, but good tunes and actors make it pleasant. 123m. **DIR:** Gordon Douglas. **CAST:** Frank Sinatra, Dean Martin, Sammy Davis Jr., Bing Crosby, Peter Falk, Barbara Rush, Victor Buono, Edward G. Robinson. 1964

ROBIN COOK'S INVASION ★★★1/2 Riveting science-fiction thriller finds a young couple living in Phoenix taking different paths during an alien invasion. When her boyfriend is infected by an alien virus, she teams up with a ragtag group of believers to combat the aliens and thwart their planned colonization of Earth. This made-for-television miniseries features engaging characters, creepy situations, and stunning special effects. Not rated; contains adult situations and violence. 179m. **DIR:** Armand Mastroianni. **CAST:** Luke Perry, Rebecca Gayheart, Kim Cattrall, Christopher Orr. 1997

ROBIN HOOD (1923) ★★★★ A rousing, fast-moving silent movie that established the character as a devil-may-care adventurer with a passion for justice and the wistful Maid Marian—in that order. Fairbanks wrote the screenplay and financed the then astronomical $1.5 million film. B&W; 118m. **DIR:** Allan Dwan. **CAST:** Douglas Fairbanks Sr., Enid Bennett, Wallace Beery, Alan Hale Sr. 1923 DVD

ROBIN HOOD (1973) ★★ A feature-length cartoon featuring Robin Hood and his gang, this is one of the lesser animated works from the Walt Disney Studios, but still good for the kiddies. Rated G. 83m. **DIR:** Wolfgang Reitherman. 1973 DVD

ROBIN HOOD (1991) ★★★ In an adventure film whose style of storytelling and atmosphere are reminiscent of John Boorman's *Excalibur*, the legend of Robin Hood is played out with most of the well-known events staged with conviction and an occasional twist. This made-for-television production doesn't have the high spirits of Errol Flynn's *The Adventures of Robin Hood* or the spectacle of Kevin Costner's *Robin Hood: Prince of Thieves*, but it's enjoyable nonetheless. 116m. **DIR:** John Irvin. **CAST:** Patrick Bergin, Uma Thurman, Jurgen Prochnow, Edward Fox, Jeroen Krabbé. 1991

ROBIN HOOD AND THE SORCERER ★★★★ While the telling of the Robin Hood legend in this film may be less straightforward than most, the added element of the mysticism enhances the all-too-familiar story and gives the dusty old characters new life. Michael Praed plays the legendary English outlaw with conviction. 115m. **DIR:** Ian Sharp. **CAST:** Michael Praed, Anthony Valentine, Nickolas Grace, Clive Mantle, Peter Williams. 1983

ROBIN HOOD GANG, THE ★★ When two young boys find a suitcase filled with cash in their apartment building's attic, they use the cash to help out the needy in their town. Too bad the loot belongs to a bank robber who will do anything to get his stash back. No big deal, yet small children may not recognize the familiar story and antics of the young cast. Rated PG. 86m. **DIR:** Eric Hendershot. **CAST:** Clayton Taylor, Steven Losack, Dalin Christiansen, Brenda Price, Scott Christopher. 1997 DVD

ROBIN HOOD: HERNE'S SON ★★★ The third in this series from the BBC begins with the death of Robin of Locksley and the choosing of Robert of Huntingdon (Jason Connery) as his successor by Herne the Hunter. The refusal of the new Robin to serve leads to the breakup of the band, followed by the abduction of Maid Marion. The new Robin must then unite his followers and save his love. 101m. **DIR:** Robert Young. **CAST:** Jason Connery, Oliver Cotton, George Baker, Michael Craig, Nickolas Grace. 1986

ROBIN HOOD: MEN IN TIGHTS ★★1/2 Director Mel Brooks's rude comic shtick seems pretty shopworn these days, although there are some genuine laughs. For more of the same, see *When Things Were Rotten*, Brooks's 1975 TV comedy featuring the same characters and ideas. Rated PG-13 for brief profanity, scatological humor, and sexual references. 104m. **DIR:** Mel Brooks. **CAST:** Cary Elwes, Richard Lewis, Roger Rees, Amy Yasbeck, Mark Blankfield, Dave Chappelle, Isaac Hayes, Megan Cavanaugh, Tracey Ullman, Patrick Stewart, Dom DeLuise, Dick Van Patten, Mel Brooks. 1993

ROBIN HOOD OF TEXAS ★★★ More of a detective story than a formula Western, Gene Autry's last film for Republic Studios finds him accused of bank robbery and keeping one step ahead of the law in order to clear his name. Better than many of his films with a nicely turned story and more action and fisticuffs than most of Autry's productions, B&W; 71m. **DIR:** Lesley Selander. **CAST:** Gene Autry, Lynne Roberts (Mary Hart), Sterling Holloway, Adele Mara. 1947

ROBIN HOOD OF THE PECOS ★★★ Roy Rogers and Gabby Hayes fight for law, order, and honest government in this history-based post–Civil War Western-drama. B&W; 50m. **DIR:** Joseph Kane. **CAST:** Roy Rogers, George "Gabby" Hayes, Marjorie Reynolds, Jay Novello, Roscoe Ates. 1941

ROBIN HOOD: PRINCE OF THIEVES ★★★★ The Robin Hood legend gets a fresh, innovative telling in this action-packed, funny, and suspenseful adult-oriented adventure, which presents Kevin Costner as the title hero. Alan Rickman is delightfully sinister as the evil Sheriff of Nottingham, and Morgan Freeman plays a Moorish warrior who aids Robin in his robbing of the rich to give to the poor. Rated PG-13 for violence and profanity. 138m. **DIR:** Kevin Reynolds. **CAST:** Kevin Costner, Morgan Freeman, Mary Elizabeth Mastrantonio, Alan Rickman, Christian Slater, Sean Connery, Brian Blessed. 1991 DVD

ROBIN HOOD: THE SWORDS OF WAYLAND ★★★★ The second of the Robin Hood series from the BBC is as good as the first, if not better. This adventure pits Robin against the forces of darkness represented by the sorceress Morgwyn of Ravenscar (Rula Lenska). The story twists and turns as the sorceress gathers the seven swords of Wayland, one of which is in Robin's hands. 105m. **DIR:** Robert Young. **CAST:** Michael Praed, Rula Lenska, Nickolas Grace. 1986

ROBIN OF LOCKSLEY ★★★1/2 The Robin Hood saga goes high-tech in this engaging family drama that concerns a precocious computer hacker who raids large business accounts for funds needed by an injured school chum. Larry Sugar's script echoes the familiar classic while maintaining reasonably proper ethics; it's a tightwire act, but Devon Sawa—as the resourceful lad—is charming enough to make it work. Rated PG for mild violence. 97m. **DIR:** Michael Kennedy. **CAST:** Devon Sawa, Joshua Jackson, Sarah Chalke, Billy O'Sullivan, Tyler Labine. 1996

ROBO C.H.I.C. 💗 Female crime fighter made in a lab has all of the right parts as played by former Playboy Playmate Kathy Shower, but film is long in the tooth and light in the budget department. Send this one back to the factory unopened. Not rated; contains violence and nudity. 101m. **DIR:** Ed Hansen, Jeff Mandel. **CAST:** Kathy Shower, Jack Carter, Burt Ward, Philip Proctor. 1990

ROBO VAMPIRE 💗 Drug smugglers vs. Asian vampires in a movie that's almost—but not quite—so bad it's good. Not rated; contains violence and brief nudity. 90m. **DIR:** Joe Livingstone. **CAST:** Harry Myles, Joe Browne. 1993

ROBOCOP ★★★★ RoboCop is the ultimate superhero movie. A stylish and stylized cop thriller set in the far future, it concerns a mortally wounded po-

liceman (Peter Weller) who is melded with a machine to become the ultimate defender of justice, RoboCop. One word of warning: this is an extremely violent motion picture. Rated R. 103m. **DIR:** Paul Verhoeven. **CAST:** Peter Weller, Nancy Allen, Dan O'Herlihy, Ronny Cox, Kurtwood Smith, Miguel Ferrer. 1987 DVD

ROBOCOP 2 ★★ Inferior, overly gory sequel pits RoboCop (Peter Weller) against a wily gang of drug dealers and the title creature, a supposedly improved version of himself that has gone berserk. Some interesting character angles but these are all too quickly abandoned in favor of mind-numbing violence. Rated R. 110m. **DIR:** Irvin Kershner. **CAST:** Peter Weller, Nancy Allen, Dan O'Herlihy, Felton Perry, Belinda Bauer. 1990 DVD

ROBOCOP 3 ★★ Completed in 1991 and unreleased for two years, this second sequel to the 1987 hit was hardly worth waiting for, although it is a slight improvement over RoboCop 2. The mayhem is a little more under control, but the story is thin and the Japanese villains are straight off a World War II recruiting poster. Rated PG-13 for violence. 104m. **DIR:** Fred Dekker. **CAST:** Robert Burke, Nancy Allen, Rip Torn, Mako, C.C.H. Pounder. 1993 DVD

ROBOT HOLOCAUST 💗 Inept attempt at a sci-fi epic that features giant worms that look like sock puppets. Not rated; contains violence and profanity. 79m. **DIR:** Tim Kincaid. **CAST:** Norris Culf, Nadine Hart, Joe Von Ornsteiner, Jennifer Delora. 1987

ROBOT IN THE FAMILY 💗 This cheap, sophomoric comedy about an ambulatory robot is one of the worst films we've ever seen; the producers apparently felt they could get away with a $1.98 budget and that kids wouldn't know the difference. (Ours did.) Rated G. 85m. **DIR:** Jack Shaoul, Mark Richardson. **CAST:** Joe Pantoliano, Amy Wright, Peter Maloney, Danny Gerard, John Rhys-Davies. 1991

ROBOT JOX ★★ Transformers-style gladiator adventure aimed at preteen boys, this futuristic tale of battles for world territorial possession will play better on home video than on the big screen. Rated PG for violence and mild profanity. 85m. **DIR:** Stuart Gordon. **CAST:** Gary Graham, Anne-Marie Johnson, Paul Koslo, Robert Sampson, Hilary Mason. 1990

ROBOT MONSTER ★★ Take a desolate-looking canyon outside of Los Angeles, borrow Lawrence Welk's bubble machine, and add a typical family on an outing and a man dressed in a gorilla suit wearing a diving helmet, and you have a serious competitor for the worst movie of all time. This absurd drama of the last days of Earth and its conquest by robot gorillas has long been considered the most inept of all science-fiction films. A must-see for all fans of truly terrible films. B&W; 63m. **DIR:** Phil Tucker. **CAST:** George Nader, Gregory Moffett, Claudia Barrett. 1953

ROBOT NINJA ★★ Robot Ninja is a superhero come to life in the form of its creator after he witnesses a brutal crime. With the help of an inventor, he builds armor to combat crime. Batman jokes abound with the character being hailed as the next Caped Crusader. Burt Ward make an in-joke appearance. Not rated; contains violence, profanity, and gore. 82m.

DIR: J. R. Bookwalter. **CAST:** Michael Todd, Bogdan Pecic, Burt Ward, Linnea Quigley, Scott Spiegel. 1989

ROBOT WARS ❤ Albert Band has a go at remaking his son Charles's film *Robot Jox*, about post-apocalyptic humanity battling it out in giant machines, and fails more miserably. Not rated, but with profanity and violence. 106m. **DIR:** Albert Band. **CAST:** Don Michael Paul, Barbara Crampton, James Staley, Yuji Okumoto, Danny Kamekona. 1993

ROCCO & HIS BROTHERS ★★★★ Compelling drama about a mother and her five sons who leave their peasant home in the south of Italy for the big city. One of Luchino Visconti's strongest screen efforts. In Italian with English subtitles. B&W; 170m. **DIR:** Luchino Visconti. **CAST:** Alain Delon, Annie Girardot, Renato Salvatori, Claudia Cardinale. 1960

ROCK, THE ★★★★ A group of Marines takes eighty-one tourists hostage on Alcatraz island and threatens to launch chemical warheads into the city of San Francisco unless the U.S. government accedes to their demands (a ransom of $100 million and proper military honors for comrades who have died in secret operations). Enter FBI lab scientist Nicolas Cage whose expertise on toxic weapons puts him at the head of a special task force that must break into the prison and neutralize the threat. It's suspenseful and occasionally beyond belief—but never boring. Rated R for violence, profanity, and simulated sex. 125m. **DIR:** Michael Bay. **CAST:** Sean Connery, Nicolas Cage, Ed Harris, David Morse, William Forsythe, John Spencer. 1996 DVD

ROCK-A-DOODLE ★★★★ Former Disney animation director Don Bluth recovers nicely from the debacle of *All Dogs Go to Heaven* with this delightfully tuneful tale of a barnyard rooster who leaves his home for the big city. It's Elvis Presley as myth, with fine voice work by Glen Campbell, Christopher Plummer, Phil Harris, Sandy Duncan, Eddie Deezen, Charles Nelson Reilly, and Ellen Greene. Rated G. 74m. **DIR:** Don Bluth. 1992 DVD

ROCK AND ROLL CIRCUS, THE ★★★★ This never-aired special made for British television by the Rolling Stones is a veritable buried treasure. All of the bands featured are in peak form, but highlights include the Who's ("A Quick One While He's Away" and an all-star jam featuring John Lennon and Eric Clapton. Made for TV. 65m. **DIR:** Michael Lindsay-Hogg. **CAST:** The Rolling Stones, John Lennon, Yoko Ono, The Who, Jethro Tull, Marianne Faithfull, Taj Mahal. 1968

ROCK 'N' ROLL HIGH SCHOOL ★★★1/2 The stern new principal tries to turn a school into a concentration camp. The popular Riff (P. J. Soles) goes against the principal by playing loud Ramones music all the time. Meanwhile, boring Tom (Vincent Van Patten) has a crush on Riff. The film includes lots of laughs and good rock 'n' roll music—a cult favorite. Rated PG. 93m. **DIR:** Allan Arkush. **CAST:** P. J. Soles, Vincent Van Patten, Clint Howard, Dey Young, The Ramones. 1979

ROCK 'N' ROLL HIGH SCHOOL FOREVER ❤ Superlame sequel to the cult hit. Rated PG-13 for profanity. 94m. **DIR:** Deborah Brock. **CAST:** Corey Feldman, Mary Woronov, Larry Linville. 1990

ROCK 'N' ROLL WRESTLING WOMEN VS. THE AZTEC APE ★★ As if your usual lady-wrestlers-battling-evil-monsters movie wasn't funny enough, this one features rockabilly songs newly dubbed in over the wrestling scenes! Sort of like *Wrestlemania* without Vince McMahon. B&W; 77m. **DIR:** René Cardona Sr. **CAST:** Elizabeth Campbell. 1962

ROCK 'N' ROLL WRESTLING WOMEN VS. THE AZTEC MUMMY ❤ Some folks found this old Mexican horror flick and attempted to turn it into a comedy by redubbing the dialogue, giving it a comical rock 'n' roll soundtrack, and retitling it. Not rated; has violence. B&W; 88m. **DIR:** René Cardona Sr., Manuel San Fernando. **CAST:** Lorena Velazquez, Armand Silvestre. 1986

ROCK AND RULE ★★1/2 Muddled fantasy of an aging rock star looking for the secret to immortality. The backgrounds are strong but the animation is static, and while the score boasts names like Lou Reed, Iggy Pop, Cheap Trick, and Blondie, the songs they contribute are mostly throwaways. Rated PG. 85m. **DIR:** Clive Smith. 1983

ROCK, BABY, ROCK IT ★★ Filmed in Dallas, this obscure feature offers a threadbare let's-put-on-a-show plot as an excuse to showcase a lot of long-forgotten doo-wop and rockabilly acts. B&W; 77m. **DIR:** Murray Douglas Sporup. **CAST:** Johnny Carroll, Kay Wheeler. 1957

ROCK HOUSE ❤ When narcotics agent Joseph Jennings loses his wife to vicious drug dealers, he takes the law into his own hands. If this guy were a football player, he would have fumbled the ball. Not rated; contains violence. 98m. **DIR:** Jack Vacek. **CAST:** Joseph Jennings. 1988

ROCK, PRETTY BABY ★★ John Saxon plays Jimmy Daley, 18-year-old leader of a struggling rock 'n' roll combo whose life is complicated by his doctor father who wants him to go into the medical profession and a difficult first-love relationship with Luana Patten. So laughably awful in spots that it becomes enjoyable. B&W; 89m. **DIR:** Richard Bartlett. **CAST:** John Saxon, Sal Mineo, Rod McKuen, Luana Patten, Edward Platt, Fay Wray, Shelley Fabares. 1957

ROCK, ROCK, ROCK ★★ If you love Tuesday Weld, Fifties rock, or entertainingly terrible movies, this nostalgic blast from the past is for you. The plot is so flimsy, Dobie Gillis would have rejected it. But watching a young Weld lip-synch to songs actually sung by Connie Francis is a wonderful treat. B&W; 83m. **DIR:** Will Price. **CAST:** Tuesday Weld, Teddy Randazzo, Alan Freed, Frankie Lymon and the Teenagers, Chuck Berry, The Flamingos, The Johnny Burnette Trio. 1956 DVD

ROCKET ATTACK USA ❤ American spies attempt to steal the plans for Sputnik from the Russians. B&W; 71m. **DIR:** Barry Mahon. **CAST:** John McKay. 1958

ROCKET GIBRALTAR ★★★ A bittersweet comedy-drama about the reunion of an eccentric family in the Hamptons, drawn by the 77th birthday of the patriarch. Burt Lancaster plays the elder, giving this slight, sentimental film credibility. Rated PG. 100m. **DIR:** Daniel Petrie. **CAST:** Burt Lancaster, Suzy Amis, John Glover, Bill Pullman. 1988

ROCKETEER, THE ★★★1/2 Bill Campbell stars as a young pilot who is transformed into a jet-propelled hero when Nazi agents attempt to steal a top-secret invention and it lands in his lap. This is Commando Cody done right; a glorious adventure for the young and the young at heart. Rated PG for violence. 110m. **DIR:** Joe Johnston. **CAST:** Bill Campbell, Alan Arkin, Jennifer Connelly, Timothy Dalton, Paul Sorvino, Terry O'Quinn, Ed Lauter. **1991 DVD**

ROCKETMAN ★★1/2 Stand-up comic Harland Williams's big-screen starring debut is about a desk-bound computer geek who winds up on NASA's first manned mission to Mars. Although wonderful with impressions and owner of the coolest T-shirts in the universe, Williams emerges as yet another adolescent in a man's body, substituting cracks about bodily functions for genuine humor. Undiscriminating 8-year-olds will love this, but all others are advised to steer clear. Rated PG for mildly disgusting humor. 94m. **DIR:** Stuart Gillard. **CAST:** Harland Williams, Jessica Lundy, Bill Sadler, Jeffrey DeMunn, Beau Bridges. **1997**

ROCKETSHIP X-M ★★1/2 A rocket heading for the moon is knocked off course by a meteor storm and is forced to land on Mars. The crewmen find Mars to be very inhospitable, as it has been devastated by atomic war and has mutated creatures inhabiting the planet. While the story is weak and the acting only passable, this is one of the first of the science-fiction films that dominated the 1950s. B&W; 77m. **DIR:** Kurt Neumann. **CAST:** Lloyd Bridges, Hugh O'Brian, Noah Beery Jr., Osa Massen, John Emery. **1950 DVD**

ROCKFORD FILES, THE (TV SERIES) ★★★★ As Jim Rockford, an ex-con turned private eye, James Garner finally breaks his typecasting as *Maverick*. In the pilot episode for this fine series, Lindsay Wagner comes to Rockford's beachside trailer with a question: was her father killed or did he commit suicide? Robert Donley was replaced in the role of Rockford's father by Noah Beery Jr. when the show began its run on NBC. Made for TV. 90m. **DIR:** Richard T. Heffron. **CAST:** James Garner, Lindsay Wagner, William Smith, Nita Talbot, Joe Santos, Robert Donley. **1974**

ROCKIN' RONNIE ★★★ Hilariously manic collage of Ronald Reagan's films, commercials, and political statements is irreverently blended. Slick, rapid-fire clips. 45m. **DIR:** Stuart Samuels. **CAST:** Ronald Reagan, Nancy Reagan. **1986**

ROCKING HORSE WINNER, THE ★★★1/2 Impressive screen adaptation of D. H. Lawrence's disturbing story about a sensitive little boy's uncanny ability to predict racehorse winners by riding his rocking horse. B&W; 91m. **DIR:** Anthony Pelissier. **CAST:** Valerie Hobson, John Howard Davies, John Mills. **1949**

ROCKTOBER BLOOD ★★ The ghost of a rock star, executed for murder, returns from the dead to avenge himself upon his former band members. The film starts off well and ends decently, but the middle wanders aimlessly. Non-horror fans will probably find this tedious. Rated R for violence, nudity, and profanity. 88m. **DIR:** Ferd Sebastian, Beverly Sebastian. **CAST:** Tray Loren. **1984**

ROCKULA ★★1/2 Entertaining but ultimately silly musical-comedy about a vampire who falls in love every twenty-two years. Shot with the look and feel of a music video, this flick has some good music and some funny lines. Rated PG-13. 90m. **DIR:** Luca Bercovici. **CAST:** Dean Cameron, Susan Tyrrell, Bo Diddley, Thomas Dolby, Toni Basil. **1990**

ROCKWELL: A LEGEND OF THE WILD WEST ★★ Low-budget and exploitative, film gets saddle sore long before calling it quits. Not rated; contains violence. 100m. **DIR:** Richard Lloyd Dewey. **CAST:** Randy Cleave, Karl Malone, George Sullivan. **1993**

ROCKY ★★★★★ Those put to sleep by the endless sequels in this series probably have forgotten the gentleness and dignity of this initial entry about Rocky Balboa, the painfully shy boxer who only "wants to go the distance" with champ Apollo Creed. One of the ultimate feel-good films, and it works every time. Rated PG for violence. 119m. **DIR:** John G. Avildsen. **CAST:** Sylvester Stallone, Burgess Meredith, Talia Shire, Burt Young, Carl Weathers. **1976 DVD**

ROCKY II ★★ The weakest entry in Sylvester Stallone's boxing series, about a down-and-out fighter attempting to prove himself through a rematch with the champ (Carl Weathers). Talia Shire, Burgess Meredith, and Burt Young reprise their series roles in this soaper in the ring. Rated PG. 119m. **DIR:** Sylvester Stallone. **CAST:** Sylvester Stallone, Carl Weathers, Talia Shire, Burgess Meredith, Burt Young. **1979 DVD**

ROCKY III ★★★ Writer-director-star Sylvester Stallone's third entry in the Rocky Balboa series is surprisingly entertaining. Though we've seen it all before, Stallone manages to make it work. Rated PG for violence and mild profanity. 99m. **DIR:** Sylvester Stallone. **CAST:** Sylvester Stallone, Talia Shire, Burgess Meredith, Mr. T, Carl Weathers. **1982**

ROCKY IV ★★★ Sylvester Stallone's Everyman returns to take on a massive Russian fighter (Dolph Lundgren) trained via computer and programmed to kill. The result is deliciously corny, enjoyably predictable entertainment. Rated PG for violence and profanity. 90m. **DIR:** Sylvester Stallone. **CAST:** Sylvester Stallone, Talia Shire, Burt Young, Carl Weathers, Brigitte Nielsen, Tony Burton, Michael Pataki, Dolph Lundgren. **1985 DVD**

ROCKY V ★★★1/2 Rocky returns home from the Soviet Union to a hero's welcome but financial ruin, thanks to naïve business decisions by brother-in-law Paulie (Burt Young). The saga of Sylvester Stallone's Rocky Balboa concludes with a suitably subdued whisper. Rated PG-13. 104m. **DIR:** John G. Avildsen. **CAST:** Sylvester Stallone, Talia Shire, Burt Young, Burgess Meredith. **1990**

ROCKY HORROR PICTURE SHOW, THE ★★★1/2 Delicious send-up of science-fiction–horror flicks, set to rock 'n' roll beat. If you're not experiencing this scintillating spoof at a midnight showing, you're missing much of the fun. Audience participation is a key. Nevertheless, this madcap musical-comedy has plenty to offer, even for the solitary viewer hunched in front of a small screen. Rated R. 100m. **DIR:** Jim Sharman. **CAST:** Tim Curry, Susan Sarandon, Barry

Bostwick, Richard O'Brien, Jonathan Adams, Patricia Quinn, Little Nell, Meat Loaf, Charles Gray. 1975

•**ROCKY MARCIANO** ★★★★ Outstanding made-for-cable bio-drama chronicles the life of championship boxer Marciano. Jon Favreau pulls no punches as Marciano, perfectly portraying the spirit of the heavyweight. The events and characters are compelling and engaging, and even though the fight scenes lack the emotional wallop of *Raging Bull*, they do convey the impact of the sport. Rated R for adult situations, language, and violence. 90m. **DIR:** Charles Winkler. **CAST:** Jon Favreau, Penelope Ann Miller, Judd Hirsch, Tony Lo Bianco, George C. Scott. 1999

ROCKY MOUNTAIN RANGERS ★★★ The Three Mesquiteers impersonate outlaws in order to avenge the murder of a young Texas Ranger comrade. Then the real outlaws show up. Bob Livingston has a meaty dual role. B&W; 54m. **DIR:** George Sherman. **CAST:** Robert Livingston, Duncan Renaldo, Raymond Hatton, Sammy McKim, LeRoy Mason. 1940

RODAN ★★★1/2 This minor classic was Japan's answer to the nuclear "big bug" films of the decade. Murderous insects are just a prelude to the main event featuring not one but *two* supersonic-speed giant pterodactyls. Released in the United States with a stock-footage preface concerning the danger of radioactive experiments, this well-constructed thriller boasts special effects by Eiji Tsuburaya that are superior to many of its American counterparts. 72m. **DIR:** Inoshiro Honda. **CAST:** Kenji Sahara. 1956

RODEO GIRL ★★★★ Katharine Ross is Sammy, the wife of rodeo champ Will Garrett (Bo Hopkins). When she decides to try her hand at roping and bronco riding, she finds that she has the potential to be a rodeo champ. But complications arise when she discovers she is pregnant. Based on a true story. 92m. **DIR:** Jackie Cooper. **CAST:** Katharine Ross, Bo Hopkins, Candy Clark, Jacqueline Brooks, Wilford Brimley. 1980

RODEO KING AND THE SENORITA ★★★ In this remake of Roy Rogers's *My Pal Trigger*, rodeo rider Rex Allen exposes the crook who's trying to bankrupt a traveling wild West show. B&W; 67m. **DIR:** Philip Ford. **CAST:** Rex Allen, Buddy Ebsen, Mary Ellen Kay, Roy Barcroft, Tristram Coffin. 1951

RODGERS & HAMMERSTEIN'S CINDERELLA ★★★ This hip, multiracial version of the classic fairy tale features Whitney Houston as a fairy godmother (with attitude) to the moping Brandy Norwood in the title role. The real show stopper is Paolo Montalban as the prince. A part as the prince's valet was created for Jason Alexander. This lavish made-for-TV production employs elaborate and colorful sets and costumes. Not rated; contains no objectionable material. 90m. **DIR:** Robert Iscove. **CAST:** Brandy Norwood, Bernadette Peters, Paolo Montalban, Whoopi Goldberg, Whitney Houston, Jason Alexander, Victor Garber. 1997

ROE VS. WADE ★★★★ Winner of two Emmy Awards—for outstanding drama special and outstanding lead actress—this fine telefilm shows the abortion issue from the point of a down-and-out, unmarried woman (Holly Hunter). Amy Madigan, as

Hunter's determined attorney, delivers an electrifyingly intense statement before the court justices. Contains frank adult discussion. 92m. **DIR:** Gregory Hoblit. **CAST:** Holly Hunter, Amy Madigan, Kathy Bates, Chris Mulkey, James Gammon. 1989

ROGER & ME ★★★★ Michael Moore's controversial documentary about the growing despair, homelessness, and crime in Flint, Michigan, where more than 30,000 autoworkers were left unemployed by the closing of General Motors plants. Scathingly funny and ultimately sobering. Rated R for brief profanity. 106m. **DIR:** Michael Moore. 1989

•**ROGUE TRADER** ★★★ Ewan McGregor stars as Nick Leeson, the British futures trader whose risky dealings eventually caused the collapse of that country's oldest bank. Based on Leeson's autobiography, the film seems a bit too sympathetic to this character, but McGregor is nonetheless fascinating to watch as he digs himself in deeper and deeper. Rated R for profanity and brief nudity. 98m. **DIR:** James Dearden. **CAST:** Ewan McGregor, Anna Friel, Betsy Brantley. 1999 DVD

ROLL OF THUNDER, HEAR MY CRY ★★★1/2 Heartwarming tale of a black family struggling to get by in Depression-era Mississippi. Made for television, this was meant to be shown in three parts, and it's best viewed that way—the pace is a little too leisurely (especially for kids) to watch this in one sitting. 150m. **DIR:** Jack Smight. **CAST:** Claudia McNeil, Janet MacLachlan, Robert Christian, Morgan Freeman. 1978

ROLL ON TEXAS MOON ★★★1/2 Gabby Hayes's standout role in Roy Rogers's Westerns as the owner of a cattle ranch at odds with encroaching sheep herders led by Dale Evans. Outlaws play the two sides against each other. First of the "new era" William Witney–directed, less-songs-more-action Rogers B Westerns. B&W; 67m. **DIR:** William Witney. **CAST:** Roy Rogers, George "Gabby" Hayes, Dale Evans, Elisabeth Risdon, Bob Nolan and the Sons of the Pioneers. 1946

ROLLERBALL ★★★★ Vastly underappreciated science-fiction film envisions a world controlled by business corporations; with no wars or other aggressive activities, the public gets its release in rollerball, a violent combination of basketball, ice hockey, and roller derby. James Caan is a top rollerball champ who refuses to quit the game in spite of threats from industrialist John Houseman, who fears that Caan may turn into a public folk hero. Rated R for violence. 128m. **DIR:** Norman Jewison. **CAST:** James Caan, John Houseman, Maud Adams, Ralph Richardson, John Beck. 1975 DVD

ROLLERBLADE 💔 *Mad Max* meets *Kansas City Bomber* and *Red Sonja*. 88m. **DIR:** Donald G. Jackson. **CAST:** Suzanne Solari, Jeff Hutchinson. 1986

ROLLERCOASTER ★★★★1/2 Fast-paced suspense film about an extortionist (Timothy Bottoms) blowing up rides in some of the nation's most famous amusement parks, and the efforts of a county safety inspector (George Segal) and an FBI agent (Richard Widmark) to nab him. Very well-done, this much-maligned film has great action, crisp dialogue, and a brilliant, nail-biting climax. Rated PG for language and violence. 119m. **DIR:** James Goldstone. **CAST:** George Segal, Richard Widmark, Timothy Bottoms, Susan Strasberg, Henry Fonda. **1977 DVD**

ROLLING THUNDER ★★★★ When a Vietnam POW returns home to Texas, he is honored with two thousand silver dollars by the local merchants for his courage and endurance under torture. (A dollar for every day served as a POW.) A gang of vicious killers attempts to rob him, but he will not tell them where the silver is, even when they begin to torture him. After some hospitalization, he recruits his Vietnam buddy and the hunt is violently and realistically played out. Rated R. 99m. **DIR:** John Flynn. **CAST:** William Devane, Tommy Lee Jones, Linda Haynes, James Best, Dabney Coleman, Lisa Richards, Luke Askew. **1977**

ROLLING VENGEANCE ★★1/2 A young trucker avenges the murder of his family and the rape of his girlfriend. A cross between a trucker movie and *Rambo*. Rated R for violence and language. 92m. **DIR:** Steven H. Stern. **CAST:** Don Michael Paul, Lawrence Dane, Ned Beatty, Lisa Howard. **1987**

ROLLOVER ★★★1/2 Jane Fonda plays an ex–film star who inherits a multimillion-dollar empire when her husband is mysteriously murdered in this gripping, but not great, film. Kris Kristofferson is the financial troubleshooter who joins forces with her to save the company. Soon both their lives are in danger. Rated R because of profanity. 118m. **DIR:** Alan J. Pakula. **CAST:** Jane Fonda, Kris Kristofferson, Hume Cronyn, Josef Sommer, Bob Gunton. **1981**

ROMAN HOLIDAY ★★★★★ Amid the beauty and mystique of Rome, an American newspaperman (Gregory Peck) is handed a news scoop on the proverbial silver platter. A princess (Audrey Hepburn) has slipped away from her stifling royal lifestyle. In her efforts to hide as one of Rome's common people, she encounters Peck. Their amiable adventures provide the basis for a charming fantasy-romance. B&W; 119m. **DIR:** William Wyler. **CAST:** Gregory Peck, Audrey Hepburn, Eddie Albert. **1953**

ROMAN SCANDALS ★★★ Old Banjo Eyes dreams himself back to ancient Rome. Busby Berkeley staged the requisite musical numbers, including one censor-baiting stanza featuring seminude chorus girls, Goldwyn Girl Lucille Ball among them. B&W; 92m. **DIR:** Frank Tuttle. **CAST:** Eddie Cantor, Ruth Etting, Alan Mowbray, Edward Arnold. **1933**

ROMAN SPRING OF MRS. STONE, THE ★★ A sensitive, elegant middle-aged actress (Vivien Leigh) has retreated to Rome to get a new focus. Warren Beatty plays a sleek, surly, wet-lipped Italian gigolo out for what he can get with the help of a crass, waspish procuress (Lotte Lenya). Banal. 104m. **DIR:** Jose Quintero. **CAST:** Vivien Leigh, Warren Beatty, Lotte Lenya, Jill St. John. **1961**

ROMANCE (1930) ★★★ Greta Garbo, even miscast as an Italian singer, brings interest to this tale of a woman of questionable character finding herself pursued by a young minister. At the 1929–30 Academy Awards Garbo and director Clarence Brown were each nominated for this movie and *Anna Christie*; both lost. B&W; 79m. **DIR:** Clarence Brown.

CAST: Greta Garbo, Lewis Stone, Gavin Gordon, Elliott Nugent. **1930 DVD**

•**ROMANCE (1999)** ★★ When a young woman is unable to arouse her boyfriend's sexual interest, she resorts to anonymous couplings with strangers and a sadomasochistic affair with her boss. Writer-director Catherine Breillat's film gained some notoriety for its graphic sex and frontal nudity, but it's just so much puerile, self-consciously "shocking" Eurotrash. Much of the dialogue (at least in translation) is hilariously silly. In French with English subtitles. Rated R for graphic sexual scenes and profanity (in subtitles). 99m. **DIR:** Catherine Breillat. **CAST:** Caroline Ducey, Sagamore Stevenin, Francois Berleand, Rocco Siffredi. **1999 DVD**

ROMANCE IN MANHATTAN ★★★ Franois Lederer as a friendly, ebullient Czech immigrant deals bravely with an inhospitable New York City and wins the love of Ginger Rogers, who befriends him. She's good, but it's his picture. B&W; 78m. **DIR:** Stephen Roberts. **CAST:** Ginger Rogers, Francis Lederer, Donald Meek, Sidney Toler. **1935**

ROMANCE ON THE HIGH SEAS ★★★ A delightful musical that introduced Doris Day to the movies. The plot is a merry mix-up about glamor gals testing their husbands' faithfulness, and Day gets third billing. Her part was originally written for Judy Garland and scaled down when Garland was unavailable. 99m. **DIR:** Michael Curtiz. **CAST:** Jack Carson, Janis Paige, Doris Day, Don DeFore, Oscar Levant, S. Z. Sakall, Franklin Pangborn, Eric Blore, Fortunio Bonanova. **1948**

ROMANCE ON THE ORIENT EXPRESS ♥ This British TV movie is ruined by insipid dialogue. 96m. **DIR:** Lawrence Gordon Clark. **CAST:** Cheryl Ladd, Stuart Wilson, John Gielgud. **1985**

ROMANCE ON THE RANGE ★★1/2 Roy Rogers's serial is marred by poor lighting and film quality. Such technical difficulties, however, can't dim his heroics in exposing a fur-trapping scam with his faithful sidekicks, Gabby Hayes and the Sons of the Pioneers. Not rated; contains violence. 53m. **DIR:** Joseph Kane. **CAST:** Roy Rogers, George "Gabby" Hayes, Sally Payne, Linda Hayes, Sons of the Pioneers. **1942**

ROMANCE WITH A DOUBLE BASS ★★★1/2 Monty Python madman John Cleese stars in this delightfully silly vignette about a double-bass player and a princess who are caught naked in a pond when a thief makes off with their clothes. The ensuing romance will tickle and charm most adult viewers with its refreshing subtlety, but a word of caution for parents: This short will not win any awards for costume design. 40m. **DIR:** Robert Young. **CAST:** John Cleese, Connie Booth, Graham Crowden, Desmond Jones, Freddie Jones, Andrew Sachs. **1974**

ROMANCING THE STONE ★★★★1/2 A rip-snorting adventure film that combines action, a love story, suspense, and plenty of laughs, this movie stars Kathleen Turner as a timid romance novelist who becomes involved in a situation more dangerous, exciting, and romantic than anything she could ever dream up. Michael Douglas plays the shotgun-wielding soldier of fortune who comes to her aid. Rated PG for violence, nudity, and profanity. 105m. **DIR:** Robert

Zemeckis. **CAST:** Kathleen Turner, Michael Douglas, Danny DeVito, Alfonso Arau, Zack Norman. **1984 DVD**

ROMANTIC COMEDY ★★★ In this enjoyable comedy, based on the 1979 Broadway play, Dudley Moore and Mary Steenburgen star as two collaborating playwrights who, during their long association, suffer from "unsynchronized passion." Rated PG for profanity and suggested sex. 103m. **DIR:** Arthur Hiller. **CAST:** Dudley Moore, Mary Steenburgen, Frances Sternhagen, Janet Eilber, Robyn Douglass, Ron Leibman. **1983**

ROMANTIC ENGLISHWOMAN, THE ★★★ Based on Thomas Wiseman's novel, this film features Michael Caine as a pulp novel writer who impels his discontented, but presumably faithful, wife into an affair with a gigolo. Rated R for language, adult situations. 115m. **DIR:** Joseph Losey. **CAST:** Glenda Jackson, Michael Caine, Helmut Berger. **1975**

ROME ADVENTURE ★★★1/2 A soap opera produced just as Hollywood was getting sexier and starring two of the sexiest women of the 1960s: Suzanne Pleshette and Angie Dickinson. The locale is romantic Rome where a visiting schoolteacher has an affair with an aging playboy, then meets a man closer to her own age she likes better. The performances are especially good. 120m. **DIR:** Delmer Daves. **CAST:** Angie Dickinson, Troy Donahue, Suzanne Pleshette, Rossano Brazzi, Chad Everett, Hampton Fancher, Al Hirt, Constance Ford. **1962**

ROMEO AND JULIET (1936) ★★★ An almost literal translation of Shakespeare's classic romance, and it would have been better with some streamlining. Both Norma Shearer and Leslie Howard are much too old to play the young lovers, but they deliver the poetic dialogue with sincerity as well as emotion. John Barrymore and Basil Rathbone take acting honors, especially Barrymore as the hapless Mercutio. B&W. 126m. **DIR:** George Cukor. **CAST:** Norma Shearer, Leslie Howard, Basil Rathbone, Edna May Oliver, Andy Devine, John Barrymore, Reginald Denny, C. Aubrey Smith. **1936**

•**ROMEO AND JULIET (1954)** ★★★1/2 Though one of the lesser-known adaptations of Shakespeare's famous tragedy, this version is one of the more beautiful to look at, thanks to location shooting around Italy. This was the only film appearance for Susan Shentall, who plays Juliet. 140m. **DIR:** Renato Castellani. **CAST:** Laurence Harvey, Susan Shentall, Flora Robson, Bill Travers, Sebastian Cabot. **1954**

ROMEO AND JULIET (1968) ★★★★1/2 Franco Zeffirelli directed this excellent version of *Romeo and Juliet*. When it was filmed, Olivia Hussey was only 15 and Leonard Whiting was only 17, keeping their characters in tune with Shakespeare's hero and heroine. Rated PG. 138m. **DIR:** Franco Zeffirelli. **CAST:** Olivia Hussey, Leonard Whiting, John McEnery, Michael York, Milo O'Shea. **1968 DVD**

ROMEO AND JULIET (1983) ★★★1/2 A first-class stage production of Shakespeare's tale of the young "star-crossed" lovers, Romeo and Juliet. Esther Rolle is interesting, and quite good, as Juliet's nurse, but the acting honors go to Dan Hamilton as the spirited, fun-loving Mercutio. A Bard Productions Ltd. release. 165m. **DIR:** William Woodman. **CAST:** Alex

Hyde-White, Blanche Baker, Esther Rolle, Dan Hamilton, Fredric Lehne, Alvah Stanley. **1983**

ROMEO AND JULIET (1988) ★★★1/2 Made for British television, this production of Shakespeare's timeless tale of star-crossed lovers is highly rewarding. Ann Hasson makes an especially sweet and beguiling Juliet. 360m. **DIR:** Joan Kemp-Welch. **CAST:** Christopher Neame, Ann Hasson, Peter Jeffrey, Peter Dyneley. **1988**

ROMEO IS BLEEDING ★★★★ In this bizarre thriller crooked cop Gary Oldman's avaricious plans come a cropper when he runs into maniacal hit woman Lena Olin. Some viewers are likely to be offended by the outrageous sex and violence, but folks who enjoyed *Reservoir Dogs* and *Bad Lieutenant* will find this nightmarish flick right up their dark alley. Rated R for violence, profanity, nudity, and simulated sex. 97m. **DIR:** Peter Medak. **CAST:** Gary Oldman, Lena Olin, Annabella Sciorra, Juliette Lewis, David Proval, Will Patton, Ron Perlman, Dennis Farina. **1994**

•**ROMEO MUST DIE** ★★ It's a shame that a performer as engaging as Jet Li must tolerate overproduced and underscripted swill such as this low-rent *West Side Story* wannabe. Mitchell Kapner's all but illiterate script is the thinnest possible retread of *Romeo and Juliet*, an homage only barely distinguishable amid the mindless violence, jive-ass dialogue and shrieking soundtrack. Only Li's personality and winning smile save this from turkeydom. Rated R for violence and profanity. 118m. **DIR:** Andrzej Bartkowiak. **CAST:** Jet Li, Aaliyah, Isaiah Washington, Russell Wong, DMX, Delroy Lindo. **2000**

ROMERO ★★★1/2 An exquisitely understated and heartfelt performance by Raul Julia in the title role enlivens this somewhat heavy-handed political and religious message movie. It chronicles the struggle of Salvadoran Archbishop Oscar Romero, who was assassinated in 1980 by representatives of the repressive government the mild-mannered cleric had been forced to fight. Rated PG-13 for violence. 105m. **DIR:** John Duigan. **CAST:** Raul Julia, Richard Jordan, Ana Alicia, Eddie Velez, Tony Plana, Harold Gould. **1989**

ROMPER STOMPER ★★★ A group of skinheads terrorizes the Asian community in Melbourne, Australia, and a bizarre love story is mixed between countless acts of violence. At first this movie may disgust the viewer, but keep watching—you could end up enjoying it. Available in R-rated and unrated versions; contains violence, profanity, nudity, and graphic sex. 83m. **DIR:** Geoffrey Wright. **CAST:** Russell Crowe, Daniel Pollock, Jacqueline McKenzie, Alex Scott. **1992**

ROMY AND MICHELE'S HIGH SCHOOL REUNION ★★1/2 Stars Mira Sorvino and Lisa Kudrow are marvelous in this tale of ditzy best friends who adopt new identities in an effort to impress former tormentors at a ten-year high-school reunion, but Robin Schiff's screenplay is too incoherent to sustain this potentially amusing premise. A lengthy, midfilm dream sequence merely emphasizes the fact that this story can't fill more than a 30-minute television sitcom slot. Rated R for profanity. 91m. **DIR:** David Mirkin. **CAST:** Mira Sorvino, Lisa Kudrow, Janeane Garofalo, Alan Cumming. **1997 DVD**

RONIN ★★★★ This is a throwback to those wonderfully complex Cold War thrillers of the 1960s and early 1970s. Director John Frankenheimer knows the territory well, having helmed numerous intelligent thrillers; and credit coscripter David Mamet, hiding behind an alias after an unsatisfying Writers Guild arbitration. The title characters, a reference to an ancient Japanese samurai legend, are mercenaries hired to retrieve a mysterious briefcase. Things go awry, during which the briefcase becomes a classic Hitchcock McGuffin: far less important for what it contains, than for who has possession of it. Special mention must be made of Jean-Claude Lagniez, who coordinated the sensational car chases. Rated R for violence, profanity, and a particularly gruesome do-it-yourself surgery. 121m. **DIR:** John Frankenheimer. **CAST:** Robert De Niro, Jean Reno, Natascha McElhone, Stellan Skarsgard, Sean Bean, Jonathan Pryce, Michel Lonsdale. **1998 DVD**

RONNIE & JULIE ★★★ This family-oriented "Shakespeare Lite" concerns an ill-fated romance between the daughter of a political incumbent and the son of a hopeful challenger: two battling families with names derived from the Montagues and Capulets. The teens, of course, care not for their parents' rivalry; to lend further spice to this meeting of dissimilar minds, she's a figure-skater, while he's on the school hockey team. Rated PG; suitable for all ages. 99m. **DIR:** Philip Spink. **CAST:** Teri Garr, Joshua Jackson, Margot Finley, Tom Butler, Alexandra Purvis. **1996**

ROOFTOPS ★★ What a coincidence! *West Side Story* director Robert Wise returns to make a film about streetwise teenagers in New York who dance, rumble, and struggle to survive. This time, star-crossed lovers (Jason Gedrick and Troy Beyer) combine kung fu with dirty dancing. Rated R for rampant profanity, violence, and brief nudity. 95m. **DIR:** Robert Wise. **CAST:** Jason Gedrick, Troy Beyer, Eddie Velez. **1989**

ROOKIE, THE ★★1/2 Clint Eastwood is a maverick detective who is saddled with the rookie (Charlie Sheen) of the title while attempting to get the goods on a German criminal. Although it delivers the goods for the action crowd, this is an otherwise disappointing effort from star-director Eastwood. Rated R for violence and profanity. 121m. **DIR:** Clint Eastwood. **CAST:** Clint Eastwood, Charlie Sheen, Raul Julia, Sonia Braga, Tom Skerritt, Pepe Serna, Tony Plana. **1990**

ROOKIE OF THE YEAR ★★★★ Sweet-natured family comedy is sure to be a hit with all ages. A 12-year-old boy achieves the ultimate fantasy: his broken arm heals oddly, leaving Thomas Ian Nicholas with a powerful pitching arm that he uses to lead the Chicago Cubs to victory. Terrific supporting cast and deft comedy bits make Daniel Stern's directorial debut memorable. Rated PG for brief profanity. 103m. **DIR:** Daniel Stern. **CAST:** Thomas Ian Nicholas, Gary Busey, Albert Hall, Amy Morton, Dan Hedaya, Bruce Altman, Eddie Bracken, Daniel Stern. **1993**

ROOM AT THE TOP ★★★★★ John Braine's powerful novel, adapted for the screen by Neil Patterson, is a smashing success. Laurence Harvey is an opportunist who will stop at nothing, including a dalliance

with his boss's daughter, to get to the top in the business world. A great cast and superb direction. This is a must-see film. B&W; 115m. **DIR:** Jack Clayton. **CAST:** Laurence Harvey, Simone Signoret, Heather Sears, Hermione Baddeley. **1959 DVD**

ROOM 43 ★★ Cabbie Eddie Constantine battles a ring of white slavers after he falls in love with one of their victims, a French girl who needs his help to remain in England. Lukewarm crime tale, featuring Michael Caine and future trash novelist Jackie Collins in small roles. B&W; 85m. **DIR:** Alvin Rakoff. **CAST:** Eddie Constantine, Diana Dors, Odile Versois, Herbert Lom. **1959**

ROOM SERVICE ★★★ After leaving his brothers (Groucho, Harpo, and Chico) to try movie producing, Zeppo Marx came up with this Broadway play about a foundering stage production and attempted to have it rewritten to suit his siblings' talents. He wasn't completely successful, but this romp does have its moments. Look for Lucille Ball and Ann Miller in early supporting roles. B&W; 78m. **DIR:** William A. Seiter. **CAST:** The Marx Brothers, Lucille Ball, Ann Miller. **1938**

ROOM WITH A VIEW, A ★★★★★ This is a triumph of tasteful, intelligent filmmaking. Director James Ivory painstakingly re-creates the milieu of 1908 Edwardian England as he explores the consequence of a tour of Florence, Italy, taken by an innocently curious young woman and her meddling aunt. Not rated, the film has one brief scene of violence and some male frontal nudity. 115m. **DIR:** James Ivory. **CAST:** Maggie Smith, Helena Bonham Carter, Denholm Elliott, Julian Sands, Daniel Day-Lewis, Simon Callow, Judi Dench, Rosemary Leach, Rupert Graves. **1986 DVD**

ROOMMATES ★★★★ Warmhearted and often humorous tearjerker about a cantankerous Polish-American baker, who raises his 5-year-old grandson after the death of the boy's parents. Falk has a field day as the tough old patriarch. Rated PG. 108m. **DIR:** Peter Yates. **CAST:** Peter Falk, D. B. Sweeney, Julianne Moore, Jan Rubes, Ellen Burstyn, Frankie Faison, Noah Fleiss. **1995**

ROOSTER COGBURN ★★★1/2 Okay, so this sequel to *True Grit* is only *The African Queen* reworked, with John Wayne playing the Humphrey Bogart part opposite the incomparable Katharine Hepburn, but we like—no, love—it. Watching these two professionals playing off each other is what movie watching is all about. The plot? Well, it's not much, but the scenes with Wayne and Hepburn are, as indicated, priceless. Rated PG. 107m. **DIR:** Stuart Millar. **CAST:** John Wayne, Katharine Hepburn, Richard Jordan, Anthony Zerbe, Strother Martin, John McIntire. **1975 DVD**

ROOSTERS ★★1/2 An ex-con (Edward James Olmos) returns to his Arizona home to resume breeding fighting cocks and ruling his poverty-stricken family. Acting is earnest and efficient (especially by Maria Conchita Alonso as Olmos's sister), but hampered by the pretentiously poetic dialogue and obvious symbolism of the script. Robert M. Young's ponderous direction doesn't help. Rated R for mature themes. 93m. **DIR:** Robert M. Young. **CAST:** Edward

James Olmos, Sonia Braga, Maria Conchita Alonso, Danny Nucci, Sarah Lassez, Valente Rodriguez. **1995**

ROOTS ★★★★★ Unique in television history is this six-volume chronicle of eighteenth and nineteenth century black life from African enslavement to and beyond Civil War emancipation. It is a triumph in every aspect—acting, writing, and production—and an illuminating look into a tragic side of American social history. Outstanding are Lou Gossett Jr., as the wise and diplomatic antebellum house servant Fiddler, and Ben Vereen as the ebullient, post–Civil War freeman Chicken George. 540m. **DIR:** Marvin J. Chomsky. **CAST:** LeVar Burton, Edward Asner, Lloyd Bridges, Cicely Tyson, Lorne Greene, Ben Vereen, Sandy Duncan, Leslie Uggams, Chuck Connors, Burl Ives, Lou Gossett Jr. **1977**

ROOTS: THE NEXT GENERATION ★★★★★ A seven-cassette, Emmy-winning continuation of *Roots*, television's most highly acclaimed dramatic series. An outstanding cast re-enacts the mesmerizing saga of slave Kunte Kinte's descendants forward from 1882 to post–World War II days, when author Alex Haley began the ancestral search for his "old African," and the beginning of his family. Like its predecessor, a fine, rewarding production. 686m. **DIR:** John Erman, Charles S. Dubin, Georg Stanford Brown, Lloyd Richards. **CAST:** Olivia de Havilland, Henry Fonda, Marlon Brando, Richard Thomas, Georg Stanford Brown, Ossie Davis, Dorian Harewood, James Earl Jones. **1979**

ROOTS OF EVIL 💗 Soft-porn, erotic thriller concerning two police detectives stalking a serial killer with a penchant for killing prostitutes. Badly acted and horrendously stereotypical. Not rated; contains violence and simulated sex. 95m. **DIR:** Gary Graver. **CAST:** Alex Cord, Delia Sheppard, Charles Dierkop. **1991**

ROOTS SEARCH ★★ Japanese animation. A spaceship crew is stalked and killed by an alien presence in this often graphically violent thriller. In Japanese with English subtitles. Not rated; contains violence and nudity. 45m. **DIR:** Hisashi Sugai. **1986**

ROOTS—THE GIFT ★★1/2 This made-for-TV spin-off from *Roots* and *Roots: The Next Generation* brings back Lou Gossett Jr. and LeVar Burton as Fiddler and Kunte Kinte to lead fellow slaves to freedom on Christmas Eve. Nice, but contrived. 100m. **DIR:** Kevin Hooks. **CAST:** Lou Gossett Jr., LeVar Burton, Michael Learned, Avery Brooks, Kate Mulgrew, Shaun Cassidy. **1988**

ROPE ★★★1/2 Recently resurrected Alfred Hitchcock film is based in part on the famous Leopold-Loeb thrill-murder case in Chicago in the 1920s. In it, the two killers divulge clues to their horrific escapade at a dinner party, to the growing suspicion of the other guests. It's one of Hitchcock's best. 80m. **DIR:** Alfred Hitchcock. **CAST:** James Stewart, John Dall, Farley Granger, Cedric Hardwicke. **1948**

RORRET ★★★ Movie buffs will enjoy this odd thriller about the murderous owner of a revival theater, if only to spot the various re-created scenes from classic suspense films. But it's a gimmick that never really leads anywhere. In Italian with English subtitles. 103m. **DIR:** Fulvio Wetzl. **CAST:** Lou Castel, Anna Galiena. **1988**

ROSALIE ★★1/2 From those thrilling days of yesteryear at MGM comes this gigantic musical about hero Nelson Eddy and his winning of a disguised Balkan princess (Eleanor Powell). It's big, colorful, and has a nice music score by Cole Porter. B&W; 122m. **DIR:** W. S. Van Dyke. **CAST:** Eleanor Powell, Nelson Eddy, Frank Morgan, Edna May Oliver, Ray Bolger, Ilona Massey. **1937**

ROSALIE GOES SHOPPING ★★★1/2 The *Bagdad Café* gang is back with another bit of quirky American-landscape comedy. German writer-director Percy Adlon and his talented German star Marianne Sägebrecht tackle consumer greed, credit card debt, and true love in this offbeat tale of an eccentric little Rock, Arkansas family. Rated PG. 94m. **DIR:** Percy Adlon. **CAST:** Marianne Sägebrecht, Brad Davis. **1990**

ROSARY MURDERS, THE ★★★ Donald Sutherland is a priest who hears the confession of a killer who is murdering nuns and priests. An interesting film, thanks to strong performances by Sutherland and Charles Durning as the bishop. Slow pacing by director Fred Walton and a needlessly murky denouement keep this murder mystery from being top rank. Rated R for violence and nudity. 107m. **DIR:** Fred Walton. **CAST:** Donald Sutherland, Charles Durning, Belinda Bauer, Josef Sommer, James Murtaugh. **1987**

ROSE, THE ★★★★ Bette Midler stars as a Janis Joplin–like rock singer who falls prey to the loneliness and temptations of superstardom. Mark Rydell directed this fine character study, which features memorable supporting performances by Alan Bates and Frederic Forrest, and a first-rate rock score. Rated R. 134m. **DIR:** Mark Rydell. **CAST:** Bette Midler, Alan Bates, Frederic Forrest, Harry Dean Stanton. **1979**

ROSE AND THE JACKAL, THE 💗 TV movie concerning the Secret Service's attempt to stop Confederate espionage in Washington, D.C., at the outbreak of the Civil War. 95m. **DIR:** Jack Gold. **CAST:** Christopher Reeve, Madolyn Smith, Carrie Snodgress, Kevin McCarthy, Jeff Corey. **1990**

ROSE GARDEN, THE ★★★1/2 In modern-day Germany, a Holocaust survivor (Maximilian Schell) is arrested for assaulting a successful elderly businessman. Defense attorney (Liv Ullmann) discovers that the businessman was a former S.S. officer who presided over a brutal Nazi death camp and was responsible for the murder of dozens of children. Engrossing psychological drama. Rated PG-13 for violence. 152m. **DIR:** Fons Rademakers. **CAST:** Liv Ullmann, Maximilian Schell, Peter Fonda. **1990**

ROSE HILL ★★★1/2 *Hallmark Hall of Fame* production features four New York street urchins circa 1866 who become law-abiding citizens after finding an abandoned baby girl. The boys head out west to start a new life and raise their new "sister." Oddly, despite their best intentions and greatest efforts, they raise a willful, spoiled brat. Overall, very watchable and entertaining. Not rated; contains violence. 91m. **DIR:** Christopher Cain. **CAST:** Jeffrey Sams, Jennifer Garner, Kristin Griffith, Justin Chambers, Zak

Orth, Tristan Tait, Casey Siemaszko, David Newsom. 1997

ROSE MARIE (1936) ★★1/2 If you enjoy MGM's perennial songbirds Nelson Eddy and Jeanette Mac-Donald, you might have fun with this musical romp into the Canadian Rockies. Unintentionally funny dialogue is created by the wooden way Eddy delivers it. B&W; 110m. **DIR:** W. S. Van Dyke. **CAST:** Nelson Eddy, Jeanette MacDonald, James Stewart, Alan Mowbray. 1936

ROSE MARIE (1954) ★★ A remake that shouldn't have been. Without the chemistry of Nelson Eddy and Jeanette MacDonald, the plot is creaky and the music sounds too old-fashioned. The highlight is the subplot between raspy-voiced Marjorie Main and Bert Lahr as "The Mountie Who Never Got His Man." 115m. **DIR:** Mervyn LeRoy. **CAST:** Howard Keel, Ann Blyth, Fernando Lamas, Marjorie Main, Bert Lahr, Ray Collins, Joan Taylor. 1954

ROSE OF WASHINGTON SQUARE ★★★1/2 Tyrone Power is a slick con artist who marries showgirl Alice Faye to cash in on her rising success. Al Jolson (performing many of his famous songs) is outstanding as Faye's mentor. Some cassettes open with an "added feature" of Faye singing "I'm Always Chasing Rainbows" and Jolson belting out both "Avalon" and "April Showers." These were deleted from the movie before its release. B&W; 86m. **DIR:** Gregory Ratoff. **CAST:** Alice Faye, Tyrone Power, Al Jolson, William Frawley, Joyce Compton, Hobart Cavanaugh. 1939

ROSE TATTOO, THE ★★★★ Making her American film debut, volatile Italian star Anna Magnani handily won a best-actress Oscar playing the widow obsessed by the memory of her stud husband. She finally lets go when she finds truck driver Burt Lancaster has a rose tattoo, the symbol of sexual prowess that the departed sported. Tangy and torrid. B&W; 117m. **DIR:** Daniel Mann. **CAST:** Anna Magnani, Burt Lancaster, Marisa Pavan, Ben Cooper, Jo Van Fleet, Virginia Grey. 1955

ROSEANNE: AN UNAUTHORIZED BIOGRAPHY ❤ Definitely one of those "What were they thinking?" excursions into tabloid-television trash. Not rated. 90m. **DIR:** Paul Schneider. **CAST:** Denny Dillon, David Graf, John Karlen. 1994

ROSEBUD BEACH HOTEL, THE (NOSTELL HOTEL, THE) ❤ Colleen Camp and Peter Scolari take over her father's failing hotel and hire prostitutes as bellgirls to improve business. Rated R. 82m. **DIR:** Harry Hurwitz. **CAST:** Colleen Camp, Peter Scolari, Christopher Lee, Hamilton Camp, Eddie Deezen, Chuck McCann, Hank Garrett. 1985

ROSELAND ★★1/2 A somewhat overly respectful triptych set in the famous, now-tattered, New York dance palace. The three stories are quietly compelling, but only Christopher Walken (certainly a good enough dancer) and Don DeNatale (who was an emcee at Roseland) give the film any vim. 103m. **DIR:** James Ivory. **CAST:** Christopher Walken, Geraldine Chaplin, Teresa Wright, Lou Jacobi, Don DeNatale, Lilia Skala. 1977

ROSEMARY'S BABY ★★★★ Mia Farrow is a young woman forced by her husband (John Cassavetes) into an unholy arrangement with a group of devil worshipers. The suspense is sustained as she is made aware that people around her are not what they seem. Ruth Gordon is priceless in her Oscar-winning role as one of the seemingly normal neighbors. Rated R. 136m. **DIR:** Roman Polanski. **CAST:** Mia Farrow, John Cassavetes, Ruth Gordon, Ralph Bellamy, Elisha Cook Jr., Maurice Evans, Patsy Kelly. 1968

ROSENCRANTZ AND GUILDENSTERN ARE DEAD ★★★1/2 Filmization of Tom Stoppard's immensely witty Shakespearean spin-off, which changes the tone of *Hamlet* from tragedy to comedy. The screen version marks the playwright's debut as a director. Rated PG. 118m. **DIR:** Tom Stoppard. **CAST:** Gary Oldman, Tim Roth, Richard Dreyfuss. 1991

ROSEWOOD ★★★★ This compelling study of events that led to the destruction of a peaceful 1923 Florida community begins when a promiscuous white woman in Sumner claims to have been beaten by a black man; her angry white-trash neighbors, jealous of the dignified black residents in neighboring Rosewood, seize this excuse to mount a massive lynching party. Oddly, director John Singleton blends this bleak slice of history with a bit of Kurosawa; Ving Rhames, cast as a heroic "man with no name," rides into Rosewood at just the right moment. The climax adopts the tone of an *Indiana Jones* adventure, but Singleton adroitly juggles these varying moods. Rated R for violence, profanity, nudity, and torture. 140m. **DIR:** John Singleton. **CAST:** Jon Voight, Ving Rhames, Don Cheadle, Bruce McGill, Loren Dean, Esther Rolle, Michael Rooker. 1997 DVD

ROSIE ★★★ Rosemary Clooney sings behind Sondra Locke's acting in this vivid, no-holds-barred rendition of the famed singer's autobiography *This for Remembrance*. Always an upfront gal, Clooney let it all hang out in telling of her rise to stardom, mental breakdown, and successful uphill fight to regain star status. Made for TV. 100m. **DIR:** Jackie Cooper. **CAST:** Sondra Locke, Tony Orlando, Katherine Helmond, Penelope Milford, Kevin McCarthy, John Karlen. 1982

ROSWELL ★★★ This purported docudrama concerns a 1947 UFO crash discovered—and subsequently buried—by army intelligence officers. Kyle MacLachlan and Martin Sheen lend stature to an otherwise pedestrian project that wallows in melodrama while taking itself far too seriously. Rated PG-13 for profanity. 91m. **DIR:** Jeremy Paul Kagan. **CAST:** Kyle MacLachlan, Martin Sheen, Dwight Yoakam, Xander Berkeley, Kim Greist, Charles Martin Smith. 1994

•ROSWELL: THE ALIENS ATTACK ❤ Pitiful made-for-TV movie about the crash of an alien spacecraft, a government cover-up, and aliens in human form, complete with glowing green eyes. Of all the films about the supposed Roswell incident, this has to be the absolute worst one. Rated PG for mild violence. 89m. **DIR:** Brad Turner. **CAST:** Steven Flynn. 1998

R.O.T.O.R. ❤ Abysmal variation on the *Robocop* theme has a part-man, part-machine police officer going berserk. Rated R for violence and profanity. 91m. **DIR:** Cullen Blaine. **CAST:** Richard Gesswein. 1988

ROUGH CUT ★★★ The screenplay, by Francis Burns, is a welcome return to the stylish romantic comedies of the 1930s and 1940s with the accent on witty dialogue, action, and suspense. Burt Reynolds and Lesley-Anne Down are a perfect screen combination. As two sophisticated jewel thieves who plot to steal $30 million in uncut diamonds, they exchange quips, become romantically entwined, and are delightful. Rated R. 112m. **DIR:** Don Siegel. **CAST:** Burt Reynolds, Lesley-Anne Down, David Niven, Patrick Magee. 1980

ROUGH JUSTICE ♥ Spaghetti Western, with Klaus Kinski as a sex-crazed outlaw. Not rated; contains violence. 95m. **DIR:** Mario Costa. **CAST:** Klaus Kinski, Steven Tedd. 1987

ROUGH MAGIC ★★★ This very strange brew of *film noir*, magic realism, and screwball adventure is an entertaining mess. Magician's assistant Myra flees to Mexico in the 1950s after her politically ambitious fiancé shoots her mentor. An American reporter hired to find Myra falls in love with her. Myra then shares an elixir with a Mayan sorceress, lays a blue egg, and transforms a menacing cantina owner into a large sausage. Rated PG-13 for language, violence, and sex between rabbits. 104m. **DIR:** Clare Peploe. **CAST:** Bridget Fonda, Russell Crowe, Jim Broadbent, D. W. Moffett, Paul Rodriguez. 1997

ROUGH NIGHT IN JERICHO ★★1/2 Former marshal George Peppard doesn't want to get involved when Jean Simmons finds her stagecoach line threatened with a takeover. Power-hungry town boss Dean Martin's brutal tactics make Peppard change his mind. Violent Western has its moments, both good and not so good. 104m. **DIR:** Arnold Laven. **CAST:** Dean Martin, Jean Simmons, George Peppard, John McIntire, Slim Pickens, Don Galloway. 1967

ROUGH RIDERS ★★★★ High production values set this TNT miniseries apart from typical TV fare. Based on Teddy Roosevelt's successful siege at San Juan Hill in Cuba circa 1898, Tom Berenger creates an annoying stereotype of our former president as an overeager military novice. Berenger is overshadowed by Sam Elliott's commanding presence and a scene-stealing Gary Busey. Brian Keith appears in his final role, as President McKinley. Epic battle scenes blend grit with glory. Not rated; contains violence and nudity. 175m. **DIR:** John Milius. **CAST:** Tom Berenger, Gary Busey, Sam Elliott, William Katt, Brad Johnson, Brian Keith, Illeana Douglas. 1997

ROUGH RIDERS' ROUNDUP ★★1/2 The accent is more on action than music in this early Roy Rogers Western about the Rough Riders reuniting to rid the range of an outlaw gang. In all, it's better than most of the Rogers vehicles that followed. B&W; 58m. **DIR:** Joseph Kane. **CAST:** Roy Rogers, Lynne Roberts (Mary Hart), Raymond Hatton, Eddie Acuff. 1939

ROUGHNECKS ★★ This TV miniseries centers around a bunch of good old boys trying to drill a geothermal well in Texas. The old-timers resent the land being disrupted. Protracted would-be-actioner. 180m. **DIR:** Bernard McEveety. **CAST:** Sam Melville, Cathy Lee Crosby, Vera Miles, Harry Morgan, Steve Forrest. 1980

ROUND MIDNIGHT ★★★★ French director Bertrand Tavernier's ode to American jazz is a long overdue celebration of that great American music and its brilliant exponents. It tells a semifictionalized story of a friendship between a self-destructive, be-bop tenor saxophonist (Dexter Gordon) and an avid French fan (Franáois Cluzet). Rated R. 133m. **DIR:** Bertrand Tavernier. **CAST:** Dexter Gordon, François Cluzet, Lonette McKee, Christine Pascal, Herbie Hancock. 1986

ROUND NUMBERS ★★ A dowdy woman suspects her husband is cheating. Uneven and frequently amateurish sex comedy. Rated R for profanity and nudity. 98m. **DIR:** Nancy Zala. **CAST:** Kate Mulgrew, Samantha Eggar. 1992

ROUND TRIP TO HEAVEN ★★1/2 Corey Feldman drags cousin Zach Galligan along to Palm Springs in a stolen Rolls to meet a super model. Typical chase film. Rated R for violence, nudity, and language. 97m. **DIR:** Alan Roberts. **CAST:** Corey Feldman, Zach Galligan, Ray Sharkey, Julie McCullough. 1991

ROUNDERS ★★★★ Director John Dahl's edgy, richly atmospheric film is a mesmerizing study of the high-stakes poker (under) world, and its impact on one young man (Matt Damon) who tries to remain honorable in the face of increasingly overwhelming odds. In terms of sheer mood, this production elicits pleasant memories of *The Cincinnati Kid*, another of the great card-playing movies of all time. Damon plays a "recovered" high-stakes poker player trying to stay clean while working his way through law school. Plans are derailed by the arrival of his best friend "Worm" (Edward Norton), freshly out of prison and determined to settle some scores. And, much to our hero's horror, Worm cheats. What follows is a study of integrity among thieves, a provocative balance between the dour grit of *Leaving Las Vegas* and the calculated insight of *Flesh and Bone*. Rated R for profanity, nudity, and violence. 120m. **DIR:** John Dahl. **CAST:** Matt Damon, Edward Norton, John Turturro, Famke Janssen, Gretchen Mol, John Malkovich, Martin Landau. 1998 DVD

ROUNDERS (1998) ★★★★ Director John Dahl's edgy film is a mesmerizing study of the high-stakes poker (under) world, and its impact on one young man (Matt Damon) who tries to remain honorable in the face of increasingly overwhelming odds. Damon plays a "recovered" high-stakes poker player trying to stay clean while working his way through law school. Plans are derailed by the arrival of his best friend "Worm" (Edward Norton), freshly out of prison and determined to settle some scores. And, much to our hero's horror, Worm cheats. What follows is a study of integrity among thieves. Rated R for profanity, nudity, and violence. 120m. **DIR:** John Dahl. **CAST:** Matt Damon, Edward Norton, John Turturro, Famke Janssen, Gretchen Mol, John Malkovich, Martin Landau. 1998

ROUNDERS, THE (1965) ★★1/2 Burt Kennedy, a solid scriptwriter of Fifties Westerns turned director in the Sixties—with hit-and-miss results. He had one of his stronger casts in this comic saga of two reluctant ranch-hand cronies. 85m. **DIR:** Burt Kennedy. **CAST:** Glenn Ford, Henry Fonda, Sue Ane Langdon, Hope Holiday, Edgar Buchanan, Chill Wills, Kathleen Freeman. 1965

ROUND-UP, THE ★★★★ In 1868, Hungarian police looking for the leaders of a political uprising subject a group of suspects to psychological warfare. A powerful, austere work; one of the most influential films in Hungarian cinema. In Hungarian with English subtitles. Not rated. B&W; 94m. **DIR:** Miklos Jancso. **CAST:** Janos Gorbe, Tibor Molnar. **1965**

ROUSTABOUT ★★1/2 Barbara Stanwyck, as the carnival owner, upgrades this typical Elvis Presley picture. In this release, Presley is a young wanderer who finds a home in the carnival as a singer. Naturally, Elvis combines romance with hard work on the midway. 101m. **DIR:** John Rich. **CAST:** Barbara Stanwyck, Elvis Presley, Leif Erickson, Sue Ane Langdon. **1964 DVD**

ROUSTERS, THE ★★★ TV pilot actioner features Chad Everett as a carnival bouncer named Wyatt Earp III. He cleverly deals with insurance fraud, domestic abuse, and an armed robbery. Fun blend of violence, humor, and crime resolution. Rated PG for violence. 72m. **DIR:** E. W. Swackhamer. **CAST:** Chad Everett, Jim Varney, Mimi Rogers. **1983**

ROUTE 9 ★★ Despite a decent cast and some genuinely suspenseful moments, this tale of two small-town deputies who stumble across a van full of dead people, drugs, and $1 million in cash fails to rise above the ordinary. Rated R for violence, language, and adult situations. 102m. **DIR:** David Mackay. **CAST:** Kyle MacLachlan, Peter Coyote, Amy Locane, Wade Andrew Williams, Roma Maffia, Miguel Sandoval. **1998**

ROVER DANGERFIELD ★★★ Rodney Dangerfield takes the plunge as an animated character in this feature-length cartoon about a city dog who ends up on a farm. Some harder-edged elements—suggestions of violence and songs about dogs "doing their business" on a Christmas tree—may offend some parents. Otherwise, it's generally enjoyable. Rated G. 71m. **DIR:** Jim George, Bob Seely. **1991**

ROWING WITH THE WIND ★★★★ Moody, atmospheric Spanish production that stars Hugh Grant as Lord Byron, who spends a fateful summer with Percy and Mary Shelley, and Claire Clairmont. When Mary Shelley begins writing *Frankenstein*, she fears that her monster has risen from the pages to bring death to their small group. Nightmarish images, lush locales, a European feel, and performances with conviction distinguish this effort. Rated R for violence, adult themes, and nudity. 120m. **DIR:** Gonzalo Suarez. **CAST:** Hugh Grant, Elizabeth Hurley, Lizzy McInnerny, Valentine Pelka. **1987**

ROXANNE ★★★★1/2 Steve Martin's most effective and rewarding comedy, based on Rostand's *Cyrano de Bergerac*. Martin plays the big-nosed fire chief who befriends a professional firefighter who has come to train the inept local firemen. While there, he meets and falls in love with the title character and enlists Martin's aid in wooing her with words. Rated PG for profanity and suggested sex. 107m. **DIR:** Fred Schepisi. **CAST:** Steve Martin, Daryl Hannah, Shelley Duvall, Rick Rossovich, Michael J. Pollard, Fred Willard. **1987 DVD**

ROXIE HART ★★★★★ Ginger Rogers stars in one of Hollywood's funniest satires. She plays a conniver who looks for as much sympathetic publicity as possible at her own murder trial. It's played for laughs and set in the Roaring Twenties before real-life criminals started doing the same thing. B&W; 75m. **DIR:** William Wellman. **CAST:** Ginger Rogers, George Montgomery, Adolphe Menjou, Phil Silvers, Iris Adrian, Spring Byington. **1942**

ROY ROGERS SHOW, THE (TV SERIES) ★★★ These six tapes contain two episodes each of the 1954–56 TV series. All the memories come back as Roy, Dale, Pat, Trigger, Bulle, and Nellybelle keep the West a safe place to live. Good fun for all. B&W; 46m. **CAST:** Roy Rogers, Dale Evans, Pat Brady. **1954–56**

ROYAL DECEIT ★★★ *Hamlet* redux, as *Babette's Feast* director Gabriel Axel spins this lush tale of a young prince's fight for his father's throne. Gabriel Byrne stars as the bloodthirsty, usurping uncle, and Christian Bale as the prince in this handsome period piece set in sixth-century Denmark. Released in Europe as *Prince of Jutland*. Rated R for nudity and violence. 85m. **DIR:** Gabriel Axel. **CAST:** Gabriel Byrne, Christian Bale, Helen Mirren, Brian Cox, Kate Beckinsale. **1994**

•ROYAL HUNT OF THE SUN ★★★1/2 There's lots of pomp and pageantry in director Irving Lerner's big screen adaptation of Peter Schaffer's stage play. An excellent cast, most notably Robert Shaw and Christopher Plummer, bring life to this tale of Spanish explorer Pizarro, and his search to find gold in South America. Rated G. 118m. **DIR:** Irving Lerner. **CAST:** Robert Shaw, Christopher Plummer, Nigel Davenport, Leonard Whiting, Michael Craig, James Donald. **1969 DVD**

ROYAL WEDDING ★★★ Brother and sister Fred Astaire and Jane Powell are performing in London when Princess Elizabeth marries Philip, and manage to find their own true loves while royalty ties the knot. 92m. **DIR:** Stanley Donen. **CAST:** Fred Astaire, Jane Powell, Sarah Churchill, Peter Lawford, Keenan Wynn. **1951 DVD**

ROYCE ★★★ Amiable spy foolishness, with James Belushi as a wisecracking agent operating for a covert U.S. organization—the Black Hand. Our hero goes into action after cutbacks disband the unit, and disgruntled members steal some nuclear warheads. Rated R for violence, profanity, and nudity. 100m. **DIR:** Rod Holcomb. **CAST:** James Belushi, Chelsea Field, Miguel Ferrer, Peter Boyle. **1994**

R.P.M. (REVOLUTIONS PER MINUTE) ★★ In this story set on a small-town college campus in the late 1960s, a liberal professor (Anthony Quinn) and his coed mistress (Ann-Margret) become involved in the efforts of a liberal student (Gary Lockwood) to have the professor made president of the university. Good intentions turn into campus unrest and violence. Rated R for violence. 92m. **DIR:** Stanley Kramer. **CAST:** Anthony Quinn, Ann-Margret, Gary Lockwood. **1970**

RSVP ★★★ This is an out-and-out sex comedy with lots of nudity and sexual situations. An author has written a novel that turns out to be based on fact. The people who inspired the "characters" have been invited to a Hollywood party to celebrate the making of a movie from the book. The writing is lively, and the puns and gags are funny. Rated R for sexual situations and language that will be offensive to some.

87m. **DIR:** John Almo, Lem Almo. **CAST:** Ray Colbert, Veronica Hart, Carey Hayes. **1984**

RUBBERFACE Comedian Jim Carrey made this Canadian story about an aspiring stand-up comedian in 1981. Carrey plays a cook at a local comedy club who yearns for the spotlight. He stinks, but with the help of a friend, he improves and gets his big chance. Slight effort plays like an after-school special on television. Rated PG. 84m. **DIR:** Glen Salzman, Rebecca Yates. **CAST:** Jim Carrey, Adah Glassbourg. **1981**

RUBDOWN ★★ In this made-for-cable original, an ex–baseball player who is now a *masseur* is paid to seduce a man's wife so the man can get a divorce. Instead, the husband winds up dead. Weak story line and mediocre acting. Not rated for violence and suggested sex. 88m. **DIR:** Stuart Cooper. **CAST:** Michelle Phillips, Jack Coleman, Kent Williams, Alan Thicke, Catherine Oxenberg, William Devane. **1993**

RUBIN & ED ★★ Wannabe salesman Howard Hesseman must bring someone—anyone—to his success seminar. The only one he can convince is a very weird Sixties throwback (Crispin Glover) who insists on burying his cat on the way. Plain strange. Rated PG-13 for profanity. 82m. **DIR:** Trent Harris. **CAST:** Crispin Glover, Howard Hesseman, Karen Black, Michael Greene. **1991**

RUBY (1977) ★★ A sleazy drive-in is the setting for this unexciting horror film about a young girl possessed by the homicidal ghost of a dead gangster. Rated R for gore. 84m. **DIR:** Curtis Harrington. **CAST:** Piper Laurie, Stuart Whitman, Roger Davis. **1977**

RUBY (1991) ★★★1/2 Superb performances help elevate this largely fictional account of the secret life of Dallas nightclub owner Jack Ruby, who became infamous for killing Lee Harvey Oswald. As with director John Mackenzie's classic British gangster film, *The Long Good Friday*, the characters and tense, realistic situations overcome the familiarity of certain key events. Rated R for violence and profanity. 100m. **DIR:** John Mackenzie. **CAST:** Danny Aiello, Sherilyn Fenn, Arliss Howard, Tobin Bell, David Duchovny, Richard Sarafian, Joe Cortese, Marc Lawrence. **1991**

RUBY GENTRY ★★★ An excellent cast and sensitive direction make this drama of a Carolina swamp girl's social progress better than might be expected. Its focus is the caste system and prejudice in a picturesque region of the great melting pot. B&W; 82m. **DIR:** King Vidor. **CAST:** Jennifer Jones, Charlton Heston, Karl Malden, Tom Tully. **1952**

RUBY IN PARADISE ★★★★ Engagingly offbeat character study about a young woman who leaves her husband and home in the Tennessee mountains for what she hopes will be a better life in Florida. The challenges faced by a young woman out on her own are thoughtfully presented in this well-made film, which benefits from an impressive big-screen debut by Ashley Judd. Rated R for brief profanity and simulated sex. 105m. **DIR:** Victor Nunez. **CAST:** Ashley Judd, Todd Field, Bentley Mitchum, Allison Dean, Dorothy Lyman, Betsy Douds, Felicia Hernandez. **1993**

RUBY JEAN AND JOE ★★★ Star–executive producer Tom Selleck obviously liked what he saw in James Lee Barrett's charming little script, and the resulting film is an engaging—if lightweight—character study. Selleck's an aging rodeo star with a fondness for classical music and an uncertain future; Rebekah Johnson is a precocious teenage hitchhiker who becomes a companion, then friend, then … ? Rated PG-13 for profanity and nudity. 100m. **DIR:** Geoffrey Sax. **CAST:** Tom Selleck, JoBeth Williams, Ben Johnson, Rebekah Johnson, Eileen Seeley, John Diehl. **1995**

RUCKUS ★★★1/2 This lighthearted adventure film is like *Rambo* without the killing. That's one of the appealing things about this tale of a Vietnam soldier, Dirk Benedict, who escapes from an army psycho ward in Mobile and ends up in a little southern town where he is harassed by the locals—but not for long. PG for violence and language. 91m. **DIR:** Max Kleven. **CAST:** Dirk Benedict, Linda Blair, Ben Johnson, Richard Farnsworth, Matt Clark. **1984**

RUDE ★★★★ This extremely well-made look at urban life interweaves stories about a woman recovering from a failed relationship, a sexually confused athlete, and an ex-con who is finding it hard to go straight. A film-festival favorite that wasn't widely distributed, this is worth seeing. Rated R for profanity, sexual situations, and violence. 90m. **DIR:** Clement Virgo. **CAST:** Sharon M. Lewis, Richard Chevolleau, Rachel Crawford. **1996 DVD**

RUDE AWAKENING (1982) ★★1/2 In another of Elvira's "Thriller Video" series, and one of the best, a real-estate broker finds himself sucked into dreams that seem like reality; or is it the other way around? It sounds standard, but it's better than you would think. 60m. **DIR:** Peter Sasdy. **CAST:** Denholm Elliott, James Laurenson, Pat Heywood. **1982**

RUDE AWAKENING (1989) ★★★ In 1969 two draft dodgers (Cheech Marin and Eric Roberts) flee from the FBI and drop out to Central America until a twist of fate fans their liberal fires and propels them to New York City in 1989. Rated R for language. 100m. **DIR:** Aaron Russo. **CAST:** Richard "Cheech" Marin, Eric Roberts, Julie Hagerty, Robert Carradine, Buck Henry, Louise Lasser, Cindy Williams, Andrea Martin, Cliff De Young. **1989**

RUDE BOY ★★★1/2 Meandering, overlong docudrama about an unemployed British teen who gets a job as a roadie with The Clash. An interesting document of the punk era, but what makes it essential viewing for music fans are plentiful performances by The Clash. Not rated, but an R equivalent for profanity. 133m. **DIR:** Jack Hazan, David Mingay. **CAST:** Ray Gange. **1980**

RUDY ★★★★1/2 Based on the life of Daniel E. (Rudy) Ruettiger, this is an excellent family film about a young man who sets a goal for himself and pursues it with dogged determination. From the people who made the equally impressive *Hoosiers*, it's a down-to-earth story with spirit-lifting rewards. Like young Rudy, played with engaging sincerity by Sean Astin, the filmmakers have us cheering them all the way. Rated PG for brief profanity. 112m. **DIR:** David Anspaugh. **CAST:** Sean Astin, Ned Beatty, Charles Dutton, Robert Prosky, Jason Miller, Lili Taylor, Greta Lind, Chelcie Ross. **1993**

RUDYARD KIPLING'S THE JUNGLE BOOK (1994) ★★★★ Terrific family adventure about a boy, Mowgli, who is lost in the jungle at the age of five and raised by animals. Returning to civilization as a young adult, our pure-hearted hero falls in love and finds himself in conflict with a rival suitor. Both parents and their children should enjoy this lavish, smartly paced film. Rated PG for violence. 110m. **DIR:** Stephen Sommers. **CAST:** Jason Scott Lee, Cary Elwes, Lena Headey, Sam Neill, John Cleese, Jason Flemyng. 1994

RUGGLES OF RED GAP ★★★1/2 Charles Laughton is superb as Ruggles, the valet who is lost in a poker game by a continental gentleman (Roland Young) to Americans (Charlie Ruggles and Mary Boland). The latter take him from Paris to the wilds of 1908 Washington State. Hilarious. B&W; 92m. **DIR:** Leo McCarey. **CAST:** Charles Laughton, Mary Boland, Charlie Ruggles, ZaSu Pitts, Roland Young, Leila Hyams. 1935

RUGRATS MOVIE, THE ★★★1/2 This feature will be adored by those who enjoy the Nickelodeon television series on which it is based. These folks deserve high fives for their successful translation of this wacky tot's-eye view of life in the big, wide world. It's a charming adventure, presented in the inventive, squiggly line art that has become the Rugrats signature style; the artwork perfectly conveys the sloppy, sticky, and unfathomable universe as experienced by a gaggle of unusually perceptive toddlers. The story concerns the arrival of Tommy Pickles's new baby brother, a shrieking little bundle of joy named Dylan (shortened to Dil). All ages will have fun with what follows. Rated G; suitable for all ages. 87m. **DIR:** Norton Virgien, Igor Kovalyov. 1998 DVD

RULE #3 ★★ If the acting weren't so atrocious, this would be a pretty slick little thriller. Alas, writer-star-director Mitchell Cox is wearing at least two hats too many; his twists on *The Sting* may keep folks guessing, but the stiff performances are strictly amateur night. Rated PG-13 for violence and profanity. 90m. **DIR:** Mitchell Cox. **CAST:** Mitchell Cox, Marcia Swayze, Jerry Rector. 1993

•**RULES OF ENGAGEMENT** ★★★★ Sent in to rescue the besieged American ambassador to Yemen, highly decorated Marine Col. Terry Childers orders his men to open fire on the crowd of seemingly peaceful demonstrators, causing the deaths of more than eighty men, women, and children, while ignoring the rooftop snipers openly firing on the embassy. An international incident results with Childers held responsible, so he asks Col. Hays Hodges, whose life he saved in Vietnam, to defend him. Director William Friedkin keeps the audience guessing along with the characters as to Childers's guilt or innocence in this gripping drama. Rated R for profanity and violence. 123m. **DIR:** William Friedkin. **CAST:** Tommy Lee Jones, Samuel L. Jackson, Guy Pearce, Bruce Greenwood, Ben Kingsley, Blair Underwood, Philip Baker Hall, Anne Archer, Mark Feuerstein. 2000

RULES OF THE GAME, THE ★★★★★ This is Jean Renoir's masterful comedy-farce that deftly exposes the moral bankruptcy of the French upper classes. A manor house is the location for a party as the shallowness of each guest is brilliantly exposed. B&W; 110m. **DIR:** Jean Renoir. **CAST:** Marcel Dalio, Nora Gregor, Mila Parely. 1939

RULING CLASS, THE ★★★★ Superbly irreverent satire about upper-crust British eccentricities. Peter O'Toole plays the heir to a peerage who proves problematic because of his insane belief that he is Jesus Christ. Rated PG. 154m. **DIR:** Peter Medak. **CAST:** Peter O'Toole, Alastair Sim, Arthur Lowe, Harry Andrews, Coral Browne. 1972

RUMBLE FISH ★★ Francis Ford Coppola's black-and-white screen portrait of S. E. Hinton's second-rate novel about a teenage boy (Matt Dillon) seeking to escape his hellish life is a disappointing misfire. Rated R. B&W; 94m. **DIR:** Francis Ford Coppola. **CAST:** Christopher Penn, Tom Waits, Matt Dillon, Dennis Hopper, Vincent Spano, Mickey Rourke. 1983 DVD

RUMBLE IN THE BRONX ★★★★ You don't have to be a Jackie Chan fan to enjoy this action-packed comedy from the Hong Kong superstar. Chan plays an innocent abroad—and he's in New York City for a very short time before a grocery store run by a friend is under siege by a biker gang. Of course, it's up to the remarkable Chan, who does all of his own stunts, to save the day. This is topflight entertainment. Rated R for profanity and violence. 97m. **DIR:** Stanley Tong. **CAST:** Jackie Chan, Anita Mui, Francoise Yip. 1996 DVD

RUMBLE IN THE STREETS 🎗 Predictable tale of a female street kid who teams up with an aspiring singer in Dallas to outwit a renegade cop who is killing street kids. It's hard to root for characters you would rather see dead. Rated R for adult situations, language, and violence. 87m. **DIR:** Bret McCormick. **CAST:** David Courtemarche, Kimberly Rowe, Patrick DeFazio. 1996

RUMIK WORLD: FIRETRIPPER ★★ In this animated feature, a young girl with the unexplained ability to time travel lives in two worlds—feudal and modern-day Japan. Not as engrossing as others in the *Rumik World* series, but it does have a few points of interest. In Japanese with English subtitles. Not rated; contains brief nudity. 50m. **DIR:** Osamu Uemura. 1992

RUMIK WORLD: LAUGHING TARGET ★★★ A suspenseful animated story of love and demonic possession (not a strange combination when compared to other Japanese animation) that moves along with the excellent pacing we expect from the *Rumik World* series. Most viewers will find this exploration of the Japanese occult world a refreshing change of pace. In Japanese with English subtitles. Not rated; contains violence and brief nudity. 50m. **DIR:** Tohru Matsuzono. 1992

RUMIK WORLD: THE SUPERGAL ★★★ Japanese animation. One of four stories from Rumiko Takahashi's imaginative *Rumik World* universe. Maris, a young woman in the service of the Space Police, lives in perpetual debt because of the inadvertent destruction of property brought about by her incredible strength. When assigned to rescue the kidnapped son of a billionaire, Maris sees her chance to finally get out of hock. In Japanese with English subtitles. Not rated; contains nudity. 50m. **DIR:** Kazuyashi Katayama, Tomoko Konparu. 1992

RUMOR MILL, THE ★★ Hokey soap opera played to the hilt by Elizabeth Taylor and Jane Alexander as rival gossip queens Louella Parsons and Hedda Hopper. Plenty of cat fights and eye-piercing high camp. Made-for-TV melodrama (that originally aired as *Malice in Wonderland*). 94m. **DIR:** Gus Trikonis. **CAST:** Elizabeth Taylor, Jane Alexander, Richard Dysart. 1988

RUMOR OF WAR, A ★★★ A well-made television movie about a Marine combat unit in Vietnam. Brad Davis plays a young officer who bravely leads his men into combat. He eventually gets charged with murder. The video version is about an hour and a half shorter than the original television print. Too bad. 105m. **DIR:** Richard T. Heffron. **CAST:** Brad Davis, Keith Carradine, Stacy Keach, Michael O'Keefe. 1980

RUMPELSTILTSKIN ★★ Inane, vicious thriller about the sadistic storybook character on the loose in modern-day Los Angeles. A young mother unleashes the devilish dwarf and then is forced into action when Rumpelstiltskin sets his sights on her son. Standard-issue horror entry brings nothing new to the genre. Rated R for violence, profanity, and adult situations. 91m. **DIR:** Mark Jones. **CAST:** Kim Johnston Ulrich, Tommy Blaze, Allyce Beasley, Max Grodenchik. 1995 DVD

RUMPOLE OF THE BAILEY (TV SERIES) ★★★★★ John Mortimer's charming and witty *Rumpole of the Bailey* is faithfully adapted in this British TV mystery series concerning a lovable old barrister who defends his clients with originality and flamboyance. Leo McKern's Horace Rumpole brings the English criminal justice system to life with the help (or hindrance) of fellow Chambers members Claude Erskine-Brown (Julian Curry), Phyllida Trant (Patricia Hodge), and Guthrie Featherstone (Peter Bowles). Rumpole's wife, Hilda, is wonderfully portrayed by Marion Mathie. Although the entire series is superb, take particular note of "Rumpole and the Alternative Society" and "Rumpole and the Blind Tasting." Each episode 52m. **DIR:** Roger Bamford, Rodney Bennett, Martyn Friend. **CAST:** Leo McKern, Marion Mathie, Julian Curry, Patricia Hodge, Peter Bowles. 1979–1981

RUN ★★★ Patrick Dempsey is a young law student who is wrongly accused of murdering the son of a mob boss, and must now avoid the vengeful father and the corrupt local police force. The action is nonstop and Dempsey's one-liners are always perfectly timed. Rated R for violence and profanity. 89m. **DIR:** Geoff Burrowes. **CAST:** Patrick Dempsey, Kelly Preston, Ken Pogue, Christopher Lawford. 1991

RUN FOR THE DREAM ★★★ This serviceable account of Olympic champion Gail Devers, who struggled to master a disease that nearly crippled her, has its heart in the right place; it's simply too pat and superficial to really engage the viewer. Focusing on her deterioration, the film sheds little insight into her hell-on-wheels battle to walk and run again. Rated PG for medical intensity. 95m. **DIR:** Neema Barnette. **CAST:** Lou Gossett Jr., Charlayne Woodard, Jeffrey Sams, Tina Lifford, Paula Kelly, Robert Guillaume. 1996

RUN FOR THE ROSES (THOROUGHBRED) ★★1/2 This is a *Rocky*-ish saga about a horse that eventually competes in the Kentucky Derby. A Puerto Rican boy, devotes himself to making the nearly lame horse a winner. Rated PG. 93m. **DIR:** Henry Levin. **CAST:** Vera Miles, Stuart Whitman, Sam Groom, Panchito Gomez. 1978

RUN FOR THE SUN ★★★1/2 There have been many adaptations of Richard Connell's masterful suspense tale, *The Most Dangerous Game*, but this crackling remake is the first one in color. Plane crash survivors Richard Widmark and Jane Greer are the quarry of fugitive Nazi Peter Van Eyck in the South American jungle. Ferocious, imaginative, and exciting. Filmed in Mexico. 99m. **DIR:** Roy Boulting. **CAST:** Richard Widmark, Jane Greer, Trevor Howard, Peter Van Eyck. 1956

RUN FOR YOUR MONEY, A ★★★★ A pair of Welsh miners in London for a day get into more than their share of misadventures. One of the best of the Ealing Studios comedies—if you're a fan of British humor, this one's a must-see. B&W; 83m. **DIR:** Charles Frend. **CAST:** Alec Guinness, Meredith Edwards, Moira Lister, Donald Houston, Hugh Griffith. 1949

RUN IF YOU CAN ★ An incomprehensible police thriller. Rated R for nudity and violence. 92m. **DIR:** Virginia Lively Stone. **CAST:** Martin Landau, Yvette Napir, Jerry Van Dyke. 1987

•**RUN LOLA RUN** ★★★1/2 You've got to love the manic energy at work here, even if the execution is rather strange. German writer-director Tom Tykwer's central gimmick in this 81-minute marvel concerns the differing paths that lives will take, as with *Sliding Doors* or *Groundhog Day*, on the basis of seemingly insignificant changes. The resulting series of varying loops will continue until a woman can get 100,000 marks to her boyfriend—in 20 minutes—and save him. If it's true that half the fun of any artistic medium is discovering those who eschew the same-old-same-old and deliver something fresh, then Tykwer clearly is a talent on the upswing. While not for all tastes—many will dismiss Tykwer as hopelessly bizarre and self-indulgent—this is an impressively vivid experience. Rated R for profanity, violence, nudity, and drug use. In German with English subtitles. 81m. **DIR:** Tom Tykwer. **CAST:** Franka Potente, Moritz Bleibtreu, Herbert Knaup, Armin Rohde. 1999 DVD

RUN OF THE ARROW ★★★ One of the strangest of all adult Westerns of the 1950s, this film tells the story of a man who joins the Sioux tribe after the Civil War rather than accept the reality of the South's defeat. Rod Steiger does a good job in a difficult role. While not entirely successful, this thought-provoking film is worth watching. 85m. **DIR:** Samuel Fuller. **CAST:** Rod Steiger, Brian Keith, Ralph Meeker, Sarita Montiel, Tim McCoy, Jay C. Flippen, Charles Bronson. 1957

RUN OF THE COUNTRY, THE ★★★★ Fabulous Irish film features Albert Finney as a crusty constable who must cope with his son, as well as his own failed dreams, after his wife's death. Superior acting, gorgeous scenery, and a fine musical score enhance the intriguing plot and add up to nonstop entertainment. Rated R for nudity, sex, violence, and profanity. 110m. DIR: Peter Yates. CAST: Albert Finney, Matt Kesslar, Anthony Brophy, Victoria Smurfit. 1995

RUN, REBECCA, RUN ★★★★ This action-filled adventure finds a brave young girl captured by an illegal alien on an Australian island. Her fear of him soon dissolves as she helps him face the Australian authorities in order to be legally admitted to their country. 81m. DIR: Peter Maxwell. CAST: Henri Szeps, Simone Buchanan, John Stanton. 1983

RUN SILENT, RUN DEEP ★★★★ Clark Gable becomes the captain of a submarine that Burt Lancaster was to command. Although he resents his new boss, Lancaster stays on. Tensions rise among Lancaster, Gable, and the crew as they set out from Pearl Harbor to destroy a Japanese cruiser. This film is noted as one of the finest World War II submarine movies. B&W; 93m. DIR: Robert Wise. CAST: Clark Gable, Burt Lancaster, Jack Warden, Don Rickles. 1958 DVD

RUN STRANGER RUN ★★★1/2 Ron Howard plays a teenager searching for his biological parents in a seaside town. Once there, he discovers that some of the town inhabitants have been disappearing. Unfortunately, the disappearances are closely linked to his past. Overall, this film keeps viewer interest without dwelling on the slash-'em-up theme. Rated PG for gore. 92m. DIR: Darren McGavin. CAST: Patricia Neal, Cloris Leachman, Ron Howard, Bobby Darin. 1973

RUNAWAY ★★★ Tom Selleck is a futuristic cop trying to track down a bunch of killer robots controlled by the evil villain (Gene Simmons, from the rock band KISS). It's a cinematic comic book and, although meant to be a thriller, never really gets the viewer involved in the story. Rated PG-13 for violence. 99m. DIR: Michael Crichton. CAST: Tom Selleck, Cynthia Rhodes, Gene Simmons, Kirstie Alley. 1984

•RUNAWAY BRIDE ★★★1/2 Julia Roberts surmounts this project's improbable script through sheer force of will, and the result—while absolutely preposterous—is reasonably entertaining. She plays a woman in rural Maryland with a habit of leaving eligible husbands at the altar; this intrigues a New York–based journalist (Richard Gere) who routinely lambastes women in a regular column intended to shed light on the battle of the sexes. He gets some facts wrong; she complains and gets him fired. And so, by way of revenge, he travels to her small community and falls in love with her. Or something like that. Not one remotely credible character inhabits this film, but Roberts is impossible to resist: a classic case of star power overwhelming pedestrian material. Rated PG for mild dramatic content. 106m. DIR: Garry Marshall. CAST: Julia Roberts, Richard Gere, Joan Cusack, Rita Wilson, Hector Elizondo, Paul Dooley. 1999 DVD

RUNAWAY FATHER ★★ Made-for-TV true story stars Donna Mills as a wife out to prove that her missing husband faked his death in order to leave his family. Standard fare gets a boost from durable cast, including Jack Scalia as the scoundrel. Not rated. 94m. DIR: John Nicolella. CAST: Donna Mills, Jack

Scalia, Chris Mulkey, Jenifer Lewis, Priscilla Pointer. 1991

RUNAWAY NIGHTMARE 🖤 Two Nevada worm ranchers are kidnapped by a gang of beautiful women. 104m. DIR: Michael Cartel. CAST: Michael Cartel, Al Valletta. 1984

RUNAWAY TRAIN ★★★★ In this riveting, pulse-pounding adventure movie, two convicts escape from prison and, accompanied by a hostage (Rebecca DeMornay), make the mistake of hopping a train speeding straight for disaster. While the story gets a bit too allegorical and philosophical on occasion, the unrelenting intensity more than makes up for it. Rated R for violence, gore, and profanity. 112m. DIR: Andrei Konchalovsky. CAST: Jon Voight, Eric Roberts, Rebecca DeMornay, John P. Ryan, Kenneth McMillan, Kyle T. Heffner, T. K. Carter. 1986 DVD

RUNESTONE ★★★ An ancient Norse runestone that contains a mythical demon is unearthed and brought to New York City. When an archaeologist discovers its forbidden curse, not even the police can stop the carnage. Rated R for violence, profanity, and nudity. 105m. DIR: Willard Carroll. CAST: Peter Riegert, Joan Severance, William Hickey, Tim Ryan, Lawrence Tierney, Chris Young, Alexander Godunov. 1990

RUNNER STUMBLES, THE ★★★ A good adaptation of Milan Stitt's play, which certainly did not deserve the scorching hatred generated during its brief box-office appearance. Dick Van Dyke plays a priest who falls in love with Kathleen Quinlan's appealing nun. The subject may make viewers uneasy, but the film is by no means tacky or exploitative. Rated PG for adult subject matter. 99m. DIR: Stanley Kramer. CAST: Dick Van Dyke, Kathleen Quinlan, Maureen Stapleton, Beau Bridges. 1979

RUNNING AGAINST TIME ★★1/2 Historian Robert Hays employs physicist Sam Wanamaker's time-travel machine in an effort to prevent Kennedy's assassination but things go horribly awry. Those accustomed to the carefully plotted intricacies of *Back to the Future* will be dismayed by this sloppy made-for-cable time-travel tale, adapted rather freely from Stanley Shapiro's *A Time to Remember*. Rated PG. 93m. DIR: Bruce Seth Green. CAST: Robert Hays, Catherine Hicks, Sam Wanamaker. 1990

RUNNING AWAY ★★ Pointless WWII film features Sophia Loren and Sydney Penny as an Italian mother and daughter team traveling from what seemed a comparatively safe Rome to the mountains. Rated PG-13 for violence. 101m. DIR: Dino Risi. CAST: Sophia Loren, Sydney Penny, Robert Loggia, Andrea Occhipinti. 1989

RUNNING BRAVE ★★★★ Robby Benson stars as Billy Mills, whose winning the ten-thousand meter race in the 1964 Olympics was one of the biggest upsets in sports history. The direction is pedestrian at best. But Benson's fine performance and the true-life drama of Mills's determination to set a positive example of achievement for his people—the Sioux and all Native Americans—is affecting. Rated PG for profanity. 105m. DIR: Donald Shebib. CAST: Robby Benson, Pat Hingle, Jeff McCracken. 1983

RUNNING COOL ★★★ Surprisingly decent biker story stars Andrew Divoff as a gallant cycle cowboy helping an old friend save wetlands from developers. Sexism mars the eco-friendly spirit, but it's fun to watch "outlaw" bikers save the day. Rated R for language and sexuality. 106m. **DIR:** Ferd Sebastian, Beverly Sebastian. **CAST:** Andrew Divoff, Dedee Pfeiffer, James Gammon, Paul Gleason. 1993

RUNNING DELILAH ★★ Kim Cattrall stars as an undercover agent who is ambushed by a notorious international arms dealer. Her partner (Billy Zane) races her body to a secret government laboratory where they turn her into a cyborg. Lifeless rip-off of TV's *The Bionic Woman*. Rated PG-13 for violence. 85m. **DIR:** Richard Franklin. **CAST:** Kim Cattrall, Billy Zane, Francois Guetary, Yorgo Voyagis, Diana Rigg. 1993

RUNNING HOT ★★★ Eric Stoltz gives a very good performance as a 17-year-old sentenced to death row. The publicity of his case arouses the interest of 30-year-old Monica Carrico, who sends him love letters in prison. His escape and bizarre affair with her have serious consequences in this fast-paced drama. Rated R for sex, violence, language, and nudity. 88m. **DIR:** Mark Griffiths. **CAST:** Eric Stoltz, Stuart Margolin, Monica Carrico, Virgil Frye. 1983

RUNNING KIND, THE ★★★★ The straitlaced scion (David Packer) of an Akron, Ohio family takes the summer off from dad's law firm to follow a sexy, free-thinking rock drummer (Brie Howard) into the bowels of Los Angeles's punk scene. A marvelously inventive comedy from writer-director Max Tash. Rated R for profanity and brief violence. 90m. **DIR:** Max Tash. **CAST:** David Packer, Brie Howard. 1989

RUNNING MAN, THE ★★★1/2 In this silly but exciting outing, Arnold Schwarzenegger is an honest cop who is framed for a crime he didn't commit and forced to fight for his life on a bizarre twenty-first-century game show. Another successful variation on the big guy's standard film formula. Rated R for profanity and violence. 101m. **DIR:** Paul Michael Glaser. **CAST:** Arnold Schwarzenegger, Maria Conchita Alonso, Richard Dawson, Yaphet Kotto, Jim Brown. 1987 DVD

RUNNING MATES (1985) ★★ Stereotyped characters populate this story of two teenagers who fall in love, only to be torn apart when their respective fathers run against each other in an election. Rated PG for adult situations. 90m. **DIR:** Thomas L. Neff. **CAST:** Gregg Webb, Barbara Howard. 1985

RUNNING MATES (1992) ★★★ Political vulnerability is the topic of A. L. Appling's script, which concerns the fallout resulting from presidential candidate Ed Harris's growing involvement with children's book author Diane Keaton (whose condescending behavior wears thin *very* quickly). Alas, this made-for-cable romantic comedy concludes unsatisfyingly, without confronting this issue of privacy versus the public's right to know. 88m. **DIR:** Michael Lindsay-Hogg. **CAST:** Diane Keaton, Ed Harris, Ed Begley Jr., Ben Masters, Russ Tamblyn. 1992

RUNNING ON EMPTY ★★★★ Extremely well-made film looks at a fugitive family that has been on the lam from the FBI for years. Unable to establish roots anywhere because of the constant fear of detection, parents Christine Lähti and Judd Hirsch must decide what to do when their son, River Phoenix, is accepted to the Juilliard School of Music. Rated PG-13. 116m. **DIR:** Sidney Lumet. **CAST:** Christine Lahti, Judd Hirsch, River Phoenix, Martha Plimpton. 1988 DVD

RUNNING SCARED (1980) ★★★ Ken Wahl and Judge Reinhold are servicemen returning home after two years in the Panama Canal Zone. Reinhold unknowingly filmed a secret base that is to be used in the Bay of Pigs operation. When their plane lands, authorities find negatives and the chase is on. Not rated. 82m. **DIR:** Paul Glicker. **CAST:** Ken Wahl, Judge Reinhold, Bradford Dillman, Pat Hingle, Lonny Chapman, John Saxon. 1980

RUNNING SCARED (1986) ★★★★ Fast, funny, and exciting, this *Beverly Hills Cop*–style comedy-cop thriller features inspired on-screen teamwork from Gregory Hines and Billy Crystal as a pair of wisecracking detectives on the trail of a devious drug dealer. Rated R for violence, nudity, and profanity. 107m. **DIR:** Peter Hyams. **CAST:** Gregory Hines, Billy Crystal, Steven Bauer, Darlanne Fluegel, Joe Pantoliano, Dan Hedaya, Jimmy Smits, Jonathan Gries, Tracy Reed. 1986

RUNNING WILD (1927) ★★ W. C. Fields is miscast and overplays his role of a toady worm suddenly turned (by hypnotism) into a coarse, violent lion—mean to family, friends, and dog. Far from vintage Fields, this film is a disappointing outing for his comic genius. Silent with titles. B&W; 68m. **DIR:** Gregory La Cava. **CAST:** W. C. Fields, Mary Brian, Claude Buchanan. 1927

RUNNING WILD (1955) ★★ Rookie cop William Campbell pretends to be a young tough to get the goods on an auto-theft gang headed by Keenan Wynn. Made to catch the teenage rock 'n' roll crowd. 81m. **DIR:** Abner Biberman. **CAST:** William Campbell, Mamie Van Doren, Keenan Wynn, Katherine Case, Jan Merlin, John Saxon. 1955

RUNNING WILD (1994) ★★ Low-budget road movie features Jennifer Barker as a woman about to marry a man twice her age when she falls for his handsome son. Then they're off and headed for Mexico with a friend in a stolen car. Some local color and a couple of offbeat moments rally to make this more than it is. Rated R for nudity, language, and violence. 97m. **DIR:** Phillippe Blot. **CAST:** Jennifer Barker, Daniel DuPont, Daniel Spector, Eliot Kenner. 1994

RUNNING WILD (1998) ★★★1/2 This charming little family film concerns a boy and a girl who join their father in Zimbabwe, befriend a baby elephant, and foil a bunch of nasty poachers. It's definitely Africa by way of Disneyland in the tradition of *Clarence, the Cross-Eyed Lion* and other similarly friendly wild-life adventures; films we don't see often enough these days. Rated PG for brief violence against animals. 90m. **DIR:** Timothy Bond. **CAST:** Gregory Harrison, Lori Hallier, Cody Jones, Brooke Nevin, Simon MacCorkindale, Themba Ndaba, Munyaradzi Kanaventi. 1998

RUSH ★★★ For her directorial debut, Lili Fini Zanuck (wife of producer Richard) chose a hard-edged story about undercover narcotics officers who become heavy users while busting other addicts in a small Texas town. It's downright dreary much of the time, with the fine acting of Sam Elliott and Max Perlich adding several bright moments. Rated R for profanity, violence, and drug use. 120m. **DIR:** Lili Fini Zanuck. **CAST:** Jason Patric, Jennifer Jason Leigh, Sam Elliott, Max Perlich, Gregg Allman, Bill Sadler. 1991

RUSH HOUR ★★★ Jackie Chan and Chris Tucker are the main attractions in this low-rent 48 Hrs.: an oil-and-vinegar "buddy thriller" where two outcasts eventually put aside petty differences and Save the Day. The advertising signature line pretty much sums it up: "The fastest hands in the East versus the biggest mouth in the West." When a Chinese consul's daughter is kidnapped while in the United States, good friend Jackie Chan is summoned. The FBI, resenting this intrusion, co-opts a reprobate LAPD officer to play nursemaid. The rest involves considerable martial arts mayhem—in Chan's signature style—and the explosive destruction of ample real estate. It's all fun, if rather soulless. Rated PG-13 for profanity and martial arts mayhem. 97m. **DIR:** Brett Ratner. **CAST:** Jackie Chan, Chris Tucker, Tom Wilkinson, Philip Baker Hall, Elizabeth Peña. 1998 DVD

RUSH WEEK ★★ A reporter (Pamela Ludwig) gets a scoop on murdered models and gets herself in the most ridiculously suicidal situations to follow her leads. Rated R for nudity, violence, and gore. 96m. **DIR:** Bob Bralver. **CAST:** Dean Hamilton, Pamela Ludwig, Gregg Allman, Roy Thinnes. 1989 DVD

RUSHMORE ★★★1/2 The parable concerns what might happen if a precocious 15-year-old geek had the talent and resources to bring his every whim to life. Max Fischer is a tenth-grader at prestigious Rushmore Academy, a preppy private school where he excels at extracurricular activities—while neglecting his "real" studies. Things get more complicated when Max meets and develops a crush on a first-grade teacher, and one of the school's primary benefactors also falls in love with the same teacher. What follows is a small treasure: funny, poignant, raw, and at times as clumsy as its protagonist . . . but no less adorable. Rated R for profanity. 93m. **DIR:** Wes Anderson. **CAST:** Jason Schwartzman, Bill Murray, Olivia Williams, Brian Cox, Seymour Cassel, Mason Gamble, Sara Tanaka. 1998 DVD

•**RUSSELL MULCAHY'S TALE OF THE MUMMY** ★★ Russell Mulcahy's low-budget adventure was once headed for the big screen, but was relegated to video after Universal beat him to the punch. Good thing. Mulcahy's film is an okay diversion, but lacks the appeal and thrills needed to make it grand entertainment. After a promising beginning, the film becomes a tired detective story set in London. The special effects are anything but special. Rated R for language and violence. 88m. **DIR:** Russell Mulcahy. **CAST:** Jason Scott Lee, Christopher Lee, Louise Lombard, Lysette Anthony, Shelley Duvall. 1999

RUSSIA HOUSE, THE ★★★★ A British book publisher (Sean Connery) becomes involved in international espionage when a Russian woman (Michelle Pfeiffer) sends him an unsolicited manuscript. This first-rate adaptation of the John Le Carre novel is a thinking-person's spy movie. Rated R for profanity. 123m. **DIR:** Fred Schepisi. **CAST:** Sean Connery, Michelle Pfeiffer, Roy Scheider, Klaus Maria Brandauer, James Fox, John Mahoney, Michael Kitchen, J. T. Walsh, Ken Russell. 1990

RUSSIAN ROULETTE ★★ George Segal plays a Royal Canadian Mountie sucked into a secret service plot to kidnap a Russian dissident prior to a visit from the Soviet premier. Good premise, but no action or thrills. Rated PG. 100m. **DIR:** Lou Lombardo. **CAST:** George Segal, Cristina Raines, Bo Brudin, Denholm Elliott, Richard Romanus, Gordon Jackson, Peter Donat, Nigel Stock, Louise Fletcher. 1975

RUSSIANS ARE COMING, THE RUSSIANS ARE COMING, THE ★★★1/2 A Russian submarine runs aground off Nantucket Island, and the townspeople go gaga, not knowing what to do first, get guns or pour vodka. Cued by Alan Arkin's engaging portrayal of an out-of-his-depth Russian sailor, the cast delivers a solid comedy as cultures clash. With Jonathan Winters aboard, things wacky. 120m. **DIR:** Norman Jewison. **CAST:** Alan Arkin, Carl Reiner, Paul Ford, Theodore Bikel, Brian Keith, Jonathan Winters, Eva Marie Saint. 1966

RUSSKIES ★★1/2 A sweet-natured Russian sailor (Whip Hubley) becomes stranded in Key West, Florida, when a raft capsizes and aborts a secret mission. He finds three youngsters who eventually agree to help him escape. The cast is appealing, but the laughs aren't frequent enough. Rated PG-13 for slight violence and profanity. 90m. **DIR:** Rick Rosenthal. **CAST:** Whip Hubley, Leaf Phoenix, Peter Billingsley, Charles Frank. 1987

RUSTLERS, THE ★★★★ Clever, sprightly paced Western has Tim Holt and his saddle pal, the everamorous Richard "Chito" Martin, tracking down Steve Brodie and his gang of rustlers. A winner. B&W; 61m. **DIR:** Lesley Selander. **CAST:** Tim Holt, Martha Hyer, Richard Martin, Steve Brodie, Addison Richards. 1949

RUSTLER'S RHAPSODY ★★★ In this fun spoof of the singing cowboy movies of the 1930s, 1940s, and 1950s, Tom Berenger plays the horseback crooner of them all, Rex O'Herlihan. Viewers need to be familiar with the old B Westerns to get the jokes. If you are, it's a hoot. Rated PG for mild violence and slight profanity. 88m. **DIR:** Hugh Wilson. **CAST:** Tom Berenger, G. W. Bailey, Marilu Henner, Andy Griffith, Fernando Rey, Patrick Wayne. 1985

RUTANGA TAPES, THE ★★1/2 A frighteningly current movie dealing with the use of chemical weapons by a government on its own people. David Dukes is the spy-economic adviser sent to the African nation with the purpose of uncovering the details. Rated R for violence. 88m. **DIR:** David Lister. **CAST:** David Dukes, Susan Anspach. 1990

RUTHERFORD COUNTY LINE ★★ Wooden acting dampens an otherwise decent script about real-life Rutherford County, North Carolina, Sheriff Damon Husky (Earl Owensby) and his efforts to police the rural Blue Ridge community. The actors appear to read their lines from cue cards. Not rated; the film contains episodes of profanity and graphic violence.

98m. **DIR:** Thom McIntyre. **CAST:** Earl Owensby, Terry Loughlin. 1985

RUTHLESS FOUR, THE ★★ This spaghetti Western could have been a lot worse, but that's no reason to watch it. Van Heflin plays a prospector who strikes gold, only to have to split the fortune with three other men less honest than he. 96m. **DIR:** Giorgio Capitani. **CAST:** Van Heflin, Gilbert Roland, Klaus Kinski, George Hilton. 1969

RUTHLESS PEOPLE ★★★★1/2 Danny DeVito decides to murder his obnoxious wife, played by Bette Midler. But when he arrives home to carry out the deed, he discovers she has been abducted. The kidnappers demand fifty thousand dollars "or else." Exactly what DeVito has in mind, so he refuses to pay a cent. A comedy classic. Rated R for nudity and profanity. 90m. **DIR:** Jim Abrahams, David Zucker, Jerry Zucker. **CAST:** Danny DeVito, Bette Midler, Judge Reinhold, Helen Slater, Anita Morris, Bill Pullman. 1986

RUTLES, THE (ALL YOU NEED IS CASH) ★★★★ Superb spoof of the Beatles has Eric Idle in a dual role as a television reporter and one of the Rutles, whose songs include "Cheese and Onions" and "Doubleback Alley." It's great stuff for fans of the Fab Four—with cameos from rock stars (including Beatle George Harrison) and members of *Saturday Night Live*'s Not Ready for Prime-Time Players. 78m. **DIR:** Eric Idle, Gary Weis. **CAST:** Eric Idle, Neil Innes, Ricky Fataar, John Halsey, Mick Jagger, Paul Simon, George Harrison, John Belushi, Dan Aykroyd, Gilda Radner. 1978

RYAN'S DAUGHTER ★★1/2 Acclaimed director David Lean took a critical beating with this release, about a spoiled woman (Sarah Miles) who shamelessly lusts after an officer (Christopher Jones). Robert Mitchum, as Miles's husband, is the best thing about this watchable misfire. Rated PG. 176m. **DIR:** David Lean. **CAST:** Sarah Miles, Christopher Jones, Robert Mitchum, Trevor Howard, John Mills, Leo McKern. 1970

SABOTAGE (1936) ★★★ One of the first of Alfred Hitchcock's characteristic thrillers. London's being terrorized by an unknown bomber, and movie theater cashier Sylvia Sidney begins to fear that her husband (Oscar Homolka) is behind it all. Hitch was still experimenting, and his use of shadows and sound effects betrays the influence of German silent films. B&W; 76m. **DIR:** Alfred Hitchcock. **CAST:** Sylvia Sidney, Oscar Homolka, John Loder. 1936 DVD

SABOTAGE (1996) ★★★ Despite the convoluted plot, Mark Dacascos and Carrie Anne Moss make a superb investigating team. He's a bodyguard trying to learn why his latest client was assassinated; she's an FBI agent trying to balance professional duty

with responsibility for her young daughter. Both are targeted by Tony Todd's sadistic villain, who brings new meaning to the phrase "big gun." Slick pacing and genuine suspense raise this several cuts above the usual genre dreck. Rated R for violence and profanity. 99m. **DIR:** Tibor Takacs. **CAST:** Mark Dacascos, Carrie Anne Moss, Tony Todd, Graham Greene, John Neville. 1996

SABOTEUR ★★★★1/2 Outstanding Alfred Hitchcock film about a World War II factory worker (Robert Cummings) turned fugitive after he's unjustly accused of sabotage. The briskly paced story follows his efforts to elude police while he tries to unmask the real culprit. A humdinger of a climax. B&W; 108m. **DIR:** Alfred Hitchcock. **CAST:** Robert Cummings, Priscilla Lane, Norman Lloyd, Otto Kruger. 1942

SABRINA (1954) ★★★★ Elfin Audrey Hepburn shines in the title role. She's the simple chauffeur's daughter who is swept off her feet by wealthy rake William Holden. Humphrey Bogart, as Holden's business-minded brother, attempts to save her from the ne'er-do-well. Director Billy Wilder paces things with his usual deft touch. B&W; 113m. **DIR:** Billy Wilder. **CAST:** Audrey Hepburn, Humphrey Bogart, William Holden, John Williams. 1954

SABRINA (1995) ★★★1/2 Samuel Taylor's delightful stage play, concerning the plain chauffeur's daughter who blossoms into a beauty and wins the heart of a millionaire, doesn't play quite as well in this remake. Julia Ormond properly updates her character to a woman of the 1990s, but it's a bit of a stretch to believe that Harrison Ford's Linus Larrabee is a "plain stiff" lacking any gentler social graces. Billy Wilder's original is the story of a mousy young woman's self-discovery, but this update is more about a rich guy's midlife crisis. Rated PG for mild sensuality. 127m. **DIR:** Sydney Pollack. **CAST:** Harrison Ford, Julia Ormond, Greg Kinnear, Nancy Marchand, John Wood. 1995

SABRINA, THE TEENAGE WITCH ★★★ The *Archie Comics* costar gets her own live-action feature, with reasonable results. Perky Melissa Joan Hart learns of her spell-casting heritage during the first full moon after her sixteenth birthday and struggles with true love and bitchy rivals while learning how to control her new powers. The subject of witchcraft notwithstanding, the film delivers strong moral lessons. Suitable for all ages. 91m. **DIR:** Tibor Takacs. **CAST:** Melissa Joan Hart, Sherry Miller, Charlene Fernetz. 1996

SACCO AND VANZETTI ★★★★ Excellent historical drama recounts the trial and eventual execution of Sacco and Vanzetti, the Italian immigrants who were convicted of murder in 1921. The case was a *cause célèbre* at the time, since many felt that they were condemned on the basis of their politics rather than on the weak evidence against them. Dubbed in English. Rated PG. 121m. **DIR:** Giuliano Montaldo. **CAST:** Gian Maria Volonté, Riccardo Cucciolla, Cyril Cusack, Milo O'Shea. 1971 DVD

SACKETTS, THE ★★★★ Fine made-for-TV Western adapted from two novels by Louis L'Amour, *The Daybreakers* and *The Sacketts*. Sam Elliott, Tom Selleck, Glenn Ford, and Ben Johnson are terrific in the lead roles, and there's plenty of action. 200m. **DIR:** Robert Totten. **CAST:** Sam Elliott, Tom Selleck, Glenn Ford, Ben Johnson, Ruth Roman, Gilbert Roland, Slim Pickens, Jack Elam, Gene Evans. **1979**

SACRED CARGO ★★★ An ex-Marine (Chris Penn) must rescue his brother, a priest (Martin Sheen), after his plan to help an order of Franciscans escape from Russia goes awry. Shot on location in Russia, this thriller is more interesting for its scenery than its rather predictable plot. Not rated; contains gore, sexual situations, and profanity. 97m. **DIR:** Alexander Buravsky. **CAST:** Christopher Penn, J. T. Walsh, Anna Karin, Martin Sheen. **1995**

SACRED GROUND ★★★1/2 Interracial marriage between a white mountain man and an Apache woman is further complicated when they have their child on the burial grounds of another Indian tribe. The trials they endure should hold viewer interest. Rated PG. 100m. **DIR:** Charles B. Pierce. **CAST:** Tim McIntire, Jack Elam, Serene Hedin. **1983**

SACRIFICE, THE ★★★★ The actors here do most of the work that expensive special effects would accomplish in an American film with a similar theme. During an approaching world holocaust, we don't see devastation. Rather, the camera records the various emotional reactions of six people in a house in the secluded countryside. Actors' faces and unpredictable actions mirror horror, pathos, and even grim humor as the plot twists in a surprisingly supernatural direction. In Swedish with English subtitles. Not rated, the film has suggested sex. 145m. **DIR:** Andrei Tarkovsky. **CAST:** Erland Josephson, Susan Fleetwood, Valerie Mairesse, Allan Edwall. **1986**

SACRILEGE ★★ Controversial drama where sin and lust take place behind the walls of a convent. An illicit affair between a nun and a nobleman escalates to a dangerous climax. Lavishly produced erotica. In Italian with English subtitles. Not rated; contains nudity and violence and is recommended for adults. 104m. **DIR:** Luciano Odorisio. **CAST:** Myriem Roussel, Alessandro Gassman. **1990**

SAD SACK, THE ★★1/2 Jerry Lewis in the army. That's all the plot there is in this better-than-average Lewis vehicle which, as usual, will please his fans and annoy all others. 98m. **DIR:** George Marshall. **CAST:** Jerry Lewis, David Wayne, Phyllis Kirk, Peter Lorre. **1957**

SADAT ★★★1/2 Although much of the great Egyptian statesman's life is left out of this two-part TV movie, what is seen is well-made and impressively acted, particularly by Lou Gossett Jr. as Sadat. 191m. **DIR:** Richard Michaels. **CAST:** Lou Gossett Jr., John Rhys-Davies, Madolyn Smith, Jeremy Kemp, Anne Heywood, Barry Morse, Nehemiah Persoff, Paul Smith, Jeffrey Tambor. **1983**

SADDLE MOUNTAIN ROUNDUP ★★★ The Range Busters set out to find the killer of a grouchy old rancher. B&W; 55m. **DIR:** S. Roy Luby. **CAST:** Ray "Crash" Corrigan, John King, Max Terhune, Jack Mulhall, George Chesebro. **1941**

SADDLE TRAMPS ★ A Casanova named Coburn (Bud Spencer) seduces Mary, the sister of a gunfighter named Sonny (Jack Palance), and Sonny pur-

sues Coburn all over the West. Good performance by Spencer, in a role where he's not his usual brutish clown, makes this a fine parody Western. Rated PG. 90m. **DIR:** Maurizio Lucidi. **CAST:** Bud Spencer, Jack Palance, Francisco Rabal, Renato Cestie. **1971**

SADIE McKEE ★★ A dated character study about a working girl who moves to the other side of the tracks, dragging her boyfriends behind her. This is the kind of movie Joan Crawford specialized in, but it is way out of style today. B&W; 89m. **DIR:** Clarence Brown. **CAST:** Joan Crawford, Franchot Tone, Edward Arnold, Gene Raymond, Esther Ralston, Leo G. Carroll, Akim Tamiroff. **1934**

SADIE THOMPSON ★★★ Screen legend Gloria Swanson is Somerset Maugham's famous South Seas floozy in this silent predecessor of the better-known 1932 Joan Crawford sound remake. Director-writer-costar Raoul Walsh more than holds his own against her, as reformer Lionel Barrymore resists but eventually succumbs to the sins of the flesh. B&W; 97m. **DIR:** Raoul Walsh. **CAST:** Gloria Swanson, Raoul Walsh, Lionel Barrymore. **1928**

SADIST, THE ♥ A serial killer and his girlfriend terrorize three teachers stranded in the middle of nowhere. Not rated; contains some violence. B&W; 90m. **DIR:** James Landis. **CAST:** Arch Hall Jr., Helen Hovey, Marilyn Manning. **1963 DVD**

SAFE ★★ San Fernando homemaker is a Stepford-like wife who is being polluted into a physical and mental meltdown by everything from car exhaust to insulting cocktail-hour jokes. She becomes a human Geiger counter to all that ails the world and seeks sanctuary at a New Age health ranch managed by an AIDS-infected motivational guru. The film is visually striking, provocative, and exasperating. Rated R for nudity, sex, and language. 119m. **DIR:** Todd Haynes. **CAST:** Julianne Moore, Xander Berkeley, Peter Friedman, Mary Carver, James LeGros, Jessica Harper. **1995**

SAFE HOUSE ★★★1/2 Just because you're paranoid doesn't mean they aren't *really* out to get you. Truer words were never spoken in this clever yarn, which concerns a senior citizen who keeps his wits sharpened with violent tactical exercises and has turned his home into a fortress. He claims it's for personal safety, because of something from his "former career"; his daughter, fearing senility, initiates a compromise in the form of a new housekeeper-companion whose efforts to gain her client's trust have unexpected results. Rated R for violence, profanity, and nudity. 112m. **DIR:** Eric Steven Stahl. **CAST:** Patrick Stewart, Kimberly Williams, Joy Kilpatrick, Craig Shoemaker, James Harlow, Hector Elizondo. **1997**

SAFE MEN ★★★1/2 Madcap comedy about two lousy lounge singers who are mistaken by the mob for a safe-cracking team. Steve Zahn and Sam Rockwell go from inept lounge singers to inept burglars, all in the name of comedy and a good time. There's a lot to admire about this quirky little exercise in mistaken identity. Rated R for language and adult situations. 89m. **DIR:** John Hamburg. **CAST:** Steve Zahn, Sam Rockwell, Harvey Fierstein, Paul Giamatti, Michael Lerner. **1998**

SAFE PASSAGE ★★★1/2 An overprotective mother is pushed to her emotional limits when she fears her son's death in a military explosion and must wait for official notice. Her care-giving eldest son tries to keep the family together while Mom is losing it. Her estranged husband just wants to return to their home and marriage. Thought-provoking look inside a family's pathos. Rated PG-13 for drug use and mature themes. 98m. **DIR:** Robert Allen Ackerman. **CAST:** Susan Sarandon, Sam Shepard, Robert Sean Leonard, Nick Stahl, Marcia Gay Harden. 1994

SAFETY LAST ★★★★ Country bumpkin Harold Lloyd sets out to make his fortune in the big city, and eventually winds up—in one of the most famous images in movie history—dangling from a clock on the side of a tall building. Outstanding silent comedy is hilarious and exciting; Lloyd knows exactly how far to push the skyscraper derring-do before whisking his hero to safety. Not rated. B&W; 78m. **DIR:** Fred Newmeyer, Sam Taylor. **CAST:** Harold Lloyd, Mildred Davis, Bill Strothers, Noah Young. 1923

SAGA OF DEATH VALLEY ★★1/2 Early Roy Rogers film finds him fighting a gang of outlaws led by a desperado who turns out to be his own brother! This well-produced Western isn't lacking in action and excitement. B&W; 56m. **DIR:** Joseph Kane. **CAST:** Roy Rogers, George "Gabby" Hayes, Don Barry. 1939

SAGA OF THE VIKING WOMEN AND THEIR VOYAGE TO THE WATERS OF THE GREAT SEA SERPENT, THE (VIKING WOMEN AND THE SEA SERPENT, THE) 🖤 Even director Roger Corman called this Nordic snoozer, "One of the biggest mistakes of my life." B&W; 66m. **DIR:** Roger Corman. **CAST:** Abby Dalton, Susan Cabot. 1957

SAGEBRUSH TRAIL ★★★ Big John Wayne, almost before he was shaving, is sent to prison for a murder he didn't commit. Naturally, our hero breaks out of the big house to clear his name. In a nice twist, he becomes friends—unknowingly—with the killer, who dies bravely in a climactic shoot-out. Good B Western. B&W; 58m. **DIR:** Armand Schaefer. **CAST:** John Wayne, Nancy Shubert, Lane Chandler, Yakima Canutt. 1933 DVD

SAHARA (1943) ★★★1/2 One of the better war films, this production contains plenty of action, suspense, and characterization. Humphrey Bogart plays the head of a British-American unit stranded in the desert. The soldiers must keep the ever-present Nazi forces at bay while searching for the precious water they need to stay alive. It's a down-to-the-bone, exciting World War II drama. B&W; 97m. **DIR:** Zoltán Korda. **CAST:** Humphrey Bogart, Bruce Bennett, Lloyd Bridges, Dan Duryea, J. Carrol Naish. 1943

SAHARA (1984) 🖤 A young heiress enters "the world's most treacherous auto race" (across the Sahara Desert). Rated PG for violence and profanity. 104m. **DIR:** Andrew V. McLaglen. **CAST:** Brooke Shields, Lambert Wilson, Horst Buchholz, John Rhys-Davies, John Mills. 1984

SAHARA (1995) ★★★1/2 James Belushi steps capably into Humphrey Bogart's shoes in this solid remake, assisted by a strong supporting cast. This old-style WWII drama pits our heroes and a temperamental tank dubbed Lulubelle against hundreds of German soldiers determined to take control of a prized desert well. Full of heroics, impossible odds, and noble deaths. Rated PG-13 for violence and profanity. 105m. **DIR:** Brian Trenchard-Smith. **CAST:** James Belushi, Alan David Lee, Simon Westaway, Mark Lee, Jerome Ehlers. 1995

SAIGON COMMANDOS ★★1/2 In Vietnam, U.S. military cop Richard Young investigates the murders of local drug dealers. Okay action drama, with more than a passing resemblance to *Off Limits* (though this was made earlier). Rated R for strong violence and profanity. 91m. **DIR:** Clark Henderson. **CAST:** Richard Young, P. J. Soles, John Allen Nelson. 1987

SAILOR WHO FELL FROM GRACE WITH THE SEA, THE ★★ Much of Japanese culture remains misunderstood, and this inept adaptation of Yukio Mishima's novel is a perfect example. Kris Kristofferson doesn't have to stretch his limited abilities as an amiable sailor who falls in love with Sarah Miles. Rated R for violence and sex. 104m. **DIR:** Lewis John Carlino. **CAST:** Sarah Miles, Kris Kristofferson, Margo Cunningham, Earl Rhodes. 1976

SAINT, THE (TV SERIES) ★★ Roger Moore honed his suavity in the series *The Saint*, and sparkled as international adventurer Simon Templar, a connoisseur of fine wine and women. The devilishly daring troubleshooter continually aided the police, who considered him a foe. Made in England, the production provided intriguing mysteries, witty dialogue, and solid action. Two episodes per tape, each. 100m. **DIR:** Roy Ward Baker, Leslie Norman. **CAST:** Roger Moore, Winsley Pithey, Norman Pitt, Ivor Dean, Percy Herbert, Ronald Radd, Lois Maxwell. 1963–1969

SAINT, THE (1997) ★★ Big budget and lofty pretensions aside, this misfired mess bears more of a resemblance to the equally bombastic, big-screen desecration of *Mission: Impossible*, than to the Leslie Charteris character who delighted readers for more than half a century. Val Kilmer is much too dour in the title role. Charteris must be spinning in his grave. Rated PG-13 for violence and profanity. 116m. **DIR:** Phillip Noyce. **CAST:** Val Kilmer, Elisabeth Shue, Rade Serbedzija, Valery Nikolaev. 1997 DVD

ST. BENNY THE DIP ★★ A good cast is about all that recommends this time-worn story of con artists who disguise their larceny behind clerics' robes and find themselves thinking clearer and walking the straight and narrow as a result of their contact with religion. B&W; 79m. **DIR:** Edgar G. Ulmer. **CAST:** Dick Haymes, Nina Foch, Roland Young, Lionel Stander, Freddie Bartholomew. 1951

ST. ELMO'S FIRE ★★★ This film would have us believe a group of college graduates are, at the age of 22, all suffering from mid-life crises. However, fine acting by some of the screen's hottest young stars helps us forgive this off-kilter premise. The movie succeeds almost in spite of itself. Rated R for suggested sex, violence, nudity, and profanity. 110m. **DIR:** Joel Schumacher. **CAST:** Emilio Estevez, Rob Lowe, Andrew McCarthy, Demi Moore, Judd Nelson, Ally Sheedy, Mare Winningham, Martin Balsam, Andie MacDowell, Joyce Van Patten. 1985

ST. ELSEWHERE (TV SERIES) ★★★ This 1980s medical drama began with a superb first season but quickly became an overly melodramatic parody of itself. The dedicated staff at St. Eligius hospital didn't always win against the Grim Reaper, which at the time was something of a novelty. With medical shows completely redefined by *ER* in the 1990s, this series hasn't dated all that well. Each episode 47m. **DIR:** Various. **CAST:** Ed Flanders, William Daniels, Norman Lloyd, David Birney, Ed Begley Jr., David Morse, Cynthia Sikes, Howie Mandel, Terence Knox, Christina Pickles, Denzel Washington, Mark Harmon. 1982–88

SAINT-EX ★★★ Made for the BBC, this biography of the French pilot who wrote the children's classic *The Little Prince* has the usual pros and cons of British television productions—nice to look at and well acted, but occasionally slow and too dry. Not rated. 90m. **DIR:** Anand Tucker. **CAST:** Bruno Ganz, Miranda Richardson, Janet McTeer, Katrin Cartlidge, Eleanor Bron. 1997

ST. HELENS ★★1/2 Very shallow look at the Mount St. Helens volcanic eruption and the following disasters. Art Carney plays Harry, the old man who refuses to move from his home. Pretty bland stuff. Rated PG for no particular reason. 90m. **DIR:** Ernest Pintoff. **CAST:** Art Carney, David Huffman, Cassie Yates, Albert Salmi, Ron O'Neal. 1981

SAINT IN LONDON, THE ★★★ George Sanders as The Saint is up to his halo in spies, murder, and intrigue in this entertaining series entry, the second to star Sanders as Simon Templar. Entrusted to protect a foreign ambassador from hired killers, The Saint fails and feels honor-bound to track down the culprits. This handsome programmer is fun to watch. B&W; 72m. **DIR:** John Paddy Carstairs. **CAST:** George Sanders, Sally Gray, David Burns, Ralph Truman. 1939

SAINT IN NEW YORK, THE ★★★ The first of Leslie Charteris's popular crime novels to hit the screen, this smooth adventure features Louis Hayward as The Saint, gentleman crime fighter, and his efforts to put an end to six gangsters who have been plaguing their metropolis. Hayward is fine in the title role. B&W; 71m. **DIR:** Ben Holmes. **CAST:** Louis Hayward, Kay Sutton, Jonathan Hale, Jack Carson, Sig Ruman. 1938

ST. IVES ★★★1/2 This is a good Charles Bronson film about a former police reporter who becomes involved in a murder. Director J. Lee Thompson pulls an understated and believable performance out of the star. Rated PG. 93m. **DIR:** J. Lee Thompson. **CAST:** Charles Bronson, Jacqueline Bisset, John Houseman, Maximilian Schell, Harry Guardino, Dana Elcar, Dick O'Neill, Elisha Cook Jr. 1976

SAINT JACK ★★★ Although an interesting film, it lacks power and a sense of wholeness. Ben Gazzara plays an oddly likable pimp plying his trade in Singapore in the 1970s who wants to become rich and powerful by running the classiest whorehouse in the Far East. Rated R. 112m. **DIR:** Peter Bogdanovich. **CAST:** Ben Gazzara, Denholm Elliott, James Villiers, Joss Ackland, Peter Bogdanovich, George Lazenby. 1979

SAINT JOAN ★★ Even a screenplay by Graham Greene can't salvage Otto Preminger's dull screen version of George Bernard Shaw's intriguing play. Jean Seberg seems at a loss and the presence of such performers as Richard Widmark and John Gielgud,

just remind one what could have been. B&W; 110m. **DIR:** Otto Preminger. **CAST:** Jean Seberg, Richard Widmark, Richard Todd, John Gielgud, Anton Walbrook, Harry Andrews, Felix Aylmer. 1957

SAINT MAYBE ★★★★ Whimsical *Hallmark Hall of Fame* special features Thomas McCarthy as a college student who blames himself for his brother's suicide. Suddenly feeling responsible for his brother's stepchildren, he begins a dramatic metamorphosis from self-centered teenager to loving parent. Although the plot is activated by the family's loss, there are a number of humorous scenes. Not rated; contains mature themes. 92m. **DIR:** Michael Pressman. **CAST:** Thomas McCarthy, Mary-Louise Parker, Blythe Danner, Edward Herrmann. 1998

SAINT OF FORT WASHINGTON, THE ★★★1/2 Well-acted drama focuses on two homeless men struggling to survive both physically and spiritually on the mean streets of New York. Matt Dillon is an emotionally troubled photographer who finds himself protected by streetwise Danny Glover in a strong film that goes somewhat astray in the last half. Rated R for violence and profanity. 103m. **DIR:** Tim Hunter. **CAST:** Matt Dillon, Danny Glover, Rick Aviles, Nina Siemaszko, Ving Rhames, Joe Seneca, Harry Ellington. 1993

SAINT STRIKES BACK, THE ★★★ A good cast, a good story, and a charming performance by George Sanders as Simon Templar, debonair crime fighter, make this one of the best of a very pleasant series. Sanders, in his first appearance as the suave adventurer, pulls out all the stops in his efforts to clear the name of a dead policeman and straighten out his wayward daughter. B&W; 67m. **DIR:** John Farrow. **CAST:** George Sanders, Wendy Barrie, Jonathan Hale, Jerome Cowan, Neil Hamilton, Barry Fitzgerald. 1939

ST. VALENTINE'S DAY MASSACRE, THE ★★ Watching the leads ham it up provides sporadic fun, but this gaudy gangster picture is long on violence and short on dramatic impact. Where's Eliot Ness when you need him? 100m. **DIR:** Roger Corman. **CAST:** Jason Robards Jr., George Segal, Ralph Meeker, Jean Hale, Frank Silvera, Joseph Campanella, Bruce Dern. 1967

SAINTS & SINNERS ★★ Best friends wind up on different sides of the law in this crime-thriller. Pooch becomes a cop. His friend "Big Boy" Baynes becomes a drug dealer. When they both fall for the same woman, Pooch uses Baynes as bait in a sting operation. When it starts to fall apart, Pooch must choose between his loyalty to his friend or his badge. Rated R for violence, nudity, adult situations, and language. 99m. **DIR:** Paul Mones. **CAST:** Damian Chapa, Jennifer Rubin, Scott Plank, William Atherton. 1994

SAINT'S VACATION, THE ★★ Simon Templar finds mystery and adventure instead of peace and quiet when he encounters intrigue on his vacation attempt. Hugh Sinclair plays the sophisticated Saint for the first time. Passable, but not up to the earlier entries in the series. B&W; 60m. **DIR:** Leslie Fenton. **CAST:** Hugh Sinclair, Sally Gray, Arthur Macrae, Cecil Parker, Gordon McLeod. 1941

SAKHAROV ★★★★ Compassionate story of the nuclear physicist and designer of the H-bomb, Andrei

Sakharov (Jason Robards), who won the Nobel Peace Prize after waking up to the global terror of the nuclear gambit and contributing to the budding human rights movement in the Soviet Union during the late 1960s. 118m. DIR: Jack Gold. CAST: Jason Robards Jr., Glenda Jackson, Michael Bryant, Paul Freeman, Anna Massey, Joe Melia, Jim Norton. **1984**

SALAAM BOMBAY! ★★★★1/2 In the most potent film about street children since Hector Babenco's *Pixote*, director Mira Nair takes us on a sobering, heartrending tour of the back alleys and gutters of India. It is there that young Krishna (Shafiq Syed) must struggle to survive among the drug dealers, pimps, and prostitutes. In Hindi with English subtitles. Not rated, the film has profanity, violence, and suggested sex. 113m. DIR: Mira Nair. CAST: Shafiq Syed, Sarfuddin Qurrassi. **1988**

SALAMANDER, THE ★ Abysmal political action-thriller. Rated R; contains violence and profanity. 101m. DIR: Peter Zinner. CAST: Franco Nero, Anthony Quinn, Martin Balsam, Sybil Danning, Christopher Lee, Cleavon Little, Paul Smith, Claudia Cardinale, Eli Wallach. **1981**

SALEM'S LOT ★★★★ This story of vampires in modern-day New England is one of the better adaptations of Stephen King's novels on film. Some real chills go along with an intelligent script in what was originally a two-part TV movie. 112m. DIR: Tobe Hooper. CAST: David Soul, James Mason, Reggie Nalder, Lance Kerwin, Elisha Cook Jr., Ed Flanders, Bonnie Bedelia. **1979 DVD**

•**SALLAH** ★★★ Haym Topol, the future star of *Fiddler on the Roof*, is the main reason to see this comedy about a Jewish family who moves to Israel only to find that life still isn't a bed of roses. Though it was nominated for the oscar for best foreign language film, it's primitively made and miscasts Topol as a man much older than he was at the time. In Hebrew with English subtitles. B&W; 105m. DIR: Ephraim Kishon. CAST: Topol, Geula Noni, Esther Greenberg. **1964**

SALLY OF THE SAWDUST ★★★★ W. C. Fields is at his brilliant best as the lovable con-man guardian of pretty Carol Dempster in this early film of his Broadway hit, *Poppy*. Knowing the identity of her wealthy grandparents, he works to restore her to her rightful place in society, does so after a variety of problems, and says farewell with the now-classic line—Fields's accepted credo—"Never give a sucker an even break." Silent. B&W; 91m. DIR: D. W. Griffith. CAST: Carol Dempster, W. C. Fields, Alfred Lunt. **1925 DVD**

SALO: 120 DAYS OF SODOM ♥ A shocking, repulsive film set during World War II in Italy, where a group of bourgeois Fascists brutalize and sexually degrade teenagers. In Italian with English subtitles. Not rated; contains scenes of graphic sex and violence. 115m. DIR: Pier Paolo Pasolini. CAST: Paolo Bonacelli. **1975**

SALOME (1923) ★★ Campy silent version of Oscar Wilde's play. Rejected and cursed by John the Baptist, Salome plans her revenge. B&W; 48m. DIR: Charles Bryant. CAST: Anna Nazimova. **1923**

SALOME (1953) ★★ Biblical belly dancer Salome (Rita Hayworth) offers herself up as a sacrifice to save John the Baptist (Stewart Granger). Inane. 109m. DIR: William Dieterle. CAST: Rita Hayworth, Stewart Granger, Judith Anderson, Charles Laughton, Cedric Hardwicke. **1953**

SALOME (1985) ★1/2 This is a strange mixture. It is the story of the famous temptress Salome, but in director Claude D'Anna's version the Roman soldiers are in World War II overcoats, there is an elevator in the palace, and the slaves are listening to portable radios. Whatever he had in mind, it doesn't make it. Rated R. 105m. DIR: Claude D'Anna. CAST: Jo Ciampa, Tomas Milian, Tim Woodward. **1985**

SALOME, WHERE SHE DANCED ♥ Yvonne De Carlo plays an exotic dancer in the American West. 90m. DIR: Charles Lamont. CAST: Yvonne De Carlo, Rod Cameron, Walter Slezak, David Bruce, Albert Dekker, Marjorie Rambeau. **1945**

SALOME'S LAST DANCE ★★★★ Ken Russell pays homage to Oscar Wilde in this outrageous dark comedy that takes place in 1895 London. A group of eccentric actors enact Wilde's play *Salome* in the most bizarre setting imaginable: a brothel. Glenda Jackson is simply remarkable, and she's supported by an equally gifted cast in this brilliantly staged surreal fantasy. Rated R for nudity and profanity. 93m. DIR: Ken Russell. CAST: Glenda Jackson, Stratford Johns, Nickolas Grace, Douglas Hodge, Imogen Millais Scott. **1988 DVD**

SALSA ♥ The music is hot, but the rest of this movie is laughably awful. Rated PG for profanity and violence. 92m. DIR: Boaz Davidson. CAST: Robby Rosa, Rodney Harvey. **1988**

SALT OF THE EARTH ★★★ Miners in New Mexico go on strike after a series of accidents and face a long, bitter battle. This once-controversial melodrama uses real mine workers in the cast and has a realistic feel. B&W; 94m. DIR: Herbert J. Biberman. CAST: Rosoura Revueltas, Will Geer. **1953 DVD**

SALT WATER MOOSE ★★★1/2 This charming family drama is set in Canada's rugged Nova Scotia, where baseball-loving city kid Johnny Morina encounters a pert local girl (Katharine Isobel) on a mission. Since a bull moose has trapped itself (during low tide) on one of the many small islands surrounding their cove, she plans to provide a mate by capturing a female moose and transporting it across the small stretch of ocean. Utterly delightful. Rated G. 100m. DIR: Stuart Margolin. CAST: Johnny Morina, Katharine Isobel, Timothy Dalton, Lolita Davidovich. **1995**

SALTMEN OF TIBET, THE ★★★ This meditative documentary chronicles a traditional spring trek to an isolated lake by Tibetan nomads. It explores the rituals, hardships, legends, and social etiquette of the journey as well as the personalities of tribesmen who perpetuate this vanishing lifestyle. Rural vistas encountered by the nomads and their yak caravan are stunning. Not rated. 110m. DIR: Ulrike Koch. **1998**

SALUT L'ARTISTE ★★★1/2 A struggling middle-aged actor, who works primarily in commercials, tries to reconcile with his ex-wife. Bittersweet comedy about the eternal appeal of show business, with

Marcello Mastroianni perfectly cast as a man finally realizing that his dreams are unlikely to come true. In French with English subtitles. Not rated; contains brief nudity. 96m. **DIR:** Yves Robert. **CAST:** Marcello Mastroianni, Françoise Fabian, Jean Rochefort. 1973

SALVADOR ★★★★ James Woods plays screenwriter-photojournalist Richard Boyle in the latter's semiautobiographical account of the events that occurred in El Salvador circa 1980–81. It is a fascinating movie despite its flaws and outrageousness. Rated R for profanity, nudity, suggested sex, drug use, and violence. 120m. **DIR:** Oliver Stone. **CAST:** James Woods, John Savage, James Belushi, Michael Murphy, Elpidia Carrillo, Tony Plana, Cynthia Gibb. 1986

SALVATION ★★★1/2 A punk's wife sends the family cash to a televangelist. Angered, the punk has his teenage sister-in-law seduce the preacher and then blackmails him into sharing his religious revenues. Beth B., who directed and shares writing and production credits, has delivered a raw, insightful film. Rated R for nudity and profanity. 80m. **DIR:** Beth B. **CAST:** Stephen McHattie, Dominique Davalos, Exene Cervenka. 1986

SALZBURG CONNECTION, THE ★★ This incredibly bad spy film set in Europe has Barry Newman playing an American lawyer on vacation who gets mixed up with Nazi spies. Rated PG for violence and language. 93m. **DIR:** Lee H. Katzin. **CAST:** Barry Newman, Anna Karina, Joe Maross, Wolfgang Preiss, Helmut Schmid, Udo Kier, Klaus Maria Brandauer. 1972

SAMANTHA ★★★ Upon learning she was adopted, a 21-year-old eccentric sets about to discover her "real" self. Martha Plimpton's acerbic lead performance helps to balance a too-cute script. A pleasant diversion. Rated PG for profanity. 101m. **DIR:** Stephen La Rocque. **CAST:** Martha Plimpton, Dermot Mulroney, Hector Elizondo, Mary Kay Place, Ione Skye. 1992

SAMARITAN: THE MITCH SNYDER STORY ★★★★ Martin Sheen portrays a nonviolent activist named Mitch Snyder, who successfully convinces city officials to deal with the problems of the homeless. Sensitive made-for-TV biography. 90m. **DIR:** Richard T. Heffron. **CAST:** Martin Sheen, Roxanne Hart, Cicely Tyson. 1986

SAME TIME NEXT YEAR ★★★★ Funny, touching film begins with an accidental meeting in 1951 between two married strangers at a rural California inn. Doris (Ellen Burstyn) is a young housewife from California, and George (Alan Alda) an accountant from New Jersey. Their meetings become an annual event. And through them, we see the changes in America and its people as we return to the same cottage every five years until 1977. Rated PG. 117m. **DIR:** Robert Mulligan. **CAST:** Ellen Burstyn, Alan Alda. 1978

SAMMY AND ROSIE GET LAID ★★★★ Excellent sexual farce set in riot-torn East London concerns a young married couple who receive an unexpected visit from Sammy's father, an arrogant politician who is fleeing from a Middle Eastern country. His world becomes shaken up by the couple's sexually liberated, anarchic friends. Outrageous comedy from the

creators of *My Beautiful Laundrette*. Not rated; contains nudity and violence. 97m. **DIR:** Stephen Frears. **CAST:** Shashi Kapoor, Frances Barber, Claire Bloom, Ayub Khan Din. 1987

SAMMY, THE WAY-OUT SEAL ★★1/2 Better than the title would imply. This series of misadventures involves two young brothers and the seal they attempt to keep as a pet. The film moves along briskly and features larger-than-life comic Jack Carson in one of his last performances. 89m. **DIR:** Norman Tokar. **CAST:** Jack Carson, Robert Culp, Patricia Barry, Billy Mumy, Ann Jillian, Michael McGreevey, Elisabeth Fraser. 1962

SAM'S SON ★★★1/2 Written and directed by Michael Landon, this sweetly nostalgic semiautobiographical family film features Timothy Patrick Murphy as the young Eugene Orowitz (Landon's real name), whose parents, Sam (Eli Wallach) and Harriet (Anne Jackson), seem destined never to realize their fondest dreams until their son lends a hand. Rated PG for brief violence. 104m. **DIR:** Michael Landon. **CAST:** Timothy Patrick Murphy, Eli Wallach, Anne Jackson. 1984

SAMSON 🐝 Samson uses his strength to restore peace in his kingdom. This dubbed film is a yawner. 99m. **DIR:** Gianfranco Parolini. **CAST:** Brad Harris, Bridgette Corey. 1960

SAMSON AND DELILAH (1949) ★★★★ This Cecil B. DeMille extravaganza still looks good today. Hedy Lamarr plays the beautiful vixen Delilah, who robs Samson (Victor Mature) of his incredible strength. Dumb but fun. 128m. **DIR:** Cecil B. DeMille. **CAST:** Hedy Lamarr, Victor Mature, George Sanders, Angela Lansbury. 1949

SAMSON AND DELILAH (1996) ★★ Disappointing biblical miniseries from the Turner Network suffers from a lack of believability on the part of the principal players. Eric Thal as Samson seems temperamental and immature rather than historically significant, and Dennis Hopper, as an enlightened Philistine, sleepwalks through his scenes. Not rated; contains sexual situations and violence. 175m. **DIR:** Nicolas Roeg. **CAST:** Eric Thal, Elizabeth Hurley, Dennis Hopper, Diana Rigg, Paul Freeman, Michael Gambon. 1996

SAMSON AND DELILAH (1984) ★★1/2 An okay TV remake of the DeMille classic that had Victor Mature in the lead. This time, Mature plays Samson's father. Mature and the other veteran actors (Max von Sydow and José Ferrer) help to save the movie. Lots of action—lions, chains, and crumbling masonry. 100m. **DIR:** Lee Philips. **CAST:** Antony Hamilton, Belinda Bauer, Max von Sydow, Stephen Macht, Maria Schell, José Ferrer, Victor Mature. 1984

SAMURAI COWBOY ★★★ A workaholic Japanese businessman who longs for a home on the range bites the bullet and buys himself a dilapidated Wyoming ranch. Veterinarian Catherine Mary Stewart provides romance and Robert Conrad is around for some old-fashioned macho wrangling. Even if the goings get goofy, straight-faced Go is such a delight you'll find this more endearing than it has a right to be. Rated PG for mild profanity and violence. 101m. **DIR:** Michael Keusch. **CAST:** Hiromi Go, Matt McCoy,

Catherine Mary Stewart, Robert Conrad, Conchata Ferrell. 1993

SAMURAI REINCARNATION ★★ Weak adventure yarn about a shogunate warrior who rises from the dead. Gory Japanese metaphysical drama. In Japanese with English subtitles. Not rated; contains nudity and graphic violence. 122m. **DIR:** Kinji Fukasaku. 1981

SAMURAI SAGA ★★★ Toshiro Mifune is in top form as a gallant samurai who challenges a powerful warrior clan in 1599 Japan while getting caught up in a love triangle involving a beautiful princess. Great action sequences. In Japanese with English subtitles. B&W; 112m. **DIR:** Hiroshi Inagaki. **CAST:** Toshiro Mifune. 1959

SAMURAI TRILOGY, THE ★★★★★ This brilliant and cinematically beautiful three-deck epic tells the story of the legendary Japanese hero Musashi Miyamoto, a sixteenth-century samurai who righted wrongs in the fashion of Robin Hood and Zorro. The film follows Miyamoto from his wild youth through spiritual discovery to the final battle with his archenemy, Sasaki Kojiro. The samurai film for the uninitiated. In Japanese with English subtitles. B&W; 303m. **DIR:** Hiroshi Inagaki. **CAST:** Toshiro Mifune, Koji Tsuruta. 1954

SAN ANTONIO ★★★ Sturdy Warner Bros. Western pits Errol Flynn against villain Victor Francen, with Alexis Smith in the middle. Nothing new, just solid action and production values. Final shoot-out at the Alamo is pretty good. 111m. **DIR:** David Butler. **CAST:** Errol Flynn, Alexis Smith, Victor Francen, S. Z. Sakall, Paul Kelly, Florence Bates. 1945

SAN ANTONIO KID ★★★1/2 Outlaws use violence and vandalism to scare ranchers off oil-rich rangeland until Red Ryder and Little Beaver intervene with blazing guns. B&W; 59m. **DIR:** Howard Bretherton. **CAST:** William Elliot, Robert Blake, Alice Fleming, Linda Stirling, Glenn Strange, Duncan Renaldo. 1944

SAN FERNANDO VALLEY ★★1/2 Cowgirls replace cowboys on a large cattle ranch. Nevertheless, Roy Rogers is brought in to rid the valley of the lawless element. Roy got his first screen kiss, from Jean Porter, in this leisurely paced oater, which was the year's number one box-office Western. B&W; 54m. **DIR:** John English. **CAST:** Roy Rogers, Dale Evans, Bob Nolan and the Sons of the Pioneers, Jean Porter. 1944

SAN FRANCISCO ★★★★ In its heyday, MGM boasted it had more stars than were in the heavens, and it made some terrific star-studded movies as a result. Take this 1936 production, starring Clark Gable, Jeanette MacDonald, and Spencer Tracy, for example. It's entertainment of the first order, with special effects—of the San Francisco earthquake—that still stand up today. B&W; 115m. **DIR:** W. S. Van Dyke. **CAST:** Clark Gable, Jeanette MacDonald, Spencer Tracy. 1936

SANCTUARY OF FEAR ★★ Barnard Hughes does a fine job of bringing G. K. Chesterton's crime-busting priest, Father Brown, to life. Unfortunately, the rest of the cast seems detached from the action. This TV movie contains violence. 98m. **DIR:** John Llewellyn Moxey. **CAST:** Barnard Hughes, Kay Lenz, Michael McGuire, George Hearn. 1979

SAND AND BLOOD ★★1/2 Brooding drama that explores the relationship between a young, gifted matador and a cultivated doctor-musician. Both leads give exceptional performances that get lost in this slow-moving drama. In French with English subtitles. Not rated; contains nudity and violence. 101m. **DIR:** Jeanne Labrune. **CAST:** Patrick Catalifo, Sami Frey. 1987

SAND PEBBLES, THE ★★★1/2 Steve McQueen is compelling as Hollman, an ordinary seaman on an American warship stationed off China in 1925. He prefers to remain below deck with his only love, the ship's engines. That way he avoids involvement or decisions. When he is forced to become involved with the world outside his engine room, the result is an enjoyable, sweeping epic with unforgettable characters. 179m. **DIR:** Robert Wise. **CAST:** Steve McQueen, Richard Crenna, Richard Attenborough, Candice Bergen, Mako, Simon Oakland, Gavin MacLeod. 1966

SANDAKAN NO. 8 ★★★★ Penetrating drama about a female journalist who becomes friends with an old woman who had been sold into prostitution and sent to Borneo in the early 1900s. Winner at the Berlin Film Festival and nominated for an Academy Award. In Japanese with English subtitles. Not rated, but is recommended for adult viewers. 121m. **DIR:** Kei Kumai. **CAST:** Kinuyo Tanaka. 1974

SANDERS OF THE RIVER ★★1/2 "Sandy the lawgiver" is the heavy right hand of the British Empire in this action-drama of colonialism in darkest Africa. Paul Robeson rises above demeaning circumstances and fills the screen with his commanding presence. Great footage of the people and terrain of Africa add to the mood of this adventure and give it an aura lacking in many jungle films. B&W; 98m. **DIR:** Zoltán Korda. **CAST:** Paul Robeson, Leslie Banks, Nina Mae McKinney, Robert Cochran. 1935

SANDLOT, THE ★★★1/2 Youngsters will get a big kick out of this kids'-eye-view story of what happens when a shy boy moves to a new neighborhood and becomes involved with a ragtag baseball team. Wonderfully funny moments mix with a few ineffective ones for a show that will even keep Mom and Dad entertained. Rated PG for scary stuff. 100m. **DIR:** David Mickey Evans. **CAST:** Karen Allen, Denis Leary, James Earl Jones, Arliss Howard, Tom Guiry. 1993

SANDMAN (1992) ★★ The director-star of this low-budget spooker died after principal photography, and we can only imagine that he might have made more sense of it in the editing stage. As it is, this story about a house that contains a door to its past has some effective moments but is too confused. Top-billed Robert Wuhl has only a cameo role, as do reunited *Dick Van Dyke Show* costars Morey Amsterdam and Rose Marie. Not rated; contains violence and profanity. 92m. **DIR:** Eric Woster. **CAST:** Eric Woster, Dedee Pfeiffer, Frank Rhodes, Stuart Whitman, Robert Wuhl. 1992

SANDMAN, THE (1996) ★★★★ An insomniac writer discovers late one night that someone or something is murdering the residents of the trailer park while they sleep. The film emerges as a triumph of suspense and terror, proving that a good horror film doesn't need elaborate gore effects to be scary. Highly recommended for horror fans, this one will leave you checking under your bed and in the closet. Not rated; contains violence and profanity. 90m. **DIR:** J. R. Bookwalter. **CAST:** A. J. Richards, Rita Gutowski, Stan Fitzgerald. **1996**

SANDPIPER, THE 🍿 Corny love triangle. 116m. **DIR:** Vincente Minnelli. **CAST:** Richard Burton, Elizabeth Taylor, Eva Marie Saint, Charles Bronson. **1965**

SANDS OF IWO JIMA ★★★★1/2 Superb war film. The Duke was never better than as the haunted Sergeant Stryker, a man hated by his men (with a few exceptions) for his unyielding toughness, but it is by that attitude that he hopes to keep them alive in combat. Watch it and see how good the Duke really was. B&W; 110m. **DIR:** Allan Dwan. **CAST:** John Wayne, John Agar, Forrest Tucker, Richard Jaeckel, Arthur Franz. **1949 DVD**

SANJURO ★★★★1/2 First-rate sequel to *Yojimbo* has the original "Man With No Name" (Toshiro Mifune) again stirring up trouble in feudal Japan. He is recruited by several young would-be samurai as their teacher and leader in exposing corruption in their clan. In his usual gentle manner, Mifune wreaks all sorts of havoc while occasionally warning, "Watch it, I'm in a bad mood." In Japanese with English subtitles. B&W; 96m. **DIR:** Akira Kurosawa. **CAST:** Toshiro Mifune, Tatsuya Nakadai, Takashi Shimura. **1962 DVD**

SANSHIRO SUGATA ★★★1/2 In this vintage film directed by Akira Kurosawa, Sanshiro Sugata (Susumu Fujita) is among the strongest practitioners of judo, but spiritually he is weak. Can he find inner strength and purity? This is an elegant film about spiritual triumph. In Japanese with English subtitles. B&W; 82m. **DIR:** Akira Kurosawa. **CAST:** Susumu Fujita, Takashi Shimura. **1943**

SANSHO THE BAILIFF ★★★ This beautifully photographed tale presents the suffering and heroism of a mother who is separated from her two children by a brutal man called Sansho. A poetic film that exhibits the humanism for which director Kenji Mizoguchi is well-known. In Japanese with English subtitles. B&W; 125m. **DIR:** Kenji Mizoguchi. **CAST:** Kinuyo Tanaka. **1954**

SANTA CLAUS CONQUERS THE MARTIANS 🍿 About a bunch of aliens abducting St. Nick because they don't have one of their own. 80m. **DIR:** Nicholas Webster. **CAST:** John Call, Leonard Hicks. **1964**

SANTA CLAUS—THE MOVIE ★★★ In this enjoyable family film, one of Santa's helpers (Dudley Moore), visits Earth and innocently joins forces with an evil toy manufacturer (delightfully played by John Lithgow). It is up to Santa (David Huddleston) to save him—and the spirit of Christmas. Rated PG for light profanity and adult themes. 105m. **DIR:** Jeannot Szwarc. **CAST:** Dudley Moore, John Lithgow, David Huddleston, Burgess Meredith, Judy Cornwell. **1985**

SANTA CLAUSE, THE ★★★★ TV star–comedian Tim Allen crosses over to the big screen in this lighthearted, humorous tale. An advertising executive finds himself filling in for Santa Claus when the big guy tumbles to his death after being caught unawares on our hero's roof. Slight story works primar-

ily because of Allen's wry wit and charm, and the result is a movie destined to be a holiday perennial. Rated PG. 97m. **DIR:** John Pasquin. **CAST:** Tim Allen, Judge Reinhold, Wendy Crewson, Eric Lloyd, David Krumholtz, Peter Boyle, Larry Brandenburg, Mary Gross, Paige Tamada. **1994 DVD**

SANTA CLAWS ★★ Not much of a shocker here with a nutcase in a Santa suit killing people. Fans of writer-director John Russo's *Night of the Living Dead* can look for Karl Hardman and Marilyn Eastman in cameos. Not rated; contains violence, nudity, and profanity. 85m. **DIR:** John Russo. **CAST:** Debbie Rochon. **1996**

SANTA FE MARSHAL ★★1/2 Hopalong Cassidy goes undercover with a medicine show. B&W; 54m. **DIR:** Lesley Selander. **CAST:** William Boyd, Russell Hayden. **1940**

SANTA FE SADDLEMATES ★★★★1/2 Government investigator Sunset Carson sets out to bust up a diamond-smuggling ring along the U.S.-Mexican border. Top-notch action makes this the best of Carson's fifteen Republic Westerns. B&W; 56m. **DIR:** Thomas Carr. **CAST:** Sunset Carson, Linda Stirling, Olin Howlin, Roy Barcroft. **1945**

SANTA FE STAMPEDE ★★1/2 The Three Mesquiteers (John Wayne, Ray Corrigan, and Max Terhune) ride to the rescue of an old friend (William Farnum) who strikes it rich with a gold mine. A villain (LeRoy Mason) is trying to steal his claim. Lightweight Western with plenty of action. B&W; 58m. **DIR:** George Sherman. **CAST:** John Wayne, Ray "Crash" Corrigan, Max Terhune, William Farnum, LeRoy Mason. **1938**

SANTA FE TRAIL ★★★1/2 Errol Flynn, Alan Hale, and Olivia de Havilland save this muddled Western, with Ronald Reagan as one of Flynn's soldier buddies who go after John Brown (Raymond Massey). B&W; 110m. **DIR:** Michael Curtiz. **CAST:** Errol Flynn, Alan Hale Sr., Olivia de Havilland, Ronald Reagan, Raymond Massey, Ward Bond, Van Heflin. **1940 DVD**

SANTA FE UPRISING ★★★★ Allan Lane takes over the role of Red Ryder for this first of seven films. Outlaws kidnap Little Beaver to stop the duchess from taking over a toll road she has inherited. B&W; 55m. **DIR:** R. G. Springsteen. **CAST:** Allan "Rocky" Lane, Robert Blake, Barton MacLane, Jack LaRue, Dick Curtis. **1946**

SANTA SANGRE ★★★1/2 A disturbed young man who kills at the behest of his armless mother. A weird and often wonderful surreal thriller that looks like a slasher film made by Federico Fellini with Salvador Dali as art director. Rated R for strong violence and sexual content. 124m. **DIR:** Alejandro Jodorowsky. **CAST:** Axel Jodorowsky, Guy Stockwell. **1990**

SANTA WITH MUSCLES ★★1/2 A health-food tycoon (Hulk Hogan) loses his memory in an accident and thinks he's Santa Claus. He then comes to the aid of an orphanage that is about to be shut down by a greedy real-estate developer. Silly holiday comedy is strictly for young kids. Rated PG for violence. 98m. **DIR:** John Murlowski. **CAST:** Hulk Hogan, Ed Begley Jr., Don Stack, Robin Curtis, Kevin West, Garrett Morris, Clint Howard. **1996**

SANTEE ★★1/2 Bounty hunter with a heart (Glenn Ford) loses his son and adopts the son of an outlaw he kills. A fine variety of old Western hands add zip to this otherwise average oater. As usual, Ford turns in a solid performance. PG. 93m. **DIR:** Gary Nelson. **CAST:** Glenn Ford, Dana Wynter, Michael Burns, Robert Donner, Jay Silverheels, Harry Townes, John Larch. 1973

SAPPHIRE ★★★ This mystery about Scotland Yard detectives searching for the murderer of a young black woman was judged a failure at the time because of the reticent way it addressed then current racial tensions. Now it can be enjoyed as a solid police procedural. 92m. **DIR:** Basil Dearden. **CAST:** Nigel Patrick, Yvonne Mitchell, Michael Craig, Paul Massie, Bernard Miles. 1959

SAPS AT SEA ★★★ Oliver Hardy contracts "hornophobia," and the only cure is rest and sea air. Comic timing is off and some of the jokes misfire, but enough of them work to make the movie enjoyable. B&W; 57m. **DIR:** Gordon Douglas. **CAST:** Oliver Hardy, Stan Laurel, Ben Turpin. 1940

SARA DANE ★★ Headstrong eighteenth-century girl manages to raise her status through marriages as well as wise business decisions. This Australian film's premise is very similar to *A Woman of Substance*. 150m. **DIR:** Rod Hardy, Gary Conway. **CAST:** Harold Hopkins, Brenton Whittle. 1981

SARAFINA! ★★★½ Both rapturous and devastating, this antiapartheid musical rockets along, alternating song and dance with the horrors of life in a South African military state. It's a film about the irreversible decision one black schoolgirl is driven to make by forces of bigotry and oppression. Whoopi Goldberg's classy, moving performance as a Soweto schoolteacher is reason enough to snatch this movie up. Rated PG-13 for violence. 101m. **DIR:** Darrell Roodt. **CAST:** Whoopi Goldberg, Leleti Khumalo, Miriam Makeba. 1992

SARAH, PLAIN AND TALL ★★★★ Heartwarming story of a headstrong New England spinster who answers an ad for a mail-order wife placed by a stoic Kansas widower with two children. Sarah says she's not looking for love, but love and special courage win the day just when it seems all is lost. First in a series of videotape releases of *Hallmark Hall of Fame* television presentations. Rated G. 98m. **DIR:** Glenn Jordan. **CAST:** Glenn Close, Christopher Walken, Lexi Randall, Margaret Sophie Stein, Jon De Vries, Christopher Bell. 1991 DVD

SARATOGA ★★★ When Jean Harlow learns her late father lost control of their racehorse farm to bookie Clark Gable, she plots to win it back. Harlow died during production; many scenes were completed by her stand-in. 92m. **DIR:** Jack Conway. **CAST:** Clark Gable, Jean Harlow, Lionel Barrymore, Frank Morgan, Walter Pidgeon, Una Merkel, Hattie McDaniel. 1937

SARDINE: KIDNAPPED ★★★ Intriguing adventure set on the Italian island of Sardinia. Peasants have traditionally obtained land by kidnapping members of wealthy families and ransoming them for land. One family has the courage to stand up to the bandits and informs the police. Directed by a former documentary filmmaker, this English-dubbed film bene-

fits from a realistic look. 110m. **DIR:** Gianfranco Mingozzi. **CAST:** Franco Nero, Charlotte Rampling. 1968

SATAN MET A LADY ★★ A pale shadow of *The Maltese Falcon*, using the same plot with different character names and a ram's horn instead of a statuette of a falcon. Bette Davis often ridiculed it as one of her worst pictures. B&W; 77m. **DIR:** William Dieterle. **CAST:** Bette Davis, Warren William, Alison Skipworth, Arthur Treacher, Marie Wilson, Winifred Shaw, Porter Hall. 1936

SATANIC RITES OF DRACULA, THE ★★½ Substantially better than the previous year's appalling *Dracula A.D. 1972*, this is the final Hammer Films *Dracula* outing to star Christopher Lee and Peter Cushing as the count and his arch-foe, Professor Van Helsing. Actually it's Van Helsing's *grandson*, since this film is set in modern London. Rated R for nudity and gore. 88m. **DIR:** Alan Gibson. **CAST:** Christopher Lee, Peter Cushing, Freddie Jones. 1973 DVD

SATAN'S BED 🦃 An unfinished film starring Yoko Ono as a Japanese woman abandoned in Manhattan is padded out with unrelated footage of juvenile delinquents molesting Long Island housewives. It's a mess. Not rated; contains strong sexual content. B&W; 71m. **DIR:** Marshall Smith. **CAST:** Yoko Ono, Val Avery, Gene Nielson. 1965

SATAN'S BREW ★★★ Wicked Rainer Werner Fassbinder comedy is dark and devious and will not sit easy with most, but for those willing to take a ride on the wild side, the trip is worth it. Fassbinder sets his sights on Artaud's Theater of Cruelty and depicts the crazy world of a hack poet who believes he is the reincarnation of a nineteenth-century German poet. His strange behavior incites family and friends. Not rated; contains adult situations. 112m. **DIR:** Rainer Werner Fassbinder. **CAST:** Kurt Raab, Helen Vita, Volker Spengler, Margit Carstensen. 1976

SATAN'S CHEERLEADERS 🦃 Cheerleaders run afoul of a cult of Satanists. Rated PG. 92m. **DIR:** Greydon Clark. **CAST:** Kerry Sherman, John Ireland, Yvonne De Carlo, John Carradine, Jack Kruschen. 1977

SATAN'S PRINCESS ★★ An ex-cop turned private detective takes on a missing-persons case that leads him straight to a centuries-old demoness, who kills people as often as she changes her wardrobe. Amateurish. Rated R for violence. 90m. **DIR:** Bert I. Gordon. **CAST:** Robert Forster, Lydie Denier, Caren Kaye. 1989

•**SATAN'S SADISTS** 🦃 Infamous biker film whose advertising campaign traded on the Manson murders is a vicious, sleazy orgy of death and gore disguised as social comment that makes you wonder how (and why) name actors ever got involved in this mess. Not rated; contains partial nudity and violence. 87m. **DIR:** Al Adamson. **CAST:** Russ Tamblyn, Scott Brady, Kent Taylor, John Cardos, Gary Kent, Graydon Clark, Regina Carrol, Jodie Taylor. 1969

SATAN'S SCHOOL FOR GIRLS ★★½ Originally made as an ABC Movie of the Week, this decent shocker concerns a series of apparent suicides at a prominent girls' school, but we all know better. Good acting and some creepy atmosphere, but the typical TV ending falls flat. 74m. **DIR:** David Lowell Rich.

CAST: Pamela Franklin, Kate Jackson, Roy Thinnes, Cheryl Ladd. **1973**

SATELLITE IN THE SKY ★★ The crew of a spaceship attempts to recover a runaway experimental bomb. Tedious sci-fi adventure memorable for a fun performance by Donald Wolfit as the bomb's eccentric inventor. B&W; 84m. **DIR:** Paul Dickson. **CAST:** Kieron Moore, Lois Maxwell, Donald Wolfit, Bryan Forbes, Shirley Lawrence. **1956**

SATISFACTION 🎬 Justine Bateman is the leader of a rock band. Rated PG-13 for profanity and suggested sex. 95m. **DIR:** Joan Freeman. **CAST:** Justine Bateman, Liam Neeson, Trini Alvarado, Julia Roberts, Deborah Harry, Chris Nash. **1988**

SATURDAY NIGHT AT THE PALACE ★★★ The fears and hatreds behind South Africa's policy of apartheid are explored in a microcosm in this intense South African film. It expands upon a real-life incident, a late-night confrontation between a white man and a black man at a suburban hamburger joint. Paul Slabolepszy, who plays the white antagonist, also wrote the screenplay. 87m. **DIR:** Robert Davies. **CAST:** Paul Slabolepszy, John Kani. **1988**

SATURDAY NIGHT FEVER ★★★★ From the first notes of "Stayin' Alive" by the Bee Gees over the opening credits, it is obvious that *Saturday Night Fever* is more than just another youth exploitation film. It is *Rebel Without a Cause* for the 1970s, with realistic dialogue and effective dramatic situations. Rated R for profanity, violence, partial nudity, and simulated sex. 119m. **DIR:** John Badham. **CAST:** John Travolta, Donna Pescow, Karen Lynn Gorney. **1977**

SATURDAY NIGHT KID, THE ★★★★ A clever comedy designed to showcase Clara Bow's perky personality. The plot involves two department-store clerks in love with the same man. The triangle gets tangled more than usual because the girls are sisters. B&W; 75m. **DIR:** Edward Sutherland. **CAST:** Clara Bow, Jean Arthur, Jean Harlow, James Hall, Edna May Oliver, Frank Ross, Ethel Wales. **1929**

SATURDAY NIGHT SHOCKERS ★★★ Each of these four tapes includes a pair of cheapo horror movies, cartoons, short subjects, and coming attractions, all from the Thirties, Forties, and Fifties. Thus seen in their proper context, these trash classics are more entertaining than they would be if viewed alone. The titles are: Volume 1, *The Creeping Terror* and *Chained for Life*; Volume 2, *Man Beast* and *Human Gorilla*; Volume 3, *Murder in the Red Barn* and *A Face at the Window*; and Volume 4, *Mesa of Lost Women* and *The Monster of Piedras Blancas*. Not rated; no objectionable content. Each tape is approximately 150m. **DIR:** Various.

SATURDAY NIGHT SPECIAL 🎬 This plotless film is just a 90-minute music video with some sex and violence thrown in. A handsome musician arrives in a small town and trouble starts. Available in R and unrated versions; contains violence, nudity, graphic sex, and profanity. 97m. **DIR:** Dan Golden. **CAST:** Billy Burnette, Maria Ford, Rick Dean, Robert Van Luik, Duane Whitaker. **1994**

SATURDAY THE 14TH 🎬 Richard Benjamin and Paula Prentiss star in this low-budget horror comedy about a family that moves into a haunted house.

Rated PG. 75m. **DIR:** Howard R. Cohen. **CAST:** Richard Benjamin, Paula Prentiss, Jeffrey Tambor, Rosemary DeCamp. **1981**

SATURN 3 ★★ Although this space shocker is endowed with a fair amount of chills and surprises, there's very little else to it. The story takes place in the distant future on the Eden-like space station Titan, which is happily inhabited by two chemists (Kirk Douglas and Farrah Fawcett). A strangely hostile newcomer (Harvey Keitel) unleashes a terror that threatens to destroy them all. Rated R. 88m. **DIR:** Stanley Donen. **CAST:** Kirk Douglas, Farrah Fawcett, Harvey Keitel. **1980 DVD**

SAVAGE ★★★ Martial arts star Olivier Gruner gets to strut his stuff as a man tracking down the scum responsible for the death of his wife and son. Aided by a policewoman, Savage (Gruner) find his prey, who deals in virtual reality and is planning the apocalypse. Exciting premise and creative computer-generated graphics. Rated R for language, nudity, and violence. 103m. **DIR:** Avi Nesher. **CAST:** Olivier Gruner, Jennifer Grant, Sam McMurray, Kario Salem, Kristin Minter. **1995**

SAVAGE ATTRACTION ★★★★ A psychotic German becomes sadistically obsessed with a lovely Australian girl in this bizarre but true tale. He uses both mental and physical cruelty to keep her with him. The suspense is never lacking. Rated R for sadism, nudity, and violence. 93m. **DIR:** Frank Shields. **CAST:** Kerry Mack, Ralph Schicha. **1983**

SAVAGE BEACH 🎬 In this sequel to *Picasso Trigger*, two female agents with the Drug Enforcement Division uncover a plot to retrieve gold lost during World War II. Rated R. 95m. **DIR:** Andy Sidaris. **CAST:** Dona Speir, Hope Marie Carlton, Bruce Penhall, John Aprea. **1990**

SAVAGE BEES, THE ★★1/2 Above-average thriller about a plague of African killer bees wreaking havoc on New Orleans during Mardi Gras. Oscar-winner Ben Johnson gives dramatic punch to this made-for-TV chiller. Some good thrills. 99m. **DIR:** Bruce Geller. **CAST:** Ben Johnson, Michael Parks, Horst Buchholz. **1976**

SAVAGE DAWN 🎬 A motorcycle gang takes over a small town in the desert. Rated R for violence, nudity, and profanity. 102m. **DIR:** Simon Nuchtern. **CAST:** George Kennedy, Richard Lynch, Lance Henriksen, Karen Black, William Forsythe. **1984**

SAVAGE GUNS 🎬 Revenge story has an outlaw destroy a saloon to prevent the owner from testifying against him. Only a gunfighter is wounded and his brother killed in the attack. The gunfighter recuperates and goes after the outlaw. Exciting action but weak story. Not rated; contains violence. 85m. **DIR:** Miles Deem. **CAST:** Robert Woods, Dean Stratford, Dennis Colt, Simone Blondell. **1971**

SAVAGE HEARTS ★★★ Offbeat thriller centers on mob assassin Maryam D'Abo, who has only six months to live. In order to enjoy her remaining days, D'Abo steals two million dollars of the mob's money. The theft enrages mob kingpin Richard Harris, who will stop at nothing to retrieve the stolen loot. Hiding out in a hotel, Baxter encounters two con artists whose fates are sealed when they attempt to help her. Rated R for violence, profanity, and adult situations. 90m. **DIR:** Mark Ezra. **CAST:** Jamie Harris, Maryam D'Abo, Richard Harris, Myriam Cir, Jerry Hall. 1995

SAVAGE INSTINCT 🖤 When Debra Sweaney accidentally walks into the dark and seedy world of a drug dealer, she is beaten and left for dead. She survives and comes back with a vengeance. Charles Bronson did it with more conviction. Not rated; contains graphic violence. 88m. **DIR:** Patrick G. Donahue. **CAST:** Debra Sweaney. 1991

SAVAGE INTRUDER, THE 🖤 An aging film star hires a male nurse who turns out to be a psycho. 90m. **DIR:** Donald Wolfe. **CAST:** Miriam Hopkins, John David Garfield, Gale Sondergaard. 1977

SAVAGE IS LOOSE, THE ★ Tedious tale strands a young man and his parents on an island for many years. Rated R. 114m. **DIR:** George C. Scott. **CAST:** George C. Scott, Trish Van Devere, John David Carson, Lee Montgomery. 1974

SAVAGE JOURNEY 🖤 Simplistic, whitewashed account of the formation of the Mormon Church. Not rated, contains some violence. 96m. **DIR:** Tom McGowan. **CAST:** Maurice Grandmaison, Charles Moll. 1983

SAVAGE JUSTICE 🖤 The daughter of an American ambassador is caught up in a revolution in a foreign country. Not rated, the film has nudity and violence. 90m. **DIR:** Joey Romero. **CAST:** Julie Montgomery, Steve Memel. 1988

SAVAGE LAND ★★★ A stagecoach on the way to Colorado is ambushed by fake Indians, and the occupants must go on the run. Mildly entertaining, with lots of lessons. Rated PG. 91m. **DIR:** Dean Hamilton. **CAST:** Corbin Bernsen, Corey Carrier, Brion James, Mercedes McNab, Charlotte Ross, Graham Greene, Vivian Schilling. 1994

SAVAGE MESSIAH ★★1/2 This flamboyant love story dramatized in the Ken Russell tradition of excess only works in part. The story of a French sculptor's affair with a much older Polish woman symbolizes the generation gap as well as the culture clash. It would have worked better as a morality play without Russell's overworked and self-indulgent camera tricks. Rated R. 100m. **DIR:** Ken Russell. **CAST:** Dorothy Tutin, Scott Anthony, Helen Mirren, John Justin, Michael Gough, Lindsay Kemp. 1972

SAVAGE NIGHTS ★★1/2 A young bisexual filmmaker with AIDS is torn between an unstable teenage girl and a shallow young boy. Despite some fine scenes and good acting, the story loses momentum and seems much longer than it is. In French with English subtitles. Rated R for mature themes and sexual scenes. 126m. **DIR:** Cyril Collard. **CAST:** Cyril Collard, Romane Bohringer, Carlos Lopez. 1992

SAVAGE SAM ★★1/2 Officially a sequel to *Old Yeller*, the film has little in common with its predecessor, except for some of the character names. Captured by Indians, the only hope of rescue for three children lies with Savage Sam, Old Yeller's son. An entertaining action film, without the depth of its predecessor. 103m. **DIR:** Norman Tokar. **CAST:** Brian

Keith, Tommy Kirk, Kevin Corcoran, Dewey Martin, Jeff York, Marta Kristen. 1963

SAVAGE STREETS 🖤 Linda Blair is the tough leader of a street gang. Rated R for everything imaginable. 90m. **DIR:** Danny Steinmann. **CAST:** Linda Blair, Robert Dryer, Sal Landi, John Vernon. 1985

SAVAGE WEEKEND ★★ Several couples head out from the big city into the backwoods to watch a boat being built, but they are killed off one by one. The only reason this movie earns any stars is for talented actor William Sanderson's performance as a demented lunatic who may or may not be the killer. Rated R for nudity, simulated sex, and violence. 88m. **DIR:** John Mason Kirby. **CAST:** Christopher Allport, James Doerr, Marilyn Hamlin, William Sanderson. 1979

SAVAGES (1973) ★★★ James Ivory's offbeat look at society, in which a naked group of primitives find their sacrificial rites disrupted by a croquet ball. This discovery leads them to a deserted mansion where an odd cluster of events culminates in a transformation in which they are civilized. Not rated, contains nudity and violence. 108m. **DIR:** James Ivory. **CAST:** Lewis J. Stadlen, Anne Francine, Thayer David, Salome Jens. 1973

SAVAGES (1974) ★★★ Man hunts man! Sam Bottoms is guiding Andy Griffith on a hunt in the desert when Griffith goes bananas and begins a savage, relentless pursuit of Bottoms. A sandy rendition of the famous short story, "The Most Dangerous Game." Thrilling, suspenseful, and intriguing to watch. Made for TV. 78m. **DIR:** Lee H. Katzin. **CAST:** Andy Griffith, Sam Bottoms, Noah Beery Jr., James Best. 1974

SAVANNAH SMILES ★★★1/2 In this surprisingly good, independently made family film, a 6-year-old runaway named Savannah (Bridgette Anderson) accidentally hides in the backseat of a car operated by two small-time crooks, Alvie (Mark Miller) and Boots (Donovan Scott). It's love at first sight for the trio, who decide to try to be a real family. The authorities, however, have other ideas. Rated G. 107m. **DIR:** Pierre DeMoro. **CAST:** Bridgette Anderson, Mark Miller, Donovan Scott, Peter Graves, Chris Robinson, Michael Parks. 1982

SAVATE ★★1/2 Here's an oddity: a post–Civil War, kick-boxing rip-off of *The Quick and the Dead*. An expatriate French soldier competes in a series of battles to help good citizens retain the rights to their two-bit town. Aside from the exotic fighting style, everything else about this film is borrowed—most notably the soundtrack, which should prompt a lawsuit from composer Ennio Morricone. Rated PG-13 for violence. 88m. **DIR:** Isaac Florentine. **CAST:** Olivier Gruner, Ian Ziering, Ashley Laurence, Marc Singer, James Brolin. 1994

SAVE ME ★★1/2 Harry Hamlin strips down for some steamy sex with a mystery woman (Lysette Anthony). Hamlin finds plenty of diversion with Anthony, whom he believes he is saving from an abusive husband, but then someone tries to kill him. Thanks to his latest tryst, the list of suspects keeps growing. R-rated and unrated versions available; both contain sex, nudity, adult language, and violence. 90m. **DIR:**

Alan Roberts. **CAST:** Harry Hamlin, Lysette Anthony, Steve Railsback, Olivia Hussey, Michael Ironside. 1993
SAVE THE LADY ★★★ Four kids set out to fight City Hall after a bureaucrat orders the historic *Lady Hope* steam ferry to be destroyed. The kids rescue *Lady Hope's* former skipper from a retirement home. Together with an expert engineer, the team valiantly repairs and repaints the boat. 76m. **DIR:** Leon Thau. **CAST:** Matthew Excell, Robert Clarkson, Miranda Cartledge, Kim Clifford. 1981
SAVE THE TIGER ★★★ Jack Lemmon won the Academy Award for best actor for his portrayal in this 1973 film as a garment manufacturer who is at the end of his professional and emotional rope. His excellent performance helps offset the fact that the picture is essentially a downer. Rated R. 101m. **DIR:** John G. Avildsen. **CAST:** Jack Lemmon, Jack Gilford, Thayer David. 1973
SAVED BY THE LIGHT ★★★1/2 Inspirational tale of a real jerk whose life is changed for the better when he is hit by lightning and visits the afterlife. Terrific performance by Eric Roberts. Not rated; contains profanity. 95m. **DIR:** Lewis Teague. **CAST:** Eric Roberts, Lynette Walden, K. Callan, Don McManus. 1995
SAVING GRACE ★★★ The pope (Tom Conti), frustrated with his lack of freedom, finds himself in the small, depressed Italian village of Montepetra where he gets back to helping people on a one-on-one basis. *Saving Grace* is very good, showing moments of conflict with the human element exposed in all its emotions. Rated PG for violence and profanity. 112m. **DIR:** Robert M. Young. **CAST:** Tom Conti, Fernando Rey, Edward James Olmos, Giancarlo Giannini, Erland Josephson. 1986
SAVING PRIVATE RYAN ★★★★★ As he did with *Schindler's List*, Steven Spielberg has delivered what probably will remain a statement of record for decades to come. The opening twenty-minute depiction of the fateful D-Day assault is mesmerizing … and very, very hard to watch. And it's merely prologue to a tale of individual courage that sends eight men into German-occupied France to rescue a soldier whose brothers all have been killed in combat. Our ground-level guide is Captain John Miller (Tom Hanks), an honorable soldier who believes in just causes and the merit of chain of command. His men are stereotypes but no less real, and their subsequent adventures unfold against Spielberg's stated desire to portray dignity and decency in the charnel house of combat. The result is not a film to be embraced frivolously: it's raw, powerful, incredibly violent … and absolutely unforgettable. Rated R for violence, profanity, and war-related gore and carnage. 170m. **DIR:** Steven Spielberg. **CAST:** Tom Hanks, Tom Sizemore, Edward Burns, Barry Pepper, Adam Goldberg, Matt Damon, Vin Diesel, Giovanni Ribisi, Jeremy Davies. 1998 DVD
SAVIOR ★★★ Grim, convoluted story about an American who becomes a mercenary for the Serbs as an act of revenge for the murder of his wife and child. He rediscovers his humanity against the atrocities and horrors of the war through a young Serb woman and her newborn daughter. Dennis Quaid's

performance is stellar. Rated R for brutal violence, profanity, and brief nudity. 104m. **DIR:** Peter Antonijevic. **CAST:** Dennis Quaid, Nastassja Kinski, Stellan Skarsgard, Natasa Ninkovic. 1997 DVD
SAWBONES ★★★ What might have been a by-the-numbers goreflick is enlivened by Nina Siemaszko, as a plucky young woman trying to solve medical-related serial killings. More howdunnit than whodunnit, Sam Montgomery's script is much smarter than usual, and the blood is surprisingly restrained for such an obvious genre entry. Rated R for brief violence, brief nudity, and a single profanity. 85m. **DIR:** Catherine Cyran. **CAST:** Adam Baldwin, Nina Siemaszko, Nicholas Sadler, Don Harvey, Don Stroud, Barbara Carrera. 1995
SAWDUST AND TINSEL ★★★1/2 A traveling circus is the background for this study of love relationships between a circus manager, the woman he loves, and her lover. Director Ingmar Bergman scores some emotional bull's-eyes in this early effort. Love triangle leads to a powerful climax, somewhat reminiscent of *The Blue Angel*. B&W; 95m. **DIR:** Ingmar Bergman. **CAST:** Harriet Andersson, Anders Ek. 1953
SAY AMEN, SOMEBODY ★★★★ This is a joyful documentary about gospel singers Thomas A. Dorsey and Willie Mae Ford Smith. Two dozen gospel songs make this modest film a treat for the ears as well as the eyes and soul. Rated G. 100m. **DIR:** George T. Nierenberg. **CAST:** Thomas A. Dorsey, Willie Mae Ford Smith, Sallie Martin. 1982
SAY ANYTHING ★★★1/2 So many things are right with this comedy-drama about first love that one can't help wincing when it takes a wrong turn. Yet everything else is honest in its depiction of a well-meaning, unexceptional guy (John Cusack) who falls in love with a seemingly unattainable beauty with brains (Ione Skye). It's a minor gem from first-time director Cameron Crowe, who wrote *Fast Times at Ridgemont High*. Rated PG-13 for suggested sex and profanity. 100m. **DIR:** Cameron Crowe. **CAST:** John Cusack, Ione Skye, John Mahoney. 1989
SAY GOODBYE, MAGGIE COLE ★★★ A retired doctor reopens her practice in a tough Chicago neighborhood after her husband dies. Standard TV movie elevated by star Susan Hayward in her final performance. 74m. **DIR:** Jud Taylor. **CAST:** Susan Hayward, Darren McGavin, Michael Constantine, Beverly Garland. 1972
SAY YES ★★1/2 A multimillionaire (Jonathan Winters) dies, leaving his estate to his son (Art Hindle) on the condition that he marry before his thirty-fifth birthday—only a day away. The comedy doesn't work most of the time, but the story is cute enough to tolerate. Rated PG-13 for sex, nudity, and profanity. 87m. **DIR:** Larry Yust. **CAST:** Art Hindle, Lissa Layng, Logan Ramsey, Jonathan Winters, Maryedith Burrell, Anne Ramsey. 1986
SAYONARA ★★★★ Marlon Brando is an American airman who engages in a romance with a Japanese actress while stationed in Japan after World War II. His love is put to the test by each culture's misconceptions and prejudices. James A. Michener's thought-provoking tragedy-romance still holds up

well. Red Buttons and Miyoshi Umeki deservedly won Oscars for their roles as star-crossed lovers "American Occupation"–style. 147m. **DIR:** Joshua Logan. **CAST:** Marlon Brando, Red Buttons, Miyoshi Umeki, Ricardo Montalban, James Garner. 1957

SCALAWAG BUNCH, THE ★★ Italian-made adaptation of the Robin Hood story is cheaply made and poorly dubbed into English. But the story is still entertaining. Not rated. 103m. **DIR:** Giorgio Ferroni. **CAST:** Mark Damon. 1975

SCALPEL 🎬 Plastic surgeon transforms a young accident victim into the spitting image of his missing daughter to pull an inheritance swindle. Rated R. 96m. **DIR:** John Grissmer. **CAST:** Robert Lansing, Judith Chapman, Arlen Dean Snyder, Sandy Martin. 1976

SCALPHUNTERS, THE ★★★1/2 Fine, old-fashioned Western finds fur-trapper Burt Lancaster and runaway slave Ossie Davis pitted against Telly Savalas and his gang of cutthroats. Frequent bits of comedy make this a solid genre entry. 102m. **DIR:** Sydney Pollack. **CAST:** Burt Lancaster, Shelley Winters, Telly Savalas, Ossie Davis, Dabney Coleman, Nick Cravat. 1968

SCALPS ★★ Early effort from Florida poverty-row director Fred Olen Ray shows him still imitating better-financed Hollywood filmmakers. Presence of experienced character actors lends novelty value to horror thriller about resurrected Indian ghost and its teenage prey. Rated R. 82m. **DIR:** Fred Olen Ray. **CAST:** Kirk Alyn, Carol Borland. 1983

SCAM ★★1/2 Sultry Lorraine Bracco, who picks up rich men only to drug and rob them, reluctantly agrees to help FBI agent Christopher Walken execute a similar sting on a specific target. Sadly, Craig Smith's twisty mystery eventually gets too convoluted for its own good, resulting in a double-reverse climax which makes no sense in view of what has taken place earlier. Rated R for profanity and violence. 102m. **DIR:** John Flynn. **CAST:** Christopher Walken, Lorraine Bracco, Miguel Ferrer, Martin Donovan. 1993

SCANDAL ★★★1/2 A remarkable motion picture, this British production takes on the Profumo affair of the 1960s and emerges as an uncommonly satisfying adult-oriented drama, rich in character and insight. John Hurt is superb as Stephen Ward, the London osteopath who groomed teenage Christine Keeler (Joanne Whalley-Kilmer) into the femme fatale who brought down the British Conservative government. Rated R for nudity, simulated sex, violence, and profanity. 105m. **DIR:** Michael Caton-Jones. **CAST:** John Hurt, Joanne Whalley, Bridget Fonda, Ian McKellen. 1989

SCANDAL IN A SMALL TOWN ★★ Predictable (and misleadingly titled) drama starring Raquel Welch as a waitress who opposes an anti-Semitic schoolteacher. Cardboard characters and situations are the real scandal in this made-for-TV movie. 90m. **DIR:** Anthony Page. **CAST:** Raquel Welch, Christa Denton, Frances Lee McCain, Ronny Cox. 1988

SCANDALOUS (1983) 🎬 Robert Hays plays an investigative reporter who gets mixed up with spies, con men, and murder in London. The cast includes Pamela Stephenson and John Gielgud, as a pair of con artists. Gielgud seems to be having a grand old time playing everything from an old Chinese man to the world's oldest punk rocker. Rated PG for profanity, nudity, and brief violence. 93m. **DIR:** Rob Byrum. **CAST:** Robert Hays, Pamela Stephenson, John Gielgud, Jim Dale, M. Emmet Walsh. 1983

SCANDALOUS (1988) 🎬 A penniless playboy is hired to find a secretary who has witnessed the murder of a renowned author. 90m. **DIR:** Robert W. Young. **CAST:** Lauren Hutton, Albert Fortell, Capucine. 1988

SCANDALOUS JOHN ★★★ Brian Keith stars as an eccentric ranch owner fighting to maintain his way of life. In his world, a cattle drive consists of one steer, and gunfights are practiced in the house with live ammunition. He must battle with the law, the world in general, and reality to keep his ranch and the life he loves. Laughs and poignancy are combined in this movie. Rated G. 113m. **DIR:** Robert Butler. **CAST:** Brian Keith, Alfonso Arau, Michele Carey, Rick Lenz, Harry Morgan, Simon Oakland. 1971

SCANDALOUS ME: THE JACQUELINE SUSANN STORY ★★★ You would think the life of Jacqueline Susann (who wrote the bestselling book *Valley of the Dolls*) would make an interesting movie, and yet something's certainly missing. Such a short film can't do justice to her complex and troubling life, but the highlights are pretty well presented here. Susann contends with an adulterous father, drug abuse, a mentally deficient son, the high price of success, an on-off relationship with her husband, and finally, cancer. Michele Lee shines as the sassy and sensitive Susann. Not rated. 95m. **DIR:** Bruce McDonald. **CAST:** Michele Lee, Peter Riegert, James Farentino, Sherry Miller. 1998

SCANNER COP ★★1/2 The filmmakers try a new tack to keep the series alive: the Scanner joins the police department. The young rookie, who has been silencing the voices in his head, is asked to uncork those feelings when members of the force are being killed, and all clues point to someone with scanning abilities. The special effects are more abstract this outing, hoping to pump some new life into the franchise. Rated R for strong violence. 94m. **DIR:** Pierre David. **CAST:** Daniel Quinn, Darlanne Fluegel, Richard Lynch, Brion James, Richard Grove. 1993

SCANNERS ★★★1/2 From its first shocking scene—in which a character's head explodes, spewing blood, flesh, and bone all over—the film poses a challenge to its viewers: How much can you take? Shock specialist David Cronenberg wrote and directed this potent film, about a bloody war among people with formidable extrasensory powers. Rated R. 102m. **DIR:** David Cronenberg. **CAST:** Jennifer O'Neill, Patrick McGoohan, Stephen Lack, Lawrence Dane, Michael Ironside. 1981

SCANNERS 2: THE NEW ORDER ★★1/2 Pretty much the same old thing, with a new breed of scanners roaming the streets, causing people to hemorrhage and explode. Good guy scanners David Hewlett and Deborah Raffin attempt to stop the bad guy scanners from controlling the city. Rated R for violence. 102m. **DIR:** Christian Duguay. **CAST:** David Hewlett, Deborah Raffin. 1991

SCANNERS 3: THE TAKEOVER 🎬 This third installment is distant from David Cronenberg's original vision. Dull. Rated R for nudity and profanity. 101m. DIR: Christian Duguay. CAST: Liliana Komorowska, Valerie Valois, Steve Parrish. 1992

SCANNERS 4: THE SHOWDOWN ★★1/2 A detective and a serial killer, both of whom are scanners, must scan to the death in this gory but passable film. Rated R for violence and profanity. 95m. DIR: Steve Barnett. CAST: Daniel Quinn, Patrick Kilpatrick, Khrystyne Haje. 1994

SCAR, THE ★★★★ Fans of hardboiled *film noir* will want to look for this lesser-known but memorable example of the genre. Paul Henreid plays two parts: a gambler fleeing from the police and a psychiatrist who is his exact double. The gambler plans to escape the law by killing the doctor and assuming his identity. Look for Jack Webb in a small role. B&W; 83m. DIR: Steve Sekely. CAST: Paul Henreid, Joan Bennett, Eduard Franz, Leslie Brooks, John Qualen. 1948

SCARAMOUCHE ★★★★ This big-screen adaptation of the Rafael Sabatini story is first-class entertainment for the whole family. Stewart Granger is perfectly cast as the swashbuckling Scaramouche, who sets out to avenge his brother's murder by a villainous master swordsman (Mel Ferrer). A wonderfully witty script, splendid cinematography, fine performances, and outstanding action scenes. 118m. DIR: George Sidney. CAST: Stewart Granger, Eleanor Parker, Mel Ferrer, Janet Leigh. 1952

SCARECROW ★★★ A real downer about two losers (Al Pacino and Gene Hackman) trying to make something of themselves, this drama is made watchable by the performances. Rated R. 115m. DIR: Jerry Schatzberg. CAST: Al Pacino, Gene Hackman, Eileen Brennan, Richard Lynch. 1973

SCARECROWS ★★★★ This is something rare—a truly frightening horror film, loaded with suspense, intelligent writing, and decent acting. The story involves a group of military deserters who have ripped off a federal money exchange and are flying south in a stolen cargo plane. They land in a secluded wilderness of cornfields filled with … scarecrows. Not recommended for the squeamish, but horror fans will find this to be a feast. Not rated; contains graphic violence. 88m. DIR: William Wesley. CAST: Ted Vernon, Michael Simms, Richard Vidan. 1988

SCARED STIFF 🎗 A newly married couple move into an old house cursed by a voodoo priest. Rated R for violence. 85m. DIR: Richard Friedman. CAST: Andrew Stevens, Mary Page Keller. 1986

SCARED TO DEATH (1946) ★★ Tepid thriller is noteworthy primarily because it is Bela Lugosi's only color film, not for the lukewarm story about a woman who dies without a traceable cause. Plenty of hocus-pocus, red herrings, and hypnosis. Directed by Christy Cabanne, a silent film pioneer. 65m. DIR: Christy Cabanne. CAST: Bela Lugosi, Douglas Fowley, Joyce Compton, George Zucco, Nat Pendleton. 1946 DVD

SCARED TO DEATH (1980) ★★1/2 Although it's an unabashed rip-off of *Alien*, this film manages to build straight through to the harrowing ending. However, little compassion for the characters ruins what could have been terrific fright fare. Rated R for vio-

lence. 95m. DIR: William Malone. CAST: John Stinston, Diana Davidson. 1980

SCARFACE (1932) ★★★★1/2 Subtitled "Shame of the Nation" when released in the 1930s, this thinly veiled account of the rise and fall (the latter being fictional) of Al Capone easily ranks as one of the very best films in the gangster genre. Paul Muni is first-rate as the Chicago gangster and receives excellent support from Ann Dvorak, George Raft, and, out standing as a rival gangster, Boris Karloff. See it. B&W; 93m. DIR: Howard Hawks. CAST: Paul Muni, Ann Dvorak, George Raft, Boris Karloff, Osgood Perkins. 1932

SCARFACE (1983) ★★★★1/2 Onetime "Godfather" Al Pacino returns to his screen beginnings with a bravura performance in the title role of this updating of Howard Hawks's 1932 gangster classic. Rather than bootleg gin as Paul Muni did in the original, Pacino imports and sells cocaine. Directed by Brian De Palma, it's the most violent, thrilling, revolting, surprising, and gruesome gangster movie ever made. Rated R for nudity, violence, sex, and profanity. 170m. DIR: Brian De Palma. CAST: Al Pacino, Steven Bauer, Robert Loggia, Paul Shenar. 1983 DVD

SCARLET AND THE BLACK, THE ★★1/2 The action in this film is centered around the Vatican during the time of the German occupation of Rome in 1943. Based on "The Scarlet Pimpernel of the Vatican," it chronicles the adventures of an Irish priest who manages to elude the German captors in true Pimpernel fashion. Moderately entertaining. 143m. DIR: Jerry London. CAST: Gregory Peck, Christopher Plummer, John Gielgud. 1983

SCARLET CLAW, THE ★★★★ Stunningly atmospheric entry in the Universal series of Sherlock Holmes mysteries has the detective journeying to Canada to find the culprit in a bizarre series of murders. This is a true whodunit, which keeps you guessing right to the end. B&W; 74m. DIR: Roy William Neill. CAST: Basil Rathbone, Nigel Bruce, Gerald Hamer, Paul Cavanagh, Arthur Hohl, Miles Mander, Ian Wolfe. 1944

SCARLET CLUE, THE ★★ Standard, workmanlike *Charlie Chan* entry in the latter-day Monogram Pictures cycle, from its most prolific hack director. A suspect is killed as Charlie investigates a plot to purloin government radar plans. Some atmosphere on a grade-C scale, but no tension. B&W; 64m. DIR: Phil Rosen. CAST: Sidney Toler, Benson Fong, Mantan Moreland, I. Stanford Jolley. 1945

SCARLET DAWN ★★ The characters bounce between coping with the Russian Revolution and sex orgies in an uneven melodrama that is as heavy as the ornate sets and garish makeup on the faces of big-time stars who should have known better. More of a curiosity piece than a satisfying film. B&W; 80m. DIR: William Dieterle. CAST: Douglas Fairbanks Jr., Lilyan Tashman, Nancy Carroll, Earle Fox. 1932

SCARLET EMPRESS, THE ★★★★1/2 This classic is a stunning cinematic achievement dominated by the seductive Marlene Dietrich. A naïve, shy girl becomes a worldly wise woman adept at court intrigue as she goes from being the unwilling bride of Czar Peter and the empress of all the Russias. Visually impressive and marvelously detailed, this is a must-see movie. B&W; 110m. DIR: Josef von Sternberg. CAST: Marlene Dietrich, Louise Dresser, Sam Jaffe, John Lodge, Maria Sieber, C. Aubrey Smith, Gavin Gordon, Olive Tell, Jane Darwell, Jameson Thomas. 1934

SCARLET LETTER, THE (1926) ★★★ Hester Prynne wears the scarlet letter A for adultery. Only her sadistic husband Roger knows that minister Arthur Dimmesdale is the father of her daughter, Pearl. Roger taunts Arthur, who plans to flee with Hester and the child but finally confesses his sin publicly. Silent. B&W; 80m. DIR: Victor Sjöström. CAST: Lillian Gish, Henry B. Walthall, Karl Dane, Lars Hanson. 1926

SCARLET LETTER, THE (1934) ★★★ Twenties-flapper star Colleen Moore proved she had acting skill in this second version (first sound) of Nathaniel Hawthorne's great classic of love, hate, jealousy, and emotional blackmail in Puritan New England. As in the 1926 silent version, D. W. Griffith star Henry B. Walthall portrays the heartless persecutor Roger Chillingworth. B&W; 69m. DIR: Robert Vignola. CAST: Colleen Moore, Hardie Albright, Henry B. Walthall. 1934

SCARLET LETTER (1973) ★★★1/2 Wim Wenders's stunning psychological portrait of bigotry and isolation, this follows a story about the social sanctions imposed upon a woman suspected of adultery in seventeenth-century Salem, Massachusetts. Based on Nathaniel Hawthorne's classic novel, this film version is given some fine contemporary touches by Wenders. In German with English subtitles. 90m. DIR: Wim Wenders. CAST: Senta Berger, Lou Castel, Hans-Christian Blech, Yella Rottlander. 1973

SCARLET LETTER, THE (1995) 💣 Little besides the title of Nathaniel Hawthorne's novel survives in this dreary, foolish film. Attempting to justify the many departures (including graphic sex, childbirth, an Indian war, and a happy ending), star Demi Moore once blurted, "Hardly anybody's read the book." Obviously, neither had she. Rated R for nudity and simulated sex. 135m. DIR: Roland Joffe. CAST: Demi Moore, Gary Oldman, Robert Duvall, Joan Plowright, Robert Prosky. 1995

SCARLET PIMPERNEL, THE (1934) ★★★ Leslie Howard plays Sir Percy, an English aristocrat engaged in the underground effort to snatch out from under the blade of the guillotine Frenchmen caught in the Reign of Terror. His ruse may throw off the French authorities, as ably represented by a sinister Raymond Massey, but he is also turning off his beautiful wife, Merle Oberon. B&W; 95m. DIR: Harold Young. CAST: Leslie Howard, Raymond Massey, Merle Oberon, Nigel Bruce. 1934 DVD

SCARLET PIMPERNEL, THE (1982) ★★★1/2 This is the made-for-TV version of the much-filmed (seven times) adventure classic. Anthony Andrews makes a dashing hero leading a double life aiding French revolutionaries while posing as a foppish member of British society. Jane Seymour is breathtakingly beautiful as his ladylove. This lavish production proves that remakes, even for television, can be worthwhile. 150m. DIR: Clive Donner. CAST: Anthony Andrews, Jane Seymour, Ian McKellen, James Villiers, Eleanor David. 1982

SCARLET RIVER ★★★ Unique movie within a movie, as Western screen star Tom Keene comes to Scarlet River ranch to shoot his next movie and ends up in a series of real shoot-outs with bad men plotting to take over the ranch. Cameo appearances by Joel McCrea and Myrna Loy as themselves. B&W; 54m. DIR: Otto Brower. CAST: Tom Keene, Lon Chaney Jr., Edgar Kennedy. 1933

SCARLET SPEAR, THE 💣 The son of an African chief undertakes a series of ritual tasks to prove his manhood. 78m. DIR: George Breakston, Ray Stahl. CAST: Ray Bentley, Martha Hyer. 1954

SCARLET STREET ★★★1/2 The director (Fritz Lang) and stars (Edward G. Robinson, Joan Bennett, and Dan Duryea) of the excellent Woman in the Window reteamed with less spectacular results for this film about a mild-mannered fellow (Robinson) seduced into a life of crime by a temptress (Bennett). B&W; 103m. DIR: Fritz Lang. CAST: Edward G. Robinson, Joan Bennett, Dan Duryea, Margaret Lindsay, Rosalind Ivan. 1945

SCARLETT ★★1/2 Prime-time soap opera fare at its gaudiest. Timothy Dalton plays a Rhett Butler whose Southern drawl is by way of London, and Joanne Whalley is just a tad coarse and screechy as the Georgia peach who drags her troubles to Ireland. The $45-million budget is evident in carriages, houses, scenery, and costumes that will take your breath away. Rated PG for mild sexual situations and violence. 360m. DIR: John Erman. CAST: Joanne Whalley, Timothy Dalton, Stephen Collins, Annabeth Gish, Colm Meaney, Jean Smart, Sean Bean. 1994

SCARS OF DRACULA ★★★ A young couple searching for the husband's brother follow the trail to Dracula's castle, and soon regret it. Compares well with other films in the series, thanks primarily to Christopher Lee's dynamite portrayal of the Count, and the first-rate direction of horror veteran Roy Ward Baker. Rated R. 94m. DIR: Roy Ward Baker. CAST: Christopher Lee, Dennis Waterman, Christopher Matthews. 1970

SCAVENGER HUNT 💣 It's a Mad Mad Mad Mad World writhes again as a bunch of wackos run hither, thither, and yawn. Rated PG. 117m. DIR: Michael Schultz. CAST: Richard Benjamin, James Coco, Scatman Crothers, Ruth Gordon, Cloris Leachman, Roddy McDowall, Cleavon Little, Robert Morley, Richard Mulligan, Tony Randall, Vincent Price. 1979

SCAVENGERS 💣 Miami University professor and his ex-girlfriend outwit the CIA, KGB, and a local African drug kingpin. Rated PG-13 for violence. 94m. DIR: Duncan McLachlan. CAST: Kenneth Gilman, Brenda Bakke, Ken Gampu. 1988

SCENE OF THE CRIME (1985) ★★ A cross between a game show and a murder mystery, this film is cut into three episodes, narrated by Orson Welles, that ask the viewers to try to solve the murder at the end of each. Originally made for network TV. 74m. DIR: Walter Grauman, Harry Falk. CAST: Orson Welles, Markie Post, Alan Thicke, Ben Piazza. 1985

SCENE OF THE CRIME (1987) ★★★ Romantic thriller with an Oedipal angle. A nightclub owner

(Catherine Deneuve) and her son get caught up in an increasingly dangerous attempt to safeguard a criminal. This watchable movie could use fast pacing and less obvious camera pyrotechnics. In French with English subtitles. 90m. DIR: André Téchiné. CAST: Catherine Deneuve, Danielle Darrieux, Wadeck Stanczak, Victor Lanoux. 1987

SCENES FROM A MALL ★★ It would be hard to imagine a drearier comedy than this uninspired tale of a married couple (Woody Allen, Bette Midler) breaking up and making up as they romp through a Beverly Hills shopping mall. Only the film's first twenty minutes—a sprightly introduction of the two main characters—make it worth watching. Rated R for profanity. 87m. DIR: Paul Mazursky. CAST: Bette Midler, Woody Allen, Bill Irwin. 1991

SCENES FROM A MARRIAGE ★★★★★ Director Ingmar Bergman successfully captures the pain and emotions of a marriage that is disintegrating. Several scenes are extremely hard to watch because there is so much truth to what is being said. Originally a six-part film for Swedish television, the theatrical version was edited by Bergman. Believable throughout, this one packs a real punch. In Swedish. No rating (contains some strong language). 168m. DIR: Ingmar Bergman. CAST: Liv Ullmann, Erland Josephson, Bibi Andersson. 1973

SCENES FROM A MURDER 🎬 Inept thriller about a killer who stalks an actress. Filmed in Italy. 90m. DIR: Alberto De Martino. CAST: Telly Savalas, Anne Heywood. 1972

SCENES FROM THE CLASS STRUGGLE IN BEVERLY HILLS ★★★★ Director Paul Bartel helms this bizarre sexual romp through the lives of the glamorous Tinseltown set. Jacqueline Bisset is delicious as a neurotic ex-sitcom star whose television comeback is complicated by her dead husband (Paul Mazursky), who keeps materializing while pledging his infernal love to her. This offbeat adult comedy is rated R for nudity and profanity. 95m. DIR: Paul Bartel. CAST: Jacqueline Bisset, Ray Sharkey, Ed Begley Jr., Paul Mazursky, Wallace Shawn, Robert Beltran. 1989

SCENES FROM THE GOLDMINE ★★1/2 Music industry exposé with Catherine Mary Stewart as a musician-composer who joins a rock band and falls in love with the lead singer. Even rock fans will find the band's performances somewhat synthetic. Rated R for sexual situations and profanity. 105m. DIR: Marc Rocco. CAST: Catherine Mary Stewart, Cameron Dye, Steve Railsback, Joe Pantoliano, Lee Ving, Lesley-Anne Down. 1987

SCENT OF A WOMAN ★★★1/2 Al Pacino's over-the-top performance in this coming-of-age movie will delight some viewers and put off others. Pacino plays a foulmouthed ex-serviceman who takes high school–age companion Chris O'Donnell on a last hurrah in New York City, where the older man intends to wine, dine, and have sex before committing suicide. Rated R for profanity and suggested sex. 157m. DIR: Martin Brest. CAST: Al Pacino, Chris O'-Donnell, James Rebhorn, Gabrielle Anwar, Richard Venture. 1992 DVD

SCENT OF GREEN PAPAYA, THE ★★★ The first Vietnamese nominee for the Best Foreign Film Oscar tells the story of a young serving girl in Saigon who grows up to be the servant, and later the lover, of a composer. The film is exquisitely photographed and graceful, but the elliptical, allusive style makes it a bit slow-moving and uneventful. In Vietnamese with English subtitles. Not rated, but suitable for mature general audiences. 103m. DIR: Tran Anh Hung. CAST: Tran Nu Yen-Khe, Lu Man San, Truong Thi Loc, Nguyen Anh Hoa. 1993

SCHINDLER ★★★ A documentary of the man who helped save Jews from Hitler during World War II. The film combines actual footage from the war, testimonials from some of the Jews who were saved, and an interview with Amon Goeth's mistress. The real Oskar Schindler is revealed here: womanizer, boozer, black-market entrepreneur, and rescuer of 1,100 Jews. Not rated; contains graphic footage of concentration camps. 80m. DIR: Jon Blair. 1981

SCHINDLER'S LIST ★★★★★ The story of one man's struggle to save the lives of one thousand Polish Jews during the Third Reich's implementation of Hitler's "final solution," this Oscar-winner for best picture may well be director Steven Spielberg's masterpiece. Skillfully shaded performances by Liam Neeson (whose Oskar Schindler evolves from a fast-living opportunist to a man of conscience) and Ben Kingsley bring humanity to this tale of real-life horror, one of the best films on the subject. Rated R for nudity and violence. 185m. DIR: Steven Spielberg. CAST: Liam Neeson, Ben Kingsley, Ralph Fiennes, Caroline Goodall, Jonathan Sagalle, Embeth Davidtz. 1993

SCHIZO 🎬 A deranged night worker freaks out when his favorite figure skater announces her wedding plans. Rated R. 109m. DIR: Pete Walker. CAST: Jack Watson, Lynne Frederick, John Leyton. 1978

SCHIZOID 🎬 This is an unimaginative slasher flick with typically gory special effects. Rated R. 91m. DIR: David Paulsen. CAST: Klaus Kinski, Marianna Hill, Craig Wasson, Christopher Lloyd. 1980

SCHIZOPOLIS ★★★ One of those movies you either love or hate, Schizopolis is virtually a home movie made by Steven Soderberg (sex, lies, and videotape). The loose plot features Soderbergh as a speechwriter for a double-talking spiritualist, but the film is more concerned with Kafkaesque examinations of the unknowable nature of modern life. There are many amusing bits but just as many that go nowhere, making this one for adventurous audiences. Not rated; contains nudity and profanity. 96m. DIR: Steven Soderbergh. CAST: Steven Soderbergh, Betsy Brantley, Mike Malone, David Jensen. 1997

SCHLOCK ★★★ Directed by and starring John Landis, this film is a spoof of not only "missing link" monster movies but other types of horror and science-fiction films. This is Landis's first film, and while it doesn't have the laughs of his later effort, Animal House, it does include some chuckles of its own. Rated PG. 80m. DIR: John Landis. CAST: John Landis, Saul Kahan, Joseph Piantadosi. 1971

SCHOOL DAZE ★★★1/2 Writer-director Spike Lee tries to get people to wake up not only to the conflict in South Africa but also to the problems that exist among different factions of the black community. Too much time is spent on a silly subplot involving a college fraternity; however, the film features some first-rate production numbers and a fine musical score by the filmmaker's father, Bill Lee. Rated R for profanity and nudity. 120m. DIR: Spike Lee. CAST: Laurence Fishburne, Giancarlo Esposito, Tisha Campbell, Spike Lee, Ossie Davis. 1988

SCHOOL FOR SCANDAL ★★1/2 Richard Sheridan's eighteenth-century comedy about philandering and infidelity became a decent but basically crude and static film in this early adaptation. The limitations of early sound techniques are painfully obvious in this stage-bound presentation. B&W; 75m. DIR: Maurice Elvey. CAST: Madeleine Carroll, Basil Gill, Ian Fleming. 1930

SCHOOL FOR SCOUNDRELS ★★★★1/2 A wry, witty British comedy about a training school for one-upmanship with some of England's most talented comics. They teach each other how to get the best of every and any situation. B&W; 94m. DIR: Robert Hamer. CAST: Alastair Sim, Terry-Thomas, Dennis Price, Ian Carmichael, Janette Scott. 1960

SCHOOL OF FLESH ★★★1/2 Intense physical attraction keeps the age, class, and cultural differences of two lovers temporarily at bay in this superbly acted French drama. A wealthy, sophisticated career woman invites a younger, bisexual hustler to live with her and seeks out his former male lovers for insights into his shady past and guarded emotions. This intriguing story is loosely based on the novel by Yukio Mishima. In French with English subtitles. Rated R for language and strong sexuality. 101m. DIR: Benoit Jacquot. CAST: Isabelle Huppert, Vincent Martinez, Vincent Lindon, Marthe Keller. 1999 DVD

SCHOOL SPIRIT 🖤 Stupid high school flick about an obnoxious libido case (Tom Nolan) who dies in an auto accident and returns as a ghost. Not rated, but an easy R for nudity and profanity. 90m. DIR: Alan Holleb. CAST: Tom Nolan, Elizabeth Foxx, Larry Linville. 1985

SCHOOL TIES ★★★★ Dick Wolf's thoughtful study of persecution for the teenage set, with Brendan Fraser just right as a 1950s-era high school senior who conceals his Jewish heritage hoping to cash in on his football skills. A compelling little sleeper. Rated PG-13 for profanity. 107m. DIR: Robert Mandel. CAST: Brendan Fraser, Chris O'Donnell, Andrew Lowery, Amy Locane, Peter Donat, Zeljko Ivanek. 1992 DVD

SCI-FIGHTERS ★★★1/2 In twenty-first century Boston, cop Roddy Piper battles a criminal who has escaped from a lunar prison and contracts a virus that transforms him into a fire-breathing mutant. Direct-to-video sci-fi action is well above average for the genre. Rated R for violence, sexual situations, and nudity. 90m. DIR: Peter Svatek. CAST: Roddy Piper, Billy Drago, Jayne Heitmeyer. 1996 DVD

SCISSORS ★★1/2 Scissors are the weapon of choice in this intense psychological thriller. Sharon Stone believes she's going insane—or is someone driving her to the edge? Rated R for violence. 105m. DIR: Frank DeFelitta. CAST: Sharon Stone, Steve Railsback, Michelle Phillips, Ronny Cox. 1990

SCORCHERS ★★ The lives of three women are tangled up in this poorly written and directed film. Not rated; contains profanity and simulated sex. 80m. DIR: David Beaird. CAST: Faye Dunaway, James Earl Jones, Emily Lloyd, Jennifer Tilly, Denholm Elliott, James Wilder, Anthony Geary. 1991

SCORCHY 🖤 Connie Stevens is an undercover cop trying to bust a major drug ring. Rated R. 99m. DIR: Howard Avedis. CAST: Connie Stevens, Cesare Danova, William Smith, Marlene Schmidt, Normann Burton, Joyce Jameson. 1976

SCORNED ★★1/2 Better-than-average sex thriller about the wife of a businessman who kills himself when a business deal goes sour. Seeking out the man responsible—a family man—she insinuates her way into his life by posing as a tutor for his son and then methodically tears the family apart. The sex is mundane, but the set-up is explosive. R-rated and unrated versions; both contain nudity, adult situations, language, and violence. 90m. DIR: Andrew Stevens. CAST: Shannon Tweed, Andrew Stevens. 1993

SCORNED 2 ★★1/2 Tane McClure takes over for Shannon Tweed as the vengeance-seeking killer who at the outset of the film has lost her memory and entered into a happy marriage to a psychiatrist. But the past catches up with her. Much of the plot won't make sense if you haven't seen the original Scorned. Rated R for sex, violence, and profanity. 97m. DIR: Rodney McDonald. CAST: Tane McClure, Andrew Stevens, Myles O'Brien, Wendy Schumacher. 1997 DVD

SCORPIO ONE 🖤 This blatant rip-off of 2001: A Space Odyssey is another tedious space-station thriller featuring lifeless performances and clumsy plotting and direction. Rated R for violence and language. 92m. DIR: Worth Keeter. CAST: Robert Carradine, Jeff Speakman, Robin Curtis, George Murdock, Steve Kanaly. 1997

SCORPION 🖤 Dim-witted martial arts film stars nonactor Tonny Tulleners, who takes on a band of terrorists. Grade Z gobbler. Rated R. 98m. DIR: William Riead. CAST: Tonny Tulleners, Don Murray. 1987 DVD

SCORPION SPRING ★★★ A cross-country traveler makes the mistake of offering a ride to a couple of drug runners. One of the better Quentin Tarantino–inspired video thrillers. Rated R for nudity, violence and profanity. 89m. DIR: Brian Cox. CAST: Patrick McGaw, Esai Morales, Matthew McConaughey, Alfred Molina, Rubén Blades, John Doe. 1996

SCORPION WOMAN, THE ★★★1/2 An interesting and intelligent May-December story with an ironic twist. A woman judge has an affair with a 23-year-old law trainee. Believable characters highlight what might have been soap-opera material. In German with English subtitles. Not rated. 101m. DIR: Susanne Zanke. CAST: Angelica Domrose, Fritz Hammel. 1989

SCOTT OF THE ANTARCTIC ★★★★ This impeccable re-creation of the race to the South Pole superbly captures the unrelenting frustration of explorer Robert Scott's ill-fated final expedition. Gorgeously lensed and orchestrated by director Charles Frend.

110m. **DIR:** Charles Frend. **CAST:** John Mills, Derek Bond, Kenneth More, Christopher Lee. **1948**

SCOUNDREL, THE ★★★1/2 After his untimely death, an arrogant writer (Noel Coward) is sent back to earth to make amends for the grief he caused. The combination of Coward and dialogue by Ben Hecht and Charles MacArthur is to die for, even if the plot is thin. B&W; 78m. **DIR:** Ben Hecht, Charles MacArthur. **CAST:** Noel Coward, Julie Haydon, Stanley Ridges, Alexander Woollcott, Lionel Stander. **1935**

SCOUT, THE ★★★★ Albert Brooks and Brendan Fraser are outstanding in this touching comedy about a down-on-his-luck major-league baseball scout and his unlikely discovery. In order to keep his job, Brooks needs to find a winner. His search ends in Mexico, where he discovers Steve Nebraska, a natural player with big emotional problems. Dianne Wiest is the psychiatrist desperate to unlock Nebraska's past. Rated PG-13 for adult situations and language. 101m. **DIR:** Michael Ritchie. **CAST:** Albert Brooks, Brendan Fraser, Dianne Wiest, Anne Twomey. **1994**

SCREAM (1982) 🎦 A group of vacationing friends spend the night in a ghost town. Rated R. 86m. **DIR:** Byron Quisenberry. **CAST:** Woody Strode, John Ethan Wayne, Hank Worden, Alvy Moore, Gregg Palmer. **1982**

SCREAM (1996) ★★★1/2 This bloody, playful slice of offbeat horror-comedy alternately spoofs and chillingly mimics the slasher film genre. Here a stalker dresses as the Grim Reaper and butchers teens just "to see what your insides look like." It's a scary, often hilarious movie about kids who have picked up all the unwritten rules of Hollywood slasher films (don't answer the door, have sex, or abuse drugs or alcohol—or you die), but break them anyway. Rated R for gore, violence, and language. 111m. **DIR:** Wes Craven. **CAST:** Neve Campbell, David Arquette, Courteney Cox, Skeet Ulrich, Matthew Lillard, Drew Barrymore, Rose McGowan. **1996 DVD**

SCREAM 2 ★★ When a tabloid TV reporter interviews survivors of the original Woodsboro massacre to promote a film based on the murders, a copycat killer renews the carnage. The self-parody here is that the latest killing spree, like this film, is a sequel and everyone knows how much sequels usually suck. The body and suspect counts go ballistic, but the wicked humor smacks more of formula than ghoulish inspiration. Rated R for gore, nudity, language, and violence. 96m. **DIR:** Wes Craven. **CAST:** Neve Campbell, Jerry O'Connell, Liev Schreiber, David Arquette, Sarah Michelle Gellar, Jamie Kennedy, Courteney Cox, Omar Epps, Jada Pinkett. **1997 DVD**

•**SCREAM 3** ★★ A serial killer plagues a movie set where the "true" events of *Scream* are being made into a movie. The second sequel to the surprise teen-slasher hit of 1996 hammers the premise even further into the ground; let's hope we can believe director Wes Craven when he promises this will be the last of the series. Carrie Fisher, Roger Corman, Jason Mewes, and Kevin Smith play uncredited cameos. Rated R for violence and profanity. 116m. **DIR:** Wes Craven. **CAST:** David Arquette, Neve Campbell, Courteney Cox Arquette, Patrick Dempsey, Parker Posey. **1999 DVD**

SCREAM AND SCREAM AGAIN ★★★1/2 A top-notch cast excels in this chilling, suspenseful story of a crazed scientist (Vincent Price) attempting to create a race of superbeings while a baffled police force copes with a series of brutal murders that may or may not be related. Complex film benefits from polished performances. Based on the novel *The Disoriented Man*, by Peter Saxon. Rated PG for violence, language, and brief nudity. 95m. **DIR:** Gordon Hessler. **CAST:** Vincent Price, Peter Cushing, Christopher Lee, Christopher Matthews, Michael Gothard. **1970**

SCREAM, BLACULA, SCREAM 🎦 William Marshall returns as the black vampire, Blacula, in this unimpressive sequel. Rated R. 96m. **DIR:** Bob Kelljan. **CAST:** William Marshall, Pam Grier, Michael Conrad. **1973**

•**SCREAM DREAM** 🎦 Recently fired musician uses witchcraft to get revenge and sends her screaming fans to commit bloody murders. Not rated; contains gore, violence, and nudity. 69m. **DIR:** Donald Farmer. **CAST:** Melissa Moore. **1989**

SCREAM FOR HELP 🎦 A suspense-thriller about a teenage girl whose stepfather is trying to kill her and her mother. Rated R for nudity, profanity, and violence. 95m. **DIR:** Michael Winner. **CAST:** Rachel Kelly, David Brooks. **1986**

SCREAM OF FEAR ★★★★ In this overlooked crackerjack thriller, Susan Strasberg plays an invalid who visits her father's Riviera mansion, only to be followed by the corpse of her away-on-business daddy. Well-crafted tale will have you second-guessing yourself to the very end. B&W; 81m. **DIR:** Seth Holt. **CAST:** Susan Strasberg, Ronald Lewis, Ann Todd, Christopher Lee. **1961**

SCREAMERS (1979) 🎦 An uncharted island, a mad doctor, a crazy inventor, and a bunch of underpaid extras in native costumes. Rated R. 90m. **DIR:** Sergio Martino, Dan T. Miller. **CAST:** Claudio Cassinelli, Richard Johnson, Joseph Cotten. **1979**

SCREAMERS (1996) ★★1/2 So-so science-fiction film features Peter Weller as the commander of a small force attempting to surive the aftermath of a full-fledged war between corporate interests and workers on a far-flung mining planet in the year 2078. Slow-paced and predictable. Rated R for violence and profanity. 107m. **DIR:** Christian Duguay. **CAST:** Peter Weller, Roy Dupuis, Jennifer Rubin, Andrew Lauer, Ron White, Charles Powell. **1996 DVD**

SCREAMING MIMI ★★★ After she is nearly murdered, burlesque dancer Anita Ekberg goes for counseling to a psychiatrist, who becomes obsessed with her. Obscure but offbeat psychological thriller atmospherically directed by Gerd Oswald, who went on to TV's *The Outer Limits*. B&W; 79m. **DIR:** Gerd Oswald. **CAST:** Anita Ekberg, Philip Carey, Gypsy Rose Lee, Harry Townes, Linda Cherney, Red Norvo. **1958**

SCREAMING SKULL, THE 🎦 The old saw about a greedy husband trying to drive his wife crazy. B&W; 68m. **DIR:** Alex Nicol. **CAST:** John Hudson, Peggy Webber, Alex Nicol. **1958 DVD**

SCREEN TEST 🎦 Teenage boys pose as film producers in order to audition beautiful women nude.

Rated R. 84m. **DIR:** Sam Auster. **CAST:** Michael Allan Bloom, Robert Bundy. 1986

SCREWBALL ACADEMY 🖤 When a production company tries to make a movie in a small beachfront town, assorted loonies come out of the closet. Reuben Rose is former *SCTV* director John Blanchard under a pseudonym. Rated R for profanity. 90m. **DIR:** Reuben Rose. **CAST:** Colleen Camp, Kenneth Welsh. 1987

SCREWBALLS 🖤 Teen-lust comedy takes place at Taft and Adams Educational Center, otherwise known as "T&A High." Rated R for nudity and profanity. 80m. **DIR:** Rafal Zielinski. **CAST:** Peter Keleghan, Linda Speciale, Linda Shayne. 1983

•**SCREWED** 🖤 A mistreated chauffeur plots to kidnap and ransom the dog belonging to his miserly employer. The title is all too appropriate in this laughless, brainless, slovenly comedy. Rated PG-13 for profanity. 85m. **DIR:** Scott Alexander, Larry Karaszewski. **CAST:** Norm MacDonald, Elaine Stritch, Dave Chappelle, Daniel Benzali, Sherman Hemsley, Danny DeVito. 2000

SCROOGE (1935) ★★★ This little-known British version of Charles Dickens's classic *A Christmas Carol* is faithful to the original story and boasts a standout performance by Seymour Hicks, who also cowrote the screenplay. A truly enjoyable film, unjustly overshadowed by Alistair Sim's bravura performance as Scrooge in the venerated 1951 version. B&W; 78m. **DIR:** Henry Edwards. **CAST:** Seymour Hicks, Donald Calthrop, Robert Cochran, Maurice Evans. 1935

SCROOGE (1970) ★★★ Tuneful retelling of Charles Dickens's classic *A Christmas Carol* may not be the best acted, but it's certainly the liveliest. Albert Finney paints old curmudgeon Ebeneezer Scrooge with a broad brush, but he makes his character come alive. Rated G. 118m. **DIR:** Ronald Neame. **CAST:** Albert Finney, Alec Guinness, Edith Evans, Kenneth More, Michael Medwin, Laurence Naismith, Kay Walsh. 1970

SCROOGED ★★1/2 The power of Charles Dickens's uncredited source material and an energetic turn by Carol Kane as the Ghost of Christmas Present save this bloated comedy from total disaster. Bill Murray waltzes through his role as a venal television executive. Rated PG-13 for language. 101m. **DIR:** Richard Donner. **CAST:** Bill Murray, Karen Allen, John Forsythe, John Glover, Bob Goldthwait, Carol Kane, Robert Mitchum, Alfre Woodard. 1988 DVD

SCRUBBERS ★★★1/2 Realistic depiction of life inside a girls' reform school. With an eye toward inspiring reform, this British film suggests that the well-intentioned but misguided treatment of troubled children puts them on a road to becoming permanently institutionalized. Rated R. 94m. **DIR:** Mai Zetterling. **CAST:** Amanda York, Elizabeth Edmonds. 1982

SCRUPLES ★★1/2 Bestseller from author Judith Krantz gets the glossy TV soap-opera treatment: an ordinary woman is thrown for a loop when she inherits a conglomerate. Edited down from the television miniseries into feature-length. 100m. **DIR:** Robert Day. **CAST:** Priscilla Barnes, Shelley Smith, Vonetta

McGee, Dirk Benedict, James Darren, Jessica Walter, Roy Thinnes. 1981

SCUM ★★1/2 Harrowing look inside a British reform school. Rated R for violence and profanity. 98m. **DIR:** Alan Clarke. **CAST:** Ray Winstone, Mick Ford, John Judd, Phil Daniels, John Blundell. 1980

SEA CHASE, THE ★★ Weak and generally uninvolving World War II story finds German sea captain John Wayne attempting to elude capture by British naval forces. Film moves at a snail's pace. 117m. **DIR:** John Farrow. **CAST:** John Wayne, Lana Turner, James Arness, Tab Hunter, Lyle Bettger, Claude Akins, David Farrar. 1955

SEA DEVILS ★★ Victor McLaglen and Ida Lupino play father and daughter in this soggy tale of Coast Guard trial and tribulation. McLaglen and Preston Foster are service rivals given to settling problems with their fists. Unfortunately, the audience can't fight back. B&W; 88m. **DIR:** Ben Stoloff. **CAST:** Victor McLaglen, Preston Foster, Ida Lupino, Donald Woods. 1937

SEA GYPSIES, THE ★★★ Director Stewart Raffill wrote this adventure movie which tells of five castaways in the Pacific who end up on a remote Aleutian island. This Disney-style tale is climaxed by a race against the approaching Alaskan winter to build a makeshift escape craft. 102m. **DIR:** Stewart Raffill. **CAST:** Robert Logan, Mikki Jamison-Olsen, Heather Rattray. 1978

SEA HAWK, THE ★★★★ Errol Flynn was the best of the screen's costumed adventurers. *The Sea Hawk* shows him at his swashbuckling peak. He plays a buccaneer sea captain who is given tacit approval by Queen Elizabeth I (Flora Robson) to wreak havoc on the Spanish fleet and their cities in the New World. B&W; 109m. **DIR:** Michael Curtiz. **CAST:** Errol Flynn, Flora Robson, Claude Rains, Donald Crisp, Alan Hale Sr., Henry Daniell, Gilbert Roland. 1940

SEA HOUND, THE ★★ Modern-day pirates searching for a buried Spanish treasure on an uncharted island find that they've bitten off more than they can chew when veteran action star Buster Crabbe shows up to spoil their plans. Every generation deserves its own pirate adventures, and with good-natured, dedicated Crabbe along, it's always an enjoyable ride. B&W; 15 episodes. **DIR:** Walter B. Eason, Mack V. Wright. **CAST:** Buster Crabbe, Jimmy Lloyd, Pamela Blake, Ralph Hodges, Robert Barron, Hugh Prosser, Rick Vallin, Jack Ingram, Spencer Chan, Pierce Lyden. 1947

SEA LION, THE ★★1/2 Stern sea story with hardbitten Hobart Bosworth as a tyrannical ship's master who vents his pent-up hatred on the men in his charge. But romance rears its head and we find out that he's not all bad; he was just acting like a sadist because he had a broken heart. Silent. B&W; 50m. **DIR:** Rowland V. Lee. **CAST:** Hobart Bosworth, Bessie Love, Richard Morris. 1921

SEA OF GRASS, THE ★★1/2 This is more soap than horse opera, where ruthless cattle baron Spencer Tracy drives his eastern-bred wife, Katharine Hepburn, into the arms of lawyer Melvyn Douglas. Disappointing. B&W; 123m. **DIR:** Elia Kazan. **CAST:** Spencer

Tracy, Katharine Hepburn, Melvyn Douglas, Robert Walker, Harry Carey. 1946

SEA OF LOVE ★★★★ Al Pacino made an explosive comeback in this sexy thriller as a New York police detective in the midst of a middle-age crisis. To forget his woes, Pacino throws himself into an investigation of some serial killings, which seems to have something to do with the lonely hearts listings in the newspaper personals columns. Rated R for violence, profanity, and simulated sex. 110m. **DIR:** Harold Becker. **CAST:** Al Pacino, Ellen Barkin, John Goodman. 1989 DVD

•SEA PEOPLE ★★★1/2 This amiable, family-oriented fable, scripted by Wendy Biller and Christopher Hawthorne, involves an adolescent girl and the two rather eccentric older folks she befriends; it seems these senior citizens have a propensity for sleeping while submerged in tanks of seawater. The story turns on the young heroine's efforts to help these oldsters "return home" when their land-based life proves unworkable; the result is both charming and bittersweet, without ever becoming unduly maudlin. Suitable for all ages. 92m. **DIR:** Vic Sarin. **CAST:** Hume Cronyn, Joan Gregson, Tegan Moss, Shawn Roberts. 1998

SEA SHALL NOT HAVE THEM, THE ★★★ Nicely done World War II film about British air rescue operations. Main story follows an RAF bomber crew shot down over the North Sea and their rescue from the ocean. B&W; 92m. **DIR:** Lewis Gilbert. **CAST:** Michael Redgrave, Dirk Bogarde, John Mitchell. 1955

SEA WOLF, THE (1941) ★★★★1/2 Rousing version of Jack London's dark seafaring adventure features a splendidly complex portrayal by Edward G. Robinson as the evil ship captain of the title. One of director Michael Curtiz's best films. B&W; 90m. **DIR:** Michael Curtiz. **CAST:** Edward G. Robinson, John Garfield, Ida Lupino, Alexander Knox, Gene Lockhart, Barry Fitzgerald, Stanley Ridges, David Bruce, Howard DaSilva. 1941

SEA WOLF, THE (1993) 🎬 Boredom washes over the deck in waves in this painful-to-watch remake of the oft-filmed Jack London novel. A flat script and poor performances combine to sink this unworthy effort. Made for TV. 96m. **DIR:** Michael Anderson. **CAST:** Charles Bronson, Christopher Reeve, Catherine Mary Stewart, Marc Singer. 1993

SEA WOLVES, THE ★★★ A World War II version of The Over the Hill Gang. Gregory Peck and Roger Moore play British officers who recruit a bunch of Boer War veterans now in their autumn years to do some espionage along the coast of India. While the film relies too heavily on comedy that doesn't work, the last twenty minutes have enough spirit to redeem it. The film is based on a true story. Rated PG for violence and sex. 120m. **DIR:** Andrew V. McLaglen. **CAST:** Gregory Peck, Roger Moore, David Niven, Trevor Howard, Barbara Kellerman, Patrick Macnee. 1980 DVD

SEANCE ON A WET AFTERNOON ★★★★1/2 This is an absolutely fabulous movie. An unbalanced medium (Kim Stanley) involves her meek husband (Richard Attenborough) in a kidnapping scheme that brings about their downfall. Brilliant acting by

all, working from a superb script. No rating, but some intense sequences. B&W; 115m. **DIR:** Bryan Forbes. **CAST:** Kim Stanley, Richard Attenborough, Patrick Magee, Nanette Newman. 1964

SEARCH AND DESTROY (1981) 🎬 Vietnam veteran is chased by a Vietnamese villain. Not rated, the film has violence and profanity. 93m. **DIR:** William Fruet. **CAST:** Perry King, Don Stroud, Tisa Farrow, George Kennedy, Park Jong Soo. 1981

SEARCH AND DESTROY (1988) ★★ There's no shortage of action, but little else noteworthy in this science-fiction action yarn about the capturing of a secret biological warfare research station. Rated R, primarily for violence. 90m. **DIR:** J. Christian Ingvordsen. **CAST:** Stuart Garrison Day. 1988

SEARCH AND DESTROY (1995) ★★ A dream team of terminally cool actors is wasted in this quirky, mostly unfunny satire about desperate hustling, pop philosophy, and big money. Rated R for language, drug use, and violence. 100m. **DIR:** David Salle. **CAST:** Griffin Dunne, Illeana Douglas, Christopher Walken, John Turturro, Ethan Hawke, Rosanna Arquette, Martin Scorsese, Dennis Hopper. 1995 DVD

SEARCH FOR BRIDEY MURPHY, THE ★★ Made quickly and cheaply (it shows) to cash in on the then-popular and controversial book by Morey Bernstein. Story of a woman under hypnosis who was able to recall her previous existence as a small girl in Ireland in the early 1800s. Dull. B&W; 84m. **DIR:** Noel Langley. **CAST:** Teresa Wright, Louis Hayward. 1956

SEARCH FOR ONE-EYE JIMMY, THE ★★★ Everyone in this Brooklyn neighborhood is too much of a character, but earthy humor and an unusual cast counteract the outrageousness. There are laugh-out-loud moments and the ending is a scream, despite the sorry budget. Worth renting just for John Turturro's debut as a disco dancer. Rated R for profanity and violence. 86m. **DIR:** Sam Henry Kass. **CAST:** Michael Badalucco, Holt McCallany, Samuel L. Jackson, John Turturro, Steve Buscemi, Jennifer Beals, Nicholas Turturro, Ray "Boom Boom" Mancini, Anne Meara. 1993

SEARCH FOR SIGNS OF INTELLIGENT LIFE IN THE UNIVERSE, THE ★★★★ As Trudy says in this film, reality "is nothing but a collective hunch." But the hunch that evolves from the fertile imaginations of actress Lily Tomlin and writer Jane Wagner is funny, perceptive, and right on target. Trudy, a bag lady in touch with alien life-forms, is just one of a dozen diverse characters brought to life in a bravura performance by Tomlin, cleverly adapted from her one-woman play. Rated PG-13. 109m. **DIR:** John Bailey. **CAST:** Lily Tomlin. 1991

SEARCH FOR THE GODS ★★ This fairly involving but failed TV-pilot about three adventurers in search of missing pieces to an ancient puzzle makes for an unfinished picture. 90m. **DIR:** Jud Taylor. **CAST:** Kurt Russell, Stephen McHattie, Victoria Racimo, Raymond St. Jacques, Albert Paulsen, Ralph Bellamy. 1975

SEARCH, THE ★★★★★ Heart-tugging story of the plight of displaced children in post–World War II Europe. One mother (Jarmila Novotna) searches for her son (Ivan Jandl), taken from her in a concentration camp. Montgomery Clift is an American soldier who finds and cares for the boy while the mother's search continues. B&W; 105m. DIR: Fred Zinnemann. CAST: Montgomery Clift, Aline MacMahon, Wendell Corey, Jarmila Novotna, Ivan Jandl. 1948

SEARCHERS, THE ★★★★ John Ford is the most celebrated director of Westerns, and *The Searchers* is considered by many to be his masterpiece. This thoughtful film follows Ethan Edwards, an embittered Indian-hating, ex-Confederate soldier as he leads the search for his niece, who was kidnapped years earlier by Indians. As time goes on, we begin to wonder whether Edwards is out to save the girl or kill her. 119m. DIR: John Ford. CAST: John Wayne, Natalie Wood, Jeffrey Hunter, Ward Bond, Vera Miles, Harry Carey Jr., Ken Curtis, Lana Wood, Patrick Wayne. 1956 DVD

SEARCHING FOR BOBBY FISCHER ★★★1/2 This film is about prodigy Josh Waitzkin, a 7-year-old boy whose understanding of chess puts him in the running to be "the next Bobby Fischer." This praise could easily be a curse—Fischer devoted his life to the game and then became a recluse after becoming the world champion. Adapted from the book by Josh's father, Fred Waitzkin, this thought-provoking commentary explores how success in America is often emphasized over decency. Rated PG for brief profanity. 107m. DIR: Steven Zaillian. CAST: Joe Mantegna, Ben Kingsley, Laurence Fishburne, Joan Allen, Max Pomeranc, Robert Stephens, David Paymer, William H. Macy, Dan Hedaya. 1993

SEASIDE SWINGERS ★★ Fans of the Sixties British invasion will want to see this comedy about a TV talent contest starring Freddie and the Dreamers. There are lots of songs by different groups. Trivia buffs may want to see costar Michael Sarne, who went on to direct *Myra Breckenridge*. 94m. DIR: James Hill. CAST: John Leyton, Michael Sarne, Freddie and the Dreamers, Ron Moody, Liz Fraser. 1965

SEASON OF FEAR ★★ Upon locating his estranged inventor father, a young man discovers Dad's latest wife to be the victim of extreme mental and physical cruelty at the homestead. Or is she? Fetid thriller has overtones of *Body Heat*. Rated R for nudity. 89m. DIR: Doug Campbell. CAST: Michael Bowen, Ray Wise, Clancy Brown, Clare Wren, Michael J. Pollard. 1989

SEASON OF GIANTS, A ★★ Slow-moving, overly long TV bio of artist Michaelangelo. With a running time of over three hours, this is rough going. 195m. DIR: Jerry London. CAST: F. Murray Abraham, Steven Berkoff, John Glover, Ian Holm, Raf Vallone, Mark Frankel. 1991

SEASON OF THE WITCH ❤ Also known as *Hungry Wives*. Rated R. 90m. DIR: George A. Romero. CAST: Jan White, Ray Lane. 1972

SECOND BEST ★★★ William Hurt plays an emotionally repressed, 42-year-old single man who decides to adopt a 10-year-old boy. The troubled new arrival doesn't mesh well with Hurt's ordered life, but before long each begins to view the other as a second shot at possible happiness. The only drawback is David Cook's script—adapted from his own novel—which concludes abruptly. Rated PG-13 for dramatic intensity. 105m. DIR: Chris Menges. CAST: William Hurt, Jane Horrocks, Prunella Scales, John Hurt, Chris Cleary Miles. 1994

SECOND CHANCE ★★1/2 Robert Mitchum plays protector to a former gangster's girlfriend (Linda Darnell) as they are pursued through South America by hit man Jack Palance. This passable chase melodrama was Howard Hughes's first excursion into wide screen, and the often-imitated climax aboard the gondola cars suspended above a deep chasm is the centerpiece of the film. 82m. DIR: Rudolph Maté. CAST: Robert Mitchum, Linda Darnell, Jack Palance, Reginald Sheffield, Roy Roberts. 1953

SECOND CHORUS ★★★ Rival trumpet players Fred Astaire and Burgess Meredith vie for the affections of Paulette Goddard, who works for Artie Shaw. The two want into Shaw's orchestra and make a comic mess of Goddard's attempts to help them. B&W; 83m. DIR: H. C. Potter. CAST: Paulette Goddard, Fred Astaire, Burgess Meredith, Charles Butterworth. 1940

SECOND CIVIL WAR, THE ★★★ In a scenario of the near future, the United States has lost its unity; California is wholly Latino, and Rhode Island is filled with Asian immigrants. Idaho governor Beau Bridges takes a stand and closes his borders to refugee third-world children, which sets up a confrontation between his National Guard troops and the U.S. Army. The whole shooting match unfolds as witnessed by the producers and reporters of one television station, and tempers flare all around as the crisis escalates. While there are some genuinely hilarious moments, the whole eventually sags beneath the weight of its disparate parts. Rated R for profanity and violence. 100m. DIR: Joe Dante. CAST: Beau Bridges, Joanna Cassidy, James Coburn, Kevin Dunn, Phil Hartman, Dan Hedaya, James Earl Jones, Denis Leary, Elizabeth Peña, Ron Perlman. 1997

SECOND FIDDLE ★★★1/2 Irving Berlin's original score makes this movie work today. It's a spoof of the search for the right actress to play Scarlett O'Hara. Talent scouts seeking "A Girl of the North" go to Minnesota to interview a pretty schoolteacher who ice skates like a dream. One of Sonja Henie's most popular films with one of her best supporting casts. B&W; 86m. DIR: Sidney Lanfield. CAST: Sonja Henie, Tyrone Power, Rudy Vallee, Edna May Oliver, Mary Healy, Lyle Talbot, Alan Dinehart, The King Sisters. 1939

SECOND JUNGLE BOOK, THE: MOWGLI AND BALOO ★★★1/2 Satisfying addition to the *Jungle Book* series (this one didn't come from the Disney factory) stars young Jamie Williams as jungle boy Mowgli, who lives with his bear friend, Baloo, in the jungle. Their serene existence is interrupted by a scout representing P. T. Barnum. When Mowgli hides out deeper in the forest, he stumbles across a lost city whose only inhabitant is a deranged soldier. Rated PG. 89m. DIR: Duncan MacLachlan. CAST: Bill Campbell, Roddy McDowall, Jamie Williams, David Paul Francis. 1997

SECOND SIGHT ★★ Silly rip-off of *Ghostbusters* stars John Larroquette as the head of a detective agency that solves its cases with the help of a mystic (Bronson Pinchot). TV-sitcom-style shtick. Rated PG for profanity and violence. 85m. DIR: Joel Zwick.

CAST: John Larroquette, Bronson Pinchot, Bess Armstrong, Stuart Pankin, John Schuck, James Tolkan. **1989**

SECOND WOMAN, THE ★★★ Is Robert Young paranoid, or is the whole world crazy? Strange and violent occurrences are plaguing the life of this talented architect. Betsy Drake, smitten with the confused fellow, is the only onlooker who doesn't doubt his sanity. This dark drama maintains a steady undercurrent of suspense. B&W; 91m. **DIR:** James V. Kern. **CAST:** Robert Young, Betsy Drake, John Sutton. **1951 DVD**

SECONDS ★★★★ Director John Frankenheimer's riveting thriller, originally released in 1966, makes its video debut with additional footage cut from the U.S. print. John Randolph costars as an older man who turns to a secret organization for a new lease on life. After extensive plastic surgery, he emerges as young and handsome Rock Hudson. Fascinating premise plays like a creepy episode of *The Twilight Zone*. Rated R for nudity. B&W; 107m. **DIR:** John Frankenheimer. **CAST:** Rock Hudson, John Randolph, Murray Hamilton, Salome Jens, Will Geer. **1996**

SECRET, THE ★★★1/2 When it is discovered that an otherwise bright and talented 9-year-old boy cannot read, family ties begin to unravel in a small town on Cape Cod. Outstanding performances, assured direction, and insightful writing transform what could have been a typical "disease-of-the-week" TV movie about dyslexia into a touching human drama. Made for TV. 92m. **DIR:** Karen Arthur. **CAST:** Kirk Douglas, Bruce Boxleitner, Brock Peters, Linda Harrington, Jesse R. Tendler. **1992**

SECRET ADMIRER ★★1/2 A sweet-natured sex comedy that suffers from predictability, this stars C. Thomas Howell as a 16-year-old who, on the last day of school before summer vacation, receives an anonymous letter from a female who swears undying love. He hopes it's from the girl of his dreams (Kelly Preston) and decides to find out. Rated R for nudity, light violence, and profanity. 100m. **DIR:** David Greenwalt. **CAST:** C. Thomas Howell, Lori Loughlin, Kelly Preston, Dee Wallace, Cliff De Young, Fred Ward, Leigh Taylor-Young. **1985**

SECRET AGENT, THE ★★★ Offbeat espionage film by the master of suspense contains many typical Alfred Hitchcock touches, but lacks the pacing and characterizations that set his best efforts apart from those of his contemporaries. Alternately grim and humorous, this uneven film (based on a novel by Somerset Maugham) is still watchable and comparable with many of the best films in the genre. B&W; 93m. **DIR:** Alfred Hitchcock. **CAST:** John Gielgud, Madeleine Carroll, Robert Young, Peter Lorre, Percy Marmont, Lilli Palmer. **1936 DVD**

SECRET AGENT, THE (1996) ★★★1/2 Slow-moving but involving, this handsome adaptation retains the ironical humor and multilayered drama of Joseph Conrad's novel. A morally challenged anarchist lives in 1894 London with his wife and brother. The story's truth is found in the wife's emotional performance as she offers up innocence at the altar of politics. Rated R for violence and profanity. 95m. **DIR:** Christopher Hampton. **CAST:** Bob Hoskins, Patricia Arquette, Gérard Depardieu, Christian Bale, Robin Williams. **1996**

SECRET AGENT CLUB ❤ Professional wrestler Hulk Hogan softens up for this completely banal exercise in warped family values, playing a toy store owner by day, secret agent by night. Rated PG for violence. 90m. **DIR:** John Murlowski. **CAST:** Hulk Hogan, Lesley-Anne Down, Richard Moll, Barry Bostwick, James Hong. **1996**

SECRET AGENT (TV SERIES) ★★★1/2 The suave and resourceful John Drake turned out to have more than one life; after the limited success of his 1961 series, *Danger Man*, he returned in 1965 with the flamboyant and popular *Secret Agent*. The new show disappeared after forty-five episodes had been aired. (But Drake would appear again—in a sense—as *The Prisoner*.) In this format, Drake worked for the British agency known as M.I.9 and took orders from an "M"-like figure named Hobbs. The hour-length dramas were grittier and more realistic than their American counterparts. B&W; each 53m. **DIR:** Don Chaffey, Peter Maxwell, Michael Truman. **CAST:** Patrick McGoohan, Peter Madden. **1965–1966**

SECRET BEYOND THE DOOR ★★1/2 Master craftsman Fritz Lang does the best he can with this melodramatic potboiler about a lonely woman (Joan Bennett) who marries a mysterious stranger (Michael Redgrave) after a whirlwind courtship. Slowly she begins to suspect that her husband may be a murderer. B&W; 99m. **DIR:** Fritz Lang. **CAST:** Joan Bennett, Michael Redgrave. **1948**

SECRET CEREMONY ★★1/2 Typical Joseph Losey psychodrama about a psychotic girl (Mia Farrow) semikidnapping an aging streetwalker (Elizabeth Taylor) who reminds her of her dead mother. Robert Mitchum plays Farrow's lecherous stepfather. With its strong sexual undertones, this film is not for kids (and probably not for some adults). 108m. **DIR:** Joseph Losey. **CAST:** Elizabeth Taylor, Mia Farrow, Robert Mitchum, Peggy Ashcroft, Pamela Brown. **1968**

SECRET DIARY OF SIGMUND FREUD, THE ★★★1/2 A consistently humorous satire on the early life of Freud. Everyone in the cast looks to be having a swell time. Sexual and psychological jokes abound. That they are flamboyantly funny is no small feat. Rated PG. 129m. **DIR:** Danford B. Greene. **CAST:** Bud Cort, Carol Kane, Klaus Kinski, Marisa Berenson, Carroll Baker, Ferdinand Mayne, Dick Shawn. **1984**

SECRET FRIENDS ★★★1/2 Dennis Potter, creator of *The Singing Detective*, made his feature directorial debut with this strange, challenging mind-game film. Alan Bates stars as an artist obsessed with doing away with his wife. Rewarding, if difficult, film. Bates, as usual, is superb. Not rated. 97m. **DIR:** Dennis Potter. **CAST:** Alan Bates, Gina Bellman, Frances Barber, Tony Doyle. **1992**

SECRET GAMES ❤ A neglected wife gets a day job at a high-class cathouse and attracts an amorous psychopath. What we have here is a video for couples unaccustomed to sharing more explicit adult films. Rated R for nudity. 90m. **DIR:** Alexander Gregory Hippolyte. **CAST:** Martin Hewitt, Michele Brin, Delia Sheppard, Billy Drago. **1992 DVD**

SECRET GAMES 3 ★★ Yet another sexy thriller about a beautiful but neglected young wife whose sexual appetite is satisfied outside of her marriage (in this case, through an upscale bordello). Unrated version reviewed here. R-rated and unrated versions available; both contain nudity and sex. 92m. DIR: Alexander Gregory Hippolyte. CAST: Woody Brown, Rochelle Swanson, May Karasun, Dean Scofield. 1995 DVD

SECRET GARDEN, THE (1949) ★★★★ A captivating adaptation of Frances Hodgson Burnett's classic. Margaret O'Brien dominates the story as the youngster who finds a beautiful garden in the midst of adult confusion in Victorian England. The story itself inspired a made-for-TV movie in 1987 and a grandiose Broadway musical in 1991. The final sequence is in Technicolor. B&W; 92m. DIR: Fred M. Wilcox. CAST: Margaret O'Brien, Dean Stockwell, Herbert Marshall, Gladys Cooper, Elsa Lanchester. 1949

SECRET GARDEN, THE (1984) ★★1/2 Slow BBC production about a little girl uprooted from India and placed in the care of her cold, stern uncle in his manor house in England. Of course the girl thaws her uncle because of her resemblance to his dear, late wife. Pretty standard stuff, although it's well acted at least. Not rated; suitable for all. 107m. DIR: Katrina Murray. CAST: Sarah Hollis Andrews, David Patterson. 1984

SECRET GARDEN, THE (1987) ★★★★ *Hallmark Hall of Fame's* adaptation of the classic children's story. Gennie James is fantastic as Mary Lennox, the spoiled girl who must live with her mean-spirited uncle after her parents die of cholera. Good acting from the entire cast, a wonderful plot, and beautiful sets make this an enjoyable film for the whole family. 100m. DIR: Alan Grint. CAST: Gennie James, Barret Oliver, Michael Hordern, Billie Whitelaw, Derek Jacobi. 1987

SECRET GARDEN, THE (1993) ★★★★ Director Agnieszka Holland creates a truly gorgeous, remarkably subtle and stately version of the children's classic. After her self-indulgent, unloving parents are killed during an earthquake in India, a spoiled, headstrong little girl is sent to live with her uncle in a house full of mysterious secrets. Magical. Rated G. 106m. DIR: Agnieszka Holland. CAST: Kate Maberly, Heydon Prowse, Andrew Knott, Maggie Smith, Laura Crossley, John Lynch. 1993 DVD

SECRET GARDEN, THE (1994) ★★★ Based on Frances Hodgson Burnett's book, this is the tale of a spoiled orphan who learns to help someone else (her bedridden cousin). She also discovers the joy of animals and the beauty to be found in an abandoned garden. Average animation is helped by riveting plot. Anndi McAffee provides the voice of Mary, the heroine. Of the five original songs written for the film, only the one about flowers blooming is a winner. Not rated, but the witchlike housekeeper/control freak may be too frightening for young viewers. 72m. DIR: Dave Edwards. 1994

SECRET HONOR ★★★★ This one-man show features Philip Baker Hall as Richard Nixon—drinking, swearing, and going completely over the top in his ravings, on such subjects as Castro, Kennedy, and Henry Kissinger. Fascinating, with Hall's performance a wonder. A one-of-a-kind movie from Robert Altman. Rated PG. 90m. DIR: Robert Altman. CAST: Philip Baker Hall. 1984

SECRET KINGDOM, THE ★★ A boy discovers a tiny kingdom hidden beneath the kitchen sink. He and his sister are drawn into the world where they find themselves battling for an evil king. So-so entertainment for the kids. Rated PG. DIR: David Schmoeller. CAST: Billie O., Jamieson K. Price, Tricia Dickson, Andrew Dicote. 1997

SECRET LIFE OF AN AMERICAN WIFE, THE ★★ Bored wife Anne Jackson decides to moonlight as a call girl. Her first client is her husband's employer. Husband walks in on wife and employer, etc. Director and writer George Axelrod had a cute idea, but it really doesn't gel. 93m. DIR: George Axelrod. CAST: Walter Matthau, Anne Jackson, Patrick O'Neal, Edy Williams, Richard Bull. 1968

SECRET LIFE OF JEFFREY DAHMER, THE ★★★ Fictional portrayal of the infamous serial killer is a low-budget effort that works despite its shortcomings. Carl Crew is magnetic as Dahmer, who invited unsuspecting men into his spider's web, took advantage of them, and then killed them. Most of the mayhem is offscreen but is effective nonetheless, giving us some insight about the loner who captivated the nation. Not rated; contains violence, adult language, and situations. 100m. DIR: David R. Bowen. CAST: Carl Crew. 1993

SECRET LIFE OF WALTER MITTY, THE ★★★★ Based on James Thurber's story, this comedy presents Danny Kaye as a timid man who dreams of being a brave, glory-bound hero. This comedy provides plenty of laughs and enjoyable moments. 105m. DIR: Norman Z. McLeod. CAST: Danny Kaye, Virginia Mayo, Boris Karloff, Reginald Denny, Florence Bates, Ann Rutherford, Thurston Hall. 1947 DVD

SECRET OBSESSIONS ❤ Maudlin, morose, melodramatic yawner. Rated PG. 82m. DIR: Henri Vart. CAST: Julie Christie, Ben Gazzara, Patrick Bruel, Jean Carmet. 1988

SECRET OF MY SUCCESS, THE ★★★1/2 The secret of this movie's success can be found in its ingredients: a witty script, vibrant direction, bouncy pop score, ingratiating star, and gifted supporting cast. Michael J. Fox is terrifically likable as a wildly ambitious Kansas lad who heads for New York City with plans to conquer the corporate world overnight. Rated PG-13. 110m. DIR: Herbert Ross. CAST: Michael J. Fox, Helen Slater, Margaret Whitton, Richard Jordan, Christopher Murney, John Pankow, Fred Gwynne. 1987 DVD

SECRET OF NIMH, THE ★★★★ Lovers of classic screen animation, rejoice! Don Bluth's *The Secret of Nimh* is the best feature-length cartoon to be released since the golden age of Walt Disney. This movie, about the adventures of a widow mouse, is more than just a children's tale. Adults will enjoy it, too. Dom DeLuise, Peter Strauss, John Carradine (voices). Rated G. 82m. DIR: Don Bluth. 1982 DVD

SECRET OF ROAN INISH, THE ★★★★ When a 10-year-old girl is sent to live with her grandparents on Ireland's rugged west coast, she hears local legends of *selkies*—half-human, half-seal Celtic beings—and becomes convinced that these strange creatures may somehow have saved her infant brother, thought lost at sea years earlier. Haskell Wexler's rich cinematography lends a sumptuous aura to a story guaranteed to delight all ages. Not rated. 103m. **DIR:** John Sayles. **CAST:** Jeni Courtney, Mick Lallay, Eileen Colgan, Richard Sheridan. 1994

SECRET OF THE BLUE ROOM, THE ★★ A woman challenges her three suitors to vie for her affections by spending the night at a castle in a room that has been sealed since three people were murdered there twenty years ago. Obviously inspired by *The Old Dark House*, but not nearly as good. B&W; 66m. **DIR:** Kurt Neumann. **CAST:** Lionel Atwill, Gloria Stuart, Paul Lukas, Edward Arnold, Onslow Stevens. 1933

SECRET OF THE SWORD, THE ♥ Characters from the television series *He-Man and the Masters of the Universe* are featured in this poorly animated, ineptly written feature-length cartoon. Rated G. 90m. **DIR:** Bill Reed, Gwen Wetzler, Ed Friedman, Lou Kachivas, Marsh Lamore. 1985

SECRET PASSION OF ROBERT CLAYTON, THE ★★★ Who really killed the stripper? If you like good court scenes, you'll enjoy this twisted plot of love, death, family, and the law. Made for cable. 91m. **DIR:** E. W. Swackhamer. **CAST:** John Mahoney, Scott Valentine, Eve Gordon, Kevin Conroy. 1992

SECRET RAPTURE, THE ★★★★ David Hare's stage play is the catalyst for this mesmerizing and haunting tale of two estranged sisters whose lives are thrown into chaos when their father dies. Not only must they contend with each other, they must also put up with their scheming, alcoholic stepmother, deliciously played by Joanne Whalley. Tensions mount as tragedy befalls the household, turning sister against sister. Rated R for adult situations. 96m. **DIR:** Howard Davies. **CAST:** Joanne Whalley, Juliet Stevenson, Penelope Wilton, Neil Pearson, Alan Howard. 1993

SECRET WAR OF HARRY FRIGG, THE ★★ A group of Allied generals has been captured by the Italians. In their vast wisdom, the high command chooses a disgruntled private (Paul Newman) to go behind the lines and free them. This is a very basic comedy, with few original laughs. Rated PG. 110m. **DIR:** Jack Smight. **CAST:** Paul Newman, Sylva Koscina, Andrew Duggan, James Gregory. 1968

SECRET WEAPON ★★ A lab technician working on Israel's secret nuclear bomb capabilities decides to go public in order to stop the arms proliferation. Predictable and slowly paced TV movie. 95m. **DIR:** Ian Sharp. **CAST:** Karen Allen, Griffin Dunne, Jeroen Krabbé. 1990

SECRET WEAPONS ♥ Sleazy made-for-TV potboiler about a Russian espionage training camp. 96m. **DIR:** Don Taylor. **CAST:** James Franciscus, Sally Kellerman, Linda Hamilton, Geena Davis. 1985

SECRETARY, THE ★★★ Another in the you-just-can't-get-good-help-these-days series of suspense thrillers. Mel Harris stars as an executive whose newly assigned secretary wants not only her job but apparently her head as well. Rated R for profanity

and violence. 94m. **DIR:** Andrew Lane. **CAST:** Mel Harris, Sheila Kelley, Barry Bostwick, James Russo. 1994

SECRETS ★★ Jacqueline Bisset's torrid sex scene is about the only interesting thing in this turgid soap opera. Rated R for nudity, suggested sex, and profanity. 86m. **DIR:** Philip Saville. **CAST:** Jacqueline Bisset, Per Oscarsson, Shirley Knight, Robert Powell. 1971 DVD

SECRETS AND LIES ★★★★★ This searing, hilarious examination of the human condition is packed with riveting dialogue as an extended working-class British family peers at the world through an enslaving veil of deceit, anxious hope, and broken dreams. A black optometrist initiates a fall of emotional dominoes when she seeks out her biological mum after the death of her adopted parents. The trail leads to the home of a frumpy white factory worker awash in self-pity, and a dark domestic storm erupts with painful but cleansing force. Rated R for language. 142m. **DIR:** Mike Leigh. **CAST:** Brenda Blethyn, Marianne Jean-Baptiste, Timothy Spall, Phyllis Logan, Claire Rushbrook, Ron Cook. 1996

SECRETS IN THE ATTIC ★★★ Independent thriller about a 12-year-old girl named Amy, whose retreat to her aunt's house unlocks a murder mystery dating back thirty years involving her grandparents. While rummaging through the attic, Amy comes across dolls representing her grandparents which seem to communicate the killer's identity, and after doing some investigative work, she comes to a startling conclusion. Creepy moments involving the haunted dollhouse and eerie flashbacks recalling the murders give this thriller the right stuff to raise goose bumps. Rated PG-13 for violence. 89m. **DIR:** Diane Haak. **CAST:** Amanda Roese, Lindsay Jackson, Rebekah Baker. 1993

SECRETS OF A MARRIED MAN ♥ TV-movie involves William Shatner's attempt at conquering the final frontier of infidelity. 100m. **DIR:** William A. Graham. **CAST:** William Shatner, Cybill Shepherd, Michelle Phillips, Glynn Turman. 1984

SECRETS OF A SOUL ★★ A chemistry professor is troubled by dream images and premonitions of murder when he learns his wife's cousin is returning from India. This early attempt to convert psychoanalysis into cinematic entertainment was bound to suffer from heavy-handed and simplistic imagery (but then, was *Spellbound* any better twenty years later?). Germany. Silent. 94m. **DIR:** G. W. Pabst. **CAST:** Werner Krauss. 1926

SECRETS OF THE WASTELAND ★★1/2 Hopalong Cassidy and his friends agree to help a group of archaeologists search some cliff dwellings but run into trouble with the local Chinese. Not as much action as some in the series but plenty of skulduggery and secret passages highlight this entry. B&W; 65m. **DIR:** Derwin Abrahams. **CAST:** William Boyd, Brad King, Andy Clyde, Barbara Britton, Douglas Fowley, Soo Young. 1941

SECRETS OF WOMEN (WAITING WOMEN) ★★★1/2 Infidelity is the theme of this early Ingmar Bergman film. Three wives (Anita Bjork, May Britt, and Eva Dahlbeck) who are staying at a summerhouse recount adventures from their marriages.

Clearly illustrates Bergman's talent for comedy and was his first commercial success. B&W; 107m. **DIR:** Ingmar Bergman. **CAST:** Anita Bjork, Jarl Kulle, Eva Dahlbeck, Gunnar Björnstrand, May Britt, Birger Malmsten. **1952**

SECT, THE ★★ The second collaboration between Dario Argento and Michele Soavi is not as good as its predecessor, *The Church*, but it still has moments. Rated R for profanity, violence, and brief nudity. 112m. **DIR:** Michele Soavi. **CAST:** Herbert Lom, Kelly Curtis. **1991**

SEDUCED ★★ The supporting cast attracts most of the attention in made-for-TV tale about an up-and-coming young politician who falls for the wife of an influential businessman. The wife gets murdered, and the politico is forced to become a sleuth. 100m. **DIR:** Jerrold Freedman. **CAST:** Gregory Harrison, Cybill Shepherd, Adrienne Barbeau, Mel Ferrer, José Ferrer. **1985**

SEDUCED AND ABANDONED ★★★1/2 This raucous Italian film takes wonderfully funny potshots at Italian life and codes of honor. It centers on a statute of Italian law that absolves a man for the crime of seducing and abandoning a girl if he marries her. This is one of the funniest movies exposing the stratagems of saving face. In Italian with English subtitles. B&W; 118m. **DIR:** Pietro Germi. **CAST:** Saro Urzi, Stefania Sandrelli. **1964**

SEDUCTION OF JOE TYNAN, THE ★★★ Alan Alda plays Senator Joe Tynan in this story of behind-the-scenes romance and political maneuvering in Washington, D.C. Tynan must face moral questions about himself and his job. It's familiar ground for Alda but still entertaining. Rated PG for language and brief nudity. 107m. **DIR:** Jerry Schatzberg. **CAST:** Alan Alda, Barbara Harris, Meryl Streep, Rip Torn, Charles Kimbrough, Melvyn Douglas. **1979**

SEDUCTION OF MIMI, THE ★★★★ Giancarlo Giannini gives an unforgettable performance as the sad-eyed Mimi, a Sicilian who migrates to the big city. He soon gets into trouble because of his obstinate character and his simple mind. Like all Wertmuller's films, sex and politics are at the heart of her dark humor. Includes one of the funniest love scenes ever filmed. Rated R for language and sex. 89m. **DIR:** Lina Wertmuller. **CAST:** Giancarlo Giannini, Mariangela Melato, Agostina Belli. **1974 DVD**

SEE NO EVIL ★★★1/2 Chilling yarn follows a young blind woman (Mia Farrow) as she tries to escape the clutches of a ruthless killer who has done away with her entire family at their quiet country farm. Mia Farrow is very convincing as the maniac's next target. Rated PG for tense moments. 90m. **DIR:** Richard Fleischer. **CAST:** Mia Farrow, Dorothy Alison, Robin Bailey. **1971**

SEE NO EVIL, HEAR NO EVIL ★★★1/2 Richard Pryor and Gene Wilder play two handicapped buddies—one deaf, one blind—who find themselves running from cops and killers alike when they "witness" a murder. Forget the contrived, stale plot and enjoy the marvelous interplay between the stars. Rated R for profanity, nudity, and violence. 103m. **DIR:** Arthur Hiller. **CAST:** Gene Wilder, Richard Pryor, Joan Severance, Kevin Spacey. **1989**

SEE YOU IN THE MORNING ★★★ A touching character study. Jeff Bridges is a New York psychiatrist whose first marriage to model Farrah Fawcett crumbles, catching him off guard. A second marriage, to Alice Krige, seems more promising, but our hero has a number of obstacles to overcome. Rated PG-13 for profanity. 115m. **DIR:** Alan J. Pakula. **CAST:** Jeff Bridges, Alice Krige, Farrah Fawcett, Drew Barrymore, Lukas Haas, David Dukes, Frances Sternhagen, Linda Lavin. **1989**

SEEDPEOPLE ★★1/2 Obviously the creators have seen *Invasion of the Body Snatchers*, because they snatch the plot from that classic almost verbatim. Intergalactic pod-people invade a small community in a film that's so awful, it's actually quite entertaining on that level. Overall, fails to take root. Rated R for violence. 87m. **DIR:** Peter Manoogian. **CAST:** Sam Hennings. **1992**

SEEKERS, THE ★★ Most melodramatic and unbelievable TV production from the John Jakes's bicentennial series, this is part three of the Kent Family Chronicles. The original French immigrant is now a cynical man of wealth (Martin Milner) whose son (Randolph Mantooth) defies him by farming in Ohio. 189m. **DIR:** Sidney Hayers. **CAST:** Randolph Mantooth, Barbara Rush, Delta Burke, Edie Adams, Brian Keith, Martin Milner, George Hamilton, Hugh O'Brian, John Carradine, Gary Merrill, Ed Harris, Stuart Whitman. **1979**

SEEMS LIKE OLD TIMES ★★★ This slick, commercial package is much better than it deserves to be. It's another predictable Neil Simon sitcom packed with one-liners. But at least it's funny most of the time. Rated PG. 121m. **DIR:** Jay Sandrich. **CAST:** Goldie Hawn, Chevy Chase, Charles Grodin, Robert Guillaume, Harold Gould. **1980**

SEIZE THE DAY ★★★ Robin Williams is watchable in this drama, but like so many comedians who attempt serious acting, he is haunted by his madcap persona. This PBS *Great Performances* entry casts Williams as Wilhelm "Tommy" Adler, the Jewish ne'er-do-well son of wealthy, unsympathetic Joseph Wiseman. The story concerns the disintegration of Tommy's life. 87m. **DIR:** Fielder Cook. **CAST:** Robin Williams, Joseph Wiseman, Jerry Stiller, Glenne Headly, John Fiedler, Tom Aldredge, Tony Roberts. **1986**

SEIZURE ★★★ In Oliver Stone's directorial debut, an author of horror stories has a recurring dream about the murder of his houseguests by a trio of diabolical characters. Dream and reality intersect. Definitely a respectable chiller. Rated PG. 93m. **DIR:** Oliver Stone. **CAST:** Jonathan Frid, Martine Beswick, Herve Villechaize, Troy Donahue. **1974**

SELENA ★★1/2 This interminable, sugarcoated portrait of the *Tejano* singer whose life was tragically cut short couldn't be more sanitized if it were produced by her father—which, in fact, it was. Jennifer Lopez certainly mimics Selena's strut and sass to good effect, and she has the body for the midriff-baring outfits that became the performer's trademark. Only Edward James Olmos, as her father, brings any depth to his performance. Rated PG for mild profanity. 127m. **DIR:** Gregory Nava. **CAST:** Jennifer Lopez,

Edward James Olmos, Jon Seda, Constance Marie, Jacob Vargas. **1997 DVD**

SELL-OUT, THE ★★1/2 Double agent Oliver Reed screws up and finds that both the Soviets and the Americans have put out contracts on him. Okay spy stuff, though a bit heavy on the shoot-outs and car chases toward the end. Filmed in Israel. Rated PG. 88m. **DIR:** Peter Collinson. **CAST:** Richard Widmark, Oliver Reed, Gayle Hunnicutt, Sam Wanamaker. **1976**

SEMI-TOUGH ★★ Semihumorous love triangle set in a professional football background is just not as funny as it should be. Some inspired moments and very funny scenes make it a highly watchable film (especially Lotte Lenya's guest bit as an untemptable masseuse), and the character actors are fine, but much of the humor relies on profanity and cruel situations. Rated R. 108m. **DIR:** Michael Ritchie. **CAST:** Burt Reynolds, Jill Clayburgh, Kris Kristofferson, Robert Preston, Bert Convy, Lotte Lenya. **1977**

SENATOR WAS INDISCREET, THE ★★★ A staid and irreproachable U.S. senator's diary disclosures cause considerable embarrassment in this satire. Urbane and suave as always, William Powell is perfect in the title role. B&W; 81m. **DIR:** George S. Kaufman. **CAST:** William Powell, Ella Raines, Peter Lind Hayes, Arleen Whelan, Hans Conried. **1947**

SEND ME NO FLOWERS ★★★ Typically bright and bubbly Doris Day vehicle has Rock Hudson as her hypochondriacal hubby, who, believing he is dying, keeps trying to find a mate for his increasingly flustered wife. This is a light, frothy comedy that provokes some solid chuckles, thanks to the two leads and Tony Randall's supporting turn. 100m. **DIR:** Norman Jewison. **CAST:** Rock Hudson, Doris Day, Tony Randall, Paul Lynde, Clint Walker, Hal March, Edward Andrews. **1964**

SENDER, THE ★★★ Those who like their horror movies with a little subtlety should have a look at this low-key but effective yarn. A young man brought to a hospital after he attempts suicide is discovered to have telepathic powers. Because of his emotional disturbances, he is unable to control himself and unleashes his nightmares into the minds of doctors and patients. Rated R for violence. 91m. **DIR:** Roger Christian. **CAST:** Kathryn Harrold, Zeljko Ivanek, Shirley Knight, Paul Freeman. **1982**

SENIORS, THE ✿ Sophomoric. 87m. **DIR:** Rod Amateau. **CAST:** Jeffrey Byron, Gary Imhoff, Dennis Quaid, Priscilla Barnes, Edward Andrews, Alan Reed. **1978**

SENSATION ★★★ Clever plot twists enliven this otherwise routine erotic thriller that finds college student Kari Wuhrer employing "psychometry" (second sight) to determine whether obsessed professor Eric Roberts actually killed a former lover. Watch this one with a date; Brian Grant's arty direction generates a fair amount of heat and passion. Rated R for nudity, simulated sex, profanity, and violence. 105m. **DIR:** Brian Grant. **CAST:** Eric Roberts, Kari Wuhrer, Ron Perlman, Paul LeMat, Claire Stansfield, Ed Begley Jr. **1994**

SENSATIONS ✿ Odd-couple love story between a prostitute and a male stripper. Rated R for strong sexual situations. 91m. **DIR:** Chuck Vincent. **CAST:** Rebecca Lynn, Blake Bahner. **1988**

SENSATIONS OF 1945 ★★ Yet another one of those all-star jumbles so popular during the mid-1940s, this uninspired musical limps along, saddled with a stale story of a producer who wants to put on a show. The great W. C. Fields isn't in his best form here, but any chance to see him and Cab Calloway in action is worth something. B&W; 87m. **DIR:** Andrew L. Stone. **CAST:** Eleanor Powell, W. C. Fields, Sophie Tucker, Dennis O'Keefe, Cab Calloway, C. Aubrey Smith, Eugene Pallette. **1944**

SENSE AND SENSIBILITY ★★★★★ A superb adaptation of Jane Austen's comedy of manners involving the potentially dire fate awaiting the newly widowed Mrs. Dashwood and her three headstrong daughters, when their estate and fortune must (by law) pass to the deceased's male heir by a previous marriage. With their social status correspondingly reduced, sisters Elinor and Marianne find that their prospects for "making a good match" are similarly dashed. Star Emma Thompson collected an Oscar for her cunning screenplay adaptation, and the result is a rich costume romp that succeeds on all levels. Rated PG for the lusty pursuit of true love. 135m. **DIR:** Ang Lee. **CAST:** Emma Thompson, Alan Rickman, Kate Winslet, Hugh Grant, James Fleet, Harriet Walter, Gemma Jones, Elizabeth Spriggs, Robert Hardy. **1995 DVD**

SENSE OF FREEDOM, A ★★★ The true story of Jimmy Boyle, a violent Scottish criminal who refused to temper his viciousness during over a decade in various prisons. The film never attempts to make a hero out of Boyle, but neither does it offer any insight into his personality. A very well-made film from John Mackenzie, whose excellent *The Long Good Friday* featured a similar protagonist. Rated R. 81m. **DIR:** John Mackenzie. **CAST:** David Hayman, Alex Norton, Jake D'Arcy, Fulton MacKay. **1983**

SENSELESS ★★ A cash-strapped student takes desperate measures to ensure his future security in this crude, uneven comedy. Daryl Witherspoon supports his single mom and younger siblings by selling his body fluids to blood and sperm banks and holding down menial college jobs. Then he volunteers to test a drug that enhances his five senses—and his chances to land a lucrative position at one of Manhattan's top financial firms. Rated R for language, nudity, and sexual content. 88m. **DIR:** Penelope Spheeris. **CAST:** Marlon Wayans, David Spade, Matthew Lillard, Brad Dourif, Rip Torn. **1998 DVD**

SENSUAL MAN, THE ★★ Unengaging dubbed comedy about the sexual exploits of an aristocratic young man (Giancarlo Giannini). Good cast never rises above the mediocre sexist script. Rated R for nudity and profanity. 98m. **DIR:** Marco Vicario. **CAST:** Giancarlo Giannini, Rossana Podesta, Lionel Stander. **1983**

SENSUOUS NURSE, THE ✿ A wealthy aristocrat has a heart attack and his two fortune-hunting, conniving nephews decide to help their lecherous uncle meet his maker. This dubbed Italian comedy is a dud. Rated R for nudity. 76m. **DIR:** Nello Rossati. **CAST:** Ursula Andress, Jack Palance, Duilio Del Prete, Luciana Paluzzi. **1978**

SENSUOUS WIFE, THE ✿ Exploitation comedy about wife-swapping notable only for an appearance by Edward D. Wood Jr. as a transvestite. Originally titled *Mrs. Stone's Thing*. Not rated. 64m. **DIR:** Joseph F. Robertson. **CAST:** Victor Rich, Karen Johnson, Edward D. Wood Jr. 1969

SENTINEL, THE ♥ A woman unknowingly moves into an apartment building over the gates of hell. Rated R for nudity, profanity, and violence. 93m. **DIR:** Michael Winner. **CAST:** Chris Sarandon, Cristina Raines, Martin Balsam, John Carradine, José Ferrer, Ava Gardner, Arthur Kennedy, Burgess Meredith, Sylvia Miles, Deborah Raffin, Eli Wallach. 1977 DVD

SEPARATE BUT EQUAL ★★★★ In one of his finest performances, Sidney Poitier stars as Thurgood Marshall, the NAACP lawyer who took the fight for racial equality to the Supreme Court via the Brown vs. Board of Education case in 1954. Richard Kiley is marvelous as Chief Justice Earl Warren, and Burt Lancaster is typically dignified and believable as the opposing counsel. Gripping drama that originally aired as a two-parter on television. 200m. **DIR:** George Stevens Jr. **CAST:** Sidney Poitier, Burt Lancaster, Richard Kiley, Cleavon Little, John McMartin. 1991

SEPARATE LIVES ★★ A transparent and silly variation on the executive-by-day/hooker-by-night theme. James Belushi is an ex-cop studying psychology, Linda Hamilton's the professor who hires him to tail her, as she "may" have a multiple-personality disorder. The sad part is that someone actually cashed a check for penning this kibble. Rated R for violence, profanity, nudity, and sexual situations. 102m. **DIR:** David Madden. **CAST:** James Belushi, Linda Hamilton, Vera Miles. 1994

SEPARATE PEACE, A ★★★ Based on John Knowles's bestselling novel, this involving story of a young man's first glimpse of adult emotions and motivations—some say homosexual frustration—is watchable for plot and performance. Gene and Finny are prep school roommates at the beginning of World War II. Jealous of Finny's popularity, Gene betrays his roommate in a moment of anger and treachery, and is responsible for a crippling accident. Rated PG. 104m. **DIR:** Larry Peerce. **CAST:** John Heyl, Parker Stevenson, Peter Brush. 1972

SEPARATE TABLES ★★★★★ This is a cable-television remake of the 1958 film with Burt Lancaster and Wendy Hiller. This time the work achieves a remarkable intimacy on tape with a top-notch British cast. Divided into two segments, this is a sort of British *Grand Hotel* room with Alan Bates and Julie Christie in dual roles. Richly engrossing adult entertainment. Rated PG for adult subject matter. 108m. **DIR:** John Schlesinger. **CAST:** Julie Christie, Alan Bates, Claire Bloom. 1983

SEPARATE VACATIONS ★★★1/2 This comedy about Richard, a bored husband (David Naughton) suddenly seeking romance outside his marriage, has some hilarious, if contrived, moments. Rated R for nudity and sexual situations. 92m. **DIR:** Michael Anderson. **CAST:** David Naughton, Jennifer Dale, Mark Keyloun, Tony Rosato. 1985

SEPTEMBER ★★★1/2 Woody Allen in his serious mode. Mia Farrow is superb as a troubled woman living in Vermont. Her houseguests are her hard-living mother (Elaine Stritch), her stepfather (Jack Warden), her best friend (Diane Wiest), and an aspiring writer (Sam Waterston). What transpires are subtle yet intense love-hate relationships. Rated PG. 82m. **DIR:** Woody Allen. **CAST:** Mia Farrow, Dianne Wiest, Sam Waterston, Denholm Elliott, Elaine Stritch, Jack Warden. 1987

SEPTEMBER AFFAIR ★★1/2 Superficial romantic tale about two married people who are reported dead after a plane crash. This gives them their chance to conduct a love affair. Bonuses: nice photography on the isle of Capri and the famous Walter Huston recording of the title song. B&W; 104m. **DIR:** William Dieterle. **CAST:** Joseph Cotten, Joan Fontaine, Françoise Rosay, Jessica Tandy, Robert Arthur, Jimmy Lydon. 1950

SEPTEMBER GUN ★★ A good cast can't save this overly talky TV Western about an aged good-hearted gunfighter reluctantly becoming the protector of a nun and some orphaned Apache children. 100m. **DIR:** Don Taylor. **CAST:** Robert Preston, Patty Duke, Christopher Lloyd, Sally Kellerman. 1983

SEPTEMBER 30, 1955 ★★★1/2 Affecting, sentimental portrait of a group of young adults and how the death of movie star James Dean changes their lives. Richard Thomas gathers up his friends for a wake and then for a celebration of Dean's spirit that ends tragically before the evening is out. Rated PG for language and violence. 107m. **DIR:** James Bridges. **CAST:** Richard Thomas, Lisa Blount, Dennis Quaid, Tom Hulce, Dennis Christopher, Deborah Benson. 1977

SERENADE ★★1/2 A James M. Cain sordid story set to music to show off Mario Lanza, but it doesn't work too well. 121m. **DIR:** Anthony Mann. **CAST:** Mario Lanza, Joan Fontaine, Sarita Montiel, Vincent Price. 1956

SERENDIPITY, THE PINK DRAGON ★★1/2 "The fates had been kind," intones the narrator with unintended irony, as a shipwrecked young boy floats to the safety of Paradise Island. That's pretty glib, considering the poor lad moments earlier had lost both his parents. Once past this questionable introduction, we settle into the pleasant little tale of the boy, his massive pink friend, and their attempts to save Paradise Island from the greedy Captain Smudge. 90m. **DIR:** Yoshikuni Nishi, Toyo Ebishima. 1989

SERGEANT RUTLEDGE ★★★1/2 Underrated and somewhat forgotten Western tells the story of a black cavalry officer on trial for rape and murder. The film's main focus is on the characters. Very good use of flashbacks to show events leading up to court-martial. B&W; 118m. **DIR:** John Ford. **CAST:** Woody Strode, Jeffrey Hunter, Constance Towers, Billie Burke. 1960

SERGEANT RYKER ★★★ This film revolves around the court-martial of Sergeant Ryker (Lee Marvin), a Korean War soldier. Ryker, accused of treason, is valiantly defended by his attorney (Bradford Dillman in a superb performance). Originally shown on television as *The Case Against Sergeant Ryker*, then released theatrically under the shortened title. 86m. **DIR:** Buzz Kulik. **CAST:** Lee Marvin, Bradford Dillman,

Vera Miles, Peter Graves, Lloyd Nolan, Murray Hamilton. 1968

SERGEANT YORK ★★★ A World War II morale booster that is still good entertainment today. Gary Cooper got an Academy Award as the deeply religious young farmer from backwoods Tennessee who tries to avoid service in World War I because of his religious convictions only to become the war's most decorated American hero! B&W; 134m. DIR: Howard Hawks. CAST: Gary Cooper, Walter Brennan, George Tobias, Ward Bond, Noah Beery Jr., June Lockhart, Joan Leslie. 1941

SERIAL ★★★1/2 Harvey Holroyd (Martin Mull) finds it difficult to go with the flow, especially when he finds out his wife, Kate (Tuesday Weld), is having an affair with a Cuban poodle-groomer while his daughter, Joan (Jennifer McAlister), has joined a religious cult. That's when the problems really begin. Rated R. 86m. DIR: Bill Persky. CAST: Martin Mull, Tuesday Weld, Jennifer McAlister, Bill Macy, Tom Smothers, Christopher Lee. 1980

SERIAL BOMBER ★★ Direct-to-video thriller apes every mad serial-bomber movie that has blown across the screen during the past five years. Lori Petty is the FBI agent who has seventy-two hours to stop a serial bomber from toasting Seattle. Rated R for adult situations, language, and violence. 89m. DIR: Keoni Waxman. CAST: Lori Petty, Jason London, James LeGros. 1996 DVD

SERIAL KILLER 🐝 The one about the female cop who goes undercover to find out who is killing her friends. Rated R for violence, adult language, and nudity. 94m. DIR: Pierre David. CAST: Kim Delaney, Gary Hudson, Tobin Bell, Pam Grier, Andrew Prine. 1995

SERIAL MOM ★★★★ Picture June Cleaver with a homicidal streak and you have Beverly Sutphin—a "perfect" mother driven to murder when her middle-class family life is even slightly jostled by outsiders. This warped social comedy skewers the media for turning killers into celebrities and turns a one-note joke into a savagely funny romp that is definitely not for everyone. Rated R for simulated sex, language, violence, and gore. 97m. DIR: John Waters. CAST: Kathleen Turner, Sam Waterston, Ricki Lake, Matthew Lillard, Scott Wesley Morgan, Walt MacPherson. 1994 DVD

SERPENT AND THE RAINBOW, THE ★★★1/2 Loosely based on the nonfiction book of the same name, this is about a sociologist who goes to Haiti to bring back a potion that reportedly resurrects the dead. Rated R for violence, language, and nudity. 98m. DIR: Wes Craven. CAST: Bill Pullman, Cathy Tyson, Zakes Mokae, Paul Winfield. 1988 DVD

SERPENT'S EGG, THE ★★ Two trapeze artists are trapped in Berlin during pre-Nazi Germany where they discover a satanic plot. Director Ingmar Bergman's nightmare vision is disappointing. 120m. DIR: Ingmar Bergman. CAST: Liv Ullmann, David Carradine, Gert Fröbe, James Whitmore. 1977

SERPENT'S LAIR ★★ Nice guy Jeff Fahey is unfortunate enough to encounter a succubus, who slowly kills him via excessive lovemaking. Scripter Marc Rosenberg drags in everything up to Satan himself, before this tawdry little chiller crashes to a wholly unsatisfying halt. Rated R for violence, profanity, nudity, and simulated sex. 90m. DIR: Jeffrey Reiner. CAST: Jeff Fahey, Lisa B., Heather Medway, Anthony Palermo, Patrick Bauchau. 1995

SERPICO ★★★★ Al Pacino is magnificent in this poignant story of an honest man who happens to be a cop. The fact that this is a true story of one man's fight against corruption adds even more punch. Rated R. 130m. DIR: Sidney Lumet. CAST: Al Pacino, Tony Roberts, John Randolph, Biff McGuire, Jack Kehoe. 1973

SERVANT, THE ★★★★ A conniving manservant (Dirk Bogarde) gradually dominates the life of his spoiled master in this psychological horror story. By preying on his sexual weaknesses, he is able to easily maneuver him to his will. The taut, well-acted adult drama holds your interest throughout, mainly because the shock value is heightened for the audience because of its plausibility. B&W; 115m. DIR: Joseph Losey. CAST: Dirk Bogarde, Sarah Miles, James Fox. 1963

SERVANTS OF TWILIGHT ★★★ Dean R. Koontz's *Twilight* is the source of this fast-paced, made-for-cable spin on *The Omen*, which features Bruce Greenwood as a dedicated private detective determined to save a little boy from a maniacal cult whose leader believes him to be the Antichrist. Violence and subdued sexual themes. 95m. DIR: Jeffrey Obrow. CAST: Bruce Greenwood, Belinda Bauer, Grace Zabriskie, Richard Bradford, Jack Kehoe. 1991

SESAME STREET PRESENTS FOLLOW THAT BIRD ★★★★ Although this kiddie film has an impressive "guest cast," the real stars are *Sesame Street* TV show regulars Big Bird, the Cookie Monster, Oscar the Grouch, Count von Count, the Telly Monster, etc. Children will love this story about Big Bird being evicted from Sesame Street. Rated G. 88m. DIR: Ken Kwapis. CAST: Sandra Bernhard, Chevy Chase, John Candy, Dave Thomas, Joe Flaherty, Waylon Jennings. 1985

SESSIONS ★★★ Veronica Hamel poses as a career woman who also takes pleasure in being a high-priced call girl in the evening. Soap-opera drama? Yes, but that's what you expect in this made-for-TV movie. And it's done with class. 100m. DIR: Richard Pearce. CAST: Veronica Hamel, Jeffrey DeMunn, Jill Eikenberry. 1983

SET IT OFF ★★ In this very violent, old-school revenge movie, four Los Angeles African American women begin robbing banks to supplement their meager janitorial paychecks. The film first focuses on the desperation of its main characters, but then wallows in sensationalism. When these women are hale, all hell breaks loose. Rated R for language, drug use, violence, and suggested sex. 105m. DIR: F. Gary Gray. CAST: Jada Pinkett, Queen Latifah, Vivica A. Fox, Kimberly Elise. 1996 DVD

SET-UP, THE (1949) ★★★★ Taut *film noir* boxing flick takes the simple story of an over-the-hill boxer who refuses to disregard his principles and throw the big fight and elevates it to true tragedy. Robert Ryan as the has-been fighter gives another of the finely drawn and fiercely independent portrayals that marked his illustrious career as one of Hollywood's finest character actors. B&W; 72m. **DIR:** Robert Wise. **CAST:** Robert Ryan, Audrey Totter, George Tobias, Alan Baxter, James Edwards, Wallace Ford. 1949

SET-UP, THE (1995) ★★★1/2 Genius burglar and programmer Billy Zane goes straight, falls in love, and—after his new paramour is kidnapped—finds himself forced to sneak past his own security devices in a supposedly impregnable bank. This spiffy little caper flick is based loosely on British author James Hadley Chase's *My Laugh Comes Last*. Good fun, although our hero goes through all seven levels of hell before turning the tables on his tormentors. Rated R for violence, nudity, simulated sex, and profanity. 91m. **DIR:** Strathford Hamilton. **CAST:** Billy Zane, James Coburn, Mia Sara, James Russo, Louis Mandylor. 1995

SEVEN ★★★★ Riveting thriller about a young detective (Brad Pitt) and an older, more experienced police officer (Morgan Freeman) attempting to track down a maniacal serial killer. The two leads are excellent, and the screenplay keeps you guessing right up to the nail-biting conclusion. Not for the faint of heart. Rated R for profanity, violence, and gruesome situations. 127m. **DIR:** David Fincher. **CAST:** Morgan Freeman, Brad Pitt, Gwyneth Paltrow, Kevin Spacey, R. Lee Ermey, Richard Roundtree. 1995 DVD

SEVEN BEAUTIES ★★★★★ Winner of many international awards, this Italian film classic is not what the title might suggest. *Seven Beauties* is actually the street name for a small-time gangster, played by Giancarlo Giannini. We watch him struggle and survive on the streets and in a World War II German prisoner-of-war camp. Excellent! Rated R. 115m. **DIR:** Lina Wertmuller. **CAST:** Giancarlo Giannini, Fernando Rey, Shirley Stoler. 1976 DVD

SEVEN BRIDES FOR SEVEN BROTHERS ★★☆ ★★★ Delightful musical. Howard Keel takes Jane Powell as his wife. The fun begins when his six younger brothers decide they want to get married, too ... immediately! 103m. **DIR:** Stanley Donen. **CAST:** Howard Keel, Jane Powell, Russ Tamblyn, Julie Newmar, Marc Platt. 1954 DVD

SEVEN BROTHERS MEET DRACULA, THE ★★1/2 Hammer Film's last Dracula movie was a coproduction with the Shaw Brothers of Hong Kong, known mainly for their kung fu films. A martial arts–horror-fantasy about Professor Van Helsing fighting a vampire cult in China. An interesting attempt, but unless you are a kung fu fan, this entry will seem all too silly. Rated R; this feature was originally titled *Legend of the Seven Golden Vampires*. 88m. **DIR:** Roy Ward Baker. **CAST:** Peter Cushing, David Chaing, Julie Ege. 1973

SEVEN CHANCES ★★★★1/2 Buster Keaton has until 7 P.M. to get married or lose a huge inheritance; a misunderstanding estranges him from his true love, and he goes wife-hunting. One of Keaton's most enjoyable silent features, climaxed by an athletic chase and the famous rock-slide scene. A few racial gags may appear in questionable taste to today's audiences. Not rated. B&W (some video releases have the opening scene in color); 56m. **DIR:** Buster Keaton.

CAST: Buster Keaton, T. Roy Barnes, Snitz Edwards, Ruth Dwyer. 1925 DVD

SEVEN CITIES OF GOLD ★★★ Michael Rennie plays an incredibly pious Father Junípero Serra, struggling to set up his first mission in California. His love of the Indians contrasts sharply with the ruthless greed of the Spanish military leaders (played by Anthony Quinn and Richard Egan). Not rated, this contains violence. 103m. **DIR:** Robert D. Webb. **CAST:** Michael Rennie, Richard Egan, Anthony Quinn, Jeffrey Hunter, Rita Moreno. 1955

SEVEN DAYS IN MAY ★★★★ A highly suspenseful account of an attempted military takeover of the U.S. government. After a slow buildup, the movie's tension snowballs toward a thrilling conclusion. This is one of those rare films that treat their audiences with respect. A working knowledge of the political process is helpful for optimum appreciation. B&W; 120m. **DIR:** John Frankenheimer. **CAST:** Burt Lancaster, Fredric March, Kirk Douglas, Ava Gardner, Edmond O'Brien, Martin Balsam. 1964 DVD

SEVEN DAY'S LEAVE ★★ Lucille Ball and Victor Mature are paired up again in this light musical comedy about two sailors on leave who seek out romantic opportunities. Lucy's charisma is unfortunately undermined by a poor script and weak direction. Some good tunes are performed by the Freddy Martin and Les Brown bands. B&W; 87m. **DIR:** Tim Whelan. **CAST:** Lucille Ball, Victor Mature, Harold Peary. 1942

SEVEN DEADLY SINS, THE ★★★ This collection of seven episodes illustrating the capital sins has its moments, but it should have been much better. Best is Jean-Luc Godard's segment on Laziness. In French with English subtitles. B&W; 113m. **DIR:** Sylvain Dhomme, Eugene Ionesco, Max Douy, Edouard Molinaro, Philippe de Broca, Jacques Demy, Jean-Luc Godard, Roger Vadim, Claude Chabrol. **CAST:** Claude Brasseur, Jean-Louis Trintignant, Eddie Constantine, Jean-Pierre Aumont, Sami Frey, Jean-Claude Brialy, Claude Berri. 1961

SEVEN DIALS MYSTERY, THE ★★★★ This lighthearted Agatha Christie whodunit concerns a group of friends who spend the weekend at The Chimneys, the ancestral home of one Lady Eileen Brent (affectionately known as Bundle). A misfired practical joke leads to an unexpectedly tragic conclusion, which somehow involves a secret society known as the Seven Dials Club. Made for TV. 110m. **DIR:** Tony Wharmby. **CAST:** Cheryl Campbell, Harry Andrews, James Warwick, John Gielgud. 1981

SEVEN DOORS OF DEATH ★★ This is the American release title (trimmed to obtain an R rating) of *The Beyond*, a stylishly gross Italian horror shocker about a Louisiana hotel situated on one of seven mythical gateways to hell. Even R-rated, this atmospheric shocker is incredibly gruesome. 86m. **DIR:** Lucio Fulci. **CAST:** Katherine MacColl, David Warbeck. 1981

◆SEVEN DOORS TO DEATH ★★ When circumstances throw a down-on-his-luck fellow and a young heiress together, he involves himself in her troubles, which include murder. The title refers to the possible suspects in a killing that occurred in a courtyard owned by the girl's dead aunt—any of the business owners there could be the culprit. Hastily edited and definitely low-budget, but entertains with red herrings, odd characters, and clever dialogue. B&W; 61m. DIR: Elmer Clifton. CAST: Chick Chandler, June Clyde, George Meeker, Michael Raffetto. 1944

7 FACES OF DR. LAO ★★★★ A first-rate fantasy taken from Charles Finney's classic story, "The Circus of Dr. Lao." Tony Randall plays multiple roles as a mysterious Chinese gentleman and his many strange circus sideshow creatures. Fabulous makeup and special effects, surrounded by a heartwarming story. Perfect for all ages, one of the few films to capture the wonder and sinister overtones of a traveling circus. 100m. DIR: George Pal. CAST: Tony Randall, Barbara Eden, Arthur O'Connell. 1964

•SEVEN FOOTPRINTS TO SATAN ★★ Footloose young heir spends a sobering night in a house of horrors where he witnesses torture, murder, devil worship, and excess of all types—all orchestrated by the man's uncle and fiancée to bring him back to his senses and to provide the audience with violence and debauchery ordinarily denied by local censors. Based on a fantasy classic by A. Merritt, this comic thriller offers a rare viewing experience for film buffs because of its source material, fabled director, and position in fantasy film lore. Silent, with Italian subtitles and musical score. B&W; 60m. DIR: Benjamin Christensen. CAST: Creighton Hale, Thelma Todd, Sheldon Lewis, William V. Mong, DeWitt Jennings, Laska Winters. 1929

SEVEN HILLS OF ROME, THE ★★★ A TV star (Mario Lanza) goes to Rome to rest, finds a pretty girl, and sings his heart out. For Lanza fans, that's enough, but this isn't one of his better films. Beautiful scenery and his voice are the only selling points. 104m. DIR: Roy Rowland. CAST: Mario Lanza, Peggie Castle, Rosella Como, Marisa Allasio, Renato Rascel. 1958

SEVEN HOURS TO JUDGMENT ★★ An action-thriller that loses much of its thrill due to its baby-faced star (and his jumpy direction). Bridges is a judge who, after letting a gang of thugs off on a technicality, must run a gauntlet through their territory. Ron Leibman steals the film as the distraught (and psychotic) husband of the gang's victim. Rated R for violence and profanity. 89m. DIR: Beau Bridges. CAST: Beau Bridges, Ron Leibman, Julianne Phillips, Reginald Vel Johnson, Al Freeman Jr. 1988

SEVEN LITTLE FOYS, THE ★★★ Deftly tailored to Bob Hope, this biography of famed vaudevillian Eddie Foy and his performing offspring is gag-filled entertainment until death makes him a widower at odds with his talented brood. A classic scene with James Cagney as George M. Cohan has Hope dancing on a tabletop. All's well that ends well—in church! 95m. DIR: Melville Shavelson. CAST: Bob Hope, Milly Vitale, George Tobias, Billy Gray, James Cagney. 1955

SEVEN MAGNIFICENT GLADIATORS, THE ❤ Seven gladiators defend the people of a small village. Rated PG. 86m. DIR: Bruno Mattei. CAST: Lou Ferrigno, Sybil Danning, Brad Harris, Dan Vadis, Mandy Rice-Davies. 1983

SEVEN MINUTES, THE ❤ Pornography is put on trial when a man claims that he was driven to commit rape after reading a sexy novel. Look for Tom Selleck in a small role. Rated R. 115m. DIR: Russ Meyer. CAST: Wayne Maunder, Marianne McAndrew, Jay C. Flippen, Edy Williams, Yvonne De Carlo, John Carradine. 1971

SEVEN MINUTES IN HEAVEN ★★1/2 When her only parent leaves town on business, 15-year-old Natalie (Jennifer Connelly) allows classmate Jeff (Byron Thames) to move into her home. Their relationship is purely platonic, but no one will believe her. Average but well-meant teen comedy. Rated PG for tastefully suggested sex. 95m. DIR: Linda Feferman. CAST: Jennifer Connelly, Byron Thames, Maddie Corman, Michael Zaslow. 1986

SEVEN-PER-CENT SOLUTION, THE ★★★★ Sherlock Holmes (Nicol Williamson) attempts to get rid of his cocaine addiction by getting treatment from Sigmund Freud (Alan Arkin). This is a fast-paced adventure with touches of humor. Robert Duvall's portrayal of Dr. Watson nearly steals the show. Great fun. Rated PG; okay for everyone. 113m. DIR: Herbert Ross. CAST: Nicol Williamson, Alan Arkin, Robert Duvall, Laurence Olivier, Vanessa Redgrave, Joel Grey. 1976 DVD

SEVEN SAMURAI, THE ★★★★★ This Japanese release—about seven swordsmen coming to the aid of a besieged peasant village—is one of those rare screen wonders that seems to end much too soon. Its timeless and appealing story served as the basis for The Magnificent Seven and other American films. In Japanese with English subtitles. Not rated; the film has violence. B&W; 197m. DIR: Akira Kurosawa. CAST: Toshiro Mifune, Takashi Shimura. 1954 DVD

SEVEN SINNERS ★★★ A brawling story of saloon life in the steamy tropics, as John Wayne and Albert Dekker vie for sultry Marlene Dietrich, who walks through this slight story with good humor as a heartbreaking "entertainer." A serviceable action tale. B&W; 87m. DIR: Tay Garnett. CAST: John Wayne, Marlene Dietrich, Albert Dekker, Broderick Crawford, Mischa Auer, Anna Lee. 1940

SEVEN THIEVES ★★★ A rousing cops-and-robbers tale told from the robbers' viewpoint with Edward G. Robinson and Rod Steiger in top form. The setting is Monte Carlo, where thieves prosper and there is a lot of competition. B&W; 103m. DIR: Henry Hathaway. CAST: Edward G. Robinson, Rod Steiger, Eli Wallach, Joan Collins, Sebastian Cabot, Michael Dante, Alexander Scourby. 1960

SEVEN-UPS, THE ★★ Hoping to cash in on the popularity of The French Connection, the producer of that film directs this slam-bang action flick in an intellectual vacuum. All that's missing are William Friedkin, Gene Hackman, and an intelligent story ... but what the hey, we've got a better car chase! Roy Scheider is, as always, quite appealing, but he can't make something out of this nothing. Rated PG for violence. 103m. DIR: Philip D'Antoni. CAST: Roy Scheider, Tony Lo Bianco, Richard Lynch. 1973

SEVEN YEAR ITCH, THE ★★★★ This movie is Marilyn Monroe's most enjoyable comedy. Marilyn lives upstairs from average American Tom Ewell. It seems his wife has escaped the heat of their New York home by going on vacation. This leaves Tom alone and unprotected, and one visit from luscious neighbor Marilyn leads him on a Walter Mitty–style adventure that is a joy to behold. 105m. DIR: Billy Wilder. CAST: Tom Ewell, Marilyn Monroe, Oscar Homolka, Carolyn Jones. 1957

SEVEN YEARS' BAD LUCK ★★★1/2 A welcome opportunity to sample the dapper comedic talents of the French master, Max Linder. He plays a bachelor who must endure all manner of misfortunes due (apparently) to the accidental smashing of a mirror. Plenty of slapstick comedy and screwball situations. Silent. B&W; 85m. DIR: Max Linder. CAST: Max Linder. 1920

SEVEN YEARS IN TIBET ★★★1/2 This study of personal growth concerns Austrian mountaineer Heinrich Harrer, who was granted the role of outside observer in the 1940s during one of this century's greatest tragedies. Initially a member of the Nazi party and part of an Aryan team climbing a Himalayan peak in 1939, Harrer endured many adventures before winding up in Tibet and befriending the young Dalai Lama. Years passed, during which Harrer eventually grew to mistrust and subsequently despise the Communist Chinese invaders bent on subjugating Tibet. The only sour note comes from star Brad Pitt, excellent at conveying Harrer's early arrogance but less convincing as a man spiritually cleansed. Rated PG-13 for violence and mild profanity. 131m. DIR: Jean-Jacques Annaud. CAST: Brad Pitt, David Thewlis, B. D. Wong, Mako, Jamyang Jamtsho Wangchuk. 1997 DVD

1776 ★★★★ Broadway's hit musical about the founding of the nation is brought to the screen almost intact. Original cast members William Daniels, as John Adams, and Howard da Silva, as Benjamin Franklin, shine anew in this unique piece. Rated G. 141m. DIR: Peter H. Hunt. CAST: William Daniels, Howard DaSilva, Ken Howard, Blythe Danner. 1972

7TH CAVALRY ★★ Randolph Scott as a cavalry officer accused of cowardice for being on leave during the battle of the Little Big Horn. Talkie and slow-moving. 75m. DIR: Joseph H. Lewis. CAST: Randolph Scott, Barbara Hale, Donald Curtis, Jay C. Flippen. 1956

SEVENTH COIN, THE ★★★1/2 Were it not for some brutality and a wholly pointless scene in a Turkish-style bath, this lively adventure would be acceptable for all ages. American Alexandra Powers and Arabian Navin Chowdhry flee through modern Jerusalem with the implacably villainous Peter O'Toole hot on their heels, all because of a rare coin. Rated PG-13 for violence, profanity, and brief nudity. 95m. DIR: Dror Soref. CAST: Alexandra Powers, Navin Chowdhry, Peter O'Toole, John Rhys-Davies, Ally Walker. 1993

SEVENTH CROSS, THE ★★★★1/2 In 1936 Germany an anti-Nazi escapee from a concentration camp turns to friends for shelter and help in fleeing the country. Suspenseful, gripping drama. B&W; 111m. DIR: Fred Zinnemann. CAST: Spencer Tracy, Signe Hasso, Hume Cronyn, Jessica Tandy, Agnes Moorehead, Felix Bressart, George Macready, Ray Collins, Steven Geray, George Zucco. 1944

SEVENTH FLOOR, THE ★★ Brooke Shields went Down Under for this routine thriller that finds her trapped in her high-tech apartment building by a madman. Even though the film is filled with plenty of action and close calls, it brings nothing new to the genre. It's hard to take Shields seriously as she stumbles over one victim after another. Rated R for violence. 99m. DIR: Ian Berry. CAST: Brooke Shields, Masaya Kato, Linda Cropper, Craig Pearce. 1993 DVD

SEVENTH SEAL, THE ★★★★1/2 This is considered by many to be Ingmar Bergman's masterpiece. It tells the story of a knight coming back from the Crusades. He meets Death, who challenges him to a chess match, the stakes being his life. The knight is brilliantly played by Max von Sydow. In Swedish with English subtitles. B&W; 96m. DIR: Ingmar Bergman. CAST: Max von Sydow, Bibi Andersson, Gunnar Björnstrand. 1956 DVD

SEVENTH SIGN, THE ★★★1/2 Finely crafted suspense film with Demi Moore portraying a woman whose unborn baby is threatened by the biblical curse of the Apocalypse. Moore is superb and Jurgen Prochnow is perfect as the avenging angel. Rated R for language and shock effects. 94m. DIR: Carl Schultz. CAST: Demi Moore, Michael Biehn, Jurgen Prochnow, John Heard. 1988 DVD

SEVENTH VEIL, THE ★★★1/2 A young woman forsakes her family and chooses to become a musician, encountering many men along the way. Safe and satisfying, this middle-brow entertainment owes much of its success to a strong performance by James Mason and an Oscar-winning screenplay. Ann Todd is just right as the freethinking heroine. B&W; 94m. DIR: Compton Bennett. CAST: James Mason, Ann Todd, Herbert Lom, Hugh McDermott, Albert Lieven. 1945

SEVENTH VICTIM, THE ★★★ Innocent Kim Hunter stumbles onto a New York City coven of devil worshipers in this eerie thriller-chiller ancestor of Rosemary's Baby. Leave the lights on. B&W; 71m. DIR: Mark Robson. CAST: Tom Conway, Kim Hunter, Jean Brooks, Evelyn Brent, Hugh Beaumont, Isabel Jewell, Barbara Hale. 1943

7TH VOYAGE OF SINBAD, THE ★★★★ Sinbad battles an evil magician who has reduced the princess, who is also Sinbad's fiancée, to six inches in height. Our hero must battle a sword-wielding skeleton, a roc (giant bird), and other dangers to restore his bride-to-be to her normal size. This film contains some of the best stop-motion animation ever created by the master in that craft, Ray Harryhausen. 87m. DIR: Nathan Juran. CAST: Kerwin Mathews, Kathryn Grant, Torin Thatcher. 1958 DVD

SEVERED ARM, THE ★★1/2 Before being rescued, a group of trapped mine explorers cut off the arm of one of the men as food for the others. Many years later, the survivors of the expedition are systematically slaughtered. This low-budget independent production is fairly suspenseful, though the acting is often listless and the gore a bit excessive. Rated R. 86m. CAST: Paul Carr, Deborah Walley, Marvin Kaplan. 1973

SEVERED TIES ★★1/2 Outrageous special effects punctuate this campy horror film about a brilliant scientist who has found a way to regenerate limbs. He becomes the first recipient of his new discovery. Rated R for violence and language. 85m. **DIR:** Damon Santostefano. **CAST:** Oliver Reed, Elke Sommer, Garrett Morris, Billy Morrissette. 1992

SEX AND THE COLLEGE GIRL ★★ This low-budget version of *Sex and the Single Girl* has two things going for it: the witty and informative intro by Joe Bob Briggs and the fact that it didn't force a happy ending. Not rated, but implied sex and immorality abound. 100m. **DIR:** Joseph Adler. **CAST:** Julie Sommars, Charles Grodin, John Gabriel, Richard Arlen, Luana Anders. 1964

SEX AND THE OTHER MAN ★★★ An impotent husband finds his interest renewed when he catches his wife in their bed with her boss, so to keep things hot he ties him up in the room for the weekend. This adaptation of a stage comedy betrays its origins in an abundance of talk, but the characters are strongly drawn. Rated R for profanity, nudity, and sex. 89m. **DIR:** Karl Slovin. **CAST:** Karl Wuhrer, Ron Eldard. 1996 DVD

SEX AND THE SINGLE GIRL ★★★ A skin magazine editor makes a play for a lady psychologist by using all the ploys espoused in his magazine. A risqué premise handled in a tastefully entertaining way. 115m. **DIR:** Richard Quine. **CAST:** Tony Curtis, Natalie Wood, Lauren Bacall, Henry Fonda, Mel Ferrer, Larry Storch, Stubby Kaye, Edward Everett Horton. 1964

SEX AND ZEN ★★★1/2 In this outrageously bawdy comedy based on an ancient Chinese story, a scholar (Lawrence Ng) bemoans his inability to satisfy his wife (Hong Kong sex star Amy Yip). A doctor cures his problem by—well, we can't describe it here, but you've never seen anything like it. The combination of high production values, directorial verve, and sheer uninhibitedness make this a one-of-a-kind film. In Cantonese with English subtitles. Not rated; absolutely not for kids. 94m. **DIR:** Michael Mak. **CAST:** Lawrence Ng, Amy Yip, Kent Chung, Elvis Tsui. 1991 DVD

SEX APPEAL ★★ A nerdish accountant makes an all-out attempt to attract the opposite sex with humorously disastrous results. Gratuitous sleaze mars an otherwise cute story. Rated R for nudity and profanity. 81m. **DIR:** Chuck Vincent. **CAST:** Louie Bonanno. 1986

SEX CRIMES ★★ After a female judge is raped, she collects the names of all known sex offenders and systematically kills them. Incredibly bad acting wrecks this revenge drama. Not rated; contains violence, profanity, and nudity. 90m. **DIR:** David Garcia. **CAST:** Jeff Osterhage, Maria Richwine. 1991 DVD

SEX, DRUGS, ROCK & ROLL ★★★★ Eric Bogosian stars as a succession of ten different characters in this aggressive, thought-provoking, often astonishing film version of his one-man off-Broadway show. Writer-actor Bogosian (of *Talk Radio* fame) creates full-bodied minidramas and comedies with varying, believable characters. Rated R with strong profanity. 100m. **DIR:** John McNaughton. **CAST:** Eric Bogosian. 1991

SEX, LIES AND VIDEOTAPE ★★★★1/2 Deliciously offbeat winner of the 1989 Palme d'Or at the Cannes Film Festival revolves around a romantic triangle. Soft-spoken James Spader visits old college chum Peter Gallagher and ends up bringing to light Gallagher's affair with the sexy sister (Laura San Giacomo) of his slightly neurotic wife (Andie MacDowell). Rated R for simulated sex, profanity, and brief violence. 104m. **DIR:** Steven Soderbergh. **CAST:** James Spader, Andie MacDowell, Peter Gallagher, Laura San Giacomo. 1989 DVD

SEX, LOVE, AND COLD HARD CASH ★★★1/2 High marks to this clever mystery from writer-director Harry S. Longstreet. Ex-con Anthony Denison teams up with call-girl JoBeth Williams to find a mob accountant who skipped with millions. Pleasant chemistry between the two leads, and Longstreet's tale moves in genuinely unexpected directions. Rated PG-13 for violence and mild sensuality. 86m. **DIR:** Harry S. Longstreet. **CAST:** JoBeth Williams, Anthony Denison, Robert Forster, Eric Pierpoint. 1993

SEX MADNESS 💔 "Educational" film about the dangers of syphilis. B&W; 50m. **DIR:** Dwain Esper. 1934

SEX WITH A SMILE ★1/2 Silly, badly dubbed Italian film featuring five short stories on sexual misunderstandings. Marty Feldman's section produces some laughs. Rated R for nudity and sex. 100m. **DIR:** Sergio Martino. **CAST:** Marty Feldman, Edwige Fenech, Sydne Rome, Barbara Bouchet, Dayle Haddon. 1976

SEXTETTE 💔 A dreadful movie that documents the vulgar campiness of the 80-year-old Mae West. Rated R. 91m. **DIR:** Ken Hughes, Irving Rapper. **CAST:** Mae West, Timothy Dalton, Dom DeLuise, Tony Curtis, Ringo Starr, George Hamilton, George Raft. 1978

SEXTON BLAKE AND THE HOODED TERROR ★★1/2 One of a series of British mysteries featuring Sexton Blake, a detective in the Sherlock Holmes tradition. He's on the trail of an international gang known as the Hooded Terror, led by a millionaire (Tod Slaughter). Slaughter, Britain's king of Grand Guignol, is the best reason to see this, even though he's relatively restrained in a supporting role. B&W; 69m. **DIR:** George King. **CAST:** George Curzon, Tod Slaughter, Greta Gynt. 1938

SEXUAL INTENT ★★ Libidinous lothario wines, dines, and rips off women for a living, but he's about to face a career crisis. Based on a true story, with Gary Hudson as the Sweetheart Scammer, who took over forty women for a ride. Now they're in the driver's seat, and what they've got planned for Mr. Romance is a vigilante feminist's dream come true. Rated R for nudity, language, and adult situations. 88m. **DIR:** Kurt Mac Carley. **CAST:** Gary Hudson, Michele Brin, Sarah Hill. 1993

SEXUAL MALICE 💔 Suspenseless erotic thriller centered around an unhappily married businesswoman who has a one-night stand with a male stripper. Rated R for sexual situations and strong language. (An "adult" version, not rated, also is available.) 93/96m. **DIR:** Jag Mundhra. **CAST:** Edward Albert, Chad McQueen, John Laughlin, Diana Barton, Samantha Phillips. 1993 DVD

S.F.W. ★★★ The media take a much deserved skewering in this angry and offbeat love story. Writer/director Jefery Levy has a lot to say about the violence and madness perpetrated by media that reduce everything to a catchphrase. Rated R for excessive profanity, off-camera violence, sexual situations, and brief nudity. 94m. **DIR:** Jefery Levy. **CAST:** Stephen Dorff, Reese Witherspoon. **1994**

SGT. BILKO (TV SERIES) ★★★1/2 Master Sergeant Ernie Bilko was indeed a master of bilking. His job was to helm the motor pool. But his mission in life was to con anyone who could cough up a buck or two. For Phil Silvers, this was the role of a lifetime. A superb supporting cast added to the hilarity. The series, originally named *You'll Never Get Rich*, became *The Phil Silvers Show* and, finally, in syndication, *SGT. Bilko*. Two episodes are included per tape. B&W; 60m. each tape. **DIR:** Al DeCaprio. **CAST:** Phil Silvers, Harvey Lembeck, Paul Ford, Joe E. Ross, Allan Melvin, Herbie Faye, Maurice Gosfield, Billy Sands, Elisabeth Fraser. **1955–1959**

SGT. BILKO ★★1/2 Phil Silvers has nothing to worry about; long after this humdrum film adaptation has vanished, he'll still be remembered for having created the part on television. Steve Martin isn't bad in the role, but Andy Breckman's screenplay doesn't provide much material. "Wild 'n' Crazy" Steve can't generate laughs in a vacuum, and that's all he has to work with here. Rated PG for mild profanity and blue humor. 94m. **DIR:** Jonathan Lynn. **CAST:** Steve Martin, Dan Aykroyd, Phil Hartman, Glenne Headly, Daryl Mitchell. **1996 DVD**

SGT. KABUKIMAN N.Y.P.D. ★★★ Wacky cop movie with a sci-fi twist. A New York detective inherits the superhuman powers of the Kabuki and changes into a colorfully dressed, if not totally competent, crime fighter. Some bad acting and a tongue-in-cheek attitude make this fun to watch with friends. Rated PG-13 for violence, profanity, and simulated sex. 99m. **DIR:** Lloyd Kaufman, Michael Herz. **CAST:** Rick Gianasi, Susan Byun, Bill Weeden, Thomas Crnkovich, Noble Lee Lester, Brick Bronsky, Larry Robinson, Pamela Alster, Shaler McClure, Fumio Furuya. **1991 DVD**

SGT. PEPPER'S LONELY HEARTS CLUB BAND 💣 Universally panned musical. Rated PG. 111m. **DIR:** Michael Schultz. **CAST:** The Bee Gees, Peter Frampton, Donald Pleasence, George Burns. **1978**

SHACK-OUT ON 101 ★★★1/2 This odd blend of character study and espionage thriller, which takes place at a highway hash house, involves some of the most colorful patrons you'll ever run across. Perky Terry Moore plays the waitress who helps the authorities close in on the men who have sabotage plans for a local chemical plant, and Lee Marvin is at his most audacious as Slob, a name he does his best to live up to. B&W; 80m. **DIR:** Edward Dein. **CAST:** Frank Lovejoy, Terry Moore, Lee Marvin, Keenan Wynn, Whit Bissell. **1955**

SHADES OF LOVE: CHAMPAGNE FOR TWO ★★★ Enjoyable romp features a likable chef who becomes the unlikely roommate of a harried architect. Made for Canadian TV, this *Shades of Love* romance has more general audience appeal than anything found in the Romance Theatre collection. Not rated; contains mild profanity, nudity, and sex. 82m. **DIR:** Lewis

Furey. **CAST:** Nicholas Campbell, Kirsten Bishop, Carol Ann Francis, Terry Haig. **1987**

SHADES OF LOVE: LILAC DREAM ★★ Mystery and romance combine in this tale of a young woman left brokenhearted. Then a storm leaves a man with no memory on the shore of her island. She nurses him back to health. Gradually, his past comes back to haunt her. 83m. **DIR:** Marc Voizard. **CAST:** Dack Rambo, Susan Almgren. **1987**

SHADES OF LOVE: SINCERELY, VIOLET ★★ In this mediocre story of love and romance, a professor (Patricia Phillips) becomes a cat burglar named Violet. She is caught in the act by Mark Janson (Simon MacCorkindale) who tries to reform her. 86m. **DIR:** Mort Ransen. **CAST:** Simon MacCorkindale, Patricia Phillips. **1987**

SHADES OF LOVE: THE ROSE CAFE ★★ Dreams can sometimes hide the truth, and in the case of Courtney Fairchild (Linda Smith), her dream of opening a restaurant has hidden her feelings for the men in her life. 84m. **DIR:** Daniele J. Suissa. **CAST:** Parker Stevenson, Linda Smith. **1987**

SHADEY ★★1/2 Mildly entertaining British comedy about Shadey (Antony Sher), a man who has the ability to "think pictures onto film." These little movies turn out to be prophecies that are ultimately fulfilled. Plodding one moment, all-out bizarre the next. Rated PG-13 for violence and profanity. 90m. **DIR:** Philip Saville. **CAST:** Antony Sher, Billie Whitelaw, Patrick Macnee, Katherine Helmond. **1987**

SHADOW, THE ★★★ Enjoyable, well-mounted, but ultimately forgettable film resurrects 1930s pulp and radio hero, The Shadow. As the one "who knows what evil lurks in the hearts of men," Alec Baldwin is more effective in makeup than out. Here, The Shadow attempts to thwart the evil plans of a descendant of Genghis Khan. Rated PG-13 for violence. 107m. **DIR:** Russell Mulcahy. **CAST:** Alec Baldwin, John Lone, Penelope Ann Miller, Peter Boyle, Ian McKellen, Tim Curry, Jonathan Winters, Sab Shimono, Andre Gregory. **1994 DVD**

SHADOW BOX, THE ★★★ A fine cast and smooth direction highlight this powerful story of one day in the lives of three terminally ill patients at an experimental hospice in California. Adapted from the prize-winning Broadway stage play. 100m. **DIR:** Paul Newman. **CAST:** Joanne Woodward, Christopher Plummer, Valerie Harper, James Broderick, Melinda Dillon, Sylvia Sidney, John Considine. **1980**

SHADOW CONSPIRACY ★★ Presidential aide Charlie Sheen suddenly finds himself the inexplicable target of steely-eyed hit man Stephen Lang. Soon Sheen is running for his life while trying to unravel the mystery, and his only ally is chief of staff Donald Sutherland (sporting his best "trust me" leer). Farfetched and silly, with a climactic attempt to assassinate the chief executive by means of a toy helicopter! Rated R for violence and profanity. 103m. **DIR:** George Pan Cosmatos. **CAST:** Charlie Sheen, Donald Sutherland, Linda Hamilton, Sam Waterston, Ben Gazzara, Stephen Lang. **1996**

SHADOW CREATURE ★★1/2 Enjoyably hokey horror spoof in which Cleveland is terrorized by a half-man, half-zebra mussel mutant. Not rated; contains gore, sexual situations, substance abuse, and profanity. 93m. DIR: James Gribbins. CAST: Shane Minor, Tracy Godard, Dennis Keefe, Anthony Chrysostom. 1995

SHADOW DANCING ★★★ Surprisingly entertaining suspense-thriller about an aspiring dancer who desperately wants to become a member of a dance ensemble. Her obsession is the perfect target for the resurrection of a former star, who died fifty years earlier in the same theater. Rated R for violence. 95m. DIR: Lewis Furey. CAST: Nadine Van Der Velde, John Colicos, Christopher Plummer. 1989

SHADOW HUNTER ★★★ After a needlessly seamy prologue, writer-director J. S. Cardone's moody made-for-cable thriller settles comfortably into territory mined by mystery author Tony Hillerman. Burned-out big city cop Scott Glenn muffs an assignment to extradite a killer from a Navajo reservation, and then joins the forces tracking the escaped maniac ... who can become a *skinwalker* and invade the dreams of his pursuers. Rated R for profanity, nudity, and violence. 98m. DIR: J. S. Cardone. CAST: Scott Glenn, Angela Alvarado, Robert Beltran. 1993

SHADOW OF A DOUBT ★★★1/2 This disturbing suburban drama, Alfred Hitchcock's personal favorite among his films, probes the hidden facets of a family with a secret. Teenager Charlie adores the uncle after whom she was named and is delighted when he comes to stay for an indefinite period ... until she begins to suspect that "dear Uncle Charlie" may be the killer wanted by the police for having sent several widows to their premature reward. Not rated; a bit intense for younger viewers. B&W; 108m. DIR: Alfred Hitchcock. CAST: Joseph Cotten, Teresa Wright, Macdonald Carey, Henry Travers, Hume Cronyn. 1943

SHADOW OF A SCREAM ★★1/2 When a police detective goes undercover to trap a suspected sex killer, she not only becomes attracted to her prey but learns that she harbors a dark nature of her own. Filmed in Ireland (but set in Boston!), this is above average for the erotic thriller genre, though the weak conclusion hurts it. Rated R for gore, nudity, sexual situations, and profanity. 84m. DIR: Howard McCain. CAST: Athena Massey, David Chokachi, Timothy Busfield, Cyril O'Reilly. 1997

SHADOW OF CHINA ★★★1/2 An idealistic Chinese revolutionary escapes to Hong Kong where he builds a financial empire. His dream of changing China through his business connections is threatened by the exposure of his early money-making schemes and his heritage. Rated PG-13 for violence. 100m. DIR: Mitsuo Yanagimachi. CAST: John Lone, Vivian Wu, Sammi Davis. 1991

SHADOW OF THE EAGLE ★★1/2 John Wayne's second serial for Mascot Pictures is another one of those stolen inventions–kidnapped scientist affairs, this time masterminded by a mysterious criminal known as The Eagle, who likes to write his threats in the sky with an airplane. Although a bit creaky, this is fun to watch. B&W; 12 chapters. DIR: Ford Beebe. CAST: John Wayne, Dorothy Gulliver, Walter Miller, Kenneth Harlan, Yakima Canutt. 1932

SHADOW OF THE THIN MAN ★★★★ Fourth in the series, with sleuths Nick and Nora Charles (William Powell and Myrna Loy) dividing their time between mysteries, Asta the wonder dog, and a stroller-bound Nick Jr. (who arrived in the previous film). Barry Nelson and Donna Reed are among the innocents this time around, and the story concerns dire deeds at the local race track. Another sumptuous serving of sophisticated fun. B&W; 97m. DIR: W. S. Van Dyke. CAST: William Powell, Myrna Loy, Sam Levene, Donna Reed, Barry Nelson. 1941

SHADOW OF THE WOLF ★★1/2 This gorgeously filmed Arctic adventure–soap about the encroachment of white men on Eskimo land and culture during the 1930s is also part mediocre crime-drama. Lou Diamond Phillips is physically convincing as an outcast Inuit hunter in a mediocre story heightened by enthralling anthropological detail and scenery. Rated PG-13 for violence and language. 108m. DIR: Jacques Dorfmann. CAST: Lou Diamond Phillips, Toshiro Mifune, Jennifer Tilly, Donald Sutherland. 1993

SHADOW PLAY ★★ Dee Wallace Stone plays a Manhattan playwright who is obsessed by the tragic death of her fiancé seven years earlier. Indeed, she becomes possessed by his ghost, which inspires her to write awful poetry. Rated R for profanity and violence. 101m. DIR: Susan Shadburne. CAST: Dee Wallace, Cloris Leachman, Ron Kuhlman, Barry Laws. 1986

SHADOW RIDERS, THE ★★★1/2 The stars of the superb made-for-television Western *The Sacketts* reunite for another adventure inspired by a Louis L'Amour tale. This time, brothers Tom Selleck, Sam Elliott, and Jeffrey Osterhage take on a white slaver. Good, old-fashioned cowboy fun. 96m. DIR: Andrew V. McLaglen. CAST: Sam Elliott, Tom Selleck, Ben Johnson, Katharine Ross, Geoffrey Lewis, Jeff Osterhage, Gene Evans, Harry Carey Jr., Jane Greer. 1982 DVD

SHADOW STRIKES, THE ★★ Loosely based on *The Ghost of the Manor*, one of hundreds of stories featuring the mysterious Shadow, this effort finds Rod La Rocque on the trail of a gang of crooks who have murdered his father, a prominent attorney. B&W; 61m. DIR: Lynn Shores. CAST: Rod La Rocque, Lynn Anders, Norman Ainsley. 1937

SHADOW WARRIORS ★★ Because it was coproduced by Roger Corman and the Russian studio Mosfilm, this *Robocop* rip-off at least has some interesting Russian settings. The special effects are okay, but the story is forgettable nonsense. Rated R for violence and profanity. 80m. DIR: Rick Jacobson. CAST: Terry O'Quinn, Patrick Cavanaugh, Evan Lurie. 1995

SHADOW ZONE: THE UNDEAD EXPRESS ★★ Juvenile horror movie features a teen who discovers vampires in the abandoned subway tunnels of New York City. No blood or violence in this made-for-cable original, so it is suitable for all audiences. But the acting is so stiff, it's hard to tell who is living and who is undead. Not rated. 95m. DIR: Stephen Williams. CAST: Ron Silver, Chauncey Leopardi, Natanya Ross, Tony T. Johnson, Ron White. 1996

SHADOWLANDS ★★★★1/2 Based on screenwriter William Nicholson's play, this exquisite film chronicles the risqué (for its time) love affair between author and lecturer C. S. Lewis (Anthony Hopkins) and an American fan/writer, Joy Gresham (Debra Winger). An emotionally fulfilling and memorable motion picture. Rated PG for brief profanity. 130m. DIR: Richard Attenborough. CAST: Anthony Hopkins, Debra Winger, Edward Hardwicke, John Wood, Michael Denison, Peter Firth. 1993 DVD

SHADOWS ★★★ A zealous young minister takes it upon himself to convert the local Chinese laundrymen. Lon Chaney as Yen Sin gives a moving performance as the man who must confront the self-righteous churchman, played by Harrison Ford (no relation to today's star). A colorful cast of good character actors help to make this a thought-provoking film. Silent. B&W; 70m. DIR: Tom Forman. CAST: Lon Chaney Sr., Harrison Ford, Marguerite de la Motte, Walter Long. 1922 DVD

SHADOWS AND FOG ★★ Only the parade of familiar faces engages much interest in this all-star, brooding misfire from writer-director-star Woody Allen. Rated PG-13 for violence. B&W; 86m. DIR: Woody Allen. CAST: Woody Allen, Kathy Bates, John Cusack, Mia Farrow, Jodie Foster, Robert Joy, Wallace Shawn, Kurtwood Smith, Josef Sommer. 1992

SHADOWS IN THE STORM ★★ Umpteenth version of a daydreaming nebbish's fatal obsession for a young beauty. Ned Beatty stars as a corporate librarian who meets vixen Mia Sara and finds himself going totally out of control. Rated R for violence and profanity. 90m. DIR: Terrell Tannen. CAST: Ned Beatty, Mia Sara. 1989

SHADOWS OF FORGOTTEN ANCESTORS ★★★★ A brilliant, epic story of star-crossed lovers set against the panoramic background of the Carpathian mountains. A visual masterpiece. In Ukrainian with English subtitles. 99m. DIR: Sergi Parajanov. CAST: Ivan Mikolaichuk, Larisa Kadochnikova. 1964

SHADOWZONE ★★1/2 A NASA dream-research experiment goes awry, releasing beings from a different dimension. Good gore effects highlight this suspenseful tale. Rated R for violence and gore. 88m. DIR: J. S. Cardone. CAST: David Beecroft, James Hong, Shawn Weatherly, Louise Fletcher. 1989 DVD

SHADRACH ★★★1/2 Notable debut for filmmaker Susanna Styron, who coadapts father William Styron's short story about an elderly black man who shows up at the Virginia plantation where he once worked as a slave hoping to be buried there. Even though the film never lacks sincerity, it does tend to skirt several important issues. Rated PG-13 for language and adult situations. 88m. DIR: Susanna Styron. CAST: Harvey Keitel, Andie MacDowell, John Franklin Sawyer, Daniel Treat, Scott Terra. 1998 DVD

SHAFT (1971) ★★★ One of the best black films from the late 1960s and early 1970s. There is plenty of action and raw energy as private eye Shaft (Richard Roundtree) battles the bad guys in order to rescue a kidnapped woman. Great musical score by Isaac Hayes. Rated PG for violence. 100m. DIR: Gordon Parks Jr. CAST: Richard Roundtree, Charles Cioffi, Moses Gunn. 1971 DVD

•SHAFT (2000) ★★★★ Ernest Tidyman's sassy, street-smart private eye gets a fresh spin in this more politically astute remake, which Samuel L. Jackson dominates like a force of nature. He's a dedicated cop who, tired of a system that tolerates racism and seems hell-bent on putting the bad guys back on the street, hands in his badge and strikes out on his own. The case that drives this taut story concerns a pampered rich snot who kills a young man and then dares our hero to do anything about it; Shaft rises to the challenge with marvelous style. The cast is strong, Isaac Hayes's Oscar-winning theme gets things off to a proper start, and director/co-scripter John Singleton concludes his tale with an unexpected moment of cynicism. Even given all these dynamic elements, you'll not be able to take your eyes off Jackson. Rated R for violence, profanity, drug use, and sexual content. 99m. DIR: John Singleton. CAST: Samuel L. Jackson, Vanessa L. Williams, Jeffrey Wright, Christian Bale, Busta Rhymes, Dan Hedaya, Toni Collette, Richard Roundtree. 2000

SHAFT'S BIG SCORE! ★★★ Obligatory first sequel to the original *Shaft* is one of the best blaxploitation action films of the Seventies. Topflight violence competes for screen time with pungent dialogue by *French Connection* scriptwriter Ernest Tidyman. Ball-of-twine plot has Shaft take on the mob. Rated R for profanity and mayhem. 104m. DIR: Gordon Parks Jr. CAST: Richard Roundtree, Moses Gunn, Joseph Mascolo. 1972 DVD

SHAG, THE MOVIE ★★★1/2 This appealing film didn't get a fair shake on the big screen, which was surprising, considering the delightful cast and solid performances. It's set in Myrtle Beach, S.C., circa 1963, and chronicles a last fling by a covey of southern belles before their society debut takes them away from the realities of their age. The title, incidentally, connotes a popular dance style. Rated PG for brief nudity, the film is harmless enough for most age-groups. 96m. DIR: Zelda Barron. CAST: Phoebe Cates, Scott Coffey, Bridget Fonda, Annabeth Gish, Page Hannah, Tyrone Power. 1989

SHAGGY D.A., THE ★★ So-so sequel to Disney's far superior *The Shaggy Dog*, this retread stars Dean Jones as the victim of an ancient curse that turns him into a canine at the worst of moments. Rated G. 91m. DIR: Robert Stevenson. CAST: Dean Jones, Tim Conway, Suzanne Pleshette. 1976

SHAGGY DOG, THE ★★★1/2 An ancient spell turns a boy into a sheepdog, and the fur flies in this slapstick Disney fantasy. Many of the gags are good, but the film sometimes drags. 104m. DIR: Charles Barton. CAST: Fred MacMurray, Jean Hagen, Tommy Kirk, Annette Funicello. 1959

SHAKA ZULU ★★★1/2 Epic chronicling the rise of Shaka, king of the Zulus. Set against the emergence of British power in Africa during the early nineteenth century, this film provides some valuable insights into comparative cultures despite some poor editing and an overly dramatic, inappropriate musical score. Not rated, this release contains graphic violence and frequent nudity. 300m. DIR: William C. Faure. CAST: Edward Fox, Robert Powell, Trevor Howard, Fiona Fullerton, Christopher Lee, Henry Cole, Roy Dotrice, Gordon Jackson. 1986 DVD

SHAKE HANDS WITH THE DEVIL ★★★★ In 1921 Dublin, an Irish-American student (Don Murray) innocently becomes involved in rebel activities and finds himself a fugitive. He joins an IRA cell led by

James Cagney, whom he at first admires, but soon comes to realize is a murderous fanatic. Another spellbinding performance by the magnificent Cagney in this hard-hitting, action-filled drama. B&W; 110m. DIR: Michael Anderson. CAST: James Cagney, Don Murray, Dana Wynter, Glynis Johns, Cyril Cusack, Michael Redgrave, Sybil Thorndike, Richard Harris. 1959

SHAKER RUN ★★ A New Zealand laboratory accidentally creates a deadly virus. Not rated, but the equivalent of a PG for violence and profanity. 91m. DIR: Bruce Morrison. CAST: Cliff Robertson, Leif Garrett, Lisa Harrow, Shane Briant. 1985

SHAKES THE CLOWN ★★1/2 Stand-up comedian Bobcat Goldthwait makes his directorial debut with this clown-out-of-circus tale. Goldthwait is the clown who hits rock bottom. Former *Brady* mom Florence Henderson is downright hilarious as a clown groupie. Rated R for profanity. 88m. DIR: Bob Goldthwait. CAST: Bob Goldthwait, Julie Brown, Paul Dooley, Florence Henderson. 1991 DVD

SHAKESPEARE IN LOVE ★★★★★ This ingenious pastiche is an erotic and enormously witty blend of history and fabrication. The setting is London in the summer of 1593, where young playwright Shakespeare has developed an acute case of writer's block which can be traced to his lack of captivating female companionship. Then the inconceivable happens: an impassioned actor reads for the role of Romeo and Shakespeare discovers that this talented thespian is actually Viola De Lesseps (Paltrow), a young woman of title and privilege unwilling to abide by the strictures of her era. Viola willingly throws herself into a double deception: tragedian in disguise by day, and clandestine lover, with Will, by night. What *fun!* Rated R for nudity and earthy sexual content. 113m. DIR: John Madden. CAST: Gwyneth Paltrow, Joseph Fiennes, Geoffrey Rush, Colin Firth, Ben Affleck, Judi Dench, Simon Callow. 1998 DVD

SHAKESPEARE WALLAH ★★★★ A family troupe of Shakespearean players performs to disinterested, dwindling audiences in the new India (*wallah* is Hindustani for *peddler*). Frustrated sensuality, social humiliation, dedication to a dying cause, and familial devotion are rendered here with the sensitivity and delicacy that we have come to expect from director James Ivory. Madhur Jaffrey won the best actress award at the Berlin Festival for her satiric rendering of a Bombay musical star. B&W; 114m. DIR: James Ivory. CAST: Shashi Kapoor, Geoffrey Kendall, Laura Liddell, Felicity Kendal, Madhur Jaffrey. 1964

SHAKIEST GUN IN THE WEST, THE ★★ This picture is a remake of *The Paleface* with Don Knotts in the Bob Hope role. A fun family film. 100m. DIR: Alan Rafkin. CAST: Don Knotts, Barbara Rhoades, Jackie Coogan, Don Barry. 1968

SHAKING THE TREE ★★1/2 This bland male-bonding film will seem familiar to anyone who's seen *Diner.* A lot of similar ground is covered in telling the story of a group of pals entering into a new era of responsibility as adults. PG-13 for profanity. 97m. DIR: Duane Clark. CAST: Arye Gross, Doug Savant, Steven Wilde, Courteney Cox, Gale Hansen. 1992

•SHAKMA ★★ Probably the world's first slasher film with a baboon as the villain. Rated R for violence. 101m. DIR: Hugh Parks, Tom Logan. CAST: Christopher Atkins, Amanda Wyss, Ari Meyers, Roddy McDowall. 1990

SHALAKO ★★ Odd British Western about European immigrants Sean Connery, Brigitte Bardot, Stephen Boyd, Jack Hawkins, and Honor Blackman menaced by Apaches in the Old West. 113m. DIR: Edward Dmytryk. CAST: Sean Connery, Brigitte Bardot, Stephen Boyd, Jack Hawkins, Honor Blackman, Woody Strode. 1968 DVD

SHALL WE DANCE? (1937) ★★★★1/2 Fred Astaire and Ginger Rogers team up (as usual) as dance partners in this musical comedy. The only twist is they must pretend to be married in order to get the job. Great songs include "Let's Call the Whole Thing Off." B&W; 109m. DIR: Mark Sandrich. CAST: Fred Astaire, Ginger Rogers, Eric Blore, Edward Everett Horton. 1937

SHALL WE DANCE? (1996) ★★★★ Writer-director Masayuki Suo's charming little drama concerns a repressed and weary businessman who secretly enrolls in a ballroom dance class and discovers that he actually enjoys the challenge and endless exercise. It's easy to see why this delightful film collected all thirteen Japanese Academy Awards. In Japanese with English subtitles. Rated PG for no particular reason. 118m. DIR: Masayuki Suo. CAST: Koji Yakusho, Tamiyo Kusakari, Naoto Takenaka, Eriko Watanabe, Akira Emoto, Yu Tokui, Hiromasa Taguchi, Reiko Kusamura. 1996

SHALLOW GRAVE (1987) 🎞 Four college girls witness a killing. Not rated; contains violence and nudity. 90m. DIR: Richard Styles. CAST: Tony March, Lisa Stahl, Tom Law. 1987

SHALLOW GRAVE (1994) ★★1/2 Although it tries for the dark satire of *Blood Simple* or *Pulp Fiction,* this extremely gory Scottish thriller just isn't as shrewd or sophisticated. Three flatmates find a suitcase filled with cash after their new tenant dies of a drug overdose, and they elect to dispose of the body and keep the money, rather than alert the police. Greed then fuels hostility and suspicion. Rated R for profanity, violence, and brief nudity. 91m. DIR: Danny Boyle. CAST: Kerry Fox, Chris Eccleston, Ewan McGregor, Ken Scott, Keith Allen. 1994 DVD

SHAME (1987) ★★★★ While on a motorcycling vacation, a lawyer (Deborra-Lee Furness) ends up in an out-of-the-way Australian town where young women are terrorized and ritually raped by a gang of young toughs. So the two-fisted Furness decides to make them pay for their crimes. It sounds corny, but *Shame* is really quite effective. Rated R for violence and profanity. 90m. DIR: Steve Jodrell. CAST: Deborra-Lee Furness, Tony Barry, Simone Buchanan. 1987

SHAME (1992) ★★1/2 Stranger in town Amanda Donohoe learns some hard lessons when she encourages a rape victim to fight back, and in return becomes the next victim of the vicious gang. This seedy little morality tale was made for cable and features a strong performance from Donohoe. Not rated; conins adult situations. 91m. DIR: Dan Lerner. CAST: manda Donohoe, Dean Stockwell. 1992

HAMELESS ★★ The culture of London drug abuse seen from the points of view of a rich young addict Elizabeth Hurley) and a cop on the breaking point Joss Ackland)—two people headed for a collision. competently made but uninvolving thriller. Rated R or nudity, sexual situations, drug use, and strong vi-lence. 99m. DIR: Henry Cole. CAST: Elizabeth Hurley, . Thomas Howell, Joss Ackland, Jeremy Brett, Claire loom. 1994 DVD

HAMELESS OLD LADY, THE ★★★1/2 Bertolt recht's reminiscences of his grandmother provided ie basis for this comedy about a 70-year-old woman, vonderfully played by the great character actress ylvie. A joyous movie. In French with English subti-es. 95m. DIR: Rene Allio. CAST: Sylvie, Malka Ri-ovska, Victor Lanoux. 1965

HAMING, THE ★★ A spinster schoolteacher is aped by a janitor and continues to have sex with him ntil she is exposed and then ostracized by the chool. This film is rated R for sex. 90m. DIR: Marvin . Chomsky. CAST: Anne Heywood, Donald Pleasence, tobert Vaughn, Carolyn Jones, Dorothy Malone, Dana lcar. 1975

HAMPOO ★★★★ Star Warren Beatty and Robert owne cowrote this perceptive comedy of morals, nost of them bad, which focuses on a hedonistic everly Hills hairdresser played by Beatty. Although ortions come perilously close to slapstick, the bal-nce is an insightful study of the pain caused by peo-le who try for no-strings-attached relationships. tated R—sexuality and adult themes. 112m. DIR: lal Ashby. CAST: Warren Beatty, Julie Christie, Lee irant, Jack Warden, Goldie Hawn, Carrie Fisher. 1975

HAMUS ★★1/2 An okay detective thriller, with 3urt Reynolds playing Burt Reynolds. Nothing new, out lots of action keeps things moving along in this tory of a private eye investigating a weapons-smug-jling ring. Rated PG. 106m. DIR: Buzz Kulik. CAST: 3urt Reynolds, Dyan Cannon, John P. Ryan. 1973

•SHANDRA, THE JUNGLE GIRL ♥ Scientists hunt a jungle queen who kills men with her physical :harms. Made-for-video soft-core erotica. Not rated; :ontains nudity and heavy sexual content. 80m. DIR: Cybil Richards. CAST: Lisa Throw, Venesa Talor. 1999

SHANE ★★★★★ Shane is surely among the best Vesterns ever made. Alan Ladd plays the title role, he mysterious stranger who helps a group of home-steaders in their struggle against the cattlemen. l18m. DIR: George Stevens. CAST: Alan Ladd, Jean \rthur, Jack Palance, Van Heflin, Ben Johnson, Elisha Cook Jr., Brandon de Wilde. 1953

SHANGHAI COBRA, THE ★★ Routine poverty-row Charlie Chan programmer, from Monogram Pic-tures. A murderer stages his killings to make them resemble snake attacks. B&W; 64m. DIR: Phil Karl-son. CAST: Sidney Toler, Benson Fong, Mantan More-land, Joan Barclay. 1945

SHANGHAI EXPRESS ★★★★ Marlene Dietrich's trademark role during the first stage of her Holly-wood career has been copied but no one has ever equaled her sultry appeal. She plays a woman of du-bious reputation who causes the downfall of a Chi-

nese warlord to save the life and reputation of the man she really loves. B&W; 80m. DIR: Josef von Sternberg. CAST: Marlene Dietrich, Warner Oland, Anna May Wong, Clive Brook, Eugene Pallette, Louise Closser Hale, Gustav von Seyffertitz. 1932

SHANGHAI GESTURE, THE ★★ Camp melo-drama—an excursion into depravity in mysterious Shanghai. Walter Huston wants to close the gam-bling casino run by Ona Munson, who has a hold over his daughter Gene Tierney. Atmospheric idiocy. B&W; 106m. DIR: Josef von Sternberg. CAST: Gene Tierney, Ona Munson, Walter Huston, Albert Basser-man, Eric Blore, Victor Mature, Maria Ouspenskaya, Mike Mazurki. 1942 DVD

SHANGHAI JOE ★★ One of the last spaghetti West-erns to incorporate martial arts. A young Chinese la-borer wants to become a cowboy, but he is faced with racial prejudice. He uses his brain and kung-fu skills to fight back, and in the meantime, uncovers an ille-gal-alien smuggling ring. Lots of kung-fu action. Rated R for violence. 97m. DIR: Mario Caiano. CAST: Chen Lee, Carla Romanelli, Klaus Kinski, Giacomo Rossi-Stuart, Gordon Mitchell. 1973

•SHANGHAI NOON ★★★ As a Chinese imperial guard, Jackie Chan teams up with a Sundance Kid–type bandit to rescue a Chinese princess. Set primarily in Nevada circa 1881, this East-meets-West actioner doesn't sweat the small stuff (such as his-torical accuracy), but focuses instead on a kaleido-scope of silly gags and corny showdowns. In a depar-ture from the Chan-dominated film format, Wilson shares center stage as the action sequences take a backseat to the comic romp. Rated PG-13 for vio-lence, profanity, and sexual innuendo. 105m. DIR: Tom Dey. CAST: Jackie Chan, Owen C. Wilson, Lucy Liu. 2000

SHANGHAI SURPRISE ♥ Madonna plays an up-tight missionary in Shanghai, 1938. She recruits a con artist (Sean Penn) to help her recover eleven hundred pounds of opium. Rated PG. 93m. DIR: Jim Goddard. CAST: Sean Penn, Madonna, Paul Freeman, Richard Griffiths, Philip Sayer, Victor Wong. 1986

SHANGHAI TRIAD ★★★1/2 A young country-bumpkin cousin to an elderly 1930s gang lord is called to Shanghai to wait on the mobster's girl-friend in this gorgeously shot crime-melodrama. The moll reluctantly takes the boy under wing until her mob sugar daddy is nearly killed in a violent power struggle. They all slip away to an isolated island hide-out where the spoiled femme fatale is dogged by tragedy. In Mandarin with English subtitles. Rated R for simulated sex and violence. 107m. DIR: Yimou Zhang. CAST: Gong Li, Li Baotian, Shun Chun, Wang Xiao, Jiang Baoying. 1995

SHANTY TRAMP ★★1/2 It's the sexy sharecrop-per's daughter versus the hypocritical evangelist in this drive-in classic. Not rated; contains nudity and simulated sex. B&W; 70m. DIR: Joseph Prieto. CAST: Lee Holland, Kenneth Douglas. 1966

SHAOLIN TEMPLE ★★★★ The best kung fu film since Enter the Dragon, this period piece, set in sev-enth-century China, traces the history of the Shaolin Temple. It stars the country's top martial arts ex-perts, yet characterization and plot are not slighted.

In Chinese with English subtitles. Not rated, the film has violence. 111m. DIR: Chang Hsin Yen. CAST: Li Lin Jei. 1982

•SHAPESHIFTER ★★ Unimpressive teen fantasy has a boy with the power to morph into whatever he can see or touch. Rated PG for mild violence. 90m. DIR: Philip Browning. CAST: Paul Nolan. 1999

SHARK! (MANEATERS!) ♥ Waterlogged undersea adventure. Rated PG. 92m. DIR: Samuel Fuller. CAST: Burt Reynolds, Barry Sullivan, Arthur Kennedy, Silvia Pinal, Enrique Lucero. 1969

•SHARK ATTACK ★★ There's not much bite in this made-for-cable adventure-thriller. Casper Van Dien plays a marine biologist who suspects that the sharks offshore may be the byproduct of a sinister experiment. The film is one awful cliché after another. Rated R for language and violence. 95m. DIR: Bob Misiorowski. CAST: Casper Van Dien, Ernie Hudson, Bentley Mitchum, Jennifer McShane. 1999 DVD

SHARK HUNTER, THE ♥ A Caribbean island recluse beats up sharks and searches for buried treasure. Not rated, but the equivalent of a PG for violence and brief nudity. 92m. DIR: Enzo G. Castellari. CAST: Franco Nero, Jorge Luke, Mike Forrest. 1984

SHARK'S TREASURE ♥ Good guys and bad guys search for sunken treasure. Rated PG for violence. 95m. DIR: Cornel Wilde. CAST: Cornel Wilde, Yaphet Kotto, John Neilson, Cliff Osmond. 1975

SHARKY'S MACHINE ★★★1/2 This is one of the best cop thrillers ever made. It's exciting, suspenseful, funny, and intelligent, so good it joins 48 Hrs., Dirty Harry, and Tightrope as the best of the genre. Burt Reynolds stars under his own direction as an undercover cop who has a compulsion to crack down on a new wave of crime in his city. Rated R because of violence and profanity. 119m. DIR: Burt Reynolds. CAST: Burt Reynolds, Rachel Ward, Brian Keith, Bernie Casey, Vittorio Gassman, Charles Durning. 1981 DVD

SHARON'S SECRET ★★★1/2 Taut thriller about a 16-year-old accused of slaughtering and mutilating her parents. The teen is almost catatonic and refuses to speak, but is she the real killer? The complex plot of this made-for-cable original will keep you guessing right to the end. Not rated; contains violence. 91m. DIR: Michael Scott. CAST: Mel Harris, Alex McArthur, Candace Cameron, Gregg Henry. 1995

SHARPE (TV SERIES) ★★★★ Twelve volumes based on the British TV series starring Sean Bean as a gutsy British soldier during the campaign against Napoleon. Each volume (Sharpe's Rifles, Sharpe's Enemy, etc.) is an exciting adventure, spellbinding, with large-scale battle scenes and believable characters. Not rated; contains violence and sexual situations. 12 volumes, each 100m. DIR: Tom Clegg. CAST: Sean Bean, Assumpta Serna, Hugh Fraser, Brian Cox. 1995

•SHATTER ★★ Stuart Whitman stars as the title character, a hip man of action who finds himself being deceived and set up as a patsy. Of course, he doesn't take this sitting down. Can't hold up to the test of time. Not rated; contains nudity and violence. 90m. DIR: Michael Carreras. CAST: Stuart Whitman, Peter Cushing, Anton Duffring. 1974

SHATTER DEAD ★★★ This zombie epic is definitely not for everyone. In this story, no one can die, so zombies walk among us. Director Scooter McCrae goes for the excess-is-good approach and in the case of the zombie stuff, this is some of the best since George Romero first woke the dead, but a sex scene goes too far. Not rated; contains violence, gore, profanity, and a graphic sex scene. 85m. DIR: Scooter McCrae. CAST: Stark Raven, Flora Fauna. 1994

SHATTERED (1972) ★★ Peter Finch plays a mild-mannered, neurotic businessman who picks up a hitchhiker (Linda Hayden) only to have her attach herself to him. As a result, he slowly begins to lose his sanity. Shelley Winters plays Finch's obnoxious wife. Like a lot of British thrillers, this one has little action until it explodes in the final fifteen minutes. Rated R for profanity and violence. 100m. DIR: Alastair Reid. CAST: Peter Finch, Shelley Winters, Colin Blakely, John Stride, Linda Hayden. 1972

SHATTERED (1991) ★★1/2 Director Wolfgang Petersen's adaptation of Richard Neely's novel is a well-acted and fairly suspenseful flick about a man who wakes up in a hospital remembering nothing of his past. Even though his wife has pictures of them together, our hero has a feeling that something isn't quite right. Rated R for violence, nudity, and profanity. 106m. DIR: Wolfgang Petersen. CAST: Tom Berenger, Bob Hoskins, Greta Scacchi, Joanne Whalley, Corbin Bernsen, Theodore Bikel. 1991

SHATTERED DREAMS ★★ Lindsay Wagner and Michael Nouri are fine as a couple who resort to abuse when things get tough, but the script and direction are so melodramatic they dilute any chance the film has of garnering our sympathy. Based on a true story. Made-for-television. Not rated; contains violence. 94m. DIR: Robert Iscove. CAST: Lindsay Wagner, Michael Nouri. 1990

SHATTERED IMAGE (1993) ★★ The FBI tries to locate the criminals who kidnapped the owner of a modeling agency. This made-for-cable movie is quite confusing and contains too many twists—it feels as if even the writer really didn't know what was going on. Not rated; contains violence and sex. 95m. DIR: Fritz Kiersch. CAST: Jack Scalia, Bo Derek, John Savage, Dorian Harewood, Ramon Franco, Michael Harris, Carol Lawrence. 1993

•SHATTERED IMAGE (1998) ★★ What could have been an involving thriller about a woman with split personalities becomes a trite exercise in overkill. Anne Parillaud is desperately shallow as a hired killer and her alter ego, a newlywed on the verge of killing herself. William Baldwin is equally uninvolved as her target and husband. The filmmakers had two opportunities to get it right and dropped the ball both times. Rated R for adult situations, language, nudity, and violence. 103m. DIR: Raúl Ruiz. CAST: Anne Parillaud, William Baldwin, Graham Greene. 1998 DVD

SHATTERED SPIRITS ★★★ Hard-hitting, made-for-television drama focuses on a father whose casual drinking problem turns into substance abuse with tragic results. When his drinking escalates to an uncontrollable rage, his family is torn apart. 93m. DIR: Robert Greenwald. CAST: Martin Sheen, Melinda

lon, Matthew Laborteaux, Lukas Haas, Roxana Zal.
86

ATTERED VOWS ★★1/2 Based on a true story, is explores a young girl's commitment to become a n—and her later decision to leave the convent. ade for TV. 95m. **DIR:** Jack Bender. **CAST:** Valerie rtinelli, David Morse, Patricia Neal, Tom Parsekian. 84

HAWSHANK REDEMPTION, THE ★★★★ Uplifting tale of a man imprisoned for the murder of his fe and her lover, who must endure the horrors of ison life until he's befriended by Morgan Freeman. ased on the short novel by Stephen King, this is a oroughly rewarding movie. Rated R for violence, rofanity, nudity, and suggested sex. 142m. **DIR:** ank Darabont. **CAST:** Tim Robbins, Morgan Freeman, ob Gunton, Bill Sadler, Clancy Brown, Gil Bellows, mes Whitmore, Mark Rolston, Jeffrey DeMunn. 994 DVD

HE (1925) ★★1/2 Statuesque vamp Betty Blythe ortrays the ageless Queen Ayesha (She) to perfecon in this seventh and final silent version of advenre novelist H. Rider Haggard's fantasy about a lost ibe and a flame of eternal life in darkest Africa. ilmed in London and Berlin. Silent, with backound music. B&W; 77m. **DIR:** G. B. Samuelson. **AST:** Betty Blythe, Carlyle Blackwell, Mary Odette. 925

HE (1935) ★★★ Adventurers brave frozen wastends in their quest for the flame of eternal life and iscover an ancient civilization ruled by a stern, ng-lived lady. Fantasy-adventure classic falls flat espite splendid sets and a strong performance by elen Gahagan as the title character. B&W; 101m. IR: Irving Pichel, Lansing C. Holden. **CAST:** Helen Gaagan, Randolph Scott, Helen Mack, Nigel Bruce, Gusav von Seyffertitz, Samuel S. Hinds, Noble Johnson, umsden Hare. **1935 DVD**

HE (1983) ♥ Sandahl Bergman is She, the leader f a post-apocalyptic nation that looks upon men as econd-class citizens. Not rated, but would be an R or violence and nudity. 90m. **DIR:** Avi Nesher. **CAST:** andahl Bergman, Quin Kessler, Harrison Muller, Goron Mitchell. 1983

.H.E. ★★★ This average made-for-TV spy-action hriller has one twist ... a female James Bond. Beauiful Cornelia Sharpe is S.H.E. (Security Hazards Exert). She pursues Robert Lansing, the U.S. syndiate boss, throughout Europe. Omar Sharif makes an ppearance as a wine baron. 105m. **DIR:** Robert ewis. **CAST:** Omar Sharif, Cornelia Sharpe, Robert ansing, Anita Ekberg. 1979

HE BEAST, THE ★★1/2 It's undeniably crude and xtremely low-budget, but this Italian-Yugoslavian orror chiller about a reincarnated witch shouldn't e dismissed. 74m. **DIR:** Michael Reeves. **CAST:** Ian gilvy, Barbara Steele, Mel Welles. 1966

HE COULDN'T SAY NO ★★ An oil-rich woman (Jean Simmons) wishes to repay the citizens of her ometown of Progress, Arkansas for the kindnesses hown her in childhood. Her idea of showering her own with money is charitable, but disrupts the dayo-day life of the citizenry. Robert Mitchum, as the own doctor, seems out of place in this picture. B&W;

89m. **DIR:** Lloyd Bacon. **CAST:** Robert Mitchum, Jean Simmons, Arthur Hunnicutt, Edgar Buchanan. 1954

SHE CREATURE, THE ★★1/2 American-International's answer to *Creature from the Black Lagoon* mixes Fifties reincarnation hocus-pocus with conventional monster lore. The eye-filling title beast is the finest creation of zero-budget makeup master Paul Blaisdell, who recycled the same suit for *Voodoo Woman* and *Ghost of Dragstrip Hollow*. B&W; 77m. **DIR:** Edward L. Cahn. **CAST:** Marla English, Tom Conway, Chester Morris. 1957

SHE DEMONS ♥ A crazed Nazi scientist holds an uncharted island in a grip of terror. B&W; 80m. **DIR:** Richard Cunha. **CAST:** Irish McCalla, Tod Griffin, Victor Sen Yung, Gene Roth. 1958

SHE-DEVIL ★★★ Meryl Streep is a hoot as a snooty romance novelist who takes Ed Begley Jr., away from frumpy Roseanne. The moments of mirth come as Roseanne methodically manages her wifely revenge. The story is predictable, and the pace is sometimes plodding and deliberate, but there are enough funny bits to make it worth watching. Rated PG-13 for profanity and suggested sex. 94m. **DIR:** Susan Seidelman. **CAST:** Meryl Streep, Roseanne, Ed Begley Jr., Sylvia Miles, Linda Hunt. 1989

SHE-DEVILS ON WHEELS ♥ Atrocious Florida biker flick. Not rated. 83m. **DIR:** Herschell Gordon Lewis. **CAST:** Cristie Wagner. 1968

SHE DONE HIM WRONG ★★★★ Mae West woos Cary Grant in this comedy classic. She is a lady saloon keeper in the Gay Nineties. He is the undercover cop assigned to bring her in. She says, "Come up and see me sometime." He does, and the result is movie magic. B&W; 66m. **DIR:** Lowell Sherman. **CAST:** Mae West, Cary Grant, Gilbert Roland, Noah Beery Sr., Rochelle Hudson, Louise Beavers. 1933

SHE FREAK, THE ♥ A remake of the classic *Freaks*. B&W; 87m. **DIR:** Byron Mabe. **CAST:** Claire Brennan, Lee Raymond. **1966 DVD**

SHE GOES TO WAR ★★ Farfetched comedy-drama about a spoiled woman who takes her fiancé's place at the front. Loaded with stereotypes, coincidences, stilted dialogue, and miserable songs. B&W; 87m. **DIR:** Henry King. **CAST:** Eleanor Boardman, John Holland, Edmund Burke. 1929

SHE WAITS ★★ Producer-director Delbert Mann tries hard but cannot breathe any real thrills into this pedestrian tale of a young wife (Patty Duke) who becomes possessed by the spirit of her husband's first wife. Made-for-TV mediocrity. 74m. **DIR:** Delbert Mann. **CAST:** Patty Duke, David McCallum, Lew Ayres, Beulah Bondi, Dorothy McGuire. 1971

SHE WORE A YELLOW RIBBON ★★★★ Lest we forget, John Wayne was one of the screen's greatest actors. The Duke gave what was arguably his greatest performance in this gorgeous color Western made by John Ford. As the aging Captain Nathan Brittles, Wayne plays a man set to retire but unwilling to leave his command at a time of impending war with the Apaches. This is one of the great Westerns. 103m. **DIR:** John Ford. **CAST:** John Wayne, Ben Johnson, Victor McLaglen, Harry Carey Jr., George O'Brien. 1949

SHEBA BABY ★★ One of Pam Grier's last blaxploitation opuses. This time, she's a private eye struggling to save the family business. Less raunchy than some entries in the series, but still mostly routine. Rated R. 90m. **DIR:** William Girdler. **CAST:** Pam Grier, Austin Stoker, D'Urville Martin. **1975**

SHEENA 🖤 Tanya Roberts as the Queen of the Jungle. Rated PG. 117m. **DIR:** John Guillermin. **CAST:** Tanya Roberts, Ted Wass, Donovan Scott. **1984**

SHEEP HAS FIVE LEGS ★★★★ The beloved French comedian Fernandel plays six roles in one of his funniest movies: five identical brothers and their father. The humor doesn't come from the plot but from watching Fernandel juggle six comic characters. Great for families, if your kids don't mind a few subtitles. B&W; 92m. **DIR:** Henri Verneuil. **CAST:** Fernandel. **1954**

SHEER MADNESS ★★★1/2 The growing friendship between two women threatens to overwhelm their respective marriages in this complex, intelligently made film. Somewhat slow, but worth the effort. In German with English subtitles. Not rated. 110m. **DIR:** Margarethe von Trotta. **CAST:** Hanna Schygulla, Angela Winkler. **1985**

SHEIK, THE ★★1/2 The story of an English lady abducted by a hot-blooded Arab promising illicit pleasure in the desert is tame today, but Rudolph Valentino made millions of female fans who love slaves. Predicted to flop by studio brass, this melodramatic blend of adventure and eroticism nonetheless catapulted the handsome Italian import to reigning stardom. Silent. B&W; 80m. **DIR:** George Melford. **CAST:** Rudolph Valentino, Agnes Ayres, Adolphe Menjou, Lucien Littlefield. **1921**

SHELTERING SKY, THE ★★1/2 So much is left unexplained, one cannot help but wonder if director Bernardo Bertolucci is trying to put something over on us. This tale of three aimless Americans becoming involved in an odd romantic triangle while enduring hardships in post–World War II North Africa mainly leaves one with the urge to read Paul Bowles's original novel and find out what the fuss was all about. Rated R for nudity, profanity, and simulated sex. 133m. **DIR:** Bernardo Bertolucci. **CAST:** Debra Winger, John Malkovich, Campbell Scott, Jill Bennett, Timothy Spall. **1990**

SHENANDOAH ★★★★ James Stewart gives a superb performance in this, director Andrew V. McLaglen's best Western. Stewart plays a patriarch determined to keep his family out of the Civil War. He ultimately fails and is forced into action to save his children from the ravages of war. It's an emotionally moving, powerful tale. 105m. **DIR:** Andrew V. McLaglen. **CAST:** James Stewart, Doug McClure, Glenn Corbett, Patrick Wayne, Katharine Ross, George Kennedy, Strother Martin. **1965**

●**SHEPHERD** ★★ Heavily armed religious cults shoot it out in a post-apocalyptic wasteland. It's hard to make much sense out of this standard Roger Corman production, which is recommended only to fans of explosions and campy acting (at which former pro wrestler "Rowdy" Roddy Piper excels). Rated R for violence, profanity, and nudity. 86m. **DIR:** Peter Hayman. **CAST:** C. Thomas Howell, Roddy Piper, David Carradine, Heidi Von Palleske, Clarence Williams III. **1998**

SHEPHERD OF THE HILLS, THE ★★★★ John Wayne's first color film has a better storyline than most of his movies. It's set in the Ozarks and tells the story of a fellow determined to kill the man who abandoned his mother. Beautiful scenery adds atmosphere and a superb cast puts life into the story. 98m. **DIR:** Henry Hathaway. **CAST:** John Wayne, Harry Carey, Betty Field, Marjorie Main, Ward Bond, Beulah Bondi, John Qualen. **1941**

SHERIFF OF LAS VEGAS ★★★ Red Ryder steps in to clear a young man framed for the murder of his father. B&W; 54m. **DIR:** Lesley Selander. **CAST:** William Elliott, Robert Blake, Peggy Stewart, Jay Kirby. **1944**

SHERLOCK HOLMES AND THE DEADLY NECKLACE ★★★ Director Terence Fisher made one of the best versions of Sir Conan Doyle's *Hound of the Baskervilles* for Hammer Films in 1959, yet only three years later he foundered with this loose, German-made (dubbed) adaptation of *The Valley of Fear*. Curt Siodmak's screenplay is sometimes silly and a bit too skewed to the tastes of German audiences. B&W; 85m. **DIR:** Terence Fisher, Frank Winterstein. **CAST:** Christopher Lee, Thorley Walters, Senta Berger. **1962**

SHERLOCK HOLMES AND THE INCIDENT AT VICTORIA FALLS ★★★1/2 A request from King George (Joss Ackland) to safeguard the Star of Africa diamond on its journey from South Africa to England brings Sherlock Holmes (Christopher Lee) and Dr. Watson (Patrick Macnee) out of retirement. First of a series. Not rated; the film has violence. 120m. **DIR:** Bill Corcoran. **CAST:** Christopher Lee, Patrick Macnee, Jenny Seagrove, Claude Akins, Richard Todd, Joss Ackland. **1991**

SHERLOCK HOLMES AND THE LEADING LADY ★★ Edited down from a miniseries that ran over three hours (sans commercials), this romantic mystery of Sherlock Holmes and Dr. Watson in retirement emerges as a fitfully coherent, highlights-only digest version. But Christopher Lee and Patrick Macnee are splendid as Holmes and Watson. 100m. **DIR:** Peter Sasdy. **CAST:** Christopher Lee, Patrick Macnee, Morgan Fairchild. **1992**

SHERLOCK HOLMES AND THE SECRET WEAPON ★★★ Although the contemporary (1940s) setting makes the Baker Street sleuth seem oddly out of place, Basil Rathbone remains one of the definitive Holmeses as he once again faces the ruthless Professor Moriarty. 68m. **DIR:** Roy William Neill. **CAST:** Basil Rathbone, Nigel Bruce, Lionel Atwill, Kaaren Verne, Dennis Hoey, Mary Gordon. **1942 DVD**

SHERLOCK HOLMES AND THE SPIDER WOMAN ★★★1/2 Originally released under the abridged title *Spider Woman*, this Sherlockian adventure is one of the better modernized versions of the Conan Doyle stories. In this one, the villain is a fiendishly evil woman who drives gambling men to suicide in order to increase her personal fortune. It's full of tension and fine performances. B&W; 62m. **DIR:** Roy William Neill. **CAST:** Basil Rathbone, Nigel Bruce, Gale Sondergaard, Dennis Hoey. **1944**

HERLOCK HOLMES AND THE VOICE OF TERROR ★★ This first entry in the Universal series is enjyable. Set during World War II, it has our heroes going after spies who are using radio broadcasts to sabtage Allied efforts. B&W; 65m. DIR: John Rawlins. **AST:** Basil Rathbone, Nigel Bruce, Evelyn Ankers, enry Daniell, Montagu Love, Thomas Gomez, Hillary rooke, Mary Gordon. **1942**

HERLOCK HOLMES FACES DEATH ★★★ Holmes Basil Rathbone) and Watson (Nigel Bruce) find nemselves back in the shadows and fog—albeit in nodern times—as they attempt to solve a murder. ased on Conan Doyle's "The Musgrave Ritual," this s a good entry in the series. B&W; 68m. DIR: Roy William Neill. **CAST:** Basil Rathbone, Nigel Bruce, Dennis Hoey, Hillary Brooke. **1943**

HERLOCK HOLMES: HANDS OF A MURDERER ★★★ This reasonable facsimile of Sir Arthur Conan Doyle's work is somewhat unevenly paced, but the erformances, set designs, and costumes capably apture the flavor of Victorian England. The complex tory involves the dread Moriarty, critical national ecrets, and a cult of Thugee murderers. Genre urists will appreciate the intelligent, self-assured r. Watson. Not rated; contains violent themes. 90m. **IR:** Stuart Orme. **CAST:** Edward Woodward, John illerman, Anthony Andrews, Kim Thomson, Peter Jefrey, Warren Clarke. **1990**

HERLOCK HOLMES IN WASHINGTON ★★1/2 Cornball wartime propaganda has Sherlock Holmes Basil Rathbone) and Dr. Watson (Nigel Bruce) hasing after spies in Washington, D.C. Strong villainy from George Zucco and Henry Daniell helps, and the stars are as watchable as ever. B&W; 71m. **DIR:** Roy William Neill. **CAST:** Basil Rathbone, Nigel Bruce, Marjorie Lord, Henry Daniell, George Zucco. **1943**

HERLOCK JR. ★★★★ In this film about film, projectionist Buster Keaton dreams about being a detective and miraculously finds himself inside the ilm he is showing. The plot involves saving his beloved from the villain, but the real thrust and appeal of the film lies in brilliant camera tricks providing some of the greatest of silent comedy sight gags. Silent. B&W; 45m. DIR: Buster Keaton. **CAST:** Buster Keaton, Kathryn McGuire. **1924 DVD**

HERLOCK: UNDERCOVER DOG ★★ Kids may oss this amateurish comedy a bone, but adults will ind it cheap and silly. Two kids spending their sumner vacation on Catalina Island find adventure when they're recruited by a talking police dog trying o save his master from kidnappers. Totally preposterous premise, executed with little flair. Rated PG. 30m. DIR: Richard Harding Gardner. **CAST:** Benjamin Eroen, Brynne Cameron, Anthony Simmons, Margy Moore. **1994**

SHERMAN'S MARCH ★★★★ In 1981 Bostonbased documentary filmmaker Ross McElwee received a $9,000 grant to make a movie about the effects of General William Tecumseh Sherman's bloody march on the South. Then McElwee's girlfriend left him. He made the film, but *Sherman's March* is only tangentially about that historic figure. Subtitled "A Meditation on the Possibility of Romantic Love in an Era of Nuclear Weapons Proliferation," it mostly deals with the filmmaker's hilarious search for the meaning of life and someone to love. Not rated, the film has brief nudity. 150m. DIR: Ross McElwee. **1987**

SHE'S ALL THAT ★★★ Surprisingly watchable teen romance features adorable Freddie Prinze Jr. as the cool dude on campus who accepts a bet to play "Professor Higgins" to a cause-conscious but nerdy "Eliza Doolittle" (Rachel Leigh Cook). Despite the lesson about looks not defining a person, which gives this film a John Hughes feel, there are plenty of fun, silly moments that guarantee at least a wide grin. Rated PG-13 for language and sexual situations. 95m. DIR: Robert Iscove. **CAST:** Freddie Prinze Jr., Rachel Leigh Cook, Matthew Lillard, Jodi O'Keefe, Kieran Culkin. **1999 DVD**

SHE'S BACK ★★1/2 Black comedy finds Carrie Fisher returning from the dead, edging her meek husband to seek retribution against the street thugs who iced her. Rated R for violence. 88m. DIR: Tim Kincaid. **CAST:** Carrie Fisher, Robert Joy. **1989**

SHE'S DRESSED TO KILL ★★ Acceptable murder mystery concerning the deaths of high-fashion models. Eleanor Parker is excellent as a garish, oncerenowned designer trying to stage a comeback. This made-for-TV movie was retitled *Someone's Killing the World's Greatest Models.* 100m. DIR: Gus Trikonis. **CAST:** Eleanor Parker, Jessica Walter, John Rubinstein, Jim McMullan, Corinne Calvet. **1979**

SHE'S GOTTA HAVE IT ★★★★ A movie about a randy young woman who's "gotta have it" might seem a bit iffy. But independent filmmaker Spike Lee— who wrote, directed, and edited this unique narrative-quasidocumentary—set up the challenge for himself and then set out to succeed *con gusto.* The beautiful lady in question, Nola Darling, is played by Tracy Camilla Johns. Rated R for language and nudity. B&W; 100m. DIR: Spike Lee. **CAST:** Tracy Camilla Johns, Redmond Hicks, John Terrell, Spike Lee. **1986**

SHE'S HAVING A BABY ★★ Director John Hughes, champion of the teenage set, advanced from the breakfast club to the breakfast table in this bland account of a young newlywed couple, played by Kevin Bacon and Elizabeth McGovern. A major (and deserved) failure. Rated PG-13 for profanity, suggested sex, and sexual themes. 110m. DIR: John Hughes. **CAST:** Kevin Bacon, Elizabeth McGovern, William Windom, James Ray, Holland Taylor. **1988**

SHE'S IN THE ARMY NOW ★★★ The distributor has labeled this made-for-TV film a comedy, but there is very little to laugh about in the story of seven weeks of basic training in a women's squadron. Kathleen Quinlan as the appointed squadron leader and Jamie Lee Curtis as the streetwise recruit with problems are both very good. 97m. DIR: Hy Averback. **CAST:** Kathleen Quinlan, Jamie Lee Curtis, Melanie Griffith, Janet MacLachlan. **1981**

SHE'S OUT OF CONTROL ★ Tony Danza overplays the father of a 15-year-old girl who suddenly blossoms into a sexy young woman. Rated PG. 97m. DIR: Stan Dragoti. **CAST:** Tony Danza, Catherine Hicks, Wallace Shawn, Ami Dolenz. **1989**

SHE'S SO LOVELY ★★1/2 The depth of characterization normally associated with a film by John Cassavetes is missing from this story of a pregnant woman who is beaten and nearly raped by her neighbor. Her husband shoots a police officer and lands in a mental institution. Ten years later, he is released to find his now-ex-wife remarried and his daughter raised by another man. In a messy resolution, the three main characters are forced to confront their emotions, loyalties, and lives. Rated R for violence, profanity, and suggested sex. 97m. DIR: Nick Cassavetes. CAST: Sean Penn, Robin Wright, John Travolta, Harry Dean Stanton, Debi Mazar, James Gandolfini, Gena Rowlands. 1997

SHE'S THE ONE ★★★1/2 Writer-director-star Edward Burns's second big-screen effort essentially reprises much of *The Brothers McMullen*. He's a shy, artistic cabby still recovering from the shock of having been cuckolded by his ex-fiancée; what he doesn't know is that she cheated on him with his own brother! Rated PG-13 for profanity and sexual candor. 96m. DIR: Edward Burns. CAST: Edward Burns, Mike McGlone, John Mahoney, Cameron Diaz, Maxine Bahns, Jennifer Aniston. 1996

SHILOH ★★★★ Top-notch family entertainment stars young Blake Heron as Marty, who befriends a mistreated beagle who has run away from his cruel owner. Marty's efforts to keep the dog are met with resistance from his father, who doesn't believe the dog is worth the trouble. With the help of a local shopkeeper, Marty follows his heart and fights for what he believes in. Solid family values and engaging performances are just the icing on this treat. Rated PG. 93m. DIR: Dale Rosenbloom. CAST: Blake Heron, Scott Wilson, Michael Moriarty, Rod Steiger. 1996

•**SHILOH 2: SHILOH SEASON** ★★ Misguided sequel fails to capture the sweetness and charm of the original. Some of the original cast is back, including Zachary Browne as Marty, the young boy who befriends Shiloh and saves him from his mean owner. The filmmakers lay it on thick and sweet, and sometimes it's too much to bear. Rated PG. 96m. DIR: Sandy Tung. CAST: Zachary Browne, Scott Wilson, Michael Moriarty, Ann Dowd, Rod Steiger. 1999

SHIN HEINKE MONOGATARI ★★★ Fans of the great Kenji Mizoguchi may be disappointed to find that this film is a historical samurai adventure rather than a story of oppressed women, his usual subject. Not one of Mizoguchi's best, though his striking use of color is memorable. In Japanese with English subtitles. 113m. DIR: Kenji Mizoguchi. CAST: Raizo Ichikawa. 1955

SHINE ★★★★ Geoffrey Rush collected a well-deserved Oscar for his galvanic portrayal of deeply troubled Australian piano prodigy David Helfgott, who suffered a crippling nervous breakdown on the verge of international fame. Anybody who has even seen Helfgott knows how superbly the actor caught his behavior and remarkable style of speaking. Rate PG-13 for nudity, sensuality, and strong dramatic content. 105m. DIR: Scott Hicks. CAST: Geoffrey Rush, Armin Mueller-Stahl, Noah Taylor, Lynn Redgrave, John Gielgud. 1996 DVD

SHINING, THE ★★1/2 A struggling writer (Jack Nicholson) accepts a position as the caretaker of large summer resort hotel during the winter season. The longer he and his family spend in the hotel, the more Nicholson becomes possessed by it. Considering the talent involved, this is a major disappointment. Director Stanley Kubrick keeps things at snail's pace, and Nicholson's performance approaches high camp. Rated R for violence and language. 146m. DIR: Stanley Kubrick. CAST: Jack Nicholson, Shelley Duvall, Scatman Crothers. 1980 DVD

SHINING HOUR, THE ★★ Soap opera about a nightclub entertainer (Joan Crawford) who fights for acceptance from her husband's small-town family with small-town values. An energetic film with good acting and a predictable plot. B&W; 81m. DIR: Frank Borzage. CAST: Joan Crawford, Margaret Sullavan, Melvyn Douglas, Robert Young, Fay Bainter, Hattie McDaniel, Allyn Joslyn, Frank Albertson. 1938

SHINING SEASON, A ★★★ Fact-based story of track star and Olympic hopeful John Baker, (Timothy Bottoms) who, when stricken by cancer, devotes his final months to coaching a girls' track team. This is very familiar territory, but director Stuart Margolin keeps things above water most of the time. Bottoms is an engaging hero-victim. Made for television. 100m. DIR: Stuart Margolin. CAST: Timothy Bottoms, Allyn Ann McLerie, Ed Begley Jr., Rip Torn, Mason Adams. 1979

SHINING THROUGH ★★★1/2 Working from the bestseller by Susan Isaacs, writer-director David Seltzer has come up with a clever and effective homage to the war films of the Forties. Melanie Griffith is a wisecracking dame who figures out that her boss (Michael Douglas) is an American spy from what she's seen in movies. In no time, she's behind enemy lines in Nazi Germany attempting to gather information. Rated R for violence, profanity, and nudity. 125m. DIR: David Seltzer. CAST: Michael Douglas, Melanie Griffith, Liam Neeson, Joely Richardson, John Gielgud. 1992

SHIP AHOY ★★★ Entertaining musical, thanks to Eleanor Powell's energetic tap dancing. The World War II plot is somewhat dated, but Powell and Red Skelton are excellent. The film showcases Tommy Dorsey's orchestra when Buddy Rich was his drummer and Sinatra his soloist. Enjoyable. B&W; 95m. DIR: Edward Buzzell. CAST: Eleanor Powell, Red Skelton, Bert Lahr, Virginia O'Brien, Tommy Dorsey, Jo Stafford, Frank Sinatra, Buddy Rich. 1942

SHIP OF FOOLS ★★★★★ In 1933, a vast and varied group of characters take passage on a German liner sailing from Mexico to Germany amidst impending doom. The all-star cast features most memorable performances in this superb screen adaptation of the Katherine Anne Porter novel. B&W; 150m. DIR: Stanley Kramer. CAST: Vivien Leigh, Oskar Werner, Simone Signoret, José Ferrer, Lee Marvin, George Segal, Michael Dunn, Elizabeth Ashley, Lilia Skala, Charles Korvin. 1965

SHIPS WITH WINGS ★★1/2 Typical patriotic British war movie, this one is set on an aircraft carrier preparing for battle. Some good character bits, but on the whole rather perfunctory. B&W; 103m.

IR: Sergei Nolbandov. **CAST:** John Clements, Ann odd, Leslie Banks, Hugh Williams, Michael Wilding, Michael Rennie, Cecil Parker. 1941

SHIPWRECKED ★★★★ A sort of *Home Alone* meets *Treasure Island*, this is a rousing adventure film based on the classic Norwegian novel, *Haakon Haakonsen* by O.V. Falck-Ytter. About a young lad who goes to sea to help get his parents out of debt, and finds himself battling a bloodthirsty pirate (Gabriel Byrne) for buried treasure. This Disney release has plenty of action, thrills, and suspense. Rated PG for light violence. 93m. **DIR:** Nils Gaup. **CAST:** Stian Smestad, Gabriel Byrne, Bjorn Sundquist. 1991

SHIRLEY VALENTINE ★★★★ Adult viewers will revel in this wise and witty movie. Pauline Collins is terrific as the title character, who one day decides to chuck it all and head for romance in the Greek isles. Tom Conti is fun as the restaurant owner who woos the wacky but sympathetic heroine. Rated R for profanity and nudity. 160m. **DIR:** Lewis Gilbert. **CAST:** Pauline Collins, Tom Conti, Julia McKenzie, Joanna Lumley, Bernard Hill, Sylvia Syms. 1989

SHIVERS, THE ★★ Plans to turn a haunted house into a dance club don't go quite as envisioned in this pawnfest from director Todd Sheets. As usual, subtlety seems to be a foreign concept to Sheets and the film would have done much better had it taken a few pointers from classier material like *The Haunting* or *The Shining*. Not rated; contains gore, violence, and profanity. 90m. **DIR:** Todd Sheets. **CAST:** Rico Love, Nick Stodden. 1999

SHOCK, THE (1923) ★★★ The legendary Lon Chaney Sr. added yet another grotesque character to his growing closet of skeletons when he played Wilse Dilling. This decent crime melodrama, no different in plot than dozens of other films over the years, has the advantage of Chaney and an exciting climax consisting of a bang-up earthquake. Corny at times, this one is still a good bet if you're interested in silent films. B&W; 96m. **DIR:** Lambert Hillyer. **CAST:** Lon Chaney Sr., Christine Mayo. 1923

SHOCK (1946) ★★★ Highly effective thriller features Vincent Price in an early performance as a murderer—in this case he's a psychiatrist who murders his wife and is then forced to silence a witness through drugs and hypnosis. This minor classic provided the framework for many subsequent suspense movies. B&W; 70m. **DIR:** Alfred Werker. **CAST:** Vincent Price, Lynn Bari, Reed Hadley, Pierre Watkin, Frank Latimore. 1946

SHOCK CORRIDOR ★★1/2 Newspaper reporter Peter Breck poses as insane to learn who committed a murder inside a state asylum, and we watch as he goes bonkers himself. Brilliant action sequences interspersed with tedium. B&W; 101m. **DIR:** Samuel Fuller. **CAST:** Peter Breck, Constance Towers, Gene Evans. 1963 DVD

SHOCK TO THE SYSTEM, A ★★★★ In this deliciously wicked black comedy, Michael Caine plays a middle-aged executive waiting impatiently for a big promotion, which goes instead to younger man Peter Riegert. So, Caine does what any man in that position would do: he plots murder. Screenwriter An-

drew Klavan's loose adaptation of Simon Brett's novel makes an uncommonly satisfying thriller. Rated R for violence and profanity. 91m. **DIR:** Jan Egleson. **CAST:** Michael Caine, Peter Riegert, Elizabeth McGovern, Swoosie Kurtz, Will Patton, John McMartin. 1990

SHOCK TREATMENT 🍂 Forgettable sequel to *The Rocky Horror Picture Show*. Janet and Brad go on a TV game show and end up trying to escape from it. Rated PG. 94m. **DIR:** Jim Sharman. **CAST:** Jessica Harper, Cliff De Young, Richard O'Brien. 1981

SHOCK WAVES (DEATH CORPS) 🍂 Vacationers stumble upon a crazed army of underwater zombies. Rated PG. 86m. **DIR:** Ken Wiederhorn. **CAST:** Peter Cushing, Brooke Adams, John Carradine. 1977

SHOCK'EM DEAD ★★ What starts out as an entirely lame scare flick ends as a completely lame scare flick. But in between are some truly frightening shocks as we see a wimp sell his soul to the devil in return for becoming the greatest rock star in the world. Rated R for violence, profanity, and gore. 94m. **DIR:** Mark Freed. **CAST:** Traci Lords, Aldo Ray, Troy Donahue. 1990

SHOCKER ★★ Wes Craven introduces Horace Pinker, a maniacal TV repairman with a Freddy Krueger personality and special powers. He spends his evenings hacking up families. Rated R for violence, profanity, and gore. 110m. **DIR:** Wes Craven. **CAST:** Mitch Pileggi, Michael Murphy. 1989 DVD

SHOES OF THE FISHERMAN 🍂 A boring film about an enthusiastic pope who single-handedly attempts to stop nuclear war, starvation, and world strife. 157m. **DIR:** Michael Anderson. **CAST:** Anthony Quinn, Laurence Olivier, Oskar Werner, David Janssen, Vittorio De Sica, John Gielgud, Leo McKern, Barbara Jefford. 1968

SHOESHINE ★★★★ Neorealist classic about two boys whose friendship gets them through hard times in Rome during the Nazi occupation. But in a harsh jail, their relationship falters. Winner of a special Academy Award. In Italian with English subtitles. 93m. **DIR:** Vittorio De Sica. **CAST:** Rinaldo Smerdoni, Franco Interlenghi. 1946

SHOGUN (FULL-LENGTH VERSION) ★★★★ This ten-hour original is the only one that does justice to James Clavell's sweeping novel. Richard Chamberlain began his reign as king of the miniseries with his portrayal of Blackthorne, the English sailor shipwrecked among the feudal Japanese. It all works, from the breathtaking cinematography to the superb acting. 600m. **DIR:** Jerry London. **CAST:** Richard Chamberlain, Toshiro Mifune, Yoko Shimada, Damien Thomas. 1980

SHOGUN ASSASSIN ★★★ Meticulously reedited, rescripted, rescored, and English-dubbed version of the original *Baby-Cart at the River Styx*: swords enter bodies at the most imaginative angles; a body count is impossible; all records are broken for bloodletting. Rated R for the violence, which really is fairly aesthetic. 90m. **DIR:** Kenji Misumi, David Weisman, Robert Hous. **CAST:** Tomisaburo Wakayama. 1980

SHOOT (1976) ★★★1/2 A group of buddies spending a weekend hunting are attacked by another group of hunters who are after game more interesting than deer. When one of their party is wounded, the attacked hunters, led by Cliff Robertson and Ernest Borgnine, want revenge and mount a military-style campaign to get it. Rated R for violence and profanity. 98m. DIR: Harvey Hart. CAST: Cliff Robertson, Ernest Borgnine, Henry Silva. 1976

SHOOT (1991) ★★1/2 Passable spoof of undercover greed features DeDee Pfeiffer as a ditzy photographer studying her crime boss's gambling operation. His real ace in the hole is a million-dollar pearl he plans to sell to the highest bidder. Surprise ending is too strange to be believed. Not rated; contains violence and criminial activity. 97m. DIR: Hugh Parks. CAST: Dedee Pfeiffer, Miles O'Keeffe, Christopher Atkins, Fred Ottaviano. 1991

SHOOT LOUD, LOUDER ... I DON'T UNDERSTAND 💖 Antique dealer confronts inept gunmen. Not rated; contains violence. 100m. DIR: Eduardo De Filippo. CAST: Marcello Mastroianni, Raquel Welch, Leopoldo Trieste. 1966

SHOOT THE LIVING ... PRAY FOR THE DEAD 💖 Overlong and nothing-new story line makes this film a waste of time. A gang hires a guide to lead them to Mexico after a bank robbery, but the guide plans to kill the gang himself for killing his family. Not rated; contains violence. 94m. DIR: Joseph Warren. CAST: Klaus Kinski, Victoria Zinni, Paul Sullivan, Dean Stratford. 1971

SHOOT THE MOON ★★ Why didn't they just call it *Ordinary People Go West?* Of course, this film isn't really a sequel to the 1980 Oscar winner. It's closer to a rip-off. None of the style, believability, or consistency of its predecessor. Rated R because of profanity, violence, and adult themes. 123m. DIR: Alan Parker. CAST: Albert Finney, Diane Keaton, Karen Allen, Dana Hill, Tracey Gold. 1982

SHOOT THE PIANO PLAYER ★★★1/2 Singer Charles Aznavour plays to perfection the antihero of this minor masterpiece directed by François Truffaut. Don't look for plot, unity of theme, or understandable mood transitions. This one's a brilliantly offbeat mix of crime, melodrama, romance, and slapstick. In French with English subtitles. B&W; 85m. DIR: François Truffaut. CAST: Charles Aznavour, Marie Dubois, Nicole Berger, Michele Mercier. 1962 DVD

SHOOT TO KILL ★★★1/2 Sidney Poitier returns to the screen after a ten-year absence to portray a streetwise FBI agent determined to track down a ruthless killer. The chase leads to the mountains of the Pacific Northwest, where Poitier teams with tracker Tom Berenger. A solid thriller. Rated R for language and violence. 110m. DIR: Roger Spottiswoode. CAST: Sidney Poitier, Tom Berenger, Kirstie Alley, Clancy Brown, Richard Masur, Andrew Robinson. 1988

SHOOTFIGHTER ★★★ Two friends in the deadly world of shootfighting—a brutal, sometimes lethal sport—team up to stay alive. A workable cast, combined with some extremely brutal fight sequences, blend together for an action film that rises above the genre. Two versions available: one rated R for violence, and one unrated with more of the same. Unrated 96m.; Rated R 94m. DIR: Pat Alan. CAST: Bolo Yeung, Maryam D'Abo, William Zabka, Martin Kove, Edward Albert. 1993

SHOOTFIGHTER 2: KILL OR BE KILLED 💖 For those who didn't get their fill of the original *Shootfighter,* more of the same. Rated R for violence. 90m. DIR: Paul Ziller. CAST: Bolo Yeung, William Zabka, Michael Bernardo, Jorge Gil. 1996

SHOOTING, THE ★★★ This early Jack Nicholson vehicle, directed by cult figure Monte Hellman, is a moody Western about revenge and murder. An interesting entry into the genre, it may not be everyone's cup of tea. No rating; contains some violence. 82m. DIR: Monte Hellman. CAST: Warren Oates, Millie Perkins, Will Hutchins, Jack Nicholson. 1967

SHOOTING ELIZABETH ★★1/2 A husband tells his friend that he is going to kill his wife during their second honeymoon. Mundane plot and acting. Not rated. 96m. DIR: Baz Taylor. CAST: Jeff Goldblum, Mimi Rogers, Burt Kwouk. 1992

SHOOTING FISH ★★★ This breezy British comedy caper focuses on two likable swindlers who are nearly exposed by peddling bogus miracle computers. They then both develop a crush on their scrappy female assistant, run a risky attic insulation scam, and get involved with a racing-horse con that may turn them into urban Robin Hoods while also making them rich. The storyline stretches credibility, but the chemistry of the characters, and the film's fizzy 1960s feel are irresistible. Rated PG. 93m. DIR: Stefan Schwartz. CAST: Dan Futterman, Stuart Townsend, Kate Beckinsale. 1998 DVD

SHOOTING PARTY, THE ★★★★ This meditation on the fading English aristocracy is an acting showcase. All main characters are played with verve, or at least the verve one would expect from English nobility in the years preceding World War I. While nothing much happens here, the rich texture of the characters, the highly stylized sets, and the incidental affairs in the plot are enough to sustain the viewer. Not rated, but equivalent to a PG for partial nudity. 97m. DIR: Alan Bridges. CAST: James Mason, Edward Fox, Dorothy Tutin, John Gielgud, Gordon Jackson, Cheryl Campbell, Robert Hardy. 1985

SHOOTIST, THE ★★★★1/2 John Wayne's final film is an intelligent tribute to the passing of the era known as the "wild West." Wayne's masterful performance is touching and bitterly ironic as well. He plays a famous gunfighter dying of cancer and seeking a place to die in peace, only to become a victim of his own reputation. Rated PG. 99m. DIR: Don Siegel. CAST: John Wayne, Lauren Bacall, James Stewart, Ron Howard, Richard Boone, Hugh O'Brian, John Carradine, Harry Morgan, Scatman Crothers. 1976

SHOP AROUND THE CORNER, THE ★★★★ A charming period comedy dealing with the lives of two people who work in the same Budapest shop and become loving pen pals. MGM later remade this picture

In the Good Old Summertime, and it formed the basis of the stage musical *She Loves Me*. B&W; 98m. DIR: Ernst Lubitsch. CAST: James Stewart, Margaret Sullavan, Frank Morgan, Joseph Schildkraut. 1939

HOP ON MAIN STREET, THE ★★★★ This film finds a Jewish woman removed from her small business and portrays her growing relationship with the man who has been put in charge of her shop. Set among the turbulent days of the Nazi occupation of Czechoslovakia, this tender film depicts the instincts of survival among the innocent pawns of brutal war. A moving film. B&W; 128m. DIR: Ján Kadár. CAST: Elmar Klos, Josef Kroner, Ida Kaminska. 1964

HOPPING ★★1/2 In the near future, the favorite sport of disaffected teens is "shopping"—stealing cars and driving them to malls, which they then loot. Early indications that this may be a comment on the nature of a spiritually dead consumer society fade as *hopping* becomes a stylish but familiar action flick. Rated R for violence and nudity. 87m. DIR: Paul Anderson. CAST: Sadie Frost, Jude Law, Sean Pertwee, Jonathan Pryce, Fraser James, Sean Bean, Marianne Faithfull. 1995

SHOPWORN ANGEL, THE ★★★1/2 Margaret Sullavan plays a callous and selfish actress who toys with the affections of shy soldier James Stewart until she is won over by his sincerity. Predictable, but this team is always a joy to watch. B&W; 85m. DIR: H. C. Potter. CAST: Margaret Sullavan, James Stewart, Walter Pidgeon, Hattie McDaniel, Nat Pendleton, Alan Curtis, Sam Levene. 1938

SHORT CIRCUIT ★★★★ In this enjoyable sci-fi comedy-adventure, a sophisticated robot, Number Five, is zapped by lightning during a storm and comes alive (à la Frankenstein's monster) to the shock of his creator (Steve Guttenberg). Created as the ultimate war weapon, the mechanical man learns the value of life from an animal lover (Ally Sheedy) and sets off on his own—with the military in hot pursuit. Rated PG for profanity and violence. 95m. DIR: John Badham. CAST: Ally Sheedy, Steve Guttenberg, Fisher Stevens, Austin Pendleton, G. W. Bailey. 1986

SHORT CIRCUIT 2 ★★ If it weren't filled with profanity, this might have been a good film for the kiddies. Indian inventor Fisher Stevens goes into the toy business with streetwise hustler Michael McKean and that lovable robot, Number Five. Rated PG for profanity and violence. 110m. DIR: Kenneth Johnson. CAST: Fisher Stevens, Michael McKean, Cynthia Gibb, Jack Weston. 1988

SHORT CUTS ★★★★★ Director Robert Altman scores again with this superb film that intertwines several of Raymond Carver's short stories into a fascinating, thought-provoking panorama of modern-day life. The performances by a huge, all-star cast are uniformly excellent. Rated R for profanity, nudity, and violence. 188m. DIR: Robert Altman. CAST: Andie MacDowell, Bruce Davison, Jack Lemmon, Julianne Moore, Matthew Modine, Tom Waits, Frances McDormand, Peter Gallagher, Annie Ross, Lori Singer, Lyle Lovett, Buck Henry, Huey Lewis. 1993

SHORT EYES ★★★★ Film version of Miguel Pinero's hard-hitting play about a convicted child molester at the mercy of other prisoners. A brutal and frightening film. Excellent, but difficult to watch. Rated R for violence and profanity. 104m. DIR: Robert M. Young. CAST: Bruce Davison, Jose Perez. 1977

SHORT FUSE 🖤 Racial tensions between the black community and the police. Rated R for violence and profanity. 91m. DIR: Blaine Novak. CAST: Art Garfunkel, Harris Yulin. 1989

SHORT GRASS ★★★★ Returning home after several years, Rod Cameron is pushed off his land by larger ranchers. Intricate script, from his own novel, by Tom Blackburn. B&W; 82m. DIR: Lesley Selander. CAST: Rod Cameron, Johnny Mack Brown, Cathy Downs, Alan Hale Jr. 1950

SHORT TIME ★★★1/2 In this sometimes hilarious action-comedy, Dabney Coleman is a soon-to-retire police officer who is incorrectly diagnosed as having a terminal disease. He spends the last few days on the force attempting to get killed to leave his wife (Teri Garr) and son a substantial insurance settlement. Rated PG-13 for violence and profanity. 102m. DIR: Gregg Champion. CAST: Dabney Coleman, Matt Frewer, Teri Garr, Barry Corbin, Joe Pantoliano. 1990

SHOT, THE ★★★ Two young actors try to break through Hollywood barriers by holding for ransom the only print of the last film by a deceased director, not realizing that they are playing into the hands of other L.A. sharks. Even viewers who don't care to see another insider-Hollywood comedy should enjoy the performances in this likable low-budget comedy. Rated R for violence and profanity. 85m. DIR: Dan Bell. CAST: Dan Bell, Michael Rivkin, Michael DeLuise, Theodore Raimi. 1995

SHOT IN THE DARK, A ★★★★ *A Shot in the Dark* is a one-man show, with Peter Sellers outdoing himself as the character he later reprised in *The Return of the Pink Panther*, *The Pink Panther Strikes Back*, and *The Revenge of the Pink Panther*. In this slapstick delight, Clouseau attempts to discover whether or not a woman (Elke Sommer) is guilty of murdering her lover. 101m. DIR: Blake Edwards. CAST: Peter Sellers, Elke Sommer, George Sanders, Burt Kwouk, Herbert Lom. 1964 DVD

SHOT THROUGH THE HEART ★★★★ Searing tale based loosely on actual events and set during the atrocious, inhumane siege of Sarajevo, Bosnia. A pair of sharpshooters, best friends, hope to qualify for the Olympics. But when the situation in Bosnia explodes, their different backgrounds place them on opposite sides as snipers. This film conveys the terrible extremes to which former friends may be driven in the face of horrifying, all-out war. Rated R for violence, profanity, nudity, and simulated sex. 112m. DIR: David Attwood. CAST: Linus Roache, Vincent Perez, Lia Williams, Adam Kotz, Soo Garay, Lothaire Bluteau. 1998

SHOTGUN ★★★ Violent melodramatic track-down story has Marshal Sterling Hayden pursuing the gun-running shotgun killer of a town sheriff. Along the way he encounters a saloon girl and a bounty hunter.

80m. **DIR:** Lesley Selander. **CAST:** Sterling Hayden, Zachary Scott, Yvonne De Carlo. **1955**

SHOUT, THE (1979) ★★★ Enigmatic British chiller about a wanderer's chilling effect on an unsuspecting couple. He possesses the ancient power to kill people by screaming. Well made, with an excellent cast. The film may be too offbeat for some viewers. Rated R. 87m. **DIR:** Jerzy Skolimowski. **CAST:** Alan Bates, Susannah York, John Hurt, Robert Stephens, Tim Curry. **1979**

SHOUT (1991) 🗨 This rock 'n' roll fantasy, in which a delinquent is reformed by the love of a good woman, has its heart in the right place; but its brain is dead. Rated PG-13 for violence and profanity. 89m. **DIR:** Jeffrey Hornady. **CAST:** James Walters, Heather Graham, John Travolta, Richard Jordan, Linda Fiorentino, Scott Coffey. **1991 DVD**

SHOUT AT THE DEVIL ★★ Good action scenes elevate this otherwise distasteful and overly complicated film about a hard-drinking American adventurer (Lee Marvin) and an upper-crust Englishman (Roger Moore) who join forces to blow up a German battleship before the breakout of World War I. Rated PG. 119m. **DIR:** Peter R. Hunt. **CAST:** Lee Marvin, Roger Moore, Barbara Parkins, Ian Holm. **1976**

SHOUT: THE STORY OF JOHNNY O'KEEFE ★★★1/2 A slow start builds up to a satisfying send-up for the man who put Australian rock music on the international map. Terry Serio is brilliant as Johnny O'Keefe, the Boomerang Kid—a man who lets conceit and self-promotion stand in the way of his happiness and sanity. Not rated, contains profanity, violence, and drug use. 192m. **DIR:** Ted Robinson. **CAST:** Terry Serio. **1985**

SHOW, THE ★★ Billed as the first "rapumentary," this hip-hop documentary is long on unenlightening talking-head commentary by noted names in the field. Performance scenes, the heart and soul of any concert film, are too short, too grainy, and too scarce. Rated R for profanity. 97m. **DIR:** Brian Robbins. **CAST:** Craig Mack, Dr. Dre, Naughty by Nature, Run DMC, Slick Rick, The Dogg Pound, Warren G, Wu-Tang Clan. **1995**

SHOW BOAT (1936) ★★★★★ The definitive film version of America's best-loved musical, it marked the first full-sound version of the 1927 Broadway hit and featured many performers in roles they played onstage. Paul Robeson sings 'Ol' Man River" the way it is *supposed* to be sung. 113m. **DIR:** James Whale. **CAST:** Irene Dunne, Allan Jones, Helen Morgan, Charles Winninger, Hattie McDaniel, Paul Robeson. **1936**

SHOW BOAT (1951) ★★★1/2 This watchable musical depicts life and love on a Mississippi showboat during the early 1900s. Kathryn Grayson, Howard Keel, and Ava Gardner try but can't get any real sparks flying. 115m. **DIR:** George Sidney. **CAST:** Kathryn Grayson, Howard Keel, Ava Gardner, Joe E. Brown, Agnes Moorehead, Marge Champion, Gower Champion. **1951 DVD**

SHOW BUSINESS ★★★ Based on incidents in Eddie Cantor's entertainment career, this slick, brassy, and nostalgic picture provides fun and good music. For Cantor and Joan Davis fans, this film is a peach.

B&W; 92m. **DIR:** Edwin L. Marin. **CAST:** Eddie Canto, George Murphy, Joan Davis, Nancy Kelly, Constanc Moore. **1944**

SHOW OF FORCE, A ★★ This engaging but occasionally unconvincing conspiracy thriller is loosel based on an infamous Puerto Rican scandal involving the fatal shooting of two pro- independence activists. Amy Irving stars as a television journalist wh finds that the incident may have been a politicall motivated murder. Rated R for language and violence. 93m. **DIR:** Bruno Barreto. **CAST:** Amy Irving Lou Diamond Phillips, Robert Duvall, Andy Garcia **1990**

SHOW PEOPLE ★★★★ Loosely based on the ca reer of Gloria Swanson, this was the justly fable Marion Davies's last silent film. Davies is warm and genuinely touching as innocent Polly Pepper, a young actress whose ambitions are thwarted a nearly every turn. As a satire on the industry, this is a glittering gem, right on the money. Charlie Chaplin John Gilbert, May Murray, and Norma Talmadge are among a coterie of stars appearing as themselves Silent. B&W; 81m. **DIR:** King Vidor. **CAST:** Marior Davies, William Haines, Polly Moran. **1928**

SHOW THEM NO MERCY ★★★ Four gangsters snatch a child and are paid off in bills that can be traced. Nobody wins in this compelling drama about a kidnapping that goes sour. B&W; 76m. **DIR:** George Marshall. **CAST:** Rochelle Hudson, Bruce Cabot, Cesar Romero, Edward Norris, Edward Brophy. **1935**

SHOWDOWN, THE (1950) ★★★★ "Wild" Bill Elliott's last Western for Republic Pictures is one of his best, a revenge story enlivened by a top-flight cast and a powerful performance by its star. Elliott is a former lawman on the trail of the man who murdered his brother, a trail that leads to a cattle drive. B&W; 86m. **DIR:** Darrell McGowan, Stuart E. McGowan. **CAST:** William Elliott, Walter Brennan, Marie Windsor, Harry Morgan, Jim Davis, Rhys Williams, Leif Erickson, Yakima Canutt. **1950**

SHOWDOWN (1973) ★★★★ Starting with the familiar tale of childhood friends who end up on opposite sides of the law, director George Seaton and his screenwriters mix inventive plot twists and sharply drawn characterizations for a compelling tale that plays especially well on the small screen. Rated PG for violence. 100m. **DIR:** George Seaton. **CAST:** Rock Hudson, Dean Martin, Susan Clark, Donald Moffat, John McLiam, Ed Begley Jr. **1973**

SHOWDOWN AT BOOT HILL ★★1/2 Stone-faced Charles Bronson does some impressive work as a lawman who finds that the criminal he has killed in the line of duty is actually a respected citizen in another community. B&W; 71m. **DIR:** Gene Fowler Jr. **CAST:** Charles Bronson, Robert Hutton, John Carradine. **1958**

SHOWDOWN AT WILLIAMS CREEK ★★★1/2 A British soldier, John Brown (Tom Burlinson), leaves Ireland for America in hopes of making his fortune and "coming back a gentleman." But the rugged, dangerous life in the frontier, with its treacherous schemers, teaches Brown what it means to be a survivor—and on trial for murder. Donnelly Rhodes gives a superb supporting turn. Fascinating, harddged Western was based on true events. Rated R for violence, nudity, and profanity. 97m. DIR: Allan Kroeker. CAST: Tom Burlinson, Donnelly Rhodes, Raymond Burr. 1991

SHOWDOWN IN LITTLE TOKYO ★★ As martial arts films go, this one is only fair. Its appeal lies in the action sequences and with the stars Dolph Lundgren and Brandon Lee. Rated R for violence, profanity, and nudity. 77m. DIR: Mark L. Lester. CAST: Dolph Lundgren, Brandon Lee, Tia Carrere. 1991 DVD

SHOWGIRL MURDERS ★★ Despite its low-budget and low-rent cast, this erotic thriller is actually better than *Showgirls* in that it never strives to be anything more than it is. Maria Ford is Tamra, a stripper on the run from a violent past, who helps turn a dingy bar into a popular hot spot. Lots of flesh with no excuses. Not rated; contains nudity, adult situations, violence, and profanity. 85m. DIR: Gene Hertel. CAST: Maria Ford, Matt Preston, Samantha Carter, Bob McFarland. 1995

SHOWGIRLS 💗 This so-called insider's glance at the life of a Las Vegas lap dancer may well be the worst big-studio production ever filmed, thanks in equal part to superstar scripter Joe Eszterhas's odious screenplay, and neophyte star Elizabeth Berkeley's atrocious acting. Rarely has so much been spent to produce so little. Rated NC-17 for nudity, simulated sex, rape, profanity, and violence. 131m. DIR: Paul Verhoeven. CAST: Elizabeth Berkeley, Kyle MacLachlan, Gina Gershon, Glenn Plummer, Robert Davi, Alan Rachins. 1995 DVD

SHOW-OFF, THE (1926) ★★★ Self-centered title character does his best to ruin his life and those of his wife and her inventor brother before being taken to task by peppery Louise Brooks in an early starring role. The first of three film versions of the popular play, this is as much melodrama as comedy and is considered to be the best. B&W; 82m. DIR: Malcolm St. Clair. CAST: Ford Sterling, Lois Wilson, Louise Brooks, Gregory Kelly, Claire McDowell. 1926

SHOW-OFF, THE (1946) ★★1/2 The third version of George Kelly's play is the weakest, but Red Skelton has the right personality for the leading role. He plays an office clerk who will do anything to impress a girlfriend and winds up getting in big trouble. Most of the laughs are supplied by the supporting cast because, strangely, Skelton has more straight lines than punch lines. B&W; 84m. DIR: Harry Beaumont. CAST: Red Skelton, Marilyn Maxwell, Marjorie Main, Eddie "Rochester" Anderson, Leon Ames, Marshall Thompson, Grady Sutton, Lila Leeds. 1946

SHRIEK IN THE NIGHT, A ★★★ Ginger Rogers and Lyle Talbot play two fast-talking reporters competing for a juicy scoop on a murder case in this entertaining low-budget whodunit. This tidy thriller makes up for its lack of production quality by the spunky, enthusiastic performances by the two leads. B&W; 66m. DIR: Albert Ray. CAST: Ginger Rogers, Lyle Talbot, Arthur Hoyt, Purnell Pratt. 1933

SHRIEKER ★★ Creaky dark-house horror-thriller about a group of six college students who meet their fate one by one when they encounter a nasty two-headed monster from another dimension. Director Victoria Sloan follows the formula that's been spoofed in *Scream* to the letter. Not much to scream about, but horror fans might be a little less demanding. Rated R for adult situations, language, nudity, and violence. 80m. DIR: Victoria Sloan. CAST: Tanya Dempsey, Jamie Gannon, Parry Allen, Alison Cuffe, Roger Crowe, Chris Boyd. 1997

SHRIEKING, THE 💗 Tedious wannabe horror-action flick about Indian witchcraft used on some good old boys on motorcycles. Rated PG for violence. 93m. DIR: Leo Garen. CAST: Keith Carradine, Gary Busey, Scott Glenn. 1974

SHRIMP ON THE BARBIE ★★ The ordinarily watchable and funny Richard "Cheech" Marin is cast in this disappointing comedy as an unemployed Mexican-American who decides to try his luck in Australia. Rated PG-13 for profanity. 90m. DIR: Alan Smithee. CAST: Richard "Cheech" Marin, Emma Samms. 1990

SHRUNKEN HEADS ★★★1/2 Off-the-wall comedy-thriller involving three teens who attempt to clean up their mean streets and wind up dead. Their heads are severed by a voodoo practitioner, reanimated, and given special powers to hunt down their killers. Outrageous special effects and great camp performances make this direct-to-video effort a cut above the rest. Rated R for violence, language, and adult situations. 86m. DIR: Richard Elfman. CAST: Aeryk Egan, Becky Herbst, A. J. Damato, Bo Sharon, Julius W. Harris, Meg Foster. 1994

SHUTTERED ROOM, THE 💗 Unfaithful shocker is yet another in a long line of disappointments for fans of H. P. Lovecraft. 99m. DIR: David Greene. CAST: Gig Young, Carol Lynley, Oliver Reed. 1967

SHY PEOPLE ★★★ Moody drama about a New York writer (Jill Clayburgh) who journeys to the Louisiana bayous to get family-background information from distant Cajun relatives. Barbara Hershey, in an offbeat role, plays a dominating Cajun mother. Clayburgh gives a strong performance, and Martha Plimpton as her troublemaking daughter is fine too. Rated R for language and sexual content. 118m. DIR: Andrei Konchalovsky. CAST: Barbara Hershey, Jill Clayburgh, Martha Plimpton, Merritt Butrick, John Philbin, Mare Winningham. 1987

SIBERIADE ★★★★ Fabulous Russian epic follows two families from 1900 to 1960. Featuring two sexy female leads, this dispels the myths about passionless and unappealing Russian women. Spectacular scenery throughout and explosive special effects for the finale make this one of the most watchable Russian films to date. In Russian with English subtitles. Not rated; contains violence, gore, and sex. Interesting mix of B&W and color. 206m. DIR: Andrei Konchalovsky. CAST: Vladimir Samoilov, Vitaly Solomin, Nikita Mikhalkov, Lyudmila Gurchenko, Sergei Shakurov. 1980

SIBLING RIVALRY ★★★1/2 Kirstie Alley gives a hilarious performance as a woman whose first affair leads to disaster. By sheer force of combined will, director Carl Reiner and Alley turn a gimmicky, cutesy story into a genuinely amusing—albeit uneven—laughfest. Rated PG-13 for profanity. 89m. DIR: Carl Reiner. CAST: Kirstie Alley, Bill Pullman, Carrie Fisher, Jami Gertz, Sam Elliott, Scott Bakula, Frances Sternhagen, John Randolph, Ed O'Neill, Paul Benedict, Bill Macy. 1990

SICILIAN, THE 🖤 This adaptation of Mario Puzo's novel becomes a tedious bore thanks to heavy-handed and pretentious direction. Rated R for violence and profanity. 105m. **DIR:** Michael Cimino. **CAST:** Christopher Lambert, Terence Stamp, Joss Ackland, John Turturro, Richard Bauer, Barbara Sukowa, Giula Boschi, Barry Miller, Andreas Katsulas, Ramon Bieri. 1987

SICK: THE LIFE AND DEATH OF BOB FLANAGAN, SUPERMASOCHIST ★★★ Flanagan, afflicted from birth with cystic fibrosis, a lung disorder that usually kills its victims by age 30, died at 43 in 1994. The premise of this strange but fascinating documentary is that Flanagan's longevity may have been due to his embracing—rather than trying to escape—a life of constant agony. Much of it was recorded on home video by his dominatrix lover and incorporated into this film. Not rated; contains extremely graphic (and completely genuine) scenes of sadomasochism. 90m. **DIR:** Kirby Dick. 1997

SID AND NANCY ★★★1/2 Leave it to Alex Cox, director of the suburban punk classic *Repo Man*, to try to make sense out of deceased punk rocker Sid Vicious and his girlfriend Nancy Spungen. Its compassionate portrait of the two famed nihilists is a powerful one, which nevertheless is not for everyone. Rated R for violence, sex, nudity, and adult subject matter. 111m. **DIR:** Alex Cox. **CAST:** Gary Oldman, Chloe Webb, Drew Schofield, David Hayman. 1986 DVD

SIDE BY SIDE: THE TRUE STORY OF THE OSMOND FAMILY ★★ If the title alone hasn't scared you away, you'll probably enjoy this schmaltzy TV movie featuring Marie Osmond as her own mother, raising nine children. It was produced by the Osmond family's own company, and it's every bit as squeaky-clean as that would indicate. 98m. **DIR:** Russ Mayberry. **CAST:** Marie Osmond, Joseph Bottoms. 1982

SIDE OUT ★★1/2 Peter Horton is a has-been volleyball pro with little going for him until he strikes up with C. Thomas Howell, who sparks his interest in a comeback. Some great contests with current pros Sinjin Smith and Randy Stoklos in this otherwise routine story. Rated PG-13. 103m. **DIR:** Peter Israelson. **CAST:** C. Thomas Howell, Peter Horton, Sinjin Smith, Randy Stoklos. 1990

SIDE SHOW ★★1/2 A young boy runs away to join the circus and discovers alcoholism, sex, and racial prejudice. When he witnesses a murder, he has to stay one step ahead of the killer. Not rated, but may not be suited for younger audiences. 98m. **DIR:** William Conrad. **CAST:** Lance Kerwin, Anthony Franciosa, Red Buttons, Connie Stevens. 1986

SIDEKICKS ★★★1/2 One of the best underdog fairy tales to emerge in years. Jonathan Brandis stars as an asthmatic high school kid who daydreams himself into elaborate, Walter Mitty–esque fantasies at the side of longtime hero Chuck Norris (who plays himself, and superbly spoofs many of his macho action hits). The supporting cast is excellent. Rated PG for fantasy-level violence. 100m. **DIR:** Aaron Norris.

CAST: Beau Bridges, Mako, Jonathan Brandis, Chuck Norris, Julia Nickson, Richard Moll, Joe Piscopo. 1993

SIDEWALKS OF LONDON ★★★ Street entertainer Charles Laughton puts pretty petty thief Vivien Leigh in his song-and-dance act, then falls in love with her. Befriended by successful songwriter Rex Harrison, she puts the streets and old friends behind her and rises to stage stardom while her rejected and dejected mentor hits the skids. Vivien Leigh is entrancing, and Charles Laughton is compelling and touching, in this dramatic sojourn in London byways. B&W; 85m. **DIR:** Tim Whelan. **CAST:** Vivien Leigh, Charles Laughton, Rex Harrison, Tyrone Guthrie. 1940

SIDEWALKS OF NEW YORK ★★ This Buster Keaton comedy would have made a very funny silent movie, but the actor gets bogged down with talk here. The camera lingers so long on his deadpan expression that the pace is irritatingly slow. The story of a rich playboy in love with a poor tenement girl turns into a sentimental cliché. B&W; 70m. **DIR:** Jules White, Zion Myers. **CAST:** Buster Keaton, Anita Page, Cliff Edwards, Syd Saylor, Clark Marshall, Frank Rowan, Frank La Rue. 1931

SIDEWINDER 1 ★★ Michael Parks is a quiet, reclusive motocross racer who becomes a partner in developing a new dirt bike. *Sidewinder 1* has good racing scenes—motocross fans will love them—but the story is studded with sexist remarks and attitudes. Rated PG. 97m. **DIR:** Earl Bellamy. **CAST:** Marjoe Gortner, Michael Parks, Susan Howard, Alex Cord. 1977

SIEGE, THE ★★★1/2 An intriguing premise is undermined by ill-defined central characters and an absurdly abrupt conclusion in this frequently disturbing urban thriller. Following the "extraction" of a Middle Eastern sheik believed responsible for an overseas terrorist incident that claimed numerous American lives, the man's fanatically devoted followers embark on a series of increasingly heinous acts in New York City. The military eventually places the Big Apple under martial law. Is it provocative? Absolutely. Is it persuasive? Regrettably … no. Rated R for violence, profanity, and sexual content. 115m. **DIR:** Edward Zwick. **CAST:** Denzel Washington, Annette Bening, Bruce Willis, Tony Shalhoub, Sami Bouajila. 1998 DVD

SIEGE OF FIREBASE GLORIA, THE ★★★ Outnumbered five to one, our Marines defended the hilltop outpost called Firebase Gloria during the Tet offensive in 1968. This is the dramatization of their seemingly hopeless struggle. Grisly scenes of death and destruction bring the Vietnam War close to home. Rated R. 95m. **DIR:** Brian Trenchard-Smith. **CAST:** Wings Hauser, R. Lee Ermey. 1988

SIEGFRIED ★★★★ Vivid, spectacular story of young god Siegfried, whose conquests and eventual murder form an intrinsic part of Teutonic legend, this nationalistic triumph for German director Fritz Lang was the most ambitious attempt to transfer folklore to film and proved an international success. Moody sets and photography give the movie an otherworldly feeling and evoke just the right atmosphere. Silent. B&W; 100m. **DIR:** Fritz Lang. **CAST:** Paul

Richter, Margarete Schon, Theodor Loos, Bernhard Goetzke. 1923

SIESTA ★★1/2 Oddly fascinating and sexually intense drama. Ellen Barkin plays a stuntwoman in love with a former trainer (Gabriel Byrne), a man who loved her but married someone else. The film plays with time, reality, and consciousness, turning them into something suspenseful. Rated R for language and sex. 90m. DIR: Mary Lambert. CAST: Ellen Barkin, Gabriel Byrne, Julian Sands, Jodie Foster, Martin Sheen, Isabella Rossellini, Grace Jones. 1987

SIGN OF FOUR, THE ★★1/2 Ian Richardson makes a fine Sherlock Holmes in this film produced for British television and fairly faithful adaptation from the story by Sir Arthur Conan Doyle. A cache of jewels brings nothing but avarice and danger to whoever possesses it, and it's up to Holmes and Dr. John H. Watson (well played by David Healy) to bring to justice a couple of creepy killers out to claim the treasure. 103m. DIR: Desmond Davis. CAST: Ian Richardson, David Healy, Cherie Lunghi, Terrence Rigby, Thorley Walters. 1983 DVD

SIGN OF ZORRO, THE ★★1/2 Baby boomers, beware. If you have fond memories of this swashbuckling Disney television series about the Z-slashing Robin Hood of Old Mexico, skip this uneven feature compilation of original episodes. It's still fine for the kiddies, however. B&W; 91m. DIR: Norman Foster, Lewis R. Foster. CAST: Guy Williams, Henry Calvin, Gene Sheldon, Britt Lomond, George J. Lewis, Lisa Gaye. 1960

SIGNAL 7 ★★★ Absorbing character study of two San Francisco cabbies features standout performances by Bill Ackridge and Dan Leegant. Entirely improvised, the film has a loose, almost documentary aproach. Not rated; contains a lot of profanity. 92m. DIR: Rob Nilsson. CAST: Bill Ackridge, Dan Leegant. 1983

SIGNS OF LIFE ★★★ When a shipyard goes out of business, its employees and owner are forced to face the inevitability of change. Rated PG-13 for profanity and violence. 95m. DIR: John David Coles. CAST: Arthur Kennedy, Beau Bridges, Vincent D'Onofrio, Kate Reid. 1989

SILAS MARNER ★★★★ Fate is the strongest character in this BBC-TV adaptation of George Eliot's novel, although Ben Kingsley gives an excellent performance as the cataleptic eighteenth-century English weaver. Betrayed by his closest friend and cast out of the church, Marner disappears into the English countryside and becomes a bitter miser, only to have his life wonderfully changed when fate brings an orphan girl to his hovel. 97m. DIR: Giles Foster. CAST: Ben Kingsley, Jenny Agutter, Patrick Ryecart, Patsy Kensit. 1985

SILENCE, THE ★★ One of Ingmar Bergman's more pretentious and claustrophobic films. Two sisters who are traveling together stop for a time in a European hotel. The film is laden with heavy-handed symbolism and banal dialogue. In Swedish with English subtitles. 95m. DIR: Ingmar Bergman. CAST: Ingrid Thulin, Gunnel Lindblom, Birger Malmsten. 1963

SILENCE LIKE GLASS ★ Disease-of-the-week movie about a ballet dancer afflicted with cancer, a giant ego, and a clichéd screenplay. Rated R for profanity. 109m. DIR: Carl Schenkel. CAST: Jami Gertz, Martha Plimpton, George Peppard, Bruce Payne, Rip Torn, Gayle Hunnicutt, James Remar. 1990

◆SILENCE OF THE HEART ★★★1/2 Powerful examination of teen suicide and the effects it has on the survivors. Mariette Hartley is exceptional as a mother and wife who is emotionally crippled but who still needs to be strong after the suicide of her son. Chad Lowe perfectly conveys the disillusionment of a teenager who feels like he's failing everyone and sees no way out. This made-for-television movie handles a tough subject with respect. Not rated. 100m. DIR: Richard Michaels. CAST: Mariette Hartley, Dana Hill, Howard Hesseman, Chad Lowe, Elizabeth Berridge, Charlie Sheen. 1984 DVD

SILENCE OF THE HAMS ★★ Half-baked attempt at spoofing *Psycho* and *Silence of the Lambs*. Director-writer-star Ezio Greggio strives to be the next Mel Brooks, but film is often uninspired and predictable. Some good jokes and an interesting cast are not enough to save this one from expiring before the big finale. Rated R for nudity, adult language, and comic violence. 85m. DIR: Ezio Greggio. CAST: Billy Zane, Dom DeLuise, Charlene Tilton, Ezio Greggio, Martin Balsam, John Astin, Phyllis Diller. 1993

SILENCE OF THE LAMBS ★★★★★ In this shock-filled powerhouse, an FBI cadet is assigned by her superior to interview an imprisoned, cannibalistic psychopath in the hopes of getting his help in capturing a crazed serial killer. Superb performances by Foster and Hopkins. From the novel by Thomas Harris. Rated R for violence, gore, nudity, and profanity. 118m. DIR: Jonathan Demme. CAST: Jodie Foster, Anthony Hopkins, Scott Glenn, Ted Levine, Tracey Walter, Charles Napier, Roger Corman. 1991 DVD

SILENCE OF THE NORTH ★★ There are some of us at the *Video Movie Guide* who would follow Ellen Burstyn anywhere. But Burstyn's narration here is pure melodrama, and ninety minutes of one catastrophe after the next is more tiring than entertaining. Burstyn portrays a woman who falls in love with a fur trapper, played by Tom Skerritt, and moves into the Canadian wilderness. Rated PG for violence. 94m. DIR: Allan Winton King. CAST: Ellen Burstyn, Tom Skerritt, Gordon Pinsent. 1981

SILENCER, THE ★★1/2 Newcomer Lynette Walden reaches the point of no return as a hit woman for a top-secret government agency. After she takes out the garbage, she drags in the trash, fulfilling her sexual desires by bedding down strangers off the street. She begins to suspect that she's on someone else's hit list. Decent action entry. Rated R for nudity, violence, and language. 85m. DIR: Amy Goldstein. CAST: Lynette Walden, Chris Mulkey, Paul Ganus, Jamie Gomez. 1992

SILENT ASSASSINS ♥ Stupid action flick about a CIA biggie gone bad. Not rated, but has violence and profanity. 91m. DIR: Lee Doo Young, Scott Thomas. CAST: Sam Jones, Linda Blair, Jun Chong, Phillip Rhee, Bill Erwin, Mako. 1987

SILENT CONFLICT ★★ A traveling charlatan hypnotizes and drugs Lucky into stealing money and trying to kill Hoppy and California. A fair series Western. B&W; 61m. **DIR:** George Archainbaud. **CAST:** William Boyd, Andy Clyde, Rand Brooks, Virginia Belmond. 1948

SILENT ENEMY, THE ★★1/2 World War II adventure has frogmen fighting it out in Gibraltar Harbor. Highlight: the underwater photography. B&W; 91m. **DIR:** William Fairchild. **CAST:** Laurence Harvey, Dawn Addams, John Clements. 1958

SILENT FALL ★★★1/2 Watchable murder-mystery has reclusive doctor Richard Dreyfuss coming out of a self-imposed exile to help an autistic 9-year-old witness to a bizarre double murder. Director Bruce Beresford brings his usual commitment to strong character development to the piece, but it is Dreyfuss's outstanding performance that holds the film together. Rated R for violence and profanity. 100m. **DIR:** Bruce Beresford. **CAST:** Richard Dreyfuss, Linda Hamilton, John Lithgow, J. T. Walsh, Ben Faulkner, Liv Tyler. 1994 DVD

SILENT HUNTER ★★★ Retired Florida cop Miles O'Keeffe gets a second crack at the crooks who murdered his family when they pull a robbery near the mountain where he now lives. Rated R for violence, profanity, and nudity. 97m. **DIR:** Fred Williamson. **CAST:** Miles O'Keeffe, Fred Williamson. 1995

SILENT MADNESS 🖤 Escaped maniac terrorizes a college campus. Rated R for nudity, violence, and profanity. 93m. **DIR:** Simon Nuchtern. **CAST:** Belinda Montgomery, Viveca Lindfors, Sidney Lassick. 1985

SILENT MOBIUS ★★ This animated story of futuristic ghostbusters is almost interesting at times, but in the end it's only mediocre. In a twenty-first century metropolis, a group of psychic policewomen track down evil spirits that infest the city. Dubbed. Not rated; contains nudity and graphic violence. 50m. **DIR:** Michitaka Kikuchi. 1991

SILENT MOTIVE ★★★ Scandalous screenwriter Patricia Wettig gets a taste of her own medicine when a copycat killer uses her scripts as a blueprint for murder. Detective Mike Farrell must prove she didn't do it, or did she? Right! Standard made-for-TV thriller gets a boost from familiar, durable cast. 90m. **DIR:** Lee Philips. **CAST:** Patricia Wettig, Edward Asner, Mike Farrell, Rick Springfield, David Packer. 1991

SILENT MOUSE ★★★★ A mouse rescued by a young village boy determines to repay his kindness by becoming the church mouse. Filmed in the magic mountains of Austria and Czechoslovakia and featuring many of Europe's most famous ensembles, choirs, and orchestras, this playful made-for-TV story will delight viewers of all ages. 50m. **DIR:** Robin Crichton. **CAST:** Lynn Redgrave, Gregor Fisher, Jack McKenzie. 1990

SILENT MOVIE ★★★1/2 Mel Brooks's *Silent Movie* is another kitchen-sink affair, with Brooks going from the ridiculous to the sublime with a beautiful idea that bears more exploring. Silent films were the best for comedy, and Brooks, along with costars Marty Feldman, Dom De Luise, and Sid Caesar, supplies numerous funny moments. Rated PG. 86m. **DIR:** Mel Brooks. **CAST:** Mel Brooks, Marty Feldman, Dom DeLuise, Bernadette Peters, Sid Caesar, James Caan, Burt Reynolds, Paul Newman, Liza Minnelli, Anne Bancroft, Marcel Marceau, Harry Ritz, Ron Carey. 1976

SILENT NIGHT, BLOODY NIGHT ★★★ Give this one an extra star for originality, even if it's not that well produced. Lawyer Patrick O'Neal and girlfriend Mary Woronov spend a few nights in an old house that he is trying to sell. But the place used to be an insane asylum, and it has quite an interesting history. Rated R, it may be a bit too strong for kids. 88m. **DIR:** Theodore Gershuny. **CAST:** Patrick O'Neal, John Carradine, Mary Woronov. 1973

SILENT NIGHT, DEADLY NIGHT 🖤 This is the one that caused such a commotion among parents' groups for its depiction of Santa Claus as a homicidal killer. No rating, but contains gobs of nudity and violent bloodshed. 92m. **DIR:** Charles E. Sellier Jr. **CAST:** Lilyan Chauvin, Gilmer McCormick, Robert Brian Wilson, Toni Nero. 1984

SILENT NIGHT, DEADLY NIGHT PART 2 🖤 The first half of this sequel is composed almost entirely of flashback scenes from the earlier movie. Rated R for nudity and gore. 88m. **DIR:** Lee Harry. **CAST:** Eric Freeman, James L. Newman, Elizabeth Cayton. 1987

SILENT NIGHT, DEADLY NIGHT III: BETTER WATCH OUT! ★★ Better than the first two in the slasher Santa series, but still nothing to get excited over. The Santa slasher awakens from a coma with a psychic connection to a young woman. Rated R for violence, profanity, and nudity. 91m. **DIR:** Monte Hellman. **CAST:** Richard Beymer, Bill Moseley, Samantha Scully, Robert Culp. 1989

SILENT NIGHT, DEADLY NIGHT 4—INITIATION ★★★ This fourth installment doesn't have any relation to the previous three films. Supernatural story that just happens to take place around Christmas. Rated R for violence and profanity. 90m. **DIR:** Brian Yuzna. **CAST:** Maud Adams, Tommy Hinkley, Allyce Beasley, Clint Howard. 1990

SILENT NIGHT, DEADLY NIGHT 5: THE TOY MAKER 🖤 An old toymaker named Joe Peto and his oddball son Pino, make deadly toys designed to kill their child owners. A twisted but silly attempt at horror. Rated R for violence, profanity, and simulated sex. 90m. **DIR:** Martin Kitrosser. **CAST:** Mickey Rooney, Jane Higginson. 1991

SILENT NIGHT, LONELY NIGHT ★★1/2 Slow-moving, but fairly interesting TV film about two lonely people (Lloyd Bridges and Shirley Jones) who share a few happy moments at Christmastime. Flashbacks to previous tragedies are distracting. Not rated. 98m. **DIR:** Daniel Petrie. **CAST:** Lloyd Bridges, Shirley Jones, Carrie Snodgress, Robert Lipton. 1969

SILENT PARTNER, THE ★★★1/2 This suspense-thriller is what they call a sleeper. It's an absolutely riveting tale about a bank teller (Elliott Gould) who, knowing of a robbery in advance, pulls a switch on a psychotic criminal (Christopher Plummer) and might not live to regret it. A real find for movie buffs, but be forewarned; it has a couple of truly unsettling scenes of violence. Rated R. 103m. **DIR:** Daryl Duke. **CAST:** Elliott Gould, Christopher Plummer, Susannah York, John Candy. 1978

•**SILENT PREDATORS** ★★ If you've seen one movie about snakes on the rampage, you've seen them all. Aggressive developing in a small town stirs up a den of deadly hybrid rattlesnakes, which then go out and kill people. Despite the best efforts of the cast, this made-for-cable original just can't struggle beyond its lame dialogue and insipid action. Not rated; contains violence. 95m. DIR: Noel Nosseck. CAST: Harry Hamlin, Shannon Sturges, David Spielberg, Patty McCormack, Jack Scalia. 1999

●SILENT PREY ✹ Incompetent action film made as a vehicle for Carol Shaya, a New York cop who was fired after she posed for *Playboy*. Not rated; contains nudity, violence, and profanity. 93m. DIR: Tom Avitabile. CAST: Carol Shaya, Frank Pelligrino, Neal Jones. 1998

SILENT RAGE ✹ A Texas sheriff is pitted against a psychotic killer. Rated R for nudity, profanity, and violence. 105m. DIR: Michael Miller. CAST: Chuck Norris, Ron Silver, Stephen Furst. 1982

SILENT REBELLION ★★ Telly Savalas plays a naturalized American who goes back to his hometown in Greece to visit. But the cross-cultural experience is not always pleasant. Some poignant moments, but lots of dull ones, too. Not rated. 90m. DIR: Charles S. Dubin. CAST: Telly Savalas, Michael Constantine, Keith Gordon. 1982

SILENT RUNNING ★★★★ True science fiction is most entertaining when it is not just glittering special effects and is, instead, accompanied by a well-developed plot and worthwhile message. This is such a picture. Bruce Dern is in charge of a futuristic space station that is entrusted with the last living remnants of Earth's botanical heritage. His efforts to preserve those trees and plants in spite of an order to destroy them makes for thoughtful moviemaking. Rated G. 89m. DIR: Douglas Trumbull. CAST: Bruce Dern, Cliff Potts, Ron Rifkin. 1971 DVD

SILENT SCREAM ★★1/2 This is a well-done shock film with a semi-coherent plot and enough thrills to satisfy the teens. Rated R. 87m. DIR: Denny Harris. CAST: Yvonne De Carlo, Barbara Steele, Avery Schreiber, Rebecca Balding. 1980

SILENT TONGUE ★★★ Talbot grieves for his Indian wife, who died during childbirth. His father tracks down the man from whom he bought Talbot's first wife. This tidy little morality play gets pretty weird at moments, but the cast and Shepard's words keep us interested. Rated PG-13 for violence and language. 101m. DIR: Sam Shepard. CAST: Richard Harris, Alan Bates, River Phoenix, Dermot Mulroney, Tantoo Cardinal, Sheila Tousey. 1991

SILENT TOUCH, THE ★★★ Max von Sydow delivers a bravura performance as an aging world-famous composer who feels his career and life have come to an end. Enter a mysterious young man who sets out to heal his wounds and give him the strength to make music again. Rated PG-13 for strong language. 92m. DIR: Krzysztof Zanussi. CAST: Max von Sydow, Lothaire Bluteau, Sarah Miles. 1992

SILENT TRIGGER ★★★ Weary contract killer Dolph Lundgren wants out of the assassination game, but his never-seen supervisor has other ideas. Rated R for violence, profanity, and brief nudity. 90m. DIR: Russell Mulcahy. CAST: Dolph Lundgren, Gina Bellman, Conrad Dunn, Christopher Heyerdahl. 1996

SILENT VICTIM ★★★1/2 Compelling true story follows distraught, pregnant wife Michele Greene, whose suicide attempt kills her unborn child. Her husband then sues her for performing an illegal abortion. Interesting idea gets plenty of mileage in the courtroom, where the issues of responsibility and morality are examined in gripping fashion. Rated R for language. 116m. DIR: Menahem Golan. CAST: Michele Greene, Kyle Secor, Alex Hyde-White, Ely Pouget. 1992

SILENT VICTORY: THE KITTY O'NEIL STORY ★★★ Better-than-average TV biography of ace stuntwoman Kitty O'Neil, who overcame the handicap of being deaf to excel in her profession. Proof positive is O'Neil doubling Channing in the stunt scenes. 100m. DIR: Lou Antonio. CAST: Stockard Channing, James Farentino, Colleen Dewhurst, Edward Albert, Brian Dennehy. 1979

SILENT WITNESS: WHAT A CHILD SAW ★★★ An African-American boy witnesses the murder of three Koreans in this made-for-cable movie. It generates interest, thanks to the plight of the young boy. Not rated; contains violence. 93m. DIR: Bruce Pittman. CAST: Mia Korf, Clark Johnson, Bill Nunn, Richard Chevolleau, Richard Yearwood, Amir Williams, Ron White. 1993

SILHOUETTE ✹ Cosmopolitan Faye Dunaway witnesses a murder in this insipid made-for-cable whodunit. 95m. DIR: Carl Schenkel. CAST: Faye Dunaway, David Rasche, John Terry. 1990

SILK DEGREES ★★ A TV star is being stalked by a terrorist, and it's up to two federal agents to keep him from discovering her whereabouts. Rated R for violence and sexual scenes. 90m. DIR: Armand Garabidian. CAST: Marc Singer, Deborah Shelton, Michael Des Barres, Mark Hamill, Adrienne Barbeau, Charles Napier, Gilbert Gottfried. 1994

SILK 'N' SABOTAGE ✹ Lamentable soft-core dreck about a curvaceous computer programmer whose ultraslick software game is stolen by a cardboard villain. If this picture has even fifteen minutes of dialogue spaced between the incessant skin scenes, we'll be amazed. Rated R for nudity, simulated sex, and profanity. 78m. DIR: Joe Cauley. CAST: Julie Skiru, Stephanie Champlin, Cherilyn Shea, Darren Foreman. 1994

SILK ROAD, THE ★★★1/2 Boasting a cast of thousands, this is actually a romance set amid turbulent China of 1026 B.C. An educated young man, enslaved in military service, saves a princess but is forced to leave her. When he returns, she is betrothed to the fierce prince whose armies have overrun her land and killed her father. In Chinese with English subtitles. Rated PG-13 for violence and gore. 99m. DIR: Junya Sato. CAST: Gohei Kogure, Kazuo Haruna, Toshiyuki Nishida, Koichi Sato, Anna Nakagawa. 1988

SILK STOCKINGS ★★★ In this remake, Greta Garbo's classic *Ninotchka* is given the Cole Porter musical treatment with a degree of success. Fred Astaire is a Hollywood producer who educates a Russian agent in the seductive allure of capitalism. Cyd Charisse plays the Garbo role. 117m. DIR: Rouben

Mamoulian. **CAST:** Fred Astaire, Cyd Charisse, Janis Paige, Peter Lorre, Barrie Chase. **1957**

SILK 2 💖 Former Playmate of the Year Monique Gabrielle plays a hard-core policewoman who will do anything to help her partner who's been kidnapped. Rated R. 76m. **DIR:** Cirio H. Santiago. **CAST:** Monique Gabrielle, Peter Nelson, Jan Merlin. **1989**

SILKWOOD ★★★★ At more than two hours, *Silkwood* is a shift-and-squirm movie that's worth it. The fine portrayals by Meryl Streep, Kurt Russell, and Cher keep the viewer's interest. Based on real events, the story focuses on 28-year-old nuclear worker and union activist Karen Silkwood, who died in a mysterious car crash while she was attempting to expose the alleged dangers in the Oklahoma plutonium plant where she was employed. Rated R for nudity, sex, and profanity. 128m. **DIR:** Mike Nichols. **CAST:** Meryl Streep, Kurt Russell, Cher, Craig T. Nelson, Fred Ward, Sudie Bond. **1984 DVD**

SILVER BEARS ★★ If *Silver Bears* was meant to be a comedy, it isn't funny. If it was meant to be a drama, it isn't gripping. It's boring. Michael Caine stars as a Mafia henchman sent to Switzerland to buy a bank. He's swindled and ends up buying two rooms over a pizza parlor. Rated PG. 113m. **DIR:** Ivan Passer. **CAST:** Michael Caine, Cybill Shepherd, Louis Jourdan, Martin Balsam, Stéphane Audran, Tom Smothers, David Warner. **1978**

SILVER BLAZE ★★★ Arthur Wontner starred as Holmes in five handsome but low-budget films; ironically, this movie was not released in America until after *Hound of the Baskervilles* introduced Basil Rathbone as the screen's most famous detective. So impressive was Rathbone's debut as Holmes, the American distributor retitled *Silver Blaze* as *Murder at the Baskervilles*. This is a loose adaptation of the original story about the disappearance of a prized racehorse. It may not be faithful, but *Silver Blaze* is fun for mystery fans. B&W; 60m. **DIR:** Thomas Bentley. **CAST:** Arthur Wontner, Ian Fleming, Lyn Harding, John Turnbull, Robert Horton, Arthur Goulet. **1937**

SILVER BULLET ★★★★ A superior Stephen King horror film, this release moves like the projectile after which it was named. From the opening scene, in which a railroad worker meets his gruesome demise at the claws of a werewolf, to the final confrontation between our heroes (Gary Busey and Corey Haim) and the hairy beast, it's an edge-of-your-seat winner. Rated R for violence and gore. 90m. **DIR:** Daniel Attias. **CAST:** Gary Busey, Everett McGill, Corey Haim, Megan Follows, James Gammon, Robin Groves. **1985**

SILVER CHALICE, THE ★★ Full of intrigue and togas, this film is notable only for two unnotable screen debuts by Paul Newman and Lorne Greene. 144m. **DIR:** Victor Saville. **CAST:** Jack Palance, Joseph Wiseman, Paul Newman, Virginia Mayo, Pier Angeli, E. G. Marshall, Alexander Scourby, Natalie Wood, Lorne Greene. **1954**

SILVER DREAM RACER ★★1/2 This so-so British drama features David Essex as a mechanic turned racer. He is determined to win not only the World Motorcycle Championship, but another man's girlfriend as well. Rated PG. 110m. **DIR:** David Wickes. **CAST:**

David Essex, Beau Bridges, Cristina Raines, Clark Peters, Harry H. Corbett. **1980**

SILVER ON THE SAGE ★★1/2 Hopalong Cassidy discovers a crooked ranch foreman and a saloon owner are actually look-alike brothers bleeding the locals and anyone else who comes their way. The crooks pin Hoppy down with hot lead until his sidekicks show up with help. B&W; 68m. **DIR:** Lesley Selander. **CAST:** William Boyd, Russell Hayden, George "Gabby" Hayes, Stanley Ridges, Jack Rockwell. **1939**

SILVER QUEEN ★★ Young and devoted daughter Priscilla Lane is determined to uphold her family's honor and pay her father's debts by gambling in San Francisco, where she develops a reputation as a real sharpie. B&W; 81m. **DIR:** Lloyd Bacon. **CAST:** George Brent, Priscilla Lane, Bruce Cabot, Lynne Overman, Eugene Pallette, Guinn Williams. **1942**

SILVER RIVER ★★1/2 Promising Western starts out well enough but becomes bogged down. A good cast of veterans manages to make things interesting, but film could have been much better. B&W; 110m. **DIR:** Raoul Walsh. **CAST:** Errol Flynn, Ann Sheridan, Thomas Mitchell, Bruce Bennett, Barton MacLane. **1948**

SILVER SPURS ★★★1/2 Better-than-average cast and strong screenplay raise the routine plot to make this one of Roy Rogers's better middle-era Westerns. Nefarious John Carradine tries to fleece Rogers's boss out of oil-rich land. B&W; 54m. **DIR:** Joseph Kane. **CAST:** Roy Rogers, Smiley Burnette, John Carradine, Phyllis Brooks, Sons of the Pioneers, Jerome Cowan. **1943**

SILVER STALLION, THE ★★1/2 Although trying for the mythic qualities and superior horsemanship of *The Man from Snowy River*, this Australian adaptation of Elyne Mitchell's *The Silver Brumby* moves at a snail's pace. Only avid horse lovers will sit still for the ponderous story-within-a-story that follows the author (played reasonably well by Caroline Goodall) as she writes of the wild stallion who roams the Australian bush. While it's nice to have wholesome family entertainment, must it be so dull? Rated G. 93m. **DIR:** John Tatoulis. **CAST:** Caroline Goodall, Russell Crowe, Ami Daemion. **1994**

SILVER STRAND ★★★ Scripter Douglas Day Stewart returns to the territory he mined so well in *An Officer and a Gentleman*, with this familiar study of a young officer finding his soul while surviving Navy SEAL training. Anjul Nigam truly shines as a jovial recruit from Bangladesh. You're likely to have trouble with the conclusion; Stewart may have intended it as triumphant, but we're not so sure. Rated R for profanity, violence, nudity, and simulated sex. 104m. **DIR:** George Miller. **CAST:** Nicollette Sheridan, Gil Bellows, Jay O. Sanders, Tony Plana, Jennifer O'Neill, Wolfgang Bodison, Anjul Nigam. **1995**

SILVER STREAK (1934) ★★ Interesting primarily for the vintage locomotives and the railway system as well as a good cast of unique personalities. B&W; 72m. **DIR:** Thomas Atkins. **CAST:** Charles Starrett, Sally Blane, Hardie Albright, William Farnum, Irving Pichel, Arthur Lake. **1934**

SILVER STREAK (1976) ★★★★1/2 Fast-paced action story laced with comedy and stars will have you cheering, laughing, and gasping. *Streak* pits neurotic Wilder, sexy Clayburgh, and shifty Pryor against a cool millionaire villain and his evil henchman in a wild high-speed chase. Rated PG. 113m. **DIR:** Arthur Hiller. **CAST:** Gene Wilder, Jill Clayburgh, Richard Pryor, Patrick McGoohan, Ray Walston, Ned Beatty, Richard Kiel. 1976

SILVERADO ★★★1/2 Scott Glenn, Kevin Kline, Kevin Costner, and Danny Glover ride side by side to clean up the town of Silverado. Excitement, laughs, thrills, and chills abound in this marvelous movie. Even those who don't ordinarily like Westerns are sure to enjoy it. Rated PG-13 for violence and profanity. 133m. **DIR:** Lawrence Kasdan. **CAST:** Kevin Kline, Scott Glenn, Kevin Costner, Danny Glover, Rosanna Arquette, John Cleese, Brian Dennehy, Linda Hunt, Jeff Goldblum. 1985 DVD

SILVERLAKE LIFE: THE VIEW FROM HERE ★★★★ Brutal but mesmerizing, this uncompromising documentary follows Mark Massi, diagnosed with AIDS, and his longtime companion, AIDS patient Tom Joslin. A "video diary" chronicles their love, shortened life span, and Tom's death. One of the most personal, and political, films ever made. Not rated; contains profanity and adult themes. 99m. **DIR:** Tom Joslin, Peter Friedman. **CAST:** Mark Massi, Tom Joslin. 1993

SIMBA ★★★★ In this hard-hitting drama, the ne'er-do-well brother (Dirk Bogarde) of a philanthropic doctor arrives in Kenya to find his brother has been murdered. Thought-provoking study of racial strife. 99m. **DIR:** Brian Desmond Hurst. **CAST:** Dirk Bogarde, Virginia McKenna, Basil Sydney. 1955

SIMON ★★ Weird, weird comedy about an average guy (Alan Arkin) who is brainwashed into thinking he's a visitor from outer space. The film has some funny moments, but it just doesn't work as a whole. Rated PG. 97m. **DIR:** Marshall Brickman. **CAST:** Alan Arkin, Madeline Kahn, Austin Pendleton, William Finley, Fred Gwynne. 1980

SIMON BIRCH ★★★★ In its own quiet way, Mark Steven Johnson's loose take on John Irving's *A Prayer for Owen Meany* will break your heart, yet leave you uplifted. The ugly-duckling title character is a little boy trying to fathom the reason for his presence on Earth. His one staunch friend knows only too well the stigma of being an outcast. This film is sentimental without becoming maudlin, upsetting without becoming intolerable, instructive without becoming didactic. Rated PG for dramatic intensity and mild profanity. 110m. **DIR:** Mark Steven Johnson. **CAST:** Joseph Mazzello, Oliver Platt, David Strathairn, Ian Michael Smith, Dana Ivey, Ashley Judd. 1998 DVD

SIMON, KING OF THE WITCHES ❤ Modern-day warlock lives in a Los Angeles sewer. Rated R. 90m. **DIR:** Bruce Kessler. **CAST:** Andrew Prine, Brenda Scott. 1971

SIMON OF THE DESERT ★★★1/2 Impossible to deny the sly pleasure we have with St. Simon Stylites, the desert anchorite who spent thirty-seven years atop a sixty-foot column (circa A.D. 400) preaching to Christian flocks and avoiding temptation. Good nasty fun for aficionados and novices alike. In Spanish with English subtitles. B&W; 40m.

DIR: Luis Buñuel. **CAST:** Claudio Brook, Silvia Pinal. 1965

●**SIMPATICO** ★★1/2 Sam Shepard's snakelike 1994 play about festering souls and secret dirty laundry doesn't quite make the leap to the big screen. A Kentucky horse breeder plunges into the aftermath of a racing scam after a derelict buddy calls from California and makes murky references to a crime from the men's past. The all-star cast is excellent but this initially intriguing story about personal demons, corruption, lost love, and emotional vengeance slowly stagnates. Rated R for language and sexual content. 106m. **DIR:** Matthew Warchus. **CAST:** Jeff Bridges, Nick Nolte, Albert Finney, Sharon Stone, Catherine Keener. 2000

SIMPLE JUSTICE ★★1/2 A team of madmen rob a bank, fatally shooting some and leaving a beautiful newlywed (Cady McClain) for dead. Her husband (Matthew Galle) and grandparents must cope with continued threats from the men who fear McClain will testify against them. Rated R for violence and profanity. 91m. **DIR:** Deborah Del Prete. **CAST:** Cesar Romero, Doris Roberts, Matthew Galle, Cady McClain. 1989

SIMPLE MEN ★★★ Director Hal Hartley's offbeat road movie is short on plot but long on eccentric behavior. Brothers Robert Burke and William Sage go looking for their father and encounter a cast of characters more off kilter than they are. One brother and the father are wanted by the law, but when they team up with mystery women Karen Sillas and Elina Lowensohn, their lives really become complicated. Rated R for language and adult situations. 105m. **DIR:** Hal Hartley. **CAST:** Robert Burke, William Sage, Karen Sillas, Elina Lowensohn, Mary Mackenzie. 1992

SIMPLE PLAN, A ★★★★ Blood bonds are strenuously tested as two midwestern brothers find over $4 million in a beer-swilling chum trots us through a bleak moral landscape soon littered with bodies. This lean crime-drama is a powder keg of surprises. Rated R for language and violence. 96m. **DIR:** Sam Raimi. **CAST:** Bill Paxton, Billy Bob Thornton, Brent Briscoe, Bridget Fonda. 1998 DVD

SIMPLE STORY, A ★★★1/2 Marie (Romy Schneider) is pregnant and decides to have an abortion. At forty, she is forced to reevaluate her life and her relationships with men. Rewarding film is paced very slowly and plot is interwoven with subplots of other characters in distress. One of Romy Schneider's best performances. In French with English subtitles. No MPAA rating. 110m. **DIR:** Claude Sautet. **CAST:** Romy Schneider, Bruno Cremer, Claude Brasseur, Roger Pigaut. 1978

SIMPLE TWIST OF FATE, A ★★★1/2 Star-writer Steve Martin updates George Eliot's *Silas Marner* for this effective tale of a man who all but cuts himself off from the world after he discovers that the child his wife is about to have is not his. Then, a baby is left on his doorstep. Rated PG-13 for profanity. 106m. **DIR:** Gillies MacKinnon. **CAST:** Steve Martin, Gabriel Byrne, Laura Linney, Catherine O'Hara, Stephen Baldwin, Bryon Jennings, Michael Des Barres, Amelia Campbell, Kellen Crosby. 1994

SIMPLE WISH, A ★★1/2 Martin Short plays a bumbling fairy godmother (yes, godmother) who tries to grant a young girl's wish for success for her struggling actor father. There are some good things here: nice performances and a clever parody of Lord Andrew Lloyd Webber. But the film is a hodgepodge, and director Michael Ritchie can't quite bring all the good things together in one coherent piece. Rated PG. 89m. **DIR:** Michael Ritchie. **CAST:** Martin Short, Mara Wilson, Kathleen Turner, Robert Pastorelli, Amanda Plummer, Ruby Dee, Teri Garr. 1997 DVD

SIN OF HAROLD DIDDLEBOCK (MAD WEDNESDAY) ★★★1/2 This is a much better film than popular Hollywood legend implies. It's a story about a middle-aged man fired from his job and set adrift with nothing but unfulfilled potential. Backer Howard Hughes rereleased it in 1950 as *Mad Wednesday* and edited it down to 79 minutes. B&W; 90m. **DIR:** Preston Sturges. **CAST:** Harold Lloyd, Frances Ramsden, Jimmy Conlin, Raymond Walburn, Edgar Kennedy, Arline Judge, Lionel Stander, Margaret Hamilton, Rudy Vallee. 1947

SIN OF MADELON CLAUDET, THE ★★★★ The heroine's sin in this unabashed tearjerker is bearing a child out of wedlock. Her redemption lies in a lifetime of devotion and sacrifice. Helen Hayes's Oscar-winning performance is a distinct plus. B&W; 73m. **DIR:** Edgar Selwyn. **CAST:** Helen Hayes, Neil Hamilton, Lewis Stone, Marie Prevost, Karen Morley, Jean Hersholt, Robert Young. 1931

SINBAD AND THE EYE OF THE TIGER ★★1/2 Sinbad seeks the hand of Princess Farah and permission from her brother, who has been turned into a baboon. Not a terrible movie (children will love it), but all the movie tricks in the world cannot disguise a bad story. Rated G. 113m. **DIR:** Sam Wanamaker. **CAST:** Patrick Wayne, Jane Seymour, Damien Thomas, Margaret Whiting, Patrick Troughton, Taryn Power. 1977

SINBAD OF THE SEVEN SEAS ★★ Lou Ferrigno stars in this mediocre Italian adaptation of the familiar fairy tale. Ferrigno, as Sinbad, must take on an evil wizard and return his Kingdom to its former bliss. Rated PG-13 for violence. 95m. **DIR:** Enzo G. Castellari. **CAST:** Lou Ferrigno, John Steiner. 1989

SINBAD THE SAILOR ★★ Aping his father, Douglas Fairbanks Jr., as Sinbad, sails forth in search of Alexander the Great's fabled treasure and hits a variety of reefs. Unfortunately, the plot not only thickens but gets murky, to boot. Some say it's all tongue-in-cheek, but it's really more foot-in-mouth. Nonetheless, it is fun. 117m. **DIR:** Richard Wallace. **CAST:** Douglas Fairbanks Jr., Walter Slezak, Maureen O'Hara, Jane Greer, Anthony Quinn, Sheldon Leonard. 1947

SINCE YOU WENT AWAY ★★ This overlong, World War II soap opera doesn't hold together despite a great cast of stars and character actors, often in minor roles. Big-budget weeper tells of life on the home front. B&W; 152m. **DIR:** John Cromwell. **CAST:** Claudette Colbert, Joseph Cotten, Jennifer Jones, Shirley Temple, Monty Woolley, Lionel Barrymore, Robert Walker, Hattie McDaniel, Agnes Moorehead, Guy Madison. 1944

SINCE YOU'VE BEEN GONE ★★1/2 *Friends* star David Schwimmer stars in and makes his directorial debut with this pedestrian comedy about a high-school reunion. The characters and situations are obvious in this made-for-cable film. Rated R for language. 96m. **DIR:** David Schwimmer. **CAST:** David Schwimmer, Lara Flynn Boyle, Teri Hatcher, Joey Slotnick, Marisa Tomei, Jennifer Grey, Jerry Springer. 1997

SINCERELY CHARLOTTE ★★★ Caroline Huppert directs her sister Isabelle in this intriguing tale of a woman with a shady past. Isabelle finds herself in trouble with the law and seeks the help of her old lover, who's now married. It's the interaction among these three characters that is fun and enticing. In French with English subtitles. 92m. **DIR:** Caroline Huppert. **CAST:** Isabelle Huppert, Neils Arestrup, Christine Pascal, Luc Beraud. 1986

SINCERELY YOURS 🦃 Ridiculous, sincerely. 115m. **DIR:** Gordon Douglas. **CAST:** Liberace, Joanne Dru, Dorothy Malone, William Demarest, Lurene Tuttle, Richard Eyer. 1955

SINFUL INTRIGUE 🦃 A masked intruder attacks the female members of a wealthy community in this supposedly "erotic" whodunit. Rated R for violence. 85m. **DIR:** Edward Holzman. **CAST:** Bobby Johnston, Beckie Mullen, Griffen Drew, Mark Zuelke. 1995

SINFUL LIFE, A 🦃 An aging chorus girl must find a husband before she is declared an unfit mother by her daughter's teacher. Based on the stage play *Just Like the Pom Pom Girls*. Rated R for profanity. 90m. **DIR:** William Schreiner. **CAST:** Anita Morris, Rick Overton, Dennis Christopher. 1989

SING ★★★ A teen film with a commendable twist: no car chases! Actually, this is a cross between *Lady and the Tramp* and *Fame*. A tough Italian punk is forced to work with an innocent Jewish girl on the class musical. You guessed it! They fall for each other. Rated PG-13 for profanity. 99m. **DIR:** Richard Baskin. **CAST:** Peter Dobson, Jessica Steen, Lorraine Bracco, Patti LaBelle, Louise Lasser. 1989

SING, COWBOY, SING ★★★★ Wagon-train raiders are thwarted by Tex Ritter and his pards masquerading as entertainers. They needn't masquerade—this one entertains with the best of the B Westerns. Look for ex–Mack Sennett clowns Snub Pollard, Chester Conklin, and Al St. John. B&W; 59m. **DIR:** Robert N. Bradbury. **CAST:** Tex Ritter, Louise Stanley, Al St. John, Karl Hackett, Charles King, Snub Pollard, Chester Conklin. 1937

SINGAPORE ★★★1/2 Stylish *film noir* in which pearl smuggler Fred MacMurray returns to Singapore and the bittersweet memories of a lost love believed to have been killed during a Japanese bombing. Credibility is stretched a bit thin, but the cinematography alone provides substance. Remade in 1957 as *Istanbul*. Not rated. B&W; 80m. **DIR:** John Brahm. **CAST:** Fred MacMurray, Ava Gardner, Richard Haydn, Thomas Gomez, George Lloyd, Porter Hall, Spring Byington, Michael Van Leyden. 1947

SINGIN' IN THE RAIN ★★★★★ In the history of movie musicals, no single scene is more fondly remembered than Gene Kelly's song-and-dance routine to the title song. This picture has more to it than Kelly's well-choreographed splash through a wet city street. It has an interesting plot based on the panic that overran Hollywood during its conversion to sound, and it has wonderful performances. 102m. **DIR:** Gene Kelly, Stanley Donen. **CAST:** Gene Kelly, Debbie Reynolds, Donald O'Connor, Jean Hagen, Cyd Charisse, Rita Moreno. **1952 DVD**

SINGING NUN, THE ★★ Unbearably cheerful little bio-pic about the Dominican nun who sang on Ed Sullivan's TV show and supposedly captured the hearts of the nation. Just as slim as you'd expect. 98m. **DIR:** Henry Koster. **CAST:** Debbie Reynolds, Ricardo Montalban, Greer Garson, Agnes Moorehead, Chad Everett, Katharine Ross, Ed Sullivan. **1966**

SINGING THE BLUES IN RED ★★★1/2 An oppressed East German protest singer is forced to defect and ply his trade in the West, only to discover new avenues of repression in the capitalist system. Exactingly scripted in English with German subtitles. Not rated. 110m. **DIR:** Kenneth Loach. **CAST:** Gerulf Pannach. **1989**

SINGLE BARS, SINGLE WOMEN ❤ A dated film that pretends to know all about the singles scene. Made for TV. 100m. **DIR:** Harry Winer. **CAST:** Tony Danza, Paul Michael Glaser, Keith Gordon, Shelley Hack, Christine Lahti, Frances Lee McCain, Kathleen Wilhoite, Mare Winningham. **1984**

SINGLE GIRL ★★★1/2 Presumably inspired by Agnes Varda's nouvelle vague classic *Cleo from 5 to 7*, this French drama takes place in real time as a young woman spends her first day on a new job in a fancy hotel pondering her life and the news that she is pregnant. Like most real-time films, it's a bit contrived, but effective due to a strong performance by Virginie Ledoyen. In French with English subtitles. Not rated; contains nudity, sexual situations, and profanity. 90m. **DIR:** Benoit Jacquot. **CAST:** Virginie Ledoyen, Benoit Magimel. **1996 DVD**

SINGLE ROOM FURNISHED ❤ Jayne Mansfield's last movie was this lurid overwrought melodrama. 93m. **DIR:** Matt Cimber. **CAST:** Jayne Mansfield, Dorothy Keller, Fabian Dean. **1968**

SINGLE STANDARD, THE ★★ Tepid Greta Garbo vehicle that, like most avowedly feminist dramas of its time, fails to deliver on its initial premise. Garbo is a woman who tosses aside her wealth and social position to seek equality with an ex–prize fighter. Of interest primarily to Garbo completists who must see *everything*. Silent. B&W; 88m. **DIR:** John S. Robertson. **CAST:** Greta Garbo, Nils Asther, Johnny Mack Brown. **1929**

SINGLE WHITE FEMALE ★★★ This entry in the stranger-from-hell subgenre gets a good start when cultivated career woman Bridget Fonda, recovering from the betrayal of an unfaithful boyfriend, accepts mousy Jennifer Jason Leigh as her new roommate. Alas, things go to pot in the third act. Rated R for language, violence, and nudity. 107m. **DIR:** Barbet Schroeder. **CAST:** Bridget Fonda, Jennifer Jason Leigh, Steven Weber, Peter Friedman. **1992 DVD**

SINGLES ★★★★ High marks to writer-director Cameron Crowe for this witty study of twentysomethings seeking romance and personal fulfillment in the Seattle rock scene. The central players often speak directly to the viewer while justifying their be-

havior. Crowe has a definite ear for the verbal byplay of young love, and his ensemble cast is superb. Rated PG-13 for profanity and suggested sex. 99m. **DIR:** Cameron Crowe. **CAST:** Bridget Fonda, Campbell Scott, Kyra Sedgwick, Matt Dillon, Sheila Kelley, Jim True, Bill Pullman. **1992 DVD**

SINGLETON'S PLUCK ★★★ In this gentle British comedy, a goose farmer, whose business has been shut down by a strike, decides to herd his gaggle to the slaughterhouse himself. Television reporters begin to cover his hundred-mile trip and he becomes a national figure. 93m. **DIR:** Richard Eyre. **CAST:** Ian Holm, Penelope Wilton. **1984**

SINISTER INVASION ❤ Boris Karloff filmed scenes for this Mexican horror film just before his death. Also available in a truncated version, *Alien Terror*. 88m. **DIR:** Juan Ibanez, Jack Hill. **CAST:** Boris Karloff. **1968**

SINISTER URGE, THE ★★ Ed *(Plan 9 From Outer Space)* Wood's last film as a writer-director is one his fans won't want to miss. The police battle a ring of pornographers and a killer who gets so worked up by looking at these "dirty pictures" that he then goes to the park to kill innocent young women. In the best early-Sixties fashion, Wood got away with flashes of nudity by claiming social significance. Look for him in a brief appearance as a participant in a fistfight. B&W; 75m. **DIR:** Edward D. Wood Jr. **CAST:** Kenne Duncan, James Moore, Jean Fontaine. **1961**

SINK OR SWIM ★★ When a group of writers learns that one of their friends has been offered a job writing for a new television series, they stoop to new lows in friendship when they try to beat him to the punch. Rated R for language and adult situations. 93m. **DIR:** Gary Rosen. **CAST:** Stephen Rea, Illeana Douglas, John Ritter, David Foley, Robert Patrick, Tom Arnold. **1997 DVD**

SINK THE BISMARCK ★★★★ True story of the British Navy's relentless search for the German "super" battleship *Bismarck* is topflight war adventure. A standout production admired by both action fans and military historians. B&W; 97m. **DIR:** Lewis Gilbert. **CAST:** Kenneth More, Dana Wynter, Carl Mohner, Laurence Naismith, Geoffrey Keen, Karel Stepanek, Michael Hordern. **1960**

SINNERS IN PARADISE ★★1/2 Survivors of a plane crash find themselves on a tropical island, where they have plenty of time to reflect on their secrets and the things in their past that haunt them. An old idea is handled effectively. B&W; 65m. **DIR:** James Whale. **CAST:** Bruce Cabot, Madge Evans, Marion Martin, Gene Lockhart, John Boles, Milburn Stone, Don Barry. **1938**

SINS OF DORIAN GRAY, THE ★★ This modern-day version of Oscar Wilde's famous horror tale manages to disappoint at nearly every turn. Only the plot—about a beautiful woman who sells her soul for eternal youth and then watches a video screen test of herself age and decay—manages to fascinate. Made for television. 98m. **DIR:** Tony Maylam. **CAST:** Anthony Perkins, Belinda Bauer, Joseph Bottoms, Olga Karlatos, Michael Ironside. **1983**

SINS OF THE MIND ★★ In this made-for-cable drama, a woman suffers from a loss of sexual inhibition after being in a car accident. Her family thinks she's now a bad girl, but her doting father believes something physical is wrong. The rest of the plot is as hard to believe as the premise. Rated R for suggested sex. 93m. DIR: James Frawley. CAST: Jill Clayburgh, Mike Farrell, Louise Fletcher. 1997

•SINYSTER ★★1/2 Imaginative haunted-house movie. First-time director Ronnie Sortor has created a tense, violent film about a killer being infected by an evil house, but poor sound quality lessons the viewing experience. Not rated; contains violence. 80m. DIR: Ronnie Sortor. CAST: Steve Kelly, Lei Renniks, Frank Alexander. 1994

SIOUX CITY ★★ Adopted at an early age by rich Caucasian parents, a Native-American medical intern is haunted by visions of his biological mom. He returns to his birthplace—a Lakota reservation—to investigate her murder, is beaten by bad cops, and uses tribal rites to solve the crime. It's *Thunderheart* meets *Dr. Kildare* on a shoestring budget in this culturally sensitive but hollow search for ethnic roots and justice. Rated PG-13 for language, suggested sex, and violence. 102m. DIR: Lou Diamond Phillips. CAST: Lou Diamond Phillips, Salli Richardson, Ralph Waite, Melinda Dillon, Adam Roarke. 1994

SIR ARTHUR CONAN DOYLE'S THE LOST WORLD ★★★ Not exactly *Jurassic Park*, this direct-to-video release features story elements and situations geared toward adults. Although some of the special effects are a little cheesy, the overall effort stays true to Doyle's vision. A heroic Patrick Bergin stars as zoologist George Challenger, who treks to Northern Mongolia with a scientific expedition to prove that dinosaurs still exist. There's lots of action, close calls, dinosaurs, and some gore in this worthy entry into the genre. Rated R for violence. 96m. DIR: Bob Keen. CAST: Patrick Bergin, Jayne Heitmeyer. 1998

SIRENS (1993) ★★★ Straitlaced young minister Hugh Grant and his wife (Tara Fitzgerald) have their eyes opened when they visit a bohemian artist (Sam Neill) at his secluded mountain estate. Writer-director John Duigan's study of art, religion, and sexual repression manages to be thoughtful, erotic, and charmingly funny all at the same time. Rated R for nudity and mature themes. 94m. DIR: John Duigan. CAST: Hugh Grant, Tara Fitzgerald, Sam Neill, Elle Macpherson, Portia de Rossi, Kate Fischer. 1993

•SIRENS (1999) ★★★1/2 Racial issues and police negligence are the subjects of this engaging made-for-cable original. The police accost a woman (Dana Delany) and her black ex-husband; misreading the situation, the cops shoot him. From then on, Delany pursues justice in any way she can, but she has a hard time convincing anyone that the police have erred. Delany and the rest put in good performances. Not rated; contains violence, profanity, and nudity. 105m. DIR: John Scaret Young. CAST: Dana Delany, Keith Carradine, Justin Theroux, Vondie Curtis-Hall, Brian Dennehy. 1999 DVD

SIRINGO ★★★ Moderately entertaining film about a marshall who goes looking for stolen money but ends up finding love. Not rated; contains violence. 90m. DIR: Kevin G. Cremin. CAST: Brad Johnson, Chad Lowe, Stephen Macht, Crystal Bernard. 1994

SIROCCO ★★★ Humphrey Bogart plays a successful crook operating in postwar Syria. He is forced to intercede in a terrorist-police situation and gets himself in trouble with both factions. One of Bogart's best later works and a representative sample of the darker side of romance and intrigue, poles apart from, but structurally related to, films like *Casablanca* and *Beat the Devil*. Give it a try. B&W; 98m. DIR: Curtis Bernhardt. CAST: Humphrey Bogart, Marta Toren, Lee J. Cobb, Everett Sloane, Zero Mostel. 1951 DVD

SISTER ACT ★★★1/2 Fast-living nightclub singer Whoopi Goldberg has to hide out in a convent after she witnesses her gangster boyfriend (Harvey Keitel) preside over the killing of a police informant. Goldberg is a delight in this surprisingly funny and heartwarming romp. Rated PG for profanity. 100m. DIR: Emile Ardolino. CAST: Whoopi Goldberg, Maggie Smith, Kathy Najimy, Wendy Makkena, Mary Wickes, Harvey Keitel, Bill Nunn. 1992

SISTER ACT 2: BACK IN THE HABIT ★★★1/2 Reacting to the surprise popularity of *Sister Act*, Disney made this family-oriented, toned-down sequel. Sister Mary Clarence goes undercover as a music teacher at an inner-city school in an attempt to reach rebellious students. Very tame—but charming. Rated PG for light profanity. 107m. DIR: Bill Duke. CAST: Whoopi Goldberg, Maggie Smith, Kathy Najimy, Mary Wickes, Wendy Makkena, Barnard Hughes, James Coburn, Michael Jeter, Robert Pastorelli, Brad Sullivan. 1993 DVD

SISTER-IN-LAW, THE (1974) ★★1/2 A struggling young singer is lured into drug smuggling by his brother's adulterous wife. Downbeat but occasionally interesting, at least as an early effort in the career of John Savage (who also wrote and sings a few songs). Rated R for nudity. 80m. DIR: Joseph Ruben. CAST: John Savage. 1974

SISTER-IN-LAW, THE (1995) ★★ A wealthy family is victimized by a woman posing as their long-lost relation. Not too many surprises in this made-for-cable original. Rated PG-13. 95m. DIR: Noel Nosseck. CAST: Kate Vernon, Shanna Reed, Craig Wasson, Kent Williams. 1995

SISTER KENNY ★★ Rosalind Russell is noble and sincere in the title role of the Australian nurse who fought polio in the bush. But the telling of her life in this dull and slow box-office flop is tiresome. B&W; 116m. DIR: Dudley Nichols. CAST: Rosalind Russell, Alexander Knox, Dean Jagger, Charles Dingle, Philip Merivale, Beulah Bondi, John Litel. 1946

SISTER, MY SISTER ★★★ Two sisters (Joely Richardson, Jodhi May) are hired as chambermaids by a snobbish widow and her pampered daughter. Based on the real-life French case that inspired Jean Genet's play *The Maids*, the film is a chilly and fascinating study of sexual repression and class conflict, well acted by all. The ending is a bit over the top. Rated R for climactic violence and several lesbian love scenes. 89m. DIR: Nancy Meckler. CAST: Joely Richardson, Jodhi May, Julie Walters, Sophie Thursfield. 1995 DVD

SISTER, SISTER ★★★ A gothic thriller set in the Louisiana bayou. Jennifer Jason Leigh is a frail lass who is haunted by a demon lover and taken care of by an overprotective older sister (Judith Ivey). Rated R for violence, nudity, simulated sex, and profanity. 91m. **DIR:** Bill Condon. **CAST:** Eric Stoltz, Jennifer Jason Leigh, Judith Ivey, Dennis Lipscomb, Anne Pitoniak. **1988**

SISTERHOOD, THE ★★1/2 Futuristic tale set in a post-apocalyptic society, where a secret society of female superwarriors battle the male establishment. Filipino-made movie is okay for fans of the genre. Rated R. 76m. **DIR:** Cirio H. Santiago. **CAST:** Rebecca Holden, Chuck Wagner, Lynn-Holly Johnson. **1988**

SISTERS, THE (1938) ★★★★ This film offered Errol Flynn, after becoming a star, his first opportunity to play something besides a hero. He portrays a writer who, unable to make a success of himself, turns to the bottle for escape, breaking wife Bette Davis's heart. B&W; 98m. **DIR:** Anatole Litvak. **CAST:** Errol Flynn, Bette Davis, Alan Hale Sr., Donald Crisp, Anita Louise, Jane Bryan, Beulah Bondi, Dick Foran. **1938**

SISTERS (1973) ★★★★1/2 A terrifying tale of twin sisters (Margot Kidder). One is normal; the other is a dangerous psychopath. It's an extremely effective thriller on all levels. Charles Durning and Jennifer Salt give the standout performances in this Brian De Palma release. Rated R for violence, nudity, and language. 93m. **DIR:** Brian De Palma. **CAST:** Margot Kidder, Charles Durning, Jennifer Salt, Barnard Hughes. **1973**

●**SISTERS OF THE GION** ★★★★ In one of his first great successes, Japanese filmmaker Kenji Mizoguchi explores the conflict between old and modern values with a story of two sisters, both geisha. The elder sister is a traditionalist who believes in her work, while the younger one sees her clients only as stepping-stones to a better life. Exquisitely filmed, giving a profound sense of a time and place long gone. In Japanese with English subtitles. B&W; 66m. **DIR:** Kenji Mizoguchi. **CAST:** Isuzu Yamada, Yôko Umemura, Benkei Shiganoya, Eitarô Shindô. **1936**

SITTING DUCKS 🐾 A Mafia accountant and his pal steal a day's payroll and hit the road. Rated R for nudity and language. 90m. **DIR:** Henry Jaglom. **CAST:** Michael Emil, Zack Norman, Patrice Townsend, Richard Romanus. **1980**

SIX DAYS, SEVEN NIGHTS ★★1/2 Star power doesn't keep this underimagined, South Seas romantic comedy-adventure buoyant. Harrison Ford and Anne Heche crash on an uncharted island, where they're chased by pirates and fall in opposites-attract love because the screenplay says they should. Rated PG-13 for violence, language, and suggested sex. 101m. **DIR:** Ivan Reitman. **CAST:** Harrison Ford, Anne Heche, David Schwimmer, Jacqueline Obradors. **1998 DVD**

SIX DEGREES OF SEPARATION ★★★1/2 Fine performances elevate this uneven comedy-drama about a young man (Will Smith) who passes himself off as Sidney Poitier's son in order to gain access to the privileged world of a wealthy couple. John Guare's screenplay gives us fascinating characters and a story with hard edges. Rated R for profanity, violence, and suggested sex. 111m. **DIR:** Fred Schepisi. **CAST:** Stockard Channing, Will Smith, Donald Suther-

land, Mary Beth Hurt, Bruce Davison, Heather Graham, Anthony Michael Hall, Eric Thal, Richard Masur, Ian McKellen. **1993**

SIX IN PARIS (PARIS VUE PAR ...) ★★★ Six *nouvelle vague* directors contributed short 16mm films about a Paris neighborhood to this collection. The shorts by Eric Rohmer and Claude Chabrol foreshadow their more mature work, though the rest is thin (Jean-Luc Godard's effort is particularly trivial). In French with English subtitles. 98m. **DIR:** Jean Douchet, Jean Rouch, Jean-Daniel Pollet, Eric Rohmer, Jean-Luc Godard, Claude Chabrol. **CAST:** Barbet Schroeder, Joanna Shimkus, Stéphane Audran, Claude Chabrol. **1965**

SIX PACK 🐾 Kenny Rogers plays a footloose stock-car racer who is latched onto by six homeless, sticky-fingered kids. Rated PG for profanity. 110m. **DIR:** Daniel Petrie. **CAST:** Kenny Rogers, Diane Lane, Erin Gray, Barry Corbin. **1982**

SIX-STRING SAMURAI ★★ Visually impressive but annoyingly arch postapocalypse nonsense. After the Russians have conquered all of an alternative-universe America except for Las Vegas, vagabond warrior/musicians cross the desert to vie for the king's crown. This low-budget student film makes an artfully grungy virtue of its staging limitations; too bad it all stages are repetitive fight scenes and pop culture posings. Rated R for violence and language. 81m. **DIR:** Lance Mungia. **CAST:** Jeffrey Falcon, Justin McGuire, Stephane Gauger. **1998 DVD**

●**SIX WAYS TO SUNDAY** ★★★ Ambitious dark comedy about a young man who gets tangled up with the mob. Norman Reedus is excellent as the young man whose close relationship with his mother is tested when his mob duties escalate into violence and a higher position in the family. Unexpected moments distinguish this offbeat effort. Rated R for violence, language, and adult situations. 97m. **DIR:** Adam Bernstein. **CAST:** Norman Reedus, Deborah Harry, Adrien Brody, Isaac Hayes. **1999 DVD**

SIX WEEKS ★★★1/2 Dudley Moore and Mary Tyler Moore star as two adults trying to make the dreams of a young girl—who has a very short time to live—come true in this tearjerker. Directed by Tony Bill, it's enjoyable for viewers who like a good cry. Rated PG for strong content. 107m. **DIR:** Tony Bill. **CAST:** Dudley Moore, Mary Tyler Moore, Katherine Healy, Joe Regalbuto. **1982**

SIX WIVES OF HENRY VIII, THE (TV SERIES) ★★★★ One of the first BBC costume dramas to appear on PBS, and still one of the best. What's really special is Keith Michell's virtuosic and sympathetic portrayal of the last Henry. Almost before your eyes, Henry is transformed from a handsome, brilliant young monarch to a corpulent, pitiable old tyrant. Each tape 90m. **DIR:** Naomi Capon. **CAST:** Keith Michell, Annette Crosbie, Dorothy Tutin, Anne Stallybrass. **1972**

SIXTH MAN, THE ★★ March Madness gets its own movie salute with this supernatural basketball comedy. Hoop star Antoine dies midway during a college game and his brother is left to lead the team to the NCAA championship. Antoine returns for unearthly assists but the running joke grows tiresome. Rated

PG-13 for language. 104m. DIR: Randall Miller. CAST: Marlon Wayans, Kadeem Hardison, Michael Michel, David Paymer. 1997

•SIXTH SENSE, THE ★★★★ A child psychologist, who failed one of his young charges with disastrous results, attempts to redeem himself by helping a young boy (Oscar nominee Haley Joel Osment), who "sees dead people." Brilliantly written and directed by M. Night Shyamalan, this is the first film since Alfred Hitchcock's *Psycho* to be so respected by moviegoers that they refused to give away the ending. And so it should be; this motion picture contains a remarkably moving twist that will leave viewers with the irresistible urge to watch it again. Osment gives a terrific performance, as does an unusually subdued Willis. Rated PG-13 for profanity, violence, and gore. 107m. DIR: M. Night Shyamalan. CAST: Bruce Willis, Toni Collette, Olivia Williams, Haley Joel Osment, Donnie Wahlberg, Glenn Fitzgerald, Mischa Barton, Trevor Morgan, Bruce Norris. 1999 DVD

SIXTEEN CANDLES ★★★★ Molly Ringwald stars in this fast and funny teen comedy as a high school student who is crushed when the whole family forgets her sixteenth birthday. Things, it seems to her, go downhill from there—that is, until the boy of her dreams suddenly starts showing some interest. Rated PG for profanity. 93m. DIR: John Hughes. CAST: Molly Ringwald, Paul Dooley, Blanche Baker, Edward Andrews, Anthony Michael Hall, Billie Bird. 1984 DVD

16 FATHOMS DEEP ★★ Sponge fisherman Creighton Chaney (Lon Chaney Jr.) borrows money to buy a boat so he and his girl can get married, but his efforts are sabotaged. Low-rent offering from Monogram uses a lot of stock underwater shots and original footage taken on Catalina Island. B&W; 59m. DIR: Armand Schaefer. CAST: Sally O'Neil, Lon Chaney Jr. 1934

633 SQUADRON ★★★ A British squadron of bomber pilots prepare for a difficult but important mission against a Nazi rocket fuel factory in Norway. Not rated, but there is graphic action. 95m. DIR: Walter Grauman. CAST: Cliff Robertson, George Chakiris, Harry Andrews, Donald Houston. 1963

'68 ★★ Hungarian immigrants settle in San Francisco, each with an idea of what America should be. While Dad tries to make it in the restaurant business, one son becomes an antiwar advocate as the other struggles with his homosexuality. This one redefines low budget. Rated R for nudity, violence, and profanity. 100m. DIR: Steven Kovacs. CAST: Eric Larson, Sandor Tecsi, Robert Locke, Terra Vandergaw, Neil Young. 1987

SIZZLE 🍿 TV movie should be called *Fizzle*. 100m. DIR: Don Medford. CAST: Loni Anderson, John Forsythe, Michael Goodwin, Leslie Uggams, Roy Thinnes, Richard Lynch, Phyllis Davis. 1981

SIZZLE BEACH, U.S.A. 🍿 Drive-in fodder about three girls who head to L.A. notable only as the debut of Kevin Costner (whose appearance isn't as prominent as the video box would lead you to believe). Rated R for nudity and sexual situations. 93m. DIR: Richard Brander. CAST: Terry Congie, Leslie Brander, Roselyn Royce, Kevin Costner. 1976 DVD

SKAG ★★★1/2 Home-ridden to recuperate after being felled by a stroke, veteran steelworker Pete Skagska must deal with family problems, his own poor health, and the chance his illness may leave him impotent. In the title role, Karl Malden gives a towering, hard-driving performance as a man determined to prevail, no matter what the emotional cost. TV movie. 152m. DIR: Frank Perry. CAST: Karl Malden, Piper Laurie, Craig Wasson, Peter Gallagher, George Voskovec. 1980

SKATEBOARD KID, THE ★★ This imbecile spin on TV's *My Mother the Car* is the sort of moronic fluff that Mother warned would stunt your growth if watched indiscriminately. Concerns a young loner who discovers a skateboard with a conscience (and the voice of Dom DeLuise) and manages to work in hidden gold and a secret map before limping to an outrageously corny conclusion. Quite a few talented players waste their time. Rated PG for mild violence. 77m. DIR: Larry Swerdlove. CAST: Timothy Busfield, Bess Armstrong, Rick Dean, Trevor Lissauer, Cliff De Young. 1993

SKATEBOARD KID 2, THE ★★★ Children into the sport of skateboarding will enjoy this fantasy about a kid desperately attempting to fit in. Rated PG. 95m. DIR: Andrew Stevens. CAST: Trent Knight, Andrew Stevens, Dee Wallace, Andrew Keegan, Bruce Davison. 1994

SKEETER 🍿 Mutant mosquitoes suck the life out of this low-rent nature-gone-awry thriller. Badly directed and poorly acted. Rated R for violence, language, and sexual situations. 95m. DIR: Clark Brandon. CAST: Tracy Griffith, Jim Youngs, Charles Napier, Michael J. Pollard. 1993

SKEEZER ★★1/2 Made-for-TV movie about a lonely young woman and her friendship with a mutt named Skeezer. This dog eventually helps her to reach emotionally disturbed children in a group home where she is a volunteer. Good for family viewing. 100m. DIR: Peter H. Hunt. CAST: Karen Valentine, Dee Wallace, Tom Atkins, Mariclare Costello. 1982

SKELETONS ★★★1/2 Ron Silver moves to a small town and learns the story of how a gay man was framed for the murder of his lover. He is quickly drawn in to the frame-up that the locals have contrived. Captivating and timely, director David DeCoteau makes the leap here from direct-to-video T&A to the big leagues and shows that he can play with the big boys and girls. Rated R for violence and profanity. 91m. DIR: David DeCoteau. CAST: Ron Silver, James Coburn, Christopher Plummer, Dee Wallace, Dennis Christopher. 1997

SKETCH ARTIST ★★1/2 Sexy made-for-cable thriller benefits from writer Michael Angeli's intriguing premise. Jeff Fahey is a police sketch artist whose rendition of a murder suspect —concocted from a description given by a briefly seen Drew Barrymore—turns out to be the spitting image of his wife (Sean Young). Alas, he then turns total fool, and plot cohesion goes right out the window. 88m. DIR: Phedon Papamichael. CAST: Jeff Fahey, Sean Young, Frank McRae, Drew Barrymore. 1992

SKETCH ARTIST II: HANDS THAT SEE ★★★1/2 Jeff Fahey, always a dynamic presence, returns for a second crack at the police-department artist with an uncanny knack for capturing faces. Scripter Michael Angeli's premise is quite intriguing: Rape victim Courteney Cox is blind, and therefore cannot evaluate the sketch in progress. As the culprit's identity is never in doubt, this evolves into a clever, *Columbo*-style courtroom drama. Rated R for nudity, rape, profanity, and violence. 95m. DIR: Jack Sholder. CAST: Jeff Fahey, Courteney Cox, Michael Beach, Brion James, James Tolkan, Jonathan Silverman. 1995

SKETCHES OF A STRANGLER ♥ Allen Garfield, in the days when he was billing himself as Allan Goorwitz, stars as a painter with a fixation on his dead mother. 91m. DIR: Paul Leder. CAST: Allen Garfield, Meredith MacRae. 1978

SKI PATROL ★★ Comedy fluff about the antics of a group of misfit skiers who work for a popular resort. Never gets off the beginners' slope. Rated PG. 91m. DIR: Richard Correll. CAST: Roger Rose, Ray Walston, Martin Mull. 1990

SKI SCHOOL ★★1/2 An obvious rip-off of *Animal House*, this teen comedy is nonetheless very funny thanks in part to Dean Cameron as the leader of a wacko class of ski bums. Not rated; contains nudity and profanity. 85m. DIR: Damien Lee. CAST: Dean Cameron, Tom Breznahan, Patrick Labyorteaux, Mark Thomas Miller. 1990

SKIN ART ★★1/2 Tattoo artist Kirk Baltz makes a living branding Oriental prostitutes at a brothel in Manhattan. When he starts to fall for his latest masterpiece, she revives memories of his days as a Vietnam POW. His obsession to turn her into a living canvas reeks of *Tattoo*, starring Bruce Dern. Kinky but not erotic. Rated R for nudity, violence, and language. 90m. DIR: W. Blake Herron. CAST: Kirk Baltz, Ariane, Jake Webber, Nora Ariffin, Hil Cato. 1993

SKIN DEEP ★★ Writer-director Blake Edwards tries for another sex farce in the *10* vein, but this one fails to rise to its potential. John Ritter's undeniable charm cannot compensate for the fact that his character—a womanizing alcoholic—is utterly lacking in redeeming social qualities. Viewers with raised consciousnesses are advised to stay away from this one. Rated R for nudity, profanity, and explicit sexual themes. 98m. DIR: Blake Edwards. CAST: John Ritter, Vincent Gardenia, Alyson Reed, Joel Brooks, Julianne Phillips, Don Gordon, Nina Foch. 1989

•**SKIN GAME, THE (1931)** ★★1/2 This early effort from Alfred Hitchcock, an adaptation of a play by John Galsworthy, is one of the last films he'd make in relative obscurity before 1935's *The Thirty-Nine Steps* shot him to fame. The story, which concerns a feud between an established landowner and an upstart newcomer, is talky and boring, despite the inclusion of a love story and a suicide. B&W; 85m. DIR: Alfred Hitchcock. CAST: C. V. France, Helen Hayes, Jill Esmond, Edmund Gwenn, John Longden, Phyllis Konstam. 1931 DVD

SKIN GAME (1971) ★★★★ Perceptive social comedy-drama set during the slave era. James Garner and Louis Gossett Jr. are con artists; Garner "sells" Gossett to unsuspecting slave owners and later helps break him free. The fleecing continues until they meet up with evil Edward Asner, who catches on to

the act ... then the story takes a chilling turn toward realism. Excellent on all levels. Rated PG for light violence. 102m. DIR: Paul Bogart. CAST: James Garner, Lou Gossett Jr., Susan Clark, Edward Asner, Andrew Duggan. 1971

SKINHEADS ♥ Three college friends and two female backpackers encounter a gang of skinheads. Rated R for violence and partial nudity. 93m. DIR: Greydon Clark. CAST: Chuck Connors, Barbara Bain, Brian Brophy, Jason Culp. 1988

SKINNED ALIVE ★★★ Similar to *Texas Chainsaw Massacre*, this film actually benefits from its ultralow budget. The story has a family selling fine leather out of the back of their van. Read the title again to see where they obtain their materials. Not rated; contains violence, gore, and profanity. 80m. DIR: Jon Killough. CAST: Mary Jackson, Scott Spiegel. 1990

SKINNER ♥ Just imagine Ted Raimi in a bloody "skin" suit and a disfigured Traci Lords limping after him for five years and you'll never have to watch this miserable movie. Rated R for profanity, violence, and nudity. 90m. DIR: Ivan Nagy. CAST: Theodore Raimi, Traci Lords, Ricki Lake. 1993 DVD

SKIRTS AHOY! ★★ Slow-moving story of three women from different backgrounds joining the WAVES, and their problems in training and the men in their lives. 109m. DIR: Sidney Lanfield. CAST: Esther Williams, Joan Evans, Vivian Blaine, Barry Sullivan. 1952

SKOKIE ★★★ The threat of neo-Nazism comes to the small, predominantly Jewish town of Skokie, Illinois in the late 1970s. An all-star cast drives this well-written TV drama, which succeeds in portraying the two sides in unemotional terms. 121m. DIR: Herbert Wise. CAST: Danny Kaye, Brian Dennehy, Eli Wallach, Kim Hunter, Carl Reiner. 1981

SKULL, THE ★★★★ A collector of occult memorabilia covets the death's-head of the infamous Marquis de Sade. Based on a fine Robert Bloch short story, this imaginative fantasy is the apex of the Amicus Productions horror cycle of the 1960s. The modern-day setting helps rather than hinders. 83m. DIR: Freddie Francis. CAST: Peter Cushing, Patrick Wymark, Christopher Lee, Jill Bennett, Nigel Green, Patrick Magee. 1965

SKULL AND CROWN ★★1/2 A border patrolman and his faithful guard dog combine talents to break up a band of smugglers. Lassie fans will love this one. B&W; 55m. DIR: Elmer Clifton. CAST: Rin Tin Tin Jr., Regis Toomey, Jack Mulhall. 1935

SKULLDUGGERY ♥ A costume store employee inherits a Satanic curse that sends him on a killing rampage. Not rated, but would earn a PG for violence and profanity. 95m. DIR: Ota Richter. CAST: Thom Haverstock, Wendy Crewson. 1983

•**SKULLS, THE** ★★ When wannabe attorney Luke McNamara is recruited to join a secret university society styled after Yale's elite Skull and Bones, his best friend warns, "If it's elite and secret, it's got to be bad." Luke joins anyway because the fraternity will pay his tuition and he is starstruck by former members that include judges and politicians. His commitment to this group soon jeopardizes his relationship with a female artist and his personal safety. Rated PG-13 for language, violence, and sexuality. 107m. DIR: Rob Cohen. CAST: Joshua Jackson, Hill Harper, Leslie Bibb, Paul Walker, Christopher McDonald, William L. Petersen, Craig T. Nelson. 2000

SKY BANDITS 🖤 An uninspired mixing of *Butch Cassidy and the Sundance Kid* and *The Blue Max*. Rated PG for violence. 95m. DIR: Zoran Perisic. CAST: Scott McGinnis, Jeff Osterhage, Ronald Lacey. 1986

SKY HEIST ★★ Frank Gorshin and Stefanie Powers hijack a police helicopter to help steal a fortune in gold bullion. Lots of familiar faces in this otherwise unmemorable TV movie. Not rated; contains no objectionable material. 96m. DIR: Lee H. Katzin. CAST: Don Meredith, Joseph Campanella, Larry Wilcox, Ken Swofford, Stefanie Powers, Frank Gorshin, Shelley Fabares, Steve Franken, Suzanne Somers, Richard Jordan. 1975

SKY IS GRAY, THE ★★★ Generosity comes from unexpected quarters in this languid TV adaptation of Ernest J. Gaines's melancholy study of a young boy's first exposure to racism, poverty, and pride in 1940s Louisiana. James Bond III is the youth, dragged to town by his strong-willed mother (Olivia Cole) to have an infected tooth removed. Introduced by Henry Fonda; suitable for family viewing. 46m. DIR: Stan Lathan. CAST: Olivia Cole, James Bond III, Margaret Avery, Cleavon Little, Clinton Derricks-Carroll. 1980

•SKY PILOT, THE ★★★ An idealistic young preacher hoping to spread the gospel in the Canadian Northwest must first win acceptance from the rough-and-tumble ranchers. Sincere, heartwarming, and well-acted, this lovely little film was based on a bestseller of the day. B&W; 63m. DIR: King Vidor. CAST: John Bowers, David Butler, Colleen Moore, James Corrigan, Kathleen Kirkham, Donald MacDonald. 1921

SKY PIRATES 🖤 Terrible acting, a stupid plot, and poorly executed stunts. Rated PG-13 for violence. 89m. DIR: Colin Eggleston. CAST: John Hargreaves, Meredith Phillips, Max Phipps. 1988

SKYLARK ★★★1/2 *Hallmark Hall of Fame's* sequel to *Sarah, Plain and Tall* combines high production values with wholesome entertainment. Glenn Close is terrific as the Maine-born, mail-order bride adapting to a difficult life on the Kansas plains. During a severe drought, she must comfort her husband (Christopher Walken) and stepchildren while coming to grips with her own ambiguous feelings about the land. Rated G. 98m. DIR: Joseph Sargent. CAST: Glenn Close, Christopher Walken, Lexi Randall, Christopher Bell. 1992 DVD

SKYLINE ★★★ Antonio Resines plays a Spanish photographer named Gustavo who comes to New York seeking international fame. Once there, he struggles to learn English, find work, and pursue friendship and romance. In Spanish and English, with subtitles it would be excellent for bilingual viewers. The twist ending really gives one a jolt. We'd rate it PG for slight profanity. 84m. DIR: Fernando Colombo. CAST: Antonio Resines, Susana Ocana. 1984

SKY'S THE LIMIT, THE ★★★★ This rare blend of comedy and drama is more than just another Fred

Astaire musical. He plays a Flying Tiger ace on leave, who meets and falls in love with magazine photographer Joan Leslie, but nixes anything permanent. Both audiences and critics misjudged this film when it debuted, seeing it as light diversion rather than incisive comment on war and its effect on people. B&W; 89m. DIR: Edward H. Griffith. CAST: Fred Astaire, Joan Leslie, Robert Benchley, Elizabeth Patterson, Clarence Kolb, Robert Ryan, Richard Davis, Peter Lawford, Eric Blore. 1943

SKYSCRAPER 🖤 The seemingly inexhaustible *Die Hard* formula hits rock bottom with this made-for-video thriller that vainly tries to make bosomy Anna Nicole Smith into an action heroine. Rated R for profanity, violence, nudity, and sexual situations. 96m. DIR: Raymond Martino. CAST: Anna Nicole Smith, Richard Steinmetz, Branko Cikatic. 1996

SKYSCRAPER SOULS ★★★1/2 A one hundred-story office building is the setting for this *Grand Hotel*–type mélange of stories. Warren William is outstanding as the industrialist who seeks to control the entire building. B&W; 99m. DIR: Edgar Selwyn. CAST: Warren William, Maureen O'Sullivan, Gregory Ratoff, Anita Page, Jean Hersholt, Hedda Hopper. 1932

SLACKER ★★★★ Imagine if you will a movie that has ninety-seven roles of equal importance, yet never spends more than five minutes with any character. Meet *Slacker*. A rogue's gallery of deadbeats, pseudointellectuals and just-plain folks is presented in this semitwisted examination of attitudes among college students in Austin, Texas. It's surprisingly entertaining. Rated R for profanity. 97m. DIR: Richard Linklater. 1991

SLAM ★★★1/2 A nickel-and-dime weed dealer and street poet-rapper gets a nasty taste of the criminal-justice system when arrested. This preachy but potent drama about the redemptive powers of art says that true liberation lies ahead in prison rather than in the gang-haunted shadows of the nation's capital. Handheld-camera effects give the film a riveting rawness and urgency. Rated R for nudity, simulated sex, profanity, and violence. 100m. DIR: Marc Levin. CAST: Saul Williams, Sonja Sohn, Bonz Malone. 1998 DVD

SLAM DANCE ★★1/2 An L.A. artist (Tom Hulce) becomes embroiled in two murders of high-priced call girls in this Hitchcockian thriller. The standard situations involving an innocent man trying to clear himself are given some fresh approaches, but there are several holes in the plot, and some events make little sense. Rated R. 99m. DIR: Wayne Wang. CAST: Tom Hulce, Mary Elizabeth Mastrantonio, Virginia Madsen, Harry Dean Stanton, Adam Ant, Don Opper. 1987

SLAM DUNK ERNEST 🖤 The least funny of the Ernest movies, this one dealing with magic shoes that turn him into a basketball star. Not even close. Rated PG. 93m. DIR: John R. Cherry III. CAST: Jim Varney, Cylk Cozart, Miguel A. Nunez Jr., Lester Barrie, Kareem Abdul-Jabbar. 1994

SLAMMER GIRLS ★★ Spoof of women's prison films. A male reporter disguises himself as a woman to prove the heroine's innocence. A few funny bits, but many more that are plain stupid. Rated R for nudity and profanity. 82m. DIR: Chuck Vincent. CAST: Devon Jenkin, Jeff Eagle, Jane Hamilton. 1987

SLAP SHOT ★★★★ When released in 1977, this comedy about a down-and-out hockey team was criticized for its liberal use of profanity. The controversy tended to obscure the fact that *Slap Shot* is a very funny, marvelously acted movie. Paul Newman, as an aging player-coach who's a loser in love and on the ice until he instructs the members of his team to behave like animals during their matches, has never been better. Rated R. 122m. DIR: George Roy Hill. CAST: Paul Newman, Strother Martin, Jennifer Warren, Lindsay Crouse, Melinda Dillon. 1977 DVD

SLAPPY AND THE STINKERS ★★ This hybrid that mixes *Our Gang* with *Andre* will please small children, who will most enjoy the slapstick shenanigans of five youngsters who steal a seal from a local aquarium with plans to set him free. Their plan is complicated by a nasty animal broker who will stop at nothing to steal the seal. Childish chaos ensues. Rated PG. 79m. DIR: Barnet Kellman. CAST: B. D. Wong, Bronson Pinchot, Sam McMurray. 1997

SLAPSTICK OF ANOTHER KIND 🐝 Jerry Lewis hasn't made a funny film in years, and this sci-fi spoof is no exception. Rated PG. 85m. DIR: Steven Paul. CAST: Jerry Lewis, Madeline Kahn, Marty Feldman. 1983

•SLASH DANCE 🐝 It's the slasher-stalking-the-dancer story yet again, this time set at Broadway auditions. Not rated; contains violence. 83m. DIR: James Shyman. CAST: Cindy Maranne, Joel Von Ornsteiner. 1989

SLASHER ★★ This routine Italian police melodrama, with former Hitchcock leading man Farley Granger hunting a serial killer, has been released in the United States under three titles: *Slasher, The Slasher Is the Sex Maniac*, and, finally, in a hard-core version (for the mid-seventies porno chic audience, with unrelated sex scenes having nothing to do with Granger) called *Penetration*. You don't need to race out and track down any of them. Rated R. 100m. DIR: Roberto Montero. CAST: Farley Granger. 1974

SLATE, WYN, AND ME 🐝 Two sociopaths kidnap a woman who witnessed a murder they committed. Rated R for endless profanities and violence. 90m. DIR: Don McLennan. CAST: Sigrid Thornton, Simon Burke, Martin Sacks. 1987

SLAUGHTER ★★1/2 The first, and tightest (thanks to the direction of underrated action specialist Jack Starrett) of two blaxploitation sagas in which Jim Brown portrays a heroic Vietnam vet who returns home to avenge his family's murder. Augmented by a cast of upscale character actors, slumming in roles far beneath them. 92m. DIR: Jack Starrett. CAST: Jim Brown, Stella Stevens, Rip Torn, Don Gordon. 1972

SLAUGHTER HIGH ★★ Ten years after disfiguring a schoolmate, several former high school friends attend a deadly reunion. The rest of the film is fairly predictable. The ending is a welcome change from the norm, though, and it's nice to see horror queen Caroline Munro still working. Not rated; contains graphic violence and adult situations. 91m. DIR:

George Dugdale. CAST: Caroline Munro, Simon Scuddamore. 1986

SLAUGHTER IN SAN FRANCISCO 🐝 Another abysmal martial arts chop-socky fest. Rated R for violence and profanity. 87m. DIR: William Lowe. CAST: Chuck Norris, Robert Jones, Daniel Ivan. 1974

SLAUGHTER OF THE INNOCENTS ★★★1/2 Thanks to a morbidly fascinating tone that is borrowed from *Silence of the Lambs*, you'll probably forgive writer-director James Glickenhaus's effort to make his grade-school son a star. An overly precocious boy shares insights overlooked by his father, an F.B.I. investigator. Rated R for graphic violence and profanity. 103m. DIR: James Glickenhaus. CAST: Scott Glenn, Jesse Cameron-Glickenhaus, Sheila Tousey, Zitto Kazann, Darlanne Fluegel, Zakes Mokae. 1993

SLAUGHTER OF THE VAMPIRES A hunted vampire bites the neck of a beautiful victim. Italian would-be thriller. B&W; 81m. DIR: Roberto Mauri. CAST: Walter Brandi. 1971

SLAUGHTER TRAIL 🐝 Good actors trapped in a clichéd story with outlaws, Indians, and cavalry. One of the hokiest soundtrack songs ever recorded. 78m. DIR: Irving Allen. CAST: Brian Donlevy, Virginia Grey, Gig Young, Andy Devine. 1951

SLAUGHTERHOUSE 🐝 A disturbed man butchers people as if they were farm animals. Rated R for violence and profanity. 85m. DIR: Rick Roessler. CAST: Joe Barton, Sherry Rendorf. 1987 DVD

SLAUGHTERHOUSE FIVE ★★★★ Based on Kurt Vonnegut's novel, which centers around the activities of Billy Pilgrim, who has become unstuck in time. This enables, or forces, him to jump back and forth among different periods in his life and even experience two separate time-space incidents simultaneously. Well done. Rated R. 104m. DIR: George Roy Hill. CAST: Michael Sacks, Valerie Perrine, Eugene Roche, John Dehner, Holly Near. 1972 DVD

SLAUGHTER'S BIG RIP-OFF ★★ The second, and less interesting, of Jim Brown's popular blaxploitation pair in which our indestructible one-man army takes on assorted sadistic criminals. Tepid entry in a waning action cycle. 93m. DIR: Gordon Douglas. CAST: Jim Brown, Ed McMahon, Brock Peters, Don Stroud. 1973

SLAVE GIRLS FROM BEYOND INFINITY ★★ A pair of space bimbos in bikinis find themselves on a weird planet whose sole occupant hunts intergalactic visitors. Low budget, but with decent effects and lighting. Not nearly campy enough. Rated R for nudity. 80m. DIR: Ken Dixon. CAST: Elizabeth Cyton, Cindy Beal, Brinke Stevens. 1987 DVD

SLAVE OF DREAMS ★★★1/2 The biblical story of Joseph gets restrained treatment in this acceptable drama, which concerns Joseph's rise from common desert slave to trusted second-in-command of the pharaoh's executioner. Rated PG-13 for nudity and simulated sex. 95m. DIR: Robert M. Young. CAST: Adrian Pasdar, Edward James Olmos, Sherilyn Fenn, Philip Newman. 1995

SLAVE OF LOVE, A ★★★★1/2 Shortly after the Bolshevik revolution, a crew of silent filmmakers attempt to complete a melodrama while fighting the forces of the changing world around them. This examines the role of the bourgeois as Olga (Elena Soloyei) changes from matinee idol to revolutionary. Politically and emotionally charged. In Russian with English subtitles. Not rated. 94m. **DIR:** Nikita Mikhalkov. **CAST:** Elena Soloyei, Rodion Nakhapetov, Alexander Kalyagin. 1978

SLAVE OF THE CANNIBAL GOD 💙 A woman encounters a cult of flesh-eaters while attempting to find her missing husband in New Guinea. Rated R for violence and nudity. 87m. **DIR:** Sergio Martino. **CAST:** Stacy Keach, Ursula Andress. 1979

SLAVERS ★★ Ray Milland plays an Arab slave trader in nineteenth-century Africa who treats his charges like cattle. Rated R for violence, nudity, and sexual situations. 102m. **DIR:** Jurgen Goslar. **CAST:** Trevor Howard, Ron Ely, Britt Ekland, Ray Milland, Cameron Mitchell. 1977

SLAVES OF NEW YORK 💙 Manhattan's downtown art scene. Rated R, with profanity and sexual situations. 125m. **DIR:** James Ivory. **CAST:** Bernadette Peters, Chris Sarandon, Mary Beth Hurt, Madeleine Potter. 1989

•**SLAVES TO THE UNDERGROUND** ★★1/2 Despite good intentions, this tale of a romantic triangle involving two girls and a guy lacks emotional drive. Director Kristine Peterson effectively captures the look and feel of the underground clubs and coffeehouses, but fails to capture the romantic entanglements with the same honesty and reality. The music is the main interest here. Rated R for adult situations, language, and nudity. 94m. **DIR:** Kristine Peterson. **CAST:** Molly Gross, Marisa Ryan, Jason Bortz. 1996 DVD

SLAYGROUND ★★ Based on the hardboiled Parker series of crime novels, this will disappoint fans of the books. The character of Parker, a tough, no-nonsense professional criminal who shoots first and walks away, has been softened into a whiny thief named Stone (Peter Coyote). Rated R. 89m. **DIR:** Terry Bedford. **CAST:** Peter Coyote, Billie Whitelaw, Philip Sayer, Bill Luhr. 1984

SLC PUNK ★★ Salt Lake City punk Stevo takes us on a rather senseless Reagan-era tour of his promiscuous, paranoid, druggie, and hardcore friends in this sometimes comic slice of life. The blue-haired anarchist wants to raze the local university instead of attending law school in the footsteps of his ex-hippie dad. Rated R for drug use, language, violence, and sexual content. 97m. **DIR:** James Marendino. **CAST:** Matthew Lillard, Michael A. Goorjian, Annabeth Gish, Jennifer Lien, Christopher McDonald. 1999 DVD

SLEAZEMANIA STRIKES BACK ★★1/2 More fast-paced, bad-taste trailers from movies—e.g., *Suburban Roulette*—you'd never be seen buying a ticket for. B&W/color; 60m. **DIR:** Johnny Legend, Jeff Vilencia. 1987

SLEAZY UNCLE, THE ★★★ Italian comedy features Vittorio Gassman as a lecherous old man. Although he is at times repulsive, there is something to be said for Gassman's obvious love of life. In Italian with English subtitles. Not rated; contains profanity and sexual innuendo. 104m. **DIR:** Franco Brusati. **CAST:** Vittorio Gassman, Giancarlo Giannini, Andrea Ferreol. 1991

SLEEP WITH ME ★★1/2 Talky love triangle is marred by its wholly unsympathetic characters, who spend all their time smoking and drinking. The only genuinely amusing moment comes when partygoer Quentin Tarantino discourses on the homoerotic subtext of *Top Gun*. Rated R for profanity, simulated sex, and brief nudity. 86m. **DIR:** Rory Kelly. **CAST:** Craig Sheffer, Eric Stoltz, Meg Tilly, Dean Cameron, June Lockhart, Quentin Tarantino. 1994

SLEEPAWAY CAMP 💙 This bloody, disgusting film is one that will make you appreciate the fast-forward feature on your VCR. 88m. **DIR:** Robert Hiltzik. **CAST:** Mike Kellin, Paul DeAngelo. 1983

SLEEPAWAY CAMP II: UNHAPPY CAMPERS ★★1/2 Gory and funny sequel about naughty kids being slaughtered by a puritanical camp counselor. Rated R for nudity, violence, and profanity. 81m. **DIR:** Michael A. Simpson. **CAST:** Pamela Springsteen, René Estevez, Brian Patrick Clarke. 1988

SLEEPAWAY CAMP III 💙 Angela (Pamela Springsteen), the murderous happy camper, returns to Camp Happy Woods. Rated R for violence and nudity. 80m. **DIR:** Michael A. Simpson. **CAST:** Pamela Springsteen, Michael J. Pollard. 1988

SLEEPER ★★★★ Writer-star-director Woody Allen finally exhibited some true filmmaking talent with this 1973 sci-fi spoof. The frenetic gag-a-minute comedy style of Allen's earlier films was replaced by nice bits of character comedy. The most enjoyable of Allen's pre-*Annie Hall* creations. Rated PG. 88m. **DIR:** Woody Allen. **CAST:** Woody Allen, Diane Keaton, John McLiam, John Beck. 1973 DVD

SLEEPERS ★★★★ Thoughtful drama which concerns four Hell's Kitchen teenagers who ruin their lives with a single, senseless act of mischief. The four enter the juvenile-detention system and emerge as wholly different people. Two become psychopathic criminals, one becomes an attorney, one remains the group's collective conscience. These divergent elements collide when fate provides an opportunity for revenge against the sadistic guard who molested them during their childhood incarceration. Director Barry Levinson has a fine touch with ensemble casts, and this film contains many powerful moments. Rated R for violence, profanity, rape, and child abuse. 152m. **DIR:** Barry Levinson. **CAST:** Jason Patric, Brad Pitt, Robert De Niro, Dustin Hoffman, Kevin Bacon, Minnie Driver, Vittorio Gassman, Billy Crudup, Ron Eldard, Brad Renfro. 1996 DVD

SLEEPING BEAUTY (1959) ★★★1/2 This Disney adaptation of Charles Perrault's seventeenth-century version of the famous fairy tale features storybook-style animation that may surprise those accustomed to the softer style of the studio's other feature-length cartoons. Nevertheless, it is the last genre classic to be supervised by Walt Disney himself and belongs in any list of the best children's films (while having the added asset of being enjoyable for adults, as well). Rated G. 75m. **DIR:** Clyde Geronimi. 1959

SLEEPING BEAUTY (1983) ★★★★ This is one of the funniest *Faerie Tale Theatre* episodes. Christopher Reeve is excellent as the handsome prince, and Bernadette Peters makes a sweet and pretty princess. Sally Kellerman is wonderful as the queen. 60m. DIR: Jeremy Paul Kagan. CAST: Beverly D'Angelo, Bernadette Peters, Christopher Reeve, Sally Kellerman. 1983

SLEEPING CAR, THE ★★ Haunted railway car converted into a rental home just may be the death of a disenchanted journalist. Stale one-liners and cheapie special effects weaken this potentially fascinating horror-comedy. Rated R for violence, language, and nudity. 96m. DIR: Douglas Curtis. CAST: David Naughton, Kevin McCarthy, Jeff Conaway. 1990

SLEEPING CAR MURDERS, THE ★★★★ An all-star French cast and crisp direction from Costa-Gavras (his first film) make this a first-rate thriller. Yves Montand stars as the detective investigating the case of a woman found dead in a sleeping compartment of a train when it pulls into Paris. Soon other occupants of the car are found murdered as well. In French with English subtitles. B&W; 92m. DIR: Constantin Costa-Gavras. CAST: Yves Montand, Simone Signoret, Pierre Mondy, Michel Piccoli, Jean-Louis Trintignant, Charles Denner. 1966

SLEEPING DOGS ★★1/2 Here's a "what if?" film set in New Zealand during a time of economic crisis. Sam Neill discovers his wife is having an affair, so he goes off to live by himself for a while. Meanwhile, a group of government agents kill innocent bystanders during demonstrations and make it look like the work of the protesters. No MPAA rating. 107m. DIR: Roger Donaldson. CAST: Sam Neill, Warren Oates, Nevan Rowe, Ian Mune. 1977

SLEEPING MURDER ★★★★ Two newlyweds fall in love with a strange old house in an English seaside town. Into this well-established mood of foreboding comes Miss Marple (Joan Hickson), who helps the young couple decipher the events behind an unsolved murder. Not rated, but suitable for family viewing. 102m. DIR: John Davies. CAST: Joan Hickson, Geraldine Alexander, John Moulder-Brown, Frederick Treves, Jack Watson. 1986

SLEEPING TIGER, THE ★★★1/2 A woman finds herself caught up in a tense triangular love affair with her psychiatrist husband and a cunning crook out on parole and released in her husband's custody. Dirk Bogarde gives a stunning performance as the ex-con. B&W; 89m. DIR: Joseph Losey. CAST: Alexis Smith, Alexander Knox, Dirk Bogarde. 1954

SLEEPING WITH STRANGERS ★★1/2 Quirky British bedroom farce offers some priceless complications: Rowdy rock star and his entourage check into a little out-of-the-way hotel for some peace and quiet, but instead encounter mistaken identities, curious neighbors and boarders, and the media. The actors seem game; it's the direction that lacks any spark. Rated R for adult situations. 103m. DIR: William T. Bolson. CAST: Adrienne Shelly, Kimberly Huffman, Neil Duncan, Shawn Thompson, Scott McNeil, Todd Warren. 1993

SLEEPING WITH THE ENEMY ★★★1/2 Battered wife Julia Roberts manages to escape from her sadistic husband (Patrick Bergin) and create a new life—but only for a short time until hubby discovers the ruse and comes for revenge. Recalls director Joseph Rubin's *The Stepfather* so much that it might have

been called *The Husband*. Rated R for violence and profanity. 99m. DIR: Joseph Ruben. CAST: Julia Roberts, Patrick Bergin, Kevin Anderson. 1991

SLEEPLESS IN SEATTLE ★★★★ When recently widowed Tom Hanks's plight is described during a radio talk show by his well-meaning son, soon-to-be-wed reporter Meg Ryan becomes obsessed with the idea of meeting him. Witty, insightful romantic comedy. Rated PG for brief profanity. 101m. DIR: Nora Ephron. CAST: Tom Hanks, Meg Ryan, Bill Pullman, Ross Malinger, Rosie O'Donnell, Gaby Hoffman, Victor Garber, Rita Wilson, Barbara Garrick, Carey Lowell, Dana Ivey, Rob Reiner. 1993 DVD

SLEEPSTALKER: THE SANDMAN'S LAST RITES 🎬 A maniacal, supernatural "sandman" puts his victims permanently to sleep, and promises to leave audiences everywhere snoozing. Rated R for profanity and violence. 101m. DIR: Turi Meyer. CAST: Jay Underwood, Kathryn Morris, Michael Harris, Bill Lucking, Michael D. Roberts. 1995

SLEEPWALKER ★★★ Bilingual computer operator translates an ancient Chinese manuscript as a free-lance job, only to find the content manifesting itself in her daily existence. Offbeat low-budget suspenser has genuine intrigue and fine values. Rated R. 78m. DIR: Sara Driver. CAST: Suzanne Fletcher, Ann Magnuson, Dexter Lee. 1987

•**SLEEPY HOLLOW** ★★★★ Paying tribute to the beloved horror movies of Universal Studios and Hammer Films, director Tim Burton creates his most lavishly atmospheric and effective motion picture to date, although fans of Washington Irving's "Legend of Sleepy Hollow" will find little to remind them of that classic tale. Johnny Depp's Ichabod Crane is a crime investigator sent by the New York justice system, tired of his "advanced" methods and theories, to the hamlet of Sleepy Hollow, where a headless horseman is killing off its inhabitants. Scare-film fans will be delighted by the appearances of genre greats Christopher Lee and Michael Gough, while casual viewers will be equally caught up in this suspenseful, exquisitely crafted movie. Rated R for violence and sex. 105m. DIR: Tim Burton. CAST: Johnny Depp, Christina Ricci, Miranda Richardson, Michael Gambon, Casper Van Dien, Jeffrey Jones, Christopher Lee, Richard Griffiths, Ian McDiarmid, Michael Gough, Christopher Walken, Martin Landau. 1999 DVD

SLENDER THREAD, THE ★★★1/2 Sidney Poitier is a psychology student working at a crisis clinic in Seattle. He fields a call from housewife Anne Bancroft, who has taken an overdose of barbiturates. Fine performances. B&W; 98m. DIR: Sydney Pollack. CAST: Sidney Poitier, Anne Bancroft, Telly Savalas, Steven Hill, Edward Asner, Dabney Coleman. 1965

SLEUTH ★★★★ Michael Caine and Laurence Olivier engage in a heavyweight acting *bataille royal* in this stimulating mystery. Both actors are brilliant as the characters engage in the struggle of one-upmanship and social game-playing. Without giving away the movie's twists and turns, we can let on that the ultimate game is being played on its audience. Rated PG. 138m. DIR: Joseph L. Mankiewicz. CAST: Michael Caine, Laurence Olivier. 1972

SLIDING DOORS ★★★1/2 A missed subway, and its impact on one woman's life, is the beguiling premise of writer-director Peter Howitt's absolutely delightful comedy-drama. You'll enjoy the story about perky London PR exec Gwyneth Paltrow and the characters involved with her two dissimilar lives, but you'll also admire the way it's all put together. Rated PG-13 for mild profanity and sensuality. 99m. **DIR:** Peter Howitt. **CAST:** Gwyneth Paltrow, John Hannah, John Lynch, Jeanne Tripplehorn. 1998 DVD

•**SLIGHT CASE OF MURDER, A** ★★★ This TNT original is a dark comedy featuring William H. Macy as a film critic caught up in the suspicious death of his girlfriend and subsequent blackmail attempts. Having a knack for making matters worse, he manages to compound his problems as he relies on old movie plots for guidance. Though the action is meant to be contemporary, there's a fortyish *film noir* feel to it. Not rated; contains violence and sexual situations. 89m. **DIR:** Steven Schachter. **CAST:** William H. Macy, Adam Arkin, Felicity Huffman, James Cromwell. 1999

SLIGHTLY HONORABLE ★★★ Wisecracks and red herrings provide the drawing cards in this fast-paced comedy-thriller. The plot's muddy, but basically it concerns a lawyer, Pat O'Brien, who is set up for a murder by crooked politician Edward Arnold. B&W. 85m. **DIR:** Tay Garnett. **CAST:** Pat O'Brien, Edward Arnold, Broderick Crawford, Evelyn Keyes, Phyllis Brooks, Eve Arden. 1939

SLIGHTLY PREGNANT MAN, A ★★ This French comedy features Marcello Mastroianni as the first pregnant man. The reversal of parenting roles provides a few laughs and the surprise ending is worth the wait in an otherwise ho-hum film. Not rated; contains adult subject matter. In French with subtitles. 92m. **DIR:** Jacques Demy. **CAST:** Catherine Deneuve, Marcello Mastroianni, Mireille Mathieu. 1973

SLIGHTLY SCARLET ★★ Confused blend of romance, crime, and political corruption focuses on good girl falling for gang leader. Forget the story. Just watch the actors interplay. 99m. **DIR:** Allan Dwan. **CAST:** John Payne, Arlene Dahl, Rhonda Fleming, Kent Taylor. 1956

SLIME PEOPLE, THE 🎬 Hideous monsters burrow up from deep inside Earth and invade Los Angeles. Grade Z. B&W; 76m. **DIR:** Robert Hutton. **CAST:** Robert Hutton, Les Tremayne, Susan Hart. 1962

SLING BLADE ★★★★ Star-writer-director Billy Bob Thornton collected a screenplay Oscar for this mesmerizing, southern Gothic study of a simpleminded killer who, after spending twenty-five years in an asylum, returns to his backwater hometown. The stage is set for further tragedy with Thornton wholly compelling in the lead role. This film is absolutely perfect in all respects. Rated R for violence, profanity, and gut-wrenching descriptions of violent behavior. 134m. **DIR:** Billy Bob Thornton. **CAST:** Billy Bob Thornton, Dwight Yoakam, John Ritter, Lucas Black, Natalie Canerday. 1996 DVD

SLINGSHOT, THE ★★★ Making slingshots from contraband condoms is one of several misadventures for 10-year-old Roland in 1920s Sweden as he learns to cope with prejudice, harsh discipline, sex, and stinging rights to the nose from his aspiring pugilist brother. Comic, dramatic, and tragic, but misses the exhilaration of a slice-of-life classic. Adapted from Roland Schutt's autobiographical novel. In Swedish with English subtitles. Rated R for violence and language. 101m. **DIR:** Ake Sandgren. **CAST:** Jesper Salen, Stellan Skarsgard, Basia Frydman, Niclas Olund, Ernst-Hugo Jaregard, Frida Hallgren. 1994

SLIPPING INTO DARKNESS ★★ An ex–motorcycle gang member's brother is murdered. So the biker gets his former buddies together to find out whodunit. Rated R for violence, nudity, and profanity. 87m. **DIR:** Eleanor Gawer. **CAST:** Michelle Johnson, Neill Barry. 1988

SLIPSTREAM ★★1/2 With its high production values and sweeping Elmer Bernstein score, this movie about a futuristic world raises high hopes. Unfortunately, the story becomes mired down in its sluggishness. Oscar-winners Ben Kingsley and F. Murray Abraham have far too brief cameos late in the film. Rated PG-13 for violence. 92m. **DIR:** Steven Lisberger. **CAST:** Bob Peck, Bill Paxton, Kitty Aldridge, Mark Hamill, Eleanor David, Ben Kingsley, F. Murray Abraham. 1989

SLITHER ★★★ In this bizarre comedy the four leads are after a cache of stolen money, carrying them on a California odyssey with a house trailer in tow, pursued by two of the most ominous looking RVs ever built. Rated PG. 92m. **DIR:** Howard Zieff. **CAST:** James Caan, Sally Kellerman, Peter Boyle, Louise Lasser. 1973

SLITHIS ★★ Okay horror tale of a gruesome monster, derived from garbage and radiation in southern California, and his reign of terror. While earnestly done, the film just can't overcome its budget restrictions. Actual on-screen title: *Spawn of the Slithis.* Rated PG. 92m. **DIR:** Stephen Traxler. **CAST:** Alan Blanchard, Judy Motulsky. 1978

SLIVER ★★1/2 Sharon Stone moves into a high-rise, Manhattan apartment building—a sliver—and ends up becoming romantically involved with Tom Berenger and William Baldwin. After a while, Stone gets the feeling she's being watched, and that's when her new life becomes a nightmare. An involving but trashy movie. Rated R for nudity, simulated sex, profanity, and violence. 115m. **DIR:** Phillip Noyce. **CAST:** Sharon Stone, Tom Berenger, William Baldwin, Martin Landau, Colleen Camp, Polly Walker, C.C.H. Pounder, Nina Foch. 1993

SLOW BULLET 🎬 Vietnam veteran and his haunting memories of combat. Rated R for violence and nudity. 95m. **DIR:** Allen Wright. **CAST:** Jim Baskin. 1988

SLOW BURN ★★ Newspaper reporter Eric Roberts is hired as a private investigator to find the son of a Palm Springs artist. Beverly D'Angelo plays the lost son's mother who may or may not know what happened to him. A muddled plot and apprentice-like direction. This made-for-cable movie is equivalent to a PG-13 for violence and profanity. 88m. **DIR:** Matthew Chapman. **CAST:** Eric Roberts, Beverly D'Angelo, Dennis Lipscomb. 1986

SLUGGER'S WIFE, THE ★★ The most shallow of Neil Simon's works to date, this is bad television situation comedy blown up to big-screen size. Darryl Palmer (Michael O'Keefe) is a self-centered baseball player who bullies his way into the affections of Debby Palmer (Rebecca DeMornay), a would-be rock star. Rated PG-13 for nudity and profanity. 105m. **DIR:** Hal Ashby. **CAST:** Michael O'Keefe, Rebecca DeMornay, Martin Ritt, Randy Quaid, Cleavant Derricks. 1985

SLUGS, THE MOVIE 🎬 Mutated slugs infest a small town, devouring anyone they can crawl across. Rated R for violence and brief nudity. 90m. **DIR:** Juan Piquer Simon. **CAST:** Michael Garfield, Kim Terry, Patty Shepard. 1988

SLUMBER PARTY 57 🎬 In this sleazy, smutty movie, six girls sit around a campfire and tell about the first time they "did it." Rated R. 89m. **DIR:** William A. Levey. **CAST:** Noelle North, Debra Winger, Rainbeaux Smith, Joe E. Ross. 1977

SLUMBER PARTY MASSACRE 🎬 A mass murderer has escaped from a mental hospital and is killing young girls with a power drill. Rated R for nudity and graphic violence. 77m. **DIR:** Amy Jones. **CAST:** Michele Michaels, Robin Stille, Michael Villella. 1982

SLUMBER PARTY MASSACRE II ★★ The driller killer is back, but this time he appears as the ghost of a 1950s rock star. His weapon: a heavy-metal guitar with a high-powered drill extending from the neck. The producers tried to be original, but they didn't go far enough. Maybe next time. Rated R for violence, nudity, and profanity. 90m. **DIR:** Deborah Brock. **CAST:** Crystal Bernard. 1987

SLUMBER PARTY MASSACRE 3 🎬 The driller killer is back yet again, boring holes into kicking and screaming scantily clad girls. Predictable gory schlock. Not rated; contains nudity, profanity, and violence. 80m. **DIR:** Sally Mattison. **CAST:** Keely Christian, M. K. Harris, David Greenlee. 1990

SLUMS OF BEVERLY HILLS ★★★1/2 Writer-director Tamara Jenkins's study of dysfunctional family life presents a portrait of American youth that is so earthy and nakedly personal that parents probably shouldn't watch with their own children. Set in the early 1970s, the story concerns a blossoming teenage girl whose financially challenged father is always one short step ahead of eviction. This isn't a film for all tastes, but there are significant truths in Jenkins's perceptive script, which honors the disenfranchised fringe-dwellers. Rated R for profanity, nudity, drug use, and strong sexual content. 91m. **DIR:** Tamara Jenkins. **CAST:** Natasha Lyonne, Alan Arkin, Marisa Tomei, Eli Marienthal, David Krumholtz, Kevin Corrigan. 1998 DVD

SMALL CHANGE ★★★★★ One of François Truffaut's best pictures, this is a charming and perceptive film viewing the joys and sorrows of young children's lives in a small French town. Wonderfully and naturally acted by a cast of children. French. 104m. **DIR:** François Truffaut. **CAST:** Geary Desmouceaux, Philippe Goldman. 1976

SMALL CIRCLE OF FRIENDS, A ★1/2 Despite a solid cast, this story of campus unrest during the 1960s never comes together. As college students at Harvard, Karen Allen, Brad Davis, and Jameson Parker play three inseparable friends living and lov-

ing their way through protests and riots. Rated PG. 112m. **DIR:** Rob Cohen. **CAST:** Karen Allen, Brad Davis, Jameson Parker, Shelley Long, John Friedrich. 1980

SMALL FACES ★★ Three adolescent brothers try to grow up in 1968 Glasgow. One is a rebellious youngster, another an aspiring artist, the oldest a stupid brute; all become embroiled in the war between teenage gangs running the city. Director Gillies MacKinnon's pseudorealistic style can't disguise the melodramatic contrivances of the script or make the characters interesting, and the thick Scottish accents are all but unintelligible to American ears. Rated R for profanity and violence. 102m. **DIR:** Gillies MacKinnon. **CAST:** Joseph McFadden, Iain Robertson, J. S. Duffy. 1996

SMALL KILLING, A ★★★1/2 This above-average made-for-TV movie gains some of its appeal from the casting. Ed Asner is a cop going undercover as a wino and Jean Simmons is a professor posing as a bag lady. They're out to bust a hit man but manage to fall in love along the way. The supporting cast is equally wonderful. 100m. **DIR:** Steven H. Stern. **CAST:** Edward Asner, Jean Simmons, Sylvia Sidney, Andrew Prine. 1981

SMALL SACRIFICES ★★★★ Farrah Fawcett delivers a fine but chilling performance as Diana Downs, the sociopathic mother who tried to kill her three children because her ex-boyfriend didn't like kids. John Shea brings intensity to the role of DA Frank Joziak who must protect the two surviving children while seeking a conviction of Downs. Absorbing made-for-TV movie. 159m. **DIR:** David Greene. **CAST:** Farrah Fawcett, John Shea, Ryan O'Neal, Gordon Clapp. 1989

SMALL SOLDIERS ★★1/2 Destructive little soldier action figures are brought to lethal life by computer chips originally designed for military applications. A sequence involving malevolent Barbie dolls (voiced by Sarah Michelle Gellar and Christina Ricci) is a stroke of demented genius. Rated PG-13 for unexpectedly grim violence. 108m. **DIR:** Joe Dante. **CAST:** Kirsten Dunst, Gregory Smith, Jay Mohr, Phil Hartman, Kevin Dunn, David Cross, Ann Magnuson, Denis Leary. 1998 DVD

SMALL TIME ★★★ Frightening look at a sociopathic young hood raised in Harlem by a mother who depends on the money he steals. Divided into five segments, this is clearly a moral play about a life of crime. Low-budget production manages to hammer home its message loudly and clearly. Not rated; contains violence and profanity. B&W; 88m. **DIR:** Norman Loftis. **CAST:** Richard Barboza, Carolyn Kinebrew, Scott Ferguson, Keith Allen, Jane Williams. 1990

•**SMALL TIME CROOKS** ★★1/2 Woody Allen's familiar character tics and directorial flourishes have grown tiresome, particularly with projects this threadbare. This film opens as a screwball heist comedy, with Allen fronting a band of hilariously inept bank robbers, and then loses its way—along with its initial roster of characters—and turns into a parable about the seductive dangers of wealth. The transition, abrupt and unsettling, feels as if Allen suddenly changed his mind about how he intended his script to proceed ... and then let the first bit remain, because he'd already filmed it. When the first-act supporting players disappear, they take all the film's energy with them; what follows, frankly, is a yawn. Rated PG for mild vulgarity. 95m. **DIR:** Woody Allen. **CAST:** Woody Allen, Tracey Ullman, Elaine May, Jon Lovitz, Hugh Grant, Michael Rapaport. **2000**

SMALL TOWN GIRL ★★1/2 Farley Granger plays a rich playboy who speeds through a small town, gets a ticket, and promptly falls in love with the judge's daughter (Jane Powell), making his fiancée (Ann Miller) so jealous she dances up a storm. Not a memorable musical, but some interesting production numbers. 93m. **DIR:** Leslie Kardos, Busby Berkeley. **CAST:** Jane Powell, Farley Granger, Ann Miller, Bobby Van, S. Z. Sakall, Billie Burke, Fay Wray, Dean Miller, William Campbell, Nat King Cole. **1953**

SMALL TOWN IN TEXAS, A ★★ Fairly effective B picture pits a revenge-lusting Timothy Bottoms against the crooked sheriff (Bo Hopkins) who framed him in a drug bust and stole his wife (Susan George). Car crashes, fights, and even a little suspense. Rated R. 95m. **DIR:** Jack Starrett. **CAST:** Timothy Bottoms, Susan George, Bo Hopkins, Art Hindle, Morgan Woodward. **1976**

SMALLEST SHOW ON EARTH, THE ★★★1/2 Warm, often hilarious comedy about a couple who inherit a run-down movie theater and their wacky attendants. Excellent performances by Peter Sellers and Margaret Rutherford. B&W; 80m. **DIR:** Basil Dearden. **CAST:** Peter Sellers, Bill Travers, Margaret Rutherford. **1957**

SMASH PALACE ★★★★ A scrap yard of crumpled and rusting automobiles serves as a backdrop to the story of a marriage in an equally deteriorated condition in this well-made, exceptionally acted film from New Zealand. Explicit sex and nude scenes may shock some viewers. It's a *Kramer vs. Kramer, Ordinary People*–style of movie that builds to a scary, nail-chewing climax. No MPAA rating; this has sex, violence, nudity, and profanity. 100m. **DIR:** Roger Donaldson. **CAST:** Bruno Lawrence, Anna Jemison, Greer Robson, Desmond Kelly. **1981**

SMASH-UP: THE STORY OF A WOMAN ★★★ Nightclub songbird Susan Hayward puts her songwriter husband's (Lee Bowman) career first. As he succeeds, she slips. His subsequent neglect and indifference make her a scenery-shedding bottle baby until near tragedy restores her sobriety and his attention. B&W; 103m. **DIR:** Stuart Heisler. **CAST:** Susan Hayward, Lee Bowman, Marsha Hunt, Eddie Albert, Carleton Young, Carl Esmond. **1947**

SMASHING THE RACKETS ★★ Chester Morris plays an easily recognizable facsimile of racket-busting Thomas E. Dewey in this cardboard melodrama about an assistant district attorney who becomes a special prosecutor and the scourge of crooks everywhere. Strictly routine. B&W; 68m. **DIR:** Lew Landers. **CAST:** Chester Morris, Frances Mercer, Bruce Cabot, Rita Johnson. **1938**

SMILE ★★★★ Don't miss this one; it's a true neglected classic. This backstage look at a teenage beauty pageant is great satirical fun every inch of the way, managing to be both tough-minded and softhearted. Rated PG. 113m. **DIR:** Michael Ritchie. **CAST:**

Bruce Dern, Barbara Feldon, Michael Kidd, Geoffrey Lewis, Nicholas Pryor, Mario O'Brien, Colleen Camp, Joan Prather, Annette O'Toole, Melanie Griffith. **1975**

SMILE, JENNY, YOU'RE DEAD ★★★1/2 Neurotic obsession triggers murder and suspense in this exceptional pilot for *Harry O*, David Janssen's follow-up television series to *The Fugitive*. Definitely a keeper. 100m. **DIR:** Jerry Thorpe. **CAST:** David Janssen, Jodie Foster, Andrea Marcovicci, Howard DaSilva, Clu Gulager, John Anderson, Martin Gabel, Zalman King. **1974**

SMILE LIKE YOURS, A ★★ This comedy suffers from an overdose of sex (in elevators, men's rooms, etc.) as a couple try to have a baby. Last half hour picks up a bit if you're willing to wade through the sludge. Rated R for profanity and sex. 97m. **DIR:** Keith Samples. **CAST:** Greg Kinnear, Lauren Holly, Joan Cusack, Jay Thomas, Jill Hennessy, Sheridan Samples. **1997**

SMILES OF A SUMMER NIGHT ★★★★★ Nowhere in Ingmar Bergman's amazing *oeuvre*, perhaps nowhere in cinema, is there such a classic of carnal comedy. An elegant roundelay that is, at heart, an enlightened boudoir farce. Used as the basis of Stephen Sondheim's *A Little Night Music*. In Swedish with English subtitles. B&W; 106m. **DIR:** Ingmar Bergman. **CAST:** Ulla Jacobsson, Gunnar Björnstrand, Eva Dahlbeck, Harriet Andersson, Jarl Kulle. **1955**

SMILIN' THROUGH (1932) ★★★1/2 The love of a soldier and an heiress is threatened by a crime his father committed against her family decades earlier. Satisfying fantasy-love story. Remade in 1941. B&W; 98m. **DIR:** Sidney Franklin. **CAST:** Norma Shearer, Fredric March, Leslie Howard, O. P. Heggie. **1932**

SMILIN' THROUGH (1941) ★★★ If you can believe it, an orphaned and brave Jeanette MacDonald falls in love with the son of a murderer. Directed and played for tear value. Best thing to come out of the picture was Jeanette's marriage to Gene Raymond. 100m. **DIR:** Frank Borzage. **CAST:** Jeanette MacDonald, Gene Raymond, Brian Aherne, Ian Hunter. **1941**

●**SMILING GHOST, THE** ★★★ Good-natured young man just shy of oafdom takes a job posing as the prospective groom of a wealthy woman whose former fiancés are either dead or crippled. Accompanied by his "valet" and a nosy newswoman who has a crush on him, the slow-witted sucker moves into the mansion of his betrothed, risking the wrath of the "smiling ghost" who terminates all potential suitors. Creepy doings, weird relatives, and all the stock "haunted house" stuff make this horror-comedy click. Willie Best as the groom's hired man comes in for his share of racial slurs, which may contribute to this film's obscurity. B&W; 72m. **DIR:** Lewis Seiler. **CAST:** Wayne Morris, Brenda Marshall, Alexis Smith, Alan Hale Sr., David Bruce, Lee Patrick, Willie Best. **1941**

SMILLA'S SENSE OF SNOW ★★★ Scientist investigates the death of a young boy—who jumped to his death—by following the scent of a crime cover-up to secrets hidden below her homeland ice. Dreamy cinematography keeps the film riveting even as it melts into a flaky James Bond–like finale. Rated R for language, violence, and sex. 121m. **DIR:** Bille August. **CAST:** Julia Ormond, Gabriel Byrne, Richard Harris, Robert Loggia, Vanessa Redgrave, Clipper Miano. 1997

SMITH! ★★★ A fine cast and sensitive screenplay distinguish this story of a strongman's efforts to secure a fair trial for an Indian accused of murder. Glenn Ford is believably rugged and righteous, and Chief Dan George is highly effective as the stoic focal point of the territory's rage. Good fare for the whole family. Rated G. 101m. **DIR:** Michael O'Herlihy. **CAST:** Glenn Ford, Nancy Olson, Dean Jagger, Keenan Wynn, Warren Oates, Chief Dan George. 1969

SMITHEREENS ★★★ An independently made feature (its budget was only $100,000), this work by producer-director Susan Seidelman examines the life of an amoral and aimless young woman (Susan Berman) living in New York. Rated R. 90m. **DIR:** Susan Seidelman. **CAST:** Susan Berman, Brad Rinn, Richard Hell, Roger Jett. 1982

SMOKE (1970) ★★★ Distraught over his father's death and his mother's remarriage, a farm boy gives his affection to an injured German shepherd instead. Well-acted, satisfying family drama from the Disney studios. 90m. **DIR:** Vincent McEveety. **CAST:** Ron Howard, Earl Holliman, Andy Devine. 1970

SMOKE (1995) ★★★★ Novelist Paul Auster's 1990 Christmas fable has been transformed into a brilliant little ensemble piece, revolving around the idiosyncratic regulars at a Brooklyn cigar shop. The film unfolds like a skillfully staged play, and the characters are fascinating. Rated R for profanity and mild violence. 112m. **DIR:** Wayne Wang. **CAST:** Harvey Keitel, William Hurt, Forest Whitaker, Stockard Channing, Harold Perrineau Jr., Ashley Judd. 1995

SMOKE SIGNALS ★★★1/2 Interesting but dramatically unfocused tale of two young Idaho Indians on a trip to Arizona. Despite fascinating cultural details and enchanting, unusual dialogue (by the fine writer Sherman Alexie, who adapted the screenplay from his short story collection *The Lone Ranger and Tonto Fistfight in Heaven*), the piece's finer points never really gel. Rated PG-13 for language. 89m. **DIR:** Chris Eyre. **CAST:** Adam Beach, Evan Adams, Gary Farmer, Irene Bedard. 1998 DVD

SMOKESCREEN ★★★ A fledgling ad executive, tired of being low man on the totem pole, becomes involved with a model who in turn involves him with a mob leader. Well acted and fairly well written, the film's main fault lies in its contrived ending. Rated R. 91m. **DIR:** Martin Lavut. **CAST:** Kim Cattrall, Matt Craven, Kim Coates, Dean Stockwell. 1990

SMOKEY AND THE BANDIT ★★★1/2 *Smokey and the Bandit* may strain credibility, but it never stops being fun. The Bandit (Burt Reynolds) is an infamous independent trucker who is hired to transport four hundred cases of Coors beer from Texarkana, Texas, where it is legal, to Atlanta, Georgia, where it is not. Hold on to your hat. Rated PG for profanity. 97m. **DIR:** Hal Needham. **CAST:** Burt Reynolds, Pat McCormick, Jerry Reed, Sally Field, Mike Henry, Jackie Gleason, Paul Williams. 1977 DVD

SMOKEY AND THE BANDIT II ★★ *Smokey II* is just more proof that "sequels aren't equal." But it isn't a

total loss. Don't turn it off until the credits roll (although you may want to fast-forward). Outtakes featuring the stars flubbing their lines are spliced together at the end, and they're hilarious. Rated PG. 101m. **DIR:** Hal Needham. **CAST:** Burt Reynolds, Jerry Reed, Pat McCormick, Paul Williams, Mike Henry, Jackie Gleason, Dom DeLuise. 1980

SMOKEY AND THE BANDIT III ♥ The Bandit may be back, but it ain't Burt. Rated PG for nudity, profanity, and scatological humor. 86m. **DIR:** Dick Lowry. **CAST:** Jerry Reed, Jackie Gleason, Paul Williams, Pat McCormick. 1983

SMOKEY BITES THE DUST ★★1/2 Jimmy McNichol stars as a mischievous teenager who takes great delight in stealing cars and making buffoons out of the sheriff and his deputies. This is pretty standard car-chase action, but it does move along and there are some laughs along the way. Rated PG. 85m. **DIR:** Charles B. Griffith. **CAST:** Jimmy McNichol, Walter Barnes, John Blythe Barrymore, William Forsythe. 1981

SMOKEY TRAILS ★★★ Once again Bob Steele is after the killer of his father—chasing him right into Lost Canyon, an outlaw den that he cleans out with plenty of fisticuffs and blazing six-shooters. Above average. B&W; 57m. **DIR:** Bernard B. Ray. **CAST:** Bob Steele, Jimmy Aubrey, Ted Adams, Carleton Young. 1939

SMOKY MOUNTAIN CHRISTMAS ★★★ Typical made-for-TV seasonal heartwarmer, this features Dolly Parton as a burned-out singer-actress who takes to the hills of Tennessee for rest and seclusion. There she rediscovers the real meaning of Christmas. Suitable for family viewing. 100m. **DIR:** Henry Winkler. **CAST:** Dolly Parton, Lee Majors, Dan Hedaya, Bo Hopkins, John Ritter. 1986

SMOOTH TALK ★★★★ Coltish Laura Dern owns this film, an uncompromising adaptation of the Joyce Carol Oates short story "Where Are You Going, Where Have You Been?" Dern hits every note as a sultry woman-child poised on the brink of adulthood and sexual maturity. Mary Kay Place does well as an exasperated mom, and Elizabeth Berridge is a sympathetic older sister. Rated PG-13 for language and sexual situations. 92m. **DIR:** Joyce Chopra. **CAST:** Laura Dern, Treat Williams, Mary Kay Place, Elizabeth Berridge, Levon Helm. 1985

SMOOTH TALKER ★★1/2 Cop Joe Guzaldo is at the end of his rope: his attorney wife just walked out and unless he can come up with a lead on a killer of 976-Phone Girls, he's about to hit the pavement, sans badge. Things heat up when the only suspect in the case winds up being prosecuted by his ex-wife. Rated R for language and violence. 89m. **DIR:** Tom E. Milo. **CAST:** Joe Guzaldo, Burt Ward, Stuart Whitman. 1991

SMURFS AND THE MAGIC FLUTE, THE ★★ Those little blue people from the popular television cartoon show are featured in their first movie. The kiddies will probably love it, but parents should read a book. Rated G. 80m. **DIR:** John Rust. 1983

SNAKE EATER ♥ Lorenzo Lamas is a lone wolf cop in pursuit of the hillbillies who killed his parents. This hybrid of *Rambo* and *The Hills Have Eyes* had us laughing at all the wrong moments. Rated R for profanity, violence, and nudity. 89m. DIR: George Erschbamer. CAST: Lorenzo Lamas. 1989

SNAKE EATER 2, THE DRUG BUSTER ★★ Mel Gibson's marketable character from the *Lethal Weapon* movies finds new merchandising life in this rip-off action flick. Lorenzo Lamas portrays Soldier, an unorthodox cop turned vigilante. Rated R for violence and profanity. 93m. DIR: George Erschbamer. CAST: Lorenzo Lamas, Michele Scarabelli, Larry B. Scott, Vittorio Rossi. 1989

SNAKE EATER III: HIS LAW ★★1/2 Renegade cop Lorenzo Lamas returns. This outing, he helps a family whose daughter was brutalized by a gang of bikers called Hell's Furies. Rated R for violence, simulated sex, and profanity. 109m. DIR: George Erschbamer. CAST: Lorenzo Lamas, Minor Mustain. 1992

SNAKE EYES ★★★1/2 Nicolas Cage owns this energetic thriller. The plot, a slight nod to Kurosawa's *Rashomon*, finds Cage as an Atlantic City police detective on hand during a televised heavyweight boxing match, when the U.S. secretary of defense is gunned down. The story itself is a mildly clever conspiracy piece, in good company with De Palma's *Blow Out.* Rated R for violence and profanity. 98m. DIR: Brian De Palma. CAST: Nicolas Cage, Gary Sinise, John Heard, Carla Gugino, Stan Shaw, Kevin Dunn. 1998 DVD

SNAKE PEOPLE 🐾 In this Mexican movie with scenes of Boris Karloff shot just before his death, the ailing actor plays a rich man whose niece is kidnapped by demon worshipers. 90m. DIR: Juan Ibanez, Jack Hill. CAST: Boris Karloff. 1968

SNAKE PIT, THE ★★★★★ One of the first and best movies about mental illness and the treatment of patients in hospitals and asylums. Olivia de Havilland turns in an exceptional performance as a woman suffering from a nervous breakdown. Based on an autobiographical novel by Mary Jane Ward. B&W; 108m. DIR: Anatole Litvak. CAST: Olivia de Havilland, Mark Stevens, Leo Genn, Celeste Holm, Betsy Blair, Ruth Donnelly, Glenn Langan, Beulah Bondi, Leif Erickson. 1948

SNAPDRAGON ★★ A detective (Chelsea Field), investigating a case involving serial murders, requests the assistance of a police psychologist (Steve Bauer). A young amnesic woman may know something about the murders or the identity of the killer. Predictable but watchable thriller. Rated R for nudity, profanity, and violence. 96m. DIR: Worth Keeter. CAST: Steven Bauer, Chelsea Field, Pamela Anderson. 1993

SNAPPER, THE ★★★1/2 The second film made from author Roddy Doyle's *Barrytown* trilogy (following *The Commitments*) is a delightful character study. The strong-willed daughter in a working-class family becomes pregnant and refuses to divulge the name of the father. This is a gem! Rated R for frank discussions of sex and brief profanity. 95m. DIR: Stephen Frears. CAST: Colm Meaney, Ruth McCabe, Tina Kellegher, Colm O'Bryne, Pat Laffan. 1994

SNATCHED ★★1/2 In this mediocre made-for-television film, the wives of three rich men are kidnapped and held for ransom. The crime is complicated when one of the husbands refuses to pay his share of the ransom. 73m. DIR: Sutton Roley. CAST: Howard Duff, Leslie Nielsen, Sheree North, Barbara Parkins, Robert Reed, John Saxon, Tisha Sterling, Anthony Zerbe, Richard Davalos. 1973

SNEAKERS ★★★★ In this slick, enjoyable piece of escapism, Robert Redford gives a star-quality performance as a computer trickster turned security expert—until government agents use his shady past to force him into a battle of wits with a former colleague. Fine acting and sly bits of humor add to the fun. Rated PG-13 for profanity and violence. 126m. DIR: Phil Alden Robinson. CAST: Robert Redford, Dan Aykroyd, Ben Kingsley, Mary McDonnell, River Phoenix, Sidney Poitier, David Strathairn, Timothy Busfield, George Hearn. 1992 DVD

SNIPER ★★1/2 Male posturing reaches ludicrous heights in this tedious jungle drama, which finds Marine sniper Tom Berenger sent into the wilds of Panama to assassinate a Colombian drug baron. Rated R for violence and profanity. 98m. DIR: Luis Llosa. CAST: Tom Berenger, Billy Zane, J. T. Walsh. 1993 DVD

SNO-LINE 🐾 A Texas cocaine operation is threatened by the mob. Rated R for violence and language. 89m. DIR: Douglas F. O'Neans. CAST: Vince Edwards, Paul Smith, June Wilkinson. 1984

SNOOPY, COME HOME ★★★1/2 Charming second entry in the "Peanuts" film series doesn't contain the childhood *angst* of the first but maintains the irreverent view of life found in the best of Charles Schulz's comic strips. Snoopy decides life at home ain't all it's cracked up to be, so he and Woodstock set off to find America. Needless to say, there's no place like home. Rated G. 70m. DIR: Bill Melendez. 1972

SNOOPY: THE MUSICAL ★★★ This is another unwieldy mix of animation and off-Broadway music, drawn from the second live-action play starring Charlie Brown and the Peanuts gang. The material was severely abridged for its original one-hour television time slot. While Larry Grossman and Hal Hackady's songs remain poignant and cute, the show feels rushed ... and it's still odd to watch an animated Snoopy actually talk (and sing). Not rated. 50m. DIR: Sam Jaimes. 1988

SNOOPY'S REUNION ★★1/2 The story of how Charlie Brown came to adopt Snoopy could have been told much better. Aside from the novelty of watching Snoopy and his doggie siblings perform in a jug band, there's little to recommend this weak Peanuts entry. Not rated. 25m. DIR: Sam Jaimes. 1991

SNOW COUNTRY ★★★1/2 A painter's romance with a lovely geisha is complicated by various friends and acquaintances. Fine Japanese love story set amidst the snowbanks of an isolated village. In Japanese with English subtitles. B&W; 134m. DIR: Shiro Toyoda. CAST: Ryo Ikebe. 1957

SNOW CREATURE, THE 🐾 Abominable Snowman movie is one of the weakest of the batch that hit American theatres in the mid-1950s. B&W; 70m. DIR: W. Lee Wilder. CAST: Paul Langton, Leslie Denison. 1954

•SNOW DAY ★★1/2 Chevy Chase takes a backseat to his children in this family film. Most of the film is devoted to his daughter's crusade to rid the streets of a maniacal snow-plow dude, and his son's romantic endeavors. Passable entertainment but unmemorable. Rated PG for comic-book violence. 89m. **DIR:** Chris Koch. **CAST:** Chevy Chase, Chris Elliott, Jean Smart. 2000

•SNOW FALLING ON CEDARS ★★1/2 In a small Pacific Northwest town shortly after World War II, the trial of a Japanese American for murder awakens slumbering racism and memories of the wartime internment camps. David Guterson's best-selling novel gets a sluggish filming by director Scott Hicks, with the characters taking a backseat to lingering shots of the scenery and weather. Some of the story's inherent drama manages to survive. Rated PG-13 for mature themes. 126m. **DIR:** Scott Hicks. **CAST:** Ethan Hawke, Youki Kudoh, Rick Yune, James Rebhorn, Max von Sydow, Sam Shepard. 1999 DVD

SNOW KILL ★★★1/2 An executive's plan for a weekend survival trip on a mountain turns into trouble when three escaped convicts try to recover their cocaine stash. Good action with David Dukes shining as the villain. Not rated, but has violence. 94m. **DIR:** Thomas Wright. **CAST:** Terence Knox, Patti D'Arbanville, David Dukes. 1990

SNOW QUEEN ★★ An exceedingly dull *Faerie Tale Theatre* tale, the Snow Queen (played by Lee Remick), teaches an unruly boy a lesson. The sets and special effects are second only to the actors' lines for their banality. 48m. **DIR:** Peter Medak. **CAST:** Melissa Gilbert, Lance Kerwin, Lee Remick, Lauren Hutton, Linda Manz, David Hemmings. 1983

SNOW WHITE AND THE SEVEN DWARFS (1938) ★★★★★ This first full-length animated film produced by Walt Disney was the culmination of a dream. *Snow White* is nothing short of breathtaking. The fairy tale, adapted from the works of the Brothers Grimm, has arrived with most of its power intact. Disney collected a special Academy Award for this film—one normal-sized statuette and seven little ones. Not rated; suitable for family viewing. 83m. **DIR:** David Hand. 1938

SNOW WHITE AND THE SEVEN DWARFS (1983) ★★★★ Both Vincent Price and Vanessa Redgrave are wickedly wonderful in this splendid adaptation of the Grimm's tale. Price plays the evil queen's (Redgrave) advising mirror. Lovely Elizabeth McGovern plays a sweet Snow White. 51m. **DIR:** Peter Medak. **CAST:** Elizabeth McGovern, Vanessa Redgrave, Vincent Price, Rex Smith. 1983

SNOW WHITE AND THE THREE STOOGES ♥ Sad entry from what was left of the Three Stooges. 107m. **DIR:** Walter Lang. **CAST:** The Three Stooges, Patricia Medina, Carol Heiss, Gil Guelfe, Buddy Baer, Edgar Barrier. 1961

SNOW WHITE: A TALE OF TERROR ★★1/2 Returning to the Brothers Grimm no doubt was intended to remove the cloying taint of Disney and other sanitized adaptations, but this rendition of the wholesome young woman and her evil stepmother trades cute forest creatures and cheerful dwarfs for pointless gore and ill-conceived characters. Rated R for violence, gore, and simulated sex. 100m. **DIR:** Michael Cohn. **CAST:** Sigourney Weaver, Sam Neill, Monica Keena, Gil Bellows, Taryn Davis, David Conrad, Brian Glover. 1996 DVD

SNOW WHITE CHRISTMAS, A ♥ The whole Charming kingdom is thrown into chaos by an evil queen who hates holiday cheer. 60m. **DIR:** Kay Wright. 1979

SNOWBALL EXPRESS ★★ This formula comedy stars the Disney stable of players from the 1960s and 1970s. Dean Jones inherits a run-down hotel and attempts to turn it into a ski resort. Standard family viewing with a ski chase to help the pace. Rated G. 99m. **DIR:** Norman Tokar. **CAST:** Dean Jones, Nancy Olson, Harry Morgan, Keenan Wynn, Johnny Whitaker. 1972

SNOWBEAST ♥ Hokey white Sasquatch–Abominable Snowman makes life miserable on the slopes. 100m. **DIR:** Herb Wallerstein. **CAST:** Bo Svenson, Yvette Mimieux, Robert Logan, Clint Walker, Sylvia Sidney. 1977

SNOWBOARD ACADEMY ♥ Troublesome snowboarders, masquerading as hip rebels, go head-to-head with the moronic staff of a ski resort. As ridiculous as it sounds. Rated PG. 89m. **DIR:** John Shephird. **CAST:** Corey Haim, Jim Varney, Brigitte Nielsen, Joe Flaherty. 1996

SNOWS OF KILIMANJARO, THE ★★★★ A broad and colorful canvas of foreign adventure with author-hero (Gregory Peck) lying injured on the slope of Africa's famous mountain reflecting on his life. From Africa to Spain to the Riviera and back again. One of the better renderings of a Hemingway novel. 117m. **DIR:** Henry King. **CAST:** Gregory Peck, Susan Hayward, Ava Gardner, Leo G. Carroll, Hildegarde Neff, Torin Thatcher. 1952 DVD

SNUFF ♥ Dull garbage cynically passed off in its theatrical debut as a genuine snuff movie—actually nothing more than an Argentinian drug smuggling pic, capped with obviously fake disemboweling climax filmed in a New York apartment. Not rated. 82m. **DIR:** Michael Findlay. 1974

SO DEAR TO MY HEART ★★★★ Loving re-creation of small-town life in the early years of this century. Young Bobby Driscoll (one of the finest of all child actors) has taken a notion to enter his black lamb Danny in the county fair. A singing blacksmith (Burl Ives in his film debut) encourages him in his dreams. This gentle film is loaded with love, goodwill, and sentiment. 84m. **DIR:** Harold Schuster. **CAST:** Burl Ives, Beulah Bondi, Harry Carey, Luana Patten, Bobby Driscoll, Matt Willis. 1949

SO ENDS OUR NIGHT ★★★★ Fredric March gives one of his best performances as a German trying to escape Nazi Germany but forced to return when he learns that his wife is terminally ill. The movie was produced before Pearl Harbor and was dismissed by critics and public alike. After the United States entered the war, it was reissued to acclaim and still has strong entertainment value. B&W; 118m. **DIR:** John Cromwell. **CAST:** Fredric March, Margaret Sullavan, Glenn Ford, Frances Dee, Erich Von Stroheim, Anna Sten. 1941

SO FINE ★★ This so-called sex comedy—about a fashion house (run by Ryan O'Neal and Jack Warden) that introduces a new line of designer jeans with see-through plastic inserts in the seat—is little more than a television situation comedy with leers. Rated R because of nudity and profanity. 91m. DIR: Andrew Bergman. CAST: Ryan O'Neal, Jack Warden, Richard Kiel, Fred Gwynne, Mike Kellin, David Rounds. 1981

SO I MARRIED AN AXE MURDERER ★★1/2 Mike Myers proves he can get some laughs outside of *Wayne's World* in this comedy about a modern-day beat poet's ill-fated marriage to a butcher's assistant. There are some good moments in this paper-thin whodunit. Rated PG-13 for violence, suggested sex, nudity, and vulgarity. 94m. DIR: Thomas Schlamme. CAST: Mike Myers, Nancy Travis, Anthony LaPaglia, Amanda Plummer, Brenda Fricker, Matt Doherty, Charles Grodin, Alan Arkin, Phil Hartman, Debi Mazar, Michael Richards, Steven Wright. 1993 DVD

SO PROUDLY WE HAIL ★★★★ Hollywood's foremost actresses worked together to make this first tribute to women in World War II a morale-builder as well as a money-maker. Nurses at the siege of Bataan in an action-filled movie with the right touch of romance to keep both men and women involved. B&W; 126m. DIR: Mark Sandrich. CAST: Claudette Colbert, Paulette Goddard, Veronica Lake, Barbara Britton, Sonny Tufts, George Reeves, Bill Goodwin, Ann Doran, Walter Abel. 1943

SO THIS IS WASHINGTON ★★1/2 From a park bench in Washington, D.C., Charles Lauck and Norris Goff, radio's cracker-barrel philosophers Lum and Abner, dispense common sense to senators and congressmen. Third in a series, this product of wartime mentality is a simpleminded feature aimed at warming the heart. B&W; 65m. DIR: Ray McCarey. CAST: Charles Lauck, Norris Goff, Alan Mowbray, Minerva Urecal. 1943

SOAPDISH ★★★1/2 Daytime soap operas get the raspberry in this often funny spoof, which features lively performances by the cast. Rated PG-13 for profanity. 97m. DIR: Michael Hoffman. CAST: Sally Field, Kevin Kline, Whoopi Goldberg, Robert Downey Jr., Cathy Moriarty, Elisabeth Shue, Teri Hatcher, Garry Marshall, Carrie Fisher. 1991

S.O.B. ★★★ Director Blake Edwards vents his resentment over Hollywood's treatment of him in the early 1970s in this failed attempt at satire. There are some good moments, but too few. Self-indulgent. Rated R. 121m. DIR: Blake Edwards. CAST: Julie Andrews, William Holden, Robert Preston, Richard Mulligan, Robert Vaughn, Loretta Swit, Larry Hagman, Craig Stevens, Shelley Winters, Rosanna Arquette. 1981

SOCCER DOG: THE MOVIE ★★1/2 Derivative rehash of *Air Bud* aimed squarely at the unassuming children's market. Young Jeremy is having a hard time fitting in with his new foster parents and at school. He turns to soccer for solace and becomes a school hero when his furry four-legged friend becomes the school's new soccer star. The usual complications follow. Rated PG. 98m. DIR: Tony Giglio. CAST: Jeremy Foley, James Marshall, Olivia D'Abo. 1998

SOCIETY ★★1/2 Every child's worst nightmare comes true for a Beverly Hills teenager who is plunged into a nightmarish world of ritual sacrifice and monstrous cruelty. Rated R for violence, profanity, and nudity. 99m. DIR: Brian Yuzna. CAST: Billy Warlock, Devin DeVasquez, Evan Richards. 1992

SODBUSTERS ★★1/2 This ponderous Western comedy isn't even fit to stand in the shadow of *Blazing Saddles*. Stone-faced Kris Kristofferson, playing a maimed gunfighter dubbed Destiny, rides into sleepy Marble Hat, Colorado, and joins local farmers hoping to thwart a greedy railroad tycoon. Only a few laughs accidentally emerge from this riff on *Shane* that wastes the talents of all involved. Rated PG-13 for profanity and a few surprisingly violent scenes. 97m. DIR: Eugene Levy. CAST: Kris Kristofferson, Fred Willard, John Vernon, Wendel Meldrum, Max Gail, Steve Landesberg. 1994

SODOM AND GOMORRAH ★★★ Better-than-average biblical epic concerning the twin cities of sin. Extremely long film contains good production values and performances. No rating, but film does contain scenes of violence and gore. 154m. DIR: Robert Aldrich. CAST: Stewart Granger, Stanley Baker, Pier Angeli, Rossana Podesta. 1963

SOFIE ★★★1/2 The great Norwegian actress Liv Ullmann directs her first film, a slow-moving but affecting family saga in turn-of-the-century Sweden. We follow the life of the title character, an enterprising and independent Jewish woman. Ullmann learned a lot from Ingmar Bergman, and layers in textures of family warmth, humor, and mystery, as well as a masterful performance by Bergman veteran Erland Josephson as Sofie's beloved father. In Swedish with English subtitles. 146m. DIR: Liv Ullmann. CAST: Karen-Lise Mynster, Erland Josephson, Ghita Norby. 1993

SOFT DECEIT ★★★ Clever little thriller about an undercover cop (Kate Vernon) who falls in love with the criminal mastermind who stole the $6 million she's supposed to recover. Although plot holes abound and numerous side issues are left unresolved, Vernon brings far more depth to her character than this genre usually supplies; you'll genuinely care about what happens to her. Rated R for nudity, simulated sex, and profanity. 95m. DIR: Jorge Montesi. CAST: Patrick Bergin, Kate Vernon, John Wesley Shipp, Gwynyth Walsh. 1994

SOFT KILL, THE ★★ When his girlfriend is found brutally murdered, a private eye discovers he's the main suspect. As the body count rises, he fights a desperate battle to prove his innocence. Another so-so crime-thriller that's predictable almost from frame one. Rated R for profanity and violence. 90m. DIR: Eli Cohen. CAST: Michael Harris, Brion James, Corbin Bernsen. 1994

SOFT SKIN, THE ★★★1/2 For some critics, this ranks as one of the new-wave master's worst; for some it remains one of his best. As usual, the truth lies in between. What keeps it from being at least a minor classic is the less-than-fresh plot. In French with English subtitles. 118m. DIR: François Truffaut. CAST: Jean Desailly, Nelly Benedetti, Françoise Dorleac. 1964 DVD

SOIS BELLE ET TAIS-TOI (JUST ANOTHER PRETTY FACE) ★★★ This French import tries to be a lighthearted, romantic adventure, but doesn't focus itself properly. Mylene Demongeot is Virginie, an 18-year-old orphan who runs away from a reformatory and falls in with a jewel-smuggling gang. Jean-Paul Belmondo and Alain Delon, both in their first film roles, are members of the teenage gang. In French with English subtitles. B&W; 110m. DIR: Marc Allegret. CAST: Mylene Demongeot, Henri Vidal, René Lefévre, Jean-Paul Belmondo, Alain Delon. 1958

SOL BIANCA ★★★★ After the pirate ship *Sol Bianca* unknowingly takes on a passenger, the five-woman crew of freebooters set their sights on a new prize: the "Gnosis," a treasure beyond price. Unfortunately the obstacle in their path, a tyrannical emperor, is determined to keep the treasure. Japanese animation from the director of *Bubblegum Crisis*. In Japanese with English subtitles. Not rated, with violence and profanity. 60m. DIR: Akiyama Katsuhito. 1990

SOLAR CRISIS ★★ The sun is the only thing that flares up in this minor effort. A solar flare-up threatens to destroy life on Earth unless a group of scientists can shoot an antimatter bomb into the sun. The direction reduces everything to bargain-basement clichés. Rated PG-13 for violence. 111m. DIR: Alan Smithee. CAST: Tim Matheson, Charlton Heston, Peter Boyle, Corin Nemec, Jack Palance, Annabel Schofield. 1992 DVD

SOLAR FORCE 💖 In this cheesy representation of the twenty-first century, Michael Paré must stop colonists from regenerating the Earth's environment, which should not be difficult, as bad guy Billy Drago has sucked up all the hot air. Rated R for violence and profanity. 91m. DIR: Boaz Davidson. CAST: Michael Paré, Billy Drago, Walker Brandt. 1994

SOLARBABIES 💖 In the far future, a group of sports teens joins forces with a mystical force. Rated PG-13 for violence. 94m. DIR: Alan Johnson. CAST: Richard Jordan, Jami Gertz, Jason Patric, Charles Durning, Lukas Haas. 1986

SOLARIS ★★★★ Based on a story by noted Polish author Stanislaw Lem, this motion picture explores the workings of a man's mind and how he deals with visions from his past. A space station situated over a water-covered planet has become almost deserted, and a scientist is sent to unravel the mysteries surrounding the death of a doctor on board the station. A milestone in the history of science-fiction cinema. In Russian with English subtitles. Not rated. 167m. DIR: Andrei Tarkovsky. CAST: Donatas Banionis, Natalya Bondarchuk. 1972

SOLDIER, THE 💖 Russian agents steal enough plutonium for a large nuclear explosion. Rated R for violence and profanity. 96m. DIR: James Glickenhaus. CAST: Ken Wahl, Klaus Kinski, William Prince. 1982

SOLDIER ★★★ Sci-fi fans will recognize this as one of the most basic plots: A supersoldier, designed to blindly follow orders without a twinge of conscience, is forced by circumstance to reevaluate his priorities and—having found his humanity—becomes the sole protector of a ragtag band of colonists facing overwhelming odds. It works because of star Kurt Russell, who is absolutely credible and wholly sympathetic in the title role. Rated R for violence. 95m. DIR: Paul Anderson. CAST: Kurt Russell, Jason Scott Lee, Connie Nielsen, Michael Chiklis, Gary Busey. 1998 DVD

SOLDIER BLUE ★★1/2 An extremely violent film that looks at the mistreatment of Indians at the hands of the U.S. Cavalry. This familiar subject has fared much better in films such as *Little Big Man*. Final attack is an exercise in excessive gore and violence. Rated R. 112m. DIR: Ralph Nelson. CAST: Candice Bergen, Peter Strauss, John Anderson, Donald Pleasence. 1970

SOLDIER BOYZ 💖 Yet another variant on *The Dirty Dozen* (and undoubtedly not the last) has ghetto punks released from prison to rescue a hostage in North Vietnam. Rated R for violence and profanity. 91m. DIR: Louis Mourneau. CAST: Michael Dudikoff, David Barry Gray, Cary-Hiroyuki Tagawa, Don Stroud. 1995

SOLDIER IN THE RAIN ★★★ *My Bodyguard* director Tony Bill is among the featured performers in this fine combination of sweet drama and rollicking comedy starring Steve McQueen, Jackie Gleason, and Tuesday Weld. Gleason is great as a high-living, worldly master sergeant, and McQueen is equally good as his protégé. B&W; 88m. DIR: Ralph Nelson. CAST: Steve McQueen, Tony Bill, Jackie Gleason, Tuesday Weld, Tom Poston. 1963

SOLDIER OF FORTUNE ★★1/2 Clark Gable helps Susan Hayward search for her husband, lost in Red China. Exotic Asian locations are the main reason to see this standard adventure-drama. Gable is virile, Hayward makes a good match for him, and Hong Kong never looked better. 96m. DIR: Edward Dmytryk. CAST: Clark Gable, Susan Hayward, Michael Rennie, Gene Barry, Tom Tully, Alex D'Arcy, Anna Sten. 1955 DVD

SOLDIER OF ORANGE ★★★★★ Rutger Hauer became an international star as a result of his remarkable performance in this Dutch release, in which he plays one of four college buddies galvanized into action when the Nazis invade the Netherlands. This is an exceptional work; an exciting, suspenseful, and intelligent war adventure. In several languages and subtitled. Rated R for nudity, profanity, implied sex, and violence. 165m. DIR: Paul Verhoeven. CAST: Rutger Hauer, Peter Faber, Jeroen Krabbé. 1979

SOLDIER OF THE NIGHT 💖 This Israeli movie about a man who kills soldiers by night while working in a toy store by day has some psychological thriller elements, but its plodding story line and poor dubbing make it almost impossible to watch. Not rated, with nudity, violence, and profanity. 89m. DIR: Dan Wolman. CAST: Iris Kaner, Hillel Neeman, Yftach Katzur. 1984

SOLDIER'S DAUGHTER NEVER CRIES, A ★★★ The autobiographical novel by Kaylie Jones, daughter of writer James Jones (*From Here to Eternity*, *The Thin Red Line*) is adapted by writer Ruth Prawer Jhabvala and director James Ivory into a tasteful, well-acted film. It's refreshing to see a film about a functional family for once; Kris Kristofferson, as the father, has seldom been better. Rated R for profanity. 124m. **DIR:** James Ivory. **CAST:** Kris Kristofferson, Barbara Hershey, LeeLee Sobieski, Anthony Roth Costanzo. **1998**

SOLDIER'S FORTUNE ★★1/2 When ex–Green Beret turned mercenary Gil Gerard finds out that his daughter has been kidnapped, he pulls together an elite fighting team in order to bring her back alive. Likable cast helps move things along. Rated R for violence. 92m. **DIR:** Arthur N. Mele. **CAST:** Gil Gerard, Charles Napier, Dan Haggerty. **1990**

SOLDIER'S HOME ★★★1/2 Melancholy adaptation of an Ernest Hemingway story. The war in question is World War I, "the war to end all wars," and young Harold Krebs (Richard Backus) learns, almost to his shame, that he'd prefer that the fighting continue; without it, he has no sense of purpose. Introduced by Henry Fonda; not rated and suitable for family viewing. 41m. **DIR:** Robert Young. **CAST:** Richard Backus, Nancy Marchand, Robert McIlwaine, Lisa Essary, Mark La Mura, Lane Binkley. **1976**

SOLDIER'S STORY, A ★★★★★ A murder mystery, a character study, and a deeply affecting drama rolled into one, based on Charles Fuller's 1981 Pulitzer Prize–winning play, this is an unforgettable viewing experience. This riveting movie examines man's inhumanity to man in one of its most venal forms: racial hatred. Rated PG for violence and profanity. 102m. **DIR:** Norman Jewison. **CAST:** Howard Rollins Jr., Adolph Caesar. **1984 DVD**

SOLDIER'S SWEETHEART, A ★★★1/2 "Vietnam is full of strange stories," the narrator tells us, and few will be more unusual than this fascinating adaptation of Tim O'Brien's short story. When one of the doctors in a M.A.S.H. unit unwisely pulls strings to bring his girlfriend over from the States for a few weeks of companionship, he's horrified to discover, as the days pass, that she *likes* the dangerous environment. Rated R for profanity, violence, simulated sex, and hospital gore. 111m. **DIR:** Thomas Michael Donnelly. **CAST:** Kiefer Sutherland, Skeet Ulrich, Georgina Cates. **1998**

SOLDIER'S TALE, A ★★★ During World War II, romance develops between a British soldier (Gabriel Byrne) and a beautiful Frenchwoman (Marianne Basler) accused of collaborating with the Germans against the French Resistance. Ending is quite a surprise. Rated R for nudity, violence, and profanity. 95m. **DIR:** Larry Parr. **CAST:** Gabriel Byrne, Judge Reinhold, Marianne Basler. **1988 DVD**

SOLE SURVIVOR ★★ A gory remake of a fine English suspense thriller of the same title—about the lone survivor of an airplane crash, haunted by the ghosts of those who died in the tragedy. A psychic tries to help this haunted woman by keeping the ghosts from killing her. Although there are some chills, this version pales in comparison to its predecessor—with Robert Powell and Jenny Agutter. Rated R for sexual situations and violence. 85m. **DIR:** Thom Eberhardt. **CAST:** Anita Skinner, Kurt Johnson. **1985**

SOLITAIRE FOR 2 ★★★ When a playboy meets a woman who can read minds, it takes more than his come-on lines to win her over. Once he does, however, her mind-reading skills threaten to sabotage

the relationship. In much the same vein as *Four Weddings and a Funeral* but not quite as charming. Rated R for profanity and a brief sex scene. 105m. **DIR:** Gary Sinyor. **CAST:** Mark Frankel, Amanda Pays, Roshan Seth, Jason Isaacs, Maryam D'Abo. **1995**

SOLO (1977) ♥ An uninteresting love story with forgettable characters. Rated PG. 90m. **DIR:** Tony Williams. **CAST:** Vincent Gil, Perry Armstrong. **1977**

SOLO (1996) ★★ Hollywood's first African American android hero is a perfect fighting machine except for one thing—he's developing feelings. This angers military brass so much that they intend to mess with his microchips, so he flees into the South American jungle where he saves local peasants from armed rebels, battles an evil android, and learns to laugh. Rated PG-13 for violence and language. 93m. **DIR:** Norberto Barba. **CAST:** Mario Van Peebles, Bill Sadler, Adrien Brody, Barry Corbin, Seidy Lopez. **1996 DVD**

SOLOMON AND SHEBA (1959) ★★★ High times in biblical times as Sheba vamps Solomon. The emphasis is on lavish spectacle. Eyewash, not brain food. 139m. **DIR:** King Vidor. **CAST:** Yul Brynner, Gina Lollobrigida, George Sanders. **1959**

SOLOMON AND SHEBA (1995) ★★ Epic love story disappoints due to Jimmy Smits's and Halle Berry's failure to exude the larger-than-life personas of a legendary king and queen. Not rated; contains sex and violence. 90m. **DIR:** Robert M. Young. **CAST:** Halle Berry, Jimmy Smits, Nickolas Grace, Kenneth Colley, Ruben Santiago Hudson. **1995**

SOME CALL IT LOVING ♥ Jazz musician buys a "Sleeping Beauty" from a circus sideshow for his own perverse enjoyment. Rated R for nudity and language. 103m. **DIR:** James B. Harris. **CAST:** Zalman King, Carol White, Tisa Farrow, Richard Pryor, Logan Ramsey. **1974**

SOME CAME RUNNING ★★★1/2 Based on James Jones's novel of life in a midwestern town, this film offers an entertaining study of some rather complex characters. Shirley MacLaine gives a sparkling performance as the town's loose woman who's in love with Frank Sinatra. The story is not strong, but the performances are fine. 136m. **DIR:** Vincente Minnelli. **CAST:** Frank Sinatra, Dean Martin, Shirley MacLaine, Arthur Kennedy, Martha Hyer. **1958**

SOME GIRLS ★★★ European tale about a young man (Patrick Dempsey) invited to join a girl and her very strange family over the Christmas season. Concentrates more on character and dramatic depth than story development. Rated R for language, nudity, and simulated sex. 95m. **DIR:** Michael Hoffman. **CAST:** Patrick Dempsey, Jennifer Connelly, Lila Kedrova, Florinda Bolkan. **1988**

SOME KIND OF HERO ★★ This Richard Pryor movie can't decide whether to tell the story of a Vietnam prisoner of war returning to American society or be another comedy caper film. As a result, it's neither very funny nor worth thinking about. Rated R for profanity, nudity, and violence. 97m. **DIR:** Michael Pressman. **CAST:** Richard Pryor, Margot Kidder, Ronny Cox, Olivia Cole. **1982**

SOME KIND OF WONDERFUL ★★★★ Eric Stoltz stars as an affable lad who can't seem to make any headway with women. Unaware of the deep affection hurled in his direction by constant companion Mary Stuart Masterson (who all but steals the show), Stoltz sets his sights high on Lea Thompson. Perceptive, thoughtful viewing. Rated PG-13 for mature situations. 93m. DIR: Howard Deutch. CAST: Eric Stoltz, Mary Stuart Masterson, Lea Thompson, Craig Sheffer, John Ashton. 1987

SOME LIKE IT HOT ★★★★ Billy Wilder's *Some Like It Hot* is the outlandish story of two men (Jack Lemmon and Tony Curtis) who accidentally witness a gangland slaying. They pose as members of an all-girl band in order to avoid the gangsters, who are now trying to silence them permanently. Marilyn Monroe is at her sensual best as the band's singer. Joe E. Brown is also hilarious as a wealthy playboy who develops an attraction for an obviously bewildered Lemmon. B&W; 119m. DIR: Billy Wilder. CAST: Marilyn Monroe, Jack Lemmon, Tony Curtis, Joe E. Brown, George Raft, Pat O'Brien, Nehemiah Persoff, Mike Mazurki. 1959

SOME MOTHER'S SON ★★★ Story of the 1981 hunger strike in Ireland is told from the point of view of the strikers' mothers, giving it a fresh poignancy. Rated R for language and violence. 112m. DIR: Terry George. CAST: Helen Mirren, Fionnula Flanagan, Aiden Gillen. 1996

SOMEBODY HAS TO SHOOT THE PICTURE ★★★★ Two mesmerizing performances fuel this gripping made-for-cable indictment of the cruel and unusual treatment that often precedes capital punishment. Roy Scheider stars as a burned-out, Pulitzer Prize–winning photojournalist who accepts convict Arliss Howard's last wish: that his final moments be captured by a photographer. Not rated, but probably too intense for younger viewers. Rated R for language and intensity. 104m. DIR: Frank Pierson. CAST: Roy Scheider, Arliss Howard, Bonnie Bedelia, Robert Carradine. 1990 DVD

SOMEBODY IS WAITING ★★★1/2 A strong cast and well-executed plot distinguish this tale of a prodigal son whose life is shattered by the death of his mother and the reappearance of his alcoholic father. Rated R for language and violence. 90m. DIR: Martin Donovan. CAST: Gabriel Byrne, Nastassja Kinski, Johnny Whitworth, Shirley Knight, Rebecca Gayheart, Valeria Golino. 1996

SOMEBODY UP THERE LIKES ME ★★★★1/2 This is a first-rate biography. Boxer Rocky Graziano's career is traced from the back streets of New York to the heights of fame in the ring. It's one of the very best fight films ever made and features a sterling performance by Paul Newman. B&W; 113m. DIR: Robert Wise. CAST: Paul Newman, Pier Angeli, Everett Sloane, Sal Mineo, Eileen Heckart, Robert Loggia, Steve McQueen. 1956

SOMEBODY TO LOVE ★★1/2 The best aspect of this independent film is bad of fire Rosie Perez as a modern-day, dollar-a-dance girl trying to break into show biz. Harvey Keitel is her sleazy lover, a former child star competing with handsome illegal alien Michael DeLorenzo for her affections. Manic plot

tangents and weak direction undermine some of the grittier and more humorous aspects. Rated R for violence, profanity, and sexual situations. 103m. DIR: Alexandre Rockwell. CAST: Rosie Perez, Harvey Keitel, Michael DeLorenzo, Steve Buscemi, Anthony Quinn, Stanley Tucci, Quentin Tarantino. 1994

SOMEONE BEHIND THE DOOR ★★1/2 A brain surgeon takes an amnesiac into his home and, during the course of his treatment, conditions him to murder his wife. Intense suspense-drama with a decent cast. The story contains too many plot twists though. Not rated; contains violence. 93m. DIR: Nicolas Gessner. CAST: Charles Bronson, Anthony Perkins, Jill Ireland, Henri Garcin. 1971

SOMEONE ELSE'S AMERICA ★★1/2 Two European immigrants patch together tragicomic family lives while pursuing the American Dream from a corner Brooklyn bar and restaurant. The thin, meandering story has several funny and tender moments but lacks deep emotional resonance. In Spanish and English with English subtitles. Rated PG. 96m. DIR: Goran Paskaljevic. CAST: Tom Conti, Miki Manojlovic, Maria Casares, Andjela Stojkovic, Sergej Trifunovic, Lazar Kalmic, Zorka Manojlovic. 1995

SOMEONE I TOUCHED ★★ The subject is VD as architect James Olson and pregnant wife Cloris Leachman trade accusations over who's to blame. The actors are far better than their material in this dated disease-of-the-week TV movie. 78m. DIR: Lou Antonio. CAST: Cloris Leachman, James Olson, Glynnis O'Connor, Andrew Robinson. 1975

SOMEONE TO DIE FOR ★★ Corbin Bernsen is the saving grace of this melodramatic thriller. He plays Jack Davis, a detective who blames three fellow officers for his daughter's death. When the three cops end up dead, Davis becomes the main suspect. Now Davis must find the real killer and prove his innocence. Been there, done that. Rated R for violence and adult language. 98m. DIR: Clay Borris. CAST: Corbin Bernsen, Ally Walker, Robert Stewart. 1995

SOMEONE TO LOVE ★★ Danny (Henry Jaglom) decides to have a filmmaking–Valentine's Day party with single people explaining directly into the camera why they are alone. Orson Welles (in his last screen appearance) sits on the balcony, commenting. One small problem: This movie wallows in all there is to detest about the Los Angeles art scene. Rated R for language. 112m. DIR: Henry Jaglom. CAST: Henry Jaglom, Michael Emil, Andrea Marcovicci, Sally Kellerman, Orson Welles. 1986

SOMEONE TO WATCH OVER ME ★★★★ This first-rate thriller benefits from director Ridley Scott's visual dynamics and an intelligent script. Ultrarich lady Mimi Rogers witnesses a horrible murder and barely escapes with her life; Tom Berenger is the down-home cop from the Bronx assigned to protect her. Rated R for language, nudity, and violence. 106m. DIR: Ridley Scott. CAST: Tom Berenger, Mimi Rogers, Lorraine Bracco, Andreas Katsulas. 1987 DVD

●**SOMETHING ABOUT SEX** ★★★1/2 Three L.A. couples are forced into discussions about what they want from marriage after a bachelor friend starts an argument about the impossibility of fidelity. This frank, funny comedy is not one to watch with someone you love unless you're ready for a heavy discussion afterwards. Also released as *Denial*. Rated R for sex, nudity, and profanity. 93m. DIR: Adam Rifkin. CAST: Jonathan Silverman, Jason Alexander, Patrick Dempsey, Amy Yasbeck, Christine Taylor. 1996 DVD

SOMETHING FOR EVERYONE ★★★ This sleeper about a manipulative, amoral young man (Michael York) and the lengths he goes to in order to advance himself might not be to everyone's tastes. Angela Lansbury gives one of her best performances as the down-on-her-luck aristocrat who falls victim to York's charms. Mature themes and situations make this film more suitable for an older audience. 112m. DIR: Harold Prince. CAST: Michael York, Angela Lansbury, Anthony Corlan, Jane Carr. 1970

SOMETHING OF VALUE ★★★ White settlers in Kenya are preyed upon by bloodthirsty Mau Mau tribesmen sick of oppression in this often too-graphic drama, which opens with a specially filmed foreword from Winston Churchill. B&W; 113m. DIR: Richard Brooks. CAST: Rock Hudson, Dana Wynter, Sidney Poitier, Wendy Hiller, Frederick O'Neal, Juano Hernandez, William Marshall, Michael Pate. 1957

SOMETHING SHORT OF PARADISE ★★★ This romantic comedy is something short of perfect but still manages to entertain. Two New Yorkers (Susan Sarandon and David Steinberg) manage to find love and happiness together despite distractions from other conniving singles. Marilyn Sokol is great as one of the obstacles. Rated PG. 91m. DIR: David Helpern Jr. CAST: Susan Sarandon, David Steinberg, Marilyn Sokol, Jean-Pierre Aumont. 1979

SOMETHING SPECIAL ★★★ Offbeat but surprisingly pleasant comedy about a 15-year-old girl named Milly (Pamela Segall) who is convinced that life would be easier if she were a boy. With the help of a magical potion and a solar eclipse, she manages to grow a penis. She changes her name to Willy to please her father and to satisfy her own curiosity. Rated PG-13. 90m. DIR: Paul Schneider. CAST: Patty Duke, Pamela Segall, Eric Gurry, Mary Tanner, John Glover, Seth Green. 1987

SOMETHING TO SING ABOUT ★★ Even the great talents of James Cagney can't lift this low-budget musical above the level of mediocrity. In it, he plays a New York bandleader who tests his mettle in Hollywood. B&W; 93m. DIR: Victor Schertzinger. CAST: James Cagney, William Frawley, Evelyn Daw, Gene Lockhart. 1937 DVD

SOMETHING TO TALK ABOUT ★★1/2 Excellent characterizations elevate the familiar story of how Julia Roberts's life is thrown into turmoil when she discovers that husband Dennis Quaid has been cheating on her. Rated R for profanity and suggested sex. 106m. DIR: Lasse Hallstrom. CAST: Julia Roberts, Dennis Quaid, Robert Duvall, Gena Rowlands, Kyra Sedgwick, Brett Cullen, Haley Aull, Muse Watson, Anne Shropshire. 1995 DVD

SOMETHING WEIRD 🖤 Tedious and bloodless time waster about a burn victim who finds he has gained extrasensory powers. There's also a subplot about a witch who restores his looks. None of it makes sense. 83m. DIR: Herschell Gordon Lewis. CAST: Tony McCabe, Elizabeth Lee. 1967 DVD

SOMETHING WICKED THIS WAY COMES ★★★ Ray Bradbury's classic fantasy novel has been fashioned into a good, but not great, movie by the Walt Disney Studios. Jason Robards Jr. stars as the town librarian whose task it is to save his family and friends from the evil temptations of Mr. Dark (Jonathan Pryce) and his Pandemonium Carnival. It's an old-fashioned, even gentle tale of the supernatural; a gothic *Wizard of Oz* that seems likely to be best appreciated by preteens. Rated PG. 94m. DIR: Jack Clayton. CAST: Jason Robards Jr., Jonathan Pryce, Pam Grier, Shawn Carson. 1983 DVD

SOMETHING WILD ★★★★1/2 Jeff Daniels stars as a desk-bound investment type whose idea of yuppie rebellion is stiffing a local diner for the price of a lunch. This petty larceny is observed by a mysterious woman (Melanie Griffith) who, to Daniels's relief and surprise, takes him not to the local police but to a seedy motel, where they share an afternoon that justifies the film's R rating. This moves from hilarious beginnings to true edge-of-the-seat terror. Rated R. 113m. DIR: Jonathan Demme. CAST: Jeff Daniels, Melanie Griffith, Ray Liotta, Margaret Colin, Tracey Walter. 1986

SOMETIMES A GREAT NOTION ★★★ Paul Newman plays the elder son of an Oregon logging family that refuses to go on strike with the other lumberjacks in the area. The family pays dearly for its unwillingness to go along. One scene in particular, which features Newman aiding Richard Jaeckel, who has been pinned in the water by a fallen tree, is unforgettable. Rated PG. 114m. DIR: Paul Newman. CAST: Paul Newman, Henry Fonda, Lee Remick, Michael Sarrazin, Richard Jaeckel. 1971

SOMETIMES AUNT MARTHA DOES DREADFUL THINGS ★★ Weird obscurity about a killer hiding out from the police by holing up in a Miami beach house dressed as a woman. He has an indecisive young male lover whom he passes off as his nephew. There are a few touches of black comedy, but not enough. Rated R for nudity. 95m. DIR: Thomas Casey. CAST: Abe Zwick, Scott Lawrence, Robin Hughes. 1971

SOMETIMES THEY COME BACK ★★★1/2 Chilling made-for-TV thriller gets good mileage from Stephen King's book. Tim Matheson is superb as the high school teacher who returns to his hometown thirty years after his brother died in a freak accident. The bullies responsible, who also died in the accident, come back one by one to seek revenge against Matheson. 97m. DIR: Tom McLoughlin. CAST: Tim Matheson, Brooke Adams, Robert Rusler. 1991 DVD

SOMETIMES THEY COME BACK AGAIN ★★★1/2 Gripping sequel finds psychologist John Porter and his teenage daughter returning to his boyhood home when his mother dies. Porter is immediately haunted by the spirit of the vicious teen who was responsible for his sister's ritualistic death thirty years earlier. Father and daughter must stand up to the evil or be lost to it forever. Rated R for violence, profanity, and nudity. 98m. DIR: Adam Grossman. CAST: Michael Gross, Alexis Arquette, Hilary Swank, Jennifer Elise Cox. 1996 DVD

SOMEWHERE I'LL FIND YOU ★★★★ A war picture that zeroes in on the dangerous lives and loves of war correspondents in the heat of battle, this movie also has the distinction of Lana Turner's sexy allure and Clark Gable's obvious appreciation of it. They play war correspondents coping with their passions. Strong dramatic scenes set the tone for this WWII drama. B&W; 108m. DIR: Wesley Ruggles. CAST: Clark Gable, Lana Turner, Robert Sterling, Keenan Wynn, Reginald Owen, Charles Dingle, Lee Patrick, Patricia Dane. 1942

SOMEWHERE IN SONORA ★★★ John Wayne, wrongly accused of cheating during a rodeo race, redeems himself by joining an outlaw gang to foil their plans. This was the first of many films to team Wayne with character actor Paul Fix, who wrote the screenplay for *Tall in the Saddle*, and played the wise old lawman on TV's *The Rifleman*. B&W; 57m. DIR: Mack V. Wright. CAST: John Wayne, Henry B. Walthall, Shirley Palmer, J. P. Macgowan, Ann Fay, Frank Rice, Paul Fix, Ralph Lewis, Billy Franey. 1933

SOMEWHERE IN THE CITY ★★ The lives of the tenants in a building on New York's Lower East Side intertwine in a number of haphazard ways. The script has several witty moments and the acting is good throughout. But there is no dramatic momentum, and the film fizzles off into two halfhearted climaxes twenty minutes apart. Not rated; contains profanity and sexual scenes. 93m. DIR: Ramin Niami. CAST: Sandra Bernhard, Robert John Burke, Bai Ling, Ornella Muti, Peter Stormare, Bulle Ogier. 1997

SOMEWHERE IN THE NIGHT ★★★1/2 An early film from Oscar-winner Joe Mankiewicz that set the stage for sinister, confusing mystery melodramas in the pre-TV era. An amnesiac tries to uncover his identity and finds out he might possibly be a murderer. B&W; 110m. DIR: Joseph L. Mankiewicz. CAST: Lloyd Nolan, John Hodiak, Richard Conte, Nancy Guild, Sheldon Leonard, Josephine Hutchinson. 1946

SOMEWHERE IN TIME ★★★ This gentle, old-fashioned film directed by Jeannot Szwarc celebrates tender passions with great style and atmosphere. The story by Richard Matheson does have a bit of a twist to it—instead of the lovers having to overcome such mundane obstacles as dissenting parents, terminal illness, or other tragedies, they must overcome time itself. Rated PG. 103m. DIR: Jeannot Szwarc. CAST: Christopher Reeve, Jane Seymour, Christopher Plummer, Bill Erwin, Teresa Wright. 1980 DVD

SOMEWHERE, TOMORROW ★★★ *The Ghost and Mrs. Muir* for a teen audience, this film is about a girl, played by Sarah Jessica Parker, who learns how to deal with her father's death by falling in love with the ghost of a teenage boy. The result is good family entertainment. 91m. DIR: Robert Wiemer. CAST: Sarah Jessica Parker, Nancy Addison, Tom Shea, Rick Weber. 1986

SOMMERSBY ★★★★ French director Daniel Vigne's brilliant *The Return of Martin Guerre* is transferred to the post–Civil War South for this involving tale of redemption. Richard Gere is fine as the returning soldier who resumes his relationship with willing wife Jodie Foster and the running of her plantation while former acquaintances marvel at his new sense of honor and responsibility. *Sommersby* retains many of the outstanding qualities of the original. Rated PG-13 for nudity and violence. 120m. DIR: Jon Amiel. CAST: Richard Gere, Jodie Foster, Bill Pullman, James Earl Jones, William Windom. 1993 DVD

SON-IN-LAW ★★★ Credit irrepressible Pauly Shore with keeping this hayseed comedy afloat, despite tired sight gags milked to death years ago on television's *Green Acres*. He plays a spaced-out valley guy who transforms the repressed and conservative parents of girlfriend Carla Gugino. Although terminally silly, the film delivers a solid, family-oriented moral. Rated PG-13 for sexual innuendo. 96m. DIR: Steve Rash. CAST: Pauly Shore, Carla Gugino, Lane Smith. 1993 DVD

SON OF ALI BABA ★★1/2 Aged Ali Baba is kidnapped by an evil caliph. His son comes to the rescue and wins a beautiful princess to boot. Juvenile, but fun. Victor Jory again plays a great villain. 85m. DIR: Kurt Neumann. CAST: Tony Curtis, Piper Laurie, Susan Cabot, William Reynolds, Hugh O'Brian, Victor Jory, Gerald Mohr. 1952

SON OF BLOB (BEWARE! THE BLOB) ★★ Larry Hagman made this sequel to *The Blob* in his low period between *I Dream of Jeannie* and *Dallas*. It looks like he just got some friends together and decided to have some fun. The result is rather lame. Rated PG. 88m. DIR: Larry Hagman. CAST: Robert Walker Jr., Godfrey Cambridge, Carol Lynley, Larry Hagman, Cindy Williams, Shelley Berman, Gerrit Graham, Dick Van Patten. 1972

SON OF CAPTAIN BLOOD ❤ Poorly produced, amateurishly acted pirate programmer. 88m. DIR: Tulio Demichell. CAST: Sean Flynn, Alessandra Panaro, Jose Nieto, Ann Todd. 1962

SON OF DRACULA (1943) ★★★1/2 Moody horror film features Lon Chaney's only turn as the Count, this time stalking a southern mansion as Alucard (spell it backward). Compelling, highly original Universal chiller boasts several eye-catching effects, dazzling camera work by George Robinson. B&W; 80m. DIR: Robert Siodmak. CAST: Lon Chaney Jr., Louise Allbritton, Robert Paige, Evelyn Ankers, Frank Craven, J. Edward Bromberg. 1943

SON OF DRACULA (1974) ❤ Addle-brained vampire musical-comedy. 90m. DIR: Freddie Francis. CAST: Harry Nilsson, Ringo Starr, Freddie Jones. 1974

SON OF FLUBBER ★★★1/2 This Disney sequel to *The Absent-Minded Professor* once again stars Fred MacMurray as the inventor of Flubber. Two new discoveries are featured: "dry rain" and "flubbergas." While not as good as the original, it does have some moments reminiscent of the original. B&W; 100m. DIR: Robert Stevenson. CAST: Fred MacMurray, Nancy Olson, Keenan Wynn, Tommy Kirk, William Demarest, Paul Lynde. 1963

SON OF FRANKENSTEIN ★★★★1/2 A strong cast (including Boris Karloff in his last appearance as the monster) makes this second sequel to *Frankenstein* memorable. This time, Frankenstein's son Wolf revives the dormant monster with the help of insane shepherd Ygor (Bela Lugosi, in his most underrated performance). Impressive, intelligent production.

B&W; 99m. **DIR:** Rowland V. Lee. **CAST:** Boris Karloff, Basil Rathbone, Bela Lugosi, Lionel Atwill, Josephine Hutchinson. **1939**

SON OF FURY ★★★★ Based on Edison Marshall's novel *Benjamin Blake*, this follows the life of a young man who's been robbed of his title and fortune by his cruel uncle. He seeks his fortune on the high seas, finds romance with a beautiful island girl, and plans revenge against his dastardly uncle. Fast-paced, filled with intrigue and adventure. B&W; 99m. **DIR:** John Cromwell. **CAST:** Tyrone Power, Roddy McDowall, Gene Tierney, George Sanders, Frances Farmer, John Carradine. **1941**

SON OF GODZILLA ★★ Juvenile production has the cute offspring of one of Japan's biggest fire-breathing stars taking on all sorts of crazy-looking monsters, with a little help from dear old Dad. Good special effects and miniature sets make this at least watchable, but the story is just too goofy for its own good. Recommended viewing age: 2 and under. Rated PG. 86m. **DIR:** Jun Fukuda. **CAST:** Tadao Takashima, Kenji Sahara. **1969**

SON OF KONG, THE ★★1/2 To cash in on the phenomenal success of *King Kong*, the producers hastily rushed this sequel into production using virtually the same cast and crew. Carl Denham (Robert Armstrong) returns to Skull Island only to find King Kong's easygoing son trapped in a pool of quicksand. Denham saves the twelve-foot albino gorilla, who becomes his protector. B&W; 70m. **DIR:** Ernest B. Schoedsack. **CAST:** Robert Armstrong, Helen Mack, Victor Wong, John Marston, Frank Reicher. **1933**

SON OF LASSIE ★★1/2 Lassie's son, Laddie, follows in his parent's pawprints by smuggling himself aboard master Peter Lawford's bomber on a mission over enemy territory. Mixture of sentiment and war action doesn't really jell. 100m. **DIR:** S. Sylvan Simon. **CAST:** Peter Lawford, Donald Crisp, June Lockhart, Nigel Bruce, Leon Ames, Nils Asther, Donald Curtis. **1945**

SON OF MONTE CRISTO, THE ★★★ True to established swashbuckler form, masked avenging hero Louis Hayward crosses wits, then swords, with would-be dictator George Sanders. Honoring tradition, he then frees imprisoned fair lady Joan Bennett from the villain's clutches. B&W; 102m. **DIR:** Rowland V. Lee. **CAST:** Louis Hayward, Joan Bennett, George Sanders, Florence Bates, Montagu Love, Ian Wolfe, Clayton Moore, Ralph Byrd. **1941**

SON OF PALEFACE ★★★1/2 Bob Hope is in top shape as he matches wits with smooth villain Douglass Dumbrille and consistently loses, only to be aided by gun-totin' Jane Russell and government agent Roy Rogers. 95m. **DIR:** Frank Tashlin. **CAST:** Bob Hope, Jane Russell, Roy Rogers, Douglass Dumbrille, Bill Williams, Harry Von Zell, Iron Eyes Cody. **1952**

SON OF THE MORNING STAR ★★★1/2 Impressively mounted, acted, and directed TV miniseries was based on the bestseller by Evan S. Connell (*Mr. Bridge, Mrs. Bridge*) and chronicles the life and times of Gen. George Armstrong Custer (Gary Cole), culminating in the Battle of the Little Bighorn. Outstanding. 183m. **DIR:** Mike Robe. **CAST:** Gary Cole,

Rosanna Arquette, Dean Stockwell, Rodney A. Grant, David Strathairn, Terry O'Quinn. **1990**

SON OF THE PINK PANTHER ★★ Writer-director Blake Edwards should quit while he's behind. Despite the usually funny Roberto Benigni (as Inspector Clouseau's illegitimate son), this leaden comedy loses its appeal after Bobby McFerrin's quirky rendition of Henry Mancini's "Pink Panther Theme." Rated PG for comic violence. 93m. **DIR:** Blake Edwards. **CAST:** Roberto Benigni, Herbert Lom, Claudia Cardinale, Jennifer Edwards, Robert Davi, Burt Kwouk. **1993**

SON OF THE SHEIK ★★1/2 This sequel to the 1921 adventure, *The Sheik*, proved to be bedroom-eyed, ex-gardener Rudolph Valentino's final film. It was released to coincide with his funeral and was an immediate hit. In the title role, the legendary Valentino acquitted himself with confidence and flair, foiling his enemies and winning the heart of nomadic dancer Vilma Banky. Silent. B&W; 62m. **DIR:** George Fitzmaurice. **CAST:** Rudolph Valentino, Vilma Banky, Bull Montana, Montagu Love, George Fawcett, Karl Dane. **1926 DVD**

SONATINE ★★★★ The survivors of a *yakuza* war hide out, assuming the worst is over. It isn't. An intriguing, stylish, well-acted drama. In Japanese with English subtitles. Rated R for violence and profanity. 94m. **DIR:** Takeshi Kitano. **CAST:** Takeshi Kitano, Aya Kikumai, Tetsu Watanabe, Masanobu Katsumura. **1993**

SONG IS BORN, A ★★ A remake of the classic comedy *Ball of Fire*, with more music and less personality. Danny Kaye heads a team of professors studying the origin of jazz. The music is sharp but the story is flat. 115m. **DIR:** Howard Hawks. **CAST:** Danny Kaye, Virginia Mayo, Steve Cochran, Benny Goodman, Louis Armstrong, Tommy Dorsey, Lionel Hampton, Hugh Herbert, Felix Bressart. **1948**

SONG OF BERNADETTE, THE ★★★★ Four Oscars, including one to Jennifer Jones for best actress, went to this beautifully filmed story of the simple nineteenth-century French peasant girl, Bernadette Soubirous, who saw a vision of the Virgin Mary in the town of Lourdes. B&W; 156m. **DIR:** Henry King. **CAST:** Jennifer Jones, Charles Bickford, William Eythe, Vincent Price, Lee J. Cobb, Gladys Cooper, Anne Revere. **1943**

SONG OF FREEDOM ★★★ A black laborer shucks his newfound fame as a singer when he discovers the medallion he has worn since babyhood entitles him to the throne of an African island. The singer and his wife return to their roots as potentates of the primitive island and find jealousy and superstition working against them. The decision to live in both worlds and "upgrade" the primitive quality of his native island smacks of colonialism and works against the positive points of the movie. Still a very interesting effort and one of Paul Robeson's favorite roles. B&W; 77m. **DIR:** J. Elder Wills. **CAST:** Paul Robeson, Elisabeth Welch, Esme Percy, Robert Adams, James Solomon, Ronald Simpson. **1936 DVD**

SONG OF LOVE ★★1/2 When the writers and producers acknowledge up front that they have taken "certain liberties," you can throw away all thoughts of a factual story of the marriage of Clara Wieck

(Katharine Hepburn) to Robert Schumann (Paul Henreid) and their close friendship with young Johannes Brahms (Robert Walker). Close your eyes and listen to the piano interludes, dubbed, uncredited, by Arthur Rubinstein. B&W; 119m. **DIR:** Clarence Brown. **CAST:** Katharine Hepburn, Paul Henreid, Robert Walker, Henry Daniell, Henry Stephenson, Leo G. Carroll. **1947**

SONG OF NEVADA ★★1/2 Roy, Dale, and the boys at the ranch come to the aid of an innocent girl who has become prey of a crook and his henchmen. This tuneful, hard-riding horse opera is chock-full of former cowboys and familiar faces. It's typical of Roy's mid-1940s movies. B&W; 75m. **DIR:** Joseph Kane. **CAST:** Roy Rogers, Dale Evans, Mary Lee, Bob Nolan and the Sons of the Pioneers, Lloyd Corrigan, Thurston Hall, John Eldredge, Forrest Taylor, George Meeker, LeRoy Mason, Kenne Duncan. **1944**

SONG OF NORWAY 🍅 If he were not dead, Norwegian composer Edvard Grieg would expire upon seeing this insult to his life and career. Rated G. 142m. **DIR:** Andrew L. Stone. **CAST:** Florence Henderson, Torval Maurstad, Edward G. Robinson, Robert Morley. **1970**

SONG OF TEXAS ★★1/2 Most of the action comes at the end of this songfest as Roy competes in a chuck-wagon race in order to win back yet another stolen ranch. Roy and the boys squeeze ten songs into this programmer. B&W; 69m. **DIR:** Joseph Kane. **CAST:** Roy Rogers, Sheila Ryan, Barton MacLane, Harry Shannon, Pat Brady, Arline Judge, Eve March, Hal Taliaferro, Bob Nolan and the Sons of the Pioneers, Tom London. **1943**

SONG OF THE EXILE ★★★★ A recent graduate of a British university returns home to Hong Kong where she is reunited with her mother and a battle of wills begins. One of the most beautiful and astonishing motion pictures of the new Asian cinema, this is director Ann Hui's finest achievement to date. In Mandarin and Japanese with English subtitles. Not rated. 100m. **DIR:** Ann Hui. **CAST:** Shwu Sen Chang, Maggie Cheung. **1990**

SONG OF THE ISLANDS ★★ A Hawaiian cattle baron feuds with a planter over land while his son romances the planter's daughter. Everyone quarrels, but love wins. En route, Betty Grable sings and dances in the standard grass skirt. Mainly a slick travelogue with singing and dancing. 75m. **DIR:** Walter Lang. **CAST:** Betty Grable, Victor Mature, Jack Oakie, Thomas Mitchell. **1942**

SONG OF THE THIN MAN ★★★1/2 Sixth and final entry in the series, a cut above the previous one because of its involvement in jazz music circles. Nick and Nora Charles (William Powell and Myrna Loy) match wits with a murderer this time out, and the setting helps their dialogue regain its crisp sparkle. All in all, a worthy effort with which to conclude things. B&W; 86m. **DIR:** Edward Buzzell. **CAST:** William Powell, Myrna Loy, Keenan Wynn, Dean Stockwell, Gloria Grahame, Patricia Morison. **1947**

SONG REMAINS THE SAME, THE ★★★ If any band is truly responsible for the genre of "heavy-metal" music, it is Led Zeppelin. Although this movie is a must for Zeppelin fans, the untrained ear may

find numbers such as the twenty-three-minute version of "Dazed and Confused" a bit tedious. Rated PG. 136m. **DIR:** Peter Clifton, Joe Massot. **CAST:** Led Zeppelin, Peter Grant. **1976**

SONG SPINNER ★★★★ Enchanting fable about a small, mythical kingdom called Shandrilan, where the king has outlawed noise. To this mythical kingdom comes Zantalalia, a mysterious woman who gives ten-year-old Aurora a "song-spinner," which makes a beautiful noise known as music. Once exposed to the wonderful music, Aurora does her best to dodge noise police and get to the king so she can convince him to change his tune. This made-for-cable fable is great family entertainment. Rated G. 95m. **DIR:** Randy Bradshaw. **CAST:** Patti LuPone, John Neville, Meredith Henderson. **1995**

SONG TO REMEMBER, A ★★★ The music is superb, but the plot of this Chopin biography is as frail as the composer's health is purported to have been. Cornel Wilde received an Oscar nomination as the ill-fated tubercular Chopin, and Merle Oberon is resolute but vulnerable in the role of his lover, French female novelist George Sand. 113m. **DIR:** Charles Vidor. **CAST:** Cornel Wilde, Merle Oberon, Paul Muni, George Coulouris, Nina Foch, Sig Arno. **1945**

SONG WITHOUT END ★★★ An Academy Award–winning score manages to save this bio-pic of composer Franz Liszt. As Liszt, Dirk Bogarde is not in his element, but perseveres. 141m. **DIR:** Charles Vidor, George Cukor. **CAST:** Dirk Bogarde, Capucine, Genevieve Page, Patricia Morison, Martita Hunt. **1960**

SONGWRITER ★★★★ Wonderfully wacky and entertaining wish-fulfillment by top country stars Willie Nelson and Kris Kristofferson, who play—what else?—top country stars who take on the recording industry and win. A delight. Rated R for profanity, nudity, and brief violence. 100m. **DIR:** Alan Rudolph. **CAST:** Willie Nelson, Kris Kristofferson, Lesley Ann Warren, Melinda Dillon, Rip Torn. **1984**

SONNY AND JED 🍅 A naive young girl seeks adventure by following a noted outlaw hunted by a determined lawman. This Western approach to the Bonnie and Clyde story doesn't work. An irritating performance by Tomas Milian. Even an effective musical score by the master Ennio Morricone can't help this film. Rated PG. 85m. **DIR:** Sergio Corbucci. **CAST:** Tomas Milian, Susan George, Telly Savalas, Eduardo Fajardo, Rosanna Yanni. **1973**

SONNY BOY ★★1/2 If you've ever wanted to see David Carradine in drag, you're in luck. As Pearl, he's the mother of a monstrous family that terrorizes a small desert town. You decide whether this one is funny on purpose or just bad: either way, it's pretty bizarre. Rated R for violence and gore. 98m. **DIR:** Robert Martin Carroll. **CAST:** David Carradine, Paul Smith, Brad Dourif, Sidney Lassick. **1987**

SONS OF KATIE ELDER, THE ★★★ John Wayne stars in this entertaining film about four brothers reunited after the death of their mother and forced to fight to get back their land. Although this Western rarely goes beyond the predictable, there's plenty of action and roughhouse comedy. 122m. **DIR:** Henry Hathaway. **CAST:** John Wayne, Dean Martin, Earl Holliman, Michael Anderson Jr., James Gregory, George Kennedy, Martha Hyer, Jeremy Slate, Paul Fix. 1965

SONS OF THE DESERT ★★★★★ Stan Laurel and Oliver Hardy scheme to get away from their wives and attend a lodge convention in Chicago. After persuading the wives that Ollie needs to sail to Honolulu for his health, they go to Chicago. The boat sinks on the way back from Hawaii, and the boys end up having to explain how they got home a day earlier than the other survivors (they ship-hiked). B&W; 69m. DIR: William A. Seiter. CAST: Stan Laurel, Oliver Hardy, Charlie Chase. 1933

SONS OF THE PIONEERS ★★★1/2 Roy Rogers plays a scientist who returns to his hometown after numerous ranches have been sabotaged. Using his scientific savvy and an occasional yodel, he saves the day. B&W; 53m. DIR: Joseph Kane. CAST: Roy Rogers, George "Gabby" Hayes, Maris Wrixon, Forrest Taylor, Pat Brady. 1942

SONS OF THE SEA ★★1/2 Made and released in Great Britain as World War II began, this topical suspense-thriller drama involves the son of a naval commander with eyes-only clearance who unknowingly aids an enemy spy. Good show, but far better things were to come as the war progressed and England geared up its propaganda machine. B&W; 83m. DIR: Maurice Elvey. CAST: Leslie Banks, Kay Walsh, Mackenzie Ward, Cecil Parker. 1939

SONS OF TRINITY, THE ★★ The offspring of the infamous Italian duo find themselves in hot water when they become the sheriff and deputy of a small town. More of the same with a different cast. Rated PG for adult situations, language, and violence. 90m. DIR: E. B. Clucher. CAST: Heath Kizzier, Keith Neubert, Yvonne De Bark, Ronald Nitschke. 1995

SOONER OR LATER ★★ This made-for-TV romance may fascinate preteens. A 13-year-old girl (Denise Miller) sets her sights on a 17-year-old rock guitarist (Rex Smith). She pretends to be older and gets caught up in her lies. 100m. DIR: Bruce Hart. CAST: Denise Miller, Rex Smith, Morey Amsterdam, Judd Hirsch, Lynn Redgrave, Barbara Feldon. 1978

SOPHIA LOREN: HER OWN STORY ★★1/2 Sophia Loren portrays herself in this television drama that chronicles her life from obscurity to international stardom. At times, it appears more like a self-parody. Interesting, but not compelling enough to justify its extreme length. 150m. DIR: Mel Stuart. CAST: Sophia Loren, John Gavin, Rip Torn. 1980

SOPHIE'S CHOICE ★★★★★ A young, inexperienced southern writer named Stingo (Peter MacNicol) learns about love, life, and death in this absorbing, wonderfully acted, and heartbreaking movie. One summer, while observing the affair between Sophie (Meryl Streep), a victim of a concentration camp, and Nathan (Kevin Kline), a charming, but sometimes explosive biologist, Stingo falls in love with Sophie, a woman with deep, dark secrets. Rated R. 157m. DIR: Alan J. Pakula. CAST: Meryl Streep, Kevin Kline, Peter MacNicol. 1982 DVD

SOPHISTICATED GENTS, THE ★★★1/2 Arguably one of the best TV movies ever made, this ensemble drama was based by Melvin Van Peebles on John A. Williams's book, The Junior Bachelor Society. A powerful production. 200m. DIR: Harry Falk. CAST: Bernie Casey, Rosey Grier, Robert Hooks, Ron O'Neal, Thalmus Rasulala, Raymond St. Jacques, Melvin Van Peebles, Dick Anthony Williams, Paul Winfield, Denise Nicholas. 1981

SORCERER ★★★★ Remake of Henri Couzot's classic, Wages of Fear, is a cult favorite. An American criminal flees to Latin America to escape prosecution but finds life there a living hell. A superb score enhances this atmospheric thriller. Rated R for violence and profanity. 122m. DIR: William Friedkin. CAST: Roy Scheider, Bruno Cremer, Francisco Rabal, Souad Amidou, Ramon Bieri. 1977 DVD

SORCERESS (1982) ❤ Twin girls are bestowed with the power of sorcery. Rated R for nudity and simulated sex. 83m. DIR: Brian Stuart. CAST: Leigh and Lynette Harris. 1982

SORCERESS, THE (1988) ★★★1/2 Visually rich, enthralling tale set in a small village in medieval France about a priest on a search for those still practicing pagan rituals. Unfortunately, the English-dubbed version kills some of the film's impact. 98m. DIR: Suzanne Schiffman. CAST: Tcheky Karyo, Christine Boisson, Jean Carmet. 1988

SORCERESS (1994) ★★ Low-budget thriller is saved by novel plot twists. Julie Strain plays the wife of an up-and-coming executive who gets rid of her husband's competition. She makes a fatal mistake when she attempts to kill his main rival, not realizing the man's wife is a witch. It's nice to see a movie where people get exactly what they deserve. Edited and unedited versions available; both contain adult situations. 93m. DIR: Jim Wynorski. CAST: Julie Strain, Linda Blair, Edward Albert, Larry Poindexter. 1994 DVD

•SORE LOSERS ★★★ Tongue-in-cheek horror-comedy about an alien who resembles a 1950s greaser who comes to Earth to kill hippies. The stars are musicians from various psychobilly bands. Definitely not for all tastes, but better than average for this kind of no-budget cult movie. Not rated; contains gore, violence, nudity, and profanity. 90m. DIR: John Michael McCathy. CAST: Jack Oblivian, Kerine Elkins, Mike Maker, Dave Friedman. 1997

•SORORITY BABES IN THE SLIMEBALL BOWL-O-RAMA ❤ Two sorority pledges find themselves trapped in a bowling alley from hell when they are forced to steal a trophy as part of their pledge in this supposed horror-comedy. Rated R for violence, profanity, and nudity. 78m. DIR: David DeCoteau. CAST: Linnea Quigley, Robin Rochelle, Brinke Stevens. 1987 DVD

SORORITY GIRL ★★ Susan Cabot is the bad girl who makes life difficult for new sorority pledge Barboura Morris. The ads promised spankings and even a hint of lesbianism, but the movie itself is tame enough for 1950s TV. B&W; 60m. DIR: Roger Corman. CAST: Susan Cabot, Dick Miller, Barboura Morris, June Kenney. 1957

•SORORITY GIRLS AND THE CREATURE FROM HELL ❤ No relation to David DeCoteau's Sorority Babes series, this flick doesn't even have those films' sleazy charm. Not rated; contains violence and adult situations. 90m. DIR: John McBrearty. CAST: Deborah Dutch, Stacy Lynn. 1990

SORORITY HOUSE MASSACRE 💖 Features a vengeful killer slashing the sexy residents of a sorority house. Rated R for profanity, nudity, and violence. 74m. DIR: Carol Frank. CAST: Angela O'Neill, Wendy Martel. 1986

SORORITY HOUSE MASSACRE 2 💖 Lame hack-and-slash thriller about busty babes fighting off a bloodthirsty killer while in various states of undress. Typical shock horror, nearly plotless and badly acted. Not rated; contains nudity, profanity, and graphic violence. 80m. DIR: Jim Wynorski. CAST: Robin Harris, Melissa Moore. 1992

SORORITY HOUSE PARTY 💖 Lamebrained trash about a rock star who tries to escape inept hit men with the help of a pair of sorority girls. Not rated; contains nudity and sexual scenes. 95m. DIR: David Michael Latt. CAST: Attila, April Lerman, Kim Little, Mark Stulce. 1994

SORRENTO BEACH ★★★★ In this involving, well-acted drama, one of three sisters is now a successful writer whose latest bestseller exposes family secrets. Rated R for language. 112m. DIR: Richard Franklin. CAST: Caroline Goodall, Joan Plowright, Tara Morice, Caroline Gillmer. 1995

SORROW AND THE PITY, THE ★★★★★ Probably the most revealing work in any medium on the subject of collaboration in World War II. Marcel Ophuls carefully and intimately examines the residents of a French town that spent the war partly under Vichy rule and partly under the Nazis. Despite its great length, there is not a single wasted moment in this perfectly realized documentary. 270m. DIR: Marcel Ophuls. 1970

SORROWFUL JONES ★★★ Bob Hope's first semi-serious film, this is a remake of the 1934 Shirley Temple hit, *Little Miss Marker*. Bob, as a bookie, gets tangled up with nightclub singer Lucille Ball and an assortment of gangsters while baby-sitting a gambler's baby daughter. A good mix of wisecracks, fast action, and sentiment. B&W; 88m. DIR: Sidney Lanfield. CAST: Bob Hope, Lucille Ball, Mary Jane Saunders, Thomas Gomez, William Demarest, Bruce Cabot. 1949

SORROWS OF SATAN, THE ★★★ Lavish surreal drama about a struggling literary critic whose engagement to an impoverished writer becomes complicated by Satan in the form of a cunning wealthy gentleman. Visually impressive. B&W; 90m. DIR: D. W. Griffith. CAST: Adolphe Menjou, Carol Dempster, Ricardo Cortez, Lya de Putti. 1926

SORRY, WRONG NUMBER (1948) ★★★★ Slick cinema adaptation, by the author herself, of Lucille Fletcher's famed radio drama. Barbara Stanwyck is superb—and received an Oscar nomination—as an invalid who, due to those "crossed wires" so beloved in fiction, overhears two men plotting the murder of a woman. Gradually Stanwyck realizes that she is the target. B&W; 89m. DIR: Anatole Litvak. CAST: Barbara Stanwyck, Burt Lancaster, Wendell Corey, Ed Begley Sr., Ann Richards. 1948

SORRY, WRONG NUMBER (1989) ★★ A made-for-TV update of the suspenseful story of an invalid who learns that her husband plans to have her killed. But it doesn't hold a candle to the Barbara Stanwyck version. Loni Anderson looks better than she acts, and that's not all bad in this case. 100m. DIR: Tony Wharmby. CAST: Loni Anderson, Patrick Macnee, Carl Weintraub, Hal Holbrook. 1989

SOS COAST GUARD ★★1/2 All-American Coast Guard stalwart Terry Kent (Ralph Byrd) has his hands full as he battles crazed inventor Boroff (Bela Lugosi). There's so much going on in this serial that it's best just to forget about the story line and sit back and enjoy the action. B&W; 12 chapters. DIR: William Witney, Alan James. CAST: Ralph Byrd, Bela Lugosi. 1937

S.O.S. TITANIC ★★★ The "unsinkable" once again goes to her watery grave in this made-for-television docudrama compounded of fiction and fact. 105m. DIR: William Hale. CAST: David Janssen, Cloris Leachman, Susan Saint James, David Warner. 1979

SOTTO SOTTO ★★★ A sexy, raucous, hilarious farce about a woman who finds herself romantically drawn to her best friend's wife. This leads to comically disastrous results. Good entertainment, especially for hard-core fans of Lina Wertmuller. In Italian with English subtitles. 104m. DIR: Lina Wertmuller. CAST: Enrico Montesano, Veronica Lario. 1984

SOUL FOOD ★★★1/2 This little film deserves your attention. It's a genuinely heartwarming study of the importance of tradition even during moments of strife and adversity. Sunday dinner is a noisy, tempestuous gathering in the massive old home of "Big Mama" Mother Joe, but in the eyes of a young grandson, they're all family. When it becomes clear that Big Mama has been ignoring her diabetes, everything crumbles … and putting matters right falls to one very scared, but nonetheless determined, little boy. Rated R for profanity, sexual content, and brief violence. 114m. DIR: George Tillman Jr. CAST: Vanessa L. Williams, Vivica A. Fox, Nia Long, Michael Beach, Mekhi Phifer, Brandon Hammon, Irma P. Hall. 1997 DVD

SOUL HUSTLER 💖 A drug-using wanderer swindles gullible hicks. Execrable. Rated PG for strong language. 81m. DIR: Burt Topper. CAST: Fabian, Nai Bonet, Tony Russell. 1986

SOUL MAN ★★★ Los Angeles preppie Mark Watson (C. Thomas Howell) masquerades as a needy black to gain entrance to Harvard Law School. Director Steve Miner keeps things moving so fast one doesn't have time to consider how silly it all is. Rated PG-13 for profanity, suggested sex, and violence. 101m. DIR: Steve Miner. CAST: C. Thomas Howell, Rae Dawn Chong, James Earl Jones, Arye Gross, James B. Sikking, Leslie Nielsen. 1986

SOUL OF THE GAME ★★★★ Strong account of the events that changed America's favorite pastime after World War II. The story involves three superstars, each superbly portrayed: Satchel Paige, who single-handedly turned every personal appearance into a major event; the doomed Josh Gibson; and dignified, young Jackie Robinson, the man to break the color barrier. Great drama. Rated PG-13 for profanity and brief nudity. 95m. DIR: Kevin Rodney Sullivan. CAST: Delroy Lindo, Mykelti Williamson, Blair Underwood,

Edward Herrmann, R. Lee Ermey, Salli Richardson, Gina Ravera. 1996

SOUL VENGEANCE (WELCOME HOME BROTHER CHARLES) ★★★ Wildly over-the-top blaxploitation film about an ex-con seeking revenge on the men who sent him to prison. A must-see for sheer weirdness, including a strangulation scene we can't describe here. Rated R for nudity, sex, profanity, and strong violence. 91m. DIR: Jamaa Fanaka. CAST: Marlo Monte, Reatha Grey. 1975

SOULER OPPOSITE, THE ★★ A low-rent riff on *Seinfeld* that concerns a condescending would-be stand-up comic who can't score with women ... and, after a scant few moments in his company, you'll understand why. Dull, dull, dull. Rated R for profanity and sexual candor. 103m. DIR: Bill Kamelson. CAST: Christopher Meloni, Janel Moloney, Timothy Busfield. 1998

SOULTAKER ✹ Moronic tale of grim-reaper types who claim souls at the moment of death. Rated R for drugs, violence, and gore. 92m. DIR: Michael Rissi. 1990 DVD

SOUND AND THE SILENCE, THE ★★★★ Superior miniseries explores the multifaceted genius of Alexander Graham Bell. Known as the inventor of the telephone, his life story has him dabbling in medicine, aeronautics, and more. John Bach plays Bell as self-absorbed and obsessive but ultimately successful at his many ventures. Exterior shots are especially breathtaking. Not rated; contains no objectionable material. 184m. DIR: John Kent Harrison. CAST: John Bach, Ian Bannen, Elizabeth Quinn, Vanessa Vaughan, Brenda Fricker. 1992

SOUND OF MUSIC, THE ★★★★1/2 Winner of the Academy Award for best picture, this musical has it all: comedy, romance, suspense. Julie Andrews plays the spunky Maria, who doesn't fit in at the convent. When she is sent to live with a large family as their governess, she falls in love with and marries her handsome boss, Baron von Trapp (Christopher Plummer). Problems arise when the Nazi invasion of Austria forces the family to flee. 172m. DIR: Robert Wise. CAST: Julie Andrews, Christopher Plummer, Eleanor Parker. 1965

SOUNDER ★★★★★ Beautifully made film detailing the struggle of a black sharecropper and his family. Director Martin Ritt gets outstanding performances from Cicely Tyson and Paul Winfield. When her husband is sent to jail, Tyson must raise her family and run the farm by herself while trying to get the eldest son an education. A truly moving and thought-provoking film. Don't miss this one. Rated G. 105m. DIR: Martin Ritt. CAST: Cicely Tyson, Paul Winfield, Kevin Hooks, Carmen Mathews, Taj Mahal, James Best, Janet MacLachlan. 1972

SOUNDSTAGE: BLUES SUMMIT IN CHICAGO ★★★★ Homage is paid to blues great Muddy Waters in this music-packed documentary. Willie Dixon, Koko Taylor, Dr. John, Mike Bloomfield, Junior Wells, Johnny Winter, Nick Gravenites, and Buddy Miles are among the students who sit in with the master of Chicago blues, who beams with pleasure at the high quality of the music. Good interview footage, too. Made for TV. 58m. DIR: Dave Erdman. 1974

SOUP FOR ONE ★★★ Marcia Strassman (formerly the wife on *Welcome Back Kotter*) stars as the dream girl to an often disappointed lover. Although there are a few slow-moving parts, it is a generally enjoyable comedy. Rated R for sexual themes. 87m. DIR: Jonathan Kaufer. CAST: Saul Rubinek, Marcia Strassman, Teddy Pendergrass. 1982

•**SOURCE, THE** ★★★★ This fascinating documentary, from filmmaker Chuck Workman (famed for his Academy Award–clip retrospectives), traces the writers' revolution during the white-bread 1950s, and the impact this movement was to have on the social unrest of the 1960s. Workman's diary of the Beat Generation is seen mostly through the eyes, commentary, and work of the movement's Unholy Trinity: Jack Kerouac, Allen Ginsberg, and William Burroughs. Watching them should forever swear viewers off mind-altering substances; these guys clearly smoked, swallowed, sniffed, and shot every drug known to humanity. But what sounds like gibberish and drug-hazed ramblings during period footage—which admittedly captures these seminal figures in far less than their best light—becomes something entirely different when interpreted by guest artists such as John Turturro and Johnny Depp. Not rated; contains considerable profanity and unapologetic depictions of drug use. 90m. DIR: Chuck Workman. CAST: Johnny Depp, Dennis Hopper, John Turturro. 1999 DVD

SOURDOUGH ★★1/2 Marvelously picturesque but dull family fare about the daily activities of a grizzled mountain man—works best as a travelogue depicting the wonders of the Northwestern wilderness. Rated G. 92m. DIR: Martin J. Spinelli. CAST: Gil Perry, Charles Brock, Slim Carlson, Carl Clark. 1975

SOUTH BEACH ✹ Has-been, ex–football players Gary Busey and Fred Williamson are wanna-be Miami private eyes, who become embroiled with mystery-woman Vanity. This slice of Miami could have used more vice. Rated R for violence and adult situations. 93m. DIR: Fred Williamson. CAST: Fred Williamson, Peter Fonda, Gary Busey, Vanity, Robert Forster. 1992

SOUTH BEACH ACADEMY ★★ If he loses a bet with a competitor, the owner of South Beach Academy—a resort for half-naked party animals—will lose his business. A pair of brothers makes sure that doesn't happen. Simply an excuse to put as many naked women on film as possible. Rated R for profanity, nudity, and sexual situations. 91m. DIR: Joe Esposito. CAST: Corey Feldman, Al Lewis, James Hong, Keith Coulouris, Elizabeth Kaitan. 1995

SOUTH CENTRAL ★★★★ Tough, uncompromising urban drama about a father's attempts to keep his son out of gangs hits home and hits hard. Explosive action coupled with hard-as-nails drama make this an exceptional film. Rated R for violence, language, and adult situations. 99m. DIR: Stephen Anderson. CAST: Glenn Plummer, Carl Lumbly, Byron Keith Minns, LaRita Shelby, Kevin Best. 1992 DVD

SOUTH OF PAGO PAGO ★★ A good title is wasted on this so-so action tale of pirates heisting native-harvested pearls and being pursued and engaged by the locals. Typical South Sea fare. B&W; 98m. DIR: Alfred E. Green. CAST: Victor McLaglen, Jon Hall, Frances Farmer, Olympe Bradna, Gene Lockhart. 1940

SOUTH OF RENO ★★★ This surreal psychodrama offers a compelling look at one man's struggle with desperation in a broiling Nevada backroads community. When he learns that his wife is carrying on an extramarital affair, he goes over the edge. Rated R; contains nudity, profanity, and violence. 98m. DIR: Mark Rezyka. CAST: Jeff Osterhage, Lisa Blount, Lewis Van Bergen, Joe Phelan. 1987

SOUTH OF ST. LOUIS ★★★ Joel McCrea, Zachary Scott, and Douglas Kennedy seek revenge for the burning of their respective spreads. Dorothy Malone and Alexis Smith provide the love interest. If you like dusty, exciting ranch epics, this film should be high on your list. 88m. DIR: Ray Enright. CAST: Joel McCrea, Zachary Scott, Douglas Kennedy, Dorothy Malone, Alexis Smith. 1949

SOUTH OF THE BORDER ★★1/2 Gene and Smiley mosey on down to Mexico as government operatives in order to quell a rebellion engineered by foreign powers who wish to control that country's oil resources. This patriotic film contains some good action scenes. B&W; 71m. DIR: George Sherman. CAST: Gene Autry, Smiley Burnette, Duncan Renaldo, June Storey. 1939

SOUTH PACIFIC ★★★ This extremely long film, adapted from the famous Broadway play about sailors during World War II, seems dated and is slowgoing for the most part. Fans of Rodgers and Hammerstein will no doubt appreciate this one more than others. 150m. DIR: Joshua Logan. CAST: Mitzi Gaynor, Rossano Brazzi, Ray Walston, John Kerr. 1958 DVD

SOUTH PARK: BIGGER, LONGER & UNCUT ★★★★ Although it features cute animated characters, parents should be aware that *this is not a movie for youngsters.* In their first big-screen romp, Kyle, Stan, Cartman, and Kenny offer a scathing indictment of the hypocrisy of American morality groups. It has something to offend everybody—and is frequently hilarious. Rated R for profanity, photos of male sex organs, implied sex acts of all descriptions, scatological humor, and violence. 81m. DIR: Trey Parker. 1999 DVD

SOUTHERN COMFORT ★★★★ Director Walter Hill's 1981 "war" film focuses on the plight of a National Guard unit lost in Cajun country while on routine training maneuvers. Armed only with M-16 rifles loaded with blanks, the soldiers (who include Keith Carradine and Powers Boothe) find themselves ill-equipped to deal with the hostile locals—and an edge-of-your-seat entertainment is the result. Rated R for violence. 106m. DIR: Walter Hill. CAST: Keith Carradine, Powers Boothe, Fred Ward, Brion James. 1981

SOUTHERN YANKEE, A ★★★ Red Skelton captures an elusive Confederate spy, then assumes his identity, going behind rebel lines with fake Union war plans. Some very good sight gags, reportedly devised by Buster Keaton. B&W; 90m. DIR: Edward

Sedgwick. CAST: Red Skelton, Brian Donlevy, Arlene Dahl, John Ireland. 1948

SOUTHERNER, THE ★★★★ Stark life in the rural South before civil rights. Dirt-poor tenant farmer (Zachary Scott) struggles against insurmountable odds to provide for his family while maintaining his dignity. Visually a beautiful film, but uneven in dramatic continuity. Nonetheless, its high rating is deserved. B&W; 91m. DIR: Jean Renoir. CAST: Zachary Scott, Betty Field, J. Carrol Naish. 1945 DVD

●**SOUTHIE** ★★ Increasingly annoying film in which a son returns home to find his family up to its eyes in debt with the local bookie. Edgy performances barely pierce the noisy atmosphere created by director John Shea. Rated R for violence and profanity. 96m. DIR: John Shea. CAST: Donnie Wahlberg, Rose McGowan, Lawrence Tierney. 1998 DVD

SOUVENIR ★★ Former German soldier returns to France for the first time in forty years to visit his daughter and come to terms with the guilt he feels. Christopher Plummer is wasted in this talky, predictable drama. Rated R for brief nudity. 93m. DIR: Geoffrey Reeve. CAST: Christopher Plummer, Catherine Hicks, Michel Lonsdale. 1988

SOYLENT GREEN ★★★ In this watchable science-fiction flick, the year is 2022, and New York City is grossly overcrowded. Food is so scarce the government creates a product, Soylent Green, for people to eat. Heston plays the policeman who discovers what it's made of. There is some violence. Rated PG. 97m. DIR: Richard Fleischer. CAST: Charlton Heston, Edward G. Robinson, Joseph Cotten, Chuck Connors. 1973

SPACE JAM ★★1/2 While it has its heart in the right place, casting Michael Jordan as a hero willing to save the cartoon world from intergalactic baddies, this is a harebrained mess. Little kids will love it, but fans of Warner Bros. toon stars are advised to steer clear. Rated PG. 81m. DIR: Joe Pytka. CAST: Michael Jordan, Wayne Knight, Theresa Randle, Bill Murray. 1996 DVD

SPACE MARINES ★★★ Fans of old sci-fi serials should love this retro action epic, which sends futuristic cousins of "the few and the proud" up against an insane pirate determined to leave a rather explosive mark in galaxial history. Robert Moreland's script has the sense not to take itself too seriously, and Billy Wirth shines as the gleefully maniacal villain. Rated R for violence and profanity. 93m. DIR: John Weidner. CAST: Billy Wirth, John Pyper-Ferguson, Edward Albert, Cady Huffman, James Shigeta, Meg Foster, Blake Boyd. 1995

SPACE 1999 (TV SERIES) ★★ An atomic explosion occurs on the Moon, throwing it out of orbit and forcing the occupants of Moon Base Alpha to wander the stars aimlessly. Low production values on this TV series hold back the occasionally original stories. This show still has a small cult following, and the producers have managed to compile some of the better episodes. Not rated. 92m. DIR: Ray Austin, Lee H. Katzin. CAST: Martin Landau, Barbara Bain, Barry Morse. 1974

SPACE RAGE ♥ Richard Farnsworth as a retired twenty-first-century cop living on a prison planet. Rated R for violence galore. 78m. DIR: Conrad E.

Palmisano. **CAST:** Richard Farnsworth, Michael Paré, John Laughlin, Lee Purcell, William Windom. **1986**

SPACE RAIDERS ★★1/2 In this low-budget sci-fi flick from B-movie king Roger Corman, a 10-year-old boy (David Mendenhall) is kidnapped by a group of space pirates led by Vince Edwards, who becomes his mentor. It's an entertaining adventure film which not-too-young youngsters will enjoy. Rated PG for profanity and violence. 82m. **DIR:** Howard R. Cohen. **CAST:** Vince Edwards, David Mendenhall. **1983**

SPACE RANGERS (TV SERIES) ★★★ Fast-paced hokum about a motley crew of outer-space good guys, whose job it is to put a stop to the activities of inter-galactic smugglers, hustlers, killers, and thieves. Good special effects and action elevate unexceptionally scripted TV fare. Each tape features three episodes of the short-lived series. 100m. **DIR:** Ben Bolt. **CAST:** Jeff Kaake, Linda Hunt, Marjorie Monaghan, Cary-Hiroyuki Tagawa, Jack McGee, Clint Howard. **1993**

SPACE TRUCKERS ★★★1/2 Great, goofy fun awaits those looking for something offbeat as space truckers are called upon to save the world from an attack by evil robots. Everything is tongue-in-cheek in this made-for-cable feature. Rated PG-13 for language and violence. 97m. **DIR:** Stuart Gordon. **CAST:** Dennis Hopper, Stephen Dorff, Debi Mazar, Charles Dance. **1997 DVD**

SPACEBALLS ★★ The plot loosely concerns planet Spaceball's attempt to "steal" the atmosphere from neighbor Druidia by kidnapping and ransoming off the royally spoiled Princess Vespa. The wacky Dark Helmet (Rick Moranis) is responsible for this dastardly plot, and he is opposed by rogue trader Lone Starr (Bill Pullman). Rated PG for mild profanity. 96m. **DIR:** Mel Brooks. **CAST:** Mel Brooks, John Candy, Rick Moranis, Bill Pullman, Daphne Zuniga, Dick Van Patten, George Wyner, Michael Winslow, Lorene Yarnell. **1987 DVD**

SPACECAMP ★★★ Kate Capshaw is a reluctant instructor at the U.S. Space Camp in Alabama. She and her independent charges—four teens and a younger child—board a real space shuttle and are accidentally launched on a perilous journey. With an attractive cast, impressive special effects, and a noble heart, the movie should inspire the astronauts of the future. Rated PG for suspense. 104m. **DIR:** Harry Winer. **CAST:** Kate Capshaw, Lea Thompson, Tom Skerritt, Kelly Preston, Tate Donovan, Leaf Phoenix. **1986**

SPACED INVADERS ★★ There are some funny moments in this spoof about inept mini-Martians who mistake a fiftieth anniversary broadcast of Orson Welles's *War of the Worlds* radio show for the real thing. Too many hick jokes drag this one down. Rated PG for vulgarity and violence. 100m. **DIR:** Patrick Read Johnson. **CAST:** Douglas Barr, Royal Dano. **1990**

SPACED OUT ★★★ In this spoof of science-fiction films, the Earth is visited by an all-female crew on a broken-down spaceship. Three men and a woman are taken hostage and the discovery of the differences between men and women make for a watchable but raunchy comedy. This film is rated R for nu-

dity and implied sex. 85m. **DIR:** Norman J. Warren. **CAST:** Barry Stokes, Tony Maiden, Glory Annen. **1985**

SPACEHUNTER: ADVENTURES IN THE FORBIDDEN ZONE ♥ A futuristic hero takes on an army of militant humanoids on a plague-infested planet. Rated PG for violence. 90m. **DIR:** Lamont Johnson. **CAST:** Peter Strauss, Molly Ringwald, Ernie Hudson, Andrea Marcovicci, Michael Ironside, Beeson Carroll. **1983**

SPACESHIP (NAKED SPACE) ♥ This "comedy" is all about an unwanted alien tagging along on a rocket full of idiots. Original title: *The Creature Wasn't Nice.* Rated PG. 88m. **DIR:** Bruce Kimmel. **CAST:** Cindy Williams, Bruce Kimmel, Leslie Nielsen, Gerrit Graham. **1981**

SPAGHETTI HOUSE ★★ Five Italian restaurant employees are held hostage in a food storage room by three crooks. Most of the film is lighthearted, though—and, unfortunately, light-headed. In Italian with English subtitles. Not rated, contains violence and profanity. 103m. **DIR:** Giulio Paradisi. **CAST:** Nino Manfredi, Rita Tushingham. **1985**

SPAGHETTI WESTERN ★★★ Typical of the genre: some big-name American actors trek to Italy for large bucks to film the kind of grade-B Western that made Clint Eastwood a household word. It's hard to tell, at times, if this is a literal send-up of the genre, but it succeeds on several levels anyway. Not rated, with violence. 90m. **DIR:** Not credited. **CAST:** Franco Nero, Martin Balsam, Sterling Hayden. **1969**

SPALDING GRAY: TERRORS OF PLEASURE ★★★★ Spalding Gray, the master storyteller, relates the humorous adventure of finding the perfect retreat and piece of land to call his own. This HBO special was filmed in concert, but some terrific editing takes you to the scenes he describes. The star of *Swimming to Cambodia* also describes his brief encounter with Hollywood. 60m. **DIR:** Thomas Schlamme. **CAST:** Spalding Gray. **1988**

SPANISH PRISONER, THE ★★★ This effort from writer-director David Mamet is simultaneously fascinating and infuriating. Its twisty script involves a convoluted con game guaranteed to please fans, but the fun is undercut by performances that are stiff and mannered to the point of absurdity. The plot concerns a genius inventor with a super-secret "process" who falls in with the wrong crowd. Rated PG for implied violence. 112m. **DIR:** David Mamet. **CAST:** Campbell Scott, Rebecca Pidgeon, Steve Martin, Ben Gazzara, Ricky Jay. **1998 DVD**

SPANKING THE MONKEY ★★★1/2 A first-year college student resents having to spend his summer nursing his mother; his anger and her frustration lead to some unexpected developments. Writer-director David O. Russell's first film is a promising debut. Not rated; contains profanity and sexual situations, including incest. 100m. **DIR:** David O. Russell. **CAST:** Jeremy Davies, Alberta Watson, Carla Gallo, Benjamin Hendrickson. **1994**

SPARKLE ★★★1/2 Largely forgotten but appealing study of a Supremes-like girl group's rise to fame in the 1960s Motown era. Lots of good musical numbers from Curtis Mayfield and the luscious Lonette McKee. Rated PG for profanity and nudity. 100m. **DIR:**

Sam O'Steen. CAST: Irene Cara, Dorian Harewood, Lonette McKee, Curtis Mayfield. 1976

SPARROWS ★★★ The legendary Mary Pickford—"Our Mary" to millions during her reign as Queen of Hollywood when this film was made—plays the resolute, intrepid champion of a group of younger orphans besieged by an evil captor. Silent melodrama at its best, folks. B&W; 84m. DIR: William Beaudine. CAST: Mary Pickford, Gustav von Seyffertitz. 1926 DVD

SPARTACUS ★★★1/2 One of the more rewarding big-budget epics that marked the late 1950s and 1960s. Even though this fictional story of an actual slave revolt against the Roman Empire is large-scale in every detail, it never lets the human drama get lost in favor of spectacle. 196m. DIR: Stanley Kubrick. CAST: Kirk Douglas, Jean Simmons, Laurence Olivier, Peter Ustinov, Charles Laughton, Tony Curtis. 1960 DVD

SPASMS ★★★ If it were not for the poor acting, this would be a top-notch horror film. Oliver Reed plays a millionaire trophy hunter who, on a hunting trip in a tropical jungle, becomes cursed by a giant monster-like snake. Peter Fonda plays the special psychologist who is hired to examine him. When the serpent is brought back to the hunter, the tension rises as the body count goes up. Not rated; contains profanity, nudity, and gore. 92m. DIR: William Fruet. CAST: Peter Fonda, Oliver Reed, Kerrie Keane, Al Waxman, Marilyn Lightstone. 1982

SPAWN ★★ This live-action adaptation of Todd McFarlane's hugely popular comic-book antihero is a mess, a veritable triumph of style over substance. Covert agent is killed, winds up in Hell, and comes back with so many snazzy powers that he's basically unbeatable. The film's minimal charm comes from John Leguizamo's comedic role as a "guardian evil clown." Rated PG-13 for violence. 90m. DIR: Mark A. Z. Dippe. CAST: John Leguizamo, Michael Jai White, Martin Sheen, Theresa Randle, Melinda Clarke. 1997 DVD

SPEAK EASILY ★★1/2 Naïve college professor Buster Keaton is falsely informed that he has inherited a large sum of money and sets out to see the world. Along the way he befriends an itinerant theater troupe, headed by Jimmy Durante. Tired and thin story. B&W; 82m. DIR: Edward Sedgwick. CAST: Buster Keaton, Jimmy Durante, Thelma Todd, Sidney Toler, Hedda Hopper, Edward Brophy, Henry Armetta. 1932

•SPEAK OF THE DEVIL ★★ Weak horror-comedy in which a phony evangelist and his nymphomaniac wife buy a haunted house and turn it into a church. Not rated; contains violence, profanity, gore, and nudity. 99m. DIR: Raphael Nussbaum. CAST: Robert Elarton, Jean Miller. 1991

SPEAKING PARTS ★★★ Stylistically offbeat drama about an actor who supports himself by working as a housekeeper in a posh hotel. Canadian filmmaker Atom Egoyan combines the media of film and video technology to create a stunning visual display. Not rated; contains nudity and profanity. 92m. DIR: Atom Egoyan. CAST: Michael McManus, Arsinée Khanjian, Gabrielle Rose. 1989

SPECIAL BULLETIN ★★★ A group of antinuclear scientists on a tugboat in Charleston, South Carolina, take a TV crew hostage then demand network airtime. They have a nuclear bomb and threaten to detonate it. Realistically effective made-for-television movie. 103m. DIR: Edward Zwick. CAST: Ed Flanders, Kathryn Walker, Roxanne Hart, Christopher Allport, David Clennon, David Rasche, Rosalind Cash. 1983

SPECIAL DAY, A ★★★★ Antonietta (Sophia Loren), a slovenly housewife, and Gabriele (Marcello Mastroianni), a depressed homosexual, meet in the spring of 1938—the same day Hitler arrives in Rome. Their experience together enriches but does not change the course of their lives. In Italian with English subtitles. No MPAA rating. 106m. DIR: Ettore Scola. CAST: Sophia Loren, Marcello Mastroianni. 1977

SPECIAL EFFECTS ♥ Low-budget horror about a film director who murders a would-be actress. Not rated, but the film contains nudity and violence. 90m. DIR: Larry Cohen. CAST: Zoe Tamerlis, Eric Bogosian, Brad Rjin, Kevin O'Connor. 1984

SPECIALIST, THE ★★ Only the action sequences and the larger-than-life supporting performance by James Woods save The Specialist from being an utter disaster. Sylvester Stallone and Sharon Stone are a woeful mismatch in this story of an explosives specialist hired by a woman seeking revenge against the Cuban-American gangsters who killed her parents. Rated R for violence, profanity, nudity, and simulated sex. 109m. DIR: Luis Llosa. CAST: Sylvester Stallone, Sharon Stone, James Woods, Rod Steiger, Eric Roberts. 1994 DVD

SPECIES ★★★ Scientific researchers blend alien DNA with a human being, and wind up with a gorgeous woman who slaughters everyone interfering with her attempts to reproduce. Logical plotting and strong characterizations are sacrificed in favor of shockcuts and gory murders. Rated R for violence, nudity, simulated sex, and profanity. 108m. DIR: Roger Donaldson. CAST: Ben Kingsley, Michael Madsen, Alfred Molina, Forest Whitaker, Marg Helgenberger, Natasha Henstridge. 1995 DVD

SPECIES II ♥ First man on Mars returns to Earth as a tentacle-sprouting sex machine that brutally copulates with human women before he crosses paths with a captive human-alien, half-alien clone named Eve. Rated R for violence, gore, sex, nudity, and language. 93m. DIR: Peter Medak. CAST: Natasha Henstridge, Justin Lazard, Michael Madsen, Marg Helgenberger, James Cromwell, Mykelti Williamson. 1998 DVD

SPECIMEN ★★1/2 A young man with strange powers learns he is only half human, part of a breeding experiment by an alien race that sends a bounty hunter to bring him back. Fairly well made as far as low-budget sci-fi goes, but the script is too lackluster to matter. Rated R for violence, nudity, sexual situations, and profanity. 85m. DIR: John Bradshaw. CAST: Mark Paul Gosselaar, Doug O'Keefe, Ingrid Kalevaars. 1997 DVD

SPECKLED BAND, THE ★★★ In his motion-picture debut, Raymond Massey makes a sturdy Sherlock

Holmes, who must bring to justice the evil villain, Dr. Grimesby Roylott (Lyn Harding). Harding, who later played Professor Moriarty in the Arthur Wontner series of Holmes mysteries, is a superb villain, and the sets are decidedly gothic. Time has not been kind to the overall production, but *The Speckled Band* has much to offer fans of the canon. B&W; 48m. DIR: Jack Raymond. CAST: Raymond Massey, Lyn Harding. 1931

SPECTER OF THE ROSE, THE ★★★★ Surreal thriller written and directed by Ben Hecht about a young ballerina who discovers that her new husband is going insane. Unique, stylish filmmaking that is reminiscent of the work of Jean Cocteau. B&W; 90m. DIR: Ben Hecht. CAST: Judith Anderson, Michael Chekhov, Lionel Stander. 1946

SPECTERS 🐕 Archaeologists uncover an ancient tomb in Rome. Not rated; contains violence and brief nudity. 95m. DIR: Marcello Avallone. CAST: Donald Pleasence, John Pepper, Erna Schurer. 1987

SPECTRE ★★ Creaky tale about a haunted manor in Ireland that won't give up the ghost. Greg Evigan plays the lucky soul who inherits the manor and immediately drags his family off to live there. Unfortunately, the spirit of a young girl who died in the house decides that she doesn't want or need the company. Typical dark-house thrills won't impress any but the clueless few. Rated R for language and violence. 87m. DIR: Scott Levy. CAST: Greg Evigan, Alexandra Paul, Briana Evigan. 1997

SPEECHLESS ★★1/2 Insomnia drives political speech writers Geena Davis and Michael Keaton to "meet cute" while arguing over the last bottle of Nytol. They begin an affair, initially unaware that they're working for rival candidates in a New Mexico senate race; they fight, they make up, they fight, they make up ... far too many times. Robert King's dialogue isn't nearly as clever as he'd like to believe, and he shamefully wastes a strong supporting cast. Rated PG-13 for profanity and suggested sex. 99m. DIR: Ron Underwood. CAST: Michael Keaton, Geena Davis, Christopher Reeve, Bonnie Bedelia, Ernie Hudson, Charles Martin Smith. 1994

SPEED ★★★★★ Action-thriller more than lives up to its name, as LAPD SWAT cops Keanu Reeves and Jeff Daniels match wits with mad bomber Dennis Hopper. Sandra Bullock gives a standout performance as a take-charge bystander who ends up piloting a runaway bus (rigged to explode if it slows to less than 50 mph), but it is Reeves, in a highly effective switch to action hero, who dominates the film. Rated R for violence and profanity. 115m. DIR: Jan De Bont. CAST: Keanu Reeves, Dennis Hopper, Sandra Bullock, Joe Morton, Jeff Daniels, Alan Ruck. 1994 DVD

SPEED 2: CRUISE CONTROL ★★ A disgruntled ex-employee of a cruise-ship line takes control of its most luxurious vessel, jeopardizing the heroine of the first film and her new SWAT-unit boyfriend. A big, loud, disappointing sequel that wastes the talent of everyone involved. Rated PG-13 for language and violence. 121m. DIR: Jan De Bont. CAST: Sandra Bullock, Jason Patric, Willem Dafoe. 1997 DVD

SPEED ZONE 🐕 Another yawner about the *Cannonball Run* cross-country road race. Rated PG. 87m.

DIR: Jim Drake. CAST: John Candy, Donna Dixon, Joe Flaherty, Eugene Levy, Tom Smothers, Tim Matheson, Jamie Farr, Peter Boyle, Brooke Shields. 1989

SPEEDWAY ★★ Elvis Presley plays a generous stock-car driver who confronts a seemingly heartless IRS agent (Nancy Sinatra). Not surprisingly, she melts in this unremarkable musical. Rated G. 94m. DIR: Norman Taurog. CAST: Elvis Presley, Nancy Sinatra, Bill Bixby, Gale Gordon. 1968

SPELLBINDER 🐕 The obsession of a lawyer for a young woman who is a Satanist. Rated R for profanity, nudity, and violence. 99m. DIR: Janet Greek. CAST: Timothy Daly, Kelly Preston, Rick Rossovich, Audra Lindley. 1988

SPELLBOUND ★★★★ Hitchcock said in his usual, understated manner that *Spellbound* "is just another manhunt story wrapped up in pseudo-psychoanalysis." The story is more than just another manhunt story; of that we can assure you. We can divulge that Ingrid Bergman plays the psychiatrist, Gregory Peck is the patient, and Salvador Dalí provides the nightmare sequences. B&W; 111m. DIR: Alfred Hitchcock. CAST: Ingrid Bergman, Gregory Peck, Leo G. Carroll, John Emery, Wallace Ford, Rhonda Fleming, Bill Goodwin. 1945 DVD

SPELLBREAKER: SECRET OF THE LEPRECHAUNS ★★ An American boy visiting his grandfather in Ireland helps local leprechauns battle the evil Queen of the Dead. A sequel to *Leapin' Leprechauns*, this low-budget fantasy (it was filmed in Romania, not Ireland) may appeal to families with a liking for Irish culture. Rated G. 84m. DIR: Ted Nicolaou. CAST: Gregory Edward Smith, John Bluthal, Godfrey James, Madeleine Potter, Sylvester McCoy. 1996

SPELLCASTER 🐕 Music television contest winners are brought to a castle to vie for a $1-million check. Tame little romp. Rated R for profanity. 83m. DIR: Rafal Zielinski. CAST: Richard Blade, Gail O'Grady, Adam Ant. 1991

SPENCER'S MOUNTAIN ★★1/2 Henry Fonda is fine as the head of a poor Wyoming family determined that his oldest son must go to college, but the movie is strangely unmoving. From the novel by Earl Hammer Jr., this is the basis for TV's *The Waltons*, and comparisons are inevitable. 118m. DIR: Delmer Daves. CAST: Henry Fonda, Maureen O'Hara, James MacArthur, Donald Crisp, Wally Cox, Virginia Gregg, Whit Bissell. 1963

SPENSER: CEREMONY ★★★★ Robert B. Parker's celebrated detective hero, Spenser, was not particularly well served by the network series bearing his name, except for the casting of Robert Urich in the lead role and Avery Brooks as the formidable Hawk. Characters get much better treatment in this made-for-TV movie in which our heroes find the runaway daughter of a powerful politician in an underworld of violence, prostitution, drugs, and blackmail—just the place where our heroes can get the job done best. 96m. DIR: Andrew Wild. CAST: Robert Urich, Avery Brooks, Barbara Williams, J. Winston Carroll, Dave Nichols. 1993

SPENSER: PALE KINGS & PRINCES ★★★1/2 When a reporter friend of Dr. Susan Silverman (Barbara Williams) is killed while investigating a story on cocaine dealers in a picturesque New England hamlet, she asks her personal private eye, Spenser (Robert Urich), to mount his white horse and slay some drug-dealing dragons. Working from a script by Robert B. Parker (the celebrated-detective-series's author) and Joan H. Parker, Urich and company take a giant step up from the original network TV series. Made for TV. 96m. **DIR:** Vic Sarin. **CAST:** Robert Urich, Avery Brooks, Barbara Williams, Sonja Smits, J. Winston Carroll. 1993

SPETTERS ★★★1/2 A study of the dreams, loves, discoveries, and tragedies of six young people in modern-day Holland, this is yet another tough, uncompromising motion picture from Paul Verhoeven. Though the sex scenes are more graphic than anything we've ever had in a major American movie, the film is never exploitative. MPAA-unrated, it contains violence, profanity, nudity. 115m. **DIR:** Paul Verhoeven. **CAST:** Hans Van Tongeren, Toon Agterberg, Renee Soutendijk. 1980

SPHERE ★★ Despite the star power of Dustin Hoffman, Sharon Stone, and Samuel L. Jackson, the direction of Barry Levinson, and a screenplay adapted from Michael Crichton's bestseller, this movie is confusing, talky and ultimately disappointing. This chronicles an expedition to the bottom of the ocean to explore the discovery of what may be an extraterrestrial vehicle. Rated PG-13. 144m. **DIR:** Barry Levinson. **CAST:** Dustin Hoffman, Sharon Stone, Samuel L. Jackson. 1998 DVD

SPHINX, THE (1933) ★★1/2 Horror-film great Lionel Atwill plays a dual role in this effective low-budget murder mystery with overtones of the supernatural. The Sphinx of the title refers to Atwill's twin brother, who is a deaf-mute. B&W; 63m. **DIR:** Phil Rosen. **CAST:** Lionel Atwill, Sheila Terry, Paul Fix. 1933

SPHINX (1981) ★★ This is a watchable film ... but not a good one. Taken from the tedious novel by Robin Cook (Coma), it concerns the plight of an Egyptologist (Lesley-Anne Down) who inadvertently runs afoul of the underworld. Rated PG. 117m. **DIR:** Franklin J. Schaffner. **CAST:** Lesley-Anne Down, Frank Langella, Maurice Ronet, John Gielgud. 1981

SPICE WORLD ★★★ This overlong rock video is unrelentingly silly and pretty much bereft of plot, but in spite of all this, it's pure dumb fun: just like its five stars. This is classic British whimsy. Rated PG for brief nudity. 93m. **DIR:** Bob Spiers. **CAST:** Spice Girls, Richard E. Grant, Claire Rushbrook, Alan Cumming, Roger Moore, George Wendt, Meat Loaf. 1997 DVD

SPICES ★★★1/2 This spirited, feminist fable from India stars Smita Patil (two-time winner of India's National Best Actress Award) in the role of an impoverished woman who struggles against oppression. Excellent direction and fine performances by some of India's top-name stars. In Hindi with English subtitles. Not rated. 98m. **DIR:** Ketan Mehta. **CAST:** Smita Patil. 1986

SPIDER AND THE FLY, THE ★★★1/2 Two writers are suspected of a murder because of a prank they played in this well-scripted made-for-cable mystery. Good acting, and you won't know who did it until the end. Rated PG-13 for violence. 87m. **DIR:** Michael

Katleman. **CAST:** Mel Harris, Ted Shackelford, Kim Coates, Colm Feore, Frankie Faison, Cynthia Belliveau, Peggy Lipton. 1994

SPIDER BABY ★★1/2 Lon Chaney Jr. plays a chauffeur caring for a family of homicidal mental defectives. An odd little film, just quirky enough to interest fans of the weird. B&W; 81m. **DIR:** Jack Hill. **CAST:** Len Chaney Jr., Carol Ohmart, Quinn Redeker. 1964 DVD

SPIDERS, THE ★★★ Long considered a lost film, The Spiders (written and directed by Fritz Lang) is an adventure story about a gang of organized criminals. Although planned as a serial, only the first two parts were completed. Fritz Lang used exotic locations, combining a labyrinth of plots. The film had its first American showing in 1978. Tinted B&W; 137m. **DIR:** Fritz Lang. **CAST:** Carl de Vogy, Ressel Orla, Lil Dagover. 1919 DVD

SPIDER'S STRATAGEM, THE ★★★★ Compelling mystery about a young man who returns to a small Italian town where his father was murdered thirty years earlier. One of director Bernardo Bertolucci's most stunning cinematic works. In Italian with English subtitles. Not rated. 97m. **DIR:** Bernardo Bertolucci. **CAST:** Giulio Brogi, Alida Valli, Tino Scotti. 1970

SPIES ★★★★ Thrilling, imaginative drama of the underworld and the dark doings of espionage agents is one of the finest of all such films and remains a classic of the genre as well as a terrific adventure movie. The camera moves in and out among the shadowy doings of the spies and their pursuers like a silent spider weaving all the components together. The final chase provides a fitting climax to this topflight entertainment from Fritz Lang. Silent. B&W; 90m. **DIR:** Fritz Lang. **CAST:** Rudolf Klein-Rogge, Gerda Maurus, Willy Fritsch, Fritz Rasp. 1928

SPIES, LIES, AND NAKED THIGHS ★★★1/2 If you laughed at The In-Laws, you should enjoy this similar made-for-TV movie. Harry Anderson plays an eccentric government agent who enlists skeptical interpreter Ed Begley Jr. in his quest to save the world from a maniac armed with ... well, we won't spoil it. 100m. **DIR:** James Frawley. **CAST:** Harry Anderson, Ed Begley Jr., Linda Purl, Wendy Crewson. 1988

SPIES LIKE US ★★1/2 Chevy Chase and Dan Aykroyd, who were co-stars on the original Saturday Night Live television show, appeared together on the big screen for the first time in this generally enjoyable comedy about two inept recruits in a U.S. intelligence organization's counterespionage mission. Rated PG for violence and profanity. 104m. **DIR:** John Landis. **CAST:** Chevy Chase, Dan Aykroyd, Bruce Davison, William Prince, Steve Forrest, Bernie Casey, Donna Dixon. 1985 DVD

SPIKE & MIKE'S FESTIVAL OF ANIMATION ★★★★ Well-balanced compilation of animated short subjects that include two Academy Award–winning efforts: "Tango" and "Charade." Impressive representation of the medium includes everything from the hilarious "Snookles" and "Bambi Meets Godzilla" to the abstract "Primiti Too

Taa." Not rated. 80m. **DIR:** Mike Gribble, Craig Decker. 1991

SPIKE OF BENSONHURST ★★ Haphazard comedy-drama about life in a Mafia-run neighborhood in New York City. Sasha Mitchell stars as a young Italian boxer trying to get his big break. Rated R for nudity, violence, and profanity. 102m. **DIR:** Paul Morrissey. **CAST:** Sasha Mitchell, Ernest Borgnine, Sylvia Miles. 1989

SPINOUT ★★ A lesser Elvis vehicle, this features a perky drummer (Deborah Walley), a spoiled heiress (Shelley Fabares), and a pushy sociologist (Diane McBain) trying to get the King to say "I do." Dated attitudes and styles don't age well. 93m. **DIR:** Norman Taurog. **CAST:** Elvis Presley, Shelley Fabares, Deborah Walley, Diane McBain, Carl Betz. 1966

SPIRAL STAIRCASE, THE (1946) ★★★★ Dorothy McGuire gives what some call the performance of her career as a mute servant in a hackle-raising household harboring a killer. Watch this one late at night, but not alone. B&W; 83m. **DIR:** Robert Siodmak. **CAST:** George Brent, Dorothy McGuire, Ethel Barrymore, Kent Smith, Elsa Lanchester, Sara Allgood. 1946

SPIRAL STAIRCASE, THE (1975) 💔 Sad remake. Not rated; contains mild violence. 89m. **DIR:** Peter Collinson. **CAST:** Jacqueline Bisset, Christopher Plummer, Sam Wanamaker, Gayle Hunnicutt. 1975

SPIRIT LOST ★★1/2 A heavy use of smoke and mirrors bogs down this sexy ghost story. An artist and his wife move into their dream house by the sea, only to find it inhabited by a two-hundred-year-old spirit desperate for sexual misadventure. There are some stylish segues and fades, but too much of this looks like soft porn and the ending is ridiculous. Rated R for nudity, profanity, and sexual situations. 90m. **DIR:** Neema Barnette. **CAST:** Leon, Regina Taylor, Cynda Williams. 1996

SPIRIT OF ST. LOUIS, THE ★★★★ Jimmy Stewart always wanted to portray Charles Lindbergh in a recreation of his historic solo flight across the Atlantic. When he finally got his chance, at age 48, many critics felt he was too old to be believable. Stewart did just fine. The action does drag at times, but this remains a quality picture for the whole family. 138m. **DIR:** Billy Wilder. **CAST:** James Stewart, Patricia Smith, Murray Hamilton, Marc Connelly. 1957

SPIRIT OF '76, THE ★★ Spoof of the Seventies has three people traveling back in time to bring back the Constitution—and thereby revive their dying culture. We found this comedy a disco drag, but it has its admirers. Rated PG for profanity. 82m. **DIR:** Lucas Reiner. **CAST:** David Cassidy, Olivia D'Abo, Leif Garrett, Barbara Bain, Julie Brown, Tommy Chong, Don Novello, Carl Reiner, Rob Reiner, Moon Zappa. 1991

SPIRIT OF THE BEEHIVE, THE ★★★★ A disturbing cinematic study of the isolation of an individual. Ana Torrent gives an unforgettable performance as a lonely girl who enters the world of fantasy when she sees the 1931 *Frankenstein* and falls in love with the monster. By far one of the most haunting films ever made about children. In Spanish with English subtitles. Not rated. 95m. **DIR:** Victor Erice. **CAST:** Fernando Fernán-Gomez, Ana Torrent. 1974

SPIRIT OF THE DEAD ★★★1/2 Originally titled *The Asphyx*, slightly edited for videocassette. Interesting tale of a scientist who discovers the spirit of death possessed by all creatures. If the spirit is trapped, its owner becomes immortal. Well-made British film with sincere performances. Rated PG for mild violence. 82m. **DIR:** Peter Newbrook. **CAST:** Robert Stephens, Robert Powell, Jane Lapotaire. 1972

SPIRIT OF THE EAGLE ★★ A widowed father takes his son into the wilderness to begin a new life, only to see the child kidnapped. This slow-moving adventure film may be rousing to youngsters, but most adults will probably nod off quickly. Not rated. 93m. **DIR:** Boon Collins. **CAST:** Dan Haggerty, William Smith. 1990 DVD

SPIRIT OF THE WEST ★★ This entertaining but primitive Western employs a tired old gimmick that Hoot Gibson had used in previous films—that of a tough hombre who masquerades as a silly fool in order to help the gal in distress and bring the greedy, land-grabbing varmints to justice. B&W; 60m. **DIR:** Otto Brower. **CAST:** Hoot Gibson, Doris Hill, Lafe McKee, Hooper Atchley. 1932

SPIRIT OF WEST POINT, THE ★★1/2 West Point football stars play themselves in this realistic saga of the Long Gray Line. B&W; 77m. **DIR:** Ralph Murphy. **CAST:** Felix "Doc" Blanchard, Anne Nagel, Alan Hale Sr., Tom Harmon. 1947

SPIRITS ★★1/2 Group of psychic researchers investigate a supposedly haunted house where a series of murders took place ten years before. Erik Estrada plays a doubting priest who must face off against the evil. As usual, things go bump in the night. Rated R for violence and nudity. 94m. **DIR:** Fred Olen Ray. **CAST:** Erik Estrada, Robert Quarry, Brinke Stevens, Oliver Darrow, Carol Lynley. 1990

SPITE MARRIAGE ★★★★ Buster Keaton is a pants presser who masquerades as a millionaire to impress actress Dorothy Sebastian. When she is spurned by her lover, she marries Keaton out of spite, and he seeks to win her true love. Silent. B&W; 77m. **DIR:** Edward Sedgwick. **CAST:** Buster Keaton, Dorothy Sebastian. 1929

SPITFIRE (1934) ★★★1/2 A girl (Katharine Hepburn) believes herself to have healing powers and is cast out from her Ozark Mountain home as a result. It's an interesting premise, and well-acted. B&W; 88m. **DIR:** John Cromwell. **CAST:** Katharine Hepburn, Robert Young, Ralph Bellamy, Sara Haden, Sidney Toler. 1934

SPITFIRE (1994) 💔 Complicated mess about a champion gymnast globe-trotting in an effort to save her superspy father. Rated R for violence, language, and adult situations. 99m. **DIR:** Albert Pyun. **CAST:** Kristie Phillips, Tim Thomerson, Lance Henriksen, Sarah Douglas. 1994

SPITFIRE GRILL, THE ★★★ Female-bonding drama that's always striving too hard for earthy sensitivity. Ex-con Alison Elliott tries to restart her life in a tiny Maine town, where she helps the women who run the local diner find themselves. From the creator of TV's *MacGyver*, which should give you some idea of how contrived this supposedly naturalistic drama plays, despite the best efforts of a fine cast. Rated PG-13. 111m. DIR: Lee David Zlotoff. CAST: Alison Elliott, Ellen Burstyn, Marcia Gay Harden, Will Patton. 1996 DVD

SPLASH ★★★★★ An uproarious comedy about a young man (Tom Hanks) who unknowingly falls in love with a mermaid (Daryl Hannah). John Candy and Eugene Levy add some marvelous bits of comedy. Rated PG for profanity and brief nudity. 111m. DIR: Ron Howard. CAST: Tom Hanks, Daryl Hannah, John Candy, Eugene Levy, Dody Goodman, Richard B. Shull. 1984 DVD

SPLATTER UNIVERSITY 🎬 Typical slasher film featuring students having sex and then getting hacked to pieces. Rated R for profanity, brief nudity, and violence. 78m. DIR: Richard W. Haines. CAST: Francine Forbes, Ric Randig. 1985

•SPLENDOR ★★★ Kathleen Robertson plays a woman without any romance in her life. In the course of one evening, all of that changes when she falls in love with two different men—and they with her. She introduces them to each other and much to her surprise, they all get along and soon find themselves living together. Then another man enters and their whole love triangle is jeopardized. Plenty of sex, including the obligatory ménage à trois. Rated R. 93m. DIR: Gregg Araki. CAST: Kathleen Robertson, Johnathon Schaech, Matt Keeslar. 1998 DVD

SPLENDOR IN THE GRASS ★★★★ Warren Beatty made his film debut in this 1961 film, as a popular, rich high school boy. Natalie Wood plays his less-prosperous girlfriend who has a nervous breakdown when he dumps her. A few tears shed by the viewer make this romantic drama all the more intriguing. 124m. DIR: Elia Kazan. CAST: Warren Beatty, Natalie Wood, Pat Hingle, Audrey Christie. 1961 DVD

SPLIT DECISIONS ★★ Gene Hackman might have been hoping for an audience-pleasing sports film on a par with *Hoosiers* when he agreed to do this fight picture, but the result is another failed takeoff on the *Rocky* series. Pure melodrama: Hackman attempts to groom one son (Craig Sheffer) for the Olympics while fearing that he, like his older brother (Jeff Fahey), will opt for the easy money offered by sleazy fight promoters. Rated R for violence and profanity. 95m. DIR: David Drury. CAST: Gene Hackman, Craig Sheffer, Jeff Fahey, Jennifer Beals, John McLiam. 1988

SPLIT IMAGE ★★★★ This is a very interesting, thought-provoking film about religious cults and those who become caught up in them. Michael O'Keefe plays a young man who is drawn into a pseudoreligious organization run by Peter Fonda. The entire cast is good, but Fonda stands out in one of his best roles. Rated R for language and nudity. 113m. DIR: Ted Kotcheff. CAST: Peter Fonda, James Woods, Karen Allen, Michael O'Keefe. 1982

SPLIT SECOND (1953) ★★★ Tense film about an escaped convict who holds several people hostage in a deserted town has a lot working for it, including the fact that the place they're holed up in is a nuclear test site. B&W; 85m. DIR: Dick Powell. CAST: Stephen McNally, Alexis Smith, Jan Sterling, Paul Kelly, Richard Egan. 1953

SPLIT SECOND (1992) 🎬 This murky sci-fi thriller—about a cop searching for the inhuman killer of his partner in twenty-first-century London—is a poor rip-off of the visuals of *Blade Runner* and the story line of *Predator*. Rated R for violence, profanity, and nudity. 90m. DIR: Tony Maylam. CAST: Rutger Hauer, Kim Cattrall, Pete Postlethwaite, Michael J. Pollard. 1992

SPLITTING HEIRS ★★★★ Wonderfully silly comedy about two babies switched at birth, resulting in the wrong baby becoming the sixteenth Duke of Bournemouth. When the real heir discovers the truth about his heritage, he plots to murder the man who stole his title. Marvelous confection of comic situations and hilarious bits. Rated PG-13 for profanity, nudity, suggested sex, and violence. 88m. DIR: Robert Young. CAST: Eric Idle, Rick Moranis, John Cleese, Barbara Hershey, Catherine Zeta Jones, Sadie Frost, Stratford Johns. 1993

SPOILERS, THE ★★★★ John Wayne is a miner who strikes gold in Nome, Alaska. An unscrupulous gold commissioner (Randolph Scott) and his cronies plot to steal the rich claim. But the Duke, his partner (Harry Carey), and their backer (Marlene Dietrich) have other ideas. This was the fourth of five screen versions of Rex Beach's novel. B&W; 87m. DIR: Ray Enright. CAST: Marlene Dietrich, Randolph Scott, John Wayne, Harry Carey, Russell Simpson, George Cleveland. 1942

SPONTANEOUS COMBUSTION 🎬 Government experiment turns Brad Dourif into a human flame thrower, but the film extinguishes itself long before any sparks ignite. Sorry effort from director Tobe Hooper. Rated R for violence. 97m. DIR: Tobe Hooper. CAST: Brad Dourif, Cynthia Bain, Melinda Dillon, Dick Butkus, Jon Cypher. 1990

SPOOKIES 🎬 Zombies of all varieties maim and kill people trapped in an old mansion. Rated R for violence and profanity. 85m. DIR: Eugine Joseph, Thomas Doran, Brenden Faulkner. CAST: Felix Ward, Dan Scott. 1985

SPOOKS RUN WILD 🎬 Bela Lugosi in another silly role that gives the aging East Side Kids a chance to humiliate him on-screen. B&W; 69m. DIR: Phil Rosen. CAST: Bela Lugosi, The East Side Kids, Dave O'Brien, Dennis Moore. 1941

SPORTING CLUB, THE 🎬 An allegory of America that takes place at an exclusive hunting club. Look for Linda Blair in a small role. 104m. DIR: Larry Peerce. CAST: Robert Fields, Nicolas Coster, Margaret Blye, Jack Warden, Richard Dysart. 1971

SPRING FEVER 🎬 Canadian production is an unbelievably dull story about a rising young tennis star (Carling Bassett). Rated PG. 100m. DIR: Joseph L. Scanlan. CAST: Jessica Walter, Susan Anton, Frank Converse, Carling Bassett, Stephen Young. 1983

SPRING PARADE ★★★★ This lilting musical confection stars Deanna Durbin as a baker's assistant in love with an army drummer. Set in Austria. B&W; 89m. DIR: Henry Koster. CAST: Deanna Durbin, Robert Cummings, S. Z. Sakall, Henry Stephenson, Mischa Auer, Reginald Denny, Allyn Joslyn. 1940

SPRING SYMPHONY ★★ A routine presentation of the lives of German composer Robert Schumann and celebrated pianist Clara Wieck. The film portrays emotion in fairy-tale fashion, simplistic and overstated. The music is the star of this show. Dubbed in English. Rated PG. 102m. **DIR:** Peter Schamoni. **CAST:** Nastassja Kinski, Herbert Gronemeyer, Bernhard Wicki. 1984 DVD

SPRINGTIME IN THE ROCKIES (1937) ★★ Foreman Gene Autry has all he can handle as a young girl arrives at his cattle ranch with a herd of sheep. Pretty tame. B&W; 54m. **DIR:** Joseph Kane. **CAST:** Gene Autry, Smiley Burnette, Polly Rowles. 1937

SPRINGTIME IN THE ROCKIES (1942) ★★★ Lake Louise and other breathtaking Canadian scenic wonders provide backgrounds for this near-plotless show-business musical. Jealous Broadway entertainers Betty Grable and John Payne fight and make up with the help of Carmen Miranda, Cesar Romero, and a bushel of songs and dances. 90m. **DIR:** Irving Cummings. **CAST:** Betty Grable, John Payne, Carmen Miranda, Cesar Romero, Edward Everett Horton, Charlotte Greenwood, Jackie Gleason, Harry James. 1942

SPRINGTIME IN THE SIERRAS ★★ Beady-eyed Roy Rogers sets his sights on stopping evil Stephanie Bachelor and her hulking henchman Roy Barcroft from shooting game animals out of season. There's more action than story in this fast-paced series entry. 75m. **DIR:** William Witney. **CAST:** Roy Rogers, Jane Frazee, Andy Devine, Stephanie Bachelor. 1947

SPRUNG ★★ A romance between two young African Americans is broken up by their jealous best friends. Then, inexplicably, the friends try to get them back together. Everyone overacts shamelessly, and the film never makes psychological sense. Rated R for profanity and raunchy humor. 105m. **DIR:** Rusty Cundieff. **CAST:** Tisha Campbell, Rusty Cundieff, Paula Jai Parker, Joe Torry, John Witherspoon, Jennifer Lee, Clarence Williams III. 1997 DVD

SPUTNIK ★★★ The memorable character actor Mischa Auer (remember the artist who imitated a gorilla in *My Man Godfrey*?) costars in this French comedy about an animal lover trying to protect a dog and a mouse that escaped from a Russian satellite. Pleasant family comedy. B&W; 80m. **DIR:** Jean Dreville. **CAST:** Noel-Noel, Denise Grey, Mischa Auer. 1960

SPY ★★1/2 A mediocre spy thriller involving a retired spy turned artist, who goes into hiding when his former colleagues decide he must die. Made for cable. 91m. **DIR:** Philip F. Messina. **CAST:** Bruce Greenwood, Jameson Parker, Tim Choate, Catherine Hicks, Ned Beatty, Michael Tucker. 1989

SPY HARD ★★ Once again, Leslie Nielsen gamely spoofs his own stalwart leading-man image; this time, he's Dick Steele, Secret Agent WD-40, on the trail of arch-villain General Rancor. Everyone tries hard to be zany, but the script is warmed-over *Get Smart*. Rated PG-13 for mild sexual humor. 85m. **DIR:** Rick Friedberg. **CAST:** Leslie Nielsen, Nicollette Sheridan, Charles Durning, Barry Bostwick, Andy Griffith, Marcia Gay Harden. 1996 DVD

SPY IN BLACK, THE ★★★ Unusual espionage-cum-romance story of German agent Conrad Veidt and his love affair with British agent Valerie Hobson. British director Michael Powell brings just the right blend of duty and tragedy to this story, set in the turmoil of World War I. B&W; 82m. **DIR:** Michael Powell.

CAST: Conrad Veidt, Valerie Hobson, Sebastian Shaw, June Duprez, Marius Goring. 1939

SPY OF NAPOLEON ★★ Heavy-handed historical hokum finds Emperor Napoleon III using his illegitimate daughter to ferret out dissidents and enemies. Amusing enough and stars former silent-screen good guy Richard Barthelmess in a meaty role. B&W; 77m. **DIR:** Maurice Elvey. **CAST:** Richard Barthelmess, Dolly Hass. 1936

SPY SMASHER ★★★ The costumed radio hero (Kane Richmond) takes on the Nazis in this fun-for-fans cliff-hanger serial. B&W; 12 chapters. **DIR:** William Witney. **CAST:** Kane Richmond, Sam Flint, Marguerite Chapman, Hans Schumm, Tristram Coffin. 1942

SPY WHO CAME IN FROM THE COLD, THE ★★★★ Realism and stark authenticity mark this sunless drama of the closing days in the career of a British cold-war spy in Berlin. Richard Burton is matchless as embittered, burned-out Alec Leamas, the sold-out agent. No 007 glamour and gimmicks here. 112m. **DIR:** Martin Ritt. **CAST:** Richard Burton, Claire Bloom, Oskar Werner, Bernard Lee, George Voskovec, Peter Van Eyck, Sam Wanamaker. 1965

SPY WHO LOVED ME, THE ★★★★ This, the tenth James Bond epic, is Roger Moore's third, and he finally hits his stride. Directed with a blend of excitement and tongue-in-cheek humor, the film teams Bond with Russian agent XXX (Barbara Bach) in an effort to stop an industrialist (Curt Jurgens) from destroying the surface world so he can rule an undersea kingdom. Rated PG for violence and sexual situations. 125m. **DIR:** Lewis Gilbert. **CAST:** Roger Moore, Barbara Bach, Curt Jurgens, Richard Kiel, Bernard Lee, Lois Maxwell, Desmond Llewellyn, Caroline Munro. 1977 DVD

SPY WITH A COLD NOSE, THE ★★★ This cute British spy spoof features Lionel Jeffries as an un-Bond-like counterintelligence agent. His plan to implant a microphone in the goodwill gift to the Soviets goes awry. The gift, a bulldog, may require an operation, and then the Soviets would be outraged. 113m. **DIR:** Daniel Petrie. **CAST:** Laurence Harvey, Daliah Lavi, Lionel Jeffries, Eric Sykes, Paul Ford. 1966

SPY WITHIN, THE ★★★ Actor Steve Railsback makes his directorial debut with this effective spy thriller. Desperate agent Theresa Russell tries to escape the clandestine government organization she worked for that now wants her dead. Rated R for nudity, violence, and profanity. 92m. **DIR:** Steve Railsback. **CAST:** Scott Glenn, Theresa Russell, Lane Smith, Terence Knox, Katherine Helmond, Alex Rocco, Joe Pantoliano. 1994

SPYMAKER: THE SECRET LIFE OF IAN FLEMING ★★★ Enjoyable fluff concentrates on writer Ian Fleming's exploits during World War II and his work with British intelligence. Jason Connery, Sean's son, is quite good as Fleming, bringing the right amounts of humor and derring-do to the character. Made for TV. 77m. **DIR:** Ferdinand Fairfax. **CAST:** Jason Connery, Kristin Scott Thomas, Joss Ackland, Patricia Hodge, David Warner, Richard Johnson, Colin Welland. 1990

S*P*Y*S 🎔 CIA agents assisting a Russian dancer wanting to defect to the West. 87m. **DIR:** Irvin Kershner. **CAST:** Donald Sutherland, Elliott Gould, Joss Ackland. **1974**

SQUANTO: A WARRIOR'S TALE ★★★ A young Indian warrior (Adam Beach) is kidnapped by seventeenth-century English traders and exhibited as a wild man back in England. The story of how he escapes and returns home makes a farfetched but enjoyable Disney family adventure, in the tradition of *The Light in the Forest* and *Tonka*. Rated PG. 97m. **DIR:** Xavier Koller. **CAST:** Adam Beach, Eric Schweig, Michael Gambon, Nathaniel Parker, Alex Norton, Stuart Pankin, Donal Donnelly, Mandy Patinkin. **1994**

SQUARE DANCE ★★★★ A coming-of-age drama about a 13-year-old Texas girl (Winona Ryder), *Square Dance* has so much atmosphere that you can almost smell the chicken-fried steaks. When the girl's loose-living mother (well played by Jane Alexander) takes her away from the comfort and care of her grandfather's (Jason Robards) ranch, the youngster's life goes from idyllic to hard-edged. Rated PG-13 for profanity and suggested sex. 110m. **DIR:** Daniel Petrie. **CAST:** Jason Robards Jr., Jane Alexander, Winona Ryder, Rob Lowe, Guich Koock. **1987**

SQUEEZE ★★1/2 Young friends try to survive the difficult life on the streets. Intense yet typical. Rated R for profanity and violence. 102m. **DIR:** Robert Patton-Spruill. **CAST:** Tyrone Burton, Eddie Cutanda, Phuong Duong, Geoffrey Rhue. **1996**

SQUEEZE, THE (1977) ★★1/2 Stacy Keach plays an alcoholic detective whose ex-wife is kidnapped for a large ransom. Good performances do not save this mediocre film. Rated R for nudity and language. 106m. **DIR:** Michael Apted. **CAST:** Stacy Keach, David Hemmings, Edward Fox, Stephen Boyd, Carol White. **1977**

SQUEEZE, THE (1987) 💣 Michael Keaton can always be counted on for at least a few laughs, but a few laughs is about all you get in this dreary comedy-thriller. It's rated PG-13 for language and violence. 101m. **DIR:** Roger Young. **CAST:** Michael Keaton, Rae Dawn Chong, Meat Loaf. **1987**

SQUEEZE PLAY ★★ Another Troma trauma from the world's cheapest movie studio, a proudly dumb comedy that transfers the battle of the sexes to a softball field. Strictly for the couchbound whose remote controls are broken. Rated R for vulgarity and brief nudity. 92m. **DIR:** Samuel Weil. **CAST:** Jim Harris. **1980**

SQUIRM 💣 Ugly film has hordes of killer worms attacking a small town. Rated PG. 92m. **DIR:** Jeff Lieberman. **CAST:** Don Scardino, Patricia Pearcy. **1976**

SQUIZZY TAYLOR ★★1/2 Fairly interesting film about the notorious Australian gangster of the 1920s. David Atkins gives a convincing performance. But the story begins to lose its edge after a while. Not rated. Has sex, nudity, and violence. 103m. **DIR:** Kevin James Dobson. **CAST:** David Atkins, Jacki Weaver, Alan Cassell, Michael Long. **1983**

S.S. HELL CAMP ★ Cheap, incredibly gross Eurotrash stomach-turner set in a Nazi compound. No rating, but sexually explicit and very sadistic. 88m. **DIR:** Ivan Katansky. **CAST:** Macha Magall, John Braun. **1975**

STACKING ★★★1/2 A cut above the righteous save-the-farm films that abound these days, because it doesn't allow for an overblown triumphant outcome and the performances are exquisite. Frederic Forrest is wonderful as a hard-drinking hired hand, and Christine Lahti really gets under the skin of her restless character. Rated PG. 95m. **DIR:** Martin Rosen. **CAST:** Christine Lahti, Frederic Forrest, Megan Follows, Jason Gedrick, Ray Baker, Peter Coyote. **1988**

STACY'S KNIGHTS ★★ Kevin Costner's career has come a long way since this early snoozer, sort of a cross between *The Karate Kid* and *The Sting* set at the blackjack tables of Reno. Rated PG. 95m. **DIR:** Jim Wilson. **CAST:** Andra Millian, Kevin Costner. **1982**

STAG ★★★ Gripping morality play about a group of successful men who gather for a bachelor stag party and find their lives turned upside down when they accidentally kill a female stripper. As they decide what action to take, several members of the group panic, escalating the situation and tension. Made-for-cable. Rated R for adult situations, language, nudity, and violence. 92m. **DIR:** Gavin Wilding. **CAST:** Mario Van Peebles, Andrew McCarthy, Kevin Dillon, Taylor Dane, John Stockwell, William McNamara, John Henson, Ben Gazzara. **1997**

STAGE DOOR ★★★★ A funny and tender taste of New York theatrical life. Katharine Hepburn and Ginger Rogers are two aspiring actresses who undergo the stifling yet stimulating life of a lodging house that caters to a vast array of prospective actresses. Eve Arden, Lucille Ball, and Ann Miller also take residence in this overcrowded and active boardinghouse. B&W; 92m. **DIR:** Gregory La Cava. **CAST:** Katharine Hepburn, Ginger Rogers, Eve Arden, Lucille Ball, Ann Miller. **1937**

STAGE DOOR CANTEEN ★★ An all-star cast play themselves in this mildly amusing romance. Unless you enjoy looking at the many stage luminaries during their early years, you will find this entire film to be ordinary, predictable, and uninspired. B&W; 85m. **DIR:** Frank Borzage. **CAST:** William Terry, Cheryl Walkers, Katharine Hepburn, Harpo Marx, Helen Hayes, Count Basie, Edgar Bergen. **1943**

STAGE FRIGHT ★★★ Another winner from Alfred Hitchcock. Drama student Jane Wyman spies on actress Marlene Dietrich to prove she murdered her husband. Alastair Sim steals his moments as Wyman's protective parent, but most of the other moments go to the hypnotic Dietrich. B&W; 110m. **DIR:** Alfred Hitchcock. **CAST:** Marlene Dietrich, Jane Wyman, Michael Wilding, Alastair Sim, Richard Todd, Kay Walsh, Patricia Hitchcock. **1950**

STAGE STRUCK (1936) ★★ A no-talent singer-dancer, Joan Blondell, makes a bid for Broadway by financing a show for herself. She hires Dick Powell to direct. They clash, fall in love, clash, and depend on good old suave Warren William to smooth it all out. Not that anyone should care too much. Below par. B&W; 86m. **DIR:** Busby Berkeley. **CAST:** Joan Blondell, Dick Powell, Warren William, Frank McHugh, Jeanne Madden, Carol Hughes, Hobart Cavanaugh, Spring Byington. **1936**

STAGE STRUCK (1958) ★★ Despite a fine cast—Susan Strasberg excepted—this rehash of *Morning*

Glory is flat and wearisome. You don't really care to pull for the young actress trying to make her mark. The late Joan Greenwood's throaty voice, however, is sheer delight. 95m. DIR: Sidney Lumet. CAST: Henry Fonda, Susan Strasberg, Joan Greenwood, Herbert Marshall, Christopher Plummer. 1958

STAGE TO CHINO ★★★1/2 In this first-rate B Western, George O'Brien is a postal inspector who goes undercover to investigate a gold-shipping scam. The always reliable Roy Barcroft is the leader of the baddies, and Virginia Vale is the not-so-helpless principal victim. O'Brien's Westerns were always marked by fine acting, lots of action, and snappy dialogue, and this is a good example. B&W; 58m. DIR: Edward Killy. CAST: George O'Brien, Virginia Vale, Roy Barcroft, Hobart Cavanaugh, Carl Stockdale, William Haade, Glenn Strange. 1940

STAGE TO MESA CITY ★★★ Lash LaRue and sidekick Fuzzy Q. Jones set out to nail bandits who are robbing stagecoaches. B&W; 56m. DIR: Ray Taylor. CAST: Lash LaRue, Al St. John, Jennifer Holt. 1947

STAGE TO TUCSON ★★★★ After several stagecoaches are stolen, two government agents are sent to lead an investigation. Well scripted, action-packed. B&W; 82m. DIR: Ralph Moody. CAST: Rod Cameron, Wayne Morris, Kay Buckley, Carl Benton Reid. 1951

STAGECOACH (1939) ★★★★★ John Ford utilized the *Grand Hotel* formula of placing a group of unrelated characters together. A stagecoach trip across the Old West provides the common setting and plenty of shared danger. Riding together with the mysterious Ringo Kid (John Wayne) is a grand assortment of some of Hollywood's best character actors. B&W; 99m. DIR: John Ford. CAST: John Wayne, Claire Trevor, Thomas Mitchell, John Carradine, Donald Meek, Andy Devine, George Bancroft, Tim Holt. 1939 DVD

STAGECOACH (1986) ★★★ This made-for-television remake of John Ford's classic 1939 Western bears little resemblance to its predecessor, but the cast of country stars seems to be enjoying itself so much you can't help but join in. Certain conceits, such as Willie Nelson substituting the character of Doc Holliday for the less glamorous original character, seem out of place, but it's enjoyable. 98m. DIR: Ted Post. CAST: Willie Nelson, Kris Kristofferson, Johnny Cash, Waylon Jennings, John Schneider, Elizabeth Ashley, Anthony Franciosa, Anthony Newley, Mary Crosby, Lash LaRue. 1986

STAGECOACH TO DENVER ★★★1/2 A supposedly good citizen resorts to murder and kidnapping in an all-out effort to get a woman's property. Red Ryder and Little Beaver put the owl hoots in their place. Action-packed. B&W; 54m. DIR: R. G. Springsteen. CAST: Allan "Rocky" Lane, Bobby Blake, Peggy Stewart, Roy Barcroft. 1946

STAGECOACH WAR ★★★1/2 Hopalong Cassidy finds himself in the middle of a contract war between rival stage lines. B&W; 63m. DIR: Lesley Selander. CAST: William Boyd, Russell Hayden, J. Farrell MacDonald. 1940

STAIRCASE ★★★ Although probably quite scandalous for its time, Charles Dyer's odd little British play-turned-film is interesting now only because of the novelty casting of Rex Harrison and Richard Burton as a couple of gay hairdressers who show their mutual affection by continuously sniping at each other. It's actually much tougher to watch Burton's character care for his invalid mother, whose confinement to bed is portrayed with graphic detail. Rated R for nudity, simulated sex, profanity, and sexual candor. 100m. DIR: Stanley Donen. CAST: Rex Harrison, Richard Burton, Cathleen Nesbitt, Beatrix Lehmann. 1969

STAKEOUT ★★★★1/2 The fastest and funniest cop thriller since the original *Beverly Hills Cop*. A pair of detectives (Richard Dreyfuss and Emilio Estevez) strive to apprehend psychotic killer Aidan Quinn, who has escaped from prison. Rated R for profanity, nudity, and suggested sex, and violence. 116m. DIR: John Badham. CAST: Richard Dreyfuss, Emilio Estevez, Madeleine Stowe, Aidan Quinn, Dan Lauria, Forest Whitaker. 1987

STALAG 17 ★★★★★ Many critics felt William Holden's Academy Award for *Stalag 17* was a gift for failing to give him proper recognition in *Sunset Boulevard*. Those critics should view this prison camp comedy-drama again. This film still holds up brilliantly today. Billy Wilder successfully alternated between suspense and comedy in this story of a World War II prison camp. Holden plays an opportunistic and cynical sergeant whose actions make him a natural suspect as the spy in the POWs' midst. B&W; 120m. DIR: Billy Wilder. CAST: William Holden, Robert Strauss, Peter Graves, Otto Preminger. 1953 DVD

STALIN ★★1/2 Robert Duvall's compelling portrayal of the infamous Soviet dictator is sabotaged by Paul Monash's haphazard script, which fails to provide the depth required to explain just how Stalin remained in power for so many years. Made for cable. 172m. DIR: Ivan Passer. CAST: Robert Duvall, Julia Ormond, Jeroen Krabbé, Joan Plowright, Maximilian Schell. 1992

STALINGRAD ★★★1/2 This German antiwar film follows the WWII Stalingrad campaign through the eyes of six German soldiers, from early triumphs through crumbling fortunes and final catastrophe. The film follows exactly the structure of *All Quiet on the Western Front*, with the comrades one by one meeting horrible ends. The characters are two-dimensional archetypes, but the film is spectacularly well made, and the horrors of war are forcefully dramatized. In German with English subtitles. Not rated; contains graphic war violence. 135m. DIR: Joseph Vilsmaier. CAST: Thomas Kreischmann, Jochen Nickel, Sebastian Rudolph, Sylvester Groth. 1993 DVD

STALKED ★★ Nothing new in this tale of an obsessed man and the lengths to which he's willing to go in order to be with the woman he loves. Rated R for violence and language. 94m. DIR: Douglas Jackson. CAST: Maryam D'Abo, Tod Fennell, Jay Underwood, Lisa Blount, Karen Robinson. 1994

STALKER ★★★★ In a decrepit future, a guide takes a scientist and a writer into the mysterious "Zone," site of a meteor crash, to find a source of great extraterrestrial knowledge. Definitely not for *Star Wars* fans, this adaptation of a Stanislaw Lem novel moves slowly but is filled with unforgettably beautiful images. In Russian with English subtitles. Not rated. 161m. **DIR:** Andrei Tarkovsky. **CAST:** Alexander Kaidanovsky, Anatoly Solanitsin. **1979**

STALKING MOON, THE ★★★ Gregory Peck is an army scout who takes in a white woman (Eva Marie Saint) and the child she bore while a captive of the Apaches. The Apache father kidnaps the child and starts a chase that lasts through most of the movie. Familiar, but captivating and with exceptional performances. 109m. **DIR:** Robert Mulligan. **CAST:** Gregory Peck, Eva Marie Saint, Robert Forster, Frank Silvera, Lou Frizell. **1969**

STAMPEDE ★★★★ Rod Cameron and his brother fight to hold on to their cattle empire against encroaching settlers. B&W; 78m. **DIR:** Lesley Selander. **CAST:** Rod Cameron, Don Castle, Gale Storm, Johnny Mack Brown. **1949**

STAND, THE ★★★1/2 Stephen King contemplated nothing less than the end of the world in his monumental novel, and it was reasonably well served by this television miniseries. After a "super-flu" virus decimates the United States, the few immune survivors gather into two camps: the forces of good and of evil. The strong ensemble cast works hard to sell the apocalyptic concept. Rated PG. 360m. **DIR:** Mick Garris. **CAST:** Gary Sinise, Molly Ringwald, Rob Lowe, Laura San Giacomo, Jamey Sheridan, Ruby Dee, Corin Nemec, Matt Frewer, Miguel Ferrer, Ossie Davis, Ray Walston, Adam Storke, Bill Faggerbakke. **1994 DVD**

STAND AND DELIVER ★★★★1/2 A *Rocky*esque interpretation of high school math teacher Jaime Escalante's true-life exploits. Edward James Olmos stars as Escalante, a man who gave up a high-paying job in electronics to make a contribution to society. Recognizing that his inner-city students need motivation to keep them from a lifetime of menial labor, he sets them a challenge: preparation for the state Advanced Placement Test … in calculus. Rated PG for language. 105m. **DIR:** Ramon Menendez. **CAST:** Edward James Olmos, Lou Diamond Phillips, Rosana De Soto, Andy Garcia. **1988 DVD**

STAND BY ME (1986) ★★★★1/2 Based on Stephen King's novella, *The Body*, the story involves four young boys in the last days of summer and their search for the missing body of a young boy believed hit by a train. Morbid as it may sound, this is not a horror movie. Rather, it is a story of ascending to manhood. Sometimes sad and often funny. Rated R. 90m. **DIR:** Rob Reiner. **CAST:** Wil Wheaton, River Phoenix, Corey Feldman, Jerry O'Connell, Kiefer Sutherland, John Cusack, Richard Dreyfuss. **1986**

STAND BY ME (1988) ★★★ This spirited AIDS Day benefit was recorded at London's Wembley Arena April 1, 1987, and features three songs sung by George Michael, including "Everything She Wants," with his onetime Wham partner, Andrew Ridgeley. The show serves as a time capsule of the mid-80s British music scene. Not rated. 60m. **DIR:** Mike Mansfield. **CAST:** George Michael, Boy George, Meat Loaf, Elton John, John Entwistle, Andy Summers, Herbie Hancock. **1988 DVD**

STAND-IN ★★★ This send-up of Hollywood rubbed more than one Tinsel Town mogul the wrong way by satirizing front office studio manipulators. Eastern financial genius Leslie Howard is sent west to "stand in" for stockholders and find out why Colossal Pictures is heading for skidsville. B&W; 91m. **DIR:** Tay Garnett. **CAST:** Leslie Howard, Humphrey Bogart, Joan Blondell, Jack Carson, Alan Mowbray. **1937**

STAND OFF ★★ An ex-convict takes the Bahamian consul in Ottawa hostage, then has to negotiate with a reasonable police chief and a trigger-happy head of the Canadian Mounties. Some suspense, but there's nothing new here. Rated R for violence and profanity. 92m. **DIR:** Murray Battle. **CAST:** David Strathairn, Dejanet Sears, Stephen Shellen, Gordon Clapp. **1995**

STAND UP AND CHEER ★★★ Depression-plagued Americans need something to bring them out of their slump. Is it jobs, money, a chicken in every pot? No! The president says it's the curly-headed little dynamo he appoints as the Secretary of Amusement. Little Shirley manages to buoy spirits through her songs, dances, and sage advice. B&W; 80m. **DIR:** Hamilton MacFadden. **CAST:** Warner Baxter, Shirley Temple, Madge Evans, James Dunn, Stepin Fetchit. **1934**

STANDING TALL ★★1/2 During the Depression, the struggling owner of a small cattle ranch refuses to sell out to a competitor and finds himself under attack. The always-watchable Robert Forster is the only reason to see this standard made-for-TV Western. 100m. **DIR:** Harvey Hart. **CAST:** Robert Forster, Will Sampson, L. Q. Jones, Buck Taylor, Linda Evans, Chuck Connors. **1978**

•STAND-INS ★★★ Fascinating character study about the women who served as stand-ins for some of Hollywood's golden-age leading ladies. Director Harvey Keith does an excellent job of evoking time and place, while his gifted actresses seem to envelop themselves in their roles. The hopes and dreams of these women who came to Hollywood to become stars but instead stand in the shadows are perfectly realized. Not rated; contains adult situations and language. 88m. **DIR:** Harvey Keith. **CAST:** Daphne Zuniga, Costas Mandylor, Charlotte Chatton, Jordan Ladd. **1997 DVD**

STANDOFF (1997) ★★★ Topical issues are addressed in this action-thriller about a botched FBI raid on a Texas cult compound. Taut without being derivative. Rated R for adult situations, language, nudity, and violence. 105m. **DIR:** Andrew Chapman. **CAST:** Robert Sean Leonard, Keith Carradine, Dennis Haysbert, Natasha Henstridge. **1997**

STANLEY ★★ A crazy Vietnam vet (Chris Robinson) uses deadly snakes to destroy his enemies in this watchable, though rather grim, horror yarn. Rated PG for violence and unpleasant situations. 106m. **DIR:** William Grefe. **CAST:** Chris Robinson, Alex Rocco, Susan Carroll, Steve Alaimo. **1972**

STANLEY AND IRIS ★★★ Jane Fonda stars as a recently widowed bakery worker who teaches an illiterate coworker (Robert De Niro) how to read. A predictable but likable low-key romance derived from Pat Banker's excellent novel, *Union Street*. Rated PG-13. 114m. **DIR:** Martin Ritt. **CAST:** Jane Fonda,

Robert De Niro, Feodor Chaliapin, Martha Plimpton, Swoosie Kurtz, Harley Cross, Jamey Sheridan. **1990**

STANLEY AND LIVINGSTONE ★★★ When Spencer Tracy delivers the historic line, "Doctor Livingstone, I presume," to Sir Cedric Hardwicke in this production, you know why he was such a great screen actor. His performance, as a reporter who journeys to Africa in order to find a lost Victorian explorer, injects life and interest into what could have been just another stodgy prestige picture. B&W; 101m. **DIR:** Henry King. **CAST:** Spencer Tracy, Cedric Hardwicke, Richard Greene, Nancy Kelly. **1939**

STAR, THE (1952) ★★★ Bette Davis earned one of her ten Oscar nominations for her role of a has-been earnestly trying to make a comeback in show business. The story of a once-famous actress on the skids resembled her career at the time, and she makes more out of the role because of it. B&W; 89m. **DIR:** Stuart Heisler. **CAST:** Bette Davis, Sterling Hayden, Natalie Wood, Warner Anderson, Barbara Lawrence, June Travis, Minor Watson. **1952**

STAR! (1968) ★★★1/2 This 1968 biopic about a fabled musical-comedy star Gertrude Lawrence has been re-mastered by director Robert Wise and restored to its original length. Though star Julie Andrews is in top form, the film is overly long and uneven. Not rated; contains mild profanity. 172m. **DIR:** Robert Wise. **CAST:** Julie Andrews, Richard Crenna, Daniel Massey, Michael Craig, Robert Reed. **1968**

STAR CHAMBER, THE ★★★★ A model group of superior court judges lose faith in the constitutional bylaws that they have sworn to uphold and decide to take the law into their own hands. Michael Douglas plays the idealistic young judge who uncovers the organization. Rated R for violence and profanity. 109m. **DIR:** Peter Hyams. **CAST:** Michael Douglas, Hal Holbrook, Yaphet Kotto, Sharon Gless, Jack Kehoe. **1983**

STAR CRASH 🖤 A vapid science-fiction space opera with but one redeeming quality: the scanty costumes worn by Caroline Munro as heroine Stella Star. Rated PG—some violence. 92m. **DIR:** Lewis Coates. **CAST:** Caroline Munro, Christopher Plummer, Joe Spinell, Marjoe Gortner, David Hasselhoff. **1979**

STAR CRYSTAL 🖤 Two astronauts encounter a rock containing a monster that feeds on and destroys humans. Rated R for nudity and violence. 93m. **DIR:** Lance Lindsay. **CAST:** Juston Campbell. **1986**

STAR 80 ★★★★ A depressing, uncompromising, but brilliantly filmed and acted portrait of a tragedy. Mariel Hemingway stars as Dorothy Stratten, the Playboy playmate of the year who was murdered in 1980 by the husband (an equally impressive portrayal by Eric Roberts) she had outgrown. The movie paints a bleak portrait of her life, times, and death. Rated R for nudity, violence, profanity, and sex. 102m. **DIR:** Bob Fosse. **CAST:** Mariel Hemingway, Eric Roberts, Cliff Robertson, Carroll Baker. **1983 DVD**

STAR HUNTER 🖤 High-school football players and cheerleaders become the prey of a group of vicious space monsters on a hunting trip. What you expect, only worse. Rated R for adult situations and violence. 84m. **DIR:** Cole McKay, Sam Newfield. **CAST:** Roddy McDowall, Stella Stevens, Rebecca Budig, Ken Stott, Zack Ward. **1995**

STAR IS BORN, A (1937) ★★★★ The first version of this thrice-filmed in-house Hollywood weeper, this is the story of an aging actor (Fredric March) whose career is beginning to go on the skids while his youthful bride's (Janet Gaynor) career is starting to blossom. Great acting and a tight script keep this poignant movie from falling into melodrama. 111m. **DIR:** William Wellman. **CAST:** Fredric March, Janet Gaynor, Adolphe Menjou, May Robson. **1937 DVD**

STAR IS BORN, A (1954) ★★★★1/2 Judy Garland's acting triumph is the highlight of this movie, which is considered to be the best version of this classic romantic tragedy. This one is well worth watching. James Mason is also memorable in the role originated by Fredric March. Be sure to get the full restored version. 154m. **DIR:** George Cukor. **CAST:** Judy Garland, James Mason, Charles Bickford, Jack Carson, Tommy Noonan. **1954 DVD**

STAR IS BORN, A (1976) ★★ The third and by far least watchable version of this venerable Hollywood war-horse has been sloppily crafted into a vehicle for star Barbra Streisand. The rocky romance between a declining star (Kris Kristofferson) and an up-and-coming new talent (Streisand) has been switched from the world of the stage to that of rock 'n' roll. Rated R. 140m. **DIR:** Frank Pierson. **CAST:** Barbra Streisand, Kris Kristofferson, Gary Busey, Oliver Clark. **1976**

STAR KID ★★★ Ignored by his dad, put down by his sister, beat up by the school bully: what's a 12-year-old to do? Save the world, of course! Costing a mere $10 million to make, this film relies on the wild imaginations of preteen viewers rather than sophisticated special effects to dazzle. This family film uses humor to teach little ones to confront their fears. Rated PG for violence. 101m. **DIR:** Manny Coto. **CAST:** Joseph Mazzello, Richard Gilliland, Corinne Bohrer, Joey Simmrin, Ashlee Levitch. **1997 DVD**

STAR KNIGHT 🖤 Medieval knights meet a visitor from outer space in a film that depicts the period with authenticity, but is pure hokum. Rated R for nudity and violence. 92m. **DIR:** Fernando Colombo. **CAST:** Klaus Kinski, Harvey Keitel, Fernando Rey. **1991**

STAR MAKER, THE ★★ A con man drives through Sicily with a truckload of motion-picture equipment, selling screen tests and promising fame and fortune to the gullible peasants he meets on his way. A grim companion piece to writer-director Giuseppe Tornatore's *Cinema Paradiso*, the film is overlong, ugly, and rather mean-spirited. In Italian with English subtitles. Rated R for (subtitled) profanity and simulated sex. 120m. **DIR:** Giuseppe Tornatore. **CAST:** Sergio Castellitto, Tiziana Lodato, Franco Scaldati, Leopoldo Trieste, Clelia Rondinella. **1995**

STAR MAPS ★★★ A young L.A. hustler harbors sweet dreams of being the next Antonio Banderas, but his pimp is also his father, and Dad is determined to keep the boy earning money on the streets. The acting is strong, especially by Douglas Spain as the hero—and Annette Murphy as the father's abused mistress. Rated R for strong sexuality, profanity, and brief violence. 86m. **DIR:** Miguel Arteta. **CAST:** Douglas Spain, Efrain Figueroa, Annette Murphy, Kandeyce Jorden, Lysa Flores, Martha Velez. **1997**

STAR OF MIDNIGHT ★★1/2 William Powell, in a role cloned from his *Thin Man* series, is a debonair, urbane lawyer accused of murder. Abetted by Ginger Rogers, he sallies forth, repartee in mouth, to catch the real culprit. The police and gangsters alike make it difficult. Not bad. B&W; 90m. **DIR:** Stephen Roberts. **CAST:** William Powell, Ginger Rogers, Paul Kelly, Gene Lockhart, Ralph Morgan. **1935**

STAR PACKER, THE ★★★ The Shadow and his band of outlaws have a group of ranchers cowed until John Wayne rides into town and turns the tables on the baddies. A good B Western that will be best appreciated by Wayne fans. B&W; 60m. **DIR:** Robert N. Bradbury. **CAST:** John Wayne, Verna Hillie, George "Gabby" Hayes, Yakima Canutt. **1934 DVD**

STAR QUEST ★★★ Better-than-average remake of *Ten Little Indians* finds eight multinational astronauts who awaken from cybersleep only to find Earth has been destroyed by a nuclear holocaust. One by one the astronauts wind up dead, leading to a suspenseful climax. Emma Samms stands out as an android who literally goes to pieces. Rated R for nudity, violence, and language. 95m. **DIR:** Rick Jacobson. **CAST:** Steven Bauer, Brenda Bakke, Alan Rachins, Emma Samms, Cliff De Young, Ming-Na Wen. **1994**

•**STAR SLAMMER** ★★ Here's an original idea: Take the standard mid-1970s women-in-prison movie and put it in outer space. Too bad the rest of the movie didn't live up to the premise. Rated R for violence, profanity, and adult situations. 88m. **DIR:** Fred Olen Ray. **CAST:** Ross Hagen, Aldo Ray, John Carradine, Bobbie Bresee, Sandy Brooke. **1986**

STAR SPANGLED RHYTHM ★★★1/2 Sailor Eddie Bracken thinks his gatekeeper father is in charge of Paramount Studios and shows up with shipmates for a deluxe tour. A good excuse to have cameos, skits, and specialty numbers by every Paramount star from William Bendix to Vera Zorina. B&W; 110m. **DIR:** George Marshall. **CAST:** Eddie Bracken, Betty Hutton, Victor Moore, Anne Revere, Walter Abel. **1942**

STAR TREK (TV SERIES) ★★★1/2 These are the voyages of the Starship *Enterprise*. Her original five-year mission was given short shrift by television executives who pulled the plug after a mere three years from late 1966 to mid-1969, and then watched in horror as fans turned it into the single most popular television series ever made. Paramount has reissued the original shows on tapes made from 35-mm masters, and the *Enterprise* and her crew never have looked lovelier. Each tape 50m. **DIR:** Marc Daniels, Joseph Pevney, James Goldstone, Gerd Oswald, Vincent McEveety. **CAST:** William Shatner, Leonard Nimoy, DeForest Kelley, George Takei, Walter Koenig, Nichelle Nichols, Majel Barrett, Grace Lee Whitney, James Doohan. **1966–1969 DVD**

STAR TREK: THE CAGE ★★★★ The first pilot episode of the *Star Trek* television series, initially rejected by NBC for being "too cerebral" and "too good for TV." This is the only recorded story of Captain Christopher Pike (Jeffrey Hunter) and his quite different *Enterprise* crew. The plot concerns a planet of aliens who entrap various forms of animal life in their interplanetary "zoo." Not rated; suitable for family viewing. 65m. **DIR:** Robert Butler. **CAST:** Jeffrey Hunter, Leonard Nimoy, Majel Barrett, John Hoyt, Susan Oliver. **1964**

STAR TREK: FIRST CONTACT ★★★★★ It's true. The even-numbered Star Trek entries are invariably the best, and this lean-and-mean face-off between the cast of *Star Trek: The Next Generation* and the Borg collective is no exception. Even if you don't know much about the Borg, a race of half-human, half-machine beings that absorb whole planet populations into their culture, it doesn't matter. The screenplay lays it all out quite clearly. Rated PG-13 for violence. 110m. **DIR:** Jonathan Frakes. **CAST:** Patrick Stewart, Jonathan Frakes, Brent Spiner, LeVar Burton, Michael Dorn, Gates McFadden, Marina Sirtis, Alfre Woodard, James Cromwell, Alice Krige, Robert Picardo, Dwight Schultz. **1996 DVD**

STAR TREK: GENERATIONS ★★★★ Fans of the two *Star Trek* TV series will be more than pleased by the big-screen teaming up of captains James T. Kirk (William Shatner) and Jean-Luc Picard (Patrick Stewart), despite the contrived circumstances under which they join forces to combat galactic evil. Rated PG for mild violence and light profanity. 118m. **DIR:** David Carson. **CAST:** Patrick Stewart, William Shatner, Malcolm McDowell, Jonathan Frakes, Brent Spiner, LeVar Burton, Michael Dorn, Gates McFadden, Marina Sirtis, James Doohan, Walter Koenig, Whoopi Goldberg, Alan Ruck. **1994 DVD**

STAR TREK: INSURRECTION ★★★★ This *Trek* adventure, while perhaps not among the best installments in this venerable series, delivers all the right moves and should keep fans quite happy. The story concerns an Eden-like planet populated by several hundred denizens who, unbeknownst to them, are being studied by a cloaked research team of Federation officers and the rather slimy and sinister Son'a. Great escapist fun. Rated PG for violence and rather ooky medical procedures. 103m. **DIR:** Jonathan Frakes. **CAST:** Patrick Stewart, Jonathan Frakes, Brent Spiner, LeVar Burton, Michael Dorn, F. Murray Abraham, Donna Murphy, Anthony Zerbe. **1998 DVD**

STAR TREK: THE MENAGERIE ★★★★ Combining the original *Star Trek* pilot, which starred Jeffrey Hunter as the captain, with footage featuring the show's eventual stars, it tells a fascinating story of how Spock brings comfort to his former commander on a planet capable of fulfilling any fantasy. It's science-fiction entertainment of the first order. 100m. **DIR:** Marc Daniels. **CAST:** William Shatner, Leonard Nimoy, Jeffrey Hunter, Susan Oliver, DeForest Kelley, James Doohan, Nichelle Nichols, George Takei. **1967**

STAR TREK—THE MOTION PICTURE ★★1/2 Even though it reunites the cast of the popular television series and was directed by Robert Wise, who made one of the best science-fiction films of all time (*The Day the Earth Stood Still*), this $35 million film is a real hit-and-miss affair. Fans of the series may find much to love, but others will be bewildered—and sometimes bored—by the overemphasis on special effects and the underemphasis on characterization. Rated G. 132m. **DIR:** Robert Wise. **CAST:** William Shatner, Leonard Nimoy, DeForest Kelley, James Doohan, Nichelle Nichols, George Takei, Walter Koenig. **1979**

STAR TREK: THE NEXT GENERATION (TV SERIES)
★★★★ The second crew of the Starship *Enterprise* "to boldly go" on a series of intergalactic adventures boasts an ensemble of fine actors. A lavishly produced, well-written program that, in our opinion, outclasses its predecessor. 96m. **DIR:** Paul Lynch. **CAST:** Patrick Stewart, Jonathan Frakes, Brent Spiner, Marina Sirtis, Gates McFadden, LeVar Burton, Denise Crosby, Michael Dorn, Wil Wheaton. **1987**

STAR TREK II: THE WRATH OF KHAN ★★★★
James T. Kirk, Mr. Spock, and the entire crew of the Starship *Enterprise* once more "boldly go where no man has gone before." It's no *Gone With the Wind*—or even *Raiders of the Lost Ark*. But it is fun to watch, and Trekkies are sure to love it. Rated PG for violence and gore. 113m. **DIR:** Nicholas Meyer. **CAST:** William Shatner, Leonard Nimoy, DeForest Kelley, Ricardo Montalban, James Doohan, George Takei, Nichelle Nichols, Walter Koenig, Kirstie Alley. **1982**

STAR TREK III: THE SEARCH FOR SPOCK ★★★★1/2 In this thrill-packed release, the crew of the U.S.S. *Enterprise* goes looking for Spock, who appeared to give his life to save his friends—at the end of *Star Trek II: The Wrath of Khan*. But is he dead? Finding out may be one of the most entertaining things you ever do in front of a TV set. Rated PG. 105m. **DIR:** Leonard Nimoy. **CAST:** Leonard Nimoy, William Shatner, DeForest Kelley, James Doohan, George Takei, Nichelle Nichols, Walter Koenig, Christopher Lloyd. **1984 DVD**

STAR TREK IV: THE VOYAGE HOME ★★★★1/2 Our stalwart heroes journey back to Earth in their "borrowed" enemy spacecraft just in time to witness a new tragedy in the making: an alien deep-space probe is disrupting our planet's atmosphere by broadcasting a message that nobody understands. When Spock identifies the "language" as that of the humpback whale, extinct in the twenty-third century, Kirk leads his crew back to the twentieth century in an attempt to locate two of the great mammals and utilize them for translation duty. Charming and lighthearted, though rated PG for somewhat intense themes. 119m. **DIR:** Leonard Nimoy. **CAST:** William Shatner, Leonard Nimoy, DeForest Kelley, James Doohan, George Takei, Walter Koenig, Nichelle Nichols, Catherine Hicks. **1986 DVD**

STAR TREK V: THE FINAL FRONTIER ★★1/2 In this entry of the big-screen series, a Vulcan (Laurence Luckinbill) takes control of the *Enterprise* to pursue his personal quest for spiritual enlightenment. Luckinbill delivers a strong performance, and the script features a number of witty exchanges between the stars. However, its ambitious, metaphysical premise is diluted by a weak, unsatisfying ending. Rated PG for profanity. 110m. **DIR:** William Shatner. **CAST:** William Shatner, Leonard Nimoy, DeForest Kelley, James Doohan, Walter Koenig, Nichelle Nichols, George Takei, David Warner, Laurence Luckinbill. **1989 DVD**

STAR TREK VI: THE UNDISCOVERED COUNTRY ★★★★ In this enjoyable piece of entertainment, Capt. Kirk and Dr. McCoy find themselves on trial for murder. Rated PG for violence. 101m. **DIR:** Nicholas Meyer. **CAST:** William Shatner, Leonard Nimoy, DeFor-est Kelley, George Takei, James Doohan, Nichelle Nichols, Walter Koenig, Kim Cattrall, David Warner, Brock Peters, Iman. **1991 DVD**

STAR WARS ★★★★★ May the Force be with you! Writer-director George Lucas blended the best of vintage pulp science fiction, old-fashioned cliffhangers, comic books, and classic fantasy to come up with the ultimate adventure "a long time ago in a galaxy far, far away." Rated PG. 121m. **DIR:** George Lucas. **CAST:** Mark Hamill, Harrison Ford, Carrie Fisher, Alec Guinness, Peter Cushing, Anthony Daniels. **1977**

STAR WARS: EPISODE I THE PHANTOM MENACE ★★★★★ Jedi Knights are dispatched to planet Naboo to help in their battle with the Trade Federation, which is being manipulated by the dark side of the Force. This prequel to writer-director George Lucas's 1977 hit ranks high in the series, second only to the original. With its eye-popping special effects and fine performances, this all-ages entertainment actually lives up to its nearly overwhelming media hype. Rated PG for violence. 131m. **DIR:** George Lucas. **CAST:** Liam Neeson, Ewan McGregor, Natalie Portman, Jake Lloyd, Ian McDiarmid, Hugh Quarshie, Anthony Daniels, Kenny Baker, Terence Stamp, Samuel L. Jackson, Frank Oz, Ray Park. **1999**

STARBIRDS ★★ Refugees from a destroyed solar system plot to invade Earth in order to survive. The fact that these aliens look suspiciously like angels is somewhat disturbing. Mediocre. 75m. **DIR:** Michael Part, Tadao Nagahama. **1986**

STARDUST MEMORIES 🎗 Absolutely unwatchable Woody Allen film, his most chaotic and Bergman-esque attempt to claim that he can't stand his fans. Rated PG—profanity. B&W; 88m. **DIR:** Woody Allen. **CAST:** Woody Allen, Charlotte Rampling, Jessica Harper, Marie-Christine Barrault. **1980 DVD**

STARFLIGHT ONE 🎗 Airport '82? 115m. **DIR:** Jerry Jameson. **CAST:** Lee Majors, Hal Linden, Lauren Hutton, Ray Milland, Gail Strickland, George DiCenzo, Tess Harper, Terry Kiser, Robert Webber. **1982**

STARGATE ★★ A surprise hit at the box office, this sci-fi epic is long on special effects and short on sense. When it is discovered that a pyramid contains a portal to the universe, an Egyptologist accompanies a military force to the other side of the galaxy where they encounter human slaves forced to serve an all-powerful alien. Silly and often boring. Rated PG-13 for profanity and violence. 121m. **DIR:** Roland Emmerich. **CAST:** Kurt Russell, James Spader, Jaye Davidson, Viveca Lindfors, Alexis Cruz, Leon Rippy, John Diehl. **1994 DVD**

STARGATE SG-1 ★★★ Made-for-cable pilot led to a series whose plot picks up about a year after the theatrical film's ending. Earthlings reenter the portal to the universe, a shortcut to other stars and planets, to rescue those who've been kidnapped by aliens inhabiting their bodies. Film relies on *Star Trek*–type adventure formula rather than extraordinary special effects to hook viewers. Rated R for violence. 97m. **DIR:** Mario Azzopardi. **CAST:** Richard Dean Anderson, Michael Shanks, Amanda Tapping, Christopher Judge. **1997 DVD**

STARK ★★★1/2 Above-average TV movie about a Kansas cop butting heads against corrupt Las Vegas politicians and mobsters as he searches for the killers of his sister. Nicolas Surovy's sure performance and Ernest Tidyman's script make this a must for private eye buffs. 95m. **DIR:** Rod Holcomb. **CAST:** Nicolas Surovy, Marilu Henner, Dennis Hopper. 1985

STARLIGHT HOTEL ★★ Familiar tale, although with a new setting: 1929 New Zealand. A 12-year-old runaway bound for Australia heads across the New Zealand countryside. Rated PG for profanity and violence. 91m. **DIR:** Sam Pillsbury. **CAST:** Peter Phelps. 1987

STARMAN ★★★★ Jeff Bridges stars as an alien who falls in love with Earthling Karen Allen. *Starman* is best described as a fairy tale for adults, but the kiddies undoubtedly will enjoy it, too. Rated PG-13 for suggested sex, violence, and profanity. 115m. **DIR:** John Carpenter. **CAST:** Jeff Bridges, Karen Allen, Charles Martin Smith, Richard Jaeckel. 1984 DVD

STARS AND BARS ★★ Inept comedy about a well-groomed British art expert who finds himself in a culture clash when he is sent to rural Georgia to acquire a priceless Renoir from an eccentric businessman. Pretty disappointing considering the fine cast. Rated R for nudity and profanity. 99m. **DIR:** Pat O'Connor. **CAST:** Daniel Day-Lewis, Harry Dean Stanton, Maury Chaykin, Joan Cusack, Keith David, Spalding Gray, Will Patton, Martha Plimpton, Steven Wright. 1988

STARS AND STRIPES FOREVER ★★★ Don't expect an in-depth biography of John Philip Sousa, the March King, and you will probably enjoy this musical tribute. Loud and stirring. Turn up the sound and we can all march around the breakfast table. Good family viewing. 89m. **DIR:** Henry Koster. **CAST:** Clifton Webb, Ruth Hussey, Debra Paget, Robert Wagner. 1952

STARS FELL ON HENRIETTA, THE ★★★★ Strong cast strikes oil in this Depression-era drama. Robert Duvall is wonderful as a prospector who discovers oil underneath the land of Aidan Quinn and family. Getting their permission to drill isn't as precarious as raising the necessary funds. Things heat up when Duvall steals the money from oil man Brian Dennehy. Rated PG for language. 110m. **DIR:** James Keach. **CAST:** Robert Duvall, Aidan Quinn, Frances Fisher, Brian Dennehy. 1995

STARS IN MY CROWN ★★★★ Joel McCrea plays a frontier minister with quiet strength in a warm, gentle tale of pioneer families in the nineteenth century. A strong cast gives the story dignity as well as charm. B&W; 89m. **DIR:** Jacques Tourneur. **CAST:** Joel McCrea, Amanda Blake, James Arness, Ellen Drew, Ed Begley Sr., Alan Hale Sr., Dean Stockwell. 1950

STARS LOOK DOWN, THE ★★★★ Classic film about a Welsh coal miner and his struggle to rise above his station and maintain his identity and the respect of his community is every bit as good today as it was when released. A coup for director Carol Reed and another great performance by Michael Redgrave as a man of quiet dignity and determination. Well worth the watching. B&W; 110m. **DIR:** Carol Reed.

CAST: Michael Redgrave, Margaret Lockwood, Edward Rigby, Emlyn Williams, Cecil Parker. 1939

STARSHIP 🦃 Rebels on a mining planet strive to overcome the evil rulers, who want to replace the workers with robots. Rated PG. 98m. **DIR:** Roger Christian. **CAST:** John Tarrant. 1985

STARSHIP INVASIONS 🦃 How did these wily Canadians get such a top cast for such a dreadful movie? By lying to them about how cheesy it would be, assert Robert Vaughn and Chris Lee. Imagine an amalgam of the worst liabilities of Monogram's early Fifties sci-fi stiffs (e.g., *Flight to Mars*) and Sunn Classics's mid-Seventies UFO schlockumentaries. Rated PG. 87m. **DIR:** Edward Hunt. **CAST:** Robert Vaughn, Christopher Lee, Helen Shaver. 1977

STARSHIP TROOPERS ★★ Some truly awesome special effects do not make up for the lack of dramatic punch in this sci-fi adventure about a group of cadets who graduate to find themselves thrust into an intergalactic war. The film only begins to get interesting at the end, where an abrupt ending seems to suggest that the filmmakers ran out of money. Rated R for violence and profanity. 129m. **DIR:** Paul Verhoeven. **CAST:** Casper Van Dien, Dina Meyer, Denise Richards, Jake Busey, Neil Patrick Harris, Clancy Brown, Michael Ironside. 1997 DVD

STARSTRUCK ★★★1/2 A 17-year-old (Jo Kennedy) wants to be a star and goes after it at top speed. Director Gillian Armstrong has taken the let's-put-on-a-show! plot and turned it into an affable punk-rock movie. Rated PG for nudity and profanity. 95m. **DIR:** Gillian Armstrong. **CAST:** Jo Kennedy, Ross O'Donovan, Max Cullen. 1982

START THE REVOLUTION WITHOUT ME ★★★★ Gene Wilder and Donald Sutherland star in this hilarious comedy as two sets of twins who meet just before the French Revolution. Cheech and Chong's *The Corsican Brothers* covered the same ground. If you want to see the story done right, check this one out. Rated PG. 98m. **DIR:** Bud Yorkin. **CAST:** Gene Wilder, Donald Sutherland, Hugh Griffith, Jack MacGowran. 1970

STARTING OVER ★★★★ Burt Reynolds and Jill Clayburgh are delightful in this Alan Pakula film about two lonely hearts trying to find romance in a cynical world. Candice Bergen is superb as Reynolds's off-key singer/ex-wife, whom he has trouble trying to forget in this winner. Rated R. 106m. **DIR:** Alan J. Pakula. **CAST:** Burt Reynolds, Jill Clayburgh, Candice Bergen, Charles Durning, Frances Sternhagen. 1979

STATE FAIR (1945) ★★★ Wholesome atmosphere marks this nostalgic Middle America story of the adventures of a farm family—Pa's prize hog, Ma's spiked mincemeat, winsome daughter, and yearning son—at the Iowa State Fair. Rodgers and Hammerstein did a standout score for it, winning an Oscar with "It Might As Well Be Spring." Donald Meek's bit as a cooking judge is cameo-sharp comedy. 100m. **DIR:** Walter Lang. **CAST:** Dana Andrews, Jeanne Crain, Vivian Blaine, Dick Haymes, Fay Bainter, Charles Winninger, Donald Meek, Frank McHugh, Percy Kilbride, Harry Morgan. 1945 DVD

STATE FAIR (1962) ★★ Lesser remake of the 1933 and 1945 films focusing on a very wholesome family's visit to the Iowa State Fair. A bit too hokey as predictable romantic situations develop. Only comic moment has Tom Ewell singing to a pig. 118m. **DIR:** José Ferrer. **CAST:** Pat Boone, Bobby Darin, Ann-Margret, Pamela Tiffin, Alice Faye, Tom Ewell. 1962

STATE OF EMERGENCY ★★★★ Overcrowded inner-city emergency wards are the focus of this taut medical drama that emphasizes the impending disintegration of the U.S. hospital network. Performances are top-notch, but you won't be left with a good feeling. Rated R for profanity and graphic surgical procedures. 97m. **DIR:** Lesli Linka Glatter. **CAST:** Joe Mantegna, Lynn Whitfield, Melinda Dillon, Paul Dooley, Richard Beymer. 1994

STATE OF GRACE ★★★ Intriguing first big-budget film from director Phil Joanou focuses on an undercover cop (Sean Penn) who comes back to his old neighborhood to bring down the Irish mob led by childhood friends Ed Harris and Gary Oldman. Oldman's performance is so over the top that he seems to have walked in from a John Waters or David Lynch movie. Rated R for violence, profanity, and nudity. 134m. **DIR:** Phil Joanou. **CAST:** Sean Penn, Ed Harris, Gary Oldman, Robin Wright, John Turturro, John C. Reilly, Burgess Meredith. 1990

STATE OF SIEGE ★★★★ This is a highly controversial but brilliant film about the kidnapping of an American A.I.D. official by left-wing guerrillas in Uruguay. The film follows step-by-step how U.S. aid is sent to fascist countries through the pretext of helping the economy and strengthening democracy. No MPAA rating. 120m. **DIR:** Constantin Costa-Gavras. **CAST:** Yves Montand, O. E. Hasse, Renato Salvatori. 1973

STATE OF THE UNION ★★★ This is a political fable about an American businessman who is encouraged by opportunities to run for the presidency, and leave his integrity behind in the process. Spencer Tracy and Katharine Hepburn are a joy to watch, as usual. B&W; 124m. **DIR:** Frank Capra. **CAST:** Spencer Tracy, Katharine Hepburn, Adolphe Menjou, Van Johnson, Angela Lansbury. 1948

STATE OF THINGS, THE ★★★★1/2 Absorbing account of a film crew stranded on an island in Portugal during the production of a movie dealing with the aftermath of a nuclear holocaust. Running out of money and film stock, the German director, who is a parody of Wim Wenders, attempts to locate an American producer who is on the lam from loan sharks. In German and English. B&W; 120m. **DIR:** Wim Wenders. **CAST:** Allen Garfield, Samuel Fuller, Paul Getty III, Viva, Roger Corman, Patrick Bauchau. 1983

STATELINE MOTEL ★★ This Italian-made film involves a jewelry store robbery by a ruthless killer (Eli Wallach) and his handsome partner, Floyd (Fabio Testi). Not much to the film except the surprise ending featuring Barbara Bach. The film is dubbed and rated R for nudity, violence, sexual situations, and obscenities. 87m. **DIR:** Maurizio Lucidi. **CAST:** Ursula Andress, Eli Wallach, Barbara Bach, Fabio Testi, Massimo Girotti. 1975

STATE'S ATTORNEY ★★1/2 John Barrymore is in good form in this barely believable story of a crooked lawyer who defends a prostitute as a lark and finds himself falling in love. Only in Hollywood, folks. B&W; 80m. **DIR:** George Archainbaud. **CAST:** John Barrymore, Helen Twelvetrees, William "Stage" Boyd. 1932

STATIC ★★★ This highly offbeat drama explores isolation and alienation in human experience and the need to believe in something greater. The story centers around a would-be inventor (Keith Gordon) who attempts to enlighten people through a device that monitors images of Heaven. Surreal film falls somewhere between *Eraserhead* and *True Stories*. Rated R. 93m. **DIR:** Mark Romanek. **CAST:** Keith Gordon, Amanda Plummer, Bob Gunton. 1985

STATION, THE ★★★ Adaptation of a popular Italian stage play takes place during one evening at a small railway station, as the manager meets a beautiful heiress on the run from her fiancé. Fresh, well-acted comic romance. In Italian with English subtitles. Not rated. 92m. **DIR:** Sergio Rubini. **CAST:** Sergio Rubini, Margherita Buy. 1990

STATION WEST ★★★ An army undercover agent (Dick Powell) attempts to find out who is responsible for a rash of gold robberies, eventually falling in love with the ringleader (Jane Greer). This sturdy Western boasts a fine supporting cast, good location cinematography, and nice action scenes. 92m. **DIR:** Sidney Lanfield. **CAST:** Dick Powell, Jane Greer, Tom Powers, Raymond Burr, Agnes Moorehead, Burl Ives, Regis Toomey, Steve Brodie, Guinn Williams. 1948

STATUE, THE 🎔 A Nobel Prize–winning linguist and a nude statue. Rated R for innuendos and nudity. 84m. **DIR:** Rod Amateau. **CAST:** David Niven, Virna Lisi, Robert Vaughn, John Cleese. 1971

STAVISKY ★★★★ Complex drama about a crafty French swindler and a brilliant con man, whose financial exploits in the Thirties brought on riots that helped topple a government. With a superb musical score by Stephen Sondheim and dazzling cinematography by Sacha Vierny. In French with English subtitles. 117m. **DIR:** Alain Resnais. **CAST:** Jean-Paul Belmondo, Anny Duperey, Charles Boyer, Gérard Depardieu. 1974

STAY AS YOU ARE ★★★★ This film begins conventionally but charmingly as the story of a romance between a 20-year-old girl, Francesca (Nastassja Kinski), and Giulio (Marcello Mastroianni), a man old enough to be her father. It remains charming, but the charm becomes mingled with a controlled anguish when it becomes evident that Giulio may indeed be her father. No MPAA rating. 95m. **DIR:** Alberto Lattuada. **CAST:** Nastassja Kinski, Marcello Mastroianni, Francisco Rabal. 1978

STAY AWAY JOE 🎔 A lesser Elvis vehicle. Rated PG for countless sexual situations. 102m. **DIR:** Peter Tewksbury. **CAST:** Elvis Presley, Burgess Meredith, Joan Blondell. 1968

STAY HUNGRY ★★★★1/2 An underrated film dealing with a young southern aristocrat's (Jeff Bridges) attempt to complete a real estate deal by purchasing a bodybuilding gym. Bridges begins to appreciate the gym as well as getting some insights into his own life. Rated R for violence, brief nudity, and language. 103m. **DIR:** Bob Rafelson. **CAST:** Jeff Bridges, Sally Field, R. G. Armstrong, Arnold Schwarzenegger. **1976**

STAY TUNED ★★★ A couch potato buys a devilish satellite dish from the prince of darkness himself. Before long, he and his wife are sucked into a nightmarish world of television where programs like "Meet the Mansons" and "Driving Over Miss Daisy" compete with game shows like "You Can't Win" and "Sadistic Hidden Videos." Dopey fun for the TV generation. Rated PG for mild violence. 98m. **DIR:** Peter Hyams. **CAST:** John Ritter, Pam Dawber, Jeffrey Jones, Eugene Levy, David Tom, Heather McComb. **1992 DVD**

STAYING ALIVE ★★ Sequel to the gutsy, effective *Saturday Night Fever* is a slick, commercial near rip-off. Six years have passed. Tony Manero (John Travolta) now attempts to break into the competitive life of Broadway dancing. Rated PG for language and suggested sex. 96m. **DIR:** Sylvester Stallone. **CAST:** John Travolta, Cynthia Rhodes, Finola Hughes, Steve Inwood. **1983**

STAYING TOGETHER ★★★★ Skillfully directed by Lee Grant, this splendid character study focuses on the McDermott family and the fried-chicken restaurant they run in Ridgeway, South Carolina. You'll be pleasantly surprised at how deeply you become involved with the characters. Rated R for profanity, nudity, and suggested sex. 91m. **DIR:** Lee Grant. **CAST:** Sean Astin, Stockard Channing, Melinda Dillon, Jim Haynie, Levon Helm, Dinah Manoff, Dermot Mulroney, Tim Quill, Keith Szarabajka, Daphne Zuniga. **1989**

STEAGLE, THE ★★★ Black comedy about how a daydreaming college professor (Richard Benjamin) deals with his mortality during the Cuban missile crisis. The week-long living spree he goes on has some hilarious consequences, but the screenplay is not handled very well despite the excellent cast. Rated PG for profanity and sex. 94m. **DIR:** Paul Sylbert. **CAST:** Richard Benjamin, Cloris Leachman, Chill Wills, Susan Tyrrell, Peter Hobbs. **1971**

STEAL BIG, STEAL LITTLE ★★ Adopted twin brothers—one a blue-collar hero full of brotherly love, the other a corporate shark driven by greed—struggle for control of a Santa Barbara lemon ranch owned by their deceased mother. This long, emotionally sluggish movie tries but fails to be a folksy comedy-drama. Rated PG-13 for language and violence. 134m. **DIR:** Andrew Davis. **CAST:** Andy Garcia, Rachel Ticotin, Alan Arkin, Holland Taylor, Joe Pantoliano, David Ogden Stiers, Kevin McCarthy. **1995**

STEAL THE SKY ★★ In this pretentious, melodramatic misfire, first telecast on HBO, Ben Cross is an Iraqi jet pilot who is targeted by Israeli intelligence for its own purposes. Mariel Hemingway is the agent assigned to seduce him into cooperating. Not rated. 110m. **DIR:** John Hancock. **CAST:** Ben Cross, Mariel Hemingway. **1988**

STEALING BEAUTY ★★★★ Tuscany's lush countryside and a gorgeous villa provide the idyllic setting for this slight but intoxicating tale of blossoming womanhood. A gawky late-teen virgin searches for love and answers to the mysteries of her mom's diary in Italy. Rated R for language, nudity, and sex. 102m.

DIR: Bernardo Bertolucci. **CAST:** Liv Tyler, Jeremy Irons, Donal McCann, Sinead Cusack, Rachel Weisz, D. W. Moffett, Stefania Sandrelli, Jean Marais. **1996**

STEALING HEAVEN ★★ Middle Ages story of a forbidden love between a member of the clergy and a beautiful young aristocrat—Abelard and Heloise. Lots of lust and guilt but little else to sustain the film. Rated R for nudity. 108m. **DIR:** Clive Donner. **CAST:** Derek de Lint, Kim Thomson, Denholm Elliott. **1988**

STEALING HOME ★★★1/2 Enjoyable and sporadically disarming character study about a gifted athlete who renews his commitment to baseball after several years of aimless drifting. An ensemble cast does a fine job with this bittersweet tale. Rated PG-13 for profanity and suggested sex. 98m. **DIR:** Steven Kampmann, Will Aldis. **CAST:** Mark Harmon, Jodie Foster, Blair Brown, John Shea, Jonathan Silverman, Harold Ramis. **1988 DVD**

STEAMBOAT BILL JR. ★★★★1/2 Buster Keaton is at his comedic-genius best in this delightful silent film as an accident-prone college student who is forced to take over his father's old Mississippi steamboat. The climax features spectacular stunts by Keaton. It is truly something to behold—and to laugh with. Silent. B&W; 71m. **DIR:** Charles F. Reisner. **CAST:** Buster Keaton, Ernest Torrence, Marion Byron. **1928 DVD**

STEAMING ★★ Nell Dunn's play takes place in an English Turkish-style bathhouse where a group of women share their feelings about life. Vanessa Redgrave lends some needed reality to this sweaty gabfest. Rated R. 112m. **DIR:** Joseph Losey. **CAST:** Vanessa Redgrave, Sarah Miles, Diana Dors, Brenda Bruce, Felicity Dean. **1984**

STEEL (1980) ★★★ Plenty of action and stunts keep this minor film popping along surprisingly well. Lee Majors stars as the head of a construction crew struggling to complete a skyscraper on schedule. Majors is almost convincing, and a strong cast of character actors are great fun to watch. Rated R. 99m. **DIR:** Steve Carver. **CAST:** Lee Majors, Jennifer O'Neill, Art Carney, George Kennedy, Harris Yulin, Terry Kiser, Richard Lynch, Roger E. Mosley, Albert Salmi, R. G. Armstrong. **1980**

STEEL (1997) ★★1/2 Following DC Comics' temporary demise of Superman, new heroes were created to protect Metropolis. One of these newcomers was Steel, an idealistic army weapons engineer named John Henry Irons. Watchable with explosive special effects. Rated PG-13 for violence. 94m. **DIR:** Kenneth Johnson. **CAST:** Shaquille O'Neal, Judd Nelson, Annabeth Gish, Richard Roundtree, Gary Graham, Eric Pierpoint, Charles Napier. **1997**

STEEL AND LACE ★★ A rather depressingly brutal sci-fi thriller involving a classical pianist's brutal gang rape. Her brother, an ex-NASA scientist, plots to reap revenge on her attackers. Rated R for language and violence. 92m. **DIR:** Ernest Farino. **CAST:** Bruce Davison, David Naughton, Clare Wren, Stacy Naiduk, Michael Cerveris, David L. Lander, Brian Backer, John J. York. **1991**

STEEL DAWN ♥ Brainless bore set in the post-apocalyptic future has martial arts warrior joining in to help widow protect a colony of peaceful settlers. Rated R for violence. 100m. **DIR:** Lance Hool. **CAST:** Patrick Swayze, Lisa Niemi, Christopher Neame, Brion James, Anthony Zerbe. 1987

STEEL FRONTIER ★★ Poor version of *The Road Warrior* in which a band of killers terrorizes a helpless town, and an unknown hero comes to save the day. Rated R for violence and profanity. 100m. **DIR:** Paul G. Volk, Jacobsen Hart. **CAST:** Joe Lara, Bo Svenson, Stacie Foster, Brion James. 1994

STEEL HELMET, THE ★★★1/2 Director-writer Samuel Fuller's war movies actually improve with age. This one, shot (as usual) on a low budget and set in the Korean War, is packed with irony, lightning pace and vivid action. A war movie made with style and authority. B&W; 84m. **DIR:** Samuel Fuller. **CAST:** Gene Evans, Robert Hutton, Steve Brodie, James Edwards. 1951

STEEL MAGNOLIAS ★★★1/2 An all-star cast in a classy tearjerker about the enduring friendships among six women in a small southern town. Rated PG for brief profanity. 118m. **DIR:** Herbert Ross. **CAST:** Sally Field, Dolly Parton, Shirley MacLaine, Daryl Hannah, Olympia Dukakis, Julia Roberts, Sam Shepard, Tom Skerritt. 1989

STEEL SHARKS ★★ The botched rescue attempt of an American scientist causes an elite commando squad to be captured and held hostage on an enemy submarine. It's up to Gary Busey and Billy Dee Williams to save the day. Derivative situations, stock characters, and unimaginative direction and special effects sabotage this murky thriller every step of the way. Rated R for language and violence. 94m. **DIR:** Rodney McDonald. **CAST:** Gary Busey, Billy Dee Williams, Billy Warlock, Shaun Toub, Barry Livingston. 1996

STEELE JUSTICE 💜 One-man-army Martin Kove is hired to wipe out the Vietnamese Mafia in Los Angeles. Rated R for profanity and violence. 94m. **DIR:** Robert Boris. **CAST:** Martin Kove, Sela Ward, Ronny Cox, Bernie Casey, Joseph Campanella, Sarah Douglas, Soon-Teck Oh. 1987

STEELE'S LAW ★★ Fred Williamson is Chicago's answer to *Dirty Harry* as he goes undercover in Texas. Williamson wears all hats—as director, producer, story-idea creator, and star—in this barely watchable actioner. Not rated, contains nudity, profanity, and violence. 90m. **DIR:** Fred Williamson. **CAST:** Fred Williamson, Bo Svenson. 1991 **DVD**

STEELYARD BLUES ★★★1/2 This is a quirky little film about a group of social misfits who band together to help one of their own against his government-employed brother. Jane Fonda, Donald Sutherland, and Peter Boyle seem to have fun playing the misfits. Boyle's imitation of Marlon Brando is a highlight. Rated PG for language. 93m. **DIR:** Alan Myerson. **CAST:** Jane Fonda, Donald Sutherland, Peter Boyle, Alan Myerson, Garry Goodrow. 1973

STELLA (1950) ★★ A family of screwballs and the suspicion of murder don't add up in this black comedy of errors. David Wayne believes he killed his uncle, buried the body, and forgot where. A moderately likable misfire. B&W; 83m. **DIR:** Claude Binyon. **CAST:** Ann Sheridan, Victor Mature, David Wayne, Leif Erickson, Frank Fontaine. 1950

●**STELLA (1955)** ★★★ Melina Mercouri made her screen debut in this melodrama as a free-spirited bar singer who leads two men to tragic ends. She's appealingly sexy, though the film (despite able work by director Michael Cacoyannis, who went on to make *Zorba the Greek*) is a bit dreary. In Greek with English subtitles. **CAST:** Melina Mercouri, Yiorgo Fountas. 1955

STELLA (1990) ★★ The Divine Miss M. takes a pratfall in this sudsy, airheaded remake of *Stella Dallas*. As in the original 1937 film, Bette Midler's Stella is a working-class gal who gives up her daughter to be raised by her wealthy father. Unfortunately for the film, the social conditions that existed during the Great Depression no longer prevail, and Stella's sacrifice seems stupid rather than noble. Rated PG-13 for profanity and frank sexual themes. 106m. **DIR:** John Erman. **CAST:** Bette Midler, John Goodman, Trini Alvarado, Stephen Collins, Marsha Mason. 1990

STELLA DALLAS ★★★★ Barbara Stanwyck's title-role performance as the small-town vulgar innocent who sacrifices everything for her daughter got her a well-deserved Oscar nomination and set the standard for this type of screen character. John Boles is the elegant wealthy heel who does her wrong. Anne Shirley is Laurel, the object of her mother's completely self-effacing conduct. B&W; 111m. **DIR:** King Vidor. **CAST:** Barbara Stanwyck, Anne Shirley, John Boles, Alan Hale Sr., Tim Holt, Marjorie Main. 1937 **DVD**

STELLA MARIS ★★★★★ Arguably Mary Pickford's masterpiece, although it stands in stark contrast to the sweetness-and-light qualities of many other popular vehicles. Some amazing double-exposure photography allows her to play *two* roles, a beautiful invalid and an ugly drab who plays an important part in the invalid's life. Silent. B&W; 70m. **DIR:** Marshall Neilan. **CAST:** Mary Pickford, Conway Tearle. 1918 **DVD**

●**STENDHAL SYNDROME, THE** ★★★1/2 One of the most complex films ever from Italian director Dario Argento, this is also his most character-driven piece. The director's daughter Asia Argento stars as a detective engaged in a game of cat and mouse with a serial rapist/killer. This film marks Argento's return to the form of his earlier *giallos* with its complexities and a brutality that seems to become an art form of its own. Haunting. Not rated; contains violence, nudity, and simulated sex. 113m. **DIR:** Dario Argento. **CAST:** Asia Argento, Thomas Kretschmann, John Quentin. 1998 **DVD**

STEP LIVELY ★★★1/2 As a jazzy, bright musical remake of the Marx Brothers film *Room Service*, this film is a very enjoyable story about George Murphy's attempt to get his show produced on Broadway. It's in this film that Frank Sinatra receives his first screen kisses (from Gloria DeHaven), which caused swoons from numerous female Sinatraphiles. As the hotel manager, Walter Slezak almost steals the show. 89m. **DIR:** Tim Whelan. **CAST:** Frank Sinatra, George Murphy, Walter Slezak, Adolphe Menjou. 1944

STEPFATHER, THE ★★★★ Jerry Blake (Terry O'Quinn) is so relentlessly cheerful that his stepdaughter, Stephanie Maine (Jill Schoelen), complains to a friend, "It's just like living with Ward Cleaver." Little does she know that the accent should be on the cleaver. Jerry, you see, is a raving maniac. A thriller of a chiller. Rated R for violence, profanity, and brief nudity. 90m. DIR: Joseph Ruben. CAST: Terry O'Quinn, Shelley Hack, Jill Schoelen, Charles Lanyer, Stephen Shellen. 1987

STEPFATHER II ★★ A misfire because it obviously tries to take advantage of its predecessor. The psychotic killer from the first film starts the same routine all over again by posing as a marriage counselor and preying on unsuspecting divorcées and widows. Rated R for gratuitous violence. 86m. DIR: Jeff Burr. CAST: Terry O'Quinn, Meg Foster, Henry Brown, Jonathan Brandis, Caroline Williams, Mitchell Laurance. 1989

STEPFATHER III: FATHER'S DAY ★★ Make room for daddy once again, as the world's worst father returns after escaping from an insane asylum, having had his face surgically altered. Obviously the filmmaker hasn't heard of family values. Rated R for violence and language. 109m. DIR: Guy Magar. CAST: Robert Wrightman, Priscilla Barnes, Season Hubley. 1992

•**STEPFORD HUSBANDS, THE** ★★1/2 Once more back to Connecticut for a tale of programmable zombies. Donna Mills stars as a wife trying to free her husband, novelist Michael Ontkean, from the experiment. The script has a been-there-done-that feel to it. Not rated; contains mild violence. 120m. DIR: Fred Walton. CAST: Donna Mills, Michael Ontkean, Sarah Douglas, Louise Fletcher, Cindy Williams. 1996

STEPFORD WIVES, THE ★★★ Ira Levin's "adult horror story" is a letdown after *Rosemary's Baby* and nowhere near as credible. Small-town newcomers can't quite figure out why all the other women in their community act so perpetually euphoric; the answer concerns a bit of misguided technology and the need to believe that all men are pigs. Rated PG for brief nudity. 115m. DIR: Bryan Forbes. CAST: Katharine Ross, Paula Prentiss, Peter Masterson, Patrick O'Neal. 1975 DVD

STEPHEN KING'S GOLDEN YEARS (TV SERIES) ★★★ Seven-episode TV miniseries about an elderly janitor who is exposed to a mysterious form of radiation during a lab accident at a secret government research facility. Soon the old man finds himself slowly growing younger and developing unexplained powers, while being pursued by a shadowy intelligence organization. Quirky, funny, and suspenseful. Not rated; contains violence and adult situations. 292m. DIR: Stephen Tolkin, Michael Gornick, Allen Coulter, Kenneth Fink. CAST: Keith Szarabajka, Felicity Huffman, Frances Sternhagen, Ed Lauter. 1991

STEPHEN KING'S GRAVEYARD SHIFT (1990) ★★ Based on a short story from King's *Night Shift* collection, this is a disappointing film about workers who are menaced by a giant mutant rat-bat while cleaning a factory basement. Rated R for violence, profanity, and gore. 90m. DIR: Ralph S. Singleton. CAST: David Andrews, Kelly Wolf, Stephen Macht, Brad Dourif, Andrew Divoff. 1990

STEPHEN KING'S SLEEPWALKERS ★★ An incestuous mother-son duo stalk virginal young women to feed their vampirelike hunger in this film of an original script from Stephen King. This film differs from his books in that it lacks all the things that make a Stephen King novel a Stephen King novel: fully fleshed out characters interacting in a cohesive plot. Rated R for violence, profanity, and gore. 91m. DIR: Mick Garris. CAST: Brian Krause, Madchen Amick, Alice Krige, Jim Haynie, Cindy Pickett, Ron Perlman. 1992

STEPHEN KING'S THE SHINING ★★★1/2 King's disappointment over Stanley Kubrick's version of his bestselling novel resulted in this spooky made-for-television miniseries that's more true to King's vision. King wrote the screenplay himself, thus fleshing out the nightmare that awaits the Torrance family when they agree to act as caretakers for the Overlook Hotel. Not rated; contains violence. 270m. DIR: Mick Garris. CAST: Steven Weber, Rebecca De-Mornay, Courtland Mead, Melvin Van Peebles. 1997

STEPMOM ★★ Fluffy little tale concerns Julia Roberts's efforts to win the respect, if not actual affection, of her fiance's two children, who'd much rather stay with divorced mom Susan Sarandon. Unfortunately, Susan Sarandon's character is so cruel and abrasive that you'll quickly cease to care about her, even when the film plunges into its lamentable third act. Rated PG-13 for profanity and sexual candor. 124m. DIR: Chris Columbus. CAST: Julia Roberts, Susan Sarandon, Ed Harris, Jena Malone, Liam Aiken. 1998 DVD

STEPMONSTER ★★★★ A Tropopkin, a comic-book monster who can assume a human form, becomes engaged to a man. His son, who's an avid comic-book reader, realizes what is happening, but no one believes him. Enjoyable for all ages, with good acting all around. Rated PG-13 for profanity and violence. 87m. DIR: Jeremy Stanford. CAST: Alan Thicke, Robin Riker, George Gaynes, Ami Dolenz, Edie McClurg, John Astin, Corey Feldman, Billy Corben, Molly Cheek. 1992

STEPPENWOLF ★★1/2 In this United States–Switzerland coproduction, director Fred Haines gives us an almost literal adaptation of Hermann Hesse's most widely read novel. It's a good try, but the source really isn't filmable. Rated PG. 105m. DIR: Fred Haines. CAST: Max von Sydow, Dominique Sanda, Pierre Clementi. 1974

STEPPING OUT ★★★1/2 Musical-comedy fans will delight in this sweet-natured, lightweight story of a struggling dance teacher (Liza Minnelli) who decides to coach her generally inept students into a crack dance troupe. A first-rate cast, and Minnelli sparkles with enthusiasm. Rated PG for profanity. 101m. DIR: Lewis Gilbert. CAST: Liza Minnelli, Shelley Winters, Bill Irwin, Ellen Greene, Julie Walters, Jane Krakowski, Sheila McCarthy, Andrea Martin. 1991

STEPSISTER, THE ★★ A young woman's father remarries, and she gains a stepsister as well as a stepmother. From the start, the stepsisters don't get along, and things soon turn nasty. This made-for-cable thriller might have been a good movie if it had a better plot, better acting, and a better script. Rated PG-13 for violence. 95m. **DIR:** Charles Correll. **CAST:** Rena Sofer, Bridgette Wilson, Richard Joseph Paul, Alan Rachins, Linda Evans. **1997**

STERILE CUCKOO, THE ★★★★ Painfully poignant story about a dedicated young college lad (Wendell Burton) and the loopy young woman (Liza Minnelli) who, unable to handle people on their own terms, demands too much of those with whom she becomes involved. Minnelli's Pookie Adams won the actress a well-deserved Academy Award nomination. Rated PG for sexual situations. 107m. **DIR:** Alan J. Pakula. **CAST:** Liza Minnelli, Wendell Burton, Tim McIntire. **1969**

STEVIE ★★★★ Glenda Jackson gives a brilliant performance as reclusive poet Stevie Smith in this stagy, but still interesting, film. Mona Washbourne is the film's true delight as Smith's doting—and slightly dotty—aunt. Trevor Howard narrates and costars in this British release. Rated PG for brief profanity. 102m. **DIR:** Robert Enders. **CAST:** Glenda Jackson, Mona Washbourne, Trevor Howard, Alec McCowen. **1978**

STEWARDESS SCHOOL ✔ Perfectly awful stewardess comedy. Rated PG. 93m. **DIR:** Ken Blancato. **CAST:** Judy Landers, Wendie Jo Sperber, Sandahl Bergman, Brett Cullen, Mary Cadorette, Vicki Frederick, Vito Scotti, Donny Most. **1987**

STICK ★★★ *Stick* is an odd mixture of comedy and violence that more than once strains the viewer's suspension of disbelief. Fans of the original novel, by Elmore Leonard, will be shocked at how far Burt Reynolds's film strays from its source. What should have been a tough, lean, and mean movie contains a surprising amount of clowning by its stars. Despite all this, it has enough action and genuine laughs to please Reynolds's fans. Rated R for profanity and violence. 109m. **DIR:** Burt Reynolds. **CAST:** Burt Reynolds, Charles Durning, George Segal, Candice Bergen. **1985**

STICK TO YOUR GUNS ★★ The old Bar-20 crowd is summoned to fight a gang of slick rustlers, and Hopalong Cassidy and California get to the trouble first. Assuming false identities, the two are invited to join the outlaw gang and then alert the Bar-20 boys. A silly subplot, too many songs, and too much Andy Clyde attempting humor mar this otherwise gritty series entry, which is a who's who of veteran actors. B&W; 63m. **DIR:** Lesley Selander. **CAST:** William Boyd, Andy Clyde, Brad King, Dick Curtis, Jacqueline Holt, Charles Middleton, Kermit Maynard. **1941**

STICK-UP, THE ✔ The alternate title, *Mud*, seems more appropriate for this dreary romance-adventure set in 1935 England. 101m. **DIR:** Jeffrey Bloom. **CAST:** David Soul, Pamela McMyler. **1977**

STICKY FINGERS ✔ Two struggling female musicians are handed $900,000 in dirty money by a drug-dealing friend. Rated PG-13 for language and sexual allusions. 89m. **DIR:** Catlin Adams. **CAST:** Helen Slater, Melanie Mayron, Eileen Brennan, Christopher Guest, Stephen McHattie, Shirley Stoler, Gwen Welles, Danitra Vance, Carol Kane. **1988**

STIGMA ✔ An ex–medical student just out of prison battles prejudice and an epidemic of VD in a shel-

tered island community. 93m. **DIR:** David E. Durston. **CAST:** Philip Michael Thomas. **1972**

●STIGMATA ★★ Atheist Pittsburgh hairdresser receives rosary beads in the mail that were stolen from a dead South American priest and experiences seizures and bloody wounds associated with the crucifixion of Jesus. A priest-scientist investigates while a cardinal emphasizes public-relations spin control over The Truth. This pretentious, mind-numbing religious thriller is a sort of MTV version of *The Exorcist* sensationalized by a Vatican conspiracy. Rated R for violence, language, and sexual content. 102m. **DIR:** Rupert Wainwright. **CAST:** Patricia Arquette, Gabriel Byrne, Jonathan Pryce, Nia Long. **1999 DVD**

STILETTO ✔ A rich jet-setter also happens to be a professional killer. Rated R. 98m. **DIR:** Bernard Kowalski. **CAST:** Alex Cord, Britt Ekland, Patrick O'Neal, Barbara McNair. **1969**

STILL CRAZY ★★1/2 This lightly amusing comedy is a sort of *Full Monty* meets *Spinal Tap*. British rock dinosaurs from the 1970s attempt a reunion tour of their group Strange Fruit to tune up for the anniversary restaging of a legendary rock concert. Trouble brews as the middle-aged lads discover they are very rusty at rocking and are still nagged by past personality conflicts. Rated R for language, sexuality, and drug content. 94m. **DIR:** Brian Gibson. **CAST:** Stephen Rea, Timothy Spall, Jimmy Nail, Bill Nighy, Juliet Aubrey, Billy Connelly. **1998 DVD**

STILL NOT QUITE HUMAN ★★1/2 While still delivering family fun, this made-for-cable film is the weakest and most unbelievable in the Disney trilogy. Chip's scientist father (Alan Thicke) is cloned by an evil scientist. Chip must find his real dad who is being tortured to reveal his computer technology secrets. 90m. **DIR:** Eric Luke. **CAST:** Alan Thicke, Jay Underwood, Christopher Neame, Rosa Nevin, Betsy Palmer. **1992**

STILL OF THE NIGHT ★★★1/2 In this well-crafted thriller by writer-director Robert Benton a psychiatrist (Roy Scheider) falls in love with an art curator (Meryl Streep) who may have killed one of his patients and may be after him next. If you like being scared out of your wits, you won't want to miss it. Rated PG for violence and adult themes. 91m. **DIR:** Robert Benton. **CAST:** Roy Scheider, Meryl Streep, Jessica Tandy, Joe Grifasi, Sara Botsford. **1982**

STILL SMOKIN' ✔ Shambles about a film festival in Amsterdam. Rated R for nudity and scatological humor. 91m. **DIR:** Thomas Chong. **CAST:** Cheech and Chong, Hansman In't Veld, Carol Van Herwijnen. **1983**

STILTS, THE (LOS ZANCOS) ★★★1/2 This film, about an aged playwright and professor (Fernando Fernán Gomez) who falls in love with a young actress (Laura Del Sol), is occasionally melodramatic. Her unwillingness to commit herself to him gives the film its tension, and the acting is good enough to overcome most of the overwrought moments. In Spanish with English subtitles. Not rated; contains nudity. 95m. **DIR:** Carlos Saura. **CAST:** Laura Del Sol, Fernando Fernán-Gomez, Francisco Rabal, Antonio Banderas. **1984**

STING, THE ★★★★1/2 Those *Butch Cassidy and the Sundance Kid* stars, Paul Newman and Robert edford, were reunited for this fast-paced entertainment as two con men who outcon a con. Winner of seven Academy Awards—including best picture—is film, directed by George Roy Hill (*A Little Romance* and *Butch Cassidy*) revived Scott Joplin's usic. For that, and the more obvious reasons, it is ot to be missed. Rated PG. 129m. **DIR:** George Roy ll. **CAST:** Paul Newman, Robert Redford, Robert haw, Charles Durning, Ray Walston, Eileen Brennan, arold Gould, Dana Elcar. **1973 DVD**

TING II, THE ★★ You could hardly expect a sequel such a joyously entertaining film as *The Sting* to easure up. True to those expectations, this film, arring Jackie Gleason, Mac Davis, Teri Garr, and arl Malden, doesn't come close. Rated PG for violence. 102m. **DIR:** Jeremy Paul Kagan. **CAST:** Jackie leason, Mac Davis, Teri Garr, Karl Malden, Oliver eed, Bert Remsen. **1983**

TINGRAY 🖤 Two young men buy a Stingray, unaware that it's filled with stolen cash and drugs. ated R for violence and profanity. 100m. **DIR:** ichard Taylor. **CAST:** Chris Mitchum, Sherry Jackson, ill Watson. **1978**

TIR CRAZY ★★★1/2 Richard Pryor and Gene Vilder work something close to a miracle, making omething out of nothing or, at least, close to nothing. It's a simpleminded spoof of crime and prison novies with, of all things, a little *Urban Cowboy* hrown in. But you have so much fun watching the tars, you don't mind. Rated R. 111m. **DIR:** Sidney oitier. **CAST:** Richard Pryor, Gene Wilder, Georg Stanord Brown, JoBeth Williams. **1980 DVD**

STIR OF ECHOES ★★★1/2 Two films released during the summer of 1999 found characters trying to elp the dead rest easy; everybody raved about *The ixth Sense*, while this one quietly came and went. It eserved better; director-scripter David Koepp intelgently adapted Richard Matheson's 1958 novel, and tar Kevin Bacon credibly plays a working-class guy vho, after an experimentation with hypnosis, finds imself "open" to all sorts of phenomena. It turns out hat his young son *also* possesses this "gift," and both and their talent utilized in an unsolved murder case hat has remained a neighborhood dark secret. Koepp displays plenty of imagination as a visual stylst; the key murder, shown through the eyes of the ictim rather than the killer, is nothing short of chillng, in terms of conveying the sheer, ghastly horror of he moment. Rated R for profanity, violence, and ape. 99m. **DIR:** David Koepp. **CAST:** Kevin Bacon, Kathryn Erbe, Illeana Douglas, Liza Weil, Kevin Dunn, Zachary David Cope. **1999 DVD**

STITCHES 🖤 Med school students playing pranks. Rated R. 92m. **DIR:** Alan Smithee. **CAST:** Parker Stevenson, Geoffrey Lewis, Eddie Albert. **1985**

STOCKS AND BLONDES 🖤 A female college student researches a paper on corporate takeovers and unearths some dirty work. Rated R. 79m. **DIR:** Arthur Greenstands. **CAST:** Leigh Wood, Veronica Hart. **1984**

STOLEN FACE ★★ Early Hammer Films sleeper from the British studio's greatest director, Terence Fisher. Imported American lead Paul Henreid plays a noted plastic surgeon who remakes a female convict's face into the image of a woman he loved and

lost. Taut and imaginative low-budget item. B&W; 72m. **DIR:** Terence Fisher. **CAST:** Paul Henreid, Lizabeth Scott, Andre Morell, Mary Mackenzie. **1952**

STOLEN HEARTS 🖤 Even the strippers are dull in this erotic thriller about a club owner who hires a private detective to find the con man who robbed her. Rated R for nudity and sexual situations. 82m. **DIR:** Ralph Portillo. **CAST:** Landon Hall, Paula Aletonis, Vincent Dale. **1995**

STOLEN HOURS ★★1/2 A fair remake of the classic 1939 Bette Davis tearjerker, *Dark Victory*. Susan Hayward is a fun-loving playgirl who learns she has only months to live and tries to make her limited time meaningful. Okay … if you haven't seen the original. 97m. **DIR:** Daniel Petrie. **CAST:** Susan Hayward, Michael Craig, Diane Baker, Edward Judd. **1963**

STOLEN KISSES ★★★★★ This is François Truffaut's third film in the continuing story about Antoine Doinel (Jean-Pierre Léaud) that began with *400 Blows*. Like the other films in the series, this work resembles Truffaut's autobiography as he romantically captures the awkwardness of Doinel and his encounters with women. This delightful comedy is often considered one of Truffaut's best movies. In French with English subtitles. 90m. **DIR:** François Truffaut. **CAST:** Jean-Pierre Léaud, Delphine Seyrig, Michel Lonsdale, Claude Jade, Daniel Ceccaldi. **1968 DVD**

STOLEN LIFE, A ★★★ Bette Davis produced this film herself. It shows her histrionic talents off to good advantage because she plays twins—one good, the other bad. When one sister takes over the other's life, she also takes the boyfriend they both want. B&W; 109m. **DIR:** Curtis Bernhardt. **CAST:** Bette Davis, Glenn Ford, Dane Clark, Bruce Bennett, Charlie Ruggles, Walter Brennan. **1946**

STONE BOY, THE ★★★★★ A superb ensemble cast elevates this rural *Ordinary People*–style film about a boy who accidentally shoots the older brother he adores and begins losing touch with reality. It's a tough subject, exquisitely handled. For some reason, this fine film was never theatrically released on a wide scale. Rated PG for brief violence and some profanity. 93m. **DIR:** Christopher Cain. **CAST:** Robert Duvall, Frederic Forrest, Glenn Close, Wilford Brimley. **1984**

STONE COLD ★★★ Ex–football player Brian Bosworth's motion picture debut is better than might be expected. "The Boz" plays an undercover cop who infiltrates a sleazy group of motorcycle outlaws. Rated R for violence, nudity, and profanity. 90m. **DIR:** Craig R. Baxley. **CAST:** Brian Bosworth, Lance Henriksen, William Forsythe, Sam McMurray. **1991**

STONE COLD DEAD ★★ This fair film, based on the novel *Sin Sniper* by Hugh Garner, centers on the investigation by Sergeant Boyd (Richard Crenna) into a bizarre series of prostitute killings. Rated R. 97m. **DIR:** George Mendeluk. **CAST:** Richard Crenna, Belinda Montgomery, Paul Williams, Linda Sorenson. **1980**

STONE FOX, THE ★★★ A boy and his dog enter a sled race hoping to win enough money to save the family farm. Predictable, made-for-TV story with some memorable race sequences. Not rated; contains no objectionable scenes. 96m. DIR: Harvey Hart. CAST: Joey Cramer, Buddy Ebsen, Belinda Montgomery, Gordon Tootoosis. 1987

STONE KILLER, THE ★★★1/2 A *Dirty Harry*–style cop thriller, this casts Charles Bronson as a no-nonsense New York cop who gets transferred to Los Angeles because of his direct way of dealing with guntoting criminals ... he shoots them. It packs a wallop. Rated R. 95m. DIR: Michael Winner. CAST: Charles Bronson, Martin Balsam, David Sheiner, Norman Fell, Ralph Waite. 1973

STONE OF SILVER CREEK ★★★★ Another of producer-star Buck Jones's superior Westerns for Universal, this offbeat, often funny movie casts Jones as a straight-shooting saloon owner who fights off a pair of persistent baddies, gives the town preacher an education in manliness, and weighs in as an all-around champion of justice. B&W; 62m. DIR: Nick Grindé. CAST: Buck Jones, Noel Francis. 1935

STONED AGE, THE ★★1/2 Somewhat enjoyable teen romp about a couple of stoner dudes out looking for drugs, babes, and parties. They run into the usual complications, but also get to listen to a cool soundtrack featuring classic 1970s rock 'n' roll. Rated R for drug use, adult situations, and language. 90m. DIR: James Melkonian. CAST: Michael Kopelow, Bradford Tatum, China Kantner, Renee Ammann, David Groh, Frankie Avalon. 1993 DVD

STONES OF DEATH 🎭 Nothing new here: teenagers getting knocked off one by one by supernatural forces. Rated R for nudity, profanity, and violence. 95m. DIR: James Bagle. CAST: Zoe Carides, Tom Jennings, Eric Oldfield. 1988

STONEWALL ★★ Director Nigel Finch's film, originally produced for British TV, is set against the background of the 1969 riots that erupted when the New York Police Department raided the Stonewall Tavern, a popular gay hangout. The film's intentions are good, but it's a trite soap opera, not very well acted, and Finch's shoestring budget is all too obvious. Rated R for profanity. 99m. DIR: Nigel Finch. CAST: Guillermo Diaz, Frederick Weller, Brendan Corbalis, Bruce MacVittie, Duane Boutte. 1996 DVD

STOOGEMANIA 🎭 It's the story of Howard F. Howard (Josh Mostel), a man whose life is controlled by watching Three Stooges films. Not rated. 83m. DIR: Chuck Workman. CAST: Josh Mostel, Melanie Chartoff, Sid Caesar, Moe Howard, Curly Howard, Larry Fine, Shemp Howard. 1985

STOP MAKING SENSE ★★★★ This has been called a star vehicle. Filmed over a three-night period in December 1983 at Hollywood's Pantages Theater, the movie is a straight recording of a Talking Heads concert that offers the movie audience front-row-center seats. It offers great fun for the band's fans. Rated PG for suggestive lyrics. 88m. DIR: Jonathan Demme. CAST: Talking Heads. 1984

STOP! OR MY MOM WILL SHOOT ★★★ Silly farce about a cop attempting to survive a visit by his overbearing mother. Anyone who is disappointed by this piece of fluff should have known better than to rent it in the first place. Rated PG. 87m. DIR: Roger Spottiswoode. CAST: Sylvester Stallone, Estelle Getty, Jo-

Beth Williams, Roger Rees, Martin Ferrero, Gailar Sartain, Dennis Burkley. 1992

STOP THE WORLD I WANT TO GET OFF ★★★1/ Filmed version of the Broadway musical, an allegoi about a little fellow who wonders if he's a fool or no because of his romantic and political adventure: Good music, lively songs, and energetic dance num bers, but not mass-appeal material. 98m. DIR: Victc Saville. CAST: Tony Tanner, Millicent Martin. 1966

STOPOVER TOKYO ★★ Based on a story by John Marquand, this ho-hum espionage tale has an Amer can spy (Robert Wagner) chasing a communist ur dercover agent all over Tokyo. Wagner is earnest, a usual, but even the cast's enthusiasm can't put lif into this one. Joan Collins is worth watching, as a ways. 100m. DIR: Richard L. Breen. CAST: Robe Wagner, Edmond O'Brien, Joan Collins, Ken Scot 1957

STORM ★★★ Thieves return years after the crim to dig up their buried cache. Suspenseful low-budge film. Rated PG-13 for violence. 100m. DIR: Davi Winning. CAST: David Palfy. 1987

STORM AND SORROW ★★1/2 Lori Singer is th "Rocky Mountain Spider Woman" who joins a 197 expedition to climb one of Russia's highest moun tains. Gorgeous scenery, but s-l-o-w going as peopl trudge through snow, pant, rest, then trudge som more. Made for TV. 96m. DIR: Richard A. Colla. CAST Lori Singer. 1990

STORM IN A TEACUP ★★★ The refusal of an ol lady to pay for a dog license touches off this amusin farrago on love, politics, and life. Rex Harrison is, o course, smashing. The dialogue is the thing. B&W 87m. DIR: Victor Saville, Ian Dalrymple. CAST: Vivier Leigh, Rex Harrison, Cecil Parker, Sara Allgood. 1937

•**STORM OF THE CENTURY** ★★★★ Quite possibl one of the best adaptations of the work of Stephei King to the screen, this TV miniseries captures th essence of what makes a King book scary: that evi can be anywhere, even in your own backyard. Colm Feore is subtly menacing as the demonic Andre Linoge, a stranger who comes to a small, isolated is land during a devastating snowstorm and begin killing the populace until they agree to give hin what he wants. The violence of Linoge and the loneli ness and despair of the townsfolk is effectively mir rored in the raging of the storm. Rated PG-13 for vio lence and intense situations. 247m. DIR: Craig R. Baxley. CAST: Tim Daly, Colm Feore, Debrah Farentino. 1999 DVD

STORM OVER ASIA ★★★★ Also known as *The Heir to Genghis Khan*, this masterpiece is from the great Russian director, Vsevolod Pudovkin. It tells the story of a young Mongol hunter who is discovered to be the heir of the great Khan. A superb example of the formal beauty of the silent film. Silent. B&W; 102m. DIR: V. I. Pudovkin. CAST: Valeri Inkizhinov. 1928 DVD

•**STORM TRACKER** ★★1/2 Luke Perry stars as a meteorologist who is developing a revolutionary new technology that can control the direction of storm fronts. Martin Sheen plays a renegade general who has commandeered this technology, and is threatening Los Angeles with a hurricane that would level the ty. Cheesy special effects combined with half-hearted performances make for a long ninety minutes. Not rated; may be inappropriate for children. **DIR:** Harris Done. **CAST:** Luke Perry, Martin sheen. **1999 DVD**

ORMQUEST ♥ Amazon women battling a band of renegade men from a neighboring tribe. Not rated. **DIR:** Alex Sessa. **CAST:** Brent Huff. **1987**

TORMY MONDAY ★★★★ In this stylish British thriller, Melanie Griffith and Sean Bean play unlikely lovers who attempt to stop ruthless American businessman Tommy Lee Jones from taking over a jazz nightclub owned by Sting. The generally strong performances, inventive filmmaking techniques, and offbeat sensibilities make the film worth watching. Rated R for violence. 93m. **DIR:** Mike Figgis. **CAST:** Melanie Griffith, Tommy Lee Jones, Sting, Sean Bean. **1988**

TORMY WATERS ★★★★ Tough rescue-ship captain Jean Gabin braves stormy waters to save hauntingly beautiful Michele Morgan. They then have a passionate love affair. This film is a fine example of French cinema at its pre–WWII zenith. 75m. **DIR:** Jean Gremillon. **CAST:** Jean Gabin, Michele Morgan, Madeleine Renaud, Fernand Ledoux. **1941**

TORMY WEATHER ★★★★ A delightful kaleidoscope of musical numbers. Lena Horne performs the title number and Fats Waller interprets his own "Ain't Misbehavin'." Dooley Wilson of *Casablanca* fame and the Nicholas Brothers are also really great. This is an overlooked 20th Century Fox classic. B&W; 77m. **DIR:** Andrew L. Stone. **CAST:** Lena Horne, Bill Robinson, Cab Calloway, Fats Waller. **1943**

TORY LADY, THE ★★★ Jessica Tandy feels worthless after coming to live with her daughter, so she buys public-access time on cable TV to share her favorite fairy tales. When an advertising executive and part-time mom decides to market Tandy's spellbinding talents, she is forced to see the damage her all-encompassing career is having on her own daughter. Heartwarming as well as thought-provoking family viewing. Not rated; contains no objectionable material. 93m. **DIR:** Larry Elikann. **CAST:** Jessica Tandy, Stephanie Zimbalist, Tandy Cronyn, Lisa Jakub, Christopher Gartin. **1991 DVD**

STORY OF A LOVE STORY ★★ In this offbeat and increasingly off-putting adaptation by screenwriter Nicholas Mosely of his novel *Impossible Object*, Alan Bates stars as an English novelist who becomes involved in an affair with a married Frenchwoman (Dominique Sanda). In English and French with some subtitles. Rated R for nudity and brief violence. 110m. **DIR:** John Frankenheimer. **CAST:** Alan Bates, Dominique Sanda, Evans Evans, Lea Massari, Michel Auclair. **1973**

STORY OF A THREE DAY PASS, THE ★★★1/2 A black soldier falls in love with a white French girl while on leave in Paris. First-time director Melvin Van Peebles makes the most of a shoestring budget on a project that contains only some of the rage that surfaced in his *Sweet Sweetback's Baadasssss Song*. 87m. **DIR:** Melvin Van Peebles. **CAST:** Harry Baird, Nicole Berger, Christian Marin. **1967**

STORY OF ADELE H, THE ★★★1/2 This basically simple story of author Victor Hugo's daughter, who loves a soldier in vain, is surprisingly textured and intriguing. Slow, exquisite unfolding of many-layered love story is arresting and pictorially beautiful. Nicely done. Some adult situations. In French with English subtitles. Rated PG. 97m. **DIR:** François Truffaut. **CAST:** Isabelle Adjani, Bruce Robinson. **1975**

STORY OF BOYS AND GIRLS ★★★★ Italian director Pupi Avati serves up a spicy, thought-provoking slice of life as thirty-plus participants in an engagement party indulge in a mouth-watering, eighteen-course meal. Set in pre–World War II Italy, this delicious import provides a feast of fascinating characters while examining the attitudes that led to the rise of fascism. In Italian with English subtitles. Not rated; the film has scenes of simulated sex. 92m. **DIR:** Pupi Avati. **CAST:** Felice Andreasi, Angiola Baggi. **1991**

STORY OF DAVID, THE ★★★1/2 The first half of this two-part TV movie tells the story of young David's defeat of the Philistine champion Goliath. The second half present David as king, in love with the forbidden Bathsheba. Lavish, respectfully produced biblical epic. Not rated; contains no objectionable material. 192m. **DIR:** Alex Segal, David Lowell Rich. **CAST:** Timothy Bottoms, Anthony Quayle, Norman Rodway, Keith Michell, Jane Seymour, Brian Blessed, Barry Morse. **1976**

STORY OF DR. WASSELL, THE ★★1/2 Plodding bio-pic about a navy doctor who risks court-martial to save the lives of severely wounded soldiers on Java during World War II. Based on the book by James Hilton. Not rated. 137m. **DIR:** Cecil B. DeMille. **CAST:** Gary Cooper, Laraine Day, Signe Hasso, Dennis O'Keefe, Carol Thurston, Carl Esmond, Stanley Ridges. **1944**

STORY OF FAUSTA, THE ★★★ A Brazilian woman, sick of her lazy and abusive husband, seeks the easy way out by befriending a wealthy old man. The more she mistreats her rescuer, the more anxious he is to please her. The humor here is deeply black. In Portuguese with English subtitles. Not rated, contains violence, profanity, and nudity. 90m. **DIR:** Bruno Barreto. **CAST:** Betty Faria, Daniel Filho, Brandao Filho. **1988**

STORY OF JACOB AND JOSEPH, THE ★★★1/2 Handsome adaptation of two Bible stories. First, Jacob battles his brother Esau over their birthright. Later, Jacob's favorite son, Joseph, has his own sibling problems when his jealous brothers sell him into slavery. Not rated; contains no objectionable material. 96m. **DIR:** Michael Cacoyannis. **CAST:** Keith Michell, Tony Lo Bianco, Colleen Dewhurst, Herschel Bernardi, Harry Andrews, Julian Glover. **1974**

STORY OF LOUIS PASTEUR, THE ★★★1/2 Master actor Paul Muni won an Oscar for his restrained portrayal of the famous French founder of bacteriology in this well-honed film biography. This is an honest, engrossing character study that avoids sentimentality. B&W; 85m. **DIR:** William Dieterle. **CAST:** Paul Muni, Josephine Hutchinson, Anita Louise, Donald Woods, Porter Hall, Akim Tamiroff. **1936**

STORY OF O, THE ★★ Adaptation of the French erotic novel. The filmmakers attempt to beautify what is basically a soft-core tale of bondage and sadomasochism. No matter how much Vaseline you apply to the camera lens, a nude whipping is still a nude whipping. Rated R (though it'd get an NC-17 today). 97m. DIR: Just Jaeckin. CAST: Udo Kier, Corinne Clery. 1975

STORY OF QIU JU, THE ★★★★★ The masterful Yimou Zhang, the first Chinese director to acquire a western following, here makes his first film about contemporary Chinese life. Viewers can observe both the marvelous and mundane in modern Chinese life. Star Gong Li proves again that she's one of the world's greatest actresses. In Chinese with English subtitles. Rated PG. 100m. DIR: Yimou Zhang. CAST: Gong Li, Lei Lao Sheng, Liu Pei Qi. 1993 DVD

STORY OF ROBIN HOOD, THE ★★★ Disney's live-action version of the Robin Hood legend has elements that give the movie its own identity. One nice touch is the use of a wandering minstrel, who draws the story together. Richard Todd is a most appealing Robin Hood, while James Robertson Justice, as Little John, and Peter Finch, as the Sheriff of Nottingham, are first-rate. 83m. DIR: Ken Annakin. CAST: Richard Todd, Joan Rice, Peter Finch, James Hayter, James Robertson Justice, Michael Hordern. 1952

STORY OF RUTH, THE ★★★ Pagan priestess Ruth renounces her graven gods to embrace the true faith of Israel but finds acceptance rough going in this static retelling of the classic Bible story. 132m. DIR: Henry Koster. CAST: Elana Eden, Stuart Whitman, Tom Tryon, Peggy Wood, Viveca Lindfors, Jeff Marrow. 1960

STORY OF SEABISCUIT, THE ★★1/2 A thoroughbred horse recovers from an injury to become a big prizewinner. Based on a true incident, this predictable family programmer gives Barry Fitzgerald as the trainer full throttle to ham and charm his way into the audience's heart. 92m. DIR: David Butler. CAST: Shirley Temple, Barry Fitzgerald, Lon McCallister, Rosemary DeCamp, Pierre Watkin, Donald MacBride. 1949

•STORY OF THE LATE CHRYSANTHEMUMS, THE ★★★★1/2 The adopted son of a family of great actors finds success only after he sets out on his own and marries the family maid, who tutors him in his craft. Director Kenji Mizoguchi's distinctive style, in which careful compositions, long takes, and a gently tracking camera impart a deep humanism, redeems this melodramatic, three-hankie story. In Japanese with English subtitles. B&W; 142m. DIR: Kenji Mizoguchi. CAST: Shotaro Hanayagi, Kakuro Mori. 1939

•STORY OF US, THE ★★1/2 Director Rob Reiner's somber study of the collapse of a fifteen-year marriage probably wasn't intended to be so depressing. In using a continual flashback/flashforward style of storytelling, he ends up putting too much emphasis on the bickering between heartbroken mates and not enough on their early years of love and harmony. This lack of balance mars what might have been a touching, involving movie. Rated R for profanity, sex, and violence. 94m. DIR: Rob Reiner. CAST: Bruce Willis, Michelle Pfeiffer, Tim Matheson, Rob Reiner, Rita Wilson, Paul Reiser, Julie Hagerty, Tom Poston, Jayne Meadows, Betty White, Red Button. 1999 DVD

STORY OF VERNON AND IRENE CASTLE, TH ★★★★ Another fine film with the flying footsies Fred Astaire and the always lovely Ginger Roger B&W; 93m. DIR: H. C. Potter. CAST: Fred Astaire, Gi ger Rogers, Edna May Oliver, Walter Brennan. 1939

STORY OF WOMEN, THE ★★★★ Excellent poli cal drama from director Claude Chabrol based on true story about the last woman to be guillotined i France, at the onset of World War II. Isabelle Hu pert delivers a powerful performance as an abortio ist who becomes the victim of an indifferent societ This riveting performance won her the best-actres prize at the Venice Film Festival. In French wit English subtitles. 112m. DIR: Claude Chabrol. CAS Isabelle Huppert, François Cluzet. 1988

STORY OF XINGHUA, THE ★★★1/2 Powerful tal of adultery finds an obedient wife looking outsid her brutal marriage for love and compassio Xinghua challenges hundreds of years of tradition a she seeks the strength to find true happiness. Engag ing performances and picture-postcard scener make this a satisfying experience. In Chinese wit English subtitles. Not rated; contains adult situa tions. 89m. DIR: Cui Junde. CAST: Jiang Wenli, Zhan Guoli, Tian Shaojun. 1993

STORYBOOK ★★★1/2 Kids will love this rom through the pages of a magical storybook, brought t life when a boy named Brandon enters the book. Be fore he can get out, he must save the magical king dom from an evil queen. Brandon is joined by som fanciful friends, including Woody the Woodsman, kangaroo, and a wise old owl. Rated G. 88m. DIR Lorenzo Doumani. CAST: William McNamara, Swoosi Kurtz, James Doohan, Richard Moll, Jack Scalia, Mil ton Berle. 1995

STOWAWAY ★★★ Tale of missionary ward Shirle Temple lost in Shanghai and befriended by Ameri can Robert Young. She holds her own against suc seasoned scene snitchers as Eugene Pallette, Arthu Treacher, and J. Edward Blomberg, while bringin playboy Young and Alice Faye together romanticall singing in Chinese, and imitating Fred Astaire, A Jolson, and Eddie Cantor. B&W; 86m. DIR: William A Seiter. CAST: Shirley Temple, Robert Young, Alice Faye Allan "Rocky" Lane, Eugene Pallette, Helen Westley Arthur Treacher, J. Edward Bromberg. 1936

STRAIGHT FOR THE HEART ★★★ Covering Con tra atrocities in Nicaragua, a Canadian photogra pher copes by repressing his emotional reactions But when he returns home, he finds that detach ment difficult to shake. A grim but involving drama featuring splendid Montreal locations. In French with English subtitles. Not rated. 92m. DIR: Lea Pool CAST: Matthias Habich, Johanne-Marie Tremblay 1988

STRAIGHT LINE ★★1/2 Laughable action film star Mr. T as a private eye who gets the job of a lifetime: track down the man brainwashing kids into enforc ing white supremacy by killing. Hokey, unbelievable and quite entertaining in a goofy sort of way. 95m.

IR: George Mihalka. **CAST:** Mr. T, Kenneth Welsh. 988

STRAIGHT OUT OF BROOKLYN ★★★1/2 Nineteen-year-old writer-producer-director Matty Rich makes a solid filmmaking debut with this thought-provoking drama about a black teenager (Lawrence Gilliard Jr.) who decides that robbing a local drug dealer is the best and quickest way to get his family out of the poverty-stricken housing projects of Red Hook in Brooklyn. Rated R for profanity, violence, and suggested sex. 91m. **DIR:** Matty Rich. **CAST:** George T. Odom, Lawrence Gilliard Jr., Matty Rich. 1991

STRAIGHT SHOOTING ★★★ John Ford's first major film holds up remarkably well today. Everything about it seems a prototype for his great Westerns to come: the authoritative presence of the solitary cowboy, Harry Carey; the striking location photography; and the rousing action scenes. Silent. B&W; 57m. **DIR:** John Ford. **CAST:** Harry Carey. 1917

STRAIGHT STORY, THE ★★★★ When 73-year-old Alvin Straight (Richard Farnsworth) learns that he may have little time left, he decides to visit his estranged brother, with whom he has not spoken in ten years. The problem is Alvin can barely walk (having to use two canes) and his eyesight is poor (making a driver's license an impossibility), so the determined senior citizen hitches up a homemade, wooden trailer to his 1966 John Deere riding mower and embarks on his quest. A superb performance from Farnsworth (who was nominated for an Oscar as best actor) and uncommonly sensitive direction by David Lynch make this an unforgettable viewing experience. Rated G. 111m. **DIR:** David Lynch. **CAST:** Richard Farnsworth, Sissy Spacek, Everett McGill, Harry Dean Stanton, Jane Galloway Heitz, Jennifer Edwards, Barbara Robertson, John Farley. 1999

STRAIGHT TALK ★★★1/2 An Arkansas country girl decides to try her luck in Chicago, where she finds her gift for gab the ticket to success as a radio talk-show host. Dolly Parton and a superb supporting cast make every scene believable. Surprisingly good. Rated PG for profanity. 87m. **DIR:** Barnet Kellman. **CAST:** Dolly Parton, James Woods, Griffin Dunne, Michael Madsen, Philip Bosco, Jerry Orbach, John Sayles, Teri Hatcher, Spalding Gray, Charles Fleischer. 1992

STRAIGHT TIME ★★★★ Well-told story of an ex-convict (Dustin Hoffman) attempting to make good on the outside only to return to crime after a run-in with his parole officer (M. Emmet Walsh). Hoffman's performance is truly chilling. A very grim and powerful film that was sadly overlooked on its initial release. Rated R for violence, nudity, and language. 114m. **DIR:** Ulu Grosbard. **CAST:** Dustin Hoffman, Harry Dean Stanton, Gary Busey, Theresa Russell, M. Emmet Walsh. 1978

STRAIGHT TO HELL 💔 Self-indulgent Western spoof with bank robbers and thugs shooting at each other in a desert town. 86m. **DIR:** Alex Cox. **CAST:** Sy Richardson, Joe Strummer, Dennis Hopper, Elvis Costello. 1987

STRAIT-JACKET ★★★1/2 Chilling vehicle for Joan Crawford as a convicted ax murderess returning home after twenty years in an insane asylum, where it appears she was restored to sanity. But was she? Genuinely frightening film features one of Joan's most powerful performances. George Kennedy is almost as good in an early role as a farmhand. B&W; 89m. **DIR:** William Castle. **CAST:** Joan Crawford, Diane Baker, Leif Erickson, George Kennedy. 1964

STRANDED ★★★ A story of bigotry and intolerance centered around aliens escaping from another world and landing in a small town. Cameron Dye is the young man who tries to help them escape from the local sheriff, a gang of good ol' boys, and an assassin from outer space. More character development and pacing than usual for a science-fiction film. Rated PG-13 for profanity and violence. 80m. **DIR:** Tex Fuller. **CAST:** Ione Skye, Joe Morton, Cameron Dye, Brendan Hughes, Maureen O'Sullivan. 1987

STRANGE AFFAIR OF UNCLE HARRY, THE ★★★★ George Sanders tried to get by the censors during the 1940s with several movies that bucked the system. This one cheats by changing the ending of Thomas Job's successful stage play about incest and murder. Hollywood kept the murder part, but you have to read between the lines to get the incest situation. The video print comes from a UCLA Archive restoration. B&W; 80m. **DIR:** Robert Siodmak. **CAST:** George Sanders, Geraldine Fitzgerald, Moyna McGill, Ella Raines, Sara Allgood, Samuel S. Hinds, Harry Von Zell. 1945

STRANGE BEDFELLOWS ★★1/2 Straightlaced American Rock Hudson marries eccentric Italian liberal Gina Lollobrigida, leaves her, then woos her again seven years later. This cornball fluff offers up some laughs, even if the plot is wildly out of control. Not rated. 114m. **DIR:** Melvin Frank. **CAST:** Rock Hudson, Gina Lollobrigida, Gig Young, Nancy Kulp, Bernard Fox, Terry-Thomas. 1965

STRANGE BEHAVIOR ★★★1/2 Michael Murphy stars as the police chief of Galesburg, Illinois, who suddenly finds himself inundated by unexplained knife murders. In all, this offbeat film is a true treat for horror-movie fans and other viewers with a yen for something spooky. Rated R. 98m. **DIR:** Michael Laughlin. **CAST:** Michael Murphy, Marc McClure, Dan Shor, Fiona Lewis, Louise Fletcher, Arthur Dignam. 1981

STRANGE BREW ★★★1/2 Okay, all you hosers and hoseheads, here come those *SCTV* superstars from the Great White North, Bob and Doug McKenzie (Rick Moranis and Dave Thomas) in their first feature film. Beauty, eh? A mad scientist employed by a brewery controls a group of mental patients by feeding them beer laced with a mind-controlling drug. Rated PG. 90m. **DIR:** Dave Thomas, Rick Moranis. **CAST:** Rick Moranis, Dave Thomas, Max von Sydow, Paul Dooley, Lynne Griffin. 1983

STRANGE CARGO ★★★ *Strange* is the best way to describe this one, but the forceful and compelling personalities make it worth watching. Clark Gable leads a group of convicts out of Devil's Island in a daring escape. 105m. **DIR:** Frank Borzage. **CAST:** Clark Gable, Joan Crawford, Ian Hunter, Albert Dekker, Peter Lorre, Paul Lukas, Eduardo Ciannelli, J. Edward Bromberg. 1940

STRANGE CASE OF DR. JEKYLL AND MR. HYDE, THE (1968) ★★ The offbeat casting of Jack Palance in the title role(s) is the main attraction in this taped-for-television production. Charles Jarrott directs with the same ponderous hand he brought to *Anne of the Thousand Days* and *Mary, Queen of Scots*, but the distinguished supporting cast is a plus. Not rated. 96m. **DIR:** Charles Jarrott. **CAST:** Jack Palance, Denholm Elliott, Torin Thatcher, Oscar Homolka, Leo Genn, Billie Whitelaw. 1968

STRANGE CASE OF DR. JEKYLL AND MR. HYDE, THE (1989) ★★★1/2 Surprisingly effective entry in Shelley Duvall's Nightmare Classics series, this does not rely on a Hulk-like transition of Dr. Jekyll (Anthony Andrews) to terrify viewers. Instead, Andrews brilliantly creates two personalities—one timid, the other frightfully uninhibited—that refuse to overlap. Not rated, contains violence. 55m. **DIR:** Michael Lindsay-Hogg. **CAST:** Anthony Andrews, George Murdock, Laura Dern, Nicholas Guest. 1989

STRANGE CASE OF DR. RX, THE ★★ Private eye Patric Knowles tracks down a vigilante killer. The best thing about this average murder mystery (misleadingly advertised as a horror movie) is the comic relief. B&W; 66m. **DIR:** William Nigh. **CAST:** Lionel Atwill, Patric Knowles, Anne Gwynne, Samuel S. Hinds, Shemp Howard, Mantan Moreland. 1942

STRANGE CASE OF THE COSMIC RAYS, THE ★★★1/2 This Bell Science educational film introduces the atom, ultraviolet radiation, and galactic phenomena. All this is explained by Dr. Frank Baxter with the help of the Bill and Cora Baird puppets and the animation of Shamus Culhane. 59m. **DIR:** Frank Capra. **CAST:** Dr. Frank Baxter. 1957

STRANGE CONFESSION ★★ Chemist Lon Chaney Jr. seeks revenge on his employer (J. Carrol Naish) in this below-average entry in the *Inner Sanctum* series. B&W; 60m. **DIR:** John Hoffman. **CAST:** Lon Chaney Jr., Brenda Joyce, J. Carrol Naish, Milburn Stone, Lloyd Bridges. 1945

STRANGE DAYS ★★ The drug of choice in 1999 is a virtual-reality setup that allows people to relive their own or someone else's experiences. During the last forty-eight hours of the twentieth century, a seedy former vice cop gets involved with two such "wire-trips."— Virtual reality greased with sleaze. Rated R for graphic violence, sex, nudity, and language. 145m. **DIR:** Kathryn Bigelow. **CAST:** Ralph Fiennes, Angela Bassett, Tom Sizemore, Juliette Lewis, Michael Wincott, Vincent D'Onofrio. 1995 DVD

STRANGE DOOR, THE ★★1/2 Charles Laughton turns up as the evil French nobleman Sire de Maletroit, who takes delight in punishing his brother, imprisoned in the dungeon after he wed the woman Maletroit loved. Not rated. B&W; 81m. **DIR:** Joseph Pevney. **CAST:** Charles Laughton, Boris Karloff, Sally Forrest, Richard Stapley, Michael Pate. 1951

STRANGE ILLUSION ★★ Following the mysterious disappearance of his father, a teenager on a fishing holiday with the family physician is disturbed by a strange dream concerning his mother. Trite. B&W; 80m. **DIR:** Edgar G. Ulmer. **CAST:** Jimmy Lydon, Sally Eilers, Regis Toomey. 1945

STRANGE INTERLUDE (1932) ★★1/2 Eugene O'Neill's plays achieve heavy-handed movies, and this is one of the heaviest. Clark Gable and Norma Shearer play lovers who grow old together while married to other people. B&W; 110m. **DIR:** Robert Z. Leonard. **CAST:** Clark Gable, Norma Shearer, Robert Young, Maureen O'Sullivan, May Robson, Henry B. Walthall, Ralph Morgan. 1932

STRANGE INTERLUDE (1988) ★★★★ Eugene O'Neill's complex love story is not for viewers seeking mindless entertainment, but for those willing to endure the considerable length, it offers ample rewards. Glenda Jackson plays a neurotic woman who in the course of twenty-five years, manages to control the lives of the three men who love her. High-class soap opera. Not rated, this PBS production contains adult themes. 190m. **DIR:** Herbert Wise. **CAST:** Glenda Jackson, José Ferrer, David Dukes, Ken Howard, Edward Petherbridge. 1988

STRANGE INVADERS ★★★★ A splendid parody of 1950s science-fiction movies, this film opens in 1958 with bug-like aliens taking over a farm town called Centerville, Illinois. The story then jumps to New York City, twenty-five years later. Rated PG for violence. 94m. **DIR:** Michael Laughlin. **CAST:** Paul LeMat, Diana Scarwid, Nancy Allen, Louise Fletcher, Michael Lerner, Kenneth Tobey, June Lockhart. 1983

•STRANGE JUSTICE ★★★1/2 If you happened to miss the Judge Clarence Thomas Senate hearing in 1991, this made-for-cable dramatization of the event will nicely sum up the key points of the whole debacle for you. The film does a good job straddling the issue, presenting both sides as compelling and truthful. Emotional reenactment of the hearing spices up the otherwise dull-as-a-post testimony, and edgy visual effects add tension to the more staid scenes. Not rated; contains profanity. 95m. **DIR:** Ernest R. Dickerson. **CAST:** Delroy Lindo, Mandy Patinkin, Regina Taylor, Lou Gossett Jr. 1999

STRANGE LOVE OF MARTHA IVERS, THE ★★★ Terrible title doesn't do this well-acted drama justice. Woman-with-a-past Barbara Stanwyck uses her this story of a secret that comes back to threaten her now-stable life and the lengths she must go to in order to ensure her security. Young Kirk Douglas in his film debut already charges the screen with electricity. B&W; 117m. **DIR:** Lewis Milestone. **CAST:** Barbara Stanwyck, Van Heflin, Kirk Douglas, Lizabeth Scott, Judith Anderson, Darryl Hickman. 1946

STRANGE LOVE OF MOLLY LOUVAIN, THE ★★★1/2 A well-played melodrama with comic overtones and almost as much sexual innuendo as movies of the 1990s. An unwed mother dallies with gangsters of every stripe and color because she just plain likes men. B&W; 80m. **DIR:** Michael Curtiz. **CAST:** Ann Dvorak, Lee Tracy, Leslie Fenton, Richard Cromwell, Guy Kibbee, Mary Doran, Frank McHugh. 1932

STRANGE NEW WORLD ★★1/2 After spending almost two centuries in suspended animation, three astronauts return to Earth to discover a *Strange New World* in this made-for-television entry. Through the miracle of cloning, Earth's inhabitants face eternal life, but with a price. 78m. **DIR:** Robert

Butler. **CAST:** John Saxon, Keene Curtis, Martine Beswick, James Olson, Kathleen Miller. **1975**

STRANGE SHADOWS IN AN EMPTY ROOM ❤ A cop investigates his sister's mysterious death. Not rated; contains violence. 97m. **DIR:** Martin Herbert. **CAST:** Stuart Whitman, John Saxon, Martin Landau, Tisa Farrow. **1976**

STRANGE TALES: RAY BRADBURY THEATER ★★★★ These three initial episodes from cable's *Ray Bradbury Theater* are noteworthy for strong casting and Bradbury's faithful adaptations of his own short stories. The most disturbing entry is "The Town Where No One Got Off," with Jeff Goldblum as a rail commuter who gets involved in a perfect murder scheme. Superior production values. 86m. **DIR:** Don McBrearty, Bruce Pittman, Douglas Jackson. **CAST:** Peter O'Toole, Charles Martin Smith, Drew Barrymore, Jeff Goldblum, Ed McNamara, Cec Linder. **1986**

STRANGE WOMAN, THE ★★ Lusty tale of a woman who conspires with her stepson to kill her husband. A strange adaptation of the Ben Ames Williams bestseller, mainly because Hedy Lamarr looks better than she acts. She bought the rights to the book, selected cast and director, and listed herself as an associate producer. B&W; 100m. **DIR:** Edgar G. Ulmer. **CAST:** Hedy Lamarr, George Sanders, Gene Lockhart, Louis Hayward, Hillary Brooke, Rhys Williams, June Storey, Ian Keith. **1946 DVD**

STRANGENESS, THE ❤ The Gold Spike Mine is haunted by a creature from down deep inside the Earth. Not rated. 90m. **DIR:** David Michael Hillman. **CAST:** Dan Lunham, Terri Berland. **1985**

STRANGER, THE (1947) ★★★★ Nazi war criminal (Orson Welles) assumes a new identity in a small New England town following World War II, unaware that a government agent (Edward G. Robinson) is tailing him. Extremely well-done film, holds the viewer's interest from start to finish. B&W; 95m. **DIR:** Orson Welles. **CAST:** Orson Welles, Edward G. Robinson, Loretta Young, Richard Long. **1946 DVD**

STRANGER, THE (1986) ★★★★ Taut psychological thriller that keeps you on the edge of your seat. Bonnie Bedelia plays a woman with amnesia trying to put the pieces together after a car accident. She thinks she may or may not have witnessed a murder. Peter Riegert is her psychiatrist who may or may not be trying to help her. This unique sleeper is fast-paced and suspenseful. Rated R for brief nudity and violence. 93m. **DIR:** Adolfo Aristarian. **CAST:** Bonnie Bedelia, Peter Riegert. **1986**

STRANGER, THE (1992) ★★★★1/2 A middle-class Calcutta husband and wife whose lives are disrupted when the wife's long-lost and unknown-to-them uncle arrives at the doorstep. The final film of the great Satyajit Ray, who died in 1992, is an entertaining, affecting modern-day fable, offering Ray's thoughtful views on families, cultural tradition, and the flaws in modern civilization. An apt reminder of Ray's place among the master filmmakers of the world. In Bengali with English subtitles. 120m. **DIR:** Satyajit Ray. **CAST:** Mamata Shankar, Deepankar De, Utpal Dutt. **1992**

STRANGER, THE (1994) ★★ Pouty Kathy Long makes a poor substitute for Clint Eastwood in this laughable biker variation on *High Plains Drifter* that mimics everything down to the mock Ennio Morricone score. Even worse, justice is hardly served by Gregory Poirier's trite script. Rated R for violence, profanity, nudity, and simulated sex. 98m. **DIR:** Fritz Kiersch. **CAST:** Kathy Long, Eric Pierpoint, Robin Lynn Heath. **1994**

STRANGER AMONG US, A ★★★1/2 Melanie Griffith becomes a tough-talkin' New York cop in this fish-out-of-water thriller. She penetrates New York's Hasidic Jewish community after a jeweler turns up dead and his sizable inventory is missing. Rated PG-13 for violence and profanity. 111m. **DIR:** Sidney Lumet. **CAST:** Melanie Griffith, Eric Thal, John Pankow, Tracy Pollan, Lee Richardson, Mia Sara, Jamey Sheridan. **1992**

STRANGER AND THE GUNFIGHTER, THE ★★1/2 The world may never be ready for this improbable mix, a tongue-in-cheek spaghetti Western by way of a standard kung-fu chop-chop flick. Lee Van Cleef, as another of his weary gunslingers, teams with martial arts master Lo Lieh. A classic this isn't, but the fast action and camp humor make it watchable. Rated PG for violence. 107m. **DIR:** Anthony M. Dawson. **CAST:** Lee Van Cleef, Lo Lieh, Patty Shepard. **1976**

STRANGER BY NIGHT ★★1/2 Proving once again that you can't trust a film that opens in a psychiatrist's office, Steven Bauer does little but look frustrated in this routine thriller about a cop who fears he may be murdering women during mental blackouts. The story deserves credit for an eleventh-hour twist, but the viewing experience is seriously marred by Ashley Irwin's god-awful music. Rated R for violence, profanity, nudity, and simulated sex. 91m. **DIR:** Gregory Brown. **CAST:** Steven Bauer, Jennifer Rubin, William Katt, Michael Parks, Luca Bercovici, Michele Greene. **1994 DVD**

STRANGER FROM VENUS ❤ The same plot and the same star (Patricia Neal) as the classic *The Day the Earth Stood Still* does not guarantee the same quality. A visitor from Venus attempts to warn Earth of the dangers of nuclear weapons but meets with suspicion and hatred. B&W; 78m. **DIR:** Burt Balaban. **CAST:** Patricia Neal, Helmut Dantine, Derek Bond. **1954**

•STRANGER IN THE KINGDOM, A ★★★ The picture-postcard town of Kingdom, Vermont, is one of those quaint places where everybody knows everyone else's name and business. Tossed into the mix are black reverend Walter Andrews and his teenage son. Set in 1952, director Jay Craven's film incorporates the themes of racism in a murder mystery that pits the town against the reverend when he is accused of killing a woman. Despite familiar themes, the film manages to carve out an identity all its own. Rated PG-13 for violence. 112m. **DIR:** Jay Craven. **CAST:** Ernie Hudson, Martin Sheen, Sean Nelson, David Lansbury, Carrie Snodgress. **1998 DVD**

STRANGER IN THE HOUSE ★★ Fate plays a hand in this story of a man whose plans to murder his wife are interrupted by a mysterious stranger—with plans of his own. Mildly entertaining. Rated R for profanity and violence. 94m. **DIR:** Rodney Gibbons.

CAST: Michele Greene, Kathleen Kinmont, Steve Railsback. 1997

STRANGER IS WATCHING, A ★★ A psychotic killer kidnaps two young ladies and keeps them prisoner in the catacombs beneath Grand Central Station. This commuter's nightmare is an ugly, dimly lit suspenser. Rated R. 92m. **DIR:** Sean S. Cunningham. **CAST:** Kate Mulgrew, Rip Torn, James Naughton. 1982

STRANGER ON MY LAND ★★★1/2 Sparks fly when the government tries to entice and then force a family of ranchers off its land in order to expand a nearby military base. Thoughtful characters on all sides of the issue, an excellent cast, and fine pacing make this story unfold nicely. Not rated; contains some violence. 94m. **DIR:** Larry Elikann. **CAST:** Tommy Lee Jones, Dee Wallace, Ben Johnson, Barry Corbin. 1990

STRANGER ON THE THIRD FLOOR ★★★★ Peter Lorre gives yet another singular performance as a disinterested murderer, a character truly alien yet strangely sympathetic. A great hallucination sequence and good performances all the way around make this a compelling treat. B&W; 64m. **DIR:** Boris Ingster. **CAST:** Peter Lorre, John McGuire, Elisha Cook Jr., Margaret Tallichet. 1940

STRANGER THAN PARADISE ★★★★1/2 In this superb independently made comedy, three oddball characters go on a spontaneous road trip through the United States, where they encounter boredom, routine problems, bad luck, and outrageous good fortune. The film, which won acclaim at the Cannes and New York film festivals, plays a lot like a Woody Allen comedy. It's a silly film for smart people. Rated R for profanity. B&W; 90m. **DIR:** Jim Jarmusch. **CAST:** John Lurie, Richard Edson, Eszter Balint. 1985

STRANGER WITHIN, THE 🎔 A housewife is mysteriously impregnated, and her unborn child begins to have a strange effect on her personality. Typical TV tripe. Not rated. 74m. **DIR:** Lee Philips. **CAST:** Barbara Eden, George Grizzard, Joyce Van Patten, David Doyle. 1979

STRANGER WORE A GUN, THE ★★1/2 Randolph Scott joins forces with evil George Macready in a plot to steal government gold shipments. Scott has a change of heart, and they end up as enemies. Initially released in 3-D; the action scenes were obviously devised for that medium. 83m. **DIR:** André de Toth. **CAST:** Randolph Scott, Claire Trevor, George Macready, Lee Marvin, Ernest Borgnine. 1953

STRANGERS ★★ Three mediocre vignettes. Too bad someone couldn't come up with just one good idea. Rated R for nudity and simulated sex. 90m. **DIR:** Daniel Vigne, Wayne Wang, Joan Tewkesbury. **CAST:** Linda Fiorentino, James Remar, François Montagut, Joan Chen, Lambert Wilson, Timothy Hutton. 1991

STRANGERS IN GOOD COMPANY ★★★ Leisurely paced coming-of-age film of the geriatric set. A group of gray foxes are stuck in the wilderness when their tour bus breaks down. There they get to know each other while revealing their secret fears and desires. Enlightening Canadian film. Rated PG. 101m. **DIR:** Cynthia Scott. **CAST:** Alice Diabo, Constance Garneau. 1990

STRANGERS IN THE CITY ★★★★ This forceful film set in a Manhattan slum paints a vivid picture of a Puerto Rican family struggling to adjust to life in a new country. When the proud father loses his job, other family members have to go to work to support themselves. The final third gives way to cheap melodrama, but the film is still well worth seeing. B&W; 83m. **DIR:** Rick Carrier. **CAST:** Robert Gentile, Camilo Delgado. 1961

STRANGERS KISS ★★1/2 Offbeat film about the making of a low-budget movie, circa 1955. A strange romantic relationship between the male and female leads develops off-camera. A good script inspired by Stanley Kubrick's *Killer's Kiss* is quite absorbing despite some production flaws. Rated R for sexual situations. 94m. **DIR:** Matthew Chapman. **CAST:** Peter Coyote, Victoria Tennant, Blaine Novak, Dan Shor. 1984

STRANGERS ON A TRAIN ★★★★★ One of the most discussed and analyzed of all of Alfred Hitchcock's films. *Strangers on a Train* was made during the height of Hitchcock's most creative period, the early 1950s. When you add a marvelous performance by Robert Walker as the stranger, you have one of the most satisfying thrillers ever. B&W; 101m. **DIR:** Alfred Hitchcock. **CAST:** Farley Granger, Robert Walker, Ruth Roman, Leo G. Carroll, Patricia Hitchcock, Marion Lorne. 1951

STRANGERS: THE STORY OF A MOTHER AND A DAUGHTER ★★★1/2 Bette Davis won an Emmy Award in this taut, made-for-television drama about a long-estranged daughter's sudden reentry into the life and home of her bitter, resentful mother. Gena Rowlands, as the daughter, holds her own matching Davis scene for scene. 100m. **DIR:** Milton Katselas. **CAST:** Bette Davis, Gena Rowlands, Ford Rainey, Royal Dano. 1979

STRANGERS WHEN WE MEET ★★1/2 An all-star cast fails to charge this overblown soap opera about an unhappily married architect who falls in love with his beautiful neighbor. Evan Hunter derived the screenplay from his novel of the same name. Not rated. 117m. **DIR:** Richard Quine. **CAST:** Kirk Douglas, Kim Novak, Ernie Kovacs, Barbara Rush, Walter Matthau, Virginia Bruce, Kent Smith, Helen Gallagher. 1960

STRANGLEHOLD ★★ Often-told tale of terrorists who take over a chemical-weapons plant and hold a congresswoman hostage. Of course, there's only one man who can stop them, and he's world kick-boxing champion Jerry Trimble. So who's going to save us from Trimble's less-than-stellar acting abilities? Rated R for violence and adult language. 73m. **DIR:** Cirio H. Santiago. **CAST:** Jerry Trimble, Jillian McWhirter, Vernon Wells. 1994

STRANGLER, THE ★★1/2 Victor Buono gives a good performance as corpulent, mother-fixated maniac who murders nurses and throws Chicago into a state of alarm. This low-budget thriller didn't get a lot of play dates as a result of the real-life horrors of Boston strangler Albert De Salvo and the senseless murder of eight nurses by Richard Speck. Not rated, but violent and gruesome. Also available at 80 minutes. B&W; 89m. **DIR:** Burt Topper. **CAST:** Victor Buono, David McLean, Ellen Corby, Jeanne Bates. 1964

STRANGLER OF THE SWAMP ★★ Ghostly revenge story about a ferryman who was unjustly lynched and who hangs his murderers one by one is atmospheric and eerie but bogged down by a cheap budget and an unnecessary love story. Considered a minor classic among fantasy fans. B&W; 60m. DIR: Frank Wisbar. CAST: Rosemary La Planche, Robert Barrat, Blake Edwards, Charles Middleton. 1946 DVD

STRAPLESS ★★★★ Deftly handled story of an American doctor in London who marries an enigmatic businessman in a moment of rapture, only to find him inscrutable and deceptive. Strong performances. Rated R. 99m. DIR: David Hare. CAST: Blair Brown, Bruno Ganz, Bridget Fonda. 1990

TRAPPED ★★★ Although intelligently scripted and artily helmed by actor Forest Whitaker (in his directorial debut), this slice of inner-city life is no different from any film by John Singleton, Spike Lee, or countless imitators: a bludgeoning indictment of failed social systems. A young man tries to help his pregnant, drug-dealing girlfriend but is hampered by a cop and gun-dealer. Rated R for incessant profanity and violence. 102m. DIR: Forest Whitaker. CAST: Boleem Woodbine, Kia Joy Goodwin, Fredro, Paul McCrane, Craig Wasson, Michael Biehn. 1993

STRATEGIC AIR COMMAND ★★1/2 Aviation and sports come together as professional baseball player Jimmy Stewart is called back to active service and forced to leave his career, his teammates, and his wife (June Allyson). Air force veterans and baseball fans will enjoy, but, otherwise, this is just routine studio fare. 114m. DIR: Anthony Mann. CAST: James Stewart, June Allyson, Frank Lovejoy, Barry Sullivan, Bruce Bennett, Rosemary DeCamp. 1955

STRATEGIC COMMAND ★★ Shameless rip-off of Executive Decision stars direct-to-video Kurt Russell wannabe Michael Dudikoff, who leads an elite commando squad aboard a hijacked airplane carrying terrorists, the vice president of the United States, and a deadly chemical. Rated R for language and violence. 95m. DIR: Rick Jacobson. CAST: Michael Dudikoff, Paul Winfield, Richard Norton. 1997

STRATTON STORY, THE ★★★★ Heartwarming true-life story of Chicago White Sox pitcher Monte Stratton, who lost a leg in a hunting accident at the height of his career. Fine performances in a "feel-good" movie. B&W; 106m. DIR: Sam Wood. CAST: James Stewart, June Allyson, Frank Morgan, Agnes Moorehead, Bill Williams. 1949

STRAW DOGS ★★★★ An American intellectual mathematician (played brilliantly by Dustin Hoffman) takes a wife (Susan George) and returns to her ancestral village on the coast of England. She taunts her former boyfriends with her wealth and power, and soon she is viciously raped. This violent, controversial shocker by Sam Peckinpah is rated R. 113m. DIR: Sam Peckinpah. CAST: Dustin Hoffman, Susan George, Peter Vaughan, T. P. McKenna, Peter Arne, David Warner. 1971 DVD

STRAWBERRY AND CHOCOLATE ★★★ This amiable sort of Odd Couple, set in 1979 Havana, focuses on the blossoming friendship between a flamboyant, art-minded gay and a determinedly straight political-science student who learns to place compassion above ideology. It's an entertaining, gingerly paced seriocomedy about tolerance. In Spanish with English subtitles. Rated R for language and suggested sex. 104m. DIR: Tomas Gutierrez Alea, Juan Carlos Tabio. CAST: Jorge Perugorria, Vladimir Cruz, Mirta Ibarra. 1994

STRAWBERRY BLONDE, THE ★★★ Sentimental flashback story of young man's unrequited love for The Strawberry Blonde (Rita Hayworth) is a change of pace for dynamic James Cagney and one of the most evocative period pieces produced in America about the innocent "Gay Nineties." Winsome Olivia de Havilland and a great cast of characters (including Alan Hale as Cagney's father) breathe life into this tragicomic tale. B&W; 97m. DIR: Raoul Walsh. CAST: James Cagney, Olivia de Havilland, Rita Hayworth, Alan Hale Sr., Jack Carson, George Tobias, Una O'Connor, George Reeves. 1941

STRAWBERRY STATEMENT, THE ★★ Inane message film attempts to make some sense (and money) out of student dissidents and rebellion. Some good performances in this hodgepodge of comedy, drama, and youth-authority confrontations. Rated R. 103m. DIR: Stuart Hagmann. CAST: Kim Darby, Bruce Davison, Bob Balaban, James Kunen. 1970

STRAY DOG ★★★★ In a fascinatingly detailed portrait of postwar Tokyo, a young detective (Toshiro Mifune) desperately searches the underworld for his stolen service revolver. Akira Kurosawa has created a tense thriller in the tradition of early Forties crime-dramas. In Japanese with English subtitles. Not rated. B&W; 122m. DIR: Akira Kurosawa. CAST: Toshiro Mifune, Takashi Shimura. 1949

STRAYS ♥ This bargain-basement critter entry attempts—and fails—to make deadly menaces of cuddly house cats. Supermom Kathleen Quinlan just looks foolish retreating in fear from a water-soaked tabby. Made for cable. Rated R for violence. 83m. DIR: John McPherson. CAST: Kathleen Quinlan, Timothy Busfield, Claudia Christian. 1991

STREAMERS ★★★1/2 This tense film is about four recruits and two veterans awaiting orders that will send them to Vietnam. The six men are a microcosm of American life in the late 1960s and early 1970s. A powerful, violent drama, this film is not suitable for everyone. Rated R. 118m. DIR: Robert Altman. CAST: Matthew Modine, Michael Wright, Mitchell Lichtenstein. 1984

STREET, THE ★★1/2 Lured by the fantasy and excitement of the street—a metaphor for elusive freedom—a husband leaves his monotonous home and is caught up in a life of gambling and murder. Classic German progenitor of a more realistic style. Silent. B&W; 87m. DIR: Karl Grune. CAST: Eugen Klopfer. 1923

•STREET ASYLUM ♥ Cops are implanted with a device that compels them to clean up the streets in the most violent fashion possible. Rated R for violence and profanity. 94m. DIR: Gregory Brown. CAST: Wings Hauser, G. Gordon Liddy, Sy Richardson, Brion James. 1987

STREET CRIMES ★★1/2 Dennis Farina adds integrity to this tale of a police officer who creates a youth center so that gang kids can settle their differences with fists and feet in the ring. A drug lord takes exception and soon both cops and kids find themselves to be targets. It's *Rocky* with a not-so-new twist. Rated R for profanity and violence. 93m. DIR: Stephen Smoke. CAST: Dennis Farina, Max Gail, Michael Worth. 1992

STREET FIGHTER (1975) ★★ Sonny Chiba first caught the attention of American audiences in this martial arts hit. But the extreme violence (so strong that the film was originally rated X) is missing from this video version: shorn of 10 minutes, what's left is often hard to follow. Rated R. 75m. DIR: S. Ozawa. CAST: Sonny Chiba. 1975

STREET FIGHTER (1994) ★★★ This entertaining action-fu adventure, based on the popular video game, is wired for grins as well as drop-kicks and shoot-outs. Jean-Claude Van Damme plays a cynical Allied Nation commando leader who must stop a wannabe world ruler from exchanging hostages for a kazillion dollars. Stephen de Souza, who penned *48 Hrs.* and *Die Hard*, makes his directorial debut and tones down the splatter. Rated PG-13 for language and violence. 95m. DIR: Stephen de Souza. CAST: Jean-Claude Van Damme, Raul Julia, Wes Studi, Ming-Na Wen, Damian Chapa. 1994 BDVD

STREET HITZ (STREET STORY) 🐱 Low-budget drama about two brothers caught up in the violent world of street gangs in South Bronx. Pretty cheesy. Not rated; contains violence. 90m. DIR: Joseph B. Vasquez. CAST: Angelo Lopez, Cookie, Lydia Ramirez, Melvin Muza. 1991

STREET HUNTER 🐱 Drugs and gang wars. Rated R for violence. 96m. DIR: John Gallagher. CAST: Steve Harris, Reb Brown. 1990

STREET JUSTICE ★★ Ex-CIA agent returns home after thirteen years of captivity to find his wife has remarried a political reformer involved in a power struggle with a corrupt political machine. Rated R for violence and profanity. 93m. DIR: Richard C. Sarafian. CAST: Michael Ontkean, Joanna Kerns, Catherine Bach. 1987

STREET KNIGHT ★★★ *Perfect Weapon*'s Jeff Speakman returns to clean up the streets of Los Angeles in this satisfying action thriller. He's a retired cop forced back into action when a mysterious group attempts to incite rival gangs into war. There's more plot than usual, so martial-artist Speakman has more to do than beat up the bad guys, led by Christopher Neame. Rated R for violence, language, and nudity. 91m. DIR: Albert Magnoli. CAST: Jeff Speakman, Christopher Neame. 1993

STREET LAW 🐱 A down-but-not-broken trial lawyer is lured into a life of crime by a childhood friend. Rated R for violence and language. 98m. DIR: Damien Lee. CAST: Jeff Wincott, Paco Christian Prieto, Christina Cox. 1994 DVD

STREET MUSIC ★★★1/2 An aspiring singer and her boyfriend, a tour guide, try to save a building full of senior citizens from eviction. Likable comedy-drama benefits from a realistic script and magnificent performances by Elizabeth Daily and Larry Breeding. Not rated; the film has sexual situations. 92m. DIR: Jenny Bowen. CAST: Elizabeth Daily, Larry Breeding, Ned Glass. 1981

STREET OF FORGOTTEN WOMEN, THE ★★ Sile exploitation movie masquerading as an exposé of ban squalor and prostitution. Entertainingly absu with an appropriately melodramatic organ score must for bad-movie buffs. B&W; 55m. DIR: Unknow 1927

STREET OF SHAME ★★★★ A penetrating study love and sex that honestly examines the dreams an problems of a group of prostitutes living in a Tok brothel. In his final film, Japan's master direct Kenji Mizoguchi creates a stirring portrait of co munal life among women trapped in a harsh and d grading existence. In Japanese with English sub tles. B&W; 88m. DIR: Kenji Mizoguchi. CAST: Machi Kyo. 1956

STREET PEOPLE 🐱 Roger Moore and Stacy Kea travel from Italy to San Francisco to rub out a mo ster. Rated R for violence. 92m. DIR: Maurizio Luci CAST: Roger Moore, Stacy Keach. 1976

STREET SCENE ★★★1/2 Playwright Elmer Ric wrote the screenplay for this fine film version of h Pulitzer Prize–winning drama of life in the New Yo tenements and the yearning and anguish of th young and hopeful who are desperate to get out. Th cast is excellent, the score classic Alfred Newma the camera work outstanding. B&W; 80m. DIR: Kin Vidor. CAST: Sylvia Sidney, William Collier Jr., Beula Bondi, David Landau, Estelle Taylor, Walter Miller. 193

STREET SMART ★★1/2 Christopher Reeve gives listless performance as a magazine writer under pressure who fabricates the life story of a New Yor pimp. Problems arise when parallels with a rea pimp under investigation by the DA surface. Morga Freeman plays the pimp Fast Black with an electrify ing mesh of elegance and sleaze. Rated R for lan guage and theme. 97m. DIR: Jerry Schatzberg. CAST Christopher Reeve, Kathy Baker, Mimi Rogers, Andr Gregory, Morgan Freeman. 1986

STREET SOLDIERS ★★1/2 Better-than-average re venge flick has a group of high school students band ing together to take out the hoodlums who killed on of their ranks. Slick production values and fast paced action sequences add up to a rousing tale Rated R for violence and language. 99m. DIR: Le Harry. CAST: Jun Chong, Jeff Rector. 1990

STREET TRASH 🐱 Filmed in New York's Lower Eas Side, it focuses on street transients who consume a new brew that's been spiked by the military and g on a gory killing spree. 90m. DIR: Jim Muro. CAST: Bi Chepil, Jane Arakawa. 1987

STREET WARS 🐱 Good intentions are not enough to save this unusual twist on the pedestrian street gang formula. 90m. DIR: Jamaa Fanaka. CAST: Alar Joseph, Bryan O'Dell, Clifford Shegog. 1994 DVD

STREET WITH NO NAME ★★★1/2 Semidocumen tary about the FBI's infiltration of a gang of young hoodlums is hard-hitting and grimly realistic Richard Widmark is at his best as the gang leader who rules his young thugs with military precision and Mark Stevens plays the agent who poses as a tough in order to get the goods on the hoods. B&W 94m. DIR: William Keighley. CAST: Mark Stevens,

Richard Widmark, Lloyd Nolan, Barbara Lawrence, Ed Begley Sr., John McIntire. **1948**

STREETCAR NAMED DESIRE, A (1951) ★★★★★ Virtuoso acting highlights this powerful and disturbing drama based on the Tennessee Williams play. Vivien Leigh once again is the southern belle. Unlike Scarlett O'Hara, however, her Blanche DuBois is no longer young. She is a sexually disturbed woman who lives in a world of illusion. Her world begins to crumble when she moves in with her sister and brutish brother-in-law (Marlon Brando). B&W; 122m. **DIR:** Elia Kazan. **CAST:** Vivien Leigh, Marlon Brando, Kim Hunter, Karl Malden. **1951 DVD**

STREETCAR NAMED DESIRE, A (1983) ★★ Some films should never be remade; watch the five-star original instead of this slow-moving, lackluster version. Not rated; contains violence. 119m. **DIR:** John Erman. **CAST:** Ann-Margret, Treat Williams, Beverly D'Angelo, Randy Quaid. **1983**

●**STREETCAR NAMED DESIRE, A (1995)** ★★1/2 Made-for-television, this is little more than a photographed version of the Broadway revival of Tennessee Williams's play. Although it uses the complete text, it runs a poor second to the 1951 film, with Alec Baldwin miscast as the brutish Stanley and Jessica Lange unsympathetic as Blanche. Not rated; contains sexual situations. 156m. **DIR:** Glenn Jordan. **CAST:** Jessica Lange, Alec Baldwin, Diane Lane, John Goodman. **1995**

STREETFIGHT (COONSKIN) ★★ Originally released in 1975 as *Coonskin*, this mixture of animation and live action was labeled racist by many. The animation tells the tale in almost *Song of the South* characterizations of a young black country rabbit caught up in Harlem's drug world. Definitely a curiosity. Rated R. 89m. **DIR:** Ralph Bakshi. **CAST:** Barry White, Scatman Crothers, Philip Michael Thomas. **1987**

STREETHAWK ★★ Only kiddies—and fans of the short-lived television series, if there are any—will find much to enjoy in this story of a police officer (Rex Smith) left for dead by drug dealers. 60m. **DIR:** Virgil Vogel. **CAST:** Rex Smith, Jayne Modean, Christopher Lloyd, Joe Regalbuto, Lawrence Pressman, Robert Beltran. **1986**

STREETS ❤ A prostitute is pursued by a psychotic cop. Rated R for violence, nudity, and depiction of drug use. 86m. **DIR:** Katt Shea Ruben. **CAST:** Christina Applegate, David Mendenhall. **1989**

STREETS OF FIRE ★★★ This comic book-style movie is a diverting compendium of nonstop action set to a rocking backbeat. In it a famous rock singer (Diane Lane) is captured by a motorcycle gang in Walter Hill's mythic world, which combines 1950s attitudes and styles with a futuristic feel. It's up to her two-fisted former boyfriend, Tom Cody (Michael Paré) to save her. Rated R for profanity and violence. 93m. **DIR:** Walter Hill. **CAST:** Diane Lane, Michael Paré, Rick Moranis, Amy Madigan, Willem Dafoe. **1984 DVD**

STREETS OF GOLD ★★★ This is a pleasant story about an ex-boxer (Klaus Maria Brandauer) who decides to regain his self-worth by passing on his skills to a pair of street boxers. Brandauer puts a lot of energy into his role, demonstrating shading and char-

acter depth far beyond what you'd expect from a routine story. Inexplicably rated R for mild language and violence. 95m. **DIR:** Joe Roth. **CAST:** Klaus Maria Brandauer, Adrian Pasdar, Wesley Snipes, Angela Molina. **1986**

STREETS OF L.A., THE ★★★1/2 Joanne Woodward plays a struggling real estate saleswoman who gets her new tires slashed by a group of angry Hispanics and decides to pursue them in the hopes of getting reimbursed. The acting is quite good even if the film is a low-budget production. A sensitive, rather quiet drama. Not rated; contains violence. 94m. **DIR:** Jerrold Freedman. **CAST:** Joanne Woodward, Robert Webber, Michael C. Gwynne, Audrey Christie, Isela Vega, Pepe Serna, Miguel Pinero, Tony Plana. **1979**

STREETS OF LAREDO ★★★★ In the official sequel to Larry McMurtry's *Lonesome Dove*, James Garner takes over the role of Capt. Woodrow Call and gives one of his greatest performances. This time, Call and his longtime deputy, Pea Eye (Sam Shepard), are on the trail of a bloodthirsty train robber—a youngster named Joey Garza—and a group of outlaws who burn their victims. A wonderful cast does memorable work, especially Sissy Spacek (as Lorena, Pea Eye's wife) and Randy Quaid (as John Wesley Hardin). Made for TV. 227m. **DIR:** Joseph Sargent. **CAST:** James Garner, Sissy Spacek, Sam Shepard, Sonia Braga, Ned Beatty, Randy Quaid, Wes Studi, Charles Martin Smith, George Carlin, Alexis Cruz, Kevin Conway, James Gammon, Anjanette Comer. **1996**

STREETWALKIN' ❤ Incoherent. Rated R for simulated sex, profanity, and violence. 84m. **DIR:** Joan Freeman. **CAST:** Julie Newmar, Melissa Leo, Leon Robinson, Antonio Fargas. **1985**

STREETWISE ★★★★★ A powerful, emotionally compelling glimpse into the lives of displaced homeless youths surviving as pimps, prostitutes, muggers, panhandlers, and small-time drug dealers on the streets of Seattle. This Oscar nominee explores its disturbing theme with great sensitivity while creating a portrait of a teenage wasteland. Highly recommended. Not rated; contains violence and profanity. 92m. **DIR:** Martin Bell, Mary Ellen Mark, Cheryl McCall. **1985**

STRICTLY BALLROOM ★★★★ Australian director Baz Luhrmann takes the garish visual style of cult director John Waters and gives it heart, in this offbeat *Cinderella* tale of a male dancer who breaks with the rules of ballroom dancing, and the wallflower who dreams of being his partner. While not for all tastes, this off-kilter musical has remarkable warmth. Rated PG for profanity. 94m. **DIR:** Baz Luhrmann. **CAST:** Paul Mercurio, Tara Morice, Bill Hunter, Pat Thomson, Barry Otto. **1992**

STRICTLY BUSINESS ★★★ Frequent laughs, deft characterizations, and fine acting save what could have been little more than a paint-by-the-numbers movie about a streetwise office boy whose success in business is connected to the rise of a junior executive. Rated PG-13 for profanity and violence. 83m. **DIR:** Kevin Hooks. **CAST:** Tommy Davidson, Joseph C. Phillips, Halle Berry, Anne-Marie Johnson, David Marshall Grant, Jon Cypher. **1991**

STRIKE (1924) ★★★★ Shot in a documentarylike style, this drama about a labor dispute during the czarist era was Sergei Eisenstein's first feature film. Advanced for its time and using techniques Eisenstein would perfect in his later masterpieces, *Strike* remains a remarkable achievement and still holds one's interest today. Silent. B&W; 82m. **DIR:** Sergei Eisenstein. **CAST:** Grigori Alexandrov, Alexander Antonov. **1924 DVD**

STRIKE! (1998) ★★★★ An exciting young cast and a sense of nostalgia fuel this invigorating film. In a private girls' school, four protagonists form a club to be true to themselves and their school, which is in dire financial straits. Fun, funny, dramatic, and beautifully realized by a stellar cast, *Strike!* is first class. A.k.a. *The Hairy Bird.* Rated PG-13 for language and adult situations. 97m. **DIR:** Sarah Kernochan. **CAST:** Gaby Hoffman, Kirsten Dunst, Rachael Leigh Cook, Lynn Redgrave, Merrit Wever, Tom Guiry. **1998**

STRIKE A POSE 💘 This so-called thriller is nothing more than thinly veiled soft-core junk, with inept performances and a laughable plot interrupted every seven minutes by sweaty love-making. Rated R for nudity, simulated sex, profanity, and violence. 87m. **DIR:** Dean Hamilton. **CAST:** Robert Eastwick, Michelle LaMothe, Margie Peterson. **1993 DVD**

STRIKE COMMANDO 💘 A Vietnam vet goes behind enemy lines. Rated R for Refuse. 92m. **DIR:** Vincent Dawn. **CAST:** Reb Brown, Christopher Connelly. **1987**

STRIKE FORCE ★★ A *French Connection* rehash, this made-for-television movie stars Richard Gere as a cop out to make a big drug bust. Lots of action, not much story. 74m. **DIR:** Barry Shear. **CAST:** Richard Gere, Cliff Gorman, Donald-Blakely, Edward Grover, Joe Spinell. **1975 DVD**

STRIKE IT RICH ★★ Whirlwind romance results in a honeymoon at Monte Carlo for a prudish British accountant (Robert Lindsay) and his young wife (Molly Ringwald). Bland romantic comedy derived from a Graham Greene novel. Rated PG. 90m. **DIR:** James Scott. **CAST:** Robert Lindsay, Molly Ringwald, John Gielgud, Simon de la Brosse. **1990**

STRIKE UP THE BAND ★★★ This encore to *Babes in Arms* has ever-exuberant Mickey Rooney leading a high school band that would shade Glenn Miller's. Second banana Judy Garland sings. "Come on, kids, let's put on a show" in a different setting. B&W; 120m. **DIR:** Busby Berkeley. **CAST:** Mickey Rooney, Judy Garland, June Preisser, Paul Whiteman. **1940**

STRIKER'S MOUNTAIN ★★ Predictable plot with suspenseless conflicts. A small-time resort owner alternately courts and repels the big corporate backing that leaves Leslie Nielsen, as a ruthless millionaire, controls. The ski scenes are the best part of the film. Not rated. 99m. **DIR:** Allen Simmonds. **CAST:** Leslie Nielsen, August Schellenberg, Mimi Kuzyk, Bruce Greenwood. **1987**

STRIKING DISTANCE ★★★1/2 An honest cop finds himself on river patrol after testifying against another police officer who brutally beat a suspect to death. Then he picks up the trail of a serial killer. While not up to the high standards of the star's *Die Hard* movies, this is still enjoyable action fare. Rated R for profanity, violence, and simulated sex. 97m. **DIR:** Rowdy Harrington. **CAST:** Bruce Willis, Sarah Jessica Parker, Dennis Farina, Tom Sizemore, Robert Pastorelli, Timothy Busfield, John Mahoney, Andr Braugher, Tom Atkins. **1993 DVD**

STRIKING POINT ★★ The Cold War may be ove but ex-KGB agents are nurturing a war of their ow by shipping deadly weapons into the United State and supplying them to street gangs. Rated R for vic lence and adult language. 93m. **DIR:** Thomas Fentor **CAST:** Chris Mitchum, Tracy Spaulding, Ivan Rogers Stan Morse. **1994**

●**STRIKING POSES** ★★1/2 A photographer wh stalks celebrities for a tabloid finds the table turned when someone starts stalking her. It's no *Th Conversation*, but this straight-to-video suspens drama is better than the box (which makes it loo like an erotic thriller) would suggest. Rated R fo profanity and violence. 99m. **DIR:** Gail Harry. **CAST** Shannen Doherty, Joseph Griffin, Tamara Gorski, Coln Feore. **1998**

STRIPES ★★★★ It's laughs aplenty when *Saturday Night Live* graduate Bill Murray enlists in the army. But hey, as Murray might say, after a guy loses his job, his car, and his girl all in the same day, what else is he supposed to do? Thanks to Murray, Harold Ramis, and John Candy, the U.S. Army may never be the same. Warren Oates also is in top form as the nononsense sergeant. Rated R. 105m. **DIR:** Ivan Reitman. **CAST:** Bill Murray, Harold Ramis, John Candy, Warren Oates, P. J. Soles, Sean Young, John Larroquette. **1981 DVD**

STRIPPER, THE ★★1/2 Somewhat engrossing account of an aging stripper (Joanne Woodward) falling in love with a teenager (Richard Beymer). Good performances by all, but the film tends to drag and become too stagy. Based on William Inge's play. 95m. **DIR:** Franklin J. Schaffner. **CAST:** Joanne Woodward, Richard Beymer, Claire Trevor, Carol Lynley, Robert Webber, Gypsy Rose Lee, Louis Nye. **1963**

STRIPTEASE ★★1/2 Carl Hiaasen's provocative bestseller stars Demi Moore as a former FBI clerk forced to earn money as a stripper, while petitioning the court to regain her daughter from a low-life former husband. Rated R for nudity, profanity, violence, and strong sexual content. 115m. **DIR:** Andrew Bergman. **CAST:** Demi Moore, Armand Assante, Ving Rhames, Robert Patrick, Burt Reynolds, Stuart Pankin. **1996 DVD**

STRIPTEASER 💘 Exotic dancer at Zipper's Clown Palace is forced to fight for her life when the club is taken over by an obsessed gunman. Just an excuse to get untalented actresses out of their clothes. Not rated; contains nudity, violence, and language. 82m. **DIR:** Dan Goldman. **CAST:** Maria Ford, Rick Dean. **1994**

STRIPTEASER 2 💘 A psycho killer stalks strippers in a cheap-looking shot-on-video sleazefest that has nothing to do with *Stripteaser*. Rated R for nudity, sex, and sexual violence. 77m. **DIR:** Karl Ernest. **CAST:** Rick Jordan, Stacey Leigh Mobley, Matt Preston, Kim Dawson. **1997**

STROKE OF MIDNIGHT ★★1/2 Filmed in Paris, this feature stars Jennifer Grey as a drab high-fashion dresser who makes a Cinderella-type transformation after a fairy godmother rewards her for a good deed. Cute fantasy is okay time-passer. Rated PG for profanity. 102m. **DIR:** Tom Clegg. **CAST:** Jennifer Grey, Rob Lowe, Andrea Ferreol. 1990

STROKER ACE ★★ Film critics all over the country jumped on this car-crash-and-corn-pone comedy. It's not all that bad. About an egotistical, woman-chasing race-car driver, it's the same old predictable nonsense. Yet it's certain to please the audience it was intended for. Rated PG for sexual innuendo and violence. 96m. **DIR:** Hal Needham. **CAST:** Burt Reynolds, Ned Beatty, Jim Nabors, Loni Anderson, Parker Stevenson. 1983 DVD

STROMBOLI ★★ This potboiler from the director of *Open City* is a brooding, sometimes boring movie about an attractive woman who marries a fisherman and attempts to adjust. Even Ingrid Bergman (by this time married to Rossellini) couldn't salvage this film. Subtitled. B&W; 81m. **DIR:** Roberto Rossellini. **CAST:** Ingrid Bergman, Mario Vitale. 1950

STRONG MAN, THE ★★★1/2 At one time silent comedy star Harry Langdon gave Charlie Chaplin, Buster Keaton, and Harold Lloyd a run for their money. *The Strong Man*, directed by a very young Frank Capra, is Langdon's best feature film. Langdon plays a young Belgian soldier who wistfully dreams of the American girl he has been corresponding with while bungling most of his assignments on the battlefield. Silent. B&W; 75m. **DIR:** Frank Capra. **CAST:** Harry Langdon, Priscilla Bonner, Robert McKim. 1926

STROSZEK ★★★★ Werner Herzog's hilarious, poignant vision of three misfits—a drunk, a soulful prostitute, and an eccentric old man—who leave Berlin and follow the American dream to rural Wisconsin. This funny, richly perceptive look at the American experience through the eyes of three German outcasts won international critical acclaim. In German with English subtitles. Not rated. 108m. **DIR:** Werner Herzog. **CAST:** Bruno S., Eva Mattes, Clemens Scheitz. 1977

STRYKER ♥ A soldier of fortune attempting to wrest a group of warrior women from the clutches of an evil tribe. Rated R. 86m. **DIR:** Cirio H. Santiago. **CAST:** Steve Sandor, Andria Savio. 1983

•**STUART LITTLE** ★★★★ Magical, heartwarming family film based on E. B. White's children's book. A couple's adoption of a second son, oblivious to the fact that he's a mouse, leads to problems with their human son which pale in comparison to the family cat's resentment. High-quality computer-generated detail allows the mouse to appear real and permits the many featured cats to talk freely. Jonathan Lipnicki is adorable as the human son and the voices of Michael J. Fox as Stuart and Nathan Lane as his nemesis Snowbell perfectly fit the roles. Rated PG for *Road Runner*-ish violence toward the cats. 86m. **DIR:** Rob Minkoff. **CAST:** Geena Davis, Hugh Laurie, Jonathan Lipnicki. 1999 DVD

STUART SAVES HIS FAMILY ★★★1/2 Al Franken re-creates his *Saturday Night Live* role of Stuart Smalley, the soft-spoken host of *Daily Affirmation* and neurotic veteran of several twelve-step foundations. In exploring Stuart's rocky history with his world-class dysfunctional family, the film is not only warmly funny but also a sweet-tempered satire of modern hang-ups. Rated PG-13 for mature themes and mild profanity. 90m. **DIR:** Harold Ramis. **CAST:** Al Franken, Laura San Giacomo, Vincent D'Onofrio, Lesley Boone, Shirley Knight, Harris Yulin. 1995

STUD, THE ♥ Sordid soft-core porn film concerning a young man's various affairs. Rated R. 95m. **DIR:** Quentin Masters. **CAST:** Joan Collins, Oliver Tobias. 1978

STUDENT BODIES ★★1/2 This comedy-horror release has something extra, because it is a parody of blood-and-guts films. Rated R. 86m. **DIR:** Mickey Rose. **CAST:** Kristin Ritter, Matthew Goldsby, Joe Flood. 1981

STUDENT CONFIDENTIAL ★★1/2 A new school counselor helps some problem children with high IQs. *Student Confidential* does not speak to teens with the self-satisfaction of *The Breakfast Club* or the brutality of *River's Edge*, but it is far better than most teen films. Rated R for violence, profanity, and nudity. 92m. **DIR:** Richard Horian. **CAST:** Eric Douglas, Marlon Jackson, Ronee Blakley. 1987

STUDENT NURSES, THE ★★★ In their last year of schooling, four young women begin to experience life in the real world of medicine and men. The first of Roger Corman's successful *Nurse* movies, this is a well-written exploitation movie that you don't have to feel guilty about liking. Rated R for nudity. 85m. **DIR:** Stephanie Rothman. **CAST:** Elaine Giftos, Karen Carlson, Barbara Leigh. 1970

STUDENT OF PRAGUE ★★★★ One of the most important films in silent German Expressionist cinema. The film is based on the myths of the Doppelgänger and Faust legends. Brilliantly photographed. Silent with English titles. B&W; 45m. **DIR:** Henrik Galeen. **CAST:** Conrad Veidt, Werner Krauss. 1926

STUDENT PRINCE, THE ★★★★ A captivating, colorful, and charming rendition of Sigmund Romberg's famous operetta, and the only talkie version made from it. Mario Lanza recorded the soundtrack but was much too fat to play the Prince of Heidelberg who lives among the commoners and falls for a barmaid (Ann Blyth). Newcomer Edmund Purdom took his place. 107m. **DIR:** Richard Thorpe. **CAST:** Ann Blyth, Edmund Purdom, John Ericson, Louis Calhern, Edmund Gwenn. 1954

STUDENT PRINCE IN OLD HEIDELBERG, THE ★★★★ The famous Lubitsch touch is in evidence in the story of a Bavarian prince eager to sow some wild oats. He enrolls at Heidelberg University, falls in love with a barmaid, and comes of age. Later versions with the famous Sigmund Romberg score turned the tale into a moodier romance. Silent. B&W; 105m. **DIR:** Ernst Lubitsch. **CAST:** Norma Shearer, Ramon Novarro, Jean Hersholt, Gustav von Seyffertitz. 1927

STUDS LONIGAN ★★ Film version of James T. Farrell's landmark first novel is a major disappointment. Depressing tale of a young man's slide into drunkenness and debauchery pulls most of the punches that the book delivered and ends up drastically changing the ending to a more conventional Hollywood fade-out. B&W; 95m. **DIR:** Irving Lerner.

CAST: Christopher Knight, Frank Gorshin, Jack Nicholson, Venetia Stevenson, Dick Foran, Jay C. Flippen, Carolyn Craig. 1960

STUDY IN SCARLET, A ★★ Bearing absolutely no resemblance to the first of Arthur Conan Doyle's Sherlock Holmes stories, this low-budget entry is perhaps the most lackluster of all the sound Holmes films. B&W; 70m. **DIR:** Edwin L. Marin. **CAST:** Reginald Owen, Anna May Wong, Alan Dinehart, June Clyde, Alan Mowbray. 1933

STUDY IN TERROR, A ★★★★ Superior Sherlock Holmes adventure pits "the original caped crusader," as the ads called him, against Jack the Ripper. John Neville is an excellent Holmes. And Donald Houston is perhaps the screen's finest Dr. John Watson. 94m. **DIR:** James Hill. **CAST:** John Neville, Donald Houston, Georgia Brown, John Fraser, Anthony Quayle, Barbara Windsor, Robert Morley, Cecil Parker. 1965

STUFF, THE ❤ A scrumptious, creamy dessert devours from within all those who eat it. Rated R for gore and profanity. 93m. **DIR:** Larry Cohen. **CAST:** Michael Moriarty, Andrea Marcovicci, Garrett Morris, Paul Sorvino, Danny Aiello. 1985

STUFF STEPHANIE IN THE INCINERATOR ❤ Excruciatingly bad stalk-and-hunt comedy that has nothing to do with an incinerator, but still deserves to get stuffed. Rated PG-13. 97m. **DIR:** Lloyd Kaufman. **CAST:** Catherine Dee. 1989

STUNT MAN, THE ★★★★1/2 Nothing is ever quite what it seems in this fast-paced, superbly crafted film. It's a Chinese puzzle of a movie and, therefore, may not please all viewers. Nevertheless, this directorial tour de force by Richard Rush has ample thrills, chills, suspense, and surprises for those with a taste for something different. Rated R. 129m. **DIR:** Richard Rush. **CAST:** Peter O'Toole, Steve Railsback, Barbara Hershey, Chuck Bail, Allen Garfield, Adam Roarke, Alex Rocco. 1980

STUPIDS, THE ★★ Dumb down the Brady Bunch a few notches and you have the Stupids, a family so out of it that they think they're on to it. While investigating the weekly theft of his garbage, Stanley Stupid (Tom Arnold) uncovers a plot to sell high-powered weapons to international tyrants. Meanwhile, his wife seeks her children, believed to have been kidnapped by the police. You'll laugh in spite of the fact that this film can only live up to its title. Rated PG for violence. 93m. **DIR:** John Landis. **CAST:** Tom Arnold, Jessica Lundy, Alex McKenna, Bug Hall, Mark Metcalf, Matt Keeslar. 1996

SUB DOWN ★★1/2 Three scientists try to help out a disabled nuclear submarine stuck below the arctic ice cap. This made-for-cable original is not a bad little action-rescue movie, but several stupid story twists and a few bad lines sink the whole film, which is probably why director Gregg Champion decided to hide behind the Alan Smithee pseudonym. Not rated. 95m. **DIR:** Alan Smithee. **CAST:** Stephen Baldwin, Gabrielle Anwar, Tom Conti. 1997

SUBJECT WAS ROSES, THE ★★★ A young soldier (Martin Sheen) returns home to his unhappily married parents (Patricia Neal, Jack Albertson). Well acted, especially by Neal in her first role after her near-fatal stroke. Vaudeville veteran Albertson won an Oscar. Rated G. 107m. **DIR:** Ulu Grosbard. **CAST:** Patricia Neal, Jack Albertson, Martin Sheen. 1968

SUBSPECIES ★★★ Two vampire brothers—one good, one evil—fight for a bloodstone left by their father. This interesting twist on the vampire legend suffers from bad acting, but benefits by holding true to many aspects of vampire lore. Not rated; contains violence, profanity, and mild gore. 90m. **DIR:** Ted Nicolaou. **CAST:** Michael Watson, Laura Tate, Angus Scrimm. 1990

SUBSTANCE OF FIRE, THE ★★★★ Manhattan publishing magnate Isaac Geldhart is descending into madness, and his once-respected literary house is "hemorrhaging money." The bitter Holocaust survivor, unable to express love to his own children, is determined to print very pricey volumes of Nazi medical atrocities that have been documented by an old friend. This compelling drama about an adult struggling with a traumatic past and an all-consuming commitment to moral and artistic excellence, blends lofty themes with fine performances. Rated R for language. 101m. **DIR:** Daniel Sullivan. **CAST:** Ron Rifkin, Sarah Jessica Parker, Tony Goldwyn, Timothy Hutton. 1996

SUBSTITUTE, THE (1993) ★★★ In this made-for-cable original, a college professor kills her husband and his lover, then resurfaces as a substitute high-school teacher. She falls in love with the father of one of her students, but people are getting suspicious, so she must kill again. Pretty predictable story line, but the acting is good. Rated R for violence and suggested sex. 86m. **DIR:** Martin Donovan. **CAST:** Amanda Donohoe, Dalton James, Natasha Gregson Wagner, Eugene Glazer, Mark Wahlberg. 1993

SUBSTITUTE, THE (1996) ★★1/2 This unintentionally wacky, reactionary urban thriller introduces the ultimate high-school disciplinarian—an unemployed mercenary soldier. Rated R for violence and language. 114m. **DIR:** Robert Mandel. **CAST:** Tom Berenger, Diane Venora, Ernie Hudson, Glenn Plummer, Raymond Cruz, William Forsythe. 1996 **DVD**

SUBSTITUTE WIFE, THE ★★★★1/2 Keep the tissue handy when you watch this charming, tender story of love and unselfishness. Peter Weller and Lea Thompson lead a stellar cast in this made-for-television tearjerker about a couple trying to keep their children and Nebraska farm together despite the odds. Set in 1869, the film is rich in period detail and strong family values. Rated PG-13 for theme. 92m. **DIR:** Peter Werner. **CAST:** Farrah Fawcett, Lea Thompson, Peter Weller. 1994

SUBURBAN COMMANDO ★★1/2 Wrestler Hulk Hogan is extremely likable as an outer-space bounty hunter in this humorous comedy. Christopher Lloyd is a nebbish architect who learns to handle his boss with the help of Hogan's commando tactics. Rated PG. 85m. **DIR:** Burt Kennedy. **CAST:** Hulk Hogan, Christopher Lloyd, Shelley Duvall, Larry Miller, Jack Elam. 1991

SUBURBAN ROULETTE ❤ Showcased by Joe Bob Briggs, this piece of trash about wife swapping is tame and boring by today's standards. Not rated.

91m. **DIR:** Herschell Gordon Lewis. **CAST:** Elizabeth Wilkinson. 1967

SUBURBIA (1983) ★★★ Penelope Spheeris, who directed the punk-rock documentary *Decline of Western Civilization*, did this low-budget film of punk rockers versus local rednecks and townspeople in a small suburban area. Not for all tastes, but a good little film for people who are bored with releases like *Cannonball Run II*. Rated R. 96m. **DIR:** Penelope Spheeris. **CAST:** Chris Pederson, Bill Coyne, Jennifer Clay. 1983

SUBURBIA (1997) ★★★1/2 Aimless 20-year-olds loiter around the parking lot of a convenience store, wondering what to do with the rest of their lives. When a former comrade, now successful rock singer, pays a visit, it sparks a night of partying spiked with outbursts of envy and hostility. Eric Bogosian's almost plotless play is smoothly transferred to the screen; the stage origins show through, but Richard Linklater's direction is sensitive and inconspicuous, with fine, well-balanced acting by the young ensemble cast. Rated R for profanity. 118m. **DIR:** Richard Linklater. **CAST:** Giovanni Ribisi, Nicky Katt, Steve Zahn, Amie Carey, Jayce Bartok, Parker Posey, Dina Spybey. 1997

SUBWAY ★★ The stunning Isabelle Adjani plays a young wife who becomes involved with a streetwise rogue played by Christopher Lambert. The plot is not very clear and the bad jokes don't help. Fast-paced action scenes keep the film interesting, but they all lead nowhere. In French with English subtitles. Rated R for profanity and violence. 110m. **DIR:** Luc Besson. **CAST:** Isabelle Adjani, Christopher Lambert, Richard Bohringer. 1985 DVD

SUBWAY STORIES ★★★ This HBO original derives from an intriguing contest that allowed "regular folks" to submit some of their more interesting experiences in the New York City subway system. The resulting ten vignettes are hit or miss, ranging from the quite funny to the provocative, to the completely pointless. Each episode comes from a different writer-director team; unfortunately, the combined whole never quite lives up to its desire to become a "subway symphony." Rated PG-13 for profanity. 83m. **DIR:** Jonathan Demme, Abel Ferrara. **CAST:** Gregory Hines, Bill Irwin, Christine Lahti, Denis Leary, Rosie Perez, Bill Rapaport, Mercedes Ruehl, Jerry Stiller. 1997

SUBWAY TO THE STARS ★★★ A near triumph of style over substance by a gifted Brazilian filmmaker. A musician searching for his girlfriend is guided through a nightmarish, Dante's Inferno–like labyrinth of Rio de Janeiro nightlife. Fascinating but overlong. 103m. **DIR:** Carlos Diegues. **CAST:** Guilherme Fontes. 1987

SUCCESS IS THE BEST REVENGE ★★★1/2 Polish exile hustles to make a film about his native country while ignoring his own family problems. Director Jerzy Skolimowski, who dazzled us with the 1982 film *Moonlighting* is in good form with this biting drama. Not rated; but has violence, profanity, and nudity. 95m. **DIR:** Jerzy Skolimowski. **CAST:** Michael York, Anouk Aimée, Michael Lyndon, John Hurt, Jane Asher, Michel Piccoli. 1984

SUDAN ★★★1/2 Good formula escapism fare, but the formula for Montez's pictures was wearing thin by the time this came out. It was one of her last. 76m. **DIR:** John Rawlins. **CAST:** Maria Montez, Jon Hall, Turhan Bey, Andy Devine, George Zucco, Robert Warwick. 1945

SUDDEN DEATH (1986) 🐨 Cheaply made rehash of *Death Wish* and *Ms. .45*. Rated R. 93m. **DIR:** Sig Shore. **CAST:** Denise Coward, Frank Runyeon, Jaime Tinelli. 1986

SUDDEN DEATH (1995) ★★1/2 *Die Hard* in a hockey arena. A fireman with a troubled past takes his kids to the Stanley Cup finals in Pittsburgh, where his daughter and the vice president of the United States are nabbed by terrorists. The film doesn't break any new ground but provides several big action thrills as the extortionists threaten to blow up the arena and parking lot. Rated R for language and violence. 110m. **DIR:** Peter Hyams. **CAST:** Jean-Claude Van Damme, Powers Boothe, Raymond J. Berry, Whittni Wright, Ross Malinger. 1995 DVD

SUDDEN FEAR ★★★★ An eerie thriller about a playwright who finds out her husband plans to kill her. She works to turn the tables on him and get his girlfriend to take the blame. Moody film that capitalizes on Joan Crawford's wide-eyed looks of shock and frustration. Because it is so well-written, the rest of the cast gets a chance to shine as well. B&W; 110m. **DIR:** David Miller. **CAST:** Joan Crawford, Jack Palance, Gloria Grahame, Mike Connors. 1952 DVD

SUDDEN IMPACT ★★★★ "Dirty Harry" Callahan (Clint Eastwood) is back, and he's meaner, nastier, and—surprise!—funnier than ever in this, his fourth screen adventure. Harry's job is to track down a female revenge killer but not until he's done away with a half-dozen villains and delivered twice as many quips including, "Go ahead, make my day." Rated R for violence and profanity. 117m. **DIR:** Clint Eastwood. **CAST:** Clint Eastwood, Sondra Locke, Pat Hingle, Bradford Dillman. 1983

SUDDEN THUNDER 🐨 Umpteenth take on the female cop avenging her father's death by taking on the mob. The only thunder is this bomb going off. Not rated; contains violence. 90m. **DIR:** David Hunt. **CAST:** Andrea Lamatsch, Corwyn Sperry, James Paoleilei, Ernie Santana. 1990

SUDDENLY ★★★★ Here's top-notch entertainment with Frank Sinatra perfectly cast as a leader of a gang of assassins out to kill the president of the United States. Film has gone largely unnoticed over the last few years, but thanks to home video, we can all enjoy this gem of a picture. B&W; 77m. **DIR:** Lewis Allen. **CAST:** Frank Sinatra, Sterling Hayden, James Gleason, Nancy Gates. 1954 DVD

SUDDENLY, LAST SUMMER ★★★ Another one of those unpleasant but totally intriguing forays of Tennessee Williams. Elizabeth Taylor is a neurotic girl being prodded into madness by the memory of her gay cousin's bizarre death, a memory that Katharine Hepburn, his adoring mother, wants to remain vague if not submerged. She prevails upon Montgomery Clift to make sure it does. B&W; 114m. **DIR:** Joseph L. Mankiewicz. **CAST:** Elizabeth Taylor, Montgomery Clift, Katharine Hepburn. 1959

SUDIE & SIMPSON ★★★1/2 This finely etched portrait of racial intolerance in a small 1940s Georgia town shows how the friendship between the kindly black Simpson and sprite Sudie teaches the locals a lesson about understanding and prejudice. Excellent performances from all in this made-for-TV movie. Not rated. 95m. **DIR:** Joan Tewkesbury. **CAST:** Lou Gossett Jr., Sara Gilbert, Frances Fisher, John Jackson. 1990

SUGAR COOKIES 💔 Two women are set up to be murdered by a porno filmmaker. Rated R for nudity, profanity, and violence. 89m. **DIR:** Michael Herz. **CAST:** Mary Woronov, Monique Van Vooren, Lynn Lowry. 1988

SUGAR HILL ★★1/2 Despite fine performances by Wesley Snipes and Michael Wright, this story of two brothers involved in the Harlem drug trade does not have the punch of *New Jack City*. Director Leon Ichaso has a great eye for detail and settings, but he is unable to add excitement to the all-too-familiar story line that has Snipes attempting to leave his gangster ways behind. Rated R for violence, profanity, and nudity. 123m. **DIR:** Leon Ichaso. **CAST:** Wesley Snipes, Michael Wright, Theresa Randle, Clarence Williams III, Abe Vigoda, Larry Joshua, Ernie Hudson, Leslie Uggams. 1994

•**SUGAR TOWN** ★★★1/2 Aging rockers seek a comeback record deal in this earthy, sweetly comic ensemble piece. Set in the fast, clogged lanes of Los Angeles's music and film scene, this sprawling stream of characters, moods, and melodrama says just as much about American culture and show business as it does individual dreams, conceits, and scruples. Its intersecting stories wheeze a bit but feel refreshingly honest. Rated R for drug content, language, and sexual content. 93m. **DIR:** Allison Anders, Kurt Voss. **CAST:** Jade Gordon, Ally Sheedy, Larry Klein, Michael Des Barres, John Taylor, Martin Kemp, John Doe. 1999

SUGARBABY ★★★1/2 In this decidedly offbeat comedy-drama from German filmmaker Percy Adlon, an overweight morgue attendant (Marianne Sägebrecht) finds new meaning in her life when she falls in love with a subway driver. In German with English subtitles. Not rated; the film has nudity. 86m. **DIR:** Percy Adlon. **CAST:** Marianne Sägebrecht. 1986

SUGARCANE ALLEY ★★★★ Set in Martinique of the 1930s, this superb French import examines the lives led by black sugarcane plantation workers. Specifically, it focuses on the hopes and dreams of José (Garry Cadenat), an 11-year-old orphan with a brilliant mind, which just may be the key to his breaking the bonds of slavery. In French with English subtitles. Not rated, the film has some scenes of violence. 100m. **DIR:** Euzhan Palcy. **CAST:** Garry Cadenat, Darling Legitimus. 1983

SUGARLAND EXPRESS, THE ★★★★ A rewarding film in many respects, this was Steven Spielberg's first feature effort. Based on an actual incident in Texas during the late 1960s, a prison escapee and his wife try to regain custody of their infant child. Their desperation results in a madcap chase across the state with a kidnapped state trooper. Rated PG. 109m. **DIR:** Steven Spielberg. **CAST:** Goldie Hawn, Ben Johnson, Michael Sacks, William Atherton. 1974

SUGARTIME ★★★ Scripter Martyn Burke's based-on-truth gangster saga is pretty ordinary compared to contemporaries such as *Bugsy* or *Casino*, but there's nonetheless a certain fascination to this study of a Vegas shark's relationship with singing star Phyllis McGuire (leader of the popular 1950s group, the McGuire Sisters). John Turturro is acceptable as the gangster with a soft spot, but Mary-Louise Parker plays Phyllis as a little fool too naïve for words. Rated R for violence and profanity. 110m. **DIR:** John N. Smith. **CAST:** John Turturro, Mary-Louise Parker, Elias Koteas, Maury Chaykin, Louis Del Grande. 1995

SUICIDE BATTALION 💔 The newsreel stock footage is more exciting than the movie itself in this stage-bound WWII programmer set at Pearl Harbor. B&W; 79m. **DIR:** Edward L. Cahn. **CAST:** Mike Connors, John Ashley, Russ Bender. 1958

SUICIDE CLUB, THE ★★ Uneven, contrived shocker features Mariel Hemingway as a bored heiress involved with a group of self-indulgent aristocrats who engage in bizarre ritualistic games. Hemingway turns in a compelling performance in this otherwise disappointing thriller. Rated R; contains nudity and violence. 90m. **DIR:** James Bruce. **CAST:** Mariel Hemingway, Robert Joy, Madeleine Potter, Michael O'Donoghue. 1988

SUICIDE KINGS ★★★ Four New York preppies kidnap a Mafia kingpin. The story is preposterous, and the telling of it is unnecessarily complicated, but it does hold your interest with dark, jittery energy, and the hypnotically menacing Christopher Walken as the mobster. Rated R for profanity and violence. 107m. **DIR:** Peter O'Fallon. **CAST:** Christopher Walken, Henry Thomas, Lara Harris, Jeremy Sisto, Sean Patrick Flanery, Jay Mohr, Denis Leary. 1998 DVD

SUICIDE RIDE ★★ Barney decides to cash it in and hires a hit man to do the job. The hit man, who's on the verge of retiring, offers Barney his job instead of killing him. Now the suicidal Barney wants to live but realizes there's no job security in his new profession. Low-budget, independent effort makes good use of its limited resources. Not rated; contains adult situations, language, nudity, and violence. 86m. **DIR:** Samer Daboul, Trever Sands. **CAST:** Tim Quill, Matthias Hues, Frank Adonis. 1994

SUITE 16 ★★★ A wealthy invalid (Peter Postlethwaite) gives refuge to a young criminal, as long as he participates in living out his host's increasingly dangerous erotic fantasies. Misleadingly marketed as a standard erotic thriller, this is a European psychodrama of a higher level that will keep even jaded viewers intrigued. Rated R for strong sexuality, language, violence, and drug use. 93m. **DIR:** Dominique Deruddere. **CAST:** Pete Postlethwaite, Antonie Kamerling, Geraldine Pailhas, Tom Jansen. 1994 DVD

SULLIVAN'S TRAVELS ★★★★ Pure genius produced this social comedy, witty and knowing spoof of Hollywood. A film director decides to find out what life outside the Tinseltown fantasyland is really like. This is a genuine Hollywood classic. B&W; 90m. **DIR:** Preston Sturges. **CAST:** Joel McCrea, Veronica Lake,

Robert Warwick, William Demarest, Franklin Pangborn, Porter Hall, Eric Blore, Jimmy Conlin. 1941

SUM OF US, THE ★★★1/2 A working-class Australian widower and his gay son live together in respectful harmony while they look for, respectively, Ms. and Mr. Right. Well acted and enjoyable, with a core of decency and right-mindedness that adds to its poignancy and charm. Not rated; contains mature themes, mild profanity, and one homosexual love scene. 100m. DIR: Kevin Dowling, Geoff Burton. CAST: Jack Thompson, Russell Crowe, John Polson, Deborah Kennedy. 1994

SUMMER ★★★★ Eric Rohmer's fifth of his six-part *Comedies and Proverbs* is the slight but emotionally resonant tale of Delphine (Marie Riviere), a Paris secretary whose vacation plans are suddenly ruined. Like the previous films in the series, *Summer* requires a commitment on the part of the viewer. Ultimately, the story touches your heart. In French with English subtitles. Rated R for nudity and profanity. 98m. DIR: Eric Rohmer. CAST: Marie Riviere, Lisa Heredia, Beatrice Romand. 1986 DVD

SUMMER AND SMOKE ★★1/2 Love-hungry spinster dominated by narrow-minded parents plays her cards wrong and can't turn a trick. Talky Tennessee Williams tale. Geraldine Page is fine, but one performance does not a hit make. 118m. DIR: Peter Glenville. CAST: Geraldine Page, Laurence Harvey, Una Merkel, Rita Moreno, John McIntire. 1961

SUMMER CAMP 🦃 The madcaps in this case are teens invited to a reunion of their old summer camp. Rated R. 85m. DIR: Chuck Vincent. CAST: Michael Abrams, Jake Barnes. 1979

SUMMER CAMP NIGHTMARE ★★ Based on *The Butterfly Revolution* and misleadingly retitled to cash in on the teen-horror market, this is actually an antifascist parable similar to *Lord of the Flies*. A young counselor at a preteen summer camp stages a revolution, overthrowing the strict director and setting himself up in charge. The ambitious premise is never resolved satisfactorily, with a particularly anticlimactic ending. Rated PG-13 for violence and nudity. 88m. DIR: Bert L. Dragin. CAST: Chuck Connors, Charles Stratton. 1986

SUMMER CITY ★★ Mel Gibson stars in this Australian teen rebel flick that lacks a fresh approach to one of the oldest stories in film: four teens go on a surfing weekend at a sleepy little seaside community only to find trouble when one of the delinquents messes around with a local's daughter. A few intense moments, and the acting is not bad, but some of the dialogue is indistinguishable in the muddy audio. Not rated, but the equivalent of PG for some sex, partial nudity, and violence. 83m. DIR: Christopher Fraser. CAST: Mel Gibson, Phil Avalon, Steve Bisley. 1976

SUMMER DREAMS ★★★ Unauthorized made-for-television biography of the rock 'n' roll group that defined the California sound: the Beach Boys. From their humble beginnings to the tumultuous years that broke up the band, this docudrama makes an honest attempt to give an overall picture of how fame and fortune can divide even the best of friends and make them crazy. Good cast, but songs were rerecorded by another group. Rated R for some additional scenes of nudity. 94m. DIR: Michael Switzer. CAST: Casey Sander, Greg Kean, Bruce Greenwood, Arlen Dean Snyder, Bo Foxworth. 1985

SUMMER FLING ★★★ Enchanting, rich story about a young Irish boy coming of age amongst his wildly eccentric family. Excellent performances throughout. Cowritten by Gabriel Byrne and director David Keating. Also known as *Last of the High Kings*. Rated R for sexuality, profanity, and adult situations. 103m. DIR: David Keating. CAST: Catherine O'Hara, Jared Leto, Christina Ricci, Gabriel Byrne, Stephen Rea, Colm Meaney. 1996

SUMMER HEAT (1983) 🦃 Bruce Davison stars as a young sheepherder who, upon being sentenced to prison, attempts to escape with his new love. Rated R for violence, profanity, and implied sex. 101m. DIR: Jack Starrett. CAST: Bruce Davison, Susan George, Anthony Franciosa. 1983

SUMMER HEAT (1987) 🦃 This is a barely lukewarm sex-and-soap sizzler. Rated R. 95m. DIR: Michie Gleason. CAST: Lori Singer, Bruce Abbott, Anthony Edwards, Clu Gulager, Kathy Bates. 1987

SUMMER HOLIDAY ★★1/2 A musical remake of Eugene O'Neill's *Ah, Wilderness*, and the music gets in the way. It just isn't hummable and takes up time the personalities could have used to flesh out this charming coming-of-age story set in the early twentieth-century in mid-America. Walter Huston is excellent as the wise head of the house. 92m. DIR: Rouben Mamoulian. CAST: Mickey Rooney, Walter Huston, Agnes Moorehead, Marilyn Maxwell, Gloria De Haven, Frank Morgan, "Butch" Jenkins, Anne Francis. 1948

SUMMER HOUSE, THE ★★★1/2 Director Waris Hussein makes mincemeat of Alice Thomas Ellis's novel, *The Clothes in the Wardrobe*. We're never quite sure why sweet, hard-drinking Margaret agreed to marry the boorish Syl, but coconspirators derailing the upcoming nuptials are so deliciously oddball that the movie succeeds almost in spite of itself. Not rated, the film has brief moments of profanity, violence, and suggested sex. 83m. DIR: Waris Hussein. CAST: Jeanne Moreau, Joan Plowright, Julie Walters, Lena Headey, David Threlfall, Maggie Steed, John Wood, Gwenyth Strong, Catherine Schell. 1993

SUMMER INTERLUDE ★★★1/2 An aging ballerina recalls a lost love from her youth and she learns through her newly reawakened memories to cope successfully with her present life. Perhaps Ingmar Bergman's first major film, and one of his most beautifully lyric. In Swedish with English subtitles. B&W; 90m. DIR: Ingmar Bergman. CAST: May Britt. 1950

SUMMER LOVERS 🦃 Study of a *ménage à trois* in Greece. Rated R for nudity, profanity, and implied sex. 98m. DIR: Randal Kleiser. CAST: Peter Gallagher, Daryl Hannah, Valerie Quennessen, Barbara Rush, Carole Cook. 1982

SUMMER MAGIC ★★1/2 Dorothy McGuire is a recent widow who finds out she has no money available. She moves her family to Maine, where they live in a fixer-upper house but are charged no rent by Burl Ives. Deborah Walley, a snobbish cousin, comes to visit and causes trouble. Lightweight and enjoyable. Rated G. 100m. DIR: James Neilson. CAST: Hayley Mills, Burl Ives, Dorothy McGuire, Deborah Walley, Eddie Hodges, Peter Brown. 1963

SUMMER NIGHT ★★★ The full title is *Summer Night, with Greek Profile, Almond Eyes and Scent of Basil*, and it's a semisequel-reprise of Wertmuller's *Swept Away . . .*, with Mariangela Melato in a similar role as a rich industrialist who captures a terrorist and holds him prisoner on a secluded island. Wertmuller fans will be disappointed; it covers nothing she hasn't done better before. In Italian with English subtitles. Rated R for nudity and sexual situations. 94m. **DIR:** Lina Wertmuller. **CAST:** Mariangela Melato, Michele Placido. 1987

SUMMER OF BEN TYLER, THE ★★★★ Heartening tale of understanding and prejudice features a winning James Woods as small southern town lawyer Temple Rayburn, whose decision to take in the black son of his late housekeeper threatens his practice and life. This *Hallmark Hall of Fame* television production, set during World War II, manages to get its message across without appearing too preachy. Rated PG. 134m. **DIR:** Arthur Allan Seidelman. **CAST:** James Woods, Elizabeth McGovern, Len Cariou. 1996

SUMMER OF FEAR ★★ Confine Wes Craven to television and his horrific abilities fly out the window. A set-upon Linda Blair is the tormented target. Originally telecast as *Stranger In Our House*. 100m. **DIR:** Wes Craven. **CAST:** Linda Blair, Macdonald Carey, Carol Lawrence, Jeff East, Lee Purcell, Jeremy Slate, Jeff McCracken. 1978

SUMMER OF '42 ★★★★ Set against the backdrop of a vacationers' resort island off the New England coast during World War II. An inexperienced young man (Gary Grimes) has a crush on the 22-year-old bride (Jennifer O'Neill) of a serviceman. His stumbling attempts to acquire sexual knowledge are handled tenderly and thoughtfully. Rated PG. 102m. **DIR:** Robert Mulligan. **CAST:** Gary Grimes, Jennifer O'Neill, Jerry Houser, Oliver Conant, Christopher Norris, Lou Frizell. 1971

SUMMER OF MY GERMAN SOLDIER ★★★★ Heartwarming tale of an open-minded girl's friendship with a German POW during World War II. Esther Rolle is superb as the family cook to whom the girl confides. Made for TV. 98m. **DIR:** Michael Tuchner. **CAST:** Kristy McNichol, Bruce Davison, Esther Rolle, Michael Constantine. 1978

•**SUMMER OF SAM** ★★★1/2 Spike Lee's ambitious ensemble drama is a fictionalized re-creation of New York City during the blistering summer of 1977, when the serial murderer dubbed "Son of Sam" erupted into full-blown homicidal fury. The resulting cauldron of suspicion and paranoia is tailor-made for Lee, who demonstrated a similar fascination with friendship under heat-induced stress in *Do the Right Thing*. The cynical director always expects people to revert to jungle savagery, and he structures the relationships in this film accordingly. The key story involves the deteriorating marriage between John Leguizamo and Mira Sorvino, and the latter's goodhearted spirit helps balance the film's often nasty tone; in a film littered with deplorable and repellent characters, Sorvino positively sparkles. Rated R for violence, profanity, drug use, nudity, and deviant sex-

ual behavior. 136m. **DIR:** Spike Lee. **CAST:** John Leguizamo, Adrien Brody, Mira Sorvino, Jennifer Esposito, Michael Rispoli, Saverio Guerra, Brian Tarantino, Al Palagonia. 1999 DVD

SUMMER OF THE MONKEYS ★★1/2 Wholesome yet ultimately staid family film set in turn-of-the-century Canada. It's there that young Jay dreams of owning his own horse. When a circus train crashes nearby and four chimpanzees escape, Jay decides to find them and collect the reward money to help his family. First he must beat a reclusive local and some cruel bullies to the punch. Slow and predictable, this effort is best left to the nondemanding viewer. Rated G. 101m. **DIR:** Michael Anderson. **CAST:** Corey Sevier, Michael Ontkean, Wilford Brimley. 1998

SUMMER PLACE, A ★★1/2 Big box-office bonanza for 1959 is a comparatively tame story of extramarital love and teenage infatuation. This mixed-audience melodrama made Troy Donahue and Sandra Dee household names. 130m. **DIR:** Delmer Daves. **CAST:** Dorothy McGuire, Richard Egan, Sandra Dee, Troy Donahue, Arthur Kennedy, Beulah Bondi, Constance Ford. 1959

SUMMER RENTAL ★★1/2 John Candy is watchable in his first film as star. Unfortunately, the film itself does not live up to his talents. It starts off well enough—with air traffic controller Candy exhibiting the kind of stress that causes his superiors to suggest a vacation—but after a fairly funny first hour, it sinks into the mire of plot resolution. Rated PG for profanity. 88m. **DIR:** Carl Reiner. **CAST:** John Candy, Richard Crenna, Karen Austin, Rip Torn, Kerri Green. 1985

SUMMER SCHOOL ★★★★ This teen comedy does something almost unheard of for its genre—it bridges the generation gap and entertains young and old alike. Director Carl Reiner knows how to milk every scene for a laugh. Mark Harmon stars as a P.E. coach forced to teach remedial English in summer school. Rated PG-13 for obscenities and gore. 95m. **DIR:** Carl Reiner. **CAST:** Mark Harmon, Kirstie Alley, Nels Van Patten, Carl Reiner, Courtney Thorne-Smith, Lucy Lee Flippin, Shawnee Smith. 1987

SUMMER SCHOOL TEACHERS ★★★ The usual Roger Corman *Nurse* movie formula: three young women of different backgrounds are devoted to their professions, but not so busy that they don't have time for a little love and lust. Director Barbara Peeters keeps it from being too exploitative, but never forgets who her true drive-in audience is. Rated R for nudity. 87m. **DIR:** Barbara Peeters. **CAST:** Candice Rialson, Pat Anderson, Dick Miller. 1975

SUMMER STOCK ★★★ An echo of the Mickey Rooney–Judy Garland talented-kids/let's-give-a-show films, this likable musical is built around a troupe of ambitious performers, led by Gene Kelly, who invade farmer Judy Garland's barn. Love blooms. Judy's "Get Happy" number, filmed long after the movie was completed and spliced in to add needed flash, is inspired. 109m. **DIR:** Charles Walters. **CAST:** Judy Garland, Gene Kelly, Eddie Bracken, Gloria De Haven, Phil Silvers, Hans Conried, Marjorie Main. 1950

SUMMER STORY, A ★★★1/2 A farm girl (Imogen Stubbs) falls for a young London barrister (James Wilby). Can their odd coupling endure class-conscious turn-of-the-century England? Strong performances draw the viewer firmly into the story. Rated PG-13 for partial nudity. 97m. **DIR:** Piers Haggard. **CAST:** James Wilby, Imogen Stubbs, Susannah York, Kenneth Colley, Sophie Ward. **1989**

SUMMER TO REMEMBER, A ★★★1/2 Heartwarming story about a deaf-mute boy. When the boy befriends an intelligent orangutan, he begins to see beyond his closed world. Rated PG for no apparent reason. 98m. **DIR:** Robert Lewis. **CAST:** James Farentino, Louise Fletcher, Burt Young. **1984 DVD**

SUMMER VACATION: 1999 💗 Pubescent awakenings, hormones, homicide, and acting so inept there should be some kind of penalty to prevent it. In Japanese with English subtitles. Not rated. 90m. **DIR:** Shusuke Kaneko. **CAST:** Eri Miyagian. **1988**

SUMMER WISHES, WINTER DREAMS 💗 Manhattan housewife's depression. Rated PG. 95m. **DIR:** Gilbert Cates. **CAST:** Joanne Woodward, Martin Balsam, Sylvia Sidney, Dori Brenner. **1973**

●**SUMMER'S END** ★★★★ A young boy, still grieving over his father's death, befriends a retired doctor living on a lake, but the racial intolerance of the other locals starts to sour their happy relationship. This simple and solid character drama works because of the chemistry between the actors, and this made-for-cable original is certainly worthwhile. Rated PG for violence. 100m. **DIR:** Helen Shaver. **CAST:** James Earl Jones, Brendan Fletcher, Jake LeDoux, Al Waxman, Wendy Crewson. **1999**

SUMMERTIME ★★★★ Katharine Hepburn is a sensitive, vulnerable spinster on holiday in Venice. She falls in love with unhappily married shopkeeper Rossano Brazzi, and the romantic idyll is beautiful. David Lean's direction is superb, Jack Hildyard's cinematography excellent. 99m. **DIR:** David Lean. **CAST:** Katharine Hepburn, Rossano Brazzi, Edward Andrews, Darren McGavin, Isa Miranda. **1955 DVD**

SUMMERTIME KILLER, THE ★★1/2 A boy witnesses the beating and drowning of his father by a gang of hoods. Twenty years pass, and we follow the grownup son as he systematically pursues and kills these men in New York, Rome, and Portugal. There are some exciting motorcycle pursuits along the way before the ending takes a slight twist. Rated R for violence and language. 100m. **DIR:** Antonio Isasi. **CAST:** Chris Mitchum, Karl Malden, Olivia Hussey, Raf Vallone, Claudine Auger, Gerard Tichy. **1972**

SUN BUNNIES 💗 A female reporter and her friends track a reclusive movie star at a beach resort in this sex comedy written by Ed Wood. Not rated; contains strong sexual situations and nudity. 89m. **DIR:** A. C. Stephen. **CAST:** Brenda Fogerty, Mariwin Roberts. **1976**

SUN COMES UP, THE ★★★ A script custom designed for Jeanette MacDonald in her later years suits her personality and gives her a chance to sing some sentimental favorites. Her character, Helen Winter, is a bitter war widow who is taken aback when an orphan enters her life and endears himself to her. So does his dog, Lassie, in this tearjerker that probably wouldn't have worked with anyone else in the primary roles. 93m. **DIR:** Richard Thorpe. **CAST:** Jeanette MacDonald, Claude Jarman Jr., Lloyd Nolan, Percy Kilbride, Lewis Stone, Margaret Hamilton. **1949**

SUN SHINES BRIGHT, THE ★★★ Lovable old curly-locked Charles Winninger steals the show in John Ford's remake of *Judge Priest*, his touching 1934 slice of small-town Americana. B&W; 92m. **DIR:** John Ford. **CAST:** Charles Winninger, Arleen Whelan, John Russell, Milburn Stone. **1953**

SUN VALLEY SERENADE ★★★1/2 John Payne agrees to care for a child refugee, who turns out to be Sonja Henie. Take it from there, but enjoy the trip. Henie is truly endearing, both on and off skates. Glenn Miller and his orchestra are on hand to help move things along. B&W; 86m. **DIR:** H. Bruce Humberstone. **CAST:** Sonja Henie, John Payne, Lynn Bari, Milton Berle, Joan Davis. **1941**

SUNBURN 💗 Farrah Fawcett pretends to be the wife of insurance investigator Charles Grodin to get the real scoop on a suicide case in Acapulco. Rated PG. 94m. **DIR:** Richard C. Sarafian. **CAST:** Farrah Fawcett, Charles Grodin, Art Carney, William Daniels, Joan Collins. **1979**

SUNCHASER ★★ When a teen gang member is diagnosed with cancer, he breaks out of prison, kidnaps a doctor, and forces him to drive to Arizona in search of a mystical lake he believes can cure him. The miscasting of Woody Harrelson as a cerebral physician is only the first mistake made by this inane combination of road thriller and male-bonding movie. Rated R for profanity and violence. 122m. **DIR:** Michael Cimino. **CAST:** Woody Harrelson, Jon Seda, Talisa Soto, Anne Bancroft. **1996**

SUNDAY ★★★★ Oliver is a dumpy IBM downsizing victim who wanders into a strange encounter with a washed-up acting beauty who thinks he is a famed art-film director. Is he or isn't he? This fascinating, disorienting character study is about loneliness, desperation, die-hard egos, and a possible case of mistaken identity. Not rated; contains profanity and frontal nudity of both sexes. 92m. **DIR:** Jonathan Nossiter. **CAST:** David Suchet, Lisa Harrow, Larry Pine. **1997**

SUNDAY, BLOODY SUNDAY ★★★ Brilliant performances by Peter Finch and Glenda Jackson are the major reason to watch this very British three-sided love story; the sides are a bit different, though ... both love Murray Head. Difficult to watch at times, but intriguing from a historical standpoint. Rated R for sexual situations. 110m. **DIR:** John Schlesinger. **CAST:** Peter Finch, Glenda Jackson, Murray Head, Peggy Ashcroft, Maurice Denham. **1971**

SUNDAY IN THE COUNTRY, A ★★★★ Filmed like an Impressionist painting, this is a romantic look at family life in pre–World War II France. Bertrand Tavernier won the best-director prize at the 1984 Cannes Film Festival for this delightful drama. In French with English subtitles. Rated G. 94m. **DIR:** Bertrand Tavernier. **CAST:** Louis Ducreux, Michel Aumont, Sabine Azema. **1984 DVD**

SUNDAY IN THE PARK WITH GEORGE ★★★★★ This is a taped version of a performance of one of the most honored musicals of the 1980s. A Pulitzer

Prize-winner, the entire play is a fabrication of plot and characters based on the Georges Seurat painting, "Sunday Afternoon on the Island of La Grande Jatte." The painting comes to life, and each of the figures has a story to tell. Seurat is played expertly by Mandy Patinkin. 147m. **DIR:** James Lapine. **CAST:** Mandy Patinkin, Bernadette Peters, Barbara Byrne, Charles Kimbrough. **1986 DVD**

SUNDAY TOO FAR AWAY ★★★1/2 An Australian film about the life and lot of a sheepshearer down under circa 1956. Jack Thompson stars as Foley, a champion shearer who finds his mantle challenged. Not rated; the film has profanity, nudity, and violence. 100m. **DIR:** Ken Hannam. **CAST:** Jack Thompson, Max Cullen, John Ewart, Reg Lye. **1983**

SUNDAYS AND CYBELE ★★★★ A shell-shocked soldier, who feels responsible for the death of a young girl in the war, seeks redemption through a friendship with a 12-year-old orphan. But he fails to see the suspicion with which the authorities view their relationship. Superb acting and direction mark this Oscar winner for best foreign film. In French with English subtitles. B&W; 110m. **DIR:** Serge Bourguignon. **CAST:** Hardy Krüger, Patricia Gozzi. **1962**

SUNDAY'S CHILDREN ★★★★★ Though Ingmar Bergman retired from film directing, he's continued to write beautiful scripts. This is a gem, entrusted into the hands of his son, director Daniel Bergman, and tells of the summer of Ingmar's eighth year, when he came to know his minister father. The film is full of warmth, the mystical and the mysterious, and is a true "Bergman film" in every way. In Swedish with English subtitles. 117m. **DIR:** Daniel Bergman. **CAST:** Thommy Berggren, Lena Endre, Henrik Linnros. **1993**

SUNDOWN (1941) ★★1/2 Fairly entertaining British drama in Africa features Bruce Cabot as a Canadian and George Sanders as the army officer who replaces him. It seems that the local tribesmen are being armed by the Germans. Although there are some bursts of energy, this is still slow-going. B&W; 90m. **DIR:** Henry Hathaway. **CAST:** Gene Tierney, Bruce Cabot, George Sanders, Harry Carey, Cedric Hardwicke, Joseph Calleia, Reginald Gardiner, Marc Lawrence. **1941**

SUNDOWN (1990) ★★1/2 Purgatory is a small desert community established by a group of vampires fed up with the old ways. They manufacture their own blood and use sun block. A new generation of bloodsuckers decides enough is enough and declares war. Unique slant on the vampire legend starts off promisingly, but then gets batty toward the end. Rated R for nudity and violence. 104m. **DIR:** Anthony Hickox. **CAST:** David Carradine, Maxwell Caulfield, Morgan Brittany, Bruce Campbell, John Ireland. **1990**

SUNDOWN RIDER, THE ★★★★ Solid, brooding Western has Buck Jones as an easygoing cowpoke who happens upon a band of rustlers. The baddies leave Jones to "guard" their camp, where he is caught and brutally branded by revenge-minded lawmen despite his protests of innocence. So Jones swears revenge. Rewarding shoot-'em-up. B&W;

66m. **DIR:** Lambert Hillyer. **CAST:** Buck Jones, Barbara Weeks, Wheeler Oakman, Ward Bond. **1933**

SUNDOWN RIDERS ★★★ First of a proposed trio series (Russell Wade, Jay Kirby, Andy Clyde) that never materialized. Too bad, because it has plenty of action. Good chance to see famed stuntman Henry Wills in an acting role. B&W; 56m. **DIR:** Lambert Hillyer. **CAST:** Russell Wade, Jay Kirby, Andy Clyde, Evelyn Finley, Jack Ingram, Marshall Reed. **1948**

SUNDOWNERS, THE (1950) ★★★ Robert Preston is the good brother and Robert Sterling is the bad one in this tolerable Western. The siblings face each other in a climactic showdown. 83m. **DIR:** George Templeton. **CAST:** Robert Preston, Cathy Downes, Robert Sterling, John Drew Barrymore, Jack Elam. **1950**

SUNDOWNERS, THE (1960) ★★★★ Robert Mitchum and Deborah Kerr were one of the great screen teams, and this is our choice as their best film together. The story of Australian sheepherders in the 1920s, it is a character study brought alive by Fred Zinnemann's sensitive direction, as well as by the fine acting of a superb cast. 113m. **DIR:** Fred Zinnemann. **CAST:** Robert Mitchum, Deborah Kerr, Peter Ustinov, Glynis Johns, Dina Merrill, Chips Rafferty. **1960**

SUNRISE ★★★★ Director F. W. Murnau's emotionally charged silent classic about a romantic triangle leading to attempted murder. Oscars went to star Janet Gaynor, cinematographers Karl Struss and Charles Rosher, and the film itself—which is stunning on a visual and narrative level. B&W; 110m. **DIR:** F. W. Murnau. **CAST:** George O'Brien, Janet Gaynor, Margaret Livingston, J. Farrell MacDonald. **1927**

SUNRISE AT CAMPOBELLO ★★★★★ Producer-writer Dore Schary's inspiring and heartwarming drama of Franklin Delano Roosevelt's public political battles and private fight against polio. Ralph Bellamy is FDR; Greer Garson is Eleanor. Both are superb. The acting is tops, the entire production sincere. Taken from Schary's impressive stage play, with all the fine qualities intact. 143m. **DIR:** Vincent J. Donehue. **CAST:** Ralph Bellamy, Greer Garson, Alan Bunce, Hume Cronyn. **1960**

SUNSET ★★★1/2 Writer-director Blake Edwards begins this charming little *soufflé* with an intriguing notion: what if legendary lawman Wyatt Earp (James Garner) had met silent-screen cowboy Tom Mix (Bruce Willis) and the two had become fast friends? The boys get involved in a seamy murder case. Rated R for language and violence. 107m. **DIR:** Blake Edwards. **CAST:** James Garner, Bruce Willis, Malcolm McDowell, Mariel Hemingway, Kathleen Quinlan, Jennifer Edwards, Patricia Hodge, M. Emmet Walsh, Joe Dallesandro. **1988 DVD**

SUNSET BOULEVARD ★★★★★ *Sunset Boulevard* is one of Hollywood's strongest indictments against its own excesses. It justly deserves its place among the best films ever made. William Holden plays an out-of-work gigolo-screenwriter who attaches himself to a faded screen star attempting a comeback. Gloria Swanson, in a stunning parody, is brilliant as the tragically deluded Norma Desmond. B&W; 110m. **DIR:** Billy Wilder. **CAST:** William Holden,

Gloria Swanson, Erich Von Stroheim, Fred Clark, Jack Webb, Hedda Hopper, Buster Keaton. **1950**

SUNSET GRILL ★★1/2 Passable private-investigator mystery features Peter Weller as a down-and-out detective trying to find his wife's assassin. Weller elevates an otherwise low-budget effort by creating a quirky, mesmerizing character. Not rated; contains nudity, sex, violence, and profanity. 105m. **DIR:** Kevin Connor. **CAST:** Peter Weller, Lori Singer, Stacy Keach, Alexandra Paul, John Rhys-Davies. **1992**

SUNSET HEAT ★★1/2 Photojournalist Michael Paré finds his former life as a drug dealer intruding on his new career when he returns to Los Angeles. A reunion with his old buddy Adam Ant results in Paré being hunted by drug lord Dennis Hopper, his former partner. Sleazy, but well acted. Rated R for profanity, nudity, and violence. 94m. **DIR:** John Nicolella. **CAST:** Michael Paré, Dennis Hopper, Adam Ant, Little Richard, Charlie Schlatter, Daphne Ashbrook. **1992**

SUNSET LIMOUSINE 💔 John Ritter plays an out-of-work comic who must make something of himself before his girlfriend (Susan Dey) will take him back. Made for TV. 92m. **DIR:** Terry Hughes. **CAST:** John Ritter, Susan Dey, Martin Short, Paul Reiser, Audrie Neenan, Lainie Kazan. **1983**

SUNSET PARK ★★ Young, charismatic actors are trapped in a familiar underdog sports drama. A woman high-school gym teacher takes the job of boys' basketball coach. Her players sort through romantic, personality, and motivation challenges and teach their rookie coach about court warfare and inner-city survival. She teaches them the aesthetics of winning. Rated R for language and drug use. 100m. **DIR:** Steve Gomer. **CAST:** Rhea Perlman, Fredro Starr, Carol Kane, Terrence DaShon Howard, Camille Saviola, De'Aundre Bonds, James Harris, Anthony Hall. **1996**

SUNSET SERENADE ★★1/2 Beady-eyed Roy Rogers and his ornery sidekick Gabby Hayes thwart the plans of a couple of no-goods who aim to murder the heir to a ranch and take it over for themselves. Enjoyable enough and not too demanding. B&W; 58m. **DIR:** Joseph Kane. **CAST:** Roy Rogers, George "Gabby" Hayes, Helen Parrish, Onslow Stevens, Joan Woodbury. **1942**

SUNSET STRIP 💔 And strip they do in this shabby tale of a young woman who has an affair with a club owner in L.A.'s exotic dance scene. Rated R for nudity and sex. 93m. **DIR:** Paul G. Volk. **CAST:** Jeff Conaway, Michelle Foreman. **1991**

SUNSHINE BOYS, THE ★★★★ The story of two feuding ex-vaudeville stars who make a TV special. Walter Matthau and Richard Benjamin, and (especially) George Burns give memorable performances. Director Herbert Ross turns this adaptation of the successful Broadway play by Neil Simon into a celluloid winner. Rated PG. 111m. **DIR:** Herbert Ross. **CAST:** Walter Matthau, Richard Benjamin, George Burns, Lee Meredith, Carol Arthur, Howard Hesseman, Ron Rifkin. **1975**

SUNSTROKE 💔 Bad accents, poor acting, and a horrible plot ruin this tale about a woman trying to locate her daughter. Rated R for violence and profanity. 91m. **DIR:** James Keach. **CAST:** Jane Seymour,

Stephen Meadows, Steve Railsback, Ray Wise, Don Ameche. **1992**

SUPER, THE ★★★ Star Joe Pesci, as a slumlord sentenced to live in his dilapidated New York tenement building, makes this thin comedy easy to take. Without him, the silly, predictable story would be painful to watch. Rated R for profanity. 98m. **DIR:** Rod Daniel. **CAST:** Joe Pesci, Vincent Gardenia, Madolyn Smith, Rubén Blades. **1991**

SUPER FORCE 💔 Despite an engaging early cameo by Patrick Macnee, this TV pilot is far from super; Ken Olandt is terminally bland as an astronaut-turned-cop who dons an ersatz RoboCop suit to battle crime in the year 2020. Although not rated, the squeaky-clean material could pass for G. 92m. **DIR:** Richard Compton. **CAST:** Ken Olandt, Larry B. Scott, Patrick Macnee, G. Gordon Liddy. **1993**

SUPER FUZZ ★★1/2 For adults, this is a silly, mindless film … but it's great fun for the kids. Terence Hill stars as Dave Speed, a police officer with supernatural powers. Rated PG. 94m. **DIR:** Sergio Corbucci. **CAST:** Terence Hill, Ernest Borgnine, Joanne Dru, Marc Lawrence. **1981**

SUPER MARIO BROTHERS, THE ★★★ A big-screen version of a popular Nintendo game, this movie is aimed at indiscriminating kids and young adults. When the dirty near-human dinos kidnap Princess Daisy, a couple of plumbers from Brooklyn save the day. Fast-moving action/comedy could have used a bit more sense. Rated PG. 118m. **DIR:** Rocky Morton, Annabel Jankel. **CAST:** Bob Hoskins, John Leguizamo, Dennis Hopper, Samantha Mathis, Fisher Stevens, Fiona Shaw, Richard Edson. **1993**

SUPER SOUL BROTHER 💔 A wino (raunchy comic Wildman Steve) is given superpowers in this lame spoof of TV's *Six Million Dollar Man*. Not rated; contains strong profanity and nudity. 80m. **DIR:** Rene Martinez. **CAST:** Steve Wildman, Joycelyn Norris, Peter Conrad. **1978**

SUPERCARRIER ★★★ This is the TV-movie premiere of the short-lived series of the same name. The action takes Top Gun graduates on a mission aboard a supercarrier. The Russians have a plane in U.S. air space and two pilots are assigned to escort it out. The flight and action scenes are engrossing, but on the ground *Supercarrier* is pretty routine. 90m. **DIR:** William A. Graham. **CAST:** Robert Hooks, Paul Gleason, Ken Olandt, Richard Jaeckel. **1988**

SUPERCOP ★★★ Following the box-office success of *Rumble in the Bronx*, this Hong Kong actioner was dubbed for American release. Part of a police-story trilogy, this has Jackie Chan teaming up with Michelle Khan, who, like himself, does her own stunt work and is an extraordinary martial artist. The two pose as brother and sister to infiltrate a vicious drug ring. Frequent comic moments, the trademark of Chan films, elevate this a notch above the kung fu flicks of the 1970s. Rated R for violence. 90m. **DIR:** Stanley Tong. **CAST:** Jackie Chan, Michelle Khan, Maggie Cheung, Yuen Wah. **1992 DVD**

SUPERDAD ★★1/2 Bob Crane doesn't approve of his daughter's boyfriend (Kurt Russell) or the crowd she runs with. She claims that he just doesn't understand them. He decides to find out about the kids first-hand. Rated G. 94m. **DIR:** Vincent McEveety. **CAST:** Bob Crane, Barbara Rush, Kurt Russell, Joe Flynn. **1973**

SUPERFLY ★★★ This exciting film follows a Harlem drug dealer's last big sale before he attempts to leave the drug world for a normal life. Rated R. 96m. **DIR:** Gordon Parks Jr. **CAST:** Ron O'Neal, Carl Lee, Sheila Frazier, Julius W. Harris. **1972**

SUPERFLY T.N.T. 💗 The first mistake connected with this sequel to *Superfly* was allowing its star, Ron O'Neal, to direct it. The second mistake was removing the title character from the tense, urban setting of the first movie. Here, the ex-drug dealer is living in exile in Europe when he decides to become involved in the plight of an African nationalist. 87m. **DIR:** Ron O'Neal. **CAST:** Ron O'Neal, Roscoe Lee Browne, Sheila Frazier, Robert Guillaume. **1973**

SUPERGIRL ★★1/2 Helen Slater makes a respectable film debut as Superman's cousin in this screen comic book, which should delight the kiddies and occasionally tickle the adults. The stellar supporting cast doesn't seem to take it seriously, so why should we? Rated PG. 105m. **DIR:** Jeannot Szwarc. **CAST:** Faye Dunaway, Peter O'Toole, Helen Slater, Mia Farrow, Brenda Vaccaro, Simon Ward, Peter Cook, Hart Bochner. **1984**

SUPERGRASS, THE ★★ The reluctant hero (Adrian Edmondson) of this English farce pretends to be an important drug dealer in order to impress his girlfriend. Ultimately, the bloke is in way over his head. So-so comedy. 96m. **DIR:** Peter Richardson. **CAST:** Adrian Edmondson, Jennifer Saunders, Peter Richardson. **1987**

SUPERMAN CARTOONS ★★★★ All other superhero cartoons pale in comparison to this collection of excellent "Man of Steel" shorts from the Max Fleischer Studios. Made between 1941 and 1943, these actually constitute the company's finest work, its Popeye cartoons notwithstanding. There are several tapes available with a selection of seven or eight shorts (approximately 75 minutes) made from 16mm prints of varying quality. One company (Video Rarities) offers a 150-minute tape with all seventeen Superman shorts taken from mint-condition 35mm Technicolor prints, and the difference is amazing. 75m. **DIR:** Dave Fleischer, Seymour Kneitel, Isadore Sparber. **1940 DVD**

SUPERMAN ★★★1/2 After a somewhat overblown introduction, which encompasses the end of Krypton and Clark Kent's adolescence in Smallville, this film takes off to provide some great moments as Superman swings into action. The action is complemented by fine tongue-in-cheek comedy. Rated PG. 143m. **DIR:** Richard Donner. **CAST:** Christopher Reeve, Margot Kidder, Jackie Cooper, Marc McClure, Marlon Brando, Glenn Ford, Gene Hackman. **1978**

SUPERMAN II ★★★★ Even better than the original, this terrific adventure of the Man of Steel includes a full-fledged—and beautifully handled—romance between Lois Lane (Margot Kidder) and Superman (Christopher Reeve) and a spectacular battle that pits our hero against three supervillains (during which the city of Metropolis is almost completely destroyed). Rated PG. 127m. **DIR:** Richard

Lester. **CAST:** Margot Kidder, Christopher Reeve, Gene Hackman, Ned Beatty, Jackie Cooper, Terence Stamp. **1980**

SUPERMAN III ★★1/2 If it weren't for Christopher Reeve's excellent performance in the title role, *Superman III* would be a total disappointment. The film features a subdued Richard Pryor as a computer whiz who is hired by bad guy Robert Vaughn to do dastardly deeds with his magic programming. Rated PG. 125m. **DIR:** Richard Lester. **CAST:** Christopher Reeve, Richard Pryor, Robert Vaughn, Annette O'Toole, Jackie Cooper, Marc McClure, Pamela Stephenson. **1983**

SUPERMAN IV: THE QUEST FOR PEACE ★★ A well-intentioned plot about Superman (Christopher Reeve) attempting to rid the Earth of nuclear weapons cannot save this overlong, overwrought, confusing, and sometimes downright dull third sequel. Rated PG for violence. 90m. **DIR:** Sidney J. Furie. **CAST:** Christopher Reeve, Gene Hackman, Mark Kidder, Jackie Cooper, Mariel Hemingway, Jon Cryer, Marc McClure, Sam Wanamaker. **1987**

SUPERMAN AND THE MOLE MEN ★★1/2 George Reeves dons the tights and cape that he was to be identified with for the rest of his life. This story concerns a huge oil well that drills too far and yields fuzzy midgets from inside the Earth. This film led to the famous television series and was subsequently shown as a two-part episode. B&W; 67m. **DIR:** Lee Sholem. **CAST:** George Reeves, Phyllis Coates, Jeff Corey, Walter Reed. **1951**

SUPERMAN—THE SERIAL ★★1/2 The first live-action Superman serial was one of the highest grossing of all chapterplays ever made, as well as Columbia's most prestigious effort in that field. The film relies on inept flying sequences and the by-now classic relationship between Clark Kent and Lois Lane for the bulk of its action. B&W; **DIR:** Spencer Gordon Bennet, Thomas Carr. **CAST:** Kirk Alyn, Noel Neill, Tommy Bond, Carol Forman, Pierre Watkin, George Meeker, Charles King, Charles Quigley, Herbert Rawlinson. **1948**

SUPERNATURAL ★★★1/2 The spirit of an executed murderess takes charge of a beautiful young socialite's body and bides its time until it can take revenge. Eerie opening credits set the tone for this somber excursion into the unknown, and decent special effects and a certain respect for the subject matter help make this one of the few Hollywood films about the occult that doesn't cheat at the end and invalidate the production. B&W; 64m. **DIR:** Victor Halperin. **CAST:** Carole Lombard, Randolph Scott, Vivienne Osborne, Alan Dinehart, H. B. Warner, Beryl Mercer, William Farnum. **1933**

SUPERNATURALS, THE ★★★1/2 A group of modern-day soldiers face off against Civil War Confederate zombies. The commanding officer (Nichelle Nichols) must find the secret to exorcise these evil spirits before they kill her and her men. Good scary entertainment. Rated R for graphic violence. 91m. **DIR:** Armand Mastroianni. **CAST:** Nichelle Nichols, Maxwell Caulfield, Talia Balsam, LeVar Burton. **1988**

●**SUPERNOVA** ★★ When a medical-rescue starship responds to a distress call from a supposedly abandoned planet, the crew find themselves faced with an evil force they can't understand. You may not understand it either, with the movie's gaping plot holes, clichés, and signs of last-minute tampering. Director Thomas Lee is actually Walter Hill, who had his name removed from the film. Rated PG-13 for violence. 91m. **DIR:** Thomas Lee. **CAST:** James Spader, Angela Bassett, Peter Facinelli, Lou Diamond Phillips, Robin Tunney, Robert Forster. 2000

•**SUPERSTAR: DARE TO DREAM** ★★ Only diehard fans of the *Saturday Night Live* character Mary Katherine Gallagher, the Catholic-school girl, will appreciate the expansion of Molly Shannon's sketch persona into a feature-length film. Here she lives with her eccentric grandmother and drools over the most popular boy at school (Will Ferrell). Some laughs and guffaws. Rated PG-13 for sexual situations and profanity. 88m. **DIR:** Bruce McCulloch. **CAST:** Molly Shannon, Will Ferrell, Glynis Johns. 1999 DVD

SUPPORT YOUR LOCAL GUNFIGHTER ★★★1/2 Although not quite as fresh or genuinely rib tickling as predecessor *Support Your Local Sheriff*, this charming Western spoof nonetheless gives James Garner another chance to modify the charming hustler honed to perfection during all those years on television's *Maverick*. This time out he's a con artist "selling" drifter Jack Elam as a professional gunfighter. Rated PG for minimal violence. 92m. **DIR:** Burt Kennedy. **CAST:** James Garner, Suzanne Pleshette, Jack Elam, Harry Morgan, John Dehner, Joan Blondell, Chuck Connors. 1971

SUPPORT YOUR LOCAL SHERIFF! ★★★★1/2 The time-honored backbone of the industry, the Western, takes a real ribbing in this all-stops-out send-up. If it can be parodied, it is—in spades. James Garner is great as a gambler "just passing through" who gets roped into being sheriff and tames a lawless mining town against all odds, including an inept deputy, a fem-lib mayor's daughter, and a snide gunman. A very funny picture. Rated G. 93m. **DIR:** Burt Kennedy. **CAST:** James Garner, Joan Hackett, Walter Brennan, Harry Morgan, Jack Elam, Bruce Dern, Henry Jones. 1969

SUPPOSE THEY GAVE A WAR AND NOBODY CAME? ★★ In this comedy involving a confrontation between a rural town and a nearby military base, Brian Keith, Tony Curtis, and Ivan Dixon play three army buddies who take it upon themselves to stop the fighting. Some funny moments. Rated PG for adult themes. 113m. **DIR:** Hy Averback. **CAST:** Brian Keith, Ernest Borgnine, Suzanne Pleshette, Tom Ewell, Tony Curtis, Bradford Dillman, Ivan Dixon, Arthur O'Connell, Don Ameche. 1970

•**SUPREME SANCTION** ★★1/2 Silly but serviceable thriller about a female assassin who breaks away from her employers only to become a target. Rated R for violence, sexuality, and profanity. 93m. **DIR:** John Terlesky. **CAST:** Kristy Swanson, Michael Madsen, Tiny Lister Jr., Donald Faison, David Dukes. 1999 DVD

SURE FIRE 💗 Heavy-handed message film moves at a snail's pace. Two men choose different paths in life—one seeks material wealth while the other is content with his modest farm. Obvious cuts are a ma-

jor distraction. Not rated; contains profanity and violence. 83m. **DIR:** Jon Jost. **CAST:** Tom Blair, Kristi Hager, Robert Ernst, Kate Dezina. 1990

SURE THING, THE ★★★1/2 This enjoyable romantic comedy, about two college freshmen who discover themselves and each other through a series of misadventures on the road, is more or less director Rob Reiner's updating of Frank Capra's *It Happened One Night*. John Cusack and Daphne Zuniga star as the unlikely protagonists. Rated PG-13 for profanity and suggested sex. 100m. **DIR:** Rob Reiner. **CAST:** John Cusack, Daphne Zuniga, Anthony Edwards, Boyd Gaines, Lisa Jane Persky. 1985

SURF NAZIS MUST DIE ★★1/2 The Surf Nazis are a gang of weirdos who rule the Los Angeles beaches. Vile, stupid, and pointless, but there's something about this film ... Rated R for violence, language, sex, and nudity. 83m. **DIR:** Peter George. **CAST:** Barry Brenner, Gail Neely, Dawn Wildsmith. 1987 DVD

SURF NINJAS ★★★ Ninja nonsense. Two California-surf dudes discover that they're actually heirs to a small South Seas kingdom. That's the good news. The bad news is that evil warlord Leslie Nielsen will stop at nothing to keep them off the throne. This mix of several different genres loses focus, but kids will get a big kick out of it. Rated PG for make-believe violence. 87m. **DIR:** Neal Israel. **CAST:** Ernie Reyes Jr., Rob Schneider, Tone Loc, Leslie Nielsen, Nicolas Cowan. 1993

SURF 2 ★★ Combination spoof of beach party and horror movies, with lunatic Eddie Deezen out for revenge on a group of surfers. Fitfully funny, with the best joke in the title: there is no *Surf 1*. Rated R for the obligatory topless beach bunnies. 91m. **DIR:** Randall Badat. **CAST:** Eddie Deezen, Linda Kerridge, Cleavon Little, Lyle Waggoner, Eric Stoltz, Corinne Bohrer, Ruth Buzzi. 1984

•**SURFACE TO AIR** 💗 Lots of military hardware and not an ounce of common sense highlight this tale of two brothers on the same aircraft carrier fighting in the Persian Gulf. First off, the military doesn't allow family to share the same duty station. Logic goes downhill from there. Rated R for language and violence. 93m. **DIR:** Rodney McDonald. **CAST:** Matthew R. Anderson, Michael Madsen, Chad McQueen. 1997

SURFACING 💗 *Deliverance* stirred with psychological mumbo jumbo and kinky sex. Rated R. 90m. **DIR:** Claude Jutra. **CAST:** Joseph Bottoms, Kathleen Beller, R. H. Thomson. 1984

SURGEON, THE ★★★1/2 A disgruntled ex-surgeon returns to the scene of the crime in order to complete his sinister experiments. Gruesome special effects, high production values, likable cast, and taut direction make this a must-see for fans of the genre. Rated R for violence, nudity, profanity, and adult situations. 90m. **DIR:** Carl Schenkel. **CAST:** Isabel Glasser, James Remar, Charles Dance, Peter Boyle, Malcolm McDowell. 1994 DVD

SURPRISE PACKAGE ★★1/2 A change of pace for Yul Brynner as a high-living gambler deported to Greece, where he meets and decides to rob an exiled king (Noel Coward, who also sings the title song). So-so comedy, based on a novel by Art Buchwald. B&W. 100m. **DIR:** Stanley Donen. **CAST:** Yul Brynner, Mitzi

Gaynor, George Coulouris, Noel Coward, Eric Pohlmann. 1960

SURRENDER ★★★ Sally Field gives a sparkling performance as a confused woman in love with Michael Caine, Steve Guttenberg, and money, not necessarily in that order. Caine and Guttenberg are superb. At times contrived and a bit forced, overall, this is an enjoyable light comedy. Rated PG-13 for language and sex. 105m. **DIR:** Jerry Belson. **CAST:** Sally Field, Michael Caine, Steve Guttenberg, Peter Boyle, Julie Kavner, Jackie Cooper. 1987

SURVIVAL GAME 🎬 Mike Norris, Chuck's son, fails to fill his father's boots. R rating for mild profanity. 89m. **DIR:** Herb Freed. **CAST:** Mike Norris, Deborah Goodrich, Seymour Cassel, Arlene Golonka. 1987

SURVIVAL QUEST ★★★1/2 Survival course students encounter a paramilitary group on maneuvers. Their adventure then turns into a genuine and compelling fight for survival. Rated R for violence. 91m. **DIR:** Don Coscarelli. **CAST:** Lance Henriksen, Dermot Mulroney. 1989

SURVIVAL ZONE 🎬 Nuclear-holocaust survivors battling evil. Not rated, contains violence and nudity. 90m. **DIR:** Percival Rubens. **CAST:** Gary Lockwood, Morgan Stevens, Camilla Sparv. 1983

SURVIVALIST, THE 🎬 A tepid action-thriller that purports to dramatize the confusion that mounts before the bombs are dropped. The real bomb is this hokey doomsday entry that literally goes up in smoke. Rated R for violence and profanity. 96m. **DIR:** Sig Shore. **CAST:** Steve Railsback, Susan Blakely, Cliff De Young, Marjoe Gortner, David Wayne. 1987

SURVIVE THE NIGHT ★★★1/2 Surprisingly believable film in which three women end up fighting for their lives in a part of New York where the police don't like to go. Stefanie Powers does a fine job portraying the mother who will do anything to protect her daughter. Not rated, made for cable, but contains violence. 95m. **DIR:** Bill Corcoran. **CAST:** Stefanie Powers, Helen Shaver, Kathleen Robertson, Lawrence Gilliard Jr., Currie Graham. 1992

SURVIVING DESIRE ★★★ Kooky made-for-TV romance based on literary ideas rather than passion ignites between an untalented college professor (Martin Donovan) and his only attentive student (Mary Ward). Ward is a comic gem especially as she halfheartedly offers to help customers in a bookstore. Also included on the tape are two other Hal Hartley shorts *Theory of Achievement* and *Ambition*. 86m. **DIR:** Hal Hartley. **CAST:** Martin Donovan, Mary Ward, Matt Malloy, Rebecca Nelson. 1991

SURVIVING PICASSO ★★★ Another portrait of the artist as a selfish pig, this one based on Françoise Gilot's memoir of her ten-year-plus affair with Pablo Picasso. Anthony Hopkins hits all the right notes of roaring egotism, but his performance is strangely passionless and uncharismatic, and the same is true of the film as a whole. Rated R for profanity and nudity. 129m. **DIR:** James Ivory. **CAST:** Anthony Hopkins, Natascha McElhone, Jane Lapotaire, Diane Venora, Julianne Moore. 1996

SURVIVING THE GAME 🎬 Homeless African-American is hunted for perverse sport by a group of men in the Pacific Northwest wilderness. Rated R for language and violence. 93m. **DIR:** Ernest R. Dickerson. **CAST:** Ice T, Rutger Hauer, Charles Dutton, John C. McGinley, Gary Busey, William McNamara, F. Murray Abraham. 1994 DVD

SURVIVOR ★★ While on a space mission, an astronaut witnesses a full-scale nuclear war. Upon return to Earth, he finds total destruction. Richard Moll plays a fine villain in this otherwise routine and violent science-fiction story. 92m. **DIR:** Michael Shackleton. **CAST:** Chris Mayer, Richard Moll, Sue Kiel, Richard Haines. 1987

SURVIVORS, THE ★★★1/2 This is an often funny movie about a goofy "survivalist" (Robin Williams), who is "adopted" by a service station owner (Walter Matthau) and pursued by a friendly but determined hit man (Jerry Reed). Generally a black comedy, this movie features a variety of comedic styles, and they all work. Rated R for vulgar language and violence. 102m. **DIR:** Michael Ritchie. **CAST:** Robin Williams, Walter Matthau, Jerry Reed, James Wainwright. 1983

SURVIVORS OF THE HOLOCAUST ★★★★ A TBS documentary capturing the heartbreaking testimonials of Nazi concentration camp survivors, this is artistically presented by producer Steven Spielberg. It works on several levels, but the emotional impact and final message of hope are what will stay with you. Also included are Spielberg and Ben Kingsley presenting a 10-minute description of the Survivors of the Shoah Visual History Foundation, a cutting-edge preservation group. Not rated; contains brief nudity and adult themes. B&W/color; 70m. **DIR:** Allan Holzman. **CAST:** Ben Kingsley, Steven Spielberg. 1995

SUSAN AND GOD ★★★ A strong cast bolsters this story of a woman who devotes herself to a new religious movement, pushing her newly adopted standards and beliefs on her family and friends. Fredric March is fine as her weak, alcoholic husband. B&W; 115m. **DIR:** George Cukor. **CAST:** Joan Crawford, Fredric March, Ruth Hussey, John Carroll, Rita Hayworth, Nigel Bruce, Marjorie Main, Gloria De Haven. 1940

SUSAN LENOX: HER FALL AND RISE ★★★ Greta Garbo flees a brutish father eager to marry her off and takes refuge with Clark Gable. The melodramatic plot's tired, but Garbo and Gable give charged performances. B&W; 76m. **DIR:** Robert Z. Leonard. **CAST:** Greta Garbo, Clark Gable, Alan Hale Sr., Jean Hersholt. 1931

SUSAN SLEPT HERE ★★1/2 Screenwriter Dick Powell must keep a tight leash on the ultrahigh-spirited vagrant teenager he protects and falls for in the course of researching a script on juvenile delinquency. Amusing dialogue and lots of innuendo mark this otherwise pedestrian sex comedy. 98m. **DIR:** Frank Tashlin. **CAST:** Dick Powell, Debbie Reynolds, Anne Francis, Glenda Farrell. 1954

SUSANNA ★★ This lurid soap opera from Luis Buñuel concerns a voluptuous young girl who escapes from a reformatory and hides out with a plantation family. Unfortunately, the movie lacks Buñuel's comic surreal touch in exploiting his characters' obsessions. In Spanish with English subtitles.

Not rated. B&W; 82m. **DIR:** Luis Buñuel. **CAST:** Rosita Quintana, Fernando Soler. 1951

SUSANNAH OF THE MOUNTIES ★★★ After her parents are killed in an Indian attack, curly Shirley is raised by a kind Canadian Mountie (Randolph Scott). Not one to hold a grudge, Shirley decides to play peacemaker for the whites and Indians by befriending the chief's son. B&W; 78m. **DIR:** William A. Seiter. **CAST:** Shirley Temple, Randolph Scott, Margaret Lockwood. 1939

SUSPECT ★★★1/2 Cher is just fine as a public defender assigned to prove a deaf and mute street bum (Liam Neeson) innocent of the murder of a Washington, D.C., secretary. One of the jurors, lobbyist Dennis Quaid, takes a liking to Cher and begins helping her with the seemingly impossible case, thus putting her career and their lives in danger. Rated R for violence and profanity. 128m. **DIR:** Peter Yates. **CAST:** Cher, Dennis Quaid, Joe Mantegna, Liam Neeson, Philip Bosco, John Mahoney, Fred Melamed. 1987

SUSPECT DEVICE ★★★1/2 Producer Roger Corman's clever thriller doesn't always make sense, but it sure moves. An analyst is the lone survivor of a hit on his espionage section and his entire life becomes a fading memory. Great, mindless fun. Rated R for violence, nudity, profanity, and drug use. 90m. **DIR:** Rick Jacobson. **CAST:** C. Thomas Howell, Stacey Travis, Jed Allan, Jonathan Fuller, John Beck. 1995

SUSPENDED ★★★1/2 Falsely accused and sentenced to death in Stalinist Poland, an ex–army officer escapes from prison and is hidden by a woman he met during the war. Their underground relationship becomes a metaphor for political repression in this provocative drama. In Polish with English subtitles. Not rated. 92m. **DIR:** Waldemar Kyzystek. **CAST:** Krystyna Janda, Jerzy Radziwilowicz. 1986

SUSPICION (1941) ★★★★ A timid woman is gradually unnerved by apprehension. Bits of evidence lead her to believe that her charming husband is a killer and that she is the intended victim. Joan Fontaine played a similar role in *Rebecca* and eventually won a best-actress Oscar for her performance in *Suspicion*. Cary Grant is excellent, too. B&W; 99m. **DIR:** Alfred Hitchcock. **CAST:** Joan Fontaine, Cary Grant, Cedric Hardwicke, Nigel Bruce, May Whitty, Isabel Jeans. 1941

SUSPICION (1987) ★★ A plain country Jane (Curtin) grows suspicious of her hubby's intentions after piecing together the plot for a murder that would benefit her penniless mate. This Alfred Hitchcock remake lacks the subtle suspense of the original. Rated PG. 97m. **DIR:** Andrew Grieve. **CAST:** Jane Curtin, Anthony Andrews, Betsy Blair, Michael Hordern, Vivian Pickles, Jonathan Lynn. 1987

SUSPICIOUS AGENDA ★★ The only thing suspicious about this crime-thriller is its resemblance to a million others like it. It helps to have Richard Grieco along as the streetwise cop tracking down a serial killer. Rated R for violence, nudity and language. 97m. **DIR:** Clay Borris. **CAST:** Richard Grieco, Nick Mancuso, Jim Byrnes. 1994

•**SUSPICIOUS MINDS** ★ A detective falls in love with the woman whose husband hired him to spy on her. This by-the-numbers pseudo *noir* understands

the conventions of the genre but can't do anything interesting with them. Rated R for violence and sex. 97m. **DIR:** Alain Zaloum. **CAST:** Patrick Bergin, Jayne Heitmeyer, Gary Busey. 1997

SUSPIRIA ★★★★ Now classic art-horror chiller is even more fearsome in the uncut version. A timid American girl enrolls in a prudish European ballet academy, only to discover it's staffed by a coven of witches who trim the roster with frightening regularity. Malevolent atmosphere steers clear of the usual camp and is genuinely apprehensive. Not rated. 97m. **DIR:** Dario Argento. **CAST:** Jessica Harper, Stefania Casini, Joan Bennett, Alida Valli, Flavio Bucci, Udo Kier. 1977

SUTURE ★★ An innocent man is unwittingly drawn into his half-brother's scheme of arson and attempted murder. A promising idea is sunk by pretentious, sophomoric filmmaking, pompous psycho-babble, and deliberately unbelievable situations and plot developments. Not rated; contains mild violence. B&W; 102m. **DIR:** David Siegel, Scott McGehee. **CAST:** Dennis Haysbert, Mel Harris, Sab Shimono, Dina Merrill, Michael Harris, Fran Ryan, David Graf, John Ingle. 1994

SUZY ★★ Cary Grant plays a WWI pilot who falls for American show girl Jean Harlow. A spy story with charismatic performers who don't seem to connect. Not up to expectations. B&W; 99m. **DIR:** George Fitzmaurice. **CAST:** Jean Harlow, Cary Grant, Franchot Tone, Lewis Stone, Benita Hume, Una O'Connor. 1936

SVENGALI (1931) ★★★★ Adapted from the George Du Maurier novel that put Svengali into the language as one who controls another. John Barrymore plays Svengali, a demonic artist obsessed with Trilby, a young artist's model. Under his hypnotic influence, she becomes a singer who obeys his every command. Bizarre sets and arresting visual effects make this a surrealistic delight. B&W; 76m. **DIR:** Archie Mayo. **CAST:** John Barrymore, Marian Marsh, Donald Crisp, Carmel Myers, Bramwell Fletcher. 1931

SVENGALI (1983) ★★ Even stars like Peter O'Toole and Jodie Foster can't help this poorly scripted remake of the classic tale. Made for cable. 96m. **DIR:** Anthony Harvey. **CAST:** Peter O'Toole, Jodie Foster, Elizabeth Ashley, Larry Joshua, Holly Hunter. 1983

SWAMP THING ★★ Kids will love this movie, about a monster-hero—part plant, part scientist—who takes on a supervillain (Louis Jourdan) and saves heroine Adrienne Barbeau. But adults may find it corny. Based on the popular 1972 comic book of the same name. Rated PG, it has some tomato-paste violence and brief nudity. 91m. **DIR:** Wes Craven. **CAST:** Louis Jourdan, Adrienne Barbeau, Ray Wise, David Hess. 1982

SWAMP WOMEN ★★ Female undercover cop infiltrates a trio of tough-talking tomatoes, engineers a prison break, and accompanies them to a danger-infested swamp to retrieve the jewels they've stashed there. Low-budget drive-in fare was shot on location in Louisiana and features "B" queens Beverly Garland and Marie Windsor in classic hardboiled roles. Cheap but fun. 70m. **DIR:** Roger Corman. **CAST:** Carole Matthews, Beverly Garland, Marie Windsor, Jill Jarmyn, Mike Connors. 1955

SWAN, THE (1925) ★★1/2 While adored by a commoner, a princess is pursued by a playboy prince in this classic comedy-drama of manners drawn from the Ferenc Molnár play. Silent. B&W; 112m. **DIR:** Dimitri Buchowetzki. **CAST:** Frances Howard, Adolphe Menjou, Ricardo Cortez. 1925

SWAN, THE (1956) ★★★ First filmed with Frances Howard in 1925, then in 1930 with Lillian Gish, this Ferenc Molnar comedy, about a princess courted by a commoner while promised to a prince, gave Hollywood princess Grace Kelly ample time to act in reel life what she shortly became in real life. 112m. **DIR:** Charles Vidor. **CAST:** Grace Kelly, Louis Jourdan, Alec Guinness, Agnes Moorehead, Brian Aherne, Jessie Royce Landis, Estelle Winwood, Leo G. Carroll, Robert Coote. 1956

SWAN PRINCESS, THE ★★★1/2 This gorgeous, animated musical-romance, based on the German *Swan Lake* legend, is about a princess who is turned into a swan by a banished magician. The charming story includes messages about how relationships between boys and girls change as they grow up and the inability of males to verbally express their emotions. Voices are provided by Sandy Duncan, Steven Wright, Jack Palance, and John Cleese. Rated G. 90m. **DIR:** Richard Rich. 1994

SWANN IN LOVE ★★★★ Slow-moving but fascinating film portrait of a Jewish aristocrat (Jeremy Irons) totally consumed by his romantic and sexual obsession with an ambitious French courtesan (Ornella Muti). It's definitely not for all tastes. However, those who can remember the overwhelming ache of first love may find it worth watching. In French with English subtitles. Rated R for nudity and suggested sex. 110m. **DIR:** Volker Schlöndorff. **CAST:** Jeremy Irons, Ornella Muti, Alain Delon, Fanny Ardant, Marie-Christine Barrault. 1985

SWAP, THE (SAM'S SONG) 💔 Robert De Niro fans, don't waste your time. This hodgepodge uses a few minutes of film from an unreleased movie De Niro made in 1969 called *Sam's Song* to pad out a story about an ex-con looking for his brother's murderer. Rated R. 87m. **DIR:** John Shade, John Broderick, Jordon Leondopoulos. **CAST:** Robert De Niro, Jennifer Warren, Lisa Blount, Sybil Danning. 1980 DVD

SWARM, THE 💔 Inept. Rated PG. 116m. **DIR:** Irwin Allen. **CAST:** Michael Caine, Katharine Ross, Richard Widmark, Henry Fonda, Olivia de Havilland, Richard Chamberlain, Fred MacMurray. 1978

SWASHBUCKLER (1976) ★★ Only a strong cast saves this pirate movie from being a total swashbuckler. Even so, it's a stylistic nightmare as a sword-wielding hero (Robert Shaw) who comes to the aid of a damsel (Genevieve Bujold) in distress. Rated PG for violence and nudity. 101m. **DIR:** James Goldstone. **CAST:** Robert Shaw, James Earl Jones, Peter Boyle, Genevieve Bujold, Beau Bridges, Geoffrey Holder, Avery Schreiber, Anjelica Huston. 1976 DVD

SWASHBUCKLER, THE (1984) 💔 Stupid story about a naturalized American who gets caught up in the French Revolution while delivering grain and seeking a divorce from his wife. 100m. **DIR:** Jean-Paul Rappeneau. **CAST:** Jean-Paul Belmondo, Marlene Jobert, Laura Antonelli, Michel Auclair, Julien Guiomar. 1984

SWEATER GIRLS 💔 Teen sexcapade. Rated R for sex and language. 84m. **DIR:** Don Jones. **CAST:** Harry Moses, Meegan King, Noelle North, Kate Sarchet, Charlene Tilton. 1984

SWEENEY TODD ★★★★★ This is not a film, but rather an eight-camera video of a Broadway musical taped during a performance before an audience. And what a musical it is, this 1979 Tony Award winner! George Hearn is terrifying as Sweeney Todd, the barber who seeks revenge on the English judicial system by slashing the throats of the unfortunate who wind up in his tonsorial chair. Angela Lansbury is spooky as Mrs. Lovett, who finds a use for Todd's leftovers by baking them into meat pies. 150m. **DIR:** Harold Prince. **CAST:** Angela Lansbury, George Hearn, Sara Woods. 1982

SWEEPER, THE ★★1/2 Star C. Thomas Howell fares well in this derivative crime-thriller. Howell plays L.A. cop Mark Goddard, whose suspects have a habit of dying. Goddard's tortured past (he witnessed his family's execution) comes into play when he's asked to join a secret police society that breaks the law in order to enforce it. When Goddard suspects the society may have been behind his family's death, havoc ensues. Rated R for violence and profanity. 101m. **DIR:** Joseph Merhi. **CAST:** C. Thomas Howell, Jeff Fahey, Ed Lauter, Cynda Williams. 1995

SWEEPERS ★★ That noise you hear isn't the numerous on-screen explosions but action star Dolph Lundgren's career hitting rock bottom. Lundgren plays a former mine-sweeping expert who is called back into duty to help stop terrorists from exporting a new deadly mine to the United States. The only bombs here are the functional script, thoughtless direction, and paper-thin performances. Rated R for violence and language. 96m. **DIR:** Darby Black. **CAST:** Dolph Lundgren, Claire Stansfield, Bruce Payne. 1997 DVD

SWEET ADELINE ★★★★ One of the first Broadway musicals transferred to the screen with most of its original score intact, this is also the first of five Jerome Kern musicals to star Irene Dunne. She gives her all to such songs as "Why Was I Born?" The story of spies and singers may be hokey, but the music is marvelous. B&W; 87m. **DIR:** Mervyn LeRoy. **CAST:** Irene Dunne, Donald Woods, Louis Calhern, Winifred Shaw, Nydia Westman, Hugh Herbert, Ned Sparks, Phil Regan, Noah Beery Sr. 1935

•**SWEET AND LOWDOWN** ★★★1/2 Bittersweet tale of a Depression-era jazz genius infatuated with himself, whose arrogant behavior and mistreatment of women become palatable only because he is, as it happens, a jazz guitarist almost without compare. (It's not hard to imagine Woody Allen lecturing us about the need to separate art from the artist.) When Samantha Morton is on camera, as a mute laundress who falls in love with Emmet, the film becomes magical and moves into Charlie Chaplin territory, specifically 1931's *City Lights*. While lacking the snap of Allen's best work, this film is nonetheless entertaining and playfully poignant. Rated PG-13 for brief profanity and sexual candor. 95m. **DIR:** Woody

Allen. **CAST:** Sean Penn, Samantha Morton, Uma Thurman, Anthony LaPaglia. **1999 DVD**

SWEET BIRD OF YOUTH (1962) ★★★ Crowds lined up to see this near-perfect big screen translation of Tennessee Williams's steamy Broadway hit about a has-been film star and her lusty, fame-hungry young lover. Director and scripter Richard Brooks got the best out of everyone in a fine cast. Definitely not for the kiddies. 120m. **DIR:** Richard Brooks. **CAST:** Geraldine Page, Paul Newman, Shirley Knight, Rip Torn, Madeleine Sherwood, Ed Begley Sr., Mildred Dunnock. **1962**

SWEET BIRD OF YOUTH (1989) ★★★1/2 Gritty adaptation of Tennessee Williams's play features Elizabeth Taylor as a fading film star often in a drunken stupor. Hitting rock bottom she takes up with a handsome gigolo (Mark Harmon). She seeks a companion, but all he wants is her connections. Harmon's performance is powerful. Made for TV, but contains nudity, violence, and adult themes. 95m. **DIR:** Nicolas Roeg. **CAST:** Mark Harmon, Elizabeth Taylor, Cheryl Paris, Valerie Perrine. **1989**

SWEET CHARITY ★★★★ This was a Broadway smash hit, and it lost nothing in transfer to the screen. Neil Simon adapted the story from Federico Fellini's *Nights of Cabiria*. Shirley MacLaine is a prostitute who falls in love with a naïve young man who is unaware of her profession. The musical numbers by Dorothy Fields and Cy Coleman are terrific. Bob Fosse, in his directorial debut, does an admirable job. Rated G. 133m. **DIR:** Bob Fosse. **CAST:** Shirley MacLaine, Chita Rivera, Paula Kelly, Ricardo Montalban, Sammy Davis Jr. **1969**

SWEET COUNTRY 💚 Chile under military rule after the murder of Allende. Rated R for violence and nudity. 105m. **DIR:** Michael Cacoyannis. **CAST:** Jane Alexander, John Cullum, Jean-Pierre Aumont, Irene Papas, Franco Nero, Carole Laure, Joanna Pettet, Randy Quaid. **1985**

SWEET DREAMS ★★★★1/2 Jessica Lange is Patsy Cline, one of the greatest country-and-western singers of all time, in this film that is much more than a response to the popularity of *Coal Miner's Daughter*. Lange's performance is flawless right down to the singing, where she perfectly mouths Cline's voice. Rated PG for profanity and sex. 115m. **DIR:** Karel Reisz. **CAST:** Jessica Lange, Ed Harris, Ann Wedgeworth, David Clennon, Gary Basaraba. **1985 DVD**

SWEET EVIL ★★ Overly familiar tale of a young couple desperate to have children. Their plan to invite a surrogate mom into their home turns deadly when the stranger unveils her own secret agenda. Adoption would have been easier and less predictable. Rated R for adult situations, language, nudity, and violence. 92m. **DIR:** Rene Eram. **CAST:** Bridgette Wilson, Peter Boyle, Scott Cohen, Seiko Matsuda. **1995 DVD**

SWEET 15 ★★★1/2 Marta's dream of a huge birthday celebration is shattered when her father fears he will be deported to Mexico in this fine family film first aired on PBS. Recommended. 110m. **DIR:** Victoria Hochberg. **CAST:** Karla Montana, Tony Plana. **1989**

SWEET HEREAFTER, THE ★★★★ Five minutes into this film and you just know it's the sort of work

that would have prompted the Cannes voters to award it the 1997 grand prize. This is a story of people seeking redemption and peace in the aftermath of a great tragedy and of the purgatory that awaits those who channel their anger and frustration in unwise directions. Based on the novel by Russell Banks. Although meticulously crafted and impeccably performed, this film lacks compelling fascination and the aftermath is unsatisfying. Rated R for nudity, profanity, and strong sexual content. 110m. **DIR:** Atom Egoyan. **CAST:** Ian Holm, Sarah Polley, Bruce Greenwood, Tom McCamus, Gabrielle Rose. **1997 DVD**

SWEET HOME CHICAGO ★★★★★ The story of Chicago's Chess Records and its timeless blues recordings is told with admirable attention to detail by filmmakers Alan and Susan Raymond. Rare footage of performances by the label's pacesetters—Muddy Waters, Howlin' Wolf, Sonny Boy Williamson, John Lee Hooker, Otis Spann, Buddy Guy, Chuck Berry, and Willie Dixon, among others—is integrated with anecdote-packed interviews for a one-of-a-kind viewing experience. Blues fans will want to own it. Made for video. 64m. **DIR:** Alan Raymond, Susan Raymond. **1993**

SWEET HOSTAGE ★★ Congenial kidnapper Martin Sheen espouses poetry and simple common sense in trying to convince captive Linda Blair that a world awaits her away from the confines of the farm. Not rated. 93m. **DIR:** Lee Philips. **CAST:** Linda Blair, Martin Sheen. **1976**

SWEET JUSTICE ★★ Women vigilantes battle small-town gangsters. Not to be taken seriously—the cast certainly didn't. Rated R for violence and nudity. 92m. **DIR:** Allen Plone. **CAST:** Finn Carter, Kathleen Kinmont, Marc Singer, Frank Gorshin, Mickey Rooney. **1991 DVD**

SWEET KILLING 💚 A strong cast is wasted in this imbecilic mess. A bored husband kills his wife and concocts a fictitious murderer, then meets a man claiming to be that very murderer. Rated R for profanity, nudity, and simulated sex. 87m. **DIR:** Eddy Matalon. **CAST:** Anthony Higgins, F. Murray Abraham, Leslie Hope, Andrea Ferreol, Michael Ironside. **1993**

SWEET LIBERTY ★★★★ Writer-director-star Alan Alda strikes again, this time with the story of a small-town historian (Alda) whose prize-winning saga of the Revolutionary War is optioned by Hollywood and turned into a movie. When the film crew descends on Alda's hometown for location shooting, predictable chaos erupts. Quite entertaining. Rated PG for mild sexual situations. 107m. **DIR:** Alan Alda. **CAST:** Alan Alda, Michael Caine, Michelle Pfeiffer, Bob Hoskins, Lise Hilboldt, Lillian Gish, Saul Rubinek, Lois Chiles, Linda Thorson. **1986**

SWEET LIES ★★ This so-called comedy contains little to laugh at, as Treat Williams plays an insurance investigator out to prove that a wheelchair-bound litigant is faking his injury. Ho-hum. Rated R for nudity and sexual situations. 96m. **DIR:** Nathalie Delon. **CAST:** Treat Williams, Joanna Pacula, Julianne Phillips. **1987**

SWEET LORRAINE ★★★★ There's a lot to like in this nostalgic stay at The Lorraine, a hotel in the Catskills. Maureen Stapleton is the owner of the 80-

year-old landmark that may be seeing its last summer. It needs extensive repairs and developers are offering a tempting price. A perfect cast makes this small-scale film a huge success. Rated PG-13. 91m. DIR: Steve Gomer. CAST: Maureen Stapleton, Trini Alvarado, Lee Richardson, John Bedford Lloyd, Giancarlo Esposito. 1987

SWEET LOVE, BITTER ★★ This film, adapted from the book *Night Song*, is loosely based on the life of Charlie Parker. Sax player (Dick Gregory) befriends a down-and-out college professor (Don Murray). Great jazz score (with Charles McPherson ghosting for Gregory on sax) and one hilarious pot-smoking scene are the only recommendations for this otherwise dated and cliché-ridden relic. Not rated; contains some violence. B&W; 92m. DIR: Herbert Danska. CAST: Dick Gregory, Don Murray, Diane Varsi, Robert Hooks. 1966

SWEET MOVIE 🎘 Incoherent, surreal comedy centers around a wealthy South African mining tycoon who purchases a virgin bride, then continues to exploit her sexually. In English and French with English subtitles. Not rated; contains sexually explicit material. 97m. DIR: Dusan Makavejev. CAST: Carole Laure, Pierre Clementi, Sami Frey. 1974

SWEET MURDER 🎘 Attractive Helene Udy allows Embeth Davidtz to move into her apartment, although Davidtz looks amazingly like the ax murderer she is. Could become infamous as the worst impersonation plot on film. Rated R for violence, profanity, and nudity. 101m. DIR: Percival Rubens. CAST: Helene Udy, Embeth Davidtz, Russell Todd. 1993

SWEET NOTHING ★★★★ The tense realism and jangling emotional honesty add up to cinema verité disguised as drama. A Wall Street exec begins a downward spiral by sampling too much of the crack he deals on the side. Watching the relentless destruction of a family is tough going, but we're left with a sliver of hope and the lingering effect of two extremely powerful performances. Rated R for violence, profanity, sexual situations, and drug use. 89m. DIR: Gary Winick. CAST: Michael Imperioli, Mira Sorvino, Paul Calderon. 1994

SWEET POISON ★★ This psychological thriller, which explores how far a decent man can be pushed, might play better if the dialogue weren't so weak and the performances so overblown. Rated R for language, sexual situations, and violence. 101m. DIR: Brian Grant. CAST: Steven Bauer, Edward Herrmann, Patricia Healy, Noble Willingham. 1991

SWEET REVENGE (1987) ★★ Nancy Allen plays a Los Angeles newswoman investigating the disappearance of several young women. She gets her story the hard way when she is kidnapped and taken to a slave market in Southeast Asia. Average action tale is marred by a disappointing ending and the miscasting of Allen. Rated R for violence, nudity, and sexual situations. 99m. DIR: Mark Sobel. CAST: Nancy Allen, Ted Shackelford, Martin Landau. 1987

SWEET REVENGE (1990) ★★★★ A newly divorced couple wrangle nonstop in this romantic comedy, originally telecast on cable. Lighthearted and pleasant, with some colorful European backgrounds. 89m.

DIR: Charlotte Brandstrom. CAST: Carrie Fisher, John Sessions, Rosanna Arquette. 1990

SWEET SIXTEEN ★★ In this static mystery, a young woman (Aliesa Shirley) from the big city reluctantly spends her summer—and her sixteenth birthday—in a small Texas town and becomes the chief suspect in a series of murders. Rated R for profanity and partial nudity. 96m. DIR: Jim Sotos. CAST: Aliesa Shirley, Bo Hopkins, Patrick Macnee, Susan Strasberg, Don Stroud. 1984

SWEET SMELL OF SUCCESS ★★★1/2 Burt Lancaster is superb as a ruthless newspaper columnist. Tony Curtis is equally great as the seedy press agent who will stop at nothing to please him. Outstanding performances by a great cast and brilliant cinematography by James Wong Howe perfectly capture the nightlife in Manhattan. Screenplay by Clifford Odets and Ernest Lehman. B&W; 96m. DIR: Alexander Mackendrick. CAST: Burt Lancaster, Tony Curtis, Martin Milner, Sam Levene, Barbara Nichols, Susan Harrison. 1957

SWEET SWEETBACK'S BAADASSSSS SONG ★★★1/2 Minor cult black film about a man running from racist white police forces. Melvin Van Peebles plays the title character, who will do anything to stay free. Very controversial when released in 1971. Lots of sex and violence gave this an X rating at the time. Probably the best of the black-produced and -directed films of the early 1970s. Rated R. 97m. DIR: Melvin Van Peebles. CAST: Melvin Van Peebles, Rhetta Hughes, Simon Chuckster, John Amos. 1971

SWEET TALKER ★★★ Ex-convict Harry Reynolds (Bryan Brown) dupes the residents of an Australian village into investing in the excavation of a bogus sunken ship filled with gold. Harry befriends the local hotel owner's son, only to have the boy see him as a surrogate father. Charming story and good acting. Rated PG. 91m. DIR: Michael Jenkins. CAST: Bryan Brown, Karen Allen, Chris Haywood, Bill Kerr. 1990 DVD

SWEET WILLIAM ★★★1/2 Sam Waterston and Jenny Agutter shine in this low-key adult comedy, which, while concerned with sex, doesn't feel the need to display any of it. She is attracted to his frenetic romanticism but slowly realizes that that same trait gets him into bed with every woman in sight. The women get the last laugh in this gentle British farce. Rated R for talk, not action. 92m. DIR: Claude Whatham. CAST: Sam Waterston, Jenny Agutter, Anna Massey, Tim Pigott-Smith. 1980

SWEETHEARTS (1938) ★★★1/2 Good acting, splendid singing, and a bright updated script make this version of the ancient Victor Herbert operetta a winning comedy about a temperamental stage duo on a collision course set by jealousy. The Technicolor cinematography won an Oscar. 120m. DIR: W. S. Van Dyke. CAST: Jeanette MacDonald, Nelson Eddy, Frank Morgan, Ray Bolger, Mischa Auer. 1938

•SWEETHEARTS (1996) ★★★ Director Aleks Horvat's frothy romantic comedy about four people looking for love in all the wrong places is filled with funny performances and equally funny dialogue. The focus is on Janeane Garofalo and Mitch Rouse, who meet as a blind date and end up spending the evening spilling their guts. Lucky for us, the script is filled with delicious slams and insights. The director manages to make this little chamber piece into an actual slice of life. Rated R for adult situations and language. 83m. DIR: Aleks Horvat. CAST: Janeane Garofalo, Mitch Rouse, Margaret Cho, Bob Goldthwait. 1996

SWEETHEARTS' DANCE ★★★ From Ernest (*On Golden Pond*) Thompson, a delightful little movie about love and relationships. High school sweethearts Don Johnson and Susan Sarandon are a married couple whose marriage has stagnated. There are subplots about male bonding, best friends, and father-son relationships. Rated R for profanity. 101m. DIR: Robert Greenwald. CAST: Don Johnson, Susan Sarandon, Jeff Daniels, Elizabeth Perkins, Justin Henry. 1988

SWEETHEARTS ON PARADE ★★ Country girl and city girl go hunting jobs and husbands. A marine and a sailor take a shine to the pair and join forces to save the country girl when she is taken in by a wealthy married man. Easygoing comedy may be sexist, but it touches on other stereotypes, too, and handles them all with good nature. One of the last silent feature films released. B&W; 66m. DIR: Marshall Neilan. CAST: Alice White, Lloyd Hughes, Marie Prevost, Kenneth Thompson, Ray Cooke, Wilbur Mack. 1930

SWEETIE ★★★1/2 Surrealistic first film by Australian writer-director Jane Campion recalls David Lynch's *Eraserhead* and *Blue Velvet* in its odd camera angles and bizarre characters. The title character (Genevieve Lemon) is a grotesque version of the spoiled daddy's girl. Rated R for profanity, nudity, and violence. 100m. DIR: Jane Campion. CAST: Genevieve Lemon, Karen Colston. 1990

SWEPT AWAY ★★★1/2 The full title is *Swept Away by an Unusual Destiny in the Blue Sea in August*, and what this Italian import addresses is a condescending, chic goddess who gets hers on a deserted island. In Italian with English subtitles. Rated R. 116m. DIR: Lina Wertmuller. CAST: Giancarlo Giannini, Mariangela Melato. 1975 DVD

SWEPT FROM THE SEA ★★★★ A shipwreck victim washes ashore and falls in love with the local "crazy lady." Effective period romance featuring a very appealing cast and a sweeping score by the legendary John Barry. Rated PG-13. 114m. DIR: Beeban Kidron. CAST: Vincent Perez, Rachel Weisz, Ian McKellen, Joss Ackland, Kathy Bates. 1997 DVD

SWIMMER, THE ★★★★ A middle-aged man in a gray flannel suit who has never achieved his potential swims from neighbor's pool to neighbor's pool on his way home on a hot afternoon in social Connecticut. Each stop brings back memories of what was and what might have been. Burt Lancaster is excellent in the title role. Rated PG. 94m. DIR: Frank Perry. CAST: Burt Lancaster, Janet Landgard, Janice Rule, Joan Rivers, Tony Bickley, Marge Champion, Kim Hunter. 1968

SWIMMING POOL, THE 🖤 This slow-moving French film features Alain Delon, Romy Schneider, and Maurice Ronet in a love triangle that leads to homicide. Dubbed into English. Not rated; contains nudity. 85m. DIR: Jacques Deray. CAST: Alain Delon, Romy Schneider, Maurice Ronet, Jane Birkin. 1970

SWIMMING TO CAMBODIA ★★★★ This low-budget movie consists of nothing more than actor-monologist Spalding Gray sitting at a desk while he tells about his experiences as a supporting actor in *The Killing Fields*. But seldom has so much come from so little. Gray is an excellent storyteller and his extended anecdotes—covering the political history of Cambodia, the filming of the movie, the sex and drugs available in Southeast Asia, and life in New York City—are often hilarious. Not rated. 87m. DIR: Jonathan Demme. CAST: Spalding Gray. 1987

SWIMMING WITH SHARKS ★★★★ Sort of a personalized *The Player* in which a misanthropic Hollywood studio executive's long-suffering assistant takes his boss hostage and tortures back. Rated R for language, violence, and sex. 93m. DIR: George Huang. CAST: Kevin Spacey, Frank Whaley, Michelle Forbes. 1995

SWIMSUIT 🖤 Lousy made-for-TV movie about the search for a model for a new swimsuit line. 95m. DIR: Chris Thomson. CAST: William Katt, Catherine Oxenberg, Nia Peeples, Tom Villard, Jack Wagner, Billy Warlock, Cyd Charisse. 1989 DVD

•**SWINDLE, THE** ★★★1/2 Con artists lure conventioneers into sharing a few cocktails, then drug them and steal their IDs and money. One mark turns out to be a bag man for the mob and the story thickens. This satirical caper about shifting and shiftless human relationships includes gorgeous globe-trotting, cheeky characterizations, and slick twists. In French with English subtitles. Not rated. 104m. DIR: Claude Chabrol. CAST: Isabelle Huppert, Michel Serrault, François Cluzet, Jean-François Balmer. 1999 DVD

SWING HIGH, SWING LOW ★★1/2 Entertainers Carole Lombard and Fred MacMurray, stranded in Panama, get married, split, and fight ennui and a variety of troubles. This is a slanted-for-comedy remake of 1929s highly successful tearjerking backstage drama, *The Dance of Life*. B&W; 95m. DIR: Mitchell Leisen. CAST: Carole Lombard, Fred MacMurray, Dorothy Lamour, Charles Butterworth, Franklin Pangborn, Anthony Quinn. 1937

SWING IT, SAILOR ★★ Envision two gobs after one gal, or make it two swabs after one skirt, and you've got this film figured out. Broad, roughhouse humor is the order of the day. The story is stale, but moves along at a decent clip. B&W; 61m. DIR: Raymond Connon. CAST: Wallace Ford, Isabel Jewell, Ray Mayer. 1937

SWING KIDS ★★1/2 The premise is certainly fascinating: young German "bop" fans resisted induction into the Hitler youth. Kenneth Branagh's ominously chilling SS officer is undercut by *Hogan's Heroes*–style cartoon Nazis (reflecting the film's Disney origins). Rated PG-13 for violence and profanity. 112m. DIR: Thomas Carter. CAST: Robert Sean Leonard, Christian Bale, Frank Whaley, Barbara Hershey, Kenneth Branagh. 1993

SWING SHIFT ★★ Goldie Hawn stars in this disappointing 1940s-era romance as Kay Walsh, the girl who's left behind when her husband, Jack (Ed Harris), goes off to fight in World War II. Rated PG for profanity and suggested sex. 100m. **DIR:** Jonathan Demme. **CAST:** Goldie Hawn, Kurt Russell, Ed Harris, Fred Ward, Christine Lahti, Sudie Bond. **1984**

SWING TIME ★★★★1/2 Fred Astaire is a gambler trying to save up enough money to marry the girl he left behind (Betty Furness). By the time he's saved the money, he and Ginger Rogers are madly in love with each other. B&W; 105m. **DIR:** George Stevens. **CAST:** Ginger Rogers, Fred Astaire, Betty Furness, Victor Moore, Helen Broderick. **1936**

SWINGERS ★★★★ The male title characters in this Cocktail Nation comedy all look "money, baby"—at least to each other if not to the "beautiful babies" they romantically stalk and covet in the retro-swing lounges of Los Angeles. This crash course in 1990s dating protocol is a hilarious ensemble piece that paints men as both desperate lechers and shell-shock victims of the singles wars. Rated R for language. 96m. **DIR:** Doug Linman. **CAST:** Jon Favreau, Vince Vaughn, Ron Livingston, Patrick Van Horn, Alex Desert, Deena Martin, Heather Graham. **1996 DVD**

SWINGIN' SUMMER, A ★★ This is one of those swingin' Sixties flicks where three swingin' teens move to a swingin' summer resort for a swingin' vacation. They start up their own swingin' dance concert schedule and book big-name acts like Gary and the Playboys, the Rip Tides, and the Righteous Brothers. Raquel Welch debuts here and also sings. 82m. **DIR:** Robert Sparr. **CAST:** Raquel Welch, James Stacy, William Wellman Jr., Quinn O'Hara, Martin West. **1965**

SWISS CONSPIRACY, THE ★★1/2 Swiss banker Ray Milland hires ex-Fed David Janssen to thwart a sophisticated blackmail scheme involving supposedly secret numbered accounts. Sexy Senta Berger and John Saxon, as a Chicago gangster double-crossing his friends, are among those being threatened with exposure and death. Rated PG. 92m. **DIR:** Jack Arnold. **CAST:** David Janssen, Senta Berger, Ray Milland, Elke Sommer, John Ireland, John Saxon. **1977 DVD**

SWISS FAMILY ROBINSON, THE ★★★1/2 Walt Disney's comedy-adventure film, adapted from the classic children's story by Johann Wyss about a family shipwrecked on a lush South Seas island. 128m. **DIR:** Ken Annakin. **CAST:** John Mills, Dorothy McGuire, James MacArthur, Tommy Kirk, Sessue Hayakawa. **1960**

SWISS MISS ★★★ Here we have Stan Laurel and Oliver Hardy in the Swiss Alps. A weak and uneven script is overcome by the stars, who seize several opportunities for brilliant comedy. For the most part, however, the film is mediocre. B&W; 72m. **DIR:** John G. Blystone. **CAST:** Stan Laurel, Oliver Hardy, Della Lind, Walter Woolf King, Eric Blore. **1938**

SWITCH ★★★ Writer-director Blake Edwards continues his exploration of the sexes with this story of a sleazy womanizer (Perry King) who is killed by his jilted ex-lovers only to come back as a woman. Ellen Barkin is wonderful as a male in a female body. Rated R for profanity and brief nudity. 104m. **DIR:** Blake Edwards. **CAST:** Ellen Barkin, Jimmy Smits, Jo-

Beth Williams, Lorraine Bracco, Tony Roberts, Perry King, Bruce Payne. **1991**

SWITCHBACK ★★★★ Intricate plotting amplifies this tricky murder mystery, and writer-director Jeb Stuart scores points for credible characters, provocative storytelling, and an underlying puzzle that'll keep everybody guessing right up to the exciting conclusion. The title reflects the film's cross-cutting style of alternating between two apparently separate narratives that we know must be related ... but how? Rated R for violence, profanity, and several close-ups of nude pinups. 121m. **DIR:** Jeb Stuart. **CAST:** Dennis Quaid, Danny Glover, Jared Leto, Ted Levine, R. Lee Ermey. **1997 DVD**

SWITCHBLADE SISTERS ★★★ Deserving of kudos for its drive-in entertainment value, this 1975 cheapie has been delivered to video by Quentin Tarantino. Doesn't matter if this cast of hot-pants-clad nobodies boasts minimal acting talent, there's more than enough campy dialogue, action, and blue eye shadow to go around. Rated R for violence, profanity, sexual situations, and brief nudity. 91m. **DIR:** Jack Hill. **CAST:** Robbie Lee, Joanne Nail, Monica Gayle, Janice Karman, Kitty Bruce, Marlene Clark. **1975 DVD**

SWITCHED AT BIRTH ★★★1/2 Above-average made-for-TV miniseries chronicles the controversial true story of two baby girls swapped at birth. When tragedy strikes and one of the girls dies, it is discovered that her blood type doesn't match that of her parents, and the search for the truth begins. Long in the tooth, but entertaining nonetheless. 200m. **DIR:** Waris Hussein. **CAST:** Bonnie Bedelia, Brian Kerwin, Ariana Richards, Edward Asner, Eve Gordon. **1991**

SWITCHING CHANNELS ★★★ Effective performances by Kathleen Turner, Burt Reynolds, and Christopher Reeve enliven this fourth big-screen version of Ben Hecht and Charles MacArthur's *The Front Page*. More specifically a remake of Howard Hawks's 1940 comedy classic, *His Girl Friday*, *Switching Channels* switches from newspapers to television but keeps many of the elements of the original's plot. Rated PG for profanity. 113m. **DIR:** Ted Kotcheff. **CAST:** Kathleen Turner, Burt Reynolds, Christopher Reeve, Ned Beatty, Henry Gibson, Joe Silver. **1988**

•**SWITCHING GOALS** ★★1/2 The Olsen twins, Mary-Kate and Ashley, mine *The Parent Trap* formula, playing identical twins who decide to switch identities. Mary-Kate is Sam, the tomboy of the two, while Ashley is Emma, rotten on the playing field but an ace at home and in school. When they wind up on opposing soccer teams, the girls are unhappy with their teammates and coach. In order not to rock the boat, they decide to impersonate each other, which means keeping up the charade both on and off the field. Rated G. 85m. **DIR:** David Steinberg. **CAST:** Mary-Kate Olsen, Ashley Olsen, Eric Lutes, Kathryn Greenwood, Joe Grifasi. **1999**

SWOON ★★★★ *Swoon* follows in the footsteps of *Rope* and *Compulsion* as films inspired by the real-life exploits of 1920s Chicago college-boy killers, Nathan Leopold Jr. and Richard Loeb. The changing climate in America, though, allows Kalin to explore a heretofore ignored aspect of the story—that Leopold and Loeb were homosexual lovers. It's stylish, original, and exciting. Rated R, with profanity and sexual content. B&W; 90m. DIR: Tom Kalin. CAST: Daniel Schlachet, Craig Chester, Ron Vawter, Michael Kirby. 1992

SWORD AND THE ROSE, THE (1953) ★★1/2 Romance, intrigue, and heroic acts of derring-do are the order of the day in this colorful Walt Disney adaptation of *When Knighthood Was in Flower*. Richard Todd makes an ideal lead and Michael Gough is a truly malevolent heavy. 93m. DIR: Ken Annakin. CAST: Richard Todd, Glynis Johns, James Robertson Justice, Michael Gough. 1953

SWORD AND THE SORCERER, THE ★★ But for the derring-do and bits of comedy provided by star Lee Horsley, this film would be a complete waste of time and talent. A soldier of fortune (Horsley) rescues a damsel in distress (Kathleen Beller) and her brother (Simon MacCorkindale) from an evil king and his powerful wizard. Rated R because of nudity, violence, gore, and sexual references. 100m. DIR: Albert Pyun. CAST: Lee Horsley, Kathleen Beller, Simon MacCorkindale, George Maharis, Richard Lynch, Richard Moll. 1982

SWORD IN THE STONE, THE ★★★1/2 The legend of King Arthur provided the story line for this animated feature film from the Walt Disney studios. Although not up to the film company's highest standards, it still provides fine entertainment for the young and the young at heart. Rated G. 80m. DIR: Wolfgang Reitherman. 1963

SWORD OF DOOM ★★★ Tatsuya Nakadai gives a fascinating performance as a brutal samurai, whose need to kill alienates even his once-devoted father. Several stories are interwoven in this film, but, surprisingly, at least two are left unresolved. This will make it disappointing—and confusing—for all but the most devoted fans of Japanese action movies. In Japanese with English subtitles. 122m. DIR: Kihachi Okamoto. CAST: Tatsuya Nakadai, Toshiro Mifune. 1967

SWORD OF GIDEON ★★★1/2 To avenge the 1972 murders of Israeli Olympic-team members in Munich, five commandos are sent on a globe-hopping mission to destroy selected leaders of the terrorist Black September movement. Location filming is a plus in this suspenseful and action-packed TV movie. Colleen Dewhurst has a touching cameo as Prime Minister Golda Meir. 150m. DIR: Michael Anderson. CAST: Steven Bauer, Michael York, Rod Steiger, Robert Joy, Leslie Hope, Laurent Malet, Linda Griffiths, Lino Ventura, Cyrielle Claire, Colleen Dewhurst. 1986

SWORD OF HONOR ★★1/2 This kung fu action flick's earnest cast tries hard but cannot overcome lackluster direction and idiotic camera tricks (notably accelerated frame speed). Dedicated Las Vegas cop Steven Vincent Leigh sets out to avenge his best friend's death and recover the prized titular object. Rated R for violence, profanity, nudity, and simulated sex. 95m. DIR: Robert Tiffe. CAST: Steven Vincent Leigh, Angelo Tiffe, Sophia Crawford, Jerry Tiffe. 1994

SWORD OF LANCELOT ★★★ Colorful production and location photography highlight this pre-*Camelot* version of life at the court of King Arthur and the forbidden love between Lancelot and Queen Guinevere (Mr. and Mrs. Cornel Wilde in real life). Long on pageantry, action, and chivalrous acts of derring-do, this is a "fun" film in the same vein as *Ivanhoe* and *The Vikings*. 116m. DIR: Cornel Wilde. CAST: Cornel Wilde, Jean Wallace, Brian Aherne, George Baker. 1963

SWORD OF THE VALIANT ★★★1/2 The Old English tale of Sir Gawain and the Green Knight is brought to the screen with an appealing blend of action-adventure and tongue-in-cheek humor. Rated PG. 162m. DIR: Stephen Weeks. CAST: Miles O'Keeffe, Sean Connery, Trevor Howard. 1984

SWORDSMAN, THE ♥ A psychic police detective sword-battles his way through a case involving stolen antiquities and mass murder, eventually discovering that he is the reincarnation of Alexander the Great. Rated R for violence and profanity. 98m. DIR: Michael Kennedy. CAST: Lorenzo Lamas, Claire Stansfield, Michael Champion. 1992

SWORN ENEMIES ★★★ Michael Paré and Peter Greene stand out in this tale of best friends and partners turned mortal enemies. Greene is hungry for power, and he's killing those who stand in his way. Paré is the local sheriff of their quiet, backwater town and will do anything to put an end to the killing spree. Rated R for adult situations, language, and violence. 101m. DIR: Shimon Dotan. CAST: Michael Paré, Peter Greene, Macha Grenon. 1996 DVD

SYBIL ★★★★ Sally Field is outstanding in this deeply disturbing but utterly fascinating made-for-TV drama of a young woman whose intense psychological childhood trauma has given her seventeen distinct personalities. Joanne Woodward is the patient, dedicated psychiatrist who sorts it all out. 116m. DIR: Daniel Petrie. CAST: Joanne Woodward, Sally Field, William Prince. 1976

SYLVESTER ★★★★ Director Tim Hunter does an admirable job with this hard-edged *National Velvet*-style drama about a tomboy (Melissa Gilbert) who rides her horse, Sylvester, to victory in the Olympics' Three-Day Event in Lexington, Kentucky. Gilbert is first-rate as the aspiring horsewoman, and Richard Farnsworth is reliable, watchable self as her cantankerous mentor. Rated PG-13 for profanity and violence. 109m. DIR: Tim Hunter. CAST: Melissa Gilbert, Richard Farnsworth, Michael Schoeffling, Constance Towers. 1985

SYLVIA ★★ About as underwhelming as a film can get and still have some redeeming qualities. Were it not for the fine performance by Eleanor David in the title role, this film about seminal educator Sylvia Ashton-Warner would be a muddled bore. It jumps from one event to another with little or no buildup or continuity. Rated PG for graphic descriptions of violence. 97m. DIR: Michael Firth. CAST: Eleanor David, Nigel Terry, Tom Wilkinson, Mary Regan. 1985

SYLVIA AND THE PHANTOM ★★★★ A delightful story concerning ghosts and the fantasies of a young lady living with her family in a castle. As the story begins, we meet Sylvia on the eve of her sixteenth birthday and find that she fantasizes about the portrait of her grandmother's lover and the rumors that he haunts the castle. In French with English subtitles. 97m. **DIR:** Claude Autant-Lara. **CAST:** Odette Joyeux, François Perier, Julien Carette. **1950**

SYLVIA SCARLETT ★★★1/2 The first screen teaming of Katharine Hepburn and Cary Grant lacks the sprightly pace and memorable humor of *Holiday* and *The Philadelphia Story*, which also were directed by George Cukor, but it's still a real find for fans of the stars. When Hepburn's con-man father (Edmund Gwenn) runs afoul of the law, they must quickly leave France while she masquerades as a boy to avert suspicion. B&W; 94m. **DIR:** George Cukor. **CAST:** Katharine Hepburn, Cary Grant, Brian Aherne, Edmund Gwenn. **1936**

SYNAPSE ★★ The quest for eternal youth is still on in the future. A company known as Life Corp. has found a way of transferring someone's mind to another body. Their first experiment, a betrayed coworker whose brain is transferred into that of a beautiful woman, backfires. The woman escapes and brings back an army of renegades anxious to put an end to Life Corp. Okay at moments, but nothing new here. Rated R for violence, nudity, and adult language. 89m. **DIR:** Allan A. Goldstein. **CAST:** Karen Duffy, Chris Makepeace, Saul Rubinek, Matt McCoy. **1994**

SYNGENOR ★★1/2 Syngenor stands for synthetic genetic organism. Starr Andreeff plays a woman fighting for her life when the beast gets loose. This slight film is fun in a no-brainer sort of way. Rated R for violence, profanity, and nudity. 98m. **DIR:** George Elanjian Jr. **CAST:** Starr Andreeff, David Gale. **1990**

SYNTHETIC PLEASURES ★★★ Occasionally intriguing documentary about virtual reality and other artifical modes of pleasure attainment (drugs not included, unless you count the "smart drinks" imbibed by some young club goers). Like the *Mondo* movies of the 1960s, all that is here passes without comment, and the film tends to stray from its theme (particularly in the case of a performance artist obsessed with plastic surgery). Not rated; contains sexual themes. 83m. **DIR:** Iara Lee. **1996**

TABLE FOR FIVE ★★★ Had it up to here with *Kramer vs. Kramer* clones about single parents coping with their kids? If you have, you'll probably decide to skip this movie—and that would be a shame, because it's a good one. Jon Voight stars as J. P. Tannen, a divorcé who takes his three youngsters on a Mediterranean cruise in hopes of getting back into their lives full-time. Rated PG for mature situations. 122m. **DIR:** Robert Lieberman. **CAST:** Jon Voight, Richard Crenna, Millie Perkins. **1983**

TABU ★★★1/2 Begun as a collaboration between F. W. Murnau and documentarian Robert Flaherty, this is an unusual but unique South Seas romance filmed with a combination of naturalistic settings and an expressionistic technique. A native girl falls in love with a young man despite the fact that she has been promised to the gods. Silent. 81m. **DIR:** F. W. Murnau. **CAST:** Anna Chevalier, Matahi. **1931**

●**TACTICAL ASSAULT** ★★★ Dazzling midair combat and lots of high-impact energy keep this direct-to-video action-thriller off the ground. Rutger Hauer is perfectly cast as an air force pilot serving in the Gulf War. When he snaps during a mission and tries to down an airliner, he comes under attack from a fellow pilot and enters a deadly game of cat-and-mouse. Rated R for language and violence. 89m. **DIR:** Mark Griffiths. **CAST:** Rutger Hauer, Robert Patrick, Isabel Glasser. **1998 DVD**

TAFFIN ★★★ The ever-watchable Pierce Brosnan plays a surprisingly tough "collector" in this fun-to-watch Irish film. The city folks approach Brosnan to get rough with the chemical plant thugs who are bulldozing their fair countryside. Rated R for violence, profanity, and nudity. 96m. **DIR:** Francis Megahy. **CAST:** Pierce Brosnan, Ray McAnally, Alison Doody. **1987 DVD**

TAG—THE ASSASSINATION GAME ★★★1/2 The short-lived fad for campus war games, in which students stalked each other with rubber darts, is the basis for this comic thriller. Student reporter Robert Carradine, smitten with star player Linda Hamilton, follows her on her hunt. Neither realizes that one player has started using a real gun. Rated PG. 92m. **DIR:** Nick Castle. **CAST:** Robert Carradine, Linda Hamilton, Bruce Abbott, Michael Winslow. **1982**

TAGGET ★★★1/2 A smooth and sympathetic lead performance from Daniel J. Travanti highlights this intriguing tale of a disabled Vietnam veteran plagued by disturbing flashbacks. His efforts to decipher the dreams reveal traces of a decade-old CIA dirty tricks cover-up. Slick, violent made-for-cable thriller. 89m. **DIR:** Richard T. Heffron. **CAST:** Daniel J. Travanti, Roxanne Hart, Peter Michael Goetz, Bill Sadler. **1991**

TAI-PAN ★★ Pretentious, overblown adaptation of James Clavell's bestseller, this disjointed mess plays like a television miniseries chopped from eight hours to two. Bryan Brown is properly stoic as the "Tai-Pan," chief trader, who dreams of establishing a colony to be named Hong Kong. Joan Chen is ludicrous as his concubine. Rated R for brief nudity and violence. 127m. **DIR:** Daryl Duke. **CAST:** Bryan Brown, John Stanton, Joan Chen, Tim Guinee. **1986**

TAILS YOU LIVE, HEADS YOU'RE DEAD ★★★ Suspenseful made-for-cable original about a stranger who picks his murder victims at random and plays mind games with them. Corbin Bernsen is excellent as the killer and Ted McGinley does a good job as his next victim. Rated R for violence and profanity. 95m. **DIR:** Tim Matheson. **CAST:** Corbin Bernsen, Ted McGinley, Tim Matheson. **1995**

TAILSPIN ★★★ Docu-style drama concerning the Soviet Union's tragic shooting down of Korean Airline's flight 007 over the Sea of Japan. A tactical error or an act of aggression? Made for TV. 82m. **DIR:** David Durlow. **CAST:** Michael Moriarty, Michael Murphy, Chris Sarandon, Harris Yulin. **1989**

TAINTED BLOOD ★★★1/2 A nationally known writer is doing research on children who inherit killer tendencies. She goes in search of a girl whose mother killed her parents and whose twin brother killed his adoptive parents. The viewer meets two families who each have an adopted daughter. At every turn, the very twisted plot keeps the viewer unsure which girl has the tainted blood. Not rated, made for cable, but contains violence. 95m. **DIR:** Matthew Patrick. **CAST:** Raquel Welch, Alley Mills, Kerri Green, Natasha Gregson Wagner, Joan Van Ark. **1993**

TAKE, THE ★★ This lurid, by-the-numbers cop thriller features Ray Sharkey as a Miami police officer who does jail time for attempting to cut himself into a drug deal, and then—surprise, surprise—faces exactly the same temptation after being released. Not rated, but with considerable violence. 95m. **DIR:** Leon Ichaso. **CAST:** Ray Sharkey, R. Lee Ermey, Larry Manetti, Lisa Hartman. **1990**

TAKE A HARD RIDE ★★1/2 When his friend and partner (Dana Andrews) dies, big Jim Brown is charged with taking the proceeds from a cattle sale to their homestead in Sonora, Mexico. On the way, a ruthless bounty hunter (Lee Van Cleef) attempts to take the money. A good cast falls prey to the shortcomings of this spaghetti Western, but there is some enjoyable action and humor. Rated R. 103m. **DIR:** Anthony M. Dawson. **CAST:** Jim Brown, Lee Van Cleef, Fred Williamson, Catherine Spaak, Dana Andrews, Barry Sullivan, Jim Kelly, Harry Carey Jr. **1975**

TAKE DOWN ★★1/2 Earnest comedy-drama set in the arena of high school wrestling. It centers on two initially reluctant participants: an intellectual teacher-turned-coach and a fiery student. The movie has enough heart to carry it to victory. Rated PG. 107m. **DIR:** Kieth Merrill. **CAST:** Edward Herrmann, Kathleen Lloyd, Lorenzo Lamas, Maureen McCormick, Kevin Hooks, Stephen Furst. **1978**

TAKE IT BIG ★★ In the early 1940s at Paramount Pictures, a B-movie unit was formed by William H. Pine and William C. Thomas. With a good track record, they tried to produce more elaborate films. This so-so musical is one of those bigger productions. Jack Haley is at the wrong end in a horse act that inherits a dude ranch. Ozzie Nelson and his band supply the musical numbers. B&W; 75m. **DIR:** Frank McDonald. **CAST:** Jack Haley, Ozzie Nelson, Harriet Nelson. **1944**

TAKE ME BACK TO OKLAHOMA ★★★★★ Top 50 B Western stars Tex Ritter who comes to the aid of a female owner of a stage line being harassed by unscrupulous competitors. This is the first Western to feature Bob Wills's fabulous Western swing music as well as a terrific rendition of Jimmy Davis's "You Are My Sunshine." B&W; 67m. **DIR:** Albert Herman. **CAST:** Tex Ritter, Bob Wills and the Texas Playboys, Arkansas Slim Andrews, Terry Walker, Karl Hackett. **1940**

TAKE ME OUT TO THE BALL GAME ★★★ Don't expect to see the usual Berkeley extravaganza in this one; this is just a run-of-the-mill musical. It does con-

tain some entertaining musical numbers, such as "O'Brien to Ryan to Goldberg." 93m. **DIR:** Busby Berkeley. **CAST:** Gene Kelly, Frank Sinatra, Esther Williams, Betty Garrett, Jules Munshin. **1949**

TAKE THE MONEY AND RUN ★★★★ Woody Allen's first original feature is still a laugh-filled delight as the star-director plays an inept criminal in a story told in pseudo-documentary-style (à la *Zelig*). It's hilarious. Rated PG. 85m. **DIR:** Woody Allen. **CAST:** Woody Allen, Janet Margolin, Marcel Hillaire. **1969 DVD**

TAKE THIS JOB AND SHOVE IT ★★★1/2 Robert Hays stars as a rising corporate executive who returns, after a ten-year absence, to his hometown to take charge of a brewery where he once worked, and winds up organizing a revolt among his fellow employees. This contemporary comedy-drama is out to raise one's spirits, and it does just that. Rated PG. 100m. **DIR:** Gus Trikonis. **CAST:** Robert Hays, Art Carney, Barbara Hershey, Martin Mull, Eddie Albert. **1981**

TAKEN AWAY ★★ Valerie Bertinelli is a waitress/student who leaves her daughter alone one night and finds the child has become a ward of the state. Extremely manipulative, as the system set up to protect children rakes Bertinelli over the legal coals. Made as a movie of the week, and it shows. Not rated. 94m. **DIR:** John Patterson. **CAST:** Valerie Bertinelli, Kevin Dunn, Juliet Sorcey. **1989**

TAKEOVER, THE ★★ Lackluster crime-drama stars Billy Drago as an East Coast crime lord looking to take over the West Coast from Nick Mancuso. Everyone involved seems to wish they were somewhere else and the low-budget, low-power gun battles don't help. Rated R for violence, nudity, and profanity. 91m. **DIR:** Troy Cook. **CAST:** Billy Drago, John Savage, Nick Mancuso, Eric DaRe, David Ramos, Cali Timmins, Gene Mitchell. **1994**

TAKING CARE OF BUSINESS ★★★ Small-time crook James Belushi finds the Filofax of high-powered businessman Charles Grodin and takes over his business dealings, with predictable results. Wastes the talents of the two stars, mainly by not giving them enough scenes together. A harmless time killer. Rated R for profanity and sexual themes. 108m. **DIR:** Arthur Hiller. **CAST:** Charles Grodin, James Belushi. **1990**

TAKING MY TURN ★★ This is a videotape of an off-Broadway musical. Unfortunately, you had to be there to really enjoy it. Sort of *A Chorus Line* for the Geritol generation, this features aging actors lamenting the way times have changed. Their song-and-dance routines are good, but for the most part this is pretty depressing. 90m. **DIR:** Robert H. Livingston. **CAST:** Margaret Whiting, Marni Nixon, Sheila Smith, Cissy Houston. **1984**

TAKING OF BEVERLY HILLS, THE ★★★ Fans of nonstop action will cheer this *Die Hard*-esque movie about a quarterback who teams up with a crooked cop to stop the looting of Beverly Hills by a clever crime boss. Rated R for violence and profanity. 102m. **DIR:** Sidney J. Furie. **CAST:** Ken Wahl, Matt Frewer, Harley Jane Kozak, Robert Davis, Lee Ving, Lyman Ward, Michael Bowen, William Prince. **1991**

TAKING OF PELHAM ONE TWO THREE, THE ★★★★ Walter Matthau is at his growling, grumbling, gum-chewing best in this edge-of-your-seat movie. He plays the chief detective of security on the New York subway who must deal with the unthinkable: the hijacking of a train by four men (with a fine Robert Shaw as their leader) and a demand by them for a $1 million ransom to prevent their killing the passengers one by one. Rated R for violence and profanity. 104m. DIR: Joseph Sargent. CAST: Walter Matthau, Robert Shaw, Martin Balsam, Tony Roberts. 1974 DVD

TAKING THE HEAT ★★★1/2 Gutsy cop Lynn Whitfield has her hands full in this entertaining thriller, when she's assigned to escort reluctant witness Tony Goldwyn to a court appointment. A routine trip across New York City becomes a nightmare thanks to a heat wave, a power blackout, and pursuing goons ordered by crime-lord Alan Arkin to eliminate Goldwyn. Rated R for profanity, violence, nudity, and suggested sex. 90m. DIR: Tom Mankiewicz. CAST: Tony Goldwyn, Lynn Whitfield, George Segal, Peter Boyle, Will Patton, Alan Arkin. 1993

TALE OF A VAMPIRE ★★★★ Julian Sands plays a scholarly vampire who thinks he's found love again in Suzanna Hamilton, a woman similar to his long-dead paramour. Archenemy Kenneth Cranham arrives and casts a pall of tragic romanticism over the lovers. Slow but effectively moody in a gothic, gory manner. Rated R for violence and gore. 93m. DIR: Shimako Sato. CAST: Julian Sands, Suzanna Hamilton, Kenneth Cranham. 1993

TALE OF RUBY ROSE, THE ★★★ Rousing frontier adventure about a woman named Ruby Rose, who has lived her entire life in the backwoods of Tasmania. Then she takes a courageous journey in search of her grandmother, a trip that causes her to look to her inner self to survive a world she never knew existed. Exhilarating. Rated PG. 101m. DIR: Roger Scholes. CAST: Melita Jurisic, Chris Haywood. 1987

TALE OF SPRINGTIME, A ★★★ A French schoolteacher is befriended by a young woman. She then becomes entangled in touchy family affairs when she's romantically paired with the girl's father. Eric Rohmer's passion for intelligent, witty discourse and subtle tension continues in a story he says "deals less with what people do than with what is going on in their minds while they are doing it." This is the third installment in his sophisticated *Tales of the Four Seasons* film series. In French with English subtitles. Rated PG. 107m. DIR: Eric Rohmer. CAST: Anne Teyssedre, Florence Darel, Hugues Quester. 1992

TALE OF TWO CITIES, A (1935) ★★★★★ A satisfactory rendition of Charles Dickens's novel. It is richly acted, with true Dickens flavor. Ronald Colman was ideally cast in the role of Sydney Carton, the English no-account who finds purpose in life amid the turmoil of the French Revolution. The photography in this film is one of its most outstanding features. The dark shadows are in keeping with the spirit of this somber Dickens story. B&W; 121m. DIR: Jack Conway. CAST: Ronald Colman, Basil Rathbone, Edna May Oliver, Elizabeth Allan. 1935

TALE OF TWO CITIES, A (1967) ★★★1/2 Impressive detailed adaptation of the Charles Dickens novel that chronicles the turmoil of the French Revolution and features some good performances by a top-notch cast. 117m. DIR: Ralph Thomas. CAST: Dirk Bogarde, Donald Pleasence, Christopher Lee, Dorothy Tutin. 1967

TALE OF TWO CITIES, A (1980) ★★★ Acceptable version of the Dickens classic, though the other versions available on video are better. There's a topflight cast, but Chris Sarandon is a bit wan for Sydney Carlton. Not rated. 216m. DIR: Jim Goddard. CAST: Chris Sarandon, Peter Cushing, Kenneth More, Barry Morse, Flora Robson, Billie Whitelaw, Alice Krige. 1980

TALE OF TWO CITIES, A (1991) ★★★★ This magnificent PBS production of Charles Dickens's classic lavishly re-creates the costumes and setting of France from 1767 to 1790. A self-imposed exile of French nobility (Xavier Deluc) finds himself helplessly drawn into the revolutionary madness of mob rule. 240m. DIR: Philippe Monnier. CAST: James Wilby, Xavier Deluc, Serena Gordon, Jean-Pierre Aumont. 1991

TALENT FOR THE GAME ★★★1/2 Little-known film is a treasure trove of wonderful performances and memorable moments. The marvelous Edward James Olmos stars as a talent scout for the California Angels. An examination of life in modern America as compared with the values inherent in the game of baseball. Rated PG for profanity. 91m. DIR: Robert M. Young. CAST: Edward James Olmos, Lorraine Bracco, Jamey Sheridan, Terry Kinney, Jeff Corbett, Tom Bower, Janet Carroll, Felton Perry, Thomas Ryan. 1991

•**TALENTED MR. RIPLEY, THE** ★★★★1/2 Matt Damon shines in the title role of this meticulously crafted character drama, adapted by scripter-director Anthony Minghella from a particularly unsettling Patricia Highsmith novel. The result is an intriguing analysis of the extremes to which one man will go to be accepted by an arrogant, class-based social strata in which he feels out of place. The setting is *La Dolce Vita* of the late 1950s, with Damon's Tom Ripley hired to "spy" on a rich American's wayward son, who's throwing his life away on jazz and expatriate girlfriend Gwyneth Paltrow. Minghella's style is strikingly Hitchcockian, but it's Damon's show: Present in absolutely every scene, he is nothing short of mesmerizing. Rated R for violence and profanity. 140m. DIR: Anthony Minghella. CAST: Matt Damon, Gwyneth Paltrow, Jude Law, Cate Blanchett, Philip Seymour Hoffman, Jack Davenport, James Rebhorn. 1999 DVD

TALES FROM A PARALLEL UNIVERSE ★★ Hokum about a group of space rebels who hijack a spaceship to find a lost planet in order to revive their leader. Their quest is jeopardized when they encounter a holographic prankster who doesn't realize the spaceship is also a deadly weapon that can destroy the universe, and will self-destruct if the occupants are killed. Made-for-cable series. Rated R for adult situations, language, and violence. 93m. DIR: Ron

Oliver. **CAST:** Brian Downey, Eva Habermann, Michael McManus, Tim Curry. **1996**

TALES FROM THE CRYPT ★★★1/2 Excellent anthology has five people gathered in a mysterious cave where the keeper (Ralph Richardson) foretells their futures, one by one, in gruesome fashion. Director Freddie Francis keeps things moving at a brisk pace, and the performances are uniformly fine, most notably Peter Cushing's in one of the better segments—"Poetic Justice." Don't miss it. Rated PG. 92m. **DIR:** Freddie Francis. **CAST:** Peter Cushing, Joan Collins, Ralph Richardson. **1972**

TALES FROM THE CRYPT (TV SERIES) ★★★1/2 Three creepy tales told with tongue firmly in cheek just as the original comic books were. Not rated; contains violence. 90m. **DIR:** Walter Hill, Robert Zemeckis, Richard Donner. **CAST:** Bill Sadler, Mary Ellen Trainor, Larry Drake, Joe Pantoliano, Robert Wuhl. **1989 DVD**

TALES FROM THE CRYPT: DEMON KNIGHT ★★1/2 On par with the TV series, this theatrical release focuses on a likable collector who has come for the key that will allow evil to take over completely. Unlike many horror films that take themselves too seriously, this pokes fun at both itself and the genre. Rated R for nudity, profanity, violence, gore, and sexual situations. 85m. **DIR:** Ernest R. Dickerson. **CAST:** Billy Zane, Bill Sadler, Jada Pinkett, Brenda Bakke. **1994 DVD**

TALES FROM THE DARKSIDE, THE MOVIE ★★★ This horror anthology (inspired by the hit TV series) features a few exceptional moments and a lot of more mundane horror-film conventions. Rated R for violence and profanity. 90m. **DIR:** John Harrison. **CAST:** Deborah Harry, Christian Slater, David Johansen, William Hickey. **1990**

TALES FROM THE DARKSIDE, VOL. I ★★ The first installment in this ongoing series of TV-episode compilations is the only one worth bothering with, largely because of the three stories adapted: Stephen King's "Word Processor of the Gods," and Harlan Ellison's "D'Jinn, No Chaser," and "Slippage." The penny-ante budget doesn't help, though. 70m. **DIR:** Michael Gornick. **1985**

TALES FROM THE CRYPT PRESENTS BORDELLO OF BLOOD 💔 A private eye searches for the missing brother of a televangelist in a mortuary staffed by half-naked, undead silicone transplantees. Bare breasts and exploding bodies are all the rage in this dull gorefest. Rated R for gore, violence, nudity, and sex. 87m. **DIR:** Gilbert Adler. **CAST:** Dennis Miller, Erika Eleniak, Angie Everhart, Chris Sarandon, Corey Feldman. **1996 DVD**

TALES FROM THE GIMLI HOSPITAL ★★★★ Blend of Scandinavian folktales, the severe look of German-expressionist silents, and a slightly skewed and surreal sense of humor. The bizarre plot line centers around a tortured character who is admitted to the primitive-looking title institution during an outbreak of plague. Singularly deadpan brand of avant-garde humor. Not rated. 68m. **DIR:** Guy Maddin. **CAST:** Kyle McCulloch, Michael Gottli, Angela Heck, Margaret Anne MacLeod, Heather Neale, David Neale. **1988**

TALES FROM THE HOOD ★★ This violent horror anthology features a mortician who spooks three gangsters searching for a missing drug stash by telling them four grisly stories. Rated R for language, violence, and gore. 97m. **DIR:** Rusty Cundieff. **CAST:** David Alan Grier, Wings Hauser, Corbin Bernsen, Joe Torry, De'Aundre Bonds, Sam Monroe. **1995 DVD**

TALES OF EROTICA ★★1/2 Four famous directors take a stab at erotic filmmaking in this uneven quartet of passionate stories. Mira Sorvino stands out as a woman who enters a painting in order to fulfill her sexual desires. Rated R for nudity, profanity, and adult situations. 103m. **DIR:** Ken Russell, Susan Seidelman, Bob Rafelson, Gus Van Sant. **CAST:** Mira Sorvino, Aida Turturro, Hetty Baynes, Simon Shepherd, Richard Barboza, Cynda Williams, Arliss Howard, Kathleen Wilhoite. **1994 DVD**

TALES OF HOFFMAN ★★★1/2 A beautifully photographed blend of opera, ballet, and cinematic effects with Jacques Offenbach's familiar score for a backdrop. Robert Rounseville stars as the tale-spinner who recalls various romantic interludes in his life. The film was a follow-up to *The Red Shoes* with the same directors, stars, and color consultants. 120m. **DIR:** Michael Powell, Emeric Pressburger. **CAST:** Moira Shearer, Robert Rounseville, Robert Helpmann, Leonide Massine, Pamela Brown. **1951**

TALES OF MANHATTAN ★★★1/2 One of the best of the many episodic films produced during the 1940s, this one uses a man's tailcoat as the link between episodes. Every new owner has an adventure associated with the coat, and they range from romance to melodrama with a little comedy thrown in. B&W; 118m. **DIR:** Julien Duvivier. **CAST:** Ginger Rogers, Henry Fonda, Edward G. Robinson, Rita Hayworth, Ethel Waters, Paul Robeson, Eddie "Rochester" Anderson, Charles Laughton, Cesar Romero, George Sanders. **1942**

TALES OF ORDINARY MADNESS 💔 Ben Gazzara in the role of infamous drunken poet Charles Bukowski, who interacts with a strange assortment of women. Rated R for profanity and nudity. 107m. **DIR:** Marco Ferreri. **CAST:** Ben Gazzara, Ornella Muti, Susan Tyrrell, Tanya Lopert. **1983 DVD**

TALES OF PARIS ★★1/2 Lightweight omnibus film featuring four stories of young women and their romantic escapades in Paris. The last segment is the most memorable, if only for a chance to see 19-year-old Catherine Deneuve in one of her first films. B&W; 85m. **DIR:** Marc Allegret, Jacques Poitrenaud, Michel Boisrone, Claude Barma. **CAST:** Dany Saval, Dany Robin, Jean Poiret, Catherine Deneuve, Johnny Hallyday. **1962**

TALES OF TERROR ★★★ An uneven anthology of horror stories adapted from the works of Edgar Allan Poe. Directed by Roger Corman, it does have a few moments. 90m. **DIR:** Roger Corman. **CAST:** Vincent Price, Basil Rathbone, Peter Lorre, Debra Paget. **1962**

TALES OF THE UNEXPECTED ★★1/2 Four half-hour made-for-television shows are included in this compilation. 101m. **DIR:** Gordon Hessler, Norman Lloyd, Paul Annett, Ray Danton. **CAST:** Don Johnson, Arthur Hill, Samantha Eggar, Sharon Gless, Dick Smothers, James Carroll Jordan, Charles Dance, Zoe

Wanamaker, Sondra Locke, Frank Converse, Charles Hallahan. 1981–1987

TALES THAT WITNESS MADNESS ★★★ Black-comic horror anthology featuring four stories told by an asylum keeper to a new psychiatrist. Most memorable is the third, in which Joan Collins fights for her husband's affections against his new lover: a possessed tree! Rated R for minor grossness. 90m. DIR: Freddie Francis. CAST: Donald Pleasence, Jack Hawkins, Suzy Kendall, Joan Collins, Kim Novak. 1973

TALES TILL THE END 🎬 If you've seen every other ultralow-budget horror flick on the planet, then this one's for you. Not rated, but contains profanity, violence, nudity, and gore. 88m. DIR: Barry Gaines, Philip Herman, Ben Stanski. CAST: Barry Gaines, Philip Herman, Ben Stanski. 1995

TALION ★★ Two bounty hunters (Robert Lansing and Patrick Wayne) go on the vengeance trail against a turncoat (Slim Pickens). The twist is that in an early gun battle, Wayne is blinded and Lansing's gun hand is crippled. Lansing looks vaguely uncomfortable in a cowboy hat, and the writing is sometimes ridiculous. 92m. DIR: Michael Moore. CAST: Robert Lansing, Patrick Wayne, Slim Pickens, Gloria Talbott, Paul Fix, Strother Martin, Clint Howard. 1966

TALK OF ANGELS ★★★ An intimate romance between a governess and her employer's son is set against an epic, sprawling civil war in this uneven yet handsome production. Polly Walker rises to the occasion as Mary Lavelle, an Irish governess who falls for the married son of her employer. Set in Spain in 1936 just before the civil war, the film's smaller moments are constantly engulfed by the grandeur of the film. Rated PG-13 for adult situations. 97m. DIR: Nick Hamm. CAST: Polly Walker, Vincent Perez, Franco Nero, Frances McDormand. 1997

TALK OF THE TOWN, THE ★★★★ Falsely accused of arson and murder, parlor radical Cary Grant escapes jail and holes up in a country house Jean Arthur is readying for law professor Ronald Colman. The radical and the egghead take to one another. Gifted direction and a brilliant cast make this topflight entertainment. B&W; 118m. DIR: George Stevens. CAST: Ronald Colman, Jean Arthur, Cary Grant, Edgar Buchanan, Glenda Farrell, Emma Dunn, Charles Dingle, Tom Tyler, Don Beddoe, Rex Ingram. 1942

TALK RADIO ★★★★ Powerful story centers on a controversial Dallas radio talk-show host's rise to notoriety—and the ultimate price he pays for it. Eric Bogosian repeats his acclaimed Broadway stage performance as the radio host who badgers and belittles callers and listeners alike. A highly cinematic, fascinating film. Director Oliver Stone keeps his camera moving and the pace rapid throughout. Rated R. 110m. DIR: Oliver Stone. CAST: Eric Bogosian, Alec Baldwin, Ellen Greene, John Pankow, John C. McGinley. 1989

TALKIN' DIRTY AFTER DARK ★★1/2 Black comedy stars Martin Lawrence as a comedian who will do anything to land a spot at the infamous Dukie's nightclub, and that includes sleeping with the main man's main squeeze. Too much jive and not enough laughs. Rated R for language and nudity. 86m. DIR: Topper Carew. CAST: Martin Lawrence, John Witherspoon. 1991

TALKING ABOUT SEX ★★1/2 At a party to promote publication of a manual to help couples nurture sexual intimacy, the guests learn more than they had anticipated about each other. Apparently designed to be similarly nurturing to viewers, this uninvolving drama tries to pack too many issues into one film. Not rated; contains nudity, sexual situations, and profanity. 87m. DIR: Aaron Speiser. CAST: Kim Wayans, Daniel Beer, Daria Lynn, Randy Powell, Kerry Ruff. 1993

TALKING WALLS ★★ Offbeat, mildly interesting comedy-drama about a student who decides to do his thesis on sexual relationships by videotaping unwitting guests as they cavort in a sleazy Hollywood motel. Not rated, contains nudity, sex, and vulgar language. 85m. DIR: Stephen F. Verona. CAST: Stephen Shellen, Marie Laurin, Sybil Danning, Sally Kirkland, Barry Primus. 1987

TALL BLOND MAN WITH ONE BLACK SHOE, THE ★★★★ If you're looking for an entertaining, easy-to-watch comedy, this is one of the best. Pierre Richard plays the bumbling blond man to hilarious perfection, especially when it comes to physical comedy. The story involves spies, murder, a mysterious sexy woman, and plenty of action. Highly recommended, but try to see the original version, with subtitles, not the dubbed version. Rated PG. 90m. DIR: Yves Robert. CAST: Pierre Richard, Bernard Blier, Mireille Darc. 1972

TALL, DARK AND DEADLY ★★ Slightly suspenseful tale about a woman stalked by a psychotic, mysterious man. Not rated; contains violence and sexual situations. 88m. DIR: Kenneth Fink. CAST: Jack Scalia, Kim Delaney, Todd Allen, Gina Mastrogiacomo. 1994

TALL GUY, THE ★★★1/2 Delightfully whacked-out comedy about an American actor (Jeff Goldblum) stuck in a dead-end London gig as a foil for a loud, obnoxious, and egotistical comedian (Rowan Atkinson). This all changes when he falls in love with a no-nonsense nurse (Emma Thompson). Rated R for profanity and nudity. 90m. DIR: Mel Smith. CAST: Jeff Goldblum, Emma Thompson, Rowan Atkinson, Geraldine Jones. 1990

TALL IN THE SADDLE ★★★★ A first-rate B Western that combines mystery with shoot-'em-up action. John Wayne is wrongly accused of murder and must find the real culprit. Helping him is Gabby Hayes, and hindering is Ward Bond. B&W; 87m. DIR: Edwin L. Marin. CAST: John Wayne, George "Gabby" Hayes, Ward Bond, Ella Raines. 1944

TALL MEN, THE ★★ Confederate army veterans Clark Gable and Cameron Mitchell join cattle baron Robert Ryan to drive his herd to market through Indian country. All three fancy Jane Russell. 122m. DIR: Raoul Walsh. CAST: Clark Gable, Jane Russell, Robert Ryan, Cameron Mitchell, Mae Marsh. 1955

TALL STORY ★★★ Jane Fonda makes a delightful college student who falls for a basketball player. This is Fonda's first movie and shows her flair for comedy. B&W; 90m. DIR: Joshua Logan. CAST: Jane Fonda, Anthony Perkins, Elizabeth Patterson, Ray Walston, Anne

Jackson, Murray Hamilton, Gary Lockwood, Marc Connelly, Tom Laughlin. **1960**

TALL T, THE ★★★★ Rancher Randolph Scott and several stagecoach passengers are captured and held by outlaws. Top-notch Burt Kennedy script from an Elmore Leonard story. Fine performances from all concerned. This is a little-known classic. 78m. **DIR:** Budd Boetticher. **CAST:** Randolph Scott, Richard Boone, Maureen O'Sullivan, Henry Silva, Skip Homeier. **1957**

TALL TALE: THE UNBELIEVABLE ADVENTURES OF PECOS BILL ★★★1/2 Youngsters will be charmed by this story of how three legendary figures—Pecos Bill (Patrick Swayze), Paul Bunyan (Oliver Platt), and John Henry (Roger Aaron Brown)—help a young boy save his family's farm from the clutches of the evil, land-grabbing J. P. Stiles. Rated PG for violence. 96m. **DIR:** Jeremiah S. Chechik. **CAST:** Patrick Swayze, Oliver Platt, Roger Aaron Brown, Nick Stahl, Scott Glenn, Stephen Lang, Jared Harris, Catherine O'Hara. **1995**

TALONS OF THE EAGLE ★★ Nothing special. Two DEA agents go undercover to bust a notorious crime lord. Once they gain his trust, they take him down in one of those extended martial-arts sequences that cap such affairs. Rated R for violence, language, and adult situations. 96m. **DIR:** Michael Kennedy. **CAST:** Billy Blanks, Jalal Merhi, James Hong, Priscilla Barnes. **1992**

TAMARIND SEED, THE ★★★ A sudsy melodrama in the old tradition, but still a lot of fun. Julie Andrews falls in love with a foreign emissary played by Omar Sharif, only to be told (by her own State Department) to stay away from him. The cold war intrigue seems pretty absurd these days, but Andrews and Sharif generate a playful chemistry that overlooks many sins. Rated PG. 123m. **DIR:** Blake Edwards. **CAST:** Omar Sharif, Julie Andrews, Anthony Quayle. **1974**

TAMING OF THE SHREW, THE (1929) ★★★ The first royal couple of Hollywood costarred in this film while under the duress of a failing marriage. Mary Pickford is properly shrewish as Katharine; Douglas Fairbanks is smug, commanding, and virile as Petruchio. Critics liked it and the public flocked to see the famous duo have at the Bard. Director Sam Taylor gave Hollywood one of its enduring anecdotes by taking screen credit for additional dialogue. B&W; 66m. **DIR:** Sam Taylor. **CAST:** Mary Pickford, Douglas Fairbanks Sr., Dorothy Jordan. **1929**

TAMING OF THE SHREW, THE (1966) ★★★★1/2 This is a beautifully mounted comedy of the battle of the sexes. Petruchio (Richard Burton), a spirited minor nobleman of the Italian Renaissance, pits his wits against the man-hating Kate (Elizabeth Taylor) in order to win her hand. The zest with which this famous play is transferred to the screen can be enjoyed even by those who feel intimidated by Shakespeare. 126m. **DIR:** Franco Zeffirelli. **CAST:** Richard Burton, Elizabeth Taylor, Cyril Cusack, Michael York. **1966 DVD**

TAMING OF THE SHREW (1982) ★★★★ Inventive and laugh-filled, a stage production of Shakespeare's best-loved comedy as the ambitious Petruchio

(Franklyn Seales) comes to wed himself well in Padua, choosing the fiery, mean-spirited Kate (Karen Austin) as his reluctant bride. Catch the running visual joke concerning Pisa. Released by Bard Productions Ltd. 115m. **DIR:** John Allison. **CAST:** Franklyn Seales, Karen Austin, Larry Drake, Kathryn Johnson, Bruce Davison, David Chemel. **1982**

TAMMY & THE T-REX ❤ Nonsense about a man who is turned into a T-Rex in order to impress a girl he wants to date. Didn't he ever hear of flowers? Not rated. 82m. **DIR:** Stewart Raffill. **CAST:** Terry Kiser, Ellen Dubin, Denise Richards, Paul Walker. **1993**

TAMMY AND THE BACHELOR ★★★ Like Debbie Reynolds's number-one hit song *Tammy*, the movie is corny but irresistible. Ingenuous country girl Reynolds falls in love with injured pilot Leslie Nielsen and nurses him back to health. The romance and humor are sweet and charming. The movie's success led to sequels and a TV series. 89m. **DIR:** Joseph Pevney. **CAST:** Debbie Reynolds, Leslie Nielsen, Walter Brennan, Mala Powers, Fay Wray, Sidney Blackmer, Mildred Natwick, Louise Beavers. **1957**

TAMMY AND THE DOCTOR ★★ Cutesy romance between country gal Sandra Dee and young Peter Fonda is relatively harmless, but this is definitely a film with a limited audience. No muss, no fuss—in fact, not much of anything at all. 88m. **DIR:** Harry Keller. **CAST:** Sandra Dee, Peter Fonda, Macdonald Carey, Beulah Bondi, Margaret Lindsay, Reginald Owen, Adam West. **1963**

TAMPOPO ★★★★ This Japanese spoof of the Italian spaghetti Western (which was, in turn, a spin-off of the samurai movie) shows a female diner owner (Nobuko Miyamoto) learning how to make perfect noodles. As silly as it sounds, this is a wonderful movie full of surprises. In Japanese with English subtitles. Not rated, with nudity and brief violence. 95m. **DIR:** Juzo Itami. **CAST:** Nobuko Miyamoto. **1987 DVD**

TANGO ★★1/2 Hard-core dance fans may enjoy this melancholy but rather monotonous story about an Argentine choreographer who tries to make a socially vital film about the sensuous tango. His project gradually becomes a reflection of his own midlife crisis, relationships with women, and political repression. In Spanish with English subtitles. Rated PG-13 for language, sexual themes, and violent images. 112m. **DIR:** Carlos Saura. **CAST:** Miguel Angel Sola, Cecilia Narova, Mia Maestro. **1998 DVD**

TANGO AND CASH ★★ Sylvester Stallone and Kurt Russell play rival L.A. detectives who find themselves framed by a powerful drug lord (Jack Palance) and must join forces to clear their names. *Tango and Cash* starts off well, with plenty of action and great comic quips, and then descends into a near parody of itself. Rated R for profanity, nudity, and violence. 98m. **DIR:** Andrei Konchalovsky. **CAST:** Sylvester Stallone, Kurt Russell, Jack Palance, Michael J. Pollard, Brion James, James Hong, Geoffrey Lewis. **1989 DVD**

TANGO BAR ★★★ Part musical, part documentary, part romantic-triangle love story, this film employs all those elements to detail the historical and cultural importance of the tango. Raul Julia and Ruben

Juarez play two tango performers who are reunited. In Spanish with English subtitles. 90m. DIR: Marcos Zurinaga. CAST: Raul Julia, Valeria Lynch, Ruben Juarez. 1988

TANGO LESSON, THE ★★★1/2 An English filmmaker (writer-director Sally Potter, playing a fictional version of herself) takes a break from writing her latest screenplay to attend a tango exhibition and becomes fascinated by the sensuous rhythms of the Argentine dance. Film is sensuous and fascinating, with fluidly hypnotic tango sequences and marvelous screen chemistry between Potter and tango master Pablo Veron. In English, French, and Spanish with English subtitles where needed. Rated PG. B&W/color; 100m. DIR: Sally Potter. CAST: Sally Potter, Pablo Veron, Carolina Lotti, Heathcote Williams, Gustavo Naveira, Fabian Salas. 1997

TANK ★★1/2 The always likable James Garner plays Sgt. Maj. Zack Carey, an army career soldier who has to use his privately owned Sherman tank to rescue his family (Shirley Jones and C. Thomas Howell) from the clutches of a mean country sheriff (G. D. Spradlin). It's all a bunch of hokum, but a sure audience pleaser. Rated PG. 113m. DIR: Marvin J. Chomsky. CAST: James Garner, Shirley Jones, C. Thomas Howell, G. D. Spradlin. 1984 DVD

TANK GIRL ★★★1/2 Alan Martin and Jamie Hewlett's savagely punk comic-book heroine gets a first-class adaptation. Although definitely not for all tastes, this should delight the midnight crowd that embraced Rocky Horror Picture Show. Rated R for profanity and violence. 104m. DIR: Rachel Talalay. CAST: Lori Petty, Malcolm McDowell, Ice T, Naomi Watts, Don Harvey, Jeff Kober. 1995

TANKS ARE COMING, THE ★★★ A hard-line war movie about the Third Amored Division's efforts to overturn Nazi onslaughts in Europe. Produced long after World War II ended so it did not have a lot of exposure. It has since become a cult favorite. B&W; 90m. DIR: Lewis Seiler. CAST: Steve Cochran, Philip Carey, Paul Picerni, Harry Bellaver, James Dobson, Mari Aldon. 1951

TANNER '88 ★★★1/2 Doonesbury creator Garry Trudeau wrote this insightful tale of a dark-horse presidential candidate (played to perfection by Michael Murphy). Along the way Tanner runs into Bob Dole, Gary Hart, and Pat Robertson. Originally aired on HBO. 120m. DIR: Robert Altman. CAST: Michael Murphy, Pamela Reed, Cynthia Nixon, Kevin J. O'Connor, Daniel H. Jenkins. 1988

TANYA'S ISLAND ★★★ This little cult oddity is one that you'll either love or hate. A woman escapes her abusive husband to a fantasy island where she spends her time with a sentient ape named Blue. Rob Bottin contributes some nifty makeup special effects. Rated R for violence, nudity, profanity, and simulated sex. 93m. DIR: Alfred Sole. CAST: D.D. Winters, Richard Sargent, Vanity. 1981

TAP ★★★★ This Flashdance-style musical-drama about a gifted tap dancer (Gregory Hines) is so good, you'll want to watch it a second time—not for the silly jewel-heist story, but for the marvelous dance sequences. See it for the eye-popping choreography and a cut contest—featuring old pros Sammy Davis Jr., Harold Nicholas, Bunny Briggs, Sandman Sims, Steve Condos, Rico, and Arthur Duncan—that will make your jaw drop. Rated PG-13 for profanity and violence. 111m. DIR: Nick Castle. CAST: Gregory Hines, Sammy Davis Jr., Joe Morton, Dick Anthony Williams. 1989

TAP DOGS ★★★ Six Australian construction-worker hunks put their feet down in this rhythmic collection of dance and noise. Decked out in hard hats, flannel shirts, and jeans, the talented cast members tap-dance through several spectacular numbers while performing live at London's Lyric Theatre. Not rated. 75m. DIR: Nigel Triffitt, Aubrey Powell. 1996

TAPEHEADS ★★★ In this off-the-wall Night Shift, John Cusack plays a pretentious and obnoxious con man who convinces Tim Robbins, a video genius, to make music videos. Weird and funny viewing, and the chemistry between the two leads is perfect. Not rated; contains offensive language and sexual situations. 94m. DIR: Bill Fishman. CAST: John Cusack, Tim Robbins, Mary Crosby, Connie Stevens, Doug McClure, Lyle Alzado. 1988

TAPS ★★★1/2 George C. Scott is an iron-jawed commander of a military academy and Timothy Hutton a gung ho cadet who leads a student revolt in this often exciting but mostly unbelievable and unnecessarily violent drama. Rated R. 118m. DIR: Harold Becker. CAST: George C. Scott, Timothy Hutton, Ronny Cox, Tom Cruise. 1981

TAR ★★ A Harlem cop falls in love with a petty thief who is being recruited to join a terrorist gang. Although attractively filmed, this low-budget effort changes directions so often that it ends up nowhere. Not rated; contains violence, nudity, sexual situations, substance abuse, and profanity. 91m. DIR: Goetz Grossman. CAST: Kevin -Thigpen, Nicole Prescott, Seth Gilliam. 1997

★TARANTELLA ★★★ A young woman rediscovers her Italian heritage while going through her mother's things shortly after her mother's death. Mira Sorvino's performance is compelling but the story moves a trifle slowly. Not rated; contains profanity. 84m. DIR: Helen DeMichel. CAST: Mira Sorvino, Rose Gregorio, Matthew Lillard, Frank Pellegrino, Antonia Rey. 1995 DVD

TARANTULA ★★★ Pretty good entry in the giant-bug subgenre of 1950s horror and science-fiction films. Heroic John Agar must deal with a mountain-sized arachnid created by well-meaning Leo G. Carroll's supergrowth formula. Don't blink during the final scenes—Clint Eastwood has a very brief bit as the fighter pilot who brings the beastie down. B&W; 80m. DIR: Jack Arnold. CAST: John Agar, Mara Corday, Leo G. Carroll, Eddie Parker, Clint Eastwood. 1955

TARANTULAS—THE DEADLY CARGO ★★ A small town is terrorized by a bumper crop of spiders in this TV movie that wastes too much time setting the viewer up for scare scenes which, when they finally arrive, aren't especially scary. 100m. DIR: Stuart Hagmann. CAST: Claude Akins, Charles Frank, Deborah Winters, Howard Hesseman. 1977

TARAS BULBA ★★★ Tony Curtis and Yul Brynner give top-notch performances in this action-packed adventure centering on Cossack life during the sixteenth century in the Ukraine. Great location photography in Argentina by Joe MacDonald, and a fine musical score by Franz Waxman. Solid entertainment. 122m. **DIR:** J. Lee Thompson. **CAST:** Tony Curtis, Yul Brynner. 1962

TARGET ★★★ In this fast-paced, entertaining suspense-thriller directed by Arthur Penn (*Bonnie and Clyde*), a father (Gene Hackman) and son (Matt Dillon) put aside their differences when they become the targets of an international spy ring. *Target* is a tad predictable, but it is the kind of predictability that adds to the viewer's enjoyment. Rated R for violence, profanity, and nudity. 117m. **DIR:** Arthur Penn. **CAST:** Gene Hackman, Matt Dillon, Gayle Hunnicutt, Josef Sommer, Victoria Fyodora, Herbert Berghof. 1985

TARGET EAGLE ❤ A mercenary is hired by a Spanish police department to infiltrate a drug-smuggling ring. Not rated, has violence. 101m. **DIR:** J. Anthony Loma. **CAST:** Jorge Rivero, Maud Adams, George Peppard, Max von Sydow, Chuck Connors. 1982

TARGET: FAVORITE SON ★★★ Television miniseries *Favorite Son* edited down to feature-length still packs quite a wallop for those into soap-opera politics. The usual collection of love, sex, politics, espionage, and assassination make this dramatic thriller as much fun as the real thing. 115m. **DIR:** Jeff Bleckner. **CAST:** Harry Hamlin, Linda Kozlowski, Robert Loggia, John Mahoney, Ronny Cox. 1988

TARGET OF SUSPICION ❤ An extremely boring and badly acted made-for-cable movie about an American who is set up while on a business trip to Paris. One to avoid. Not rated; contains violence. 95m. **DIR:** Bob Swaim. **CAST:** Tim Matheson, Lysette Anthony, Agnes Soral. 1994

TARGETS ★★★★★ The stunning filmmaking debut of critic-turned-director Peter Bogdanovich juxtaposes real-life terror, in the form of an unhinged mass murderer (Tim O'Kelly), with its comparatively subdued and safe screen counterpart, as represented by the scare films of Byron Orlock (Boris Karloff in a brilliant final bow). Rated PG. 90m. **DIR:** Peter Bogdanovich. **CAST:** Tim O'Kelly, Boris Karloff, Nancy Hsueh, Peter Bogdanovich. 1968

•**TARNISHED ANGELS, THE** ★★★1/2 William Faulkner's novel *Pylon* was the basis for this assured melodrama starring Robert Stack as a WWI flying ace who becomes a daredevil stunt pilot. Rock Hudson is a reporter who gradually comes under the spell of Stack and his traveling family. 91m. **DIR:** Douglas Sirk. **CAST:** Robert Stack, Rock Hudson, Dorothy Malone. 1958

TARO, THE DRAGON BOY ★★★★ Distinctive animation, reminiscent of Japanese silkscreens, provides an engaging forum for introducing young viewers to Japanese mythology and culture. Here, young Taro makes a pilgrimage to a faraway lake to rescue his mother, who has been turned into a dragon. 75m. **DIR:** K. Urayama. 1985

TARTUFFE ★★★ Let's be upfront about this one: It's a sophisticated version of Molière's play about religious hypocrisy. The satire is funny and biting, but this Royal Shakespeare Company production is not for everyone. The performances, especially Antony Sher's interpretation of Tartuffe, are brilliant, but very subtle. 110m. **DIR:** Bill Alexander. **CAST:** Antony Sher, Nigel Hawthorne, Alison Steadman. 1984

TARZAN (1999) ★★★★★ Superb animation and clever storytelling make this one of Disney's true, timeless classics. While Edgar Rice Burroughs's original tale is shunted aside once again by the filmmakers, the joys of this all-ages entertainment are many. Rated G. 88m. **DIR:** Kevin Lima, Chris Buck. 1999 DVD

TARZAN AND HIS MATE ★★★★★ Tarzan against ivory hunters. The best MGM Tarzan movie is a bona fide film classic, one of the few sequels to surpass the original. A marvelously entertaining motion picture. B&W; 105m. **DIR:** Cedric Gibbons. **CAST:** Johnny Weissmuller, Maureen O'Sullivan, Neil Hamilton, Paul Cavanagh. 1934

•**TARZAN AND THE GOLDEN LION** ★★1/2 In this last silent Tarzan feature, the Lord of the Jungle tracks a look-alike who has ransacked his estate and absconded with his friend's fiancée. Then a lost race of diamond hoarders seizes her and plans to sacrifice her to their sun god. This long-lost minor epic is the only one of four full-length presound movies about the twentieth century's best-known noble savage that exists in anything near its original form. Silent, with musical score. B&W; 58m. **DIR:** J. P. McGowan. **CAST:** James Pierce, Dorothy Dunbar, Edna Murphy, Harold Goodwin, Fred Peters, Boris Karloff. 1927

TARZAN AND THE GREEN GODDESS ★★ Olympic champion Herman Brix (a.k.a. Bruce Bennett) makes one of the best-looking of all movie Tarzans as he journeys to South America to help secure a priceless stone image known as the "Green Goddess." Primitive filming conditions and a horrible soundtrack hinder the jungle nonsense. B&W; 72m. **DIR:** Edward Kull. **CAST:** Bruce Bennett, Ula Holt, Frank Baker. 1938

TARZAN AND THE LEOPARD WOMAN ★★1/2 Above-average Tarzan entry pits him against legendary bad actress Acquanetta (*Captive Wild Woman*) as the titular villainess, leader of a murderous jungle cult. B&W; 72m. **DIR:** Kurt Neumann. **CAST:** Johnny Weissmuller, Johnny Sheffield, Brenda Joyce, Acquanetta, Dennis Hoey. 1946

TARZAN AND THE LOST CITY ★★1/2 Compared to most of the other Tarzan films that Hollywood has butchered from Edgar Rice Burroughs's original classics, this one is generally tolerable. But the vine swinging and annoying yell are still here so as not to leave out those raised on the Johnny Weissmuller films. Poor acting by the leads, however, brings down what could have been an enjoyable romp. Rated PG for violence. 84m. **DIR:** Carl Schenkel. **CAST:** Casper Van Dien, Jane March. 1998 DVD

TARZAN AND THE TRAPPERS ★★ This oddity is actually three television pilots that producer Sol Lesser was unable to sell to networks back in 1958. This is pretty ordinary, uninspired stuff, but it's a one-of-a-kind Tarzan film, unavailable for years. B&W; 74m. **DIR:** H. Bruce Humberstone. **CAST:** Gordon Scott, Evelyn Brent, Rickie Sorenson, Maurice Marsac. 1958

TARZAN ESCAPES ★★★ Once again greed spurs an expedition but instead of ivory, Tarzan is the prize. This troubled production took two years and three directors before it reached the screen due to negative audience reaction to the grim nature of many scenes as well as the inevitable pressure brought on all productions by the Breen Office and the Legion of Decency. B&W; 95m. DIR: Richard Thorpe. CAST: Johnny Weissmuller, Maureen O'Sullivan, Benita Hume, William Henry, E. E. Clive. **1936**

TARZAN FINDS A SON ★★★1/2 Tarzan and Jane find an infant, the only survivor of a plane crash, and raise him as their "Boy." Five years later, relatives of his rich parents arrive and attempt to return him to civilization. Plenty of jungle action. B&W; 82m. DIR: Richard Thorpe. CAST: Johnny Weissmuller, Maureen O'Sullivan, Johnny Sheffield, Ian Hunter, Henry Stephenson, Frieda Inescort, Henry Wilcoxon, Laraine Day. **1939**

TARZAN OF THE APES ★★★1/2 The first filmed version of Edgar Rice Burroughs's classic tells the story of the Greystokes. Their child is raised by a she-ape and becomes Tarzan of the Apes. Barrel-chested Elmo Lincoln portrayed Tarzan and actually killed the lion he fights in one of the film's more exciting moments. This silent extravaganza is well worth the watch. Silent. B&W; 130m. DIR: Scott Sidney. CAST: Elmo Lincoln, Enid Markey, George French. **1918**

TARZAN THE APE MAN (1932) ★★★1/2 *Tarzan the Ape Man* is the film that made Johnny Weissmuller a star and Tarzan an idiot. That classic "Me Tarzan, you Jane" blasphemy is here in its original splendor. Maureen O'Sullivan seduces the dumb beast, and it's all great fun. Hollywood at its peak ... but no relation to Edgar Rice Burroughs's hero. B&W; 99m. DIR: W. S. Van Dyke. CAST: Johnny Weissmuller, Maureen O'Sullivan, Neil Hamilton. **1932**

TARZAN THE APE MAN (1981) 🖤 Even counting the lowest of the Tarzan flicks, this remake is the absolute worst. Rated R for profanity and nudity. 112m. DIR: John Derek. CAST: Bo Derek, Richard Harris, Miles O'Keeffe, John Phillip Law. **1981**

TARZAN THE FEARLESS 🖤 Leave this one on the vine. B&W; 85m. DIR: Robert Hill. CAST: Buster Crabbe, Jacqueline Wells, E. Alyn Warren, Edward Woods. **1933 DVD**

TARZAN THE MIGHTY ★★1/2 Tarzan number five Frank Merrill once earned the title of "World's Most Perfect Man" and his jungle heroics made this Universal serial the hit of 1928. It was expanded from twelve to fifteen episodes by astute executives who correctly gauged a receptive audience. Merrill pioneered many of the stunts associated with the series, especially the vine swinging and aerial acrobatics. Silent. B&W; 15 chapters. DIR: Jack Nelson. CAST: Frank Merrill, Natalie Kingston, Al Ferguson. **1928**

TARZAN THE TIGER ★★ Based loosely on Edgar Rice Burroughs's *Tarzan and the Jewels of Opar*, this serial was shot as a silent but released with synchronized musical score and sound effects. Frank Merrill as Tarzan inaugurated the popular vine swing used by later ape-men and was the first to give his rendition of the famous cry of the bull ape—sans mixer and dubbers. This sequel to *Tarzan the Mighty* was long considered a lost film. B&W; 15 chapters. DIR: Henry McRae. CAST: Frank Merrill, Natalie Kingston, Lillian Worth, Al Ferguson. **1929**

TARZAN TRIUMPHS 🖤 Just like Sherlock Holmes, Tarzan was called on to do his part for the war effort by battling Nazis in this, one of the worst of the Johnny Weissmuller series. B&W; 78m. DIR: William Thiele. CAST: Johnny Weissmuller, Johnny Sheffield, Frances Gifford, Stanley Ridges, Sig Ruman. **1943**

TARZAN'S NEW YORK ADVENTURE ★★★1/2 Boy is kidnapped by a circus owner and taken to New York to be put on display. Tarzan and Jane follow. Lots of fun with the jungle man out of his element, then scaling skyscrapers, swinging on flagpole lines until chased atop the Brooklyn Bridge. Maureen O'Sullivan's sixth and last appearance as Jane. B&W; 72m. DIR: Richard Thorpe. CAST: Johnny Weissmuller, Maureen O'Sullivan, Johnny Sheffield, Virginia Grey, Charles Bickford, Paul Kelly, Chill Wills. **1942**

TARZAN'S REVENGE 🖤 Back-lot nonsense. B&W; 70m. DIR: D. Ross Lederman. CAST: Glenn Morris, Eleanor Holm, George Barbier, C. Henry Gordon, Hedda Hopper, George Meeker. **1938**

TARZAN'S SECRET TREASURE ★★★ Members of a scientific expedition are corrupted by gold found in Tarzan's paradise. By this fifth teaming of Johnny Weissmuller and Maureen O'Sullivan as Tarzan and Jane, the situations were becoming predictable. Yet, there is lots of terrific action. B&W; 81m. DIR: Richard Thorpe. CAST: Johnny Weissmuller, Maureen O'Sullivan, Johnny Sheffield, Barry Fitzgerald, Reginald Owen, Tom Conway, Philip Dorn. **1941**

TASK FORCE ★★1/2 Standard military soap opera tracing the development of the aircraft carrier. Predictable script, with all the usual heroics, but the stalwart cast holds it up. B&W; 116m. DIR: Delmer Daves. CAST: Gary Cooper, Jane Wyatt, Wayne Morris, Walter Brennan, Julie London, Jack Holt. **1949 DVD**

TASTE FOR KILLING, A ★★1/2 Two rich boys spend their summer vacation on an offshore oil rig only to become involved in a murder. Of course it looks like they did the killing. A boring premise, but nicely acted made-for-cable thriller. 96m. DIR: Lou Antonio. CAST: Michael Biehn, Jason Bateman, Henry Thomas, Helen Cates, Blue Deckert. **1992**

TASTE OF BLOOD, A 🖤 The most ambitious film by Herschell Gordon Lewis, "The Godfather of Gore." The plot involves an American descendant of Dracula. 120m. DIR: Herschell Gordon Lewis. CAST: Bill Rogers. **1967**

TASTE OF CHERRY ★★ An Iranian businessman, determined to commit suicide, tries to find someone who will help him end it all. The film won the Palme d'Or at Cannes, but the prize must have been a political statement (the film was banned in Iran, where the subject of suicide is taboo), because the film is a windy, interminable bore. In Farsi with English subtitles. Not rated; suitable for general audiences. 95m. DIR: Abbas Kiarostami. CAST: Homayon Ershadi, Abdolrahman Bagheri, Afshin Khorshid Bakhtiari, Safar Ali Moradi. **1997 DVD**

TASTE OF HONEY, A ★★★1/2 Offbeat comedy-drama memorably tells the story of a lower-class teenager (Rita Tushingham) made pregnant by a black sailor. Tough but tender, this piece of attempted social realism by new-wave British director Tony Richardson is based on a successful stage play. B&W; 100m. DIR: Tony Richardson. CAST: Rita Tushingham, Dora Bryan, Murray Melvin, Robert Stephens. 1961

TASTE THE BLOOD OF DRACULA ★★★ This fourth entry in Hammer Films's *Dracula* cycle is a big improvement over *Dracula Has Risen from the Grave*, but there's a problem: where's Dracula? We're almost half an hour into the movie before three Victorian family men revive the Count (unwittingly, natch). Stylish and creepy, but with more for the indefatigable Chris Lee to do, this might've been a four-star film. Rated PG. 95m. DIR: Peter Sasdy. CAST: Christopher Lee, Linda Hayden, Geoffrey Keen, Anthony Higgins, Roy Kinnear, Ralph Bates, Gwen Watford, John Carson, Isla Blair. 1970

TATIE DANIELLE ★★★1/2 While in the process of destroying the lives and home of her great-nephew and his sweet-natured wife, a cranky old lady manages to make them look like the culprits. This black comedy is exceedingly dark, and, therefore, not for all tastes. In French with English subtitles. Not rated; the film has profanity and nudity. 107m. DIR: Étienne Chatiliez. CAST: Tsilla Chelton, Catherine Jacob, Isabelle Nanty, Neige Dolsky, Eric Prat. 1991

TATTLE TALE ★★1/2 C. Thomas Howell is a struggling actor whose ex-wife writes a "kiss and tell" book. Ally Sheedy is fabulous as the bitchy, egocentric hack, but Howell is lost amid silly disguises and a thin plot. Some clever moments but too unbelievable overall. Rated PG for profanity. 93m. DIR: Baz Taylor. CAST: C. Thomas Howell, Ally Sheedy. 1993

TATTOO 💔 Simply the most vile, reprehensible, sexist, and misogynistic piece of tripe ever released under the guise of a mainstream film. Bruce Dern is a demented tattoo artist who kidnaps Maud Adams to use as a "living tableau." Rated R for gross violence and kinky sex. 103m. DIR: Bob Brooks. CAST: Bruce Dern, Maud Adams, John Getz. 1981

TATTOO CONNECTION 💔 Typical chop-phooey fare. Rated R for violence, profanity, and nudity. 95m. DIR: Lee Tso-Nan. CAST: Jim Kelly. 1978

TAXI BLUES ★★★1/2 This Russian film details the volatile love-hate relationship between a fiercely independent, undisciplined Jewish jazz artist and a stern, muscular, narrow-minded cabdriver. It's as aggressive and stimulating as the hard-driving sax solos that permeate the soundtrack. In Russian with English subtitles. Not rated. 100m. DIR: Pavel Lounguine. CAST: Piotr Zaitchenko, Piotr Mamonov. 1991

TAXI DANCERS 💔 Small-town girl must turn to dancing in a seedy club when her Hollywood dreams fail to materialize. Not rated; contains adult situations, language, and violence. 97m. DIR: Norman Thaddeus Vane. CAST: Sonny Ladham, Robert Miano, Brittany McCrena, Michelle Hess. 1993

TAXI DRIVER ★★★★★ Robert De Niro plays an alienated Vietnam-era vet thrust into the nighttime urban sprawl of New York City. In his despair after a romantic rejection by an attractive political campaign aide, he focuses on "freeing" a 12-year-old prostitute by unleashing violent retribution on her pimp. It's unnerving and realistic. Rated R for violence and profanity. 113m. DIR: Martin Scorsese. CAST: Robert De Niro, Harvey Keitel, Cybill Shepherd, Jodie Foster, Peter Boyle. 1976 DVD

TAXI ZUM KLO (TAXI TO THE TOILET) ★★★1/2 Sexually explicit film by and about Frank Ripploh, a restless and promiscuous gay elementary-school teacher in Berlin. Ripploh pulls absolutely no punches in his portrait of his sexual encounters, and that should be a fair warning. Get through the sex, however, and the humor will seem refreshing compared to a lot of other films that try to capture gay life. In German with English subtitles. Not rated; contains profanity and frank sexual content. 92m. DIR: Frank Ripploh. CAST: Frank Ripploh, Bernd Broaderup. 1981

TAXING WOMAN, A ★★★ After exposing the world to the inner workings of the noodle business in *Tampopo*, director Juzo Itami focused on Japan's nasty Internal Revenue Service. Nobuko Miyamoto plays a hard-line tax inspector. Nicely offbeat. In Japanese with English subtitles. Not rated, with adult themes. 118m. DIR: Juzo Itami. CAST: Nobuko Miyamoto, Tsutomu Yamazaki. 1988 DVD

TAXING WOMAN'S RETURN, A ★★★ In this follow-up to his 1987 hit, director Juzo Itami scores another high. This time the diligent heroine, tax inspector Nobuko Miyamoto, tackles a corrupt fundamentalist religious order. In Japanese with English subtitles. Rated R for nudity and violence. 127m. DIR: Juzo Itami. CAST: Nobuko Miyamoto. 1988

TBONE N WEASEL ★★ Lame story follows the misadventures of two not-so-smart criminals. The film is played for laughs that never really come off. Stars try hard, but to no avail. 105m. DIR: Lewis Teague. CAST: Gregory Hines, Christopher Lloyd, Ned Beatty, Larry Hankin, Graham Jarvis. 1992

TC 2000 💔 In the year 2020, the atmosphere is gone, so the worthy inhabitants of the Earth live underground. A female cop is killed, turned into a powerful evil android, and sent to destroy all the surface people. Extremely bad acting. Rated R for violence and profanity. 92m. DIR: T.J. Scott. CAST: Bolo Yeung, Jalal Merhi, Billy Banks, Bobbie Phillips, Matthias Hues. 1993

TCHAO PANTIN ★★★★1/2 Violent *film noir* about an ex-cop suffering from alienation as a result of the tragic death of his son from narcotics. He befriends a young stranger who deals heroin. The two form an odd relationship that eventually leads to disaster. This movie swept the French Oscars. In French with English subtitles. 94m. DIR: Claude Berri. CAST: Coluche, Richard Anconina, Philippe Léotard. 1985

TEA AND SYMPATHY ★★★★ Well-crafted story (from the Broadway play) of an introverted student who finds understanding and love with the wife of the school's headmaster. Sensitively directed and with convincing acting, this is a must-see film. 123m. DIR: Vincente Minnelli. CAST: Deborah Kerr, John Kerr, Leif Erickson, Edward Andrews, Darryl Hickman, Dean Jones. 1959

TEA FOR TWO ★★★ Doris Day planning to back and star in a musical play, finds she has lost her wealth in the stock market crash. To win a $25,000 bet, she must say "No" to every question for forty-eight hours, even those asked by amorous Gordon MacRae. Loosely based on *No, No, Nanette*. 98m. DIR: David Butler. CAST: Doris Day, Gordon MacRae, Gene Nelson, Eve Arden, Billy DeWolfe, S. Z. Sakall. 1950

TEA WITH MUSSOLINI ★★★ Odd assortment of English and American women in 1935 Florence, Italy, take illegitimate 7-year-old Luca into their fold after his mother dies. Tender if somewhat uneven piece of time travel as Mussolini's Fascists rise to power in the 1940s and Luca joins the Resistance. Rated PG. 116m. DIR: Franco Zeffirelli. CAST: Joan Plowright, Cher, Judi Dench, Maggie Smith, Lily Tomlin, Charlie Lucas. 1999 DVD

TEACH ME 💗 Erotic writer offers to teach a couple how to spruce up their sex life. Just an excuse to expose as much flesh as possible. Not rated; contains adult situations, language, and nudity. 90m. DIR: Gary Delfiner. CAST: Raasa Leela Shields, Greg Provance, Shannon Leahy. 1997

•**TEACH ME TONIGHT** ★★ The plot of this erotic thriller, about a woman's attempt to find the killer of her philandering boyfriend, is only there to space out the endless sex scenes (they're even more endless in the 93-minute unrated version). Rated R for profanity, nudity, and sexual situations. 74m. DIR: Rick Blaine. CAST: Judy Thompson, Kim Yates, Jack Becker. 1998 DVD

TEACHERS ★★ This satirical look at a contemporary urban high school flunks as a film. Teachers will hate it because it's not serious enough; students will hate it because it's just terrible. It's no more interesting than a dull day in high school. Rated R for sexual innuendo, violence, and profanity. 106m. DIR: Arthur Hiller. CAST: Nick Nolte, JoBeth Williams, Judd Hirsch, Richard Mulligan, Ralph Macchio. 1984

TEACHER'S PET ★★★ Winsome journalism instructor Doris Day fascinates and charms hardboiled city editor Clark Gable in this near plotless but most diverting comedy of incidents. The two are terrific, but Gig Young, as the teacher's erudite but liquor-logged boyfriend, is the one to watch. B&W; 120m. DIR: George Seaton. CAST: Clark Gable, Doris Day, Gig Young, Mamie Van Doren, Nick Adams, Jack Albertson, Marion Ross. 1958

•**TEACHING MRS. TINGLE** ★★ Three high-school students hold their meanest teacher hostage to teach her some humanity. This film panders shamelessly to the whining of spoiled mall rats (parents are clueless, teachers are evil, teenagers are pure, decent, and loyal). Helen Mirren easily outacts her callow costars, literally with her hands tied. Rated PG-13 for profanity and brief violence. 96m. DIR: Kevin Williamson. CAST: Helen Mirren, Katie Holmes, Marisa Coughlan, Barry Watson, Michael McKean. 1999 DVD

TEAHOUSE OF THE AUGUST MOON, THE ★★★1/2 The post–World War II Americanizing of Okinawa gets sent up in faultless style in this screen version of the 1952 Broadway stage comedy hit. Marlon Brando is amusing as the clever Okinawan interpreter who binds it all together, but it is blustering Paul Ford, from the stage production, who comes knife-edge close to stealing this memorable film.

123m. DIR: Daniel Mann. CAST: Marlon Brando, Glenn Ford, Eddie Albert, Machiko Kyo, Paul Ford. 1956

TEAMSTER BOSS: THE JACKIE PRESSER STORY ★★★1/2 Brian Dennehy's larger-than-life performance as self-made Teamster president Jackie Presser fuels this strawberry-lensed TV adaptation of James Neff's *Mobbed Up*. Abby Mann's script works far too hard at glossing over the controversial figure's unpleasant qualities. Rated R for violence, suggested sex, and profanity. 110m. DIR: Alastair Reid. CAST: Brian Dennehy, Jeff Daniels, Maria Conchita Alonso, Eli Wallach, Robert Prosky, Donald Moffat. 1992

TEARAWAY ★★ In this film from Australia, the young streetwise son of an alcoholic father rescues a rich girl from a gang of lecherous toughs. Regrettably, tragic but predictable events cause this otherwise gritty study to degenerate into another ordinary tale of revenge. Rated R for violence and strong language. 100m. DIR: Bruce Morrison. CAST: Matthew Hunter, Mark Pilisi. 1987

TED & VENUS ★★ Quirky, offbeat love story from director Bud Cort, who knows the territory well (he was Harold in *Harold & Maude*). This time he plays a poet whose fascination with the girl of his dreams forces him to go to extremes in order to get her attention. Some funny moments, but it's just too cordial to be crazy. Rated R for nudity and adult language. 100m. DIR: Bud Cort. CAST: Bud Cort, Carol Kane, James Brolin, Rhea Perlman, Andrea Martin, Martin Mull, Woody Harrelson. 1990

TEEN ALIEN 💗 A group of kids put on a Halloween spook show in an abandoned mining mill. Rated PG for mild violence. 88m. DIR: Peter Senelka. CAST: Vern Adix. 1988

TEEN VAMP 💗 High school nerd is transformed into a vampire by a bloodsucking prostitute. Rated R for violence and profanity. 87m. DIR: Samuel Bradford. CAST: Clu Gulager, Karen Carlson. 1988

TEEN WITCH ★★ Robyn Lively plays Louise, a high school wallflower who discovers on her sixteenth birthday that she has the powers of witchcraft. Some blandly catchy songs (by Larry Weir) are patched in for the music-video market. Rated PG-13 for mild profanity. 90m. DIR: Dorian Walker. CAST: Robyn Lively, Zelda Rubinstein, Dick Sargent, Shelley Berman. 1989

TEEN WOLF 💗 Pitifully bad film about a teenager who discovers he has the ability to change into a werewolf. Rated PG. 95m. DIR: Rod Daniel. CAST: Michael J. Fox, James Hampton, Scott Paulin. 1985

TEEN WOLF, TOO 💗 In this painfully dull sequel, the original Teen Wolf's cousin goes to college on a sports scholarship. Rated PG. 95m. DIR: Christopher Leitch. CAST: Jason Bateman, Kim Darby, John Astin, James Hampton. 1987

TEENAGE BONNIE AND KLEPTO CLYDE ★★1/2 Minor hoods Scott Wolf and Maureen Flannigan chuck their comfortable lives for a little excitement. What starts off as teen rebellion quickly turns deadly as the pair rob and kill their way to mythic status. Rated R for violence, nudity, language, and adult situations. 90m. DIR: John Shepphird. CAST: Scott Wolf,

Maureen Flannigan, Bentley Mitchum, Don Novello. 1993

TEENAGE CONFIDENTIAL 🎬 A rip-off, advertised as "an in-depth study," wherein Mamie Van Doren introduces a couple of short, juvenile delinquency documentaries from the 1940s, followed by "Previews of Coming Attractions" of rock 'n' roll, high school, and biker movies that packed the drive-ins during the 1950s. B&W/color; 60m. **DIR:** Various. **1987**

TEENAGE EXORCIST ★★ When a reserved young woman (Brinke Stevens, who also wrote the screenplay) moves into a haunted house, a lustier side of her personality comes to the fore. Not rated; contains nudity, violence, and adult situations. 90m. **DIR:** Grant Austin Waldman. **CAST:** Brinke Stevens, Eddie Deezen, Oliver Darrow, Jay Richardson, Elena Sahagun, Robert Quarry, Michael Berryman. **1991**

TEENAGE MUTANT NINJA TURTLES ★★★★ Cowabunga, dude, the movie debut of the *Teenage Mutant Ninja Turtles* is a fun- and action-packed comic book for the screen. Leonardo, Raphael, Michelangelo, and Donatello come to the aid of a female newscaster (Judith Hoag) when her life is threatened by the minions of the evil Shredder. Rated PG for comicbook-style violence and vulgarity. 93m. **DIR:** Steve Barron. **CAST:** Judith Hoag, Elias Koteas. **1990 DVD**

TEENAGE MUTANT NINJA TURTLES II: THE SECRET OF THE OOZE ★★★1/2 The lean, green teens return to face their archenemy Shredder, and find the secret to their origins in the sewers of New York. David Warner costars as the professor who developed the toxic green ooze responsible for the Turtles' large size and superpowers. Rated PG for mild violence. 88m. **DIR:** Michael Pressman. **CAST:** Paige Turco, David Warner, Ernie Reyes Jr. **1991**

TEENAGE MUTANT NINJA TURTLES III ★★ This franchise has been taken to the well once too often. Although writer-director Stuart Gillard gets off to a good start by sending our youthful ninjas-on-the-half-shell back in time to feudal Japan, the setting is wasted on wafer-thin foes who don't even prompt our heroes to work up a sweat. Rated PG for comic-book violence. 95m. **DIR:** Stuart Gillard. **CAST:** Elias Koteas, Paige Turco, Stuart Wilson, Sab Shimono, Vivian Wu. **1993**

TEKWAR: THE ORIGINAL MOVIE ★★★ Telefilm was the springboard for syndicated series about an ex-cop, falsely accused of murder, who was sentenced to a cryogenic prison. Not rated; contains some violence. 92m. **DIR:** William Shatner. **CAST:** Greg Evigan, William Shatner, Sheena Easton, Eugene Clark. **1993**

TELEFON ★★★ In this good suspense film, Charles Bronson is a KGB agent who, with the help of the CIA's Lee Remick, is out to stop some preprogrammed Soviet spies from blowing up the United States. Rated PG. 102m. **DIR:** Don Siegel. **CAST:** Charles Bronson, Lee Remick, Donald Pleasence, John Mitchum, Patrick Magee. **1977**

TELEGRAPH TRAIL, THE ★★★1/2 Before moving on, John Wayne made a series of quality B Westerns for Warner Bros.—this film about the stringing of telegraph lines is one of the best. The scenes featuring Wayne's "miracle horse," Duke, do strain credi-

bility, however. B&W; 54m. **DIR:** Tenny Wright. **CAST:** John Wayne, Marceline Day, Frank McHugh, Otis Harlan, Albert J. Smith, Yakima Canutt, Lafe McKee. **1933**

TELEPHONE, THE ★★ It's hard to like, but even harder to walk away from, this uneven comedydrama. Whoopi Goldberg stars as an out-of-work actress who is more than a little nuts. Definitely for the midnight-movie junkie who will enjoy the bizarre ending. Rated R for profanity. 96m. **DIR:** Rip Torn. **CAST:** Whoopi Goldberg, Elliott Gould, Amy Wright, John Heard, Severn Darden. **1987**

TELEVISION PARTS HOME COMPANION ★★★ This is more of Mike Nesmith's *Elephant Parts* style of variety-show entertainment. Again, he has hilarious skits and mock commercials, as well as choreographed stories to accompany his songs. 40m. **DIR:** William Dear, Alan Myerson. **CAST:** Mike Nesmith, Joe Allain, Bill Martin. **1984**

TELL IT TO THE JUDGE ★★★ Robert Cummings tries to talk ex-wife Rosalind Russell into remarrying him, not Gig Young. Amiable comedy coasts on star power. B&W; 87m. **DIR:** Norman Foster. **CAST:** Rosalind Russell, Robert Cummings, Gig Young, Marie McDonald, Louise Beavers. **1949**

TELL IT TO THE MARINES ★★★ Lon Chaney Sr. is good in a rare nonhorror role as a marine sergeant training new recruits in the Philippines. Silent. B&W; 75m. **DIR:** George Hill. **CAST:** Lon Chaney Sr., William Haines, Warner Oland. **1926**

TELL ME A RIDDLE ★★★1/2 Melvyn Douglas and Lila Kedrova give memorable performances as an elderly married couple whose relationship has grown bitter. Their love for each other is rekindled when they take a cross-country trip. This poignant drama marked the directorial debut of actress Lee Grant. Rated PG. 94m. **DIR:** Lee Grant. **CAST:** Melvyn Douglas, Lila Kedrova, Brooke Adams, Dolores Dorn, Zalman King. **1980**

TELL-TALE HEART, THE ★★1/2 Fascinating, if extremely low-budget, study in sexual obsession and murder. A shy recluse, lured out of his dismal lifestyle by the new woman in his Victorian neighborhood, goes murderously mad when he spies her bedding down (shades of *Rear Window!*) with his best pal. B&W; 81m. **DIR:** Ernest Morris. **CAST:** Laurence Payne, Adrienne Corri, Dermot Walsh. **1961**

TELL THEM WILLIE BOY IS HERE ★★★ Robert Redford is a southwestern sheriff in the early days of this country. He is pursuing an Indian (Robert Blake) who is fleeing to avoid arrest. The story is elevated from a standard Western chase by the dignity and concern shown to the Indian's viewpoint. Rated PG. 96m. **DIR:** Abraham Polonsky. **CAST:** Robert Redford, Robert Blake, Katharine Ross. **1969**

TELLING LIES IN AMERICA ★★★★1/2 This is a gently sentimental coming-of-age saga set in 1961 at an expensive private Catholic high school where Hungarian-born Karchy comes under the spell of a slick radio deejay (Kevin Bacon, absolutely perfect), the nearest thing to an honest-to-God celebrity Cleveland kids might reasonably expect to meet. What follows is one young man's encounter with questionable ethics and the dawning awareness that ultimately compels him to do the right thing. Rated

PG-13 for profanity and sexual content. 102m. **DIR:** Guy Ferland. **CAST:** Brad Renfro, Kevin Bacon, Calista Flockhart, Maximilian Schell, Paul Dooley. **1997 DVD**

•**TELLING YOU** ★★ Dreadful tale of two college graduates who stand behind the counter of a pizzeria while their friends all go on to bigger and better things. Rated R for profanity and sexuality. 90m. **DIR:** Robert DeFranco. **CAST:** Jennifer Love Hewitt, Peter Facinelli, Richard Libertini, Rick Rossovich. **1998 DVD**

TEMP, THE ★★ There's been kids from hell. Cops from hell. Dates from hell. And nannies from hell. Now comes the temporary office assistant from you know where—a femme fatale way beyond bitch who is just as efficient and sexy as she may be ruthless and insane. More of a slick crowd teaser than an actual thriller. Rated R for language and violence. 100m. **DIR:** Tom Holland. **CAST:** Lara Flynn Boyle, Timothy Hutton, Dwight Schultz, Oliver Platt, Faye Dunaway. **1993**

TEMPEST (1928) ★★1/2 Set during the 1914 Bolshevik uprising in Russia, this richly romantic drama has army officer John Barrymore stepping out of place to court his aristocratic commandant's daughter. As a result, both are undone and must flee for their lives and love. Silent, with music track. B&W; 105m. **DIR:** Sam Taylor. **CAST:** John Barrymore, Camilla Horn, Louis Wolheim, George Fawcett. **1928**

TEMPEST (1982) ❤ An architect has prophetic dreams. Rated PG; the film has nudity and profanity. 140m. **DIR:** Paul Mazursky. **CAST:** John Cassavetes, Gena Rowlands, Vittorio Gassman, Molly Ringwald, Susan Sarandon. **1982**

TEMPEST, THE (1983) ★★1/2 A slow-moving stage production of Shakespeare's tale of sorcery and revenge on a desolate island controlled by the mystical Prospero (Efrem Zimbalist Jr.). Zimbalist is interesting but very wooden in the role. A Bard Productions Ltd. release. 126m. **DIR:** William Woodman. **CAST:** Efrem Zimbalist Jr., William H. Bassett, Ted Sorel, Kay E. Kuter, Edward Edwards, Nicholas Hammond. **1983**

TEMPTATION ★★★ An ex-con (Jeff Fahey) gets his chance for revenge when the partner who left him for the cops ten years ago inadvertently hires him to captain his pleasure yacht. Loads of action and a couple of steamy love scenes make it fairly easy to overlook the film's Swiss-cheese plot. David Keith gives an exceptional performance as Fahey's Australian buddy. Rated R for violence, profanity, nudity, and sexual situations. 91m. **DIR:** Strathford Hamilton. **CAST:** Jeff Fahey, David Keith, Alison Doody, Philip Casnoff. **1994**

TEMPTATION OF A MONK ★★★★ An elaborate epic set in seventh-century China in which a pair of generals battle to the death and a beautiful princess (Joan Chen) becomes a destructive temptress. Grandly visual, stunningly powerful filmmaking. In Mandarin with English subtitles. Not rated, but features many bloody battle scenes. 118m. **DIR:** Clara Law. **CAST:** Joan Chen, Hsin Kuo Wu, Zhang Fengyi, Michael Lee, Lisa Lu. **1993 DVD**

TEMPTER, THE ❤ Lurid Italian demonic-possession flick about a crippled woman who is the reincarnation of a witch. Rated R for profanity and violence.

96m. **DIR:** Alberto De Martino. **CAST:** Carla Gravina, Mel Ferrer, Arthur Kennedy. **1978**

TEMPTRESS ★★ The spirit of a mythical goddess invades the body of a sexy female photographer and all hell breaks loose. Not nearly as suspenseful, erotic, or entertaining as it should be. Rated R for profanity and sexuality. 93m. **DIR:** Lawrence Lanoff. **CAST:** Kim Delaney, Chris Sarandon, Corbin Bernsen, Ben Cross. **1995**

TEMPTRESS MOON ★★★1/2 Hardened gigolo in 1920s Shanghai specializes in blackmailing rich women. The ravishing-looking film needs more momentum and a few strategically placed emotional depth charges. In Mandarin with English subtitles. Rated R for drug use and intense sexual content. 115m. **DIR:** Chen Kaige. **CAST:** Leslie Cheung, Gong Li, Kevin Lin, Saifei He, Zhang Shi. **1997**

10 ★★★1/2 Ravel's "Bolero" enjoyed a renewed popularity, and Bo Derek rocketed to stardom because of this uneven but generally entertaining sex comedy, directed by Blake Edwards (*The Pink Panther*). Most of the film's funny moments come from the deftly timed physical antics of Dudley Moore, who plays a just-turned-40 songwriter who at long last meets the girl (Bo Derek) of his dreams—on her wedding day. Rated R. 122m. **DIR:** Blake Edwards. **CAST:** Dudley Moore, Bo Derek, Julie Andrews, Robert Webber. **1979 DVD**

TEN BENNY ★★1/2 Standard-issue drama about a young New Jersey salesman whose hopes of turning a tip on a racehorse into a nest egg for his future go awry when he loses. Too bad he borrowed the seed money from a hood. Rated R for language, violence, adult situations, and nudity. 98m. **DIR:** Eric Bross. **CAST:** Adrien Brody, Sybil Temchin, Tony Gillian, Michael Gallagher, Frank Vincent. **1996 DVD**

TEN COMMANDMENTS, THE (1923) ★★★ Master showman Cecil B. DeMille's monumental two-phase silent version of the Book of Exodus and the application of the Ten Commandments in modern life. Part One, set in ancient times, is in early color; Part Two, set in the modern (1923) period, is in black and white. Impressive special effects, including the parting of the Red Sea. In scope, this is the film that foreshadows DeMille's great spectacles of the sound era. B&W; 140m. **DIR:** Cecil B. DeMille. **CAST:** Theodore Roberts, Charles de Roche, Estelle Taylor, James Neill, Noble Johnson, Richard Dix, Rod La Rocque, Leatrice Joy, Nita Naldi. **1923**

TEN COMMANDMENTS, THE (1956) ★★★1/2 A stylish, visually stunning, epic-scale biblical study as only Cecil B. DeMille could make 'em (until William Wyler came along three years later with *Ben Hur*). Charlton Heston, as Moses, in charge of "God's people," holds the lengthy film together. Not rated; suitable for family viewing. 219m. **DIR:** Cecil B. DeMille. **CAST:** Charlton Heston, Yul Brynner, Edward G. Robinson, Cedric Hardwicke, John Derek, Anne Baxter, Debra Paget. **1956 DVD**

TEN DAYS WONDER ★★★★ One of Claude Chabrol's superb *hommages* to the American detective thriller. Originally titled *La Decade Prodigieuse*, it is based on one of Ellery Queen's finest psychological studies of a serial murderer. Typically, Chabrol is more interested in characterization and mood than in pacing and graphic violence. 100m. **DIR:** Claude Chabrol. **CAST:** Orson Welles, Marlene Jobert, Anthony Perkins, Michel Piccoli. **1972**

10 FROM YOUR SHOW OF SHOWS ★★★★ Ten skits from the early 1950s television program that set the pace for all variety shows. Granted, the style is dated and far from subtle, but as a joyful look at television's formative years, it can't be beat. Not rated. B&W; 92m. **DIR:** Max Liebman. **CAST:** Sid Caesar, Imogene Coca, Carl Reiner, Howard Morris, Louis Nye. **1973**

TEN LITTLE GALL FORCE/SCRAMBLE WARS ★★★ This animated double feature is a sound spoof of the genre in a "superdeformed" format (caricatures of animated characters). The first feature includes animated "outtakes" of *Gall Force* and a live-action short about the story's creator Shonora Kenichi. In the second, characters from three different animation stories compete in a contest reminiscent of *Cannonball Run*. In Japanese with English subtitles. Not rated; contains nudity and violence. 67m. **DIR:** Yatagai Kenichi, Fukushima Hiroyuki. **1988**

TEN LITTLE INDIANS (1966) ★★★1/2 A good retelling of the Agatha Christie classic with ten complete strangers trapped in an Alpine chateau, one among them having murder in mind. B&W; 92m. **DIR:** George Pollock. **CAST:** Hugh O'Brian, Shirley Eaton, Fabian, Leo Genn, Stanley Holloway, Marianne Hoppe, Wilfrid Hyde-White, Daliah Lavi, Dennis Price, Mario Adorf. **1966**

TEN LITTLE INDIANS (1975) ✪ Absolutely dismal third version of the Agatha Christie classic. This one completely mucks up the plot, switching from an isolated island mansion to a hotel deep in the Iranian desert(!). Rated PG—mild violence. 98m. **DIR:** Peter Collinson. **CAST:** Oliver Reed, Richard Attenborough, Elke Sommer, Herbert Lom, Gert Fröbe. **1975**

TEN LITTLE INDIANS (1989) ★★ Agatha Christie's suspenseful whodunit loses much of its flair in this slow-moving, poorly acted rendition. A group of ten is systematically picked off at an isolated African campsite. Rated PG. 99m. **DIR:** Alan Birkinshaw. **CAST:** Donald Pleasence, Frank Stallone, Brenda Vaccaro. **1989**

10 RILLINGTON PLACE ★★★★ This bleak true-crime drama is based on one of England's most famous murder cases and was actually shot in the house and the neighborhood where the crimes took place. The seamy squalor of the surroundings perfectly mirrors the poverty of mind and soul that allowed John Christy to murder and remain undetected for over ten years. 111m. **DIR:** Richard Fleischer. **CAST:** Richard Attenborough, Judy Geeson, John Hurt, Andre Morell. **1971**

10 THINGS I HATE ABOUT YOU ★★★1/2 This engaging little film, which borrows heavily from Shakespeare's *Taming of the Shrew*, starts off like a slapstick teen comedy, but eventually becomes genuinely funny, compelling, and charming. Bianca has been told by their single-parent father that she cannot date until older sister Kat does ... and no one expects that to happen until hell freezes over. Bianca and her new beau orchestrate a scheme whereby an other school outcast is paid to squire Kat about town. What follows plays out with deft wit—and strong sexual chemistry—against a zesty collection of pop tunes. Rated PG-13 for profanity and crude sexual commentary. 94m. **DIR:** Gil Junger. **CAST:** Heath Ledger, Julia Stiles, Joseph Gordon Levitt, Larisa Oleynik, David Krumholtz, Andrew Keegan, Larry Miller, Susan May Pratt, Gabrielle Union. **1999 DVD**

TEN TO MIDNIGHT ✪ Old "Death Wish" himself goes up against a *Friday the 13th*–type killer. Rated R for nudity, profanity, and violence. 101m. **DIR:** J. Lee Thompson. **CAST:** Charles Bronson, Andrew Stevens, Lisa Eilbacher, Cosie Costa. **1983**

10 VIOLENT WOMEN ✪ Female coal miners land in jail after a jewel robbery and a cocaine deal go bad. Rated R for violence and a little nudity. 95m. **DIR:** Ted V. Mikels. **CAST:** Sherri Vernon, Dixie Lauren, Georgia Morgan. **1982**

TEN WANTED MEN ★★★1/2 Small Arizona landowner Richard Boone attempts to wrest control of the territory by framing cattle baron Randolph Scott's nephew. 80m. **DIR:** H. Bruce Humberstone. **CAST:** Randolph Scott, Richard Boone, Dennis Weaver, Lee Van Cleef, Skip Homeier, Leo Gordon. **1955**

TEN WHO DARED ✪ In 1869, Major John Wesley Powell and nine other explorers set out to explore the wild Colorado River. 92m. **DIR:** William Beaudine. **CAST:** Brian Keith, John Beal, James Drury, David Stollery. **1960**

10 MILLION DOLLAR GETAWAY, THE ★★★1/2 Doug Feiden's published account of the infamous Lufthansa robbery is transformed by scripter Christopher Canaan into a slick (made-for-cable) character study that unequivocally proves that crime does not pay. The excellent cast is led by John Mahoney. Rated PG-13. 93m. **DIR:** James A. Contner. **CAST:** John Mahoney, Joseph Carberry, Terrence Mann, Karen Young, Tony Lo Bianco. **1991**

TENTH MAN, THE ★★★★ Superb made-for-TV adaptation of Graham Greene's novel starring Anthony Hopkins as a wealthy French attorney taken hostage by the Nazis during the occupation of France. When the French Resistance kills some Nazi officers, the Nazis order every tenth man held in prison executed in retaliation. Hopkins strikes a bargain when he becomes the tenth man. 87m. **DIR:** Jack Gold. **CAST:** Anthony Hopkins, Kristin Scott Thomas, Derek Jacobi, Cyril Cusack. **1992**

TENTH MONTH, THE ★★1/2 Tiresome overlong drama about a middle-aged divorcée who has an affair with a married man and becomes pregnant. Good performances by Carol Burnett and Keith Michell are the only bright spots in this made-for-TV film. 130m. **DIR:** Joan Tewkesbury. **CAST:** Carol Burnett, Keith Michell, Dina Merrill. **1979**

TENTH VICTIM, THE ★★★1/2 A weird little science-fiction film that has achieved minor cult status, thanks to droll performances and an intriguing plot taken from the novel by Robert Sheckley. The setting is the near future, and pop culture has embraced an assassination/hunt game with only one winner. Not rated, contains sexual situations. 92m. **DIR:** Elio Petri. **CAST:** Marcello Mastroianni, Ursula Andress, Elsa Martinelli, Massimo Serato. **1965**

TENANT, THE ★★★ Roman Polanski is superb in this cryptic thriller about a bumbling Polish expatriate in France who leases an apartment owned previously by a young woman who committed suicide. Increasingly, Polanski believes the apartment's tenants conspired demonically to destroy the woman and are attempting to do the same to him. Rated R. 125m. **DIR:** Roman Polanski. **CAST:** Roman Polanski, Melvyn Douglas, Shelley Winters. **1976**

TENDER COMRADE ★★★ This sentimental melodrama, in which Ginger Rogers ably portrays one of several wives left at home while their men are fighting in World War II, demonstrates that she was underrated as a dramatic actress. The film later attracted unwarranted controversy after its writer, Dalton Trumbo, and director, Edward Dmytryk, fell victim to the anticommunist blacklist. 102m. **DIR:** Edward Dmytryk. **CAST:** Ginger Rogers, Robert Ryan, Ruth Hussey. **1943**

TENDER MERCIES ★★★★★ Robert Duvall more than deserved his best-actor Oscar for this superb character study about a down-and-out country singer trying for a comeback. His Mac Sledge is a man who still has songs to sing, but barely the heart to sing them. That is, until he meets up with a sweet-natured widow (Tess Harper) who gives him back the will to live. Rated PG. 89m. **DIR:** Bruce Beresford. **CAST:** Robert Duvall, Tess Harper, Ellen Barkin. **1983** DVD

TENDER TRAP, THE ★★★ Swinging bachelor Frank Sinatra takes aim at a young actress (Debbie Reynolds) who turns out less naïve (and more marriage-minded) than she seems. Sprightly stage-derived romantic comedy has clever dialogue, attractive stars, and a solid supporting cast. 111m. **DIR:** Charles Walters. **CAST:** Frank Sinatra, Debbie Reynolds, Celeste Holm, David Wayne, Carolyn Jones, Lola Albright. **1955**

TENDER YEARS, THE ★★1/2 The fight against cruelty to animals is at the heart of this sentimental film about a small-town minister who steals the dog his son loves, to save it from being used in illicit dogfighting. B&W; 81m. **DIR:** Harold Schuster. **CAST:** Joe E. Brown, Josephine Hutchinson, Charles Drake. **1948**

TENDRES COUSINES ★★ Okay soft-core sex comedy about two pubescent cousins. Directed by renowned photographer, David Hamilton. In French with English subtitles. Rated R. 90m. **DIR:** David Hamilton. **CAST:** Thierry Tevini, Anja Shute. **1980**

TENNESSEE STALLION ★★★ Interesting background, beautiful photography, and more than competent acting save this otherwise ordinary action-adventure film set in the world of the Tennessee walking-horse show circuit. Jimmy Van Patten is excellent as a man who makes it to the big time with his outstanding horse and the help of the woman who loves him. 87m. **DIR:** Don Hulette. **CAST:** Audrey Landers, Judy Landers, James Van Patten. **1978**

TENNESSEE'S PARTNER ★★1/2 Allan Dwan directed this minor Western featuring Ronald Reagan as a stranger who steps into the middle of a fight between gamblers and ends up befriending one (John Payne). This is one of Payne's better roles. Good little drama; better than the title suggests. 87m. **DIR:**

Allan Dwan. **CAST:** John Payne, Ronald Reagan, Rhonda Fleming, Coleen Gray. **1955**

TENTACLES ✦ Rotten monster movie from Italy about a phony-looking octopus attacking and devouring some famous Hollywood stars. Rated PG. 90m. **DIR:** Ovidio Assonitis (Oliver Hellman). **CAST:** John Huston, Shelley Winters, Henry Fonda, Bo Hopkins, Cesare Danova. **1977**

TEOREMA ★★★ The title translates as *Theorem,* which indicates the mathematical style of this attack on bourgeois values. A handsome young man enters the home of a middle-class family, whose members are unable to cope with life after he leaves. In Italian with English subtitles. Not rated; contains strong sexual content. 93m. **DIR:** Pier Paolo Pasolini. **CAST:** Terence Stamp, Silvana Mangano, Massimo Girotti. **1968**

TEQUILA SUNRISE ★★★★1/2 Screenwriter Robert Towne *(Chinatown, The Last Detail)* takes an oft-used plot and makes it new. Childhood friends end up on opposite sides of the law with a beautiful woman the object of their affections. A fascinating and often surprising movie. Rated R for profanity, violence, suggested sex, and drug use. 116m. **DIR:** Robert Towne. **CAST:** Mel Gibson, Kurt Russell, Michelle Pfeiffer, Raul Julia. **1988** DVD

TERESA'S TATTOO ★★★ Likable, familiar cast fleshes out this dark comedy about a kidnapping that goes haywire. When an accident kills their hostage, three goofball kidnappers must come up with a replacement or face the wrath of her gangster brother. The kidnappers find a dead ringer in college student Adrienne Shelly, with just one exception. The woman needs a tattoo in order to pull off the charade. The comic complications that ensue are moderately funny. Rated R for adult situations. 95m. **DIR:** Julie Cypher. **CAST:** C. Thomas Howell, Nancy McKeon, Adrienne Shelly, Lou Diamond Phillips, Jonathan Silverman, Casey Siemaszko. **1980**

TERMINAL BLISS ★★1/2 A slow-moving and utterly depressing story of a group of rich teenagers who overindulge in drugs and angst. Despite its deep undercurrent of despair, this is a watchable film that will have you worried about the future of our youth. Rated R for nudity, profanity, and drug use. 93m. **DIR:** Jordan Alan. **CAST:** Luke Perry, Timothy Owen. **1990**

TERMINAL CHOICE ★★ If it's blood you want, you'll get your money's worth with this one—by the gallons! There's some real tension in this film about a hospital staff that secretly bets on the mortality of its patients—not exactly family entertainment. Rated R for nudity, language, and plenty of gore. 98m. **DIR:** Sheldon Larry. **CAST:** Joe Spano, Diane Venora, David McCallum, Robert Joy, Don Francks, Nicholas Campbell, Ellen Barkin. **1984**

TERMINAL ENTRY ★★ This *War Games* clone is only moderately entertaining. Three teenage couples tap into a computer game called Terminal Entry. It turns out that the game is real and they're caught in the middle of a U.S. antiterrorist strike force and foreign invaders. Rated R for nudity and violence. 95m. **DIR:** John Kincade. **CAST:** Edward Albert, Paul Smith, Yaphet Kotto, Patrick Labyorteaux. **1986**

TERMINAL IMPACT ★★ A pair of federal marshals find themselves battling a group of genetically-engineered and computer-enhanced superwarriors when they try to find a missing news reporter. Bad performances, sloppy direction, and corny writing overwhelm the dazzling fire effects and stunts that save this film from getting a turkey. Rated R for violence and profanity. 94m. **DIR:** Yossi Wein. **CAST:** Frank Zagarino, Bryan Genesse, Jennifer Miller, Ian Roberts, Justin Illusion, Michael Brunner. **1995**

TERMINAL ISLAND 💔 Trite piece of exploitation. Rated R. 88m. **DIR:** Stephanie Rothman. **CAST:** Phyllis Davis, Tom Selleck, Don Marshall, Marta Kristen. **1977**

TERMINAL JUSTICE ★★★ Clever plotting lifts this futuristic action saga above its genre cousins. Loner cop Lorenzo Lamas tracks a particularly nasty criminal fronting a new black-market sensation: cloned lovers who won't care how they're abused. The emphasis is on high-tech gadgetry rather than graphic violence, and that's a nice switch. Rated R for profanity, nudity, simulated sex, and violence. 95m. **DIR:** Rick King. **CAST:** Lorenzo Lamas, Chris Sarandon, Kari Wuhrer, Peter Coyote. **1995**

TERMINAL JUSTICE, CYBERTECH P.D. ★★ In the future, a special division of police is formed to prevent the misuse of virtual reality. Dull and just plain silly. Rated R for profanity, nudity, and violence. 94m. **DIR:** Rick King. **CAST:** Lorenzo Lamas, Peter Coyote, Chris Sarandon. **1995**

TERMINAL MAN, THE ★★ A dreary adaptation of the crackling novel by Michael Crichton, although George Segal tries hard to improve the film's quality. He stars as a paranoid psychotic who undergoes experimental surgery designed to quell his violent impulses; unfortunately (and quite predictably), he becomes even worse. Rated R for violence. 104m. **DIR:** Mike Hodges. **CAST:** George Segal, Joan Hackett, Jill Clayburgh. **1974**

TERMINAL VELOCITY ★★★1/2 A spectacular stunt in which a daredevil sky diver attempts a midair rescue—by opening the trunk of a plummeting automobile—is one of the key elements that help save this big, dumb but enjoyable espionage thriller. Entertaining for those willing to turn off their logic centers and go with the flow. Rated PG-13 for violence and profanity. 100m. **DIR:** Deran Sarafian. **CAST:** Charlie Sheen, Nastassja Kinski, James Gandolfini, Christopher McDonald, Gary Bullock, Hans R. Howes, Mario Van Peebles, Richard Sarafian. **1994 DVD**

TERMINAL VIRUS 💔 This poverty-row quickie, about a post-apocalyptic virus that has rendered sexual contact between men and women fatal to both, is just another dumb excuse for women to shed clothes and men to shoot guns. Rated R for nudity, rape, violence, profanity, and simulated sex. 81m. **DIR:** Dan Golden. **CAST:** James Brolin, Bryan Genesse, Kehli O'Byrne, Elena Sahagun, Richard Lynch. **1995**

TERMINATOR, THE ★★★1/2 In this science-fiction–time-travel adventure, Arnold Schwarzenegger stars as a cyborg (part man, part machine) sent from the future to present-day Los Angeles to murder a woman (Linda Hamilton). Her offspring will play an important part in the world from which the killer came. Michael Biehn is the rebel soldier sent to thwart Schwarzenegger's plans. Rated R for nudity, simulated sex, violence, and profanity. 108m. **DIR:** James Cameron. **CAST:** Arnold Schwarzenegger, Linda Hamilton, Michael Biehn. **1984 DVD**

TERMINATOR 2: JUDGMENT DAY ★★★★★ A rip-roaring juggernaut of a thriller that far surpasses the original *Terminator*. What elevates this one are elements you may not expect: a fascinating continuation of the original time-travel plot and an engrossing human story about the conflict between man and machine. Rated R, with strong violence and profanity. 135m. **DIR:** James Cameron. **CAST:** Arnold Schwarzenegger, Linda Hamilton, Robert Patrick, Joe Morton, Edward Furlong. **1991 DVD**

TERMINI STATION ★★★1/2 Mom's a drunk, her daughter can't sustain relationships, and her son will sacrifice anything to get a promotion. Probing into this dysfunctional family's past reveals the root of everyone's problems. Colleen Dewhurst is terrific as the formerly passionate woman drowning her loneliness in a bottle. Not rated; this Canadian film contains profanity and violence. 105m. **DIR:** Allan Winton King. **CAST:** Colleen Dewhurst, Megan Follows, Gordon Clapp. **1989**

TERMS OF ENDEARMENT ★★★★ This stylish soap opera, written, produced, and directed by James L. Brooks, covers thirty years in the lives of a Houston matron, played by Shirley MacLaine, and her daughter, played by Debra Winger, who marries an English teacher with a wandering eye. Jack Nicholson is also on hand, to play MacLaine's neighbor, an astronaut with the wrong stuff. Rated PG for profanity and suggested sex. 132m. **DIR:** James L. Brooks. **CAST:** Shirley MacLaine, Debra Winger, Jack Nicholson, Danny DeVito, Jeff Daniels. **1983**

TERRIFIED ★★1/2 A young woman is stalked by an assailant she can never quite see. Kudos to the makers of this thriller for having the sense to emulate such classic intelligent shockers as *Repulsion* and *Carnival of Souls*. Too bad the film never lives up to its potential. Rated R for profanity, violence, and sexual situations. 95m. **DIR:** James Merendino. **CAST:** Heather Graham, Lisa Zane, Rustam Branaman, Tom Breznahan, Max Perlich, Richard Lynch. **1996 DVD**

TERROR, THE ★ This is an incomprehensible sludge of mismatched horror scenes even Boris Karloff can't save. 81m. **DIR:** Roger Corman. **CAST:** Boris Karloff, Jack Nicholson, Sandra Knight. **1963 DVD**

•**TERROR ABOARD** ★★★ The grim events on a derelict yacht boarded by salvagers reveal a man willing to kill his passengers and crew to escape the justice awaiting him at the end of his voyage. The cold-blooded killer almost does away with all the witnesses and escapes his fate. Almost. Sometimes gruesome, precode independent is a mystery-horror-thriller with running humor that works well on all levels. B&W; 67m. **DIR:** Paul Sloane. **CAST:** John Halliday, Charlie Ruggles, Shirley Grey, Neil Hamilton, Verree Teasdale, Jack LaRue, Stanley Fields, Eila Bennett. **1933**

TERROR AT LONDON BRIDGE ★★ Jack the Ripper is mystically resurrected in contemporary Arizona and goes on a killing spree in the British-style tourist trap. Only one man suspects that this is more than the work of a serial killer, and he must convince someone before it's too late. Predictable made-for-TV movie with some schlock gore effects. 96m. **DIR:** E. W. Swackhamer. **CAST:** David Hasselhoff, Stephanie Kramer, Randolph Mantooth, Adrienne Barbeau. 1985

TERROR AT THE OPERA ★★1/2 In this stylish and suspenseful Italian production, a beautiful young diva is terrorized by a hooded maniac who makes her watch him murder the members of her opera company. An intense musical score, realistic effects, and the killer's brutality make this a disturbing experience. The movie fizzles out with a senseless conclusion. Not rated, but with extreme violence and some nudity. 107m. **DIR:** Dario Argento. **CAST:** Cristina Marsillach, Ian Charleson, Daria Nicolodi. 1991

TERROR AT THE RED WOLF INN (TERROR HOUSE) ★★★ This is a sometimes ghoulishly funny horror-comedy about a college student who is chosen as the winner of a free vacation at an inn owned by a sweet old couple. Not all of the scenes work, but we guarantee it will give you the willies and the sillies. Rated R. (Also known as *The Folks at the Red Wolf Inn* and *Terror House.*) 98m. **DIR:** Bud Townsend. **CAST:** Linda Gillin, Arthur Space, John Neilson, Mary Jackson. 1972

TERROR BY NIGHT ★★★ Penultimate entry in the Rathbone/Bruce Sherlock Holmes series, with the master sleuth and his loyal companion up against a series of murders on a train bound from London to Edinburgh. The culprit ultimately turns out to be Col. Sebastian Moran, but you'll have to watch the film to discover which of the passengers he impersonates! B&W; 69m. **DIR:** Roy William Neill. **CAST:** Basil Rathbone, Nigel Bruce, Alan Mowbray, Renee Godfrey, Billy Bevan, Dennis Hoey. 1946 DVD

TERROR CREATURES FROM THE GRAVE ★★1/2 Grade-Z title tacked onto what is actually a fairly stately, decorous Barbara Steele vehicle from Italy. She plays the wife of an occult scientist who summons zombies from the grounds of their Gothic estate. Atmospheric and fun. B&W; 83m. **DIR:** Ralph Zucker (Massimo Pupillo). **CAST:** Barbara Steele, Walter Brandi. 1966

TERROR FROM THE YEAR 5,000 ★★ Not-bad cheapjack sci-fi about contemporary scientists who bring a woman from A.D. 5,000 to their own time and soon regret it. Fast-paced. B&W; 74m. **DIR:** Robert Gurney Jr. **CAST:** Ward Costello, Joyce Holden, Salome Jens. 1958

TERROR IN PARADISE ❤ Grade-Z thriller finds an American couple battling terrorists on a small island getaway. Paradise lost! Rated R for nudity and violence. 81m. **DIR:** Peer J. Oppenheimer. **CAST:** Gary Lockwood, Joanna Pettet, David Anthony Smith, Leslie Ryan, David McKnight. 1992

TERROR IN THE HAUNTED HOUSE ★★★ Although the title of this movie makes it sound as if it's a horror film, it is actually a psychological thriller along the Hitchcock line. It is the story of a young newlywed woman who has a recurring nightmare about a house she has never seen. She fears that something in the attic will kill her. The terror starts when her new husband takes her from Switzerland, where she has been since childhood, to the United States and ... the house in her horrid dream. 90m. **DIR:** Harold Daniels. **CAST:** Gerald Mohr, Cathy O'Donnell. 1958

TERROR IN THE SWAMP ❤ A Sasquatch-like creature is stalking the swamp. Rated PG for violence. 87m. **DIR:** Joe Catalanotto. **CAST:** Billy Holiday. 1984

TERROR IN THE WAX MUSEUM ★★ The all-star cast from yesteryear looks like a sort of Hollywood wax museum. Their fans will suffer through this unsuspenseful murder mystery. Rated PG. 93m. **DIR:** Georg Fenady. **CAST:** Ray Milland, Broderick Crawford, Elsa Lanchester, Maurice Evans, Shani Wallis, John Carradine, Louis Hayward, Patric Knowles. 1973

TERROR OF MECHAGODZILLA ★★ Another outlandish Godzilla epic from the 1970s with the big guy battling his own robot double, Mechagodzilla. Nothing special, but a lot of flashy effects and explosions. As always, the kids will love it. Rated G. 89m. **DIR:** Inoshiro Honda. **CAST:** Katsuhiko Sasaki. 1978 DVD

TERROR OF THE TONGS, THE ★★★ In 1910 Hong Kong, sea captain Geoffrey Toone's daughter is killed by Christopher Lee's Red Dragon Tong. Competent, atmospheric revenge adventure. Not rated; contains violence. 80m. **DIR:** Anthony Bushell. **CAST:** Christopher Lee, Geoffrey Toone, Yvonne Monlaur, Marne Maitland. 1961

TERROR OF TINY TOWN, THE ❤ The definitive all-midget Western, with action, gunplay, romance, and a happy ending to boot. B&W; 63m. **DIR:** Sam Newfield. **CAST:** Billy Curtis, Yvonne Moray, Little Billy. 1938

TERROR ON ALCATRAZ ❤ A group of teenagers split off from a tour of a former prison and end up locked in overnight. Not rated; contains violence. 96m. **DIR:** Philip Marcus. **CAST:** Aldo Ray. 1987

TERROR ON THE 40TH FLOOR ★★ A typical disaster film, this deals with a skyscraper fire. Not rated. 100m. **DIR:** Jerry Jameson. **CAST:** John Forsythe, Joseph Campanella, Don Meredith. 1974 DVD

TERROR OUT OF THE SKY ★★ This made-for-television film is a sequel to *The Savage Bees* (1976). Here two bee experts and a gung ho pilot try everything to stop another infestation of the flying killers in the United States. Stick with the original. 100m. **DIR:** Lee H. Katzin. **CAST:** Efrem Zimbalist Jr., Dan Haggerty, Tovah Feldshuh, Lonny Chapman, Ike Eisenmann, Steve Franken. 1978

TERROR SQUAD ★★★ Better-than-average action movie about small-town Indiana police chief Chuck Connors battling Libyan terrorists. This offers some thrills and style despite the obvious low budget. Not rated. 92m. **DIR:** Peter Maris. **CAST:** Chuck Connors, Kerry Brennan. 1987

TERROR STALKS THE CLASS REUNION ★★ The closing of a school on a German army base attracts a couple of psychos, one of whom still has a deadly crush on a former teacher. Geraint Wyn Davies captures Kate Nelligan, chains her to his wall, and plans their wedding. This Mary Higgins Clark story is clichéd, but Nelligan's performance is interesting. Rated PG for violence. 95m. **DIR:** Clive Donner. **CAST:**

Jennifer Beals, Kate Nelligan, Geraint Wyn Davies. **1992**

TERROR TRAIN ★★★ This is perhaps the best slasher film made in the eighties. The story involves a New Year's Eve frat party taking place on a moving train, with everyone having a great time until students start showing up murdered. This film relies on true suspense and good performances for its thrills. Rated R for violence. 97m. **DIR:** Roger Spottiswoode. **CAST:** Ben Johnson, Jamie Lee Curtis, Hart Bochner, David Copperfield. **1980**

TERROR VISION ★★★ An imaginative spoof of sci-fi films, with a hip slant. A family of swinging yuppies accidentally beam down a hostile alien through their satellite dish. Horror fans will be delighted. Rated R for violence and adult situations. 84m. **DIR:** Ted Nicolaou. **CAST:** Diane Franklin, Gerrit Graham, Mary Woronov, Chad Allen. **1986**

TERROR WITHIN, THE ★★1/2 A moderately scary terror film in the *Alien* mold. A group of scientists deep underground are the only people left after a plague wipes out mankind. Rated R for violence and profanity. 89m. **DIR:** Thierry Notz. **CAST:** George Kennedy, Andrew Stevens. **1988**

TERROR WITHIN 2, THE 🎔 It's sort of *Alien* meets *Mad Max Beyond Thunderdome* this time around as scientists battle superhuman mutants and a killer virus. Dopey. Rated R for nudity, profanity, and violence. 89m. **DIR:** Andrew Stevens. **CAST:** Andrew Stevens, Stella Stevens, Chick Vennera, R. Lee Ermey, Burton Gilliam. **1990**

•**TERRORIST, THE** ★★★1/2 A young guerrilla fighter in some unnamed struggle for independence volunteers for a suicide mission to assassinate an important politician, but as the appointed day draws near she begins to doubt her dedication for the cause. Writer-director Santosh Sivan uses his well-constructed story, evocative photography, and the expressive face of Ayesha Dharkar in the title role to draw us into the thoughts of this young woman as she prepares herself for a martyr's death. In Hindi with English subtitles. Not rated; contains brief violence. 95m. **DIR:** Santosh Sivan. **CAST:** Ayesha Dharkar, Vinshwa, Bhanu Prakash, Sonu Sisupal, Vishnu Vardhan. **1998**

TERRORISTS, THE ★★★★ Solid suspense-thriller has Sean Connery as the bullheaded commander of Norway's national security force, which is galvanized into action when a group of English terrorists takes over the British embassy. Rated PG for violence. 100m. **DIR:** Caspar Wrede. **CAST:** Sean Connery, Ian McShane, James Maxwell, Isabel Dean, Jeffrey Wickham, John Quentin, Robert Harris. **1975**

TERRORNAUTS, THE ★★ A British scientist succeeds in contacting an alien civilization. They beam the entire building in which he works to their galaxy. British science fiction tends to be talky, and this is no exception. 75m. **DIR:** Montgomery Tully. **CAST:** Simon Oates, Zena Marshall, Charles Hawtrey, Max Adrian. **1967**

TERRY FOX STORY, THE ★★★ This made-for-HBO film chronicles the "Marathon of Hope" undertaken by amputee Terry Fox (Eric Fryer), who jogged 3,000 miles across Canada before collapsing in Ontario. Based on a true story, this uplifting film is helped by solid performances, direction, and writing. 96m. **DIR:** Ralph L. Thomas. **CAST:** Eric Fryer, Robert Duvall, Chris Makepeace, Rosalind Chao, Michael Zelniker. **1983**

TESS ★★★★1/2 A hypothetically beautiful adaptation of Thomas Hardy's late-nineteenth-century novel *Tess of the D'Urbervilles*, this is director Roman Polanski's finest artistic achievement. Nastassja Kinski is stunning as the country girl who is "wronged" by a suave aristocrat and the man she marries. The story unfolds at the pace of a lazy afternoon stroll, but Polanski's technical skills and the cinematography are spellbinding. Rated PG. 170m. **DIR:** Roman Polanski. **CAST:** Nastassja Kinski, Peter Firth, John Bett. **1979**

TEST OF LOVE, A ★★ This tearjerker, taken from the Australian bestselling novel *Annie's Coming Out*, vividly displays the love and determination a therapist (Angela Punch McGregor) has in fighting for the rights of Anne O'Farrell, a severely disabled teenager who was misdiagnosed as being retarded. Yet the makers of this movie lack the finesse it takes to make the antagonists of this story more than one-dimensional. Rated PG for profanity. 93m. **DIR:** Gil Brealey. **CAST:** Angela Punch McGregor, Drew Forsythe, Tina Arhondis. **1984**

TEST PILOT ★★★1/2 A top-notch cast playing believable characters made this drama of daredevils who try out new aircraft a big winner with critics and at the box office as World War II loomed. Cinematographer Ray June's aerial sequences are stunning. One of the biggest hits in MGM history. B&W; 118m. **DIR:** Victor Fleming. **CAST:** Clark Gable, Spencer Tracy, Myrna Loy, Marjorie Main, Lionel Barrymore, Louis Jean Heydt. **1938**

TESTAMENT ★★★★★ In its own quiet, unspectacular way, this film tells a simple story about what happens to one family when World War III begins and ends in a matter of minutes. Jane Alexander is superb as the mother attempting to cope with the unthinkable, and this fine movie is one you won't soon forget. Rated PG. 90m. **DIR:** Lynne Littman. **CAST:** Jane Alexander, William Devane, Ross Harris, Roxana Zal, Lukas Haas, Lila Kedrova, Leon Ames, Kevin Costner, Rebecca DeMornay. **1983**

TESTAMENT OF DR. CORDELIER, THE ★★★1/2 This is the great Jean Renoir's exploration of the Jekyll/Hyde theme, and of interest primarily for that unique departure. Made for French TV but released to theaters, it has a certain flatness that belies its director's talent. The transformation scenes, however, have an almost transcendent energy. B&W; 74m. **DIR:** Jean Renoir. **CAST:** Jean-Louis Barrault. **1959**

TESTAMENT OF DR. MABUSE ★★★1/2 In this sequel to *Dr. Mabuse the Gambler* by Thea Von Harboll and the director Fritz Lang, the infamous criminal mastermind dies in an asylum, and his assistant takes over his identity. It's a fast-moving picture, said by Lang to be a diatribe against Adolf Hitler. Whatever it is, it rates as slick entertainment. B&W; 122m. **DIR:** Fritz Lang. **CAST:** Rudolf Klein-Rogge, Otto Wernicke. **1933**

TESTAMENT OF ORPHEUS, THE ★★★ Jean Cocteau's last film, it marks the final installment of an Orpheus Trilogy, began with *The Blood of the Poet* (1930) and continued with *Orpheus* (1949). While its nonlinear sequence of events is quite incomprehensible, the fifteen episodes are generally concerned with an eighteenth-century poet (Jean Cocteau) who dies and is reborn into modern times. In French with English subtitles. 80m. **DIR:** Jean Cocteau. **CAST:** Jean Cocteau, Jean Marais. **1959 DVD**

TETSUO II: BODY HAMMER ★★1/2 Less a sequel than a variant on the same film, *Tetsuo II* has more of a plot as a frustrated "salary man" is driven by the pressures of Tokyo life to mutate into a half-metal being. As in the first film, the imagery is wildly bizarre, but a little of this goes a long, long way. Not rated; contains strong violence, nudity, and sexual situations. In Japanese with English subtitles. 90m. **DIR:** Shinya Tsukamoto. **CAST:** Tomoroh Taguchi, Nodu Kanaoka, Shinya Tsukamoto. **1991**

TETSUO: THE IRON MAN ★★★ There's hardly any story in this hyperkinetic cult hit about an office worker mutating into a part-human, part-metal being. Grotesque makeup, stop-action animation, and time-lapse photography make this the perfect visual equivalent of the industrial-music soundtrack. In Japanese with English subtitles. B&W; 67m. **DIR:** Shinya Tsukamoto. **CAST:** Tomoroh Taguchi, Kei Fujiwara. **1989 DVD**

•TEVYE ★★★1/2 The stories of writer Sholem Aleichem that were later adapted for the stage and film hit *Fiddler on the Roof* also inspired this feature made for the once-flourishing Yiddish film industry that operated out of New York. Despite some technical limitations and hammy acting, it's worth seeing as a peek into the past, with nineteenth-century Russia re-created by people who came to America from there. In Yiddish with English subtitles. B&W; 93m. **DIR:** Maurice Schwartz. **CAST:** Maurice Schwartz, Miriam Riselle. **1939**

TEX ★★★★1/2 Matt Dillon, Jim Metzler, and Ben Johnson star in this superb coming-of-age adventure about the struggles and conflicts of two teenage brothers growing up in the Southwest without parental guidance. 103m. Rated PG for violence and mature situations. **DIR:** Tim Hunter. **CAST:** Matt Dillon, Jim Metzler, Ben Johnson, Emilio Estevez, Meg Tilly. **1982 DVD**

TEX AND THE LORD OF THE DEEP ★★ Based on the Italian cartoon-character Tex Willer. Tex fights an Indian uprising spurred on by a medicine man who has discovered a glowing green rock that turns people into instant mummies. Good performances by spaghetti Western veterans Giuliano Gemma and William Berger are not enough to overcome the concept. Not rated, contains violence. 90m. **DIR:** Duccio Tessari. **CAST:** Giuliano Gemma, William Berger, Carlo Mucari, Isabel Russinova, Aldo Sambrell. **1985**

TEXAS (1941) ★★★ Friends William Holden and Glenn Ford are rivals for the affections of Claire Trevor in this lively, action-jammed Western pitting cattleman against cattle rustler. It might have been an epic, but a cost-conscious producer kept a tight rein. Good, though! B&W; 93m. **DIR:** George Marshall.

CAST: William Holden, Glenn Ford, Claire Trevor, George Bancroft, Edgar Buchanan, Raymond Hatton. **1941**

TEXAS (1994) ★★1/2 In an interesting twist, this two-part James A. Michener miniseries about the founding of our twenty-eighth state debuted on video before going to television. A $12 million historical soap opera, it's chock-full of romance, politics, and adventure, but never feels gritty enough. Perhaps it's those nudie shots intercut with the battle scenes. Not rated; contains profanity, violence, and nudity. Each tape 90m. **DIR:** Richard Lang. **CAST:** Maria Conchita Alonso, Benjamin Bratt, Patrick Duffy, Chelsea Field, Anthony Michael Hall, Stacy Keach, David Keith, John Schneider, Grant Show, Randy Travis, Rick Schroder. **1994**

TEXAS ACROSS THE RIVER ★★1/2 Low-brow Western comedy has the dubious distinction of being the only movie to feature Joey Bishop as an Indian. That said, the film was a sizable hit and has its fans, despite inept postproduction work that is glaringly obvious on the small screen. A Spanish nobleman, officer Peter Graves, and a con-man save a small Texas settlement from an inept Comanche tribe. 101m. **DIR:** Michael Gordon. **CAST:** Dean Martin, Alain Delon, Rosemary Forsyth, Joey Bishop, Tina Marquand, Peter Graves, Michael Ansara, Andrew Prine, Roy Barcroft. **1966**

TEXAS CARNIVAL ★★★ When down-and-out carnival workers, Red Skelton and Esther Williams are mistaken for brother and sister cattle millionaires, they go along with the mix-up. 77m. **DIR:** Charles Walters. **CAST:** Esther Williams, Red Skelton, Howard Keel, Ann Miller, Keenan Wynn. **1951**

TEXAS CHAINSAW MASSACRE, THE ★★★ This, the first film about a cannibalistic maniac by horror specialist Tobe Hooper, went pretty much unnoticed in its original release. That's probably because it sounds like the run-of-the-mill drive-in exploitation fare. While it was made on a very low budget, it nevertheless has been hailed as a ground-breaking genre work by critics and film buffs and became a cult classic. Rated R for extreme violence. 83m. **DIR:** Tobe Hooper. **CAST:** Marilyn Burns, Gunnar Hansen, Edwin Neal. **1974 DVD**

TEXAS CHAINSAW MASSACRE 2, THE ★★1/2 Leatherface is back! In fact, so is most of the family in this maniacal sequel. Dennis Hopper stars as a retired lawman out to avenge the gruesome murder of his nephew, and Caroline Williams plays the disc jockey who helps him locate the butchers. Not rated, but loaded with repulsive gore. 95m. **DIR:** Tobe Hooper. **CAST:** Dennis Hopper, Caroline Williams. **1986**

TEXAS CHAINSAW MASSACRE: THE NEXT GENERATION ★★ Virtual remake of Tobe Hooper's trend-setting horror–thriller is most notable as the springboard from which current hot stars Matthew McConaughey and Renee Zellweger made their first leap into film. Instead of bringing anything new to the party, writer-director Kim Henkel completely apes Hooper's film, this time in color. Rated R for language and violence. 93m. **DIR:** Kim Henkel. **CAST:** Matthew McConaughey, Renee Zellweger, Robert Jacks. **1994 DVD**

TEXAS CYCLONE ★★★ An easygoing cowpoke (Tim McCoy) is mistaken for a straight-shooting rancher and sticks around to help the rancher's wife (Shirley Grey) fight off cattle rustlers. A top-notch McCoy gets some solid support from a couple of newcomers, John Wayne and Walter Brennan. B&W; 63m. **DIR:** D. Ross Lederman. **CAST:** Tim McCoy, Shirley Grey, John Wayne, Walter Brennan, Wheeler Oakman, Harry Cording. **1932**

TEXAS GUNS ★★★ Enjoyable romp from veteran Western helmer Burt Kennedy, who lassos a bevy of old stable hands to tell the tale of a group of aging train robbers whose efforts are thwarted by a senior citizen posse and a young upstart played by Shaun Cassidy. Made-for-television film also known as *Once Upon a Texas Train*. 100m. **DIR:** Burt Kennedy. **CAST:** Willie Nelson, Richard Widmark, Shaun Cassidy, Angie Dickinson, Chuck Connors, Stuart Whitman. **1988**

TEXAS JOHN SLAUGHTER: STAMPEDE AT BITTER CREEK ★★1/2 Former Texas Ranger John Slaughter is falsely accused of rustling as he attempts to drive his cattle into New Mexico despite threats from a rival rancher and his hired gun. Tom Tryon is ruggedly heroic in this Disney adventure Western culled from episodes originally featured on *Walt Disney Presents* from 1958 to 1962. 52m. **DIR:** Harry Keller. **CAST:** Tom Tryon, Harry Carey Jr., Adeline Harris, Annette Gorman, Betty Lynn. **1962**

TEXAS LADY ★★ An out-of-her-element Claudette Colbert is a crusading newspaper editor in the Old West. If you're a Western fan, you'll like it. 86m. **DIR:** Tim Whelan. **CAST:** Claudette Colbert, Barry Sullivan, John Litel. **1955**

TEXAS MASQUERADE ★★★★ Hopalong Cassidy masquerades as an eastern Milquetoast to get the goods on badmen in this slam-bang Western that is one of the best of the series. B&W; 59m. **DIR:** George Archainbaud. **CAST:** William Boyd, Andy Clyde, Jimmy Rogers, Don Costello. **1944**

TEXAS PAYBACK ★★ Familiar faces flesh out this pedestrian action-thriller about an escaped convict out to even the score with the Texas Ranger who put him away. Rated R for nudity, violence, and profanity. 96m. **DIR:** Richard W. Munchkin. **CAST:** Sam Jones, Gary Hudson, Bo Hopkins, Kathleen Kinmont. **1994**

TEXAS RANGERS (1936) ★★★1/2 Outlaw buddies Fred MacMurray, Jack Oakie, and Lloyd Nolan rob trains and then part ways when MacMurray and Oakie join the Texas Rangers. A few years go by and the two rangers are assigned to track down the most notorious outlaw of the day: their old buddy, Nolan. If the plot sounds familiar, it's been used several times, most notably in the official remake, *Streets of Laredo*. But this is the original, and fans of shoot-'em-ups will enjoy it despite some uneven moments. B&W; 95m. **DIR:** King Vidor. **CAST:** Fred MacMurray, Jack Oakie, Jean Parker, Lloyd Nolan, George "Gabby" Hayes, Fred Kohler Sr. **1936**

TEXAS RANGERS, THE (1951) ★★★★ George Montgomery and the Texas Rangers vs. Sam Bass, the Sundance Kid and their band of outlaws. Superior B filmmaking. 74m. **DIR:** Phil Karlson. **CAST:** George Montgomery, Gale Storm, Jerome Courtland, William Bishop, John Dehner, Douglas Kennedy, Noah Beery Jr. **1951**

TEXAS TERROR ★★1/2 John Wayne hangs up his guns (for a while) in this Lone Star Western about a lawman falsely accused of the death of his friend. Wayne finds the real culprits and gets a chance to do some hard ridin' and fancy sluggin'. B&W; 58m. **DIR:** Robert N. Bradbury. **CAST:** John Wayne, Lucille Brown, LeRoy Mason, George "Gabby" Hayes, Yakima Canutt. **1935**

TEXAS TRAIL ★★1/2 It's 1898 and Hopalong Cassidy and the boys are chomping at the bit to get into the fight in Cuba, but the government needs horses more than fighting men. They round up the required horses but crooks rustle the herd. With the help of the U.S. Cavalry, Hoppy and his "rough riders" settle things with the bad guys, get into their uniforms, and sail for the fray with Spain. B&W; 59m. **DIR:** David Selman. **CAST:** William Boyd, George "Gabby" Hayes, Russell Hayden, Judith Allen. **1937**

TEXASVILLE ★★★★ This much-maligned sequel to *The Last Picture Show* is surprisingly good—an absorbing tale of people facing the truth about themselves. The naïveté, manipulation, and hope that propelled the characters' lives in the original film (when they were decades younger) have given way to wisdom and sober truth. An uncommonly rich motion picture. Rated R for profanity. 125m. **DIR:** Peter Bogdanovich. **CAST:** Jeff Bridges, Cybill Shepherd, Annie Potts, Timothy Bottoms, Cloris Leachman, Randy Quaid, Eileen Brennan. **1990**

T-FORCE ★★★1/2 When a squad of robotic crime fighters becomes more of a problem than the bad guys they're supposed to be fighting, detective Jack Scalia is hired to rein them in. Rated R for profanity and violence. 101m. **DIR:** Richard Pepin. **CAST:** Jack Scalia, Erin Gray, Evan Lurie. **1995**

THANK GOD IT'S FRIDAY ★★ This film is episodic and light in mood and features a cast primarily of newcomers. Donna Summer plays an aspiring singer who pesters a disc jockey, Bobby Speed (Ray Vitte), to let her sing. Rated PG. 90m. **DIR:** Robert Klane. **CAST:** Donna Summer, The Commodores, Ray Vitte, Debra Winger, Jeff Goldblum. **1978**

THANK YOU, MR. MOTO ★★★ The Japanese detective races with villains in search of Chinese scrolls that reveal the location of the treasure-laden tomb of Genghis Khan. The second and best of the Mr. Moto movies, with Peter Lorre in peak form as the wily sleuth. B&W; 66m. **DIR:** Norman Foster. **CAST:** Peter Lorre, Thomas Beck, Pauline Frederick, John Carradine. **1937**

THANK YOUR LUCKY STARS ★★★1/2 Practically nonexistent plot—involving banjo-eyed Eddie Cantor as a cabdriver and the organizer of this gala affair—takes a backseat to the wonderful array of Warner Bros. talent gathered together for the first and only time in one film. Lots of fun for film buffs. B&W; 127m. **DIR:** David Butler. **CAST:** Eddie Cantor, Dennis Morgan, Joan Leslie, Bette Davis, Olivia de Havilland, Ida Lupino, Ann Sheridan, Humphrey Bogart, Errol Flynn, John Garfield. **1943**

THANKSGIVING STORY, THE ★★1/2 Originally a TV holiday special, this features the wholesome Walton family. John-boy (Richard Thomas) tries to impress the girl of his dreams while applying for a college scholarship. An accident causing brain damage threatens his future. A bit slow-paced and overly sweet. 95m. **DIR:** Philip Leacock. **CAST:** Richard Thomas, Ralph Waite, Michael Learned, Ellen Corby, Will Geer. 1973

THAT BRENNAN GIRL ★★★1/2 A forerunner of the juvenile-delinquency movies of the 1950s and 1960s, this film tells the story of a young woman who learns that money isn't everything, and she learns it the hard way. Dated in style but not content. B&W; 95m. **DIR:** William Nigh. **CAST:** Mona Freeman, James Dunn, William Marshall. 1946

THAT CERTAIN THING ★★★ When a poor working-class girl (Viola Dana) marries a wealthy idler (Ralph Graves), they are cut off from his inheritance. Fairy-tale romance with more than a touch of the screwball comedies to come from director Frank Capra. Silent. B&W; 70m. **DIR:** Frank Capra. **CAST:** Viola Dana, Ralph Graves. 1928

THAT CERTAIN WOMAN ★★1/2 A gangster's widow marries a weak alcoholic playboy, and his father forces an annulment. When they learn she has a child, they try to take him from her. Enough self-sacrifice by lovely Bette Davis to fill four movies. B&W; 96m. **DIR:** Edmund Goulding. **CAST:** Bette Davis, Henry Fonda, Ian Hunter, Donald Crisp, Anita Louise. 1937

THAT CHAMPIONSHIP SEASON (1982) ★★1/2 Former high school basketball stars (Bruce Dern, Stacy Keach, Martin Sheen, and Paul Sorvino) and their coach (Robert Mitchum) get together for the twenty-fourth annual celebration of their championship season. While there's nothing wrong with a sobering look at broken dreams and the pain of midlife crisis, we've seen it all on screen before. Rated R for profanity, racial epithets, violence, and adult content. 110m. **DIR:** Jason Miller. **CAST:** Bruce Dern, Stacy Keach, Martin Sheen, Paul Sorvino, Robert Mitchum. 1982

●**THAT CHAMPIONSHIP SEASON (1999)** ★★★ Jason Miller's Pulitzer-winning play made a disappointing transition to the big screen in 1982; this interminable new adaptation isn't any better . . . possibly because it's directed by and stars Paul Sorvino, who also appeared in the original. His tunnel-visioned handling of the material merely amplifies its flaws, resulting in yet another tedious tale of male bonding that goes awry when too much alcohol loosens tongues and inhibitions. The setting is the twenty-fourth annual reunion of a small-town high-school basketball coach and the now-grown students he motivated toward success; the predictable climax, long in coming, is that these men haven't done anything significant with their lives ever since. Their so-called camaraderie is quick to evaporate amid increasingly spiteful bickering, leaving us to wonder how they ever functioned as a team in the first place. While the savage and brittle dialogue might fuel formidable performances on a live stage, it becomes only so much sniping in the confines of a screen. Rated R for profanity, racial epithets, and sexual candor. 127m. **DIR:** Paul Sorvino. **CAST:** Vincent

D'Onofrio, Terry Kinney, Tony Shalhoub, Gary Sinise, Paul Sorvino. 1999

THAT COLD DAY IN THE PARK ★★ This claustrophobic study of an emotionally disturbed woman and her obsessive interest in a young man is just about as strange as they come. It nonetheless gives gifted Sandy Dennis one of her most memorable roles. This film focuses on repressed sexuality, but also hints at incest and other subjects considered taboo when this Canadian-made movie was released. 113m. **DIR:** Robert Altman. **CAST:** Sandy Dennis, Michael Burns, Suzanne Benton, John Garfield Jr., Luana Anders, Michael Murphy. 1969

THAT DARN CAT (1965) ★★1/2 Trust Disney to take a great book—*Undercover Cat*, by Gordon and Mildred Gordon—and turn it into a moronic slapstick farce. A fulsome feline returns from his nightly rounds with a watch belonging to a woman taken hostage in a recent bank robbery. Enter an ailurophobic FBI agent. 116m. **DIR:** Robert Stevenson. **CAST:** Dean Jones, Hayley Mills, Dorothy Provine, Roddy McDowall, Elsa Lanchester, Neville Brand, William Demarest, Ed Wynn, Frank Gorshin. 1965

THAT DARN CAT (1997) 💙 Even this comedy's stale feline looks indignant and bored as its teen owner teams up with an inept rookie FBI agent to crack a kidnapping case. Rated PG. 89m. **DIR:** Bob Spiers. **CAST:** Christina Ricci, Doug E. Doug, Dyan Cannon, Michael McKean, Dean Jones, Peter Boyle. 1997

THAT FORSYTE WOMAN ★★ Greer Garson has the central role of a woman trapped in a marriage of convenience. She flouts the rigid social taboos of nineteenth-century England. Based on the first book of John Galsworthy's epic *Forsyte Saga*. A dull movie with little conviction. B&W; 114m. **DIR:** Compton Bennett. **CAST:** Greer Garson, Errol Flynn, Janet Leigh, Walter Pidgeon, Robert Young, Harry Davenport. 1949

THAT HAMILTON WOMAN ★★★1/2 The legendary acting duo of Mr. and Mrs. Laurence Olivier re-creates one of England's legendary romantic scandals: the love of naval hero Horatio Nelson for the alluring Lady Emma Hamilton. B&W; 128m. **DIR:** Alexander Korda. **CAST:** Vivien Leigh, Laurence Olivier. 1941

THAT LUCKY TOUCH ★★★ This romantic comedy features unlikely neighbors falling in love. Roger Moore plays Michael Scott, a weapons merchant. Susannah York, on the other hand, is an antimilitary writer. Shelley Winters provides a few laughs as the airhead wife of a NATO general (Lee J. Cobb). Comparable to a PG, but basically pretty tame. 93m. **DIR:** Christopher Miles. **CAST:** Roger Moore, Susannah York, Shelley Winters, Lee J. Cobb, Sydne Rome. 1975

THAT MAN FROM RIO ★★★★ This fast-moving comedy-action-thriller about a stolen artifact—with Jean-Paul Belmondo as a cross between James Bond and Indiana Jones—never lets up. In French with English subtitles. 115m. **DIR:** Philippe de Broca. **CAST:** Jean-Paul Belmondo, Françoise Dorleac, Simone Renant, Adolfo Celi. 1964

THAT MIDNIGHT KISS ★★★ Mario Lanza makes his film debut as an ex-GI making it as a truck driver when he gets involved with an heiress who wants to be an opera star. Slight plot, but it's the music that counts. A fine rendition of "They Won't Believe Me,"

96m. DIR: Norman Taurog. CAST: Mario Lanza, Kathryn Grayson, José Iturbi, Ethel Barrymore, Keenan Wynn, J. Carrol Naish, Thomas Gomez, Marjorie Reynolds, Arthur Treacher. 1949

THAT NIGHT ★★★ Nostalgic slice of life finds young Eliza Dushku acting as a go-between for popular Juliette Lewis and tough guy C. Thomas Howell. The year is 1961, and when Lewis becomes pregnant, it's up to Dushku to keep them together. Period soundtrack, an eye for detail, and sensitive, likable characters. Rated PG-13 for adult situations. 89m. DIR: Craig Bolotin. CAST: C. Thomas Howell, Juliette Lewis, Eliza Dushku. 1993

THAT OBSCURE OBJECT OF DESIRE ★★★★1/2 Luis Buñuel's last film cunningly combines erotic teasing, wit, and social comment. Mathieu (Fernando Rey) is a 50-year-old man who falls hopelessly in love with a young woman. Buñuel, a master of surrealism, tantalizes the viewer by casting two actresses to play the heroine and a third actress to do the voice of both. Rated R for profanity and nudity. 100m. DIR: Luis Buñuel. CAST: Fernando Rey, Carole Bouquet, Angela Molina. 1977

THAT OLD FEELING ★★★★ Bette Midler and Dennis Farina, divorced for years and unable to speak a civil word to each other, suddenly relight the old torch at their daughter's wedding. Leslie Dixon's sly script is equal parts farce, romantic comedy, and satire, and is directed with madcap grace by Carl Reiner. Rated PG-13 for profanity. 107m. DIR: Carl Reiner. CAST: Bette Midler, Dennis Farina, Paula Marshall, Gail O'Grady, David Rasche, Danny Nucci, Jamie Denton. 1997 DVD

THAT SINKING FEELING ★★★★ Following Scottish director Bill Forsyth's box-office success with *Gregory's Girl* and *Local Hero*, his first feature was resurrected for release in America. It's a typically wry and dry comic affair about a group of unemployed young men deciding on a life of crime. The result is engaging silliness. Rated PG. 92m. DIR: Bill Forsyth. CAST: Robert Buchanan, John Hughes, Billy Greenlees, Gordon John Sinclair. 1979

THAT SUMMER OF WHITE ROSES ★★★ Guests at an isolated Yugoslavian summer resort clash with Nazis during WWII. A well-seasoned drama that simmers at the start, but eventually comes to a full boil. Rated R for profanity and violence. 98m. DIR: Rajko Grlic. CAST: Tom Conti, Susan George, Rod Steiger. 1990

THAT THING YOU DO! ★★★★★ It seems one of the hardest things to do is make a fully convincing and entertaining movie about rock 'n' roll, but that's exactly what first-time director Tom Hanks has done with this light, fluffy but knowing tale of the one-hit "Wonders." Every detail, from the player's attitudes to the bottom line of the record companies, is right on the mark. Hanks himself is on board to add his distinctive brand of humor. It's a hoot. Rated PG. 110m. DIR: Tom Hanks. CAST: Tom Everett Scott, Liv Tyler, Johnathon Schaech, Steve Zahn, Ethan Embry, Tom Hanks, Alex Rocco, Bill Cobbs, Rita Wilson, Chris Isaak, Kevin Pollak. 1996

THAT TOUCH OF MINK ★★★1/2 This 1962 romantic comedy is enjoyable, but only as escapist fare.

Doris Day stars as an unemployed girl pursued by a wealthy businessman (Cary Grant). 99m. DIR: Delbert Mann. CAST: Doris Day, Cary Grant, Gig Young, Audrey Meadows, John Astin. 1962 DVD

THAT UNCERTAIN FEELING ★★1/2 This is an amusing film about marital unrest until the midpoint, when the time-tried romantic triangle plot thins rather than thickens. Burgess Meredith all but filches the film in a supporting role. Merle Oberon is devastatingly beautiful, even when she has the hiccups—an important plot device. B&W; 86m. DIR: Ernst Lubitsch. CAST: Merle Oberon, Melvyn Douglas, Alan Mowbray, Burgess Meredith, Eve Arden, Sig Ruman. 1941 DVD

THAT WAS ROCK ★★★★★ Compilation of two previous films, *The T.A.M.I. Show* and *The Big T.N.T. Show*, which were originally shot in the mid-1960s in black and white. The video is muddy, the simulated stereo is annoying, and the audience nearly drowns out the performers, but it's one of the best collections of rock 'n' roll and R&B talent you will ever see. Not rated. 92m. DIR: Steve Binder, Larry Peerce. CAST: The Rolling Stones, Chuck Berry, Tina Turner, Marvin Gaye, The Supremes, Smokey Robinson and the Miracles, James Brown, Ray Charles, Gerry and the Pacemakers, The Ronettes. 1984

THAT WAS THEN ... THIS IS NOW ★★★★ Adapted from a novel by S. E. Hinton (*The Outsiders*; *Rumble Fish*). The cuteness and condescension that mar most coming-of-age films are laudably absent in its tale of two working-class teenagers (Emilio Estevez and Craig Sheffer) coming to grips with adulthood. A work that teens and adults alike can appreciate. Rated R for violence and profanity. 103m. DIR: Christopher Cain. CAST: Emilio Estevez, Craig Sheffer, Kim Delaney, Morgan Freeman, Larry B. Scott, Barbara Babcock. 1985

THAT'LL BE THE DAY ★★★★ A provocative character study. Charismatic David Essex stars as a British working-class youth whose adolescent restlessness points him toward rock music. Ringo Starr contributes an engaging performance as a roughhewn lad who eventually proves to be less morally suspect than the protagonist. The film's sequel *Stardust* offers some of filmdom's most fascinating glimpses into the rock 'n' roll world. 90m. DIR: Claude Whatham. CAST: David Essex, Ringo Starr, Rosemary Leach, James Booth, Billy Fury, Keith Moon. 1974

THAT'S ADEQUATE ★★ This mock documentary rapidly exhausts its welcome. The sixty-year examination of the Adequate Pictures Studio includes glimpses of its many exploitation fiascos, such as *Singing in the Synagogue* and *Sigmund Freud in Sherwood Forest*. Rated R for raunchy language and brief nudity. 80m. DIR: Harry Hurwitz. CAST: Tony Randall, James Coco, Jerry Stiller, Anne Meara, Bruce Willis, Richard Lewis. 1989

THAT'S ENTERTAINMENT ★★★★★ A feast of screen highlights. Culled from twenty-nine years of MGM classics, this release truly has something for everybody. Taken from Metro-Goldwyn-Mayer's glory days when it boasted "more stars than there are in heaven," nearly every sequence is a showstopper.

Rated G. 135m. **DIR:** Jack Haley Jr. **CAST:** Judy Garland, Fred Astaire, Frank Sinatra, Gene Kelly, Esther Williams. 1974

THAT'S ENTERTAINMENT PART II ★★★★ More wonderful scenes from the history of MGM highlight this compilation, hosted by director Gene Kelly and Fred Astaire. It's a real treat for film buffs. Rated G. 132m. **DIR:** Gene Kelly. **CAST:** Gene Kelly, Fred Astaire. 1976

THAT'S ENTERTAINMENT! III ★★★½ This fourth compilation of old MGM musical routines feels a bit repetitious, but it's gussied up with a treasury of outtakes, previously unseen production numbers, and behind-the-scenes footage. It's proof positive why MTV will never be MGM. Rated G. 113m. **DIR:** Bud Friedgen, Michael J. Sheridan. **CAST:** June Allyson, Cyd Charisse, Lena Horne, Howard Keel, Gene Kelly, Ann Miller, Debbie Reynolds, Mickey Rooney, Esther Williams. 1994

THAT'S LIFE ★★★ Jack Lemmon and Julie Andrews play a married couple enduring a torrent of crises during one fateful weekend. The film is a mixture of good and bad, funny and sad, tasteful and tasteless. That it ends up on the plus side is to the credit of its lead players. Rated PG-13 for profanity and scatological humor. 102m. **DIR:** Blake Edwards. **CAST:** Julie Andrews, Jack Lemmon, Sally Kellerman, Robert Loggia, Jennifer Edwards, Chris Lemmon. 1986 DVD

THAT'S MY BABY 💙 Unemployed man wants his career-oriented girlfriend to have his baby. Rated PG-13 for nudity. 97m. **DIR:** Edie Yolles, John Bradshaw. **CAST:** Timothy Webber, Sonja Smits. 1989

THAT'S SINGING: THE BEST OF BROADWAY ★★½ You'll find this on the shelf with *That's Dancing* and *That's Entertainment*. It should be with *The Adventures of Ozzie and Harriet*. This is a television show where stars present an offering from Broadway musicals in which they appeared. The highlight is Jerry Orbach, singing "Try To Remember" from *The Fantasticks*. The star rating is for Broadway diehards only. 117m. **DIR:** Robert Iscove. **CAST:** Tom Bosley, Diahann Carroll, Glynis Johns, Ethel Merman, Jerry Orbach, Robert Morse, Debbie Reynolds. 1982

•**THAT'S THE WAY I LIKE IT** ★★★½ Delightful Singapore comedy about a young man who idolizes the film *Saturday Night Fever* and enters a disco-dance contest in order to buy a Triumph motorcycle. Fans of the John Travolta film and early Woody Allen comedies will appreciate the irony and similarities in the story, while the likable cast will win over everyone else. Totally charming and funny. Rated PG for language and violence. 95m. **DIR:** Glen Goei. **CAST:** Adrian Pang, Madeline Tan, Pierre Png, Anna Belle Francis, Steven Lim. 1998 DVD

THEATRE OF BLOOD ★★★★ Deliciously morbid horror-comedy about a Shakespearean actor (Vincent Price) who, angered by the thrashing he receives from a series of critics, decides to kill them in uniquely outlandish ways. He turns to the Bard for inspiration, and each perceived foe is eliminated in a manner drawn from one of Shakespeare's plays. Rated R for violence. 104m. **DIR:** Douglas Hickox. **CAST:** Vincent Price, Diana Rigg, Robert Morley. 1973

THEATRE OF DEATH ★★½ Mildly interesting mystery succeeds mainly due to Christopher Lee's assured performance and some well-timed scares as a series of gruesome murders is committed in Paris with an apparent connection to the local theater company. Good title sequence deserves mention. 90m. **DIR:** Samuel Gallu. **CAST:** Christopher Lee, Julian Glover, Lelia Goldoni. 1967

THEIR ONLY CHANCE ★★ True-life adventure film about a young man (Steve Hoddy) who has a way with wild animals. Former Tarzan Jock Mahoney has a dual role as a rancher and a mountain man. A nice, quiet wildlife film suitable for the entire family. 84m. **DIR:** David Siddon. **CAST:** Jock Mahoney, Steve Hoddy. 1975

THELMA & LOUISE ★★★★ Director Ridley Scott and screenwriter Callie Khouri skillfully interweave suspense and comedy in this distaff *Easy Rider*, in which two buddies set off on a vacation and end up running from the law after one of them shoots a would-be rapist. Entertaining action-movie/road-picture. Rated R for violence, profanity, and suggested sex. 128m. **DIR:** Ridley Scott. **CAST:** Susan Sarandon, Geena Davis, Harvey Keitel, Michael Madsen, Christopher McDonald, Brad Pitt. 1991 DVD

THEM! ★★★★ Classic 1950s sci-fi about colossal mutant ants, at large in a New Mexico desert, threatening to take over the world. Frightening special effects and lightning pace make this a supercharged entertainment, with Edmund Gwenn delivering a standout performance as the scientist who foretells the danger. Great. B&W; 94m. **DIR:** Gordon Douglas. **CAST:** Edmund Gwenn, James Arness, James Whitmore, Fess Parker. 1954

•**THEODORA GOES WILD** ★★★ The usually serious Irene Dunne tries her hand at screwball comedy and plays a small-town writer who visits New York after her *Peyton Place*-ish novel becomes a bestseller. Melvyn Douglas is a good foil as the big city sophisticate who becomes her guide. B&W; 94m. **DIR:** Richard Boleslawski. **CAST:** Irene Dunne, Melvyn Douglas, Thomas Mitchell, Thurston Hall. 1936

THEODORE REX 💙 Whoopi Goldberg proves what a good actress she is by making it through this science-fiction comedy with a straight face. Goldberg plays futuristic police officer Katie Coltrane, who exists in a future where dinosaurs have been reanimated and live among humans. When a dinosaur is found murdered, Coltrane is paired with a Tyrannosaurus Rex named Teddy, and together they set out to solve the case. A disaster. Rated PG. 92m. **DIR:** Jonathan Betuel. **CAST:** Whoopi Goldberg, Armin Mueller-Stahl, Juliet Landau, Richard Roundtree. 1996

•**THEORY OF FLIGHT, THE** ★★★★ Kenneth Branagh and Helena Bonham Carter are outstanding in this tale of true friendship. Branagh is the disillusioned man who doesn't mind risking his life for a thrill. Bonham Carter is the woman suffering from Lou Gehrig's disease who turns to him for one last favor. Even though the film attempts to deal with serious subject matters, a clunky script and direction almost detract from the marvelous performances. Rated R for language and adult situations. 98m. **DIR:** Paul

Greengrass. **CAST:** Kenneth Branagh, Helena Bonham Carter, Gemma Jones, Holly Aird. **1998**

THERE GOES MY BABY ★★★ Although trying for the youthful angst of *American Graffiti*, writer-director Floyd Mutrux's farewell glimpse of the 1965 Westwood High senior class is a bit overwrought. The B-level ensemble cast tries hard, but never rises above the facile stereotypes: surfer, draft dodger, flower girl, earnest valedictorian, etc. Rated R for profanity and violence. 99m. **DIR:** Floyd Mutrux. **CAST:** Dermot Mulroney, Rick Schroder, Kelli Williams, Noah Wyle, Jill Schoelen, Kristin Minter, Lucy Deakins. **1994**

THERE GOES THE NEIGHBORHOOD ★★★★ Prison shrink Jeff Daniels learns of $8.5 million of Mafia loot buried in the suburbs. Catherine O'Hara is the woman living over said loot. Quirky and cute, this breezy comedy is unpredictable and sweetly enjoyable. Rated PG-13 for profanity. 88m. **DIR:** Bill Phillips. **CAST:** Jeff Daniels, Catherine O'Hara, Dabney Coleman, Hector Elizondo, Judith Ivey, Rhea Perlman. **1992**

THERE WAS A CROOKED MAN ★★★1/2 Crooked-as-they-come Kirk Douglas bides and does his time harried by holier-than-thou Arizona prison warden Henry Fonda, who has more than redemption on his mind. A good plot and clever casting make this oater well worth the watching. And, yes, rattlesnakes do make good watchdogs. Rated R. 123m. **DIR:** Joseph L. Mankiewicz. **CAST:** Kirk Douglas, Henry Fonda, Hume Cronyn, Warren Oates, Burgess Meredith, Arthur O'-Connell. **1970**

•**THERE'S SOMETHING ABOUT MARY** ★★★ The late 1990s resurgence in "moron comedy" probably saw its finest hour with this effort, which blends low humor, bad taste, and slapstick silliness with an unexpectedly touching love story. Geeky Ben Stiller, madly in love since high school with Cameron Diaz, eventually wonders what has become of her, now that both have reached adulthood. He hires a private detective who decides to court the fair lady himself; as the story progresses, it seems that everybody who ever encountered Mary now wants to become a permanent part of her life. Some of the bits are hilarious, others forced and unfunny, but it's great fun for an undemanding Friday evening. Rated R for profanity and strong sexual content. 119m. **DIR:** Bobby Farrelly, Peter Farrelly. **CAST:** Cameron Diaz, Matt Dillon, Ben Stiller, Lee Evans, Chris Elliott, Jeffrey Tambor. **1998 DVD**

THEREMIN: AN ELECTRONIC ODYSSEY ★★★ Russian scientist who virtually created the field of electronic music in the 1920s and later was devastatingly suppressed by the U.S.S.R. Just as fascinating is the story of Clara Rockmore, the woman who loved Theremin and helped popularize his musical instruments. Highly unusual and intriguing on several levels. B&W/color; 85m. **DIR:** Steven M. Martin. **CAST:** Leon Theremin, Clara Rockmore, Robert Moog, Brian Wilson. **1994**

THERE'S A GIRL IN MY SOUP ★★1/2 Goldie Hawn hadn't completely shed her *Laugh-In* image when this British sex farce came out, and it didn't do her career any good. Quite a letdown, after her Oscar-

winning performance in *Cactus Flower*. Peter Sellers is a middle-aged boob who falls in lust with flower child Hawn. A low point for all concerned. Rated R. 95m. **DIR:** Roy Boulting. **CAST:** Peter Sellers, Goldie Hawn, Diana Dors, Tony Britton. **1970**

THERE'S NO BUSINESS LIKE SHOW BUSINESS ★★ Even the strength of the cast can't save this marginally entertaining musical comedy about a show-biz family. Irving Berlin's tunes and Monroe's scenes are the only redeeming qualities in this one. 117m. **DIR:** Walter Lang. **CAST:** Ethel Merman, Dan Dailey, Marilyn Monroe, Donald O'Connor, Johnnie Ray, Mitzi Gaynor, Hugh O'Brian, Frank McHugh. **1954**

THERE'S NOTHING OUT THERE ★★★ Independent filmmaker Rolf Kanefsky sends up haunted house, hockey-mask groaners. His teens visiting a cabin in the middle of nowhere are in for a surprise. Sure, there's the alien creature patroling the woods, but there's also plenty of humor. One low-budget entry that defies its origins. Not rated; contains nudity and adult language. 91m. **DIR:** Rolf Kanefsky. **CAST:** Craig Peck, Wendy Bednarz, John Carhart III. **1990**

THERESE ★★★★1/2 French director Alain Cavalier's breathtakingly beautiful film is the story of St. Theresa of Lisieux, who entered a Carmelite nunnery in the late nineteenth century at the age of 15 and lived there for eight years until she died of tuberculosis. She was declared a saint by Pope Pius XI in 1925, twenty-eight years after her death. In French with English subtitles. 90m. **DIR:** Alain Cavalier. **CAST:** Catherine Mouchet, Helene Alexandridis. **1986**

THERESE AND ISABELLE (1967) ★★★ Tender, gorgeously filmed tale of young love in a French private school. As the new girl in school, Therese finds herself an outsider. When she meets Isabelle, she finds a friend and then a lover as she explores her sexual desires. One of the first films to deal openly with lesbian relationships, this blast from the past is both titillating and honest in its portrayal of the subject matter. Not rated; contains nudity. B&W; 118m. **DIR:** Radley Metzger. **CAST:** Essy Presson, Anna Gael, Barbara Laage, Anne Vernon. **1967**

THESE GIRLS WON'T TALK ★★ As a series of three silent short stories, this Mack Sennett–produced series is short of inspiration. The shorts are called *Her Bridal Nightmare*, *Campus Carmen*, and *As Luck Would Have It*. The most interesting thing about this compilation is seeing Carole Lombard long before she was a star. B&W; 50m. **DIR:** Mack Sennett. **CAST:** Colleen Moore, Carole Lombard, Betty Compson. **1920**

THESE THREE ★★★★ A superb cast brings alive this story of two upright and decent schoolteachers victimized by the lies of a malicious student. Miriam Hopkins and Merle Oberon are the pair brutally slandered; Bonita Granville is the evil liar. Script by Lillian Hellman, loosely based on her play *The Children's Hour*, under which title the film was remade in 1961. B&W; 93m. **DIR:** William Wyler. **CAST:** Miriam Hopkins, Merle Oberon, Joel McCrea, Bonita Granville, Marcia Mae Jones. **1936**

•**THESIS** ★★★★ A young university student searches for extreme examples of violence in the media—the subject of her thesis. She gets more than she asks for when she comes across a snuff film in which the murder of a young woman is actually captured on video. The tension escalates when she realizes that the victim was just one of many female students missing from her university, and some of the faculty must be involved. In Spanish with English subtitles. Rated R for violence. 121m. **DIR:** Alejandro Amenabar. **CAST:** Ana Torrent, Fele Martinez, Eduardo Noriega, Nieves Herranz. **1996 DVD**

THEY (THEY WATCH) ★★★ Rudyard Kipling's eerie short story gets stretched too far in this study of a distraught father (Patrick Bergin) who can't stop grieving for his dead daughter. He's got good reason, since the girl's spirit seems to be trapped in a house owned by weird southern mystic Vanessa Redgrave. Although everybody tries hard, there's just not enough plot to keep this feature going. Rated PG. 100m. **DIR:** John Korty. **CAST:** Patrick Bergin, Vanessa Redgrave, Valerie Mahaffey. **1993**

THEY ALL LAUGHED ★★★★ This is director Peter Bogdanovich at his best. A very offbeat comedy that looks at four New York private eyes' adventures and love lives. Final film of ex–Playboy bunny Dorothy Stratten. Worth a look. Rated PG. 115m. **DIR:** Peter Bogdanovich. **CAST:** Audrey Hepburn, Ben Gazzara, John Ritter, Dorothy Stratten. **1981**

•**THEY BITE** ★★ Cheesy low-budget chiller echoes *Horror of Party Beach* with its tale of scaly sea creatures that are really from outer space. The effects are cheap and the acting passable, but it is all in good fun. Rated R for gore, violence, and nudity. 96m. **DIR:** Brett Piper. **CAST:** Donna Frotscher, Charlie Barnett, Ron Jeremy, Susie Owens. **1995**

THEY CALL IT SIN ★★1/2 A four-sided romance that uses top character stars to play stereotypes. The heroine is engaged to a womanizer, fights off an aging playboy, and cries on the shoulder of an uptight doctor in her search for lasting romance. Good but not great. B&W; 75m. **DIR:** Thornton Freeland. **CAST:** Loretta Young, George Brent, David Manners, Louis Calhern, Una Merkel, Helen Vinson, Nella Walker. **1932**

THEY CALL ME BRUCE? ★★ In this unsophisticated kung fu comedy, Johnny Yune portrays an Asian immigrant who, because of his "resemblance" to Bruce Lee and an accidental exhibition of craziness (misinterpreted as martial arts expertise), gets a reputation as a mean man with fists and feet. But it is Ralph Mauro, playing Bruce's chauffeur, who steals the show. Rated PG. 88m. **DIR:** Elliot Hong. **CAST:** Johnny Yune, Ralph Mauro, Margaux Hemingway. **1982**

THEY CALL ME MISTER TIBBS ★★★ An inferior follow-up, this contains the further adventures of the character Sidney Poitier created for the film *In the Heat of the Night.* Detective Virgil Tibbs is again investigating a murder and trying to clear his friend, as well. Rated PG—contains strong language and some violence. 108m. **DIR:** Gordon Douglas. **CAST:** Sidney Poitier, Barbara McNair, Martin Landau. **1970**

THEY CALL ME TRINITY ★★1/2 This Western-comedy can be best described as an Italian *Blazing Saddles.* Terence Hill and Bud Spencer team up as half brothers trying to protect a colony from cattle rustlers and a shady sheriff. Rated G. 109m. **DIR:** E. B. Clucher. **CAST:** Terence Hill, Bud Spencer, Farley Granger. **1971 DVD**

THEY CAME FROM BEYOND SPACE ★★★ Enjoyable tale of formless aliens landing in Cornwall and taking over the minds and bodies of a group of scientists in an effort to preserve their dissipating race. Robert Hutton plays the one man who can't be controlled because of a metal plate in his skull. Based on *The Gods Hate Kansas* by Joseph Millard. 86m. **DIR:** Freddie Francis. **CAST:** Robert Hutton, Jennifer Jayne, Zia Mohyeddin, Bernard Kay, Michael Gough. **1967**

THEY CAME FROM WITHIN ★★★ This is David Cronenberg's commercial feature-film debut. Even at this early stage in his career, his preoccupation with violence and biological rebellion is very much in evidence. Slimy, disgusting parasites invade the sterile orderliness of a high-rise apartment complex, turning the inhabitants into raving sex maniacs. Rated R. 87m. **DIR:** David Cronenberg. **CAST:** Paul Hampton, Joe Silver, Lynn Lowry, Barbara Steele. **1975**

THEY CAME TO CORDURA ★★ This film, which examines the true character of the war hero, is not one of Gary Cooper's best. The story has Cooper in Mexico during World War I as one of six military men returning to base. The hardships they encounter on the way create the drama. The movie has a nice look, but just not enough action. 123m. **DIR:** Robert Rossen. **CAST:** Gary Cooper, Rita Hayworth, Van Heflin, Tab Hunter, Richard Conte. **1959**

THEY DIED WITH THEIR BOOTS ON ★★★★ Errol Flynn gives a first-rate performance as General George Custer in this Warner Bros. classic directed by Raoul Walsh. The superb supporting cast adds to this Western epic. B&W; 138m. **DIR:** Raoul Walsh. **CAST:** Errol Flynn, Olivia de Havilland, Arthur Kennedy, Gene Lockhart, Anthony Quinn, Sydney Greenstreet. **1941**

THEY DO IT WITH MIRRORS ★★★ When told there is something very strange going on at a childhood friend's country estate (which serves as a reform institution for young criminals), Miss Marple promptly pays a visit. Numerous scene shifts and a large cast make this BBC Agatha Christie adaptation unnecessarily convoluted and confusing. Not rated; suitable for family viewing. 100m. **DIR:** Norman Stone. **CAST:** Joan Hickson, Jean Simmons, Joss Ackland, Faith Brook, Gillian Barge, David Horovitch. **1991**

THEY DRIVE BY NIGHT ★★★★ Here's a Warner Bros. gem! George Raft and Humphrey Bogart star as truck-driving brothers who cope with crooked bosses while wooing Ann Sheridan and Ida Lupino. The dialogue is terrific, and the direction by Raoul Walsh is crisp. B&W; 93m. **DIR:** Raoul Walsh. **CAST:** George Raft, Humphrey Bogart, Ann Sheridan, Ida Lupino. **1940**

THEY GOT ME COVERED ★★1/2 Typical Bob Hope vehicle of the 1940s is full of gals, gags, goofy situations, snappy dialogue, and one-line zingers, and boasts an incredible supporting cast of great character actors and actresses. Thin story about spy nonsense in Washington, D.C., is secondary to the zany antics of Paramount's ski-nosed comedian. B&W; 95m. **DIR:** David Butler. **CAST:** Bob Hope, Dorothy Lamour, Lenore Aubert, Otto Preminger, Eduardo Ciannelli, Marion Martin, Donald MacBride, Donald Meek, Philip Ahn. **1943 DVD**

THEY KNEW WHAT THEY WANTED ★★★ This film is a fine example of offbeat casting that somehow succeeds. Charles Laughton and Carole Lombard were required to submerge their usual histrionics in order to bring off a low-key little tragedy. The story is of the unrequited love of an Italian wine grower for the opportunistic hash house waitress that he marries. B&W; 96m. **DIR:** Garson Kanin. **CAST:** Charles Laughton, Carole Lombard, William Gargan, Harry Carey. **1940**

THEY LIVE ★★ The first two-thirds of this science-fiction–horror hybrid is such harebrained fun that one is truly disappointed when it falls apart at the end. Roddy Piper is a drifter in the not-so-distant future who discovers that the human population of Earth is being hypnotized into subservience by alien-created television signals. Rated R for nudity and violence. 95m. **DIR:** John Carpenter. **CAST:** Roddy Piper, Keith David, Meg Foster. **1988 DVD**

THEY LIVE BY NIGHT ★★★1/2 A seminal film dealing with youth, alienation, and the concept of the loner who operates outside the confines of conventional behavior and morality. This postwar crime drama gave American youth a minor cultural folk hero in Farley Granger and began the directing career of young Nicholas Ray, who would in turn provide the world with the ultimate image of teenage alienation: *Rebel Without a Cause*. B&W; 95m. **DIR:** Nicholas Ray. **CAST:** Farley Granger, Cathy O'Donnell, Howard DaSilva, Jay C. Flippen. **1949**

THEY MADE ME A CRIMINAL ★★1/2 John Garfield's film persona is a direct result of this Warner Bros. story about the redemption of a loner on the lam from the law for a crime he didn't commit. A great cast still doesn't change the fact that this remake of 1933s *The Life of Jimmy Dolan* is muddled and not too solidly constructed. B&W; 92m. **DIR:** Busby Berkeley. **CAST:** John Garfield, Claude Rains, Ann Sheridan, Gloria Dickson, The Dead End Kids, Ward Bond. **1939 DVD**

THEY MEET AGAIN ★★ In this film, the last in the popular Dr. Christian series about a snoopy small-town doctor, genial Jean Hersholt is upset because a man he feels is innocent is serving time. The good doctor finds out who embezzled the missing money. B&W; 69m. **DIR:** Erle C. Kenton. **CAST:** Jean Hersholt, Robert Baldwin, Neil Hamilton, Dorothy Lovett, Arthur Hoyt. **1941**

THEY MET IN BOMBAY ★★★ Clark Gable and Rosalind Russell are jewel thieves pursued from Bombay to Hong Kong. He is mistaken for a British officer and becomes a reluctant war hero in this odd mixture of light comedy and action-drama. The stars are fun to watch. B&W; 93m. **DIR:** Clarence Brown. **CAST:** Clark Gable, Rosalind Russell, Peter Lorre, Jessie Ralph, Reginald Owen, Eduardo Ciannelli. **1941**

THEY MIGHT BE GIANTS ★★★★ Stylish and engaging study of a retired judge (George C. Scott) who imagines himself to be Sherlock Holmes. With visions of dollar-signs floating before his eyes, the judge's brother hopes to have this ersatz detective committed; to this end, the brother brings in a female psychiatrist whose name happens to be—you guessed it—Watson. Rated PG. 88m. **DIR:** Anthony Harvey. **CAST:** George C. Scott, Joanne Woodward, Jack Gilford. **1971 DVD**

THEY ONLY KILL THEIR MASTERS ★★★ Pretty solid whodunit (if a bit TV-ish), with James Garner terrific as always, playing a small-town California sheriff. He solves a pregnant woman's murder. The title refers to a deadly Doberman pinscher. Rated PG. 97m. **DIR:** James Goldstone. **CAST:** James Garner, Katharine Ross, Hal Holbrook, Harry Guardino, June Allyson, Peter Lawford, Edmond O'Brien, Arthur O'-Connell, Christopher Connelly, Tom Ewell, Ann Rutherford. **1972**

THEY SAVED HITLER'S BRAIN 🎗 This bargain-basement bomb is actually a used movie since a major portion of it was lifted from an entirely different film made ten years earlier. B&W; 74m. **DIR:** David Bradley. **CAST:** Walter Stocker, Audrey Caire, Carlos Rivas, John Holland, Marshall Reed, Nestor Paiva. **1963 DVD**

THEY SHALL HAVE MUSIC ★★★ Good cast and great music increase the appeal of this attempt to make concert violinist Jascha Heifetz a film star. Simple plot has a group of poor kids convincing him to play a benefit and save Walter Brennan's music school in the slums. B&W; 101m. **DIR:** Archie Mayo. **CAST:** Jascha Heifetz, Joel McCrea, Andrea Leeds, Walter Brennan, Marjorie Main, Porter Hall. **1939**

THEY SHOOT HORSES, DON'T THEY? ★★★★★ The desperation and hopelessness of the Great Depression are graphically shown in this powerful drama, through a pitiful collection of marathon dancers. Some of the group will endure this physical and mental assault on their human spirit; some will not. Jane Fonda, as a cynical casualty of the Depression, and Gig Young, as the uncaring master of ceremonies, give stunning performances. Rated PG. 121m. **DIR:** Sydney Pollack. **CAST:** Jane Fonda, Gig Young, Michael Sarrazin. **1969 DVD**

THEY STILL CALL ME BRUCE 🎗 Perhaps one of the least-anticipated sequels ever, this attempt by Korean comic Johnny Yune to follow up his 1982 nonhit *They Call Me Bruce?* is completely hopeless. It's rated PG for Yune's occasionally off-color humor. 91m. **DIR:** Johnny Yune, James Orr. **CAST:** Johnny Yune, David Mendenhall, Joey Travolta. **1987**

THEY WENT THAT-A-WAY AND THAT-A-WAY ★★ Tim Conway wrote and stars in this comedy. He plays a small-town deputy who follows the governor's orders by being secretly placed in a maximum-security prison as an undercover agent. Fellow deputy (Chuck McCann) is his partner. When the governor suddenly dies, the two must escape from the prison. There are some silly gags, but this film does provide a few laughs and no deep plots. Rated PG. 106m. **DIR:** Edward Montagne, Stuart E. McGowan. **CAST:** Tim Conway, Chuck McCann, Reni Santoni, Richard Kiel, Dub Taylor. **1978**

THEY WERE EXPENDABLE ★★★★1/2 First-rate action-drama about American PT boat crews fighting a losing battle against advancing Japanese forces in the Philippines. Director John Ford based this film, his most personal, on his war experiences and the people he knew in the conflict. No phony heroics or glory here, but a realistic, bleak, and ultimately inspiring picture of men in war. B&W; 136m. DIR: John Ford. CAST: John Wayne, Robert Montgomery, Donna Reed, Jack Holt, Ward Bond, Marshall Thompson, Louis Jean Heydt. 1945 DVD

THEY WON'T BELIEVE ME ★★★1/2 Robert Young is a grade-A stinker in this classic *film noir* of deceit, mistaken murder, suicide, and doomed romance. Rita Johnson is especially fine as the wronged wife. B&W; 95m. DIR: Irving Pichel. CAST: Robert Young, Susan Hayward, Jane Greer, Rita Johnson, Tom Powers, Don Beddoe, Frank Ferguson. 1947

THEY'RE PLAYING WITH FIRE 💔 A high school student is seduced by a teacher in this gobbler. Rated R. 96m. DIR: Howard Avedis. CAST: Sybil Danning, Eric Brown, Andrew Prine. 1983

THICKER THAN WATER ★★★1/2 An intriguing use of vignettes, combined with the talents of Jonathan Pryce and Theresa Russell, rescue this BBC thriller from narrative hell. She plays telepathic twins, one of whom is happily married. The other twin is, naturally, rather naughty. The film is too long and is weakened by a switch in the focus from one of the twins to Pryce. Honest, well-written dialogue and bold editing ease some of the narrative flaws. Not rated; contains profanity and violence. 150m. DIR: Marc Evans. CAST: Theresa Russell, Jonathan Pryce. 1993 DVD

THIEF, THE (1952) ★★1/2 A scientist for the Atomic Energy Commission tries to flee the country when the FBI discovers he's been selling information to enemy spies. Filmed entirely without dialogue, this *noir* thriller has strong visuals and an intense performance by Ray Milland, but the silence becomes a burdensome gimmick before long. B&W; 87m. DIR: Russell Rouse. CAST: Ray Milland, Martin Gabel, Rita Gam. 1952

THIEF (1981) ★★★★ James Caan stars in this superb study of a jewel thief. Caan's character tries desperately to create the life he visualized while in prison—one complete with a car, money, house, wife, and kids. But as soon as he manages to acquire these things, they start slipping away. It's an interesting plot, and Michael Mann's direction gives it a sense of realism. Visually stunning, with a great score by Tangerine Dream. Rated R for violence, language, and brief nudity. 122m. DIR: Michael Mann. CAST: James Caan, Tuesday Weld, James Belushi, Willie Nelson. 1981 DVD

THIEF, THE (1997) ★★★★ Homeless woman with a young son meets a soldier on a train in Stalin's Russia and falls in love. Then a dark side seeps through his air of respectability that threatens to destroy them all. This entrancing story uses domestic dynamics as a metaphor for a political system that cannibalizes its own people. In Russian with English subtitles. Rated R for violence, language, and sexual content. 93m. DIR: Pavel Chukhrai. CAST: Yehaterina Rednikova, Vladimir Mashkov, Misha Philipchuk. 1997 DVD

THIEF OF BAGDAD, THE (1924) ★★★1/2 The first of four spectacular versions of this classic Arabian Nights–ish fantasy-adventure of derring-do with magically flying carpets, giant genies, and crafty evil sorcery. The now-fabled Douglas Fairbanks Sr. is the thief, Julanne Johnson the beautiful princess he carries away on an airborne rug. Of all silent epics, this one is rated the most imaginative. The sets rival everything filmed before and since. Silent. B&W; 140m. DIR: Raoul Walsh. CAST: Douglas Fairbanks Sr., Julanne Johnson, Anna May Wong, Sojin. 1924 DVD

THIEF OF BAGDAD, THE (1940) ★★★★★ With its flying carpets, giant genies, magic spells, and evil wizards, this film ranks as one of the finest fantasy films of all time. John Justin plays a young king, Ahmad, who is duped by his Grand Vizier, Jaffar, and loses his throne. With the aid of a colossal genie (excellently played by Rex Ingram) and other magical devices, Ahmad must do battle with Jaffar in a rousing fairy tale of good versus evil. 106m. DIR: Ludwig Berger, Tim Whelan, Michael Powell. CAST: Sabu, John Justin, June Duprez, Rex Ingram, Conrad Veidt. 1940

THIEF OF BAGHDAD (1978) ★★ A passable television version of the Arabian Nights fable made bland by low-budget special effects but offset, if marginally, by an excellent cast. Not rated, it's certainly suitable for family viewing. 100m. DIR: Clive Donner. CAST: Peter Ustinov, Terence Stamp, Roddy McDowall, Ian Holm, Pavla Ustinov. 1978

THIEF OF HEARTS ★★★ A young, upwardly mobile married woman loses her intimate diary of sexual fantasies to a thief who has broken into her home. In an interesting premise, the woman becomes a willing participant in the thief's sexual manipulations without knowing that he is the man who stole her secrets. Rated R. 100m. DIR: Douglas Day Stewart. CAST: Steven Bauer, Barbara Williams. 1984

THIEF WHO CAME TO DINNER, THE ★★★ Silly stuff about Ryan O'Neal leading a double life: as a bookish computer programmer by day and a jewel thief by night. The film's most interesting performance comes from Jill Clayburgh in an early screen role. It's mindless fluff and inoffensive. Rated PG. 102m. DIR: Bud Yorkin. CAST: Ryan O'Neal, Jacqueline Bisset, Warren Oates, Jill Clayburgh, Charles Cioffi, Ned Beatty. 1973

THIEVES (LES VOLEURS) ★★★1/2 Catherine Deneuve and Daniel Auteuil are scintillating in this erotic crime caper. An intelligent professor and police detective both fall under the spell of a young car thief who leads them into her world of crime and murder. Nothing is what it seems in this tale of a lovers' triangle. In French with English subtitles. Rated R for adult situations, language, nudity, and violence. 116m. DIR: André Téchiné. CAST: Catherine Deneuve, Daniel Auteuil, Laurence Cote, Benoit Magimel, Julien Riviere. 1996

THIEVES LIKE US ★★★★ A classic melodrama about gangsters that relies more on story and characters than gunfire and bloodshed. Robert Altman turns the story of survivors during the Depression into a heartfelt love story with sensitive acting and exceptional production values. It plays like a documentary and looks like a movie because of Altman's unique storytelling style. Rated R. 123m. DIR: Robert Altman. CAST: Keith Carradine, Shelley Duvall, Louise

Fletcher, Bert Remsen, Tom Skerritt, John Schuck. **1974**

THIEVES OF FORTUNE ★★1/2 Shawn Weatherly attempts to win a $28 million bet that involves outrageous cliff-hanging stunts. Rated R for language and violence. 100m. **DIR:** Michael McCarthy. **CAST:** Michael Nouri, Shawn Weatherly, Lee Van Cleef, Liz Torres. **1989**

THIN BLUE LINE, THE ★★★★ Fascinating look into the 1976 murder of a Dallas policeman that led to a highly debated conviction of a drifter. Filmmaker Errol Morris's terrifying account of this incident raises some serious questions about the misuse of our current justice system. Not rated. 90m. **DIR:** Errol Morris. **1988**

THIN ICE ★★★★ One of Sonja Henie's most successful films. She stars as an ice-skating teacher who meets a European prince traveling in her country incognito. Naturally, they fall in love and she helps him solve his political problems. Of course, she also skates well. One of the movie's highlights is the performance of comedienne Joan Davis as an orchestra leader. B&W; 78m. **DIR:** Sidney Lanfield. **CAST:** Sonja Henie, Tyrone Power, Joan Davis, Arthur Treacher, Raymond Walburn, Alan Hale Sr., Sig Ruman, Leah Ray. **1937**

THIN LINE BETWEEN LOVE AND HATE, A ★★ Never say "I love you" to a lady—no matter what the circumstance—is the rule that a slick womanizer makes, breaks, and then pays for heavily in this sporadically comic, crude *Fatal Attraction*. The film tries to be both a hip, bawdy sitcom and a film with real heart as two partners in crimes of the heart use their jobs as nightclub promoters to score dates. Rated R for language and violence. 97m. **DIR:** Martin Lawrence. **CAST:** Martin Lawrence, Bobby Brown, Lynn Whitfield, Regina King, Della Reese. **1996 DVD**

THIN MAN, THE ★★★★1/2 Viewers and critics alike were captivated by William Powell and Myrna Loy in this first (and best) of a series based on Dashiell Hammett's mystery novel about his "other" detective and wife, Nick and Nora Charles. The thin man is a murder victim. But never mind. The delight of this fun film is the banter between its stars. You'll like their little dog, too. B&W; 89m. **DIR:** W. S. Van Dyke. **CAST:** William Powell, Myrna Loy, Edward Brophy, Porter Hall, Maureen O'Sullivan. **1934**

THIN MAN GOES HOME, THE ★★1/2 Fifth and weakest entry in the series. Nick Charles (William Powell) returns to his old hometown, accompanied by Nora (Myrna Loy) and young Nick Jr. Still entertaining, but a lesser effort. B&W; 101m. **DIR:** Richard Thorpe. **CAST:** William Powell, Myrna Loy, Lucile Watson, Gloria De Haven, Anne Revere, Helen Vinson, Harry Davenport, Leon Ames, Donald Meek, Edward Brophy. **1944**

THIN RED LINE, THE ★★★ Eclectic director-scripter Terence Malick's ponderous style destroys any dramatic impact in this dull WWII-based drama, adapted from James Jones's novel. It's wrapped in artificially symbolic narration, needlessly melancholy cinematography, and far too much time wasted on atmosphere-establishing shots. You're left with a film that apparently *knows* that it's pretentious.

Rated R for violence, profanity, and the charnel-house atrocities of war. 170m. **DIR:** Terence Malick. **CAST:** Sean Penn, Nick Nolte, Adrien Brody, Jim Caviezel, Ben Chaplin, Arie Verveen, Dash Mihok. **1998 DVD**

THING (FROM ANOTHER WORLD), THE (1951) ★★★★ A highly entertaining film, this was based on a John W. Campbell's story about a hostile visitor from space at large at an army radar station in the Arctic. Considered by many to be a classic, this relies on the unseen rather than the seen for its power, and as such it is almost unbearably suspenseful. James Arness, in an early role, plays the monster. B&W; 87m. **DIR:** Christian Nyby. **CAST:** Kenneth Tobey, Margaret Sheridan, James Arness. **1951**

THING, THE (1982) ★★★★ The modern master of fright, John Carpenter, has created a movie so terrifying, it'll crawl right up your leg. Rather than a remake, this updated version of Howard Hawks's 1951 science-fiction–horror classic is closer to a sequel, with Kurt Russell and his crew arriving at the Antarctic encampment after the chameleon-like creature from outer space has finished off its inhabitants. It's good ol' "tell me a scary story" fun. Rated R for profanity and gore. 108m. **DIR:** John Carpenter. **CAST:** Kurt Russell, Wilford Brimley, Richard Dysart. **1982 DVD**

THING CALLED LOVE, THE ★★★1/2 River Phoenix, in his last role, is well cast as a frustrated singer trying to make it in Nashville. Director Peter Bogdanovich's film follows four young aspiring stars, and the exciting cast, fleshed out by real country stars, turns up the heat on and off the stage. Rated PG-13 for adult language and situations. 116m. **DIR:** Peter Bogdanovich. **CAST:** River Phoenix, Samantha Mathis, Sandra Bullock, Dermot Mulroney. **1993**

THING THAT COULDN'T DIE, THE ✿ Severed head of a devil worshiper takes over the minds of those who dig it up from its ancient tomb. B&W; 69m. **DIR:** Will Cowan. **CAST:** William Reynolds, Andra Martin, Carolyn Kearney. **1958**

THINGS ARE TOUGH ALL OVER ✿ Richard "Cheech" Marin and Tommy Chong up to no good. Rated R for profanity. 92m. **DIR:** Tom Avildsen. **CAST:** Cheech and Chong, Rikki Marin, Rip Taylor. **1982**

THINGS CHANGE ★★★★ Director David Mamet and his coscreenwriter, Shel Silverstein, have fashioned a marvelously subtle and witty comedy about an inept, low-level gangster (Joe Mantegna). He goes against orders to take an old shoe-shine "boy" (Don Ameche) on one last fling before the latter goes to prison for a crime he didn't commit. Rated PG for profanity and violence. 100m. **DIR:** David Mamet. **CAST:** Don Ameche, Joe Mantegna, Robert Prosky. **1988 DVD**

THINGS TO COME ★★★★ The world of the future as viewed from the perspective of the 1930s, this is an interesting screen curio based on the book by H. G. Wells. Special effects have come a long way since then, but sci-fi fans will still enjoy the spectacular sets in this honorable, thoughtful production. B&W; 92m. **DIR:** William Cameron Menzies. **CAST:** Raymond Massey, Cedric Hardwicke, Ralph Richardson. **1936 DVD**

THINGS TO DO IN DENVER WHEN YOU'RE DEAD ★★★1/2 Although this slick entry in the wiseguy-noir subgenre is an obvious imitation of *Pulp Fiction*, scripter Scott Rosenberg has a lot of fun with the hard-luck gangsters populating his story. When smooth-talking Jimmy the Saint and his gang muff an easy assignment, there's hell to pay ... but at least they go out with style. Rated R for violence and profanity. 117m. **DIR:** Gary Fleder. **CAST:** Andy Garcia, Christopher Walken, William Forsythe, Christopher Lloyd, Bill Nunn, Treat Williams, Gabrielle Anwar. 1995 DVD

THINGS WE DID LAST SUMMER ★★1/2 A mixed bag used to supplement *Saturday Night Live* episodes in the show's first golden era, this features some of The Not Ready For Prime Time Players in skits of varying quality. The highlights are provided by John Belushi and Dan Aykroyd performing live in concert as the Blues Brothers. 50m. **DIR:** Gary Weis. **CAST:** John Belushi, Dan Aykroyd, Bill Murray, Gilda Radner, Garrett Morris, Laraine Newman. 1977

THINK BIG ★★1/2 The perpetually late Barbarian Brothers (Peter and David Paul) are sent to L.A. to deliver a truckload of toxic waste, and a stowaway throws a wrench into their gears. Surprisingly good-natured in the dubious tradition of the all-star *Gumball Rally/Cannonball Run* films. PG-13. 86m. **DIR:** Jon Turteltaub. **CAST:** Martin Mull, Richard Moll, Michael Winslow, David Carradine, Richard Kiel, Ari Meyers, Claudia Christian, Peter Paul, David Paul. 1988

THINK FAST, MR. MOTO ★★★ German actor Peter Lorre may have seemed an odd choice to play a Japanese detective, but he was so popular in this film that seven sequels were made in two years, and Mr. Moto nearly eclipsed Charlie Chan. Here he's on the trail of jewel smugglers on a ship to Shanghai. B&W; 66m. **DIR:** Norman Foster. **CAST:** Peter Lorre, Virginia Field, Sig Ruman, J. Carrol Naish. 1937

THINKIN' BIG ★★ Soft-core beach romp with the usual horny teens heading for spring-break fun in the sun. Rated R for nudity. 94m. **DIR:** S. F. Brownrigg. **CAST:** Bruce Anderson, Nancy Buechler. 1986

THINNER ★★ Stephen King's skinny horror novel (under the pen name Richard Bachman) was funnier and scarier as a quick midnight read. Chubby Maine attorney Billy Halleck is getting oral sex from his wife while driving in a rainstorm when he runs over an elderly gypsy woman. Billy's judge and cop buddies keep him out of jail, but the woman's ancient father puts a curse on him that makes him lose weight no matter how much he eats. Rated R for violence, gore, language, and sexual references. 92m. **DIR:** Tom Holland. **CAST:** Robert Burke, Joe Mantegna, Lucinda Jenney, Joy Lenz, Michael Constantine. 1996 DVD

THIRD DEGREE BURN ★★★ Debt-ridden ex-cop reluctantly accepts a domestic investigation, only to fall headlong for the blonde subject. (Virginia Madsen is the perfect Monroe-like sex bomb.) Steamy mystery twists like a snake. Made for HBO. 97m. **DIR:** Roger Spottiswoode. **CAST:** Treat Williams, Virginia Madsen, C.C.H. Pounder, Richard Masur. 1989

THIRD MAN, THE ★★★★★ Considered by many to be the greatest suspense film of all time, this classic inevitably turns up on every best-film list. It rivals any Hitchcock thriller as being the ultimate master piece of film suspense. A writer (Joseph Cotten) discovers an old friend he thought dead to be the head of a vicious European black market organization. Unfortunately for him, that information makes him a marked man. B&W; 104m. **DIR:** Carol Reed. **CAST:** Joseph Cotten, Orson Welles, Alida Valli, Trevor Howard. 1949 DVD

THIRD MAN ON THE MOUNTAIN ★★★ James MacArthur stars as a young man whose father was killed in a climbing accident. The Citadel (actually the Matterhorn) has never been scaled. Miraculously, he finds the secret passage his father had been seeking. Breathtaking scenery and an excellent script make this an excellent adventure story for the family. Not rated. 106m. **DIR:** Ken Annakin. **CAST:** Michael Rennie, James MacArthur, Janet Munro, Herbert Lom. 1959

●**THIRD MIRACLE, THE** ★★★★ A priest investigates a candidate for sainthood while grappling with his own crisis of faith; meanwhile, he is strongly attracted to the candidate's daughter, who has her own doubts about her late mother's saintliness. This strong, subtle drama deals intelligently with issues of faith and cynicism, with fine acting throughout. Rated R for mature themes, brief profanity, and violence. 119m. **DIR:** Agnieszka Holland. **CAST:** Ed Harris, Anne Heche, Barbara Sukowa, Armin Mueller-Stahl. 1999 DVD

THIRD SOLUTION, THE ♥ Don't let the (usually) talented cast sucker you into sampling this laughably convoluted, poorly dubbed Italian political melodrama. Rated R for violence and brief nudity. 113m. **DIR:** Pasquale Squiteri. **CAST:** F. Murray Abraham, Treat Williams, Danny Aiello, Rita Rusic. 1989

THIRST ♥ An innocent young woman is kidnapped by a Satanic brotherhood and subjected to diabolical torture. Rated R for nudity and violence. 96m. **DIR:** Rod Hardy. **CAST:** Chantal Contouri, David Hemmings, Henry Silva, Rod Mullinar. 1988

THIRSTY DEAD, THE ♥ Charles Mansonesque figure lives in the jungle and sacrifices young women in bloody rituals. Rated PG. 90m. **DIR:** Terry Becker. **CAST:** John Considine, Jennifer Billingsley. 1975

THIS BOY'S LIFE ★★★ Young Tobias Wolff is trapped when his mother tries to do the right thing by marrying "a good provider." The boy's life slowly becomes a nightmare. Screenwriter Robert Getchell's adaptation of Wolff's autobiographical book skimps on character depth, leaving us a good—but not great—film. Rated R for profanity, violence, nudity, and simulated sex. 114m. **DIR:** Michael Caton-Jones. **CAST:** Robert De Niro, Ellen Barkin, Leonardo DiCaprio, Chris Cooper. 1993

THIS COULD BE THE NIGHT ★★★ A timid schoolteacher becomes a secretary to two nightclub owners and finds herself pursued by one of them. A fair try at a Damon Runyon atmosphere. Joan Blondell and J. Carrol Naish steal the movie. B&W; 103m. **DIR:** Robert Wise. **CAST:** Jean Simmons, Paul Douglas, Anthony Franciosa, Julie Wilson, Joan Blondell, J. Carrol Naish, ZaSu Pitts. 1957

THIS GUN FOR HIRE (1942) ★★★★ Alan Ladd made his first big impression in this 1942 gangster film as a bad guy who turns good guy in the end. Robert Preston and Veronica Lake costar in this still enjoyable revenge film. B&W; 80m. DIR: Frank Tuttle. CAST: Alan Ladd, Robert Preston, Veronica Lake. **1942**

THIS GUN FOR HIRE (1991) ★★★ Graham Greene's moody thriller gets another go-around, this time with Robert Wagner reprising the role that made Alan Ladd a star. Wagner's implacable hired gunman who finds his soul at the wrong moment. Greene's cynical view of humanity remains seductive. Made for cable TV. Rated R for violence and sexual themes. 89m. DIR: Lou Antonio. CAST: Robert Wagner, Nancy Everhard, Fredric Lehne, John Harkins. **1991**

THIS HAPPY BREED ★★★★ Slice of British nostalgia chronicles the lives of a working-class family from 1919 to 1939. Adapted from a Noel Coward play, this is an extraordinary film of collector caliber. 114m. DIR: David Lean. CAST: Robert Newton, Celia Johnson, John Mills, Kay Walsh, Stanley Holloway. **1944**

THIS HAPPY FEELING ★★ Curt Jurgens is an aging actor, Debbie Reynolds is the young girl who develops a crush on him, and John Saxon is Jurgens's handsome young neighbor who falls hard for Reynolds. The film is truly reflective of the 1950s, with its unreal colors and a musical score inundating every scene. Alexis Smith as "the other woman" is enjoyable. 92m. DIR: Blake Edwards. CAST: Debbie Reynolds, Curt Jurgens, John Saxon, Alexis Smith, Mary Astor, Estelle Winwood, Troy Donahue. **1958**

THIS IS AMERICA, CHARLIE BROWN ★★★1/2 This eight-part miniseries employs the Peanuts gang to teach viewers about seminal moments in American history, from the Mayflower voyages and signing of the Constitution, to a NASA space station and an overview of American music. The soundtracks are superbly scored by jazz greats such as Dave Brubeck, Wynton Marsalis, George Winston, and David Benoit. Sadly, the uneven animation occasionally spoils the package. Not rated. Each 25m. DIR: Evert Brown, Sam Jaimes, Bill Melendez, Sam Nicholson. **1988**

THIS IS ELVIS ★★★★ A blend of film footage of the "real" Elvis with other portions, played by convincing stand-ins. The result is a warm, nostalgic portrait of a man who touched the hearts of young and old throughout the world. Rated PG because of slight profanity. 101m. DIR: Malcolm Leo, Andrew Solt. CAST: Elvis Presley, David Scott, Paul Boensh III. **1981**

THIS IS MY AFFAIR ★★1/2 A turn-of-the-century melodrama produced to take advantage of the real-life romantic pairing of Robert Taylor and Barbara Stanwyck in Hollywood. He is the navy man accused of a crime. She is the saloon singer who appeals directly to President McKinley for help. B&W; 100m. DIR: William A. Seiter. CAST: Robert Taylor, Barbara Stanwyck, Brian Donlevy, Victor McLaglen, John Carradine, Sidney Blackmer. **1937**

•**THIS IS MY FATHER** ★★1/2 A middle-aged schoolteacher travels to Ireland to learn about the starcrossed courtship between his parents (Aidan Quinn, Moya Farrelly) during the 1930s. The film is a sincere, well-intentioned labor of love for the Quinn brothers (star Aidan, cinematographer Declan, and writer-director Paul) and well-acted by all, but it's also clumsy and plodding. The modern-day "framing" story is less interesting than the flashbacks. Rated R for sexual scenes and mature themes. 120m. DIR: Paul Quinn. CAST: James Caan, Aidan Quinn, Moya Farrelly, John Cusack, Jacob Tierney, Stephen Rea. **1998 DVD**

THIS IS MY LIFE ★★★ Sparkling dialogue and memorable characters help elevate this comedy about conflicting mother-daughter perspectives. The low spots involve onstage comedy routines by Mom (Julie Kavner). As with most movies about stand-up comics, these bits aren't really funny. Rated PG-13 for profanity. 94m. DIR: Nora Ephron. CAST: Julie Kavner, Samantha Mathis, Gaby Hoffman, Carrie Fisher, Dan Aykroyd. **1992**

THIS IS SPINAL TAP ★★★★1/2 This is one of the funniest movies ever made about rock 'n' roll. This is a satire of rock documentaries that tells the story of Spinal Tap, an over-the-hill British heavy-metal group that's fast rocketing to the bottom of the charts. *This Is Spinal Tap* isn't consistently funny, but does it ever have its moments. Some of the song lyrics are hysterical, and the performances are perfect. Rated R for profanity. 82m. DIR: Rob Reiner. CAST: Michael McKean, Christopher Guest, Harry Shearer, Rob Reiner. **1984**

THIS IS THE ARMY ★★★ Hoofer (later U.S. senator) George Murphy portrays Ronald Reagan's father in this musical mélange penned by Irving Berlin to raise funds for Army Emergency Relief during World War II. It's a star-studded, rousing show of songs and skits from start to finish, but practically plotless. 121m. DIR: Michael Curtiz. CAST: George Murphy, Joan Leslie, Ronald Reagan, George Tobias, Alan Hale Sr., Joe Louis, Kate Smith, Irving Berlin, Frances Langford, Charles Butterworth. **1943**

THIS IS THE SEA ★★★ This film about star-crossed lovers on opposite sides of the Irish conflict arrives too late to make an impact. Writer-director Mary McGuckian's efforts to transplant *Romeo and Juliet* in the middle of war-torn Northern Ireland fall considerably short of other recent efforts like *Some Mother's Son*. Ross McDade and Samantha Morton are the ill-fated lovers, one a Catholic, the other a Protestant, whose love affair brings about tragic consequences. Decent supporting cast includes Richard Harris and Gabriel Byrne. Rated R for language. 104m. DIR: Mary McGuckian. CAST: Gabriel Byrne, Richard Harris, John Lynch, Samantha Morton, Ross McDade. **1998**

THIS ISLAND EARTH ★★★ A fine 1950s sci-fi flick about scientists kidnapped by aliens to help them save their planet, this has good makeup and effects for the era. 86m. DIR: Joseph M. Newman. CAST: Jeff Morrow, Rex Reason, Faith Domergue, Russell Johnson. **1955 DVD**

THIS LAND IS MINE ★★★ Charles Laughton performs another fine characterization, this time as a timid French teacher who blossoms as a hero when he is incited to vigorous action by the Nazi occupation. Time has dulled this wartime film, but the artistry of the director and players remains sharp. B&W; 103m. DIR: Jean Renoir. CAST: Charles Laughton, Maureen O'Hara, George Sanders, Walter Slezak. 1943

THIS MAN CAN'T DIE ★★★ Yet another "revenge for a slaughtered family" sadistic spaghetti Western with Guy Madison as a government agent avenger on the trail of an outlaw who murdered his parents. 90m. DIR: Gianfranco Baldanello. CAST: Guy Madison, Lucienne Bridou, Rik Battaglia. 1968

THIS MAN MUST DIE ★★★★ Claude Chabrol pays homage to Alfred Hitchcock with this outstanding thriller about a man who sets out to find the hit-and-run driver responsible for the death of his son. Complications ensue as the father encounters the murderer's sister, whom he seduces. A riveting shocker with a startling climax. French, dubbed into English. 112m. DIR: Claude Chabrol. CAST: Michel Duchaussoy, Jean Yanne, Caroline Cellier. 1970

THIS PROPERTY IS CONDEMNED ★★1/2 Marginal film interpretation of Tennessee Williams's play. Owen Legate (Robert Redford) is a stranger in town, there for the purpose of laying off local railroaders. Alva (Natalie Wood) is a flirtatious southern girl who casts her spell of romance on the stranger. 109m. DIR: Sydney Pollack. CAST: Natalie Wood, Robert Redford, Charles Bronson, Kate Reid, Robert Blake. 1966

THIS SPECIAL FRIENDSHIP ★★1/2 At a boys' boarding school, a relationship between an older student and a younger, innocent boy is broken up by teachers. Once-controversial story of homoeroticism now seems merely sentimental and self-consciously sensitive. In French with English subtitles. B&W; 105m. DIR: Jean Delannoy. CAST: Francis Lacombrade, Didier Haudepin, Michel Bouquet. 1964

THIS SPORTING LIFE ★★★1/2 Richard Harris and Rachel Roberts shine in this stark, powerful look into the life and dreams of a Yorkshire coal miner who seeks to become a professional rugby player. The squeamish will not like all the game scenes. 129m. DIR: Lindsay Anderson. CAST: Rachel Roberts, Richard Harris, Colin Blakely. 1963 DVD

THIS TIME FOR KEEPS ★★★ A typical Esther Williams swimming event with more musical variety than usual pits her allure against the comedy of Jimmy Durante and the sophistication of opera-star Lauritz Melchior. On Mackinac Island Melchior's son promptly falls in love with Williams, and the movie dissolves into a series of musical numbers. More padding than plot, but the padding is classy stuff. 105m. DIR: Richard Thorpe. CAST: Esther Williams, Lauritz Melchior, Jimmy Durante, May Whitty, Johnnie Johnston, Sharon MacManus, Kenneth Tobey, Esther Dale, Ludwig Stossel, Xavier Cugat. 1947

THIS WORLD, THEN THE FIREWORKS ★★★ Decent stab at *film noir* stars Billy Zane as an investigative reporter in Chicago in the 1950s whose latest story is too hot for the local law. Filled with unsavory characters doing unsavory things to each other and a voice-over narration that pulls it all together, this film is at times dark and depressing, but never boring. Rated R for violence, language, nudity, and adult situations. 99m. DIR: Michael Oblowitz. CAST:

Billy Zane, Gina Gershon, Sheryl Lee, Rue McClanahan. 1996

THOMAS CROWN AFFAIR, THE (1968) ★★★★ Combine an engrossing bank-heist cpaer with an offbeat romance and you have the ingredients for a fun-filled movie. Steve McQueen and Faye Dunaway are at their best as the sophisticated bank robber and unscrupulous insurance investigator. The emotional tricks and verbal sparring between these two are a joy. This is one of the few films where the split-screen technique really moves the story along. 102m. DIR: Norman Jewison. CAST: Steve McQueen, Faye Dunaway, Paul Burke. 1968

•**THOMAS CROWN AFFAIR, THE (1999)** ★★★★ This striking, stylish remake succeeds on its own merits, in great part because of the playful chemistry between Pierce Brosnan and René Russo. The material is updated and reworked—and considerably more erotic—but the central premise remains intact: that of a successful corporate playboy who moonlights as an art thief, and draws the attention of a vibrantly sophisticated insurance investigator determined to nail him. The resulting capers, crosses, and double crosses are a joy: sleek and loaded with charm and savoir faire. Brosnan and Russo are perfectly suited to these characters: dueling titans who must appear icily superficial and above common worldly concerns. Director John McTiernan has crafted a delicious bit of cat-and-mouse whimsy: a worthy successor to *To Catch a Thief*, *How to Steal a Million*, and *The Thief Who Came to Dinner*. Rated R for nudity, strong sexual content, and profanity. 113m. DIR: John McTiernan. CAST: Pierce Brosnan, René Russo, Denis Leary, Ben Gazzara, Frankie Faison, Fritz Weaver, Faye Dunaway. 1999 DVD

THOMAS GRAAL'S BEST CHILD ★★★★ The best of the Thomas Graal films. Newlyweds Victor Sjöström and Karin Molander bicker about the best ways to rear their child. Among the many subjects satirized is the so-called liberated woman of contemporary Sweden. Silent. B&W; 94m. DIR: Mauritz Stiller. CAST: Victor Sjöström, Karin Molander. 1918

THOMAS GRAAL'S BEST FILM ★★★★ One of a popular series of Thomas Graal films, all starring Victor Sjöström and his wife. They all presented satiric jabs at contemporary life, much in the same way as today's television sitcoms do. In this one Graal is a screenwriter distracted by a romance with a rich man's daughter. Sweden. Silent. B&W; 67m. DIR: Mauritz Stiller. CAST: Victor Sjöström, Karin Molander. 1917

THOMAS JEFFERSON ★★★1/2 The first in a projected series of films on great Americans by Ken Burns, this two-tape documentary is similar in style to his past projects, relying on famous voices, narrated letters, and careful research. However, there are not enough interviews, the reenactments are limited to two repetitive scenes and far too many of the shots are stagnant. Burns tackles the enigma that was Jefferson, and there is much here of quality, but the overall production is not up to his usually high standards. Narrated by Ossie Davis. Not rated. 180m. DIR: Ken Burns. 1997

THOMPSON'S LAST RUN ★★★1/2 Robert Mitchum plays a criminal who is being transferred to a new prison by a school friend who chose the right side of the law and is ready to retire. Bittersweet story with solid performances by all. 95m. DIR: Jerrold Freedman. CAST: Robert Mitchum, Wilford Brimley, Kathleen York. 1986

THORNBIRDS, THE ★★★ Originally a ten-hour TV miniseries, this much-edited film is still worth a watch. Richard Chamberlain plays an ambitious priest who falls in love with an innocent, trusting young woman (Rachel Ward). It's all played out against shifting backgrounds of outback Australia, Vatican Rome, and idyllic Greece. This has been released for a limited time and copies may be hard to locate. 150m. DIR: Daryl Duke. CAST: Richard Chamberlain, Rachel Ward, Christopher Plummer, Bryan Brown, Barbara Stanwyck, Richard Kiley, Jean Simmons, John Friedrich, Philip Anglim. 1983

THOROUGHBREDS DON'T CRY ★★★ In this first teaming of Mickey Rooney and Judy Garland, he is a discredited jockey (sound familiar?), and they help a young English boy win a big race with his horse, The Pookah. Garland does get to sing, but Sophie Tucker, as her agent, is wasted in a nonsinging role. B&W; 80m. DIR: Alfred E. Green. CAST: Judy Garland, Mickey Rooney, Sophie Tucker, C. Aubrey Smith. 1937

THOROUGHLY MODERN MILLIE ★★★ First-rate music characterizing America's Jazz Age dominates this harebrained-plotted, slapstick-punctuated spoof of the 1920s, complete with villains, a bordello, and a cooing flapper so smitten with her stuffedshirt boss that she can't see her boyfriend for beans. It's toe-tapping entertainment, but a tad too long. 138m. DIR: George Roy Hill. CAST: Julie Andrews, Mary Tyler Moore, Carol Channing, James Fox, Beatrice Lillie, John Gavin, Noriyuki "Pat" Morita, Jack Soo. 1967

THOSE CALLOWAYS ★★★★ Sensitive, sentimental film about a family in New England. Man battles townspeople and nature to preserve a safe haven for geese. Marvelous scenes of life in a small town and the love between individuals. Rated G. 131m. DIR: Norman Tokar. CAST: Brian Keith, Vera Miles, Brandon de Wilde, Linda Evans. 1965

THOSE DARING YOUNG MEN IN THEIR JAUNTY JALOPIES ★★★ Director Ken Annakin's follow up to *Those Magnificent Men In Their Flying Machines* lacks that certain spark it takes to make a classic, but there are some hilarious moments in this tale of a European road rally in the 1920s. Peter Cook and Dudley Moore as two very, very British officers are the best of the international cast. Rated G. 125m. DIR: Ken Annakin. CAST: Tony Curtis, Susan Hampshire, Peter Cook, Gert Fröbe, Dudley Moore, Terry-Thomas. 1969

THOSE ENDEARING YOUNG CHARMS ★★★ Heroine Laraine Day brings smoothie Robert Young to bay and then to heel in this cliché-plotted, but sprightly played, romantic comedy. Public hunger for wholesome laughter and sentimental tears as World War II wound down made this a box-office bonanza. Ann Harding is perfect as the wise mother. B&W; 82m. DIR: Lewis Allen. CAST: Robert Young, Laraine Day, Bill Williams, Ann Harding, Anne Jeffreys, Lawrence Tierney. 1945

THOSE GLORY GLORY DAYS ★★ A group of young girls idolize the members of their school's soccer team. Tired nostalgia from the British television anthology *First Love*. 77m. DIR: Philip Saville. CAST: Julia McKenzie, Elizabeth Spriggs. 1984

THOSE LIPS, THOSE EYES ★★ So-so "let's put on a show" musical features Frank Langella as a wouldbe stage star forced to play to small towns, though he longs to appear on Broadway. Rated R for profanity and brief nudity. 106m. DIR: Michael Pressman. CAST: Frank Langella, Glynnis O'Connor, Tom Hulce, Jerry Stiller, Kevin McCarthy. 1980

THOSE MAGNIFICENT MEN IN THEIR FLYING MACHINES ★★★★ An air race between London and Paris in the early days of flight is this comedy's centerpiece. Around it hang an enjoyable number of ribtickling vignettes. A large international cast, each get their chance to shine as the contest's zany participants. Terry-Thomas stands out as the hapless villain. 132m. DIR: Ken Annakin. CAST: Terry-Thomas, Stuart Whitman, Sarah Miles, Gert Fröbe. 1965

THOU SHALT NOT KILL ... EXCEPT 🖤 A violent cult (complete with a Charles Manson look-alike) goes on a killing spree. Not rated, but has violence, profanity, and comic-book gore. 84m. DIR: Josh Becker. CAST: Brian Schulz, Tim Quill, Sam Raimi. 1987

THOUSAND ACRES, A ★★1/2 Jane Smiley's Pulitzer-winning novel descends into relentless male-bashing. Jessica Lange and Michelle Pfeiffer are sensational as the dissimilar sisters drawn together by a land dispute involving their cruel and bellicose father. Rated R for profanity and strong sexual content. 104m. DIR: Jocelyn Moorhouse. CAST: Michelle Pfeiffer, Jessica Lange, Jason Robards Jr., Jennifer Jason Leigh, Colin Firth, Keith Carradine, Kevin Anderson, Pat Hingle. 1997 DVD

THOUSAND CLOWNS, A ★★★★ Famous Broadway play comes to the screen with memorable performances by all the principals and standout jobs by Jason Robards as a talented nonconformist and Barry Gordon as his precocious ward. They struggle against welfare bureaucracy in order to stay together. Very funny in spots and equally poignant in others. B&W; 118m. DIR: Fred Coe. CAST: Jason Robards Jr., Barry Gordon, Barbara Harris, Martin Balsam, Gene Saks, William Daniels. 1965

THOUSAND EYES OF DR. MABUSE, THE ★★1/2 Famed suspense *auteur* Fritz Lang's return to Germany and his attempt to revive Dr. Mabuse, his notorious master criminal, is a middling success. But a Lang near miss is better than a triumph by almost anyone else, so this intricately plotted mystery should delight film buffs. Ignore the dopey romantic subplot. Also titled: *Eyes of Evil, The Secret of Dr. Mabuse* and *The Diabolical Dr. Mabuse*. B&W; 103m. DIR: Fritz Lang. CAST: Dawn Addams, Peter Van Eyck, Gert Fröbe, Wolfgang Preiss. 1960

THOUSAND HEROES, A ★★★ Exciting docudrama about the events leading up to the United Airlines flight that lost its hydraulics over Iowa on July 19, 1989, and was forced to make a crash landing. How nearly two hundred passengers lived through this horrendous event was credited to the ground crew, who had prepared for such an emergency. While Charlton Heston attempts to stabilize the plane in the air, Richard Thomas and James Coburn play members of the ground team. Rated PG. 95m. DIR: Lamont Johnson. CAST: Charlton Heston, Richard Thomas, James Coburn. 1992

THOUSAND PIECES OF GOLD ★★★★ Ah, the joys of independent cinema: no formulas, no studio-policy compromises, no catering to star's images—just solid storytelling and committed filmmaking. Encompassing a story that begins in China and settles in Idaho's gold country in 1880, this wonderful movie about a woman who goes from slavery to fierce independence, offers a fresh perspective on the Old West. Not rated, the film has profanity and suggested sex. 105m. DIR: Nancy Kelly. CAST: Rosalind Chao, Chris Cooper, Dennis Dun. 1991

THOUSANDS CHEER ★★★ The typical story about someone putting together a talent show for some good cause who gets a major shot in the arm by the appearances of top MGM performers. 126m. DIR: George Sidney. CAST: John Boles, Kathryn Grayson, Mickey Rooney, Judy Garland, Gene Kelly, Red Skelton, Lucille Ball, Ann Sothern, Eleanor Powell, Frank Morgan, Lena Horne, Virginia O'Brien. 1943

THRASHIN' 💔 Hotshot skateboarder comes to L.A. and gets on the bad side of a gang of street skaters. Rated PG-13 for sexual situations. 92m. DIR: David Winters. CAST: Josh Brolin, Robert Rusler, Chuck McCann. 1986

THREADS ★★★★ Unforgettable British TV depiction of the effects of nuclear war on two small-town families makes *The Day After* look like a Hollywood musical. It doesn't indulge in shock or false sentimentality, rendering a chillingly plausible account of life after the end. 110m. DIR: Mick Jackson. CAST: Karen Meagher, Reece Dinsdale. 1984

THREAT, THE ★★★1/2 Underrated suspense feature packs every minute with tension as vengeance-minded Charles McGraw escapes from jail and kidnaps the police detective and district attorney as well as snatches a singer he thinks may have told on him for good measure. The police put the pressure on the kidnapper, and he puts the squeeze on his captives. B&W; 65m. DIR: Felix Feist. CAST: Charles McGraw, Michael O'Shea, Frank Conroy, Virginia Grey, Julie Bishop, Robert Shayne, Anthony Caruso, Don McGuire. 1949

THREE AGES, THE ★★★1/2 Frozen-faced Buster Keaton coproduced and codirected this parody on the films of that master of excessiveness, Cecil B. DeMille. A funny and very enjoyable silent film. Not Keaton's best, but far from mundane. B&W; 89m. DIR: Buster Keaton, Eddie Cline. CAST: Buster Keaton, Wallace Beery, Oliver Hardy. 1923 DVD

THREE AMIGOS ★★1/2 In this send-up of *The Cowboy Star*, Steve Martin, Chevy Chase, and Martin Short play three silent-screen cowboys who attempt to save a Mexican village from bloodthirsty banditos. Steve Martin, in particular, has some very funny moments. Overall, it's pleasant—even amusing—but nothing more. Rated PG. 105m. DIR: John Landis.

CAST: Steve Martin, Chevy Chase, Martin Short, Alfonso Arau, Patrice Martinez, Joe Mantegna, Jon Lovitz. 1986 DVD

THREE BROADWAY GIRLS ★★★ Three streetwise gold diggers stalk their prey among New York's socially prominent in this comedy adapted from Zoe Atkins's 1930 Broadway hit. Also titled *The Greeks Had a Word for Them.* B&W; 78m. DIR: Lowell Sherman. CAST: Joan Blondell, Ina Claire, Madge Evans, David Manners, Betty Grable. 1932

THREE BROTHERS ★★★★ Francesco Rosi directed this thoughtful, emotionally powerful movie that details the effect of a mother's recent death on her family. A drama with great insight and compassion. In Italian with English subtitles. Not rated; the film has a few scenes of violence. 113m. DIR: Francesco Rosi. CAST: Philippe Noiret, Michele Placido, Vittorio Mezzogiorno. 1980

THREE BULLETS FOR A LONG GUN 💔 A gunfighter and a Mexican bandit join forces to find a hidden Confederate treasure, but there isn't enough for both of them. Boring story line and bad acting. Not rated; contains violence. 89m. DIR: Peter Henkel. CAST: Beau Brummel, Keith Van Der Wat, Don McCorkindale, Janis Reinhardt. 1970

3 X 3 EYES, VOLS. 1–4 ★★★ Japanese animation. Bizarre but intriguing horror series. Pai, the last surviving member of her mythic three-eyed race, goes in search of the artifact that will at last transform her into a human being. Violent but entertaining. 30m. each. DIR: Daisuke Nishio. 1991

THREE CABALLEROS, THE ★★★ In Walt Disney's first attempt at combining animation and live action, Donald Duck is joined by two Latin feathered friends. Originally designed as a World War II propaganda piece promoting inter-American unity, it still holds up well today and remains a timeless learning experience for the kids. 72m. DIR: Walt Disney. 1942 DVD

THREE CAME HOME ★★★ During World War II, British families residing in Borneo are forced into prison camps by Japanese troops. The courage and suffering of the confined women make for compelling drama. Claudette Colbert delivers one of her finest performances. 106m. DIR: Jean Negulesco. CAST: Claudette Colbert, Patric Knowles, Sessue Hayakawa. 1950

THREE CASES OF MURDER ★★★★ Presented in a letter-box format, these three eerie stories are a wonderfully written collection of the macabre. Most effective is the opening tale in which we see a museum painting from the other side of the canvas. The final episode is by W. Somerset Maugham and stars Orson Welles as a brilliant but cold foreign minister who learns a harsh lesson about heartlessness. Not rated; contains implied violence. B&W; 99m. DIR: Wendy Toye, David Eady, George More O'Ferrall. CAST: Orson Welles, Alan Badel, John Gregson, Elizabeth Sellars. 1954

THREE CHARLIES AND A PHONEY! ★★★ Two early Keystone comedies, "Recreation" and "His Musical Career," a special World War I bond sales promotion, "The Bond," and "His Day Out" make up this slapstick anthology. Silent. 1914–1918 with organ music; B&W; 69m. **DIR:** Charles Chaplin. **CAST:** Charlie Chaplin, Mack Swain, Edna Purviance, Sydney Chaplin.

THREE COMRADES ★★★1/2 Three friends in Germany have romantic designs on the same woman, and she has an incurable disease. A real weeper, but the acting is terrific. F. Scott Fitzgerald cowrote the screenplay with E. E. Paramore and got screen credit. It was Fitzgerald's only credit during his entire Hollywood stay. B&W; 98m. **DIR:** Frank Borzage. **CAST:** Robert Taylor, Margaret Sullavan, Robert Young, Franchot Tone, Monty Woolley, Lionel Atwill, Charley Grapewin, Guy Kibbee. 1938

THREE DARING DAUGHTERS ★★★ Divorcée Jeanette MacDonald meets and weds pianist Jose Iturbi—her daughters object until they learn he can play boogie-woogie. Slight plot but wonderful music. A joke is that Iturbi plays himself. 115m. **DIR:** Fred M. Wilcox. **CAST:** Jeanette MacDonald, José Iturbi, Jane Powell, Edward Arnold, Harry Davenport, Elinor Donahue. 1948

THREE DAYS OF THE CONDOR ★★★★ Robert Redford is a CIA information researcher who is forced to flee for his life when his New York cover operation is blown and all of his coworkers brutally murdered. What seems at first to be a standard man-on-the-run drama gradually deepens into an engrossing mystery as to who is chasing him and why. Faye Dunaway expertly handles a vignette as the stranger Redford uses to avoid capture. Rated R. 117m. **DIR:** Sydney Pollack. **CAST:** Robert Redford, Cliff Robertson, Max von Sydow, Faye Dunaway, John Houseman. 1975 DVD

THREE DAYS TO A KILL ★★ Serviceable macho heroics from some old (and we do mean old) familiar faces. Seasoned mercenaries Fred Williamson and Bo Svenson rescue a U.S. diplomat from sneering drug lord Henry Silva. Rated R for violence. 90m. **DIR:** Fred Williamson. **CAST:** Fred Williamson, Bo Svenson, Henry Silva, Chuck Connors, Van Johnson, Sonny Landham. 1991

THREE FACES OF EVE, THE ★★★★★ This distinguished movie boasts Joanne Woodward's Oscar-winning performance as a woman with multiple personalities. Woodward progresses through all three personalities in one amazing scene. Based on a true-life case. 91m. **DIR:** Nunnally·Johnson. **CAST:** Joanne Woodward, Lee J. Cobb, David Wayne, Vince Edwards. 1957

THREE FACES WEST ★★★ John Wayne is the leader of a group of Dust Bowl farmers attempting to survive in this surprisingly watchable Republic release. Sigrid Gurie and Charles Coburn co-star as the European immigrants who show them what courage means. B&W; 79m. **DIR:** Bernard Vorhaus. **CAST:** John Wayne, Charles Coburn, Sigrid Gurie, Spencer Charters. 1940

3:15—THE MOMENT OF TRUTH ★★1/2 *High Noon* in high school, as Adam Baldwin prepares for a showdown. Director Larry Gross, a Walter Hill protégé, doesn't have Hill's ability to rise above the too plentiful action clichés. Rated R for violence. 85m. **DIR:** Larry Gross. **CAST:** Adam Baldwin, Deborah Foreman, René Auberjonois, Ed Lauter, Mario Van Peebles, Wings Hauser. 1985

THREE FOR BEDROOM C ★★★ Adequate farce that was the first film made by Gloria Swanson after her stunning comeback in *Sunset Boulevard*. She portrays a movie star who books a compartment on a train that is also occupied by a Harvard scientist. Predictable. 74m. **DIR:** Milton H. Bren. **CAST:** Gloria Swanson, James Warren, Fred Clark, Hans Conried, Margaret Dumont. 1952

THREE FOR THE ROAD ★★ Dull comedy about a senator's aide (Charlie Sheen) who is assigned to take his employer's difficult daughter (Kerri Green) to a reform school. Rated PG. 95m. **DIR:** B.W.L. Norton. **CAST:** Charlie Sheen, Kerri Green, Alan Ruck, Sally Kellerman. 1987

THREE FUGITIVES ★★★ France's current master of film comedy, Francois Veber, made his American debut with this overly sentimental but often hilarious comedy about a hardened criminal (Nick Nolte) thrown together with a mute girl (Sarah Rowland Doroff) and her down-and-out dad (Martin Short) when the latter robs a bank and takes Nolte hostage. Rated PG-13 for profanity and violence. 90m. **DIR:** Francis Veber. **CAST:** Nick Nolte, Martin Short, James Earl Jones, Kenneth McMillan, Sarah Rowland Doroff. 1989

THREE GODFATHERS, THE ★★★1/2 Director John Ford's second version of Peter B. Kyne's biblically oriented Western features John Wayne, Harry Carey Jr., and Pedro Armendariz as three good-hearted outlaws who discover a baby in the desert and dedicate themselves to saving its life. The three leads work well together, and Ford's stock company—Ward Bond in particular—adds grit to the sentimental story. 103m. **DIR:** John Ford. **CAST:** John Wayne, Harry Carey Jr., Pedro Armendariz, Ward Bond, Mae Marsh, Jane Darwell, Ben Johnson. 1949

THREE IN THE ATTIC ★★ Three women kidnap the college Lothario and get revenge by making him their sex slave. The titillating premise of this curio soon gives way to tired debates about relationships. Rated R. 91m. **DIR:** Richard Wilson. **CAST:** Christopher Jones, Yvette Mimieux, Judy Pace. 1968

THREE IN THE CELLAR 💔 Wes Stern as a college student who has just lost his scholarship. Not rated, this low-budget yawner contains nudity and sexual situations. 93m. **DIR:** Theodore J. Flicker. **CAST:** Wes Stern, Joan Collins, Larry Hagman, David Arkin, Judy Pace. 1970

•**THREE KINGS** ★★★★ What appears at first to be a cynical take on *Kelly's Heroes* set during the 1991 Gulf War is actually an intelligent, thought-provoking study of America's role as police force to the world and the evils it fosters. That said, there's action, horror, and humor aplenty as George Clooney leads a band of renegade soldiers on a quest for Sadam Hussein's hidden cache of Kuwaiti gold. The twist comes when our antiheroes decide to help the innocent people being victimized by Iraq's Republican Guard, thus adding a dash of adrenaline-pumping heroism to the mix. It's a thrilling war picture—with a conscience. Rated R for violence, profanity, and sex. 115m. **DIR:** David O. Russell. **CAST:** George Clooney, Mark Wahlberg, Ice Cube, Spike Jonze, Nora

Dunn, Jamie Kennedy, Mykelti Williamson, Clifford Curtis. **1999 DVD**

THREE LITTLE WORDS ★★1/2 That this is supposedly Fred Astaire's favorite among his numerous films says little for his taste. He and Red Skelton thoroughly enjoyed playing ace songwriters Bert Kalmar and Harry Ruby in this semiaccurate bio-pic, but, overall, the film lacks luster. 102m. **DIR:** Richard Thorpe. **CAST:** Fred Astaire, Red Skelton, Vera-Ellen, Gloria De Haven, Arlene Dahl, Debbie Reynolds, Keenan Wynn. **1950**

THREE LIVES AND ONLY ONE DEATH ★★★★ Marcello Mastroianni gives one of his best performances in this comedy as three very different people who may in fact be the same person. The first relatively mainstream work by veteran filmmaker Raoul Ruiz shows that he is perfectly able to adapt the structural playfulness of his avant-garde work in order to entertain (but not condescend to) a general audience. in French with English subtitles. Not rated; contains no objectionable material. 125m. **DIR:** Raúl Ruiz. **CAST:** Marcello Mastroianni, Arielle Dombasle, Chiara Mastroianni, Lou Castel. **1996**

THREE LIVES OF KAREN, THE ★★★ A woman about to be married gets the shock of her life when the husband and daughter she doesn't remember come back into her life. Amnesia is suspected, but how many other lives is this woman suppressing? This made-for-cable drama is moving, despite the trite plotline. Rated PG-13. 95m. **DIR:** David Burton Morris. **CAST:** Gail O'Grady, Dennis Boutsikaris, Tim Guinee. **1997**

THREE LIVES OF THOMASINA, THE ★★★★ An excellent cast and innovative ways of telling the story highlight this tale of love and caring. A young girl's cat is brought back to life by a woman who also teaches the girl's father to let others into his life. The cat's trip to cat heaven is outstandingly executed. 97m. **DIR:** Don Chaffey. **CAST:** Patrick McGoohan, Susan Hampshire, Karen Dotrice, Vincent Winter. **1964**

THREE MEN AND A BABY ★★★1/2 Tom Selleck, Steve Guttenberg, and Ted Danson are three carefree bachelors in this energetic remake of the French *Three Men and a Cradle*. The trio find an unexpected bundle at the door of their impeccably furnished apartment. The conclusion (changed from the French original) is hopelessly hokey, but getting there's a lot of fun. Rated PG for language. 102m. **DIR:** Leonard Nimoy. **CAST:** Tom Selleck, Steve Guttenberg, Ted Danson, Nancy Travis, Margaret Colin. **1987**

THREE MEN AND A CRADLE ★★★★ In this sweet-natured character study from France, three high-living bachelors become the guardians of a baby girl. In addition to turning their life-styles inside out, she forces them to confront their values—with heartwarming results. Rated PG for profanity and nudity. In French with English subtitles. 105m. **DIR:** Coline Serreau. **CAST:** Roland Giraud, Michel Boujenah, André Dussolier. **1985**

THREE MEN AND A LITTLE LADY ★★★ Amiable, lightweight sequel to *Three Men and a Baby*, in which the title trio (Tom Selleck, Steve Guttenberg, and Ted Danson) must confront the possibility of losing their ward when her mother (Nancy Travis) de-

cides to marry. Rated PG for brief profanity. 106m. **DIR:** Emile Ardolino. **CAST:** Tom Selleck, Steve Guttenberg, Ted Danson, Nancy Travis, Robin Weisman, Christopher Cazenove. **1990**

THREE MEN FROM TEXAS ★★★★★ A likely contender for the best Hopalong Cassidy film made. This one breaks every rule in the book as the romantic interest is killed off. Sidekick Andy Clyde is a reformed outlaw as he and Hoppy bust up Morris Ankrum's plot to gain control of the Mexican border territory. B&W; 75m. **DIR:** Lesley Selander. **CAST:** William Boyd, Russell Hayden, Andy Clyde, Morris Ankrum (Stepen Morris), Dick Curtis. **1940**

THREE MEN IN A BOAT ★★★ A male-bonding comedy that shows how men on a boat trip down the Thames River are quick to desert their buddies when a pretty girl enters the scene. 84m. **DIR:** Ken Annakin. **CAST:** Laurence Harvey, David Tomlinson, Jimmy Edwards, Martita Hunt, Jill Ireland, Shirley Eaton, Adrienne Corri. **1956**

THREE MEN ON A HORSE ★★★1/2 Frank McHugh, a timid greeting-card writer, handicaps winning horses as a hobby. Some small-time gamblers, led by Sam Levene, learn of his talent and turn it to their advantage. Stagy, but fun to watch. B&W; 87m. **DIR:** Mervyn LeRoy. **CAST:** Frank McHugh, Joan Blondell, Sam Levene, Guy Kibbee, Carol Hughes, Allen Jenkins, Edgar Kennedy, Eddie "Rochester" Anderson. **1936**

•**THREE MUSKETEERS, THE (1921)** ★★★1/2 Lavish silent adaptation of the classic tale with Douglas Fairbanks as the character he was born to play—D'Artagnan, the fledgling musketeer who proves his skills with a sword and foils the nefarious efforts of the dastardly Cardinal Richelieu. B&W; 119m. **DIR:** Fred Niblo. **CAST:** Douglas Fairbanks Sr., Leon Barry, Marguerite de la Motte, Eugene Pallette, Adolphe Menjou. **1921 DVD**

THREE MUSKETEERS, THE (1933) ★★ The weakest and least-seen of John Wayne's three serials for Mascot Studios. This desert-bound story presents four friends who fight against a harsh environment and the evil Devil of the Desert. Standard Foreign Legion stuff. B&W; 12 chapters. **DIR:** Armand Schaefer, Colbert Clark. **CAST:** John Wayne, Ruth Hall, Jack Mulhall, Raymond Hatton, Francis X. Bushman, Noah Beery Jr. **1933 DVD**

THREE MUSKETEERS, THE (1935) ★★★ With middle-aged actors in the swashbuckling roles, this is the most sedate of the many versions of the story. They don't swash as many buckles as those who followed, but they do tell a good story and keep it on a very serious level. Author Alexandre Dumas would be pleased with the attention paid to the details of his story. B&W; 90m. **DIR:** Rowland V. Lee. **CAST:** Walter Abel, Paul Lukas, Moroni Olsen, Onslow Stevens, Heather Angel, Margot Grahame, Ian Keith, Ralph Forbes, Rosamond Pinchot, John Qualen, Nigel de Brulier. **1935**

THREE MUSKETEERS, THE (1939) ★★★ The Ritz Brothers as Dumas's famous trio? Yes, it's true. As a comedy-musical, this picture rides a moderate course, sticking closely to the original story but never taking anything too seriously. Don Ameche is very sharp as D'Artagnan and Binnie Barnes is charming as Lady DeWinter. B&W; 73m. DIR: Allan Dwan. CAST: Don Ameche, The Ritz Brothers, Lionel Atwill, Binnie Barnes. 1939

THREE MUSKETEERS, THE (1948) ★★ MGM's all-star version of the classic swashbuckler by Alexandre Dumas gets its swords crossed up, primarily due to some blatant miscasting. Gene Kelly as D'Artagnan and June Allyson playing the queen's seamstress are never convincing as French citizens during the reign of Louis XIII. Fans of Lana Turner may find the movie worthwhile, because hidden in this fluff is one of her finest performances as the villainous Lady DeWinter. B&W; 128m. DIR: George Sidney. CAST: Gene Kelly, Lana Turner, June Allyson, Van Heflin, Vincent Price, Gig Young, Angela Lansbury, Keenan Wynn. 1948

THREE MUSKETEERS, THE (1973) ★★★★★ Alexandre Dumas's oft-filmed swashbuckler classic—there may have been as many as ten previous versions—finally came to full life with this 1973 release. It is a superb adventure romp with scrumptious moments of comedy, character, and action. Rated PG. 105m. DIR: Richard Lester. CAST: Michael York, Oliver Reed, Raquel Welch, Richard Chamberlain, Faye Dunaway, Charlton Heston. 1973 DVD

THREE MUSKETEERS, THE (1993) ★★★1/2 The Brat Pack tackles Dumas's swashbuckling classic with generally pleasing results. We still prefer the Richard Lester triptych, but every generation needs a cast of its own to proclaim, "All for one, one for all." Rated PG for light violence. 105m. DIR: Stephen Herek. CAST: Charlie Sheen, Kiefer Sutherland, Chris O'Donnell, Oliver Platt, Tim Curry, Rebecca DeMornay, Gabrielle Anwar, Paul McGann, Julie Delpy, Hugh O'Connor. 1993 DVD

THREE NINJAS ★★★1/2 Kids will love this Karate Kid knockoff about youngsters who help their mentor-grandfather take on a criminal and his army of evil ninjas. Rated PG for light violence. 85m. DIR: Jon Turteltaub. CAST: Victor Wong, Michael Treanor, Max Elliott Slade, Chad Power. 1992

THREE NINJAS KICK BACK ★★★1/2 More kid-pleasing entertainment has our three youthful heroes forced to choose between playing in a championship baseball game and accompanying their all-wise grandfather to Japan for a martial arts tournament. It's The Karate Kid, The Three Stooges, The Bad News Bears, and Indiana Jones all crammed into one fast-paced movie that works surprisingly well. Rated PG for goofy violence. 99m. DIR: Mark Saltzman. CAST: Victor Wong, Sab Shimono, Max Elliott Slade, Evan Bonifant, Caroline Junko King, Alan McRae, Margarita Franco. 1994

THREE NINJAS KNUCKLE UP ★★ More of the same as the three brothers team up to take on a toxic-waste dumper. Younger kids will enjoy this third entry in the series, but older kids will be bored. Rated PG-13 for violence. 93m. DIR: Simon S. Sheen. CAST: Victor Wong, Charles Napier, Michael Treanor, Max Elliott Slade, Chad Power. 1995

THREE NUTS IN SEARCH OF A BOLT ❤ Three loonies, too poor to see a psychiatrist on their own, hire an out-of-work actor to pretend he has each of their symptoms. Not rated, but equal to PG-13 for nu-

dity and adult situations. 78m. DIR: Tommy Noonan. CAST: Mamie Van Doren, Tommy Noonan, Paul Gilbert, Ziva Rodann. 1964

THREE O'CLOCK HIGH ★★1/2 Director Phil Joanou leaves no doubt of his technical skill in his first film. Too bad his story is just a teen variation on High Noon. Jerry Mitchell (Casey Siemaszko) is an average high schooler who ends up having the worst day of his life. Rated PG-13 for profanity and violence. 95m. DIR: Phil Joanou. CAST: Casey Siemaszko, Anne Ryan, Richard Tyson, Jeffrey Tambor, Philip Baker Hall, John P. Ryan. 1987

THREE OF HEARTS ★★★ A lesbian hires a male escort to break the heart of her former lover, but this film handles the premise with sensitivity, warmth, and humor. William Baldwin is endearing and Kelly Lynch is a revelation as the stereotype-busting lesbian. The buddy relationship the two develop makes the movie memorable. Rated R for language and suggested sex. 93m. DIR: Yurek Bogayevicz. CAST: William Baldwin, Kelly Lynch, Sherilyn Fenn, Joe Pantoliano, Gail Strickland. 1993

THREE ON A MATCH ★★★ Tough direction, a nifty script, and snappy editing make a winner of this tale of the reunion of three slum girls who ignore superstition to tempt fate and court tragedy by lighting their cigarettes from the same match. Ann Dvorak lights up last, and is outstanding in an outstanding cast. B&W; 68m. DIR: Mervyn LeRoy. CAST: Joan Blondell, Bette Davis, Ann Dvorak, Humphrey Bogart, Glenda Farrell, Edward Arnold. 1932

THREE ON A MEATHOOK ★ Hillbilly horror about a rural psychopath and his reign of terror. Can't decide if it's a spoof or a conventional gore movie. Rated R. 90m. DIR: William Girdler. CAST: Charles Kissinger. 1973

THREE ON THE TRAIL ★★★ A crooked sheriff and the local vice lord fool a British rancher into taking sides against Hopalong Cassidy. Pleasant musical interludes, good interplay among the friends, and lots of action and gunplay place this early entry on the list of best of series. B&W; 67m. DIR: Howard Bretherton. CAST: William Boyd, James Ellison, Onslow Stevens, Muriel Evans, George "Gabby" Hayes, Claude King, William Duncan. 1936

•THREE SEASONS ★★★ Several characters briefly cross paths in Saigon as their lives change and the city's past rubs shoulders with the present in this delicately woven drama. A bicycle taxi driver becomes emotionally attached to a hooker; an American who fought in the Vietnam War searches for a daughter he has never met; a street kid tries to find his stolen case of tourist trinkets; a woman flower vendor sings her way into the home of a hermitlike Buddhist master. In Vietnamese with English subtitles. Rated PG-13 for adult themes. 113m. DIR: Tony Bui. CAST: Don Duong, Nguyen Ngoc Hiep, Tran Manh, Harvey Keitel. 1999

THREE SECRETS ★★★ Three women, each with her own reason for believing she is his mother, anxiously await the rescue of a five-year-old boy, the sole survivor of a plane crash in rugged mountains. B&W; 98m. DIR: Robert Wise. CAST: Eleanor Parker, Patricia

Neal, Ruth Roman, Frank Lovejoy, Leif Erickson, Ted de Corsia. 1950

THREE SMART GIRLS ★★★★ Starring debut of fourteen-year-old Deanna Durbin as Penny Craig, who with her two sisters, saves their easygoing father from the clutches of a gold digger. Fast-moving musical, with some fine comedy touches, particularly by Mischa Auer. B&W; 84m. DIR: Henry Koster. CAST: Deanna Durbin, Binnie Barnes, Alice Brady, Ray Milland, Charles Winninger, Mischa Auer, Nan Gray, Barbara Read, Lucile Watson. 1937

THREE SMART GIRLS GROW UP ★★★1/2 Deanna Durbin returns in this sequel, this time acting as matchmaker for her two sisters and their assorted beaux. Nice mixture of light comedy and song. B&W; 90m. DIR: Henry Koster. CAST: Deanna Durbin, Charles Winninger, Nan Gray, Helen Parrish, Robert Cummings, William Lundigan. 1939

THREE SOVEREIGNS FOR SARAH ❤ Salem witch trials. Supposedly a true story about the real motivations that led to this dark spot in American history. 171m. DIR: Philip Leacock. CAST: Vanessa Redgrave, Ronald Hunter, Patrick McGoohan, Will Lyman, Kim Hunter. 1987

THREE STOOGES, THE (VOLUMES 1–10) ★★★★ The Three Stooges made 190 two-reel short subjects between 1934 and 1959. For over fifty years, people have either loved them or hated them. If you are a fan, you'll find these collections the answer to a knucklehead's dream. Each cassette features three shorts of impeccable quality, transferred from brand-new, complete 35-mm prints. All of the films are from the classic "Curly" period, when the team was at the peak of its energy and originality. B&W; 60m. DIR: Various. CAST: Moe Howard, Curly Howard, Larry Fine. 1934

THREE STRANGE LOVES ★★1/2 Three former ballerinas struggle to find happiness in their private lives. Ingmar Bergman's gloomy style is the perfect backdrop for the disappointment and heartache the women face. In Swedish with subtitles that flicker by at a pace suitable only for a speed reader. B&W; 84m. DIR: Ingmar Bergman. CAST: Eva Henning, Birger Malmsten. 1949

•3 STRIKES ❤ This tedious, vulgar crime comedy is about a two-time loser who, immediately upon release from prison, is chased by police and thugs throughout South Central Los Angeles. Rated R for drug use, profanity, nudity, suggested sex, and sexual references. 82m. DIR: D. J. Pooh. CAST: Brian Hooks, Starletta Dupois, George Wallace, N'Bushe Wright, David Alan Grier. 2000

3:10 TO YUMA ★★★★ This first-rate adult Western draws its riveting drama and power from the interaction of well-drawn characters rather than gun-blazing action. A farmer (Van Heflin) captures a notorious gunman (Glenn Ford) and, while waiting for the train to take them to Yuma prison, must hole up in a hotel and overcome the killer's numerous ploys to gain his freedom. B&W; 92m. DIR: Delmer Daves. CAST: Glenn Ford, Van Heflin, Felicia Farr, Leora Dana, Henry Jones, Richard Jaeckel, Robert Emhardt. 1957

THREE TEXAS STEERS ★★★ The Three Mesquiteers ride to the rescue of Carole Landis

when bad guys try to force her to sell her ranch. Their solution is to enter her horse into a trotting race, which produces some amusing footage of John Wayne spitting the horse's tail out of his mouth while being pursued by the baddies. Max Terhune's last appearance as a Mesquiteer. B&W; 59m. DIR: George Sherman. CAST: John Wayne, Ray "Crash" Corrigan, Max Terhune, Carole Landis, Ralph Graves, Roscoe Ates, Billy Curtis, David Sharpe. 1939

THREE THE HARD WAY ★★★ A white supremacist (Jay Robinson) attempts to wipe out the black race by putting a deadly serum in the country's water supply. Fred Williamson, Jim Brown and Jim Kelly team up to stop him in this action-packed movie. Rated PG for violence. 93m. DIR: Gordon Parks Jr. CAST: Fred Williamson, Jim Brown, Jim Kelly, Sheila Frazier, Jay Robinson. 1974

•THREE TO TANGO ★★★1/2 This utterly delightful, gender-bending screwball romp proves that the romantic comedy is far from dead. Credit scripters Rodney Vaccaro and Aline Brosh McKenna, and Neve Campbell, displaying the spunky personality and deft comic timing of, say, Irene Dunne or Jean Arthur. Although impossible to condense, the complicated plot involves a Chicago architect (Matthew Perry) who gets a chance to design a cultural center for a pretentious tycoon, who has the mistaken impression that our hero is gay … and thus selects the guy to spy on his mistress (Campbell). What follows is fun-fun-fun. If the conclusion seems a bit rushed and trite, well … some things are inevitable. Rated PG-13 for sensuality and brief profanity. 98m. DIR: Damon Santostefano. CAST: Matthew Perry, Neve Campbell, Dylan McDermott, Oliver Platt, John C. McGinley, Bob Balaban. 1999 DVD

THREE VIOLENT PEOPLE ★★★ Charlton Heston returns to Texas after the Civil War with his bride and finds himself fighting land grabbers. Should have been better but Elaine Stritch is colorful as a saloon hostess. 100m. DIR: Rudolph Maté. CAST: Charlton Heston, Anne Baxter, Gilbert Roland, Tom Tryon, Forrest Tucker, Bruce Bennett, Elaine Stritch, Barton MacLane. 1956

THREE WISHES ★★1/2 A minor but cute fairy tale that tries to enchant, but travels down territory everyone but kids will find too familiar. A mysterious drifter enters the life of a widow and her two sons at a time when they really could use a helping hand. This does make a good case for listening to your own heart, as the story is set in 1955, when conformity was a way of life. Rated PG for brief nudity and suggested sex. 115m. DIR: Martha Coolidge. CAST: Patrick Swayze, Mary Elizabeth Mastrantonio, Joseph Mazzello, Seth Mumy. 1995

THREE-WORD BRAND, THE ★★★ Indians murder a homesteader, thus orphaning his twin sons. The brothers become separated—going their own ways—until circumstances reunite them many years later. William S. Hart deftly portrays the father and the sons in this silent sagebrush drama. B&W; 75m. DIR: Lambert Hillyer. CAST: William S. Hart, Jane Novak. 1921

THREE WORLDS OF GULLIVER, THE ★★★ Following a violent storm at sea, Dr. Lemuel Gulliver

(Kerwin Mathews) finds himself ashore on Lilliput, an island with miniature people. A biting satire on human nature, featuring seamless special effects by Ray Harryhausen and an ear-filling Bernard Herrmann score. Based on the classic by Jonathan Swift. Great fun. 100m. **DIR:** Jack Sher. **CAST:** Kerwin Mathews, June Thorburn, Jo Morrow, Gregoire Aslan. 1960

THREEPENNY OPERA, THE ★★★★ Based on John Gay's *The Beggar's Opera.* Classic gangster musical features mob leader Mack the Knife, his moll, and the hordes of the underworld. This Bertolt Brecht satire (with music by Kurt Weill), although not too popular with the Nazis or their predecessors, is always a favorite with the audience. B&W; 113m. **DIR:** G. W. Pabst. **CAST:** Rudolph Forster, Lotte Lenya, Reinhold Schunzel, Carola Neher. 1931

THREE'S TROUBLE ★★★1/2 Screenwriter David Williamson often hits the bull's-eye with this warm, witty *Mr. Mom* Australian style. When a much put upon housewife hires a baby-sitter (handsome Steven Vidler), her know-it-all husband is forced to reassess his contributions to the family. Not rated, contains profanity. 93m. **DIR:** Chris Thomson. **CAST:** Jacki Weaver, John Waters, Steven Vidler. 1985

THREESOME ★★ A woman (Lara Flynn Boyle) is assigned two male roommates in a college dorm. This clumsy film tries to mix leering sex farce with soulful sensitivity—*Porky's* meets *A Separate Peace.* The muttered dialogue is often inaudible. Rated R for profanity and simulated sex. 93m. **DIR:** Andrew Fleming. **CAST:** Lara Flynn Boyle, Stephen Baldwin, Josh Charles. 1994

13 AT DINNER ★★★1/2 Above-average made-for-TV Agatha Christie mystery, with Peter Ustinov reprising his big-screen role as fastidious Belgian sleuth Hercule Poirot. This time out, the dapper detective contends with a murdered British lord and his thespian widow (Faye Dunaway). Notable for the presence of David Suchet as Scotland Yard's Inspector Japp, a few years before Suchet took over the role of Poirot himself. 100m. **DIR:** Lou Antonio. **CAST:** Peter Ustinov, Faye Dunaway, David Suchet, Lee Horsley, Amanda Pays. 1985

13 GHOSTS ★★★ Lighthearted horror tale of an average family inheriting a haunted house complete with a creepy old housekeeper (Margaret Hamilton) who may also be a witch, and a secret fortune hidden somewhere in the place. William Castle directs with his customary style and flair. Pretty neat. B&W; 88m. **DIR:** William Castle. **CAST:** Charles Herbert, Donald Woods, Martin Milner, Rosemary DeCamp, Jo Morrow, Margaret Hamilton. 1960

13 RUE MADELEINE ★★★ Espionage thriller, inspired by the *March of Time* series, shot in semidocumentary style. James Cagney is an OSS chief who goes to France to complete a mission when one of his men is killed. B&W; 95m. **DIR:** Henry Hathaway. **CAST:** James Cagney, Annabella, Walter Abel, Frank Latimore, Melville Cooper, E. G. Marshall, Karl Malden, Sam Jaffe, Richard Conte. 1946

THIRTEENTH FLOOR, THE (1990) ★★ A young girl watches as her ruthless politician father has a man and his son executed. Years later, on the run from her father, she takes refuge in the same building where

the killing took place. She soon discovers it's haunted by the spirit of the murdered boy. Rated R for violence and profanity. 86m. **DIR:** Chris Roach. **CAST:** Lisa Hensley, Tim McKenzie. 1990

THIRTEENTH FLOOR, THE (1999) ★★★ Yet another of the many cyberspace/virtual reality scenarios released by Hollywood in the spring of 1999, and among the least interesting. A wealthy software programmer, investigating the murder of his mentor, begins to suspect that his world isn't quite all it seems. A B-effort at best. Rated R—rather unfairly—for brief profanity and fairly mild violence. 120m. **DIR:** Josef Rusnak. **CAST:** Craig Bierko, Gretchen Mol, Vincent D'Onofrio, Dennis Haysbert, Armin Mueller-Stahl. 1999 DVD

THIRTEENTH GUEST, THE ★★★ A gathering of relatives in a spooky old mansion invites murder in this superior thriller. When a storm rages outside, the reading of a strange will is interrupted by a mysterious figure, and when the lights come on there's a corpse. B&W; 65m. **DIR:** Albert Ray. **CAST:** Ginger Rogers, Lyle Talbot, J. Farrell MacDonald. 1932

•13TH WARRIOR, THE ★★★★ Taken from Michael Crichton's fact-based, 1976 novel, *Eaters of the Dead,* this is the epic tale of an Arabian prince and poet (Antonio Banderas) who finds himself conscripted by a band of Vikings off to battle supernatural monsters. Although this film was shelved for two years and allegedly underwent some editorial changes against the wishes of director John McTiernan, it nevertheless emerges as a blood-stirring epic. Rated R for nudity, violence, and gore. 103m. **DIR:** John McTiernan. **CAST:** Antonio Banderas, Diane Venora, Dennis Storhoi, Vladmir Kulich, Omar Sharif, Anders T. Anderson, Richard Bremmer, Tony Curran. 1999 DVD

30-FOOT BRIDE OF CANDY ROCK, THE ★★ A nebbish inventor turns his girlfriend into a giant. A mild comedy with a certain amount of charm, this was the last film made by Columbia's B-picture unit, and Lou Costello's only feature film after breaking up with Bud Abbott. He died before the film was released. B&W; 75m. **DIR:** Sidney Miller. **CAST:** Lou Costello, Dorothy Provine, Gale Gordon, Charles Lane, Doodles Weaver. 1959

30 IS A DANGEROUS AGE, CYNTHIA ★★ Dated British comedy features Dudley Moore as a pianist-composer who intends to find a bride and write a musical before he turns 30. 83m. **DIR:** Joseph McGrath. **CAST:** Dudley Moore, Suzy Kendall, Eddie Foy Jr., John Bird, Patricia Routledge. 1967

THIRTY SECONDS OVER TOKYO ★★★★ Spencer Tracy is in top form as General Doolittle, who led the first bombing attack on Tokyo during World War II. A true-life adventure that, despite its length, never bogs down. B&W; 138m. **DIR:** Mervyn LeRoy. **CAST:** Spencer Tracy, Van Johnson, Robert Walker, Phyllis Thaxter, Scott McKay, Robert Mitchum, Stephen McNally. 1944

THIRTY-TWO SHORT FILMS ABOUT GLENN GOULD ★★★★★ This innovative portrayal of the eccentric, controversial Canadian pianist—one of the greatest musicians of the twentieth century— won four Genie Awards (Canadian Oscars) including best picture and best director. As refreshing and visionary as the man himself. Not rated. 90m. DIR: Francois Girard. CAST: Colm Feore. 1994

35 UP ★★★1/2 When he's not working on mainstream films, English director Michael Apted returns to the brilliant, ongoing documentary with which he first made his reputation. The filming of the lives and times of a select group of fourteen English men and women. They've been interviewed and depicted on film at seven-year intervals, starting when they were seven, in 1963. You don't have to be familiar with earlier segments to gain a lot from *35 Up*. Not rated. 127m. DIR: Michael Apted. 1991

36 FILLETTE ★★★ A sexually charged comedy-drama from France, about a 14-year-old girl and her frustrated efforts to cast off her virginity. Delphine Zentout is most impressive as the girl. The title is a reference to a French adolescent dress size. In French with English subtitles. 92m. DIR: Catherine Breillat. CAST: Delphine Zentout, Etienne Chicot. 1988 DVD

36 HOURS ★★★1/2 An intriguing psychological war-drama. James Garner, a designer of the secret Allied invasion plans, is kidnapped by Nazis and brainwashed into believing the war is long over. Rod Taylor is so likable as the doctor leading the ruse that you almost hope his plan succeeds. Remade for cable as *Breaking Point*. 115m. DIR: George Seaton. CAST: James Garner, Eva Marie Saint, Rod Taylor, Werner Peters, Alan Napier. 1964

36 HOURS TO DIE ★★★1/2 Tense drama unfolds when mobsters make a high-tech takeover attempt of a family-owned brewery. Treat Williams is terrific in this TNT original as he is forced to outsmart vicious Saul Rubinek. Unrated, contains violence and nudity. 89m. DIR: Yves Simoneau. CAST: Treat Williams, Kim Cattrall, Saul Rubinek, Carroll O'Connor. 1999

38 VIENNA BEFORE THE FALL ★★★ The romance between a Jewish theatrical producer and a beautiful Aryan woman becomes threatened by the prejudicial climate of Nazi Germany. In German with English subtitles. Rated R for nudity, profanity, and violence. 97m. DIR: Wolfgang Gluck. CAST: Tobias Engel, Sunnyi Melles. 1989

THIRTY-NINE STEPS, THE (1935) ★★★★★ Alfred Hitchcock was assigned to direct what was intended to be a simple, low-budget spy-chase thriller. Using the style and technique that were to make him famous, he gained immediate audience sympathy for the plight of his central character, an innocent Canadian (Robert Donat) who while visiting England is implicated in the theft of national secrets and murder. The result was a big hit. B&W; 87m. DIR: Alfred Hitchcock. CAST: Robert Donat, Madeleine Carroll, Lucie Mannheim. 1935 DVD

THIRTY-NINE STEPS, THE (1959) ★★1/2 Inferior remake of Alfred Hitchcock's suspense classic has Kenneth More as the hapless fellow who innocently becomes involved in a spy plot. The 1978 version with Robert Powell also has its beat. 93m. DIR: Ralph Thomas. CAST: Kenneth More, Taina Elg, Brenda de Banzie, Barry Jones,.Sidney James. 1959

THIRTY-NINE STEPS, THE (1978) ★★★1/2 An innocent man stumbles onto a spy plot in pre–World War I London with nowhere to turn. The best of several Hitchcock remakes in the 1970s. It can't compete with the original, of course. Rated PG. 102m. DIR: Don Sharp. CAST: Robert Powell, David Warner, Eric Porter, Karen Dotrice, John Mills. 1978

301/302 ★★★ A pair of neighbors—one a cook, the other a writer—share a strange relationship that ends in wild culinary exploration. Fascinating character study with a bizarre story to boot. Not rated; contains nudity, violence, and profanity. 98m. DIR: Chui-Soo Park. CAST: Eun-Jin Bang, Sin-Hye Hwang, Chu-Ryun Kim. 1996

317TH PLATOON, THE ★★★ Near the end of the French involvement in Vietnam, a group of soldiers tries to make its way back to its squadron after a failed offensive. Filmed in Cambodia, this is an eerie precursor to recent American films about Vietnam. In French with English subtitles. 100m. DIR: Pierre Schoendoerffer. CAST: Jacques Perrin, Bruno Cremer. 1965

365 NIGHTS IN HOLLYWOOD ★★1/2 Washed-up movie director gets a chance to make a comeback picture and defies crooks who want to plunder the budget. A young Alice Faye plays a Jean Harlow look-alike who carhops by day and sings and acts her way into this slightly goofy movie about moviemaking. Interesting musical productions and Faye's sparkling performance compensate for some low-level comedy that slows the film. B&W; 74m. DIR: George Marshall. CAST: James Dunn, Alice Faye, Frank Mitchell, John Bradford, Grant Mitchell, John Qualen. 1934

THRESHOLD ★★ Donald Sutherland stars in this film about the first artificial-heart transplant. Rated PG. 106m. DIR: Richard Pearce. CAST: Donald Sutherland, John Marley, Jeff Goldblum, Michael Lerner. 1981

THRILL KILLERS, THE ❤ Psycho killer Cash Flagg (a.k.a. writer-director Ray Dennis Steckler) and three escaped mental patients meet up at a diner, where they terrorize the patrons. Pretty dull. B&W; 69m. DIR: Ray Dennis Steckler. CAST: Cash Flagg, Liz Renay, Carolyn Brandt, Atlas King. 1965

THRILL OF A ROMANCE ★★ Esther Williams's groom deserts her on their wedding night to close a business deal. Opera star Lauritz Melchior feels she could do better with war hero Van Johnson, so he acts as cupid. 104m. DIR: Richard Thorpe. CAST: Van Johnson, Esther Williams, Lauritz Melchior, Spring Byington. 1946

THRILL OF IT ALL, THE ★★★ Married life is perfect for housewife and mother Doris Day and doctor James Garner until she accepts a high-paying television commercial job in this witty observation of television, advertising, and domestic bliss, as scripted by Carl Reiner. 103m. DIR: Norman Jewison. CAST: Doris Day, James Garner, Arlene Francis, Edward Andrews, ZaSu Pitts, Elliott Reid, Reginald Owen, Alice Pearce. 1963

THRILLED TO DEATH ★★ An unsuspecting couple is framed for murder and drug running. The dupes are so incredibly naïve that you'll find yourself yelling at them to wake up. Rated R for nudity and violence. 93m. DIR: Chuck Vincent. CAST: Blake Bahner. 1988

THRILLER (TV SERIES) ★★★1/2 As was true of this television anthology series during its brief network run in the early 1960s, host and sometimes star Boris Karloff is the main draw. Fortunately, three of the first six episodes released on tape feature the venerated horror actor and are recommended. Made for TV. B&W; 58m. DIR: Robert Florey, John Brahm, Douglas Heyes. CAST: Boris Karloff, John Carradine, Hazel Court, William Shatner, Sidney Blackmer, Patricia Medina, Elizabeth Montgomery, Tom Poston, Dick York, Guy Rolfe, Audrey Dalton. 1960–62

THRILLKILL 🐾 Woman has a falling-out with her partners after stealing $3 million via computer. Not rated; contains some violence and frank language. 88m. DIR: Anthony Kramreither, Anthony D'Andrea. CAST: Robin Ward, Gina Massey. 1986

THRONE OF BLOOD ★★★★★ Japanese director Akira Kurosawa's retelling of *Macbeth* may be the best film adaptation of Shakespeare ever made. Kurosawa uses the medium to present Shakespeare's themes in visual images. When Birnam Wood literally comes to Dunsinane, it is a truly great moment you would have believed could only happen in the limitless landscapes of a dream. In Japanese with English subtitles. B&W; 105m. DIR: Akira Kurosawa. CAST: Toshiro Mifune, Minoru Chiaki, Takashi Shimura. 1957

THRONE OF FIRE, THE 🐾 The son of Satan must overthrow the king and marry his daughter to sit upon the legendary Throne of Fire. Not rated; contains violence that might be unsuitable for younger viewers. 91m. DIR: Franco Prosperi. CAST: Sabrina Siani. 1973

THROUGH A GLASS DARKLY ★★ Two siblings compete for their father's love. The father, who happens to be a famous writer, sits back and observes. Ingmar Bergman goes overboard this time with endless monologues on God and love. In Swedish with English subtitles, this film is unrated but contains mature themes. B&W; 90m. DIR: Ingmar Bergman. CAST: Harriet Andersson, Gunnar Björnstrand, Max von Sydow. 1961

THROUGH NAKED EYES ★★★ A pretty good made-for-TV mystery thriller with voyeurism in high-rise apartments as the pivotal plot line. David Soul is watching Pam Dawber across the way, but she's also been watching him. When a series of murders occurs in their buildings, it appears someone else is watching, too. Not rated. 91m. DIR: John Llewellyn Moxey. CAST: David Soul, Pam Dawber, Rod McCary. 1983

THROUGH THE LOOKING GLASS ★★1/2 A likable adaptation of the adventures of Alice after her trip to Wonderland. This production loses some of its charm due to a more contemporary telling, but voice characterizations by Phyllis Diller, Mr. T, and Jonathan Winters help. No rating. 70m. DIR: Andrea Bresciani, Richard Slapczynski. 1987

THROW MOMMA FROM THE TRAIN ★★★ Gravel-voiced Anne Ramsey, as the titular Momma, is by far the best element of this comedy, which marks the directing debut of star Danny DeVito. He's a would-be writer in novelist Billy Crystal's class, and the two

concoct a scheme to trade murders *à la* Hitchcock's *Strangers on a Train*. The finished film just doesn't provide the manic delight promised by its two stars. Rated PG-13 for language. 88m. DIR: Danny DeVito. CAST: Danny DeVito, Billy Crystal, Anne Ramsey, Kim Greist, Kate Mulgrew. 1987

•THUGS 🐾 If this movie were any more of a dog, it would have a tail. Uninspired low-budget effort about a street punk anxious to impress the local syndicate. Been there, done that. Rated R for adult situations, language, nudity, and violence. 93m. DIR: Travis Milloy. CAST: Justin Pagel, Scott Cooke, Michael Egan. 1998

THUMBELINA (1983) ★★★★ This is an *Alice in Wonderland*–type tale of a thumb-size girl (Carrie Fisher) and her adventures as she tries to find her way home. The creatures she meets along the way are well characterized. This is one of the more rewarding *Faerie Tale Theatre* productions. David Hemmings, Carrie Fisher, William Katt, Burgess Meredith (voices). 48m. DIR: Michael Lindsay-Hogg. 1983

THUMBELINA (1989) ★★★★ David Johnson's exquisitely delicate illustrations are the primary appeal here. The Hans Christian Andersen tale concerns a little girl—no larger than the tip of one's thumb. Kelly McGillis narrates the story, and background music is provided by Mark Isham. 30m. DIR: Tim Raglin. 1989

THUNDER ALLEY 🐾 Midwestern teenagers form a rock band. Rated R. 102m. DIR: J. S. Cardone. CAST: Roger Wilson, Jill Schoelen, Scott McGinnis, Leif Garrett. 1985

THUNDER AND LIGHTNING ★★ Weak "action film" about moonshiners. Stars David Carradine and Kate Jackson are watchable enough, but a few touches of originality wouldn't have hurt. Rated PG for profanity and violence. 95m. DIR: Corey Allen. CAST: David Carradine, Kate Jackson, Roger C. Carmel, Sterling Holloway. 1977

THUNDER BAY ★★★1/2 James Stewart plays an oil driller forced to take on a nasty group of Louisiana shrimp fishermen. The story is full of action and fine characterizations from a talented cast. 102m. DIR: Anthony Mann. CAST: James Stewart, Dan Duryea, Joanne Dru, Jay C. Flippen, Gilbert Roland. 1953

THUNDER IN PARADISE ★★★ A hotel owner must marry within two days or she will lose her hotel to her greedy uncle. A nice mix of kidnapping and treasure hunting, plus an amazing high-speed boat race make for an enjoyable film. Even Hulk Hogan manages to perform well in a likable role. Rated PG. 104m. DIR: Douglas Schwartz. CAST: Hulk Hogan, Felicity Waterman, Carol Alt, Robin Weisman, Chris Lemmon, Patrick Macnee, Sam Jones, Charlotte Rae. 1993

THUNDER IN PARADISE II 🐾 Inane full-length version of the syndicated TV show featuring Hulk Hogan and Chris Lemmon as soldiers of fortune. Real star is their high-tech super boat. Unbelievable, uninteresting, and unwatchable. Rated PG for comic book violence. 89m. DIR: Douglas Schwartz. CAST: Hulk Hogan, Chris Lemmon, Carol Alt, Ashley Correll, Patrick Macnee. 1994

THUNDER IN THE CITY ★★ Time severely dates this comedy-drama about a brash, fast-talking American promotor (Edward G. Robinson) who goes to staid London to promote modern U.S. advertising methods. Nigel Bruce fared far better as Holmes's Dr. Watson. B&W; 85m. **DIR:** Marion Gering. **CAST:** Edward G. Robinson, Nigel Bruce, Ralph Richardson. 1937

THUNDER PASS ★★ A good cast wasted as cavalry captain Dane Clark leads settlers out of Indian Territory. B&W; 80m. **DIR:** Frank McDonald. **CAST:** Dane Clark, Dorothy Patrick, Raymond Burr, Andy Devine, John Carradine, Mary Ellen Kay. 1954

THUNDER POINT ★★★ Lackluster telling of an intriguing Jack Higgins story stars Kyle MacLachlan as a former IRA terrorist pressed into duty by the British government to find a potentially world-shattering secret document. Rated R for violence, nudity, and profanity. 95m. **DIR:** George Mihalka. **CAST:** Kyle MacLachlan, Alan Thicke, Michael Sarrazin. 1996

THUNDER ROAD ★★★★ Robert Mitchum wrote the original story and hit theme song for this fast-paced, colorful tale of a bootlegger (Mitchum) who attempts to outwit revenuer Gene Barry. It's one of Mitchum's few all-around, big-screen successes and a tribute to his talents in front of and behind the camera. The star's son, Jim Mitchum, made his film debut as Robert's younger brother. B&W; 92m. **DIR:** Arthur Ripley. **CAST:** Robert Mitchum, Gene Barry, Keely Smith, Jim Mitchum. 1958 DVD

THUNDER RUN 🎦 Grade Z action flick. Rated R for nudity, profanity, suggested sex, and violence. 89m. **DIR:** Gary Hudson. **CAST:** Forrest Tucker, John Ireland, John Shepherd, Jill Whitlow, Cheryl M. Lynn. 1986

THUNDER TRAIL ★★1/2 Gilbert Roland and James Craig, two brothers, are separated as youngsters by outlaws. Years later they are on opposite sides of the law. An A cast fails to lift this Zane Grey story out of a B-movie mold. B&W; 58m. **DIR:** Charles Barton. **CAST:** Gilbert Roland, Charles Bickford, Marsha Hunt, J. Carrol Naish, James Craig. 1937

THUNDER WARRIOR 🎦 In this shameless rip-off of the action scenes in *First Blood*, a tough Indian goes on a one-man rampage. Rated R for profanity, violence, and nudity. 84m. **DIR:** Larry Ludman. **CAST:** Mark Gregory, Bo Svenson. 1983

THUNDER WARRIOR II 🎦 Sleazy, Italian-made action flick. Rated R. 84m. **DIR:** Larry Ludman. **CAST:** Mark Gregory, Bo Svenson. 1985

THUNDERBALL ★★★ When originally released in 1965, this fourth entry in the James Bond series suffered from comparison to its two admittedly superior predecessors, *From Russia with Love* and *Goldfinger*. However, time has proved it to be one of the more watchable movies based on the books by Ian Fleming, with Sean Connery in top form as 007 and assured direction by Terence Young. 129m. **DIR:** Terence Young. **CAST:** Sean Connery, Claudine Auger, Adolfo Celi. 1965 DVD

THUNDERBOLT AND LIGHTFOOT ★★★★ Clint Eastwood's right-on-target performance is equaled by those of his costars in this decidedly offbeat caper picture. *Thunderbolt and Lightfoot* proved a little too offbeat when originally released in 1974. However, movie buffs have since proclaimed it a cinematic gem, a reputation it deserves. Rated R. 114m. **DIR:** Michael Cimino. **CAST:** Clint Eastwood, Jeff Bridges, George Kennedy, Geoffrey Lewis, Gary Busey. 1974 DVD

THUNDERHEART ★★★1/2 FBI agent Val Kilmer is assigned to help veteran agent Sam Shepard investigate the murder of an Oglala Sioux on a reservation in the badlands of South Dakota. Michael Apted's richest and most compelling movie since *Coal Miner's Daughter*. Rated R for violence and profanity. 127m. **DIR:** Michael Apted. **CAST:** Val Kilmer, Sam Shepard, Graham Greene, Fred Ward, Fred Dalton Thompson. 1992 DVD

THUNDERING HOOFS ★★1/2 A rancher's son wins a horse and a beautiful señorita. Chock-full of daring stunts, winning performances, and unbridled enthusiasm, this early Fred Thomson series entry shows why he was one of the highest regarded of all cowboy stars before his untimely death. Stunt legend Yakima Canutt doubled Thomson in a daring horse-to-stagecoach transfer that predates Canutt's similar stunts in bigger-budgeted films a dozen years later. B&W; 53m. **DIR:** Albert S. Rogell. **CAST:** Fred Thomson, Fred Huntley, Charles Mailes, Ann May. 1924

THURSDAY'S GAME ★★★ Engaging made-for-television film about two ordinary guys (Gene Wilder and Bob Newhart) who continue to get together on Thursday nights after their weekly poker game collapses. Both make the most of this small rebellion. The supporting cast is excellent. Not rated; adult themes. 74m. **DIR:** Robert Moore. **CAST:** Gene Wilder, Bob Newhart, Ellen Burstyn, Cloris Leachman, Rob Reiner, Nancy Walker, Valerie Harper. 1974

THX 1138 ★★★1/2 Science-fiction and movie buffs may want to rent this moody, atmospheric picture, starring Robert Duvall and Donald Pleasence, to see an example of the type of work director George Lucas was doing pre–*Star Wars*. It was the fabulously successful filmmaker's first. Interesting. Rated PG. 88m. **DIR:** George Lucas. **CAST:** Robert Duvall, Donald Pleasence, Maggie McOmie. 1971

TICK, THE (TV SERIES) ★★★ Based on the underground comic book of the same name, this entertaining animated series unmercifully parodies the typical superhero fare with irreverent glee as clueless Tick and his pal Arthur save the world from an assortment of oddball villains. Not rated. Each 50m. **DIR:** Richard Bowman. 1994–1995

TICK … TICK … TICK … ★★★ Newly elected sheriff Jim Brown struggles against racism, ignorance, and some good-ole-boys to keep a rural southern community from exploding. Dated but still entertaining. Rated PG for violence. 100m. **DIR:** Ralph Nelson. **CAST:** Jim Brown, George Kennedy, Fredric March, Don Stroud, Clifton James, Lynn Carlin, Janet MacLachlan. 1970

TICKET, THE ★★1/2 A family on the verge of poverty wins the lottery but must fly across snow-packed mountains to claim the prize. Their plane is sabotaged, and the bad guys start chasing them to steal the winning ticket. It's a fairly moronic plot in this made-for-cable original, but there are one or two adequately acted scenes sprinkled through the action.

Rated PG-13 for violence. 95m. **DIR:** Stuart Cooper. **CAST:** Shannen Doherty, James Marshall, Heidi Swedberg, Al Mancini. 1997

TICKET OF LEAVE MAN, THE ★★ British horror star Tod Slaughter gleefully plays a maniacal killer who swindles rich philanthropists with a phony charity organization he has established. Slaughter single-handedly presided as Great Britain's unofficial hobgoblin during the 1930s and early 1940s. The majority of his films have been unavailable for years in America. B&W; 71m. **DIR:** George King. **CAST:** Tod Slaughter, John Warwick, Marjorie Taylor. 1937

TICKET TO HEAVEN ★★★ This Canadian film presents a lacerating look at the frightening phenomenon of contemporary religious cults. Nick Mancuso is riveting as the brainwashed victim. Saul Rubinek and Meg Foster are splendid in support. But R. H. Thomson almost steals the show as a painfully pragmatic deprogrammer. Nice touches of humor give the movie balance. Rated PG. 107m. **DIR:** Ralph L. Thomas. **CAST:** Nick Mancuso, Saul Rubinek, Meg Foster, Kim Cattrall, R. H. Thomson. 1981 DVD

TICKLE ME ★★ The plot falls below that found in a standard Elvis vehicle in this unfunny comedy-musical, which has Elvis working and singing at an all-female health ranch. Mindless fluff. 90m. **DIR:** Norman Taurog. **CAST:** Elvis Presley, Jocelyn Lane, Julie Adams, Jack Mullaney, Merry Anders. 1965

TIDES OF WAR ★★1/2 Clichéd wartime intrigue concerning a German naval officer who lands on a Caribbean island to secure it as a Nazi missile site and gradually discovers he sympathizes with the Allied cause. Rated PG-13 for violence and brief nudity. 91m. **DIR:** Nello Rossati. **CAST:** David Soul, Yvette Heyden, Rod Obregon, Ernest Borgnine, Stephen Luotto, Bo Svenson. 1990

TIDY ENDINGS ★★★★ Tender, touching AIDS drama deals with the confrontation between the victim's wife, wonderfully played by Stockard Channing, and the man's gay lover, sensitively played by Harvey Fierstein. Both wife and lover must come to grips with each other, and what each other meant to the deceased. Insightful and human. 54m. **DIR:** Gavin Millar. **CAST:** Stockard Channing, Harvey Fierstein, Nathaniel Moreau, Jean De Baer. 1989

TIE ME UP! TIE ME DOWN! ★★★1/2 From Spain's hot cult director Pedro Almodóvar, concerning the unorthodox romance between a soft-core porno star named Marina (Victoria Abril) and a recently released psychiatric patient named Ricky (Antonio Banderas). This film exists in both R and unrated versions, due to profanity and explicit sexual content. In Spanish with English subtitles. 105m. **DIR:** Pedro Almodóvar. **CAST:** Victoria Abril, Antonio Banderas. 1990

TIE THAT BINDS, THE ★★ Two psycho serial killers set out to retrieve their 6-year-old daughter from the decent couple who have adopted her. This wildly implausible melodrama has only its middle-class-nightmare premise to recommend it; not even the performances of the usually reliable cast can redeem the film's tawdry excesses. Rated R for extreme violence (even the little girl winds up with blood on her hands). 98m. **DIR:** Wesley Strick. **CAST:** Daryl Hannah,

Keith Carradine, Moira Kelly, Vincent Spano, Julia Devin. 1995 DVD

TIE-DIED: ROCK 'N' ROLL'S MOST DEDICATED FANS ★★1/2 An almost entertaining intro into the land of the Dead, where Jerry Garcia was king and the 1960s never ended. It really is about the fans and not the group, and director Andrew Behar does reveal the downside to life's longest road trip. Rated R for profanity and drug use. 88m. **DIR:** Andrew Behar. 1995 DVD

TIEFLAND ★★★1/2 A shepherd and a marquis vie for the affections of a Spanish dancer in this atmospheric, visually poetic melodrama featuring gorgeous black-and-white photography. Leni Riefenstahl did most of the filming in 1935 but was unable to complete it for nineteen years because of the war and later problems with the French government. B&W; 98m. **DIR:** Leni Riefenstahl. **CAST:** Leni Riefenstahl, Franz Eichberger. 1954

TIGER AND THE PUSSYCAT, THE ★★1/2 Male menopause comedy-drama of middle-aged Vittorio Gassman entranced with Ann-Margret, an American student living and loving in Italy. Pretty dated; the stars make it bearable. In English. Not rated, with some innocuous sex talk. 105m. **DIR:** Dino Risi. **CAST:** Ann-Margret, Vittorio Gassman, Eleanor Parker. 1967

TIGER BAY ★★★1/2 Young Hayley Mills began her film career—in a part originally written for a boy—as an imaginative girl who witnesses a murder and then befriends the killer. Since the child is a known liar, nobody believes her until events escalate to the point of desperation. Horst Buchholz is excellent as the remorseful murderer. A thoughtful drama for all ages. Not rated; suitable for family viewing. B&W; 105m. **DIR:** J. Lee Thompson. **CAST:** John Mills, Horst Buchholz, Hayley Mills, Yvonne Mitchell, Anthony Dawson. 1959 DVD

TIGER HEART ★★ Sort of a grittier take on *The Karate Kid*, with T. J. Roberts as a teenage martial arts champion who helps protect his girlfriend's uncle from thugs trying to make him sell his supermarket. Designed for teen viewers who are too old for cartoons but too young for most action films. Rated PG-13 for mild profanity and violence. 90m. **DIR:** Georges Chamchoum. **CAST:** Ted Jan Roberts, Robert LaSardo, Jennifer Lyons. 1996

TIGER TOWN ★★1/2 In this passable movie, made for the Disney Channel, Roy Scheider stars as a legendary baseball player whose final year with the Detroit Tigers looks dismal until a young boy (Justin Henry) "wishes" him to success. At least, that's what the boy believes. Both Scheider and Henry give good performances, but the overall effect is not as impressive as it could have been. Rated G. 76m. **DIR:** Alan Shapiro. **CAST:** Roy Scheider, Justin Henry. 1984

TIGER WALKS, A ★★1/2 This Disney drama about an escaped circus tiger and the impact his fate has on a small town boasts a good cast of veteran film personalities as well as a jaundiced view of politics and mass hysteria. 88m. **DIR:** Norman Tokar. **CAST:** Brian Keith, Vera Miles, Pamela Franklin, Sabu, Kevin Corcoran, Peter Brown, Una Merkel, Frank McHugh. 1964

TIGER WARSAW ★★ Members of a family torn apart by a tragic incident struggle through their lives—all the while unable to forgive and forget. Patrick Swayze is Tiger Warsaw, a man haunted by the memory of shooting his father. Vague film lacking in substance and direction. Rated R for violence and profanity. 92m. **DIR:** Amin Q. Chaudhri. **CAST:** Patrick Swayze, Barbara Williams, Lee Richardson, Piper Laurie. 1987

TIGER'S TALE, A 💐 Grievously unfunny comedy about a not-so-bright teenage stud from Texas. Rated R for nudity. 97m. **DIR:** Peter Douglas. **CAST:** Ann-Margret, C. Thomas Howell, Charles Durning, Kelly Preston, William Zabka, Ann Wedgeworth, Tim Thomerson. 1988

•**TIGGER MOVIE, THE** ★★★ Don't expect the latest dazzling animation in this sweet, mild adaptation of author A. A. Milne's *Hundred Acre Woods* characters. The background scenery is flat, giving the film a booklike feel. What isn't flat is Tigger's over-the-top personality as he seeks companionship and receives help from Winnie the Pooh and pals. Adorable Roo steals every scene. Rated G. 85m. **DIR:** Jun Falkenstein. 2000

TIGHT LITTLE ISLAND ★★★★ A World War II transport laden with whiskey founders just off the shore of a Scottish island. Hilarious hell breaks loose as delirious lads and lassies seek to salvage the water of life before authorities can claim it. One of the great comedies that revived the British film industry after the war. B&W; 82m. **DIR:** Alexander Mackendrick. **CAST:** Basil Radford, Joan Greenwood, James Robertson Justice, Gordon Jackson. 1949

TIGHTROPE ★★★★★ A terrific, taut suspense-thriller, this ranks with the best films in the genre. Written and directed by Richard Tuggle, it casts Clint Eastwood as Wes Block, homicide inspector for the New Orleans Police Department. His latest assignment is to track down a Jack the Ripper–style sex murderer. This case hits disturbingly close to home in more ways than one. Rated R for violence. 115m. **DIR:** Richard Tuggle. **CAST:** Clint Eastwood, Genevieve Bujold, Dan Hedaya, Alison Eastwood. 1984

TIGRERO: A FILM THAT WAS NEVER MADE ★★★★ In 1954, maverick director Sam Fuller went to the jungles of Brazil to scout locations for a film he was going to make, *Tigrero*, starring John Wayne, Ava Gardner, and Tyrone Power. For insurance reasons the studio canceled the project. Forty years later Fuller, accompanied by fellow filmmaker Jim Jarmusch, returns to visit the members of the Karaja tribe he met on his original trip and shows them the films he took of them and their now-dead relatives. A fascinating cultural document. Not rated; contains no objectionable material. 75m. **DIR:** Mika Kaurismaki. **CAST:** Samuel Fuller, Jim Jarmusch. 1995

TIGRESS, THE ★★ Tired blood makes this kitty roll over and play dead. Sultry Valentina Vargas gets involved with con man James Remar. Available in two versions: unrated for less-than-titillating sex scenes, and rated R for less of the same. Unrated 89m.; Rated R 87m. **DIR:** Karin Howard. **CAST:** James Remar, Valentina Vargas, George Peppard, Hannes Jaenicke. 1992 DVD

'TIL THERE WAS YOU ★★1/2 Searching for Mr. Right is a test of stamina for audiences and leading ladies alike, in this sugary romantic comedy. The tease here is that it takes twenty years for two strangers to cross paths several times and then sort of fall in love at first sight. The story bulges with group-hug humanity, but is rather uninvolving. Rated PG-13 for profanity and mature themes. 114m. **DIR:** Scott Winant. **CAST:** Jeanne Tripplehorn, Dylan McDermott, Sarah Jessica Parker, Jennifer Aniston, Craig Bierko, Michael Tucker, Karen Allen. 1997

TILL DEATH DO US PART ★★★1/2 Made-for-TV film based on Los Angeles DA Vincent Bugliosi's brilliant case against spouse killer Alan Palliko in 1966. All the evidence against Palliko and his gal pal was circumstantial. Suspenseful and spellbinding moments. Not rated; contains violence and nudity. 93m. **DIR:** Yves Simoneau. **CAST:** Treat Williams, Arliss Howard, Rebecca Jenkins. 1991

TILL MARRIAGE DO US PART ★★ Although a slight Italian sex comedy, its star, Laura Antonelli, is as delicious as ever. It's a treat for her fans only. Rated R. 97m. **DIR:** Luigi Comencini. **CAST:** Laura Antonelli. 1974

TILL MURDER DO US PART ★★★ Meredith Baxter-Birney is good as convicted murderess Betty Broderick in this made-for-television docudrama. When a devoted wife's husband leaves her for another woman, she goes off the deep end and begins a campaign of terror that culminates in murder. Stephen Collins and Michelle Johnson costar as the unfaithful husband and mistress whose affair is the catalyst for Broderick's breakdown. Not rated. 82m. **DIR:** Dick Lowry. **CAST:** Meredith Baxter-Birney, Stephen Collins, Michelle Johnson, Kelli Williams. 1992

TILL THE CLOUDS ROLL BY ★★1/2 Biography of songwriter Jerome Kern is a barrage of MGM talent that includes Judy Garland, Frank Sinatra, Lena Horne, Dinah Shore, Kathryn Grayson, and many more in short, tuneful vignettes that tie this all-out effort together. Not too bad as musical bio-pics go, but singing talent is definitely the star in this production. 137m. **DIR:** Richard Whorf. **CAST:** Robert Walker, Van Heflin, Judy Garland, Lucille Bremer. 1946 DVD

TILL THE END OF THE NIGHT ★★★ Scott Valentine gives an effective performance as a man who discovers that his wife's past includes a marriage to a hardened criminal. Of course, he discovers this when that hardened criminal is released from prison and begins to harass his family. Sure, it's silly at times but performances throughout are solid and the film does offer some suspense and action. Rated R for profanity and violence. 90m. **DIR:** Larry Brand. **CAST:** Scott Valentine, Katherine Kelly Lang, Roger Clinton. 1994

TILL THE END OF TIME ★★★ Three veterans of World War II come home to find life, in general, and how it was when they left, considerably changed. Readjustment is tough, and the love they left has soured. A good drama. B&W; 105m. **DIR:** Edward Dmytryk. **CAST:** Dorothy McGuire, Guy Madison, Robert Mitchum, Jean Porter. 1946

TILL THERE WAS YOU ★★ A lackluster film about an American saxophonist (Mark Harmon) who goes to the island nation of Vanuatu. An almost plotless mystery. Rated PG-13 for violence and nudity. 94m. **DIR:** John Seale. **CAST:** Mark Harmon, Deborah Unger, Jeroen Krabbé, Briant Shane. **1991**

TILT 💔 Brooke Shields's third movie (after *Alice, Sweet Alice* and *Pretty Baby*) is a mess. Rated PG. 104m. **DIR:** Rudy Durand. **CAST:** Brooke Shields, Ken Marshall, Charles Durning, Geoffrey Lewis. **1978**

TIM ★★★1/2 An unforgettable character study from down under, this features Mel Gibson in his film debut as a simpleminded young adult and Piper Laurie as the older woman who finds herself falling in love with him. Superb supporting performances by the Australian cast—especially Alwyn Kurts and Pat Evison, as Tim's parents. Rated PG for suggested sex. 108m. **DIR:** Michael Pate. **CAST:** Mel Gibson, Piper Laurie, Alwyn Kurts. **1979**

TIME AFTER TIME ★★★★ H. G. Wells (Malcolm McDowell) pursues Jack the Ripper (David Warner) into modern-day San Francisco via a time machine. It's an enjoyable pastiche that has quite a few nice moments. Rated PG. 112m. **DIR:** Nicholas Meyer. **CAST:** Malcolm McDowell, David Warner, Mary Steenburgen. **1979**

TIME BANDITS ★★★★ Anyone with a sense of adventure will find a lot to like about this delightful tale of a boy and six dwarves—no, this isn't *Snow White*—who travel back in time through holes in the fabric of the universe. Rated PG for violence and adult themes. 110m. **DIR:** Terry Gilliam. **CAST:** Sean Connery, Shelley Duvall, Ralph Richardson, Ian Holm, David Warner, John Cleese, Michael Palin. **1981 DVD**

TIME BOMB ★★ Michael Biehn plays an amnesiac who suddenly finds himself a target for assassination. Patsy Kensit costars as a psychiatrist who Biehn first abducts and persuades to restore his memory. Rated R for violence, profanity, and simulated sex. 96m. **DIR:** Avi Nesher. **CAST:** Michael Biehn, Patsy Kensit, Tracy Scoggins, Robert Culp, Richard Jordan. **1991**

TIME CHASERS ★★★1/2 After the time machine he invented destroys the future of mankind, a physics teacher tries to go back in time to undo the damage. Clever low-budget sci-fi tale proves you don't need a $100 million budget if you have imagination and a good story. Not rated; contains nothing objectionable. 90m. **DIR:** David Giancola. **CAST:** Matthew Burch, Bonnie Pritchard, Peter Harrington. **1995**

TIME FLIES WHEN YOU'RE ALIVE ★★★★ Actor Paul Linke's monologue chronicling his wife's battle with cancer and how it affected his family is a wonderful mix of humor and sorrow. Linke takes the audience on a roller coaster ride of emotions from heartbreaking tales of death and loss to amusing anecdotes celebrating life. Not rated; contains profanity. 80m. **DIR:** Roger Spottiswoode. **CAST:** Paul Linke. **1990**

TIME GUARDIAN, THE 💔 Enemies of the future—man and metallic man—go back in time to prepare to do battle. Rated PG for violence. 80m. **DIR:** Brian Hannant. **CAST:** Carrie Fisher, Tom Burlinson, Dean Stockwell. **1987**

TIME MACHINE, THE ★★★★ Rod Taylor plays a scientist in the early 1900s who invents a device that can transport him within the dimensions of time. He goes forward past three world wars and into the year 802,701, where he encounters a world very different from the one he left. This movie has all the elements that make up a classic in science fiction. 103m. **DIR:** George Pal. **CAST:** Rod Taylor, Yvette Mimieux, Alan Young, Sebastian Cabot. **1960**

TIME OF DESTINY, A ★★1/2 Old-fashioned tale of love, hate, and revenge set against the backdrop of World War II. William Hurt is the guilt-ridden son of a Basque family in San Diego out to avenge the accidental death of his father. Timothy Hutton is the subject of Hurt's revenge. Beautiful photography, terrific editing and pacing help keep you from noticing the weak spots in the familiar plot. Rated PG-13 for violence and profanity. 118m. **DIR:** Gregory Nava. **CAST:** William Hurt, Timothy Hutton, Melissa Leo, Stockard Channing. **1988**

TIME OF THE GYPSIES ★★★★ A young psychic gypsy learns the meaning of life the hard way. Absorbing character study, brilliantly photographed. The film weaves magical realism, visual humor, and pathos. A must-see! In Yugoslavian with English subtitles. Rated R. 136m. **DIR:** Emir Kusturica. **CAST:** Davor Dujmovic, Bora Todorovic. **1989**

TIME OF THEIR LIVES, THE ★★1/2 Bearing more than a passing resemblance to *The Canterville Ghost* and *I Married a Witch*, this story of ghostly goings-on is one of Abbott and Costello's most unusual features. Costello plays a man mistakenly shot as a traitor during the Revolutionary War and doomed to haunt a Colonial mansion until proved innocent. B&W; 82m. **DIR:** Charles Barton. **CAST:** Bud Abbott, Lou Costello, Marjorie Reynolds, Binnie Barnes, John Shelton, Gale Sondergaard, Robert Barrat, Donald MacBride. **1946**

TIME OF YOUR LIFE, THE ★★★1/2 Originally a prize-winning play by the brilliant William Saroyan. Director H. C. Potter and a talented group of actors have created a pleasing film about the diverse characters who are regulars at Nick's Saloon, Restaurant and Entertainment Palace on San Francisco's Barbary Coast. A charmer, this picture grows on you. B&W; 109m. **DIR:** H. C. Potter. **CAST:** James Cagney, Wayne Morris, Broderick Crawford, Jeanne Cagney, Ward Bond, Jimmy Lydon, Gale Page. **1948 DVD**

TIME OUT FOR LOVE ★★ Romantic roundelay with Jean Seberg as an American girl who gets caught in the middle of a failed love affair between a race-car driver and a suicidal fashion designer. In French with English subtitles. 93m. **DIR:** Jean Valère. **CAST:** Jean Seberg, Micheline Presle. **1961**

TIME RUNNER ★★ Story alternates between the year 2022, when Earth is at war with aliens, and 1992, when a man from 2022 has arrived on Earth. Of course his actions during 1992 will determine the outcome of the future war. Predictable. Rated R for profanity and violence. 90m. **DIR:** Michael Mazo. **CAST:** Mark Hamill, Brion James, Marc Baur, Gordon Tipple, Rae Dawn Chong. **1992**

•**TIME SERVED** 💔 A woman sent to prison agrees to participate in a work-release program so that she can dance topless at the club frequented by the psychotic judge who sentenced her. No one here gets time off for good behavior. Rated R for adult situations, language, nudity, and violence. 94m. **DIR:** Glen Pitre. **CAST:** Catherine Oxenberg, Jeff Fahey, Bo Hopkins, Larry Manetti, Louise Fletcher. 1999

•**TIME SHIFTERS, THE** ★★★ Watchable sci-fi feature focuses on a tabloid journalist's discovery that futuristic tourists are visiting historic disaster sites. After the journalist prevents a plane crash, the Thrill Seeker "tour company" must stop him from further altering their time line. Not rated; contains violence and language. 91m. **DIR:** Mario Azzopardi. **CAST:** Casper Van Dien, Catherine Bell, Theresa Saldana, Peter Outerbridge. 1999

TIME STALKERS ★★★ A mildly entertaining made-for-TV movie about a modern-day Old West buff who helps a scientist from the future track a villain into the past. An exciting conclusion. Not rated; contains mild violence. 96m. **DIR:** Michael Schultz. **CAST:** William Devane, Lauren Hutton, John Ratzenberger, Forrest Tucker, Klaus Kinski. 1986

TIME STANDS STILL ★★1/2 This Hungarian export dwells so much on the "art for art's sake" credo that it nearly destroys some of the life the film tries to depict. It's about restless youths at the threshold of adulthood in Hungary. The film is presented in the original language with subtitles. Not rated, but the equivalent of an R for nudity and language. 99m. **DIR:** Peter Gothar. **CAST:** Ben Barenholtz, Albert Schwartz. 1982

TIME TO DIE, A (1983) ★★ Despite the name actors and source material by Mario Puzo, this vengeance flick has a story as dog-eared as they come. An American spy returns to Europe after World War II to hunt the Nazis who killed his French wife. The twists unravel too easily to make for a thrilling affair. Rated R for nudity and violence. 89m. **DIR:** Matt Cimber. **CAST:** Rex Harrison, Rod Taylor, Edward Albert, Raf Vallone. 1983

TIME TO DIE, A (1990) 💗 The only mystery in this tale of a female photographer (former porn star Traci Lords) who catches a cop in a compromising position, is why anyone would want to watch it in the first place. Rated R for violence and profanity. 90m. **DIR:** Charles Kanganis. **CAST:** Traci Lords, Richard Roundtree, Jeff Conaway. 1991

TIME TO KILL (1990) ★★ Nicolas Cage stars as Enrico, an Italian officer stationed in Africa who accidentally kills a woman. Rated R for violence and nudity. 100m. **DIR:** Giuliano Montaldo. **CAST:** Nicolas Cage. 1990 DVD

TIME TO KILL, A (1996) ★★1/2 John Grisham's overwrought first novel gets equally melodramatic treatment in this *too*-faithful adaptation. Mississippi attorney defends a factory worker who killed the two racist thugs guilty of raping his 10-year-old daughter; the subsequent case becomes a media sensation involving the KKK, the National Guard, and several kitchen sinks. Rated R for violence, profanity, and rape. 145m. **DIR:** Joel Schumacher. **CAST:** Sandra Bullock, Samuel L. Jackson, Matthew McConaughey, Kevin Spacey, Brenda Fricker, Oliver Platt, Charles Dut-

ton, Ashley Judd, Patrick McGoohan, Donald Sutherland, Kiefer Sutherland. 1996 DVD

TIME TO LOVE AND A TIME TO DIE, A ★★1/2 A well-intentioned but preachy and largely unsatisfying antiwar film adapted from the novel by Erich Maria Remarque who also portrays the professor. John Gavin is a German soldier who receives a furlough from the Russian front in 1944. He returns home to find his town a bombed-out shell and his parents missing. 133m. **DIR:** Douglas Sirk. **CAST:** John Gavin, Lilo Pulver, Jock Mahoney, Don DeFore, Keenan Wynn, Erich Maria Remarque, Jim Hutton, Klaus Kinski. 1958

TIME TRACKERS ★★ Scientists from the future chase one of their own through time in an effort to stop him from changing the course of history. Great medieval costumes, but the production is too amateurish to soar very high. Rated PG. 86m. **DIR:** Howard R. Cohen. **CAST:** Wil Shriner, Ned Beatty, Kathleen Beller, Bridget Hoffman, Lee Bergere, Alex Hyde-White. 1989

TIME TRAVELERS, THE ★★★1/2 Imaginative story of scientists who plunge into a time corridor to rescue a colleague and find themselves stuck in the wreckage of the Earth of the future. Similar in many respects to other survival-after-nuclear-holocaust films, this entertaining film boasts vicious mutants, intelligent survivors who live under the surface of Earth, and a trick ending that is unique and intriguing. 82m. **DIR:** Ib Melchior. **CAST:** Preston Foster, Philip Carey, Merry Anders, Steve Franken, John Hoyt, Joan Woodbury. 1964

TIME WALKER 💗 Egyptologist accidentally brings an ancient mummy back to life. Avoid it. Rated PG. 83m. **DIR:** Tom Kennedy. **CAST:** Ben Murphy, Nina Axelrod, Kevin Brophy, Shari Belafonte. 1982

TIME WITHOUT PITY ★★★★ Suspenseful British thriller with a clear anti-capital-punishment message. An alcoholic just out of the hospital has twenty-four hours to save his son from the gallows. It all gets a bit overwrought by the end. Not rated; contains violence. B&W; 88m. **DIR:** Joseph Losey. **CAST:** Michael Redgrave, Ann Todd, Leo McKern, Peter Cushing, Alec McCowen, Renee Houston, Joan Plowright, Lois Maxwell. 1957

TIMECOP ★★★1/2 Jean-Claude Van Damme is the Timecop, a law-enforcement officer whose job it is to prevent crooks from using a new time-travel technology to get rich. Some plot twists lead to lapses in logic; however, an affecting subplot concerning the death of Van Damme's wife works well enough to redeem the whole affair. Rated R for violence, profanity, nudity, and simulated sex. 98m. **DIR:** Peter Hyams. **CAST:** Jean-Claude Van Damme, Mia Sara, Ron Silver, Bruce McGill, Gloria Reuben, Scott Bellis, Jason Schombing. 1994 DVD

TIMEMASTER ★★ Another vanity production from director James Glickenhaus, starring his son Jesse as an orphan who believes his parents are alive but are being held prisoner in another galaxy. He enlists the aid of a wise, old inventor to help him defeat the evil dictator, free his parents, and save the world from an evil virtual-reality game. Rated PG-13 for violence. 110m. **DIR:** James Glickenhaus. **CAST:**

Noriyuki "Pat" Morita, Jesse Cameron-Glickenhaus, Joanna Pacula, Michael Dorn, Michelle Williams. **1995**

TIMERIDER 💗 A motorcycle rider and his motorcycle break the time barrier and end up being chased by cowboys in the Old West. Rated PG. 94m. **DIR:** William Dear. **CAST:** Fred Ward, Belinda Bauer, Peter Coyote, L. Q. Jones, Ed Lauter. **1983**

TIMES SQUARE 💗 A totally unbelievable story involving two New York teens who hang out in Times Square. Rated R for profanity. 111m. **DIR:** Alan Moyle. **CAST:** Tim Curry, Robin Johnson, Trini Alvarado, Peter Coffield. **1980**

TIMES TO COME ★★★ When an innocent man is accidentally shot during a demonstration, this act hurls him into a nightmarish world where he must struggle to survive. A futuristic city plagued with political unrest and violence provides the backdrop for this baffling science-fiction thriller. In Spanish with English subtitles. Not rated; the film has profanity, nudity, and violence. 98m. **DIR:** Gustavo Mosquera. **CAST:** Hugo Soto, Juan Leyrado. **1988**

TIN CUP ★★★1/2 Director Ron Shelton touches all the bases in this look at the game of golf and the personalities drawn to it. Kevin Costner is terrific as the burned-out pro, now a golf instructor in the middle of nowhere, whose attraction to René Russo revives an old rivalry with circuit champ Don Johnson. A thought-provoking drama with real insight and romance. Rated R for profanity and brief nudity. 135m. **DIR:** Ron Shelton. **CAST:** Kevin Costner, René Russo, Don Johnson, Richard "Cheech" Marin, Linda Hart, Dennis Burkley, Rex Linn. **1996 DVD**

TIN DRUM, THE ★★★1/2 Günter Grass's bizarre tale of 3-year-old Oskar, who stops growing as the Nazis rise to power in Germany. Oskar expresses his outrage by banging on a tin drum. This unique film has a disturbing dreamlike quality, while its visuals are alternately startling and haunting. Received the Academy Award for best foreign film. In German with English subtitles. Rated R for nudity and gore. 142m. **DIR:** Volker Schlöndorff. **CAST:** David Bennent, Mario Adorf, Angela Winkler, Daniel Olbrychski. **1979 DVD**

TIN MAN ★★★ For the most part, this is an intriguing drama about a deaf auto mechanic who invents a computer with which he can hear and speak. When he attempts to get the device manufactured, the computer company sets out to exploit him. Timothy Bottoms is extraordinary, and the story holds your attention, but the film is hurt by cardboard villains and a pat ending. Not rated. 95m. **DIR:** John G. Thomas. **CAST:** Timothy Bottoms, Deana Jurgens, John Phillip Law, Troy Donahue. **1983**

TIN MEN ★★★★ Writer-director Barry Levinson takes a simple subject—the vendetta between two aluminum-siding salesmen in the 1950s—and fashions it into an insightful, witty comedy. The tone is similar to Levinson's earlier *Diner*. He has elicited top-notch performances from his trio of stars. Barbara Hershey is convincing as she transforms her character from mousy pawn to attractive, assertive woman. Rated R. 110m. **DIR:** Barry Levinson. **CAST:** Richard Dreyfuss, Danny DeVito, Barbara Hershey. **1987**

TIN PAN ALLEY ★★★1/2 Showgirl sisters Alice Faye and Betty Grable cross romantic paths with song pluggers John Payne and Jack Oakie from the turn of the century until World War I. Many wonderful songs from that era and an Oscar for Alfred Newman's score. Some cassettes open with an "added feature" of Faye singing "Get Out and Get Under." This was deleted from the movie before its release. B&W; 94m. **DIR:** Walter Lang. **CAST:** Alice Faye, Betty Grable, Jack Oakie, John Payne, Allen Jenkins, Billy Gilbert, Elisha Cook Jr., John Loder. **1940**

TIN SOLDIER, THE ★★1/2 This inane update of Hans Christian Andersen's fairy tale was one of the silliest results of 1995s Voices Against Violence Week. Rated PG for mild violence. 100m. **DIR:** Jon Voight. **CAST:** Jon Voight, Ally Sheedy, Dom DeLuise, Trent Knight. **1995**

TIN STAR, THE ★★★★ Solid Anthony Mann–directed adult Western has Anthony Perkins as the inexperienced sheriff of a wild-and-woolly town seeking the help of hardened gunfighter Henry Fonda. Although it contains some unconvincing moments, it succeeds overall thanks to the skilled playing of its cast. B&W; 93m. **DIR:** Anthony Mann. **CAST:** Henry Fonda, Anthony Perkins, Betsy Palmer, John McIntire, Michel Ray, Neville Brand, Lee Van Cleef. **1957**

TINGLER, THE ★★★ Director William Castle's stylish thriller is probably best known for its theatrical gimmick—joy buzzers installed in seats. The jolt was to create hysteria in theaters to match the panic on the screen. On video, the film is a campy treat, thanks to Vincent Price's coroner, who discovers that fear creates a creepy parasite on the spinal cord. The terror comes when the parasites break free. Fun blast from the past. 82m. **DIR:** William Castle. **CAST:** Vincent Price, Judith Evelyn, Darryl Hickman, Philip Coolidge. **1959 DVD**

TINTORERA 💗 Interminable *Jaws* rip-off. Rated R for gore and T&A. 91m. **DIR:** René Cardona Jr. **CAST:** Susan George, Hugo Stiglitz, Fiona Lewis. **1977**

TINY TOON ADVENTURES ★★★★ Downsized classic cartoon characters have not always been successful—*The Flintstone Kids* being a nauseous example—but the pint-sized inhabitants of Warner Bros. Tiny Toons universe are wisecracking strokes of genius. Elmyra, a shrill little girl who *loooooves* her "fuzzy-wuzzy buddies," is a wholly original character clearly shaped by executive producer Steven Spielberg. Certain parodies may be too scary for small fry. Each collection includes a mix of shorter and longer stories. 40m. **DIR:** Various. **1993**

TINY TOONS ADVENTURES: HOW I SPENT MY VACATION ★★★★ The Warner Bros. cartoon legacy lives on, thanks to producer Steven Spielberg's lovingly crafted pint-sized renditions of the classic animated superstars. This made-for-video feature concerns the various members of ACME Acres, as school lets out for summer. Babs and Buster Bunny take a river journey through the deep South; Plucky Duck and Hampton Pig share the family car-trip from hell; holy terror Elmira (who "wuvs kitties") has a close encounter with the big cats of a safari park. 80m. **DIR:** Steven Spielberg. **1992**

•**TITAN A.E.** ★★★1/2 This ambitious space saga, something of an animated riff on *Star Wars*, delivers solid characters and dramatic conflict in a package that feels like an American take on traditional Japanese *anime*. The year is 3028, and Earth has been destroyed by a race of energy beings bent on eradicating humans from the universe; one of the few survivors, a young man whose father invented a massive spaceship rumored to be mankind's only hope, is sucked into a series of dangerous adventures while trying to find this near-mythical craft. Although the characters here (thankfully) never break into song, the score is laced with cutting-edge rock from bands such as Powerman 5000, Electrasy, Bliss, The Urge, and Fun Lovin' Criminals; at times you'll wonder if the sound track album was deemed more important than the film itself. Rated PG for dramatic content. 94m. **DIR:** Don Bluth, Gary Goldman. 2000

TITANIC (1953) ★★1/2 The sinking of the "unsinkable" 1912 luxury liner on its maiden voyage dramatically solves the domestic problems of a rich but unhappy couple, Barbara Stanwyck and Clifton Webb, in this powerful fiction and fact re-creation of the most famous peacetime sea tragedy of this century. Superb acting, special effects, and a first-rate story make this film a classic. 97m. **DIR:** Jean Negulesco. **CAST:** Barbara Stanwyck, Clifton Webb, Robert Wagner, Audrey Dalton, Thelma Ritter, Allyn Joslyn, Brian Aherne. 1953

TITANIC (1995) ★★★★ The fascinating story of the dream that became a nightmare is vividly told through interviews with survivors, diary excerpts, still photos, and newsreels. Narrated by David McCallum. Not rated. 200m. on four cassettes DIR: Melissa Peltier. 1995

TITANIC (1996) ★★★ Once again the greatest steamship in the world sails majestically to her tragic end in the deep Atlantic. This account, a blend of fiction and fact, adds little to the legend, but should please fans of the ship and her sad history. 173m. **DIR:** Robert Lieberman. **CAST:** Peter Gallagher, George C. Scott, Eva Marie Saint, Tim Curry, Marilu Henner. 1996 DVD

TITANIC (1997) ★★★★★ Writer-director James Cameron has, against all odds, come up with an old-fashioned-style classic in the oft-told tale of the sinking of the luxury liner. Leonardo DiCaprio and Kate Winslet are perfectly cast as the vulnerable young lovers from opposite ends of the social strata who find true passion before the ship inevitably collides with an iceberg. As are *Gone with the Wind* and *Casablanca*, *Titanic* is a touching story against a cataclysmic backdrop with universal emotions and timeless grace. Rated PG-13 for violence, nudity, and language. 194m. **DIR:** James Cameron. **CAST:** Leonardo DiCaprio, Kate Winslet, Billy Zane, Kathy Bates, Frances Fisher, Gloria Stuart, Bill Paxton, Bernard Hill, Jonathan Hyde, Victor Garber, David Warner, Suzy Amis, Bernard Fox. 1997 DVD

TITANIC: A QUESTION OF MURDER ★★★ The greatest sea disaster of the twentieth century is again scrutinized. This time the focus is on new evidence about the *Titanic* and how the hundreds of lives lost when she went down in April 1912 might

have been saved. Produced for television and reported by Peter Williams; footage includes interviews with survivors vividly recalling the tragedy. 53m. **DIR:** Alan Ravenscroft. 1983

TITANIC: THE NIGHTMARE AND THE DREAM ★★★ The nightmare is the tragic sinking of the *Titanic*, on her maiden voyage from England to New York. The dream, realized more than seventy years later, is that of undersea geologist Dr. Robert D. Ballard, who sought and found the grave of the great steamship lost more than two miles beneath the Atlantic Ocean off Newfoundland. 56m. **DIR:** Graham Hurley. 1986

TITANICA ★★★ This fascinating documentary tells the story of the greatest of all modern sea disasters, the cruel sinking of the unsinkable *Titanic* on her 1912 maiden voyage, through the eyes of survivor Eva Hart and deep-sea photography exploring the ship where she lies, two-and-a-half miles below the surface of the icy Atlantic. B&W/color; 95m. **DIR:** Stephen Low. 1991

TITO AND ME ★★★★ In 1954 Yugoslavia, Zoran, a 10-year-old underachiever tries to impress a girl and finds himself on a state-sponsored hike through the homeland of President Tito. Political satire shares the screen with broad comedy, as Zoran's extended family lives in an apartment that's far too small for them. In Croatian with English subtitles. Not rated; contains no objectionable material. 104m. **DIR:** Goran Markovic. **CAST:** Dimitrie Vojnov, Lazar Ristovski. 1992

•**TITUS** ★★★★ A Roman general becomes embroiled in a spiraling web of vengeance with a malevolent queen. Shakespeare's first and bloodiest tragedy, *Titus Andronicus*, is also one of his least produced, mainly because it offers a parade of horrors—rape, murder, mutilation, cannibalism—in place of the poetry, power, and insight that would be the hallmark of the mature Bard. Even so, it gets a stylish, energetic filming from director Julie Taymor and a first-rate cast. Rated R for violence, nudity, and sexual scenes. 162m. **DIR:** Julie Taymor. **CAST:** Anthony Hopkins, Jessica Lange, Alan Cumming, Colm Feore, Angus MacFadyen, Laura Fraser, James Frain. 1999

T-MEN ★★1/2 Two undercover operatives for the Treasury Department infiltrate a master counterfeiting ring and find themselves on opposite sides when the lead starts to fly. Unable to save the life of his partner without exposing himself, agent Dennis O'-Keefe courageously continues the work of both men. B&W; 92m. **DIR:** Anthony Mann. **CAST:** Dennis O'-Keefe, Alfred Ryder, Mary Meade, Wallace Ford, June Lockhart, Charles McGraw, Jane Randolph. 1948

TNT JACKSON 🎞 A sexy kung fu expert who comes to Hong Kong to exact revenge on her brother's killer. Rated R for nudity, profanity, and violence. 73m. **DIR:** Cirio H. Santiago. **CAST:** Jeanne Bell, Stan Shaw, Pat Anderson. 1975

TO ALL A GOOD NIGHT ★★ In this typical slasher film, a group of young teenage girls gets away from supervision, and the mad killer shows up with a sharp weapon. A slightly above-average film of its genre. Rated R; has nudity, violence, and profanity.

90m. **DIR:** David Hess. **CAST:** Jennifer Runyon, Forrest Swenson. 1983

TO ALL MY FRIENDS ON SHORE ★★★★ The dreams of two working-class parents to move their family out of the city fade when they learn that their son has sickle-cell anemia. Much better than the usual disease-of-the-week TV movie, with strong performances and a heartfelt script. 75m. **DIR:** Gilbert Cates. **CAST:** Bill Cosby, Gloria Foster, Dennis Hines. 1972

TO BE OR NOT TO BE (1942) ★★★½ After gaining early stardom in *Twentieth Century*, Carole Lombard returned to another black comedy and another role as an oddball theater performer, for the last film of her life. One of Hollywood's premier comedy directors, Ernst Lubitsch, coached excellent performances from Carole Lombard and costar Jack Benny in this hilarious farce about a theater couple who outwit the Nazis. B&W; 99m. **DIR:** Ernst Lubitsch. **CAST:** Carole Lombard, Jack Benny, Robert Stack. 1942

TO BE OR NOT TO BE (1983) ★★★★ In this hilarious remake of the Jack Benny–Carole Lombard classic from 1942, Mel Brooks and Anne Bancroft are Polish actors who foil the Nazis at the outbreak of World War II. It's producer-star Brooks's best film since *Young Frankenstein* and was directed by Alan Johnson, who choreographed *Springtime for Hitler* for Brooks's first film, *The Producers*. Rated PG. 108m. **DIR:** Alan Johnson. **CAST:** Mel Brooks, Anne Bancroft, Charles Durning, Tim Matheson. 1983

TO CATCH A KILLER ★★★ Much-edited, former miniseries chronicles the mounting evidence against—and eventual arrest of—serial killer John Wayne Gacy. Brian Dennehy is truly frightening as Gacy, the man responsible for the deaths of thirty-two teenage boys. Michael Riley is also convincing as the dedicated lieutenant who would stop at nothing to halt Gacy's reign of terror. 95m. **DIR:** Eric Till. **CAST:** Brian Dennehy, Michael Riley, Margot Kidder, David Eisner. 1991 DVD

TO CATCH A KING ★★ Made-for-cable spy thriller that fails to live up to its promising premise. In 1940, cunning Nazis plot to kidnap the Duke and Duchess of Windsor during the romantic couple's respite in Lisbon. Robert Wagner plays a café owner, a more debonair version of *Casablanca*'s Rick. Teri Garr is a nightclub singer. The film is neither convincing nor exciting. 113m. **DIR:** Clive Donner. **CAST:** Robert Wagner, Teri Garr, Horst Janson, Barbara Parkins. 1984

TO CATCH A THIEF ★★★★ John Robie (Cary Grant) is a retired cat burglar living in France in peaceful seclusion. When a sudden rash of jewel thefts hits the Riviera, he is naturally blamed. He sets out to clear himself, and the fun begins. This is certainly one of director Alfred Hitchcock's most amusing films. 103m. **DIR:** Alfred Hitchcock. **CAST:** Cary Grant, Grace Kelly, John Williams, Jessie Royce Landis. 1955

TO CATCH A YETI ★★½ Made-for-cable children's movie about the search for the Himalayan yeti. Meat Loaf plays the hunter looking for the creature, who turns out to be a cuddly pet of a millionaire's spoiled son. It's up to a little girl to save the yeti and release

him back into the wild. Cute creature, cute kids, cute endings. You get the idea. Rated PG. 87m. **DIR:** Bob Keen. **CAST:** Meat Loaf, Chantellese Kent, Jeff Moser, Rick Howland, Jim Gordon, Leigh Lewis. 1993

TO DANCE WITH THE WHITE DOG ★★★★ Hume Cronyn delivers the performance of a lifetime in this moving *Hallmark Hall of Fame* special. When his wife dies, he befriends a white dog only seen by him, and his daughters fear that he's losing his mind. Exceptional acting and superior production values do justice to Terry Kay's novel about eternal love. 95m. **DIR:** Glenn Jordon. **CAST:** Hume Cronyn, Jessica Tandy, Esther Rolle, Christine Baranski. 1993

TO DIE FOR (1989) ★★ Tooth-and-neck story stays fairly close to traditional vampire values, as warring brothers resolve a 500-year-old family feud in downtown L.A. Rated R for nudity and profanity. 94m. **DIR:** Deran Sarafian. **CAST:** Steve Bond, Sydney Walsh, Amanda Wyss, Duane Jones, Scott Jacoby, Brendan Hughes. 1989

TO DIE FOR (1995) ★★★★ Vapid, would-be media celebrity marries a nice guy and, after discovering his family values cramp her style, seduces a stoned teenager into killing him. Joyce Maynard's wonderfully nasty novel has been turned by veteran scribe Buck Henry into an equally dark and funny movie. Rated R for profanity, violence, simulated sex, and drug use. 103m. **DIR:** Gus Van Sant. **CAST:** Nicole Kidman, Matt Dillon, Joaquin Phoenix, Casey Affleck, Illeana Douglas, Alison Foland, Dan Hedaya. 1995 DVD

TO DIE FOR 2: SON OF DARKNESS ★★ The 500-year-old bloodsuckers are back, and it's up to the hero from the first film to put an end to their horror once and for all. Rated R for violence, profanity, and nudity. 95m. **DIR:** David F. Price. **CAST:** Rosalind Allen, Steve Bond, Scott Jacoby, Michael Praed, Amanda Wyss. 1991

TO DIE STANDING ★★★ Easily irritated FBI agent Cliff De Young goes to Peru to extradite a drug boss. Thrilling, intertwined tale of love and power. Rated R for violence and profanity. 85m. **DIR:** Louis Morneau. **CAST:** Cliff De Young, Robert Beltran, Jamie Rose, Gerald Anthony. 1990

TO FORGET VENICE ★★★★ Character-driven drama puts two pairs of gay lovers (one male, one female) in a quiet country house for a weekend. Prompted by the death of the woman who raised three of them, they are forced to come to grips with their lives. Beautifully acted. Dubbed in English. 110m. **DIR:** Franco Brusati. **CAST:** Erland Josephson, Mariangela Melato, Eleonora Giorgi, David Pontremoli. 1979

TO GILLIAN ON HER 37TH BIRTHDAY ★★½ A thirtysomething widower (Peter Gallagher) can't let go of his dead wife (Michelle Pfeiffer), even as his teenage daughter starves for affection. The film entirely misses the point of Michael Brady's original play (the dead wife wasn't the flawless saint the husband remembers), no doubt because Pfeiffer's husband, David E. Kelley, produced and wrote the screenplay. All that's left is the play's blubbery sentimentality, and it gets old in a hurry. Rated PG-13 for mild profanity. 92m. **DIR:** Michael Pressman. **CAST:**

Peter Gallagher, Michelle Pfeiffer, Claire Danes, Kathy Baker, Wendy Crewson, Bruce Altman. **1996**

TO HAVE AND HAVE NOT ★★★1/2 Director Howard Hawks once bet Ernest Hemingway he could make a good film from one of the author's worst books. Needless to say, he won the bet with this exquisite entertainment, which teamed Humphrey Bogart and Lauren Bacall for the first time. B&W; 100m. **DIR:** Howard Hawks. **CAST:** Humphrey Bogart, Lauren Bacall, Walter Brennan. **1944**

TO HEAL A NATION ★★★ Touching TV drama about the attempts of three Vietnam veterans to have the memorial wall built recounts the opposition and the enthusiasm. 100m. **DIR:** Michael Pressman. **CAST:** Eric Roberts, Glynnis O'Connor, Marshall Colt, Scott Paulin, Lee Purcell, Laurence Luckinbill. **1988**

TO HELL AND BACK ★★1/2 Real-life war hero Audie Murphy plays himself in this sprawling World War II action film. Murphy received twenty-four medals, including the Congressional Medal of Honor, which made him the most decorated soldier in World War II. Good performances and true-life drama make up for a static script. 106m. **DIR:** Jesse Hibbs. **CAST:** Audie Murphy, Marshall Thompson, Charles Drake, Gregg Palmer, Jack Kelly, Paul Picerni, Susan Kohner, David Janssen. **1955**

TO KILL A CLOWN 💐 A husband and wife move from the big city to a remote island in an effort to save their marriage. Rated R for violence. 82m. **DIR:** George Bloomfield. **CAST:** Alan Alda, Blythe Danner. **1983**

TO KILL A MOCKINGBIRD ★★★★★ *To Kill a Mockingbird* is a leisurely paced, flavorful filming of Harper Lee's bestselling novel. Gregory Peck earned an Oscar as a small-town southern lawyer who defends a black man accused of rape. Mary Badham, Philip Alford, and John Megna are superb as Peck's children and a visiting friend who are trying to understand life in a small town. B&W; 129m. **DIR:** Robert Mulligan. **CAST:** Gregory Peck, Mary Badham, Philip Alford, John Megna. **1962 DVD**

TO KILL A PRIEST ★★ Set in Warsaw, Poland, in 1984, this story tells of a secret police officer (Ed Harris) obsessed with a Catholic priest (Christopher Lambert) who is aiding the Solidarity movement. An interesting story is hampered by a mishmash of French, American, and British accents. Rated R for violence and profanity. 117m. **DIR:** Agnieszka Holland. **CAST:** Christopher Lambert, Ed Harris, David Suchet, Joanne Whalley, Joss Ackland. **1990**

TO LIVE ★★★★ Spanning thirty years of Chinese history beginning in the 1940s, this intimate, compassionate, sometimes humorous epic of survival focuses on the common folk who were emotionally and physically bloodied by civil war, Mao's Great Leap Forward, and the Cultural Revolution. Their resiliency becomes the heart of the film. In Mandarin with English subtitles. Not rated; contains violence. 135m. **DIR:** Yimou Zhang. **CAST:** Ge You, Gong Li. **1994**

TO LIVE AND DIE IN L.A. 💐 Overly violent account of lone wolf William L. Petersen's attempt to shut down counterfeiter Willem Dafoe. Rated R for nudity and excessive violence. 114m. **DIR:** William Friedkin.

CAST: William L. Petersen, Willem Dafoe, John Pankow, Dean Stockwell, Debra Feuer, John Turturro, Darlanne Fluegel. **1985**

TO PARIS WITH LOVE ★★1/2 Alec Guinness stands out like a pumpkin in a pea patch in this average comedy about a rich and indulgent father who takes his son to gay Paree to learn the facts of life. 78m. **DIR:** Robert Hamer. **CAST:** Alec Guinness, Odile Versois, Austin Trevor, Vernon Gray. **1955**

TO PLEASE A LADY ★★★ Racing film designed to sustain Clark Gable's macho image didn't win at the box office but looks pretty good today. The star-powered love/hate relationship between Gable's devil-may-care driver and Barbara Stanwyck's tough newspaper columnist is more exciting than the speedway scenes. B&W; 91m. **DIR:** Clarence Brown. **CAST:** Clark Gable, Barbara Stanwyck, Adolphe Menjou, Will Geer, Roland Winters. **1950**

TO PROTECT AND SERVE ★★★ C. Thomas Howell is quite effective in this hard-hitting, gritty thriller about a renegade group of killer cops who are being picked off themselves by someone who's in on their scheme. The cast is both attractive and believable. Rated R for nudity, violence, and language. 93m. **DIR:** Eric Weston. **CAST:** C. Thomas Howell, Lezlie Deane, Richard Romanus, Joe Cortese. **1992**

TO SEE SUCH FUN ★★ This is a compilation of a vast number of comedy film clips from 1930 to 1970. Many of the clips illustrate the British love of puns, rhymes, and slapstick. Viewers hoping to see a lot of Peter Sellers, Benny Hill, and Marty Feldman clips will be disappointed because most of the footage comes from films of the 1930s and 1940s. 90m. **DIR:** Jon Scoffield. **CAST:** Peter Sellers, Marty Feldman, Benny Hill, Eric Idle, Margaret Rutherford, Alec Guinness, Dirk Bogarde, Spike Milligan, Norman Wisdom. **1977**

TO SIR WITH LOVE ★★★★ A moving, gentle portrait of the influence of a black teacher upon a classroom of poverty-ridden teenagers in London's East End, this stars Sidney Poitier, in one of his finest performances, as the teacher. He instills in his pupils a belief in themselves and respect for one another. 105m. **DIR:** James Clavell. **CAST:** Sidney Poitier, Judy Geeson, Christian Roberts, Suzy Kendall, Lulu. **1967 DVD**

TO SLEEP WITH A VAMPIRE ★★★ Better-than-average slant on the vampire legend finds lonely bloodsucker Scott Valentine longing for the pleasures of daylight. When he meets lonely stripper Charlie Spradling, he finds a willing tutor. As the night comes to a close, the two have a difficult decision to make. Stylish thriller with fangs. Rated R for nudity, violence, and adult situations. 81m. **DIR:** Adam Friedman. **CAST:** Scott Valentine, Charlie Spradling, Richard Zobel, Ingrid Vold. **1993**

TO SLEEP WITH ANGER ★★★★1/2 Writer-director Charles Burnett based much of this superb, offbeat film on the southern folktales told to him by his grandmother. Its most unusual character, Harry (Danny Glover), is what she called a trickster, "a man who comes to town to steal your soul, and you have to trick him out of it." Rated PG for profanity. 101m. **DIR:** Charles Burnett. **CAST:** Danny Glover, Paul

...ler, Mary Alice, Carl Lumbly, Vonetta McGee, ...hard Brooks, Sheryl Lee Ralph, Julius W. Harris. ...90

■ THE DEVIL, A DAUGHTER ★★★1/2 Based on ...nnis Wheatley's book this above-average thriller ...about occult novelist John Verney, who finds him-...f pitted against Satanists. Rated R for nudity, pro-...ity, and violence in small quantities. 95m. DIR: ...ter Sykes. CAST: Richard Widmark, Christopher Lee, ...nor Blackman, Denholm Elliott, Nastassja Kinski. ...76

■ THE LAST MAN ★★★★ Feudin' and fussin' in ...e Old West, Zane Grey style. Based on an actual ...an clash that took place in Arizona during the ...80s, this is a top-quality oater from Paramount ...ctures' series of films based on Grey's novels. Ran-...lph Scott was directed in several of these by Henry ...athaway, and they made a potent team. Look for ...irley Temple in one of her earliest roles. B&W; ...m. DIR: Henry Hathaway. CAST: Randolph Scott, ...chard Dix, Esther Ralston, Noah Beery Sr., Buster ...abbe, Jack LaRue. 1933

■ THE LIGHTHOUSE ★★★ Virginia Woolf's exper-...ental novel about a family and their hidden trou-...es makes for a rather dry film. Director Colin ...egg (We Think the World of You) is unable to make ...e talky script very interesting, though he does get ...iformly strong performances from his cast. Noth-...ted; contains nothing offensive. 115m. DIR: Colin ...egg. CAST: Rosemary Harris, Michael Gough, Ken-...th Branagh, T. P. McKenna. 1983

...) THE LIMIT ★★1/2 Supermodel Anna Nicole ...nith had her first starring vehicle with this improb-...le crime-drama about a no-nonsense CIA agent ...mith) who becomes allied with a Mafia chieftain ... oppose a renegade agency operative. Delivers ...enty of shoot-'em-up action, but somehow the true ...cus seems to be Smith's hygienic habits, as evi-...nced in numerous shower scenes. Rated R for ...ult situations, nudity, violence, and strong lan-...age. 96m. DIR: Raymond Martino. CAST: Anna ...cole Smith, Joey Travolta, John Aprea, David Proval, ...ranscombe Richmond, Michael Nouri. 1995

...O THE SHORES OF TRIPOLI ★★★ This wartime ...ibute to the Marines has smart-aleck recruit John ...ayne earning the love of navy nurse Maureen ...'Hara after learning some humility and respect for ...e Corps. 87m. DIR: H. Bruce Humberstone. CAST: ...aureen O'Hara, John Payne, Randolph Scott, Nancy ...elly, Maxie Rosenbloom, Alan Hale Jr. 1942

...O WONG FOO, THANKS FOR EVERYTHING, ...ULIE NEWMAR ★★★1/2 Don't let the documen-...ary-type intro to transvestites prevent you from en-...oying what becomes a delightful comedy. When ...aree fairy godbrothers—Patrick Swayze, Wesley ...nipes, and John Leguizamo—descend on a sleepy ...ebraska town, they manage to turn lives around for ...e better. Surprisingly uplifting. Watch for cameos ...y RuPaul, Robin Williams, and Julie Newmar. Rated ...G-13 for language, alternate lifestyles, and vio-...ence. 109m. DIR: Beeban Kidron. CAST: Wesley ...nipes, Patrick Swayze, John Leguizamo, Stockard ...hanning, Blythe Danner, Arliss Howard, Christopher ...enn. 1995

TOAST OF NEW ORLEANS ★★1/2 Don't look for too much plot in this colorful showcase for the considerable vocal talent of the late Mario Lanza. Aided and abetted by the engaging soprano of Kathryn Grayson, Lanza sings up a storm. "Be My Love" was the film's and record stores' big number. 97m. DIR: Norman Taurog. CAST: Kathryn Grayson, Mario Lanza, Thomas Mitchell, David Niven, J. Carrol Naish, Rita Moreno. 1950

TOAST OF NEW YORK, THE ★★★ Semiaccurate biography of legendary post–Civil War Wall Street wheeler-dealer James Fisk. But, even so, it is a good film. Edward Arnold superbly plays Fisk. Jack Oakie does a fine turn. Don't expect the Cary Grant you know and love, however. B&W; 109m. DIR: Rowland V. Lee. CAST: Edward Arnold, Cary Grant, Frances Farmer, Jack Oakie, Donald Meek, Clarence Kolb, Billy Gilbert. 1937

TOBE HOOPER'S NIGHT TERRORS ★★ The infamous Marquis de Sade is back, and he has his sights set on a young woman living in New York. Except for the creative set design, which provides an impressive backdrop for the madness and mayhem, this film really doesn't have much to recommend it. Rated R for nudity, violence, and language. 98m. DIR: Tobe Hooper. CAST: Robert Englund, Zoe Trilling, William Finley. 1993

TOBOR THE GREAT ★★ Kids foil commie plot to steal secret robot plans. Terrific-looking robot is only saving grace. B&W; 77m. DIR: Lee Sholem. CAST: Charles Drake, Karin Booth, Billy Chapin. 1954

TOBRUK ★★★ Rock Hudson, Nigel Green, and George Peppard lead a ragtag group of British soldiers and homeless Jews against the Nazi and Italian armies in the North African desert during World War II. An exciting climax, beautiful photography, and good performances help offset a farfetched script. 110m. DIR: Arthur Hiller. CAST: Rock Hudson, George Peppard, Guy Stockwell, Nigel Green. 1966

TOBY AND THE KOALA BEAR ★★ Adventure tale from Australia in which cartoon characters are placed in real-life settings. Toby is a youngster living in the Australia of yesteryear, in a camp for convicts. After he adopts an adorable pet koala bear, he sets off on a walkabout. 76m. DIR: Yoram Gross. CAST: Rolf Harris. 1981

TOBY MCTEAGUE ★★★ Solid children's story about Canadian teenager Toby McTeague, who has to take over the reins of his father's dog-racing team for the big race. Some profane language, but otherwise suitable for almost everyone. 94m. DIR: Jean-Claude Lord. CAST: Winston Rekert, Yannick Bisson, Timothy Webber. 1987

TOBY TYLER ★★★1/2 Disney version of the popular juvenile book about a young runaway and his adventures with the circus is breezy entertainment and a showcase for young Kevin Corcoran (Moochie of many Disney television shows and the Mickey Mouse Club). 96m. DIR: Charles Barton. CAST: Kevin Corcoran, Henry Calvin, Gene Sheldon, Bob Sweeney, James Drury. 1960

TODAY WE LIVE ★★ A typical Joan Crawford movie of the 1930s, this film has all the right ingredients but doesn't come off well. It's set during World War I with Gary Cooper, Robert Young, and Franchot Tone competing for Crawford's affections between wartime exploits. The battle scenes are better than the love scenes and include some daredevil air sequences and a very exciting torpedo run. B&W; 113m. DIR: Howard Hawks. CAST: Gary Cooper, Joan Crawford, Robert Young, Franchot Tone, Roscoe Karns, Louise Closser Hale. 1933

TODD KILLINGS, THE ★★1/2 Harrowing fact-based drama about a rebellious young murderer (Robert F. Lyons) and the alienated kids who protect him. This film offers a penetrating look into the pathological mind of a 23-year-old killer who seeks out teenage girls. Shocking, disturbing portrait of a thrill-seeking psychopath. Rated R, contains nudity and violence. 93m. DIR: Barry Shear. CAST: Robert F. Lyons, Richard Thomas, Belinda Montgomery, James Broderick, Gloria Grahame, Holly Near, Edward Asner, Barbara Bel Geddes. 1971

TOKYO DECADENCE ★★★1/2 Decadent study of a 22-year-old Tokyo call girl who longs for a better life but must perform kinky sex in order to survive. Ali (Miho Nikhaido) sees her life as a steady stream of deviate johns. Then she meets a dominatrix who opens the door to her dreams. The degradation Ali is forced to endure makes for kinky viewing. In Japanese with English subtitles. Rated NC-17 for strong sexual content. 92m. DIR: Ryu Murakami. CAST: Miho Nikhaido, Sayoko Amano, Chie Sema. 1991 DVD

TOKYO-GA ★★★ German filmmaker Wim Wenders presents an absorbing film diary of his visit to Japan, where he attempts to define his relationship to a culture and city he knows only through the cinematic work of Yasujiro Ozu, the director of *Tokyo Story*. A great introspective account of Ozu's career is much of the film's focus. In Japanese with English subtitles. 92m. DIR: Wim Wenders. CAST: Chishu Ryu, Yuharu Atsuta, Werner Herzog. 1983

TOKYO JOE ★★ Sinister intrigue in postwar Japan has Humphrey Bogart dealing with a blackmailing Sessue Hayakawa. Definitely not vintage Bogie. B&W; 88m. DIR: Stuart Heisler. CAST: Humphrey Bogart, Alexander Knox, Sessue Hayakawa. 1949

TOKYO POP ★★ If you want a gander at modern-day Japan and its pop-music world, this is just the ticket. When Wendy (Carrie Hamilton) leaves her punk band in New York and flies to Tokyo, she finds herself pursued by a would-be rocker who has decided his group needs a Western girl. Despite a maudlin love story, the film is worth watching for its revealing depictions of Tokyo street life and Japanese traditions. Rated R. 101m. DIR: Fran Rubel Kuzui. CAST: Carrie Hamilton, Yutaka Tadokoro. 1988

TOKYO STORY ★★★★★ Yasujiro Ozu's overpowering masterpiece is a deeply felt human drama about an elderly couple who travel to Tokyo, where they are unenthusiastically received by their grown-up children. Outstanding black-and-white cinematography brilliantly captures the landscape of Tokyo. In Japanese with English subtitles. B&W; 139m. DIR: Yasujiro Ozu. CAST: Chishu Ryu, Chiyeko Higashiyama. 1953

TOL'ABLE DAVID ★★1/2 Though it creaks a bit with age, this stalwart tale of good besting evil deserves

attention and rewards it. Silent. B&W; 80m. DIR: King Vidor. CAST: Richard Barthelmess, Gladys Hulette, Ernest Torrence, Warner Richmond. 1921 DVD

TOLLBOOTH ★★★1/2 Quirky, offbeat comedy about a tollbooth operator named Jack (Lenny Von Dohlen), who's in love with a gas-station attendant named Doris (Fairuza Balk). Unfortunately, Doris won't marry Jack and leave their Florida Keys stomping grounds until her long-lost daddy final returns home. Get a clue, Doris. Daddy's been gone for ten years, and his departure has left Doris and her mom a wreck. Outrageously novel dark comedy features wonderful performances and tight direction. Rated R for profanity, nudity, and violence. 108m. DIR: Salome Breziner. CAST: Lenny Von Dohlen, Fairuza Balk, Will Patton, Seymour Cassel, Louise Fletcher. 1994

TOM AND HUCK ★★★ Mark Twain's classic story about friendship and loyalty is revived with all its familiar characters and misadventures intact. Rated PG. 92m. DIR: Peter Hewitt. CAST: Jonathan Taylor Thomas, Brad Renfro, Amy Wright, Charles Rocket, Rachel Leigh, Eric Schweig. 1995

TOM & JERRY: THE MOVIE ★★ This full-length animated feature begins with the manic intensity expected of the dueling cat and mouse, but everything goes awry about ten minutes in when our hitherto mute heroes begin to *talk*. It's bad enough that Tom and Jerry suddenly lose their Buster Keaton-style charm—then they become another tedious, smarmy couple of chums determined to reunite a girl with her missing father. Rated G. 84m. DIR: Phil Roman. 1993

TOM & VIV ★★★ At first glance, this appears to be nothing but a talkfest aimed at the menstrual problems created by T. S. Eliot's wife, Vivien Haigh-Wood. As the story unfolds, you realize it is an astute, even maddening commentary on the treatment of women. Miranda Richardson is dead-on as the clever but imbalanced woman who finds herself trampled under the ego of her poetic, uptight husband. Rated PG-13 for profanity and adult themes. 115m. DIR: Brian Gilbert. CAST: Willem Dafoe, Miranda Richardson, Rosemary Harris, Tim Dutton, Nickolas Grace. 1995

TOM BROWN'S SCHOOL DAYS (1940) ★★1/2 "Old school tie" story mixes top Hollywood production values and minor classic of British secondary schools into an enjoyable froth filled with all the clichés. Better than one would think and not the creaky old groaner it could have been. B&W; 86m. DIR: Robert Stevenson. CAST: Cedric Hardwicke, Freddie Bartholomew, Gale Storm, Jimmy Lydon, Josephine Hutchinson, Polly Moran, Billy Halop. 1940

TOM BROWN'S SCHOOLDAYS (1950) ★★★1/2 Tom, played by John Howard Davies, brings a civilizing influence to his peers in this engaging account of life in a Victorian England boys' school. Robert Newton, of course, is superb. An excellent cast, under good direction, makes this a particularly fine film. B&W; 93m. DIR: Gordon Parry. CAST: Robert Newton, John Howard Davies, James Hayter, Hermione Baddeley. 1950

TOM, DICK AND HARRY ★★★1/2 An energetic comic delight has Ginger Rogers trying to decide ich very eligible bachelor to have for her beau. e entire cast comes through with solid performances, but Phil Silvers almost walks off with the ow in his role as an obnoxious ice-cream man. Gar-n Kanin's direction is sharp. B&W; 86m. DIR: Gar-n Kanin. CAST: Ginger Rogers, George Murphy, rgess Meredith, Alan Marshal, Phil Silvers. 1941

M HORN ★★1/2 Steve McQueen doesn't give a eat performance in his next-to-last motion picture, out the last days of a real-life Wyoming bounty inter, nor does director William Wiard craft a mem-able Western. Rated R. 98m. DIR: William Wiard. AST: Steve McQueen, Richard Farnsworth, Billy een Bush, Slim Pickens, Elisha Cook Jr. 1980

M JONES ★★★★★ Rarely has a movie captured e spirit and flavor of its times or the novel on which was based. This is a rambunctious, witty, and often wdy tale of a youth's misadventures in eighteenth-ntury England. Albert Finney is a perfect rascal as m. We joyously follow him through all levels of ritish society as he tries to make his fortune and in the lovely Sophie (Susannah York). The entire st is brilliant. 129m. DIR: Tony Richardson. CAST: bert Finney, Susannah York, Hugh Griffith, Edith ans. 1963 DVD

OM SAWYER (1917) ★★★1/2 This faithful adap-tion of Mark Twain's nineteenth-century American assic includes most of his familiar vignettes of nall-town life and boyish behavior, but the film ds partway into the novel and omits the famous ection of Injun' Joe's cave. This title is one of the w available that William Desmond Taylor directed. lent, with musical score. B&W; 59m. DIR: William esmond Taylor. CAST: Jack Pickford, Helen Gilmore, ara Horton, Antrum Short, Robert Gordon, Carl oetz. 1917

OM SAWYER (1930) ★★1/2 Adequate version of ne famous Mark Twain novel. It's worth seeing for hild star Jackie Coogan in the title role, but parents eware: kids will find this dull. B&W; 85m. DIR: John romwell. CAST: Jackie Coogan, Junior Durkin, Jane arwell. 1930

OM SAWYER (1973) ★★★ This musical version f Mark Twain's classic has a few contrived moments ere and there, but it is, on the whole, enjoyable. ated G. 102m. DIR: Don Taylor. CAST: Johnny Vhitaker, Celeste Holm, Jeff East, Jodie Foster, Warren ates. 1973

OM SAWYER (1973) ★★ Mark Twain's classic tory loses its satirical edge in this homogenized nade-for-television production about the adven-ures of Tom Sawyer (Josh Albee) and Huckleberry 'inn (Jeff Tyler). The kids may enjoy it, but adults vill want to reread the book. Better yet, read the ook to your kids. Rated G. 78m. DIR: James Neilson. AST: Josh Albee, Jeff Tyler, Jane Wyatt, Buddy Ebsen, ic Morrow, John McGiver. 1973

OM THUMB ★★★1/2 This underrated George Pal antasy is a treat for young and old viewers. Good ef-ects, pleasant tunes, and a distinguished cast of vet-ran British performers combine with Russ Tam-blyn's infectious lead to make this a surefire choice or the kids. 98m. DIR: George Pal. CAST: Russ Tam-

blyn, June Thorburn, Peter Sellers, Terry-Thomas, Alan Young, Jessie Matthews, Bernard Miles. 1958

TOMB, THE ★★ Typical high-energy (and low-bud-get) Fred Olen Ray production, with the veteran stars on hand for B-movie marquee value, while a largely unknown young cast handles the strenuous mayhem. The plot centers on a curse that follows the desecrators of an Egyptian tomb. Rated R. 84m. DIR: Fred Olen Ray. CAST: Cameron Mitchell, John Carra-dine, Fred Olen. 1985

TOMB OF LIGEIA ★★★ A grieving widower is dri-ven to madness by the curse of his dead wife. This was Roger Corman's final Poe-inspired movie. The most subtle and atmospheric entry in the series, it was photographed by Nicolas Roeg on sets left over from *Becket*. The screenplay was by Robert Towne, who went on to write *Chinatown*. 81m. DIR: Roger Corman. CAST: Vincent Price, Elizabeth Shepherd. 1964

TOMBOY 💘 Mindless nonsense (with plenty of skin) about a female race car driver. Rated R. 91m. DIR: Herb Freed. CAST: Betsy Russell, Kristi Somers, Jerry Dinome. 1985

TOMBOY AND THE CHAMP 💘 The kids will hate this overwrought story of a young Texas tomboy and her pet heifer. But adults who cherish really bad movies are sure to love its inane melodramatics, with tunes from cowboy singer Rex Allen. Not rated. 92m. DIR: Francis D. Lyon. CAST: Candy Moore, Ben Johnson, Rex Allen, Jesse White. 1961

TOMBS OF THE BLIND DEAD ★★★ First entry in an entertaining exploitation-horror series, center-ing on the periodic resurrection of thirteenth-cen-tury Knights Templar and their quest for victims. Vi-sually breathtaking—and one of the few examples of a Spanish horror film that has appeal for U.S. view-ers. Rated R. 86m. DIR: Amando de Ossorio. CAST: Oscar Burner. 1971 DVD

TOMBSTONE ★★★★ After cleaning up Dodge City, the Earp brothers attempt to settle down in Tomb-stone, but a marauding outlaw gang forces them to put their guns back on. Val Kilmer may well be the screen's best Doc Holliday. Rated R for violence and profanity. 130m. DIR: George Pan Cosmatos. CAST: Kurt Russell, Val Kilmer, Michael Biehn, Powers Boothe, Robert Burke, Dana Delany, Sam Elliott, Stephen Lang, Terry O'Quinn, Jason Priestley, Joanna Pacula, Dana Wheeler-Nicholson, Harry Carey Jr., Billy Zane. 1993 DVD

TOMCAT: DANGEROUS DESIRES ★★ Richard Grieco is purr-fectly cast as a handsome loner whose rare blood disease leads him to scientist Maryam D'Ado. After being injected with a new serum, he de-velops unusual catlike tendencies. The good news is that he's an animal in bed. The bad news is that he uses people who discover his secret as a scratching post. Made-for-cable erotic sci-fi thriller just man-ages to keep its paws out of the litter box. Rated R for nudity and violence. 96m. DIR: Paul Donovan. CAST: Richard Grieco, Maryam D'Abo, Natalie Radford. 1993

TOMMY ★★1/2 In bringing The Who's ground-breaking rock opera to the screen, director Ken Rus-sell let his penchant for bad taste and garishness run wild. The result is an outrageous movie about a deaf, dumb, and blind boy who rises to prominence as a "Pinball Wizard" and then becomes the new Messiah. Rated PG. 111m. DIR: Ken Russell. CAST: Roger Daltrey, Ann-Margret, Jack Nicholson, Oliver Reed, Elton John, Tina Turner. **1975 DVD**

TOMMY BOY ★★1/2 Basically a takeoff of *Planes, Trains and Automobiles*, this buddy and coming-of-age film features Chris Farley as the unlikely proprietor of an auto-parts factory. *Saturday Night Live* creator Lorne Michaels's production offers some incredibly funny scenes. Rated PG-13 for profanity, brief nudity, and comic-book violence. 98m. DIR: Peter Segal. CAST: Chris Farley, David Spade, Bo Derek, Brian Dennehy, Julie Warner, Rob Lowe, Dan Aykroyd. **1995 DVD**

TOMMYKNOCKERS, THE ★★1/2 This network-television miniseries about a town taken over by long-dormant aliens suffers from the same flaws that plagued Stephen King's novel: second-rate characters and a slow, rambling narrative. King fans are destined to howl over the altered conclusion. Rated R for violence, profanity, and sensuality. 120m. DIR: John Power. CAST: Jimmy Smits, Marg Helgenberger, John Ashton, Allyce Beasley, Robert Carradine, Joanna Cassidy, Traci Lords, E. G. Marshall. **1993 DVD**

TOMORROW ★★★★★ Robert Duvall gives yet another sensitive, powerful, and completely convincing performance in this superb black-and-white character study about a caretaker who finds himself caring for—in both senses—a pregnant woman (Olga Bellin) who turns up one day at the lumber mill where he works. Rated PG for violence. B&W; 103m. DIR: Joseph Anthony. CAST: Robert Duvall, Olga Bellin, Sudie Bond. **1972**

TOMORROW AT SEVEN ★★ Obscure murder drama pits crime novelist Chester Morris and bumbling policemen Allen Jenkins and Frank McHugh against the mysterious Ace, who sends his victims a calling card and tells them where to go to die, which they inevitably do. This routine whodunit has little to offer. B&W; 62m. DIR: Ray Enright. CAST: Chester Morris, Vivienne Osborne, Allen Jenkins, Frank McHugh, Henry Stephenson, Grant Mitchell, Charles Middleton. **1933**

TOMORROW IS FOREVER ★★★★ Orson Welles is tempermentally suited for the role of the man who has disappeared for twenty years. When he returns, he finds out his wife (Claudette Colbert) has remarried and has children by her second husband (George Brent). Weepy (but wonderful) melodrama. B&W; 105m. DIR: Irving Pichel. CAST: Claudette Colbert, Orson Welles, George Brent, Natalie Wood, Lucile Watson, Richard Long. **1946**

TOMORROW NEVER COMES 💔 Absolutely brainless movie about a weirdo who goes on a rampage. Not rated; the film has violence. 109m. DIR: Peter Collinson. CAST: Oliver Reed, Susan George, Stephen McHattie, Raymond Burr, John Ireland, Donald Pleasence, Paul Koslo. **1977**

TOMORROW NEVER DIES ★★★★ Pierce Brosnan demonstrates more of the right stuff in his second outing as not-so-secret agent James Bond, this time opposed by a media mogul hoping to goose his satellite network's ratings by starting a world war. Better still, though, is Asian action costar Michelle Yeoh Bond's true equal: a tough-talking, tougher-fighting agent from the People's Republic of China who matches him stunt for stunt. Further good news is the properly 007-flavored soundtrack. Rated PG-13 for violence and sensuality. 119m. DIR: Roger Spottiswoode. CAST: Pierce Brosnan, Jonathan Pryce, Michelle Yeoh, Teri Hatcher, Judi Dench, Joe Don Baker, Gotz Otto, Ricky Jay. **1997 DVD**

TOMORROW'S CHILD ★★ Made during television's cause-of-the-week period, this saga deals with the topics of in vitro fertilization and surrogate motherhood. *Remington Steele* charmer Stephanie Zimbalist is acceptably overwrought, as is most of the cast of familiar TV faces. 100m. DIR: Joseph Sargent. CAST: Stephanie Zimbalist, Arthur Hill, William Atherton, Bruce Davison, James Shigeta, Susan Oliver, Ed Flanders, Salome Jens. **1982**

TONGS ★★★ Set in Manhattan's teeming Chinatown, this variation on *Scarface* stars current Hong Kong superstar Simon Yam as an immigrant who schemes and kills his way to the top of a drug empire. Not rated; contains strong violence. 89m. DIR: Phil Chan. CAST: Simon Yam, Tony Leung Chiu-Wai. **1988**

TONI ★★★★ In story, style, and mood, *Toni* anticipates the methods of the future master postwar directors. A love quadrangle, a murder, a trial, an execution, a confession—these are the everyday elements director Jean Renoir chose to show as objectively as possible, Renoir was proud of his film and it holds up well. In French with English subtitles. B&W; 90m. DIR: Jean Renoir. CAST: Charles Blavette, Max Dalban. **1934**

TONIGHT AND EVERY NIGHT ★★★ Another Fox ties song-and-dance extravaganza—this time in war-torn London. In spite of bomb raids and uncertainty in their private lives, a determined troupe keeps their show alive. Seems a bit dated now, but Rita Hayworth is worth watching. 92m. DIR: Victor Saville. CAST: Rita Hayworth, Lee Bowman, Janet Blair, Leslie Brooks, Marc Platt. **1945**

TONIO KROGER ★★ This adaptation of Thomas Mann's semiautobiographical novel, about a young writer wandering Europe while trying to choose between bourgeois comfort and the excitement of the unchained life, never comes alive on screen. In German with English subtitles. 92m. DIR: Rolf Thiele. CAST: Jean-Claude Brialy, Nadja Tiller, Werner Hinz, Gert Fröbe. **1965**

TONKA ★★★ Sal Mineo is White Bull, a Sioux Indian who captures and tames a wild stallion and names it Tonka Wakan—The Great One. Tribal law requires him to give the horse to his older Indian cousin, a bully who would mistreat the animal. Rather than do so, Mineo frees the horse. Thus begins an enjoyable adventure story for the family. 97m. DIR: Lewis R. Foster. CAST: Sal Mineo, Philip Carey, Jerome Courtland. **1958**

TONY ROME ★★★ Pretty good private eye film has detective Frank Sinatra looking for clues into the disappearance of a wealthy man's daughter. Good atmosphere and a fine cast lend support as well. 110m. DIR: Gordon Douglas. CAST: Frank Sinatra, Jill St.

hn, Sue Lyon, Richard Conte, Simon Oakland, Gena
owlands. 1967

OO BEAUTIFUL FOR YOU ★★★★1/2 Bertrand
ier's subtle, surprising French comedy about an
beat romantic triangle. Gérard Depardieu stars as
married automobile dealer who falls for the rather
wdy secretary who works in his office. In French
th English subtitles. Rated R for profanity. 91m.
R: Bertrand Blier. CAST: Gérard Depardieu, Carole
ouquet, Josiane Balasko. 1990

OO FAST TOO YOUNG ★★ A teen is forced by the
usin who raised him to help out with an armored-
ar robbery. Nothing here you haven't seen before,
nd probably done much better. Rated R for vio-
ence, strong profanity, nudity, and sexual situations.
2m. DIR: Tim Everitt. CAST: Michael Ironside, Kasia
gura, James Wellington, Patrick Tiller, Marshall Bell,
ichard Riehle. 1996

OO HOT TO HANDLE ★★★ Daredevil newsreel
hotographer Clark Gable and spunky pilot Myrna
oy team up in this fast-paced comedy-adventure
at bounces from China to Borneo. Gable and Loy,
e "king and queen" of Hollywood that year, make
is screwy adventure click. B&W; 105m. DIR: Jack
onway. CAST: Clark Gable, Myrna Loy, Walter Pid-
eon, Leo Carrillo, Virginia Weidler, Marjorie Main.
938

OO LATE THE HERO ★★★1/2 Great World War II
ction-drama about two reluctant soldiers who are
ent on a suicide mission to an island in the Pacific.
hown on network TV as *Suicide Run*. Rated PG.
33m. DIR: Robert Aldrich. CAST: Michael Caine, Cliff
obertson, Henry Fonda. 1970

OO MANY GIRLS ★★★1/2 Four young men are
ired by prestigious Pottawatomie College in Stop-
ap, New Mexico, to keep an eye on carefree student
ucille Ball. This marked the debut of Eddie
racken, Desi Arnaz, *and*, in the chorus, Van John-
on. A trivia lover's delight, this is pure fun to watch.
&W; 85m. DIR: George Abbott. CAST: Lucille Ball,
ichard Carlson, Eddie Bracken, Ann Miller, Desi Arnaz
r. 1940

OO MUCH SUN ❤ Utterly tasteless comedy about
he gay son and lesbian daughter of a multimillion-
ire (Howard Duff) whose will decrees that one or
he other of his offspring must produce a son. Rated
R for profanity and simulated sex. 97m. DIR: Robert
owney. CAST: Robert Downey Jr., Laura Ernst, Jim
aynie, Eric Idle, Ralph Macchio, Andrea Martin, Leo
Rossi, Howard Duff. 1991

OO OUTRAGEOUS ★★ In this disappointing se-
uel to 1977s surprise hit *Outrageous*, Craig Russell
eprises his role as the gay hairdresser, now having
ealized his dreams of becoming a successful female
mpersonator. Hollis McLaren is his schizophrenic
riend. Rated R for language and sexual content.
00m. DIR: Richard Benner. CAST: Craig Russell, Hollis
McLaren, David McIlwraith. 1987

OO SHY TO TRY ★★★ Director Pierre Richard
stars in this romantic comedy about a man who takes
a crash course in romance after meeting the girl of
his dreams. Some genuinely funny moments. In
French with English subtitles. Not rated; contains

nudity. 89m. DIR: Pierre Richard. CAST: Pierre
Richard, Aldo Maccioni, Jacques François. 1982

TOO YOUNG TO DIE ★★ Brad Pitt and Juliette
Lewis dismally reprise their roles from the film *Kalifornia*. Rated R for violence, nudity, and profanity.
92m. DIR: Robert Markowitz. CAST: Brad Pitt, Juliette
Lewis, Michael Tucker, Michael O'Keefe. 1994

TOOTSIE ★★★★★ Dustin Hoffman is Michael
Dorsey, an out-of-work actor who disguises himself
as a woman—Dorothy Michaels—to get a job and
becomes a big star on a popular television soap
opera. An absolute delight, *Tootsie* is hilarious,
touching, and marvelously acted. Rated PG for adult
content. 119m. DIR: Sydney Pollack. CAST: Dustin
Hoffman, Bill Murray, Jessica Lange, Teri Garr, Dabney
Coleman, Sydney Pollack, George Gaynes, Charles
Durning. 1982

TOP DOG ★★ Chuck Norris teams up with a canine
partner to bring down a white supremacist group. A
derivative buddy film that's long on violence and
short on charm. Rated PG-13 for violence. 93m. DIR:
Aaron Norris. CAST: Chuck Norris, Timothy Bottoms,
Michele Lamar Richards. 1994 DVD

TOP GUN ★★★1/2 Tom Cruise stars as a student at
the navy's Fighter Weapons School, where fliers are
turned into crack fighter pilots. While competing for
the title of Top Gun there, he falls in love with an instructor (Kelly McGillis of *Witness*). Rated PG for
light profanity, suggested sex, and violence. 110m.
DIR: Tony Scott. CAST: Tom Cruise, Kelly McGillis, Val
Kilmer, Anthony Edwards, Tom Skerritt, Michael Ironside, John Stockwell, Rick Rossovich, Barry Tubb,
Whip Hubley. 1986 DVD

TOP HAT ★★★★★ The most delightful and enduring of the Fred Astaire–Ginger Rogers musicals of
the 1930s. This movie has an agreeable wisp of a plot
and amusing, if dated, comedy dialogue. B&W; 99m.
DIR: Mark Sandrich. CAST: Fred Astaire, Ginger
Rogers, Edward Everett Horton, Eric Blore, Helen Bro-
erick. 1935

TOP SECRET ★★1/2 By the makers of *Airplane!*,
this film makes up for its flimsy plot with one gag after another. Nick Rivers (Val Kilmer), a rock 'n' roll
star, visits East Germany. There he falls in love with
Hilary and becomes involved in the plot to free her
scientist father. Lots of lively old Beach Boys and
Elvis Presley tunes. Rated PG for some profanity and
sexually oriented gags. 90m. DIR: Jim Abrahams,
David Zucker, Jerry Zucker. CAST: Val Kilmer, Omar
Sharif, Peter Cushing, Lucy Gutteridge. 1984

TOPAZ ★★★ Medium-to-rare Hitchcock suspense-
thriller about cloak-and-dagger intrigue concerning
Russian involvement in Cuba and infiltration of the
French government. Constant shift of scene keeps
viewers on their toes. Rated PG. 127m. DIR: Alfred
Hitchcock. CAST: John Forsythe, Frederick Stafford,
Dany Robin, John Vernon. 1969

TOPAZE (1933) ★★★1/2 John Barrymore gives one
of his finest comic performances in this engaging
film about a college professor who is innocently in-
veigled into a swindle and ends up turning the tables
on the crooks. Witty and often moving. B&W; 80m.
DIR: Harry D'Arrast. CAST: John Barrymore, Myrna
Loy. 1933

TOPAZE (1951) ★★★ Another version of Marcel Pagnol's perennially popular satirical play (it was also adapted as a vehicle for John Barrymore and Peter Sellers) about a lowly schoolteacher who is dismissed from his job but finds success in the business world. The best and most faithful adaptation of the play makes a fine showcase for French-comedian Fernandel. In French with English subtitles. Not rated. B&W; 135m. **DIR:** Marcel Pagnol. **CAST:** Fernandel, Marcel Vallee, Jacqueline Pagnol. 1951

TOPKAPI ★★★★★ This is one of the finest and funniest of the "big heist" genre. Director Jules Dassin assembled a highly talented international cast. They are members of a charming group of jewel thieves whose target is a priceless jeweled dagger in a Turkish museum. The execution of their clever plan is both humorous and exciting. 120m. **DIR:** Jules Dassin. **CAST:** Peter Ustinov, Melina Mercouri, Maximilian Schell. 1964

TOPPER ★★★★ This is the original feature of what became a delightful fantasy movie series and television series. Cary Grant and Constance Bennett are the Kirbys, a duo of social high livers who, due to an unfortunate auto accident, become ghosts. They now want to transfer their spirit of living the good life to a rather stodgy banker, the fellow they are now haunting, one Cosmo Topper (Roland Young). Good fun all around. B&W; 97m. **DIR:** Norman Z. McLeod. **CAST:** Cary Grant, Constance Bennett, Roland Young, Billie Burke. 1937

TOPPER RETURNS ★★★ Cary Grant and Constance Bennett have gone on to their heavenly rewards, but Roland Young, as Cosmo Topper, is still seeing ghosts. This time the spooky personage is that of Joan Blondell, who helps our hero solve a murder in this entertaining comedy. B&W; 87m. **DIR:** Roy Del Ruth. **CAST:** Roland Young, Joan Blondell, Eddie "Rochester" Anderson, Carole Landis, Dennis O'Keefe, H. B. Warner. 1941

TOPPER TAKES A TRIP ★★★ Second film in the original series finds Cosmo and Henrietta Topper on the French Riviera accompanied by their ghostly friend Marion Kirby, portrayed by the star of the original film, Constance Bennett. Topper and Marion pool forces to stop Mrs. Topper from being victimized by a smooth-talking confidence man. Cary Grant makes a brief appearance in a flashback sequence. Harmless fun. B&W; 85m. **DIR:** Norman Z. McLeod. **CAST:** Constance Bennett, Roland Young, Billie Burke, Alan Mowbray, Franklin Pangborn. 1939

TOPSY TURVY (1984) ★★ A conservative young man finds his world turned topsy-turvy when a swinging neighbor girl takes him on vacation. This European sex comedy, dubbed into English is mediocre. 90m. **DIR:** Edward Fleming. **CAST:** Lisbet Dahl, Ebbe Rode. 1984 DVD

•**TOPSY-TURVY** (1999) ★★★★1/2 Writer-director Mike Leigh's film deals with the touchy partnership of Gilbert and Sullivan and the creation of their most popular work, *The Mikado*. It's a loving, minutely-detailed examination of the creative process and one of the best movies ever made about the theater. It's also an incisive portrait of life in London at the zenith of the British Empire, with every detail so convincing

that it feels like a trip in a time machine. The ic on the cake is the marvelous rendition of severa Gilbert and Sullivan's songs. Rated R for brief nuc 161m. **DIR:** Mike Leigh. **CAST:** Jim Broadbent, A Corduner, Timothy Spall, Lesley Manville, Ron Co Wendy Nottingham. 1999 DVD

TORA! TORA! TORA! ★★★★ An American-Jap ese cooperative venture reenacts the events up and including the December 7 attack on Pearl H bor. Although many well-known actors contrib their skills, they are overshadowed by the techni brilliance of the realistic re-creation of the climac attack. Rated G. 143m. **DIR:** Richard Fleischer, Tos Masuda, Kinji Fakasaku. **CAST:** Jason Robards Martin Balsam, James Whitmore, Joseph Cotten. 1S DVD

TORCH SONG ★★ A muddled melodrama made show off Joan Crawford's form and figure when s was approaching fifty. She plays a tough chorus-g turned-Broadway-dancer. 90m. **DIR:** Charles Walte **CAST:** Joan Crawford, Michael Wilding, Gig You Marjorie Rambeau, Harry Morgan. 1953

TORCH SONG TRILOGY ★★★ Harvey Fierstei prize-winning play of the same title couldn't be b ter suited to film, but this comedy-drama is not everyone. Fierstein plays Arnold Beckoff, an in cure female impersonator looking for that one, a encompassing relationship. Anne Bancroft is his u bending Jewish mama. The musical numbers in t gay nightclub are classy and clever. Rated R. 120 **DIR:** Paul Bogart. **CAST:** Harvey Fierstein, Anne Ba croft, Matthew Broderick, Brian Kerwin. 1988

TORMENT ★★ Low-budget slasher film starts slow and, if it weren't for one interesting plot tw halfway through, would be an exercise in boredom The story revolves around a man who becomes a p chotic killer when he is rejected by a young woman. R for violence and gore. 90m. **DIR:** Sams Aslanian, John Hopkins. **CAST:** Taylor Gilbert. 1986

TORN APART ★★1/2 An Israeli soldier and an Ar girl incur the wrath of their friends and famili when they fall in love. Based on Chayym Zeldi novel *A Forbidden Love*. A tolerable time-wast Rated R for violence. 120m. **DIR:** Jack Fisher. **CAS** Adrian Pasdar, Cecilia Peck. 1987

TORN BETWEEN TWO LOVERS ★★★1/2 Th made-for-TV romantic triangle features a marrie Lee Remick who finds herself having an affair with divorced architect. She must finally tell her husban the truth and choose between the two. Nothing bo ing about this soap! 100m. **DIR:** Delbert Mann. **CAS** Lee Remick, Joseph Bologna, George Peppard, Giorg Tozzi. 1979

TORN CURTAIN ★★★ Just-okay film was directe by Alfred Hitchcock in 1966. Paul Newman plays a American scientist posing as a defector, with Jul Andrews as his secretary-lover. Somehow we aren moved by the action or the characters. 128m. **DIR:** A fred Hitchcock. **CAST:** Paul Newman, Julie Andrew Lila Kedrova, David Opatoshu. 1966

TORNADO! 🎬 The very reason some directors kee their projects under wraps. This rip-off of *Twiste* features the same plot and identical characters, bu is poorly executed and the special effects are a re

...ke. Television may have beaten *Twister* to the ...nch, but it's a sucker punch at best. Rated PG. ...m. **DIR:** Noel Nosseck. **CAST:** Bruce Campbell, Shan-...n Sturges, Ernie Hudson, L. Q. Jones. **1996 DVD**

...RPEDO ALLEY ★★ World War II pilot Bob Bing-...m (Mark Stevens) is haunted by guilt after the ...aths of his flight crew. He gets a second chance to ...ove himself when he applies for submarine duty ...ring the Korean War. B&W; 84m. **DIR:** Lew Landers. **...ST:** Mark Stevens, Dorothy Malone, Charles Win-...ager, Bill Williams. **1953**

...RPEDO RUN ★★★1/2 A driving pace marks this ...utly exciting World War II mouse-chases-cat story ...out a navy submarine tracking, catching, and de-...roying a Japanese aircraft carrier in Kiska Harbor. ...m. **DIR:** Joseph Pevney. **CAST:** Glenn Ford, Ernest ...rgnine, Dean Jones, Diane Brewster. **1958**

...RRENTS OF SPRING 💔 Beautifully pho-...graphed but uninvolving costume drama set in Eu-...pe during the 1840s. Rated R. 97m. **DIR:** Jerzy ...kolimowski. **CAST:** Timothy Hutton, Nastassja Kinski, ...aleria Golino, William Forsythe, Urbano Barberini. ...990

...RSO ★★1/2 Who's bumping off (and hacking ...art) the pretty coeds at an Italian university? It ...kes forever to find out in this mechanical stalk-...d-slash melodrama. However, the film springs to ...'e for a climactic battle to the death between hero ...d masked villain. Rated R. 86m. **DIR:** Sergio Mar-...io. **CAST:** Suzy Kendall, John Richardson, Tina Au-...ont, Luc Merenda. **1973 DVD**

...ORTILLA FLAT ★★1/2 A watered-down (under-...andable for the times) adaptation of John Stein-...eck's lusty novel of a group of *paisanos* on the Cali-...rnia coast, led by Spencer Tracy, whose main pur-...ose in life is to avoid any form of work or ...sponsibility. One, John Garfield, inherits two run-...own houses and his outlook changes, much to the ...oncern of his friends. B&W; 105m. **DIR:** Victor Flem-...g. **CAST:** Spencer Tracy, Hedy Lamarr, John Garfield, ...ank Morgan, Akim Tamiroff, Sheldon Leonard. **1942**

...ORTURE CHAMBER OF BARON BLOOD, THE ★★ ...oring Italian production is basically nonsense as a ...rg-dead nobleman (Joseph Cotten) is inadver-...ently restored to life, only to (naturally) embark on ...horrendous killing spree. Worth watching for Mario ...ava's unique directorial style. Originally titled ...*aron Blood.* Rated R. 90m. **DIR:** Mario Bava. **CAST:** ...oseph Cotten, Elke Sommer, Massimo Girotti. **1972 ...VD**

...ORTURE CHAMBER OF DR. SADISM, THE ★★ ...ased on Poe's "The Pit and the Pendulum," this ...erman production has Christopher Lee as a count ...ho lures Lex Barker and Karin Dor to his forebod-...ng castle. Although containing some good shock ...cenes, *Torture Chamber* doesn't live up to its ...ource material or title. Not rated; contains violence ...nd torture. 90m. **DIR:** Harald Reinl. **CAST:** Christo-...her Lee, Lex Barker, Karin Dor. **1967**

...ORTURE DUNGEON 💔 Unwatchable garbage from ...ndy Milligan, Staten Island's *auteur*, whose forays ...nto medieval horror have all the entertainment ...alue of a lobotomy. Rated R. 80m. **DIR:** Andy Milli-...an. **CAST:** Susan Cassidy, Jeremy Brooks. **1970**

TORTURE GARDEN ★★★1/2 A group of patrons at a carnival sideshow has their possible futures exposed to them by a screwball barker (Burgess Meredith) who exclaims, "I've promised you horror ... and I intend to keep that promise." He does more than this in this frightening film laced with plenty of shock, plot twists, and intense situations. Rated PG. 93m. **DIR:** Freddie Francis. **CAST:** Burgess Meredith, Jack Palance, Beverly Adams, Peter Cushing, Maurice Denham, Robert Hutton. **1968**

TOTAL ECLIPSE ★★★ Writer Christopher Hampton (adapting one of his early plays) dramatizes the sadomasochistic, destructive relationship between nineteenth-century French poets Arthur Rimbaud and Paul Verlaine. Acting is excellent; unfortunately, the central characters are such cruel, selfish boors that many viewers will be turned off. Rated R for profanity, nudity, and simulated sex. 110m. **DIR:** Agnieszka Holland. **CAST:** Leonardo DiCaprio, David Thewlis, Romane Bohringer, Dominique Blanc. **1995 DVD**

TOTAL EXPOSURE ★★★ When fashion photographer Season Hubley is framed for murdering a model, she turns to private eye Michael Nouri to clear her name. Nouri begins to suspect that his client might actually be guilty. Watch this one to see what develops. Rated R for nudity, strong language, and violence. 96m. **DIR:** John Quinn. **CAST:** Michael Nouri, Season Hubley, Christian Bocher, Jeff Conaway, Robert Prentiss. **1990**

TOTAL RECALL ★★★★1/2 Arnold Schwarzenegger flexes plenty of action-movie muscle in this terrific sci-fi adventure. The film has impressive bloodlines: it's adapted from a short story by Philip K. Dick (who also inspired *Blade Runner*), with a screenplay from the *Alien* creators, and direction by the creator of *RoboCop*. A thrill-a-minute futuristic tale. Rated R, with strong violence and profanity. 109m. **DIR:** Paul Verhoeven. **CAST:** Arnold Schwarzenegger, Rachel Ticotin, Sharon Stone, Ronny Cox, Michael Ironside. **1990 DVD**

TOTO THE HERO ★★★★ In Belgian director Jaco Van Dormael's inventive black comedy, a cranky old man's reveries are made to seem the universal story of modern man. Toto's reminiscences are colored by his perspective, which, as the story unfolds, is proven to be somewhat askew. Rated PG-13 for nudity and violence. 90m. **DIR:** Jaco Van Dormael. **CAST:** Michel Bouquet, Mireille Perrier. **1991**

TOUCH ★★★1/2 Skeet Ulrich works miracles in this dark comedy about the exploitation of religion. He plays Juvenal, a miracle healer who catches the attention of a former evangelist who sees Juvenal as his ticket to the big time. His plan backfires when the woman he sends to lure Juvenal into his fold falls in love with him. Sharp, witty dialogue. Rated R for adult situations, language, and nudity. 96m. **DIR:** Paul Schrader. **CAST:** Skeet Ulrich, Bridget Fonda, Christopher Walken, Tom Arnold. **1997**

TOUCH AND DIE 💔 Martin Sheen stars as an American journalist in Rome assigned to cover the murders of three people. His investigation reveals a conspiracy. Warning: title tells it all. Rated R for violence, profanity, and nudity. 108m. **DIR:** Piernico

Solinas. **CAST:** Martin Sheen, René Estevez, David Birney, Franco Nero. 1991

TOUCH AND GO ★★1/2 A comedy that sat on the shelf for two years. Chicago hockey player falls in love with the mother of a young delinquent who mugged him. Michael Keaton is appealing, Maria Conchita Alonso is fiery, and the script contains sharp dialogue, a few good laughs, and a number of sweet moments. Rated PG for profanity. 101m. **DIR:** Robert Mandel. **CAST:** Michael Keaton, Maria Conchita Alonso, Ajay Naidu. 1984

TOUCH OF CLASS, A ★★★★★ In one of the best romantic comedies of recent years, George Segal and Glenda Jackson are marvelously paired as a sometimes loving—sometimes bickering—couple who struggle through an extramarital affair. They begin their oddball romance when he runs over one of her children while chasing a fly ball in a baseball game. Fine acting and witty dialogue. Rated PG. 105m. **DIR:** Melvin Frank. **CAST:** George Segal, Glenda Jackson, Paul Sorvino, Hildegard Neil. 1972

TOUCH OF EVIL ★★★★1/2 In 1958, director-actor Orson Welles proved that he was still a filmmaking genius, with this dark and disturbing masterpiece about crime and corruption in a border town. B&W; 108m. **DIR:** Orson Welles. **CAST:** Orson Welles, Charlton Heston, Marlene Dietrich, Janet Leigh, Zsa Zsa Gabor. 1958

TOUCH OF FROST, A (TV SERIES) ★★★★ A gripping series based upon British author Rodney Wingfield's Detective Frost novels. The disorganized and disheveled (yet amazingly perceptive) Detective Inspector solves relentlessly complicated crimes, unconcerned with bad publicity or suspects with bruised feelings. The witty scripts, and occasional spark of humor make this a superior series. Not rated; contains violent themes. Each 95m. **DIR:** Don Leaver, Ross Devenish. **CAST:** David Jason, Bruce Alexander, Sally Dexter. 1995

TOUCHED ★★★ This sensitive drama involves the struggle of two young psychiatric patients who try to make it outside the hospital walls. Robert Hays and Kathleen Beller are terrific as the frightened couple who must deal with numerous unforeseen obstacles. Rated R for mature topic. 89m. **DIR:** John Flynn. **CAST:** Robert Hays, Kathleen Beller, Gilbert Lewis, Ned Beatty. 1982

TOUCHED BY LOVE ★★★ Strong performances make this affecting sentimental drama about a teenage cerebral palsy victim given hope through correspondence with singer Elvis Presley. Deborah Raffin is excellent as the nurse who nurtures patient Diane Lane from cripple to functioning teenager. Originally titled *From Elvis with Love*. Rated PG. 95m. **DIR:** Gus Trikonis. **CAST:** Deborah Raffin, Diane Lane, Michael Learned, Cristina Raines, Mary Wickes, Clu Gulager, John Amos. 1980

TOUGH AND DEADLY ★★★ Action heroes Roddy Piper and Billy Blanks team up again, the former as a seedy private investigator and the latter as a rogue CIA agent with amnesia. Naturally, both must punch and kick all sorts of nefarious folks, although the predictable action is kept palatable thanks to tongue-in-cheek performances and lighthearted direction. Rated R for violence and profanity. 9█ **DIR:** Steve Cohen. **CAST:** Billy Blanks, Roddy P█ Richard Norton, James Karen. 1994

TOUGH ENOUGH ★★1/2 Dennis Quaid plays "Country-and-Western Warrior," a singer-fighter w slugs his way through taxing "Toughman" conte from Fort Worth to Detroit in a quest for fame fortune. It's *Rocky* meets *Honeysuckle Rose*, yet s mildly enjoyable. Rated PG for profanity and lence. 106m. **DIR:** Richard Fleischer. **CAST:** Der Quaid, Warren Oates, Stan Shaw, Pam Grier, Wilf Brimley. 1983

TOUGH GUYS ★★★ This enjoyable movie featu Burt Lancaster and Kirk Douglas as two flamboy train robbers who are released from prison aft thirty years to find they have no place in soci They decide to strike back by doing what they best. It's featherweight, but the stars make it f Rated PG for light profanity, suggested sex, and m violence. 103m. **DIR:** Jeff Kanew. **CAST:** Burt L caster, Kirk Douglas, Charles Durning, Alexis Sm Dana Carvey, Darlanne Fluegel, Eli Wallach. 1986

TOUGH GUYS DON'T DANCE ★★ Interesting uneven attempt at *film noir*. Strenuous dialogue a bizarre acting makes this excursion into experim tal filmmaking confusing. Ryan O'Neal is an ex-c who wants to be a writer. Newcomer Debra Sundla is stunning as an obnoxious southern belle. Rate for nudity, language, and violence. 110m. **DIR:** N man Mailer. **CAST:** Ryan O'Neal, Isabella Rossell Wings Hauser, Debra Sundland, Frances Fisher. 198

TOUR OF DUTY ★★★ Pilot for the TV series of t same name, *Tour of Duty* is like a 90-minute cou in Vietnam War history with prime-time cleanline And while the cleanliness hinders the film's credib ity, the action scenes make it worth watching. N rated, has violence. 93m. **DIR:** B.W.L. Norton. **CA** Terence Knox, Stephen Caffrey, Joshua Maurer, Ke Conroy. 1987

TOURNAMENT TEMPO ★★ Professional hock player catches the eye of a beautiful talent scout w signs him up to make films. When his team's chanc at the championship are jeopardized the star has choose which career to concentrate on. B&W; 67 **DIR:** George Blair. **CAST:** Allen Lane, Jean Rogers, E ward Ashley, Frank Albertson, Anne Robertson, Pa Harvey. 1946

TOUS LES MATINS DU MONDE ★★★ Music for own sake is the prevailing metaphor in this sump ously photographed biography of little-known seve teenth-century viol player and composer Monsie de Sainte Colombe. Music lovers will be awed by t richly textured soundtrack, but mainstream viewe are apt to nod off. Not rated, with brief nudity a simulated sex. 114m. **DIR:** Alain Corneau. **CAST:** Jea Pierre Marielle, Gérard Depardieu, Anne Brochet, Gu laume Depardieu, Caroline Sihol, Carole Richert. 19█

TOUTE UNE NUIT ★★ Overly fragmented mov about the various stages and states of relationsh The end product is ultimately creatively arid. N one of Akerman's finer efforts. In French with En lish subtitles. Rated R for nudity. 90m. **DIR:** Chan█ Akerman. **CAST:** Aurore Clement, Tcheky Karyo. 198█

TOVARITCH ★★★1/2 A Russian duchess and her consort flee the revolution to Paris while entrusted with the tzar's fortune of forty billion francs. Too honest to spend any of it, they hire themselves out as domestics. Good farce. B&W; 98m. DIR: Anatole Litvak. CAST: Claudette Colbert, Charles Boyer, Basil Rathbone, Anita Louise, Melville Cooper, Isabel Jeans, Montagu Love, Curt Bois. 1937

TOWARD THE TERRA ★★ In the far future a group of telepaths are driven from society and forced to fight the computer-controlled human majority for their inheritance. Although entertaining to a point, this animated feature loses what impact the story should have by simply taking too long. In Japanese with English subtitles. Not rated; contains violence and brief nudity. 112m. DIR: Hideo Onchi. 1980

TOWER OF LONDON (1939) ★★★1/2 Basil Rathbone really sinks his teeth into the role of Richard III (and some of the scenery) in this historical drama about the evil prince's bloody rise to power. Despite a weak ending, this is an enjoyable movie of terror. In one of his all-too-rare leading roles, Rathbone is wonderful to watch, as are Boris Karloff (properly menacing as the executioner, Mord) and Vincent Price (as the conniving but ineffectual Duke of Clarence). B&W; 92m. DIR: Rowland V. Lee. CAST: Basil Rathbone, Boris Karloff, Vincent Price, Barbara O'Neil, Ian Hunter, Nan Grey, Leo G. Carroll, Miles Mander. 1939

TOWER OF LONDON (1962) ★★★ A bloody update of the 1939 classic. Vincent Price plays Richard III, who systematically murders everyone who stands in his way to the throne of England. One can feel the chills crawling up the spine. Roger Corman's melodramatic style works well in this gothic setting. Not rated. B&W; 79m. DIR: Roger Corman. CAST: Vincent Price, Michael Pate, Joan Freeman. 1962

TOWER OF SCREAMING VIRGINS, THE ★★ Lush, stately, sex-filled, and often sadistic medieval horror—supposedly based on an Alexander Dumas novel—set in and around a Gothic castle and its chamber of tortures. Despite the ad copy and lurid box art, the virgins are a bunch of young *men*, who fall prey to a sinister group of femmes fatales. Rated R. 89m. DIR: François Legrand. CAST: Terry Torday, Jean Piat, Uschi Glas. 1971

TOWERING INFERNO, THE ★★★★ This is the undisputed king of the disaster movies of the 1970s. An all-star cast came together for this big-budget thriller about a newly constructed San Francisco high-rise hotel and office building that is set ablaze due to substandard materials. Rated PG. 165m. DIR: John Guillermin, Irwin Allen. CAST: Steve McQueen, Paul Newman, William Holden, Faye Dunaway, Fred Astaire, Richard Chamberlain. 1974 DVD

TOWN CALLED HELL, A 🎬 Confusing action yarn about a manhunt for a Mexican revolutionary. Rated R. 95m. DIR: Robert Parrish. CAST: Robert Shaw, Telly Savalas, Stella Stevens. 1971

TOWN LIKE ALICE, A ★★★★1/2 This outstanding PBS series is even more enjoyable to watch in one viewing than during a six-week period. It is the story of female British POWs in Malaysia and their incredible struggle. Helen Morse is wonderful as the one who takes charge to help maintain the sanity and welfare of the group. Bryan Brown is the soldier who risks his life to help the women and falls in love with Morse. 301m. DIR: David Stevens. CAST: Helen Morse, Bryan Brown, Gordon Jackson. 1980

TOWN THAT DREADED SUNDOWN, THE ★★★1/2 The fact that this is based on actual events makes this effective little film all the more chilling. The story takes place in the year 1946 in the small border town of Texarkana. It begins in documentary style, with a narrator describing the post–World War II atmosphere, but soon gets to the unsettling business of the Phantom, a killer who terrorized the locals. Rated R for violence. 90m. DIR: Charles B. Pierce. CAST: Ben Johnson, Andrew Prine, Dawn Wells. 1977

TOXIC AVENGER, THE ★★★ Just another "nerdy" pool attendant tossed into a tub of toxic waste becomes mutant crime-fighter" picture. Actually, this low-budget horror spoof has a number of inspired moments. If you are looking for sick humor and creative bloodshed. Enjoy. Rated R for violence. 100m. DIR: Michael Herz, Samuel Weil. CAST: Mitchell Cohen. 1985 DVD

TOXIC AVENGER PART II, THE ★★1/2 The makers of the original are back with another tongue-in-cheek bloodfest. Toxie goes to Japan in search of the man who might be his father. Not as bad as it sounds but just as weird. Rated R for violence and nudity. 96m. DIR: Michael Herz, Lloyd Kaufman. CAST: Ron Fazio, Lisa Gaye. 1989 DVD

TOXIC AVENGER PART III, THE: THE LAST TEMPTATION OF TOXIE ★★★1/2 With nothing to do after ridding the town of Tromaville of all the bad guys, the Toxic Avenger unknowingly gets a job promoting a corporation bent on polluting the world. It's all in good fun. An unrated version runs a minute longer. Rated R for violence, profanity, and nudity. 102m. DIR: Michael Herz, Lloyd Kaufman. CAST: Ron Fazio, Lisa Gaye. 1989

TOY, THE ★★ You would think any comedy that combines the talents of Richard Pryor and Jackie Gleason would have to be exceptionally good, to say nothing of funny. But that's simply not true of this movie, about a spoiled rich kid (Scott Schwartz) whose father (Gleason) allows him to buy the ultimate toy (Pryor). Rated PG for profanity and adult themes. 99m. DIR: Richard Donner. CAST: Richard Pryor, Jackie Gleason, Scott Schwartz, Ned Beatty. 1982

TOY SOLDIERS (1983) 🎬 Inept film about a group of vacationing college students in Latin America. Rated R. 85m. DIR: David Fisher. CAST: Jason Miller, Cleavon Little, Rodolfo DeAnda. 1983

TOY SOLDIERS (1991) ★★★1/2 In what might be called *The Godfather Meets Taps*, a group of rich-kid rejects take on a band of terrorists who are holding them hostage to force the release of a South American drug lord. The preposterous story line benefits from assured performances by Denholm Elliott and young leads Sean Astin, Keith Coogan, Wil Wheaton, and George Perez. Rated R for violence and profanity. 112m. DIR: Daniel Petrie Jr. CAST: Sean Astin, Wil Wheaton, Keith Coogan, Lou Gossett Jr., Denholm Elliott, R. Lee Ermey, Jerry Orbach, George Perez. 1991

TOY STORY ★★★★★ Ground-breaking, state-of-the-art moviemaking meets a delightful, all-ages story in this instant classic from Disney. Whenever humans aren't around, the toys in Andy's room spring to life. A birthday present of spaceman Buzz Lightyear creates more than a few problems for cowboy Woody, who, up to that point, was king of the toy shelf. Excellent voice work by Tom Hanks and Tim Allen, Don Rickles, Jim Varney, Annie Potts, Wallace Shawn, John Ratzenberger, and R. Lee Ermey. Rated G. 80m. DIR: John Lasseter. 1995

•**TOY STORY 2** ★★★★★ The folks at Pixar and Disney do the impossible—by coming up with a computer-animated sequel that's even better than the original. This time, cowboy Woody (voiced by Tom Hanks) is sold during a garage sale to a toy collector, thus sending Buzz Lightyear (Tim Allen) and the other toys on a quest to save their buddy. It's delightful, with so many memorable bits that there's not enough room to call attention to them here. Suffice to say, you won't want to miss the ending credits, where the filmmakers send up the outtake "blooper" clips made popular by director Hal Needham in his Smokey and the Bandit days. Rated G. 92m. DIR: John Lasseter. 1999

TOYS 💔 Idiotic waste of Robin Williams's talents. He's a toy manufacturer's whimsical, spacey son. Dad Donald O'Connor's death results in a battle between Williams and militaristic uncle Michael Gambon, who is bent on making lethal war toys. A rare misfire from director Barry Levinson. Rated PG-13 for violence. 121m. DIR: Barry Levinson. CAST: Robin Williams, Michael Gambon, Joan Cusack, Robin Wright, Donald O'Connor, Arthur Malet, Jack Warden. 1992

TOYS IN THE ATTIC ★★ A man brings his baby doll bride home to confront his two overly protective spinster sisters in this watered-down screen version of the Lillian Hellman stage play. As the sisters, Geraldine Page and Wendy Hiller are superb, as always. B&W; 90m. DIR: George Roy Hill. CAST: Dean Martin, Geraldine Page, Wendy Hiller, Yvette Mimieux, Gene Tierney, Nan Martin, Larry Gates. 1963

TRACES OF RED ★★ Half-baked erotic thriller—narrated by the fresh corpse of a homicide detective—features a Palm Beach serial killer who slashes women with a letter opener, smears their faces with Yves Saint Laurent lipstick, steals their clothes, and mails out lousy poetry that warns of further mayhem. Rated R for language, nudity, simulated sex, and violence. 104m. DIR: Andy Wolk. CAST: James Belushi, Lorraine Bracco, Tony Goldwyn, William Russ. 1993

TRACK OF THE MOON BEAST 💔 A mineralogist comes into contact with a fragment of a meteor. 90m. DIR: Richard Ashe. CAST: Chase Cordell. 1976

TRACK 29 ★★ British director Nicolas Roeg continues his downhill creative slide with this psycho-silly story of a bored, alcoholic housewife (Theresa Russell) who takes up with a strange hitchhiker (Gary Oldman) who may or may not be her son. Rated R for violence and gore. 90m. DIR: Nicolas Roeg. CAST: Theresa Russell, Gary Oldman, Christopher Lloyd,

Colleen Camp, Sandra Bernhard, Seymour Cassel. 1988

TRACKED ★★ Made-for-cable action-drama about a prisoner who is punished by becoming a "dog boy," human bait for the prison's attack dogs. While Bryan Brown is efficient as a scrupulous guard, Tia Carrere is totally miscast as an assistant district attorney. Some exciting moments early on, but the film becomes one long chase at the end. A.k.a. Dogboys. Rated PG-13 for language and violence. 92m. DIR: Ken Russell. CAST: Dean Cain, Bryan Brown, Tia Carrere, Ken James, Sean McCann. 1998

TRACKER, THE ★★★ In this generally effective made-for-HBO Western, Kris Kristofferson stars as famed tracker Noble Adams. He hunts down a blood-thirsty religious zealot–turned–outlaw (Scott Wilson) wanted for multiple murders and the kidnapping of a teenage girl. The film is sometimes slow and a bit too talky, but it's sporadically inventive. 90m. DIR: John Guillermin. CAST: Kris Kristofferson, Scott Wilson, Mark Moses, David Huddleston, Karen Kopins. 1988

TRACKERS, THE ★★ Ernest Borgnine plays a vengeful rancher out to get the men who killed his son and kidnapped his daughter. He reluctantly enlists the aid of a black professional tracker (Sammy Davis Jr.). It's a mildly entertaining Western made for TV. 73m. DIR: Earl Bellamy. CAST: Sammy Davis Jr., Ernest Borgnine. 1971

TRACKS 💔 A Vietnam War veteran escorts his dead buddy on a train cross-country and goes crazy in the process. Rated R. 90m. DIR: Henry Jaglom. CAST: Dennis Hopper, Taryn Power, Dean Stockwell, Topo Swope, Michael Emil. 1977

TRACKS OF A KILLER ★★ A high-powered executive invites his protégé to his wilderness retreat to see if the young man has the right stuff to take over the company. He finds out the hard way that his replacement has the killer instinct—in spades. So-so suspense thriller. Rated R for violence and profanity. 100m. DIR: Harvey Frost. CAST: Kelly LeBrock, Wolf Larson, James Brolin, Courtney Taylor, George Touliatos. 1995

TRADE OFF ★★ Theresa Russell "accidentally" bumps into Adam Baldwin at a trade show and suggests they knock off each other's spouses. Baldwin's character is an idiotic bungler and the jazz score is annoying. Feels like a setup from the opening credits and then spins completely out of control. Rated R for profanity, violence, nudity, and sexual situations. 92m. DIR: Andrew Lane. CAST: Theresa Russell, Adam Baldwin, Barry Primus, Megan Gallagher. 1994

TRADE SECRETS ★★ Picture-postcard locations set the tone for this sophisticated but uninvolving French whodunit, as ex-Interpol policeman Sam Waterston probes the suspicious demise of a Bordeaux-wine heiress. Rated R for nudity and adult situations. 91m. DIR: Claude Feraldo. CAST: Sam Waterston, Marisa Berenson, Bernard Pierre Donnadieu, Lauren Hutton, Arielle Dombasle. 1986

TRADING FAVORS ★★ Tired tale of young college jock who gets involved with a wild woman. She ends up stealing his car and taking him on a crime-laden road trip. It was a match made in heaven, which gets real hot toward the end when the woman's volatile ex-boyfriend enters the picture. Rated R for adult situations, language, nudity, and violence. 103m. **DIR:** Sondra Locke. **CAST:** Rosanna Arquette, Devon Gummersal, Peter Greene, George Dzundza. **1997**

TRADING HEARTS ★★★ A period charmer written by Don Deford casts Raul Julia as a washed-up baseball player who's lured into the sedate Florida family life of a single mother and her precocious child. Predictable and occasionally schmaltzy, but entertaining. Rated PG. 88m. **DIR:** Neil Leifer. **CAST:** Raul Julia, Beverly D'Angelo, Nina Axelrod, Jenifer Lewis. **1987**

TRADING MOM ★★★1/2 Delightful family movie, based on the short story "The Mommy Market," finds Sissy Spacek playing four different roles. She plays the mother of three who decide they want another mommy. They go to the Mommy market, where they are given the chance to test-drive three candidates, also played by Spacek. Children will enjoy the whimsical situations, while parents will appreciate the life lessons. Rated PG. 83m. **DIR:** Tia Brelis. **CAST:** Sissy Spacek, Anna Chlumsky, Maureen Stapleton, Aaron Michael Metchik, Asher Metchik. **1993**

TRADING PLACES ★★★★ Here's an uproarious comedy about what happens when uptight Philadelphia broker (Dan Aykroyd) and dynamic black street hustler (Eddie Murphy) change places. Rated R for nudity and profanity. 117m. **DIR:** John Landis. **CAST:** Dan Aykroyd, Eddie Murphy, Ralph Bellamy, Don Ameche, Jamie Lee Curtis, Denholm Elliott. **1983**

TRAFFIC ★★★ Mr. Hulot is back, and this time his escapades revolve around an international auto show. The sight and sound gags are quite amusing. Multilingual with some English dubbed in, but the spoken word is not needed to enjoy the film. Not rated. 89m. **DIR:** Jacques Tati. **CAST:** Jacques Tati, Marla Kimberly. **1971**

TRAFFIC IN SOULS ★★★1/2 One of the first exploitation films ever made, this makes great use of New York City locations and natives as it uncovers the "true crime" horrors of forced prostitution. The documentarylike realism is still gripping, but the film is so cropped that telegrams and newspapers are illegible. Somewhat overblown by today's standards, but the timeless social commentary never undermines the plot. Silent. Not rated; contains adult themes. B&W; 88m. **DIR:** George Loane Tucker. **CAST:** Matt Moore, Jane Gail, Ethel Grandin. **1913**

•**TRAFFIC JAM** ★★★ A road trip slowly turns into a disaster when a hard-working Japanese man decides to take his family to visit his parents. The humor isn't as broad as in the *National Lampoon Vacation* series and an undercurrent of strong affection among the characters makes this enjoyable viewing. Original title: *Jutai*. In Japanese with English subtitles. Not rated; contains no objectionable material. 108m. **DIR:** Mitsuo Kurotsuchi. **CAST:** Junko Takarada, Shingo Yuzawa, Eiji Okada. **1992**

TRAGEDY OF A RIDICULOUS MAN ★★★1/2 A wealthy businessman struggles with the most difficult decision of his life: Should he sell his beloved cheese factory to raise the ransom money for his kidnapped son, or should he assume that his son has already been murdered? Ugo Tognazzi won the Cannes best-actor award for his role as the distraught father. In Italian with English subtitles. Not rated; contains nudity and profanity. 117m. **DIR:** Bernardo Bertolucci. **CAST:** Ugo Tognazzi, Anouk Aimée, Laura Morante, Victor Cavallo. **1981**

TRAGEDY OF FLIGHT 103, THE: THE INSIDE STORY ★★★★ A tragic and riveting account of the events leading up to the destruction of Pan Am Flight 103, resulting in the deaths at Christmastime in 1988 of 270 people over Lockerbie, Scotland. This dramatized reconstruction exposes the inner workings of international terrorists, ineffectual cosmetic airport security, and how communication failures between intelligence agencies and airport officials have led to the loss of innocent lives. Made for TV. 89m. **DIR:** Leslie Woodhead. **CAST:** Peter Boyle, Ned Beatty, Vincent Gardenia. **1990**

TRAIL BEYOND, THE ★★1/2 Once again, John Wayne rides to the rescue in a low-budget Western from the 1930s. It's pretty typical stuff as the Duke fights outlaws who are attempting to steal a gold mine. But this B Western has lots of action and a rare appearance of father and son actors Noah Beery Sr. and Noah Beery Jr. B&W; 55m. **DIR:** Robert N. Bradbury. **CAST:** John Wayne, Verna Hillie, Noah Beery Sr., Noah Beery Jr. **1934 DVD**

TRAIL BLAZERS ★★★ The Three Mesquiteers stop a bandit gang run by a newspaper editor trying to halt the westward development of the telegraph. B&W; 54m. **DIR:** George Sherman. **CAST:** Robert Livingston, Bob Steele, Rufe Davis, Pauline Moore. **1940**

TRAIL DRIVE ★★★★ Cattleman Ken Maynard brings to justice an unscrupulous rancher on a thrill packed cattle drive. B&W; 60m. **DIR:** Alan James. **CAST:** Ken Maynard, Cecilia Parker, Bob Kortman. **1933**

TRAIL DUST ★★★ People up north are crying for beef, but a group of unscrupulous cattlemen are ignoring the crisis and holding out for top dollar. Hopalong Cassidy and some of the smaller ranchers combine herds and make a cattle drive marked by murder and sabotage by the rogue cowboys. There's plenty of action, a few songs, some funny business between Hoppy and Windy, and a great ending. B&W; 77m. **DIR:** Nate Watt. **CAST:** William Boyd, James Ellison, George "Gabby" Hayes, Morris Ankrum (Stepen Morris), Gwynne Shipman. **1936**

TRAIL OF ROBIN HOOD ★★★ This star-studded oddity finds Roy Rogers and a handful of contemporary Western heroes aiding screen great Jack Holt (playing himself) in his effort to provide Christmas trees to needy families in time for the holidays. Enjoyable film for all ages and a special treat for fans of the genre. 67m. **DIR:** William Witney. **CAST:** Roy Rogers, Penny Edwards, Gordon Jones, Jack Holt, Emory Parnell, Clifton Young, Rex Allen, Allan "Rocky" Lane, Monte Hale, Kermit Maynard, Tom Keene, Ray "Crash" Corrigan, William Farnum. **1950**

TRAIL OF THE LONESOME PINE, THE ★★★1/2 Railroad builder gets caught in the crossfire between feuding families in Virginia's Blue Ridge Mountains. Based on John Fox, Jr.'s popular turn-of-the-century novel this is old-fashioned but powerful, and it put young Henry Fonda on the map. Noteworthy as the first outdoor film shot in full Technicolor. Not rated; suitable for general audiences. 102m. **DIR:** Henry Hathaway. **CAST:** Sylvia Sidney, Fred MacMurray, Henry Fonda, Fred Stone, Beulah Bondi, Spanky McFarland, Nigel Bruce, Fuzzy Knight. **1936**

TRAIL OF THE PINK PANTHER, THE ★★1/2 Through the magic of editing, the late Peter Sellers "stars" as the bumbling Inspector Clouseau. Writer-director Blake Edwards uses outtakes of Sellers from previous films and combines them with new footage featuring David Niven, Herbert Lom, and Capucine. Disappointing. Rated PG for nudity and scatological humor. 97m. **DIR:** Blake Edwards. **CAST:** Peter Sellers, David Niven, Herbert Lom, Capucine, Robert Wagner. **1982**

TRAIL OF THE SILVER SPURS ★★★ The Range Busters investigate hidden passages, salted mines, and a mysterious ghost-town killer known as the Jingler. B&W; 58m. **DIR:** S. Roy Luby. **CAST:** Ray "Crash" Corrigan, John King, Max Terhune, Dorothy Short, I. Stanford Jolley. **1941**

TRAIL STREET ★★★ Randolph Scott plays Bat Masterson in this well-acted story of conflicting western philosophies as Robert Ryan defends the farmers against gambler Steve Brodie and the cattle-rancher faction. Gabby Hayes lends some levity to this otherwise dramatic adult Western. Skillful repackaging of a familiar story. B&W; 84m. **DIR:** Ray Enright. **CAST:** Randolph Scott, Robert Ryan, Anne Jeffreys, George "Gabby" Hayes, Steve Brodie. **1947**

TRAILIN' NORTH ★★ Texas Ranger Bob Steele heads to Canada where he works with the Mounties to bring back a prisoner. Every B-Western cliché in the book. B&W; 57m. **DIR:** John P. McCarthy. **CAST:** Bob Steele, Doris Hill, George "Gabby" Hayes. **1933**

TRAIN, THE ★★★★ A suspenseful World War II adventure about the French Resistance's attempt to stop a train loaded with fine art, seized from French museums, from reaching its destination in Nazi Germany. Burt Lancaster is fine as the head of the French railway system, but he is far outclassed by the performance of Paul Scofield as the unrelenting German commander. B&W; 133m. **DIR:** John Frankenheimer. **CAST:** Burt Lancaster, Paul Scofield, Michel Simon, Jeanne Moreau. **1965 DVD**

TRAIN KILLER, THE ★★ The true story of Sylvester Matushka, the Hungarian businessman who was responsible for a number of train wrecks in 1931. What is frustrating about this film is that it prepares the viewer for political intrigue that is never fully explained by the end of the film. Towje Kleiner is superb as Dr. Epstein, investigator of the train wrecks. Not rated; contains sex, nudity, and violence. 90m. **DIR:** Sandor Simo. **CAST:** Michael Sarrazin, Towje Kleiner. **1983**

•TRAIN OF LIFE ★★1/2 The inhabitants of a Jewish village in Nazi-occupied Europe try to smuggle themselves to Palestine disguised as a deportation train, with some of them dressed in German uniforms to complete the ruse. This bizarre mixture of *Fiddler on the Roof* and *Von Ryan's Express* is energetic and pretty to look at, but there's a spurious implication behind the premise: that the Holocaust was no big

deal if you could just keep a cheerful attitude. In French with English subtitles. Rated R for nudity. 102m. **DIR:** Radu Mihaileanu. **CAST:** Lionel Abelanski, Rufus, Clement Harari, Marie-Jose Nat. **1998**

TRAIN ROBBERS, THE ★★1/2 John Wayne and Ben Johnson join Ann-Margret in a search for a lost train and gold. Some nice moments but generally unsatisfying. For hard-core Wayne fans only. Rated PG for violence, but nothing extreme. 92m. **DIR:** Burt Kennedy. **CAST:** John Wayne, Ben Johnson, Ann-Margret, Rod Taylor, Ricardo Montalban. **1973**

TRAINED TO FIGHT ★★ Average martial arts actioner features a college freshman pursuing his interest in kung fu. He must win the $25,000 tournament money to help underprivileged kids. His master tries to explain why his moves are meant to promote nonviolence, but that's stretching it. Not rated; contains violence. 95m. **DIR:** Eric Sherman. **CAST:** Ken McLeod, Tang Tak Wing, Matthew Roy Cohen, Mark Williams. **1991**

TRAINSPOTTING ★★★★ Exuberant movie about the rigors and rushes of Scottish-junkie life. Working from Irvine Welsh's novel, director Danny Boyle doesn't flinch from depicting the horrid consequences of heroin use, but he never lets you forget that most people do it because it feels better than anything else. Surrealistic and speedy in a glib, rock-video kind of way, the film doesn't cover any new ground, but it does approach the dead-end scene with an irrepressible style and audacious visual wit. Rated R. 90m. **DIR:** Danny Boyle. **CAST:** Ewan McGregor, Ewen Bremner, Jonny Lee Miller, Kevin McKidd, Robert Carlyle. **1996 DVD**

TRAITOR, THE ★★1/2 Marshal Tim McCoy goes undercover to catch a gang of cutthroats. He succeeds in his plan of joining the outlaws, but his life is in constant danger. A game performance by McCoy, but the story is too typical and the direction is plodding. B&W; 56m. **DIR:** Sam Newfield. **CAST:** Tim McCoy, Frances Grant, Wally Wales, Karl Hackett. **1936**

TRAMP AT THE DOOR ★★★★ Poignant story of a transient who poses as a distant relative of a family to gain shelter and food from them. The script is solid, especially the stories that the tramp (played brilliantly by Ed McNamara) weaves for the astonished family. Not rated; for all ages. 81m. **DIR:** Allan Kroeker. **CAST:** Ed McNamara, August Schellenberg, Monique Mercure. **1985**

TRAMPLERS, THE ★★ Gordon Scott returns from the Civil War to find his father (Joseph Cotten) trying to preserve the prewar South by burning out settlers and starting mass lynchings. Scott and his younger brother (Jim Mitchum) join up with their father's enemies. 105m. **DIR:** Albert Band. **CAST:** Gordon Scott, Joseph Cotten, Jim Mitchum, Franco Nero. **1966**

TRANCERS ★★ Tim Thomerson is Jack Deth, a police officer in the 2280s who is sent to bring back a violent cult leader who escaped into the twentieth century. Rated PG-13 for profanity and lots of violence. 76m. **DIR:** Charles Band. **CAST:** Tim Thomerson, Helen Hunt, Michael Stefani, Art Le Fleur, Telma Hopkins, Richard Herd, Anne Seymour. **1985 DVD**

TRANCERS II (THE RETURN OF JACK DETH) ✔ Jack Deth returns to Los Angeles to battle zompielike creatures in this technically abysmal production. Rated R for nudity and violence. 86m. DIR: Charles Band. CAST: Tim Thomerson, Helen Hunt. 1991

TRANCERS III: DETH LIVES ★★★ In this third installment, Trancer tracker Jack Deth, played with aplomb by Tim Thomerson, is back to hunt down some new Trancers in town, and this time they're tougher and tougher. This series from Full Moon Productions is one of their highlights and is entertaining in a brutal, self-mocking sort of way. Rated R for violence and language. 83m. DIR: C. Courtney Joyner. CAST: Tim Thomerson, Melanie Smith, Andrew Robinson, Helen Hunt, Megan Ward. 1992

TRANCERS 4: JACK OF SWORDS ★★1/2 In his fourth outing as Trancer hunter Jack Deth, Tim Thomerson is transported to another dimension where the locals are being bred as food. Trapped in a medieval world, Deth must utilize knowledge from his time to end the Trancers' reign of terror. New setting and swordplay breathe life into the series. Rated R for violence, nudity, and adult situations. 74m. DIR: David Nutter. CAST: Tim Thomerson, Stacie Randall, Ty Miller, Stephen Macht, Alan Oppenheimer. 1993

TRANCERS 5: SUDDEN DETH ★★★ This (supposedly) closes out the Jack Deth flicks with a final battle with the life-sucking Trancers. A quick rundown of past installments shows us that time-traveler Deth has been stuck in a sword-and-sorcery universe in which everyone is named after a Shakespearean character. This is hardly art, but Deth's unflappability and cynical humor, combined with a fast pace, make for an enjoyable romp. Rated R for profanity and violence. 73m. DIR: David Nutter. CAST: Tim Thomerson, Stacie Randall, Ty Miller, Terri Ivens, Mark Arnold, Stephen Macht. 1994

TRANSATLANTIC MERRY-GO-ROUND ★★ Jack Benny is the emcee of this transatlantic showboat, the S.S. Progress, en route from New York to Paris. This tub is loaded with romance, blackmail, chicanery, and murder. But it's rather lightweight overall. B&W; 90m. DIR: Ben Stoloff. CAST: Gene Raymond, Nancy Carroll, Jack Benny, Mitzi Green, Boswell Sisters. 1934

TRANSATLANTIC TUNNEL ★★1/2 A truly splendid cast still manages to get bogged down a bit in this heavy-handed account of the building of a passageway under the Atlantic Ocean. Richard Dix plays the stalwart engineer who can get the job done and Walter Huston plays the president of the United States. B&W; 90m. DIR: Maurice Elvey. CAST: Richard Dix, Leslie Banks, Madge Evans, C. Aubrey Smith, George Arliss, Walter Huston, Helen Vinson. 1935

TRANSFORMATIONS 🎬 An AIDS subtext runs through this sci-fi film, but the similarities to David Cronenberg's remake of The Fly overpower any good intentions. Rated R for violence, profanity, nudity, gore, and simulated sex. 84m. DIR: Jay Kamen. CAST: Rex Smith, Patrick Macnee, Lisa Langlois, Christopher Neame. 1988

TRANSFORMERS, THE MOVIE 🎬 Animated vehicle for violence and destruction. Rated PG for violence and occasional obscenities. 80m. DIR: Nelson Shin. 1986

TRANSMUTATIONS ★★ Much-lauded horror writer Clive Barker disowned this, the first of his stories to be filmed. A retired London mobster, searching for his missing girlfriend, discovers an underground society of mutants, the victims of drug experiments. The strong cast has little to do, and the story is more mystery than horror. Rated R. 103m. DIR: George Pavlou. CAST: Larry Lamb, Denholm Elliott, Nicola Cowper, Steven Berkoff, Miranda Richardson, Ingrid Pitt. 1985

TRANSYLVANIA 6-5000 ★★ Sometimes amusing but ultimately silly horror spoof focusing on an inept pair of tabloid reporters (Jeff Goldblum and Ed Begley Jr.) sent to Transylvania to investigate the Frankenstein monster. Rated PG for mild profanity. 93m. DIR: Rudy DeLuca. CAST: Jeff Goldblum, Ed Begley Jr., Joseph Bologna, Carol Kane, Jeffrey Jones, John Byner, Michael Richards. 1985

TRANSYLVANIA TWIST ★★1/2 No horror movie is safe in this lampoon from producer Roger Corman. Scenes from classics like Frankenstein and Dracula, along with more recent entries in the genre (Friday the 13th and Nightmare on Elm Street) are parodied in this tale of the search for a book that will raise the "evil one." Rated PG-13. 82m. DIR: Jim Wynorski. CAST: Robert Vaughn, Teri Copley, Steve Altman, Angus Scrimm, Jay Robinson, Howard Morris, Steve Franken. 1990

TRAP, THE ★★★1/2 Fast pace and taut suspense mark this thriller about as fine a gaggle of fleeing gangsters as ever menaced the innocent inhabitants of a small California desert town. This is edge-of-chair stuff. It was in films such as this that Richard Widmark made his name praisingly hissable. 84m. DIR: Norman Panama. CAST: Richard Widmark, Lee J. Cobb, Earl Holliman, Tina Louise, Carl Benton Reid, Earl Holliman, Tina Louise, Lorne Greene. 1958

TRAP THEM AND KILL THEM 🎬 Originally titled Emmanuelle and the Last Cannibals, this gross out extravaganza merges the sexploitation Emmanuelle series of porn pictures with the Italian cannibal horror genre. Not rated, but sexually explicit and very gruesome. 85m. DIR: Joe D'Amato (Aristide Massaccesi). CAST: Laura Gemser, Gabriele Tinti, Susan Scott. 1977

TRAPEZE ★★1/2 Overly familiar tale of professional (Burt Lancaster) who takes young protégé (Tony Curtis) under his wing only to have scheming opportunist Gina Lollobrigida come between them is okay but nothing out of the ordinary. Solid performances and competent stunts performed by the stars. 105m. DIR: Carol Reed. CAST: Burt Lancaster, Tony Curtis, Gina Lollobrigida, Katy Jurado, Thomas Gomez. 1956

TRAPPED ★★1/2 Kathleen Quinlan's resourceful businesswoman saves this low-rent stuck-in-a-deserted-building-with-a-maniac programmer from complete turkeydom, but there's little to admire in Fred Walton's inane script or hackneyed direction. Made for cable. 88m. DIR: Fred Walton. CAST: Kathleen Quinlan, Bruce Abbott, Katy Boyer. 1989

TRAPPED BY TELEVISION ★★1/2 Collection agent hooks up with a penniless inventor who is just about to complete a "televisor" that can transmit action to a receiver miles away! Our heroes battle the crooks who want to destroy the machine and corner the market with their own device. A low-budget treat. B&W; 64m. DIR: Del Lord. CAST: Lyle Talbot, Mary Astor, Nat Pendleton, Joyce Compton, Thurston Hall, Robert Strange. **1936**

TRAPPED BY THE MORMONS ★★ Isoldi Keene chooses Nora for his next wife and uses hypnotic powers to recruit her girlfriends. Lured from home and into the "Mormon net," their fate is set. Silent British oddity. B&W; 70m. DIR: H. B. Parkinson. CAST: Evelyn Brent, Lewis Willoughby, Ward McAllister, George Wynn, Olive Sloan. **1922**

TRAPPED IN PARADISE ★★ Three bumbling brothers (Nicolas Cage, Dana Carvey, Jon Lovitz) rob a small-town bank on Christmas Eve, then botch their getaway and wind up spending the holiday with the bank president and his wonderful family. Aimless, leaden farce wastes the talents of its three stars, then shamelessly and ineptly fumbles at your heartstrings. Rated PG-13 for comic violence and mild profanity. 111m. DIR: George Gallo. CAST: Nicolas Cage, Dana Carvey, Jon Lovitz, Donald Moffat, Madchen Amick, Florence Stanley, John Ashton. **1994**

TRAPPED IN SPACE ★★★ Entertaining, involving sci-fi drama about a group of space travelers who discover that—due to the unexpected rupture of their oxygen tanks—they've only got enough air left for one of them to return home. Who will it be? The cast is very good, displaying their various levels of paranoia and panic with precision. Based on the short story "Breaking Strain" by Arthur C. Clarke. Rated PG for violence. 87m. DIR: Arthur Allan Seidelman. CAST: Jack Wagner, Jack Coleman, Kay Lenz, Kevin Colson, Craig Wasson, Sigrid Thornton. **1994**

TRAPPER COUNTY WAR ★★ Two city boys trigger a blood feud when one of them falls for a country girl who's already spoken for. An oft-told tale of backwoods romance and revenge. Rated R for violence and profanity. 98m. DIR: Worth Keeter. CAST: Rob Estes, Betsy Russell, Bo Hopkins, Ernie Hudson. **1989** DVD

TRASH ★★1/2 Favorite Andy Warhol actor Joe Dallesandro faces the squalor of New York once again. This is one of Warhol's more palatable productions. It contains some truly amusing scenes and insightful dialogue, as well as good performances by Dallesandro and Holly Woodlawn, whose relationship is the highlight of the film. Nudity, language, and open drug use fill the frames of this freewheeling life study. 110m. DIR: Paul Morrissey. CAST: Joe Dallesandro, Holly Woodlawn, Jane Forth. **1970** DVD

TRAUMA ★★ American cast gets lost in this weak effort from noted Italian horror-director Dario Argento. A woman is traumatized when she sees her parents decapitated by a serial killer. Argento keeps things creepy, but the film is slow and the characters are uninteresting. Not rated and R-rated versions available; unrated contains more gore. 106m. DIR: Dario Argento. CAST: James Russo, Frederic Forrest, Brad Dourif, Piper Laurie, Christopher Rydell, Asia Argento. **1992**

TRAVELING MAN ★★★1/2 John Lithgow puts heart and soul into this engaging portrayal of a congenial road-bound salesman pushing foam insulation. Lithgow winds up chaperoning a wet-behind-the-ears trainee (Jonathan Silverman)—who then makes a grab for his mentor's route. Originally made for cable, it is unrated, but contains nudity. 105m. DIR: Irvin Kershner. CAST: John Lithgow, Jonathan Silverman, John Glover, Margaret Colin. **1989**

TRAVELLER ★★★★ Star-producer Bill Paxton shepherded this clever little drama to the screen and it's easy to see why he cared so much. He's one of a roving band of modern-day Celtic gypsies, whose life grows complicated when he takes a surly young man under his wing, and falls in love with a spirited barmaid who's "outside the clan." Rich characterization and an excellent use of music are just a few of this film's many charms. Rated R for profanity and violence. 101m. DIR: Jack Green. CAST: Bill Paxton, Mark Wahlberg, Julianna Margulies, James Gammon, Luke Askew. **1996** DVD

TRAVELLING NORTH ★★★1/2 Fine Australian romance focuses on the love of two senior citizens. Touching, delightful, and definitely worth watching. Rated PG-13 for profanity and adult themes. 97m. DIR: Carl Schultz. CAST: Leo McKern, Julia Blake. **1988**

TRAVELS WITH MY AUNT ★★1/2 Director George Cukor's screen version of Graham Greene's comic novel is only slightly above average. Maggie Smith's overbearing and overplayed aunt knocks what could have been a delightful *Auntie Mame*-style farce completely off-kilter. Alec McCowen gives an affecting performance as the bank executive who finds his tidy world disrupted. Rated PG. 109m. DIR: George Cukor. CAST: Maggie Smith, Alec McCowen, Lou Gossett Jr., Robert Stephens, Cindy Williams. **1972**

TRAXX ★★★ Wacky, often funny tale about a mercenary turned cookie maker who cleans the criminal element out of Hadleyville, Texas. Shadoe Stevens is Traxx, a man who derives simple pleasure from shooting people, causing mayhem—and baking the oddest-flavored cookies he can imagine. Rated R for cartoon violence and slight nudity. 85m. DIR: Jerome Gray. CAST: Shadoe Stevens, Priscilla Barnes, Robert Davi, John Hancock. **1988**

TREACHEROUS ★★ Tired thriller about a couple who find passion and intrigue while on vacation at a paradise resort. Rated R for violence, language, and sensuality. 90m. DIR: Kevin Brodie. CAST: C. Thomas Howell, Tia Carrere, Adam Baldwin, Kevin Bernhardt. **1993**

TREACHEROUS CROSSING ★★★1/2 Lindsay Wagner is a newlywed who goes on a honeymoon cruise with her new husband, only to have him disappear right after boarding. Wagner portrays the unstable character quite convincingly, and the story is twisted enough, so that one does not know who to believe. Made for cable. 95m. DIR: Tony Wharmby. CAST: Lindsay Wagner, Angie Dickinson, Grant Show, Joseph Bottoms, Karen Medak, Charles Napier, Jeffrey DeMunn. **1992**

TREASURE ISLAND (1934) ★★★★ This is an MGM all-star presentation of Robert Louis Stevenson's classic of a young boy's adventure with pirates, buried treasure, and that delightful rogue of fiction Long John Silver. It seems all the great character actors of the 1930s put in an appearance, including Wallace Beery, as Silver, and Lionel Barrymore, as

Billy Bones. B&W; 105m. DIR: Victor Fleming. CAST: Wallace Beery, Lionel Barrymore, Jackie Cooper, Lewis Stone. 1934

TREASURE ISLAND (1950) ★★★★ Disney remake of the Robert Louis Stevenson pirate adventure is powered by a memorable Robert Newton as Long John Silver. 87m. DIR: Byron Haskin. CAST: Robert Newton, Bobby Driscoll, Basil Sydney. 1950

TREASURE ISLAND (1990) ★★★1/2 Robert Louis Stevenson's classic adventure yarn receives its best treatment in this rousing made-for-cable adaptation. The location photography is gorgeous, the sailing ship *Hispaniola* is a beauty, and the pirates look like N. C. Wyeth and Howard Pyle illustrations come to life. 132m. DIR: Fraser Heston. CAST: Charlton Heston, Christian Bale, Oliver Reed, Julian Glover, Richard Johnson, Clive Wood, Christopher Lee. 1990

TREASURE OF ARNE ★★ Swedish master Mauritz Stiller forsook his flair for comedy and wrought this grim tale of crime, guilt, and sacrifice—famous in its day but unrelievedly tedious today. Based on Selma Lagerlöf's tale about escaped prisoners who steal a treasure with a curse on it. Silent. B&W; 100m. DIR: Mauritz Stiller. CAST: Richard Lund, Mary Johnson, Hjalmar Selander. 1919

TREASURE OF PANCHO VILLA, THE ★★1/2 Rory Calhoun and Gilbert Roland pull off a gold robbery with the intention of giving the loot to the Mexican revolutionary forces. However, Calhoun begins to think the money would be better in his pocket. Complications ensue. Calhoun carries a great machine gun in this watchable Western, and Roland is fascinating as always. Good action scenes. 96m. DIR: George Sherman. CAST: Rory Calhoun, Shelley Winters, Gilbert Roland, Joseph Calleia. 1955

TREASURE OF THE AMAZON ♥ Mexican-made action flick about a fortune in diamonds. Not rated; contains some violence. 105m. DIR: René Cardona Jr. CAST: Stuart Whitman, Bradford Dillman, Donald Pleasence, John Ireland. 1983

TREASURE OF THE SIERRA MADRE ★★★★★ Humphrey Bogart gives a brilliant performance in this study of greed. The setting is rugged mountains in Mexico where Bogart, with Tim Holt and a grizzled prospector, played marvelously by Walter Huston, set out to make a fortune in gold prospecting. They do, with their troubles getting worse. Seamless script and magnificent performances add up to a classic. B&W; 126m. DIR: John Huston. CAST: Humphrey Bogart, Tim Holt, Walter Huston, Bruce Bennett. 1948

TREASURE OF THE YANKEE ZEPHYR ★★1/2 When an old trapper (Donald Pleasence) discovers a sunken treasure of military medals and liquor, he enlists the aid of his partner (Ken Wahl) and his daughter (Lesley Ann Warren) to bring in the haul. A ruthless claim jumper (George Peppard) and his henchmen follow. Rated PG for violence. 97m. DIR: David Hemmings. CAST: Ken Wahl, Lesley Ann Warren, Donald Pleasence, George Peppard, Bruno Lawrence. 1981

TREASURE OF PIRATE'S POINT ★★ Nondiscerning children might enjoy this harmless but halfhearted family romp about a group of kids who suspect that a pirate's treasure is buried in their small town. They're *Goonies* wannabes. Rated PG. 88m.

DIR: Richard Stanley. CAST: Asher Metchik, Brittany Alyse Smith, Sam Gifaldi, William Sheppard. 1998

TREASURE OF THE MOON GODDESS ♥ Indifferent direction and a poor script sink this Indiana Jones clone. Rated R for violence, profanity, and nudity. 89m. DIR: Joseph Louis Agraz. CAST: Don Calfa, Linnea Quigley. 1987

TREASURE OF THE FOUR CROWNS ♥ Logic is the victim of this steal from *Raiders of the Lost Ark*. Rated PG for violence. 97m. DIR: Ferdinando Baldi. CAST: Tony Anthony, Gene Quintano. 1983

TREASURES OF THE *TITANIC* ★★★ Two miles beneath the Atlantic Ocean lie the remains of RMS *Titanic*, lost April 14, 1912. This film of the 1987 French-American exploration of the famous wreck and retrieval of a variety of artifacts, such as a ship's safe, a bell, navigation equipment, and china, brings the haunting tragedy into greater and sharper focus. Included in the film is an interview with a survivor. Doug Llewelyn narrates. 60m. DIR: Steve Kroopnick. 1988

TREE GROWS IN BROOKLYN, A ★★★★ A richly detailed and sentimental evocation of working-class Brooklyn at the turn of the century. The story focuses on the happiness and tragedies of a poor family ruled by a kindly but alcoholic father and a strong-willed mother. B&W; 128m. DIR: Elia Kazan. CAST: Dorothy McGuire, James Dunn, Joan Blondell, Peggy Ann Garner, Lloyd Nolan, James Gleason. 1945

TREE OF THE WOODEN CLOGS, THE ★★★★★ Stunning, epic masterpiece about the hardships in the life of a community of peasants in northern Italy, just before the turn of the century. In Italian with English subtitles. Not rated. 185m. DIR: Ermanno Olmi. CAST: Luigi Ornaghi, Francesca Moriggi, Omar Brignoli. 1978

•TREEHOUSE HOSTAGE ★★ Jim Varney is the main attraction here, playing an escaped con who ends up being held hostage in a treehouse by a kid who plans to use him as a class project. The idea is totally inane, yet young children may find some of this entertaining. Rated PG. 90m. DIR: Sean McNamara. CAST: Jim Varney, Joey Zimmerman, Todd Bosley, Mark Moses, Debby Boone. 1999 DVD

TREES LOUNGE ★★★★ This seriocomic movie is the best road map to an alcoholic lifestyle since 1987's *Barfly*. Tommy has been fired, lost his pregnant girlfriend, and heads for disaster when he gets mixed up with a 17-year-old girl. Rated R for drug use, language, and suggested sex. 96m. DIR: Steve Buscemi. CAST: Steve Buscemi, Anthony LaPaglia, Chloe Sevigny, Elizabeth Bracco, Michael Buscemi, Daniel Baldwin, Mark Boone Jr. 1996 DVD

TREKKIES ★★★1/2 Documentarian Roger Nygard takes a bemused look at the *Star Trek* fan phenomenon, loosely tracing its development from the first convention in the early 1970s to the present. On the whole this is one of affection rather than disdain. With guest appearances from most of the cast of all four *Star Trek* series. Rated PG. 86m. DIR: Roger Nygard. 1998 DVD

TREMORS ★★★★1/2 Here's a terrific, old-fashioned monster movie with great performances, a witty and suspenseful screenplay, and masterful direction. Kevin Bacon and Fred Ward are hilarious as a couple of independent cusses. One day our heroes discover a decapitated sheep rancher and his gruesomely devoured flock, and are forced to fight for their lives against a pack of flesh-eating, giant worms. Rated PG-13 for light profanity and remarkably limited violence. 90m. DIR: Ron Underwood. CAST: Kevin Bacon, Fred Ward, Finn Carter, Michael Gross, Reba McEntire, Victor Wong. 1990 DVD

TREMORS 2: AFTERSHOCKS ★★★1/2 Although not quite as much fun as its predecessor, this engaging sequel doesn't miss by much. Monster-worm hunter Fred Ward returns and accepts an assignment to rid a Mexican oil refinery of the earth-burrowing "graboids" that munch everything in their path. Survivalist Michael Gross also reappears, but Christopher Gartin is a weak replacement for Kevin Bacon. While our heroes get off to a good start, the worms turn clever and adapt into even more lethal forms. Very entertaining, particularly for folks who like monster flicks without the gore. Rated PG-13 for violence and profanity. 100m. DIR: S. S. Wilson. CAST: Fred Ward, Christopher Gartin, Helen Shaver, Michael Gross, Marcelo Tubert. 1995 DVD

TRENCHCOAT ★★ No one is what he appears to be in this inept spoof of the detective genre. While there are moments that evoke some chuckles, *Trenchcoat* rarely hits the mark. Rated PG. 91m. DIR: Michael Tuchner. CAST: Margot Kidder, Robert Hays, Daniel Faraldo. 1983

TRESPASS ★★★★ Nobody directs action better than Walter Hill, and, by working from a tight script by Bob Gale and Robert Zemeckis, this rough-and-tumble, modern-day shoot-'em-up ranks as one of his best films. Two Arkansas firemen's search for lost treasure leads them to a taut battle of wits, fists, and flying bullets that will have fans of the genre cheering. Rated R for profanity and violence. 101m. DIR: Walter Hill. CAST: Bill Paxton, Ice T, Bill Sadler, Ice Cube, Art Evans. 1992 DVD

TRESPASSES 🞰 A beautiful woman is raped by two degenerate transients while her banker husband watches. Rated R for nudity and violence. 90m. DIR: Adam Roarke, Loren Bivens. CAST: Ben Johnson, Robert Kuhn, Mary Pillot, Van Brooks, Adam Roarke. 1986

TRIAL, THE (1963) ★★★1/2 A man in an unnamed country is arrested for an unexplained crime he is never told about. It is never made too clear to the audience, either. Orson Welles's unique staging and direction nevertheless make it all fascinating, if disturbing, entertainment. B&W; 118m. DIR: Orson Welles. CAST: Anthony Perkins, Jeanne Moreau, Romy Schneider, Orson Welles, Elsa Martinelli, Akim Tamiroff. 1963 DVD

TRIAL, THE (1992) ★★★★ Powerful story of persecution and paranoia as written by Harold Pinter and based on Franz Kafka's novel, this film is more effective than Orson Welles's 1963 version. Set in an unnamed country in some past time, a hapless bank clerk is accused of an unspecified crime, set for an unrevealed trial date. Rife with sexual tension and shadows of police states past and present. Not rated; contains profanity. 120m. DIR: David Jones. CAST:

Kyle MacLachlan, Anthony Hopkins, Jason Robards Jr., Juliet Stevenson, Polly Walker, Alfred Molina. 1992 DVD

TRIAL & ERROR (1992) ★★★ A prosecutor who sent a man to death row starts to have doubts about the man's guilt right before his execution. Tim Matheson does a fine job portraying the prosecutor. Not rated, made for cable, but contains violence. 95m. DIR: Mark Sobel. CAST: Tim Matheson, Helen Shaver Sean McCann, Page Fletcher, Michael J. Reynolds, Ian D. Clark, Eugene A. Clark. 1992

TRIAL AND ERROR (1997) ★★★1/2 Director Jonathan Lynn makes another courtroom delight following the success of *My Cousin Vinny*. This time he features Michael Richards as an actor who fills in for his hungover attorney buddy (Jeff Daniels). Richards delivers the expected Kramer-esque slapstick he became famous for on *Seinfeld*, but then allows his character a more serious and rational side. Rated PG-13 for profanity and sexual situations. 98m. DIR: Jonathan Lynn. CAST: Michael Richards, Jeff Daniels, Charlize Theron, Jessica Steen, Austin Pendleton, Rip Torn. 1997 DVD

TRIAL BY JURY ★★ Manhattan antiques dealer does her civic duty on a jury considering the fate of powerful, crazed mob boss who turns out to be the embodiment of pure evil. Soon becomes so contrived that it's difficult to watch. Rated R for violence, profanity, and suggested sex. 92m. DIR: Heywood Gould. CAST: Joanne Whalley, Armand Assante, Gabriel Byrne, William Hurt, Kathleen Quinlan, Margaret Whitton, Ed Lauter, Richard Ortnow, Joe Santos, Stuart Whitman. 1994 DVD

TRIAL OF THE CANTONSVILLE NINE, THE ★★ This film is a claustrophobic adaptation of a play about nine Baltimore antiwar protesters (two are priests), who faced trial in 1968. It's high-minded and self-righteous. 85m. DIR: Gordon Davidson. CAST: Ed Flanders, Douglas Watson, William Schallert, Peter Strauss, Richard Jordan, Barton Heyman. 1972

TRIAL OF THE INCREDIBLE HULK ★★★ The green goliath hits New York City, only to be jailed on murder charges. Defending him is blind attorney, Matt Murdock, whose alter ego is the swashbuckling superhero, Daredevil. Together they team up to bring down the city's biggest crime lord, The Kingpin. Made for TV. 93m. DIR: Bill Bixby. CAST: Bill Bixby, Lou Ferrigno, Rex Smith. 1989

TRIBES ★★★1/2 Long-haired peacenik Jan-Michael Vincent is drafted into the Marines and faces a tough time from drill instructor Darren McGavin. TV movie is far above the usual television schlock, with insightful script and solid acting. One of Vincent's best performances. Seems a bit dated by today's standards, but still worth a look. 74m. DIR: Joseph Sargent. CAST: Jan-Michael Vincent, Darren McGavin, Earl Holliman. 1970

TRIBUTE ★★★1/2 A moving portrait of a man in crisis, *Tribute* bestows a unique gift to its audience: the feeling that they have come to know a very special man. Jack Lemmon stars as a Broadway press agent who has contracted a terminal blood disease and is feted by his friends in show business. Though adjusted to his fate, Lemmon finds that he has some unfinished business: to make peace with his son, Robby Benson. Rated PG. 121m. DIR: Bob Clark. CAST: Jack Lemmon, Robby Benson, Lee Remick, Colleen Dewhurst, John Marley. 1980

TRIBUTE TO A BAD MAN ★★★★ A mean-spirited Western that works because of the personalities. James Cagney chews the scenery as a ruthless land baron who defies everyone to take advantage of him and his holdings. Cagney treats the role as if it were written for him, even though it was meant for Spencer Tracy, who passed on the project. 95m. DIR: Robert Wise. CAST: James Cagney, Irene Papas, Lee Van Cleef, Vic Morrow, Don Dubbins, Royal Dano, Stephen McNally. 1956

•TRICK ★★1/2 Two young gay men looking for a place to have a one-night stand, find themselves genuinely falling in love. The script takes some amusing turns, but Jim Fall's direction is flat. Rated R for sexual themes and profanity. 89m. DIR: Jim Fall. CAST: Christian Campbell, John Paul Pitoc, Tori Spelling, Steve Hays, Clinton Leupp. 1999 DVD

TRICK OR TREAT (1982) 🎬 A slow-moving mess about a baby-sitter and a spoiled brat on Halloween. Not rated; contains violence and profanity. 90m. DIR: Gary Graver. CAST: Peter Jason, Chris Graver, David Carradine, Carrie Snodgress, Steve Railsback. 1982

TRICK OR TREAT (1986) ★★1/2 Perhaps it was inevitable that someone would make a horror film about the supposed Satanic messages found in heavy-metal rock music. While not a classic of the genre, *Trick or Treat* is both clever and funny. Marc Price's performance is one of the film's pluses. Rated R for profanity, nudity, suggested sex, and violence. 97m. DIR: Charles Martin Smith. CAST: Marc Price, Doug Savant, Elaine Joyce, Gene Simmons, Ozzy Osbourne. 1986

TRICKS ★★★ Mimi Rogers stars as a former Reno showgirl who has to resort to prostitution in order to stay alive. Excellent performances help buoy an otherwise unoriginal script. Rated R for sexuality, nudity, violence, and profanity. 96m. DIR: Kenneth Fink. CAST: Mimi Rogers, Tyne Daly, Ray Walston. 1997

TRICKS OF THE TRADE ★★ Short-on-laughs comedy features Cindy Williams as a well-to-do housewife involved with a Hollywood prostitute (Markie Post) after her husband is murdered in Post's apartment. Made for TV. 94m. DIR: Jack Bender. CAST: Cindy Williams, Markie Post, Scott Paulin, John Ritter. 1988

TRIGGER EFFECT, THE ★★★ A suburban neighborhood falls apart during a massive power failure. The simplistic civics-lesson premise isn't terribly original (a Baby Boomer rehash of *Lord of the Flies*), and performances are constricted into stereotypes to make specific dramatic points. Still, writer-director David Koepp manages some passable suspense. Rated R for profanity and violence. 93m. DIR: David Koepp. CAST: Kyle MacLachlan, Elisabeth Shue, Dermot Mulroney, Richard T. Jones. 1996 DVD

TRIGGER FAST ★★ Low-budget Civil War–era action film aims high but fails. Martin Sheen plays Confederate Gen. Jackson Baines Hardin, assigned by the president to head down to Mexico to pardon some Southern soldiers. Rated R for violence. 96m.

DIR: David Lister. CAST: Martin Sheen, Jurgen Prochnow, Christopher Atkins, Corbin Bernsen. 1993

TRIGGER HAPPY (MAD DOG TIME) ★★1/2 Offbeat gangster comedy about a mob boss whose outrageous behavior lands him in a mental hospital and when released he systematically begins rubbing out the competition and trusted friends. All-star cast breathes life into this quirky effort that's more talk than action. Rated R for violence, language, and sexuality. 92m. DIR: Larry Bishop. CAST: Richard Dreyfuss, Jeff Goldblum, Ellen Barkin, Gabriel Byrne, Diane Lane, Gregory Hines, Kyle MacLachlan, Burt Reynolds. 1996

TRIGGER, JR. ★★★ Trucolor Roy Rogers film has everything going for it in the form of plot, songs, character actors, and hard ridin'. Roy, Dale, and the gang battle an unscrupulous gang of blackmailers as well as teach a young boy to overcome his fear of horses. 68m. DIR: William Witney. CAST: Roy Rogers, Dale Evans, Pat Brady, Gordon Jones, Grant Withers. 1950

TRILOGY OF TERROR ★★★ Karen Black stars in this trio of horror stories, the best of which is the final episode, about an ancient Indian doll coming to life and stalking Black. It's often very frightening, and well worth wading through the first two tales. Originally made as an ABC Movie of the Week. 78m. DIR: Dan Curtis. CAST: Karen Black, Robert Burton, John Karlen. 1974 DVD

TRILOGY OF TERROR II ★★★ Director Dan Curtis returns to a familiar format, with Lysette Anthony starring—as different characters—in three deliciously grim little shockers. Rated PG-13 for violence, gore, and profanity. 95m. DIR: Dan Curtis. CAST: Lysette Anthony, Geraint Wyn Davies, Geoffrey Lewis, Matt Clark, Blake Heron, Richard Fitzpatrick, Thomas Mitchell. 1996

TRINITY IS STILL MY NAME ★★ In this comedy sequel to *They Call Me Trinity*, Bud Spencer and Terence Hill again team up as the unlikely heroes of an Italian Western. Rated G. 117m. DIR: E. B. Clucher. CAST: Bud Spencer, Terence Hill, Harry Carey Jr. 1972 DVD

TRIO ★★★★ Wonderful collection of Somerset Maugham's short stories, introduced by Maugham. Each has a nice twist ending. "The Verger" centers on a man's decisions after being fired for his illiteracy. "Mr. Know-All" is an obnoxious bore who is shunned by the others on his cruise. Finally, Michael Rennie and Jean Simmons co-star as TB patients who fall in love while they live in the sanitorium. B&W; 88m. DIR: Ken Annakin, Harold French. CAST: Jean Simmons, Michael Rennie, Nigel Patrick, Wilfrid Hyde-White. 1950

TRIP, THE ★★ Peter Fonda plays a director of TV commercials who discovers the kaleidoscopic pleasures of LSD. This features outdated special effects and sensibilities. Screenplay by Jack Nicholson. 85m. DIR: Roger Corman. CAST: Peter Fonda, Susan Strasberg, Bruce Dern, Dennis Hopper, Dick Miller, Luana Anders, Peter Bogdanovich. 1967

TRIP TO BOUNTIFUL, THE ★★★★1/2 In 1947, an elderly widow (wonderfully played by Oscar-winner Geraldine Page) leaves the cramped apartment where she lives with her loving but weak son and his demanding wife to return to the small town where she had spent her happy youth ... unaware that it no longer exists. A joyous celebration of life. Rated PG. 105m. DIR: Peter Masterson. CAST: Geraldine Page, John Heard, Carlin Glynn, Richard Bradford, Rebecca DeMornay. 1986

TRIPLE IMPACT 🦃 Tedious entry in kick-fighting series has three world champions battling the usual array of bad guys. Even three stars can't kick start this mess. Not rated; contains violence. 97m. DIR: David Hunt. CAST: Ron Hall, Dale "Apollo" Cook, Bridget "Baby Doll" Riley, Robert Marius. 1992

TRIPLE JUSTICE ★★★1/2 Once again, star George O'Brien and director David Howard take a standard B Western plot and infuse it with intelligence, character, and excitement. O'Brien is a peaceable cowpoke who innocently joins a gang of bank robbers. Silly, but surprisingly effective. B&W; 65m. DIR: David Howard. CAST: George O'Brien, Virginia Vale, Paul Fix, Glenn Strange. 1940

TRIPLECROSS (1985) ★★★ Harmless made-for-TV comedy about a trio of former police detectives who, after being left sizable fortunes by a grateful crime victim, now battle each other as to who can solve the crime *du jour*. 97m. DIR: David Greene. CAST: Ted Wass, Markie Post, Gary Swanson, Shannon Wilcox, Barbara Horan, Robert Costanzo, Ric Mancini, Mike Genovese, Dennis Farina. 1985

TRIPLECROSS (1995) ★★★ Ambitious convict Michael Paré is released to set up former partner Patrick Bergin on a phony diamond heist, all so obsessed FBI agent Billy Dee Williams can finally lay his fixation to rest. J. A. Rosen's twisty script tries for too many surprises during its final act. Rated R for profanity, violence, nudity, and simulated sex. 95m. DIR: Jeno Hodi. CAST: Michael Paré, Billy Dee Williams, Ashley Laurence, Patrick Bergin, James Hong. 1995

TRIPODS ★★1/2 Though a bit hard to follow because it is a compilation of episodes from the middle of a BBC science-fiction TV series, this is an interesting release about a young man's attempts to escape alien conquerors of Earth in the far future. Once free, our hero decides to join the rebel forces. 150m. DIR: Graham Theakston, Christopher Barry. CAST: John Shackley, Jim Baker, Ceri Seel, Richard Wordsworth. 1984

TRIPPIN' ★★1/2 Procrastinating high school senior "G" Reed spends more time daydreaming than filling out college applications in this swirl of social messages, sexual fantasies, and street profanity. G's hilarious scenes with his mom, dad, and grandfather highlight this hip-hop comedy. Rated R for language and sexual content. 92m. DIR: David Raynr. CAST: Dean Richmond, Donald Faison, Maia Campbell, Aloma Wright, Harold Sylvester, Bill Henderson. 1999 DVD

TRIPWIRE ★★★ During a gun exchange, a terrorist leader's son is killed by a special agent. Fast-paced and well-acted adventure that allows for character development as well. Rated R for violence. 92m. DIR: James Lemmo. CAST: Terence Knox, David Warner, Isabella Hoffman, Yaphet Kotto. 1989

TRISTANA ★★★★ Luis Buñuel's hilarious, surreal drama about a young woman who becomes a victim of her own captivating beauty as she becomes the object of desire between two men. The film is a brilliant examination of moral decay through the dispassionate eye of Luis Buñuel. In Spanish with English subtitles. Not rated. 98m. DIR: Luis Buñuel. CAST: Catherine Deneuve, Fernando Rey, Franco Nero. 1970

TRIUMPH OF SHERLOCK HOLMES, THE ★★★1/2 A candle is the clue that unlocks the secret of a murder in this superior Sherlock Holmes film featuring Arthur Wontner and Ian Fleming as the infallible consulting detective and his friend and assistant Dr. John Watson. Made by an independent production company on a limited budget, this rendering of Conan Doyle's *Valley of Fear* retains much of the story's original dialogue. B&W; 75m. DIR: Leslie S. Hiscott. CAST: Arthur Wontner, Ian Fleming, Lyn Harding, Leslie Perrins. 1935

TRIUMPH OF THE SPIRIT ★★★1/2 Willem Dafoe plays a Greek Jew imprisoned at Auschwitz who boxes for the entertainment of the Nazi officers. Dafoe's limp performance makes the film soft in the center, but the innate drama of the story, fine performances by Edward James Olmos and Robert Loggia, and Robert M. Young's firmly understated direction make it compelling. Rated R. 120m. DIR: Robert M. Young. CAST: Willem Dafoe, Edward James Olmos, Robert Loggia. 1990

TRIUMPH OF THE WILL ★★★★1/2 World-renowned German documentary of the rise of Hitler's Third Reich is a masterpiece of propaganda and remains a chilling testament to the insanity that can lurk in great art. Director Leni Riefenstahl created a powerful and noble image of a German empire that was already threatening Europe and would eventually engulf the world in a devastating war. B&W; 110m. DIR: Leni Riefenstahl. 1935

TRIUMPHS OF A MAN CALLED HORSE 🦃 Richard Harris only makes a brief appearance in the title role as John Morgan, an English nobleman who was captured by the Sioux in 1825. Instead, the story focuses on his bland warrior son. Rated PG for violence and implied sex. 86m. DIR: John Hough. CAST: Richard Harris, Michael Beck, Ana De Sade. 1983

TROJAN WAR ★★ A high-school nerd spends an eventful night when he sets out in search of a condom after the cheerleader of his dreams makes him a one-night-only offer. Strained comedy isn't as offensive as it sounds, but (aside from a brief appearance by Anthony Michael Hall as a cranky bus driver) it isn't very funny, either. Rated PG-13 for sexual themes and profanity. 84m. DIR: George Huang. CAST: Will Friedle, Jennifer Love Hewitt, Marley Shelton, Anthony Michael Hall, Lee Majors. 1997

TROJAN WOMEN, THE ★★ This Greek-American film is worth seeing for the four female leads. Unfortunately, the plot (revolving around the Trojan War and their defeat) is lost. Rated PG. 105m. DIR: Michael Cacoyannis. CAST: Katharine Hepburn, Vanessa Redgrave, Genevieve Bujold, Irene Papas. 1972

TROLL 🦃 A family besieged by evil little creatures. Rated PG-13 for profanity, violence, and gore. 95m.

IR: John Carl Buechler. **CAST:** Noah Hathaway, Michael Moriarty, Shelley Hack, Jenny Beck, June Lockhart, Anne Lockhart, Sonny Bono, Brad Hall. 1986

ROLL II 💗 Flat sequel-of-sorts to producer Charles Band's original spoof. Family unleashes malevolent specter who wreaks havoc before being banished to late-night cable outlets everywhere. Rated PG-13 for violence. 95m. **DIR:** Drago Floyd. **CAST:** Michael Stephenson, Connie McFarland. 1992

ROLL IN CENTRAL PARK, A ★★ Brightly animated but uninvolving story of a pair of city kids who find a wealth of wonder in Stanley, the troll with a green thumb. Like some of producer-director Don Bluth's previous work, the story can't hold a candle to the animation. Featuring songs from the songwriters of *An American Tail*. Voices of Dom DeLuise, Cloris Leachman, Charles Nelson Reilly. Rated G. 79m. **DIR:** Don Bluth, Gary Goldman. 1994

ROMA'S WAR ★★1/2 A shoot-'em-up about a group of air-crash survivors stranded on a deserted island. This ragtag bunch soon find themselves fighting terrorists bent on taking over the United States with the AIDS virus. Made by the people responsible for *The Toxic Avenger*, this frequently tasteless flick combines violent action with totally deadpan comedy. Not rated. 105m. **DIR:** Michael Herz, Samuel Weil. **CAST:** Carolyn Beauchamp, Sean Bowen. 1988

VD

RON ★★★ An enjoyable, if somewhat lightheaded, piece of escapism, this science-fiction adventure concerns a computer genius (Jeff Bridges) who suspects evil doings by a corporate executive (David Warner). During his investigation, Bridges is trapped into another dimension and finds himself a player in a gladiatorial video game. Rated PG. 96m. **DIR:** Steven Lisberger. **CAST:** Jeff Bridges, David Warner, Bruce Boxleitner, Cindy Morgan, Barnard Hughes. 1982 **DVD**

ROOP BEVERLY HILLS 💗 Shelley Long as a ditsy Beverly Hills mom who agrees to act as the troop leader for her daughter's Wilderness Girls group. Rated PG. 105m. **DIR:** Jeff Kanew. **CAST:** Shelley Long, Craig T. Nelson, Betty Thomas, Mary Gross. 1989

ROPIC OF CANCER ★★ Want to see what an X-rated movie looked like when major stars would appear in one and it wasn't box-office poison? Here you are. Henry Miller's account of a hedonistic American in Paris finds an eager interpreter in Rip Torn. Pretentious and dated. X-rated for profanity, full nudity, and simulated sex. 87m. **DIR:** Joseph Strick. **CAST:** Rip Torn, James Callahan, Ellen Burstyn. 1970

TROPICAL HEAT ★★1/2 Exotic locales enhance this sultry mystery, as insurance-investigator Rick Rossovich travels to India to track down the widow of a maharaja killed on a hunting safari. What starts off as a job becomes an infatuation as dangerous as the woman he has fallen for. Sexual content in unrated version really turns up the *Tropical Heat*. Rated R for sex, nudity, adult situations, and violence; unrated version contains more of the same. 86m./88m. **DIR:** Jag Mundhra. **CAST:** Rick Rossovich, Maryam D'Abo, Lee Anne Beaman, Asha Siewkumar. 1993

TROPICAL SNOW ★★★★ Realistic story about two lovers from South America whose dream is to get

to America and make enough money to support their families. Suspenseful and harrowing. Rated R for nudity. 87m. **DIR:** Ciro Duran. **CAST:** Nick Corri, Madeleine Stowe, David Carradine. 1988

TROUBLE ALONG THE WAY ★★★ Disillusioned, divorced ex–football coach John Wayne cares about only one thing: his young daughter. So when the Probation Bureau decides that he's an unfit father, Duke decides to fight back—by coaching a ragtag team for a run-down Catholic college. Sentimental Hollywood stuff played and directed with no-nonsense expertise. B&W; 110m. **DIR:** Michael Curtiz. **CAST:** John Wayne, Donna Reed, Charles Coburn, Sherry Jackson, Marie Windsor, Tom Tully, Leif Erickson, Chuck Connors. 1953

TROUBLE BOUND ★★ Michael Madsen is a luckless gambler who wins a car with a body in the trunk. Then he hooks up with sexy waitress Patricia Arquette, who turns out to be the granddaughter of a Mafia kingpin. Decent performances, but a thriller should never be wacky. Rated R for profanity and violence. 90m. **DIR:** Jeffrey Reiner. **CAST:** Michael Madsen, Patricia Arquette. 1992

TROUBLE IN MIND ★★★★ An ex-cop, Kris Kristofferson, is paroled from prison and returns to Rain City, hoping to rekindle his romance with café owner Genevieve Bujold. Once there, he falls in love with the wife (Lori Singer) of a thief (Keith Carradine). Director Alan Rudolph's ultrabizarre, semifuturistic tale is an unusual screen experience that almost defies description. Rated R. 111m. **DIR:** Alan Rudolph. **CAST:** Kris Kristofferson, Keith Carradine, Genevieve Bujold, Lori Singer, Joe Morton, Divine. 1986

TROUBLE IN PARADISE ★★ Made for TV, a reworking of *Swept Away*, with a diplomat's widow and a roughneck Australian sailor castaway on a tropical island. When opposites begin to attract, drug smugglers intrude. A joy only for Raquel Welch watchers. 100m. **DIR:** Di Drew. **CAST:** Raquel Welch, Jack Thompson, Nicholas Hammond. 1988

TROUBLE IN TEXAS ★★1/2 Two-fisted singing rodeo cowboy Tex Ritter investigates crooked rodeo contests and seeks the men responsible for the death of his brother. Future glamour girl Rita Hayworth appears on-screen for the last time under her real name (Cansino). This enjoyable oater boasts a wild chase on a dynamite-laden wagon for a finale. B&W; 53m. **DIR:** Robert N. Bradbury. **CAST:** Tex Ritter, Rita Hayworth, Earl Dwire, Yakima Canutt. 1937

TROUBLE IN THE GLEN ★★ A white-haired, cigar-chomping Orson Welles in Scots kilts is farfetched, to say the least. The film turns on a feud over a closed road. Thoroughly scotched by poor pacing and a script that misses the mark. Deep-dyed Welles fans will like it. 91m. **DIR:** Herbert Wilcox. **CAST:** Orson Welles, Margaret Lockwood, Victor McLaglen, Forrest Tucker. 1953

•**TROUBLE ON THE CORNER** ★★★1/2 This smartly made indie takes us into the mind of a psychiatrist who is starting to lose his grip after years of listening to his patients' problems. A strong cast of familiar faces and intelligent direction by newcomer Alan Madison make this a good bet for film buffs with a taste for the unusual. Not rated; contains nudity, sexual situations, profanity, and violence. 104m. DIR: Alan Madison. CAST: Tony Goldwyn, Edie Falco, Debi Mazar, Tammy Grimes, Charles Busch, Giancarlo Esposito, Joe Morton, Roger Rees, Daniel Von Bargen. 1997

TROUBLE WITH ANGELS, THE ★★★ Rosalind Russell stars as the Mother Superior at the St. Francis Academy for Girls. Her serenity and the educational pursuits of the institution are coming apart at the seams due to the pranks of two rambunctious teenagers, Hayley Mills and June Harding. This comedy's humor is uninspired, but the warmth and humanity of the entire production make it worthwhile family viewing. 112m. DIR: Ida Lupino. CAST: Rosalind Russell, Hayley Mills, June Harding. 1966

TROUBLE WITH DICK, THE ♥ Study of frustrated author's peculiar work habits becomes self-consciously banal after the first five minutes. 86m. DIR: Gary Walkow. CAST: Tom Villard, Susan Dey, Elaine Giftos, Elizabeth Gorcey. 1986

TROUBLE WITH GIRLS, THE ★★★1/2 First of all, forget the stupid title, which has nothing to do with this charming tale of the Chautauqua Players of 1927. It's sort of a *Music Man*–ish tale about a troupe of entertainers. Elvis is the manager of the troupe. Sheree North is the tainted woman who is ruthlessly pursued by her lecherous boss (Dabney Coleman). Refreshingly above Elvis's inane girly films. Rated G. 105m. DIR: Peter Tewksbury. CAST: Elvis Presley, Sheree North, Vincent Price, Dabney Coleman. 1969

TROUBLE WITH HARRY, THE ★★★★ Shirley MacLaine made her film debut in this wickedly funny black comedy, directed by Alfred Hitchcock. This is the last of long-unseen screen works by the master of suspense to be rereleased, and the most unusual, because the accent is on humor instead of tension-filled drama. In it, a murdered man causes no end of problems for his neighbors in a peaceful New England community. Rated PG when it was rereleased. 100m. DIR: Alfred Hitchcock. CAST: John Forsythe, Edmund Gwenn, Shirley MacLaine, Mildred Natwick, Jerry Mathers. 1955

TROUBLE WITH SPIES, THE ★★ Even Donald Sutherland's amiable charm can't save this inept secret-agent spoof, which makes no sense at all. Producer-director Burt Kennedy, who also adapted the script from Marc Lovell's *Apple Spy in the Sky*, lacks the simplest knowledge of pacing, shading, or tonal consistency. Rated PG-13 for partial nudity. 91m. DIR: Burt Kennedy. CAST: Donald Sutherland, Ned Beatty, Ruth Gordon, Lucy Gutteridge, Michael Hordern, Robert Morley. 1984

TROUBLEMAKERS ★★ Italian Western-comedy looks like it has been plucked from the 1970s, when stars Terence Hill and Bud Spencer teamed up for several *Trinity* films. Hill directs himself as a famous gunfighter forced to reunite with his bounty-hunter brother for Christmas. Some serviceable laughs, but the presence of Ruth Buzzi makes this film seem even more dated. Rated PG. 98m. DIR: Terence Hill. CAST: Terence Hill, Bud Spencer, Ruth Buzzi. 1994 DVD

TRUCE, THE ★★★1/2 Based on the memoir of Italian writer Primo Levi, who spent ten months in Auschwitz during World War II and, after being liberated by the Red Army, joined the millions of displaced persons trying to make their way home in the chaos of peace. The episodic film is slow-paced but compelling, and the acting is fine. Rated R for mature themes and frank portrayal of the Holocaust. 116m. DIR: Francesco Rosi. CAST: John Turturro, Massimo Ghini, Rade Serbedzija, Agnieszka Wagner, Stefano Dionisi. 1996

TRUCK TURNER ★★ Singer Isaac Hayes traded in his gold chains for guns in this disappointing action thriller. He and Alan Weeks play bounty hunters on the run from vengeful gangster Yaphet Kotto. Rated R for violence, profanity, and sexual situations. 91m. DIR: Jonathan Kaplan. CAST: Isaac Hayes, Yaphet Kotto, Alan Weeks, Scatman Crothers, Stan Shaw. 1974

TRUCKS ★★ Trucks come to life and start killing people in this made-for-cable thriller. Based on a Stephen King story, this version is not as intelligent or scary as the original tale. Poor acting and a silly plot are only partly redeemed by a chilling ending. Not rated; contains violence. 95m. DIR: Chris Thomson. CAST: Timothy Busfield, Brenda Bakke. 1997 DVD

TRUCKSTOP WOMEN ♥ A truck-stop prostitution racket. Rated R. 82m. DIR: Mark L. Lester. CAST: Claudia Jennings, Lieux Dressler, John Martino. 1974

TRUE BELIEVER ★★★★ James Woods gives a powerhouse performance in this gripping thriller, tautly directed by Joseph Ruben. Woods plays a maverick lawyer who takes on the case of a convicted killer only to find himself bucking the powers-that-be in New York City. Robert Downey Jr. gives an effective performance as Woods's assistant. Rated R for violence and profanity. 103m. DIR: Joseph Ruben. CAST: James Woods, Robert Downey Jr., Margaret Colin, Kurtwood Smith. 1989

TRUE COLORS ★★★1/2 John Cusack and James Spader give impressive performances in this thought-provoking drama about how the desire for power corrupts a political hopeful. Strong support from Richard Widmark, as a hard-nosed senator, and Mandy Patinkin, as a sleazy developer, adds to this morality tale. Rated R for violence and profanity. 111m. DIR: Herbert Ross. CAST: John Cusack, James Spader, Richard Widmark, Imogen Stubbs, Mandy Patinkin. 1991

TRUE CONFESSIONS ★★★★1/2 This is the thoughtful, powerful story of two brothers (Robert De Niro and Robert Duvall)—one a priest, the other a jaded detective—caught in the sordid world of power politics in post–World War II Los Angeles. It's a brilliant and disturbing film. Rated R. 108m. DIR: Ulu Grosbard. CAST: Robert De Niro, Robert Duvall, Charles Durning, Burgess Meredith. 1981

TRUE CRIME (1995) ★★★ Alicia Silverstone plays an amateur teen sleuth, looking for leads in the death of a classmate. With the help of police cadet Kevin Dillon, she uncovers the trail of a serial killer. As she digs deeper, she learns that the truth lies close to home, and she can't trust anyone, including the cadet. Rated R for violence and language. 94m. DIR: Pat Verducci. CAST: Alicia Silverstone, Kevin Dillon, Bill Nunn. 1995 DVD

TRUE CRIME (1999) ★★1/2 It's unfortunate that this film's lethargic style and pacing make it seem as slow and tired as leading man Clint Eastwood. Self-indulgent behavior distracts the audience right out of a tidy little thriller about a gung-ho reporter who realizes he has less than a day to prevent an innocent man from being executed. Rated R for profanity, coarse dialogue, and dramatic impact. 127m. **DIR:** Clint Eastwood. **CAST:** Clint Eastwood, Isaiah Washington, Denis Leary, Lisa Gay Hamilton, James Woods, Diane Venora, Bernard Hill, Michael McKean, Michael Jeter. 1999 DVD

TRUE GRIT ★★★★ John Wayne finally won his best-actor Oscar for his 1969 portrayal of a boozy marshal helping a tough-minded girl (Kim Darby) track down her father's killers. Well-directed by Henry Hathaway, it's still not one of the Duke's classics—although it does have many good scenes, the best of which is the final shoot-out between Wayne's Rooster Cogburn and chief baddie, Ned Pepper (Robert Duvall). Rated G. 128m. **DIR:** Henry Hathaway. **CAST:** John Wayne, Kim Darby, Robert Duvall, Glen Campbell. 1969 DVD

•**TRUE HEART** ★★★1/2 Enjoyable story about a pair of siblings, plane-wrecked in Canada, and the forest-dwelling native who helps them survive. Perfect for family viewing. Rated PG. 92m. **DIR:** Catherine Cyran. **CAST:** Kirsten Dunst, Zachary Ty Bryan, August Schellenberg, Dey Young, Michael Gross. 1997

TRUE HEART SUSIE ★★★ Lillian Gish and Robert Herron are sweethearts in a small, rural, bedrock-solid American town in this sentimental silent film account of a young girl's transition from scatter-brained, uninhibited adolescent to dignified, self-assured woman. Sensitive acting and directing make what could have been cloying mush a touching, charming excursion back to what are nostalgically recalled as "the good old days." B&W; 62m. **DIR:** D. W. Griffith. **CAST:** Lillian Gish, Robert Herron, Wilbur Higby, George Fawcett, Carol Dempster. 1919

TRUE IDENTITY ★★★ British comedian Lenny Henry makes his film debut in this generally enjoyable entry about an aspiring black actor who must masquerade as a white hit man. It's the little insights provided by director Charles Lane and the occasional big laughs from Henry's clowning that make this movie worth watching. Rated R for violence and profanity. 106m. **DIR:** Charles Lane. **CAST:** Lenny Henry, Frank Langella, Charles Lane, J. T. Walsh, Anne-Marie Johnson, Andreas Katsulas, Michael McKean, Peggy Lipton. 1991

TRUE LIES ★★★★ Secret agent Arnold Schwarzenegger is content to pose as a dull computer salesman until he's forced to give his wife a taste of the real thing when he attempts to stop an Arab terrorist. Thrill-packed, special effects–laden, and little touches make it work. Rated R for violence, profanity, and suggested sex. 141m. **DIR:** James Cameron. **CAST:** Arnold Schwarzenegger, Jamie Lee Curtis, Tom Arnold, Bill Paxton, Tia Carrere, Art Malik, Charlton Heston. 1994 DVD

TRUE LOVE ★★★★ A very funny yet sometimes painful look at the preparations for a New York wedding. From the engagement party to the wedding day, director Nancy Savoca finds all the comedy and drama involved between two people who probably shouldn't get married—and the family and friends around them. Rated R for profanity. 100m. **DIR:** Nancy Savoca. **CAST:** Annabella Sciorra, Ron Eldard. 1990

TRUE ROMANCE ★★★★ Quentin Tarantino supplied the screenplay for this outrageously violent black comedy about a modern-day Bonnie and Clyde (albeit of the naïve and innocent variety) who get chased across the United States by the police and the mob. Wild performances by an all-star cast are certainly something to see and the story constantly surprises. Rated R for violence, profanity, simulated sex, and drug use. 120m. **DIR:** Tony Scott. **CAST:** Christian Slater, Patricia Arquette, Dennis Hopper, Christopher Walken, Val Kilmer, Gary Oldman, Brad Pitt, Bronson Pinchot, Conchata Ferrell, Saul Rubinek, Samuel L. Jackson, Michael Rapaport, Tom Sizemore, Christopher Penn. 1993 DVD

TRUE STORIES ★★1/2 *True Stories* is Talking Heads leader David Byrne's satirical look at the imaginary town of Virgil, Texas. It's a mixture of *The National Enquirer* and deadpan cinematic humor. Some of the bits are truly funny, but the lethargic tone becomes an aggravating artistic conceit. Rated PG. 89m. **DIR:** David Byrne. **CAST:** David Byrne, John Goodman, Annie McEnroe, Swoosie Kurtz, Spalding Gray. 1986 DVD

TRUE STORY OF FRANKENSTEIN, THE ★★★1/2 Well-written and -executed documentary surveys public fascination with Mary Shelley's unique gothic horror story through interviews with scholars and cinema personalities connected with the story over the years. Mel Brooks, Gene Wilder, Kenneth Branagh, John Cleese, and Robert De Niro are among film luminaries interviewed along with a coterie of English literature professors. A must for horror fans. 100m. **DIR:** Richard Brown. 1995

TRUE WEST ★★★★ Sam Shepard's powerful play about sibling rivalry and responsibility is masterfully performed by members of the Steppenwolf Theater Company for public television. John Malkovich stars as a reclusive drifter who returns home to make his brother, a Hollywood screenwriter, sit up and take notice. Not rated. 110m. **DIR:** Gary Sinise. **CAST:** John Malkovich, Gary Sinise. 1983

TRUE WOMEN ★★★★ Soaring Hallmark Productions presentation depicts the heartaches and struggles that faced pioneer women when their husbands were off winning independence from Mexico. Dana Delany and Annabeth Gish are superb as sisters Sarah and Euphemia, who are forced to summon up all of the courage within themselves and each other in order to fend off intruders and death. Both heroic and somber, this handsome period piece was originally broadcast as a television miniseries. Rated PG for violence. 170m. **DIR:** Karen Arthur. **CAST:** Dana Delany, Annabeth Gish, Angelina Jolie, Powers Boothe, Michael York, Charles Dutton. 1997

TRUEBLOOD ★★1/2 Writer-director Frank Kerr gives a 1980s spin to urban underworld dramas of the 1940s like *The Naked City* and *Kiss of Death*. Jeff Fahey and Chad Lowe are brothers, estranged for ten years, who try to rebuild their relationship on the mean streets of Brooklyn. Rated R for profanity and graphic violence. 100m. **DIR:** Frank Kerr. **CAST:** Jeff Fahey, Chad Lowe. **1989**

TRULY, MADLY, DEEPLY ★★★1/2 British writer-director Anthony Minghella's directorial debut is a truly, madly, deeply wonderful motion picture. Juliet Stevenson gives a remarkable performance as a young woman whose overpowering grief over the death of her lover turns to joy and maturity when he returns to help her back to the world of the living. Not rated, the film has brief profanity. 107m. **DIR:** Anthony Minghella. **CAST:** Juliet Stevenson, Alan Rickman, Bill Paterson, Michael Maloney. **1991**

TRUMAN ★★★★ Gary Sinise dominates this stylish adaptation of David McCullough's presidential biography, as a resolutely moral and dignified gentleman who can give 'em hell. More than anything, this made-for-HBO film evokes nostalgia for simpler times, and for the accidental ascension of a president. Rated PG-13 for profanity. 130m. **DIR:** Frank Pierson. **CAST:** Gary Sinise, Diana Scarwid, Richard Dysart, Colm Feore, James Gammon, Tony Goldwyn, Pat Hingle, Harris Yulin. **1995 DVD**

TRUMAN SHOW, THE ★★★★ Profound and wildly outrageous bit of "theater of the absurd" boasts a cleverly crafted script, a frankly astonishing performance from Jim Carrey, and shrewd direction by Aussie Peter Weir. Carrey's Truman Burbank lives the American dream in a postcard-perfect small town, little realizing that he's the "star" of his own life, being broadcast twenty-four hours a day to an engrossed world. He's the only one who doesn't know it … although his suspicions are mounting. Rated PG for mild profanity. 104m. **DIR:** Peter Weir. **CAST:** Jim Carrey, Laura Linney, Ed Harris, Noah Emmerich. **1998 DVD**

TRUST ★★★★ Surprisingly touching tale of a pregnant high school dropout (whose father keels over dead with the baby news) and a somewhat older nihilistic electronics whiz (whose mother died giving birth to him). Surreal, but somehow believable. Rated R for language. 90m. **DIR:** Hal Hartley. **CAST:** Adrienne Shelly, Martin Donovan. **1991**

TRUST ME ★★★ Ex-rocker Adam Ant is an L.A. art dealer who loves the high life, but is on the verge of bankruptcy. Observing that dead artists' works seem to sell better than live ones, he starts looking for some talent that might be suicidal or terminal. Interesting black comedy. Rated R for language. 94m. **DIR:** Bobby Houston. **CAST:** Adam Ant, Talia Balsam, Barbara Bain. **1989**

TRUTH ABOUT CATS AND DOGS, THE ★★★★ Janeane Garofalo's starring debut is a delightful romantic comedy with echoes of *Cyrano de Bergerac*. She's a plain-Jane radio veterinarian who fears her reality won't live up to expectations. All sorts of entanglements ensue when she sends a blonde friend on a date in her place. The human performers receive able assistance from one of the greatest dogs in the world. Rated PG-13 for profanity and strong sexual content. 97m. **DIR:** Michael Lehmann. **CAST:** Janeane Garofalo, Uma Thurman, Ben Chaplin, Jamie Foxx, James McCaffrey. **1996**

TRUTH ABOUT WOMEN, THE ★★1/2 Playboy Laurence Harvey flirts with every woman in sight in this comedy-drama. This British production has a fine cast, especially Julie Harris, and the production design is also quite good, but it's sooo slow. 98m. **DIR:** Muriel Box. **CAST:** Laurence Harvey, Julie Harris, Eva Gabor, Diane Cilento, Mai Zetterling, Wilfrid Hyde-White. **1958**

TRUTH OR CONSEQUENCES, N.M. ★★★★ A group of petty criminals steals a shipment of drugs and finds themselves fleeing not only the cops but the mob as well. Kiefer Sutherland's directing debut is a stylish, edgy thriller with taut performances by all. Rated R for violence and language. 101m. **DIR:** Kiefer Sutherland. **CAST:** Vincent Gallo, Mykelti Williamson, Kiefer Sutherland, Kevin Pollak, Kim Dickens, Grace Phillips. **1997 DVD**

TRUTH OR DARE ★★★★ Pop superstar Madonna allowed first-time filmmaker Alek Keshishian complete access—both onstage and backstage—to her 1990 Blond Ambition tour. The result is a fascinating, not-so-flattering look at one of contemporary music's true phenomena. Rated R for nudity and profanity. 118m. **DIR:** Alek Keshishian. **CAST:** Madonna, Warren Beatty, Sandra Bernhard, Kevin Costner. **1991 DVD**

TRUTH OR DARE? A CRITICAL MADNESS 🎬 The old grade-school game turns deadly in this unrelentingly bad movie credited to director Yale Wilson, although the culprit is really Tim Ritter. Not rated; contains violence, profanity, and gore. 87m. **DIR:** Yale Wilson. **CAST:** John Brace, Mary Fanaro. **1987**

TRUTH OR DIE ★★★1/2 Tony Danza delivers a powerful performance as convicted killer Jerry Rosenberg, sentenced to the electric chair, who turns his life around while on death row. Made-for-TV film, also known as *Doing Life*. 100m. **DIR:** Gene Reynolds. **CAST:** Tony Danza, Lisa Langlois, Alvin Epstein, Jon De Vries. **1986**

TRY AND GET ME ★★★1/2 A desperate, unemployed husband and father (Frank Lovejoy) teams up with a ruthless thief and murderer (Lloyd Bridges) but can't live with his guilt after their crime spree. Interesting analysis of criminality, yellow journalism, and mob rule. Not rated; contains violence. 91m. **DIR:** Cy Endfield. **CAST:** Frank Lovejoy, Lloyd Bridges, Kathleen Ryan, Richard Carlson. **1950**

TRYST 🎬 Ludicrous and laughable tale about a rich woman (Barbara Carrera), her jealous husband (David Warner), and their housemaid's son (Steve Bond). Completely unsuccessful attempt to take a new angle on the *Double Indemnity* and *Body Heat* types of filmmaking. Rated R for profanity, nudity, sexual situations, and violence. 101m. **DIR:** Peter Foldy. **CAST:** Barbara Carrera, Louise Fletcher, David Warner, Steve Bond. **1994**

TUCK EVERLASTING ★★★1/2 Entertaining family film about a 12-year-old girl who discovers a family of immortals living in the woods on her father's property. She becomes involved in their lives and is eventually entrusted with their secret. Rated G. 100m. **DIR:** Frederick King Keller. **CAST:** Margaret Chamberlain, Fred A. Keller, James McGuire, Sonia Raimi. **1980**

TUCKER: A MAN AND HIS DREAM ★★★1/2 Francis Ford Coppola has always admired Preston Tucker, entrepreneurial genius and designer of a Forties automobile built to challenge the big three automakers. This movie catches the spirit of postwar times when everything seemed possible. Rated PG for language. 130m. **DIR:** Francis Ford Coppola. **CAST:** Jeff Bridges, Frederic Forrest, Joan Allen, Dean Stockwell, Martin Landau, Mako, Lloyd Bridges, Christian Slater. **1988**

TUFF TURF ★★ A forgettable movie about young love as the new kid in town falls for a streetwise young woman with a dangerous lover. Rated R for violence, profanity, and suggested sex. 112m. **DIR:** Fritz Kiersch. **CAST:** James Spader, Kim Richards, Paul Mones. **1984**

TULIPS 🖤 Canadian-made comedy casts Gabe Kaplan and Bernadette Peters as would-be suicides. Rated PG. 91m. **DIR:** Stan Ferris. **CAST:** Gabe Kaplan, Bernadette Peters, Henry Gibson, Al Waxman. **1981**

TULSA ★★1/2 Typical potboiler has feisty Susan Hayward as a strong-willed woman intent on drilling oil wells on her property no matter who tries to interfere. Standard soap situations made more palatable by fine cast of character actors. 90m. **DIR:** Stuart Heisler. **CAST:** Susan Hayward, Robert Preston, Pedro Armendariz, Chill Wills, Ed Begley Sr. **1949**

TULSA KID ★★★1/2 Don Barry deserts his gunfighter heritage to aid defenseless pioneers threatened by a ruthless racketeer and his hired gunman—who turns out to be Barry's foster father. B&W; 57m. **DIR:** George Sherman. **CAST:** Don Barry, Noah Beery Sr., Luana Walters. **1940**

TUMBLEWEEDS ★★★1/2 One of silent films' greatest action sequences, the Oklahoma Land Rush along the Cherokee Strip, highlights this prestigious Western, famed cowboy star William S. Hart's final film. He retired to write novels. This version, which was introduced with a prologue spoken by Hart—his only venture into sound film—was released in 1939. Silent, with musical score. B&W; 114m. **DIR:** William S. Hart, King Baggott. **CAST:** William S. Hart, Barbara Bedford, Lucien Littlefield, Lillian Leighton. **1925 DVD**

TUNE, THE ★★★ Animator Bill Plympton's first feature is a whimsical endeavor. He uses his trademark style to tell the tale of a songwriter at a creative crossroads, who gets swept into the imaginary world of Flooby Nooby. Plympton experiments with various musical styles, each one complimented by his strange, surreal animation. Most unusual. Not rated. 72m. **DIR:** Bill Plympton. **1993 DVD**

TUNE IN TOMORROW ★★★ Thoroughly enjoyable romp has young, impressionable Keanu Reeves falling for spinster aunt Barbara Hershey, while assisting writer Peter Falk on a radio serial. Freewheeling adaptation of Mario Vargas Llosa's *Aunt Julia and the Scriptwriter*—worth turning the dial for. Rated PG-13 for profanity. 102m. **DIR:** Jon Amiel. **CAST:** Peter Falk, Keanu Reeves, Barbara Hershey, Bill McCutcheon. **1990**

TUNES OF GLORY ★★★★ Gripping drama of rivalry between embittered older soldier Alec Guinness and his younger replacement John Mills is a classic study of cruelty as Guinness loses no opportunity to bully and belittle the competent but less aggressive Mills. Superb acting highlights this tragic story. 107m. **DIR:** Ronald Neame. **CAST:** Alec Guinness, John Mills, Susannah York, Dennis Price, Duncan Macrae, Kay Walsh, Gordon Jackson, John Fraser, Allan Cuthbertson. **1960**

TUNNEL, THE 🖤 Married woman and her obsessive lover. Rated R for nudity, simulated sex, and violence. 99m. **DIR:** Antonio Drove. **CAST:** Jane Seymour, Peter Weller, Fernando Rey. **1987**

TUNNEL OF LOVE, THE ★★★1/2 A mild sex farce, with Doris Day and Richard Widmark tied up in the adoption process. He considers adopting his own child as a result of his fling with social worker Gia Scala. B&W; 98m. **DIR:** Gene Kelly. **CAST:** Doris Day, Richard Widmark, Gig Young, Gia Scala. **1958**

TUNNEL VISION (1994) ★★★ Australian thriller focuses on a team of police officers (Patsy Kensit and Robert Reynolds) as they pursue a serial killer. Their relationship to each other takes center stage with a very surprising twist at the end. Gratuitous nudity and gore cheapen the film a bit, but edge-of-your-seat suspense keeps you watching. Not rated; contains nudity, violence, profanity, and gore. 100m. **DIR:** Clive Fleury. **CAST:** Patsy Kensit, Robert Reynolds, Rebecca Rigg, Gary Day, Shane Briant. **1994**

TUNNELVISION (1976) ★★1/2 Here is a lightweight spoof of television. Sometimes it is funny, and other times it is just gross. The "stars," like Chevy Chase, have small bits. Still, there are some funny moments. *Tunnelvision* is like *The Groove Tube* in most respects, the good equally in proportion to the bad. Rated R. 67m. **DIR:** Neal Israel, Brad Swirnoff. **CAST:** Chevy Chase, Howard Hesseman, Betty Thomas, Laraine Newman. **1976**

TURBO: A POWER RANGERS ADVENTURE 🖤 Abundantly cleavaged space pirate Divatox is pursued by the Rangers as she kidnaps a cuddly wizard (a cross between Yoda and a Troll doll) and tries to release a monster from an island lava pit in this fantasy adventure ripe with cheesy special effects, bad acting, and lame pseudorock music. Morph me outta here. Rated PG. 90m. **DIR:** David Winning, Shuki Levy. **CAST:** Jason David Frank, Steve Cardenas, Johnny Yong Bosch, Catherine Sutherland, Nakia Burrise, Blake Foster, Hilary Shepard Turner. **1997**

TURBULENCE ★★1/2 Ray Liotta riffs wickedly on the cunning psychotic groove he developed in *Unlawful Entry* in this implausible but tense thriller. A convicted serial killer shoots his cop escorts and takes over a 747 en route from New York to Los Angeles on Christmas Eve. A feisty flight attendant locks herself in the cockpit (while the twisted felon and a level-six thunderstorm stalk her), then tries to get home safely. Rated R for suspense, violence, and language. 103m. **DIR:** Robert Butler. **CAST:** Ray Liotta, Lauren Holly, Ben Cross, Rachel Ticotin, Hector Elizondo, Brendan Gleeson. **1997 DVD**

TURK 182 ★★ Timothy Hutton stars as a young man who embarks on a personal crusade against injustice. His older brother (Robert Urich), a fireman, has been denied his pension after being injured while saving a child from a burning building when he was off-duty. This is one of those manipulative movies thought by their makers to be a surefire hit. It's anything but. Rated PG-13 for violence, profanity, and suggested sex. 102m. DIR: Bob Clark. CAST: Timothy Hutton, Robert Urich, Kim Cattrall, Robert Culp, Darren McGavin, Peter Boyle. **1985**

TURKISH BATH, THE ★★★1/2 When an Italian goes to Istanbul to sell the Turkish bath he inherited from his expatriate aunt, he finds himself irresistibly drawn to the people and culture of Turkey. Released in America as *Steam: The Turkish Bath* and promoted as a gay romance, this film is actually about the contrast of cultures on several levels, including sexuality. In Italian and Turkish with English subtitles. Not rated; contains mature themes and brief scenes of homosexuality. 98m. DIR: Ferzan Ozpetek. CAST: Alessandro Gassman, Francesca D'Aloja, Carlo Cecchi, Halil Ergun. **1997**

TURKISH DELIGHT ★★★1/2 Those already familiar with the work of Dutch director Paul Verhoeven (*Spetters, The 4th Man*) will be the most appreciative audience for this drama about a bohemian artist and his wife. Others may be put off by the graphic sexuality and crude behavior. Dubbed in English. 96m. DIR: Paul Verhoeven. CAST: Rutger Hauer, Monique van de Ven. **1974**

TURN OF THE SCREW, THE (1989) ★★★ This chilling entry in Shelley Duvall's *Nightmare Classics* features Amy Irving as the heroine of Henry James's novel. As a new governess, she tries to instill her two new charges with morality. In the process she must take on the evil spirit that possesses them. Not rated; contains nudity and violence. 55m. DIR: Graeme Clifford. CAST: Amy Irving, David Hemmings, Balthazar Getty, Micole Mercurio. **1989**

TURN OF THE SCREW (1992) ★★★★ Updated to the 1960s, this is an intense and intelligent adaptation of Henry James's moody masterpiece. Julian Sands hires Patsy Kensit to tutor his odd niece and nephew, without revealing the secrets of his country house. Heavy doses of eroticism help build the tension to a creepy, albeit overly symbolic conclusion. Rated R for brief nudity and simulated sex. 95m. DIR: Rusty Lemorande. CAST: Patsy Kensit, Stéphane Audran, Julian Sands, Marianne Faithfull. **1992**

TURNER AND HOOCH ★★★ K-9 redux! Tom Hanks is a fussy police detective who finds himself stuck with a mean junkyard dog who is the only witness to a murder. Once again the Hanks magic elevates a predictable story into a fun film. Rated PG. 110m. DIR: Roger Spottiswoode. CAST: Tom Hanks, Mare Winningham. **1989**

TURNING POINT, THE ★★★★1/2 Well-crafted drama about a pair of dancers both blessed and cursed with the aftermaths of their own personal turning points. Blended with the story is a series of beautifully rendered ballet sequences featuring Mikhail Baryshnikov, in his film debut. Rated PG for intensity of theme. 119m. DIR: Herbert Ross. CAST: Anne Bancroft, Shirley MacLaine, Mikhail Baryshnikov, Leslie Browne, Tom Skerritt. **1977**

TURTLE BEACH (KILLING BEACH) ★★★ Shocking images propel this sobering, thought-provoking movie about the plight of the Vietnamese boat people. Set on the east Malaysian coast, it depicts an on-going human tragedy, which two women, a journalist and a courtesan attempt to stop. Rated R for violence, suggested sex, and nudity. 88m. DIR: Stephen Wallace. CAST: Greta Scacchi, Joan Chen, Jack Thompson, Art Malik, Norman Kaye. **1992**

TURTLE DIARY ★★★★1/2 Deliciously offbeat bit of British whimsy about people living side by side but rarely touching. An author of children's books and a bookstore assistant share an obsession for turtles and devise a plan to free creatures from a nearby zoo. Rated PG for nudity. 97m. DIR: John Irvin. CAST: Glenda Jackson, Ben Kingsley, Richard Johnson, Michael Gambon, Rosemary Leach, Eleanor Bron, Harriet Walter, Jeroen Krabbé. **1986**

TUSKEGEE AIRMEN, THE ★★★★ Inspirational docudrama about the first all-black WWII pilot squadron to actually face aerial combat. The flying footage is impressive, as are the facts revealed just prior to the closing credits. Rated PG-13 for profanity and wartime violence. 107m. DIR: Robert Markowitz. CAST: Laurence Fishburne, Allen Payne, Malcolm-Jamal Warner, Courtney B. Vance, Andre Braugher, Christopher McDonald, Daniel Hugh Kelly, John Lithgow, Cuba Gooding Jr. **1995**

TUSKS ★★1/2 Shot in the African wilderness, this tale of a conservationist kidnapped by a poacher to act as bait for the game warden is sometimes bogged down by bad writing and uneven pacing. When it is in stride, though, it is a tense and vicious look at man against animal. Rated R for nudity and profanity. 99m. DIR: Tara Moore. CAST: Lucy Gutteridge, Andrew Stevens, John Rhys-Davies, Julian Glover. **1990**

TUTTLES OF TAHITI, THE ★★★ Captain Bligh goes native in this comedy of arch indolence and planned sloth in beautiful, bountiful Tahiti. Impoverished Charles Laughton and Florence Bates are rivals whose son Jon Hall and daughter Peggy Drake respectively fall in love. A good-natured, congenial film of leisure life. B&W; 91m. DIR: Charles Vidor. CAST: Charles Laughton, Jon Hall, Peggy Drake, Mala, Florence Bates, Alma Ross, Victor Francen, Curt Bois, Gene Reynolds. **1942**

TUXEDO WARRIOR ★★ Trite story about a bar owner/soldier of fortune (John Wyman) who becomes embroiled with diamond thieves in South Africa. Two stars for the British accents and some decent action. Not rated; contains violence and profanity. 93m. DIR: Andrew Sinclair. CAST: John Wyman, Carol Royle, Holly Palance, James Coburn Jr. **1982**

TV'S BEST ADVENTURES OF SUPERMAN ★★★1/2 Excellent series of tapes combines two episodes of the TV series from the 1950s, one color and one black-and-white, with a Superman cartoon from the Max Fleischer Studios. This series is highly collectible for fans. B&W; Each 60m. DIR: Thomas Carr, George Reeves, Harry Gerstad, Dave Fleischer. CAST: George Reeves, Noel Neill, Phyllis Coates, Jack Larson, John Hamilton. **1950**

TWICE A JUDAS 🖤 Another case of amnesia on the prairie. Luke, suffering from amnesia, is set upon by a local swindler who, after murdering Luke's family, passes himself off as Luke's brother. An unbelievable story and lack of action make this a dull film, even with Klaus Kinski in a leading role. Not rated; contains violence. 96m. DIR: Nando Cicero. CAST: Klaus Kinski, Antonio Sabato, Cristina Galbo, Pepe Calvo. 1968

TWICE DEAD ★★★ An all-American family moves into an old mansion inhabited by a street gang. The gang, furious about losing their clubhouse, starts terrorizing the family. This movie is highlighted by good performances, above-average effects, and a sharp wit. Rated R for violence and nudity. 90m. DIR: Bert L. Dragin. CAST: Tom Breznahan, Jill Whitlow, Todd Bridges. 1988

TWICE IN A LIFETIME ★★★★★ Superior slice-of-life drama about a Washington mill worker who reaches a mid-life crisis. The cast is uniformly fine, the story poignant without being sugary. Rated R for adult situations. 111m. DIR: Bud Yorkin. CAST: Gene Hackman, Ann-Margret, Ellen Burstyn, Amy Madigan, Ally Sheedy, Brian Dennehy. 1985

TWICE-TOLD TALES ★★ With all his usual feeling, Vincent Price lurks, leers, and hams his nefarious way through a trilogy of nineteenth-century novelist Nathaniel Hawthorne's most vivid horror stories, including *The House of the Seven Gables*. 119m. DIR: Sidney Salkow. CAST: Vincent Price, Sebastian Cabot, Joyce Taylor, Brett Halsey, Beverly Garland, Mari Blanchard. 1963

TWICE UPON A TIME ★★★★ Sardonic wit is laced throughout this wild and wacky animated fairy tale from producer George Lucas. Filmmakers utilize a cut-and-paste animation process called Lumage to present intrepid heroes attempting to stop the evil Murkworks from blanketing the world in nightmares. Rated PG. 75m. DIR: John Korty, Charles Swenson. 1983

•**TWICE UPON A YESTERDAY** ★★1/2 Familiar themes are woven through this British romantic drama about a man who finds a way to turn back time and win back his girlfriend, who left him after he cheated. The film succumbs to the traditions of the genre, but with a little tweaking, it could have been something special. Rated R for adult situations and language. 94m. DIR: Maria Ripoll. CAST: Lena Headey, Douglas Henshall, Penelope Cruz, Elizabeth McGovern. 1998 DVD

TWILIGHT ★★★ Mannered, updated *film noir* detective thriller. Paul Newman's weary private investigator and all the supporting players' every action is so calculated and slow that they seem to exist in a different universe. Rated R for profanity, violence, nudity, and sexual content. 94m. DIR: Robert Benton. CAST: Paul Newman, Susan Sarandon, Gene Hackman, James Garner, Stockard Channing, Reese Witherspoon, Giancarlo Esposito. 1998 DVD

TWILIGHT MAN ★★★ Pretty good thriller about a university professor whose life is thrown into a shambles when a mysterious stranger begins futzing with his computer records—and killing his friends. Rated R for profanity and violence. 99m. DIR: Craig R. Baxley. CAST: Tim Matheson, Dean Stockwell, L. Scott Caldwell, Joel Polis, Yvette Nipar, Georgann Johnson. 1996

TWILIGHT OF THE GOLDS, THE ★★1/2 Jonathan Tolin's stage play should have been a thoughtful drama but is a shrill polemic. Thanks to an experi-

mental scientific procedure, a newly pregnant woman learns that her child will be born gay; the resulting "crisis" draws battle lines within her marriage and family. The shrieking tone isn't helped by the film's wretched soundtrack. Rated PG-13 for profanity. 95m. DIR: Ross Marks. CAST: Jennifer Beals, Faye Dunaway, Brendan Fraser, Garry Marshall, Sean O'Bryan, Jon Tenney. 1996 DVD

TWILIGHT ON THE TRAIL ★★ An old friend needs a hand so Hopalong Cassidy and his pals impersonate British detectives to throw a curve to the cattle rustlers they're seeking. B&W; 58m. DIR: Howard Bretherton. CAST: William Boyd, Brad King, Andy Clyde, Jack Rockwell, Wanda McKay, Tom London. 1941

TWILIGHT PEOPLE 🦃 Mad scientist on remote island dabbles with things better left unfilmed. Rated R for violence. 84m. DIR: Eddie Romero. CAST: John Ashley, Jan Merlin, Pam Grier. 1972

TWILIGHT ZONE, THE (TV SERIES) ★★★★1/2 Writer-producer Rod Serling's precedent-shattering anthology series, which ruled television during the early 1960s, earned its place in history thanks to a deft blend of credible human emotions amid incredible situations. Each video includes two episodes; Volume One is by far the strongest. 55m. DIR: Richard Donner, Douglas Heyes, Lamont Johnson, Buzz Kulik. CAST: Robert Redford, Agnes Moorehead, Lee Marvin, Burgess Meredith, Jack Klugman, Gladys Cooper, William Shatner. 1959 DVD

TWILIGHT ZONE—THE MOVIE ★★★ A generally enjoyable tribute to the 1960s television series created by Rod Serling, this film, directed by Steven Spielberg, John Landis, Joe Dante, and George Miller, is broken into four parts. Miller brings us the best: a tale about a white-knuckled air traveler (John Lithgow) who sees a gremlin doing strange things on the wing of a jet. Rated PG. 102m. DIR: Steven Spielberg, John Landis, Joe Dante, George Miller. CAST: Vic Morrow, Scatman Crothers, Kathleen Quinlan, John Lithgow, Dan Aykroyd, Albert Brooks. 1983

TWILIGHT'S LAST GLEAMING ★★★ Although this is another maniac-at-the-button doomsday chronicle, it is so convincing that it makes the well-worn premise seem new. From the moment a group of ex-cons (Burt Lancaster, Paul Winfield, Burt Young, and William Smith) seize control of an air force pickup truck, it becomes obvious that the audience is in the front seat of a nonstop roller coaster. Rated R for violence and profanity. 146m. DIR: Robert Aldrich. CAST: Burt Lancaster, Paul Winfield, Burt Young, William Smith, Charles Durning, Richard Widmark, Melvyn Douglas, Joseph Cotten. 1977

TWIN DRAGONS ★★ This one's a stinker. And small wonder: It's merely the American rerelease of a lesser 1992 effort originally called *Shuang Long Hui*, and has been trimmed which explains why so little makes sense. Identical brothers are separated at birth and grow up to become radically different people. The obligatory mistaken-identity gags are rendered as clumsily as the often poor split-screen effects. Even the fight scenes are less imaginative than usual. Rated PG-13 for comic mayhem and grade-school sexual content. 89m. DIR: Tsui Hark, Ringo Lam. CAST: Jackie Chan, Maggie Cheung, Teddie Robin, Nina Li Chi. 1999 DVD

•TWIN FALLS IDAHO ★★★ When a good-hearted hooker befriends a pair of conjoined twins, she causes the first stirrings of conflict in the brothers' intimate relationship. The film is a real oddity, cowritten by brothers Michael and Mark Polish, who are identical twins (though not conjoined) in real life. Slow-paced and a bit overcontrolled, it's nevertheless compelling, offering a glimpse into a world where it's the so-called normal people who are the outsiders. Rated R for profanity and mature themes. 110m. DIR: Michael Polish. CAST: Michael Polish, Mark Polish, Michele Hicks, Garrett Morris, William Katt, Lesley Ann Warren. 1999 DVD

TWIN PEAKS (MOVIE) ★★★ The television pilot for the mystery–soap opera thinking fan. The series went off in too many directions, but this still is a fascinating opening, where the logging town of Twin Peaks is stunned when a teenage girl is kidnapped, tortured, raped, and murdered. Contains added footage to wrap up the crime. 113m. DIR: David Lynch. CAST: Kyle MacLachlan, Michael Ontkean, Joan Chen, Richard Beymer, Peggy Lipton, Jack Nance, Piper Laurie, Russ Tamblyn. 1989

TWIN PEAKS (TV SERIES) ★★ These seven episodes, following one of the most talked-about television pilot movies in years, became the shaggiest of all dogs when writers David Lynch and Mark Frost tried to attack our senses from too many directions, losing focus on an intriguing mystery. Those not familiar with the pilot will find these episodes valueless; those initially hooked may want to reflect on what might have been. Each 48m. DIR: Various. CAST: Kyle MacLachlan, Michael Ontkean, Joan Chen, Richard Beymer, Peggy Lipton, Jack Nance, Piper Laurie, Russ Tamblyn. 1990

TWIN PEAKS: FIRE WALK WITH ME ★★★ Fans of David Lynch's self-indulgent television series will no doubt be thrilled with this prequel; the rest of America is advised to steer clear. Angelo Badalamenti's main theme still brings a chill. Rated R for nudity and language. 135m. DIR: David Lynch. CAST: Kyle MacLachlan, Sheryl Lee, Moira Kelly, David Bowie, Chris Isaak, Harry Dean Stanton, Ray Wise, Kiefer Sutherland, Peggy Lipton. 1992

TWIN SITTERS ★★★ A couple of muscle-bound morons are hired to watch over the nephews of a rich, former mob member. The brats-from-hell almost prove too much for the Barbarian Brothers but eventually turn the tables. Innocent family fare that offers laughs, action, and a message. Rated PG-13 for violence and mild profanity. 93m. DIR: John Paragon. CAST: Peter Paul, David Paul, Christian Cousins, Joseph Cousins, Rena Sofer, Jared Martin, Barry Dennen, George Lazenby. 1994

TWIN TOWN ★★★ Fans of *Trainspotting* will enjoy this Welsh comedy about unemployed twin brothers out for revenge against their father's crooked boss, whom they blame for the injuries he suffered on the job. The broad, crude humor will appeal to an audience that doesn't normally go in for "foreign films." Not rated, but an R equivalent for profanity, nudity,

violence, and adult situations. 98m. DIR: Kevin Allen. CAST: Llyr Evan, Rhys Hans, Huw Ceredig. 1997

•TWIN WARRIORS ★★★1/2 Jet Li's *The Tai Chi Masters* has been reedited and dubbed to become *Twin Warriors.* Fortunately, much of the action and pageantry remain intact. Li and Chi Sui Hou star as best friends who grow up together in a monastery. When they are expelled for fighting, the two go their separate ways. Their inevitable reunion years later—one sides with political rebels, the other with a desperate and ruthless ruler—is filled with lots of action and emotion. Rated R. 91m. DIR: Yuen Woo-Ping. CAST: Jet Li, Michelle Yeoh, Chi Sui Hou. 1993 DVD

TWINS ★★★★ Arnold Schwarzenegger and Danny DeVito play the title roles in this marvelously silly movie, which has the far-from-identical twins—products of a supersecret scientific experiment—meeting as adults after being separated at birth. This could easily have been a one-joke movie, but director Ivan Reitman and the stars keep it warm, funny, and fast-paced right up to the nicely satisfying conclusion. Rated PG for profanity and violence. 105m. DIR: Ivan Reitman. CAST: Arnold Schwarzenegger, Danny DeVito, Kelly Preston, Chloe Webb. 1988 DVD

TWINS OF EVIL ★★★ *Playboy* magazine's first twin Playmates, Madeleine and Mary Collinson, were tapped for this British Hammer Films horror entry about a good girl and her evil, blood-sucking sister. Peter Cushing adds class to what should in theory have been a forgettable exploitation film but provides surprisingly enjoyable entertainment for genre buffs. Rated R for nudity, violence, and gore. 85m. DIR: John Hough. CAST: Peter Cushing, Madeleine Collinson, Mary Collinson, Dennis Price. 1972

TWINSANITY ★★★ Twins (Judy Geeson and Martin Potter) who still play games together are lured into London's underbelly. Sleazy sexual encounters lead the twins to concoct a game of murder. Though dated by its music and costuming, this film (originally released as *Goodbye Gemini*) does include some fine acting and a complex story line. Rated R for violence. 91m. DIR: Alan Gibson. CAST: Judy Geeson, Martin Potter, Alexis Kanner, Michael Redgrave, Mike Pratt, Freddie Jones, Peter Jeffrey. 1970

TWIST AND SHOUT ★★★★1/2 An exceptional coming-of-age story about two friends, a drummer with a pseudo-Beatles group, and a quiet sort with severe problems at home, circa 1964. It is a true-to-life movie that will leave no viewer unmoved. In Danish with English subtitles. Not rated; contains profanity, nudity, and suggested sex. 99m. DIR: Bille August. CAST: Adam Tonsberg, Lars Simonsen. 1986

•TWIST AROUND THE CLOCK ★★1/2 The plot, about a concert promoter trying to cash in on the Twist dance craze, is just here to fill time between musical performances. The best are from Dion, who sings "Runaround Sue" and "The Wanderer." Give it an extra star if you're a big fan of the post-Elvis, pre-Beatles era. B&W; 86m. DIR: Oscar Rudolph. CAST: Chubby Checker, Dion, The Marcels. 1961

TWISTED ★★1/2 Early Christian Slater thriller has the budding star playing a troubled teen who torments the new baby-sitter. Not rated, contains strong language and violence. 87m. DIR: Adam Holender. CAST: Christian Slater, Lois Smith, Tandy Cronyn, Dina Merrill, Noelle Parker. 1985 DVD

TWISTED LOVE ★★ Former television teen stars can't breathe any life into this derivative story about a teen crush that goes too far. Rated R for violence. 80m. DIR: Eb Lottimer. CAST: Lisa Dean Ryan, Mark Paul Gosselaar, Soleil Moon Frye, Sasha Jenson. 1995

TWISTED NIGHTMARE ❤ A group of young people at a camp near a lake are menaced by a mysterious homicidal maniac. Sound familiar? Rated R for violence. 95m. DIR: Paul Hunt. CAST: Rhonda Gray, Cleve Hall. 1982

TWISTED OBSESSION ★★ A screenwriter becomes infatuated with a film director's sister in this very offbeat tale of obsession and brother-sister domination. Not rated, but with nudity, profanity, and violence. 109m. DIR: Fernando Trueba. CAST: Jeff Goldblum, Miranda Richardson, Dexter Fletcher. 1990

TWISTED TALES ❤ Anthology of tales that wouldn't scare a 5-year-old. Not rated; contains violence and profanity. 90m. DIR: Mick McCleery, Kevin J. Lindenmuth, Rita Klus. CAST: Mick McCleery, Laura McLaughlin, Theresa Oliver. 1993

TWISTER (1988) ★★ Patriarch Harry Dean Stanton presides over a mansion filled with the spoiled, eccentric, and just plain lunatic members of his extended family. This adaptation of Mary Robison's *Oh* lacks the central point of view needed to make it palatable. Rated PG-13 for profanity. 95m. DIR: Michael Almereyda. CAST: Harry Dean Stanton, Suzy Amis, Crispin Glover, Dylan McDermott, Jenny Wright, Lois Chiles. 1988

TWISTER (1996) ★★★1/2 This undeniably exciting drama, which gets most of its juice from awesome tornado sequences, won't play nearly as well on a small screen ... and more's the pity. Absent that raw fury, Michael Crichton and Anne-Marie Martin's superficial script will be exposed as an anemic reworking of *His Girl Friday*. Rated PG-13 for wind-driven violence. 117m. DIR: Jan De Bont. CAST: Helen Hunt, Bill Paxton, Jami Gertz, Cary Elwes, Lois Smith. 1996 DVD

TWISTS OF TERROR ★★1/2 This 1996 made-for-television omnibus takes its cue from the original *Trilogy of Terror*. Joseph Ziegler is the creepy host who introduces three tales of terror, including a wicked little story about a man on the run from a vicious dog who finds himself trapped in a hospital where you can't check out. As with all short-story collections, some stories are better than others, but all suffer from the restrictions of broadcast television standards. Not rated; contains violence. 90m. DIR: Douglas Jackson. CAST: Jennifer Rubin, Nick Mancuso, Carl Marotte, Andrew Jackson, Joseph Ziegler. 1996

TWITCH OF THE DEATH NERVE ★★★ Also known as *Bay of Blood, Carnage*, and *Last House on the Left, Part II*, this is the ultimate splatter film, and it comes from an unexpected source: Mario Bava. The director was Italy's pioneer horror stylist, blending elegant visuals with gothic gore. In contrast, this *Ten Little Indians* clone is jarringly contemporary and

features the most bloodletting ever in a non–X-rated shocker. Rated R. 87m. DIR: Mario Bava. CAST: Claudine Auger, Chris Avran, Laura Betti. 1970

TWO BITS ★★★1/2 Newcomer Jerry Barone is excellent as a Depression-era 12-year-old who desperately wants to attend the opening of a South Philadelphia movie house. In order to raise the two bits he needs for admission, he embarks on a number of schemes. Al Pacino shines as the boy's dying grandfather who dispenses words of wisdom. Rated PG-13 for adult situations. 83m. DIR: James Foley. CAST: Jerry Barone, Al Pacino, Mary Elizabeth Mastrantonio, Andy Romano. 1995

TWO BITS & PEPPER ★★ In an odd bit of casting, Joe Piscopo plays a duo of bumbling kidnappers who abduct two girls and hold them for ransom. The girls outwit the pair with the help of two talking horses. Honest. And they say there's nothing new coming out of Hollywood. Rated PG. 90m. DIR: Corey Michael Eubanks. CAST: Joe Piscopo, Dennis Weaver, Lauren Eckstrom, Rachel Crane, Perry Stephens. 1995

TWO BY SCORSESE ★★★ Interesting duet of early works by Martin Scorsese, one of the most prolific American film directors. *Italianamerican*, made in 1974, is a penetrating look at the filmmakers' parents. *The Big Shave*, made in 1968, is a black comedy musical about a man having a bloody shave to the tune of Bunny Berigan's "I Can't Get Started." Not rated; contains mild violence. 54m. DIR: Martin Scorsese. 1991

TWO DAUGHTERS ★★★★ Satyajit Ray's beautiful two-part film is based on tales by Nobel Prize–winning author Rabindranath Tagore. With Chekhovian delicacy and pathos, Ray explores the hopes and disappointments of two young women experiencing first love. Ray's stories transcend the surface of Indian culture while creating a universally felt character study. In Bengali with English subtitles. B&W; 114m. DIR: Satyajit Ray. CAST: Anil Chatterjee, Chandana Bannerjee, Soumitra Chatterjee. 1961

TWO DAYS IN THE VALLEY ★★1/2 Writer-director John Herzfeld attempts a Quentin Tarantino with this gory comedy-drama, but one *Pulp Fiction* was enough. Danny Aiello is the standout as a hit man left for dead by his partner. Rated R for violence, profanity, nudity, and simulated sex. 107m. DIR: John Herzfeld. CAST: Danny Aiello, James Spader, Teri Hatcher, Jeff Daniels, Greg Cruttwell, Glenne Headly, Peter Horton, Marsha Mason, Paul Mazursky, Charlize Theron, Eric Stoltz, Keith Carradine, Louise Fletcher, Austin Pendleton. 1996

TWO DEATHS ★★★ In 1989 Romania, as civil war rages outside the door, four men gather for their yearly reunion. They reveal shocking secrets, but none more shocking than that of their host, who tells the story of why his beautiful housekeeper endures his abuse. Typically murky (but impeccably acted and filmed) psychodrama from Nicolas Roeg. Rated R for nudity, violence, and sexual situations. 102m. DIR: Nicolas Roeg. CAST: Michael Gambon, Sonia Braga, Patrick Malahide. 1994 DVD

TWO ENGLISH GIRLS ★★★★1/2 Twenty-two minutes were later added to this very civilized and rewarding film. Set in pre–World War I Europe and based on the Henri-Pierre Roché novel (his only other being *Jules et Jim*, the modern flip side of the arrangement here), Truffaut's work has Frenchman Léaud the object of two English sisters' desire. In French with English subtitles. 130m. DIR: François Truffaut. CAST: Jean-Pierre Léaud, Kiki Markham, Stacey Tendeter. 1972 DVD

TWO EVIL EYES ★★ A two-part Edgar Allan Poe film shot in Pittsburgh. The first story, George Romero's version of "The Facts in the Case of M. Valdemar," is a total washout—shrill, derivative, and boring. The second, Dario Argento's adaptation of "The Black Cat," has some narrative shortcomings (principally its ending), but contains a powerful performance by Harvey Keitel and offers a scary study in obsession. 121m. DIR: Dario Argento, George A. Romero. CAST: Harvey Keitel, Adrienne Barbeau, E. G. Marshall, John Amos. 1990

TWO-FACED WOMAN ★★★ Garbo's last film is better than its reputation. She has an infectious sense of humor as the woman who tests her husband's faithfulness by posing as her own seductive twin sister. Fast-moving, full of clever dialogue, and professionally acted by the entire cast. 94m. DIR: George Cukor. CAST: Greta Garbo, Melvyn Douglas, Constance Bennett, Roland Young, Robert Sterling, Ruth Gordon. 1941

TWO-FISTED LAW ★★★★ A couple of young whippersnappers, John Wayne and Walter Brennan, add zest to this tale of a rancher (Tim McCoy in top form) out to get the goods on the crooks who cheated him out of his ranch. The screenplay by Three Mesquiteers creator William Colt MacDonald makes this one of McCoy's best; an outstanding B-plus Western. B&W; 64m. DIR: D. Ross Lederman. CAST: Tim McCoy, Wheeler Oakman, Tully Marshall, John Wayne, Walter Brennan. 1932

TWO FOR THE ROAD ★★★★ Clever editing and Frederic Raphael's inventive script highlight this delightful study of a marriage on the rocks, illuminated by deftly inserted flashbacks that occur each time the vacationing couple passes another car on the road. Albert Finney and Audrey Hepburn are the tempestuous lovers; the sweetly romantic score comes from Henry Mancini. 112m. DIR: Stanley Donen. CAST: Audrey Hepburn, Albert Finney, Jacqueline Bisset. 1967

TWO FOR THE SEESAW ★★1/2 While reevaluating his life and previous marriage, a Nebraska attorney moves to New York City and has an affair with a quirky modern dancer. Candid dialogue and touching humor but a little too long to be fully recommended. B&W; 120m. DIR: Robert Wise. CAST: Robert Mitchum, Shirley MacLaine, Edmon Ryan, Elisabeth Fraser. 1962

TWO FRIENDS ★★1/2 Jane Campion fans will be disappointed by this early effort, produced for Australian TV. The lives of two high-school girls unfold from the present to the past as we witness the small shifts in circumstance that alter their paths. A weird blend of styles and an awkward presentation make this feel like an experiment instead of a finished film. Letterboxed. Not rated; contains profanity.

76m. DIR: Jane Campion. CAST: Emma Coles, Kris Bidenko, Kris McQuade. 1986

TWO GIRLS AND A SAILOR ★★★ June Allyson and Gloria De Haven run a canteen for servicemen and both fall for sailor Van Johnson. Their romantic triangle is resolved, but not before guest stars perform specialty numbers to give the movie its entertainment value. The personalities are potent enough to keep the film entertaining beyond its era. 124m. DIR: Richard Thorpe. CAST: Van Johnson, June Allyson, Gloria De Haven, Tom Drake, Jimmy Durante, José Iturbi, Gracie Allen, Harry James, Xavier Cugat, Ben Blue. 1944

TWO-GUN MAN FROM HARLEM ★★1/2 Framed for murder, a cowboy leaves town and heads to the big city to lose himself. One year later a two-fisted deacon arrives to bring the real culprit to justice. Lensed on weekends at a dude ranch, this was the first in a series of "all-colored" Westerns featuring Herbert Jeffrey as singing cowboy Bob Blake. B&W; 65m. DIR: Richard C. Kahn. CAST: Herbert Jeffrey (Herbert Jeffries), Clarence Brooks, Margaret Whitten, Mantan Moreland, Spencer Williams, Stymie Beard, Mae Turner. 1938

TWO IF BY SEA ★★ A small-time thief (Denis Leary) steals a valuable painting, then he and his put-upon girlfriend (Sandra Bullock) hide out in a Cape Cod mansion waiting to sell the art to a mysterious buyer. Bullock is charming once again, but her forced Brooklyn accent is a distraction and her surroundings are unworthy of her—the plot is farfetched, the supporting characters are unlikable, and the jokes aren't funny. Rated R for profanity. 96m. DIR: Bill Bennett. CAST: Sandra Bullock, Denis Leary, Yaphet Kotto. 1996 DVD

TWO JAKES, THE ★★1/2 Okay, so this sequel is not as good as its predecessor, *Chinatown*, but how many movies are? We loved the performances in this detective thriller set in 1948, when private eye Jake Gittes (Jack Nicholson, who also directed) is hired by another Jake (Harvey Keitel) to follow his wife. A convoluted, but noble effort. Rated R for violence and profanity. 133m. DIR: Jack Nicholson. CAST: Jack Nicholson, Harvey Keitel, Meg Tilly, Madeleine Stowe, Eli Wallach, Rubén Blades, Frederic Forrest, David Keith, Richard Farnsworth, Perry Lopez. 1990 DVD

TWO LOST WORLDS 🎬 Pointless story involving pirates and kidnapping. B&W; 61m. DIR: Norman Dawn. CAST: James Arness, Laura Elliot, Bill Kennedy, Gloria Petroff, Tom Hubbard, Pierre Watkin, James Guilfoyle. 1950 DVD

TWO MEN AND A WARDROBE ★★★1/2 Roman Polanski's award-winning short made while he was a student at the Polish Film Institute is a bitter parable blending slapstick and the absurd. Two men emerge from the sea sporting a single wardrobe. Also included in the package is a second short, *The Fat and the Lean*, an outrageously funny attack on governmental tyranny. Silent. B&W; 35m. DIR: Roman Polanski. CAST: Henlyk Kluga, Jakub Goldberg. 1958

TWO-MINUTE WARNING ★★★ An all-star disaster film about a sniper loose in a crowded football stadium that is more exciting on video than it was on the big screen. The main reason is the lingering close-ups of the crowd and individual reactions are more impressive on a smaller screen. Rated R for violence, but the violence is tame by today's movie standards. 112m. **DIR:** Larry Peerce. **CAST:** John Cassavetes, Charlton Heston, Beau Bridges, Gena Rowlands, Marilyn Hassett, Martin Balsam, David Janssen, Walter Pidgeon, Jack Klugman, Brock Peters, Merv Griffin. **1976 DVD**

TWO MOON JULY ★★ The Kitchen, a New York City center for visual and performing arts, pays homage to the avant-garde with a diverse but uneven program of music, theater, dance, and film. An adventurous but uneven endeavor. 60m. **DIR:** Tom Bowes. **CAST:** Laurie Anderson, David Byrne. **1985**

TWO MOON JUNCTION ★★ Two weeks before her marriage, a young, well-to-do southern woman falls for a muscular carnival worker. A pattern in their relationship soon develops. They argue, they make love, and then she cries. Rated R for nudity, profanity, and violence. 104m. **DIR:** Zalman King. **CAST:** Sherilyn Fenn, Richard Tyson, Louise Fletcher, Burl Ives, Kristy McNichol. **1988 DVD**

TWO MRS. CARROLLS, THE ★★1/2 It won't take you as long as it takes Barbara Stanwyck to realize that the moody artist she has married is a self-made repeat widower. No real suspense, just hysteria galore. B&W; 99m. **DIR:** Peter Godfrey. **CAST:** Humphrey Bogart, Barbara Stanwyck, Alexis Smith, Nigel Bruce. **1947**

TWO MUCH ★★1/2 Donald E. Westlake's hilarious and inventive novel gets ho-hum treatment. Conniving South Florida art dealer gets swept away by a daffy socialite and then must inhabit the role of a fictitious twin brother when he falls genuinely in love with her sister. Sounds funny; plays dumb. Rated PG-13 for profanity, mild violence, and adult themes. 118m. **DIR:** Fernando Trueba. **CAST:** Antonio Banderas, Melanie Griffith, Daryl Hannah, Danny Aiello, Joan Cusack, Eli Wallach, Gambino Diego, Austin Pendleton. **1995**

TWO MULES FOR SISTER SARA ★★★ Clint Eastwood returns in his role of the "Man With No Name" (originated in Sergio Leone's Italian spaghetti Westerns) and Shirley MacLaine as an unlikely nun in this entertaining comedy-Western. Rated PG. 105m. **DIR:** Don Siegel. **CAST:** Clint Eastwood, Shirley MacLaine. **1970**

TWO OF A KIND (1951) ★★ Average suspense-drama concerning a con-artist team who attempt to steal the inheritance of two elderly people. Both the cast and script are okay, but that's just the problem. B&W; 75m. **DIR:** Henry Levin. **CAST:** Edmond O'Brien, Lizabeth Scott, Terry Moore, Alexander Knox. **1951**

TWO OF A KIND (1982) ★★★★ This heartwarming TV film features George Burns as a discarded senior citizen and Robby Benson as his retarded grandson. The two come together when the boy decides to help his seemingly disabled grandpa play golf again. Cliff Robertson and Barbara Barrie play Benson's parents. All in all, this is a fine film with a positive message about family unity. 102m. **DIR:** Roger Young. **CAST:** George Burns, Robby Benson, Cliff Robertson, Barbara Barrie, Ronny Cox. **1982**

TWO OF A KIND (1983) ★★ John Travolta and Olivia Newton-John, who first teamed on-screen in the box-office smash Grease, are reunited in this 1980s-style screwball comedy, which mixes clever ideas with incredibly stupid ones. Young viewers probably won't rave, but neither will they be too disappointed. Others, however, should stay away. Rated PG for profanity and violence; 87m. **DIR:** John Herzfeld. **CAST:** John Travolta, Olivia Newton-John, Charles Durning. **1983**

TWO OF US, THE ★★★1/2 This story of generational and religious differences joins an 8-year-old Jewish boy (Alain Cohen) and an irascible Catholic grandpa (Michel Simon). The boy is fleeing Nazi-occupied France in 1944 and comes to live with the anti-Semitic old man who is a family friend's relative. Beautifully acted, this is a different kind of movie for parents to enjoy with their older children. In French with English subtitles. 86m. **DIR:** Claude Berri. **CAST:** Alain Cohen, Michel Simon. **1968**

TWO ON A GUILLOTINE ★★ A woman has to spend the night in the spooky house of her father, a magician who claimed he would return from the dead, in order to inherit his estate. About as scary as one might expect for a film starring Connie Stevens and Dean Jones. B&W; 107m. **DIR:** William Conrad. **CAST:** Connie Stevens, Dean Jones, Cesar Romero, Parley Baer. **1964**

•**TWO OR THREE THINGS I KNOW ABOUT HER** ★★★★ French director Jean-Luc Godard all but abandoned the conventions of narrative film with this "film essay" about both the city of Paris (the "Her" of the title) and his filmmaking process. Godard's musings on anything and everything (he narrates the film) are held together by the story of a housewife who works one day a week as a prostitute in order to support her shopping habit. A good introduction to this challenging but often difficult filmmaker. In French with English subtitles. Not rated; contains sexual themes. 90m. **DIR:** Jean-Luc Godard. **CAST:** Marina Vlady, Anny Duperey. **1977**

TWO RODE TOGETHER ★★★ In this variation of The Searchers, director John Ford explores the anguish of settlers over the children they have lost to Indian raiding parties and the racial prejudice that arises when one boy, now a full-blown warrior, is returned to his "people." It is not a fully effective film, but it does have its moments. 109m. **DIR:** John Ford. **CAST:** James Stewart, Richard Widmark, Shirley Jones, John McIntire, Woody Strode, Linda Cristal, Andy Devine. **1961**

TWO SISTERS FROM BOSTON ★★★1/2 Turn-of-the-century fun. Kathryn Grayson comes to New York to seek an operatic career, but she and sister June Allyson end up working at a Bowery honky-tonk owned by Jimmy Durante. The whole cast shines and Durante really shows the talent that endeared him to millions. B&W; 112m. **DIR:** Henry Koster. **CAST:** Kathryn Grayson, June Allyson, Lauritz Melchior, Jimmy Durante, Peter Lawford, Ben Blue. **1946**

TWO SMALL BODIES ★★★1/2 A cop thinks that a single mother/strip-bar hostess may have murdered her children. As he investigates, he finds himself being further and inexplicably drawn to her, despite the mounting evidence. Based on the play by Neal Bell. Not rated; contains violence, profanity, and sexual situations. 85m. DIR: Beth B. CAST: Fred Ward, Suzy Amis. 1993

TWO TICKETS TO BROADWAY ★★ Clichéd let's-put-on-a-show film features Janet Leigh as a small-town ingenue who heads for New York. Ann Miller's dance routines and Tony Martin's songs are highlights. 106m. DIR: James V. Kern. CAST: Tony Martin, Janet Leigh, Gloria De Haven, Ann Miller. 1951

TWO TO TANGO ★★1/2 Satisfying little thriller starring Don Stroud as a burned-out hit man for an ominous organization called the Company. He's terminated one too many targets and bargains with his superior to do one last hit in Buenos Aires, Argentina; then he'll retire to Nepal. Rated R for violence and nudity. 87m. DIR: Hector Olivera. CAST: Don Stroud, Adrienne Sachs, Michael Cavanaugh, Dulio Marzio. 1988

TWO-WAY STRETCH ★★★★ Delightful British caper comedy about a group of thieves plotting to break out of their lenient prison just long enough to pull a huge robbery and then return to their cells, leaving them with the perfect alibi. First-rate. 84m. DIR: Robert Day. CAST: Peter Sellers, Wilfrid Hyde-White, David Lodge, Bernard Cribbins, Lionel Jeffries. 1961

TWO WEEKS IN ANOTHER TOWN ★★1/2 Kirk Douglas is uptight as a former movie actor who had a bout with the bottle and is trying for a comeback. A downer based on an Irwin Shaw novel. 107m. DIR: Vincente Minnelli. CAST: Kirk Douglas, Edward G. Robinson, Cyd Charisse, Claire Trevor, George Hamilton, Daliah Lavi, Rosanna Schiaffino, George Macready, James Gregory, Leslie Uggams. 1962

TWO WEEKS WITH LOVE ★★ An old-fashioned musical set in a bygone age when corsets and long bathing suits were the norm. Debbie Reynolds and Carleton Carpenter sing "Abba Dabba Honeymoon," the novelty song that catapulted them to fame. Songs like "On Moonlight Bay" add to the romantic atmosphere. 92m. DIR: Roy Rowland. CAST: Jane Powell, Debbie Reynolds, Ricardo Montalban, Ann Harding, Louis Calhern, Carleton Carpenter. 1950

TWO WOMEN ★★★★ In the performance that won her an Oscar, Sophia Loren is a widow who, with her 13-year-old daughter, escapes war-torn Rome, eventually finding solace in her native village. This uncompromising drama was a Grand Prize winner at the Cannes Film Festival. In Italian with English subtitles. Not rated. 99m. DIR: Vittorio De Sica. CAST: Sophia Loren, Eleanora Brown, Jean-Paul Belmondo, Raf Vallone. 1960 DVD

TWO WORLDS OF JENNIE LOGAN, THE ♥ A young woman is magically transported one hundred years into the past. Made for TV. 99m. DIR: Frank DeFelitta. CAST: Lindsay Wagner, Marc Singer, Linda Gray, Alan Feinstein, Irene Tedrow, Henry Wilcoxon. 1979

12 ANGRY MEN (1957) ★★★★★ A superb cast under inspired direction makes this film brilliant in every aspect. Henry Fonda is the holdout on a jury who desperately seeks to convince his eleven peers to reconsider their hasty conviction of a boy accused of murdering his father. The struggle behind closed doors is taut, charged, and fascinating. B&W; 95m.

DIR: Sidney Lumet. CAST: Henry Fonda, Lee J. Cobb, Ed Begley Sr., E. G. Marshall, Jack Klugman, Jack Warden, Martin Balsam, John Fiedler, Robert Webber, George Voskovec, Edward Binns, Joseph Sweeney. 1957

12 ANGRY MEN (1997) ★★★★★ Reginald Rose's compelling story hasn't lost any of its power and this sizzling remake retains the clever premise and all the piquant dialogue while updating the concept with an integrated cast … and what a cast! A lone juror isn't necessarily convinced that a young man is guilty of killing his father; the other eleven men react with varying degrees of curiosity, disbelief, and outrage. As time passes in the hot, non-air-conditioned room the hold-out gradually wears away at his companions' resolve, setting in motion what turns into a murder mystery by proxy. Absolutely sensational. Rated PG-13 for profanity. 116m. DIR: William Friedkin. CAST: Courtney B. Vance, Ossie Davis, George C. Scott, Armin Mueller-Stahl, Dorian Harewood. 1997

TWELVE CHAIRS, THE ★★★ Based on a Russian comedy fable about an impoverished nobleman seeking jewels secreted in one of a dozen fancy dining room chairs. Ron Moody is the anguished Russian, Dom DeLuise his chief rival in the hunt. Mel Brooks's direction keeps things moving with laughs. Rated G. 94m. DIR: Mel Brooks. CAST: Mel Brooks, Dom DeLuise, Frank Langella, Ron Moody. 1970 DVD

TWELVE MILES OUT ★★1/2 Rumrunners on the lam break into a house and kidnap a man and his bored young fiancée. Just as rogue John Gilbert and captive Joan Crawford are warming up to each other, Gilbert's outlaw pal shows up and wants part of the action—and all of Joan. The two outlaws shoot it out, and when the law finally does arrive, it's too late. Originally released at 85 minutes, this version is all that is currently available. B&W; 60m. DIR: Jack Conway. CAST: John Gilbert, Joan Crawford, Ernest Torrence, Edward Earle. 1927

12 MONKEYS ★★★★1/2 Bruce Willis gives a terrific performance as a time traveler from the future sent to the past to save mankind from extinction. You don't dare miss a single minute of Terry Gilliam's masterpiece, a work on a par with the best in the genre. Rated R for violence, profanity, and nudity. 130m. DIR: Terry Gilliam. CAST: Bruce Willis, Madeleine Stowe, Brad Pitt, Christopher Plummer, Jon Seda, Joseph Melito. 1995 DVD

TWELVE MONTHS ★★1/2 A good-hearted waif is rewarded for her kindness by the incarnations of each month of the year when she is sent on an impossible errand by her evil stepmother. What might have been an entertaining tale is marred by a dragging pace. 90m. DIR: Kimio Yabuki. 1985

TWELVE O'CLOCK HIGH ★★★★ Gregory Peck is the flight commander who takes over an England-based bomber squadron during World War II. He begins to feel the strain of leadership and becomes too involved with the men in his command. This is a well-produced and well-acted film. Dean Jagger won an Oscar for supporting actor for his fine performance. B&W; 132m. DIR: Henry King. CAST: Gregory Peck, Dean Jagger, Gary Merrill, Hugh Marlowe. 1950

12:01 ★★★★ Surprisingly effective science-fiction thriller has accountant Jonathan Silverman trapped in time when an electrical shock "saves" him as the Earth is destroyed by a controversial experiment. Like Bill Murray in *Groundhog Day*, Silverman is fated to live the same day over and over again—unless he can change the course of history. Made for TV. 96m. **DIR:** Jack Sholder. **CAST:** Jonathan Silverman, Helen Slater, Martin Landau, Nicolas Surovy, Robin Bartlett, Jeremy Piven. **1993**

TWENTY BUCKS ★★1/2 Money—what it does to people and what people do with it—is the subject of this low-budget comedy-drama. A single twenty-dollar bill gets lost, found, stolen, lent, spent, and ironically shuffled about by a bag lady, teen skateboarder, emigrant chewing-gum magnate, bride and groom, stripper, crooks, and aspiring writer in a series of quirky, uneven vignettes. Not consistently memorable. Rated R for nudity, violence, and language. 91m. **DIR:** Keva Rosenfeld. **CAST:** Brendan Fraser, Christopher Lloyd, Steve Buscemi, Linda Hunt, Elisabeth Shue. **1994**

•**20 DATES** ★★ Sometimes funny, sometimes just plain annoying "documentary" in which director Myles Berkowitz goes on twenty dates in search of his perfect woman. Rated R for profanity. 92m. **DIR:** Myles Berkowitz. **CAST:** Myles Berkowitz, Tia Carrere. **1998**

TWENTY-ONE ★★★ Irreverent glimpse inside the life of an adventurous young woman (Patsy Kensit). Kensit carries on a monologue chronicling her simultaneous affairs with a drug addict and a married man. Rated R for nudity, violence, profanity, and drug use. 92m. **DIR:** Don Boyd. **CAST:** Patsy Kensit, Jack Shepherd, Patrick Ryecart. **1990**

TWENTY-FOUR EYES ★★★1/2 Beauty and innocence are lost as war and progress intrude upon a rural village in this poignant, touching drama. The story concerns a progressive schoolteacher from Tokyo who changes the lives of students in an elementary school on a remote island off Japan in the late 1920s. In Japanese with English subtitles. B&W; 158m. **DIR:** Keisuke Kinosita. **CAST:** Keisuke Kinosita, Chishu Ryu. **1954**

•**24-HOUR WOMAN** ★★1/2 What begins as a smart comedy-drama about a harried television producer trying to juggle pregnancy and her job turns into melodrama with obvious results. Rosie Perez is fine as the producer, whose pregnancy becomes a ratings bonanza for her news program. Once the baby arrives, director Nancy Savoca loses focus and the film becomes a wasteland of clichés. Rated R for language and adult situations. 93m. **DIR:** Nancy Savoca. **CAST:** Rosie Perez, Marianne Jean-Baptiste, Karen Duffy, Patti LuPone, Diego Serrano. **1998**

TWENTYFOURSEVEN ★★★ The title of this familiar but richly textured drama reflects the daily rut of small-town English teens in the 1980s. A loner resurrects a boxing club he hopes will replace the anger and despair of local youth with dignity, discipline, and fitness. Rated R for language, violence, and drug use. B&W; 96m. **DIR:** Shane Meadows. **CAST:** Bob Hoskins, Frank Harper, Pamela Cundell, Danny Nussbaum, James Hooton, Darren Campbell, Justin Brady. **1998**

25 X 5: THE CONTINUING HISTORY OF THE ROLLING STONES ★★★★★ The definitive history lesson on the Rolling Stones. Using extensive interviews and rare never-before-seen video footage, director Nigel Finch chronicles twenty-five years of the band—beginning in the early Sixties and ending with the Steel Wheels Tour. Not rated. Contains adult language and brief nudity. 130m. **DIR:** Nigel Finch. **1989**

25, FIREMEN'S STREET ★★★★ The troubled history of post–World War II Hungary is recounted in the memories of people living in an old house slated for demolition. Political upheavals take on personal resonance in this innovative, fascinating film. In Hungarian with English subtitles. Not rated. 93m. **DIR:** Istvan Szabo. **CAST:** Rita Bekes. **1973**

27TH DAY, THE ❦ Anticommunist propaganda disguised as science fiction, in the less-than-capable hands of the director who created the TV show *Bewitched*. B&W; 75m. **DIR:** William Asher. **CAST:** Gene Barry, Valerie French, George Voskovec. **1957**

•**28 DAYS** ★★ Sandra Bullock tries gamely, but she's no match for this clumsy, ill-advised "comedy." Director Betty Thomas betrays a serious subject—one woman's struggle to overcome her addictions to alcohol and pills—by turning it into wincingly uncomfortable burlesque. Every time Susannah Grant's script threatens to become serious, every time a cast member struggles to deliver a poignant moment of genuine emotion, Thomas yanks the rug out and buries all concerned beneath a cheap giggle. Rated PG-13 for brief profanity and drug use. 103m. **DIR:** Betty Thomas. **CAST:** Sandra Bullock, Viggo Mortensen, Dominic West, Diane Ladd, Elizabeth Perkins, Steve Buscemi, Alan Tudyk. **2000**

28 UP ★★★★★ A riveting and innovative British documentary that follows the woes and wonders of fourteen young people, reuniting them for new interviews every seven years. The result is a movie that exposes human vulnerability, while exposing the ludicrous and pompous British class system. Not rated. 120m. **DIR:** Michael Apted. **1985**

29TH STREET ★★★★ Imagine winning the first New York state lottery of $6.2 million and being unhappy about it—that's what happens to Frank Pesce (Anthony LaPaglia) in this warmhearted, often hilarious movie. Frank has always been lucky, and now it seems his luck may destroy his family. The real Pesce plays older brother Vito. Rated R for profanity and violence. 105m. **DIR:** George Gallo. **CAST:** Danny Aiello, Anthony LaPaglia, Lainie Kazan, Robert Forster. **1991**

200 CIGARETTES ★★ There's a lot of hot, young Hollywood talent on display in this drama-comedy, but they're saddled with a talkative script and pedestrian direction. It's a labored concept about a group of people trying to make the best of New Year's Eve in 1981. Rated R for language. 97m. **DIR:** Risa Bramon Garcia. **CAST:** Ben Affleck, Janeane Garofalo, Courtney Love, Christina Ricci, Gaby Hoffman. **1999 DVD**

200 MOTELS ★★1/2 Weird blend of comedy and music written and performed by Frank Zappa and the Mothers of Invention. This bizarre opera set against an even stranger backdrop of completely berserk gags. The film never really finds its center. Rated R for nudity and profanity. 98m. **DIR:** Frank Zappa, Tony Palmer. **CAST:** Frank Zappa, Theodore Bikel, Ringo Starr, Keith Moon. **1971**

2,000 MANIACS 🦃 Full of cruel tortures and mutilation, this drive-in hit was the prototype of today's sick-humor slasher films. 84m. **DIR:** Herschell Gordon Lewis. **CAST:** Thomas Wood, Jeffrey Allen. **1964**

2001: A SPACE ODYSSEY ★★★★★ There's no denying the visual magnificence of Stanley Kubrick's science-fiction epic. Ponderous, ambiguous, and arty, it's nevertheless considered a classic of the genre by many film buffs. The set design, costumes, cinematography, and Oscar-winning special effects combine to create unforgettable imagery. Rated G. 139m. **DIR:** Stanley Kubrick. **CAST:** Keir Dullea, William Sylvester, Gary Lockwood. **1968 DVD**

2010 ★★★★ The exciting sequel stars Roy Scheider, John Lithgow, Helen Mirren, and Bob Balaban as participants in a joint American-Russian space mission. We finally find out what really happened to astronaut Dave Bowman (Keir Dullea); the computer, HAL 9000; and the spaceship, *Discovery*, near the planet Jupiter. Rated PG. 116m. **DIR:** Peter Hyams. **CAST:** Roy Scheider, John Lithgow, Helen Mirren, Bob Balaban, Keir Dullea. **1984 DVD**

2020 TEXAS GLADIATORS 🦃 Alternately hilarious and just plain boring *Road Warrior* clone. Rated R for sex and gore, but turns up in censored version on Saturday-afternoon TV. 91m. **DIR:** Kevin Mancuso (Joe d'Amato). **CAST:** Harrison Muller. **1984**

20,000 LEAGUES UNDER THE SEA (1916) ★★1/2 Confusing blend of three tales (Jules Verne's *Mysterious Island* and *20,000 Leagues Under the Sea* as well as the creation of an original past for Captain Nemo) forces viewers to jump back and forth trying to get a handle on what's actually happening. Further, the director's fascination with underwater photography reduces this to a lesser entry of a Jacques Cousteau documentary. Silent. B&W; 105m. **DIR:** Stuart Paton. **CAST:** Allan Holubar. **1916 DVD**

20,000 LEAGUES UNDER THE SEA (1954) ★★★★ In this Disney version of the famous Jules Verne adventure-fantasy, a sailor (Kirk Douglas) and a scientist (Paul Lukas) get thoroughly involved with Captain Nemo, played by James Mason, and his fascinating submarine of the future. The cast is great, the action sequences ditto. 127m. **DIR:** Richard Fleischer. **CAST:** Kirk Douglas, James Mason, Paul Lukas, Peter Lorre. **1954**

TWENTY THOUSAND LEAGUES UNDER THE SEA (1972) ★★ Less than thrilling adaptation of the Jules Verne classic. Here, Captain Nemo and his amazing submarine, the *Nautilus*, are the centerpiece of a number of deep-sea adventures. 60m. **DIR:** Arthur Rankin Jr., Jules Bass. **1972**

20,000 LEAGUES UNDER THE SEA (1996) ★★★ Michael Caine makes a stalwart Captain Nemo in this sporadically engaging television miniseries that goes back to the source material to tell the story of the obsessed sea captain and his dream of conquering the ocean. Not rated; contains violence. 180m. **DIR:** Rod Hardy. **CAST:** Michael Caine, Patrick Dempsey, Bryan Brown, Mia Sara, Adewale Akinnouye-Agbaje. **1996**

20 MILLION MILES TO EARTH ★★★★ An egg from outer space grows into a giant monster that terrorizes Rome. Ray Harryhausen's stop-motion special effects are still impressive as the gargantuan Ymir battles an elephant and meets its fate in the ruins of the Colosseum. B&W; 84m. **DIR:** Nathan Juran. **CAST:** William Hopper, Joan Taylor. **1957**

TWELFTH NIGHT ★★★★ Shakespeare's gender comedy gets a delightful spin in scripter-director Trevor Nunn's lavish adaptation, with sensational Imogen Stubbs as the bereft young woman who disguises herself as a man in order to make her way in a country at war with her homeland. Rated PG for mild sensuality. 134m. **DIR:** Trevor Nunn. **CAST:** Imogen Stubbs, Helena Bonham Carter, Richard E. Grant, Nigel Hawthorne, Ben Kingsley, Mel Smith, Toby Stephens, Nicolas Farrell. **1996**

TWENTIETH CENTURY ★★★★ A screwball-comedy masterpiece, scripted from the hit play by Ben Hecht and Charles MacArthur. Egocentric Broadway producer, John Barrymore, turns shop girl Carole Lombard into a star, gets dumped, and pulls out all stops to win her back during a cross-country train trip. The fun is fast and furious as the miles fly by. Barrymore and Lombard couldn't be funnier. B&W; 91m. **DIR:** Howard Hawks. **CAST:** Carole Lombard, John Barrymore, Roscoe Karns, Walter Connolly, Edgar Kennedy. **1934**

TWOGETHER ★★★ A lustful couple deals with a pregnancy. Though neither wants marriage, they agree to move in together and their unique lifestyles begin to clash. Complex, ambiguous tale is long on plot and short on characterization despite a hard-working cast. A feisty soundtrack contains songs from Duran Duran, Pat Benatar, Camouflage, and Primal Scream. Not rated; contains profanity, nudity, and strong sexual content. 123m. **DIR:** Andrew Chiaramonte. **CAST:** Nick Cassavetes, Brenda Bakke, Jeremy Piven, Jim Beaver. **1992**

TWONKY, THE ★★1/2 A television set literally takes over the life of a philosophy professor (Hans Conreid)—it walks, does chores, and even tells him what books to read! Bizarre, but not as much fun as it sounds—writer-director Arch Oboler (*Five*) truly hated television, and the film is a humorless harangue about the evils of the "magic box." B&W; 72m. **DIR:** Arch Oboler. **CAST:** Hans Conried, Billy Lynn, Gloria Blondell, Janet Warren. **1953**

TYCOON 🦃 A would-be epic about the building of a railroad through the Andes. 128m. **DIR:** Richard Wallace. **CAST:** John Wayne, Laraine Day, Cedric Hardwicke, Judith Anderson, Anthony Quinn, James Gleason. **1947**

TYSON ★★★ Scripter Robert Johnson's adaptation of José Torres's *Fire and Fear* presents a sanitized biography of championship boxer Mike Tyson, and this made-for-cable drama earns most of its respect from the strong supporting cast. Paul Winfield is a hoot as flamboyant promoter Don King, and George C. Scott is amiably irascible as Tyson's trainer and surrogate father, Cus D'Amato. Rated R for profanity, violence, and simulated sex. 105m. **DIR:** Uli Edel.

CAST: George C. Scott, Paul Winfield, Michael Jai White, James B. Sikking, Malcolm-Jamal Warner, Tony Lo Bianco. 1995

UBU AND THE GREAT GIDOUILLE ★★★1/2 Impressive animation feature by world-renowned animator Jan Lenica, loosely based on Alfred Jarry's bizarre play that recounts the grotesque adventures of Pére Ubu, who with his ignorance and greed seizes the throne of Poland and tyrannizes the people. A masterpiece of animation and black humor. In French with English subtitles. Not rated. 80m. DIR: Jan Lenica. 1979

•U-571 ★★★1/2 This claustrophobic WWII sub thriller is an old-fashioned, high-testosterone epic, where cast members "do the right thing" at the right moment, and address each other with nicknames such as Rabbit and Tank. In April 1942, with Hitler's U-boats pounding the hell out of Allied supply lines in the Atlantic, word comes down that the crew of an American sub will pull a "Trojan Horse" ploy and impersonate Germans during a rendezvous with a stranded U-boat, the goal being to snag the coding device that is standard equipment on all Nazi subs. The resulting mission is laden with melodrama and nail-biting tension. Rated PG-13 for war-related violence. 115m. DIR: Jonathan Mostow. CAST: Matthew McConaughey, Bill Paxton, Harvey Keitel, Jon Bon Jovi, Jake Webber, Matthew Settle, Erik Palladino, David Keith. 2000

UFORIA ★★★★ Like *Repo Man* and *Stranger Than Paradise*, this low-budget American film deserved better treatment than it was given. Cindy Williams is hilarious as a born-again Christian who believes that salvation will come to Earth in the form of a flying saucer. Harry Dean Stanton plays a crooked evangelist who exploits the Jesus-in-a-spaceship concept for every penny he can get. Rated PG for profanity. 100m. DIR: John Binder. CAST: Cindy Williams, Harry Dean Stanton, Fred Ward, Harry Carey Jr., Darrell Larson. 1984

UGETSU ★★★★1/2 Set in sixteenth-century Japan, this film follows the lives of two Japanese peasants as their greed and ambition brings disaster upon their families. There is a fine blending of action and comedy in this ghostly tale. In Japanese with English subtitles. 94m. DIR: Kenji Mizoguchi. CAST: Machiko Kyo, Masayuki Mori. 1953

UGLY, THE ★★★ Writer-director Scott Reynolds has created a familiar yet ultimately chilling tale of a court-appointed psychiatrist whose interview with a convicted serial killer opens up a Pandora's box of evil. Paolo Rotundo is mesmerizing as the tormented killer who claims that demons called "The Ugly" are responsible for his reprehensible behavior. Not rated; contains graphic violence, language, and adult situations. 94m. DIR: Scott Reynolds. CAST: Paolo Rotundo, Rebecca Hobbs, Jennifer Ward-Leland, Roy Ward. 1996 DVD

UGLY AMERICAN, THE ★★1/2 With Marlon Brando playing an American ambassador newly arrived at his Asian post, more is expected of this film than just a routine potboiler. However, the film attempts to focus on the political interworkings of Brando's struggle with rising communist elements, but fails to generate any excitement. 120m. DIR: George Englund. CAST: Marlon Brando, Pat Hingle, Sandra Church, Arthur Hill, Eiji Okada, Jocelyn Brando. 1963

UGLY DACHSHUND, THE ★★ In this Disney movie, Dean Jones and Suzanne Pleshette are husband and wife; she loves dachshunds and owns a number of puppies. Charlie Ruggles convinces Jones to take a Great Dane puppy to raise. Since all of its peers are dachshunds, the Great Dane tries to act like them. Somewhat entertaining along the lines of a made-for-TV-movie. Not rated. 93m. DIR: Norman Tokar. CAST: Dean Jones, Suzanne Pleshette, Charlie Ruggles, Parley Baer, Kelly Thordsen. 1966

UHF ★★★1/2 A daydreamer finally lands in the right habitat: Channel 62, a UHF station with the lowest ratings in the country. Tastelessly innocent and funny. Rated PG-13 for profanity and violence. 95m. DIR: Jay Levey. CAST: "Weird Al" Yankovic, Victoria Jackson, Kevin McCarthy, Michael Richards, David Bowe, Anthony Geary, Billy Barty. 1989

ULEE'S GOLD ★★★★1/2 Outstanding character study about an aging Florida beekeeper who comes out of his self-imposed emotional shell when his dysfunctional family reaches a crisis point. Peter Fonda gives the performance of his career as the taciturn Ulee (short, significantly, for Ulysses), a decent guy damaged almost beyond repair by the irresponsibility of his imprisoned son and drug-addicted daughter-in-law. Rated R. 113m. DIR: Victor Nunez. CAST: Peter Fonda, Patricia Richardson, Christine Dunford. 1997 DVD

ULTERIOR MOTIVES ★★ A reporter pursuing a story about a research scientist stumbles onto a complex espionage plot involving the Japanese and the *yakuza*. Rated R for nudity, violence, and profanity. 95m. DIR: Terry Becker. CAST: Thomas Ian Griffith, Mary Page Keller, Joe Yamanaka, Ellen Crawford, M. C. Gainey, Ken Howard. 1992

ULTIMATE DECEPTION ★★★ In this made-for-cable original, a woman wants a baby more than anything, and her husband is all too willing to oblige, but he commits a terrible crime to fulfill her wish. After a slow start, the story (inspired by true events) picks up momentum and builds tension to the end. Richard Grieco does a good job as the seemingly great guy who hides a dark side. Not rated, but contains violence. 95m. DIR: Richard A. Colla. CAST: Yasmine Bleeth, Richard Grieco. 1998

ULTIMATE DESIRES 🗡 A public defender poses as a prostitute to solve a murder mystery. Low-budget time waster with an overdose of sleaze. Rated R for drug use, violence, nudity, and profanity. 90m. DIR: Lloyd A. Simandl. CAST: Tracy Scoggins, Marc Singer, Brion James. 1991

ULTIMATE WARRIOR, THE ★★1/2 The payoff doesn't match the promise of the premise in this less-than-thrilling science-fiction thriller. In the not-so-distant future, ragged residents of devastated New York City battle vicious gangs. Initially intriguing, the film stumbles to a ludicrous conclusion. Rated R. 94m. DIR: Robert Clouse. CAST: Yul Brynner, Max von Sydow, Joanna Miles, William Smith, Stephen McHattie. 1975

ULTRAVIOLET ★★ A reconciling couple is forcibly separated by a sadistic madman in the vast expanse of Death Valley. A *Dead Calm* variation. Rated R for nudity and profanity. 80m. DIR: Mark Griffiths. CAST: Esai Morales, Patricia Healy, Stephen Meadows. 1992

ULTRAWARRIOR 🎦 Another patchwork film from Roger Corman that has scenes stolen from other films to pad the slight story. Rated R for profanity, violence, and nudity. 75m. DIR: Augusto Tamayo, Kevin Tent. CAST: Meshach Taylor, Clare Beresford. 1992

ULYSSES ★★ One of Kirk Douglas's least successful independent productions, this heavily dubbed Italian epic emphasizes dialogue over thrills. Kirk Douglas does his best, but he gets mired down in this slow retelling of Ulysses's long voyage home after the Trojan War. 104m. DIR: Mario Camerini. CAST: Kirk Douglas, Silvana Mangano, Anthony Quinn, Rossana Podesta, Sylvie. 1955 DVD

ULYSSES' GAZE ★★★1/2 The first of Theo Angelopoulos's films to be seen widely in the United States, *Ulysses' Gaze* is not the best introduction to the work of the renowned Greek filmmaker. This story of a historian (Harvey Keitel) searching the war-torn Balkans for three reels of film shot there in 1904 is, at three hours, rather slow-going. But it offers much of great beauty for those with the patience to stick with it. In English and Greek with English subtitles. Not rated; contains nudity, sexual situations, violence, and profanity. 178m. DIR: Theo Angelopoulos. CAST: Harvey Keitel, Maia Morgenstern, Erland Josephson. 1995 DVD

ULZANA'S RAID ★★★★ A tense and absorbing film. Burt Lancaster and an expert cast and director take a fine screenplay penned by Alan Sharp and create a cavalry-Indians tale that is far from ordinary. Burt Lancaster plays an Indian scout who helps an inexperienced cavalry officer try to roust renegade Apache Ulzana and his tribe. Rated R. 103m. DIR: Robert Aldrich. CAST: Burt Lancaster, Bruce Davison, Jorge Luke, Richard Jaeckel, Lloyd Bochner. 1972 DVD

UMBERTO D ★★★★★ Seems as poignant now as when it was initially released. Quite simply, the plot centers upon a retired civil servant trying to maintain some sort of dignity and life for himself and his dog on his meager government pension. The film is agonizingly candid. A Vittorio De Sica masterpiece. In Italian with English subtitles. B&W; 89m. DIR: Vittorio De Sica. CAST: Carlo Battisti, Maria Pia Casilio. 1955

UMBRELLAS OF CHERBOURG, THE ★★★★ Simply the most romantic film to come from France in the 1960s. Catherine Deneuve made her first popular appearance, and we've been madly in love with her ever since. Simple story—boy meets girl—but played against a luxuriously photographed backdrop. Exquisite score from Michel Legrand. Watch this with somebody you love. 91m. DIR: Jacques Demy. CAST: Catherine Deneuve, Nino Castelnuovo, Marc Michel. 1964 DVD

UN CHIEN ANDALOU ★★★★★ Possibly the only film ever made completely according to surrealist principles, this famous short consists of a series of shocking and humorous images. Luis Buñuel and Salvador Dali wrote down some of their dreams and then photographed them. Sixty years later this seventeen-minute film retains the power to startle. The videotape includes four other avant-garde shorts. Of interest to the serious cinema student. B&W; 74m. DIR: Luis Buñuel, Salvador Dali. 1928

UN COEUR EN HIVER ★★★★1/2 The delicacy and detail with which the French view romantic relationships often make for intoxicating viewing, as amply evidenced by this superb study of heartbreak. Enhanced by the glorious music of Ravel's sonatas and trios. In French with English subtitles. Not rated, the film has profanity, suggested sex, and light violence. DIR: Claude Sautet. CAST: Daniel Auteuil, Emmanuelle Beart, André Dussolier, Elisabeth Bourgnine, Brigitte Catillon, Maurice Garrel, Myriam Boyer. 1993

UN SINGE EN HIVER (A MONKEY IN WINTER) ★★1/2 Alcoholic Jean Gabin vows to swear off if he and his wife survive the bombing of their village during World War II. They do, and he does. Years pass. A young version of Gabin arrives and rekindles the older man's memories of drink and dreams. In French with English subtitles. Originally released in the U.S. as *A Monkey in Winter*. Marred by murky photography. B&W; 105m. DIR: Henri Verneuil. CAST: Jean Gabin, Jean-Paul Belmondo, Suzanne Flon, Paul Frankeur, Noel Roquevert. 1962

UNAPPROACHABLE, THE 🎦 A completely unwatchable film about a young man obsessed with a reclusive aging starlet. Not rated; contains profanity. 100m. DIR: Krzysztof Zanussi. CAST: Leslie Caron, Daniel Webb, Leslie Magon. 1982

UNBEARABLE LIGHTNESS OF BEING, THE ★★★★★ One of the most playfully alive films ever made. Philip Kaufman calls his film a "variation" of Milan Kundera's novel about a womanizing neurosurgeon from Prague. What results is something poetic, erotic, funny, and exuberant. Rated R for sexual content. 164m. DIR: Phil Kaufman. CAST: Daniel Day-Lewis, Juliette Binoche, Lena Olin, Derek de Lint, Erland Josephson. 1988 DVD

UNBELIEVABLE TRUTH, THE ★★1/2 When Robert Burke returns home after an extended vacation in prison, his presense gets the whole town talking. Offbeat film with an edge. Rated R for its profanity. 90m. DIR: Hal Hartley. CAST: Adrienne Shelly, Robert Burke, Christopher Cooke, Gary Sauer, Julia McNeal, Mark Bailey. 1990

UNBORN, THE 🎦 Title says it all: another ferocious fetus movie that's unfortunately not stillborn. Rated R for nudity, violence, and profanity. 84m. DIR: Rodman Flender. CAST: Brooke Adams, Jeff Hayenga, James Karen, K. Callan, Jane Cameron. 1991

UNBORN II, THE 🎦 Ferocious fetus returns for more mayhem, as Mom and a friend try to stop a fanatic from destroying the offspring. Just as bad as the first one. Rated R for violence and language. 84m. **DIR:** Rick Jacobson. **CAST:** Michele Greene, Scott Valentine, Robin Curtis, Michael James McDonald. **1994**

UNCANNY, THE 💔 A paranoid writer tells three tales of cat-related horror. Rated R. 88m. **DIR:** Denis Heroux. **CAST:** Peter Cushing, Ray Milland, Susan Penhaligon, Joan Greenwood, Donald Pleasence, Samantha Eggar, John Vernon. **1977**

UNCERTAIN GLORY ★★ A curiosity piece from World War II days and a pale imitation of previous war melodramas. The movie has the advantage of Errol Flynn as its roguish leading man who turns himself into a hero. But it takes him much too long to do it. B&W; 102m. **DIR:** Raoul Walsh. **CAST:** Errol Flynn, Paul Lukas, Jean Sullivan, Lucile Watson, Faye Emerson. **1944**

UNCLE BUCK ★★★★ If you enjoyed John Candy in *Planes, Trains and Automobiles*, you'll love him here as the slobbish *Uncle Buck* who is called upon to take care of his brother's three kids when their mother's father has a heart attack. The results are hilarious and heartwarming. Rated PG for profanity. 106m. **DIR:** John Hughes. **CAST:** John Candy, Amy Madigan, Jean Kelly, Gaby Hoffman. **1989 DVD**

UNCOMMON VALOR ★★★★ In this action-packed adventure film, retired Marine Gene Hackman learns that his son may still be alive in a Vietnamese prison camp ten years after being listed as missing in action. He decides to go in after him. Rated R for profanity and violence. 105m. **DIR:** Ted Kotcheff. **CAST:** Gene Hackman, Fred Ward, Reb Brown, Randall "Tex" Cobb, Harold Sylvester, Robert Stack. **1983**

UNCONQUERED ★★★½ A colorful adventure set in colonial times with a sizzling romance between a soldier and the woman he rescues from slavery. Well-staged battle scenes and lush Technicolor landscapes give the film authenticity. Personable performers make it fun to watch in spite of its length. 146m. **DIR:** Cecil B. DeMille. **CAST:** Gary Cooper, Paulette Goddard, Boris Karloff, Howard DaSilva, Ward Bond, Mike Mazurki, C. Aubrey Smith. **1947**

UNDEAD, THE ★★★ Psychiatrist delving into the past lives of a prostitute gets taken for a ride back to the Middle Ages, where he tries to thwart his patient's impending execution but discovers that you can't alter history. A thinking fan's drive-in movie—a moody, offbeat melodrama—this is absolutely the best horror film with a trick ending ever shot in an abandoned grocery store. B&W; 71m. **DIR:** Roger Corman. **CAST:** Pamela Duncan, Richard Garland, Allison Hayes, Val Dufour, Dorothy Neuman, Billy Barty, Richard Devon. **1957**

UNDEFEATABLE 💔 Kung fu queen Cynthia Rothrock is at it again, She's out to avenge the murder of her sister by a serial killer, who's also a martial arts expert. Rated R for nudity, violence, and profanity. 95m. **DIR:** Godfrey Hall. **CAST:** Cynthia Rothrock, Don Niam, John Miller, Donna Jason, Emilie Davazac, Hang Yip Kim, Gerald Klein. **1993**

UNDEFEATED, THE ★★ Lumbering large-scale Western has Yankee colonel John Wayne forming an uneasy alliance with Confederate colonel Rock Hud-

son to sell wild horses in Mexico. This film has little to recommend it—even to die-hard Wayne fans. Even the action is minimal. Rated PG. 119m. **DIR:** Andrew V. McLaglen. **CAST:** John Wayne, Rock Hudson, Bruce Cabot, Ben Johnson, Antonio Aguilar, Harry Carey Jr., Lee Meriwether, Jan-Michael Vincent. **1969**

UNDER CALIFORNIA STARS ★★½ Trigger, the "Smartest Horse in the Movies," is the victim of a horse-napping plot in this enjoyable Roy Rogers oater. 71m. **DIR:** William Witney. **CAST:** Roy Rogers, Jane Frazee, Andy Devine, Michael Chapin. **1948**

UNDER CAPRICORN ★★★ This film is about a nineteenth-century Australian household that is hiding some dark secrets. Michael Wilding is drawn into solving the family's mystery because of his attraction to the lady of the house, Ingrid Bergman. This is not a typical Alfred Hitchcock movie. It lacks his customary suspense, and its pace could be called leisurely at best. 117m. **DIR:** Alfred Hitchcock. **CAST:** Michael Wilding, Ingrid Bergman, Joseph Cotten. **1949**

UNDER FIRE ★★½ Nick Nolte, Gene Hackman, and Joanna Cassidy are journalists covering political upheaval in Central America circa 1979. While *Under Fire* has its moments (found primarily in the superb supporting performances of Ed Harris and French actor Jean-Louis Trintignant), you have to wade through a bit of sludge to get to them. Rated R for profanity, violence, and gore. 128m. **DIR:** Roger Spottiswoode. **CAST:** Nick Nolte, Gene Hackman, Joanna Cassidy, Ed Harris, Jean-Louis Trintignant. **1983**

UNDER INVESTIGATION ★★ Harry Hamlin stars as a grungy L.A. detective in this sordid murder mystery. His main suspect is the wife of a famous murdered artist who stands to inherit a small fortune. Lustful looks, heavy breathing, and panting are substituted for plot and dialogue. Rated R for nudity, simulated sex, violence, and profanity. 99m. **DIR:** Kevin Meyer. **CAST:** Harry Hamlin, Joanna Pacula, Ed Lauter, Richard Beymer, John Mese, Lydie Denier. **1993**

UNDER LOCK AND KEY ★★ To get the goods on a powerful drug lord, an FBI agent goes undercover in a women's prison. Rated R for sexual scenes, violence, and strong language. 90m. **DIR:** Henri Charr. **CAST:** Wendi Westbrook, Barbara Niven, Taylor Leigh, Stephanie Ann Smith, Sai Tyler. **1995**

UNDER MEXICALI STARS ★★★ Modern-day Western involves counterfeiters and gold smugglers using helicopters to transport their contraband. B&W; 67m. **DIR:** George Blair. **CAST:** Rex Allen, Buddy Ebsen, Dorothy Patrick, Roy Barcroft. **1950**

UNDER MILK WOOD ★★ Welsh poet Dylan Thomas's play loses its vitality in this slow, stuffy, dry, image-burdened film version. All the queen's men plus the beautiful Elizabeth Taylor, cannot infuse it with life. 90m. **DIR:** Andrew Sinclair. **CAST:** Elizabeth Taylor, Richard Burton, Peter O'Toole, Glynis Johns, Vivien Merchant, Sian Phillips. **1973**

•UNDER PRESSURE ★★½ Mostly ludicrous thriller is buoyed by Charlie Sheen's portrayal of a psycho neighbor who's on the edge of exploding into violence. Also known as *Bad Day on the Block*. Rated R for profanity and violence. 88m. **DIR:** Craig R. Baxley. **CAST:** Charlie Sheen, Mare Winningham,

David Andrews, Dawnn Lewis, John Ratzenberger. 1997

UNDER SIEGE ★★★1/2 Reuniting with director Andrew Davis, Steven Seagal comes up with another winner. A gang of terrorists take over a naval ship with nuclear capabilities only to discover that one-man-army Seagal is on board to give 'em hell. Rip-roaring entertainment. Rated R for profanity, nudity, and violence. 103m. **DIR:** Andrew Davis. **CAST:** Steven Seagal, Tommy Lee Jones, Gary Busey, Nick Mancuso, Erika Eleniak, Patrick O'Neal, Colm Meaney. **1992** DVD

UNDER SIEGE 2: DARK TERRITORY ★★★1/2 While not as good as the original entry in the series, this sequel still has much to offer fans of Steven Seagal and action movies. This time, series hero Casey Ryback (Seagal) is escorting his niece by rail from her father's funeral when a group of terrorists take over the train. It's up to the ultimate one-man army to save the day. Rated R for violence and profanity. 100m. **DIR:** Geoff Murphy. **CAST:** Steven Seagal, Eric Bogosian, Katherine Heigl, Everett McGill, Morris Chestnut, Kurtwood Smith, Nick Mancuso. **1995** DVD

UNDER SUSPICION ★★★ Womanizing private investigator Liam Neeson's wife and client are murdered, he becomes the prime suspect. Multiple plot twists and an edge-of-your-seat climax that border on the unbelievable. Rated R for nudity, violence, and profanity. 100m. **DIR:** Simon Moore. **CAST:** Liam Neeson, Laura San Giacomo, Kenneth Cranham, Maggie O'Neill. **1991**

UNDER TEXAS SKIES ★★★ Bob Steele's first with the Three Mesquiteers finds him suspected of killing a sheriff. B&W; 54m. **DIR:** George Sherman. **CAST:** Robert Livingston, Bob Steele, Rufe Davis, Henry Brandon. **1940**

UNDER THE BILTMORE CLOCK ★★★ This acceptable TV adaptation of F. Scott Fitzgerald's "Myra Meets His Family" presents Sean Young as a young woman who decides to marry for wealth; she then has the task of meeting fiancé Lenny Von Dohlen's eccentric family. 70m. **DIR:** Neal Miller. **CAST:** Sean Young, Lenny Von Dohlen, Barnard Hughes. **1985**

UNDER THE BOARDWALK 💙 In this *West Side Story* update, the *lowks* (local dudes) take on the *vals* to see who will rule the local waves and babes. Rated R for violence and profanity. 102m. **DIR:** Fritz Kiersch. **CAST:** Danielle von Zerneck, Keith Coogan, Richard Joseph Paul, Sonny Bono. **1988**

UNDER THE CHERRY MOON ★★ Prince plays a gigolo-type singer who pursues a debutante, Mary (Kristin Scott Thomas). Rated PG-13 for language and mature theme. B&W; 100m. **DIR:** Prince. **CAST:** Prince, Jerome Benton, Steven Berkoff, Alexandra Stewart, Kristin Scott Thomas, Francesca Annis. **1986**

UNDER THE DOMIM TREE ★★★ Slow-moving, loosely structured movie set in 1950s Israel, at a village for children whose parents died in Nazi death camps. Despite the unusual setting, it's not much different from many other coming-of-age movies, though obviously deeply felt. Not rated; no objectionable material. 102m. **DIR:** Eli Cohen. **CAST:** Kaipo Cohen, Juliano Mer. **1996**

UNDER THE GUN (1988) 💙 A hotheaded St. Louis cop comes to Los Angeles to investigate the murder

of his brother. Rated R for language, violence, and nudity. 90m. **DIR:** James Sbardellati. **CAST:** Vanessa L. Williams, Sam Jones, John Russell. **1988**

UNDER THE GUN (1995) 💙 Deadly dull Australian-lensed action film about a retiring nightclub owner who pulls a double cross on local gangsters on his final night in the business. Rated R for violence, drug use, and strong language. 90m. **DIR:** Matthew George. **CAST:** Richard Norton, Kathy Long, Jane Badler, Peter Lindsey, Robert Bruce. **1995** DVD

UNDER THE HULA MOON ★★★1/2 Offbeat romance about a luckless couple living in a trailer park in Arizona who dream of something better. Interesting characters and outrageous situations make this little slice of white-trash humor worth a look. Rated R for violence, adult situations, and language. 96m. **DIR:** Jeff Celentano. **CAST:** Stephen Baldwin, Emily Lloyd, Christopher Penn. **1995**

UNDER THE RAINBOW ★★1/2 While this comedy is not quite jam-packed with laughs, it certainly keeps your interest. Set in 1938, the improbable story centers around the making of *The Wizard of Oz*, assassination attempts on a duke and duchess, the nefarious doings of Nazi and Japanese spies prior to World War II, and the life span of a dog named Streudel. Rated PG because of slight nudity and suggestive dialogue. 98m. **DIR:** Steve Rash. **CAST:** Chevy Chase, Carrie Fisher, Eve Arden, Joseph Maher. **1981**

UNDER THE ROOFS OF PARIS ★★★★ This simple Parisian love story of a street singer and a young girl is less important for its plot than for its style: at a time when most movies were overdosing on dialogue, director René Clair used music and other types of sound to advance his story. It is also, like most of Clair's films, a charming depiction of his home city. In French with English subtitles. B&W; 92m. **DIR:** René Clair. **CAST:** Albert Préjean, Pola Illery. **1929**

UNDER THE SKIN ★★★ Two sisters grow apart when their mother's death sends their sibling rivalry spinning out of control. The film's chief asset is a riveting performance by Samantha Morton as the younger, more unstable sister. Not rated; contains profanity and graphic sexual scenes. 85m. **DIR:** Carine Adler. **CAST:** Samantha Morton, Claire Rushbrook, Rita Tushingham, Stuart Townsend. **1997**

UNDER THE SUN OF SATAN ★★ Though well-acted and emotionally complex, this drama about a wavering French priest will only reach viewers willing to wade through the film's murky, slow-moving style. In French with English subtitles. Not rated. 97m. **DIR:** Maurice Pialat. **CAST:** Gérard Depardieu, Sandrine Bonnaire, Maurice Pialat. **1987**

UNDER THE VOLCANO ★★★★ Brilliant, but disturbing, adaptation of the Malcolm Lowry novel about a suicidal, alcoholic British consul in Mexico on the eve of World War II. Rated R for suggested sex, violence, and profanity. 109m. **DIR:** John Huston. **CAST:** Albert Finney, Jacqueline Bisset, Anthony Andrews. **1984**

UNDER WESTERN STARS ★★★1/2 Roy Rogers, in his first feature, plays a young congressman trying to obtain waterpower for the Dust Bowl area. Academy Award nomination for the song "Dust." B&W; 54m.

DIR: Joseph Kane. **CAST:** Roy Rogers, Smiley Burnette, Carol Hughes. **1938**

UNDERCOVER (1987) ★★ Cliché-ridden cop story. David Neidorf is a policeman who goes undercover in a South Carolina high school. Rated R for language and nudity. 92m. **DIR:** John Stockwell. **CAST:** David Neidorf, Jennifer Jason Leigh, Barry Corbin, David Harris, Kathleen Wilhoite. **1987**

UNDERCOVER (1995) 💔 Half-baked crime and sexploitation hybrid about a police detective who poses as a hooker. Rated R for sexual scenes and nudity. An "adult" version, not rated, is also available. 93/101m. **DIR:** Alexander Gregory Hippolyte. **CAST:** Athena Massey, Tom Tayback, Anthony Guidera, Meg Foster. **1995 DVD**

•**UNDERCOVER ANGEL** ★★★1/2 A struggling writer's bachelor life is interrupted when he's forced to take care of the six-year-old daughter of an ex-girlfriend. The moppet soon wins over the writer, and begins playing matchmaker for him. Likable cast makes this an engaging romantic comedy. Rated PG-13 for adult situations. 93m. **DIR:** Bryan Michael Stoller. **CAST:** Yasmine Bleeth, Dean Winters, Emily Mae Young, Casey Kasem, James Earl Jones. **2000 DVD**

UNDERCOVER BLUES ★★★ Sometimes stupid films are so charming that you can't help enjoying them—Ian Abrams's terminally silly update of *The Thin Man* is a perfect example. Superspies Jane and Jeff Blue are called out of retirement and child-rearing to save the world from a master villainess. Stanley Tucci steals the show. Rated PG-13 for cartoon violence and sensuality. 89m. **DIR:** Herbert Ross. **CAST:** Kathleen Turner, Dennis Quaid, Fiona Shaw, Stanley Tucci, Larry Miller, Obba Babatundé. **1993**

UNDERCURRENT ★★ A bride (Katharine Hepburn) comes to realize her husband (Robert Taylor) is a scoundrel. Considering the talent involved, this is a peculiarly dull drama. B&W; 116m. **DIR:** Vincente Minnelli. **CAST:** Katharine Hepburn, Robert Taylor, Robert Mitchum, Edmund Gwenn, Jayne Meadows, Marjorie Main. **1946 DVD**

UNDERGRADS, THE ★★★1/2 This made-for-cable Disney film has only sporadic funny moments. Art Carney plays a spunky senior citizen whose son would like to put him into a rest home. Chris Makepeace (Carney's movie grandson) refuses to allow this. Instead, he and his grandfather become college roommates. A good film with some heavy moments. 102m. **DIR:** Steven H. Stern. **CAST:** Art Carney, Chris Makepeace, Jackie Burroughs, Len Birman, Alfie Scopp. **1984**

UNDERGROUND (1990) 💔 A young woman takes a job as a waitress in a sleazy strip joint where she falls in love with a disc jockey searching for his missing sister, last seen in the bar. Not rated, with violence and nudity. 87m. **DIR:** Bret Carr. **CAST:** Rachel Carr, Clement von Franckenstein, Sean Rankin. **1990 DVD**

UNDERGROUND (1997) ★★★★ A manufacturer of black-market arms in World War II keeps his business going after the war by tricking his workers—all political refugees—into remaining in their underground factory by telling them that the war is still going on. Winner of the Palme d'Or at the 1995 Cannes Film Festival, *Underground* is a lively blend of absurd humor and political allegory. Not rated; contains nudity, strong violence, and sexual situations. 169m. **DIR:** Emir Kusturica. **CAST:** Miki Manojlovic, Mirjana Jokovic. **1995**

UNDERGROUND ACES 💔 Big-city hotel parking attendants run amok. Rated PG for profanity and nudity. 93m. **DIR:** Robert Butler. **CAST:** Dirk Benedict, Melanie Griffith, Kario Salem, Robert Hegyes, Audrey Landers, Frank Gorshin. **1980**

UNDERNEATH, THE ★★★ Director Steven Soderbergh's tale of an ex-con who reverts to his old ways in order to be with the woman he loves. Uneven but often intriguing film isn't a complete success but is entertaining for the most part. Sadly, Elisabeth Shue is all but wasted as a local girl. Rated R for profanity. 100m. **DIR:** Steven Soderbergh. **CAST:** Peter Gallagher, Alison Elliott, Elisabeth Shue, Joe Don Baker, Paul Dooley. **1994 DVD**

UNDERSEA KINGDOM ★★1/2 "Crash" Corrigan plays himself in this science-fiction serial of the 1930s as he attempts to thwart the evil plans of Unga Khan and his followers, who live under the ocean in the ancient city of Atlantis. Filled with gadgetry, robots, and futuristic machines, this cliff-hanger was extremely popular with young audiences, and it's still a lot of fun today. B&W; 12 chapters. **DIR:** B. Reeves "Breezy" Eason, Joseph Kane. **CAST:** Ray "Crash" Corrigan, Lois Wilde, Monte Blue, William Farnum, Lee Van Atta, Smiley Burnette, Lon Chaney Jr. **1936**

UNDERSTUDY, THE: GRAVEYARD SHIFT II ★★ Silvio Oliviero returns in this sequel, playing an actor who gets the lead role in a vampire film without the rest of the cast knowing he really *is* a vampire. Rated R for nudity and gore. 88m. **DIR:** Gerard Ciccoritti. **CAST:** Wendy Gazelle, Mark Soper, Silvio Oliviero. **1988**

UNDERTAKER AND HIS PALS, THE 💔 A mortician and two diner owners team up in a money-making venture, using human legs, breasts, etc., as the daily specials. Not rated. 70m. **DIR:** David C. Graham. **CAST:** Ray Dannis. **1967**

UNDERTAKER'S WEDDING, THE ★★★ Unexpectedly offbeat dark comedy about a young mortician working for the mob. Thanks to a long-standing rivalry, business is booming. Adrien Brody is deliciously wry as the young man who gets more than he bargained for when he's involved in a double cross. Kari Wuhrer shows maturity as an actress, playing the fiancée who is as understanding as she is good looking. Rated R for adult situations, language, and violence. 90m. **DIR:** John Bradshaw. **CAST:** Adrien Brody, Jeff Wincott, Kari Wuhrer, Burt Young. **1996**

UNDERTOW ★★1/2 Personable drifter Lou Diamond Phillips gets stranded during a hellish rainstorm with a wacko survivalist and his fearful wife. The cabin is crammed with guns and bear traps; you can work out the rest. The already sluggish film is made even more tedious by countless shots of both men bellowing in slow-motion frustration. Rated R for profanity, violence, nudity, and simulated sex.

93m. **DIR:** Eric Red. **CAST:** Lou Diamond Phillips, Mia Sara, Charles Dance. **1995**

UNDERWATER! ★★ The best stories about this sopping-wet adventure center around the elaborate publicity launched by reclusive millionaire Howard Hughes to sell it to the public. Hughes's original idea of supplying the press with Aqualungs and screening the film in an underwater theater didn't help the reviews and only made this costly, overblown story of sea scavengers more of a hoot than it already was. 99m. **DIR:** John Sturges. **CAST:** Jane Russell, Gilbert Roland, Richard Egan, Jayne Mansfield, Lori Nelson. **1955**

UNDERWORLD (1927) ★★★ After being rescued from prison by his moll and right-hand man, a gangster soon realizes that the two are having an affair. One of the first movies to look at crime through the gangster's point of view. Silent. B&W; 82m. **DIR:** Josef von Sternberg. **CAST:** George Bancroft, Evelyn Brent. **1927**

UNDERWORLD (1996) ★★★ Therapeutic revenge thriller about an ex-con trying to clear his thoughts by killing everyone responsible for taking out his old man. Denis Leary stars as Johnny Crown, fresh out of prison, who puts his future on hold in order to hunt down the responsible parties. Rated R for adult situations, language, and violence. 95m. **DIR:** Roger Christian. **CAST:** Denis Leary, Joe Mantegna, Annabella Sciorra, Traci Lords, Abe Vigoda. **1996 DVD**

UNDERWORLD STORY ★★1/2 Hardboiled story of a mercenary reporter who exposes a ruthless publisher who is attempting to frame an innocent man for murder. The story is full of holes, and the portrait of journalism is about as sordid as anything done on the subject before or since. B&W; 90m. **DIR:** Cy Endfield. **CAST:** Dan Duryea, Herbert Marshall, Gale Storm, Howard DaSilva, Michael O'Shea, Mary Anderson, Melville Cooper, Gar Moore, Frieda Inescort, Art Baker. **1950**

UNDERWORLD U.S.A. ★★★1/2 Impressive crime-drama from writer-director Sam Fuller about a man (Cliff Robertson) who, after witnessing his father's death at the hands of mobsters, develops a lifetime obsession to get even with the murderers. Great cinematography and exceptional performances rise above the weak script. B&W; 99m. **DIR:** Samuel Fuller. **CAST:** Cliff Robertson, Dolores Dorn. **1961**

•**UNDYING MONSTER, THE** ★★★1/2 A criminologist employs modern techniques to rid the moors of a murderous monster and free the local gentry from a centuries-old curse. Atmospheric thriller gives the impression of a British film shot on location. Actually, it's an intelligent, supernatural film that dignifies its subject. Little known to the general public, this beauty is one of the best werewolf movies and the only good horror film to come from Twentieth Century Fox in the 1940s. B&W; 64m. **DIR:** John Brahm. **CAST:** James Ellison, Heather Angel, John Howard, Bramwell Fletcher, Heather Thatcher, Aubrey Mather, Halliwell Hobbes. **1942**

UNE PARTIE DE PLAISIR (PIECE OF PLEASURE) ★★★ Life and art uncomfortably commingle in this loosely fictionalized look at the troubled marriage of Paul Gegauff, director Claude Chabrol's usual scriptwriter. Gegauff plays himself (opposite his real ex-wife)—one can only hope that the brutal behav-

ior he displays here was exaggerated. (A few years later, he was murdered by his second wife.) Occasionally fascinating, it may leave the viewer feeling voyeuristic. In French with English subtitles. Not rated. 100m. **DIR:** Claude Chabrol. **CAST:** Paul Gegauff, Danielle Gegauff. **1975**

UNEARTHING, THE 🎗 Young, unwed pregnant girl accepts offer of a young heir to a wealthy estate to be his bride so his ailing mother can die happy. The girl's there for the money; the rest of the family wants to sacrifice her baby. Rated R for violence and language. 83m. **DIR:** Wrye Martin, Barry Poltermann. **CAST:** Norman Moses, Tina Ona Paukstelis. **1993**

UNEARTHLY, THE 🎗 Mad scientist goes back into the lab to torture more innocent victims. 73m. **DIR:** Brooke L. Peters. **CAST:** John Carradine, Allison Hayes, Myron Healey. **1957**

UNEXPECTED ENCOUNTERS 🎗 This couples-only, after-hours rental is little more than a tease. Not rated (however there's partial nudity). 60m. **DIR:** Mannie Marshall. **CAST:** Giselle Wilder, Justin Dylan. **1988**

UNEXPECTED FAMILY, AN ★★1/2 An unmarried woman inherits two children from her sister, who abandons them to pursue a love interest in London. Predictably, the woman and the kids don't get along, then slowly work things out. This made-for-cable original may have sounded like a good idea, but simply ends up boring. Not rated. 95m. **DIR:** Larry Elikann. **CAST:** Stockard Channing, Stephen Collins, Christine Ebersole, Noah Fleiss. **1996**

UNEXPECTED LIFE, AN ★★1/2 This overbearing drama is about a woman and her makeshift family—her boyfriend and her sister's two kids—and how they adjust to a new baby in the family. Everyone has issues in this made-for-cable original, and predictably, everything is patched up by the end. Not rated. 95m. **DIR:** David Jones. **CAST:** Stockard Channing, Stephen Collins, Christine Ebersole, Noah Fleiss, Elaine Stritch. **1997**

UNFAITHFULLY YOURS (1948) ★★★ Symphony conductor Rex Harrison suspects his wife of infidelity and contemplates several solutions to his "problem." This film follows all the prerequisites of screwball comedies—mistaken identities, misinterpreted remarks. Harrison has fun, but his energy cannot sustain a film that runs about fifteen minutes too long. Not rated—family fare. B&W; 105m. **DIR:** Preston Sturges. **CAST:** Rex Harrison, Linda Darnell, Kurt Kreuger, Barbara Lawrence, Rudy Vallee, Lionel Stander. **1948**

UNFAITHFULLY YOURS (1984) ★★★ In this entertaining and sometimes hilarious remake of Preston Sturges's 1948 comedy, Dudley Moore plays a symphony orchestra conductor who suspects his wife (Nastassja Kinski) of fooling around with a violinist (Armand Assante) and decides to get revenge. Rated PG for nudity and profanity. 96m. **DIR:** Howard Zieff. **CAST:** Dudley Moore, Nastassja Kinski, Armand Assante, Albert Brooks. **1984**

UNFINISHED PIECE FOR THE PLAYER PIANO, AN (UNFINISHED PIECE FOR A MECHANICAL PIANO, AN) ★★★★ Based on the writing of Anton Chekhov, this film is alive with intimate character portraits. A group of aristocrats gather for an annual family reunion where they find their traditional values and way of life are slipping away, poisoned by their own excesses. In Russian with English subtitles. 100m. **DIR:** Nikita Mikhalkov. **CAST:** Alexander Kalyagin, Elena Soloyei, Yevgenta Clushenko, Oleg Tabakov. **1977**

UNFORGETTABLE ★★ This chilling, crackpot thriller involves several transfers of brain fluid between dead and living people but no credible smarts of its own. A Seattle forensic pathologist steals an experimental memory-retrieval potion and injects himself with his dead wife's cerebral juices in hopes of finding his wife's killer. The warped story unravels. Rated R for nudity and violence. 111m. **DIR:** John Dahl. **CAST:** Ray Liotta, Linda Fiorentino, Peter Coyote, Kim Cattrall, David Paymer, Christopher McDonald. **1996**

UNFORGETTABLE SUMMER, AN ★★★ In 1925, a Bulgarian officer and his wife are assigned to an untamed outpost on the Bulgarian/Romanian border, where tribal hatreds seem impossible to overcome. While it is an effective history lesson, it is hurt by thin characterizations. In Swedish and Romanian with English subtitles. Not rated; contains nudity, violence, and adult themes. 81m. **DIR:** Lucian Pintilie. **CAST:** Claudiu Bleont, George Constantin, Kristin Scott Thomas, Marcel Iures. **1992**

UNFORGIVEN, THE (1960) ★★★1/2 This tough Texas saga is filled with pride, prejudice, and passion. Audrey Hepburn, as a troubled Indian girl raised by whites, is at the center of the turmoil. In addition to some intriguing relationships, the movie provides plenty of thrills with intense cowboy-versus-Indian action scenes. The cast is uniformly excellent. 125m. **DIR:** John Huston. **CAST:** Burt Lancaster, Audrey Hepburn, Audie Murphy, John Saxon, Charles Bickford, Lillian Gish, Doug McClure, Joseph Wiseman, Albert Salmi. **1960**

UNFORGIVEN (1992) ★★★★ A former outlaw returns to violence in order to bring down a corrupt sheriff in the troubled town of Big Whiskey. Actor-director Clint Eastwood returns to the Western genre in high style by going up against a strong adversary in the always reliable Gene Hackman. Rated R for violence and profanity. 127m. **DIR:** Clint Eastwood. **CAST:** Clint Eastwood, Gene Hackman, Morgan Freeman, Richard Harris. **1992 DVD**

UNHOLY, THE ❤ A priest attempts to battle a demon that prolongs its existence by killing sinners in the act of sinning. Rated R for gore, nudity, and profanity. 99m. **DIR:** Camilo Vila. **CAST:** Ben Cross, Hal Holbrook, Ned Beatty, Trevor Howard, William Russ. **1988**

UNHOLY THREE ★★★1/2 With his last film and first talkie, Lon Chaney became the man of a thousand voices. If he hadn't, in an ironic twist, died of cancer of the throat, Chaney would have starred in *Dracula* and maybe even *Frankenstein*. As it is, we have this early sound remake of Tod Browning's 1925 silent thriller, in which Chaney's carnival ventriloquist teams up with a midget and a strong man to commit crimes. B&W; 73m. **DIR:** Jack Conway. **CAST:**

Lon Chaney Sr., Lila Lee, Elliott Nugent, Harry Earles. **1930**

UNHOOK THE STARS ★★★1/2 Class struggle, family conflict, and personal responsibility are the core of this well-acted dramatic comedy. Marisa Tomei, desperate for a baby-sitter for her young son, is a wild woman who crashes into the dignified and lonely life of neighbor Gena Rowlands. Directed by Rowland's son Nick Cassavetes with both sympathy and humor, this is a fascinating character study, though it sometimes lacks credibility. Rated R for profanity. 105m. **DIR:** Nick Cassavetes. **CAST:** Gena Rowlands, Marisa Tomei, Gérard Depardieu, Jake Lloyd. **1996**

UNICORN, THE ★★★ An innocent boy learns that even the magical powers of the Unicorn's horn can't change the world. Sadly, he learns this by buying a one-horned goat instead of the mythical beast. 29m. **DIR:** Carol Reed. **CAST:** Celia Johnson, Diana Dors, David Kossoff. **1983**

UNIDENTIFIED FLYING ODDBALL ★★1/2 Inept astronaut is transported to the court of King Arthur in his spacecraft. Once there, he discovers that Merlin and a knight are plotting against the king and sets out to expose them. Uneven script with situations not fully developed or explored hampers this Disney trifle. Rated G. 92m. **DIR:** Russ Mayberry. **CAST:** Dennis Dugan, Jim Dale, Ron Moody, Kenneth More. **1979 DVD**

UNINVITED, THE (1944) ★★★★★ Probably the greatest ghost-haunted house film ever made, all the terror being in the unseen, with a particularly satisfying and logical conclusion to the mystery. When brother and sister Ray Milland and Ruth Hussey buy a house on the English coast, a moody girl from the nearby village finds herself being drawn to it, although she has not lived there since she was a small child. Don't see this alone. B&W; 98m. **DIR:** Lewis Allen. **CAST:** Ray Milland, Ruth Hussey, Gail Russell, Donald Crisp, Cornelia Otis Skinner, Alan Napier. **1944**

UNINVITED, THE (1987) ❤ A group of college kids take staff jobs on a yacht and spend their spring break cruising to the Caribbean. Rated R for violence and nudity. 92m. **DIR:** Greydon Clark. **CAST:** George Kennedy, Alex Cord, Clu Gulager, Toni Hudson. **1987**

UNINVITED, THE (1993) ❤ Embarrassingly bad Western finds a ragtag group of prospectors looking for gold on sacred Indian burial ground. Top-billed Jack Elam disappears before the opening credits are over. Not rated; contains violence and adult situations. 90m. **DIR:** Michael Bohusz. **CAST:** Jack Elam, Christopher Boyer, Erin Noble. **1993**

UNION CITY ★★★ Called the "punk rock *film noir*," *Union City* is a quietly disturbing tale of murder and paranoia circa 1953. Deborah Harry (of the rock group Blondie) stars as a bored housewife; Dennis Lipscomb is her high-strung, paranoid husband. The mood, tone, and feel of the film are spooky, though it may be too oblique for some. Rated PG for adult themes and violence. 87m. **DIR:** Mark Reichert. **CAST:** Deborah Harry, Dennis Lipscomb, Pat Benatar. **1980 DVD**

UNION PACIFIC ★★★1/2 Lots of action in this fast-moving tale of the building of the transcontinental railroad, with a stellar cast playing the heroes and villains. With Cecil B. DeMille at the helm, you know it is an epic, in every sense, for the entire family. B&W; 135m. **DIR:** Cecil B. DeMille. **CAST:** Barbara Stanwyck, Joel McCrea, Brian Donlevy, Robert Preston, Akim Tamiroff, Anthony Quinn. **1939**

UNION STATION ★★★ A big, bustling railroad terminal is the backdrop of this suspense-thriller centering on the manhunt that ensues following the kidnapping of a blind girl for ransom. William Holden is the hero, Lyle Bettger is the villain, Allene Roberts is the victim. The plot's tired, but ace cinematographer-turned-director Rudolph Maté keeps everything moving fast and frantic. B&W; 80m. **DIR:** Rudolph Maté. **CAST:** William Holden, Nancy Olson, Allene Roberts, Barry Fitzgerald, Lyle Bettger, Jan Sterling. **1950**

U.S. MARSHALS ★★★1/2 Action-packed follow-up to *The Fugitive* brings back main character Chief Deputy Marshal Sam Gerard (Tommy Lee Jones) and pits him against a crafty, well-trained government operative accused of murdering two of his fellow agents. Full of surprises, suspense, and elaborate set pieces. Rated R for violence and profanity. 127m. **DIR:** Stuart Baird. **CAST:** Tommy Lee Jones, Wesley Snipes, Robert Downey Jr., Kate Nelligan, Joe Pantoliano, Irène Jacob. **1998 DVD**

UNIVERSAL SOLDIER ★★1/2 Jean-Claude Van Damme and Dolph Lundgren are part of a top-secret, scientific project to create perfect human fighting machines from dead soldiers. The program goes awry when Van Damme begins remembering his past, and a personal war develops between him and Lundgren. Average. Rated R for violence and profanity. 98m. **DIR:** Roland Emmerich. **CAST:** Jean-Claude Van Damme, Dolph Lundgren, Ally Walker, Ed O'Ross, Jerry Orbach. **1992 DVD**

•**UNIVERSAL SOLDIER II: BROTHERS IN ARMS** ★★ Mediocre by-the-numbers action-thriller picks up where the Dolph Lundgren/Jean Claude Van Damme original left off. Only things missing are Lundgren and Van Damme, which leaves precious little. Rated R for violence. 93m. **DIR:** Jeff Woolnough. **CAST:** Matt Battaglia, Chandra West, Jeff Wincott, Gary Busey. **1998**

UNKISSED BRIDE 💘 Tom Kirk plays the groom who passes out every time he and his wife (Anne Helm) contemplate lovemaking. 82m. **DIR:** Jack H. Harris. **CAST:** Tommy Kirk, Danica D'Hondt, Anne Helm, Jacques Bergerac, Joe Pyne. **1966**

UNKNOWN, THE ★★★1/2 Armless knife thrower (Lon Chaney Sr.) falls in love with another performer at his circus, a Gypsy horse rider (Joan Crawford) who despises being touched. Sounds like a perfect match, except that the circus strong man has eyes for her as well. Typically bizarre collaboration between director Tod Browning and the amazing Chaney, who throws knives and plays guitar with his feet! Silent. B&W; 61m. **DIR:** Tod Browning. **CAST:** Lon Chaney Sr., Joan Crawford, Norman Kerry. **1927**

UNKNOWN CHAPLIN ★★★★ In three parts—"My Happiest Years," "The Great Director," and "Hidden Treasures"—this is a fascinating excursion into the creative techniques and art of Charlie Chaplin. James Mason narrates. B&W; each part. 60m. **DIR:** Kevin Brownlow, David Gill. **1983**

UNKNOWN ORIGIN ★★★ Lots of fun 10,000 feet under the sea as deep-sea miners encounter an alien life force in the year 2050. Good cast, decent special effects, and a quaint 1960s drive-in feel give this made-for-cable thriller its appeal. Rated R for violence. 95m. **DIR:** Scott Levy. **CAST:** Roddy McDowall, Alex Hyde-White, Melanie Shatner, Don Stroud, Roger Halston. **1995**

UNKNOWN TERROR, THE 💘 Scientist turns tropical natives into fungus men. Appropriately titled film in which terror is indeed unknown. B&W; 76m. **DIR:** Charles Marquis Warren. **CAST:** John Howard, Mala Powers, Paul Richards, Charles Gray. **1957**

UNKNOWN WORLD ★★ Low-budget science-fiction story about an inventor who builds a drill capable of exploring inner Earth seems to borrow from Edgar Rice Burroughs's *Pellucidar* series, but it is actually closer to the nuclear-holocaust films of the postwar period. Short on thrills, this effort uses extensive footage of Carlsbad Caverns to simulate the interior of our planet. B&W; 74m. **DIR:** Terrel O. Morse. **CAST:** Victor Kilian, Bruce Kellogg, Marilyn Nash. **1950**

UNLAWFUL ENTRY ★★★1/2 After finding an intruder in their home, upscale L.A. suburbanites Kurt Russell and Madeleine Stowe are grateful for the arrival of police officers Ray Liotta and Roger E. Mosley. But when Liotta becomes fixated on Stowe being his "perfect woman," he turns into the cop from hell. Suspense-flick fans will get a good fix from this formula thriller. Rated R for violence, profanity, and nudity. 111m. **DIR:** Jonathan Kaplan. **CAST:** Kurt Russell, Ray Liotta, Madeleine Stowe, Roger E. Mosley. **1992**

UNLIKELY ANGEL ★★1/2 Dolly Parton and the late Roddy McDowall are the main attractions of the heavenly made-for-television family film about a country-and-western singer (guess who) who dies in a car crash. Before she can be granted her wings she must heal a family's wounds back on Earth. Not rated. 90m. **DIR:** Michael Switzer. **CAST:** Dolly Parton, Roddy McDowall, Brian Kerwin, Allison Mack, Eli Marienthal, Gary Sandy. **1996 DVD**

•**UNMADE BEDS** ★★★ This mixture of documentary and fiction was concocted from interviews with New Yorkers who had tried and failed to find mates through the personal ads. The four people featured play themselves, re-creating incidents from their experiences. Odd but often compelling, it's a refreshingly open view of modern romance. Not rated; contains strong adult situations, nudity, and profanity. 95m. **DIR:** Nicholas Barker. **CAST:** Aimee Copp, Michael DeStefano, Brenda Monte, Michael Russo. **1997**

UNMARRIED WOMAN, AN ★★★★★ Jill Clayburgh's Erica has settled into a comfortable rut and barely notices it when things begin to go wrong. One day, after lunch with her husband, Martin (Michael Murphy), she is shocked by his sobbing admission that he is in love with another woman. Her world is shattered. This first-rate film concerns itself with her attempts to cope with the situation. Rated R for sex, nudity, and profanity. 124m. **DIR:** Paul Mazursky. **CAST:** Jill Clayburgh, Michael Murphy, Alan Bates, Pat Quinn. **1978**

UNMASKED PART 25 🐢 Spoof of the Jason and Freddy films is even more lame than they were. Rated R for violence, gore, nudity, and profanity. 85m. **DIR:** Anders Palm. **CAST:** Gregory Cox. **1990**

UNNAMABLE, THE ★★★ College students spend the night in a haunted house in this adaptation of H. P. Lovecraft short story. While there, the promiscuous teens must contend with a family curse and a monstrous she-beast that delights in tearing humans limb from limb. There's a fair amount of good humor and some genuine chills. Horror fans should have a good time. Not rated; contains nudity and graphic violence. 87m. **DIR:** Jean Paul Ouellette. **CAST:** Charles King, Mark Kinsey Stephenson, Alexandra Durrell. **1988**

UNNAMABLE II, THE ★★ Sequels are usually worse than the originals, and this is no exception. A 300-year-old winged demon is separated from the body and soul of the young, beautiful woman. So, of course, a bloody chase ensues. Not rated; contains violence and nudity. 95m. **DIR:** Jean Paul Ouellette. **CAST:** John Rhys-Davies, Mark Kinsey Stephenson, Julie Strain, Peter Breck, David Warner. **1992**

UNNATURAL ★★1/2 Gothic fantasy about a scientist who creates a beautiful femme fatale through artificial insemination. This German production is laced with impressive cinematography, giving the film an impressionistic look reminiscent of the early silent-film period. Unfortunately, it suffers from a weak script. B&W; 90m. **DIR:** Arthur Maria Rabenalt. **CAST:** Erich Von Stroheim, Hildegarde Neff, Carl Boehm. **1952**

UNNATURAL CAUSES ★★★★ Alfre Woodard stars in this made-for-TV movie about a Veterans Administration counselor who takes up the cause of linking Agent Orange to stricken vets under her care. John Ritter gives a sensitive performance as one of the Vietnam vets. This fact-based story is given maximum impact thanks to the intelligent script of John Sayles. 100m. **DIR:** Lamont Johnson. **CAST:** John Ritter, Alfre Woodard, Patti LaBelle, John Sayles. **1986**

UNNATURAL PURSUITS ★★★1/2 This BBC production sends up artists, particularly writers, and America in general. Alan Bates is excellent as a talented but drunken playwright who breaks into song when the going gets tough. Bates pursues his play through several transformations on both sides of the Atlantic before finding tragedy and renewal. Bizarre, black, terribly clever, and far too long. Not rated; contains profanity and nudity. 143m. **DIR:** Christopher Morahan. **CAST:** Alan Bates, Bob Balaban, John Mahoney. **1994**

UNREMARKABLE LIFE, AN ★★★ Two elderly sisters who still live together in their family home find themselves at odds when one of them starts dating. Polished performances highlight what is an otherwise overwrought melodrama. Rated PG for racial epithets. 95m. **DIR:** Amin Q. Chaudhri. **CAST:** Patricia Neal, Shelley Winters, Mako. **1989**

UNSANE ★★★1/2 American fans of stylish Italian director Dario Argento had been awaiting his 1984 film *Tenebrae* for years. Although it never played theatrically in the U.S., it snuck onto video with a new title, *Unsane*. A mystery novelist discovers that a series of killings seems to be based on those in his latest book. Argento's trademarks—violent murders, a complex plot, and a pulsing synthesizer score—are all here in abundance. Not rated; the film contains nudity and violence. 92m. **DIR:** Dario Argento. **CAST:** Anthony Franciosa, Daria Nicolodi, John Saxon, Giuliano Gemma, John Steiner. **1984 DVD**

UNSEEN, THE 🐢 A cellar-dwelling invisible critter that does what you'd expect. Rated R. 89m. **DIR:** Peter Foleg. **CAST:** Barbara Bach, Sidney Lassick, Stephen Furst. **1981**

UNSETTLED LAND 🐢 Israeli-made production concerning a commune of young Jews from Europe establishing a settlement in the Sinai Desert after World War I. Overblown saga. Rated PG for violence. 109m. **DIR:** Uri Barbash. **CAST:** Kelly McGillis, John Shea. **1987**

UNSINKABLE MOLLY BROWN, THE ★★★ Noisy, big-budget version of hit Broadway musical has Debbie Reynolds at her spunkiest as the tuneful gal from Colorado who survives the sinking of the *Titanic* and lives to sing about it. High-stepping dance numbers and the performances by Reynolds and Harve Presnell make this a favorite with musicals fans, but it does drag a bit for the casual viewer. 128m. **DIR:** Charles Walters. **CAST:** Debbie Reynolds, Harve Presnell, Ed Begley Sr., Hermione Baddeley, Jack Kruschen. **1964**

UNSPEAKABLE, THE ★★1/2 Scripter Christopher Wood's police thriller gets a few points for keeping us guessing, but the central plot remains pretty silly. Cute cop Athena Massey goes deep undercover to entrap a suspected serial rapist/killer, then falls in love with him. Only in the movies. Rated R for nudity, violence, gore, profanity, and simulated sex. 90m. **DIR:** Howard McCain. **CAST:** David Chokachi, Cyril O'Reilly, Athena Massey, Timothy Busfield. **1996**

UNSPEAKABLE ACTS ★★★1/2 This TV dramatization of the landmark day-care sexual-abuse case in 1984 Miami features Jill Clayburgh and Brad Davis as the child psychologists who interviewed the abused children. Though disturbing, the film is a must-see for everyone seeking qualified child care. Contains mature themes. 94m. **DIR:** Linda Otto. **CAST:** Jill Clayburgh, Brad Davis, Season Hubley, Gregory Sierra. **1989**

UNSTRUNG HEROES ★★★★ Franz Lidz's poignant book becomes a compelling little comedy-drama in director Diane Keaton's hands. Andie MacDowell is the one sane member of a family of misfits, but when she turns up with cancer, it's the screwball men who show their young nephew the values of faith, heritage, and family ties. A genuine tearjerker. Rated PG for dramatic intensity. 93m. **DIR:** Diane Keaton. **CAST:** Andie MacDowell, John Turturro, Michael Richards, Maury Chaykin, Nathan Watt, Kendra Krull. **1995**

UNTAMED HEART ★★★★ Tom Sierchio's poignant urban love story becomes a career-making vehicle for Marisa Tomei, in her first starring role. She's a perky Minneapolis twentysomething working as a waitress. She eventually connects with the diner's introverted busboy (Christian Slater, very good in a part completely unlike his usual work). Rated PG-13 for profanity. 102m. DIR: Tony Bill. CAST: Christian Slater, Marisa Tomei, Rosie Perez, Kyle Secor. 1993

UNTIL SEPTEMBER ★★ A midwestern divorcée (Karen Allen) falls in love with a married Parisian banker (Thierry Lhermitte) during the summer vacation in this unabashed soap opera. Rated R. 95m. DIR: Richard Marquand. CAST: Karen Allen, Thierry Lhermitte, Christopher Cazenove. 1984

UNTIL THE END OF THE WORLD ★★ Futuristic folly follows a good-time girl as she pursues a fugitive (William Hurt). Bounty hunters, bank robbers, her boyfriend, and a private eye become entangled in her cross-continental chase. New wave soundtrack and directionless plot make this nearly impossible to enjoy. Rated R for violence, nudity, and profanity. 158m. DIR: Wim Wenders. CAST: William Hurt, Solveig Dommartin, Sam Neill, Max von Sydow, Jeanne Moreau. 1991

UNTIL THEY SAIL ★★★1/2 Romantic drama about a quartet of sisters and the men they meet during World War II in New Zealand. Based on a James Michener novel, so there's plenty of meat to the story, including a murder and some mismatched lovers. B&W; 96m. DIR: Robert Wise. CAST: Paul Newman, Jean Simmons, Joan Fontaine, Sandra Dee, Piper Laurie, Dean Jones, Charles Drake, Patrick Macnee. 1957

UNTOLD STORY, THE ★★★ Like *Silence of the Lambs*, this Hong Kong tale of a gruesome serial killer won that country's equivalent of the Oscar for best actor (Anthony Wong) and best film. But it is a much more graphic film, with injections of comedy that are as shocking as they are tasteless. Not rated, but absolutely not for kids, or anyone with a weak stomach! In Cantonese with English subtitles. 95m. DIR: Herman Yau. CAST: Anthony Wong, Danny Lee. 1993 DVD

UNTOUCHABLES, THE ★★★★1/2 An absolutely superb retelling of the beloved television series, with director Brian De Palma working his stylish magic in tandem with a deft script from Pulitzer-winning playwright David Mamet. Prohibition-era Chicago has been beautifully re-created to emphasize big-city decadence. Al Capone was the populist hero for providing alcohol for the masses; Eliot Ness was the arrow-straight federal agent who rose to the challenge. (Look for Sean Connery in the performance of his career as a beat cop who assists Ness.) Rated R for language and extreme violence. 119m. DIR: Brian De Palma. CAST: Kevin Costner, Sean Connery, Robert De Niro, Charles Martin Smith, Andy Garcia, Billy Drago, Richard Bradford. 1987

UNTOUCHABLES, THE: SCARFACE MOB ★★★ This violence-ridden film was released theatrically in 1962 but was actually the original two-part pilot for the popular TV series. Steely-eyed Robert Stack as Eliot Ness gets the government's go-ahead to form his own special team of incorruptible agents. B&W; 90m. DIR: Phil Karlson. CAST: Robert Stack, Keenan

Wynn, Barbara Nichols, Pat Crowley, Neville Brand, Bruce Gordon, Anthony George, Abel Fernandez, Nick Giorgiade. 1962

UNVEILED ★★1/2 While on vacation in Marrakech, a young woman learns that her childhood friend has been murdered. With the assistance of a handsome government official, she uses her feminine wiles to draw out the killer. Things get complicated when she begins to fall for the suspect. Rated R for nudity, adult situations, and violence. 103m. DIR: William Cole. CAST: Lisa Zane, Nick Chinlund, Whip Hubley, Martha Gehman, Amidou. 1993

UNZIPPED ★★★ Fashion designer Isaac Mizrahi develops his fall 1994 collection in a film that is less documentary than infomercial and it's frankly adoring. Fortunately, Mizrahi has the dynamic presence of a born star. Rated R for profanity and brief nudity. 76m. DIR: Douglas Keeve. CAST: Isaac Mizrahi, Sarah Mizrahi, Sandra Bernhard, Cindy Crawford, Naomi Campbell, Eartha Kitt. 1995

UP AGAINST THE WALL ★★ Black teenager has his moral code challenged when he moves from his mother's modest home to his brother's house in the affluent suburbs in this well-meaning but amateurish drama. Rated PG-13 for language and violence. 103m. DIR: Ron O'Neal. CAST: Marla Gibbs, Ron O'Neal, Stoney Jackson. 1991

UP CLOSE AND PERSONAL ★★★★ Old-fashioned Hollywood movies are hard to come by these days, and that is what makes this big-screen love story such a treasure. Writers Joan Didion and John Gregory Dunne, who based the screenplay on Alanna Nash's biography of ill-fated TV newswoman Jessica Savitch, have gone with a largely fictional tale, and this works very much in the film's favor. Rated PG-13 for profanity, violence, and suggested sex. 124m. DIR: Jon Avnet. CAST: Robert Redford, Michelle Pfeiffer, Stockard Channing, Joe Mantegna, Kate Nelligan, Glenn Plummer, Dedee Pfeiffer, Noble Willingham. 1996 DVD

UP FROM THE DEPTHS 🐾 Perfunctory remake of *Creature from the Haunted Sea*. Rated R. 80m. DIR: Charles B. Griffith. CAST: Sam Bottoms, Susanne Reed, Virgil Frye. 1979

UP IN ARMS ★★1/2 Danny Kaye's first film will not disappoint his fans, as he sings and mugs his way through the war. Dinah Shore loves the hypochondriac Kaye; the war takes a backseat to entertainment. 105m. DIR: Elliott Nugent. CAST: Danny Kaye, Dinah Shore, Dana Andrews, Constance Dowling. 1944

UP IN SMOKE ★★★★ This is Cheech and Chong's first, and best, film. Forget about any plot as Cheech and Chong go on the hunt for good weed, rock 'n' roll, and good times. Several truly hysterical moments, with Stacy Keach's spaced-out cop almost stealing the show. Rated R for language, nudity, and general raunchiness. 87m. DIR: Lou Adler. CAST: Cheech and Chong, Strother Martin, Stacy Keach, Edie Adams, Tom Skerritt. 1978

UP PERISCOPE ★★1/2 Edmond O'Brien is a by-the-book sub commander who risks his command and men on a dangerous mission. Well-done, but too familiar. 111m. DIR: Gordon Douglas. CAST: James Garner, Edmond O'Brien, Alan Hale Sr., Carleton Carpenter. 1959

UP THE ACADEMY 💙 This was *Mad* magazine's first and only attempt to emulate *National Lampoon*'s film success. Rated R for profanity and general disgustingness. 88m. DIR: Robert Downey. CAST: Ron Leibman, Wendell Brown, Ralph Macchio, Tom Citera, Tom Poston, Stacey Nelkin, Barbara Bach. **1980**

UP THE CREEK (1958) ★★★★ Left in charge of an unimportant naval base without a commanding officer, junior officer Peter Sellers turns it into a fountain for personal money-making schemes. Dryly funny British farce with a plethora of amusing supporting players. 86m. DIR: Val Guest. CAST: Peter Sellers, David Tomlinson, Wilfrid Hyde-White, Vera Day, Lionel Jeffries. **1958**

UP THE CREEK (1984) ★★★ Two stars from *Animal House*, Tim Matheson ("Otter") and Stephen Furst ("Flounder"), are reunited in this mostly entertaining raft-race comedy. It doesn't beg you to laugh at it the way *Police Academy* does. Matheson is charismatic enough to carry the film. Rated R for nudity, profanity, scatalogical humor, and violence. 95m. DIR: Robert Butler. CAST: Tim Matheson, Stephen Furst, Dan Monahan, John Hillerman, James B. Sikking, Tom Nolan. **1984**

UP THE DOWN STAIRCASE ★★★1/2 Sandy Dennis perfectly captures the flighty teacher of Bel Kaufman's hilarious novel about the New York City high school scene, but the students and minor plot crises do not wear as well as her performance. Although Dennis smoothly enacts the teacher we'd all like to have, Tad Mosel's script never quite catches the book's inspired lunacy. 124m. DIR: Robert Mulligan. CAST: Sandy Dennis, Eileen Heckart, Jean Stapleton. **1967**

UP THE SANDBOX ★★ A weird, uneven comedy about a neglected housewife (Barbra Streisand). Its fantasy sequences are among the strangest ever put on film. Rated R. 97m. DIR: Irvin Kershner. CAST: Barbra Streisand, David Selby, Jane Hoffman. **1972**

UP TO A CERTAIN POINT ★★★1/2 It's one thing to talk about sexual and social liberation, but quite another to live up to it. So discovers a writer as he does research among working-class Cubans for a film on Latino machismo. A pointed satire from Cuba's best-known filmmaker. Not rated; contains no objectionable material. 68m. DIR: Tomas Gutierrez Alea. CAST: Oscar Alvarez, Mirta Ibarra. **1983**

UP YOUR ALLEY 💙 L.A. street dwellers. Rated R for profanity. 90m. DIR: Bob Logan. CAST: Linda Blair, Murray Langston, Ruth Buzzi. **1988**

UP YOUR ANCHOR 💙 Ever wonder what one of the beach films of the 1960s or *Love Boat* would be like with nudity and rampant sexual encounters? 89m. DIR: Dan Wolman. CAST: Yftach Katzur, Zachi Nay. **1985**

UP/DOWN/FRAGILE ★★★1/2 This musical about three young women in modern-day Paris is a tribute to the spirit of classic Hollywood musicals that aims to take out much of the starch by making the singing and dancing more ordinary. In French with English subtitles. Not rated; contains adult themes. 169m.

DIR: Jacques Rivette. CAST: Marianne Denicourt, Nathalie Richard, Laurence Cote. **1995**

UPHILL ALL THE WAY 💙 Ridiculous film concerns two down-and-outers mistaken for bank robbers. Rated PG. 86m. DIR: Frank Q. Dobbs. CAST: Roy Clark, Mel Tillis, Glen Campbell. **1985**

UPSTAIRS, DOWNSTAIRS ★★★★★ Life in a fashionable London town house between 1904 and 1930 is depicted with insight, wit, and charm through the activities and thoughts of the patrician family upstairs and the servants downstairs in this superb *Masterpiece Theater* series. The late Gordon Jackson is perfect as the unflappable.butler Hudson, closely rivaled by Jean Marsh as the unpredictable maid Rose. 900m. DIR: Simon Langton. CAST: Gordon Jackson, Jean Marsh, Pauline Collins, Rachel Gurney, Ian Ogilvy, Raymond Huntley, Lesley-Anne Down. **1971**

UPTOWN NEW YORK ★★ Sobby melodrama about a doctor whose family forces him to jilt the girl he loves and marry for money. B&W; 80m. DIR: Victor Schertzinger. CAST: Jack Oakie, Shirley Grey. **1932**

UPTOWN SATURDAY NIGHT ★★★1/2 Sidney Poitier (who also directed), Bill Cosby, Harry Belafonte, Richard Pryor, and Flip Wilson head an all-star cast in this enjoyable comedy about a couple of buddies (Poitier and Cosby) who get into all sorts of trouble. Rated PG. 104m. DIR: Sidney Poitier. CAST: Sidney Poitier, Bill Cosby, Harry Belafonte, Richard Pryor, Flip Wilson. **1974**

URANUS ★★★★ Sumptuous character study of a group of villagers immediately following the Nazi occupation of France. The town has been torn into three camps: those who joined the Nazis, those who joined the resistance, and those who just minded their own business. In French with English subtitles. Not rated; contains nudity and violence. 100m. DIR: Claude Berri. CAST: Gérard Depardieu, Michel Blanc, Jean-Pierre Marielle, Philippe Noiret, Michel Galabru. **1992**

URBAN COWBOY ★★★ The film is a slice-of-life *Saturday Night Fever*–like look at the after-hours life of blue-collar cowboys. Overall, the film works because of excellent directing by James Bridges and the fine acting of John Travolta, Debra Winger, and Scott Glenn. Rated PG. 132m. DIR: James Bridges. CAST: John Travolta, Debra Winger, Scott Glenn, Madolyn Smith, Charlie Daniels Band. **1980**

URBAN CROSSFIRE ★★1/2 Gritty crime-drama about a cop whose partner is killed by a vicious drug dealer, and whose desire to apprehend the killer shoves him over the edge. If the film wasn't so exploitative, it would be a good reminder of the high wire that cops are forced to walk. Rated R for violence and language. 95m. DIR: Dick Lowry. CAST: Mario Van Peebles, Ray Sharkey, Peter Boyle, Courtney B. Vance, Michael Patrick Boatman. **1994**

URBAN JUNGLE ★★ Although the performances are uneven, viewers may enjoy some of the characters in this story about a young man trying to escape a life of crime in the inner city. Not rated; contains violence. 76m. DIR: Daniel Matmor. CAST: Brian Paul, McKinley Winston. **1990**

URBAN LEGEND ★★★1/2 First-time filmmakers Jamie Blanks and screenwriter Silvio Horta have quickly established their names with this thrilling chiller that takes the slasher film in its own new direction. As the anniversary of a university massacre—which may or may not have occurred—draws near, students find themselves caught up in a series of murders. Dark comedy abounds and you'll be guessing right up until the climactic moment as to who the killer is. Rated R for violence, profanity, sexual dialogue, and simulated sex. 108m. **DIR:** Jamie Blanks. **CAST:** Alicia Witt, Jared Leto, Rebecca Gayheart, Joshua Jackson, Tara Reid, Robert Englund, Danielle Harris, Natasha Gregson Wagner, Brad Dourif. 1998 DVD

•**URBAN MENACE** ★★ After his family is killed and his church burned to the ground, a preacher seeks revenge on those who wronged him—with bad direction and godawful acting, both of which are plentiful in this film. Rated R for violence and profanity. 97m. **DIR:** Albert Pyun. **CAST:** Snoop Dog, Ice T, Big Pun, Fat Joe. 1999 DVD

URBAN WARRIORS 🎬 A group of scientists survive a nuclear holocaust. Rated R for violence. 90m. **DIR:** Joseph Warren. **CAST:** Karl Landgren. 1989

URGE TO KILL ★★★★ A top-notch cast shines in this drama about a convicted killer who, upon release from a mental institution, comes home to face prejudice and violent recriminations. Well written and acted, the film's focus is on the quality of justice versus the quality of mercy and what people will do to subvert both. Holly Hunter is outstanding as the sister of the murder victim. Not rated; contains mature themes. 96m. **DIR:** Mike Robe. **CAST:** Karl Malden, Holly Hunter, Alex McArthur, Paul Sorvino, Catherine Mary Stewart, William Devane. 1984

URINAL ★★★1/2 Structurally imaginative semi-documentary in which the ghosts of gay artists (including Sergey Eisenstein, Frida Kahlo, and Yukio Mishima) return to Canada to help combat police harassment of gays who meet in public washrooms. Not rated; contains nudity and strong sexual themes. 100m. **DIR:** John Greyson. **CAST:** Pauline Carey, Paul Bettis. 1988

UROTSUKIDOJI: LEGEND OF THE OVERFIEND ★★★ An unbelievably violent and perverse animated Japanese feature based on *The Wandering Kid* comics and representative of the violent/erotic subgenre. Every 3,000 years the Overfiend returns to unite the three separate worlds of man, demon, and animal-man—but is the creature a healer or a destroyer? Dubbed in English. Rated NC-17; contains explicit sexual scenes and violence. 108m. An uncut, subtitled version in three parts also is available and runs 40 minutes longer. **DIR:** Hideki Takayama. 1989

UROTSUKIDOJI II: LEGEND OF THE DEMON WOMB ★★ Less interesting than the original, this animated sequel has the Overfiend dealing with his beloved cousin, who has become the Evil King and is being manipulated by the crazed son of a Nazi scientist. Sound ridiculous? It is. Dubbed in English. Not rated; contains gratuitous violence and explicit sexual scenes. 88m. A director's cut of this film combines this with *Urotsukidoji: Legend of the Over-*

fiend and runs 40 extra minutes. **DIR:** Hideki Takayama. 1991

URUSEI YATSURA (TV SERIES) VOLS. 1–45 ★★★1/2 Japanese animation. Entertaining mixture of love triangles, humor, and science fiction. The main characters include teenage Romeo, Ataru Morobishi, his main girlfriend, Shinobu, and Lum the alien princess who lives in Ataru's closet. In Japanese with English subtitles. 80m. **DIR:** Kazuo Yamazaki, Yuuji Moriyama. 1980–1982

URUSEI YATSURA: BEAUTIFUL DREAMER ★★★★ Japanese animation. This is the second movie from the *Urusei Yatsura* collection. Strong, constantly developing characterizations make these feature films consistently enjoyable and a delightful change from the giant robots that transform into everything but the kitchen sink. In Japanese with English subtitles. Not rated. 90m. **DIR:** Mamoru Oshii. 1984

URUSEI YATSURA: INABA THE DREAMMAKER ★★★1/2 Japanese animation. The further adventures of Ataru, Shinobu, and Lum as they are presented with several of their possible futures, not all of which are desirable. Holds to the high standards of comedy found in the original series episodes and movies. In Japanese with English subtitles. 57m. **DIR:** Dezuki Tetsu. 1987

URUSEI YATSURA: ONLY YOU ★★★★ Japanese animation. How long has our hero Ataru had his obsession with girls? Find out as his associates plan to attend a reunion with his first flirtation. The fast-paced story line is reminiscent of Blake Edwards's early Pink Panther films. In Japanese with English subtitles. 101m. **DIR:** Kazuo Yamazaki, Yuuji Moriyama. 1983

URUSEI YATSURA: REMEMBER LOVE ★★★★ Japanese animation. Once again, Ataru's twisted charm enmeshes him in extraterrestrial difficulties and involves his associates in situations that stretch the imagination. The vocal characterizations, expressive artwork, and excellent subtitling allow the viewer to easily follow the story. In Japanese with English subtitles. 93m. **DIR:** Kazuo Yamazaki. 1985

USED CARS ★★★★ This is a riotous account of two feuding used-car businesses. Jack Warden and Kurt Russell are both excellent in this overlooked comedy. Fine support is offered by Frank McRae, Gerrit Graham, and Deborah Harmon. Rated R for language, nudity, and some violence. 111m. **DIR:** Robert Zemeckis. **CAST:** Jack Warden, Kurt Russell, Frank McRae, Gerrit Graham, Deborah Harmon. 1980

USED PEOPLE ★★★1/2 Shirley MacLaine and Marcello Mastroianni are up to their tried-and-true tricks in this story of an Italian ne'er-do-well whose love for a Jewish woman is given full flower when her husband dies. The old pros manage to carry if off. Rated PG-13 for profanity and suggested sex. 116m. **DIR:** Beeban Kidron. **CAST:** Shirley MacLaine, Marcello Mastroianni, Jessica Tandy, Kathy Bates, Marcia Gay Harden, Sylvia Sidney, Bob Dishy, Joe Pantoliano. 1992

USERS, THE ★★ Another bloated TV movie boasts a fine cast and little else. Jaclyn Smith stars as a beautiful girl who plays a major role in the resurgence of a down-and-out movie star's career. Standard "television" production values and "television" dialogue do this one in. 125m. DIR: Joseph Hardy. CAST: Jaclyn Smith, Tony Curtis, Joan Fontaine, Red Buttons. 1978

USUAL SUSPECTS, THE ★★★★★ When five career criminals are picked up by the New York City police for a lineup, they decide to make use of their chance meeting and pull off a big job. Wild, crazy, gripping movie with terrific performances, assured direction, and brilliant writing. Bet you can't watch it just once. Rated R for profanity and violence. 105m. DIR: Bryan Singer. CAST: Gabriel Byrne, Kevin Spacey, Kevin Pollak, Stephen Baldwin, Chazz Palminteri, Benicio Del Toro, Suzy Amis, Dan Hedaya, Giancarlo Esposito. 1995 DVD

UTAH ★★★ Roy Rogers tries to prevent show girl Dale Evans from selling her ranch to raise money to back a Broadway musical. B&W; 78m. DIR: John English. CAST: Roy Rogers, George "Gabby" Hayes, Dale Evans, Peggy Stewart, Grant Withers. 1945

UTILITIES ★★★1/2 Despite some rather crude humor once in a while, this modest comedy has a lot of charm and the heart of a Frank Capra film. Robert Hays plays a fed-up social worker who turns vigilante against the public utility companies. Rated PG for profanity and sex. 94m. DIR: Harvey Hart. CAST: Robert Hays, Brooke Adams, John Marley. 1983

UTU ★★★★★ This stunner from New Zealand contains all the action of the great American Westerns, but with a moral message that leaves most of that genre's best in the dust. A Maori corporal in the nineteenth-century British army finds his family slaughtered by his own army and vows "utu" (Maori for revenge) to rid his land of white people. Rated R for violence. 100m. DIR: Geoff Murphy. CAST: Anzac Wallace, Bruno Lawrence, Kelly Johnson, Tim Elliot. 1985

U-TURN ★★ Oliver Stone's adaptation of John Ridley's novel—with the author contributing his own script—is a parade of degenerate freaks given sham mythic status. This tale quickly becomes intolerable, since "victim" Sean Penn is every bit as amoral and deranged as the absurd residents of the tiny Arizona town where his 1964- Mustang breaks down. Rated R for profanity, violence, nudity, gore, and extremely strong sexual content. 125m. DIR: Oliver Stone. CAST: Sean Penn, Jennifer Lopez, Nick Nolte, Powers Boothe, Claire Danes, Joaquin Phoenix, Billy Bob Thornton, Jon Voight. 1997 DVD

U2: RATTLE AND HUM ★★★★1/2 More than just a concert movie. It's an eloquent cry for change. The Irish rock quartet and 26-year-old director Phil Joanou have combined forces to create a remarkably moving screen work. Filmed in black and white and color during the group's American tour in support of its ground-breaking *Joshua Tree* album, it captures the excitement of the live shows while underlining U2s timely message. Rated PG-13 for profanity. 99m. DIR: Phil Joanou. CAST: U2. 1988 DVD

UTZ ★★★1/2 The director of *The Vanishing* here attempts a more subtle, complex film. Armin Mueller-Stahl stars as an obsessive collector of fine porcelain figures living in Prague. The Communist Czech government decides the collection belongs to the state. Peter Riegert costars as an American collector who unravels Utz's story in flashbacks; the masterful Paul Scofield contributes a tasty bit as Utz's closest old friend. 101m. DIR: George Sluizer. CAST: Armin Mueller-Stahl, Brenda Fricker, Peter Riegert, Paul Scofield. 1992

V ★★★1/2 Exciting science-fiction thriller began as a television miniseries and then evolved into a full-fledged series. The action begins immediately as several large saucers hover over all of the Earth's major cities, their occupants promising peace, but planning to use humans as food. A series of massive battles between freedom fighters and aliens ensues. Features outstanding special effects, extensive character development, and enough subplots to fuel several movies. 205m. DIR: Kenneth Johnson. CAST: Marc Singer, Jane Badler, Faye Grant, Michael Durrell, Andrew Prine, Richard Herd, Robert Englund. 1983

VAGABOND ★★★1/2 French new wave writer-director Agnes Varda's dispassionate but beautifully photographed "investigation"—via flashbacks—of a young misfit's meandering trek through the French countryside features a superb performance by Sandrine Bonnaire. Her *Vagabond* is presented as rude, lazy, ungrateful. Yet in some subliminal way the film draws one into the alienation that fuels this outsider's journey into death. In French with English subtitles. Rated R for profanity and suggested sex. 105m. DIR: Agnes Varda. CAST: Sandrine Bonnaire, Macha Meril. 1986 DVD

VAGABOND LOVER, THE ★★★ Rudy Vallee portrays an orchestra conductor who has fallen deeply in love with the daughter (Sally Blane) of a dotty dowager (Marie Dressler). Conventional but entertaining. B&W; 69m. DIR: Marshall Neilan. CAST: Rudy Vallee, Sally Blane, Marie Dressler. 1929

VAGRANT, THE ★★1/2 Bill Paxton is a Yuppie homeowner driven out of his mind by an intrusive, repulsive derelict. This weird, low-budget flick is riddled with a black humor that turns eerie as Paxton unravels. Not for everyone. Rated R for profanity and violence. 91m. DIR: Chris Walas. CAST: Bill Paxton, Michael Ironside. 1992

VALDEZ IS COMING ★★★1/2 Burt Lancaster is superb as Valdez, an aging town constable who takes it upon himself to collect $100 from a ruthless rancher after the senseless killing of an innocent black man. Rated R for violence, profanity, and simulated sex. 90m. DIR: Edwin Sherin. CAST: Burt Lancaster, Susan Clark, Richard Jordan, Jon Cypher, Barton Heyman, Frank Silvera, Maria Montez, Nick Cravat, Hector Elizondo. 1971

VALENTINA ★★★ Subtle drama based on a novel by Ramon Sender about Jose Garce's love for Valentina that lasted from childhood until his death. Produced by Anthony Quinn. In Spanish with English subtitles. 90m. DIR: Antonio J. Betancor. CAST: Jorge Sanz, Paloma Gomez. 1984

VALENTINO ★★1/2 This outrageous biography of one of the screen's greatest legends uses selective facts and historical settings in an attempt to isolate the real nature of the adulation of Rudolph Valentino. Director Ken Russell freely mixes fruit and wild hallucinations. Rudolf Nureyev is somehow an apt choice to play Valentino, and the rest of the cast and production seems to fit. 132m. DIR: Ken Russell. CAST: Rudolf Nureyev, Leslie Caron, Michelle Phillips, Carol Kane, Felicity Kendal, Seymour Cassel, Huntz Hall, Alfred Marks, David De Keyser. 1977

VALENTINO RETURNS ★★1/2 Small Town, U.S.A., 1955, proves too confining for Wayne Gibbs (Barry Tubb). He takes off in his new pink Cadillac and manages to take on a biker gang, ruin his car, and find love (lust) in short order. Rated R for violence, profanity, and nudity. 97m. DIR: Peter Hoffman. CAST: Frederic Forrest, Veronica Cartwright, Barry Tubb, Jenny Wright. 1988

VALLEY, THE ★★1/2 The plot of this dated movie—hip young people travel to New Guinea—is forgettable. But the exquisite Nestor Almendros photography and the Pink Floyd score make it a pleasant viewing experience. In French with English subtitles. Not rated; contains nudity and sexual situations. 114m. DIR: Barbet Schroeder. CAST: Bulle Ogier, Jean-Pierre Kalfon, Michael Gothard. 1972

VALLEY GIRL ★★★1/2 The story of a romance between a San Fernando Valley girl and a Hollywood punker, *Valley Girl* claims the distinction of being one of the few teen movies directed by a woman: Martha Coolidge. And, perhaps for that reason, it's a little treasure: a funny, sexy, appealing story that contains something for nearly everyone. Rated R. 95m. DIR: Martha Coolidge. CAST: Nicolas Cage, Deborah Foreman, Colleen Camp, Frederic Forrest, Lee Purcell. 1983

VALLEY OF GWANGI ★★★ Prehistoric reptiles are found in Mexico in the early 1900s; attempts are made to capture them alive to be put on display. A cross between *King Kong* and *Hatari!*, with a Western flavor. Fine special effects by Ray Harryhausen. Rated PG. 95m. DIR: Jim O'Connolly. CAST: James Franciscus, Richard Carlson, Gila Golan. 1969

VALLEY OF THE DOLLS ❤ Trash film of Jacqueline Susann's trashy bestseller about the effect of drugs (the *dolls* of the title) on ladies from show business and society. John Williams was Oscar-nominated for his score. 123m. DIR: Mark Robson. CAST: Barbara Parkins, Patty Duke, Sharon Tate, Susan Hayward, Paul Burke, Martin Milner, Lee Grant. 1967

VALLEY OF THE SUN ★★★ A discredited army scout runs into conflict with an unscrupulous government agent responsible for the maltreatment of Indians in the Arizona Territory in the 1800s. A Western that mixes in comedy. B&W; 84m. DIR: George Marshall. CAST: Lucille Ball, Cedric Hardwicke, Dean Jagger, James Craig. 1942

●**VALLEY OF THE ZOMBIES** ★★ A former mental patient with a craving for blood leaves cadavers everywhere in this low-budget comedy-thriller. Gallows humor, grim doings, and a spooky old house spice up this little oddity with head creep Ian Keith a standout. B&W; 57m. DIR: Philip Ford. CAST: Ian Keith, Robert Livingston, Adrian Booth, Thomas Jackson, Charles Trowbridge. 1946

VALMONT ★★★★ Milos Forman took a great artistic risk in directing what amounts to a one-year-later remake of Stephen Frears's Oscar-winning *Dangerous Liaisons*, but the result is captivating, with a young cast bringing poignance and innocence to its tale of seduction and deceit. Rated R for nudity and violence. 137m. DIR: Milos Forman. CAST: Colin Firth, Annette Bening, Meg Tilly, Sian Phillips, Jeffrey Jones, Henry Thomas, Fabia Drake, Fairuza Balk. 1989

VALS, THE ★★ Not as totally grody as one would expect, this teen flick features bored valley girls who transform from shop-aholics into charitable drug busters. Rated R for profanity. 96m. DIR: James Polakof. CAST: Jill Carroll, Elena Stratheros. 1982

VAMP ★★★ Effective comedy shocker concerns a pair of college kids (Chris Makepeace and Robert Rusler) who must find a stripper for a big party being thrown that night. Upon arriving at the After Dark Club, the duo quickly decide on the outrageous Katrina (Grace Jones), little realizing that she is a vicious, bloodthirsty vampire in disguise. Rated R for gore and brief nudity. 93m. DIR: Richard Wenk. CAST: Chris Makepeace, Grace Jones, Robert Rusler, Sandy Baron, Gedde Watanabe, Dedee Pfeiffer. 1986

VAMPING ★★ Dreary attempt to update *film noir*, with Patrick Duffy as a down-and-out musician persuaded to break into the home of a dead man. Once there, he falls in love with a photo of the man's widow. Overlong. Rated R for profanity. 110m. DIR: Frederick King Keller. CAST: Patrick Duffy, Catherine Hyland, Rod Arrants. 1984

VAMPIRE, THE ★★1/2 Here it is, the first in a long line of late-Fifties/early-Sixties Mexican monster movies—all of them variously atmospheric, technically primitive, culturally eccentric . . . , and often compulsively watchable. German Robles was Mexico's Christopher Lee, although this first of his many vampire movies was shot a full year before Lee's *Horror of Dracula* debut. B&W; 84m. DIR: Fernando Mendez. CAST: German Robles, Abel Salazar. 1957

VAMPIRE AT MIDNIGHT ★★ A young woman becomes the object of adoration of a brutal vampire posing as a motivational psychologist. This tries hard to be a character study rather than a horror movie, but it misses the mark. Rated R for violence and nudity. 94m. DIR: Greggor McClatchy. CAST: Jason Williams, Gustav Vintas, Leslie Milne, Jenie Moore, Robert Random. 1988

VAMPIRE BAT, THE ★★★ Prolific director Frank Strayer gave low-rent Majestic Studios their biggest hit with this eerie thriller reminiscent of the great horror films. Lionel Atwill and Fay Wray reunite to share the screen with distinguished Melvyn Douglas as a skeptical magistrate out to solve several mysterious deaths. It seems the victims have all been drained of blood and great hordes of bats have been hovering about. . . . B&W; 63m. DIR: Frank Strayer. CAST: Lionel Atwill, Fay Wray, Melvyn Douglas, Dwight Frye, Maude Eburne. 1933 DVD

•VAMPIRE COP ★★ Low-budget direct-to-video tale of a vampire who becomes a cop and uses his position to evoke red from the criminals. They'll let just about anyone be a cop these days. Rated PG for violence. 86m. DIR: Donald Farmer. CAST: William Lucas, Melissa Moore, Donald Farmer. 1990

VAMPIRE HAPPENING ♥ A Hollywood sexpot vacations in Europe and learns her grandmother was a vampire. Not rated, 97m. DIR: Freddie Francis. CAST: Pia Dagermark, Ferdinand Mayne, Thomas Hunter. 1971

VAMPIRE HOOKERS (SENSUOUS VAMPIRES) ♥ Aging vampire lords over a bevy of beauteous bloodsuckers. (Also known as Sensuous Vampires.) Rated R for violence and nudity. 82m. DIR: Cirio H. Santiago. CAST: John Carradine. 1979

VAMPIRE IN BROOKLYN ★★ This anemic vampire comedy is yet another misfire by star Eddie Murphy, apparently more concerned with playing multiple roles than with delivering a coherent film. His riff on the classic Dracula myth is neither funny nor scary; it's all pretty familiar as Murphy's faux-sophisticated fangster travels to New York City to find his "perfect mate." Ho hum. Rated R for profanity, violence, and gore. 100m. DIR: Wes Craven. CAST: Eddie Murphy, Angela Bassett, Allen Payne, Kadeem Hardison, John Witherspoon. 1995

VAMPIRE JOURNALS ★★1/2 Anne Rice fans are the target audience for this overwrought tale of a junior vampire, the older bloodsucker who took his life, and the woman they both desire. Like many Full Moon productions, authentic European locations help provide plenty of atmosphere. Rated R for nudity, violence and sex. 92m. DIR: Ted Nicolaou. CAST: Jonathan Morris, David Gunn, Starr Andreeff. 1997 DVD

VAMPIRE LOVERS, THE ★★★ Hammer Films of England revitalized the Frankenstein and Dracula horror series in the late 1950s. But by 1971, when this film was released, Hammer's horrors had become passé. Even adding sex to the mix, as the studio did in this faithful screen version of Sheridan LeFanu's Camilla, didn't help much. Nonetheless, sexy Ingrid Pitt makes a voluptuous vampire. Rated R for violence, nudity, suggested sex, and gore. 88m. DIR: Roy Ward Baker. CAST: Ingrid Pitt, Peter Cushing, Pippa Steele, Madeleine Smith, George Cole, Dawn Addams, Kate O'Mara. 1971

VAMPIRE OVER LONDON ♥ This is one of many titles appended to Bela Lugosi's last British film, shot as Old Mother Riley Meets the Vampire, and starring Arthur Lucan as the washerwoman character he designed decades earlier for a drag act on the music hall circuit. Finally released in the United States in the Sixties as My Son, the Vampire. B&W; 74m. DIR: John Gilling. CAST: Bela Lugosi, Arthur Lucan. 1952

VAMPIRE PRINCESS MIYU ★★ Spiritual investigator Himiko encounters strange happenings in two melodramatic, animated tales of the occult, Japan-

ese style. In Japanese with English subtitles. 60m. DIR: Toshihiro Hirano. 1988

VAMPIRE VIXENS FROM VENUS ♥ Totally lame horror-sex comedy noteworthy only for a cameo by comic Charlie Callas. Not rated; contains nudity and gore. 85m. DIR: Ted A. Bohus. CAST: Leon Head, Michelle Bauer, Charlie Callas. 1994

VAMPIRELLA ★★ Talisa Soto makes a woefully anemic Vampirella in this laughable adaptation of the long-running comic-book series. Soto doesn't convey any of the character's innate menace or sensuality, and her costume's all wrong! Roger Daltrey is much better as the scenery-chewing villain; too bad he couldn't have played the hero. Rated R for violence, profanity, and nudity. 80m. DIR: Jim Wynorski. CAST: Talisa Soto, Roger Daltrey, Richard Joseph Paul, Brian Bloom. 1996

VAMPIRES, THE (1915) (LES VAMPIRES) ★★★★ Generally considered the crowning achievement of Louis Feuillade, who took the form of the movie serial to its peak. The Vampires are a gang of costumed criminals led by the beautiful Musidora. Accused of glorifying crime, Feuillade and cast actually improvised much of the action in this ten-part silent serial. Still impressive today. B&W; 420m. DIR: Louis Feuillade. CAST: Musidora, Edouard Mathé. 1915–1916

VAMPIRES ALWAYS RING TWICE ♥ A couple attempts to get away from it all and find themselves trying to get away from Postal vampires. Bottom of the barrel. Not rated. 118m. DIR: Steve Postal. CAST: Alan Ramey, Jennifer Tuck, Angela Shepard. 1990

VAMPIRES & OTHER STEREOTYPES ★★ When in doubt, take a small group of people, put them in a confined place, and besiege them with something. That's the road taken here in this film, which tries hard but never quite succeeds. Not rated; contains violence, gore, and profanity. 88m. DIR: Kevin J. Lindenmuth. CAST: Bill White, Ed Hubbard. 1995

VAMPIRES FROM OUTER SPACE ♥ An undead bride from the planet Cirrus takes her unwitting groom to a strange island in this entirely amateurish shot-on-video production. Not rated. 114m. DIR: Steve Postal. CAST: Alan Ramey, Angela Shepard, Jennifer Tuck. 1990

VAMPIRE'S KISS ♥ A ranting, obnoxious literary agent becomes convinced that he is a vampire. Rated R for violence, profanity, and brief nudity. 103m. DIR: Robert Bierman. CAST: Nicolas Cage, Maria Conchita Alonso, Jennifer Beals, Elizabeth Ashley. 1989

•VAMPS: DEADLY DREAM GIRLS ★★1/2 A priest frequents a strip club (!) in an attempt to save the souls of the dancers. Instead he gets mixed up in a struggle with vampires for one girl's soul. An enjoyable, though under-budgeted film. Not rated; contains violence, profanity, and nudity. 90m. DIR: Mark Burchett, Michael D. Fox. CAST: Jennifer Huss, Paul Morris, Lorissa McComas. 1996

VAMPYR (1931) ★★★★★ Director Carl Dreyer believed that horror is best implied. By relying on the viewer's imagination, he created a classic. A young man at a very bizarre inn discovers an unconscious woman, who had been attacked by a vampire in the form of an old woman. This outstanding film is one of the few serious films of the macabre. B&W; 68m. **DIR:** Carl Dreyer. **CAST:** Julian West, Sybille Schmitz. 1931 DVD

VAMPYR, THE (1992) ★★ An operetta based on a nineteenth-century score, this misogynistic witches' brew of gore, sex, and surrealism features a vampire released from an icy grave beneath London's skyscrapers. He must renew his pact with Satan by slaying three women within three days, all the while singing of his troubles. Difficult to sit through, very little narrative, and the structure is too stagy for the format. Not rated; contains violence, nudity, gore, sexual situations, and profanity. 115m. **DIR:** Nigel Finch. **CAST:** Omar Ebrahim, Richard van Allan, Fiona O'Neill, Philip Salmon, Colenton Freeman. 1992

●**VAMPYRE (1990)** ★★1/2 Director Bruce G. Hallenbeck remakes Carl Dreyer's silent classic with only so-so results. Here a village is plagued by vampirism and a mysterious slayer arrives to confront the bloodsuckers. Not rated; contains violence. 90m. **DIR:** Bruce G. Hallenbeck. **CAST:** Cathy Seyler, John Brant, John McCarty. 1990

VAMPYRES ★★1/2 This tale of two beautiful female vampires living in an old mansion and sharing their male victims sexually before drinking their blood was considered pornographic in its time. It's pretty tame by current standards, and also easier to appreciate as a piece of serious, if low-budget, erotica. There are two versions available on video; the longer, unrated one has elongated sexual situations, though both feature abundant nudity. 87m. **DIR:** Joseph Larraz. **CAST:** Marianne Morris, Anulka, Murray Brown, Brian Deacon, Bessie Love. 1974

VAN, THE (1976) 💣 Inept teenager uses his impressive new van to seduce bimbos. Rated PG. 92m. **DIR:** Sam Grossman. **CAST:** Stuart Getz, Danny DeVito. 1976 DVD

VAN, THE (1997) ★★★1/2 The final entry in Irish novelist Roddy Doyle's *Barrytown* trilogy is no less entertaining as it follows the ups and downs of two best friends and pubmates who unwisely go into business together. Rated R for profanity and sexual candor. 100m. **DIR:** Stephen Frears. **CAST:** Colm Meaney, Donal O'Kelly, Ger Ryan, Carolyn Rothwell, Brendan O'Carroll. 1997

VAN GOGH ★★ If they keep telling the story of Vincent van Gogh, perhaps somebody will finally get it right. Maurice Pialat did not get it right in this long, dull exercise. Pialat's point with the story of the famous painter is to emphasize the mundane. It's a noble idea, but how do you make the mundane interesting for observers? Especially for nearly three hours? In French with English subtitles. 158m. **DIR:** Maurice Pialat. **CAST:** Jacques Dutronc, Bernard Le Coq, Gérard Séty, Alexandra London. 1991

●**VANINA VANINI** ★★1/2 Set in Italy in the 1800s, this film mixes politics and romance when a princess falls in love with a revolutionary on a mission to kill a traitor. One of director Roberto Rossellini's least memorable films: at the very least, it's difficult to understand fully unless you're a student of Italian history. Originally released in America as *The Betrayer*. In Italian with English subtitles. B&W; 125m. **DIR:** Roberto Rossellini. **CAST:** Martine Carol, Olimpia Cava, Sandra Milo, Laurent Terzieff. 1961

VANISHING, THE (1988) ★★★★★ Superb thriller as well as an insightful portrait of a sociopath. The mysterious disappearance of his girlfriend leads Rex on an obsessive quest that results in a confrontation with her killer. The violence (including an unforgettable ending) is understated. Donnadieu's portrayal of the villain quietly freezes the blood. In Dutch and French with English subtitles. Rated R for adult content. 107m. **DIR:** George Sluizer. **CAST:** Bernard Pierre Donnadieu, Gene Bervoets, Johanna ter Steege. 1988

VANISHING, THE (1993) ★★★1/2 Director George Sluizer's Americanized remake of his superb, 1988 Dutch thriller suffers from an imbalance caused by an overemphasis on the sociopathic killer. Rated R for profanity and violence. 120m. **DIR:** George Sluizer. **CAST:** Jeff Bridges, Kiefer Sutherland, Nancy Travis, Sandra Bullock, Park Overall, Maggie Linderman, Lisa Eichhorn. 1993

VANISHING ACT ★★★1/2 A tense psychological drama with a knockout ending. Mike Farrell's wife of one week is missing. He routinely reports this to town cop Elliot Gould. Before the investigation begins, the wife reappears. But Farrell says she's not his wife. Rated PG. 95m. **DIR:** David Greene. **CAST:** Mike Farrell, Margot Kidder, Elliott Gould, Fred Gwynne, Graham Jarvis. 1987

VANISHING AMERICAN, THE ★★★1/2 One of the few major studio releases of the silent era to treat the American Indian with compassion and dignity, this is a beautifully photographed silent gem from Paramount. Based on Zane Grey's popular melodramatic adventure, this landmark film is still historically important as well as being a fine job by director George Seitz. Silent. B&W; 114m. **DIR:** George B. Seitz. **CAST:** Richard Dix, Lois Wilson, Noah Beery Sr., Charles Stevens. 1925

VANISHING POINT ★★1/2 Interesting story of a marathon car chase through Colorado and California. Cleavon Little gives a standout performance as the disc jockey who helps a driver (Barry Newman) elude the police. Richard Sarafian's direction is competent, but the story eventually runs out of gas before the film ends. Rated PG. 107m. **DIR:** Richard C. Sarafian. **CAST:** Cleavon Little, Barry Newman, Dean Jagger. 1971

VANISHING PRAIRIE, THE ★★★1/2 Award-winning true-life adventure from Walt Disney ranks with *The Living Desert* as the finest (and certainly most widely seen) nature film of the 1950s. Beautifully photographed, this is a fun but sobering movie the whole family can enjoy. 75m. **DIR:** James Algar. 1954

VANITY FAIR 💣 In updating Thackeray's classic *Vanity Fair*, screenwriter F. Hugh Herbert and director Chester M. Franklin have created a disaster. B&W; 78m. **DIR:** Chester M. Franklin. **CAST:** Myrna Loy, Conway Tearle, Barbara Kent, Anthony Bushell. 1938

VANYA ON 42ND STREET ★★★★★ A workshop production of Anton Chekhov's *Uncle Vanya*, performed in an abandoned Manhattan theater by actors in modern dress. Without the distraction of period sets and costumes, the splendid ensemble cast cuts right to the heart of Chekhov's great (and surprisingly modern) play. A filmed experiment in which everything goes marvelously right. Rated PG. 119m. **DIR:** Louis Malle. **CAST:** Wallace Shawn, Julianne Moore, Larry Pine, Brooke Smith, George Gaynes. **1994**

VARAN, THE UNBELIEVABLE ★★1/2 Another Godzilla rip-off with better-than-average effects. B&W; 70m. **DIR:** Inoshiro Honda. **CAST:** Jerry Baerwitz, Myron Healey, Tsuruko Kobayashi. **1962**

VARIETY ★★★★★ A milestone of cinema art. It tells a simple, tragic tale of a famous and conceited vaudeville acrobat whose character flaw is cowardice; a clever and entirely unscrupulous girl; and a trusting waterfront circus boss—made a fool of by love—who murders because of that hollow love. The cast is incredible, the cinematography superb. Silent. B&W; 104m. **DIR:** E. A. Dupont. **CAST:** Emil Jannings, Lya de Putti. **1926**

VARIETY LIGHTS ★★★★ This is Federico Fellini's first film, though it's not entirely his. (It's codirected by Alberto Lattuada.) Still, Fellini fans will recognize themes of fantasy and illusion and the pursuit of impossible-to-capture dreams, as well as the presence of the sublime Giulietta Masina. In Italian with English subtitles. 93m. **DIR:** Federico Fellini, Alberto Lattuada. **CAST:** Peppino De Filippo, Carla Del Poggio, Giulietta Masina. **1950**

VARSITY BLUES ★★★1/2 This raucous high-school fantasy rises above stereotypes, thanks to W. Peter Iliff's thoughtful script about restless young men—and women—desperately trying to escape their dead-end, small-town environments. In West Canaan, Texas, the best hope is football, and the players are elevated to the status of local gods. The tale may be wholly predictable, but it's told with honesty, conviction, and a sound moral foundation. Rated R for profanity, nudity, and sexual content. 106m. **DIR:** Brian Robbins. **CAST:** James van der Beek, Jon Voight, Paul Walker, Ron Lester, Scott Caan, Richard Lineback, Tiffany C. Love, Amy Smart. **1999 DVD**

VASECTOMY ★★1/2 A bank vice president (Paul Sorvino) is having plenty of family problems. After bearing their eighth child, his wife urges him to have a vasectomy while other family members are stealing from his bank. This comedy is rated R for nudity and obscenities. 92m. **DIR:** Robert Burge. **CAST:** Paul Sorvino, Abe Vigoda, Cassandra Edwards, Lorne Greene. **1986**

VAULT OF HORROR ★★ British sequel to *Tales from the Crypt* boasts a fine cast and five short stories borrowed from the classic EC comics line of the early 1950s, but delivers very little in the way of true chills and atmosphere. Not nearly as effective as the earlier five-story thriller *Dr. Terror's House of Horrors* and not as much fun as the most recent homage to the EC horror story, *Creepshow.* Rated R. 87m. **DIR:** Roy Ward Baker. **CAST:** Daniel Massey, Anna Massey, Terry-Thomas, Glynis Johns, Curt Jurgens, Dawn Addams, Tom Baker, Denholm Elliott, Michael Craig, Edward Judd. **1973**

VEGA$ ★★1/2 A few days in the life of a high-flying, T-Bird-driving private eye whose beat is highways, byways, and gambling casinos of Las Vegas. Robert Urich, an ex-cop, is hired to find a runaway teenage girl who's gotten in too deep with the sleazy side of Fortune Town. 104m. **DIR:** Richard Lang. **CAST:** Robert Urich, Judy Landers, Tony Curtis, Will Sampson, Greg Morris. **1978**

VEGAS IN SPACE 🎬 Bad acting, bad sets, bad costumes, and bad dialogue are the high points of this outer space dragfest. Not rated; contains profanity, nudity, and adult situations. 85m. **DIR:** Philip Ford. **CAST:** Doris Fish, Miss X, Ginger Quest, Ramona Fisher. **1995**

VEGAS VACATION ★★★ The Griswolds arrive in Las Vegas: Dad becomes a gambling addict, Mom is courted by Wayne Newton, their son hooks up with hood-type high rollers, and their daughter goes out with a stripper. All this is fun but pales in comparison to Randy Quaid's performance as their unbalanced cousin. Rated PG for sexual situations. 90m. **DIR:** Stephen Kessler. **CAST:** Chevy Chase, Beverly D'Angelo, Randy Quaid, Wayne Newton, Ethan Embry, Wallace Shawn. **1997 DVD**

●**VELOCITY OF GARY, THE** ★★1/2 Vincent D'Onofrio is the main reason to watch this conventional drama revolving around a love triangle between two men and a woman. He plays a porno star who attracts a telephone sex operator and a waitress, who can't stand each other, but are forced to reconcile their differences when D'Onofrio becomes ill. Director Dan Ireland creates lots of pretty pictures but not much heat or heart. Rated R for adult situations, language, and violence. 110m. **DIR:** Dan Ireland. **CAST:** Vincent D'Onofrio, Thomas Jane, Salma Hayek. **1998**

●**VELOCITY TRAP** 🎬 In this very bad sci-fi movie, Olivier Gruner plays a man framed for murder, who must come to the rescue of a multibillion dollar starship that is threatened by space pirates and asteroids. Rated R for violence, language, and sexual situations. 89m. **DIR:** Phillip Roth. **CAST:** Olivier Gruner, Alicia Coppola, Bruce Weitz. **1998 DVD**

VELVET GOLDMINE ★★ This lurid fantasy revisits the world of 1970s glam rock associated with David Bowie, Marc Bolan, and Iggy Pop. It is awash in sultry leers of androgynous male rockers and star power, nostalgia, decadence, self-identity, and obsession. Fascinating only in spurts. Rated R for sex, nudity, profanity, and drug use. 117m. **DIR:** Todd Haynes. **CAST:** Christian Bale, Jonathan Rhys-Meyers, Ewan McGregor, Toni Collette, Eddie Izzard. **1998 DVD**

VELVET TOUCH, THE ★★★★1/2 This is a marvelous suspense-drama featuring Rosalind Russell as a stage actress. In a fit of rage, she kills her jealous producer, a blackmailer. Leo Rosten's screenplay crackles with spirit and polish. B&W; 97m. **DIR:** John Gage. **CAST:** Rosalind Russell, Leo Genn, Claire Trevor, Leon Ames, Sydney Greenstreet, Frank McHugh, Lex Barker. **1948**

VELVET VAMPIRE, THE ★★ Marginally unconventional low-budget horror about a young married couple vampirized by a sultry femme fatale. A few scenes are effective, but overall film is so slackly paced that it never generates any suspense. Rated R. 79m. **DIR:** Stephanie Rothman. **CAST:** Sherry Miles, Michael Blodgett, Celeste Yarnall. **1971**

VENDETTA (1985) 🎬 A laughably bad women's prison flick. Rated R. 89m. **DIR:** Bruce Logan. **CAST:**

Karen Chase, Sandy Martin, Roberta Collins, Kin Shriner. 1985

•VENDETTA (1999) ★★★1/2 Italian immigrants run afoul of racism and entrenched backroom politics in this sprawling, fact-based account of the largest lynching in U.S. history, which took place in New Orleans in 1890, when businessmen decided that they wanted to take over the docks controlled—mostly peacefully—by hard-working Italians. The story is seen through the eyes of a newly arrived young man who further compounds his plight by falling in love with an Irish girl. It all boils into a full-blown riot and racial bloodbath on par with the worst deep-South lynchings. Director Nicholas Meyer, always intrigued by little-known historical events, deserves credit for helping bring this atrocity to light; scripter Timothy Prager commendably condenses the events of Richard Gambino's far more ambitious book, which no doubt will be embraced by viewers wanting to learn more after seeing this film. Rated R for violence and torture. 117m. DIR: Nicholas Meyer. CAST: Luke Askew, Clancy Brown, Andrew Connolly, Bruce Davison, Joaquim de Almeida, Andrea di Stefano, Edward Herrmann, Richard Libertini, Christopher Walken. 1999 DVD

VENGEANCE ♥ Dull account of an escape from a Latin American prison camp. Not rated, the film has graphic violence and sex. 114m. DIR: Antonio Isasi. CAST: Jason Miller, Lea Massari, Marisa Peredes. 1987

VENGEANCE IS MINE (1976) ★★ A stark and brutal story of backcountry justice. Murderous bank robbers run into Ernest Borgnine, who matches brutality with brutality. A bleak and stilted movie. Not rated; contains violence and profanity. 90m. DIR: John Trent. CAST: Ernest Borgnine, Michael J. Pollard, Hollis McLaren. 1976

VENGEANCE IS MINE (1979) ★★★★ Terrifying, complex portrait of a mass murderer, played with chilling detachment by Ken Ogata. Shohei Imamura, Japan's most controversial director, has created a nightmarish film that is both poignant and disturbing in its depiction of a psychopathic mind at work. In Japanese with English subtitles. Not rated but contains scenes of graphic violence and nudity. 129m. DIR: Shohei Imamura. CAST: Ken Ogata. 1979

•VENGEANCE OF SHE, THE ★★★ Loose sequel to the Ursula Andress film version of H. Rider Haggard's She is an enjoyable romp with all the prerequisites for a fun adventure movie. Sexy Olinka Berova doesn't remember who she is. All she knows is that she is drawn to a lost city in the mountains where an evil priest is trying to lure her to her death. Rated G. 100m. DIR: Cliff Owen. CAST: Olinka Berova, Edward Judd, John Richardson, Andre Morell, George Sewell. 1968 DVD

VENGEANCE VALLEY ★★ Slow-moving story of no-good cattle heir Robert Walker and his protective foster brother Burt Lancaster lacks suspense and doesn't have enough action. 83m. DIR: Richard Thorpe. CAST: Burt Lancaster, Robert Walker, Joanne Dru, Ray Collins, John Ireland, Sally Forrest. 1951 DVD

VENICE/VENICE ★★★★ Henry Jaglom portrays a filmmaker at the Venice Film Festival doing the usual rounds of publicity until he's introduced to a

female journalist from France. Their mutual interest continues through the festival and back at the filmmaker's home in Venice, California. (Hence, Venice/Venice). Highly enjoyable. Rated PG. 108m. DIR: Henry Jaglom. CAST: Henry Jaglom, Nelly Alard, Suzanne Bertish, Daphna Kastner, David Duchovny. 1992

VENOM ♥ This combination horror film and police thriller doesn't really work as either. Rated R for nudity and violence. 98m. DIR: Piers Haggard. CAST: Nicol Williamson, Klaus Kinski, Susan George, Oliver Reed, Sterling Hayden, Sarah Miles. 1982

VENUS IN FURS ♥ Poor mystery involving a musician and a mutilated woman who washes ashore. Rated R. 86m. DIR: Jess (Jesus) Franco. CAST: James Darren, Barbara McNair, Klaus Kinski, Dennis Price. 1970

VENUS RISING ★★ When a man and woman escape from a brutal, futuristic prison, they travel back to civilization where they discover a world controlled by drugs and virtual reality. Maybe prison was better. Rated R for profanity, violence, and nudity. 91m. DIR: Leora Barish. CAST: Billy Wirth, Audie England, Costas Mandylor, Meredith Salenger, Morgan Fairchild, Joel Grey. 1995

VENUS WARS, THE ★★★★ Outstanding example of the art of Japanese animation, certainly one of the finest available in America. Set on barren Venus in the twenty-first century, the story follows young Hiro and his friends, members of a racing team. All the excitement of Akira, with a better (and more coherent) story. In Japanese with English subtitles. Not rated; contains violence. 104m. DIR: Yoshikazu Yasuhiko. 1989 DVD

VERA CRUZ ★★★ Two American soldiers of fortune find themselves in different camps during one of the many Mexican revolutions of the 1800s. Gary Cooper is the good guy, but Burt Lancaster steals every scene as the smiling, black-dressed baddie. The plot is pretty basic but holds your interest until the traditional climactic gunfight. 94m. DIR: Robert Aldrich. CAST: Gary Cooper, Burt Lancaster, Denise Darcel, Ernest Borgnine. 1954

VERDICT, THE ★★★★1/2 In this first-rate drama, Paul Newman brilliantly plays an alcoholic Boston lawyer who redeems himself by taking on slick James Mason in a medical malpractice suit. Rated R for profanity and adult situations. 129m. DIR: Sidney Lumet. CAST: Paul Newman, James Mason, Charlotte Rampling, Jack Warden. 1982

VERMONT IS FOR LOVERS ★★ A couple of New York yuppies decide to tie the knot at a Vermont farm, but nearly talk us to death before the ceremony. Writer-director John O'Brien's casual, improvisational style is interesting enough to make you wonder what he could do with real actors and a viable budget. Not rated. 88m. DIR: John O'Brien. CAST: George Thrush, Marya Cohn, Ann O'Brien, Euclid Farnham. 1993

VERNE MILLER ★★ Scott Glenn stars as the infamous gunman who masterminded and executed the violent Kansas City massacre at the insistence of crime czar Al Capone. Too many dull gunfights and too little story line or character development. Rated

R for nudity and violence. 95m. **DIR:** Rod Hewitt. **CAST:** Scott Glenn, Barbara Stock, Thomas Waites, Lucinda Jenney, Sonny Carl Davis, Andrew Robinson. **1988**

VERNON, FLORIDA ★★★ Weirdos of the world seem to have united and set up housekeeping in Vernon, Florida. This unique and off-the-wall film comes from the strange vision of director Errol Morris. In this slice of life, the viewers become acquainted with (and amused by) the citizens of this slightly off-center small town. Not rated. 60m. **DIR:** Errol Morris. **1988**

VERONIKA VOSS ★★ A famous German actress tries to revive her flagging career with alcohol and drugs in this final addition to Rainer Werner Fassbinder's trilogy about the collapse of the West German postwar dream. While technically a well-made movie, Fassbinder's point is lost amid the bleak shadow life of the losers he so skillfully captures. In German with English subtitles. Rated R. 105m. **DIR:** Rainer Werner Fassbinder. **CAST:** Rosel Zech, Hilmar Thate. **1982**

VERTIGO ★★★★1/2 The first hour of this production is slow, gimmicky, and artificial. However, the rest of this suspense picture takes off at high speed. James Stewart stars as a San Francisco detective who has a fear of heights and is hired to shadow an old friend's wife (Kim Novak). He finds himself falling in love with her—then tragedy strikes. 128m. **DIR:** Alfred Hitchcock. **CAST:** James Stewart, Kim Novak, Barbara Bel Geddes. **1958 DVD**

VERY BAD THINGS ★★ The accidental killing of a hooker at a bachelor party snowballs into a nightmare of murder and mutilation. Writer-director Peter Berg clearly means this to be an outrageous black comedy, but there's not a laugh to be had from beginning to end; Berg shows little flair for even conventional comedy, let alone the kind that hinges on death and dismemberment. Rated R for profanity, sexual scenes, and several gruesome deaths. 101m. **DIR:** Peter Berg. **CAST:** Christian Slater, Jon Favreau, Cameron Diaz, Daniel Stern, Jeremy Piven, Jeanne Tripplehorn, Leland Orser. **1998 DVD**

VERY BRADY CHRISTMAS, A ★★★★ One of television's most revered families decides to get together for Christmas. All of the kids have grown up, and all but one of the original stars return to help. A little sappy, a little corny, but part of the American culture. 94m. **DIR:** Peter Baldwin. **CAST:** Robert Reed, Florence Henderson, Ann B. Davis. **1988**

VERY BRADY SEQUEL, A ★★★ While *The Brady Bunch Movie* drew guffaws, the sequel elicits genuine belly laughs. While Marcia and Greg have the hots for each other, a handsome stranger appears claiming to be Carol's first husband. Comic highlights include the teens' angst and the entire family's outdated trust and good cheer. Rated PG-13 for mild profanity and sexual innuendo. 90m. **DIR:** Arlene Sanford. **CAST:** Shelley Long, Gary Cole, Tim Matheson, Christine Taylor, Christopher Daniel Barnes. **1996**

VERY BRITISH COUP, A ★★★1/2 A very confusing tale about a socialist prime minister who succeeds at maintaining his ideals against the established British government. Ray McAnally does a wonderful job portraying the prime minister, and the editing is excellent, but the plot needs some work. Not rated. 180m. **DIR:** Mick Jackson. **CAST:** Ray McAnally, Alan MacNaughton, Keith Allen, Geoffrey Beevers, Jim Carter, Philip Madoc, Tim McInnerny, Marjorie Yates. **1988**

VERY CURIOUS GIRL, A ★★★ A village girl who has been sexually exploited by the town fathers gets revenge by charging for her "services." Broad (sometimes too broad) social satire. In French with English subtitles. Rated R for sexual content. 105m. **DIR:** Nelly Kaplan. **CAST:** Bernadette Lafont, Georges Geret, Michel Constantin. **1970**

VERY EDGE, THE ★★★ An ex-model loses the child she is carrying after she is raped. Her trauma puts a strain on her marriage, while her attacker is still on the loose. Effective psychological suspense, marred slightly by a contrived ending. B&W; 82m. **DIR:** Cyril Frankel. **CAST:** Anne Heywood, Richard Todd, Jack Hedley, Maurice Denham, Patrick Magee. **1963**

VERY NATURAL THING, A ★★1/2 A blast from the past, this 1973 drama was one of the first gay films to be released into the mainstream. Robert Joel stars as Jason, a 26-year-old gay man who leaves the priesthood and moves to New York in search of true love. What may have been daring more than twenty years ago now appears tame and campy. Film's depiction of uninhibited behavior in the pre-AIDS era may make some nostalgic. Not rated; contains nudity and adult situations. 85m. **DIR:** Christopher Larkin. **CAST:** Robert Joel, Curt Gareth, Bo White. **1973 DVD**

VERY OLD MAN WITH ENORMOUS WINGS, A ★★★★ A winged man lands inexplicably in a tiny Colombian village. People flock in droves to the new attraction, and a huge carnival is born, spewed forth from the womb of human superstition and curiosity. A frenetically frenzied furor full of fantastic, colorful absurdity. In Spanish with English subtitles. Rated R for nudity and simulated sex. 90m. **DIR:** Fernando Birri. **CAST:** Daisy Granados, Asdrubal Melendez. **1988**

VERY PRIVATE AFFAIR, A ★★★ Bardot fan, or just never had a chance to see her? In this romantic drama she plays a famous movie star who can no longer cope with notoriety, so she retreats from public scrutiny. Marcello Mastroianni is equally appealing as a director coming to her aid. In French with English subtitles. 95m. **DIR:** Louis Malle. **CAST:** Brigitte Bardot, Marcello Mastroianni. **1962**

VIBES ★★ This sad misfire should have been much better, given the track record of scripters Lowell Ganz and Babaloo Mandel, but the talented parts simply don't make an impressive whole. Cyndi Lauper and Jeff Goldblum play psychic hotshots hired by shifty Peter Falk, but everything plods along to a foolish finale. Rated PG. 99m. **DIR:** Ken Kwapis. **CAST:** Cyndi Lauper, Jeff Goldblum, Julian Sands, Peter Falk. **1988**

VIBRATIONS ♥ A recently crippled rock 'n' roller finds a friend in a metaphysical good Samaritan who unwittingly helps him come to terms with his new condition. Contrived, overplayed, and loaded with clichés. Rated R for language. 103m. **DIR:** Michael Paseornek. **CAST:** James Marshall, Christina Applegate, Faye Grant, Paige Turco. **1994**

VICE SQUAD ★★★1/2 Slick, fast-paced thriller set in the seamy world of pimps and prostitutes. Season Hubley is an adorable mom by day and a smart-mouthed hooker by night forced to help cop Gary Swanson capture a sicko killer, played with frightening intensity by Wings Hauser. A total fairy tale, but it moves quickly enough to mask improbabilities. Not for the squeamish. Rated R. 97m. **DIR:** Gary A. Sherman. **CAST:** Season Hubley, Wings Hauser, Gary Swanson, Beverly Todd. **1982**

VICE VERSA ★★★1/2 Young Fred Savage nearly steals the show from Judge Reinhold in this surprisingly entertaining comedy about a father who changes bodies with his son. We've seen it all many times before in lesser films such as *Freaky Friday* and *Like Father, Like Son*. However, the writing of Dick Clement and Ian De Frenais and the chemistry of the players make it seem almost fresh. Rated PG for profanity. 98m. **DIR:** Brian Gilbert. **CAST:** Judge Reinhold, Fred Savage, Swoosie Kurtz, Jane Kaczmarek, David Proval, William Prince. **1988**

VICIOUS ★★ In this bland Australian film a young man is unwittingly the provocateur of a sadistic attack on his wealthy girlfriend and her parents by a trio of thugs. The ensuing revenge is predictable. Rated R for graphic violence. 90m. **DIR:** Karl Zwicky. **CAST:** Tamblyn Lord, Craig Pearce. **1988**

VICIOUS CIRCLES ★★★ Kinky tale of an American woman who is forced to work as a prostitute for a mysterious gentleman in order to raise money to free her brother, who is in jail on drug-possession charges. Available in R-rated and not-rated versions; both contain adult situations, language, nudity, and violence. 90m. **DIR:** Alexander Whitelaw. **CAST:** Carolyn Lowery, Ben Gazzara, Paul Hipp, Jerome Davis. **1997**

VICIOUS SWEET, THE ★★★ Scream queen Sasha Graham finds herself kidnapped by an obsessed fan. The powerplay that goes on between these two never lets the momentum lag. Not rated; contains profanity and violence. 93m. **DIR:** Ron Bonk. **CAST:** Sasha Graham, Robert Licata. **1997**

VICTIM ★★★ One of the first films to deal with homosexuality, this well-made British effort has Dirk Bogarde as a lawyer confronting blackmailers who killed his lover. It was daring then, but not now. The story, though, is still interesting. B&W; 100m. **DIR:** Basil Dearden. **CAST:** Dirk Bogarde, Sylvia Syms, Dennis Price, John Barrie. **1961**

VICTIM OF LOVE ★★1/2 Psychologist JoBeth Williams finds herself in a quandary when she falls for professor Pierce Brosnan, who is having an affair with her patient Virginia Madsen. Director Jerry London keeps this made-for-television thriller on its toes, and additional footage added to the video adds just the right risqué touch. 92m. **DIR:** Jerry London. **CAST:** Pierce Brosnan, JoBeth Williams, Virginia Madsen. **1991 DVD**

VICTIMLESS CRIMES ★★1/2 Conspiracy and betrayal in the art world. Everyone from the gallery owner to the insurance company are making a buck off stolen paintings, until the artist decides that he's about to make a killing, too! Rated R for violence.

85m. **DIR:** Peter Hawley. **CAST:** Debra Sandlund, Craig Bierko. **1990**

VICTOR/VICTORIA ★★★★ Director Blake Edwards takes us on a funny, off-the-wall romp through 1930s Paris. Julie Andrews plays a down-on-her-luck singer who poses as a gay Polish count to make ends meet. Rated PG because of adult situations. 133m. **DIR:** Blake Edwards. **CAST:** Julie Andrews, James Garner, Robert Preston, Lesley Ann Warren. **1982**

•**VICTORY (1919)** ★★★ Man who lives a life of solitude on an island surrounded by books and ideas faces change when romance and danger invade his privacy. Silent version of Joseph Conrad's oft-filmed story is a mature drama with some very heavyweight scoundrels sleazing up the tropics. Lon Chaney as a knife-wielding sadist is outstanding. B&W; 51m. **DIR:** Maurice Tourneu. **CAST:** Jack Holt, Seena Owen, Ben Deely, Wallace Beery, Lon Chaney Sr., Bull Montana. **1919**

VICTORY (1981) ★★★ Sylvester Stallone and Michael Caine star in this entertaining but predictable World War II drama about a soccer game between Allied prisoners of war and the Nazis. With a title like *Victory*, guess who wins. Rated PG. 110m. **DIR:** John Huston. **CAST:** Sylvester Stallone, Michael Caine, Pelé, Max von Sydow. **1981 DVD**

VICTORY AT ENTEBBE ★★ All-star cast helps made-for-television film about the raid by Israeli commandos to free Jewish hostages being held by Arab terrorists in Uganda. Docudrama fails to capture the truth of the moment and instead relies on cardboard characters to tell the story. 150m. **DIR:** Marvin J. Chomsky. **CAST:** Kirk Douglas, Burt Lancaster, Helen Hayes, Helmut Berger, Theodore Bikel, Elizabeth Taylor, Linda Blair, Anthony Hopkins, Jessica Walter. **1976**

VIDEODROME ★★1/2 Director David Cronenberg strikes again with a clever, gory nightmare set in the world of television broadcasting. James Woods and Deborah Harry (of the rock group Blondie) star in this eerie, occasionally sickening horror film about the boss (Woods) of a cable TV station. Rated R for profanity, nudity, violence, gore, and pure nausea. 88m. **DIR:** David Cronenberg. **CAST:** James Woods, Deborah Harry, Sonja Smits. **1983 DVD**

VIETNAM, TEXAS ★★1/2 A Texas priest, haunted by guilt over the pregnant woman he abandoned when he was a soldier in Vietnam, tracks her down in Houston. He determines to save her from the drug-running mobster she has married. Shoot-'em-up with a social conscience. Rated R for violence. 92m. **DIR:** Robert Ginty. **CAST:** Robert Ginty, Haing S. Ngor, Tim Thomerson. **1990**

VIETNAM WAR STORY ★★★★ This is a collection of three outstanding episodes from HBO's short-term series. *The Pass* dramatizes one soldier's reluctance to return to duty. *The Mine* is about an independent soldier's reliance on others when he is trapped on a land mine. *Home* concerns disabled veterans in a hospital. All are heart-wrenching. There are no stars in the cast, but all performances are top-rate. Not rated, but for mature audiences. 90m. **DIR:** Kevin Hooks, Georg Stanford Brown, Ray

Danton. CAST: Eriq La Salle, Nicholas Cascone, Tony Becker. 1988

VIETNAM WAR STORY—PART TWO ★★★★ Three more segments of the HBO series: *An Old Ghost Walks the Earth; R&R* and *The Flagging.* Not rated, but for mature audiences. 90m. DIR: Michael Toshiyuki Uno, David Morris, Jack Sholder. CAST: Tim Guinee, Cynthia Bain. 1988

VIEW TO A KILL, A ★★★ Despite a spectacular opening sequence, the James Bond series is starting to look a little old and tired—just like Roger Moore. Christopher Walken costars as the maniacal villain who plans to corner the world's microchip market by flooding the San Andreas Fault. For fans only. Rated PG for violence and suggested sex. 131m. DIR: John Glen. CAST: Roger Moore, Tanya Roberts, Christopher Walken, Grace Jones. 1985

VIGIL ★★★ After the death of her father, a New Zealand farm girl observes the positive changes in her family brought on by the arrival of a young drifter. Compelling film is rich in visual imagery and texture. 90m. DIR: Vincent Ward. CAST: Penelope Stewart, Fiona Kay, Frank Whitten, Bill Kerr. 1984

VIGILANTE ★★ After the death of his son, a cop joins a vigilante group to clean up the streets. It's all been done before, but the cast is game and the direction crisp. Rated R for violence and profanity. 91m. DIR: William Lustig. CAST: Fred Williamson, Carol Lynley, Robert Forster, Joe Spinell, Rutanya Alda. 1982 DVD

VIGILANTES ARE COMING! ★★1/2 This early Republic serial features Robert Livingston in a story suspiciously similar to the Zorro legend: A young man returns to 1840s California and finds that an evil despot has taken his family's lands so he dons a mask and robe and finds the oppressor under the name of The Eagle. Action-packed and with impressive stunts. B&W; 12 chapters. DIR: Mack V. Wright, Ray Taylor. CAST: Robert Livingston, Kay Hughes, Guinn Williams, Raymond Hatton, Fred Kohler Sr., William Farnum, Bob Kortman, Ray "Crash" Corrigan, Yakima Canutt. 1936

VIGILANTES OF BOOMTOWN ★★★1/2 Factions oppose the sanctioning of the heavyweight boxing bout between James Corbett and Bob Fitzsimmons in 1897 Carson City, Nevada. It takes Red Ryder to keep peace between the two pugilists as well as rout bank robbers and foil a kidnapping. B&W; 54m. DIR: R. G. Springsteen. CAST: Allan "Rocky" Lane, Bobby Blake, Peggy Stewart, Roy Barcroft, George Chesebro. 1947

VIKING SAGAS, THE ★★1/2 Gorgeously filmed but rather pedestrian tale of revenge and redemption. Cinematographer Michael Chapman (*Raging Bull*) directed this familiar tale of one man's quest for revenge after his father has been killed and his people are run off their land. Lots of swordplay enhances the action scenes, but the performances are pretty dull. Rated R for violence and nudity. 83m. DIR: Michael Chapman. CAST: Ralph Moeller, Ingibjorg Stefansdottir, Sven-Ole Thorsen. 1995

VIKINGS, THE ★★★1/2 Well-done action film following the exploits of a group of Vikings (led by Tony Curtis and Kirk Douglas). Many good battle scenes and beautiful photography and locations make the picture a standout. Ernest Borgnine gives a great performance. Don't miss it. 114m. DIR: Richard Fleischer. CAST: Kirk Douglas, Tony Curtis, Ernest Borgnine, Janet Leigh. 1958

VILLA RIDES ★★ Uneven rehash of the Pancho Villa legend ignores the wealth of the real story and becomes yet another comic-book adventure. Good cast, but this ill-fated production doesn't deliver what it should. 125m. DIR: Buzz Kulik. CAST: Yul Brynner, Robert Mitchum, Charles Bronson, Herbert Lom, Jill Ireland, Alexander Knox, Fernando Rey. 1968

VILLAGE OF THE DAMNED (1960) ★★★★ A science-fiction thriller about twelve strangely emotionless children all born at the same time in a small village in England. George Sanders plays their teacher, who tries to stop their plans for conquest. This excellent low-budget film provides chills. B&W; 78m. DIR: Wolf Rilla. CAST: George Sanders, Barbara Shelley, Michael C. Gwynne. 1960

VILLAGE OF THE DAMNED (1995) ★★1/2 Although reasonably faithful to its predecessor and John Wyndham's original novel (*The Midwich Cuckoos*), this updated remake is remarkably lifeless. Rather than radiating menace, the malevolent "children from space" evoke laughter. Inexplicably rated R for restrained violence. 98m. DIR: John Carpenter. CAST: Christopher Reeve, Kirstie Alley, Linda Kozlowski, Mark Hamill, Meredith Salenger, Michael Paré. 1995 DVD

VILLAGE OF THE GIANTS ★★ Utterly ridiculous story of a gang of teenage misfits taking over a small town after they ingest a bizarre substance and grow to gigantic heights. What makes this worth watching, though, are the famous faces of the many young stars-to-be. 80m. DIR: Bert I. Gordon. CAST: Tommy Kirk, Beau Bridges, Ron Howard, Johnny Crawford. 1965

•**VILLAIN, THE** ★★★ Live action *Road Runner* spoof features Kirk Douglas as the much abused Coyote figure and Arnold Schwarzenegger as the clever Road Runner type. There is a noticeable lack of lines for Schwarzenegger, whose English was not yet refined. Ann-Margret plays sort of a damsel in distress. Cameos by Paul Lynde, Ruth Buzzi, Strother Martin, and more add a number of sight gags and one-liners giving this a *Laugh In* feel. This should tickle your funny bone if silliness doesn't turn you off. Rated PG for cartoonish violence. 89m. DIR: Hal Needham. CAST: Kirk Douglas, Arnold Schwarzenegger, Ann-Margret. 1979

VILLAIN STILL PURSUED HER, THE 💙 Dull, old-fashioned melodrama. B&W; 66m. DIR: Eddie Cline. CAST: Anita Louise, Richard Cromwell, Hugh Herbert, Alan Mowbray, Buster Keaton, Billy Gilbert, Margaret Hamilton. 1940

VINCENT AND THEO ★★★★ Based on letters written by the celebrated painter Vincent van Gogh (Tim Roth) to his art-dealer brother, Theo (Paul Rhys), this is a first-rate cinematic biography; perhaps the best ever to be made about the life of a painter. Rated PG-13 for profanity and nudity. 138m. DIR: Robert Altman. CAST: Tim Roth, Paul Rhys, Johanna ter Steege. 1990

VINCENT, FRANÇOIS, PAUL AND THE OTHERS
★★★★★ A deeply moving film about friendship as a band of buddies survive marriage, affairs, and career challenges. Claude Sautet, one of France's most respected directors, gets superb performances from leading and supporting roles. Don't miss this one! In French with English subtitles. Not rated. 118m. **DIR:** Claude Sautet. **CAST:** Yves Montand, Michel Piccoli, Serge Reggiani, Gérard Depardieu, Stéphane Audran, Marie Dubois. **1974**

VINDICATOR, THE ★★ A comic-bookish story about a scientist who is blown up by his evil employers and put back together using cybernetic systems and a nearly indestructible futuristic space suit. Overall, it's a pretty typical story with some thrills and a fair amount of action and graphic violence. Rated R for violence, adult language, and brief nudity. 92m. **DIR:** Jean-Claude Lord. **CAST:** Teri Austin, Richard Cox, Pam Grier, Maury Chaykin. **1984**

VIOLATED 💘 Soap-opera starlets are invited to Mafia parties, where they are brutally raped. Rated R for violence and nudity. 90m. **DIR:** Richard Cannistraro. **CAST:** J. C. Quinn, John Heard. **1984**

VIOLENCE AT NOON ★★★1/2 Complex drama about two rape victims and their rapist set against the socialist movement in postwar Japan. Director Nagisa Oshima explores the pathology of a society in which the criminal and victim reside. In Japanese with English subtitles. B&W; 100m. **DIR:** Nagisa Oshima. **CAST:** Saeda Kawaguchi, Akiko Koyama, Kei Sato. **1966**

VIOLENT BREED, THE 💘 The CIA goes into Vietnam to stop a guerrilla gang. Gratuitous nudity and violence galore. 91m. **DIR:** Fernando Di Leo. **CAST:** Henry Silva, Harrison Muller, Woody Strode, Carole André. **1983**

•**VIOLENT COP** ★★★1/2 For his debut as a film director, "Beat" Takeshi Kitano, a popular comedian on Japanese television, plays a *Dirty Harry*–like cop out to uncover a narcotics dealer with links to the police department. This film is better than the average *Dirty Harry* entry, with Kitano fascinating as a man of unshakable ideals. In Japanese with English subtitles. Not rated; but an R equivalent for violence, rape, and drug use. 103m. **DIR:** Takeshi Kitano. **CAST:** Takeshi Kitano, Maiko Kawakami, Shiro Sano. **1989** **DVD**

VIOLENT MEN, THE ★★★ Edward G. Robinson is a crippled cattle baron, manipulated by his greedy wife and brother into a range war with a peace-loving rancher and valley settlers. Good action sequences. 96m. **DIR:** Rudolph Maté. **CAST:** Glenn Ford, Barbara Stanwyck, Edward G. Robinson, Brian Keith, Richard Jaeckel. **1954**

•**VIOLENT NEW BREED** 💘 Vile, repulsive film from goremeister Todd Sheets as a group of demons tries to bring about the birth of the Antichrist in the form of a little girl. Not rated; contains gore, violence, nudity, and profanity. 121m. **DIR:** Todd Sheets. **CAST:** Mark Glover, Nick Stodden, Jennifer Geigel, Rudy Ray Moore. **1996**

VIOLENT YEARS, THE ★★ The screenwriter of this camp classic was Edward D. Wood Jr., and it bears his unmistakable touch. A gang of rich girls don men's clothing and rob gas stations. In their spare time, they pet heavily at a combination pajama-cocktail party, rape a lover's-lane Lothario, and even get involved in an international communist conspiracy! Their response to every query is a sneered "So what?" A must-see for buffs of bad movies! 65m. **DIR:** Franz Eichorn. **CAST:** Jean Moorehead, Barbara Weeks, Glenn Corbett, I. Stanford Jolley. **1956**

VIOLETS ARE BLUE ★★★1/2 In this watchable screen soap opera, former sweethearts Sissy Spacek and Kevin Kline are reunited when she, a successful photojournalist, returns to her hometown. Their romance is rekindled although he is now married (to Bonnie Bedelia, who is terrific in her all-too-brief on-screen bits). Rated PG for suggested sex and light profanity. 89m. **DIR:** Jack Fisk. **CAST:** Sissy Spacek, Kevin Kline, Bonnie Bedelia, Augusta Dabney. **1986**

•**VIOLETTE** ★★★★ Based on a true story that scandalized Paris in the 1930s, Isabelle Huppert plays a promiscuous young woman who tried to murder her parents in order to get their money. Her performance (for which she was awarded Best Actress at Cannes) is the best thing about this well-crafted but somewhat chilly movie. In French with English subtitles. Not rated, but an R equivalent for violence and sexual themes. 123m. **DIR:** Claude Chabrol. **CAST:** Isabelle Huppert, Stéphane Audran, Jean Carmet. **1997**

VIPER 💘 A CIA operation breaks into a university and kills the members of the administration. Rated R for language and violence. 96m. **DIR:** Peter Maris. **CAST:** Linda Purl, James Tolkan, Jeff Kober, Chris Robinson. **1988**

V.I.P.S, THE ★★★ The problems of an assortment of passengers stranded at a London airport get glossy treatment in this drama thrown together to cash in on the real-life romance of Elizabeth Taylor and Richard Burton. The stars are easily upstaged by the solid supporting cast, especially Maggie Smith and Oscar-winner Margaret Rutherford. Not rated. 119m. **DIR:** Anthony Asquith. **CAST:** Elizabeth Taylor, Richard Burton, Margaret Rutherford, Maggie Smith, Rod Taylor, Louis Jourdan, Orson Welles. **1963**

VIRGIN AMONG THE LIVING DEAD, A 💘 Available only in a severely cut version, this sub-gothic, damsel-in-distress snoozer is an atypical entry from its director's most prolific period—although the undead attack footage was shot eight years later by Jean Rollin during the making of *Zombie Lake*, and spliced in to make this English-language print releasable! 90m. **DIR:** Jess (Jesus) Franco. **CAST:** Christina von Blanc, Anne Libert, Howard Vernon. **1971**

VIRGIN AND THE GYPSY, THE ★★★1/2 The title tells the tale in this stylish, effective screen adaptation of the D. H. Lawrence novella. Franco Nero and Joanna Shimkus exude sexual tension as the gypsy and his love, a minister's daughter. Rated R for nudity. 95m. **DIR:** Christopher Miles. **CAST:** Franco Nero, Joanna Shimkus, Honor Blackman, Mark Burns, Maurice Denham. **1970**

VIRGIN HIGH 💘 Inane tale of a girl sent to a Catholic boarding school in order to protect her virginity. Her boyfriend pursues her, disguising himself as a priest. Gratuitous sleaze downgrades an extremely mediocre teen romance. Rated R for nudity, sex, and profanity. 90m. **DIR:** Richard Gabai. **CAST:** Chris Dempsey, Burt Ward, Linnea Quigley, Tracy Dali. 1990

VIRGIN OF NUREMBERG (HORROR CASTLE) 💘 A hooded killer lurking in an ancient German castle. (Alternate title: *Horror Castle*.) 82m. **DIR:** Anthony M. Dawson. **CAST:** Rossana Podesta, George Riviere, Christopher Lee. 1963

VIRGIN QUEEN, THE ★★★ Bette Davis reprises her memorable 1939 *Elizabeth and Essex* portrayal of Elizabeth I of England in this rehashing of majestic might and young love. This time around the queen dotes on Sir Walter Raleigh, who crosses her up, but survives to sail away to happiness. A fine example of Hollywood film history. 92m. **DIR:** Henry Koster. **CAST:** Bette Davis, Richard Todd, Joan Collins, Herbert Marshall. 1955

VIRGIN QUEEN OF ST. FRANCIS HIGH, THE ★★★ This teen market release has more depth and interest than most in its genre. There's nothing much new in the first half hour, but the two leads, Joseph R. Straface and Stacy Christensen, have winning personalities. The ending is too pat and saccharine, though. Rated PG for profanity. 89m. **DIR:** Francesco Lucente. **CAST:** Joseph R. Straface, Stacy Christensen. 1988

VIRGIN SOLDIERS, THE ★★★★ This outstanding drama of young British recruits in 1950 Singapore has some great performances. Hywel Bennett is one of the recruits who is as green with his first sexual encounter as he is on the battlefield. 96m. **DIR:** John Dexter. **CAST:** Hywel Bennett, Nigel Patrick, Lynn Redgrave, Nigel Davenport. 1969

VIRGIN SPRING, THE ★★★★ Ingmar Bergman's scenario is based on a fourteenth-century Swedish legend. Accompanied by her jealous older stepsister, a young girl is raped and killed while on a journey to her church—and the three killers make the mistake of seeking shelter with the parents. Won an Oscar for best foreign language film. In Swedish with English subtitles. B&W; 87m. **DIR:** Ingmar Bergman. **CAST:** Max von Sydow, Birgitta Pettersson, Gunnel Lindblom. 1960

●**VIRGIN SUICIDES, THE** ★★★1/2 This sweet, sad, dreamlike adaptation of Jeffery Eugenides's novel tackles the issues of budding sexual attraction and teen suicide. The film begins as the youngest of five sisters in an upscale 1970s Michigan suburb kills herself. A former neighborhood boy guides us through a whisper of a mystery propelled by raging hormones, overprotective parents, and the ache of puppy love. Rated R for mature themes. 97m. **DIR:** Sofia Coppola. **CAST:** Kirsten Dunst, Josh Hartnett, Hanna Hall, Kathleen Turner, James Woods, Chelse Sain, A. J. Cook, Leslie Hayman, Jonathan Tucker, Anthony DeSimone. 2000

VIRGINIA CITY ★★★1/2 Errol Flynn's second big-budget Western for Warner Bros. is a hit-and-miss affair about three groups vying for a shipment of gold during the Civil War. B&W; 121m. **DIR:** Michael Curtiz. **CAST:** Errol Flynn, Miriam Hopkins, Randolph Scott, Humphrey Bogart, Alan Hale Sr., Guinn Williams, Frank McHugh, Douglass Dumbrille, John Litel, Ward Bond, Charles Middleton, Paul Fix, Russell Simpson. 1940

VIRGINIAN, THE (1923) ★★ Lackluster version of Owen Wister's classic Western play and novel features good photography and some nice panoramas of the wide-open spaces, but the leads are stiff and the action is lacking. Kenneth Harlan doesn't cut it as the Virginian, and he brings the film down with him. Silent. B&W; 73m. **DIR:** Tom Forman. **CAST:** Kenneth Harlan, Florence Vidor, Russell Simpson, Pat O'Malley, Raymond Hatton. 1923

VIRGINIAN, THE (1929) ★★★★ Although a bit slow in parts, this early Western still impresses today. Gary Cooper is terrific in the title role as a fun-loving but tough ranch foreman who has to face the worst task of his life when a friend falls in with an outlaw. B&W; 90m. **DIR:** Victor Fleming. **CAST:** Gary Cooper, Walter Huston, Mary Brian, Richard Arlen, Eugene Pallette, Chester Conklin. 1929

VIRGINIAN, THE (1946) ★★★ OK remake of the Gary Cooper classic with Joel McCrea in the title role and Brian Donlevy properly menacing as the villain. Even as creaky as it may seem to some viewers, the 1929 version is by far the superior film. 90m. **DIR:** Stuart Gilmore. **CAST:** Joel McCrea, Brian Donlevy, Barbara Britton, Sonny Tufts, Tom Tully, William Frawley, Fay Bainter, Henry O'Neill, Paul Guilfoyle, Marc Lawrence, Minor Watson. 1946

●**VIRGINIAN, THE (1999)** ★★★ Based on Owen Wister's novel, this TNT original allows the cowboy to become a crime-stopping hero. Director Bill Pullman also stars in the title role playing a cowpuncher working a Wyoming ranch in the late 1800s. When he's not struggling with cattle rustlers, he's pursuing the new schoolmarm (Diane Lane) who can't relate to the vigilante justice practiced in the territory. A cameo appearance by TV series *Virginian* James Drury adds a nice touch to a decent time passer. Not rated; contains violence. 95m. **DIR:** Bill Pullman. **CAST:** Bill Pullman, Diane Lane, Dennis Weaver, John Savage, Colm Feore. 1999

VIRIDIANA ★★★★★ Angelic Viridiana (Silvia Pinal) visits her sex-obsessed uncle (Fernando Rey) prior to taking her religious vows. The film was an amazing *cause célèbre* at the time. Much to Spain's and the Catholic Church's consternation, it won the Palme d'Or at Cannes. In Spanish with English subtitles. B&W; 90m. **DIR:** Luis Buñuel. **CAST:** Silvia Pinal, Fernando Rey, Francisco Rabal, Margarita Lozano. 1961

VIRTUAL ASSASSIN ★★ Michael Dudikoff jumps on the information superhighway to come to the aid of a father-daughter team of scientists whose new virus has attracted the interest of a madman who wants to control the world. Rated R for violence, language, and nudity. 99m. **DIR:** Robert Lee. **CAST:** Michael Dudikoff, Suki Kaiser, Brion James, James Thom, Jon Cuthbert. 1995

VIRTUAL COMBAT 💘 Pitiful cyber-thriller about a virtual-reality villain who becomes flesh and blood and challenges the gatekeeper of the grid to a fight to the death. Please! Rated R for violence, nudity, and adult language. 91m. **DIR:** Andrew Stevens.

CAST: Don "The Dragon" Wilson, Athena Massey, Stella Stevens, Loreen Avedon. 1994 DVD

VIRTUAL DESIRE ❤ Ridiculously predictable erotic thriller concerning a cheating husband who must find out which of the lovers he met over the Internet has murdered his wife. Rated R for sexual situations. 90m. DIR: Henri Noble. CAST: Michael Meyer, Ross Hagen, Julie Strain, Gail Harris, Marcia Gray, Tammy Parks, Catherine Weber. 1995 DVD

VIRTUAL ENCOUNTERS ❤ A woman vicariously lives out her sexual fantasies using the latest in virtual-reality technology. It's a thin excuse for a series of soft-core couplings. Available in R and unrated versions, both featuring nonstop nudity and sex. 86m. DIR: Cybil Richards. CAST: Elizabeth Kaitan, Taylore St. Claire, Rob Lee. 1996 DVD

VIRTUAL SEDUCTION ★★★1/2 Until derailed by its bewildering climax, this intriguing little science-fiction drama deftly illustrates the addictive perils of too much virtual reality. Test subject Jeff Fahey finds he prefers the VR simulation of his deceased girlfriend to the real-life charms of his current paramour. Fortunately, the latter's not willing to give up quite that easily. Rated R for nudity, simulated sex, and violence. 90m. DIR: Paul Ziller. CAST: Jeff Fahey, Ami Dolenz, Carrie Genzel, Meshach Taylor. 1995

•VIRTUAL SEXUALITY ★★ This British import plays like a female version of *Weird Science*, without the sense of fun. Tired of losing every guy to her rival, 17-year-old Justine attends a techno fair to find a date, but ends up instead creating the perfect man in a virtual-reality booth. The situation becomes preposterous when a freak explosion turns Justine into her dream date. Rated R for adult situations, language, and nudity. 92m. DIR: Nick Hurran. CAST: Laura Fraser, Rupert Penry-Jones, Luke De Lacey, Kieran O'Brien. 1999 DVD

VIRTUOSITY ★★ Computer-generated killer Russell Crowe breaks free of his cyberspace boundaries and wreaks all sorts of havoc in this futuristic thriller, and only one man—jailed cop Denzel Washington—will be able to stop him. This obnoxiously noisy actionfest is long on violence and short on common sense, and you'll wonder what an actor of Washington's stature is doing in such a mess. Rated R for violence, profanity, and nudity. 105m. DIR: Brett Leonard. CAST: Denzel Washington, Kelly Lynch, Russell Crowe, Stephen Spinella, William Forsythe, Louise Fletcher. 1995 DVD

VIRUS (1980) ★★★ Japan goes Hollywood. Film provides some moments of high drama and decent special effects, not to mention panoramic location shots in Antarctica. The story concerns a polar expedition that becomes the last vestige of humanity when a plague and nuclear war decimate the population. Rated PG. 155m. DIR: Kinji Fukasaku. CAST: George Kennedy, Chuck Connors, Glenn Ford, Sonny Chiba, Olivia Hussey, Henry Silva. 1980

VIRUS (1996) ★★ Secret service agent Brian Bosworth tries to keep the president out of a national park where biological warfare chemicals have leaked. Of a long line of action heroes clogging video racks these days, Bosworth may be the dullest. Rated

PG-13 for violence and profanity. 90m. DIR: Allan A. Goldstein. CAST: Brian Bosworth, Leah Pinsent. 1996

•VIRUS (1999) ★★ This bland, big-budget gorefest is about as stupid as horror thrillers can get. The story concerns the crew of a salvage tug who board a deserted Russian science ship and discover that an outer-space whatsis has "infected" all the on-board computers and machinery. Rated R for violence, profanity, and gobs o'gore. DIR: John Bruno. CAST: Jamie Lee Curtis, William Baldwin, Donald Sutherland, Joanna Pacula. 1999

VIRUS KNOWS NO MORALS, A ★★★1/2 A comedy about AIDS may sound like the ultimate in tastelessness, but gay filmmaker Rosa von Praunheim's aim is to educate audiences while making them laugh. This loosely structured film, featuring a non-professional cast, makes fun of the public misconceptions and hysteria surrounding the disease. In German with English subtitles. Not rated. 82m. DIR: Rosa von Praunheim. CAST: Rosa von Praunheim, Dieter Dicken, Eva Kurz. 1985

VISION QUEST ★★★1/2 A young athlete makes good against all odds. If you can get past the familiarity of the plot, it isn't bad. It benefits particularly from a charismatic lead performance by Matthew Modine. Rated R for nudity, suggested sex, violence, and profanity. 96m. DIR: Harold Becker. CAST: Matthew Modine, Linda Fiorentino, Michael Schoeffling, Ronny Cox, Harold Sylvester. 1985 DVD

VISITANTS, THE ❤ Two aliens move into a house in an American suburb. Not rated. 93m. DIR: Rick Sloane. CAST: Marcus Vaughter, Johanna Grika, Nicole Rio. 1987

VISITING HOURS ❤ Here's a Canadian production that actually forces the viewer to wallow in the degradation, humiliation, and mutilation of women. Rated R for blood, gore, violence, and general unrelenting ugliness. 103m. DIR: Jean-Claude Lord. CAST: Lee Grant, William Shatner, Linda Purl, Michael Ironside. 1982

VISITOR, THE ★★ An 8-year-old girl, gifted with incredible powers, uses her abilities maliciously. As she formulates a plan that could lead the world toward destruction, an ancient alien mystic comes to Earth to stop her evil scheme. Great premise, flawed execution. Rated R for violence. 96m. DIR: Michael J. Paradise. CAST: Mel Ferrer, John Huston, Glenn Ford, Shelley Winters. 1979

VISITORS, THE ★★ An American family moves to Sweden, and strange things begin to happen in their new home. While the climax of this standard possessed-house movie is above par, it's too bad the rest is so boring. Rated R for violence and profanity. 102m. DIR: Joakim Ersgard. CAST: Keith Berkeley, Lena Endre, John Force, John Olsen, Joanna Berg, Brent Landiss, Patrick Ersgard. 1989

VITAL SIGNS ❤ Third-year med students struggling through hospital training. Rated R for sexual situations and profanity. 102m. DIR: Marisa Silver. CAST: Jimmy Smits, Adrian Pasdar, Diane Lane. 1990

VIVA KNIEVEL ❤ Evel Knievel (playing himself) is duped by a former buddy into doing a stunt tour of Mexico. Rated PG. 106m. DIR: Gordon Douglas.

CAST: Evel Knievel, Marjoe Gortner, Leslie Nielsen, Gene Kelly, Lauren Hutton. 1977

VIVA LAS VEGAS ★★ In this romantic musical, Elvis Presley plays a race-car driver who also sings. Ann-Margret is a casino dancer. Eventually Elvis and Ann-Margret get together, which is no surprise to any viewer who is awake. 86m. DIR: George Sidney. CAST: Elvis Presley, Ann-Margret, Cesare Danova, William Demarest, Jack Carter. 1964 DVD

VIVA MARIA! ★★★★ Great slapstick and hilarious situations abound as two song-and-dance girls traveling with a carnival become involved with Mexican revolutionaries during the time of Pancho Villa. A fast-moving comedy gem. In French with English subtitles. 125m. DIR: Louis Malle. CAST: Jeanne Moreau, Brigitte Bardot, George Hamilton, Paulette Dubost. 1965

VIVA MAX! ★★★ Skip credibility and enjoy. Peter Ustinov is a contemporary Mexican general who leads his men across the border to reclaim the Alamo as a tourist attraction. Jonathan Winters all but steals this romp, playing a bumbling, confused National Guard officer in the face of an audacious "enemy." Rated G. 92m. DIR: Jerry Paris. CAST: Peter Ustinov, Jonathan Winters, Keenan Wynn, Pamela Tiffin. 1969

VIVA VILLA! ★★★★ Even though he left the project before completion, director Howard Hawks's breezy style is still in evidence throughout this, Wallace Beery's best starring vehicle. A whitewashed account of Pancho Villa's activities from 1910 to 1916, it allows Beery to do some hard riding, fast shooting, and a whole lot of mugging as he leads his *bandido* revolutionaries against the Federales. B&W; 115m. DIR: Jack Conway, Howard Hawks. CAST: Wallace Beery, Leo Carrillo, Fay Wray, Donald Cook, Stu Erwin, George E. Stone, Joseph Schildkraut, Katherine DeMille, Henry B. Walthall, Arthur Treacher. 1934

VIVA ZAPATA! ★★★★1/2 This film chronicles Mexican revolutionary leader Emiliano Zapata from his peasant upbringing until his death as a weary, disillusioned political liability. Marlon Brando won an Oscar nomination for his insightful portrayal of Zapata. Anthony Quinn, as Zapata's brother, did manage to hold his own against the powerful Brando characterization and was rewarded with a supporting actor Oscar. B&W; 113m. DIR: Elia Kazan. CAST: Marlon Brando, Anthony Quinn, Jean Peters, Joseph Wiseman. 1952

VIVACIOUS LADY ★★★ Cultures clash when small-town professor James Stewart impulsively weds New York nightclub singer Ginger Rogers, brings her back to the campus, and cannot tell his father, upright and stuffy college president Charles Coburn, who the new lady is. B&W; 90m. DIR: George Stevens. CAST: Ginger Rogers, James Stewart, Charles Coburn, Frances Mercer, James Ellison, Beulah Bondi, Franklin Pangborn, Grady Sutton, Jack Carson, Willie Best. 1938

VIVE L'AMOUR ★★★ An empty apartment in bustling Taiwan becomes a microcosm of urban life for three people whose lives intersect there—a real-estate agent, the street vendor she sleeps with, and the homeless gay man who spies on them. The title is ironic in this elegant but chilly look at modern alienation. In Chinese with English subtitles. Not rated; contains nudity and sexual situations. DIR: Mingliang Tsai. CAST: Kuei-Mei Yang, Chao-jung Chen, Kang-sheng Lee. 1996 DVD

V. I. WARSHAWSKI ★★★1/2 The mystery novels by Sara Paretsky are better, but we enjoyed this *Thin Man*-ish movie romp with Kathleen Turner as the wisecracking, two-fisted female detective of the title. In what, sadly, may be her only on-screen adventure because of a poor showing at the box office, V. I. Warshawski is hired by the daughter of a murdered pro hockey player to find his killer. Rated R for violence and profanity. 95m. DIR: Jeff Kanew. CAST: Kathleen Turner, Jay O. Sanders, Charles Durning, Angela Goethals, Frederick Coffin. 1991

VOICES ★★★ A sentimental love story that manages to maintain a sensitive tone that ultimately proves infectious. Amy Irving stars as a deaf young woman who wants to become a dancer; Michael Ontkean is a young man who would rather be a singer. They meet, fall in love. The material is sugary, but Irving and Ontkean make it work. Rated PG for language and adult themes. 107m. DIR: Robert Markowitz. CAST: Amy Irving, Michael Ontkean, Herbert Berghof, Viveca Lindfors. 1979

•VOICES FROM A LOCKED ROOM ★★ In this true story, about composer Peter Warlock—the toast of London, circa 1930s—Warlock's work is music to everyone's ear except notorious music critic Philip Heseltine, who constantly rides Warlock. The verbal war escalates when Warlock threatens Heseltine. His new lover, chanteuse Lily Buxton, steps in and discovers a dark secret that threatens her existence. Nice period touches and exquisite score, but not much else. Rated R for adult situations and language. 92m. DIR: Malcolm Clarke. CAST: Jeremy Northam, Tushka Bergen. 1995

VOLCANO ★★1/2 The La Brea Tar Pits in Los Angeles suddenly begin spouting molten lava, and it's up to iron-jawed disaster-agency manager Tommy Lee Jones and spunky seismologist Anne Heche to save the day. Director Mick Jackson stages the cataclysm with headlong efficiency; the film hits the ground running almost before the opening credits are over. It's painfully predictable, with suspicious traces of last-minute editing, but it's briskly paced and easy to take. Rated PG-13 for profanity and violence. 104m. DIR: Mick Jackson. CAST: Tommy Lee Jones, Anne Heche, Don Cheadle, John Corbett, Keith David, Gaby Hoffman, Jacqueline Kim, John Carroll Lynch, Michael Rispoli. 1997 DVD

VOLCANO: FIRE ON THE MOUNTAIN ★★ Television tries to cash in on the volcano craze with this molten mess about a ski resort threatened by an active volcano. Clichéd characters and situations, low-budget special effects, and leisurely direction do little to help the cause. Rated PG-13 for violence. 98m. DIR: Graeme Campbell. CAST: Dan Cortese, Cynthia Gibb, Brian Kerwin. 1997

VOLERE VOLARE ★★★1/2 A sexy woman who makes her living fulfilling fantasies falls in love with a nerdy cartoon sound man in this delightful romp. Like *Who Framed Roger Rabbit*, this hilarious comedy skillfully mixes live action and animation. Maurizio Nichetti writes, directs, and stars as the sound genius. In Italian with English subtitles. Rated R for nudity and sexual situations. 92m. DIR: Guido Manuli, Maurizio Nichetti. CAST: Maurizio Nichetti, Angela Finocciaro, Mariella Valentini, Patrizio Roversi. 1991

VOLPONE ★★★★ Filmed in 1939, this superb screen version of Shakespeare contemporary Ben Jonson's classic play of greed was not released until after World War II, by which time star Harry Baur, a titan of French cinema, was mysteriously dead, having probably been killed by the Nazis. Aided by his avaricious and parasitic servant, Mosca, Volpone, an old Venetian, pretends he is dying and convinces his greedy friends that each of them is his heir. In French with English subtitles. B&W; 80m. DIR: Maurice Tourneur. CAST: Harry Baur, Louis Jouvet. 1939

VOLUNTEERS ★★ This comedy reunites Tom Hanks and John Candy, who were so marvelously funny together in Ron Howard's *Splash*. However, this film about high jinks in the Peace Corps in Thailand circa 1962 has very little going for it. Hanks and Candy do their best, but the laughs are few and far between. Rated R for profanity, violence, and sexual innuendo. 105m. DIR: Nicholas Meyer. CAST: Tom Hanks, John Candy, Rita Wilson, Tim Thomerson, Gedde Watanabe. 1985 DVD

VON RYAN'S EXPRESS ★★★★ This is a first-rate World War II tale of escape from a prisoner-of-war camp aboard a German train to neutral Switzerland. Trevor Howard is the officer in charge until a feisty Frank Sinatra takes over the escape plan. This is a great action story, with Sinatra playing the hero's role perfectly. 117m. DIR: Mark Robson. CAST: Frank Sinatra, Trevor Howard, Edward Mulhare, James Brolin, Luther Adler. 1965

VOODOO ★★ Pledging a fraternity can be murder. That's what student Corey Feldman learns when he takes the pledge, only to discover that he's joined a cult dedicated to the black arts. Making matters worse is that the cult has decided to use Feldman's girlfriend as its next human sacrifice. It's amazing what you have to do to get a good education today. Rated R for nudity, violence, and adult language. 91m. DIR: Rene Eram. CAST: Corey Feldman, Sara Douglas, Jack Nance. 1995 DVD

VOODOO DAWN ★★ The old story of good versus evil played out in a small town in the South. Two college buddies take a road trip to visit a friend, who unfortunately is in the process of being transformed into a zombie. Rated R for violence and nudity. 83m. DIR: Steven Fierberg. CAST: Raymond St. Jacques, Theresa Merritt, Gina Gershon. 1990 DVD

VOODOO DOLLS ♥ Tender, young schoolgirls are seduced by the spirit residents of their old private academy. Rated R for profanity, nudity, suggested sex, and violence. 90m. DIR: Andre Pelletier. CAST: Maria Stanton. 1990

VOODOO ISLAND ♥ In what is probably his dullest movie, Boris Karloff plays a scientist investigating claims of supernatural occurrences on a tropical island. B&W; 76m. DIR: Reginald LeBorg. CAST: Boris Karloff, Beverly Tyler, Murvyn Vye, Elisha Cook Jr., Rhodes Reason. 1957

VOODOO MAN ★★1/2 So low-budget and corny it unintentionally funny, this Monogram cheapie fe tures Bela Lugosi as a doctor attempting to revive h wife from a twenty-year zombie state by stealing th "life force" from a group of young women. A remak of *The Corpse Vanishes*. B&W; 62m. DIR: Willia Beaudine. CAST: Bela Lugosi, John Carradine, Georg Zucco, Wanda McKay, Louise Currie, Ellen Hall. 1945

VOODOO WOMAN ★★ Typical—if irresistible— American-International mixture of phony sets, to much talk, and an occasional outburst of mayhem a a jungle monster (AIP's *She Creature* suit, slight reworked) is summoned by mad scientist Tom Co way. B&W; 77m. DIR: Edward L. Cahn. CAST: Mar English, Tom Conway, Mike Connors. 1957

VOULEZ VOUS DANSER AVEC MOI? (WILL YO DANCE WITH ME?) ♥ This is another interminabl Brigitte Bardot film, one in which a marital squabbl lands her in the center of a murder investigation. I French with English subtitles. 89m. DIR: Michel Bois rone. CAST: Brigitte Bardot, Henri Vidal, Dawn Ac dams, Noel Roquevert. 1959

VOW TO KILL, A ★★ The daughter of a medi mogul marries a poor photographer and goes on th honeymoon from hell. Not rated; contains violenc and sexual situations. 93m. DIR: Harry S. Longstree CAST: Richard Grieco, Julianne Phillips, Gordon Pir sent, Peter MacNeill. 1994

VOYAGE ★★★ A middle-aged couple, trying to fin the love they once felt, takes a world trip on thei yacht in this made-for-cable original. They pick u another couple along the way. Now starts the voyag from hell. Good acting all around, but the story does n't move quickly enough. Not rated; contains implie sex. 95m. DIR: John Mackenzie. CAST: Rutger Haue Eric Roberts, Karen Allen, Connie Nielsen. 1993

VOYAGE EN BALLON (STOWAWAY TO TH STARS) ★★★ This endearing French film is some what of a follow-up to *The Red Balloon* (also di rected by Albert Lamorisse and starring son Pasca this time allowing that boy to ascend into th clouds—in the basket of a hot-air balloon). Unfortu nately, Lamorisse *père* is a far better director tha writer, and this film lacks the drama needed to sus tain its greater length. Not rated, suitable for famil viewing. 82m. DIR: Albert Lamorisse. CAST: Andr Gille, Maurice Baquet, Pascal Lamorisse. 1959

VOYAGE EN DOUCE ★★★★ A look into the heart and minds of two lifelong friends, this involvin French import is a character study in which plo plays little part. This is intentional, and all is eventu ally revealed and explained. In other words, *Voyag en Douce* offers exactly what fans of foreign films ex pect. In French with English subtitles. Not rated 95m. DIR: Michel Deville. CAST: Dominique Sanda Geraldine Chaplin, Jacques Zabor, Valerie Masterson 1981

VOYAGE IN ITALY ★★★ A married couple drive through Italy to inspect a property they have inher ited. Removed from their usual routine, they begin t inspect their life together. Much admired by fans o director Roberto Rossellini, this slow neorealist drama is recommended only for the most patien viewers. In English. B&W; 97m. DIR: Robert

Rossellini. **CAST:** Ingrid Bergman, George Sanders. **1953**

VOYAGE OF TERROR: THE ACHILLE LAURO AFFAIR ★★ Beware of falling asleep during this telefilm based on the true story of the hijacking of a cruise ship. The viewer views most of the ordeal through an older American couple. 95m. **DIR:** Alberto Negrin. **CAST:** Burt Lancaster, Eva Marie Saint, Rebecca Schaeffer, Bernard Fresson, Robert Culp. **1990**

VOYAGE OF THE DAMNED ★★★★ This fine drama takes place in 1939 as a shipload of Jewish refugees are refused refuge in Havana and are forced to return to Germany for certain imprisonment or death. Rated PG. 134m. **DIR:** Stuart Rosenberg. **CAST:** Oskar Werner, Faye Dunaway, Max von Sydow, Orson Welles, Malcolm McDowell, James Mason, Julie Harris, Lee Grant. **1976 DVD**

VOYAGE 'ROUND MY FATHER, A ★★★★ Writer John Mortimer, famed for creating British barrister Horace Rumpole, composed this play to honor his rather idiosyncratic father. Laurence Olivier, who essays the lead, turns eccentricity into an art form. The younger Mortimer is played by Alan Bates. Originally made for British television and suitable for family viewing. 85m. **DIR:** Alvin Rakoff. **CAST:** Laurence Olivier, Alan Bates, Jane Asher, Elizabeth Sellars. **1983**

VOYAGE TO THE BOTTOM OF THE SEA ★★ An atomic submarine rushes to save Earth from destruction by a burning radiation belt. Intrigue, adventure, and hokey fun, with a low-level all-star cast. Much better than the subsequent television show. Not rated, the film has mild violence. 105m. **DIR:** Irwin Allen. **CAST:** Walter Pidgeon, Joan Fontaine, Robert Sterling, Barbara Eden, Michael Ansara, Peter Lorre, Frankie Avalon, Henry Daniell. **1961**

VOYAGE TO THE PREHISTORIC PLANET 💙 Wisely hiding behind a pseudonym, director Curtis Harrington cobbled together this deadly dull space opera by mixing footage from a Soviet sci-fi movie (*Planet of Storms*) with a few talky scenes involving Basil Rathbone and Faith Domergue. Released directly to TV. 80m. **DIR:** Jonathan Sebastian. **CAST:** Basil Rathbone, Faith Domergue. **1965**

VOYAGER ★★ Slow-moving tale of a man, the woman he loves, and the forbidden secret they share. Although well acted, this is a dull and soapy nostalgia piece. Rated PG-13 for adult themes. 113m. **DIR:** Volker Schlöndorff. **CAST:** Sam Shepard, Julie Delpy, Barbara Sukowa. **1991**

VUKOVAR ★★★★ By turns gentle and horrifying, the film adopts a decidedly Shakespearean manner while revealing how even the purest love—between a Croatian man and a Serbian woman—can be tainted, battered, and finally eradicated by the horrors of war. It's a searing, unforgettable portrait of a country devouring itself. In Serbian with English subtitles. Rated R for violence, profanity, and brief nudity. 96m. **DIR:** Boro Draskovic. **CAST:** Boris Isakovic, Monika Romic, Nebojsa Glogovac, Predrag Ejdus, Mira Banjac. **1994**

VULTURES ★★ A murder mystery with slasher undertones. Poorly written and acted, but has some suspense. Not rated; contains graphic violence and adult situations. 101m. **DIR:** Paul Leder. **CAST:** Stuart Whitman, Greg Mullavey, Carmen Zapata, Yvonne De Carlo, Maria Perschy. **1983**

W ★★★1/2 Someone is trying to kill the Lewises, Katy (Twiggy) and Ben (Michael Witney). Each gets into a car and finds too late that it has been tampered with and nearly is killed in a headlong, high-speed crash. On each vehicle, the letter *W* is scrawled in the dust. Who could be after them? This is a highly involving, Hitchcockian thriller that will keep mystery lovers captivated. Rated PG. 95m. **DIR:** Richard Quine. **CAST:** Twiggy, Michael Witney, Eugene Roche, John Vernon, Dirk Benedict. **1974**

WABASH AVENUE ★★★★ A delightful musical that pokes fun at show-business stereotypes and uses romance, glamour, and colorful production numbers to keep them in perspective. 92m. **DIR:** Henry Koster. **CAST:** Betty Grable, Victor Mature, Phil Harris, Margaret Hamilton, Reginald Gardiner, Henry Kulky. **1950**

WACKIEST SHIP IN THE ARMY, THE ★★★ A battered ship becomes an unlikely implement for World War II heroism. The situation is played mostly for laughs, but dramatic moments are smoothly included. Jack Lemmon sets his performance at just the right pitch. Ricky Nelson is amiable and amusing. 99m. **DIR:** Richard Murphy. **CAST:** Jack Lemmon, Ricky Nelson, John Lund, Chips Rafferty, Tom Tully, Joby Baker, Warren Berlinger. **1960**

WACKO 💙 Excruciating parody of *Halloween*. Rated PG. 90m. **DIR:** Greydon Clark. **CAST:** Joe Don Baker, Stella Stevens, George Kennedy, Jeff Altman. **1981**

WACKY WORLD OF WILLS AND BURKE, THE ★★1/2 Incongruously lighthearted parody of the true story of the explorers who set out to cross Australia by camel in 1860. (A straight version of the ill-fated expedition, *Burke and Wills*, was made at the same time as this.) Some funny Monty Python-ish satire will be lost on those unfamiliar with Australian history. Not rated. 97m. **DIR:** Bob Weis. **CAST:** Garry McDonald, Kim Gyngell, Nicole Kidman, Colin Hay. **1985**

WAG THE DOG ★★★★★ Deliciously clever story of how the public's attention is diverted from an incident involving the president molesting a young girl in the White House. Political consultant invents a phony war with Armenia and, despite snafu after snafu, keeps the ruse going long enough to accomplish his goal. This is a wry, hilarious satire on just about everything in American culture. From the novel *American Hero* by Larry Beinhart. Woody Harrelson is especially effective in a cameo as an American hero unlike any you've ever seen before. Rated R for language. 97m. **DIR:** Barry Levinson. **CAST:** Dustin

Hoffman, Robert De Niro, Anne Heche, Woody Harrelson, Denis Leary, Willie Nelson, Andrea Martin, Michael Belson, Craig T. Nelson, James Belushi, Suzanne Cryer, Kirsten Dunst, William H. Macy. 1997 DVD

WAGES OF FEAR, THE ★★★★★ This masterpiece of suspense pits four seedy and destitute men against the challenge of driving two nitroglycerin-laden trucks over crude and treacherous Central American mountain roads to quell a monstrous oil-well fire. Incredible risk and numbing fear ride along as the drivers, goaded by high wages, cope with dilemma after dilemma. In French with English subtitles. B&W; 128m. DIR: Henri-Georges Clouzot. CAST: Yves Montand, Charles Vanel, Peter Van Eyck, Vera Clouzot. 1953 DVD

WAGNER ★★★ This five-hour film gives you an idea of what the greatest opera composer may have been like, but the legendary supporting cast, although credible, is not up to his reputation. Not rated, but equal to an R for violence, profanity, and nudity. 300m. DIR: Tony Palmer. CAST: Richard Burton, Vanessa Redgrave, Gemma Craven, John Gielgud, Ralph Richardson, Laurence Olivier, Marthe Keller, Ronald Pickup. 1982

WAGON TRAIN (TV SERIES) ★★★1/2 John Ford's Wagonmaster inspired the creation of this Western series, which starred Ward Bond as Major Seth Adams, the no-nonsense leader of a wagon train headed West, and Robert Horton, a scout Flint McCullough. In the premiere episode of this anthology-oriented show, Ernest Borgnine plays a former soldier from Adams's command. B&W; 60m. DIR: Herschel Daugherty. CAST: Ward Bond, Robert Horton, Ernest Borgnine, Marjorie Lord, Andrew Duggan, Beverly Washburn, Frank McGrath, Terry Wilson. 1957

WAGON WHEELS ★★★ Scout Randolph Scott guides a wagon train to Oregon against all the Westward trek odds—the worst of which is a half-breed inciting the Indians into an uprising. Remake of Fighting Caravans (with Gary Cooper), including much stock footage. B&W; 56m. DIR: Charles Barton. CAST: Randolph Scott, Gail Patrick, Raymond Hatton, Monte Blue. 1934

WAGON WHEELS WESTWARD ★★★ Red Ryder leads a wagon train of settlers into a seemingly deserted town, only to find it is inhabited by a gang of vicious outlaws. B&W; 56m. DIR: R. G. Springsteen. CAST: William Elliott, Robert Blake, Linda Stirling, Roy Barcroft. 1945

WAGONMASTER ★★★★1/2 John Ford was unquestionably the greatest director of Westerns. This release ranks with the best of Ford's work. Ward Bond, who plays the elder in this story of a Mormon congregation migrating west, became a star, thanks to the popular television series it inspired: Wagon Train. And Ben Johnson, who won the best-supporting-actor Oscar in 1971 for The Last Picture Show, is excellent in his first starring role. B&W; 86m. DIR: John Ford. CAST: Ben Johnson, Ward Bond, Harry Carey Jr., Joanne Dru, James Arness. 1950

WAGONS EAST ♥ John Candy died on the set of this lame Western-comedy in which he plays a melancholy wagon-train master who gets a chance to recover his sobriety and self-respect by leading group of disgruntled frontier settlers back eas Rated PG-13 for language. 101m. DIR: Peter Markl CAST: John Candy, Richard Lewis, John C. McGinle Robert Picardo, Ellen Greene, William Sanderso 1994

●WAGONS ROLL AT NIGHT, THE ★★ Circus own promotes an untried young man as his prize lio tamer but goes off the deep end when his kid siste falls for his new star. Humphrey Bogart was on th verge of greatness after several false starts, and tire rewrites of old films like this fueled his disputes wit studio boss Jack Warner. B&W; 84m. DIR: Ray En right. CAST: Humphrey Bogart, Eddie Albert, Sylv Sidney, Joan Leslie, Sig Ruman, Cliff Clark, Charle Foy. 1941

WAIKIKI WEDDING ★★★ This typical Bing Crost musical, which produced the Oscar-winning son "Sweet Leilani," has all the ingredients of Depres sion-era escapist fare. It works, thanks to the pe sonable talented combo of Bing Crosby, Marth Raye, and Bob Burns. B&W; 89m. DIR: Frank Tuttl CAST: Bing Crosby, Shirley Ross, Martha Raye, Bo Burns, Anthony Quinn, Grady Sutton. 1937

WAIT UNTIL DARK ★★★★ Suspense abounds i this chiller about a blind housewife (Audrey Hep burn) who is being pursued by a gang of criminals She has inadvertently gotten hold of a doll filled wit heroin. Alan Arkin is especially frightening as th psychotic gang's mastermind who alternates be tween moments of deceptive charm and sudden vic lence in his attempt to separate Hepburn from th doll. 108m. DIR: Terence Young. CAST: Audrey Hep burn, Alan Arkin, Richard Crenna, Efrem Zimbalist J 1967

WAIT UNTIL SPRING, BANDINI ★★★ Author Joh Fante's fond remembrance of his youth is lovingl brought to the screen in this nostalgic look at an im migrant family beating the odds in Colorado, circ 1920. Handsome production benefits from a warm cast, especially Joe Mantegna as the clan head dere. CAST: Joe Mantegna, Ornella Muti, Faye Dun away, Burt Young, Daniel Wilson. 1989

WAITING ★★★1/2 Imagine an Australian Bi Chill, as told from a woman's perspective. Writer-di rector Jackie McKimmie has fashioned a charming tale of diverse female friends who come from aroun the world to help their friend with the forthcoming birth of her child. An entertaining film. 90m. DIR Jackie McKimmie. CAST: Noni Hezelhurst, Deborra Lee Furness. 1992

WAITING FOR GUFFMAN ★★★★ This deadpan mockumentary spoofs amateur theater productions Middle America values, and small-town booster ism—and celebrates tackiness. The result is hilari ous. Rated R for language and sex talk. 84m. DIR Christopher Guest. CAST: Christopher Guest, Frec Willard, Catherine O'Hara, Eugene Levy, Parker Posey Bob Balaban. 1997

WAITING FOR THE LIGHT ★★★1/2 A single mother of two children inherits and reopens a run down roadside café. When her aunt, an ex-circus magician, pulls a nighttime prank on their mean pirited neighbor, he mistakes it for a heavenly visit. Set during the uneasy time of the Cuban missile crisis, the troubled and the faithful flock to the scene of the "miracle," and business booms. Rated PG for sanity. 94m. DIR: Christopher Monger. CAST: Shirley MacLean, Teri Garr, Vincent Schiavelli, Clancy Brown, John Bedford Lloyd. 1991

WAITING FOR THE MOON ★★ Linda Hunt is Alice B. Toklas and Linda Bassett is Gertrude Stein in this idiosyncratic, self-indulgent, and frustrating film. The stars' performances are fine, but the impressionistic style of cowriter-director Jill Godmilow tends to be more irritating than artistic. Rated PG-13 for profanity and adult themes. 88m. DIR: Jill Godmilow. CAST: Linda Hunt, Linda Bassett, Bruce McGill, Andrew McCarthy, Bernadette Lafont. 1987

WAITING TO EXHALE ★★1/2 Four African American women support and comfort each other through a year of romantic ups and downs. This glossy, expensive-looking soap opera is self-conscious and affected, and awkwardly directed by actor Forest Whitaker. Rated R for profanity and simulated sex. 123m. DIR: Forest Whitaker. CAST: Whitney Houston, Angela Bassett, Lela Rochon, Loretta Devine, Dennis Haysbert, Gregory Hines, Mykelti Williamson. 1995 DVD

WAKE ISLAND ★★★★ Hard-hitting tale of a small gallant detachment of U.S. Marines holding out against attack after attack by the Japanese army, navy, and air force. A true story from the early dark days of World War II. Brian Donlevy commands the troops, and William Bendix and Robert Preston fight each other as much as the Japanese. Wake Island received four Academy Award nominations and was the first realistic American film made about World War II. B&W; 88m. DIR: John Farrow. CAST: Brian Donlevy, Macdonald Carey, Robert Preston, Albert Dekker, William Bendix, Walter Abel. 1942

WAKE OF THE RED WITCH ★★★★ Good, seafaring adventure tale with John Wayne outstanding as a wronged ship's captain seeking justice and battling an octopus for sunken treasure. B&W; 106m. DIR: Edward Ludwig. CAST: John Wayne, Gail Russell, Gig Young, Luther Adler. 1948

WAKING NED DEVINE ★★★★ A national-lottery win transforms a small town in writer-director Kirk Jones's droll and charming British comedy, which is every bit as earthy and enchanting as the rugged Irish seacoast where it takes place. Study of an isolated group of people confronted by an event that could change their lives forever … and the somewhat unorthodox manner in which they react to it. Rated PG for mild sensuality and geezer nudity. 91m. DIR: Kirk Jones. CAST: Ian Bannen, David Kelly, Fionnula Flanagan, Susan Lynch, James Nesbitt. 1998 DVD

WALK, DON'T RUN ★★★ During the summer Olympics in Tokyo, Samantha Eggar agrees to share her apartment in the crowded city with businessman Cary Grant and athlete Jim Hutton. Happy, wholesome havoc results. Cary Grant's last film, a remake of 1943's The More the Merrier. 114m. DIR: Charles Walters. CAST: Cary Grant, Samantha Eggar, Miiko Taka, Jim Hutton, John Standing, George Takei. 1966

WALK IN THE CLOUDS, A ★★★ Keanu Reeves returns home after World War II and finds himself participating in a gallant lie: pretending to be the husband of a fellow bus traveler who cannot otherwise admit her pregnancy (by a departed lover) to old-fashioned father Giancarlo Giannini. Although the Napa Valley wine-country setting provides a suitably sensuous palate, the overly contrived story ultimately overwhelms the budding romance. Rated PG-13 for sexual content. 103m. DIR: Alfonso Arau. CAST: Keanu Reeves, Aitana Sanchez-Gijon, Anthony Quinn, Giancarlo Giannini, Angelica Aragon, Debra Messing. 1995

WALK IN THE SPRING RAIN, A ★★1/2 Two well-into-middle-age people find romance while on vacation in the country. Their problem is that both are married to other people. From such a fine cast you expect more. Rated PG. 100m. DIR: Guy Green. CAST: Anthony Quinn, Ingrid Bergman, Fritz Weaver, Katherine Crawford. 1970

WALK IN THE SUN, A ★★★★1/2 Based on Harry Brown's novel, this picture really gets to the heart of the human reaction to war. The story of an American army unit's attack on a German stronghold in World War II Italy is a first-rate character study. B&W; 117m. DIR: Lewis Milestone. CAST: Dana Andrews, Richard Conte, Sterling Holloway, John Ireland. 1945 DVD

WALK INTO HELL ★★★ Popular Australian star Chips Rafferty is something of a precursor to "Crocodile" Dundee in this outback adventure. He plays a bush explorer who helps a businessman find oil in New Guinea. Of course, the aborigines aren't all too happy about this. Plenty of National Geographic-type footage pads out this okay adventure. 93m. DIR: Les Robinson. CAST: Chips Rafferty, Françoise Christophe, Reg Lye. 1957

WALK LIKE A MAN 🌢 Unfunny, forced attempt at a comic version of The Jungle Book. Rated PG-13 for language. 86m. DIR: Melvin Frank. CAST: Howie Mandel, Christopher Lloyd, Cloris Leachman, Amy Steel. 1987

WALK ON THE MOON, A ★★★ In the summer of 1969, between the Apollo 11 moon landing and the Woodstock festival, a bored young housewife has an affair with a footloose hippie. This understated slice-of-life soap opera profits from intelligent writing and honest acting. Rated R for nudity and sexual scenes. 106m. DIR: Tony Goldwyn. CAST: Diane Lane, Viggo Mortensen, Liev Schreiber, Anna Paquin, Tovah Feldshuh. 1999 DVD

WALK ON THE WILD SIDE ★★ Trashy tale of a young man's attempt to find his girlfriend, only to discover she's working in a New Orleans brothel. Extremely slow-paced film wastes a first-rate cast and a great musical score by Elmer Bernstein. For lovers of soap operas only. B&W; 114m. DIR: Edward Dmytryk. CAST: Laurence Harvey, Jane Fonda, Capucine, Barbara Stanwyck, Anne Baxter. 1962

WALK SOFTLY, STRANGER ★★1/2 Joseph Cotten plays a calculating predator who falls for crippled victim Alida Valli and decides to call the swindle off. The plot thickens when a tough gambler Cotten had robbed in the past shows up to cut himself in and put our hero out—permanently. B&W; 81m. DIR: Robert Stevenson. CAST: Joseph Cotten, Alida Valli, Spring Byington, Paul Stewart, Jack Paar, Jeff Donnell, John McIntire. 1950

WALKABOUT ★★★1/2 Mesmerizing, haunting tale of paradise lost and found. When their crazed father drives them to the middle of the Australian outback and then commits suicide, a teenage girl and her young brother must struggle to survive and find civilization. They are escorted on their journey by a young Aborigine man on a quest to prove his manhood. Explores the sexual awakening of young people without making it seem exploitative. Not rated; contains nudity, violence, and adult situations. 100m. DIR: Nicolas Roeg. CAST: Jenny Agutter, David Gulpilil, Lucien John, John Meillon. 1971 DVD

WALKER ★★★ True story of William Walker and his takeover of Nicaragua in 1855 by director Alex Cox. Ed Harris has a great time with the broad character of Walker and makes clear that power corrupts. For those with a taste for something out of the ordinary, Walker is worth viewing. Rated R for language, nudity, and simulated sex. 98m. DIR: Alex Cox. CAST: Ed Harris, Richard Masur, René Auberjonois, Marlee Matlin, Sy Richardson, Peter Boyle. 1988

WALKER: TEXAS RANGER ★★★ Chuck Norris stars as the title character, a rough-and-tumble Texas Ranger, complete with holster and cowboy hat. When he's assigned to protect a U.S. senator, he and a retired buddy unwittingly uncover an assassination plot. Not rated. 96m. DIR: Michael Preece. CAST: Chuck Norris, Clarence Gilyard Jr., Stuart Whitman, Sheree Wilson. 1994

WALKING AND TALKING ★★★★ Two lifelong pals (Catherine Keener, Anne Heche) feel the strain in their friendship when one decides to marry. After a slow, talky start, writer-director Nicole Holofcener begins playfully and patiently fleshing out her characters, and the film grows stronger with every scene. Acting is excellent, especially Keener as the friend staying single, and Kevin Corrigan as a nerdy videostore clerk. Michael Spiller's cheerful cinematography is another plus. Rated R for profanity and mature themes. 90m. DIR: Nicole Holofcener. CAST: Catherine Keener, Anne Heche, Liev Schreiber, Todd Field, Kevin Corrigan. 1996

WALKING DEAD, THE ★★1/2 A squad of marines in Vietnam, ambushed and stranded, must fight their way through the jungle to rendezvous with another unit and escape to safety. Standard "lost patrol" heroics, interspersed with trite flashbacks to the home front. Rated R for violence and profanity. 90m. DIR: Preston A. Whitmore II. CAST: Allen Payne, Eddie Griffin, Joe Morton. 1995

WALKING ON AIR ★★★★ Uplifting Ray Bradbury tale about a paralyzed boy who refuses to submit to the law of gravity. Inspired by his zany science teacher (played to perfection by Lynn Redgrave), he petitions NASA for a chance to float in space. This WonderWorks production is suitable for the entire family. 58m. DIR: Ed Kaplan. CAST: Lynn Redgrave, Jordan Marder. 1986

WALKING TALL ★★1/2 Poor Joe Don Baker never outrun his one-note performance as Buford Pusser,

the baseball bat–toting southern sheriff who decided to take the law into his own hands in his fight against the cancerous scum of society. Unpleasantly brutal and difficult to enjoy for any reason. Talented Elizabeth Hartman is completely wasted. Not a family picture. Rated R. 125m. DIR: Phil Karlson. CAST: Joe Don Baker, Elizabeth Hartman, Noah Beery Jr. Rosemary Murphy. 1973 DVD

WALKING TALL PART II ★★ This follow-up to the successful Walking Tall proves that sequels are better off not being made at all. This story line gives Bo Svenson a chance to look mean, but that's about it. Rated R for violence and language. 109m. DIR: Earl Bellamy. CAST: Bo Svenson, Luke Askew, Richard Jaeckel, Noah Beery Jr. 1975

WALL, THE (1998) (FOREIGN) ★★★ Based-on-fact story of life in a brutal Turkish prison where prisoners of all ages, genders, and types (political and criminal) are incarcerated together. Director Yilmaz Guney spent much of his life in such prisons before escaping in 1981. Not rated, but too brutal for children. 117m. DIR: Yilmaz Guney. CAST: Tuncel Kurtiz. 1983

WALL, THE (1998) (U.S.) ★★★ The gimmick in this trilogy of stories might make a good TV series if viewers could get beyond the depressing concept. Each tale concerns one of the mementos left at the base of the Vietnam War memorial and how it relates to the characters whose fates we follow. Sadly, the premise is better than the execution; each story is underscripted, each character lamentably underdeveloped. Rated R for profanity and violence. 95m. DIR: Joseph Sargent. CAST: Edward James Olmos, Savion Glover, Ruby Dee, Frank Whaley, Michael De Lorenzo. 1998

WALL STREET ★★★★ The same energy and insight that propelled writer-director Oliver Stone's Oscar-winning Platoon helps make this look at double-dealing in the stock market much more entertaining than one would expect. Chief among its pleasures is Michael Douglas's deliciously evil character of Gordon Gekko, a hotshot financier who takes novice Bud Fox (Charlie Sheen) under his wing. Rated R for profanity, nudity, and violence. 120m. DIR: Oliver Stone. CAST: Michael Douglas, Charlie Sheen, Daryl Hannah, Martin Sheen, Terence Stamp, Sean Young, Hal Holbrook, James Spader. 1987

WALL STREET COWBOY ★★★ Roy Rogers takes to the concrete canyons when a trial requires his presence in New York in his first contemporary Western of many to come. Often good-naturedly pokes fun at Roy's image. B&W; 54m. DIR: Joseph Kane. CAST: Roy Rogers, George "Gabby" Hayes, Raymond Hatton, Ann Baldwin. 1939

WALLACE & GROMIT: A GRAND DAY OUT ★★★★ Claymation animator Nick Park clearly was perfecting his skills during this, the first saga to star fussy, cheese-loving Wallace, and his wise but quiet canine companion, Gromit. The figure animation is a bit uneven, reflecting the years Park required to complete his first short feature, but the character interaction is already wonderful. Not rated. 25m. DIR: Nick Park. 1990 DVD

WALLACE & GROMIT: THE WRONG TROUSERS
★★★★★ This Oscar-winning short subject may be one of the most perfect little films ever made, blending inventive clay animation with deliciously droll scripting and a simply astonishing climax. This wildly amusing short captures the very essence of dry British humor. Not rated. 30m. **DIR:** Nick Park. **1993 DVD**

WALLACE & GROMIT: A CLOSE SHAVE ★★★★★ Nick Park's third clay animation Wallace and Gromit adventure is every bit as entertaining as its predecessors, and quite worthy of its Academy Award. Not to be missed. Not rated, but acceptable for all ages. 30m. **DIR:** Nick Park. **1995 DVD**

WALLS OF GLASS ★★★1/2 A New York cabdriver who aspires to be an actor exposes us to the many characters of his life: his gambling family, his troubled youth, and the colorful customers in his cab. A truly warm and insightful drama with a bravura performance by Philip Bosco. Rated R for language. 85m. **DIR:** Scott Goldstein. **CAST:** Philip Bosco, Geraldine Page, Olympia Dukakis, William Hickey. **1988**

WALPURGIS NIGHT ★★★ This sudsy romance features a secretary in love with her married boss. In Swedish with English subtitles that are not grammatically correct in translation. B&W; 75m. **DIR:** Gustaf Edgren. **CAST:** Ingrid Bergman, Victor Sjöström, Lars Hanson. **1935**

WALTZ KING, THE ★★★1/2 The wonderful music of Johann Strauss Jr. is the real star of this Walt Disney biography filmed on location in Vienna. A treat to the eyes and ears, this is a good family film. 94m. **DIR:** Steve Previn. **CAST:** Kerwin Mathews, Brian Aherne, Senta Berger, Peter Kraus, Fritz Eckhardt. **1963**

WALTZ OF THE TOREADORS ★★★★ The unique Peter Sellers is superb as a retired military officer who can't subdue his roving eye. Margaret Leighton is fine, as always. Dany Robin is adorable. It's saucy and sex-shot, but intellectually stimulating nonetheless. A charming film, and not just for Sellers's fans. 105m. **DIR:** John Guillermin. **CAST:** Peter Sellers, Margaret Leighton, Dany Robin. **1962 DVD**

WALTZ THROUGH THE HILLS ★★★1/2 Two Australian orphans, fearing separation, set off for a ship to take them to their grandparents in England. They are helped by an outback native (Ernie Dingo) who is both frightening and endearing. A WonderWorks production, this is fine family fare. 116m. **DIR:** Frank Arnold. **CAST:** Tina Kemp, Andre Jansen, Ernie Dingo, Dan O'Herlihy. **1988**

WALTZES FROM VIENNA ★★ Alfred Hitchcock ... directing a musical? Not really. This biopic of the Strauss family is more of a romantic comedy. By any category, it's a misfire. Not rated; suitable for family viewing. B&W; 80m. **DIR:** Alfred Hitchcock. **CAST:** Jessie Matthews, Esmond Knight, Edmund Gwenn. **1933**

WANDA NEVADA ★★1/2 Interesting little film with Peter Fonda as a shifty, amoral gambler who wins Brooke Shields in a poker game. They come into the possession of a map that marks a gold strike. If you watch carefully, you'll see Henry Fonda as a gold prospector. It's the only film that father and son ever did together. Rated PG for violence and mature situations. 105m. **DIR:** Peter Fonda. **CAST:** Peter Fonda, Brooke Shields, Fiona Lewis. **1979**

WANDERER, THE ★★1/2 An exciting newcomer turns a girl's life upside down, but her loyalty to him is a mystery since a more worthwhile man loves her. Marvelous music and imaginative surreal sequences cannot completely compensate for the slow pace and confusion that permeate this arty film. In French with English subtitles. 107m. **DIR:** Jean Gabriel Albicocco. **CAST:** Brigitte Fossey, Jean Blaise, Alain Noury. **1967**

WANDERERS, THE ★★★★ This enjoyable film is set in the early 1960s and focuses on the world of teenagers. Though it has ample amounts of comedy and excitement, because it deals with life on the streets of the Bronx there is an atmosphere of ever-present danger and fear. The Wanderers are a gang of Italian-American youths who have banded together for safety and good times. Rated R. 113m. **DIR:** Phil Kaufman. **CAST:** Ken Wahl, John Friedrich, Karen Allen, Tony Ganios. **1979**

WANNABES ★★1/2 Japanese animation. This one does have a certain charm. The *Wannabes* are a duo of determined women wrestlers that become the unknowing test subjects of genetic research. Sounds like a stretch (and it is), but it has the flavor of a Fifties drive-in classic. In Japanese with English subtitles. Not rated. 45m. **DIR:** Masuzumi Matsumiya. **1986**

WANNSEE CONFERENCE, THE ★★★★ This is a fascinating historical drama about a meeting held on January 20, 1942, with the fourteen members of Hitler's hierarchy. Wannsee is the Berlin suburb where they met to decide "the final solution" to the Jewish problem. Chillingly told from the actual minutes taken at the conference. A must-see film. In German with subtitles. 87m. **DIR:** Keinz Schirk. **CAST:** Dietrich Mattausch. **1984**

WANTED: DEAD OR ALIVE ★★★ In this lean action thriller, Rutger Hauer stars as Nick Randall, the great-grandson of Old West bounty hunter Josh Randall (played by Steve McQueen in the *Wanted: Dead or Alive* television series). Nick is a former CIA agent who is brought out of retirement when an international terrorist (Gene Simmons) begins leaving a bloody trail across Los Angeles. Rated R for profanity and violence. 104m. **DIR:** Gary A. Sherman. **CAST:** Rutger Hauer, Gene Simmons, Robert Guillaume, Mel Harris, William Russ. **1987**

WANTED: DEAD OR ALIVE (TV SERIES) ★★★1/2 The public was first captivated by Steve McQueen's cool, tough, intense persona with this top-notch Western series. McQueen plays dedicated bounty hunter Josh Randall, who travels the country searching for outlaws. The first video releases feature "Reunion for Revenge" with James Coburn and Ralph Meeker and "Medicine Man" with J. Pat O'Malley and Cloris Leachman. 30m. **DIR:** Thomas Carr, Richard Donner. **CAST:** Steve McQueen, Wright King. **1958–1961**

WANTON CONTESSA, THE ★★★★1/2 Luchino Visconti—aristocrat by birth, Marxist by conviction—offers one of the lushest and most expressive Italian films ever made (known there as *Senso*). The large-budget spectacular is operatic in scope and look. Venice, 1866. A countess (the alluring Alida Valli) finds herself passionately in love with a young Austrian officer (Farley Granger). Dubbed in English (with dialogue by Tennessee Williams and Paul Bowles). 120m. **DIR:** Luchino Visconti. **CAST:** Alida Valli, Farley Granger, Massimo Girotti. **1954**

WAR, THE ★★★ This early 1970s lesson in tolerance is also a coming-of-age story that bogs down in syrupy sincerity. A Vietnam vet tortured by war memories has as much trouble keeping his son out of fistfights in a rural Mississippi town as he does keeping a job. Rated PG-13 for violence and language. 127m. **DIR:** Jon Avnet. **CAST:** Kevin Costner, Elijah Wood, Mare Winningham, Lexi Randall, Christine Baranski, Raynor Scheine. **1994 DVD**

WAR AND PEACE (1956) ★★1/2 Mammoth international effort to film this classic novel results in an overlong, unevenly constructed melodrama. The massive battle scenes and outdoor panoramas are truly impressive, as are the performers on occasion. But the whole production seems to swallow up the principals and the action, leaving a rather lifeless film. 208m. **DIR:** King Vidor. **CAST:** Henry Fonda, Audrey Hepburn, Mel Ferrer, John Mills. **1956**

WAR AND PEACE (1968) ★★★★★ Many film versions of great books take liberties that change important plot situations, and more. This Academy Award–winning Soviet production stays as close to the book as possible, making it terribly long, but one of the greatest re-creations of great literature ever done. It took five years to make at enormous cost; it is a cinematic treasure. Poorly dubbed. 373m. **DIR:** Sergei Bondarchuk. **CAST:** Lyudmila Savelyeva, Sergei Bondarchuk. **1968**

WAR AND REMEMBRANCE ★★★ Drawn-out sudsy TV docudrama is Herman Wouk's sequel to *Winds of War*. Action begins with Pearl Harbor and eventual battles with Hitler. 96–146m. **DIR:** Dan Curtis. **CAST:** Robert Mitchum, Jane Seymour, Polly Bergen, Hart Bochner, Victoria Tennant. **1988**

WAR ARROW ★★ Pure cowboy-and-Indian pulp, this movie is more of an excuse to show that good guys always end up with good girls—even when the good guy bucks authority and tries to pit one tribe of Indians against another. OK, but not very original. 78m. **DIR:** George Sherman. **CAST:** Maureen O'Hara, Jeff Chandler, Susan Ball, Charles McIntire, Jay Silverheels, Charles Drake. **1953**

WAR BOY, THE ★★★1/2 A 12-year-old boy (Jason Hopely) living in World War II Germany suffers the experiences of growing up amid the brutalities of conflict. Hopely's performance is terrific. The story and production are nowhere near as ambitious as *Hope and Glory* or *Empire of the Sun*, but *The War Boy* is a good film in its own right. Rated PG for violence and some sex. 96m. **DIR:** Allan Eastman. **CAST:** Helen Shaver, Kenneth Welsh, Jason Hopely. **1985**

WAR GAME, THE ★★★★★ Pseudo-documentary depicts the events preceding and following a nuclear attack. Originally made for the BBC, which never ran it because it was thought to be too unsettling for viewers. Not rated. 47m. **DIR:** Peter Watkins. **1965**

WAR LORD, THE ★★★1/2 In the eleventh century, the warlord (Charlton Heston) of the Duke of Normandy moves to secure the coastline against invaders and to claim a maiden. The battle scenes are great and Richard Boone, as the title character's right hand, turns in a fine performance. 120m. **DIR:** Franklin J. Schaffner. **CAST:** Charlton Heston, Richard Boone, Rosemary Forsyth, Maurice Evans, Guy Stockwell, Henry Wilcoxon, James Farentino. **1965 DVD**

WAR LOVER, THE ★★1/2 This is a very slow-moving account of pilots (Steve McQueen and Robert Wagner) in England during World War II. Both pilots are seeking the affections of the same woman. Nothing in the film raises it above the level of mediocrity. B&W; 105m. **DIR:** Philip Leacock. **CAST:** Steve McQueen, Robert Wagner, Shirley Anne Field. **1962**

WAR OF THE BUTTONS ★★★★ Engaging family film about the children of two Irish villages, who begin feuding for no particular reason and allow matters to escalate into a full-scale war. The children use buttons as the prize and set into motion an increasingly violent series of skirmishes that leave their parents completely mystified. The kids are wonderful, the scenery to die for, and the message heartfelt. Rated PG for mild language and nudity. 95m. **DIR:** John Roberts. **CAST:** Greg Fitzgerald, Gerard Kearney, Darag Naughton, Brendan McNamara, John Coffey, Paul Batt, Karl Byrne. **1995**

WAR OF THE COLOSSAL BEAST ★★1/2 This sequel to *The Amazing Colossal Man* actually restores the long missing color ending, in which our oversize friend (now looking like the title character of *The Cyclops*, after being mutilated in the climax to the previous film) stumbles into high-tension electrical wires. That lends this American-International cheapie some stature as a video keeper. B&W/color; 68m. **DIR:** Bert I. Gordon. **CAST:** Sally Fraser, Roger Pace, Russ Bender. **1958**

WAR OF THE GARGANTUAS ★★ Giant, furry monsters—one good, one evil—slug it out in mountainous and eventually urban Japan. Eye-filling, braindead Toho Films sci fi. 93m. **DIR:** Inoshiro Honda. **CAST:** Russ Tamblyn, Kumi Mizuno, Kipp Hamilton. **1966**

WAR OF THE ROSES, THE ★★★★★ A brilliant black comedy from director Danny DeVito, this frightening and funny film stars Michael Douglas and Kathleen Turner as a couple whose marriage collapses into a vicious divorce battle over material possessions. The acting is superb, and the direction is stunning. Rated R for profanity, seminudity, and violence. 100m. **DIR:** Danny DeVito. **CAST:** Michael Douglas, Kathleen Turner, Danny DeVito, Marianne Sägebrecht, Sean Astin, G. D. Spradlin, Peter Donat. **1989**

WAR OF THE SATELLITES 🞬 Confusing and boring Roger Corman sci-fi thriller of note only for having been conceived and produced in eight weeks in order to cash in on the launching of the first American space satellite. B&W; 66m. **DIR:** Roger Corman. **CAST:** Dick Miller, Susan Cabot, Richard Devon, Robert Shayne, Bruno Ve Sota. **1958**

WAR OF THE WILDCATS ★★★ Big John Wayne takes on bad guy Albert Dekker in this story of oil drillers at the turn of the century. Gabby Hayes adds a vintage touch to this standard-formula Republic feature. B&W; 102m. **DIR:** Albert S. Rogell. **CAST:** John Wayne, Martha Scott, Albert Dekker, George "Gabby" Hayes, Sidney Blackmer, Dale Evans. **1943**

WAR OF THE WORLDS, THE ★★★★ Gene Barry stars as a scientist who is among the first Earthlings to witness the Martian invasion of Earth. The film is an updated version of H. G. Wells's classic story, with the action heightened by excellent special effects. 85m. **DIR:** Byron Haskin. **CAST:** Gene Barry, Les Tremayne, Ann Robinson. **1953 DVD**

WAR PARTY ★★ An interesting idea, but not suitably developed, this film details what happens when a group of disgruntled, modern-day native Americans go on the warpath. They disrupt a summer festival by taking the cowboy-and-Indian war games seriously—and use real ammunition. Rated R, with strong violence. 100m. **DIR:** Franc Roddam. **CAST:** Kevin Dillon, Billy Wirth, Tim Sampson, M. Emmet Walsh. **1988**

WAR REQUIEM ★★★ Arty, at times surrealistic view of war as seen through the eyes of World War II soldiers, nurses, and children. All action is without dialogue using Wilfred Owen's poetry and Benjamin Britten's music with emotional and thought-provoking results. Not rated; contains violence. 92m. **DIR:** Derek Jarman. **CAST:** Laurence Olivier, Tilda Swinton, Owen Teale, Nathaniel Parker. **1988**

WAR ROOM, THE ★★★★ Nominated for an Oscar for best documentary in 1993, this film follows Bill Clinton's 1992 presidential campaign staff (including James Carville and George Stephanopoulos) from the first primary to the acceptance speech. The viewer gets a firsthand look at the inner workings of a campaign, including mudslinging. Very well done and quite fascinating. Rated PG for profanity. 96m. **DIR:** Chris Hegedus, D. A. Pennebaker. **1993 DVD**

WAR WAGON, THE ★★★ While not John Wayne at his best, this Western, costarring Kirk Douglas and directed by Burt Kennedy, does have plenty of laughs and action. It's guaranteed to keep fans of the Duke pleasantly entertained. 101m. **DIR:** Burt Kennedy. **CAST:** John Wayne, Kirk Douglas, Howard Keel, Keenan Wynn. **1967 DVD**

•**WAR ZONE, THE** ★★1/2 A teenage boy (Freddie Cunliffe) suspects his father (Ray Winstone) is sexually abusing his sister (Lara Belmont). The theme of the film, from Alexander Stuart's novel, is the destruction of a family. But in director Tim Roth's relentlessly bleak and sullen film, the family is miserable and joyless even before the boy's suspicions are confirmed, so there seems no great loss. Rated R for profanity and graphic scenes of incest. 98m. **DIR:** Tim Roth. **CAST:** Ray Winstone, Tilda Swinton, Lara Belmont, Freddie Cunliffe. **1999**

WARBIRDS ★★ Inept action flick concerns American intervention in a Middle Eastern revolution. Rated R for violence and profanity. 88m. **DIR:** Ulli Lommel. **CAST:** Jim Eldbert. **1988**

WARBUS ★★ A Vietnam adventure about a motley crew fleeing a mission in a school bus, heading south during the closing days of the war. Hardly realistic, but the characters are likable and the action is tightly paced. Rated R for violence and profanity.

90m. **DIR:** Ted Kaplan. **CAST:** Daniel Stephen, Rom Kristoff, Urs Althaus, Gwendoline Cook, Ernie Zarte, Don Gordon. **1985**

WARGAMES ★★★1/2 A young computer whiz (Matthew Broderick) who thinks he's hooking into a game manufacturer's computer accidentally starts World War III when he decides to "play" a selection titled "Global Thermonuclear Warfare." Though the movie contains almost no violence or any other sensationalistic content (apart from a wee bit of vulgar language), it still grips the viewer. Rated PG. 114m. **DIR:** John Badham. **CAST:** Matthew Broderick, Dabney Coleman, Ally Sheedy, John Wood, Barry Corbin. **1983 DVD**

WARHEAD ★★★ Special forces ranger tries to stop a white supremacist who has stolen a nuclear warhead and pointed it at Washington, D.C. Obviously inspired by *Broken Arrow*, this is weak on plot but features two extended action sequences that make it worthwhile for genre fans. Rated R for violence and profanity. 97m. **DIR:** Mark Roper. **CAST:** Frank Zagarino, Joe Lara, Elizabeth Giordano. **1996**

WARLOCK (1959) ★★★ Even a high-voltage cast cannot energize this slow-paced "adult" Western. Lack of action hurts this film, which concentrates on psychological homosexual aspects of the relationship between gunfighter Henry Fonda and gambler Anthony Quinn. Richard Widmark is all but lost in the background as the town sheriff. 121m. **DIR:** Edward Dmytryk. **CAST:** Henry Fonda, Richard Widmark, Anthony Quinn, Dorothy Malone. **1959**

WARLOCK (1988) ★★★ An ancient witch-hunter follows an evil warlock to the streets of contemporary Los Angeles. Some great one-liners and a streamlined story help this entry. Rated R for violence, profanity, and gore. 102m. **DIR:** Steve Miner. **CAST:** Julian Sands, Lori Singer, Richard E. Grant, Mary Woronov, Allan Miller, Anna Levine, David Carpenter. **1988 DVD**

WARLOCK: THE ARMAGEDDON 🎬 The son of Satan returns for the final battle between good and evil in this rock-bottom stinker. Rated R for extreme violence and gore. 93m. **DIR:** Anthony Hickox. **CAST:** Julian Sands, Joanna Pacula. **1993 DVD**

•**WARLOCK III: THE END OF INNOCENCE** 🎬 Tedious sequel brings nothing new to the party and finds itself falling back on the old haunted house theme with lackluster results. Not nearly as exciting or terrifying as the original. Rated R for adult situations, language, and violence. 94m. **DIR:** Eric Freiser. **CAST:** Bruce Payne, Ashley Laurence, Angel Boris. **1999 DVD**

WARLORDS 🎬 Genetic engineering goes awry in a postnuclear holocaust world. Rated R for graphic violence and profanity. 87m. **DIR:** Fred Olen Ray. **CAST:** David Carradine, Sid Haig, Ross Hagen, Robert Quarry. **1988**

WARLORDS OF HELL 🎬 Two dirt bike–riding brothers wander into a marijuana plantation south of the border. Rated R for nudity, violence, and profanity. 76m. **DIR:** Clark Henderson. **CAST:** Brad Henson, Jeffrey D. Rice. **1987**

WARLORDS OF THE 21ST CENTURY 🎬 A cold-blooded killer leads his band of roving outlaws in a siege against a peaceful community. Rated R for violence. 91m. DIR: Harley Cokliss. CAST: James Wainwright, Annie McEnroe, Michael Beck. 1982

WARM NIGHTS ON A SLOW MOVING TRAIN ★★1/2 In this offbeat drama, Wendy Hughes portrays a schoolteacher who spends many of her nights as a prostitute on a passenger train in order to support her ailing, morphine-dependent brother. Rated R for simulated sex. 91m. DIR: Bob Ellis. CAST: Wendy Hughes, Colin Friels, Norman Kaye. 1989

WARM SUMMER RAIN ❤ Self-destructive woman botches a suicide attempt, flees to a roadside bar, purchases a five-legged iguana, uses it to belt a persistent fellow trying to pick her up, and then spends the rest of the film having her way with the same guy. Rated R for nudity. 96m. DIR: Joe Gayton. CAST: Kelly Lynch, Barry Tubb. 1989

WARNING, THE ❤ Convoluted dirty-cop flick from Italy. Not rated, but probably equal to an R for violence, profanity, and nudity. 101m. DIR: Damiano Damiani. CAST: Martin Balsam, Giuliano Gemma, Giancarlo Zanetti. 1985

WARNING SHADOWS (1923) ★★★★ An insane husband's jealousy of his wife's lover comes to a head when a hypnotist performs a shadow play mirroring the trio's emotions and passions. A classic post–World War I German cinema drama laced with mystery, fantasy, romance, and psychological terror. Silent with English and German titles. B&W; 93m. DIR: Arthur Robison. CAST: Fritz Kortner, Ruth Weyher. 1923

WARNING SHADOWS (1933) ★★ Bela Lugosi hams it to the hilt as the curator of the House of Mystery. He's the tainted genius behind the lifelike wax figures that move and speak like human creatures. But is he the mysterious Whispering Shadow who jams the airwaves and can eavesdrop and even murder people by remote-control radio and television? This Mascot serial, though stilted and creaky, is worth a watch. B&W; 12 chapters. DIR: Albert Herman, Colbert Clark. CAST: Bela Lugosi, Henry B. Walthall, Karl Dane, Roy D'Arcy, Bob Kortman, Tom London, Lafe McKee, Ethel Clayton. 1933

WARNING SIGN ★★★ This is a passable science-fiction thriller about what happens when an accident occurs at a plant, producing a particularly virulent microbe for germ warfare. Rated R for violence and gore. 99m. DIR: Hal Barwood. CAST: Sam Waterston, Kathleen Quinlan, Yaphet Kotto, Jeffrey DeMunn, Richard Dysart, G. W. Bailey, Rick Rossovich. 1985

WARRIOR AND THE SORCERESS, THE ❤ Sword-and-sorcery version of *A Fistful of Dollars.* Rated R for gore and nudity. 81m. DIR: John Broderick. CAST: David Carradine, Luke Askew, Maria Socas. 1984

WARRIOR OF THE LOST WORLD ❤ A lone warrior is convinced to help find a woman's father who has been kidnapped by their enemy in a post-apocalyptic world. Not rated; contains violence. 90m. DIR: David Worth. CAST: Robert Ginty, Persis Khambatta, Donald Pleasence, Fred Williamson. 1988

WARRIOR QUEEN ❤ This stinker robs footage from an Italian epic about the eruption of Mount Vesuvius and pads it out with a nonstory about an emissary from Rome inspecting the city of Pompeii. There are

two different versions, an R-rated one with nudity and violence and an unrated one with more nudity. 69/79m. DIR: Chuck Vincent. CAST: Sybil Danning, Donald Pleasence, Richard Hill, Josephine Jacqueline Jones. 1987

WARRIOR SPIRIT ★★★ Two boys become friends in a school for boys. Their differing races (one's white, one's Indian) make their friendship a difficult but ultimately rewarding one. Rated PG. 82m. DIR: Rene Manzor. CAST: Lukas Haas, Allan Musy, Jimmy Herman, Jean-Pierre Matte. 1994

WARRIORS, THE (1955) ★★★ In this, his last swashbuckling role, Errol Flynn looks older than his 46 years. Cast as a British prince, he seems more qualified to battle the bulge and the bottle than the murderous hordes of nasty Peter Finch. Nevertheless, even in his decline, Flynn was more adept with a sword and a leer than anyone else in Hollywood. Though the movie is predictable, it's also quite entertaining. 85m. DIR: Henry Levin. CAST: Errol Flynn, Joanne Dru, Peter Finch, Yvonne Furneaux, Michael Hordern. 1955

WARRIORS, THE (1979) ★★★★ Comic book–style violence and sensibilities made this Walter Hill film an unworthy target for those worried about its prompting real-life gang wars. It's just meant for fun, and mostly it is, as a group of kids try to make their way home through the territories of other, less understanding gangs in a surrealistic New York. Rated R. 94m. DIR: Walter Hill. CAST: Michael Beck, James Remar, Thomas Waites, Deborah Van Valkenburgh. 1979

WARRIORS (1994) ★★ Routine action entry about a highly trained government antiterrorist squad so volatile it's kept behind lock and key and its existence is denied. When the squad's leader escapes, only one man, his protégé, can track him down and defuse him. Gary Busey and Michael Paré walk through this one as hunted and hunter. Rated R for violence and adult language. 100m. DIR: Shimon Dotan. CAST: Gary Busey, Michael Paré, Wendi Fulford. 1994

WARRIORS FROM HELL ❤ When ruthless rebels take over a small African country, a ragtag group of commandos save the day. War truly is hell. Rated R for violence and language. 90m. DIR: Ronnie Isaacs. CAST: Deon Stewardson, Glen Gabela, Shayne Leith, Adrian Pearce. 1990

WARRIORS OF THE APOCALYPSE ★★ Another low-rent post-apocalyptic adventure. Fifty years after war has killed most of the Earth's population, a band of nomads search for a mountain that is said to hold the secret of survival. Rated R for violence and brief nudity. 96m. DIR: Bobby A. Suarez. CAST: Michael James, Deborah Moore. 1985

WARRIORS OF THE WASTELAND ❤ Cheap Italian copy of *Road Warrior*, with nuclear-holocaust survivors battling the evil Templars. Not rated, contains violence and slight nudity. 92m. DIR: Enzo G. Castellari. CAST: Fred Williamson, Timothy Brent, George Eastman, Anna Kanakis, Thomas Moore. 1983

WARRIORS OF VIRTUE ★★ Fantasy world struggle between good and evil. The heroes have sort of a Barney persona until they punch, swat, and join forces to overcome their drug-ingesting, youth-corrupting, ultraviolent adversary. This wouldn't interest adults, and who'd want kids to see it? Rated PG for violence. 95m. DIR: Ronny Yu. CAST: Angus MacFadyen, Mario Yedidia, Marley Shelton. **1997 DVD**

WASH, THE ★★★ A straightforward story of a fading marriage and the rekindling of love, unusual for the advanced age of its characters and the film's offbeat setting among Asian-Americans in California. The talented Mako is memorable as a gruff, seemingly unaffectionate retiree who can't understand why his wife (Nobu McCarthy) wants a separation. Rated PG. 100m. DIR: Michael Toshiyuki Uno. CAST: Mako, Nobu McCarthy. **1988**

WASHINGTON AFFAIR, THE ★★★ Jim Hawley (Tom Selleck) is an incorruptible federal agent who must award a government contract. Walter Nicholson (Barry Sullivan) tries to blackmail Hawley. There are enough surprises in this film to keep most viewers on the edge of their couch. Rated R for simulated sex. 104m. DIR: Victor Stoloff. CAST: Tom Selleck, Barry Sullivan, Carol Lynley. **1977**

WASHINGTON SQUARE ★★★ Henry James's novel was filmed before by William Wyler as *The Heiress*. This version follows the book more closely (except for a bizarre ending that reeks of the 1990s). Wyler's 1949 classic remains unsurpassed. Rated PG. 115m. DIR: Agnieszka Holland. CAST: Jennifer Jason Leigh, Albert Finney, Ben Chaplin, Maggie Smith, Judith Ivey. **1997**

WASP WOMAN (1960) 💗 Laughable cult favorite centers around a cosmetics magnate who turns into a wasp-monster. B&W; 66m. DIR: Roger Corman. CAST: Susan Cabot, Anthony Eisley, Barboura Morris. **1960**

WASP WOMAN, THE (1995) 💗 An aging model and businesswoman takes a dose of wasp venom to regain her youth, but instead turns into a you-know-what in this poorly acted, low-budget horror movie. Rated R for profanity, violence, nudity, and simulated sex. 90m. DIR: Jim Wynorski. CAST: Jennifer Rubin, Doug Wert, Maria Ford, Melissa Brasselle, Daniel J. Travanti. **1995**

WATCH IT ★★★ Peter Gallagher stars in this bittersweet drama about a young man who returns to his hometown to attempt a reconciliation with his male cousin. Moving in with the embittered relative and his roommates, Gallagher falls in love with his cousin's girlfriend. Rated R for nudity and profanity. 105m. DIR: Tom Flynn. CAST: Peter Gallagher, Suzy Amis, John C. McGinley, Jon Tenney, Cynthia Stevenson, Lili Taylor, Tom Sizemore. **1992**

WATCH ME WHEN I KILL 💗 Sylvia Kramer plays a woman who is witness to a murder and is now in danger of becoming one of the killer's next victims. Dubbed in English. Not rated; has violence and profanity. 94m. DIR: Anthony Bido. CAST: Richard Stewart, Sylvia Kramer. **1981**

WATCH ON THE RHINE ★★★★ Lillian Hellman's exposé of Nazi terrorism was brought from Broadway to the screen in first-rate form. Paul Lukas won a best-actor Oscar for his role of an underground leader who fled Germany for the United States, only to be hunted down by Nazi agents. Bette Davis is

wonderful in what was one of her few small supporting roles. B&W; 114m. DIR: Herman Shumlin. CAST: Paul Lukas, Bette Davis, Geraldine Fitzgerald. **1943**

WATCH THE BIRDIE ★★1/2 Red Skelton runs a photo shop and, with a borrowed newsreel camera, unknowingly films crooks. Passable family fodder. B&W; 71m. DIR: Jack Donohue. CAST: Red Skelton, Arlene Dahl, Ann Miller. **1950**

WATCHED! 💗 A former U.S. attorney suffers a drug-related mental breakdown and kills a narcotics agent. Not rated. 95m. DIR: John Parsons. CAST: Stacy Keach, Harris Yulin, Brigid Polk, Tony Serra. **1973**

WATCHER IN THE WOODS, THE ★★ This typical teenage gothic plot (family moves into old mansion and strange things begin to happen) is completely obscure and ends by defiantly refusing to explain itself. Rated PG because of minor violence. 84m. DIR: John Hough. CAST: Bette Davis, Lynn-Holly Johnson, Carroll Baker, David McCallum. **1980**

WATCHERS ★★★1/2 Based on the novel by Dean R. Koontz, this is a refreshing sci-fi–horror film. About a boy (Corey Haim) who finds a superintelligent dog and becomes the target of a scientifically created monster, it plays fair with the viewer throughout. Director Jon Hess even leaves quite a bit to the imagination, building the kind of suspense so seldom seen in this age of gore-infested hack-'em-ups. Rated R for violence and profanity. 91m. DIR: Jon Hess. CAST: Corey Haim, Barbara Williams, Michael Ironside. **1988**

WATCHERS II ★★★ Huge fun for animal lovers, as a computer-literate dog aids a hapless couple in thwarting the activities of a murderous runaway biological experiment, reminiscent of Ridley Scott's *Alien*. Littered with classic horror homage, including a climax under L.A.'s storm drains. Rated R. 101m. DIR: Thierry Notz. CAST: Marc Singer, Tracy Scoggins, Irene Miracle, Mary Woronov. **1989**

WATER ★★★ In this delightful British comedy, Michael Caine is the governor of the small English colony located on the island of Cascara. The governor's wife (Brenda Vaccaro) is bored until an oil company sends out a famous actor to film a commercial. Pleasant craziness accompanied by a great soundtrack featuring the music of Eddy Grant, and a jam session with Ringo Starr, George Harrison, and Eric Clapton. Rated PG-13. 91m. DIR: Dick Clement. CAST: Michael Caine, Brenda Vaccaro, Valerie Perrine, Fred Gwynne. **1986**

WATER BABIES, THE ★★★ Big fans of *Mary Poppins* should enjoy this. In Victorian England a chimney sweep's apprentice has a series of adventures with animated characters who live underwater. Designed more for kids than for families, though adults can enjoy the cast of fine British character actors. Rated G. 93m. DIR: Lionel Jeffries. CAST: James Mason, Billie Whitelaw, Bernard Cribbins, Joan Greenwood, David Tomlinson. **1979**

WATER ENGINE, THE ★★★1/2 What happens when an assembly-line worker invents an engine that runs on water for its only fuel is the main thrust of this fine drama written by David Mamet. Greed, back-stabbing, and other selfish motives come into play as word of the engine begins to circulate. Set in

Chicago during the 1930s, the film boasts several very good performances and fine production values. 108m. **DIR:** Steven Schachter. **CAST:** Charles Durning, Patti LuPone, John Mahoney, Joe Mantegna, Treat Williams, William H. Macy, Joanna Miles. **1992**

WATERBOY, THE ★★★1/2 Adam Sandler is at his comedic best as the product of a deranged mother (Kathy Bates) and the back bayous of Louisiana. While serving as a much-abused waterboy, he's discovered for his inner rage by a desperate football coach (Henry Winkler). Hilarious scenes as both the coach and Sandler's sexy girlfriend take on momma. Rated PG-13 for language and sexual innuendo. 88m. **DIR:** Frank Coraci. **CAST:** Adam Sandler, Henry Winkler, Kathy Bates, Fairuza Balk. **1998 DVD**

WATERDANCE, THE ★★★★ Eric Stoltz, Wesley Snipes, and William Forsythe are superb in writer-codirector Neal Jimenez's fictionalized retelling of the aftermath of a hiking accident that left him permanently paralyzed from the waist down. An absorbing, emotional, and often suprisingly humorous story of confronting the unthinkable. Rated R for profanity and violence. 106m. **DIR:** Neal Jimenez, Michael Steinberg. **CAST:** Eric Stoltz, Wesley Snipes, William Forsythe, Helen Hunt, Elizabeth Peña. **1992**

WATERFRONT ★★ Classic film villains John Carradine and J. Carrol Naish are properly menacing as Nazi spies who try to convert German-Americans to their cause in this low-budget wartime espionage drama. Uninspired. B&W; 68m. **DIR:** Steve Sekely. **CAST:** John Carradine, J. Carrol Naish, Terry Frost. **1944**

WATERHOLE #3 ★★★ Amusing Western-comedy follows the misadventures of three outlaws, led by James Coburn, who rob the Union Army of a fortune in gold. 95m. **DIR:** William A. Graham. **CAST:** James Coburn, Carroll O'Connor, Margaret Blye, Bruce Dern, Claude Akins, Joan Blondell, James Whitmore. **1967**

WATERLAND ★★★★ Jeremy Irons gives a superb performance as an Englishman suffering a nervous breakdown while teaching history at American high school. At a loss to reach his disaffected students, let alone his increasingly manic-depressive wife, Irons turns to his past in an effort to explain the present. Rated R for nudity and profanity. 95m. **DIR:** Stephen Gyllenhaal. **CAST:** Jeremy Irons, Ethan Hawke, John Heard, Sinead Cusack, Grant Warnock, Lena Headley, David Morrissey. **1992**

WATERLOO ★★ Spectacular action and a confusing plot make a muddled movie. The story of Napoleon's defeat is staged in detail with the deft touch of Russia's Sergei Bondarchuk making it look larger than life. But the characters are cardboard and the dialogue lifeless. 123m. **DIR:** Sergei Bondarchuk. **CAST:** Rod Steiger, Orson Welles, Christopher Plummer, Jack Hawkins, Dan O'Herlihy, Virginia McKenna, Michael Wilding. **1971**

WATERLOO BRIDGE ★★★★ A five-hanky romance about the lives of two people caught in the turmoil of World War II. This is a poignant tale of a beautiful ballerina (Vivien Leigh) who falls in love with a British officer (Robert Taylor) and how her life is altered when he leaves for the battlefields of Europe. This is one of Leigh's best performances, although

she rarely gave a bad one. B&W; 103m. **DIR:** Mervyn LeRoy. **CAST:** Vivien Leigh, Robert Taylor, Lucile Watson. **1941**

WATERMELON MAN ★★ A bigoted white man wakes up one morning and finds himself black. Using the late, great black comedian Godfrey Cambridge in the title role shows that someone in production had his head on right, The film makes a statement. Trouble is, it makes it over and over and over again. Rated R. 97m. **DIR:** Melvin Van Peebles. **CAST:** Godfrey Cambridge, Estelle Parsons. **1970**

WATERSHIP DOWN ★★★★ Although it's a full-length cartoon about the adventures of a group of rabbits, you'll find no cutesy, Disney-styled Thumpers à la *Bambi*. About the odyssey that a small group of rabbits undertakes after one of them has a vision of evil things coming to destroy their homes. Their arduous journey is full of surprises and rewards. Rated PG. 92m. **DIR:** Martin Rosen. **1978**

WATERWORLD ★★★1/2 This futuristic adventure tale is better than its reputation would suggest. Costner stars as a "fish man" in the far future fighting for survival on an Earth that is almost completely covered by water. Although the story is a bit too reminiscent of George Miller's *Mad Max* trilogy there are still enough memorable moments in this science-fiction–adventure movie to make it well worth watching. Rated PG-13 for violence, nudity, and profanity. 135m. **DIR:** Kevin Reynolds. **CAST:** Kevin Costner, Dennis Hopper, Jeanne Tripplehorn, Tina Majorino, Michael Jeter, Gerard Murphy, R. D. Call, Kim Coates, Robert Joy, John Toles-Bey. **1995 DVD**

WAVELENGTH (1983) ★★★★ You've seen it all many times before in science-fiction movies of wide-ranging quality: the innocent visitors from outer space, the callous government officials who see them as guinea pigs instead of guests, the handful of compassionate Earthlings, even the race to the mother ship. But rarely has the plot been used so effectively. Rated PG. 87m. **DIR:** Mike Gray. **CAST:** Robert Carradine, Cherie Currie, Keenan Wynn. **1983**

WAVELENGTH (1995) ★★★ Romantic comedy stars Jeremy Piven as an Oxford professor desperately trying to unlock the mysteries of the universe. Too bad he can't unlock the mysteries of love, having both a wonderful wife (Kelli Williams) and a girlfriend (Liza Walker). Under pressure at work and in bed, Piven has only one person he can turn to—"The Visitor," played by Richard Attenborough. Nice little slice-of-life comedy. Rated R for profanity and adult situations. 94m. **DIR:** Benjamin Fry. **CAST:** Jeremy Piven, Kelli Williams, Liza Walker, Richard Attenborough. **1995**

WAX ★★1/2 Bizarre, hallucinatory film about a NASA weapons-guidance programmer and beekeeper. He enters an alternative reality after his bees drill a hole in his head and install a mirrored crystal that sends strange images to his brain. Shot on videotape, with film spliced in, plus some nifty computer simulated graphics. This film can either fascinate or disconcert, depending on the viewer's taste. Not rated. 85m. **DIR:** David Blair. **CAST:** David Blair, Meg Savlov, William S. Burroughs. **1993**

WAXWORK ★★★ In this thrilling tongue-in-cheek horror film, six college students are invited to a midnight show at a mysterious wax museum. The sets of wax figures, famous monsters and killers, are missing one ingredient that can bring them all back to life: a dead victim. Rated R. 100m. **DIR:** Anthony Hickox. **CAST:** Zach Galligan, Deborah Foreman, Michelle Johnson, Miles O'Keeffe, Patrick Macnee, David Warner. **1988**

WAXWORK II: LOST IN TIME ★★ The two survivors of the previous film embark on a journey through time and meet various famous movie monsters. Fairly entertaining, especially to fans of classic horror films. Not rated; contains violence. 104m. **DIR:** Anthony Hickox. **CAST:** Zach Galligan, Alexander Godunov, Bruce Campbell. **1991**

WAXWORKS ★★★ A young poet dreams about the wax figures he sees in a fair booth: an Oriental sultan (Harun-al-Rashid), Ivan the Terrible, and Jack the Ripper. Outstanding example of the German Expressionist cinema in the 1920s. Silent. B&W; 63m. **DIR:** Paul Leni. **CAST:** William Dieterle, Emil Jannings, Conrad Veidt, Werner Krauss. **1924**

WAY BACK HOME ♥ Whatever cornball charm this folksy little radio-related oddity can claim relies on rural amusements, songs, hymns, and a plot line old as the hills. Bette Davis was originally billed seventh. B&W; 81m. **DIR:** William A. Seiter. **CAST:** Bette Davis, Phillips Lord, Frankie Darro. **1932**

WAY DOWN EAST ★★★ Classic story of a young woman ostracized by her family and community was an audience favorite of the early part of this century but old hat even by 1920, when this melodrama was released. Justly famous for the exciting and dangerous flight of the beautiful Lillian Gish across the ice floes, pursued and eventually rescued by stalwart yet sensitive Richard Barthelmess, this was one of classic director D. W. Griffith's last solid critical and commercial blockbusters. Silent. B&W; 119m. **DIR:** D. W. Griffith. **CAST:** Lillian Gish, Richard Barthelmess, Lowell Sherman. **1920 DVD**

WAY OUT WEST ★★★★★ Stan Laurel and Oliver Hardy travel west to deliver a gold mine map to the daughter of a friend. The map is given to an imposter, and the boys have to retrieve it and ensure correct delivery. A delightful, marvelous film that demonstrates the team's mastery of timing and characterization. B&W; 65m. **DIR:** James W. Horne. **CAST:** Stan Laurel, Oliver Hardy, Sharon Lynn. **1937**

WAY WE WERE, THE ★★★1/2 The popular theme song somewhat obscures the fact that this is a rather slow-moving romance about a Jewish girl (Barbra Streisand) who marries a WASPish writer (Robert Redford). The film has its moments, but a portion dealing with the McCarthy Communist witch-hunt falls flat. Rated PG. 118m. **DIR:** Sydney Pollack. **CAST:** Barbra Streisand, Robert Redford, Patrick O'Neal, Viveca Lindfors, Bradford Dillman, Lois Chiles. **1973 DVD**

WAY WEST, THE (1967) ★★ A strong cast cannot buoy this bloated Western about a wagon train inching its way along the Oregon Trail in 1843. Director Andrew McLaglen is obviously trying to make an epic in the style of his mentor, John Ford, but he fails miserably. 122m. **DIR:** Andrew V. McLaglen. **CAST:** Robert Mitchum, Kirk Douglas, Richard Widmark, Sally Field, Lola Albright, Stubby Kaye, John Mitchum. **1967**

WAY WEST, THE (1995) ★★★★ This four-part PBS miniseries is a detailed and informative look at an era that shaped our nation's character, the westward movement and the devastation of the Native Americans. Hosted by Russell Baker. Not rated. 360m. **DIR:** Ric Burns. **1995**

WAYNE'S WORLD ★★★1/2 Mike Myers and Dana Carvey re-create and flesh out their characters from the recurring *Saturday Night Live* sketch in this comedy that will appeal primarily to the show's fans. The familiar story has our heroes fighting a sleazy promoter to maintain the integrity of their cable show when it is moved to commercial television. Rated PG-13 for profanity and sexual humor. 95m. **DIR:** Penelope Spheeris. **CAST:** Mike Myers, Dana Carvey, Rob Lowe, Tia Carrere, Brian Doyle-Murray, Lara Flynn Boyle, Ed O'Neill, Colleen Camp, Donna Dixon, Alice Cooper, Meat Loaf. **1992**

WAYNE'S WORLD 2 ★★ More idiocy from the goofy head-banger hosts of cable-access TV—but not as infectiously funny. *Saturday Night Live* characters Wayne Campbell and Garth Algar return to stage a massive rock concert (Waynestock) amid misadventures filled with more movie spoofs than memorable laughs. Rated PG-13 for language and suggested sex. 91m. **DIR:** Stephen Surjik. **CAST:** Mike Myers, Dana Carvey, Tia Carrere, Olivia D'Abo, Aerosmith, Christopher Walken, Chris Farley, Kim Basinger, James Hong. **1993**

WE ALL LOVED EACH OTHER SO MUCH ★★★★ Exceptional high-spirited comedy about three friends and their lives and loves over the course of three decades. A wonderful homage to Fellini, De Sica, and postwar neorealism. In Italian with English subtitles. 124m. **DIR:** Ettore Scola. **CAST:** Nino Manfredi, Vittorio Gassman, Stefania Sandrelli. **1977**

WE ARE NO ANGELS ★★ Another *Trinity* wannabe. In 1910 a race is set to determine which company will obtain a transport concession. Of course the villains try to stop our heroes Rafael and Angel, but they invent hanggliders and win the race. A good cast makes this enjoyable. Rated PG. 90m. **DIR:** Frank Kramer. **CAST:** John Ireland, Woody Strode, Michael Coby, Paul Smith. **1976**.

WE ARE THE CHILDREN ★★★ This made-for-television story—about an American doctor (Ally Sheedy) who goes to famine-torn Ethiopia and meets up with a globe-trotting television reporter (Ted Danson)—suffers from preachiness. Despite that, Sheedy and Danson, along with Judith Ivey as a nun, give credible performances that make this a film worth watching. 92m. **DIR:** Robert M. Young. **CAST:** Ted Danson, Ally Sheedy, Judith Ivey, Zia Mohyeddin. **1987**

WE DIVE AT DAWN ★★★1/2 Tense story about a British submarine's duel with a German battleship during World War II is top-notch entertainment with a documentary feel. A fine cast and sensitive direction by Anthony Asquith lend this film dignity. B&W; 93m. **DIR:** Anthony Asquith. **CAST:** John Mills, Eric Portman. **1943**

WE OF THE NEVER NEVER ★★★1/2 The compelling story of a woman's year in the Australian outback, where she learns about aborigines and they learn about her, is based on a true-life account written by Jeannie Gunn and published in 1908. Rated G. 132m. **DIR:** Igor Auzins. **CAST:** Angela Punch McGregor, Arthur Dignam, Tony Barry. **1983**

WE THE JURY ★★★★ This excellent court drama focuses on the perspective of the jury in a murder trial involving a media icon. Emotions rage in this made-for-cable original, as very different people try to hash out the facts of the murder and reach a consensus. This conflict, with a little mystery thrown in, compels you to watch to the very end. Not rated. 95m. **DIR:** Sturla Gunnarsson. **CAST:** Kelly McGillis, Lauren Hutton, Nicholas Campbell, Christopher Plummer. **1996**

WE THE LIVING ★★1/2 Weak adaptation of Ayn Rand's compelling novel about a headstrong young Soviet woman who becomes romantically involved with a counterrevolutionary. In Italian with English subtitles. Not rated. B&W; 174m. **DIR:** Goffredo Alessandrini. **CAST:** Fosco Giachetti, Alida Valli, Rossano Brazzi. **1942**

WE THINK THE WORLD OF YOU ★★★1/2 A bittersweet British comedy, set in the 1950s, and based on the autobiographical novel by Joseph R. Ackerley. Alan Bates plays a frustrated and emotionally abused homosexual who can't seem to reconcile his relationship with an ex-sailor/ex-con (Gary Oldman). This is a quirky, gentle, offbeat film, elevated by strong performances. Rated PG. 100m. **DIR:** Colin Gregg. **CAST:** Alan Bates, Gary Oldman, Frances Barber, Max Wall. **1988**

WEAPONS OF MASS DISTRACTION ★★★ Scripter Larry Gelbart tries for the same darkly savage tone he nailed so effectively in *Barbarians at the Gate*, but this study of rival media tycoons is simply too nasty to be all that amusing. Rated R for profanity, violence, and brief nudity. 95m. **DIR:** Stephen Surjik. **CAST:** Gabriel Byrne, Ben Kingsley, Mimi Rogers, Jeffrey Tambor, Illeana Douglas, Chris Mulkey. **1997**

WEB OF DECEIT ★★1/2 West Coast lawyer Linda Purl gets summoned back to the aristocratic Atlanta of her youth, to defend a young man (Paul de Souza) accused of rape and murder. Writer-director Sandor Stern's by-the-numbers mystery is redeemed by the performances. Rated PG-13 for violence. 93m. **DIR:** Sandor Stern. **CAST:** Linda Purl, James Read, Paul de Souza, Larry Black, Barbara Rush. **1990**

WEBBER'S WORLD (AT HOME WITH THE WEBBERS) ★★★1/2 Desperately in need of cash, a dysfunctional family gathers to turn their everyday lives into a twenty-four-hour-a-day cable show. Some moments are downright hilarious. Not rated; contains nudity, adult situations, and strong language. 109m. **DIR:** Brad Marlowe. **CAST:** Jeffrey Tambor, Rita Taggart, Jennifer Tilly, David Arquette, Brian Bloom, Caroline Goodall, Robby Benson. **1993**

•**WEBMASTER** ★★ A computer hacker is drawn further into the cyberworld when another mysterious hacker starts interfering with his online presence. Even computer experts probably won't understand this confusing sci-fi film, notable mostly for its special effects. Rated R for profanity and violence. 102m. **DIR:** Thomas Birch Nielsen. **CAST:** Lars Bom, Lars Borch Nielsen, Jorgen Kiil, Dorthe Westh Lerhmann, Mads Parsum. **1998 DVD**

WEDDING, A (1978) ★★★ The story deals with a wedding between two relatively wealthy families and the comic implications that follow. Fine acting keeps things afloat. Rated PG. 125m. **DIR:** Robert Altman. **CAST:** Carol Burnett, Desi Arnaz Jr., Geraldine Chaplin, Vittorio Gassman, Lillian Gish, Lauren Hutton, Paul Dooley, Howard Duff, Pam Dawber, Dina Merrill, John Considine. **1978**

WEDDING, THE (1972) ★★★★ A wedding between a farm girl and a poet works as an allegory of the internal problems that have troubled Poland for centuries. One of director Andrzej Wajda's most cinematic films, its atmospheric virtuosity will be appreciated even by those who find its themes too obscure. In Polish with English subtitles. Not rated. B&W; 103m. **DIR:** Andrzej Wajda. **CAST:** Eva Zietek, Daniel Olbrychski, Wojiech Pszoniak. **1972**

WEDDING BANQUET, THE ★★★1/2 Gentle comedy about a New York real estate dealer who agrees to marry one of his tenants to help her get a green card and put an end to his parents' attempts to find him "the perfect Chinese wife." This is all done with the knowledge and consent of his male lover. Not rated, the film has brief profanity and suggested sex. 112m. **DIR:** Ang Lee. **CAST:** Winston Chao, May Chin, Mitchell Lichtenstein. **1993**

WEDDING BELL BLUES ★★★ On the verge of age 30, three female friends impulsively decide to head to Las Vegas, find husbands, and divorce them in the same day, just to stop their friends and families from badgering them about being unhitched. This implausible plot serves as a framework for a sharply observed buddy comedy that is well acted by its stars. Rated R for profanity and sexual situations. 101m. **DIR:** Dana Lustig. **CAST:** Illeana Douglas, Julie Warner, Paulina Porizkova, Charles Martin Smith, Richard Edson, Stephanie Beacham. **1996 DVD**

WEDDING GIFT, THE ★★★ A middle-class English couple (Jim Broadbent, Julie Walters) tries to cope with the wife's mysterious, debilitating illness. The film is a pretty standard disease-of-the-week drama, but worth watching for its fine acting, especially by the Walters as the wife and Thora Hird as the dotty old mother-in-law. Rated PG-13 for adult themes and mild profanity. 87m. **DIR:** Richard Loncraine. **CAST:** Julie Walters, Jim Broadbent, Thora Hird, Sian Thomas. **1993**

WEDDING IN BLOOD ★★★★ As in the best of Hitchcock, no one can be trusted in this elegantly perverse murder mystery. Two unhappily married people having an affair plan to rid themselves of their spouses. The spouses, however, have their own plans. In French with English subtitles. 98m. **DIR:** Claude Chabrol. **CAST:** Michel Piccoli, Stéphane Audran, Claude Pieplu. **1973**

WEDDING IN GALILEE, A ★★★★★ A Palestinian village elder is determined to give his son a grand traditional wedding, but to do so he must agree to invite the occupying Israeli leaders as guests of honor.

Exceptional drama works on many levels. Filmed on location in the occupied West Bank. In Arabic and Hebrew with English subtitles. Not rated; contains nudity. 113m. DIR: Michel Khleifi. CAST: Ali Mohammed El Akili. 1987

WEDDING IN WHITE ★★ It's World War II and Carol Kane is the young naïve daughter of an authoritative father who only shows affection for his son. The film succeeds in making you feel outrage, but is bleak from beginning to end. 103m. DIR: William Fruet. CAST: Donald Pleasence, Carol Kane, Doris Petrie. 1972

WEDDING MARCH, THE ★★★1/2 The story is simple: the corrupt, money-hungry family of an Austrian prince forces him to forsake his true love, a penniless musician, and marry a dull, crippled heiress. The telling is incredibly overblown. Critics and big-city audiences acclaimed this film, but it laid eggs by the gross in the hinterlands. Silent. B&W; 140m. DIR: Erich Von Stroheim. CAST: Erich Von Stroheim, Fay Wray, ZaSu Pitts, George Fawcett. 1928

WEDDING PARTY, THE ♥ Plodding and irksome, this is about a groom who develops cold feet. Filmed in 1963, but not released until 1969; B&W; 92m. DIR: Cynthia Munroe, Wilford Leach, Brian De Palma. CAST: Robert De Niro, Jill Clayburgh, Jennifer Salt. 1969

WEDDING REHEARSAL ★★ There's not much magic or comedy in this shaky farce. Director Alexander Korda shows poor directorial technique in this story of an officer whose grandmother plans to get him married. You can catch the whole thing with one eye closed and your favorite radio station on. B&W; 84m. DIR: Alexander Korda. CAST: Roland Young, George Grossmith, John Loder, Lady Tree, Wendy Barrie, Maurice Evans, Merle Oberon. 1932

WEDDING SINGER, THE ★★★1/2 This delightful little love story admirably displays the skills of Adam Sandler and Drew Barrymore. The setting is 1985, and Sandler plays a musician making ends meet by performing as a host/singer at suburban weddings. Barrymore is the perky waitress who catches his eye. Rated PG-13 for profanity and sexual content. 96m. DIR: Frank Coraci. CAST: Adam Sandler, Drew Barrymore, Christine Taylor, Allen Covert, Angela Featherstone. 1998 DVD

WEE WILLIE WINKIE ★★★★ The best of Shirley Temple's features from her star period is this adaptation of a Rudyard Kipling tale. Temple and her screen mother Constance Collier go to live with her disapproving grandfather C. Aubrey Smith in India. It's a real charmer and a fine adventure film to boot. B&W; 100m. DIR: John Ford. CAST: Shirley Temple, Victor McLaglen, C. Aubrey Smith, Cesar Romero, Constance Collier. 1937

WEEDS ★★★ Nick Nolte gives one of his finest performances in this uneven but generally rewarding film as a San Quentin inmate doing "life without possibility" until he secures his release by writing a play that impresses a reporter. Rated R for profanity, nudity, and violence. 115m. DIR: John Hancock. CAST: Nick Nolte, Lane Smith, William Forsythe, Joe Mantegna, Ernie Hudson. 1987

WEEKEND ★★★ Jean-Luc Godard's apocalyptic film can best be described as a dark comic vision of the decline and fall of consumer society through the eyes of a young perverted bourgeois couple. Recommended only for hard-core fans of Godard. Others may find this movie too disgusting and very confusing. In French with English subtitles. Not rated; contains sexual situations and violence. 105m. DIR: Jean-Luc Godard. CAST: Mireille Darc, Jean-Pierre Léaud, Jean Yanne. 1967

WEEKEND AT BERNIE'S ★★1/2 In this tolerable comedy with some hilarious moments, Andrew McCarthy and Jonathan Silverman play upwardly mobile young executives all set to have a wild, wild weekend at their boss's swank beach house—until they find the murdered body of said boss. Terry Kiser steals the show as the dead man, which gives our an idea of how silly it all is. Rated PG-13 for profanity and tasteless humor. 110m. DIR: Ted Kotcheff. CAST: Andrew McCarthy, Jonathan Silverman, Catherine Mary Stewart, Terry Kiser. 1989 DVD

WEEKEND AT BERNIE'S II ★★1/2 More of the same as yuppie junior executives Andrew McCarthy and Jonathan Silverman resurrect their dead boss (Terry Kiser) for another adventure. The plot is pretty lame, but Kiser is hilarious. He shows more life as a corpse—made more animate this time by a voodoo spell—than his supposedly livelier costars. Rated PG for light profanity and sexual violence. 89m. DIR: Robert Klane. CAST: Andrew McCarthy, Jonathan Silverman, Terry Kiser, Barry Bostwick, Tom Wright, Steve James, Troy Beyer. 1993

WEEKEND AT THE WALDORF ★★★ 1932s *Grand Hotel* updated to World War II and transplanted to New York's classiest hotel. Can't touch the original, of course, but well made and polished to a fine gloss. B&W; 130m. DIR: Robert Z. Leonard. CAST: Ginger Rogers, Lana Turner, Walter Pidgeon, Van Johnson, Edward Arnold, Keenan Wynn, Robert Benchley. 1945

WEEKEND IN HAVANA ★★★ To keep salesgirl Alice Faye from suing over a mishap, a luxury-liner company sends executive John Payne to Havana to see she has a good vacation. Lots of songs and some good laughs, particularly from Cesar Romero as a two-bit lothario. Some cassettes open with an "added feature" of Faye singing "I'll See You in My Dreams." This was deleted from the movie before its release. 80m. DIR: Walter Lang. CAST: Alice Faye, Carmen Miranda, John Payne, Cesar Romero, Cobina Wright Jr., George Barbier, Sheldon Leonard, Leonid Kinskey, Crispin Martin, Billy Gilbert. 1941

WEEKEND IN THE COUNTRY, A ★★★ Assorted neurotic characters converge in California's Napa Valley wine country in this West Coast cousin of Woody Allen's ensemble comedies. Although written and directed by the team responsible for *Peter's Friends*, the various elements here don't mesh quite as well. Rated PG for profanity and sexual candor. 95m. DIR: Martin Bergman. CAST: Jennifer Elise Cox, Faith Ford, Christine Lahti, Jack Lemmon, Richard Lewis, Dudley Moore, Rita Rudner, John Shea, Betty White. 1995

WEEKEND WAR ★★ A group of National Guardsmen are assigned to repair a bridge in Honduras near the Nicaraguan border. Effective but bland antiwar drama. 100m. DIR: Steven H. Stern. CAST:

Stephen Collins, Daniel Stern, Michael Beach, James Tolkan, Charles Haid. **1988**

WEEKEND WARRIORS ★★ Mildly amusing, excessively wacky tale of Hollywood actors, writers, and singers circa 1961—avoiding combat by enlisting in the reserves. Rated R for profanity and sexual innuendo. 90m. **DIR:** Bert Convy. **CAST:** Chris Lemmon, Lloyd Bridges, Vic Tayback, Graham Jarvis, Tom Villard. **1986**

WEEP NO MORE MY LADY ★★1/2 Agreeable adaptation of Mary Higgins Clark's bestselling mystery about the murder of a popular actress, with a French chateau full of suspects. Made-for-Canadian-cable effort maintains its level of suspense thanks to a tight script and a strong leading performance by Daniel J. Travanti. Rated PG-13 for violence and drug content. 92m. **DIR:** Michel Andrieu. **CAST:** Daniel J. Travanti, Shelley Winters, Kristin Scott Thomas, Francesca Annis. **1992**

WEIRD SCIENCE ★★★ In this wacky comedy by writer-director John Hughes, two put-upon nerds (Anthony Michael Hall and Ilan Mitchell-Smith), desperate for a date, cop an idea from James Whale's *Frankenstein* and create a sexy woman via computer. Thus begins a roller-coaster ride of hit-and-miss humor as the nerds get class fast. Rated PG-13 for slight violence, partial nudity, and profanity. 94m. **DIR:** John Hughes. **CAST:** Anthony Michael Hall, Kelly LeBrock, Ilan Mitchell-Smith, Bill Paxton. **1985 DVD**

WEIRD WOMAN ★★★ Second and best of the *Inner Sanctum* movies has Lon Chaney Jr. as a college professor who suspects that his new wife (Anne Gwynne) is using voodoo to advance his career. Later remade as *Burn Witch Burn!* and *Witches' Brew.* B&W; 62m. **DIR:** Reginald LeBorg. **CAST:** Lon Chaney Jr., Anne Gwynne, Evelyn Ankers, Ralph Morgan. **1944**

WELCOME HOME ★★★1/2 This unjustly neglected drama makes ample use of Kris Kristofferson (in perhaps his best performance ever) as a Vietnam soldier presumed killed in action, who fourteen years later turns up in Thailand needing medical assistance. Once back stateside, he learns his wife has remarried. Rated R for language and brief nudity. 90m. **DIR:** Franklin J. Schaffner. **CAST:** Kris Kristofferson, JoBeth Williams, Sam Waterston, Brian Keith. **1990**

WELCOME HOME, ROXY CARMICHAEL ★★★★ Although shunned at the box office, Karen Leigh Hopkins's perceptive and poignant little tale says a great deal about friendship, love, and the dangers of idol worship. Winona Ryder stars as Dinky Bossetti, a small-town girl attaching special significance to the return of Roxy Carmichael, a local legend who achieved fame and fortune on the West Coast. Rated PG-13 for language. 98m. **DIR:** Jim Abrahams. **CAST:** Winona Ryder, Jeff Daniels, Laila Robins, Dinah Manoff. **1990**

WELCOME, STRANGER ★★★ Made to cash in on the popularity of Bing Crosby's successful teamwork with Barry Fitzgerald after both won Oscars for *Going My Way,* this movie casts them as doctors instead of priests. B&W; 107m. **DIR:** Elliott Nugent. **CAST:** Bing

Crosby, Barry Fitzgerald, Joan Caulfield, Percy Kilbride, Charles Dingle, Elizabeth Patterson. **1947**

WELCOME TO 18 ♥ This low-budget film's only point of interest is that it marks the big-screen debut of Mariska Hargitay, the daughter of Jayne Mansfield. Rated PG-13 for profanity and nudity. 91m. **DIR:** Terry Carr. **CAST:** Mariska Hargitay, Courtney Thorne-Smith, Jo Ann Willette. **1986**

WELCOME TO L.A. ★★★1/2 Extremely well-made film concerning the disjointed love lives of several of Los Angeles's nouveaux riches. The film's focal point is songwriter Keith Carradine, whose romantic interludes set the wheels in motion. Entire cast is first-rate, with Richard Baskin's musical score the only drawback. Rated R. 106m. **DIR:** Alan Rudolph. **CAST:** Keith Carradine, Geraldine Chaplin, Harvey Keitel, Sally Kellerman, Sissy Spacek, Lauren Hutton. **1977**

WELCOME TO SARAJEVO ★★★★1/2 Using a seamless blend of graphic news footage and impassioned drama, this scathing drama crawls under the skin of the international press corps and inhabitants of battle-ravaged Sarajevo in the summer of 1992. A television newsman smuggles a young girl out of the country to reawaken his numb humanity. Inspired by the true story of British journalist Michael Nicholson. Rated R for violence, war atrocities, and language. 101m. **DIR:** Michael Winterbottom. **CAST:** Stephen Dillane, Woody Harrelson, Marisa Tomei, Emira Nusevic, Kerry Fox. **1997**

WELCOME TO SPRING BREAK ★★ Two of the least reputable movie genres—beach party and slasher—meet as an executed biker returns from the dead to wreak vengeance. *Where the Boys Are* it ain't. Rated R for violence and nudity. 92m. **DIR:** Harry Kirkpatrick. **CAST:** Nicolas de Toth, Sarah Buxton, Michael Parks, John Saxon. **1989**

WELCOME TO THE DOLLHOUSE ★★★★★ An awkward, unattractive New Jersey 11-year-old is degraded at school and dismissed at home by parents who like her siblings better. Writer-director Todd Solondz finds scathing humor in nasty, heartbreaking behavior, and his cast of mostly unknowns creates a superbly observed tapestry of tacky self-absorption. A scream in every sense of the word. Rated R. 87m. **DIR:** Todd Solondz. **CAST:** Heather Matarazzo, Brendan Sexton Jr., Daria Kalinina, Matthew Faber, Eric Mabius. **1996 DVD**

WELCOME TO WOOP WOOP ★★★ Madcap whimsy in the small Australian outback town of Woop Woop, where everyone is welcome, but no one is allowed to leave. Woop Woop is a destination filled with laughs and heart. Rated R for language and adult situations. 97m. **DIR:** Stephan Elliott. **CAST:** Johnathon Schaech, Rod Taylor, Susie Porter, Paul Mercurio, Rachel Griffiths, Dee Smart. **1997**

WELL, THE ★★★ When a small black child becomes trapped in the bottom of a well, the gathering crowd's reactions say a lot about the small town in which they live. Powerful stuff. B&W; 85m. **DIR:** Leo Popkin, Russell Rouse. **CAST:** Harry Morgan, Barry Kelley, Ernest Anderson, Christine Larson. **1951**

WELL-DIGGER'S DAUGHTER, THE ★★★1/2 A well digger disowns his daughter when she is seduced and abandoned, but they are reunited by his assistant. As in all of the films of Marcel Pagnol, a melodramatic story becomes something greater. In French with English subtitles. B&W; 142m. DIR: Marcel Pagnol. CAST: Raimu, Fernandel, Charpin. 1940

WE'RE BACK! A DINOSAUR'S STORY ★★1/2 Jumbled animated adaptation of the popular book by Hudson Talbott. A quartet of dinosaurs are fed intelligence-increasing Brain Grain by an intergalactic traveler and brought forward in time to fulfill the wishes of modern-day kids. The animation is first-rate, but the screenplay by John Patrick Shanley will confuse even adults. In addition, scenes set in a scary circus may be too frightening for the small fry. Rated G. 72m. DIR: Dick Zondag, Ralph Zondag, Phil Nibbelink, Simon Wells. 1993

WE'RE GOING TO EAT YOU! ★★ A gross, stylish horror-comedy about an island inhabited by cannibals and the predictably grisly fate that awaits those who stray into their clutches. If you thought there was nothing new in the cannibal subgenre, see this wild low-budget item. Not rated, but with plenty of gore on an NC-17 level. 90m. DIR: Tsui Hark. 1980

WE'RE NO ANGELS (1955) ★★1/2 The *New York Times* dubbed this "a slow, talky reprise of the delightful stage comedy" and was right. Three Devil's Island convicts "adopt" an island family and protect it against an uncle it can do without. There is a roguishness about the trio that almost makes them endearing, but the film does drag. 106m. DIR: Michael Curtiz. CAST: Humphrey Bogart, Peter Ustinov, Aldo Ray, Basil Rathbone, Joan Bennett, Leo G. Carroll. 1955

WE'RE NO ANGELS (1989) ★★★1/2 The screenplay by David Mamet is a goofy send-up of the old Warner Bros. gangster melodramas, with Robert De Niro and Sean Penn mugging it up as a couple of escaped convicts mistaken for priests, who find themselves involved in a miracle. Director Neil Jordan couldn't decide whether he was making a crime-drama or a comedy. Rated PG-13 for nudity, profanity, and violence. 106m. DIR: Neil Jordan. CAST: Robert De Niro, Sean Penn, Demi Moore, James Russo, Ray McAnally, Hoyt Axton, Wallace Shawn, Bruno Kirby. 1989

WE'RE NOT DRESSING ★★★1/2 A shipwreck strands an heiress and her snob friends on an island. They are taught how to survive by an easygoing sailor (Bing Crosby). Short, fast-moving musical comedy based on James Barrie's classic, *The Admirable Crichton*. Barrie is not credited, but his play is mentioned. B&W; 74m. DIR: Norman Taurog. CAST: Bing Crosby, Carole Lombard, George Burns, Gracie Allen, Ethel Merman, Leon Errol, Ray Milland. 1934

WE'RE NOT MARRIED ★★★1/2 Assorted couples learn their marriages were performed illegally, so now they have certain options. Great episodic comedy. B&W; 85m. DIR: Edmund Goulding. CAST: Fred Allen, Eve Arden, Eddie Bracken, Louis Calhern, Paul Douglas, Zsa Zsa Gabor, Mitzi Gaynor, Marilyn Monroe, Victor Moore, Ginger Rogers, David Wayne. 1952

WE'RE TALKING SERIOUS MONEY ★★ Two con artists cheat a mob boss in New York and end up running to California. Unbelievable characters and bad acting make this a disappointing film. Rated PG-13

for profanity and violence. 92m. DIR: James Lemmo. CAST: Dennis Farina, Leo Rossi, Fran Drescher. 1991

WEREWOLF 🖤 Archaeological team in the Mexican desert digs up the bones of an ancient werewolf, starting the predictable results. Rated R for nudity, violence, and profanity. 99m. DIR: Tony Zarindast. CAST: Jorge Rivero, Fred Cavalli, Adrianna Miles, Joe Estevez, Jules Desjarlais, Richard Lynch. 1996 DVD

WEREWOLF OF LONDON ★★★ Universal's first attempt at a werewolf film is full of fog, atmosphere, and laboratory shots but short on chills and horror. Henry Hull just doesn't make the grade when his fangs grow. B&W; 75m. DIR: Stuart Walker. CAST: Henry Hull, Warner Oland, Valerie Hobson, Lester Matthews, Spring Byington. 1935

WEREWOLF OF WASHINGTON ★★ Dean Stockwell plays the president's press secretary, who becomes a werewolf after a visit to eastern Europe. Although it was made at the height of the Watergate scandal, this satire is surprisingly lacking in bite. Stockwell gives a game performance, but the script doesn't give him much to work with. Rated PG. 90m. DIR: Milton Moses Ginsberg. CAST: Dean Stockwell, Biff McGuire, Clifton James, Michael Dunn. 1973

•**WEREWOLF REBORN!** ★★ Second in the *Filmonsters* series is a shadow of its predecessor. While technically well made, the film lacks plausible situations and sensible characters. Here, a young girl travels to Romania to visit her uncle, who has become a werewolf. Rated PG for violence. 70m. DIR: Jeff Burr. CAST: Ashley Cafagna, Robin Downes, Len Lesser. 1998

WEREWOLVES ON WHEELS 🖤 Cursed bikers become werewolves. The worst of two genres. Rated R for nudity and violence. 85m. DIR: Michel Levesque. CAST: Steven Oliver, Barry McGuire, Billy Gray. 1971

WES CRAVEN'S NEW NIGHTMARE ★★★ Director Wes Craven and his cast star as themselves in this wicked spin on the horror genre. Key players from earlier *Nightmare on Elm Street* installments are terrorized by Freddy Krueger and his razor-fingered glove as he crosses over into their offscreen lives. It's a life-imitating-art twist that's ghoulishly fun. Rated R for language, violence, and gore. 109m. DIR: Wes Craven. CAST: Robert Englund, Heather Langenkamp, Miko Hughes, Matt Winston, Rob LaBelle, David Newsom, Wes Craven. 1994 DVD

WES CRAVEN'S WISHMASTER 🖤 Genies don't get much nastier than the Djinn who is released from an ancient Persian opal and tricks people into making requests that he can twist into hideous punishments. Rated R for gore, violence, and language. 96m. DIR: Robert Kurtzman. CAST: Tammy Lauren, Andrew Divoff, Wendy Benson, Kane Hodder, Robert Englund, Tony Todd. 1997 DVD

•**WEST BEIRUT** ★★★★ This autobiographical coming-of-age story of a teen Lebanese boy vividly paints human faces on the victims of the 1975 Beirut bloodshed and anarchy. News footage and splashes of humor provide both a chilling edge to, and affectionate taste of, what it's like to be young and reckless in a war zone. The film takes us into an Arab family under siege as Beirut divides into warring Muslim and Christian camps and a brothel becomes the city's only demilitarized zone. In Arabic with English subtitles. Not rated. 105m. **DIR:** Ziad Doueiri. **CAST:** Rami Doueiri, Mohamad Chamas, Rola Al Amin, Carmen Lebbos, Joseph Bou Nassar. **1999**

WEST OF THE DIVIDE ★★★ John Wayne is on the trail of his father's murderer (again) in this standard B Western, which has the slight twist of having the Duke also searching for his younger brother, who has been missing since dear old Dad took the fatal bullet. Looks as if it was made in a day—and probably was. Good stunt work, though. B&W; 54m. **DIR:** Robert N. Bradbury. **CAST:** John Wayne, Virginia Brown Faire, George "Gabby" Hayes, Yakima Canutt, Earl Dwire. **1934**

WEST OF THE LAW ★★★ The last of the Rough Riders Westerns, this entry takes the series out in style. The heroes help the townspeople defeat a band of rustlers. Buck Jones handles most of the horseback heroics while Tim McCoy instills fear in the bad guys with his steely-eyed stare. B&W; 60m. **DIR:** Howard Bretherton. **CAST:** Buck Jones, Tim McCoy, Raymond Hatton, Evelyn Cooke, Harry Woods, Jack Daley, Roy Barcroft. **1942**

WEST OF ZANZIBAR ★★★ Over-the-top melodrama casts Lon Chaney Sr. as a crippled magician in a jungle village plotting revenge against the man who caused his injuries. The plot is corny, but thanks to Chaney and director Tod Browning (*Freaks*) this is one intense film. Silent. B&W; 63m. **DIR:** Tod Browning. **CAST:** Lon Chaney Sr., Lionel Barrymore, Warner Baxter. **1928**

WEST POINT STORY, THE ★★★ James Cagney is an athletic Broadway hoofer reluctantly becoming involved in the West Point annual cadet review, even trying out dorm life. Oscar nomination for the score by Ray Heindorf. B&W; 107m. **DIR:** Roy Del Ruth. **CAST:** James Cagney, Virginia Mayo, Doris Day, Gordon MacRae, Gene Nelson, Roland Winters, Jerome Cowan, Alan Hale Jr. **1950**

WEST SIDE STORY ★★★★★ The Romeo-and-Juliet theme is updated to 1950s New York and given an endearing music score. The story of rival white and Puerto Rican youth gangs first appeared as a hit Broadway musical and none of the brilliance of the play was lost in its transformation to the screen. It received the Oscar for best picture. (Wood's vocals were dubbed by Marni Nixon.) 151m. **DIR:** Robert Wise, Jerome Robbins. **CAST:** Natalie Wood, Richard Beymer, Rita Moreno, George Chakiris, Russ Tamblyn. **1961 DVD**

WESTERN UNION ★★★1/2 Randolph Scott's strong performance as an outlaw trying to go straight elevates this somewhat predictable Western epic about the coming of telegraph lines to the Wild West. 94m. **DIR:** Fritz Lang. **CAST:** Randolph Scott, Robert Young, Dean Jagger, Virginia Gilmore, John Carradine, Slim Summerville, Chill Wills, Barton MacLane. **1941**

WESTERNER, THE ★★★★ The plot revolves around earnest settlers being run off their land. But the heart of this classic yarn rests in the complex relationship that entwines Judge Roy Bean (Walter Brennan) and a lanky stranger (Gary Cooper). Bean is a fascinating character, burdened with a strange sense of morality and an obsession for actress Lily

Langtry. Brennan won an Oscar for his portraya Cooper is at his laconic best. B&W; 100m. **DIR** William Wyler. **CAST:** Gary Cooper, Walter Brenna Forrest Tucker, Chill Wills, Dana Andrews, Tom Tyle Fred Stone. **1940 DVD**

WESTFRONT 1918 ★★★★ G. W. Pabst's firs sound film chronicles the agonies suffered by fou German soldiers sent to the French front during th last months of World War I. Brilliant use of mobil camera gives the battle scenes a shocking look of re alism. In German with English subtitles. B&W; 98m **DIR:** G. W. Pabst. **CAST:** Gustav Diessl. **1930**

WESTING GAME, THE ★★★ Ellen Raskin's de lightful children's book becomes one of thos equally darling little films made from the viewpoir of a child. Residents in an apartment complex be come involved in a most unusual treasure hunt: on involving lots of money and secrets about the neigh bors. Suitable for all ages. 95m. **DIR:** Terence H. Wink less. **CAST:** Ray Walston, Ashley Peldon, Sally Kirk land, Cliff De Young, Diane Lane. **1997**

WESTWARD HO ★★★ Better production values i this John Wayne B Western, an enjoyable outing i which the star is once again seeking revenge on th outlaws who killed his parents and (in an extra twist kidnapped his brother. B&W; 60m. **DIR:** Robert N. Brad bury. **CAST:** John Wayne, Sheila Manners, Frank Mc Glynn Jr., Jack Curtis, Yakima Canutt, Dickie Jones. **193**

WESTWARD HO, THE WAGONS ★★1/2 Episodi film about a wagon train traveling west. The basi appeal is seeing Fess Parker in another Davy Crock ett–type role and four of the Mouseketeers as chil dren in the train. Devoid of a real beginning or end this movie just rambles along. Not rated. 90m. **DIR** William Beaudine. **CAST:** Fess Parker, Kathleen Crow ley, Jeff York, David Stollery, Sebastian Cabot, George Reeves. **1956**

WESTWARD THE WOMEN ★★★★1/2 A rousing Western that emphasizes the problems of women or the frontier. Indian attacks, cat fights among th women, and accidental deaths can't keep these strong women from finding lonesome cowpokes and populating the frontier. 118m. **DIR:** William Wellman **CAST:** Robert Taylor, Denise Darcel, Hope Emerson Julie Bishop, John McIntire, Marilyn Erskine. **1951**

WESTWORLD ★★★★ This is another science-fic tion yarn from the author Michael Crichton. The film concerns an expensive world for well-to-do vacation ers. They can live out their fantasies in the Old West or King Arthur's Court with the aid of programmed robots repaired nightly by scientists so they can be "killed" the next day by tourists. Richard Benjamin and James Brolin are tourists who come up against a rebellious robot (Yul Brynner). Rated PG. 88m. **DIR:** Michael Crichton. **CAST:** Yul Brynner, Richard Benjamin, James Brolin. **1973 DVD**

WET AND WILD SUMMER 💘 Vulgar Aussie version of Frankie-and-Annette beach movies is sexist, badly acted, and buffoonish. Rated R for nudity, profanity, and general bad taste. 95m. **DIR:** Maurice Murphy, Martin McGrath. **CAST:** Christopher Atkins, Elliott Gould, Julian McMahon, Rebecca Cross. **1993**

WET GOLD 💘 A waitress who follows an old alcoholic's lead to sunken gold. Substandard made-for-

✔ film. 95m. **DIR:** Dick Lowry. **CAST:** Brooke Shields, urgess Meredith, Tom Byrd, Brian Kerwin. 1984

ETHERBY ★★1/2 Buried under *Wetherby*'s dismally portentous attitudes about England and loneliness is a pretty interesting story. The film unfolds ike a thriller, but it doesn't satisfy in the end. √anessa Redgrave in the lead is characteristically excellent. 104m. **DIR:** David Hare. **CAST:** Vanessa Redrave, Ian Holm, Judi Dench, Marjorie Yates, Joely ichardson, Tom Wilkinson, Stuart Wilson. 1985

HALE FOR THE KILLING, A ★★★ Peter Strauss's ramatic, powerful personal statement against the aughter of whales off the rugged coast of Newundland. Based on Canadian environmentalist-ature writer Farley Mowat's noted book indicting he practice. Overlong, but engrossing, TV movie. 50m. **DIR:** Richard T. Heffron. **CAST:** Peter Strauss, ichard Widmark, Dee Wallace, Kathryn Walker, Bruce icGill. 1981

HALES OF AUGUST, THE ★★★ The joy of seeing wo screen legends, Bette Davis and Lillian Gish, together in a film tailor-made for them is considerably nuted by the uneventfulness of playwright David arry's story. Essentially, we watch Davis and Gish lay two elderly sisters who cope, bicker, and reminisce at their summer home on an island off the oast of Maine. Rated PG for profanity. 90m. **DIR:** indsay Anderson. **CAST:** Bette Davis, Lillian Gish, Vinent Price, Ann Sothern, Harry Carey Jr., Mary Steenurgen. 1987

HARF RAT, THE ★★★1/2 Although it starts out low, keep watching this film about two brothers—ne a cop and one a criminal—and you'll be pleasantly surprised. Good acting all around and enteraining action. Rated R for profanity and violence. 90m. **DIR:** Jimmy Huston. **CAST:** Lou Diamond ²hillips, Judge Reinhold, Rachel Ticotin. 1995

HAT ABOUT BOB? ★★★1/2 Fitfully hilarious tale f a deranged but lovable neurotic (Bill Murray) who attaches himself to the family of a high-profile psychiatrist (Richard Dreyfuss) while they're on vacaion. Murray is typically goofy, but Dreyfuss gives a masterfully comic performance. Rated PG for brief profanity. 97m. **DIR:** Frank Oz. **CAST:** Bill Murray, Richard Dreyfuss, Julie Hagerty, Charlie Korsmo. 1991 DVD

HAT COMES AROUND ★★ Jerry Reed stars as a world-famous country-western singer who is strung out on booze and pills. Bo Hopkins plays the younger brother who kidnaps Reed to save him from his own self-destruction. This all-American action-comedy-drama features the country music of Jerry Reed. A must-see for his fans. Rated PG. 92m. **DIR:** Jerry Reed. **CAST:** Jerry Reed, Bo Hopkins, Barry Corbin, Arte Johnson. 1985

WHAT DO YOU SAY TO A NAKED LADY? 💋 Allen Funt's R-rated version of *Candid Camera*. 90m. **DIR:** Allen Funt. **CAST:** Allen Funt, Richard Roundtree. 1970

WHAT DREAMS MAY COME ★★1/2 A physician (Robin Williams) marries the woman of his dreams and starts a family, only to have both children taken away in a tragic accident. Williams dies shortly thereafter, leaving behind a widow who cannot begin to cope. Our hero's adventures in an afterlife of his

own design—apparently we create our own visions of heaven—are interrupted when his Earth-bound wife commits an understandable but selfish act, which threatens to place her beyond reach through all eternity. What follows is a spiritual journey to the borders of heaven and hell. Not everybody will embrace this film: The story—adapted from Richard Matheson's novel—is slow, at times ponderously so, but it will appeal to those who celebrate the preeminent power of devotion. Rated PG-13 for dramatic intensity and brief nudity. 113m. **DIR:** Vincent Ward. **CAST:** Robin Williams, Cuba Gooding Jr., Annabella Sciorra, Max von Sydow. 1998 DVD

WHAT EVER HAPPENED TO . . . ? ★★1/2 Wholly unnecessary TV-movie remake of the 1962 shocker *What Ever Happened to Baby Jane?* The Redgrave sisters earnestly incarnate the Hudson sisters, but Vanessa remains far too passive in the role of the victimized Blanche, while Lynn goes strictly over the top as the grotesquely looney Jane. 100m. **DIR:** David Greene. **CAST:** Lynn Redgrave, Vanessa Redgrave, John Glover, Bruce A. Young, Amy Steel, John Scott Clough, Samantha Jordon, Erinn Canavan. 1991

WHAT EVER HAPPENED TO BABY JANE? ★★★1/2 One of the last hurrahs of screen giants Bette Davis and Joan Crawford in a chillingly unpleasant tale of two aged sisters. Davis plays a former child movie star who spends her declining years dreaming of lost fame and tormenting her sister (Crawford). Victor Buono deserves special notice in a meaty supporting role. B&W; 132m. **DIR:** Robert Aldrich. **CAST:** Bette Davis, Joan Crawford, Victor Buono. 1962 DVD

WHAT HAPPENED WAS . . . ★★★1/2 There are a million stories in the naked city, but few so effectively capture the loneliness accompanying them, even if the execution is a little self-conscious. Writer-director Tommy Noonan shares the screen with Karen Sillas as a couple of colleagues hoping to connect on another level. The script explores and then transcends first-date awkwardness as it strips away the protective layers these two don like clothing. Not rated; contains profanity. 90m. **DIR:** Tommy Noonan. **CAST:** Karen Sillas, Tommy Noonan. 1993

WHAT HAVE I DONE TO DESERVE THIS? ★★★★ Outrageously funny black comedy about a working-class housewife who struggles to maintain her sanity while keeping her crazy family afloat. This perverse fable on contemporary life is superbly directed by Pedro Almodóvar and features a brilliant performance by Carmen Maura. In Spanish with English subtitles. Not rated; contains nudity and profanity. 100m. **DIR:** Pedro Almodóvar. **CAST:** Carmen Maura. 1984

WHAT NEXT, CHARLIE BROWN? ★★★ Poor Charlie Brown has a mighty tough time in these thirteen tales battling kite-eating trees and Lucy's big mouth. Several of the vignettes (all taken from *The Charlie Brown and Snoopy Show*) are rather cruel, and others are quickie blackouts united by common themes such as snow fights and Schroeder's piano. 47m. **DIR:** Bill Melendez, Sam Jaimes, Sam Nicholson, Phil Roman. 1983–1985

WHAT! NO BEER? ★★1/2 Then topical, now dated comedy, with Jimmy Durante pulling his friend, taxidermist Buster Keaton, and his money, into a plan to brew beer and have it ready for sale upon the end of Prohibition. Not enough deadpan Keaton antics. B&W; 66m. **DIR:** Edward Sedgwick. **CAST:** Buster Keaton, Jimmy Durante, Roscoe Ates, Edward Brophy, John Miljan. 1933

•**WHAT PLANET ARE YOU FROM?** ★★★★ This crisply written, science-fiction comedy about the Mars-Venus aspect of human relationships is hilarious. An all-male race of aliens on a distant planet tries to save itself from extinction by sending a "chosen one" called Harold to mate with an Earth woman. Harold is an ET sperm bank who is outfitted with a male reproductive organ that hums when stimulated. He poses as a Phoenix loan officer and tries to connect with several females while befriending a promiscuous married man. Rated R for sexuality and language. 100m. **DIR:** Mike Nichols. **CAST:** Garry Shandling, Annette Bening, Greg Kinnear, Ben Kingsley, Linda Fiorentino, John Goodman. 2000

WHAT PRICE GLORY? (1926) ★★★1/2 Two rough-edged fighting men compete for women all over the world and get down to serious business in France during World War I. A masterly blend of sex, humor, and action set against the carnage of war makes this one of the first and most effective pacifist statements from the American cinema. One of the great silent films. B&W; 116m. **DIR:** Raoul Walsh. **CAST:** Victor McLaglen, Edmund Lowe, Dolores Del Rio, William H. Mong, Phyllis Haver, Leslie Fenton, Barry Norton, Sammy Cohen, Ted McNamara. 1926

WHAT PRICE GLORY (1952) ★★★ James Cagney is Captain Flagg, Dan Dailey is Sergeant Quirt in this rough-and-tumble tale of rivalry in romance set against the sobering background of World War I in France. The feisty pair of Marines vies for the affections of adorable Charmaine (Corinne Calvet). Between quarrels, they fight in the trenches. 109m. **DIR:** John Ford. **CAST:** James Cagney, Dan Dailey, Corinne Calvet, William Demarest, Robert Wagner, Marisa Pavan, James Gleason. 1952

WHAT PRICE HOLLYWOOD? ★★★★ This first production of *A Star Is Born* packs the same punch as the two more famous versions and showcases Constance Bennett as a tough but tender girl who wants to reach the top. Bennett seems somehow less martyred and long-suffering than either Janet Gaynor or Judy Garland, and that gives this version an edge that the others lack. B&W; 88m. **DIR:** George Cukor. **CAST:** Constance Bennett, Lowell Sherman, Neil Hamilton, Gregory Ratoff. 1932

WHAT THE DEAF MAN HEARD ★★★1/2 This *Hallmark Hall of Fame* made-for-TV film is a delightful survival tale of a suddenly orphaned boy who must make a life for himself in a new town. His decision to say nothing about himself leads people to believe that he is deaf and mute. Twenty years later he exacts his revenge on the town bully. Unbelievable plot is nonetheless too much fun to turn off. Not rated; contains adult themes. 90m. **DIR:** John Kent Harrison. **CAST:** Matthew Modine, Tom Skerritt, Judith Ivey, Jake Webber, Jerry O'Connell, James Earl Jones. 1997

WHAT WAITS BELOW 💔 A group of military and scientific researchers explore a cave and find a race of mutants. Rated PG; 88m. **DIR:** Don Sharp. **CAST:** Robert Powell, Lisa Blount, Richard Johnson, Anne Heywood, Timothy Bottoms. 1983

WHATEVER ★★1/2 A smart but confused high school senior goes through the standard movie growing pains. Director Susan Skoog's script lacks originality—it's essentially a gender-switching update of *The Catcher in the Rye*—but the acting is strong. Rated R for profanity and sexual scenes. 112m. **DIR:** Susan Skoog. **CAST:** Liza Weil, Chad Morgan, Frederic Forrest, Kathryn Rossetter. 1998

WHATEVER HAPPENED TO AUNT ALICE ★★★1/2 Entertaining black comedy about an eccentric woman (impeccably performed by Geraldine Page) who stays wealthy by killing off her housekeepers and stealing their savings. Ruth Gordon equally impressive as an amateur sleuth trying to solve the missing-persons mystery. 101m. **DIR:** Lee Katzin. **CAST:** Geraldine Page, Ruth Gordon, Rosemary Forsyth, Robert Fuller, Mildred Dunnock. 1969

•**WHATEVER IT TAKES** 💔 This lame modernization of *Cyrano de Bergerac* is another teen comedy which messy affairs of the heart and loins are all resolved on prom night. Rated PG-13 for language and sexual references. 92m. **DIR:** David Raynr. **CAST:** Shane West, James Franco, Marla Sokoloff, Jodi Lyn O'Keefe, Julia Sweeney. 2000 DVD

WHAT'S EATING GILBERT GRAPE? ★★★1/2 Small-town grocery clerk—the passive anchor of an odd Iowa family—cares for his 500-pound recluse mom and mentally challenged brother but gets an emotional jump start from a free-spirited, vacationing lass. It's a strange, sad, melancholy story about how personal happiness can take a backseat to family responsibility, that is also sometimes very funny. Rated PG-13 for suggested sex and language. 118m. **DIR:** Lasse Hallstrom. **CAST:** Johnny Depp, Leonardo DiCaprio, Juliette Lewis, Mary Steenburgen, Kevin Tighe, John C. Reilly, Crispin Glover. 1994

WHAT'S LOVE GOT TO DO WITH IT? ★★★★ The story of Ike and Tina Turner is based on Tina Turner's autobiography and stars two of Hollywood's most respected black performers. Even though biographical films can't rely on surprise elements, they can use strong personalities to advantage. Angela Bassett stars as Tina Turner from her teen years to the present. 120m. **DIR:** Brian Gibson. **CAST:** Angela Bassett, Laurence Fishburne. 1993 DVD

WHAT'S NEW, PUSSYCAT? ★★★ Peter O'Toole is a fashion editor who can't stop becoming romantically involved with his models. In spite of a strong, supporting cast, this dated 1960s "hip" comedy has few genuine laughs. Mostly, it's just silly. 108m. **DIR:** Clive Donner. **CAST:** Peter Sellers, Peter O'Toole, Woody Allen, Ursula Andress, Romy Schneider, Capucine, Paula Prentiss. 1965

WHAT'S THE MATTER WITH HELEN? ★★★1/2 Circa 1930, Debbie Reynolds and Shelley Winters flee to Hollywood to escape public hounding after their sons are involved in a brutal murder. They soon begin to fear they may have been followed by someone with revenge in mind. Good suspense and a fine feel for the era. Rated PG. 101m. **DIR:** Curtis Harring-

n. CAST: Debbie Reynolds, Shelley Winters, Dennis eaver, Agnes Moorehead. 1971

HAT'S UP, DOC? ★★★★ A virtual remake of oward Hawks's classic *Bringing Up Baby*, this anages to recapture much of the madcap charm nd nonstop action of the original story. The zany fi- l chase through the streets of San Francisco is one ' filmdom's best. Rated G. 94m. DIR: Peter Bog- anovich. CAST: Ryan O'Neal, Barbra Streisand, Ken- eth Mars, Austin Pendleton. 1972

HAT'S UP, TIGER LILY? ★★★ A dreadful Japan- se spy movie has been given a zany English-lan- uage soundtrack by Woody Allen in one of his earli- st movie productions. You are left with an offbeat oof of the whole genre of spy films. The results are ten amusing, but its one-joke premise gets rather dious before it's over. 80m. DIR: Woody Allen. CAST: atsuya Mihashi, Miya Hana, Woody Allen. 1966

HEEL OF FORTUNE ★★1/2 John Wayne in a crewball comedy? Yep. Also titled *A Man Betrayed*, he surprise is that this low-budget production is atchable. B&W; 83m. DIR: John H. Auer. CAST: John ayne, Frances Dee, Ward Bond. 1941

HEELER DEALERS, THE ★★★1/2 Texas million- ires risk huge sums without getting their grins or en-gallon hats out of place. James Garner is at his elightfully devious best in this briskly paced romp. ee Remick is a treat for the eyes. A gang of talented haracter actors lends strong support. 106m. DIR: rthur Hiller. CAST: Lee Remick, James Garner, Jim ackus, Phil Harris, Chill Wills, John Astin, Louis Nye. 963

HEELS: AN INLINE STORY ★★ A collection of so- o in-line skating stunts linked together with inane arration that's supposed to be a story. Remarkable nly in that it is the product of three teenage broth- rs. Features music by Hanson. Not rated, but suit- ble for all ages. 30m. DIR: The Klein Brothers. CAST: ndrew Flack, Mathew Alexander, Merideth Ward, pencer Rauum, Nic Klein. 1998

HEELS OF FIRE 🖤 Shameless rip-off of *The Road Warrior*. Rated R for nudity, violence, and profanity. 1m. DIR: Cirio H. Santiago. CAST: Gary Watkins, aura Banks, Lynda Wiesmeiser, Linda Grovenor. 1984

HEELS OF TERROR 🖤 Interminable trash that its spunky school-bus driver Joanna Cassidy gainst an unseen child molester who uses his dirty lack sedan as a weapon, clearly having seen Steven pielberg's *Duel* a few too many times. Unwatchable ade-for-cable junk. 85m. DIR: Christopher Cain. AST: Joanna Cassidy, Marcie Leeds, Arlen Dean Sny- er. 1990

WHEN A MAN LOVES A WOMAN ★★★★ A weeper with a cast of pros who make it work. Meg Ryan plays Andy Garcia's alcoholic wife. She gets help, but it takes its toll on their marriage. They try to pick up the pieces, but it's tough on both of them. Rated PG- 13 for mature themes. 122m. DIR: Luis Mandoki. CAST: Meg Ryan, Andy Garcia, C.C.H. Pounder, Tina Majorino, Mae Whitman. 1994 DVD

WHEN A MAN SEES RED ★★★★ Writer-director Alan James gives producer-star Buck Jones a mar- velous story line, and Jones gives a breezy, authorita- tive performance. Peggy Campbell plays the spoiled

rich girl who is heir to the California ranch that Jones oversees, and he is charged with looking after her interests. B&W; 60m. DIR: Alan James. CAST: Buck Jones, Peggy Campbell, LeRoy Mason. 1934

WHEN A STRANGER CALLS ★★★ A *Psycho II*- style atmosphere pervades this film when the mur- derer of two children returns after seven years to complete his crime. Rated R. 97m. DIR: Fred Walton. CAST: Carol Kane, Charles Durning, Colleen Dewhurst, Tony Beckley, Rachel Roberts, Ron O'Neal. 1979 DVD

WHEN A STRANGER CALLS BACK ★★★ Writer-di- rector Fred Walton's sequel to the 1979 chiller be- gins superbly, with Jill Schoelen just right as a cau- tious baby-sitter being taunted by someone. Sadly, the momentum flags once the girl makes contact with psychologist Jill Johnson (Carol Kane) and in- vestigator John Clifford (Charles Durning), who see parallels to the events they survived years earlier. Rated R for violence and nudity. 94m. DIR: Fred Wal- ton. CAST: Carol Kane, Charles Durning, Jill Schoelen, Gene Lythgow. 1993

WHEN A WOMAN ASCENDS THE STAIRS ★★★★1/2 As in many of his films, Mikio Naruse ex- amines a woman trying to make her own way in the world, in this case a bar hostess struggling with debt and loneliness. Clearly influenced by Hollywood melodramas of the 1950s, he adapts their conven- tions (including the wide-screen format, preserved in this letter-boxed video transfer) to good effect. In Japanese with English subtitles. B&W; 110m. DIR: Mikio Naruse. CAST: Hideko Takamine. 1960

WHEN COMEDY WAS KING ★★★★ A nostalgic, sidesplitting look back to the screen comedy days of yesteryear when absurdity and the sight gag reigned supreme. This clutch of classic comedy scenes from silent days is outstanding. B&W; 81m. DIR: Robert Youngson. CAST: Charlie Chaplin, Buster Keaton, Glo- ria Swanson, Mabel Normand, Oliver Hardy, Stan Lau- rel. 1960

WHEN DANGER FOLLOWS YOU HOME ★★★ A psychology intern meddles a little too much into the life of a mentally unbalanced criminal, and the man follows her home. She befriends him, disaster strikes, and she's accused of murder. This made-for- cable thriller is well written, and has a solid plot, but doesn't rise much above the average. Not rated; con- tains violence. 95m. DIR: David Peckinpah. CAST: Jo- Beth Williams, William Russ, Michael Manasseri, Nico- las Surovy. 1997

WHEN DINOSAURS RULED THE EARTH ★★★ British novelist and fantasy author J. G. Ballard (*Empire of the Sun*) wrote the treatment for this un- usually ambitious Hammer Films epic, shot in the Canary Islands. Director Val Guest (one of Hammer's top talents) and effects wizard Jim Danforth suc- ceed, possibly for the first time, in integrating the stop-motion dinosaur sequences seamlessly into the narrative—they aren't mere "stop-the-show" set pieces. Rated G. 96m. DIR: Val Guest. CAST: Victoria Vetri, Robin Hawdon, Patrick Allen. 1969

WHEN FATHER WAS AWAY ON BUSINESS ★★★ Seen through the eyes of a young boy, the film deals with the sudden disappearance of a father from a family. Tension mounts when it becomes clear that it is the father's brother-in-law who turned him in and had him sent to a work camp. The film received the Palm D'Or at the 1985 Cannes Film Festival. Rated R for sex and nudity. In Slavic with English subtitles. 144m. DIR: Emir Kusturica. CAST: Moreno De Bartolli, Miki Manojlovic. 1985

WHEN GANGLAND STRIKES ★★ Stale story of a lawman who has to knuckle under to hoodlums who have some dirt on him is adequate but nothing dynamic. B&W; 70m. DIR: R. G. Springsteen. CAST: Raymond Greenleaf, Marjie Millar, John Hudson, Anthony Caruso. 1956

WHEN HARRY MET SALLY ★★★★1/2 Wonderful character comedy stars Billy Crystal and Meg Ryan as longtime acquaintances who drift from mild animosity to friendship to love. Director Rob Reiner skillfully tickles our funny bones and touches our hearts with this semiautobiographical tale, which was scripted by Nora Ephron. Rated R for profanity and suggested sex. 110m. DIR: Rob Reiner. CAST: Billy Crystal, Meg Ryan, Carrie Fisher, Bruno Kirby. 1989

WHEN HE'S NOT A STRANGER ★★★1/2 Date rape is sensitively handled in this made-for-TV drama. College freshman Annabeth Gish accepts an offer from popular John Terlesky to come up to his room and get acquainted, but what starts off innocently leads to a harrowing act. Gish must come to grips with the incident and seek the courage to fight back. Kevin Dillon is the friend who lends support. Not rated; contains adult situations. 90m. DIR: John Gray. CAST: Annabeth Gish, Kevin Dillon, John Terlesky. 1989

WHEN LADIES MEET ★★★1/2 A spasmodically delightful high-society romantic romp. A writer falls in love with her married publisher, much to the dismay of her jealous suitor, who befriends the publisher's wife and invites her to the writer's home for the weekend. B&W; 105m. DIR: Robert Z. Leonard. CAST: Joan Crawford, Robert Taylor, Greer Garson, Herbert Marshall, Spring Byington. 1941

WHEN NIGHT IS FALLING ★★★★ Provocative romantic triangle exists when a prim religious college teacher can't decide between her reserved minister boyfriend and a passionate and unpredictable female circus performer. Sensual, erotic, handsomely mounted production. R-rated and unrated versions; both contain nudity and adult situations. 94m. DIR: Patricia Rozema. CAST: Pascale Bussières, Rachel Crawford, Don McKellar, Tracy Wright, Henry Czerny. 1995

WHEN THE BOUGH BREAKS ★★★ Competent thriller stars Martin Sheen as a Houston police chief who's on the trail of a serial killer. His only hope lies with a forensic expert played by Ally Walker, and a mentally disturbed child who is psychically connected to the killer. Decent performances and plenty of dark, twisted turns. Rated R for violence and adult language. 103m. DIR: Michael Cohn. CAST: Martin Sheen, Ally Walker, Ron Perlman. 1993

WHEN THE BULLET HITS THE BONE ★★ When emergency-room doctor Jack Davies decides he's seen enough human carnage, he does something about it. Davies goes after the drug dealers causing the human misery, and in doing so, stumbles across a

coverup that goes straight to the top of the Unit- States government. Star Jeff Wincott has done many of these lone-avenger films it's almost hard tell one from the other. Rated R for violence, profa- ity, and adult situations. 92m. DIR: Damien L- CAST: Jeff Wincott, Michelle Johnson, Doug O'Kee 1995

WHEN THE CAT'S AWAY ★★★★ Timid Parisia model makeup artist Chloe leaves her cat with an e derly neighborhood lady while she vacations at th seaside. The feline is missing when Chloe returr and her attempts to find it slowly nudge her out of hollow singles funk. The story, which is about th many shades of loneliness, is spare but rich in atmo phere. In French with English subtitles. Rated R f simulated sex and language. 95m. DIR: Cedr Klapisch. CAST: Garance Clavel, Renee Le Calm, Zin dine Soualem, Olivier Py, Romain Duris. 1996

WHEN THE CLOUDS ROLL BY ★★★★ If you hav to choose the outstanding example of the preco tume Douglas Fairbanks comedies, surely this is It's a satire on hypochondriacs. The highlight is chase in a revolving room and a subsequent scuff in slow-motion photography. Silent. B&W; 77m. DII Victor Fleming. CAST: Douglas Fairbanks Sr. 1919

WHEN THE DARK MAN CALLS ★★1/2 This slight suspenseful made-for-cable original is about woman who is haunted by suppressed memories the murder of her parents. Not rated; contains vie lence. 89m. DIR: Nathaniel Gutman. CAST: Joan Va Ark, Chris Sarandon, James Read, Geoffrey Lewi 1995

WHEN THE LEGENDS DIE ★★★1/2 A young Ute Ir dian is taken from his home in the Colorado Rockie after his parents die. In the modern white world he taught the "new ways." His extraordinary riding abi ities make him a target for exploitation as Red Dillo (Richard Widmark) trains him as a rodeo bronc rider, then proceeds to cash in on his protégé's suc cess. A touching story that finds Widmark in one his better roles and introduces a young Frederic For rest. Rated PG for some mild profanity. 105m. DIR Stuart Millar. CAST: Richard Widmark, Frederic For rest. 1972

WHEN THE PARTY'S OVER ★★★★ Twenty-some things share a house and some life lessons in thi comedy-drama. At the center is Rae Dawn Chong, successful businesswoman with a disastrous per sonal life. Though there are several intriguing char acters, Fisher Stevens is especially good as a charis matic performance artist. Engrossing, but a bi rough around the edges. Rated R for profanity and sexual situations. 114m. DIR: Matthew Irmas. CAST Rae Dawn Chong, Fisher Stevens, Elizabeth Berridge Sandra Bullock, Kris Kamm, Brian McNamara. 1993

WHEN THE SCREAMING STOPS ★★★ A woman who lives under the Rhine must turn into a monster and eat people's hearts to remain the ruler of a mag nificent underwater kingdom. Cheap monster ef fects and amateur gore do not detract from the wild story. Rated R for violence and nudity. 86m. DIR: Amando de Ossorio. CAST: Tony Kendall, Helga Line. 1974

HEN THE TIME COMES ★★★ A 34-year-old 'oman dying from cancer decides to take her own 'e, much to the dismay of her friends and family. etter-than-average made-for-TV suds, thanks to a rong performance by Bonnie Bedelia. 94m. DIR: hn Erman. CAST: Bonnie Bedelia, Brad Davis, Terry Quinn, Karen Austin. 1987

HEN THE WHALES CAME ★★★1/2 Paul Scofield ays a deaf islander known as the birdman because f his fine carvings. Befriended by two village chil'en, the three must save a beached whale that the llagers are hungrily eyeing. Rated PG. 100m. DIR: 'ive Rees. CAST: Helen Mirren, Paul Scofield, David uchet, Jeremy Kemp. 1989

HEN THE WIND BLOWS ★★★ Ironic full-length ritish cartoon that chronicles the preparations of a etired English couple for the coming nuclear holoaust. Their ignorance of the facts and innocent aith in the "powers that be" make this a touching nd moving statement about the nuclear Armagedon. 80m. DIR: Jimmy T. Murakami. 1988

HEN THINGS WERE ROTTEN (TV SERIES) ★★★ his compilation of three episodes from the shortved television series of the same name is sure to lease fans of *Blazing Saddles*-style humor. Dick 'autier's nearly serious portrayal of Robin Hood is a erfect foil for the slapstick antics of the rest of the ast. 78m. DIR: Coby Ruskin, Marty Feldman, Peter onerz. CAST: Dick Gautier, Dick Van Patten, Bernie opell, Richard Dimitri, Henry Polic II, Misty Rowe, avid Sabin. 1975

WHEN TIME EXPIRES ★★★ Engaging if somewhat onvoluted sci-fi tale about a man from the future 'ho must intervene in the past in order to prevent n impending nuclear war. Rated R for violence and ensuality. 93m. DIR: David Bourla. CAST: Richard rieco, Cynthia Geary, Mark Hamill, Tim Thomerson, :had Everett. 1997

WHEN TIME RAN OUT! ♥ Time never seems to run out as we wait and wait for a volcano to erupt and put he all-star cast out of its misery. Rated PG. 121m. DIR: James Goldstone. CAST: Paul Newman, Jacqueine Bisset, William Holden, James Franciscus, Edward Albert, Red Buttons, Ernest Borgnine, Burgess Mereith, Valentina Cortese, Alex Karras, Barbara Carrera. 1980

WHEN TRUMPETS FADE ★★★★ *Saving Private Ryan* got all the attention during the summer of 1998, but this more intimate WWII drama—origially cablecast on HBO—is nearly as compelling. It concerns the little-known Battle of the Hurtgen Forest, and demonstrated a level of Allied stupidity perhaps matched only by the events depicted in *Gallipoli*. A grunt is the sole survivor when his squad is decimated by Germans; whether this results from luck or cowardice is very much the point, as he keeps climbing in rank after his superiors are killed. A searing indictment of war's senseless brutality. Rated R for violence, gore, profanity, and nudity. 92m. DIR: John Irvin. CAST: Ron Eldard, Frank Whaley, Zak Orth, Dylan Bruno, Martin Donovan, Timothy Olyphant, Dan Futterman, Dwight Yoakam. 1998 DVD

WHEN WE WERE KINGS ★★★1/2 Muhammad Ali and George Foreman's Rumble in the Jungle, the 1974 heavyweight championship fight that spotlighted Zaire, is revisited in this provocative documentary. A melting pot of history, sports drama, music, and culture. Rated PG. 87m. DIR: Leon Gast. 1996 DVD

WHEN WOLVES CRY ♥ A 10-year-old boy is diagnosed as being terminally ill. Originally titled *The Christmas Tree*. Rated G. 108m. DIR: Terence Young. 1983

WHEN WOMEN HAD TAILS ★★ Italian comedy about five cavemen discovering the delightful difference of the sexes when pretty Senta Berger suddenly appears in their midst. Despite plenty of potential, this farce falls flat. Rated R for language and nudity. 99m. DIR: Pasquale Festa Campanile. CAST: Senta Berger, Frank Wolff, Giuliano Gemma, Lando Buzzanca. 1970

WHEN WOMEN LOST THEIR TAILS ★★1/2 Most of the cast of *When Women Had Tails* returns in a much more sophisticated sex comedy set in prehistoric times. This slapstick sequel takes a broader view, poking fun at the earliest manifestations of civilization. The Stone Age jabs are still silly, but many of the observations are surprisingly enlightening. Rated R. 94m. DIR: Pasquale Festa Campanile. CAST: Senta Berger, Frank Wolff, Lando Buzzanca, Francesco Mule. 1971

WHEN WORLDS COLLIDE ★★ Interesting end-of-the-world sci-fi fable from George Pal has dated badly since its original release in 1951. Final scene of Earth pilgrims landing on the planet and walking into an obvious superimposed painting is laughable today, but many of the other Oscar-winning effects are still quite convincing. 81m. DIR: Rudolph Maté. CAST: Richard Derr, Barbara Rush, Peter Hanson, Larry Keating, John Hoyt. 1951

WHEN YOUR LOVER LEAVES ♥ Valerie Perrine plays the other woman who's just lost out to her lover's wife. Hideous TV movie. 96m. DIR: Jeff Bleckner. CAST: Valerie Perrine, Betty Thomas, David Ackroyd, Ed O'Neill, Dwight Schultz. 1983

WHEN'S YOUR BIRTHDAY? ★★★ Joe E. Brown stars as a student of astrology who doubles as a boxer. The stars tell him when he'll win in the ring. Unfortunately, a gangster gets wind of his abilities and tries to turn them to his own ends. It's all a showcase for Brown, though Edgar Kennedy steals his scenes with his hilarious slow burn. B&W; 76m. DIR: Harry Beaumont. CAST: Joe E. Brown, Marian Marsh, Edgar Kennedy, Edgar Hamilton. 1937

WHERE ANGELS FEAR TO TREAD ★★★ Adapted from E. M. Forster's less mature first novel, British director Charles Sturridge fails to find the central core of the story and weave the comic and tragic elements into a seamless whole. However, this story of English arrogance and class attitude in Italy offers well-crafted performances. Not rated. 112m. DIR: Charles Sturridge. CAST: Helena Bonham Carter, Judy Davis, Helen Mirren, Rupert Graves. 1991

WHERE ARE THE CHILDREN? ★★★ On the ninth anniversary of the murder of her previous children, a mother's children from her new marriage disappear. Jill Clayburgh is very good as the mother attempting to piece together the reason for this second occurrence. This film has a crackerjack surprise ending. Rated R. 97m. DIR: Bruce Malmuth. CAST: Jill Clayburgh, Max Gail, Clifton James, Elizabeth Wilson, Barnard Hughes, Frederic Forrest. 1988

WHERE EAGLES DARE ★★★ Clint Eastwood and Richard Burton portray Allied commandos in this World War II adventure film which is short on realism. Instead we have farfetched but exciting shootouts, explosions, and mass slaughter. Our heroes must break out an American general being held captive in a heavily fortified German castle. 158m. DIR: Brian G. Hutton. CAST: Richard Burton, Clint Eastwood, Mary Ure, Michael Hordern, Patrick Wymark, Anton Diffring, Robert Beatty, Donald Houston, Ingrid Pitt. 1969

WHERE EAST IS EAST ★★★ Despite the presence of director Tod Browning and silent star Lon Chaney, this isn't a horror movie. It's an Oriental revenge melodrama, set in Indochina. Full of kinky sexual peccadilloes that would have had a rough time getting by the censors had it been made a decade later. B&W; 68m. DIR: Tod Browning. CAST: Lon Chaney Sr., Lupe Velez, Lloyd Hughes. 1925

WHERE EVIL LIES 💔 A strip club turns out to be the headquarters of a white-slavery ring in this lurid women-in-jeopardy opus. Not rated; contains adult situations and violence. 83m. DIR: Kevin Alber. CAST: Nikki Fritz, Emile Levisetti, Melissa Park, Mark Kinsey Stephenson, Roma Court. 1995

WHERE LOVE HAS GONE ★★ Hilariously anachronistic throwback to late-1940s "women's picture" histrionics, but the sleaze and vulgarity are vintage 1960s, as Joey Heatherton murders the lover of her mother, Susan Hayward. Adapted from Harold Robbins's novel, which echoed the Lana Turner–Johnny Stompanato killing, and anything else he could think of. Low camp. 114m. DIR: Edward Dmytryk. CAST: Bette Davis, Susan Hayward, Joey Heatherton, Michael Connors, Jane Greer. 1964

WHERE SLEEPING DOGS LIE ★★★ Investigating a brutal murder, writer Dylan McDermott moves into the house where it took place. He gets more than he bargained for when a mysterious stranger, chillingly played by Tom Sizemore, arrives, offering information that only the killer could know. Respectful attempt at *film noir* costars Sharon Stone as McDermott's sultry editor. Rated R for violence, language, and adult situations. 92m. DIR: Charles Finch. CAST: Dylan McDermott, Tom Sizemore, Sharon Stone. 1991

WHERE THE BOYS ARE (1960) ★★★ Connie Francis warbled the title tune and made her movie debut in this frothy, mildly entertaining film about teenagers doing what's natural during Easter vacation in Fort Lauderdale. It's miles ahead of the idiotic remake. 99m. DIR: Henry Levin. CAST: Dolores Hart, George Hamilton, Yvette Mimieux, Jim Hutton, Barbara Nichols, Connie Francis. 1960 DVD

WHERE THE BOYS ARE '84 💔 Poor remake. Rated R. 96m. DIR: Hy Averback. CAST: Lisa Hartman, Russell Todd, Lorna Luft, Lynn-Holly Johnson, Wendy Schaal, Howard McGillin, Louise Sorel. 1984

WHERE THE BUFFALO ROAM 💔 Horrendous film about the exploits of gonzo journalist Hunter S.

Thompson. Rated R. 96m. DIR: Art Linson. CAST: B Murray, Peter Boyle, Bruno Kirby, René Auberjonois, G. Armstrong, Rafael Campos, Leonard Frey. 198 DVD

WHERE THE DAY TAKES YOU ★★ This fil switches between recorded interviews with parolee and his life on the streets of Los Angele The viewer comes away feeling nothing for the cha acters in the film. Rated R for violence, profanit and suggested sex. 107m. DIR: Marc Rocco. CAS Sean Astin, Lara Flynn Boyle, Dermot Mulroney, Pet Dobson, Balthazar Getty, Kyle MacLachlan, Adam Bal win, Nancy McKeon, Alyssa Milano, Leo Rossi, Rach Ticotin, Laura San Giacomo, Christian Slater. 1992

WHERE THE GREEN ANTS DREAM ★★★★ A other stark, yet captivating vision from perhaps th most popular director of modern German cinem The film, set in Australia, is basically an ecologica tug of war between progress and tradition, namel uranium mining interests against aborigines an their practices. 100m. DIR: Werner Herzog. CAS Bruce Spence, Ray Barrett, Norman Kaye. 1984

WHERE THE HEART IS (1990) 💔 Mindless driv about a successful demolition expert's fall fror wealth. Rated R for profanity and adult situation 111m. DIR: John Boorman. CAST: Dabney Colema Joanna Cassidy, Uma Thurman, Christopher Plumme 1990

•**WHERE THE HEART IS (2000)** ★★1/2 For a while this film overcomes its melodramatic trappings an becomes an engaging if unlikely account of a youn woman, seventeen and pregnant, who is abandone by her boyfriend at an Oklahoma Wal-Mart; once he baby is born, she befriends a series of colorful an eccentric characters who become the surrogate fam ily she never had. Unfortunately, contrivance an heavy dollops of bathos eventually turn this adapta tion of Billie Letts's novel into soap-opera swil Rated PG-13 for profanity, sexual candor, and dra matic intensity. 120m. DIR: Matt Williams. CAST: Na talie Portman, Ashley Judd, Stockard Channing, Joar Cusack, James Frain, Dylan Bruno, Keith David. 2000

WHERE THE LILIES BLOOM ★★★1/2 Heartwarm ing melodrama about four orphaned children ir rural America who pretend their father is still alive in order to keep the authorities from separating them. The settings are beautiful, and the actors are all fine, especially Harry Dean Stanton. Background score by bluegrass legend Earl Scruggs. 96m. DIR: William A. Graham. CAST: Julie Gholson, Jan Smithers, Harry Dean Stanton, Sudie Bond. 1974

•**WHERE THE MONEY IS** ★★★ For all its charm, this mildly comic heist film is an oddly unsatisfying experience, as if we've just watched a picture that was heavily truncated for television broadcast. The setup is clever, with Paul Newman as a career bank robber who feigns a stroke to get into a lesser-security nursing home; attendant Linda Fiorentino, smelling a rat, penetrates the facade and then announces that the price for her silence is involvement in a new caper. The subsequent character dynamics are intriguing, but the film fades away instead of delivering a proper third act. Rated PG-13 for brief nudity, brief violence, and sexual candor. 89m. DIR

Marek Kanievska. **CAST:** Paul Newman, Linda Fiorentino, Dermot Mulroney. **2000**

WHERE THE RED FERN GROWS ★★★★ Fine family fare about a boy's love for two hunting dogs and his coming of age in Oklahoma in the 1930s. Rated G. 90m. **DIR:** Norman Tokar. **CAST:** James Whitmore, Beverly Garland, Jack Ging, Lonny Chapman, Stewart Peterson. **1974 DVD**

WHERE THE RIVER RUNS BLACK ★★★1/2 A primitive child is snatched from his home in the Amazon rain forest and brought into the modern world of corruption and violence. Sumptuous images, courtesy of Juan Ruiz-Anchia's superb cinematography, fill the screen as its eerie, fanciful, and finally suspenseful tale is told. Rated PG for violence and suggested sex. 105m. **DIR:** Christopher Cain. **CAST:** Charles Durning, Peter Horton, Ajay Naidu, Conchata Ferrell. **1986**

WHERE THE RIVERS FLOW NORTH ★★★ Despite generous offers and promises, a stubborn timber man refuses to sell his land so that a new dam can be built. This circa-1920s drama boasts excellent performances and scenery as well as a usually engrossing storyline. Rated PG-13. 106m. **DIR:** Jay Craven. **CAST:** Rip Torn, Tantoo Cardinal, Bill Raymond, Michael J. Fox, John Griesemer, Mark Margolis. **1993 DVD**

WHERE THE SPIRIT LIVES ★★★ Stirring reenactment of Indian children in Canada being kidnapped and forced to live in terrifying residential schools in which physical, emotional, and sexual abuse were the order of the day. Michelle St. John stars as a defiant newcomer who decides that the only way to survive is to escape. Aided by Bruce Pittman. **CAST:** Michelle St. John, Anne-Marie Macdonald. **1989**

WHERE TRAILS END ★★1/2 World War II is in full swing. Aided by his wonder horse Prince, U.S. Marshal Tom Keene, in glaring white from hat to boots, protects ranchers from ruthless outlaws working for Nazis. B&W; 58m. **DIR:** Robert Emmett Tansey. **CAST:** Tom Keene, Joan Curtis, Charles King. **1942**

WHERE WERE YOU WHEN THE LIGHTS WENT OUT? 🎬 Bad attempt at farce and sexual mix-ups and misunderstandings. Backfires all the way. 94m. **DIR:** Hy Averback. **CAST:** Doris Day, Robert Morse, Terry-Thomas, Patrick O'Neal, Lola Albright, Steve Allen, Jim Backus, Ben Blue, Pat Paulsen. **1968**

WHERE'S PICCONE? ★★★★ Highly entertaining comedy starring Giancarlo Giannini as a small-time hustler searching for a respectable Italian businessman who inexplicably vanished in an ambulance on the way to the hospital. In Italian with English subtitles. Not rated; contains nudity, violence, and profanity. 110m. **DIR:** Nanni Loy. **CAST:** Giancarlo Giannini. **1984**

WHERE'S POPPA? ★★★★ One of George Segal's best comic performances is found in this cult favorite. Ruth Gordon co-stars as the senile mother whom Segal tries to scare into having a cardiac arrest. Director Carl Reiner's son, Rob, makes a short appearance as a fervent draft resister. Rated R. 82m. **DIR:** Carl Reiner. **CAST:** George Segal, Ruth Gordon, Trish Van Devere, Ron Leibman, Rae Allen, Vincent Gardenia, Barnard Hughes, Rob Reiner, Garrett Morris. **1970**

WHERE'S THE MONEY, NOREEN? ★★1/2 Just when you think this made-for-cable original might get interesting, it doesn't. Julianne Phillips portrays a recently paroled convict looking for the man who set her up. Rated PG-13 for violence and suggested sex. 93m. **DIR:** Artie Mandelberg. **CAST:** Julianne Phillips, A Martinez, Nigel Bennett, Nancy Warren. **1995**

WHICH WAY HOME ★★1/2 In 1979, a Red Cross nurse flees to Thailand and Australia with a small group of Cambodian and Vietnamese orphans. Often implausible, overlong cable-TV production. 141m. **DIR:** Carl Schultz. **CAST:** Cybill Shepherd, John Waters. **1991**

WHICH WAY IS UP? ★★★★ This irreverent, ribald farce reunites the talented comedy team of director Michael Shultz and star Richard Pryor (*Greased Lightning*) for one of the funnier movies of the 1970s. Pryor plays three major roles. His ability to create totally separate and distinctive characters contributes greatly to the success of this oft-tried but rarely believable gimmick. Rated R. 94m. **DIR:** Michael Schultz. **CAST:** Richard Pryor, Lonette McKee, Margaret Avery, Dolph Sweet, Morgan Woodward. **1977**

WHICH WAY TO THE FRONT? 🎬 Jerry Lewis directs and stars in this pathetic story about a rich 4-F American who enlists other such unfortunates into a military unit to combat Nazi Germany. 96m. **DIR:** Jerry Lewis. **CAST:** Jerry Lewis, John Wood, Jan Murray, Kaye Ballard, Robert Middleton, Paul Winchell, Gary Crosby. **1970**

WHIFFS 🎬 Army private is a human guinea pig suffering annoying side effects from biological and chemical-weapons testing. Not rated. 92m. **DIR:** Ted Post. **CAST:** Elliott Gould, Eddie Albert, Jennifer O'Neill, Harry Guardino. **1975**

WHILE THE CITY SLEEPS ★★1/2 An impressive cast and the talents of director Fritz Lang can't transform this standard newspaper-crime story into a great film. Rival newspaper executives compete with each other and the police in an effort to come up with the identity of a mad killer. Convoluted gabfest quickly bogs down. B&W; 100m. **DIR:** Fritz Lang. **CAST:** Dana Andrews, Ida Lupino, Rhonda Fleming, George Sanders, Vincent Price, John Drew Barrymore, Thomas Mitchell, Howard Duff, Mae Marsh. **1956**

WHILE YOU WERE SLEEPING ★★★★1/2 A series of misunderstandings leaves a coma victim's family believing a Good Samaritan to be his fiancée, only she's falling for someone else. The plot may be predictable, but this extremely entertaining romance owes all to Sandra Bullock's subtle, heartfelt performance. Rated PG for mild profanity. 100m. **DIR:** Jon Turteltaub. **CAST:** Sandra Bullock, Bill Pullman, Peter Gallagher, Jack Warden, Micole Mercurio, Michael Rispoli. **1995 DVD**

WHISKERS ★★★1/2 Winsome family fun ensues as a 10-year-old boy turns to an Egyptian cat goddess for help when his parents want to get rid of his furry friend Whiskers. The cat is turned into a 30-year-old man who helps teach young Jed some important lesssons about life. This tale of friendship and fun stars an enjoyable Brent Carver as the feline-turned-man. Made for cable. Rated G. 94m. DIR: James Kaufman. CAST: Brent Carver, Michael Caloz. 1996

WHISPER KILLS, A ❤️ Weak made-for-TV slasher film about a killer who warns the potential victim by phone before the inevitable murder. 96m. DIR: Christian I. Nyby II. CAST: Loni Anderson, Joe Penny, June Lockhart. 1988 DVD

WHISPERING, THE ❤️ An insurance investigator learns that a demon is responsible for a recent series of suicides. Rated R for adult situations, language, and violence. 88m. DIR: Gregory Gieras. CAST: Cedrick Terrell, Mette Holt, Scott Johnson, Leslie Danon. 1996

WHISPERS ★★ A woman is repeatedly attacked by a man with the perfect alibi, prompting the police to disbelieve her. Mediocre. Rated R for violence and nudity. 96m. DIR: Douglas Jackson. CAST: Victoria Tennant, Jean Leclerc, Chris Sarandon. 1990

WHISPERS IN THE DARK ★★ Psychiatrist Annabella Sciorra finds herself drawn into a murder investigation, during which she enlists the aid of mentors Jill Clayburgh and Alan Alda. Over-the-top, campy, contrived suspense. Rated R for violence and profanity. 112m. DIR: Christopher Crowe. CAST: Annabella Sciorra, Jamey Sheridan, Anthony LaPaglia, Jill Clayburgh, Alan Alda, John Leguizamo, Deborah Unger. 1992

WHISTLE BLOWER, THE ★★★★ Taut suspense-thriller from England combines the elements of a murder mystery with real-life human drama. Michael Caine, in one of his finest performances, stars as a stoic British subject whose tidy life is disrupted when his son (Nigel Havers) discovers what he believes are immoral acts on the part of the government. Rated PG for suspense. 100m. DIR: Simon Langton. CAST: Michael Caine, Nigel Havers, James Fox, Felicity Dean, John Gielgud, Kenneth Colley, Gordon Jackson, Barry Foster. 1987

WHISTLE DOWN THE WIND ★★★1/2 Bryan Forbes's first film is a thoughtful, allegorical tale about three children who encounter an accused murderer hiding in a barn and take him to be a Christ figure fleeing from his persecutors. Based on Mary Hayley Bell's popular novel, this is one of the best films ever made dealing with the fragile nature of childhood trust and beliefs. B&W; 99m. DIR: Bryan Forbes. CAST: Hayley Mills, Alan Bates, Bernard Lee, Norman Bird, Elsie Wagstaff. 1961

WHISTLE STOP ❤️ Small-town girl returns from the big city. Tripe. B&W; 85m. DIR: Leonide Moguy. CAST: George Raft, Ava Gardner, Tom Conway, Victor McLaglen, Charles Drake, Jimmy Conlin. 1946

WHISTLING IN BROOKLYN ★★★ Red Skelton returns as the radio sleuth, The Fox, this time pursued by the police from one Brooklyn landmark to another, and ending up at Ebbets Field pitching against the Dodgers. More slapstick than usual. B&W; 87m. DIR: S. Sylvan Simon. CAST: Red Skelton, Ann Rutherford, Rags Ragland, Jean Rogers, Ray Collins, Henry O'Neill, William Frawley, Sam Levene. 1943

WHISTLING IN DIXIE ★★★1/2 Red Skelton's second outing as the radio detective, The Fox, plunges him and his bride into mysterious doings at an old southern mansion. Some good chills mixed in with lots of laughs. B&W; 74m. DIR: S. Sylvan Simon. CAST: Red Skelton, Ann Rutherford, George Bancroft, Guy Kibbee. 1942

WHISTLING IN THE DARK ★★★1/2 Red Skelton is a radio criminologist, The Fox, noted for devising and solving ingenious crimes. He's pursued and kidnapped by Conrad Veidt, who wants him to construct a perfect murder. Lots of laughs in Skelton's first starring role, aided and abetted by the hilariously sinister Veidt. B&W; 77m. DIR: S. Sylvan Simon. CAST: Red Skelton, Conrad Veidt, Ann Rutherford, Virginia Grey, Rags Ragland, Eve Arden, Henry O'Neill, Reed Hadley. 1941

WHITE ★★1/2 The second part of director Krzysztof Kieslowski's *Three Colors* trilogy. This one takes a hapless Pole from rags to riches, as he rebuilds his life after being dumped by his French wife. Interesting, but the progress of the story isn't always clear, and the ending is confusing and unsatisfying. In Polish and French with English subtitles. Rated R for simulated sex. 92m. DIR: Krzysztof Kieslowski. CAST: Zbigniew Zamachowski, Julie Delpy. 1994

WHITE BALLOON, THE ★★★1/2 This Iranian import is short on plot—a little girl keeps losing her money on the way to market to buy a goldfish—but long on charm and sweet, gentle comedy. Given the simplicity of the story, it's also surprisingly suspenseful. Seven-year-old Aida Mohammadkhani gives an amazingly natural performance, by turns adorable and exasperating—just like a real little girl. In Farsi with English subtitles. Not rated; suitable for general audiences. 85m. DIR: Jafar Panahi. CAST: Aida Mohammadkhani, Mohsen Kalifi, Fereshteh Sadr Orfani. 1995

WHITE BUFFALO ❤️ All-star cast wallows in weird *Jaws*-inspired Western, which has Wild Bill Hickok (Charles Bronson) on the trail of a mythical beast. Myth thith one. Rated R for violence. 97m. DIR: J. Lee Thompson. CAST: Charles Bronson, Kim Novak, Clint Walker, Jack Warden, Will Sampson, Stuart Whitman, Slim Pickens, John Carradine. 1977

WHITE CARGO ★★1/2 Hedy Lamarr is Tondelayo, a sultry African native girl who sets about seducing a group of British plantation managers. Considered daring when released, the movie is pretty corny today. Lamarr has never been lovelier, reason enough to give this one a look. B&W; 90m. DIR: Richard Thorpe. CAST: Hedy Lamarr, Walter Pidgeon, Frank Morgan, Richard Carlson, Reginald Owen, Henry O'Neill. 1942

WHITE CHRISTMAS ★★★ This attempt to capitalize on the title tune is an inferior remake of 1942s *Holiday Inn* (in which the song "White Christmas" first appeared). It's another in that long line of let's-put-on-a-show stories, with the last several reels showcasing the singing, dancing, and mugging talents of the cast. 120m. DIR: Michael Curtiz. CAST: Bing Crosby, Danny Kaye, Vera-Ellen, Rosemary Clooney. 1954

WHITE CLIFFS OF DOVER, THE ★★★★ Taking advantage of the patriotic pro-British sentiment of World War II, MGM successfully crafted an all-star, big-budget tearjerker very similar in content and texture to their popular *Mrs. Miniver*. The movie follows Irene Dunne as an American woman who marries into English aristocracy. She and her family are forced to endure the hardships of two world wars. B&W; 126m. **DIR:** Clarence Brown. **CAST:** Irene Dunne, Alan Marshal, Roddy McDowall, Frank Morgan, C. Aubrey Smith, May Whitty, Van Johnson. **1943**

WHITE COMANCHE ★★ Twin sons of an Indian mother and a white settler fight amongst themselves. One, Notah, leads a band of renegade Comanches while the other, Johnny Moon, lives among the whites. William Shatner plays dual roles and is aided by Joseph Cotten as the sheriff. Not rated; contains violence. 90m. **DIR:** Gilbert Kay. **CAST:** William Shatner, Joseph Cotten, Rossana Yani, Perla Cristal. **1967 DVD**

WHITE DAWN, THE ★★★★ This is a gripping and thought-provoking adventure film. Three whalers (Warren Oates, Lou Gossett Jr., and Timothy Bottoms) get lost in the Arctic and are rescued by Eskimos, whom they end up exploiting. Rated PG. 109m. **DIR:** Phil Kaufman. **CAST:** Warren Oates, Lou Gossett Jr., Timothy Bottoms. **1974**

WHITE DOG ★★★ In this adaptation of the Romain Gary novel, Kristy McNichol finds a dog and decides to keep it—unaware that it has been trained by white supremacists to attack black people. An intriguing premise, although not entirely successful in the telling. Rated R for profanity and violence. 89m. **DIR:** Samuel Fuller. **CAST:** Kristy McNichol, Paul Winfield, Burl Ives, Jameson Parker, Lynne Moody, Marshall Thompson, Paul Bartel, Dick Miller, Parley Baer. **1982**

WHITE DWARF ★★1/2 Almost-good futristic fantasy was a TV-pilot film for a proposed series. Circa A.D. 3040 a young doctor is stationed on a planet in the White Dwarf star system and he soon discovers the violent division between the light and dark sides of his new world. The problem with this film is its uneven pacing: bursts of action followed by long boring segments and an unsatisfactory ending. The plus is the decent special-effects work. Not rated; contains violence and gore. 91m. **DIR:** Peter Markle. **CAST:** Paul Winfield, Neal McDonough, C.C.H. Pounder, Ele Keats. **1995**

WHITE FANG ★★★★ A young man travels to Alaska in search of his father's lost gold mine and meets up with an old miner, an evil dogfight promoter, and a wolf. A wonderful Disney adventure film. Rated PG for violence. 104m. **DIR:** Randal Kleiser. **CAST:** Klaus Maria Brandauer, Ethan Hawke, Seymour Cassel, James Remar, Susan Hogan. **1991**

WHITE FANG 2: MYTH OF THE WHITE WOLF ★★1/2 This disappointing sequel banishes former star Ethan Hawke to cameo status and replaces him with overly wholesome Scott Bairstow. The insufferably politically correct story finds our hero and his loyal pooch battling greedy miners and helping Alaskan Native Americans. The stupid story line will annoy adults, and kids will be put off by the film's length and lack of action. Rated PG for mild violence. 105m. **DIR:** Ken Olin. **CAST:** Scott Bairstow, Charmaine Craig, Al Harrington, Alfred Molina, Geoffrey Lewis, Ethan Hawke. **1994**

WHITE FANG AND THE HUNTER ★★ A dog, White Fang, and his master, Daniel (Robert Wood), are attacked by wolves. They are taken in by a young widow who is being forced to marry. So Daniel and the dog come to her aid. Poor acting and directing hamper this familiar story. Rated G. 87m. **DIR:** Alfonso Brescia. **CAST:** Robert Wood, Pedro Sanchez. **1985**

WHITE GHOST 💙 William Katt does an embarrassing Rambo imitation in this miserable rip-off. Rated R for violence and profanity. 93m. **DIR:** B. J. Davis. **CAST:** William Katt, Rosalind Chao, Martin Hewitt, Wayne Crawford, Reb Brown. **1988**

WHITE GOLD ★★★★ Remarkable drama about a woman condemned to a boring life on a sheep ranch. She is caught between a resentful father-in-law and a timid husband; and when she commits murder to fend off a would-be rapist, everyone can only believe the worst of her. Silent. B&W; 70m. **DIR:** William K. Howard. **CAST:** Jetta Goudal, Kenneth Thompson, George Bancroft. **1927**

WHITE HEAT ★★★1/2 James Cagney gives one of his greatest screen performances as a totally insane mama's boy and gangster, Cody Jarrett. Margaret Wycherly is chillingly effective as the evil mom, and Virginia Mayo is uncommonly outstanding as the bad man's moll. But it is Cagney's picture pure and simple as he ironically makes it to "the top of the world, Ma!" B&W; 114m. **DIR:** Raoul Walsh. **CAST:** James Cagney, Margaret Wycherly, Virginia Mayo, Edmond O'Brien, Steve Cochran. **1949**

WHITE HOT ★★1/2 A quick-paced drama about a yuppie couple's fall from grace. Robby Benson (in his directorial debut) and Tawny Kitaen take over a drug lord's trade and become hopelessly immersed in the high life. Rated R for violence and drug use. 95m. **DIR:** Robby Benson. **CAST:** Robby Benson, Tawny Kitaen, Danny Aiello. **1989**

WHITE HOT: THE MYSTERIOUS MURDER OF THELMA TODD ★★ Melodramatic staging and dialogue mar what could have been compelling in this made-for-TV speculation on the death of Thirties starlet Thelma Todd. Loni Anderson is ever so glamorous in the title role of the siren who captivated men even after her death. 90m. **DIR:** Paul Wendkos. **CAST:** Loni Anderson, Robert Davi, Scott Paulin, Robin Strasser, Paul Dooley. **1991**

WHITE HUNTER BLACK HEART ★★★★ Director-star Clint Eastwood boldly impersonates flamboyant director John Huston (renamed John Wilson) in Peter Vietel's fictionalized account of the filming of *The African Queen*—during which Huston/Wilson is more interested in shooting an elephant than shooting his movie. Fascinating. Rated PG for profanity and violence. 112m. **DIR:** Clint Eastwood. **CAST:** Clint Eastwood, Jeff Fahey, George Dzundza, Marisa Berenson. **1990**

WHITE LEGION ★★ The White Legion were doctors who fought to find a cure for the yellow fever that plagued workers building the Panama Canal. Unfortunately, their story doesn't make for much of a movie; it's artificially padded with melodramatic situations. B&W; 81m. DIR: Karl Brown. CAST: Ian Keith, Tala Birell, Snub Pollard. 1936

WHITE LIE ★★★★ Samuel Charters's *Louisiana Black* gets first-cabin treatment from director Bill Condon and scripter Nevin Schreiner, who send New York mayoral press adviser Gregory Hines to the Deep South to investigate the events that led to his father's lynching thirty years earlier. Hines finds sympathetic pediatrician Annette O'Toole ... who may have her own reasons for getting involved. Made for cable, with highly unsettling images and attitudes. Rated PG-13 for mild profanity and mild violence. 93m. DIR: Bill Condon. CAST: Gregory Hines, Annette O'Toole, Bill Nunn, Gregg Henry. 1991

WHITE LIGHT ★★1/2 When cop Martin Kove bites the bullet, he meets the woman of his dreams on the other side. Weird fantasy directed by Kove's *Cagney and Lacey* costar, Al Waxman. Rated R for profanity and violence. 96m. DIR: Al Waxman. CAST: Martin Kove, Martha Henry. 1990

WHITE LIGHTNING ★★ Good old boy Burt Reynolds as a speed-loving moonshiner fights the inevitable mean and inept cops and revenue agents in this comic-book chase and retribution film. A good cast of character actors makes this stock drive-in movie entertaining, although it is just like the majority of Burt Reynolds's car films—gimmicky and predictable. Rated PG. 101m. DIR: Joseph Sargent. CAST: Burt Reynolds, Jennifer Billingsley, Ned Beatty, Bo Hopkins, Matt Clark, Louise Latham, Diane Ladd. 1973

WHITE LINE FEVER ★★★ Jan-Michael Vincent plays an incorruptible young trucker in this film. He is angered when forced to smuggle goods in his truck. He fights back after he and his pregnant wife (Kay Lenz) are attacked. Rated PG. 92m. DIR: Jonathan Kaplan. CAST: Jan-Michael Vincent, Kay Lenz, Slim Pickens, L. Q. Jones, Leigh French, Don Porter. 1975

WHITE MAMA ★★★ Aging widow Bette Davis, living on a shoestring in a condemned tenement, is befriended by a streetwise black youth (Ernest Harden) and becomes the mother he can't remember when she provides him with a home in return for protection. A good story, touchingly told. Made for TV. 105m. DIR: Jackie Cooper. CAST: Bette Davis, Ernest Harden, Eileen Heckart, Lurene Tuttle, Virginia Capers. 1980

WHITE MAN'S BURDEN ★★1/2 In an alternate-world Los Angeles, a white underclass struggles in the squalid inner city while wealthy blacks live in secure, gated mansions. In this atmosphere, a frustrated, out-of-work John Travolta kidnaps rich Harry Belafonte to show him how the other half lives. Writer-director Desmond Nakano sets up that gimmicky premise, then does nothing with it; the film wanders aimlessly with only the performances of the two stars to hold our interest. Rated R for profanity and violence. 90m. DIR: Desmond Nakano. CAST: John Travolta, Harry Belafonte, Tom Bower, Margaret Avery, Kelly Lynch. 1995 DVD

WHITE MEN CAN'T JUMP ★★★★ As with writer-director Ron Shelton's *Bull Durham*, this movie

about a pair of hoop hustlers (Wesley Snipes, Woody Harrelson) is smart, sassy, sexy, and rich in characterization. Deceptively adept at basketball, Harrelson arrives in Venice, California, to hook up with local hotshot Snipes for a big score. The dialogue is lightning fast, and the performances are just as electric. Rated R for profanity, nudity, and brief violence. 115m. DIR: Ron Shelton. CAST: Wesley Snipes, Woody Harrelson, Rosie Perez, Tyra Ferrell. 1992

WHITE MILE ★★★★ Rapacious executive Alan Alda bullies staff and clients into a disastrous whitewater rafting expedition, and then attempts to evade personal responsibility for the inevitable tragedy. After years of playing amiable good guys, this film casts Alda in an entirely new light ... and he's positively chilling. Rated R for profanity and dramatic intensity. 96m. DIR: Robert Butler. CAST: Alan Alda, Peter Gallagher, Bruce Altman, Robert Loggia, Fionnula Flanagan. 1994

WHITE MISCHIEF ★★1/2 In the early Forties while Britain was being pounded to rubble by German bombs, a group of wealthy colonials carried on with alcohol, drugs, and spouse swapping in Kenya. A stunning backdrop—complete with giraffes roaming in the backyards of opulent mansions—is the film's greatest asset. But James Fox's script is flat. Rated R for language and explicit sex scenes. 100m. DIR: Michael Radford. CAST: Charles Dance, Sarah Miles, Greta Scacchi, John Hurt, Joss Ackland. 1987

WHITE NIGHTS (1957) ★★★★ In this stylish melodrama, a shy young man encounters a mysterious girl whose lover has not returned from a journey across the sea. Based on a story by Dostoyevski. In Italian with English subtitles. B&W; 107m. DIR: Luchino Visconti. CAST: Marcello Mastroianni, Maria Schell, Jean Marais. 1957

WHITE NIGHTS (1985) ★★★1/2 Russian defector and ballet star Mikhail Baryshnikov, finding himself back in the U.S.S.R., joins forces with American defector Gregory Hines to escape to freedom in this soap opera–styled thriller. The plot is contrived, but the dance sequences are spectacular. Rated PG-13 for violence and profanity. 135m. DIR: Taylor Hackford. CAST: Mikhail Baryshnikov, Gregory Hines, Geraldine Page, Jerzy Skolimowski, Isabella Rossellini. 1985

WHITE OF THE EYE ★★1/2 Tense film deals with a serial killer on the loose in Arizona. David Keith plays a commercial-stereo whiz who becomes a suspect in a series of bizarre and brutal murders of affluent women. Director Donald Cammell avoids the usual slasher pitfalls, although this one is saddled with a truly abysmal finale. Rated R. 113m. DIR: Donald Cammell. CAST: David Keith, Cathy Moriarty, Art Evans. 1988

WHITE PALACE ★★★ Twitchy, blank-eyed James Spader is a widowed yuppie who slowly falls for burger-slingin' country gal Susan Sarandon. It's one of those movies that is terrific in the early-to-middle scenes and just so-so in the conclusion. Rated R for nudity and profanity. 106m. DIR: Luis Mandoki. CAST: Susan Sarandon, James Spader, Jason Alexander, Kathy Bates, Eileen Brennan, Steven Hill, Renee Taylor. 1990 DVD

WHITE PHANTOM ★★ A Ninja gang attempts to deliver a plutonium weapon to terrorists. Bo Svenson is out to break up the plan and blackmails a dancer into infiltrating the gang. Not rated, but with the usual genre violence. 89m. **DIR:** Dusty Nelson. **CAST:** Jay Roberts Jr., Page Leong, Bo Svenson. **1987**

WHITE PONGO (BLOND GORILLA) 💔 Reverently referred to by fans of genre films as the worst of all crazed-gorilla–missing link jungle movies. B&W; 74m. **DIR:** Sam Newfield. **CAST:** Richard Fraser, Lionel Royce, Al Ebon, Gordon Richards. **1945**

WHITE ROSE, THE (1923) ★★★ Bessie Williams (Mae Marsh) is seduced and abandoned by an aristocratic Southerner (Ivor Novello). Sheer melodrama, although the production is salvaged by the soft-focus photography of Billy Bitzer and Hendrik Sartov. Not one of the major Griffith efforts, its appeal is limited to Griffith purists and silent-film specialists. Silent. B&W; 100m. **DIR:** D. W. Griffith. **CAST:** Mae Marsh, Carol Dempster, Ivor Novello. **1923**

WHITE ROSE, THE (1983) ★★★ Based on a true story about a group of youths in wartime Germany who revolted against Hitler by printing and distributing subversive leaflets to the public. All of the young actors are good, especially Lena Stolze, who plays the protagonist. In German. Not rated. 108m. **DIR:** Michael Verhoeven. **CAST:** Lena Stolze, Wulf Kessler, Martin Benrath. **1983**

WHITE SANDS ★★★1/2 Willem Dafoe is a small-town sheriff whose investigation of a murder leads him deep inside an FBI sting. Lots of plot twists and turns will keep viewers interested, although the middle of this film drags a bit. Rated R for violence, profanity, and nudity. 105m. **DIR:** Roger Donaldson. **CAST:** Willem Dafoe, Samuel L. Jackson, Mickey Rourke, Mary Elizabeth Mastrantonio, M. Emmet Walsh, Mimi Rogers. **1992 DVD**

WHITE SHADOWS IN THE SOUTH SEAS ★★1/2 Documentary director Robert Flaherty worked on this South Seas romance (ultimately without credit), which in certain ways is a more conventional dry run for his later *Tabu*. The location cinematography is this turgid soap opera's main strength. B&W; 88m. **DIR:** W. S. Van Dyke. **CAST:** Monte Blue, Raquel Torres. **1927**

WHITE SHEIK, THE ★★★ A warm salute to romantic movie heroes. When a recently wed couple go to Rome, the bride sneaks off to a movie set where her idol, the White Sheik, is making a film. Federico Fellini manages to create an original cinematic piece with great satirical precision. In Italian with English subtitles. B&W; 86m. **DIR:** Federico Fellini. **CAST:** Brunella Bovo, Leopoldo Trieste, Alberto Sordi, Giulietta Masina. **1952**

WHITE SISTER, THE ★★★ Cheated out of an inheritance, Italian aristocrat Lillian Gish falls in love with an army officer. When he is reported dead, she joins a convent, only to be faced with renouncing her vows when he returns. Only about half of the original film remains, but that's more than enough. Silent. B&W; 68m. **DIR:** Henry King. **CAST:** Lillian Gish, Ronald Colman, Charles Lane, Juliette la Violette. **1923**

WHITE SQUALL ★★★ This oceanbound *Dead Poets Society*, set in the early 1960s, concerns a group of young men who forgo their senior year at a conventional high school in favor of a season in the Ocean Academy: crewing and studying on a square-rigged brigantine sailing the oceans. The titular disaster is suspensefully staged, but the film remains oddly uninvolving. Rated PG-13 for violence, profanity, and brief nudity. 127m. **DIR:** Ridley Scott. **CAST:** Jeff Bridges, Caroline Goodall, John Savage, Scott Wolf, Jeremy Sisto, Ryan Philippe, David Lascher. **1996 DVD**

WHITE TIGER ★★★ Brother and sister separated since childhood are reunited thirteen years later as thieves. Teaming up with the man responsible for their father's death, the three steal a fortune in jewels and hide out in a remote cabin where secrets long hidden are revealed. B&W; 81m. **DIR:** Tod Browning. **CAST:** Priscilla Dean, Raymond Griffith, Wallace Beery, Matt Moore. **1923**

WHITE TOWER, THE ★★1/2 Symbolic melodrama of a weird group of people who attempt the ascension of an Alpine mountain. The action scenes are good, but the actors seem to walk through their parts. 98m. **DIR:** Ted Tetzlaff. **CAST:** Glenn Ford, Claude Rains, Alida Valli, Oscar Homolka, Cedric Hardwicke, Lloyd Bridges. **1950**

WHITE WATER SUMMER ★★★ Kevin Bacon plays a ruthless wilderness guide who intends to transform four boys into men. Sean Astin is the boy most abused by Bacon and he must decide what to do when Bacon is seriously injured. Interesting coming-of-age adventure. Rated PG for profanity. 87m. **DIR:** Jeff Bleckner. **CAST:** Kevin Bacon, Sean Astin, Jonathan Ward, Matt Adler. **1987**

WHITE WOLVES: A CRY IN THE WILD II ★★1/2 During a camping trip a teacher falls over a cliff and his students must find and save him. Very predictable film about teenagers learning to understand and like each other. The young cast needs acting lessons. Rated PG. 74m. **DIR:** Catherine Cyran. **CAST:** Ami Dolenz, Mark Paul Gosselaar, David Moscow, Amy O'Neill, Marc Riffon, Matt McCoy. **1993 DVD**

WHITE ZOMBIE ★★★★ This eerie little thriller is the consummate zombie film, with hordes of the walking dead doing the bidding of evil Bela Lugosi as their overseer and master. A damsel-in-distress story with a new twist, this independently produced gem features sets and production standards usually found in films by the major studios. A minor classic, with a standout role by Lugosi. B&W; 73m. **DIR:** Victor Halperin. **CAST:** Bela Lugosi, Madge Bellamy, Robert Frazer. **1932 DVD**

◆**WHITEBOYZ** ★★★ In the rolling cornfields of Iowa, the only gangster rapper to be found is a stark white teenager named Flip Dogg. When he takes his posse on a road trip to Chicago in order to experience a real hood and get connections with some drug pushers, Flip Dogg gets himself into more trouble than he can deal with. Often funny, this movie has many cameo appearances by popular rap stars that also add to the soundtrack. Rated R for profanity, violence, and simulated sex. 88m. **DIR:** Marc Levin. **CAST:** Danny Hoch, Dash Mihok, Mark Webber. **1999**

WHITEWATER SAM ★★1/2 Keith Larsen wrote, directed, coproduced, and stars in this wilderness adventure. He plays the legendary Whitewater Sam, the first white man to survive the harsh Rocky Mountain winters. The real star, however, seems to be his dog, Sybar. The beautiful scenery makes this film more than watchable. Rated PG for violence. 85m. DIR: Keith Larsen. CAST: Keith Larsen. 1978

WHO AM I? ★★★ This Jackie Chan entry went straight to cable, which is odd. This time our hero's a mercenary-for-hire who loses his memory following an assignment in South Africa and is unable to trust anybody. As usual, the action is played for laughs, and Chan finds plenty of outlets for his signature fight scenes with everyday objects … not to mention the climactic stunt, which is a real heart-stopper. Rated PG-13 for violence. 108m. DIR: Benny Chan, Jackie Chan. CAST: Jackie Chan, Michelle Ferre, Mirai Yamamoto. 1998 DVD

WHO AM I THIS TIME? ★★★1/2 The new girl in town, Helene Shaw (Susan Sarandon), gets a part in the local theater group production of *A Streetcar Named Desire* opposite Harry Nash (Christopher Walken). Dreadfully shy, Harry only comes to life in every part he plays on the stage. Helene sets out to win him. This is a pleasing Kurt Vonnegut Jr. story played by a capable cast. 60m. DIR: Jonathan Demme. CAST: Susan Sarandon, Christopher Walken, Robert Ridgely. 1982

WHO ARE THE DEBOLTS AND WHERE DID THEY GET 19 KIDS? ★★★★★ This Academy Award–winning documentary features Dorothy and Bob Debolt and their nineteen children—some natural, most adopted. Their family is unique not only for its great size but for the multiple physical disabilities their adopted children have, the positive way these problems are dealt with, and the fantastic organizational system under which their daily lives are run. This is an excellent and inspirational film. Rated G. 73m. DIR: John Korty. 1978

WHO DONE IT? ★★1/2 Standard Abbott and Costello programmer about a pair of soda jerks who witness an on-the-air murder during a radio broadcast and pose as detectives. B&W; 75m. DIR: Erle C. Kenton. CAST: Bud Abbott, Lou Costello, Patric Knowles, William Gargan, Louise Allbritton, William Bendix, Thomas Gomez, Jerome Cowan. 1942

WHO FRAMED ROGER RABBIT ★★★★1/2 In this innovative and vastly entertaining motion picture, which seamlessly blends animated characters with live action, cartoon character Roger Rabbit (voice by Charles Fleischer) is accused of murder and turns to a hardboiled private detective (Bob Hoskins) for help. As with his *Back to the Future* and *Romancing the Stone*, director Robert Zemeckis has come up with a wonderful movie for all ages. Rated PG for vulgar language. 103m. DIR: Robert Zemeckis. CAST: Bob Hoskins, Christopher Lloyd, Joanna Cassidy, Stubby Kaye. 1988 DVD

WHO IS KILLING THE GREAT CHEFS OF EUROPE? ★★★★ Scripter Peter Stone, working from Nan and Ivan Lyons' deliciously funny novel, whips up a droll entrée in that most difficult of genres: the comic mystery. Internationally renowned dessert chef Jacqueline Bisset wins a commission as the final course in the meal of the century, while fending off the boorish advances of her ex-husband, a fast-food mogul. Rated PG for imaginative violence. 112m. DIR: Ted Kotcheff. CAST: George Segal, Jacqueline Bisset, Robert Morley, Jean-Pierre Cassel, Madge Ryan. 1978

WHO IS THE BLACK DAHLIA? ★★★★ An above-average semidocumentary crime-drama based on one of the Los Angeles Police Department's most famous unsolved cases: the 1947 murder and gruesome dissection of a mysterious young woman whose lifestyle and mode of dress earned her the nickname of Black Dahlia. An excellent cast performs a first-rate script in this gripping telemovie. 100m. DIR: Joseph Pevney. CAST: Lucie Arnaz, Efrem Zimbalist Jr., Ronny Cox, Macdonald Carey, Gloria De Haven, Tom Bosley, Mercedes McCambridge, Donna Mills, June Lockhart. 1975

WHO KILLED BABY AZARIA? ★★★★ Made-for-Australian-TV version of the true story, told in the American *A Cry in the Dark*, about a woman accused of murdering a baby that she claims was dragged away by a wild dog in the outback. Less polished than the remake, but still compelling. Not rated. 96m. DIR: Judy Rymer. CAST: Elain Hudson, John Hamblin. 1983

WHO KILLED MARY WHAT'S 'ER NAME? ★★1/2 Gritty detective melodrama about an ex-boxer who solves the murder of a prostitute when no one else seems to care. Above-average low-budget thriller. Rated PG. 90m. DIR: Ernest Pintoff. CAST: Red Buttons, Sylvia Miles, Conrad Bain, David Doyle, Ron Carey, Alice Playten, Sam Waterston. 1971

WHO KILLED PASOLINI? ★★★1/2 Riveting docudrama about the 1975 murder of the infamous Italian director/poet. The film suggests that Pasolini, who made enemies with his homosexual lifestyle and attacks on political decadence, was the victim of an unholy conspiracy. The case's circumstances and shoddy investigation are teasingly open-ended. In Italian with English subtitles. Not rated; contains adult themes. 100m. DIR: Marco Tuillo Giordana. CAST: Carlo De Filippi, Nicoletta Braschi, Toni Bertorelli, Guilio Scarpati. 1995

WHO SHOT PAT? ✿ A plotless, nostalgic return to the narrator's last year at vocational school and the harsh realities of growing up in Brooklyn. Not rated; contains profanity and violence. 111m. DIR: Robert Brooks. CAST: David Knight, Sandra Bullock. 1991 DVD

WHO SLEW AUNTIE ROO? ★★ Ghoulish horror version of *Hansel and Gretel*, with Shelley Winters as the madwoman who lures two children (Mark Lester and Chloe Franks) into her evil clutches. Rated R for violence. 89m. DIR: Curtis Harrington. CAST: Shelley Winters, Mark Lester, Chloe Franks, Ralph Richardson, Lionel Jeffries, Hugh Griffith. 1971

WHODUNIT? ✿ Low-budget murder mystery in which characters are being systematically eliminated at a place called Creep Island. Rated R for violence and profanity. 82m. DIR: Bill Naud. CAST: Rick Bean, Gary Phillips. 1982

•WHOLE NINE YARDS, THE ★★★1/2 Canadian dentist Matthew Perry's already miserable life takes a turn for the worse when a well-known, mob hit man

Bruce Willis) moves in next door. Suddenly, Perry finds himself involved in all sorts of intrigue, thanks primarily to his scheming, money-hungry wife who talks him into betraying Willis in the hopes of getting her husband killed so she can collect a $1 million insurance policy. Several intertwining plots feature some fine bits of physical comedy by Perry and a dry, understated turn from Willis. Rated R for profanity, violence, and simulated sex. 97m. DIR: Jonathan Lynn. CAST: Bruce Willis, Matthew Perry, Rosanna Arquette, Michael Clarke Duncan, Natasha Henstridge, Amanda Peet, Kevin Pollak. 1999

WHOLE WIDE WORLD, THE ★★★1/2 Writer Robert E. Howard (creator of *Conan the Barbarian*) who committed suicide in 1936, had a turbulent, unconsummated romance with schoolteacher Novaline Price, which she chronicled in a 1988 memoir. This film, based on her book, takes an uncritical view of Howard's writing and features fine performances. Rated PG-13 for mild profanity and mature themes. 113m. DIR: Dan Ireland. CAST: Vincent D'Onofrio, Renee Zellweger, Ann Wedgeworth, Harve Presnell. 1996

WHO'LL STOP THE RAIN ★★★1/2 In this brilliant film, Nick Nolte gives one of his finest performances as a hardened vet who agrees to smuggle drugs for a buddy (the always effective Michael Moriarty). What neither of them knows is that it's a setup, so Nolte and Moriarty's neurotic wife, played to perfection by Tuesday Weld, have to hide out from the baddies (Anthony Zerbe, Richard Masur, and Ray Sharkey). Rated R. 126m. DIR: Karel Reisz. CAST: Nick Nolte, Michael Moriarty, Tuesday Weld, Anthony Zerbe, Richard Masur, Ray Sharkey, David Opatoshu, Gail Strickland. 1978

WHOLLY MOSES! ★★1/2 *Wholly Moses!* pokes fun at Hollywood biblical epics in a rapid-fire fashion. While the film is sometimes very funny, it is also loaded with a fair share of predictable, flat, and corny moments. It's so-so viewing fare. Rated R. 109m. DIR: Gary Weis. CAST: Dudley Moore, Richard Pryor, Laraine Newman, James Coco, Paul Sand, Jack Gilford, Dom DeLuise, John Houseman, Madeline Kahn, David L. Lander, John Ritter. 1980

WHOOPEE ★★1/2 The first of six Eddie Cantor musical films of the 1930s, this one's a two-color draft of his 1928 Broadway hit of the same name. The big-eyed comic plays a superhypochondriac on an Arizona dude ranch. Cowpokes and chorines abound. Busby Berkeley production numbers make it palatable. B&W; 93m. DIR: Thornton Freeland. CAST: Eddie Cantor, Eleanor Hunt, Paul Gregory, Ethel Shutta. 1930

WHOOPEE BOYS, THE ❤ A pair of obnoxious—and supposedly lovable—misfits attempt to save a school for needy children. Rated R for profanity. 94m. DIR: John Byrum. CAST: Michael O'Keefe, Paul Rodriguez, Lucinda Jenney, Denholm Elliott, Eddie Deezen. 1986

WHOOPS APOCALYPSE ★★1/2 This overlong but sometimes rewarding British comedy consists of a news coverage spoof on events leading up to World War III. The plot centers around the theft of a U.S. nuclear bomb. Many viewers may get fidgety during the second, less successful half. Not rated, it contains nudity and obscene language. 137m. DIR: John

Reardon. CAST: John Barron, John Cleese, Richard Griffiths, Peter Jones, Barry Morse. 1981

WHORE ★★ This lurid walk on the wild side is just as harsh, brash, and uncompromising as the title implies. Sensationalism runs rampant as a streetwalker (Theresa Russell) talks directly into the camera between tricks about the intricacies of her profession, and hides out from her knife-wielding pimp. This film exists in both R and NC-17 versions, both due to profanity and explicit sexual content. 92m. DIR: Ken Russell. CAST: Theresa Russell, Benjamin Mouton, Antonio Fargas. 1991

WHORE 2 ★★★★ Though it has little (read: nothing) to do with Ken Russell's 1991 *Whore*, this is a surprisingly engrossing drama about an author (Amos Kollek) who spends a couple of months in a red-light district to do research on prostitution. There he discovers a startling subculture whose existence seems impossible until the film's final moments reveal the majority of the cast are real hookers. Engrossing, enlightening, and disturbing. Not rated; contains profanity, violence, and sexual situations. 85m. DIR: Amos Kollek. CAST: Amos Kollek, Marla Sucharetza, Mari Nelson. 1993

WHO'S AFRAID OF VIRGINIA WOOLF? ★★★★★ Edward Albee's powerful play about the love-hate relationship of a college professor and his bitchy wife was brilliantly transferred to the screen. Elizabeth Taylor gives one of her best acting performances and Richard Burton is equally stunning. B&W; 129m. DIR: Mike Nichols. CAST: Elizabeth Taylor, Richard Burton, Sandy Dennis, George Segal. 1966 DVD

WHO'S GOT THE ACTION? ★★ One of Lana Turner's less glamorous roles teams her with Dean Martin in a spoof of gambling movies. The twist is that they are married, and she tries to keep his gambling losses in the family by being his bookie—incognito, of course. When he starts winning, she has to sell his assets to pay him. The comic twists are diluted by the posturing of the stars. 93m. DIR: Daniel Mann. CAST: Lana Turner, Dean Martin, Walter Matthau, Eddie Albert, Margo, Nita Talbot, Paul Ford. 1962

WHO'S HARRY CRUMB? ❤ Inept private eye Harry Crumb bumbles his way through the case of a kidnapped heiress. Rated PG-13 for profanity and suggested sex. 87m. DIR: Paul Flaherty. CAST: John Candy, Jeffrey Jones, Annie Potts, Tim Thomerson, Barry Corbin. 1989 DVD

WHO'S MINDING THE MINT? ★★★1/2 When a U.S. Mint employee (Jim Hutton) accidentally destroys thousands of newly printed bills, a group of misfits bands together to help him out. This film is often hilarious and always enjoyable. 97m. DIR: Howard Morris. CAST: Milton Berle, Jim Hutton, Dorothy Provine, Joey Bishop, Walter Brennan, Jamie Farr, Victor Buono. 1967

WHO'S THAT GIRL ❤ A warped, pseudoremake of the 1938 comedy classic *Bringing Up Baby*. Rated PG for profanity. 95m. DIR: James Foley. CAST: Madonna, Griffin Dunne, Haviland Morris, John McMartin, John Mills. 1987

WHO'S THAT KNOCKING AT MY DOOR? ★★★ All the trademark obsessional concerns—women, money, peer pressure—of better-known Martin Scorsese melodramas are evident in this first feature by the distinctive director. Harvey Keitel fumbles violently through his stormy relationship with a free-thinking, elusive young woman while shedding the shackles of strict Catholicism. B&W; 90m. DIR: Martin Scorsese. CAST: Zina Bethune, Harvey Keitel. 1968

WHO'S THE MAN? ★★★ Two inept Harlem haircutters reluctantly become inept Harlem cops and investigate the murder of their former barbershop boss in this funny, sassy, streetwise comedy but MTV rap hosts Dr. Dre and Ed Lover bring to the party the most rhythmic and natural comic chemistry since Cheech and Chong. Rated R for language. 100m. DIR: Ted Demme. CAST: Doctor Dre, Ed Lover, Jim Moody, Denis Leary, Colin Quinn, Badja Djola, Cheryl James, Andre Blake, Rozwill Young. 1993

WHO'S WHO ★★★★★ This brilliant, ascerbic comedy deals with the violent differences in lifestyle and attitude that exist within the British class system. A pathetic, vacuous clerk in a stockbroker's office is obsessed with the aristocracy, who regard his social advances with facial expressions similar to the expressions of those who have just discovered fresh canine excrement on their shoes. Brilliant. Not rated. 75m. DIR: Mike Leigh. CAST: Bridget Kane, Sam Kelly, Simon Chandler, Adam Norton, Philip Davis. 1978

WHOSE CHILD AM I? 🎬 Artificial insemination is the pitiful excuse for this ridiculously sordid film. 90m. DIR: Lawrence Britten. CAST: Kate O'Mara, Paul Freeman, Edward Judd. 1974

WHOSE LIFE IS IT, ANYWAY? ★★★★ Richard Dreyfuss is superb as a witty and intellectually dynamic sculptor who is paralyzed after an auto accident and fights for his right to be left alone to die. John Cassavetes and Christine Lahti costar as doctors in this surprisingly upbeat movie. Rated R. 118m. DIR: John Badham. CAST: Richard Dreyfuss, John Cassavetes, Christine Lahti, Bob Balaban, Kenneth McMillan, Kaki Hunter, Janet Eilber. 1981

WHY, CHARLIE BROWN, WHY? ★★★★ The Peanuts kids perform a superb public service in this poignant tale when one of Linus's best friends—a little girl named Janice—is hospitalized with leukemia. Aside from its sugar-coated conclusion, the instructive script doesn't pull any punches. Not rated. 25m. DIR: Sam Jaimes. 1990

WHY DIDN'T THEY ASK EVANS? ★★★★ A famous explorer's dying question sends amateur sleuths Lady Derwent and Bobby Jones (Francesca Annis and James Warwick, who later teamed up for the popular *Partners in Crime* series) on the trail in this entertaining Agatha Christie TV yarn. That cryptic query, an attempt on Bobby's life, and an apparent suicide are just a few of the mysteries tackled by the energetic duo. The 1930s setting is re-created faithfully, and the costume design is excellent. Suitable for family viewing. 180m. DIR: John Davies. CAST: Francesca Annis, James Warwick, Eric Porter, John Gielgud, Joan Hickson. 1980

WHY DO FOOLS FALL IN LOVE ★★★★ Three faces of rock legend Frankie Lymon are revealed during a heated courtroom battle over his estate.

The marrying kind, with three wives before he overdosed at twenty-five, Lymon never divorced any of them. In this film, at least, Lymon played second fiddle to the strong-willed women who claimed separate aspects of the man. Heavy doses of humor are sprinkled with heartbreak. Rated R for violence, drug use, sex, nudity, language, and animal cruelty. 115m. DIR: Gregory Nava. CAST: Larenz Tate, Halle Berry, Vivica A. Fox, Lela Rochon, Paul Mazursky. 1998 DVD

•**WHY DOES HERR R. RUN AMOK?** ★★★ With an unmoving camera lending a sense of emotional claustrophobia, this film depicts the dreary life of a middle-class German family, culminating in murder and suicide. It's an experimental film that imparts the misery of the characters to the viewer, though that doesn't make it much fun to watch. In German with English subtitles. Not rated. 88m. DIR: Rainer Werner Fassbinder, Michael Fengler. CAST: Kurt Raab, Lilith Ungerer, Hanna Schygulla. 1970

•**WHY HAS BHODI DHARMA LEFT FOR THE EAST?** ★★★★ Essentially plotless, this South Korean film attempts to guide the viewer through the central tenets of Buddhism via a series of incidents in the lives of an adult and a child. You don't have to be interested in religion, however, to enjoy this beautifully photographed and elegantly paced movie, which was filmed over a period of seven years by an art professor with no previous filmmaking experience. In Korean with English subtitles. Not rated; contains no objectionable material. 137m. DIR: Yong-Kyun Bae. CAST: Hae-Jin Huang, Su-Myong Ko, Yi Pan-Yong, Sin Won-Sop. 1989 DVD

WHY ME? 🎬 Two career burglars steal a cursed ruby. Badly acted, poorly written adventure. Rated R for profanity. 87m. DIR: Gene Quintano. CAST: Christopher Lambert, Kim Greist, Christopher Lloyd. 1989

WHY SHOOT THE TEACHER? ★★★ Bud Cort stars in this intimate and simple film about a young instructor whose first teaching position lands him in the barren plains of Canada. Lean realism and bright dashes of humor give the picture some memorable moments, but this story develops with a disengaging slowness. Rated PG. 101m. DIR: Silvio Narizzano. CAST: Bud Cort, Samantha Eggar, Chris Wiggins, Gary Reineke. 1977

WICKED, THE ★★1/2 The Terminus family are bloodsuckers who are more than thrilled when strangers visit their quaint small town. Okay shocker. Rated R for nudity and violence. 87m. DIR: Colin Eggleston. CAST: Brett Cumo, Richard Morgan, Angela Kennedy, John Doyle. 1987

WICKED CITY, THE (1992) ★★★ The imagery is dazzling, but the plot is nearly impossible to follow in this over-the-top live-action fantasy based on a Japanese cartoon. The story line seems to revolve around a race of shape-shifting creatures intent on taking over the Earth. The film races along at a fast clip, and features an array of eye-catching FX. Dubbed. Not rated; contains violence and nudity. 88m. DIR: Mak Tai-Kit. CAST: Jacky Cheung, Leon Lai, Michelle Reis, Tatsuya Nakadai. 1992

WICKED CITY (1995) ★★★ Exciting Japanese animated film about a race of shape shifters and their ties to Earth, which is presently at risk unless a treaty is signed. Creatures have a style reminiscent of Rob Bottin's work on John Carpenter's remake of *The Thing*, but some viewers may be shocked by the sexuality expressed in the film. Not rated; contains violence, profanity, nudity, and simulated sex. 90m. **DIR:** Yoshiaki Kawajiri. **1995 DVD**

•**WICKED GAMES** 🖤 The copper-masked serial killer from *Truth or Dare?* returns in this sleazy sequel coproduced by the local Shakespearean company (?!). Not rated; contains gore and violence. 80m. **DIR:** Tim Ritter. **CAST:** Joel Wynkoop, Kermit Christman. **1994**

WICKED LADY, THE (1945) ★★ Margaret Lockwood's scruples dip as low as her neckline in this somewhat tedious period piece about a vixen who masquerades as an outlaw. James Mason is appropriately evil as her companion in crime. B&W; 104m. **DIR:** Leslie Arliss. **CAST:** Margaret Lockwood, James Mason, Patricia Roc, Michael Rennie, Martita Hunt. **1945**

WICKED LADY, THE (1983) 🖤 An absolutely awful swashbuckler. Rated R. 98m. **DIR:** Michael Winner. **CAST:** Faye Dunaway, Alan Bates, John Gielgud, Denholm Elliott, Prunella Scales, Oliver Tobias, Glynis Barber. **1983**

WICKED STEPMOTHER, THE 🖤 A lame horror-comedy about an old woman who moves in with a family and turns their lives upside down with her evil powers. Rated PG-13 for profanity. 95m. **DIR:** Larry Cohen. **CAST:** Bette Davis, Barbara Carrera, Richard Moll, Tom Bosley. **1989**

WICKER MAN, THE ★★★1/2 An anonymous letter that implies a missing girl has been murdered brings Sergeant Howie of Scotland Yard, to Summerisle, an island off the coast of England. Lord Summerisle, the ruler and religious leader of the island, seems to take it all as a joke, so Howie swears to find the truth. Rated R. 95m. **DIR:** Robin Hardy. **CAST:** Edward Woodward, Christopher Lee, Britt Ekland, Diane Cilento, Ingrid Pitt. **1973**

WIDE AWAKE ★★ Fifth-grader is on a spritual quest and questions his faith in God after the death of his widowed grandfather. The most intriguing rub of the film—that the boy's search for enlightenment is frustrated rather than simplified by his attendance at a boys-only Catholic school—is sapped of its potency by a rather saccharine script. Rated PG. 90m. **DIR:** M. Night Shyamalan. **CAST:** Joseph Cross, Robert Loggia, Timothy Reifsnyder, Dana Delany, Denis Leary, Julia Stiles, Rosie O'Donnell. **1998 DVD**

WIDE SARGASSO SEA ★★★1/2 Lush, gothic romance, based on Jean Rhys's celebrated novel, acts as a prequel to Charlotte Brontë's *Jane Eyre*. Englishman sets sail to Jamaica for an arranged marriage to a mysterious and sensual woman that leads him on an erotic journey that crosses all boundaries and eventually leads to betrayal. One hot film. Rated R and unrated versions available; both contain nudity and adult situations. 100m. **DIR:** John Duigan. **CAST:** Karina Lombard, Nathaniel Parker, Claudia Robinson, Michael York, Rachel Ward. **1993**

WIDE-OPEN TOWN ★★★ A saloon-based gang run by a beautiful woman and her cold-blooded henchman steals Hopalong Cassidy's cattle and kills an old prospector. Hopalong and ace villain Victor Jory duke it out in a no-holds-barred finale that puts a satisfying end to this superior series entry. B&W; 79m. **DIR:** Lesley Selander. **CAST:** William Boyd, Russell Hayden, Andy Clyde, Evelyn Brent, Victor Jory, Morris Ankrum (Stepen Morris), Roy Barcroft, Glenn Strange. **1941**

WIDOW COUDERC ★★★ Tense, well-acted thriller about a small-town woman's affair with an escaped killer. From a novel by Georges Simenon. In French with English subtitles. Not rated; contains no objectionable material. 92m. **DIR:** Pierre Granier-Deferre. **CAST:** Simone Signoret, Alain Delon. **1974**

WIDOW'S KISS ★★★ Beverly D'Angelo plays the black widow who beds, weds, and then disposes of her husbands. Unfortunately, her latest victim (Bruce Davison) has a son (MacKenzie Astin) who will stop at nothing to prove dear old stepmom is really a killer. That means having to get close to the woman who put Dad in the grave. Decent acting saves this formula thriller from falling through the cracks. Rated R for violence, profanity, and nudity. 103m. **DIR:** Peter Foldy. **CAST:** Beverly D'Angelo, Mackenzie Astin, Dennis Haysbert, Bruce Davison, Barbara Rush. **1996**

WIDOW'S PEAK ★★★★ Fabulous Irish film perfectly showcases Mia Farrow's talents. She plays the village oddball who is provided for by the upper-crust ladies. Joan Plowright also excels as the queen bee and manipulator extraordinaire. A number of plot twists and turns lead to a satisfying, surprise ending, rich in irony. Lush Irish countryside is a bonus. Rated PG for adult situations. 105m. **DIR:** John Irvin. **CAST:** Mia Farrow, Joan Plowright, Natasha Richardson, Adrian Dunbar. **1994**

WIFE, THE ★★★ A New Age version of *Who's Afraid of Virginia Woolf?* that is a vicious and darkly funny exploration of marriage and psychotherapy. Therapist couple find their remote Vermont home disturbed by the unexpected appearance of a patient and his trashy, outspoken wife. The performances and dialogue are delectably spiky and unexpectedly creepy. Letterboxed. Not rated; contains profanity and nudity. 101m. **DIR:** Tommy Noonan. **CAST:** Julie Hagerty, Tommy Noonan, Wallace Shawn, Karen Young. **1994 DVD**

WIFE! BE LIKE A ROSE! ★★★★ A young woman travels from Tokyo to rural Japan in search of her father, hoping to persuade him to abandon his mistress and return home to his wife. Gentle comedy–drama. In Japanese with English subtitles. B&W; 73m. **DIR:** Mikio Naruse. **CAST:** Sachiko Chiba. **1935**

WIFE VS. SECRETARY ★★ Jean Harlow is a super secretary to publisher Clark Gable. Friends and family of his wife (Myrna Loy) convince her that Harlow is kept around for more than efficiency, so she files for divorce. B&W; 88m. **DIR:** Clarence Brown. **CAST:** Clark Gable, Jean Harlow, Myrna Loy, May Robson, James Stewart. **1936**

WIFEMISTRESS ★★★1/2 Marcello Mastroianni stars as a husband in hiding, and Laura Antonelli as his repressed wife. When Mastroianni is falsely accused of murder, he hides out in a building across the street from his own home. His wife, not knowing where he is, begins to relive his sexual escapades. There are some comic moments as the former philandering husband must deal with his wife's new sexual freedom. 110m. DIR: Marco Vicario. CAST: Marcello Mastroianni, Laura Antonelli, Leonard Mann. 1977

WIGSTOCK: THE MOVIE ★★1/2 A hoot to watch, just don't expect any substance. Wigstock is an annual drag festival that's a combination concert, revue, and gay-pride forum. The movie, however, is little more than a home-video rendition of the festival. Rated R for profanity and adult themes. 82m. DIR: Barry Shils. CAST: Alexis Arquette, RuPaul, Lypsinka, Crystal Waters, Deee-Lite, Jackie Beat, John Kelly. 1995

WILBY CONSPIRACY, THE ★★★1/2 This underappreciated political thriller tackled the issue of apartheid years before its worldwide recognition as a serious problem. Michael Caine stars as an apolitical Brit who gains social consciousness after encountering an idealistic revolutionary (Sidney Poitier). Somewhat implausible, but entertaining nonetheless. Rated PG. 104m. DIR: Ralph Nelson. CAST: Michael Caine, Sidney Poitier, Nicol Williamson. 1975

WILD AMERICA ★★★ Three teen Stouffer brothers—armed with a 16mm camera—leave their rural Arkansas home in the summer of 1967 for the wilds. This lightweight, fact-based story is a rather sloppy outdoor adventure that says more about American myth building than it does about the animal kingdom. Rated PG. 106m. DIR: William Dear. CAST: Scott Bairstow, Devon Sawa, Jonathan Taylor Thomas, Jamey Sheridan, Frances Fisher. 1997 DVD

WILD AND WOOLLY ★★★★ It's always fun to watch a performer spoof himself, and Douglas Fairbanks Sr. was especially good at it. He plays an easterner fascinated with the Old West and fantasies of adventure. When he gets the chance to go west, it's not what he imagined. Very entertaining. B&W; 90m. DIR: John Emerson. CAST: Douglas Fairbanks Sr., Eileen Percy, Sam de Grasse. 1917

WILD ANGELS, THE ★★ It's 1960s hip, low-budget Hollywood style. If they gave Oscars for cool, Peter Fonda—in shades, three-day growth of beard, and leather—would win for sure. This cool motorcycle gang leader needs a hot mama. Unfortunately, he has to make do with Nancy ("These Boots Are Made for Walkin'") Sinatra. But the movie's greatest asset is "Blue's Theme," which revs up the proceedings with wonderfully tacky fuzz-tone guitar. 85m. DIR: Roger Corman. CAST: Peter Fonda, Nancy Sinatra, Bruce Dern, Michael J. Pollard, Diane Ladd, Gayle Hunnicutt. 1966

WILD AT HEART ★★★ One's gag reflex gets a real workout in this off-the-edge movie about a pair of young lovers (Nicolas Cage, Laura Dern) on the run. Director David Lynch explores the dark side of the American dream in a road picture that often seems to have been written and acted by the inmates of an insane asylum. Rated R for nudity, simulated sex, profanity, gore, and violence. 125m. DIR: David Lynch. CAST: Nicolas Cage, Laura Dern, Diane Ladd, Willem Dafoe, Isabella Rossellini, Harry Dean Stanton, Crispin Glover. 1990

WILD BEASTS, THE ★★1/2 After PCP infects their water supply, animals and children go on a rampage killing anyone in sight. Made in Europe, where they must not have any animal-rights laws. Not rated; contains violence and nudity. 92m. DIR: Franco Prosperi. CAST: John Aldrich. 1985

WILD BILL ★★★★ Episodic but engaging biopic on the lawman years of Old West legend Wild Bill Hickok features a marvelously twitchy performance by Jeff Bridges in the title role and the idiosyncratic filmmaking style of director Walter Hill. It's never boring. Rated R for violence, profanity, and simulated sex. 97m. DIR: Walter Hill. CAST: Jeff Bridges, Ellen Barkin, John Hurt, Diane Lane, David Arquette, Christina Applegate, Bruce Dern, James Gammon, Marjoe Gortner, James Remar, Keith Carradine, Steve Reevis. 1995

WILD BUNCH, THE ★★★★1/2 A classic Western brilliantly directed by Sam Peckinpah. He created a whole new approach to violence in this landmark film about men making a last stand. It is without a doubt Peckinpah's greatest film and is bursting with action, vibrant characters, and memorable dialogue. Good acting, too, by a first-rate cast. Rated R. 145m. DIR: Sam Peckinpah. CAST: William Holden, Ernest Borgnine, Robert Ryan, Ben Johnson, Edmond O'Brien, Warren Oates, Strother Martin, L. Q. Jones, Emilio Fernandez. 1969 DVD

WILD CACTUS ★★ Desert-bound thriller features many erotic encounters in a sordid plot line about a young wife held hostage by a murderous ex-con and his girlfriend. Available in R and unrated versions; both feature sex, violence, and profanity. 92m./96m. DIR: Jag Mundhra. CAST: David Naughton, India Allen, Gary Hudson, Michelle Moffett, Kathy Shower, Robert Z'dar. 1993

WILD CARD ★★★ A former preacher is asked to investigate the mysterious death of a Texas landowner. Made for cable. 95m. DIR: Mel Damski. CAST: Powers Boothe, Cindy Pickett, Terry O'Quinn, René Auberjonois, M. Emmet Walsh. 1992

WILD CHILD, THE (L'ENFANT SAUVAGE) ★★★★ Based on fact. In 1798 a boy, believed to be about 12, is found running wild in the French woods, apparently abandoned there when little more than an infant. A doctor–teacher of deaf mutes, sensitively played by director François Truffaut, takes over the task of domesticating the snarling, bewildered youth. Completely absorbing from start to finish. In French with English subtitles. Not rated, but suitable for all. B&W; 86m. DIR: François Truffaut. CAST: François Truffaut, Jean-Pierre Cargol. 1970

WILD DUCK, THE ★★1/2 Despite the cast, or maybe because of it, this poignant story of love and tragedy falls short of its ambitious mark. Jeremy Irons and Liv Ullmann are struggling parents whose child (Lucinda Jones) is slowly going blind. An idealistic friend (Arthur Dignam) complicates matters by nearthing truths that were better off buried. Derived from the classic Henrik Ibsen stage play. Rated G for profanity. 96m. DIR: Henri Safran. CAST: Liv Ullmann, Jeremy Irons, Lucinda Jones, Arthur Dignam, John Meillon, Michael Pate. 1963

WILD FLOWER (1991) ★★ A backwoods family tries to bring a mentally disabled girl (Patricia Arquette) out of her shell to join the rest of humanity. Although somewhat touching, this TV film tries to be all things and ends up never being compelling. 94m. DIR: Diane Keaton. CAST: Beau Bridges, Patricia Arquette, Susan Blakely, William McNamara. 1991

WILD FLOWER (1993) (FIORILE) ★★★★ Directors Paolo and Vittorio Taviani once again have woven a colorful tapestry of several generations of an Italian family, as told from the point of view of grandfather Luigi. Funny, touching, and at times heartbreaking. Rated PG-13 for adult situations. 118m. DIR: Paolo Taviani, Vittorio Taviani. CAST: Claudio Bigagli, Michael Vartan, Lino Capolicchio, Constanze Engelbrecht. 1993

WILD FRONTIER ★★★★ Sheriff Rocky Lane goes after the outlaws responsible for his father's death, aided by the town's dishonest saddle shop owner. First in the Rocky Lane series. B&W; 59m. DIR: Philip Ford. CAST: Allan "Rocky" Lane, Jack Holt, Eddy Waller, Roy Barcroft. 1947

WILD GEESE, THE ★★★ Features the unlikely combination of Richard Burton, Roger Moore, and Richard Harris as three mercenaries hired by a rich British industrialist (Stewart Granger) to go into Rhodesia and free a captured humanist leader. Better than you would expect. Rated R. 134m. DIR: Andrew V. McLaglen. CAST: Richard Burton, Roger Moore, Richard Harris, Stewart Granger, Hardy Krüger, Jack Watson, Frank Finlay. 1978

WILD GEESE II 🎦 A new group of mercenaries attempts to break into a Berlin prison to free Nazi war criminal Rudolf Hess. Rated R for violence and language. 118m. DIR: Peter R. Hunt. CAST: Scott Glenn, Barbara Carrera, Edward Fox, Laurence Olivier, Stratford Johns. 1985

WILD GUITAR 🎦 An exploitative record company gets its comeuppance from hell-raising Arch Hall Jr., a motorcycle-riding rock `n' roller who couldn't act if his life depended on it. Incredibly bad. 87m. DIR: Ray Dennis Steckler. CAST: Arch Hall Jr., Nancy Czar, William Watters (Arch Hall Sr.), Cash Flagg. 1962

WILD HEARTS CAN'T BE BROKEN ★★★★ A rebellious teenager (Gabrielle Anwar) in the 1920s runs away to join a traveling show, where she learns to leap on horseback into a water tank from a forty-foot-high platform. Sparkling family film from the folks at Disney. Rated G. 90m. DIR: Steve Miner. CAST: Gabrielle Anwar, Michael Schoeffling, Cliff Robertson. 1991

WILD HORSE HANK ★★1/2 Linda Blair is a horse lover pitted against a family that is stampeding wild horses. Richard Crenna plays her father. This Canadian feature is not rated. 94m. DIR: Eric Till. CAST: Linda Blair, Richard Crenna, Al Waxman, Michael Wincott. 1978

WILD IN THE COUNTRY ★★★ Elvis Presley is encouraged to pursue a literary career when counseled during his wayward youth. Most viewers will find it interesting to see Elvis in such a serious role. The supporting cast also—Hope Lange, Millie Perkins, John Ireland, and (especially) Tuesday Weld—add to the okay script. 114m. DIR: Philip Dunne. CAST: Elvis Presley, Hope Lange, Tuesday Weld, Millie Perkins, John Ireland. 1961

WILD IN THE STREETS ★★ Ridiculous what-if? film about future America when youth runs the show, the voting age is lowered to 14, and a rock singer involved in drug selling sits as president in the White House. This dated daydream of the 1960s was considered lame at the time of its release, but has gathered a following over the years. Rated PG. 97m. DIR: Barry Shear. CAST: Christopher Jones, Shelley Winters, Hal Holbrook, Diane Varsi, Ed Begley Sr., Millie Perkins, Richard Pryor, Bert Freed. 1968

WILD LIFE, THE ★★ From some of the same people who brought you Fast Times at Ridgemont High comes a film set in a world where your "cool" is measured by how many cigarettes you can smoke (and eat) and how many girls you can bed. Christopher Penn offers a believable performance as the leader of a pack of teens trying to grow up too fast. Rated R for suggested sex and language. 96m. DIR: Art Linson. CAST: Christopher Penn, Lea Thompson, Rick Moranis, Randy Quaid, Ian Mitchell-Smith. 1984

WILD MAN 🎦 An ex-CIA agent Eric Wild who is pressured to take on one more assignment. Rated R for nudity, profanity, and violence. 105m. DIR: F. J. Lincoln. CAST: Don Scribner. 1989

WILD MAN BLUES ★★★ Two-time Academy Award winner Barbara Kopple presents a lovely look of Woody Allen's European tour with his New Orleans jazz band. It's more a concert film than a documentary about Allen, with several good performances by the band (Allen's talent as a clarinetist is modest but real) interspersed with scenes of the celebrated filmmaker generally carrying on like a character in one of his movies. Rated PG. 106m. DIR: Barbara Kopple. CAST: Woody Allen, Soon-Yi Previn, Eddy Davis. 1998

WILD ONE, THE ★★★1/2 This classic film (based loosely on a real event in Hollister, California) about rival motorcycle gangs taking over a small town is pretty tame stuff these days and provides more laughs than thrills. Marlon Brando and his brooding Johnny are at the heart of this film's popularity; that coupled with the theme of motorcycle nomads have assured the film a cult following. B&W; 79m. DIR: Laslo Benedek. CAST: Marlon Brando, Mary Murphy, Robert Keith, Lee Marvin, Jay C. Flippen, Jerry Paris, Alvy Moore. 1953 DVD

WILD ORCHID ★★1/2 Mickey Rourke does Rio de Janeiro in this sexual adventure that's as short on provocative eroticism as it is on plot. Screenplay by Patricia Louisianna Knap and director Zalman King. Rated R for language and nudity. 105m. DIR: Zalman King. CAST: Mickey Rourke, Carré Otis, Jacqueline Bisset. 1990

WILD ORCHID 2: TWO SHADES OF BLUE ★★ Not a sequel, but another exploration into the sexual awakening of a young woman. Nina Siemaszko stars as Blue, a teenage beauty sent off to live in a house of ill repute. How she redeems herself nicely offsets the decadence she must endure. Rated R for nudity, violence, and strong language. Unrated version contains more sexual content. The original *Wild Orchid* seems like a timeless classic by comparison. 111m. DIR: Zalman King. CAST: Wendy Hughes, Tom Skerritt, Robert Davi, Nina Siemaszko. 1992

WILD ORCHIDS ★★★ A beautiful, young Greta Garbo is the highlight of this familiar story of tropic love. Plantation owner Lewis Stone busies himself with overseeing his property in Java, but local prince Nils Asther finds himself overseeing the owner's wife and the usual complications ensue. Silent. B&W; 103m. DIR: Sidney Franklin. CAST: Greta Garbo, Lewis Stone, Nils Asther. 1928

WILD PAIR, THE ★★ Beau Bridges, a yuppie FBI agent, and Bubba Smith, a streetwise city cop, are assigned to investigate a drug-related murder. The two clash as they find surprises around each corner. Bridges's acting, even as Smith's, is fine, but his directing is wanting. Rated R for profanity, violence, and nudity. 89m. DIR: Beau Bridges. CAST: Beau Bridges, Bubba Smith, Lloyd Bridges, Raymond St. Jacques, Gary Lockwood, Danny De La Paz. 1987

WILD PALMS ★★★1/2 James Belushi is a lawyer-turned-television-executive whose life becomes a nightmarish power struggle involving mind control. Twenty-five years in the future, a pseudoreligious government tries to alter reality through drugs and television. Eerie because it is so plausible, this made-for-TV miniseries looks great, but it's too dense and too slow. Not rated; contains violence. Two 150m. episodes. DIR: Paul Hewitt, Keith Gordon, Kathryn Bigelow, Phil Joanou. CAST: James Belushi, Dana Delany, Robert Loggia, Kim Cattrall, Angie Dickinson. 1993

WILD PARTY, THE (1929) ★★★ Legendary silent star Clara Bow, the "It" girl, made her talkie debut in this fast-paced story of a sexy, uninhibited college coed. Critics panned the film, but the public loved it, finding Bow's Brooklyn accent perfectly suited to her vivacious personality. B&W; 76m. DIR: Dorothy Arzner. CAST: Clara Bow, Fredric March, Jack Oakie. 1929

WILD PARTY, THE (1975) ★★★1/2 This is a very grim look at how Hollywood treats its fading stars. James Coco plays a one-time comedy star trying to come back with a hit film. Raquel Welch plays Coco's girlfriend who plans a party for Hollywood's elite in order to push his film. The film is based on the career of Fatty Arbuckle. Rated R. 107m. DIR: James Ivory. CAST: James Coco, Raquel Welch, Perry King, David Dukes. 1975

WILD REEDS ★★★★ Involving coming-of-age story in which three young men and a young woman find their sexuality, their love, and their lives. Enlightening feature is well written and performed. In French with English subtitles. Not rated; contains profanity and sexual situations. 110m. DIR: André Téchiné. CAST: Elodie Bouchez, Gael Morel, Stephane Rideau, Frederic Gorny. 1995 DVD

WILD RIDE, THE ♥ Early Jack Nicholson. Here he appears as a hedonistic hot-rodder who casually kills

people. B&W; 63m. DIR: Harvey Berman. CAST: Jack Nicholson, Robert Bean. 1960

WILD ROSE ★★ This low-budget film, shot in and around the Minnesota iron ore fields, floats between being a love story and a social commentary on mining conditions. By trying to cover all the bases, writer-director John Hanson fails to cover even one satisfactorily. 96m. DIR: John Hanson. CAST: Lisa Eichhorn, Tom Bower. 1984

WILD ROVERS, THE ★★★★ Sadly overlooked Western tells the story of two cowboys running from the law after robbing a bank. Holden is perfect as the older and not so wiser of the two, and O'Neal gives one of his best performances as the young partner. Rich in texture and smoothly directed by Blake Edwards. Rated PG. 109m. DIR: Blake Edwards. CAST: William Holden, Ryan O'Neal, Karl Malden, Tom Skerritt, Lynn Carlin, Joe Don Baker, Moses Gunn. 1971

WILD SIDE ♥ Amazingly chintzy, dialogue-heavy bomb about a nympho who works in a bank by day and turns tricks at night; the whole dreary mess is filmed in a handful of cheap sets and motel rooms. Rated R for nudity, profanity, rape, simulated sex, and violence. 85m. DIR: Franklin Brauner. CAST: Anne Heche, Christopher Walken, Joan Chen, Steven Bauer. 1995 DVD

WILD STRAWBERRIES ★★★★ This film is probably Ingmar Bergman's least ambiguous. Superbly photographed and acted, the film tells the story of an elderly professor facing old age and reviewing his life's disappointments. The use of flashbacks is very effective. B&W; 90m. DIR: Ingmar Bergman. CAST: Victor Sjöström, Ingrid Thulin, Bibi Andersson, Gunnar Björnstrand. 1957

WILD THING ★★★1/2 Screenwriter (and sometimes director) John Sayles creates another wonderfully offbeat tale: A young boy witnesses the murder of his parents and escapes to grow up in the streets of New York as kind of an urban Tarzan. Lots of fun. Rated PG-13 for violence. 92m. DIR: Max Reid. CAST: Rob Knepper, Kathleen Quinlan, Robert Davi, Betty Buckley. 1987

WILD THINGS ★★1/2 Mainstream taboos (male frontal nudity, bisexuality) abound in this kinky trash *noir* about a high-school counselor accused of raping a wealthy student. Testimony sends yacht-club society into a snit as detectives poke at the case until it oozes dark secrets. The top-notch cast has fun but the script is so enamored with its cleverness that several flashbacks during the closing credits are needed to explain its twists. Rated R for nudity, sex, and violence. 106m. DIR: John McNaughton. CAST: Matt Dillon, Denise Richards, Neve Campbell, Kevin Bacon, Daphne Rubin-Vega, Theresa Russell, Carrie Snodgress, Robert Wagner. 1998 DVD

WILD TIMES ★★★ A two-cassette Western originally made for television. Sam Elliott plays sharpshooter Hugh Cardiff, whose life is anything but easy as he makes his way across the Old West. This could have been helped by some trimming. 200m. DIR: Richard Compton. CAST: Sam Elliott, Ben Johnson, Timothy Scott, Harry Carey Jr., Bruce Boxleitner, Penny Peyser, Dennis Hopper. 1980

WILD WEST (1946) ★★★★1/2 Eddie Dean and his pals string the Western telegraph against all odds including Indians and outlaws. The absolute best of Eddie Dean's Westerns with plenty of great action and good songs. 70m. DIR: Robert Emmett Tansey. CAST: Eddie Dean, Lash LaRue, Roscoe Ates, Buzz Henry, Louise Currie. 1946

WILD WEST (1993) ★★1/2 Offbeat comedy about a group of Pakistani country-and-western musicians eking out a living in West London while hoping to travel to Nashville and make it big. Perhaps his British style of outrageous comedy doesn't travel well, but there is something in this film to offend nearly everyone. Not rated, the film has profanity, violence, and suggested sex. 85m. DIR: David Attwood. CAST: Naveen Andrews, Sarita Choudhury. 1993

WILD WILD WEST, THE (TV SERIES) ★★★★ The mid-60s spy craze produced a lot of TV shows, none more inventive than this Civil War–era adventure series starring Robert Conrad as James T. West, an undercover agent for President Ulysses Grant. Operating out of a gadget-laden railroad car and paired with Ross Martin's often-disguised Artemus Gordon, West tackled numerous foes bent on creating havoc or fomenting rebellion in the still-youthful United States. Look for the black-and-white first-season episodes, vastly superior to those that followed during the full-color remainder of the show's five-year run. 52m. each. DIR: Various. CAST: Robert Conrad, Ross Martin, Michael Dunn. 1965–1870

WILD WILD WEST REVISITED, THE ★★★ That diminutive genius, Miguelito Loveless, has a new plan for world domination. He's cloning heads of state. It's worked in England, Spain, and Russia. The United States and President Cleveland could be next. Those legendary agents James West and Artemus Gordon are called out of retirement to save the day. This revival of the Sixties series is breezily entertaining. 95m. DIR: Burt Kennedy. CAST: Robert Conrad, Ross Martin, Paul Williams, Harry Morgan, René Auberjonois, Robert Shields, Lorene Yarnell. 1979

WILD WILD WEST (1999) 🎭 Hollywood never learns. This overblown re-creation of the famed Robert Conrad/Ross Martin TV series is a miserable failure in all respects: a slipshod, incoherent mess that bears all the hallmarks of a doomed picture consigned to heavy eleventh-hour editing in an attempt to salvage something from the carnage … an effort that failed. Rated PG-13 for violence and brief nudity. 107m. DIR: Barry Sonnenfeld. CAST: Will Smith, Kevin Kline, Kenneth Branagh, Salma Hayek, Ted Levine. 1999 DVD

WILD WOMEN OF WONGO 🎭 This early sex-exploitation adventure pits two primitive tribes against each other. 72m. DIR: James L. Wolcott. CAST: Jean Hawkshaw, Johnny Walsh, Ed Fury, Pat Crowley. 1958

WILD WORLD OF BATWOMAN, THE (SHE WAS A HAPPY VAMPIRE) 🎭 Execrable James Bond spoof. B&W; 70m. DIR: Jerry Warren. CAST: Katherine Victor, George Andre, Steve Brodie. 1966

WILDCATS ★★ Standard Goldie Hawn vehicle, with her playing high school football coach to a rowdy group of inner-city kids who need to prove their worth as much as she needs to raise her self-esteem and prove her skill to chauvinistic athletic directors. Director Michael Ritchie shows little of the tension he brought to The Bad News Bears. Rated R for nudity and language. 107m. DIR: Michael Ritchie. CAST: Goldie Hawn, Swoosie Kurtz, James Keach, Nipsey Russell, Woody Harrelson, M. Emmet Walsh. 1986

WILDE ★★1/2 Irish-born writer, social satirist, and notorious public personality Oscar Wilde was convicted in late 1890s London of "gross indecency" (engaging in sodomy) after recklessly pursuing a defamation suit against his male lover's father. This rather stuffy drama covers Wilde's preceding adult years and the trial's crushing impact on his wife, private life, public acceptance, and creativity. It is excellently acted but still far from gripping. Rated R for simulated sex, nudity, and language. 115m. DIR: Brian Gilbert. CAST: Stephen Fry, Jude Law, Vanessa Redgrave, Jennifer Ehle, Michael Sheen, Gemma Jones, Tom Wilkinson. 1998

WILDER NAPALM ★★★ Everything works in this quirky comedy except the show-offy script, which wants to be screwball but is merely screwed up. Two feuding brothers, both in love with the same woman, share the power to start fires at will. Eventually everything in this movie turns out to be window dressing covering a brick wall. Rated PG-13 for sexual situations. 110m. DIR: Glenn Gordon Caron. CAST: Debra Winger, Dennis Quaid, Arliss Howard, Jim Varney, M. Emmet Walsh, Glenn Gordon Caron. 1993

WILDERNESS FAMILY, PART 2, THE ★★★ Taken on its own terms, The Wilderness Family, Part 2 isn't a bad motion picture. Film fans who want thrills and chills or something challenging to the mind should skip it. Rated G. 105m. DIR: Frank Zuniga. CAST: Robert Logan, Susan D. Shaw, Heather Rattray, Ham Larsen, George "Buck" Flower, Brian Cutler. 1978

WILDFIRE (1945) ★★★ Bob Steele—in color—protecting the rights of wild horses. 57m. DIR: Robert Emmett Tansey. CAST: Bob Steele, Sterling Holloway, William Farnum, Eddie Dean. 1945

WILDFIRE (1988) ★★1/2 When a bank robbery goes wrong, a teen groom is imprisoned for eight years. In his absence his pregnant bride remarries a wealthy man. The imprisoned man returns for his woman with predictably disastrous results. Rated PG for profanity. 98m. DIR: Zalman King. CAST: Steven Bauer, Linda Fiorentino, Will Patton, Marshall Bell. 1988

WILDING, THE CHILDREN OF VIOLENCE 🎭 Taking its name from the highly publicized rape in New York City's Central Park, this film trivializes the case. By associating itself with that factual incident with its opening scene, the film hints at condemning that crime while depicting an unrelated series of fictional beatings by a band of suburbanite youths on a rampage against L.A.'s police and residents. Not rated, though there is partial nudity, violence, and profanity. 92m. DIR: Eric Louzil. CAST: Wings Hauser, Joey Travolta. 1990

WILL, G. GORDON LIDDY ★★★1/2 Robert Conrad is transformed into the fanatic, strong-willed Watergate mastermind Liddy. The first half lacks excitement or revelation. Liddy's stay in prison, however, is a fascinating study. 100m. **DIR:** Robert Leiberman. **CAST:** Robert Conrad, Katherine Cannon, Gary Bayer, James Rebhorn. **1982**

WILL PENNY ★★★★1/2 Charlton Heston gives the finest performance of his distinguished career in this gritty, unsentimental look at the life of an illiterate cowboy in the American West. Equivalent to a PG-13. 108m. **DIR:** Tom Gries. **CAST:** Charlton Heston, Joan Hackett, Donald Pleasence, Lee Majors, Bruce Dern, Anthony Zerbe, Clifton James, Ben Johnson, Slim Pickens. **1968**

WILL SUCCESS SPOIL ROCK HUNTER? ★★★★ A comedy about the early days of TV that isn't as dated as you might think. Jayne Mansfield created the part on Broadway and no one else has done it as well as she. 95m. **DIR:** Frank Tashlin. **CAST:** Jayne Mansfield, Tony Randall, Mickey Hargitay, Joan Blondell, Betsy Drake, John Williams, Henry Jones, Lili Gentle. **1957**

WILLA ★★1/2 Made-for-TV movie has something of a cult reputation for feminist themes, but it's a pretty standard drama about a waitress who wants to become a trucker. 95m. **DIR:** Joan Darling, Claudio Guzman. **CAST:** Deborah Raffin, Clu Gulager, Cloris Leachman, Diane Ladd, Nancy Marchand, John Amos, Hank Williams Jr., Corey Feldman. **1979**

WILLARD ★★1/2 This worked far better as a novel. Bruce Davison plays a put-upon wimp who identifies more with rodents than people. When nasty Ernest Borgnine becomes too unpleasant, Davison decides to make him the bait in a better rattrap. It was destined to get worse in the sequel, entitled *Ben.* Rated PG—mild violence. 95m. **DIR:** Daniel Mann. **CAST:** Bruce Davison, Ernest Borgnine, Sondra Locke. **1971**

WILLIAM SHAKESPEARE'S A MIDSUMMER NIGHT'S DREAM ★★★1/2 Director-scripter Michael Hoffman has made his rendition of the Bard's bawdy comedy into an earthy and erotic tale. The tale is transposed to northern Italy, toward the end of the 19th century and turns on two young lovers who flee into a nearby forest. Havoc is wreaked when the king and queen of the fairies misuse magic spells. It's all rather inconsequential when all is said and done. Rated PG-13 for considerable nudity, although it remains most discreet. 110m. **DIR:** Michael Hoffman. **CAST:** Kevin Kline, Michelle Pfeiffer, Rupert Everett, Stanley Tucci, Calista Flockhart, Anna Friel, Christian Bale, Dominic West, David Strathairn, Sophie Marceau. **1999 DVD**

WILLIAM SHAKESPEARE'S ROMEO AND JULIET ★★1/2 This latest take on Shakespeare's ill-starred lovers has raucous MTV-style editing, frantic gun battles, a kitschy vision of urban apocalypse, and hot teen actors in the title roles. But director Baz Luhrmann gets mainly floundering high-school performances from his talented cast. Rated PG-13 for violence. 121m. **DIR:** Baz Luhrmann. **CAST:** Leonardo DiCaprio, Claire Danes, John Leguizamo, Harold Perrineau Jr., Paul Sorvino, Brian Dennehy, Miriam Margolyes. **1996 DVD**

WILLIE AND PHIL ★★1/2 Director Paul Mazursky's "hip" take on Truffaut's *Jules and Jim*, this story of a love triangle now seems quite dated. Margot Kidder is the love interest of two best friends who share her affections for nine years. Kidder's character is generally unsympathetic and, as a result, much of the film seems artificial. Rated R for nudity and profanity. 116m. **DIR:** Paul Mazursky. **CAST:** Michael Ontkean, Margot Kidder, Ray Sharkey, Jan Miner. **1980**

WILLIE MCBEAN AND HIS MAGIC MACHINE ★★ Saddled with a slow story line in which the hero must thwart the efforts of a mad scientist to change history, *Willie* lacks the charm and style of better animated characters and has little to offer compared to more sophisticated contemporary productions. 94m. **DIR:** Arthur Rankin Jr. **1959**

WILLIES, THE ★★1/2 Lies, tall tales, and boyish machismo abound in this silly yet watchable movie as three kids try to out-gross each other with wild stories. Rated PG-13. 92m. **DIR:** Brian Peck. **CAST:** James Karen, Sean Astin, Kathleen Freeman, Jeremy Miller. **1990**

WILLOW ★★★ A formulaic but entertaining fantasy epic, this focuses on the quest of an apprentice sorcerer, Willow (Warwick Davis), to keep a magical child safe from the minions of the wicked queen (Jean Marsh) she is destined to destroy. The first half tends to drag as the characters and situations are somewhat laboriously introduced. However, things pick up midway. Rated PG for violence. 120m. **DIR:** Ron Howard. **CAST:** Val Kilmer, Joanne Whalley, Jean Marsh, Warwick Davis, Patricia Hayes, Billy Barty. **1988**

WILLY WONKA AND THE CHOCOLATE FACTORY ★★★ Gene Wilder plays a candy company owner who allows some lucky kids to tour the facility. However, a few of his guests get sticky fingers (pun intended) and suffer the consequences. This essentially entertaining movie has its memorable moments—as well as bad. Rated G. 98m. **DIR:** Mel Stuart. **CAST:** Gene Wilder, Jack Albertson, Peter Ostrum, Roy Kinnear. **1971 DVD**

WILMA ★★1/2 This made-for-TV film chronicles the early years of Olympic star Wilma Rudolph (Cicely Tyson) and follows her career up to her winning the gold. Film fails to do justice to its subject matter. Lackluster production. 100m. **DIR:** Bud Greenspan. **CAST:** Cicely Tyson, Shirley Jo Finney, Joe Seneca, Jason Bernard. **1977**

WILSON ★★★★1/2 Outstanding film biography of the adult years of Woodrow Wilson (Alexander Knox) as dean of Princeton, governor of New Jersey, and president of the United States, with emphasis on World War I and his later determination to join the League of Nations. Winner of five Oscars, including Lamar Trotti's screenplay, with nominations for best picture, Knox's portrayal, and Henry King's direction. 154m. **DIR:** Henry King. **CAST:** Alexander Knox, Charles Coburn, Geraldine Fitzgerald, Thomas Mitchell, Ruth Nelson, Cedric Hardwicke, Vincent Price, William Eythe. **1944**

WIMPS 🐱 *Animal House* meets *Cyrano de Bergerac.* Rated R for language, nudity, and sexual situaons. 94m. DIR: Chuck Vincent. CAST: Louie Bonanno, eborah Blaisdell, Jim Abele, Jane Hamilton. **1986**

WIN, PLACE OR STEAL 🍂 Slow, boring comedy about three aging adolescents who prefer playing the ponies to working. Not rated. 88m. DIR: Richard Bailey. CAST: Dean Stockwell, Russ Tamblyn, Alex Karras, McLean Stevenson. **1972**

WINCHELL ★★★ Biography of Walter Winchell, the great newspaper and radio journalist, is mostly loss without much dirt. The film paints Winchell as an egotistical hothead and genius with a well-deserved reputation, but leaves out much of the controversy of his life. Fine performances all around, and his made-for-cable production looks slick, but entertainment-wise, some crucial dimension is missing. Rated R for violence, profanity, and simulated sex. 105m. DIR: Paul Mazursky. CAST: Stanley Tucci, Glenne Headly, Paul Giamatti, Xander Berkeley, Kevin Tighe, Christopher Plummer. **1998**

WINCHESTER '73 ★★★ Cowboy James Stewart acquires the latest iron from the East, a Winchester '73 rifle, loses it to a thief, and pursues the prized weapon as it passes from hand to hand. Simple, brisk-paced, direct, action-packed, tongue-in-cheek, mean, sweaty, suspenseful, and entirely entertaining. B&W; 82m. DIR: Anthony Mann. CAST: James Stewart, Shelley Winters, Dan Duryea, Stephen McNally, Will Geer, Rock Hudson, Tony Curtis, John McIntire. **1950**

WIND, THE (1928) ★★★★ A gentle girl marries a brutish farmhand in order to escape from relatives who do not understand her sensitive nature. She finds no peace. As the girl, Lillian Gish joined Victor Seastrom (né Sjöström) in scoring an artistic triumph. An incredible film. Silent. B&W; 82m. DIR: Victor Sjöström. CAST: Lillian Gish, Lars Hanson, Montagu Love. **1928**

WIND, THE (1986) ★★1/2 There's some solid suspense in this tale of a mystery novelist on a secluded Mediterranean island who is terrorized by a psychopath. Director Nico Mastorakis makes good use of the Greek locations. Unfortunately, he lets his two stars overact. 92m. DIR: Nico Mastorakis. CAST: Meg Foster, Wings Hauser, Robert Morley. **1986 DVD**

WIND (1992) ★★★ This gorgeously photographed and highly romanticized *Rocky* of the seven seas stars Matthew Modine as a sailing enthusiast who pursues the America's Cup and an ex-girlfriend. The story has the feel of an ancient John Wayne action-comedy, but manages to stay rather dreamily afloat. Rated PG-13 for language. 123m. DIR: Carroll Ballard. CAST: Matthew Modine, Stellan Skarsgard, Rebecca Miller, Cliff Robertson, Jack Thompson, Jennifer Grey. **1992**

WIND AND THE LION, THE ★★★★ In the 1970s, Sean Connery made a trio of memorable adventure movies, one being this release, impressively directed by John Milius. In the other two films—*The Man Who Would Be King* and *Robin and Marian*—*The Wind and the Lion*, in which Connery plays a dashing Arab chieftain, is a thoroughly satisfying motion picture. Rated PG. 119m. DIR: John Milius. CAST: Sean Connery, Brian Keith, Candice Bergen, John Hus-

ton, Geoffrey Lewis, Steve Kanaly, Vladek Sheybal. **1975**

WIND IN THE WILLOWS, THE (1949) ★★★★ One of Disney's finest. This adaptation of Kenneth Grahame's classic deals with the adventures of J. Thaddeus Toad and his friends Cyril, Mole, Rat, and Mac Badger. Basil Rathbone narrates this classic short. 75m. DIR: Wolfgang Reitherman. **1949**

WIND IN THE WILLOWS, THE (1983) ★★★1/2 Based on the famous Kenneth Grahame book, this collection of three separate stories is a delight of stop-motion animation. The much-loved characters of Mole, Ratty, and of course, Toad, are brought beautifully to life in miniature Edwardian settings. 60m. DIR: Mark Hall. **1983**

WINDHORSE ★★★ This amateurish but engrossing melodrama begins as a young Tibetan girl's life is shattered by the murder of her Buddhist grandfather after he protests against the country's occupation by Chinese communists. The girl grows up to reassess her assimilation into repressive foreign rule after another family tragedy. The film was shot clandestinely on location in Tibet. In Tibetan and Mandarin with English subtitles. Not rated. 98m. DIR: Paul Wagner. CAST: Dadon, Hampa Kelsang, Richard Chang, Lu Yu. **1998**

WINDJAMMER ★★★1/2 Western hero George O'Brien trades the wide open spaces of the range for vast wastes of the Pacific Ocean in this story of high-seas smuggling. Solid adventure. B&W; 58m. DIR: Ewing Scott. CAST: George O'Brien, Constance Worth. **1937**

WINDMILLS OF THE GODS ★★★ Author Sidney Sheldon's bestselling novel gets the small-screen treatment, with mixed results. There's plenty to look at, from exotic locales, to Jaclyn Smith as a lady professor assigned as Ambassador to Romania. Cast is likable, locations are great, but film suffers from melodrama-itis. 95m. DIR: Lee Philips. CAST: Jaclyn Smith, Robert Wagner, Franco Nero, Ruby Dee, Ian McKellen. **1987**

WINDOM'S WAY ★★★ In this British drama set on an island in the Far East, a struggle ensues between the natives and plantation owners over civil rights. A doctor (Peter Finch) is enlisted as the spokesperson for the natives. Set against the backdrop of World War II, it is enjoyable entertainment. 104m. DIR: Ronald Neame. CAST: Peter Finch, Mary Ure, Natasha Parry, Robert Flemyng, Michael Hordern, Marne Maitland, Gregoire Aslan. **1957**

WINDOW, THE ★★★1/2 This chilling drama about a young boy who witnesses a murder and finds himself unable to convince any authority figures of what he has seen is one of the classic nightmare films of the postwar period. Bobby Driscoll (who earned a special Academy Award for this film) is kidnapped by the murderers and the film becomes one taut encounter after another. B&W; 73m. DIR: Ted Tetzlaff. CAST: Bobby Driscoll, Arthur Kennedy, Barbara Hale, Paul Stewart, Ruth Roman. **1949**

WINDOW SHOPPING ★★★ With tongue firmly entrenched in cheek, this French musical-comedy of romantic error concerns Lilli, the belle of the shopping mall. Somewhat like a cross between *Romeo* *and Juliet* and *Grease*, this buoyant movie is a cinematographic curiosity piece. In French with English subtitles. Rated R for nudity. 96m. **DIR:** Chantal Akerman. **CAST:** Delphine Seyrig, Myriam Boyer, Fanny Cottençon, Charles Denner, John Berry. **1986**

WINDOW TO PARIS ★★★1/2 East meets West with hilarious results in this delightful fantasy that skewers human nature and post–cold war nationalism. A young Russian music teacher moves into an apartment house where he and his landlord discover a magic window that opens onto a Paris rooftop. A riotous culture clash ensues as the Russians explore their new backyard. In Russian and French with English subtitles. Rated PG-13 for violence and language. 87m. **DIR:** Yuri Mamin. **CAST:** Sergei Dontsov, Viktor Mikhailov, Agnes Soral. **1995**

WINDRIDER 🎬 A self-centered windsurfer becomes obsessed with his quest to perform a 360-degree flip on his sailboard. Rated R for profanity and simulated sex. 83m. **DIR:** Vincent Morton. **CAST:** Tom Burlinson. **1986**

WINDRUNNER ★★★1/2 Warm, inspirational tale of high-school student fighting personal demons and a new low when he's cut from the football team. Then he encounters an Indian in the desert who agrees to help him. The boy learns many lessons from the wise stranger, and in exchange, tracks down and captures a white stallion for him. Revelations about who the Indian is, and why he is here, make for captivating entertainment. Rousing finale will leave viewers cheering. Rated PG. 110m. **DIR:** William Clark. **CAST:** Russell Means, Jason Wiles, Margot Kidder, Amanda Peterson, Bruce Weitz. **1994**

WINDS OF JARRAH, THE ★★ At the close of World War II, an Englishwoman on the rebound from a bad love affair takes a position in Australia as a nanny. Her employer is a bitter, lonely man who hates women. Readers of paperback romances will guess what happens within the first two minutes, and the rest of the audience won't be far behind. Not rated. 78m. **DIR:** Mark Egerton. **CAST:** Terence Donovan, Sue Lyon, Harold Hopkins. **1983**

WINDS OF KITTY HAWK, THE ★★★★ This made-for-TV movie is beautifully photographed, quietly acted, and gives a wonderful insight into the lives of the Wright brothers and the period in which they lived. A treat for the entire family. 100m. **DIR:** E. W. Swackhamer. **CAST:** Michael Moriarty, David Huffman, Kathryn Walker. **1978**

WINDS OF THE WASTELAND ★★★ Big John Wayne is the head of a stagecoach company that competes for a government mail contract in the days after the pony express. Better than most B Westerns made by the Duke, because he was beginning to show more polish and confidence, but still no classic. B&W; 57m. **DIR:** Mack V. Wright. **CAST:** John Wayne, Phyllis Fraser, Yakima Canutt, Lane Chandler. **1936 DVD**

WINDS OF WAR, THE ★★★1/2 Mega WWII epic follows the lives of a naval officer turned ambassador to Germany (Robert Mitchum) and his family from 1939 to 1941 within Hitler's conquests as a backdrop. Originally a TV miniseries, this adaptation of Herman Wouk's novel spared no expense in production

and features dozens of well-known stars. 880m. **DIR:** Dan Curtis. **CAST:** Robert Mitchum, Polly Bergen, Jan-Michael Vincent, Ali MacGraw, John Houseman. **1983**

WINDSOR PROTOCOL, THE ★★★ A former IRA terrorist teams up with the British government to thwart a plan to revive the Third Reich. Interesting to see Alan Thicke play a bad guy. Rated R for violence, profanity, and nudity. 96m. **DIR:** George Mihalka. **CAST:** Kyle MacLachlan, Macha Grenon, Alan Thicke. **1996**

WINDWALKER ★★★★ Trevor Howard plays the title role in this superb film which spans three generations of a Cheyenne Indian family. It refutes the unwritten rule that family entertainment has to be bland and predictable and is proof that films don't need to include sensationalism to hold the attention of modern filmgoers. Rated PG. 108m. **DIR:** Kieth Merrill. **CAST:** Trevor Howard, Nick Ramus, James Remar, Serene Hedin. **1980**

WINDY CITY ★★ Very uneven, very frustrating attempt to chronicle the story of a group of young adults who have known one another since they were kids. It has the feel of being based on real-life experiences but is embarrassingly true to rude and off-putting behavior most people would rather have private memories of. Rated R. 103m. **DIR:** Armyan Bernstein. **CAST:** John Shea, Kate Capshaw, Josh Mostel, Jeffrey DeMunn, Lewis J. Stadlen, James Sutorius. **1984**

WING AND A PRAYER, A (1944) ★★★★ An all-male cast in an excellent film about the war in the South Pacific. A combination of actual wartime action photography and soundstage settings give the film an unusual look. One of the most successful propaganda films to be released during World War II. B&W; 98m. **DIR:** Henry Hathaway. **CAST:** Don Ameche, William Eythe, Dana Andrews, Charles Bickford, Cedric Hardwicke, Richard Jaeckel, Harry Morgan, Glenn Langan, Richard Crane. **1944**

WING AND A PRAYER, A (1997) ★★★1/2 This tense disaster thriller follows a burned-out air-traffic controller on his return flight to Salt Lake City. His wife is the head controller at Salt Lake, and she deals with all sorts of catastrophes when the computer goes down, but the worst is trying to get her husband's plane landed without radio or transponder. Not rated. 95m. **DIR:** Paul Wendkos. **CAST:** Claudia Christian, Jeff Yagher, Jessica Tuck, Christopher Cousins, Leon Russom. **1997**

WING CHUN ★★★ Top-notch vehicle for Hong Kong action star Michelle Yeoh (AKA Michelle Khan, star of Jackie Chan's *Police Story III—Super Cop*). As Wing Chun, Yeoh uses her brains as well as her fighting skills to deal with the bandits making trouble in her village. Engaging comedy sequences and fight scenes that are more clever than violent make this one of the best of the Hong Kong action films. Not rated. Available dubbed or in Chinese with English subtitles. 93m. **DIR:** Yuen Wo Ping. **CAST:** Michelle Khan, Donnie Yen, Waise Lee. **1994 DVD**

WING COMMANDER 🎬 In the year 2564, two brash rookie pilots and their female military girlfriends blast aliens into space debris. Based on the popular computer game. Rated PG-13 for language, sexual references, and violence. 100m. DIR: Chris Roberts. CAST: Freddie Prinze Jr., Matthew Lillard, Jurgen Prochnow, Saffron Burrows, Ginny Holder, David Suchet, David Warner. 1999 DVD

WINGS ★★★★ First recipient of the Academy Award for best picture. The story concerns two buddies who join the Air Corps in World War I and go to France to battle the Germans. War scenes are excellent, even by today's standards. B&W; 139m. DIR: William Wellman. CAST: Clara Bow, Charles "Buddy" Rogers, Richard Arlen, Jobyna Ralston, Gary Cooper, Arlette Marchal, El Brendel. 1927

WINGS OF DESIRE ★★★★ Angels see in black-and-white; mortals see in color. Wim Wenders's follow-up to Paris, Texas is a stark and moving story set in Berlin about two angels (Bruno Ganz and Otto Sander) who travel through the city listening to people's thoughts. Ganz grows weary of comforting others and decides to reenter the world as a human. Rated PG-13 for adult subject matter. In German and French with English subtitles. 130m. DIR: Wim Wenders. CAST: Bruno Ganz, Solveig Dommartin, Curt Bois, Peter Falk, Otto Sander. 1988

WINGS OF EAGLES, THE ★★★★ An often moving bio-pic about navy-flier-turned-screenwriter Frank "Spig" Wead (They Were Expendable), this film features fine dramatic performances from John Wayne and Maureen O'Hara. Features the usual John Ford elements of sentimentality and brawling slapstick, but there's also an underlying poignance that makes this a treat. 107m. DIR: John Ford. CAST: John Wayne, Maureen O'Hara, Dan Dailey, Ward Bond, Ken Curtis, Edmund Lowe, Kenneth Tobey. 1957

WINGS OF FAME ★★★ Peter O'Toole delivers a deliciously droll performance as Cesar Valetin, an actor who's being stalked by Brian Smith, a young fan played by Colin Firth. When Brian kills Valetin during a film festival, he finds Valetin and himself trapped in a spiritual hotel where the famous and near-famous go after they die. The film takes great delight in exposing pretentions and how they relate to those we put on a pedestal. Insightful, imaginative, and very funny. Rated R for adult language and situations. 109m. DIR: Otakar Votocek. CAST: Peter O'Toole, Colin Firth, Marie Trintignant. 1990

WINGS OF THE DOVE, THE ★★1/2 Two penniless English lovers conspire for the man to woo and wed a dying American heiress, expecting to live on her money after she's gone, but their scheme is undone by his conscience, her jealousy, and the heiress's genuine goodness. Henry James's novel of thwarted passion gets a strangely dispassionate filming. Rated R for nudity and sexual scenes. 101m. DIR: Iain Softley. CAST: Helena Bonham Carter, Linus Roache, Allison Elliot, Charlotte Rampling, Elizabeth McGovern, Michael Gambon. 1997 DVD

WINNER, THE ★★★ This fresh, sassy, and unusual drama, based on the play A Darker Purpose by Wendy Riss, is the story of a Las Vegas man who can't lose and all the real losers around him. Great cast propels the strange story along nicely. Rated R for language and violence. 89m. DIR: Alex Cox. CAST: Rebecca DeMornay, Vincent D'Onofrio, Delroy Lindo, Michael Madsen, Billy Bob Thornton. 1996

WINNERS OF THE WEST ★★★ The white hats of the railroad fight it out with the black hats of the unscrupulous land baron in this classic thirteen-part oater jammed with gunplay, burning work trains, dynamited bridges, and a kidnapped heroine. B&W; 234m. DIR: Ford Beebe, Ray Taylor. CAST: Dick Foran, James Craig, Anne Nagel, Harry Woods. 1940

WINNERS TAKE ALL ★★1/2 A California teen decides to compete in a Texas regional motocross competition. All of the usual sports-movie clichés are present and accounted for, though the final grudge race is full of high-spirited stunts that even nonracing fans should enjoy. Rated PG-13. 103m. DIR: Fritz Kiersch. CAST: Don Michael Paul, Kathleen York, Robert Krantz. 1986

WINNING ★★★1/2 Paul Newman is very good as a race car driver who puts winning above all else, including his family. Some very good racing sequences and fine support from Joanne Woodward and Richard Thomas. Rated PG. 123m. DIR: James Goldstone. CAST: Paul Newman, Joanne Woodward, Robert Wagner, Richard Thomas. 1969 DVD

WINNING OF THE WEST ★★ Same old stuff about a brave newspaper publisher who enlists the aid of no-nonsense Gene Autry and all-nonsense Smiley Burnette. B&W; 57m. DIR: George Archainbaud. CAST: Gene Autry, Smiley Burnette, Gail Davis, Robert Livingston. 1953

WINNING TEAM, THE ★★ This film biography of baseball pitcher Grover Cleveland Alexander would have worked better with a different cast. Ronald Reagan's inept acting is a distraction. B&W; 99m. DIR: Lewis Seiler. CAST: Doris Day, Ronald Reagan, Frank Lovejoy, Russ Tamblyn, Eve Miller, James Millican. 1952

WINSLOW BOY, THE (1950) ★★★★ A proper British barrister defends a young naval cadet, wrongly accused of theft, against the overbearing pomp and indifferent might of the Crown. At stake is the long-cherished democratic right to be regarded as innocent until proven guilty by a fair trial. Based on an actual 1912 case, this is a superb courtroom melodrama. B&W; 118m. DIR: Anthony Asquith. CAST: Robert Donat, Margaret Leighton, Cedric Hardwicke, Basil Radford, Frank Lawton, Wilfrid Hyde-White, Neil North. 1950

WINSLOW BOY, THE (1999) ★★★ American playwright David Mamet wrote and directed this adaptation of Terence Rattigan's play about a British youth falsely accused of petty theft. Edwardian England is a real change of pace for Mamet, and stiff upper lips may not be his style. The film is meticulously produced and generally well acted. Rated G. 104m. DIR: David Mamet. CAST: Nigel Hawthorne, Jeremy Northam, Rebecca Pidgeon, Gemma Jones, Guy Edwards. 1999 DVD

WINTER GUEST, THE ★★1/2 Actor Alan Rickman's first directorial effort, adapted from Sharman Macdonald's play, concerns a day in the life of a recently widowed photographer, her strong-willed mother, son, and his new girlfriend, with barely relevant sidebars. The actors all do their best, but the film is uneventful and monumentally dull. Rated R for profanity and brief nudity. 110m. DIR: Alan Rickman.

CAST: Phyllida Law, Emma Thompson, Gary Hollywood, Arlene Cockburn, Sheila Reid, Sandra Voe. **1997**

WINTER KILLS ★★★★ An all-star cast is featured in this sometimes melodramatic, but often wry, account of a presidential assassination. Rated R. 97m. **DIR:** William Richert. **CAST:** Jeff Bridges, John Huston, Belinda Bauer, Richard Boone, Anthony Perkins, Toshiro Mifune, Sterling Hayden, Eli Wallach, Ralph Meeker, Dorothy Malone, Tomas Milian, Elizabeth Taylor. **1979**

WINTER LIGHT ★★★ Second film in director Ingmar Bergman's "faith" trilogy (it follows *Through a Glass Darkly* and precedes *The Silence*) centers on a disillusioned priest who attempts to come to grips with his religion and his position in the inner workings of the church. This effort to explore the psyche of a cleric is a thoughtful, incisive drama with great performances. In Swedish with English subtitles. B&W; 80m. **DIR:** Ingmar Bergman. **CAST:** Ingrid Thulin, Gunnar Björnstrand, Max von Sydow, Gunnel Lindblom. **1962**

WINTER MEETING ★★1/2 Talky, slow-moving story of a spinsterish writer falling for a war hero, learning he plans to join the priesthood. Jim Davis's debut. B&W; 115m. **DIR:** Bretaigne Windust. **CAST:** Bette Davis, Jim Davis, Janis Paige, John Hoyt, Florence Bates. **1948**

WINTER OF OUR DREAMS ★★ An all-too-typical soaper about a married man (Bryan Brown) who tries to help a lost soul (Judy Davis). This downbeat film has good acting but less-than-adequate direction. Rated R. 90m. **DIR:** John Duigan. **CAST:** Judy Davis, Bryan Brown, Cathy Downes. **1981**

WINTER PEOPLE ★★★1/2 Kelly McGillis's outstanding performance in this drama elevates what is essentially a Hatfields-and-McCoys rehash. Kurt Russell stars as a clock maker in the Depression who ends up in the Blue Ridge Mountains, where unwed mother McGillis is about to stir up the feudin' locals. Somehow, director Ted Kotcheff and his cast help us forget how silly the film is for most of its running time. Rated PG-13 for violence. 110m. **DIR:** Ted Kotcheff. **CAST:** Kurt Russell, Kelly McGillis, Lloyd Bridges, Mitchell Ryan. **1989**

●**WINTERBEAST** ★★ Shot-on-video thriller concerns a winter resort built on ancient Indian burial grounds. Predictably enough, folks start to disappear. Not rated; contains violence and profanity. 80m. **DIR:** Christopher Thies. **CAST:** Tim R. Morgan, Mike Magri, Dori May Kelly. **1993**

●**WINTER'S END** ★★★1/2 Final entry in the *Sarah, Plain and Tall* trilogy presented by *Hallmark Hall of Fame* features Glenn Close in a battle to survive both a blizzard and the sudden reappearance of her husband's father (Jack Palance). The winter of 1918 falls particularly hard on the Wittings and their Kansas farm but they rely on their Walton-ish bond to empower them. Close and Palance play well off each other in this memorable film. Not rated; contains mature themes. 95m. **DIR:** Glenn Jordan. **CAST:** Glenn Close, Christopher Walken, Jack Palance. **1999** DVD

WINTERSET ★★1/2 Heavy-duty drama of a bitter young man's efforts to clear his father's name boasts

a great cast of distinguished character actors and marks the screen debut of the versatile Burgess Meredith. Long on moralizing and short on action. B&W; 78m. **DIR:** Alfred Santell. **CAST:** Burgess Meredith, Margo, Eduardo Ciannelli, John Carradine, Paul Guilfoyle, Stanley Ridges, Mischa Auer. **1936**

WINTERTIME ★★ Sonja Henie's weakest movie and her last for a major studio. Her showy routines attract people to an old run-down hotel so the owners can afford to turn it into a profitable resort. The musical numbers are better than the dialogue and almost as good as the skating scenes. B&W; 82m. **DIR:** John Brahm. **CAST:** Sonja Henie, Cornel Wilde, Jack Oakie, Cesar Romero, Carole Landis, S. Z. Sakall, Helene Reynolds, Geary Steffen, Woody Herman. **1943**

WIRED 🐼 John Belushi (Michael Chiklis) clambers from a body bag in the morgue after his fatal drug overdose and is escorted through his past by a Puerto Rican angel/cabbie (Ray Sharkey). Rated R. 112m. **DIR:** Larry Peerce. **CAST:** Michael Chiklis, J. T. Walsh, Patti D'Arbanville, Alex Rocco, Ray Sharkey. **1989**

WIRED TO KILL 🐼 The year is 1998, and 120 million Americans are dead from a killer plague. Rated R for violence and raw language. 90m. **DIR:** Franky Schaefer. **CAST:** Emily Longstreth, Deven Holescher, Merritt Buttrick. **1986**

WISDOM 🐼 Writer-director Emilio Estevez plays a modern-day Robin Hood who comes to the aid of farmers. Rated R for violence. 109m. **DIR:** Emilio Estevez. **CAST:** Emilio Estevez, Demi Moore, Tom Skerritt, Veronica Cartwright, William Allen Young. **1986**

WISE BLOOD ★★★★ While there are many laughs in this fascinating black comedy about a slow-witted country boy (Brad Dourif) who decides to become a man of the world, they tend to stick in your throat. This searing satire on southern do-it-yourself religion comes so close to the truth, it is almost painful to watch at times. Rated PG. 108m. **DIR:** John Huston. **CAST:** Brad Dourif, Harry Dean Stanton, Ned Beatty, Amy Wright, Dan Shor. **1979**

WISE GUYS ★★★1/2 Director Brian De Palma, apparently tired of derivative Hitchcockian thrillers, returned to his roots with this send-up of gangster movies. Danny DeVito and Joe Piscopo play Harry and Moe, a couple of goofball syndicate gofers. When they muck up a bet on the ponies; as punishment, the boss secretly instructs each to kill the other. Inexplicably rated R for language. 91m. **DIR:** Brian De Palma. **CAST:** Danny DeVito, Joe Piscopo, Harvey Keitel, Ray Sharkey, Dan Hedaya. **1986**

WISH ME LUCK 🐼 A genie tries to help a schlemiel lose his virginity. Not rated; contains nudity and adult situations. 91m. **DIR:** Philip J. Jones. **CAST:** Avalon Anders, Zen Gesner, Christine Harte, Raymond Storti, Stephanie Champlin, David Sobel. **1995**

WISH YOU WERE HERE ★★★★ The heroine of this British production is a foulmouthed, promiscuous 16-year-old (superbly played by Emily Lloyd), who raises hackles in the straitlaced world of 1940s England. Her story is shocking, funny, and ultimately touching. Writer-director David Leland has created a hilarious comedy. Rated R for profanity, nudity, and simulated sex. 92m. **DIR:** David Leland. **CAST:** Emily

Lloyd, Tom Bell, Jesse Birdsall, Geoffrey Durham, Pat Heywood. 1987

WISHFUL THINKING (1992) ★★ A recluse receives a magical notebook. With it, he can have anything he wants, and he wants a beautiful woman. Sight gags are overdone. Not rated; contains nudity and violence. 94m. **DIR:** Murray Langston. **CAST:** Murray Langston, Michelle Johnson, Ruth Buzzi, Billy Barty, Ray "Boom Boom" Mancini. 1992 DVD

•**WISHFUL THINKING (1997)** ★★ Tepid love story told from the viewpoints of three of its main characters. Excellent performances throughout can't shake the dull out of this one. Rated R for profanity. 91m. **DIR:** Adam Park. **CAST:** Drew Barrymore, Jennifer Beals, Jon Stewart, James LeGros. 1997 DVD

•**WISHMASTER 2: EVIL NEVER DIES** ★★ Sloppy made-for-video sequel delivers more of the same, but with less style and logic. Andrew Divoff returns as the evil Djinn, and seems to have a ball as he grants unsuspecting victims their wishes. Unfortunately, writer-director Jack Sholder fails to realize any real suspense or terror, even though the prison setting is ripe for both. A low budget keeps the filmmakers from fulfilling their vision. Rated R for violence, language, and nudity. 96m. **DIR:** Jack Sholder. **CAST:** Andrew Divoff, Holly Fields, Paul Johansson, Bokeem Woodbine. 1999 DVD

WISTFUL WIDOW OF WAGON GAP, THE ★★★ Back in the old West a salesman accidentally kills a man and finds that legally he must support the widow and her six children. This doesn't sound like a comedy, but when the salesman is Lou Costello and the widow is Marjorie Main laughs come easily. B&W; 77m. **DIR:** Charles Barton. **CAST:** Bud Abbott, Lou Costello, Marjorie Main, Audrey Young, George Cleveland, Gordon Jones, William Ching. 1947

WITCH HUNT ★★★1/2 This entertaining sequel to *Cast a Deadly Spell* finds Dennis Hopper playing world-weary investigator H. Phillip Lovecraft, the only "regular guy" in a universe where everybody practices magic. Good sight gags and clever dialogue. Rated R for profanity and brief nudity. 100m. **DIR:** Paul Schrader. **CAST:** Dennis Hopper, Penelope Ann Miller, Eric Bogosian, Sheryl Lee Ralph, Julian Sands. 1994

WITCHBOARD ★★ Some good moments buoy this horror film about a group of people who play with a Ouija board at a party and find themselves haunted into becoming murderers and victims. Rated R for profanity and violence. 100m. **DIR:** Kevin S. Tenney. **CAST:** Todd Allen, Tawny Kitaen, Stephen Nicholas, Kathleen Wilhoite, Rose Marie. 1987 DVD

WITCHBOARD 2 ❤ Wannnabe artist moves into a new apartment, toys with an abandoned Ouija board, and unleashes the spirit of a murdered former tenant. A sequel "which bored, too." Rated R for nudity, violence, and profanity. 96m. **DIR:** Kevin S. Tenney. **CAST:** Ami Dolenz, Timothy Gibbs, Laraine Newman. 1993

WITCHCRAFT ❤ A new mother can't understand the strange nightmares she begins to have after she moves in with her mother-in-law. R rating. 90m. **DIR:** Robert Spera. **CAST:** Anat Topol-Barzilai. 1988 DVD

WITCHCRAFT II: THE TEMPTRESS ❤ This sequel to the original *Witchcraft* is as lame and ridiculous

as its predecessor. Rated R for violence, profanity, and simulated sex. 88m. **DIR:** Mark Woods. **CAST:** Charles Solomon. 1990 DVD

WITCHCRAFT III, THE KISS OF DEATH ★★ Two forces of evil confront each other over the love of a woman in this extremely sexy plot thinly disguised as a horror movie. Offers great-looking young men, sex kittens with breast implants, and mediocre-to-bad acting. Rated R for language. 85m. **DIR:** R. L. Tillmans. **CAST:** Charles Solomon. 1991

WITCHCRAFT IV ❤ A lawyer is lured into the world of witchcraft and devil worship, and seeks the help of a stripper. As banal as it sounds. Rated R for nudity. 92m. **DIR:** Kevin Morrissey. **CAST:** Charles Solomon, Julie Strain. 1992

WITCHCRAFT V: DANCE WITH THE DEVIL ★★ Caine (David Huffman), chief cook and bottle washer for Satan, uses unwilling warlock William (Marklen Kennedy) to bring about the release of his evil master. You find yourself wishing that Caine could open the gates of Hell so something interesting would happen. Rated R for violence, nudity, and sexual situations. 94m. **DIR:** Talun Hsu. **CAST:** Marklen Kennedy, Carolyn Taye-Loren, Nicole Sassaman, David Huffman. 1993

WITCHCRAFT VI: THE DEVIL'S MISTRESS ❤ More supernatural shenanigans with lawyer/warlock Will Spanner. Rated R for violence, nudity, simulated sex, and profanity. 86m. **DIR:** Julie Davis. **CAST:** Jerry Spicer, Bryan Nutter, Debra Beatty. 1994

WITCHCRAFT 7: JUDGMENT HOUR ❤ Bad-as-they-get sequel about an attorney who is drawn to the dark world of vampires. Rated R for nudity, violence, and language. 89m. **DIR:** Michael Paul Girard. **CAST:** David Byrnes, April Breneman, Alisa Christensen. 1995

•**WITCHCRAFT XI: SISTERS IN BLOOD** ❤ An evil Satanist tries to resurrect three ancient witches by utilizing the bodies of three topless drama students that star in his sacrilegious rendition of *Macbeth*. As terrible a movie as this is, it actually has better production values than *Witchcraft X*. Not rated; not for children. 90m. **DIR:** Ron Ford. **CAST:** Miranda Odell, Don Donason, Lauren Ian Richards. 2000

WITCHCRAFT THROUGH THE AGES (HAXAN) ★★★1/2 After seventy years of notoriety, this controversial film is still unique as one of the most outrageous movies of all time. Envisioned by director Benjamin Christensen as a study of black magic, witchcraft, and demonology from the Middle Ages to the present, this silent Scandinavian epic fluctuates between lecture material and incredibly vivid footage that gave the censors ulcers in the 1920s. B&W; 82m. **DIR:** Benjamin Christensen. **CAST:** Maren Pedersen. 1921

WITCHERY ★★ A fairly typical, somewhat suspenseful, demonic-possessions flick about a group of real-estate speculators trapped in a haunted hotel. Not rated. 96m. **DIR:** Martin Newlin. **CAST:** David Hasselhoff, Linda Blair, Catherine Hickland. 1988

•**WITCHES, THE (1967)** ★★★ Decent chiller from Hammer concerning witchcraft at a private school. While the plot is a fairly well-used subgenre, the wonderful work by the cast really brings the film to life. Joan Fontaine plays the headmistress of the school. 90m. DIR: Cyril Frankel. CAST: Joan Fontaine, Kay Walsh, Alec McCowen. 1967

WITCHES, THE (1990) ★★★★ Everyone over the age of eight will be fascinated by this spooky tale of a 9-year-old boy who attempts to thwart the evil designs of the Grand High Witch (Anjelica Huston in top form) as she embarks on a campaign to turn all children into mice. The special effects and makeup are marvelous in this wonderfully spooky adaptation of a Roald Dahl story. Rated PG for scary stuff. 90m. DIR: Nicolas Roeg. CAST: Anjelica Huston, Mai Zetterling, Jasen Fisher. 1990 DVD

WITCHES' BREW ★★ Margret (Teri Garr) and her two girlfriends have been dabbling in witchcraft to help their university professor husbands to succeed. It's supposed to be a horror spoof but turns out to be more of a horror rip-off of *Burn Witch Burn!* Lana Turner has a small role as the witchcraft mentor to the three young women. Rated PG. 98m. DIR: Richard Shoor, Herbert L. Strock. CAST: Richard Benjamin, Teri Garr, Lana Turner, Kathryn Leigh Scott. 1980

WITCHES OF EASTWICK, THE ★★★★1/2 In this wickedly funny comedy, Jack Nicholson gives one of his finest—and funniest—performances as a self-described "horny little devil" who comes to a tiny hamlet at the behest of three women (Cher, Susan Sarandon, and Michelle Pfeiffer). Only trouble is, these "witches" have no idea of what they've done until it is very nearly too late. Rated R for profanity and suggested sex. 121m. DIR: George Miller. CAST: Jack Nicholson, Cher, Susan Sarandon, Michelle Pfeiffer, Veronica Cartwright, Richard Jenkins. 1987 DVD

WITCHING, THE (NECROMANCY) 🎗 An embarrassment. Rated PG. 82m. DIR: Bert I. Gordon. CAST: Orson Welles, Pamela Franklin, Michael Ontkean, Lee Purcell. 1972

WITCHING, THE (1994) ★★ A teen discovers he is the descendant of a witch hunter and is the only one who can stop the queen of the witches. Highly silly, but watchable. Not rated; contains violence and profanity. 70m. DIR: Eric Black. CAST: Auggi Alvarez, Mike Hellman, Veronica Orr, Frank Dunlay. 1994

WITCHING OF BEN WAGNER, THE ★★★ Magical tale of 13-year-old Ben's encounter with Regina, a young girl who lives with her kind grandmother. Ben doesn't believe the town's rumors that Regina and her grandmother are witches, but when Ben's father falls under a spell that leads to disaster, he doesn't know what to believe. How Ben copes with the town's prejudices and his father set the scene for a magical encounter. Rated G. 96m. DIR: Paul Annett. CAST: Sam Bottoms, Justin Gocke, Harriet Hall, Bettina Rae, Sylvia Sydney. 1995

WITCHING TIME ★★ Another entry from "Thriller Video," hosted by TV's Elvira, "Mistress of the Dark." The owner of an English farmhouse is visited by a previous occupant, a seventeenth-century witch. Unfortunately for him, after three hundred years, the old gal is hot to trot. Originally filmed for the British television series *Hammer House of Horror*. Not rated; nudity edited out of the print used for this cassette. 60m. DIR: Don Leaver. CAST: Jon Finch, Patricia Quinn, Prunella Gee, Ian McCulloch. 1985

WITCH'S MIRROR, THE ★★ One of the better entries in the early-Sixties rash of low-budget Mexican horror movies that will bore the pants off some viewers, while entertaining the devotees. In the nineteenth century, the mirror of the title curses an unscrupulous surgeon. Weird and atmospheric, but unevenly dubbed into English. B&W; 75m. DIR: Chano Urveta. CAST: Rosita Arenas, Armando Calvo. 1960

WITCHTRAP ★★ Takes place in a mansion haunted by its former owner, who practiced Satanic rituals in the attic. When the new owner hires a team of expert psychics to rid the mansion of its evil, a horrifying chain of events occurs. Rated R for nudity and profanity. 92m. DIR: Kevin S. Tenney. CAST: James W. Quinn, Kathleen Bailey, Linnea Quigley. 1989

WITH HONORS ★★★ Joe Pesci plays a homeless philosopher who teaches blue-blooded Harvard student Brendan Fraser about life and compassion. The story is predictable, even when it takes a tearjerking turn, but Pesci's cocky charm and the remarkably attractive supporting ensemble keep things interesting. Rated PG-13 for profanity and mild nudity. 96m. DIR: Alek Keshishian. CAST: Joe Pesci, Brendan Fraser, Moira Kelly, Patrick Dempsey, Josh Hamilton, Gore Vidal. 1994 DVD

WITH SIX YOU GET EGGROLL ★★ Widow Doris Day has three kids; widower Brian Keith has a daughter. They get together. Awwwww! *Bachelor Father* meets *Mother Knows Best*. The two stars refer to Doris and Brian, neither of whom helped their cause with this turkey. Strictly a picture for the 1960s. Not rated. 99m. DIR: Howard Morris. CAST: Doris Day, Brian Keith, Barbara Hershey. 1968

WITHIN THE ROCK ★★★ A team of miners is sent to intercept a meteor and push it off its course with Earth by planting charges at its core. What they find at the center is a nasty alien just awakened from a million-year slumber. What could have been a cheesy *Alien* rip-off instead turns out to be an enjoyable romp thanks in large part to a decent script, atmospheric direction, and a great creature. Rated R for violence and profanity. 91m. DIR: Gary J. Tunnicliffe. CAST: Xander Berkeley, Caroline Barclay, Bradford Tatum, Brian Krause, Barbara Patrick, Duane Whitaker, Earl Boen. 1996 DVD

WITHNAIL AND I ★★★★ A funny but sometimes grim comedy set in the Great Britain of the late 1960s. Two friends, whose decadent lifestyle of booze and drugs has hit bottom, try to make a new start by taking a holiday in the country. The performances are excellent, period details are perfect, and the movie is well made. Rated R for profanity and adult themes. 110m. DIR: Bruce Robinson. CAST: Richard E. Grant, Paul McGann, Richard Griffiths. 1987

WITHOUT A CLUE ★★★★ In this delightful send-up of Conan Doyle's mysteries, it is revealed that Holmes was nothing more than a fictional creation of the real crime-fighting genius, Dr. John H. Watson (Ben Kingsley). The Great Detective was actually an inept, clumsy, and often inebriated actor, Reginald Kincaid (Michael Caine), hired by Watson. An overlooked gem of a comedy. Rated PG for violence. 106m. DIR: Thom Eberhardt. CAST: Michael Caine, Ben

Kingsley, Jeffrey Jones, Lysette Anthony, Paul Freeman, Nigel Davenport, Peter Cook. 1988

WITHOUT A TRACE ★★★ A drama about a boy who vanishes and his mother's unrelenting faith that he will return, this is yet another entry in the family-in-trouble movie genre. Well-acted but sometimes overwrought and predictable. Rated PG for mature content. 120m. **DIR:** Stanley Jaffe. **CAST:** Kate Nelligan, Judd Hirsch, David Dukes, Stockard Channing, Jacqueline Brooks, Kathleen Widdoes. 1983

WITHOUT LOVE ★★★★ Widow Katharine Hepburn enters into a marriage of convenience with scientist Spencer Tracy. Great fun, with this wonderful team being matched every step of the way by wise-cracking Lucille Ball and likable lush Keenan Wynn. B&W; 111m. **DIR:** Harold S. Bucquet. **CAST:** Spencer Tracy, Katharine Hepburn, Lucille Ball, Keenan Wynn, Patricia Morison, Felix Bressart. 1945

WITHOUT MERCY ★★ Tedious actioner tells the story of a former Marine who—after seeing his fellow Marines murdered in an ambush—leaves the military and hits the streets of Somalia. There he winds up enmeshed with a brutal drug kingpin and the kingpin's girlfriend. Nothing new or unique to recommend this shabby direct-to-video release. Rated R for violence, profanity, and sexual situations. 88m. **DIR:** Robert Anthony. **CAST:** Frank Zagarino, Ayu Azhari, Frans Tumbuan, Martin Kove. 1995

WITHOUT RESERVATIONS ★★★ Wartime comedy about an author and her plan to turn a soldier into the leading man of her filmed novel is light and enjoyable and sprinkled with guest appearances by Hollywood celebrities. B&W; 107m. **DIR:** Mervyn LeRoy. **CAST:** John Wayne, Claudette Colbert, Don DeFore, Phil Brown, Thurston Hall, Louella Parsons. 1946

WITHOUT WARNING 🎔 Hollywood veterans battle with an intergalactic alien hunter (a rubber-faced leftover from the *Outer Limits* television series) and his hungry pets. 89m. **DIR:** Greydon Clark. **CAST:** Jack Palance, Martin Landau, Cameron Mitchell, Larry Storch, Sue Ane Langdon. 1980

WITHOUT WARNING: THE JAMES BRADY STORY ★★★★ Scripter Robert Bolt, drawing from Mollie Dickenson's book *Thumbs Up*, provides Beau Bridges with a plum role. He's absolutely splendid as press secretary James Brady in this TV-movie re-creation of John Hinckley's assassination attempt on Ronald Reagan, which left the president wounded and Brady crippled for life. 120m. **DIR:** Michael Toshiyuki Uno. **CAST:** Beau Bridges, Joan Allen, Bryan Clark, Steven Flynn, David Strathairn. 1991

WITHOUT YOU I'M NOTHING ★★★★ Comedian and social satirist Sandra Bernhard stars in an adaptation (cowritten with director John Boskovich) of her celebrated one-woman show. Not for the prudish or easily offended, but there are many thought-provoking laughs as Bernhard pokes wicked fun at middle-class life, love, and sexual politics. Rated R for profanity. 89m. **DIR:** John Boskovich. **CAST:** Sandra Bernhard. 1990

WITNESS ★★★★1/2 This is three terrific movies in one: an exciting cop thriller, a touching romance, and a fascinating screen study of a modern-day clash of cultures. Harrison Ford is superb as a detective who must protect an 8-year-old Amish boy, the only witness to a drug-related murder. Rated R for violence, profanity, and nudity. 112m. **DIR:** Peter Weir. **CAST:** Harrison Ford, Kelly McGillis, Josef Sommer, Lukas Haas, Alexander Godunov, Danny Glover. 1985 DVD

WITNESS FOR THE PROSECUTION (1957) ★★🅐 ★★★ Superb performances help make this gripping courtroom drama an enduring favorite of film buffs. The screenplay was adapted from a play by Agatha Christie and features Charles Laughton as an aging lawyer called upon to defend an alleged murderer (Tyrone Power). It is Dietrich, in one of her greatest screen performances, who nearly steals the show. B&W; 114m. **DIR:** Billy Wilder. **CAST:** Tyrone Power, Charles Laughton, Marlene Dietrich, Elsa Lanchester, John Williams, Henry Daniell, Una O'Connor. 1957

WITNESS FOR THE PROSECUTION (1982) ★★★ An enjoyable made-for-television remake of Agatha Christie's courtroom drama. Ralph Richardson and Deborah Kerr are adequate as the wily yet ailing barrister and his continually frustrated nurse. Unfortunately, they lack the rich humor brought to the roles by Charles Laughton and Elsa Lanchester in the original. Beau Bridges is particularly outstanding as the defendant. 100m. **DIR:** Alan Gibson. **CAST:** Ralph Richardson, Beau Bridges, Diana Rigg, Deborah Kerr. 1982

•**WITNESS PROTECTION** ★★★★ Taut, intense drama about a family forced into the government's witness protection program and the havoc it wreaks upon their lives. Excellent performances throughout. Rated R for violence and profanity. 105m. **DIR:** Richard Pearce. **CAST:** Tom Sizemore, Mary Elizabeth Mastrantonio, Shawn Hatosy, Sky McCole Bartusiak, Forest Whitaker, William Sandler. 1999 DVD

WITNESS TO THE EXECUTION ★★★1/2 Enthralling made-for-television thriller about a TV executive who hits upon the next big thing: broadcasting an execution. The executive needs the perfect star, and she finds one in a handsome and personable death row inmate. There's just one problem: he may not be guilty. Rated PG-13 for some intense situations. 92m. **DIR:** Tommy Lee Wallace. **CAST:** Sean Young, Timothy Daly, Len Cariou, George Newbern, Alan Fudge, Dee Wallace. 1993

WIVES UNDER SUSPICION ★★★ Fanatical district attorney whose sole purpose in life is executing murderers is slapped into reality when a case he is prosecuting bears an uneasy similarity to his own situation at home. Warren William is fine as the zealous avenger, and Gail Patrick shines as his ignored and restless wife. B&W; 68m. **DIR:** James Whale. **CAST:** Warren William, Gail Patrick, William Lundigan, Constance Moore, Ralph Morgan, Samuel S. Hinds. 1938

WIZ, THE ★★ Ineffective updating of *The Wizard of Oz* with an all-black cast, including Diana Ross (who is too old for the part), Richard Pryor, and Michael Jackson. Adapted from a successful Broadway play, this picture should have been better. Rated G. 133m. **DIR:** Sidney Lumet. **CAST:** Diana Ross, Richard Pryor, Michael Jackson, Nipsey Russell, Ted Ross, Mabel

King, Theresa Merritt, Thelma Carpenter, Lena Horne. **1978 DVD**

WIZ KID, THE ★★ Teenage high jinks find young computer whiz Martin Forbes cloning himself so his hipper alter self can make out with the prettiest girl in school. Predictable problems don't help this obviously dubbed foreign import. Rated PG for adult situations. 90m. **DIR:** Gloria Behrens. **CAST:** Martin Forbes, Gary Forbes, Heiner Lauterbach. 1993

WIZARD, THE ★★ It's *Rain Man* meets the *Pinball Wizard* as Fred Savage takes his emotionally disturbed half brother (Luke Edwards) to the national video game championship. Little more than a cleverly disguised advertisement for Nintendo games and the Universal Studios Tour. Rated PG for light violence and profanity. 100m. **DIR:** Todd Holland. **CAST:** Fred Savage, Beau Bridges, Christian Slater, Luke Edwards, Jenifer Lewis. 1989

WIZARD OF GORE, THE 💔 Blood and guts galore as a sideshow magician takes the old "saw the girl in half" trick a bit too far. Rated R. 80m. **DIR:** Herschell Gordon Lewis. **CAST:** Ray Sager. **1970 DVD**

WIZARD OF LONELINESS, THE ★★★1/2 After his mom dies and his dad goes off to war (World War II), young Wendall Oler (Lukas Haas) is forced to live with his grandparents, aunt, uncle, and cousin. Good acting and excellent Forties sets and costumes add to John Nichols's thought-provoking novel. Rated PG-13 for violence and profanity. 110m. **DIR:** Jenny Bowen. **CAST:** Lukas Haas, Lea Thompson, John Randolph, Anne Pitoniak. 1988

WIZARD OF MARS, THE ★★ Low-budget interplanetary version of *The Wizard of Oz* finds a rocketship full of Earthlings on the planet Mars where magic and fantasy are the prevalent forces. Written, directed, and produced by David Hewitt, with technical assistance from famed science-fiction–fantasy expert Forrest J. Ackerman, this doesn't really compare to major science-fiction or fantasy films. 81m. **DIR:** David L. Hewitt. **CAST:** John Carradine, Vic McGee, Roger Gentry. 1964

WIZARD OF OZ, THE ★★★★★ Fifty years old and still going strong—on a fresh, bright Technicolor print with special rare footage additions—this alltime classic continues to charm audiences of all ages. In this case, for watching great movies, "there is no place like home." Right, Toto? It's 119m. **DIR:** Victor Fleming. **CAST:** Judy Garland, Ray Bolger, Bert Lahr, Jack Haley, Frank Morgan, Billie Burke, Margaret Hamilton, Charley Grapewin, Clara Blandick. **1939 DVD**

WIZARD OF SPEED AND TIME, THE ★★★ Based on Mike Jittlov's own difficulties in breaking into show business, this tongue-in-cheek success story features him producing a special-effects masterpiece on a shoestring budget. Silly gags and slapstick surround five stop-motion shorts. Rated PG for language. 92m. **DIR:** Mike Jittlov. **CAST:** Mike Jittlov, Paige Moore, Richard Kaye, Philip Michael Thomas. 1986

WIZARD OF THE LOST KINGDOM 💔 Bo Svenson as a master swordsman who comes to the aid of a sorcerer's son. Rated PG for violence. 76m. **DIR:** Hector Olivera. **CAST:** Bo Svenson, Vidal Peterson, Thom Christopher. 1985

WIZARD OF THE LOST KINGDOM II 💔 In medieval times, a boy wizard is sent on a quest to bring freedom to three kingdoms. Rated PG. 80m. **DIR:** Charles B. Griffith. **CAST:** David Carradine, Bobby Jacoby, Mel Wells. 1989

WIZARDS ★★★ Director-animator Ralph Bakshi's cost-cutting corners, which had not been that evident in his *Fritz the Cat* films, become a bit too noticeable in this charming little tale of ultimate good versus ultimate evil. Our hero is an aged wizard who relies on magic; his evil doppelgänger resorts to the horrors of technology. The conflict builds well until its climax, which (sadly) negates the premise of the entire battle. Rated PG for occasionally graphic violence. 81m. **DIR:** Ralph Bakshi. 1977

WOLF ★★★★ A clever combination of horror film, social comment, and character study as publishing-house editor Jack Nicholson finds himself trapped as his company changes hands and a smarmy protégé co-opts his job. An accidental encounter with a wolf gives Nicholson a new edge. It's genre fun for smart people, with first-rate performances. Rated R for profanity, violence, and suggested sex. 125m. **DIR:** Mike Nichols. **CAST:** Jack Nicholson, Michelle Pfeiffer, James Spader, Kate Nelligan, Richard Jenkins, Christopher Plummer, Om Puri, Ron Rifkin, Prunella Scales. **1994 DVD**

WOLF AT THE DOOR ★★ Pompous and heavy-handed, this film gnaws away at painter Paul Gauguin's life in a rather self-conscious fashion, despite some beautiful photography. Predictable and ponderous, and Gauguin's love life with 13-year-old girls is downright depressing. English-dubbed. 94m. **DIR:** Henning Carlsen. **CAST:** Donald Sutherland, Fanny Bastien. 1987

WOLF CALL ★★ Jack London's story of a dog brought from the city to join a wolf pack somehow evolves into a musical-adventure-drama in this curious film. Playboy John Carroll falls in love with Indian maiden Movita while investigating his father's radium mine. B&W; 61m. **DIR:** George Waggner. **CAST:** John Carroll, Movita. 1939

WOLF MAN, THE ★★★★ Classic horror film featuring a star-making performance by Lon Chaney Jr. as Lawrence Talbot (a role he would go on to play five times). Upon attempting to save a young woman from a wolf's vicious attack, Talbot is bitten by a werewolf. Now he too will become a bloodthirsty creature of the night whenever the full moon rises. B&W; 70m. **DIR:** George Waggner. **CAST:** Lon Chaney Jr., Evelyn Ankers, Claude Rains, Patric Knowles, Ralph Bellamy, Bela Lugosi, Maria Ouspenskaya, Warren William. **1941 DVD**

WOLFEN ★★ The best features of this sluggish horror film are its innovative visual work and actors who make the most of an uneven script. Directed by Michael Wadleigh, it follows a sequence of mysterious murders that are sometimes disturbingly bloody. This explains the R rating. 115m. **DIR:** Michael Wadleigh. **CAST:** Albert Finney, Diane Venora, Gregory Hines, Tommy Noonan, Edward James Olmos, Dick O'Neill. 1981

WOLFHEART'S REVENGE ★★1/2 Wolfheart, a Rin-Tin-Tin look-alike, helps Guinn "Big Boy" Williams bring a killer to justice and win the girl in this silent oater. B&W; 64m. **DIR:** Fritz Lang. **CAST:** Guinn Williams, Helen Walton. 1925

WOLFMAN 🎬 A young man inherits his ancestral home, only to be transformed into a wolfman by a cult of Satanists. Not rated; contains violence. 91m. **DIR:** Worth Keeter. **CAST:** Earl Owensby. 1978

WOLVES, THE (1981) ★★★ Three gangsters fight for survival in this stylish but slightly overlong *yakuza* story set in pre–World War II Japan, when the old samurai-based ways were beginning to collapse. In Japanese with English subtitles. Not rated. 132m. **DIR:** Hideo Gosha. **CAST:** Tatsuya Nakadai. 1981

WOLVES, THE (1994) ★★1/2 Gorgeous scenery outshines this simplistic story about a brother and sister's plans to thwart a developer who seeks to turn the untamed wilderness into a toxic-dump site. The children are aided by a Native American, who wants to protect a pack of wolves that inhabit the area. Rated PG-13 for violence. 87m. **DIR:** Steve Carver. **CAST:** Darren Dalton, Raimund Harmstorf, Ben Cardinal, John Furey, Kristen Hocking. 1994

WOMAN AT HER WINDOW, A ★★★ A wealthy woman is drawn into political intrigue when she aids a revolutionary in his escape from Greece. Focus is primarily on her relationships with her philandering husband, an adoring fan, and the handsome man on the run. Suspense and romance make for a winning formula and Romy Schneider, as passion's plaything, is absolutely mesmerizing. In French with English subtitles. Not rated. 110m. **DIR:** Pierre Granier-Deferre. **CAST:** Romy Schneider, Philippe Noiret, Victor Lanoux, Umberto Orsini. 1977

WOMAN AT WAR, A ★★★★ Well-conceived, taut drama about a young woman whose parents are arrested by the Gestapo in war-torn Brussels. Determined to survive, she goes undercover and infiltrates Gestapo headquarters, a move that could cost her life. Martha Plimpton and Eric Stoltz shine in this made-for-British-television drama. Not rated. 115m. **DIR:** Edward Bennett. **CAST:** Martha Plimpton, Eric Stoltz. 1991

WOMAN CALLED GOLDA, A ★★★1/2 Ingrid Bergman won an Emmy for her outstanding performance as Israeli Prime Minister Golda Meir. Leonard Nimoy costars in this highly watchable film, which was originally made for TV. 200m. **DIR:** Alan Gibson. **CAST:** Ingrid Bergman, Judy Davis, Leonard Nimoy. 1982

WOMAN CALLED MOSES, A ★★★ Cicely Tyson plays Harriet Tubman to perfection in this made-for-TV dramatization of her life. Unfortunately, this TV movie is soured by unnecessary narration by Orson Welles. 200m. **DIR:** Paul Wendkos. **CAST:** Cicely Tyson, Will Geer, Robert Hooks, James Wainwright, Hari Rhodes. 1978

WOMAN, HER MEN AND HER FUTON, A 🎬 Pointless film about a shallow woman who uses men for sex, money, and her career. She's so insipid and unsympathetic that it's painful to watch. Rated R for nudity, suggested sex, and profanity. 92m. **DIR:**

Mussef Sibay. **CAST:** Jennifer Rubin, Lance Edwards, Grant Show, Robert Lipton. 1991

WOMAN IN FLAMES, A ★★★★ A male and a female prostitute fall in love and decide to set up shop in the same household, insisting that their business trysts will not interfere with their personal relationship. If erotic drama and bizarre twists are your fancy, this should be your film. Rated R for sexual situations and language. 104m. **DIR:** Robert Van Ackeren. **CAST:** Gudrun Landgrebe, Mathieu Carriere. 1984

WOMAN IN GREEN, THE ★★★ This is a grisly little entry in the Rathbone/Bruce Sherlock Holmes series, with the master sleuth investigating a series of severed fingers sent to Scotland Yard. The culprit is, once again, Professor Moriarty (Henry Daniell). Careful viewers will detect moments from *The Adventure of the Empty House.* B&W; 68m. **DIR:** Roy William Neill. **CAST:** Basil Rathbone, Nigel Bruce, Hillary Brooke, Henry Daniell, Paul Cavanagh. 1945 DVD

WOMAN IN QUESTION ★★★1/2 When a fortune teller is murdered, the police detective who investigates tries to decide what to believe from conflicting testimony offered by five people who knew her. This structurally complex drama has aged well and will be appreciated by Quentin Tarantino fans as well as English-mystery buffs. B&W; 84m. **DIR:** Anthony Asquith. **CAST:** Jean Kent, Dirk Bogarde, Hermione Baddeley. 1949

WOMAN IN RED, THE ★★★★ Gene Wilder's funniest film in years, this is best described as a bittersweet romantic comedy. Wilder, who also adapted the screenplay and directed, plays an advertising executive and heretofore happily married man who becomes obsessed with a beautiful woman. The results are hilarious. Rated PG-13 for partial nudity, brief violence, and profanity. 87m. **DIR:** Gene Wilder. **CAST:** Gene Wilder, Charles Grodin, Joseph Bologna, Gilda Radner, Judith Ivey, Michael Huddleston, Kelly LeBrock. 1984

WOMAN IN THE DUNES ★★★★★ An entomologist collecting beetles on the dunes misses his bus back to the city. Some locals offer him assistance, and he is lowered by a ladder down into a sand pit where he finds a woman willing to provide food and lodging in her shack. The ladder is removed, however, and he is trapped. A classic thriller. In Japanese with English subtitles. B&W; 123m. **DIR:** Hiroshi Teshigahara. **CAST:** Eiji Okada. 1964 DVD

WOMAN IN THE MOON (GIRL IN THE MOON; BY ROCKET TO THE MOON) ★★★ Fritz Lang's last silent film is actually a futuristic melodrama written by his wife and collaborator, Thea von Harbou. Admired by science-fiction aficionados for Lang's imaginative visual sense, not the content of the story. German, silent. B&W; 115m. **DIR:** Fritz Lang. **CAST:** Gerda Maurus, Willy Fritsch, Fritz Rasp, Gustav von Waggenheim. 1929

●**WOMAN IN THE WINDOW** ★★★★1/2 A mild-mannered college professor (Edward G. Robinson) who would never dream of cheating on his wife indulges in an innocent conversation with a beautiful woman (Joan Bennett). Before he knows it, he's sucked into a spiral of murder and blackmail. One of the best from the classic period of Hollywood *film noir*, this is grippingly directed by Fritz Lang. Its only weakness is the ending, which many viewers may see as a Hollywood cop-out, even though it was planned by Lang. B&W; 99m. **DIR:** Fritz Lang. **CAST:** Edward G. Robinson, Joan Bennett, Raymond Massey, Dan Duryea. 1945

WOMAN IS A WOMAN, A ★★★★ One of Jean-Luc Godard's most accessible movies is built around a love triangle involving a stripper (Anna Karina, whom Godard married after filming), her lover, and his best friend. Unlike much of Godard's later work, this tribute cum parody of Hollywood musicals keeps your attention even when the literal meaning is unclear. In French with English subtitles. 85m. **DIR:** Jean-Luc Godard. **CAST:** Anna Karina, Jean-Paul Belmondo, Jean-Claude Brialy, Jeanne Moreau. 1961 DVD

WOMAN NAMED JACKIE, A ★★★ Made-for-television miniseries based on the best-selling biography by C. David Heymann, features a winning Roma Downey as the First Lady whose life was plagued by heartbreak. While Downey shines, the rest of the docudrama plays like a prime-time soap opera. Handsome production values and period detail. Three tapes. 289m. **DIR:** Larry Peerce. **CAST:** Roma Downey, William Devane, Stephen Collins, Joss Ackland, Wendy Hughes. 1993

WOMAN NEXT DOOR, THE ★★★½ François Truffaut is on record as one of the greatest admirers of Alfred Hitchcock, and the influence shows in this gripping, well-made film about guilt, passion, and the influence of a small sin that grows. In French with English subtitles. MPAA not rated, but contains nudity and violence. 106m. **DIR:** François Truffaut. **CAST:** Gérard Depardieu, Fanny Ardant, Henri Garcin. 1981 DVD

WOMAN OBSESSED, A ★★ When a mentally unstable woman who had been forced to give up her son for adoption meets him as an adult, she goes crazy and kidnaps him, thinking he is her dead husband. Lurid melodrama takes too long to get going, though the later scenes are suspenseful. Rated R for violence and sexual situations. 103m. **DIR:** Chuck Vincent. **CAST:** Ruth Raymond, Gregory Patrick, Troy Donahue, Linda Blair. 1989

WOMAN OF AFFAIRS, A ★★★ Young woman with wild tendencies loses her true love and enters into a disastrous marriage. Watered-down version of Michael Arelen's *The Green Hat*. Greta Garbo steals the show. Silent with synchronized score and effects. B&W; 90m. **DIR:** Clarence Brown. **CAST:** Greta Garbo, John Gilbert, Lewis Stone, Johnny Mack Brown, Douglas Fairbanks Jr., Hobart Bosworth. 1928

WOMAN OF DESIRE ★★ The South African scenery and Robert Mitchum's shrewd defense attorney are the sole attractions in this relentlessly silly erotic thriller. It's impossible to determine who did what to whom, except that Bo Derek who still acts with her fingers in her mouth—does it with nearly everybody. Rated R for profanity, nudity, and simulated sex. 97m. **DIR:** Robert Ginty. **CAST:** Jeff Fahey, Bo Derek, Steven Bauer, Robert Mitchum. 1993 DVD

WOMAN OF DISTINCTION, A ★★★½ Though minor, this is really a quite enjoyable film. Rosalind Russell portrays a college dean who must face a tough decision involving a professor (Ray Milland). Familiar but fun. B&W; 85m. **DIR:** Edward Buzzell. **CAST:** Rosalind Russell, Ray Milland, Edmund Gwenn, Janis Carter, Francis Lederer. 1950

WOMAN OF INDEPENDENT MEANS, A ★★★½ Disappointing conclusion mars an otherwise spellbinding adaptation of Elizabeth Forsythe Hailey's novel. Always terrific Sally Field plays Bess Alcott, a plucky southern belle. Having her own money, she challenges female norms from the time of her marriage in 1907 until 1963. Conflicts with her daughter are more annoying than plot enriching. A TV miniseries, this is unrated but contains adult themes. 270m. **DIR:** Robert Greenwald. **CAST:** Sally Field, Ron Silver, Charles Durning, Brenda Fricker, Tony Goldwyn, Jack Thompson. 1995

WOMAN OF PARIS, A ★★★★ In this now-classic silent, a simple country girl (Edna Purviance) goes to Paris and becomes the mistress of a wealthy philanderer (Adolphe Menjou). In her wake follow her artist sweetheart and his mother. Director Charles Chaplin surprised everyone with this film by suddenly forsaking, if only momentarily, his Little Tramp comedy for serious caustic drama. B&W; 112m. **DIR:** Charles Chaplin. **CAST:** Edna Purviance, Adolphe Menjou, Henry Bergman. 1923 DVD

WOMAN OF SUBSTANCE, A ★★★½ This TV miniseries retells Barbara Taylor Bradford's best-selling novel of love and revenge. Multimillionairess Emma Hart recalls her humble beginnings as a poor servant girl, her struggle to survive, and finding the love of her life. Fine entertainment. Three tapes. 300m. **DIR:** Don Sharp. **CAST:** Jenny Seagrove, Deborah Kerr, Barry Bostwick, John Mills, Barry Morse. 1984

WOMAN OF THE TOWN ★★½ Albert Dekker, as famed sheriff Bat Masterson, is forced to choose between his job and his love for saloon girl Claire Trevor. Good supporting cast can't save the slow pace of this Western soap opera. B&W; 87m. **DIR:** George Archainbaud. **CAST:** Albert Dekker, Claire Trevor, Barry Sullivan, Henry Hull. 1943

WOMAN OF THE YEAR ★★★★★ This is the film that first teamed Spencer Tracy and Katharine Hepburn, and it's impossible to imagine anybody else doing a better job. He's a sports reporter; she's a famed political journalist who needs to be reminded of life's simple pleasures. Like baseball … and her attempts to learn the game are priceless. The witty script garnered an Oscar for Ring Lardner Jr. and Michael Kanin. Not rated—family fare. B&W; 112m. **DIR:** George Stevens. **CAST:** Spencer Tracy, Katharine Hepburn, Fay Bainter, Reginald Owen, William Bendix. 1942

WOMAN REBELS, A ★★★★ Surprisingly valid today despite its 1936 vintage. Katharine Hepburn plays a rebellious woman of Victorian England who flouts convention and becomes a fighter for women's rights. Van Heflin makes his film debut. B&W; 88m. **DIR:** Mark Sandrich. **CAST:** Katharine Hepburn, Herbert Marshall, Donald Crisp, Elizabeth Allan, Van Heflin. **1936**

WOMAN TIMES SEVEN ★★ Shirley MacLaine assays seven different roles in this episodic stew and is not as good as she could have been in any of them. There are some funny moments, but they do not a film make. 99m. **DIR:** Vittorio De Sica. **CAST:** Shirley MacLaine, Peter Sellers, Alan Arkin, Rossano Brazzi, Robert Morley, Michael Caine, Vittorio Gassman, Anita Ekberg. **1967**

WOMAN UNDER THE INFLUENCE, A ★★★★ Gena Rowlands is fascinating as a housewife mother swinging back and forth over the edge of insanity, with mood changes from vamp to childlike innocence. Peter Falk is her husband, trying to cope and be understanding, but often lashing out in utter frustration. The movie has been designated a "National Treasure" by the National Film Registry of the Library of Congress. Rated R for adult situations. 147m. **DIR:** John Cassavetes. **CAST:** Gena Rowlands, Peter Falk. **1974 DVD**

WOMAN UNDONE ★★1/2 Mary McDonnell provides more talent than this project deserves, as a philandering wife whose husband dies under very mysterious circumstances. It's absolutely impossible to identify with this self-centered sufferer, although McDonnell tries to make her sympathetic. Rated R for profanity, violence, and simulated sex. 92m. **DIR:** Evelyn Purcell. **CAST:** Mary McDonnell, Randy Quaid, Sam Elliott, Benjamin Bratt. **1995**

WOMAN WITH A PAST ★★★1/2 Forced to flee an abusive marriage with her two children, Pamela Reed (in a stellar performance) takes some drastic measures and becomes a fugitive of the law. After she establishes another identity, federal agents come knocking at her door and her perfect world begins to crumble. Torn from today's headlines, this film is a tour de force for Reed. Rated R for violence, language, and adult situations. 95m. **DIR:** Mimi Leder. **CAST:** Pamela Reed, Dwight Schultz, Richard Lineback, Carrie Snodgress, Paul LeMat. **1994**

WOMAN WITHOUT LOVE, A ★★★ Absorbing melodrama about a neglected housewife who indulges in an affair with an engineer only to return to her wealthy old husband. Twenty years later, the husband leaves a fortune to her son's lover, causing a family castastrophe. In Spanish with English subtitles. Not rated. B&W; 91m. **DIR:** Luis Buñuel. **CAST:** Rosario Granados, Julio Villarreal. **1952**

WOMAN'S FACE, A ★★★1/2 Joan Crawford is the heroine accused of villain Conrad Veidt's murder. Her personality undergoes an amazing transformation following plastic surgery in this taut, strongly plotted melodrama. B&W; 105m. **DIR:** George Cukor. **CAST:** Joan Crawford, Conrad Veidt, Melvyn Douglas, Osa Massen, Reginald Owen, Albert Basserman, Marjorie Main, Charles Quigley, Henry Daniell, George Zucco, Robert Warwick. **1941**

WOMAN'S SECRET, A ★★ Confusing story about a once-popular singer who confesses to the shooting of her protégé; done with flashbacks and testimonials. Second-rate whodunit. B&W; 85m. **DIR:** Nicholas Ray. **CAST:** Maureen O'Hara, Melvyn Douglas, Gloria Gra-

hame, Victor Jory, Bill Williams, Jay C. Flippen, Ellen Corby. **1949**

WOMAN'S TALE, A ★★★★★ A superb film from the highly individual Australian director, Paul Cox. It focuses on Martha, a modern, young-at-heart, fiercely independent woman, trapped in an 80-year-old body. This sensitive, humane, and gently profound film portrays Martha as she approaches the end of her life, refusing to give in to cynicism. Not rated. 94m. **DIR:** Paul Cox. **CAST:** Sheila Florance, Norman Kaye. **1992**

WOMAN'S WORLD ★★★★ A movie that paints a pretty picture of business and businessmen, this one is a curiosity piece as well as an entertaining film. Clever comedy about businesses and office politics. 94m. **DIR:** Jean Negulesco. **CAST:** June Allyson, Clifton Webb, Lauren Bacall, Fred MacMurray, Cornel Wilde, Arlene Dahl, Elliott Reid, Margalo Gilmore. **1954**

WOMEN, THE ★★★1/2 Director George Cukor and some of Hollywood's finest female stars combine for a winning screen version of Clare Boothe's stage hit. This look at the state of matrimony is great entertainment. The script is full of witty, stinging dialogue. B&W; 132m. **DIR:** George Cukor. **CAST:** Norma Shearer, Joan Crawford, Rosalind Russell, Joan Fontaine, Paulette Goddard. **1939 DVD**

WOMEN & MEN: STORIES OF SEDUCTION ★★★★ Three short vignettes, adapted for HBO from noted American short stories, are given first-class treatment. 90m. **DIR:** Ken Russell, Frederic Raphael, Tony Richardson. **CAST:** Elizabeth McGovern, Beau Bridges, Peter Weller, Molly Ringwald, James Woods, Melanie Griffith. **1990**

WOMEN & MEN 2 ★★★★ The second entry in HBO's American short story anthology series follows a theme that finds well-meaning men at a crossroads. Another class act by cast and crew. 90m. **DIR:** Walter Bernstein, Mike Figgis, Kristi Zea. **CAST:** Matt Dillon, Kyra Sedgwick, Ray Liotta, Andie MacDowell, Scott Glenn, Juliette Binoche. **1991**

WOMEN FROM DOWN UNDER ★★★1/2 Female sexuality is the subject of four short films by directors from Australia and New Zealand (hence the title). The best of the four, *Just Desserts*, is a humorous look at a girl who discovers the joys of Italian food and sex at just about the same time. Not rated; contains profanity and sexual situations. 52m. **DIR:** Christine Parker, Monica Pellizzari, Christina Andrees, Jane Schneider. **CAST:** Lucy Lawless, Tania Simon, Joel Tobeck. **1994**

WOMEN FROM THE LAKE OF THE SCENTED SOULS ★★★1/2 One woman's business savvy and success can't make up for a lifetime of abuse by her drunken husband. Ironically, she seals a similar fate for a poor village girl by buying her as a bride for her demented son. Eerily and peaceful scenes contrast sharply with the women's despair. In Mandarin with English subtitles. Not rated; contains violence, sex, adult themes, and profanity. 106m. **DIR:** Xie Fei. **CAST:** Sigin Gaowa, Wu Yujuan, Lei Lao Sheng, Chen Baoguo. **1993**

WOMEN IN CELL BLOCK 9 🎭 Sleazy women's prison melodrama. Filmed in Spain; poorly dubbed into English. No rating, but packed with nudity and gore. 78m. DIR: Jess (Jesus) Franco. CAST: Susan Hemingway, Howard Vernon. **1977**

WOMEN IN LOVE ★★★★1/2 Glenda Jackson won an Oscar for her performance in this British film. Two love affairs are followed simultaneously in this excellent adaptation of D. H. Lawrence's novel. Rated R. B&W; 129m. DIR: Ken Russell. CAST: Glenda Jackson, Oliver Reed, Alan Bates, Eleanor Bron, Jennie Linden, Alan Webb. **1970**

WOMEN OF BREWSTER PLACE, THE ★★★1/2 Marvelous made-for-TV soap about black women sharing a tenement and endless problems. Producer Oprah Winfrey comes across as a near saint both in raising her son and helping out the women around her. 195m. DIR: Donna Deitch. CAST: Oprah Winfrey, Jackée, Robin Givens, Cicely Tyson. **1989**

WOMEN OF THE PREHISTORIC PLANET ❤ Not only is this outer-space saga incredibly cheap, it's also misleadingly titled. There is only one woman, and she's not from the prehistoric planet. 92m. DIR: Arthur C. Pierce. CAST: Wendell Corey, John Agar, Keith Larsen, Merry Anders, Paul Gilbert, Adam Roarke, Stuart Margolin, Gavin MacLeod, Lyle Waggoner. **1966**

WOMEN OF VALOR ★★1/2 This made-for-television feature about a group of army nurses who are captured by the invading Japanese in the Philippines of early World War II is merely average, but the stars raise it up a notch. 100m. DIR: Buzz Kulik. CAST: Susan Sarandon, Kristy McNichol, Alberta Watson, Valerie Mahaffey. **1986**

WOMEN ON THE ROOF, THE ★★1/2 Early in the twentieth century, a shy young woman learns about life when she is befriended by bohemians. Director Carl-Gustav Nykvist shows little eye for imagery or color and the film is adequately played but surprisingly unerotic. In Swedish with English subtitles. Not rated; contains nudity and sexual situations. 86m. DIR: Carl-Gustav Nykvist. CAST: Helena Bergstrom, Stellan Skarsgard, Amanda Ooms. **1997**

WOMEN ON THE VERGE OF A NERVOUS BREAKDOWN ★★★★ Delightful Spanish comedy features Carmen Maura as a pregnant soap-opera star who has just been dumped by her longtime lover. A madcap farce. In Spanish with bright yellow English subtitles. Rated R for profanity. 88m. DIR: Pedro Almodóvar. CAST: Carmen Maura, Fernando Guillen, Antonio Banderas. **1988**

WOMEN'S CLUB, THE ❤ Rated R for profanity, brief nudity, and excessive sexual situations. 89m. DIR: Sandra Weintraub. CAST: Michael Paré, Maud Adams, Eddie Velez. **1986**

WONDER BAR ★★ All the ingredients for a great Warner Bros.–Busby Berkeley musical, but the mixture falls flat this time. Berkeley's musical numbers are as spectacular as ever, but one, "Goin' to Heaven on a Mule" (with Al Jolson in blackface), is perhaps the most colossally tasteless number in movie history. B&W; 84m. DIR: Lloyd Bacon. CAST: Al Jolson, Kay Francis, Dolores Del Rio, Ricardo Cortez, Guy Kibbee. **1934**

•**WONDER BOYS** ★★★★ Among the wittiest and most benevolently caustic indictments of writers and writing ever captured on screen, Steve Kloves's script—adapted from Michael Chabon's novel—is certain to be enjoyed and embraced by book people … and particularly by anybody who ever withered beneath a barrage of superficial "criticism" from a creative writing classroom filled with no-talent hacks who wouldn't know parallel structure from parallel parking. Michael Douglas is marvelous as the rumpled Grady Tripp, a disheveled and eccentric university professor whose latest novel passed the 2,000-page mark several months back. During a single tumultuous weekend, he will deal with a pregnant (and married) lover; an impatient editor; a forlorn and slightly warped young man; and a cutesy-pie coed with a serious crush. Although the film sags a bit in the third act, its rarefied collegiate atmosphere remains palatable to all viewers. Rated R for profanity. 112m. DIR: Curtis Hanson. CAST: Michael Douglas, Tobey Maguire, Frances McDormand, Robert Downey Jr., Katie Holmes. **2000**

WONDER MAN ★★★ Deftly doubling, Danny Kaye plays identical twins with personalities as far apart as the polar regions. One, Buzzy Bellew, is a brash, irrepressible nightclub comic; his mirror, Edwin Dingle, is a mousy double-dome full of tongue-twisting erudition. Identities are switched, of course. Thin on plot, this is mostly a tailored showcase for Kaye's brilliant talents. 98m. DIR: H. Bruce Humberstone. CAST: Danny Kaye, Vera-Ellen, Virginia Mayo, Donald Woods, S. Z. Sakall, Allen Jenkins, Edward Brophy. **1945 DVD**

WONDERFUL HORRIBLE LIFE OF LENI RIEFENSTAHL ★★★★1/2 Leni Riefenstahl, probably one of the greatest filmmakers of all time, is also the most controversial. Among her works are some appalling, though brilliant, propaganda films for the Nazis. After World War II her life was in ruins. She makes a fascinating subject for this long, engrossing documentary. In German with English subtitles. Not rated; suitable for general audiences. 181m. DIR: Ray Müller. **1993 DVD**

WONDERFUL ICE CREAM SUIT, THE ★★★★ Ray Bradbury's celebrated short story was the basis for this wonderfully engaging tale of five Hispanic gentlemen who pool their resources in order to buy a white suit that seems to have magical powers. A change of pace for director Stuart Gordon, who proves equally adept at comedy-drama as he does horror. The cast couldn't be better in this made-for-cable, culturally rich film. Rated PG. 77m. DIR: Stuart Gordon. CAST: Edward James Olmos, Joe Mantegna, Esai Morales, Gregory Sierra, Clifton González González, Sid Caesar. **1998**

WONDERFUL WORLD OF THE BROTHERS GRIMM, THE ★★★ Excellent adaptations of the Grimm tales, featuring brilliant animation by Puppetoon master George Pal and Oscar-winning costumes by Mary Willis. One of the standout sequences has Buddy Hackett battling a fire-breathing dragon in a toy shop. Originally shown in Cinerama. 129m. DIR: Henry Levin, George Pal. CAST: Laurence Harvey, Claire Bloom, Karlheinz Böhm, Oscar Homolka, Barbara Eden, Russ Tamblyn, Buddy Hackett, Terry-Thomas. **1962**

WONDERLAND ★★★1/2 Meandering comedy-drama starts out as a romance between two gay teens, but turns into a thriller after they witness a gangland murder. Too overstuffed to be completely satisfying, though there are many nice bits. Originally known as *The Fruit Machine*. Rated R for sexual discussions. 103m. DIR: Philip Saville. CAST: Emile Charles, Tony Forsyth, Robert Stephens, Robbie Coltrane. 1988

WONDERWALL ★★1/2 Experimental curiosity piece depicts the fantasies of an entomologist as he spies on the woman in the apartment next to his. Electronic music score by George Harrison. Not rated, the film includes some nudity. 93m. DIR: Joe Massot. CAST: Jack MacGowran, Jane Birkin, Irene Handl. 1968

WOO ★★ A blind date between two young, urban Brooklynites (Jada Pinkett, Tommy Davidson) begins in misunderstanding but finally blossoms into romance. The script is repetitive, the direction is plodding, the jokes are stale; the film's only real assets are the appealing performances of Pinkett and Davidson and handsome photography by Jean Lapine. Rated R for profanity. 84m. DIR: Daisy von Scherler Mayer. CAST: Jada Pinkett, Tommy Davidson, Duane Martin, Michael Ralph, LL Cool J. 1998

•**WOOD, THE** ★★★ Three male friends reminisce about their formative years in Inglewood, California, in this meandering, clumsy but entertaining comedy-drama. When one buddy is missing in action on his wedding day, his two pals have two hours to fetch him from the home of a former flame, sober him up, and cure his case of cold feet. The film then flashes back to the trio's 1980s school days where they shared their first brushes with crime, sex, and love. Rated R for language and sexual content. 106m. DIR: Rick Famuyiwa. CAST: Taye Diggs, Omar Epps, Richard T. Jones, Trent Cameron, Sean Nelson, Duane Finley. 1999 DVD

WOODEN HORSE, THE ★★★ Good casting and taut direction make this tale of British POWs tunneling out of a Nazi prison camp well worth watching. Made when memories were fresh, the film glows with reality as English cunning, grit, and timing vie with Nazi suspicion, assumed superiority, and complacency. B&W; 101m. DIR: Jack Lee. CAST: Leo Genn, David Tomlinson, Anthony Steel, Peter Finch. 1950

WOODEN MAN'S BRIDE, THE ★★★★ Gorgeously filmed, epic tale of forbidden love finds a young bride forced to marry a wooden effigy of her fiancé when he is killed in an accident. Tradition and a stern mother-in-law force the bride into the union, but she finds solace and love in the arms of the young peasant Kui. Exquisite period detail, mesmerizing performances, and intense subject matter make this foreign import a real treat. In Chinese with English subtitles. Not rated; contains violence and adult situations. 114m. DIR: Huang Jianxin. CAST: Chang Shih, Wang Lan, Ku Paoming, Wang Yumei. 1995

WOODSTOCK ★★★1/2 Woodstock is probably, along with *Gimme Shelter*, the most important film documentation of the late 1960s counterculture in the United States. The bulk of the film consists of footage of the bands and various other performers who played at the festival. There are some great split-screen sequences and some imaginative interviews. Well worth viewing. Rated R. 184m. DIR: Michael Wadleigh. CAST: Country Joe and the Fish, Jimi Hendrix, Jefferson Airplane. 1970 DVD

WOODY GUTHRIE—HARD TRAVELIN' ★★★1/2 Woody Guthrie's musical presence will be felt for many years. This tribute traces his brilliant songwriting career from the dust bowl of the Midwest to California in the early 1940s. Many performers, including Joan Baez and Arlo Guthrie, Woody's son, sing and discuss the Guthrie influence on their own music. 74m. DIR: Jim Brown. CAST: Hoyt Axton, Joan Baez, Judy Collins, Pete Seeger, Arlo Guthrie. 1984

WORD, THE ★★★ In a catacomb beneath Ostia, Italy, an archaeologist discovers an ancient manuscript that could cause chaos in the Christian world. The manuscript is said to contain the writings of Christ's younger brother, James the Just. A good story, with wonderful actors. Not rated. 188m. DIR: Richard Lang. CAST: David Janssen, John Huston, James Whitmore. 1978

WORDS AND MUSIC ★★1/2 Fictionalized biography of the song-writing team of Richard Rogers and Lorenz Hart, dwelling mostly on the short and tormented life of the latter. As long as there's music, song, and dance, everything is great. The rest should have been silence. 119m. DIR: Norman Taurog. CAST: Mickey Rooney, Tom Drake, June Allyson, Betty Garrett, Judy Garland, Gene Kelly, Ann Sothern, Vera-Ellen, Cyd Charisse, Allyn Ann McLerie, Mel Torme, Janet Leigh, Perry Como. 1948

WORKING GIRL ★★★★ Clever, sophisticated comedy makes up for a lack of all-out belly laughs with the ring of truth. Melanie Griffith is terrific as the good-hearted gal attempting to work her way up but is thwarted by her scheming boss. A high-powered deal maker rides to the rescue. Rated R for nudity and profanity. 120m. DIR: Mike Nichols. CAST: Harrison Ford, Sigourney Weaver, Melanie Griffith, Alec Baldwin, Joan Cusack. 1988

WORKING GIRLS ★★★★ The sex in this feminist docudrama about prostitution is about as appealing as the smell of dirty socks. The story, on the other hand, is compelling, thought-provoking, oddly touching, and often funny. The main character, Molly (Louise Smith), is a Yale graduate who lives with a female lover and is working toward becoming a professional photographer. Not rated, the film has simulated sex, profanity, nudity, and violence. 90m. DIR: Lizzie Borden. CAST: Louise Smith, Ellen McElduff. 1987

WORKING STIFFS ★★★ This video is composed of the first three episodes of the 1979 TV series about two brothers working as janitors. Good scripts and great timing between the two leads make you wonder why it was canceled. Not rated. 75m. DIR: Penny Marshall, Norman Abbott. CAST: James Belushi, Michael Keaton. 1979

WORLD ACCORDING TO GARP, THE ★★★1/2 Director George Roy Hill and screenwriter Steven Tesich have captured the quirky blend of humor and pathos of John Irving's bestseller. The acting is impressive, with first-rate turns by Robin Williams (in the title role), Glenn Close as his mother, Jenny Fields, and John Lithgow as a kindly transsexual. Rated R for nudity, profanity, sexual situations, and violence. 136m. **DIR:** George Roy Hill. **CAST:** Robin Williams, Glenn Close, John Lithgow, Mary Beth Hurt, Hume Cronyn, Jessica Tandy, Swoosie Kurtz, Amanda Plummer. 1982

WORLD APART, A ★★★1/2 Based on a true story, this is an emotionally charged drama about an antiapartheid South African journalist (Barbara Hershey) who becomes the first white woman to be held under that country's infamous ninety-day detention law. Seen largely through the half-understanding eyes of the woman's daughter. The musical score enhances the searing brutality of this "world apart." Rated PG. 135m. **DIR:** Chris Menges. **CAST:** Barbara Hershey, Jodhi May. 1988

WORLD GONE MAD, THE ★★ This features Wall Street types of questionable character versus a district attorney and his investigators during the Prohibition era. A great cast, but the viewer loses interest. B&W; 73m. **DIR:** Christy Cabanne. **CAST:** Pat O'Brien, Evelyn Brent, Neil Hamilton, Mary Brian, Louis Calhern, J. Carrol Naish. 1933

WORLD GONE WILD ❤ On Earth after the nuclear holocaust, a group of flower children live in Lost Wells, a desert oasis. Rated R for violence, profanity, and nudity. 84m. **DIR:** Lee H. Katzin. **CAST:** Bruce Dern, Michael Paré, Catherine Mary Stewart, Adam Ant. 1988

WORLD IS FULL OF MARRIED MEN, THE ★★ Neglected wife Carroll Baker sets out for revenge on her womanizing husband (Anthony Franciosa) in this pseudofeminist soap opera, written by Jackie Collins at her trashiest. Fun for those who don't take it too seriously. Rated R for sexual situations. 107m. **DIR:** Robert Young. **CAST:** Anthony Franciosa, Carroll Baker. 1979

•**WORLD IS NOT ENOUGH, THE** ★★★1/2 Pierce Brosnan continues to fit the role of 007 with aplomb, and his work here—his third outing as Ian Fleming's "Bond . . . James Bond"—is smooth and assured. The film's production values are superb as always, the locales properly exotic, the action sequences smartly staged, and Sophie Marceau's supporting role intriguingly layered. But Denise Richards's clumsy and wholly unbelievable performance as nuclear weapons expert (!) Christmas Jones ranks at the bottom of the barrel, alongside brain-dead bimbettes Britt Ekland (*The Man with the Golden Gun*) and Tanya Roberts (*A View to a Kill*). Similarly, the story's pacing is uneven. Call this one a midlevel Bond, with Brosnan, Marceau, and composer David Arnold overcoming many of the film's shortcomings through sheer energy. Rated PG-13 for violence, and Bondian mayhem and sensuality. 128m. **DIR:** Michael Apted. **CAST:** Pierce Brosnan, Sophie Marceau, Robert Carlyle, Denise Richards, Robbie Coltrane, Judi Dench, Desmond Llewellyn, Samantha Bond. 1999 DVD

WORLD OF ANDY PANDA, THE ★★1/2 The black-and-white Mickey Mouse look-alike, Andy Panda, went through a number of changes in appearance, and these cartoons from 1941 to 1946 reflect this. Many of his animated adventures often feature other, less bland critters. That said, "Apple Andy" is a near-classic, and the rest aren't bad. 62m. **DIR:** Walter Lantz.

WORLD OF APU, THE ★★★★ The concluding part of director Satyajit Ray's famed *Apu* trilogy covering the life and growth of a young man in India. In this last film, Apu marries and helps bring life into the world himself, completing the cycle amid realizations about himself and his limitations in this world. This movie and its predecessors form a beautiful tapestry of existence in a different culture and were among the most influential of all Indian films for many years. In Bengali with English subtitles. B&W; 103m. **DIR:** Satyajit Ray. **CAST:** Soumitra Chatterjee, Sharmila Tagore, Alok Charkravarty, Swapan Mukherji. 1959

WORLD OF HENRY ORIENT, THE ★★★★ A quirky comedy for the whole family. Peter Sellers is a woman-crazy New York pianist who finds himself being followed by two teenage girls who have come to idolize him. Loads of fun, with a great performance by Angela Lansbury. 106m. **DIR:** George Roy Hill. **CAST:** Peter Sellers, Paula Prentiss, Angela Lansbury, Phyllis Thaxter. 1964

WORLD OF STRANGERS, A ★★★ When a London publisher is transferred to South Africa, he finds new friends among both the black and white communities, gradually becoming aware of the tensions and inequities around him. An intelligent and often disturbing treatment from the novel by Nadine Gordimer. B&W; 89m. **DIR:** Henning Carlsen. **CAST:** Zakes Mokae, Gideon Nxomalo, Evelyn Frank, Ivan Jackson. 1962

WORLD OF SUZIE WONG, THE ★★ William Holden is an artist living a bohemian life in Hong Kong. He falls in love with Nancy Kwan, a prostitute. Tepid and without much action. Nancy Kwan is very good, but she can't save the slow romantic melodrama. 129m. **DIR:** Richard Quine. **CAST:** William Holden, Nancy Kwan, Sylvia Syms, Michael Wilding, Laurence Naismith, Jaqui Chan. 1960

WORLD OF THE VAMPIRES ★★ One of the weaker Mexican-monster movies imported and dubbed into English by K. Gordon Murray, this convoluted melodrama *looks* marvelously atmospheric, but collapses midway along. Unintentionally funny. B&W; 85m. **DIR:** Alfonso Corona. **CAST:** Guillermo Murray. 1960

WORLD WAR III ★★★1/2 In this made-for-TV thriller, Rock Hudson, as a U.S. president, must send a crack military unit to Alaska to stop the Russians from capturing the Alaska pipeline. The battle scenes are tense and effective, and Brian Keith, as the Russian secretary-general, is terrific. It's long but certainly worth a view. 200m. **DIR:** David Greene. **CAST:** Rock Hudson, David Soul, Brian Keith, Cathy Lee Crosby, Katherine Helmond, Jeroen Krabbé. 1982

•**WORLD WITHOUT END** ★★1/2 First manned spaceflight to Mars goes awry and the crew is propelled five centuries into the future. They find themselves on an Earth slowly recovering from nuclear holocaust and inhabited by things dear to such films: giant spiders, primitive mutants, and beautiful women in high heels. Optimistic, decently acted, and well-produced, this is one of the better efforts of its decade and solid second-tier science fiction. 81m. **DIR:** Edward L. Bernds. **CAST:** Hugh Marlowe, Nancy Gates, Rod Taylor, Nelson Leigh, Shawn Smith, Lisa Montell. 1956

WORLD'S GREATEST ATHLETE, THE ★★★ John Amos is the athletics instructor at Merrivale College. He and his assistant, Tim Conway, travel to Africa to get away from their troubles and come across Nanu (Jan-Michael Vincent), the greatest natural athlete in the world. One of the better Disney college films. Rated G. 89m. **DIR:** Robert Scheerer. **CAST:** Jan-Michael Vincent, John Amos, Tim Conway, Roscoe Lee Browne. 1973

WORLD'S GREATEST LOVER, THE ★★1/2 Gene Wilder plays a would-be silent-movie star who tests for the part of the "new Valentino" while his wife (Carol Kane) runs off with the real Rudolph. Dom De-Luise is around to brighten things up, but writer-director Wilder's ideas of what's funny aren't quite right. Rated PG. 89m. **DIR:** Gene Wilder. **CAST:** Gene Wilder, Carol Kane, Dom DeLuise, Fritz Feld, Carl Ballantine, Michael Huddleston, Matt Collins, Ronny Graham. 1977

WORM EATERS, THE 🗜 Stomach-turning flick about southern town infested with night crawlers. Not rated. 75m. **DIR:** Herb Robins. 1977

WORST WITCH, THE ★★★★ Jill Murphy's charming children's book gets first-cabin treatment in this delightful made-for-cable adaptation that features Fairuza Balk as hapless young Mildred Hubble, the only student at Miss Cackle's International Academy for Witches who cannot properly perform her spells. Screenwriter Mary Pleshette Willis retains the book's whimsical tone, and Diana Rigg is deliciously spooky as the imperious head mistress. 70m. **DIR:** Robert Young. **CAST:** Diana Rigg, Charlotte Rae, Tim Curry, Fairuza Balk, Sabina Franklyn. 1986

WORTH WINNING 💘 TV weatherman thinks he's the ultimate ladies' man. Rated PG-13 for profanity and suggested sex. 104m. **DIR:** Will Mackenzie. **CAST:** Mark Harmon, Madeleine Stowe, Lesley Ann Warren, Maria Holvoe, Mark Blum, Andrea Martin, David Brenner. 1989

WOUNDED ★★1/2 A forest ranger hunts down the man who killed her fiancé in this routine chase-through-the-woods film. Rated R for violence and profanity. 91m. **DIR:** Richard Martin. **CAST:** Madchen Amick, Graham Greene, Adrian Pasdar. 1996

WOUNDED HEART ★★1/2 A ruthless businesswoman goes to Texas to secure her inheritance, but instead ends up falling in love in this made-for-cable original. Simplistic and hackneyed storyline. Not rated; contains violence. 95m. **DIR:** Vic Sarin. **CAST:** Paula DeVicq, Jon Hensley, Stuart Whitman. 1995

WOYZECK ★★★1/2 Powerful yet uneven adaptation of Georg Buchner's haunting, absurd opera. Klaus Kinski plays a man who plunges into madness and murder. In German with English subtitles. Not rated; contains nudity and violence. 82m. **DIR:** Werner Herzog. **CAST:** Klaus Kinski, Eva Mattes. 1978

WR: MYSTERIES OF THE ORGANISM ★★★★ Once-controversial film still has an anarchic kick, with too many ideas flying around to catch them all in one viewing. Writer-director Dusan Makavejev mixes documentary and fictional elements to explore the theories of sexologist Wilhelm Reich, with a number of amusing detours along the way. In Serbian with English subtitles. Not rated. 84m. **DIR:** Dusan Makavejev. **CAST:** Milena Dravic, Jagoda Kaloper. 1971

WRAITH, THE ★★ A small town in Arizona is visited by a spirit taking revenge on a gang of road pirates. Some nice car wrecks and explosions. Car buffs will like the Wraith Mobile. A typical shallow revenge picture without style, substance, or surprises. Rated PG. 93m. **DIR:** Mike Marvin. **CAST:** Charlie Sheen, Randy Quaid, Clint Howard, Griffin O'Neal. 1986

WRANGLER ★★1/2 Set in the Aussie outback, B-movie hunkster Jeff Fahey is the dashing businessman out to save Tushka Bergen from an evil rancher and a dangerous drover. The plot could have been lifted from a dime novel, but very pretty fluff. 93m. **DIR:** Ian Barry. **CAST:** Jeff Fahey, Tushka Bergen, Steven Vidler. 1993

WRECK OF THE MARY DEARE, THE ★★★ Sea captain Gary Cooper, in attempting to prove the crew and owners of his ship were involved in an insurance scam, is himself accused of dereliction. After a suspenseful start, this bogs down and becomes predictable. 100m. **DIR:** Michael Anderson. **CAST:** Gary Cooper, Charlton Heston, Michael Redgrave, Emlyn Williams, Cecil Parker, Alexander Knox, Virginia McKenna, Richard Harris. 1959

WRESTLING ERNEST HEMINGWAY ★★★1/2 Robert Duvall and Richard Harris show excellent teamwork in this easygoing drama about a Cuban barber and an Irish sea captain retired to a small Florida town. Director Randa Haines smooths out the aimless spots in Steve Conrad's episodic script, and the acting is first-rate. Sandra Bullock as a kindly waitress all but steals the show. Rated PG-13 for mild profanity. 122m. **DIR:** Randa Haines. **CAST:** Robert Duvall, Richard Harris, Sandra Bullock, Shirley MacLaine, Piper Laurie. 1993

WRITE TO KILL ★★1/2 Routine vendetta thriller has writer Scott Valentine tracking down the gang of counterfeiters who killed his brother. Rated R for violence and profanity. 94m. **DIR:** Reuben Preuss. **CAST:** Scott Valentine, Joan Severance, Chris Mulkey, G. W. Bailey. 1990

WRITTEN ON THE WIND ★★★1/2 Tame by today's standards, this film still provides quite a few good moments and an Academy Award–winning performance by Dorothy Malone. Rock Hudson and Robert Stack play good friends who meet, respectively, Dorothy Malone who has a problem just saying no and Lauren Bacall who is nice and loves Stack but loves his oil-dipped money even more. High-quality Hollywood soap opera. 99m. **DIR:** Douglas Sirk. **CAST:** Rock Hudson, Lauren Bacall, Robert Stack, Dorothy Malone, Robert Keith. 1956

WRONG ARM OF THE LAW, THE ★★★★ Peter Sellers is hilarious as Pearly Gates, the Cockney leader of a group of bandits. Sellers and his gang join forces with police inspector Parker (Lionel Jeffries) after a group of Australians pose as police and capture Sellers's stolen goods. This British comedy contains enough to keep most viewers in stitches. B&W;

94m. DIR: Cliff Owen. CAST: Peter Sellers, Lionel Jeffries, Bernard Cribbins, Davy Kaye, Nanette Newman. 1962

WRONG BOX, THE ★★★★ Some of Britain's best-known comics appear in this screwball farce about two zany families who battle over an inheritance in Victorian England. The film borders on black humor and is a delightful comedy. 105m. DIR: Bryan Forbes. CAST: John Mills, Ralph Richardson, Dudley Moore, Peter Sellers, Peter Cook, Michael Caine, Nanette Newman, Wilfrid Lawson, Tony Hancock. 1966

WRONG GUYS, THE ★★ Low-energy farce about the camping-trip reunion of a 1962 Cub Scout Troop. The troop is mistaken for FBI agents by a crazed convict, and therein lies the comedy. Rated PG for language and comic-book violence. 86m. DIR: Danny Bilson. CAST: Louie Anderson, Richard Lewis, Richard Belzer, Franklin Ajaye, Tim Thomerson, John Goodman, Brion James, Ernie Hudson, Alice Ghostley, Kathleen Freeman. 1988

WRONG IS RIGHT ★★★★ Sean Connery, as a globe-trotting television reporter, gives what may be the best performance of his career, in this gorgeous, thoroughly entertaining end-of-the-world black comedy, written, produced, and directed by Richard Brooks. It's an updated combination of *Network* and *Dr. Strangelove*, and wickedly funny. Rated R because of profanity and violence. 117m. DIR: Richard Brooks. CAST: Sean Connery, Robert Conrad, George Grizzard, Katharine Ross, G. D. Spradlin, John Saxon, Henry Silva, Leslie Nielsen, Robert Webber, Rosalind Cash, Hardy Krüger, Dean Stockwell, Ron Moody. 1982

WRONG MAN, THE (1956) ★★★★ In this frightening true-life tale, Henry Fonda plays a man falsely accused of robbery. Vera Miles is his wife, who can't handle the changes wrought in their lives by this gross injustice. Fonda is excellent. B&W; 105m. DIR: Alfred Hitchcock. CAST: Henry Fonda, Vera Miles, Anthony Quayle, Harold J. Stone, Nehemiah Persoff. 1956

WRONG MAN, THE (1993) ★★★★ Raymond Chandler's *film noir* sensibilities blend with Tennessee Williams's earthy sensuality in this delicious drama that finds a ship-hand on the run for a murder he didn't commit. Includes a wonderfully eerie Los Lobos soundtrack. 98m. DIR: Jim McBride. CAST: Rosanna Arquette, Kevin Anderson, John Lithgow, Jorge Cervera Jr. 1993

WRONG MOVE, THE ★★ Rudiger Vogler is cast as a would-be writer in this slow-moving character drama. It concerns a soul-searching odyssey across Germany by a diverse group of misfits. Initially absorbing, yet too disconcerting to recommend. German with English subtitles. 103m. DIR: Wim Wenders. CAST: Rudiger Vogler, Hanna Schygulla, Nastassja Kinski. 1978

WRONGFULLY ACCUSED 💔 Leslie Nielsen finds himself wrongfully accused of murder in this parody of *The Fugitive*. Endless sight gags and toilet humor fail to measure up to Nielsen's successful spoofs (*Airplane*, *Naked Gun*). Rated PG-13 for sexual situations. 85m. DIR: Pat Proft. CAST: Leslie Nielsen, Kelly LeBrock, Melinda McGraw, Richard Crenna. 1998 DVD

WUTHERING HEIGHTS (1939) ★★★★ Taken from the Emily Brontë novel, this is a haunting, mesmerizing film. Set on the murky, isolated moors, it tells the tale of Heathcliff, a foundling Gypsy boy who loves Cathy, the spoiled daughter of the house. Their affair, born in childhood, is doomed. As the star-crossed lovers, Laurence Olivier and Merle Oberon are impressive. B&W; 103m. DIR: William Wyler. CAST: Merle Oberon, Laurence Olivier, Flora Robson, David Niven. 1939 DVD

WUTHERING HEIGHTS (1953) ★★1/2 Luis Buñuel's film of the Emily Brontë classic. This Spanish version in no way measures up to the 1939 original. The Richard Wagner music, however, is perfect for the melodramatic performances. 90m. DIR: Luis Buñuel. CAST: Iraseme Dilian, Jorge Mistral. 1953

WUTHERING HEIGHTS (1971) ★★1/2 Inventive but not great rendition of Emily Brontë's classic about the star-crossed lovers, Heathcliff (Timothy Dalton) and Cathy (Anna Calder-Marshall). Dalton is especially good as Cathy's smoldering, abused, and later vengeful love. The 1939 version is still the best. Rated G. 105m. DIR: Robert Fuest. CAST: Timothy Dalton, Anna Calder-Marshall, Harry Andrews, Hugh Griffith. 1971

WYATT EARP ★★★1/2 Perhaps if this hadn't followed the energetic *Tombstone* into release, *Wyatt Earp* might have seemed fresher. The film moves in fits and starts as it covers more of Earp's life than we've previously seen. That said, it is most definitely a good film, though not the great one its makers had intended. Rated PG-13 for violence, profanity, and suggested sex. DIR: Lawrence Kasdan. CAST: Kevin Costner, Dennis Quaid, Gene Hackman, Jeff Fahey, Mark Harmon, Michael Madsen, Catherine O'Hara, Bill Pullman, Isabella Rossellini, Tom Sizemore, JoBeth Williams, Mare Winningham, David Andrews, Linden Ashby, James Gammon, Adam Baldwin, Annabeth Gish, Betty Buckley. 1994

WYATT EARP: RETURN TO TOMBSTONE ★★★1/2 An original Wyatt Earp (Hugh O'Brian) looks back on the highlights of his life as a frontier lawman. Made-for-TV production is a surprisingly effective combination of new footage and colorized sequences from O'Brian's classic TV series, *The Life and Legend of Wyatt Earp*. A timely tribute. 96m. DIR: Frank McDonald, Paul Landres. CAST: Hugh O'Brian, Bruce Boxleitner, Harry Carey Jr., Paul Brinegar, Bo Hopkins, Alex Hyde-White, Martin Kove, Don Meredith, Jay Underwood, Douglas Fowley, Rayford Barnes, Trevor Bardette, Morgan Woodward, Lloyd Corrigan. 1994

WYOMING OUTLAW ★★★1/2 One of the best episodes in the popular "Three Mesquiteers" cowboy series. Silent-era *Tarzan* Elmo Lincoln, in a rare return to the screen, appears as a marshal. B&W; 62m. DIR: George Sherman. CAST: John Wayne, Ray "Crash" Corrigan, Raymond Hatton, Pamela Blake, Don Barry, LeRoy Mason, Yakima Canutt, Charles Middleton, Elmo Lincoln, David Sharpe. 1939

X (THE MAN WITH THE X-RAY EYES) ★★★ Intriguing, offbeat tale of a scientist (Ray Milland) who discovers a drug that gives him the power to see through objects. He has a great time at first, but soon becomes addicted and begins seeing more and more, until.... This production is highly enjoyable, with a surprisingly effective role by comedian Don Rickles as a carnival barker. 80m. DIR: Roger Corman. CAST: Ray Milland, Diana Van Der Vlis, Harold J. Stone, John Hoyt, Don Rickles. 1963

X—THE UNKNOWN ★★★★ Scientist Dean Jagger, in one of his best performances, battles a deadly substance from the center of the earth in this outstanding Hammer Studios production. While not officially an entry in the similar *Quatermass* series, it is very much on a par—productionwise and in first-rate storytelling—with *The Creeping Unknown*, *Enemy from Space*, and *Five Million Years to Earth*. It was Hammer stalwart Jimmy Sangster's first produced screenplay. B&W; 80m. DIR: Leslie Norman. CAST: Dean Jagger, Leo McKern, Edward Judd, Anthony Newley, Edward Chapman, William Lucas, Peter Hammond. 1956 DVD

X FROM OUTER SPACE, THE ★★1/2 A mission to Mars returns with an alien spore that grows into Guilala, a huge, energy-absorbing monster that looks like a giant chicken with scales. Abundant destruction of model cities and planes highlights this none-too-professional entry in the Japanese big-rubber-monster movie category. Rated PG. 88m. DIR: Kazui Nihonmatzu. CAST: Toshiya Wazaki, Peggy Neal. 1967

X, Y AND ZEE 🐾 Pointless tale of sexual relationships. Rated R. 110m. DIR: Brian G. Hutton. CAST: Elizabeth Taylor, Michael Caine, Susannah York, Margaret Leighton, John Standing. 1972

X-FILES, THE (1998) ★★★1/2 Based on the popular television series, this feature film is both a culmination of and an expansion on many of the themes of the show's first five seasons. This ambitious science-fiction tale generates a few seat-jumping moments even for the uninitiated. Oh yes: Scully and Mulder discover the real intentions of alien visitors throughout history. Rated PG-13 for violence and creepy images. 117m. DIR: Rob Bowman. CAST: David Duchovny, Gillian Anderson, Martin Landau, Blythe Danner, Armin Mueller-Stahl, Mitch Pileggi, William B. Davis, John Neville. 1998 DVD

X-FILES, THE (TV SERIES) ★★★1/2 FBI agents Fox Mulder (David Duchovny) and Dana Scully (Gillian Anderson) investigate bizarre occurrences around the globe in this cult favorite from the Fox television network. Created by Chris Carter, the series covers all aspects of the outré, from voodoo to alien abductions. Made for TV. 90m. DIR: Various. CAST: David Duchovny, Gillian Anderson, Mitch Pileggi, Jerry Hardin, William B. Davis, Nicholas Lea, John Neville, Bruce Harwood, Steven Williams. 1993

XANADU ★★1/2 This musical lacks inspiration and story line. It is basically a full-length video that includes some good numbers by Olivia Newton-John and Gene Kelly. See it for the musical entertainment, not for the story. Rated PG. 88m. DIR: Robert Greenwald. CAST: Olivia Newton-John, Gene Kelly, Michael Beck, James Sloyan, Sandahl Bergman. 1980 DVD

•XIU XIU: THE SENT DOWN GIRL ★★★ During Mao Zedong's Cultural Revolution, a city girl is sent to the country to learn horse wrangling; homesickness and hardship eventually break her spirit. Director Joan Chen draws a sharp contrast between the utopian myth of Maoist propaganda and the grim reality of the young girl's life. Acting by Lu Lu as the heroine and Lopsang as her grizzled mentor is excellent. In Mandarin with English subtitles. Rated R for sexual scenes. 99m. DIR: Joan Chen. CAST: Lu Lu, Lopsang, Jie Gao, Wengqiang Wang. 1998 DVD

XTRO 🐾 Grotesquely slimy sci-fi horror flick with an idiotic plot that revolves around a series of repulsive bladder effects. Rated R. 84m. DIR: Harry Davenport. CAST: Philip Sayer, Bernice Stegers, Maryam D'Abo. 1982 DVD

XTRO II ★★★ If you saw the original *Xtro*, forget all about it. *Xtro II* has a whole new exciting plot that doesn't even follow the original. The Nexus computer program transports three scientists to a parallel universe, only to have one return with a hideous creature inside of it. The few remaining scientists inside the project attempt to kill off the beast. Rated R for violence. 92m. DIR: Harry Davenport. CAST: Jan-Michael Vincent, Paul Kosto, Tara Buckman. 1991

XTRO: WATCH THE SKIES (XTRO 3) 🐾 Familiar UFO-conspiracy story about a misfit band of Marines who journey to an uncharted island on a top-secret mission only to encounter a bloodthirsty alien. Rated R. 97m. DIR: Harry Davenport. CAST: Sal Landi, Andrew Divoff, Karen Moncrieff, David M. Parker, Jim Hanks, Andrea Lauren-Herz. 1995

YAKUZA, THE ★★★★★ In this superb blending of the American gangster and Japanese samurai genres, Robert Mitchum plays Harry Kilmer, an ex-G.I. who returns to Japan when a friend's daughter has been kidnapped and is held for ransom. This forces Kilmer to call on a onetime enemy who owes him a debt. Thus begins a clash of cultures and a web of intrigue that keep the viewers on the edge of their seats. Rated R. 112m. DIR: Sydney Pollack. CAST: Robert Mitchum, Brian Keith, Ken Takakura, Herb Edelman, Richard Jordan. 1975

YANK IN THE RAF, A ★★1/2 Title is misleading in this story of an American pilot, Tyrone Power, enlisting in the British air force and falling in love with

Betty Grable. Standard plot lines and lack of any real action do not help matters in this slow-moving, generally uninteresting film. 98m. **DIR:** Henry King. **CAST:** Tyrone Power, Betty Grable, Reginald Gardiner, John Sutton. 1941

YANKEE DOODLE DANDY ★★★★ Magnetic James Cagney, stepping out of his gangster roles, gives a magnificent performance in the life story of dancing vaudevillian George M. Cohan. An outstanding show-business story with unassuming but effective production. B&W; 126m. **DIR:** Michael Curtiz. **CAST:** James Cagney, Joan Leslie, Walter Huston, Irene Manning, Rosemary DeCamp, Richard Whorf, Jeanne Cagney. 1942

YANKS ★★★1/2 Director John Schlesinger re-created classic Hollywood, when smiling men went bravely off to battle while dedicated women stayed behind, in this World War II saga of England's reaction to young American GIs. Richard Gere (who cemented his pretty-boy image with this role) and Lisa Eichhorn handle the primary boy-meets-girl subplot, while William Devane and Vanessa Redgrave embark on a more subdued relationship. Rated R for nudity. 140m. **DIR:** John Schlesinger. **CAST:** Richard Gere, Vanessa Redgrave, William Devane, Lisa Eichhorn. 1979

YARN PRINCESS, THE ★★★1/2 Jean Smart delivers a triumphant performance in this made-for-television drama about a mentally challenged mother who is forced to become the main care provider of her home and family when her husband becomes seriously ill. Dalene Young's screenplay allows her to grow as a person and maintain her dignity without resorting to melodrama. Not rated. 92m. **DIR:** Tom McLoughlin. **CAST:** Jean Smart, Robert Pastorelli, Dennis Boutsikaris, Shirley Knight, Jared Rushton. 1993

YEAR IN PROVENCE, A ★★★★1/2 Based on Peter Mayle's delightful book, this four-part TV series is a visual, breezy delight. John Thaw and Lindsay Duncan are the British escapees who set up house in the south of France and chronicle their first year. Humorous and full of élan, but it presents a caricatured British view of the French villagers. Not rated. Four 90-minute episodes. **DIR:** David Tucker. **CAST:** John Thaw, Lindsay Duncan. 1992

YEAR MY VOICE BROKE, THE ★★★★ A likable Australian coming-of-age drama with echoes of *The Last Picture Show* and the novels of S. E. Hinton. Though the film market has been saturated with adolescent dramas circa 1962, this movie's refreshing honesty makes it a welcome addition to the genre. Rated PG-13, with profanity and some mild sexual situations. 103m. **DIR:** John Duigan. **CAST:** Noah Taylor. 1988 DVD

YEAR OF LIVING DANGEROUSLY, THE ★★★★1/2 Set in 1965 Indonesia when the Sukarno regime was toppling from pressures left and right. Mel Gibson and Sigourney Weaver star as an Australian journalist and a British diplomatic attaché, respectively. The film, however, belongs to Linda Hunt, in her Academy Award–winning role as free-lance photographer Billy Kwan. Rated R for profanity, nudity, and violence. 115m. **DIR:** Peter Weir. **CAST:** Mel Gibson,

Sigourney Weaver, Linda Hunt, Michael Murphy, Bill Kerr, Noel Ferrier. 1983 DVD

YEAR OF THE COMET ★★1/2 In this slightly silly romantic adventure-comedy, Penelope Ann Miller finds a huge bottle of the world's finest and rarest wine—Lafitte 1811—only to have to rely on a boorish troubleshooter (Timothy Daly) to keep it out of the hands of thieves. This determinedly lightweight film was written by William Goldman. Rated PG-13 for profanity and violence. 91m. **DIR:** Peter Yates. **CAST:** Penelope Ann Miller, Timothy Daly, Louis Jourdan, Art Malik, Ian Richardson. 1992

YEAR OF THE DRAGON 🦃 Youth gangs in New York's Chinatown. Rated R for violence, profanity, gore, simulated sex, and nudity. 136m. **DIR:** Michael Cimino. **CAST:** Mickey Rourke, John Lone, Ariane, Leonard Termo. 1985

YEAR OF THE GUN ★★★ An American novelist (Andrew McCarthy) returns to terrorist-plagued Italy in 1978, hoping to free a married woman (Valeria Golino) from her abusive, politically powerful husband. A chance meeting with a photojournalist (Sharon Stone) puts our hero's life in danger, and a series of crosses and double crosses leads him to the truth. Rated R for violence, nudity, and profanity. 111m. **DIR:** John Frankenheimer. **CAST:** Andrew McCarthy, Valeria Golino, Sharon Stone, John Pankow. 1991 DVD

YEAR OF THE QUIET SUN ★★★★ A beautifully orchestrated meditation on the nature of love, this import is about a Polish widow after World War II who becomes romantically involved with an American soldier during a war-crimes investigation. In Polish with English subtitles. 106m. **DIR:** Krzysztof Zanussi. **CAST:** Scott Wilson, Maja Komorowska. 1985

YEARLING, THE ★★★★1/2 A beautiful film version of Marjorie Kinnan Rawlings's sensitive story of a young boy's love for a pet fawn that his father must destroy. Simply told, this emotionally charged drama has been rated one of the finest films ever made. 134m. **DIR:** Clarence Brown. **CAST:** Gregory Peck, Jane Wyman, Claude Jarman Jr., Chill Wills. 1946

YELLOW ★★★★ Refreshingly insightful take on the teen comedy genre, and not just because they're all Korean Americans here. Writer-director Lee balances typical graduation-night high jinks with serious character drama, a little mystery, and a marvelous agenda about building bridges across age, racial, cultural, and gender divides. A little rough in places, but by and large an outstanding first feature. Not rated; contains language and mild violence. 101m. **DIR:** Chris Chan Lee. **CAST:** Michael Daeho Chung, Burt Bulos, Angie Suh, Mia Suh, Soon-Teck Oh. 1998

YELLOW CAB MAN, THE ★★★1/2 Red Skelton is a bumbling cabdriver who develops a process for a new unbreakable safety glass. Crooks see the potential and come after it. Good sight gags. B&W; 85m. **DIR:** Jack Donohue. **CAST:** Red Skelton, Gloria De Haven, Walter Slezak, Edward Arnold, James Gleason, Jay C. Flippen. 1950

YELLOW EARTH ★★★★ In 1939, a communist soldier is sent to a remote province to collect folk songs and learn about rural life. The first film from direc-

Chen Kaige (*Farewell My Concubine*) is a small rk of beautiful simplicity, in which the faces of raracters communicate to the viewer feelings they annot share with each other. In Chinese with English subtitles. Not rated, contains no objectionable terial. 89m. **DIR:** Chen Kaige. **CAST:** Xue Bai, Wang eqi. **1984**

LLOW HAIR AND THE FORTRESS OF GOLD ★★ de to look like a 1940s serial, this film is more like emale *Indiana Jones.* Yellow Hair is a famed fe- le Indian warrior, who is sent to find a lost trea- e. Along the way she fights arrows, avalanches, l greedy gringos. Cameo appearances by ghetti Western character actors make this a fun n. Rated R for violence. 102m. **DIR:** Matt Cimber. **ST:** Laurene Landon, Ken Roberson, Luis Lorenzo, o Sambrell, Claudia Gravy, Frank Brana, Eduardo ardo. **1984**

LLOW SUBMARINE ★★★★ Clever cartoon ver- ns of John, Paul, George, and Ringo journey into pperland to save it from the Blue Meanies in this lightful blend of psychedelic animation and flight Beatles music. "All You Need Is Love," hen I'm 64," "Lucy in the Sky with Diamonds," and ellow Submarine" provide the background and wer the action in a film that epitomized the flower neration. 85m. **DIR:** George Dunning. **1968 DVD**

LLOWBEARD ★★1/2 This pirate comedy barely ntains a boatload of laughs under the directorship first-timer Mel Damski. Rated PG for profanity, dity, violence, gore, and scatological humor. 101m. **R:** Mel Damski. **CAST:** Graham Chapman, Eric Idle, hn Cleese, Peter Cook, Cheech and Chong, Peter yle, Madeline Kahn, Marty Feldman, Kenneth Mars. 83

NTL ★★1/2 Barbra Streisand, who also pro- ced, coscripted, and directed, stars as a woman o must disguise herself as a man in order to pur- e an education among Orthodox Jews in turn-of- e-century eastern Europe. The story is fine, but the ngs all sound the same. Still, *Yentl* is, overall, a atchable work. Rated PG for brief nudity. 134m. **R:** Barbra Streisand. **CAST:** Barbra Streisand, Mandy atinkin, Amy Irving, Nehemiah Persoff, Steven Hill. **483**

ES, GIORGIO ★★ In this old-fashioned star vehi- e, Luciano Pavarotti makes a less-than-memorable reen debut as Giorgio Fini, a macho Italian tenor ho meets a pretty Boston throat specialist Kathryn Harrold) when his voice suddenly fails m. They fall in love and the viewer falls asleep. ated PG for adult themes. 110m. **DIR:** Franklin J. haffner. **CAST:** Luciano Pavarotti, Kathryn Harrold, ldie Albert, James Hong. **1982**

ES, PRIME MINISTER ★★★ British sitcom man- ges to lampoon not only its own government but the orld at large. Paul Eddington stars as the novice rime minister who works more on his photo oppor- nities than his governing policies. He falls easy rey to his ever crafty, power-hungry Cabinet secre- ry, played to perfection by Nigel Hawthorne. Not ated, its aim is to offend all. Each tape contains ree to four episodes. each 90m. **DIR:** Sydney Lot-

terby. **CAST:** Paul Eddington, Nigel Hawthorne, Derek Fowlds. **1987**

YESTERDAY MACHINE, THE ♥ Nazi scientist has invented a time machine that can move people to the past and the future. 85m. **DIR:** Russ Marker. **CAST:** Tim Holt, Jack Herman. **1962**

YESTERDAY, TODAY AND TOMORROW ★★★1/2 Hilarious three-vignette romp teaming Sophia Loren and Marcello Mastroianni. The first (and best) story features Loren as an impoverished woman who con- tinues to have babies in order to avoid a jail sen- tence, with Mastroianni as her husband who gives in to the scheme. Italian dubbed into English. 119m. **DIR:** Vittorio De Sica. **CAST:** Sophia Loren, Marcello Mastroianni, Tina Plca. **1964**

YESTERDAY'S HERO ★★★ Ian McShane plays a washed-up alcoholic ex-soccer star who wants to make a comeback. He gets assistance from his old flame (Suzanne Somers), a pop star, and her singing partner (Paul Nicolas). Not rated. 95m. **DIR:** Neil Leifer. **CAST:** Ian McShane, Adam Faith, Paul Nicolas, Suzanne Somers. **1979**

YESTERDAY'S TARGET ★★ David Bourla's con- fused and rambling time-travel script plays like the pilot of an unsold series, which failed for obvious rea- sons. Four future metahumans with psi talents travel back to our present in an effort to change their past. Been there, done that. Rated R for violence and pro- fanity. 84m. **DIR:** Barry Samson. **CAST:** Daniel Bald- win, Stacy Haiduk, T. K. Carter, LeVar Burton, Malcolm McDowell. **1996**

YIN AND YANG OF MR. GO, THE ★★ Jeff Bridges would probably like to forget that he made his debut in this confusing comic thriller about a Hong Kong weapons dealer who becomes a good guy due to the intervention of Buddha. Rated PG; contains brief nu- dity and violence. 89m. **DIR:** Burgess Meredith. **CAST:** James Mason, Jeff Bridges, Peter Lind Hayes, Burgess Meredith, Broderick Crawford. **1970**

YODELIN' KID FROM PINE RIDGE ★★★ Plot is reminiscent of his first film, *Tumbling Tumble- weeds,* as Gene Autry is banished by his father only to return to his Georgia hometown with a Wild West show five years later to find his father murdered. B&W; 54m. **DIR:** Joseph Kane. **CAST:** Gene Autry, Smi- ley Burnette, Betty Bronson, Charles Middleton. **1937**

YOJIMBO ★★★★1/2 Viewed from different per- spectives this can be the most devastating comedy ever made; Kurosawa's parody of the American West- ern; or his satire on the United States and Soviet Union's achieving peace through nuclear prolifera- tion. The plot: an unemployed samurai in nine- teenth-century Japan sells his services to two rival merchants, each with killer gangs that are tearing the town apart. The film is boisterous and exuberant. (Remade by Sergio Leone as *A Fistful of Dollars.*) No rating, but very violent. B&W; 110m. **DIR:** Akira Kuro- sawa. **CAST:** Toshiro Mifune, Eijiro Tono. **1961 DVD**

YOL ★★★1/2 Winner of the Grand Prix at the Cannes Film Festival, this work written by Turkish filmmaker and political prisoner Yilmaz Guney fol- lows several inmates of a minimum-security prison who are granted a few days' leave, telling their sto- ries in parallel scenes. Guney—who smuggled instructions out of prison to his trusted assistants, then escaped from prison and edited the film—was hailed at Cannes for creating an eloquent protest against suppression and totalitarian government. Not rated, but the film has violence and suggested sex. 111m. DIR: Serif Goren. CAST: Tarik Akan, Serif Sezer. 1982

YOLANDA AND THE THIEF ★★ An exotic fantasy, staged with near-cloying opulence, and now a cult favorite. Down on his luck con man Fred Astaire finds beautiful, rich, convent-bred Lucille Bremer praying to her guardian angel. His eye on her money, he claims to be the angel. 108m. DIR: Vincente Minnelli. CAST: Fred Astaire, Lucille Bremer, Frank Morgan, Mildred Natwick, Ludwig Stossel, Leon Ames, Gigi Perreau. 1945

YONGARY—MONSTER FROM THE DEEP ★★ A Korean entry in the big-rubber-monster movie genre. An earthquake-causing monster (a dead ringer for Godzilla) rises to wage a destructive path across the country. Bad miniatures and a poor script make this more funny than scary. Rated PG. 79m. DIR: Kim Ki-duk. CAST: Oh Young Il. 1969

YOU'RE A BIG BOY NOW ★★★1/2 Francis Ford Coppola not only directed this (his first) film but also wrote the screenplay. Peter Kastner, the product of overprotective parents, learns about life from streetwise go-go dancer Elizabeth Hartman. Fast-paced and very entertaining. 96m. DIR: Francis Ford Coppola. CAST: Peter Kastner, Elizabeth Hartman, Geraldine Page, Julie Harris, Rip Torn, Michael Dunn, Tony Bill, Karen Black. 1966

YOU'RE JINXED FRIEND, YOU JUST MET SACRAMENTO ★★ A peaceful cowboy and his children are forced into a showdown with a spiteful town boss. Unimaginative, mindless spaghetti oater with Ty Hardin, made after his successful Warner Bros. *Bronco* TV series ended. 90m. DIR: Giorgio Cristallini. CAST: Ty Hardin, Christian Hay, Jenny Atkins. 1970

YOU'RE NOT ELECTED, CHARLIE BROWN ★★★★ This school-themed special includes some classic material, from Sally's troubles with her locker (she can't reach it), to Linus's bid for class president ... which seems a guaranteed success until the candidate extols the virtues of the Great Pumpkin. Listen for one of Vince Guaraldi's jazziest soundtracks. Not rated. 25m. DIR: Bill Melendez. 1972

YOU BET YOUR LIFE (TV SERIES) ★★★1/2 Over the years, two different game formats were devised for this show, but it was the interview segment that made the program a winner. In grilling the contestants, who ranged from average folks to celebrities to bizarre characters, Groucho Marx invariably got off a number of clever quips. B&W; 30m. DIR: Robert Dwan, Bernie Smith. CAST: Groucho Marx, George Fenneman. 1950–1961

YOU CAN'T CHEAT AN HONEST MAN ★★★1/2 Nearly plotless, this is, star W. C. Fields admitted, "a jumble of vaudeville skits"—which, nonetheless, brings together, with hilarious results, a cast of exquisite comedians. Fields fans will relish it all, of course. B&W; 76m. DIR: George Marshall. CAST: W. C.

Fields, Edgar Bergen, Constance Moore, Mary Forbe Thurston Hall, Eddie "Rochester" Anderson. 1939

YOU CAN'T FOOL YOUR WIFE ★★★ A disil sioned Lucille Ball leaves her husband (James El son) and then tries to patch things up at a costur party. This is an average comedy with Ball playi two parts. B&W; 68m. DIR: Ray McCarey. CAST: L cille Ball, Robert Coote, James Ellison. 1940

YOU CAN'T HURRY LOVE ★★ A young man leav Ohio to live with his hip cousin in Los Angeles. The he meets assorted women through a video datii service. Rated R for nudity and profanity. 92m. DI Richard Martini. CAST: David Leisure, Scott McGinn Anthony Geary, Bridget Fonda, Frank Bonner, Kris McNichol. 1987

YOU CAN'T TAKE IT WITH YOU (1938) ★★★★ Frank Capra's adaptation of the beloved Kaufma and Hart stage classic continues to charm auc ences. The fun starts when James Stewart and Jea Arthur fall in love and announce their desire to we This zany romp won 1938s Oscar for best pictur B&W; 126m. DIR: Frank Capra. CAST: James Stewa Lionel Barrymore, Jean Arthur, Edward Arnold, Sprin Byington, Mischa Auer, Ann Miller. 1938

YOU CAN'T TAKE IT WITH YOU (1984) ★★★★1 Filmed on one set before a live audience, th Pulitzer Prize-winning Kaufman and Hart play fe tures Jason Robards as the head of a very eccentr family. Now they must be on their best behavior meet the parents of their daughter's beau. 116r DIR: Kirk Browning. CAST: Jason Robards Jr., Georg Rose, Elizabeth Wilson, Colleen Dewhurst. 1984

•**YOU KNOW MY NAME** ★★★1/2 TNT original pay tribute to lawman Bill Tilghman (played by Sam E liott), the famed marshal called out of retirement become a small Oklahoma town's police chief 1924. Elliott takes on a Gary Cooper-ish persona the quiet, relentless good guy. Showdown is rivetin Not rated; contains profanity and violence. 91m. DII John Kent Harrison. CAST: Sam Elliott, Arliss Howar Carolyn McCormick, Walter Olkewicz. 1999

YOU LIGHT UP MY LIFE ★★1/2 Pretty weak stor concerning a young girl, Didi Conn, trying to make in show business. Notable for the title song, fili proves it's tough to make a hit song stretch into a fea ture film. Rated PG. 90m. DIR: Joseph Brooks. CAS Didi Conn, Michael Zaslow, Joe Silver, Stephen Nathar 1977

YOU MUST REMEMBER THIS ★★1/2 Heavy handed message film exposes the shameful portray als of black actors in early films. Robert Guillaum delivers a wooden performance as a former film d rector who could not exploit his black actors Though not overly entertaining, this—being a Wor derworks Production—is worthy of family viewin and discussion. Not rated; contains no objectionabl material. 102m. DIR: Helaine Head. CAST: Robert Guil laume, Tim Reid, Maria Celedonio, Vonte Swee Vonetta McGee. 1992

YOU ONLY LIVE ONCE ★★ About a three-time lose (Henry Fonda) who can't even be saved by the love o a good woman (Sylvia Sidney) because society won' allow him to go straight. This film is a real downer recommended for Fonda fans only. B&W; 86m. DIR:

tz Lang. **CAST:** Henry Fonda, Sylvia Sidney, William rgan, Barton MacLane, Jerome Cowan, Margaret milton, Ward Bond, Guinn Williams. **1937**

OU ONLY LIVE TWICE ★★★ Sean Connery as mes Bond—who could expect more? Well, a better ot and more believable cliff-hanger situations me to mind. Still, this entry isn't a bad 007, and it es star the best Bond. 116m. **DIR:** Lewis Gilbert. **ST:** Sean Connery, Akiko Wakabayashi, Tetsuro mba, Mie Hama, Karin Dor, Bernard Lee, Lois Max- ll, Desmond Llewellyn, Donald Pleasence. **1967**

OU SO CRAZY ★★ Martin Lawrence's crude, wd, sometimes very funny stand-up comedy is not daring or as fresh as he may want us to think. Act cludes riffs on Caucasians reacting to African mericans who talk at movies, racism, crack, the odney King beating, male and female genitalia, east infections, and the inner strength of his other. Filmed at the Brooklyn Academy of Music's ajestic Theatre. Not rated by the MPAA. 86m. **R:** Thomas Schlamme. **CAST:** Martin Lawrence. 994

OU TALKIN' TO ME ★★★ A struggling young New ork actor whose idol is Robert De Niro (particularly e Niro's performance in *Taxi Driver*) moves to Los ngeles seeking his big break. Quirky offbeat film at eventually succeeds despite weak direction and umsy dialogue. Rated R for violence and profanity. 7m. **DIR:** Charles Winkler. **CAST:** Jim Youngs, Faith ord, Mykelti Williamson, James Noble. **1987**

OU WERE NEVER LOVELIER ★★★★ In this in- eresting story, Fred Astaire goes stepping about ith the most glamorous of all the stars—Rita Hay- orth. This film's worth seeing twice. B&W; 97m. **IR:** William A. Seiter. **CAST:** Fred Astaire, Rita Hay- orth, Adolphe Menjou, Leslie Brooks, Adele Mara. 942

OU'LL FIND OUT ★★★ Three titans of terror— oris Karloff, Peter Lorre, and Bela Lugosi—men- ce bandleader Kay Kyser and heiress Helen Parrish n this silly but amiable comedy. Kyser isn't much of screen personality, but director David Butler keeps he comedy, music, and suspense nicely balanced. &W; 97m. **DIR:** David Butler. **CAST:** Kay Kyser, Peter orre, Boris Karloff, Bela Lugosi, Dennis O'Keefe, He- en Parrish. **1940**

OU'LL NEVER GET RICH ★★★1/2 Musical com- dy has play producer Fred Astaire getting drafted ight before his big show. Somehow he manages to erve his country and put the show on while romanc- ng Rita Hayworth. B&W; 88m. **DIR:** Sidney Lanfield. **AST:** Fred Astaire, Rita Hayworth, John Hubbard, Robert Benchley, Osa Massen, Frieda Inescort, Guinn Villiams. **1941**

YOUNG AMERICANS, THE ★★★1/2 Hard-hitting rime-drama about a Los Angeles narcotics cop who's loaned to Scotland Yard in an attempt to put an end to the reign of terror of an American drug ealer intent on taking over the drug trade in Lon- lon. Rated R for extreme violence, language, and dult situations. 108m. **DIR:** Danny Cannon. **CAST:** Harvey Keitel, Viggo Mortensen, John Wood. **1993**

YOUNG AND INNOCENT ★★★ Reputedly director Alfred Hitchcock's favorite of the films he made in

Great Britain, this film employs one of his favorite devices, that of an innocent man avoiding the police while attempting to catch the real criminal and prove his innocence. Not as well-known as many of his other films, this seldom-seen movie is vintage Hitchcock and on a par with much of his best work. B&W; 80m. **DIR:** Alfred Hitchcock. **CAST:** Derrek de Marney, Nova Pilbeam, Percy Marmont, Edward Rigby, Mary Clare, Basil Radford. **1937 DVD**

YOUNG AND WILLING ★★1/2 Hope springs eternal in the hearts of a gaggle of show business neophytes living and loving in a New York theatrical boarding- house. Cute and entertaining, but formula. B&W; 82m. **DIR:** Edward H. Griffith. **CAST:** William Holden, Susan Hayward, Eddie Bracken, Barbara Britton, Robert Benchley. **1943**

YOUNG AT HEART ★★★1/2 A glossy remake of the Warner Bros. 1938 success *Four Daughters*. The plot presents Doris Day as a refined New England lass from a respected family who marries a down-on-his- luck musician (Frank Sinatra). 117m. **DIR:** Gordon Douglas. **CAST:** Doris Day, Frank Sinatra, Gig Young, Ethel Barrymore, Dorothy Malone. **1955**

YOUNG AT HEART COMEDIANS, THE ★★ Some of America's most famous comedians join together for this cable special. Moderately funny but dated mate- rial marks their routines. Not rated. 77m. **DIR:** Joe Hostettler. **CAST:** Carl Ballantine, Shelley Berman, Norm Crosby, Jackie Gayle, George Gobel, Jackie Ver- non, Henny Youngman, David Brenner. **1984**

YOUNG BESS ★★★1/2 Lavish, colorful, beauti- fully acted historical tale about England's Henry VIII and his tempestuous young daughter, Elizabeth. Charles Laughton repeats his Oscar-winning turn as the egotistical king. Good action and fiery perfor- mances. 112m. **DIR:** George Sidney. **CAST:** Charles Laughton, Jean Simmons, Stewart Granger, Deborah Kerr, Leo G. Carroll. **1953**

YOUNG BILL HICKOK ★★1/2 Highly fictionalized tale of Wild Bill Hickok takes place after the Civil War when Roy Rogers (as Hickok) goes after foreign agents trying to gain control of California land. Mud- dled. B&W; 54m. **DIR:** Joseph Kane. **CAST:** Roy Rogers, George "Gabby" Hayes, Julie Bishop, Sally Payne. **1940**

YOUNG CATHERINE ★★★ Lavish cable-TV cos- tume drama focuses on the early life of Russia's Catherine the Great and her ascent to the throne. Political intrigue and romance take center stage in this rather lengthy but always interesting film. 165m. **DIR:** Michael Anderson. **CAST:** Julia Ormond, Vanessa Redgrave, Christopher Plummer, Franco Nero, Marthe Keller, Maximilian Schell, Mark Frankel, Reece Dinsdale. **1991**

YOUNG DOCTORS IN LOVE ★★★ This comedy at- tempts to do for medical soap operas what *Airplane!* did for disaster movies—and doesn't quite make it. Director Garry Marshall has nevertheless created an enjoyable movie for open-minded adults. The R- rated film is a bit too raunchy and suggestive for the younger set. 95m. **DIR:** Garry Marshall. **CAST:** Michael McKean, Sean Young, Harry Dean Stanton, Patrick Macnee, Hector Elizondo, Dabney Coleman, Pamela

Reed, Michael Richards, Taylor Negron, Saul Rubinek, Titos Vandis. **1982**

YOUNG EINSTEIN 💔 Einstein discovers how to split the atom and thus puts the bubbles into beer. Rated PG. 91m. **DIR:** Yahoo Serious. **CAST:** Yahoo Serious. **1989**

YOUNG FRANKENSTEIN ★★★★1/2 This is one of Mel Brooks's best. *Young Frankenstein* is the story of Dr. Frankenstein's college professor descendant who abhors his family history. This spoof of the old Universal horror films is hilarious from start to finish. Rated PG. B&W; 105m. **DIR:** Mel Brooks. **CAST:** Gene Wilder, Marty Feldman, Peter Boyle, Teri Garr, Madeline Kahn, Cloris Leachman, Kenneth Mars, Richard Haydn, Gene Hackman. **1974 DVD**

YOUNG GRADUATES 💔 Misadventures of a high school girl who falls in love with her teacher. 99m. **DIR:** Robert Anderson. **CAST:** Patricia Wymer, Tom Stewart, Dennis Christopher. **1971**

YOUNG GUNS ★★ The Brat Pack attempts to ape the Wild Bunch in this disappointing Western. Emilio Estevez seems to be having a great time playing Billy the Kid, while his brother Charlie Sheen makes a more convincing cowboy. But it's all for naught because the story lacks any authenticity. The only bright moments are provided by genre veterans Jack Palance, Brian Keith, and Patrick Wayne in all-too-brief supporting roles. Rated R for violence and profanity. 102m. **DIR:** Christopher Cain. **CAST:** Emilio Estevez, Kiefer Sutherland, Charlie Sheen, Lou Diamond Phillips, Dermot Mulroney, Casey Siemaszko, Jack Palance, Brian Keith, Patrick Wayne. **1988 DVD**

YOUNG GUNS II ★★ More pop Western nonsense. This time Billy the Kid and his gang find themselves pursued by an old saddle pal, Pat Garrett. *Lonesome Dove* it ain't. Rated PG-13 for violence and profanity. 109m. **DIR:** Geoff Murphy. **CAST:** Emilio Estevez, Kiefer Sutherland, Lou Diamond Phillips, William L. Petersen, Christian Slater, James Coburn, Alan Ruck, Balthazar Getty. **1990 DVD**

YOUNG HERCULES ★★★★ The creators of the popular *Hercules* television series take a look at the strongest man in his younger days. Fans of the series won't be disappointed in this feature film that may not star Kevin Sorbo but is obviously of the same stuff. Rated PG-13. 93m. **DIR:** T.J. Scott. **CAST:** Ian Bohen, Dean O'Gorman, Chris Conrad, Johna Stewart, Kevin Smith. **1997 DVD**

YOUNG IN HEART, THE ★★★1/2 This delightful romp has a fortune-hunting family finding a change of heart when they meet a nice old lady, appropriately named Miss Fortune. The entire cast is wonderful in this lavish production. 91m. **DIR:** Richard Wallace. **CAST:** Janet Gaynor, Douglas Fairbanks Jr., Paulette Goddard, Roland Young, Billie Burke. **1938**

YOUNG LIONS, THE ★★★1/2 The impact of love and war on young lives is the focus of this gripping drama of World War II told from the German and American points of view. Marlon Brando is superb as the Aryan soldier who comes to question his Nazi beliefs. Recommended. 167m. **DIR:** Edward Dmytryk. **CAST:** Marlon Brando, Montgomery Clift, Dean Martin, Hope Lange, Barbara Rush, May Britt, Maximilian Schell, Arthur Franz. **1958**

YOUNG LOVE, FIRST LOVE ★★ Boy loves girl, g loves boy. Does girl love boy enough to go all the wa Nothing better to do? Then watch and find out. V lerie Bertinelli is supercute as the girl. Timothy Hu ton is wasted as the boy with the sweats. Not rate 100m. **DIR:** Steven H. Stern. **CAST:** Valerie Bertine Timothy Hutton. **1979**

YOUNG MAGICIAN, THE ★★ Trite tale of a your man (Rusty Jedwab) who discovers he has magic powers and has a run-in with society. Special effec are good, but the dubbing in this Polish-Canadia production detracts a lot from the story. Not rate suitable for the entire family. 99m. **DIR:** Waldem Dziki. **CAST:** Rusty Jedwab. **1986**

YOUNG MAN WITH A HORN ★★★1/2 Interestir dramatic portrayal of a young horn player who figh to fill his need for music. Story becomes too melodr matic as Kirk Douglas becomes trapped in a roma tic web between Lauren Bacall and Doris Day. Hor work by Harry James. B&W; 112m. **DIR:** Michael Cu tiz. **CAST:** Kirk Douglas, Lauren Bacall, Doris Da Hoagy Carmichael, Juano Hernandez. **1950**

YOUNG MR. LINCOLN ★★★1/2 Director Joh Ford's tribute to the Great Emancipator is splen didly acted by Henry Fonda in the title role, with typ ically strong support from a handpicked supportin cast. This homespun character study develops into suspenseful courtroom drama for a rousing conclu sion. B&W; 100m. **DIR:** John Ford. **CAST:** Henry Fond Alice Brady, Marjorie Weaver, Donald Meek, Richar Cromwell, Eddie Quillan, Milburn Stone, Ward Bond **1939**

YOUNG NURSES, THE ★★ There's more sex tha plot in the next-to-last of producer Roger Corman' *Nurse* movies. Look for director Sam Fuller in cameo as a villainous doctor. Rated R for nudity 77m. **DIR:** Clinton Kimbrough. **CAST:** Jean Mansor Ashley Porter, Dick Miller, Sally Kirkland, Manta Moreland. **1973**

YOUNG NURSES IN LOVE 💔 A foreign spy poses a a nurse to steal the sperm from the sperm bank tha was donated by world leaders, celebrities, and ge niuses. Rated R for nudity. 82m. **DIR:** Chuck Vincen **CAST:** Jeanne Marie. **1989**

YOUNG ONES, THE ★★★ Three episodes of the in ventive, anarchic British TV series (you may hav seen it on MTV) about a quartet of impoverished col lege students. Raucous, obnoxious, shrill—and of ten very funny. 96m. **DIR:** Geoffrey Posner. **CAST:** Ri Mayall, Adrian Edmondson, Nigel Planer, Alexei Sayle **1982**

YOUNG PHILADELPHIANS, THE ★★★★ In thi excellent film, Robert Vaughn stars as a rich young man accused of murder. Paul Newman, a young lawyer, defends Vaughn while pursuing society gir Barbara Rush. B&W; 136m. **DIR:** Vincent Sherman **CAST:** Robert Vaughn, Paul Newman, Barbara Rush Alexis Smith, Brian Keith, Adam West, Billie Burke John Williams, Otto Kruger. **1959**

YOUNG POISONER'S HANDBOOK, THE ★★ British amateur chemist Graham Young spices up hi stale teen life by spiking the tea of his family and fel low Londoners with lethal powders. This black com edy about a remorseless psychopath who charts the

ealth of his victims in a diary begins with a wicked
allop but becomes monotonous about halfway
rough its dark, sick route. Rated R for language
nd the macabre. 105m. DIR: Benjamin Ross. CAST:
ugh O'Connor, Roger Lloyd Pack, Ruth Sheen,
amantha Edmonds, Antony Sher, Charlotte Coleman.
996

OUNG SAVAGES, THE ★★★1/2 Members of an
alian-American gang are charged with the murder
' a seemingly innocent blind Puerto Rican boy, and
A Burt Lancaster begins to wonder if everything is
s it seems. Good adaptation of Evan Hunter's novel,
 Matter of Conviction. B&W; 110m. DIR: John
ankenheimer. CAST: Burt Lancaster, Shelley Winters,
dward Andrews, Vivian Nathan, Larry Gates, Telly
avalas. 1961

OUNG SHERLOCK HOLMES ★★1/2 This disap-
ointingly derivative Steven Spielberg production
peculates on what might have happened if Sherlock
olmes and Dr. Watson had met during their student
ays in 1870 England. A better name for it might be
herlock Holmes and the Temple of Doom. Young-
ters are likely to enjoy it. Rated PG-13 for violence
nd scary stuff. 115m. DIR: Barry Levinson. CAST:
icholas Rowe, Alan Cox, Sophie Ward, Anthony Hig-
ins, Freddie Jones. 1985

OUNG SOUL REBELS ★★★★ Two black English
oul DJ's attempt to break into mainstream radio
tardom during the 1977 British punk explosion.
'his film accurately depicts the hazy sexual bound-
ries of the era. Rated R for nudity and profanity.
5m. DIR: Isaac Julien. CAST: Valentine Nonyela, Mo
esau, Dorian Healy. 1991

'OUNG TOM EDISON ★★★1/2 The first half of
4GM's two-part tribute to Thomas Alva Edison (fol-
owed in months by Edison, the Man), geared to a
ubdued Mickey Rooney as the inquisitive teenage
inventor. Mixture of fact and myth presented with re-
pect. B&W; 86m. DIR: Norman Taurog. CAST: Mickey
Rooney, Fay Bainter, George Bancroft, Virginia Weidler,
ugene Pallette, Clem Bevans. 1940

OUNG WARRIORS, THE ★★ Revenge exploita-
ion with James Van Patten leading his college-frat
rothers on a hunt for the psychos who raped and
illed his sister. Rated R for violence. 105m. DIR:
awrence D. Foldes. CAST: Ernest Borgnine, Richard
Roundtree, Lynda Day George, James Van Patten,
nne Lockhart, Mike Norris, Dick Shawn, Linnea
Quigley. 1983

OUNG WINSTON ★★★ Rousing and thoroughly
ntertaining account of this century's man for all
easons, England's indomitable Winston Churchill.
'he film takes him from his often wretched school
days to his beginnings as a journalist of resource and
daring in South Africa during the Boer War, up to his
irst election to Parliament. Simon Ward is excellent
n the title role. Rated PG. 145m. DIR: Richard Attenborough. CAST: Simon Ward, Anne Bancroft, Robert
Shaw, John Mills, Jack Hawkins, Robert Flemyng,
Patrick Magee, Laurence Naismith. 1972

YOUNGER AND YOUNGER ★★1/2 Percy Adlon's
love story desperately wants to be enchantingly
quirky but is more strained than sweet. A wife drops
dead listening to her husband's latest infidelity. She

begins to haunt him, looking increasingly beautiful,
growing ever younger, until she exacts a fitting revenge. Rated R for profanity, sexual situations, and
brief nudity. 97m. DIR: Percy Adlon. CAST: Donald
Sutherland, Lolita Davidovich, Brendan Fraser, Sally
Kellerman, Julie Delpy, Linda Hunt. 1993

YOUR FRIENDS & NEIGHBORS ★★ The coupling
of a married woman and a weaselly drama teacher
compounds the misery of six grating characters in
this ugly black comedy. The film is a springboard for
social commentary, savage satire, and introspection
that has us wallow in—rather than squirm at—the
current state of the human condition. Rated R for
graphic sexual dialogue and profanity. 97m. DIR: Neil
LaBute. CAST: Jason Patric, Aaron Eckhart, Amy Brenneman, Ben Stiller, Catherine Keener, Nastassja Kinski.
1998 DVD

YOURS, MINE AND OURS ★★★ A widow with
eight children marries a widower with ten of his own.
This works as a harbinger of The Brady Bunch.
Wholesome but never sterile or overly sentimental,
this comedy-drama is probably Lucille Ball's best
post–I Love Lucy vehicle. Rated G. 111m. DIR:
Melville Shavelson. CAST: Lucille Ball, Henry Fonda,
Van Johnson, Tom Bosley. 1968

YOU'VE GOT MAIL ★★★★ Meg Ryan rules the
screen in this mostly delightful update of Ernst Lubitsch's The Shop Around the Corner. She's the
owner-proprietor of a much beloved children's bookstore tucked away in New York's Upper West Side
while Tom Hanks—the apparent villain—owns a
monolithic book superstore poised to open its
newest branch across the street. But the slash-and-
burn campaign soon to erupt is only half the story:
our two heroes have been maintaining a strictly
anonymous E-mail correspondence with each other
despite other romatic ties and the certain knowledge that they'd hate each other on sight should the
truth emerge. Rated PG for no particular reason.
119m. DIR: Nora Ephron. CAST: Tom Hanks, Meg
Ryan, Parker Posey, Jean Stapleton, Greg Kinnear,
Dave Chappelle, Steve Zahn. 1998 DVD

YO-YO MAN ★★★★ This is ostensibly an instruction video on the development of yo-yo skills, but it is
much more. The actual instruction consists of the
basic tricks, tips on using the yo-yo, plus advanced
skills that are great fun to watch and can be accomplished with practice. There are clips from The
Smothers Brothers Comedy Hour series and new
footage with Tommy Smothers and yo-yo expert
Daniel Volk. Dick Smothers adds narrative and humor, and there is a catchy soundtrack. 38m. DIR:
David Grossman. CAST: Tom Smothers, Dick Smothers, Daniel Volk. 1988

YUMA ★★1/2 Big Clint Walker fights most of the
rowdy elements of a tough town and has to expose a
plan to undermine his authority as a lawman in this
enjoyable made-for-television Western. 73m. DIR:
Ted Post. CAST: Clint Walker, Barry Sullivan, Edgar
Buchanan, Kathryn Hays, Peter Mark Richman, Morgan Woodward. 1970

YURI NOSENKO, KGB ★★★1/2 This ably directed
spy drama is based on the transcripts of public hear-
ings, interviews, and published sources relating to

the defection of KGB agent Yuri Nosenko in 1964. The filmmakers have filled in the gaps where direct evidence was unavailable. Tommy Lee Jones gives a tremendous performance as CIA agent Steve Daley. Oleg Rudnik is also good as Nosenko. 89m. **DIR:** Mick Jackson. **CAST:** Tommy Lee Jones, Josef Sommer, Ed Lauter, Oleg Rudnik. **1986**

Z ★★★★ Director Costa-Gavras first explored political corruption in this taut French thriller. Yves Montand plays a political leader who is assassinated. Based on a true story. Academy Award for best foreign film. Well worth a try. No rating, with some violence and coarse language. 127m. **DIR:** Constantin Costa-Gavras. **CAST:** Yves Montand, Irene Papas, Jean-Louis Trintignant, Charles Denner. **1969 DVD**

ZABRISKIE POINT ★★1/2 An interesting but confusing story of a young college radical who shoots a policeman during a campus demonstration in the late 1960s. This film does not really say too much. Rated R. 112m. **DIR:** Michelangelo Antonioni. **CAST:** Mark Frechette, Daria Halprin, Rod Taylor. **1970**

ZACHARIAH ★★1/2 Forget the story line in this midnight movie Western and sit back and enjoy the music and the images. Television performers, a variety of musicians and actors, (including a youthful Don Johnson), populate this minor cult favorite and take every opportunity to be cool and break into song. There are tunes for most tastes and the fast-moving nature of the film makes it a good choice for company or a party. 93m. **DIR:** George Englund. **CAST:** John Rubinstein, Pat Quinn, Don Johnson, Country Joe and the Fish, Doug Kershaw. **1971 DVD**

ZANDALEE ★★ A sexually frustrated wife starts an affair with her husband's old friend. Unfortunately, writer Mari Kornhauser did a lousy job with an interesting idea. If you like graphic sex, you will love this film. Available in both R and unrated versions. 100m. **DIR:** Sam Pillsbury. **CAST:** Nicolas Cage, Judge Reinhold, Erika Anderson, Viveca Lindfors, Aaron Neville, Joe Pantoliano. **1990 DVD**

ZANDY'S BRIDE ★★1/2 Gene Hackman takes Liv Ullmann as a mail-order bride, uses (and abuses) her as chattel until shared hardships bring about respect and devotion. Also released as *For Better, For Worse*. Rated PG. 116m. **DIR:** Jan Troell. **CAST:** Gene Hackman, Liv Ullmann, Eileen Heckart, Harry Dean Stanton, Susan Tyrrell, Sam Bottoms, Joe Santos. **1974**

ZANY ADVENTURES OF ROBIN HOOD, THE ★★ Made-for-TV spoof of the legendary hero of Sherwood Forest. George Segal is likable as Robin Hood. Okay time passer but nothing more. 90m. **DIR:** Ray Austin. **CAST:** George Segal, Morgan Fairchild, Roddy McDowall, Janet Suzman. **1984**

ZAPPED! ★★ A campy takeoff on high school movies that doesn't work. *Zapped* is a bore. Rated R for nudity and sexual situations. 96m. **DIR:** Robert J. Rosenthal. **CAST:** Scott Baio, Willie Aames, Felice Schachter, Heather Thomas, Scatman Crothers, Robert Mandan, Greg Bradford. **1982**

ZAPPED AGAIN ★★1/2 A new student inspires the science club to take on the jocks. His secret potion allows him to defy the law of gravity and manipulate people and things around him. As teen comedies go this is not too bad. Rated R for nudity, profanity, and violence. 93m. **DIR:** Doug Campbell. **CAST:** Todd Eric Andrews, Kelli Williams, Linda Blair, Lyle Alzado. **1989**

ZARDOZ ★★1/2 Cult sci-fi about a strange society of the future and Sean Connery's attempts to free the people from the evil rulers. Murky plot is hard to follow, but it is amusing to watch Connery running around in a diaper for two hours. Rated R. 105m. **DIR:** John Boorman. **CAST:** Sean Connery, Charlotte Rampling. **1974**

ZARKORR! THE INVADER 🦃 Inspired by Japanese monster flicks and presuperhero comic legends, the man in the monster suit thrashing about among the miniature cities looks pretty good. Unfortunately, he appears in very few scenes and, in the end, we're still unsure about Zarkorr's mission—and we no longer care. Rated PG for violence and profanity. 81m. **DIR:** Aaron Osborne. **CAST:** Rees Christian Pugh, DePrise Grossman, Mark Hamilton, Eileen Wesson, Charles Schneider. **1996**

ZATOICHI: MASSEUR ICHI AND A CHEST OF GOLD ★★★ Popular samurai series from Japan features a blind swordsman-masseur on an endless quest through the Japanese countryside. Zatoichi travels to pay his respects at the grave of a gambler he killed years ago. He is framed for robbery and murder. Zatoichi's character requires the viewer to suspend disbelief for enjoyment, but it's well worth it. In Japanese with English subtitles. Not rated; contains violence. 83m. **DIR:** Kazuo Ikehiro. **CAST:** Shintaro Katsu, Mikiko Tsubouchi, Machiko Hasgawa, Kenzaburo Joh, Shogo Shimada. **1964**

ZATOICHI: THE BLIND SWORDSMAN AND THE CHESS EXPERT ★★★★ The ragged, endearing character of the long-running Japanese series returns. This time he's on a gambling junket to Mt. Fuji. and incurs the wrath of gangsters when he wins all their money. In Japanese with English subtitles. Not rated; contains violence. 87m. **DIR:** Kenji Misumi. **CAST:** Shintaro Katsu, Mikio Narita, Chizu Hayashi, Kaneko Iwasaki, Gayo Kamamoto. **1965**

ZATOICHI: THE BLIND SWORDSMAN'S VENGEANCE ★★★★ Wandering blind swordsman-masseur Zatoichi chances upon a dying man who entrusts to him a bag of money to be delivered to someone named Taichi. When Zatoichi finally locates the mysterious Taichi, he finds more than he bargained for. Unique blend of action, comedy, and drama gives these films a Zen-like quality. In Japanese with English subtitles. Not rated; contains violence. 83m. **DIR:** Tokuzo Tanaka. **CAST:** Shintaro Katsu, Shigeru Amachi, Mayumi Ogawa, Kei Sato, Jun Hamamura. **1966**

ZATOICHI VS. YOJIMBO ★★★1/2 Two of the giants of the Japanese samurai genre square off in this omic entry in the long-running blind-swordsman eries. Shintaro Katsu is Zatoichi, an almost superuman hero. The story is a send-up of Akira Kuroawa's *Yojimbo*, with Toshiro Mifune doing a omedic turn on his most famous character. It's fun or fans, but far from classic. In Japanese with English subtitles. 116m. **DIR:** Kihachi Okamoto. **CAST:** Shintaro Katsu, Toshiro Mifune. **1970**

'AZIE DANS LE METRO ★★★★ Hilarious, offbeat ale of a foulmouthed 11-year-old who comes to Paris o visit her drag-queen uncle (Philippe Noiret). 'reewheeling fun. In French with English subtitles. 2m. **DIR:** Louis Malle. **CAST:** Catherine Demongeot, 'hilippe Noiret. **1960**

EBRA IN THE KITCHEN ★★ When a family moves o the city, their tame pet wildcat must go to an overrowded zoo to comply with local regulations. Feelng a little mischievous, young star Jay North lets the nimals loose. One-dimensional. 92m. **DIR:** Ivan Tors. **CAST:** Jay North, Martin Milner, Andy Devine, Joyce Meadows, Jim Davis. **1965**

EBRAHEAD ★★★★1/2 Michael Rapaport is a white, Jewish kid who is preoccupied with black culure. This low-budget but well-made examination of 'ers a truthful, often funny peek at teenagers in the 990s and pulsates with a taut undercurrent of anger. Rated R for profanity, violence, and sexual sitations. 102m. **DIR:** Anthony Drazan. **CAST:** Michael Rapaport, Ray Sharkey, DeShonn Castle, N'Bushe Wright. **1992**

ZED AND TWO NOUGHTS, A ★★ Bizarre, unpleasant, but beautifully photographed (by Sacha Vierny) oddity about a woman who loses her leg in an auto accident, then becomes involved with the husbands of two women killed in the same wreck. A good deal of frontal nudity earned the film its R rating. 115m. **DIR:** Peter Greenaway. **CAST:** Andrea Ferreol, Brian Deacon, Eric Deacon, Frances Barber, Joss Ackland. **1985 DVD**

ZELDA ★★ Silly, contrived drama of F. Scott Fitzgerald's romance and marriage to Zelda. Zelda descends into mental illness while attempting to steer Fitzgerald toward his writing and away from his drinking. Natasha Richardson gives it her all in the title role, but she can't save this drivel. Made for cable TV. 94m. **DIR:** Pat O'Connor. **CAST:** Timothy Hutton, Natasha Richardson, Jon De Vries, Spalding Gray, Rob Knepper. **1993**

ZELIG ★★★★★ Woody Allen plays Leonard Zelig, a remarkable man who can fit anywhere in society because he can change his appearance at will. The laughs come fast and furious in this account of his adventures in the 1920s, when he became all the rage and hung out with the likes of F. Scott Fitzgerald, Jack Dempsey, and Babe Ruth. Allen seamlessly weds black-and-white newsreel footage with his humorous tale, allowing Zelig to be right in the thick of history. Rated PG. B&W; 79m. **DIR:** Woody Allen. **CAST:** Woody Allen, Mia Farrow. **1984**

ZELLY AND ME ★★ In this drama, we witness the turbulent life of a rich orphan played by Alexandra Johnes. She is overprotected and minus the knowledge of the ways of the real world. Isabella Rossellini and Glynis Johns are outstanding in secondary leads.

The basic problem with this film, though, is that we never learn what happens to our orphan. Rated PG. 87m. **DIR:** Tina Rathborne. **CAST:** Isabella Rossellini, Alexandra Johnes, Glynis Johns, Kaiulani Lee. **1988**

ZENOBIA ★★★★ A cute comedy about a doctor called to treat an elephant. He treats the animal so well it refuses to leave him. One of Oliver Hardy's few appearances without Stan Laurel, and he's good enough to keep the elephant from upstaging him. B&W; 93m. **DIR:** Gordon Douglas. **CAST:** Oliver Hardy, Harry Langdon, Billie Burke, James Ellison, Jean Parker, Hattie McDaniel, Stepin Fetchit. **1939**

ZENTROPA ★★★ This surreal odyssey, whose chief attribute is style, follows a young man into a new job as a railway conductor in Germany immediately after the end of World War II. Often enigmatic, this Danish film uses the railway as a complex metaphor for the emerging of Europe after the war. Stunning photography and startling imagery abound. In Danish with English subtitles. 114m. **DIR:** Lars von Trier. **CAST:** Jean-Marc Barr, Barbara Sukowa, Lawrence Hartman, Udo Kier, Eddie Constantine. **1991**

ZEPPELIN ★★★ An emotionally wrought Michael York must choose between homeland and duty in this story of a German-born British aviator during World War I. Cast, design, and special effects blend to make this fine fare. 101m. **DIR:** Etienne Perier. **CAST:** Michael York, Elke Sommer, Marius Goring, Peter Carsten, Anton Diffring. **1971**

ZERAM ★★ A female bounty hunter with a powerful computer must go into another universe to capture an evil alien being. Two stooges from the power company are accidently transported with her and must help her battle the alien. Dubbed in English. Not rated; contains excessive violence and gore. 92m. **DIR:** Keita Amamiya. **CAST:** Yuko Moriyama, Kunihiko Ida, Yukijiro Hotaru. **1991 DVD**

ZERO EFFECT ★★★ Daryl Zero is the world's greatest living private detective, and he's hired to end an ongoing extortion. The eccentric investigator uses his "deeply nuanced understanding of human nature" in this goofy, fragile spin on the private eye genre. Rated R for language. 115m. **DIR:** Jake Kasdan. **CAST:** Bill Pullman, Kim Dickens, Ben Stiller, Ryan O'Neal, Angela Featherstone. **1998 DVD**

ZERO FOR CONDUCT ★★★★1/2 Unique fantasy about the rebellion of boys in a French boarding school is told from the point of view of the students and provides perhaps the purest picture in the history of cinema of what authority appears to be to young minds. This all-too-short gem was sadly one of only four films made by terminally ill director Jean Vigo, at the age of 29. Banned across the Continent when first released, this film provided much of the story line for Lindsay Anderson's 1969 update *If...* In French with English subtitles. B&W; 44m. **DIR:** Jean Vigo. **CAST:** Jean Dasté. **1933**

ZERO KELVIN ★★★1/2 Unusual psychological drama set in 1925 Norway. A young writer accepts an assignment to write about fur trappers in the Arctic. Anticipating a rich adventure à la Jack London, he gets something rather different at a bleak tundra outpost where his only companions are a brooding scientist and a crude, bullying sailor. In Norwegian with English subtitles. Not rated; contains profanity, violence, nudity, and sexual situations. 113m. **DIR:** Hans Petter Moland. **CAST:** Stellan Skarsgard, Gard B. Eidsvold, Camilla Martins. **1995**

ZERO TOLERANCE ★★★ Although an early scene is needlessly sadistic, this explosive revenge saga certainly provides high-octane action and good, mindless fun. Robert Patrick delivers considerable tormented anguish as an FBI man who vows to terminate the so-called White Hand drug cartel: five mainstream businessmen who ordered his family's execution. The results are much better than this genre usually provides. Rated R for violence and profanity. 92m. **DIR:** Joseph Merhi. **CAST:** Robert Patrick, Titus Welliver, Kristen Meadows, Mick Fleetwood, Miles O'-Keeffe. **1994**

ZEUS AND ROXANNE ★★ This bland and blatantly cute family film features single parents—a rock composer and a marine-biologist researcher—who get tricked into falling in love by their precocious kids while interspecies communication blossoms between the title's dog and dolphin. Rated PG. 98m. **DIR:** George Miller. **CAST:** Steve Guttenberg, Kathleen Quinlan, Arnold Vosloo, Dawn McMillan, Miko Hughes, Majandra Delfino, Jessica Howell. **1996 DVD**

ZIEGFELD FOLLIES ★★★ MGM tries to imitate a Ziegfeld-style stage show. Don't get confused; this is not the Oscar-winning *The Great Ziegfeld* (with William Powell). 110m. **DIR:** Vincente Minnelli. **CAST:** Fred Astaire, Lucille Ball, William Powell, Judy Garland, Fanny Brice, Lena Horne, Red Skelton, Victor Moore, Virginia O'Brien, Cyd Charisse, Gene Kelly, Edward Arnold, Esther Williams. **1946**

ZIEGFELD GIRL ★★★ Judy Garland becomes a star, Hedy Lamarr weds rich, and poor Lana Turner hits the bottle. This all-stops-out musical-drama is jammed with show girls, lavish sets and costumes, and songs no one but trivia buffs recall. B&W; 131m. **DIR:** Robert Z. Leonard. **CAST:** Judy Garland, Hedy Lamarr, Lana Turner, Edward Everett Horton, Eve Arden, James Stewart, Jackie Cooper, Dan Dailey. **1941**

ZIPPERFACE 🎞 Beautiful cop must go undercover to catch a serial killer who preys on prostitutes. Been there, done that. Not rated; contains nudity, violence, and language. 90m. **DIR:** Mansour Pourmand. **CAST:** Dona Adams, David Clover, Jonathan Mandell. **1992**

ZOLTAN—HOUND OF DRACULA 🎞 Dracula's faithful servant journeys to Los Angeles in search of the last surviving member of the Dracula clan. Rated R for violence. 85m. **DIR:** Albert Band. **CAST:** Michael Pataki, Reggie Nalder, José Ferrer. **1977**

ZOMBIE 🎞 Gruesome, gory, and ghastly unauthorized entry in George Romero's zombie series. Rated X for gore and nudity. 91m. **DIR:** Lucio Fulci. **CAST:** Tisa Farrow, Ian McCulloch, Richard Johnson. **1979 DVD**

•ZOMBIE ARMY 🎞 Disgusting film has soldiers turned into the shuffling dead. Not rated; contains violence, gore, nudity, and profanity. 72m. **DIR:** Betty Stapleford. **CAST:** Eileen Saddow. **1993**

ZOMBIE BLOODBATH 🎞 No one makes a zombie movie like George Romero and this woefully inept film proves that point. Not rated; contains graphic violence and gore. 98m. **DIR:** Todd Sheets. **CAST:** Augg Alvarez, Frank Dunlay, Tonia Monahan. **1993**

ZOMBIE BLOODBATH 2 ★★ While Todd Sheets has come a long way as a filmmaker, he still has to learn that a story is more important than elaborate gore effects. This time around, teens return home to find it overrun by criminals and the living dead. Not rated; contains graphic violence, gore, and profanity. 90m. **DIR:** Todd Sheets. **CAST:** Kathleen McSweeney, Matthew Jason Walsh. **1995**

ZOMBIE COP 🎞 After being turned into a zombie by a Haitian voodoo doctor, a cop teams up with his partner to hunt down the man responsible. Fails to generate any real thrills. The director is actually a pseudonym for cult fave J. R. Bookwalter. Not rated; contains violence, profanity, and gore. 75m. **DIR:** Lance Randas. **CAST:** Michael Kemper, Bill Morrison, James L. Edwards, Bogdan Pecic. **1991**

ZOMBIE HIGH 🎞 Low-rent horror movie set at a prep school where the administration consists of 100-year-old men who have kept their youth through a potion made with live brain tissue obtained from their students. Rated R. 93m. **DIR:** Ron Link. **CAST:** Virginia Madsen, Richard Cox, James Wilder. **1987**

ZOMBIE ISLAND MASSACRE 🎞 Tourists in the Caribbean run into a pack of natives practicing voodoo. Rated R for violence, profanity, and nudity. 89m. **DIR:** John Carter. **CAST:** David Broadnax, Rita Jenrette. **1984**

ZOMBIE LAKE 🎞 Third Reich storm troopers return from their watery graves in this cheesy Eurotrash gorefest. Rated R. 90m. **DIR:** Jean Rollin. **CAST:** Howard Vernon. **1982**

ZOMBIE NIGHTMARE ★★ This film—about an innocent boy who is killed by some "savage suburban teens" only to rise again as a zombie to avenge his murder—tries to be more mystical than gory. But it never becomes atmospheric enough to be interesting. Rated R for violence and profanity. 89m. **DIR:** Jack Brauman. **CAST:** Adam West, Tia Carrere, Linda Singer. **1986**

ZOMBIES OF MORA TAV ★★ Laughable, low-budget time waster about zombies and sunken treasure. Shows how dull zombies were before *Night of the Living Dead*. Not rated, but timid enough for your aunt Sally. B&W. 70m. **DIR:** Edward L. Cahn. **CAST:** Gregg Palmer, Allison Hayes. **1957**

ZOMBIES OF THE STRATOSPHERE (SATAN'S SATELLITES) (SERIAL) ★★ The Inter-Planetary Patrol tracks down part-human zombies and a renegade scientist who plan to blow Earth off its orbit. Balsa wood rocket ships and stock footage from the other "Rocket Man" serials make this one of the more ludicrous entries. B&W; 12 chapters. **DIR:** Fred Brannon. **CAST:** Judd Holdren, Aline Towne, Wilson Wood, Lane Bradford. **1952**

ZOMBIES ON BROADWAY ★★ Near–poverty row comedy starring Wally Brown and Alan Carney. The dim-witted duo portray press agents trying to book a zombie—a scheme that drops them into Bela Lugosi's clutches. B&W; 68m. **DIR:** Gordon Douglas. **CAST:** Wally Brown, Alan Carney, Bela Lugosi, Anne Jeffreys. **1945**

ONE TROOPERS ★★ This is a dumb comic-book tale about an American troop in World War II lost behind German lines. Eventually, soldiers encounter space aliens who have crash-landed in the woods. Rated PG for mild violence. 86m. **DIR:** Danny Bilson. **AST:** Tim Thomerson, Timothy Van Patten. 1985

OO GANG, THE ★★ An oddball gang of crooks sets out to discover whether crime pays and winds up with more than it bargained for. Distinguished by Ben Vereen's excellent performance. Rated PG-13 or violence. 96m. **DIR:** John Watson, Pen Densham. **AST:** Ben Vereen, Jason Gedrick, Eric Gurry. 1985

OO RADIO ★★ This sophomoric comedy deals with dueling Los Angeles radio stations. A continuous stream of one-line jokes and sight gags—some work, some don't. Rated R for strong language. 88m. **IR:** M. Ray Roach. **CAST:** Peter Feig, Ron Dickinson, avid Pires, Terra Mays. 1990

ZOOMAN ★★★1/2 Potent adaptation of Charles Fuller's play about an inner-city gangbanger who accidentally kills a little girl. The grieving father, angered by scared neighbors who saw the murder but refuse to identify the killer, hangs a sign that collectively indicts the neighborhood ... and then things really get interesting. Rated R for violence and incessant profanity. 95m. **DIR:** Leon Ichaso. **CAST:** Lou Gossett Jr., Cynthia Martellis, C.C.H. Pounder, Charles Dutton, Khalil Kain, Hill Harper. 1995

ZOOT SUIT ★★★★ Adapted from his stage drama–musical by writer-director Luis Valdez, this innovative film presents a fictionalized version of the Sleepy Lagoon murder case that took place in 1942. Rated R for profanity and violence. 104m. **DIR:** Luis Valdez. **CAST:** Edward James Olmos, Charles Aidman, John Anderson, Tyne Daly, Daniel Valdez. 1981

ZORBA THE GREEK ★★★★ A tiny Greek village in Crete is the home of Zorba, a zesty, uncomplicated man whose love of life is a joy to his friends and an eye-opener to a visiting stranger. Anthony Quinn is a delight as Zorba. Lila Kedrova was to win an Oscar for her poignant role as an aging courtesan in this drama. B&W; 146m. **DIR:** Michael Cacoyannis. **CAST:** Anthony Quinn, Alan Bates, Irene Papas, Lila Kedrova. 1963

ZORRO ★★★ The dashing swordsman with the black mask and the flashing rapier rides against injustice, though in this version he rides in South America instead of California. Suitably swashbuckling, if a notch below the 1940 *Mark of Zorro.* Rated G. 88m. **DIR:** Duccio Tessari. **CAST:** Alain Delon, Stanley Baker, Enzo Cerusico, Ottavia Piccolo, Adriana Asti. 1975 DVD

ZORRO RIDES AGAIN ★★★ A modern-day Zorro, played by John Carroll, lends his hand to a railway under siege by ruthless Noah Beery Sr., one of the cinema's greatest heavies. Constant harassment keeps Zorro on his toes. A great cast keeps this serial moving at a rapid clip. B&W; 12 chapters. **DIR:** William Witney, John English. **CAST:** John Carroll, Helen Christian, Reed Howes, Duncan Renaldo, Noah Beery Sr., Nigel de Brulier, Bob Kortman, Tom London. 1937

ZORRO, THE GAY BLADE ★★★★ Here's another delight from (and starring) actor-producer George Hamilton. As with *Love at First Bite,* in which Hamilton played a slightly bent Count Dracula to great effect, the accent in *Zorro, the Gay Blade* is on belly-wrenching laughs ... and there are plenty of them. Rated PG because of sexual innuendo. 93m. **DIR:** Peter Medak. **CAST:** George Hamilton, Lauren Hutton, Brenda Vaccaro, Ron Leibman, Donovan Scott. 1981

ZORRO'S FIGHTING LEGION ★★★ Quality serial places Reed Hadley (as Zorro) at the helm of a determined band of patriotic ranchers eager to ensure safe passage of the gold shipments needed to continue Juarez's rule. B&W; 12 chapters. **DIR:** William Witney, John English. **CAST:** Reed Hadley, Sheila Darcy, C. Montague Shaw, Budd Buster, Carleton Young, Charles King. 1939

ZOTZ! ★★★1/2 Charming, underrated little fantasy about a college professor (Tom Poston) who finds a magical coin blessed with three bizarre powers: sudden pain, slow motion, and explosive destruction. An excellent opportunity for Poston to control a film in one of his rare leading parts. Give this a try; you won't be disappointed. B&W; 87m. **DIR:** William Castle. **CAST:** Tom Poston, Jim Backus, Julia Meade. 1962

ZOU ZOU ★★★ Josephine Baker's debut in talkies and a huge success in France. Baker's rendition of "Haiti" is the highlight. In French with English subtitles. B&W; 92m. **DIR:** Marc Allegret. **CAST:** Josephine Baker, Jean Gabin. 1934

Z.P.G. (ZERO POPULATION GROWTH) 🎭 In the pre–*Star Wars* 1970s, science fiction languished, and dreary films like this were a dime a dozen. Overpopulation imposes severe restrictions on life in the future. We guarantee no moviegoer will want to suffer through it. Rated PG. 95m. **DIR:** Michael Campus. **CAST:** Oliver Reed, Geraldine Chaplin, Don Gordon, Diane Cilento. 1972

ZU: WARRIORS FROM THE MAGIC MOUNTAIN ★★★★ A must-see for all fans of action and fantasy films. The plot can be hard to follow as a young swordsman and a monk battle a demon queen intent on taking over the world. A wild, wonderfully imaginative movie. Available dubbed or in Cantonese with English subtitles. Not rated; contains no objectionable material. 98m. **DIR:** Tsui Hark. **CAST:** Yuen Biao, Adam Cheng, Brigitte Lin, Moon Lee, Sammo Hung. 1983

ZULU ★★★★1/2 Several films have been made about the British army and its exploits in Africa during the nineteenth century. *Zulu* ranks with the finest. A stellar cast headed by Stanley Baker and Michael Caine who charge through this story of an outmanned British garrison laid to siege by several thousand Zulu warriors. Based on fact, this one delivers the goods for action and tension. 138m. **DIR:** Cy Endfield. **CAST:** Stanley Baker, Michael Caine, Jack Hawkins, Nigel Green. 1964

ZULU DAWN ★★★ This prequel to the film *Zulu,* which was made fifteen years earlier, seems quite pale when compared with the first. Based on the crushing defeat of the British army at the hands of the Zulu warriors, *Zulu Dawn* depicts the events leading up to the confrontation portrayed in *Zulu.* Considering all involved, this is a disappointment. Rated PG for violence. 121m. **DIR:** Douglas Hickox.

CAST: Burt Lancaster, Peter O'Toole, Simon Ward, John Mills, Nigel Davenport. **1979**

ZVENIGORA ★★★★ Prompted by their grandfather's stories, two young peasants dream of the legendary treasure buried in the hills of Zvenigora. Alexander Dovzhenko was the cinema's great epic poet, and in this, his first feature, he seamlessly blends mythology and his own personal beliefs with the history of the Ukraine. Silent. B&W; 73m. **DIR:** Alexander Dovzhenko. **1928**

Adams, Mason: Assault at West Point; Final Conflict, The; F/X; Kid with the Broken Halo, The; Night They Saved Christmas, The; Revenge of the Stepford Wives; Shining Season, A

Adams, Maud: Deadly Intent; Girl in Blue, The; Hostage Tower, The; Intimate Power; Jane and the Lost City; Killer Force; Man of Passion, A; Man with the Golden Gun, The; Nairobi Affair; Octopussy; Playing for Time; Rollerball; Silent Night, Deadly Night 4—Initiation; Target Eagle; Tattoo; Women's Club, The

Adams, Nick: Die, Monster, Die!; FBI Story, The; Godzilla vs. Monster Zero; Hell Is for Heroes; Interns, The; Mission Mars; No Time for Sergeants; Picnic; Rebel Without a Cause; Teacher's Pet

Adams, Robert: Song of Freedom

Adams, Ted: Arizona Gunfighter; Desert Phantom; Smokey Trails

Adams, Tom: Fighting Prince of Donegal, The

Adams, Wendy: Fool and His Money, A

Adamson, Amy: Last Stop

Adamson, Christopher: Razor Blade Smile

Adamson, Dave: City in Panic

Adamson, George: Christian the Lion

Addabbo, Tony: Gunfighters, The

Addams, Dawn: King in New York, A; Liars, The; Moon Is Blue, The; Robe, The; Silent Enemy, The; Thousand Eyes of Dr. Mabuse, The; Vampire Lovers, The; Vault of Horror; Voulez Vous Danser avec Moi? (Will You Dance with Me?)

Addison, Nancy: Somewhere, Tomorrow

Addy, Mark: Flintstones in Viva Rock Vegas, The; Full Monty, The; Jack Frost (1998)

Addy, Wesley: Bostonians, The; Europeans, The; Hiroshima

Adele, Jan: High Tide

Adell, Traci: Life 101

Adix, Vern: Teen Alien

Adjani, Isabelle: Camille Claudel; Diabolique (1996); Driver, The; Ishtar; Next Year If All Goes Well; One Deadly Summer; Quartet (1981); Queen Margot; Story of Adele H, The; Subway

Adkins, Seth: ... First Do No Harm

Adler, Jerry: Manhattan Murder Mystery

Adler, Kim: Edgar Allan Poe's Madhouse

Adler, Luther: Brotherhood, The; Cornered; Crashout; Desert Fox, The; D.O.A. (1949); Hoodlum Empire; House of Strangers; Kiss Tomorrow Goodbye; Last Angry Man, The; Loves of Carmen, The; Man in the Glass Booth; Murph the Surf; Von Ryan's Express; Wake of the Red Witch

Adler, Matt: Diving In; Flight of the Navigator; North Shore; White Water Summer

Adler, Stella: My Girl Tisa

Admire, Jenny: Bimbos B.C.; Dominion (1994); Edgar Allan Poe's Madhouse; Goblin; Prehistoric Bimbos in Armageddon City

Adolphson, Edvin: Only One Night

Adonis, Frank: Suicide Ride

Adorée, Renée: Big Parade, The; Blackbird, The; Buster Keaton Festival Vol. 1–3

Adorf, Mario: Holcroft Covenant, The; Invitation au Voyage; King, Queen and Knave; Lola (1982); Manhunt (1973) (The Italian Connection); Ten Little Indians (1966); Tin Drum, The

Adrian, Iris: Blue Hawaii; Bluebeard (1944); Horror Island; Lady of Burlesque; Road to Zanzibar; Roxie Hart

Adrian, Max: Boy Friend, The; Devils, The; Music Lovers, The; Terrornauts, The

Adrian, Patricia: I'm the One You're Looking For

Adu, Robinson Frank: Heart

Adu, Sade: Absolute Beginners

Aerosmith: Wayne's World 2

Affleck, Ben: Armageddon; Boiler Room; Chasing Amy; Dogma; Forces of Nature; Going All the Way; Good Will Hunting; No Looking Back; Phantoms; Reindeer Games; Shakespeare in Love; 200 Cigarettes

Affleck, Casey: Drowning Mona; Good Will Hunting; Race the Sun; To Die For (1995)

Affleck, Neil: My Bloody Valentine

Agar, John: Along the Great Divide; Attack of the Puppet People; Brain from Planet Arous, The; Daughter of Dr. Jekyll; Fort Apache; Invisible Invaders; Jet Attack; Johnny Reno; Miracle Mile; Mole People, The; Perfect Bride, The;

Revenge of the Creature; Sands of Iwo Jima; Tarantula; Women of the Prehistoric Planet

Agbayani, Tetchie: Deathfight; Gymkata

Agee, Arthur: Hoop Dreams

Agostino, Pierre: Hollywood Strangler Meets the Skid Row Slasher

Agren, Janet: Aladdin (1987); Emerald Jungle; Hands of Steel; Lobster for Breakfast

Agterberg, Toon: Spetters

Aguilar, Antonio: Undefeated, The

Agutter, Jenny: American Werewolf in London, An; Amy; Child's Play 2; Dark Tower; Dominique Is Dead; Equus; Gunfire; King of the Wind; Logan's Run; Man in the Iron Mask, The (1977); Not a Penny More, Not a Penny Less; Othello (1982); Railway Children, The; Riddle of the Sands; Silas Marner; Sweet William; Walkabout

Aherne, Brian: Beloved Enemy; Forever and a Day; I Confess; I Live My Life; Juarez; Lady in Question; Night to Remember, A (1943); Prince Valiant (1954); Smilin' Through (1941); Swan, The (1956); Sword of Lancelot; Sylvia Scarlett; Titanic (1953); Waltz King, The

Aherne, Michael: Commitments, The

Ahlstedt, Borje: Emma's Shadow; I Am Curious Blue; I Am Curious Yellow

Ahmed, Kamal: Jerky Boys, The

Ahmed, Lalita: Bhaji on the Beach

Ahn, Philip: Battle Circus; Betrayal from the East; Buck Rogers: Destination Saturn (Planet Outlaws); Halls of Montezuma; His Majesty O'Keefe; Kung Fu (1971); They Got Me Covered

Aidman, Charles: Countdown; Hour of the Gun, The; King Lear (1982); Kotch; Menace on the Mountain; Prime Suspect (1982) (Feature); Zoot Suit

Aiello, Danny: Alone in the Neon Jungle; Anything for Love; Brooklyn State of Mind, A; Cemetery Club, The; City Hall; Closer, The; Defiance; Do the Right Thing; Harlem Nights; Hudson Hawk; Jacob's Ladder; January Man, The; Key Exchange; Last Don, The; Man on Fire; Me and the Kid; Mistress (1992); Mojave Moon; Moonstruck; Old Enough; Once Around; Pickle, The; Power of Attorney; Preppie Murder, The; Professional, The; Protector, The; Purple Rose of Cairo, The; Question of Honor, A; Road Home, The; Ruby (1991); Stuff, The; Third Solution, The; Two Days in the Valley; Two Much; 29th Street; White Hot

Aiello, Rick: Brooklyn State of Mind, A; Endangered; Hollywood Confidential; Me and the Kid

Aiken, Liam: I Dreamed of Africa; Stepmom

Aimée, Anouk: Dr. Bethune; 8 ½; Head Against the Wall; Justine; La Dolce Vita; Lola (1960); Man and a Woman, A; Man and a Woman, A: 20 Years Later; Paris Express, The; Ready to Wear; Success Is the Best Revenge; Tragedy of a Ridiculous Man

Aimone, Gene: Freakshow

Ainsley, Norman: Shadow Strikes, The

Aird, Holly: Overindulgence; Theory of Flight, The

Airlie, Andrew: Hard Evidence

Aitchison, Suzy: Bloody New Year

Aitken, Spottiswoode: Eagle, The; Home, Sweet Home (1914)

Ajaye, Franklin: American Yakuza; Car Wash; Get Crazy; Wrong Guys, The

Akan, Tarik: Yol

Akili, Ali Mohammed El: Wedding in Galilee, A

Akinnouye-Agbaje, Adewale: Legionnaire; 20,000 Leagues Under the Sea (1996)

Akins, Claude: Battle for the Planet of the Apes; Burning Hills, The; Curse, The; Death Squad, The; Devil's Brigade, The; Eric; Falling from Grace; Gambler Returns, The; Luck of the Draw; Inherit the Wind (1960); Manhunt for Claude Dallas; Monster in the Closet; Night Stalker, The (1971); Onionhead; Return of the Seven; Ride Beyond Vengeance; Rio Bravo; Sea Chase, The; Sherlock Holmes and the Incident at Victoria Falls; Tarantulas—The Deadly Cargo; Waterhole #3

Akiyama, Denis: Johnny Mnemonic

Akutagawa, Hiroshi: Mistress, The (1953)

Alaimo, Marc: Arena; Avenging Force; Fence, The

Alaimo, Steve: Stanley

Alan, Craig: Game, The (1988)

Alan-Lee, Jeff: Beniker Gang, The

Alansu, John: Love Serenade

Alard, Nelly: Eating; Venice/Venice

Alaskey, Joe: Gross Jokes; Lucky Stiff

Alba, Jessica: Idle Hands

Alba, Maria: Mr. Robinson Crusoe; Return of Chandu (Magician, The)

Albano, Lou: Body Slam; It's a Complex World

Albasiny, John: Kipperbang

Albee, Josh: Tom Sawyer (1973)

Alber, Kevin: Bram Stoker's Burial of the Rats

Alberghetti, Anna Maria: Cinderella; Last Command, The (1955)

Alberni, Luis: Big Stampede, The; Madame X (1937); Man from Monterey, The; Road to Zanzibar

Alberoni, Sherry: Nightmare Circus (Barn of the Living Dead) (Terror Circus)

Albers, Hans: Baron Münchhausen (1943)

Albert, Eddie: Act, The; Actors and Sin; Airport '79: The Concorde; Attack!; Beulah Land; Birch Interval, The; Bombardier; Captain Newman, M.D.; Carrie (1952); Crash of Flight 401; Devil's Rain, The; Dreamscape; Dress Gray; Escape to Witch Mountain; Foolin' Around; Fuller Brush Girl, The; Goliath Awaits; Head Office; Heartbreak Kid, The; Hustle; I'll Cry Tomorrow; Longest Yard, The; McQ; Miracle of the White Stallions; Moving Violation; Oklahoma!; Perfect Marriage; Roman Holiday; Smash-Up: The Story of a Woman; Stitches; Take This Job and Shove It; Teahouse of the August Moon, The; Wagons Roll at Night, The; Whiffs; Who's Got the Action?; Yes, Giorgio

Albert, Edward: Body Language (1992); Butterflies Are Free; Demon Keeper; Distortions; Exiled in America; Fist Fighter; Fool Killer, The; Forty Carats; Galaxy of Terror; Getting Even; Greek Tycoon, The; Guarding Tess; Hard Drive; House Where Evil Dwells, The; Ice Runner; Midway; Mindgames; Out of Sight Out of Mind; Purple Taxi, The; Red Sun Rising; Rescue, The; Sexual Malice; Shootfighter; Silent Victory: The Kitty O'Neil Story; Sorceress (1994); Space Marines; Terminal Entry; Time to Die, A (1983); When Time Ran Out!

Albert, Laura: Blood Games

Albert, Maxine: Home Remedy

Albert, Robert: Clean Shaven

Albertazzi, Giorgio: Last Year at Marienbad

Alberti, Lima: Clowns, The

Albertson, Frank: Ah, Wilderness; Alice Adams; Bachelor Mother; Connecticut Yankee, A; Dr. Christian Meets the Women; Doubting Thomas; Enemy Below, The; Hucksters, The; Louisiana Purchase; Man Made Monster (The Atomic Monster); Navy Blue and Gold; Psycho (1960); Shining Hour, The; Tournament Tempo

Albertson, Jack: Big Business Girl; Dead and Buried; Don't Go Near the Water; Flim-Flam Man, The; How to Murder Your Wife; Justine; Kissin' Cousins; Lover Come Back; Period of Adjustment; Rabbit Run; Subject Was Roses, The; Teacher's Pet; Willy Wonka and the Chocolate Factory

Albrecht, Marcy: Hollywood High

Albright, Ariana: Bloodletting; Polymorph

Albright, Brad: Don't Let Your Meat Loaf

Albright, Hardie: Mom and Dad; Scarlet Letter, The (1934); Silver Streak (1934)

Albright, Lola: Impossible Years, The; Joy House; Kid Galahad (1962); Lord Love a Duck; Monolith Monsters, The; Peter Gunn (TV Series); Tender Trap, The; Way West, The (1967); Where Were You When the Lights Went Out?

Alcaide, Chris: Gunslinger

Alcazar, Damian: Men with Guns

Alcroft, Jamie: Million Dollar Mystery

Alda, Alan: And the Band Played On; Betsy's Wedding; California Suite; Canadian Bacon; Crimes and Misdemeanors; Everyone Says I Love You; Flirting with Disaster; Four Seasons, The; Glass House, The; Mad City; Manhattan Murder Mystery; M*A*S*H (TV Series); Mephisto Waltz, The; Murder at 1600; New Life, A; Object of My Affection, The; Paper Lion; Playmates; Purlie Victorious; Same Time Next Year; Seduction of Joe Tynan, The; Sweet Liberty; To Kill a Clown; Whispers in the Dark; White Mile

Alda, Antony: Hot Child in the City

Alda, Beatrice: New Life, A

Alda, Robert: Beast with Five Fingers, The; Bittersweet Love; Cloak and Dagger (1946); Devil in the House of Exorcism, The; House of Exorcism, The; I Will, I Will … for Now; Imitation of Life; Man I Love, The; Rhapsody in Blue

Alda, Rutanya: Amityville II: The Possession; Apprentice to Murder; Dark Half, The; Racing with the Moon; Vigilante

Alden, Ginger: Lady Grey

Alden, Matt: Doin' Time on Planet Earth

Alden, Norman: Red Line 7000

Alden, Priscilla: Criminally Insane

Alden, Terry: Last Game, The

Alderman, John: Pink Angels

Aldon, Mari: Distant Drums; Tanks Are Coming, The

Aldredge, Tom: Man That Corrupted Hadleyburg, The; O Pioneers!; Rain People, The; Seize the Day

Aldrich, John: Wild Beasts, The

Aldrich, Matthew: My Sweet Suicide

Aldridge, Kitty: African Dream, An; American Roulette; Slipstream

Aldridge, Michael: Bullshot (Bullshot Crummond)

Aleandro, Norma: Cousins; Gaby, a True Story; Official Story, The; One Man's War

Aleman, Julio: Green Wall, The

Alentova, Vera: Moscow Does Not Believe in Tears

Aleong, Aki: Braddock: Missing in Action III; Out for Blood

Alerme, Andre: Carnival in Flanders

Ales, John: Nutty Professor, The (1996)

Aless, Jean: Homicidal

Aletonis, Paula: Stolen Hearts

Alexander, Alphonso: Bustin' Loose

Alexander, Barbara Lee: Illegal Entry; Psycho Cop 2

Alexander, Ben: Dragnet (1954); Hearts of the World

Alexander, Bruce: Touch of Frost, A (TV Series)

Alexander, Denise: Lindbergh Kidnapping Case, The

Alexander, Frank: Gladiator Cop II: The Swordsman; Sinyster

Alexander, Geraldine: Sleeping Murder

Alexander, Jane: All the President's Men; Betsy, The; Brubaker; Calamity Jane (1984); City Heat; Friendship in Vienna, A; Great White Hope, The; Gunfight, A; In Love and War; Kramer vs. Kramer; Love and War; New Centurions, The; Night Crossing; Playing for Time; Rumor Mill, The; Square Dance; Sweet Country; Testament

Alexander, Jason: Coneheads; Dunston Checks In; For Better or Worse; I Don't Buy Kisses Anymore; Jacob's Ladder; Love! Valour! Compassion!; Paper, The; Rodgers & Hammerstein's Cinderella; Something About Sex; White Palace

Alexander, John: Alien P.I.; Horn Blows at Midnight, The

Alexander, Katharine: Great Man Votes, The; Operator 13

Alexander, Khandi: House Party 3

Alexander, Liz: Killing of Angel Street, The

Alexander, Mathew: Wheels: An Inside Story

Alexander, Ross: Captain Blood; Flirtation Walk

Alexander, Spike: Brain Donors

Alexander, Terence: Frankenstein (1984)

Alexander, Terry: Day of the Dead

Alexander, Tiana: Catch the Heat

Alexandridis, Helene: Therese

Alexandrov, Grigori: Strike (1924)

Alexiadis, Anna: Fantasies

Alexi-Malle, Adam: Bowfinger

Alexio, Dennis: Kickboxer

Alfonso, Kristian: Army of One; Blindfold: Acts of Obsession

Alford, Philip: To Kill a Mockingbird

Alfredson, Hans: Adventures of Picasso, The

Algeria: Ramparts of Clay

Ali, Muhammad: Greatest, The

Ali, Tatyana: Clown at Midnight, The

Alice, Mary: Down in the Delta; Laurel Avenue; Road to Freedom: The Vernon Johns Story; To Sleep with Anger

Alicia, Ana: Coward of the County; Romero

Aliff, Lisa: Playroom

Alighiero, Carlo: Cat O'Nine Tails

Alison, Dorothy: Amazing Mr. Blunden, The; See No Evil

Allain, Joe: Television Parts Home Companion

Allan, Andrea: House That Vanished, The

Allan, Elizabeth: Ace of Aces; Camille; Haunted Strangler, The; Mark of the Vampire; Tale of Two Cities, A (1935); Woman Rebels, A

Allan, Jed: Suspect Device

Allasio, Marisa: Seven Hills of Rome, The

Alyse-Smith, Brittany: Pinocchio's Revenge

Alzado, Lyle: Club Fed; Comrades in Arms; Destroyer; Double McGuffin, The; Ernest Goes to Camp; Neon City; Oceans of Fire; Tapeheads; Zapped Again

Amachi, Shigeru: Zatoichi: The Blind Swordsman's Vengeance

Amano, Sayoko: Tokyo Decadence

Amar, Leonora: Captain Scarlett

Amastutz, Roland: Eyes of the Birds

Ambrose, Lauren: Can't Hardly Wait

Ambrosini, Philippe: Bye-Bye

Ameche, Don: Alexander's Ragtime Band; Cocoon; Cocoon: The Return; Corrina, Corrina; Down Argentine Way; Folks; Guest Wife; Happy Landing; Harry and the Hendersons; Heaven Can Wait (1943); Hollywood Cavalcade; In Old Chicago; It's in the Bag; Midnight (1939); Moon over Miami; Oddball Hall; One in a Million; Oscar (1991); Pals; Picture Mommy Dead; Sunstroke; Suppose They Gave a War and Nobody Came; Things Change; Three Musketeers, The (1939); Trading Places; Wing and a Prayer, A

Amendola, Claudio: Forever Mary; La Scorta

America, Paul: Ciao! Manhattan

Ames, Adrienne: Death Kiss, The; Harmony Lane

Ames, Leon: Any Number Can Play; Big Hangover, The; By the Light of the Silvery Moon; Date with Judy, A; Deadly Encounter (1975); From the Terrace; Iron Major, The; Jake Speed; Lady in the Lake; Marshal of Mesa City; Merton of the Movies; Misadventures of Merlin Jones, The; Mr. Moto in Danger Island; Monkey's Uncle, The; Murders in the Rue Morgue (1932); Mysterious Mr. Moto; On Moonlight Bay; Peggy Sue Got Married; Peyton Place; Show-Off, The (1946); Son of Lassie; Testament; Thin Man Goes Home, The; Velvet Touch, The; Yolanda and the Thief

Ames, Ramsay: Mummy's Ghost, The

Ames, Rosemary: Our Little Girl

Amick, Madchen: Bombshell (1997); Courtyard, The; Don't Tell Her It's Me; Dream Lover (1994); French Exit; Heartless; Hunted (1997); I'm Dangerous Tonight; Love, Cheat & Steal; Stephen King's Sleepwalkers; Trapped in Paradise; Wounded

Amidou: Unveiled

Amidou, Souad: Petit Con; Sorcerer

Amin, Rola Al: West Beirut

Amis, Suzy: Ballad of Little Jo, The; Beneficiary, The; Big Town, The; Blown Away (1994); Cadillac Ranch; Ex, The; Firestorm; Judgment Day; Last Stand at Saber River; Nadja; One Good Turn; Plain Clothes; Rich in Love; Rocket Gibraltar; Titanic (1997); Twister (1988); Two Small Bodies; Usual Suspects, The; Watch It

Ammann, Renee: Number One Fan; Stoned Age, The

Amos, David: Flipping

Amos, John: American Flyers; Beastmaster, The; Coming to America; Die Hard 2: Die Harder; Jungle Heat; Let's Do It Again; Lock Up; Mac; Mardi Gras for the Devil; Sweet Sweetback's Baadasssss Song; Touched by Love; Two Evil Eyes; Willa; World's Greatest Athlete, The

Amos, Keith: Breach of Conduct

Amphlett, Christina: Monkey Grip

Amplas, John: Martin; Midnight (1980)

Amrani, Gabi: Lupo; Madron

Amsterdam, Morey: Beach Party; Dick Van Dyke Show, The (TV Series); Gay Purr-ee; Machine-Gun Kelly; Muscle Beach Party; Sooner or Later

Anbeh, Susan: French Kiss

Anchoriz, Leo: Bullet for Sandoval, A; Finger on the Trigger

Anconina, Richard: Love Songs (Paroles et Musique); Police; Tchao Pantin

Anders, Avalon: Wish Me Luck

Anders, Donna: Count Yorga, Vampire

Anders, Glenn: Lady from Shanghai

Anders, Luana: Border Radio; Dementia 13; Easy Rider; Greaser's Palace; Manipulator, The; One from the Heart; Pit and the Pendulum, The (1961); Sex and the College Girl; That Cold Day in the Park; Trip, The

Anders, Lynn: Shadow Strikes, The

Anders, Merry: Farmer Takes a Wife, The; Hypnotic Eye, The; Tickle Me; Time Travelers, The; Women of the Prehistoric Planet

Andersen, Dana: Ginger Ale Afternoon

Andersen, Elga: Global Affair, A

Andersen, Isa: Night Angel

Andersen, Suzy: Black Sabbath; Gangster's Law

Anderson, Adisa: Daughters of the Dust

Anderson, Anders T.: 13th Warrior, The

Anderson, Anthony: Life

Anderson, Bridgette: Fever Pitch; Savannah Smiles

Anderson, Bruce: Thinkin' Big

Anderson, Carl: Jesus Christ, Superstar

Anderson, Daniel: Body of Influence 2

Anderson, Daphne: Hobson's Choice (1954)

Anderson, Dave: No Dead Heroes

Anderson, Eddie "Rochester": Birth of the Blues; Brewster's Millions (1945); Buck Benny Rides Again; Cabin in the Sky; Green Pastures; Honolulu; It Happened in New Orleans; Jack Benny Program, The (TV Series); Meanest Man in the World, The; Show-Off, The (1946); Tales of Manhattan; Three Men on a Horse; Topper Returns; You Can't Cheat an Honest Man

Anderson, Erich: Love Kills

Anderson, Erika: Object of Obsession; Quake; Zandalee

Anderson, Ernest: Well, The

Anderson, Erville: Haunted Gold

Anderson, Gabrych: Edge of Seventeen

Anderson, Gillian: Hellcab; Mighty, The; Playing by Heart; X-Files, The (1998); X-Files, The (TV Series)

Anderson, Harry: It (1991); Spies, Lies, and Naked Thighs

Anderson, Haskell A.: Brotherhood of Death

Anderson, Herbert: Benny Goodman Story, The; I Bury the Living

Anderson, James: Hunt the Man Down

Anderson, Jean: Back Home

Anderson, Jeff: Clerks

Anderson, Jill: Omaha (The Movie)

Anderson, John: Deerslayer, The (1920); Donner Pass: The Road to Survival; Executive Action; Firehouse (1987); In Search of Historic Jesus; Man and Boy; Medicine Hat Stallion, The; Namu, the Killer Whale; Psycho (1960); Ride the High Country; Smile, Jenny, You're Dead; Soldier Blue; Zoot Suit

Anderson, Judith: All Through the Night; And Then There Were None; Blood Money; Edge of Darkness (1943); King's Row; Lady Scarface; Laura; Macbeth (1961); Man Called Horse, A; Pursued; Rebecca; Red House, The; Salome (1953); Specter of the Rose, The; Strange Love of Martha Ivers, The; Tycoon

Anderson, Kenneth: Feast of July

Anderson, Kevin: Hoffa; In Country; Liebestraum; Miles from Home; Night We Never Met, The; Orphans; Orpheus Descending; Pink Nights; Rising Sun; Sleeping with the Enemy; Thousand Acres, A; Wrong Man, The (1993)

Anderson, Laurie: Two Moon July

Anderson, Lindsay: O Lucky Man!; Prisoner of Honor

Anderson, Loni: Jayne Mansfield Story, The; Munchie; My Mother's Secret Life; Night at the Roxbury, A; Sizzle; Sorry, Wrong Number (1989); Stroker Ace; Whisper Kills, A; White Hot: The Mysterious Murder of Thelma Todd

Anderson, Louie: Ratboy; Wrong Guys, The

Anderson, Mary: Hunt the Man Down; Underworld Story

Anderson, Matthew R.: Surface to Air

Anderson, Melissa Sue: Chattanooga Choo Choo; Dead Men Don't Die; Equalizer, The: "Memories of Manon"; First Affair; Happy Birthday to Me; Little House on the Prairie (TV Series)

Anderson, Melody: Dead and Buried; Elvis—The Movie; Final Notice; Firewalker; Flash Gordon; Hitler's Daughter; Landslide; Marilyn & Bobby: Her Final Affair

Anderson, Michael J.: Great Land of Small, The

Anderson Jr., Michael: Dear Heart; In Search of the Castaways; Legacy for Leonette; Sons of Katie Elder, The

Anderson, Mitchell: Back to Hannibal: The Return of Tom Sawyer and Huckleberry Finn; Deadly Dreams; Goodbye, Miss 4th of July; Relax ... It's Just Sex

Anderson, Pamela: Baywatch: The Movie; Raw Justice; Snapdragon

Anderson, Pat: Summer School Teachers; TNT Jackson

Anderson, Richard: Bionic Woman, The; Escape from Fort Bravo; Gettysburg; Glass Shield, The; I Love Melvin; It's a Dog's Life; Magnificent Yankee, The; Night Strangler, The; Rich, Young and Pretty

Anderson, Richard Dean: Ordinary Heroes; Past the Bleachers; Stargate SG-1

Arliss, George: Disraeli; Dr. Syn; Iron Duke, The; Transatlantic Tunnel

Armendariz, Pedro: Captain Sinbad; Conqueror, The; El Bruto (The Brute); Flor Sylvestre; Fugitive, The (1947); Littlest Outlaw, The; Pearl, The; Three Godfathers, The; Tulsa

Armendariz Jr., Pedro: Bandits (1967); Don't Be Afraid of the Dark; Le Chèvre (The Goat)

Armetta, Henry: Devil's Brother, The; Everybody Sing; Make a Wish; Manhattan Merry-Go-Round; Poor Little Rich Girl (1936); Speak Easily

Arms, Russell: By the Light of the Silvery Moon; Loaded Pistols

Armstrong, Alun: Awfully Big Adventure, An

Armstrong, Bess: Dream Lover (1994); High Road to China; Jaws 3; Jekyll & Hyde—Together Again; Nothing in Common; Perfect Daughter, The; Second Sight; Skateboard Kid, The

Armstrong, Curtis: Adventures of Huck Finn, The (1993); Bad Medicine; Elvis Meets Nixon; One Crazy Summer; Revenge of the Nerds; Revenge of the Nerds II: Nerds in Paradise; Revenge of the Nerds III: The Next Generation; Revenge of the Nerds IV: Nerds in Love; Risky Business

Armstrong, Jack: Guyver, The

Armstrong, Kerry: Hunting

Armstrong, Lee: Leprechaun 3

Armstrong, Louis: Cabin in the Sky; Every Day's a Holiday; Five Pennies, The; Glenn Miller Story, The; High Society; Man Called Adam, A; Paris Blues; Song Is Born, A

Armstrong, Neil: Killing Time (1996)

Armstrong, Perry: Solo (1977)

Armstrong, R. G.: Angels Die Hard; Best of Times, The; Boss; Bulletproof (1988); Children of the Corn; Dick Tracy (1990); Dixie Dynamite; El Dorado; Evilspeak; Ghetto Blaster; Great Northfield Minnesota Raid, The; Hammett; Invasion of Privacy (1996); Lone Wolf McQuade; Pack, The; Payback (1994); Predator; Pursuit of D. B. Cooper; Red-Headed Stranger, The; Ride the High Country; Stay Hungry; Steel (1980); Where the Buffalo Roam

Armstrong, Robert: Action in Arabia; Be Yourself; Big News; Blood on the Sun; Danger Lights; Dive Bomber; Ex-Mrs. Bradford, The; Fugitive, The (1947); Girl in Every Port, A (1928); Hold 'em Jail; Kansan, The; King Kong (1933); Lost Squadron; Mighty Joe Young (1949); Mr. Winkle Goes to War; Most Dangerous Game, The; Paleface, The; Palooka; Racketeer; Son of Kong, The; Tournament Tempo

Armstrong, Ronald K.: Bugged!

Armstrong, Todd: Jason and the Argonauts

Arnaz Jr., Desi: Fakeout; House of the Long Shadows; Joyride (1977); Lucy and Desi: A Home Movie; Mambo Kings, The; Wedding, A (1978)

Arnaz Sr., Desi: Bataan; Escape Artist, The; Forever Darling; Four Jacks and a Jill; I Love Lucy (TV Series); Long, Long Trailer, The; Lucy and Desi: A Home Movie; Too Many Girls

Arnaz, Lucie: Jazz Singer, The (1980); Lucy and Desi: A Home Movie; Mating Season, The; Who Is the Black Dahlia?

Arndt, Denis: Amelia Earhart: The Final Flight

Arndt, Jurgen: Celeste

Arne, Peter: Return of the Pink Panther, The; Straw Dogs

Arness, James: Alamo, The; Thirteen Days to Glory; Big Jim McLain; Farmer's Daughter, The; Gunsmoke (TV Series); Gunsmoke: Return to Dodge; Hondo; Island in the Sky; Sea Chase, The; Stars in My Crown; Them!; Thing (From Another World), The (1951); Two Lost Worlds; Wagonmaster

Arnez, Eva: Ferocious Female Freedom Fighters

Arngrim, Stephan: Fear No Evil

Arno, Alice: Erotikill

Arno, Sig: Melody Master (The Great Awakening) (New Wine); Palm Beach Story, The; Song to Remember, A

Arnold, Edward: Ambassador's Daughter, The; Annie Get Your Gun; Broken Trust (1992); City That Never Sleeps; Come and Get It; Command Decision; Crime and Punishment (1935); Dear Wife; Devil and Daniel Webster, The; Hucksters, The; Idiot's Delight; I'm No Angel; Johnny Apollo; Johnny Eager; Kismet (1944); Let Freedom Ring; Mrs. Parkington; Roman Scandals; Sadie McKee; Secret of the Blue Room, The; Slightly Honorable; Three Daring Daughters; Three on a Match; Toast of New York, The;

Weekend at the Waldorf; Yellow Cab Man, The; You Can't Take it with You (1938); Ziegfeld Follies

Arnold, Jesse: Hard Hombre

Arnold, Mark: Trancers 5: Sudden Deth

Arnold, Steve: Apart from Hugh

Arnold, Tom: Backfield in Motion; Big Bully; Carpool; Hero (1992); McHale's Navy; National Lampoon's Golf Punks; Nine Months; Sink or Swim; Stupids, The; Touch; True Lies

Arnott, David: Crisscross (1992)

Arnott, Mark: Return of the Secaucus 7

Arnoul, Françoise: Forbidden Fruit; Jacko and Lise; Little Theatre of Jean Renoir, The

Aronson, Judie: American Ninja; Desert Kickboxer

Arp, Philip: Last Five Days, The

Arquette, Alexis: Children of the Corn V: Fields of Terror; Dead Weekend; Don't Do It; Grief; I Think I Do; Jack Be Nimble; Jumpin' at the Boneyard; Sometimes They Come Back Again; Wigstock: The Movie

Arquette, David: Alarmist, The; Dead Man's Walk; Dream with the Fishes; Fall Time; Free Money; Johns; Never Been Kissed; Ravenous; Ready to Rumble; Roadracers; Scream (1996); Scream 2; Scream 3; Webber's World (At Home with the Webbers); Wild Bill

Arquette, Patricia: Beyond Rangoon; Bringing Out the Dead; Dillinger (1990); Ed Wood; Ethan Frome; Far North; Flirting with Disaster; Goodbye Lover; Hi-Lo Country, The; Holy Matrimony; Indian Runner, The; Infinity; Inside Monkey Zetterland; Lost Highway; Nightmare on Elm Street 3, A: The Dream Warriors; Nightwatch; Prayer of the Rollerboys; Pretty Smart; Secret Agent, The (1996); Stigmata; Trouble Bound; True Romance; Wild Flower (1991)

Arquette, Rosanna: After Hours; ... Almost; Amazon Women on the Moon; Aviator, The; Baby, It's You; Big Blue, The; Black Rainbow; Crash (1996); Dark Secret of Harvest Home, The; Desperately Seeking Susan; Don't Hang Up; 8 Million Ways to Die; Executioner's Song, The; Fathers & Sons; Flight of the Intruder, The; Floating Away; Gone Fishin'; Gorp; I'm Losing You; In the Deep Woods; Linguini Incident, The; More American Graffiti; New York Stories; Nobody's Fool (1986); Nowhere to Run (1993); Off the Wall; One Cooks, the Other Doesn't; Promised a Miracle; Pulp Fiction; Search and Destroy (1995); Silverado; S.O.B.; Son of the Morning Star; Sweet Revenge (1990); Trading Favors; Whole Nine Yards, The; Wrong Man, The (1993)

Arrants, Rod: Vamping

Arrindell, Lisa: Livin' Large

Arroyave, Karina: 187

Artaud, Antonin: Napoleon (1927); Passion of Joan of Arc, The

Arthur, Anna: Alley Cats, The

Arthur, Bea: Lovers and Other Strangers; Mame

Arthur, Carol: Sunshine Boys, The

Arthur, Jean: Arizona; Danger Lights; Devil and Miss Jones, The; Ex-Mrs. Bradford, The; History Is Made at Night; Lady Takes a Chance, A; Mr. Deeds Goes to Town; Mr. Smith Goes to Washington; More the Merrier, The; Mysterious Dr. Fu Manchu; Only Angels Have Wings; Plainsman, The; Return of Dr. Fu Manchu; Saturday Night Kid, The; Shane; Talk of the Town, The; You Can't Take it with You (1938)

Arthur, Johnny: Ghost Walks, The; Masked Marvel, The; Road to Singapore

Arthur, Maureen: How to Succeed in Business without Really Trying; Love God?, The

Arthur, Robert: Mother Wore Tights; September Affair

Artura, Michael: Killer Looks

Ashbrook, Dana: Girlfriend from Hell; Return of the Living Dead Part II

Ashbrook, Daphne: Automatic; Deadman's Revenge; Gimme an "F"; Intruders; Love Letter, The (1998); Quiet Cool; Sunset Heat

Ashby, Linden: Beneficiary, The; Blast; Cadillac Ranch; Mortal Kombat; Night Angel; Perfect Bride, The; Wyatt Earp

Ashcroft, Peggy: Hullabaloo over George and Bonnie's Pictures; Jewel in the Crown, The; Joseph Andrews; Madame Sousatzka; Nun's Story, The; Passage to India, A; Rhodes of Africa (Rhodes); Secret Ceremony; Sunday, Bloody Sunday

Asher, Jane: Deep End; Dreamchild; Masque of the Red Death, The (1964); Success Is the Best Revenge; Voyage 'Round My Father, A

the Vampire; Mr. Moto Takes a Vacation; Murders in the Zoo; Mystery of the Wax Museum; Night Monster; Pardon My Sarong; Secret of the Blue Room, The; Sherlock Holmes and the Secret Weapon; Son of Frankenstein; Sphinx, The (1933); Strange Case of Dr. Rx, The; Three Comrades; Three Musketeers, The (1939); Vampire Bat, The

Atzorn, Robert: From the Lives of the Marionettes

Auberjonois, René: Ballad of Little Jo, The; Eyes of Laura Mars, The; Feud, The; Lone Justice; Lost Language of Cranes, The; More Wild Wild West; My Best Friend Is a Vampire; Police Academy 5: Assignment: Miami Beach; 3:15—The Moment of Truth; Walker; Where the Buffalo Roam; Wild Card; Wild Wild West Revisited, The

Aubert, Lenore: Abbott and Costello Meet the Killer, Boris Karloff; They Got Me Covered

Aubrey, Cecile: Manon

Aubrey, James: Forever Young (1983); Lord of the Flies (1963)

Aubrey, Jimmy: Smokey Trails

Aubrey, Juliet: Go Now; Middlemarch; Still Crazy

Aubry, Danielle: Operation C.I.A.

Auclair, Michel: Funny Face; Manon; Story of a Love Story; Swashbuckler, The (1984)

Audran, Stéphane: Violette

Audran, Stéphane: Babette's Feast; Bad Girls (1969); Black Bird, The; Blood of Others, The; Blood Relatives; Brideshead Revisited; Clean Slate (Coup de Torchon) (1981); Discreet Charm of the Bourgeoisie, The; Eagle's Wing; La Cage aux Folles III, The Wedding; Le Boucher (The Butcher); Les Biches; Maximum Risk; Mistral's Daughter; Silver Bears; Six in Paris (Paris Vue par …); Turn of the Screw (1992); Vincent, François, Paul and the Others; Wedding in Blood

Auer, Mischa: Around the World; Brewster's Millions (1945); Crusades, The (1935); Destry Rides Again; Drums of Jeopardy; Hellzapoppin; Just Imagine; Mr. Arkadin (Confidential Report); Monster Walks, The; One Rainy Afternoon; One Hundred Men and a Girl; Rage of Paris, The; Seven Sinners; Spring Parade; Sputnik; Sweethearts; Three Smart Girls; Winterset; You Can't Take it with You (1938)

Auffay, Patrick: 400 Blows, The

Auger, Claudine: Associate, The (1982); Lobster for Breakfast; Summertime Killer, The; Thunderball; Twitch of the Death Nerve

Augger, Perito: Bugsy Malone

August, Pernilla: Best Intentions, The; Jerusalem

August, Robert: Endless Summer, The

Auld, Georgie: New York, New York

Aulin, Ewa: Blood Castle (1972)

Auli, Haley: Something to Talk About

Ault, Marie: Lodger, The

Aumiller, Gary: Murdered Innocence

Aumont, Jean-Pierre: Bizarre, Bizarre; Blackout (1978); Blood of Others, The; Cat and Mouse; Catherine & Co.; Cauldron of Blood; Devil at 4 O'Clock, The; Happy Hooker, The; Horse Without a Head, The; John Paul Jones; Lili; Proprietor, The; Seven Deadly Sins, The; Something Short of Paradise; Sweet Country; Tale of Two Cities, A (1991)

Aumont, Michel: La Vie Continue; Sunday in the Country, A

Aumont, Tina: Lifespan; Malicious (1974); Partner; Torso

Aurelius, Marcus: Apex; Full Contact

Austin, Al: Pay or Die

Austin, Albert: Charlie Chaplin—The Early Years Vol. 1–4; Charlie Chaplin Cavalcade; Charlie Chaplin Festival

Austin, Charlotte: Bride and the Beast, The; Gorilla at Large

Austin, Jerry: Adventures of Don Juan, The

Austin, Karen: Assassin; Far from Home; Girl to Kill For, A; Ladies Club; Summer Rental; Taming of the Shrew (1982); When the Time Comes

Austin, Lois: Mom and Dad

Austin, Teri: Vindicator, The

Austin, William: Fig Leaves; It (1927); Mysterious Dr. Fu Manchu; Return of Dr. Fu Manchu

Auteuil, Daniel: Eighth Day, The; Elegant Criminal, The; Jean De Florette; La Separation; Les Voleurs; Ma Saison Preferée; Mama, There's a Man in Your Bed; Manon of the Spring; Queen Margot; Thieves (Les Voleurs); Un Coeur en Hiver

Autry, Alan: Great Los Angeles Earthquake, The; Roadhouse 66

Autry, Gene: Beyond the Purple Hills; Big Sombrero, The; Blue Montana Skies; Colorado Sunset; Cow Town; Git Along, Little Dogies; Hills of Utah, The; In Old Santa Fe; Last of the Pony Riders; Last Round-Up; Loaded Pistols; Man from Music Mountain; Man of the Frontier (Red River Valley); Manhattan Merry-Go-Round; Melody Ranch; Melody Trail; Mexicali Rose; Mule Train; Oh! Susanna!; Old Corral; Phantom Empire (1935); Public Cowboy #1; Radio Ranch (Men with Steel Faces, Phantom Empire); Ride, Ranger, Ride; Riders of the Whistling Pines; Rim of the Canyon; Robin Hood of Texas; South of the Border; Springtime in the Rockies (1937); Winning of the West; Yodelin' Kid from Pine Ridge

Avalon, Frankie: Alamo, The; Back to the Beach; Beach Blanket Bingo; Beach Party; Bikini Beach; Dr. Goldfoot and the Bikini Machine; How to Stuff a Wild Bikini; I'll Take Sweden; Muscle Beach Party; Panic in the Year Zero; Stoned Age, The; Voyage to the Bottom of the Sea

Avalon, Phil: Summer City

Avalos, Luis: Fires Within; Ghost Fever; Lone Justice; Lone Justice 2

Avedon, Loreen: No Retreat, No Surrender II; No Retreat, No Surrender 3: Blood Brothers; Operation Golden Phoenix; Virtual Combat

Avellana, José Mari: Deathfight

Avery, Linda: Hitchhikers

Avery, Margaret: Blueberry Hill; Color Purple, The; For Us the Living; The Medgar Evers Story; Heat Wave (1990); Hell Up in Harlem; Jacksons, The: An American Dream; Mardi Gras for the Devil; Return of Superfly, The; Sky Is Gray, The; Which Way is Up?; White Man's Burden

Avery, Val: Black Caesar; Dream of Kings, A; Firehouse (1972); Heroes; Satan's Bed

Avery, Vicci: Return of the Sand Fairy, The

Aviles, Angel: Mi Vida Loca

Aviles, Rick: Mondo New York; Saint of Fort Washington, The

Avital, Mili: Invasion of Privacy (1996); Kissing a Fool

Avran, Chris: Captive Planet; Twitch of the Death Nerve

Awashima, Chikage: Human Condition, The, Part One: No Greater Love

Axelrod, Nina: Cross Country; Motel Hell; Time Walker; Trading Hearts

Axman, Hanne: Red Menace, The

Axton, Hoyt: Act of Vengeance; Black Stallion, The; Buried Alive (1990); Disorganized Crime; Dixie Lanes; Endangered Species; Gremlins; Heart Like a Wheel; King Cobra; Liar's Moon; Number One Fan; Retribution; We're No Angels (1989); Woody Guthrie—Hard Travelin'

Ayashi, Sachiko: 8Man

Aykroyd, Dan: Blues Brothers, The; Blues Brothers 2000; Caddyshack II; Canadian Bacon; Celtic Pride; Chaplin (1987); Conehands; Couch Trip, The; Doctor Detroit; Dragnet (1987); Driving Miss Daisy; Exit to Eden; Feeling Minnesota; Getting Away with Murder; Ghostbusters; Ghostbusters II; Great Outdoors, The; Grosse Pointe Blank; Into the Night; Loose Cannons; Love at First Sight; My Fellow Americans; My Girl; My Girl 2; My Stepmother Is an Alien; Neighbors; 1941; Nothing But Trouble (1991); Rutles, The (All You Need Is Cash); Sgt. Bilko; Sneakers; Spies Like Us; Things We Did Last Summer; This Is My Life; Tommy Boy; Trading Places; Twilight Zone—The Movie

Aykroyd, Peter: Gas

Aylmer, Felix: As You Like It; Citadel, The; From the Terrace; Ghosts of Berkeley Square; Hamlet (1948); Henry V (1944); Iron Duke, The; Knights of the Round Table; Nine Days a Queen; Quo Vadis (1951); Saint Joan

Aymerie, Catherine: Rabid Grannies

Ayres, Agnes: Sheik, The

Ayres, Jo Ann: In the Time of Barbarians

Ayres, Leah: Bloodsport; Burning, The; Eddie Macon's Run; Hot Child in the City

Ayres, Lew: Advise and Consent; All Quiet on the Western Front (1930); Battlestar Galactica; Broadway Serenade; Carpetbaggers, The; Cast the First Stone; Damien: Omen II; Dark Mirror, The; Dr. Kildare's Strange Case; Donovan's Brain; End of the World; Fingers at the Window; Francis Gary Powers: The True Story of the U-2 Spy Incident; Holiday; Johnny Belinda; Of Mice and Men (1981); She Waits

Ayres, Robert: Battle Beneath the Earth

Ayres, Rosalind: Beautiful People

Azaria, Hank: Birdcage, The; Cradle Will Rock; Godzilla (1998); Great Expectations (1998); Grosse Pointe Blank; Homegrown; Mystery, Alaska; Mystery Men; Quiz Show

Azema, Sabine: Life and Nothing But; Melo; Sunday in the Country, A

Azhari, Ayu: Without Mercy

Azito, Tony: Private Resort

Aznavour, Charles: Blockhouse, The; Head Against the Wall; Shoot the Piano Player

Azorin, Eloy: All About My Mother

Azzara, Candy: Doin' Time on Planet Earth; Easy Money; Fatso; Pandemonium

B., Lisa: Serpent's Lair

Baal, Karin: Dead Eyes of London

Babatundé, Obba: Introducing Dorothy Dandridge; Life; Miss Evers' Boys; Reason to Believe, A; Undercover Blues

Babb, Sean: Pig's Tale, A

Babcock, Barbara: Christmas Coal Mine Miracle, The; Far and Away; News at Eleven; Quarterback Princess; That Was Then . . . This Is Now

Bacall, Lauren: All I Want for Christmas; Appointment with Death; Big Sleep, The (1946); Blood Alley; Dark Passage; Designing Woman; Dinner at Eight (1990); Fan, The; Flame over India; Foreign Field, A; From the Mixed-Up Files of Mrs. Basil E. Frankweiler; Harper; How to Marry a Millionaire; Innocent Victim; Key Largo; Mirror Has Two Faces, The; Misery; Mr. North; Murder on the Orient Express; My Fellow Americans; Portrait, The; Ready to Wear; Sex and the Single Girl; Shootist, The; To Have and Have Not; Woman's World; Written on the Wind; Young Man with a Horn

Baccaloni: Fanny (1961)

Bach, Barbara: Caveman; Force Ten from Navarone; Give My Regards to Broad Street; Great Alligator, The; Princess Daisy; Spy Who Loved Me, The; Stateline Motel; Unseen, The; Up the Academy

Bach, Catherine: Masters of Menace; Rage and Honor; Street Justice

Bach, John: Crimebroker; Georgia (1987); Lost Tribe, The; Sound and the Silence, The

Bachar, Dian: Orgazmo

Bachchan, Amitabh: God Is My Witness

Bacholor, Stephanie: I've Always Loved You; Springtime in the Sierras

Bachmann, Hans: Beyond the Rising Moon (Star Quest); Invader

Baci, Michael: Rebecca's Secret

Backer, Brian: Burning, The; Fast Times at Ridgemont High; Steel and Lace

Backus, Jim: Above and Beyond; Androcles and the Lion; Ask Any Girl; Billie; C.H.O.M.P.S.; Crazy Mama; Critic's Choice; Francis in the Navy; Good Guys Wear Black; Great Lover, The; His Kind of Woman; Horizontal Lieutenant, The; I Love Melvin; I Married Joan (TV Series); Ice Palace; I'll See You in My Dreams; Ma and Pa Kettle Go to Town; Man of a Thousand Faces; Meet Me in Las Vegas; Now You See Him, Now You Don't; Opposite Sex, The (1956); Pete's Dragon; Rebel Without a Cause; Wheeler Dealers, The; Where Were You When the Lights Went Out?; Zotz!

Backus, Richard: Deathdream; Soldier's Home

Baclanova, Olga: Docks of New York, The; Freaks; Man Who Laughs, The

Bacon, Irving: Blondie Takes a Vacation; Blondie Has Servant Trouble; Caught in the Draft; Dreaming Out Loud; Guest Wife; Howards of Virginia, The; Interns Can't Take Money; It's a Great Life

Bacon, Kevin: Air Up There, The; Apollo 13; Balto; Big Picture, The; Criminal Law; Digging to China; Diner; End of the Line; Few Good Men, A; Flatliners; Footloose; Friday the 13th; He Said, She Said; JFK; Murder in the First; My Dog Skip; Picture Perfect; Pyrates; Queens Logic; Quicksilver; River Wild, The; She's Having a Baby; Sleepers; Stir of Echoes; Telling Lies in America; Tremors; White Water Summer; Wild Things

Bacon, Lloyd: Charlie Chaplin . . . Our Hero; Charlie Chaplin—The Early Years Vol. 1–4; Charlie Chaplin Carnival; Charlie Chaplin Cavalcade

Bad, Steven: Evil Laugh

Badal, Tom: Out on Bail

Badalucco, Michael: Mac; Professional, The; Search for One-Eye Jimmy, The

Baddeley, Hermione: Adventures of Bullwhip Griffin, The; Belles of St. Trinian's, The; Mary Poppins; Passport to Pimlico; Pickwick Papers, The; Quartet (1948); Room at the Top; Tom Brown's Schooldays (1950); Unsinkable Molly Brown, The; Woman in Question

Badel, Alan: Arabesque; Children of the Damned; Day of the Jackal, The; Three Cases of Murder

Badema: Close to Eden

Bader, Diedrich: Beverly Hillbillies, The (1993)

Bader, John: J. Lyle

Badford, Basil: Quartet (1948)

Badham, Mary: To Kill a Mockingbird

Badia, Nuria: Barcelona

Badland, Annette: Angels and Insects; Twentyfourseven (boxing)

Badler, Jane: Under the Gun (1995); V

Baer, Buddy: Giant from the Unknown; Jubilee Trail; Quo Vadis (1951); Snow White and the Three Stooges

Baer, Harry: Fox and His Friends

Baer, Max: Africa Screams; Beverly Hillbillies, The (TV Series); Beverly Hillbillies Go Hollywood, The; Harder They Fall, The

Baer Jr., Max: Macon County Line

Baer, Meredith: Chicken Chronicles, The

Baer, Parley: Two on a Guillotine; Ugly Dachshund, The; White Dog

Baerwitz, Jerry: Varan, the Unbelievable

Baez, Joan: Don't Look Back (1967); Woody Guthrie—Hard Travelin'

Baeza, Paloma: Kid in King Arthur's Court, A

Baff, Regina: Below the Belt

Bagdasarian, Carol: Aurora Encounter

Baggett, Lynne: D.O.A. (1949)

Baggetta, Vincent: Man Who Wasn't There, The

Baggi, Angiola: Story of Boys and Girls

Bagheri, Abdolrahman: Taste of Cherry

Bagley, Ross Elliot: Little Rascals, The (1994)

Bagwell, Marcus: Day of the Warrior

Bahner, Blake: Blackbelt 2: Fatal Force; Sensations; Thrilled to Death

Bahns, Maxine: Brothers McMullen, The; She's the One

Bai, Xue: Yellow Earth

Bailey, Bill: On the Edge

Bailey, Blake: Head of the Family; Lurking Fear

Bailey, G. W.: Burglar (U.S.); Capture of Grizzly Adams, The; Doublecrossed; Mannequin (1987); Police Academy 4: Citizens on Patrol; Police Academy 6: City Under Siege; Rustler's Rhapsody; Short Circuit; Warning Sign; Write to Kill

Bailey, Jimmy: Penitentiary III

Bailey, Kathleen: Witchtrap

Bailey, Marion: Meantime

Bailey, Mark: Unbelievable Truth, The

Bailey, Pearl: Carmen Jones; Norman . . . Is That You?

Bailey, Raymond: Beverly Hillbillies, The (TV Series); Beverly Hillbillies Go Hollywood, The

Bailey, Robin: See No Evil

Baily, Joel: King Lear (1982)

Baily, Matt: Blood Thirsty

Bain, Barbara: Skinheads; Space 1999 (TV Series); Spirit of '76, The; Trust Me

Bain, Conrad: Child Bride of Short Creek; C.H.O.M.P.S.; Last Summer; Postcards from the Edge; Who Killed Mary What's 'Er Name?

Bain, Cynthia: Spontaneous Combustion; Vietnam War Story—Part Two

Bain, Ron: Experience Preferred . . . But Not Essential

Bainter, Fay: Babes on Broadway; Children's Hour, The; Dark Waters; Human Comedy, The; Journey for Margaret; June Bride; Our Town (1940); Presenting Lily Mars; Shining Hour, The; State Fair (1945); Virginian, The (1946); Woman of the Year; Young Tom Edison

Baio, Jimmy: Brass; Playing for Keeps

Baio, Scott: Alice in Wonderland (1985); Bugsy Malone; Foxes; I Love N.Y.; Zapped!

Baird, Harry: Story of a Three Day Pass, The

Baird, Roxanne: Blackbelt 2: Fatal Force

Bairstow, Scott: Black Circle Boys; White Fang 2: Myth of the White Wolf; Wild America

Baisho, Mitsuko: Eijanaika (Why Not?)

Baitz, Jon Robin: Last Summer in the Hamptons

Bajpai, Maoj: Bandit Queen

Bakalyan, Dick: Blame It on the Night; Paratroop Command

Baker, Annie: Halloween Tree, The

Baker, Art: Underworld Story

Baker, Blanche: Cold Feet (1984); French Postcards; Livin' Large; Mary and Joseph: A Story of Faith; Romeo and Juliet (1983); Sixteen Candles

Baker, Carroll: Andy Warhol's Bad; Baby Doll; Big Country, The; But Not for Me; Captain Apache; Carpetbaggers, The; Cheyenne Autumn; Easy to Love; Game, The (1997); Giant; Greatest Story Ever Told, The; Harlow; How the West Was Won; Ironweed; Just Your Luck; Kindergarten Cop; Miracle, The (1959); Native Son (1986); North Shore Fish; Paranoia; Secret Diary of Sigmund Freud, The; Star 80; Watcher in the Woods, The; World Is Full of Married Men, The

Baker, Colin: Dr. Who (TV series)

Baker, Diane: Baker's Hawk; Best of Everything, The; Closer, The; Horse in the Gray Flannel Suit, The; Journey to the Center of the Earth (1959); Marnie; Mirage (1965); Net, The; Pilot, The; Prize, The; Stolen Hours; Strait-Jacket

Baker, Dylan: Delirious; Disclosure; Happiness; Long Walk Home, The; Oxygen

Baker, Fay: Chain Lightning; Double Deal

Baker, Frank: New Adventures of Tarzan; Tarzan and the Green Goddess

Baker, George: At Bertram's Hotel; Curse of the Fly; For Queen and Country; Goodbye, Mr. Chips (1969); Robin Hood: Herne's Son; Sword of Lancelot

Baker, Gregg: Kleptomania

Baker, James: Ferngully 2: The Magical Rescue

Baker, Jamie: Ferngully 2: The Magical Rescue

Baker, Jay: April Fool's Day; Naked Lies

Baker, Jim: Tripods

Baker, Joby: Last Angry Man, The; Wackiest Ship in the Army, The

Baker, Joe Don: Adam at 6 A.M.; Cape Fear (1991); Charley Varrick; Citizen Cohn; Congo; Criminal Law; Distinguished Gentleman, The; Edge of Darkness (1986); Felony; Final Justice (1984); Fletch; Framed (1975); George Wallace; Getting Even; Goldeneye; Guns of the Magnificent Seven; Joy Sticks; Junior Bonner; Killing Time, The (1987); Leonard Part 6; Living Daylights, The; Natural, The; Pack, The; Panther; Poodle Springs; Ring of Steel; Tomorrow Never Dies; Underneath, The; Wacko; Walking Tall; Wild Rovers, The

Baker, Josephine: French Way, The; Princess Tam Tam; Zou Zou

Baker, Kathy: Article 99; Clean and Sober; Dad; Edward Scissorhands; Image, The; Inventing the Abbotts; Jackknife; Jennifer 8; Killing Affair, A; Lush Life; Mad Dog and Glory; Mr. Frost; Not In This Town; Street Smart; To Gillian on Her 37th Birthday

Baker, Kenny: At the Circus; Goldwyn Follies, The; Harvey Girls, The; Mikado, The (1939); Star Wars: Episode I The Phantom Menace

Baker, Kirsten: Gas Pump Girls

Baker, Lee Anne: Necropolis

Baker, Lenny: Next Stop, Greenwich Village

Baker, Nellie Bly: Red Kimono, The

Baker, Pamela: Bloody Wednesday

Baker, Phil: Gang's All Here, The

Baker, Ray: Anywhere But Here; Disaster at Silo 7; Final Cut, The; Hard Truth; Hexed; Masters of Menace; Stacking

Baker, Robekah: Secrets in the Attic

Baker, Renee: Delirious

Baker, Scott: Broadcast Bombshells

Baker, Sharon: Captive Planet

Baker, Stanley: Accident; Concrete Jungle, The (1962) (Criminal, The); Cruel Sea, The; Dingaka; Guns of Navarone, The; Helen of Troy; Knights of the Round Table; Robbery; Sodom and Gomorrah; Zorro; Zulu

Baker, Tom: Angels Die Hard; Canterbury Tales, The; Curse of King Tut's Tomb, The; Dr. Who: Revenge of the Cybermen; Dr. Who (TV series); Freakmaker; Golden Voyage of Sinbad, The; Nicholas and Alexandra; Vault of Horror

Bakewell, Gary: BackBeat

Bakhtiari, Afshin Khorshid: Taste of Cherry

Bakke, Brenda: Death Spa; Fixer, The; Hot Shots Part Deux; Lone Justice 2; Scavengers; Star Quest; Tales from the Crypt: Demon Knight; Trucks; Twogether

Bako, Brigitte: Dark Tide; Double Take; Escape, The; Man in Uniform, A; Paranoia (1998); Red Shoe Diaries; Replikator: Cloned to Kill

Bakri, Muhamad: Beyond the Walls; Double Edge

Bakula, Scott: Color of Night; Invaders, The; Last Fling, The; Lord of Illusions; Mean Streak; Mercy Mission (The Rescue of Flight 711); Necessary Roughness; Passion to Kill, A; Quantum Leap (TV Series); Sibling Rivalry

Balaban, Bob: Absence of Malice; Altered States; City Slickers II; Dead-Bang; Deconstructing Harry; End of the Line; For Love or Money; Greedy; Jakob the Liar; Late Shift, The; Strawberry Statement, The; Three to Tango; 2010; Unnatural Pursuits; Waiting for Guffman; Whose Life Is It Anyway?

Balan, Ovidiu: Mondo

Balaski, Belinda: Bobbie Jo and the Outlaw; Cannonball; Proud Men

Balasko, Josiane: French Twist; Too Beautiful for You

Balasz, Samu: Cat's Play

Balding, Rebecca: Boogens, The; Gathering, Part II, The; Silent Scream

Baldwin, Adam: Bad Guys; Bitter Harvest (1993); Blind Justice; Chocolate War, The; Cohen and Tate; Cold Sweat (1993); D.C. Cab; Deadbolt; Digital Man; 800 Leagues Down the Amazon; Full Metal Jacket; Hadley's Rebellion; Indiscreet (1998); Lover's Knot; My Bodyguard; Next of Kin (1989); Poison Ivy (1985); Predator 2; Radio Flyer; Reckless (1984); Sawbones; 3:15—The Moment of Truth; Trade Off; Treacherous; Where the Day Takes You; Wyatt Earp

Baldwin, Alec: Alamo, The; Thirteen Days to Glory; Alice (1990); Beetlejuice; Confession, The; Dress Gray; Edge, The; Forever Lulu; Getaway, The (1994); Ghosts of Mississippi; Glengarry Glen Ross; Great Balls of Fire; Heaven's Prisoners; Hunt for Red October, The; Juror, The; Looking for Richard; Malice; Marrying Man, The; Mercury Rising; Miami Blues; Outside Providence; Prelude to a Kiss; Shadow, The; Streetcar Named Desire, A (1995); Talk Radio; Working Girl

Baldwin, Ann: Wall Street Cowboy

Baldwin, Daniel: Attack of the 50-Foot Woman (1993); Dead on Sight; Family of Cops; Heroes of Desert Storm; Invader, The; John Carpenter's Vampires; Knight Moves; Lone Justice; Love Kills (1999); Pandora Project, The; Phoenix; Trees Lounge; Yesterday's Target

Baldwin, Dick: Mr. Moto's Gamble

Baldwin, Michael: Phantasm; Phantasm III: Lord of the Dead; Phantasm IV: Oblivion

Baldwin, Peter: Ghost, The (1963)

Baldwin, Robert: Courageous Dr. Christian, The; Meet Dr. Christian; They Meet Again

Baldwin, Stephen: Bio-Dome; Bitter Harvest (1993); Crimetime; Crossing the Bridge; Dead Weekend; 8 Seconds; Fall Time; Fled; Flintstones in Viva Rock Vegas, The; Great American Sex Scandal, The; Mr. Murder; Mrs. Parker and the Vicious Circle; New Eden; One Tough Cop; Posse (1993); Simple Twist of Fate, A; Sub Down; Threesome; Under the Hula Moon; Usual Suspects, The

Baldwin, William: Backdraft; Curdled; Fair Game (1995); Flatliners; Internal Affairs; Preppie Murder, The; Pyromaniac's Love Story, A; Shattered Image (1998); Sliver; Three of Hearts; Virus (1999)

Bale, Christian: American Psycho; Empire of the Sun; Little Women (1994); Metroland; Newsies; Royal Deceit; Secret Agent, The (1996); Shaft (2000); Swing Kids; Treasure Island (1990); Velvet Goldmine; William Shakespeare's A Midsummer Night's Dream

Balenda, Carla: Hunt the Man Down

Balfour, Betty: Champagne

Balin, Ina: Black Orchid, The; Charro!; Children of An Lac, The; Comancheros, The; From the Terrace; Patsy, The; Projectionist, The

Balin, Mireille: Pepe Le Moko

Balint, Andras: Father (1966)

Balint, Eszter: Bail Jumper; Linguini Incident, The; Stranger Than Paradise

Balk, Fairuza: American History X; Craft, The; Danger of Love; Gas, Food, Lodging; Imaginary Crimes; Island of Dr. Moreau, The; Outside Chance of Maximilian Glick, The; Re-

Bengell, Norma: Hellbenders, The; Planet of the Vampires

Benichou, Maurice: A La Mode

Benigni, Roberto: Down by Law; Johnny Stecchino; Life Is Beautiful; Monster, The (1996); Night on Earth; Son of the Pink Panther

Bening, Annette: American President, The; Bugsy; Grifters, The; Guilty by Suspicion; In Dreams; Love Affair (1994); Mars Attacks!; Postcards from the Edge; Regarding Henry; Richard III (1995); Siege, The; Valmont; What Planet Are You From?

Benjamin, Paul: Education of Sonny Carson, The; Fence, The; Mr. Inside/Mr. Outside

Benjamin, Richard: Catch-22; Diary of a Mad Housewife; First Family; Goodbye Columbus; House Calls; How to Beat the High Co$t of Living; Last of Sheila, The; Love at First Bite; Packin' It In; Pentagon Wars, The; Portnoy's Complaint; Saturday the 14th; Scavenger Hunt; Steagle, The; Sunshine Boys, The; Westworld; Witches' Brew

Benji: Benji; Benji the Hunted; For the Love of Benji; Oh, Heavenly Dog!

Bennett, David: Legend; Tin Drum, The

Bennett, Heinz: From the Lives of the Marionettes

Bennett, Bruce: Alligator People, The; Before I Hang; Clones, The; Cosmic Man, The; Daniel Boone, Trail Blazer; Dark Passage; Lone Ranger, The (1938); Man I Love, The; Mildred Pierce; New Adventures of Tarzan; Sahara (1943); Silver River; Stolen Life, A; Strategic Air Command; Tarzan and the Green Goddess; Three Violent People; Treasure of the Sierra Madre

Bennett, Constance: Common Law, The; Goose Woman, The; Madame X (1966); Topper; Topper Takes a Trip; Two-Faced Woman; What Price Hollywood?

Bennett, Eila: Terror Aboard

Bennett, Enid: Robin Hood (1923)

Bennett, Fran: King of the Carnival

Bennett, Hywel: Deadline (1987); Endless Night; Loot; Murder Elite; Virgin Soldiers, The

Bennett, Jill: Charge of the Light Brigade, The (1968); Concrete Jungle, The (1962) (Criminal, The); I Want What I Want; Lady Jane; Nanny, The; Old Curiosity Shop, The (1975); Sheltering Sky, The; Skull, The

Bennett, Joan: Best of Dark Shadows, The; Bulldog Drummond; Colonel Effingham's Raid; Dark Shadows (TV Series); Disraeli; Father of the Bride (1950); Father's Little Dividend; House Across the Bay, The; House of Dark Shadows; Little Women (1933); Man Hunt (1941); Man in the Iron Mask, The (1939); Mississippi; Scar, The; Scarlet Street; Secret Beyond the Door; Son of Monte Cristo, The; Suspiria; We're No Angels (1955); Woman in the Window

Bennett, Leila: Emma

Bennett, Marion: Lantern Hill

Bennett, Nigel: Where's the Money, Noreen?

Bennett, Ray: Lovers' Lovers

Bennett, Richard: Arrowsmith; If I Had a Million

Bennett, Tony: Oscar, The (1966)

Bennett, Zachary: By Way of the Stars; Looking for Miracles

Benny, Jack: Broadway Melody of 1936; Buck Benny Rides Again; George Washington Slept Here; Guide for the Married Man, A; Hollywood Canteen; Horn Blows at Midnight, The; It's in the Bag; Jack Benny Program, The (TV Series); Meanest Man in the World, The; To Be or Not to Be (1942); Transatlantic Merry-Go-Round

Benrath, Martin: White Rose, The (1983)

Benrubi, Abraham: Program, The

Benson, Deborah: Danger of Love; Just Before Dawn; Mutant on the Bounty; September 30, 1955

Benson, Lucille: Private Parts

Benson, Martin: Battle Beneath the Earth; Gorgo; Hitchhiker's Guide to the Galaxy, The; Istanbul (1956)

Benson, Robby: All the Kind Strangers; Chosen, The; City Limits; Die Laughing; End, The; Harry and Son; Homewrecker; Ice Castles; Invasion of Privacy; Jory; Last of Mrs. Lincoln, The; Modern Love; Ode to Billy Joe; One on One; Our Town (1980); Rent-a-Cop; Running Brave; Tribute; Two of a Kind (1982); Webber's World (At Home with the Webbers); White Hot

Benson, Wendy: Wes Craven's Wishmaster

Benson, William C.: Redneck Zombies

Bentine, Michael: Down Among the "Z" Men

Bentley, John: Chair, The; Flight from Vienna; Istanbul (1956)

Bentley, Ray: Scarlet Spear, The

Benton, Barbi: Deathstalker; For the Love of It; Hospital Massacre

Benton, Eddie: Dr. Strange

Benton, Helen: Bloodbeat

Benton, Jerome: Graffiti Bridge; Under the Cherry Moon

Benton, Kevin: No Escape, No Return

Benton, Mark: Career Girls

Benton, Suzanne: Boy and His Dog, A; That Cold Day in the Park

Benussi, Femi: Rattler Kid

Ben-Victor, Paul: Corruptor, The; Evil Lives; Red Scorpion 2

Benz, Donna Kei: Pray for Death

Benz, Julie: Jawbreaker

Benzali, Daniel: Murder at 1600; Screwed

Beradino, John: Moon of the Wolf

Beraud, Luc: Sincerely Charlotte

Bercovici, Luca: Drop Zone; Frightmare; K2; Mirror Images II; Mission of Justice; Mortal Passions; Pacific Heights; Parasite; Stranger by Night

Berenger, Eric: Monsieur Hire

Berenger, Tom: At Play in the Fields of the Lord; Avenging Angel, The (1995); Betrayed (1988); Beyond Obsession; Big Chill, The; Body Language (1995); Born on the Fourth of July; Butch and Sundance: The Early Days; Chasers; Diplomatic Siege; Dogs of War, The; Eddie and the Cruisers; Fear City; Field, The; Gettysburg; Gingerbread Man, The; In Praise of Older Women; In the Company of Spies; Last of the Dogmen; Last Rites (1988); Looking for Mr. Goodbar; Love at Large; Major League; Major League II; Murder of Crows, A; Occasional Hell, An; One Man's Hero; Platoon; Rough Riders; Rustler's Rhapsody; Shattered (1991); Shoot to Kill; Sliver; Sniper; Someone to Watch Over Me; Substitute, The (1996)

Berenson, Marisa: Barry Lyndon; Death in Venice; Killer Fish; Night of the Cyclone; Secret Diary of Sigmund Freud, The; Trade Secrets; White Hunter Black Heart

Beresford, Clare: Ultrawarrior

Berfield, Lorne: Double Blast

Berg, Joanna: Visitors, The

Berg, Peter: Across the Moon; Aspen Extreme; Case for Murder, A; Copland; Crooked Hearts; Fire in the Sky; Girl 6; Great White Hype, The; Last Ride, The (1994); Last Seduction, The; Late for Dinner; Midnight Clear, A; Never on Tuesday; Race for Glory

Berge, Colette: Les Abysses

Berge, Francine: Judex; Les Abysses; Mr. Klein

Bergen, Candice: Bite the Bullet; Carnal Knowledge; Domino Principle, The; 11 Harrowhouse; Gandhi; Getting Straight; Mayflower Madam; Merlin & the Sword; Night Full of Rain, A; Oliver's Story; Rich and Famous; Sand Pebbles, The; Soldier Blue; Starting Over; Stick; Wind and the Lion, The

Bergen, Edgar: Fun and Fancy Free; Goldwyn Follies, The; Letter of Introduction; Look Who's Laughing; Muppet Movie, The; Stage Door Canteen; You Can't Cheat an Honest Man

Bergen, Frances: Eating

Bergen, Patrick: Proposition, The

Bergen, Polly: Across the Rio Grande; At War with the Army; Cape Fear (1962); Cry-Baby; Escape from Fort Bravo; Haunting of Sarah Hardy, The; Kisses for My President; Lightning Incident, The; Making Mr. Right; Murder on Flight 502; My Brother's Wife; Once Upon a Time … When We Were Colored; War and Remembrance; Winds of War, The

Bergen, Tushka: Barcelona; Voices From a Locked Room; Wrangler

Berger, Helmut: Ash Wednesday; Battle Force; Code Name: Emerald; Conversation Piece; Damned, The; Dorian Gray; Garden of the Finzi-Continis, The; Godfather, Part III, The; Romantic Englishwoman, The; Victory at Entebbe

Berger, Nicole: Shoot the Piano Player; Story of a Three Day Pass, The

Berger, Sarah: Green Man, The

Berger, Senta: Ambushers, The; Cast a Giant Shadow; Diabolically Yours; Full Hearts and Empty Pockets; Killing Cars; Quiller Memorandum, The; Scarlet Letter (1973);

Sherlock Holmes and the Deadly Necklace; Swiss Conspiracy, The; Waltz King, The; When Women Had Tails; When Women Lost Their Tails

Berger, Sidney: Carnival of Souls

Berger, William: Dial: Help; Tex and the Lord of the Deep

Bergerac, Jacques: Gigi; Hypnotic Eye, The; Les Girls; Unkissed Bride

Bergere, Lee: Time Trackers

Berggren, Thommy: Elvira Madigan; Sunday's Children

Berghof, Herbert: Belarus File, The; Target; Voices

Bergin, Patrick: Double Cross; Durango; Eye of the Beholder; Frankenstein (1992); Highway to Hell; Lawnmower Man 2: Jobe's War (Lawnmower Man); Beyond Cyberspace); Love Crimes; Map of the Human Heart; Mountains of the Moon; Patriot Games; Ripper, The (1997); Robin Hood (1991); Sir Arthur Conan Doyle's The Lost World; Sleeping with the Enemy; Soft Deceit; Suspicious Minds; They (They Watch); Triplecross (1995)

Bergi, Emily: Rage, The; Carrie 2

Bergman, Henry: Charlie Chaplin—The Early Years Vol. 1–4; Charlie Chaplin Cavalcade; Charlie Chaplin Festival; Circus, The/A Day's Pleasure; Woman of Paris, A

Bergman, Ingrid: Adam Had Four Sons; Anastasia (1956); Arch of Triumph; Autumn Sonata; Bells of St. Mary's, The; Cactus Flower; Casablanca; Dr. Jekyll and Mr. Hyde (1941); Dollar; Elena and Her Men; Fear (1955); For Whom the Bell Tolls; Gaslight (1944); Goodbye Again; Hideaways, The; Indiscreet (1958); Inn of the Sixth Happiness, The; Intermezzo (1936); Intermezzo (1939); Joan of Arc; June Night; Matter of Time, A; Murder on the Orient Express; Notorious; Only One Night; Spellbound; Stromboli; Under Capricorn; Voyage in Italy; Walk in the Spring Rain, A; Walpurgis Night; Woman Called Golda, A

Bergman, Peter: Phantom of the Ritz

Bergman, Sandahl: Body of Influence; Conan the Barbarian; Getting Physical; Hell Comes to Frogtown; Inner Sanctum 2; Kandyland; Lipstick Camera; Possessed by the Night; Programmed to Kill; Raw Nerve; Red Sonja; She (1983); Stewardess School; Xanadu

Bergmann, Erik: Ferngully 2: The Magical Rescue

Bergner, Elisabeth: As You Like It; Catherine the Great; Cry of the Banshee

Bergryd, Ulla: Bible, The

Bergstrom, Helena: House of Angels; Women on the Roof, The

Bergstrom, Linda: Children of Noisy Village, The

Berkeley, Elizabeth: First Wives Club, The; Real Blonde, The; Showgirls

Berkeley, Keith: Visitors, The

Berkeley, Xander: Air Force One; Candyman (1992); Dead to Rights; If These Walls Could Talk; Persons Unknown; Poison Ivy 2: Lily; Roswell; Safe; Winchell; Within the Rock

Berkoff, Steven: Another 9 Weeks; Barry Lyndon; Fair Game (1995); Legionnaire; Rambo: First Blood II; Season of Giants, A; Transmutations; Under the Cherry Moon

Berkowitz, Myles: 20 Dates

Berland, Terri: Pink Motel; Strangeness, The

Berle, Milton: Broadway Danny Rose; Cracking Up; Evil Roy Slade; It's a Mad Mad Mad Mad World; Legend of Valentino; Lepke; Loved One, The; Muppet Movie, The; Storybook; Sun Valley Serenade; Who's Minding the Mint?

Berleand, Francois: Romance (1999)

Berlin Comic Opera Ballet: Cinderella (1987)

Berlin, Irving: This Is the Army

Berlin, Jeannie: Baby Maker, The; Heartbreak Kid, The; Housewife; In the Spirit; Portnoy's Complaint

Berling, Charles: Dry Cleaning; Ridicule

Berlingame, Tiffany: Miami Hot Talk

Berlinger, Warren: Billie; Four Deuces, The; Free Ride; I Will, I Will … for Now; Lepke; Long Goodbye, The; Magician of Lublin, The; Outlaw Force; Wackiest Ship in the Army, The

Berman, Shelley: Best Man, The (1964); Son of Blob (Beware! The Blob); Teen Witch; Young at Heart Comedians, The

Berman, Susan: Smithereens

Bern, Thomas: Dreamaniac

Bernard, Crystal: As Good as Dead; Face to Kill For, A; Siringo; Slumber Party Massacre II

Bernard, Jason: Liar, Liar; Wilma

Bernard, Maurice: Lucy and Desi: Before the Laughter

Bernard, Paul: Pattes Blanches (White Paws)

Bernard, Thelonious: Little Romance, A

Bernardi, Herschel: Irma La Douce; Love with the Proper Stranger; No Deposit, No Return; Peter Gunn (TV Series); Story of Jacob and Joseph, The

Bernardo, Michael: Shootfighter 2: Kill or Be Killed

Bernhard, Joachim: Last Five Days, The

Bernhard, Sandra: Anything for Love; Apocalypse, The; Hudson Hawk; Inside Monkey Zetterland; King of Comedy, The; Sesame Street Presents Follow That Bird; Somewhere in the City; Track 29; Truth or Dare; Unzipped; Without You I'm Nothing

Bernhardt, Daniel: Bloodsport II; Bloodsport III; Bloodsport IV: The Dark Kumite

Bernhardt, Kevin: Beauty School; Hellraiser 3: Hell On Earth; Kick or Die; Treacherous

Bernhardt, Sarah: Queen Elizabeth

Bernsen, Collin: Puppet Master II

Bernsen, Corbin: Baja; Bert Rigby, You're a Fool; Bloodhounds; Bloodhounds II; Breaking Point (1989); Brilliant Disguise, A; Cover Me; Dead on the Money; Dentist, The; Dentist 2, The; Brace Yourself; Disorganized Crime; Final Mission (1994); Frozen Assets; Ghost Brigade; Hello Again; Inhumanoid; Kounterfeit; L.A. Law; Major League; Major League II; Ring of the Musketeer; Savage Land; Shattered (1991); Soft Kill, The; Someone to Die For; Tails You Live, Heads You're Dead; Tales from the Hood; Temptress; Trigger Fast

Bernstein, Caron: Business for Pleasure

Bernstein, Sheryl: Gross Jokes

Beron, David: Honor Thy Father & Mother: The Menendez Killings

Berova, Olinka: Vengeance of She, The

Berri, Claude: Le Sex Shop; Seven Deadly Sins, The

Berridge, Elizabeth: Amadeus; Funhouse, The; Montana (1990); Silence of the Heart; Smooth Talk; When the Party's Over

Berry, Amanda: Palm Beach

Berry, Bill: High Country, The

Berry, Chuck: American Hot Wax; Chuck Berry Hail! Hail! Rock'n'Roll; Go, Johnny, Go!; Rock, Rock, Rock; That Was Rock

Berry, Halle: B.A.P.S.; Boomerang (1992); Bulworth; Executive Decision; Father Hood; Flintstones, The; Introducing Dorothy Dandridge; Losing Isaiah; Program, The; Race the Sun; Rich Man's Wife, The; Solomon and Sheba (1995); Strictly Business; Why Do Fools Fall in Love

Berry, John: Man in Love, A; Window Shopping

Berry, Jules: Crime of Monsieur Lange, The; Le Jour Se Leve (Daybreak) (1939); Les Visiteurs Du Soir

Berry, Ken: Cat from Outer Space, The; Herbie Rides Again

Berry, Raymond J.: Sudden Death (1995)

Berry, Richard: Caged Heart, The (L'Addition); Day of Atonement; Honeymoon; La Balance; Man and a Woman, A: 20 Years Later

Berry, Vincent: Amnesia; Free Willy 3: The Rescue; Fury Within, The

Berryman, Dorothee: Decline of the American Empire, The; Paper Wedding

Berryman, Michael: Auntie Lee's Meat Pies; Barbarians, The; Cut and Run; Guyver, The; Hills Have Eyes, The: Part Two; Teenage Exorcist

Berteloot, Jean-Yves: Deep Trouble

Berthelsen, Anders W.: Mifune

Berti, Aldo: Big Rip-off, The

Bertin, Roland: Hairdresser's Husband, The; L'Homme Blessé (The Wounded Man)

Bertinelli, Valerie: C.H.O.M.P.S.; Number One with a Bullet; Ordinary Heroes; Pancho Barnes; Shattered Vows; Taken Away; Young Love, First Love

Bertish, Suzanne: Venice/Venice

Berto, Juliet: Celine and Julie Go Boating; Le Gai Savoir (The Joy of Knowledge); Le Sex Shop; Mr. Klein

Bertorelli, Toni: Who Killed Pasolini?

Bertrand, Janette: Big Red

Bervoets, Gene: Vanishing, The (1988)

Berz, Michael: Hot Resort

Besch, Bibi: Beast Within, The; Betrayal (1978); Kill Me Again; Lonely Lady, The; Medicine Hat Stallion, The; Rattled

Besnehard, Dominique: A Nos Amours

Besse, Ariel: Beau Pere

Bessell, Ted: Billie; Breaking Up Is Hard to Do; Don't Drink the Water

Besser, Joe: Abbott and Costello Show, The (TV Series); Hey Abbott!

Best, Alyson: Dark Forces; Man of Flowers

Best, Edna: Ghost and Mrs. Muir, The; Man Who Knew Too Much, The (1934)

Best, James: Comanche Territory; Firecreek; Grey Matter; Killer Shrews, The; Left Handed Gun, The; Ma and Pa Kettle at the Fair; Ride Lonesome; Rolling Thunder; Savages (1974); Sounder

Best, Kevin: South Central

Best, Willie: Face of Marble, The; Littlest Rebel, The; Mr. Moto Takes a Vacation; Monster Walks, The; Smiling Ghost, The; Vivacious Lady

Bestar, Barbara: Man with the Steel Whip

Beswick, Martine: Bullet for the General, A; Cyclone; Dr. Jekyll and Sister Hyde; Happy Hooker Goes Hollywood, The; Prehistoric Women (1967); Seizure; Strange New World

Bethune, Zina: Who's That Knocking at My Door?

Betsworth, Gary: Cutting Moments

Bett, John: Gregory's Girl; Tess

Bettger, Lyle: All I Desire; Gundown at Sandoval; Johnny Reno; Lone Ranger, The (1956); Sea Chase, The; Union Station

Betti, Laura: Canterbury Tales, The; Lovers and Liars; Twitch of the Death Nerve

Bettina: Journey to Spirit Island

Bettis, Paul: Urinal

Bettles, Robert: Fourth Wish, The

Bettoia, Franca: Last Man on Earth, The

Betz, Carl: Deadly Encounter (1975); Spinout

Bevan, Billy: Cavalcade; High Voltage (1929); Li'l Abner (1940); Lost Patrol, The; Terror by Night

Bevans, Clem: Of Human Hearts; Young Tom Edison

Bevis, Leslie: November Men, The

Bey, Turhan: Ali Baba and the Forty Thieves; Amazing Mr. X; Arabian Nights (1942); Background to Danger; Climax, The; Dragon Seed; Mad Ghoul, The; Mummy's Tomb, The; Out of the Blue; Sudan

Beyer, Troy: Let's Talk About Sex; Rooftops; Weekend at Bernie's II

Beymer, Richard: Blackbelt; Cross Country; Elvis Meets Nixon; Indiscretion of an American Wife; Johnny Tremain; Little Death, The; Presence, The; Silent Night, Deadly Night III: Better Watch Out!; State of Emergency; Stripper, The; Twin Peaks (Movie); Twin Peaks (TV Series); Under Investigation; West Side Story

Bezace, Didier: Little Thief, The

Bezer, Amber: Appointment with Death

Bhaskar: Dragon Chow; I Drink Your Blood

Bhat, Rishi: Indian in the Cupboard, The

Biagli, Claudio: Mediterraneo

Bianca, Raquel: Abducted II

Bianchi, Daniela: From Russia with Love

Biao, Yuen: Eastern Condors; Millionaire's Express (Shanghai Express); Mr. Vampire (Vol. 1–4); Zu: Warriors from the Magic Mountain

Bibb, Leslie: Skulls, The

Bibby, Charles K.: Order of the Black Eagle

Biberman, Abner: Betrayal from the East; Panama Lady

Bickford, Charles: Anna Christie (1930); Babe Ruth Story, The; Big Country, The; Big Hand for the Little Lady, A; Branded; Brute Force; Command Decision; Court-martial of Billy Mitchell, The; Days of Wine and Roses (1962); East of Borneo; Farmer's Daughter, The; Four Faces West; Jim Thorpe—All American; Johnny Belinda; Little Miss Marker (1934); Not as a Stranger; Plainsman, The; Reap the Wild Wind; Riders of Death Valley; Riding High; Song of Bernadette, The; Star Is Born, A (1954); Tarzan's New York Adventure; Thunder Trail; Unforgiven, The (1960); Wing and a Prayer, A

Bickley, Tony: Swimmer, The

Bicknell, Andrew: Buffalo Girls; Moving Finger, The

Bicknell, Gene: Gypsy Angels

Bideau, Jean-Luc: Jonah Who Will Be 25 in the Year 2000; Revenge of the Musketeers

Bidenko, Kris: Two Friends

Bidonde, Hector: Funny Dirty Little War (No Habra Mas Penas ni Olvido)

Biehn, Michael: Abyss, The; Aliens; Blood of the Hunter; Breach of Trust; Coach; Conundrum; Dead Men Can't Dance; Deadfall; Deep Red (1994); Fan, The; Frame by Frame; In a Shallow Grave; Jade; K2; Magnificent Seven, The (TV Series); Mojave Moon; Navy Seals; Rampage; Seventh Sign, The; Strapped; Taste for Killing, A; Terminator, The; Time Bomb; Tombstone

Biel, Jessica: I'll Be Home for Christmas

Bierbichler, Josef: Heart of Glass

Bieri, Ramon: Badlands (1973); Christmas without Snow, A; Frisco Kid, The; Grandview, U.S.A.; It's Good to Be Alive; Sicilian, The; Sorcerer

Bierko, Craig: Long Kiss Goodnight, The; Thirteenth Floor, The (1999); 'Til There Was You; Victimless Crimes

Bigagli, Claudio: Wild Flower (1993) (Fiorile)

Biggs, Jason: American Pie

Biggs, Roxann: Broken Angel; Darkman III: Die, Darkman, Die; Mortal Sins (1992)

Bignamini, Nino: All Screwed Up

Bikel, Theodore: African Queen, The; Assassination Game, The; Colditz Story, The; Dark Tower; Defiant Ones, The; Dog of Flanders, A; Enemy Below, The; Final Days, The; Flight from Vienna; I Bury the Living; I Want to Live!; Murder on Flight 502; My Side of the Mountain; Never Let Me Go; Pride and the Passion, The; Russians Are Coming, the Russians Are Coming, The; Shattered (1991); 200 Motels; Victory at Entebbe

Bill, Tony: Are You in the House Alone?; Come Blow Your Horn; Haunts of the Very Rich; Ice Station Zebra; Initiation of Sarah, The; Killing Mind, The; Less Than Zero; None But the Brave; Soldier in the Rain; You're a Big Boy Now

Billerey, Raoul: Revenge of the Musketeers

Billings, Dawn Ann: Human Desires

Billingsley, Barbara: Eye of the Demon

Billingsley, Jennifer: C.C. & Company; Thirsty Dead, The; White Lightning

Billingsley, Peter: Arcade; Beverly Hills Brats; Christmas Story, A; Dirt Bike Kid, The; Russkies

Billington, Francis: Blind Husbands

Billington, Michael: Invasion UFO

Bindon, John: Man in the Wilderness

Bing, Herman: Bitter Sweet; Bluebeard's Eighth Wife; Guardsman, The

Binge, Rob: Dead Is Dead

Binkley, Lane: Bernice Bobs Her Hair; Soldier's Home

Binns, Edward: Hunter (1971); Oliver's Story; Pilot, The; 12 Angry Men (1957)

Binoche, Juliette: Blue (1993); Couch in New York, A; Damage; Emily Bronte's Wuthering Heights; English Patient, The; Horseman on the Roof, The; Lovers on the Bridge; Rendez-Vous; Unbearable Lightness of Being, The; Women & Men 2

Birch, Paul: Apache Woman; Queen of Outer Space

Birch, Thora: Alaska; All I Want for Christmas; Hocus Pocus; Monkey Trouble; Night Ride Home; Now and Then; Paradise (1991)

Birchall, Jeremy: Heaven (1998)

Bird, Billie: End of Innocence, The; Ernest Saves Christmas; Sixteen Candles

Bird, John: 30 Is a Dangerous Age, Cynthia

Bird, Norman: Whistle Down the Wind

Birdsall, Jesse: Getting It Right; Wish You Were Here

Birdsong, Lori: Blood Salvage

Birell, Tala: Purple Heart, The; White Legion

Birkin, Jane: Beethoven's Nephew; Catherine & Co.; Daddy Nostalgia; Dark Places; Dust; Evil Under the Sun; La Belle Noiseuse; Le Petit Amour; Make Room for Tomorrow; Swimming Pool, The; Wonderwall

Birkin, Ned: Cement Garden, The

Birman, Len: Captain America (1979); Captain America II: Death Too Soon; Lies My Father Told Me; Man Inside, The (1984); Undergrads, The

Birman, Matt: Born in Action

Birney, David: Caravan to Vaccares; King Richard II; Night of the Fox; Nightfall; Oh, God! Book II; Only with Married Men; Pretty Kill; Ray Bradbury's Chronicles: The Martian Episodes; St. Elsewhere (TV Series); Touch and Die

Birney, Reed: Greatest Man in the World, The

Birt, Christopher: Reason to Believe, A

Bishop, Debby: Blue Money

Bishop, Ed: Invasion UFO

Highway; Marshal of Cripple Creek; Money Train; Of Mice and Men (1981); Out California Way; Phantom of the Plains; PT 109; San Antonio Kid; Santa Fe Uprising; Sheriff of Las Vegas; Tell Them Willie Boy Is Here; This Property Is Condemned; Wagon Wheels Westward

Blake, Stephen: Mad at the Moon

Blake, Teresa: Payback (1990)

Blake, Valerie: Blastfighter

Blake, Whitney: Hazel Christmas Show, The (TV Series)

Blakely, Colin: Dogs of War, The; Equus; Evil Under the Sun; Little Lord Fauntleroy (1980); Loophole; Pink Panther Strikes Again, The; Private Life of Sherlock Holmes, The; Shattered (1972); This Sporting Life

Blakely, Donald: Strike Force

Blakely, Susan: Airport '79: The Concorde; Blackmail (1991); Broken Angel; Bunker, The; Cry for Love, A; Dead Reckoning (1990); Dreamer; Incident, The (1989); Intruders; Lady Killers; Lords of Flatbush, The; Make Me an Offer; My Mom's a Werewolf; Out of Sight Out of Mind; Over the Top; Report to the Commissioner; Survivalist, The; Wild Flower (1991)

Blakemore, Michael: Country Life

Blakiston, Caroline: At Bertram's Hotel

Blakley, Ronee: Baltimore Bullet, The; Desperate Women; Driver, The; Murder by Numbers; Nashville; Nightmare on Elm Street, A; Private Files of J. Edgar Hoover, The; Student Confidential

Blanc, Dominique: Total Eclipse

Blanc, Erica: Django Shoots First; Longest Hunt, The; Mark of the Devil, Part 2

Blanc, Manuel: Beaumarchais the Scoundrel

Blanc, Mel: Gay Purr-ee; Jack Benny Program, The (TV Series); Neptune's Daughter

Blanc, Michel: Dead Tired (Grosse Fatigue); Favor, the Watch and the Very Big Fish, The; Ménage; Merci La Vie; Monsieur Hire; Monster, The (1996); Prospero's Books; Uranus

Blanchar, Pierre: Crime and Punishment (1935); Man from Nowhere, The

Blanchard, Alan: Slithis

Blanchard, Felix "Doc": Spirit of West Point, The

Blanchard, Mari: Abbott and Costello Go to Mars; Twice-Told Tales

Blanchard, Rachel: Road Trip

Blanchett, Cate: Elizabeth; Paradise Road; Pushing Tin; Talented Mr. Ripley, The

Blanck, Gerry: Full Contact

Blanco, Roberto: Hell Hounds of Alaska

Bland, Peter: Came a Hot Friday

Blandick, Clara: Can't Help Singing; Drums of Jeopardy; Girl from Missouri, The; Wizard of Oz, The

Blane, Sally: Silver Streak (1934); Vagabond Lover, The

Blankfield, Mark: Dracula: Dead and Loving It; Frankenstein General Hospital; Incredible Shrinking Woman, The; Jekyll & Hyde—Together Again; Robin Hood: Men in Tights

Blanks, Billy: Back in Action; Balance of Power; Expect No Mercy; Talons of the Eagle; Tough and Deadly

Blanton, Arell: House of Terror

Blatchford, Ed: Birthday Boy, The

Blavette, Charles: Toni

Blaze, Tommy: Rumpelstiltskin

Bleachman, Jonah: Fall Time

Blech, Hans-Christian: Scarlet Letter (1973)

Bledsoe, Tempestt: Dance 'Til Dawn; Dream Date

Bledsoe, Will: Dark Side of the Moon, The

Blee, Debra: Beach Girls, The; Malibu Bikini Shop, The; Movie; Hawaii Five-O; Ultimate Deception; Undercover Angel

Bleibtreu, Moritz: Run Lola Run

Bleont, Claudiu: Unforgettable Summer, An

Blessed, Brian: Hamlet (1996); High Road to China; Hound of the Baskervilles, The (1983); I, Claudius; King Arthur, The Young Warlord; Much Ado About Nothing; Prisoner of Honor; Return to Treasure Island; Robin Hood: Prince of Thieves; Story of David, The

Blessing, Jack: Game of Love, The; Last of His Tribe, The

Blethyn, Brenda: Music from Another Room; River Runs Through It, A; RKO 281; Secrets and Lies

Blier, Bernard: Buffet Froid (Cold Cuts); By the Blood of Others; Daydreamer, The (1970) (Le Distrait); Dedee D'An-

vers; Jenny Lamour; L'Ecole Buissonniere; Les Miserables (1957); Organizer, The; Passion for Life; Passion of Love; Tall Blond Man with One Black Shoe, The

Block, Larry: Dead Man Out

Blocker, Dan: Bonanza (TV Series); Come Blow Your Horn; Lady in Cement

Blocker, Dirk: Night of the Scarecrow

Blodgett, Michael: Velvet Vampire, The

Blom, Dan: Mind Ripper

Blondell, Gloria: Twonky, The

Blondell, Joan: Adventure; Battered; Big Business Girl; Blonde Crazy; Bullets or Ballots; Dames; Dead Don't Die, The; Death at Love House; Desk Set; Footlight Parade; Gold Diggers of 1933; Illicit; Lady for a Night; Night Nurse; Opening Night; Opposite Sex, The (1956); Rebels, The; Ride Beyond Vengeance; Stage Struck (1936); Stand-In; Stay Away Joe; Support Your Local Gunfighter; This Could Be the Night; Three Broadway Girls; Three Men on a Horse; Three on a Match; Topper Returns; Tree Grows in Brooklyn, A; Waterhole #3; Will Success Spoil Rock Hunter?

Blondell, Simone: Savage Guns

Bloom, Anne: Dirt Bike Kid, The

Bloom, Brian: Escape from Atlantis; Knocking on Death's Door; Vampirella; Webber's World (At Home with the Webbers)

Bloom, Claire: Alexander the Great; Brainwashed; Brideshead Revisited; Brothers Karamazov, The; Buccaneer, The; Charly; Daylight; Deja Vu (1984); Doll's House, A (1989); Haunting, The (1963); Illustrated Man, The; Intimate Contact; Islands in the Stream; Limelight; Look Back in Anger (1959); Mighty Aphrodite; Mirror Crack'd from Side to Side, The; Queenie; Richard III (1955); Sammy and Rosie Get Laid; Separate Tables; Shameless; Spy Who Came in from the Cold, The; Wonderful World of the Brothers Grimm, The

Bloom, John: Brain of Blood; Casino (1995)

Bloom, Michael Allan: Screen Test

Bloom, Verna: After Hours; Badge 373; Blue Knight, The (1975); High Plains Drifter; Hired Hand, The; Last Temptation of Christ, The; Medium Cool

Bloomfield, Don: Lost Angels

Bloomfield, George: And Then You Die

Blore, Eric: Ex-Mrs. Bradford, The; Gay Divorcée, The; I Dream Too Much; Lady Scarface; Moon and Sixpence, The; Quality Street; Road to Zanzibar; Romance on the High Seas; Shall We Dance? (1937); Shanghai Gesture, The; Sky's the Limit, The; Sullivan's Travels; Swiss Miss; Top Hat

Blossom, Roberts: American Clock, The; Christine; Citizen's Band; Deranged; Escape from Alcatraz; Home Alone; Resurrection; Reuben, Reuben

Blouin, Michael: Great Land of Small, The

Blount, Lisa: Blind Fury; Box of Moonlight; Cease Fire; Cut and Run; Judicial Consent; Nightflyers; Prince of Darkness; Radioactive Dreams; September 30, 1955; South of Reno; Stalked; Swap, The (Sam's Song); What Waits Below

Blow, Kurtis: Krush Groove

Blue, Ben: Big Broadcast of 1938, The; Broadway Rhythm; College Swing; Two Girls and a Sailor; Two Sisters from Boston; Where Were You When the Lights Went Out?

Blue, Edgar Washington: Beggars of Life

Blue, Monte: Apache; Hawk of the Wilderness; Hell Town; Intolerance; Lives of a Bengal Lancer, The; Marriage Circle, The; Orphans of the Storm; Ride, Ranger, Ride; Riders of Death Valley; Road to Morocco; Undersea Kingdom; Wagon Wheels; White Shadows in the South Seas

Bluestone, Abby: Night of the Juggler

Bluhm, Brady: Alone in the Woods; Crazysitter, The

Blum, Mark: Blind Date (1987); "Crocodile" Dundee; Defenders, The; Desperately Seeking Susan; Just Between Friends; Presidio, The; Worth Winning

Blum, Steven: Bram Stoker's Shadowbuilder

Blumenfeld, Alan: Dark Side of the Moon, The; Instant Karma; Night Life

Blundell, John: Scum

Bluteau, Lothaire: Bent; Black Robe; Jesus of Montreal; Shot Through the Heart; Silent Touch, The

Bluthal, John: Leapin' Leprechauns; Spellbreaker: Secret of the Leprechauns

Blyden, Larry: On a Clear Day, You Can See Forever

Blye, Margaret: Ash Wednesday; Final Chapter—Walking Tall; Melvin Purvis: G-Man; Sporting Club, The; Waterhole #3

Blystone, Stanley: Ivory-Handled Gun, The

Blyth, Ann: All the Brothers Were Valiant; Great Caruso, The; Helen Morgan Story, The; Kismet (1955); Mildred Pierce; Mr. Peabody and the Mermaid; One Minute to Zero; Rose Marie (1954); Student Prince, The

Blythe, Benedick: Little Riders, The

Blythe, Betty: Gangster's Boy; Nomads of the North; She (1925)

Blythe, Catherine: Hawk's Vengeance

Blythe, John: Alfred Hitchcock's Bon Voyage and Aventure Malgache

Blythe, Robert: Experience Preferred … But Not Essential

Blythe, Robin: Deathrow Gameshow

Boa, Bruce: Murder Story

Boardman, Eleanor: Crowd, The; She Goes to War

Boatman, Michael Patrick: China Beach (TV Series); Fourth Story; Glass Shield, The; Hamburger Hill; Urban Crossfire

Bob Wills and the Texas Playboys: Take Me Back to Oklahoma

Bobochkin, Boris: Chapayev

Boccardo, Delia: Assisi Underground, The

Bocher, Christian: Total Exposure

Bochner, Hart: Apartment Zero; Break Up; Die Hard; Fellow Traveler; Having It All; Islands in the Stream; Mad at the Moon; Making Mr. Right; Mr. Destiny; Rich and Famous; Supergirl; Terror Train; War and Remembrance

Bochner, Lloyd: Crystal Heart; Good Idea; Horse in the Gray Flannel Suit, The; Landslide; Lonely Lady, The; Man in the Glass Booth; Mary and Joseph: A Story of Faith; Mazes and Monsters; Morning Glory (1992); Night Walker, The; Point Blank (1967); Ulzana's Raid

Bodison, Wolfgang: Criminal Passion; Few Good Men, A; Freeway (1996); Silver Strand

Bodner, Jenna: Cellblock Sisters; Friend of the Family II; Huntress: Spirit of the Night

Bodrov Jr., Sergei: East-West; Prisoner of the Mountains

Boehm, Carl: Peeping Tom; Unnatural

Boen, Earl: Dentist, The; Within the Rock

Boensh III, Paul: This Is Elvis

Bogarde, Dirk: Accident; Bridge Too Far, A; Daddy Nostalgia; Damn the Defiant!; Damned, The; Darling; Death in Venice; Despair; Doctor at Large; Doctor at Sea; Doctor in Distress; Doctor in the House; I Could Go On Singing; Ill Met by Moonlight; Justine; Night Ambush; Night Flight from Moscow; Night Porter, The; Permission to Kill; Providence; Quartet (1948); Sea Shall Not Have Them, The; Servant, The; Simba; Sleeping Tiger, The; Song Without End; Tale of Two Cities, A (1967); To See Such Fun; Victim; Woman in Question

Bogardus, Stephen: Love! Valour! Compassion!

Bogart, Humphrey: Across the Pacific; Action in the North Atlantic; African Queen, The; All Through the Night; Amazing Dr. Clitterhouse, The; Angels with Dirty Faces; Barefoot Contessa, The; Battle Circus; Beat the Devil; Big Sleep, The (1946); Black Legion; Brother Orchid; Bullets or Ballots; Caine Mutiny, The; Casablanca; Chain Lightning; Conflict; Dark Passage; Dark Victory; Dead End; Dead Reckoning (1947); Deadline USA; Desperate Hours, The (1955); Enforcer, The (1951); Harder They Fall, The; High Sierra; In a Lonely Place; Key Largo; Kid Galahad (1937); Knock on Any Door; Left Hand of God, The; Maltese Falcon, The; Marked Woman; Midnight (1934); Oklahoma Kid, The; Passage to Marseilles; Petrified Forest, The; Return of Dr. X; Roaring Twenties, The; Sabrina (1954); Sahara (1943); Sirocco; Stand-In; Thank Your Lucky Stars; They Drive by Night; Three on a Match; To Have and Have Not; Tokyo Joe; Treasure of the Sierra Madre; Two Mrs. Carrolls, The; Virginia City; Wagons Roll at Night, The; We're No Angels (1955)

Bogdanova, Elena: Adam's Rib (1993)

Bogdanovich, Peter: Saint Jack; Targets; Trip, The

Bogmaz, Dmitri: Forbidden Zone: Alien Abduction

Bogosian, Eric: Bright Shining Lie, A; Caine Mutiny Court Martial, The; Dolores Claiborne; Gossip; Sex, Drugs, Rock & Roll; Special Effects; Talk Radio; Under Siege 2: Dark Territory; Witch Hunt

Bohannon, Kelly: Idaho Transfer

Bohen, Ian: Frankenstein Sings; Young Hercules

Böhm, Karlheinz: Fox and His Friends; Wonderful World of the Brothers Grimm, The

Bohnen, Roman: Hard Way, The (1942)

Bohnet, Folker: Bridge, The

Bohrer, Corinne: Dead Solid Perfect; Operation Intercept; Star Kid; Surf 2

Bohringer, Richard: Accompanist, The; Barjo; Bolero (1982); Caged Heart, The (L'Addition); Cook, the Thief, His Wife & Her Lover, The; Le Grand Chemin (The Grand Highway); Peril; Subway

Bohringer, Romane: Accompanist, The; Chambermaid on the Titanic, The; Mina Tannenbaum; Savage Nights; Total Eclipse

Bois, Curt: Caught (1949); Gypsy Wildcat; Tovaritch; Tuttles of Tahiti, The; Wings of Desire

Bois, Elaine: Legacy of Horror

Boisson, Christine: Sorceress, The (1988)

Bok, Sarel: Far Off Place, A

Bolam, James: Crucible of Terror; End of the Affair, The

Boland, Mary: If I Had a Million; Julia Misbehaves; New Moon; Nothing But Trouble (1944); Ruggles of Red Gap

Bolder, Cal: Jesse James Meets Frankenstein's Daughter

Boles, John: Craig's Wife; Curly Top; Frankenstein (1931); King of Jazz, The; Last Warning, The; Littlest Rebel, The; Sinners in Paradise; Stella Dallas; Thousands Cheer

Bolger, John: Parting Glances

Bolger, Ray: April in Paris; Babes in Toyland (1961); Daydreamer, The (1966); Four Jacks and a Jill; Harvey Girls, The; Just You and Me, Kid; Look for the Silver Lining; Rosalie; Sweethearts; Wizard of Oz, The

Bolkan, Florinda: Aqua E Sapone; Collector's Item; Day that Shook the World, The; Some Girls

Bolling, Tiffany: Bonnie's Kids; Centerfold Girls; Kingdom of the Spiders; Open House

Bologna, Joseph: Alligator II; Big Bus, The; Blame It on Rio; Chapter Two; Citizen Cohn; Cops and Robbers; Danger of Love; Deadly Rivals; Don's Analyst, The; Honor Thy Father; Jersey Girl; Love Is All There Is; My Favorite Year; Not Quite Human; One Cooks, the Other Doesn't; Rags to Riches; Revenge of the Nerds IV: Nerds in Love; Torn Between Two Lovers; Transylvania 6-5000; Woman in Red, The

Ballet, Bolshoi: Anna Karenina (1974)

Bolt, David: Killing Man, The

Bom, Dor Zweigen: Late Summer Blues

Bom, Lars: Webmaster

Bon Jovi, Jon: Homegrown; Leading Man, The; Little City; Moonlight and Valentino; No Looking Back; U-571

Bonacelli, Paolo: Johnny Stecchino; Mille Bolle Blu; Salo: 120 Days of Sodom

Bonaduce, Danny: America's Deadliest Home Video; H.O.T.S.

Bonanno, Louie: Sex Appeal; Wimps

Bonanova, Fortunio: Ali Baba and the Forty Thieves; Fiesta; Romance on the High Seas

Bond, Derek: Nicholas Nickleby; Scott of the Antarctic; Stranger from Venus

Bond, Graham: Fast Lane Fever

Bond, Lilian: Old Dark House, The (1932)

Bond, Raymond: Man from Planet X, The

Bond, Rene: Fugitive Girls

Bond, Samantha: World Is Not Enough, The

Bond, Steve: Magdalene; Prey, The; To Die For (1989); To Die For 2: Son of Darkness; Tryst

Bond, Sudie: Come Back to the Five and Dime, Jimmy Dean, Jimmy Dean; Greatest Man in the World, The; Silkwood; Swing Shift; Tomorrow; Where the Lilies Bloom

Bond, Tommy: Atom Man vs. Superman; Superman—The Serial

Bond, Ward: Blowing Wild; Bride Walks Out, The; Broadway Bill; Dakota (1945); Devil Dogs of the Air; Dodge City; Drums Along the Mohawk; Falcon Takes Over, The; Fighting Code; Fighting Ranger, The; Fighting Shadows; Fighting Sullivans, The (Sullivans, The); Fort Apache; Fugitive, The (1947); Gentleman Jim; Great Missouri Raid, The; Guy Named Joe, A; Gypsy Colt; Hello, Frisco, Hello; Hitler—Dead or Alive; Hondo; It Happened One Night; It's a Wonderful Life; Joan of Arc; Johnny Guitar; Kiss Tomorrow Goodbye; Law West of Tombstone; Long Gray Line, The; Maltese Falcon, The; Man Alone, A; Mr. Moto's Gamble; Mister Roberts; Mortal Storm, The; My Darling Clementine;

Bostwick, Barry: Danielle Steel's Once in a Lifetime; 800 Leagues Down the Amazon; George Washington; George Washington: The Forging of a Nation; Hitchhiker, The (Series); I Worship His Shadow; In the Heat of Passion II: Unfaithful; Megaforce; Movie Movie; Praying Mantis; Project: Metalbeast; Red Flag: The Ultimate Game; Rocky Horror Picture Show, The; Secret Agent Club; Secretary, The; Spy Hard; Weekend at Bernie's II; Woman of Substance, A

Boswell Sisters: Transatlantic Merry-Go-Round

Boswell, Charles: Kiss Me a Killer

Bosworth, Brian: Back in Business; Blackout (1995); One Man's Justice; Stone Cold; Virus (1996)

Bosworth, Hobart: Abraham Lincoln; Big Parade, The; General Spanky; Just Imagine; Sea Lion, The; Woman of Affairs, A

Botes, Costa: Forgotten Silver

Botsford, Sara: By Design; Deadly Eyes; Gunrunner, The; Still of the Night

Bottoms, John: Blue Hotel

Bottoms, Joseph: Black Hole, The; Blind Date (1984); Born to Race; Celebrity; Cloud Dancer; Crime & Passion; High Rolling; Inner Sanctum; Intruder Within, The; King of the Mountain; Open House; Side by Side: The True Story of the Osmond Family; Sins of Dorian Gray, The; Surfacing; Treacherous Crossing

Bottoms, Sam: Bronco Billy; Dolly Dearest; Gardens of Stone; Hunter's Blood; Prime Risk; Project Shadowchaser 3000; Savages (1974); Up from the Depths; Witching of Ben Wagner, The; Zandy's Bride

Bottoms, Timothy: Ava's Magical Adventure; Deathgame; Diamondbacks; Digger; Drifter, The; East of Eden (1982); Fantasist, The; Gift of Love, The; Hambone and Hillie; High Country, The; Hourglass; In the Shadow of Kilimanjaro; Invaders from Mars (1986); Istanbul: Keep Your Eyes Open; Johnny Got His Gun; Land of Faraway, The; Last Picture Show, The; Love's Leading the Way; Other Side of the Mountain, Part II, The; Paper Chase, The; Ripper Man; Rollercoaster; Shining Season, A; Small Town in Texas, A; Story of David, The; Texasville; Tin Man; Top Dog; What Waits Below; White Dawn, The

Bottone, Bonaventura: Mikado, The (1987)

Bouajila, Sami: Bye-Bye; Siege, The

Bouchet, Barbara: Sex with a Smile

Bouchey, Willis: Bridges at Toko-Ri, The

Bouchez, Elodie: Dreamlife of Angels, The; Wild Reeds

Bouchitey, Patrick: Great, My Parents Are Divorcing

Bouise, Jean: Final Combat, The; I Am Cuba; Mr. Klein

Bouix, Evelyne: Edith and Marcel; Jacko and Lise

Boujenah, Michel: Les Misérables (1995); Three Men and a Cradle

Boulanger, Jamieson: Frankenstein and Me

Bould, Sam: End of the Affair, The; Hollow Reed

Boulting, Ingrid: Last Tycoon, The

Boundin, Bo: Great Waldo Pepper, The

Bouquet, Carole: Business Affair, A; Dead Tired (Grosse Fatigue); For Your Eyes Only; That Obscure Object of Desire; Too Beautiful for You

Bouquet, Michel: Beyond Fear; Borsalino; Bride Wore Black, The; Le Complot (The Conspiracy); Mississippi Mermaid; This Special Friendship; Toto the Hero

Bourdon, Didier: La Machine

Bourgeois, John: Gift of Love: The Daniel Huffman Story; Ms. Scrooge

Bourgnine, Elisabeth: Un Coeur en Hiver

Bourseiller, Antoine: Cleo from 5 to 7

Bourvil: Crazy For Love; Four Bags Full; La Grande Vadrouille; Les Grandes Gueules (Jailbirds' Vacation); Les Miserables (1957); When Wolves Cry

Bouton, Jim: Long Goodbye, The

Boutsikaris, Dennis: Dream Team, The; Three Lives of Karen, The; Yarn Princess, The

Boutte, Duane: Stonewall

Bouvier, Jean Pierre: Goodbye Emmanuelle

Bovasso, Julie: Gentleman Bandit, The; Moonstruck

Bovo, Brunella: White Sheik, The

Bow, Clara: Call Her Savage; Dancing Mothers; Down to the Sea in Ships; Hula; It (1927); Saturday Night Kid, The; Wild Party, The (1929); Wings

Bow, Simmy: Doberman Gang, The

Bowe, David: UHF

Bowe, John: Prime Suspect 1

Bowen, Rosemarie: Big Bluff, The

Bowen, Dennis: Gas Pump Girls

Bowen, Julie: American Werewolf in Paris, An; Happy Gilmore; Multiplicity

Bowen, Lori: Pumping Iron II: The Women

Bowen, Michael: Check Is in the Mail, The; Echo Park; Excess Baggage; Jackie Brown; Less Than Zero; Mortal Passions; New Eden; Season of Fear; Taking of Beverly Hills, The

Bowen, Roger: Playmates

Bowen, Sean: Troma's War

Bowens, Malick: Out of Africa

Bower, David: Four Weddings and a Funeral

Bower, Tom: Avenging Angel, The (1995); Ballad of Gregorio Cortez, The; Dillinger (1990); Far From Home: The Adventures of Yellow Dog; Poodle Springs; Riders of the Purple Sage; River's Edge; Talent for the Game; White Man's Burden; Wild Rose

Bowers, John: Ace of Hearts; Sky Pilot, The

Bowie, David: Absolute Beginners; Basquiat; Hunger, The (1983); Into the Night; Just a Gigolo; Labyrinth; Last Temptation of Christ, The; Linguini Incident, The; Man Who Fell to Earth, The; Merry Christmas, Mr. Lawrence; Twin Peaks: Fire Walk with Me

Bowie, Trixxie: Fraternity Demon

Bowker, Judi: Brother Sun, Sister Moon; Clash of the Titans; East of Elephant Rock

Bowles, Peter: Day in the Death of Joe Egg, A; Prisoner, The (1968) (TV Series); Rumpole of the Bailey (TV Series)

Bowman, Don: Hillbillys in a Haunted House

Bowman, Jessica: Remote

Bowman, Lee: Buck Privates; Having a Wonderful Time; House by the River; Interns Can't Take Money; Love Affair (1939); My Dream Is Yours; Next Time I Marry; Smash-Up: The Story of a Woman; Tonight and Every Night

Bowman, Loretta Leigh: Offerings

Bowz, Eddie: Fear, The (1994)

Boxer, Stephen: Prime Suspect: Scent of Darkness

Boxleitner, Bruce: Babe, The (1992); Babylon 5 (TV Series); Baltimore Bullet, The; Diplomatic Immunity; Double Jeopardy (1992); East of Eden (1982); From the Dead of Night; Gambler, The (1980); Gambler, Part II—The Adventure Continues, The; Gambler, Part III—The Legend Continues, The; Kuffs; Murderous Vision; Passion Flower; Perfect Family; Secret, The; Tron; Wild Times; Wyatt Earp: Return to Tombstone

George, Boy: Stand by Me (1988)

Boyar, Sully: Car Wash

Boyce, Alan: Permanent Record

Boyd, Blake: Space Marines

Boyd, Brittany: Lassie

Boyd, Chris: Shrieker

Boyd, Guy: Dark Wind; Doctor Quinn Medicine Woman; Ewok Adventure, The; Eyes of Fire; Kiss Me a Killer; Past Midnight; Pride of Jesse Hallman, The

Boyd, Jan Gan: Assassination; Chorus Line, A

Boyd, Rick: Guns for Dollars; Place Called Trinity, A

Boyd, Sarah: Old Enough

Boyd, Stephen: Ben-Hur (1959); Best of Everything, The; Bravados, The; Caper of the Golden Bulls, The; Fall of the Roman Empire, The; Fantastic Voyage; Jumbo; Man Called Noon, The; Man Who Never Was, The; Oscar, The (1966); Shalako; Squeeze, The (1977)

Boyd, William: Bar-20 Rides Again; Border Patrol; Border Vigilantes; Borderland; Call of the Prairie; Dangerous Venture; Doomed Caravan; Eagle's Brood; False Colors; Flying Fool, The; Forty Thieves; Heart of Arizona; Hidden Gold; High Voltage (1929); Hills of Old Wyoming; Hopalong Cassidy Returns; Hopalong Rides Again; Hoppy Serves a Writ; In Old Colorado; In Old Mexico; King of Kings, The (1927); Law of the Pampas; Leather Burners, The; Mystery Man; North of the Rio Grande; Outlaws of the Desert; Painted Desert, The; Pirates on Horseback; Range War; Renegade Trail; Riders of the Timberline; Road to Yesterday, The; Santa Fe Marshal; Secrets of the Wasteland; Silent Conflict; Silver on the Sage; Stagecoach War; Stick to Your Guns; Texas Masquerade; Texas Trail; Three Men from Texas; Three on the Trail; Trail Dust; Twilight on the Trail; Wide-Open Town

Boyd, William "Stage": Lost City, The; Oliver Twist (1933); State's Attorney

Boyer, Charles: Adorable Julia; All This and Heaven Too; April Fools, The; Arch of Triumph; Barefoot in the Park; Break of Hearts; Buccaneer, The; Casino Royale (1967); Conquest; Earrings of Madame De ... , The; Fanny (1961); Four Horsemen of the Apocalypse; Garden of Allah, The; Gaslight (1944); History Is Made at Night; How to Steal a Million; Is Paris Burning?; Love Affair (1939); Madwoman of Chaillot, The; Matter of Time, A; Mayerling; Nana; Stavisky; Tovaritch

Boyer, Christopher: Uninvited, The (1993)

Boyer, Katy: Trapped

Boyer, Marie-France: Le Bonheur

Boyer, Myriam: Jonah Who Will Be 25 in the Year 2000; Un Coeur en Hiver; Window Shopping

Boyer, Tom: Massive Retaliation

Boykin, Nancy: Plants Are Watching, The

Boyle, Alan: Butcher Boy, The

Boyle, Brandon: Public Access

Boyle, Lara Flynn: Afterglow; Baby's Day Out; Big Squeeze, The; Cafe Society; Dark Backward, The; Equinox (1993); Eye of the Storm; Farmer and Chase; Happiness; Jacob; May Wine; Past Tense; Preppie Murder, The; Red Rock West; Road to Wellville, The; Since You've Been Gone; Temp, The; Threesome; Wayne's World; Where the Day Takes You

Boyle, Lissa: Friend of the Family; Night That Never Happened, The

Boyle, Peter: Beyond the Poseidon Adventure; Born to Be Wild; Brinks Job, The; Bulletproof Heart; Candidate, The; Disaster at Silo 7; Dr. Dolittle (1998); Dream Team, The; Echoes in the Darkness; F.I.S.T.; Ghost in the Noonday Sun; Hammett; Hardcore; Honeymoon in Vegas; Joe; Kickboxer 2: The Road Back; Men of Respect; Nervous Ticks; Outland; Red Heat (1988); Royce; Santa Clause, The; Shadow, The; Slither; Solar Crisis; Speed Zone; Steelyard Blues; Surgeon, The; Surrender; Swashbuckler (1976); Sweet Evil; Taking the Heat; Taxi Driver; That Darn Cat (1997); Tragedy of Flight 103, The: The Inside Story; Turk 182; Urban Crossfire; Walker; Where the Buffalo Roam; While You Were Sleeping; Yellowbeard; Young Frankenstein

Bozo: Life and Times of Grizzly Adams, The

Bozyk, Reizl: Crossing Delancey

Bozzuffi, Marcel: Caravan to Vaccares

Bracco, Elizabeth: Trees Lounge

Bracco, Lorraine: Basketball Diaries, The; Being Human; Dream Team, The; Even Cowgirls Get the Blues; Getting Gotti; Goodfellas; Hackers; Lifeline; Medicine Man; Radio Flyer; Scam; Sing; Someone to Watch Over Me; Switch; Talent for the Game; Traces of Red

Brace, John: Truth or Dare? A Critical Madness

Bracken, Eddie: American Clock, The; Baby's Day Out; Caught in the Draft; Hail the Conquering Hero; Home Alone 2: Lost in New York; Miracle of Morgan's Creek, The; Oscar (1991); Rookie of the Year; Star Spangled Rhythm; Summer Stock; Too Many Girls; We're Not Married; Young and Willing

Braconnier, Liza: Dirty Dishes

Bradbury, Ray: Halloween Tree, The

Bradford, Greg: Lovelines; Zapped!

Bradford, Jesse: Far From Home: The Adventures of Yellow Dog; King of the Hill

Bradford, John: 365 Nights in Hollywood

Bradford, Lane: Man with the Steel Whip; Zombies of the Stratosphere (Satan's Satellites) (Serial)

Bradford, Richard: Ambition; Arctic Blue; Chinatown Murders, The: The Man Against the Mob; Cold Heaven; Dr. Giggles; Hoodlum; Little Nikita; Milagro Beanfield War, The; Night Game; Permanent Record; Servants of Twilight; Trip to Bountiful, The; Untouchables, The

Bradley, Cathleen: Closer You Get, The

Bradley, Chris: Killer Instinct; Leather Jacket Love Story

Bradley, David: American Ninja III; American Ninja IV: The Annihilation; Blood Warriors; Cyborg Cop; Cyborg Soldier; Exit; Hard Justice; Lower Level; Outside the Law (1994)

Bradley, Doug: Clive Barker's Salome and The Forbidden; Hellraiser 3: Hell On Earth; Hellraiser: Bloodline; Proteus

Bradna, Olympe: South of Pago Pago

Bradshaw, Booker: Coffy

Bradshaw, Cathryn: Bert Rigby, You're a Fool

Bradshaw, Terry: Magic Christmas Tree, The

Brady, Alice: Gay Divorcée, The; Go West, Young Man; In Old Chicago; My Man Godfrey (1936); One Hundred Men and a Girl; Three Smart Girls; Young Mr. Lincoln

Brady, Janelle: Allnighter, The; Class of Nuke 'em High

Brady, Justin: Twentyfourseven (English)

Brady, Pat: Bells of Coronado; Down Dakota Way; Golden Stallion, The; Roy Rogers Show, The, (TV Series); Song of Texas; Sons of the Pioneers; Trigger, Jr.

Brady, Ruth: Caught (1949)

Brady, Scott: Arizona Bushwhackers; Bonnie's Kids; Castle of Evil; China Syndrome, The; Five Bloody Graves; Gremlins; Gun Riders, The; He Walked by Night; Johnny Guitar; Journey to the Center of Time (Time Warp); Kansas City Massacre, The; Maverick Queen, The; Mohawk; Montana Belle; Nightmare in Wax (Crimes in the Wax Museum); Port of New York; Restless Breed, The; Satan's Sadists

Braeden, Eric: Adultress, The; Ambulance, The; Colossus: The Forbin Project; Escape from the Planet of the Apes; Herbie Goes to Monte Carlo; Meet the Deedles

Braekman, Caroline: Rabid Grannies

Braga, Sonia: Burning Season, The; Dona Flor and Her Two Husbands; Gabriela; I Love You (Eu Te Amo); Kiss of the Spider Woman; Lady on the Bus; Last Prostitute, The; Man Who Broke 1000 Chains, The; Milagro Beanfield War, The; Moon over Parador; Rookie, The; Roosters; Streets of Laredo; Two Deaths

Bragadottir, Byrndia Petra: Juniper Tree, The

Bragg, Melvyn: Dennis Potter: The Last Interview

Brambell, Wilfred: Adventures of Picasso, The; Hard Day's Night, A

Bramley, Flora: College

Brana, Frank: Yellow Hair and the Fortress of Gold

Branagh, Kenneth: Celebrity (1998); Dead Again; Fortunes of War (1987); Gingerbread Man, The; Hamlet (1996); Henry V (1989); High Season; Look Back In Anger (1989); Mary Shelley's Frankenstein; Month in the Country, A; Much Ado About Nothing; Othello (1995); Peter's Friends; Swing Kids; Theory of Flight, The; To the Lighthouse; Wild Wild West (1999)

Branaman, Rustam: Terrified

Brancato, Lillo: Bronx Tale, A; Crimson Tide; Provocateur

Brand, Neville: Adventures of Huckleberry Finn, The (1960); Cahill—US Marshal; Deadly Trackers, The; Desperados, The; D.O.A. (1949); Eaten Alive; Evils of the Night; Fire!; Gun Fury; Kansas City Confidential; Kiss Tomorrow Goodbye; Lonely Man, The; Mad Bomber, The; Man from the Alamo, The; Mohawk; Ninth Configuration, The; Prince Valiant (1954); Prodigal, The; Psychic Killer; Return, The (1980); Riot in Cell Block Eleven; That Darn Cat (1965); Tin Star, The; Untouchables, The: Scarface Mob

Brandauer, Klaus Maria: Becoming Colette; Burning Secret; Colonel Redl; Hanussen; Introducing Dorothy Dandridge; Lightship, The; Mephisto; Never Say Never Again; Out of Africa; Quo Vadis? (1985); Russia House, The; Salzburg Connection, The; Streets of Gold; White Fang

Brandenburg, Larry: Santa Clause, The

Brandenburg, Otto: Kingdom, The

Brander, Leslie: Sizzle Beach, U.S.A.

Brandi, Walter: Slaughter of the Vampires; Terror Creatures from the Grave

Brandis, Jonathan: Ladybugs; NeverEnding Story II, The; Outside Providence; Sidekicks; Stepfather II

Brandise, Thomas: Gravesend

Brando, Jocelyn: Big Heat, The; Dark Night of the Scarecrow; Ugly American, The

Brando, Luisina: I Don't Want to Talk About It

Brando, Marion: Apocalypse Now; Appaloosa, The; Bedtime Story; Burn!; Chase, The, (1966); Christopher Columbus: The Discovery (1992); Countess from Hong Kong, A; Désirée; Don Juan DeMarco; Dry White Season, A; Formula, The; Free Money; Freshman, The; Fugitive Kind, The; Godfather, The; Godfather Epic, The; Guys and Dolls; Island of Dr. Moreau, The; Julius Caesar (1953); Last Tango in Paris; Men, The, (1950); Missouri Breaks, The; Morituri; Mutiny on the Bounty (1962); Night of the Following Day, The; Nightcomers, The; On the Waterfront; One-Eyed Jacks; Reflections in a Golden Eye; Roots: The Next Generation; Sayonara; Streetcar Named Desire, A (1951); Superman; Teahouse of the August Moon, The; Ugly American, The; Viva Zapata!; Wild One, The; Young Lions, The

Brando, Rikki: Bikini Carwash Company 2; Buford's Beach Bunnies

Brando, Yasusuka: Mishima: A Life in Four Chapters

Brandon, David: Beyond Darkness

Brandon, Henry: Bad Man of Deadwood; Black Legion; Captain Sinbad; Drums of Fu Manchu; Marshal of Mesa City; Okefenokee; Ranger and the Lady, The; Under Texas Skies

Brandon, Michael: Change of Seasons, A; FM; James Dean—A Legend in His Own Time; Lovers and Other Strangers; Promises in the Dark; Queen of the Stardust Ballroom; Red Alert; Rich and Famous

Brandsteder, Ron: Field of Honor (1986)

Brandt, Carolyn: Hollywood Strangler Meets the Skid Row Slasher; Incredibly Strange Creatures Who Stopped Living and Became Mixed-Up Zombies, The; Rat Pfink a Boo Boo; Thrill Killers, The

Brandt, Walker: Solar Force

Brandy: I Still Know What You Did Last Summer

Brandy, Moya: Neverending Story III, The: Escape to Fantasia

Branham, Craig: One Last Run

Branigan, Laura: Mugsy's Girls

Bransfield, Marjorie: Abraxas Guardian of the Universe

Branski, David: 9 1/2 Weeks

Brant, John: Vampyre (1990)

Brantley, Betsy: Dreams Lost, Dreams Found; Five Days One Summer; I Come in Peace; Rogue Trader; Schizopolis

Braoude, Patrick: Great, My Parents Are Divorcing

Braschi, Nicoletta: Johnny Stecchino; Life Is Beautiful; Monster, The (1996); Who Killed Pasolini?

Brascia, Dominick: Evil Laugh

Brass, Lorne: Eye of the Wolf; Northern Passage

Brasselle, Keefe: It's a Big Country; Not Wanted; Place in the Sun, A; Railroaded

Brasselle, Melissa: Wasp Woman, The (1995)

Brasseur, Claude: Act of Aggression; Band of Outsiders; Elusive Corporal, The; Josepha; La Boum; Liars, The; Pardon Mon Affaire; Pardon Mon Affaire, Too!; Seven Deadly Sins, The; Simple Story, A

Brasseur, Pierre: Candide; Children of Paradise, The; Eyes Without a Face; Head Against the Wall; Le Schpountz

Bratt, Benjamin: Bound by Honor; Next Best Thing, The; River Wild, The; Texas (1994); Woman Undone

Brauer, Josh: Doll in the Dark, A

Braugher, Andre: City of Angels; Class of '61; Court-martial of Jackie Robinson, The; Frequency; Get on the Bus; Passing Glory; Striking Distance; Tuskegee Airmen, The

Braun, John: S.S. Hell Camp

Brauner, Asher: American Eagle; Boss' Son, The

Brauss, Arthur: Goalie's Anxiety at the Penalty Kick

Braverman, Bart: Alligator; Gladiator, The (1986) (Television); Hit and Run

Bravo, Carlos: Gunfire

Bray, Gillian: Animal Called Man, An

Bray, Thomas: Lady Mobster

Brazaele, Mark: Ravage

Brazeau, Jay: Double Jeopardy (1999); Kissed; Prisoner of Zenda, Inc.

Brazzi, Rossano: Barefoot Contessa, The; Bobo, The; Dr. Frankenstein's Castle of Freaks; Far Pavilions, The; Fear City; Final Conflict, The; Italian Job, The; Legend of the Lost; One Step to Hell; Rome Adventure; South Pacific; Summertime; We the Living; Woman Times Seven

Breck, Peter: Benji; Big Valley, The (TV Series); Crawling Hand, The; Shock Corridor; Unnamable II, The

Breeding, Larry: Street Music

Breen, Bobby: Breaking the Ice; It Happened in New Orleans; Make a Wish

Breen, Joe: Angela's Ashes

Breen, Patrick: For Love or Money

Brega, Mario: Death Rides a Horse; Fistful of Dollars, A

Bregman, Tracy: Concrete Jungle, The (1982)

Brejchova, Hana: Baron Munchausen (1961); Loves of a Blonde

Brel, Jacques: Assassins de L'Ordre, Les (Law Breakers); Franz; Pain in the A——, A

Bremer, Lucille: Till the Clouds Roll By; Yolanda and the Thief

Bremmer, Richard: 13th Warrior, The

Bremner, Ewen: Trainspotting

Brendel, El: Big Trail, The; Captain Caution; Happy Landing; Just Imagine; Little Miss Broadway; Wings

Brendler, Julie: Moondance

Breneman, April: Witchcraft 7: Judgment Hour

Breneman, Tom: Breakfast in Hollywood

Brennan, Brid: Four Days in July

Brennan, Claire: She Freak, The

Brennan, Eileen: Babes in Toyland (1986); Blood Vows: The Story of a Mafia Wife; Changing Habits; Cheap Detective, The; Clue; Daisy Miller; FM; Fourth Wise Man, The; Great Smokey Roadblock, The; I Don't Buy Kisses Anymore; Last Picture Show, The; Murder So Sweet; My Old Man; New Adventures of Pippi Longstocking, The; Playmates; Private Benjamin; Reckless (1995); Rented Lips; Scarecrow; Sticky Fingers; Sting, The; Texasville; White Palace

Brennan, John H.: Galaxis

Brennan, Johnny: Jerky Boys, The

Brennan, Kerry: Party Camp; Terror Squad

Brennan, Stephen: Eat the Peach

Brennan, Tom: Gore Vidal's Lincoln

Brennan, Walter: Adventures of Tom Sawyer, The; Along the Great Divide; At Gunpoint; Bad Day at Black Rock; Barbary Coast, The; Best of the Badmen; Brimstone; Come and Get It; Cowboy and the Lady, The; Dakota (1945); Far Country, The; Fury (1936); Gnome-Mobile, The; Goodbye, My Lady; Green Promise, The; Hangmen Also Die; Home for the Holidays (1972) (Television); How the West Was Won; Long Long Trail; Meet John Doe; My Darling Clementine; Northwest Passage; One and Only, Genuine, Original Family Band, The; Pride of the Yankees, The; Princess and the Pirate, The; Red River; Rio Bravo; Sergeant York; Showdown, The (1950); Stolen Life, A; Story of Vernon and Irene Castle, The; Support Your Local Sheriff!; Tammy and the Bachelor; Task Force; Texas Cyclone; They Shall Have Music; To Have and Have Not; Two-Fisted Law; Westerner, The; Who's Minding the Mint?

Brenneman, Amy: Daylight; Fear (1996); Heat (1995); Nevada; Your Friends & Neighbors

Brenner, Barry: Surf Nazis Must Die

Brenner, David: Worth Winning; Young at Heart Comedians, The

Brenner, Dori: Summer Wishes, Winter Dreams

Brenner, Hans: Knife in the Head

Brent, Evelyn: Framed (1930); Hopalong Cassidy Returns; Last Command, The (1928); Law West of Tombstone; Mr. Wong, Detective; Panama Lady; Riders for Justice; Seventh Victim, The; Tarzan and the Trappers; Trapped by the Mormons; Underworld (1927); Wide-Open Town; World Gone Mad, The

Brent, George: Baby Face; Dark Victory; Female; Fighting 69th, The; Great Lie, The; In Person; In This Our Life; Jezebel; Luxury Liner; Montana Belle; Old Maid, The; Out of the Blue; Painted Veil, The; Purchase Price, The; Rains Came, The; Silver Queen; Spiral Staircase, The (1946); They Call It Sin; Tomorrow Is Forever

Brent, Linda: Below the Border

Brent, Romney: Adventures of Don Juan, The; Dinner at the Ritz

Brent, Timothy: Warriors of the Wasteland

Brentano, Amy: Blood Sisters

Brenton, Gilbert: Class of Nuke 'em High

Breon, Edmund: Dressed to Kill (1946)

Bresee, Bobbie: Evil Spawn; Mausoleum; Pre-Madonnas (Social Suicide); Star Slammer

Breslin, Jimmy: If Ever I See You Again

Breslin, Patricia: Homicidal

Bressart, Felix: Bitter Sweet; Comrade X; Iceland; I've Always Loved You; Seventh Cross, The; Song Is Born, A; Without Love

Brett, Jeremy: Adventures of Sherlock Holmes, The (Series); Macbeth (1981); Shameless

Breuer, Jacques: Berlin Tunnel 21

Breuer, Jim: Half Baked

Breuer, Jerry: Offerings

Brewster, Diane: Fugitive, The: The Last Episode (TV Series); Invisible Boy, The; Maverick (TV Series); Torpedo Run

Brewster, Paget: Let's Talk About Sex

Brewton, Maia: Adventures in Babysitting

Breznahan, Tom: Brain, The (1988); Diplomatic Immunity; Ski School; Terrified; Twice Dead

Brialy, Jean-Claude: Bride Wore Black, The; Burning Court, The; Catherine & Co.; Circle of Love; Claire's Knee; Judge and the Assassin, The; Le Beau Serge; Les Cousins; Monster, The (1996); Paris Belongs to Us; Phantom of Liberty, The; Robert et Robert; Seven Deadly Sins, The; Tonio Kroger; Woman Is a Woman, A

Brian, David: Beyond the Forest; Blade Rider; Castle of Evil; Flamingo Road; High and the Mighty, The; Intruder in the Dust; Million Dollar Mermaid

Brian, Mary: Amazing Adventure; Blessed Event; Charlie Chan in Paris; Dragnet (1947); Front Page, The (1931); Peter Pan (1924); Running Wild (1927); Virginian, The (1929); World Gone Mad, The

Briand, Ludwig: Little Indian, Big City

Briant, Shane: Captain Kronos: Vampire Hunter; Cassandra; Frankenstein and the Monster from Hell; Grievous Bodily Harm; Shaker Run; Tunnel Vision (1994)

Brice, Fanny: Be Yourself; Everybody Sing; Great Ziegfeld, The; Ziegfeld Follies

Brice, Pierre: Mill of the Stone Women

Brice, Ron: Fly by Night; Horse for Danny, A; Ripe

Bridge, Alan: Badmen of the Hills; Forty-Niners

Bridges, Al: Call of the Prairie

Bridges, Beau: Alice Through the Looking Glass (1985); Daddy's Dyin' and Who's Got the Will; Dangerous Company; Defenders, The: Taking the First; Defenders, The; Fabulous Baker Boys, The; Fifth Musketeer, The; For Love of Ivy; Four Feathers, The (1978); Greased Lightning; Hammersmith Is Out; Heart Like a Wheel; Hidden in America; Honky Tonk Freeway; Hotel New Hampshire, The; Incident, The (1967); Inherit the Wind (1999); Iron Triangle, The; Killing Time, The (1987); Kissinger and Nixon; Losing Chase; Love Child; Married to It; Night Crossing; Nightjohn; Norma Rae; Other Side of the Mountain, The; Outer Limits: Sandkings; Outrage!; Positively True Adventures of the Alleged Texas Cheerleader-Murdering Mom, The; Red Light Sting, The; Rocketman; Runner Stumbles, The; Second Civil War, The; Seven Hours to Judgment; Sidekicks; Signs of Life; Silver Dream Racer; Swashbuckler (1976); Two-Minute Warning; Village of the Giants; Wild Flower (1991); Wild Pair, The; Without Warning: The James Brady Story; Witness for the Prosecution (1982); Wizard, The; Women & Men: Stories of Seduction

Bridges, Dylan: Outer Limits: Sandkings

Bridges, Jeff: Against All Odds (1984); American Heart; Arlington Road; Bad Company (1972); Big Lebowski, The; Blown Away (1994); Cutter's Way; 8 Million Ways to Die; Fabulous Baker Boys, The; Fat City; Fearless (1993); Fisher King, The; Hearts of the West; Heaven's Gate; Hidden in America; Jagged Edge; King Kong (1976); Kiss Me Goodbye; Last American Hero, The; Last Picture Show, The; Mirror Has Two Faces, The; Morning After, The; Muse, The; Nadine; Rancho Deluxe; See You in the Morning; Simpatico; Starman; Stay Hungry; Texasville; Thunderbolt and Lightfoot; Tron; Tucker: A Man and His Dream; Vanishing, The (1993); White Squall; Wild Bill; Winter Kills; Yin and Yang of Mr. Go, The

Bridges, Krista: Bloodknot

Bridges, Lloyd: Abilene Town; Airplane!; Alice Through the Looking Glass (1985); Apache Woman; Around the World Under the Sea; Bear Island; Blown Away (1994); Blue and the Gray, The; Cousins; Daring Game; Devlin; Dress Gray; East of Eden (1982); Fifth Musketeer, The; George Washington; Goddess, The; Great Wallendas, The; Haunts of the Very Rich; Heat's On, The; High Noon; Honey, I Blew Up the Kid; Hot Shots; Hot Shots Part Deux; Jane Austen's Mafia; Joe Versus the Volcano; Last of the Comanches; Little Big Horn; Master Race, The; Moonrise; Outer Limits: Sandkings; Rainmaker, The (1956); Ramrod; Rocketship X-M; Roots; Sahara (1943); Silent Night, Lonely Night; Strange Confession; Try and Get Me; Tucker: A Man and His Dream; Weekend Warriors; White Tower, The; Wild Pair, The; Winter People

Bridges, Todd: Homeboys; Twice Dead

Bridou, Lucienne: This Man Can't Die

Briers, Richard: Midwinter's Tale, A; Norman Conquests, The, Episode 1: Table Manners; Norman Conquests, The, Episode 2: Living Together; Norman Conquests, The, Episode 3: Round and Round the Garden

Brieux, Bernard: Petit Con; Rascals, The

Briggs, Donald: Panama Lady

Bright, Richard: Cut and Run; Godfather, Part III, The; On the Yard; Panic in Needle Park; Red Heat (1988); Ref, The

Brignoli, Omar: Tree of the Wooden Clogs, The

Brill, Fran: Look Back in Anger (1980)

Brill, Jason: Hell High

Brill, Robert: Look Back in Anger (1980)

Brilli, Nancy: Demons 2

Brimble, Nick: Gone Fishin'

Brimhall, Cynthia: Fit to Kill

Brimley, Wilford: Absence of Malice; Act of Vengeance; American Justice; Borderline; Cocoon; Cocoon: The Return; Country; Death Valley; Electric Horseman, The; End of the Line; Eternity; Ewoks: The Battle for Endor; Firm, The; Good Old Boys, The; Gore Vidal's Billy the Kid; Hard Target; Harry and Son; High Road to China; In & Out; Murder in Space; Mutant Species; My Fellow Americans; Natural, The; Progeny; Remo Williams: The Adventure Begins; Rodeo Girl; Stone Boy, The; Summer of the Monkeys; Thing, The (1982); Thompson's Last Run; Tough Enough

Brin, Michele: Secret Games; Sexual Intent

Brinegar, Paul: Gambler Returns, The: Luck of the Draw; How to Make a Monster; Rawhide (TV Series); Wyatt Earp: Return to Tombstone

Brink, Irvin: On Deadly Ground

Brinkley, Christie: National Lampoon's Vacation

Brinkley, Ritch: Cabin Boy

Brion, Françoise: French Lessons

Brisco, Gwen: Getting Over

Briscoe, Brent: Simple Plan, A

Brisebois, Danielle: Big Bad Mama II; Premonition, The

Brisson, Carl: Manxman, The; Murder at the Vanities; Ring, The

Bristow, Michael: Karate Cop

Britt, May: Secrets of Women (Waiting Women); Summer Interlude; Young Lions, The

Brittain, Charlotte: Get Real

Brittany, Morgan: Body Armor; In Search of Historic Jesus; Initiation of Sarah, The; LBJ: The Early Years; Legend of the Spirit Dog; Sundown (1990)

Britton, Barbara: Captain Kidd; Champagne for Caesar; Loaded Pistols; Secrets of the Wasteland; So Proudly We Hail; Virginian, The (1946); Young and Willing

Britton, Connie: Brothers McMullen, The; Escape Clause

Britton, Pamela: D.O.A. (1949); If It's Tuesday, This Must Be Belgium; Key to the City

Britton, Tony: Day of the Jackal, The; Dr. Syn, Alias the Scarecrow; Horsemasters; Night Watch; Operation Amsterdam; There's a Girl in My Soup

Brix, Herman: Hawk of the Wilderness; Hi-Yo Silver

Broadbent, Jim: Avengers, The; Borrowers, The (1997); Bullets over Broadway; Crying Game, The; Enchanted April; Good Father, The; Life Is Sweet; Princess Caraboo; Richard III (1995); Rough Magic; Topsy-Turvy; Wedding Gift, The

Broaderup, Bernd: Taxi Zum Klo (Taxi to the Toilet)

Broadhurst, Kent: Dark Half, The

Broadnax, David: Zombie Island Massacre

Broche, Mario Gonzales: I Am Cuba

Brochet, Anne: Barjo; Cyrano De Bergerac (1990); Tous les Matins du Monde

Brock, Charles: Sourdough

Brock, Phil: Dollman vs. Demonic Toys

Brockius, Lawrence: Deadmate

Brockman, Jay: Penpal Murders

Brocksmith, Roy: Kull the Conqueror

Brockwell, Gladys: Oliver Twist (1922)

Broderick, Beth: Are You Lonesome Tonight; In the Deep Woods; Maternal Instincts

Broderick, Chris: Legacy of Horror

Broderick, Helen: Bride Walks Out, The; My Love for Yours (Honeymoon in Bali); No, No Nanette; Rage of Paris, The; Swing Time; Top Hat

Broderick, James: Alice's Restaurant; Group, The; Shadow Box, The; Todd Killings, The

Broderick, Jocelyn: My Daughter's Keeper

Broderick, Matthew: Addicted to Love; Biloxi Blues; Cable Guy, The; Cinderella (1985); Family Business; Ferris Bueller's Day Off; Freshman, The; Glory; Godzilla (1998); Infamous Dorothy Parker, The; Infinity; Inspector Gadget; Ladyhawke; Life in the Theater, A; Master Harold and the

rousek, Otakar: Lies & Whispers

rousse, Liliane: Paranoiac

ower, Jordan: Forest Warrior

own Jr., Gilbert: Raising the Heights

rown, Andre: Bronx War, The

rown, Barbara: Ma and Pa Kettle Back on the Farm

rown, Barry: Bad Company (1972); Daisy Miller

rown, Blair: Altered States; And I Alone Survived; Choir-
oys, The; Continental Divide; Day My Parents Ran Away,
he; Flash of Green, A; Kennedy (TV Miniseries); One Trick
ony; Passed Away; Stealing Home; Strapless

rown, Bobby: Thin Line Between Love and Hate, A

rown, Bryan: Blame It on the Bellboy; Breaker Morant;
ocktail; Dead Heart; Dead in the Water; Devlin; Full Body
Massage; F/X; F/X 2: The Deadly Art of Illusion; Good Wife,
he; Gorillas in the Mist; Last Hit, The; Odd Angry Shot,
he; Palm Beach; Prisoners of the Sun; Rebel (1985);
weet Talker; Tai-Pan; Thornbirds, The; Town Like Alice, A;
racked; 20,000 Leagues Under the Sea (1996); Winter of
ur Dreams

rown, Caitlin: Babylon 5 (TV Series)

rown, Carlos: Dangerous Company

rown, Charles: Old Swimmin' Hole, The

rown, Christopher M.: Aliens Among Us

rown, Clancy: Ambition; Blue Steel (1990); Bride, The;
ast a Deadly Spell; Donor Unknown; Extreme Prejudice;
emale Perversions; Flubber; Highlander; In the Company
f Spies; Last Light; Love, Lies and Murder; Past Midnight;
et Sematary Two; Season of Fear; Shawshank Redemp-
on, The; Shoot to Kill; Starship Troopers; Vendetta; Wait-
ng for the Light

rown, D. W.: Mischief

rown, David: Chasing Dreams; Deadly Harvest

rown, Dwier: Cutting Edge, The; Galaxies Are Colliding;
uardian, The (1990); Intimate Betrayal

rown, Dyann: Lone Wolf

rown, Eleanora: Two Women

rown, Eric: Private Lessons; They're Playing with Fire

rown, Georg Stanford: Ava's Magical Adventure; Day-
on's Devils; House Party 2; Jesse Owens Story, The; Kid
with the Broken Halo, The; Night the City Screamed, The;
Roots: The Next Generation; Stir Crazy

rown, Georgia: Bawdy Adventures of Tom Jones, The;
Devil's Undead, The; Long Ago Tomorrow; Study in Terror, A

rown, Gibran: Marvin and Tige

rown, Henry: Stepfather II

rown, James: Adios Amigo; Chain Lightning; Objective,
urma!; That Was Rock

rown, Jim: Crack House; Dark of the Sun (Mercenaries)
1968); Dirty Dozen, The; El Condor; Fingers; Grasshopper,
he; Ice Station Zebra; I'm Gonna Git You Sucka!; Kid
Vengeance; One Down, Two to Go; 100 Rifles; Original
Gangstas; Pacific Inferno; Rio Conchos; Riot (1969); Run-
ing Man, The; Slaughter; Slaughter's Big Rip-Off; Take a
Hard Ride; Three the Hard Way; Tick . . . Tick . . . Tick . . .

rown, Joe E.: Beware of Spooks; Comedy of Terrors; Dar-
ng Young Man, The; Earthworm Tractors; Pin-Up Girl; Rid-
ng on Air; Show Boat (1951); Some Like It Hot; Tender
Years, The; When's Your Birthday?

rown, Johnny Mack: Belle of the Nineties; Between Men;
Coquette; Deep in the Heart of Texas; Desert Phantom; Fe-
male; Hell Town; Lawman Is Born, A; Lone Star Trail; Our
Dancing Daughters; Ride 'em Cowboy; Short Grass; Single
Standard, The; Stampede; Woman of Affairs, A

rown, Juanita: Caged Heat

rown, Julie: Aliens Among Us; Earth Girls Are Easy; Na-
ional Lampoon's Attack of the 5' 2" Women; Nervous
Ticks; Opposite Sex (And How to Live with Them), The
1993); Raining Stones; Shakes the Clown; Spirit of '76,
The

rown, Katie: Bloodfist IV—Die Trying; Last Way Out, The

rown, Ken: Palm Beach

rown, Lawrence: Big Fella

rown, Lou: Alison's Birthday; Irishman, The

rown, Lowell: High School Caesar

rown, Lucille: Mystery Squadron; Rainbow Valley; Texas
Terror

Brown, Matthew: God's Army

Brown, Murray: Vampyres

Brown, Olivia: Memories of Murder; Miami Vice; Miami
Vice: "The Prodigal Son"

Brown Jr., Oscar: Original Gangstas

Brown, Pamela: Becket; Cleopatra (1963); Dracula (1973);
Half a Sixpence; Lust for Life; One of Our Aircraft Is Missing; Secret Ceremony; Tales of Hoffman

Brown, Peter: Asylum (1996); Aurora Encounter; Concrete
Jungle, The (1982); Foxy Brown; Summer Magic; Tiger
Walks, A

Brown, Phil: Jungle Captive; Without Reservations

Brown, Ralph: Crying Game, The; Ivanhoe (1997)

Brown, Reb: Cage; Cage II: Arena of Death, The; Captain
America (1979); Captain America II: Death Too Soon; Death
of a Soldier; Fast Break; Firing Line, The; Howling II . . . Your
Sister Is a Werewolf; Last Flight to Hell; Mercenary Fight-
ers; Street Hunter; Strike Commando; Uncommon Valor;
White Ghost

Brown, Ritza: McGuffin, The

Brown, Roger: Paper Lion

Brown, Roger Aaron: China Moon; Tall Tale: The Unbelievable Adventures of Pecos Bill

Brown, Ron: Charlie, the Lonesome Cougar

Brown, Sara Suzanne: Killer Looks

Brown, Terry: Bloodbeat

Brown, Tim: Pacific Inferno

Brown, Timothy: Girls Are for Loving

Brown, Tom: Anne of Green Gables (1934); Buck Privates
Come Home; In Old Chicago; Judge Priest; Navy Blue and
Gold

Brown, Vanessa: Bless the Beasts and Children; Heiress,
The; I've Always Loved You

Brown, Violet: Firehouse (1987)

Brown, Wally: Girl Rush; High and the Mighty, The; Zombies on Broadway

Brown, Wendell: Up the Academy

Brown, Woody: Accused, The; Animal Instincts 2; Rain
Killer, The; Secret Games 3

Browne, Coral: Auntie Mame; Courtney Affair, The; Dreamchild; Eleanor: First Lady of the World; Englishman Abroad,
An; Killing of Sister George, The; Ruling Class, The

Browne, Joe: Robo Vampire

Browne, Kathie: Hondo and the Apaches

Browne, Leslie: Dancers; Nijinsky; Turning Point, The

Browne, Roscoe Lee: Black Like Me; Connection, The
(1961); Cowboys, The; Dear God; For Us the Living: The
Medgar Evers Story; Forest Warrior; Jumpin' Jack Flash;
King; Legal Eagles; Liberation of L. B. Jones, The; Moon 44;
Nothing Personal (1980); Superfly T.N.T.; World's Greatest
Athlete, The

Browne, Suzanne: Bikini Carwash Company 2

Browne, Zachary: Shiloh 2: Shiloh Season

Browning, Emily Jane: Echo of Thunder, The

Browning, Rod: Double McGuffin, The

Browning, Tod: Intolerance

Bruce, Angela: Charlie Boy

Bruce, Brenda: Back Home; Nightmare (1964); Steaming

Bruce, Cheryl Lynn: Daughters of the Dust

Bruce, David: Calling Dr. Death; Can't Help Singing; Gung
Ho! (1943); Lady on a Train; Mad Ghoul, The; Salome,
Where She Danced; Sea Wolf, The (1941); Smiling Ghost,
The

Bruce, Ed: Fire Down Below

Bruce, Kitty: Switchblade Sisters

Bruce, Lenny: Dance Hall Racket; Lenny Bruce Performance Film, The

Bruce, Nigel: Adventures of Sherlock Holmes, The; Becky
Sharp; Blue Bird, The; Chocolate Soldier, The; Corn Is
Green, The (1945); Dressed to Kill (1946); Follow the Boys;
Gypsy Wildcat; Hound of the Baskervilles, The (1939);
House of Fear; Journey for Margaret; Julia Misbehaves;
Lassie Come Home; Last of Mrs. Cheney, The; Limelight;
Pearl of Death, The; Pursuit to Algiers; Rains Came, The;
Rebecca; Scarlet Claw, The; Scarlet Pimpernel, The (1934);
She (1935); Sherlock Holmes and the Secret Weapon;
Sherlock Holmes and the Spider Woman; Sherlock Holmes
and the Voice of Terror; Sherlock Holmes Faces Death;
Sherlock Holmes in Washington; Son of Lassie; Susan and
God; Suspicion (1941); Terror by Night; Thunder in the
City; Trail of the Lonesome Pine, The; Two Mrs. Carrolls,
The; Woman in Green, The

Bruce, Robert: Under the Gun (1995)

Bruce, Virginia: Action in Arabia; Born to Dance; Great
Ziegfeld, The; Invisible Woman, The; Jane Eyre (1934); Let

Jimmy, The; Somebody to Love; Trees Lounge; Twenty Bucks; 28 Days

Busch, Charles: Trouble on the Corner

Busch, Ernest: Kameradschaft

Busch, Mae: Foolish Wives; Keystone Comedies: Vol. 1–5; Laurel and Hardy Classics: Vol. 1–9

Busey, Gary: Act of Piracy; Angels Hard as They Come; Barbarosa; Big Wednesday; Black Sheep; Breaking Point (1993); Buddy Holly Story, The; Bulletproof (1988); Canvas; Carny; Carried Away; Chain, The; Chasers; Chrome Soldiers; Dangerous Life, A; D.C. Cab; Detour (1999); Diary of a Serial Killer; Drop Zone; Execution of Private Slovik, The; Eye of the Tiger; Fallen Angels; Fear and Loathing in Las Vegas; Firm, The; Foolin' Around; Gumball Rally, The; Hider in the House; Hitchhiker, The (Series); Insignificance; Last American Hero, The; Let's Get Harry; Lethal Tender; Lethal Weapon; Man with a Gun; My Heroes Have Always Been Cowboys; Neon Empire, The; Point Break; Predator 2; Real Thing, The; Rookie of the Year; Rough Riders; Shrieking, The; Silver Bullet; Soldier; South Beach; Star Is Born, A (1976); Steel Sharks; Straight Time; Surviving the Game; Suspicious Minds; Thunderbolt and Lightfoot; Under Siege; Universal Soldier II: Brothers in Arms; Warriors (1994)

Busey, Jake: Black Cat Run; Enemy of the State; Frighteners, The; Home Fries; Starship Troopers

Busfield, Timothy: Dream House; Erasable You; Fade to Black (1993); Field of Dreams; First Kid; Revenge of the Nerds; Revenge of the Nerds II: Nerds in Paradise; Sneakers of a Scream; Skateboard Kid, The; Sneakers; Souler Opposite, The; Strays; Striking Distance; Trucks; Unspeakable, The

Bush, Billy Green: Alice Doesn't Live Here Anymore; Conagher; Culpepper Cattle Co., The; Electra Glide in Blue; Elvis and Me; Five Easy Pieces; Jericho Mile, The; Tom Horn

Bush, Chuck: Fandango

Bush, Owen: Prehysteria 2

Bush, Rebeccah: Hunk

Bushell, Anthony: Dark Journey; Disraeli; Quatermass and the Pit; Vanity Fair

Bushey, Trent: American Shaolin: King of the Kickboxers II

Bushman, Francis X.: Ben-Hur (1926); Dick Tracy (1937); Three Musketeers, The (1933)

Bushman, Ralph: Our Hospitality

Busia, Akosua: Color Purple, The; George McKenna Story, The; Low Blow; Native Son (1986)

Busia, Marion: Gone in 60 Seconds

Busker, Ricky: Big Shots

Bussières, Pascale: When Night is Falling

Buster, Budd: Arizona Days; Zorro's Fighting Legion

Buster, Michael: God's Army

Bustric, Sergio: Life Is Beautiful

Butkus, Dick: Cracking Up; Deadly Games; Hamburger—The Motion Picture; Spontaneous Combustion

Butler, Calvin: Drying Up the Streets

Butler, Cindy: Boggy Creek II

Butler, David: Sky Pilot, The

Butler, Dean: Desert Hearts; Kid with the 200 I.Q., The; Little House on the Prairie (TV Series)

Butler, Holly: Looking for Trouble

Butler, Jean: Brylcreem Boys, The

Butler, Kent: Curse of the Queerwolf

Butler, Paul: To Sleep with Anger

Butler, Tom: Ronnie & Julie

Butler, William: Inner Sanctum; Leatherface—the Texas Chainsaw Massacre III

Butler, Yancey: Drop Zone; Ex, The; Fast Money (1996); Hard Target; Hit List, The (1992); Ravager

Butrick, Merritt: Death Spa; Head Office; Shy People

Butterworth, Charles: Cat and the Fiddle, The; Dixie Jamboree; Every Day's a Holiday; Forsaking All Others; Illicit; It Happened in New Orleans; Let Freedom Ring; Love Me Tonight; Second Chorus; Swing High, Swing Low; This Is the Army

Butterworth, Peter: Carry on Doctor; Carry on Emmanuelle; Follow That Camel

Butterworth, Tyler: Consuming Passions

Buttle, Stephanie: Couch in New York, A

Buttons, Red: Alice in Wonderland (1985); Alice Through the Looking Glass (1985); C.H.O.M.P.S.; 18 Again; Five

Weeks in a Balloon; Gay Purr-ee; Harlow; Hatari!; It Could Happen to You; Leave 'em Laughing; Movie Movie; One, Two, Three; Pete's Dragon; Poseidon Adventure, The; Sayonara; Side Show; Story of Us, The; Users, The; When Time Ran Out!; Who Killed Mary What's 'Er Name?

Buttram, Pat: Beyond the Purple Hills; Hills of Utah, The; Mule Train

Buttrick, Merritt: Wired to Kill

Buxton, Sarah: Listen; Welcome to Spring Break

Buy, Margherita: Station, The

Buzby, Zane: Americathon; Cracking Up; National Lampoon's Class Reunion

Buzzanca, Lando: Playing the Field; When Women Had Tails; When Women Lost Their Tails

Buzzard, Eddie: Bulldog Courage

Buzzi, Ruth: Apple Dumpling Gang Rides Again, The; Bad Guys; Being, The; Boys Will Be Boys; Chu Chu and the Philly Flash; Dixie Lanes; Freaky Friday; My Mom's a Werewolf; Surf 2; Troublemakers; Up Your Alley; Wishful Thinking (1992)

Byers, Kate: Career Girls

Byington, Spring: Big Wheel, The; Blue Bird, The; Devil and Miss Jones, The; Dodsworth; Enchanted Cottage, The; Heaven Can Wait (1943); In the Good Old Summertime; Jezebel; Little Women (1933); Living in a Big Way; Lucky Partners; Meet John Doe; Please Don't Eat the Daisies; Presenting Lily Mars; Roxie Hart; Singapore; Stage Struck (1936); Thrill of a Romance; Walk Softly, Stranger; Werewolf of London; When Ladies Meet; You Can't Take it with You (1938)

Bykov, Rolan: Overcoat, The

Byner, John: Great Smokey Roadblock, The; Man in the Santa Claus Suit, The; Transylvania 6-5000

Byrd, Ralph: Dick Tracy (1937); Dick Tracy Meets Gruesome; Dick Tracy Returns; Dick Tracy vs. Crime Inc.; Dick Tracy's Dilemma; Dick Tracy's G-Men; Son of Monte Cristo, The; SOS Coast Guard

Byrd, Tom: Wet Gold

Byrd-Nethery, Miriam: Civil War Diary

Byrne, Barbara: Sunday in the Park with George

Byrne, Catherine: Eat the Peach

Byrne, David: True Stories; Two Moon July

Byrne, Debbie: Rebel (1985)

Byrne, Eddie: Jack the Ripper (1959)

Byrne, Gabriel: Buffalo Girls; Christopher Columbus (1985); Cool World; Dangerous Woman, A; Dark Obsession; Dead Man; Defense of the Realm; End of Days; End of Violence, The; Frankie Starlight; Gothic; Hanna K.; Hello Again; Into the West; Julia and Julia; Lionheart (1986); Little Women (1994); Miller's Crossing; Point of No Return; Polish Wedding; Royal Deceit; Shipwrecked; Siesta; Simple Twist of Fate, A; Smilla's Sense of Snow; Soldier's Tale, A; Somebody's Waiting; Stigmata; Summer Fling; This Is the Sea; Trial by Jury; Trigger Happy (Mad Dog Time); Usual Suspects, The; Weapons of Mass Distraction

Byrne, Karl: War of the Buttons

Byrne, Martha: Anna to the Infinite Power; Eyes of the Amaryllis

Byrne, Michael: Battlefield Earth; Infiltrator, The

Byrne, Niall: Miracle, The (1990)

Byrnes, David: Witchcraft 7: Judgment Hour

Byrnes, Edd: Final Defeat, The; Go Kill and Come Back; Mankillers; Reform School Girl

Byrnes, Jim: Bloodhounds II; Dirty Work; Dream Man; Harmony Cats; Suspicious Agenda

Byrnes, Josephine: Brides of Christ; Frauds

Byron, David: Based on an Untrue Story; Fade to Black (1993)

Byron, Jean: Invisible Invaders; Magnetic Monster, The

Byron, Jeffrey: Dungeonmaster, The; Metalstorm: The Destruction of Jared-Syn; Seniors, The

Byron, Marion: Steamboat Bill Jr.

Byrska, Irene: Man of Iron

Byun, Susan: Sgt. Kabukiman N.Y.P.D.

Caan, James: Alien Nation; Another Man, Another Chance; Bolero (1982); Bottle Rocket; Boy Called Hate, A; Brian's Song; Bridge Too Far, A; Bulletproof (1996); Chapter Two; Cinderella Liberty; Comes a Horseman; Countdown; Dark Backward, The; Dick Tracy (1990); El Dorado; Eraser; Flesh and Bone; For the Boys; Freebie and the Bean; Funny Lady; Gambler, The (1974); Gardens of Stone; Godfather, The;

Godfather Epic, The; Gone with the West; Harry and Walter Go to New York; Hide in Plain Sight; Honeymoon in Vegas; Killer Elite, The; Kiss Me Goodbye; Lady in a Cage; Little Moon & Jud McGraw; Mickey Blue Eyes; Misery; North Star (1996); Poodle Springs; Program, The; Rabbit Run; Rain People, The; Red Line 7000; Rollerball; Silent Movie; Slither; Thief (1981); This Is My Father

Caan, Scott: Boy Called Hate, A; Ready to Rumble; Varsity Blues

Cabezas, Oyanka: Carla's Song

Cabot, Bruce: Angel and the Badman; Ann Vickers; Best of the Badmen; Big Jake; Captain Caution; Chisum; Comancheros, The; Diamonds Are Forever; Dodge City; Fancy Pants; Finishing School; Fury (1936); Goliath and the Barbarians; Green Berets, The; Hellfighters; John Paul Jones; King Kong (1933); Last of the Mohicans, The (1936); Show Them No Mercy; Silver Queen; Sinners in Paradise; Smashing the Rackets; Sorrowful Jones; Sundown (1941); Undefeated, The

Cabot, Sebastian: Family Jewels, The; Ivanhoe (1952); Johnny Tremain; Omar Khayyam; Romeo and Juliet (1954); Seven Thieves; Time Machine, The; Twice-Told Tales; Westward Ho, the Wagons

Cabot, Susan: Carnival Rock; Machine-Gun Kelly; Saga of the Viking Women and Their Voyage to the Waters of the Great Sea Serpent, The (The Viking Women and the Sea Serpent, The); Son of Ali Baba; Sorority Girl; War of the Satellites; Wasp Woman (1960)

Cadell, Jean: Love from a Stranger (1937)

Cadell, Simon: Cold Light of Day, The

Cadenat, Garry: Sugarcane Alley

Cadieux, Jason: Iron Eagle IV; Lilies

Cadillacs, The: Go, Johnny, Go!

Cadorette, Mary: Stewardess School

Caesar, Adolph: Club Paradise; Color Purple, The; Fortune Dane; Soldier's Story, A

Caesar, Shirley: Gospel

Caesar, Sid: Airport 1975; Alice in Wonderland (1985); Barnaby and Me; Cheap Detective, The; Fiendish Plot of Dr. Fu Manchu, The; Grease; Guide for the Married Man, A; It's a Mad Mad Mad Mad World; Munsters' Revenge, The; Over the Brooklyn Bridge; Silent Movie; Stoogemania; 10 from Your Show of Shows; Wonderful Ice Cream Suit, The

Cafagna, Ashley: Midas Touch, The; Mystery Monsters; Werewolf Reborn!

Caffaro, Cheri: Abductors, The; Ginger; Girls Are for Loving; Place Called Today, A

Caffrey, Peter: I Went Down

Caffrey, Stephen: Buried Alive II; Tour of Duty

Cage, Nicolas: Amos & Andrew; Birdy; Boy in Blue, The; Bringing Out the Dead; City of Angels; Con Air; Deadfall; 8MM; Face/Off; Fast Times at Ridgemont High; Fire Birds; Gone in 60 Seconds; Guarding Tess; Honeymoon in Vegas; Industrial Symphony No. 1 The Dream of the Broken Hearted; It Could Happen to You; Kiss of Death (1995); Leaving Las Vegas; Moonstruck; Peggy Sue Got Married; Racing with the Moon; Raising Arizona; Red Rock West; Rock, The; Snake Eyes; Time to Kill (1990); Trapped in Paradise; Valley Girl; Vampire's Kiss; Wild at Heart; Zandalee

Cagen, Andrea: Hot Box, The

Cagney, James: Angels with Dirty Faces; Blonde Crazy; Blood on the Sun; Boy Meets Girl; Bride Came C.O.D., The; Captains of the Clouds; Ceiling Zero; City for Conquest; Devil Dogs of the Air; Each Dawn I Die; Fighting 69th, The; Footlight Parade; Gallant Hours, The; Great Guy; Johnny Come Lately; Kiss Tomorrow Goodbye; Lady Killer; Lion Is in the Streets, A; Love Me or Leave Me; Man of a Thousand Faces; Midsummer Night's Dream, A (1935); Mister Roberts; Never Steal Anything Small; Oklahoma Kid, The; One, Two, Three; Public Enemy; Ragtime; Roaring Twenties, The; Seven Little Foys, The; Shake Hands with the Devil; Something to Sing About; Strawberry Blonde, The; 13 Rue Madeleine; Time of Your Life, The; Tribute to a Bad Man; West Point Story, The; What Price Glory; White Heat; Yankee Doodle Dandy

Cagney, Jeanne: Kentucky Rifle; Lion Is in the Streets, A; Man of a Thousand Faces; Rhythm on the River; Time of Your Life, The; Yankee Doodle Dandy

Cagney, William: Palooka

Cain, Dean: Best Men; Futuresport; Tracked

Caine, Michael: Alfie; Ashanti; Battle of Britain; Beyond the Limit; Beyond the Poseidon Adventure; Black Windmill, The; Blame It on Rio; Blood and Wine; Blue Ice; Bridge Too Far, A; Bullet to Beijing; Bullseye; Cider House Rules, The; Deathtrap; Destructors, The; Dirty Rotten Scoundrels; Dressed to Kill (1980); Eagle Has Landed, The; Educating Rita; Fourth Protocol, The; Funeral in Berlin; Gambit; Get Carter; Half-Moon Street; Hand, The; Hannah and Her Sisters; Harry and Walter Go to New York; Holcroft Covenant, The; Ipcress File, The; Island, The; Italian Job, The; Jack the Ripper (1988); Jaws: The Revenge; Jekyll & Hyde; Jigsaw Man, The; Last Valley, The; Man Who Would Be King, The; Mandela and De Klerk; Mr. Destiny; Mona Lisa; Muppet Christmas Carol, The; Noises Off; On Deadly Ground; Pulp; Romantic Englishwoman, The; Shock to the System, A; Silver Bears; Sleuth; Surrender; Swarm, The; Sweet Liberty; Too Late the Hero; 20,000 Leagues Under the Sea (1996); Victory; Water; Whistle Blower, The; Wilby Conspiracy, The; Without a Clue; Woman Times Seven; Wrong Box, The; X, Y and Zee; Zulu

Caire, Audrey: They Saved Hitler's Brain

Cairns, Jason: Eye of the Snake

Calabro, Thomas: Lady Killers

Calamai, Clara: Ossessione

Calder-Marshall, Anna: King Lear (1984); Wuthering Heights (1971)

Calderon, Paul: Bad Lieutenant; Condition Red; Sweet Nothing

Caldwell, Janette Allyson: Mandroid; Night Screams

Caldwell, L. Scott: Twilight Man

Caldwell, Zoe: Lantern Hill

Cale, Paula: Milo

Calegory, Jade: Mac and Me

Calfa, Don: Bank Shot; Blue Movies; Chopper Chicks in Zombietown; Greaser's Palace; Me, Myself & I; Return of the Living Dead, The; Treasure of the Moon Goddess

Calfan, Nicole: Permission to Kill

Calhern, Louis: Annie Get Your Gun; Arch of Triumph; Asphalt Jungle, The; Athena; Betrayed (1954); Blonde Crazy; Bridge of San Luis Rey, The; Count of Monte Cristo, The (1934); Diplomaniacs; Duck Soup; Executive Suite; Forever Darling; Heaven Can Wait (1943); Julius Caesar (1953); Last Days of Pompeii, The (1935); Latin Lovers; Life of Emile Zola, The; Life of Her Own, A; Magnificent Yankee, The; Men of the Fighting Lady; Nancy Goes to Rio; Night after Night; Notorious; Prisoner of Zenda, The (1952); Prodigal, The; Red Pony, The; Rhapsody; Student Prince, The; Sweet Adeline; They Call It Sin; Two Weeks with Love; We're Not Married; World Gone Mad, The

Calhoun, Monica: Best Man, The (1999); Players Club, The

Calhoun, Rory: Avenging Angel (1985); Bad Jim; Blue and the Gray, The; Dayton's Devils; Finger on the Trigger; Flatbed Annie and Sweetie Pie: Lady Truckers; Hell Comes to Frogtown; How to Marry a Millionaire; Mission to Glory; Motel Hell; Pure Country; Red House, The; River of No Return; Treasure of Pancho Villa, The

Call, Brandon: Blind Fury

Call, John: Santa Claus Conquers the Martians

Call, R. D.: Last Man Standing (1996); Waterworld

Callahan, James: Outlaw Blues; Tropic of Cancer

Callan, K.: Saved by the Light; Unborn, The

Callan, Michael: Bon Voyage!; Cat and the Canary, The (1978); Cat Ballou; Donner Pass: The Road to Survival; Double Exposure (1982); Frasier the Lovable Lion (Frasier the Sensuous Lion); Freeway (1988); Gidget Goes Hawaiian; Interns, The; Lepke; Mysterious Island

Callard, Rebecca: Borrowers, The (1993)

Callas, Charlie: Vampire Vixens from Venus

Callas, Maria: Medea

Calleia, Joseph: After the Thin Man; Branded; Five Came Back; For Whom the Bell Tolls; Four Faces West; Gilda; Jungle Book (1942); Littlest Outlaw, The; My Little Chickadee; Noose Hangs High, The; RiffRaff (1936); Sundown (1941); Treasure of Pancho Villa, The

Callen, John: Rainbow Warrior

Callie, Dayton: Executive Target; Last Days of Frankie the Fly, The

Callow, Simon: Ace Ventura: When Nature Calls; Bedrooms and Hallways; Crucifer of Blood; Four Weddings and a Funeral; Good Father, The; Jefferson in Paris; Manifesto;

Comfort; Standoff (1997); Thieves Like Us; Thousand Acres, A; Tie That Binds, The; Trouble in Mind; Two Days in the Valley; Welcome to L.A.; Wild Bill

Carradine, Robert: All's Fair; As Is; Big Red One, The; Bird of Prey; Blackout (1998); Breakout (1998); Buy and Cell; Cannonball; Clarence; Coming Home; Conspiracy: The Trial of the Chicago 8; Disappearance of Christina, The; Double-crossed; Gunfighter (1997); Heartaches; Humanoids from the Deep (1996); Illusions; Incident, The (1989); Jackson County Jail; John Carpenter Presents: Body Bags; Joyride (1977); Long Riders, The; Massacre at Central High; Mean Streets; Number One with a Bullet; Orca; Revenge of the Nerds; Revenge of the Nerds II: Nerds in Paradise; Revenge of the Nerds III: The Next Generation; Revenge of the Nerds IV: Nerds in Love; Rude Awakening (1989); Scorpio One; Somebody Has to Shoot the Picture; Tag—The Assassination Game; Tommyknockers, The; Wavelength (1983)

Carrara, Chris: Remote

Carrera, Barbara: Adventures of Young Brave, The; Condorman; Embryo; I, the Jury; Island of Dr. Moreau, The; Lone Wolf McQuade; Love at Stake; Love Is All There Is; Loverboy; Masada; Never Say Never Again; Point of Impact; Sawbones; Tryst; When Time Ran Out!; Wicked Stepmother, The; Wild Geese II

Carrere, Tia: Aloha Summer; Fatal Mission; High School High; Hollow Point; Hostile Intentions; Immortals, The; Jury Duty; Kull the Conqueror; My Teacher's Wife; Natural Enemy; Quick; Rising Sun; Showdown in Little Tokyo; Tracked; Treacherous; True Lies; 20 Dates; Wayne's World; Wayne's World 2; Zombie Nightmare

Carrey, Jim: Ace Ventura: Pet Detective; Ace Ventura: When Nature Calls; Batman Forever; Cable Guy, The; Dumb and Dumber; Earth Girls Are Easy; High Strung; Liar, Liar; Man on the Moon; Mask, The (1994); Me, Myself & Irene; Once Bitten; Rubberface; Truman Show, The

Carrico, Monica: Running Hot

Carrier, Corey: Savage Land

Carriere, Mathieu: Beethoven's Nephew; Bilitis; Coup De Grace; Woman in Flames, A

Carrillo, Elpidia: Beyond the Limit; Border, The; Lightning Incident, The; My Family; Predator; Salvador

Carrillo, Leo: American Empire; Captain Caution; Cisco Kid (TV Series); Fugitive, The (1947); Ghost Catchers, The; Girl of the Golden West, The; Gypsy Wildcat; History Is Made at Night; Horror Island; Manhattan Melodrama; Manhattan Merry-Go-Round; One Night in the Tropics; Riders of Death Valley; Too Hot to Handle; Viva Villa!

Carroi, Regina: Satan's Sadists

Carroll, Barbara: Last Days of Pompeii (1960)

Carroll, Beeson: Spacehunter: Adventures in the Forbidden Zone

Carroll, Diahann: Carmen Jones; Eve's Bayou; Five Heartbeats, The; From the Dead of Night; Goodbye Again; I Know Why the Caged Bird Sings; Paris Blues; That's Singing: The Best of Broadway

Carroll, Helena: Man Upstairs, The

Carroll, J. Winston: Spenser: Ceremony; Spenser: Pale Kings & Princes

Carroll, Janet: Talent for the Game

Carroll, Jill: Vals, The

Carroll, John: Decision at Sundown; Fabulous Texan, The; Farmer Takes a Wife, The; Fiesta; Flying Tigers, The; Go West; Only Angels Have Wings; Rio Rita; Susan and God; Wolf Call; Zorro Rides Again

Carroll, Johnny: Rock, Baby, Rock It

Carroll, Justin: Dark Secrets

Carroll, Kevin: E's Next Move

Carroll, Lane: Crazies, The

Carroll, Leo G.: Adventures of Topper, The; Bulldog Drummond's Secret Police; Charlie Chan in City in Darkness; Charlie Chan's Murder Cruise; Christmas Carol, A (1938); Enchantment; Father of the Bride (1950); Forever Amber; House on 92nd Street, The; Man from U.N.C.L.E., The (TV Series); Paradine Case, The; Prize, The; Sadie McKee; Snows of Kilimanjaro, The; Song of Love; Spellbound; Strangers on a Train; Swan, The (1956); Tarantula; Tower of London (1939); We're No Angels (1955); Young Bess

Carroll, Lisa Hart: Midnight Cabaret

Carroll, Madeleine: General Died at Dawn, The; Lloyd's of London; My Favorite Blonde; My Love for Yours (Honeymoon in Bali); Northwest Mounted Police; On the Avenue;

Prisoner of Zenda, The (1937); School for Scandal; Secret Agent, The; Thirty-Nine Steps, The (1935)

Carroll, Matthew: Dance with a Stranger

Carroll, Nancy: Scarlet Dawn; Transatlantic Merry-Go-Round

Carroll, Regina: Brain of Blood

Carroll, Susan: Stanley

Carrot Top (Scott Thompson): Chairman of the Board; Future Shock; Hijacking Hollywood; Kids in the Hall: Brain Candy; Rest in Pieces

Carson, Charles: Cry, the Beloved Country (1952)

Carson, Hunter: Invaders from Mars (1986); Paris, Texas

Carson, Jack: Arsenic and Old Lace; Bride Came C.O.D., The; Carefree; Cat on a Hot Tin Roof (1958); Dangerous When Wet; Doughgirls, The; Gentleman Jim; Hard Way, The (1942); Having a Wonderful Time; It's a Great Feeling; King of the Roaring Twenties; Love Crazy; Lucky Partners; Mildred Pierce; Mr. and Mrs. Smith; My Dream Is Yours; Red Garters; Romance on the High Seas; Saint in New York, The; Sammy, the Way-Out Seal; Stand-In; Star Is Born, A (1954); Strawberry Blonde, The; Vivacious Lady

Carson, John: After Julius; Taste the Blood of Dracula

Carson, John David: Captain Kronos: Vampire Hunter; Creature from Black Lake; Savage Is Loose, The

Carson, Johnny: Johnny Carson: His Favorite Moments

Carson, L. M. "Kit": David Holzman's Diary; Hurricane Streets

Carson, Lisa Nicole: Love Jones

Carson, Shawn: Something Wicked This Way Comes

Carson, Sunset: Bells of Rosarita; Cherokee Flash; El Paso Kid; Red River Renegades; Santa Fe Saddlemates

Carsen, Terrence "T. C.": Firehawk; Livin' Large

Carsten, Peter: And God Said to Cain; Dark of the Sun (Mercenaries) (1968); Mr. Superinvisible; Zeppelin

Carstensen, Margit: Bitter Tears of Petra Von Kant, The; Chinese Roulette; Mother Kusters Goes to Heaven; Satan's Brew

Cartaxo, Marcelia: Hour of the Star

Cartel, Michael: Runaway Nightmare

Cartellieri, Carmen: Hands of Orlac

Carter, Alex: Man in the Attic, The; Moonshine Highway

Carter, Alice: Dangerous Heart

Carter, Ben: Dressed to Kill (1941)

Carter, Bruce: Laser Moon

Carter, Crispin Bonham: Pride and Prejudice (1996)

Carter, Dixie: Killing of Randy Webster, The

Carter, Finn: Sweet Justice; Tremors

Carter, Helena: Bugles in the Afternoon; Invaders from Mars (1953)

Carter, Helena Bonham: Dark Adapted Eye, A; Fight Club; Francesco; Getting It Right; Hamlet (1990); Howards End; Lady Jane; Margaret's Museum; Mary Shelley's Frankenstein; Merry War, A; Mighty Aphrodite; Room with a View, A; Theory of Flight, The; Twelfth Night; Where Angels Fear to Tread; Wings of the Dove, The

Carter, Jack: Alligator; Amazing Dobermans; Deadly Embrace; Happy Hooker Goes to Washington, The; Horizontal Lieutenant, The; Hustle; In the Heat of Passion; Octagon, The; Opposite Sex (And How to Live with Them), The (1993); Red Nights; Robo C.H.I.C.; Viva Las Vegas

Carter, Janis: Half-Breed, The; Miss Grant Takes Richmond; My Forbidden Past; Woman of Distinction, A

Carter, Jim: Very British Coup, A

Carter, Karen: Big Bust Out, The

Carter, Lynda: Bobbie Jo and the Outlaw; Danielle Steel's Daddy; I Posed for Playboy; Prayer in the Dark, A; Rita Hayworth: The Love Goddess

Carter, Michael Patrick: Milk Money

Carter, Nell: Grass Harp, The; Proprietor, The

Carter, Samantha: Showgirl Murders

Carter, T. K.: Doctor Detroit; Runaway Train; Yesterday's Target

Carter, Terry: Foxy Brown

Carteris, Gabrielle: Beverly Hills 90210

Cartier, Carlo: Dangerous Prey; Month by the Lake, A

Cartier, Miranda: Save the Lady

Cartledge, Miranda: Before the Rain; Breaking the Waves; Career Girls; Naked; Saint Ex

Cartwright, Angela: High School, USA; Lost in Space (TV Series); Lost in Space (1998)

ered Country; 36 Hours to Die; Ticket to Heaven; Turk 182; Unforgettable; Wild Palms

Caubère, Philippe: My Father's Glory; My Mother's Castle

Cauchy, Daniel: Bob le Flambeur

Caudell, Lane: Archer: Fugitive from the Empire; Hanging on a Star

Caudell, Toran: Johnny Mysto; Max Is Missing

Caulfield, Joan: Blue Skies; Buckskin; Daring Dobermans, The; Dear Wife; Hatfields and the McCoys, The; Monsieur Beaucaire; Pony Express Rider; Welcome, Stranger

Caulfield, Maxwell: Alien Intruder; Animal Instincts; Beverly Hills 90210; Boys Next Door, The (1985); Dance with Death; Empire Records; Exiled in America; Gettysburg; Grease 2; In a Moment of Passion; Midnight Witness; Mindgames; No Escape, No Return; Project: Alien; Real Blonde, The; Sundown (1990); Supernaturals, The

Cava, Olimpia: Vanina Vanini

Cavagnaro, Gary: Drive-In

Cavalli, Fred: Werewolf

Cavallo, Victor: Tragedy of a Ridiculous Man

Cavanagh, Paul: Bill of Divorcement, A; Bride of the Gorilla; Francis in the Haunted House; Goin' to Town; Scarlet Claw, The; Tarzan and His Mate; Woman in Green, The

Cavanaugh, Hobart: Kismet (1944); Rose of Washington Square; Stage Struck (1936); Stage to Chino

Cavanaugh, Megan: League of Their Own, A; Robin Hood: Men in Tights

Cavanaugh, Michael: Forced Vengeance; Full Fathom Five; Two to Tango

Cavanaugh, Patrick: Shadow Warriors

Cavazos, Lumi: Bottle Rocket; Like Water for Chocolate; Manhattan Merengue

Cave, Des: Paddy

Cave, Nick: Johnny Suede

Caven, Ingrid: In a Year of 13 Moons; Malou; Mother Kusters Goes to Heaven

Cavender, Glen: General, The (1927); Keystone Comedies: Vol. 1–5

Cavett, Dick: Jimi Hendrix

Caviezel, Jim: Frequency; Thin Red Line, The

Cawthorn, Joseph: Dixiana

Cayton, Elizabeth: Necromancer; Silent Night, Deadly Night Part 2

Cazale, John: Conversation, The; Deer Hunter, The; Dog Day Afternoon; Godfather, The; Godfather, Part II, The; Godfather Epic, The

Cazenove, Christopher: Aces: Iron Eagle III; Children of the Full Moon; Eye of the Needle; Fantasist, The; Heat and Dust; Jenny's War; Mata Hari (1985); Proprietor, The; Three Men and a Little Lady; Until September

Ceccaldi, Daniel: Holiday Hotel; Stolen Kisses

Cecchi, Carlo: Turkish Bath, The

Cederna, Giuseppi: Mediterraneo

Celarie, Clementine: Great, My Parents Are Divorcing

Celedonio, Maria: Freeway 2: Confessions of a Trickbaby; You Must Remember This

Celi, Adolfo: Cafe Express; Danger: Diabolik; Grand Prix; Hitler, the Last Ten Days; Manhunt (1973) (The Italian Connection); Murders in the Rue Morgue (1971); Phantom of Liberty, The; That Man from Rio; Thunderball

Celli, Teresa: Black Hand, The

Cellier, Antoinette: River of Unrest

Cellier, Caroline: L'Année des Meduses; Petit Con; This Man Must Die

Cellier, Peter: Bhaji on the Beach

Celozzi, Nicholas: Hidden Obsession

Celulari, Edson: Opera do Malandro

Cerdan Jr., Marcel: Edith and Marcel

Ceredig, Huw: Twin Town

Cerny, Daniel: Children of the Corn III: Urban Harvest

Cerusico, Enzo: Zorro

Cervantes, Gandong: Midnight Dancer (1994)

Cervantes, Gary: Low Down Dirty Shame, A

Cervenka, Exene: Salvation

Cervera Jr., Jorge: Wrong Man, The (1993)

Cerveris, Michael: Steel and Lace

Cervi, Gino: Full Hearts and Empty Pockets; Indiscretion of an American Wife; Little World of Don Camillo, The; Naked Maja, The

Cervi, Valentina: Artemisia

Cesak, Brian: Fandango

Cestie, Renato: Saddle Tramps

Chabat, Alain: French Twist

Chabert, Lacey: Lost in Space (1998)

Chabrol, Claude: Six in Paris (Paris Vue par …)

Chabrol, Thomas: Rascals, The

Chadwick, June: Distortions; Forbidden World; Quiet Thunder; Rebel Storm

Chadwick, Justin: London Kills Me

Chadwick, Sarah: Adventures of Priscilla, Queen of the Desert, The

Chaffee, Suzy: Fire and Ice (1987)

Chaffin, Aimee: Pariah

Chaing, David: Seven Brothers Meet Dracula, The

Chakiris, George: Diamond Head; Pale Blood; Return to Fantasy Island; 633 Squadron; West Side Story

Chaia, George: Kameradschaft

Chaliapin, Feodor: Church, The; Curse IV: The Ultimate Sacrifice; Don Quixote (1933); King's Whore, The; Moonstruck; Name of the Rose, The; Stanley and Iris

Chalimon, Andrej: Kolya

Chalke, Sarah: Dead Ahead; I've Been Waiting for You; Our Mother's Murder; Robin of Locksley

Chamas, Mohamad: West Beirut

Chamberlain, Margaret: Tuck Everlasting

Chamberlain, Richard: Allan Quartermain and the Lost City of Gold; Bird of Prey; Bourne Identity, The; Casanova (1987); Count of Monte Cristo, The (1975); Four Musketeers, The; Julius Caesar (1970); King Solomon's Mines (1985); Lady Caroline Lamb; Last Wave, The; Madwoman of Chaillot, The; Man in the Iron Mask, The (1977); Murder by Phone; Music Lovers, The; Ordeal in the Arctic; Petulia; Return of the Musketeers; Shogun (Full-Length Version); Swarm, The; Thornbirds, The; Three Musketeers, The (1973); Towering Inferno, The

Chamberlain, Wilt: Conan the Destroyer

Chambers, Carrie: Karate Cop

Chambers, Emma: Notting Hill

Chambers, Jill: Rose Hill

Chambers, Marilyn: Angel of H.E.A.T.; Bikini Bistro; Party Girls (Party Inc.); Rabid

Chambers, Michael: Breakin'; Breakin' 2 Electric Boogaloo

Chambliss, Woodrow: Glen and Randa

Champa, Jo: Direct Hit

Champion, Beth: One Crazy Night

Champion, Gower: Give a Girl a Break; Jupiter's Darling; Lovely to Look At; Show Boat (1951)

Champion, Marge: Give a Girl a Break; Jupiter's Darling; Lovely to Look At; Party, The; Show Boat (1951); Swimmer, The

Champion, Michael: Private Wars; Swordsman, The

Champlin, Stephanie: Silk 'n' Sabotage; Wish Me Luck

Chan, Dennis: Kickboxer; Kickboxer 2: The Road Back; Kickboxer Three—Art of War

Chan, Frances: Meeting at Midnight

Chan, Jackie: Alan Smithee Film, An—Burn Hollywood Burn; Armour of God; Big Brawl, The; Crime Story; Dragons Forever; Heart of Dragon; Jackie Chan's First Strike; Jackie Chan's Police Force; Mr. Nice Guy; Operation Condor (Jackie Chan); Police Story III—Super Cop; Project A (Part I); Project A (Part II); Protector, The; Rumble in the Bronx; Rush Hour; Shanghai Noon; Supercop; Twin Dragons; Who Am I?

Chan, Jaqui: World of Suzie Wong, The

Chan, Kim: American Shaolin: King of the Kickboxers II

Chan, Mike: Cardiac Arrest

Chan, Spencer: Sea Hound, The

Chancellor, Anna: Four Weddings and a Funeral; Pride and Prejudice (1996)

Chanda: Angel of Destruction

Chandler, Andrew: La Petite Bande

Chandler, Chick: Blood Money; Dangerous Charter; Hollywood Cavalcade; Lost Continent, The (1951); Seven Doors to Death

Chandler, George: Arizona; Dead Reckoning (1947); High and the Mighty, The; Island in the Sky

Chandler, Helen: Christopher Strong; Dracula (1931)

Chandler, Jeff: Away all Boats; Broken Arrow (1950); Jayhawkers, The; Return to Peyton Place; War Arrow

Chandler, John Davis: Good Guys and the Bad Guys, The

Chandler, Kyle: Angel's Dance; Convict Cowboy

Chowdhry, Ranjit: Lonely in America

Christ, Chad: No Laughing Matter

Christensen, Alisa: Witchcraft 7: Judgment Hour

Christensen, Stacy: Virgin Queen of St. Francis High, The

Christensen, Ute: Berlin Tunnel 21

Christian, Claudia: Adventures of a Gnome Named Gnorm, The; Arena; Babylon 5 (TV Series); Danielle Steel's Kaleidoscope; Hexed; Hidden, The; Mad About You; Maniac Cop 2; Mercenary 2: Thick and Thin; Never on Tuesday; Strays; Think Big; Wing and a Prayer, A (1997)

Christian, Helen: Zorro Rides Again

Christian, John: Little Patriot, The

Christian, Keely: Slumber Party Massacre 3

Christian, Leigh: Beyond Atlantis

Christian, Linda: Athena; Casino Royale (1954); Full Hearts and Empty Pockets; Holiday in Mexico

Christian, Michael: Private Obsession

Christian, Paul: Beast from 20,000 Fathoms, The

Christian, Robert: Bustin' Loose; Roll of Thunder, Hear My Cry

Christians, Mady: All My Sons (1948); Letter from an Unknown Woman

Christians, Rudolph: Foolish Wives

Christiansen, Dalin: Robin Hood Gang, The

Christie, Audrey: Frankie and Johnny (1966); Splendor in the Grass; Streets of L.A., The

Christie, Julie: Afterglow; Billy Liar; Darling; Demon Seed; Dr. Zhivago; Don't Look Now; Dragonheart; Fahrenheit 451; Far from the Madding Crowd; Fools of Fortune; Go-Between, The; Hamlet (1996); Heat and Dust; Heaven Can Wait (1978); McCabe and Mrs. Miller; Miss Mary; Petulia; Power (1986); Railway Station Man, The; Return of the Soldier, The; Secret Obsessions; Separate Tables; Shampoo

Christine, Virginia: Billy the Kid vs. Dracula; Guess Who's Coming to Dinner; Mummy's Curse, The; Not as a Stranger; One Man's Way; Phantom of the Plains; Prize, The

Christman, Kermit: Wicked Games

Christmas, Eric: Air Bud; Challengers, The; Home Is Where the Hart Is; Philadelphia Experiment, The

Christophe, Françoise: Walk into Hell

Christopher, Dennis: Alien Predators; Bernice Bobs Her Hair; Breaking Away; California Dreaming; Chariots of Fire; Circuitry Man; Circuitry Man II: Plughead Rewired; Don't Cry, It's Only Thunder; Fade to Black (1980); It (1991); Jake Speed; Last Word, The (1979); September 30, 1955; Sinful Life, A; Skeletons; Young Graduates

Christopher, Jean: Playgirl Killer, The

Christopher, Jordan: Return of the Seven

Christopher, Kay: Dick Tracy's Dilemma

Christopher, Scott: Robin Hood Gang, The

Christopher, Thom: Deathstalker III—The Warriors from Hell; Wizard of the Lost Kingdom

Christopherson, Kathy: Executive Target; Guyver 2: Dark Hero

Christy, Dorothy: Big Business Girl; Parlor, Bedroom and Bath; Radio Ranch (Men with Steel Faces, Phantom Empire)

Christy, Vic: Challenge to Be Free

Chrysostom, Anthony: Shadow Creature

Chu, Emily: Heart of Dragon

Chuck D: Alan Smithee Film, An—Burn Hollywood Burn

Chuckles, The: Girl Can't Help It, The

Chuckster, Simon: Sweet Sweetback's Baadasssss Song

Chun, Shun: Shanghai Triad

Chung, Cherie: Once a Thief; Peking Opera Blues

Chung, David: Ballad of Little Jo, The

Chung, Kent: Sex and Zen

Chung, Michael Daeho: Yellow

Church, Sandra: Ugly American, The

Church, Thomas Haden: Free Money; Mr. Murder

Churchill, Berton: Big Stampede, The

Churchill, Donald: Hound of the Baskervilles, The (1983)

Churchill, Marguerite: Ambassador Bill; Big Trail, The; Dracula's Daughter

Churchill, Sarah: Royal Wedding

Churikova, Inna: Adam's Rib (1993)

Chuvelov, Ivan: End of St. Petersburg, The

Ciampa, Jo: Salome (1985)

Ciannelli, Eduardo: Bulldog Drummond's Bride; Creeper, The; Dillinger (1945); Gunga Din; Kitty Foyle; Lost Moment, The; Marked Woman; Monster from Green Hell; Mummy's

Hand, The; Mysterious Dr. Satan; Strange Cargo; They Got Me Covered; They Met in Bombay; Winterset

Ciardi, Francesca: Cannibal Holocaust

Cielpielewska, Anna: Passenger, The (1963)

Ciesar, Jennifer: Lovers' Lovers

Cikatic, Branko: Skyscraper

Cilento, Diane: Admirable Crichton, The; Agony and the Ecstasy, The; Hitler, the Last Ten Days; Hombre; Naked Edge, The; Rattle of a Simple Man; Truth About Women, The; Wicker Man, The; Z.P.G. (Zero Population Growth)

Cimino, Leonardo: Rappaccini's Daughter

Cinkozoev, Mirlan: Beshkempir, The Adopted Son

Cinnante, Kelly: Christmas in Connecticut (1992)

Cintra, Luis Miguel: Convent, The

Cioffi, Charles: Don Is Dead, The; Lucky Luciano; Remo Williams: The Adventure Begins; Shaft; Thief Who Came to Dinner, The

Cir, Myriam: Savage Hearts

Citera, Tom: Up the Academy

Citrinti, Michael: Hideous

Citti, Franco: Accattone; Arabian Nights (1974); Decameron, The; Mamma Roma; Oedipus Rex (1967); Pigsty

Clabbers, Rein: Last Broadcast, The

Claire, Cyrielle: Code Name: Emerald; Sword of Gideon

Claire, Ina: Three Broadway Girls

Claire, Jennifer: Right Hand Man, The

Claire, Marion: Make a Wish

Clairiond, Aimée: Monsieur Vincent

Clanton, Jimmy: Go, Johnny, Go!

Clanton, Rony: Education of Sonny Carson, The

Clapp, Gordon: Kurt Vonnegut's Monkey House; Morrison Murders, The, Rage, The; Carrie 2; Return of the Secaucus 7; Small Sacrifices; Stand Off; Termini Station

Clapton, Eric: Chuck Berry Hail! Hail! Rock 'n' Roll; Jimi Hendrix; Last Waltz, The

Clare, Diane: Plague of the Zombies

Clare, Mary: Citadel, The; Evil Mind, The (The Clairvoyant); Young and Innocent

Clark Sisters: Gospel

Clark, Alexander: No Time for Sergeants (Television)

Clark, Andrew: Anzacs

Clark, Anthony: Dogfight; Hourglass

Clark, Brett: Alien Warrior; Deathstalker IV: Match of the Titans; Eye of the Eagle; Inner Sanctum; Malibu Express

Clark, Bryan: Without Warning: The James Brady Story

Clark, Candy: American Graffiti; Amityville III: The Demon; Big Sleep, The (1978); Blob, The (1988); Blue Thunder; Cat's Eye; Citizen's Band; Cool As Ice; Fat City; Hambone and Hillie; James Dean—A Legend in His Own Time; Man Who Fell to Earth, The; More American Graffiti; Original Intent; Q; Rodeo Girl

Clark, Carl: Sourdough

Clark, Carol Higgins: Cry in the Night, A

Clark, Carolyn Ann: Cradle Will Fall, The; Mutator

Clark, Cliff: Wagons Roll at Night, The

Clark, Dane: Action in the North Atlantic; Destination Tokyo; Hollywood Canteen; Moonrise; Murder on Flight 502; Stolen Life, A; Thunder Pass

Clark, Dick: Deadman's Curve

Clark, Doran: Black Eagle

Clark, Eugene: Tekwar: The Original Movie

Clark, Eugene A.: Trial & Error (1992)

Clark, Fred: Auntie Mame; Bells Are Ringing; Boys' Night Out; Caddy, The; Curse of the Mummy's Tomb, The; Dr. Goldfoot and the Bikini Machine; Don't Go Near the Water; George Burns and Gracie Allen Show, The, (TV Series); Here Come the Girls; Horse in the Gray Flannel Suit, The; It Started With a Kiss; Laugh for Joy (Passionate Thief (1954)); Lemon Drop Kid, The; Mating Game, The; Passionate Thief, The (1961); Sunset Boulevard; Three for Bedroom C

Clark, Graydon: Satan's Sadists

Clark, Harry: No Time for Sergeants (Television)

Clark, Harvey: Law for Tombstone

Clark, Ian D.: Lilies; Trial & Error (1992)

Clark, Jameson: Battle of the Sexes, The

Clark, Ken: Attack of the Giant Leeches

Clark, Kerric: Angel 4: Undercover

Clark, Liddy: Blue Fin; Kitty and the Bagman

Clark, Marlene: Night of the Cobra Woman; Switchblade Sisters

Cluzet, François: French Kiss; Horse of Pride, The; L'Enfer; One Deadly Summer; Round Midnight; Story of Women, The; Swindle, The

Clyde (the ape): Every Which Way but Loose

Clyde, Andy: Bad Lands (1939); Border Patrol; Border Vigilantes; Dangerous Venture; Doomed Caravan; False Colors; Forty Thieves; Hoppy Serves a Writ; In Old Colorado; Leather Burners, The; Little Minister, The; Mystery Man; Outlaws of the Desert; Pirates on Horseback; Riders of the Timberline; Secrets of the Wasteland; Silent Conflict; Stick to Your Guns; Sundown Riders; Texas Masquerade; Three Men from Texas; Twilight on the Trail; Wide-Open Town

Clyde, June: Seven Doors to Death; Study in Scarlet, A

Coates, Kim: Amityville Curse, The; Battlefield Earth; Breach of Trust; Club, The (1993); Cold Front; Dead Silence (1996); Harmony Cats; Lethal Tender; Model by Day; Red-Blooded American Girl; Smokescreen; Spider and the Fly, The; Waterworld

Coates, Phyllis: I Was a Teenage Frankenstein; Incredible Petrified World, The; Invasion USA (1952); Longhorn; Marshal of Cedar Rock; Panther Girl of the Congo; Superman and the Mole Men; TV's Best Adventures of Superman

Cobanoglu, Necmettin: Journey of Hope

Cobb, Lee J.: Anna and the King of Siam; Boomerang (1947); Brothers Karamazov, The; Buckskin Frontier; But Not for Me; Cali Northside 777; Come Blow Your Horn; Coogan's Bluff; Dark Past, The; Exodus; Exorcist, The; Four Horsemen of the Apocalypse; Golden Boy; Gorilla at Large; Green Mansions; In Like Flint; Lawman; Left Hand of God, The; Liberation of L. B. Jones, The; Macho Callahan; Mackenna's Gold; Man in the Gray Flannel Suit, The; Man of the West; Man Who Cheated Himself, The; Man Who Loved Cat Dancing, The; Meanest Men in the West, The; Men of Boys Town; Miracle of the Bells, The; North of the Rio Grande; On the Waterfront; Our Man Flint; Party Girl (1958); Racers, The; Sirocco; Song of Bernadette, The; That Lucky Touch; Three Faces of Eve, The; Trap, The; 12 Angry Men (1957)

Cobb, Randall "Tex": Blind Fury; Buy and Cell; Collision Course (1989); Critical Condition; Diggstown; Dirty Dozen, The: The Deadly Mission; Ernest Goes to Jail; Fletch Lives; Golden Child, The; Liar, Liar; Raising Arizona; Uncommon Valor

Cobbs, Bill: Air Bud; Always Outnumbered; Bodyguard, The; Decoration Day; Ed; Hudsucker Proxy, The; I Still Know What You Did Last Summer; Nightjohn; Out There; That Thing You Do!

Cobo De Garcia, Eva: Operation Condor (Jackie Chan)

Cobo, Roberto: Los Olvidados

Coburn, Charles: Bachelor Mother; Colonel Effingham's Raid; Devil and Miss Jones, The; Edison, The Man; Gentlemen Prefer Blondes; George Washington Slept Here; Heaven Can Wait (1943); Idiot's Delight; Impact; In Name Only; In This Our Life; John Paul Jones; King's Row; Knickerbocker Holiday; Lady Eve, The; Made for Each Other; Mr. Music; Monkey Business (1952); More the Merrier, The; Of Human Hearts; Paradine Case, The; Road to Singapore; Three Faces West; Trouble Along the Way; Vivacious Lady; Wilson

Coburn, David: Born American

Coburn, James: Affliction; Americanization of Emily, The; Avenging Angel, The (1995); Baltimore Bullet, The; Bite the Bullet; Bronco (TV Series); Bruce Lee: Curse of the Dragon; Charade; Cherokee Kid, The; Christmas Reunion, A; Cross of Iron; Dain Curse, The; Dead Heat on a Merry-Go-Round; Deadfall; Death of a Soldier; Draw; Eraser; Firepower (1979); Fistful of Dynamite, A; Goldengirl; Great Escape, The; Hard Times; Hell Is for Heroes; High Risk; Hit List, The (1992); Hudson Hawk; In Like Flint; Internecine Project, The; Keys to Tulsa; Last of Sheila, The; Looker; Loved One, The; Loving Couples; Magnificent Seven, The; Major Dundee; Martin's Day; Massacre at Fort Holman (Reason to Live … A Reason to Die, A); Maverick; Missing Pieces (2000); Mr. Murder; Muppet Movie, The; Nutty Professor, The (1996); Our Man Flint; Pat Garrett and Billy the Kid; Pinocchio (1983); President's Analyst, The; Ride Lonesome; Second Civil War, The; Set-Up, The (1995); Sister Act 2: Back in the Habit; Skeletons; Thousand Heroes, A; Waterhole #3; Young Guns II

Coburn Jr., James: Tuxedo Warrior

Coby, Michael: Bitch, The; We Are No Angels

Coca, Imogene: Alice in Wonderland (1985); 10 from Your Show of Shows

Coca, Richard: Hitz; Only the Strong

Cochran, Eddie: Girl Can't Help It, The; Go, Johnny, Go!

Cochran, Robert: I Stand Condemned; Sanders of the River; Scrooge (1935)

Cochran, Steve: Carnival Story; Chase, The (1946); Copacabana; Deadly Companions, The; I, Mobster; Il Grido (Outcry, The); Jim Thorpe—All American; Kid from Brooklyn, The; Private Hell 36; Song Is Born, A; Tanks Are Coming, The; White Heat

Cochrane, Rory: Adventures of Sebastian Cole, The; Dazed and Confused; Empire Records; Fathers & Sons; Love & a .45; Low Life, The

Cockburn, Arlene: Winter Guest, The

Cocker, Joe: Mad Dogs and Englishmen

Coco, James: Chair, The; Cheap Detective, The; Generation; Hunk; Littlest Angel, The; Man of La Mancha; Murder by Death; New Leaf, A; Only When I Laugh; Scavenger Hunt; That's Adequate; Wholly Moses!; Wild Party, The (1975)

Cocquyt, Connie: Dead Is Dead

Cocteau, Jean: Testament of Orpheus, The

Cody, Iron Eyes: Ernest Goes to Camp; Grayeagle; Son of Paleface

Cody, Kyle: Life 101

Cody, Lew: Dishonored

Coe, Barry: But Not for Me; Cat, The (1966); Dr. Death: Seeker of Souls; Peyton Place

Coe, George: Blind Date (1987); End of Innocence, The; Flash of Green, A; Hollywood Detective, The; Listen to Your Heart; My Name Is Bill W; Red Flag: The Ultimate Game; Remo Williams: The Adventure Begins

Coe, Peter: Mummy's Curse, The; Okefenokee

Coffey, Colleen: Mosaic Project, The

Coffey, John: War of the Buttons

Coffey, Scott: Amazing Stories (TV Series); Montana (1990); Shag, the Movie; Shout (1991)

Coffield, Peter: Times Square

Coffin, Frederick: V. I. Warshawski

Coffin, Tristram: Corpse Vanishes, The; Forbidden Trails; King of the Rocketmen; Ma Barker's Killer Brood; Pirates of the High Seas; Rodeo King and the Senorita; Spy Smasher

Coggio, Roger: Immortal Story

Coghill, Nikki: Dark Age

Coghlan Jr., Frank: Adventures of Captain Marvel, The; Drum Taps; Hell's House

Cohen, Alain: Two of Us, The

Cohen, Emma: Cut Throats Nine; Horror Rises from the Tomb

Cohen, Jeff: Goonies, The

Cohen, Kaipo: Under the Domim Tree

Cohen, Matthew Roy: Trained to Fight

Cohen, Mitchell: Toxic Avenger, The

Cohen, Sammy: Office Picture Glory? (1926)

Cohen, Scott: Sweet Evil

Cohn, Marya: Vermont Is for Lovers

Cohn, Mindy: Boy Who Could Fly, The

Coinman, John: Laughing Horse

Colagrande, Stefano: Misunderstood (1988)

Colantoni, Enrico: Galaxy Quest; Member of the Wedding, The (1996)

Colao, Manuel: Flight of the Innocent

Colasanto, Nicholas: Fat City; Mad Bull; Raging Bull

Colbert, Claudette: Bluebeard's Eighth Wife; Boom Town; Cleopatra (1934); Drums Along the Mohawk; Egg and I, The; Guest Wife; I Cover the Waterfront; It Happened One Night; Let's Make It Legal; Midnight (1939); Palm Beach Story, The; Parrish; Since You Went Away; So Proudly We Hail; Texas Lady; Three Came Home; Tomorrow Is Forever; Tovaritch; Without Reservations

Colbert, Ray: RSVP

Colbourne, Maurice: Littlest Horse Thieves, The

Cole, Alexandra: Dr. Butcher, M.D. (Medical Deviate)

Cole, Dennis: Connection (1973); Death House; Powderkeg; Pretty Smart

Cole, Gary: Brady Bunch Movie, The; Echoes in the Darkness; Fall from Grace; Fatal Vision; I'll Be Home for Christmas; In the Line of Fire; Kiss the Sky; Office Space; Son of the Morning Star; Very Brady Sequel, A

Cole, George: Adventures of Sadie; Belles of St. Trinian's, The; Blue Murder at St. Trinian's; Dr. Syn, Alias the Scarecrow; Gone in 60 Seconds; Mary Reilly; Vampire Lovers, The

Cole, Henry: Shaka Zulu

Cole, Michael: Mod Squad, The (TV Series)

Cole, Nat King: China Gate; Istanbul (1956); Small Town Girl

Cole, Natalie: Always Outnumbered; Freak City

Cole, Olivia: Sky Is Gray, The; Some Kind of Hero

Cole, Skyler: Adventures Beyond Belief

Coleby, Robert: Archer's Adventure; Great Expectations—The Untold Story; Now and Forever; Plumber, The

Coleman, Charlotte: Beautiful People; Four Weddings and a Funeral; Oranges Are Not the Only Fruit; Young Poisoner's Handbook, The

Coleman, Dabney: Amos & Andrew; Bad Ronald; Beverly Hillbillies, The (1993); Bite the Bullet; Callie and Son; Clifford; Cloak and Dagger (1984); Dragnet (1987); Hot to Trot; How to Beat the High Co$t of Living; I Love My Wife; Inspector Gadget; Judicial Consent; Man with One Red Shoe, The; Meet the Applegates; Muppets Take Manhattan, The; Murrow; Never Forget; Nine to Five; Nothing Personal (1980); Pray TV (1980); President's Plane Is Missing, The; Rolling Thunder; Scalphunters, The; Short Time; Slender Thread, The; There Goes the Neighborhood; Tootsie; Trouble with Girls, The; Wargames; Where the Heart Is; Young Doctors in Love

Coleman, Frank J.: Charlie Chaplin Cavalcade

Coleman, Gary: Jimmy the Kid; Kid from Left Field, The; Kid with the Broken Halo, The; Kid with the 200 I.Q., The; On the Right Track

Coleman, Jack: Beneath the Bermuda Triangle; Daughter of Darkness; Foreign Student; Landlady, The; Return of Eliot Ness, The; Rubdown; Trapped in Space

Coleman, Jimmy: Riff-Raff (1992)

Coleman, Nancy: Edge of Darkness (1943)

Coleman, Patricia: Habit

Coleman, Signy: Reientless 3

Colen, Beatrice: Night Stalker, The: Two Tales of Terror (TV Series)

Coleridge, Tania: Rain Killer, The

Coles, Emma: Two Friends

Coles, Michael: Dracula A.D. 1972; I Want What I Want

Coley, Thomas: Dr. Cyclops

Colgan, Eileen: Quackser Fortune Has a Cousin in the Bronx; Secret of Roan Inish, The

Colicos, John: Drum; King Solomon's Treasure; No Contest; Nowhere to Hide; Phobia; Postman Always Rings Twice, The (1981); Raid on Rommel; Shadow Dancing

Colin Jr., David: Beyond the Door; Beyond the Door 2

Colin, Gregoire: Before the Rain; Dreamlife of Angels, The; Olivier, Olivier

Colin, Jean: Mikado, The (1939)

Colin, Margaret: Adventures of Sebastian Cole, The; Amos & Andrew; Butcher's Wife, The; Devil's Own, The; Independence Day (1996); Like Father, Like Son; Martians Go Home; Something Wild; Three Men and a Baby; Traveling Man; True Believer

Coll, Melanie: Lust for Freedom

Collard, Cyril: Savage Nights

Collazo, Luz Maria: I Am Cuba

Collet, Christopher: Langoliers, The; Manhattan Project, The; Prayer of the Rollerboys

Collette, Toni: Clockwatchers; Cosi; Efficiency Expert, The (Spotswood); Emma (1996); Muriel's Wedding; Pallbearer, The; Shaft (2000); Sixth Sense, The; Velvet Goldmine

Colley, Kenneth: And Nothing But the Truth; Music Lovers, The; Plot to Kill Hitler, The; Return to Treasure Island; Solomon and Sheba (1995); Summer Story, A; Whistle Blower, The

Collier, Constance: Damsel in Distress, A; Monsieur Beaucaire; Perils of Pauline, The (1947); Wee Willie Winkie

Collier, Lois: Naughty Nineties, The; Night in Casablanca, A

Collier Jr., William: Cimarron (1931); Street Scene

Collin, Maxime: Leolo

Collins Jr., Clifton: Light It Up; Price of Glory

Collins, Alan: And God Said to Cain; Ark of the Sun God ... Temple of Hell, The; Exterminators of the Year 3000

Collins, Gary: Hangar 18; Kid from Left Field, The

Collins, Joan: Adventures of Sadie; Annie, a Royal Adventure!; Bawdy Adventures of Tom Jones, The; Bitch, The; Bravados, The; Cartier Affair, The; Dark Places; Decameron Nights; Devil Within Her, The; Dynasty of Fear; Empire of the Ants; Executioner, The; Fear in the Night (Dynasty of Fear); Fearless (1978); Game for Vultures; Great Adventure, The; Homework; Land of the Pharaohs; Midwinter's Tale, A; Monte Carlo; Oh, Alfie; Opposite Sex, The (1956); Playing the Field; Revenge (1971) (Joan Collins); Road to Hong Kong, The; Seven Thieves; Stopover Tokyo; Stud, The; Sunburn; Tales from the Crypt; Tales that Witness Madness; Three in the Cellar; Virgin Queen, The

Collins, Judy: Junior (1994); Woody Guthrie—Hard Travelin'

Collins, Kevin: Garden, The

Collins, Lewis: Code Name: Wild Geese; Final Option, The; Jack the Ripper (1988)

Collins, Lisa: Danger Zone (1995); Deep Red (1994); Going Overboard

Collins, Matt: World's Greatest Lover, The

Collins, Patricia: Phobia

Collins, Patrick: Dirt Bike Kid, The

Collins, Pauline: City of Joy; Paradise Road; Shirley Valentine; Upstairs, Downstairs

Collins, Phil: And the Band Played On; Balto; Buster; Frauds; Hook

Collins, Ray: Badman's Territory; Big Street, The; Can't Help Singing; Citizen Kane; Commandos Strike at Dawn; Double Life, A; Francis, the Talking Mule; Heiress, The; Homecoming (1948); Human Comedy, The; It Happens Every Spring; Ma and Pa Kettle Back on the Farm; Ma and Pa Kettle on Vacation; Man from Colorado, The; Racket, The; Rose Marie (1954); Seventh Cross, The; Vengeance Valley; Whistling in Brooklyn

Collins, Roberta: Arousers; Hardbodies; Vendetta (1985)

Collins, Russell: Enemy Below, The; Matchmaker, The (1958)

Collins, Ruth: Doom Asylum; Galactic Gigolo

Collins, Stephen: Between the Lines; Brewster's Millions (1985); Chiefs; Choke Canyon; First Wives Club, The; Hold the Dream; Jumpin' Jack Flash; Loving Couples; My New Gun; Promise, The (1978); Scarlett; Stella (1990); Till Murder Do Us Part; Unexpected Family, An; Unexpected Life, An; Weekend War; Woman Named Jackie, A

Collins, Steve: Hitchhiker, The (Series)

Collinson, Madeleine: Twins of Evil

Collinson, Mary: Twins of Evil

Collyer, June: Drums of Jeopardy; Ghost Walks, The; Murder by Television

Colman, Renee: Pentathlon

Colman, Ronald: Arrowsmith; Bulldog Drummond; Champagne for Caesar; Double Life, A; If I Were King; Kismet (1944); Lady Windermere's Fan; Lost Horizon; Lucky Partners; Prisoner of Zenda, The (1937); Random Harvest; Tale of Two Cities, A (1935); Talk of the Town, The; White Sister, The

Colodner, Joel: Plants Are Watching, The

Colomby, Scott: Porky's; Porky's II: The Next Day; Porky's Revenge

Colonna, Jerry: College Swing; Road to Rio; Road to Singapore

Colosimo, Clara: Orchestra Rehearsal

Colson, Kevin: Trapped in Space

Colston, Karen: Sweetie

Colt, Dennis: Savage Guns

Colt, Marshall: Beverly Hills Madam; To Heal a Nation

Coltrane, Robbie: Adventures of Huck Finn, The (1993); Alice in Wonderland (1999); Bert Rigby, You're a Fool; Buddy; Chinese Boxes; Cracker (TV Series); Danny, The Champion of the World; Frogs for Snakes; Goldeneye; Message in a Bottle; Montana (1997); Nuns on the Run; Oh, What a Night; Perfectly Normal; Pope Must Diet, The; Wonderland; World Is Not Enough, The

Coluche: My Best Friend's Girl; Tchao Pantin

Columbu, Franco: Beretta's Island; Desperate Crimes; Last Man Standing (1988)

Colvin, Jack: Incredible Hulk, The

Colyar, Michael: Jugular Wine

Combes, Norman: Kill or Be Killed

Constantine, Michael: Beyond Fear; Cold Sweat (1970); Don't Drink the Water; Family, The (1970); If It's Tuesday, This Must Be Belgium; In the Mood; Justine; My Life; North Avenue Irregulars, The; Prancer; Question of Faith; Reivers, The; Say Goodbye, Maggie Cole; Silent Rebellion; Summer of My German Soldier; Thinner

Conte, Richard: Assault on a Queen; Big Combo, The; Blue Gardenia, The; Call Northside 777; Circus World; Godfather, The; Guadalcanal Diary; Hotel; House of Strangers; I'll Cry Tomorrow; Lady in Cement; Purple Heart, The; Somewhere in the Night; They Came to Cordura; 13 Rue Madeleine; Tony Rome; Walk in the Sun, A

Conti, Tom: American Dreamer; Beyond Therapy; Deep Cover (1980); Duellists, The; Dumb Waiter, The; Gospel According to Vic, The; Haunting of Julia, The; Merry Christmas, Mr. Lawrence; Miracles; Norman Conquests, The, Episode 1: Table Manners; Norman Conquests, The, Episode 2: Living Together; Norman Conquests, The, Episode 3: Round and Round the Garden; Quick and the Dead, The (1987); Reuben, Reuben; Saving Grace; Shirley Valentine; Someone Else's America; Sub Down; That Summer of White Roses

Contouri, Chantal: Goodbye, Miss 4th of July; Thirst

Converse, Frank: Bushido Blade; Cruise into Terror; Hour of the Gun, The; Pilot, The; Spring Fever; Tales of the Unexpected

Converse-Roberts, William: Courtship; Kiss the Girls; 1918; On Valentine's Day

Convy, Bert: Hero at Large; Jennifer; Man in the Santa Claus Suit, The; Semi-Tough

Conway, Deborah: Fast Lane Fever

Conway, Gary: American Ninja II; How to Make a Monster; I Was a Teenage Frankenstein

Conway, Kevin: Calm at Sunset; Elephant Man, The (1982); Flashpoint; Gettysburg; Homeboy; Jennifer 8; Lawnmower Man 2: Jobe's War (Lawnmower Man: Beyond Cyberspace); One Good Cop; Prince Brat and the Whipping Boy; Quick and the Dead, The (1995); Rage of Angels; Rambling Rose; Streets of Laredo

Conway, Morgan: Brother Orchid; Dick Tracy versus Cueball

Conway, Pat: Brighty of the Grand Canyon

Conway, Russ: Interval

Conway, Tim: Apple Dumpling Gang, The; Apple Dumpling Gang Rides Again, The; Billion Dollar Hobo, The; Dear God; Longshot, The (1985); Private Eyes, The; Prizefighter, The; Shaggy D.A., The; They Went That-A-Way and That-A-Way; World's Greatest Athlete, The

Conway Jr., Tim: Beverly Hills Vamp

Conway, Tom: Atomic Submarine, The; Bride of the Gorilla; Cat People (1942); Death of a Scoundrel; Falcon in Mexico, The; Falcon's Brother, The; I Walked with a Zombie; Prince Valiant (1954); Rio Rita; Seventh Victim, The; She Creature, The; Tarzan's Secret Treasure; Voodoo Woman; Whistle Stop

Cooder, Joachim: Buena Vista Social Club, The

Cooder, Ry: Buena Vista Social Club, The

Coogan, Jackie: Addams Family, The (TV Series); Dr. Heckyl and Mr. Hype; Kid, The/The Idle Class; Lonelyhearts; Marlowe; Oliver Twist (1922); Peck's Bad Boy; Prey, The; Shakiest Gun in the West, The; Tom Sawyer (1930)

Coogan, Keith: Adventures in Babysitting; Book of Love; Cheetah; Cousins; Don't Tell Mom the Babysitter's Dead; Downhill Willie; Forever; Hiding Out; Life 101; Power Within, The; Reason to Believe, A; Toy Soldiers (1991); Under the Boardwalk

Coogan, Steve: Indian in the Cupboard, The

Cook, A. J.: Virgin Suicides, The

Cook, Barbara: Killing 'Em Softly

Cook, Ben: Little Men (1998)

Cook, Carole: Grandview, U.S.A.; Incredible Mr. Limpet, The; Summer Lovers

Cook, Dale "Apollo": Double Blast; Fist of Steel; Raw Target; Triple Impact

Cook, Donald: Baby Face; Viva Villa!

Cook Jr., Elisha: Big Sleep, The (1946); Born to Kill; Dark Waters; Dillinger (1945); Don't Bother to Knock; Drum Beat; Electra Glide in Blue; Gangster, The; Great Northfield Minnesota Raid, The; Hammett; Harry's War; Haunted Palace, The; Hellzapoppin; House on Haunted Hill; Killing, The; Leave 'em Laughing; Lonely Man, The; Mad Bull; Mal-

tese Falcon, The; One-Eyed Jacks; Papa's Delicate Condition; Pat Garrett and Billy the Kid; Rosemary's Baby; St. Ives; Salem's Lot; Shane; Stranger on the Third Floor; Tin Pan Alley; Tom Horn; Voodoo Island

Cook, Gwendoline: Warbus

Cook, Kelly: Hollywood Dreams

Cook, Paul: Great Rock and Roll Swindle, The

Cook, Penny: Deadly Possession

Cook, Peter: Bedazzled; Find the Lady; Getting It Right; Hound of the Baskervilles, The (1977); Supergirl; Those Daring Young Men in Their Jaunty Jalopies; Without a Clue; Wrong Box, The; Yellowbeard

Cook, Rachael Leigh: Baby-Sitters Club, The; Bumblebee Flies Anyway, The; Carpool; Eighteenth Angel, The; Naked Man, The; She's All That; Strike! (1998)

Cook, Roger: Garden, The

Cook, Ron: Secrets and Lies; Topsy-Turvy

Cook, Tommy: Adventures of Red Ryder; Missile to the Moon

Cooke, Christopher: Unbelievable Truth, The

Cooke, Evelyn: West of the Law

Cooke, Gregory: Gore Vidal's Lincoln

Cooke, Jennifer: Friday the 13th, Part VI: Jason Lives; Gimme an "F"

Cooke, John: Invader

Cooke, Keith: Heatseeker

Cooke, Ray: Sweethearts on Parade

Cooke, Scott: Thugs

Cookie: Street Hitz (Street Story)

Cool J, LL: Deep Blue Sea; In Too Deep

Coolidge, Philip: Tingler, The

Coolidge, Rita: Mad Dogs and Englishmen

Coolio: Alan Smithee Film, An—Burn Hollywood Burn; Judgment Day; Leprechaun in the Hood; Phat Beach

Coombs, Jeffrey: House on Haunted Hill (1999)

Cooney, Kevin: Arctic Blue; Full Moon in Blue Water

Cooper, Alice: Monster Dog; Prince of Darkness; Wayne's World

Cooper, Barrett: Buford's Beach Bunnies

Cooper, Ben: Arizona Raiders; Rose Tattoo, The

Cooper, Chris: Great Expectations (1998); Horse Whisperer, The; Lone Justice; Lone Star (1996); Lonesome Dove; Matewan; Me, Myself & Irene; Money Train; October Sky; Patriot, The; Pharaoh's Army; Return to Lonesome Dove; This Boy's Life; Thousand Pieces of Gold

Cooper, Clancy: Distant Drums

Cooper, Gary: Adventures of Marco Polo, The; Along Came Jones; Ball of Fire; Beau Geste; Blowing Wild; Bluebeard's Eighth Wife; Casanova Brown; Cloak and Dagger (1946); Court-martial of Billy Mitchell, The; Cowboy and the Lady, The; Distant Drums; Farewell to Arms, A; Fighting Caravans; For Whom the Bell Tolls; Fountainhead, The; Friendly Persuasion; General Died at Dawn, The; Good Sam; Hanging Tree, The; High Noon; If I Had a Million; It (1927); It's a Big Country; Lives of a Bengal Lancer, The; Love in the Afternoon; Man of the West; Meet John Doe; Mr. Deeds Goes to Town; Morocco; Naked Edge, The; Northwest Mounted Police; Operator 13; Plainsman, The; Pride of the Yankees, The; Real Glory, The; Return to Paradise (1953); Sergeant York; Story of Dr. Wassell, The; Task Force; They Came to Cordura; Today We Live; Unconquered; Vera Cruz; Virginian, The (1929); Westerner, The; Wings; Wreck of the Mary Deare, The

Cooper, Gladys: At Sword's Point; Happiest Millionaire, The; Homecoming (1948); Iron Duke, The; Kitty Foyle; Mrs. Parkington; Nice Girl Like Me, A; Pirate, The; Secret Garden, The (1949); Song of Bernadette, The; Twilight Zone, The (TV Series)

Cooper, Jackie: Champ, The (1931); Gangster's Boy; Love Machine, The; Return of Frank James, The; Superman; Superman II; Superman III; Superman IV: The Quest for Peace; Surrender; Treasure Island (1934); Ziegfeld Girl

Cooper, Jeanne: Intruder, The (1961); Plunder Road

Cooper, Jeff: Circle of Iron; Impossible Years, The

Cooper, Jeremy: Reflecting Skin, The

Cooper, Joe: Mississippi Blues

Cooper, Justin: Liar, Liar

Cooper, Kenn: Pre-Madonnas (Social Suicide)

Cooper, Maggie: And Baby Makes Six; Eye for an Eye (1981)

Cox, Paul: Careful

Cox, Richard: Between the Lines; Cruising; King of the Mountain; Vindicator, The; Zombie High

Cox, Ronny: Beast Within, The; Beverly Hills Cop II; Bound for Glory; Captain America (1990); Connection (1973); Deliverance; Fallen Angel; FBI Murders, The; Forces of Nature; Gray Lady Down; Harper Valley P.T.A.; Hollywood Vice Squad; Kavik the Wolf Dog; Loose Cannons; Mind Snatchers, The; Murder at 1600; One-Man Force; Onion Field, The; Our Town (1980); Raw Courage; RoboCop; Scandal in a Small Town; Scissors; Some Kind of Hero; Steele Justice; Taps; Target; Favorite Son; Total Recall; Two of a Kind (1982); Vision Quest; Who Is the Black Dahlia?

Cox, Veanne: National Lampoon's Class of '86

Cox, Wally: Bedford Incident, The; Morituri; Night Strangler, The; Spencer's Mountain

Coy, Jonathan: Rector's Wife, The

Coyne, Bill: Suburbia (1983)

Coyne, Roxanne: Alien Force

Coyote, Peter: Baja Oklahoma; Basket, The; Best Kept Secrets; Bitter Moon; Blue Yonder, The; Breach of Conduct; Buffalo Girls; Crooked Hearts; Cross Creek; Echoes in the Darkness; E.T.—The Extra-Terrestrial; Exposure; Heart of Midnight; Heartbreakers; Hitchhiker, The (Series); Indiscreet (1998); Jagged Edge; Keeper of the City; Kika; Legend of Billie Jean, The; Man in Love, A; Man Inside, The (1990); Moonlight and Valentino; Out; Outrageous Fortune; People vs. Jean Harris; Road Ends; Route 9; Slayground; Stacking; Strangers Kiss; Terminal Justice; Terminal Justice, Cybertech P.D.; Timerider; Unforgettable

Cozart, Cylk: Conspiracy Theory; Slam Dunk Ernest

Crabbe, Buster: Alien Dead; Arizona Raiders; Buck Rogers: Destination Saturn (Planet Outlaws); Buffalo Stampede; Colorado Sunset; Flash Gordon Conquers the Universe; Flash Gordon: Rocketship (Spaceship to the Unknown; Perils from Planet Mongo); Forlorn River; His Brother's Ghost; Last of the Redmen; Man of the Forest; Pirates of the High Seas; Prairie Rustlers; Red Barry; Sea Hound, The; Tarzan the Fearless; To the Last Man

Cracknell, Ruth: Alice to Nowhere; Island Trader

Craig, Carolyn: House on Haunted Hill; Studs Lonigan

Craig, Charmaine: White Fang 2: Myth of the White Wolf

Craig, Daimon: Claire of the Moon

Craig, Daniel: Love is the Devil; Moll Flanders (1996); Power of One, The

Craig, James: Cyclops, The; Devil and Daniel Webster, The; Drums in the Deep South; Hell Town; Human Comedy, The; Kismet (1944); Kitty Foyle; Naked in the Sun; Our Vines Have Tender Grapes; Revenge of Dr. X, The; Thunder Trail; Valley of the Sun; Winners of the West

Craig, Josh: Freakshow

Craig, Michael: Escape 2000; Irishman, The; Mysterious Island; Ride a Wild Pony; Robin Hood: Herne's Son; Royal Hunt of the Sun; Sapphire; Star! (1968); Stolen Hours; Vault of Horror

Craig, Roger: Hooked Obsession

Craig, Wendy: Joseph Andrews; Nanny, The

Craig, Yvonne: Gene Krupa Story, The; How to Frame a Figg; It Happened at the World's Fair

Craigie, Ingrid: Dead, The

Crain, Jeanne: Fastest Gun Alive, The; Leave Her to Heaven; Letter to Three Wives, A; Man without a Star; People Will Talk; Pinky; State Fair (1945)

Cramer, Grant: Hardbodies; Killer Klowns from Outer Space; Leapin' Leprechauns

Cramer, Joey: Stone Fox, The

Crampton, Barbara: Castle Freak; From Beyond; Re-Animator; Robot Wars

Crandall, Edward: Glorifying the American Girl

Crane, Bob: Hogan's Heroes (TV Series); Return to Peyton Place; Superdad

Crane, Norman: Fiddler on the Roof

Crane, Rachel: Two Bits & Pepper

Crane, Richard: Alligator People, The; Neanderthal Man, The; Wing and a Prayer, A

Cranham, Kenneth: Hellraiser II: Hellbound; Midnight Man; On Dangerous Ground (1995); Oranges Are Not the Only Fruit; Tale of a Vampire; Under Suspicion

Cranshaw, Patricia: Broken Vessels

Cranston, Bryan: Dead Space

Crater, Rich: Carnal Crimes

Crauchet, Paul: King's Whore, The

Cravat, Nick: Crimson Pirate, The; Flame and the Arrow, The; Scalphunters, The; Valdez Is Coming

Craven, Frank: Barbary Coast, The; City for Conquest; Dreaming Out Loud; In This Our Life; Jack London; Our Town (1940); Pittsburgh; Son of Dracula (1943)

Craven, Gemma: Wagner

Craven, James: Green Archer; Project Moon Base

Craven, Matt: Agent on Ice; Bulletproof Heart; Crimson Tide; Few Good Men, A; Final Cut, The; Happy Birthday to Me; Indian Summer; Jacob's Ladder; Kingfish: A Story of Huey P. Long; K2; Masterminds; Palais Royale; Smokescreen

Craven, Mimi: Last Gasp; Midnight Heat

Craven, Wes: Fear, The (1994); Wes Craven's New Nightmare

Crawford, Broderick: All the King's Men; Beau Geste; Between Heaven and Hell; Born Yesterday (1950); Dark Forces; Eternally Yours; Fastest Gun Alive, The; Goliath and the Dragon; Human Desire; Il Bidone; Last of the Comanches; Little Romance, A; Lone Star (1952); Not as a Stranger; Private Files of J. Edgar Hoover, The; Real Glory, The; Seven Sinners; Slightly Honorable; Terror in the Wax Museum; Time of Your Life, The; Yin and Yang of Mr. Go, The

Crawford, Cindy: Fair Game (1995); Unzipped

Crawford, Ellen: Ulterior Motives

Crawford, H. Marion: Adventures of Sherlock Holmes, The (TV Series)

Crawford, Joan: Above Suspicion (1943); Autumn Leaves; Berserk; Best of Everything, The; Bride Wore Red, The; Chained; Dance, Fools, Dance; Dancing Lady; Flamingo Road; Forsaking All Others; Gorgeous Hussy, The; Grand Hotel; Hollywood Canteen; Humoresque; I Live My Life; Johnny Guitar; Last of Mrs. Cheney, The; Laughing Sinners; Love on the Run (1936); Mannequin (1937); Mildred Pierce; Night Gallery; Our Dancing Daughters; Our Modern Maidens; Possessed (1931); Possessed (1947); Rain; Reunion in France; Sadie McKee; Shining Hour, The; Straitjacket; Strange Cargo; Sudden Fear; Susan and God; Today We Live; Torch Song; Twelve Miles Out; Unknown, The; What Ever Happened to Baby Jane?; When Ladies Meet; Woman's Face, A; Women, The

Crawford, John: Devil's Messenger, The; Grave Secrets

Crawford, Johnny: El Dorado; Gambler, Part II—The Adventure Continues, The; Gambler Returns, The: Luck of the Draw; Great Texas Dynamite Chase, The; Macbeth (1981); Rifleman, The (TV Series); Village of the Giants

Crawford, Katherine: Riding with Death; Walk in the Spring Rain, A

Crawford, Michael: Barnum (1986); Condorman; Funny Thing Happened on the Way to the Forum, A; Hello, Dolly!; How I Won the War; Knack . . . and How to Get It, The

Crawford, Rachel: In His Father's Shoes; Rude; When Night is Falling

Crawford, Sophia: Sword of Honor

Crawford, Wayne: American Cop; Crime Lords; Jake Speed; Quiet Thunder; Rebel Storm; White Ghost

Craze, Galaxy: Nadja

Creed-Miles, Charlie: Nil by Mouth

Creer, Erica: Circle of Iron

Cregar, Laird: Black Swan, The; Hangover Square; Heaven Can Wait (1943); Hello, Frisco, Hello; I Wake Up Screaming; Joan of Paris

Creley, Jack: Reincarnate, The

Cremer, Bruno: Josepha; Ménage; Simple Story, A; Sorcerer; 317th Platoon, The

Crenna, Richard: Body Heat; Breakheart Pass; Case of Deadly Force, A; Catlow; Deathship; Deserter, The; Devil Dog: The Hound of Hell; Doctors' Wives; Evil, The; First Blood; Flamingo Kid, The; Hillside Stranglers, The; Hot Shots Part Deux; Intruders; Jade; Leviathan; Man Called Noon, The; Marooned; Montana (1990); On Wings of Eagles; Our Miss Brooks (TV Series); Pride of St. Louis, The; Rambo: First Blood II; Rambo III; Sand Pebbles, The; Star! (1968); Stone Cold Dead; Summer Rental; Table for Five; Wait Until Dark; Wild Horse Hank; Wrongfully Accused

Crew, Carl: Blood Diner; Secret Life of Jeffrey Dahmer, The

Crew, Eddie: Queen Victoria and the Zombies

Crew, Robin: Mark of Cain

Crews, Laura Hope: Camille; Idiot's Delight

terview with the Vampire; Jerry Maguire; Legend; Losin' It;
Magnolia; Mission: Impossible 2; Mission: Impossible;
Outsiders, The; Rain Man; Risky Business; Taps; Top Gun

Crumb, Robert: Crumb

Crumpacker, Amy: Revenge of the Teenage Vixens from
Outer Space

Crutchley, Jeremy: Mangler, The

Cruttwell, Greg: Naked; Two Days in the Valley

Cruz, Alexis: Old Man and the Sea, The (1990); Riot (1996)
(TV Movie); Stargate; Streets of Laredo

Cruz, Carlos: Guantanamera!

Cruz, Charmain: Bronx War, The

Cruz, Penelope: All About My Mother; Belle Epoque; Hi-Lo
Country, The; Jamon, Jamon; Open Your Eyes; Twice Upon
A Yesterday

Cruz, Raymond: Alien Resurrection; Substitute, The
(1996)

Cruz, Tania: Men with Guns

Cruz, Vladimir: Strawberry and Chocolate

Cruz, Wilson: All over Me; Joyride (1997)

Cryer, Jon: Dudes; Heads; Hiding Out; Holy Man; Hot
Shots; Morgan Stewart's Coming Home; No Small Affair;
Noon Wine; O.C. & Stiggs; Plan B; Pompatus of Love, The;
Pretty in Pink; Superman IV: The Quest for Peace

Cryer, Suzanne: Wag the Dog

Crystal, Billy: Analyze This; Breaking Up Is Hard to Do; City
Slickers; City Slickers II; Deconstructing Harry; Enola Gay:
The Men, the Mission, the Atomic Bomb; Father's Day; For-
get Paris; Hamlet (1996); Memories of Me; Mr. Saturday
Night; My Giant; Princess Bride, The; Rabbit Test; Running
Scared (1986); Throw Momma from the Train; When Harry
Met Sally

Cubitt, David: I Shot a Man in Vegas

Cucciola, Riccardo: Sacco and Vanzetti

Cucinotta, Maria Grazia: Postman, The (Il Postino)

Cudutz, Michael: Liars' Club, The

Cuervo, Frank: Indio 2: The Revolt

Cuff, John Haslett: Psycho Girls

Cuffe, Alison: Shrieker

Cugat, Xavier: Date with Judy, A; Heat's On, The; Holiday in
Mexico; Luxury Liner; Neptune's Daughter; This Time For
Keeps; Two Girls and a Sailor

Cuka, Frances: Attic: The Hiding of Anne Frank

Culf, Norris: Robot Holocaust

Culkin, Christian: My Summer Story

Culkin, Kieran: Mighty, The; My Summer Story; Nowhere
to Run (1993); She's All That

Culkin, Macaulay: George Balanchine's The Nutcracker;
Getting Even with Dad; Good Son, The; Home Alone; Home
Alone 2: Lost in New York; Jacob's Ladder; My Girl; Only
the Lonely; Pagemaster, The; Richie Rich

Culkin, Michael: Candyman (1992)

Culkin, Quinn: Good Son, The

Cullen, Brett: In a Stranger's Hands; Killing Jar, The; Prehysteria; Something to Talk About; Stewardess School

Cullen, Max: Fast Lane Fever; Starstruck; Sunday Too Far
Away

Culliver, Katheryn: Biohazard: The Alien Force

Cullum, John: Day After, The; Held Up; Inherit the Wind
(1999); Northern Exposure (TV Series); Quantum Leap (TV
Series); Sweet Country

Cullum, Kimberly: Grave Secrets: The Legacy of Hilltop
Drive; Rapture, The

Culp, Jason: Skinheads

Culp, Joseph: Arrival, The (1990)

Culp, Nancy: Beverly Hillbillies Go Hollywood, The

Culp, Robert: Big Bad Mama II; Blue Lighting, The; Bob &
Carol & Ted & Alice; Castaway Cowboy, The; Flood!; Gladia-
tor, The (1986) (Television); Goldengirl; Great Scout and
Cathouse Thursday, The; Hannie Caulder; I Spy (TV Series);
Inside Out (1975); Key to Rebecca, The; Mercenary; Mur-
derous Vision; Night the City Screamed, The; Outer Limits,
The (TV Series); Pelican Brief, The; PT 109; Pucker Up and
Bark Like a Dog; Sammy, the Way-Out Seal; Silent Night,
Deadly Night III: Better Watch Out!; Time Bomb; Turk 182;
Voyage of Terror: The Achille Lauro Affair

Culp, Steven: Gore Vidal's Lincoln; Jason Goes to Hell: The
Final Friday

Culver, Michael: Moving Finger, The; Philby, Burgess and
Maclean: Spy Scandal of the Century

Culver, Roland: Betrayed (1954); Emperor Waltz, The; Encore; Great Lover, The; On Approval

Cumbuka, Ji-Tu: Bound for Glory

Cumming, Alan: Buddy; Circle of Friends; Eyes Wide Shut;
Romy and Michele's High School Reunion; Spice World; Titus

Cumming, Dorothy: Dancing Mothers

Cummings, Burton: Melanie

Cummings, Constance: Battle of the Sexes, The; Behind
the Mask; Blithe Spirit; Night after Night

Cummings, Jim: Balto (voice)

Cummings, Quinn: Babysitter, The (1980); Goodbye Girl,
The

Cummings Jr., Richard: Beverly Hills 90210

Cummings, Robert: Beach Party; Carpetbaggers, The;
Chase, The (1946); College Swing; Devil and Miss Jones,
The; Dial M for Murder; Everything Happens at Night; Five
Golden Dragons; Forever and a Day; It Started with Eve;
King's Row; Lost Moment, The; Lucky Me; Moon over Mi-
ami; My Geisha; One Night in the Tropics; Promise Her Any-
thing; Saboteur; Spring Parade; Tell It to the Judge; Three
Smart Girls Grow Up

Cummins, Gregory: Blood Games

Cummins, Martin: Poltergeist: The Legacy

Cummins, Peggy: Captain's Table; Carry on Admiral; Curse
of the Demon; Gun Crazy (1950)

Cummins, Peter: Blue Fire Lady

Cumo, Brett: Wicked, The

Cundell, Pamela: Twentyfourseven (English)

Cundieff, Rusty: Fear of a Black Hat; Sprung

Cunliffe, Freddie: War Zone, The

Cunningham, Beryl: Exterminators of the Year 3000

Cunningham, Liam: Little Princess, A (1995)

Cunningham, Margo: Sailor Who Fell from Grace with the
Sea, The

Cunninghame, June: Horrors of the Black Museum

Cuny, Alain: Camille Claudel; Christ Stopped at Eboli; Emmanuelle; Les Visiteurs Du Soir; Lovers, The (1958); Milky
Way, The (1970)

Curcio, E. J.: Hard Rock Zombies

Curnow, Graham: Horrors of the Black Museum

Curran, Lynette: Bliss (1986)

Curran, Pamela: Mutiny in Outer Space

Curran, Tony: 13th Warrior, The

Curreri, Lee: Crystal Heart; Fame

Currie, Cherie: Foxes; Wavelength (1983)

Currie, Finlay: Billy Liar; Bonnie Prince Charlie; 49th Parallel, The; Great Expectations (1946); People Will Talk; Quo
Vadis (1951); Rob Roy, the Highland Rogue

Currie, Gordon: Blood & Donuts; Fear, The: Halloween
Night; Listen; Puppet Master Four; Puppet Master 5: The Final Chapter

Currie, Louise: Adventures of Captain Marvel, The; Ape
Man, The; Forty Thieves; Masked Marvel, The; Voodoo
Man; Wild West (1946)

Curry, Christopher: C.H.U.D.; Return of Superfly, The

Curry, Don (DC): Next Friday

Curry, Julian: Rumpole of the Bailey (TV Series)

Curry, Stephen: Castle, The (1997)

Curry, Steven: Glen and Randa

Curry, Tim: Addams Family Reunion; Annie; Blue Money;
Clue; Congo; Home Alone 2: Lost in New York; Hunt for Red
October, The; It (1991); Legend; Lover's Knot; McHale's
Navy; Muppet Treasure Island; National Lampoon's Loaded
Weapon 1; Oliver Twist (1982); Oscar (1991); Pass the
Ammo; Passed Away; Ploughman's Lunch, The; Rocky
Horror Picture Show, The; Shadow, The; Shout, The
(1979); Tales from a Parallel Universe; Three Musketeers,
The (1993); Times Square; Titanic (1996); Worst Witch,
The

Curtin, Jane: Coneheads; How to Beat the High Co$t of Liv-
ing; O.C. & Stiggs; Suspicion (1987)

Curtin, Valerie: Big Trouble; Christmas without Snow, A;
Different Story, A; Maxie

Curtis, Alan: Buck Privates; Gung Ho! (1943); High Sierra;
Hollywood Cavalcade; Invisible Man's Revenge, The; Mannequin (1937); Melody Master (The Great Awakening)
(New Wine); Naughty Nineties, The; Renegade Girl; Shopworn Angel, The

Curtis, Billy: Hellzapoppin; Terror of Tiny Town, The; Three
Texas Steers

Curtis, Clifford: Desperate Remedies; Three Kings

Curtis, Dick: Santa Fe Uprising; Stick to Your Guns; Three Men from Texas

Curtis, Donald: Earth vs. the Flying Saucers; It Came from Beneath the Sea; Riders for Justice; 7th Cavalry; Son of Lassie

Curtis, Jack: Westward Ho

Curtis, Jamie Lee: Amazing Grace and Chuck; As Summers Die; Blue Steel (1990); Death of a Centerfold; Dominiok and Eugene; Drowning Mona; Fierce Creatures; Fish Called Wanda, A; Fog, The; Forever Young (1992); Grandview, U.S.A.; Halloween; Halloween II; Halloween: H20; Heidi Chronicles, The; Homegrown; House Arrest; Love Letters; Man in Love, A; Mother's Boys; My Girl; My Girl 2; Perfect; Prom Night; Queens Logic; Road Games; She's in the Army Now; Terror Train; Trading Places; True Lies; Virus (1999)

Curtis, Joan: Where Trails End

Curtis, Keene: Blade (1973); Strange New World

Curtis, Kelly: Sect, The

Curtis, Ken: California Gold Rush; Conagher; Gunsmoke (TV Series); Killer Shrews, The; Pony Express Rider; Searchers, The; Wings of Eagles, The

Curtis, Liane: Critters 2: The Main Course; Girlfriend from Hell

Curtis, Robin: Bloodfist VI: Ground Zero; Dark Breed; Santa with Muscles; Scorpio One; Unborn II, The

Curtis, Sonia: Evil Lives

Curtis, Susan: Octavia

Curtis, Todd: Chain of Command; Out for Blood

Curtis, Tony: Bad News Bears Go to Japan, The; Balboa; Boeing, Boeing; Boston Strangler, The; Brainwaves; Captain Newman, M.D.; Center of the Web; Chamber of Horrors; Christmas in Connecticut (1992); Club Life; Count of Monte Cristo, The (1975); Defiant Ones, The; Forty Pounds of Trouble; Francis, the Talking Mule; Great Impostor, The; Great Race, The; Houdini (1953); Immortals, The; Insignificance; It Rained All Night the Day I Left; Kings Go Forth; Last of Philip Banter, The; Last Tycoon, The; Lepke; Little Miss Marker (1980); Lobster Man from Mars; Mafia Princess; Manitou, The; Midnight (1989); Mirror Crack'd, The; Operation Petticoat; Perfect Furlough; Persuaders, The (TV Series); Portrait of a Showgirl; Prime Target; Sex and the Single Girl; Sextette; Some Like It Hot; Son of Ali Baba; Spartacus; Suppose They Gave a War and Nobody Came?; Sweet Smell of Success; Taras Bulba; Those Daring Young Men in Their Jaunty Jalopies; Trapeze; Users, The; Vega$; Vikings, The; Winchester '73

Curtis-Hall, Vondie: Deadman's Revenge; Don King: Only in America; Drop Squad, The; Freedom Song; Passion Fish; Sirens (1999)

Curzi, Pierre: Blind Trust (Pouvoir Intime)

Curzon, George: Sexton Blake and the Hooded Terror

Cusack, Anne: Multiplicity

Cusack, Cyril: Children of Rage; Cry of the Innocent; Danny, the Champion of the World; Day of the Jackal, The; Elusive Pimpernel, The; Fahrenheit 451; Harold and Maude; Homecoming, The (1973); Ill Met by Moonlight; King Lear (1971); Les Miserables (1978); Love Spell; Manhunt (1973) (The Italian Connection); My Left Foot; Night Ambush; 1984 (1984); Sacco and Vanzetti; Shake Hands with the Devil; Taming of the Shrew, The (1966); Tenth Man, The

Cusack, Joan: Addams Family Values; Allnighter, The; Arlington Road; Broadcast News; Corrina, Corrina; Cradle Will Rock; Grosse Pointe Blank; Hero (1992); High Fidelity; In & Out; Men Don't Leave; Mr. Wrong; My Blue Heaven; Nine Months; Runaway Bride; Smile Like Yours, A; Stars and Bars; Toys; Two Much; Where the Heart Is (2000); Working Girl

Cusack, John: Anastasia (1997); Being John Malkovich; Better Off Dead (1985); Bullets over Broadway; City Hall; Con Air; Cradle Will Rock; Eight Men Out; Fat Man and Little Boy; Floundering; Grifters, The; Grosse Pointe Blank; Hellcab; High Fidelity; Hot Pursuit; Jack Bull, The; Journey of Natty Gann, The; Map of the Human Heart; Midnight in the Garden of Good and Evil; Money for Nothing; One Crazy Summer; Pushing Tin; Road to Wellville, The; Roadside Prophets; Say Anything; Shadows and Fog; Stand by Me (1986); Sure Thing, The; Tapeheads; This Is My Father; True Colors

Cusack, Niamh: Closer You Get, The

Cusack, Sinead: Bad Behaviour; Cement Garden, The; Revenge (1971) (Joan Collins); Stealing Beauty; Waterland

Cushing, Peter: Abominable Snowman of the Himalayas, The; And Now the Screaming Starts; Asylum (1972); At the Earth's Core; Beast Must Die, The; Biggles—Adventures in Time; Blood Beast Terror, The; Brides of Dracula; Creeping Flesh, The; Curse of Frankenstein, The; Daleks—Invasion Earth 2150 A.D.; Devil's Undead, The; Dr. Phibes Rises Again; Dr. Terror's House of Horrors; Dr. Who and the Daleks; Dracula A.D. 1972; Dynasty of Fear; Evil of Frankenstein, The; Fear in the Night (Dynasty of Fear); Frankenstein and the Monster from Hell; Frankenstein Created Woman; From Beyond the Grave; Ghoul, The (1975); Gorgon, The; Hamlet (1948); Hellfire Club, The; Horror Express; Horror of Dracula; Hound of the Baskervilles, The (1959); House of the Long Shadows; House That Dripped Blood, The; Island of Terror; John Paul Jones; Land of the Minotaur; Legend of the Werewolf; Madhouse (1972); Mania; Masks of Death; Moulin Rouge; Mummy, The (1959); Naked Edge, The; Revenge of Frankenstein; Satanic Rites of Dracula, The; Scream and Scream Again; Seven Brothers Meet Dracula, The; Shatter; Shock Waves (Death Corps); Skull, The; Star Wars; Tale of Two Cities, A (1980); Tales from the Crypt; Time Without Pity; Top Secret; Torture Garden; Twins of Evil; Uncanny, The; Vampire Lovers, The

Cutanda, Eddie: Squeeze

Cuthbert, Elisha: Believe

Cuthbert, Jon: Virtual Assassin

Cuthbertson, Allan: Tunes of Glory

Cuthbertson, Ian: Railway Children, The

Cutler, Allen: Halfback of Notre Dame, The

Cutler, Brian: Wilderness Family, Part 2, The

Cutt, Michael: Night of the Demon

Cutter, Lise: Fleshtone

Cutts, Dale: Cyborg Soldier

Cwiklinska, M.: Border Street

Cybulski, Zbigniew: Ashes and Diamonds

Cypher, Jon: Blade (1973); Off the Mark; Spontaneous Combustion; Strictly Business; Valdez Is Coming

Cyphers, Charles: Halloween; Halloween II

Cyton, Elizabeth: Slave Girls from Beyond Infinity

Czar, Nancy: Wild Guitar

Czerny, Harry: Mission: Impossible

Czerny, Henry: Boys of St. Vincent; Clear and Present Danger; When Night Is Falling

Czyzewska, Elzbieta: Misplaced

D., Chris: Border Radio

D'Angelo, Beverly: Illuminata

D'Arcy, Roy: Last Warning, The; Merry Widow, The (1925)

D'Errico, Donna: Candyman 3: Day of the Dead

D'Onofrio, Vincent: That Championship Season; Velocity of Gary, The

Dabney, Augusta: Violets Are Blue

D'Abo, Maryam: Double Obsession; Immortal Sins; Leon the Pig Farmer; Living Daylights, The; Money; Nightlife; Not a Penny More, Not a Penny Less; Red Shoe Diaries 3: Another Woman's Lipstick; Savage Hearts; Shootfighter; Solitaire for 2; Stalked; Tomcat: Dangerous Desires; Tropical Heat; Xtro

D'Abo, Olivia: Bank Robber; Beyond the Stars; Big Green, The; Bolero (1984); Bullies; Dream to Believe; Greedy; Into the Fire; Kicking and Screaming; Last Good Time, The; Live Nude Girls; Midnight's Child; Point of No Return; Really Weird Tales; Soccer Dog: The Movie; Spirit of '76, The; Wayne's World 2

Dacascos, Mark: Base, The; Boogie Boy; Deadly Past; DNA; Double Dragon; Kickboxer 5: Redemption; Only the Strong; Redline; Sabotage (1996)

Dacqumine, Jacques: Phedre

Daddo, Andrew: Body Melt

Dade, Frances: Daughter of the Dragon; Phantom Thunderbolt

Dadon: Windhorse

Daemion, Ami: Silver Stallion, The

Dafoe, Willem: Affliction; American Psycho; Body of Evidence; Born on the Fourth of July; Clear and Present Danger; Cry-Baby; English Patient, The; eXistenZ; Faraway, So Close; Flight of the Intruder, The; Hitchhiker, The (Series); Last Temptation of Christ, The; Light Sleeper; Loveless, The; Lulu on the Bridge; Mississippi Burning; New Rose Hotel; Night and the Moment, The; Off Limits (1988); Platoon; Roadhouse 66; Speed 2: Cruise Control; Streets of Fire; To Live and Die in L.A.; Tom & Viv; Triumph of the Spirit; White Sands; Wild at Heart

Dagermark, Pia: Vampire Happening

Daggett, Jensen: Friday the 13th, Part VIII: Jason Takes Manhattan

Dagher, Laila: Angel in Training

D'Agostino, Liza: Bar Girls

Dagover, Lil: Cabinet of Doctor Caligari, The; Destiny; Spiders, The

Dahl, Arlene: Here Come the Girls; Journey to the Center of the Earth (1959); Kisses for My President; Land Raiders; Night of the Warrior; Slightly Scarlet; Southern Yankee, A; Three Little Words; Watch the Birdie; Woman's World

Dahl, Lisbet: Topsy Turvy

Dahlbeck, Eva: Brink of Life; Counterfeit Traitor, The; Dreams; Lesson in Love, A; Secrets of Women (Waiting Women); Smiles of a Summer Night

Daichi, Yasuo: Minbo, or The Gentle Art of Japanese Extortion

Dailey, Dan: It's Always Fair Weather; Lady Be Good; Meet Me in Las Vegas; Mortal Storm, The; Mother Wore Tights; Pride of St. Louis, The; Private Files of J. Edgar Hoover, The; There's No Business Like Show Business; What Price Glory; Wings of Eagles, The; Ziegfeld Girl

Dailey, Irene: Grissom Gang, The

Daily, Elizabeth: One Dark Night; Pee-Wee's Big Adventure; Street Music

Daimon, Masaaki: Godzilla vs. Mechagodzilla

Dain, Joseph: Public Enemy #1

Dainaro, Neil: Dawson Patrol, The

Dajani, Nadia: Breathing Room

Dalban, Max: Boudu Saved from Drowning; Toni

Dalbes, Alberto: Cut Throats Nine

Dale, Colin: Diamond's Edge

Dale, Cynthia: Boy in Blue, The; Heavenly Bodies

Dale, Esther: Blondie Has Servant Trouble; Ma and Pa Kettle (The Further Adventures of Ma and Pa Kettle); Ma and Pa Kettle at the Fair; Ma and Pa Kettle Back on the Farm; This Time For Keeps

Dale, Jennifer: Dream House; John Woo's Once a Thief; Of Unknown Origin; Separate Vacations

Dale, Jim: American Clock, The; Carry on Cleo; Carry on Cowboy; Carry on Doctor; Follow That Camel; Hot Lead and Cold Feet; Joseph Andrews; Pete's Dragon; Scandalous (1983); Unidentified Flying Oddball

Dale, Tony: Fix, The

Dale, Vincent: Stolen Hearts

Dale, Virginia: Buck Benny Rides Again; Dragnet (1947); Holiday Inn

Daley, Cass: Red Garters

Daley, Jack: West of the Law

Dali, Tracy: Virgin High

Dalio, Marcel: Black Jack; Cartouche; Grand Illusion; Lady L; Pepe Le Moko; Rules of the Game, The

Dall, John: Corn Is Green, The (1945); Gun Crazy (1950); Man Who Cheated Himself, The; Rope

Dalle, Beatrice: Betty Blue

Dallesandro, Joe: Andy Warhol's Dracula; Andy Warhol's Frankenstein; Bad Love; Critical Condition; Cry-Baby; Double Revenge; Flesh; Guncrazy (1992); Heat (1972); Hollywood Detective, The; Limey, The; Private War; Sunset; Trash

Dallimore, Maurice: Collector, The

D'Aloja, Francesca: Turkish Bath, The

Dalton, Abby: Cyber Tracker; Maverick (TV Series); Saga of the Viking Women and Their Voyage to the Waters of the Great Sea Serpent, The (Viking Women and the Sea Serpent, The)

Dalton, Audrey: Casanova's Big Night; Drum Beat; Elfego Baca: Six Gun Law; Monster That Challenged the World, The; Thriller (TV Series); Titanic (1953)

Dalton, Darren: Wolves, The (1994)

Dalton, Kristen: Digital Man

Dalton, Timothy: Antony and Cleopatra (1981); Beautician and the Beast, The; Brenda Starr; Chanel Solitaire; Cromwell; Doctor and the Devils, The; Flash Gordon; Hawks; Informant, The; Jane Eyre (1983); King's Whore, The; License to Kill; Lion in Winter, The; Living Daylights, The; Mistral's Daughter; Permission to Kill; Rocketeer, The;

Daltrey, Roger: Buddy's Song; Cold Justice; Forgotten Prisoners; If Looks Could Kill (1991); Legacy, The; Lisztomania; Mack the Knife; McVicar; Tommy; Vampirella

Daly, Eileen: Razor Blade Smile

Daly, Timothy: Associate, The (1996); Caroline at Midnight; Dangerous Heart; Denise Calls Up; Dr. Jekyll and Ms. Hyde; I Married a Centerfold; In the Line of Duty: Ambush in Waco; Love or Money?; Mirrors; Spellbinder; Storm of the Century; Witness to the Execution; Year of the Comet

Daly, Tyne: Adultress, The; Aviator, The; Better Late than Never; Enforcer, The (1976); Intimate Strangers; Money Kings; Movers and Shakers; Tricks; Zoot Suit

Damato, A. J.: Shrunken Heads

d'Amboise, Charlotte: American Blue Note

d'Amboise, Jacques: Carousel

Damevsky, Mony: 5 Dead on the Crimson Canvas

Damian, Leo: Ghosts Can't Do It; Hard Drive

Damita, Lily: Fighting Caravans

Dammett, Blackie: Nine Deaths of the Ninja

Damon, Mark: Anzio; Black Sabbath; Crypt of the Living Dead; Devil's Wedding Night, The; Fall of the House of Usher, The (1960); Scalawag Bunch, The

Damon, Matt: Courage Under Fire; Dogma; Geronimo: An American Legend (1993); Good Old Boys, The; Good Will Hunting; Mystic Pizza; Rainmaker, The; Rising Son; Rounders; Rounders (1998); Saving Private Ryan; Talented Mr. Ripley, The

Damon, Stuart: Cinderella (1964)

Damon, Una: Race

Damone, Vic: Athena; Hell to Eternity; Hit the Deck; Kismet (1955); Rich, Young and Pretty

Damus, Mike: Pig's Tale, A

Dana, Barbara: Matter of Principle, A; Necessary Parties

Dana, Bill: Murder in Texas

Dana, Leora: Kings Go Forth; 3:10 to Yuma

Dana, Viola: That Certain Thing

Dance, Charles: Alien 3; Century; China Moon; Golden Child, The; Good Morning, Babylon; Hilary and Jackie; In the Presence of Mine Enemies; Jewel in the Crown, The; Last Action Hero, The; McGuffin, The; Out on a Limb (1986); Pascali's Island; Plenty; Space Truckers; Surgeon, The; Tales of the Unexpected; Undertow; White Mischief

Dando, Evan: Heavy

Dandridge, Dorothy: Carmen Jones

Dane, Karl: Scarlet Letter, The (1926); Son of the Sheik; Warning Shadows (1933)

Dane, Lawrence: Case of Libel, A; Clown Murders, The; Fatal Attraction (1985); Find the Lady; Good Fight, The; Good Idea; Nothing Personal (1980); Of Unknown Origin; Rituals; Rolling Vengeance; Scanners

Dane, Patricia: Johnny Eager; Somewhere I'll Find You

Dane, Shelton: Hidden in America

Dane, Taylor: Stag

Danes, Claire: Brokedown Palace; Home for the Holidays (1995); How to Make an American Quilt; Les Misérables (1998); Little Women (1994); Mod Squad, The; Polish Wedding; Rainmaker, The; To Gillian on Her 37th Birthday; U-Turn; William Shakespeare's Romeo and Juliet

D'Angelo, Beverly: American History X; Big Trouble; Coal Miner's Daughter; Cold Front; Crazysitter, The; Daddy's Dyin' and Who's Got the Will; First Love (1977); Hair; High Spirits; Highpoint; Honky Tonk Freeway; In the Mood; Lansky; Lightning Jack; Lonely Hearts (1991); Maid to Order; Man Trouble; Miracle, The (1990); National Lampoon's Christmas Vacation; National Lampoon's European Vacation; National Lampoon's Vacation; Pacific Heights; Paternity; Pope Must Diet, The; Sleeping Beauty (1983); Slow Burn; Streetcar Named Desire, A (1983); Trading Hearts; Vegas Vacation; Widow's Kiss

Dangerfield, Rodney: Back to School; Caddyshack; Casper: A Spirited Beginning; Easy Money; Godson, The; Ladybugs; Meet Wally Sparks; Moving; Natural Born Killers; Projectionist, The

Daniel, Brittany: On Hostile Ground

Daniel, Jennifer: Kiss of the Vampire

Daniel, Trudik: Castle, The (1963)

Danieli, Emma: Last Man on Earth, The

Danieli, Isa: Ciao Professore

Daniell, Henry: All This and Heaven Too; Body Snatcher, The (1945); Camille; Castle in the Desert; Diane; Dressed to Kill (1941); Firefly, The; Five Weeks in a Balloon; Four Jacks and a Jill; Four Skulls of Jonathan Drake, The; Holiday; Jane Eyre (1944); Madame X (1937); Private Lives of Elizabeth and Essex, The; Sea Hawk, The; Sherlock Holmes and the Voice of Terror; Sherlock Holmes in Washington; Song of Love; Voyage to the Bottom of the Sea; Witness for the Prosecution (1957); Woman in Green, The; Woman's Face, A

Danielle, Suzanne: Carpathian Eagle; Carry on Emmanuelle

Daniels, Alex: Meridian (Kiss of the Beast)

Daniels, Anthony: Empire Strikes Back, The; Return of the Jedi; Star Wars; Star Wars: Episode I The Phantom Menace

Daniels, Bebe: Dixiana; Feel My Pulse; Harold Lloyd's Comedy Classics; Reaching for the Moon (1931)

Daniels, Ben: Beautiful Thing; Passion in the Desert

Daniels, Danny D.: Outing, The

Daniels, Gary: Bloodmoon (1997); Deadly Target; Firepower (1993); Fist of the North Star (1995); Hawk's Vengeance; Heatseeker; Rage (1995); Riot (1996)

Daniels, J. D.: Beanstalk

Daniels, Jeff: Arachnophobia; Butcher's Wife, The; Caine Mutiny Court Martial, The; Checking Out; Dumb and Dumber; Fly Away Home; Gettysburg; Grand Tour: Disaster in Time; Heartburn; House on Carroll Street, The; Love Hurts; Marie; My Favorite Martian; 101 Dalmatians (1996); Pleasantville; Purple Rose of Cairo, The; Rain Without Thunder; Redwood Curtain; Something Wild; Speed; Sweethearts' Dance; Teamster Boss: The Jackie Presser Story; Terms of Endearment; There Goes the Neighborhood; Trial and Error (1997); Two Days in the Valley; Welcome Home, Roxy Carmichael

Daniels, Jennifer: Reptile, The

Daniels, John: Bare Knuckles; Getting Over

Daniels, Lisa: Glass Slipper, The

Daniels, Phil: Bad Behaviour; Breaking Glass; Meantime; Quadrophenia; Scum

Daniels, William: Blind Date (1987); Blue Lagoon, The; City in Fear; Francis Gary Powers: The True Story of the U-2 Spy Incident; Her Alibi; Marlowe; Night Stalker, The: Two Tales of Terror (TV Series); One and Only, The; Parallax View, The; Rehearsal for Murder; 1776; St. Elsewhere (TV Series); Sunburn; Thousand Clowns, A

Danielson, Lynn: Mortuary Academy

Danner, Blythe: Alice (1990); Another Woman; Are You in the House Alone?; Brighton Beach Memoirs; Call to Remember, A; Forces of Nature; Futureworld; Great Santini, The; Hearts of the West; Homage; Inside the Third Reich; Judgment; Mad City; Man, Woman and Child; Mr. and Mrs. Bridge; Myth of Fingerprints, The; Never Forget; No Looking Back; Prince of Tides, The; Saint Maybe; 1776; To Kill a Clown; To Wong Foo, Thanks for Everything, Julie Newmar; X-Files, The (1998)

Danning, Sybil: Amazon Women on the Moon; Chained Heat; Hercules (1983); Hitchhiker, The (Series); Howling II . . . Your Sister Is a Werewolf; Jungle Warriors; Kill Castro (Cuba Crossing, Mercenaries (1978), Sweet Violent Tony); L.A. Bounty; Malibu Express; Man with Bogart's Face, The; Phantom Empire, The (1986); Reform School Girls; Salamander, The; Seven Magnificent Gladiators, The; Swap, The (Sam's Song); Talking Walls; They're Playing with Fire; Warrior Queen

Dannis, Ray: Undertaker and His Pals, The

Dano, Royal: Cimarron (1960); Cocaine Wars; Crime of Passion; Culpepper Cattle Co., The; Electra Glide in Blue; Ghoulies II; House II: The Second Story; Huckleberry Finn (1975); Killer Inside Me, The; Killer Klowns from Outer Space; King of Kings (1961); Never Steal Anything Small; Red Badge of Courage, The; Red-Headed Stranger, The; Spaced Invaders; Strangers: The Story of a Mother and a Daughter; Tribute to a Bad Man

Danon, Leslie: Blood Thirsty; Whispering, The

Danova, Cesare: Chamber of Horrors; Scorchy; Tentacles; Viva Las Vegas

Danson, Ted: Body Heat; Chinese Web, The; Cousins; Dad; Fine Mess, A; Getting Even with Dad; Gulliver's Travels (1996) (Television); Homegrown; Just Between Friends; Little Treasure; Loch Ness; Made in America; Mumford; Onion Field, The; Our Family Business; Pontiac Moon; Three Men and a Baby; Three Men and a Little Lady; We Are the Children

Dante, Michael: Beyond Evil; Big Score, The; Cage; Naked Kiss, The; Seven Thieves

Dantes, Roland: Pacific Connection, The

Dantine, Helmut: Bring Me the Head of Alfredo Garcia; Edge of Darkness (1943); Operation Crossbow; Stranger from Venus

Danton, Ray: Centerfold Girls; I'll Cry Tomorrow; Majority of One, A; Onionhead; Rise and Fall of Legs Diamond, The

Danza, Tony: Angels in the Outfield (1994); Brooklyn State of Mind, A; Going Ape!; Hollywood Knights, The; Illtown; Love to Kill; Mob Justice; Noah; North Shore Fish; She's Out of Control; Single Bars, Single Women; Truth or Die

Dao, Catherine: Femme Fontaine: Killer Babe for the CIA

Dao-Lin, Sun: Go-Masters, The

Dapkounaite, Ingeborga: Burnt by the Sun; On Dangerous Ground (1995)

D'Arbanville, Patti: Big Wednesday; Bilitis; Boys Next Door, The (1985); Call Me; Fan, The (1996); Fifth Floor, The; Flesh; Fresh Horses; Modern Problems; Rancho Deluxe; Snow Kill; Wired

Darbo, Patrika: Fast Money (1996)

Darby, Kim: Better Off Dead (1985); Capture of Grizzly Adams, The; Don't Be Afraid of the Dark; Enola Gay: The Men, the Mission, the Atomic Bomb; Flatbed Annie and Sweetie Pie: Lady Truckers; Generation; Grissom Gang, The; One and Only, The; People, The; Strawberry Statement, The; Teen Wolf, Too; True Grit

Darc, Mireille: Icy Breasts; Return of the Tall Blond Man with One Black Shoe, The; Tall Blond Man with One Black Shoe, The; Weekend

Darcel, Denise: Battleground; Dangerous When Wet; Vera Cruz; Westward the Women

D'Arcy, Alex: Blood of Dracula's Castle; Soldier of Fortune

D'Arcy, Jake: Gregory's Girl; Sense of Freedom, A

D'Arcy, Roy: Revolt of the Zombies; Warning Shadows (1933)

Darcy, Sheila: Zorro's Fighting Legion

Darden, Severn: Back to School; Battle for the Planet of the Apes; Conquest of the Planet of the Apes; Dead Heat on a Merry-Go-Round; Disappearance of Aimee, The; Hired Hand, The; Justine; Legend of Hillbilly John, The; Luv; Playmates; Telephone, The

Dare, Debra: Hard to Die

DaRe, Eric: Takeover, The

Darel, Florence: A La Mode; Tale of Springtime, A

Darie, Frederic: Deep Trouble

Darin, Bobby: Captain Newman, M.D.; Come September; Hell Is for Heroes; Pressure Point; Run Stranger Run; State Fair (1962)

Darlene, Gigi: Bad Girls Go to Hell

Darling, Candy: Flesh

Darmon, Gerard: Obsession: A Taste for Fear

Darnell, Linda: Anna and the King of Siam; Blackbeard the Pirate; Blood and Sand (1941); Buffalo Bill; City Without Men; Dakota Incident; Forever Amber; Hangover Square; Island of Desire; Letter to Three Wives, A; Mark of Zorro, The (1940); My Darling Clementine; Second Chance; Unfaithfully Yours (1948)

Darnoux, George: Day in the Country, A

Darr, Lisa: Plan B

Darren, James: Boss' Son, The; Diamond Head; Gene Krupa Story, The; Gidget; Gidget Goes Hawaiian; Gidget Goes to Rome; Guns of Navarone, The; Scruples; Venus in Furs

Darrieux, Danielle: Alexander the Great; Bluebeard (1963); Club des Femmes; Earrings of Madame De . . . , The; Five Fingers; La Ronde; Lady Chatterley's Lover (1959); Le Plaisir; Le Rouge et le Noir; Mauvaise Graine (Bad Seed); Mayerling; Rage of Paris, The; Rich, Young and Pretty; Scene of the Crime (1987)

Darro, Frankie: Broadway Bill; Devil Horse, The; Little Men (1935); Phantom Empire (1935); Radio Ranch (Men with Steel Faces, Phantom Empire); Way Back Home

Darrough, Al: Fraternity Demon

Darrow, Henry: Attica; Badge 373; Criminal Passion; In Dangerous Company; L.A. Bounty; Last of the Finest, The

Darrow, Oliver: Bad Girls from Mars; Spirits; Teenage Exorcist

Darrow, Paul: Blake's 7 (TV Series)

Darrow, Tony: Me and the Mob; Mickey Blue Eyes

Dartez, Gail: Out

Darvas, Lili: Love; Meet Me in Las Vegas

Darvi, Bella: Racers, The

Darwell, Jane: Aggie Appleby, Maker of Men; All Through the Night; Bigamist, The; Captain January; Craig's Wife; Curly Top; Devil and Daniel Webster, The; Grapes of Wrath, The; Jesse James; Last Hurrah, The; Lemon Drop Kid, The; Little Miss Broadway; Mary Poppins; Ox-Bow Incident, The; Poor Little Rich Girl (1936); Rains Came, The; Scarlet Empress, The; Three Godfathers, The; Tom Sawyer (1930)

Dary, Rene: Grisbi

Das, Nandita: Earth (1998)

Dash, Stacey: Black Water; Clueless; Cold Around the Heart; Illegal in Blue; Mo' Money; Renaissance Man

Da Silva, Eric: Delta of Venus

Da Silva, Fernando Ramos: Pixote

DaSilva, Howard: Blue Dahlia, The; David and Lisa; Garbo Talks; Greatest Man in the World, The; Keeper of the Flame; Lost Weekend, The; Missiles of October, The; Nevada Smith; Sea Wolf, The (1941); 1776; Smile, Jenny, You're Dead; They Live By Night; Unconquered; Underworld Story

Dassin, Jules: Never on Sunday

Dassule, Helene: La Petite Bande

Dasté, Jean: Boudu Saved from Drowning; Green Room, The; L'Atalante; Zero for Conduct

Datcher, Alex: Expert, The

Dauden, Marlene: Combat Killers

Daughton, James: Blind Date (1984); Girlfriend from Hell; House of the Rising Sun

Daugirda, Jerry: Gone in 60 Seconds

Dauphin, Claude: April in Paris; Is Paris Burning?; Lady L; Les Miserables (1978); Little Boy Lost; Madame Rosa

Davalos, Dominique: Salvation

Davalos, Elyssa: House in the Hills, A; Jericho Fever

Davalos, Richard: Snatched

Davao, Charlie: Blind Rage

Davazac, Emilie: Undefeatable

Davenport, Alice: Keystone Comedies: Vol. 1–5

Davenport, Harry: Adventure; All This and Heaven Too; Courage of Lassie; Cowboy and the Lady, The; December 7th: The Movie; Enchanted Forest, The; Jack London; Kismet (1944); Lucky Partners; Made for Each Other; Ox-Bow Incident, The; Rage of Paris, The; That Forsyte Woman; Thin Man Goes Home, The; Three Daring Daughters

Davenport, Jack: Talented Mr. Ripley, The

Davenport, Mark: Criminal Mind, The

Davenport, Nigel: Chariots of Fire; Cry of the Innocent; Dracula (1973); Living Free; Phase IV; Royal Hunt of the Sun; Virgin Soldiers, The; Without a Clue; Zulu Dawn

Davi, Robert: Amazon; Beneficiary, The; Blind Justice; Center of the Web; Christopher Columbus: The Discovery (1992); Cops and Robbersons; Dangerous, The (1994); Dogfighters, The; Illicit Behavior; License to Kill; Maniac Cop 2; Maniac Cop 3: Badge of Silence; Mardi Gras for the Devil; No Contest; November Men, The; Occasional Hell, An; Peacemaker (1990); Predator 2; Quick; Raw Deal; Showgirls; Son of the Pink Panther; Traxx; White Hot: The Mysterious Murder of Thelma Todd; Wild Orchid 2: Two Shades of Blue; Wild Thing

David, Angel: Mixed Blood

David, Clifford: Agent on Ice; Resurrection

David, Eleanor: Comfort and Joy; King's Whore, The; Scarlet Pimpernel, The (1982); Slipstream; Sylvia

David, Elizabeth: Gruesome Twosome

David, Jody: Merlin of the Crystal Cave

David, Keith: Armageddon; Bird; Clockers; Dead Presidents; Executive Target; Final Analysis; Flipping; Grave, The; Johns; Marked for Death; Men at Work; Nails; Pitch Black; Puppet Masters, The; Quick and the Dead, The (1995); Stars and Bars; They Live; Volcano; Where the Heart Is (2000)

David, Lawrence: Midnight Dancer (1994)

David, Thayer: Duchess and the Dirtwater Fox, The; Eiger Sanction, The; Savages (1973); Save the Tiger

Davidovich, Lolita: Blaze; Boiling Point (1993); Cobb; Dead Silence (1996); For Better or Worse; Harvest of Fire; Indictment: The McMartin Trial; Inner Circle, The; Intersection; Jungle 2 Jungle; Keep the Change; Leap of Faith; Mystery, Alaska; Play It to the Bone; Prison Stories: Women on

the Inside; Raising Cain; Salt Water Moose; Younger and Younger

Davidson, Diana: Scared to Death (1980)

Davidson, Doug: Mr. Write

Davidson, Eileen: Easy Wheels; Eternity; House on Sorority Row

Davidson, Jaye: Crying Game, The; Stargate

Davidson, Jim: Reasons of the Heart

Davidson, John: Captain America (1944); Dick Tracy vs. Crime Inc.; Happiest Millionaire, The; One and Only, Genuine, Original Family Band, The; Perils of Pauline, The (1933)

Davidson, Tommy: Booty Call; Strictly Business; Woo

Davidtz, Embeth: Army of Darkness; Bicentennial Man; Fallen; Feast of July; Garden of Redemption, The; Gingerbread Man, The; Last Rites; Mansfield Park; Matilda (1996); Murder in the First; Schindler's List; Sweet Murder

Davies, Ann: Midwinter's Tale, A

Davies, Freddie: Funnybones

Davies, Geraint Wyn: Conspiracy of Fear, The; Hush Little Baby; Terror Stalks the Class Reunion; Trilogy of Terror II

Davies, Jeremy: Going All the Way; Locusts; Ravenous; Saving Private Ryan; Spanking the Monkey

Davies, John: Positive I.D.

Davies, John Howard: Oliver Twist (1948); Rocking Horse Winner, The; Tom Brown's Schooldays (1950)

Davies, Kate Emma: Queenie

Davies, Lane: Funland; Impure Thoughts; Magic of Lassie, The

Davies, Lindy: Malcolm

Davies, Marion: Going Hollywood; MGM's The Big Parade of Comedy; Operator 13; Show People

Davies, Ray: Absolute Beginners

Davies, Rudi: Object of Beauty, The

Davies, Rupert: Dracula Has Risen from the Grave; Five Golden Dragons; Night Visitor, The (1970); Oblong Box, The

Davies, Sian Leisa: Heaven on Earth

Davies, Stephen: Berlin Conspiracy, The; Ladykiller (1996); Nest, The (1988)

Davion, Alexander: Paranoiac

Davis, Amy: All-American Murder

Davis, Ann B.: Brady Bunch, The (TV series); Lover Come Back; Very Brady Christmas, A

Davis, Bette: All About Eve; All This and Heaven Too; As Summers Die; Beyond the Forest; Bride Came C.O.D., The; Bureau of Missing Persons; Burnt Offerings; Cabin in the Cotton; Catered Affair, The; Corn Is Green, The (1945); Dangerous (1935); Dark Secret of Harvest Home, The; Dark Victory; Dead Ringer; Death on the Nile; Deception (1946); Disappearance of Aimee, The; Empty Canvas, The; Ex-Lady; Great Lie, The; Hell's House; Hollywood Canteen; Hush . . . Hush, Sweet Charlotte; In This Our Life; Jezebel; John Paul Jones; Juarez; June Bride; Kid Galahad (1937); Letter, The; Little Foxes, The; Little Gloria, Happy at Last; Madame Sin; Man Who Came to Dinner, The; Marked Woman; Mr. Skeffington; Murder with Mirrors; Nanny, The; Now, Voyager; Of Human Bondage (1934); Old Maid, The; Petrified Forest, The; Phone Call from a Stranger; Piano for Mrs. Cimino, A; Pocketful of Miracles; Private Lives of Elizabeth and Essex, The; Return from Witch Mountain; Right of Way; Satan Met a Lady; Sisters, The (1938); Star, The (1952); Stolen Life, A; Strangers: The Story of a Mother and a Daughter; Thank Your Lucky Stars; That Certain Woman; Three on a Match; Virgin Queen, The; Watch on the Rhine; Watcher in the Woods, The; Way Back Home; Whales of August, The; What Ever Happened to Baby Jane?; Where Love Has Gone; White Mama; Wicked Stepmother, The; Winter Meeting

Davis, Brad: Blood Ties (1987); Caine Mutiny Court Martial, The; Chariots of Fire; Chiefs; Child of Darkness, Child of Light; Cold Steel; Greatest Man in the World, The; Habitation of Dragons, The; Heart; Midnight Express; Plot to Kill Hitler, The; Querelle; Rosalie Goes Shopping; Rumor of War, A; Small Circle of Friends, A; Unspeakable Acts; When the Time Comes

Davis, Clifton: Don't Look Back: The Story of Leroy "Satchel" Paige; Dream Date; Night the City Screamed, The

Davis, Cynthia: Cooley High

Davis, Daniel: Glen or Glenda

Dayrit, Dina: Infested (Ticks)

Dayton, Danny: Mad Bull

de Bankole, Isaach: Ghost Dog: The Way of the Samurai

de Bray, Yvonne: Les Parents Terribles

de Grasse, Sam: Man Who Laughs, The

De La Bretonere, Esmee: Johnsons, The

de la Motte, Marguerite: Nut, The; Three Musketeers, The (1921)

De Lacey, Luke: Virtual Sexuality

De, Deepankar: Stranger, The (1992)

Dea, Marie: Les Visiteurs Du Soir

Deacon, Brian: Jesus; Vampyres; Zed and Two Noughts, A

Deacon, Eric: Zed and Two Noughts, A

Deacon, Richard: Abbott and Costello Meet the Mummy; Awakening of Cassie, the; Dick Van Dyke Show, The (TV Series); Happy Hooker Goes Hollywood, The; My Sister Eileen

Dead End Kids, The: They Made Me a Criminal

Deakins, Lucy: Boy Who Could Fly, The; Cheetah; Little Nikita; There Goes My Baby

de Almeida, Joaquim: Clear and Present Danger; Desperado; Good Morning, Babylon; Only You (1994)

Dean, Allison: Ruby in Paradise

Dean, Bill: Family Life

Dean, Billy: Face to Kill, A

Dean, Eddie: Caravan Trail; Colorado Serenade; Wild West (1946); Wildfire (1945)

Dean, Fabian: Single Room Furnished

Dean, Felicity: Steaming; Whistle Blower, The

Dean, Isabel: Terrorists, The

Dean, Ivor: Saint, The (TV Series)

Dean, James: East of Eden (1955); Giant; Rebel Without a Cause

Dean, Jimmy: Big Bad John

Dean, Laura: Fame

Dean, Loren: American Clock, The; Billy Bathgate; End of Violence, The; Enemy of the State; 1492: The Conquest of Paradise; Gattaca; JFK: Reckless Youth; Mrs. Winterbourne; Mumford; Passion of Darkly Noon, The; Rosewood

Dean, Priscilla: Outside the Law (1921); White Tiger

Dean, Rick: Carnosaur 2; Carnosaur 3: Primal Species; Cheyenne Warrior; Max Is Missing; Naked Obsession; New Crime City; Los Angeles 2020; One Man Army; Saturday Night Special; Skateboard Kid, The; Stripteaser

Dean, Ron: Birthday Boy, The; Cold Justice

DeAnda, Rodolfo: Toy Soldiers (1983)

Deane, Lezlie: To Protect and Serve

DeAngelo, Paul: Sleepaway Camp

Deas, Justin: Dream Lover (1986); Montana (1990)

De Baer, Jean: Tidy Endings

de Banzie, Brenda: Doctor at Sea; Entertainer, The; Hobson's Choice (1954); Thirty-Nine Steps, The (1959)

De Bark, Yvonne: Sons of Trinity, The

De Bartolli, Moreno: When Father Was Away on Business

Debby Boone: Hollywood Safari

DeBell, Kristine: Big Brawl, The

DeBello, James: Detroit Rock City

DeBenning, Burr: Incredible Melting Man, The

de Beranger, Andre: Fig Leaves

De Boeck, Antje: Daens

De Boer, Nikki: Cube; Prom Night IV—Deliver Us from Evil

De Borg, Beatrice: Dangerous Prey

de Bruiler, Nigel: Iron Mask, The; Three Musketeers, The (1935); Zorro Rides Again

Debucourt, Jean: La Chute de la Maison Usher; Monsieur Vincent

De Cadanet, Amanda: Fall

DeCamp, Rosemary: Big Hangover, The; By the Light of the Silvery Moon; Look For The Silver Lining; Main Street to Broadway; On Moonlight Bay; Saturday the 14th; Story of Seabiscuit, The; Strategic Air Command; 13 Ghosts; Yankee Doodle Dandy

DeCarlo, Mark: Angel 4: Undercover

De Carlo, Yvonne: American Gothic; Arizona Bushwhackers; Band of Angels; Cabash; Captain's Paradise, The; Cellar Dweller; Criss Cross (1948); Death of a Scoundrel; Global Affair, A; Good Idea; Hostile Guns; Liar's Moon; McLintock!; Mirror Mirror; Munsters' Revenge, The; Nocturna; Oscar (1991); Passion (1954); Road to Morocco; Salome, Where She Danced; Satan's Cheerleaders; Seven Minutes, The; Shotgun; Silent Scream; Vultures

Deckert, Blue: Taste for Killing, A

Decleir, Jan: Antonia's Line; Character (Karakter)

DeCleir, Jan: Daens

Declie, Xavier: Nemesis 3: Time Lapse

De Coff, Linda: Hurry Up or I'll Be 30

Decombie, Guy: Jour de Fête

De Cordoba, Pedro: Before I Hang; Law of the Pampas; Mexican Hayride

De Cordova, Arturo: El (This Strange Passion); For Whom the Bell Tolls

de Corsia, Ted: Buccaneer, The; Enforcer, The (1951); It Happens Every Spring; Lady from Shanghai; Mohawk; Naked City, The; Neptune's Daughter; Three Secrets

Dee, Catherine: Stuff Stephanie in the Incinerator

Dee, Frances: Becky Sharp; Blood Money; Finishing School; Four Faces West; Gypsy Colt; I Walked with a Zombie; If I Had a Million; If I Were King; Little Women (1933); Of Human Bondage (1934); Private Affairs of Bel Ami, The; So Ends Our Night; Wheel of Fortune

Dee, Ruby: All God's Children; Baby Geniuses; Buck and the Preacher; Cat People (1982); Cop and a Half; Courtmartial of Jackie Robinson, The; Decoration Day; Do the Right Thing; Ernest Green Story, The; Gore Vidal's Lincoln; I Know Why the Caged Bird Sings; Incident, The (1967); It's Good to Be Alive; Jackie Robinson Story, The; Jungle Fever; Just Cause; Mr. and Mrs. Loving; Passing Glory; Purlie Victorious; Raisin in the Sun, A (1961); Simple Wish, A; Stand, The; Wall, The (1998) (U.S.); Windmills of the Gods

Dee, Sandra: Come September; Dunwich Horror, The; Fantasy Island; Gidget; Imitation of Life; Reluctant Debutante, The; Summer Place, A; Tammy and the Doctor; Until They Sail

Deee-Lite: Wigstock: The Movie

Deely, Ben: Victory (1919)

Deering, Olive: Danger

Dees, Kevin: Jet Benny Show, The

Deezen, Eddie: Beverly Hills Vamp; Desperate Moves; Hollywood Boulevard II; I Wanna Hold Your Hand; Midnight Madness; Million Dollar Mystery; Mob Boss; Mugsy's Girls; Polish Vampire in Burbank, A; Rosebud Beach Hotel, The (Nostell Hotel, The); Surf 2; Teenage Exorcist; Whoopee Boys, The

DeFazio, Patrick: Rumble in the Streets

De Filippi, Carlo: Who Killed Pasolini?

De Filippo, Peppino: Variety Lights

DeFoe, Diane: Deceit

DeFore, Don: Adventures of Ozzie and Harriet, The (TV Series); Battle Hymn; Facts of Life; Girl in Every Port, A (1952); Hazel Christmas Show, The (TV Series); Jumping Jacks; My Friend Irma; Romance on the High Seas; Time to Love and a Time to Die, A; Without Reservations

de Funes, Louis: Candide; Delusions of Grandeur; Four Bags Full; La Grande Vadrouille

DeGeneres, Ellen: Dr. Dolittle (1998); EDtv; Goodbye Lover; Love Letter, The (1999); Mr. Wrong

Degermark, Pia: Elvira Madigan; Looking Glass War, The

de Graaf, Marina: Antonia's Line

de Grasse, Sam: Blind Husbands; Wild and Woolly

DeGruccio, Nick: Josh Kirby ... Time Warrior: Journey to the Magic Cavern

Deguy, Marie-Armelle: Elegant Criminal, The

De Haven, Gloria: Best Foot Forward; Bog; Broadway Rhythm; Out to Sea; Summer Holiday; Summer Stock; Susan and God; Thin Man Goes Home, The; Three Little Words; Two Girls and a Sailor; Two Tickets to Broadway; Who Is the Black Dahlia?; Yellow Cab Man, The

DeHaven, Lisa: Redneck Zombies

de Havilland, Olivia: Adventures of Robin Hood, The; Ambassador's Daughter, The; Anastasia: The Mystery of Anna; Anthony Adverse; Captain Blood; Charge of the Light Brigade, The (1936); Dark Mirror, The; Dodge City; Fifth Musketeer, The; Gone with the Wind; Heiress, The; Hollywood Canteen; Hush ... Hush, Sweet Charlotte; In This Our Life; Lady in a Cage; Midsummer Night's Dream, A (1935); Not as a Stranger; Private Lives of Elizabeth and Essex, The; Proud Rebel, The; Roots: The Next Generation; Santa Fe Trail; Snake Pit, The; Strawberry Blonde, The; Swarm, The; Thank Your Lucky Stars; They Died with Their Boots On

Dehner, John: Apache; California Gold Rush; Creator; Dynamite Pass; Girl in Black Stockings, The; Golden Earrings;

out; Stand by Me (1986); Tin Men; Trigger Happy (Mad Dog Time); What About Bob?; Whose Life Is It, Anyway?

Driggs, Deborah: Night Rhythms

Drillinger, Brian: Brighton Beach Memoirs

Drinkwater, Carol: Father (1990)

Driscoll, Bobby: Fighting Sullivans, The (Sullivans, The); So Dear to My Heart; Treasure Island (1950); Window, The

Driscoll, Mark: Concealed Weapon

Driscoll, Martha: Li'l Abner (1940)

Driscoll, Robin: Mr. Bean

Drivas, Robert: Cool Hand Luke; Illustrated Man, The

Driver, Minnie: Big Night; Circle of Friends; Good Will Hunting; Governess, The; Grosse Pointe Blank; Hard Rain; Return to Me; Sleepers

Dru, Joanne: All the King's Men; Hell on Frisco Bay; Light in the Forest, The; Pride of St. Louis, The; Red River; Sincerely Yours; Super Fuzz; Thunder Bay; Vengeance Valley; Wagonmaster; Warriors, The (1955)

Drummond, Alice: Daybreak (1993)

Druou, Claire: Le Bonheur

Druou, Jean-Claude: Le Bonheur; Light at the End of the World, The

Drury, James: Elfego Baca: Six Gun Law; Gambler Returns, The: The Luck of the Draw; Meanest Men in the West, The; Ride the High Country; Ten Who Dared; Toby Tyler

Dryden, Darren: Lie Down with Dogs

Dryden, Mack: Million Dollar Mystery

Drye, Jenny: Man Bites Dog

Dryer, Fred: Death Before Dishonor

Dryer, Robert: Savage Streets

Dryhurst, Nia: Hedd Wyn

Drynan, Jeanie: Muriel's Wedding

Duane, Michael: City Without Men

Duarte, Regina: Happily Ever After

Dubarry, Denise: Monster in the Closet

Dubbins, Don: D.I., The; Enchanted Island; Fix, The; From the Earth to the Moon; Prize, The; Tribute to a Bad Man

Dubin, Ellen: Tammy & the T-Rex

Dubois, Marie: Les Grandes Gueules (Jailbirds' Vacation); Shoot the Piano Player; Vincent, François, Paul and the Others

DuBois, Marta: Blackout (1995); Boulevard Nights

Dubost, Paulette: May Fools; Viva Maria!

Dubov, Paul: Ma Barker's Killer Brood

Ducasse, Cecile: Chocolat

Ducati, Kristi: Bikini Carwash Company 2

Ducaux, Annie: Abel Gance's Beethoven

Duce, Sharon: Buddy's Song

Ducey, Caroline: Romance (1999)

Duchamp, Marcel: Avant Garde Program #2

Duchaussoy, Michel: May Fools; Road to Ruin (1991); This Man Must Die

Duchesne, Roger: Bob le Flambeur

Duchovny, David: Beethoven; Julia Has Two Lovers; California; Playing God; Red Shoe Diaries; Red Shoe Diaries II: Double Dare; Red Shoe Diaries 4: Auto Erotica; Red Shoe Diaries 5: Weekend Pass; Return to Me; Ruby (1991); Venice/Venice; X-Files, The (1998); X-Files, The (TV Series)

Ducommun, Rick: Blank Check; 'Burbs, The

Ducreux, Louis: Sunday in the Country, A

Dudgeon, Neil: Different for Girls

Dudikoff, Michael: American Ninja; American Ninja II; American Ninja IV: The Annihilation; Avenging Force; Bounty Hunters; Chain of Command; Crash Dive; Human Shield, The; Midnight Ride; Moving Target (1996); Platoon Leader; Radioactive Dreams; Rescue Me; Ringmaster; River of Death; Soldier Boyz; Strategic Command; Virtual Assassin

Dudley, Doris: Moon and Sixpence, The

Duel, Peter: Generation

Duering, Carl: Arabesque

Duez, Sophie: Eye of the Wolf

Duff, Amanda: Devil Commands, The; Mr. Moto in Danger Island

Duff, Debbie: Helter-Skelter Murders, The

Duff, Denice: Bloodfist V: Human Target; Bloodlust: Subspecies III; Bloodstone: Subspecies II; Return to Frogtown

Duff, Howard: All My Sons (1948); Battered; Boys' Night Out; Brute Force; Deadly Companion; East of Eden (1982); Kramer vs. Kramer; Late Show, The; Naked City, The; No

Way Out; Oh, God! Book II; Private Hell 36; Snatched; Too Much Sun; Wedding, A (1978); While the City Sleeps

Duffey, Todd: Civil War Diary

Duffring, Anton: Shatter

Duffy, Dee: Hellcats, The

Duffy, J. S.: Small Faces

Duffy, Jack: Madame Behave

Duffy, Karen: Blank Check; Dumb and Dumber; Synapse; 24-Hour Woman

Duffy, Patrick: Alice Through the Looking Glass (1985); Danielle Steel's Daddy; Enola Gay: The Men, the Mission, the Atomic Bomb; Last of Mrs. Lincoln, The; Man from Atlantis, The; Texas (1994); Vamping

Dufilho, Jacques: Black and White in Color; Horse of Pride, The

Dufour, Val: Undead, The

Du Fresne, Georges: Ma Vie En Rose

Dugan, Dennis: Can't Buy Me Love; Howling, The; New Adventures of Pippi Longstocking, The; Norman ... Is That You?; Unidentified Flying Oddball

Duggan, Andrew: Firehouse (1972); Frankenstein Island; Housewife; In Like Flint; Incredible Journey of Dr. Meg Laurel, The; Incredible Mr. Limpet, The; It Lives Again; It's Alive!; Palm Springs Weekend; Return to Salem's Lot, A; Secret War of Harry Frigg, The; Skin Game; Wagon Train (TV Series)

Duggan, Tom: Frankenstein 1970

Dujmovic, Davor: Time of the Gypsies

Dukakis, John: Delusion (1980)

Dukakis, Olympia: Cemetery Club, The; Dad; Dead Badge; Digger; I Love Trouble; In the Spirit; Jane Austen's Mafia!; Jeffrey; Jerusalem; Look Who's Talking; Look Who's Talking Too; Mighty Aphrodite; Mr. Holland's Opus; Moonstruck; Mother (1994); Over the Hill; Pentagon Wars, The; Picture Perfect; Steel Magnolias; Walls of Glass

Duke, Bill: Action Jackson; Always Outnumbered; Bird on a Wire; Limey, The; Menace II Society; No Man's Land; Predator

Duke, Patty: Amityville 4: The Evil Escapes; Babysitter, The (1980); Best Kept Secrets; Billie; By Design; Curse of the Black Widow; Daydreamer, The (1966); Family Upside Down, A; 4D Man; George Washington; George Washington: The Forging of a Nation; Grave Secrets: The Legacy of Hilltop Drive; Harvest of Fire; Miracle Worker, The (1962); Miracle Worker, The (1979); My Sweet Charlie; Prelude to a Kiss; September Gun; She Waits; Something Special; Valley of the Dolls

Duke, Robin: Blue Monkey; Hostage for a Day

Dukes, David: Cat on a Hot Tin Roof (1985); Catch the Heat; Date with an Angel; First Deadly Sin, The; Fled; George Washington; Josephine Baker Story, The; Little Romance, A; Love Letter, The (1998); Me and the Kid; Men's Club, The; Norma Jean and Marilyn; Rawhead Rex; Rutanga Tapes, The; See You in the Morning; Snow Kill; Strange Interlude (1988); Supreme Sanction; Wild Party, The (1975); Without a Trace

Dulany, Caitlin: Class of 1999 II: The Substitute; Maniac Cop 3: Badge of Silence

Dullea, Keir: Black Christmas; Blind Date (1984); Brainwaves; David and Lisa; Haunting of Julia, The; Hoodlum Priest, The; Leopard in the Snow; Next One, The; Oh, What a Night; 2001: A Space Odyssey; 2010

Du Maurier, Gerald: Catherine the Great

Dumbrille, Douglass: Abbott and Costello in the Foreign Legion; Baby Face; Big Store, The; Broadway Bill; Buccaneer, The; Castle in the Desert; Dragnet (1947); False Colors; Female; Firefly, The; Gypsy Wildcat; It's a Joke, Son!; Lady Killer; Lost in a Harem; Mr. Deeds Goes to Town; Naughty Marietta; Operator 13; Princess Comes Across, The; Ride 'em Cowboy; Road to Utopia; Road to Zanzibar; Son of Paleface; Virginia City

DuMond, Hayley: Hunter's Moon

Dumont, Margaret: Animal Crackers; At the Circus; Bathing Beauty; Big Store, The; Cocoanuts; Day at the Races, A; Duck Soup; Horn Blows at Midnight, The; Night at the Opera, A; Three for Bedroom C

Dun, Dennis: Big Trouble in Little China; Last Emperor, The; Prince of Darkness; Thousand Pieces of Gold

Dunarie, Malcolm: Heaven Help Us

Dunaway, Faye: Albino Alligator; Arizona Dreams; Arrangement, The; Barfly; Beverly Hills Madam; Bonnie and

Not to Be (1983); Tootsie; Tough Guys; True Confessions; Twilight's Last Gleaming; Two of a Kind (1983); V. I. Warshawski; Water Engine, The; When a Stranger Calls; When a Stranger Calls Back; Where the River Runs Black; Woman of Independent Means, A

Durock, Dick: Return of the Swamp Thing

Durr, Jason: Killer Tongue

Durrell, Alexandra: Unnamable, The

Durrell, Lawrence: Henry Miller Odyssey

Durrell, Michael: V

Dury, Ian: Different for Girls

Duryea, Dan: Along Came Jones; Bamboo Saucer (Collision Course); Battle Hymn; Criss Cross (1948); Five Golden Dragons; Flight of the Phoenix, The; Great Flamarion, The; Gundown at Sandoval; Lady on a Train; Little Foxes, The; Mrs. Parkington; None But the Lonely Heart; Platinum High School; Pride of the Yankees, The; Sahara (1943); Scarlet Street; Thunder Bay; Underworld Story; Winchester '73; Woman in the Window

Dusenberry, Ann: Cutter's Way; Desperate Women; Heart Beat; Lies; Possessed, The (1977)

Dushku, Eliza: Journey; Race the Sun; That Night

Dusic, Joe: Bikini Carwash Company, The

Dussault, Nancy: Nurse, The

Dussolier, André: And Now, My Love; Le Beau Mariage; Melo; Three Men and a Cradle; Un Coeur en Hiver

Dutch, Deborah: Sorority Girls and the Creature from Hell

Dutcher, Richard: God's Army

Dutronc, Jacques: Les Tricheurs; L'Etat Sauvage (The Savage State); Van Gogh

Dutt, Utpal: Stranger, The (1992)

Dutton, Charles: Alien 3; Black Dog; Blind Faith; Cookie's Fortune; "Crocodile" Dundee II; Deadlocked; Distinguished Gentleman, The; Foreign Student; Get on the Bus; Low Down Dirty Shame, A; Menace II Society; Mimic; Mississippi Masala; Nick of Time; Piano Lesson, The; Random Hearts; Rudy; Surviving the Game; Time to Kill, A (1996); True Women; Zooman

Dutton, Simon: Lion and the Hawk, The

Dutton, Tim: Tom & Viv

Duval, James: Clown at Midnight, The; Doom Generation, The; Nowhere

DuVall, Clea: Faculty, The; Girl, Interrupted

Duvall, Robert: Apocalypse Now; Apostle, The; Badge 373; Betsy, The; Breakout (1975); Chase, The (1966); Civil Action, A; Colors; Countdown; Days of Thunder; Deep Impact; Detective, The (1968); Eagle Has Landed, The; Falling Down; Family Thing, A; Geronimo: An American Legend (1994); Gingerbread Man, The; Godfather, The; Godfather, Part II, The; Godfather Epic, The; Gone in 60 Seconds; Great Northfield Minnesota Raid, The; Great Santini, The; Greatest, The; Handmaid's Tale, The; Hotel Colonial; Ike: The War Years; Joe Kidd; Killer Elite, The; Lady Ice; Lawman; Let's Get Harry; Lightship, The; Lonesome Dove; Man Who Captured Eichmann, The; M*A*S*H; Natural, The; Network; Newsies; Outer Limits, The (TV Series); Paper, The; Phenomenon; Plague, The; Pursuit of D. B. Cooper; Rain People, The; Rambling Rose; Scarlet Letter, The (1995); Seven-Per-Cent Solution, The; Show of Force, A; Something to Talk About; Stalin; Stars Fell on Henrietta, The; Stone Boy, The; Tender Mercies; Terry Fox Story, The; THX 1138; Tomorrow; True Confessions; True Grit; Wrestling Ernest Hemingway

Duvall, Shelley: Annie Hall; Bernice Bobs Her Hair; Changing Habits; Frankenweenie; Home Fries; McCabe and Mrs. Miller; Popeye; Portrait of a Lady, The; Roxanne; Russell Mulcahy's Tale of the Mummy; Shining, The; Suburban Commando; Thieves Like Us; Time Bandits

Dux, Pierre: La Vie Continue

Dvorak, Ann: Abilene Town; Case of the Stuttering Bishop, The; Flame of the Barbary Coast; Life of Her Own, A; Manhattan Merry-Go-Round; Out of the Blue; Private Affairs of Bel Ami, The; Return of Jesse James, The; Scarface (1932); Strange Love of Molly Louvain, The; Three on a Match

Dwire, Earl: Arizona Days; Assassin of Youth (Marijuana); Lawless Frontier; Man from Music Mountain; Mystery of the Hooded Horsemen; New Frontier; Randy Rides Alone; Riders of Destiny; Trouble in Texas; West of the Divide

Dwyer, Hilary: Conqueror Worm, The

Dwyer, Karyn: Better Than Chocolate

Dwyer, Ruth: Seven Chances

Dyall, Franklyn: Easy Virtue

Dyall, Valentine: Body in the Library, The

Dye, Cameron: Apocalypse, The; Body Rock; Fraternity Vacation; Heated Vengeance; Joy of Sex, The; Out of the Dark; Scenes from the Goldmine; Stranded

Dye, Dale: Cover Story; Operation Delta Force 2; Relentless II: Dead On

Dye, John: Campus Man

Dyer, Danny: Human Traffic

Dyktynski, Matthew: Love and Other Catastrophes

Dylan, Bob: Backtrack; Don't Look Back (1967); Hearts of Fire; Last Waltz, The; Pat Garrett and Billy the Kid

Dylan, Justin: Unexpected Encounters

Dyneley, Peter: Manster, The; Romeo and Juliet (1988)

Dysart, Richard: Autobiography of Miss Jane Pittman, The; Back to the Future III; Bitter Harvest (1981); Day One; Falcon and the Snowman, The; L.A. Law; Last Days of Patton, The; Marilyn & Bobby: Her Final Affair; Ordeal of Dr. Mudd, The; Pale Rider; People vs. Jean Harris; Prophecy (1979); Riding with Death; Rumor Mill, The; Sporting Club, The; Thing, The (1982); Truman; Warning Sign

Dytri, Mike: Living End, The

Dzandzanovic, Edin: Beautiful People

Dzhylkychiev, Bakit: Beshkempir, The Adopted Son

Dzundza, George: Act of Passion; Basic Instinct; Beast, The (1988); Best Defense; Brotherly Love; Butcher's Wife, The; Crimson Tide; Dangerous Minds; Enemy Within, The; Glory Years; Impulse (1990); Instinct; Limbic Region, The; No Mercy; Trading Favors; White Hunter Black Heart

Eadie, Nicholas: Return to Snowy River, Part II

Eagan, Daisy: Ripe

Eagle, Jeff: Slammer Girls

Earl, Elizabeth: Fairy Tale: A True Story

Earle, Edward: Twelve Miles Out

Earles, Harry: Unholy Three

Easley, Richert: Outrageous

East Side Kids, The: Ghosts on the Loose; Spooks Run Wild

East, Jeff: Deadly Blessing; Huckleberry Finn (1974); Mary and Joseph: A Story of Faith; Pumpkinhead; Summer of Fear; Tom Sawyer (1973)

Easterbrook, Leslie: Police Academy III: Back in Training; Police Academy 5: Assignment: Miami Beach

Eastin, Steve: Last Man Standing (1994)

Eastland, Todd: Pledge Night

Eastman, George: Blastfighter; Detective School Dropouts; Hands of Steel; Warriors of the Wasteland

Easton, Michael: Coldfire

Easton, Robert: Comin' Round the Mountain

Easton, Rodney: Deadly Weapon

Easton, Sheena: John Carpenter Presents: Body Bags; Tekwar: The Original Movie

Eastwick, Robert: Strike a Pose

Eastwood, Alison: Black & White; Midnight in the Garden of Good and Evil; Tightrope

Eastwood, Clint: Absolute Power; Any Which Way You Can; Beguiled, The; Bridges of Madison County, The; Bronco Billy; City Heat; Coogan's Bluff; Dead Pool, The; Dirty Harry; Eiger Sanction, The; Enforcer, The (1976); Escape from Alcatraz; Every Which Way But Loose; Firefox; Fistful of Dollars, A; For a Few Dollars More; Francis in the Navy; Gauntlet, The; Good the Bad and the Ugly, The; Hang 'em High; Heartbreak Ridge; High Plains Drifter; Honkytonk Man; In the Line of Fire; Joe Kidd; Kelly's Heroes; Magnum Force; Maverick (TV Series); Outlaw Josey Wales, The; Paint Your Wagon; Pale Rider; Perfect World, A; Pink Cadillac; Play Misty for Me; Rawhide (TV Series); Revenge of the Creature; Rookie, The; Sudden Impact; Tarantula; Thunderbolt and Lightfoot; Tightrope; True Crime (1999); Two Mules for Sister Sara; Unforgiven (1992); Where Eagles Dare; White Hunter Black Heart

Eastwood, Jayne: Hostile Take Over

Eastwood, Kyle: Honkytonk Man

Eaton, Mary: Glorifying the American Girl

Eaton, Shirley: Against All Odds (1968) (Kiss and Kill, Blood of Fu Manchu); Around the World Under the Sea; Doctor at Large; Girl Hunters, The; Naked Truth (Your Past Is Showing); Ten Little Indians (1966); Three Men in a Boat

Eaves, John: Fire and Ice (1987)

Eberhardt, Norma: Return of Dracula

Eberly, Bob: I Dood It

Eisenberg, Aron: Playroom

Eisenberg, Avner: Jewel of the Nile, The

Eisenberg, Hallie Kate: Bicentennial Man

Eisenberg, Ned: Hiding Out; Path to Paradise

Eisenmann, Ike: Escape to Witch Mountain; Return from Witch Mountain; Terror Out of the Sky

Eisenstadt, Debra: Oleanna

Eisermann, Andre: Brother of Sleep

Eisley, Anthony: Deep Space; Journey to the Center of Time (Time Warp); Mummy and the Curse of the Jackals, The; Naked Kiss, The; Navy vs. the Night Monsters, The; Wasp Woman (1960)

Eisner, David: To Catch a Killer

Ejdus, Predrag: Vukovar

Ejogo, Carmen: Metro

Ek, Anders: Sawdust and Tinsel

Ekberg, Anita: Abbott and Costello Go to Mars; Alphabet Murders, The; Artists and Models; Back from Eternity; Boccaccio 70; Call Me Bwana; Cobra, The (1967); Four for Texas; Hollywood or Bust; La Dolce Vita; Northeast of Seoul; Paris Holiday; Red Dwarf, The; Screaming Mimi; S.H.E.; Woman Times Seven

Ekland, Britt: After the Fox; Baxter (1973); Beverly Hills Vamp; Bobo, The; Cold Heat; Endless Night; Get Carter; Great Wallendas, The; High Velocity; King Solomon's Treasure; Man with the Golden Gun, The; Monster Club, The; Moon in Scorpio; Night They Raided Minsky's, The; Slavers; Stiletto; Wicker Man, The

Eklund, Bengt: Port of Call

Ekman, Gosta: Adventures of Picasso, The; Faust; Inside Man, The; Intermezzo (1936)

El Sawy, Khaled: Legend of the Lost Tomb

Elam, Jack: Apple Dumpling Gang Rides Again, The; Appointment in Honduras; Aurora Encounter; Big Bad John; Cattle Queen of Montana; Creature from Black Lake; Dynamite and Gold; Firecreek; Grayeagle; Hannie Caulder; Hawmps!; Hot Lead and Cold Feet; Huckleberry Finn (1975); Jubilee Trail; Kansas City Confidential; Man from Laramie, The; Man without a Star; Night of the Grizzly, The; Once Upon a Time in the West; Pocketful of Miracles; Pony Express Rider; Rancho Notorious; Rare Breed, The (1966); Rawhide (1951); Rio Lobo; Sacketts, The; Sacred Ground; Suburban Commando; Sundowners, The (1950); Support Your Local Gunfighter; Support Your Local Sheriff!; Uninvited, The (1993)

Elarton, Robert: Speak of the Devil

Elcar, Dana: Blue Skies Again; Fool Killer, The; Great Northfield Minnesota Raid, The; Inside Out (1986); Jungle Warriors; Learning Tree, The; Nude Bomb, The (Return of Maxwell Smart, The); Quarterback Princess; St. Ives; Shaming, The; Sting, The

Eldard, Ron: Bastard Out of Carolina; Drop Dead Fred; Last Supper, The (1996); Mystery, Alaska; Sex and the Other Man; Sleepers; True Love; When Trumpets Fade

Eldbert, Jim: Warbirds

Eldor, Gabi: Boy Takes Girl

Eldredge, John: Dangerous (1935); Flirtation Walk; Song of Nevada

Eldridge, Florence: Divorcee, The; Les Miserables (1935)

Electra, Carmen: Mating Habits of the Earthbound Human, The

Eleniak, Erika: Beverly Hillbillies, The (1993); Chasers; Girl in the Cadillac; Pandora Project, The; Pyromaniac's Love Story, A; Tales from the Crypt Presents Bordello of Blood; Under Siege

Eles, Sandor: And Soon the Darkness

Elfman, Jenna: Can't Hardly Wait; EDtv; Keeping the Faith; Krippendorf's Tribe

Elfman, Marie-Pascale: Forbidden Zone

Elg, Taina: Diane; Great Wallendas, The; Les Girls; Prodigal, The; Thirty-Nine Steps, The (1959)

Elhers, Jerome: Fatal Bond

Elian, Yona: Last Winter, The

Elias, Alix: Citizen's Band; Munchies

Eliasdottir, Soley: Remote Control (1992)

Elise, Christine: Body Snatchers, The (1993); Boiling Point (1993); Child's Play 2; Escape from Mars

Elise, Kimberly: Beloved; Set It Off

Elizabeth, Monet: Island Fury

Elizondo, Hector: American Gigolo; Backstreet Justice; Being Human; Beverly Hills Cop 3; Born to Win; Chains of

Gold; Cuba; Dain Curse, The; Dear God; Entropy; Exit to Eden; Final Approach; Flamingo Kid, The; Forgotten Prisoners; Frankie and Johnny (1991); Getting Even with Dad; Honeyboy; Leviathan; Necessary Roughness; Nothing in Common; Out of the Darkness; Perfect Alibi; Power, Passion, and Murder; Private Resort; Report to the Commissioner; Runaway Bride; Safe House; Samantha; There Goes the Neighborhood; Turbulence; Valdez Is Coming; Young Doctors in Love

Elkin, Karen: Great Land of Small, The

Elkins, Kerine: Sore Losers

Elle, Daniella: Facade

Ellerbe, Harry: Magnetic Monster, The

Ellers, Sally: Doughboys

Elliman, Yvonne: Jesus Christ, Superstar

Ellington, Duke: Belle of the Nineties; Murder at the Vanities

Ellington, Harry: Saint of Fort Washington, The

Elliot, Alison: Wings of the Dove, The

Elliot, Jane: Change of Habit

Elliot, John: Heart of Arizona

Elliot, Laura: Two Lost Worlds

Elliot, Shawn: Crossover Dreams

Elliot, Tim: Utu

Elliot, William: San Antonio Kid

Elliott, Alison: Buccaneers, The; Eternal, The; Monkey Trouble; Spitfire Grill, The; Underneath, The

Elliott, Chris: Cabin Boy; CB4; Groundhog Day; Kingpin; Snow Day; There's Something About Mary

Elliott, David James: Holiday Affair (1996)

Elliott, Denholm: Apprenticeship of Duddy Kravitz, The; Bleak House; Bourne Identity, The; Brimstone and Treacle; Child's Christmas in Wales, A; Codename: Kyril; Cuba; Deep Cover (1980); Defense of the Realm; Doll's House, A (1989); Hound of the Baskervilles, The (1977); Hound of the Baskervilles, The (1983); House That Dripped Blood, The; Indiana Jones and the Last Crusade; Madame Sin; Maurice; Missionary, The; Noises Off; Overindulgence; Private Function, A; Raiders of the Lost Ark; Robin and Marian; Room with a View, A; Rude Awakening (1982); Russian Roulette; Saint Jack; Scorchers; September; Stealing Heaven; Strange Case of Dr. Jekyll and Mr. Hyde, The (1968); To the Devil, a Daughter; Toy Soldiers (1991); Trading Places; Transmutations; Vault of Horror; Whoopee Boys, The; Wicked Lady, The (1983)

Elliott, Patricia: Natural Enemies

Elliott, Peter: Missing Link

Elliott, Peter Anthony: Pre-Madonnas (Social Suicide)

Elliott, Ross: Dynamite Pass; Hot Lead; Indestructible Man

Elliott, Sam: Blue Knight, The (1973); Blue Lighting, The; Blue River; Buffalo Girls; Conagher; Desperate Trail; Fatal Beauty; Final Cut, The; Frogs; Gettysburg; Gone to Texas; Hi-Lo Country, The; I Will Fight No More Forever; Legacy, The; Lifeguard; Mask (1985); Murder in Texas; Prancer; Quick and the Dead, The (1987); Road House (1989); Rough Riders; Rush; Sacketts, The; Shadow Riders, The; Sibling Rivalry; Tombstone; Wild Times; Woman Undone; You Know My Name

Elliott, Shawn: Hurricane Streets

Elliott, Stephen: Arthur; Arthur 2: On the Rocks; Assassination; Golden Honeymoon, The; Prototype; Roadhouse 66

Elliott, William: Bells of Rosarita; Calling Wild Bill Elliott; Death Valley Manhunt; Fabulous Texan, The; Hellfire; Hidden Valley Outlaws; In Early Arizona; Longhorn; Mojave Firebrand; Phantom of the Plains; Sheriff of Las Vegas; Showdown, The (1950); Wagon Wheels Westward

Ellis, Aunjanue: Girls Town (1996)

Ellis, Diane: High Voltage (1929)

Ellis, Edward: Fury (1936); Return of Peter Grimm, The

Ellis, Jack: Prime Suspect 2

Ellis, James: Leapin' Leprechauns; No Surrender

Ellis, Patricia: Block-Heads; Case of the Lucky Legs, The; Postal Inspector

Ellis, Paul R.: In the Name of Justice

Ellis, Robin: Curse of King Tut's Tomb, The; Elizabeth R; Europeans, The

Ellison, Gwen: Luggage of the Gods

Ellison, James: Bar-20 Rides Again; Borderland; Call of the Prairie; Eagle's Brood; Fifth Avenue Girl; Gang's All Here, The; I Walked with a Zombie; Next Time I Marry; Three on

pent's Lair; Sketch Artist; Sketch Artist II: Hands That See; Split Decisions; Sweeper, The; Temptation; Time Served; Trueblood; Virtual Seduction; White Hunter Black Heart; Woman of Desire; Wrangler; Wyatt Earp

Fahey, Mary: Mutant Hunt

Fahey, Myrna: Fall of the House of Usher, The (1960)

Fai, Leung Ka: Prison on Fire

Fails, J. W.: No Retreat, No Surrender

Fair, Jody: Brain Eaters, The

Fairbairn, Bruce: Nightstick

Fairbanks Jr., Douglas: Angels over Broadway; Catherine the Great; Corsican Brothers, The (1941); Ghost Story; Gunga Din; Having a Wonderful Time; Hostage Tower, The; Joy of Living; Little Caesar; Morning Glory (1933); Our Modern Maidens; Prisoner of Zenda, The (1937); Rage of Paris, The; Scarlet Dawn; Sinbad the Sailor; Woman of Affairs, A; Young in Heart, The

Fairbanks Sr., Douglas: American Aristocracy, An; Black Pirate, The; Days of Thrills and Laughter; Don Q, Son of Zorro; Down to Earth; Great Chase, The; His Picture in the Papers; Iron Mask, The; Man from Painted Post, The; Mark of Zorro, The (1920); Mr. Robinson Crusoe; Nut, The; Private Life of Don Juan, The; Reaching for the Moon (1917); Reaching for the Moon (1931); Robin Hood (1923); Taming of the Shrew, The (1929); Thief of Bagdad, The (1924); Three Musketeers, The (1921); When the Clouds Roll By; Wild and Woolly

Fairbrass, Bruce: Killing Time (1996)

Fairbrass, Craig: Galaxis; Nightscare; Proteus

Fairchild, Margaret: For Love of Angela

Fairchild, Morgan: Based on an Untrue Story; Bimbo Movie Bash; Campus Man; Criminal Hearts; Haunting of Sarah Hardy, The; Honeyboy; Mob Boss; Phantom of the Mall—Eric's Revenge; Red-Headed Stranger, The; Sherlock Holmes and the Leading Lady; Venus Rising; Zany Adventures of Robin Hood, The

Faire, Virginia Brown: Peter Pan (1924); West of the Divide

Fairman, Michael: Glory Years

Faison, Donald: Supreme Sanction; Trippin'

Faison, Frankie: Exterminator 2, The; Roommates; Spider and the Fly, The; Thomas Crown Affair, The (1999)

Faith, Adam: Beat Girl; McVicar; Yesterday's Hero

Faith, Dolores: Mutiny in Outer Space

Faithfull, Marianne: Assault on Agathon; Hamlet (1969); Moondance; Rock and Roll Circus, The; Shopping; Turn of the Screw (1992)

Fajardo, Eduardo: Adios, Hombre; Gentleman Killer; Long Live Your Death; Oasis of the Zombies; Sonny and Jed; Yellow Hair and the Fortress of Gold

Falana, Lola: Klansman, The; Liberation of L. B. Jones, The; Man Called Adam, A

Falcao, Luzia: Luzia

Falco, Edie: Hurricane Streets; Judy Berlin; Laws of Gravity; Trouble on the Corner

Falcon, Jeffrey: Six-String Samurai

Falconetti, Maria: Passion of Joan of Arc, The

Faldaas, Morten: Heart of Darkness

Falk, Peter: All the Marbles; Anzio; Balcony, The; Big Trouble; Brinks Job, The; Cheap Detective, The; Columbo: Murder by the Book; Cookie; Faraway, So Close; Great Muppet Caper, The; Great Race, The; Griffin and Phoenix: A Love Story; Happy New Year (1987); In-Laws, The; In the Spirit; It's a Mad Mad Mad Mad World; Luv; Mikey and Nicky; Money Kings; Murder by Death; Pocketful of Miracles; Pressure Point; Princess Bride, The; Pronto; Robin & the Seven Hoods; Roommates; Tune in Tomorrow; Vibes; Wings of Desire; Woman Under the Influence, A

Fallender, Deborah: Jabberwocky

Fan, Jing-Ma: Madame Butterfly

Fanaro, Mary: Truth or Dare? A Critical Madness

Fancher, Hampton: Rome Adventure

Fancy, Richard: Nick Knight

Fanfan, Li: Not One Less

Fantoni, Sergio: Prize, The

Faracy, Stephanie: Great Outdoors, The

Faraldo, Daniel: Above the Law; Trenchcoat

Farber, Arlene: All the Kind Strangers

Farentino, Debrah: Capone; Dead Air; Mortal Sins (1990) (Dangerous Obsession); Storm of the Century

Farentino, James: Bulletproof (1996); Cop for the Killing, A; Cradle Will Fall, The; Dead and Buried; Honor Thy Father & Mother: The Menendez Killings; Possessed, The (1977); Scandalous Me: The Jacqueline Susann Story; Silent Victory: The Kitty O'Neil Story; Summer to Remember, A; War Lord, The

Fargas, Antonio: Ambush Murders, The; Borrower, The; Florida Straits; Howling VI: The Freaks; Huckleberry Finn (1975); I'm Gonna Git You Sucka!; Milo; Night of the Sharks; Pretty Baby; Putney Swope; Streetwalkin'; Whore

Faria, Betty: Bye Bye Brazil; Story of Fausta

Faridany, Franchesca: Conceiving Ada

Farina, Carolyn: Age of Innocence, The; Metropolitan

Farina, Dennis: Another Stakeout; Bella Mafia; Birthday Boy, The; Code of Silence; Eddie; Get Shorty; Hillside Stranglers, The; Manhunter; Men of Respect; Midnight Run; Mod Squad, The; Out of Annie's Past; Out of Sight; Reindeer Games; Romeo Is Bleeding; Street Crimes; Striking Distance; That Old Feeling; Triplecross (1985); We're Talking Serious Money

Farley, Chris: Almost Heroes; Beverly Hills Ninja; Black Sheep; Coneheads; Tommy Boy; Wayne's World 2

Farley, Jim: General, The (1927)

Farley, John: Straight Story, The

Farley, Teresa: Breeders (1986)

Farmer, Donald: No Justice; Vampire Cop

Farmer, Frances: Among the Living; Come and Get It; Rhythm on the Range; Son of Fury; South of Pago Pago; Toast of New York, The

Farmer, Gary: Blown Away (1992); Dark Wind; Dead Man; Moonshine Highway; Powwow Highway; Smoke Signals

Farmer, Ken: Last of the Warriors

Farmer, Mark: Mr. Corbett's Ghost

Farmer, Mimsy: Allonsanfan; Autopsy; Black Cat, The (1981); Code Name: Wild Geese; More

Farmer, Suzan: Die, Monster, Die!; Dracula—Prince of Darkness

Farnham, Euclid: Vermont Is for Lovers

Farnsworth, Richard: Anne of Green Gables (1985); Comes a Horseman; Fire Next Time, The; Getaway, The (1994); Grey Fox, The; Highway to Hell; Independence Day; Into the Night; Lassie; Misery; Natural, The; Resurrection; Rhinestone; River Pirates, The; Ruckus; Space Rage; Straight Story, The; Sylvester; Tom Horn; Two Jakes, The

Farnum, William: Between Men; Connecticut Yankee, A; Eagle's Brood; Git Along, Little Dogies; Kid Ranger; Law of the Sea; Lone Ranger, The (1938); Mexicali Rose; Mr. Robinson Crusoe; Painted Desert, The; Powdersmoke Range; Public Cowboy #1; Santa Fe Stampede; Silver Streak (1934); Supernatural; Trail of Robin Hood; Undersea Kingdom; Vigilantes Are Coming!; Wildfire (1945)

Farr, Felicia: Charley Varrick; Jubal; Kiss Me, Stupid; Kotch; Onionhead; 3:10 to Yuma

Farr, Jamie: Blue Knight, The (1973); Curse II—The Bite; Fearless Tiger; Happy Hour; Speed Zone; Who's Minding the Mint?

Farrar, David: Beat Girl; Black Narcissus; Escape to Burma; John Paul Jones; Lilacs in the Spring (Let's Make Up); Pearl of the South Pacific; Sea Chase, The

Farrell, Charles: Aggie Appleby, Maker of Men; City Girl; Convoy (1940); Just Around the Corner; Old Ironsides

Farrell, Glenda: Bureau of Missing Persons; City Without Men; Disorderly Orderly, The; Go into Your Dance; Gold Diggers of 1935; Hollywood Hotel; I Am a Fugitive from a Chain Gang; Johnny Eager; Lady for a Day; Middle of the Night; Mystery of the Wax Museum; Rage of Paris, The; Susan Slept Here; Talk of the Town, The; Three on a Match

Farrell, Kenneth: It's a Joke, Son!

Farrell, Mike: Battered; Dark River: A Father's Revenge; Incident at Dark River; Memorial Day; Prime Suspect (1982) (Feature); Silent Motive; Sins of the Mind; Vanishing Act

Farrell, Nicolas: Beautiful People; Berlin Tunnel 21; Chariots of Fire; Legionnaire; Midwinter's Tale, A; Twelfth Night

Farrell, Sharon: Arcade; Can't Buy Me Love; Fifth Floor, The; It's Alive!; Marlowe; Premonition, The; Rage (1980); Reivers, The

Farrell, Terry: Beverly Hills Madam; Off the Mark; Reasons of the Heart; Red Sun Rising

Farrell, Timothy: Glen or Glenda; Jail Bait (1954)

Farrell, Tommy: Pirates of the High Seas

Farrelly, Moya: This Is My Father

Farrington, Debbie: Black Panther, The

Farrington, Hugh: Arizona Heat

Farrow, Mia: Alice (1990); Another Woman; Avalanche; Broadway Danny Rose; Crimes and Misdemeanors; Dandy in Aspic, A; Death on the Nile; Great Gatsby, The; Hannah and Her Sisters; Haunting of Julia, The; High Heels (1972); Hurricane (1979); Husbands and Wives; Miami Rhapsody; Midsummer Night's Sex Comedy, A; New York Stories; Purple Rose of Cairo, The; Radio Days; Reckless (1995); Rosemary's Baby; Secret Ceremony; See No Evil; September; Shadows and Fog; Supergirl; Widow's Peak; Zelig

Farrow, Tisa: And Hope to Die; Fingers; Grim Reaper, The (1980); Search and Destroy (1981); Some Call It Loving; Strange Shadows in an Empty Room; Zombie

Farugia, Lena: Gods Must Be Crazy II, The

Fassbinder, Rainer Werner: Ali: Fear Eats the Soul; American Soldier, The; Fox and His Friends; Germany In Autumn; Kamikaze 89; Querelle

Fastinetti, Nikki: Alien P.I.

Fat Boys, The: Disorderlies; Knights of the City; Krush Groove

Fataar, Ricky: Rutles, The (All You Need Is Cash)

Faulkner, Ben: Silent Fall

Faulkner, Graham: Brother Sun, Sister Moon

Faulkner, James: Albino; Maid, The

Faulkner, Sally: Alien Prey

Faulkner, Stephanie: Bus Is Coming, The

Fauna, Flora: Shatter Dead

Faustina: Original Sins

Faustino, David: Perfect Harmony

Faustino, Michael: Blank Check; Judgment

Faversham, William: Arizona Days

Favreau, Jon: Just Your Luck; Persons Unknown; Rocky Marciano; Swingers; Very Bad Things

Fawcett, Allen: Blindside

Fawcett, Farrah: Apostle, The; Between Two Women; Burning Bed, The; Cannonball Run; Children of the Dust; Double Exposure (1989); Extremities; Man of the House; Murder in Texas; Murder on Flight 502; Myra Breckenridge; Poor Little Rich Girl: The Barbara Hutton Story; Red Light Sting, The; Saturn 3; See You in the Morning; Small Sacrifices; Substitute Wife, The; Sunburn

Fawcett, George: Son of the Sheik; Tempest (1928); True Heart Susie; Wedding March, The

Fay, Ann: Somewhere in Sonora

Fay, Frank: Love Nest

Fay, Hugh: Little Annie Rooney

Faye, Alice: Alexander's Ragtime Band; Four Jills in a Jeep; Gang's All Here, The; Hello, Frisco, Hello; Hollywood Cavalcade; In Old Chicago; Magic of Lassie, The; On the Avenue; Poor Little Rich Girl (1936); Rose of Washington Square; State Fair (1962); Stowaway; 365 Nights in Hollywood; Tin Pan Alley; Weekend in Havana

Faye, Frances: Pretty Baby

Faye, Herbie: Sgt. Bilko (TV Series)

Faylen, Frank: Copper Canyon; Flustered Comedy of Leon Errol, The; Gunfight at the O.K. Corral; Kid Galahad (1937); Lost Weekend, The; McConnell Story, The; Monkey's Uncle, The; Perils of Pauline, The (1947); Red Garters; Riot in Cell Block Eleven; Road to Rio

Fazenda, Louise: Keystone Comedies: Vol. 1–5; Noah's Ark

Fazio, Ron: Toxic Avenger Part II, The; Toxic Avenger Part III, The: The Last Temptation of Toxie

Feast, Michael: Caribbean Mystery, A

Featherstone, Angela: Dark Angel: The Ascent; Family of Cops; Wedding Singer, The; Zero Effect

Feder, Frederique: Red

Feeney, Caroleen: Cadillac Ranch; Denise Calls Up

Fehmiu, Bekim: Deserter, The; Permission to Kill

Fehr, Oded: Deuce Bigalow: Male Gigolo

Feig, Peter: Zoo Radio

Feinstein, Alan: Two Worlds of Jennie Logan, The

Fejto, Raphael: Au Revoir, Les Enfants

Feld, Fritz: Affairs of Annabel, The; Everything Happens at Night; Four Jacks and a Jill; Iceland; It's a Date; I've Always Loved You; Mexican Hayride; Noose Hangs High, The; Promises, Promises; World's Greatest Lover, The

Felder, Clarence: Hidden, The; Killing Floor, The

Feldman, Andrea: Heat (1972)

Feldman, Corey: Blown Away (1992); Born Bad; 'Burbs, The; Dangerous Place, A; Dream a Little Dream; Dream a Little Dream 2; Edge of Honor; Evil Obsession; Friday the 13th—The Final Chapter; Goonies, The; License to Drive; Lipstick Camera; Lost Boys, The; Meatballs 4; National Lampoon's Last Resort; Red Line; Rock 'n' Roll High School Forever; Round Trip to Heaven; South Beach Academy; Stand by Me (1986); Stepmonster; Tales from the Crypt Presents Bordello of Blood; Voodoo; Willa

Feldman, Marty: Adventure of Sherlock Holmes' Smarter Brother, The; Last Remake of Beau Geste, The; Sex with a Smile; Silent Movie; Slapstick of Another Kind; To See Such Fun; Yellowbeard; Young Frankenstein

Feldon, Barbara: Get Smart Again; No Deposit, No Return; Playmates; Smile; Sooner or Later

Feldshuh, Tovah: Amazing Howard Hughes, The; Blue Iguana; Brewster's Millions (1985); Cheaper to Keep Her; Day in October, A; Holocaust; Idolmaker, The; Terror Out of the Sky; Walk on the Moon, A

Feliciano, Jose: Fargo

Feliciano, Nancy: Jacker 2: Descent to Hell

Fell, Norman: Boatniks, The; Boneyard, The; Bullitt; C.H.U.D. II (Bud the C.H.U.D.); Cleopatra Jones and the Casino of Gold; For the Boys; For the Love of It; Hexed; If It's Tuesday, This Must Be Belgium; On the Right Track; Paternity; Stone Killer, The

Fellini, Federico: Alex in Wonderland; Ciao Federico!; Fellini's Roma

Fellowes, Rockcliffe: Regeneration

Felmy, Hansjor: Brainwashed

Felt, Asbestos: Killing Spree

Felton, Tom: Anna and the King; Borrowers, The (1997)

Felton, Verna: Oklahoman, The

Fenech, Edwige: Phantom of Death; Sex with a Smile

Feng, Ku: Mighty Peking Man

Fengyi, Zhang: Emperor and the Assassin, The; Farewell My Concubine; Temptation of a Monk

Fenn, Sherilyn: Assassination File, The; Backstreet Dreams; Boxing Helena; Crime Zone; Desire and Hell at Sunset Motel; Diary of a Hitman; Dillinger (1990); Don's Analyst, The; Fatal Instinct (1993); Just Write; Lovelife; Meridian (Kiss of the Beast); Of Mice and Men (1992); Outside Ozona; Ruby (1991); Slave of Dreams; Three of Hearts; Two Moon Junction

Fennell, Tod: Stalked

Fenneman, George: You Bet Your Life (TV Series)

Fenton, Frank: Clay Pigeon, The

Fenton, Leslie: Strange Love of Molly Louvain, The; What Price Glory? (1926)

Fenton, Sarah Jane: Good Man in Africa, A

Fenton, Simon: Matinee

Feore, Colm: Beautiful Dreamers; Blades of Courage; Dr. Bethune; Escape, The; Hostile Waters; Lesser Evil, The; Night Falls on Manhattan; Red Violin, The; Spider and the Fly, The; Storm of the Century; Striking Poses; Thirty-Two Short Films About Glenn Gould; Titus; Truman; Virginian, The (1999)

Feraco, Scott: Nasty Hero

Ferency, Adam: Interrogation

Ferguson, Al: Roamin' Wild; Tarzan the Mighty; Tarzan the Tiger

Ferguson, Andrew: Miracle Down Under

Ferguson, Chloe: Quiet Room, The

Ferguson, Colin: Prayer in the Dark, A

Ferguson, Craig: Big Tease, The

Ferguson, Frank: Caught (1949); They Won't Believe Me

Ferguson, Helen: Miss Lulu Bett

Ferguson, Jane: Mystery Mansion

Ferguson, Matthew: Lilies

Ferguson, Phoebe: Quiet Room, The

Ferguson, Sandra: Interlocked

Ferguson, Scott: Messenger, The; Small Time

Ferguson, Tom: Biohazard: The Alien Force

Fergusson, Karen: Angel at My Table, An

Fernán-Gomez, Fernando: Belle Epoque; Half of Heaven; Spirit of the Beehive, The; Stilts, The (Los Zancos)

Fernandel: Angele; Fernandel the Dressmaker; Forbidden Fruit; Harvest; Le Schpountz; Little World of Don Camillo, The; Nais; Pantaloons; Paris Holiday; Sheep Has Five Legs, The; Topaze (1951); Well-Digger's Daughter, The

Flanders, Ed: Amazing Howard Hughes, The; Citizen Cohn; Exorcist III: Legion; Final Days, The; MacArthur; Ninth Configuration, The; Pursuit of D. B. Cooper; Salem's Lot; Special Bulletin; St. Elsewhere (TV Series); Tomorrow's Child; Trial of the Cantonsville Nine, The

Flanders, Michael: Long Ago Tomorrow

Flanery, Sean Patrick: Best Men; Body Shots; Eden; Just Your Luck; Powder; Raging Angels; Suicide Kings

Flannigan, Maureen: Teenage Bonnie and Klepto Clyde

Flatley, Nigel: I Want What I Want

Flavin, James: Abbott and Costello Meet the Killer, Boris Karloff; Cloak and Dagger (1946); Fingers at the Window

Flea: Dudes; Just Your Luck; Motorama

Fleet, James: Four Weddings and a Funeral; Sense and Sensibility

Fleetwood, Mick: Zero Tolerance

Fleetwood, Susan: Heat and Dust; Krays, The; Persuasion (1995); Sacrifice, The

Fleischer, Charles: Back to the Future II; Gridlock'd; Straight Talk

Fleiss, Heidi: Doom Generation, The

Fleiss, Jane: Kent State

Fleiss, Noah: Josh and S.A.M.; Mother's Prayer, A; Roommates; Unexpected Family, An; Unexpected Life, An

Fleming, Alice: Phantom of the Plains; San Antonio Kid

Fleming, Craig: Dead Silence (1989)

Fleming, Eric: Curse of the Undead; Queen of Outer Space; Rawhide (TV Series)

Fleming, Ian: School for Scandal; Silver Blaze; Triumph of Sherlock Holmes, The

Fleming, Rhonda: Abilene Town; Bullwhip; Cry Danger; Great Lover, The; Gunfight at the O.K. Corral; Nude Bomb, The (Return of Maxwell Smart, The); Out of the Past; Pony Express; Slightly Scarlet; Spellbound; Tennessee's Partner; While the City Sleeps

Fleming, Susan: Range Feud

Flemyng, Jason: Alive & Kicking; Hollow Reed; Lock, Stock and Two Smoking Barrels; Red Violin, The; Rudyard Kipling's The Jungle Book (1994)

Flemyng, Robert: Blood Beast Terror, The; Conspirator; Horrible Dr. Hichcock, The (Terror of Dr. Hichcock, The); Kafka; Man Who Never Was, The; Windom's Way; Young Winston

Fletcher, Bramwell: Bill of Divorcement, A; Daughter of the Dragon; Svengali (1931); Undying Monster, The

Fletcher, Brendan: Floating Away; Summer's End

Fletcher, Dexter: Lionheart (1986); Lock, Stock and Two Smoking Barrels; Rachel Papers; Raggedy Rawney, The; Twisted Obsession

Fletcher, Jay: Born to Win

Fletcher, Louise: Blind Vision; Blue Steel (1990); Brainstorm; Cheap Detective, The; Cruel Intentions; Devil's Arithmetic, The; Exorcist II: The Heretic; Final Notice; Flowers in the Attic; Frankenstein and Me; Haunting of Sea Cliff Inn, The; Heartless; High School High; Invaders from Mars (1986); Lady in Red; Love Kills (1999); Love to Kill; Magician of Lublin, The; Mamma Dracula; Map of the World, A; Natural Enemies; Nightmare on the 13th Floor; Nobody's Fool (1986); One Flew over the Cuckoo's Nest; Return to Two-Moon Junction; Russian Roulette; Shadowzone; Sins of the Mind; Stepford Husbands, The; Strange Behavior; Strange Invaders; Summer to Remember, A; Thieves Like Us; Time Served; Tollbooth; Tryst; Two Days in the Valley; Two Moon Junction; Virtuosity

Fletcher, Page: Buying Time; Friends, Lovers & Lunatics; Hitchhiker, The (Series); Trial & Error (1992)

Fletcher, Suzanne: Sleepwalker

Flint, Helen: Black Legion

Flint, Sam: Monster Maker, The; New Frontier; Spy Smasher

Flippen, Jay C.: Carnival Story; Cat Ballou; Elfego Baca: Six Gun Law; Far Country, The; Firecreek; Flying Leathernecks; Killing, The; King and Four Queens, The; Las Vegas Story, The; Lemon Drop Kid, The; Restless Breed, The; Run of the Arrow; Seven Minutes, The; 7th Cavalry; Studs Lonigan; They Live By Night; Thunder Bay; Wild One, The; Woman's Secret, A; Yellow Cab Man, The

Flippin, Lucy Lee: Summer School

Flockhart, Calista: Birdcage, The; Telling Lies in America; William Shakespeare's A Midsummer Night's Dream

Flohe, Charles: Rappin'

Flon, Suzanne: Moulin Rouge; One Deadly Summer; Un Singe en Hiver (A Monkey in Winter)

Flood, Joe: Blue Yonder, The; Student Bodies

Florance, Sheila: Woman's Tale, A

Flores, Lysa: Star Maps

Floria, Holly: Bikini Island; Private Wars

Flory, Agata: Guns for Dollars

Flower, George "Buck": Across the Great Divide; Adventures of the Wilderness Family; Wilderness Family, Part 2, The

Flowers, Bess: One in a Million

Flowers, Kim: Alien Resurrection

Floyd, Charles R.: P.O.W.: The Escape

Floyd, Robert: Darwin Conspiracy, The

Fluegel, Darlanne: Border Heat; Breaking Point (1993); Bulletproof (1988); Darkman III: Die, Darkman, Die; Deadly Stranger; Freeway (1988); Lock Up; Project: Alien; Relative Fear; Running Scared (1986); Scanner Cop; Slaughter of the Innocents; To Live and Die in L.A.; Tough Guys

Flygenring, Vladimir Orn: Juniper Tree, The

Flynn, Barbara: Cracker (TV Series)

Flynn, Colleen: Incident at Deception Ridge; Late for Dinner

Flynn, Errol: Adventures of Don Juan, The; Adventures of Robin Hood, The; Against All Flags; Assault of the Rebel Girls (Cuban Rebel Girls); Captain Blood; Case of the Curious Bride, The; Charge of the Light Brigade, The (1936); Cry Wolf; Dawn Patrol, The; Desperate Journey; Dive Bomber; Dodge City; Edge of Darkness (1943); Escape Me Never; Footsteps in the Dark; Gentleman Jim; Hollywood Canteen; Istanbul (1956); Kim; Lilacs in the Spring (Let's Make Up); Master of Ballantrae, The; Never Say Goodbye; Northern Pursuit; Objective, Burma!; Prince and the Pauper, The (1937); Private Lives of Elizabeth and Essex, The; San Antonio; Santa Fe Trail; Sea Hawk, The; Silver River; Sisters, The (1938); Thank Your Lucky Stars; That Forsyte Woman; They Died with Their Boots On; Uncertain Glory; Virginia City; Warriors, The (1955)

Flynn, Joe: Computer Wore Tennis Shoes, The; Divorce American Style; Gentle Savage; How to Frame a Figg; Love Bug, The; Lover Come Back; Million Dollar Duck, The; Now You See Him, Now You Don't; Superdad

Flynn, Miriam: 18 Again; For Keeps

Flynn, Sean: Son of Captain Blood

Flynn, Steven: Roswell: The Aliens Attack; Without Warning: The James Brady Story

Foch, Nina: American in Paris, An; Cash McCall; Child of Glass; Dark Past, The; Executive Suite; Jennifer; Morning Glory (1992); Return of the Vampire, The; St. Benny the Dip; Skin Deep; Sliver; Song to Remember, A

Fogel, Vladimir: Bed and Sofa; By the Law; Girl with the Hatbox, The

Fogerty, Brenda: Sun Bunnies

Foland, Alison: To Die For (1995)

Foley, David: Blast from the Past; High Stakes (1986); It's Pat: The Movie; Kids in the Hall: Brain Candy; Sink or Swim

Foley, Jake: Octavia

Foley, Jeremy: Dante's Peak; Soccer Dog: The Movie

Foley, Michael M.: Prison Planet

Folk, Abel: All Tied Up

Folland, Alison: All over Me; Boys Don't Cry

Follows, Megan: Anne of Avonlea; Anne of Green Gables (1985); Back to Hannibal: The Return of Tom Sawyer and Huckleberry Finn; Cry in the Wind; Silver Bullet; Stacking; Termini Station

Folsom, Megan: Heartland

Fonda, Bridget: Aria; Balto; Bodies, Rest & Motion; Break Up; Camilla (1994); City Hall; Doc Hollywood; Finding Graceland; Frankenstein Unbound; Grace of My Heart; In the Gloaming; Iron Maze; It Could Happen to You; Jackie Brown; Jacob I Have Loved; Lake Placid; Leather Jackets; Little Buddha; Mr. Jealousy; Out of the Rain; Point of No Return; Road to Wellville, The; Rough Magic; Scandal; Shag, the Movie; Simple Plan, A; Single White Female; Singles; Strapless; Touch; You Can't Hurry Love

Fonda, Henry: Advise and Consent; Ash Wednesday; Battle Force; Battle of the Bulge; Best Man, The (1964); Big Hand for the Little Lady, A; Big Street, The; Boston Strangler, The; Cheyenne Social Club, The; Clarence Darrow; Drums Along the Mohawk; Fail-Safe; Firecreek; Fort Apache; Fugitive, The (1947); Gideon's Trumpet; Grapes of Wrath, The; Great

Smokey Roadblock, The; How the West Was Won; I Dream Too Much; Immortal Sergeant, The; In Harm's Way; Jesse James; Jezebel; Lady Eve, The; Longest Day, The; Mad Miss Manton, The; Madigan; Meteor; Midway; Mister Roberts; My Darling Clementine; My Name Is Nobody; Night Flight from Moscow; Oldest Living Graduate, The; On Golden Pond; Once Upon a Time in the West; Ox-Bow Incident, The; Return of Frank James, The; Rollercoaster; Roots: The Next Generation; Rounders, The (1965); Sex and the Single Girl; Sometimes a Great Notion; Spencer's Mountain; Stage Struck (1958); Swarm, The; Tales of Manhattan; Tentacles; That Certain Woman; There Was a Crooked Man; Tin Star, The; Too Late the Hero; Trail of the Lonesome Pine, The; 12 Angry Men (1957); War and Peace (1956); Warlock (1959); Wrong Man, The (1956); You Only Live Once; Young Mr. Lincoln; Yours, Mine and Ours

Fonda, Jane: Agnes of God; Any Wednesday; Barbarella; Barefoot in the Park; California Suite; Cat Ballou; Chase, The (1966); China Syndrome; Circle of Love; Comes a Horseman; Coming Home; Dollmaker, The; Doll's House, A (1973); Electric Horseman, The; Fun with Dick and Jane; Game Is Over, The; Joy House; Julia; Klute; Morning After, The; Nine to Five; Old Gringo; On Golden Pond; Period of Adjustment; Rollover; Stanley and Iris; Steelyard Blues; Tall Story; They Shoot Horses, Don't They?; Walk on the Wild Side

Fonda, Peter: Certain Fury; Deadfall; Dirty Mary, Crazy Larry; Don't Look Back (1996); Easy Rider; Fatal Mission; Fighting Mad; Futureworld; High-Ballin'; Hired Hand, The; Hostage Tower, The; John Carpenter's Escape from L.A.; Jungle Heat; Killer Force; Last Movie, The (Chinchero); Lilith; Limey, The; Mercenary Fighters; Molly & Gina; Montana (1990); Nadja; 92 in the Shade; Outlaw Blues; Passion of Ayn Rand, The; Race with the Devil; Rose Garden, The; South Beach; Spasms; Split Image; Tammy and the Doctor; Trip, The; Ulee's Gold; Wanda Nevada; Wild Angels, The

Fondacaro, Phil: Creeps, The; Dollman vs. Demonic Toys

Fong, Benson: Charlie Chan in the Secret Service; Chinese Cat, The; Chinese Web, The; First Yank into Tokyo; Flower Drum Song; Girls! Girls! Girls!; Jinxed; Kung Fu—The Movie (1986); Scarlet Clue, The; Shanghai Cobra, The

Fong, Leo: Blind Rage; Low Blow

Fontaine, Frank: Stella (1950)

Fontaine, Jean: Sinister Urge, The

Fontaine, Joan: Beyond a Reasonable Doubt (1956); Bigamist, The; Born to Be Bad; Casanova's Big Night; Damsel in Distress, A; Decameron Nights; Emperor Waltz, The; Gunga Din; Ivanhoe (1952); Jane Eyre (1944); Letter from an Unknown Woman; Maid's Night Out, The; Quality Street; Rebecca; September Affair; Serenade; Suspicion (1941); Until They Sail; Users, The; Voyage to the Bottom of the Sea; Witches, The (1967); Women, The

Fontanel, Genevieve: Grain of Sand, The

Fontanne, Lynn: Guardsman, The

Fontes, Guilherme: Subway to the Stars

Foody, Ralph: Code of Silence

Foote, Hallie: Courtship; Habitation of Dragons, The; 1918; On Valentine's Day

Foran, Dick: Atomic Submarine, The; Black Legion; Boy Meets Girl; Brighty of the Grand Canyon; Dangerous (1935); Earthworm Tractors; Empty Holsters; Fighting 69th, The; Guest Wife; Horror Island; House of the Seven Gables, The; Mummy's Hand, The; My Little Chickadee; Petrified Forest, The; Private Buckaroo; Ride 'em Cowboy; Riders of Death Valley; Sisters, The (1938); Studs Lonigan; Winners of the West

Forbes, Brenda: Man Upstairs, The

Forbes, Bryan: Colditz Story, The; League of Gentlemen, The; Satellite in the Sky

Forbes, Francine: Splatter University

Forbes, Gary: Wiz Kid, The

Forbes, Martin: Wiz Kid, The

Forbes, Mary: You Can't Cheat an Honest Man

Forbes, Michelle: Black Day Blue Night; John Carpenter's Escape from L.A.; Kalifornia; Swimming with Sharks

Forbes, Ralph: Lilies of the Field (1930); Phantom Broadcast, The; Riptide; Three Musketeers, The (1935)

Forbes, Scott: Operation Pacific

Force, John: Visitors, The

Ford, Anitra: Big Bird Cage, The; Invasion of the Bee Girls

Ford, Bette: Landlady, The

Ford, Carol Ann: Dr. Who (TV series)

Ford, Constance: Last Hunt, The; Rome Adventure; Summer Place, A

Ford, Faith: Murder So Sweet; Weekend in the Country, A; You Talkin' to Me

Ford, Francis: Bad Lands (1939); Man from Monterey, The

Ford, Glenn: Affair in Trinidad; Americano, The; Appointment in Honduras; Big Heat, The; Blackboard Jungle, The; Border Shootout; Cimarron (1960); Courtship of Eddie's Father, The; Day of the Assassin; Dear Heart; Don't Go Near the Water; Experiment in Terror; Fastest Gun Alive, The; Final Verdict; Four Horsemen of the Apocalypse; Gazebo, The; Gilda; Happy Birthday to Me; Human Desire; Interrupted Melody; Is Paris Burning?; It Started With a Kiss; Jubal; Lady in Question; Loves of Carmen, The; Lust for Gold; Man from Colorado, The; Man from the Alamo, The; Pocketful of Miracles; Raw Nerve; Return of October, The; Rounders, The (1965); Sacketts, The; Santee; Smith!; So Ends Our Night; Stolen Life, A; Superman; Teahouse of the August Moon, The; Texas (1941); 3:10 to Yuma; Torpedo Run; Violent Men, The; Virus (1980); Visitor, The; White Tower, The

Ford, Harrison: Air Force One; American Graffiti; Apocalypse Now; Blade Runner; Clear and Present Danger; Conversation, The; Devil's Own, The; Empire Strikes Back, The; Force Ten from Navarone; Frantic (1988); Frisco Kid, The; Fugitive, The (1993); Hanover Street; Heroes; Indiana Jones and the Last Crusade; Indiana Jones and the Temple of Doom; More American Graffiti; Mosquito Coast, The; Patriot Games; Possessed, The (1977); Presumed Innocent; Raiders of the Lost Ark; Random Hearts; Regarding Henry; Return of the Jedi; Sabrina (1995); Shadows; Six Days, Seven Nights; Star Wars; Witness; Working Girl

Ford, Julia: Fatal Inversion, A

Ford, Maria: Alien Terminator; Angel of Destruction; Black Rose of Harlem; Bram Stoker's Burial of the Rats; Dance of the Damned; Dark Planet; Deathstalker IV: Match of the Titans; Final Judgment; Future Fear; Naked Obsession; Night Hunter; Saturday Night Special; Showgirl Murders; Stripteaser; Wasp Woman, The (1995)

Ford, Mick: Scum

Ford, Paul: Advise and Consent; Big Hand for the Little Lady, A; Comedians, The; Matchmaker, The (1958); Music Man, The; Naked City, The; Russians Are Coming, the Russians Are Coming, The; Sgt. Bilko (TV Series); Spy with a Cold Nose, The; Teahouse of the August Moon, The; Who's Got the Action?

Ford, Ross: Jungle Patrol; Project Moon Base; Reform School Girl

Ford, Ruth: Eyes of the Amaryllis

Ford, Terrence: Escape from Survival Zone

Ford, Val: Dead Man Out

Ford, Wallace: All Through the Night; Ape Man, The; Backdoor to Heaven; Blood on the Sun; Dead Reckoning (1947); Employees' Entrance; Freaks; Jericho; Last Hurrah, The; Lawless Street, A; Lost Patrol, The; Matchmaker, The (1958); Maverick Queen, The; Mummy's Hand, The; Mysterious Mr. Wong, The; One Frightened Night; Patch of Blue, A; Possessed (1931); Rainmaker, The (1956); Set-Up, The (1949); Spellbound; Swing It, Sailor; T-Men

Forde, Jessica: Four Adventures of Reinette and Mirabelle

Foree, Ken: Dawn of the Dead; From Beyond; Leatherface—the Texas Chainsaw Massacre III

Foreman, Darren: Silk 'n' Sabotage

Foreman, Deborah: April Fool's Day; Destroyer; Experts, The; Friends, Lovers & Lunatics; Lobster Man from Mars; Love in the Present Tense; Lunatics: A Love Story; My Chauffeur; 3:15—The Moment of Truth; Valley Girl; Waxwork

Foreman, Michelle: Sunset Strip

Forest, Andy J.: Bridge to Hell

Forest, Delphine: Europa, Europa

Forest, Mark: Goliath and the Dragon

Forest, Michael: Atlas

Forlani, Claire: Basil; Last Time I Committed Suicide, The; Mall Rats; Meet Joe Black

Forman, Carol: Superman—The Serial

Forman, Joey: Nude Bomb, The (Return of Maxwell Smart, The)

Forman, Milos: Heartburn; Keeping the Faith; New Year's Day

Blooded; Doc Hollywood; For Love or Money; Frighteners, The; Greedy; Hard Way, The (1991); High School, USA; Life with Mikey; Light of Day; Poison Ivy (1985); Secret of My Success, The; Teen Wolf; Where the Rivers Flow North

Fox, Morgan: Flesh Gordon 2: Flesh Gordon meets the Cosmic Cheerleaders

Fox, Peter: Minor Miracle, A

Fox, Samantha: Night to Dismember, A

Fox, Sidney: Midnight (1934); Murders in the Rue Morgue (1932)

Fox, Virginia: Buster Keaton Festival Vol. 1–3

Fox, Vivica A.: Booty Call; Set It Off; Soul Food; Why Do Fools Fall In Love

Foxworth, Bo: Summer Dreams

Foxworth, Robert: Ants!; Beyond the Stars; Black Marble, The; Deathmoon; Double Standard; Frankenstein (1973); Invisible Strangler; Prophecy (1979)

Foxx, Elizabeth: School Spirit

Foxx, Jamie: Any Given Sunday; Booty Call; Great White Hype, The; Held Up; Players Club, The; Truth About Cats and Dogs, The

Foxx, Redd: Cotton Comes to Harlem; Harlem Nights; Norman ... Is That You?

Foy, Charley: Wagons Roll at Night, The

Foy Jr., Eddie: Bells Are Ringing; Farmer Takes a Wife, The; Four Jacks and a Jill; Gidget Goes Hawaiian; Lucky Me; Pajama Game, The; 30 Is a Dangerous Age, Cynthia

Foyt, Victoria: Babyfever; Déjà Vu (1998); Last Summer in the Hamptons

Frailey, David: Love Street

Frain, James: Hillary and Jackie; Loch Ness; Nothing Personal (1997); Rasputin (1996); Reindeer Games; Titus; Where the Heart Is (2000)

Frakes, Jonathan: Journey's End: The Saga of Star Trek: The Next Generation; Star Trek: First Contact; Star Trek: Generations; Star Trek: Insurrection; Star Trek: The Next Generation (TV Series)

Frampton, Peter: Sgt. Pepper's Lonely Hearts Club Band

France, C. V.: Skin Game, The (1931)

France, Ronald: Dirty Games

Francen, Victor: J'Accuse; Madame Curie; San Antonio; Tuttles of Tahiti, The

Franchi, Franco: Dr. Goldfoot and the Girl Bombs

Francine, Anne: Savages (1973)

Franciosa, Anthony: Across 110th Street; Assault on a Queen; Backstreet Dreams; Career; City Hall; Cricket, The; Curse of the Black Widow; Death House; Death Wish II: Double Threat; Drowning Pool, The; Face in the Crowd, A; Firepower (1979); Ghost in the Noonday Sun; Long Hot Summer, The (1958); Naked Maja, The; Period of Adjustment; Rio Conchos; Side Show; Stagecoach (1986); Summer Heat (1983); This Could Be the Night; Unsane; World is Full of Married Men, The

Francis, Anna Belle: That's the Way I Like It

Francis, Anne: Bad Day at Black Rock; Battle Cry; Blackboard Jungle, The; Born Again; Don't Go Near the Water; Double-O Kid, The; Forbidden Planet; Haunts of the Very Rich; Laguna Heat; Lion Is in the Streets, A; Little Vegas; Love God?, The; Pancho Villa; Return (1984); Summer Holiday; Susan Slept Here

Francis, Arlene: All My Sons (1948); Murders in the Rue Morgue (1932); One, Two, Three; Thrill of It All, The

Francis, Bev: Pumping Iron II: The Women

Francis, Carol Ann: Shades of Love: Champagne for Two

Francis, Connie: Where the Boys Are (1960)

Francis, David Paul: Second Jungle Book, The: Mowgli and Baloo

Francis, Jan: Champions; Dracula (1979)

Francis, Kay: Cocoanuts; Four Jills in a Jeep; In Name Only; It's a Date; Little Men (1940); Wonder Bar

Francis, Noel: Stone of Silver Creek

Francis, Robert: Caine Mutiny, The; Long Gray Line, The

Francis, Ryan: River Pirates, The

Franciscus, James: Amazing Dobermans; Beneath the Planet of the Apes; Cat O'Nine Tails; Good Guys Wear Black; Greek Tycoon, The; Killer Fish; Man Inside, The (1984); Marooned; Miracle of the White Stallions; Nightkill; Secret Weapons; Valley of Gwangi; When Time Ran Out!

Francks, Don: Christmas Wife, The; Drying Up the Streets; Finian's Rainbow; Fish Hawk; Heck's Way Home; Terminal Choice

Francks, Rainbow Sun: Junior's Groove

Franco, James: Whatever It Takes

Franco, Jess: Demoniac; Ilsa, the Wicked Warden

Franco, Margarita: Three Ninjas Kick Back

Franco, Ramon: Kiss Me a Killer; Shattered Image

François, Jacques: North Star (1996); Too Shy to Try

Franey, Billy: Somewhere in Sonora

Frank, Charles: Guide for the Married Woman, A; LBJ: The Early Years; Russkies; Tarantulas—The Deadly Cargo

Frank, Diana: Eyes of the Serpent; In the Time of Barbarians II

Frank, Evelyn: World of Strangers, A

Frank, Gary: Enemy Territory; Enola Gay: The Men, the Mission, the Atomic Bomb

Frank, Horst: Head, The (1959)

Frank, Jason David: Mighty Morphin Power Rangers: The Movie; Turbo: A Power Rangers Adventure

Frank, Joanna: Always (1984)

Frankel, Mark: For Roseanna; Leon the Pig Farmer; Season of Giants, A; Solitaire for 2; Young Catherine

Franken, Al: One More Saturday Night; Stuart Saves His Family

Franken, Steve: Can't Buy Me Love; Hardly Working; Sky Heist; Terror Out of the Sky; Time Travelers, The; Transylvania Twist

Frankeur, Paul: Jour de Fête; Le Gentleman D'Espom (Duke of the Derby); Milky Way, The (1970); Un Singe en Hiver (A Monkey in Winter)

Frankham, David: Return of the Fly, The

Frankie Lymon and the Teenagers: Rock, Rock, Rock

Franklin, Carl: Eye of the Eagle 3

Franklin, Diane: Better Off Dead (1985); Terror Vision

Franklin, Don: Fast Forward

Franklin, George: Maximum Security

Franklin, Gloria: Drums of Fu Manchu

Franklin, Joe: Ghoul School

Franklin, John: Children of the Corn; Children of the Corn 666: Isaac's Return

Franklin, Pamela: And Soon the Darkness; Flipper's New Adventure; Food of the Gods; Horse Without a Head, The; Innocents, The (1961); Legend of Hell House, The; Night of the Following Day, The; Prime of Miss Jean Brodie, The; Satan's School for Girls; Tiger Walks, A; Witching, The (Necromancy)

Franklyn, Sabina: Worst Witch, The

Franklyn, William: Enemy from Space

Franks, Chloe: Littlest Horse Thieves, The; Who Slew Auntie Roo?

Frann, Mary: Fatal Charm

Franz, Arthur: Abbott and Costello Meet the Invisible Man; Amazing Howard Hughes, The; Atomic Submarine, The; Flight to Mars; Hellcats of the Navy; Invaders from Mars (1953); Jungle Patrol; Member of the Wedding, The; Monster on the Campus; Sands of Iwo Jima; Young Lions, The

Franz, Dennis: American Buffalo; Blow Out; Children of Fury; City of Angels; Die Hard 2: Die Harder; Kiss Shot; Package, The; Psycho II

Franz, Eduard: Burning Hills, The; Four Skulls of Jonathan Drake, The; Jazz Singer, The (1953); Latin Lovers; Magnificent Yankee, The; Scar, The

Fraser, Bill: Captain's Paradise, The; Corn Is Green, The (1979)

Fraser, Brendan: Airheads; Blast from the Past; Dudley Do-Right; Encino Man; George of the Jungle; Gods and Monsters; Mrs. Winterbourne; Mummy, The (1999); Passion of Darkly Noon, The; School Ties; Scout, The; Twilight of the Golds, The; Twenty Bucks; With Honors; Younger and Younger

Fraser, Brent: Little Death, The

Fraser, Duncan: Call of the Wild (1992); Captains Courageous (1995)

Fraser, Elisabeth: Sammy, the Way-Out Seal; Sgt. Bilko (TV Series); Two for the Seesaw

Fraser, Hugh: Poirot (Series); Sharpe (TV Series)

Fraser, John: Repulsion; Study in Terror, A; Tunes of Glory

Fraser, Laura: Titus; Virtual Sexuality

Fraser, Liz: Adventures of a Private Eye; Carry on Cruising; Chicago Joe and the Showgirl; Seaside Swingers

Fraser, Phyllis: Winds of the Wasteland

Fraser, Richard: Bedlam; White Pongo (Blond Gorilla)

Fraser, Ronald: Flight of the Phoenix, The; Moll Flanders (1996)

Fraser, Sally: Dangerous Charter; It's a Dog's Life; War of the Colossal Beast

Fraser, Shane: Angel 4: Undercover

Frates, Robin: Arrival, The (1990)

Fratkin, Stuart: Remote

Frawley, William: Abbott and Costello Meet the Invisible Man; Adventures of Huckleberry Finn, The (1939); Babe Ruth Story, The; Blondie in Society; Fighting Seabees, The; Flame of the Barbary Coast; Footsteps in the Dark; Harmony Lane; I Love Lucy (TV Series); Lady on a Train; Lemon Drop Kid, The; Mad About Music; Monsieur Verdoux; Mother Wore Tights; Princess Comes Across, The; Rancho Notorious; Rhythm on the River; Rose of Washington Square; Something to Sing About; Virginian, The (1946); Whistling in Brooklyn

Frazee, Jane: Buck Privates; Hellzapoppin; Springtime in the Sierras; Under California Stars

Frazer, Robert: From a Far Country; Gangs of Sonora; White Zombie

Frazer, Rupert: Back Home; Girl in a Swing, The

Frazier, Ron: Dead Ahead: The Exxon Valdez Disaster; Head Office

Frazier, Sheila: Firehouse (1972); Lazarus Syndrome, The; Superfly; Superfly T.N.T.; Three the Hard Way

Frechette, Mark: Zabriskie Point

Frechette, Peter: Empire City

Freddie and the Dreamers: Seaside Swingers

Frederick, Lynne: Amazing Mr. Blunden, The; Phase IV; Prisoner of Zenda, The (1979); Schizo

Frederick, Pauline: Thank You, Mr. Moto

Frederick, Tara: Lotus Eaters, The

Frederick, Vicki: All the Marbles; Body Rock; Chopper Chicks in Zombietown; Stewardess School

Fredro: Strapped

Freed, Alan: Go, Johnny, Go!; Rock, Rock, Rock

Freed, Bert: Billy Jack; Gazebo, The; Wild in the Streets

Freed, Sam: Call Me

Freeman Jr., Al: Detective, The (1968); Down in the Delta; Malcolm X; My Sweet Charlie; Once Upon a Time ... When We Were Colored; Seven Hours to Judgment

Freeman, Colenton: Vampyr, The (1992)

Freeman, Eric: Silent Night, Deadly Night Part 2

Freeman, J. E.: Alien Resurrection; Copycat; Hard Traveling; Memphis

Freeman, Joan: Fastest Guitar Alive, The; Friday the 13th—The Final Chapter; Mooncussers; Panic in the Year Zero; Reluctant Astronaut, The; Tower of London (1962)

Freeman, Kathleen: Adventures of Topper, The; Blues Brothers 2000; Disorderly Orderly, The; Dragnet (1987); House by the River; In the Mood; Ladies' Man, The; Love Is Better Than Ever; Nutty Professor, The; Reckless Kelly; Rounders, The (1965); Willies, The; Wrong Guys, The

Freeman, Mona: Black Beauty (1946); Branded; Copper Canyon; Dear Wife; Heiress, The; Jumping Jacks; Mother Wore Tights; That Brennan Girl

Freeman, Morgan: Amistad; Bonfire of the Vanities; Chain Reaction (1996); Clean and Sober; Clinton and Nadine; Death of a Prophet; Deep Impact; Driving Miss Daisy; Glory; Hard Rain; Johnny Handsome; Kiss the Girls; Lean on Me; Moll Flanders; Outbreak; Power of One, The; Robin Hood: Prince of Thieves; Roll of Thunder, Hear My Cry; Seven; Shawshank Redemption, The; Street Smart; That Was Then ... This Is Now; Unforgiven (1992)

Freeman, Paul: Aces: Iron Eagle III; Devil's Arithmetic, The; Eminent Domain; Hit Woman: The Double Edge; Just Like a Woman; May Wine; Mighty Morphin Power Rangers: The Movie; Only Love; Raiders of the Lost Ark; Sakharov; Samson and Delilah (1996); Sender, The; Shanghai Surprise; Whose Child Am I?; Without a Clue

Frehley, Ace: Kiss Meets the Phantom of the Park

Freiss, Stephane: Does This Mean We're Married?; King's Whore, The

French, Bill: Killing Edge, The

French, Bruce: Pipe Dreams

French, Ed: Breeders (1986)

French, George: Tarzan of the Apes

French, Leigh: Hollywood Knights, The; White Line Fever

French, Valerie: Four Skulls of Jonathan Drake, The; Jubal; 27th Day, The

French, Victor: Charro!; House on Skull Mountain; Little House on the Prairie (TV Series)

Fresh, Dave: Ganjasaurus Rex

Fresnay, Pierre: César; Fanny (1932); Grand Illusion; Le Corbeau (The Raven (1943)); Marius; Monsieur Vincent

Fresson, Bernard: French Connection II, The; Hiroshima, Mon Amour; Voyage of Terror: The Achille Lauro Affair

Frewer, Matt: Day My Parents Ran Away, The; Far from Home; Honey, I Shrunk the Kids; Kissinger and Nixon; Lawnmower Man 2: Jobe's War (Lawnmower Man: Beyond Cyberspace); Max Headroom; National Lampoon's Senior Trip; Positively True Adventures of the Alleged Texas Cheerleader-Murdering Mom, The; Quicksilver Highway; Short Time; Stand, The; Taking of Beverly Hills, The

Frey, Glenn: Let's Get Harry

Frey, Leonard: Boys in the Band, The; Fiddler on the Roof; Where the Buffalo Roam

Frey, Sami: Band of Outsiders; Black Widow; César and Rosalie; My Life and Times with Antonin Artaud; Nea (A Young Emmanuelle); Revenge of the Musketeers; Sand and Blood; Seven Deadly Sins, The; Sweet Movie

Freyd, Bernard: Alexina

Friberg, Ulf: Jerusalem

Fricke, Grayson: Past the Bleachers

Fricker, Brenda: Angels in the Outfield (1994); Brides of Christ; Deadly Advice; Durango; Field, The; Home Alone 2: Lost in New York; Journey; Man of No Importance, A; Masterminds; My Left Foot; Resurrection Man; So I Married an Axe Murderer; Sound and the Silence,The; Time to Kill, A (1996); Utz; Woman of Independent Means, A

Frid, Jonathan: Best of Dark Shadows, The; Dark Shadows (TV Series); House of Dark Shadows; Seizure

Fridbjornsson, Bjorn Jorundur: Remote Control (1992)

Fridell, Squire: Pink Motel

Friedle, Will: Trojan War

Friedman, Brad: Dead Boyz Can't Fly

Friedman, Budd: Gross Jokes

Friedman, Dave: Sore Losers

Friedman, Michael: Forest Warrior

Friedman, Peter: Blink; Heidi Chronicles, The; Safe; Single White Female

Friedrich, John: Final Terror, The; Small Circle of Friends, A; Thornbirds, The; Wanderers, The

Friel, Anna: Land Girls, The; Rogue Trader; William Shakespeare's A Midsummer Night's Dream

Friell, Vincent: Restless Natives

Friels, Colin: Angel Baby; Back of Beyond; Class Action; Cosi; Darkman; Dingo; Good Man in Africa, A; Grievous Bodily Harm; Ground Zero; High Tide; Kangaroo; Malcolm; Mr. Reliable; Monkey Grip; Warm Nights on a Slow Moving Train

Friend, Philip: Pimpernel Smith

Frijda, Nelly: Question of Silence, A

Frisco, Joe: Riding High

Frith, Rebecca: Love Serenade

Fritsch, Thomas: Full Hearts and Empty Pockets

Fritsch, Willy: Spies; Woman in the Moon (Girl in the Moon; By Rocket to the Moon)

Fritz, Nikki: Where Evil Lies

Frizell, Lou: Stalking Moon, The; Summer of '42

Fröbe, Gert: $ (Dollars); Goldfinger; I Killed Rasputin; Is Paris Burning?; Serpent's Egg, The; Ten Little Indians (1975); Those Daring Young Men in Their Jaunty Jalopies; Those Magnificent Men in Their Flying Machines; Thousand Eyes of Dr. Mabuse, The; Tonio Kroger

Froler, Samuel: Best Intentions, The

Frome, Milton: Ride 'em Cowgirl

Fromholz, Steve: Positive I.D.

Fromin, Troy: Adventures of the Kung Fu Rascals, The

Fronsoe, Susan: Biohazard: The Alien Force

Frost, Lindsay: Dead Heat; Monolith

Frost, Sadie: Bram Stoker's Dracula; Cisco Kid, The; Crimetime; Magic Hunter; Pyromaniac's Love Story, A; Shopping; Splitting Heirs

Frost, Terry: Atom Man vs. Superman; Ghost Town Renegades; Man Who Cheated Himself, The; Waterfront

Frot, Catherine: Dinner Game, The

Frotscher, Donna: They Bite

Froud, Toby: Labyrinth

Fry, Stephen: I.Q.; Jeeves and Wooster (TV Series); Peter's Friends; Wilde

Frydman, Basia: Slingshot, The

Frye, Brittein: Hide and Go Shriek

Frye, Dwight: Black Camel, The; Bride of Frankenstein; Crime of Dr. Crespi, The; Dead Men Walk; Dracula (1931); Drums of Fu Manchu; Invisible Man, The; Vampire Bat, The

Frye, Soleil Moon: I've Been Waiting for You; Piranha (1995); Pumpkinhead II: Bloodwings; Twisted Love

Frye, Virgil: Running Hot; Up from the Depths

Fryer, Eric: Terry Fox Story, The

Fuchs, Jason: Flipper (1996)

Fuchsberger, Joachim: Curse of the Yellow Snake, The

Fudge, Alan: Children of An Lac, The; My Demon Lover; Witness to the Execution

Fuentes, Daisy: Curdled

Fuerstein, Mark: Muse, The

Fugard, Athol: Meetings with Remarkable Men; Road to Mecca, The

Fuizat, Allen: For the Love of Benji

Fuji, Tatsuya: In the Realm of Passion; In the Realm of the Senses

Fujioka, Hiroshi: Ghost Warrior; K2

Fujita, Susumu: Sanshiro Sugata

Fujiwara, Kei: Tetsuo: The Iron Man

Fulci, Lucio: Cat in the Brain, A

Fulford, Wendi: Warriors (1994)

Force, Full: House Party

Fuller, Barbara: Red Menace, The

Fuller, Brook: When Wolves Cry

Fuller, Dolores: Glen or Glenda; Jail Bait (1954)

Fuller, Jonathan: Bloodfist VI: Ground Zero; Castle Freak; Last Man Standing (1994); Pit and the Pendulum, The (1991); Suspect Device

Fuller, Kurt: Moonbase

Fuller, Lance: Apache Woman; Bride and the Beast, The; Kentucky Rifle

Fuller, Penny: Cat on a Hot Tin Roof (1985); Elephant Man, The (1982); George Washington: The Forging of a Nation; Lois Gibbs and the Love Canal; Miss Rose White; Piano for Mrs. Cimino, A

Fuller, Robert: Brain from Planet Arous, The; Donner Pass: The Road to Survival; Maverick; Return of the Seven; Whatever Happened to Aunt Alice?

Fuller, Samuel: Last Movie, The (Chinchero); Pierrot Le Fou; Return to Salem's Lot, A; State of Things, The; Tigrero: A Film That Was Never Made

Fullerton, Fiona: Alice's Adventures in Wonderland; Ghost in Monte Carlo, A; Shaka Zulu

Fulton, Christina: Girl with the Hungry Eyes, The; Hard Drive; Red Shoe Diaries 3: Another Woman's Lipstick

Felton, Rikki: Girl in the Picture, The

Fulton, Todd: Escapes

Fultz, Ronda: I Drink Your Blood

Funakoshi, Elji: Fires on the Plain

Fung, Stephen: Gen-X Cops

Funicello, Annette: Babes in Toyland (1961); Back to the Beach; Beach Blanket Bingo; Beach Party; Bikini Beach; Elfego Baca: Six Gun Law; Escapade in Florence; Horsemasters; How to Stuff a Wild Bikini; Lots of Luck; Misadventures of Merlin Jones, The; Monkey's Uncle, The; Muscle Beach Party; Shaggy Dog, The

Funt, Allen: What Do You Say to a Naked Lady?

Furey, John: Friday the 13th, Part II; Mutant on the Bounty; Wolves, The (1994)

Furlan, Mira: Babylon 5 (TV Series)

Furlong, Edward: American Heart; American History X; Before and After; Brainscan; Detroit Rock City; Grass Harp, The; Home of our Own, A; Little Odessa; Pecker; Pet Sematary Two; Terminator 2: Judgment Day

Furman, Roger: Georgia, Georgia

Furneaux, Yvonne: Master of Ballantrae, The; Mummy, The (1959); Repulsion; Warriors, The (1955)

Furness, Betty: Aggie Appleby, Maker of Men; Swing Time

Furness, Deborra-Lee: Angel Baby; Shame (1987); Waiting

Furst, Stephen: Dream Team, The; Magic Kid; Magic Kid 2; Midnight Madness; National Lampoon's Class Reunion; Silent Rage; Take Down; Unseen, The; Up the Creek (1984)

Furuya, Fumio: Sgt. Kabukiman N.Y.P.D.

Fury, Billy: That'll Be the Day

Fury, Ed: Wild Women of Wongo

Futterman, Dan: Birdcage, The; Breathing Room; Class of '61; Shooting Fish; When Trumpets Fade

Fyfe, Mak: Excalibur Kid, The

Fyodora, Victoria: Target

Gabai, Richard: Hot Under the Collar

Gabay, Sasson: Escape: Human Cargo; Impossible Spy, The

Gabel, Martin: First Deadly Sin, The; Lady in Cement; Lord Love a Duck; Marnie; Smile, Jenny, You're Dead; Thief, The (1952)

Gabel, Michael: On the Block

Gabel, Scilla: Mill of the Stone Women

Gabela, Glen: Warriors from Hell

Gabi, Richard: Dinosaur Island

Gabin, Jean: Cat, The (1971) (Le Chat); Four Bags Full; French Can Can; Golgotha; Grand Illusion; Grisbi; La Bête Humaine; Le Cas du Dr. Laurent; Le Gentleman D'Espom (Duke of the Derby); Le Jour Se Leve (Daybreak) (1939); Le Plaisir; Les Miserables (1957); Lower Depths (1936); Melodie en Sous-Sol (The Big Grab) (Any Number Can Win); Pepe Le Moko; Stormy Waters; Un Singe en Hiver (A Monkey in Winter); Zou Zou

Gable, Christopher: Boy Friend, The; Music Lovers, The; Rainbow, The

Gable, Clark: Across the Wide Missouri; Adventure; Any Number Can Play; Band of Angels; Betrayed (1954); Boom Town; But Not for Me; Chained; China Seas; Command Decision; Comrade X; Dance, Fools, Dance; Dancing Lady; Forsaking All Others; Free Soul, A; Gone with the Wind; Hold Your Man; Homecoming (1948); Honky Tonk; Hucksters, The; Idiot's Delight; It Happened One Night; It Started in Naples; Key to the City; King and Four Queens, The; Laughing Sinners; Lone Star (1952); Love on the Run (1936); Manhattan Melodrama; Misfits, The; Mogambo; Mutiny on the Bounty (1935); Never Let Me Go; Night Nurse; No Man of Her Own; Painted Desert, The; Possessed (1931); Red Dust; Run Silent, Run Deep; San Francisco; Saratoga; Soldier of Fortune; Somewhere I'll Find You; Strange Cargo; Strange Interlude (1932); Susan Lenox: Her Fall and Rise; Tall Men, The; Teacher's Pet; Test Pilot; They Met in Bombay; To Please a Lady; Too Hot to Handle; Wife vs. Secretary

Gable, John Clark: Bad Jim

Gabor, Eva: Artists and Models; Don't Go Near the Water; Gigi; It Started with a Kiss; Last Time I Saw Paris, The; My Man Godfrey (1957); New Kind of Love, A; Princess Academy, The; Truth About Women, The

Gabor, Miklos: Father (1966)

Gabor, Zsa Zsa: Beverly Hillbillies, The (1993); Boys' Night Out; Death of a Scoundrel; For the First Time; Lili; Lovely to Look At; Moulin Rouge; Picture Mommy Dead; Queen of Outer Space; Touch of Evil; We're Not Married

Gabriel, John: Sex and the College Girl

Gabrielle, Monique: Deathstalker II: Duel of the Titans; Silk 2

Gabrio, Gabriel: Harvest

Gades, Antonio: Blood Wedding; El Amor Brujo

Gadsden, Jacqueline: It (1927)

Gael, Anna: Therese and Isabelle (1967)

Gage, Kevin: Double Tap; Gunshy; Point Blank (1998)

Gage, Michael: Dee Snider's Strangeland

Gage, Patricia: Little Kidnappers; Rabid

Gagnon, Jacques: Mon Oncle Antoine

Gago, Jenny: My Family

Gahagan, Helen: She (1935)

Gaigalas, Regina: Body Melt

Gail, Jane: Traffic in Souls

Gail, Max: Cardiac Arrest; Dangerous Touch; D.C. Cab; Deadly Target; Forest Warrior; Game of Love, The; Good Luck; Heartbreakers; Judgment in Berlin; Sodbusters; Street Crimes; Where Are the Children?

Gail, Tim: If Looks Could Kill (1986)

Gaines, Barry: Burglar From Hell; Jacker 2: Descent to Hell; Tales Till the End

Gaines, Boyd: Call Me; Sure Thing, The

Gainey, M. C.: Breakdown; Citizen Ruth; El Diablo; Leap of Faith; Ulterior Motives

Gains, Courtney: Can't Buy Me Love; King Cobra; Memphis Belle

Gainsbourg, Charlotte: Cement Garden, The; Jane Eyre (1996); Le Petit Amour; Little Thief, The; Merci La Vie

the Iguana, The; On the Beach; One Touch of Venus; Pandora and the Flying Dutchman; Permission to Kill; Priest of Love; Regina; Sentinel, The; Seven Days in May; Show Boat (1951); Singapore; Snows of Kilimanjaro, The; Whistle Stop

Gardner, Daniel: How U Like Me Now

Gardner, David: Bethune

Gardner, Devin: Kid Called Danger, A

Gardner, Hy: Girl Hunters, The

Gardner, Joan: Catherine the Great; Dark Journey; Man Who Could Work Miracles, The; Private Life of Don Juan, The

Gardner, Richard Harding: Deadly Daphne's Revenge

Gareth, Curt: Very Natural Thing, A

Garfield, Allen: Beverly Hills Cop II; Black Stallion Returns, The; Brinks Job, The; Candidate, The; Club Fed; Continental Divide; Conversation, The; Crime of the Century; Cry Uncle!; Cyborg 2; Desert Bloom; Diabolique (1996); Family Prayers; Front Page, The (1974); Get Crazy; Greetings; Hi Mom; Let It Ride; Night Visitor (1989); One from the Heart; Putney Swope; Sketches of a Strangler; State of Things, The; Stunt Man, The

Garfield, Frank: Night of the Zombies (1983)

Garfield, John: Air Force; Body and Soul (1947); Destination Tokyo; Fallen Sparrow, The; Force of Evil; Four Daughters; Gentlemen's Agreement; Hollywood Canteen; Humoresque; Juarez; Postman Always Rings Twice, The (1946); Sea Wolf, The (1941); Thank Your Lucky Stars; They Made Me a Criminal; Tortilla Flat

Garfield, John David: Savage Intruder, The

Garfield Jr., John: Golden Voyage of Sinbad, The; That Cold Day in the Park

Garfield, Michael: Slugs, the Movie

Garfunkel, Art: Boxing Helena; Carnal Knowledge; Catch-22; Short Fuse

Gargan, William: Aggie Appleby, Maker of Men; Animal Kingdom, The; Black Fury; Broadway Serenade; Canterville Ghost, The (1944); Cheers for Miss Bishop; I Wake Up Screaming; Miss Annie Rooney; Rain; They Knew What They Wanted; Who Done It?; You Only Live Once

Gario, Gabriel: Pepe Le Moko

Garko, Gianni: Night of the Devils

Garko, John: Have a Nice Funeral

Garland, Beverly: Alligator People, The; Blood Song (Haunted Symphony); Gamble on Love; Gundown at Sandoval; Gunslinger; It Conquered the World; It's My Turn; Pretty Poison; Say Goodbye, Maggie Cole; Swamp Women; Twice-Told Tales; Where the Red Fern Grows

Garland, Judy: Andy Hardy Meets a Debutante; Babes in Arms; Babes on Broadway; Broadway Melody of 1938; Child Is Waiting, A; Clock, The; Easter Parade; Everybody Sing; For Me and My Gal; Gay Purr-ee; Girl Crazy; Harvey Girls, The; I Could Go on Singing; In the Good Old Summertime; Judgment at Nuremberg; Life Begins for Andy Hardy; Listen, Darling; Little Nellie Kelly; Love Finds Andy Hardy; Meet Me in St. Louis; Pirate, The; Presenting Lily Mars; Star Is Born, A (1954); Strike Up the Band; Summer Stock; That's Entertainment; Thoroughbreds Don't Cry; Thousands Cheer; Till the Clouds Roll By; Wizard of Oz, The; Words and Music; Ziegfeld Follies; Ziegfeld Girl

Garland, Richard: Attack of the Crab Monsters; Mutiny in Outer Space; Panic in the Year Zero; Undead, The

Garlick, Sean: Fortress (1985)

Garlicki, Piotr: Camouflage

Garlington, Lee: Babysitter, The (1995)

Garlington, Mary: Polyester

Garmon, Huw: Hedd Wyn

Garms, Justin: Gordy

Garneau, Constance: Strangers in Good Company

Garner, Alice: Love and Other Catastrophes

Garner, James: Americanization of Emily, The; Barbarians at the Gate; Boys' Night Out; Breathing Lessons; Cash McCall; Castaway Cowboy, The; Children's Hour, The; Dead Silence (1996); Decoration Day; Distinguished Gentleman, The; Duel at Diablo; Fan, The; Fire in the Sky; Glitter Dome, The; Grand Prix; Great Escape, The; Hour of the Gun, The; Legalese; Marlowe; Maverick; Maverick (TV Series); Murphy's Romance; My Fellow Americans; My Name Is Bill W; Rockford Files, The (TV Series); Sayonara; Skin Game; Streets of Laredo; Sunset; Support Your Local Gunfighter; Support Your Local Sheriff!; Tank; They Only Kill Their Mas-

ters; 36 Hours; Thrill of It All, The; Twilight; Up Periscope; Victor/Victoria; Wheeler Dealers, The

Garner, Jennifer: Rose Hill

Garner, Peggy Ann: Betrayal (1978); Cat, The (1966); In Name Only; Jane Eyre (1944); Tree Grows in Brooklyn, A

Garnett, Gale: Children, The; Mad Monster Party

Garofalo, Janeane: Bumblebee Flies Anyway, The; Bye Bye, Love; Clay Pigeons; Cold-Blooded; Copland; I Shot a Man in Vegas; Larger than Life; Matchmaker, The (1997); Minus Man, The; Mystery Men; Reality Bites; Romy and Michele's High School Reunion; Sweethearts (1996); Truth About Cats and Dogs; 200 Cigarettes

Garofolo, Ettore: Mamma Roma

Garr, Teri: After Hours; Black Stallion, The; Black Stallion Returns, The; Changing Habits; Close Encounters of the Third Kind; Dumb and Dumber; Escape Artist, The; Firstborn; Full Moon in Blue Water; Head (1968); Honky Tonk Freeway; Let It Ride; Michael; Miracles; Mr. Mom; Mom and Dad Save the World; Oh, God!; One from the Heart; Out Cold; Perfect Alibi; Perfect Little Murder, A; Prime Suspect (1982) (Feature); Ronnie & Julie; Short Time; Simple Wish, A; Sting II, The; To Catch a King; Tootsie; Waiting for the Light; Witches' Brew; Young Frankenstein

Garralaga, Martin: Big Sombrero, The

Garrani, Ivo: Black Sunday (1961); Hercules (1959)

Garrel, Maurice: Un Coeur en Hiver

Garrett, Betty: My Sister Eileen; Neptune's Daughter; On the Town; Take Me Out to the Ball Game; Words and Music

Garrett, Brad: Facade

Garrett, Hank: Blood Frenzy; Boys Next Door, The (1985); Rosebud Beach Hotel, The (Nostell Hotel, The)

Garrett, Leif: Cheerleader Camp; Kid Vengeance; Longshot (1981); Medicine Hat Stallion, The; Outsiders, The; Party Line; Shaker Run; Spirit of '76, The; Thunder Alley

Garrett, Lesley: Mikado, The (1987)

Garrett, Patsy: Benji; Dennis the Menace: Dinosaur Hunter; For the Love of Benji

Garrett, Teresa: It's in the Water (1996); It's in the Water (1998)

Garrick, Barbara: Ellen Foster; Sleepless in Seattle

Garrick, John: Just Imagine

Garrison, David: Homeboys

Garrone, Riccardo: Bang Bang Kid, The

Garson, Greer: Adventure; Goodbye, Mr. Chips (1939); Happiest Millionaire, The; Julia Misbehaves; Julius Caesar (1953); Madame Curie; Miniver Story, The; Mrs. Miniver; Mrs. Parkington; Pride and Prejudice (1940); Random Harvest; Singing Nun, The; Sunrise at Campobello; That Forsyte Woman; When Ladies Meet

Garth, Daniel: Behind Locked Doors

Garth, Jennie: Beverly Hills 90210; Power 98

Gartin, Christopher: Matters of the Heart; No Big Deal; Story Lady, The; Tremors 2: Aftershocks

Garvey, Steve: Bloodfist VI: Ground Zero

Garvie, Elizabeth: Pride and Prejudice (1985)

Garvin, Anita: Chump at Oxford, A; Laurel and Hardy Classics: Vol. 1–9

Garwood, John: Hell's Angels on Wheels

Gary, Lorraine: Jaws; Jaws 2; Jaws: The Revenge; Just You and Me, Kid; Pray for the Wildcats

Gascon, Jean: Man Called Horse, A

Gassman, Alessandro: Month by the Lake, A; Sacrilege; Turkish Bath, The

Gassman, Vittorio: Abraham; Big Deal on Madonna Street; Bitter Rice; Catch as Catch Can; Family, The (1987); Immortal Bachelor, The; Mambo; Miracle, The (1959); Nude Bomb, The (Return of Maxwell Smart, The); Palermo Connection, The; Rhapsody; Sharky's Machine; Sleazy Uncle, The; Sleepers; Tempest (1982); Tiger and The Pussycat, The; We All Loved Each Other So Much; Wedding, A (1978); Woman Times Seven

Gates, Anthony: L.A. Crackdown II

Gates, B. J.: Midnight Kiss

Gates, Larry: Hoodlum Priest, The; Hour of the Gun, The; Toys in the Attic; Young Savages, The

Gates, Nancy: Cheyenne Takes Over; Death of a Scoundrel; Suddenly; World Without End

Gates, William: Hoop Dreams

Gateson, Marjorie: Goin' to Town

Gatins, John: Leprechaun 3

Gatti, Jennifer: Double Exposure (1993)

the White Stallion; Mandingo; Out of Season; Small Town in Texas, A; Sonny and Jed; Straw Dogs; Summer Heat (1983); That Summer of White Roses; Tintorera; Tomorrow Never Comes; Venom

Georgeson, Tom: Fish Called Wanda, A; No Surrender

Georges-Picot, Olga: Children of Rage

Geralds, Jim: Le Voyage Imaginaire

Gerard, Charles: Bandits (1987); Happy New Year (1973) (La Bonne Année)

Gerard, Danny: Robot in the Family

Gerard, George: Metamorphosis: The Alien Factor

Gerard, Gil: Buck Rogers in the 25th Century; Final Notice; Soldier's Fortune

Gerardi, Joan: Bikini Bistro

Garay, Steven: French Line, The; Gilda; Seventh Cross, The

Gerber, Jay: Cartier Affair, The

Gere, Richard: American Gigolo; And the Band Played On; Beyond the Limit; Bloodbrothers; Breathless (1983); Cotton Club, The; Days of Heaven; Final Analysis; First Knight; Internal Affairs; Intersection; Jackal, The; King David; Looking for Mr. Goodbar; Miles from Home; Mr. Jones; No Mercy; Officer and a Gentleman, An; Power (1986); Pretty Woman; Primal Fear; Red Corner; Report to the Commissioner; Rhapsody in August; Runaway Bride; Sommersby; Strike Force; Yanks

Geret, Georges: Diary of a Chambermaid (1964); Very Curious Girl, A

Gerini, Claudia: Iris Blond

German, Gretchen: Man Called Sarge, A

Gerrish, Frank: Partners in Crime

Gerroll, Daniel: Big Business; Eyes of a Witness

Gerron, Kurt: Blue Angel, The

Gerry and the Pacemakers: That Was Rock

Gerry, Alex: Bellboy, The

Gersak, Savina: Iron Warrior; Lone Runner; Midnight Ride

Gershon, Gina: Black & White; Bound; Face/Off; Flinch; Guinevere; Insider, The; Joey Breaker; Legalese; Lies & Whispers; Love Matters; Lulu on the Bridge; One Tough Cop; Palmetto; Red Heat (1988); Showgirls; This World, Then the Fireworks; Voodoo Dawn

Gerson, Betty Lou: Red Menace, The

Gerstein, Lisa: My Life's in Turnaround

Gerstle, Frank: Gang Busters

Gert, Valeska: Diary of a Lost Girl

Gertz, Jami: Crossroads; Don't Tell Her It's Me; Jersey Girl; Less Than Zero; Listen to Me; Lost Boys, The; Quicksilver; Renegades; Sibling Rivalry; Silence Like Glass; Solarbabies; Twister (1996)

Gesner, Zen: Wish Me Luck

Gesswein, Richard: R.O.T.O.R.

Getty, Balthazar: Dead Beat; December; Don't Do It; Habitat; Judge Dredd; Lord of the Flies (1989); Lost Highway; My Heroes Have Always Been Cowboys; Pope Must Diet, The; Red Hot; Turn of the Screw, The (1989); Where the Day Takes You; Young Guns II

Getty, Estelle: Mannequin (1987); Stop! Or My Mom Will Shoot

Getty III, Paul: State of Things, The

Getz, John: Blood Simple; Curly Sue; Don't Tell Mom the Babysitter's Dead; Fly, The (1986); Fly II, The; Kent State; Men at Work; Painted Hero; Passion to Kill, A; Playmaker; Tattoo

Getz, Stuart: Van, The (1976)

Geva, Tamara: Manhattan Merry-Go-Round

Gevedon, Stephen: Paranoia (1998)

Ghia, Dana: Big Rip-off, The

Ghiglíotti, Marilyn: Clerks

Ghini, Massimo: Truce, The

Gholson, Julie: Where the Lilies Bloom

Ghosal, Smaran: Aparajito

Ghostley, Alice: Addams Family Reunion; Gator; New Faces; Wrong Guys, The

Giachetti, Fosco: We the Living

Giamatti, Paul: Big Momma's House; Man on the Moon; Safe Men; Winchell

Giambalvo, Louis: Dead to Rights; Fade to Black (1993); Illegal in Blue; Question of Faith; Ratings Game, The

Gian, Joe: Mad About You; Night Stalker, The (1986)

Gianasi, Rick: Escape from Safehaven; Mutant Hunt; Occultist, The; Sgt. Kabukiman N.Y.P.D.

Giannini, Giancarlo: American Dreamer; Blood Feud; Blood Red; Disappearance of García Lorca, The; Fever Pitch; Heaven Before I Die; How Funny Can Sex Be?; Immortal Bachelor, The; Innocent, The (1976); Jacob; La Grande Bourgeoise; Lili Marleen; Love and Anarchy; Lovers and Liars; Mimic; New York Stories; Night Full of Rain, A; Once Upon a Crime; Saving Grace; Seduction of Mimi, The; Sensual Man, The; Seven Beauties; Sleazy Uncle, The; Swept Away; Walk in the Clouds, A; Where's Piccone?

Gibb, Cynthia: Death Warrant; Drive Like Lightning; Gypsy (1993); Holiday Affair (1996); Jack's Back; Malone; Modern Girls; Salvador; Short Circuit 2; Volcano: Fire on the Mountain

Gibb, Donald: Bloodsport; Bloodsport II; Magic Kid 2; Revenge of the Nerds IV: Nerds in Love

Gibbs, Maria: Foolish; Meteor Man; Up Against the Wall

Gibbs, Rick: Buckeye and Blue

Gibbs, Timothy: Witchboard 2

Gibet, Michel: Blue Jeans

Gibney, Rebecca: I Live With Me Dad; Paperback Romance

Gibney, Susan: Cabin by the Lake; Evolution's Child

Gibson, Donal: Fatal Bond

Gibson, Henry: Asylum (1996); Bio-Dome; 'Burbs, The; Cyber Bandits; Evil Roy Slade; For the Love of It; Incredible Shrinking Woman, The; Innerspace; Long Gone; Long Goodbye, The; Monster in the Closet; Nashville; Switching Channels; Tulips

Gibson, Hoot: Hard Hombre; Horse Soldiers, The; Last Outlaw, The (1936); Long Long Trail; Painted Stallion, The; Powdersmoke Range; Spirit of the West

Gibson, Mel: Air America; Attack Force Z; Bird on a Wire; Bounty, The; Braveheart; Conspiracy Theory; Forever Young (1992); Gallipoli; Hamlet (1990); Lethal Weapon; Lethal Weapon 2; Lethal Weapon 3; Lethal Weapon 4; Mad Max; Mad Max Beyond Thunderdome; Man without a Face, The; Maverick; Mrs. Soffel; Patriot, The; Payback (1999); Ransom (1996); River, The (1984); Road Warrior, The; Summer City; Tequila Sunrise; Tim; Year of Living Dangerously, The

Gibson, Paulette: Getting Over

Gibson, Thomas: Far and Away; Love and Human Remains

Gibson, Virginia: Athena

Gibson, Wynne: Aggie Appleby, Maker of Men; Night after Night

Gidley, Pamela: Aberration; Bad Love; Bombshell (1997); Cheatin' Hearts; Crew, The; Disturbed; Freefall; Jane Austen's Mafia; Liebestraum; Little Death, The

Gidwani, Kitu: Earth (1998)

Gielgud, John: Appointment with Death; Arthur; Arthur 2: On the Rocks; Brideshead Revisited; Canterville Ghost, The (1986); Charge of the Light Brigade, The (1968); Chariots of Fire; Chimes at Midnight (Falstaff); 11 Harrowhouse; First Knight; Formula, The; Frankenstein (1984); Gandhi; Getting It Right; Haunted; Human Factor, The; Hunchback (1982); Inside the Third Reich; Invitation to the Wedding; Joseph Andrews; Julius Caesar (1953); Julius Caesar (1970); Les Miserables (1978); Loved One, The; Murder by Decree; Plenty; Portrait of a Lady, The; Portrait of the Artist as a Young Man, A; Power of One, The; Priest of Love; Prospero's Books; Providence; Richard III (1955); Romance on the Orient Express; Saint Joan; Scandalous (1983); Scarlet and the Black, The; Secret Agent, The; Seven Dials Mystery, The; Shine; Shining Through; Shoes of the Fisherman; Shooting Party, The; Sphinx (1981); Strike It Rich; Wagner; Whistle Blower, The; Why Didn't They Ask Evans?; Wicked Lady, The (1983)

Gierasch, Stefan: Jack the Bear; Jeremiah Johnson

Gifaldi, Sam: Treasure of Pirate's Point

Gifford, Frances: American Empire; Border Vigilantes; Luxury Liner; Our Vines Have Tender Grapes; Riding High; Tarzan Triumphs

Giftos, Elaine: Gas-s-s-s; Student Nurses, The; Trouble with Dick, The

Gigante, Tony: Metamorphosis: The Alien Factor

Gil, Ariadna: Belle Epoque; Celestial Clockwork

Gil, Jorge: Shootfighter 2: Kill or Be Killed

Gil, Vincent: Encounter at Raven's Gate; Solo (1977)

Gilbert, Andrew S.: Kiss or Kill

Gilbert, Billy: Arabian Nights (1942); Block-Heads; Breaking the Ice; Bride Walks Out, The; Broadway Melody of

Goldthwait, Bob: Burglar (U.S.); Freaked; Hot to Trot; One Crazy Summer; Police Academy III: Back in Training; Police Academy 4: Citizens on Patrol; Scrooged; Shakes the Clown; Sweethearts (1996)

Goldwyn, Tony: Boys Next Door, The (1996); Doomsday Gun; Ghost (1990); Iran Days of Crisis; Kiss the Girls; Kuffs; Last Word, The (1995); Lesser Evil, The; Love Matters; Pelican Brief, The; Reckless (1995); Substance of Fire, The; Taking the Heat; Traces of Red; Trouble on the Corner; Truman; Woman of Independent Means, A

Goleen, Frank Rozelaar: Goodnight, God Bless

Golino, Valeria: Big Top Pee-Wee; Clean Slate (1994); Detective School Dropouts; Four Rooms; Hot Shots; Hot Shots Part Deux; Immortal Beloved; Indian Runner, The; John Carpenter's Escape from L.A.; King's Whore, The; Occasional Hell, An; Rain Man; Somebody is Waiting; Torrents of Spring; Year of the Gun

Golisano, Francesco: Miracle in Milan

Golonka, Arlene: Dr. Alien; Foxtrap; Hang 'em High; Last Married Couple in America, The; Survival Game

Golovine, Marina: Olivier, Olivier

Golubkina, Maria: Adam's Rib (1993)

Gombell, Minna: Block-Heads; Doomed Caravan; Pagan Love Song

Gomez, Carlos: Fools Rush In; Hostile Intentions

Gomez, Consuelo: El Mariachi

Gomez, Jamie: Silencer, The

Gomez, Jose Luis: Roads to the South

Gomez, Paloma: Valentina

Gomez, Panchito: Mi Vida Loca; Run for the Roses (Thoroughbred)

Gomez, Thomas: But Not for Me; Casbah; Force of Evil; Kim; Macao; Pittsburgh; Pony Soldier; Sherlock Holmes and the Voice of Terror; Singapore; Sorrowful Jones; That Midnight Kiss; Trapeze; Who Done It?

Gonzales, Barbara: Lotto Land

Gonzales, Dan Rivera: Men with Guns

Gonzales, Peter: Fellini's Roma

González González, Clifton: Wonderful Ice Cream Suit, The

Gonzalez, Clifton: 187

González, Rubén: Buena Vista Social Club, The

Good, Maurice: Five Million Years to Earth

Goodall, Caroline: Casualties; Disclosure; Ring of Scorpio; Schindler's List; Silver Stallion, The; Sorrento Beach; Webber's World (At Home with the Webbers); White Squall

Goodall, Louise: My Name is Joe

Goodfellow, Joan: Buster and Billie; Flash of Green, A

Gooding Jr., Cuba: As Good as It Gets; Boyz N the Hood; Chill Factor; Daybreak (1993); Few Good Men, A; Gladiator (1992); Instinct; Jerry Maguire; Judgment Night; Lightning Jack; Losing Isaiah; Murder of Crows, A; Outbreak; Tuskegee Airmen, The; What Dreams May Come

Goodlife, Michael: One That Got Away, The

Goodman, Benny: Gang's All Here, The; Song is Born, A

Goodman, Dody: Cool As Ice; Private Resort; Splash

Goodman, John: Always (1989); Arachnophobia; Babe, The (1992); Barton Fink; Big Easy, The; Big Lebowski, The; Blues Brothers 2000; Born Yesterday (1993); Borrowers, The (1997); Bringing Out the Dead; Everybody's All-American; Fallen; Flintstones, The; Jack Bull, The; King Ralph; Kingfish: A Story of Huey P. Long; Matinee; Mother Night; Pie in the Sky; Punchline; Raising Arizona; Revenge of the Nerds; Sea of Love; Stella (1990); Streetcar Named Desire, A (1995); True Stories; What Planet Are You From?; Wrong Guys, The

Goodrich, Deborah: Remote Control (1987); Survival Game

Goodrow, Garry: Almos' a Man; Cardiac Arrest; Connection, The (1961); Glen and Randa; Steelyard Blues

Goodwin, Bill: Bathing Beauty; House of Horrors; It's a Great Feeling; Jolson Sings Again; Jolson Story, The; So Proudly We Hail; Spellbound

Goodwin, Harold: Abbott and Costello Meet the Keystone Kops; Tarzan and the Golden Lion

Goodwin, Kia Joy: Strapped

Goodwin, Laurel: Girls! Girls! Girls!; Papa's Delicate Condition

Goodwin, Michael: Sizzle

Goorjian, Michael A.: SLC Punk

Gora, Claudio: Catch as Catch Can

Goranson, Alicia: Boys Don't Cry

Gorbe, Janos: Round-Up, The

Gorcey, Bernard: Bowery Boys, The (Series)

Gorcey, David: Bowery Boys, The (Series); Pride of the Bowery

Gorcey, Elizabeth: Trouble with Dick, The

Gorcey, Leo: Bowery Boys, The (Series); Boys of the City; Pride of the Bowery; Road to Zanzibar

Gordon, Barry: Body Slam; Girl Can't Help It, The; Hands of a Stranger; Thousand Clowns, A

Gordon, Ben: Goof Balls

Gordon, Bobby: Big Business Girl

Gordon, Bruce: Curse of the Undead; Elephant Boy; Untouchables, The; Scarface Mob

Gordon, C. Henry: Charlie Chan at the Wax Museum; Gabriel over the White House; Tarzan's Revenge

Gordon, Carl: Piano Lesson, The

Gordon, Claire: Konga

Gordon, Colin: One That Got Away, The

Gordon, Dexter: Round Midnight

Gordon, Don: Beast Within, The; Borrower, The; Bullitt; Education of Sonny Carson, The; Final Conflict, The; Mack, The; Papillon; Skin Deep; Slaughter; Warbus; Z.P.G. (Zero Population Growth)

Gordon, Eve: Honey, We Shrunk Ourselves; I'll Be Home for Christmas; Paradise (1991); Secret Passion of Robert Clayton, The; Switched at Birth

Gordon, Gale: All in a Night's Work; Our Miss Brooks (TV Series); Speedway; 30 Foot Bride of Candy Rock, The

Gordon, Gavin: Bat, The; Bitter Tea of General Yen, The; Matchmaker, The (1958); Romance; Scarlet Empress, The

Gordon, Gerald: Force Five; Judas Project, The

Gordon, Hannah: Oh, Alfie

Gordon, Hannah Taylor: Jakob the Liar

Gordon, Jade: Sugar Town

Gordon, Jim: To Catch a Yeti

Gordon, Joyce: Killing 'Em Softly

Gordon, Julius: D.P.

Gordon, Keith: Back to School; Christine; Dressed to Kill (1980); Home Movies; Kent State; Legend of Billie Jean, The; Silent Rebellion; Single Bars, Single Women; Static

Gordon, Leo: Haunted Palace, The; Hondo; Hostile Guns; Intruder, The (1961); Maverick; Maverick (TV Series); My Name is Nobody; Rage (1980); Riot in Cell Block Eleven; Ten Wanted Men

Gordon, Mary: Double Wedding; Hound of the Baskervilles, The (1939); Pearl of Death, The; Pot O' Gold; Sherlock Holmes and the Secret Weapon; Sherlock Holmes and the Voice of Terror; Texas Cyclone

Gordon, Philip: Bridge to Nowhere; Came a Hot Friday

Gordon, Robert: Loveless, The; Tom Sawyer (1917)

Gordon, Ruth: Abe Lincoln in Illinois; Action in the North Atlantic; Any Which Way You Can; Big Bus, The; Don't Go to Sleep; Every Which Way But Loose; Harold and Maude; Inside Daisy Clover; Lord Love a Duck; Maxie; Mugsy's Girls; My Bodyguard; North Star, The (1943); Prince of Central Park, The; Rosemary's Baby; Scavenger Hunt; Trouble with Spies, The; Two-Faced Woman; Whatever Happened to Aunt Alice?; Where's Poppa?

Gordon, Serena: Tale of Two Cities, A (1991)

Gordon, Stuart: Age of Innocence, The

Gordon, Susan: Picture Mommy Dead

Gordon-Levitt, Joseph: Angels in the Outfield (1994); Great Elephant Escape, The; Holy Matrimony; Juror, The

Gore, Sandy: Brides of Christ

Gorg, Galyn: Living the Blues

Gorg, Gwyn: Living the Blues

Gorham, Mel: Blue in the Face; Curdled

Goring, Marius: Barefoot Contessa, The; Circle of Danger; Ill Met by Moonlight; Night Ambush; Paris Express, The; Red Shoes, The (1948); Spy in Black, The; Zeppelin

Gorman, Annette: Texas John Slaughter: Stampede at Bitter Creek

Gorman, Cliff: Angel; Boys in the Band, The; Cops and Robbers; Down Came a Blackbird; Hoffa; Justine; Night and the City (1992); Night of the Juggler; Strike Force

Gorme, Eydie: Alice Through the Looking Glass (1985)

Gormley, Felim: Commitments, The

Gorney, Karen Lynn: Saturday Night Fever

Gorny, Frederic: Wild Reeds

Gorshin, Frank: Batman (1966); Beverly Hills Bodysnatchers; Bloodmoon (1997); Goliath Awaits; Hail Caesar; Hollywood Vice Squad; Hot Resort; Invasion of the Saucer Men; Meteor Man; Midnight (1989); Sky Heist; Studs Lonigan; Sweet Justice; That Darn Cat (1965); Underground Aces

Gorski, Tamara: Lost World, The (1992); Picture Windows; Return to the Lost World; Striking Poses

Gortner, Marjoe: American Ninja III; Bobbie Jo and the Outlaw; Food of the Gods; Hellhole; Jungle Warriors; Marjoe; Mausoleum; Pray for the Wildcats; Sidewinder 1; Star Crash; Survivalist, The; Viva Knievel; Wild Bill

Gorton, Brad: Get Real

Gosch, Christopher: Last Season, The

Gosden, Freeman: Check and Double Check

Gosfield, Maurice: Sgt. Bilko (TV Series)

Goss, David: Hollywood Cop

Gosselaar, Mark Paul: Dead Man on Campus; Kounterfeit; Necessary Parties; Specimen; Twisted Love; White Wolves: A Cry in the Wild II

Gossett Jr., Lou: Aces: Iron Eagle III; Bram Stoker's The Mummy; Carolina Skeletons; Choirboys, The; Cover-Up; Curse of the Starving Class; Dangerous Relations; Deep, The; Diggstown; Don't Look Back: The Story of Leroy "Satchel" Paige; El Diablo; Enemy Mine; Firewalker; Flashfire; Good Man in Africa, A; Goodbye, Miss 4th of July; Guardian, The (1984); In His Father's Shoes; Inside; Inspectors, The; Iron Eagle; Iron Eagle II; Iron Eagle IV; It Rained All Night the Day I Left; It's Good to Be Alive; Jaws 3; J.D.'s Revenge; Josephine Baker Story, The; Keeper of the City; Laughing Policeman, The; Lazarus Syndrome, The; Little Ladies of the Night; Managua; Monolith; Murder on the Bayou; Officer and a Gentleman, An; Principal, The; Punisher, The; Raisin in the Sun, A (1961); Return to Lonesome Dove; Roots; Roots—The Gift; Run for the Dream; Sadat; Skin Game; Strange Justice; Sudie & Simpson; Toy Soldiers (1991); Travels with My Aunt; White Dawn, The; Zooman

Gostukhin, Vladimir: Close to Eden

Gotestam, Staffan: Brothers Lionheart, The

Gothard, Michael: King Arthur, The Young Warlord; Lifeforce; Scream and Scream Again; Valley, The

Gottfried, Gilbert: Aladdin & the King of Thieves; Problem Child; Silk Degrees

Gottli, Michael: Tales from the Gimli Hospital

Gottlieb, Carl: Cannonball

Gottschalk, Thomas: Driving Me Crazy; Ring of the Musketeer

Goudal, Jetta: White Gold

Goude, Ingrid: Killer Shrews, The

Gough, Lloyd: All My Sons (1948); Green Hornet, The (TV Series); It's Good to Be Alive; Rancho Notorious

Gough, Michael: Advocate, The; Age of Innocence, The; Anna Karenina (1947); Batman (1989); Batman Returns; Batman & Robin; Berserk; Caravaggio; Crucible of Horror; Curse of the Crimson Altar; Horror Hospital; Horror of Dracula; Horrors of the Black Museum; Horse's Mouth, The; Konga; Out of Africa; Phantom of the Opera (1962); Rob Roy, the Highland Rogue; Savage Messiah; Sleepy Hollow; Sword and the Rose, The (1953); They Came from Beyond Space; To the Lighthouse

Gould, Ben: Frankenstein Reborn!

Gould, Elliott: American History X; Beyond Justice; Big Hit, The; Bob & Carol & Ted & Alice; Boy Called Hate, A; Bugsy; Capricorn One; Conspiracy: The Trial of the Chicago 8; Cover Me; Dangerous, The (1994); Dangerous Love; Dead Men Don't Die; Devil and Max Devlin, The; Dirty Tricks; Escape to Athena; Falling in Love Again; Getting Straight; Glass Shield, The; Harry and Walter Go to New York; Hitz; I Love My Wife; I Will, I Will … for Now; Inside Out (1986); Johns; Lady Vanishes, The (1979); Last Flight of Noah's Ark; Lemon Sisters, The; Lethal Obsession; Little Murders; Long Goodbye, The; M*A*S*H; Matilda; Mean Johnny Barrows; Muppet Movie, The; Muppets Take Manhattan, The; My Wonderful Life; Naked Face, The; Night They Raided Minsky's, The; Night Visitor (1989); November Conspiracy, The; Over the Brooklyn Bridge; Quick, Let's Get Married; Silent Partner, The; S*P*Y*S; Telephone, The; Vanishing Act; Wet and Wild Summer; Whiffs

Gould, Harold: Better Late than Never; Big Bus, The; Brown's Requiem; Fourth Wise Man, The; Front Page, The (1974); Gambler, The (1980); Gambler, Part II—The Adventure Continues, The; How to Break Up a Happy Divorce; Love and Death; Man in the Santa Claus Suit, The; My Giant; One and Only, The; Playing for Keeps; Red Light Sting, The; Romero; Seems Like Old Times; Sting, The

Gould, Jason: Prince of Tides, The

Goulet, Arthur: Silver Blaze

Goulet, Robert: Based on an Untrue Story; Gay Purr-ee; Naked Gun 2, The

Gourmet, Olivier: La Promesse

Goutine, Andrei: Luna Park

Gow, David: Hiroshima

Gowa, Siqin: Day the Sun Turned Cold, The

Gower, Andre: Monster Squad, The

Gowland, Gibson: Blind Husbands; Greed; Hell Harbor

Goya, Chantal: Masculine Feminine

Gozlino, Paolo: Guns for Dollars

Gozzi, Patricia: Sundays and Cybèle

Graas, John Christian: Philadelphia Experiment 2, The

Grable, Betty: Beautiful Blonde from Bashful Bend, The; College Swing; Dolly Sisters, The; Down Argentine Way; Farmer Takes a Wife, The; Follow the Fleet; Footlight Serenade; Four Jills in a Jeep; Gay Divorcée, The; Give Me a Sailor; Hold 'em Jail; How to Marry a Millionaire; I Wake Up Screaming; Moon over Miami; Mother Wore Tights; Pin-Up Girl; Song of the Islands; Springtime in the Rockies (1942); Three Broadway Girls; Tin Pan Alley; Wabash Avenue; Yank in the RAF, A

Grabol, Sofie: Mifune

Grace, Anna: Girls Town (1996)

Grace, Carol: Gangster Story

Grace, Nickolas: Max Headroom; Robin Hood and the Sorcerer; Robin Hood: Herne's Son; Robin Hood: The Swords of Walyand; Salome's Last Dance; Solomon and Sheba (1995); Tom & Viv

Gracen, Elizabeth: Final Mission (1994); Lower Level

Grady, Ed L.: Last Game, The

Graf, David: Police Academy II: Their First Assignment; Police Academy III: Back in Training; Police Academy 4: Citizens on Patrol; Police Academy 5: Assignment: Miami Beach; Police Academy 6: City Under Siege; Police Academy: Mission to Moscow; Roseanne: An Unauthorized Biography; Suture

Graff, Ilene: Ladybugs

Graff, Todd: Dominick and Eugene; Fly by Night; Framed (1990); Opportunity Knocks

Graham, Bill: Bugsy

Graham, Cameron: Dream House

Graham, Currie: Survive the Night

Graham, Gary: Alien Nation, Dark Horizon; Arrogant, The; Dirty Dozen, The: The Deadly Mission; Last Warrior, The; Presence, The; Robot Jox; Steel (1997)

Graham, Gerrit: Annihilators, The; Bobbie Jo and the Outlaw; Break, The; Cannonball; Child's Play 2; C.H.U.D. II (Bud the C.H.U.D.); Demon Seed; Game of Love, The; Greetings; Home Movies; It's Alive III: Island of the Alive; Love Matters; National Lampoon's Class Reunion; National Lampoon's Favorite Deadly Sins; Philadelphia Experiment 2, The; Ratboy; Ratings Game, The; Son of Blob (Beware! The Blob); Spaceship (Naked Space); Terror Vision; Used Cars

Graham, Heather: Austin Powers: The Spy Who Shagged Me; Boogie Nights; Bowfinger; Diggstown; Don't Do It; Drugstore Cowboy; Entertaining Angels; Guilty as Charged; License to Drive; Lost in Space (1998); Nowhere; O Pioneers!; Shout (1991); Six Degrees of Separation; Swingers; Terrified

Graham, Kirsty: Loch Ness

Graham, Lauren: One True Thing

Graham, Marcus: Dangerous Game (1990)

Graham, Ronny: New Faces; Ratings Game, The; World's Greatest Lover, The

Graham, Samaria: Children of the Corn IV: The Gathering

Graham, Sasha: Addicted to Murder; Alien Agenda, The (TV Series); Bloodletting; Polymorph; Vicious Sweet, The

Graham, Sheilah: Girls Town (1959)

Graham, William: Just William's Luck

Grahame, Gloria: Bad and the Beautiful, The; Big Heat, The; Chilly Scenes of Winter; Crossfire (1947); Greatest Show on Earth, The; Human Desire; In a Lonely Place; It Happened in Brooklyn; Macao; Man Who Never Was, The; Mansion of the Doomed; Merry Wives of Windsor, The; Merton of the Movies; Nesting, The; Not as a Stranger; Ok-

Gray, Marcia: Housewife from Hell; Virtual Desire

Gray, Nadia: Captain's Table; La Dolce Vita; Maniac (1962)

Gray, Nan: Three Smart Girls; Three Smart Girls Grow Up

Gray, Rhonda: Twisted Nightmare

Gray, Sally: Dangerous Moonlight (Suicide Squadron); Green for Danger; Keeper, The; Saint in London, The; Saint's Vacation, The

Gray, Sam: Heart

Gray, Spalding: Bad Company (1995); Beaches; Beyond Rangoon; Clara's Heart; Diabolique (1996); Drunks; Hard Choices; King of the Hill; Monster in a Box; Paper, The; Spalding Gray: Terrors of Pleasure; Stars and Bars; Straight Talk; Swimming to Cambodia; True Stories; Zelda

Gray, Vernon: To Paris with Love

Grayson, Kathryn: Anchors Aweigh; Andy Hardy's Private Secretary; Desert Song, The; It Happened in Brooklyn; Kiss Me Kate; Kissing Bandit, The; Lovely to Look At; Rio Rita; Show Boat (1951); That Midnight Kiss; Thousands Cheer; Toast of New Orleans; Two Sisters from Boston

Greco, Jose: Proud and the Damned, The

Greco, Juliette: Elena and Her Men

Green, Abel: Copacabana

Green, Adolph: Lily in Love

Green, Brian Austin: American Summer, An; Kid

Green, D. L.: Dear Santa

Green, Gilbert: Executive Action

Green, Harry: Be Yourself

Green, Janet Laine: Bullies; Primo Baby

Green, Josh: Curse of the Puppet Master

Green, Kerri: Blue Flame; Goonies, The; Lucas; Summer Rental; Tainted Blood; Three for the Road

Green, Leif: Joy Sticks

Green, Marika: Emmanuelle; Pickpocket

Green, Martyn: Mikado, The (1939)

Green, Mitzi: Little Orphan Annie; Lost in Alaska; Transatlantic Merry-Go-Round

Green, Nigel: Corridors of Blood; Ipcress File, The; Skull, The; Tobruk; Zulu

Green, Seth: Airborne; Austin Powers: The Spy Who Shagged Me; Can't Hardly Wait; Can't Buy Me Love; Idle Hands; Infested (Ticks); Radio Days; Something Special

Green, Tom: Road Trip

Greenberg, Esther: Lupo; Sallah

Greenblatt, William: Homecoming (1996)

Greenbush, Lindsay and Sidney: Little House on the Prairie (TV Series)

Greene, Angela: At War with the Army; Cosmic Man, The

Greene, Daniel: American Tiger; Elvira, Mistress of the Dark; Hands of Steel; Opponent, The

Greene, Elizabeth: Offerings

Greene, Ellen: Dinner at Eight (1990); Glory! Glory!; Killer: A Journal of Murder; Little Shop of Horrors (1986); Me and Him; Next Stop, Greenwich Village; Professional, The; Pump Up the Volume; Stepping Out; Talk Radio; Wagons East

Greene, Graham: Benefit of the Doubt; Broken Chain, The; Clearcut; Cooperstown; Dances with Wolves; Die Hard with a Vengeance; Education of Little Tree, The; Huck and the King of Hearts; Last of His Tribe, The; Maverick; Medicine River; Pathfinder, The; Rain Without Thunder; Sabotage (1996); Savage Land; Shattered Image (1998); Thunderheart; Wounded

Greene, Kim Morgan: Grizzly Mountain

Greene, Lorne: Alamo, The; Thirteen Days to Glory; Autumn Leaves; Battlestar Galactica; Bonanza (TV Series); Buccaneer, The; Earthquake; Mission Galactica: The Cylon Attack; Peyton Place; Roots; Silver Chalice, The; Trap, The; Vasectomy

Greene, Michael: Americana; Clones, The; Eve of Destruction; Johnny Be Good; Kill Me Again; Rubin & Ed

Greene, Michele: Daddy's Girl; Double Standard; I Posed for Playboy; Nightmare on the 13th Floor; Silent Victim; Stranger by Night; Stranger in the House; Unborn II, The

Greene, Peter: Big Bang Theory, The; Black Cat Run; Blue Streak; Clean Shaven; Double Tap; Judgment Night; Laws of Gravity; Mask, The (1994); Rich Man's Wife, The; Sworn Enemies; Trading Favors

Greene, Richard: Against All Odds (1968) (Kiss and Kill, Blood of Fu Manchu); Black Castle, The; Captain Scarlett; Castle of Fu Manchu; Forever Amber; Hound of the

Baskervilles, The (1939); Island of the Lost; Little Princess, The (1939); My Lucky Star; Stanley and Livingstone

Greene, Shecky: Love Machine, The

Greenlea, Raymond: When Gangland Strikes

Greenlee, David: Slumber Party Massacre 3

Greenlees, Billy: That Sinking Feeling

Greenquist, Brad: Mutants in Paradise

Greenstreet, Sydney: Across the Pacific; Background to Danger; Casablanca; Christmas in Connecticut (1945); Conflict; Flamingo Road; Hollywood Canteen; Hucksters, The; Maltese Falcon, The; Passage to Marseilles; They Died with Their Boots On; Velvet Touch, The

Greenwald, Alex: Halloween Tree, The

Greenwood I, Bruce: Double Jeopardy (1999)

Greenwood, Bruce: Adrift; Another Chance; Bitter Vengeance; Climb, The; Color of Courage, The; Companion, The; Disturbing Behavior; Dream Man; Exotica; Father's Day; FBI Murders, The; Here on Earth; Hide & Seek; Little Kidnappers; Malibu Bikini Shop, The; Passenger 57; Rio Diablo; Rules of Engagement; Servants of Twilight; Spy; Striker's Mountain; Summer Dreams; Sweet Hereafter, The

Greenwood, Charlotte: Dangerous When Wet; Down Argentine Way; Great Dan Patch, The; Moon over Miami; Opposite Sex, The (1956); Parlor, Bedroom and Bath; Springtime in the Rockies (1942)

Greenwood, Joan: At Bertram's Hotel; Detective, The (1954); Hound of the Baskervilles, The (1977); Importance of Being Earnest, The; Little Dorrit; Man in the White Suit, The; Moonspinners, The; Mysterious Island; Stage Struck (1958); Tight Little Island; Uncanny, The; Water Babies, The

Greenwood, Kathryn: Switching Goals

Greer, Gregory A.: Midnight Kiss

Greer, Jane: Big Steal, The; Billie; Clown, The; George White's Scandals; Man of a Thousand Faces; Out of the Past; Prisoner of Zenda, The (1952); Run for the Sun; Shadow Riders, The; Sinbad the Sailor; Station West; They Won't Believe Me; Where Love Has Gone

Greer, Judy: Jawbreaker

Greer, Michael: Fortune and Men's Eyes

Greeson, Timothy: Disturbance, The

Gregg, Bradley: Class of 1999; Eye of the Storm

Gregg, Clark: Adventures of Sebastian Cole, The

Gregg, Julie: From Hell to Borneo

Gregg, Mitchell: House of Terror

Gregg, Virginia: Casbah; D.I., The; Hanging Tree, The; Spencer's Mountain

Greggio, Ezio: Silence of the Hams

Gregory, Pascal: Pauline at the Beach; Queen Margot

Gregor, Nora: Rules of the Game, The

Gregorio, Rose: Tarantella

Gregory, Andre: Last Summer in the Hamptons; Last Temptation of Christ, The; Linguini Incident, The; Mosquito Coast, The; My Dinner with Andre; Shadow, The; Street Smart

Gregory, Celia: Agatha; Children of the Full Moon; Inside Man, The

Gregory, David: Deadmate

Gregory, Dick: Sweet Love, Bitter

Gregory, James: Al Capone; Ambushers, The; Beneath the Planet of the Apes; Clambake; Comeback Kid, The; Francis Gary Powers: The True Story of the U-2 Spy Incident; Love God?, The; Manchurian Candidate, The; Murderers' Row; Naked City, The; Onionhead; PT 109; Secret War of Harry Frigg, The; Sons of Katie Elder, The; Two Weeks in Another Town

Gregory, Lola: Coming Up Roses

Gregory, Mark: 1990: The Bronx Warriors; Thunder Warrior; Thunder Warrior II

Gregory, Natalie: Alice in Wonderland (1985); Alice Through the Looking Glass (1985)

Gregory, Nick: Last Summer in the Hamptons

Gregory, Paul: Whoopee

Gregson, Joan: Sea People

Gregson, John: Captain's Table; Genevieve; Hans Brinker; Pursuit of the Graf Spee; Three Cases of Murder

Greif, Stephen: Great Riviera Bank Robbery, The

Greist, Kim: Duplicates; Homeward Bound: The Incredible Journey; Homeward Bound II: Lost in San Francisco; Houseguest; Last Exit to Earth; Manhunter; Payoff; Roswell; Throw Momma from the Train; Why Me?

Grellier, Michel: Holiday Hotel

renfell, Joyce: Americanization of Emily, The; Belles of t. Trinian's, The; Blue Murder at St. Trinian's; Old Dark ouse, The (1963); Pickwick Papers, The

renier, Adrian: Adventures of Sebastian Cole, The

renier, Adrian: Drive Me Crazy

renon, Macha: Legends of the North; Sworn Enemies; Vindsor Protocol, The

revill, Laurent: Camille Claudel

rey, Anne: Number 17

rey, Denise: Devil in the Flesh (1946); Sputnik

rey, Jennifer: Bloodhounds of Broadway; Case for Murder, A; Criminal Justice; Dirty Dancing; Eyes of a Witness; erris Bueller's Day Off; Lover's Knot; Since You've Been one; Stroke of Midnight; Wind (1992)

rey, Joel: Buffalo Bill and the Indians; Cabaret; Christmas arol, A (1999); Come September; Dangerous, The (1994); afka; Man on a String; Music of Chance, The; Queenie; emo Williams: The Adventure Begins; Seven-Per-Cent olution, The; Venus Rising

rey, Nan: House of the Seven Gables, The; Invisible Man eturns; Tower of London (1939)

rey, Reatha: Soul Vengeance (Welcome Home Brother harles)

rey, Samantha: Night of the Zombies (1981)

rey, Shirley: Hurricane Express; Mystery of the Marie Ceeste, The (The Phantom Ship); Riding Tornado, The; Terror board; Texas Cyclone; Uptown New York

rey, Virginia: Another Thin Man; Big Store, The; Broadway Serenade; House of Horrors; Idiot's Delight; Jungle im; Love Has Many Faces; Mexican Hayride; Naked Kiss, he; Rose Tattoo, The; Slaughter Trail; Tarzan's New York dventure; Threat, The; Whistling in the Dark

reyeyes, Michael: Crazy Horse; Dance Me Outside; Magnificent Seven, The (TV Series)

reyn, Clinton: Raid on Rommel

ribbon, Harry: Ride Him Cowboy

rieco, Richard: Born to Run; Demolitionist, The; Heaven or Vegas; It Looks Could Kill (1991); Inhumanoid; Mobsters; Mutual Needs; Suspicious Agenda; Tomcat: Dangerous Desires; Ultimate Deception; Vow to Kill, A; When Time Expires

riem, Helmut: Cabaret; Children of Rage; Damned, The; es Rendez-Vous D'Anna; Malou

rier, David Alan: Beer; Blankman; Boomerang (1992); In he Army Now; Jumanji; McHale's Navy; Return to Me; ales from the Hood; 3 Strikes

rier, Pam: Above the Law; Big Bird Cage, The; Bill and ed's Bogus Journey; Bucktown; Class of 1999; Coffy; Drum; Fortress 2: Re-entry; Foxy Brown; Friday Foster; reased Lightning; Holy Smoke; In Too Deep; Jackie Brown; John Carpenter's Escape from L.A.; Miami Vice: The Prodigal Son"; On the Edge; Original Gangstas; Package, The; Scream, Blacula, Scream; Serial Killer; Sheba Baby; Something Wicked This Way Comes; Tough Enough; Twilight People; Vindicator, The

rier, Rosey: Reggie's Prayer; Sophisticated Gents, The

ries, Jonathan: Casualties; Four Eyes and Six Guns; Fright Night II; Get Shorty; Kill Me Again; Pucker Up and Bark Like a Dog; Running Scared (1986)

riesemer, John: Where the Rivers Flow North

rieve, Russ: Hills Have Eyes, The

rifasi, Joe: Bad Medicine; Benny & Joon; Feud, The; Gentleman Bandit, The; Heavy; Hide in Plain Sight; Money Train; Naked Man, The; On the Yard; Still of the Night; Switching Goals

riffeth, Simone: Hot Target; Patriot

riffies, Ethel: Billy Liar; Billy the Kid; Birds, The

riffin, Eddie: Deuce Bigalow: Male Gigolo; Foolish; Meteor Man; Walking Dead, The

riffin, Joseph: First Degree; Striking Poses

riffin, Kathy: It's Pat: The Movie

riffin, Lynne: Strange Brew

riffin, Merv: Alice Through the Looking Glass (1985); Lonely Guy, The; Two-Minute Warning

riffin, Rhonda: Creeps, The; Hideous

riffin, Tod: She Demons

riffith, Andy: Andy Griffith Show, The (TV Series); Face in the Crowd, A; Fatal Vision; Hearts of the West; Murder in Coweta County; Murder in Texas; No Time for Sergeants; No Time for Sergeants (Television); Onionhead; Pray for

the Wildcats; Return to Mayberry; Rustler's Rhapsody; Savages (1974); Spy Hard

Griffith, Corinne: Lilies of the Field (1930)

Griffith, Geraldine: Experience Preferred … But Not Essential

Griffith, Hugh: Abominable Dr. Phibes, The; Canterbury Tales, The; Counterfeit Traitor, The; Cry of the Banshee; Diary of Forbidden Dreams; Dr. Phibes Rises Again; Hound of the Baskervilles, The (1977); How to Steal a Million; Joseph Andrews; Last Days of Man on Earth, The; Legend of the Werewolf; Lucky Jim; Luther; Mutiny on the Bounty (1962); Oliver; Run for Your Money, A; Start the Revolution Without Me; Tom Jones; Who Slew Auntie Roo?; Wuthering Heights (1971)

Griffith, James: Amazing Transparent Man, The; Blonde Ice; Bullwhip; Double Deal; Dynamo; Guns of Fort Petticoat

Griffith, Katharine: Pollyanna (1920)

Griffith, Kenneth: Englishman Who Went up a Hill But Came down a Mountain, The; Koroshi

Griffith, Kristin: Europeans, The; Rose Hill

Griffith, Melanie: Another Day in Paradise; Body Double; Bonfire of the Vanities; Born Yesterday (1993); Buffalo Girls; Cherry 2000; Crazy in Alabama; Drowning Pool, The; Fear City; In the Spirit; Joyride (1977); Lolita (1997); Milagro Beanfield War, The; Milk Money; Mulholland Falls; Night Moves; Nobody's Fool (1994); Now and Then; Pacific Heights; Paradise (1991); RKO 281; She's in the Army Now; Shining Through; Smile; Something Wild; Stormy Monday; Stranger Among Us, A; Two Much; Underground Aces; Women & Men: Stories of Seduction; Working Girl

Griffith, Raymond: White Tiger

Griffith, Rhiana: Pitch Black

Griffith, Thomas Ian: Blood of the Innocent; Crackerjack; Excessive Force; Hollow Point; John Carpenter's Vampires; Ulterior Motives

Griffith, Tom: Alien Factor, The

Griffith, Tracy: All Tied Up; Finest Hour, The; First Power, The; Skeeter

Griffiths, Linda: Lianna; Reno and the Doc; Sword of Gideon

Griffiths, Rachel: Children of the Revolution; Cosi; Hilary and Jackie; Muriel's Wedding; My Son the Fanatic; Welcome to Woop Woop

Griffiths, Richard: Blame It on the Bellboy; Funnybones; Guarding Tess; King Ralph; Private Function, A; Shanghai Surprise; Sleepy Hollow; Whoops Apocalypse; Withnail and I

Griggs, Camilla: Bar Girls; Forced Vengeance

Griggs, Jeff: Forbidden Games (1995)

Grika, Johanna: Visitants, The

Grimaldi, Dan: Don't Go in the House

Grimes, Frank: Crystalstone; Dive, The

Grimes, Gary: Cahill—US Marshal; Class of '44; Culpepper Cattle Co., The; Gus; Summer of '42

Grimes, Scott: Critters; Critters 2: The Main Course; It Came Upon a Midnight Clear; Mystery, Alaska; Night Life

Grimes, Steven: Fatal Past

Grimes, Tammy: America; Can't Stop the Music; Modern Affair, A; No Big Deal; Trouble on the Corner

Grimm, Dick: Night of the Bloody Transplant

Grinberg, Anouk: Merci la Vie; Mon Homme (My Man); My Man (Mon Homme)

Grisham, Jerry: Escapes

Grives, Steven: Dangerous Game (1990)

Grizzard, George: Attica; Bachelor Party; Caroline?; Comes a Horseman; Deliberate Stranger, The; From the Terrace; Iran Days of Crisis; Oldest Living Graduate, The; Stranger Within, The; Wrong Is Right

Groce, Larry: Heroes of the Heart

Grodenchik, Max: Rumpelstiltskin

Grodin, Charles: Beethoven; Beethoven's 2nd; Clifford; Couch Trip, The; Dave; 11 Harrowhouse; Grass Is Always Greener over the Septic Tank, The; Great Muppet Caper, The; Grown-Ups; Heart and Souls; Heartbreak Kid, The; Heaven Can Wait (1978); Incredible Shrinking Woman, The; Ishtar; It's My Turn; King Kong (1976); Last Resort; Lonely Guy, The; Meanest Men in the West, The; Midnight Run; Movers and Shakers; My Summer Story; Real Life; Seems Like Old Times; Sex and the College Girl; So I Married an Axe Murderer; Sunburn; Taking Care of Business; Woman in Red, The

Grody, Kathryn: Lemon Sisters, The

Grogan, C. P.: Comfort and Joy

Grogan, Clare: Gregory's Girl

Groh, David: Acts of Betrayal; Broken Vows; King Lear (1982); Last Exit to Earth; Return of Superfly, The; Stoned Age, The

Gronemeyer, Herbert: Das Boot (The Boat); Spring Symphony

Groom, Sam: Baby Maker, The; Deadly Eyes; Deadly Games; Run for the Roses (Thoroughbred)

Gross, Arye: Arthur's Quest; Couch Trip, The; Coupe De Ville; Experts, The; For the Boys; Hexed; House II: The Second Story; In the Company of Spies; Matter of Degrees, A; Midnight Clear, A; Opposite Sex (And How to Live with Them), The (1993); Shaking the Tree; Soul Man

Gross, Edan: And You Thought Your Parents Were Weird; Halloween Tree, The

Gross, Loretta: Kill-Off, The

Gross, Mary: Casual Sex?; Couch Trip, The; Feds; Hot to Trot; Santa Clause, The; Troop Beverly Hills

Gross, Michael: Alan and Naomi; Big Business; Cool As Ice; FBI Murders, The; Ground Control; Kounterfeit; Little Gloria, Happy at Last; Midnight Murders; Sometimes They Come Back Again; Tremors; Tremors 2: Aftershocks; True Heart

Gross, Molly: Slaves to the Underground

Gross, Paul: Aspen Extreme; Buffalo Jump; Northern Extremes

Grossman, DePrise: Zarkorr! The Invader

Grossmith, George: Wedding Rehearsal

Grosso, Sonny: French Connection, The

Groth, Sylvester: Stalingrad

Grove, Richard: Army of Darkness; Scanner Cop

Grovenor, Linda: Die Laughing; Wheels of Fire

Grover, Edward: Strike Force

Groves, Robin: Nesting, The; Silver Bullet

Groves, Stewart: Raising Heroes

Grubb, Robert: Gallipoli

Grubbs, Gary: Ernest Green Story, The; Fatal Vision; JFK

Grunberg, Klaus: More

Grundgens, Gustav: M

Gruner, Olivier: Angel Town; Automatic; Mercenary; Mercenary 2: Thick and Thin; Nemesis (1992); Savage; Savate; Velocity Trap

Gryglaszewska, Halina: Double Life of Veronique, The

Gschnitzer, Julia: Inheritors, The

Guadagni, Nicky: Cube

Guard, Christopher: Return to Treasure Island

Guard, Dominic: Absolution; Picnic at Hanging Rock

Guard, Pippa: Daisies in December

Guardino, Harry: Adventures of Bullwhip Griffin, The; Dirty Harry; Enforcer, The (1976); Five Pennies, The; Get Christie Love!; Hell Is for Heroes; Houseboat; Lovers and Other Strangers; Madigan; Matilda; Neon Empire, The; Pork Chop Hill; St. Ives; They Only Kill Their Masters; Whiffs

Guarnica, Lupe: Gloria (1980)

Gudmundsdottir, Bjork: Juniper Tree, The

Guedj, Vanessa: Le Grand Chemin (The Grand Highway)

Guerin, Michael: Curse of the Puppet Master

Guerra, Blanca: Danzon

Guerra, Danny: Plutonium Baby

Guerra, Ruy: Aguirre: Wrath of God

Guerra, Saverio: Summer of Sam

Guerrero, Evelyn: Cheech and Chong's Next Movie; Nice Dreams

Guerrero, Franco: Deathfight

Guesmi, Samir: Halfmoon

Guessan, Albertine: Faces of Women

Guest, Christopher: Beyond Therapy; Few Good Men, A; Girlfriends; Last Word, The (1979); Little Shop of Horrors (1986); Long Riders, The; Piano for Mrs. Cimino, A; Return of Spinal Tap, The; Sticky Fingers; This Is Spinal Tap; Waiting for Guffman

Guest, Lance: Halloween II; Jaws: The Revenge; Last Starfighter, The; Plan B

Guest, Nicholas: Adrenalin: Fear the Rush; Brain Smasher ... A Love Story; Chrome Soldiers; Dollman; Long Riders, The; My Daughter's Keeper; Night Hunter; Puppet Master 5: The Final Chapter; Strange Case of Dr. Jekyll and Mr. Hyde, The (1989)

Guetary, Francois: Running Delilah

Guevara, Nacha: Miss Mary

Guffey, Cary: Mutant

Gugino, Carla: Buccaneers, The; Judas Kiss; Miami Rhapsody; Murder Without Motive; Red Hot; Snake Eyes; Son-in-Law

Guidera, Anthony: Undercover (1995)

Guier, Adam: Pistol, The: The Birth of a Legend

Guilbert, Ann: Grumpier Old Men

Guilbert, Ann Morgan: Dick Van Dyke Show, The (TV Series)

Guild, Nancy: Abbott and Costello Meet the Invisible Man; Black Magic (1949); Somewhere in the Night

Guilfoyle, James: Two Worlds

Guilfoyle, Paul: Air Force One; Amelia Earhart: The Final Flight; Brother Orchid; Celtic Pride; Couch in New York, A; Crime of Dr. Crespi, The; Curiosity Kills; Final Analysis; Hoffa; In Dreams; L.A. Confidential; One Tough Cop; Random Hearts; Ransom (1996); Virginian, The (1946); Winterset

Guillaume, Robert: Cosmic Slop; Death Warrant; First Kid; His Bodyguard; Kid with the Broken Halo, The; Kid with the 200 I.Q., The; Lean on Me; Meteor Man; North and South; Penthouse, The; Run for the Dream; Seems Like Old Times; Superfly T.N.T.; Wanted: Dead or Alive; You Must Remember This

Guillen, Fernando: Women on the Verge of a Nervous Breakdown

Guinan, Francis: Mortal Sins (1992)

Guinee, Tim: Chain of Desire; John Carpenter's Vampires; Lily Dale; Pompatus of Love, The; Tai-Pan; Three Lives of Karen, The; Vietnam War Story—Part Two

Guinness, Alec: Bridge on the River Kwai, The; Brother Sun, Sister Moon; Captain's Paradise, The; Comedians, The; Cromwell; Damn the Defiant!; Detective, The (1954); Dr. Zhivago; Fall of the Roman Empire, The; Foreign Field, A; Great Expectations (1946); Handful of Dust, A; Hitler, the Last Ten Days; Horse's Mouth, The; Hotel Paradiso; Kafka; Kind Hearts and Coronets; Ladykillers, The; Last Holiday; Lavender Hill Mob, The; Lawrence of Arabia; Little Dorrit; Little Lord Fauntleroy (1980); Lovesick; Majority of One, A; Malta Story, The; Man in the White Suit, The; Monsignor Quixote; Murder by Death; Mute Witness; Oliver Twist (1948); Passage to India, A; Prisoner, The (1955); Promoter, The; Quiller Memorandum, The; Raise the Titanic; Run for Your Money, A; Scrooge (1970); Star Wars; Swan, The (1956); To Paris with Love; To See Such Fun; Tunes of Glory

Guiomar, Julien: Leolo; Swashbuckler, The (1984)

Guirardeau, Bernard: Ridicule

Guiry, Tom: Lassie; Sandlot, The; Strike! (1998)

Guitierrez, Lorena: Crier, The

Guitry, Sacha: Pearls of the Crown, The

Gulager, Clu: Gambler, The (1980); Glass House, The; Gunfighter (1997); Hidden, The; Hit Lady; Hunter's Blood; I'm Gonna Git You Sucka!; Lies; Living Proof: The Hank Williams, Jr., Story; McQ; My Heroes Have Always Been Cowboys; Nightmare on Elm Street 2, A: Freddy's Revenge Offspring, The; Other Side of Midnight, The; Prime Risk; Return of the Living Dead, The; Smile, Jenny, You're Dead; Summer Heat (1987); Teen Vamp; Touched by Love; Uninvited, The (1987); Willa

Gulette, Sean: Pi

Gulliver, Dorothy: Galloping Ghost, The; In Old Cheyenne; Shadow of the Eagle

Gulpilil, David: "Crocodile" Dundee; Mad Dog Morgan; Walkabout

Guma, Antonio: Lola's Game

Gummersal, Devon: Trading Favors

Gunn, David: Vampire Journals

Gunn, Jane: Carnosaur 3: Primal Species

Gunn, Janet: Dark Prince: The Intimate Diary of the Marquis de Sade; Dark Prince: The Intimate Tales of Marquis de Sade; Marquis de Sade; Night of the Running Man; Nurse, The

Gunn, Moses: Aaron Loves Angela; Amityville II: The Possession; Certain Fury; Cornbread, Earl and Me; Dixie Lanes; Haunts of the Very Rich; Heartbreak Ridge; Hot Rock, The; Killing Floor, The; Leonard Part 6; Memphis; Ninth Configuration, The; Perfect Harmony; Shaft; Shaft's Big Score!; Wild Rovers, The

Gunning, Paul: Hollywood Hot Tubs

inton, Bob: Ace Ventura: When Nature Calls; Broken Arrow (1996); Buffalo Soldiers; Elvis Meets Nixon; Father ood; Glimmer Man, The; In Pursuit of Honor; Ladykiller; is Gibbs and the Love Canal; Patch Adams; Perfect orm, The; Rollover; Shawshank Redemption, The; Static

ioli, Zhang: Story of Xinghua, The

ipia, Kamlesh: Crystalstone

irchenko, Lyudmilla: Siberiade

irie, Sigrid: Adventures of Marco Polo, The; Three Faces est

irney, Rachel: Upstairs, Downstairs

irry, Eric: Bad Boys (1983); Something Special; Zoo ang, The

irwitch, Annabelle: Changing Habits; Intimate Betrayal; zza Man

uthrie, Arlo: Alice's Restaurant; Roadside Prophets; oody Guthrie—Hard Travellin'

uthrie, Tyrone: Beachcomber, The; Sidewalks of London utierrez, Miguel: Bitter Sugar

utierrez, Zaide Silvia: El Norte

utowski, Rita: Sandman, The (1996)

uttenberg, Steve: Amazon Women on the Moon; Bad edicine; Bedroom Window, The; Big Green, The; Can't top the Music; Casper: A Spirited Beginning; Chicken hronicles, The; Cocoon; Cocoon: The Return; Day After, he; Diner; Don't Tell Her It's Me; High Spirits; Home for the olidays (1995); It Takes Two (1995); Man Who Wasn't here, The; Miracle on Ice; Police Academy; Police Academy II: Their First Assignment; Police Academy III: Back in raining; Police Academy 4: Citizens on Patrol; Short Circuit; Surrender; Three Men and a Baby; Three Men and a ittle Lady; Zeus and Roxanne

utteridge, Lucy: Little Gloria, Happy at Last; Top Secret; rouble with Spies, The; Tusks

uve, Bertil: Fanny and Alexander

uy, DeJuan: One Man's Justice

uy, Jasmine: America's Dream; Perfect Crime

uzaldo, Joe: Evil Has a Face; Smooth Talker

uzman, Luis: Bone Collector, The; Carlito's Way; Jumpin' t the Boneyard; Limey, The; Mr. Wonderful

wenn, Edmund: Anthony Adverse; Bigamist, The; Challenge to Lassie; Cheers for Miss Bishop; Doctor Takes a Wife, The; Foreign Correspondent; Green Dolphin Street; Hills of Home; If I Were Rich; It's a Dog's Life; Lassie Come Home; Life with Father; Meanest Man in the World, The; Miracle on 34th Street (1947); Skin Game, The (1931); Student Prince, The; Sylvia Scarlett; Them!; Trouble with Distinction, A

wyndaf, Gweirydd: Christmas Reunion, A

wynn, Michael: Revenge of Frankenstein

wynn, Peter: Nostradamus Kid, The

wynne, Anne: Arson Inc.; Black Friday; Dick Tracy Meets Gruesome; House of Frankenstein; King of the Bullwhip; Meteor Monster (Teenage Monster); Ride 'em Cowboy; Strange Case of Dr. Rx, The; Weird Woman

wynne, Fred: Any Friend of Nicholas Nickleby Is a Friend of Mine; Boy Who Could Fly, The; Car 54 Where Are You? (TV Series); Disorganized Crime; Ironweed; Littlest Angel, The; Man That Corrupted Hadleyburg, The; Munsters' Revenge, The; My Cousin Vinny; Mysterious Stranger, The; Pet Sematary; Secret of My Success, The; Simon; So Fine; Vanishing Act; Water

Gwynne, Michael C.: Cherry 2000; Deadly Encounter (1972); Guyana Tragedy, The: The Story of Jim Jones; Harry Tracy; Last of the Finest, The; Payday; Streets of L.A., The; Village of the Damned (1960)

Gyllenhaal, Jake: October Sky

Gyngell, Kim: Boulevard of Broken Dreams; Heaven Tonight; Wacky World of Wills and Burke, The

Gynt, Greta: Human Monster, The (Dark Eyes of London); Sexton Blake and the Hooded Terror

Haade, William: Days of Old Cheyenne; Kid Galahad (1937); Stage to Chino

Haas, Hugo: Casbah; Holiday in Mexico; King Solomon's Mines (1950); Merton of the Movies; Northwest Outpost; Private Affairs of Bel Ami, The

Haas, Lukas: Alan and Naomi; Boys (1996); Everyone Says I Love You; Johns; Lady in White; Leap of Faith; Mars Attacks!; Music Box, The; Rambling Rose; See You in the

Morning; Shattered Spirits; Solarbabies; Testament; Warrior Spirit; Witness; Wizard of Loneliness, The

Haase, Cathy: Kill-Off, The

Habbema, Cox: Question of Silence, A

Habeck, Michael: Gigashadow

Habermann, Eva: Eating Pattern; Gigashadow; I Worship His Shadow; Tales from a Parallel Universe

Habich, Matthias: Coup De Grace; Straight for the Heart

Hack, Shelley: Finishing Touch, The; If Ever I See You Again; Me, Myself & I; Single Bars, Single Women; Stepfather, The; Troll

Hacker, George: Manhattan Baby

Hackett, Buddy: Babe (1982); Bud and Lou; God's Little Acre; It's a Mad Mad Mad Mad World; Loose Shoes; Love Bug, The; Muscle Beach Party; Music Man, The; Paulie; Wonderful World of the Brothers Grimm, The

Hackett, Claire: Gallowglass

Hackett, Joan: Escape Artist, The; Group, The; One Trick Pony; Only When I Laugh; Possessed, The (1977); Reflections of Murder; Support Your Local Sheriff!; Terminal Man, The; Will Penny

Hackett, John: Dead of Night (1977)

Hackett, Karl: Border Phantom; Desert Phantom; His Brother's Ghost; Prairie Rustlers; Sing, Cowboy, Sing; Take Me Back to Oklahoma; Traitor, The

Hackett, Sandy: Hamburger—The Motion Picture

Hackford, Taylor: First Works, Volumes 1 & 2

Hackl, Karl Heinz: Assisi Underground, The

Hackman, Gene: Absolute Power; All Night Long; Another Woman; Bat 21; Birdcage, The; Bite the Bullet; Bonnie and Clyde; Class Action; Company Business; Conversation, The; Crimson Tide; Doctors' Wives; Domino Principle, The; Downhill Racer; Enemy of the State; Eureka; Extreme Measures; Firm, The; French Connection, The; French Connection II, The; Full Moon in Blue Water; Geronimo: An American Legend (1994); Get Shorty; Hawaii; Hoosiers; I Never Sang for My Father; Lilith; Loose Cannons; March or Die; Marooned; Mississippi Burning; Misunderstood (1984); Narrow Margin (1990); Night Moves; No Way Out; Package, The; Poseidon Adventure, The; Postcards from the Edge; Power (1986); Prime Cut; Quick and the Dead, The (1995); Reds; Riot (1969); Scarecrow; Split Decisions; Superman: Superman II; Superman III: The Quest for Peace; Target; Twice in a Lifetime; Twilight; Uncommon Valor; Under Fire; Unforgiven (1992); Wyatt Earp; Young Frankenstein; Zandy's Bride

Hada, Michiko: Mystery of Rampo, The

Hadary, Jonathan: As Is

Haddon, Dayle: Bedroom Eyes; Cyborg; French Woman, The; North Dallas Forty; Sex with a Smile

Haden, Sara: Anne of Green Gables (1934); Life Begins for Andy Hardy; Life of Her Own, A; Love Laughs at Andy Hardy; Mad Love (1935); Mr. Ace; Our Vines Have Tender Grapes; Poor Little Rich Girl (1936); Spitfire (1934)

Hadji-Lazaro, François: Dellamorte, Dellamore

Hadley, Reed: Baron of Arizona, The; Half-Breed, The; Kansas Pacific; Little Big Horn; Rimfire; Shock (1946); Whistling in the Dark; Zorro's Fighting Legion

Hafner, Ingrid: Philby, Burgess and Maclean: Spy Scandal of the Century

Hagalin, Sigridur: Children of Nature

Hagan, Jennifer: Gallagher's Travels

Hagan, Marianne: Halloween: The Curse of Michael Myers; I Think I Do

Hagan, Molly: French Exit; Ringmaster

Hagar, Ivan: Behind Locked Doors

Hagen, Jean: Asphalt Jungle, The; Danny Thomas Show, The (TV Series); Dead Ringer; Latin Lovers; Life of Her Own, A; Panic in the Year Zero; Shaggy Dog, The; Singin' in the Rain

Hagen, Ross: Armed Response; Attack of the 60 Ft. Centerfold; B.O.R.N.; Commando Squad; Cyberzone; Dinosaur Island; Hellcats, The; Night Creature; Phantom Empire, The (1986); Star Slammer; Virtual Desire; Warlords

Hagen, Uta: Other, The; Reversal of Fortune

Hager, Kristi: Sure Fire

Hagerty, Julie: Airplane!; Airplane II: The Sequel; Bad Medicine; Beyond Therapy; Bloodhounds of Broadway; Boys Will Be Boys; Goodbye New York; Lost in America; Midsummer Night's Sex Comedy, A; Necessary Parties;

Marlow, Jean: Bombshell (1933); China Seas; Dinner at Eight (1933); Girl from Missouri, The; Hold Your Man; Laurel and Hardy Classics: Vol. 1–9; Libeled Lady; Personal Property; Platinum Blonde; Public Enemy; Reckless 1935); Red Dust; Red-Headed Woman; RiffRaff (1936); Saratoga; Saturday Night Kid, The; Suzy; Wife vs. Secretary

Harmon, Deborah: Used Cars

Harmon, Mark: After the Promise; Casualties; Cold Heaven; Deliberate Stranger, The; Dillinger (1990); Fear and Loathing in Las Vegas; Fourth Story; Goliath Awaits; Let's Get Harry; Long Road Home, The; Magic in the Water, The; Presidio, The; Prince of Bel Air; St. Elsewhere (TV Series); Stealing Home; Summer School; Sweet Bird of Youth 1989); Till There Was You; Worth Winning; Wyatt Earp

Harmon, Tom: Spirit of West Point, The

Harmstorf, Raimund: Wolves, The (1994)

Harnett, Josh: Faculty, The; Halloween: H20

Harnick, Aaron: Judy Berlin

Harnos, Christine: Bloodhounds

Harnos, Kristina: Rescue, The

Harolde, Ralf: I'm No Angel

Harper, Frank: Twentyfourseven (English)

Harper, Hill: He Got Game; Skulls, The; Zooman

Harper, James: Mortal Sins (1990) (Dangerous Obsession)

Harper, Jessica: Blue Iguana; Imagemaker, The; Inserts; Mr. Wonderful; Pennies from Heaven; Phantom of the Paradise; Safe; Shock Treatment; Stardust Memories; Suspiria

Harper, Kamie: Friendship in Vienna, A

Harper, Kyra: Project: Genesis

Harper, Marjory: Life and Times of Grizzly Adams, The

Harper, Paul: Bloody Trail

Harper, Robert: My Name Is Bill W; Nick Knight; Not Quite Human; Payoff

Harper, Samantha: Oh! Calcutta!

Harper, Tess: Amityville III: The Demon; Chiefs; Children of Fury; Crimes of the Heart; Criminal Law; Daddy's Dyin' and Who's Got the Will; Dark River: A Father's Revenge; Far North; Flashpoint; Her Alibi; Incident at Dark River; Ishtar; Man in the Moon, The; My Heroes Have Always Been Cowboys; My New Gun; Road to Galveston, The; Starflight One; Tender Mercies

Harper, Valerie: Blame It on Rio; Chapter Two; Don't Go to Sleep; Execution, The; Freebie and the Bean; Last Married Couple in America, The; Night Terror; Shadow Box, The; Thursday's Game

Harrelson, Brett: Dee Snider's Strangeland; From Dusk Till Dawn 2: Texas Blood Money; People vs. Larry Flynt, The

Harrelson, Woody: Cool Blue; Cowboy Way, The; Doc Hollywood; EDtv; Eye of the Demon; Hi-Lo Country, The; Indecent Proposal; Kingpin; Money Train; Natural Born Killers; Palmetto; People vs. Larry Flynt, The; Play It to the Bone; Sunchaser; Ted & Venus; Wag the Dog; Welcome to Sarajevo; White Men Can't Jump; Wildcats

Harring, Laura: Rio Diablo

Harrington, Al: White Fang 2: Myth of the White Wolf

Harrington, Kate: Rachel, Rachel

Harrington, Laura: Dead Air; Linda; Maximum Overdrive; Midnight Cabaret; Perfect Witness

Harrington, Linda: Secret, The

Harrington, Pat: Affair, The (1973); President's Analyst, The

Harrington, Peter: Time Chasers

Harris, Adeline: Texas John Slaughter: Stampede at Bitter Creek

Harris, Anita: Follow That Camel; Martians Go Home

Harris, Barbara: Dirty Rotten Scoundrels; Family Plot; Freaky Friday; Movie Movie; Nice Girls Don't Explode; North Avenue Irregulars, The; Oh Dad, Poor Dad—Mama's Hung You in the Closet and I'm Feeling So Sad; Peggy Sue Got Married; Plaza Suite; Seduction of Joe Tynan, The; Thousand Clowns, A

Harris, Barbara Eve: In His Father's Shoes

Harris, Brad: Fury of Hercules, The; Hercules (1983); Rattler Kid; Samson; Seven Magnificent Gladiators, The

Harris, Bruklin: Dangerous Minds; Girls Town (1996)

Harris, Bud: Moon over Harlem

Harris, Christi: Night of the Demons 2

Harris, Cynthia: Edward and Mrs. Simpson; Izzy & Moe; Pancho Barnes; Reuben, Reuben

Harris, Danielle: Halloween IV: The Return of Michael Myers; Halloween V: The Revenge of Michael Myers; Nightmare (1991); Urban Legend

Harris, David: Badge of the Assassin; Dangerous Relations; Undercover (1987)

Harris, Dina: Ravage

Harris, Ed: Absolute Power; Abyss, The; Alamo Bay; Apollo 13; Borderline; China Moon; Code Name: Emerald; Eye for an Eye (1995); Firm, The; Flash of Green, A; Glengarry Glen Ross; Jacknife; Just Cause; Knightriders; Last Innocent Man, The; Milk Money; Needful Things; Nixon; Paris Trout; Places in the Heart; Riders of the Purple Sage; Right Stuff, The; Rock, The; Running Mates (1992); Seekers, The; State of Grace; Stepmom; Sweet Dreams; Swing Shift; Third Miracle, The; To Kill a Priest; Truman Show, The; Under Fire; Walker

Harris, Estelle: Addams Family Reunion; Chairman of the Board; Downhill Willie

Harris, Fred: Exterminators of the Year 3000

Harris, Gail: Cellblock Sisters; Forbidden Games (1995); Virtual Desire

Harris, George: Prime Suspect 2

Harris, James: Sunset Park

Harris, Jamie: Savage Hearts

Harris, Jared: B. Monkey; Blue in the Face; Eternal, The; Happiness; I Shot Andy Warhol; Public Eye, The; Tall Tale: The Unbelievable Adventures of Pecos Bill

Harris, Jim: Squeeze Play

Harris, Jo Ann: Beguiled, The; Deadly Games

Harris, Jonathan: Lost in Space (TV Series)

Harris, Julie: Bell Jar, The; Carried Away; Christmas Wife, The; Dark Half, The; East of Eden (1955); Ellen Foster; Gorillas in the Mist; Harper; Haunting, The (1963); Hiding Place, The; Home for the Holidays (1972) (Television); Housesitter; I Am a Camera; Last of Mrs. Lincoln, The; Member of the Wedding, The; Reflections in a Golden Eye; Requiem for a Heavyweight (1962); Truth About Women, The; Voyage of the Damned; You're a Big Boy Now

Harris, Julius W.: Black Caesar; Friday Foster; Harley Davidson and the Marlboro Man; Hell Up in Harlem; Islands in the Stream; Shrunken Heads; Superfly; To Sleep with Anger

Harris, Kathryn: Broken Trust (1992)

Harris, Lara: All Tied Up; Dogfighters; The; Habitat; Inhumanoid; No Man's Land; Suicide Kings

Harris, Laura: Faculty, The

Harris, Leigh and Lynette: Sorceress (1982)

Harris, Lynn: Pleasure Unlimited

Harris, M. K.: Horseplayer; Slumber Party Massacre 3

Harris, Mel: Cameron's Closet; Desperate Motive; K-9; My Brother's Wife; Secretary, The; Sharon's Secret; Spider and the Fly, The; Suture; Wanted: Dead or Alive

Harris, Michael: Bar Girls; Dead Air; I Love You, Don't Touch Me!; Shattered Image; Sleepstalker: The Sandman's Last Rites; Soft Kill, The; Suture

Harris, Moira: Hellcab; One More Saturday Night

Harris, Neil Patrick: Clara's Heart; Cold Sassy Tree; Man in the Attic, The; My Antonia; Purple People Eater; Starship Troopers

Harris, Phil: Buck Benny Rides Again; Dreaming Out Loud; Goodbye, My Lady; High and the Mighty, The; Melody Cruise; Wabash Avenue; Wheeler Dealers, The

Harris, Priscilla: Nights in White Satin

Harris, Richard: Abraham; Bible, The; Camelot; Cassandra Crossing, The; Cromwell; Cry, the Beloved Country (1995); Deadly Trackers, The; Field, The; Game for Vultures; Gladiator (2000); Gulliver's Travels (1977); Hawaii; Hero, The (1971); Highpoint; Hunchback, The (1997); Juggernaut (1974); King of the Wind; Last Word, The (1979); Mack the Knife; Major Dundee; Man Called Horse, A; Man in the Wilderness; Martin's Day; Molly Maguires, The; Mutiny on the Bounty (1962); 99 and 44/100 Percent Dead; Orca; Patriot Games; Red Desert; Return of a Man Called Horse, The; Robin and Marian; Savage Hearts; Shake Hands with the Devil; Silent Tongue; Smilla's Sense of Snow; Tarzan the Ape Man (1981); This Is the Sea; This Sporting Life; Triumphs of a Man Called Horse, The; Unforgiven (1992); Wild Geese, The; Wreck of the Mary Deare, The; Wrestling Ernest Hemingway

Harris, Robert: Terrorists, The

Harris, Robert H.: How to Make a Monster

Harris, Robin: House Party; Mo' Better Blues; Sorority House Massacre 2

Harris, Robyn: Hard to Die

Harris, Rolf: Toby and the Koala Bear

Harris, Rosalind: Fiddler on the Roof

Harris, Rosemary: Beau Brummell (1954); Chisholms, The; Heartbreak House; Little Riders, The; Ploughman's Lunch, The; To the Lighthouse; Tom & Viv

Harris, Ross: Dog Trouble; Nightmare House; Testament

Harris, Steve: Street Hunter

Harris Jr., Wendell B.: Chameleon Street

Harris, Zelda: Clover; Crooklyn

Harrison, Andrew: Littlest Horse Thieves, The

Harrison, Catherine: Blue Fire Lady; Empire State

Harrison, Emily: Curse of the Puppet Master

Harrison, Gavin: Public Enemy #1

Harrison, George: Imagine: John Lennon; Rutles, The (All You Need Is Cash)

Harrison, Gregory: Air Bud: Golden Receiver; Bare Essentials; Caught in the Act; Dangerous Pursuit; Duplicates; Enola Gay: The Men, the Mission, the Atomic Bomb; For Ladies Only; Hard Evidence; Hasty Heart; It's My Party; North Shore; Oceans of Fire; Razorback; Running Wild (1998); Seduced

Harrison, Jenilee: Curse III: Blood Sacrifice; Fist of Iron; Illicit Behavior; Prime Target

Harrison, Kathleen: Christmas Carol, A (1951); Ghoul, The (1933); Night Must Fall

Harrison, Linda: Beneath the Planet of the Apes

Harrison, Noel: Déjà Vu (1998)

Harrison, Rex: Agony and the Ecstasy, The; Anastasia: The Mystery of Anna; Anna and the King of Siam; Ashanti; Blithe Spirit; Citadel, The; Cleopatra (1963); Doctor Dolittle; Fifth Musketeer, The; Ghost and Mrs. Muir, The; Heartbreak House; Honey Pot, The; King Richard and the Crusaders; Major Barbara; Midnight Lace; My Fair Lady; Night Train to Munich (Night Train); Prince and the Pauper, The (1978); Reluctant Debutante, The; Sidewalks of London; Staircase; Storm in a Teacup; Time to Die, A (1983); Unfaithfully Yours (1948)

Harrison, Richard: Between God, the Devil and a Winchester; Empire of the Dark; His Name Was King; Place Called Trinity, A; Rescue Force

Harrison, Sandra: Blood of Dracula

Harrison, Schae: Interlocked

Harrison, Susan: Sweet Smell of Success

Harrod, David: Blood on the Badge

Harrold, Kathryn: Best Legs in the 8th Grade, The; Bogie; Companion, The; Dead Solid Perfect; Deadly Desire; Heartbreakers; Hunter, The (1980); Into the Night; Modern Romance; Nightwing; Pursuit of D. B. Cooper; Rainbow Drive; Raw Deal; Sender, The; Yes, Giorgio

Harron, Dan: Really Weird Tales

Harron, Robert: Avenging Conscience, The; Hearts of the World; Home, Sweet Home (1914); Intolerance; Judith of Bethulia; Mother and the Law, The

Harrow, Lisa: Final Conflict, The; From a Far Country; Last Days of Chez Nous, The; Shaker Run; Sunday

Harry, Deborah: Forever Lulu; Hairspray; Heavy; Intimate Stranger; John Carpenter Presents: Body Bags; Satisfaction; Six Ways to Sunday; Tales from the Darkside, The Movie; Union City; Videodrome

Hart, Christopher J.: Lady Terminator

Hart, Dolores: King Creole; Lonelyhearts; Loving You; Where the Boys Are (1960)

Hart, Dorothy: Naked City, The

Hart, Ian: BackBeat; Closer You Get, The; End of the Affair, The; Frogs for Snakes; Hollow Reed; Hours and Times; Land and Freedom; Michael Collins; Monument Ave.; Nothing Personal (1997)

Hart, John: Blackenstein; Longhorn

Hart, Kevin: Lone Wolf

Hart, Linda: Get Shorty; Tin Cup

Hart, Melissa Joan: Drive Me Crazy; Sabrina, the Teenage Witch

Hart, Nadine: Robot Holocaust

Hart, Pam: Pi

Hart, Richard: Green Dolphin Street

Hart, Roxanne: Last Innocent Man, The; Meteorites!; Oh, God, You Devil!; Our Mother's Murder; Pulse; Samaritan: The Mitch Snyder Story; Special Bulletin; Tagget

Hart, Stacy: Get Real

Hart, Susan: Dr. Goldfoot and the Bikini Machine; Slime People, The

Hart, Teddy: Ma and Pa Kettle on Vacation

Hart, Veronica: RSVP; Stocks and Blondes

Hart, William S.: Hell's Hinges; Narrow Trail, The; Three Word Brand, The; Tumbleweeds

Harte, Christine: Wish Me Luck

Harte, Jennifer: Prehysteria 2

Hartford, Glen: Hell Squad (1985)

Hartley, Daniel: Mystery Monsters

Hartley, Hal: Flirt

Hartley, Mariette: Encino Man; Improper Channels; M.A.D.D.: Mothers Against Drunk Driving; 1969; O'Hara's Wife; Ride the High Country; Silence of the Heart

Hartman, David: Island at the Top of the World, The

Hartman, Elizabeth: Beguiled, The; Group, The; Patch o' Blue, A; Walking Tall; You're a Big Boy Now

Hartman, Jesse: Habit

Hartman, Lawrence: Zentropa

Hartman, Lisa: Bare Essentials; Bodily Harm; Full Exposure; Return of Eliot Ness, The; Take, The; Where the Boys Are '84

Hartman, Phil: Blind Date (1987); CB4; Coneheads; Greedy; Houseguest; Jingle All the Way; Pagemaster, The; Pee-Wee Herman Show, The; Second Civil War, The; Sgt Bilko; Small Soldiers; So I Married an Axe Murderer

Hartmann, Paul: Haunted Castle

Hartnell, William: Battle Hell; Dr. Who (TV series)

Hartner, Rona: Gadjo Dilo

Hartnett, Josh: Here on Earth; Virgin Suicides, The

Haruna, Kazuo: Silk Road, The

Harvest, Rainbow: Mirror Mirror; Old Enough

Harvey, Don: American Flyers; Atom Man vs. Superman; Batman and Robin (Adventures of Batman and Robin); Better Off Dead (1993); Casualties of War; Con, The; Gang Busters; Prey of the Chameleon; Sawbones; Tank Girl

Harvey, Forrester: Chump at Oxford, A; Mystery Ranch

Harvey, Georgette: Chloe: Love is Calling You

Harvey, Joan: Hands of a Stranger

Harvey, John: Pin-Up Girl

Harvey, Laurence: Alamo, The; Butterfield 8; Dandy in Aspic, A; Darling; Escape to the Sun; I Am a Camera; King Richard and the Crusaders; Manchurian Candidate, The; Night Watch; Of Human Bondage (1964); Romeo and Juliet (1954); Room at the Top; Silent Enemy, The; Spy with a Cold Nose, The; Summer and Smoke; Three Men in a Boat; Truth About Women, The; Walk on the Wild Side; Wonderful World of the Brothers Grimm, The

Harvey, Paul: Call Northside 777; Helldorado (1946); Meet Dr. Christian; Tournament Tempo

Harvey, Rodney: Guncrazy (1992); Mixed Blood; Salsa

Harvey, Tom: And Then You Die

Harwood, Bruce: X-Files, The (TV Series)

Hasegawa, Kazuo: Actor's Revenge, An; Chikamatsu Monogatari

Hasgawa, Machiko: Zatoichi: Masseur Ichi and a Chest of Gold

Hashemian, Mir Farrokh: Children of Heaven

Haskell, Peter: Christina; Cracker Factory; Riding the Edge

Hass, Dolly: Spy of Napoleon

Hasse, O. E.: Betrayed (1954); Big Lift, The; State of Siege

Hasselhoff, David: Bail Out; Baywatch: The Movie; Cartier Affair, The; Final Alliance; Revenge of the Cheerleaders; Ring of the Musketeer; Star Crash; Terror at London Bridge; Witchery

Hassett, Marilyn: Bell Jar, The; Body Count (1988); Gypsy Angels; Massive Retaliation; Messenger of Death; Other Side of the Mountain, The; Other Side of the Mountain, Part II, The; Two-Minute Warning

Hasso, Signe: Heaven Can Wait (1943); House on 92nd Street, The; Johnny Angel; Picture Mommy Dead; Reflection of Fear; Seventh Cross, The; Story of Dr. Wassell, The; Woman's Face, A

Hasson, Ann: Romeo and Juliet (1988)

Hatch, Richard: Battlestar Galactica; Charlie Chan and the Curse of the Dragon Queen; Deadman's Curve; Delta Force, The; Ghetto Blaster; Hatfields and the McCoys, The; Heated Vengeance; Party Line; Prisoners of the Lost Universe

Hatcher, Teri: All Tied Up; Brain Smasher ... A Love Story; Cool Surface, The; Dead in the Water; Heaven's Prisoners;

Since You've Been Gone; Soapdish; Straight Talk; Tomorrow Never Dies; Two Days in the Valley

Hatfield, Hurd: Boston Strangler, The; Crimes of the Heart; Dragon Seed; El Cid; Her Alibi; King of Kings (1961); Left Handed Gun, The; Lies of the Twins; Picture of Dorian Gray, The

Hathaway, Amy: Last Exit to Earth

Hathaway, Noah: NeverEnding Story, The; Troll

Hatosy, Shawn: Anywhere But Here; Faculty, The; Outside Providence; Witness Protection

Hattie, Hilo: Ma and Pa Kettle at Waikiki

Hatton, Raymond: Ace of Hearts; Arizona Bound; Below the Border; Covered Wagon Days; Dawn on the Great Divide; Down Texas Way; Forbidden Trails; Frontier Horizon; Frontier Pony Express; Ghost Town Law; Gunman from Bodie; Kansas Terrors; Lady Killer; Law and Order; Peck's Bad Boy; Rocky Mountain Rangers; Rough Riders' Roundup; Texas (1941); Three Musketeers, The (1933); Vigilantes Are Coming!; Virginian, The (1923); Wagon Wheels; Wall Street Cowboy; West of the Law; Wyoming Outlaw

Hatton, Rondo: Brute Man, The; House of Horrors; In Old Chicago; Pearl of Death, The

Haudepin, Didier: Assassins de L'Ordre, Les (Law Breakers); This Special Friendship

Hauer, Rutger: Amelia Earhart: The Final Flight; Arctic Blue; Beyond Justice; Blade Runner; Blast; Bleeders; Blind Fury; Blind Side; Blood of Heroes; Blood of the Innocent; Bloodhounds of Broadway; Bone Daddy; Breed Apart, A; Buffy, the Vampire Slayer; Call of the Wild: The Dog of the Yukone; Chanel Solitaire; Crossworlds; Dandelions; Deadlock; Eating Pattern; Escape from Sobibor; Eureka; Fatherland; Flesh and Blood (Sword and the Rose, the (1985)); Forbidden Choices; Hitcher, The; Hostile Waters; Inside the Third Reich; Katie's Passion; Ladyhawke; Mr. Stitch; Mysteries; Nighthawks; Nostradamus; Omega Doom; Osterman Weekend, The; Partners in Crime; Past Midnight; Precious Find; Redline; Soldier of Orange; Split Second (1992); Surviving the Game; Tactical Assault; Turkish Delight; Voyage; Wanted: Dead or Alive

Hauff, Thomas: Climb, The

Haughton, David: Caligula, the Untold Story

Hauman, Constance: Madame Butterfly

Hauser, Cole: All over Me; Good Will Hunting; Hi-Lo Country, The; Pitch Black

Hauser, Fay: Christmas Lilies of the Field; Jimmy the Kid; Jo Jo Dancer, Your Life Is Calling; Marvin and Tige

Hauser, Wings: Art of Dying, The; Beastmaster 2: Through the Portal of Time; Bedroom Eyes II; Carpenter, The; Coldfire; Dead Man Walking (1987); Deadly Force; Exiled in America; Frame Up; Homework; Hostage (1987); Jo Jo Dancer, Your Life Is Calling; L.A. Bounty; Living to Die; Long Hot Summer, The (1985); Mutant; Nightmare at Noon; No Safe Haven; Original Gangstas; Out of Sight Out of Mind; Pale Blood; Reason to Die; Siege of Firebase Gloria, The; Street Asylum; Tales from the Hood; 3:15—The Moment of Truth; Tough Guys Don't Dance; Vice Squad; Wilding, The Children of Violence; Wind, The (1986)

Haustein, Thomas: Christiane F.

Hautesserre, Francois: A La Mode

Havens, Richie: Greased Lightning

Haver, June: Dolly Sisters, The; Look For The Silver Lining; Love Nest

Haver, Phyllis: Buster Keaton Festival Vol. 1–3; Fig Leaves; What Price Glory? (1926)

Havers, Nigel: Burke and Wills; Burning Season, The; Chariots of Fire; Empire of the Sun; Farewell to the King; Little Princess, A (1986); Whistle Blower, The

Haverstock, Thom: Skullduggery

Haverty, Liz: Dance on the Crimson Canvas

Havoc, June: Brewster's Millions (1945); Can't Stop the Music; Four Jacks and a Jill; Gentlemen's Agreement; Hello, Frisco, Hello

Hawdon, Robin: When Dinosaurs Ruled the Earth

Hawke, Ethan: Alive; Before Sunrise; Dad; Dead Poets Society; Explorers; Floundering; Gattaca; Great Expectations (1998); Midnight Clear, A; Mystery Date; Newton Boys, The; Reality Bites; Rich in Love; Search and Destroy (1995); Snow Falling on Cedars; Waterland; White Fang; White Fang 2: Myth of the White Wolf

Hawkes, Chesney: Buddy's Song

Hawkes, John: Roadracers

Hawkes, Steve: Blood Freak

Hawkes, Terri: Killing Man, The

Walter Hawkins and the Hawkins Family: Gospel

Hawkins, Corwin: Low Down Dirty Shame, A

Hawkins, Georgia: Doomed Caravan

Hawkins, Jack: Ben-Hur (1959); Bonnie Prince Charlie; Bridge on the River Kwai, The; Cruel Sea, The; Elusive Pimpernel, The; Escape to the Sun; Fallen Idol, The; Land of the Pharaohs; League of Gentlemen, The; Malta Story, The; No Highway in the Sky; Prisoner, The (1955); Shalako; Tales that Witness Madness; Waterloo; Young Winston; Zulu

Hawkins, Jimmy: Annie Oakley (TV Series)

Hawkins, Screamin' Jay: Mystery Train

Hawkshaw, Jean: Wild Women of Wongo

Hawley, Richard: Captives

Hawn, Goldie: Best Friends; Bird on a Wire; Butterflies Are Free; Cactus Flower; Crisscross (1992); Death Becomes Her; Deceived; $ (Dollars); Duchess and the Dirtwater Fox, The; Everyone Says I Love You; First Wives Club, The; Foul Play; Girl from Petrovka, The; Housesitter; Lovers and Liars; One and Only, Genuine, Original Family Band, The; Out-of-Towners, The (1999); Overboard; Private Benjamin; Protocol; Seems Like Old Times; Shampoo; Sugarland Express, The; Swing Shift; There's a Girl in My Soup; Wildcats

Haworth, Jill: Exodus; Home for the Holidays (1972) (Television); In Harm's Way

Haworth, Vinton: Riding on Air

Hawthorne, Elizabeth: Alex

Hawthorne, Nigel: Amistad; Big Brass Ring, The; Demolition Man; Inside; Madeline (1998); Madness of King George, The; Mapp & Lucia; Murder in Mind; Object of My Affection, The; Pope John Paul II; Tartuffe; Twelfth Night; Winslow Boy, The (1999); Yes, Prime Minister

Hawtrey, Charles: Carry on at Your Convenience; Carry on Cleo; Carry on Doctor; Carry on Nurse; Follow That Camel; Terrornauts, The

Hawtrey, Kay: Funeral Home

Hay, Christian: You're Jinxed Friend, You Just Met Sacramento

Hay, Colin: Wacky World of Wills and Burke, The

Hayakawa, Sessue: Bridge on the River Kwai, The; Cheat, The; Daughter of the Dragon; Green Mansions; Hell to Eternity; Swiss Family Robinson, The; Three Came Home; Tokyo Joe

Hayashi, Chizu: Zatoichi: The Blind Swordsman and the Chess Expert

Hayashi, Marc: Chan Is Missing; Laser Man, The

Hayden, Dennis: One Man Army

Hayden, Julie: It's Pat: The Movie

Hayden, Linda: Blood on Satan's Claw; Madhouse (1972); Shattered (1972); Taste the Blood of Dracula

Hayden, Nora: Angry Red Planet, The

Hayden, Russell: Badmen of the Hills; Border Vigilantes; Doomed Caravan; Heart of Arizona; Heritage of the Desert; Hidden Gold; Hills of Old Wyoming; Hopalong Rides Again; In Old Colorado; In Old Mexico; Law of the Pampas; North of the Rio Grande; Pirates on Horseback; Range War; Renegade Trail; Santa Fe Marshal; Silver on the Sage; Stagecoach War; Texas Trail; Three Men from Texas; Wide-Open Town

Hayden, Sterling: Asphalt Jungle, The; Blue and the Gray, The; Crime of Passion; Denver and Rio Grande, The; Dr. Strangelove or How I Learned to Stop Worrying and Love the Bomb; Fighter Attack; Flat Top; Gas; Godfather, The; Johnny Guitar; Kansas Pacific; Killing, The; King of the Gypsies; Last Command, The (1955); Last Days of Man on Earth, The; Long Goodbye, The; Prince Valiant (1954); Shotgun; Spaghetti Western; Star, The (1952); Suddenly; Venom; Winter Kills

Haydn, Richard: Adventures of Bullwhip Griffin, The; And Then There Were None; Ball of Fire; Clarence, the Cross-Eyed Lion; Emperor Waltz, The; Five Weeks in a Balloon; Forever Amber; Jupiter's Darling; Mr. Music; Mutiny on the Bounty (1962); Never Let Me Go; Please Don't Eat the Daisies; Singapore; Young Frankenstein

Haydon, Julie: Scoundrel, The

Hayek, Salma: Breaking Up; Desperado; Dogma; Faculty, The; 54; Fled; Fools Rush In; Hunchback, The (1997); Roadracers; Velocity of Gary, The; Wild Wild West (1999)

Hayenga, Jeff: Unborn, The

Hayes, Allan: Neon Maniacs

Hayes, Allison: Attack of the 50-Foot Woman (1958); Disembodied, The; Gunslinger; Hypnotic Eye, The; Mohawk; Undead, The; Unearthly, The; Zombies of Mora Tav

Hayes, Billie: Li'l Abner (1959)

Hayes, Carey: RSVP

Hayes, George "Gabby": Along the Navajo Trail; Arizona Kid; Bad Man of Deadwood; Badman's Territory; Bar-20 Rides Again; Bells of Rosarita; Blue Steel (1934); Borderland; Broadway to Cheyenne; Call of the Prairie; Calling Wild Bill Elliott; Cariboo Trail; Carson City Kid; Dark Command; Death Valley Manhunt; Don't Fence Me In; Eagle's Brood; Heart of Arizona; Heart of the Golden West; Helldorado (1946); Hidden Valley Outlaws; Hills of Old Wyoming; Hopalong Cassidy Returns; Hopalong Rides Again; In Old Caliente; In Old Mexico; In Old Santa Fe; Jesse James at Bay; Lawless Frontier; Lawless Nineties, The; Lights of Old Santa Fe; Lost City, The; Lucky Texan; Man from Utah, The; Melody Ranch; Mojave Firebrand; My Pal Trigger; 'Neath Arizona Skies; North of the Rio Grande; Phantom Broadcast, The; Plainsman, The; Rainbow Valley; Randy Rides Alone; Ranger and the Lady, The; Renegade Trail; Return of the Bad Men; Riders of Destiny; Robin Hood of the Pecos; Roll on Texas Moon; Romance on the Range; Saga of Death Valley; Silver on the Sage; Sons of the Pioneers; Star Packer, The; Sunset Serenade; Tall in the Saddle; Texas Rangers (1936); Texas Terror; Texas Trail; Three on the Trail; Trail Dust; Trail Street; Trailin' North; Utah; Wall Street Cowboy; War of the Wildcats; West of the Divide; Young Bill Hickok

Hayes, Helen: Airport; Anastasia (1956); Arrowsmith; Candleshoe; Family Upside Down, A; Farewell to Arms, A; Herbie Rides Again; Murder with Mirrors; One of Our Dinosaurs Is Missing; Sin of Madelon Claudet, The; Skin Game, The (1931); Stage Door Canteen; Victory at Entebbe

Hayes, Isaac: Acting on Impulse; Counterforce; Final Judgment; Flipper (1996); Good Idea; Guilty as Charged; Illtown; I'm Gonna Git You Sucka!; It Could Happen to You; Oblivion; Oblivion 2: Backlash; Prime Target; Robin Hood: Men in Tights; Six Ways to Sunday; Truck Turner

Hayes, Jerri: Black Sister's Revenge

Hayes, Linda: Romance on the Range

Hayes, Maggie: Girls Town (1959)

Hayes, Margaret: In Old Colorado

Hayes, Patricia: Corn Is Green, The (1979); Fish Called Wanda, A; Willow

Hayes, Peter Lind: Five Thousand Fingers of Dr. T, The; Senator Was Indiscreet, The; Yin and Yang of Mr. Go, The

Hayes, Sean P.: Billy's Hollywood Screen Kiss

Hayes, Susan Seaforth: Dream Machine

Haygarth, Tony: Infiltrator, The

Hayman, Cyd: After Julius; Godsend, The

Hayman, David: Gospel According to Vic, The; Hope and Glory; My Name is Joe; Sense of Freedom, A; Sid and Nancy

Hayman, Leslie: Virgin Suicides, The

Haymer, John: Four Deuces, The

Haymes, Dick: Four Jills in a Jeep; St. Benny the Dip; State Fair (1945)

Hayner, Daniel: Hallelujah!

Haynes, Linda: Drowning Pool, The; Human Experiments; Latitude Zero; Rolling Thunder

Haynes, Lloyd: Good Guys Wear Black

Haynes, Roberta: Hell Ship Mutiny; Return to Paradise (1953)

Haynie, Jim: Bridges of Madison County, The; From Hollywood to Deadwood; Grand Tour: Disaster in Time; On the Edge; Out; Peacemaker, The (1997); Staying Together; Stephen King's Sleepwalkers; Too Much Sun

Hays, Kathryn: Ride Beyond Vengeance; Yuma

Hays, Lauren: Rebecca's Secret

Hays, Robert: Airplane!; Airplane II: The Sequel; California Gold Rush; Cat's Eye; Cyber Bandits; Fall of the House of Usher, The (1979); Fifty/Fifty; Homeward Bound: The Incredible Journey; Homeward Bound II: Lost in San Francisco; Honeymoon Academy; Hot Chocolate; No Dessert Dad Until You Mow the Lawn; Raw Justice; Running Against Time; Scandalous (1983); Take This Job and Shove It; Touched; Trenchcoat; Utilities

Hays, Robert:

Hays, Steve: Trick

Haysbert, Dennis: Love and Basketball; Love Field; Minus Man, The; Mr. Baseball; Random Hearts; Return to Lonesome Dove; Standoff (1997); Suture; Thirteenth Floor, The (1999); Waiting to Exhale; Widow's Kiss

Hayshi, Henry: Pushed to the Limit

Hayter, David: Guyver 2: Dark Hero

Hayter, James: Big Fella; Pickwick Papers, The; Story of Robin Hood, The; Tom Brown's Schooldays (1950)

Hayward, Chad: Killing Game, The

Hayward, Chris: In Search of Anna

Hayward, David: Accidental Meeting; Delusion (1980); Fallen Angel; Red Alert

Hayward, Leland: Fear, The (1994)

Hayward, Louis: And Then There Were None; Anthony Adverse; Black Arrow, The (1948); Christmas Kid, The; Chuka; Dance, Girl, Dance; House by the River; Man in the Iron Mask, The (1939); Rage of Paris, The; Saint in New York, The; Search for Bridey Murphy, The; Son of Monte Cristo, The; Strange Woman, The; Terror in the Wax Museum

Hayward, Susan: Adam Had Four Sons; Among the Living; Back Street; Beau Geste; Conqueror, The; David and Bathsheba; Deadline at Dawn; Demetrius and the Gladiators; Fighting Seabees, The; Hairy Ape, The; Honey Pot, The; House of Strangers; I Want to Live!; I'll Cry Tomorrow; Jack London; Lost Moment, The; Lusty Men, The; My Foolish Heart; Rawhide (1951); Reap the Wild Wind; Say Goodbye, Maggie Cole; Smash-Up: The Story of a Woman; Snows of Kilimanjaro, The; Soldier of Fortune; Stolen Hours; They Won't Believe Me; Tulsa; Valley of the Dolls; Where Love Has Gone; Young and Willing

Haywood, Chris: Alex; Attack Force Z; Dogs in Space; Heatwave (1983); Kiss or Kill; Malcolm; Man of Flowers; Navigator: A Medieval Odyssey, The; Sweet Talker; Tale of Ruby Rose, The

Hayworth, Rita: Affair in Trinidad; Angels over Broadway; Blood and Sand (1941); Charlie Chan in Egypt; Circus World; Cover Girl; Gilda; Hit the Saddle; Lady from Shanghai; Lady in Question; Loves of Carmen, The; Miss Sadie Thompson; Only Angels Have Wings; Pal Joey; Poppy Is Also a Flower, The; Renegade Ranger; Salome (1953); Strawberry Blonde, The; Susan and God; Tales of Manhattan; They Came to Cordura; Tonight and Every Night; Trouble in Texas; You Were Never Lovelier; You'll Never Get Rich

Haze, Jonathan: Little Shop of Horrors, The (1960); Poor White Trash

Hazeldine, James: Business As Usual

Hazlehurst, Noni: Monkey Grip

He, Saifei: Temptress Moon

Head, Leon: Vampire Vixens from Venus

Head, Murray: French Woman, The; Sunday, Bloody Sunday

Headey, Lena: Gossip; Mrs. Dalloway; Rudyard Kipling's The Jungle Book (1994); Summer House, The; Twice Upon A Yesterday

Headley, Lena: Waterland

Headly, Glenne: Bastard Out of Carolina; Dick Tracy (1990); Dirty Rotten Scoundrels; Getting Even with Dad; Grand Isle; Hotel Room; Lonesome Dove; Making Mr. Right; Mr. Holland's Opus; Mortal Thoughts; My Own Country; Nadine; Ordinary Magic; Paperhouse; Pronto; Seize the Day; Sgt. Bilko; Two Days in the Valley; Winchell

Heald, Anthony: Deep Rising; 8MM

Healey, Myron: Gang Busters; Incredible Melting Man, The; Kansas Pacific; Longhorn; Monsoon; Panther Girl of the Congo; Rage at Dawn; Unearthly, The; Varan, the Unbelievable

Healy, David: Sign of Four, The

Healy, Dorian: Young Soul Rebels

Healy, Katherine: Six Weeks

Healy, Mary: Five Thousand Fingers of Dr. T, The; Second Fiddle

Healy, Patricia: Sweet Poison; Ultraviolet

Healy, Ted: Dancing Lady; Hollywood Hotel; Lost Stooges, The; Mad Love (1935); Operator 13

Healy-Louie, Miriam: No Telling

Heames, Darin: Fear, The (1994)

Heard, John: After Hours; Awakenings; Beaches; Best Revenge; Betrayed (1988); Between the Lines; Big; Cat People (1982); Chilly Scenes of Winter; C.H.U.D.; Cutter's Way; Dead Ahead: The Exxon Valdez Disaster; Deceived; End of Innocence, The; Executive Power; First Love (1977); Gladiator (1992); Heart Beat; Heaven Help Us; Home Alone; Home Alone 2: Lost in New York; Men; Milagro Beanfield War, The; Mindwalk; My Fellow Americans; On the Yard; 187; Out on a Limb (1986); Package, The; Pelican Brief, The; Radio Flyer; Rambling Rose; Seventh Sign, The; Snake Eyes; Telephone, The; Trip to Bountiful, The; Violated; Waterland

Hearn, Ann: Dollmaker, The

Hearn, George: Annie, a Royal Adventure!; Barney's Great Adventure; Durango; Piano for Mrs. Cimino, A; Sanctuary of Fear; Sneakers; Sweeney Todd

Hearst, Patty: Bio-Dome; Cry-Baby

Hearst, Rick: Crossing the Line (1990)

Heath, Charlie: Leprechaun 2

Heath, Darrell: Don't Be a Menace to South Central while Drinking Your Juice in the 'Hood

Heath, Robin Lynn: Stranger, The (1994)

Heather, Jean: Last Round-Up

Heatherton, Joey: Bluebeard (1972); Cry-Baby; Happy Hooker Goes to Washington, The; Where Love Has Gone

Heavener, David: L.A. Goddess; Outlaw Force; Prime Target

Heche, Anne: Adventures of Huck Finn, The (1993); Donnie Brasco; Girls in Prison; I Know What You Did Last Summer; If These Walls Could Talk; Juror, The; Kingfish: A Story of Huey P. Long; O Pioneers!; Pie in the Sky; Psycho (1998); Return to Paradise (1998); Six Days, Seven Nights; Third Miracle, The; Volcano; Wag the Dog; Walking and Talking; Wild Side

Hecht, Donatella: Flesh Eating Mothers

Hecht, Gina: One Night Stand (1995)

Hecht, Jessica: Intimate Betrayal

Heck, Angela: Tales from the Gimli Hospital

Heckart, Eileen: Bad Seed, The; Burnt Offerings; Butterflies Are Free; First Wives Club, The; Heller in Pink Tights; Hiding Place, The; Hot Spell; No Way to Treat a Lady; Somebody Up There Likes Me; Up the Down Staircase; White Mama; Zandy's Bride

Hedaya, Dan: Addams Family, The; Alien Resurrection; Based on an Untrue Story; Benny & Joon; Blood Simple; Boiling Point (1993); Clueless; Commando; Daylight; Dick; First Wives Club, The; For Love or Money; Four Eyes and Six Guns; Freeway (1996); Garden of Redemption, The; Hurricane, The (1999); Joe Versus the Volcano; Life Less Ordinary, A; Locked in Silence; Mr. Wonderful; Night at the Roxbury, A; Picture Windows; Ransom (1996); Reckless (1984); Rookie of the Year; Running Scared (1986); Searching for Bobby Fischer; Second Civil War, The; Shaft (2000); Smoky Mountain Christmas; Tightrope; To Die For (1995); Usual Suspects, The; Wise Guys

Heden, Herten: Deerslayer

Hedin, Serene: Sacred Ground; Windwalker

Hedison, Alexandra: Max Is Missing

Hedison, David: Awakening of Cassie, The; Enemy Below, The; ffolkes; Fly, The (1958)

Hedley, Jack: New York Ripper, The; Very Edge, The

Hedren, Tippi: Birds, The; Birds II, The: Land's End; Countess from Hong Kong, A; Deadly Spygames; Foxfire Light; Harrad Experiment, The; In the Cold of the Night; Marnie; Pacific Heights

Hedwall, Deborah: Alone in the Dark

Heffner, Kyle T.: Runaway Train

Heflin, Marta: Come Back to the Five and Dime, Jimmy Dean, Jimmy Dean

Heflin, Van: Airport; Backdoor to Heaven; Battle Cry; Cry of Battle; East Side, West Side; Greatest Story Ever Told, The; Green Dolphin Street; Johnny Eager; Madame Bovary (1949); Patterns; Possessed (1947); Presenting Lily Mars; Ruthless Four, The; Santa Fe Trail; Shane; Strange Love of Martha Ivers, The; They Came to Cordura; 3:10 to Yuma; Three Musketeers, The (1948); Till the Clouds Roll By; Woman Rebels, A

Hegelin, Ken: A La Mode

Heggie, O. P.: Anne of Green Gables (1934); Count of Monte Cristo, The (1934); Devotion; Midnight (1934); Mysterious Dr. Fu Manchu; Return of Dr. Fu Manchu; Smilin' Through (1932)

Hegyes, Robert: Underground Aces

Heidt, Horace: Pot O' Gold

Heifetz, Jascha: They Shall Have Music

Heigl, Katherine: Bride of Chucky; Bug Buster; My Father, the Hero; Prince Valiant (1997); Under Siege 2: Dark Territory

Heilbron, Lorna: Creeping Flesh, The

Heilvell, Elayne: Birds of Prey; Payday

Heinle, Amelia: Black Cat Run; Limey, The

Heinrich, Mimi: Reptilicus

Heinz, Werner: Tonio Kroger

Heiss, Carol: Snow White and the Three Stooges

Heit, Michael: Bare Knuckles

Heitmeyer, Jayne: Beyond Redemption; Dead End (1997); Face the Evil; Hawk's Vengeance; Sci-Fighters; Sir Arthur Conan Doyle's The Lost World; Suspicious Minds

Heitz, Jane Galloway: Straight Story, The

Heldren, Judd: Lost Planet, The

Heigenberger, Marg: After Midnight; Blind Vengeance; Conundrum; Crooked Hearts; Death Dreams; Desperate Motive; Erin Brockovich; Fire Down Below; Frame by Frame; Gold Coast; Last Time I Committed Suicide, The; Species; Species II; Tommyknockers, The

Helger, Annemarie: Ladies on the Rocks

Hell, Richard: Smithereens

Heller, Randee: Can You Hear the Laughter? The Story of Freddie Prinze

Hellman, Mike: Edgar Allan Poe's Madhouse; Witching, The (1994)

Hellstrom, Gunnar: Return to Peyton Place

Hellwig, Jim: Firepower (1993)

Helm, Anne: Follow That Dream; Magic Sword, The; Nightmare in Wax (Crimes in the Wax Museum); Unkissed Bride

Helm, Brigitte: Love of Jeanne Ney; Metropolis (1926); Metropolis (1984 Musical Version)

Helm, Fay: Blondie Has Servant Trouble

Helm, Levon: Best Revenge; Coal Miner's Daughter; Dollmaker, The; End of the Line; Fire Down Below; Right Stuff, The; Smooth Talk; Staying Together

Helmer, Heidi: Beachballs

Helmond, Katherine: Brazil; Diary of a Teenage Hitchhiker; Family Plot; Inside Monkey Zetterland; Lady in White; Ms. Scrooge; Overboard; Rosie; Shadey; Spy Within, The; World War III

Helmore, Tom: Flipper's New Adventure

Helmuth, Frits: Memories of a Marriage

Helpmann, Robert: Patrick; Quiller Memorandum, The; Tales of Hoffman

Helpmann, Sheila: Getting of Wisdom, The

Hemblen, David: Family Viewing; Man in Uniform, A

Hemingway, Margaux: Bad Love; Deadly Rivals; Double Obsession; Inner Sanctum; Killer Fish; Lipstick; Over the Brooklyn Bridge; They Call Me Bruce?

Hemingway, Mariel: Bad Moon; Creator; Crying Child, The; Delirious; Falling from Grace; Into the Badlands; Lipstick; Little Men (1998); Manhattan; Mean Season, The; Personal Best; Road Ends; Star 80; Steal the Sky; Suicide Club, The; Sunset; Superman IV: The Quest for Peace

Hemingway, Susan: Women in Cell Block 9

Hemmings, David: Beyond Reasonable Doubt (1983); Blood Relatives; Blow-Up; Calamity Jane (1984); Camelot; Charge of the Light Brigade, The (1968); Dark Forces; Deep Red (1975); Disappearance, The; Islands in the Stream; Juggernaut (1974); Just a Gigolo; Key to Rebecca, The; Love Machine, The; Murder by Decree; Old Curiosity Shop, The (1975); Rainbow, The; Snow Queen; Squeeze, The (1977); Thirst; Turn of the Screw, The (1989)

Hemsley, Sherman: Alice in Wonderland (1985); Club Fed; Ghost Fever; Mr. Nanny; Screwed

Hendershott, Adam: Celtic Pride

Henderson, Bill: Get Crazy; Trippin'

Henderson, Florence: Brady Bunch, The (TV series); Shakes the Clown; Song of Norway; Very Brady Christmas, A

Henderson, Jo: Lianna

Henderson, Marcia: All I Desire; Hypnotic Eye, The

Henderson, Meredith: Song Spinner

Henderson, Sarah: Kids

Hendricks, Cheryl: Regenerated Man, The

Hendricks, Gorman: On the Bowery

Hendrickson, Benjamin: Spanking the Monkey

Hendrickson, Nancy: Mother's Day

Hendrix, Elaine: Here on Earth; Last Dance (1991); Parent Trap, The (1998)

Hendrix, Jimi: Jimi Hendrix; Monterey Pop; Woodstock

Hendrix, Wanda: Admiral Was a Lady, The
Hendry, Gloria: Bare Knuckles; Black Belt Jones; Black Caesar; Hell Up in Harlem
Hendry, Ian: Children of the Damned; Get Carter; Hill, The; Internecine Project, The; Journey to the Far Side of the Sun; Passenger, The (1975); Repulsion
Henie, Sonja: Everything Happens at Night; Happy Landing; Iceland; My Lucky Star; One in a Million; Second Fiddle; Sun Valley Serenade; Thin Ice; Wintertime
Henn, Carrie: Aliens
Henner, Marilu: Between the Lines; Bloodbrothers; Cannonball Run II; Chains of Gold; Chasers; Grand Larceny; Grown-Ups; Hammett; Johnny Dangerously; L.A. Story; Lady Killers; Love with a Perfect Stranger; Man Who Loved Women, The (1983); Noises Off; Perfect; Rustler's Rhapsody; Stark; Titanic (1996)
Hennessy, Jill: Smile Like Yours, A
Hennessy, Mark: Double Exposure (1987)
Hennessy, Jill: Molly
Henning, Eva: Three Strange Loves
Henning, Linda: Dog Trouble
Hennings, Sam: Seedpeople
Henreid, Paul: Battle Shock; Casablanca; Deception (1946); Deep in My Heart; Four Horsemen of the Apocalypse; Joan of Paris; Madwoman of Chaillot, The; Never So Few; Night Train to Munich (Night Train); Now, Voyager; Operation Crossbow; Scar, The; Song of Love; Stolen Face
Henrey, Bobby: Fallen Idol, The
Henriksen, Lance: Aliens; Baja; Boulevard; Choke Canyon; Color of Night; Comrades in Arms; Criminal Mind, The; Dead Man; Deadly Intent; Delta Heat; Excessive Force; Face the Evil; Felony; Gunfighter's Moon; Hard Target; Hit List (1988); Horror Show, The; Jennifer 8; Johnny Handsome; Knights; Last Assassins; Man's Best Friend (1993); Mansion of the Doomed; Millennium (1996); Mind Ripper; Nature of the Beast; Near Dark; Nightmares; No Escape; Operation Intercept; Outfit, The; Piranha Part Two: The Spawning; Pit and the Pendulum, The (1991); Powder; Profile for Murder; Pumpkinhead; Quick and the Dead, The (1995); Savage Dawn; Spitfire (1994); Stone Cold; Survival Quest
Henry, Buck: Aria; Defending Your Life; Even Cowgirls Get the Blues; Gloria (1980); Grumpy Old Men; Harrison Bergeron; Heaven Can Wait (1978); Keep the Change; Linguini Incident, The; Man Who Fell to Earth, The; Old Boyfriends; Rude Awakening (1989); Short Cuts
Henry, Buzz: Wild West (1946)
Henry, Charlotte: Charlie Chan at the Opera; March of the Wooden Soldiers (Babes in Toyland (1934))
Henry, Gloria: Rancho Notorious
Henry, Gloria Lynn: Phantasm III: Lord of the Dead
Henry, Gregg: Body Double; Last of Philip Banter, The; Nightmare (1991); Patriot; Payback (1999); Positively True Adventures of the Alleged Texas Cheerleader-Murdering Mom, The; Sharon's Secret; White Lie
Henry, Justin: Martin's Day; Sweethearts' Dance; Tiger Town
Henry, Laura: Heavenly Bodies
Henry, Lenny: Bernard and the Genie; True Identity
Henry, Linda: Beautiful Thing
Henry, Martha: Dancing in the Dark; White Light
Henry, Mike: Adios Amigo; Rio Lobo; Smokey and the Bandit; Smokey and the Bandit II
Henry, Thomas Browne: Beginning of the End
Henry, Tim: Dawson Patrol, The
Henry, Tom: Lone Wolf
Henry, William: Dance Hall; Denver Kid; Fury of the Congo; Marshal of Cedar Rock; Tarzan Escapes
Henshall, Douglas: Angels and Insects; Twice Upon A Yesterday
Hensley, Jon: Wounded Heart
Hensley, Lisa: Thirteenth Floor, The (1990)
Hensley, Pamela: Buck Rogers in the 25th Century; Doc Savage . . . , The Man of Bronze; Double Exposure (1982)
Henson, Brad: Warlords of Hell
Henson, Elden: Gift of Love: The Daniel Huffman Story; Idle Hands
Henson, John: Stag
Henson, Nicky: Bawdy Adventures of Tom Jones, The; Number One of the Secret Service; Psychomania

Henstridge, Natasha: Adrenalin: Fear the Rush; Jason and the Argonauts (2000); Maximum Risk; Species; Species II; Standoff (1997); Whole Nine Yards, The
Henteloff, Alex: Dog Trouble; Red Light Sting, The
Hepburn, Audrey: Always (1989); Bloodline; Breakfast at Tiffany's; Charade; Children's Hour, The; Funny Face; Green Mansions; How to Steal a Million; Love in the Afternoon; My Fair Lady; Nun's Story, The; Paris When It Sizzles; Robin and Marian; Roman Holiday; Sabrina (1954); They All Laughed; Two for the Road; Unforgiven, The (1960); Wait Until Dark; War and Peace (1956)
Hepburn, Dee: Gregory's Girl
Hepburn, Doreen: Da
Hepburn, Katharine: Adam's Rib (1949); African Queen, The; Alice Adams; Bill of Divorcement, A; Break of Hearts; Bringing Up Baby; Christopher Strong; Corn Is Green, The (1979); Desk Set; Dragon Seed; Grace Quigley; Guess Who's Coming to Dinner; Holiday; Keeper of the Flame; Lion in Winter, The; Little Minister, The; Little Women (1933); Long Day's Journey into Night (1962); Love Affair (1994); Love Among the Ruins; Madwoman of Chaillot, The; Man Upstairs, The; Mary of Scotland; Morning Glory (1933); On Golden Pond; Pat and Mike; Philadelphia Story, The; Quality Street; Rainmaker, The (1956); Rooster Cogburn; Sea of Grass, The; Song of Love; Spitfire (1934); Stage Door; Stage Door Canteen; State of the Union; Suddenly, Last Summer; Summertime; Sylvia Scarlett; Trojan Women, The; Undercurrent; Without Love; Woman of the Year; Woman Rebels, A
Hepton, Bernard: Emma (1996)
Herbert, Charles: Colossus of New York, The; 13 Ghosts
Herbert, Chris: Check Is in the Mail, The
Herbert, Dorothy: Mysterious Dr. Satan
Herbert, Hugh: Beautiful Blonde from Bashful Bend, The; Bureau of Missing Persons; Dames; Danger Lights; Diplomaniacs; Eternally Yours; Footlight Parade; Hellzapoppin; Hollywood Hotel; Hook, Line and Sinker; It's a Great Life; Kismet (1944); One Rainy Afternoon; Song Is Born, A; Sweet Adeline; Villain Still Pursued Her, The
Herbert, Leon: Girl with the Hungry Eyes, The
Herbert, Percy: Captain Apache; Saint, The (TV Series)
Herbert, Sidney: Orphans of the Storm
Herbst, Becky: Shrunken Heads
Herbst, Rich: Brain Damage
Herd, Carla: Deathstalker III—The Warriors from Hell
Herd, Richard: Gleaming the Cube; I Married A Monster; Judas Project, The; Marciano; Trancers; V
Herder, Andreas: Blue Hour, The
Heredia, Lisa: Summer
Herlie, Eileen: Hamlet (1948); Hungry Hill
Herlihy, James Leo: Four Friends
Herlin, Jacques: Adios, Hombre
Herman, Jack: Yesterday Machine, The
Herman, Jimmy: Geronimo (1993); Medicine River; Warrior Spirit
Herman, Pee-wee: Big Top Pee-Wee; Nice Dreams; Pee-Wee Herman Show, The; Pee-Wee's Big Adventure; Pinocchio (1983)
Herman, Philip: Jacker 2: Descent to Hell; Tales Till the End
Herman, Woody: Wintertime
Hermann, Irm: Last Five Days, The; Merchant of Four Seasons, The
Hermits, Herman's: Mrs. Brown You've Got a Lovely Daughter
Hermine, Pepi: Putney Swope
Hermine, Ruth: Putney Swope
Hermosa, Leila: Blind Rage
Hernandez, Ernesto: Price of Glory
Hernandez, Felicia: Ruby in Paradise
Hernandez, Juano: Intruder in the Dust; Mark of the Hawk, The; Something of Value; Young Man with a Horn
Hernandez, Sophia Adella: Knockout
Heron, Blake: Shiloh; Trilogy of Terror II
Herranz, Nieves: Thesis
Herrera, Anthony: Foreign Student
Herrier, Mark: Porky's; Porky's II: The Next Day; Porky's Revenge
Herring, Laura: Forbidden Dance, The
Herrmann, Edward: Annie; Big Business; Born Yesterday (1993); Compromising Positions; Electric Grandmother, The; Foreign Field, A; Foreign Student; Harry's War;

Lawrenceville Stories, The; Little Sex, A; Lost Boys, The; Man with One Red Shoe, The; Memorial Day; Mrs. Soffel; Murrow; My Boyfriend's Back; North Avenue Irregulars, The; Overboard; Portrait of a Stripper; Purple Rose of Cairo, The; Reds; Richie Rich; Saint Maybe; Soul of the Game; Sweet Poison; Take Down; Vendetta

Herron, Robert: True Heart Susie

Herschberger, Gary: Free Ride; Paradise Motel

Hershey, Barbara: Abraham; Americana; Angel on My Shoulder (1980); Baby Maker, The; Beaches; Boxcar Bertha; Dangerous Woman, A; Defenseless; Diamonds; Entity, The; Falling Down; Flood!; Frogs for Snakes; Hannah and Her Sisters; Hoosiers; Killing in a Small Town; Last of the Dogmen; Last Summer; Last Temptation of Christ, The; Liberation of L. B. Jones, The; My Wicked, Wicked Ways; Pallbearer, The; Paris Trout; Passion Flower; Portrait of a Lady, The; Public Eye, The; Pursuit of Happiness, The; Return to Lonesome Dove; Right Stuff, The; Shy People; Soldier's Daughter Never Cries, A; Splitting Heirs; Stunt Man, The; Swing Kids; Take This Job and Shove It; Tin Men; Tune in Tomorrow; With Six You Get Eggroll; World Apart, A

Hersholt, Jean: Cat and the Fiddle, The; Courageous Dr. Christian, The; Dr. Christian Meets the Women; Emma; Greed; Happy Landing; Heidi (1937); Hell Harbor; Mask of Fu Manchu, The; Meet Dr. Christian; Melody for Three; Mr. Moto in Danger Island; One in a Million; Painted Veil, The; Remedy for Riches; Sin of Madelon Claudet, The; Skyscraper Souls; Student Prince in Old Heidelberg, The; Susan Lenox: Her Fall and Rise; They Meet Again

Herter, Gerard: Caltiki, the Immortal Monster; Go Kill and Come Back; Machine Gun Killers

Hervey, Irene: Charlie Chan in Shanghai; Count of Monte Cristo, The (1934); Dude Ranger; Mr. Peabody and the Mermaid; Night Monster; Play Misty for Me

Herzog, Werner: Burden of Dreams; Man of Flowers; Tokyo-Ga

Heskin, Kam: Blackjack

Heslov, Grant: Dante's Peak

Hess, David: Last House on the Left; Let It Rock; Swamp Thing

Hess, Joe: Master Blaster

Hess, Michelle: Taxi Dancers

Hess, Sandra: Beastmaster III: The Eye of Braxus; Endangered; Mortal Kombat: Annihilation

Hess, Susan: Dress Gray

Hesseman, Howard: Amazon Women on the Moon; Big Bus, The; Diamond Trap, The; Doctor Detroit; Flight of the Navigator; Gridlock'd; Heat (1987); Hot Chocolate; Inside Out (1986); Little Miss Millions; Loose Shoes; Murder in New Hampshire; My Chauffeur; One Shoe Makes It Murder; Out of Sync; Police Academy II: Their First Assignment; Princess Who Had Never Laughed, The; Private Lessons; Rubin & Ed; Silence of the Heart; Sunshine Boys, The; Tarantulas—The Deadly Cargo; Tunnelvision (1976)

Heston, Charlton: Agony and the Ecstasy, The; Airport 1975; Alaska; Antony and Cleopatra (1973); Arrowhead; Avenging Angel, The (1995); Awakening, The; Ben-Hur (1959); Beneath the Planet of the Apes; Big Country, The; Buccaneer, The; Call of the Wild (1972); Chiefs; Crucifer of Blood; Diamond Head; Earthquake; El Cid; 55 Days at Peking; Four Musketeers, The; Gray Lady Down; Greatest Show on Earth, The; Greatest Story Ever Told, The; Hamlet (1996); In the Mouth of Madness; Julius Caesar (1970); Khartoum; Little Kidnappers; Major Dundee; Midway; Mother Lode; Mountain Men, The; Nairobi Affair; Naked Jungle, The; Omega Man, The; Planet of the Apes; Pony Express; Prince and the Pauper, The (1978); Proud Men; Ruby Gentry; Solar Crisis; Soylent Green; Ten Commandments, The (1956); Thousand Heroes, A; Three Musketeers, The (1973); Three Violent People; Touch of Evil; Treasure Island (1990); True Lies; Two-Minute Warning; War Lord, The; Will Penny; Wreck of the Mary Deare, The

Hewett, Christopher: Producers, The; Ratboy

Hewett, Lauren: Echo of Thunder, The

Hewitt, Alan: Misadventures of Merlin Jones, The

Hewitt, Barbara: Equinox (1971) (The Beast)

Hewitt, Jennifer Love: Can't Hardly Wait; I Know What You Did Last Summer; I Still Know What You Did Last Summer; Little Miss Millions; Telling You; Trojan War

Hewitt, Martin: Alien Predators; Carnal Crimes; Crime Lords; Endless Love; Killer Party; Night Fire; Night

Rhythms; Out of Control; Private War; Secret Games; White Ghost

Hewlett, David: Boys of St. Vincent; Cube; Desire and Hell at Sunset Motel; Penthouse, The; Pin; Scanners 2: The New Order

Hext, Tamera: Gates of Hell Part II: Dead Awakening

Hey, Virginia: Obsession: A Taste for Fear

Heyden, Yvette: Tides of War

Heydt, Louis Jean: Great McGinty, The; Great Moment, The; Test Pilot; They Were Expendable

Heyerdahl, Christopher: Silent Trigger

Heyl, John: Separate Peace, A

Heyman, Barton: Billy Galvin; Let's Scare Jessica to Death; Trial of the Cantonsville Nine, The; Valdez Is Coming

Heyman, Elizabeth: Broadcast Bombshells

Heywood, Anne: Brain, The (1965); I Want What I Want; Ninety Degrees in the Shade; Sadat; Scenes from a Murder; Shaming, The; Very Edge, The; What Waits Below

Heywood, Colin: Bloody New Year

Heywood, Pat: Girly; Rude Awakening (1982); Wish You Were Here

Hezelhurst, Noni: Waiting

Hickey, Barry: Las Vegas Weekend

Hickey, Brendan: I Married a Vampire

Hickey, John Benjamin: Love! Valour! Compassion!; Only You (1994)

Hickey, Marguerite: Mirrors

Hickey, Tom: Raining Stones

Hickey, William: Any Man's Death; Bright Lights, Big City; Da; Forget Paris; Jerky Boys, The; Maddening, The; Major Payne; Mob Boss; Name of the Rose, The; Pink Cadillac; Prizzi's Honor; Puppet Master, The; Runestone; Tales from the Darkside, The Movie; Walls of Glass

Hickland, Catherine: Ghost Town; Witchery

Hickman, Darryl: Any Number Can Play; Fighting Father Dunne; Human Comedy, The; Island in the Sky; Johnny Shiloh; Keeper of the Flame; King Lear (1982); Leave Her to Heaven; Men of Boys Town; Strange Love of Martha Ivers, The; Tea and Sympathy; Tingler, The

Hickman, Dwayne: Dr. Goldfoot and the Bikini Machine; High School, USA; How to Stuff a Wild Bikini

Hickman, Howard: Civilization; Kansas Terrors

Hicks, Catherine: Child's Play; Death Valley; Eight Days a Week; Fever Pitch; Laguna Heat; Like Father, Like Son; Peggy Sue Got Married; Razor's Edge, The (1984); Redwood Curtain; Running Against Time; She's Out of Control; Souvenir; Spy; Star Trek IV: The Voyage Home

Hicks, Danny: Intruder (1988)

Hicks, Greg: Deadline (1988)

Hicks, Hilly: Amazing Spiderman, The; Cartier Affair, The

Hicks, Kevin: Blood Relations; Dance Me Outside; Final Notice

Hicks, Leonard: Santa Claus Conquers the Martians

Hicks, Michele: Twin Falls Idaho

Hicks, Redmond: She's Gotta Have It

Hicks, Russell: Captain America (1944); Devil Dogs of the Air; Flying Saucer, The

Hicks, Seymour: Scrooge (1935)

Hicks, Taral: Belly; Bronx Tale, A

Hicks, William T.: Day of Judgment, A; Order of the Black Eagle

Hickson, Joan: At Bertram's Hotel; Body in the Library, The; Caribbean Mystery, A; Clockwise; 4:50 From Paddington; Great Expectations (1988); Mirror Crack'd from Side to Side, The; Moving Finger, The; Murder at the Vicarage; Murder Is Announced, A; Murder She Said; Nemesis (1986); Pocketful of Rye, A; Sleeping Murder; They Do It with Mirrors; Why Didn't They Ask Evans?

Hidalgo-Gato, Raymundo: El Super

Hidari, Sachiko: Insect Woman

Hiep, Nguyen Ngoc: Three Seasons

Higashiyama, Chieko: Tokyo Story

Higby, Mary Jane: Honeymoon Killers, The

Higby, Wilbur: True Heart Susie

Higgins, Anthony: Alive & Kicking; Bride, The; Cold Room, The; Draughtman's Contract, The; For Love or Money; Max Mon Amour; Quartet (1981); Sweet Killing; Taste the Blood of Dracula; Young Sherlock Holmes

Higgins, Clare: Hellraiser; Hellraiser II: Hellbound

Higgins, Joel: First Affair; Killing at Hell's Gate

Hocking, Kristen: Bitter Vengeance; Wolves, The (1994)

Hodder, Kane: Jason Goes to Hell: The Final Friday; Wes Craven's Wishmaster

Hoddy, Steve: Their Only Chance

Hode, Kate: Hidden II, The

Hodge, Charlie: Elvis—The Movie

Hodge, Douglas: Dark Obsession; Fatal Inversion, A; Middlemarch; Salome's Last Dance

Hodge, Patricia: Betrayal (1983); Diamond's Edge; Lies & Whispers; Naked Civil Servant, The; Rumpole of the Bailey (TV Series); Spymaker: The Secret Life of Ian Fleming; Sunset

Hodges, Eddie: Adventures of Huckleberry Finn, The (1960); Hole in the Head, A; Summer Magic

Hodges, Ralph: Sea Hound, The

Hodges, Tom: Excessive Force; Going Overboard; Heavyweights

Hodgins, Earle: Law for Tombstone

Hodiak, John: Across the Wide Missouri; Battleground; Command Decision; Harvey Girls, The; Homecoming (1948); I Dood It; Lifeboat; Love from a Stranger; Miniver Story, The; Somewhere in the Night

Hodson, Donal: Lone Runner

Hoesl, Tobias: Mines of Kilimanjaro; Polar Bear King, The

Hoey, Dennis: Golden Earrings; House of Fear; Pearl of Death, The; Sherlock Holmes and the Secret Weapon; Sherlock Holmes and the Spider Woman; Sherlock Holmes Faces Death; Tarzan and the Leopard Woman; Terror by Night

Hoff, John: Howling, The: New Moon Rising

Hoffman, Basil: Double-O Kid, The; Ice Runner

Hoffman, Bridget: Time Trackers

Hoffman, Dustin: Agatha; Alfredo Alfredo; All the President's Men; American Buffalo; Billy Bathgate; Death of a Salesman; Dick Tracy (1990); Family Business; Graduate, The; Hero (1992); Hook; Ishtar; Kramer vs. Kramer; Lenny; Little Big Man; Mad City; Madigan's Millions; Marathon Man; Messenger: The Story of Joan of Arc, The; Midnight Cowboy; Outbreak; Papillon; Rain Man; Sleepers; Sphere; Straight Time; Straw Dogs; Tootsie; Wag the Dog

Hoffman, Elizabeth: Dante's Peak; Fear No Evil

Hoffman, Erika: Last Days of Patton, The

Hoffman, Gaby: Everyone Says I Love You; Man without a Face, The; Now and Then; Sleepless in Seattle; Strike! (1998); This Is My Life; 200 Cigarettes; Uncle Buck; Volcano

Hoffman, Gertrude: Ape, The

Hoffman, Isabella: Tripwire

Hoffman, Jane: Up the Sandbox

Hoffman, Linda: Dentist, The

Hoffman, Otto: Haunted Gold

Hoffman, Pato: Cheyenne Warrior; Meteorites!

Hoffman, Philip Seymour: Big Lebowski, The; Flawless; Happiness; Leap of Faith; Magnolia; Montana (1997); Next Stop Wonderland; Patch Adams; Talented Mr. Ripley, The

Hoffman, Robert: Black Veil for Lisa, A; Eyes Behind the Stars

Hoffman, Shawn: Adventures in Dinosaur City

Hoffman, Thom: Lily Was Here; Orlando

Hoffmann, Isabella: In a Stranger's Hands

Hoffman, Jutta: Bandits (1997)

Hoffs, Susanna: Allnighter, The

Hofheimer, Charlie: Father's Day

Hofmann, Isabella: Atomic Dog

Hofschneider, Marco: Foreign Student

Hogan, Bosco: Portrait of the Artist as a Young Man, A

Hogan, Gabriel: Halfback of Notre Dame, The

Hogan, Hulk: McCinsey's Island; Mr. Nanny; No Holds Barred; Santa with Muscles; Secret Agent Club; Suburban Commando; Thunder in Paradise II; Thunder in Paradise

Hogan, Michael: Clearcut; Lost!; Pathfinder, The

Hogan, Paul: Almost an Angel; Anzacs; "Crocodile" Dundee; "Crocodile" Dundee II; Flipper (1996); Floating Away; Lightning Jack

Hogan, Robert: Gone Are the Days; Lady in Red

Hogan, Susan: Phobia; White Fang

Hoger, Hannelore: Germany in Autumn

Hohl, Arthur: Lady by Choice; Scarlet Claw, The

Holbrook, Ashely: Ringmaster

Holbrook, Hal: Bachelor, The (1999); Capricorn One; Carried Away; Creepshow; Dress Gray; Firm, The; Fletch Lives;

Fog, The; Girl from Petrovka, The; Great White Hope, The; Group, The; Judas Kiss; Kidnapping of the President, The; Killing of Randy Webster, The; Magnum Force; Midway; My Own Country; Natural Enemies; North and South; Operation Delta Force; Our Town (1980); Rituals; Sorry, Wrong Number (1989); Star Chamber, The; They Only Kill Their Masters; Unholy, The; Wall Street; Wild in the Streets

Holden, Bob: Deadly Vengeance

Holden, Fay: Andy Hardy Gets Spring Fever; Andy Hardy Meets a Debutante; Andy Hardy's Double Life; Andy Hardy's Private Secretary; Big Hangover, The; Bulldog Drummond Escapes; Life Begins for Andy Hardy; Love Finds Andy Hardy; Love Laughs at Andy Hardy

Holden, Gloria: Dracula's Daughter; Having a Wonderful Crime; Life of Emile Zola, The; Miss Annie Rooney

Holden, Joyce: Terror from the Year 5,000

Holden, Laurie: Expect No Mercy; Magnificent Seven, The (TV Series); Past Perfect; Pathfinder, The

Holden, Marjean: Ballistic; Philadelphia Experiment 2, The

Holden, Mark: Blue Fire Lady; Lovely But Deadly

Holden, Peter: Great Man Votes, The

Holden, Rebecca: Sisterhood, The

Holden, William: Alvarez Kelly; Arizona; Ashanti; Blue Knight, The (1973); Boots Malone; Born Yesterday (1950); Bridge on the River Kwai, The; Bridges at Toko-Ri, The; Casino Royale (1967); Counterfeit Traitor, The; Country Girl, The (1954); Damien: Omen II; Dark Past, The; Dear Wife; Devil's Brigade, The; Earthling, The; Escape from Fort Bravo; Executive Suite; Fedora; Force of Arms; Golden Boy; Horse Soldiers, The; Key, The; Love Is a Many-Splendored Thing; Man from Colorado, The; Miss Grant Takes Richmond; Moon Is Blue, The; Network; Our Town (1940); Paris When It Sizzles; Picnic; Rachel and the Stranger; Sabrina (1954); S.O.B.; Stalag 17; Sunset Boulevard; Texas (1941); Towering Inferno, The; Union Station; When Time Ran Out!; When Wolves Cry; Wild Bunch, The; Wild Rovers, The; World of Suzie Wong, The; Young and Willing

Holder, Geoffrey: Boomerang (1992); Live and Let Die; Swashbuckler (1976)

Holder, Ginny: Wing Commander

Holdren, Judd: Zombies of the Stratosphere (Satan's Satellites) (Serial)

Holescher, Deven: Wired to Kill

Holiday, Billie: Ladies Sing the Blues, The

Holiday, Billy: Terror in the Swamp

Holiday, Hope: Ladies' Man, The; Rounders, The (1965)

Holiday, Kene: Dangerous Company; Josephine Baker Story, The

Holland, Agnieszka: Interrogation

Holland, Betty Lou: Goddess, The

Holland, John: Blonde Ice; Hell Harbor; She Goes to War; They Saved Hitler's Brain

Holland, Lee: Shanty Tramp

Holland, Nicholas: Dusty

Holland, Pamela: Dorm That Dripped Blood, The (Pranks)

Hollander, David: Call to Glory

Hollander, Tom: Bedrooms and Hallways

Holliday, Judy: Adam's Rib (1949); Bells Are Ringing; Born Yesterday (1950); It Should Happen to You

Holliday, Polly: Bernice Bobs Her Hair; Catamount Killing, The; Gremlins; Lots of Luck; Mrs. Doubtfire; Moon over Parador

Holliman, Earl: Anzio; Bridges at Toko-Ri, The; Broken Lance; Burning Hills, The; Don't Go Near the Water; Gunsmoke: Return to Dodge; Hot Spell; I Died a Thousand Times; Last Train from Gun Hill; Rainmaker, The (1956); Smoke (1970); Sons of Katie Elder, The; Trap, The; Tribes

Holliman, Tina: Beach Babes 2: Cave Girl Island

Hollis, Tommy: Piano Lesson, The

Holloman, Laurel: Incredibly True Adventure of Two Girls in Love, The; Myth of Fingerprints, The

Holloway, Stanley: Brief Encounter (1945); Dr. Jekyll and Mr. Hyde (1973); Hamlet (1948); Immortal Battalion, The (The Way Ahead); In Harm's Way; Journey into Fear (1975); Lavender Hill Mob, The; Mrs. Brown You've Got a Lovely Daughter; My Fair Lady; No Love for Johnnie; Passport to Pimlico; Private Life of Sherlock Holmes, The; Ten Little Indians (1989); This Happy Breed

Holloway, Sterling: Adventures of Huckleberry Finn, The (1960); Beautiful Blonde from Bashful Bend, The; Cheers for Miss Bishop; Dancing Lady; Doubting Thomas; Gold

Diggers of 1933; International House; Kentucky Rifle; Little Men (1940); Melody Master (The Great Awakening) (New Wine); Remember the Night; Robin Hood of Texas; Thunder and Lightning; Walk in the Sun, A; Wildfire (1945)

Holloway, W. E.: Elephant Boy

Holly, Lauren: Band of the Hand; Dangerous Heart; Down Periscope; Dragon: The Bruce Lee Story; Dumb and Dumber; Entropy; Money Kings; No Looking Back; Smile Like Yours, A; Turbulence

Hollywood, Gary: Winter Guest, The

Holm, Astrid: Master of the House (Du Skal Aere Din Hustru)

Holm, Celeste: All About Eve; Bittersweet Love; Champagne for Caesar; Cinderella (1964); Gentlemen's Agreement; High Society; Private Files of J. Edgar Hoover, The; Road House (1948); Snake Pit, The; Tender Trap, The; Tom Sawyer (1973)

Holm, Eleanor: Tarzan's Revenge

Holm, Ian: Alien; All Quiet on the Western Front (1979); Another Woman; Big Night; Blue Ice; Borrowers, The (1993); Brazil; Chariots of Fire; Dance with a Stranger; Dreamchild; eXistenZ; Fifth Element, The; Greystoke: The Legend of Tarzan, Lord of the Apes; Hamlet (1990); Henry V (1989); Homecoming, The (1973); Inside the Third Reich; Joe Gould's Secret; Juggernaut (1974); Kafka; Life Less Ordinary, A; Loch Ness; Madness of King George, The; Mary Shelley's Frankenstein; Midsummer Night's Dream, A (1968); Naked Lunch; Night Falls on Manhattan; Return of the Soldier, The; Robin and Marian; Season of Giants, A; Shout at the Devil; Singleton's Pluck; Sweet Hereafter, The; Thief of Baghdad (1978); Time Bandits; Wetherby

Holman, Chaz: Alley Cats, The

Holmes, Brittany Ashton: Little Rascals, The (1994)

Holmes, Helen: Gentleman from California

Holmes, Hollye: Adventures of the Wilderness Family

Holmes, Katie: Disturbing Behavior; Go; Teaching Mrs. Tingle; Wonder Boys

Holmes, Michelle: Rita, Sue and Bob Too

Holmes, Phillips: Criminal Code, The; General Spanky

Holmes, Taylor: Beware, My Lovely; Double Deal; Hoodlum Empire

Holmes, Tina: Edge of Seventeen

Holmes, Wendell: Lotto Land

Holms, Stuart: Man Who Laughs, The

Holotik, Rosie: Encounter with the Unknown

Holschneider, Marco: Europa, Europa

Holt, Anthony: Deadly Daphne's Revenge

Holt, Charlene: El Dorado; Man's Favorite Sport?; Red Line 7000

Holt, Hans: Almost Angels; Mozart Story, The

Holt, Jack: Across the Wide Missouri; Arizona Ranger; Behind the Mask; Brimstone; King of the Bullwhip; Littlest Rebel, The; Loaded Pistols; My Pal Trigger; Renegade Girl; Task Force; They Were Expendable; Trail of Robin Hood; Victory (1919); Wild Frontier

Holt, Jacqueline: Stick to Your Guns

Holt, Jennifer: Private Buckaroo; Stage to Mesa City

Holt, Mette: Whispering, The

Holt, Patrick: Psychomania

Holt, Sandrine: Black Robe; Dance Me Outside; John Woo's Once a Thief; Rapa Nui

Holt, Steven: Preppies

Holt, Tim: Arizona Ranger; Brothers in the Saddle; Dynamite Pass; Fifth Avenue Girl; Gun Smugglers; Guns of Hate; His Kind of Woman; Hitler's Children; Hot Lead; Land of the Open Range; Law West of Tombstone; Magnificent Ambersons, The; Monster That Challenged the World, The; My Darling Clementine; Mysterious Desperado; Pirates of the Prairie; Renegade Ranger; Rider from Tucson; Road Agent; Rustlers, The; Stagecoach (1939); Stella Dallas; Treasure of the Sierra Madre; Yesterday Machine, The

Holt, Ula: New Adventures of Tarzan; Tarzan and the Green Goddess

Holton, Mark: Leprechaun; Pee-Wee's Big Adventure

Holubar, Allan: 20,000 Leagues Under the Sea (1916)

Holvoe, Maria: Worth Winning

Holyfield, Evander: Blood Salvage

Holzboer, Max: Blue Light, The

Holzbog, Arabella: Evil Lives

Holzer, Baby Jane: Ciao! Manhattan

Homar, Lluis: Celestial Clockwork

Homeier, Skip: At Gunpoint; Between Heaven and Hell; Burning Hills, The; Ghost and Mr. Chicken, The; Gunfighter, The (1950); Johnny Shiloh; Tall T, The; Ten Wanted Men

Homolka, Oscar: Ball of Fire; Boys' Night Out; Comrade X; Executioner, The; Funeral in Berlin; I Remember Mama; Invisible Woman, The; Key, The; Madwoman of Chaillot, The; Mooncussers; Rhodes of Africa (Rhodes); Sabotage (1936); Seven Year Itch, The; Strange Case of Dr. Jekyll and Mr. Hyde, The (1968); White Tower, The; Wonderful World of the Brothers Grimm, The

Hong, James: Bethune; Big Trouble in Little China; Bloodsport II; Bloodsport III; Breakout (1998); Broken Vessels; China Girl; Cyber Bandits; Femme Fontaine: Killer Babe for the CIA; Framed (1990); Gladiator Cop II: The Swordsman; Golden Child, The; Merlin; Missing in Action; New Adventures of Charlie Chan, The (TV Series); Operation Golden Phoenix; Red Corner; Secret Agent Club; Shadowzone; South Beach Academy; Talons of the Eagle; Tango and Cash; Triplecross (1995); Wayne's World 2; Yes, Giorgio

Hongo, Kojiro: Gamera Versus Barugon; Gamera Versus Gaos

Hood, Darla: Bat, The

Hooks, Brian: Phat Beach; 3 Strikes

Hooks, Jan: Coneheads; Dangerous Woman, A; Funland

Hooks, Kevin: Aaron Loves Angela; Can You Hear the Laughter? The Story of Freddie Prinze; Sounder; Take Down

Hooks, Robert: Aaron Loves Angela; Execution, The; Fast-Walking; Fled; Free of Eden; Passenger 57; Sophisticated Gents, The; Supercarrier; Sweet Love, Bitter; Woman Called Moses, A

Hooten, Peter: Dr. Strange; Fantasies

Hootkins, William: Biggles—Adventures in Time; Death Machine; Hear My Song

Hooton, James: Twentyfourseven (English)

Hoover, Danielle: Alien Arsenal

Hoover, Dave: Fast, Cheap and Out of Control

Hoover, Phil: Black Gestapo, The

Hoover, Tom: Galaxy of the Dinosaurs; Ozone

Hope, Bob: Bachelor in Paradise; Big Broadcast of 1938, The; Boy, Did I Get a Wrong Number!; Call Me Bwana; Cancel My Reservation; Casanova's Big Night; Cat and the Canary, The (1939); Caught in the Draft; College Swing; Critic's Choice; Facts of Life; Fancy Pants; Ghost Breakers; Give Me a Sailor; Global Affair, A; Great Lover, The; Here Come the Girls; I'll Take Sweden; Lemon Drop Kid, The; Louisiana Purchase; Monsieur Beaucaire; Muppet Movie, The; My Favorite Blonde; My Favorite Brunette; Off Limits (1953); Paleface, The; Paris Holiday; Princess and the Pirate, The; Private Navy of Sgt. O'Farrell, The; Road to Bali; Road to Hong Kong, The; Road to Morocco; Road to Rio; Road to Singapore; Road to Utopia; Road to Zanzibar; Seven Little Foys, The; Son of Paleface; Sorrowful Jones; They Got Me Covered

Hope, Leslie: Sweet Killing

Hope, Leslie: Avenging Angel, The (1995); Big Slice, The; Caught in the Act; Conspiracy of Fear, The; First Degree; Kansas; Men at Work; Paris France; Prep School; Sword of Gideon

Hope, Margot: Femme Fontaine: Killer Babe for the CIA

Hope, Richard: Bellman and True

Hopely, Jason: War Boy, The

Hopkins, Anthony: Amistad; Audrey Rose; August; Bounty, The; Bram Stoker's Dracula; Bunker, The; Change of Seasons, A; Chaplin; Chorus of Disapproval, A; Dawning, The; Desperate Hours (1990); Doll's House, A (1989); Edge, The; Efficiency Expert, The (Spotswood); 84 Charing Cross Road; Elephant Man, The (1980); Freejack; Girl from Petrovka, The; Good Father, The; Great Expectations (1989); Hamlet (1969); Howards End; Hunchback (1982); Innocent, The (1993); Instinct; International Velvet; Juggernaut (1974); Legends of the Fall; Lindbergh Kidnapping Case, The; Lion in Winter, The; Looking Glass War, The; Magic; Married Man, A; Mask of Zorro, The; Meet Joe Black; Mussolini and I; Nixon; One Man's War; QB VII; Remains of the Day; Road to Wellville, The; Shadowlands; Silence of the Lambs; Surviving Picasso; Tenth Man, The; Titus; Trial, The (1992); Victory at Entebbe

Hopkins, Barrett: Firehouse (1987)

Hopkins, Bo: American Graffiti; Ballad of Little Jo, The; Big Bad John; Blood Ties (1993); Bounty Hunter; Center of the Web; Cheyenne Warrior; Culpepper Cattle Co., The; Day of the Locust, The; Fever Lake; Final Alliance; Fifth Floor, The; From Dusk Till Dawn 2: Texas Blood Money; Inside Monkey Zetterland; Kansas City Massacre, The; Killer Elite, The; Last Ride of the Dalton Gang, The; Macho Callahan; Mark of the Beast, The; More American Graffiti; Mutant; Nightmare at Noon; November Conspiracy, The; Painted Hero; Posse (1975); Rodeo Girl; Small Town in Texas, A; Smoky Mountain Christmas; Sweet Sixteen; Tentacles; Texas Payback; Time Served; Trapper County War; What Comes Around; White Lightning; Wyatt Earp: Return to Tombstone

Hopkins, Harold: Club, The (1985); Sara Dane; Winds of Jarrah, The

Hopkins, Jermaine: Juice

Hopkins, Jermaine "Huggy": Phat Beach

Hopkins, Miriam: Barbary Coast, The; Becky Sharp; Carrie (1952); Chase, The (1966); Children's Hour, The; Dr. Jekyll and Mr. Hyde (1932); Heiress, The; Old Maid, The; Savage Intruder, The; These Three; Virginia City

Hopkins, Telma: Bosom Buddies (TV Series); Kid with the Broken Halo, The; Trancers

Hoppe, Marianne: Ten Little Indians (1966)

Hoppe, Rolf: Palmetto

Hopper, Dennis: American Friend, The; Apocalypse Now; Backtrack; Basquiat; Black Widow; Blood Red; Blue Velvet; Boiling Point (1993); Carried Away; Chasers; Chattahoochee; Cheyenne (TV Series); Doublecrossed; Easy Rider; EDtv; Eye of the Storm; Flashback; Giant; Glory Stompers, The; Heart of Justice; Hoosiers; Inside Man, The; Jason and the Argonauts (2000); King of the Mountain; Last Days of Frankie the Fly, The; Last Movie, The (Chinchero); Let It Rock; Mad Dog Morgan; Meet the Deedles; My Science Project; Nails; Night Tide; O.C. & Stiggs; Osterman Weekend, The; Paris Trout; Pick-Up Artist, The; Planet of Blood (Queen of Blood); Rebel Without a Cause; Red Rock West; Riders of the Storm; River's Edge; Road Ends; Rumble Fish; Samson and Delilah (1996); Search and Destroy (1995); Source, The; Space Truckers; Speed; Stark; Straight to Hell; Sunset Heat; Super Mario Brothers, The; Texas Chainsaw Massacre 2, The; Tracks; Trip, The; True Romance; Waterworld; Wild Times; Witch Hunt

Hopper, Hal: Mudhoney

Hopper, Hedda: Alice Adams; As You Desire Me; Common Law, The; Maid's Night Out, The; Midnight (1939); One Frightened Night; Racketeer; Skyscraper Souls; Speak Easily; Sunset Boulevard; Tarzan's Revenge

Hopper, William: Bad Seed, The; Deadly Mantis, The; Goodbye, My Lady; 20 Million Miles to Earth

Hopton, Russell: Lady Killer

Horan, Barbara: Malibu Bikini Shop, The; Triplecross (1985)

Horan, Gerard: Look Back In Anger (1989)

Horan, James: Image of Passion

Hordern, Michael: Christmas Carol, A (1951); Danny, The Champion of the World; Dark Obsession; Green Man, The; How I Won the War; Joseph Andrews; Lady Jane; Man Who Never Was, The; Middlemarch; Missionary, The; Old Curiosity Shop, The (1975); Oliver Twist (1982); Secret Garden, The (1987); Sink the Bismarck; Story of Robin Hood, The; Suspicion (1987); Trouble with Spies, The; Warriors, The (1955); Where Eagles Dare; Windom's Way

Horino, Tad: Pacific Inferno

Horn, Camilla: Faust; Tempest (1928)

Horn, Patrick Van: Swingers

Horne, Lena: Broadway Rhythm; Cabin in the Sky; Death of a Gunfighter; Duchess of Idaho; I Dood It; Ladies Sing the Blues, The; Panama Hattie; Stormy Weather; That's Entertainment! III; Thousands Cheer; Wiz, The; Ziegfeld Follies

Horneff, Wil: Born to Be Wild

Horner, Penelope: Half a Sixpence

Horney, Brigitte: Baron Münchhausen (1943)

Horoks, Zbigniew: Dr. Petiot

Horovitch, David: 4:50 from Paddington; Mirror Crack'd from Side to Side, The; Murder at the Vicarage; They Do It with Mirrors

Horovitz, Adam: Lost Angels; Roadside Prophets

Horrocks, Jane: Absolutely Fabulous; Deadly Advice; Dressmaker, The; Getting It Right; Life Is Sweet; Second Best

Horse, Michael: Avenging, The; House of Cards; Legend of the Lone Ranger, The; Passenger 57

Horsford, Anna Maria: Murder Without Motive

Horsley, Lee: French Silk; Sword and the Sorcerer, The; 13 at Dinner

Horton, Clara: Tom Sawyer (1917)

Horton, Edward Everett: Bluebeard's Eighth Wife; Cold Turkey; Front Page, The (1931); Gang's All Here, The; Gay Divorcée, The; Here Comes Mr. Jordan; Holiday; I Married an Angel; Lady on a Train; Lost Horizon; Merry Widow, The; Pocketful of Miracles; Reaching for the Moon (1931); Sex and the Single Girl; Shall We Dance? (1937); Springtime in the Rockies (1942); Top Hat; Ziegfeld Girl

Horton, Peter: Children of the Corn; Death Benefit; Side Out; Two Days in the Valley; Where the River Runs Black

Horton, Robert: Green Slime, The; Men of the Fighting Lady; Pony Soldier; Silver Blaze; Wagon Train (TV Series)

Hosea, Bobby: O. J. Simpson Story, The

Hoshi, Yuriko: Ghidrah, the Three-Headed Monster; Godzilla vs. Mothra; Kojiro

Hoskins, Bob: Balto; Beyond the Limit; Blue Ice; Brazil; Cousin Bette; Cry Terror; Don Quixote (2000); Dunera Boys, The; Favor, the Watch and the Very Big Fish, The; Felicia's Journey; Heart Condition; Hook; Inner Circle, The; Inserts; Lassiter; Lonely Passion of Judith Hearne, The; Long Good Friday, The; Mermaids; Michael; Mona Lisa; Mussolini and I; Nixon; Passed Away; Pink Floyd: The Wall; Prayer for the Dying, A; Raggedy Rawney, The; Secret Agent, The (1996); Shattered (1991); Super Mario Brothers, The; Sweet Liberty; Twentyfourseven (English); Twentyfourseven (boxing); Who Framed Roger Rabbit

Hossack, Allison: Escape from Mars

Hossein, Robert: Battle of El Alamein, The; Bolero (1982); Double Agents; Le Repos du Guerrier (Warrior's Rest)

Hotaru, Yukijiro: Zeram

Hotchkis, Joan: Last Game, The; Ode to Billy Joe

Hotton, Donald: Hearse, The

Hou, Chi Sui: Twin Warriors

Houdini, Harry: Man from Beyond, The

Houghton, Katharine: Ethan Frome; Guess Who's Coming to Dinner; Night We Never Met, The

Hounsou, Djimon: Amistad; Gladiator (2000)

House, Billy: People Will Talk

House, Ron: Bullshot (Bullshot Crummond)

Houseman, John: Another Woman; Babysitter, The (1980); Bright Lights, Big City; Cheap Detective, The; Christmas without Snow, A; Displaced Person, The; Fog, The; Ghost Story; Gideon's Trumpet; Merry Wives of Windsor, The; Murder by Phone; Old Boyfriends; Our Town (1980); Paper Chase, The; Rollerball; St. Ives; Three Days of the Condor; Wholly Moses!; Winds of War, The

Houser, Jerry: Bad Company (1972); Class of '44; Summer of '42

Houser, Patrick: Hot Dog … The Movie

Houston, Alan: Black and White (2000)

Houston, Cissy: Taking My Turn

Houston, Donald: Battle Hell; Doctor in the House; Maniac (1962); Run for Your Money, A; 633 Squadron; Study in Terror, A; Where Eagles Dare

Houston, Renee: Horse's Mouth, The; Time Without Pity

Houston, Robert: Hills Have Eyes, The

Houston, Whitney: Bodyguard, The; Preacher's Wife, The; Rodgers & Hammerstein's Cinderella; Waiting to Exhale

Hove, Anders: Bloodlust: Subspecies III; Bloodstone: Subspecies II

Hoven, Adrian: Castle of the Creeping Flesh; Cave of the Living Dead

Hovey, Helen: Sadist, The

Hovey, Natasha: Aqua E Sapone

Hovis, Larry: Hogan's Heroes (TV Series)

Howard, Adam Coleman: No Secrets; Quiet Cool

Howard, Alan: Cook, the Thief, His Wife & Her Lover, The; Return of the Musketeers; Secret Rapture, The

Howard, Andrea: Nude Bomb, The (Return of Maxwell Smart, The)

Howard, Arliss: Beyond the Call; Crisscross (1992); Door to Door; For the Boys; Full Metal Jacket; Infiltrator, The; Iran Days of Crisis; Johns; Lesser Evil, The; Lost World, The; Jurassic Park; Man Who Captured Eichmann, The; Map of the World, A; Men Don't Leave; Old Man; Plain Clothes; Ruby (1991); Sandlot, The; Somebody Has to Shoot the

Crow, The; Dirty Dozen, The: The Fatal Mission; Ghostbusters; Ghostbusters II; Hand That Rocks the Cradle, The; Just Your Luck; Leviathan; Mr. Magoo; Never 2 Big; No Escape; Operation Delta Force; Penitentiary II; Shark Attack; Spacehunter: Adventures in the Forbidden Zone; Speechless; Stranger in the Kingdom, A; Substitute, The (1996); Sugar Hill; Tornado!; Trapper County War; Weeds; Wrong Guys, The

Hudson, Gary: Force, The; Lights, Camera, Action, Love; Martial Outlaw; Mindtwister; Serial Killer; Sexual Intent; Texas Payback; Wild Cactus

Hudson, John: Screaming Skull, The; When Gangland Strikes

Hudson, Kate: Gossip

Hudson, Mark: Hysterical

Hudson, Rochelle: Curly Top; Mr. Moto Takes a Chance; Mr. Skitch; She Done Him Wrong; Show Them No Mercy

Hudson, Rock: All That Heaven Allows; Ambassador, The; Avalanche; Battle Hymn; Bend of the River; Come September; Darling Lili; Devlin Connection III, The; Embryo; Giant; Gun Fury; Hornet's Nest; Ice Station Zebra; Lover Come Back; Magnificent Obsession; Man's Favorite Sport?; Martian Chronicles, Parts I-III, The; Mirror Crack'd, The; Pillow Talk; Seconds; Send Me No Flowers; Showdown (1973); Something of Value; Strange Bedfellows; Tarnished Angels, The; Tobruk; Undefeated, The; Winchester '73; World War III; Written on the Wind

Hudson, Ruben Santiago: Rear Window (1998); Solomon and Sheba (1995)

Hudson, Stephanie: Beach Babes 2: Cave Girl Island

Hudson, Toni: Just One of the Guys; Prime Risk; Uninvited, The (1987)

Hudson, William: Amazing Colossal Man, The; Attack of the 50-Foot Woman (1958); Hysterical

Hues, Matthias: Alone in the Woods; Blackbelt; Bounty Tracker; Cyberzone; Digital Man; Fist of Iron; Mission of Justice; Suicide Ride; TC 2000

Huff, Brent: Armed Response; Final Justice (1994); Nine Deaths of the Ninja; Stormquest

Huff, Shawn: Final Justice (1994)

Huffman, Cady: Space Marines

Huffman, David: Firefox; F.I.S.T.; Jane Doe; St. Helens; Winds of Kitty Hawk, The; Witchcraft V: Dance with the Devil

Huffman, Felicity: Slight Case of Murder, A; Stephen King's Golden Years (TV Series)

Huffman, Kimberly: Sleeping with Strangers

Hufsey, Billy: Magic Kid; Off the Wall

Hugeny, Sharon: Majority of One, A

Hughes, Barnard: Cold Turkey; Da; First Monday in October; Hospital, The; Incident, The (1989); Lost Boys, The; Maxie; Midnight Cowboy; Odd Couple II, The; Past the Bleachers; Primal Secrets; Pursuit of Happiness, The; Rage (1972); Sanctuary of Fear; Sister Act 2: Back in the Habit; Sisters (1973); Tron; Under the Biltmore Clock; Where Are the Children?; Where's Poppa?

Hughes, Brendan: Howling VI: The Freaks; Stranded; To Die For (1989)

Hughes, Carol: Flash Gordon Conquers the Universe; Man from Music Mountain; Stage Struck (1936); Three Men on a Horse; Under Western Stars

Hughes, Finola: Above Suspicion (1994); Aspen Extreme; Crying Child, The; Dark Side of Genius; Staying Alive

Hughes, Helen: Locked in Silence; Peanut Butter Solution, The

Hughes, John: That Sinking Feeling

Hughes, Kathleen: Cult of the Cobra

Hughes, Kay: Dick Tracy (1937); Ride, Ranger, Ride; Vigilantes Are Coming!

Hughes, Kenneth: Adventures of Young Brave, The

Hughes, Kristen: Jane and the Lost City

Hughes, Lloyd: Drums of Jeopardy; Ella Cinders; Sweethearts on Parade; Where East Is East

Hughes, Mary Beth: Charlie Chan in Rio; Dressed to Kill (1941); Great Flamarion, The; Ox-Bow Incident, The; Rimfire

Hughes, Miko: Cops and Robbersons; Fly Boy; Jack the Bear; Mercury Rising; Wes Craven's New Nightmare; Zeus and Roxanne

Hughes, Rhetta: Sweet Sweetback's Baadasssss Song

Hughes, Robin: Sometimes Aunt Martha Does Dreadful Things

Hughes, Stuart: Blades of Courage

Hughes, Wendy: Careful He Might Hear You; Dangerous Summer, A; Happy New Year (1987); Heist, The; Indecent Obsession, An; Kostas; Lonely Hearts (1981); My Brilliant Career; My First Wife; Newsfront; Princess Caraboo; Return to Eden; Warm Nights on a Slow Moving Train; Wild Orchid 2: Two Shades of Blue; Woman Named Jackie, A

Hughs, Sandy: High Rolling

Hugo, Mauritz: Man with the Steel Whip

Hui, Michael: Chinese Box

Hui, Ricky: Mr. Vampire (Vol. 1–4)

Hui, Samuel: Aces Go Places (1–3) (Mad Mission 1–3)

Huike, Zhang: Not One Less

Huison, Steve: Full Monty, The

Hulce, Tom: Amadeus; Animal House; Black Rainbow; Dominick and Eugene; Echo Park; Fearless (1993); Heidi Chronicles, The; Inner Circle, The; Mary Shelley's Frankenstein; Parenthood; September 30, 1955; Slam Dance; Those Lips, Those Eyes

Hulette, Gladys: Tol'able David

Hull, Dianne: Aloha, Bobby and Rose; Fifth Floor, The; New Adventures of Pippi Longstocking, The; Onion Field, The

Hull, Henry: Babes in Arms; Boys' Town; Fool Killer, The; High Sierra; Jesse James; Lifeboat; Master of the World; Midnight (1934); Objective, Burma!; Portrait of Jennie; Proud Rebel, The; Return of Frank James, The; Return of Jesse James, The; Rimfire; Werewolf of London; Woman of the Town

Hull, Josephine: Arsenic and Old Lace; Harvey

Hulswit, Mart: Island of the Lost

Humbert, George: I Cover the Waterfront

Hume, Benita: It Happened in New Orleans; Last of Mrs. Cheney, The; Peck's Bad Boy with the Circus; Private Life of Don Juan, The; Suzy; Tarzan Escapes

Humphrey, Mark: Iron Eagle II

Humphrey, Renee: Cadillac Ranch; Fun; Jailbait (1992)

Humphreys, Judith: Hedd Wyn

Humphreys, Michael Connor: Forrest Gump

Humphries, Barry: Barry McKenzie Holds His Own; Leading Man, The; Les Patterson Saves the World

Humphries, Tessa: Cassandra

Hundar, Robert: Cut Throats Nine

Hung, Sammo: Eastern Condors; Heart of Dragon; Millionaire's Express (Shanghai Express); Painted Faces; Paper Marriage (1988); Project A (Part I); Zu: Warriors from the Magic Mountain

Hunnicutt, Arthur: Big Sky, The; Bounty Man, The; Broken Arrow (1950); Devil's Canyon; Distant Drums; El Dorado; French Line, The; Harry and Tonto; Last Command, The (1955); Lusty Men, The; Pinky; Red Badge of Courage, The; She Couldn't Say No

Hunnicutt, Gayle: Dream Lover (1986); Legend of Hell House, The; Marlowe; Martian Chronicles, Parts I-III, The; Once in Paris; Return of the Man from U.N.C.L.E., The; Sell-Out, The; Silence Like Glass; Spiral Staircase, The (1975); Target; Wild Angels, The

Hunt, Bonnie: Beethoven; Beethoven's 2nd; Getting Away with Murder; Green Mile, The; Jumanji; Kissing a Fool; Only You (1994); Random Hearts; Return to Me

Hunt, Brad: Blindsided; Dream with the Fishes; Fire Down Below

Hunt, Eleanor: Blue Steel (1934); Whoopee

Hunt, Gareth: Bloodbath at the House of Death; It Couldn't Happen Here

Hunt, Helen: As Good as It Gets; Bill: On His Own; Dark River: A Father's Revenge; Incident at Dark River; Into the Badlands; Kiss of Death (1995); Mr. Saturday Night; Murder in New Hampshire; Next of Kin (1989); Only You (1991); Pioneer Woman; Project X; Quarterback Princess; Trancers; Trancers II (The Return of Jack Deth); Trancers III: Deth Lives; Twister (1996); Waterdance, The

Hunt, Jay: in Old Cheyenne

Hunt, Jimmy: Invaders from Mars (1953)

Hunt, Linda: Bostonians, The; Eleni; If Looks Could Kill (1991); Kindergarten Cop; Rain Without Thunder; Ready to Wear; She-Devil; Silverado; Space Rangers (TV Series); Twenty Bucks; Waiting for the Moon; Year of Living Dangerously, The; Younger and Younger

Hunt, Marsha: Actors and Sin; Hell Town; Human Comedy, The; Johnny Got His Gun; Panama Hattie; Pride and Prejudice (1940); Smash-Up: The Story of a Woman; Thunder Trail

Hunt, Martita: Admirable Crichton, The; Becket; Brides of Dracula; Great Expectations (1946); Man in Grey, The; Song Without End; Three Men in a Boat; Wicked Lady, The (1945)

Hunter, Bill: Adventures of Priscilla, Queen of the Desert, The; Custodian, The; Death of a Soldier; Heatwave (1983); Hit, The (1984); In Search of Anna; Last Days of Chez Nous, The; Muriel's Wedding; Newsfront; Race the Sun; Rebel (1985); Strictly Ballroom

Hunter, Ciara: Dangerous Prey

Hunter, Debra: Nightmare Weekend

Hunter, Holly: Always (1989); Animal Behavior; Broadcast News; Copycat; Crash (1996); Crazy in Love; End of the Line; Firm, The; Home for the Holidays (1995); Life Less Ordinary, A; Living Out Loud; Miss Firecracker; Murder on the Bayou; Once Around; Piano, The; Positively True Adventures of the Alleged Texas Cheerleader-Murdering Mom, The; Raising Arizona; Roe vs. Wade; Svengali (1983); Urge to Kill

Hunter, Ian: Adventures of Robin Hood, The; Andy Hardy's Private Secretary; Billy the Kid; Bitter Sweet; Broadway Melody of 1940; Broadway Serenade; Easy Virtue; Flame over India; Little Princess, The (1939); Order of the Black Eagle; Pursuit of the Graf Spee; Ring, The; Smilin' Through (1941); Strange Cargo; Tarzan Finds a Son; That Certain Woman; Tower of London (1939)

Hunter, Jeffrey: Christmas Kid, The; Great Locomotive Chase, The; Guide for the Married Man, A; Hell to Eternity; King of Kings (1961); Last Hurrah, The; Private Navy of Sgt. O'Farrell, The; Searchers, The; Sergeant Rutledge; Seven Cities of Gold; Star Trek: The Cage; Star Trek: The Menagerie

Hunter, Kaki: Just the Way You Are; Porky's II: The Next Day; Porky's Revenge; Whose Life Is It, Anyway?

Hunter, Kim: Bad Ronald; Beneath the Planet of the Apes; Born Innocent; Comedian, The; Deadline USA; Escape from the Planet of the Apes; Kindred, The; Lilith; Planet of the Apes; Requiem for a Heavyweight (1956) (Television); Seventh Victim, The; Skokie; Streetcar Named Desire, A (1951); Swimmer, The; Three Sovereigns for Sarah

Hunter, Matthew: Tearaway

Hunter, Morgan: Cyborg Soldier

Hunter, Ron: Rage of Angels

Hunter, Ronald: Lazarus Syndrome, The; Three Sovereigns for Sarah

Hunter, Tab: Arousers, The; Battle Cry; Burning Hills, The; Cameron's Closet; Damn Yankees; Dark Horse; Grotesque; Hostile Guns; Island of Desire; Kid from Left Field, The; Loved One, The; Lust in the Dust; Pandemonium; Polyester; Ride the Wild Surf; Sea Chase, The; They Came to Cordura

Hunter, Thomas: Battle of the Commandos; Escape from the KGB; Vampire Happening

Hunter, Tony: Naked in the Sun

Huntington, Sam: Detroit Rock City; Jungle 2 Jungle

Huntley, Fred: Thundering Hoofs

Huntley, Raymond: I See a Dark Stranger; Immortal Battalion, The (The Way Ahead); Upstairs, Downstairs

Huppert, Isabelle: Amateur (1995); Bedroom Window, The; Cactus; Clean Slate (Coup de Torchon) (1981); Entre Nous (Between Us); Going Places; Heaven's Gate; Judge and the Assassin, The; La Cérémonie; La Separation; La Truite (The Trout); Lacemaker, The; Loulou; Madame Bovary (1991); My Best Friend's Girl; School of Flesh; Sincerely Charlotte; Story of Women, The; Swindle, The; Violette

Hurdle, James: Climb, The

Hurkos, Peter: Boxoffice

Hurley, Elizabeth: Austin Powers: International Man of Mystery; Dangerous Ground; EDtv; Kill Cruise; My Favorite Martian; Nightscare; Permanent Midnight; Rowing with the Wind; Samson and Delilah (1996); Shameless

Hursey, Sherry: Avenging, The

Hurst, Brandon: Man Who Laughs, The

Hurst, Margaret: Meet the Navy

Hurst, Marguerite: Forgotten Silver

Hurst, Michael: Death Warmed Up; Desperate Remedies; Hercules and the Amazon Women; Hercules in the Underworld

Hurst, Paul: Big Stampede, The; Gun Smugglers; Missourians, The; Racketeer

Hurt, John: After Darkness; Alien; Aria; Champions; Contact; Dead Man; Deadline (1988); Disappearance, The; East of Elephant Rock; Elephant Man, The (1980); Even Cowgirls Get the Blues; Field, The; Frankenstein Unbound; From the Hip; Ghoul, The (1975); Heaven's Gate; Hit, The (1984); I, Claudius; Jake Speed; King Lear (1984); King Ralph; Little Sweetheart; Love and Death on Long Island; Midnight Express; Monolith; Naked Civil Servant, The; New Blood; Night Crossing; 1984 (1984); Osterman Weekend, The; Partners; Rob Roy; Scandal; Second Best; Shout, The (1979); Success Is the Best Revenge; 10 Rillington Place; White Mischief; Wild Bill

Hurt, Mary Beth: Affliction; Age of Innocence, The; Baby Girl Scott; Chilly Scenes of Winter; Compromising Positions; D.A.R.Y.L.; Defenseless; From the Journals of Jean Seberg; Light Sleeper; My Boyfriend's Back; Parents; Six Degrees of Separation; Slaves of New York; World According to Garp, The

Hurt, Wesley Ivan: Popeye

Hurt, William: Accidental Tourist, The; Alice (1990); Altered States; Big Brass Ring, The; Big Chill, The; Body Heat; Broadcast News; Children of a Lesser God; Couch in New York, A; Dark City; Doctor, The; Eyewitness; Gorky Park; I Love You to Death; Jane Eyre (1996); Kiss of the Spider Woman; Lost in Space (1998); Michael; Mr. Wonderful; One True Thing; Plague, The; Second Best; Smoke (1995); Time of Destiny, A; Trial by Jury; Until the End of the World

Husky, Ferlin: Hillbillys in a Haunted House; Las Vegas Hillbillys

Huss, Jennifer: Polymorph; Vamps: Deadly Dream Girls

Hussey, Olivia: Bastard, The; Black Christmas; Cat and the Canary, The (1978); Distortions; Escape 2000; Ivanhoe (1982); Jesus of Nazareth; Man with Bogart's Face, The; Psycho 4: The Beginning; Quest of the Delta Knights; Romeo and Juliet (1968); Save Me; Summertime Killer, The; Virus (1980)

Hussey, Ruth: Another Thin Man; Facts of Life; Honolulu; Madame X (1937); Marine Raiders; Mr. Music; Northwest Passage; Philadelphia Story, The; Stars and Stripes Forever; Susan and God; Tender Comrade; Uninvited, The (1944)

Huster, Francis: Another Man, Another Chance; Dinner Game, The; Edith and Marcel

Huston, Anjelica: Addams Family, The; Addams Family Values; And the Band Played On; Buffalo Girls; Buffalo '66; Cowboy and the Ballerina, The; Crimes and Misdemeanors; Crossing Guard, The; Dead, The; Enemies—A Love Story; Ever After; Gardens of Stone; Grifters, The; Handful of Dust, A; Ice Pirates; Lonesome Dove; Manhattan Murder Mystery; Mr. North; Perez Family, The; Phoenix; Postman Always Rings Twice, The (1981); Prizzi's Honor; Swashbuckler (1976); Witches, The (1990)

Huston, Cissy: Road to Freedom: The Vernon Johns Story

Huston, Danny: Leo Tolstoy's Anna Karenina (1997)

Huston, James: Outing, The

Huston, John: Angela; Battle for the Planet of the Apes; Battle Force; Bible, The; Breakout (1975); Cardinal, The; Casino Royale (1967); Chinatown; Deserter, The; Fatal Attraction (1985); Lovesick; Man in the Wilderness; Minor Miracle, A; Mr. Corbett's Ghost; Myra Breckenridge; Tentacles; Visitor, The; Wind and the Lion, The; Winter Kills; Word, The

Huston, Virginia: Flight to Mars; Nocturne

Huston, Walter: Abraham Lincoln; And Then There Were None; Ann Vickers; Criminal Code, The; December 7th: The Movie; Devil and Daniel Webster, The; Dodsworth; Dragon Seed; Duel in the Sun; Edge of Darkness (1943); Gabriel over the White House; Law and Order; North Star, The (1943); Of Human Hearts; Outlaw, The; Rain; Rhodes of Africa (Rhodes); Shanghai Gesture, The; Summer Holiday; Transatlantic Tunnel; Treasure of the Sierra Madre; Virginian, The (1929); Yankee Doodle Dandy

Hutchence, Michael: Dogs in Space

Hutchins, Will: Clambake; Maverick; Shooting, The

Hutchinson, Jeff: Rollerblade

Hutchinson, Josephine: Love Is Better Than Ever; Somewhere in the Night; Son of Frankenstein; Story of Louis Pasteur, The; Tender Years, The; Tom Brown's School Days (1940)

Hutchison, Doug: Green Mile, The

Hutchison, Fiona: Biggles—Adventures in Time; Rage (1995)

Hutton, Betty: Annie Get Your Gun; Greatest Show on Earth, The; Here Come the Waves; Let's Dance; Miracle of Morgan's Creek, The; Perils of Pauline, The (1947); Star Spangled Rhythm

Hutton, Brian: Carnival Rock

Hutton, Jim: Bachelor in Paradise; Don't Be Afraid of the Dark; Green Berets, The; Hallelujah Trail, The; Hellfighters; Honeymoon Machine, The; Horizontal Lieutenant, The; Major Dundee; Period of Adjustment; Psychic Killer; Time to Love and a Time to Die, A; Walk, Don't Run; Where the Boys Are (1960); Who's Minding the Mint?

Hutton, Lauren: American Gigolo; Cradle Will Fall, The; Fear (1990); Forbidden Sun; Gambler, The (1974); Gator; Guilty as Charged; Lassiter; Malone; Millions; Missing Pieces; Monte Carlo; Once Bitten; Paper Lion; Paternity; Scandalous (1988); Snow Queen; Starflight One; Time Stalkers; Trade Secrets; Viva Knievel; We the Jury; Wedding, A (1978); Welcome to L.A.; Zorro, the Gay Blade

Hutton, Marion: In Society

Hutton, Robert: Big Bluff, The; Casanova's Big Night; Hollywood Canteen; Invisible Invaders; Man in the Eiffel Tower, The; Naked Youth; Racket, The; Showdown at Boot Hill; Slime People, The; Steel Helmet, The; They Came from Beyond Space; Torture Garden

Hutton, Timothy: Aldrich Ames: Traitor Within; And Baby Makes Six; Beautiful Girls; City of Industry; Daniel; Dark Half, The; Everybody's All-American; Falcon and the Snowman, The; French Kiss; Friendly Fire; General's Daughter, The; Iceman; Last Word, The (1995); Made in Heaven (1987); Mr. and Mrs. Loving; Money Kings; Oldest Living Graduate, The; Ordinary People; Playing God; Q & A; Strangers; Substance of Fire, The; Taps; Temp, The; Time of Destiny, A; Torrents of Spring; Turk 182; Young Love, First Love; Zelda

Huy-Quan, Ke: Goonies, The

Hvenegaard, Pelle: Pelle the Conqueror

Hwang, Sin-Hye: 301/302

Hyams, Leila: Big House, The; Freaks; Girl in Every Port, A (1928); Island of Lost Souls; Red-Headed Woman; Ruggles of Red Gap

Hyde, Jonathan: Anaconda; Jumanji; Plot to Kill Hitler, The; Richie Rich; Titanic (1997)

Hyde, Tracy: Melody

Hyde-White, Alex: Alien Within, The; Biggles—Adventures in Time; Ironclads; Phantom of the Opera (1989); Romeo and Juliet (1983); Silent Victim; Time Trackers; Unknown Origin; Wyatt Earp: Return to Tombstone

Hyde-White, Wilfrid: Adam and Evalyn; Betrayed (1954); Browning Version, The (1951); Chamber of Horrors; Conspirator; Flame over India; Ghosts of Berkeley Square; In Search of the Castaways; Last Holiday; Let's Make Love; Ten Little Indians (1966); Trio; Truth About Women, The; Two-Way Stretch; Up the Creek (1958); Winslow Boy, The

Hyer, Martha: Abbott and Costello Go to Mars; Battle Hymn; Best of Everything, The; Catch as Catch Can; Chase, The (1966); Clay Pigeon, The; Delicate Delinquent, The; First Men in the Moon; Francis in the Navy; Gun Smugglers; House of 1,000 Dolls; Houseboat; Ice Palace; Lucky Me; My Man Godfrey (1957); Night of the Grizzly, The; Paris Holiday; Picture Mommy Dead; Rustlers, The; Scarlet Spear, The; Some Came Running; Sons of Katie Elder, The

Hyland, Catherine: Vamping

Hyland, Diana: Boy in the Plastic Bubble, The; One Man's Way

Hylands, Scott: Coming Out Alive; Daddy's Gone A-Hunting; Fools; Halfback of Notre Dame, The

Hylton, Jane: Manster, The

Hyman, Flo: Order of the Black Eagle

Hymer, Warren: Case of the Curious Bride, The; Hitler—Dead or Alive; Kid Millions

Hynson, Mike: Endless Summer, The

Hyser, Joyce: Greedy; Just One of the Guys

Hytten, Olaf: Drums of Fu Manchu

Hywel, Dafydd: Coming Up Roses

Iandoli, Dean: Monster High

Ibarra, Mirta: Guantanamera!; Strawberry and Chocolate; Up to a Certain Point

Ice Cube: Anaconda; Boyz N the Hood; Dangerous Ground; Friday; Glass Shield, The; Higher Learning; Next Friday; Players Club, The; Three Kings; Trespass

Ice T: Agent of Death; Body Count (1997) (direct to video); Johnny Mnemonic; Judgment Day; Leprechaun in the Hood; Mean Guns; New Jack City; Ricochet; Surviving the Game; Tank Girl; Trespass; Urban Menace

Ichikawa, Raizo: Enjo; Shin Heinke Monogatari

Ida, Hiroki: Cyber Ninja

Ida, Kunihiko: Zeram

Idle, Eric: Adventures of Baron Münchausen, The; Alan Smithee Film, An—Burn Hollywood Burn; And Now for Something Completely Different; Around the World in 80 Days (1989); Casper; Dudley Do-Right; Life of Brian; Mikado, The (1987); Missing Pieces; Mom and Dad Save the World; Monty Python Live at the Hollywood Bowl; Monty Python's Flying Circus (TV Series); Monty Python's The Meaning of Life; National Lampoon's European Vacation; Nuns on the Run; Rutles, The (All You Need Is Cash); Splitting Heirs; To See Such Fun; Too Much Sun; Yellowbeard

Idol, Billy: Doors, The

Ieracitano, Guiseppe: Il Ladro Di Bambini (Stolen Children)

Ifans, Rhys: Notting Hill

Igawa, Hisashi: Rhapsody in August

Igughi, Takahito: Boiling Point (1990)

Igus, Darrow: Horrible Doctor Bones, The

Ihara, Tsuyoshi: Gamera: Guardian of the Universe

Ihnat, Steve: Hour of the Gun, The; Hunter (1971); Madigan

Ikebe, Ryo: Snow Country

Ikeda, Shoko: Operation Condor (Jackie Chan)

Illery, Pola: Under the Roofs of Paris

Illusion, Justin: Terminal Impact

Iman: Exit to Eden; Heart of Darkness; Human Factor, The; Lies of the Twins; No Way Out; Star Trek VI: The Undiscovered Country

Imasheva, Albina: Beshkempir, The Adopted Son

Imhoff, Gary: Angel in Training; Seniors, The

Imperioli, Michael: Flirt; Sweet Nothing

Imrie, Celia: Dark Adapted Eye, A; Hilary and Jackie; Oranges Are Not the Only Fruit

Incontrera, Annabella: Badlands Drifter (Challenge of McKenna); Bullet for Sandoval, A

Inescort, Frieda: Beauty for the Asking; Casanova's Big Night; Judge Steps Out, The; Return of the Vampire, The; Tarzan Finds a Son; Underworld Story; You'll Never Get Rich

Ingalls, Joyce: Deadly Force

Ingels, Marty: Horizontal Lieutenant, The; If It's Tuesday, This Must Be Belgium

Ingerman, Randi: Desperate Crimes; Let's Talk About Sex

Ingersoll, Amy: Knightriders

Ingham, Barrie: Antony and Cleopatra (1981); Dr. Who and the Daleks; Josh Kirby, Time Warrior (Series); Josh Kirby … Time Warrior: Journey to the Magic Cavern; Josh Kirby … Time Warrior: Trapped on Toy World

Ingle, John: Suture

Ingraham, Bill: Butch Camp

Ingram, Jack: Atom Man vs. Superman; Ghost Town Renegades; Sea Hound, The; Sundown Riders

Ingram, Rex: Adventures of Huckleberry Finn, The (1939); Cabin in the Sky; Dark Waters; Green Pastures; Talk of the Town, The; Thief of Bagdad, The (1940)

Inkizhinov, Valeri: Storm over Asia

Innes, Neil: Rutles, The (All You Need Is Cash)

Innocent, Harold: Canterville Ghost, The (1986)

Inosanto, Danny: Game of Death

Interlenghi, Franco: I Vitelloni; Little World of Don Camillo, The; Shoeshine

Inwood, Steve: Human Shield, The; Staying Alive

Iorio, Jeffrey R.: Deadly Obsession

Ip, Grace: Gen-X Cops

Ipale, Aharon: Invisible: The Chronicles of Benjamin Knight

Irazoque, Enrique: Gospel According to Saint Matthew, The

Ireland, Jill: Assassination; Breakheart Pass; Breakout (1975); Chato's Land; Chino; Cold Sweat (1970); Death Wish II; Family, The (1970); Hard Times; Love and Bullets; Mechanic, The; Rider on the Rain; Someone Behind the Door; Three Men in a Boat; Villa Rides

Ireland, John: All the King's Men; Arizona Bushwhackers; Badlands Drifter (Challenge of McKenna); Bushwhackers; Dead for a Dollar; Delta Fox; Doolins of Oklahoma; Escape to the Sun; Fall of the Roman Empire, The; Farewell My Lovely; 55 Days at Peking; Gangster, The; Gunfight at the O.K. Corral; Gunslinger; House of Seven Corpses, The; Kavik the Wolf Dog; Little Big Horn; Machine Gun Killers; Martin's Day; Messenger of Death; Miami Horror; Northeast of Seoul; Party Girl (1958); Railroaded; Ransom (1977); Red River; Return of Jesse James, The; Satan's Cheerleaders; Southern Yankee, A; Sundown (1990); Swiss Conspiracy, The; Thunder Run; Tomorrow Never Comes; Treasure of the Amazon; Vengeance Valley; Walk in the Sun, A; We Are No Angels; Wild in the Country

Ireland, Kathy: Alien from L.A.; Amore! (1993); Backfire (1994); Journey to the Center of the Earth (1987); Miami Hustle; National Lampoon's Loaded Weapon 1; Necessary Roughness; Presence, The

Irissari, Tina: Devil, Probably, The

Irizarry, Vincent: Jackie Collins' Lucky Chances

Irlen, Steve: On the Make

Irons, Jeremy: Betrayal (1983); Brideshead Revisited; Chinese Box; Chorus of Disapproval, A; Damage; Danny, The Champion of the World; Dead Ringers; Die Hard with a Vengeance; French Lieutenant's Woman, The; House of the Spirits, The; Kafka; Lolita (1997); Man in the Iron Mask, The (1998); M. Butterfly; Mission, The; Moonlighting (1983); Nijinsky; Reversal of Fortune; Stealing Beauty; Swann in Love; Waterland; Wild Duck, The

Irons, Samuel: Danny, The Champion of the World

Irons, Shaun: Jugular Wine

Ironside, Michael: Beyond Redemption; Black Ice; Coming Out Alive; Common Bonds; Cross Country; Deadly Surveillance; Deadman's Revenge; Destiny to Order; Drop Dead Gorgeous (1991); Extreme Prejudice; Father Hood; Ford: The Man & The Machine; Fortunes of War (1993); Free Willy; Glass Shield, The; Guncrazy (1992); Hellcab; Hello, Mary Lou: Prom Night II; Highlander 2: The Quickening; Hostile Take Over; Jo Jo Dancer, Your Life Is Calling; Johnny 2.0; Killer Image; Killing Man, The; Major Payne; Mardi Gras for the Devil; McBain; Mind Field; Murder in Space; Neon City; Next Karate Kid, The; Nowhere to Hide; Payback (1990); Point of Impact; Probable Cause; Red Scorpion 2; Red Sun Rising; Save Me; Scanners; Sins of Dorian Gray, The; Spacehunter: Adventures in the Forbidden Zone; Starship Troopers; Sweet Killing; Too Fast Too Young; Top Gun; Total Recall; Vagrant, The; Visiting Hours; Watchers

Irving, Amy: Anastasia: The Mystery of Anna; Benefit of the Doubt; Carrie (1976); Carried Away; Competition, The; Confession, The; Crossing Delancey; Deconstructing Harry; Far Pavilions, The; Fury, The (1978); Heartbreak House; Honeysuckle Rose; I'm a Fool; I'm Not Rappaport; James Dean—A Legend in His Own Time; Kleptomania; Micki & Maude; Rage, The; Carrie 2; Show of Force, A; Turn of the Screw, The (1989); Voices; Yentl

Irving, Christopher: Dedicated Man, A

Irving, Clifford: F for Fake

Irving, George S.: Deadly Hero

Irwin, Bill: My Blue Heaven; Popeye; Scenes from a Mall; Stepping Out; Subway Stories

Irwin, Tom: Holiday Affair (1996); Ladykiller

Isaacs, Jason: End of the Affair, The; Patriot, The; Solitaire for 2

Isaak, Chris: Grace of My Heart; Little Buddha; That Thing You Do!; Twin Peaks: Fire Walk with Me

Isakovic, Boris: Vukovar

Isfeld, Justin: Ice Cream Man

Ishibashi, Ryo: Blue Tiger

Ishida, Yuriko: Boiling Point (1990)

Ishikawa, Hiroshi: Godzilla vs. Gigan

Isobel, Katharine: Salt Water Moose

Isomura, Kenji: Heaven's Burning

Isunza, Agustin: Illusion Travels by Streetcar

Itami, Juzo: Family Game, The

Itanzo, Antonio: Cut Throats Nine

Ito, Robert: John Woo's Once a Thief

Itonia: Blood Harvest

Iturbi, José: Holiday in Mexico; That Midnight Kiss; Three Daring Daughters; Two Girls and a Sailor

Itzin, Gregory: Fly Boy

Iures, Marcel: Unforgettable Summer, An

Iures, Michael: Peacemaker, The (1997)

Ivan, Daniel: Slaughter in San Francisco

Ivan, Rosalind: Pursuit to Algiers; Scarlet Street

Ivanek, Zeljko: Julian Po; Mass Appeal; Our Sons; Rat Pack, The; School Ties; Sender, The

Ivanov, Ivan: Bloodsport IV: The Dark Kumite

Ivar, Stan: Creature

Ivashov, Vladimir: Ballad of a Soldier

Ivens, Terri: Trancers 5: Sudden Death

Ivernel, Daniel: Diary of a Chambermaid (1964)

Ives, Burl: Baker's Hawk; Big Country, The; Cat on a Hot Tin Roof (1958); Daydreamer, The (1966); Desire under the Elms; East of Eden (1955); Ensign Pulver; Just You and Me, Kid; Roots; So Dear to My Heart; Station West; Summer Magic; Two Moon Junction; White Dog

Ivey, Dana: Adventures of Huck Finn, The (1993); Impostors, The; Mumford; Simon Birch; Sleepless in Seattle

Ivey, Judith: Brighton Beach Memoirs; Compromising Positions; Decoration Day; Devil's Advocate; Everybody Wins; Hello Again; In Country; Long Hot Summer, The (1985); Love Hurts; Mystery, Alaska; Sister, Sister; There Goes the Neighborhood; Washington Square; We Are the Children; What the Deaf Man Heard; Woman in Red, The

Ivgi, Moshe: Cup Final

Ivy, Bob: Phantasm IV: Oblivion

Iwai, Sharon: Great Wall, A

Iwasaki, Kaneko: Zatoichi: The Blind Swordsman and the Chess Expert

Iwashita, Shima: Autumn Afternoon, An; Double Suicide; Red Lion

Izewska, Teresa: Kanal

Izumiya, Shigeru: Eijanaika (Why Not?)

Izzard, Eddie: Mystery Men; Velvet Goldmine

Jablonska, Linda: Last Butterfly, The

Jackée: Ladybugs; Women of Brewster Place, The

Jacks, Robert: Texas Chainsaw Massacre: The Next Generation

Jackson, Andrew: Twists of Terror

Jackson, Anne: Bell Jar, The; Folks; Funny About Love; Leave 'em Laughing; Lovers and Other Strangers; Out on a Limb (1986); Rescuers, Stories of Courage, "Two Women"; Sam's Son; Secret Life of an American Wife, The; Tall Story

Jackson, Barry: Mr. Love

Jackson, Ernestine: Aaron Loves Angela

Jackson, Freda: Brides of Dracula

Jackson, Glenda: And Nothing But the Truth; Baby-Sitters Club, The; Beyond Therapy; Boy Friend, The; Business as Usual; Class of Miss MacMichael, The; Elizabeth R; Hedda; Hopscotch; House Calls; Incredible Sarah, The; King of the Wind; Lost and Found (1979); Marat/Sade; Music Lovers, The; Nasty Habits; Negatives; Rainbow, The; Return of the Soldier, The; Romantic Englishwoman, The; Sakharov; Salome's Last Dance; Stevie; Strange Interlude (1988); Sunday, Bloody Sunday; Touch of Class, A; Turtle Diary; Women in Love

Jackson, Gordon: Fighting Prince of Donegal, The; Hamlet (1969); Ipcress File, The; Madame Sin; Medusa Touch, The; Mutiny on the Bounty (1962); Prime of Miss Jean Brodie, The; Russian Roulette; Shaka Zulu; Shooting Party, The; Tight Little Island; Town Like Alice, A; Tunes of Glory; Upstairs, Downstairs; Whistle Blower, The

Jackson, Ivan: World of Strangers, A

Jackson, Janet: Poetic Justice

Jackson, John: Glimmer Man, The; Sudie & Simpson

Jackson, John M.: Deadman's Revenge; Ginger Ale Afternoon

Jackson, Jonathan: Camp Nowhere; Deep End of the Ocean, The; Prisoner of Zenda, Inc.

Jackson, Joshua: Cruel Intentions; Digger; Magic in the Water, The; Robin of Locksley; Ronnie & Julie; Skulls, The; Urban Legend

Jackson, Kate: Adrift; Best of Dark Shadows, The; Death at Love House; Dirty Tricks; Listen to Your Heart; Loverboy; Making Love; Night of Dark Shadows; Satan's School for Girls; Thunder and Lightning

...arned to Stop Worrying and Love the Bomb; Empire
...rikes Back, The (voice); End of the Road; Excessive
...rce; Exorcist II: The Heretic; Family Thing, A; Field of
...reams; Gang Related; Gardens of Stone; Great White
...ope, The; Greatest, The; Grim Prairie Tales; Heat Wave
...990); Hunt for Red October, The; Ivory Hunters; Jeffer-
...n in Paris; Matewan; Meteor Man; My Little Girl; Our
...iend, Martin; Patriot Games; Percy & Thunder; Piece of
...e Action, A; Rebound; Return of the Jedi; Road to Free-
...om: The Vernon Johns Story; Roots: The Next Generation;
...andlot, The; Scorchers; Second Civil War, The; Som-
...ersby; Soul Man; Summer's End; Swashbuckler (1976);
...ree Fugitives; Undercover Angel; What the Deaf Man
...eard

...ones, Janet: American Anthem; Flamingo Kid, The; Police
...cademy 5: Assignment: Miami Beach
...ones, Jeffrey: Avenging Angel, The (1995); Beetlejuice;
...evil's Advocate; Ed Wood; Ferris Bueller's Day Off; Gam-
...er, Part III—The Legend Continues, The; George Wash-
...gton: The Forging of a Nation; Hanoi Hilton, The; House-
...est; Howard the Duck; Hunt for Red October, The; Mom
...nd Dad Save the World; Out on a Limb (1992); Over Her
...ead Body; Pest, The; Ravenous; Sleepy Hollow; Stay
...uned; Transylvania 6-5000; Valmont; Who's Harry
...rumb?; Without a Clue
...ones, Jennifer: Beat the Devil; Carrie (1952); Dick Tracy's
...-Men; Duel in the Sun; Frontier Horizon; Indiscretion of an
...merican Wife; Love Is a Many-Splendored Thing;
...ladame Bovary (1949); Man in the Gray Flannel Suit, The;
...ortrait of Jennie; Ruby Gentry; Since You Went Away;
...ong of Bernadette, The
...ones, Jerry: Dolemite
...ones, Jocelyn: Great Texas Dynamite Chase, The
...ones, Josephine Jacqueline: Black Venus; Warrior
...ueen
...ones, Ken: Melody
...ones, L. Q.: Ballad of Cable Hogue, The; Brotherhood of
...atan; Bulletproof (1988); Edge, The; Jack Bull, The; Light-
...ing Jack; Lone Wolf McQuade; Ride the High Country;
...iver of Death; Standing Tall; Timerider; Tornado!; White
...ine Fever; Wild Bunch, The
...ones, Lisa: Life and Times of Grizzly Adams, The
...ones, Lucinda: Wild Duck, The
...ones, Marcia Mae: Mad About Music; Meet Dr. Christian;
...Misadventures of Buster Keaton, The; Old Swimmin' Hole,
...he; These Three
...ones, Marilyn: On the Block
...ones, Neal: Day at the Beach; Silent Prey
...ones, Nicholas: Not a Penny More, Not a Penny Less
...ones, Norman: Inspector Morse (TV Series)
...ones, Paul: Demons of the Mind
...ones, Peter: Hitchhiker's Guide to the Galaxy, The;
...Whoops Apocalypse
...ones, Richard: Good Old Boys, The
...ones, Richard T.: Black Rose of Harlem; Event Horizon;
...Kiss the Girls; Renaissance Man; Trigger Effect, The; Wood,
...he
...ones, Robert: Slaughter in San Francisco
...ones, Robert Earl: Displaced Person, The
...ones, Ronalda: Alligator Shoes
...ones, Rosie: Alice to Nowhere; Ganjasaurus Rex
...ones, Sam: American Strays; Ballistic; Davincl's War; Fist
...of Iron; Flash Gordon; In Gold We Trust; Jane and the Lost
...City; Lady Dragon 2; Maximum Force; My Chauffeur; Night
...Rhythms; Other Woman, The; Silent Assassins; Texas Pay-
...back; Thunder in Paradise; Under the Gun (1988)
...ones, Samantha: Get to Know Your Rabbit
...ones, Sharon Lee: Josh Kirby ... Time Warrior: Trapped
...on Toy World; Leapin' Leprechauns; Princess Warrior
...ones, Shirley: Bedtime Story; Carousel; Cheyenne Social
...Club, The; Children of An Lac, The; Courtship of Eddie's Fa-
...ther, The; Elmer Gantry; Girls of Huntington House; Music
...Man, The; Never Steal Anything Small; Oklahoma!; Silent
...Night, Lonely Night; Tank; Two Rode Together
...ones, Simon: Brideshead Revisited; For Love or Money;
...Hitchhiker's Guide to the Galaxy, The; Miracle on 34th
...Street (1994); Operation Delta Force 2; Privates on Parade
...ones, Steve: Great Rock and Roll Swindle, The
...ones, Tamala: Booty Call
...ones, Tammi: Hav Plenty

Jones, Terry: And Now for Something Completely Differ-
ent; Crusades, The (1995); Erik the Viking; Life of Brian;
Monty Python and the Holy Grail; Monty Python Live at the
Hollywood Bowl; Monty Python's Flying Circus (TV Series);
Monty Python's The Meaning of Life
Jones, Tim: Gross Jokes
Jones, Tommy Lee: Amazing Howard Hughes, The; Back
Roads; Barn Burning; Batman Forever; Betsy, The; Big
Town, The; Black Moon Rising; Blown Away (1994); Blue
Sky; Broken Vows; Cat on a Hot Tin Roof (1985); Client,
The; Coal Miner's Daughter; Cobb; Double Jeopardy
(1999); Executioner's Song, The; Eyes of Laura Mars, The;
Fire Birds; Fugitive, The (1993); Good Old Boys, The;
Gotham; Heaven and Earth (1993); House of Cards; Jack-
son County Jail; JFK; Lonesome Dove; Men in Black; Nate
and Hayes; Natural Born Killers; Package, The; Park is
Mine, The; River Rat, The; Rolling Thunder; Rules of En-
gagement; Stormy Monday; Stranger on My Land; Under
Siege; U.S. Marshals; Volcano; Yuri Nosenko, KGB
Jones, Vinnie: Lock, Stock and Two Smoking Barrels
Jones-Moreland, Betsy: Creature from the Haunted Sea,
The
Jonsson, Nine-Christine: Port of Call
Jonz, Jo D.: Deadlocked
Jonze, Spike: Three Kings
Joplin, Janis: Monterey Pop
Jordan: Jubilee
Jordan, Bobby: Angels with Dirty Faces; Bowery Boys, The
(Series); Boys of the City; Pride of the Bowery
Jordan, Dorothy: Cabin in the Cotton; Lost Squadron; Min
and Bill; Taming of the Shrew, The (1929)
Jordan, James Carroll: Diary of a Teenage Hitchhiker;
Dirty Dozen, The: The Fatal Mission; Tales of the Unex-
pected
Jordan, Jeremy: Never Been Kissed
Jordan, Jim: Look Who's Laughing
Jordan, Louis: Reet, Petite and Gone
Jordan, Marion: Look Who's Laughing
Jordan, Michael: Space Jam
Jordan, Richard: Bunker, The; Chato's Land
Jordan, Richard: Dune; Flash of Green, A; Gettysburg;
Heaven Is a Playground; Hunt for Red October, The; Hunt
for the Night Stalker; Interiors; Lawman; Les Miserables
(1978); Logan's Run; Mean Season, The; Men's Club, The;
Murder of Mary Phagan, The; Old Boyfriends; Primary Mo-
tive; Raise the Titanic; Romero; Rooster Cogburn; Secret of
My Success, The; Shout (1991); Sky Heist; Solarbabies;
Time Bomb; Trial of the Cantonsville Nine, The; Valdez Is
Coming; Yakuza, The
Jordan, Rick: Stripteaser 2
Jordan, Will: I Wanna Hold Your Hand
Jordano, Daniel: Playing for Keeps
Jordan, Kandeyce: Star Maps
Jordon, Samantha: What Ever Happened To ... ?
Jorgensen, Ben: Break, The
Jory, Victor: Adventures of Tom Sawyer, The; Border Vigi-
lantes; Buckskin Frontier; Cariboo Trail; Cat Women of the
Moon; Charlie Chan in Rio; Death of a Scoundrel; Devil
Dog: The Hound of Hell; Fugitive Kind, The; Green Archer;
Hoppy Serves a Writ; Kansan, The; Leather Burners, The;
Loves of Carmen, The; Man from the Alamo, The; Manfish;
Papillon; Riders of the Timberline; Son of Ali Baba; Wide-
Open Town; Woman's Secret, A
Joseph, Alan: Street Wars
Joseph, Don: Color Me Blood Red
Joseph, Jackie: Gremlins 2: The New Batch; Little Shop of
Horrors, The (1960)
Josephs, Tony: Lady Avenger
Josephson, Erland: After the Rehearsal; Brink of Life;
Hanusson; Nostalghia; Passion of Anna, The; Sacrifice,
The; Saving Grace; Scenes from a Marriage; Sofie; To For-
get Venice; Ulysses' Gaze; Unbearable Lightness of Being,
The
Joshua, Larry: Sugar Hill; Svengali (1983)
Joslin, Tom: Silverlake Life: The View from Here
Joslyn, Allyn: Colonel Effingham's Raid; Fastest Gun Alive,
The; Heaven Can Wait (1943); Horn Blows at Midnight,
The; I Love Melvin; If You Knew Susie; Immortal Sergeant,
The; Island in the Sky; Jazz Singer, The (1953); Only Angels
Have Wings; Shining Hour, The; Spring Parade; Titanic
(1953)

Joslyn, Don: Hoodlum Priest, The
Joston, Darwin: Assault on Precinct 13
Jostyn, Jennifer: Milo
Jouanneau, Jacques: Judex
Joujon-Roche, Gregory: Hard Rock Nightmare
Jourdan, Jimi: Chains
Jourdan, Louis: Best of Everything, The; Beverly Hills Madam; Can-Can; Count of Monte Cristo, The (1975); Counterforce; Decameron Nights; Gigi; Grand Larceny; Julie; Letter from an Unknown Woman; Madame Bovary (1949); Man in the Iron Mask, The (1977); Octopussy; Paradine Case, The; Return of the Swamp Thing; Silver Bears; Swamp Thing; Swan, The (1956); V.I.P.s, The; Year of the Comet
Jourdan, Raymond: Rise of Louis XIV, The
Jouvet, Louis: Bizarre, Bizarre; Carnival in Flanders; Jenny Lamour; La Marseillaise; Lower Depths (1936); Volpone
Jovovich, Milla: Chaplin; Dazed and Confused; Fifth Element, The; He Got Game; Kuffs; Messenger: The Story of Joan of Arc, The; Return to the Blue Lagoon
Joy, Leatrice: Ace of Hearts; Old Swimmin' Hole, The; Ten Commandments, The (1923)
Joy, Mark: Perfect Daughter, The
Joy, Robert: Amityville III: The Demon; Big Shots; Dark Half, The; Death Wish V: The Face of Death; Desperately Seeking Susan; Judgment; Lawrenceville Stories, The; Millennium (1989); Modern Affair, A; Pharaoh's Army; Resurrection (1998); Shadows and Fog; She's Back; Suicide Club, The; Sword of Gideon; Terminal Choice; Waterworld
Joyce, Alice: Dancing Mothers
Joyce, Brenda: Enchanted Forest, The; Little Giant; Pillow of Death; Rains Came, The; Strange Confession; Tarzan and the Leopard Woman
Joyce, Elaine: Guide for the Married Woman, A; How to Frame a Figg; Motel Hell; Trick or Treat (1986)
Joyce, Peggy Hopkins: International House
Joyeux, Odette: Sylvia and the Phantom
Joyner, Frank: Chloe: Love is Calling You
Joyner, Mario: Hangin' with the Homeboys
Joyner, Michelle: Painted Hero
Juarez, Ruben: Tango Bar
Judd, Ashley: Double Jeopardy (1999); Eye of the Beholder; Heat (1995); Kiss the Girls; Locusts, The; Norma Jean and Marilyn; Normal Life; Our Friend, Martin; Passion of Darkly Noon, The; Ruby in Paradise; Simon Birch; Smoke (1995); Time to Kill, A (1996); Where the Heart Is (2000)
Judd, Craig: Chain, The
Judd, Edward: Concrete Jungle, The (1962) (Criminal, The); Day the Earth Caught Fire, The; First Men in the Moon; Hound of the Baskervilles, The (1983); Island of Terror; Stolen Hours; Vault of Horror; Vengeance of She, The; Whose Child Am I?; X—The Unknown
Judd, John: Scum
Judd, Naomi: Rio Diablo
Judge, Arline: Here Comes Trouble; Lady Is Willing, The; Mad Wednesday (see also Sin of Harold Diddlebook); Mysterious Mr. Wong, The; One in a Million; Sin of Harold Diddlebook (Mad Wednesday); Song of Texas
Judge, Christopher: Stargate SG-1
Judge, Mike: Beavis and Butt-head Do America
Juhlin, Niklas: Mystery Island
Julia, Raul: Addams Family, The; Addams Family Values; Alamo, The: Thirteen Days to Glory; Burning Season, The; Compromising Positions; Down Came a Blackbird; Escape Artist, The; Florida Straits; Frankenstein Unbound; Gumball Rally, The; Havana; Kiss of the Spider Woman; Mack the Knife; Moon over Parador; Morning After, The; Onassis: The Richest Man in the World; One from the Heart; Organization, The; Panic in Needle Park; Penitent, The; Plague, The; Presumed Innocent; Romero; Rookie, The; Street Fighter (1994); Tango Bar; Tequila Sunrise; Trading Hearts
Julian, Janet: Choke Canyon; Ghost Warrior; Humongous; King of New York
Julien, Max: Getting Straight; Mack, The
Jump, Gordon: Bitter Vengeance
Jurado, Katy: Badlanders, The; Barabbas; Broken Lance; Bullfighter and the Lady, The; El Bruto (The Brute); High Noon; One-Eyed Jacks; Racers, The; Trapeze
Jurasik, Peter: Late Shift, The

Jurgens, Curt: And God Created Woman (1957); Battle Britain; Battle of the Commandos; Brainwashed; Brea through; Enemy Below, The; Goldengirl; Inn of the Six Happiness, The; Just a Gigolo; Mephisto Waltz, The; Mir cle of the White Stallions; Mozart Story, The; Spy Wh Loved Me, The; This Happy Feeling; Vault of Horror
Jurgens, Deana: Tin Man
Jurisic, Melita: Tale of Ruby Rose, The
Juross, Albert: Les Carabiniers
Justice, James Robertson: Captain Horatio Hornblowe Doctor at Large; Doctor at Sea; Doctor in Distress; Docto in the House; Land of the Pharaohs; Le Repos du Guerrie (Warrior's Rest); Murder She Said; Rob Roy, the Highlan Rogue; Story of Robin Hood, The; Sword and the Rose, Th (1953); Tight Little Island
Justice, Katherine: Five Card Stud; Frasier the Lovabl Lion (Frasier the Sensuous Lion)
Justin, John: Savage Messiah; Thief of Bagdad, The (194C
Justin, Larry: Hollywood Meatcleaver Massacre
Justine, William: Bride and the Beast, The
Jutra, Claude: Mon Oncle Antoine
Kaake, Jeff: Border Shootout; Space Rangers (TV Series
Kaaren, Suzanne: Devil Bat, The
Kabler, Roger: Alligator Eyes
Kabo, Olga: Ice Runner
Kaczmarek, Jane: All's Fair; D.O.A. (1988); Door to Doo Heavenly Kid, The; Vice Versa
Kadler, Karen: Devil's Messenger, The
Kadochnikova, Larisa: Shadows of Forgotten Ancestors
Kagan, Diane: Barn Burning
Kagan, Elaine: Babyfever
Kagawa, Kyoko: Chikamatsu Monogatari
Kahan, Saul: Schlock
Kahler, Wolf: Dirty Dozen, The: The Deadly Mission Raiders of the Lost Ark
Kahmhadze, Teimour: Chef in Love, A
Kahn, Madeline: Adventure of Sherlock Holmes' Smarte Brother, The; American Tail, An; Betsy's Wedding; Blazin Saddles; Cheap Detective, The; City Heat; Clue; First Family For Richer, for Poorer; Happy Birthday, Gemini; Hideaways The; High Anxiety; History of the World, Part One, The Judy Berlin; Mixed Nuts; Muppet Movie, The; Paper Moon Simon; Slapstick of Another Kind; Wholly Moses!; Yellow beard; Young Frankenstein
Kaidanovsky, Alexander: Magic Hunter; Stalker
Kain, Amber: Mercy
Kain, Khalil: Juice; Love Jones; Zooman
Kaiser, Erwin: Dressed to Kill (1941)
Kaiser, Suki: Bloodhounds II; Virtual Assassin
Kaitan, Elizabeth: Assault of the Killer Bimbos; Desperate Crimes; Petticoat Planet; South Beach Academy; Virtua Encounters
Kalem, Toni: Billy Galvin
Kalember, Patricia: Danielle Steel's Kaleidoscope
Kalevaars, Ingrid: Specimen
Kalfon, Jean-Pierre: Confidentially Yours; Valley, The
Kalifi, Mohsen: White Balloon, The
Kalinina, Daria: Welcome to the Dollhouse
Kalipha, Stefan: Born of Fire
Kallo, John: My Samurai
Kalmic, Lazar: Someone Else's America
Kaloper, Jagoda: WR: Mysteries of the Organism
Kalyagin, Alexander: Slave of Love, A; Unfinished Piece for the Player Piano, An (Unfinished Piece for a Mechanical Piano, An)
Kamamoto, Gayo: Zatoichi: The Blind Swordsman and the Chess Expert
Kaman, Bob: Bloodfist
Kam-bo: Painted Faces
Kamekona, Danny: Robot Wars
Kamei, Stanley: Dancing with Danger
Kamerling, Antonie: Suite 16
Kaminska, Ida: Shop on Main Street, The
Kamm, Kris: Heroes of Desert Storm; When the Party's Over
Kanakis, Anna: After the Fall of New York; Warriors of the Wasteland
Kanaly, Steve: Balboa; Dillinger (1973); Double Trouble (1991); Eye of the Eagle 3; Fleshburn; Pumpkinhead II: Bloodwings; Scorpio One; Wind and the Lion, The
Kanan, Sean: Rich Girl

Keena, Monica: Ripe; Snow White: A Tale of Terror
Keene, Tom: Driftin' Kid; Dynamite Canyon; Lights of Old Santa Fe; Our Daily Bread; Plan 9 from Outer Space; Scarlet River; Trail of Robin Hood; Where Trails End
Keener, Catherine: Being John Malkovich; Box of Moonlight; 8MM; Johnny Suede; Living in Oblivion; Real Blonde, The; Simpatico; Walking and Talking; Your Friends & Neighbors
Keeslar, Matt: Durango; Last Days of Disco, The; Last Days of Disco, The; Splendor; Stupids, The
Kehkaial, Vladimir: Jugular Wine
Kehler, Jack: Blindsided
Kehoe, Jack: On the Nickel; Paper, The; Serpico; Servants of Twilight; Star Chamber, The
Keir, Andrew: Absolution; Catholics; Daleks—Invasion Earth 2150 A.D.; Dracula—Prince of Darkness; Dragonworld; Five Million Years to Earth; Rob Roy
Keitel, Harvey: Alice Doesn't Live Here Anymore; Bad Lieutenant; Blindside; Blue Collar; Blue in the Face; Border, The; Buffalo Bill and the Indians; Bugsy; Camorra; City of Industry; Copland; Corrupt; Dangerous Game, A 1993); Death Watch; Duellists, The; Eagle's Wing; Exposed; Fairy Tale: A True Story; Falling in Love; Finding Graceland; Fingers; From Dusk Till Dawn; Holy Smoke; Imaginary Crimes; Inquiry, The; January Man, The; La Nuit de Varennes; Last Temptation of Christ, The; Lulu on the Bridge; Mean Streets; Men's Club, The; Monkey Trouble; Mortal Thoughts; Mother, Jugs, and Speed; Off Beat; Piano, The; Pick-Up Artist, The; Point of No Return; Pulp Fiction; Reservoir Dogs; Rising Sun; Saturn 3; Shadrach; Sister Act; Smoke (1995); Somebody to Love; Star Knight; Taxi Driver; Thelma & Louise; Three Seasons; Two Evil Eyes; Two Jakes, The; U-571; Ulysses' Gaze; Welcome to L.A.; Who's That Knocking at My Door?; Wise Guys; Young Americans, The
Keith, Brian: Alamo, The: Thirteen Days to Glory; Arrowhead; Deadly Companions, The; Death Before Dishonor; Dino; Entertaining Angels; Gambler Returns, The: Luck of the Draw; Hallelujah Trail, The; Hooper; Johnny Shiloh; Meteor; Moon Pilot; Mountain Men, The; National Lampoon's Favorite Deadly Sins; Nevada Smith; Parent Trap, The (1961); Rare Breed, The (1966); Reflections in a Golden Eye; Rough Riders; Run of the Arrow; Russians Are Coming, the Russians Are Coming, The; Savage Sam; Scandalous John; Seekers, The; Sharky's Machine; Suppose They Gave a War and Nobody Came?; Ten Who Dared; Those Calloways; Tiger Walks, A; Violent Men, The; Welcome Home; Wind and the Lion, The; With Six You Get Eggroll; World War III; Yakuza, The; Young Guns; Young Philadelphians, The
Keith, Clete: Dead Silence (1989)
Keith, David: Back Roads; Born Wild; Caged Fear; Desperate Motive; Family Thing, A; Firestarter; Further Adventures of Tennessee Buck, The; Gold Diggers: The Secret of Bear Mountain; Gulag; Heartbreak Hotel; Independence Day; Indian in the Cupboard, The; Invasion of Privacy (1996); Judge and Jury; Lords of Discipline, The; Major League II; Off and Running; Officer and a Gentleman, An; Poodle Springs; Raw Justice; Temptation; Texas (1994); Two Jakes, The; U-571; White of the Eye
Keith, Ian: Abraham Lincoln; Big Trail, The; Chinese Cat, The; Corregidor; Crusades, The (1935); Dick Tracy's Dilemma; It Came from Beneath the Sea; Phantom of the Plains; Strange Woman, The; Three Musketeers, The (1935); Valley of the Zombies; White Legion
Keith, Michael: King Kong vs. Godzilla
Keith, Penelope: Norman Conquests, The, Episode 1: Table Manners; Norman Conquests, The, Episode 2: Living Together; Norman Conquests, The, Episode 3: Round and Round the Garden; Priest of Love
Keith, Robert: Battle Circus; Branded; Cimarron (1960); Drum Beat; Duel of Champions; Love Me or Leave Me; My Foolish Heart; My Man Godfrey (1957); Object of Obsession; Rites of Passage; Wild One, The; Written on the Wind
Keleghan, Peter: Screwballs
Kellard, Robert: Drums of Fu Manchu
Kellaway, Cecil: Adventures of Bullwhip Griffin, The; Beast from 20,000 Fathoms, The; Brother Orchid; Francis Goes to the Races; Guess Who's Coming to Dinner; Harvey; Hush ... Hush, Sweet Charlotte; I Married a Witch; Intermezzo (1939); Interrupted Melody; Invisible Man Returns, The; Kim;

Maid's Night Out, The; Mrs. Parkington; Monsieur Beaucaire; Postman Always Rings Twice, The (1946); Prodigal, The
Kellegher, Tina: Snapper, The
Kellen, Mike: King Lear (1982)
Keller, Dorothy: Single Room Furnished
Keller, Fred A.: Tuck Everlasting
Keller, Hiram: Ciao Federico!; Countryman; Fellini Satyricon; Lifespan
Keller, Marthe: Amateur, The (1982); Amnesia; And Now, My Love; Black Sunday (1977); Bobby Deerfield; Dark Eyes; Fedora; Formula, The; Marathon Man; Nightmare Years, The; Red Kiss (Rouge Baiser); School of Flesh; Wagner; Young Catherine
Keller, Mary Page: Any Place But Home; Colony, The (1995); Dirty Little Secret; Scared Stiff; Ulterior Motives
Kellerman, Barbara: Quatermass Conclusion, The; Sea Wolves, The
Kellerman, Sally: All's Fair; April Fools, The; Back to School; Big Bus, The; Boris and Natasha; Boston Strangler, The; Brewster McCloud; Dempsey; Drop Dead Gorgeous (1991); Fatal Attraction (1985); Foxes; It Rained All Night the Day I Left; Last of the Red Hot Lovers; Little Romance, A; M*A*S*H; Meatballs III; Mirror, Mirror 2: Raven Dance; Moving Violations; Rafferty and the Gold Dust Twins; Ready to Wear; Reflection of Fear; Reform School Girl; Secret Weapons; September Gun; Sleeping Beauty (1983); Slither; Someone to Love; That's Life; Three for the Road; Welcome to L.A.; Younger and Younger
Kellerman, Susan: Elvira, Mistress of the Dark
Kelley, Barry: Ma and Pa Kettle (The Further Adventures of Ma and Pa Kettle); Well, The
Kelley, DeForest: Law and Jake Wade, The; Star Trek (TV Series); Star Trek: The Menagerie; Star Trek—The Motion Picture; Star Trek II: The Wrath of Khan; Star Trek III: The Search for Spock; Star Trek IV: The Voyage Home; Star Trek V: The Final Frontier; Star Trek VI: The Undiscovered Country
Kelley, Sheila: Pure Luck; Secretary, The; Singles
Kellin, Mike: At War with the Army; Boston Strangler, The; Demon (God Told Me To); Hell Is for Heroes; Lonelyhearts; On the Yard; Riot (1969); Sleepaway Camp; So Fine
Kellner, Catherine: Day at the Beach
Kellogg, Bruce: Unknown World
Kellogg, John: Jacob I Have Loved
Kelly, Andrew: For a Lost Soldier
Kelly, Brian: Around the World Under the Sea; Crinoline Head; Flipper's New Adventure; Flipper's Odyssey; Longest Hunt, The
Kelly, Brian D.: Freakshow
Kelly, Craig: Nightscare
Kelly, Daniel Hugh: Atomic Dog; Bad Company (1995); Chill Factor; Cujo; Nowhere to Hide; Tuskegee Airmen, The
Kelly, David: Into the West; Waking Ned Devine
Kelly, David Patrick: Cafe Society; Cheap Shots; Crooklyn; Crow, The; 48 Hrs.; Last Man Standing (1996); Misfit Brigade, The; Penn & Teller Get Killed
Kelly, Desmond: Smash Palace
Kelly, Dori May: Winterbeast
Kelly, Gene: American in Paris, An; Anchors Aweigh; Black Hand, The; Brigadoon; Cover Girl; Du Barry Was a Lady; For Me and My Gal; Forty Carats; Inherit the Wind (1960); Invitation to the Dance; It's a Big Country; It's Always Fair Weather; Les Girls; Living In A Big Way; Marjorie Morningstar; North and South; On the Town; Pirate, The; Singin' in the Rain; Summer Stock; Take Me Out to the Ball Game; That's Entertainment; That's Entertainment Part II; That's Entertainment! III; Thousands Cheer; Three Musketeers, The (1948); Viva Knievel; Words and Music; Xanadu; Ziegfeld Follies
Kelly, Grace: Bridges at Toko-Ri, The; Country Girl, The (1954); Dial M for Murder; High Noon; High Society; Mogambo; Poppy Is Also a Flower, The; Rear Window; Swan, The (1956); To Catch a Thief
Kelly, Gregory: Show-Off, The (1926)
Kelly, Jack: Commandos; Cult of the Cobra; Forbidden Planet; Gambler Returns, The: The Luck of the Draw; Maverick (TV Series); To Hell and Back
Kelly, James F.: Marilyn & Bobby: Her Final Affair
Kelly, James T.: Charlie Chaplin—The Early Years Vol. 1–4
Kelly, Jean: Uncle Buck

Kilgour, Melanie: Last of the Warriors
Kilian, Victor: Dangerous Passage; Dr. Cyclops; Mary Hartman, Mary Hartman (TV Series); Unknown World
Killion, Cynthia: Killing Game, The
Kilmer, Val: At First Sight (1999); Batman Forever; Doors, The; Ghost and the Darkness, The; Gore Vidal's Billy The Kid; Heat (1995); Island of Dr. Moreau, The; Kill Me Again; Man Who Broke 1000 Chains, The; Real Genius; Real Mc-Coy, The; Saint, The (1997); Thunderheart; Tombstone; Top Gun; Top Secret; True Romance; Willow
Kilner, Kevin: Home Alone 3
Kilpatrick, Joy: Safe House
Kilpatrick, Lincoln: Hollywood Cop; Prison
Kilpatrick, Patrick: Cellar, The; Free Willy 3: The Rescue; Last Stand at Saber River; Scanners 4: The Showdown
Kim, Chu-Ryun: 301/302
Kim, Daniel Dae: American Shaolin: King of the Kickboxers II
Kim, Eva: Magic Stone, The
Kim, Evan: Dead Pool, The; Kentucky Fried Movie
Kim, Hang Yip: Undefeatable
Kim, Jacqueline: Brokedown Palace; Volcano
Kim, Miki: Primary Target
Kimball, Anne: Monster from the Ocean Floor, The
Kimball, Bruce: Pink Angels
Kimberley, Maggie: Mummy's Shroud, The
Kimberly, Marla: Traffic
Kimbrough, Charles: Seduction of Joe Tynan, The; Sunday in the Park with George
Kimmel, Bruce: First Nudie Musical, The; Spaceship (Naked Space)
Kimmel, Dana: Friday the 13th, Part III
Kimura, Kazuya: Gonin
Kincaid, Aron: Proud and the Damned, The
Kinchev, Konstantin: Burglar (Russian)
Kind, David: Quest of the Delta Knights
Kind, Richard: All-American Murder
Kindlon, Kevin: Heartstopper; Majorettes, The
Kinebrew, Carolyn: Messenger, The; Small Time
King Sisters, The: Second Fiddle
King, Adrienne: Friday the 13th; Friday the 13th, Part II
King, Alan: Author! Author!; Cat's Eye; Enemies—A Love Story; I, the Jury; Infiltrator, The; Just Tell Me What You Want; Memories of Me; Night and the City (1992)
King, Andrea: Beast with Five Fingers, The; Lemon Drop Kid, The; Man I Love, The; Red Planet Mars
King, Atlas: Incredibly Strange Creatures Who Stopped Living and Became Mixed-Up Zombies, The; Thrill Killers, The
King, B. B.: Amazon Women on the Moon
King, Bernard: Fast Break
King, Billy: Hopalong Rides Again
King, Brad: Outlaws of the Desert; Riders of the Timberline; Secrets of the Wasteland; Stick to Your Guns; Twilight on the Trail
King, Brenda: Dawn of the Mummy
King, Caroline Junko: Three Ninjas Kick Back
King, Charles: Arizona Stagecoach; Below the Border; Broadway Melody, The; Caravan Trail; Desert Phantom; Enemy of the Law; Forbidden Trails; Ghost Town Law; His Brother's Ghost; In Early Arizona; Kid Ranger; Lawless Nineties, The; Lightnin' Crandall; Mystery of the Hooded Horsemen; Riders of the Rio Grande; Riders of the Rockies; Sing, Cowboy, Sing; Superman—The Serial; Unnamable, The; Where Trails End; Zorro's Fighting Legion
King, Claude: Behind the Mask; Three on the Trail
King, Dennis: Devil's Brother, The; Miracle, The (1959)
King, Dexter: Our Friend, Martin
King, Erik: Desperate Measures; Joey Breaker
King, John: Ace Drummond; Arizona Stagecoach; Boothill Bandits; Fugitive Valley; Renegade Girl; Saddle Mountain Roundup; Trail of the Silver Spurs
King, Lawrence: Abducted II
King, Loretta: Bride of the Monster
King, Mabel: Dead Men Don't Die; Wiz, The
King, Meegan: Sweater Girls
King, Perry: Andy Warhol's Bad; Choirboys, The; City in Fear; Class of 1984; Cracker Factory; Cry in the Night, A; Danielle Steel's Kaleidoscope; Different Story, A; Disaster at Silo 7; Hasty Heart; Jericho Fever; Killing Hour, The; Lipstick; Lords of Flatbush, The; Love's Savage Fury;

Mandingo; Prize Pulitzer, The: The Roxanne Pulitzer St[…] Search and Destroy (1981); Switch; Wild Party, The (19[…]
King, Regina: Enemy of the State; Friday; How Stella Her Groove Back; Poetic Justice; Thin Line Between L and Hate, A
King, Scott: Double Exposure (1987)
King, Stephen: Creepshow
King, Tony: Bucktown; Gordon's War; Report to the C[…] missioner
King, Walter Woolf: Go West; Swiss Miss
King, Wright: Wanted: Dead or Alive (TV Series)
King, Yolanda: Death of a Prophet; Our Friend, Martin
King, Zalman: Blue Sunshine; Smile, Jenny, You're De[…] Some Call It Loving; Tell Me a Riddle
Kingsford, Walter: Fingers at the Window
Kingsley, Ben: Alice in Wonderland (1999); Assignme[…] The; Betrayal (1983); Bugsy; Confession, The; Dave; De[…] and the Maiden; Fifth Monkey, The; Gandhi; Har[…] Joseph; Moses (1996); Murderers Among Us: The Sim[…] Wiesenthal Story; Pascali's Island; Photographing Fair[…] Rules of Engagement; Schindler's List; Searching [...] Bobby Fischer; Silas Marner; Slipstream; Sneake[…] Species; Survivors of the Holocaust; Turtle Diary; Twe[…] Night; Weapons of Mass Distraction; What Planet Are Y[…] From?; Without a Clue
Kingsley, Danitza: Amazons
Kingsley, Susan: Dollmaker, The
Kingston, Alex: Moll Flanders (1996)
Kingston, Mark: Intimate Contact
Kingston, Natalie: His Private Secretary; Tarzan t[…] Mighty; Tarzan the Tiger
Kinkade, Amelia: Night of the Demons 2; Night of [...] Demons 3
Kinmont, Kathleen: Art of Dying, The; CIA Codena[…] Alexa; CIA II: Target: Alexa; Corporate Ladder; Final Impa[…] Final Round; Night of the Warrior; Renegade; Stranger [...] the House; Sweet Justice; Texas Payback
Kinnaman, Melanie: Friday the 13th, Part V—A New E[…] ginning
Kinnear, Greg: As Good as It Gets; Dear God; Mystery M[…] Sabrina (1995); Smile Like Yours, A; What Planet Are Y[...] From?; You've Got Mail
Kinnear, Roy: Diamond's Edge; Herbie Goes to Mor[…] Carlo; Hound of the Baskervilles, The (1977); Juggerna[…] (1974); Madame Sin; Melody; Pirates; Return of the Mu[...] keteers; Taste the Blood of Dracula; Willy Wonka and t[…] Chocolate Factory
Kinney, Kathy: Parting Glances
Kinney, Terry: Body Snatchers, The (1993); Devil in a Bl[…] Dress; Fly Away Home; George Wallace; Good Old Boy[…] The; JFK: Reckless Youth; No Mercy; Oxygen; Talent for t[…] Game; That Championship Season
Kinosita, Keisuke: Twenty-four Eyes
Kinsella, Neil: Octavia
Kinsey, Lance: Club Fed
Kinskey, Leonid: Can't Help Singing; Everything Happe[…] at Night; Weekend in Havana
Kinski, Klaus: Aguirre: Wrath of God; And God Said Cain; Android; Buddy, Buddy; Bullet for the General, A; Bu[…] den of Dreams; Circus of Fear; Code Name: Wild Gees[…] Count Dracula; Counterfeit Traitor, The; Crawlspace; Cre[...] ture; Dead Eyes of London; Deadly Sanctuary; Fitzcarrald[…] For a Few Dollars More; French Woman, The; Gangster[…] Law; His Name Was King; Jack the Ripper (1979); Lifespa[…] Little Drummer Girl, The; Operation Thunderbolt; Roug[…] Justice; Ruthless Four, The; Schizoid; Secret Diary of Sig[…] mund Freud, The; Shanghai Joe; Shoot the Living … Pra[…] for the Dead; Soldier, The; Star Knight; Time Stalkers; Tim[…] to Love and a Time to Die, A; Twice a Judas; Venom; Ven[…] in Furs; Woyzeck
Kinski, Nastassja: Bella Mafia; Boarding School; Cat Peo[...] ple (1982); Crackerjack; Exposed; Faraway, So Close; Fa[…] ther's Day; For Your Love Only; Harem; Hotel New Hamp[...] shire, The; Magdalene; Maria's Lovers; Moon in the Gutte[…] The; One from the Heart; One Night Stand (1997); Paris[…] Texas; Revolution; Savior; Somebody is Waiting; Sprin[…] Symphony; Stay as You Are; Terminal Velocity; Tess; To th[...] Devil, a Daughter; Torrents of Spring; Unfaithfully Your[…] (1984); Wrong Move, The; Your Friends & Neighbors
Kirby, Bruce: Mr. Wonderful

rby, Bruno: Basketball Diaries, The; Between the Lines;

rdy; Borderline; City Slickers; Donnie Brasco; Fallen An-
els; Freshman, The; Golden Gate; Good Morning, Viet-
am; Harrad Experiment, The; Modern Romance; Nitti: The
nforcer; We're No Angels (1989); When Harry Met Sally;
here the Buffalo Roam

rby, Jay: Sheriff of Las Vegas; Sundown Riders

rby, Leonard: Return of the Sand Fairy, The

rby, Michael: Swoon

rk, Jack: Pals of the Saddle

rk, James: National Lampoon's Golf Punks

rk, Justin: Love! Valour! Compassion!

rk, Phyllis: Back from Eternity; House of Wax; Life of Her
wn, A; Sad Sack, The

rk, Tommy: Absent-Minded Professor, The; Babes in
oyland (1961); Bon Voyage!; Escapade in Florence;
orsemasters; Mars Needs Women; Misadventures of
erlin Jones, The; Monkey's Uncle, The; Old Yeller; Savage
am; Shaggy Dog, The; Son of Flubber; Swiss Family
obinson, The; Unkissed Bride; Village of the Giants

rkham, Kathleen: Sky Pilot, The

rkland, Sally: Amnesia; Anna; Best of the Best; Blue
1968); Bullseye; Cheatin' Hearts; Cold Feet (1989); Double
eopardy (1992); Double Threat; EDtv; Fatal Games; For-
ver; Futz; Gunmen; High Stakes (1989); Hit the Dutchman;
n the Heat of Passion; JFK; Little Ghost; Paint It Black;
aranoia (1998); Picture Windows; Primary Motive; Prime
ime Murder; Revenge (1990); Talking Walls; Westing
ame, The; Young Nurses, The

.irkwood, Gene: Highlander: The Gathering

irsch, Stan: Highlander: The Gathering

irshner, Mia: Crow: City of Angels, The; Exotica; Johnny's
irl; Leo Tolstoy's Anna Karenina (1997); Love and Human
Remains; Mad City

.irsten, Dorothy: Great Caruso, The

.irtadze, Nino: Chef in Love, A

.irwin, William: Playgirl Killer, The

.iser, Terry: Forest Warrior; Friday the 13th, Part VII: The
New Blood; Hourglass; Into the Sun; Mannequin Two: On
he Move; Offspring, The; Pet Shop; Rich Kids; Starflight
One; Steel (1980); Tammy & the T-Rex; Weekend at
3ernie's; Weekend at Bernie's II

.ishi, Keiko: Kwaidan

.ishimoto, Kayoko: Fireworks

.issinger, Charles: Asylum of Satan; Three on a Meathook

.issner, Jeremy James: Dogs of Flanders, A (1999)

.istler, Darci: George Balanchine's The Nutcracker

.itaen, Tawny: Bachelor Party; Crystal Heart; Dead Tides;
Glory Years; Happy Hour; Hercules and the Circle of Fire;
Hercules in the Underworld; Instant Justice; Playback;
White Hot; Witchboard

.itano, Takeshi: Boiling Point (1990); Fireworks; Gonin;
Johnny Mnemonic; Sonatine; Violent Cop

.itaoji, Kinya: Himatsuri

.itchen, Michael: Doomsday Gun; Enchanted April; Fatherland; Fools of Fortune; Mrs. Dalloway; Out of Africa;
Russia House, The

.itt, Eartha: Boomerang (1992); Erik the Viking; Ernest
Scared Stupid; Fatal Instinct (1993); Friday Foster; Harriet
the Spy; Mark of the Hawk, The; New Faces; Pink Chiquitas,
The; Unzipped

.itzmiller, John: Cave of the Living Dead

.izzier, Heath: Sons of Trinity, The

.lar, Norman: Hitchhikers

.larwein, Eleonore: Peppermint Soda

.lausmeyer, Charles: Can It Be Love

.lein, Chris: American Pie; Here on Earth

.lein, Gerald: Honor and Glory; Undefeatable

.lein, Larry: Sugar Town

.lein, Nic: Wheels: An Inline Story

.lein, Nita: Muriel

.lein, Robert: Bell Jar, The; Dangerous Curves; Labor
Pains; Mixed Nuts; Next Stop Wonderland; Nobody's Perfekt; Owl and the Pussycat, The; Poison Ivy (1985); Pursuit
of Happiness, The

.leiner, Towje: Train Killer, The

.lein-Rogge, Rudolf: Destiny; Dr. Mabuse, the Gambler
(Parts I and II); Kriemhilde's Revenge; Spies; Testament of
Dr. Mabuse

.lemp, Anna: Blue Sky

Klemperer, Werner: Hogan's Heroes (TV Series); Istanbul
(1956)

Klenck, Margaret: Hard Choices

Kline, Kevin: Big Chill, The; Chaplin; Consenting Adults
(1992); Cry Freedom; Dave; Fierce Creatures; Fish Called
Wanda, A; French Kiss; Grand Canyon; I Love You to Death;
Ice Storm, The; In & Out; January Man, The; Pirates of Penzance, The; Princess Caraboo; Silverado; Soapdish; Sophie's Choice; Violets Are Blue; Wild Wild West (1999);
William Shakespeare's A Midsummer Night's Dream

Kline, Val: Beach Girls, The

Kling, Heidi: D3: The Mighty Ducks; Mighty Ducks, The;
Out on a Limb (1992)

Klintoe, Hanne: Loss of Sexual Innocence, The

Klisser, Evan J.: Hellgate

Klopfer, Eugen: Street, The

Klos, Elmar: Shop on Main Street, The

Kluga, Henlyk: Two Men and a Wardrobe

Klugman, Jack: Days of Wine and Roses (1962); Detec-
tive, The (1968); Goodbye Columbus; I Could Go On
Singing; Parallel Lives; Twilight Zone, The (TV Series);
Two-Minute Warning; 12 Angry Men (1957)

Klusak, Jan: Report on the Party and the Guests, A

Knapp, Dave: Honeymoon Murders

Knapp, Evalyn: His Private Secretary; In Old Santa Fe; Perils of Pauline, The (1933); Rawhide (1938)

Knaup, Herbert: Run Lola Run

Knell, David: Life on the Mississippi

Knepper, Rob: Kidnapped in Paradise; Red Shoe Diaries II:
Double Dare; Wild Thing; Zelda

Knievel, Evel: Viva Knievel

Knight, Christopher: Studs Lonigan

Knight, David: Demons 2; Nightmare (1964); Who Shot
Pat?

Knight, Esmond: Element of Crime, The; Waltzes from Vienna

Knight, Fuzzy: Adventures of Gallant Bess; Egg and I, The;
Horror Island; Lone Star Trail; Operator 13; Rimfire; Trail of
the Lonesome Pine, The

Knight, Gladys: Pipe Dreams

Knight, Jack: Class of 1999 II: The Substitute

Knight, Michael E.: Date with an Angel; Hexed

Knight, Nic: Prince Brat and the Whipping Boy

Knight, Sandra: Frankenstein's Daughter; Terror, The

Knight, Shirley: As Good as It Gets; Endless Love; Group,
The; If These Walls Could Talk; Indictment: The McMartin
Trial; Juggernaut (1974); Outer Limits, The (TV Series);
Petulia; Playing for Time; Rain People, The; Secrets;
Sender, The; Somebody is Waiting; Stuart Saves His Fam-
ily; Sweet Bird of Youth (1962); Yarn Princess, The

Knight, Stephen: Black Room, The (1985)

Knight, Ted: Caddyshack

Knight, Trent: Charlie's Ghost; Forest Warrior; Invisible
Mom; Skateboard Kid 2, The; Tin Soldier, The

Knight, Tuesday: Cover Story

Knight, Wayne: Chameleon (1995); For Richer or Poorer;
Jurassic Park; Space Jam

Knight, Wyatt: Porky's; Porky's II: The Next Day; Porky's
Revenge

Knipper, Robert: Getting Out

Knittle, Kristen: Body Strokes (Siren's Call)

Knopf, Sascha: Black Male

Knott, Andrew: Black Beauty (1994); Secret Garden, The
(1993)

Knotts, Don: Andy Griffith Show, The (TV Series); Apple
Dumpling Gang, The; Apple Dumpling Gang Rides Again,
The; Big Bully; Ghost and Mr. Chicken, The; Gus; Herbie
Goes to Monte Carlo; Hot Lead and Cold Feet; How to
Frame a Figg; Incredible Mr. Limpet, The; Love God?, The;
No Deposit, No Return; No Time for Sergeants; Private
Eyes, The; Prizefighter, The; Reluctant Astronaut, The; Re-
turn to Mayberry; Shakiest Gun in the West, The

Knowles, Patric: Beauty for the Asking; Big Steal, The;
Charge of the Light Brigade, The (1936); Chisum; Elfego
Baca: Six Gun Law; Five Came Back; Frankenstein Meets
the Wolf Man; Hit the Ice; Monsieur Beaucaire; Strange
Case of Dr. Rx, The; Terror in the Wax Museum; Three
Came Home; Who Done It?; Wolf Man, The

Knox, Alexander: Commandos Strike at Dawn; Cry of the
Innocent; Gorky Park; Judge Steps Out, The; Khartoum;
Man in the Saddle; Operation Amsterdam; Puppet on a

Lawrence, Mark Christopher: Fear of a Black Hat

Lawrence, Martin: Bad Boys (1995); Big Momma's House; Blue Streak; Boomerang (1992); House Party 2; Life; Nothing to Lose; Talkin' Dirty After Dark; Thin Line Between Love and Hate, A; You So Crazy

Lawrence, Matthew: Mrs. Doubtfire; Pulse

Lawrence, Michael: Came a Hot Friday

Lawrence, Ronald William: Blackbelt 2: Fatal Force

Lawrence, Rosina: Charlie Chan's Secret; General Spanky

Lawrence, Scott: Laurel Avenue; Perfect Crime; Sometimes Aunt Martha Does Dreadful Things

Lawrence, Shirley: Satellite in the Sky

Lawrence, Steve: Alice Through the Looking Glass (1985); Blues Brothers 2000; Express to Terror

Laws, Barry: Shadow Play

Lawson, Adam: Apex

Lawson, Charles: Four Days in July

Lawson, Cheryl: Dead Pit, The

Lawson, Leigh: Charlie Boy; Fire and Sword; Love Among the Ruins

Lawson, Linda: Night Tide

Lawson, Priscilla: Flash Gordon: Rocketship (Spaceship to the Unknown; Perils from Planet Mongo)

Lawson, Shannon: Heck's Way Home

Lawson, Wilfrid: Danny Boy (1941); Night Has Eyes, The; Pygmalion; Wrong Box, The

Lawton, Frank: Cavalcade; David Copperfield; Devil Doll, The (1936); Invisible Ray, The; Night to Remember, A (1958); Winslow Boy, The

Laxdal, Jon: Polar Bear King, The

Laydu, Claude: Diary of a Country Priest

Layng, Lissa: Say Yes

Layton, Marcia: Cthulhu Mansion

Lazar, John: Night of the Scarecrow

Lazar, Paul: Buffalo Girls; Mickey Blue Eyes

Lazard, Justin: Brutal Truth, The; Dead Center; Species II

Lazarev, Alexander: Friend of the Deceased, A

Lazarev, Eugene: Ice Runner

Lazenby, George: Eyes of the Beholder; Fatally Yours; Gettysburg; Never Too Young to Die; On Her Majesty's Secret Service; Return of the Man from U.N.C.L.E., The; Saint Jack; Twin Sitters

Lazure, Gabrielle: Joshua Then and Now

Le Clainche, Charles: Man Escaped, A

Le, Hiep Thi: Heaven and Earth (1993)

Lea, Nicholas: John Woo's Once a Thief; Raffle, The; X-Files, The (TV Series)

Lea, Ron: Neighbor, The

Leach, Rosemary: D.P.; Hawk, The; Room with a View, A; That'll Be the Day; Turtle Diary

Leachman, Cloris: Beverly Hillbillies, The (1993); Charley and the Angel; Crazy Mama; Daisy Miller; Danielle Steel's Fine Things; Dillinger (1973); Dixie Changing Habits; Fade to Black (1993); Foolin' Around; Hanging Up; Haunts of the Very Rich; Herbie Goes Bananas; High Anxiety; History of the World, Part One, The; Kiss Me Deadly; Last Picture Show, The; Love Hurts; Lovers and Other Strangers; Migrants, The; Muppet Movie, The; Music of the Heart; My Boyfriend's Back; Nobody's Girls; North Avenue Irregulars, The; Oldest Living Graduate, The; Prancer; Run Stranger Run; Scavenger Hunt; Shadow Play; Someone I Touched; S.O.S. Titanic; Steagle, The; Texasville; Thursday's Game; Walk Like a Man; Willa; Young Frankenstein

Leah, Leslie: Fix, The

Leahy, Shannon: Teach Me

Leake, Damien: Killing Floor, The

Learned, Michael: All My Sons (1986); Dragon: The Bruce Lee Story; Roots—The Gift; Thanksgiving Story, The; Touched by Love

Leary, Denis: Gunmen; Judgment Night; Matchmaker, The (1997); Monument Ave.; National Lampoon's Favorite Deadly Sins; Neon Bible, The; Operation Dumbo Drop; Ref, The; Sandlot, The; Second Civil War, The; Small Soldiers; Subway Stories; Suicide Kings; Thomas Crown Affair, The (1999); True Crime (1999); Two If By Sea; Underworld (1996); Wag the Dog; Who's the Man?; Wide Awake

Leary, Timothy: Conceiving Ada; Hold Me, Thrill Me, Kiss Me; Roadside Prophets

Lease, Rex: Cyclone in the Saddle; Helldorado (1946); In Old Cheyenne; Monster Walks, The

Léaud, Jean-Pierre: Day for Night; 400 Blows, The; Diary of a Seducer; Irma Vep; Last Tango in Paris; Le Départ; Le Gai Savoir (The Joy of Knowledge); Love on the Run (1979); Masculine Feminine; Mother and the Whore, The; Oldest Profession, The; Pierrot Le Fou; Pigsty; Stolen Kisses; Two English Girls; Weekend

Leavins, Chris: Hanging Garden, The

Lebbos, Carmen: West Beirut

Lebedef, Ivan: Goin' to Town

LeBlanc, Diana: Madonna: Innocence Lost

LeBlanc, Matt: Ed; Lost in Space (1998)

Lebowitz, Fran: Infamous Dorothy Parker, The

Le Brock, Gene: Fortress of Amerikkka; Metamorphosis

LeBrock, Kelly: Betrayal of the Dove; Hard Bounty; Hard to Kill; Tracks of a Killer; Weird Science; Woman in Red, The; Wrongfully Accused

Lebrun, Francoise: Mother and the Whore, The

Le Calm, Renee: When the Cat's Away

Leclerc, Ginette: Baker's Wife, The; Man from Nowhere, The

Leclerc, Jean: Blown Away (1992); Whispers

Le Coq, Bernard: Van Gogh

Led Zeppelin: Song Remains the Same, The

Lederer, Francis: Bridge of San Luis Rey, The; Lisbon; Midnight (1939); One Rainy Afternoon; Return of Dracula; Romance in Manhattan; Woman of Distinction, A

Ledger, Heath: Patriot, The; 10 Things I Hate About You

Ledingham, David: Final Judgment

Ledoux, Fernand: La Bête Humaine; Stormy Waters

LeDoux, Jake: Summer's End

Ledoyen, Virginie: Beach, The; La Cérémonie; Single Girl

Leduc, Richard: Nous N'Irons Plus Au Bois

Leduke, Harrison: Laser Moon

Lee, Alan David: Sahara (1995)

Lee, Anna: Bedlam; Commandos Strike at Dawn; Ghost and Mrs. Muir, The; Hangmen Also Die; King Solomon's Mines (1937); Man Who Lived Again, The; Prize, The; Seven Sinners

Lee, Bernard: Brain, The (1965); Detective, The (1954); Dr. No; Fallen Idol, The; Frankenstein and the Monster from Hell; Key, The; Last Holiday; Long Ago Tomorrow; Man with the Golden Gun, The; Pursuit of the Graf Spee; Rhodes of Africa (Rhodes); Spy Who Came in from the Cold, The; Spy Who Loved Me, The; Whistle Down the Wind; You Only Live Twice

Lee, Brandon: Bruce Lee: Curse of the Dragon; Crow, The; Kung Fu—The Movie (1986); Laser Mission; Rapid Fire; Showdown in Little Tokyo

Lee, Britton: Ironheart

Lee, Bruce: Bruce Lee: Curse of the Dragon; Chinese Connection, The; Enter the Dragon; Fists of Fury; Game of Death; Green Hornet, The (TV Series); Marlowe; Return of the Dragon

Lee, Canada: Cry, the Beloved Country (1952); Lifeboat

Lee, Carl: Gordon's War; Superfly

Lee, Chen: Shanghai Joe

Lee, Christian: Invasion Earth: The Aliens Are Here

Lee, Christopher: Against All Odds (1968) (Kiss and Kill, Blood of Fu Manchu); Airport '77; Albino; Bear Island; Beat Girl; Captain America II: Death Too Soon; Caravans; Castle of Fu Manchu; Castle of the Living Dead; Circle of Iron; Circus of Fear; Corridor of Mirrors; Corridors of Blood; Count Dracula; Creeping Flesh, The; Crimson Pirate, The; Curse III: Blood Sacrifice; Curse of Frankenstein, The; Curse of the Crimson Altar; Dark Places; Death Train; Desperate Moves; Devil Rides Out, The; Devil's Undead, The; Dr. Terror's House of Horrors; Double Vision; Dracula A.D. 1972; Dracula and Son; Dracula Has Risen from the Grave; Dracula—Prince of Darkness; End of the World; Eye for an Eye (1981); Far Pavilions, The; Five Golden Dragons; Four Musketeers, The; Funnyman; Girl, The; Goliath Awaits; Gorgon, The; Gremlins 2: The New Batch; Hannie Caulder; Hercules in the Haunted World; Hollywood Meatcleaver Massacre; Horror Express; Horror Hotel; Horror of Dracula; Hound of the Baskervilles, The (1959); House of the Long Shadows; House That Dripped Blood, The; Howling II . . . Your Sister Is a Werewolf; Jocks; Journey of Honor; Julius Caesar (1970); Keeper, The; Killer Force; Land of Faraway, The;

Lockhart, June: All This and Heaven Too; Capture of Grizzly Adams, The; C.H.U.D. II (Bud the C.H.U.D.); Colony, The (1995); Deadly Games; Gift of Love, The; It's a Joke, Son!; Lost in Space (TV Series); Lost in Space (1998); Night They Saved Christmas, The; Out There; Rented Lips; Sergeant York; Sleep with Me; Son of Lassie; Strange Invaders; T-Men; Troll; Whisper Kills, A; Who Is the Black Dahlia?

Lockhart, Kathleen: Blondie; Christmas Carol, A (1938); Mother Wore Tights

Locklear, Heather: Big Slice, The; Body Language (1992); Double Tap; Fade to Black (1993); Great American Sex Scandal, The; Illusions; Lethal Charm; Money Talks; Return of the Swamp Thing

Locklin, Loryn: Fortress (1993)

Lockwood, Gary: Firecreek; Incredible Journey of Dr. Meg Laurel, The; It Happened at the World's Fair; Magic Sword, The; Night of the Scarecrow; R.P.M. (Revolutions per Minute); Survival Zone; Tall Story; Terror in Paradise; 2001: A Space Odyssey; Wild Pair, The

Lockwood, Margaret: Dr. Syn; Hungry Hill; Lady Vanishes, The (1938); Man in Grey, The; Night Train to Munich (Night Train); Stars Look Down, The; Susannah of the Mounties; Trouble in the Glen; Wicked Lady, The (1945)

Lockwood, Preston: At Bertram's Hotel

Lodato, Tiziana: Star Maker, The

Loder, John: Brighton Strangler, The; Dishonored Lady; Dr. Syn; Hairy Ape, The; How Green Was My Valley; King Solomon's Mines (1937); Man Who Lived Again, The; Racketeer; River of Unrest; Sabotage (1936); Tin Pan Alley; Wedding Rehearsal

Lodge, David: Edge of Sanity; Two-Way Stretch

Lodge, John: Murders in the Zoo; River of Unrest; Scarlet Empress, The

Lodolo, Massimo: Flight of the Innocent

Lodro, Jamyang: Cup, The

Loeh, Tennyson: Lady of the Lake

Loewi, Fiona: Love and Death on Long Island; National Lampoon's Senior Trip

Lofbergh, Pete: Evil Ed

Loft, Arthur: My Friend Flicka

Logan, Jacqueline: King of Kings, The (1927)

Logan, Janice: Dr. Cyclops

Logan, Phyllis: Another Time, Another Place (1984); Doctor and the Devils, The; Inquiry, The; Kitchen Toto, The; McGuffin, The; Secrets and Lies

Logan, Robert: Across the Great Divide; Adventures of the Wilderness Family; Born to Race; Mountain Family Robinson; Night in Heaven, A; Sea Gypsies, The; Snowbeast; Wilderness Family, Part 2, The

Loggia, Robert: Afterburn; Armed and Dangerous; Bad Girls (1994); Believers, The; Big; Code Name: Chaos; Cold-Blooded; Conspiracy: The Trial of the Chicago 8; Don's Analyst, The; Echoes in the Darkness; Elfego Baca: Six Gun Law; First Love (1977); Gaby, a True Story; Gladiator (1992); Hard Time; Holy Man; Hot Pursuit; I Love Trouble; Independence Day (1996); Innocent Blood; Intrigue; Jagged Edge; Joe Torre: Curveballs Along the Way; Lifepod; Lost Highway; Lost Missile, The; Man with a Gun; Marrying Man, The; Mercy Mission (The Rescue of Flight 711); Mistrial; Necessary Roughness; Nine Lives of Elfego Baca, The; Ninth Configuration, The; Opportunity Knocks; Over the Top; Prizzi's Honor; Psycho II; Relentless; Return to Me; Revenge of the Pink Panther, The; Right to Remain Silent, The; Running Away; Scarface (1983); Smilla's Sense of Snow; Somebody Up There Likes Me; Target: Favorite Son; That's Life; Triumph of the Spirit; White Mile; Wide Awake; Wild Palms

Logue, Donal: Baja; Blade (1998); Bright Shining Lie, A; Crew, The; Grave, The; Reindeer Games

Lohan, Lindsay: Parent Trap, The (1998)

Lohr, Marie: Pygmalion

Loiselle, Rachel: Mosquito

Lokey, Ben: Breakin'

Lollobrigida, Gina: Bad Man's River; Beat the Devil; Beauties of the Night; Buono Sera, Mrs. Campbell; Come September; Fanfan the Tulip; Hotel Paradiso; King, Queen and Knave; Never So Few; Private Navy of Sgt. O'Farrell, The; Solomon and Sheba (1959); Strange Bedfellows; Trapeze

Lolly, Teri: Restless Natives

Lom, Herbert: And Now the Screaming Starts; Asylum (1972); Brass Monkey, The; Count Dracula; Curse of the

Pink Panther, The; Dark Places; Dead Zone, The; Dorian Gray; Flame over India; Gambit; Going Bananas; Horse Without a Head, The; Hotel Reserve; Journey to the Far Side of the Sun; King Solomon's Mines (1985); Lady Vanishes, The (1979); Lion and the Hawk, The; Man with Bogart's Face, The; Mark of the Devil; Murders in the Rue Morgue (1971); Mysterious Island; Night and the City (1950); 99 Women; Paris Express, The; Phantom of the Opera (1962); Pink Panther Strikes Again, The; Pope Must Diet, The; Return of the Pink Panther, The; Revenge of the Pink Panther, The; River of Death; Room 43; Sect, The; Seventh Veil, The; Shot in the Dark, A; Son of the Pink Panther; Ten Little Indians (1975); Third Man on the Mountain; Trail of the Pink Panther, The; Villa Rides

Lombard, Carole: Big News; Golden Age of Comedy, The; Hands Across the Table; High Voltage (1929); In Name Only; Lady by Choice; Made for Each Other; Mr. and Mrs. Smith; My Man Godfrey (1936); No Man of Her Own; Nothing Sacred; Princess Comes Across, The; Racketeer; Supernatural; Swing High, Swing Low; These Girls Won't Talk; They Knew What They Wanted; To Be or Not to Be (1942); Twentieth Century; We're Not Dressing

Lombard, Karina: Kull the Conqueror; Last Man Standing

Lombard, Louise: Russell Mulcahy's Tale of the Mummy

Lombard, Michael: Clinton and Nadine; "Crocodile" Dundee

Lommel, Ulli: Boogeyman 2; Chinese Roulette; Effi Briest

Lomnicki, Tadeusz: Contract; Generation, A

Lomond, Britt: Sign of Zorro, The

Londez, Guilaine: Night and Day (1991)

London, Alexandra: Van Gogh

London, Daniel: Patch Adams

London, Jason: Blood Ties (1993); Broken Vessels; Dazed and Confused; Fall Time; Jason and the Argonauts (2000); Man in the Moon, The; My Teacher's Wife; Rage, The; Carrie 2; Serial Bomber

London, Jeremy: Babysitter, The (1995); Breaking Free; Defenders, The; Taking the First; Mall Rats

London, Julie: Girl Can't Help It, The; Man of the West; Red House, The; Task Force

London, Lisa: H.O.T.S.

London, Tom: Cherokee Flash; Red River Renegades; Song of Texas; Twilight on the Trail; Warning Shadows (1933); Zorro Rides Again

Lone, John: Hunted, The; Iceman; Last Emperor, The; M. Butterfly; Moderns, The; Shadow, The; Shadow of China; Year of the Dragon

Long, Audrey: Adventures of Gallant Bess; Born to Kill; Desperate; Indian Uprising

Long, Howie: Broken Arrow (1996); Firestorm

Long, Joseph: Queen of Hearts

Long, Kathryn: Goosebumps: The Haunted Mask

Long, Kathy: Knights; Stranger, The (1994); Under the Gun (1995)

Long, Michael: Squizzy Taylor

Long, Nia: Best Man, The (1999); Big Momma's House; Boiler Room; Boyz N the Hood; Friday; Held Up; In Too Deep; Love Jones; Made in America; Never 2 Big; Soul Food; Stigmata

Long, Richard: Big Valley, The (TV Series); Criss Cross (1948); Cult of the Cobra; Dark Mirror, The; House on Haunted Hill; Ma and Pa Kettle (The Further Adventures of Ma and Pa Kettle); Ma and Pa Kettle Back on the Farm; Ma and Pa Kettle Go to Town; Maverick (TV Series); Stranger, The (1947); Tomorrow Is Forever

Long, Robert: Neanderthal Man, The

Long, Shelley: Brady Bunch Movie, The; Caveman; Cracker Factory; Don't Tell Her It's Me; Frozen Assets; Hello Again; Irreconcilable Differences; Losin' It; Money Pit, The; Night Shift; Outrageous Fortune; Small Circle of Friends, A; Troop Beverly Hills; Very Brady Sequel, A

Long, Walter: Laurel and Hardy Classics: Vol. 1–9; Shadows

Longbois, Frederic: Celestial Clockwork

Longden, John: Blackmail (1929); Skin Game, The (1931)

Longden, Terence: Carry on Nurse

Longenecker, Jane: Coroner, The

Longet, Claudine: Party, The

Longo, Tony: Remote

Lund, Richard: Treasure of Arne

Lundgren, Dolph: Army of One; Blackjack; Bridge of Dragons; Cover-Up; Hidden Assassin; I Come in Peace; Johnny Mnemonic; Masters of the Universe; Men of War; Pentathlon; Punisher, The; Red Scorpion; Rocky IV; Showdown in Little Tokyo; Silent Trigger; Sweepers; Universal Soldier

Lundigan, William: Andy Hardy's Double Life; Dishonored Lady; Fabulous Dorseys, The; Fighting 69th, The; Follow Me Quietly; Love Nest; Pinky; Three Smart Girls Grow Up; Wives Under Suspicion

Lundquist, Steve: Killer Tomatoes Eat France

Lundy, Jessica: Madhouse (1990); Rocketman; Stupids, The

Lung, Sihung: Eat Drink Man Woman; Pushing Hands

Lung, Ti: Better Tomorrow, A; Better Tomorrow 2, A; People's Hero

Lunghi, Cherie: Buccaneers, The; Excalibur; Jack and Sarah; Letters to an Unknown Lover; Sign of Four, The

Lunham, Dan: Strangeness, The

Lunt, Alfred: Guardsman, The; Sally of the Sawdust

Luotto, Andy: Excellent Cadavers

Luotto, Stephen: Tides of War

Lupino, Ida: Adventures of Sherlock Holmes, The; Beware, My Lovely; Bigamist, The; Devil's Rain, The; Escape Me Never; Food of the Gods; Forever and a Day; Hard Way, The (1942); High Sierra; Hollywood Canteen; Junior Bonner; Lust for Gold; Man I Love, The; My Boys Are Good Boys; On Dangerous Ground (1951); One Rainy Afternoon; Private Hell 36; Road House (1948); Sea Devils; Sea Wolf, The (1941); Thank Your Lucky Stars; They Drive by Night; While the City Sleeps

Lupo, Alberto: Atom Age Vampire; Django Shoots First

LuPone, Patti: Driving Miss Daisy; Family Prayers; Fighting Back; LBJ: The Early Years; Song Spinner; 24-Hour Woman; Water Engine, The

LuPone, Robert: High Stakes (1989)

Luppi, Federico: Cocaine Wars; Cronos; Funny Dirty Little War (Ni Habra Mas Penas ni Olvido); Men with Guns

Lupton, John: Escape from Fort Bravo; Great Locomotive Chase, The; Jesse James Meets Frankenstein's Daughter

Lurie, Evan: Shadow Warriors; T-Force

Lurie, John: Down by Law; Just Your Luck; Stranger Than Paradise

Lush, Valerie: Nemesis (1986)

Lussier, Jacques: Norman's Awesome Experience

Lustig, Aaron: Bad Channels

Lutes, Eric: Bram Stoker's The Mummy; Distant Justice; Switching Goals

Lutter, Alfred: Alice Doesn't Live Here Anymore; Bad News Bears, The; Love and Death

Lutz, Adelle: Beyond Rangoon

Luz, Franc: Don Juan DeMarco; Ghost Town; Nest, The (1988)

Lyden, Pierce: Sea Hound, The

Lydon, Jimmy: Island in the Sky; Life with Father; Little Men (1940); Magnificent Yankee, The; September Affair; Strange Illusion; Time of Your Life, The; Tom Brown's School Days (1940)

Lydon, John: Corrupt; Great Rock and Roll Swindle, The

Lye, Reg: Killing of Angel Street, The; Sunday Too Far Away; Walk into Hell

Lyman, Dorothy: Ollie Hopnoodle's Haven of Bliss; Ruby in Paradise

Lyman, Will: Three Sovereigns for Sarah

Lynas, Jeffrey: Lies My Father Told Me

Lynch, Barry: Infested (Ticks)

Lynch, Jimmy: Avenging Disco Godfather

Lynch, John: Angel Baby; Cal; Hardware; Moll Flanders; Nothing Personal (1997); Railway Station Man, The; Secret Garden, The (1993); Sliding Doors; This Is the Sea

Lynch, John Carroll: Volcano

Lynch, Kate: Def-Con 4; Meatballs

Lynch, Kelly: Cold Around the Heart; Curly Sue; Desperate Hours (1990); Drugstore Cowboy; For Better and for Worse; Forbidden Choices; Heaven's Prisoners; Homegrown; Imaginary Crimes; Mr. Magoo; Persons Unknown; Three of Hearts; Virtuosity; Warm Summer Rain; White Man's Burden

Lynch, Ken: I Married a Monster from Outer Space

Lynch, Pierrette: Lethal Lolita—Amy Fisher: My Story

Lynch, Richard: Alligator II; Bad Dreams; Barbarians, The; Cut and Run; Cyborg 3: The Recycler; Deathsport; Delta Fox; Double Threat; Enemy Action; Forbidden Dance, The; High Stakes (1989); Invasion U.S.A. (1985); Little Nikita; Maximum Force; Merlin; Midnight Confessions; Nightforce; Premonition, The; Proposition, The; Puppet Master III: Toulon's Revenge; Savage Dawn; Scanner Cop; Scarecrow; Seven-Ups, The; Sizzle; Steel (1980); Sword and the Sorcerer, The; Terminal Virus; Terrified; Werewolf

Lynch, Susan: Ivanhoe (1997); Waking Ned Devine

Lynch, Valeria: Tango Bar

Lynde, Paul: Beach Blanket Bingo; Bye Bye Birdie; Glass Bottom Boat, The; New Faces; Send Me No Flowers; Son of Flubber

Lyndon, Michael: Lightship, The; Success Is the Best Revenge

Lynley, Carol: Balboa; Blackout (1990); Cardinal, The; Cat and the Canary, The (1978); Dark Tower; Fantasy Island; Flood!; Four Deuces, The; Howling VI: The Freaks; Light in the Forest, The; Night Stalker, The (1971); Return to Peyton Place; Shuttered Room, The; Son of Blob (Beware! The Blob); Spirits; Stripper, The; Vigilante; Washington Affair, The

Lynn, Betty: Return to Mayberry; Texas John Slaughter: Stampede at Bitter Creek

Lynn, Billy: Twonky, The

Lynn, Cheryl M.: Emanon; Fate; Thunder Run

Lynn, Daria: Talking About Sex

Lynn, Diana: Annapolis Story, An; Bedtime for Bonzo; Every Girl Should Be Married; Kentuckian, The; Miracle of Morgan's Creek, The; My Friend Irma

Lynn, Donna: Hollywood High, Part II

Lynn, Emmet: Days of Old Cheyenne

Lynn, Jeffrey: All This and Heaven Too; Fighting 69th, The; Letter to Three Wives, A; Roaring Twenties, The

Lynn, Jonathan: Suspicion (1987)

Lynn, Kelly: Dinosaur Babes

Lynn, Meredith: Billy's Hollywood Screen Kiss; Forces of Nature; I Love You, Don't Touch Me!

Lynn, Rebecca: Sensations

Lynn, Sharon: Way Out West

Lynn, Stacy: Sorority Girls and the Creature from Hell

Lynn, Theresa: Psycho Sisters (1998)

Lynn, Traci: Fright Night II

Lynskey, Melanie: Heavenly Creatures

Lyon, Alice: Horror of Party Beach, The

Lyon, Ben: I Cover the Waterfront; Indiscreet (1931); Night Nurse

Lyon, Steve: Campus Man

Lyon, Sue: Crash! (1977); End of the World; Evel Knievel; Flim-Flam Man, The; Four Rode Out; Lolita (1962); Night of the Iguana, The; Tony Rome; Winds of Jarrah, The

Lyon, Wendy: Hello, Mary Lou: Prom Night II

Lyonne, Natasha: Everyone Says I Love You; Freeway 2: Confessions of a Trickbaby; Krippendorf's Tribe; Slums of Beverly Hills

Lyons, Bruce: Navigator: A Medieval Odyssey, The

Lyons, James: Poison

Lyons, Jennifer: Tiger Heart

Lyons, Phyllis: Casualties of Love: The Long Island Lolita Story

Lyons, Robert F.: American Eagle; Cease Fire; Getting Straight; Platoon Leader; Todd Killings, The

Lyons, Susan: Ebbtide

Lypsinka: Wigstock: The Movie

Lys, Lya: Age of Gold; L'Age D'Or

Lythgow, Gene: When a Stranger Calls Back

M., Monika: Nekromantik 2

Maazel, Lincoln: Martin

Mabe, Byron: Doberman Gang, The

Mabe, Ricky: Screamers

Maberly, Kate: Langoliers, The; Secret Garden, The (1993)

Mabius, Eric: Black Circle Boys; Harvest of Fire; Welcome to the Dollhouse

Mabry, Zachary: Little Rascals, The (1994)

Mac, Bernie: Above the Rim; Friday; House Party 3; Players Club, The

Macario, Jacqueline: Murdered Innocence

MacArthur, James: Cry of Battle; Interns, The; Kidnapped (1960); Light in the Forest, The; Ride Beyond Vengeance;

Spencer's Mountain; Swiss Family Robinson, The; Third Man on the Mountain

MacBride, Donald: Annabel Takes a Tour; Blondie Takes a Vacation; Buck Privates Come Home; Egg and I, The; Murder over New York; Story of Seabiscuit, The; They Got Me Covered; Time of Their Lives, The

Macchio, Ralph: Crossroads; Dangerous Company; Distant Thunder (1988); Karate Kid, The; Karate Kid Part II, The; Karate Kid Part III, The; My Cousin Vinny; Naked in New York; Outsiders, The; Teachers, The; Too Much Sun; Up the Academy

Maccioni, Aldo: Loves and Times of Scaramouche, The; Too Shy to Try

MacColl, Katherine: Gates of Hell; House by the Cemetery; Seven Doors of Death

MacCorkindale, Simon: Jaws 3; Macbeth (1981); Obsessive Love; Quatermass Conclusion, The; Riddle of the Sands; Robbers of the Sacred Mountain; Running Wild (1998); Shades of Love: Sincerely, Violet; Sword and the Sorcerer, The

MacDonald, Aimi: Number One of the Secret Service

Macdonald, Anne-Marie: I've Heard the Mermaids Singing; Where the Spirit Lives

MacDonald, Bruce: Return of the Secaucus 7

MacDonald, Dan: Gift of Love: The Daniel Huffman Story

MacDonald, Donald: Sky Pilot, The

MacDonald, Gordon: Brain Damage

MacDonald, J. Farrell: In Old Arizona; Painted Desert, The; Riders of the Timberline; Stagecoach War; Sunrise; Thirteenth Guest, The

MacDonald, Jeanette: Bitter Sweet; Broadway Serenade; Cairo; Cat and the Fiddle, The; Firefly, The; Follow the Boys; Girl of the Golden West, The; I Married an Angel; Love Me Tonight; Maytime; Merry Widow, The; Naughty Marietta; New Moon; Rose Marie (1936); San Francisco; Smilin' Through (1941); Sun Comes Up, The; Sweethearts; Three Daring Daughters

MacDonald, Jennifer: Alien Chaser; Headless Body in Topless Bar

MacDonald, Kelly: Cousin Bette; Entropy

Macdonald, Michael: Oddballs

MacDonald, Norm: Dirty Work (1998); Dr. Dolittle (1998); Screwed

MacDonald, Phillip: Garden, The

MacDonald, Wendy: Blood Frenzy

MacDonell, Sarah: Fatally Yours

MacDowell, Andie: Bad Girls (1994); Deception (1993); End of Violence, The; Four Weddings and a Funeral; Green Card; Greystoke: The Legend of Tarzan, Lord of the Apes; Groundhog Day; Hudson Hawk; Just the Ticket; Michael; Multiplicity; Muppets From Space; Muse, The; Object of Beauty, The; St. Elmo's Fire; sex, lies and videotape; Shadrach; Short Cuts; Unstrung Heroes; Women & Men 2

Mace, Paul: Lords of Flatbush, The

MacFadyen, Angus: Braveheart; Brylcreem Boys, The; Cradle Will Rock; Facade; Lost Language of Cranes, The; Nevada; Rat Pack, The; Titus; Warriors of Virtue

MacGinnis, Niall: Betrayed (1954); Curse of the Demon; Helen of Troy; Martin Luther; River of Unrest

Macgowan, J. P.: Somewhere in Sonora

MacGowran, Jack: Brain, The (1965); Cul-de-Sac; Fearless Vampire Killers, or, Pardon Me, But Your Teeth Are in My Neck, The; Giant Behemoth, The; How I Won the War; King Lear (1971); Quiet Man, The; Start the Revolution Without Me; Wonderwall

MacGraw, Ali: Convoy (1978); Getaway, The (1972); Goodbye Columbus; Just Tell Me What You Want; Love Story; Murder Elite; Natural Causes; Players; Winds of War, The

MacGreevy, Thomas: Love in the Present Tense

Machiavelli, Nicoletta: Minute to Pray, A Second to Die, A

Macht, Stephen: Adventures of Galgameth, The; Amityville 1992: It's About Time; Contract for Life: The S.A.D.D. Story; Friendship in Vienna, A; Galaxina; Last Winter, The; Mountain Men, The; Samson and Delilah (1984); Siringo; Stephen King's Graveyard Shift (1990); Trancers 4: Jack of Swords; Trancers 5: Sudden Serb

MacIntosh, Keegan: Don't Talk to Strangers; Road Home, The

Mack, Allison: No Dessert Dad Until You Mow the Lawn; Unlikely Angel

Mack, Betty: Forty-Niners

Mack, Charles Emmett: Dream Street

Mack, Craig: Show, The

Mack, Helen: His Girl Friday; Melody Cruise; Milky Way, The (1936); Return of Peter Grimm, The; She (1935); Son of Kong, The

Mack, Kerry: Savage Attraction

Mack, Marion: General, The (1927)

Mack, Wilbur: Sweethearts on Parade

MacKay, Fulton: Defense of the Realm; Local Hero; Sense of Freedom, A

MacKay, John: Rejuvenator, The

Mackay, Mathew: Peanut Butter Solution, The

Mackenzie, Alex: Greyfriars Bobby

Mackenzie, Evan: Ghoulies III

MacKenzie, Jan: Gator Bait II—Cajun Justice

Mackenzie, Mary: Simple Men; Stolen Face

Mackenzie, Patch: Goodbye, Norma Jean

Mackenzie, Philip Charles: Red Light Sting, The

Mackenzie, Phillip: Blackjack

MacKenzie, Sam: Dragonworld

Mackie, Allison: Lurking Fear

Mackintosh, Steven: Different for Girls; Land Girls, The; London Kills Me; Return of the Native, The

MacLachlan, Janet: Pinocchio's Revenge; Roll of Thunder, Hear My Cry; She's in the Army Now; Sounder; Tick . . . Tick . . . Tick . . .

MacLachlan, Kyle: Against the Wall; Blue Velvet; Don't Tell Her It's Me; Doors, The; Dune; Flintstones, The; Hidden, The; Moonshine Highway; One Night Stand (1997); Rich in Love; Roswell; Route 9; Showgirls; Thunder Point; Trial, The (1992); Trigger Effect, The; Trigger Happy (Mad Dog Time); Twin Peaks (Movie); Twin Peaks (TV Series); Twin Peaks: Fire Walk with Me; Where the Day Takes You; Windsor Protocol, The

MacLaine, Shirley: All in a Night's Work; Apartment, The; Around the World in 80 Days (1956); Artists and Models; Ask Any Girl; Being There; Bliss of Mrs. Blossom, The; Can-Can; Cannonball Run II; Career; Change of Seasons, A; Children's Hour, The; Evening Star, The; Gambit; Guarding Tess; Hot Spell; Irma La Douce; Loving Couples; Madame Sousatzka; Matchmaker, The (1958); Mrs. Winterbourne; My Geisha; Out on a Limb (1986); Postcards from the Edge; Some Came Running; Steel Magnolias; Sweet Charity; Terms of Endearment; Trouble with Harry, The; Turning Point, The; Two for the Seesaw; Two Mules for Sister Sara; Used People; Waiting for the Light; Woman Times Seven; Wrestling Ernest Hemingway

MacLane, Barton: All Through the Night; Big Street, The; Black Fury; Bombardier; Buckskin; Bugles in the Afternoon; Bullets or Ballots; Case of the Lucky Legs, The; Ceiling Zero; Go into Your Dance; Half-Breed, The; Jubilee Trail; Kansas Pacific; Kiss Tomorrow Goodbye; Marine Raiders; Melody Ranch; Naked in the Sun; Prince and the Pauper, The (1937); Santa Fe Uprising; Silver River; Song of Texas; Three Violent People; Western Union; You Only Live Once

MacLaren, Fawna: Cover Girl Murders, The

MacLean, Peter: King Richard II; Othello (1982)

MacLellan, Elizabeth: Puppet Master II

MacLeod, Gavin: Kelly's Heroes; Only with Married Men; Party, The; Sand Pebbles, The; Women of the Prehistoric Planet

MacLeod, Margaret Anne: Tales from the Gimli Hospital

MacLiammoir, Micheal: Othello (1952)

MacMahon, Aline: Ah, Wilderness; Backdoor to Heaven; Cimarron (1960); Gold Diggers of 1933; Guest in the House; Heroes for Sale; I Could Go On Singing; I Live My Life; Lady Is Willing, The; Search, The

MacManus, Sharon: This Time For Keeps

MacMurray, Fred: Above Suspicion (1943); Absent-Minded Professor, The; Alice Adams; Apartment, The; At Gunpoint; Bon Voyage!; Caine Mutiny, The; Charley and the Angel; Dive Bomber; Double Indemnity; Egg and I, The; Follow Me, Boys!; Hands Across the Table; Happiest Millionaire, The; Kisses for My President; Lady Is Willing, The; Miracle of the Bells, The; My Love for Yours (Honeymoon in Bali); Princess Comes Across, The; Remember the Night; Shaggy Dog, The; Singapore; Son of Flubber; Swarm, The; Swing High, Swing Low; Texas Rangers (1936); Trail of the Lonesome Pine, The; Woman's World

MacNaughton, Alan: Dark Angel, The; Very British Coup, A

MacNaughton, Robert: E.T.—The Extra-Terrestrial; I Am the Cheese

Macnee, Patrick: Avengers, The (TV Series); Avengers, The; Club Med; Dead of Night (1977); Down Under; Gambler Returns, The: The Luck of the Draw; Howling, The; King Solomon's Treasure; Lobster Man from Mars; Masque of the Red Death (1989); Pursuit of the Graf Spee; Rehearsal for Murder; Return of the Man from U.N.C.L.E., The; Sea Wolves, The; Shadey; Sherlock Holmes and the Incident at Victoria Falls; Sherlock Holmes and the Leading Lady; Sorry, Wrong Number (1989); Super Force; Sweet Sixteen; Thunder in Paradise II; Thunder in Paradise; Transformations; Until They Sail; Waxwork; Young Doctors in Love

MacNeill, Peter: Conundrum; Hanging Garden, The; Vow to Kill, A

MacNicol, Peter: American Blue Note; Baby Geniuses; Bean; By Dawn's Early Light; Dracula: Dead and Loving It; Dragonslayer; Heat (1987); Housesitter; Sophie's Choice

Macollum, Barry: Interns Can't Take Money

Macpherson, Elle: Edge, The; If Lucy Fell; Jane Eyre (1996); Sirens

MacPherson, Joe: Bay Boy, The

MacPherson, Walt: Serial Mom

Macrae, Arthur: Saint's Vacation, The

Macrae, Duncan: Tunes of Glory

MacRae, Gordon: By the Light of the Silvery Moon; Carousel; Desert Song, The; Look for the Silver Lining; Oklahoma!; On Moonlight Bay; Pilot, The; Tea for Two; West Point Story, The

MacRae, Meredith: Sketches of a Strangler

MacRae, Michael: Dear Detective; Don't Talk to Strangers; Madhouse (1987)

Macready, George: Alligator People, The; Black Arrow, The (1948); Coroner Creek; Dead Ringer; Doolins of Oklahoma; Gilda; Human Duplicators, The; Nevadan, The; Paths of Glory; Seventh Cross, The; Stranger Wore a Gun, The; Two Weeks in Another Town

MacVittie, Bruce: Stonewall

Macy, Bill: Bad Medicine; Death at Love House; Doctor, The; Jerk, The; Late Show, The; Movers and Shakers; My Favorite Year; Oh! Calcutta!; Serial; Sibling Rivalry

Macy, William H.: Above Suspicion (1994); Air Force One; Andersonville; Being Human; Benny & Joon; Boogie Nights; Civil Action, A; Client, The; Con, The; Down Periscope; Fargo; Ghosts of Mississippi; Happy, Texas; Heart of Justice; Homicide; Magnolia; Mr. Holland's Opus; Murder in the First; Mystery Men; Oleanna; Pleasantville; Psycho (1998); Searching for Bobby Fischer; Slight Case of Murder, A; Wag the Dog; Water Engine, The

Madaras, Josef: Red and the White, The

Madden, Ciaran: Married Man, A

Madden, Dave: Eat My Dust

Madden, Donald: Life on the Mississippi

Madden, Jeanne: Stage Struck (1936)

Madden, John: Little Giants; P.K. & the Kid

Madden, Peter: Loneliness of the Long Distance Runner, The; Secret Agent (TV Series)

Maddern, Victor: Carrington, V. C.

Maddox, Billy: Adventures of Young Brave, The

Madigan, Amy: Alamo Bay; Ambush Murders, The; Bright Shining Lie, A; Dark Half, The; Female Perversions; Field of Dreams; Love Child; Love Letters; Nowhere to Hide; Prince of Pennsylvania; Riders of the Purple Sage; Roe vs. Wade; Streets of Fire; Twice in a Lifetime; Uncle Buck

Madigan, Reese: American Shaolin: King of the Kickboxers II

Madio, James: Basketball Diaries, The

Madison, Elina: L.I.P. Service

Madison, Gloria: Native Son (1950)

Madison, Guy: Bang Bang Kid, The; Bullwhip; Drums in the Deep South; Final Defeat, The; Pacific Connection, The; Since You Went Away; This Man Can't Die; Till the End of Time

Madison, Mae: Big Stampede, The

Madison, Rock: Man Beast

Madoc, Philip: Very British Coup, A

Madonna: Bloodhounds of Broadway; Blue in the Face; Body of Evidence; Dangerous Game, A (1993); Desperately Seeking Susan; Dick Tracy (1990); Evita; Four Rooms; League of Their Own, A; Next Best Thing, The; Shanghai Surprise; Truth or Dare; Who's That Girl

Madorsky, Bryan: Parents

Madou, Malou: Man Bites Dog

Madruga, Teresa: In the White City

Madsen, Michael: Agent of Death; Almost Blue; Beyond the Law (1992); Dead Connection; Detour (1999); Diary of a Serial Killer; Donnie Brasco; Executive Target; Fatal Instinct (1992); Free Willy; Free Willy 2: The Adventure Home; Getaway, The (1994); House in the Hills, A; Kill Me Again; Last Days of Frankie the Fly, The; Love to Kill; Man with a Gun; Money for Nothing; Mulholland Falls; Red Line; Reservoir Dogs; Species; Species II; Straight Tale; Supreme Sanction; Surface to Air; Thelma & Louise; Trouble Bound; Winner, The; Wyatt Earp

Madsen, Virginia: Becoming Colette; Bitter Vengeance; Blue Tiger; Candyman (1992); Caroline at Midnight; Creator; Electric Dreams; Fire with Fire; Gotham; Hearst and Davies Affair, The; Heart of Dixie, The; Highlander 2: The Quickening; Hot Spot; Hot to Trot; Ironclads; Just Your Luck; Linda; Long Gone; Love Kills; Modern Girls; Prophecy, The (1995); Slam Dance; Third Degree Burn; Victim of Love; Zombie High

Maelen, Christian: I Think I Do

Maes, Michele: Eighth Day, The

Maestro, Mia: Tango

Maffay, Peter: Lethal Obsession

Maffei, Robert: Magic Christmas Tree, The

Maffia, Roma: Defenders, The; Disclosure; Mistrial; Nick of Time; Route 9

Magalhaeds, Yona: Black God (White Devil)

Magall, Macha: S.S. Hell Camp

Magda, Cass: Hawk's Vengeance

Magee, Patrick: And Now the Screaming Starts; Anzio; Asylum (1972); Barry Lyndon; Black Cat, The (1981); Clockwork Orange, A; Cromwell; Dementia 13; King Lear (1971); King Lear (1988); Lady Ice; Last Days of Man on Earth, The; Luther; Marat/Sade; Masque of the Red Death, The (1964); Rough Cut; Seance on a Wet Afternoon; Skull, The; Telefon; Very Edge, The; Young Winston

Mager, Jad: Blue Flame

Maggart, Brandon: Christmas Evil

Maggio, Pupella: Amarcord

Maggiorani, Lamberto: Bicycle Thief, The

Magimel, Benoit: Les Voleurs; Single Girl; Thieves (Les Voleurs)

Magnani, Anna: Amore (1948); Bellissima; Fugitive Kind, The; Golden Coach, The; Laugh for Joy (Passionate Thief (1954)); Mamma Roma; Open City; Passionate Thief, The (1961); Rose Tattoo, The

Magnier, Pierre: Cyrano de Bergerac (1925)

Magnuson, Ann: Before and After; Checking Out; Love at Large; Making Mr. Right; Night in the Life of Jimmy Reardon, A; Sleepwalker; Small Soldiers

Magon, Leslie: Unapproachable, The

Magri, Mike: Winterbeast

Maguire, Mary: Mysterious Mr. Moto

Maguire, Tobey: Cider House Rules, The; Fear and Loathing in Las Vegas; Ice Storm, The; Joyride (1997); Pleasantville; Revenge of the Red Baron; Wonder Boys

Mahaffey, Valerie: National Lampoon's Senior Trip; They (They Watch); Women of Valor

Mahal, Taj: Outside Ozona; Rock and Roll Circus, The; Sounder

Mahan, Larry: Good Old Boys, The

Maharis, George: Desperados, The; Land Raiders; Murder on Flight 502; Return to Fantasy Island; Sword and the Sorcerer, The

Maher, Bill: Cannibal Women in the Avocado Jungle of Death; Club Med; House II: The Second Story; Pizza Man

Maher, Joseph: Evil That Men Do, The; Frankenweenie; Funny Farm; Going Ape!; I.Q.; Under the Rainbow

Maheu, Gilles: Night Zoo

Mahler, Bruce: Funland; Police Academy II: Their First Assignment

Mahmud-Bey, Shiek: Night Falls on Manhattan

Mahoney, Jock: Away all Boats; Battle Hymn; Cow Town; Glory Stompers, The; Land Unknown, The; Nevadan, The; Rim of the Canyon; Their Only Chance; Time to Love and a Time to Die, A

Mahoney, John: Article 99; Barton Fink; Dinner at Eight (1990); Frantic (1988); Hudsucker Proxy, The; Image, The; In the Line of Fire; Love Hurts; Moonstruck; Primal Fear;

Mareze, Janie: La Chienne

Margo: Behind the Rising Sun; Lost Horizon; Who's Got the Action?; Winterset

Margolin, Janet: David and Lisa; Enter Laughing; Game of Love, The; Last Embrace, The; Morituri; Planet Earth; Pray for the Wildcats; Take the Money and Run

Margolin, Stuart: Class; Fine Mess, A; Futureworld; Guilty by Suspicion; Iron Eagle II; Running Hot; Women of the Prehistoric Planet

Margolis, Mark: End of Days; Pi; Where the Rivers Flow North

Margolis, Miriam: End of Days

Margolyes, Miriam: Age of Innocence, The; Different for Girls; Ed & His Dead Mother; James and the Giant Peach; William Shakespeare's Romeo and Juliet

Margulies, David: Last Breath; Out on a Limb (1992)

Margulies, Julianna: Newton Boys, The; Paradise Road; Price Above Rubies, A; Traveller

Margulies, Lynne: Aftermath, The

Marian, Ferdinand: Jud Suss

Marie, Anne-Laure: Aviator's Wife, The

Marie, Baby Rose: International House

Marie, Constance: My Family; Selena

Marie, Jeanne: International House; Young Nurses in Love

Marie, Lisa: Frogs for Snakes

Marie, Rose: Dick Van Dyke Show, The (TV Series); Lunch Wagon; Witchboard

Marielle, Jean-Pierre: One Wild Moment; Tous les Matins du Monde; Uranus

Marienthal, Eli: Slums of Beverly Hills; Unlikely Angel

Marietta: Nudes on the Moon

Marin, Christian: Story of a Three Day Pass, The

Marin, Jacque: Herbie Goes to Monte Carlo

Marin, Richard "Cheech": After Hours; Born in East L.A.; Charlie's Ghost; Cisco Kid, The; Courtyard, The; Desperado; Echo Park; Far Out Man; From Dusk Till Dawn; Great White Hype, The; Million to Juan, A; Paulie; Ring of the Musketeer; Rude Awakening (1989); Shrimp on the Barbie; Tin Cup

Marin, Rikki: Gas Pump Girls; Things Are Tough All Over

Marinaro, Ed: Dancing with Danger; Diamond Trap, The; Game of Love, The; Gift of Love: The Daniel Huffman Story; Lethal Lolita—Amy Fisher: My Story

Marino, Dan: Ace Ventura: Pet Detective

Marion, Beth: Between Men

Marion, George F.: Anna Christie (1922)

Marioni, Saverio: Padre Padrone

Maris, Mona: Camila (1984); Falcón in Mexico, The

Marius, Robert: Triple Impact

Markel, Daniel: Dark Angel: The Ascent

Marken, Jane: Crazy For Love

Markes, Tony: In the Aftermath: Angels Never Sleep

Markey, Enid: Civilization; Tarzan of the Apes

Markham, Barbara: House of Whipcord

Markham, David: Richard's Things

Markham, Kiki: Two English Girls

Markham, Monte: Defense Play; Ginger in the Morning; Guns of the Magnificent Seven; Hot Pursuit; Hour of the Gun, The; Hustling; Jake Speed; Off the Wall; Piranha (1995)

Markov, Margaret: Hot Box, The

Marks, Alfred: Valentino

Marks, Shae: Day of the Warrior; Return to Savage Beach

Markus, Winnie: Mozart Story, The

Marlaud, Philippe: Aviator's Wife, The

Marley, Ben: Mosaic Project, The; Pride of Jesse Hallman, The

Marley, Cedella: Joey Breaker

Marley, John: Amateur, The (1982); Blade (1973); Car, The; Deathdream; Framed (1975); Glitter Dome, The; Godfather, The; Greatest, The; It Lives Again; Joe Louis Story, The; Jory; Kid Vengeance; Love Story; Mother Lode; On the Edge; Robbers of the Sacred Mountain; Threshold; Tribute; Utilities

Marlier, Carla: Melodie en Sous-Sol (The Big Grab) (Any Number Can Win)

Marlowe, Alan: Deadly Vengeance

Marlowe, Hugh: Bugles in the Afternoon; Casanova's Big Night; Castle of Evil; Day the Earth Stood Still, The; Earth vs. the Flying Saucers; Mrs. Parkington; Monkey Business

(1952); Night and the City (1950); Rawhide (1951); Twelve O'Clock High; World Without End

Marlowe, Linda: Green Man, The

Marlowe, Scott: Journey into Fear (1975)

Marly, Florence: Dr. Death: Seeker of Souls; Planet of Blood (Queen of Blood)

Marmont, Percy: Lisbon; Rich and Strange; Secret Agent, The; Young and Innocent

Marnhout, Heidi: Phantasm IV: Oblivion

Maroney, Kelli: Chopping Mall; Face Down; Night of the Comet

Maross, Joe: Salzburg Connection, The

Marotte, Carl: Breaking All the Rules; Twists of Terror

Marquand, Christian: And God Created Woman (1957); Flight of the Phoenix, The

Marquand, Tina: Game Is Over, The; Texas Across the River

Marquardt, Peter: El Mariachi

Marques, Maria Elena: Pearl, The

Marquette, Chris: Noah

Marquette, Ron: Deadly Past; Public Access; Red Shoe Diaries 5: Weekend Pass

Marquez, Esteban: Ascent to Heaven (Mexican Bus Ride)

Marquez, Evaristo: Burn!

Marriott, David: Operation War Zone

Marriott, Moore: Frozen Limits, The

Marrow, Jeff: Story of Ruth, The

Mars, Kenneth: Apple Dumpling Gang Rides Again, The; Beer; For Keeps; Illegally Yours; Police Academy 6: City Under Siege; Producers, The; What's Up, Doc?; Yellowbeard; Young Frankenstein

Marsac, Maurice: Tarzan and the Trappers

Marsden, James: Disturbing Behavior; Gossip; Public Enemy #1

Marsden, Jimmy: No Dessert Dad Until You Mow the Lawn

Marsh, Garry: Just William's Luck

Marsh, Jean: Changeling, The; Danny, The Champion of the World; Dark Places; Fatherland; Goliath Awaits; Return to Oz; Upstairs, Downstairs; Willow

Marsh, Joan: Charlie Chan on Broadway; Road to Zanzibar

Marsh, Mae: Avenging Conscience, The; Birth of a Nation, The; D. W. Griffith Triple Feature; Home, Sweet Home (1914); Intolerance; Judith of Bethulia; Mother and the Law, The; Tall Men, The; Three Godfathers, The; While the City Sleeps; White Rose, The (1923)

Marsh, Marian: Black Room, The (1935); Crime and Punishment (1935); Svengali (1931); When's Your Birthday?

Marsh, Michele: Evil Town

Marsh, William: Proteus

Marshal, Alan: Conquest; House on Haunted Hill; Howards of Virginia, The; Lydia; Night Must Fall; Tom, Dick and Harry; White Cliffs of Dover, The

Marshal, Dodie: Easy Come, Easy Go

Marshall, Brenda: Background to Danger; Captains of the Clouds; Footsteps in the Dark; Smiling Ghost, The

Marshall, Bryan: Hot Target; Persuasion (1971); Return to Snowy River, Part II

Marshall, Clark: Sidewalks of New York

Marshall, Connie: Mother Wore Tights

Marshall, Don: Terminal Island

Marshall, E. G.: Absolute Power; Bridge at Remagen, The; Cash McCall; Chase, The (1966); Compulsion; Consenting Adults (1992); Defenders; Eleanor: First Lady of the World; Interiors; Ironclads; Kennedy (TV Miniseries); Lazarus Syndrome, The; Littlest Angel, The; Miss Evers' Boys; Mountain, The; My Chauffeur; National Lampoon's Christmas Vacation; Nixon; Poppy Is Also a Flower, The; Power (1986); Pursuit of Happiness, The; Silver Chalice, The; 13 Rue Madeleine; Tommyknockers, The; Two Evil Eyes; 12 Angry Men (1957)

Marshall, Everett: Dixiana

Marshall, Garry: League of Their Own, A; Lost in America; Never Been Kissed; Soapdish; Twilight of the Golds, The

Marshall, Georges: French Way, The

Marshall, Herbert: Black Jack; Blonde Venus; Crack-Up; Enchanted Cottage, The; Five Weeks in a Balloon; Fly, The (1958); Foreign Correspondent; Letter, The; List of Adrian Messenger, The; Little Foxes, The; Mad About Music; Midnight Lace; Moon and Sixpence, The; Murder; Painted Veil, The; Razor's Edge, The (1946); Riptide; Secret Garden, The

(1949); Stage Struck (1958); Underworld Story; Virgin Queen, The; When Ladies Meet; Woman Rebels, A

Marshall, James: Don't Do It; Few Good Men, A; Gladiator (1992); Soccer Dog: The Movie; Ticket, The; Vibrations

Marshall, Ken: Feds; Krull; Tilt

Marshall, Marion: I Was a Male War Bride

Marshall, Mike: La Grande Vadrouille

Marshall, Nancy: Frankenstein Meets the Space Monster

Marshall, Patricia: Good News

Marshall, Paula: Hellraiser 3: Hell on Earth; That Old Feeling

Marshall, Penny: Challenge of a Lifetime; Hard Way, The (1991); Movers and Shakers

Marshall, Peter: Guide for the Married Woman, A

Marshall, Ruth: Love and Human Remains

Marshall, Sarah: Lord Love a Duck

Marshall, Sean: Pete's Dragon

Marshall, Trudy: Married Too Young

Marshall, Tully: Ball of Fire; Cat and the Canary, The (1927); Covered Wagon, The; Hurricane Express; Intolerance; Night of Terror; Red Dust; Two-Fisted Law

Marshall, William: Blacula; Dinosaur Valley Girls; Othello (1982); Scream, Blacula, Scream; Something of Value; That Brennan Girl

Marshall, Zena: Terrornauts, The

Marsillach, Cristina: Every Time We Say Goodbye; Terror at the Opera

Marston, John: Son of Kong, The

Marta, Darcy: Living End, The

Martel, Chris: Gruesome Twosome

Martel, June: Forlorn River

Martel, Wendy: Sorority House Massacre

Martell, Donna: Hills of Utah, The; Project Moon Base

Martell, Peter: Cobra, The (1967)

Martellis, Cynthia: Zooman

Marti, Luisito: Nueba Yol

Martin, Andra: Thing that Couldn't Die, The

Martin, Andrea: Believe; Boris and Natasha; Harrison Bergeron; Rude Awakening (1989); Stepping Out; Ted & Venus; Too Much Sun; Wag the Dog; Worth Winning

Martin, Anne-Marie: Boogens, The; Hammered: The Best of Sledge

Martin, Barney: Arthur 2: On the Rocks; Pucker Up and Bark Like a Dog

Martin, Bill: Television Parts Home Companion

Martin, Christopher: Class Act; House Party 2; House Party 3

Martin, Crispin: Ali Baba and the Forty Thieves; Weekend in Havana

Martin, Damon: Amityville 1992: It's About Time; Ghoulies II

Martin, Dan: Laurel Avenue

Martin, Dean: Airport; All in a Night's Work; Ambushers, The; Artists and Models; At War with the Army; Bandolero!; Bells Are Ringing; Caddy, The; Cannonball Run; Cannonball Run II; Career; Five Card Stud; Four for Texas; Hollywood or Bust; Jumping Jacks; Kiss Me, Stupid; Murderers' Row; My Friend Irma; Ocean's Eleven; Rio Bravo; Robin & the Seven Hoods; Rough Night in Jericho; Showdown (1973); Some Came Running; Sons of Katie Elder, The; Texas Across the River; Toys in the Attic; Who's Got the Action?; Young Lions, The

Martin, Dean Paul: Backfire (1987); Heart Like a Wheel; Misfits of Science; Players

Martin, Deena: Swingers

Martin, Dewey: Big Sky, The; Flight to Fury; Land of the Pharaohs; Men of the Fighting Lady; Savage Sam

Martin, Dick: Carbon Copy

Martin, Duane: Above the Rim; Woo

Martin, D'Urville: Black Caesar; Blind Rage; Boss; Dolemite; Final Comedown, The; Hell Up in Harlem; Sheba Baby

Martin, George: Drunks

Martin, Jared: Quiet Cool; Twin Sitters

Martin, Jean: Battle of Algiers

Martin, Jill: Hawk of the Wilderness

Martin, John: Black Roses

Martin, Keil: Hill Street Blues (TV Series)

Martin, Kellie: Matinee

Martin, Lori: Cape Fear (1962)

Martin, Maribel: Blood Spattered Bride, The

Martin, Marion: Sinners in Paradise; They Got Me Covered

Martin, Marji: Hollywood Harry

Martin, Mary: Birth of the Blues; Night and Day (1946); Peter Pan (1960); Rhythm on the River

Martin, Millicent: Alfie; Stop the World I Want to Get Off

Martin, Nan: Doctor Detroit; For Love of Ivy; Golden Honeymoon, The; King Richard II; Other Side of the Mountain, Part II, The; Toys in the Attic

Martin, Pamela Sue: Buster and Billie; Cry in the Wild, A; Eye of the Demon; Girls of Huntington House; Lady in Red

Martin, Richard: Arizona Ranger; Brothers in the Saddle; Dynamite Pass; Gun Smugglers; Guns of Hate; Hot Lead; Marine Raiders; Mysterious Desperado; Rider from Tucson; Road Agent; Rustlers, The

Martin, Ross: Colossus of New York, The; Dead Heat on a Merry-Go-Round; Experiment in Terror; More Wild Wild West; Wild Wild West, The (TV series); Wild Wild West Revisited, The

Martin, Rudolf: Fall

Martin, Sallie: Say Amen, Somebody

Martin, Sandy: Scalpel; Vendetta (1985)

Martin, Steve: All of Me; And the Band Played On; Bowfinger; Dead Men Don't Wear Plaid; Dirty Rotten Scoundrels; Father of the Bride (1991); Father of the Bride Part II; Grand Canyon; Houseslitter; Jerk, The; Joe Gould's Secret; Kids Are Alright, The; L.A. Story; Leap of Faith; Little Shop of Horrors (1986); Lonely Guy, The; Man with Two Brains, The; Mixed Nuts; Movers and Shakers; Muppet Movie, The; My Blue Heaven; Out-of-Towners, The (1999); Parenthood; Pennies from Heaven; Planes, Trains and Automobiles; Roxanne; Sgt. Bilko; Simple Twist of Fate, A; Spanish Prisoner, The; Three Amigos

Martin, Strother: Attack!; Ballad of Cable Hogue, The; Better Late than Never; Brotherhood of Satan; Cool Hand Luke; Great Scout and Cathouse Thursday, The; Hannie Caulder; Hard Times; Love and Bullets; Magnetic Monster, The; Man Who Shot Liberty Valance, The; Nightwing; Pocket Money; Rooster Cogburn; Shenandoah; Slap Shot; Talion; Up in Smoke; Wild Bunch, The

Martin, Todd: Finger on the Trigger

Martin, Tony: Big Store, The; Casbah; Easy to Love; Here Come the Girls; Hit the Deck; Two Tickets to Broadway

Martindale, Margo: Critical Care

Martine, Daniel: Cause of Death

Martinelli, Elsa: Blood and Roses; Hatari!; Madigan's Millions; Maroc 7; Oldest Profession, The; Tenth Victim, The; Trial, The (1963)

Martines, Alessandra: Les Misérables (1995)

Martinez, A: Cherokee Kid, The; Double Tap; Hunt for the Night Stalker; Last Rites; One Night Stand (1995); Powwow Highway; Where's the Money, Noreen?

Martinez, Fele: Lovers of the Arctic Circle; Open Your Eyes; Thesis

Martinez, Jorge: Catch the Heat

Martinez, Mario Ivan: Like Water for Chocolate

Martinez, Olivier: Chambermaid on the *Titanic*, The; Horseman on the Roof, The; IP5: The Island of Pachyderms; Mon Homme (My Man)

Martinez, Patrice: Three Amigos

Martinez, Reinol: El Mariachi

Martinez, Vanessa: Limbo

Martinez, Vincent: School of Flesh

Martino, John: Truckstop Women

Martins, Camilla: Zero Kelvin

Martling, Jackie: Ghoul School

Martyn, Greg: Ellis Island

Marut, Marc: Paperboy, The

Marvin, Lee: Attack!; Bad Day at Black Rock; Big Heat, The; Big Red One, The; Cat Ballou; Comancheros, The; Death Hunt; Delta Force, The; Dirty Dozen, The; Dirty Dozen, The: The Next Mission; Dog Day; Donovan's Reef; Gorilla at Large; Gorky Park; Great Scout and Cathouse Thursday, The; Gun Fury; Hangman's Knot; Hell in the Pacific; I Died a Thousand Times; Killers, The; Klansman, The; Man Who Shot Liberty Valance, The; Meanest Men in the West, The; Monte Walsh; Not as a Stranger; Paint Your Wagon; Pete Kelly's Blues; Pocket Money; Point Blank (1967); Prime Cut; Professionals, The; Raintree County; Sergeant Ryker; Shack-Out on 101; Ship of Fools; Shout at the Devil; Stranger Wore a Gun, The; Twilight Zone, The (TV series); Wild One, The

Marwa, Emil: East Is East

Marx Brothers, The: Animal Crackers; At the Circus; Big Store, The; Cocoanuts; Day at the Races, A; Duck Soup; Go West; Horse Feathers; Love Happy; Monkey Business (1931); Night at the Opera, A; Night in Casablanca, A; Room Service

Marx, Groucho: Copacabana; Double Dynamite; Girl in Every Port, A (1952); Mr. Music; You Bet Your Life (TV Series)

Marx, Harpo: Stage Door Canteen

Marzio, Dulio: Two to Tango

Masak, Ron: Harper Valley P.T.A.

Mascarino, Pierrino: Clockmaker (1998)

Mascolo, Joseph: Shaft's Big Score!

Masé, Marino: Commandos; Les Carabiniers

Mashkov, Vladimir: Thief, The (1997)

Masina, Giulietta: Ginger and Fred; Il Bidone; Juliet of the Spirits; La Strada; Madwoman of Chaillot, The; Nights of Cabiria; Variety Lights; White Sheik, The

Maskell, Virginia: Only Two Can Play

Mason, Connie: Blood Feast

Mason, Eric: Kiss of the Tarantula

Mason, Hilary: Dolls; Meridian (Kiss of the Beast); Robot Jox

Mason, Jackie: Caddyshack II; Jerk, The

Mason, James: Assisi Underground, The; Autobiography of a Princess; Bad Man's River; Bloodline; Blue Max, The; Botany Bay; Boys from Brazil, The; Caught (1949); Cold Sweat (1970); Cross of Iron; Dangerous Summer, A; Desert Fox, The; Desert Rats, The; Destructors, The; East Side, West Side; 11 Harrowhouse; Evil Under the Sun; Fall of the Roman Empire, The; ffolkes; Five Fingers; Forever Darling; Georgy Girl; Heaven Can Wait (1978); High Command, The; Hotel Reserve; Inside Out (1975); Ivanhoe (1982); Jesus of Nazareth; Journey to the Center of the Earth (1959); Julius Caesar (1953); Kidnap Syndicate, The; Last of Sheila, The; Lolita (1962); Lord Jim; Mackintosh Man, The; Madame Bovary (1949); Man in Grey, The; Mandingo; Mill on the Floss, The; Murder by Decree; Night Has Eyes, The; North by Northwest; Odd Man Out; Pandora and the Flying Dutchman; Prince Valiant (1954); Prisoner of Zenda, The (1952); Salem's Lot; Seventh Veil, The; Shooting Party, The; Star Is Born, A (1954); 20,000 Leagues Under the Sea (1954); Verdict, The; Voyage of the Damned; Water Babies, The; Wicked Lady, The (1945); Yin and Yang of Mr. Go, The

Mason, LeRoy: Apache Rose; Federal Operator 99; Helldorado (1946); Hidden Valley Outlaws; Mojave Firebrand; Painted Stallion, The; Rainbow Valley; Rocky Mountain Rangers; Santa Fe Stampede; Song of Nevada; Texas Terror; When a Man Sees Red; Wyoming Outlaw

Mason, Madison: Dangerously Close

Mason, Marlyn: Christina

Mason, Marsha: Audrey Rose; Blume in Love; Broken Trust (1995); Chapter Two; Cheap Detective, The; Cinderella Liberty; Dinner at Eight (1990); Drop Dead Fred; Goodbye Girl, The; Heartbreak Ridge; I Love Trouble; Image, The; Lois Gibbs and the Love Canal; Max Dugan Returns; Nick of Time; Only When I Laugh; Promises in the Dark; Stella (1990); Two Days in the Valley

Mason, Pamela: Navy vs. the Night Monsters, The

Mason, Tom: F/X 2: The Deadly Art of Illusion; Men Don't Leave; Return of the Man from U.N.C.L.E., The

Mason, Vivian: Lost Planet, The

Massari, Lea: Allonsonfan; And Hope to Die; Christ Stopped at Eboli; L'Aventura; Les Choses de la Vie (Things in Life, The); Les Rendez-Vous D'Anna; Murmur of the Heart; Story of a Love Story; Vengeance

Massen, Osa: Background to Danger; Iceland; Jack London; Master Race, The; My Love for Yours (Honeymoon in Bali); Rocketship X-M; Woman's Face, A; You'll Never Get Rich

Massey, Anna: Angels and Insects; Corn Is Green, The (1979); Déjà Vu (1998); Five Days One Summer; Frenzy; Haunted; Peeping Tom; Sakharov; Sweet William; Vault of Horror

Massey, Athena: Shadow of a Scream; Undercover (1995); Unspeakable, The; Virtual Combat

Massey, Daniel: Incredible Sarah, The; Intimate Contact; Love with a Perfect Stranger; Star! (1968); Vault of Horror

Massey, Dick: Commitments, The

Massey, Edith: Desperate Living; Female Trouble; Multiple Maniacs; Mutants in Paradise; Pink Flamingos; Polyester

Massey, Gina: Thrillkill

Massey, Ilona: Balalaika; Frankenstein Meets the Wolf Man; Holiday in Mexico; Invisible Agent; Melody Master (The Great Awakening) (New Wine); Northwest Outpost; Rosalie

Massey, Raymond: Abe Lincoln in Illinois; Action in the North Atlantic; Arsenic and Old Lace; Chain Lightning; David and Bathsheba; Desert Song, The; Desperate Journey; Drums; East of Eden (1955); Fountainhead, The; 49th Parallel, The; Hurricane, The (1937); Naked and the Dead, The; Old Dark House, The (1932); Omar Khayyam; Possessed (1947); President's Plane Is Missing, The; Prisoner of Zenda, The (1937); Reap the Wild Wind; Santa Fe Trail; Scarlet Pimpernel, The (1934); Speckled Band, The; Things to Come; Woman in the Window

Massi, Mark: Silverlake Life: The View from Here

Massie, Paul: Sapphire

Massine, Leonide: Tales of Hoffman

Master P: Foolish; I Got the Hook Up

Masters, Ben: Celebrity; Deliberate Stranger, The; Dream Lover (1986); Key Exchange; Making Mr. Right; Running Mates (1992)

Masterson, Chase: In a Moment of Passion; Married People, Single Sex

Masterson, Fay: Avenging Angel, The (1995); Cops and Robbersons; Man without a Face, The; Power of One, The

Masterson, Mary Stuart: Amazing Stories (TV Series); Bad Girls (1994); Bed of Roses; Benny & Joon; Chances Are; Digging to China; Fried Green Tomatoes; Funny About Love; Gardens of Stone; Heaven's Prisoners; Immediate Family; Lily Dale; Mad at the Moon; Married to It; My Little Girl; Radioland Murders; Some Kind of Wonderful

Masterson, Peter: Stepford Wives, The

Masterson, Rod: Delta Heat

Masterson, Valerie: Voyage en Douce

Mastrantonio, Mary Elizabeth: Abyss, The; Class Action; Color of Money, The; Consenting Adults (1992); Fools of Fortune; January Man, The; Limbo; Perfect Storm, The; Robin Hood: Prince of Thieves; Slam Dance; Three Wishes; Two Bits; White Sands; Witness Protection

Mastroglacomo, Gina: Tall, Dark and Deadly

Mastroianni, Chiara: Diary of a Seducer; Ma Saison Preferée; Nowhere; Three Lives and Only One Death

Mastroianni, Marcello: Allonsonfan; Beyond Obsession; Big Deal on Madonna Street; Blood Feud; City of Women; Dark Eyes; Diary of Forbidden Dreams; Divine Nymph, The; Divorce—Italian Style; 8 ½; Everybody's Fine; Fine Romance, A; Gabriela; Ginger and Fred; Henry IV; I Don't Want to Talk About It; La Dolce Vita; La Nuit de Varennes; Lunatics & Lovers; Macaroni; Marriage Italian Style; Massacre in Rome; Organizer, The; Poppy Is Also a Flower, The; Ready to Wear; Salut L'Artiste; Shoot Loud, Louder … I Don't Understand; Slightly Pregnant Man, A; Special Day, A; Stay as You Are; Tenth Victim, The; Three Lives and Only One Death; Used People; Very Private Affair, A; White Nights (1957); Wifemistress; Yesterday, Today and Tomorrow

Masur, Richard: Adam; Believers, The; Betrayal (1978); Burning Bed, The; Cast the First Stone; Encino Man; Fallen Angel; Far from Home; Fire Down Below; Flashback; Forget Paris; George McKenna Story, The; Head Office; Heartburn; Hiroshima; It (1991); License to Drive; Man without a Face, The; Mean Season, The; Mr. Horn; Multiplicity; My Girl; My Girl 2; My Science Project; Rent-a-Cop; Risky Business; Shoot to Kill; Six Degrees of Separation; Third Degree Burn; Walker; Who'll Stop the Rain

Matahi: Tabu

Matarazzo, Heather: Deli, The; Welcome to the Dollhouse

Mateos, Julian: Four Rode Out; Hellbenders, The

Materhofer, Ferdinand: Orphan Boy of Vienna, An

Mathé, Edouard: Vampires, The (1915) (Les Vampires)

Mather, Aubrey: House of Fear; Undying Monster, The

Mathers, James: Dr. Jekyll's Dungeon of Death

Mathers, Jerry: Trouble with Harry, The

Matheson, Hans: Les Misérables (1998)

Matheson, Michelle: Howling VI: The Freaks

Matheson, Tim: Animal House; Best Legs in the 8th Grade, The; Black Sheep; Buried Alive (1990); Buried Alive II; Dreamer; Drop Dead Fred; Eye of the Demon; Fletch; Impulse (1984); Listen to Your Heart; Little Sex, A; Little White

Neck, The; River of Diamonds; Secret Diary of Sigmund Freud, The; Vampire Happening

Mayniel, Juliette: Eyes Without a Face; Les Cousins

Maynor, Virginia: Man Beast

Mayo, Christine: Shock, The (1923)

Mayo, Virginia: Along the Great Divide; Best Years of Our Lives, The; Captain Horatio Hornblower; Castle of Evil; Devil's Canyon; Flame and the Arrow, The; French Quarter; Jack London; Kid from Brooklyn, The; King Richard and the Crusaders; Midnight Witness; Out of the Blue; Pearl of the South Pacific; Princess and the Pirate, The; Secret Life of Walter Mitty, The; Silver Chalice, The; Song Is Born, A; West Point Story, The; White Heat; Wonder Man

Mayron, Melanie: Boss' Wife, The; Checking Out; Girlfriends; Missing; My Blue Heaven; Ordeal in the Arctic; Sticky Fingers

Mays, Terra: Zoo Radio

Maza, Bob: Fringe Dwellers, The

Mazar, Debi: Bad Love; Beethoven's 2nd; Empire Records; Frogs for Snakes; Girl 6; Inside Monkey Zetterland; Meet Wally Sparks; Money for Nothing; Nowhere; She's So Lovely; So I Married an Axe Murderer; Space Truckers; Trouble on the Corner

Mazur, Monet: Raging Angels

Mazurki, Mike: Blood Alley; Challenge to Be Free; Four for Texas; Hell Ship Mutiny; Incredible Rocky Mountain Race, The; Magic of Lassie, The; Man with Bogart's Face, The; Mob Boss; Neptune's Daughter; Night and the City (1950); Noose Hangs High, The; Shanghai Gesture, The; Some Like It Hot; Unconquered

Mazursky, Paul: Alex in Wonderland; Enemies—A Love Story; Faithful; First Works, Volumes 1 & 2; Into the Night; Man, a Woman and a Bank, A; Man Trouble; Miami Rhapsody; Scenes from the Class Struggle in Beverly Hills; Two Days in the Valley; Why Do Fools Fall In Love

Mazzarelli, Carmelo Di: L'America

Mazzello, Joseph: Cure, The; Jurassic Park; Radio Flyer; River Wild, The; Simon Birch; Star Kid; Three Wishes

MC Lyte: Fly by Night

McAfee, Anndi: Ice Cream Man

McAleer, Desmond: Four Days in July

McAlister, Jennifer: Serial

McAllister, Shawn: Looking for Trouble

McAllister, Ward: Trapped by the Mormons

McAnally, Ray: Danny Boy (1982); Death of Adolf Hitler, The; Empire State; Great Expectations (1989); Jack the Ripper (1988); Mission, The; My Left Foot; No Surrender; Taffin; Very British Coup, A; We're No Angels (1989)

McAndrew, Marianne: Bat People; Hello, Dolly!; Seven Minutes, The

McArdle, John: Gallowglass

McArthur, Alex: Devil in the Flesh (1998); Kiss the Girls; Ladykiller (1996); Perfect Alibi; Race for Glory; Rampage; Sharon's Secret; Urge to Kill

McAteer, Desmond: Butterfly Kiss

McAuley, Annie: Recruits

McAvoy, May: Ben-Hur (1926); Jazz Singer, The (1927); Lady Windermere's Fan

McBain, Diane: Donner Pass: The Road to Survival; Parrish; Spinout

McBain, Robert: Deadline (1988)

McBeath, Tom: Quarantine

McBee, Deron Michael: In the Time of Barbarians; Killing Zone, The

McBride, Alex: Rats

McBride, Chi: Cosmic Slop; Mercury Rising

McBroom, Marcia: Beyond the Valley of the Dolls

McCabe, Ruth: Snapper, The

McCabe, Tony: Something Weird

McCafferty, John: Deathrow Gameshow

McCaffrey, James: Truth About Cats and Dogs, The

McCain, Frances Lee: Gremlins; Lookalike, The; Question of Faith; Real Life; Scandal in a Small Town; Single Bars, Single Women

McCall, Katherine: Crystal Force

McCall, Mitzi: Opposite Sex (And How to Live with Them), The (1993)

McCalla, Irish: Hands of a Stranger; She Demons

McCatlany, Holt: Search for One-Eye Jimmy, The

McCallister, Lon: Big Cat, The; Red House, The; Story of Seabiscuit, The

McCallum, David: Around the World Under the Sea; Deathgame; Haunting of Morella, The; King Solomon's Treasure; Man from U.N.C.L.E., The (TV Series); Night to Remember, A (1958); Outer Limits, The (TV Series); Return of the Man from U.N.C.L.E., The; She Waits; Terminal Choice; Watcher in the Woods, The

McCambridge, Mercedes: All the King's Men; Cimarron (1960); Deadly Sanctuary; Girls of Huntington House; Johnny Guitar; 99 Women; President's Plane Is Missing, The; Who Is the Black Dahlia?

McCamey, Shane: Legacy for Leonette

McCamus, Tom: First Degree; Man in Uniform, A; Norman's Awesome Experience; Passion of Ayn Rand, The; Sweet Hereafter, The

McCann, Chuck: Cameron's Closet; C.H.O.M.P.S.; Dracula: Dead and Loving It; Hamburger—The Motion Picture; Heart Is a Lonely Hunter, The; Projectionist, The; Rosebud Beach Hotel, The (Nostell Hotel, The); They Went That-A-Way and That-A-Way; Thrashin'

McCann, Donal: Cal; Danny Boy (1982); Dead, The; December Bride; Hard Way, The (1979); Miracle, The (1990); Stealing Beauty

McCann, Sean: Mind Field; Tracked; Trial & Error (1992)

McCardle, Brian: Ghost and the Darkness, The

McCann, Tara: Dracula Rising

McCarren, Fred: Boogens, The; Red Flag: The Ultimate Game

McCarthy, Andrew: Beniker Gang, The; Beyond Redemption; Class; Club Extinction; Courtyard, The; Dead Funny; Dream Man; Escape Clause; Fresh Horses; Getting In; Heaven Help Us; I'm Losing You; Kansas; Less Than Zero; Mannequin (1987); Mrs. Parker and the Vicious Circle; Night of the Running Man; Only You (1991); Pretty in Pink; St. Elmo's Fire; Stag; Waiting for the Moon; Weekend at Bernie's; Weekend at Bernie's II; Year of the Gun

McCarthy, Holis: Civil War Diary

McCarthy, Jenny: Basketball

McCarthy, Kevin: Ace High; Addams Family Reunion; Annapolis Story, An; Buffalo Bill and the Indians; Dan Candy's Law (Alien Thunder); Dark Tower; Dead on the Money; Distinguished Gentleman, The; Duplicates; Final Approach; Ghoulies III; Greedy; Hero at Large; Hostage (1987); Hotel; Innerspace; Invasion of the Body Snatchers (1956); Invitation to Hell; Judicial Consent; Just Cause; LBJ: The Early Years; Love or Money?; Midnight Hour; Mirage (1965); My Tutor; Piranha (1978); Poor Little Rich Girl: The Barbara Hutton Story; Prize, The; Ratings Game, The; Rose and the Jackal, The; Rosie; Sleeping Car, The; Steal Big, Steal Little; Those Lips, Those Eyes; UHF

McCarthy, Lin: D.I., The

McCarthy, Nobu: Karate Kid Part II, The; Pacific Heights; Wash, The

McCarthy, Sheila: Beautiful Dreamers; Friends, Lovers & Lunatics; George's Island; I've Heard the Mermaids Singing; Lotus Eaters, The; Paradise (1991); Private Matter, A; Really Weird Tales; Stepping Out

McCarthy, Steven: Locked in Silence

McCarthy, Thomas: Saint Maybe

McCartney, Linda: Give My Regards to Broad Street

McCartney, Paul: Give My Regards to Broad Street

McCarty, John: Vampyre (1990)

McCary, Mary: French Line, The

McCary, Rod: Girl to Kill For, A; Through Naked Eyes

McCashin, Constance: Nightmare at Bittercreek; Obsessive Love

McClain, Cady: Simple Justice

McClanahan, Rue: Baby of the Bride; Modern Love; Pursuit of Happiness, The; This World, Then the Fireworks

McClanahan, Michael: Alice's Restaurant

McClarin, Curtis: Murder Without Motive

McCleery, Gary: Hard Choices

McCleery, Mick: Addicted to Murder; Twisted Tales

McCleister, Tom: Haunting of Sea Cliff Inn, The

McClements, Catherine: Desperate Prey

McClinton, Delbert: Kleptomania

McClory, Sean: Dead, The; Fools of Fortune; Island in the Sky; My Chauffeur

McCloskey, Leigh: Accidental Meeting; Cameron's Closet; Dirty Laundry; Double Revenge; Fraternity Vacation; Hamburger—The Motion Picture; Inferno (1980)

McClung, Susan: Birch Interval, The

McClure, Doug: At the Earth's Core; Deadman's Revenge; Enemy Below, The; Firebird 2015 AD; Gambler Returns, The; Luck of the Draw; Gidget; Hell Hounds of Alaska; House Where Evil Dwells, The; Land That Time Forgot, The; Maverick; Omega Syndrome; People That Time Forgot, The; Playmates; Rebels, The; Shenandoah; Tapeheads; Unforgiven, The (1960)

McClure, Marc: After Midnight; Grim Prairie Tales; I Wanna Hold Your Hand; Perfect Match, The; Strange Behavior; Superman; Superman III; Superman IV: The Quest for Peace

McClure, Shaler: Sgt. Kabukiman N.Y.P.D.

McClure, Tane: Lap Dancing; Scorned 2

McClurg, Edie: Cinderella (1985); Dance 'Til Dawn; Flubber; River Runs Through It, A; Stepmonster

McCluskey, Kenneth: Commitments, The

McCollum, Warren: Reefer Madness

McColm, Matt: Acts of Betrayal; Body Armor; Red Scorpion 2

McComas, Lorissa: Vamps: Deadly Dream Girls

McComass, Lorissa: Lap Dancing

McComb, Heather: New York Stories; Stay Tuned

McConaughey, Matthew: Amistad; Boys on the Side; Contact; EDtv; Larger than Life; Lone Star (1996); Newton Boys, The; Scorpion Spring; Texas Chainsaw Massacre: The Next Generation; Time to Kill, A (1996); U-571

McCord, Hugh: Blood, Guts, Bullets & Octane

McCord, Kent: Accidental Meeting; Illicit Behavior; Predator 2; Return of the Living Dead 3

McCorkindale, Don: Three Bullets for a Long Gun

McCormack, Catherine: Dancing at Lughnasa; Dangerous Beauty; Land Girls, The; Loaded; North Star (1996)

McCormack, Eric: Free Enterprise; Lost World, The (1992); Return to the Lost World

McCormack, Leigh: Long Day Closes, The

McCormack, Mary: Alarmist, The; Backfire (1994); Big Tease, The; Mystery, Alaska; Private Parts (1997)

McCormack, Patty: Adventures of Huckleberry Finn, The (1960); All Mine to Give; Awakening of Cassie, The; Bad Seed, The; Mommy; Mommy 2: Mommy's Day; Silent Predators

McCormick, Carolyn: You Know My Name

McCormick, Gilmer: Silent Night, Deadly Night

McCormick, Maureen: Idolmaker, The; Pony Express Rider; Take Down

McCormick, Michelle: Fatal Pulse

McCormick, Myron: Hustler, The; Jolson Sings Again; No Time for Sergeants

McCormick, Pat: Doin' Time; Mr. Horn; Rented Lips; Smokey and the Bandit; Smokey and the Bandit II; Smokey and the Bandit III

McCourt, Emer: Boston Kickout; London Kills Me; Riff-Raff (1992)

McCowen, Alec: Age of Innocence, The; Dedicated Man, A; Forever Young (1983); Frenzy; Hanover Street; Henry V (1989); Loneliness of the Long Distance Runner, The; Never Say Never Again; Night to Remember, A (1958); Personal Services; Stevie; Time Without Pity; Travels with My Aunt; Witches, The (1967)

McCoy, H.: Regeneration

McCoy, Matt: Bigfoot: The Unforgettable Encounter; Cool Surface, The; Dead On; Deepstar Six; Eyes of the Beholder; Fast Money (1996); Hand That Rocks the Cradle, The; Hard Bounty; Hard Drive; Little Bigfoot; Rent-A-Kid; Samurai Cowboy; Synapse; White Wolves: A Cry in the Wild II

McCoy, Steve: I Was a Teenage Zombie

McCoy, Sylvester: Dr. Who (TV series); Leapin' Leprechauns; Spellbreaker: Secret of the Leprechauns

McCoy, Tim: Aces and Eights; Arizona Bound; Below the Border; Bulldog Courage; Down Texas Way; End of the Trail; Fighting Shadows; Forbidden Trails; Ghost Patrol; Ghost Town Law; Gun Code; Gunman from Bodie; Riding Tornado, The; Roaring Guns; Run of the Arrow; Texas Cyclone; Traitor, The; Two-Fisted Law; West of the Law

McCoy, Tony: Bride of the Monster

McCracken, Jeff: Kent State; Running Brave; Summer of Fear

McCracken, Joan: Good News

McCrae, Scooter: Original Sins

McCrane, Paul: Fame; Portrait, The; Strapped

McCrary, Darius: Big Shots

McCrea, Jody: Beach Blanket Bingo; Beach Party; Cry Blood, Apache; Glory Stompers, The; Muscle Beach Party

McCrea, Joel: Barbary Coast, The; Bird of Paradise; Buffalo Bill; Come and Get It; Common Law, The; Cry Blood, Apache; Dead End; Foreign Correspondent; Four Faces West; Great Man's Lady, The; Great Moment, The; Interns Can't Take Money; Lost Squadron; More the Merrier, The; Most Dangerous Game, The; Oklahoman, The; Our Little Girl; Palm Beach Story, The; Primrose Path; Ramrod; Ride the High Country; South of St. Louis; Stars in My Crown; Sullivan's Travels; These Three; They Shall Have Music; Union Pacific; Virginian, The (1946)

McCrena, Brittany: Taxi Dancers

McCulloch, Bruce: KIds in the Hall: Brain Candy

McCulloch, Ian: Dr. Butcher, M.D. (Medical Deviate); Witching Time; Zombie

McCulloch, Kyle: Careful; Tales from the Gimli Hospital

McCullough, Julie: Big Bad Mama II; Round Trip to Heaven

McCullough, Lisa: Bloodsport II

McCullough, Suli: Don't Be a Menace to South Central while Drinking Your Juice in the 'Hood

McCurley, Matthew: North

McCurry, Natalie: Dead-End Drive-In

McCusker, Frank: Railway Station Man, The

McCutcheon, Bill: Tune in Tomorrow

McDade, Ross: This Is the Sea

McDaniel, Donna: Hollywood Hot Tubs

McDaniel, Hattie: Alice Adams; Bride Walks Out, The; George Washington Slept Here; Gone with the Wind; Great Lie, The; In This Our Life; Johnny Come Lately; Judge Priest; Murder by Television; Never Say Goodbye; Operator 13; Saratoga; Shining Hour, The; Shopworn Angel, The; Show Boat (1936); Since You Went Away; Zenobia

McDaniel, James: Road to Galveston, The

McDaniel, Tim: Ghost Chase

McDermott, Colleen: Night That Never Happened, The

McDermott, Dylan: Blue Iguana; Cowboy Way, The; Destiny Turns on the Radio; Fear Inside, The; Hamburger Hill; Hardware; Home for the Holidays (1995); In the Line of Fire; Into the Badlands; Jersey Girl; Miracle on 34th Street (1994); Neon Empire, The; Three to Tango; 'Til There Was You; Twister (1988); Where Sleeping Dogs Lie

McDermott, Hugh: Devil Girl from Mars; Pimpernel Smith; Seventh Veil, The

McDermott, Shane: Airborne

McDevitt, Ruth: Homebodies

McDiarmid, Ian: Chernobyl: The Final Warning; Sleepy Hollow; Star Wars: Episode I The Phantom Menace

McDonagh, Sean: Closer You Get, The

McDonald, Christopher: Benefit of the Doubt; Boys Next Door, The (1985); Chances Are; Conflict of Interest; Dirty Work (1998); Eighteenth Angel, The; Fair Game (1995); Fatal Exposure; Fatal Instinct (1993); Happy Gilmore; House Arrest; Lawn Dogs; Leave It to Beaver; Monkey Trouble; My Teacher's Wife; Paramedics; Playroom; Quiz Show; Rich Man's Wife, The; Skulls, The; SLC Punk; Terminal Velocity; Thelma & Louise; Tuskegee Airmen, The; Unforgettable

McDonald, Francis: Bad Lands (1939); Girl in Every Port, A (1928); Nomads of the North

McDonald, Garry: Wacky World of Wills and Burke, The

McDonald, Grace: Gung Ho! (1943)

McDonald, Ian: Ramrod

McDonald, Jack: Don Q, Son of Zorro

McDonald, Jennifer: Clean Shaven

McDonald, Joe: Mind Killer

McDonald, Kenneth: Coast Patrol, The

McDonald, Kevin: Godson, The; Kids in the Hall: Brain Candy

McDonald, Marie: Living in a Big Way; Promises, Promises; Tell It to the Judge

McDonald, Mary Ann: Love at First Sight

McDonald, Michael James: Unborn II, The

McDonald, Peter: Felicia's Journey; I Went Down

McDonald, Scott: Jack Frost

McDonnell, Mary: American Clock, The; Blue Chips; Dances with Wolves; Evidence of Blood; Grand Canyon; Independence Day (1996); Matewan; Mumford; Passion Fish; Sneakers; Woman Undone

McDonough, Mary: Mom

McDonough, Neal: Blue River; Grace and Glorie; White Dwarf

McDonough, Robert: Magic Stone, The

McDormand, Frances: Beyond Rangoon; Blood Simple; Butcher's Wife, The; Chattahoochee; Crazy in Love; Darkman; Fargo; Good Old Boys, The; Hidden Agenda; Hidden in America; Madeline (1998); Mississippi Burning; Palookaville; Paradise Road; Passed Away; Primal Fear; Short Cuts; Talk of Angels; Wonder Boys

McDowall, Roddy: Adventures of Bullwhip Griffin, The; Alice in Wonderland (1985); Alice Through the Looking Glass (1985); Alien Within, The; Angel 4: Undercover; Arnold; Battle for the Planet of the Apes; Bedknobs and Broomsticks; Carmilla; Cat from Outer Space, The; Circle of Iron; Class of 1984; Cleopatra (1963); Conquest of the Planet of the Apes; Cutting Class; Dead of Winter; Deadly Game; Dirty Mary, Crazy Larry; Double Trouble (1991); Escape from the Planet of the Apes; Evil Under the Sun; Fatally Yours; Five Card Stud; Flood!; Fright Night; Fright Night II; Grass Harp, The; Heads; Holiday in Mexico; How Green Was My Valley; Inside Daisy Clover; It's My Party; Keys to the Kingdom, The; Laserblast; Lassie Come Home; Legend of Hell House, The; Lord Love a Duck; Macbeth (1948); Mae West; Martian Chronicles, Parts I–III, The; Mean Johnny Barrows; Midnight Lace; Mirror, Mirror 2: Raven Dance; My Friend Flicka; Night Gallery; Planet of the Apes; Poseidon Adventure, The; Rabbit Test; Scavenger Hunt; Second Jungle Book, The: Mowgli and Baloo; Shakma; Son of Fury; Star Hunter; That Darn Cat (1965); Thief of Baghdad (1978); Unknown Origin; Unlikely Angel; White Cliffs of Dover, The; Zany Adventures of Robin Hood, The

McDowell, Claire: Show-Off, The (1926)

McDowell, Malcolm: Asylum (1996); Blue Thunder; Bopha!; Britannia Hospital; Buy and Cell; Caligula; Caller, The; Cat People (1982); Chain of Desire; Class of 1999; Clockwork Orange, A; Collection, The; Compleat Beatles, The; Cyborg 3: The Recycler; Dangerous Indiscretion; Disturbed; Eye of the Snake; First 9 Weeks, The; Fist of the North Star (1995); Get Crazy; Gigashadow; Gulag; Hugo Pool; If ... ; Jezebel's Kiss; Light in the Jungle, The; Little Riders, The; Long Ago Tomorrow; Look Back in Anger (1980); Merlin & the Sword; Milk Money; Monte Carlo; Moon 44; My Life So Far; Night Train to Venice; O Lucky Man!; Star Trek: Generations; Sunset; Surgeon, The; Tank Girl; Time After Time; Voyage of the Damned; Yesterday's Target

McDowell, Trevyn: Middlemarch

McEachin, James: Christina; Double Exposure (1993); Honeyboy

McElduff, Ellen: Maximum Overdrive; Working Girls

McElhone, Natascha: Mrs. Dalloway; Ronin; Surviving Picasso

McEnery, John: Bartleby; Land That Time Forgot, The; One Russian Summer; Pope John Paul II; Romeo and Juliet (1968)

McEnery, Peter: Entertaining Mr. Sloane; Fighting Prince of Donegal, The; Game Is Over, The; I Killed Rasputin; Moonspinners, The; Negatives

McEnroe, Annie: Hand, The; Howling II ... Your Sister is a Werewolf; True Stories; Warlords of the 21st Century

McEntire, Reba: Buffalo Girls; Gambler Returns, The: Luck of the Draw; Little Rascals, The (1994); Man from Left Field, The; Tremors

McEwan, Geraldine: Henry V (1989); Mapp & Lucia; Moses (1996); Oranges Are Not the Only Fruit

McFadden, Gates: Star Trek: First Contact; Star Trek: Generations; Star Trek: The Next Generation (TV Series)

McFadden, Joseph: Small Faces

McFadden, Stephanie: Love Field

McFarland, Bob: Showgirl Murders

McFarland, Connie: Troll II

McFarland, Monica: Back Street Jane

McFarland, Spanky: General Spanky; Kentucky Kernels; Peck's Bad Boy with the Circus; Trail of the Lonesome Pine, The

McFarlane, Andrew: Boulevard of Broken Dreams

McGaharin, Michael: Blondes Have More Guns

McGann, Mark: Business As Usual; John & Yoko: A Love Story

McGann, Paul: Afraid of the Dark; Alien 3; Dealers; Fairy Tale: A True Story; Paper Mask; Rainbow, The; Three Musketeers, The (1993); Withnail and I

McGavin, Darren: American Clock, The; Billy Madison; Blood and Concrete, A Love Story; By Dawn's Early Light; Captain America (1990); Child in the Night; Christmas Story, A; Court-martial of Billy Mitchell, The; Cyborg: The Six Million Dollar Man; Dead Heat; Delicate Delinquent, The; Diamond Trap, The; Firebird 2015 AD; From the Hip; Hangar 18; Hitchhiker, The (Series); Hot Lead and Cold Feet; Ike: The War Years; Man with the Golden Arm, The; Martian Chronicles, Parts I–III, The; Mission Mars; My Wicked, Wicked Ways; Night Stalker, The (1971); Night Stalker, The: Two Tales of Terror (TV Series); Night Strangler, The; No Deposit, No Return; Perfect Harmony; Raw Deal; Say Goodbye, Maggie Cole; Summertime; Tribes; Turk 182

McGaw, Patrick: Amongst Friends; Basketball Diaries, The; Forbidden Choices: Malicious (1995); Scorpion Spring

McGee, Jack: Space Rangers (TV Series)

McGee, Michi: In Gold We Trust

McGee, Vic: Wizard of Mars, The

McGee, Vonetta: Big Bust Out, The; Blacula; Detroit 9000 (Detroit Heat); Eiger Sanction, The; Repo Man; Scruples; To Sleep with Anger; You Must Remember This

McGee, William: Don't Look in the Basement

McGill, Bruce: As Summers Die; Citizen's Band; End of the Line; Good Old Boys, The; Hand, The; Last Boy Scout, The; Last Innocent Man, The; Little Vegas; My Cousin Vinny; No Mercy; Rosewood; Timecop; Waiting for the Moon; Whale for the Killing, A

McGill, Everett: Field of Honor (1986); Heartbreak Ridge; Jezebel's Kiss; My Fellow Americans; People Under the Stairs, The; Quest for Fire; Silver Bullet; Straight Story, The; Under Siege 2: Dark Territory

McGill, Moyna: Strange Affair of Uncle Harry, The

McGillin, Howard: Where the Boys Are '84

McGillis, Kelly: Accused, The; At First Sight (1999); Babe, The (1992); Cat Chaser; Grand Isle; Ground Control; House on Carroll Street, The; Made in Heaven (1987); Reuben, Reuben; Top Gun; Unsettled Land; We the Jury; Winter People; Witness

McGinley, John C.: Article 99; Born to Be Wild; Car 54, Where Are You? (1991); Highlander 2: The Quickening; Jack Bull, The; Johns; Last Outlaw, The (1993); Midnight Clear, A; Nothing to Lose; On Deadly Ground; Pentagon Wars, The; Platoon; Point Break; Prisoners of Inertia; Surviving the Game; Talk Radio; Three to Tango; Wagons East; Watch It

McGinley, Sean: Closer You Get, The; General, The (1998)

McGinley, Ted: Blue Tornado; Covert Assassin; Every Mother's Worst Fear; Linda; Revenge of the Nerds; Revenge of the Nerds III: The Next Generation; Revenge of the Nerds IV: Nerds in Love; Tails You Live, Heads You're Dead

McGinnis, Scott: Sky Bandits; Thunder Alley; You Can't Hurry Love

McGiver, John: Arnold; Gazebo, The; I Married a Woman; Love in the Afternoon; Man's Favorite Sport?; Period of Adjustment; Tom Sawyer (1973)

McGlone, Mike: Brothers McMullen, The; One Tough Cop; She's the One

McGlynn Jr., Frank: Westward Ho

McGlynn, Mary Elizabeth: Invisible Dad

McGoohan, Patrick: Baby—Secret of the Lost Legend; Braveheart; Danger Man (TV Series); Dr. Syn, Alias the Scarecrow; Escape from Alcatraz; Hard Way, The (1979); I Am a Camera; Ice Station Zebra; Kings and Desperate Men: A Hostage Incident; Koroshi; Man in the Iron Mask, The (1977); Of Pure Blood; Phantom, The (1996); Prisoner, The (1968) (TV Series); Scanners; Secret Agent (TV Series); Silver Streak (1976); Three Lives of Thomasina, The; Three Sovereigns for Sarah; Time to Kill, A (1996)

McGovern, Elizabeth: Bedroom Window, The; Broken Trust (1995); Clover; Favor, The; Handmaid's Tale, The; Johnny Handsome; King of the Hill; Lovesick; Me & Veronica; Native Son (1986); Once Upon a Time in America (Long Version); Ordinary People; Racing with the Moon; Ragtime; She's Having a Baby; Shock to the System, A; Snow White and the Seven Dwarfs (1983); Summer of Ben Tyler, The; Twice Upon a Yesterday; Wings of the Dove, The; Women & Men: Stories of Seduction

McGovern, Michael: Dirty Games

McGowan, Rose: Devil in the Flesh (1998); Doom Generation, The; Going All the Way; Jawbreaker; Last Stop; Phantoms; Ready to Rumble; Scream (1996); Southie

McGowan, Tom: Heavyweights

McGrady, Michael: Malevolence; Operation Delta Force 2

McGrath, Derek: Bloodsport IV: The Dark Kumite; Chameleon (1995)

McGrath, Frank: Wagon Train (TV Series)

McGraw, Charles: Away all Boats; Bridges at Toko-Ri, The; Cimarron (1960); Defiant Ones, The; Gangster, The; His Kind of Woman; Horizontal Lieutenant, The; Killer Inside Me, The; Ma and Pa Kettle Go to Town; Mad Ghoul, The; Narrow Margin, The (1952); One Minute to Zero; Pendulum; Threat, The; T-Men

McGraw, Melinda: Wrongfully Accused

McGreevey, Michael: Sammy, the Way-Out Seal

McGregor, Angela Punch: Island, The; Test of Love, A; We of the Never Never

McGregor, Ewan: Brassed Off; Eye of the Beholder; Life Less Ordinary, A; Nightwatch; Pillow Book, The; Rogue Trader; Shallow Grave (1994); Star Wars: Episode I The Phantom Menace; Trainspotting; Velvet Goldmine

McGregor, Kenneth: Primal Scream

McGuire, Barry: Werewolves on Wheels

McGuire, Biff: Child of Glass; Last Word, The (1979); Serpico; Werewolf of Washington

McGuire, Don: Fuller Brush Man, The; Threat, The

McGuire, Dorothy: Enchanted Cottage, The; Friendly Persuasion; Gentlemen's Agreement; Greatest Story Ever Told, The; Incredible Journey of Dr. Meg Laurel, The; Last Best Year, The; Make Haste to Live; Old Yeller; She Waits; Spiral Staircase, The (1946); Summer Magic; Summer Place, A; Swiss Family Robinson, The; Till the End of Time; Tree Grows in Brooklyn, A

McGuire, James: Tuck Everlasting

McGuire, Jason: Pet Sematary Two

McGuire, John: Bells of San Angelo; Invisible Ghost; Stranger on the Third Floor

McGuire, Justin: Six-String Samurai

McGuire, Kathryn: Art of Buster Keaton, The; Navigator, The (1924); Sherlock Jr.

McGuire, Michael: Blade (1973); Great Wallendas, The; Sanctuary of Fear

McHattie, Stephen: Belizaire the Cajun; Beverly Hills Cop 3; Call Me; Caribe; Convict Cowboy; Dark, The (1994); Death Valley; James Dean—A Legend in His Own Time; Moving Violation; Salvation; Search for the Gods; Sticky Fingers; Tomorrow Never Comes; Ultimate Warrior, The

McHugh, Darren: Broken Harvest

McHugh, Frank: All Through the Night; Boy Meets Girl; Bullets or Ballots; City for Conquest; Devil Dogs of the Air; Ex-Lady; Fighting 69th, The; Footlight Parade; Going My Way; I Love You Again; Last Hurrah, The; Marine Raiders; Mighty Joe Young (1949); Miss Grant Takes Richmond; Mystery of the Wax Museum; Roaring Twenties, The; Stage Struck (1936); State Fair (1945); Strange Love of Molly Louvain, The; Telegraph Trail, The; There's No Business Like Show Business; Three Men on a Horse; Tiger Walks, A; Tomorrow at Seven; Velvet Touch, The; Virginia City

McHugh, Jason: Cannibal! The Musical

McIlwaine, Robert: Soldier's Home

McIlwraith, David: Too Outrageous

McInnerny, Lizzy: Rowing with the Wind

McInnerny, Tim: Very British Coup, A

McIntire, Charles: War Arrow

McIntire, James: Gone in 60 Seconds

McIntire, John: As Summers Die; Away all Boats; Call Northside 777; Cloak and Dagger (1984); Command Decision; Far Country, The; Flaming Star; Fugitive, The (TV Series); Heroes of the Heart; Honkytonk Man; Mark of the Hawk, The; Psycho (1960); Rooster Cogburn; Rough Night in Jericho; Street with No Name; Summer and Smoke; Tin Star, The; Two Rode Together; Walk Softly, Stranger; Westward the Women; Winchester '73

McIntire, Tim: Aloha, Bobby and Rose; American Hot Wax; Fast-Walking; Gumball Rally, The; Sacred Ground; Sterile Cuckoo, The

McIntosh, Judy: Ebbtide

McKamy, Kim: Dreamaniac

McKay, David: Girl in the Picture, The; My Name is Joe

McKay, Doreen: Night Riders, The; Pals of the Saddle

McKay, John: Assault of the Rebel Girls (Cuban Rebel Girls); Niagara Niagara; Rocket Attack USA

McKay, Scott: Thirty Seconds Over Tokyo

McKay, Wanda: Black Raven, The; Bowery at Midnight; Corrigidor; Monster Maker, The; Twilight on the Trail; Voodoo Man

McKean, Michael: Across the Moon; Big Picture, The; Book of Love; Brady Bunch Movie, The; Casper: A Spirited Beginning; Clue; Coneheads; D.A.R.Y.L.; Earth Girls Are Easy; Edie & Pen; Flashback; Hider in the House; Light of Day; Man Trouble; Memoirs of an Invisible Man; Nothing to Lose; Planes, Trains and Automobiles; Pompatus of Love, The; Return of Spinal Tap, The; Short Circuit 2; Teaching Mrs. Tingle; That Darn Cat (1997); This Is Spinal Tap; True Crime (1999); True Identity; Young Doctors in Love

McKee, Lafe: Big Stampede, The; Man from Monterey, The; Mystery of the Hooded Horsemen; Rawhide (1938); Ride Him Cowboy; Spirit of the West; Telegraph Trail, The; Warning Shadows (1933)

McKee, Lonette: Blind Faith; Brewster's Millions (1985); Cotton Club, The; Cuba; Dangerous Passion; Gardens of Stone; Jungle Fever; Malcolm X; Round Midnight; Sparkle; Which Way Is Up?

McKee, Robin: DNA

McKeehan, Luke: Concrete Angels

McKellar, Don: eXistenZ; Exotica; Highway 61; In the Presence of Mine Enemies; Last Night; Red Violin, The; When Night is Falling

McKellen, Ian: And the Band Played On; Apt Pupil; Ballad of Little Jo, The; Bent; Cold Comfort Farm; Gods and Monsters; Jack and Sarah; Keep, The; Plenty; Priest of Love; Rasputin (1996); Richard III (1995); Scandal; Scarlet Pimpernel, The (1982); Shadow, The; Six Degrees of Separation; Swept from the Sea; Windmills of the Gods

McKelvey, Mark: On the Make

McKenna, Alex: Joey; Stupids, The

McKenna, Seana: Hanging Garden, The

McKenna, Siobhan: Hungry Hill; King of Kings (1961); Of Human Bondage (1964); Playboy of the Western World

McKenna, T. P.: Beast in the Cellar, The; Bleak House; Caribbean Mystery, A; Portrait of the Artist as a Young Man, A; Straw Dogs; To the Lighthouse

McKenna, Virginia: Born Free; Christian the Lion; Cruel Sea, The; Gathering Storm; Ring of Bright Water; Simba; Waterloo; Wreck of the Mary Deare, The

McKennon, Dallas: Mystery Mansion

McKenzie, Jack: Silent Mouse

McKenzie, Jacqueline: Angel Baby; Deep Blue Sea; Mr. Reliable; Romper Stomper

McKenzie, Julia: Shirley Valentine; Those Glory Glory Days

McKenzie, Tim: Dead Easy; Gallipoli; Thirteenth Floor, The (1990)

McKeon, Doug: Breaking Home Ties; Comeback Kid, The; Heart of a Champion: The Ray Mancini Story; Mischief; On Golden Pond

McKeon, Nancy: Lightning Incident, The; Poison Ivy (1985); Teresa's Tattoo; Where the Day Takes You

McKeon, Philip: Red Surf

McKern, Leo: Blue Lagoon, The; Candleshoe; Day the Earth Caught Fire, The; Foreign Field, A; French Lieutenant's Woman, The; Help!; Horse Without a Head, The; House on Garibaldi Street; King Lear (1984); Ladyhawke; Massacre in Rome; Monsignor Quixote; Mouse That Roared, The; Murder with Mirrors; Nativity, The; Prisoner, The (1968) (TV Series); Reilly: The Ace of Spies; Rumpole of the Bailey (TV Series); Ryan's Daughter; Shoes of the Fisherman; Time Without Pity; Travelling North; X—The Unknown

McKidd, Kevin: Bedrooms and Hallways; Trainspotting

McKim, Robert: Hell's Hinges; Mark of Zorro, The (1920); Strong Man, The

McKim, Sammy: Painted Stallion, The; Rocky Mountain Rangers

McKinney, Bill: Bronco Billy; City Slickers II; Final Justice (1984); Heart Like a Wheel; Outlaw Josey Wales, The; Pink Cadillac

McKinney, Gregory: Brilliant Disguise, A

McKinney, Kurt: No Retreat, No Surrender

McKinney, Mark: Kids in the Hall: Brain Candy

McKinney, Nina Mae: Hallelujah!; Sanders of the River

McKinnon, Mona: Hellborn; Plan 9 from Outer Space

eadows, Jayne: Alice in Wonderland (1985); Alice
rough the Looking Glass (1985); Enchantment; James
ean—A Legend in His Own Time; Lady in the Lake; Mur-
r by Numbers; Norman ... Is That You?; Story of Us, The;
ndercurrent

eadows, Joyce: Brain from Planet Arous, The; Zebra in
e Kitchen

eadows, Kristen: Zero Tolerance

eadows, Stephen: Sunstroke; Ultraviolet

eager, Jill: 4:50 From Paddington

eagher, Karen: Experience Preferred ... But Not Essen-
al; Threads

eaney, Colm: Con Air; Doctor Quinn Medicine Woman;
nglishman Who Went up a Hill But Came down a Moun-
in, The; Far and Away; Into the West; Money Kings; Mon-
ment Ave.; Mystery, Alaska; Road to Wellville, The; Scar-
tt; Snapper, The; Summer Fling; Under Siege; Van, The
997)

eans, Angela: House Party 3
eans, Russell: Buffalo Girls; Last of the Mohicans, The
992); Pathfinder, The; Windrunner
eara, Anne: Daytrippers, The; Heavyweights; Longshot,
ne (1985); Lovers and Other Strangers; My Little Girl; Out
Towners, The (1970); Search for One-Eye Jimmy, The;
nat's Adequate
eat Loaf: Black Dog; Crazy in Alabama; Everything That
ises; Fight Club; Leap of Faith; Mighty, The; Motorama;
utside Ozona; Rocky Horror Picture Show, The; Spice
Vorld; Squeeze, The (1987); Stand by Me (1988); To Catch
Yeti; Wayne's World
edak, Karen: Galaxies Are Colliding; Girl to Kill For, A;
reacherous Crossing
edeiros, Michale: Infested (Ticks)
ederov, Talai: Beshkempir, The Adopted Son
edford, Kay: Ensign Pulver; Face in the Crowd, A; Funny
irl
edina, Ofelia: Frida
edina, Patricia: Abbott and Costello in the Foreign Le-
ion; Botany Bay; Francis, the Talking Mule; Hotel Reserve;
ackpot, The; Latitude Zero; Mr. Arkadin (Confidential Re-
ort); Snow White and the Three Stooges; Thriller (TV Sees)
edway, Heather: Serpent's Lair
edwetz, Anthony: Clockmaker (1998)
edwin, Michael: Rattle of a Simple Man; Scrooge (1970)
eed, Geoff: Kickboxer 5: Redemption
eehan, Danny: Don't Drink the Water
eek, Donald: Air Raid Wardens; Bathing Beauty; Blondie
akes a Vacation; Colonel Effingham's Raid; Du Barry Was a
ady; Hollywood Cavalcade; Jesse James; Keeper of the
lame; Little Miss Broadway; Love on the Run (1936);
Make a Wish; Mrs. Wiggs of the Cabbage Patch; Murder at
he Vanities; Return of Frank James, The; Return of Peter
rimm, The; Romance in Manhattan; Stagecoach (1939);
State Fair (1945); They Got Me Covered; Thin Man Goes
lome, The; Toast of New York, The; Young Mr. Lincoln
eek, Jeff: Night of the Cyclone
eeker, George: Apache Rose; Hips, Hips, Hooray; Murder by Television; Night of Terror; Seven Doors to Death;
Song of Nevada; Superman—The Serial; Tarzan's Revenge
eeker, Ralph: Alpha Incident, The; Anderson Tapes, The;
Battle Shock; Birds of Prey; Brannigan; Dead Don't Die,
he; Detective, The (1968); Food of the Gods; Four in a
Jeep; Gentle Giant; Kiss Me Deadly; Mind Snatchers, The;
My Boys Are Good Boys; Naked Spur, The; Night Games;
Paths of Glory; Run of the Arrow; St. Valentine's Day Massacre, The; Winter Kills
eeks, Edith: Poison
eeks, Edward: Blood of the Hunter
eiffre, Armand: Blue Country; Here Comes Santa Claus
egna, John: Ratings Game, The; To Kill a Mockingbird
egowan, Don: Creation of the Humanoids; Lawless
Street, A
ehaffey, Blanche: Battling Orioles, The
ehler, Tobias: Inspectors, The
ehri, Jalal: Fearless Tiger
eier, Shane: Andre
eighan, Thomas: Male and Female
eillon, John: Cars That Eat People (The Cars That Ate
Paris); "Crocodile" Dundee; "Crocodile" Dundee II; Ever-

lasting Secret Family, The; Fourth Wish, The; Frenchman's
Farm; Ride a Wild Pony; Walkabout; Wild Duck, The
Meineke, Eva Marie: César and Rosalie
Meininger, Frederique: Lover, The
Meira, Tarcisio: Boca
Meisner, Gunter: In a Glass Cage
Mejia, Alfonso: Los Olvidados
Mekhralieva, Susanna: Prisoner of the Mountains
Melamed, Fred: Suspect
Melato, Mariangela: By the Blood of Others; Love and An-
archy; Seduction of Mimi, The; Summer Night; Swept
Away; To Forget Venice
Melchior, Lauritz: Luxury Liner; This Time For Keeps; Thrill
of a Romance; Two Sisters from Boston
Meldrum, Wendel: Hush Little Baby; Sodbusters
Melendez, Asdrubal: Very Old Man with Enormous Wings,
A
Melendez, Ron: Children of the Corn III: Urban Harvest
Melford, Kim: Corvette Summer
Melia, Joe: Hitchhiker's Guide to the Galaxy, The; Privates
on Parade; Sakharov
Melito, Joseph: 12 Monkeys
Mell, Marisa: Danger: Diabolik
Mellaney, Victor: Cyborg Soldier
Mellencamp, John: Falling from Grace
Melles, Sunnyi: 38 Vienna Before the Fall
Mellinger, Leonie: Lion and the Hawk, The
Mello, Breno: Black Orpheus
Melonas, Mac: Kid Called Danger, A
Meloni, Christopher: Bound; Souler Opposite, The
Melson, Sara: Low Life, The
Melton, Sid: Lost Continent, The (1951)
Melville, Sam: Roughnecks
Melvin, Allan: Sgt. Bilko (TV Series)
Melvin, Murray: Taste of Honey, A
Memel, Steve: Savage Justice
Memphis, Ricky: La Scorta
Menchikov, Oleg: Burnt by the Sun; East-West
Mendaille, David: Kameradschaft
Mendel, Stephen: Midnight Heat; Provocateur
Mendelsohn, Ben: Cosi; Efficiency Expert, The
(Spotswood)
Mendelson, Braddon: Nudist Colony of the Dead
Mendenhall, David: Going Bananas; Over the Top; Space
Raiders; Streets; They Still Call Me Bruce
Mendez, Eva: Children of the Corn V: Fields of Terror
Mendez, Ray: Fast, Cheap and Out of Control
Mendiesolin, Bob: Devil's Gift, The
Mendonca, George: Fast, Cheap and Out of Control
Mendonca, Mauro: Dona Flor and Her Two Husbands
Menese, Jose: Flamenco
Ménez, Bernard: Dracula and Son
Mengatti, John: Knights of the City; Meatballs Part II
Menglet, Alex: Georgia (1987)
Menina, Asha: House of Cards
Menjou, Adolphe: Across the Wide Missouri; Ambas-
sador's Daughter, The; Are Parents People?; Bundle of Joy;
Farewell to Arms, A; Front Page, The (1931); Gold Diggers
of 1935; Golden Boy; Goldwyn Follies, The; Hucksters, The;
I Married a Woman; Letter of Introduction; Little Miss
Marker (1934); Marriage Circle, The; Milky Way, The
(1936); Morning Glory (1933); Morocco; My Dream Is
Yours; One in a Million; One Hundred Men and a Girl; Paths
of Glory; Pollyanna (1960); Roxie Hart; Sheik, The; Sor-
rows of Satan, The; Star Is Born, A (1937); State of the
Union; Step Lively; Swan, The (1925); Three Musketeers,
The (1921); To Please a Lady; Woman of Paris, A; You Were
Never Lovelier
Menshikov, Oleg: Prisoner of the Mountains
Menuhin, Yehudi: Magic Bow, The
Menzies, Heather: Captain America (1979); Piranha
(1978)
Menzies, Robert: Cactus
Meoli, Christian: Low Life, The
Mer, Juliano: Under the Domim Tree
Merasty, Bill: Legends of the North
Mercado, Patrick: Dreamlife of Angels, The
Merce, Jose: Flamenco
Mercer, Beryl: Cavalcade; Public Enemy; Supernatural
Mercer, Frances: Annabel Takes a Tour; Mad Miss Manton,
The; Smashing the Rackets; Vivacious Lady

Mercer, Marian: Out on a Limb (1992)

Merchant, Veronica: Deep Crimson

Merchant, Vivien: Homecoming, The (1973); Offence, The; Under Milk Wood

Mercier, Michele: Call of the Wild (1972); Global Affair, A; Shoot the Piano Player

Merckens, Marijke: Flight of Rainbirds, A

Mercouri, Melina: Dream of Passion, A; Nasty Habits; Never on Sunday; Once Is Not Enough; Stella (1955); Topkapi

Mercure, Jean: Baxter (1988)

Mercure, Monique: Tramp at the Door

Mercurio, Micole: Turn of the Screw, The (1989); While You Were Sleeping

Mercurio, Paul: Anything for Love; Back of Beyond; Dark Planet; Exit to Eden; First 9 Weeks, The; Joseph; Strictly Ballroom; Welcome to Woop Woop

Mereader, Maria: Pardon My Trunk (Hello Elephant!)

Meredith, Burgess: Advise and Consent; Batman (1966); Big Hand for the Little Lady, A; Burnt Offerings; Clash of the Titans; Day of the Locust, The; Diary of a Chambermaid (1946); Foul Play; Full Moon in Blue Water; Great Bank Hoax, The; Grumpier Old Men; Grumpy Old Men; Hindenburg, The; Idiot's Delight; In Harm's Way; Last Chase, The; Madame X (1966); Magic; Man in the Eiffel Tower, The; Manitou, The; Mine Own Executioner; Mr. Corbett's Ghost; 92 in the Shade; Oddball Hall; Outrage!; Probe; Rocky; Rocky II; Rocky III; Rocky V; Santa Claus—The Movie; Second Chorus; Sentinel, The; State of Grace; Stay Away Joe; That Uncertain Feeling; There Was a Crooked Man; Tom, Dick and Harry; Torture Garden; True Confessions; Twilight Zone, The (TV Series); Wet Gold; When Time Ran Out!; Winterset; Yin and Yang of Mr. Go, The

Meredith, Don: Express to Terror; Night the City Screamed, The; Sky Heist; Terror on the 40th Floor; Wyatt Earp: Return to Tombstone

Meredith, Iris: Green Archer; Lawman Is Born, A; Mystery of the Hooded Horsemen

Meredith, Judi: Jack the Immortal Monster

Meredith, Lee: Producers, The; Sunshine Boys, The

Meredith, Lois: Headless Horseman, The

Merenda, Luc: Kidnap Syndicate, The; Torso

Merhar, Stanislas: Dry Cleaning

Merhi, Jalal: Expect No Mercy; Operation Golden Phoenix; Talons of the Eagle; TC 2000

Meril, Macha: Double Vision; Married Woman, A; Robert et Robert; Vagabond

Merivale, John: Caltiki, the Immortal Monster

Merivale, Philip: Sister Kenny

Meriwether, Lee: Batman (1966); Cruise into Terror; 4D Man; Namu, the Killer Whale; Undefeated, The

Merkel, Una: Abraham Lincoln; Bank Dick, The; Bat Whispers, The; Bombshell (1933); Born to Dance; Broadway Melody of 1936; Destry Rides Again; Evelyn Prentice; 42nd Street; Girl Most Likely, The; I Love Melvin; It's a Joke, Son!; Kentuckian, The; Mad Doctor of Market Street, The; Mating Game, The; Merry Widow, The; On Borrowed Time; Private Lives; Red-Headed Woman; Rich, Young and Pretty; RiffRaff (1936); Road to Zanzibar; Saratoga; Summer and Smoke; They Call It Sin; Tiger Walks, A

Merkerson, S. Epatha: Place for Annie, A

Merlet, Valentin: La Cérémonie

Merli, Maurizio: Fearless (1978); Priest of Love

Merlin, Jan: Guns of Diablo; Running Wild (1955); Silk 2; Twilight People

Merlin, Joanna: Class Action; Mr. Wonderful

Merlo, Ismael: Hunt, The

Merman, Ethel: Alexander's Ragtime Band; Happy Landing; It's a Mad Mad Mad Mad World; Kid Millions; That's Singing: The Best of Broadway; There's No Business Like Show Business; We're Not Dressing

Merrall, Mary: Love on the Dole

Merrick, Doris: Neanderthal Man, The

Merrick, Lynn: Days of Old Cheyenne; Dead Man's Gulch; Kansas Cyclone

Merrill, Dina: Anna to the Infinite Power; Butterfield 8; Courtship of Eddie's Father, The; Deadly Encounter (1975); Desk Set; I'll Take Sweden; Just Tell Me What You Want; Operation Petticoat; Player, The; Sundowners, The (1960); Suture; Tenth Month, The; Twisted; Wedding, A (1978)

Merrill, Frank: Tarzan the Mighty; Tarzan the Tiger

Merrill, Gary: All About Eve; Clambake; Great Imposter, The; Huckleberry Finn (1974); Incident, The (1967); Mysterious Island; Phone Call from a Stranger; Ride Beyond Vengeance; Seekers, The; Twelve O'Clock High

Merrill, Joan: Iceland

Merrill, Julie: Mirror of Death

Merriman, Ryan: Deep End of the Ocean, The; Everything That Rises

Merrison, Clive: Pocketful of Rye, A

Merritt, Theresa: Voodoo Dawn; Wiz, The

Merrow, Jane: Appointment, The; Hands of the Ripper

Merton, John: Boothill Bandits; Cherokee Flash

Mervyn, William: Railway Children, The

Merwin, David: Apart from Hugh

Meryl, Riba: Beyond the Doors

Mese, John: Excessive Force II: Force on Force; Night the Scarecrow; Under Investigation

Messemer, Hannes: General Della Rovere

Messier, Marc: Boys, The (1997)

Messina, Gabriella: Everything Relative

Messing, Debra: McHale's Navy; Walk in the Clouds, A

Metcalf, Laurie: Always Outnumbered; Blink; Dangerous Woman, A; Dear God; Desperately Seeking Susan; Hellcab; Internal Affairs; JFK; Making Mr. Right; Mistress (1992); Pacific Heights

Metcalf, Mark: Hijacking Hollywood; Stupids, The

Metchik, Aaron Michael: Trading Mom

Metchik, Asher: Trading Mom; Treasure of Pirate's Point

Methot, Mayo: Case of the Curious Bride, The

Metrano, Art: Beverly Hills Bodysnatchers; Breathless (1983); Cheaper to Keep Her; Going Ape!; Malibu Express; Matilda; Police Academy III: Back in Training

Mette, Nancy: Meet the Hollowheads

Metzier, Jim: Circuitry Man; Circuitry Man II: Plughead Rewired; Delusion (1991); French Silk; Love Kills; 976-EVIL; On Wings of Eagles; One False Move; Tex

Meurisse, Paul: Diabolique (1955); Picnic on the Grass

Meury, Anne-Laure: Boyfriends and Girlfriends

Mewes, Jason: Chasing Amy

Meyer, Breckin: Dancer, Texas: Pop. 81; Road Trip

Meyer, Daniel: Locusts, The

Meyer, Dina: Bats; Dragonheart; Johnny Mnemonic; Poodle Springs; Starship Troopers

Meyer, Emile: Hostile Guns; Riot in Cell Block Eleven

Meyer, Jean: Le Bourgeois Gentilhomme

Meyer, Johannes: Master of the House (Du Skal Aere Di Hustru)

Meyer, Michael: Virtual Desire

Meyer, Russ: Amazon Women on the Moon

Meyer, Thom: Blood Suckers from Outer Space

Meyers, Ari: Dark Horse; Shakma; Think Big

Meyers, Jonathan Rhys: Governess, The

Meyers, Mike: Mystery, Alaska

Meyrink, Michelle: Joy of Sex, The; Nice Girls Don't Explode; Real Genius; Revenge of the Nerds

Mezzogiorno, Vittorio: Cafe Express; L'Homme Blesse (The Wounded Man); Mussolini and I; Three Brothers

Mhlope, Geina: Place of Weeping

Miano, Clipper: Smilla's Sense of Snow

Miano, Robert: Ministry of Vengeance; Taxi Dancers

Miao, Cora: Eat a Bowl of Tea

Miao, Nora: Fists of Fury; Return of the Dragon

Michael, Bill: Farmer's Other Daughter, The

Michael, Christopher: Guyver 2: Dark Hero

Michael, George: Stand by Me (1988)

Michael, Gertrude: I'm No Angel

Michael, Jordan Christopher: Motorama

Michael, Ralph: Diary of a Mad Old Man

Michaels, Michele: Slumber Party Massacre

Michaels, Seth: Freeze Frame

Michaelson, Kari: Kid with the 200 I.Q., The

Michalski, Jeff: Pet Shop

Michel, Dominique: Decline of the American Empire, The

Michel, Marc: Lola (1960); Umbrellas of Cherbourg, The

Michel, Michael: Sixth Man, The

Michel, Odile: Peppermint Soda

Michelangeli, Calla: And God Said to Cain

Michell, Helena: At Bertram's Hotel

Michell, Keith: Executioner, The; Grendel, Grendel, Grendel; Hellfire Club, The; Six Wives of Henry VIII, The (TV Series)

Miller, Eve: Big Trees, The; Kansas Pacific; Winning Team, The

Miller, Frank: Jugular Wine

Miller, Garry: Amazing Mr. Blunden, The

Miller, Gary: Darkness

Miller, Glenn: Orchestra Wives

Miller, Helen: Being Human

Miller, Henry: Henry Miller Odyssey

Miller, Jason: Best Little Girl in the World, The; Dain Curse, The; Eternal, The; Exorcist, The; Light of Day; Mommy; Monsignor; Murdered Innocence; Ninth Configuration, The; Rudy; Toy Soldiers (1983); Vengeance

Miller, Jean: Speak of the Devil

Miller, Jennifer: Never Say Die; Terminal Impact

Miller, Jeremy: Emanon; Willies, The

Miller, John: Undefeatable

Miller, Jonny Lee: Afterglow; Dead Man's Walk; Hackers; Mansfield Park; Plunkett & Macleane; Trainspotting

Miller, Joshua: And You Thought Your Parents Were Weird

Miller, Kathleen: Fighting Mad; Strange New World

Miller, Kristine: Jungle Patrol

Miller, Larry: Big Tease, The; Chairman of the Board; Corrina, Corrina; Dream Lover (1994); Favor, The; For Richer or Poorer; Necessary Roughness; Nutty Professor, The (1996); Suburban Commando; 10 Things I Hate About You; Undercover Blues

Miller, Linda G.: Night of the Juggler

Miller, Lydia: Backlash

Miller, Mark: Ginger in the Morning; Mr. Sycamore; Savannah Smiles

Miller, Mark Thomas: Blue de Ville; Misfits of Science; Mom; Ski School

Miller, Marvin: Dead Reckoning (1947); Hell Squad (1985); Off Limits (1953); Red Planet Mars

Miller, Mary: After Pilkington

Miller, Michael: Doc Savage … , The Man of Bronze

Miller, Mike: Blastfighter

Miller, Patsy Ruth: Hunchback of Notre Dame, The (1923)

Miller, Penelope Ann: Adventures in Babysitting; Awakenings; Break Up; Carlito's Way; Chaplin; Dead-Bang; Downtown; Freshman, The; Gun In Betty Lou's Handbag, The; Kindergarten Cop; Last Don, The; Little City; Other People's Money; Outside Ozona; Relic, The; Rocky Marciano; Shadow, The; Witch Hunt; Year of the Comet

Miller, Rebecca: Consenting Adults (1992); Murder of Mary Phagan, The; Wind (1992)

Miller, Roger: Lucky Luke

Miller, Sherry: Rent-A-Kid; Sabrina, the Teenage Witch; Scandalous Me: The Jacqueline Susann Story

Miller, Stephen E.: Home Is Where the Hart Is

Miller, Ty: Trancers 4: Jack of Swords; Trancers 5: Sudden Deth

Miller, Walter: Dick Tracy's G-Men; Ghost Patrol; Ivory-Handled Gun, The; Lawless Valley; Lone Defender, The; Shadow of the Eagle; Street Scene

Millian, Andra: Stacy's Knights

Millican, James: Beyond the Purple Hills; Rimfire; Winning Team, The

Milligan, Spike: Alice's Adventures in Wonderland; Down Among the "Z" Men; Ghost in the Noonday Sun; To See Such Fun

Milliken, Angie: Dead Heart

Mills, Alley: Going Berserk; Tainted Blood

Mills, Donna: Alice Through the Looking Glass (1985); Bunco; Curse of the Black Widow; False Arrest; Fire!; Haunts of the Very Rich; Incident, The (1967); Murph the Surf; Play Misty for Me; Runaway Father; Stepford Husbands, The; Who Is the Black Dahlia?

Mills, Eddie: Dancer, Texas: Pop. 81

Mills, Hayley: Appointment with Death; Back Home; Chalk Garden, The; Daydreamer, The (1966); Endless Night; In Search of the Castaways; Moonspinners, The; Parent Trap, The (1961); Pollyanna (1960); Summer Magic; That Darn Cat (1965); Tiger Bay; Trouble with Angels, The; Whistle Down the Wind

Mills, Hayword: Mississippi Blues

Mills, John: Africa—Texas Style!; Bean; Black Veil for Lisa, A; Cats; Chalk Garden, The; Chuka; Colditz Story, The; Dr. Strange; Frankenstein (1992); Gandhi; Goodbye, Mr. Chips (1939); Grave Indiscretion; Great Expectations (1946); Hobson's Choice (1954); In Which We Serve; King Rat;

Lady Caroline Lamb; Martin Chuzzlewit; Masks of Death; Murder with Mirrors; Night of the Fox; Nine Days a Queen; Operation Crossbow; Quatermass Conclusion, The; Rocking Horse Winner, The; Ryan's Daughter; Sahara (1984); Scott of the Antarctic; Swiss Family Robinson, The; Thirty Happy Breed; Thirty-Nine Steps, The (1978); Tiger Bay; Tunes of Glory; War and Peace (1956); We Dive at Dawn; Who's That Girl; Woman of Substance, A; Wrong Box, The; Young Winston; Zulu Dawn

Mills, Johnny: Garden, The

Mills, Juliet: Avanti!; Barnaby and Me; Beyond the Door; Rare Breed, The (1966)

Mills, Kiri: Desperate Remedies

Mills, Samantha: Prehysteria

Mills, Tom: Luther, The Geek

Mills, Walter: High Country, The

Milne, Leslie: Vampire at Midnight

Milner, Martin: Columbo: Murder by the Book; Compulsion; Flood!; Francis in the Navy; Life with Father; Marjorie Morningstar; Operation Pacific; Pete Kelly's Blues; Seekers, The; Sweet Smell of Success; 13 Ghosts; Valley of the Dolls; Zebra in the Kitchen

Milo, Sandra: Bang Bang Kid, The; Dead for a Dollar; 8 1/2; General Della Rovere; Juliet of the Spirits; Vanina Vanini

Milot, Charles: French Connection II, The

Miltsakakis, Stefanos: Bloodsport IV: The Dark Kumite

Milushev, Boyan: Bird of Prey

Miluwi, John Omirah: Gorillas in the Mist

Mimieux, Yvette: Black Hole, The; Caper of the Golden Bulls, The; Dark of the Sun (Mercenaries) (1968); Devil Dog: The Hound of Hell; Diamond Head; Hit Lady; Jackson County Jail; Journey into Fear (1975); Legend of Valentino; Monkeys Go Home; Neptune Factor, The; Obsessive Love; Platinum High School; Snowbeast; Three in the Attic; Time Machine, The; Toys in the Attic; Where the Boys Are (1960)

Minardos, Nico: Assault on Agathon; Daring Game

Minciotti, Esther: Marty (1953) (Television)

Mineau, Charlotte: Charlie Chaplin—The Early Years Vol. 1–4

Mineo, Sal: Cheyenne Autumn; Dino; Exodus; Gene Krupa Story, The; Rebel Without a Cause; Rock, Pretty Baby; Somebody Up There Likes Me; Tonka

Miner, Jan: Lenny; Willie and Phil

Ming, Lau Siu: Eat a Bowl of Tea

Minevich, Borrah: One in a Million

Mingand, Pierre: Mauvaise Graine (Bad Seed)

Minjarez, Mike: Escape to White Mountain

Mink, Claudette: Deadly Heroes

Minnelli, Liza: Arthur; Arthur 2: On the Rocks; Cabaret; Matter of Time, A; Muppets Take Manhattan, The; New York, New York; Parallel Lives; Rent-a-cop; Silent Movie; Stepping Out; Sterile Cuckoo, The

Minns, Byron Keith: South Central

Minogue, Dannii: One Crazy Night

Minor, Bob: Delinquent School Girls

Minor, Shane: Shadow Creature

Minter, Kelly Jo: People Under the Stairs, The; Popcorn

Minter, Kristin: Cool As Ice; Flashfire; Savage; There Goes My Baby

Minzhi, Wei: Not One Less

Miou-Miou: Dog Day; Dry Cleaning; Eighth Day, The; Entre Nous (Between Us); Going Places; Jonah Who Will Be 25 in the year 2000; Josepha; La Lectrice (The Reader); Little Indian, Big City; May Fools; Ménage; My Other Husband; Roads to the South

Mira, Brigitte: Ali: Fear Eats the Soul; Chinese Roulette; Every Man for Himself and God Against All; Kamikaze 89; Mother Kusters Goes to Heaven

Miracle, Irene: In the Shadow of Kilimanjaro; Last of Philip Banter, The; Laughing Horse; Puppet Master, The; Watchers II

Miranda, Carmen: Copacabana; Date with Judy, A; Doll Face; Down Argentine Way; Four Jills in a Jeep; Gang's All Here, The; Nancy Goes to Rio; Springtime in the Rockies (1942); Weekend in Havana

Miranda, Isa: Dog Eat Dog; La Signora di Tutti; Man from Nowhere, The; Night Porter, The; Summertime

Miranda, John: Bloodthirsty Butchers

Miranda, Robert: Chips, the War Dog; Monkey Trouble

Mironova, Olga: Come and See

Moffett, D. W.: Danielle Steel's Fine Things; In the Deep Woods; Lisa; Little Death, The; Misfit Brigade, The; Molly; Rough Magic; Stealing Beauty

Moffett, Gregory: Robot Monster

Moffett, Michelle: Deathstalker IV: Match of the Titans; Wild Cactus

Mog, Aribert: Ecstasy

Mogila, Linda: Cyrano de Bergerac (1925)

Mohammadi, Azize: Apple, The

Mohammadkhani, Aida: White Balloon, The

Mohner, Carl: Last Gun, The; Rififi; Sink the Bismarck

Mohr, Gerald: Angry Red Planet, The; Hunt the Man Down; Invasion USA (1952); King of the Cowboys; Son of Ali Baba; Terror in the Haunted House

Mohr, Jay: For Better or Worse; Go; Jane Austen's Mafia; Picture Perfect; Small Soldiers; Suicide Kings

Mohyeddin, Zia: Bombay Talkie; They Came from Beyond Space; We Are the Children

Moir, Alison: Johnny Suede

Moir, Richard: Heatwave (1983); In Search of Anna; Indecent Obsession, An

Mok, Karen: Black Mask

Mokae, Zakes: Dry White Season, A; Dust Devil; Master Harold and the Boys; Percy & Thunder; Rage in Harlem, A; Serpent and the Rainbow, The; Slaughter of the Innocents; World of Strangers, A

Mol, Gretchen: Music from Another Room; New Rose Hotel; Rounders; Rounders (1998); Thirteenth Floor, The (1999)

Molander, Karin: Thomas Graal's Best Child; Thomas Graal's Best Film

Moldovan, Florin: Gadjo Dilo

Moldovan, Jeff: Master Blaster

Molière Players, The: Alfred Hitchcock's Bon Voyage and Aventure Malgache

Molina, Alfred: American Friends; Before and After; Dead Man; Dudley Do-Right; Enchanted April; Hideaway; Impostors, The; Leo Tolstoy's Anna Karenina (1997); Letter to Brezhnev; Man Who Knew Too Little, The; Manifesto; Maverick; Meantime; Not Without My Daughter; Perez Family, The; Prick Up Your Ears; Scorpion Spring; Species; Trial, The (1992); White Fang 2: Myth of the White Wolf

Molina, Angela: Camorra; Demons in the Garden; 1492: The Conquest of Paradise; Half of Heaven; Live Flesh; Streets of Gold; That Obscure Object of Desire

Molina, Mariano Vidal: Gentleman Killer

Moll, Charles: Savage Journey

Moll, Georgia: Misunderstood (1988)

Moll, Richard: Beanstalk; Dream Date; Dungeonmaster, The; Galaxis; Glass Cage, The; Highlander: The Gathering; House; Night Train to Terror; No Dessert Dad Until You Mow the Lawn; Secret Agent Club; Sidekicks; Storybook; Survivor; Sword and the Sorcerer, The; Think Big; Wicked Stepmother, The

Molloy, Patrick: Plutonium Baby

Molnar, Tibor: Red and the White, The; Round-Up, The

Molone, Steve: Big Sweat, The

Moloney, Janel: Souler Opposite, The

Moltke, Alexandra: Dark Shadows (TV Series)

Momo, Alessandro: Malicious (1974)

Momoi, Kaori: Eijanaika (Why Not?)

Monaghan, Marjorie: Nemesis (1992); Space Rangers (TV Series)

Monahan, Dan: Porky's; Porky's II: The Next Day; Porky's Revenge; Up the Creek (1984)

Monahan, Tonia: Dominion (1994); Edgar Allan Poe's Madhouse; Goblin; Prehistoric Bimbos in Armageddon City; Zombie Bloodbath

Moncrieff, Karen: Deathfight; Midnight Witness; Xtro: Watch the Skies (Xtro 3)

Mondy, Pierre: Gift, The; Sleeping Car Murders, The

Mones, Paul: Tuff Turf

Monfort, Sylvia: Le Cas du Dr. Laurent

Mong, William V.: Seven Footprints to Satan; What Price Glory? (1926)

Monk, Debra: Center Stage; Ellen Foster; Redwood Curtain

Monks, Kathy: Invasion for Flesh and Blood

Monlaur, Yvonne: Brides of Dracula; Terror of the Tongs, The

Monnier, Antoine: Devil, Probably, The

Monnier, Valentine: After the Fall of New York; Devilfish

Monoson, Lawrence: Black Rose of Harlem; Dangerous Love; Gaby, a True Story

Monot, Roland: Man Escaped, A

Monro, Truan: Prince Brat and the Whipping Boy

Monroe, Lochlan: Downhill Willie

Monroe, Marilyn: All About Eve; As Young as You Feel; Asphalt Jungle, The; Bus Stop; Clash by Night; Don't Bother to Knock; Gentlemen Prefer Blondes; How to Marry a Millionaire; Ladies of the Chorus; Let's Make It Legal; Let's Make Love; Love Happy; Love Nest; Misfits, The; Monkey Business (1952); Niagara; Prince and the Showgirl, The; River of No Return; Seven Year Itch, The; Some Like It Hot There's No Business Like Show Business; We're Not Married

Monroe, Sam: Tales from the Hood

Monroe, Steve: Kill-Off, The

Montagut, François: Strangers

Montalban, Carlos: Bananas

Montalban, Paolo: Rodgers & Hammerstein's Cinderella

Montalban, Ricardo: Across the Wide Missouri; Alice Through the Looking Glass (1966); Battleground; Blue (1968); Cheyenne Autumn; Conquest of the Planet of the Apes; Deserter, The; Escape from the Planet of the Apes; Fantasy Island; Fiesta; Kissing Bandit, The; Latin Lovers; Madame X (1966); Mission to Glory; Naked Gun, The; Neptune's Daughter; On an Island with You; Return to Fantasy Island; Sayonara; Singing Nun, The; Star Trek II: The Wrath of Khan; Sweet Charity; Train Robbers, The; Two Weeks with Love

Montana, Bull: Son of the Sheik; Victory (1919)

Montana, Karla: Sweet 15

Montana, Monte: Down Dakota Way

Montanary, Michel: Jacko and Lise

Montand, Yves: César and Rosalie; Choice of Arms, A; Delusions of Grandeur; Goodbye Again; Grand Prix; IP5: The Island of Pachyderms; Is Paris Burning?; Jean De Florette; Let's Make Love; Manon of the Spring; My Geisha; Napoleon (1955); On a Clear Day, You Can See Forever; Roads to the South; Sleeping Car Murders, The; State of Siege; Vincent, François, Paul and the Others; Wages of Fear, The; Z

Monte, Brenda: Unmade Beds

Monte, Mario: Soul Vengeance (Welcome Home Brother Charles)

Monte, Mike: No Dead Heroes

Monteith, Kelly: Hollywood Boulevard II

Montell, Lisa: Nine Lives of Elfego Baca, The; World Without End

Montenegro, Fernanda: Central Station

Monteros, Rosenda: Battle Shock

Montesano, Enrico: Sotto Sotto

Montesi, Jorge: Death Target

Montesinos, Gino: Magic Stone, The

Montez, Maria: Ali Baba and the Forty Thieves; Arabian Nights (1942); Cobra Woman; Follow the Boys; Gypsy Wildcat; Sudan; Valdez Is Coming

Montgomery, Belinda: Blackout (1978); Man from Atlantis, The; Marciano; Miami Vice; Other Side of the Mountain, Part II, The; Silent Madness; Stone Cold Dead; Stone Fox, The; Todd Killings, The

Montgomery, Douglass: Cat and the Canary, The (1939); Harmony Lane; Mystery of Edwin Drood, The

Montgomery, Elizabeth: Court-martial of Billy Mitchell, The; Thriller (TV Series)

Montgomery, George: From Hell to Borneo; Hostile Guns; Indian Uprising; Lone Ranger, The (1938); Orchestra Wives; Roxie Hart; Texas Rangers, The (1951)

Montgomery, Julie: Revenge of the Nerds; Savage Justice

Montgomery, Lee: Baker's Hawk; Ben; Burnt Offerings; Girls Just Want to Have Fun; Into the Fire; Midnight Hour; Mutant; Prime Risk; Savage Is Loose, The

Montgomery, Robert: Big House, The; Divorcee, The; Forsaking All Others; Free and Easy; Here Comes Mr. Jordan; Inspiration; June Bride; Lady in the Lake; Last of Mrs. Cheney, The; Mr. and Mrs. Smith; Night Must Fall; Private Lives; Riptide; They Were Expendable

Monti, Ivana: Contraband

Monti, Maria: Fistful of Dynamite, A

Montiel, Sarita: Run of the Arrow; Serenade

Montorsi, Stefania: Mille Bolle Blu

Moran, Nick: Lock, Stock and Two Smoking Barrels; New Blood

Moran, Patrick: Biohazard: The Alien Force

Moran, Pauline: Poirot (Series)

Moran, Peggy: Horror Island; King of the Cowboys; Mummy's Hand, The

Moran, Polly: Red River Range; Show People; Tom Brown's School Days (1940)

Morane, Jacqueline: Picnic on the Grass

Moranis, Rick: Big Bully; Club Paradise; Flintstones, The; Ghostbusters; Ghostbusters II; Head Office; Honey, I Blew Up the Kid; Honey, I Shrunk the Kids; Honey, We Shrunk Ourselves; Last Polka, The; Little Giants; Little Shop of Horrors (1986); My Blue Heaven; Parenthood; Spaceballs; Splitting Heirs; Strange Brew; Streets of Fire; Wild Life, The

Morant, Richard: John & Yoko: A Love Story; Mahler

Morante, Laura: Tragedy of a Ridiculous Man

Moray, Yvonne: Terror of Tiny Town, The

Mordyukova, Nonna: Commissar, The

More, Camilla: In Search of the Serpent of Death

More, Kenneth: Admirable Crichton, The; Adventures of Sadie; Battle of Britain; Dark of the Sun (Mercenaries) (1968); Doctor in the House; Flame over India; Genevieve; Leopard in the Snow; Never Let Me Go; Night to Remember, A (1958); Scott of the Antarctic; Scrooge (1970); Sink the Bismarck; Tale of Two Cities, A (1980); Thirty-Nine Steps, The (1959); Unidentified Flying Oddball

Moreau, Jeanne: Alberto Express; Alex in Wonderland; Bride Wore Black, The; Chimes at Midnight (Falstaff); Diary of a Chambermaid (1964); Elevator to the Gallows; Ever After; Fire Within, The; Foreign Field, A; Going Places; Heat of Desire; Immortal Story; Jules and Jim; Last Tycoon, The; Les Liaisons Dangereuses; Little Theatre of Jean Renoir, The; Lovers, The (1958); Lumiere; Mademoiselle; Map of the Human Heart; Mr. Klein; Monte Walsh; Old Lady Who Walked in the Sea, The; Proprietor, The; Querelle; Summer House, The; Train, The; Trial, The (1963); Until the End of the World; Viva Maria!; Woman Is a Woman, A

Moreau, Nathaniel: Kissing Place, The; Tidy Endings

Morehead, Elizabeth: Interceptor

Morel, Gael: Wild Reeds

Moreland, Mantan: Charlie Chan in the Secret Service; Chinese Cat, The; Dressed to Kill (1941); Jade Mask, The; King of the Zombies; Meeting at Midnight; Next Time I Marry; Revenge of the Zombies; Scarlet Clue, The; Shanghai Cobra, The; Strange Case of Dr. Rx, The; Two-Gun Man from Harlem; Young Nurses, The

Moreland, Sherry: Fury of the Congo

Morell, Andre: Dark of the Sun (Mercenaries) (1968); Giant Behemoth, The; Hound of the Baskervilles, The (1959); Mummy's Shroud, The; Plague of the Zombies; Quatermass and the Pit; Stolen Face; 10 Rillington Place; Vengeance of She, The

Morell, Joshua: Making Contact

Morelli, Lino: Lunatics & Lovers

Moreno, Antonio: Bohemian Girl, The; Creature from the Black Lagoon; It (1927)

Moreno, Lisa: From Hell to Borneo

Moreno, Rita: Age Isn't Everything; Boss' Son, The; Cry of Battle; Four Seasons, The; Happy Birthday, Gemini; I Like It Like That; King and I, The (1956); Latin Lovers; Ma and Pa Kettle on Vacation; Marlowe; Night of the Following Day, The; Pagan Love Song; Popi; Portrait of a Showgirl; Ritz, The; Seven Cities of Gold; Singin' in the Rain; Summer and Smoke; Toast of New Orleans; West Side Story

Morente, Enrique: Flamenco

Moretti, Linda: Postman, The (Il Postino)

Moretti, Nanni: Caro Diario; Palombella Rossa

Morevski, Abraham: Dybbuk, The

Morey, Bill: Real Men

Morgan, Alexandra: Deadly Games

Morgan, Audrey: Love Your Mama

Morgan, Chad: Whatever

Morgan, Cindy: Tron

Morgan, Debbi: Eve's Bayou; Jesse Owens Story, The; Love and Basketball

Morgan, Dennis: Captains of the Clouds; Christmas in Connecticut (1945); Fighting 69th, The; Great Ziegfeld, The; Hard Way, The (1942); In This Our Life; It's a Great Feeling; Kitty Foyle; Pearl of the South Pacific; Return of Dr. X; Thank Your Lucky Stars

Morgan, Emily: French Lieutenant's Woman, The

Morgan, Frank: Any Number Can Play; Balalaika; Bombshell (1933); Boom Town; Broadway Melody of 1940; Broadway Serenade; Casanova Brown; Cat and the Fiddle, The; Courage of Lassie; Dimples; Great Ziegfeld, The; Green Dolphin Street; Hallelujah, I'm A Bum; Honky Tonk; Human Comedy, The; I Live My Life; Key to the City; Last of Mrs. Cheney, The; Mortal Storm, The; Naughty Marietta; Rosalie; Saratoga; Shop Around the Corner, The; Strattor Story, The; Summer Holiday; Sweethearts; Thousands Cheer; Tortilla Flat; White Cargo; White Cliffs of Dover, The; Wizard of Oz, The; Yolanda and the Thief

Morgan, Georgia: 10 Violent Women

Morgan, Harry: All My Sons (1948); Apple Dumpling Gang, The; Apple Dumpling Gang Rides Again, The; Better Late than Never; Boots Malone; Cat from Outer Space, The; Charley and the Angel; Cimarron (1960); Dragnet (1987); Far Country, The; Flim-Flam Man, The; Frankie and Johnny (1966); Gangster, The; Glenn Miller Story, The; Incident, The (1989); It Started With a Kiss; More Wild Wild West; Not as a Stranger; Ox-Bow Incident, The; Roughnecks; Scandalous John; Shootist, The; Showdown, The (1950); Snowball Express; State Fair (1945); Support Your Local Gunfighter; Support Your Local Sheriff!; Torch Song; Well, The; Wild Wild West Revisited, The; Wing and a Prayer, A

Morgan, Helen: Applause; Frankie and Johnny (1934); Glorifying the American Girl; Go into Your Dance; Show Boat (1936)

Morgan, Jane: Our Miss Brooks (TV Series)

Morgan, Jaye P.: Night Patrol

Morgan, Mariana: Private Lessons—Another Story

Morgan, Michele: Bluebeard (1963); Cat and Mouse; Chase, The (1946); Everybody's Fine; Fallen Idol, The; Higher and Higher; Joan of Paris; Lost Command; Naked Heart, The; Stormy Waters

Morgan, Nancy: Americathon; Grand Theft Auto; Lucky Luke; Nest, The (1988); Pray TV (1980)

Morgan, Priscilla: Pride and Prejudice (1985)

Morgan, Ralph: Dick Tracy vs. Crime Inc.; General Spanky; Kennel Murder Case, The; Last Round-Up; Little Men (1935); Mannequin (1937); Monster Maker, The; Night Monster; Rasputin and the Empress; Star of Midnight; Strange Interlude (1932); Weird Woman; Wives Under Suspicion

Morgan, Read: Hollywood Harry

Morgan, Rhian: August

Morgan, Richard: Wicked, The

Morgan, Scott Wesley: Serial Mom

Morgan, Shelley Taylor: Malibu Express

Morgan, Sidney: Juno and the Paycock

Morgan, Terence: Curse of the Mummy's Tomb, The; Hamlet (1948); Lifetaker, The

Morgan, Tim R.: Winterbeast

Morgan, Trevor: Barney's Great Adventure; Sixth Sense, The

Morganti, Claudio: Palombella Rossa

Morgenstern, Madeleine: Francois Truffaut: Stolen Moments

Morgenstern, Maia: Ulysses' Gaze

Morghen, John: Make Them Die Slowly

Morguia, Ana Ofelia: Mary My Dearest

Mori, Claudia: Lunatics & Lovers

Mori, Kakuro: Story of the Late Chrysanthemums, The

Mori, Masayuki: Bad Sleep Well, The; Idiot, The; Princess Yang Kwei Fei; Rashomon; Ugetsu

Mori, Toshia: Bitter Tea of General Yen, The

Moriarty, Cathy: Another Stakeout; Burndown; Casper; Crazy in Alabama; Digging to China; Dream with the Fishes; Gloria (1999); Gun in Betty Lou's Handbag, The; Hugo Pool; Kindergarten Cop; Mambo Kings, The; Matinee; Me and the Kid; Neighbors; Opposite Corners; Pontiac Moon; P.U.N.K.S.; Raging Bull; Soapdish; White of the Eye

Moriarty, Michael: Bang the Drum Slowly; Blood Link; Calm at Sunset; Children of the Dust; Courage Under Fire; Crime of the Century; Dark Tower; Full Fathom Five; Hanoi Hilton, The; Holocaust; It's Alive III: Island of the Alive; Last Detail, The; Managua; My Old Man's Place; Nitti: The Enforcer; Pale Rider; Q; Report to the Commissioner; Return to Salem's Lot, A; Shiloh; Shiloh 2: Shiloh Season; Stuff, The; Tailspin; Troll; Who'll Stop the Rain; Winds of Kitty Hawk, The

Moriarty, P. H.: Lock, Stock and Two Smoking Barrels

Morice, Tara: Sorrento Beach; Strictly Ballroom

Morier-Genoud, Philippe: Au Revoir, Les Enfants

Moriggi, Francesca: Tree of the Wooden Clogs, The

Morin, Mayo: Clowns, The

Morina, Johnny: Boys of St. Vincent; Salt Water Moose

Morishita, Eri: Cyber Ninja

Morison, Patricia: Calling Dr. Death; Dressed to Kill (1946); Fallen Sparrow, The; Lady on a Train; Song of the Thin Man; Song Without End; Without Love

Morita, Noriyuki "Pat": Alice Through the Looking Glass (1985); Auntie Lee's Meat Pies; Babes in Toyland (1986); Bloodsport II; Bloodsport III; Captive Hearts; Collision Course (1989); Desert Heat; Even Cowgirls Get the Blues; For the Love of It; Hiroshima: Out of the Ashes; Honeymoon in Vegas; Karate Kid, The; Karate Kid Part II, The; Karate Kid Part III, The; King Cobra; Miracle Beach; Next Karate Kid, The; Reggie's Prayer; Thoroughly Modern Millie; Timemaster

Moritz, Louisa: Death Race 2000

Moritzen, Henning: Celebration, The; Memories of a Marriage

Moriyama, Yuko: Zeram

Morley, Karen: Beloved Enemy; Black Fury; Gabriel over the White House; Littlest Rebel, The; Mask of Fu Manchu, The; Mata Hari (1931); Our Daily Bread; Sin of Madelon Claudet, The

Morley, Natasha: Kissed

Morley, Rita: Flesh Eaters, The

Morley, Robert: African Queen, The; Alice in Wonderland (1985); Alice Through the Looking Glass (1985); Alphabet Murders, The; Battle of the Sexes, The; Beat the Devil; Beau Brummell (1954); Cromwell; Ghosts of Berkeley Square; Great Muppet Caper, The; High Road to China; Hot Millions; Hotel Paradiso; Human Factor, The; Istanbul: Keep Your Eyes Open; Loved One, The; Major Barbara; Marie Antoinette; Murder at the Gallop; Of Human Bondage (1964); Oh, Heavenly Dog!; Old Dark House, The (1963); Road to Hong Kong, The; Scavenger Hunt; Song of Norway; Study in Terror, A; Theatre of Blood; Trouble with Spies, The; Who Is Killing the Great Chefs of Europe?; Wind, The (1986); Woman Times Seven

Mornell, Sara: Plan B

Moro, Alicia: Exterminators of the Year 3000

Morra, Gigio: Ciao Professore

Morrell, Leo: Crime Killer, The

Morrill, Priscilla: Last of Mrs. Lincoln, The; Right of Way

Morris, Adrian: Fighting Marines, The

Morris, Anita: Absolute Beginners; Aria; Bloodhounds of Broadway; Blue City; 18 Again; Little Miss Millions; Me and the Kid; Ruthless People; Sinful Life, A

Morris, Ann: Honolulu

Morris, Barboura: Atlas; Bucket of Blood, A; Sorority Girl; Wasp Woman (1960)

Morris, Chester: Bat Whispers, The; Big House, The; Divorcee, The; Five Came Back; Frankie and Johnny (1934); Red-Headed Woman; She Creature, The; Smashing the Rackets; Tomorrow at Seven

Morris, Garrett: Black Rose of Harlem; Black Scorpion II: Aftershock; Cooley High; Critical Condition; Motorama; Santa with Muscles; Severed Ties; Stuff, The; Things We Did Last Summer; Twin Falls Idaho; Where's Poppa?

Morris, Glenn: Tarzan's Revenge

Morris, Greg: Vega$

Morris, Haviland: Home Alone 3; Love or Money?; Who's That Girl

Morris, Howard: Andy Griffith Show, The (TV Series); Boys' Night Out; End of the Line; Forty Pounds of Trouble; Life Stinks; Portrait of a Showgirl; 10 from Your Show of Shows; Transylvania Twist

Morris, Jane: Frankie and Johnny (1991); Pet Shop

Morris, Jonathan: Vampire Journals

Morris, Judy: Between Wars; In Search of Anna; Plumber, The

Morris, Kathryn: Inherit the Wind (1999); Sleepstalker: The Sandman's Last Rites

Morris, Kirk: Maciste in Hell

Morris, Marianne: Vampyres

Morris, Mary: Pimpernel Smith

Morris, Paul: Vamps: Deadly Dream Girls

Morris, Phil: Legal Deceit

Morris, Phyllis: Adventures of Tartu

Morris, Richard: Sea Lion, The

Morris, Stepen (Ankrum, Morris): North of the Rio Grande

Morris, Stephen: Hopalong Cassidy Returns

Morris, Theresa: Private Lessons—Another Story

Morris, Wayne: Bushwhackers; Kid Galahad (1937); Plunder Road; Return of Dr. X; Smiling Ghost, The; Stage to Tucson; Task Force; Time of Your Life, The

Morrisey, Betty: Circus, The/A Day's Pleasure

Morrison, Bill: Maximum Impact; Ozone; Zombie Cop

Morrison, Christine: Galaxy of the Dinosaurs

Morrison, Kenny: NeverEnding Story II, The; Quick and the Dead, The (1987)

Morrison, Temuera: Barb Wire; Once Were Warriors

Morrison, Van: Last Waltz, The

Morrissette, Billy: Severed Ties

Morrissey, David: Hilary and Jackie; Waterland

Morrissey, Eamon: Eat the Peach

Morrow, Doretta: Because You're Mine

Morrow, Jeff: Creature Walks Among Us, The; Giant Claw, The; Kronos; Octaman; This Island Earth

Morrow, Jo: Dr. Death: Seeker of Souls; Three Worlds of Gulliver, The; 13 Ghosts

Morrow, Joshua: My Stepson, My Lover

Morrow, Rob: Labor Pains; Last Dance (1996); Mother (1996); Northern Exposure (TV Series); Only Love; Private Resort; Quiz Show

Morrow, Vie: Bad News Bears, The; Blackboard Jungle, The; Cimarron (1960); Dirty Mary, Crazy Larry; Glass House, The; Men in War; 1990: The Bronx Warriors; Tom Sawyer (1973); Tribute to a Bad Man; Twilight Zone—The Movie

Morse, Barry: Asylum (1972); Changeling, The; Fugitive, The (TV Series); Fugitive, The: The Last Episode (TV Series); Funeral Home; Love at First Sight; Sadat; Space 1999 (TV Series); Story of David, The; Tale of Two Cities, A (1980); Whoops Apocalypse; Woman of Substance, A

Morse, David: Brotherhood of the Rose; Contact; Crazy in Alabama; Crossing Guard, The; Cry in the Wind; Desperate Hours (1990); Extreme Measures; Getaway, The (1994); Green Mile, The; Indian Runner, The; Inside Moves; Langoliers, The; Long Kiss Goodnight, The; Prototype; Rock, The; Shattered Vows; St. Elsewhere (TV Series)

Morse, Helen: Caddie; Picnic at Hanging Rock; Town Like Alice, A

Morse, Laila: Nil by Mouth

Morse, Robert: Boatniks, The; Guide for the Married Man, A; How to Succeed in Business without Really Trying; Hunk; Loved One, The; Matchmaker, The (1958); Oh Dad, Poor Dad—Mama's Hung You in the Closet and I'm Feeling So Sad; That's Singing: The Best of Broadway; Where Were You When the Lights Went Out?

Morse, Stan: Striking Point

Morshower, Glen: Drive-In

Mortensen, Viggo: Albino Alligator; American Yakuza; Boiling Point (1993); Carlito's Way; Crew, The; Crimson Tide; Daylight; Deception (1993); G.I. Jane; Indian Runner, The; Leatherface—the Texas Chainsaw Massacre III; Passion of Darkly Noon, The; Perfect Murder, A; Prophecy, The (1995); Psycho (1998); Reflecting Skin, The; 28 Days; Walk on the Moon, A; Young Americans, The

Mortimer, Caroline: Death of Adolf Hitler, The

Morton, Amy: Rookie of the Year

Morton, Dee Dee: Dakota (1988)

Morton, Gary: Postcards from the Edge

Morton, Greg: Adultress, The

Morton, Joe: Alone in the Neon Jungle; Astronaut's Wife, The; Between the Lines; Blues Brothers 2000; Brother from Another Planet, The; City of Hope; Crossroads; Executive Decision; Forever Young (1992); Inkwell, The; Legacy of Lies; Lone Star (1996); Miss Evers' Boys; Speed; Stranded; Tap; Terminator 2: Judgment Day; Trouble in Mind; Trouble on the Corner; Walking Dead, The

Morton, Samantha: Dreaming of Joseph Lees; Emma (1996); Sweet and Lowdown; This Is the Sea; Under the Skin

Mosby, John: Backfire (1994)

Moschin, Gastone: Joke of Destiny; Mr. Superinvisible; Oldest Profession, The

Moscovich, Maurice: Everything Happens at Night

Moscow, David: Big; Newsies; White Wolves: A Cry in the Wild II

Moseley, Bill: Silent Night, Deadly Night III: Better Watch Out!

Moser, Jeff: To Catch a Yeti

Moses, David: Daring Dobermans, The

Moses, Harry: Sweater Girls

Moses, Mark: Dead Men Don't Die; Hollywood Heartbreak; Tracker, The; Treehouse Hostage

Moses, Norman: Unearthing, The

Moses, William R.: Alien from L.A.; Circumstances Unknown; Double Exposure (1993); Evil Has a Face; Fiancé, The; Fun; Haunting of Sea Cliff Inn, The; Mystic Pizza; Nurse, The

Moskow, Kenny: Overkill (1996)

Mosley, Roger E.: Greatest, The; Heart Condition; I Know Why the Caged Bird Sings; Jericho Mile, The; Mack, The; Pentathlon; Pray TV (1980); Steel (1980); Unlawful Entry

Moss, Arnold: Caper of the Golden Bulls, The; Loves of Carmen, The

Moss, Carrie Anne: Matrix, The; New Blood; Sabotage (1996)

Moss, Darcy De: Forbidden Zone: Alien Abduction

Moss, Elizabeth: Earthly Possessions; Girl, Interrupted; Midnight's Child

Moss, George: Riff-Raff (1992)

Moss, Jesse: Noah

Moss, Ronn: Hard Ticket to Hawaii; Hearts and Armour; Hot Chili in the City

Moss, Stewart: Bat People

Moss, Tegan: Sea People

Most, Donny: Huckleberry Finn (1975); Stewardess School

Mostel, Josh: Animal Behavior; Beverly Hills 90210; Billy Madison; City Slickers; City Slickers II; Compromising Positions; Great Expectations (1998); Little Man Tate; Maddening, The; Matewan; Money Pit, The; Naked Tango; Radio Days; Stoogemania; Windy City

Mostel, Zero: Du Barry Was a Lady; Enforcer, The (1951); Front, The; Funny Thing Happened on the Way to the Forum, A; Hot Rock, The; Journey into Fear (1975); Mastermind; Panic in the Streets; Producers, The; Sirocco

Motoki, Masahiro: Gonin; Mystery of Rampo, The

Motulsky, Judy: Slithis

Mouchet, Catherine: Therese

Moulder-Brown, John: Deep End; King, Queen and Knave; Sleeping Murder

Moulin, Charles: Baker's Wife, The

Mouton, Benjamin: Whore

Movin, Lisbeth: Day of Wrath

Movita: Wolf Call

Mowbray, Alan: Androcles and the Lion; Charlie Chan in London; Doughgirls, The; Every Girl Should Be Married; Girl from Missouri, The; Hollywood Hotel; In Person; It Happened in New Orleans; Ma and Pa Kettle at Home; Majority of One, A; Merton of the Movies; My Dear Secretary; On the Avenue; Roman Scandals; Rose Marie (1936); So This Is Washington; Stand-In; Study in Scarlet, A; Terror by Night; That Uncertain Feeling; Topper Takes a Trip; Villain Still Pursued Her, The

Mower, Patrick: Black Beauty (1971)

Moy, Wood: Chan Is Missing

Moya, Pay: In the Soup

Moyer, Stephen: Prince Valiant (1997)

Moyer, Tawny: House of the Rising Sun

Moynihan, Bill: Creeps, The

Moyo, Alois: Power of One, The

Mr. T: D.C. Cab; Freaked; Penitentiary II; Rocky III; Straight Line

Mucari, Carlo: Tex and the Lord of the Deep

Mudugno, Enrica Maria: Kaos

Muel, Jean-Paul: House That Mary Bought, The

Mueller, Cookie: Female Trouble; Multiple Maniacs

Mueller, Dick: Omaha (The Movie)

Mueller, Maureen: In a Shallow Grave; Over Her Dead Body

Mueller-Stahl, Armin: Angry Harvest; Avalon; Colonel Redl; Forget Mozart; Game, The (1997); Holy Matrimony; House of the Spirits, The; In the Presence of Mine Enemies; Jakob the Liar; Kafka; Last Good Time, The; Lola (1982); Music Box, The; Night on Earth; Peacemaker, The (1997); Power of One, The; Red Hot; Shine; Theodore Rex; Third

Miracle, The; Thirteenth Floor, The (1999); 12 Angry Men (1997); Utz; X-Files, The (1998)

Mui, Anita: Better Tomorrow 3, A: Love and Death in Saigon; Jet Li's the Enforcer; Rumble in the Bronx

Muir, David: Doctor Hackenstein

Muir, Gavin: Night Tide

Mukherji, Swapan: World of Apu, The

Mulcahy, Jack: Brothers McMullen, The

Muldaur, Diana: Beyond Reason; McQ; Other, The; Planet Earth; Return of Frank Cannon, The

Muldoon, Patrick: Arrival II, The; Black Cat Run; Rage and Honor II: Hostile Takeover

Mule, Francesco: When Women Lost Their Tails

Mulford, Nancy: Act of Piracy

Mulgrew, Kate: Danielle Steel's Daddy; Love Spell; Manions of America, The; Remo Williams: The Adventure Begins; Roots—The (TV Series); Round Numbers; Stranger Is Watching, A; Throw Momma from the Train

Mulhall, Jack: Buck Rogers: Destination Saturn (Planet Outlaws); Flesh and Blood (1922); Invisible Ghost; Mysterious Dr. Satan; Mystery Squadron; Outlaws of Sonora; Saddle Mountain Roundup; Skull and Crown; Three Musketeers, The (1933)

Mulhare, Edward: Our Man Flint; Out to Sea; Outer Limits, The (TV Series); Von Ryan's Express

Mulhern, Matt: Biloxi Blues

Mulkey, Chris: Bound and Gagged: A Love Story; Dead Cold; Deadbolt; Ghost in the Machine; Heartbreak Hotel; Hometown Boy Makes Good; In Dangerous Company; Jack's Back; Patti Rocks; Roe vs. Wade; Runaway Father; Silencer, The; Weapons of Mass Distraction; Write to Kill

Mull, Martin: Bad Manners; Boss' Wife, The; Clue; Cutting Class; Dance with Death; Day My Parents Ran Away, The; Edie & Pen; Far Out Man; FM; Home Is Where the Hart Is; How the West Was Fun; Lots of Luck; Mary Hartman, Mary Hartman (TV Series); Mr. Mom; Mr. Write; Mrs. Doubtfire; My Bodyguard; O.C. & Stiggs; Private School; Rented Lips; Serial; Ski Patrol; Take This Job and Shove It; Ted & Venus; Think Big

Mullally, Megan: Last Resort

Mullan, Carrie: Hideous Kinky

Mullan, Peter: Miss Julie (1999); My Name is Joe

Mullaney, Jack: Honeymoon Machine, The; Tickle Me

Mullany, Mitch: Breaks, The

Mullavey, Greg: Body Count (1988); C.C. & Company; I Dismember Mama; Mary Hartman, Mary Hartman (TV Series); Vultures

Mullen, Barbara: Corridor of Mirrors

Mullen, Beckie: Sinful Intrigue

Mullen, Patty: Doom Asylum; Frankenhooker

Muller, Harrison: Final Executioner, The; She (1983); 2020 Texas Gladiators; Violent Breed, The

Muller, Paul: Devil's Commandment, The; Nightmare Castle

Mulligan, Richard: Babes in Toyland (1986); Big Bus, The; Doin' Time; Fine Mess, A; Gore Vidal's Lincoln; Group, The; Heavenly Kid, The; Hideaways, The; Little Big Man; Meatballs Part II; Poker Alice; Scavenger Hunt; S.O.B.; Teachers

Mulligan, Terry David: Hard Core Logo

Mullinar, Rod: Thirst

Mullins, Robin: Nell

Mulloney, Joe: Restless Natives

Mullowney, Deborah: Cellar Dweller

Mulroney, Dermot: Bad Girls (1994); Bastard Out of Carolina; Bright Angel; Career Opportunities; Copycat; Goodbye Lover; Heart of Justice; How to Make an American Quilt; Kansas City; Last Outlaw, The (1993); Living in Oblivion; Longtime Companion; My Best Friend's Wedding; Point of No Return; Samantha; Silent Tongue; Staying Together; Survival Quest; There Goes My Baby; Thing Called Love, The; Trigger Effect, The; Where the Day Takes You; Where the Money Is; Young Guns

Mulroney, Kieran: Career Opportunities

Mulrooney, Lee: Resurrection Man

Mummert, Danny: It's a Great Life

Mumy, Billy: Bless the Beasts and Children; Dear Brigitte; Lost in Space (TV Series); Sammy, the Way-Out Seal

Mumy, Seth: Three Wishes

Munch, Richard: Of Pure Blood

Munchkin, R. W.: L.A. Vice

Mundra, Michael Aniel: Across the Moon

Mundy, Kevin: Better Than Chocolate

Mune, Ian: Sleeping Dogs

Muni, Paul: Angel on My Shoulder (1946); Black Fury; Commandos Strike at Dawn; Good Earth, The; I Am a Fugitive from a Chain Gang; Juarez; Last Angry Man, The; Life of Emile Zola, The; Scarface (1932); Song to Remember, A; Story of Louis Pasteur, The

Muniz, Frankie: My Dog Skip

Muniz, Tommy: Crazy from the Heart

Munro, Caroline: At the Earth's Core; Captain Kronos: Vampire Hunter; Devil Within Her, The; Don't Open Till Christmas; Golden Voyage of Sinbad, The; Last Horror Film, The; Maniac (1980); Night Owl; Slaughter High; Spy Who Loved Me, The; Star Crash

Munro, Janet: Crawling Eye, The; Darby O'Gill and the Little People; Day the Earth Caught Fire, The; Horsemasters; Third Man on the Mountain

Munro, Lochlyn: Dead Man on Campus

Munro, Neil: Confidential; Dancing in the Dark

Munroe, Fred: Longest Hunt, The

Munroe, Steve: Comic, The (1985)

Munshin, Jules: Easter Parade; Mastermind; On the Town; Take Me Out to the Ball Game

Munson, Ona: Lady from Louisiana; Red House, The; Shanghai Gesture, The

Munzuk, Maxim: Dersu Uzala

Muppets: Great Muppet Caper, The; Muppet Movie, The; Muppets Take Manhattan, The

Murase, Sachiko: Rhapsody in August

Murat, Jean: Carnival in Flanders; Eternal Return, The

Murata, Takehiro: Minbo, or The Gentle Art of Japanese Extortion

Muravyova, Irina: Moscow Does Not Believe in Tears

Murdocco, Vince: Deathgame; Flesh Gordon 2: Flesh Gordon meets the Cosmic Cheerleaders

Murdock, George: Breaker! Breaker!; Certain Fury; Scorpio One; Strange Case of Dr. Jekyll and Mr. Hyde, The (1989)

Muresan, Gheorghe: My Giant

Murney, Christopher: Grace Quigley; Last Dragon, The; Secret of My Success, The

Murphy, Annette: Star Maps

Murphy, Audie: Arizona Raiders; Guns of Fort Petticoat; Red Badge of Courage, The; To Hell and Back; Unforgiven, The (1960)

Murphy, Ben: Chisholms, The; Cradle Will Fall, The; Riding with Death; Time Walker

Murphy, Brittany: Clueless; Devil's Arithmetic, The; Girl, Interrupted; Prophecy II, The

Murphy, Carolyn: Liberty Heights

Murphy, Charlie: CB4

Murphy, Donald: Frankenstein's Daughter; Lord Love a Duck

Murphy, Donna: Center Stage; Star Trek: Insurrection

Murphy, Eddie: Another 48 Hrs.; Best Defense; Beverly Hills Cop; Beverly Hills Cop II; Beverly Hills Cop 3; Boomerang (1992); Bowfinger; Coming to America; Distinguished Gentleman, The; Dr. Dolittle (1998); 48 Hrs.; Golden Child, The; Harlem Nights; Holy Man; Life; Metro; Nutty Professor, The (1996); Trading Places; Vampire in Brooklyn

Murphy, Edna: Tarzan and the Golden Lion

Murphy, George: Bataan; Battleground; Broadway Melody of 1938; Broadway Melody of 1940; Broadway Rhythm; For Me and My Gal; Girl, a Guy and a Gob, A; Having a Wonderful Time; It's a Big Country; Kid Millions; Letter of Introduction; Little Miss Broadway; Little Nellie Kelly; Show Business; Step Lively; This Is the Army; Tom, Dick and Harry

Murphy, Gerard: Waterworld

Murphy, Jack: Peter Pan (1924)

Murphy, Johnny: Commitments, The; Into the West

Murphy, Mary: Main Street to Broadway; Man Alone, A; Maverick Queen, The; Wild One, The

Murphy, Michael: Autobiography of Miss Jane Pittman, The; Breaking the Surface: The Greg Louganis Story; Caine Mutiny Court Martial, The; Class of Miss MacMichael, The; Clean Slate (1994); Cloak and Dagger (1984); Count Yorga, Vampire; Dead Ahead: The Exxon Valdez Disaster; Folks; Great Bank Hoax, The; Kansas City; Manhattan; Mesmerized (Shocked); Phase IV; Salvador; Shocker; Strange Be-

havior; Tailspin; Tanner '88; That Cold Day in the Park; Unmarried Woman, An; Year of Living Dangerously, The

Murphy, Reilly: Body Snatchers, The (1993)

Murphy, Rosemary: Any Wednesday; Ben; For the Boys; Walking Tall

Murphy, Shannon: Firehouse (1987)

Murphy, Steve: No Justice

Murphy, Timothy Patrick: Sam's Son

Murray, Bill: Caddyshack; Cradle Will Rock; Ed Wood; Ghostbusters; Ghostbusters II; Groundhog Day; Kingpin; Larger than Life; Little Shop of Horrors (1986); Loose Shoes; Mad Dog and Glory; Man Who Knew Too Little, The; Meatballs; Quick Change; Razor's Edge, The (1984); Rushmore; Scrooged; Space Jam; Stripes; Things We Did Last Summer; Tootsie; What About Bob?; Where the Buffalo Roam

Murray, Chic: Gregory's Girl

Murray, Christopher: Just Cause

Murray, Don: Advise and Consent; Baby the Rain Must Fall; Bus Stop; Conquest of the Planet of the Apes; Deadly Hero; Endless Love; Ghosts Can't Do It; Hearts Adrift; Hoodlum Priest, The; I Am the Cheese; Justin Morgan Had a Horse; Mistress (1987); One Man's Way; Peggy Sue Got Married; Quarterback Princess; Radioactive Dreams; Scorpion; Shake Hands with the Devil; Sweet Love, Bitter

Murray, Guillermo: World of the Vampires

Murray, James: Crowd, The

Murray, Jan: Night Stalker, The: Two Tales of Terror (TV Series); Which Way to the Front?

Murray, John: Moving Violations

Murray, Mae: Bachelor Apartment; Merry Widow, The (1925)

Murray, Mick: Midnight Witness

Murtaugh, James: Rosary Murders, The

Murton, Lionel: Meet the Navy

Murton, Tom: Main Street to Broadway

Musante, Tony: Bird with the Crystal Plumage, The; Breaking Up Is Hard to Do; Collector's Item; Grissom Gang, The; Incident, The (1967)

Muscat, Angelo: Prisoner, The (1968) (TV Series)

Muse, Clarence: Black Stallion, The; Murder over New York

Musgrave, Robert: Bottle Rocket

Musidora: Vampires, The (1915) (Les Vampires)

Mustain, Minor: Snake Eater III: His Law

Musy, Allan: Warrior Spirit

Mutchie, Marjorie Ann: It's a Great Life

Muti, Ornella: Casanova (1987); Once Upon a Crime; Oscar (1991); Somewhere in the City; Swann in Love; Tales of Ordinary Madness; Wait Until Spring, Bandini

Muza, Melvin: Street Hitz (Street Story)

Myers, Bruce: Governess, The

Myers, Carmel: Beau Brummell (1924); Ben-Hur (1926); Svengali (1931)

Myers, Cynthia: Beyond the Valley of the Dolls

Myers, Harrison: Dear Santa

Myers, Harry: City Lights

Myers, Kathleen: Dick Turpin

Myers, Kim: Illegally Yours; Nightmare on Elm Street 2, A: Freddy's Revenge

Myers, Mike: Austin Powers: International Man of Mystery; Austin Powers: The Spy Who Shagged Me; 54; So I Married an Axe Murderer; Wayne's World; Wayne's World 2

Myerson, Alan: Steelyard Blues

Myles, Harry: Robo Vampire

Mynster, Karen-Lise: Sofie

N!Xau: Gods Must Be Crazy II, The

Renhua, Na: Girl from Hunan

Nabors, Jim: Andy Griffith Show, The (TV Series); Return to Mayberry; Stroker Ace

Nachtergaele, Matheus: Four Days in September

Nader, George: Away all Boats; Carnival Story; House of 1,000 Dolls; Human Duplicators, The; Lady Godiva; Monsoon; Robot Monster

Nader, Michael: Finishing Touch, The; Flash, The; Fled; Jackie Collins' Lucky Chances; Lady Mobster; Nick Knight

Naderi, Massoumeh: Apple, The

Naderi, Qorban Ali: Apple, The

Naderi, Zahra: Apple, The

Nagase, Masatochi: Cold Fever; Mystery Train

Nagel, Anne: Black Friday; Case of the Stuttering Bishop, The; Hoosier Schoolboy; Mad Doctor of Market Street, The; Mad Monster; Man Made Monster (The Atomic Monster); Spirit of West Point, The; Winners of the West

Nagel, Conrad: All That Heaven Allows; Ann Vickers; Divorcee, The; Kiss, The (1929); Mysterious Lady, The

Nagy, Bill: Countess from Hong Kong, A

Naidu, Ajay: Touch and Go; Where the River Runs Black

Naiduk, Stacy: Steel and Lace

Nail, Jimmy: Diamond's Edge; Evita; Still Crazy

Nail, Joanne: Switchblade Sisters

Naish, J. Carrol: Across the Wide Missouri; Ann Vickers; Annie Get Your Gun; Beast with Five Fingers, The; Beau Geste; Behind the Rising Sun; Black Hand, The; Bulldog Drummond Comes Back; Bulldog Drummond in Africa; Calling Dr. Death; Clash by Night; Corsican Brothers, The (1941); Denver and Rio Grande, The; Down Argentine Way; Dracula vs. Frankenstein; Fighter Attack; Fugitive, The (1947); Gung Ho! (1943); House of Frankenstein; Humoresque; Joan of Arc; Jungle Woman; Kissing Bandit, The; Last Command, The (1955); Monster Maker, The; New Adventures of Charlie Chan, The (TV Series); Rage at Dawn; Rio Grande; Sahara (1943); Southerner, The; Strange Confession; That Midnight Kiss; Think Fast, Mr. Moto; This Could Be the Night; Thunder Trail; Toast of New Orleans; Waterfront; World Gone Mad, The

Naismith, Laurence: Amazing Mr. Blunden, The; Carrington, V. C.; Concrete Jungle, The (1962) (Criminal, The); Greyfriars Bobby; Man Who Never Was, The; Night to Remember, A (1958); Persuaders, The (TV Series); Scrooge (1970); Sink the Bismarck; World of Suzie Wong, The; Young Winston

Naito, Takashi: After Life

Naito, Taketoshi: After Life

Najee-ullah, Mansoor: Death of a Prophet

Naji, Amir: Children of Heaven

Najimy, Kathy: Hocus Pocus; Jeffrey; Nevada; Sister Act; Sister Act 2: Back in the Habit

Nakadai, Tatsuya: Face of Another, The; High and Low; Human Condition, The, Part One: No Greater Love; Human Condition, The, Part Two: The Road to Eternity; Human Condition, The, Part Three: A Soldier's Prayer; Hunter in the Dark; Kagemusha; Kojiro; Kwaidan; Odd Obsession; Ran; Sanjuro; Sword of Doom; Wicked City, The (1992); Wolves, The (1981)

Nakagawa, Anna: Silk Road, The

Nakagawa, Ken: Living on Tokyo Time

Nakagawa, Roger: Escapade in Japan

Nakamura, Atsuo: Highest Honor, The

Nakamura, Ganjiro: Drifting Weeds

Nakamura, Kichiemon: Double Suicide

Nakamura, Knemon: Forty Seven Ronin

Nakamura, Toru: Blue Tiger; Gen-X Cops; New York Cop

Nakhapetov, Rodion: Slave of Love, A

Nalbach, Daniel: Gig, The

Nalder, Reggie: Day And The Hour; Mark of the Devil; Mark of the Devil, Part 2; Salem's Lot; Zoltan—Hound of Dracula

Naldi, Nita: Blood and Sand (1922); Dr. Jekyll and Mr. Hyde (1920); Ten Commandments, The (1923)

Namath, Joe: C.C. & Company; Chattanooga Choo Choo

Nance, Jack: Eraserhead; Little Witches; Meatballs 4; Twin Peaks (Movie); Twin Peaks (TV Series); Voodoo

Nance, John: Ghoulies

'Nann, Erika: Mindtwister

Nanty, Isabelle: Tatie Danielle

Napaul, Neriah: Bikini Carwash Company 2

Naper, Marshall: Georgia (1987)

Napier, Alan: Across the Wide Missouri; Challenge to Lassie; Hangover Square; Hills of Home; House of the Seven Gables, The; Invisible Man Returns; Mademoiselle Fifi; Mole People, The; 36 Hours; Uninvited, The (1944)

Napier, Charles: Big Tease, The; Center of the Web; Citizen's Band; Deep Space; Ernest Goes to Jail; Eyes of the Beholder; Future Zone; Grifters, The; Hard Justice; Homicidal Impulse; Hunter's Moon; Incredible Hulk Returns, The; Indio 2: The Revolt; Instant Justice; Jury Duty; Last Embrace, The; Macon County Jail; Max Is Missing; Miami Blues; Night Stalker, The (1986); One-Man Force; Philadelphia; Rambo: First Blood II; Renegade; Return to Frogtown; Riot (1996); Silence of the Lambs; Silk Degrees; Skeeter; Sol-

dier's Fortune; Steel (1997); Three Ninjas Knuckle Up; Treacherous Crossing

Napir, Yvette: Run If You Can

Naples, Toni: Dinosaur Island

Nardi, Tony: Good Night, Michelangelo

Nardini, Tom: Africa—Texas Style!

Narelle, Brian: Dark Star

Narita, Darling: Big Bang Theory, The

Narita, Mikio: Zatoichi: The Blind Swordsman and the Chess Expert

Narova, Cecilia: Tango

Nas: Belly

Naschak, Andrea: Hold Me, Thrill Me, Kiss Me

Naschy, Paul: Blood Moon (Werewolf Versus the Vampire Woman, The); Craving, The; Dracula's Great Love; Fury of the Wolf Man; Horror Rises from the Tomb; House of Psychotic Women; Night of the Howling Beast

Nash, Chris: Mischief; Modern Girls; Satisfaction

Nash, Jennifer: Invisible: The Chronicles of Benjamin Knight

Nash, Marilyn: Monsieur Verdoux; Unknown World

Nash, Mary: Cobra Woman; Men of Boys Town

Nash, Noreen: Lone Ranger and the Lost City of Gold, The

Nassar, Joseph Bou: West Beirut

Nat, Marie-Jose: Les Violons du Bal; Train of Life

Natale, Anthony: His Bodyguard

Nathan, Adam: Parting Glances

Nathan, Stephen: First Nudie Musical, The; You Light Up My Life

Nathan, Vivian: Young Savages, The

Natsuki, Yosuke: Dagora, the Space Monster; Ghidrah, the Three-Headed Monster

Natwick, Mildred: Against All Flags; Barefoot in the Park; Court Jester, The; Daisy Miller; Dangerous Liaisons; If It's Tuesday, This Must Be Belgium; Kissing Bandit, The; Long Voyage Home, The; Quiet Man, The; Tammy and the Bachelor; Trouble with Harry, The; Yolanda and the Thief

Naughton, Charlie: Frozen Limits, The

Naughton, Darag: War of the Buttons

Naughton, David: American Werewolf in London, An; Amityville: A New Generation; Beanstalk; Boy in Blue, The; Getting Physical; Hot Dog … The Movie; Midnight Madness; Not for Publication; Overexposed; Private Affairs; Separate Vacations; Sleeping Car, The; Steel and Lace; Wild Cactus

Naughton, James: Birds II, The: Land's End; Glass Menagerie, The; Good Mother, The; Stranger Is Watching, A

Naughty by Nature: Show, The

Navarro, Carlos: Illusion Travels by Streetcar

Navarro, Gustavo: Tango Lesson, The

Naveira, Anna: Blood and Sand (1941); Bridge of San Luis Rey, The; Salome (1923)

Nay, Zachi: Up Your Anchor

Nazimova, Anna: Blood and Sand (1941); Bridge of San Luis Rey, The; Salome (1923)

Nazzari, Amedeo: Naked Maja, The; Nights of Cabiria

Ndaba, Themba: Running Wild (1998)

Neagle, Anna: Courtney Affair, The; Forever and a Day; Lilacs in the Spring (Let's Make Up); London Melody; No, No Nanette; Nurse Edith Cavell

Neal, Billie: Mortal Thoughts

Neal, Edwin: Future-Kill; Texas Chainsaw Massacre, The

Neal, Ella: Mysterious Dr. Satan

Neal, Elsie: Restaurant

Neal, Frances: Lady Scarface

Neal, Patricia: All Quiet on the Western Front (1979); Bastard, The; Baxter (1973); Breakfast at Tiffany's; Caroline?; Cookie's Fortune; Day the Earth Stood Still, The; Eric; Face in the Crowd, A; Fountainhead, The; Ghost Story; Hud; In Harm's Way; Operation Pacific; Run Stranger Run; Shattered Vows; Stranger from Venus; Subject Was Roses, The; Three Secrets; Unremarkable Life, An

Neal, Peggy: X from Outer Space, The

Neal, Scott: Beautiful Thing

Neal, Tom: Another Thin Man; Behind the Rising Sun; Bowery at Midnight; Brute Man, The; Courageous Dr. Christian, The; Detour (1945); First Yank into Tokyo; Hatbox Mystery, The; King of the Bullwhip

Neale, David: Tales from the Gimli Hospital

Neale, Heather: Tales from the Gimli Hospital

Nealon, Kevin: All I Want for Christmas

Neame, Christopher: Diplomatic Immunity; Dracula A.D. 1972; Edge of Honor; Hellbound; Romeo and Juliet (1988);

Steel Dawn; Still Not Quite Human; Street Knight; Transformations

Near, Holly: Dogfight; Slaughterhouse Five; Todd Killings, The

Neckar, Vaclav: Closely Watched Trains; Larks on a String

Needham, Tracey: Backlash (1998); Buried Alive II; Lush Life

Neeley, Ted: Hard Country; Jesus Christ, Superstar

Neely, Cam: Dumb and Dumber

Neely, Gail: Surf Nazis Must Die

Neely, Mark: Off the Mark

Neeman, Hillel: Boy Takes Girl; Soldier of the Night

Neenan, Audrie: Sunset Limousine

Neeson, Liam: Before and After; Big Man; Bounty, The; Darkman; Dead Pool, The; Deception (1993); Ethan Frome; Excalibur; Good Mother, The; Gun Shy; Haunting, The (1999); High Spirits; Husbands and Wives; Leap of Faith; Les Misérables (1998); Michael Collins; Mission, The; Nell; Next of Kin (1989); Rob Roy; Satisfaction; Schindler's List; Shining Through; Star Wars: Episode I The Phantom Menace; Suspect; Under Suspicion

Neff, Hildegarde: Bluebeard (1963); Fedora; Snows of Kilimanjaro, The; Unnatural

Negami, Jun: Golden Demon

Negoda, Natalya: Back in the U.S.S.R.; Comrades of Summer, The; Little Vera

Negret, Francois: Night and Day (1991)

Negri, Pola: Gypsy Blood; Moonspinners, The; One Arabian Night; Passion (1919)

Negro, Del: Aguirre: Wrath of God

Negro, Mary Joan: King Richard II; No Big Deal

Negron, Olivia: Everything Relative

Negron, Taylor: Angels in the Outfield (1994); Bad Medicine; Bio-Dome; Changing Habits; Last Boy Scout, The; Young Doctors in Love

Neher, Carola: Threepenny Opera, The

Nehm, Kristina: Fringe Dwellers, The

Neidorf, David: Undercover (1987)

Neil, Christopher: Adventures of a Private Eye

Neil, Hildegard: Antony and Cleopatra (1973); Man Who Haunted Himself, The; Touch of Class, A

Neil, Roger: Oracle, The

Neill, James: Ten Commandments, The (1923)

Neill, Noel: Atom Man vs. Superman; Invasion USA (1952); Superman—The Serial; TV's Best Adventures of Superman

Neill, Sam: Attack Force Z; Bicentennial Man; Blood of Others, The; Children of the Revolution; Country Life; Cry in the Dark, A; Dead Calm; Death in Brunswick; Enigma; Event Horizon; Fever; Final Conflict, The; For Love Alone; Forgotten Silver; From a Far Country; Good Wife, The; Horse Whisperer, The; Hostage (1992); Hunt for Red October, The; In the Mouth of Madness; Ivanhoe (1982); Jurassic Park; Memoirs of an Invisible Man; My Brilliant Career; One Against the Wind; Piano, The; Plenty; Question of Faith; Rainbow Warrior; Reilly: The Ace of Spies; Restoration; Rudyard Kipling's The Jungle Book (1994); Sirens; Sleeping Dogs; Snow White: A Tale of Terror; Until the End of the World

Neilson, Agnes: Buster and Fatty

Neilson, John: Terror at the Red Wolf Inn (Terror House)

Nelkin, Stacey: Everything Relative; Get Crazy; Going Ape!; Halloween III: Season of the Witch; Up the Academy

Nell, Little: Jubilee; Rocky Horror Picture Show, The

Nell, Nathalie: Rape of Love (L'Amour Violé)

Nelligan, Kate: Bethune; Calm at Sunset; Cider House Rules, The; Diamond Fleece, The; Eleni; Eye of the Needle; Fatal Instinct (1993); Frankie and Johnny (1991); How to Make an American Quilt; Love and Hate; Margaret's Museum; Mother's Prayer, A; Prince of Tides, The; Terror Stalks the Class Reunion; U.S. Marshals; Up Close and Personal; Without a Trace; Wolf

Neilson, John: Shark's Treasure

Nelson, Barry: Bataan; Casino Royale (1954); Island Claws; Johnny Eager; Pete 'n' Tillie; Rio Rita; Shadow of the Thin Man

Nelson, Bob: Brain Donors

Nelson, Bobby: Cyclone in the Saddle

Nelson, Craig T.: Action Jackson; All the Right Moves; ... And Justice for All; Call to Glory; Devil's Advocate; Diary of a Teenage Hitchhiker; Fire Next Time, The; Ghosts of Mis-

sissippi; Huntress, The; I'm Not Rappaport; Josephine Baker Story, The; Killing Fields, The; Me and Him; Murderers Among Us: The Simon Wiesenthal Story; Poltergeist; Poltergeist II: The Other Side; Probable Cause; Rachel River; Rage (1980); Silkwood; Skulls, The; Troop Beverly Hills; Wag the Dog

Nelson, Danny: Blood Salvage

Nelson, David: Adventures of Ozzie and Harriet, The (TV Series); Cry-Baby; Peyton Place

Nelson, Dick: Great Guns

Nelson, Ed: Attack of the Crab Monsters; Boneyard, The; Brain Eaters, The; Bucket of Blood, A; Cries of Silence; For the Love of Benji; Return of Frank Cannon, The

Nelson, Gene: Lullaby of Broadway; Tea for Two; West Point Story, The

Nelson, Guy: Invasion of the Space Preachers

Nelson, Harriet: Adventures of Ozzie and Harriet, The (TV Series); Follow the Fleet; Kid with the 200 I.Q., The; Take It Big

Nelson, John Allen: Criminal Passion; Deathstalker III—The Warriors from Hell; Hunk; Killer Klowns from Outer Space; Saigon Commandos

Nelson, Judd: Billionaire Boys Club; Blackwater Trail; Blindfold: Acts of Obsession; Blue City; Breakfast Club, The; Cabin by the Lake; Caroline at Midnight; Circumstances Unknown; Conflict of Interest; Dark Backward, The; Entangled; Every Breath; Fandango; Far Out Man; Flinch; From the Hip; Hail Caesar; Hiroshima: Out of the Ashes; Light It Up; Making the Grade; New Jack City; Primary Motive; Relentless; St. Elmo's Fire; Steel (1997)

Nelson, June: Adventures of Ozzie and Harriet, The (TV Series)

Nelson, Kenneth: Boys in the Band, The

Nelson, Kris: Adventures of Ozzie and Harriet, The (TV Series)

Nelson, Lori: All I Desire; Day the World Ended, The; I Died a Thousand Times; Ma and Pa Kettle at the Fair; Ma and Pa Kettle at Waikiki; Mohawk; Revenge of the Creature; Underwater!

Nelson, Mari: Whore 2

Nelson, Michael J.: Mystery Science Theatre 3000: The Movie

Nelson, Ozzie: Adventures of Ozzie and Harriet, The (TV Series); Impossible Years, The; People Are Funny; Take It Big

Nelson, Peter: Crime Zone; Eye of the Eagle 3; Silk 2

Nelson, Rebecca: Surviving Desire

Nelson, Ricky: Adventures of Ozzie and Harriet, The (TV Series); Rio Bravo; Wackiest Ship in the Army, The

Nelson, Ruth: Awakenings; Haunting Passion, The; Wilson

Nelson, Sandra: Halfback of Notre Dame, The

Nelson, Sean: American Buffalo; Fresh; Stranger in the Kingdom, A; Wood, The

Nelson, Steven: Little Ninjas

Nelson, Tracy: Down and Out in Beverly Hills; Game of Love, The

Nelson, Willie: Amazons; Another Pair of Aces; Barbarosa; Coming Out of the Ice; Dynamite and Gold; Electric Horseman, The; Honeysuckle Rose; Last Days of Frank and Jesse James; Pair of Aces; Red-Headed Stranger, The; Songwriter; Stagecoach (1986); Texas Guns; Thief (1981); Wag the Dog

Nemec, Corin: Drop Zone; Lifeforce Experiment, The; Operation Dumbo Drop; Solar Crisis; Stand, The

Nene, Sibongile: Jit

Neri, Francesca: Flight of the Innocent; Live Flesh; Outrage (1994)

Nero, Franco: Camelot; Challenge to White Fang; Confessions of a Police Captain; Die Hard 2: Die Harder; Django; Enter the Ninja; Force Ten from Navarone; Girl, The; High Crime; Kamikaze 89; Legend of Valentino; Long Live Your Death; Magdalene; Man with Bogart's Face, The; Querelle; Redneck; Salamander, The; Sardine: Kidnapped; Shark Hunter, The; Spaghetti Western; Sweet Country; Talk of Angels; Touch and Die; Tramplers, The; Tristana; Virgin and the Gypsy, The; Windmills of the Gods; Young Catherine

Nero, Toni: No Dead Heroes; Silent Night, Deadly Night

Nervo, Jimmy: Frozen Limits, The

Nesbitt, Cathleen: Affair to Remember, An; Desirée; Family Plot; Nicholas Nickleby; Staircase

Nesbitt, Derren: Horrors of Burke and Hare

Nesbitt, James: Go Now; Waking Ned Devine

Nesmith, Mike: Head (1968); Television Parts Home Companion

Nettleton, Lois: Bamboo Saucer (Collision Course); Brass; Butterfly; Deadly Blessing; Good Guys and the Bad Guys, The; Man in the Glass Booth; Manhunt for Claude Dallas; Period of Adjustment

Neubert, Keith: Sons of Trinity, The

Neufeld, Martin: Relative Fear

Neufield, Marc: Highlander: The Final Dimension

Neuman, Dorothy: Undead, The

Neuman, Jenny: Delos Adventure, The; Hell Night

Neuwirth, Bebe: Adventures of Pinocchio, The; Associate, The (1996); Bugsy; Faculty, The; Green Card; Jumanji; Liberty Heights; Malice; Paint Job, The

Neville, Aaron: Zandalee

Neville, John: Adventures of Baron Münchausen, The; Baby's Day Out; Johnny 2.0; Sabotage (1996); Song Spinner; Study in Terror, A; X-Files, The (1998); X-Files, The (TV Series)

Nevin, Brooke: Running Wild (1998)

Nevin, Robyn: Careful He Might Hear You; Fourth Wish, The; Irishman, The

Nevin, Rosa: Still Not Quite Human

Nevins, Claudette: Mask, The (1961); Possessed, The (1977)

Nevinson, Gennie: Muriel's Wedding

New, Nancy: Bostonians, The

Newark, Derek: Bellman and True; Offence, The

Newbern, George: Doppelganger: The Evil Within; Evening Star, The; Father of the Bride (1991); Father of the Bride Part II; It Takes Two (1988); Little Sister; Paramedics; Witness to the Execution

Newbigin, Flora: Borrowers, The (1997)

Newburger, Marc: Curse of the Puppet Master

Newcomb, Jamie: Lone Wolf

Newell, William: Mysterious Dr. Satan

Newhart, Bob: Cold Turkey; First Family; Hell Is for Heroes; Hot Millions; In & Out; Little Miss Marker (1980); Marathon; On a Clear Day, You Can See Forever; Thursday's Game

Newland, Michael: Big Bang Theory, The

Newley, Anthony: Alice in Wonderland (1985); Alice Through the Looking Glass (1985); Boris and Natasha; Doctor Dolittle; Garbage Pail Kids Movie, The; Good Idea; Old Curiosity Shop, The (1975); Outrage!; Stagecoach (1986); X—The Unknown

Newman, Barry: Amy; Bowfinger; Brown's Requiem; Having It All; Limey, The; Mirror Crack'd from Side to Side, The; Night Games; Salzburg Connection, The; Vanishing Point

Newman, James L.: Silent Night, Deadly Night Part 2

Newman, Laraine: Alone in the Woods; American Hot Wax; Coneheads; Invaders from Mars (1986); Perfect; Problem Child 2; Revenge of the Red Baron; Things We Did Last Summer; Tunnelvision (1976); Wholly Moses!; Witchboard 2

Newman, Nanette: Endless Game, The; Long Ago Tomorrow; Madwoman of Chaillot, The; Of Human Bondage (1964); Seance on a Wet Afternoon; Wrong Arm of the Law, The; Wrong Box, The

Newman, Paul: Absence of Malice; Blaze; Buffalo Bill and the Indians; Butch Cassidy and the Sundance Kid; Cat on a Hot Tin Roof (1958); Color of Money, The; Cool Hand Luke; Drowning Pool, The; Exodus; Fat Man and Little Boy; Fort Apache—The Bronx; From the Terrace; Harper; Harry and Son; Helen Morgan Story, The; Hombre; Hud; Hudsucker Proxy, The; Hustler, The; Lady L; Left Handed Gun, The; Life and Times of Judge Roy Bean, The; Long Hot Summer, The (1958); Mackintosh Man, The; Message in a Bottle; Mr. and Mrs. Bridge; New Kind of Love, A; Nobody's Fool (1994); Paris Blues; Pocket Money; Prize, The; Quintet; Secret War of Harry Frigg, The; Silent Movie; Silver Chalice, The; Slap Shot; Somebody Up There Likes Me; Sometimes a Great Notion; Sting, The; Sweet Bird of Youth (1962); Torn Curtain; Towering Inferno, The; Twilight; Until They Sail; Verdict, The; When Time Ran Out!; Where the Money Is; Winning; Young Philadelphians, The

Newman, Philip: No Justice; Slave of Dreams

Newman, Tom: Fortune, The

Newmar, Julie: Deep Space; Evils of the Night; Ghosts Can't Do It; Hysterical; Li'l Abner (1959); Mackenna's Gold;

Nudity Required; Oblivion; Oblivion 2: Backlash; Seven Brides for Seven Brothers; Streetwalkin'

Newsom, David: Rose Hill; Wes Craven's New Nightmare

Newton, Bert: Fatty Finn

Newton, John Haymes: Desert Kickboxer

Newton, Margie: Bronx Executioner, The; Night of the Zombies (1983)

Newton, Robert: Androcles and the Lion; Around the World in 80 Days (1956); Beachcomber, The; Blackbeard the Pirate; Desert Rats, The; Gaslight (1940); Henry V (1944); High and the Mighty, The; Jamaica Inn; Long John Silver; Major Barbara; Odd Man Out; Oliver Twist (1948); This Happy Breed; Tom Brown's Schooldays (1950); Treasure Island (1950)

Newton, Thandie: Beloved; Besieged; Flirting; Gridlock'd; Jefferson in Paris; Journey of August King, The; Leading Man, The; Loaded; Mission: Impossible 2

Newton, Wayne: Adventures of Ford Fairlane, The; Best of the Best 2; Dark Backward, The; Night of the Running Man; Vegas Vacation

Newton-John, Olivia: Grease; It's My Party; Two of a Kind (1983); Xanadu

Ney, Richard: Mrs. Miniver; Premature Burial, The

Neyland, Anne: Motorcycle Gang

Neyland, Dixie: Merry Wives of Windsor, The

Nezu, Jimpachi: Gonin

Ng, Christine: Crime Story

Ng, Lawrence: Sex and Zen

Ng, Richard: Mr. Vampire (Vol. 1–4)

Nghieu, Tieu Quan: China, My Sorrow

Ngor, Haing S.: Eastern Condors; Fortunes of War (1993); Heaven and Earth (1993); In Love and War; Iron Triangle, The; Killing Fields, The; Love and War; My Life; Vietnam, Texas

Niam, Don: Undefeatable

Nicastro, Michelle: Bad Guys

Nichetti, Maurizio: Icicle Thief, The; Volere Volare

Nicholas, Anna: Mutants in Paradise

Nicholas, Denise: Blacula; Ghost Dad; Marvin and Tige; Piece of the Action, A; Sophisticated Gents, The

Nicholas, Harold: Five Heartbeats, The

Nicholas, Paul: Alice (1981); Invitation to the Wedding; Lisztomania

Nicholas, Stephen: Witchboard

Nicholas, Thomas Ian: Kid in King Arthur's Court, A; Rookie of the Year

Nicholls, Anthony: Burn, Witch, Burn

Nicholls, Phoebe: Fairy Tale: A True Story

Nichols, Barbara: Human Duplicators, The; King and Four Queens, The; Manfish; Pajama Game, The; Pal Joey; Sweet Smell of Success; Untouchables, The; Scarface Mob; Where the Boys Are (1960)

Nichols, Conrad: Man Called Rage, A

Nichols, Dave: Spenser: Ceremony

Nichols, David B.: Johnny & Clyde

Nichols, Kyra: George Balanchine's The Nutcracker

Nichols, Nichelle: Antony and Cleopatra (1981); Star Trek (TV Series); Star Trek: The Menagerie; Star Trek—The Motion Picture; Star Trek II: The Wrath of Khan; Star Trek III: The Search for Spock; Star Trek IV: The Voyage Home; Star Trek V: The Final Frontier; Star Trek VI: The Undiscovered Country; Supernaturals, The

Nichols, Red: Gene Krupa Story, The

Nichols, Stephen: Glass Cage, The

Nichols, Taylor: Barcelona; Evolution's Child; Headless Body in Topless Bar; Metropolitan

Nicholson, Jack: As Good as It Gets; Batman (1989); Blood and Wine; Border, The; Broadcast News; Carnal Knowledge; Chinatown; Crossing Guard, The; Easy Rider; Ensign Pulver; Evening Star, The; Few Good Men, A; Five Easy Pieces; Flight to Fury; Fortune, The; Goin' South; Heartburn; Hell's Angels on Wheels; Hoffa; Ironweed; King of Marvin Gardens, The; Last Detail, The; Last Tycoon, The; Little Shop of Horrors, The (1960); Man Trouble; Mars Attacks!; Missouri Breaks, The; On a Clear Day, You Can See Forever; One Flew over the Cuckoo's Nest; Passenger, The (1975); Postman Always Rings Twice, The (1981); Prizzi's Honor; Psych-Out; Raven, The (1963); Rebel Rousers; Reds; Ride in the Whirlwind; Shining, The; Shooting, The; Studs Lonigan; Terms of Endearment; Terror, The; Tommy;

O'Connor, Kevin: Bogie; Special Effects

O'Connor, Kevin J.: Candy Mountain; Deep Rising; F/X 2: The Deadly Art of Illusion; Hellcab; Lord of Illusions; Moderns, The; Mummy, The (1999); No Escape; Peggy Sue Got Married; Tanner '88

O'Connor, Matt: Burglar From Hell

O'Connor, Renee: Darkman II: The Return of Durant; Hercules and the Lost Kingdom

O'Connor, Sinead: Butcher Boy, The

O'Connor, Terry: Breaker! Breaker!

O'Connor, Tim: Buck Rogers in the 25th Century

O'Conor, Una: Adventures of Don Juan, The; Cavalcade; Chained; Christmas in Connecticut (1945); Invisible Man, The; Personal Property; Strawberry Blonde, The; Suzy; Witness for the Prosecution (1957)

O'Conor, Joseph: Black Windmill, The

Oda, Erika: After Life

O'Daniels, Barrie: Devil Horse, The

O'Day, Mollie: Chloe: Love is Calling You

O'Day, Nell: Arizona Stagecoach

O'Dea, Dennis: Captain Horatio Hornblower

O'Dea, Jimmy: Darby O'Gill and the Little People

O'Dea, Judith: Night of the Living Dead (1968)

O'Dell, Bryan: Street Wars

Odell, Miranda: Witchcraft XI: Sisters in Blood

O'Dell, Tony: Chopping Mall; Evils of the Night

Odetta: Autobiography of Miss Jane Pittman, The

Odette, Mary: She (1925)

Odom, George T.: Straight out of Brooklyn

O'Donnell, Cathy: Amazing Mr. X; Best Years of Our Lives, The; Man from Laramie, The; Miniver Story, The; Terror in the Haunted House; They Live By Night

O'Donnell, Chris: Bachelor, The (1999); Batman Forever; Batman & Robin; Blue Sky; Circle of Friends; Cookie's Fortune; Fried Green Tomatoes; In Love and War (1996); Mad Love (1995); Scent of a Woman; School Ties; Three Musketeers, The (1993)

O'Donnell, Rosie: Another Stakeout; Beautiful Girls; Car 54, Where Are You? (1991); Exit to Eden; Flintstones, The; Harriet the Spy; League of Their Own, A; Now and Then; Sleepless in Seattle; Wide Awake

O'Donnell, Spec: Little Annie Rooney

O'Donoghue, Michael: Suicide Club, The

O'Donovan, Ross: Starstruck

O'Driscoll, Martha: Fallen Sparrow, The; Ghost Catchers, The; Here Come the Co-Eds; House of Dracula

Oedekerk, Steve: High Strung

Ogata, Ken: Ballad of Narayama, The; Eijanaika (Why Not?); Mishima: A Life in Four Chapters; Vengeance Is Mine (1979)

Ogawa, Mayumi: Zatoichi: The Blind Swordsman's Vengeance

Ogier, Bulle: Candy Mountain; Celine and Julie Go Boating; Discreet Charm of the Bourgeoisie, The; Irma Vep; Les Tricheurs; Maitresse; Somewhere in the City; Valley, The

Ogier, Pascale: Full Moon in Paris

Ogilvy, Ian: And Now the Screaming Starts; Anna Karenina (1985); Conqueror Worm, The; Death Becomes Her; Invasion of Privacy; She Beast, The; Upstairs, Downstairs

O'Gorman, Dean: Young Hercules

O'Grady, Gail: Blackout (1990); Celtic Pride; Nobody's Perfect; Spellcaster; That Old Feeling; Three Lives of Karen, The

O'Grady, Timothy E.: James Joyce's Women

Ogumbanjo, Femi: Loss of Sexual Innocence, The

Oh, Sandra: Double Happiness; Last Night

Oh, Soon-Teck: Death Wish IV: The Crackdown; Home of our Own, A; Legend of the White Horse; Missing in Action 2: The Beginning; Red Sun Rising; Steele Justice; Yellow

O'Halloran, Brian: Clerks

O'Halloran, Jack: Dragnet (1987); Hero and the Terror; Mob Boss

Ohana, Claudia: Erendira; Erotique; Luzia; Opera do Malandro

O'Hara, Brett: Incredibly Strange Creatures Who Stopped Living and Became Mixed-Up Zombies, The

O'Hara, Catherine: After Hours; Beetlejuice; Betsy's Wedding; Heartburn; Home Alone; Home Alone 2: Lost in New York; Home Fries; Hope; Last Polka, The; Little Vegas; Paper, The; Really Weird Tales; Simple Twist of Fate, A; Summer Fling; Tall Tale: The Unbelievable Adventures of Pecos

Bill; There Goes the Neighborhood; Waiting for Guffman; Wyatt Earp

O'Hara, David: Braveheart; Matchmaker, The (1997); Oliver Twist (1997)

O'Hara, Jenny: Angie

O'Hara, Kareen: Go Kill and Come Back

O'Hara, Maureen: Against All Flags; At Sword's Point; Big Jake; Black Swan, The; Buffalo Bill; Comanche Territory; Dance, Girl, Dance; Deadly Companions, The; Fallen Sparrow, The; How Green Was My Valley; Hunchback of Notre Dame, The (1939); Immortal Sergeant, The; Jamaica Inn; Lady Godiva; Lisbon; Long Gray Line, The; McLintock!; Miracle on 34th Street (1947); Mr. Hobbs Takes a Vacation; Only the Lonely; Parent Trap, The (1961); Quiet Man, The; Rare Breed, The (1966); Redhead from Wyoming, The; Rio Grande; Sinbad the Sailor; Spencer's Mountain; This Land is Mine; To the Shores of Tripoli; War Arrow; Wings of Eagles, The; Woman's Secret, A

O'Hara, Quinn: Swingin' Summer, A

O'Hara, Terence: Devastator, The

O'Hare, Michael: Babylon 5 (TV Series)

Ohashi, Minako: Living on Tokyo Time

O'Heaney, Caitlin: He Knows You're Alone

O'Herlihy, Dan: Actors and Sin; At Sword's Point; Dead, The; Halloween III: Season of the Witch; Imitation of Life; Invasion USA (1952); Last Starfighter, The; Longest Drive, The; MacArthur; Macbeth (1948); Odd Man Out; 100 Rifles; People, The; Rat Pack, The; RoboCop; RoboCop 2; Waltz Through the Hills; Waterloo

O'Herlihy, Gavan: Conagher

O'Herne, Pete: Bad Taste

Ohmart, Carol: House on Haunted Hill; Naked Youth; Spider Baby

Ohtomo, Osamu: 8Man

O'Hurley, John: Mirror Images; Power Within, The

Oida, Yoshi: Pillow Book, The

Okada, Eiji: Hiroshima, Mon Amour; Traffic Jam; Ugly American, The; Woman in the Dunes

Okamura, Gerald: Power Within, The

O'Keefe, Alexis: Angel in Training

O'Keefe, Anne-Marie: City of the Vampires

O'Keefe, Dennis: Brewster's Millions (1945); Broadway Bill; Dishonored Lady; Doll Face; Fighting Seabees, The; Great Dan Patch, The; Hangmen Also Die; I'm No Angel; Lady Scarface; Leopard Man, The; Sensations of 1945; Story of Dr. Wassell, The; T-Men; Topper Returns; You'll Find Out

O'Keefe, Doug: Specimen; When the Bullet Hits the Bone

O'Keefe, Jodi: She's All That

O'Keefe, Jodi Lyn: Halloween: H20; Whatever It Takes

O'Keefe, John: Conceiving Ada

O'Keefe, John E.: Out of the Rain

O'Keefe, Michael: Bridge to Silence; Caddyshack; Dark Secret of Harvest Home, The; Disaster at Silo 7; Edie & Pen; Fear (1990); Great Santini, The; Hitchhiker, The (Series); Incident at Deception Ridge; Ironweed; Me & Veronica; Nate and Hayes; Nina Takes a Lover; Out of the Rain; Rumor of War, A; Slugger's Wife, The; Split Image; Too Young to Die; Whoopee Boys, The

O'Keefe, Paul: Daydreamer, The (1966)

O'Keefe, Miles: Ator: The Fighting Eagle; Blade Master, The; Campus Man; Dead Tides; Diamondbacks; Drifter, The; Iron Warrior; Liberty and Bash; Lone Runner; Marked Man; Relentless II: Dead On; Shoot (1991); Silent Hunter; Sword of the Valiant; Tarzan the Ape Man (1981); Waxwork; Zero Tolerance

O'Kelly, Donal: Van, The (1997)

O'Kelly, Tim: Targets

Okking, Jens: Kingdom, The

Okumoto, Yuji: Hard Justice; Nemesis (1992); Robot Wars

Olaf, Pierre: Little Theatre of Jean Renoir, The

Oland, Warner: Black Camel, The; Charlie Chan in Shanghai; Charlie Chan at Monte Carlo; Charlie Chan at the Olympics; Charlie Chan at the Opera; Charlie Chan at the Racetrack; Charlie Chan in Egypt; Charlie Chan in London; Charlie Chan in Paris; Charlie Chan on Broadway; Charlie Chan's Secret; Daughter of the Dragon; Dishonored; Drums of Jeopardy; Jazz Singer, The (1927); Mysterious Dr. Fu Manchu; Painted Veil, The; Return of Dr. Fu Manchu; Shanghai Express; Tell It to the Marines; Werewolf of London

Olandt, Ken: Digital Man; Leprechaun; Super Force; Super-carrier

Olbrychski, Daniel: Birch Wood; Bolero (1982); Deluge, The (Potop) (1973); Tin Drum, The; Wedding, The (1972)

Oldfield, Eric: Island Trader; Stones of Death

Oldham, Will: Matewan

Oldman, Gary: Air Force One; Basquiat; Bram Stoker's Dracula; Chattahoochee; Criminal Law; Fallen Angels; Fifth Element, The; Immortal Beloved; JFK; Lost in Space (1998); Meantime; Murder in the First; Prick Up Your Ears; Professional, The; Romeo Is Bleeding; Rosencrantz and Guildenstern Are Dead; Scarlet Letter, The (1995); Sid and Nancy; State of Grace; Track 29; True Romance; We Think the World of You

Olds, Gabriel: Calendar Girl

O'Leary, Ann: Kiss the Girls Goodbye

O'Leary, Celine: Quiet Room, The

O'Leary, William: Flight of Black Angel; Hot Shots; In the Line of Duty: Ambush in Waco; Nice Girls Don't Explode

Olen, Fred: Tomb, The

Oleynik, Larisa: 10 Things I Hate About You

Oliensis, Adam: Pompatus of Love, The

Olin, Ken: Evolution's Child; Game of Love, The; Queens Logic

Olin, Lena: Enemies—A Love Story; Havana; Mr. Jones; Mystery Men; Night and the Moment, The; Night Falls on Manhattan; Ninth Gate, The; Polish Wedding; Romeo Is Bleeding; Unbearable Lightness of Being, The

Olita, Joseph: Amin: The Rise and Fall

Oliver, Barret: Cocoon; D.A.R.Y.L.; Frankenweenie; Never-Ending Story, The; Secret Garden, The (1987)

Oliver, David: Defense Play

Oliver, Edna May: Ann Vickers; David Copperfield; Drums Along the Mohawk; Little Miss Broadway; Lydia; Nurse Edith Cavell; Romeo and Juliet (1936); Rosalie; Saturday Night Kid, The; Second Fiddle; Story of Vernon and Irene Castle, The; Tale of Two Cities, A (1935)

Oliver, Gordon: Blondie

Oliver, Michael: Problem Child; Problem Child 2

Oliver, Robert Lee: Flesh Eating Mothers

Oliver, Rochelle: Courtship; 1918; On Valentine's Day

Oliver, Steven: Werewolves on Wheels

Oliver, Susan: Disorderly Orderly, The; Fugitive, The (TV Series); Gene Krupa Story, The; Ginger in the Morning; Guns of Diablo; Hardly Working; Star Trek: The Cage; Star Trek: The Menagerie; Tomorrow's Child

Oliver, Theresa: Twisted Tales

Oliveri, Robert: Honey, I Blew Up the Kid

Olivery, Jody: Delivery Boys

Olivier, Laurence: As You Like It; Battle of Britain; Betsy, The; Bounty, The; Boys from Brazil, The; Brideshead Revisited; Bridge Too Far, A; Carrie (1952); Clash of the Titans; Clouds over Europe; Collection, The; Devil's Disciple, The; Divorce of Lady X, The; Dracula (1979); Ebony Tower, The; Entertainer, The; Fire over England; 49th Parallel, The; Hamlet (1948); Henry V (1944); I Stand Condemned; Jazz Singer, The (1980); Jigsaw Man, The; Khartoum; King Lear (1984); Lady Caroline Lamb; Little Romance, A; Love Among the Ruins; Marathon Man; Mr. Halpern and Mr. Johnson; Nicholas and Alexandra; Othello (1965); Pride and Prejudice (1940); Prince and the Showgirl, The; Rebecca; Richard III (1955); Seven-Per-Cent Solution, The; Shoes of the Fisherman; Sleuth; Spartacus; That Hamilton Woman; Voyage 'Round My Father, A; Wagner; War Requiem; Wild Geese II; Wuthering Heights (1939)

Oliviero, Silvio: Graveyard Shift (1987); Understudy, The: Graveyard Shift II

Olkewicz, Walter: Pronto; You Know My Name

Olmos, Edward James: American Me; Ballad of Gregorio Cortez, The; Blade Runner; Burning Season, The; Caught (1996); Dead Man's Walk; Disappearance of Garcia Lorca, The; Gossip; Hollywood Confidential; Limbic Region, The; Miami Vice: "The Prodigal Son"; Million to Juan, A; Mirage (1995); My Family; Roosters; Saving Grace; Selena; Slave of Dreams; Stand and Deliver; Talent for the Game; Triumph of the Spirit; Wall, The (1998) (U.S.); Wolfen; Wonderful Ice Cream Suit, The; Zoot Suit

Olmstead, Gertrude: Monster, The (1925)

O'Loughlin, Gerald S.: Pleasure Palace; Riot (1969)

Olsen, Ashley: Billboard Dad; How the West Was Fun; It Takes Two (1995); Switching Goals

Olsen, Eric Christian: Arthur's Quest

Olsen, John: Visitors, The

Olsen, Mary-Kate: Billboard Dad; How the West Was Fun; It Takes Two (1995); Switching Goals

Olsen, Moroni: Cobra Woman; Three Musketeers, The (1935)

Olsen, Ole: All over Town; Country Gentlemen; Ghost Catchers, The; Hellzapoppin

Olson, James: Amityville II: The Possession; Andromeda Strain, The; Commando; My Sister, My Love (The Mafu Cage); Rachel, Rachel; Rachel River; Someone I Touched; Strange New World

Olson, Nancy: Absent-Minded Professor, The; Big Jim McLain; Force of Arms; Mr. Music; Pollyanna (1960); Smith!; Snowball Express; Son of Flubber; Union Station

Olund, Niclas: Slingshot, The

Olyphant, Timothy: Go; Gone in 60 Seconds; When Trumpets Fade

Omaggio, Maria Rosaria: Cop in Blue Jeans, The

O'Malley, Jason: Backstreet Dreams

O'Malley, Pat: Fighting Marines, The; Virginian, The (1923)

O'Mara, Kate: Horror of Frankenstein; Nativity, The; Vampire Lovers, The; Whose Child Am I?

Omori, Yoshiyuki: MacArthur's Children

Ondra, Anny: Blackmail (1929); Manxman, The

O'Neal, Frederick: Free, White, and 21; Something of Value

O'Neal, Griffin: April Fool's Day; Assault of the Killer Bimbos; Escape Artist, The; Evil Lives; Hadley's Rebellion; Wraith, The

O'Neal, Patrick: Alvarez Kelly; Chamber of Horrors; El Condor; For the Boys; From the Terrace; In Harm's Way; Like Father, Like Son; Make Me an Offer; New York Stories; Q & A; Secret Life of an American Wife, The; Silent Night, Bloody Night; Stepford Wives, The; Stiletto; Under Siege; Way We Were, The; Where Were You When the Lights Went Out?

O'Neal, Ron: As Summers Die; Guyana Tragedy, The; Mercenary Fighters; Original Gangstas; Red Dawn; St. Helens; Sophisticated Gents, The; Story of Jim Jones, The; Superfly; Superfly T.N.T.; Up Against the Wall; When a Stranger Calls;

O'Neal, Ryan: Alan Smithee Film, An—Burn Hollywood Burn; Barry Lyndon; Chances Are; Driver, The; Faithful; Fever Pitch; Green Ice; Irreconcilable Differences; Love Story; Main Event, The; Man Upstairs, The; Oliver's Story; Paper Moon; Partners; Small Sacrifices; So Fine; Thief Who Came to Dinner, The; Tough Guys Don't Dance; What's Up, Doc?; Wild Rovers, The; Zero Effect

O'Neal, Shaquille: Blue Chips; Kazaam; Steel (1997)

O'Neal, Tatum: Bad News Bears, The; Certain Fury; Circle of Two; International Velvet; Little Darlings; Little Noises; Paper Moon

O'Neil, Barbara: All This and Heaven Too; I Am the Law; Tower of London (1939)

O'Neil, Colette: Dreams Lost, Dreams Found

O'Neil, Sally: 16 Fathoms Deep

O'Neil, Tricia: Are You in the House Alone?; Piranha Part Two: The Spawning

O'Neill, Amy: White Wolves: A Cry in the Wild II

O'Neill, Angela: River of Diamonds; Sorority House Massacre

O'Neill, Chris: BackBeat; James Joyce's Women

O'Neill, Dick: Buddy Holly Story, The; St. Ives; Wolfen

O'Neill, Ed: Adventures of Ford Fairlane, The; Bone Collector, The; Disorganized Crime; Dutch; Little Giants; Prefontaine; Sibling Rivalry; Wayne's World; When Your Lover Leaves

O'Neill, Fiona: Vampyr, The (1992)

O'Neill, Henry: Anthony Adverse; Case of the Lucky Legs, The; Girl Crazy; Honky Tonk; It Happened in New Orleans; Lady Killer; Return of October, The; Virginian, The (1946); Whistling in Brooklyn; Whistling in the Dark; White Cargo

O'Neill, James: Count of Monte Cristo, The (1912)

O'Neill, Jennifer: Bad Love; Caravans; Cloud Dancer; Committed; Corporate Ladder; Cover Girl Murders, The; Force of One; Full Exposure; I Love N.Y.; Innocent, The (1976); Invasion of Privacy; Lady Ice; Love's Savage Fury; Perfect Family; Psychic, The; Reincarnation of Peter Proud,

The; Rio Lobo; Scanners; Silver Strand; Steel (1980); Summer of '42; Whiffs

O'Neill, Maggie: Under Suspicion

O'Neill, Ryan J.: Hollywood Safari

O'Neill, Shannon: Creeping Terror, The

O'Neill, Willa: One Crazy Night

Ong, Alannah: Double Happiness

Ono, Masahiko: Boiling Point (1990)

Ono, Yoko: Imagine: John Lennon; Rock and Roll Circus, The; Satan's Bed

Onodera, Akira: Gamera: Guardian of the Universe

Onoe, Kikunosuke: Kojiro

Onorati, Peter: Dead Ahead; Donor Unknown; Firehouse (1987); Not Like Us

Ontiveros, Lupe: Candyman 3: Day of the Dead

Ontkean, Michael: Blood of Others, The; Clara's Heart; Cold Front; Just the Way You Are; Legacy of Lies; Maid to Order; Making Love; Stepford Husbands, The; Street Justice; Summer of the Monkeys; Twin Peaks (Movie); Twin Peaks (TV Series); Voices; Willie and Phil; Witching, The (Necromancy)

Ooms, Amanda: Women on the Roof, The

Opatoshu, David: Forced Vengeance; Torn Curtain; Who'll Stop the Rain

Ophuls, Marcel: Francois Truffaut: Stolen Moments

Opiana, Marian: Man of Iron

Opinato, Mario: Muse, The

Oppenheimer, Alan: Invisible: The Chronicles of Benjamin Knight; Macbeth (1981); Riding with Death; Trancers 4: Jack of Swords

Opper, Don: Android; Critters; Critters 2: The Main Course; Critters 3; Critters 4; Slam Dance

O'Quinn, Terry: Amityville: A New Generation; Black Widow; Blind Fury; Company Business; Cutting Edge, The; Don't Talk to Strangers; Forgotten One, The; Good Fight, The; Lipstick Camera; Millennium (1996); My Samurai; My Stepson, My Lover; Pin; Prisoners of the Sun; Rocketeer, The; Shadow Warriors; Son of the Morning Star; Stepfather, The; Stepfather II; Tombstone; When the Time Comes; Wild Card

O'Rawe, Geraldine: Circle of Friends

Orbach, Jerry: Adventures of a Gnome Named Gnorm, The; Aladdin & the King of Thieves; California Casanova; Crimes and Misdemeanors; Delirious; Delusion (1991); Dirty Dancing; F/X; Imagemaker, The; Last Exit to Brooklyn; Mr. Saturday Night; Out for Justice; Out on a Limb (1986); Prince of the City; Straight Talk; That's Singing: The Best of Broadway; Toy Soldiers (1991); Universal Soldier

Orbach, Ron: Love Crimes

Orbison, Roy: Fastest Guitar Alive, The

Ordung, Wyott: Monster from the Ocean Floor, The

O'Reilly, Cyril: Cool Surface, The; Dance of the Damned; Eruption; Shadow of a Scream; Unspeakable, The

O'Reilly, Harry: Hamburger Hill

O'Reilly, Robert: Moonbase

Orfani, Fereshteh Sadr: White Balloon, The

Oriel, Ray: Infested (Ticks)

Orla, Ressel: Spiders, The

Orlando, Tony: Rosie

Orlov, Dmitri: Alexander Nevsky

Ormeny, Tom: Agent on Ice

Ormond, Julia: Captives; First Knight; Legends of the Fall; Sabrina (1995); Smilla's Sense of Snow; Stalin; Young Catherine

Ormsby, Alan: Children Shouldn't Play with Dead Things

Ormsby, Anya: Children Shouldn't Play with Dead Things; Deathdream

Ornaghi, Luigi: Tree of the Wooden Clogs, The

O'Ross, Ed: Another 48 Hrs.; Full Metal Jacket; Hidden, The; Play Nice; Power Within, The; Red Heat (1988); Universal Soldier

O'Rourke, Heather: Poltergeist II: The Other Side; Poltergeist III

O'Rourke, Rachel: Eternal, The

Orozco, Regina: Deep Crimson

Orr, Christopher: Calm at Sunset; Robin Cook's Invasion

Orr, Veronica: Bimbos B.C.; Prehistoric Bimbos in Armageddon City; Witching, The (1994)

Orser, Leland: Cover Story; Resurrection (1998); Very Bad Things

Orsi, Leigh Ann: Pet Shop

Orsini, Marini: Eddie and the Cruisers II: Eddie Lives!

Orsini, Umberto: César and Rosalie; Goodbye Emmanuelle; Mademoiselle; Woman at Her Window, A

Orth, Debra: Billy the Kid Meets the Vampires

Orth, Zak: Rose Hill; When Trumpets Fade

Ortnow, Richard: Trial by Jury

Orwig, Bob: No Justice

Osborn, Les: Mosaic Project, The

Osborne, John: Get Carter

Osborne, Vivienne: Captain Caution; Supernatural; Tomorrow at Seven

Osbourne, Ozzy: Trick or Treat (1986)

Oscarsson, Per: Doll; House of Angels; Hunger (1966); Night Visitor, The (1970); Secrets

O'Shea, Daniel: Hamburger Hill

O'Shea, Michael: Big Wheel, The; It Should Happen to You; Jack London; Lady of Burlesque; Last of the Redmen; Threat, The; Underworld Story

O'Shea, Milo: Barbarella; Broken Vows; Butcher Boy, The; Loot; Matchmaker, The (1997); Medicine Hat Stallion, The; Once a Hero; Only the Lonely; Opportunity Knocks; Paddy; Pilot, The; Playboys, The; Romeo and Juliet (1968); Sacco and Vanzetti

O'Shea, Paul: Among the Cinders

Oshima, Yukari: Millionaire's Express (Shanghai Express)

Osment, Haley Joel: Bogus; Sixth Sense, The

Osmond, Cliff: Fortune Cookie, The; Invasion of the Bee Girls; Kiss Me, Stupid; Shark's Treasure

Osmond, Marie: Gift of Love, The; Side by Side: The True Story of the Osmond Family

Osorio, Yelba: Riot (1996) (TV Movie)

Osterhage, Jeff: Big Bad John; Buckeye and Blue; Masque of the Red Death (1989); Sex Crimes; Shadow Riders, The; Sky Bandits; South of Reno

Ostrander, William: Red Heat (1985)

Ostrum, Peter: Willy Wonka and the Chocolate Factory

Osugi, Ren: Fireworks

O'Sullivan, Billy: Robin of Locksley

O'Sullivan, Maureen: All I Desire; Anna Karenina (1935); Barretts of Wimpole Street, The; Connecticut Yankee, A; Day at the Races, A; Devil Doll, The (1936); Hannah and Her Sisters; Habitation of Dragons, The; Just Imagine; Peggy Sue Got Married; Pride and Prejudice (1940); River Pirates, The; Skyscraper Souls; Stranded; Strange Interlude (1932); Tall T, The; Tarzan and His Mate; Tarzan Escapes; Tarzan Finds a Son; Tarzan the Ape Man (1932); Tarzan's New York Adventure; Tarzan's Secret Treasure; Thin Man, The

Oteri, Cheri: Inspector Gadget

Otis, Carré: Exit in Red; Wild Orchid

O'Toole, Annette: Best Legs in the 8th Grade, The; Broken Vows; Cat People (1982); Cross My Heart (1987); Foolin' Around; 48 Hrs.; Here on Earth; Huntress, The; It (1991); King of the Gypsies; Love at Large; Love Matters; One on One; Smile; Superman III; White Lie

O'Toole, Peter: Becket; Caligula; Club Paradise; Creator; Dark Angel, The; Fairy Tale: A True Story; Foxtrot; Goodbye, Mr. Chips (1969); Gulliver's Travels (1996) (Television); High Spirits; How to Steal a Million; King Ralph; Last Emperor, The; Lawrence of Arabia; Lion in Winter, The; Lord Jim; Man of La Mancha; Masada; Murphy's War; My Favorite Year; Night of the Generals; Phantoms; Rainbow Thief, The; Ruling Class, The; Seventh Coin, The; Strange Tales: Ray Bradbury Theater; Stunt Man, The; Supergirl; Svengali (1983); Under Milk Wood; What's New, Pussycat?; Wings of Fame; Zulu Dawn

Otowa, Nobuko: Island, The (1962); Onibaba

Ott, Angelica: Hell Hounds of Alaska

Ottaviano, Fred: Shoot (1991)

Otto, Barry: Bliss (1986); Cosi; Custodian, The; Howling III; Kiss or Kill; Strictly Ballroom

Otto, Gotz: Tomorrow Never Dies

Otto, Miranda: Jack Bull, The; Last Days of Chez Nous, The; Love Serenade; Nostradamus Kid, The

Ottoson, Carl: Reptilicus

Ouedraogo, Assita: La Promesse

Ouedraogo, Rasmane: La Promesse

Ouimet, Daniele: Daughters of Darkness

Ousdal, Sverre Anker: Insomnia

Ouspenskaya, Maria: Beyond Tomorrow; Dodsworth; Frankenstein Meets the Wolf Man; I've Always Loved You;

Love Affair (1939); Mortal Storm, The; Rains Came, The; Shanghai Gesture, The; Wolf Man, The

Outerbridge, Peter: Better Than Chocolate; Drop Dead Gorgeous (1991); Escape from Mars; Kissed; Time Shifters, The

Outlaw, Geoff: Alice's Restaurant

Overall, Park: Gambler Returns, The: Luck of the Draw; House of Cards; Vanishing, The (1993)

Overman, Lynne: Broadway Bill; Caught in the Draft; Edison, The Man; Little Miss Marker (1934); Midnight (1934); Northwest Mounted Police; Silver Queen

Overton, Frank: Desire under the Elms; Fail-Safe; Lonely-hearts

Overton, Rick: Galaxies Are Colliding; Sinful Life, A

Owen, Chris: Angus; October Sky

Owen, Clive: Bent; Century; Class of '61; Close My Eyes; Lorna Doone; Nobody's Children; Return of the Native, The; Rich Man's Wife, The

Owen, Garry: Blondie in Society

Owen, Granville: Li'l Abner (1940)

Owen, Megan: Clean Shaven

Owen, Michael: Dick Tracy vs. Crime Inc.

Owen, Patty: Portfolio

Owen, Reginald: Above Suspicion (1943); Anna Karenina (1935); Bride Wore Red, The; Cairo; Canterville Ghost, The (1944); Captain Kidd; Challenge to Lassie; Christmas Carol, A (1938); Conquest; Five Weeks in a Balloon; Great Ziegfeld, The; Hills of Home; I Married an Angel; Love on the Run (1936); Madame Curie; Madame X (1937); Miniver Story, The; Mrs. Miniver; Monsieur Beaucaire; National Velvet; Personal Property; Pirate, The; Queen Christina; Random Harvest; Real Glory, The; Red Garters; Reunion in France; Somewhere I'll Find You; Study in Scarlet, A; Tammy and the Doctor; Tarzan's Secret Treasure; They Met in Bombay; Thrill of It All, The; White Cargo; Woman of the Year; Woman's Face, A

Owen, Rena: Once Were Warriors

Owen, Seena: Victory (1919)

Owen, Timothy: Terminal Bliss

Owen, Tony: Norman Loves Rose

Owens, Ciaran: Angela's Ashes

Owens, Eamonn: Butcher Boy, The

Owens, Mark: Friday the 13th: The Orphan

Owens, Michelle: Midnight Kiss

Owens, Patricia: Fly, The (1958); Hell to Eternity; Law and Jake Wade, The

Owens, Susie: They Bite

Owensby, Earl: Dogs of Hell; Rutherford County Line; Wolfman

Owsley, Monroe: Call Her Savage; Goin' to Town

Oxenberg, Catherine: Arthur's Quest; Lair of the White Worm; Overexposed; Ring of Scorpio; Rubdown; Swimsuit; Time Served

Oxenbould, Ben: Fatty Finn

Oxley, David: Ill Met by Moonlight; Night Ambush

Oz, Frank: Blues Brothers 2000; Star Wars: Episode I The Phantom Menace

Ozanne, Robert: Circonstances Attenuantes

Ozawa, Shoichi: Pornographers, The

P, Postmaster: Leprechaun in the Hood

Paar, Jack: Love Nest; Walk Softly, Stranger

Pace, Judy: Brian's Song; Cotton Comes to Harlem; Three in the Attic; Three in the Cellar

Pace, Roger: War of the Colossal Beast

Pace, Tom: Blood Orgy of the She Devils

Pacific, Mark: Princess Warrior

Pacifici, Federico: Flight of the Innocent

Pacino, Al: ... And Justice for All; Any Given Sunday; Author! Author!; Bobby Deerfield; Carlito's Way; City Hall; Cruising; Devil's Advocate; Dick Tracy (1990); Dog Day Afternoon; Donnie Brasco; Frankie and Johnny (1991); Glengarry Glen Ross; Godfather, The; Godfather, Part II, The; Godfather, Part III, The; Godfather Epic, The; Heat (1995); Insider, The; Looking for Richard; Panic in Needle Park; Revolution; Scarecrow; Scarface (1983); Scent of a Woman; Sea of Love; Serpico; Two Bits

Pack, Roger Lloyd: Young Poisoner's Handbook, The

Pack, Stephanie: Hours and Times

Packard, Kelly: Little Bigfoot

Packer, David: Courtyard, The; Heartless; Running Kind, The; Silent Motive

Pacome, Maria: Daydreamer, The (1970) (Le Distrait)

Pacula, Joanna: Black Ice; Body Puzzle; Breaking Point (1989); Business for Pleasure; Captain Nuke and the Bomber Boys; Death Before Dishonor; Deep Red (1994); Escape from Sobibor; Every Breath; Eyes of the Beholder; Gorky Park; Haunted Sea, The; Heaven Before I Die; Husbands and Lovers; Kiss, The (1988); Last Gasp; Marked for Death; My Giant; Not Like Us; Not Quite Paradise; Options; Sweet Lies; Timemaster; Tombstone; Under Investigation; Virus (1999); Warlock: The Armageddon

Padden, Sarah: Lone Star Raiders

Padron, Ana: My Daughter's Keeper

Pagan, Michael J.: How Stella Got Her Groove Back

Pagano, Bartolomeo: Cabiria

Page, Amy: Buford's Beach Bunnies

Page, Anita: Broadway Melody, The; Free and Easy; Our Modern Maidens; Sidewalks of New York; Skyscraper Souls

Page, Anthony: Rebel (1973)

Page, Corey: Dead Man on Campus

Page, Diamond Dallas: Ready to Rumble

Page, Dorothy: Ride 'em Cowgirl

Page, Gale: Amazing Dr. Clitterhouse, The; Four Daughters; Time of Your Life, The

Page, Genevieve: Belle de Jour; Day and the Hour; Private Life of Sherlock Holmes, The; Song Without End

Page, Geraldine: Beguiled, The; Blue and the Gray, The; Bride, The; Dear Heart; Dollmaker, The; Happiest Millionaire, The; Harry's War; Hitchhiker, The (Series); Hondo; Honky Tonk Freeway; I'm Dancing As Fast As I Can; Interiors; My Little Girl; Native Son (1986); Pete 'n' Tillie; Pope of Greenwich Village, The; Summer and Smoke; Sweet Bird of Youth (1962); Toys in the Attic; Trip to Bountiful, The; Walls of Glass; Whatever Happened to Aunt Alice?; White Nights (1985); You're a Big Boy Now

Page, Grant: Road Games

Page, Harrison: Hammered: The Best of Sledge; Lionheart (1991)

Page, Joy: Bullfighter and the Lady, The; Fighter Attack; Kismet (1944)

Page, Ken: Cats

Page, Patti: Boys' Night Out

Page, Rebecca: Danny

Pagel, Justin: Thugs

Pages, Jean-François: Deep Trouble

Paget, Debra: Broken Arrow (1950); Demetrius and the Gladiators; From the Earth to the Moon; Haunted Palace, The; Last Hunt, The; Love Me Tender; Omar Khayyam; Prince Valiant (1954); Stars and Stripes Forever; Tales of Terror; Ten Commandments, The (1956)

Pagett, Nicola: Oliver's Story; Privates on Parade

Pagliero, Marcel: Dedee D'Anvers

Pagnol, Jacqueline: Nais; Topaze (1951)

Paige, Elaine: Cats

Paige, Janis: Angel on My Shoulder (1980); Bachelor in Paradise; Hollywood Canteen; Love at the Top; Please Don't Eat the Daisies; Romance on the High Seas; Silk Stockings; Winter Meeting

Paige, Robert: Abbott and Costello Go to Mars; Blonde Ice; Can't Help Singing; Green Promise, The; Hellzapoppin; Monster and the Girl, The; Pardon My Sarong; Son of Dracula (1943)

Pailhas, Geraldine: Don Juan DeMarco; IP5: The Island of Pachyderms; Suite 16

Pain, Didier: My Father's Glory; My Mother's Castle

Paiva, Nestor: Ballad of a Gunfighter; Creature from the Black Lagoon; Falcon in Mexico, The; Nine Lives of Elfego Baca, The; Purple Heart, The; They Saved Hitler's Brain

Pajala, Turo: Ariel

Palagonia, Al: Summer of Sam

Palance, Holly: Best of Times, The; Tuxedo Warrior

Palance, Jack: Alice Through the Looking Glass (1966); Alone in the Dark; Arrowhead; Attack!; Bagdad Café; Barabbas; Batman (1989); Battle of the Commandos; Buffalo Girls; Chato's Land; City Slickers; City Slickers II; Cocaine Cowboys; Contempt; Cop in Blue Jeans, The; Cops and Robbersons; Cyborg 2; Deadly Sanctuary; Desperados, The; Dracula (1973); Ebenezer; Four Deuces, The; Gor; Great Adventure, The; Halls of Montezuma; Hatfields and the McCoys, The; Hawk the Slayer; Hell's Brigade; Horsemen, The; I Died a Thousand Times; Keep the Change; Last

Contract, The; Last Ride of the Dalton Gang, The; Lonely Man, The; Monte Walsh; Outlaw of Gor; Panic in the Streets; Requiem for a Heavyweight (1956) (Television); Saddle Tramps; Second Chance; Sensuous Nurse, The; Shane; Silver Chalice, The; Solar Crisis; Strange Case of Dr. Jekyll and Mr. Hyde, The (1968); Sudden Fear; Tango and Cash; Torture Garden; Winter's End; Without Warning; Young Guns

Palazzolo, Michael: Curse of the Queerwolf

Palermo, Anthony: Serpent's Lair

Paley, Phillip: Beachballs

Palfy, David: Storm

Palillo, Ron: Committed; Hellgate

Palin, Michael: American Friends; And Now for Something Completely Different; Brazil; Fierce Creatures; Fish Called Wanda, A; How to Irritate People; Jabberwocky; Life of Brian; Missionary, The; Monty Python and the Holy Grail; Monty Python Live at the Hollywood Bowl; Monty Python's Flying Circus (TV Series); Private Function, A; Ripping Yarns; Time Bandits

Palladino, Aleksa: Huntress, The; Manny & Lo

Palladino, Erik: U-571

Pallenberg, Anita: Barbarella; Performance

Pallette, Eugene: Adventures of Robin Hood, The; Bride Came C.O.D., The; Fighting Caravans; First Love (1939); Gang's All Here, The; Heaven Can Wait (1943); Intolerance; It's a Date; Kansan, The; Kennel Murder Case, The; Mark of Zorro, The (1940); Mr. Skitch; My Man Godfrey (1936); One Hundred Men and a Girl; Pin-Up Girl; Sensations of 1945; Shanghai Express; Silver Queen; Stowaway; Three Musketeers, The (1921); Virginian, The (1929); Young Tom Edison

Pallister, Joseph: Broadcast Bombshells

Pallodino, Aleksa: Adventures of Sebastian Cole, The

Palme, Ulf: Dreams; Miss Julie

Palmer, Betsy: Fear, The; Halloween Night; Friday the 13th; Friday the 13th, Part II; Last Angry Man, The; Long Gray Line, The; Marty (1953) (Television); Still Not Quite Human; Tin Star, The

Palmer, Byron: Ma and Pa Kettle at Waikiki

Palmer, Geoffrey: Mrs. Brown

Palmer, Gregg: From Hell It Came; Scream (1982); To Hell and Back; Zombies of Mora Tav

Palmer, Gretchen: I Got the Hook Up

Palmer, Lilli: Adorable Julia; Body and Soul (1947); Boys from Brazil, The; But Not for Me; Chamber of Horrors (1940); Cloak and Dagger (1946); Counterfeit Traitor, The; Holcroft Covenant, The; Miracle of the White Stallions; Murders in the Rue Morgue (1971); My Girl Tisa; Operation Crossbow; Secret Agent, The

Palmer, Maria: Days of Glory

Palmer, Peter: Li'l Abner (1959)

Palmer, Shirley: Somewhere in Sonora

Palminteri, Chazz: Analyze This; Bronx Tale, A; Bullets over Broadway; Diabolique (1996); Excellent Cadavers; Faithful; Hurlyburly; Jade; Last Word, The (1995); Mulholland Falls; Oscar (1991); Perez Family, The; Usual Suspects, The

Palomino, Carlos: Geronimo: An American Legend (1994)

Paltrow, Gwyneth: Emma (1996); Flesh and Bone; Great Expectations (1998); Hard Eight; Jefferson in Paris; Mrs. Parker and the Vicious Circle; Moonlight and Valentino; Pallbearer, The; Perfect Murder, A; Seven; Shakespeare in Love; Sliding Doors; Talented Mr. Ripley, The

Paluzzi, Luciana: Black Veil for Lisa, A; Carlton-Browne of the F.O.; Chuka; Green Slime, The; Manhunt (1973) (The Italian Connection); Muscle Beach Party; 99 Women; Powderkeg; Return to Peyton Place; Sensuous Nurse, The

Pan Chacon, Thales: Quilombo

Pan-Andreas, George: Crime Killer, The

Panaro, Alessandra: Son of Captain Blood

Pandey, Nirmal: Bandit Queen

Panebianco, Richard: China Girl; Dogfight

Paneque, Miguel: Letters from the Park

Pang, Adrian: That's the Way I Like It

Pang, Andrew: Corruptor, The

Pangborn, Franklin: All over Town; Call Out the Marines; Christmas in July; Great Moment, The; Hail the Conquering Hero; Horn Blows at Midnight, The; International House; My Dream Is Yours; Palm Beach Story, The; Romance on

the High Seas; Sullivan's Travels; Swing High, Swing Low; Topper Takes a Trip; Vivacious Lady

Panjabi, Archie: East Is East

Pankin, Stuart: Beanstalk; Betrayal of the Dove; Dirt Bike Kid, The; Father & Scout; Hollywood Knights, The; Honey, We Shrunk Ourselves; Life Stinks; Love at Stake; Mannequin Two: On the Move; Second Sight; Squanto: A Warrior's Tale; Striptease

Pankow, John: Monkey Shines: An Experiment in Fear; Mortal Thoughts; Object of My Affection, The; Secret of My Success, The; Stranger Among Us, A; Talk Radio; To Live and Die in L.A.; Year of the Gun

Pankratov-Tchiorny, Alexandre: Jazzman

Pannach, Gerulf: Singing the Blues in Red

Pantoliano, Joe: Baby's Day Out; Bad Boys (1995); Bound; Downtown; El Diablo; Fugitive, The (1993); Hoods; Immortals, The; Last of the Finest, The; Last Word, The (1995); Matrix, The; Me and the Kid; Natural Enemy; New Blood; Ready to Rumble; Risky Business; Robin in the Family; Running Scared (1986); Scenes from the Goldmine; Short Time; Spy Within, The; Steal Big, Steal Little; Tales from the Crypt (TV Series); Three of Hearts; U.S. Marshals; Used People; Zandalee

Pan-Yong, Yi: Why Has Bhodi Dharma Left for the East?

Paolelei, James: Sudden Thunder

Paoli, Cecile: Near Misses

Paoming, Ku: Wooden Man's Bride, The

Papa, Anny: Blade in the Dark, A

Papas, Helen: Graveyard Shift (1987)

Papas, Irene: Assisi Underground, The; Brotherhood, The; Christ Stopped at Eboli; Dream of Kings, A; Erendira; Guns of Navarone, The; High Season; Into the Night; Iphigenia; Message, The (Mohammad, Messenger of God); Moonspinners, The; Moses (1975); Sweet Country; Tribute to a Bad Man; Trojan Women, The; Z; Zorba the Greek

Papas, Laslo: Crazed

Paquin, Anna: Amistad; Fly Away Home; Hurlyburly; Jane Eyre (1996); Member of the Wedding, The (1996); Piano, The; Walk on the Moon, A

Paragon, John: Echo Park

Paramore, Kiri: Last Days of Chez Nous, The

Parducci, Michael: Gravesend

Paré, Michael: Bad Moon; Blink of an Eye; Closer, The; Dangerous, The (1994); Deadly Heroes; Eddie and the Cruisers; Eddie and the Cruisers II: Eddie Lives!; Empire City; Hope Floats; Instant Justice; Into the Sun; Killing Streets; Last Hour, The; Moon 44; Philadelphia Experiment, The; Point of Impact; Raging Angels; Solar Force; Space Rage; Streets of Fire; Sunset Heat; Sworn Enemies; Triple-cross (1995); Village of the Damned (1995); Warriors (1994); Women's Club, The; World Gone Wild

Paredes, Marisa: All About My Mother; Deep Crimson; Flower of My Secret, The; High Heels (1992)

Parely, Mila: Rules of the Game, The

Parent, Monique: Blood Thirsty; Buford's Beach Bunnies; Dark Secrets; Midnight Confessions

Parfitt, Judy: Dolores Claiborne; Hamlet (1969); Jewel in the Crown, The; Office Romances

Parillaud, Anne: Frankie Starlight; Innocent Blood; La Femme Nikita; Man in the Iron Mask, The (1998); Map of the Human Heart; Shattered Image (1998)

Paris, Cheryl: Sweet Bird of Youth (1989)

Paris, Jerry: Dick Van Dyke Show, The (TV Series); Wild One, The

Parish, Dick: Magic Christmas Tree, The

Parisy, Andrea: La Grande Vadrouille

Park, Melissa: Where Evil Lies

Park, Ray: Star Wars: Episode I The Phantom Menace

Park, Reg: Hercules and the Captive Women; Hercules in the Haunted World; Hercules, Prisoner of Evil

Parker, Cecil: Admirable Crichton, The; Citadel, The; Heavens Above; Indiscreet (1958); Ladykillers, The; Magic Bow, The; Man in the White Suit, The; Quartet (1948); Saint's Vacation, The; Ships with Wings; Sons of the Sea; Stars Look Down, The; Storm in a Teacup; Study in Terror, A; Wreck of the Mary Deare, The

Parker, Cecilia: Ah, Wilderness; Andy Hardy Gets Spring Fever; Andy Hardy Meets a Debutante; Andy Hardy's Double Life; Love Finds Andy Hardy; Mystery Ranch; Painted Veil, The; Riders of Destiny; Trail Drive

Parker, Charlie: Celebrating Bird: The Triumph of Charlie Parker

Parker, Christopher: Red Nights

Parker, Cindy: Lovers' Lovers

Parker, Corey: Big Man on Campus; How I Got into College; Lost Language of Cranes, The; Mr. and Mrs. Loving

Parker, David M.: Xtro: Watch the Skies (Xtro 3)

Parker, Eddie: Tarantula

Parker, Eleanor: Above and Beyond; Chain Lightning; Dead on the Money; Escape from Fort Bravo; Escape Me Never; Hans Brinker; Hole in the Head, A; Home for the Holidays (1972) (Television); Home from the Hill; Interrupted Melody; King and Four Queens, The; Man with the Golden Arm, The; Naked Jungle, The; Never Say Goodbye; Oscar, The (1966); Panic Button; Return to Peyton Place; Scaramouche; She's Dressed to Kill; Sound of Music, The; Three Secrets; Tiger and The Pussycat, The

Parker, Ellen: Lost Missile, The

Parker, F. William: Jack Frost

Parker, Fess: Davy Crockett and the River Pirates; Davy Crockett, King of the Wild Frontier; Great Locomotive Chase, The; Hell Is for Heroes; Jayhawkers, The; Light in the Forest, The; Old Yeller; Them!; Westward Ho, the Wagons

Parker, Jameson: American Justice; Callie and Son; Curse of the Crystal Eye; Gathering, Part II, The; Prince of Darkness; Small Circle of Friends, A; Spy; White Dog

Parker, Jean: Beyond Tomorrow; Bluebeard (1944); Dead Man's Eyes; Flying Blind; Flying Deuces; Gabriel over the White House; Ghost Goes West, The; Gunfighter, The (1950); Lawless Street, A; Little Women (1933); One Body Too Many; Operator 13; Texas Rangers (1936); Zenobia

Parker, Kim: Fiend without a Face

Parker, Lara: Best of Dark Shadows, The; Foxfire Light; Night of Dark Shadows; Race with the Devil

Parker, Mary-Louise: Boys on the Side; Bullets over Broadway; Client, The; Cupid and Cate; Fried Green Tomatoes; Goodbye Lover; Grand Canyon; Legalese; Longtime Companion; Mr. Wonderful; Murder in Mind; Naked in New York; Place for Annie, A; Reckless (1995); Saint Maybe; Sugartime

Parker, Molly: In the Shadows; Kissed

Parker, Monica: Coming Out Alive; Improper Channels

Parker, Nathaniel: Beverly Hills Ninja; Othello (1995); Squanto: A Warrior's Tale; War Requiem; Wide Sargasso Sea

Parker, Nicole: Incredibly True Adventure of Two Girls in Love, The

Parker, Noelle: Lethal Lolita—Amy Fisher: My Story; Twisted

Parker, Norman: Killing Hour, The

Parker, Paula Jai: Breaks, The; Cosmic Slop; Sprung

Parker Jr., Ray: Enemy Territory

Parker, Sarah Jessica: Dudley Do-Right; Ed Wood; Extreme Measures; First Wives Club, The; Flight of the Navigator; Footloose; Girls Just Want to Have Fun; Hocus Pocus; Honeymoon in Vegas; If Lucy Fell; L.A. Story; Mars Attacks!; Miami Rhapsody; Somewhere, Tomorrow; Striking Distance; Substance of Fire, The; 'Til There Was You

Parker, Suzy: Chamber of Horrors; Interns, The

Parker, Trey: Basketball; Orgazmo

Parker, Wes: Cry from the Mountain

Parker, Willard: Hunt the Man Down

Parkes, Shaun: Human Traffic

Parkins, Barbara: Asylum (1972); Christina; Puppet on a Chain; Shout at the Devil; Snatched; To Catch a King; Valley of the Dolls

Parks, Larry: Jolson Sings Again; Jolson Story, The; Love Is Better than Ever

Parks, Michael: Arizona Heat; Bible, The; China Lake Murders, The; Club Life; Death Wish V: The Face of Death; Deceiver; Dial M for Murder (1981); ffolkes; Hard Country; Hitman, The; Julian Po; Niagara Niagara; Private Files of J. Edgar Hoover, The; Return of Josey Wales; Savage Bees, The; Savannah Smiles; Sidewinder 1; Stranger by Night; Welcome to Spring Break

Parks, Tammy: Attack of the 60 Ft. Centerfold; Virtual Desire

Parks, Tom: Ladybugs

Parks, Tricia: L.A. Crackdown

Parlavecchio, Steve: Amongst Friends

Parlo, Dita: L'Atalante

Parnell, Emory: Ma and Pa Kettle at the Fair; Ma and Pa Kettle Back on the Farm; Trail of Robin Hood

Parrish, Helen: First Love (1939); In Old California; Sunset Serenade; Three Smart Girls Grow Up; You'll Find Out

Parrish, Julie: Doberman Gang, The

Parrish, Leslie: Candyman, The (1968); Li'l Abner (1959); Manchurian Candidate, The

Parrish, Max: Hold Me, Thrill Me, Kiss Me

Parrish, Steve: Scanners 3: The Takeover

Parry, David: Lost Platoon

Parry, Natasha: Windom's Way

Parsekian, Tom: Hot Resort; Shattered Vows

Parsons, Estelle: American Clock, The; Bonnie and Clyde; Come Along with Me; Don't Drink the Water; For Pete's Sake; Freak City; Gentleman Bandit, The; I Never Sang for My Father; Looking for Richard; Love Letter, The (1998); Private Matter, A; Rachel, Rachel; Watermelon Man

Parsons, Karyn: Major Payne

Parsons, Louella: Hollywood Hotel; Without Reservations

Parsons, Nancy: Motel Hell; Porky's II: The Next Day

Parsons, Shannon Michelle: Freakshow

Parsum, Mads: Webmaster

Parton, Dolly: Best Little Whorehouse in Texas, The; Beverly Hillbillies, The (1993); Nine to Five; Rhinestone; Smoky Mountain Christmas; Steel Magnolias; Straight Talk; Unlikely Angel

Parton, Julia: Naked Detective, The

Partridge, Laurie Tait: Deadly Daphne's Revenge

Partridge, Ross: Amityville: A New Generation

Pas, Michael: Daens

Pascal, Christine: Clockmaker, The (1973); Round Midnight; Sincerely Charlotte

Pascal, Olivia: Bloody Moon

Pascaud, Nathale: Mr. Hulot's Holiday

Pasco, Isabelle: Deep Trouble; Prospero's Books

Pasco, Richard: Gorgon, The; Mrs. Brown

Pasdar, Adrian: Carlito's Way; Cookie; Ghost Brigade; Just Like a Woman; Last Good Time, The; Lost Capone, The; Made in USA; Near Dark; Pompatus of Love, The; Slave of Dreams; Streets of Gold; Torn Apart; Vital Signs; Wounded

Pashin, Yevgeni: Friend of the Deceased, A

Pasolini, Pier Paolo: Canterbury Tales, The

Pass, Cyndi: Bounty Tracker

Passalia, Antonio: Le Boucher (The Butcher)

Passanante, Jean: Return of the Secaucus 7

Passi, Christopher: Marvelous Land of Oz, The

Pastko, Earl: Highway 61

Pastore, Louis: Agent on Ice

Pastore, Vincent: Mickey Blue Eyes

Pastorelli, Robert: Eraser; Michael; Paint Job, The; Simple Wish, A; Sister Act 2: Back in the Habit; Striking Distance; Yarn Princess, The

Pataki, Michael: Amazing Spiderman, The; Bat People; Delinquent School Girls; Graduation Day; Grave of the Vampire; Last Word, The (1979); Pink Angels; Rocky IV; Zoltan—Hound of Dracula

Pate, Michael: Black Castle, The; Curse of the Undead; Hondo; Lawless Street, A; Mad Dog Morgan; Something of Value; Strange Door, The; Tower of London (1962); Wild Duck, The

Paterson, Bill: Comfort and Joy; Coming Up Roses; Defense of the Realm; Diamond's Edge; Dutch Girls; Odd Job, The; Return of the Musketeers; Truly, Madly, Deeply

Paterson, Pat: Charlie Chan in Egypt

Patey, Christian: L'Argent

Patil, Smita: Spices

Patinkin, Mandy: Adventures of Elmo in Grouchland, The; Alien Nation; Daniel; Dick Tracy (1990); Doctor, The; House on Carroll Street, The; Hunchback, The (1997); Impromptu; Lulu on the Bridge; Maxie; Music of Chance, The; Night of the Juggler; Princess Bride, The; Squanto: A Warrior's Tale; Strange Justice; Sunday in the Park with George; True Colors; Yentl

Paton, Angela: Con, The

Paton, Charles: Blackmail (1929)

Paton, Laurie: Norman's Awesome Experience

Patric, Jason: After Dark, My Sweet; Denial; Frankenstein Unbound; Geronimo: An American Legend (1994); Incognito; Journey of August King, The; Lost Boys, The; Rush;

Sleepers; Solarbabies; Speed 2: Cruise Control; Your Friends & Neighbors

Patrick, Barbara: Within the Rock

Patrick, Butch: Adventures of Milo in the Phantom Tollbooth, The

Patrick, Dennis: Dear Dead Delilah; Heated Vengeance; Joe

Patrick, Dorothy: Follow Me Quietly; Road Agent; Thunder Pass; Under Mexicali Stars

Patrick, Gail: Brewster's Millions (1945); Death Takes a Holiday; Doctor Takes a Wife, The; Love Crazy; Mad About Music; Mississippi; Murder at the Vanities; Murders in the Zoo; My Man Godfrey (1936); Phantom Broadcast, The; Wagon Wheels; Wives Under Suspicion

Patrick, Gregory: Bad Blood (1988); Woman Obsessed, A

Patrick, Lee: Adventures of Topper, The; Black Bird, The; City for Conquest; Footsteps in the Dark; Fuller Brush Girl, The; In This Our Life; Mildred Pierce; Mrs. Parkington; Smiling Ghost, The; Somewhere I'll Find You

Patrick, Nigel: Battle of Britain; Browning Version, The (1951); Encore; Executioner, The; League of Gentlemen, The; Mackintosh Man, The; Pandora and the Flying Dutchman; Pickwick Papers, The; Raintree County; Sapphire; Trio; Virgin Soldiers, The

Patrick, Robert: Asylum (1996); Body Language (1995); Body Shot; Cool Surface, The; Copland; Decoy; Double Dragon; Eye of the Eagle; Faculty, The; Fire in the Sky; From Dusk Till Dawn 2: Texas Blood Money; Future Hunters; Hong Kong '97; Last Gasp; Only Thrill, The; Sink or Swim; Striptease; Tactical Assault; Terminator 2: Judgment Day; Zero Tolerance

Patry, Cherie: Kingdom of the Vampire

Patte, Jean-Marie: Rise of Louis XIV, The

Patten, Luana: Fun and Fancy Free; Home from the Hill; Johnny Tremain; Rock, Pretty Baby; So Dear to My Heart

Patterson, David: Secret Garden, The (1984)

Patterson, Elizabeth: Bill of Divorcement, A; Bluebeard's Eighth Wife; Colonel Effingham's Raid; Hold Your Man; Intruder in the Dust; I've Always Loved You; Love Me Tonight; Sky's the Limit, The; Tall Story; Welcome, Stranger

Patterson, Hank: El Paso Kid

Patterson, J. G. "Pat": Doctor Gore

Patterson, Jay: Double Exposure (1989); Double Jeopardy (1992); Excessive Force II: Force on Force

Patterson, Lee: Jack the Ripper (1959)

Patterson, Lorna: Imposter, The

Patterson, Neva: David and Lisa; Desk Set

Patterson, Sarah: Company of Wolves, The

Patterson, Scott: Alien Nation, Dark Horizon

Patton, Mark: Anna to the Infinite Power; Nightmare on Elm Street 2, A: Freddy's Revenge

Patton, Will: Armageddon; Belizaire the Cajun; Chinese Boxes; Client, The; Cold Heaven; Copycat; Deadly Desire; Dillinger (1990); Entrapment; Everybody Wins; Fled; Gone in 60 Seconds; In the Deep Woods; In the Soup; Inventing the Abbotts; Judicial Consent; Midnight Edition; Murder on the Bayou; Natural Causes; No Way Out; Paint Job, The; Postman, The; Puppet Masters, The; Romeo Is Bleeding; Shock to the System, A; Spitfire Grill, The; Stars and Bars; Taking the Heat; Tollbooth; Wildfire (1988)

Patton-Hall, Michael: Escapes

Paukstelis, Tina Ona: 5 Dark Souls; Unearthing, The

Paul, Adrian: Cover Girl Murders, The; Dead Men Can't Dance; Highlander: The Gathering

Paul, Alexandra: American Flyers; Baywatch: The Movie; Christine; Cyber Bandits; Death Train; Detonator II: Night Watch; Dragnet (1987); 8 Million Ways to Die; Getting Physical; Millions; Paperboy, The; Piranha (1995); Prey of the Chameleon; Spectre; Sunset Grill

Paul, Brian: Urban Jungle

Paul, David: Barbarians, The; Double Trouble (1991); Think Big; Twin Sitters

Paul, Don Michael: Aloha Summer; Heart of Dixie, The; Rich Kid; Robot Wars; Rolling Vengeance; Winners Take All

Paul, Eugenia: Disembodied, The

Paul, Megan: Forest Warrior

Paul, Patricia: Creep

Paul, Peter: Barbarians, The; Double Trouble (1991); Think Big; Twin Sitters

Paul, Richard: Bloodfist III: Forced to Fight

Paul, Richard Joseph: Oblivion; Oblivion 2: Backlash; Stepsister, The; Under the Boardwalk; Vampirella

Paul, Rosemary: Dead Easy

Paul, Stuart: Emanon; Falling in Love Again; Fate

Paul, Zoe: L.I.P. Service

Pauley, Rebecca: Near Misses

Paulin, Scott: Captain America (1990); Cat People (1982); Deceit; From Hollywood to Deadwood; Grim Prairie Tales; Last of Philip Banter, The; Pump Up the Volume; Teen Wolf; To Heal a Nation; Tricks of the Trade; White Hot: The Mysterious Murder of Thelma Todd

Pauli, Morgan: Fade to Black (1980)

Pauli, Nicki: Boulevard of Broken Dreams

Paulsen, Albert: Gypsy Warriors, The; Laughing Policeman, The; Search for the Gods

Paulsen, Pat: Blood Suckers from Outer Space; Night Patrol; Where Were You When the Lights Went Out?

Paulsen, Rob: Perfect Match, The

Pavan, Marisa: Diane; Drum Beat; John Paul Jones; Man in the Gray Flannel Suit, The; Rose Tattoo, The; What Price Glory

Pavarotti, Luciano: Yes, Giorgio

Pavlovsky, Tato: Miss Mary

Pavlow, Muriel: Doctor in the House; Malta Story, The; Murder She Said

Pawley, Edward: Hoosier Schoolboy

Paxinou, Katina: For Whom the Bell Tolls; Miracle, The (1959)

Paxton, Bill: Apollo 13; Back to Back; Boxing Helena; Brain Dead; Bright Shining Lie, A; Dark Backward, The; Evening Star, The; Frank & Jesse; Future Shock; Indian Summer; Last of the Finest, The; Mighty Joe Young (1998); Monolith; Near Dark; Next of Kin (1989); One False Move; Pass the Ammo; Predator 2; Simple Plan, A; Slipstream; Titanic (1997); Traveller; Trespass; True Lies; Twister (1996); U-571; Vagrant, The; Weird Science

Payan, Ilka Tanya: Florida Straits

Payant, Gilles: Big Red

Paymer, David: American President, The; Amistad; Carpool; Chill Factor; City Hall; Crime of the Century; Gang Related; Get Shorty; Heart and Souls; Lesser Evil, The; Mighty Joe Young (1998); Mr. Saturday Night; Mumford; Nixon; Outside Ozona; Payback (1999); Quiz Show; Searching for Bobby Fischer; Sixth Man, The; Unforgettable

Payne III, Carl Anthony: Breaks, The

Payne, Allen: CB4; Jason's Lyric; Price Above Rubies, A; Tuskegee Airmen, The; Vampire in Brooklyn; Walking Dead, The

Payne, Bruce: Cisco Kid, The; Face the Evil; Full Eclipse; H. P. Lovecraft's Necronomicon: Book of the Dead; Counterfeit; Nemesis (1986); One Man's Justice; Operation Intercept; Passenger 57; Ravager; Silence Like Glass; Sweepers; Switch; Warlock III: The End of Innocence

Payne, Eric: Gridlock'd

Payne, John: College Swing; Dodsworth; Dolly Sisters, The; Footlight Serenade; Hello, Frisco, Hello; Iceland; Kansas City Confidential; Razor's Edge, The (1946); Slightly Scarlet; Springtime in the Rockies (1942); Sun Valley Serenade; Tennessee's Partner; Tin Pan Alley; To the Shores of Tripoli; Weekend in Havana

Payne, Julie: Private School

Payne, Laurence: Tell-Tale Heart, The

Payne, Sally: Bad Man of Deadwood; Jesse James at Bay; Man from Music Mountain; Romance on the Range; Young Bill Hickok

Payne, Sandra: Moving Finger, The

Pays, Amanda: Cold Room, The; Dead on the Money; Exposure; Flash, The; Kindred, The; Leviathan; Max Headroom; Off Limits (1988); Oxford Blues; Solitaire for 2; 13 at Dinner

Payton, Barbara: Bride of the Gorilla; Drums in the Deep South; Kiss Tomorrow Goodbye; Only the Valiant

Payton-Wright, Pamela: Going in Style; Resurrection

Payvar, Puya: Life and Nothing More ...

Pazos, Felipe: Old Man and the Sea, The (1958)

Pazzafini, Nello: Adios, Hombre

Peña, Candela: All About My Mother

Peach, Mary: No Love for Johnnie

Peacock, Trevor: Merlin of the Crystal Cave

Peaker, E. J.: Four Deuces, The; Graduation Day; Hello, Dolly!

Pereio, Paulo Cesar: I Love You (Eu Te Amo)

Perella, Marco: Man with the Perfect Swing, The

Perera, Fia: Raising the Heights

Perez, George: Manhattan Merengue; Toy Soldiers (1991)

Perez, Jose: Off and Running; One Shoe Makes It Murder; Short Eyes

Perez, Rosie: Criminal Justice; Fearless (1993); It Could Happen to You; Night on Earth; Somebody to Love; Subway Stories; 24-Hour Woman; Untamed Heart; White Men Can't Jump

Perez, Vincent: Crow: City of Angels, The; Cyrano De Bergerac (1990); I Dreamed of Africa; Indochine; Queen Margot; Shot Through the Heart; Swept from the Sea; Talk of Angels

Perier, François: Gervaise; Le Samourai; Nights of Cabiria; Sylvia and the Phantom

Perkins, Anthony: Black Hole, The; Catch-22; Crimes of Passion; Daughter of Darkness; Deadly Companion; Demon in My View, A; Desire under the Elms; Destroyer; Edge of Sanity; Fear Strikes Out; ffolkes; Fool Killer, The; Friendly Persuasion; Glory Boys, The; Goodbye Again; Green Mansions; I'm Dangerous Tonight; In the Deep Woods; Les Miserables (1978); Lonely Man, The; Mahogany; Matchmaker, The (1958); Napoleon and Josephine: A Love Story; On the Beach; Pretty Poison; Psycho (1960); Psycho II; Psycho III; Psycho 4: The Beginning; Ravishing Idiot, The; Sins of Dorian Gray, The; Someone Behind the Door; Tall Story; Ten Days Wonder; Tin Star, The; Trial, The (1963); Winter Kills

Perkins, Elizabeth: About Last Night … ; Avalon; Big; Doctor, The; Flintstones, The; From the Hip; He Said, She Said; I'm Losing You; Indian Summer; Love at Large; Miracle on 34th Street (1994); Moonlight and Valentino; Over Her Dead Body; Rescuers, Stories of Courage, "Two Women"; Sweethearts' Dance; 28 Days

Perkins, Millie: Cockfighter; Diary of Anne Frank, The; Ensign Pulver; Gun in the House, A; Haunting Passion, The; Love in the Present Tense; Macbeth (1981); Pistol, The: The Birth of a Legend; Ride in the Whirlwind; Shooting, The; Table for Five; Wild in the Country; Wild in the Streets

Perkins, Osgood: Scarface (1932)

Perles, Alfred: Henry Miller Odyssey

Perlich, Max: Born Yesterday (1993); Georgia (1995); Gummo; House on Haunted Hill (1999); Lansky; Maverick; Real Thing, The; Rush; Terrified

Perlman, Rhea: Amazing Stories (TV Series); Canadian Bacon; Carpool; Houdini (1998); Matilda (1996); Over Her Dead Body; Ratings Game, The; Sunset Park; Ted & Venus; There Goes the Neighborhood

Perlman, Ron: Adventures of Huck Finn, The (1993); Beauty and the Beast (TV Series); Blindman's Bluff; Body Armor; Cisco Kid, The; City of Lost Children, The; Cronos; Double Exposure (1993); Frogs for Snakes; Island of Dr. Moreau, The; Last Supper, The (1996); Magnificent Seven, The (TV Series); Name of the Rose, The; Price of Glory; Prince Valiant (1997); Quest for Fire; Romeo Is Bleeding; Second Civil War, The; Sensation; Stephen King's Sleepwalkers; When the Bough Breaks

Pernel, Florence: Blue (1993)

Perra, J. W.: Head of the Family

Perreau, Gigi: Girls Town (1959); Journey to the Center of Time (Time Warp); Mr. Skeffington; My Foolish Heart; Yolanda and the Thief

Perri, Paul: Hit and Run

Perrier, Mireille: Love Without Pity; Toto the Hero

Perrin, Francis: Billy Ze Kick

Perrin, Jack: Painted Stallion, The

Perrin, Jacques: Cinema Paradiso; Donkey Skin (Peau D'Ane); Flight of the Innocent; Girl with a Suitcase; Le Crabe Tambour; Love Songs (Paroles et Musique); 317th Platoon, The

Perrine, Valerie: Agency; Boiling Point (1993); Border, The; Break, The; Bright Angel; Brown's Requiem; Can't Stop the Music; Electric Horseman, The; Last American Hero, The; Lenny; Magician of Lublin, The; Maid to Order; Mr. Billion; Slaughterhouse Five; Sweet Bird of Youth (1989); Water; When Your Lover Leaves

Perrineau Jr., Harold: Edge, The; Smoke (1995); William Shakespeare's Romeo and Juliet

Porrino, Joseph: Bumblebee Flies Anyway, The

Perrins, Leslie: Nine Days a Queen; Triumph of Sherlo Holmes, The

Perry, Felton: Dumb and Dumber; RoboCop 2; Talent f¹ the Game

Perry, Gil: Sourdough

Perry, Jeff: Hard Promises; Kingfish: A Story of Huey Long; Playmaker

Perry, John Bennett: Fools Rush In; Last Fling, The

Perry, Luke: American Strays; Buffy, the Vampire Slayer Seconds; Fifth Element, The; Indiscreet (1998); La Breath; Normal Life; Riot (1996) (TV Movie); Robin Cook Invasion; Storm Tracker; Terminal Bliss

Perry, Margaret: Go West, Young Man

Perry, Matthew: Almost Heroes; Fools Rush In; Three Tango; Whole Nine Yards, The

Perry, Natasha: Midnight Lace

Perry, Rod: Black Gestapo, The; Black Godfather, The

Perry, Roger: Cat, The (1966); Count Yorga, Vampire; R¹ venge (1971) (Shelley Winters)

Perry, Susan: Knock on Any Door

Perryman, Clara: Escape to Love

Perschy, Maria: Castle of Fu Manchu; Horror of the Zor bies; Man's Favorite Sport?; Vultures

Persky, Lisa Jane: Big Easy, The; Coneheads; Peggy Su Got Married; Sure Thing, The

Persoff, Nehemiah: Al Capone; American Tail, An; Badla ders, The; Comancheros, The; Deadly Harvest; Eric; Franc Gary Powers: The True Story of the U-2 Spy Incident; Gree Mansions; In Search of Historic Jesus; Marty (1953) (Tele vision); Never Steal Anything Small; Psychic Killer; Sada Some Like It Hot; Wrong Man, The (1956); Yentl

Persson, Essy: Mission Stardust

Pertwee, Jon: Adventures of a Private Eye; Carry on Cle¹ Dr. Who (TV series); House That Dripped Blood, The; Nuri ber One of the Secret Service

Pertwee, Sean: Deadly Voyage; Shopping

Peru, Dana: Gal Young 'Un

Perugorria, Jorge: Guantanamera!; Strawberry an Chocolate

Pesce, Franco: Have a Nice Funeral

Pesci, Joe: Betsy's Wedding; Bronx Tale, A; Casino (1995 Easy Money; 8 Heads in a Duffel Bag; Eureka; Gone Fishin Goodfellas; Home Alone; Home Alone 2: Lost in New York JFK; Jimmy Hollywood; Lethal Weapon 2; Lethal Weapo 3; Lethal Weapon 4; Man on Fire; My Cousin Vinny; Publ Eye, The; Raging Bull; Super, The; With Honors

Pescow, Donna: Glory Years; Jake Speed; Saturday Nig¹ Fever

Peters, Bernadette: Alice (1990); Annie; Heartbeeps; Im promptu; Jerk, The; Last Best Year, The; Longest Yard, Th¹ Martian Chronicles, Parts I–III, The; Odyssey, The; Pennie from Heaven; Pink Cadillac; Rodgers & Hammerstein's Cir derella; Silent Movie; Slaves of New York; Sleeping Beaut (1983); Sunday in the Park with George; Tulips

Peters, Brock: Ace High; Adventures of Huckleberry Finr The (1978); Broken Angel; Carmen Jones; Framed (1975 Incredible Journey of Dr. Meg Laurel, The; Pawnbroke The; Secret, The; Slaughter's Big Rip-Off; Star Trek VI: Th Undiscovered Country; Two-Minute Warning

Peters, Clark: Mona Lisa; Silver Dream Racer

Peters, Erika: Heroes Die Young

Peters, Fred: Tarzan and the Golden Lion

Peters, House: Human Hearts

Peters, Jean: Apache; As Young as You Feel; Broke Lance; It Happens Every Spring; Man Called Peter, A; Nla¹ gara; Pickup on South Street; Viva Zapata!

Peters, Kelly Jean: Pocket Money

Peters, Lauri: For Love of Ivy

Peters, Noel: Invisible Maniac

Peters, Rick: Elvis Meets Nixon

Peters, Scott: Girl Hunters, The

Peters, Werner: Corrupt Ones, The; 36 Hours

Petersen, Amy: Foolish

Petersen, Paul: Mommy 2: Mommy's Day

Petersen, William: Kiss the Sky

Petersen, William L.: Amazing Grace and Chuck; Anythin¹ for Love; Beast, The (1996); Cousins; Deadly Currents; Fea (1996); Gunshy; Hard Promises; Keep the Change; Long Gone; Manhunter; Passed Away; Rat Pack, The; Return t Lonesome Dove; Skulls, The; To Live and Die in L.A.; Young Guns II eterson, Amanda: Can't Buy Me Love; Fatal Charm; I osed for Playboy; Windrunner

eterson, Cassandra (Elvira): Allan Quartermain and the ost City of Gold; Echo Park

eterson, Kimberlee: Homecoming (1996); Legend of the ost Tomb

eterson, Margie: Strike a Pose

eterson, Robert: Crude Oasis, The

eterson, Stewart: Against a Crooked Sky; Pony Express der; Where the Red Fern Grows

eterson, Vidal: Wizard of the Lost Kingdom

etersons, Alexannder: Desperate Prey

etherbridge, Edward: Lovers of Their Time; Strange Inrlude (1988)

etit, Philippe: Mondo

etit, Victor: Night of the Death Cult; Return of the Evil ead

etrella, Ian: Christmas Story, A

etrenko, Alexei: Rasputin (1985)

etrie, Doris: Wedding in White

etrillo, Sammy: Boys from Brooklyn, The

etroff, Gloria: Two Lost Worlds

etrusic, Luka: I Want You

ettersson, Birgitta: Virgin Spring, The

ettet, Joanna: Blue (1968); Casino Royale (1967); Cry of the Innocent; Double Exposure (1982); Evil, The; Group, he; Night of the Generals; Pioneer Woman; Robbery; weet Country; Terror in Paradise

ettiet, Christopher: Goodbye Bird, The

ettifer, Brian: Gospel According to Vic, The

etty, Lori: Free Willy; Glass Shield, The; In the Army Now; eague of Their Own, A; Point Break; Relax ... It's Just Sex; erial Bomber; Tank Girl

etty, Rose: Housekeeper, The

etty, Tom: Postman, The

ettyjohn, Angelique: Biohazard

evney, Joseph: Nocturne

eyser, Penny: Frisco Kid, The; In-Laws, The; Wild Times feiffer, Dedee: Allnighter, The; Deadly Past; Double Exposure (1993); Red Surf; Running Cool; Sandman (1992); hoot (1991); Up Close and Personal; Vamp

feiffer, Michelle: Age of Innocence, The; Batman Reurns; Callie and Son; Dangerous Liaisons; Dangerous Minds; Deep End of the Ocean, The; Fabulous Baker Boys, he; Falling in Love Again; Frankie and Johnny (1991); rease 2; Hollywood Knights, The; Into the Night; Ladyawke; Love Field; Married to the Mob; One Fine Day; ower, Passion, and Murder; Russia House, The; Story of ls, The; Sweet Liberty; Tequila Sunrise; Thousand Acres, ; To Gillian on Her 37th Birthday; Up Close and Personal; Villiam Shakespeare's A Midsummer Night's Dream; Vitches of Eastwick, The; Wolf

flug, Jo Ann: Catlow; M*A*S*H; Night Strangler, The

helan, Joe: South of Reno

helps, Buster: Little Orphan Annie

helps, Peter: Blackwater Trail; Lighthorsemen, The; Merin; Starlight Hotel

helps, Robert: Lights, Camera, Action, Love

henice, Michael: 9 Ninjas

hifer, Mekhi: Clockers; High School High; I Still Know Vhat You Did Last Summer; Soul Food

hilbin, John: Crew, The; Martians Go Home; North Shore; Shy People

hilbin, Mary: Human Hearts; Man Who Laughs, The; Merry-Go-Round, The; Phantom of the Opera (1925)

hilbrook, James: Finger on the Trigger

hilipchuk, Misha: Thief, The (1997)

hilipe, Gérard: Beauties of the Night; Devil in the Flesh 1946); Fanfan the Tulip; Le Rouge et le Noir; Les Liaisons Dangereuses

hilippe, Ryan: Cruel Intentions; I Know What You Did ast Summer; Lifeform; White Squall

hilips, Emo: Journey to the Center of the Earth (1987)

hilips, Lee: Peyton Place

hilips, Mary: Farewell to Arms, A; Leave Her to Heaven

hillip, Lawrence King: Abducted

hillippe, Ryan: 54; Playing by Heart

hillips, Angie: Manny & Lo

hillips, Bijou: Black and White (2000)

hillips, Bill: Flat Top

Phillips, Bobbie: Back in Action; Chameleon (1998); Cover Girl Murders, The; Ring of Fire 3: Lion Strike; TC 2000

Phillips, Chynna: Goodbye, Miss 4th of July; Prize Pulitzer, The: The Roxanne Pulitzer Story

Phillips, Courtney: Return to the Blue Lagoon

Phillips, Gary: Whodunit?

Phillips, Gina: Breaking Free

Phillips, Grace: All the Vermeers in New York; Truth or Consequences, N.M.

Phillips, Howard: Last Mile, The

Phillips, James: In Gold We Trust; Prison Planet

Phillips, Jean: Among the Living; Outlaws of the Desert

Phillips, John: Mummy's Shroud, The

Phillips, Joseph C.: Strictly Business

Phillips, Julianne: Big Bully; Fletch Lives; Seven Hours to Judgment; Skin Deep; Sweet Lies; Vow to Kill, A; Where's the Money, Noreen?

Phillips, Kristie: Spitfire (1994)

Phillips, Leslie: August; Gamma People, The

Phillips, Lou Diamond: Ambition; Bats; Big Hit, The; Boulevard; Courage Under Fire; Dakota (1988); Dangerous Touch; Dark Wind; Disorganized Crime; Extreme Justice; First Power, The; Harley; La Bamba; Renegades; Shadow of the Wolf; Show of Force, A; Sioux City; Stand and Deliver; Supernova; Teresa's Tattoo; Undertow; Wharf Rat, The; Young Guns; Young Guns II

Phillips, Mackenzie: American Graffiti; Love Child; More American Graffiti; Rafferty and the Gold Dust Twins

Phillips, Meredith: Sky Pirates

Phillips, Michelle: American Anthem; Assault & Matrimony; Death Squad, The; Dillinger (1973); Man with Bogart's Face, The; Rubdown; Scissors; Secrets of a Married Man; Valentino

Phillips, Patricia: Shades of Love: Sincerely, Violet

Phillips, Peg: Northern Exposure (TV Series)

Phillips, Samantha: Deceit; Sexual Malice

Phillips, Sian: Age of Innocence, The; Borrowers, The (1993); Carpathian Eagle; Doctor and the Devils, The; Goodbye, Mr. Chips (1969); I, Claudius; Murphy's War; Under Milk Wood; Valmont

Phillips, Sydney Coale: Cause of Death

Phillips, Wendy: Bugsy

Phipps, Bill: Red River Shore

Phipps, Max: Dark Age; Nate and Hayes; Sky Pirates

Phoenix, Gemma: Raining Stones

Phoenix, Joaquin: Clay Pigeons; 8MM; Gladiator (2000); Inventing the Abbotts; Return to Paradise (1998); To Die For (1995); U-Turn

Phoenix, Leaf: Russkies; SpaceCamp

Phoenix, Rain: Even Cowgirls Get the Blues

Phoenix, River: Dogfight; Explorers; I Love You to Death; Indiana Jones and the Last Crusade; Little Nikita; Mosquito Coast, The; My Own Private Idaho; Night in the Life of Jimmy Reardon, A; Running on Empty; Silent Tongue; Sneakers; Stand by Me (1986); Thing Called Love, The

Phuntsok, Sonam: Kundun

Piałat, Maurice: A Nos Amours; Under the Sun of Satan

Piantadosi, Joseph: Schlock

Piat, Jean: Tower of Screaming Virgins, The

Piazza, Ben: Children of An Lac, The; Consenting Adults (1985); Guilty by Suspicion; Hanging Tree, The; Scene of the Crime (1985)

Pica, Tina: Yesterday, Today and Tomorrow

Picardo, Robert: Explorers; Gremlins 2: The New Batch; Jack's Back; 976-EVIL; Star Trek: First Contact; Wagons East

Picato, Alexandra: Colony, The (1995)

Piccoli, Michel: Beaumarchais the Scoundrel; Belle de Jour; Beyond Obsession; Contempt; Danger: Diabolik; Dangerous Moves; Day and the Hour; Death in the Garden; Diary of a Chambermaid (1964); Discreet Charm of the Bourgeoisie, The; Game Is Over, The; Genealogies of a Crime; Infernal Trio, The; La Belle Noiseuse; La Passante; La Puritaine; Lady L; Le Doulos; Les Choses de la Vie (Things in Life, The); L'Etat Sauvage (The Savage State); Mado; May Fools; Milky Way, The (1970); Passion in the Desert; Peril; Phantom of Liberty, The; Sleeping Car Murders, The; Success Is the Best Revenge; Ten Days Wonder; Vincent, François, Paul and the Others; Wedding in Blood

Piccolo, Ottavia: Mado; Zorro

Picerni, Paul: Operation Pacific; Tanks Are Coming, The; To Hell and Back

Pichel, Irving: Dick Tracy's G-Men; Dracula's Daughter; General Spanky; Oliver Twist (1933); Silver Streak (1934)

Pickens Jr., James: Gridlock'd

Pickens, Slim: Apple Dumpling Gang, The; Blazing Saddles; Cowboys, The; Deserter, The; Dr. Strangelove or How I Learned to Stop Worrying and Love the Bomb; Ginger in the Morning; Hawmps!; Honeysuckle Rose; Howling, The; Mr. Billion; 1941; One-Eyed Jacks; Pink Motel; Pony Express Rider; Rancho Deluxe; Red River Shore; Rough Night in Jericho; Sacketts, The; Talion; Tom Horn; White Buffalo; White Line Fever; Will Penny

Picker, Josh: Alex

Pickering, Sarah: Little Dorrit

Pickett, Blake: Dark Universe, The

Pickett, Bobby: Frankenstein Sings

Pickett, Cindy: Atomic Dog; Call to Glory; Crooked Hearts; Deepstar Six; Echoes in the Darkness; Evolver; Ferris Bueller's Day Off; Goodbye Bird, The; Hot to Trot; Hysterical; Into the Homeland; Men's Club, The; Painted Hero; Stephen King's Sleepwalkers; Wild Card

Pickford, Jack: Goose Woman, The; Tom Sawyer (1917)

Pickford, Mary: Coquette; D. W. Griffith Triple Feature; Little Annie Rooney; Pollyanna (1920); Poor Little Rich Girl, The (1917); Pride of the Clan, The; Rebecca of Sunnybrook Farm (1917); Sparrows; Stella Maris; Taming of the Shrew, The (1929)

Pickles, Carolyn: Letting the Birds Go Free

Pickles, Christina: St. Elsewhere (TV Series)

Pickles, Vivian: Candleshoe; Elizabeth R; Harold and Maude; Suspicion (1987)

Pickup, Ronald: Danny, The Champion of the World; Fortunes of War (1987); Pope John Paul II; Rector's Wife, The; Wagner

Picon, Molly: Come Blow Your Horn; Fiddler on the Roof; For Pete's Sake; Murder on Flight 502

Picot, Genevieve: Proof

Pidgeon, Rebecca: Dawning, The; Spanish Prisoner, The; Winslow Boy, The (1999)

Pidgeon, Walter: Advise and Consent; Bad and the Beautiful, The; Big Red; Cinderella (1964); Command Decision; Dark Command; Deep in My Heart; Executive Suite; Forbidden Planet; Funny Girl; Girl of the Golden West, The; Hit the Deck; Holiday in Mexico; House Across the Bay, The; How Green Was My Valley; It's a Date; Julia Misbehaves; Last Time I Saw Paris, The; Lindbergh Kidnapping Case, The; Listen, Darling; Madame Curie; Man Hunt (1941); Men of the Fighting Lady; Million Dollar Mermaid; Miniver Story, The; Mrs. Miniver; Mrs. Parkington; Murder on Flight 502; Neptune Factor, The; Saratoga; Shopworn Angel, The; That Forsyte Woman; Too Hot to Handle; Two-Minute Warning; Voyage to the Bottom of the Sea; Weekend at the Waldorf; White Cargo

Pieplu, Claude: Wedding in Blood

Pierce, Bradley: Borrowers, The (1997); Jumanji

Pierce, Brock: First Kid; Legend of the Lost Tomb

Pierce Jr., Charles B.: Norseman, The

Pierce, Chuck: Boggy Creek II

Pierce, David: Little Man Tate

Pierce, David Hyde: Isn't She Great; Mating Habits of the Earthbound Human, The; Nixon

Pierce, James: Tarzan and the Golden Lion

Pierce, Jill: Cyborg Soldier

Pierce, Justin: Black Male; First Time Felon; Kids

Pierce, Maggie: Fastest Guitar Alive, The

Pierce, Stack: Enemy Unseen; Low Blow; Patriot

Pierce, Wendell: It Could Happen to You

Pierini, David: Last Way Out, The

Pierpoint, Eric: Alien Nation, Dark Horizon; Sex, Love, and Cold Hard Cash; Steel (1997); Stranger, The (1994)

Pierre, Roger: Mon Oncle d'Amerique

Pigaut, Roger: Simple Story, A

Pigg, Alexandra: Chicago Joe and the Showgirl; Letter to Brezhnev

Piggins, Chris: Lady of the Lake

Pigott-Smith, Tim: Hunchback (1982); Jewel in the Crown, The; Remains of the Day; Sweet William

Pilato, Joseph: Day of the Dead; Married People, Single Sex

Pilbeam, Nova: Man Who Knew Too Much, The (1934); Nine Days a Queen; Young and Innocent

Pileggi, Mitch: Shocker; X-Files, The (TV Series)

Pilisi, Mark: Tearaway

Pilkington, Lorraine: Human Traffic; Miracle, The (1990)

Pillars, Jeffrey: Ernest Rides Again

Pileggi, Mitch: X-Files, The (1998)

Pillot, Mary: Trespasses

Pilmark, Soren: Kingdom, The

Pilon, Daniel: Obsessed

Pilon, Donald: Left for Dead; Pyx, The

Pinal, Silvia: Exterminating Angel, The; Shar (Maneaters!); Simon of the Desert; Viridiana

Pinchette, Jean-François: Being at Home with Claude

Pinchot, Bronson: Beverly Hills Cop 3; Blame It on the Be boy; Courage Under Fire; First Wives Club, The; Gre American Sex Scandal, The; Hot Resort; It's My Party; La goliers, The; Risky Business; Second Sight; Slappy and th Stinkers; True Romance

Pinchot, Rosamond: Three Musketeers, The (1935)

Pine, Larry: Sunday; Vanya on 42nd Street

Pine, Philip: Lost Missile, The

Pine, Robert: Apple Dumpling Gang Rides Again, The; A You Lonesome Tonight; Empire of the Ants

Pinero, Miguel: Miami Vice; Streets of L.A., The

Pinkett, Jada: If These Walls Could Talk; Inkwell, The; Ja son's Lyric; Low Down Dirty Shame, A; Menace II Societ Nutty Professor, The (1996); Scream 2; Set It Off; Tale from the Crypt: Demon Knight; Woo

Pinon, Dominique: Alien Resurrection; City of Lost Chil dren, The; Delicatessen

Pinsent, Gordon: Case of Libel, A; John and the Missus; Si lence of the North; Vow to Kill, A

Pinsent, Leah: Virus (1996)

Pintauro, Danny: Beniker Gang, The; Cujo

Pinter, Harold: Mansfield Park

Pinto, Dan: Captured Alive

Pinto, Johnny: Off and Running

Pinza, Ezio: Mr. Imperium

Piper, Kelly: Maniac (1980); Rawhead Rex

Piper, Roddy: Back in Action; Body Slam; Dead Tides; He Comes to Frogtown; Immortal Combat; Jungleground Marked Man; No Contest; Sci-Fighters; Shepherd; The Live; Tough and Deadly

Piranha, P. Floyd: Redneck Zombies

Pires, David: Zoo Radio

Pirrie, Bruce: Pink Chiquitas, The

Pirro, Mark: Polish Vampire in Burbank, A

Piscopo, Joe: Captain Nuke and the Bomber Boys; Dea Heat; Huck and the King of Hearts; Joe Piscopo Live Johnny Dangerously; Sidekicks; Two Bits & Pepper; Wis Guys

Pisier, Marie-France: Celine and Julie Go Boating; Chane Solitaire; Cousin, Cousine; Francois Truffaut: Stolen Mo ments; French Postcards; Love on the Run (1979); Mis Right; Nous N'Irons Plus Au Bois; Other Side of Midnigh The

Pistone, Kimberly: Blue de Ville

Pithey, Winsley: Saint, The (TV Series)

Pitillo, Maria: Dear God; Frank & Jesse; Godzilla (1998)

Pltoc, John Paul: Trick

Pitoeff, Sacha: Last Year at Marienbad

Pitoniak, Anne: Agnes of God; Sister, Sister; Wizard o Loneliness, The

Pitt, Brad: Across the Tracks; Cool World; Cutting Class Devil's Own, The; Favor, The; Fight Club; Interview with th Vampire; Johnny Suede; Kalifornia; Legends of the Fall Meet Joe Black; River Runs Through It, A; Seven; Seven Years in Tibet; Sleepers; Thelma & Louise; Too Young t Die; True Romance; 12 Monkeys

Pitt, Ingrid: House That Dripped Blood, The; Transmuta tions; Vampire Lovers, The; Where Eagles Dare; Wicke Man, The

Pitt, Norman: Saint, The (TV Series)

Pitts, ZaSu: Aggie Appleby, Maker of Men; Dames; Denve and Rio Grande, The; Eternally Yours; Francis Joins the Wacs; Francis, the Talking Mule; Greed; Guardsman, The Life with Father; Mr. Skitch; Mrs. Wiggs of the Cabbage Patch; No, No Nanette; Nurse Edith Cavell; Perfect Mar riage; Ruggles of Red Gap; This Could Be the Night; Thrill o It All, The; Wedding March, The

Itzalis, Federico: Devil in the Flesh (1987)

Iven, Jeremy: Don King: Only in America; Grosse Pointe Blank; Judgment Night; Just Write; Kiss the Girls; Music from Another Room; PCU; Phoenix; Real Thing, The; 12:01; Twogether; Very Bad Things; Wavelength (1995)

lace, Mary Kay: Being John Malkovich; Big Chill, The; Bright Angel; Captain Ron; Citizen Ruth; Crazy from the Heart; Girl Who Spelled Freedom, The; Manny & Lo; Mary Hartman, Mary Hartman (TV Series); Modern Problems; More American Graffiti; New Life, A; New York, New York; Pecker; Rainmaker, The; Samantha; Smooth Talk

lacido, Michele: Big Business; Forever Mary; L'America; Private Affairs; Summer Night; Three Brothers

lana, Tony: Backlash (1998); Break of Dawn; Disorderlies; Havana; Hillside Stranglers, The; Knockout; Listen to Your Heart; Live Wire; One Good Cop; Romero; Rookie, The; Salvador; Silver Strand; Streets of L.A., The; Sweet 15

lanchon, Roger: Return of Martin Guerre, The

laner, Nigel: Young Ones, The

lank, Scott: Dying to Remember; Marshal Law; Moonbase; Pastime; Saints & Sinners

latt, Edward: Rebel Without a Cause; Rock, Pretty Baby

latt, Louise: Captain Caution

latt, Marc: Seven Brides for Seven Brothers; Tonight and Every Night

latt, Oliver: Benny & Joon; Bicentennial Man; Bulworth; Dangerous Beauty; Diggstown; Dr. Dolittle (1998); Executive Decision; Flatliners; Funnybones; Gun Shy; Impostors, The; Indecent Proposal; Infiltrator, The; Lake Placid; Ready to Rumble; Simon Birch; Tall Tale: The Unbelievable Adventures of Pecos Bill; Temp, The; Three Musketeers, The (1993); Three to Tango; Time to Kill, A (1996)

latters, The: Girl Can't Help It, The

layton, Alice: Who Killed Mary What's 'Er Name?

leasence, Angela: Christmas Carol, A (1984); Favor, the Watch and the Very Big Fish, The; Godsend, The

leasence, Donald: Advocate, The; All Quiet on the Western Front (1979); Alone in the Dark; Ambassador, The; American Tiger; Barry McKenzie Holds His Own; Better Late than Never; Black Arrow (1984); Black Windmill, The; Blood Relatives; Breed Apart, A; Caribbean Mystery, A; Circus of Horrors; Count of Monte Cristo, The (1975); Creepers; Cul-de-Sac; Deep Cover (1980); Devil Within Her, The; Devonville Terror, The; Dr. Jekyll and Mr. Hyde (1973); Dracula (1979); Escape from New York; Fantastic Voyage; Freakmaker; From Beyond the Grave; Great Escape II, The; Ground Zero; Hallelujah Trail, The; Halloween; Halloween II; Halloween IV: The Return of Michael Myers; Halloween V: The Revenge of Michael Myers; Halloween: The Curse of Michael Myers; Hanna's War; Horsemasters; House of Usher, The; Journey into Fear (1975); Land of the Minotaur; Last Tycoon, The; Madwoman of Chaillot, The; Mania; Millions; Monster Club, The; Night Creatures; Night of the Generals; 1984 (1955); No Love for Johnnie; Nothing Underneath; Operation 'Nam; Outer Limits, The (TV Series); Phantom of Death; Prince of Darkness; Puma Man, The; Raw Meat; River of Death; Sgt. Pepper's Lonely Hearts Club Band; Shaming, The; Soldier Blue; Specters; Tale of Two Cities, A (1967); Tales that Witness Madness; Telefon; Ten Little Indians (1989); THX 1138; Tomorrow Never Comes; Treasure of the Amazon; Treasure of the Yankee Zephyr; Uncanny, The; Warrior of the Lost World; Warrior Queen; Wedding in White; Will Penny; You Only Live Twice

leshette, John: Kid with the Broken Halo, The; Paramedics

leshette, Suzanne: Adventures of Bullwhip Griffin, The; Alone in the Neon Jungle; Belarus File, The; Birds, The; Blackbeard's Ghost; Dixie Changing Habits; Forty Pounds of Trouble; Fugitive, The (TV Series); Hot Stuff; If It's Tuesday, This Must Be Belgium; Legend of Valentino; Nevada Smith; Oh, God! Book II; One Cooks, the Other Doesn't; Rome Adventure; Shaggy D.A., The; Support Your Local Gunfighter; Suppose They Gave a War and Nobody Came?; Ugly Dachshund, The

limpton, George: Easy Wheels; Fool and His Money, A; If Ever I See You Again; Just Cause

limpton, Martha: Beautiful Girls; Chantilly Lace; Daybreak (1993); Defenders, The: Taking the First; Defenders, The; Forbidden Choices; Goonies, The; I Shot Andy Warhol; I'm Not Rappaport; Inside Monkey Zetterland; Josh and S.A.M.; Last Summer in the Hamptons; Mosquito Coast, The; Music from Another Room; Parenthood; Pecker; River Rat, The; Running on Empty; Samantha; Shy People; Silence Like Glass; Stanley and Iris; Stars and Bars; Woman at War, A

Plimpton, Shelley: Glen and Randa

Plotnick, Jack: Chairman of the Board

Plowman, Melinda: Billy the Kid vs. Dracula

Plowright, Joan: Aldrich Ames: Traitor Within; Avalon; Brimstone and Treacle; Britannia Hospital; Dance with Me; Dedicated Man, A; Dennis the Menace; Dressmaker, The; Drowning by Numbers; Enchanted April; Entertainer, The; Equus; I Love You to Death; Jane Eyre (1996); Last Action Hero, The; Mr. Wrong; 101 Dalmatians (1996); Place for Annie, A; Pyromaniac's Love Story, A; Return of the Native, The; Scarlet Letter, The (1995); Sorrento Beach; Stalin; Summer House, The; Tea with Mussolini; Time Without Pity; Widow's Peak

Pluhar, Erika: Goalie's Anxiety at the Penalty Kick

Plumb, Eve: ... And God Spoke

Plummer, Amanda: Butterfly Kiss; Courtship; Daniel; Dollmaker, The; Don't Look Back (1996); Drunks; Final Cut, The; Fisher King, The; Freeway (1996); Hotel New Hampshire, The; Last Light; Miss Rose White; Needful Things; Nostradamus; Prisoners of Inertia; Prophecy, The (1995); Pulp Fiction; Right to Remain Silent, The; Simple Wish, A; So I Married an Axe Murderer; Static; World According to Garp, The

Plummer, Christopher: Amateur, The (1982); American Tail, An (voice); Battle of Britain; Boss' Wife, The; Boy in Blue, The; Clown at Midnight, The; Conduct Unbecoming; Conspiracy of Fear, The; Crackerjack; Day that Shook the World, The; Dial M for Murder (1981); Disappearance, The; Dolores Claiborne; Dragnet (1987); Dreamscape; Eyewitness; Fall of the Roman Empire, The; Firehead; Ghost in Monte Carlo, A; Hanover Street; Harrison Bergeron; Highpoint; I Love N.Y.; Inside Daisy Clover; Insider, The; International Velvet; Lily in Love; Man Who Would Be King, The; Mind Field; Money; Murder by Decree; Night of the Generals; Ordeal by Innocence; Prototype; Pyx, The; Red-Blooded American Girl; Return of the Pink Panther, The; Royal Hunt of the Sun; Scarlet and the Black, The; Shadow Box, The; Shadow Dancing; Silent Partner, The; Skeletons; Somewhere in Time; Sound of Music, The; Souvenir; Spiral Staircase, The (1975); Stage Struck (1958); Star Crash; Star Trek VI: The Undiscovered Country; Thornbirds, The; 12 Monkeys; Waterloo; We the Jury; Where the Heart Is; Winchell; Wolf; Young Catherine

Plummer, Glenn: Menace II Society; Pastime; Pronto; Showgirls; South Central; Substitute, The (1996); Up Close and Personal

Png, Pierre: That's the Way I Like It

Podemski, Jennifer: Dance Me Outside

Podesta, Alejandra: I Don't Want to Talk About It

Podesta, Rossana: Helen of Troy; Hercules (1983); Sensual Man, The; Sodom and Gomorrah; Ulysses; Virgin of Nuremberg (Horror Castle)

Podobed: Extraordinary Adventures of Mr. West in the Land of the Bolsheviks, The

Poelvoorde, Benoit: Man Bites Dog

Pogson, Kathryn: Overindulgence

Pogue, Ken: Blindman's Bluff; Climb, The; Contagious; Dead of Winter; Grey Fox, The; Keeping Track; One Magic Christmas; Run

Pohlmann, Eric: Horsemen, The; Surprise Package

Pohnel, Ron: No Retreat, No Surrender

Poindexter, Larry: American Ninja II; Blue Movies; Sorceress (1994)

Pointer, Priscilla: Disturbed; Runaway Father

Poiret, Jean: Elegant Criminal, The; Last Metro, The; Tales of Paris

Poitier, Sidney: Band of Angels; Bedford Incident, The; Blackboard Jungle, The; Brother John; Buck and the Preacher; Children of the Dust; Cry, the Beloved Country (1952); Defiant Ones, The; Duel at Diablo; For Love of Ivy; Free of Eden; Goodbye, My Lady; Greatest Story Ever Told, The; Guess Who's Coming to Dinner; In the Heat of the Night; Jackal, The; Let's Do It Again; Lilies of the Field (1963); Little Nikita; Mandela and De Klerk; Mark of the Hawk, The; Organization, The; Paris Blues; Patch of Blue, A; Piece of the Action, A; Pressure Point; Raisin in the Sun, A

Prevert, Pierre: Age of Gold

Previn, Soon-Yi: Wild Man Blues

Prevost, Daniel: Dinner Game, The

Prevost, Marie: Flying Fool, The; Hands Across the Table; Ladies of Leisure; Marriage Circle, The; Sin of Madelon Claudet, The; Sweethearts on Parade

Price, Alan: Don't Look Back (1967); O Lucky Man!; Oh, Alfie

Price, Brenda: Robin Hood Gang, The

Price, Dennis: Five Golden Hours; Horror Hospital; Horror of Frankenstein; Hungry Hill; Kind Hearts and Coronets; Magic Bow, The; Murder Most Foul; Naked Truth (Your Past Is Showing); No Love for Johnnie; School for Scoundrels; Ten Little Indians (1966); Tunes of Glory; Twins of Evil; Venus in Furs; Victim

Price, Hai: Desert Phantom

Price, Jamieson K.: Secret Kingdom, The

Price, Marc: Killer Tomatoes Eat France; Rescue, The; Trick or Treat (1986)

Price, Molly: Jersey Girl

Price, Rosalinda: Roaring Guns

Price, Stanley: Driftin' Kid

Price, Sue: Nemesis 2; Nemesis 3: Time Lapse; Nemesis 4

Price, Vincent: Abominable Dr. Phibes, The; Backtrack; Baron of Arizona, The; Bat, The; Bloodbath at the House of Death; Champagne for Caesar; Comedy of Terrors; Conqueror Worm, The; Cry of the Banshee; Dangerous Mission; Dead Heat; Diary of a Madman; Dr. Goldfoot and the Bikini Machine; Dr. Goldfoot and the Girl Bombs; Dr. Phibes Rises Again; Edward Scissorhands; Escapes; Fall of the House of Usher, The (1960); Fly, The (1958); Haunted Palace, The; Heart of Justice; His Kind of Woman; House of 1,000 Dolls; House of the Long Shadows; House of the Seven Gables, The; House of Wax; House on Haunted Hill; Invisible Man Returns; Journey into Fear (1975); Keys to the Kingdom, The; Las Vegas Story, The; Last Man on Earth, The; Laura; Leave Her to Heaven; Madhouse (1972); Masque of the Red Death, The (1964); Master of the World; Monster Club, The; Oblong Box, The; Offspring, The; Pit and the Pendulum, The (1961); Private Lives of Elizabeth and Essex, The (1939); Return of the Fly, The; Scavenger Hunt; Scream and Scream Again; Serenade; Shock (1946); Snow White and the Seven Dwarfs (1983); Song of Bernadette, The; Tales of Terror; Theatre of Blood; Three Musketeers, The (1948); Tingler, The; Tomb of Ligeia; Tower of London (1939); Tower of London (1962); Trouble with Girls, The; Twice-Told Tales; Whales of August, The; While the City Sleeps; Wilson

Prichard, Robert: Alien Space Avenger

Priest, Martin: Plot Against Harry, The

Priest, Pat: Easy Come, Easy Go; Incredible Two-Headed Transplant, The

Priestley, Jason: Beverly Hills 90210; Calendar Girl; Cold-Blooded; Eye of the Beholder; Love and Death on Long Island; Nowhere to Run (1989); Quantum Leap (TV Series); Tombstone

Prieto, Paco Christian: Only the Strong; Street Law

Prim, Suzy: Mayerling

Prima, Barry: Ferocious Female Freedom Fighters

Prima, Louis: Manhattan Merry-Go-Round

Prime, Cheryl: Lovers of Their Time

Primus, Barry: Autopsy; Big Business; Black & White; Boxcar Bertha; Brotherly Love; Cannibal Women in the Avocado Jungle of Death; Crime of the Century; Denial; Flipping; Gold Coast; Jake Speed; Macbeth (1981); Night and the City (1992); Portrait of a Showgirl; Talking Walls; Trade Off

Prince: Graffiti Bridge; Purple Rain; Under the Cherry Moon

Prince, Clayton: Hairspray

Prince, Faith: My Father, the Hero

Prince, John T.: Battling Orioles, The

Prince, William: Blade (1973); City in Fear; Cyrano De Bergerac (1950); Gauntlet, The; Greatest Man in the World, The; Objective, Burma!; Soldier, The; Spies Like Us; Sybil; Taking of Beverly Hills, The; Vice Versa

Principal, Victoria: I Will, I Will ... for Now; Life and Times of Judge Roy Bean, The; Mistress (1987); Nightmare (1991); Pleasure Palace

Prine, Andrew: Bandolero!; Callie and Son; Centerfold Girls; Christmas Coal Mine Miracle, The; Crypt of the Living Dead; Donner Pass: The Road to Survival; Eliminators, The; Evil, The; Generation; Gettysburg; Grizzly; Last of the Mohicans (1985); Miracle Worker, The (1962); Nightmare Circus (Barn of the Living Dead) (Terror Circus); Possums; Riding with Death; Serial Killer; Simon, King of the Witches; Small Killing, A; Texas Across the River; They're Playing with Fire; Town That Dreaded Sundown, The; V

Pringle, Joan: J.D.'s Revenge

Prinsloo, Sandra: African Rage; Gods Must Be Crazy, The

Prinz, Dietmar: Beethoven's Nephew

Prinze Jr., Freddie: House of Yes, The; I Know What You Did Last Summer; I Still Know What You Did Last Summer; Money Kings; She's All That; Wing Commander

Prior, Ted: Born Killer; Center of the Web; Future Zone; Los Platoon; Possessed by the Night; Raw Nerve

Pritchard, Bonnie: Time Chasers

Prival, Lucien: Mr. Wong, Detective; Return of Chandu (Magician, The)

Prochnow, Jurgen: Beverly Hills Cop II; Body of Evidence; Cop and the Girl, The; Das Boot (The Boat); DNA; Dry Whit Season, A; Dune; English Patient, The; Fire Next Time, The; Forbidden; Fourth War, The; Hurricane Smith; In the Mout of Madness; Interceptor; Judge Dredd; Keep, The; Ki Cruise; Killing Cars; Last Stop; Man Inside, The (1990); O Dangerous Ground (1995); Robin Hood (1991); Seventh Sign, The; Trigger Fast; Wing Commander

Procter, Emily: Body Shots

Proctor, Philip: Dr. Dolittle (1998); Robo C.H.I.C.

Prokhorenko, Shanna: Ballad of a Soldier

Prokhorova, Olga: Project: Genesis

Prophet, Melissa: Invasion U.S.A. (1985)

Prosky, Robert: Age Isn't Everything; Big Shots; Broadcas News; Christine; Dangerous Pursuit; Dead Man Walking (1995); Dudley Do-Right; Far and Away; From the Dead o Night; Funny About Love; Gremlins 2: The New Batch Hanky Panky; Hit Woman: The Double Edge; Hoffa; Las Action Hero, The; Loose Cannons; Lords of Discipline, The Mad City; Miracle on 34th Street (1994); Mrs. Doubtfire Murder of Mary Phagan, The; Natural, The; Outrageou Fortune; Rudy; Scarlet Letter, The (1995); Teamster Bos The Jackie Presser Story; Things Change

Prosser, Hugh: Sea Hound, The

Protheroe, Brian: Not a Penny More, Not a Penny Less

Prouty, Jed: Hollywood Cavalcade

Proval, David: Flipping; Romeo Is Bleeding; To The Limit Vice Versa

Provance, Greg: Teach Me

Provine, Dorothy: Good Neighbor Sam; It's a Mad Mad Mad Mad World; Never a Dull Moment; That Darn Ca (1965); 30 Foot Bride of Candy Rock, The; Who's Minding the Mint?

Provost, Jon: Escapade in Japan

Prowse, Dave: Empire Strikes Back, The; Frankenstein and the Monster from Hell; Return of the Jedi

Prowse, Heydon: Secret Garden, The (1993)

Prowse, Juliet: Can-Can; Dingaka; G.I. Blues

Prud'homme, Cameron: Rainmaker, The (1956)

Pruett, Harold: Precious Find

Pryce, Jonathan: Age of Innocence, The; Barbarians at the Gate; Brazil; Breaking Glass; Business Affair, A; Carrington Consuming Passions; Deadly Advice; Doctor and the Devils, The; Evita; Glengarry Glen Ross; Haunted Honeymoon Jumpin' Jack Flash; Man on Fire; Ploughman's Lunch, The Rachel Papers; Ronin; Shopping; Something Wicked This Way Comes; Stigmata; Thicker Than Water; Tomorrow Never Dies

Pryor, Mowava: Cover Girl Murders, The

Pryor, Nicholas: Happy Hooker, The; Hoffa; Less Than Zero; Life and Assassination of the Kingfish, The; Morgan Stewart's Coming Home; Night Terror; Risky Business, Smile

Pryor, Nick: Force Five

Pryor, Richard: Adios Amigo; Another You; Bingo Long Traveling All-Stars and Motor Kings, The; Blue Collar; Brewster's Millions (1985); Bustin' Loose; California Suite; Car Wash; Critical Condition; Greased Lightning; Harlem Nights; Hit! (1973); Jo Jo Dancer, Your Life Is Calling; Lady Sings the Blues; Mack, The; Moving; Muppet Movie, The; See No Evil, Hear No Evil; Silver Streak (1976); Some Call It Loving; Some Kind of Hero; Stir Crazy; Superman III; Toy,

der on the Orient Express; Orpheus Descending; Out of Season; Playing for Time; Prick Up Your Ears; Seven-Per-Cent Solution, The; Smilla's Sense of Snow; Snow White and the Seven Dwarfs (1983); Steaming; They (They Watch); Three Sovereigns for Sarah; Trojan Women, The; Wagner; Wetherby; What Ever Happened To ... ?; Wilde; Yanks; Young Catherine

Redman, Amanda: For Queen and Country; Richard's Things

Redmond, Liam: Ghost and Mr. Chicken, The; I See a Dark Stranger

Redmond, Moira: Nightmare (1964)

Redmond, Siobhan: Look Back In Anger (1989)

Rednikova, Yekaterina: Thief, The (1997)

Redondo, Emiliano: Black Venus

Redwine, Ted: Mystery Monsters; P.U.N.K.S.

Reed, Alan: Actors and Sin; Days of Glory; Seniors, The

Reed, Alyson: Chorus Line, A; Manhattan Merengue; Skin Deep

Reed, Dolores: Invasion of the Star Creatures

Reed, Donald: Man from Monterey, The

Reed, Donna: Babes on Broadway; Benny Goodman Story, The; Caddy, The; From Here to Eternity (1953); Green Dolphin Street; Gun Fury; Hangman's Knot; Human Comedy, The; It's a Wonderful Life; Last Time I Saw Paris, The; Picture of Dorian Gray, The; Shadow of the Thin Man; They Were Expendable; Trouble Along the Way

Reed, Hal: Doberman Gang, The

Reed, Jennifer A.: Apart from Hugh

Reed, Jerry: Bat 21; Gator; High-Ballin'; Hot Stuff; Smokey and the Bandit; Smokey and the Bandit II; Smokey and the Bandit III; Survivors, The; What Comes Around

Reed, Kevin: Last Way Out, The

Reed, Laura: Prime Time Murder

Reed, Lou: Blue in the Face; Faraway, So Close; Get Crazy; One Trick Pony

Reed, Marshall: Sundown Riders; They Saved Hitler's Brain

Reed, Oliver: Adventures of Baron Münchausen, The; Beat Girl; Big Sleep, The (1978); Black Arrow (1984); Blood in the Streets; Brood, The; Burnt Offerings; Captive; Captive Rage; Castaway; Christopher Columbus (1985); Class of Miss MacMichael, The; Condorman; Curse of the Werewolf, The; Dante's Inferno; Devils, The; Dr. Heckyl and Mr. Hype; Four Musketeers, The; Funnybones; Ghost in Monte Carlo, A; Gladiator (2000); Gor; Great Scout and Cathouse Thursday, The; Hired to Kill; House of Usher, The; Lion of the Desert; Misfit Brigade, The; Oliver; One Russian Summer; Paranoiac; Prince and the Pauper, The (1978); Prisoner of Honor; Ransom (1977); Return of the Musketeers; Return to Lonesome Dove; Sell-Out, The; Severed Ties; Shuttered Room, The; Spasms; Sting II, The; Ten Little Indians (1975); Three Musketeers, The (1973); Tommy; Tomorrow Never Comes; Treasure Island (1990); Venom; Women in Love; Z.P.G. (Zero Population Growth)

Reed, Pamela: Bean; Best of Times, The; Cadillac Man; Caroline?; Chattahoochee; Clan of the Cave Bear; Critical Choices; Goodbye People, The; Junior (1994); Kindergarten Cop; Melvin and Howard; Passed Away; Rachel River; Right Stuff, The; Tanner '88; Woman with a Past; Young Doctors in Love

Reed, Paul: Car 54 Where Are You? (TV Series)

Reed, Penelope: Amazons

Reed, Phillip: Klondike Annie; Last of the Mohicans, The (1936); Madame X (1937)

Reed, Rachel: Midnight Tease

Reed, Ralph: Reform School Girl

Reed, Rex: Myra Breckenridge

Reed, Robert: Boy in the Plastic Bubble, The; Brady Bunch, The (TV series); Bud and Lou; Casino (1980); Death of a Centerfold; Haunts of the Very Rich; Pray for the Wildcats; Prime Target; Snatched; Star! (1968); Very Brady Christmas, A

Reed, Shanna: Don't Talk to Strangers; Mirrors; Rattled; Sister-In-Law, The (1995)

Reed, Susanne: Up from the Depths

Reed, Tracy: All the Marbles; Night Rhythms; Running Scared (1986)

Reed, Walter: Superman and the Mole Men

Reeder, Mark: Nekromantik 2

Reedus, Norman: Dark Harbor; Gossip; Reach the Rock; Six Ways to Sunday

Rees, Angharad: Hands of the Ripper

Rees, Donough: Crush (1994)

Rees, Roger: Black Male; Bumblebee Flies Anyway, The; If Looks Could Kill (1991); Mountains of the Moon; Robin Hood: Men in Tights; Stop! Or My Mom Will Shoot; Trouble on the Corner

Reese, Della: Harlem Nights; Kid Who Loved Christmas, The; Psychic Killer; Thin Line Between Love and Hate, A

Reese, Michelle: Night Stalker, The (1986)

Reeve, Christopher: Above Suspicion (1994); Anna Karenina (1985); Aviator, The; Black Fox; Blood Horse; Bostonians, The; Death Dreams; Deathtrap; Good Men and Bad; Great Escape II, The; Monsignor; Morning Glory (1992); Mortal Sins (1992); Noises Off; Rear Window (1998); Remains of the Day; Rose and the Jackal, The; Sea Wolf, The (1993); Sleeping Beauty (1983); Somewhere in Time; Speechless; Street Smart; Superman; Superman II; Superman III; Superman IV: The Quest for Peace; Switching Channels; Village of the Damned (1995)

Reeves, Eve: Behind Locked Doors

Reeves, George: Blue Gardenia, The; Bugles in the Afternoon; Great Lover, The; Hoppy Serves a Writ; Jungle Jim; Rancho Notorious; So Proudly We Hail; Strawberry Blonde, The; Superman and the Mole Men; TV's Best Adventures of Superman; Westward Ho, the Wagons

Reeves, Keanu: Babes in Toyland (1986); Bill and Ted's Bogus Journey; Bill and Ted's Excellent Adventure; Bram Stoker's Dracula; Brotherhood of Justice; Chain Reaction (1996); Devil's Advocate; Dream to Believe; Even Cowgirls Get the Blues; Feeling Minnesota; I Love You to Death; Johnny Mnemonic; Last Time I Committed Suicide, The; Little Buddha; Matrix, The; Much Ado About Nothing; My Own Private Idaho; Night Before, The; Parenthood; Permanent Record; Point Break; Prince of Pennsylvania; River's Edge; Speed; Tune in Tomorrow; Walk in the Clouds, A

Reeves, Lisa: Chicken Chronicles, The

Reeves, Mathonwy: Child's Christmas in Wales, A

Reeves, Saskia: Antonia & Jane; Butterfly Kiss; Close My Eyes; December Bride; Different for Girls

Reeves, Scott: Edge of Honor; Friday the 13th, Part VIII: Jason Takes Manhattan; Hearts Adrift

Reeves, Steve: Athena; Goliath and the Barbarians; Hercules (1959); Hercules Unchained; Jail Bait (1954); Last Days of Pompeii (1960); Morgan the Pirate

Reevis, Steve: Geronimo: An American Legend (1994); Last of the Dogmen; Wild Bill

Regalbuto, Joe: Deadly Weapon; Raw Deal; Six Weeks; Streethawk

Regan, Mary: Heart of the Stag; Midnight Dancer; Sylvia

Regan, Phil: Go into Your Dance; Manhattan Merry-Go-Round; Sweet Adeline

Regehr, Duncan: Monster Squad, The; My Wicked, Wicked Ways; Primo Baby

Regent, Benoit: Blue (1993)

Reggiani, Serge: Cat and Mouse; La Ronde; Le Doulos; Paris Blues; Vincent, François, Paul and the Others

Regina, Paul: Bounty Tracker; It's My Party

Regine: My New Partner; Robert et Robert

Regnier, Natacha: Dreamlife of Angels, The

Reicher, Frank: Captain America (1944); Jade Mask, The; King Kong (1933); Son of Kong, The

Reichmann, Wolfgang: Beethoven's Nephew

Reid, Beryl: Beast in the Cellar, The; Carry on Emmanuelle; Doctor and the Devils, The; Dr. Phibes Rises Again; Entertaining Mr. Sloane; Joseph Andrews; Killing of Sister George, The; Psychomania

Reid, Carl Benton: Athena; Indian Uprising; Pressure Point; Stage to Tucson

Reid, Christopher: Class Act; House Party 2; House Party 3

Reid, Elliott: Gentlemen Prefer Blondes; Thrill of It All, The; Woman's World

Reid, Kate: Andromeda Strain, The; Atlantic City; Circle of Two; Death of a Salesman; Deathship; Deceived; Fire with Fire; Heaven Help Us; Highpoint; Last Best Year, The; Signs of Life; This Property Is Condemned

Reid, Lehua: Point of Impact

Reid, Sheila: Winter Guest, The

Reid, Tara: Big Lebowski, The; Body Shots; Urban Legend

Reid, Tim: Dead-Bang; Fourth War, The; It (1991); You Must Remember This

Reid, Wallace: Roaring Road, The

Reifsnyder, Timothy: Wide Awake

Reilly, John C.: Boogie Nights; Boys (1996); Casualties of War; Dolores Claiborne; For Love of the Game; Georgia (1995); Hard Eight; Hoffa; Incredible Journey of Dr. Meg Laurel, The; Magnolia; Never Been Kissed; Out on a Limb (1992); Perfect Storm, The; River Wild, The; State of Grace; What's Eating Gilbert Grape?

Reilly, Robert: Frankenstein Meets the Space Monster

Reilly, Tom: Mirror Images II

Reineke, Gary: Why Shoot the Teacher?

Reiner, Carl: Dead Men Don't Wear Plaid; Dick Van Dyke Show, The (TV Series); Fatal Instinct (1993); Gazebo, The; Generation; Gidget Goes Hawaiian; Guide for the Married Man, A; Pinocchio (1983); Right to Remain Silent, The; Russians Are Coming, the Russians Are Coming, The; Skokie; Spirit of '76, The; Summer School; 10 from Your Show of Shows

Reiner, Rob: Bullets over Broadway; Bye Bye, Love; EDtv; Enter Laughing; Mixed Nuts; Muse, The; Postcards from the Edge; Sleepless in Seattle; Spirit of '76, The; Story of Us, The; This Is Spinal Tap; Thursday's Game; Where's Poppa?

Reiner, Tracy: League of Their Own, A

Reinhardt, Janis: Three Bullets for a Long Gun

Reinhold, Judge: As Good as Dead; Baby on Board; Bank Robber; Beverly Hills Cop; Beverly Hills Cop II; Beverly Hills Cop 3; Black Magic (1992); Coming Unglued; Daddy's Dyin' and Who's Got the Will; Fast Times at Ridgemont High; Floating Away; Four Eyes and Six Guns; Head Office; Homegrown; Hostage Train; Near Misses; Off Beat; Over Her Dead Body; Promised a Miracle; Right to Remain Silent, The; Roadhouse 66; Running Scared (1980); Ruthless People; Santa Clause, The; Soldier's Tale, A; Vice Versa; Wharf Rat, The; Zandalee

Reiniger, Scot: Dawn of the Dead

Reinking, Ann: All That Jazz; Micki & Maude; Movie Movie

Reis, Michelle: Wicked City, The (1992)

Reiser, Paul: Aliens; Bye Bye, Love; Crazy People; Cross My Heart (1987); Family Prayers; Marrying Man, The; Mr. Write; Story of Us, The; Sunset Limousine

Rekert, Winston: Agnes of God; Cooler Climate, A; Eternal Evil; Glory! Glory!; Heartaches; High Stakes (1986); Toby McTeague

Rekin, Dwayne: Cat, The (1966)

Remar, James: Across the Moon; Band of the Hand; Blink; Born Bad; Boys on the Side; Confessions of a Hitman; Cotton Club, The; Deadlock; Drugstore Cowboy; Fatal Charm; Fatal Instinct (1993); 48 Hrs.; Indecency; Inferno (1998); Miracle on 34th Street (1994); One Good Turn; Phantom, The (1996); Quest, The (1996); Quiet Cool; Renaissance Man; Rent-a-Cop; Rites of Passage; Silence Like Glass; Strangers; Surgeon, The; Tigress, The; Warriors, The (1979); White Fang; Wild Bill; Windwalker

Remarque, Erich Maria: Time to Love and a Time to Die, A

Remay, Albert: Children of Paradise, The

Remberg, Erika: Cave of the Living Dead; Circus of Horrors

Remick, Lee: Anatomy of a Murder; Baby the Rain Must Fall; Blue Knight, The (1973); Bridge to Silence; Competition, The; Days of Wine and Roses (1962); Detective, The (1968); Europeans, The; Experiment in Terror; Face in the Crowd, A; Hallelujah Trail, The; Hennessy; Hustling; I Do! I Do!; Ike: The War Years; Jesse; Long Hot Summer, The (1958); Loot; Medusa Touch, The; Mistral's Daughter; No Way to Treat a Lady; Of Pure Blood; Omen, The; QB VII; Snow Queen; Sometimes a Great Notion; Telefon; Torn Between Two Lovers; Tribute; Wheeler Dealers, The

Remsen, Bert: Borderline; Carny; Code of Silence; Daddy's Dyin' and Who's Got the Will; Dead Ringer; Hobson's Choice (1983); Hugo Pool; Jack the Bear; Jezebel's Kiss; Ladykiller; Lies; Lookin' to Get Out; M.A.D.D.: Mothers Against Drunk Driving; Only the Lonely; Payback (1990); Road Ends; Sting II, The; Thieves Like Us

Remsen, Kerry: Appointment with Fear

Remy, Albert: 400 Blows, The

Renaldo, Duncan: Border Patrol; Cisco Kid (TV Series); Covered Wagon Days; Fighting Seabees, The; Kansas Terrors; Outlaws of the Desert; Painted Stallion, The; Rocky Mountain Rangers; San Antonio Kid; South of the Border; Zorro Rides Again

Renan, Sergio: Debajo del Mundo (Under Earth)

Renant, Simone: Les Liaisons Dangereuses; That Man from Rio

Renaud, Madeleine: Stormy Waters

Renaud, Georges: East of Borneo

Renay, Liz: Desperate Living; Thrill Killers, The

Renderer, Scott: Poison

Rendorf, Sherry: Slaughterhouse

Renfro, Brad: Apt Pupil; Client, The; Cure, The; Sleepers; Telling Lies in America; Tom and Huck

Renler, Jeremie: La Promesse

Renko, Serge: Rendezvous in Paris

Renna, Patrick: Address Unknown; Beanstalk; Blue River; Johnny Mysto; P.U.N.K.S.

Rennard, Deborah: Lionheart (1991)

Renner, Jeremy: National Lampoon's Senior Trip

Rennie, Callum Keith: Hard Core Logo; Last Night

Rennie, James: Illicit

Rennie, Michael: Battle of El Alamein, The; Day the Earth Stood Still, The; Demetrius and the Gladiators; Desirée; Devil's Brigade, The; Five Fingers; Hondo and the Apaches; Hotel; Mambo; Omar Khayyam; Phone Call from a Stranger; Ride Beyond Vengeance; Robe, The; Seven Cities of Gold; Ships with Wings; Soldier of Fortune; Third Man on the Mountain; Trio; Wicked Lady, The (1945)

Renniks, Lei: Sinyster

Reno, Ginetta: Leolo

Reno, Jean: Big Blue, The; Final Combat, The; For Roseanna; French Kiss; Godzilla (1998); Mission: Impossible; Professional, The; Ronin

Reno, Kelly: Black Stallion, The; Black Stallion Returns, The; Brady's Escape

Renoir, Jean: La Bête Humaine

Renoir, Pierre: La Marseillaise; Madame Bovary (1934)

Renoir, Sophie: Boyfriends and Girlfriends

Renucci, Robin: King's Whore, The

Renvail, Johan: Dance

Renying, Zhou: King of Masks, The

Renzi, Eva: Bird with the Crystal Plumage, The; Funeral in Berlin

Renzi, Maggie: City of Hope; Passion Fish; Return of the Secaucus 7

Repo-Martell, Liisa: Critical Choices

Resines, Antonio: Skyline

Resnick, Judith: Carnival of Blood

Ressel, Frank: Have a Nice Funeral

Rettig, Tommy: At Gunpoint; Five Thousand Fingers of Dr. T, The; Jackpot, The; River of No Return

Reuben, Gloria: Dead Air; Indiscreet (1998); Nick of Time; Timecop

Reubens, Paul: Buddy; Dunston Checks In; Mystery Men; Pandemonium

Revach, Zeev: Escape: Human Cargo

Revere, Anne: Birch Interval, The; Body and Soul (1947); Devil Commands, The; Forever Amber; Gentlemen's Agreement; Howards of Virginia, The; Meanest Man in the World, The; National Velvet; Place in the Sun, A; Song of Bernadette, The; Star Spangled Rhythm; Thin Man Goes Home, The

Revill, Clive: Avanti!; Ghost in the Noonday Sun; Legend of Hell House, The; Matilda; One of Our Dinosaurs Is Missing; Private Life of Sherlock Holmes, The

Revueltas, Rosaura: Salt of the Earth

Rey, Alejandro: Fun in Acapulco; High Velocity; Ninth Configuration, The; Pacific Connection, The; Rita Hayworth: The Love Goddess

Rey, Antonia: Tarantella

Rey, Fernando: Antony and Cleopatra (1973); Black Arrow (1984); Discreet Charm of the Bourgeoisie, The; 1492: Conquest of Paradise; French Connection, The; French Connection II, The; High Crime; Hit, The (1984); Immortal Story; La Grande Bourgeoise; Last Days of Pompeii (1960); Light at the End of the World, The; Monsignor; Moon over Parador; Naked Tango; Pantaloons; Quintet; Rustler's Rhapsody; Saving Grace; Seven Beauties; Star Knight; That Obscure Object of Desire; Tristana; Tunnel, The; Villa Rides; Viridiana

Rey, Mony: Mademoiselle

Reyes Jr., Ernie: Red Sonja; Surf Ninjas; Teenage Mutant Ninja Turtles II: The Secret of the Ooze

Reyes, Pia: Forbidden Zone: Alien Abduction

Reynal, Madeleine: Dr. Caligari

Reynaud, Janine: Castle of the Creeping Flesh

Reyne, James: Return to Eden

Reynolds, Adeline de Walt: Iceland

Reynolds, Burt: Armored Command; Best Friends; Best Little Whorehouse in Texas, The; Blade Rider; Boogie Nights; Breaking In; Cannonball Run; Cannonball Run II; Cherokee Kid, The; Citizen Ruth; City Heat; Cop and a Half; Deliverance; End, The; Everything You Always Wanted to Know About Sex but Were Afraid to Ask; Frankenstein and Me; Fuzz; Gator; Gunsmoke (TV Series); Hard Time; Heat (1987); Hooper; Hunter's Moon; Hustle; Longest Yard, The; Maddening, The; Malone; Man from Left Field, The; Man Who Loved Cat Dancing, The; Man Who Loved Women, The (1983); Meet Wally Sparks; Modern Love; Mystery, Alaska; 100 Rifles; Operation C.I.A.; Paternity; Physical Evidence; Raven; Rent-a-Cop; Rough Cut; Semi-Tough; Shamus; Shark! (Maneaters!); Sharky's Machine; Silent Movie; Smokey and the Bandit; Smokey and the Bandit II; Starting Over; Stick; Striptease; Stroker Ace; Switching Channels; Trigger Happy (Mad Dog Time); White Lightning

Reynolds, Debbie: Affairs of Dobie Gillis, The; Athena; Bundle of Joy; Catered Affair, The; Detective Sadie and Son; Divorce American Style; Gazebo, The; Gift of Love: The Daniel Huffman Story; Give a Girl a Break; Heaven and Earth (1993); Hit the Deck; How the West Was Won; I Love Melvin; In & Out; It Started With a Kiss; Mating Game, The; Mr. Imperium; Mother (1996); Singin' in the Rain; Singing Nun, The; Susan Slept Here; Tammy and the Bachelor; Tender Trap, The; That's Entertainment! III; That's Singing: The Best of Broadway; This Happy Feeling; Three Little Words; Two Weeks with Love; Unsinkable Molly Brown, The; What's the Matter with Helen?

Reynolds, Gene: Andy Hardy's Private Secretary; Bridges at Toko-Ri, The; Diane; Jungle Patrol; Mortal Storm, The; Of Human Hearts; Tuttles of Tahiti, The

Reynolds, Hayley: Lifeforce Experiment, The

Reynolds, Helene: Wintertime

Reynolds, Jacob: Gummo

Reynolds, Jay: Reincarnate, The

Reynolds, Joyce: Adventures of Mark Twain, The (1944)

Reynolds, Marjorie: Doomed to Die; Fatal Hour, The; His Kind of Woman; Holiday Inn; Mr. Wong in Chinatown; Monsieur Beaucaire; Robin Hood of the Pecos; That Midnight Kiss; Time of Their Lives, The

Reynolds, Michael J.: Lifeforce Experiment, The; Trial & Error (1992)

Reynolds, Nicola: Human Traffic

Reynolds, Patrick: Eliminators, The

Reynolds, Paul: Angelic Conversation; Let Him Have It

Reynolds, Quentin: Golden Earrings

Reynolds, Robert: Daughter of Darkness; Tunnel Vision (1994)

Reynolds, Ryan: Alarmist, The; Ordinary Magic

Reynolds, Simon: Gate II

Reynolds, Vera: Monster Walks, The; Road to Yesterday, The

Reynolds, William: Away all Boats; Land Unknown, The; Son of Ali Baba; Thing that Couldn't Die, The

Rhames, Ving: Body Count (1997); Bringing Out the Dead; Con Air; Dangerous Ground; Dave; Don King: Only in America; Drop Squad; Entrapment; Homicide; Kiss of Death (1995); Long Walk Home, The; Mission: Impossible 2; Mission: Impossible; Out of Sight; Patty Hearst; People Under the Stairs, The; Pulp Fiction; Rising Son; Rosewood; Saint of Fort Washington, The; Striptease

Rhee, Phillip: Best of the Best; Best of the Best 2; Silent Assassins

Rhoades, Barbara: Shakiest Gun in the West, The

Rhodes, Cynthia: Curse of the Crystal Eye; Dirty Dancing; Runaway; Staying Alive

Rhodes, Donnelly: After the Promise; Dirty Work; Kurt Vonnegut's Monkey House; Showdown at Williams Creek

Rhodes, Earl: Sailor Who Fell from Grace with the Sea, The

Rhodes, Erik: Charlie Chan in Paris; Gay Divorcée, The; One Rainy Afternoon

Rhodes, Frank: Sandman (1992)

Rhodes, Hari: Detroit 9000 (Detroit Heat); Dream for Christmas, A; Woman Called Moses, A

Rhodes, Marjorie: Decameron Nights

Rhodin, Olof: Evil Ed

Rhue, Geoffrey: Squeeze

Rhue, Madlyn: Majority of One, A

Rhymes, Busta: Shaft (2000)

Rhys, Paul: Becoming Colette; Chaplin; Gallowglass; Nina Takes a Lover; Vincent and Theo

Rhys, Phillip: Fear, The; Halloween Night

Rhys-Davies, John: Aladdin & the King of Thieves (voice); Best Revenge; Blood of the Innocent; Bloodsport III; Body Armor; Canvas; Cyborg Cop; Dark Prince: The Intimate Diary of the Marquis de Sade; Dark Prince: The Intimate Tales of Marquis de Sade; Double-O Kid, The; Firewalker; Great Expectations (1989); In the Shadow of Kilimanjaro; Indiana Jones and the Last Crusade; Journey of Honor; King Solomon's Mines (1985); Living Daylights, The; Lost World, The (1992); Marquis de Sade; Nativity, The; Raiders of the Lost Ark; Rebel Storm; Return to the Lost World; Ring of the Musketeer; Robot in the Family; Sadat; Sahara (1984); Seventh Coin, The; Sunset Grill; Tusks; Unnamable II, The

Rhys-Meyers, Jonathan: Loss of Sexual Innocence, The; Velvet Goldmine

Ri'chard, Robert: Light It Up

Rialson, Candice: Hollywood Boulevard; Summer School Teachers

Ribeiro, Alfonso: Infested (Ticks)

Ribisi, Giovanni: Boiler Room; Gone in 60 Seconds; Mod Squad, The; Saving Private Ryan; SubUrbia (1997)

Ribon, Diego: Evil Clutch

Ribovska, Malka: Shameless Old Lady, The

Ricci, Christina: Addams Family, The; Bastard Out of Carolina; Buffalo '66; Casper; Cemetery Club, The; Gold Diggers: The Secret of Bear Mountain; Ice Storm, The; Mermaids; Now and Then; Opposite of Sex, The; Pecker; Sleepy Hollow; Summer Fling; That Darn Cat (1997); 200 Cigarettes

Ricci, Rona De: Pit and the Pendulum, The (1991)

Ricciarelli, Katia: Otello

Rice, Diana: Barney's Great Adventure

Rice, Florence: Double Wedding; Navy Blue and Gold; Riding on Air

Rice, Frank: Fiddlin' Buckaroo; Fighting Ranger, The; Ivory-Handled Gun, The; Somewhere in Sonora

Rice, Jeffrey D.: Warlords of Hell

Rice, Joan: His Majesty O'Keefe; Story of Robin Hood, The

Rice, Joel S.: Final Exam

Rice-Davies, Mandy: Absolute Beginners; Seven Magnificent Gladiators, The

Rich, Adam: Devil and Max Devlin, The

Rich, Allan: Miami Hustle

Rich, Buddy: Ship Ahoy

Rich, Christina: Midnight Confessions

Rich, Christopher: Prisoners of Inertia

Rich, Claude: Bride Wore Black, The; Elusive Corporal, The; Le Crabe Tambour; Revenge of the Musketeers

Rich, Debra: Dear Santa

Rich, Irene: Angel and the Badman; Beau Brummell (1924); Champ, The (1931); Lady in Question; Lady Windermere's Fan; Mortal Storm, The

Rich, Matty: Straight out of Brooklyn

Rich, Ron: Fortune Cookie, The

Rich, Victor: Sensuous Wife, The

Richard, Eric: Home Sweet Home (1982)

Richard, Fir-mine: Mama, There's a Man in Your Bed

Richard, Jean: Candide

Richard, Nathalie: Irma Vep; Up/Down/Fragile

Richard, Pierre: Chef in Love, A; Daydreamer, The (1970) (Le Distrait); Le Chèvre (The Goat); Les Comperes; Return of the Tall Blond Man with One Black Shoe, The; Tall Blond Man with One Black Shoe, The; Too Shy to Try

Richard, Robert: In His Father's Shoes

Ri-Chard, Robert: Our Friend, Martin

Richards, A. J.: Sandman, The (1996)

Richards, Addison: Bad Lands (1939); Our Daily Bread; Rustlers, The

Richards, Ann: Badman's Territory; Sorry, Wrong Number (1948)

Riley, Jack: Attack of the Killer Tomatoes; Night Patrol

Riley, Jeannine: Electra Glide in Blue

Riley, Larry: Dead Solid Perfect

Riley, Lisa Jane: Butterfly Kiss

Riley, Michael: ... And God Spoke; Heck's Way Home; Perfectly Normal; To Catch a Killer

Rilla, Walter: Adventures of Tartu; Days of Wrath; Gamma People, The

Rin Tin Tin: Lone Defender, The

Rin Tin Tin Jr.: Adventures of Rex and Rinty; Skull and Crown

Rinaldi, Gerard: For Better and for Worse

Ringwald, Molly: Baja; Betsy's Wedding; Breakfast Club, The; Brutal Truth, The; Face the Music; For Keeps; Fresh Horses; Malicious (1995); Office Killer; Packin' It In; Pick-Up Artist, The; P.K. & the Kid; Pretty in Pink; Sixteen Candles; Spacehunter: Adventures in the Forbidden Zone; Stand, The; Strike It Rich; Tempest (1982); Women & Men: Stories of Seduction

Rinn, Brad: Smithereens

Rintoul, David: Pride and Prejudice (1985)

Rio, Nicole: Visitants, The

Riordan, Marjorie: Pursuit to Algiers

Ripley, Fay: Mute Witness

Ripper, Michael: Curse of the Mummy's Tomb, The; Quatermass and the Pit

Ripploh, Frank: Taxi Zum Klo (Taxi to the Toilet)

Rippy, Leon: Eye of the Storm; Stargate

Risdon, Elisabeth: Crime and Punishment (1935); Roll on Texas Moon

Riselle, Miriam: Tevye

Rispoli, Michael: Summer of Sam; Volcano; While You Were Sleeping

Ristanovski, Nikola: Cabaret Balkan

Ristovski, Lazar: Cabaret Balkan; Tito and Me

Ritchard, Cyril: Blackmail (1929); Half a Sixpence; Hans Brinker; Peter Pan (1960)

Ritchie, Clint: Against a Crooked Sky

Ritchie, June: Kind of Loving, A

Ritchie, Lionel: Preacher's Wife, The

Ritt, Martin: Slugger's Wife, The

Ritter, Brent: Curse of the Blue Lights

Ritter, Jason: Mumford

Ritter, John: Americathon; Colony, The (1995); Comeback Kid, The; Dead Husbands; Hero at Large; In Love with an Older Woman; It (1991); Last Fling, The; Mercenary; Montana (1997); My Brother's Wife; Noises Off; Nowhere; Other, The; Pray TV (1982); Prison for Children; Problem Child; Problem Child 2; Real Men; Sink or Swim; Skin Deep; Sling Blade; Smoky Mountain Christmas; Stay Tuned; Sunset Limousine; They All Laughed; Tricks of the Trade; Unnatural Causes; Wholly Moses!

Ritter, Kristin: Student Bodies

Ritter, Tex: Arizona Days; Deep in the Heart of Texas; Enemy of the Law; Lone Star Trail; Mystery of the Hooded Horsemen; Riders of the Rockies; Sing, Cowboy, Sing; Take Me Back to Oklahoma; Trouble in Texas

Ritter, Thelma: As Young as You Feel; Bird Man of Alcatraz; Boeing, Boeing; Daddy Long Legs; Farmer Takes a Wife, The; Hole in the Head, A; Incident, The (1967); Misfits, The; New Kind of Love, A; Pickup on South Street; Pillow Talk; Rear Window; Titanic (1953)

Ritz Brothers, The: Goldwyn Follies, The; Gorilla, The; On the Avenue; One in a Million; Three Musketeers, The (1939)

Ritz, Harry: Silent Movie

Riva, Emmanuelle: Hiroshima, Mon Amour

Rivas, Carlos: They Saved Hitler's Brain

Rivas, Geoffrey: Above Suspicion (1994)

Rivera, Chita: Mayflower Madam; Sweet Charity

Rivera, Rick: Body Moves

Rivero, Enrique: Blood of a Poet

Rivero, Jorge: Counterforce; Day of the Assassin; Fist Fighter; Priest of Love; Rio Lobo; Target Eagle; Werewolf

Rivers, Joan: Muppets Take Manhattan, The; Swimmer, The

Rivers, Victor: Chain, The; Fled

Riviere, George: Castle of Blood (Castle of Terror); Virgin of Nuremberg (Horror Castle)

Riviere, Julien: Ma Vie En Rose; Thieves (Les Voleurs)

Riviere, Marie: Autumn Tale; Aviator's Wife, The; Summer

Rivkin, Michael: Shot, The; Shot, The

Riza, Bella: Hideous Kinky

Rizzo, Gianni: Mission Stardust

Rjin, Brad: Special Effects

Roach, Bert: Last Warning, The

Roach, Rickey: Black Devil Doll from Hell

Roache, Linus: Priest; Shot Through the Heart; Wings of the Dove, The

Roanne, André: Diary of a Lost Girl

Roarke, Adam: Dirty Mary, Crazy Larry; Four Deuces, The; Hell's Angels on Wheels; Losers, The; Psych-Out; Sioux City; Stunt Man, The; Trespasses; Women of the Prehistoric Planet

Roarke, John: Mutant on the Bounty

Robards Jr., Jason: Adventures of Huck Finn, The (1993); All the President's Men; Any Wednesday; Ballad of Cable Hogue, The; Big Hand for the Little Lady, A; Black Rainbow; Boy and His Dog, A; Breaking Home Ties; Bright Lights, Big City; Burden of Dreams; By Love Possessed; Cabo Blanco; Chernobyl: The Final Warning; Christmas to Remember, A; Christmas Wife, The; Comes a Horseman; Day After, The; Divorce American Style; Dream a Little Dream; Enemy Within, The; Fools; Good Mother, The; Hour of the Gun, The; Hurricane (1979); Inconvenient Woman, An; Isadora (1969); Johnny Got His Gun; Journey; Julia; Julius Caesar (1970); Laguna Heat; Legend of the Lone Ranger, The; Long Day's Journey into Night (1962); Long Hot Summer, The (1985); Magnolia; Max Dugan Returns; Melvin and Howard; Mr. Sycamore; Murders in the Rue Morgue (1971); My Antonia; Night They Raided Minsky's, The; Once Upon a Time in the West; Paper, The; Parenthood; Pat Garrett and Billy the Kid; Philadelphia; Quick Change; Raise the Titanic; Reunion; St. Valentine's Day Massacre, The; Sakharov; Something Wicked This Way Comes; Square Dance; Thousand Acres, A; Thousand Clowns, A; Tora! Tora! Tora!; Trial, The (1992); You Can't Take it with You (1984)

Robards Sr., Jason: Abraham Lincoln; Bedlam; Broadway Bill; Fighting Marines, The; Isle of the Dead; Mademoiselle Fifi; Rimfire

Robards, Sam: Donor Unknown; Fandango; Man Who Captured Eichmann, The; Not Quite Paradise; Pancho Barnes

Robay, Terrance: Let It Rock

Robb, David: Dreams Lost, Dreams Found

Robb, R. D.: Eight Days a Week

Robbins, Brian: C.H.U.D. II (Bud the C.H.U.D.)

Robbins, Christmas: Demon Lover, The

Robbins, Marty: Ballad of a Gunfighter

Robbins, Skeeter Bill: Hard Hombre

Robbins, Tim: Arlington Road; Bob Roberts; Bull Durham; Cadillac Man; Erik the Viking; Five Corners; High Fidelity; Howard the Duck; Hudsucker Proxy, The; I.Q.; Jacob's Ladder; Jungle Fever; Miss Firecracker; Mission to Mars; Nothing to Lose; Player, The; Ready to Wear; Shawshank Redemption, The; Tapeheads

Rober, Richard: Port of New York

Roberson, David: O. J. Simpson Story, The

Roberson, Ken: Yellow Hair and the Fortress of Gold

Robert Mitchell Boys Choir: Blondie in Society

Roberts, Allene: Knock on Any Door; Red House, The; Union Station

Roberts, Arthur: Deadly Vengeance; Femme Fontaine: Killer Babe for the CIA; Friend of the Family II; Illegal Entry; Not of This Earth; Revenge of the Ninja

Roberts, Christian: Desperados, The; To Sir with Love

Roberts, Conrad: Mosquito Coast, The

Roberts, Darryl: How U Like Me Now

Roberts, Doris: Love in the Present Tense; My Giant; Number One with a Bullet; Once in Paris; Ordinary Heroes; Simple Justice

Roberts, Eliza: Dead End (1997); Love Is a Gun

Roberts, Eric: Agent of Death; Ambulance, The; American Strays; Babyfever; Best of the Best; Best of the Best 2; Blood Red; By the Sword; Coca Cola Kid, The; Dead End (1997); Descending Angel; Facade; Family Matter, A; Final Analysis; Freefall; Glass Cage, The; Grave, The; Hard Truth; Heaven's Prisoners; Immortals, The; It's My Party; King of the Gypsies; Lansky; Lonely Hearts (1991); Lost Capone, The; Love, Cheat & Steal; Love Is a Gun; Nature of the Beast; Nobody's Fool (1986); Odyssey, The; Past Perfect; Paul's Case; Pope of Greenwich Village, The; Power 98;

Prophecy II, The; Public Enemy #1; Purgatory; Raggedy Man; Rude Awakening (1989); Runaway Train; Saved by the Light; Sensation; Slow Burn; Specialist, The; Star 80; To Heal a Nation; Voyage

Roberts, Eliden: Crater Lake Monster, The

Roberts, Ian: Power of One, The; Terminal Impact

Roberts Jr., J. Jay: White Phantom

Roberts, Jessica: Angel Fist

Roberts, Joe: Buster Keaton Festival Vol. 1–3

Roberts, Jordan: Butch Camp

Roberts, Julia: Conspiracy Theory; Dying Young; Erin Brockovich; Everyone Says I Love You; Flatliners; Hook; I Love Trouble; Mary Reilly; Michael Collins; My Best Friend's Wedding; Mystic Pizza; Notting Hill; Pelican Brief, The; Pretty Woman; Ready to Wear; Runaway Bride; Satisfaction; Sleeping with the Enemy; Something to Talk About; Steel Magnolias; Stepmom

Roberts, Ken: Fatal Pulse; Great Land of Small, The

Roberts, Leonard: Love Jones

Roberts, Lynne (Hart, Mary): Billy the Kid Returns; Dick Tracy Returns; Dynamite Pass; Eyes of Texas; Frontier Pony Express; Heart of the Rockies; Hi-Yo Silver; Hunt the Man Down; In Old Caliente; Lone Ranger, The (1938); Robin Hood of Texas; Rough Riders' Roundup

Roberts, Mariwin: Sun Bunnies

Roberts, Mark: Night of the Devils; Posse (1975)

Roberts, Michael D.: Sleepstalker: The Sandman's Last Rites

Roberts, Pernell: Bonanza (TV Series); Checkered Flag; Desire under the Elms; Four Rode Out; High Noon, Part Two; Magic of Lassie, The; Night Train to Katmandu; Ride Lonesome

Roberts, Rachel: Belstone Fox, The; Hostage Tower, The; O Lucky Man!; Picnic at Hanging Rock; This Sporting Life; When a Stranger Calls

Roberts, Rick: Love and Human Remains

Roberts, Roy: Enforcer, The (1951); Force of Evil; He Walked by Night; King and Four Queens, The; Second Chance

Roberts, Shawn: Sea People

Roberts, Tanya: Almost Pregnant; Beastmaster, The; Body Slam; California Dreaming; Hearts and Armour; Inner Sanctum; Sheena: Viva to a Kill, A

Roberts, Teal: Fatal Games; Hardbodies

Roberts, Ted Jan: Dangerous Place, A; Magic Kid; Magic Kid 2; Power Within, The; Tiger Heart

Roberts, Theodore: Miss Lulu Bett; Ten Commandments, The (1923)

Roberts, Tony: American Clock, The; Amityville III: The Demon; Annie Hall; 18 Again; Just Tell Me What You Want; Key Exchange; Midsummer Night's Sex Comedy, A; Million Dollar Duck, The; Our Sons; Packin' It In; Play It Again, Sam; Popcorn; Question of Honor, A; Seize the Day; Serpico; Switch; Taking of Pelham One Two Three, The

Robertson, Andrew: Cement Garden, The

Robertson, Barbara: Straight Story, The

Robertson, Cliff: All in a Night's Work; Autumn Leaves; Best Man, The (1964); Charly; Days of Wine and Roses, The (1958); Dead Reckoning (1990); Devil's Brigade, The; Dominique Is Dead; Ford: The Man & the Machine; Gidget; Girl Most Likely, The; Great Northfield Minnesota Raid, The; Honey Pot, The; Interns, The; John Carpenter's Escape from L.A.; Key to Rebecca, The; Love Has Many Faces; Malone; Midway; Naked and the Dead, The; Obsession; Out of Season; Outer Limits, The (TV Series); Picnic; Pilot, The; PT 109; Race; Renaissance Man; Shaker Run; Shoot (1976); 633 Squadron; Star 80; Three Days of the Condor; Too Late the Hero; Two of a Kind (1982); Underworld U.S.A.; Wild Hearts Can't Be Broken; Wind (1992)

Robertson, Dale: Cariboo Trail; Dakota Incident; Devil's Canyon; Farmer Takes a Wife, The; Kansas City Massacre, The; Last Ride of the Dalton Gang, The; Melvin Purvis: G-Man

Robertson, George R.: Dawson Patrol, The

Robertson, Iain: Small Faces

Robertson, Jenny: Danger of Love; Jacob I Have Loved; Nightman, The

Robertson, Kathleen: Splendor; Survive the Night

Robertson, Patricia: Attack of the Swamp Creature

Robertson, Robbie: Carny

Robeson, Paul: Big Fella; Body and Soul (1924); Emperor Jones, The; Jericho; King Solomon's Mines (1937); Sanders of the River; Show Boat (1936); Song of Freedom; Tales of Manhattan

Robie, Wendy: People Under the Stairs, The

Robin, Dany: Tales of Paris; Topaz; Waltz of the Toreadors

Robin, Michel: Investigation; Le Chèvre (The Goat)

Robin, Teddie: Twin Dragons

Robins, Barry: Bless the Beasts and Children

Robins, Laila: Female Perversions; Innocent Man, An; Live Nude Girls; Planes, Trains and Automobiles; Welcome Home, Roxy Carmichael

Robins, Oliver: Poltergeist II: The Other Side

Robinson and the Miracles, Smokey: That Was Rock

Robinson, Alexia: Candyman 3: Day of the Dead

Robinson, Amy: Mean Streets

Robinson, Andrew: Charley Varrick; Cobra (1986); Dirty Harry; Fatal Charm; Hellraiser; Into the Badlands; Not My Kid; Prime Target; Pumpkinhead II: Bloodwings; Shoot to Kill; Someone I Touched; Trancers III: Deth Lives; Verne Miller

Robinson, Ann: Dragnet (1954); Midnight Movie Massacre; War of the Worlds, The

Robinson, Bill: Just Around the Corner; Little Colonel, The; Littlest Rebel, The; Rebecca of Sunnybrook Farm (1938); Stormy Weather

Robinson, Bruce: Story of Adele H, The

Robinson, Charles Knox: Daring Dobermans, The; Psychic Sisters (1972)

Robinson, Charles P.: Black Gestapo, The

Robinson, Chris: Amy; Savannah Smiles; Stanley; Viper

Robinson, Claudia: Wide Sargasso Sea

Robinson, David: Buford's Beach Bunnies

Robinson, Edward G.: Actors and Sin; All My Sons (1948); Amazing Dr. Clitterhouse, The; Barbary Coast, The; Brothers Orchid; Bullets or Ballots; Cheyenne Autumn; Cincinnat Kid, The; Double Indemnity; Good Neighbor Sam; Hell or Frisco Bay; Hole in the Head, A; House of Strangers; I Am the Law; Key Largo; Kid Galahad (1937); Little Caesar; Mr. Winkle Goes to War; My Geisha; Never a Dull Moment; Our Vines Have Tender Grapes; Prize, The; Red House, The; Robin & the Seven Hoods; Scarlet Street; Sea Wolf, The (1941); Seven Thieves; Song of Norway; Soylent Green; Stranger, The (1947); Tales of Manhattan; Ten Commandments, The (1956); Thunder in the City; Two Weeks in Another Town; Violent Men, The; Woman in the Window

Robinson, Frances: Red Barry

Robinson, Holly: Jacksons, The: An American Dream; Killers in the House

Robinson, Jackie: Jackie Robinson Story, The

Robinson, Jackson: Bikini Island

Robinson, Jay: Born Again; Demetrius and the Gladiators; Dying to Remember; King Richard II; Macbeth (1981); Malibu Bikini Shop, The; My Man Godfrey (1957); Othello (1982); Robe, The; Three the Hard Way; Transylvania Twist

Robinson, Karen: Stalked

Robinson, Larry: Sgt. Kabukiman N.Y.P.D.

Robinson, Leon: Band of the Hand; Streetwalkin'

Robinson, Lucy: Emma (1996)

Robinson, Madeleine: Le Gentleman D'Espom (Duke of the Derby)

Robinson, Michael: Beware! Children at Play

Robinson, Paul Michael: Capitol Conspiracy, The; Friend of the Family II; Maximum Security

Robinson, Roger: Newman's Law

Robinson, Tony: Neverending Story III, The: Escape to Fantasia

Robinson, Wendy Raquel: Ringmaster

Robles, Frank: Crossover Dreams

Robles, German: Vampire, The

Robson, Flora: Beast in the Cellar, The; Black Narcissus; Caesar and Cleopatra; Catherine the Great; Dominique Is Dead; Fire over England; Great Day; Les Miserables (1978); Murder at the Gallop; Restless; Romeo and Juliet (1954); Sea Hawk, The; Tale of Two Cities, A (1980); Wuthering Heights (1939)

Robson, Greer: Smash Palace

Robson, May: Adventures of Tom Sawyer, The; Anna Karenina (1935); Bringing Up Baby; Dancing Lady; It Happened in New Orleans; Joan of Paris; Lady by Choice; Lady for a Day; Little Orphan Annie; Nurse Edith Cavell; Reckless

Rojas, Eduardo Lopez: My Family

Rojas, Victor: It Could Happen to You; Max Is Missing

Rojo, Gustavo: Christmas Kid, The

Rojo, Helena: Aguirre: Wrath of God; Foxtrot; Mary, Mary, Bloody Mary

Rojo, Maria: Break of Dawn; Danzon; Mary My Dearest

Rojo, Ruben: Great Madcap, The

Roland Petit Dance Company: Black Tights

Roland, Eugenie Cisse: Faces of Women

Roland, Gilbert: Bad and the Beautiful, The; Barbarosa; Beneath the 12-Mile Reef; Between God, the Devil and a Winchester; Bullfighter and the Lady, The; Call Her Savage; Captain Kidd; French Line, The; Go Kill and Come Back; Miracle of Our Lady of Fatima, The; Pacific Connection, The; Poppy Is Also a Flower, The; Racers, The; Ruthless Four, The; Sacketts, The; Sea Hawk, The; She Done Him Wrong; Three Violent People; Thunder Bay; Thunder Trail; Treasure of Pancho Villa, The; Underwater!

Roland, Jeanne: Curse of the Mummy's Tomb, The

Rolfe, Guy: Alphabet Murders, The; Dolls; Puppet Master III: Toulon's Revenge; Puppet Master Four; Puppet Master 5: The Final Chapter; Snow White and the Three Stooges; Thriller (TV Series)

Rolffes, Kirsten: Kingdom, The

Rolin, Judy: Alice Through the Looking Glass (1966)

Rollan, Henri: Crazy Ray, The

Rolle, Esther: Age-Old Friends; Down in the Delta; Driving Miss Daisy; House of Cards; I Know Why the Caged Bird Sings; My Fellow Americans; Nobody's Girls; P.K. & the Kid; Raisin in the Sun, A (1988); Romeo and Juliet (1983); Rosewood; Summer of My German Soldier; To Dance with the White Dog

Rolling Stones, The: Gimme Shelter; Let's Spend the Night Together; Rock and Roll Circus, The; That Was Rock

Rollins, Henry: Chase, The (1994); Johnny Mnemonic; Jugular Wine

Rollins Jr., Howard: Children of Times Square, The; Drunks; For Us the Living: The Medgar Evers Story; King; On the Block; Soldier's Story, A

Rolston, Mark: Comrades of Summer, The; Shawshank Redemption, The

Romain, Yvonne: Circus of Horrors; Curse of the Werewolf, The; Devil Doll (1963)

Romaine, Katherine: Metamorphosis: The Alien Factor

Roman, Cathrine: Bloody New Year

Roman, Ruth: Baby, The; Beyond the Forest; Blowing Wild; Champion; Day of the Animals; Far Country, The; Impulse (1974); Love Has Many Faces; Sacketts, The; Strangers on a Train; Three Secrets; Window, The

Romance, Viviane: Melodie en Sous-Sol (The Big Grab) (Any Number Can Win); Panique

Romand, Beatrice: Autumn Tale; Chloe in the Afternoon; Claire's Knee; Le Beau Mariage; Summer

Romanelli, Carla: Shanghai Joe

Romano, Andy: Chameleon (1995); Heaven or Vegas; Two Bits

Romano, Rino: Club, The (1993)

Romans, Pierre: Dr. Petiot

Romanus, Richard: Couch Trip, The; Night Terror; Point of No Return; Protocol; Russian Roulette; Sitting Ducks; To Protect and Serve

Romanus, Robert: Bad Medicine; Dangerous Curves

Romay, Lina: Adventure; Demoniac; Erotikill; Heat's On, The; Ilsa, the Wicked Warden; Oasis of the Zombies

Rome, Sydne: Diary of Forbidden Dreams; Just a Gigolo; Puma Man, The; Sex with a Smile; That Lucky Touch

Romer, Fred: Great Adventure, The

Romero, Cesar: Americano, The; Batman (1966); Beautiful Blonde from Bashful Bend, The; Charlie Chan at Treasure Island; Computer Wore Tennis Shoes, The; Crooks and Coronets (Sophie's Place); Dance Hall; Happy Go Lovely; Happy Landing; Hot Millions; Julia Misbehaves; Latitude Zero; Little Princess, The (1939); Lost Continent, The (1951); Lust in the Dust; Madigan's Millions; Mission to Glory; My Lucky Star; Now You See Him, Now You Don't; Ocean's Eleven; Orchestra Wives; Proud and the Damned, The; Racers, The; Show Them No Mercy; Simple Justice; Springtime in the Rockies (1942); Tales of Manhattan; Two on a Guillotine; Wee Willie Winkie; Weekend in Havana; Wintertime

Romero, Ned: Children of the Corn II: The Final Sacrifice; Deerslayer, The (1920); I Will Fight No More Forever; Last of the Mohicans (1985); Magnificent Seven, The (TV Series); Medicine Hat Stallion, The

Romic, Monika: Vukovar

Rommel, Dave: Colony (1996)

Romney, Edana: Corridor of Mirrors

Romo, Daniela: One Man's Hero

Rondinella, Clelia: Star Maker, The

Ronet, Maurice: Beau Pere; Circle of Love; Elevator to the Gallows; Fire Within, The; La Balance; L'Odeur Des Fauves (Scandal Man); Purple Noon; Sphinx (1981); Swimming Pool, The

Ronettes, The: That Was Rock

Ronstadt, Linda: Chuck Berry Hail! Hail! Rock 'n' Roll; Pirates of Penzance, The

Rooker, Michael: Afterburn; Bastard Out of Carolina; Bone Collector, The; Bram Stoker's Shadowbuilder; Brown's Requiem; Cliffhanger; Dark Half, The; Days of Thunder; Deceiver; Hard Truth; Henry: Portrait of a Serial Killer; Here on Earth; JFK; Johnny & Clyde; Keys to Tulsa; Mall Rats; Rosewood

Rooney, Mickey: Adventures of Huckleberry Finn, The (1939); Ah, Wilderness; Andy Hardy Gets Spring Fever; Andy Hardy Meets a Debutante; Andy Hardy's Double Life; Andy Hardy's Private Secretary; Atomic Kid, The; Babe: Pig in the City; Babes in Arms; Babes on Broadway; Big Wheel, The; Bill; Bill: On His Own; Black Stallion, The; Boys' Town; Boys Will Be Boys; Breakfast at Tiffany's; Bridges at Toko-Ri, The; Captains Courageous (1937); Care Bears Movie, The; Chained; Comedian, The; Domino Principle, The; Erik the Viking; Evil Roy Slade; Find the Lady; Francis in the Haunted House; Fugitive, The (TV Series); Gambler Returns, The: The Luck of the Draw; Home for Christmas; Hoosier Schoolboy; How to Stuff a Wild Bikini; Human Comedy, The; It Came Upon a Midnight Clear; It's a Mad Mad Mad Mad World; King of the Roaring Twenties; Leave 'em Laughing; Life Begins for Andy Hardy; Lightning, the White Stallion; Little Lord Fauntleroy (1936); Love Finds Andy Hardy; Love Laughs at Andy Hardy; Magic of Lassie, The; Manhattan Melodrama; Manipulator, The; Maximum Force; Men of Boys Town; Midsummer Night's Dream, A (1935); My Heroes Have Always Been Cowboys; My Pal, the King; National Velvet; Off Limits (1953); Pete's Dragon; Platinum High School; Pulp; Reckless (1935); Requiem for a Heavyweight (1962); Revenge of the Red Baron; Road Home, The; Silent Night, Deadly Night 5: The Toy Maker; Strike Up the Band; Summer Holiday; Sweet Justice; That's Entertainment! III; Thoroughbreds Don't Cry; Thousands Cheer; Words and Music; Young Tom Edison

Roos, Camilla Overbye: Facade

Roose, Thorkild: Day of Wrath

Root, Amanda: Persuasion (1995)

Root, Stephen: Night of the Scarecrow; Office Space

Rooymans, Huib: Flight of Rainbirds, A

Roquevert, Noel: Fanfan the Tulip; Un Singe en Hiver (A Monkey in Winter); Voulez Vous Danser avec Moi? (Will You Dance with Me?)

Rosa, Robby: Salsa

Rosa, Donna: Master Blaster

Rosario, Alex Del: Midnight Dancer (1994)

Rosato, Tony: Busted Up; City of Shadows; Diamond Fleece, The; Separate Vacations

Rosay, Françoise: Bizarre, Bizarre; Carnival in Flanders; Full Hearts and Empty Pockets; Naked Heart, The; Quartet (1948); September Affair

Roscoe, Albert: Last of the Mohicans, The (1920)

Rose, Gabrielle: Adjuster, The; Speaking Parts; Sweet Hereafter, The

Rose, George: Devil's Disciple, The; Hideaways, The; Jack the Ripper (1959); Night to Remember, A (1958); Pirates of Penzance, The; You Can't Take It with You (1984)

Rose, James: Chain, The

Rose, Jamie: Chopper Chicks in Zombietown; In Love with an Older Woman; Rebel Love; To Die Standing

Rose, Lenny: Beach Babes 2: Cave Girl Island

Rose, Michael: Naked Lies

Rose, Robin Pearson: Last Resort

Rose, Roger: Ski Patrol

Rose, Sherrie: Black Scorpion II: Aftershock; Devil in the Flesh (1998); Double Threat; In Gold We Trust; Maximum Force; New Crime City: Los Angeles 2020

Roseanne: Backfield in Motion; Blue in the Face; Even Cowgirls Get the Blues; She-Devil

Rosenberg, Sarah: Foxfire (1996)

Rosenberg, Saturday: Encounter at Raven's Gate

Rosenberg, Stephen: Jacob Two-Two Meets the Hooded Fang

Rosenbloom, Maxie: Abbott and Costello Meet the Keystone Kops; Each Dawn I Die; I Married a Monster from Outer Space; Louisiana Purchase; Mr. Moto's Gamble; To the Shores of Tripoli

Rosenthal, Sheila: Not Without My Daughter

Ross, Alma: Tuttles of Tahiti, The

Ross, Andrew: Party Camp

Ross, Annie: Basket Case 3: The Progeny; Short Cuts

Ross, Anthony: Country Girl, The (1954)

Ross, Betsy King: Phantom Empire (1935); Radio Ranch (Men with Steel Faces, Phantom Empire)

Ross, Beverly: Crazed

Ross, Charlotte: Foreign Student; Kidnapped in Paradise; Savage Land

Ross, Chelcie: Amos & Andrew; Chain Reaction (1996); Legacy of Lies; Rudy

Ross, Diana: Lady Sings the Blues; Mahogany; Wiz, The

Ross, Frank: Saturday Night Kid, The

Ross, Gene: Encounter with the Unknown; Poor White Trash II

Ross, Joe E.: Car 54 Where Are You? (TV Series); Sgt. Bilko (TV Series); Slumber Party 57

Ross, Katharine: Betsy, The; Butch Cassidy and the Sundance Kid; Climate for Killing, A; Conagher; Final Countdown, The; Fools; Get to Know Your Rabbit; Graduate, The; Hellfighters; Legacy, The; Murder in Texas; Red-Headed Stranger, The; Rodeo Girl; Shadow Riders, The; Shenandoah; Singing Nun, The; Stepford Wives, The; Swarm, The; Tell Them Willie Boy Is Here; They Only Kill Their Masters; Wrong Is Right

Ross, Lee: Dreaming of Joseph Lees; Metroland

Ross, Marion: Evening Star, The; Teacher's Pet

Ross, Matt: Ed's Next Move

Ross, Matthew: Last Days of Disco, The

Ross, Merrie Lynn: Bobbie Jo and the Outlaw; Class of 1984

Ross, Natanya: Shadow Zone: The Undead Express

Ross, Ricco: Proteus

Ross, Shirley: Big Broadcast of 1938, The; Waikiki Wedding

Ross, Ted: Bingo Long Traveling All-Stars and Motor Kings, The; Fighting Back; Wiz, The

Rossellini, Isabella: Big Night; Blue Velvet; Cousins; Crime of the Century; Death Becomes Her; Don Quixote (2000); Fallen Angels; Fearless (1993); Funeral, The (1996); Immortal Beloved; Impostors, The; Innocent, The (1993); Ivory Hunters; Lies of the Twins; Matter of Time, A; Odyssey, The; Siesta; Tough Guys Don't Dance; White Nights (1985); Wild at Heart; Wyatt Earp; Zelly and the Rossetter, Kathryn: Whatever

Rossi, Frank: Criminal Mind, The

Rossi, Leo: Accused, The; Casualties of Love: The Long Island Lolita Story; Fast Getaway; Fast Getaway II; Felony; Heart Like a Wheel; Hit List (1988); Maniac Cop 2; Mutant Species; Rave Review; Relentless; Relentless II: Dead On; Relentless 3; River's Edge; Too Much Sun; We're Talking Serious Money; Where the Day Takes You

Rossi, Vittorio: Snake Eater 2, the Drug Buster

Rossi-Stuart, Giacomo: Curse of the Living Dead (Kill, Baby, Kill); Last Man on Earth, The; Shanghai Joe

Rossiter, Leonard: Britannia Hospital; Luther

Rossman, Charley: Buford's Beach Bunnies

Rossovich, Rick: Black Scorpion; Cover Me; Fatally Yours; Gambler Returns, The: The Luck of the Draw; Legend of the Lost Tomb; Lords of Discipline, The; Navy Seals; New Crime City: Los Angeles 2020; Paint It Black; Roxanne; Spellbinder; Telling You; Top Gun; Tropical Heat; Warning Sign

Rotaeta, Felix: Pepi, Luci, Bom and Other Girls

Roth, Andrea: Club, The (1993); Crossworlds; Divided by Hate; Executive Power

Roth, Celia: All About My Mother; Labyrinth of Passion

Roth, Gene: Big Sombrero, The; Earth vs. the Spider; Marshal of Cripple Creek; Pirates of the High Seas; She Demons

Roth, Joan: Luther, The Geek

Roth, Johnny: Bride and the Beast, The

Roth, Lillian: Alice, Sweet Alice (Communion, Holy Terror); Animal Crackers; Ladies They Talk About; Madame Satan

Roth, Matt: Blink

Roth, Tim: Bodies, Rest & Motion; Captives; Deceiver; Everyone Says I Love You; Four Rooms; Gridlock'd; Heart of Darkness; Hit, The (1984); Hoodlum; Jumpin' at the Boneyard; Legend of 1900, The; Little Odessa; Meantime; No Way Home; Pulp Fiction; Reservoir Dogs; Rob Roy; Rosencrantz and Guildenstern Are Dead; Vincent and Theo

Rothe, Bendt: Gertrude

Rothman, John: Copycat

Rothrock, Cynthia: Angel of Fury; China O'Brien; China O'Brien 2; Fast Getaway; Fast Getaway II; Guardian Angel; Honor and Glory; Lady Dragon; Lady Dragon 2; Martial Law; Martial Law Two—Undercover; Millionaire's Express (Shanghai Express); Rage and Honor; Rage and Honor II: Hostile Takeover; Undefeatable

Rothwell, Carolyn: Van, The (1997)

Rottlander, Yella: Alice in the City; Scarlet Letter (1973)

Rotundo, Paolo: Ugly, The

Rouan, Brigitte: Overseas; Post Coitum

Rouffe, Alida: Marius

Rounds, David: So Fine

Roundtree, Richard: Amityville: A New Generation; Any Place But Home; Bad Jim; Ballistic; Big Score, The; Bloodfist III: Forced to Fight; Body of Influence; Christmas in Connecticut (1992); City Heat; Crack House; Day of the Assassin; Deadly Rivals; Diamonds; Escape to Athena; Eye for an Eye (1981); Firehouse (1972); Game for Vultures; Gypsy Angels; Jocks; Last Contract, The; Maniac Cop; Miami Cops; Mindtwister; Night Visitor (1989); Once Upon a Time … When We Were Colored; One Down, Two to Go; Opposing Force; Original Gangstas; Party Line; Q; Seven; Shaft; Shaft (2000); Shaft's Big Score!; Steel (1997); Theodore Rex; Time to Die, A (1990); What Do You Say to a Naked Lady?; Young Warriors, The

Rounseville, Robert: Carousel; Tales of Hoffman

Rourke, Mickey: Angel Heart; Another 9 1/2 Weeks; Barfly; Body Heat; Bullet; Desperate Hours (1990); Diner; Double Team; Eureka; Exit in Red; Fall Time; Francesco; Harley Davidson and the Marlboro Man; Homeboy; Johnny Handsome; Last Outlaw, The (1993); Last Ride, The (1994); 9 Weeks; Point Blank (1998); Pope of Greenwich Village, The; Prayer for the Dying, A; Rainmaker, The; Rape and Marriage: The Rideout Case; Rumble Fish; White Sands; Wild Orchid; Year of the Dragon

Rouse, Mitch: Sweethearts (1996)

Roussel, Anne: Music Teacher, The

Roussel, Myriem: First Name: Carmen; Hail Mary; Sacrilege

Roussel, Nathalie: My Father's Glory; My Mother's Castle

Routledge, Alison: Bridge to Nowhere; Quiet Earth, The

Routledge, Jordan: East Is East

Routledge, Patricia: 30 Is a Dangerous Age, Cynthia

Rouvel, Catherine: Assassins de l'Ordre, Les (Law Breakers); Black and White in Color; Borsalino; Picnic on the Grass

Rouverol, Jean: Bar-20 Rides Again

Rouyer, Andre: Maitresse

Rovensky, Joseph: Diary of a Lost Girl

Roversi, Patrizio: Volere volare

Roveryre, Liliane: Dirty Dishes

Rowan, Dominic: Emma (1996)

Rowan, Frank: Sidewalks of New York

Rowan, Kelly: Adrift; Candyman: Farewell to the Flesh; 187

Rowe, Brad: Billy's Hollywood Screen Kiss; Body Shots; Purgatory

Rowe, David: Overkill (1996)

Rowe, Douglas: Appointment with Fear

Rowe, Greg: Blue Fin

Rowe, Kimberly: Knocking on Death's Door; Rumble in the Streets

Rowe, Misty: Goodbye, Norma Jean; Hitchhikers; Man with Bogart's Face, The; Meatballs Part II; When Things Were Rotten (TV Series)

Rowe, Nevan: Sleeping Dogs

Rowe, Nicholas: Lawrenceville Stories, The; Young Sherlock Holmes

Rowe, Stephen: Cyber Tracker 2

Rowell, Victoria: Barb Wire; Dumb and Dumber

Rowland, Dan: Ravage

Rowland, Duane: Longest Hunt, The

Rowland, Leesa: Class of Nuke 'em High III

Rowland, Paige: Riot (1996)

Rowlands, Gena: Another Woman; Brinks Job, The; Child Is Waiting, A; Crazy in Love; Early Frost, An; Gloria (1980); Grace and Glorie; Hope Floats; Light of Day; Lonely Are the Brave; Love Streams; Mighty, The; Montana (1990); Neon Bible, The; Night on Earth; Once Around; Opening Night; Parallel Lives; Paulie; Playing by Heart; She's So Lovely; Something to Talk About; Strangers: The Story of a Mother and a Daughter; Tempest (1982); Tony Rome; Two-Minute Warning; Unhook the Stars; Woman Under the Influence, A

Rowles, Polly: Springtime in the Rockies (1937)

Roxburgh, Richard: Children of the Revolution; Mission: Impossible 2

Roy, Lise: Boys of St. Vincent

Royale, Allan: Man Inside, The (1984)

Royce, Lionel: White Pongo (Blond Gorilla)

Royce, Roselyn: Sizzle Beach, U.S.A.

Royle, Carol: Tuxedo Warrior

Royle, Selena: Big Hangover, The; Courage of Lassie; Fighting Sullivans, The (The Sullivans, The); Mrs. Parkington

Royle, William: Hawk of the Wilderness

Rozakis, Gregory: Abduction

Rubes, Jan: Believe; Birds II, The: Land's End; Blood Relations; By Way of the Stars; Class Action; D2: The Mighty Ducks; Dead of Winter; Deceived; Descending Angel; Devlin; Flood: A River's Rampage; Outside Chance of Maximillian Glick, The; Roommates

Rubin, Andrew: Police Academy

Rubin, Benny: Go into Your Dance

Rubin, Jennifer: Bad Dreams; Bitter Harvest (1993); Crush, The (1993); Delusion (1991); Drop Dead Gorgeous (1991); Fear Inside, The; Little Witches; Playmaker; Red Scorpion 2; Saints & Sinners; Screamers (1996); Stranger by Night; Twists of Terror; Wasp Woman, The (1995); Woman, Her Men and Her Futon, A

Rubin, Michael: I Was a Teenage Zombie

Rubinek, Saul: Agency; Android Affair, The; Blackjack; Bonfire of the Vanities; By Design; Color of Justice; Deathship; Getting Even with Dad; Highpoint; Hostile Intent; I Love Trouble; Man Trouble; Nothing Personal (1980); Obsessed; Outside Chance of Maximilian Glick, The; Past Perfect; Quarrel, The; Soup for One; Sweet Liberty; Synapse; 36 Hours to Die; Ticket to Heaven; True Romance; Young Doctors in Love

Rubini, Giulia: Adios, Hombre; Goliath and the Barbarians

Rubini, Sergio: Station, The

Rubinstein, John: Another Stakeout; Car, The; In Search of Historic Jesus; M.A.D.D.: Mothers Against Drunk Driving; Make Me an Offer; Mercy; She's Dressed to Kill; Zachariah

Rubinstein, Zelda: Anguish; Little Witches; Poltergeist II: The Other Side; Poltergeist III; Teen Witch

Rubin-Vega, Daphne: Wild Things

Rubio, Pablo Alvarez: Dracula (Spanish)

Ruck, Alan: Ferris Bueller's Day Off; Speed; Star Trek: Generations; Three for the Road; Young Guns II

Rudd, Bob: Married People, Single Sex

Rudd, Paul: Cider House Rules, The; Clueless; Locusts, The; Object of My Affection, The; Overnight Delivery

Rudd, Paul Stephen: Halloween: The Curse of Michael Myers

Rudder, Michael: Lifeforce Experiment, The

Ruddock, John: Martin Luther

Rudley, Herbert: Jayhawkers, The

Rudner, Rita: Peter's Friends; Weekend in the Country, A

Rudnik, Oleg: Yuri Nosenko, KGB

Rudolph, Alan: Infamous Dorothy Parker, The

Rudolph, Lars: Inheritors, The

Rudolph, Sebastian: Stalingrad

Rudulph, Ken: Blood, Guts, Bullets & Octane

Rudy, Reed: Free Ride

Ruebeck, Johan: Evil Ed

Ruehl, Mercedes: Another You; Fisher King, The; For Roseanna; Indictment: The McMartin Trial; Last Action Hero, The; Leader of the Band; Lost in Yonkers; Married to the Mob; Minus Man, The; North Shore Fish; Subway Stories

Ruff, Kerry: Talking About Sex

Rufus: Jonah Who Will Be 25 in the Year 2000; Train of Life

Ruggles, Charlie: All in a Night's Work; Balalaika; Breaking the Ice; Bringing Up Baby; Doughgirls, The; If I Had a Million; Invisible Woman, The; Look For The Silver Lining; Love Me Tonight; Melody Cruise; Murders in the Zoo; Papa's Delicate Condition; Perfect Marriage; Ramrod; Ruggles of Red Gap; Stolen Life, A; Terror Aboard; Ugly Dachshund, The

Ruggles, Derya: Remote

Ruggles, Wesley: Charlie Chaplin Cavalcade

Ruginis, Vyto: Last Gasp

Ruhmann, Heinz: Faraway, So Close

Rui, Zhao Xiao: Red Firecracker, Green Firecracker

Ruick, Barbara: Carousel; I Love Melvin

Ruivivar, Anthony: Race the Sun

Rule, Janice: Alvarez Kelly; Ambushers, The; American Flyers; Battle Shock; Chase, The (1966); Doctors' Wives; Gumshoe; Invitation to a Gunfighter; Missing; Swimmer, The

Rulu, Francesco: Grim Reaper, The (1962)

Ruman, Sig: Bitter Sweet; Bold Caballero, The; Comrade X; Emperor Waltz, The; Errand Boy, The; Honolulu; House of Frankenstein; Love Crazy; Ma and Pa Kettle on Vacation; Maytime; Night at the Opera, A; On the Avenue; Only Angels Have Wings; Saint in New York, The; Tarzan Triumphs; That Uncertain Feeling; Think Fast, Mr. Moto; Wagons Roll at Night, The

Run DMC: Krush Groove; Show, The

Runacre, Jenny: Jubilee; Last Days of Man on Earth, The; Passenger, The (1975)

Running Fox, Joseph: Avenging, The; Geronimo (1993); Lakota Woman: Siege at Wounded Knee

Runyeon, Frank: Sudden Death (1986)

Runyon, Jennifer: Blue de Ville; Carnosaur; 18 Again; Killing Streets; Man Called Sarge, A; Quantum Leap (TV Series); To All a Good Night

Ruocheng, Ying: Last Emperor, The; Little Buddha

RuPaul: Mother's Prayer, A; Wigstock: The Movie

Rupe, Katja: Germany In Autumn

Ruscio, Elizabeth: Cast the First Stone; Death Benefit; Hider in the House

Rush, Barbara: Between Friends; Bramble Bush, The; Can't Stop the Music; Come Blow Your Horn; Hombre; It Came from Outer Space; Moon of the Wolf; Robin & the Seven Hoods; Seekers, The; Strangers When We Meet; Summer Lovers; Superdad; Web of Deceit; When Worlds Collide; Widow's Kiss; Young Lions, The; Young Philadelphians, The

Rush, Deborah: Big Business; In & Out; My Blue Heaven

Rush, Elizabeth: Invasion of the Girl Snatchers

Rush, Geoffrey: Children of the Revolution; Elizabeth; House on Haunted Hill (1999); Les Misérables (1998); Mystery Men; Shakespeare in Love; Shine

Rush, Sarah: For Love of Angela

Rushbrook, Claire: Secrets and Lies; Spice World; Under the Skin

Rushton, Jared: Big; Cry in the Wild, A; Honey, I Shrunk the Kids; Pet Sematary Two; Yarn Princess, The

Rusic, Rita: Third Solution, The

Ruskin, Joseph: Firepower (1993); Gypsy Warriors, The

Ruskin, Sheila: Caribbean Mystery, A

Rusler, Robert: Assassination Game, The; Final Embrace; Game of Love, The; Sometimes They Come Back; Thrashin'; Vamp

Russ, Tim: Heroes of Desert Storm

Russ, William: Aspen Extreme; Beer; Crazy from the Heart; Crisis at Central High; Dead of Winter; Disorganized Crime; Drive Like Lightning; Pastime; Raw Courage; Traces of Red; Unholy, The; Wanted: Dead or Alive; When Danger Follows You Home

Russell, Andy: Copacabana

Russell, Betsy: Avenging Angel (1985); Cheerleader Camp; Delta Heat; Out of Control; Tomboy; Trapper County War

Russell, Bryan: Adventures of Bullwhip Griffin, The; Charlie, the Lonesome Cougar; Emil and the Detectives

Russell, Clive: Margaret's Museum

Salmi, Albert: Ambushers, The; Born American; Breaking In; Brothers Karamazov, The; Empire of the Ants; Hard to Hold; Hour of the Gun, The; Jesse; Kill Castro (Cuba Crossing, Mercenaries (1978), Sweet Violent Tony); Lawman; Meanest Men in the West, The; Menace on the Mountain; Night Games; St. Helens; Steel (1980); Unforgiven, The (1960)

Salmon, Colin: Prime Suspect 2

Salmon, Philip: Vampyr, The (1992)

Saionga, Lea: Redwood Curtain

Salt, Jennifer: Gargoyles (1972); Hi Mom; Sisters (1973); Wedding Party, The

Salt, Karen: Prince Brat and the Whipping Boy

Saltarelli, Elizabeth: Bound and Gagged: A Love Story

Salvador, Phillip: Fight for Us

Salvatori, Renato: Big Deal on Madonna Street; Burn!; Organizer, The; Rocco & His Brothers; State of Siege

Salzberg, Brian: Begotten

Salzman, Mark: Iron & Silk

Sambrell, Aldo: Tex and the Lord of the Deep; Yellow Hair and the Fortress of Gold

Samms, Emma: Goliath Awaits; Humanoids from the Deep (1996); Illusions; More Wild Wild West; Shrimp on the Barbie; Star Quest

Samoilov, Vladimir: Siberiade

Samoilova, Tatyana: Cranes Are Flying, The

Samples, Sheridan: Smile Like Yours, A

Sampson, Robert: Arrival, The (1990); Dark Side of the Moon, The; Gates of Hell; Re-Animator; Robot Jox

Sampson, Tim: War Party

Sampson, Will: Buffalo Bill and the Indians; Fish Hawk; Insignificance; One Flew over the Cuckoo's Nest; Orca; Poltergeist II: The Other Side; Standing Tall; Vega$; White Buffalo

Sams, Jeffrey: Fly by Night; Hope; Just Write; Rose Hill; Run for the Dream

Samten, Lobsang: Kundun

Samuel, Joanne: Alison's Birthday; Gallagher's Travels; Mad Max

Samuels, Haydon: I Live With Me Dad

San Giacomo, Laura: Apocalypse, The; Nina Takes a Lover; Once Around; Pretty Woman; Quigley Down Under; Right to Remain Silent, The; sex, lies and videotape; Stand, The; Stuart Saves His Family; Under Suspicion; Where the Day Takes You

San Juan, Antonia: All About My Mother

San Juan, Olga: Beautiful Blonde from Bashful Bend, The; Blue Skies

San, Lu Man: Scent of Green Papaya, The

Sanchez, Jaime: Florida Straits

Sanchez, Pedro: Final Defeat, The; Go Kill and Come Back; White Fang and the Hunter

Sanchez-Gijon, Aitana: Chambermaid on the *Titanic*, The; Walk in the Clouds, A

Sancho, Fernando: Boldest Job in the West, The; Django Shoots First

Sand, Paul: Can't Stop the Music; Great Bank Hoax, The; Hot Rock, The; Last Fling, The; Main Event, The; Wholly Moses!

Sanda, Dominique: Cabo Blanco; Conformist, The; Damnation Alley (Survival Run); Garden of the Finzi-Continis, The; Mackintosh Man, The; 1900; Nobody's Children; Steppenwolf; Story of a Love Story; Voyage en Douce

Sander, Casey: Crosscut; Summer Dreams

Sander, Otto: Wings of Desire

Sanders, George: Action in Arabia; All About Eve; Allegheny Uprising; Amorous Adventures of Moll Flanders, The; Bitter Sweet; Black Jack; Black Swan, The; Candyman, The (1968); Death of a Scoundrel; Doomwatch; Endless Night; Falcon Takes Over, The; Falcon's Brother, The; Five Golden Hours; Foreign Correspondent; Forever Amber; From the Earth to the Moon; Ghost and Mrs. Muir, The; Hangover Square; House of the Seven Gables, The; In Search of the Castaways; Ivanhoe (1952); Jupiter's Darling; King Richard and the Crusaders; Last Voyage, The; Lloyd's of London; Man Hunt (1941); Mr. Moto's Last Warning; Moon and Sixpence, The; Nurse Edith Cavell; One Step to Hell; Picture of Dorian Gray, The; Private Affairs of Bel Ami, The; Psychomania; Quiller Memorandum, The; Rebecca; Saint in London, The; Saint Strikes Back, The; Samson and Delilah (1949); Shot in the Dark, A; Solomon and Sheba

(1959); Son of Fury; Son of Monte Cristo, The; Strange Affair of Uncle Harry, The; Strange Woman, The; Sundown (1941); Tales of Manhattan; This Land Is Mine; Village of the Damned (1960); Voyage in Italy; While the City Sleeps

Sanders, Henry G.: Boss' Son, The; Rebel (1973)

Sanders, Hugh: Pride of St. Louis, The

Sanders, Jay O.: Angels in the Outfield (1994); Big Green, The; Confession, The; Daylight; Down Came a Blackbird; Earthly Possessions; For Richer or Poorer; Hostages; JFK; Kiss the Girls; Matchmaker, The (1997); Misfit Brigade, The; Nobody's Children; Silver Strand; V. I. Warshawski

Sanders, Otto: Faraway, So Close

Sanders, Paul Austin: Dark Universe, The

Sanders, Peggie: Lady Avenger

Sanders, Richard: Neon City

Sanderson, William: Client, The; Deadly Weapon; Forest Warrior; George Wallace; Last Man Standing (1988); Last Man Standing (1996); Lonesome Dove; Mirror Mirror; Mirror, Mirror 2: Raven Dance; Raggedy Man; Return to Lonesome Dove; Savage Weekend; Wagons East

Sandler, Elizabeth: Animal Instincts 2

Sandler, Adam: Airheads; Big Daddy; Billy Madison; Bulletproof (1996); Going Overboard; Happy Gilmore; Mixed Nuts; Waterboy, The; Wedding Singer, The

Sandler, William: Witness Protection

Sandlund, Debra: Victimless Crimes

Sandor, Steve: Bonnie's Kids; Dynamo; Stryker

Sandoval, Miguel: Breach of Trust; Dancing with Danger; Fixer, The; Get Shorty; Mrs. Winterbourne; Route 9

Sandre, Didier: Autumn Tale

Sandrelli, Stefania: Alfredo Alfredo; Conformist, The; Divorce—Italian Style; Family, The (1987); Jamon, Jamon; Of Love and Shadows; Partner; Seduced and Abandoned; Stealing Beauty; We All Loved Each Other So Much

Sandrini, Luis: El Professor Hippie

Sands, Diana: Georgia, Georgia; Raisin in the Sun, A (1961)

Sands, Johnny: Admiral Was a Lady, The

Sands, Julian: After Darkness; Black Water; Boxing Helena; Browning Version, The (1994); Circle of Passion; Crazy in Love; Doctor and the Devils, The; End of Summer; Gothic; Grand Isle; Great Elephant Escape, The; Husbands and Lovers; Impromptu; Killing Fields, The; Leaving Las Vegas; Loss of Sexual Innocence, The; Mercy (1999); Murder by Moonlight; Naked Lunch; Phantom of the Opera (1998); Room with a View, A; Siesta; Tale of a Vampire; Turn of the Screw (1992); Vibes; Warlock (1988); Warlock: The Armageddon; Witch Hunt

Sands, Sonny: Bellboy, The

Sands, Tommy: Babes in Toyland (1961); Ensign Pulver; None But the Brave

Sands, Walter: Blonde Ice

Sandweiss, Ellen: Evil Dead, The

Sandy, Gary: Mommy 2: Mommy's Day; Unlikely Angel

Sanford, Erskine: Lady from Shanghai; Letter from an Unknown Woman

Sanford, Garwin: Maternal Instincts; Quarantine

Sanford, Isabel: Desperate Moves; Pucker Up and Bark Like a Dog

Sanford, Stanley: Laurel and Hardy Classics: Vol. 1–9

Sano, Shiro: Violent Cop

Sanoussi-Bliss, Pierre: Nobody Loves Me

Sansone, Patricia: Merlin's Shop of Mystical Wonders

Santagata, Alfonso: Palombella Rossa

Santamaria, Claudio: Besieged

Santana, Ernie: Sudden Thunder

Santiago, Saundra: Miami Vice

Santini, Pierre: Dirty Dishes

Santoni, Reni: Anzio; Bad Boys (1983); Cobra (1986); Dead Men Don't Wear Plaid; Dirty Harry; Dr. Dolittle (1998); Enter Laughing; Late Shift, The; They Went That-A-Way and That-A-Way

Santos, Joe: Blade (1973); Blue Knight, The (1973); Deadly Desire; Mo' Money; Rockford Files, The (TV Series); Trial by Jury; Zandy's Bride

Sanville, Michael: Dreams Come True; First Turn-on, The

Sanz, Jorge: Belle Epoque; Lovers (1992); Valentina

Sapara, Ade: Crusoe

Sara, Mia: Any Man's Death; Apprentice to Murder; Black Day Blue Night; Blindsided; Bullet to Beijing; By the Sword;

Call of the Wild (1992); Caroline at Midnight; Climate for Killing, A; Daughter of Darkness; Ferris Bueller's Day Off; Hard Time; Legend; Maddening, The; Pompatus of Love, The; Queenie; Set-Up, The (1995); Shadows in the Storm; Stranger Among Us, A; Timecop; 20,000 Leagues Under the Sea (1996); Undertow

Sarafian, Richard: Bound; Bugsy; Don Juan DeMarco; Gotti; Gunmen; Miami Hustle; Ruby (1991); Terminal Velocity

Sarandon, Chris: Child's Play; Collision Course (1989); Cuba; Dark Tide; Dog Day Afternoon; Forced March; Fright Night; Goodbye, Miss 4th of July; Just Cause; Lipstick; Little Men (1998); Mayflower Madam; Osterman Weekend, The; Princess Bride, The; Protocol; Resurrected, The; Road Ends; Sentinel, The; Slaves of New York; Tailspin; Tale of Two Cities, A (1990); Tales from the Crypt Presents Bordello of Blood; Temptress; Terminal Justice; Terminal Justice, Cybertech P.D.; When the Dark Man Calls; Whispers

Sarandon, Susan: Anywhere But Here; Atlantic City; Buddy System, The; Bull Durham; Client, The; Compromising Positions; Cradle Will Rock; Dead Man Walking (1995); Dry White Season, A; Earthly Possessions; Front Page, The (1974); Great Smokey Roadblock, The; Great Waldo Pepper, The; Hunger, The (1983); Illuminata; January Man, The; Joe; Joe Gould's Secret; King of the Gypsies; Light Sleeper; Little Women (1994); Lorenzo's Oil; Loving Couples; Mussolini and I; Other Side of Midnight, The; Our Friend, Martin; Pretty Baby; Rocky Horror Picture Show, The; Safe Passage; Something Short of Paradise; Stepmom; Sweethearts' Dance; Tempest (1982); Thelma & Louise; Twilight; White Palace; Who Am I This Time?; Witches of Eastwick, The; Women of Valor

Sarasohn, Lane: Groove Tube, The

Sarchet, Kate: Sweater Girls

Sardà, Rosa Maria: All About My Mother

Sardou, Fernand: Little Theatre of Jean Renoir, The

Sarelle, Leilani: Breach of Trust; Harvest, The; Neon Maniacs

Sargent, Dick: Billie; Body Count (1988); Clonus Horror, The; Ghost and Mr. Chicken, The; Hardcore; Live a Little, Love a Little; Melvin Purvis: G-Man; Murder by Numbers; Operation Petticoat; Teen Witch

Sargent, Richard: Tanya's Island

Sarky, Daniel: Emmanuelle

Sarne, Michael: Seaside Swingers

Sarrazin, Michael: Beulah Land; Bullet to Beijing; Captive Hearts; Caravans; Deadly Companion; Doomsday Flight, The; Fighting Back; Flim-Flam Man, The; For Pete's Sake; Groundstar Conspiracy, The; Gumball Rally, The; Hostage Train; Joshua Then and Now; Keeping Track; Lena's Holiday; Loves and Times of Scaramouche, The; Malarek; Mascara; Pursuit of Happiness, The; Reincarnation of Peter Proud, The; Sometimes a Great Notion; They Shoot Horses, Don't They?; Thunder Point; Train Killer, The

Sarsgaard, Peter: Boys Don't Cry; Freak City

Sartain, Gailard: Ernest Goes to Jail; Fried Green Tomatoes; Getting Even with Dad; Grifters, The; Guilty by Suspicion; Leader of the Band; Murder in Mind; One Riot, One Ranger; Open Season; Real McCoy, The; Stop! or My Mom Will Shoot

Sasaki, Katsuhiko: Terror of Mechagodzilla

Sassaman, Nicole: Witchcraft V: Dance with the Devil

Sassard, Jacqueline: Accident; Bad Girls (1969); Les Biches

Sassoon, Cat: Angel Fist; Bloodfist IV—Die Trying; Bloodfist VI: Ground Zero

Sastre, Ines: Best Man, The (1997)

Sastri, Lina: Excellent Cadavers; Good Night, Michelangelo

Satie, Erik: Avant Garde Program #2

Sato, Kei: Violence at Noon; Zatoichi: The Blind Swordsman's Vengeance

Sato, Koichi: Gonin; Silk Road, The

Saucier, Jason: Crawlers

Sauer, Gary: Unbelievable Truth, The

Saunders, Jennifer: Absolutely Fabulous; Midwinter's Tale, A; Muppet Treasure Island; Supergrass, The

Saunders, Justine: Fringe Dwellers, The

Saunders, Mary Jane: Sorrowful Jones

Saunders, Michael K.: Billy the Kid Meets the Vampires

Saunders, Pamela: Alien Warrior

Savage, Ann: Detour (1945); Renegade Girl

Savage, Ben: Little Monsters

Savage, Brad: Islands in the Stream

Savage, Fred: Boy Who Could Fly, The; Little Monsters; Princess Bride, The; Vice Versa; Wizard, The

Savage, John: All the Kind Strangers; Amateur, The (1982); American Strays; Amnesia; Any Man's Death; Bad Company (1972); Brady's Escape; Caribe; Carnosaur 2; CIA II: Target: Alexa; Club Vampire; Coming Out of the Ice; Dangerous, The (1994); Daybreak (1993); Deer Hunter, The; Do the Right Thing; Eric; Godfather, Part III, The; Hair; Hostile Intent; Hotel Colonial; Hunting; Inside Moves; Jack Bull, The; Managua; Maria's Lovers; Message in a Bottle; Nairobi Affair; One Good Turn; Onion Field, The; Primary Motive; Red Scorpion 2; Salvador; Shattered Image; Sister-in-Law, The (1974); Takeover, The; Virginian, The (1999); White Squall

Savage, Vic: Creeping Terror, The

Saval, Dany: Boeing, Boeing; Moon Pilot; Tales of Paris

Savalas, George: Belarus File, The; Family, The (1970)

Savalas, Telly: Alice in Wonderland (1985); Backfire (1994); Battle of the Bulge; Belarus File, The; Beyond Reason; Beyond the Poseidon Adventure; Bird Man of Alcatraz; Buono Sera, Mrs. Campbell; Cannonball Run II; Cape Fear (1962); Capricorn One; Cartier Affair, The; Crooks and Coronets (Sophie's Place); Devil in the House of Exorcism, The; Dirty Dozen, The; Deadly Mission; Dirty Dozen, The: The Fatal Mission; Escape to Athena; Fakeout; Family, The (1970); Greatest Story Ever Told, The; Hollywood Detective, The; Horror Express; House of Exorcism, The; Inside Out (1975); Interns, The; Kelly's Heroes; Killer Force; Land Raiders; Mackenna's Gold; Massacre at Fort Holman (Reason to Live . . . A Reason to Die, A); Mindtwister; Muppet Movie, The; On Her Majesty's Secret Service; Pancho Villa; Redneck; Scalphunters, The; Scenes from a Murder; Silent Rebellion; Slender Thread, The; Sonny and Jed; Town Called Hell, A; Young Savages, The

Savant, Doug: Face To Kill For, A; Masquerade (1988); Paint It Black; Red Surf; Shaking the Tree; Trick or Treat (1986)

Savelyeva, Lyudmila: War and Peace (1968)

Savident, John: Brain Donors

Savidge, Jennifer: Magic Kid 2

Savini, Tom: Dawn of the Dead; From Dusk Till Dawn; Heartstopper; Knightriders; Maniac (1980)

Savio, Andria: Stryker

Saviola, Camille: Sunset Park

Savlov, Meg: Wax

Savoy, Suzanne: Cellar, The; Man with the Perfect Swing, The

Savoy, Teresa Ann: Caligula

Savvina, Iya: Lady and the Dog, The

Sawa, Devon: Boys Club, The; Final Destination; Idle Hands; Robin of Locksley; Wild America

Sawalha, Julia: Absolutely Fabulous; Martin Chuzzlewit; Pride and Prejudice (1996)

Sawyer, Joe: Black Legion; Buckskin Frontier; Comin' Round the Mountain; Indian Uprising; Naughty Nineties, The; Roaring Twenties, The

Sawyer, John Franklin: Shadrach

Saxon, Glenn: Django Shoots First

Saxon, John: Appaloosa, The; Arrival, The (1990); Baby Doll Murders, The; Battle Beyond the Stars; Bees, The; Beverly Hills Cop 3; Beyond Evil; Big Score, The; Black Christmas; Blackmail (1991); Blood Beach; Blood Salvage; Crossing the Line (1990); Death House; Death of a Gunfighter; Doomsday Flight, The; Electric Horseman, The; Enter the Dragon; Fever Pitch; Final Alliance; Hands of Steel; Hellmaster; Invasion of the Flesh Hunters; Joe Kidd; Maximum Force; Mr. Hobbs Takes a Vacation; Moonshine County Express; My Mom's a Werewolf; Night Caller from Outer Space; Nightmare on Elm Street, A; No Escape, No Return; Payoff; Planet Earth; Planet of Blood (Queen of Blood); Prisoners of the Lost Universe; Raid on Entebbe; Reluctant Debutante, The; Rock, Pretty Baby; Running Scared (1980); Running Wild (1955); Snatched; Strange New World; Strange Shadows in an Empty Room; Swiss Conspiracy, The; This Happy Feeling; Unforgiven, The (1960); Unsane; Welcome to Spring Break; Wrong Is Right

Saxon, Vin: Rat Pfink a Boo Boo

Sayer, Philip: Shanghai Surprise; Slayground; Xtro

Schneider, Maria: Jane Eyre (1996); Last Tango in Paris; Mamma Dracula; Passenger, The (1975)

Schneider, Rob: Adventures of Pinocchio, The; Beverly Hillbillies, The (1993); Big Daddy; Deuce Bigalow: Male Gigolo; Down Periscope; Judge Dredd; Knock Off; Muppets From Space; Surf Ninjas

Schneider, Romy: Assassination of Trotsky, The; Boccaccio 70; Cardinal, The; César and Rosalie; Death Watch; Good Neighbor Sam; Hero, The (1971); Infernal Trio, The; La Passante; Les Choses de La Vie (Things in Life, The); Mado; Simple Story, A; Swimming Pool, The; Trial, The (1963); What's New, Pussycat?; Woman at Her Window, A

Schock, Barbara: From Hollywood to Deadwood

Schoeffling, Michael: Belizaire the Cajun; Let's Get Harry; Mermaids; Sylvester; Vision Quest; Wild Hearts Can't Be Broken

Schoelen, Jill: Adventures in Spying; Babes in Toyland (1986); Chiller; Curse II—The Bite; Cutting Class; Phantom of the Opera (1989); Popcorn; Rich Girl; Stepfather, The; There Goes My Baby; Thunder Alley; When a Stranger Calls Back

Schoene, Reiner: Gunfighters, The; Nobody's Children

Schoener, Ingeborg: Mr. Superinvisible

Schofield, Annabel: Body Armor; Exit in Red; Solar Crisis

Schofield, Drew: Sid and Nancy

Schofield, Katharine: Lion of Africa, The

Schofield, Nell: Puberty Blues

Schombing, Jason: Timecop

Schon, Margarete: Kriemhilde's Revenge; Siegfried

Schoppert, Bill: Personals, The

Schrader, Maria: Nobody Loves Me

Schrage, Lisa: China White; Hello, Mary Lou: Prom Night II

Schreck, Max: Nosferatu

Schreiber, Avery: Dracula: Dead and Loving It; Galaxina; Hunk; Loose Shoes; Silent Scream; Swashbuckler (1976)

Schreiber, Liev: Daytrippers, The; Denise Calls Up; Hurricane, The (1999); Jakob the Liar; Phantoms; Ransom (1996); RKO 281; Scream 2; Walk on the Moon, A; Walking and Talking

Schreier, Tom: Ripper, The (1985)

Schroder, Rick: Across the Tracks; Call of the Wild (1992); Champ, The (1979); Crimson Tide; Earthling, The; Ebenezer; Last Flight of Noah's Ark; Little Lord Fauntleroy (1980); Lonesome Dove; Return to Lonesome Dove; Texas (1994); There Goes My Baby

Schroeder, Barbet: Celine and Julie Go Boating; Six in Paris (Paris Vue par ...)

Schub, Steven: Caught (1996)

Schubert, Heinz: Emil and the Detectives

Schubert, Karin: Bluebeard (1972)

Schuck, John: Blade (1973); Butch and Sundance: The Early Days; Four Eyes and Six Guns; Hammersmith Is Out; Holy Matrimony; Outrageous Fortune; Second Sight; Thieves Like Us

Schue, Matt: Femalien

Schull, Amanda: Center Stage

Schulter, Ariane: 1-900

Schultz, Albert: Ebenezer

Schultz, Dwight: Alone in the Dark; Fat Man and Little Boy; Long Walk Home, The; Star Trek: First Contact; Temp, The; When Your Lover Leaves; Woman with a Past

Schultz, Jeff: Buying Time

Schultz, Tom: Eyes of the Serpent; In the Time of Barbarians II

Schulz, Brian: Thou Shalt Not Kill ... Except

Schulze, Paul: Grind; Hand Gun

Schumacher, Wendy: Animal Instincts: The Seductress; Capitol Conspiracy, The; Fugitive Rage; Scorned 2

Schumm, Hans: Spy Smasher

Schunzel, Reinhold: Fortune's Fool; Golden Earrings; Threepenny Opera, The

Schurer, Erna: Blood Castle (1970); Specters

Schuurman, Betty: Character (Karakter)

Schuyler, Lonnie: Cybernator

Schwan, Ivyann: Problem Child 2

Schwartz, Aaron: Heavyweights

Schwartz, Albert: Time Stands Still

Schwartz, Maurice: Tevye

Schwartz, Scott: Toy, The

Schwartz, Simon: Inheritors, The

Schwartzman, Jason: Rushmore

Schwarzenegger, Arnold: Batman & Robin; Beretta's Island; Commando; Conan the Barbarian; Conan the Destroyer; Dave; End of Days; Eraser; Hercules Goes Bananas; Jayne Mansfield Story, The; Jingle All the Way; Junior (1994); Kindergarten Cop; Last Action Hero, The; Predator; Pumping Iron; Raw Deal; Red Heat (1988); Red Sonja; Running Man, The; Stay Hungry; Terminator, The; Terminator 2: Judgment Day; Total Recall; True Lies; Twins; Villain, The

Schwedop, Lisa: Revenge of the Teenage Vixens from Outer Space

Schweig, Eric: Broken Chain, The; Last of the Mohicans, The (1992); Pontiac Moon; Squanto: A Warrior's Tale; Tom and Huck

Schweiger, Til: Judas Kiss; Maybe, Maybe Not

Schwimmer, David: Apt Pupil; Kissing a Fool; Pallbearer, The; Since You've Been Gone; Six Days, Seven Nights

Schwimmer, Rusty: Little Princess, A (1995)

Schygulla, Hanna: Barnum (1987); Berlin Alexanderplatz; Beware of a Holy Whore; Bitter Tears of Petra Von Kant, The; Casanova (1987); Circle of Deceit; Dead Again; Delta Force, The; Effi Briest; Forever Lulu; Gods of the Plague; Lili Marleen; Love in Germany, A; Marriage of Maria Braun, The; Merchant of Four Seasons, The; Sheer Madness; Why Does Herr R. Run Amok?; Wrong Move, The

Scio, Yvonne: Redline

Sciorra, Annabella: Addiction, The; Copland; Cure, The; Funeral, The (1996); Hand That Rocks the Cradle, The; Hard Way, The (1991); Jungle Fever; Little City; Mr. Jealousy; Mr. Wonderful; National Lampoon's Favorite Deadly Sins; New Rose Hotel; Night We Never Met, The; Prison Stories: Women on the Inside; Reversal of Fortune; Romeo Is Bleeding; True Love; Underworld (1996); What Dreams May Come; Whispers in the Dark

Scob, Edith: Eyes Without a Face; Judex

Scofield, Dean: Last Assassins; Prehysteria 2; Secret Games 3

Scofield, Paul: Anna Karenina (1985); Attic: The Hiding of Anne Frank; Bartleby; Crucible, The; Hamlet (1990); Henry V (1989); King Lear (1971); Little Riders, The; Man for All Seasons, A; Martin Chuzzlewit; Mr. Corbett's Ghost; Quiz Show; Train, The; Utz; When the Whales Came

Scoggins, Tracy: Alien Intruder; Babylon 5 (TV Series); Dead On; Demonic Toys; Dollman vs. Demonic Toys; Great American Sex Scandal, The; Gumshoe Kid, The; In Dangerous Company; One Last Run; Time Bomb; Ultimate Desires; Watchers II

Scolari, Peter: Bosom Buddies (TV Series); Corporate Affairs; Infested (Ticks); Perfect Harmony; Rosebud Beach Hotel, The (Nostell Hotel, The)

Scooler, Zvee: Love and Death

Scopp, Alfie: Undergrads, The

Scorsese, Martin: Akira Kurosawa's Dreams; First Works, Volumes 1 & 2; Guilty by Suspicion; Muse, The; Quiz Show; Search and Destroy (1995)

Scorupco, Izabella: Goldeneye

Scott Thomas, Kristin: Angels and Insects; Bachelor, The (1993); Bitter Moon; English Patient, The; Four Weddings and a Funeral; Framed (1990); Handful of Dust, A; Horse Whisperer, The; Mission: Impossible; Pompatus of Love, The; Richard III (1995); Spymaker: The Secret Life of Ian Fleming; Tenth Man, The; Under the Cherry Moon; Unforgettable Summer, An; Weep No More My Lady

Scott, Alex: Romper Stomper

Scott, Bainbridge: Death Chase; Hell Squad (1985)

Scott, Brenda: Simon, King of the Witches

Scott, Campbell: Dead Again; Dying Young; Hi Life; Infamous Dorothy Parker, The; Innocent, The (1993); Longtime Companion; Love Letter, The (1998); Mrs. Parker and the Vicious Circle; Sheltering Sky, The; Singles; Spanish Prisoner, The

Scott, Carey: Making the Grade

Scott, Cherie: Dark Universe, The

Scott, Dan: Spookies

Scott, David: This Is Elvis

Scott, Debralee: Mary Hartman, Mary Hartman (TV Series); Pandemonium

Scott, Donovan: Savannah Smiles; Sheena; Zorro, the Gay Blade

Scott, Dougray: Ever After; Mission: Impossible 2

Scott, Geoffrey: First and Ten

Scott, George C.: Anatomy of a Murder; Angus; Bank Shot; Changeling, The; Christmas Carol, A (1984); Day of the Dolphin, The; Deadly Currents; Descending Angel; Dr. Strangelove or How I Learned to Stop Worrying and Love the Bomb; Exorcist III: Legion; Firestarter; Flim-Flam Man, The; Formula, The; Gloria (1999); Hanging Tree, The; Hardcore; Hindenburg, The; Hospital, The; Hustler, The; Inherit the Wind (1999); Islands in the Stream; Last Days of Patton, The; List of Adrian Messenger, The; Malice; Movie Movie; Murders in the Rue Morgue (1986); New Centurions, The; Oliver Twist (1982); Pals; Patton; Petulia; Prince and the Pauper, The (1978); Prince Brat and the Whipping Boy; Rage (1972); Rocky Marciano; Savage Is Loose, The; Taps; They Might Be Giants; Titanic (1996); 12 Angry Men (1997); Tyson

Scott, Gordon: Goliath and the Vampires; Tarzan and the Trappers; Tramplers, The

Scott, Hazel: Broadway Rhythm; Heat's On, The; I Dood It

Scott, Howard: Revenge of the Teenage Vixens from Outer Space

Scott, Imogen Millais: Salome's Last Dance

Scott, Janette: Day of the Triffids, The; Devil's Disciple, The; Old Dark House, The (1963); Paranoiac; School for Scoundrels

Scott, John: Horror of Party Beach, The

Scott, Joseph: Dead Silence (1989)

Scott, Kathryn Leigh: Best of Dark Shadows, The; Dark Shadows (TV Series); House of Dark Shadows; Murrow; Witches' Brew

Scott, Ken: Shallow Grave (1994); Stopover Tokyo

Scott, Kimberly: Caught in the Act; Client, The

Scott, Kirk: Cinderella (1976)

Scott, Larry B.: Children of Times Square, The; Fear of a Black Hat; Hero Ain't Nothin' But a Sandwich, A; Revenge of the Nerds II: Nerds in Paradise; Revenge of the Nerds IV: Nerds in Love; Snake Eater 2, the Drug Buster; Super Force; That Was Then . . . This Is Now

Scott, Lizabeth: Dead Reckoning (1947); Easy Living; Loving You; Pitfall; Pulp; Racket, The; Stolen Face; Strange Love of Martha Ivers, The; Two of a Kind (1951)

Scott, Martha: Cheers for Miss Bishop; Desperate Hours, The (1955); Doin' Time on Planet Earth; Howards of Virginia, The; Our Town (1940); War of the Wildcats

Scott, Pippa: Bad Ronald; Cold Turkey

Scott, Randolph: Abilene Town; Badman's Territory; Bombardier; Buffalo Stampede; Captain Kidd; Cariboo Trail; China Sky; Coroner Creek; Decision at Sundown; Doolins of Oklahoma; Fighting Westerner, The; Follow the Fleet; Go West, Young Man; Gung Ho! (1943); Hangman's Knot; Jesse James; Last of the Mohicans, The (1936); Lawless Street, A; Man in the Saddle; Man of the Forest; Murders in the Zoo; My Favorite Wife; Nevada, The; Pittsburgh; Rage at Dawn; Rebecca of Sunnybrook Farm (1938); Return of the Bad Men; Ride Lonesome; Ride the High Country; Roberta; 7th Cavalry; She (1935); Spoilers, The; Stranger Wore a Gun, The; Supernatural; Susannah of the Mounties; Tall T, The; Ten Wanted Men; To the Last Man; To the Shores of Tripoli; Trail Street; Virginia City; Wagon Wheels; Western Union

Scott, Raymond: Happy Landing

Scott, Sarah: Horrible Doctor Bones, The

Scott, Seann William: Final Destination; Road Trip

Scott, Susan: Trap Them and Kill Them

Scott, Timothy: Ballad of Gregorio Cortez, The; Gettysburg; Kid Vengeance; Lonesome Dove; Return to Lonesome Dove; Wild Times

Scott, Tom Everett: American Werewolf in Paris, An; Boiler Room; Dead Man on Campus; Inherit the Wind (1999); Love Letter, The (1999); One True Thing; That Thing You Do!

Scott, William Lee: October Sky

Scott, Zachary: Appointment in Honduras; Born to Be Bad; Cass Timberlane; Flamingo Road; Let's Make It Legal; Mildred Pierce; Shotgun; South of St. Louis; Southerner, The

Scotti, Nick: Kiss Me Guido

Scotti, Tino: Spider's Stratagem, The

Scotti, Vito: Caper of the Golden Bulls, The; Head (1968); Stewardess School

Scott-Thomas, Serena: Relax . . . It's Just Sex

Scourby, Alexander: Affair in Trinidad; Big Heat, The; Redhead from Wyoming, The; Seven Thieves; Silver Chalice, The

Scratch, Derf: Du-Beat-E-O

Scribner, Don: Wild Man

Scrimm, Angus: Mindwarp; Phantasm II; Phantasm III: Lord of the Dead; Phantasm IV: Oblivion; Subspecies; Transylvania Twist

Scruggs, Linda: Las Vegas Lady

Scuddamore, Simon: Slaughter High

Scully, Samantha: Silent Night, Deadly Night III: Better Watch Out!

Scully, Sean: Almost Angels

Seacat, Sandra: Baby Dance, The

Seagal, Steven: Above the Law; Executive Decision; Fire Down Below; Glimmer Man, The; Hard to Kill; Marked for Death; My Giant; On Deadly Ground; Out for Justice; Under Siege; Under Siege 2: Dark Territory

Seago, Howie: Beyond Silence

Seagrave, Jocelyn: Moonbase

Seagrove, Jenny: Appointment with Death; Chorus of Disapproval, A; Deadly Game; Guardian, The (1990); Hold the Dream; Sherlock Holmes and the Incident at Victoria Falls; Woman of Substance, A

Seal, Elizabeth: Philby, Burgess and Maclean: Spy Scandal of the Century

Seale, Douglas: Ernest Saves Christmas

Seales, Franklyn: Onion Field, The; Taming of the Shrew (1982)

Seamens, Sueanne: Majorettes, The

Searcy, Nick: Nell; Perfect Crime

Sears, Dejanet: In His Father's Shoes; Stand Off

Sears, Heather: Phantom of the Opera (1962); Room at the Top

Seay, James: Amazing Colossal Man, The; Killers from Space

Sebanek, Josef: Loves of a Blonde

Sebastian, Dorothy: Free and Easy; Spite Marriage

Sebastian, Lobo: 187

Seberg, Jean: Airport; Bonjour Tristesse; Breathless (1959); Fine Madness, A; Lilith; Macho Callahan; Mouse That Roared, The; Paint Your Wagon; Pendulum; Saint Joan; Time Out For Love

Secombe, Harry: Down Among the "Z" Men

Secor, Kyle: Children of Fury; Delusion (1991); Drop Zone; Late for Dinner; Silent Victim; Untamed Heart

Seda, Jon: Dear God; I Like It Like That; Price of Glory; Selena; Sunchaser; 12 Monkeys

Sedaka, Neil: Playgirl Killer, The

Sedden, Margaret: Headin' Home

Seddiqi, Bahare: Children of Heaven

Sedgewick, Edna: Red Barry

Sedgwick, Edie: Ciao! Manhattan

Sedgwick, Kyra: Born on the Fourth of July; Critical Care; Heart and Souls; Kansas; Labor Pains; Losing Chase; Low Life, The; Man Who Broke 1000 Chains, The; Miss Rose White; Mr. and Mrs. Bridge; Montana (1997); Phenomenon; Pyrates; Singles; Something to Talk About; Women & Men 2

Sedgwick, Robert: Nasty Hero

Seeger, Pete: Woody Guthrie—Hard Travelin'

Seel, Ceri: Tripods

Seeley, Blossom: Blood Money

Seeley, Eileen: Ruby Jean and Joe

Seely, Sybil: Buster Keaton Festival Vol. 1–3

Seff, Brian: Pee-Wee Herman Show, The

Segal, George: All's Fair; Army of One; Babysitter, The (1995); Black Bird, The; Blume in Love; Born to Win; Bridge at Remagen, The; Carbon Copy; Cold Room, The; Direct Hit; Duchess and the Dirtwater Fox, The; Endless Game, The; Flirting with Disaster; For the Boys; Fun with Dick and Jane; Hot Rock, The; Houdini (1998); Invitation to a Gunfighter; It's My Party; Killing 'Em Softly; King Rat; Last Married Couple in America, The; Look Who's Talking; Lost and Found (1979); Lost Command; Me, Myself & I; Mirror Has Two Faces, The; No Way to Treat a Lady; Not My Kid; November Conspiracy, The; Owl and the Pussycat, The; Picture Windows; Quiller Memorandum, The; Rollercoaster; Russian Roulette; St. Valentine's Day Massacre, The; Ship of Fools; Stick; Taking the Heat; Terminal Man, The; Touch of Class, A; Where's Poppa?; Who Is Killing the Great Chefs of Europe?; Who's Afraid of Virginia Woolf?; Zany Adventures of Robin Hood, The

Segal, Howard: Last Game, The

Segal, Robbin Zohra: Harem

Segal, Zohra: Bhaji on the Beach; Masala

Segall, Pamela: After Midnight; Bed of Roses; Gate II; Something Special

Segda, Dorotha: My 20th Century

Seghers, Mil: Antonia's Line

Segundo, Compay: Buena Vista Social Club, The

Seidel, Ileana: Beach House

Seidelman, Susan: First Works, Volumes 1 & 2

Seigner, Emmanuelle: Bitter Moon; Frantic (1988); Ninth Gate, The

Seigner, Louis: Le Bourgeois Gentilhomme

Seigner, Mathilde: Dry Cleaning

Seitz, John: Forced March; Hard Choices; Out of the Rain

Sekka, Johnny: Message, The (Mohammad, Messenger of God)

Selander, Hjalmar: Treasure of Arne

Selby, David: Best of Dark Shadows, The; Dying Young; Girl in Blue, The; Grave Secrets: The Legacy of Hilltop Drive; Headless Body in Topless Bar; Intersection; Night of Dark Shadows; Raise the Titanic; Rich and Famous; Up the Sandbox

Selby, Nicholas: Elizabeth R; Macbeth (1971)

Selby, Sarah: Huckleberry Finn (1975)

Self, Doug: Men in Love

Sell, Jack M.: Deadly Spygames

Sellars, Elizabeth: Chalk Garden, The; Mummy's Shroud, The; Never Let Go; Three Cases of Murder; Voyage 'Round My Father, A

Sellecca, Connie: Brotherhood of the Rose; Captain America II: Death Too Soon; Last Fling, The

Selleck, Tom: Broken Trust (1995); Bunco; Christopher Columbus: The Discovery (1992); Daughters of Satan; Folks; Gypsy Warriors, The; Her Alibi; High Road to China; In & Out; Innocent Man, An; Lassiter; Last Stand at Saber River; Love Letter, The (1999); Mr. Baseball; Most Wanted (1976); Myra Breckenridge; Quigley Down Under; Ruby Jean and Joe; Runaway; Sacketts, The; Shadow Riders, The; Terminal Island; Three Men and a Baby; Three Men and a Little Lady; Washington Affair, The

Sellers, Mary: Crawlers

Sellers, Peter: After the Fox; Alice's Adventures in Wonderland; Battle of the Sexes, The; Being There; Blockhouse, The; Bobo, The; Carlton-Browne of the F.O.; Casino Royale (1967); Dr. Strangelove or How I Learned to Stop Worrying and Love the Bomb; Down Among the "Z" Men; Fiendish Plot of Dr. Fu Manchu, The; Ghost in the Noonday Sun; Heavens Above; I Love You Alice B. Toklas!; I'm All Right Jack; Ladykillers, The; Lolita (1962); Magic Christian, The; Mouse That Roared, The; Murder by Death; Naked Truth (Your Past Is Showing); Never Let Go; Only Two Can Play; Party, The; Pink Panther, The; Pink Panther Strikes Again, The; Prisoner of Zenda, The (1979); Return of the Pink Panther, The; Revenge of the Pink Panther, The; Road to Hong Kong, The; Shot in the Dark, A; Smallest Show on Earth, The; There's a Girl in My Soup; To See Such Fun; Tom Thumb; Trail of the Pink Panther, The; Two-Way Stretch; Up the Creek (1958); Waltz of the Toreadors; What's New, Pussycat?; Woman Times Seven; World of Henry Orient, The; Wrong Arm of the Law, The; Wrong Box, The

Sellier, Georges: Red Balloon, The

Sellner, Gustav Rudolph: Pedestrian, The

Selzer, Milton: Miss Rose White

Sema, Chie: Tokyo Decadence

Sembera, Tricia: Flash and the Firecat

Gupta, Pinaki Sen: Aparajito

Seneca, Joe: Blob, The (1988); Crossroads; Mississippi Masala; Murder on the Bayou; Road to Freedom: The Vernon Johns Story; Saint of Fort Washington, The; Wilma

Sennett, Mack: Abbott and Costello Meet the Keystone Kops; Hollywood Cavalcade

Serato, Massimo: Catch as Catch Can; Tenth Victim, The

Serban, Isidor: Gadjo Dilo

Serbedzija, Rade: Before the Rain; Broken English; Eyes Wide Shut; Lies & Whispers; Mighty Joe Young (1998); Polish Wedding; Saint, The (1997); Truce, The

Sergei, Ivan: John Woo's Once a Thief; Opposite of Sex, The

Serio, Terry: Fast Lane Fever; Shout: The Story of Johnny O'Keefe

Serious, Yahoo: Reckless Kelly; Young Einstein

Serling, Rod: Encounter with the Unknown

Serna, Assumpta: Hidden Assassin; Managua; Matador; Sharpe (TV Series)

Serna, Pepe: American Me; Break of Dawn; Conagher; Force of One; Killer Inside Me, The; Rookie, The; Streets of L.A., The

Sernas, Jacques: Goliath and the Vampires; Helen of Troy

Serner, Halan: Man on the Roof

Serra, Raymond: Alphabet City; Nasty Hero

Serra, Tony: Watched!

Serrano, Diego: 24-Hour Woman

Serrault, Michel: Artemisia; Associate, The (1982); Beaumarchais the Scoundrel; Dr. Petiot; Holes, The; La Cage aux Folies; La Cage aux Folies II; La Cage aux Folies III, The Wedding; Love and the Frenchwoman; Nelly and Monsieur Arnaud; Old Lady Who Walked in the Sea, The; Swindle, The

Serrdakue, John: Crystal Force

Serre, Henri: Jules and Jim

Serres, Jacques: Blue Country; French Detective, The

Servaes, Daguey: Fortune's Fool

Servais, Jean: Angele; Liars, The; Rififi

Sesau, Mo: Young Soul Rebels

Sessions, Almira: Oklahoma Annie

Sessions, John: Sweet Revenge (1990)

Seth, Roshan: Gandhi; Little Dorrit; London Kills Me; Mississippi Masala; My Beautiful Laundrette; Not Without My Daughter; Solitaire for 2

Sethna, Maia: Earth (1998)

Seton, Bruce: Demon Barber of Fleet Street, The; Love from a Stranger (1937)

Settle, Matthew: Lansky; U-571

Séty, Gérard: Van Gogh

Severance, Joan: Almost Pregnant; Another Pair of Aces; Bird on a Wire; Black Scorpion; Black Scorpion II: Aftershock; Criminal Passion; Dangerous Indiscretion; Hard Evidence; Illicit Behavior; In Dark Places; Lake Consequence; No Holds Barred; Payback (1994); Profile for Murder; Red Shoe Diaries II: Double Dare; Runestone; See No Evil, Hear No Evil; Write to Kill

Severn, Billy: Enchanted Forest, The

Sevier, Corey: Summer of the Monkeys

Sevigny, Chloe: American Psycho; Boys Don't Cry; Gummo; Kids; Last Days of Disco, The; Map of the World, A; Palmetto; Trees Lounge

Seville, Carmen: Boldest Job in the West, The; Pantaloons

Seward, Jim: Last Broadcast, The

Sewell, George: Invasion UFO; Vengeance of She, The

Sewell, Rufus: Carrington; Cold Comfort Farm; Dangerous Beauty; Dark City; Hamlet (1996); Illuminata; Man of No Importance, A; Middlemarch

Sexton III, Brendan: Boys Don't Cry; Hurricane Streets

Sexton Jr., Brendan: Welcome to the Dollhouse

Seyler, Athene: Make Mine Mink

Seyler, Cathy: Vampyre (1990)

Seymour, Anne: Desire under the Elms; Misty; Trancers

Seymour, Caroline: Gumshoe

Seymour, Clarine: Idol Dancer, The

Seymour, Jane: Are You Lonesome Tonight; Battlestar Galactica; Doctor Quinn Medicine Woman; East of Eden (1982); Four Feathers, The (1978); Haunting Passion, The; Head Office; Jack the Ripper (1988); Lassiter; Live and Let Die; Matters of the Heart; Oh, Heavenly Dog!; Onassis: The Richest Man in the World; Praying Mantis; Scarlet Pimpernel, The (1982); Sinbad and the Eye of the Tiger; Somewhere in Time; Story of David, The; Sunstroke; Tunnel, The; War and Remembrance

Seymour, Ralph: Longshot (1981)

Seyrig, Delphine: Black Windmill, The; Daughters of Darkness; Discreet Charm of the Bourgeoisie, The; Donkey Skin (Peau D'Ane); Grain of Sand, The; I Sent a Letter to My Love; Last Year at Marienbad; Milky Way, The (1970); Muriel; Stolen Kisses; Window Shopping

Sezer, Serif: Yol

Shackelford, Ted: Baby of the Bride; Dying to Remember; Spider and the Fly, The; Sweet Revenge (1987)

Shackley, John: Tripods

Class Struggle in Beverly Hills; Shadows and Fog; She's Out of Control; Vanya on 42nd Street; Vegas Vacation; We're No Angels (1989); Wife, The

Shay, Dorothy: Comin' Round the Mountain

Shaya, Carol: Silent Prey

Shayne, Linda: Screwballs

Shayne, Robert: Dynamite Pass; Face of Marble, The; I, Mobster; King of the Carnival; Loaded Pistols; Marshal of Cedar Rock; Neanderthal Man, The; Rider from Tucson; Threat, The; War of the Satellites

Shea, Cherilyn: Silk 'n' Sabotage

Shea, Eric: Castaway Cowboy, The

Shea, John: Adventures of Sebastian Cole, The; Backstreet Justice; Case of Deadly Force, A; Honey, I Blew Up the Kid; Honeymoon; Hussy; Impossible Spy, The; Kennedy (TV Miniseries); Ladykiller; Missing; Nativity, The; New Life, A; Small Sacrifices; Stealing Home; Unsettled Land; Weekend in the Country, A; Windy City

Shea, Katt: Barbarian Queen; Devastator, The; Preppies

Shea, Tom: Somewhere, Tomorrow

Shearer, Harry: Blood and Concrete, A Love Story; Godzilla (1998); Oscar (1991); Plain Clothes; Pure Luck; Return of Spinal Tap, The; Right Stuff, The; This Is Spinal Tap

Shearer, Moira: Black Tights; Peeping Tom; Red Shoes, The (1948); Tales of Hoffman

Shearer, Norma: Barretts of Wimpole Street, The; Divorcee, The; Free Soul, A; He Who Gets Slapped; Idiot's Delight; Marie Antoinette; Private Lives; Riptide; Romeo and Juliet (1936); Smilin' Through (1932); Strange Interlude (1932); Student Prince in Old Heidelberg, The; Women, The

Shearman, Alan: Bullshot (Bullshot Crummond)

Sheedy, Ally: Amnesia; Bad Boys (1983); Betsy's Wedding; Blue City; Breakfast Club, The; Buried Alive II; Chantilly Lace; Fear (1990); Fury Within, The; Haunting of Sea Cliff Inn, The; Heart of Dixie, The; High Art; Invader; Lost Capone, The; Macon County Jail; Maid to Order; Man's Best Friend (1993); One Night Stand (1995); Only the Lonely; Parallel Lives; Red Shoe Diaries 4: Auto Erotica; St. Elmo's Fire; Short Circuit; Sugar Town; Tattle Tale; Tin Soldier, The; Twice in a Lifetime; Wargames; We Are the Children

Sheehan, Doug: FBI Murders, The

Sheeler, Todd: McCinsey's Island

Sheen, Charlie: Arrival, The (1996); Being John Malkovich; Beyond the Law (1992); Boys Next Door, The (1985); Cadence; Chase, The (1994); Courage Mountain; Deadfall; Eight Men Out; Ferris Bueller's Day Off; Free Money; Hot Shots; Hot Shots Part Deux; Lucas; Major League; Major League II; Men at Work; Money Talks; National Lampoon's Loaded Weapon 1; Navy Seals; No Man's Land; Platoon; Red Dawn; Rookie, The; Shadow Conspiracy; Silence of the Heart; Terminal Velocity; Three for the Road; Three Musketeers, The (1993); Under Pressure; Wall Street; Wraith, The; Young Guns

Sheen, Lucy: Ping Pong

Sheen, Martin: American President, The; Andersonville Trial, The; Apocalypse Now; Badlands (1973); Believers, The; Beverly Hills Brats; Beyond the Stars; Boca; Born Wild; Break, The; Cadence; Captain Nuke and the Bomber Boys; Cassandra Crossing, The; Catholics; Cold Front; Consenting Adults (1985); Conspiracy: The Trial of the Chicago 8; Da; Dead Zone, The; Dillinger & Capone; Eagle's Wing; Enigma; Entertaining Angels; Execution of Private Slovik, The; Final Countdown, The; Firestarter; Fourth Wise Man, The; Gandhi; Gettysburg; Ghost Brigade; Guardian, The (1984); Gunfighter (1997); Hear no Evil; Hostile Waters; Incident, The (1967); Judgment in Berlin; Kennedy (TV Miniseries); Little Girl Who Lives Down the Lane, The; Loophole; Maid, The; Man, Woman and Child; Missiles of October, The; Monument Ave.; News at Eleven; Nightbreaker; No Drums, No Bugles; Original Intent; Out of the Darkness; Outer Limits, The, (TV Series); Rage (1972); Roswell; Sacred Cargo; Samaritan: The Mitch Snyder Story; Shattered Spirits; Siesta; Spawn; Storm Tracker; Stranger in the Kingdom, A; Subject Was Roses, The; Sweet Hostage; That Championship Season (1982); Touch and Die; Trigger Fast; Wall Street; When the Bough Breaks

Sheen, Michael: Gallowglass; Wilde

Sheen, Ramon: Man of Passion, A

Sheen, Ruth: High Hopes; Young Poisoner's Handbook, The

Sheer, William: Headin' Home; Regeneration

Sheffer, Craig: Baby Cakes; Bliss (1997); Bloodknot; Blue Desert; Desperate Trail; Double Take; Executive Power; Eye of the Storm; Fire in the Sky; Fire with Fire; Grave, The; In Pursuit of Honor; Instant Karma; Miss Evers' Boys; Night Breed; Program, The; River Runs Through It, A; Road Killers, The; Sleep with Me; Some Kind of Wonderful; Split Decisions; That Was Then . . . This Is Now

Sheffield, Johnny: Tarzan and the Leopard Woman; Tarzan Finds a Son; Tarzan Triumphs; Tarzan's New York Adventure; Tarzan's Secret Treasure

Sheffield, Reginald: Second Chance

Shegog, Clifford: Street Wars

Sheila E.: Krush Groove

Sheilds, Frank: Hoosier Schoolboy

Sheiner, David: Stone Killer, The

Shelby, LaRita: South Central

Sheldon, Barbara: Lucky Texan

Sheldon, Gene: Sign of Zorro, The; Toby Tyler

Shellen, Stephen: Casual Sex?; Damned River; Drop Dead Gorgeous (1991); Gimme an "F"; Lifeline; Model by Day; Modern Girls; Murder One; River Runs Through It, A; Stand Off; Stepfather, The; Talking Walls

Shelley, Barbara: Blood of the Vampire; Cat Girl; Dracula—Prince of Darkness; Five Million Years to Earth; Gorgon, The; Rasputin: The Mad Monk; Village of the Damned (1960)

Shelley, Joshua: Front, The

Shelly, Adrienne: Big Girls Don't Cry—They Get Even; Grind; Hexed; Hold Me, Thrill Me, Kiss Me; Sleeping with Strangers; Teresa's Tattoo; Trust; Unbelievable Truth, The

Shelton, Deborah: Blind Vision; Body Double; Circuitry Man II: Plughead Rewired; Hunk; Nemesis (1992); Silk Degrees

Shelton, John: Time of Their Lives, The

Shelton, Marley: Hercules in the Underworld; Trojan War; Warriors of Virtue

Shelton, Reid: First and Ten

Shenar, Paul: Bedroom Window, The; Best Seller; Brass; Deadly Force; Dream Lover (1986); King Richard II; Raw Deal; Scarface (1983)

Shenkman, Ben: Pi

Shentall, Susan: Romeo and Juliet (1954)

Shepard, Angela: Billy the Kid Meets the Vampires; Curse of the House Surgeon, The; Honeymoon Murders; Penpal Murders; Queen Victoria and the Zombies; Vampires Always Ring Twice; Vampires from Outer Space

Shepard, Jewel: Caged Heat 2: Stripped of Freedom

Shepard, Patty: Blood Moon (Werewolf Versus the Vampire Woman, The); Man Called Noon, The; Rest in Pieces; Slugs, the Movie; Stranger and the Gunfighter, The

Shepard, Sam: Baby Boom; Bright Angel; Country; Crimes of the Heart; Days of Heaven; Defenseless; Fool for Love; Frances; Good Old Boys, The; Lily Dale; Only Thrill, The; Pelican Brief, The; Purgatory; Raggedy Man; Resurrection; Right Stuff, The; Safe Passage; Snow Falling on Cedars; Steel Magnolias; Streets of Laredo; Thunderheart; Voyager

Shephard, Hilary: Last Exit to Earth

Shephard, O-Lan: Out

Shepherd, Amanda: Hocus Pocus

Shepherd, Cybill: Alice (1990); Chances Are; Daisy Miller; Guide for the Married Woman, A; Heartbreak Kid, The; Lady Vanishes, The (1979); Last Picture Show, The; Last Word, The (1995); Long Hot Summer, The (1985); Married to It; Memphis; Moonlighting (1985) (TV Pilot); Muse, The; Once Upon a Crime; Return, The (1980); Secrets of a Married Man; Seduced; Silver Bears; Taxi Driver; Texasville; Which Way Home

Shepherd, Elizabeth: Invitation to the Wedding; Tomb of Ligeia

Shepherd, Jack: Twenty-One

Shepherd, Jean: Ollie Hopnoodle's Haven of Bliss

Shepherd, John: Friday the 13th, Part V—A New Beginning; Thunder Run

Shepherd, Morgan: Elvira, Mistress of the Dark; Max Headroom

Shepherd, Simon: Tales of Erotica

Sheppard, Delia: Animal Instincts; Dead Boyz Can't Fly; Homeboys II: Crack City; Mirror Images; Roots of Evil; Secret Games

Sheppard, Patty: Crypt of the Living Dead

Sheppard, Paula E.: Alice, Sweet Alice (Communion, Holy Terror); Liquid Sky

Sheppard, W. Morgan: Escape, The

Sheppard, William: Treasure of Pirate's Point

Sher, Antony: Alive & Kicking; Erik the Viking; Genghis Cohn; Mrs. Brown; Shadey; Tartuffe; Young Poisoner's Handbook, The

Sherbedgia, Rade: Mission: Impossible 2

Sheridan, Ann: Angels with Dirty Faces; Appointment in Honduras; Black Legion; City for Conquest; Dodge City; Doughgirls, The; Edge of Darkness (1943); Fighting Westerner, The; George Washington Slept Here; Good Sam; I Was a Male War Bride; King's Row; Letter of Introduction; Man Who Came to Dinner, The; Mississippi; Murder at the Vanities; Opposite Sex, The (1956); Silver River; Stella (1950); Thank Your Lucky Stars; They Drive by Night; They Made Me a Criminal

Sheridan, Dinah: Genevieve; Railway Children, The

Sheridan, Gail: Hills of Old Wyoming; Hopalong Cassidy Returns

Sheridan, Jamey: All I Want for Christmas; Echo of Thunder, The; Stand, The; Stanley and Iris; Stranger Among Us, A; Talent for the Game; Whispers in the Dark; Wild America

Sheridan, Margaret: Thing (From Another World), The (1951)

Sheridan, Nicollette: Beverly Hills Ninja; Dead Husbands; Jackie Collins' Lucky Chances; Noises Off; Silver Strand; Spy Hard

Sheridan, Richard: Secret of Roan Inish, The

Sherman, Bobby: Get Crazy

Sherman, Ellen: Dr. Tarr's Torture Dungeon

Sherman, Kerry: Satan's Cheerleaders

Sherman, Lowell: Bachelor Apartment; Ladies of Leisure; Way Down East; What Price Hollywood?

Sherwood, David: Curse of the Crystal Eye

Sherwood, Madeleine: Broken Vows; Sweet Bird of Youth (1962)

Sherwood, Roberta: Courtship of Eddie's Father, The

Shevtsov, George: Love Serenade

Sheybal, Vladek: Wind and the Lion, The

Shi, Zhang: Temptress Moon

Shields, Aaron: Crude Oasis, The

Shields, Arthur: Daughter of Dr. Jekyll; Enchanted Island; King and Four Queens, The; Little Nellie Kelly; Quiet Man, The; River, The (1951)

Shields, Brooke: Alice, Sweet Alice (Communion, Holy Terror); Bachelor, The (1999); Backstreet Dreams; Black and White (2000); Blue Lagoon, The; Born Wild; Brenda Starr; Diamond Trap, The; Endless Love; Freaked; Freeway (1996); Just You and Me, Kid; King of the Gypsies; Muppets Take Manhattan, The; Pretty Baby; Sahara (1984); Seventh Floor, The; Speed Zone; Tilt; Wanda Nevada; Wet Gold

Shields, Nicholas: Princes in Exile

Shields, Raasa Leela: Teach Me

Shields, Robert: Wild Wild West Revisited, The

Shiganoya, Benkei: Sisters of the Gion

Shigeta, James: Cage II: Arena of Death, The; China Cry; Die Hard; Flower Drum Song; Space Marines; Tomorrow's Child

Shih, Chang: Wooden Man's Bride, The

Shiina, Kippei: Gonin

Shilling, Marion: Common Law, The

Shiloh, Shmuel: Double Edge; Goodbye New York

Shimada, Shogo: Zatoichi: Masseur Ichi and a Chest of Gold

Shimada, Yoko: Hunted, The; Shogun (Full-Length Version)

Shimizu, Jenny: Foxfire (1996)

Shimizu, Misa: Eel, The

Shimkus, Joanna: Six in Paris (Paris Vue par ...); Virgin and the Gypsy, The

Shimono, Sab: Come See the Paradise; Shadow, The; Suture; Teenage Mutant Ninja Turtles III; Three Ninjas Kick Back

Shimura, Takashi: Bad Sleep Well, The; Drunken Angel; Godzilla, King of the Monsters; High and Low; Ikiru; No Regrets for Our Youth; Sanjuro; Sanshiro Sugata; Seven Samurai, The; Stray Dog; Throne of Blood

Shinas, Sofia: Hostile Intent; Hourglass

Shindô, Eitarô: Sisters of the Gion

Shiner, Ronald: Carry on Admiral

Shintaro, Katsu: Razor, The: Sword of Justice

Shipman, Gwynne: Trail Dust

Shipp, John Wesley: Flash, The; NeverEnding Story II, The; Soft Deceit

Shirakawa, Yumi: H-Man, The

Shire, Talia: Bed and Breakfast; Blood Vows: The Story of a Mafia Wife; Chantilly Lace; Cold Heaven; Deadfall; Dunwich Horror, The; For Richer, for Poorer; Godfather, The; Godfather, Part II, The; Godfather, Part III, The; Godfather Epic, The; Landlady, The; New York Stories; Old Boyfriends; Prophecy (1979); Rad; Rocky; Rocky II; Rocky III; Rocky IV; Rocky V

Shirley, Aliesa: Sweet Sixteen

Shirley, Anne: Anne of Green Gables (1934); Bombardier; Devil and Daniel Webster, The; Four Jacks and a Jill; Murder My Sweet; Stella Dallas

Shirt, J. C. White: Broken Chain, The

Shishido, Joe: 8Man

Shishido, Kai: 8Man

Shoaib, Samia: Pi

Shoemaker, Ann: House by the River

Shoemaker, Craig: Safe House

Shor, Dan: Mesmerized (Shocked); Strange Behavior; Strangers Kiss; Wise Blood

Shore, Dinah: Fun and Fancy Free; Up in Arms

Shore, Pauly: Bio-Dome; Curse of Inferno, The; Dream Date; Encino Man; In the Army Now; Jury Duty; Son-in-Law

Short, Antrum: Tom Sawyer (1917)

Short, Bobby: Blue Ice

Short, Dorothy: Reefer Madness; Trail of the Silver Spurs

Short, Kathryn: Goosebumps: The Haunted Mask

Short, Martin: Alice in Wonderland (1999); Big Picture, The; Captain Ron; Clifford; Cross My Heart (1987); Father of the Bride (1991); Father of the Bride Part II; Innerspace; Jungle 2 Jungle; Mars Attacks!; Mumford; Pure Luck; Really Weird Tales; Simple Wish, A; Sunset Limousine; Three Amigos; Three Fugitives

Short, Pat: Closer You Get, The

Shou, Robin: Mortal Kombat; Mortal Kombat: Annihilation

Show, Grant: Texas (1994); Treacherous Crossing; Woman, Her Men and Her Futon, A

Showalter, Max: Lord Love a Duck

Shower, Kathy: Commando Squad; Further Adventures of Tennessee Buck, The; L.A. Goddess; Out on Bail; Robo C.H.I.C.; Wild Cactus

Shriner, Kin: Crying Child, The; Cyberzone; Obsessive Love; Vendetta (1985)

Shriner, Wil: Time Treasures

Shrody, Eric: Big Bang Theory, The

Shropshire, Anne: Something to Talk About

Shubert, Nancy: Sagebrush Trail

Shue, Elisabeth: Adventures in Babysitting; Back to the Future II; Back to the Future III; Blind Justice; Call to Glory; Cocktail; Cousin Bette; Deconstructing Harry; Heart and Souls; Howling, The: New Moon Rising; Karate Kid, The; Leaving Las Vegas; Link; Marrying Man, The; Molly; Palmetto; Radio Inside; Saint, The (1997); Soapdish; Trigger Effect, The; Twenty Bucks; Underneath, The

Shuford, Stephanie: Dreams Come True

Shull, Richard B.: Big Bus, The; Cockfighter; Fortune, The; Pack, The; Splash

Shum, Frankie: Crippled Masters, The

Shute, Anja: Tendres Cousines

Shutta, Ethel: Whoopee

Slani, Sabrina: Ator: The Fighting Eagle; Throne of Fire, The

Sibbett, Jane: Arrival II, The; It Takes Two (1995); Noah; Resurrected, The

Sicari, Joseph R.: Night School

Sidahl, Viveka: House of Angels

Sidney, Sylvia: Blood on the Sun; Come Along with Me; Corrupt; Damien: Omen II; Dead End; Death at Love House; Demon (God Told Me To); Early Frost, An; Finnegan Begin Again; Fury (1936); Having It All; Love from a Stranger; Mr. Ace; Pals; Sabotage (1936); Shadow Box, The; Small Killing, A; Snowbeast; Street Scene; Summer Wishes, Winter Dreams; Trail of the Lonesome Pine, The; Used People; Wagons Roll at Night, The; You Only Live Once

Sieber, Maria: Scarlet Empress, The

Siebert, Charles: Blue Sunshine; Cry for Love, A; Incredible Hulk, The; Miracle Worker, The (1979)

Siemaszko, Casey: Amazing Stories (TV Series); Big Slice, The; Biloxi Blues; Breaking In; Limbo; Miracle of the Heart; Near Misses; Of Mice and Men (1992); Rose Hill; Teresa's Tattoo; Three O'Clock High; Young Guns

Siemaszko, Nina: Power of Attorney; Red Shoe Diaries 3: Another Woman's Lipstick; Saint of Fort Washington, The; Sawbones; Wild Orchid 2: Two Shades of Blue

Sierra, Gregory: Clones, The; Code Name: Dancer; Deep Cover (1992); Gambler, Part II—The Adventure Continues, The; Low Down Dirty Shame, A; Miami Vice; Unspeakable Acts; Wonderful Ice Cream Suit, The

Siewkumar, Asha: Tropical Heat

Siffredi, Rocco: Romance (1999)

Signorelli, Tom: Alice, Sweet Alice (Communion, Holy Terror); Crossover Dreams

Signoret, Simone: Cat, The (1971) (Le Chat); Day And The Hour; Death in the Garden; Dedee D'Anvers; Diabolique (1955); I Sent a Letter to My Love; Is Paris Burning?; La Ronde; Madame Rosa; Room at the Top; Ship of Fools; Sleeping Car Murders, The; Widow Couderc

Sihol, Caroline: Tous les Matins du Monde

Sikes, Brenda: Cleopatra Jones; Mandingo

Sikes, Cynthia: Arthur 2: On the Rocks; Love Hurts; Oceans of Fire; Possums; St. Elsewhere (TV Series)

Sikharulidze, Jemal: Prisoner of the Mountains

Sikking, James B.: Dead Badge; Final Approach; Hill Street Blues (TV Series); In Pursuit of Honor; Man on a String; Morons from Outer Space; Narrow Margin (1990); Ollie Hopnoodle's Haven of Bliss; Ordinary People; Pelican Brief, The; Soul Man; Tyson; Up the Creek (1984)

Silbar, Adam: Hot Moves

Silberg, Joshua: Ebenezer

Sillas, Karen: Beast, The (1996); Female Perversions; Flirt; Reach the Rock; Simple Men; What Happened Was …

Sills, Milton: Miss Lulu Bett

Silva, Henry: Above the Law; Allan Quartermain and the Lost City of Gold; Alligator; Almost Human; Bravados, The; Buck Rogers in the 25th Century; Bulletproof (1988); Code of Silence; Day of the Assassin; Ghost Dog: The Way of the Samurai; Green Mansions; Harvest, The; Jayhawkers, The; Law and Jake Wade, The; Love and Bullets; Lust in the Dust; Man and Boy; Manhunt (1973) (The Italian Connection); Megaforce; Never a Dull Moment; Possessed by the Night; Shoot (1976); Tall T, The; Thirst; Three Days to a Kill; Violent Breed, The; Virus (1980); Wrong Is Right

Silva, Trinidad: Night Before, The

Silvain, Eugene: Passion of Joan of Arc, The

Silveira, Lenor: Convent, The

Silver, Joe: Gig, The; Rabid; Switching Channels; They Came from Within; You Light Up My Life

Silver, Ron: Arrival, The (1996); Beneficiary, The; Best Friends; Betrayal (1978); Billionaire Boys Club; Black & White; Blind Side; Blue Steel (1990); Danger Zone (1995); Deadly Outbreak; Dear Detective; Eat and Run; Enemies—A Love Story; Entity, The; Father's Revenge, A; Fellow Traveler; Forgotten Prisoners; Garbo Talks; Goodbye People, The; In the Company of Spies; Kissinger and Nixon; Lifepod; Live Wire; Married to It; Mr. Saturday Night; Oh, God, You Devil!; Reversal of Fortune; Shadow Zone: The Undead Express; Silent Rage; Skeletons; Timecop; Woman of Independent Means, A

Silvera, Frank: Appaloosa, The; Killer's Kiss; Miracle of Our Lady of Fatima, The; St. Valentine's Day Massacre, The; Stalking Moon, The; Valdez Is Coming

Silverheels, Jay: Broken Arrow (1950); Lone Ranger, The (1956); Lone Ranger, The (TV Series); Lone Ranger and the Lost City of Gold, The; Santee; War Arrow

Silverman, Jonathan: Age Isn't Everything; At First Sight (1995); Breaking the Rules; Brighton Beach Memoirs; Caddyshack II; Challenge of a Lifetime; Class Action; For Richer, for Poorer; Freak City; French Exit; Girls Just Want to Have Fun; Inspectors, The; Little Sister; Odd Couple II, The; Sketch Artist II: Hands That See; Something About Sex; Stealing Home; Teresa's Tattoo; Traveling Man; 12:01; Weekend at Bernie's; Weekend at Bernie's II

Silvers, Phil: All Through the Night; Boatniks, The; Buono Sera, Mrs. Campbell; Cheap Detective, The; Chicken Chronicles, The; Cover Girl; Follow That Camel; Footlight Serenade; Four Jills in a Jeep; Forty Pounds of Trouble; Funny Thing Happened on the Way to the Forum, A; Guide for the Married Man, A; Happy Hooker Goes Hollywood, The; Hey Abbott!; It's a Mad Mad Mad Mad World; Lady Be Good; Lady Takes a Chance, A; Lucky Me; Roxie Hart; Sgt. Bilko (TV Series); Summer Stock; Tom, Dick and Harry

Silverston, Ben: Browning Version, The (1994)

Silverstone, Alicia: Babysitter, The (1995); Batman & Robin; Blast from the Past; Clueless; Crush, The (1993); Excess Baggage; Hideaway; True Crime (1995)

Silverstone, Ben: Get Real

Silvestre, Armand: Rock 'n' Roll Swinging Women vs. the Aztec Mummy

Sim, Alastair: Belles of St. Trinian's, The; Blue Murder at St. Trinian's; Christmas Carol, A (1951); Green for Danger; Littlest Horse Thieves, The; Ruling Class, The; School for Scoundrels; Stage Fright

Sim, Gerald: Dr. Jekyll and Sister Hyde; Long Ago Tomorrow

Sim, Sheila: Great Day

Simko, Anthony: Castle, The (1997)

Simm, John: Boston Kickout; Human Traffic

Simmons, Anthony: Sherlock: Undercover Dog

Simmons, Beverly: Buck Privates Come Home

Simmons, Gene: Kiss Meets the Phantom of the Park; Never Too Young to Die; Red Surf; Runaway; Trick or Treat (1986); Wanted: Dead or Alive

Simmons, Jaason: Frankenstein Reborn!

Simmons, Jean: Adam and Evalyn; Androcles and the Lion; Big Country, The; Black Narcissus; Clouded Yellow, The; Dain Curse, The; Daisies in December; Dawning, The; Desirée; Divorce American Style; Dominique Is Dead; Egyptian, The; Elmer Gantry; Going Undercover; Grass Is Greener, The; Great Expectations (1946); Great Expectations (1989); Guys and Dolls; Hamlet (1948); How to Make an American Quilt; Hungry Hill; Mr. Sycamore; Robe, The; Rough Night in Jericho; She Couldn't Say No; Small Killing, A; Spartacus; They Do It with Mirrors; This Could Be the Night; Thornbirds, The; Trio; Until They Sail; Young Bess

Simmons, Richard: Man with the Steel Whip

Simmrin, Joey: Midas Touch, The; Star Kid

Simms, Ginny: Broadway Rhythm

Simms, Hilda: Joe Louis Story, The

Simms, Larry: Blondie; Blondie Has Servant Trouble; Blondie in Society; Blondie Knows Best; Blondie Hits the Jackpot

Simms, Michael: Scarecrows

Simms, Mike: Bus Is Coming, The

Simon, François: Basileus Quartet; Christ Stopped at Eboli; Lumiere

Simon, Luc: Lancelot of the Lake

Simon, Michel: Bizarre, Bizarre; Boudu Saved from Drowning; Candide; Circonstances Attenuantes; Head, The (1959); L'Atalante; La Chienne; Panique; Train, The; Two of Us, The

Simon, Paul: Annie Hall; One Trick Pony; Rutles, The (All You Need Is Cash)

Simon, Robert F.: Benny Goodman Story, The; Chinese Web, The; Nine Lives of Elfego Baca, The

Simon, Simone: Cat People (1942); Curse of the Cat People, The; Devil and Daniel Webster, The; La Bête Humaine; La Ronde; Le Plaisir; Mademoiselle Fifi

Simon, Tania: Women from Down Under

Simonetti, Michelle: Benedette

Simons, Frank: Blue Yonder, The

Simonsen, Lars: Twist and Shout

Simonson, Renée: Nothing Underneath

Simpson, Monica: Concealed Weapon

Simpson, O. J.: Capricorn One; CIA Codename Alexa; Firepower (1979); Hambone and Hillie; Killer Force; Klansman, The; Naked Gun, The; Naked Gun 2 , The; Naked Gun 33 1/3, The—The Final Insult; No Place To Hide

Simpson, Raeanin: Little Heroes

Simpson, Ronald: Song of Freedom

Simpson, Russell: Border Patrol; Cabin in the Cotton; Grapes of Wrath, The; Human Hearts; Ma and Pa Kettle at the Fair; Spoilers, The; Virginia City; Virginian, The (1923)

Simpson, Sandy: Glory Years

Simpson, Tina May: Final Equinox

Sims, Aaron: Adventures of the Kung Fu Rascals, The

Sims, George: High Country, The

Sims, Jackson: Kill-Off, The

Sims, Joan: Carry on at Your Convenience; Carry on Behind; Carry on Cleo; Carry on Cowboy; Carry on Doctor; Carry on Emmanuelle; Follow That Camel; Love Among the Ruins; Murder Is Announced, A

Sinatra, Frank: Anchors Aweigh; Assault on a Queen; Can-Can; Cannonball Run II; Come Blow Your Horn; Detective, The (1968); Devil at 4 O'Clock, The; Double Dynamite; First Deadly Sin, The; Four for Texas; From Here to Eternity (1953); Guys and Dolls; High Society; Higher and Higher; Hole in the Head, A; It Happened in Brooklyn; Kings Go Forth; Kissing Bandit, The; Lady in Cement; Man with the Golden Arm, The; Manchurian Candidate, The; Meet Danny Wilson; Miracle of the Bells, The; Never So Few; None But the Brave; Not as a Stranger; Ocean's Eleven; On the Town; Pal Joey; Pride and the Passion, The; Robin & the Seven Hoods; Ship Ahoy; Some Came Running; Step Lively; Suddenly; Take Me Out to the Ball Game; Tender Trap, The; That's Entertainment; Tony Rome; Von Ryan's Express; Young at Heart

Sinatra Jr., Frank: Man Called Adam, A

Sinatra, Nancy: Speedway; Wild Angels, The

Sinbad: Cherokee Kid, The; Coneheads; First Kid; George of the Jungle; Good Burger; Houseguest; Jingle All the Way; Meteor Man; Necessary Roughness

Sinclair, Gordon John: Girl in the Picture, The; Gregory's Girl; That Sinking Feeling

Sinclair, Hugh: Circle of Danger; Corridor of Mirrors; Saint's Vacation, The

Sinclair, Kristian: Countryman

Sinclair, Madge: Almos' a Man; Coming to America; Conrack; Convoy (1978); Cornbread, Earl and Me

Sinden, Donald: Captain's Table; Cruel Sea, The; Doctor in the House; Island at the Top of the World, The

Singer, Linda: Junior (1984); Zombie Nightmare

Singer, Lori: Falcon and the Snowman, The; Footloose; Last Ride, The (1994); Made in USA; Man with One Red Shoe, The; Short Cuts; Storm and Sorrow; Summer Heat (1987); Sunset Grill; Trouble in Mind; Warlock (1988)

Singer, Marc: Beastmaster, The; Beastmaster 2: Through the Portal of Time; Beastmaster III: The Eye of Braxus; Berlin Conspiracy, The; Born to Race; Cyberzone; Dead Space; Deadly Game; Go Tell the Spartans; High Desert Kill; If You Could See What I Hear; Man Called Sarge, A; Savate; Sea Wolf, The (1993); Silk Degrees; Sweet Justice; Two Worlds of Jennie Logan, The; Ultimate Desires; V; Watchers II

Singer, Ritchie: Encounter at Raven's Gate

Singer, Susie: Landlady, The

Singh, Greishma Makar: Little Buddha

Singhammer, Eva Maria: Heidi (1965)

Singleton, Penny: Blondie; Blondie Takes a Vacation; Blondie Has Servant Trouble; Blondie in Society; Blondie's Blessed Event; Blondie Knows Best; Blondie Hits the Jackpot; Boy Meets Girl; It's a Great Life

Singleton, Sam: Death of a Prophet

Sinise, Gary: Albino Alligator; Apollo 13; Forrest Gump; George Wallace; Jack the Bear; Midnight Clear, A; Mission to Mars; My Name Is Bill W; Of Mice and Men (1992); Ransom (1996); Reindeer Games; Snake Eyes; Stand, The; That Championship Season; True West; Truman

Sinniger, Christina: Evil Within, The

Sirianni, Nancy: Ghoul School; Psycho Sisters (1998)

Sirico, Tony: New York Cop

Sirola, Joseph: Love Is a Gun

Sirtis, Marina: Journey's End: The Saga of Star Trek: The Next Generation; Star Trek: First Contact; Star Trek: Generations; Star Trek: The Next Generation (TV Series)

Sisk, Kathleen: Girl Who Spelled Freedom, The

Sistillio, Troy: Raising Heroes

Sisto, Jeremy: Crew, The; Hideaway; Suicide Kings; White Squall

Sisupal, Sonu: Terrorist, The

Sivero, Frank: Cop and a Half

Sizemore, Tom: American Story, An; Bad Love; Bringing Out the Dead; Devil in a Blue Dress; Heart and Souls; Heat (1995); Matter of Degrees, A; Passenger 57; Play It to the Bone; Relic, The; Saving Private Ryan; Strange Days; Striking Distance; True Romance; Watch It; Where Sleeping Dogs Lie; Witness Protection; Wyatt Earp

Sjoman, Vilgot: I Am Curious Blue

Sjöström, Victor: Outlaw and His Wife, The; Phantom Chariot; Thomas Graal's Best Child; Thomas Graal's Best Film; Walpurgis Night; Wild Strawberries

Skaggs, Jimmie F.: Lost Capone, The

Skala, Lilia: Charly; Deadly Hero; Flashdance; Heartland; House of Games; Lilies of the Field (1963); Men of Respect; Probe; Roseland; Ship of Fools

Skarsgard, Stellan: Amistad; Breaking the Waves; Deep Blue Sea; Good Evening Mr. Wallenberg; Good Will Hunting; Insomnia; My Son the Fanatic; Noon Wine; Ronin; Savior; Slingshot, The; Wind (1992); Women on the Roof, The; Zero Kelvin

Skarvellis, Jackie: Rats are Coming! The Werewolves Are Here!, The

Skelton, Red: Bathing Beauty; Clown, The; Du Barry Was a Lady; Fuller Brush Man, The; Having a Wonderful Time; I Dood It; Lady Be Good; Lovely to Look At; Merton of the Movies; Neptune's Daughter; Panama Hattie; Ship Ahoy; Show-Off, The (1946); Southern Yankee, A; Texas Carnival; Thousands Cheer; Three Little Words; Watch the Birdie; Whistling in Brooklyn; Whistling in Dixie; Whistling in the Dark; Yellow Cab Man, The; Ziegfeld Follies

Skerla, Lena: Fire Within, The

Skerritt, Tom: Alien; Big Bad Mama; Big Man on Campus; Big Town, The; Child in the Night; China Lake Murders, The; Contact; Dangerous Summer, A; Dead Zone, The; Devil's Rain, The; Divided by Hate; Fighting Back; Fuzz; Heist, The; Hitchhiker, The (Series); Ice Castles; Knight Moves; Maid to Order; M*A*S*H; Miles to Go; Nightmare at Bittercreek; Opposing Force; Poison Ivy (1992); Poker Alice; Poltergeist III; Red King, White Knight; River Runs Through It, A; Rookie, The; Silence of the North; SpaceCamp; Steel Magnolias; Thieves Like Us; Top Gun; Turning Point, The; Up in Smoke; What the Deaf Man Heard; Wild Orchid 2: Two Shades of Blue; Wild Rovers, The; Wisdom

Skinner, Anita: Girlfriends; Sole Survivor

Skinner, Cornelia Otis: Uninvited, The (1944)

Skinner, Keith: Mademoiselle

Skipper, Pat: Dancing with Danger

Skipworth, Alison: Becky Sharp; Dangerous (1935); Doubting Thomas; If I Had a Million; Night after Night; Princess Comes Across, The; Satan Met a Lady

Skiru, Julie: Silk 'n' Sabotage

Skjonberg, Espen: One Day in the Life of Ivan Denisovich

Skoliar, Igor: Jazzman

Skolimowski, Jerzy: Big Shots; Circle of Deceit; White Nights (1985)

Skomarovsky, Vladimir: Black Eagle

Skye, Ione: Carmilla; Gas, Food, Lodging; Girls in Prison; Guncrazy (1992); Mindwalk; Night in the Life of Jimmy Reardon, A; Rachel Papers; River's Edge; Samantha; Say Anything; Stranded

Slabolepszy, Paul: Saturday Night at the Palace

Slade, Max Elliott: Three Ninjas; Three Ninjas Kick Back; Three Ninjas Knuckle Up

Sladen, Elizabeth: Dr. Who: Revenge of the Cybermen; Gulliver in Lilliput

Slaska, Aleksandra: Passenger, The (1963)

Slate, Jeremy: Born Losers; Centerfold Girls; Dead Pit, The; Dream Machine; Girls! Girls! Girls!; Hell's Angels '69; Mr. Horn; Sons of Katie Elder, The; Summer of Fear

Slater, Christian: Basil; Bed of Roses; Beyond the Stars; Broken Arrow (1996); Gleaming the Cube; Hard Rain; Heathers; Interview with the Vampire; Jimmy Hollywood; Julian Po; Kuffs; Legend of Billie Jean, The; Mobsters; Murder in the First; Name of the Rose, The; Pump Up the Volume; Robin Hood: Prince of Thieves; Tales from the Darkside, The Movie; True Romance; Tucker: A Man and His Dream; Twisted; Untamed Heart; Very Bad Things; Where the Day Takes You; Wizard, The; Young Guns II

Slater, Helen: Betrayal of the Dove; Chantilly Lace; City Slickers; Happy Together; House in the Hills, A; Lassie; Legend of Billie Jean, The; No Way Back; Parallel Lives; Ruthless People; Secret of My Success, The; Sticky Fingers; Supergirl; 12:01

Slater, Justine: Bar Girls

Slater, Ryan: Amazing Panda Adventure, The

Slater, Suzanne: Mindtwister

Slattery, John: Lily Dale

Slattery, Tony: Heaven's a Drag; Peter's Friends

Slaughter, Sgt.: Bad Guys

Slaughter, Tod: Crimes at the Dark House; Crimes of Stephen Hawke, The; Demon Barber of Fleet Street, The; Face at the Window, The; Never Too Late; Sexton Blake and the Hooded Terror; Ticket of Leave Man, The

Slavens, Darla: Married People, Single Sex

Slavin, Slick: Invasion of the Star Creatures

Slayton, Bobby: Rat Pack, The

Sledge, Tommy: Gross Jokes; Movie, In Your Face!

Siezak, Leo: Baron Münchhausen (1943)

Siezak, Victor: Bridges of Madison County, The

Siezak, Walter: Abbott and Costello in the Foreign Legion; Bedtime for Bonzo; Black Beauty (1971); Born to Kill; Caper of the Golden Bulls, The; Come September; Cornered; Emil and the Detectives; Fallen Sparrow, The; Inspector General, The; Lifeboat; Miracle, The (1959); Once Upon a Honeymoon; People Will Talk; Pirate, The; Princess and the Pirate, The; RiffRaff (1947); Salome, Where She Danced; Sinbad the Sailor; Step Lively; This Land Is Mine; Yellow Cab Man, The

Slick Rick: Show, The

Sloan, Olive: Trapped by the Mormons

Sloane, Everett: By Love Possessed; Citizen Kane; Disorderly Orderly, The; Enforcer, The (1951); Journey into Fear (1942); Lady from Shanghai; Marjorie Morningstar; Patsy, The; Patterns; Sirocco; Somebody Up There Likes Me

Slotnick, Joey: Pirates of Silicon Valley; Since You've Been Gone

Slowe, Georgia: Black Arrow (1984)

Sloyan, James: Callie and Son; Prime Suspect (1982) (Feature); Xanadu

Small, Marya: Fade to Black (1980)

Smart, Amy: Outside Providence; Varsity Blues

Smart, Dee: Back of Beyond; Welcome to Woop Woop

Smart, Jean: Fire with Fire; Guinevere; Homeward Bound: The Incredible Journey; Mistress (1992); Odd Couple II, The; Scarlett; Snow Day; Yarn Princess, The

Smart, Rebecca: Celia, Child of Terror

Smerczak, Ron: Return of the Family Man

Smerdoni, Rinaldo: Shoeshine

Smestad, Stian: Shipwrecked

Smit, Maarten: For a Lost Soldier

Smit, Rulle: Littlest Viking, The

Smith, A. Thomas: Invader

Smith, Al: Forbidden Trail

Smith, Albert J.: Telegraph Trail, The

Smith, Alexis: Adventures of Mark Twain, The (1944); Age of Innocence, The; Any Number Can Play; Casey's Shadow; Conflict; Dive Bomber; Doughgirls, The; Gentleman Jim; Here Comes the Groom; Hollywood Canteen; Horn Blows at Midnight, The; Little Girl Who Lives Down the Lane, The; Night and Day (1946); Once Is Not Enough; Rhapsody in Blue; San Antonio; Sleeping Tiger, The; Smiling Ghost, The; South of St. Louis; Split Second (1953); This Happy Feeling; Tough Guys; Two Mrs. Carrolls, The; Young Philadelphians, The

Smith, Allison: At First Sight (1995); Jason Goes to Hell: The Final Friday; Reason to Believe, A

Smith, Amber: Faithful

Smith, Anna Deavere: American President, The

Smith, Anna Nicole: Skyscraper; To The Limit

Smith, Art: Letter from an Unknown Woman

Smith, Bessie: Ladies Sing the Blues, The

Smith, Brittany Alyse: Treasure of Pirate's Point

Smith, Brooke: Vanya on 42nd Street

Smith, Bubba: Black Moon Rising; My Samurai; Police Academy; Police Academy II: Their First Assignment; Police Academy III: Back in Training; Police Academy 4: Citizens on Patrol; Police Academy 5: Assignment: Miami Beach; Police Academy 6: City Under Siege; Wild Pair, The

Smith, C. Aubrey: Adventures of Mark Twain, The (1944); And Then There Were None; Another Thin Man; Balalaika; Beyond Tomorrow; Bombshell (1933); Cleopatra (1934); Dr. Jekyll and Mr. Hyde (1941); Eternally Yours; Five Came Back; Four Feathers, The (1939); Little Lord Fauntleroy (1936); Lives of a Bengal Lancer, The; Lloyd's of London; Love Me Tonight; Madame Curie; Morning Glory (1933); Prisoner of Zenda, The (1937); Queen Christina; Romeo and Juliet (1936); Scarlet Empress, The; Sensations of 1945; Thoroughbreds Don't Cry; Transatlantic Tunnel; Unconquered; Wee Willie Winkie; White Cliffs of Dover, The

Smith, Caleb: Escape to White Mountain

Smith, Cedric: Penthouse, The

Smith, Charles Martin: American Graffiti; Beast, The (1996); Buddy Holly Story, The; Dead Silence (1996); Deep Cover (1992); Experts, The; Final Cut, The; Fifty/Fifty; Herbie Goes Bananas; Hot Spot; I Love Trouble; More American Graffiti; Never Cry Wolf; Rafferty and the Gold Dust Twins; Road Home, The; Roswell; Speechless; Starman; Strange Tales: Ray Bradbury Theater; Streets of Laredo; Untouchables, The; Wedding Bell Blues

Smith, Cheryl: Cinderella (1976); Laserblast; Lemora—Lady Dracula

Smith, Cotter: Bunny's Tale, A; Cameron's Closet; Lady Beware; Last Prostitute, The; Lifeform; Midnight's Child

Smith, Cynthia: For the Love of Benji

Smith, Danny: Hollywood Dreams

Smith, David Anthony: Terror in Paradise

Smith, Ebbe Roe: Big Easy, The

Smith, Forry: Black Cobra 3

Smith, G. Michael: Offerings

Smith, Geraldine: Flesh; Mixed Blood

Smith, Gregory: Small Soldiers

Smith, Gregory Edward: Harriet the Spy; Krippendorf's Tribe; Leapin' Leprechauns; Spellbreaker: Secret of the Leprechauns

Smith, Hal: Andy Griffith Show, The (TV Series)

Smith, Howard: Call Northside 777

Smith, Ian: Body Melt

Smith, Ian Michael: Simon Birch

Smith, Jack: On Moonlight Bay

Smith, Jaclyn: Bourne Identity, The; Danielle Steel's Kaleidoscope; Deja Vu (1984); George Washington; Lies Before Kisses; Night They Saved Christmas, The; Nightkill; Rage of Angels; Users, The; Windmills of the Gods

Smith, Jacob: Evolution's Child

Smith, Jada Pinkett: Return to Paradise (1998)

Smith, Jamie: Killer's Kiss

Smith, Jamie Renée: Dante's Peak; Magic in the Mirror

Smith, John: Circus World; High and the Mighty, The; Hondo and the Apaches

Smith, Julie K.: Day of the Warrior; Return to Savage Beach

Smith, Kate: This Is the Army

Smith, Keely: Thunder Road

Smith, Kent: Affair, The (1973); Badlanders, The; Cat People (1942); Curse of the Cat People, The; Death of a Gunfighter; Forever and a Day; Fountainhead, The; Hitler's Children; My Foolish Heart; Party Girl (1958); Spiral Staircase, The (1946); Strangers When We Meet

Smith, Kerr: Final Destination

Smith, Kevin: Desperate Remedies; Young Hercules

Smith, Kurtwood: Boxing Helena; Bright Shining Lie, A; Citizen Ruth; Company Business; Dead on Sight; Delos Adventure, The; Fortress (1993); Last of the Dogmen; Magnificent Seven, The (TV Series); Nightmare Years, The; Rambo III; RoboCop; Shadows and Fog; Star Trek VI: The Undiscovered Country; True Believer; Under Siege 2: Dark Territory

Smith, Lane: Between the Lines; Blind Vengeance; Displaced Person, The; Distinguished Gentleman, The; Duplicates; False Arrest; Final Days, The; Inherit the Wind (1999); Mighty Ducks, The; My Cousin Vinny; Native Son (1986); Prime Suspect (1982) (Feature); Prison; Race for Glory; Son-in-Law; Spy Within, The; Weeds

Smith, Lewis: Fulfillment; Heavenly Kid, The

Smith, Linda: Shades of Love: The Rose Cafe

Smith, Lois: Eternal, The; Falling Down; Fried Green Tomatoes; How to Make an American Quilt; Keep the Change; Next Stop, Greenwich Village; Reckless (1984); Reuben, Reuben; Twisted; Twister (1996)

Smith, Loring: Clown, The

Smith, Louise: Working Girls

Smith, Madeleine: Bawdy Adventures of Tom Jones, The; Frankenstein and the Monster from Hell; Vampire Lovers, The

Smith, Madolyn: Caller, The; Final Approach; Funny Farm; Plot to Kill Hitler, The; Pray TV (1982); Rose and the Jackal, The; Sadat; Super, The; Urban Cowboy

Smith, Maggie: California Suite; Clash of the Titans; Evil Under the Sun; First Wives Club, The; Honey Pot, The; Hook; Hot Millions; Lily in Love; Lonely Passion of Judith

Hearne, The; Missionary, The; Murder by Death; Othello (1965); Prime of Miss Jean Brodie, The; Private Function, A; Quartet (1981); Richard III (1995); Room with a View, A; Secret Garden, The (1993); Sister Act; Sister Act 2: Back in the Habit; Tea with Mussolini; Travels with My Aunt; V.I.P.s, The; Washington Square

Smith, Mel: Brain Donors; Misadventures of Mr. Wilt, The; Morons from Outer Space; Twelfth Night

Smith, Melanie: Baby Doll Murders, The; Night Hunter; Trancers III: Deth Lives

Smith, Mittie: Blue Yonder, The

Smith, Pam: Misty

Smith, Patricia: Spirit of St. Louis, The

Smith, Paul: Death Chase; Desert Kickboxer; Gor; Haunted Honeymoon; Jungle Warriors; Madron; Outlaw Force; Popeye; Red Sonja; Sadat; Salamander, The; Sno-Line; Sonny Boy; Terminal Entry; We Are No Angels

Smith, Queenie: Mississippi; My Sister Eileen

Smith, Rainbeaux: Revenge of the Cheerleaders; Slumber Party 57

Smith, Ray: King Lear (1998)

Smith, Rex: Danielle Steel's Once in a Lifetime; Passion to Kill, A; Pirates of Penzance, The; Snow White and the Seven Dwarfs (1983); Sooner or Later; Streethawk; Transformations; Trial of the Incredible Hulk

Smith, Robert: Call Out the Marines

Smith, Roger: Never Steal Anything Small

Smith, Roger Guenveur: Color of Courage, The; Facade

Smith, Sammy: How to Succeed in Business without Really Trying

Smith, Shawn: Land Unknown, The; World Without End

Smith, Shawnee: Blob, The (1988); Desperate Hours (1990); Summer School

Smith, Shelley: Taking My Turn

Smith, Shelley: Scruples

Smith, Sinjin: Side Out

Smith, Stephanie: Kiss the Girls Goodbye

Smith, Stephanie Ann: Under Lock and Key

Smith, T. Ryder: Brainscan

Smith, Ted: Adventures of the Kung Fu Rascals, The

Smith, Terri Susan: Basket Case

Smith, Will: Bad Boys (1995); Enemy of the State; Independence Day (1996); Made in America; Men in Black; Six Degrees of Separation; Wild Wild West (1999)

Smith, William: Angels Die Hard; Any Which Way You Can; B.O.R.N.; Boss; C.C. & Company; Commando Squad; Cybernator; Deadly Trackers, The; Fever Pitch; Frisco Kid, The; Gas Pump Girls; Gentle Savage; Grave of the Vampire; Invasion of the Bee Girls; L.A. Vice; Last American Hero, The; Last of the Warriors; Losers, The; Maniac Cop; Moon in Scorpio; Platoon Leader; Red Dawn; Red Nights; Rockford Files, The (TV Series); Scorchy; Spirit of the Eagle; Twilight's Last Gleaming; Ultimate Warrior, The

Smith, Willie E.: Legend of Boggy Creek

Smith, Willie Mae Ford: Say Amen, Somebody

Smith, Yeardley: Ginger Ale Afternoon; Just Write; Maximum Overdrive

Smith-Cameron, J.: Gal Young 'Un; Harriet the Spy; Rage, The; Carrie 2

Smithers, Jan: Where the Lilies Bloom

Smitrovich, Bill: Futuresport; Killing Affair, A; Miami Vice; Millennium (1996)

Smits, Jimmy: Believers, The; Cisco Kid, The; Fires Within; Glitz; L.A. Law; Last Word, The (1995); Marshal Law; Murder in Mind; My Family; Old Gringo; Price of Glory; Running Scared (1986); Solomon and Sheba (1995); Switch; Tommyknockers, The; Vital Signs

Smits, Sonja: Dead Husbands; Spenser: Pale Kings & Princes; That's My Baby; Videodrome

Smollett, Jurnee: Eve's Bayou

Smothers, Dick: Alice Through the Looking Glass (1966); Tales of the Unexpected; Yo-Yo Man

Smothers, Tom: Alice Through the Looking Glass (1966); Get to Know Your Rabbit; Kids Are Alright, The; Pandemonium; Serial; Silver Bears; Speed Zone; Yo-Yo Man

Smurfit, Victoria: Ivanhoe (1997); Run of the Country, The

Snaider, Meredith: Habit

Snape, William: Full Monty, The

Sneider, Eric: Captains Courageous (1995)

Snider, Dee: Dee Snider's Strangeland

Snipes, Wesley: America's Dream; Blade (1998); Boiling Point (1993); Demolition Man; Down in the Delta; Drop Zone; Fan, The (1996); Futuresport; Jungle Fever; King of New York; Mo' Better Blues; Money Train; Murder at 1600; New Jack City; One Night Stand (1997); Passenger 57; Rising Sun; Streets of Gold; Sugar Hill; To Wong Foo, Thanks for Everything, Julie Newmar; U.S. Marshals; Waterdance, The; White Men Can't Jump

Snodgrass, Carrie: Across the Tracks; Attic, The; Ballad of Little Jo, The; Blueberry Hill; Death Benefit; Diary of a Mad Housewife; 8 Seconds; Mission of the Shark; Murphy's Law; Night in Heaven, A; Pale Rider; Rabbit Run; Rose and the Jackal, The; Silent Night, Lonely Night; Stranger in the Kingdom, A; Trick or Treat (1982); Wild Things; Woman with a Past

Snow, Victoria: Kissing Place, The

Snowden, Jane: French Lessons

Snowden, Leigh: Creature Walks Among Us, The

Snowflake: Lawless Nineties, The; Lonely Trail, The

Snyder, Arlen Dean: Dear Detective; No Man's Land; Scalpel; Summer Dreams; Wheels of Terror

Snyder, Deb: Pushing Hands

Snyder, Drew: Blindfold: Acts of Obsession; Dance with Death; Night School; Project: Eliminator

Snyder, Maria: Prophecy, The (1995)

Snyder, Nancy: Plants Are Watching, The

Snyder, Suzanne: Killer Klowns from Outer Space

Snyder, Valerie Sedle: Merry Wives of Windsor, The

Sobel, David: Wish Me Luck

Sobieski, LeeLee: Eyes Wide Shut; Here on Earth; Horse for Danny, A; Never Been Kissed; Soldier's Daughter Never Cries, A

Socas, Maria: Warrior and the Sorceress, The

Soderbergh, Steven: Schizopolis

Soderdahl, Lars: Brothers Lionheart, The

Soeberg, Camilla: Erotique; Manifesto

Sofaer, Abraham: Captain Sinbad; Elephant Walk; His Majesty O'Keefe; Journey to the Center of Time (Time Warp); Naked Jungle, The; Quo Vadis (1951)

Sofer, Rena: Stepsister, The; Twin Sitters

Softley, Ellen: I, Zombie

Sohn, Sonja: Slam

Sojin: Thief of Bagdad, The (1924)

Sokol, Marilyn: Foul Play; Something Short of Paradise

Sokoloff, Marla: Whatever It Takes

Sokoloff, Vladimir: Baron of Arizona, The

Sola, Miguel Angel: Tango

Solanitsin, Anatoly: Stalker

Solar, Silvia: Finger on the Trigger; Gentleman Killer

Solari, Rudy: Boss' Son, The

Solari, Suzanne: Rollerblade

Soler, Andres: El Bruto (The Brute)

Soler, Fernando: Great Madcap, The; Susanna

Soles, P. J.: Alienator; Awakening of Cassie, The; B.O.R.N.; Halloween; Little Bigfoot; Power Within, The; Rock 'n' Roll High School; Saigon Commandos; Stripes

Solli, Sergio: Ciao Professore

Solntseva, Yulia: Aelita: Queen of Mars; Cigarette Girl from Mosselprom, The

Sologne, Madeleine: Eternal Return, The

Solomin, Vitaly: Siberiade

Solomin, Yuri: Dersu Uzala

Solomon, Charles: Witchcraft III, The Kiss of Death; Witchcraft IV: Witchcraft II: The Temptress

Solomon, James: Song of Freedom

Solondz, Todd: Fear, Anxiety and Depression

Soloyei, Elena: Oblomov; Slave of Love, A; Unfinished Piece for the Player Piano, An (Unfinished Piece for a Mechanical Piano, An)

Somack, Jack: Portnoy's Complaint

Somers, Kristi: Tomboy

Somers, Suzanne: Ants!; Bullitt; Magnum Force; No Laughing Matter; Nothing Personal (1980); Sky Heist; Yesterday's Hero

Somerville, Geraldine: Cracker (TV Series)

Sommars, Julie: Herbie Goes to Monte Carlo; Sex and the College Girl

Sommer, Elke: Adventures Beyond Belief; Boy, Did I Get a Wrong Number!; Carry on Behind; Corrupt Ones, The; Daniella by Night; Devil in the House of Exorcism, The; Double McGuffin, The; House of Exorcism, The; Inside the

Third Reich; Invisible Strangler; Jenny's War; Left for Dead; Lily in Love; No One Cries Forever; Oscar, The (1966); Prisoner of Zenda, The (1979); Prize, The; Probe; Severed Ties; Shot in the Dark, A; Swiss Conspiracy; Ten Little Indians (1975); Torture Chamber of Baron Blood, The; Zeppelin

Sommer, Josef: American Story, An; Assault at West Point; Bridge to Silence; Brotherly Love; Chances Are; D.A.R.Y.L.; Dracula's Widow; Enemy Within, The; Forced March; Hidden in America; Hostages; Iceman; Malice; Mistrial; Moonlight and Valentino; Next Best Thing, The; Nobody's Fool (1994); Rollover; Rosary Murders, The; Shadows and Fog; Target; Witness; Yuri Nosenko, KGB

Sondergaard, Gale: Anna and the King of Siam; Anthony Adverse; Cat and the Canary, The (1939); Climax, The; East Side, West Side; Gypsy Wildcat; Life of Emile Zola, The; Mark of Zorro, The (1940); My Favorite Blonde; Night to Remember, A (1943); Return of a Man Called Horse, The; Road to Rio; Savage Intruder, The; Sherlock Holmes and the Spider Woman; Time of Their Lives, The

Sonkkila, Paul: Mr. Reliable

Sons of the Pioneers: King of the Cowboys; Romance on the Range; Silver Spurs

Soo, Jack: Flower Drum Song; Green Berets, The; Thoroughly Modern Millie

Soo, Park Jong: Search and Destroy (1981)

SooHan, Master Bong: Kentucky Fried Movie

Soper, Mark: Blood Rage; Understudy, The; Graveyard Shift II

Sopkiw, Michael: After the Fall of New York; Blastfighter; Devilfish

Soral, Agnes: Target of Suspicion; Window to Paris

Sorbas, Elga: American Soldier, The

Sorbo, Kevin: Hercules and the Amazon Women; Hercules and the Circle of Fire; Hercules and the Lost Kingdom; Hercules in the Underworld; Kull the Conqueror

Sorcey, Juliet: Taken Away

Sordi, Alberto: I Vitelloni; White Sheik, The

Sorel, Edmond: Raising Heroes

Sorel, Jean: Adorable Julia; Belle de Jour; Circle of Love

Sorel, Louise: Get Christie Love!; Mazes and Monsters; Where the Boys Are '84

Sorel, Ted: Tempest, The (1983)

Soremekun, Kai: Back in Action

Sorensen, Cindy L.: Josh Kirby … Time Warrior: Journey to the Magic Cavern

Sorenson, Linda: Joshua Then and Now; Kavik the Wolf Dog; Stone Cold Dead

Sorenson, Rickie: Tarzan and the Trappers

Sorina, Alexandra: Hands of Orlac

Sorvino, Mira: Amongst Friends; At First Sight (1999); Barcelona; Beautiful Girls; Blue in the Face; Buccaneers, The; Free Money; Lulu on the Bridge; Mighty Aphrodite; Mimic; New York Cop; Norma Jean and Marilyn; Replacement Killers, The; Romy and Michele's High School Reunion; Summer of Sam; Sweet Nothing; Tales of Erotica; Tarantella

Sorvino, Paul: Age Isn't Everything; Backstreet Justice; Bloodbrothers; Brinks Job, The; Bulworth; Chiefs; Chiller; Cover Me; Cruising; Day of the Dolphin, The; Dick Tracy (1990); Escape Clause; Fine Mess, A; Gambler, The (1974); Goodfellas; Houdini (1998); I Will, I Will … for Now; Joe Torre: Curveballs along the Way; Knock Off; Love Is All There Is; Melanie; Money Talks; My Mother's Secret Life; Nightmare (1991); Nixon; Off the Wall; Panic in Needle Park; Parallel Lives; Question of Honor, A; Rocketeer, The; Stuff, The; That Championship Season (1982); That Championship Season; Touch of Class, A; Urge to Kill; Vasectomy; William Shakespeare's Romeo and Juliet

Sothern, Ann: Best Man, The (1964); Blue Gardenia, The; Brother Orchid; Crazy Mama; Judge Steps Out, The; Kid Millions; Lady Be Good; Lady in a Cage; Letter to Three Wives, A; Manitou, The; Nancy Goes to Rio; Panama Hattie; Thousands Cheer; Whales of August, The; Words and Music

Sothern, Hugh: Captain America (1944)

Soto, Hugo: Man Facing Southeast; Times to Come

Soto, Talisa: Corporate Ladder; Don Juan DeMarco; Hostage (1992); Mortal Kombat; Mortal Kombat: Annihilation; Sunchaser; Vampirella

Sou, Robin: Beverly Hills Ninja

Soualem, Zinedine: When the Cat's Away

Souchon, Alain: One Deadly Summer

Soul, David: Appointment with Death; Cry in the Wind; Dogpound Shuffle; FBI Murders, The; Grave Secrets: The Legacy of Hilltop Drive; Hanoi Hilton; In the Cold of the Night; Johnny Got His Gun; Key to Rebecca, The; Little Ladies of the Night; Magnum Force; Manions of America, The; Pentathlon; Rage (1980); Salem's Lot; Stick-Up, The; Through Naked Eyes; Tides of War; World War III

Soutendijk, Renee: Eve of Destruction; Forced March; Fourth Man, The; Grave Secrets; Keeper of the City; Murderers Among Us: The Simon Wiesenthal Story; Spetters

Southwood, Charles: Guns for Dollars

Soyka, Doris Anne: Dead Silence (1989)

Spaak, Catherine: Cat O'Nine Tails; Empty Canvas, The; Hotel; Take a Hard Ride

Space, Arthur: Panther Girl of the Congo; Terror at the Red Wolf Inn (Terror House)

Spacek, Sissy: Affliction; Badlands (1973); Beyond the Call; Blast from the Past; Carrie (1976); Coal Miner's Daughter; Crimes of the Heart; Ginger in the Morning; Girls of Huntington House; Good Ol' Boys, The; Grass Harp, The; Hard Promises; Heart Beat; If These Walls Could Talk; JFK; Katherine; Long Walk Home, The; Marie; Migrants, The; Missing; Night, Mother; Place for Annie, A; Prime Cut; Private Matter, A; Raggedy Man; River, The (1984); Straight Story, The; Streets of Laredo; Trading Mom; Violets Are Blue; Welcome to L.A.

Spacey, Kevin: Consenting Adults (1992); Dad; Doomsday Gun; Glengarry Glen Ross; Henry & June; Hurlyburly; Iron Will; L.A. Confidential; Long Day's Journey into Night (1987); Looking for Richard; Midnight in the Garden of Good and Evil; Murder of Mary Phagan, The; Negotiator, The; Outbreak; Ref, The; See No Evil, Hear No Evil; Seven; Swimming with Sharks; Time to Kill, A (1996); Usual Suspects, The

Spade, David: Black Sheep; Coneheads; 8 Heads in a Duffel Bag; Lost & Found (1999); PCU; Senseless; Tommy Boy

Spader, James: Bad Influence; Cocaine: One Man's Seduction; Crash (1996); Critical Care; Discovery Program; Dream Lover (1994); Jack's Back; Keys to Tulsa; Less Than Zero; Music of Chance, The; New Kids, The; Pretty in Pink; sex, lies and videotape; Stargate; Supernova; True Colors; Tuff Turf; Two Days in the Valley; Wall Street; White Palace; Wolf

Spain, Douglas: Star Maps

Spain, Fay: Al Capone; Flight to Fury; God's Little Acre; Hercules and the Captive Women

Spalding, B. J.: Bail Jumper

Spall, Timothy: Dutch Girls; Gothic; Home Sweet Home (1982); Life Is Sweet; Secrets and Lies; Sheltering Sky, The; Still Crazy; Topsy-Turvy

Spano, Joe: Apollo 13; Cast the First Stone; Disaster at Silo 7; Dunera Boys, The; Fever; Great Los Angeles Earthquake, The; Hill Street Blues (TV Series); Northern Lights; Rave Review; Terminal Choice

Spano, Vincent: Afterburn; Alive; Alphabet City; And God Created Woman (1987); Ascent, The; Baby, It's You; Black Stallion Returns, The; Blood Ties (1987); Brooklyn State of Mind, A; City of Hope; Creator; Double McGuffin, The; Downdraft; Gentleman Bandit, The; Good Morning, Babylon; Indian Summer; Maria's Lovers; Oscar (1991); Prophecy 3: The Ascent; Rumble Fish; Tie That Binds, The

Sparks, Don: Fairy Tales

Sparks, Ned: Bureau of Secret; Bride Walks Out, The; Going Hollywood; Magic Town; One in a Million; Sweet Adeline

Sparks, Tom: Movie, in Your Face!

Sparrowhawk, Leo: Out on Bail

Sparv, Camilla: Dead Heat on a Merry-Go-Round; Downhill Racer; Greek Tycoon, The; Survival Zone

Spaulding, Tracy: Striking Point

Speakman, Jeff: Deadly Outbreak; Escape from Atlantis; Expert, The; Perfect Weapon; Scorpio One; Street Knight

Spears, Aries: Out of Sync

Speciale, Linda: Screwballs

Speck, David: Client, The

Spector, Daniel: Running Wild (1994)

Speed, Carol: Avenging Disco Godfather

Speer, Hugo: Full Monty, The

Speir, Dona: Fit to Kill; Hard Ticket to Hawaii; Savage Beach

Spell, George: Dream for Christmas, A; Man and Boy

Spelling, Tori: House of Yes, The; Trick

Spelvin, Georgina: I Spit on Your Corpse

Spence, Bruce: ... Almost; Mad Max Beyond Thunderdome; Rikki and Pete; Road Warrior, The; Where the Green Ants Dream

Spence, Sebastian: Boys of St. Vincent

Spencer, Bud: Ace High; Aladdin (1987); Beyond the Law (1968); Boot Hill; Massacre at Fort Holman (Reason to Live ... A Reason to Die, A); Miami Supercops; Saddle Tramps; They Call Me Trinity; Trinity Is Still My Name; Troublemakers

Spencer, Chris: Don't Be a Menace to South Central while Drinking Your Juice in the 'Hood

Spencer, Danielle: Crossing, The

Spencer, Jeremy: Prince and the Showgirl, The

Spencer, John: Albino Alligator; Cafe Society; Cold Around the Heart; Negotiator, The; Presumed Innocent; Rock, The

Spencer, Marv: Killing Edge, The

Spengler, Volker: In a Year of 13 Moons; Satan's Brew

Sperandeo, Tony: La Scorta

Sperber, Wendie Jo: Bosom Buddies (TV Series); First Time, The; I Wanna Hold Your Hand; Mr. Write; Moving Violations; Stewardess School

Sperberg, Fritz: Lucky Luke

Sperry, Corwyn: Sudden Thunder

Spice Girls: Spice World

Spicer, Jerry: Witchcraft VI: The Devil's Mistress

Spiegel, Scott: Dead Next Door, The; Robot Ninja; Skinned Alive

Spielberg, David: Effect of Gamma Rays on Man-in-the-Moon Marigolds, The; Silent Predators

Spielberg, Steven: Survivors of the Holocaust

Spiesser, Jacques: Baxter (1988); Black and White in Color; La Truite (The Trout)

Spill, Stormy: Mutant Hunt

Spillane, Mickey: Girl Hunters, The

Spilsbury, Klinton: Legend of the Lone Ranger, The

Spindler, Will: Last Five Days, The

Spinell, Joe: Big Score, The; Hollywood Harry; Last Horror Film, The; Maniac (1980); Ninth Configuration, The; Operation War Zone; Star Crash; Strike Force; Vigilante

Spinella, Stephen: Love! Valour! Compassion!; Virtuosity

Spiner, Brent: Independence Day (1996); Introducing Dorothy Dandridge; Out to Sea; Phenomenon; Pie in the Sky; Star Trek: First Contact; Star Trek: Generations; Star Trek: Insurrection; Star Trek: The Next Generation (TV Series)

Spinetti, Victor: Hard Day's Night, A; Help!

Spitz, Mark: Challenge of a Lifetime

Spitzer, Peter M.: Meateater, The

Spolt, William: Rattler Kid

Spoonauer, Lisa: Clerks

Spottiswood, Greg: Looking for Miracles

Spradlin, G. D.: And I Alone Survived; Ed Wood; Formula, The; Long Kiss Goodnight, The; Lords of Discipline, The; North Dallas Forty; One on One; Riders of the Purple Sage, Tank; War of the Roses, The; Wrong Is Right

Spradling, Charlie: Angel of Destruction; Puppet Master II; To Sleep With a Vampire

Spriggs, Elizabeth: Sense and Sensibility; Those Glory Glory Days

Spring, Helen: Hazel Christmas Show, The (TV Series)

Springer, Gary: Bernice Bobs Her Hair

Springer, Jerry: Ringmaster; Since You've Been Gone

Springfield, Rick: Dead Reckoning (1990); Hard to Hold; Nick Knight; Silent Motive

Springsteen, Pamela: Sleepaway Camp II: Unhappy Campers; Sleepaway Camp III

Sprinkle, Annie: My Father Is Coming

Sprouse, Cole: Big Daddy

Sprouse, Dylan: Big Daddy

Spybey, Dina: Julian Po; SubUrbia (1997)

Squire, Ronald: Encore

Squire, Sean: Passing Glory

Sridevi: God Is My Witness

St. Alban, Nancy: Durango

St. Louis, Dean: Coroner, The

Stabile, Nick: Bride of Chucky

Stack, Don: Santa with Muscles

Stack, Joanna Leigh: Paradise Motel

Stack, Robert: Airplane!; Beavis and Butt-head Do America (voice); Big Trouble; Bullfighter and the Lady, The; Cad-

dyshack II; Corrupt Ones, The; Dangerous Curves; Date with Judy, A; First Love (1939); George Washington; High and the Mighty, The; Is Paris Burning?; Joe Versus the Volcano; John Paul Jones; Last Voyage, The; Mr. Music; Mortal Storm, The; Most Wanted (1976); Murder on Flight 502; Plain Clothes; Return of Eliot Ness, The; Tarnished Angels, The; To Be or Not to Be (1942); Uncommon Valor; Untouchables, The: Scarface Mob; Written on the Wind

Stacy, James: Double Exposure (1982); Matters of the Heart; Posse (1975); Swingin' Summer, A

Stadlen, Lewis J.: Between the Lines; Savages (1973); Windy City

Staff, Kathy: Mary Reilly

Stafford, Chris: Edge of Seventeen

Stafford, Frederick: Battle of El Alamein, The; Topaz

Stafford, Jo: Ship Ahoy

Stafford, Jon: Crossing the Line (1990)

Stahelski, Chad: Nemesis 2

Stahl, Lisa: Shallow Grave (1987)

Stahl, Nick: Blue River; Disturbing Behavior; Man without a Face, The; Safe Passage; Tall Tale: The Unbelievable Adventures of Pecos Bill

Staiola, Enzo: Bicycle Thief, The

Staley, James: Robot Wars

Staley, Joan: Ghost and Mr. Chicken, The

Stallone, Frank: Barfly; Fear (1988); Heart of Midnight; Lethal Games; Order of the Eagle; Outlaw Force; Pink Chiquitas, The; Public Enemy #1; Ten Little Indians (1989)

Stallone, Jacqueline: Beach Babes from Beyond

Stallone, Sage: Fatally Yours

Stallone, Sylvester: Alan Smithee Film, An—Burn Hollywood Burn; Assassins; Cannonball; Cliffhanger; Cobra (1986); Copland; Daylight; Death Race 2000; Demolition Man; First Blood; F.I.S.T.; Judge Dredd; Lock Up; Lords of Flatbush, The; Nighthawks; Oscar (1991); Over the Top; Paradise Alley; Rambo: First Blood II; Rambo III; Rebel (1973); Rhinestone; Rocky; Rocky II; Rocky III; Rocky IV; Rocky V; Specialist, The; Stop! Or My Mom Will Shoot; Tango and Cash; Victory

Stallybrass, Anne: Six Wives of Henry VIII, The (TV Series)

Stalmaster, Hal: Johnny Tremain

Stamos, John: Alice Through the Looking Glass (1985); Born to Ride; Disappearance of Christina, The; Never Too Young to Die

Stamp, Terence: Adventures of Priscilla, Queen of the Desert, The; Alien Nation; Billy Budd; Bliss (1997); Blue (1968); Bowfinger; Collector, The; Divine Nymph, The; Far from the Madding Crowd; Genuine Risk; Hit, The (1984); Kiss the Sky; Legal Eagles; Limey, The; Link; Meetings with Remarkable Men; Real McCoy, The; Sicilian, The; Star Wars: Episode I The Phantom Menace; Superman II; Teorema; Thief of Baghdad (1978); Wall Street

Stanczak, Wadeck: Rendez-Vous; Scene of the Crime (1987)

Stander, Lionel: Beyond the Law (1968); Black Bird, The; Boot Hill; Cul-de-Sac; Dandy in Aspic, A; Last Good Time, The; Loved One, The; Mad Wednesday (see also Sin of Harold Diddlebook); Matilda; Mr. Deeds Goes to Town; New York, New York; Once Upon a Time in the West; Pulp; St. Benny the Dip; Scoundrel, The; Sensual Man, The; Sin of Harold Diddlebook (Mad Wednesday); Specter of the Rose, The; Unfaithfully Yours (1948)

Standing, Guy: Bulldog Drummond Escapes; Death Takes a Holiday; Lives of a Bengal Lancer, The

Standing, John: Legacy, The; Man Who Knew Too Little, The; Mrs. Dalloway; Nightflyers; Privates on Parade; Walk, Don't Run; X, Y and Zee

Stanford, Nathania: Return to the Lost World

Stang, Arnold: Hercules Goes Bananas; Man with the Golden Arm, The

Stanley, Alvah: Romeo and Juliet (1983)

Stanley, Edwin: Mysterious Dr. Satan

Stanley, Florence: Fortune, The; Prisoner of Second Avenue, The; Trapped in Paradise

Stanley, Forrest: Outlaws of the Desert

Stanley, Kim: Cat on a Hot Tin Roof (1985); Danger; Frances; Goddess, The; Right Stuff, The; Seance on a Wet Afternoon

Stanley, Louise: Riders of the Rockies; Sing, Cowboy, Sing

Stanley, Mike: Dead Is Dead

Stanley, Pat: Ladies' Man, The

Stanley, Paul: I Heard the Owl Call My Name; Kiss Meets the Phantom of the Park

Stanley, Rebecca: Eyes of Fire

Stansbury, Hope: Rats are Coming! The Werewolves Are Here!, The

Stansfield, Claire: Mind Ripper; Sensation; Sweepers; Swordsman, The

Stanski, Ben: Burglar From Hell; Jacker 2: Descent to Hell; Tales Till the End

Stanton, Harry Dean: Against the Wall; Alien; Black Marble, The; Blue Tiger; Christine; Cockfighter; Dead Man's Walk; Death Watch; Dillinger (1973); Down Periscope; Farewell My Lovely; Fire Down Below; Flatbed Annie and Sweetie Pie: Lady Truckers; Fool for Love; Fourth War, The; Hostages; Hotel Room; Last Temptation of Christ, The; Man Trouble; Mighty, The; Missouri Breaks, The; Mr. North; Never Talk to Strangers; 92 in the Shade; Oldest Living Graduate, The; One from the Heart; One Magic Christmas; Paris, Texas; Payoff; Playback; Pretty in Pink; Rafferty and the Gold Dust Twins; Rancho Deluxe; Rebel Rousers; Red Dawn; Repo Man; Ride in the Whirlwind; Rose, The; She's So Lovely; Slam Dance; Stars and Bars; Straight Story, The; Straight Time; Twin Peaks: Fire Walk with Me; Twister (1988); Uforia; Where the Lilies Bloom; Wild at Heart; Wise Blood; Young Doctors in Love; Zandy's Bride

Stanton, John: Dusty; Great Expectations—The Untold Story; Kitty and the Bagman; Naked Country, The; Run, Rebecca, Run; Tai-Pan

Stanton, Maria: Voodoo Dolls

Stanton, Robert: Abbott and Costello in Hollywood; Dennis the Menace

Stanwyck, Barbara: All I Desire; Baby Face; Ball of Fire; Big Valley, The (TV Series); Bitter Tea of General Yen, The; Blowing Wild; Bride Walks Out, The; Cattle Queen of Montana; Christmas in Connecticut (1945); Clash by Night; Crime of Passion; Cry Wolf; Double Indemnity; East Side, West Side; Escape to Burma; Executive Suite; Golden Boy; Great Man's Lady, The; Hollywood Canteen; Illicit; Interns Can't Take Money; Ladies of Leisure; Ladies They Talk About; Lady Eve, The; Lady of Burlesque; Mad Miss Manton, The; Maverick Queen, The; Meet John Doe; Night Nurse; Night Walker, The; Purchase Price, The; Remember the Night; Roustabout; Sorry, Wrong Number (1948); Stella Dallas; Strange Love of Martha Ivers, The; This Is My Affair; Thornbirds, The; Titanic (1953); To Please a Lady; Two Mrs. Carrolls, The; Union Pacific; Violent Men, The; Walk on the Wild Side

Stapel, Huub: Amsterdamned; Attic: The Hiding of Anne Frank; Lift, The

Stapleton, Jean: Cinderella (1985); Eleanor: First Lady of the World; Grown-Ups; Habitation of Dragons, The; Lily Dale; Michael; Up the Down Staircase; You've Got Mail

Stapleton, Maureen: Addicted to Love; Cocoon; Cocoon: The Return; Electric Grandmother, The; Fan, The; Gathering, The; Gathering, Part II, The; Heartburn; Johnny Dangerously; Last Good Time, The; Little Gloria, Happy at Last; Lonelyhearts; Lost and Found (1979); Made in Heaven (1987); Money Pit, The; Nuts; On the Right Track; Passed Away; Plaza Suite; Queen of the Stardust Ballroom; Reds; Runner Stumbles, The; Sweet Lorraine; Trading Mom

Stapley, Richard: Strange Door, The

Star, Holly: Prehistoric Bimbos in Armageddon City

Stark, Jonathan: House II: The Second Story; Project X

Stark, Koo: Emily

Starke, Anthony: Magnificent Seven, The (TV Series); Return of the Killer Tomatoes

Starr, Beau: Check Is in the Mail, The; Dead Air; Empire City; Glory Years; Halloween V: The Revenge of Michael Myers; Prisoner of Love

Starr, Blaze: Blaze Starr: The Original

Starr, Emerald: Men in Love

Starr, Fredro: Ride; Sunset Park

Starr, Mike: Clockers; Deli, The; Dumb and Dumber; Ed Wood; Gloria (1999); Just Your Luck; Mad Dog and Glory; Mardi Gras for the Devil

Starr, Ringo: Alice in Wonderland (1985); Caveman; Give My Regards to Broad Street; Kids Are Alright, The; Lisztomania; Magic Christian, The; Princess Daisy; Sextette; Son of Dracula (1974); That'll Be the Day; 200 Motels

Starret, Jennifer: Frightmare

Starrett, Charles: Badmen of the Hills; Mask of Fu Manchu The; Silver Streak (1934)

Starrett, Jack: Brothers in Arms; Cry Blood, Apache; Death Chase; First Blood; Mr. Horn; Nightwish

Statham, Jason: Lock, Stock and Two Smoking Barrels

Staunton, Imelda: Antonia & Jane; Deadly Advice; Much Ado About Nothing; Peter's Friends

Stavin, Mary: Opponent, The

Steadman, Alison: Abigail's Party; Blame It on the Bellboy Clockwise; Kipperbang; Life Is Sweet; Misadventures of Mr Wilt, The; Pride and Prejudice (1996); Tartuffe

Steadman, Lynda: Career Girls

Steafel, Sheila: Bloodbath at the House of Death

Steckler, Ray Dennis: Las Vegas Weekend

Steed, Maggie: Intimate Contact; Summer House, The

Steel, Amy: April Fool's Day; Friday the 13th, Part II; Walk Like a Man; What Ever Happened To . . . ?

Steel, Anthony: Malta Story, The; Master of Ballantrae The; Wooden Horse, The

Steele, Barbara: Black Sunday (1961); Caged Heat; Capitol Conspiracy, The; Castle of Blood (Castle of Terror) Curse of the Crimson Altar; 8 ; Ghost, The (1963); Horrible Dr. Hichcock, The (Terror of Dr. Hichcock, The); La Dolce Vita; Nightmare Castle; Pit and the Pendulum, The (1961) She Beast, The; Silent Scream; Terror Creatures from the Grave; They Came from Within

Steele, Bob: Arizona Gunfighter; Atomic Submarine, The Bandits of Dark Canyon; Big Sleep, The (1946); Border Phantom; Carson City Kid; Comancheros, The; Decision at Sundown; Gangs of Sonora; Giant from the Unknown; Island in the Sky; Kid Ranger; Lightnin' Crandall; Lone Star Raiders; Mystery Squadron; Northwest Trail; Pork Chop Hill; Powdersmoke Range; Revenge of the Zombies; Riders for Justice; Riders of the Rio Grande; Rio Bravo; Smokey Trails; Trail Blazers; Trailin' North; Under Texas Skies; Wild-fire (1945)

Steele, Karen: Decision at Sundown; Hazel Christmas Show, The (TV Series); Ride Lonesome; Rise and Fall of Legs Diamond, The

Steele, Pippa: Vampire Lovers, The

Steele, Tom: Dangers of the Canadian Mounted; King of the Rocketmen

Steele, Tommy: Finian's Rainbow; Half a Sixpence; Happiest Millionaire, The

Steelman, Ron: Out for Blood

Steen, Irving: Fall of the House of Usher, The (1949)

Steen, Jessica: On Hostile Ground; Sing; Trial and Error (1997)

Steen, Paprika: Celebration, The

Steenburgen, Mary: Attic: The Hiding of Anne Frank; Back to the Future III; Butcher's Wife, The; Clifford; Cross Creek Dead of Winter; End of the Line; Goin' South; Grass Harp The; Gulliver's Travels (1996) (Television); Melvin and Howard; Midsummer Night's Sex Comedy, A; Miss Firecracker; My Summer Story; Nixon; One Magic Christmas Parenthood; Philadelphia; Pontiac Moon; Powder; Ragtime; Romantic Comedy; Time After Time; Whales of August, The; What's Eating Gilbert Grape?

Stefani, Michael: Trancers

Stefansdottir, Ingibjorg: Viking Sagas, The

Steffen, Anthony: Gentleman Killer

Steffen, Geary: Wintertime

Stegers, Bernice: Frozen Terror; Girl, The; Xtro

Steiger, Rod: Al Capone; American Gothic; Amityville Horror, The; Back from Eternity; Ballad of the Sad Cafe, The; Black Water; Breakthrough; Captain Nuke and the Bomber Boys; Carpool; Catch the Heat; Chosen, The; Court-martial of Billy Mitchell, The; Dr. Zhivago; End of Days; F.I.S.T.; Fistful of Dynamite, A; Glory Boys, The; Guilty as Charged; Harder They Fall, The; Hennessy; Illustrated Man, The; In Pursuit of Honor; In the Heat of the Night; Incognito; January Man, The; Jesus of Nazareth; Jubal; Kindred, The; Last Contract, The; Lion of the Desert; Longest Day, The; Love and Bullets; Loved One, The; Lucky Luciano; Marty (1953) (Television); Men of Respect; Midnight Murders; Naked Face, The; Neighbor, The; No Way to Treat a Lady; Oklahoma!; On the Waterfront; Out There; Pawnbroker, The; Real Thing, The; Run of the Arrow; Seven Thieves; Shiloh; Shiloh 2: Shiloh Season; Specialist, The; Sword of Gideon; That Summer of White Roses; Waterloo

Stein, Ken: Killer Instinct

Stein, Margaret Sophie: Enemies—A Love Story; Sarah, Plain and Tall

Stein, Mary: Babe: Pig in the City

Stein, Saul: Beer; New Jersey Drive; No Way Home

Steinberg, David: End, The; Something Short of Paradise

Steinem, Gloria: Infamous Dorothy Parker, The

Steiner, John: Ark of the Sun God ... Temple of Hell, The; Beyond the Door 2; Blood and Guns (Tepepa); Cut and Run; Devil Within Her, The; Massacre in Rome; Operation 'Nam; Sinbad of the Seven Seas; Unsane

Steinmetz, Richard: Skyscraper

Steinmiller, Robert J.: Jack the Bear; Ref, The

Steis, William: Demon of Paradise; Eye of the Eagle

Stelfox, Shirley: Personal Services

Stelling, Frans: Rembrandt—1669

Sten, Anna: Girl with the Hatbox, The; So Ends Our Night; Soldier of Fortune

Stenborg, Helen: Flash of Green, A

Stensgaard, Yutte: Lust for a Vampire

Stepanek, Karel: Sink the Bismarck

Stephane, Nicole: Les Enfants Terribles

Stephen, Daniel: Warbus

Stephens, Harvey: Evelyn Prentice; Forlorn River; Oklahoma Kid, The

Stephens, James: Getaway, The (1994); Gone to Texas; Pancho Barnes

Stephens, Martin: Innocents, The (1961)

Stephens, Matt: Dead Hate the Living, The

Stephens, Perry: Two Bits & Pepper

Stephens, Robert: American Roulette; Century; Duellists, The; Henry V (1989); High Season; Morgan; Prime of Miss Jean Brodie, The; Private Life of Sherlock Holmes, The; Searching for Bobby Fischer; Shout, The (1979); Spirit of the Dead; Taste of Honey, A; Travels with My Aunt; Wonderland

Stephens, Toby: Photographing Fairies; Twelfth Night

Stephenson, Henry: Animal Kingdom, The; Bill of Divorcement, A; Captain Blood; Challenge to Lassie; Charge of the Light Brigade, The (1936); Conquest; Down Argentine Way; Julia Misbehaves; Mutiny on the Bounty (1935); Private Lives of Elizabeth and Essex, The; Red-Headed Woman; Song of Love; Spring Parade; Tarzan Finds a Son; Tomorrow at Seven

Stephenson, James: Beau Geste; Letter, The

Stephenson, Mark Kinsey: Unnamable, The; Unnamable II, The; Where Evil Lies

Stephenson, Michael: Troll II

Stephenson, Pamela: Bloodbath at the House of Death; Les Patterson Saves the World; Scandalous (1983); Superman III

Sterling, David Michael: Eyes of the Serpent

Sterling, Ford: Keystone Comedies: Vol. 1–5; Show-Off, The (1926)

Sterling, Jan: First Monday in October; Harder They Fall, The; High and the Mighty, The; High School Confidential!; 1984 (1955); Pony Express; Split Second (1953); Union Station

Sterling, Lesli Kay: Forbidden Games (1995)

Sterling, Mindy: Austin Powers: The Spy Who Shagged Me

Sterling, Philip: Death of the Incredible Hulk, The

Sterling, Robert: Adventures of Topper, The; Global Affair, A; Johnny Eager; Return to Peyton Place; Somewhere I'll Find You; Sundowners, The (1950); Two-Faced Woman; Voyage to the Bottom of the Sea

Sterling, Tisha: Coogan's Bluff; Killer Inside Me, The; Powderkeg; Snatched

Stern, Daniel: Born in East L.A.; Boss' Wife, The; Breaking Away; Bushwhacked; Celtic Pride; C.H.U.D.; City Slickers; City Slickers II; Coupe De Ville; Court-martial of Jackie Robinson, The; Diner; D.O.A. (1988); Frankenweenie; Friends, Lovers & Lunatics; Get Crazy; Hannah and Her Sisters; Home Alone; Home Alone 2: Lost in New York; Key Exchange; Leviathan; Little Monsters; Milagro Beanfield War, The; Rookie of the Year; Very Bad Things; Weekend War

Stern, Deborah: Nudist Colony of the Dead

Stern, Erik: Love Butcher

Stern, Howard: Private Parts (1997)

Stern, Miroslava: Criminal Life of Archibaldo de la Cruz, The

Stern, Tom: Hell's Angels '69

Stern, Wes: Three in the Cellar

Sternhagen, Frances: Bright Lights, Big City; Communion; Con, The; Independence Day; Man That Corrupted Hadleyburg, The; Misery; Outland; Prototype; Raising Cain; Romantic Comedy; See You in the Morning; Sibling Rivalry; Starting Over; Stephen King's Golden Years (TV Series)

Stevenin, Sagamore: Romance (1999)

Stevens, Andrew: Bastard, The; Boys in Company C, The; Counterforce; Deadly Rivals; Death Hunt; Double Threat; Down the Drain; Fury, The (1978); Massacre at Central High; Miracle on Ice; Munchie; Munchie Strikes Back; Rebels, The; Red-Blooded American Girl; Scared Stiff; Scorned; Scorned 2; Skateboard Kid 2, The; Ten to Midnight; Terror Within, The; Terror Within 2, The; Tusks

Stevens, Bill: Federal Operator 99

Stevens, Brinke: Bad Girls from Mars; Cyberzone; Grandma's House; Mommy; Mommy 2: Mommy's Day; Slave Girls from Beyond Infinity; Sorority Babes in the Slimeball Bowl-O-Rama; Spirits; Teenage Exorcist

Stevens, Casey: Prom Night

Stevens, Charles: Bold Caballero, The; Mystery Ranch; Vanishing American, The

Stevens, Connie: Back to the Beach; Littlest Angel, The; Love Is All There Is; Love's Savage Fury; Palm Springs Weekend; Parrish; Playmates; Scorchy; Side Show; Tapeheads; Two on a Guillotine

Stevens, Craig: Deadly Mantis, The; Dive Bomber; Doughgirls, The; Drums in the Deep South; French Line, The; Humoresque; Man I Love, The; Peter Gunn (TV Series); Phone Call from a Stranger; S.O.B.

Stevens, Fisher: Boss' Wife, The; Cold Fever; Hackers; Marrying Man, The; My Science Project; Mystery Date; Nina Takes a Lover; Only You (1994); Right to Remain Silent, The; Short Circuit; Short Circuit 2; Super Mario Brothers, The; When the Party's Over

Stevens, Inger: Dream of Kings, A; Firecreek; Five Card Stud; Guide for the Married Man, A; Hang 'em High; Madigan

Stevens, K. T.: Great Man's Lady, The; Missile to the Moon; Port of New York

Stevens, Kimberly: Evil Obsession

Stevens, Mark: Dark Corner, The; Snake Pit, The; Street with No Name; Torpedo Alley

Stevens, Morgan: Survival Zone

Stevens, Onslow: Angel on My Shoulder (1946); Creeper, The; Hills of Utah, The; House of Dracula; Lonelyhearts; Secret of the Blue Room, The; Sunset Serenade; Three Musketeers, The (1935); Three on the Trail

Stevens, Paul: Get Christie Love!; Mask, The (1961)

Stevens, Rise: Chocolate Soldier, The; Going My Way

Stevens, Shadoe: Death Artist; Traxx

Stevens, Stella: Adventures Beyond Belief; Arnold; Ballad of Cable Hogue, The; Chained Heat; Cleopatra Jones and the Casino of Gold; Courtship of Eddie's Father, The; Cruise into Terror; Exiled in America; Express to Terror; Girls! Girls! Girls!; Granny, The; Invisible Mom; Jake Spanner Private Eye; Las Vegas Lady; Last Call; Li'l Abner (1959); Longshot, The (1985); Make Me an Offer; Manitou, The; Molly & Gina; Monster in the Closet; Nutty Professor, The; Poseidon Adventure, The; Slaughter; Star Hunter; Terror Within 2, The; Town Called Hell, A; Virtual Combat; Wacko

Stevens, Tabitha: Major Rock

Stevenson, Charles: Grandma's Boy

Stevenson, Cynthia: Air Bud; Golden Receiver; Forget Paris; Happiness; Live Nude Girls; Player, The; Watch It

Stevenson, Juliet: Drowning by Numbers; Emma (1996); Secret Rapture, The; Trial, The (1992); Truly, Madly, Deeply

Stevenson, McLean: M*A*S*H (TV Series); Win, Place or Steal

Stevenson, Parker: Are You Lonesome Tonight; Lifeguard; Not of This Earth (1995); Official Denial; Separate Peace, A; Shades of Love: The Rose Cafe; Stitches; Stroker Ace

Stevenson, Ray: Return of the Native, The

Stevenson, Venetia: Horror Hotel; Studs Lonigan

Stewardson, Deon: Warriors from Hell

Stewart, Alexandra: Fire Within, The; Full Hearts and Empty Pockets; In Praise of Older Women; Under the Cherry Moon

Stewart, Brian Paul: Homeboys II: Crack City

Stewart, Catherine Mary: Cafe Romeo; Dudes; Last Starfighter, The; Mischief; Night of the Comet; Nightflyers;

Taggart, Rita: Horror Show, The; Webber's World (At Home with the Webbers)

Taghmaoui, Said: Hate; Hideous Kinky

Tagore, Sharmila: Days and Nights in the Forest; World of Apu, The

Taguchi, Hiromasa: Shall We Dance? (1996)

Taguchi, Tomoroh: Tetsuo II: Body Hammer; Tetsuo: The Iron Man

Taimak: Last Dragon, The

Tainsh, Tracy: Frenchman's Farm

Tait, Tristan: Rose Hill

Taka, Miiko: Walk, Don't Run

Takahashi, Etsushi: 8Man

Takaki, Mio: Berlin Affair, The

Takakura, Ken: Antarctica; Black Rain (1989); Mr. Baseball; Yakuza, The

Takamine, Hideko: Mistress, The (1953); When a Woman Ascends the Stairs

Takarada, Akira: Godzilla vs. Monster Zero; Godzilla vs. Mothra; Latitude Zero; Minbo, or The Gentle Art of Japanese Extortion

Takarada, Junko: Traffic Jam

Takashima, Tadao: King Kong vs. Godzilla; Son of Godzilla

Takayama, Akira: Picture Bride

Takei, George: Bug Buster; Green Berets, The; Kissinger and Nixon; Live by the Fist; Oblivion; Oblivion 2: Backlash; Prisoners of the Sun; Red Line 7000; Star Trek (TV Series); Star Trek: The Menagerie; Star Trek—The Motion Picture; Star Trek II: The Wrath of Khan; Star Trek III: The Search for Spock; Star Trek IV: The Voyage Home; Star Trek V: The Final Frontier; Star Trek VI: The Undiscovered Country; Walk, Don't Run

Takenaka, Naoto: Gonin; Mystery of Rampo, The; Shall We Dance? (1996)

Takle, Darien: Lost Tribe, The

Takle, Emma: Lost Tribe, The

Talbert, Charlie: Angus

Talbot, Helen: Federal Operator 99

Talbot, Lyle: Adventures of Ozzie and Harriet, The (TV Series); Atom Man vs. Superman; Batman and Robin (Adventures of Batman and Robin); Case of the Lucky Legs, The; Dixie Jamboree; Fury of the Congo; Glen or Glenda; Go West, Young Man; Jail Bait (1954); Ladies They Talk About; One Body Too Many; One Night of Love; Our Little Girl; Purchase Price, The; Second Fiddle; Shriek in the Night, A; Thirteenth Guest, The; Trapped by Television

Talbot, Nita: Amityville 1992: It's About Time; Chained Heat; Concrete Jungle, The (1982); Frightmare; I Married a Woman; Island Claws; Puppet Master II; Rockford Files, The (TV Series); Who's Got the Action?

Talbott, Gloria: Arizona Raiders; Cyclops, The; Daughter of Dr. Jekyll; Girls Town (1959); I Married a Monster from Outer Space; Leech Woman, The; Talion

Talbott, Michael: Miami Vice

Taliaferro, Hal: Federal Operator 99; Hi-Yo Silver; Lone Ranger, The (1938); Painted Stallion, The; Song of Texas

Talking Heads: Stop Making Sense

Tallichet, Margaret: Stranger on the Third Floor

Talmadge, Constance: Intolerance

Talmadge, Natalie: Art of Buster Keaton, The; Our Hospitality

Talman, William: City That Never Sleeps; Crashout; One Minute to Zero; Racket, The

Talor, Venesa: Femalien; Shandra, The Jungle Girl

Tam, Alex: Armour of God

Tamada, Paige: Santa Clause, The

Tamara: No, No Nanette

Tamba, Tetsuro: You Only Live Twice

Tamblyn, Amber: Johnny Mysto

Tamblyn, Russ: Attack of the 60 Ft. Centerfold; Blood Screams; Cimarron (1960); Don't Go Near the Water; Fastest Gun Alive, The; Haunting, The (1963); High School Confidential!; Hit the Deck; Invisible Mom; Johnny Mysto; Last Hunt, The; My Magic Dog; Necromancer; Peyton Place; Phantom Empire, The (1986); Retreat Hell; Running Mates (1992); Satan's Sadists; Seven Brides for Seven Brothers; Tom Thumb; Twin Peaks (Movie); Twin Peaks (TV Series); War of the Gargantuas; West Side Story; Win, Place or Steal; Winning Team, The; Wonderful World of the Brothers Grimm, The

Tambor, Jeffrey: Big Bully; Cocaine: One Man's Seduction; Girl, Interrupted; Gun in the House, A; House in the Hills, A; Life Stinks; Man Who Captured Eichmann, The; Man Who Wasn't There, The; Meet Joe Black; Muppets From Space; My Teacher's Wife; Pastime; Sadat; Saturday the 14th; There's Something about Mary; Three O'Clock High; Weapons of Mass Distraction; Webber's World (At Home with the Webbers)

Tamerlis, Zoe: Ms. .45; Special Effects

Tamiroff, Akim: Alphaville; Anastasia (1956); Battle Hell; Black Magic (1949); Bridge of San Luis Rey, The; Can't Help Singing; Chained; Corsican Brothers, The (1941); Deadly Sanctuary; For Whom the Bell Tolls; Gangster, The; General Died at Dawn, The; Great McGinty, The; His Butler's Sister; Hotel Paradiso; Lt. Robin Crusoe, U.S.N.; Miracle of Morgan's Creek, The; Mr. Arkadin (Confidential Report); My Girl Tisa; My Love for Yours (Honeymoon in Bali); Naughty Marietta; Northwest Mounted Police; Outpost in Morocco; Panic Button; Sadie McKee; Story of Louis Pasteur, The; Tortilla Flat; Trial, The (1963); Union Pacific

Tan, Madeline: That's the Way I Like It

Tan, Philip: Bloodsport II

Tanaka, Kinuyo: Life of Oharu; Mother (1952); Sandakan No. 8; Sansho the Bailiff

Tanaka, Kunie: Evil of Dracula

Tanaka, Sara: Rushmore

Tanaka, Shinji: Island, The (1962)

Tanaka, Yoshiko: Black Rain (1988)

Tandy, Jessica: Batteries Not Included; Best Friends; Birds, The; Bostonians, The; Camilla (1994); Cocoon; Cocoon: The Return; Desert Fox, The; Driving Miss Daisy; Forever Amber; FoxFire; Fried Green Tomatoes; Gin Game, The; House on Carroll Street, The; Nobody's Fool (1994); September Affair; Seventh Cross, The; Still of the Night; Story Lady, The; To Dance with the White Dog; Used People; World According to Garp, The

Tandy, Mark: Railway Station Man, The

Tanner, Mary: Something Special

Tanner, Tony: Stop the World I Want to Get Off

Tapping, Amanda: Stargate SG-1

Tara, Suzanne: Danger Zone, The (1986)

Tarantino, Brian: Summer of Sam

Tarantino, Quentin: Desperado; Destiny Turns on the Radio; Four Rooms; From Dusk Till Dawn; Reservoir Dogs; Sleep with Me; Somebody to Love

Taratorkin, Georgi: Crime and Punishment (1970)

Tardif, Rene: National Lampoon's Golf Punks

Tarding, Emil: Mifune

Tari, Le: Brotherhood of Death

Tarkenton, Fran: First and Ten

Tarkovsky, Andrei: Andrei Rublev

Tarrant, John: Starship

Tarrin: Monster from a Prehistoric Planet

Tashman, Lilyan: Bulldog Drummond; Frankie and Johnny (1934); Riptide; Scarlet Dawn

Tassoni, Carolina C.: Evil Clutch

Tataryn, Sean: Leather Jacket Love Story

Tate, Larenz: Dead Presidents; Inkwell, The; Love Jones; Menace II Society; Postman, The; Why Do Fools Fall In Love

Tate, Laura: Dead Space; Subspecies

Tate, Sharon: Ciao Federico!; Fearless Vampire Killers, or, Pardon Me, But Your Teeth Are in My Neck, The; Valley of the Dolls

Tati, Jacques: Jour de Fête; Mr. Hulot's Holiday; My Uncle (Mon Oncle); Parade; Playtime; Traffic

Tattoli, Elda: China Is Near

Tatum, Bradford: Stoned Age, The; Within the Rock

Taube, Sven-Bertil: Jerusalem; Puppet on a Chain

Tauber, Richard: Heart's Desire

Tavernier, Bertrand: Francois Truffaut: Stolen Moments

Tavernier, Nils: Beatrice; Post Coitum

Tavi, Tuvia: Paradise (1982)

Taxier, Arthur: Cover Girl Murders, The

Tayback, Tom: Undercover (1995)

Tayback, Vic: Alice Doesn't Live Here Anymore; Beverly Hills Bodysnatchers; Cheap Detective, The; Horseplayer; Lepke; Portrait of a Stripper; Rage (1980); Weekend Warriors

Taye-Loren, Carolyn: Witchcraft V: Dance with the Devil

Covenant, The; L.A. Story; Strangers Kiss; War and Remembrance; Whispers

Tenney, Anne: Castle, The (1997)

Tenney, Jon: Fools Rush In; Lassie; Lovelife; Music from Another Room; Twilight of the Golds, The; Watch It

Tenuta, Judy: Butch Camp

Tepper, William: Miss Right

ter Steege, Johanna: Immortal Beloved; Vanishing, The (1988); Vincent and Theo

Terajima, Susumu: After Life; Fireworks

Terao, Akira: Akira Kurosawa's Dreams; Ran

Terekhova, Margarita: Mirror, The

Teresina: On the Make

Terhune, Max: Arizona Stagecoach; Black Market Rustlers; Boothill Bandits; Fugitive Valley; Heart of the Rockies; Hit the Saddle; Manhattan Merry-Go-Round; Night Riders, The; Outlaws of Sonora; Overland Stage Raiders; Pals of the Saddle; Range Defenders; Red River Range; Ride, Ranger, Ride; Riders of the Black Hills; Riders of the Whistling Skull; Saddle Mountain Roundup; Santa Fe Stampede; Three Texas Steers; Trail of the Silver Spurs

Terkel, Studs: Eight Men Out

Terlesky, John: Allnighter, The; Chopping Mall; Damned River; Deathstalker II: Duel of the Titans; When He's Not a Stranger

Termo, Leonard: Year of the Dragon

Terra, Scott: Shadrach

Terral, Boris: Post Coitum

Terrell, Cedrick: Whispering, The

Terrell, John: Five Heartbeats, The; She's Gotta Have It

Terrell, Steve: Invasion of the Saucer Men; Motorcycle Gang

Terrence, John: Merlin's Shop of Mystical Wonders

Tramp, Terry the: Hell's Angels '69

Terry, Carl: Firing Line, The

Terry, DeSean: God's Army

Terry, Edward: Luther, The Geek

Terry, John: Big Green, The; Dangerous Woman, A; Hawk the Slayer; Killing in a Small Town; Resurrected, The; Silhouette

Terry, Kim: Slugs, the Movie

Terry, Nigel: Caravaggio; Deja Vu (1984); Edward II; Excalibur; Lion in Winter, The; Sylvia

Terry, Paul: James and the Giant Peach

Terry, Philip: Balalaika; Born to Kill; George White's Scandals; Lost Weekend, The

Terry, Ruth: Heart of the Golden West

Terry, Sheila: Haunted Gold; Lawless Frontier; 'Neath Arizona Skies; Sphinx, The (1933)

Terry, William: Stage Door Canteen

Terry-Thomas: Abominable Dr. Phibes, The; Blue Murder at St. Trinian's; Brothers In Law; Carlton-Browne of the F.O.; Danger: Diabolik; Daydreamer, The (1966); Dr. Phibes Rises Again; Don't Raise the Bridge, Lower the River; Hound of the Baskervilles, The (1977); How to Murder your Wife; I'm All Right Jack; Lucky Jim; Make Mine Mink; Naked Truth (Your Past Is Showing); School for Scoundrels; Strange Bedfellows; Those Daring Young Men in Their Jaunty Jalopies; Those Magnificent Men in Their Flying Machines; Tom Thumb; Vault of Horror; Where Were You When the Lights Went Out?; Wonderful World of the Brothers Grimm, The

Terzieff, Laurent: A Coeur Joie (Head over Heels); Milky Way, The (1970); Vanina Vanini

Tesreau, Krista: Breaking the Rules

Tessier, Genevieve: Real Howard Spritz, The

Tessier, Robert: Born Losers; Deep, The; Double Exposure (1982); Fix, The; Last of the Mohicans (1985); Lost Empire, The; Nightwalk; No Safe Haven

Tessier, Valentine: Club des Femmes; Madame Bovary (1934)

Testi, Fabio: Ambassador, The; Blood in the Streets; Contraband; Garden of the Finzi-Continis, The; Gunfire; Mussolini and I; Stateline Motel

Testud, Sylvie: Beyond Silence

Teterson, Pete: Cold River

Tethong, Gyurme: Kundun

Tevini, Thierry: Tendres Cousines

Tewes, Lauren: China Lake Murders, The; Eyes of a Stranger

Texiere, Jacob: Leaves from Satan's Book

Teyssedre, Anne: Tale of Springtime, A

Tha Dogg Pound: Show, The

Thai, Eric: Gun in Betty Lou's Handbag, The; Prisoner of Love; Puppet Masters, The; Samson and Delilah (1996); Six Degrees of Separation; Stranger Among Us, A

Thalbach, Katharina: Good Evening Mr. Wallenberg

Thall, Benj: Homeward Bound: The Incredible Journey; Homeward Bound II: Lost in San Francisco

Thames, Byron: Blame It on the Night; Seven Minutes in Heaven

Thatcher, Heather: Undying Monster, The

Thatcher, Torin: Affair in Trinidad; Crimson Pirate, The; Diane; From Hell to Borneo; Houdini (1953); Istanbul (1956); Jack the Giant Killer; 7th Voyage of Sinbad, The; Snows of Kilimanjaro, The; Strange Case of Dr. Jekyll and Mr. Hyde, The (1968)

Thate, Hilmar: Veronika Voss

Thaw, John: Business As Usual; Chaplin; Inspector Morse (TV Series); Killing Heat; Year in Provence, A

Thaxter, Phyllis: Jim Thorpe—All American; Living In A Big Way; Thirty Seconds Over Tokyo; World of Henry Orient, The

Thayer, Brynn: Game of Love, The; Hero and the Terror

Thayer, Max: No Dead Heroes; No Retreat, No Surrender II

Thayer, Meg: Omega Cop

Thayer, Tina: Jive Junction

Theirse, Darryl: I Love You, Don't Touch Me!

Thelen, Jodi: Four Friends; One Night Stand (1995)

Theremin, Leon: Theremin: An Electronic Odyssey

Theriault, Serge: Boys, The (1997)

Theron, Charlize: Astronaut's Wife, The; Celebrity (1998); Cider House Rules, The; Devil's Advocate; Hollywood Confidential; Mighty Joe Young (1998); Reindeer Games; Trial and Error (1997); Two Days in the Valley

Theroux, Justin: Body Count (1997) (direct to video); Sirens (1999)

Thesiger, Ernest: Brass Monkey, The; Bride of Frankenstein; Ghosts of Berkeley Square; Ghoul, The (1933); Old Dark House, The (1932)

Thewlis, David: Besieged; Black Beauty (1994); Dragonheart; Island of Dr. Moreau, The; Naked; Prime Suspect 3; Restoration; Seven Years in Tibet; Total Eclipse

Thibeau, Jack: Escape from Alcatraz

Thibeault, Debi: Cemetery High; Galactic Gigolo; Psychos in Love

Thicke, Alan: And You Thought Your Parents Were Weird; Any Place But Home; Betrayal of the Dove; Dance 'Til Dawn; Great American Sex Scandal, The; Not Quite Human; Not Quite Human 2; Obsessed; Rubdown; Scene of the Crime (1985); Stepmonster; Still Not Quite Human; Thunder Point; Windsor Protocol, The

Thierry, Melanie: Legend of 1900, The

Thiess, Ursula: Monsoon

Thiessen, Tiffani-Amber: Love Stinks

Thigpen, Kevin: Just Another Girl on the I.R.T.; Tar

Thinnes, Roy: Hindenburg, The; Invaders, The; Journey to the Far Side of the Sun; Rush Week; Satan's School for Girls; Scruples; Sizzle

Thirloway, Gregory: Inspectors, The; National Lampoon's Golf Punks

Thivisol, Victoire: Ponette

Thom, James: Virtual Assassin

Thomas, B. J.: Jory

Thomas, Betty: Hill Street Blues (TV Series); Homework; Prison for Children; Troop Beverly Hills; Tunnelvision (1976); When Your Lover Leaves

Thomas, Buckwheat: General Spanky

Thomas, Damien: Shogun (Full-Length Version); Sinbad and the Eye of the Tiger

Thomas, Danny: Danny Thomas Show, The (TV Series); I'll See You in My Dreams; Jazz Singer, The (1953)

Thomas, Dave: Boris and Natasha; Cold Sweat (1993); Coneheads; Love at Stake; Moving; My Man Adam; Sesame Street Presents Follow That Bird; Strange Brew

Thomas, Doug: Hangmen

Thomas, Frank: Frank and Ollie

Thomas, Gareth: Blake's 7 (TV Series)

Thomas, George: Hide and Go Shriek

Thomas, Heather: Cyclone; Dirty Dozen, The: The Fatal Mission; Ford: The Man & the Machine; Hidden Obsession; Red-Blooded American Girl; Zapped!

Thomas, Henry: Bombshell (1997); Cloak and Dagger (1984); Curse of the Starving Class; E.T.—The Extra-Terrestrial; Fire in the Sky; Hijacking Hollywood; Indictment: The McMartin Trial; Legends of the Fall; Misunderstood (1984); Moby Dick (1998); Murder One; Niagara Niagara; Psycho 4: The Beginning; Quest, The (1985); Raggedy Man; Riders of the Purple Sage; Suicide Kings; Taste for Killing, A; Valmont

Thomas, Isa: Flash of Green, A

Thomas, Jameson: Farmer's Wife, The; Scarlet Empress, The

Thomas, Jay: Mr. Holland's Opus; Mork & Mindy (TV Series); Smile Like Yours, A

Thomas, Jennifer: Desolation Angels

Thomas, Jonathan Taylor: Adventures of Pinocchio, The; I'll Be Home for Christmas; Man of the House; Tom and Huck; Wild America

Thomas, Kristin Scott: Random Hearts

Thomas, Kurt: Gymkata

Thomas, Marcus: Drowning Mona

Thomas, Marlo: Act of Passion; Consenting Adults (1985); In the Spirit; Real Blonde, The

Thomas, Philip Michael: Death Drug; Miami Vice; Miami Vice: "The Prodigal Son"; Stigma; Streetfight (Coonskin); Wizard of Speed and Time, The

Thomas, Richard: All Quiet on the Western Front (1979); Battle Beyond the Stars; Berlin Tunnel 21; Down, Out & Dangerous; Flood: A River's Rampage; Glory! Glory!; Hobson's Choice (1983); Invaders, The; It (1991); Last Summer; Linda; Living Proof: The Hank Williams, Jr., Story; Mission of the Shark; Roots: The Next Generation; September 30, 1955; Thanksgiving Story, The; Thousand Heroes, A; Todd Killings, The; Winning

Thomas, Robin: Amityville Dollhouse; Chameleon (1995); From the Dead of Night; Memories of Murder

Thomas, Ron: Night Screams

Thomas, Sian: Wedding Gift, The

Thomas, Tressa: Five Heartbeats, The

Thomassin, Florence: Mina Tannenbaum

Thomerson, Tim: Brain Smasher ... A Love Story; Cherry 2000; Detour (1999); Die Watching; Dollman; Dollman vs. Demonic Toys; Escape from Atlantis; Fade to Black (1980); Flash, The; Fleshtone; Glory Years; Harvest, The; Hong Kong '97; Incredible Hulk Returns, The; Intimate Stranger; Iron Eagle; Metalstorm: The Destruction of Jared-Syn; Natural Causes; Near Dark; Nemesis (1992); Nemesis 3: Time Lapse; Prime Time Murder; Spitfire (1994); Tiger's Tale, A; Trancers; Trancers II (The Return of Jack Deth); Trancers III: Deth Lives; Trancers 4: Jack of Swords; Trancers 5: Sudden Deth; Vietnam, Texas; Volunteers; When Time Expires; Who's Harry Crumb?; Wrong Guys, The; Zone Troopers

Thompson, Gregg: Soultaker

Thompson, Alina: Marked Man

Thompson, Andrea: Doin' Time on Planet Earth

Thompson, Brian: Catch the Heat; Commando Squad; Doctor Mordrid; Hired to Kill; Mortal Kombat: Annihilation; Nightwish; Rage and Honor

Thompson, Cindy Ann: Cave Girl

Thompson, David L.: Cat in the Brain, A

Thompson, Deborah: Prison Planet

Thompson, Derek: Belfast Assassin

Thompson, Emma: Carrington; Dead Again; Fortunes of War (1987); Henry V (1989); Howards End; Impromptu; In the Name of the Father; Judas Kiss; Junior (1994); Look Back in Anger (1989); Much Ado About Nothing; My Father, the Hero; Peter's Friends; Primary Colors; Remains of the Day; Sense and Sensibility; Tall Guy, The; Winter Guest, The

Thompson, Fred Dalton: Aces: Iron Eagle III; Baby's Day Out; Barbarians at the Gate; Born Yesterday (1993); Cape Fear (1991); Class Action; Curly Sue; Die Hard 2: Die Harder; In the Line of Fire; Keep the Change; Thunderheart

Thompson, Gordon: Donor, The

Thompson, Jack: Breaker Morant; Broken Arrow (1996); Burke and Wills; Caddie; Club, The (1985); Earthling, The; Excess Baggage; Far Off Place, A; Flesh and Blood (Sword and the Rose, the, 1985); Ground Zero; Last Dance (1996); Mad Dog Morgan; Man from Snowy River, The; Midnight in the Garden of Good and Evil; Sum of Us, The; Sunday Too Far Away; Trouble in Paradise; Turtle Beach

(Killing Beach); Wind (1992); Woman of Independent Means, A

Thompson, Jody: Deathgame

Thompson, Judy: Teach Me Tonight

Thompson, Kay: Funny Face

Thompson, Kenan: Good Burger; Heavyweights

Thompson, Kenneth: Just Imagine; Sweethearts on Parade; White Gold

Thompson, Lea: All the Right Moves; Article 99; Back to the Future; Back to the Future II; Back to the Future III; Beverly Hillbillies, The (1993); Casual Sex?; Dennis the Menace; Going Undercover; Howard the Duck; Montana (1990); Nightbreaker; Red Dawn; Right to Remain Silent, The; Some Kind of Wonderful; SpaceCamp; Substitute Wife, The; Wild Life, The; Wizard of Loneliness, The

Thompson, Marshall: Around the World Under the Sea; Bog; Clarence, the Cross-Eyed Lion; Crashout; Cult of the Cobra; East of Kilimanjaro; Fiend without a Face; First Man into Space, The; Homecoming (1948); It! The Terror from Beyond Space; Show-Off, The (1946); They Were Expendable; To Hell and Back; White Dog

Thompson, Michelle: My Sweet Suicide

Thompson, Rex: Eddy Duchin Story, The

Thompson, Sada: Indictment: The McMartin Trial; Our Town (1980); Princess Daisy; Pursuit of Happiness, The

Thompson, Shawn: Bram Stoker's Shadowbuilder; Future Fear; Hairspray; Heads; Sleeping with Strangers

Thompson, Sophie: Dancing at Lughnasa; Emma (1996)

Thompson, Susann: Ghosts of Mississippi

Thompson, Teri: Breakaway; Married People, Single Sex

Thompson, Weyman: Hot Shot

Thomsen, Ulrich: Celebration, The

Thomsett, Sally: Railway Children, The

Thomson, Anna: Cafe Society; Outside the Law (1994)

Thomson, Fred: Thundering Hoofs

Thomson, Kim: Great Expectations (1989); Murder 101; Sherlock Holmes: Hands of a Murderer; Stealing Heaven

Thomson, Pat: Strictly Ballroom

Thomson, R. H.: And Then You Die; Bone Daddy; Ford: The Man & the Machine; Heaven on Earth; If You Could See What I Hear; Lotus Eaters, The; Quarrel, The; Surfacing; Ticket to Heaven

Thor, Cameron: Face Down

Thor, Larry: Amazing Colossal Man, The

Thorburn, June: Three Worlds of Gulliver, The; Tom Thumb

Thordsen, Kelly: Ugly Dachshund, The

Thorley, Ken: Escapes; Ghost in the Machine

Thorliefsson, Eggert: Remote Control (1992)

Thornbury, Bill: Phantasm; Phantasm IV: Oblivion

Thorndike, Sybil: Major Barbara; Nine Days a Queen; Prince and the Showgirl, The; Shake Hands with the Devil

Thorne, Callie: Ed's Next Move; Next Stop Wonderland

Thorne, Dyanne: Ilsa, the Wicked Warden

Thorne-Smith, Courtney: Breach of Conduct; Chairman of the Board; Lucas; Revenge of the Nerds II: Nerds in Paradise; Summer School; Welcome to 18

Thornhill, Lisa: Enemy Action

Thornton, Billy Bob: Apostle, The; Armageddon; Don't Look Back (1996); Homegrown; Primary Colors; Pushing Tin; Simple Plan, A; Sling Blade; U-Turn; Winner, The

Thornton, Brad: Kickboxer 4: Aggressor, The

Thornton, David: Breathing Room; Off and Running

Thornton, Noley: Danielle Steel's Fine Things; Little Riders, The

Thornton, Sigrid: Great Expectations—The Untold Story; Lighthorsemen, The; Over the Hill; Return to Snowy River, Part II; Slate, Wyn, and Me; Trapped in Space

Thorogood, Maurice: House That Mary Bought, The

Thorsen, Sven-Ole: Abraxas Guardian of the Universe; Fatal Combat; Viking Sagas, The

Thorson, Linda: Act of Passion; Avengers, The (TV Series); Curtains; Sweet Liberty

Three Stooges, The: Dancing Lady; Snow White and the Three Stooges

Threlfall, David: Summer House, The

Thring, Frank: Mad Max Beyond Thunderdome

Throne, Malachi: It Takes a Thief (TV Series)

Throw, Lisa: Shandra, The Jungle Girl

Thrush, George: Vermont Is for Lovers

Thual, Jean-Yves: Red Dwarf, The

Thuillier, Luc: Monsieur Hire; Old Lady Who Walked in the Sea, The

Thulin, Ingrid: Brink of Life; Cries and Whispers; Damned, The; Four Horsemen of the Apocalypse; Hour of the Wolf; Magician, The; Moses (1975); Silence, The; Wild Strawberries; Winter Light

Thundercloud, Chief: Badman's Territory; Hi-Yo Silver; Lone Ranger, The (1938); Riders of the Whistling Skull

Thurman, Bill: Mountaintop Motel Massacre

Thurman, Uma: Adventures of Baron Münchausen, The; Avengers, The; Batman & Robin; Beautiful Girls; Dangerous Liaisons; Even Cowgirls Get the Blues; Final Analysis; Gattaca; Henry & June; Jennifer 8; Johnny Be Good; Kiss Daddy Good Night; Les Misérables (1998); Mad Dog and Glory; Month by the Lake, A; Pulp Fiction; Robin Hood (1991); Sweet and Lowdown; Truth About Cats and Dogs, The; Where the Heart Is

Thurseon, Debbie: Prey, The

Thursfield, Sophie: Sister, My Sister

Thurston, Carol: Story of Dr. Wassell, The

Tichy, Gerard: Summertime Killer, The

Ticotin, Rachel: Con Air; Critical Condition; Don Juan De Marco; Falling Down; First Time Felon; Fort Apache—The Bronx; F/X 2: The Deadly Art of Illusion; Keep the Change; One Good Cop; Prison Stories: Women on the Inside; Steal Big, Steal Little; Total Recall; Turbulence; Wharf Rat, The; Where the Day Takes You

Tidof, Max: Harmonists, The

Tien, James: Fists of Fury

Tiernan, Andrew: Edward II

Tierney, Gene: Advise and Consent; Egyptian, The; Ghost and Mrs. Muir, The; Heaven Can Wait (1943); Laura; Leave Her to Heaven; Left Hand of God, The; Never Let Me Go; Night and the City (1950); Razor's Edge, The (1946); Return of Frank James, The; Shanghai Gesture, The; Son of Fury; Sundown (1941); Toys in the Attic

Tierney, Jacob: Dead End (1997); Josh and S.A.M.; Neon Bible, The; This Is My Father

Tierney, Lawrence: Abduction; Born to Kill; Bushwhackers; Devil Thumbs a Ride, The; Dillinger (1945); Dillinger (1990); Female Jungle; Midnight (1980); Prowler, The; Reservoir Dogs; Runestone; Southie; Those Endearing Young Charms

Tierney, Maura: Forces of Nature; Instinct; Liar, Liar; Mercy; Oxygen; Primary Colors

Tierney, Patrick: Next of Kin (1984)

Tiffe, Angelo: Sword of Honor

Tiffe, Jerry: Sword of Honor

Tiffin, Pamela: One, Two, Three; State Fair (1962); Viva Max!

Tifo, Marie: Blind Trust (Pouvoir Intime)

Tigar, Kenneth: Gypsy Warriors, The; Little Bigfoot; Rage (1995)

Tighe, Kevin: Another 48 Hrs.; Avenging Angel, The (1995); Better Off Dead (1993); Caught in the Act; City of Hope; Darwin Conspiracy, The; Double Cross; Geronimo: An American Legend (1994); Jade; K-9; Man in Uniform, A; Men of War; Mumford; Race the Sun; What's Eating Gilbert Grape?; Winchell

Tikaram, Ramon: Kama Sutra: A Tale of Love

Tilbury, Peter: Nemesis (1986)

Tiller, Nadja: Burning Court, The; Tonio Kroger

Tiller, Patrick: Too Fast Too Young

Tillis, Mel: Uphill All the Way

Tilly, Jennifer: American Strays; Bella Mafia; Bird of Prey; Bound; Bride of Chucky; Bullets over Broadway; Double Cross; Edie & Pen; Embrace of the Vampire; Fabulous Baker Boys, The; Far from Home; Getaway, The (1994); Heads; Hide & Seek; High Spirits; Hoods; House Arrest; Inside Out (1986); Inventing the Abbotts; Let It Ride; Liar, Liar; Made in America; Man with a Gun; Moving Violations; Muse, The; Music from Another Room; Pompatus of Love, The; Relax ... It's Just Sex; Remote Control (1987); Rented Lips; Scorchers; Shadow of the Wolf; Webber's World (At Home with the Webbers)

Tilly, Meg: Agnes of God; Big Chill, The; Body Snatchers, The (1993); Carmilla; Girl in a Swing, The; Impulse (1984); Journey; Leaving Normal; Masquerade (1988); Off Beat; One Dark Night; Primal Secrets; Psycho II; Sleep with Me; Tex; Two Jakes, The; Valmont

Tilton, Charlene: Border Shootout; Center of the Web; Deadly Bet; Diary of a Teenage Hitchhiker; Fall of the House of Usher, The (1979); Silence of the Hams; Sweater Girls

Timbrook, Corbin: Forbidden Sins

Timko, Johnny: Hot Moves

Timmins, Cali: Hard Evidence; Takeover, The

Timmons, James: Kissed

Timothy, Christopher: All Creatures Great and Small

Timsit, Patrick: Little Indian, Big City

Tinapp, Barton: Dennis the Menace: Dinosaur Hunter

Tindall, Hilary: Max Headroom

Tinelli, Jaime: Sudden Death (1986)

Tingwell, Charles: Breaker Morant; Castle, The (1997); Cry in the Dark, A; Miracle Down Under; Murder Ahoy; Murder at the Gallop; Murder Most Foul; Murder She Said

Tinti, Gabriele: Trap Them and Kill Them

Tiny Tim: Blood Harvest

Tiplady, Brittany: Millennium (1996)

Tippitt, Wayne: Pipe Dreams

Tipple, Gordon: Time Runner

Tippo, Patti: Omega Syndrome

Tishman, Keren: Chain of Command

Tittle, Bently: Dark Universe, The

Tobeck, Joel: Women from Down Under

Tobey, Kenneth: Beast from 20,000 Fathoms, The; Bigamist, The; Davy Crockett and the River Pirates, The; Davy Crockett, King of the Wild Frontier; Elfego Baca: Six Gun Law; I Was a Male War Bride; It Came from Beneath the Sea; Kiss Tomorrow Goodbye; Strange Invaders; Thing (From Another World), The (1951); This Time For Keeps; Wings of Eagles, The

Tobgyal, Orgyen: Cup, The

Tobias, George: Air Force; Balalaika; Bride Came C.O.D., The; Captains of the Clouds; City for Conquest; Judge Steps Out, The; Mildred Pierce; New Kind of Love, A; Objective, Burma!; Rawhide (1951); Sergeant York; Set-Up, The (1949); Seven Little Foys, The; Strawberry Blonde, The; This Is the Army

Tobias, Oliver: Breeders (1996); King Arthur, The Young Warlord; Mata Hari (1985); Operation 'Nam; Stud, The; Wicked Lady, The (1983)

Tobin, Genevieve: Case of the Lucky Legs, The

Tobolowsky, Stephen: Basic Instinct; Black Dog; Dr. Jekyll and Ms. Hyde; Funny About Love; Glimmer Man, The; Grifters, The; Groundhog Day; Josh and S.A.M.; Memoirs of an Invisible Man; Mr. Magoo; My Father, the Hero; Power 98

Todd, Ann: All This and Heaven Too; Danny Boy (1941); Human Factor, The; Paradine Case, The; Scream of Fear; Seventh Veil, The; Ships with Wings; Son of Captain Blood; Time Without Pity

Todd, Beverly: Brother John; Clara's Heart; Don't Look Back: The Story of Leroy "Satchel" Paige; Jericho Mile, The; Ladies Club; Lean on Me; Moving; Vice Squad

Todd, Hallie: Check Is in the Mail, The

Todd, Harry: Jack Knife Man, The

Todd, Michael: Robot Ninja

Todd, Richard: Asylum (1972); Battle Hell; Dam Busters, The; D-Day the Sixth of June; Dorian Gray; Man Called Peter, A; Never Let Go; Number One of the Secret Service; Operation Crossbow; Rob Roy, the Highland Rogue; Saint Joan; Sherlock Holmes and the Incident at Victoria Falls; Stage Fright; Story of Robin Hood, The; Sword and the Rose, The (1953); Very Edge, The; Virgin Queen, The

Todd, Russell: Chopping Mall; One Last Run; Sweet Murder; Where the Boys Are '84

Todd, Saira: Bad Behaviour; Fatal Inversion, A

Todd, Thelma: Bohemian Girl, The; Call Her Savage; Cockeyed Cavaliers; Devil's Brother, The; Hips, Hips, Hooray; Horse Feathers; Monkey Business (1931); Palooka; Seven Footprints to Satan; Speak Easily

Todd, Tony: Beastmaster III: The Eye of Braxus; Black Fox; Blood Horse; Bram Stoker's Shadowbuilder; Candyman (1992); Candyman 3: Day of the Dead; Candyman: Farewell to the Flesh; Good Men and Bad; Ivory Hunters; Night of the Living Dead (1990); Pandora Project, The; Sabotage (1996); Wes Craven's Wishmaster

Todd, Trisha: Claire of the Moon

Todorovic, Bora: Time of the Gypsies

Toffalo, Lino: Lunatics & Lovers

Tognazzi, Ricky: Blood Ties (1987)

Tognazzi, Ugo: Joke of Destiny; La Cage aux Folles; La Cage aux Folles II; La Cage aux Folles III, The Wedding; Pigsty; Tragedy of a Ridiculous Man

Toibin, Niall: Eat the Peach; Rawhead Rex

Tokui, Yu: Shall We Dance? (1996)

Tol, Henriette: Flight of Rainbirds, A

Tolan, Michael: Hour of the Gun, The

Tolbe, Joe: Men in Love

Toler, Sidney: Castle in the Desert; Charlie Chan in City in Darkness; Charlie Chan at the Wax Museum; Charlie Chan at Treasure Island; Charlie Chan in Honolulu; Charlie Chan in Panama; Charlie Chan in Reno; Charlie Chan in Rio; Charlie Chan in the Secret Service; Charlie Chan's Murder Cruise; Chinese Cat, The; Dead Men Tell; Double Wedding; Heritage of the Desert; It's in the Bag; Jade Mask, The; Law of the Pampas; Meeting at Midnight; Murder over New York; Night to Remember, A (1943); Our Relations; Romance in Manhattan; Scarlet Clue, The; Shanghai Cobra, The; Speak Easily; Spitfire (1934)

Toles-Bey, John: Leap of Faith; Rage in Harlem, A; Waterworld

Tolkan, James: Bloodfist IV—Die Trying; Bolling Point (1993); Masters of the Universe; Ministry of Vengeance; Opportunity Knocks; Question of Faith; Second Sight; Sketch Artist II: Hands That See; Viper; Weekend War

Tolo, Marilu: Beyond Fear; Confessions of a Police Captain; Long Live Your Death; Marriage Italian Style

Tom, David: Stay Tuned

Tom, Lauren: Joy Luck Club, The

Tom, Nicholle: Beethoven's 2nd

Tomanovich, Dara: Amnesia; Back in Business

Tomasina, Jeana: Beach Girls, The

Tomei, Adam: My Own Country

Tomei, Marisa: Chaplin; Four Rooms; My Cousin Vinny; My Own Country; Only Love; Only You (1994); Oscar (1991); Paper, The; Perez Family, The; Since You've Been Gone; Slums of Beverly Hills; Unhook the Stars; Untamed Heart; Welcome to Sarajevo

Tomelty, Frances: Bellman and True; Blue Money; Bullshot (Bullshot Crummond); Field, The

Tomita, Tamlyn: Come See the Paradise; Joy Luck Club, The; Killing Jar, The; Picture Bride

Tomlin, Lily: All of Me; And the Band Played On; Beverly Hillbillies, The (1993); Big Business; Blue in the Face; Flirting with Disaster; Getting Away with Murder; Incredible Shrinking Woman, The; Krippendorf's Tribe; Late Show, The; Nashville; Nine to Five; Search for Signs of Intelligent Life in the Universe, The; Tea with Mussolini

Tomlins, Jason: Live! From Death Row

Tomlinson, David: Bedknobs and Broomsticks; Carry on Admiral; Fiendish Plot of Dr. Fu Manchu, The; Made in Heaven (1948); Mary Poppins; Pimpernel Smith; Three Men in a Boat; Up the Creek (1958); Water Babies, The; Wooden Horse, The

Tomlinson, Ricky: Raining Stones; Riff-Raff (1992)

Tompkins, Angel: Don Is Dead, The; I Love My Wife; Prime Cut

Tompkins, Joan: I Love My Wife

Tompkinson, Stephen: Brassed Off

Tonby, Kristian: Littlest Viking, The

Tone, Franchot: Advise and Consent; Bombshell (1933); Bride Wore Red, The; Dancing Lady; Dangerous (1935); Dark Waters; Every Girl Should Be Married; Five Graves to Cairo; Gabriel over the White House; Girl from Missouri, The; Gorgeous Hussy, The; Here Comes the Groom; His Butler's Sister; In Harm's Way; Lives of a Bengal Lancer, The; Love on the Run (1936); Man in the Eiffel Tower, The; Mutiny on the Bounty (1935); Quality Street; Reckless (1935); Sadie McKee; Suzy; Three Comrades; Today We Live

Tong, Jacqueline: How to Get Ahead in Advertising

Tong, Kam: Have Gun, Will Travel (TV Series)

Tono, Eijiro: Yojimbo

Tonsberg, Adam: Twist and Shout

Toomey, Regis: Arizona; Betrayal from the East; Beyond the Forest; Dive Bomber; Doughgirls, The; Dynamite Pass; Framed (1930); High and the Mighty, The; Island in the Sky; Phantom Creeps, The; Skull and Crown; Station West; Strange Illusion

Toone, Geoffrey: Captain Sinbad; Terror of the Tongs, The

Tootoosis, Gordon: Call of the Wild, The (1992); Stone Fox, The

Topaz, David: Goodbye New York

Topol: Fiddler on the Roof; Flash Gordon; For Your Eyes Only; House on Garibaldi Street; Queenie; Sallah

Topol-Barzilai, Anat: Witchcraft

Torday, Terry: Tower of Screaming Virgins, The

Toren, Marta: Casbah; Paris Express, The; Sirocco

Torey, Roberta: Hans Brinker

Torgan, Kendra: Killing Time (1996)

Torgov, Sarah: Drying Up the Streets; If You Could See What I Hear

Tork, Peter: Head (1968)

Torme, Mel: Comedian, The; Girls Town (1959); Good News; Higher and Higher; Man Called Adam, A; Words and Music

Tormey, John: Ghost Dog: The Way of the Samurai

Torn, Rip: Another Pair of Aces; Baby Doll; Beastmaster, The; Beautiful Dreamers; Beer; Betrayal (1978); Birch Interval, The; Blue and the Gray, The; By Dawn's Early Light; Canadian Bacon; Cat on a Hot Tin Roof (1985); City Heat; Cold Feet (1989); Coma; Critic's Choice; Cross Creek; Dead Ahead: The Exxon Valdez Disaster; Defending Your Life; Dolly Dearest; Down Periscope; Extreme Prejudice; First Family; Flashpoint; Heartland; Hit List (1988); How to Make an American Quilt; Jinxed; King of Kings (1961); Laguna Heat; Letter to My Killer; Man Who Fell to Earth, The; Manhunt for Claude Dallas; Men in Black; Nadine; One Trick Pony; Pair of Aces; Passing Glory; Payday; Pork Chop Hill; President's Plane Is Missing, The; Private Files of J. Edgar Hoover, The; Rape and Marriage: The Rideout Case; Robo-Cop 3; Seduction of Joe Tynan, The; Senseless; Shining Season, A; Silence Like Glass; Slaughter; Songwriter; Sophia Loren: Her Own Story; Stranger Is Watching, A; Summer Rental; Sweet Bird of Youth (1962); Trial and Error (1997); Tropic of Cancer; Where the Rivers Flow North; You're a Big Boy Now

Torne, Regina: Like Water for Chocolate

Toro, Benicio Del: Basquiat; China Moon; Fan, The (1996); Fearless (1993); Funeral, The (1996); Usual Suspects, The

Torocsik, Mari: Love

Torrence, David: City Girl

Torrence, Ernest: Covered Wagon, The; Fighting Caravans; Hunchback of Notre Dame, The (1923); I Cover the Waterfront; King of Kings, The (1927); Peter Pan (1924); Steamboat Bill Jr.; Tol'able David; Twelve Miles Out

Torrent, Ana: ¡Cría!; Nest, The (1981); Spirit of the Beehive, The; Thesis

Torres, Fernanda: One Man's War

Torres, Liz: America; Bloodfist IV—Die Trying; Just Cause; More Wild Wild West; Thieves of Fortune

Torres, Raquel: Duck Soup; White Shadows in the South Seas

Torry, Joe: Back in Business; Poetic Justice; Sprung; Tales from the Hood

Toto: Big Deal on Madonna Street; Gold of Naples, The; Hawks and the Sparrows, The; Laugh for Joy (Passionate Thief (1954)); Passionate Thief, The (1961)

Totter, Audrey: Any Number Can Play; Carpetbaggers, The; Jet Attack; Lady in the Lake; Set-Up, The (1949)

Toub, Shaun: Steel Sharks

Touliatos, George: Crackerjack; Firebird 2015 AD; Firepower (1979); Heartaches; Left for Dead; Mortal Sins (1992); Robbers of the Sacred Mountain; Tracks of a Killer

Toumanova, Tamara: Days of Glory

Tousey, Sheila: Medicine River; Silent Tongue; Slaughter of the Innocents

Toussaint, Beth: Armed and Deadly; Blackmail (1991); Breach of Conduct; Nightsiege-Project: Shadowchaser 2

Toussaint, Lorraine: America's Dream; Nightjohn

Tovar, Lupita: Dracula (Spanish)

Tower, Wade: Ripper, The (1985)

Towers, Constance: Horse Soldiers, The; Naked Kiss, The; Next Karate Kid, The; On Wings of Eagles; Sergeant Rutledge; Shock Corridor; Sylvester

Towles, Tom: Mad Dog and Glory

Towne, Aline: Radar Men from the Moon; Zombies of the Stratosphere (Satan's Satellites) (Serial)

Townes, Harry: Santee; Screaming Mimi

Townsend, Anna: Grandma's Boy

Townsend, Jill: Awakening, The; Oh, Alfie

Townsend, Omar: Party Girl (1995)

Townsend, Patrice: Always (1984); Sitting Ducks

Trotter, Laura: Miami Horror

Troughton, David: Norman Conquests, The, Episode 1: Table Manners; Norman Conquests, The, Episode 2: Living Together; Norman Conquests, The, Episode 3: Round and Round the Garden

Troughton, Patrick: Dr. Who (TV series); Frankenstein and the Monster from Hell; Sinbad and the Eye of the Tiger

Troup, Bobby: Five Pennies, The

Trowbridge, Charles: Captain America (1944); Fatal Hour, The; Valley of the Zombies

Troxell, Richard: Madame Butterfly

Troy, Ellen: Dance

Troy, Phillip: Ice

Truax, Maude: Hula

Trudeau, Margaret: Kings and Desperate Men: A Hostage Incident

True, Jim: Affliction; Hudsucker Proxy, The; Normal Life; Singles

True, Rachel: Craft, The; Half Baked; Nowhere

Truex, Ernest: Adventures of Marco Polo, The; Bachelor Mother; Christmas in July; His Girl Friday

Truffaut, Ewa: Francois Truffaut: Stolen Moments

Truffaut, François: Close Encounters of the Third Kind; Day for Night; Green Room, The; Wild Child, The (L'Enfant Sauvage)

Truffaut, Laura: Francois Truffaut: Stolen Moments

Trujillo, Raul: Black Fox; Blood Horse; Clearcut; Good Men and Bad; Highlander: The Final Dimension; Medicine River

Truman, Jeff: Bliss (1986)

Truman, Ralph: Saint in London, The

Trumbo, Karen: Claire of the Moon

Trump, Marla Maples: Executive Decision

Truswell, Chris: Fast Talking

Tryon, Glenn: Battling Orioles, The

Tryon, Tom: Cardinal, The; Color Me Dead; Gundown at Sandoval; I Married a Monster from Outer Space; In Harm's Way; Moon Pilot; Story of Ruth, The; Texas John Slaughter: Stampede at Bitter Creek; Three Violent People

Trzepiecinska, Joanna: Blood of the Innocent

Tsang, Eric: Gen-X Cops

Tsang, Ken: Police Story III—Super Cop

Tsarong, Tenzin Thuthob: Kundun

Tschechowa, Olga: Haunted Castle; Italian Straw Hat, The

Tse, Nicholas: Gen-X Cops

Tse, Yang: Enter the Dragon

Tselikovskaya, Ludmila: Ivan the Terrible—Part I & Part II

Tsopei, Corinna: Man Called Horse, A

Tsubouchi, Mikiko: Zatoichi: Masseur Ichi and a Chest of Gold

Tsuchiya, Yoshio: Human Vapor, The

Tsui, Elvis: Sex and Zen

Tsukamoto, Shinya: Tetsuo II: Body Hammer

Tsuneta, Fujio: Eel, The

Tsuruta, Koji: Samurai Trilogy, The

Tubb, Barry: Consenting Adults (1985); Top Gun; Valentino Returns; Warm Summer Rain

Tubert, Marcelo: Tremors 2: Aftershocks

Tucci, Stanley: Alarmist, The; Beethoven; Big Night; Billy Bathgate; Daytrippers, The; Impostors, The; In the Soup; In Too Deep; It Could Happen to You; Joe Gould's Secret; Jury Duty; Kiss of Death (1995); Life Less Ordinary, A; Men of Respect; Modern Affair, A; Montana (1997); Pelican Brief, The; Public Eye, The; Somebody to Love; Undercover Blues; William Shakespeare's A Midsummer Night's Dream; Winchell

Tucci, Tony: Gravesend

Tuck, Jennifer: Curse of the House Surgeon, The; Penpal Murders; Queen Victoria and the Zombies; Vampires Always Ring Twice; Vampires from Outer Space

Tuck, Jessica: Lifepod; Mr. Write; O. J. Simpson Story, The; Wing and a Prayer, A (1997)

Tucker, Chris: Dead Presidents; Fifth Element, The; Friday; Jackie Brown; Money Talks; Rush Hour

Tucker, Forrest: Abominable Snowman of the Himalayas, The; Adventures of Huckleberry Finn, The (1978); Auntie Mame; Big Cat, The; Brimstone; Bugles in the Afternoon; Cancel My Reservation; Chisum; Coroner Creek; Cosmic Monsters, The; Crawling Eye, The; Final Chapter—Walking Tall; Finger Man (1955); Hellfire; Hoodlum Empire; Incredible Rocky Mountain Race, The; Jubilee Trail; Keeper of the Flame; Melody Master (The Great Awakening) (New Wine);

Montana Belle; Nevadan, The; Never Say Goodbye; Pony Express; Rage at Dawn; Real American Hero, The; Sands of Iwo Jima; Three Violent People; Thunder Run; Time Stalkers; Trouble in the Glen; Westerner, The

Tucker, Jerry: Dick Tracy Returns

Tucker, Jonathan: Virgin Suicides, The

Tucker, Michael: Assault & Matrimony; Checking Out; D2: The Mighty Ducks; Day One; For Love or Money; Goodbye People, The; L.A. Law; Radio Days; Spy; 'Til There Was You; Too Young to Die

Tucker, Sophie: Broadway Melody of 1938; Follow the Boys; Sensations of 1945; Thoroughbreds Don't Cry

Tucker, Tanya: Follow That Car; Hard Country; Rebels, The

Tudor, Christine: Final Mission (1984)

Tudyk, Alan: 28 Days

Tufts, Sonny: Cat Women of the Moon; Easy Living; Glory at Sea; Here Come the Waves; So Proudly We Hail; Virginian, The (1946)

Tull, Jethro: Rock and Roll Circus, The

Tull, Patrick: Parting Glances

Tulleners, Tonny: Scorpion

Tullis Jr., Dan: Private Wars

Tully, Tom: Adventure; Branded; Coogan's Bluff; Jazz Singer, The (1953); June Bride; Lady in the Lake; Love Is Better Than Ever; Love Me or Leave Me; Moon Is Blue, The; Northern Pursuit; Ruby Gentry; Soldier of Fortune; Trouble Along the Way; Virginian, The (1946); Wackiest Ship in the Army, The

Tumbuan, Frans: Rage and Honor II: Hostile Takeover; Without Mercy

Tune, Tommy: Boy Friend, The

Tung, Bill: Police Story III—Super Cop

Tunney, Robin: Craft, The; Empire Records; End of Days; Julian Po; Montana (1997); Niagara Niagara; Riders of the Purple Sage; Supernova

Turano, Robert: Federal Hill

Turco, Paige: Dead Funny; November Conspiracy, The; Teenage Mutant Ninja Turtles II: The Secret of the Ooze; Teenage Mutant Ninja Turtles III; Vibrations

Turkel, Ann: Deep Space; Fear, The (1994); Last Contract, The; 99 and 44/100 Percent Dead; Paper Lion

Turlington, Christy: Catwalk

Turman, Glynn: Attica; Blue Knight, The (1975); Buffalo Soldiers; Cooley High; Freedom Song; Gremlins; Hero Ain't Nothin' But a Sandwich, A; Inkwell, The; J.D.'s Revenge; Out of Bounds; Penitentiary II; Secrets of a Married Man

Turnbull, John: Silver Blaze

Turner, Barbara: Monster from Green Hell

Turner, Claramae: Carousel

Turner, Clive: Howling, The: New Moon Rising

Turner, Fred: Jack Knife Man, The

Turner, Guinevere: Go Fish

Turner, Hilary Shepard: Turbo: A Power Rangers Adventure

Turner, Isaac: Girl with the Hungry Eyes, The

Turner, Janine: Ambulance, The; Cliffhanger; Curse of Inferno, The; Leave It to Beaver; Northern Exposure (TV Series); Quantum Leap (TV Series)

Turner, Jim: My Samurai

Turner, Kathleen: Accidental Tourist, The; Baby Geniuses; Body Heat; Breed Apart, A; Crimes of Passion; House of Cards; Jewel of the Nile, The; Julia and Julia; Legalese; Man with Two Brains, The; Moonlight and Valentino; Naked in New York; Peggy Sue Got Married; Prizzi's Honor; Romancing the Stone; Serial Mom; Simple Wish, A; Switching Channels; Undercover Blues; Virgin Suicides, The; V. I. Warshawski; War of the Roses, The

Turner, Lana: Adventures of Marco Polo, The; Another Time, Another Place (1958); Bachelor in Paradise; Bad and the Beautiful, The; Betrayed (1954); Bittersweet Love; By Love Possessed; Cass Timberlane; Diane; Dr. Jekyll and Mr. Hyde (1941); Green Dolphin Street; Homecoming (1948); Honky Tonk; Imitation of Life; Johnny Eager; Latin Lovers; Life of Her Own, A; Love Finds Andy Hardy; Love Has Many Faces; Madame X (1966); Mr. Imperium; Persecution; Peyton Place; Postman Always Rings Twice, The (1946); Prodigal, The; Sea Chase, The; Somewhere I'll Find You; Three Musketeers, The (1948); Weekend at the Waldorf; Who's Got the Action?; Witches' Brew; Ziegfeld Girl

Turner, Mae: Two-Gun Man from Harlem

Urquhart, Robert: Battle Hell; Curse of Frankenstein, The; Knights of the Round Table

Urquidez, Benny: Bloodmatch; Kick Fighter

Urzi, Saro: Seduced and Abandoned

Usher, Guy: Devil Bat, The; Doomed to Die

Ustinov, Pavla: Thief of Baghdad (1978)

Ustinov, Peter: Alice in Wonderland (1999); Appointment with Death; Around the World in 80 Days (1989); Ashanti; Beau Brummell (1954); Billy Budd; Blackbeard's Ghost; Charlie Chan and the Curse of the Dragon Queen; Comedians, The; Death on the Nile; Egyptian, The; Evil Under the Sun; Great Muppet Caper, The; Grendel, Grendel, Grendel; Hammersmith Is Out; Hot Millions; Immortal Battalion, The (The Way Ahead); Lady L; Lion and the Hawk, The; Logan's Run; Lola Montes; Lorenzo's Oil; Old Curiosity Shop, The (1994); One of Our Aircraft Is Missing; One of Our Dinosaurs Is Missing; Purple Taxi, The; Quo Vadis (1951); Spartacus; Sundowners, The (1960); Thief of Baghdad (1978); 13 at Dinner; Topkapi; Viva Max!; We're No Angels (1955)

Utley, Darrell Thomas: Danielle Steel's Once in a Lifetime

Utsunomiya, Masayo: Irezumi (Spirit of Tattoo)

Vaananen, Kari: Amazon

Vaccaro, Brenda: Cookie; Dear Detective; Death Weekend; First Deadly Sin, The; For Keeps; Guyana Tragedy, The: The Story of Jim Jones; Heart of Midnight; Honor Thy Father; I Love My Wife; Lethal Games; Midnight Cowboy; Mirror Has Two Faces, The; Once Is Not Enough; Pride of Jesse Hallman, The; Red Shoe Diaries; Supergirl; Ten Little Indians (1989); Water; Zorro, the Gay Blade

Vadas, Kenny: Captains Courageous (1995)

Vadim, Annette: Blood and Roses; Les Liaisons Dangereuses

Vadim, Roger: Ciao! Manhattan

Vadis, Dan: Bronco Billy; Seven Magnificent Gladiators, The

Vahanian, Marc: Prince of Central Park, The

Vahle, Timothy: Forbidden Sins

Valandrey, Charlotte: House That Mary Bought, The; Orlando; Red Kiss (Rouge Baiser)

Valdez, Daniel: Zoot Suit

Vale, Virginia: Flustered Comedy of Leon Errol, The; Marshal of Mesa City; Stage to Chino; Triple Justice

Valen, Nancy: Final Embrace

Valens, Ritchie: Go, Johnny, Go!

Valenti, Chuck: Bronx Executioner, The

Valentine, Anthony: Carpathian Eagle; Dirty Dozen, The: The Fatal Mission; Father's Revenge, A; Robin Hood and the Sorcerer

Valentine, Karen: Hot Lead and Cold Feet; Jane Doe; North Avenue Irregulars, The; Power Within, The; Return to Fantasy Island; Skeezer

Valentine, Kim: Grandma's House

Valentine, Scott: After the Shock; Carnosaur 3: Primal Species; Dangerous Pursuit; Deadtime Stories; Double Obsession; Homicidal Impulse; My Demon Lover; Object of Obsession; Out of Annie's Past; Paranoia (1998); Secret Passion of Robert Clayton, The; Till the End of the Night; To Sleep With a Vampire; Unborn II, The; Write to Kill

Valentini, Mariella: Volere Volare

Valentino, Rudolph: Blood and Sand (1922); Eagle, The; Moran of the Lady Letty; Sheik, The; Son of the Sheik

Valenza, Tasia: Rappin'

Valerie, Jeanne: Les Liaisons Dangereuses

Vallai, Peter: Magic Hunter

Vallance, Louise: Robbers of the Sacred Mountain

Vallee, Marcel: Topaze (1951)

Vallee, Rudy: Admiral Was a Lady, The; Bachelor and the Bobby-Soxer, The; Beautiful Blonde from Bashful Bend, The; How to Succeed in Business without Really Trying; It's in the Bag; Mad Wednesday (see also Sin of Harold Diddlebook); Palm Beach Story, The; People Are Funny; Second Fiddle; Sin of Harold Diddlebock (Mad Wednesday); Unfaithfully Yours (1948); Vagabond Lover, The

Valletta, Al: Runaway Nightmare

Valli, Alida: Eyes Without a Face; Il Grido (Outcry, The); Miracle of the Bells, The; Month by the Lake, A; Oedipus Rex (1967); Paradine Case, The; Spider's Stratagem, The; Suspiria; Third Man, The; Walk Softly, Stranger; Wanton Contessa, The; We the Living; White Tower, The

Valli, Frankie: Dirty Laundry; Opposite Corners

Valli, Romolo: Bobby Deerfield; Fistful of Dynamite, A

Vallin, Rick: Ghosts on the Loose; Jungle Jim; King of the Carnival; Last of the Redmen; Riders of the Rio Grande; Sea Hound, The

Vallone, Raf: Almost Perfect Affair, An; Bitter Rice; Catholics; Christopher Columbus (1985); El Cid; Greek Tycoon, The; Gunfight, A; Harlow; Honor Thy Father; Nevada Smith; Other Side of Midnight, The; Season of Giants, A; Summertime Killer, The; Time to Die, A (1983); Two Women

Vallone, Saverio: Grim Reaper, The (1980)

Valois, Valerie: Scanners 3: The Takeover

Van, Bobby: Affairs of Dobie Gillis, The; Bunco; Kiss Me Kate; Navy vs. the Night Monsters, The; Small Town Girl

van Allan, Richard: Vampyr, The (1992)

Van Ammelrooy, Willeke: Antonia's Line; On Top of the Whale

Van Ark, Joan: Frogs; Red Flag: The Ultimate Game; Tainted Blood; When the Dark Man Calls

Van Atta, Lee: Dick Tracy (1937); Undersea Kingdom

Van Bergen, Lewis: Pinocchio's Revenge; South of Reno

Van Buren, Mabel: Miss Lulu Bett

Vance, Courtney B.: Adventures of Huck Finn, The (1993); Affair, The (1995); Blind Faith; Boys Next Door, The (1996); Cookie's Fortune; Dangerous Minds; Hamburger Hill; Last Supper, The (1996); Panther; Percy & Thunder; Piano Lesson, The; Preacher's Wife, The; Tuskegee Airmen, The; 12 Angry Men (1997); Urban Crossfire

Vance, Danitra: Jumpin' at the Boneyard; Limit Up; Sticky Fingers

Vance, Pruitt Taylor: Mumford

Vance, Vivian: Great Race, The; I Love Lucy (TV Series)

Van Cleef, Lee: Bad Man's River

Van Cleef, Lee: Armed Response; Beast from 20,000 Fathoms, The; Beyond the Law (1968); Blade Rider; Bravados, The; Captain Apache; China Gate; Code Name: Wild Geese; Commandos; Days of Wrath; Death Rides a Horse; El Condor; Escape from New York; For a Few Dollars More; Good the Bad and the Ugly, The; Gunfight at the O.K. Corral; Gypsy Colt; Hard Way, The (1979); It Conquered the World; Jungle Raiders; Kansas City Confidential; Kid Vengeance; Lonely Man, The; Man Alone, A; Man Who Shot Liberty Valance, The; Octagon, The; Ride Lonesome; Stranger and the Gunfighter, The; Take a Hard Ride; Ten Wanted Men; Thieves of Fortune; Tin Star, The; Tribute to a Bad Man

Van Dam, José: Music Teacher, The

van Damme, Gabrielle: Marquis

Van Damme, Jean-Claude: Black Eagle; Bloodsport; Cyborg; Death Warrant; Desert Heat; Double Impact; Double Team; Hard Target; Kickboxer; Knock Off; Legionnaire; Lionheart (1991); Maximum Risk; No Retreat, No Surrender; Nowhere to Run (1993); Quest, The (1996); Street Fighter (1994); Sudden Death (1995); Timecop; Universal Soldier

Van Den Bergh, Gert: Naked Prey, The

van den Elsen, Sylvie: L'Argent

Vander, Musetta: Project Shadowchaser 3000

van der Beek, James: Angus; Varsity Blues

Vandergaw, Terra: '68

Vandernoot, Alexandra: Blood of the Hunter; Dinner Game, The; Highlander: The Gathering

Van Der Velde, Nadine: Shadow Dancing

Van Der Vlis, Diana: X (The Man with the X-Ray Eyes)

Van Der Wat, Keith: Three Bullets for a Long Gun

van de Ven, Monique: Amsterdamned; Assault, The; Johnsons, The; Katie's Passion; Lily Was Here; Turkish Delight

Van Devere, Trish: Changeling, The; Day of the Dolphin, The; Deadly Currents; Hearse, The; Hollywood Vice Squad; Messenger of Death; Movie, Movie; Savage Is Loose, The; Where's Poppa?

Van Dien, Casper: Beastmaster III: The Eye of Braxus; Shark Attack; Sleepy Hollow; Starship Troopers; Tarzan and the Lost City; Time Shifters

Vandis, Titos: Young Doctors in Love

Van Doren, Mamie: Francis Joins the Wacs; Free Ride; Girl in Black Stockings, The; Girls Town (1959); High School Confidential!; Las Vegas Hillbillys; Navy vs. the Night Monsters, The; Running Wild (1955); Teacher's Pet; Three Nuts in Search of a Bolt

van Dreelen, John: Great Wallendas, The

Van Dyke, Barry: Casino (1980); Foxfire Light

Van Dyke, Conny: Framed (1975); Hell's Angels '69

Van Dyke, Dick: Bye Bye Birdie; Chitty Chitty Bang Bang; Cold Turkey; Country Girl, The (1982); Dick Tracy (1990); Dick Van Dyke Show, The (TV Series); Divorce American Style; Lt. Robin Crusoe, U.S.N.; Mary Poppins; Never a Dull Moment; Runner Stumbles, The

Van Dyke, Jerry: Courtship of Eddie's Father, The; Run If You Can

Vanel, Charles: Death in the Garden; Diabolique (1955); Wages of Fear, The

Van Eyck, Peter: Brain, The (1965); Bridge at Remagen, The; Run for the Sun; Spy Who Came in from the Cold, The; Thousand Eyes of Dr. Mabuse, The; Wages of Fear, The

Van Fleet, Jo: East of Eden (1955); Gunfight at the O.K. Corral; I Love You Alice B. Toklas!; I'll Cry Tomorrow; Four Queens, The: Rose Tattoo, The

Van Hentenryck, Kevin: Basket Case; Basket Case 2; Basket Case 3: The Progeny

Van Herwijnen, Carol: Still Smokin'

Van Horn, Patrick: Free Enterprise

van Huet, Fedja: Character (Karakter)

Vanilla Ice: Cool As Ice

Vanity: Action Jackson; Davinci's War; 52 Pick-Up; Highlander: The Gathering; Last Dragon, The; Memories of Murder; Neon City; Never Too Young to Die; South Beach; Tanya's Island

Van Kamp, Merete: Princess Daisy

VanKamp, Merete: Lethal Woman

Van Kempen, Ad: 1-900

Van Lent, Amber: Bloodsport III

Van Lidth, Erland: Alone in the Dark

Van Loon, Robert: Paisan

Van Luik, Robert: Saturday Night Special

Van Ness, Jon: Bostonians, The; Hospital Massacre

Vannicola, Joanne: Iron Eagle IV; Love and Human Remains

Van Pallandt, Nina: American Gigolo; Assault on Agathon; Jungle Warriors; Long Goodbye, The

Van Patten, Dick: Charly; Dangerous Place, A; Diary of a Teenage Hitchhiker; Final Embrace; Gus; High Anxiety; Jake Spanner Private Eye; Love Is All There Is; Midnight Hour; Robin Hood: Men in Tights; Son of Blob (Beware! The Blob); Spaceballs; When Things Were Rotten (TV Series)

Van Patten, James: Nightforce; Tennessee Stallion; Young Warriors, The

Van Patten, Joyce: Billy Galvin; Breathing Lessons; Eleanor: First Lady of the World; Goddess, The; Housewife; Mikey and Nicky; Monkey Shines: An Experiment in Fear; St. Elmo's Fire; Stranger Within, The

Van Patten, Nels: Mirror Images; One Last Run; Summer School

Van Patten, Timothy: Class of 1984; Curse IV: The Ultimate Sacrifice; Zone Troopers

Van Patten, Vincent: Break, The; Charley and the Angel; Chino; Hell Night; Rock 'n' Roll High School

Van Peebles, Mario: Delivery Boys; Exterminator 2, The; Full Eclipse; Gang in Blue; Gunmen; Heartbreak Ridge; Highlander: The Final Dimension; Hot Shot; Identity Crisis; Jaws: The Revenge; Judgment Day; Killers in the House; Love Kills (1999); New Jack City; Posse (1993); Rappin'; Riot (1996) (TV Movie); Solo (1996); Stag; Terminal Velocity; 3:15—The Moment of Truth; Urban Crossfire

Van Sickel, Dale: Dangers of the Canadian Mounted; King of the Rocketmen; Man with the Steel Whip

Van Sloan, Edward: Before I Hang; Behind the Mask; Death Kiss, The; Deluge (1933); Dracula (1931); Dracula's Daughter; Mummy, The (1932); Riders of the Rio Grande

Van Thijn, Marion: Lily Was Here

Van Tieghem, David: No Telling

Van Tongeren, Hans: Spetters

van Uchelen, Marc: Assault, The

Van Valkenburgh, Deborah: Brain Smasher ... A Love Story; Bunny's Tale, A; Phantom of the Ritz; Rampage; Warriors, The (1979)

Van Vooren, Monique: Andy Warhol's Frankenstein; Ash Wednesday; Sugar Cookies

Van Wormer, Steve: Meet the Deedles

Varconi, Victor: Everything Happens at Night

Varden, Evelyn: Athena

Varden, Norma: Mademoiselle Fifi

Vardhan, Vishnu: Terrorist, The

Varela, Amanda: Falcon's Brother, The

Vargas, Jacob: Mi Vida Loca; Selena

Vargas, John: In Dark Places

Vargas, Valentina: Dirty Games; Hellraiser: Bloodline; Tigress, The

Varma, Indira: Kama Sutra: A Tale of Love

Varney, Jim: Beverly Hillbillies, The (1993); Dr. Otto and the Riddle of the Gloom Beam; Ernest Goes to Africa; Ernest Goes to Camp; Ernest Goes to Jail; Ernest in the Army; Ernest Rides Again; Ernest Saves Christmas; Ernest Scared Stupid; Expert, The; Fast Food; Rousters, The; Slam Dunk Ernest; Snowboard Academy; Treehouse Hostage; Wilder Napalm

Varney, Reg: Great St. Trinian's Train Robbery, The

Varsi, Diane: Compulsion; I Never Promised You a Rose Garden; Johnny Got His Gun; People, The; Peyton Place; Sweet Love, Bitter; Wild in the Streets

Vartan, Michael: Dead Man's Curve; Myth of Fingerprints, The; Wild Flower (1993) (Fiorile)

Varty, John: Born Wild

Vasconcelos, Tito: Danzon

Vasquez, José Luis Lopez: Garden of Delights, The

Vasquez, Roberta: Fit to Kill

Vasut, Marek: Delta of Venus

Vattier, Robert: Le Schpountz

Vaughan, Alberta: Randy Rides Alone

Vaughan, Greg: Children of the Corn V: Fields of Terror; Poison Ivy: The New Seduction

Vaughan, Peter: Bleak House; Blockhouse, The; Die! Die! My Darling!; Fatherland; Forbidden; Haunted Honeymoon; Les Misérables (1998); Remains of the Day; Straw Dogs

Vaughan, Sarah: Ladies Sing the Blues, The

Vaughan, Vanessa: Crazy Moon; Sound and the Silence,The

Vaughn, Martin: Phar Lap

Vaughn, Ned: Chips, the War Dog

Vaughn, Robert: Baseketball; Battle Beyond the Stars; Black Moon Rising; Blind Vision; Blue and the Gray, The; Brass Target; Bridge at Remagen, The; Bullitt; Captive Rage; C.H.U.D. II (Bud the C.H.U.D.); City in Fear; Delta Force, The; Going Under; Hangar 18; Hitchhiker, The (Series); Hour of the Assassin; Inside the Third Reich; Julius Caesar (1970); Kill Castro (Cuba Crossing; Mercenaries (1978), Sweet Violent Tony); Magnificent Seven, The; Man from U.N.C.L.E., The (TV Series); McGinsey's Island; Nightstick; Nobody's Perfect; Prince of Bel Air; Question of Honor, A; Return of the Man from U.N.C.L.E., The; River of Death; Shaming, The; S.O.B.; Starship Invasions; Statue, The; Superman III; Transylvania Twist; Young Philadelphians, The

Vaughn, Vince: Clay Pigeons; Cool, Dry Place, A; Just Your Luck; Locusts, The; Lost World, The: Jurassic Park; Psycho (1998); Return to Paradise (1998); Swingers

Vaughter, Marcus: Visitants, The

Vaugier, Emmanuelle: Halfback of Notre Dame, The

Vavrova, Dana: Brother of Sleep

Vawter, Ron: Philadelphia; Swoon

Ve Sota, Bruno: Attack of the Giant Leeches; Daughter of Horror; War of the Satellites

Vega, Isela: Barbarosa; Bring Me the Head of Alfredo Garcia; Deadly Trackers, The; Streets of L.A., The

Vega, Vladimir: Ladybird, Ladybird

Veidt, Conrad: Above Suspicion (1943); All Through the Night; Beloved Rogue; Cabinet of Doctor Caligari, The; Dark Journey; Hands of Orlac; Man Who Laughs, The; Spy in Black, The; Student of Prague; Thief of Bagdad, The (1940); Waxworks; Whistling in the Dark; Woman's Face, A

Vel Johnson, Reginald: Die Hard; Die Hard 2: Die Harder; Great American Sex Scandal, The; Posse (1993); Seven Hours to Judgment

Velasquez, Andres: Littlest Outlaw, The

Velasquez, Andy: Heaven Before I Die

Velasquez, Patricia: Eruption

Velazquez, Lorena: Rock 'n' Roll Wrestling Women vs. the Aztec Mummy

Veld, Hansman In't: Still Smokin'

Velez, Eddie: Bitter Vengeance; Doin' Time; Romero; Rooftops; Women's Club, The

Velez, Lauren: I Like It Like That; I Think I Do

Velez, Lupe: Hell Harbor; Hollywood Party; Mexican Spitfire; Palooka; Where East Is East

Velez, Martha: Star Maps

Wagner, Cristie: She-Devils on Wheels

Wagner, David: Pet Shop

Wagner, Jack: Dirty Little Secret; Swimsuit; Trapped in Space

Wagner, Kristina Malandro: Double Dragon

Wagner, Lindsay: Bionic Woman, The; Callie and Son; Contagious; Convicted; Danielle Steel's Once in a Lifetime; From the Dead of Night; High Risk; Incredible Journey of Dr. Meg Laurel, The; Martin's Day; Nighthawks; Nightmare at Bittercreek; Paper Chase, The; Princess Daisy; Ricochet; Rockford Files, The (TV Series); Shattered Dreams; Treacherous Crossing; Two Worlds of Jennie Logan, The

Wagner, Natasha Gregson: Another Day in Paradise; Dead Beat; Mind Ripper; Molly & Gina; Substitute, The (1993); Tainted Blood; Urban Legend

Wagner, Robert: Affair, The (1973); Airport '79: The Concorde; Austin Powers: International Man of Mystery; Austin Powers: The Spy Who Shagged Me; Beneath the 12-Mile Reef; Between Heaven and Hell; Broken Lance; Curse of the Pink Panther, The; Death at Love House; Deep Trouble; Dragon: The Bruce Lee Story; False Arrest; Halls of Montezuma; Harper; I Am the Cheese; It Takes a Thief (TV Series); Let's Make It Legal; Longest Day, The; Madame Sin; Mountain, The; Pink Panther, The; Prince Valiant (1954); Stars and Stripes Forever; Stopover Tokyo; This Gun for Hire (1991); Titanic (1953); To Catch a King; Trail of the Pink Panther, The; War Lover, The; What Price Glory; Wild Things; Windmills of the Gods; Winning

Wagner, Thomas: Dead On; Marilyn & Bobby: Her Final Affair; Pinocchio's Revenge

Wagner, Wende: Green Hornet, The (TV Series)

Wagstaff, Elsie: Whistle Down the Wind

Wah, Yuen: Police Story III—Super Cop; Supercop

Wahl, Adam: Deadmate

Wahl, Ken: Dirty Dozen, The: The Next Mission; Favor, The; Fort Apache—The Bronx; Gladiator, The (1986) (Television); Jinxed; Omega Syndrome; Purple Hearts; Running Scared (1980); Soldier, The; Taking of Beverly Hills, The; Treasure of the Yankee Zephyr; Wanderers, The

Wahlberg, Donnie: Black Circle Boys; Body Count (1997); Never 2 Big; Purgatory; Sixth Sense, The; Southie

Wahlberg, Mark: Big Hit, The; Boogie Nights; Corruptor, The; Fear (1996); Perfect Storm, The; Renaissance Man; Substitute, The (1993); Three Kings; Traveller

Wainwright, James: Private Files of J. Edgar Hoover, The; Survivors, The; Warlords of the 21st Century; Woman Called Moses, A

Waitaire, Gnarnay Yarrahe: Dead Heart

Waite, Ralph: Bodyguard, The; Crash and Burn; Five Easy Pieces; Gentleman Bandit, The; Last Summer; Lawman; On the Nickel; Red Alert; Sioux City; Stone Killer, The; Thanksgiving Story, The

Waites, Thomas: Clan of the Cave Bear; On the Yard; Verne Miller; Warriors, The (1979)

Waits, Tom: At Play in the Fields of the Lord; Bram Stoker's Dracula; Candy Mountain; Cold Feet (1989); Down by Law; Ironweed; Mystery Men; Rumble Fish; Short Cuts

Wajnberg, Marc-Henri: Mamma Dracula

Wakabayashi, Akiko: You Only Live Twice

Wakao, Ayako: Geisha, A

Wakayama, Tomisaburo: Bad News Bears Go to Japan, The; Irezumi (Spirit of Tattoo); Lone Wolf and Cub: Sword of Vengeance; Shogun Assassin

Wakeham, Deborah: House of the Rising Sun

Wakely, Jimmy: Across the Rio Grande

Walbrook, Anton: Dangerous Moonlight (Suicide Squadron); 49th Parallel, The; Gaslight (1940); La Ronde; Life and Death of Colonel Blimp, The; Lola Montes; Red Shoes, The (1948); Saint Joan

Walburn, Raymond: Christmas in July; Count of Monte Cristo, The (1934); Hail the Conquering Hero; Key to the City; Let Freedom Ring; Louisiana Purchase; Mad Wednesday (see also Sin of Harold Diddlebook); Sin of Harold Diddlebook (Mad Wednesday); Thin Ice

Walcott, Gregory: Jet Attack; Plan 9 from Outer Space; Prime Cut

Walcott, Jersey Joe: Harder They Fall, The

Walcott, William: Down to the Sea in Ships

Walcutt, John: Return (1984)

Walczewski, Marek: Passenger, The (1963)

Walden, Lynette: Almost Blue; Saved by the Light; Silencer, The

Walden, Robert: Bloody Mama; Blue Sunshine; Kansas City Massacre, The; Memorial Day

Waldhorn, Gary: After Pilkington

Waldron, Shawna: Little Giants

Walerstein, Marcela: Disappearance of Garcia Lorca, The

Wales, Ethel: Border Vigilantes; Saturday Night Kid, The

Wales, Wally: Traitor, The

Walken, Christopher: Addiction, The; All-American Murder; At Close Range; Batman Returns; Biloxi Blues; Blast from the Past; Brainstorm; Business Affair, A; Comfort of Strangers, The; Communion; Day of Atonement; Dead Zone, The; Deadline (1987); Deer Hunter, The; Dogs of War, The; Eternal, The; Excess Baggage; Funeral, The (1996); Heaven's Gate; Homeboy; Illuminata; King of New York; Last Embrace, The; Last Man Standing (1996); McBain; Milagro Beanfield War, The; Mind Snatchers, The; Mistress (1992); Mouse Hunt; New Rose Hotel; Next Stop, Greenwich Village; Nick of Time; Prophecy, The (1995); Prophecy II, The; Prophecy 3: The Ascent; Pulp Fiction; Roseland; Sarah, Plain and Tall; Scam; Search and Destroy (1995); Skylark; Sleepy Hollow; Suicide Kings; Things to Do in Denver When You're Dead; Touch; True Romance; Vendetta; View to a Kill, A; Wayne's World 2; Who Am I This Time?; Wild Side; Winter's End

Walker, Albertina: Leap of Faith

Walker, Ally: Happy, Texas; Kazaam; Seventh Coin, The; Someone to Die For; Universal Soldier; When the Bough Breaks

Walker, Arnetia: Love Crimes

Walker, Christopher: Echo Park

Walker, Clint: Baker's Hawk; Bounty Man, The; Cheyenne (TV Series); Deadly Harvest; Dirty Dozen, The; Gambler Returns, The: The Luck of the Draw; Hysterical; Maya; Night of the Grizzly, The; None But the Brave; Pancho Villa; Send Me No Flowers; Snowbeast; White Buffalo; Yuma

Walker, Corban: Frankie Starlight

Walker, Dominic: Power of One, The

Walker, Eric: Ewok Adventure, The

Walker, Fiona: Norman Conquests, The, Episode 1: Table Manners; Norman Conquests, The, Episode 2: Living Together; Norman Conquests, The, Episode 3: Round and Round the Garden

Walker, Helen: Brewster's Millions (1945); Call Northside 777; Impact; My Dear Secretary; People Are Funny

Walker, Jimmie: Doin' Time; Frankenstein Sings; Going Bananas; Let's Do It Again

Walker, Joyce: Education of Sonny Carson, The

Walker, Justin: Born Bad; Humanoids from the Deep (1996)

Walker, Kathryn: Blade (1973); Dangerous Game (1990); Murder of Mary Phagan, The; Neighbors; Rich Kids; Special Bulletin; Whale for the Killing, A; Winds of Kitty Hawk, The

Walker, Kim: Deadly Weapon; Heathers; Reason to Believe, A

Walker, Liza: Wavelength (1995)

Walker, Lou: Nightman, The

Walker, Marcy: Hot Resort; Midnight's Child

Walker, Matthew: Intimate Relations

Walker, Nancy: Best Foot Forward; Forty Carats; Girl Crazy; Lucky Me; Thursday's Game

Walker, Nella: They Call It Sin

Walker, Nicholas: Amnesia

Walker, Paul: Meet the Deedles; Skulls, The; Tammy & the T-Rex; Varsity Blues

Walker, Polly: Dark Harbor; Enchanted April; For Roseanna; Lorna Doone; Sliver; Talk of Angels; Trial, The (1992)

Walker, Robert: Bataan; Clock, The; Madame Curie; One Touch of Venus; Sea of Grass, The; Since You Went Away; Song of Love; Strangers on a Train; Thirty Seconds Over Tokyo; Till the Clouds Roll By; Vengeance Valley

Walker Jr., Robert: Angkor: Cambodia Express; Ensign Pulver; Evil Town; Gone with the West; Hambone and Hillie; Heated Vengeance; Little Moon & Jud McGraw; Son of Blob (Beware! The Blob)

Walker, Sarah: Gloriana; Housekeeping

Walker, Sydney: Mrs. Doubtfire; Prelude to a Kiss

Walker, Terry: Take Me Back to Oklahoma

(1999); Natural Enemy; Night in Heaven, A; One and Only, Genuine, Original Family Band, The; Portrait of a Showgirl; Portrait of a Stripper; Pure Country; Songwriter; Treasure of the Yankee Zephyr; Twin Falls Idaho; Victor/Victoria; Worth Winning

Warren, Marc: Boston Kickout

Warren, Michael: Hill Street Blues (TV Series); Norman ... Is That You?

Warren, Mike: Butterflies Are Free; Fast Break; Heaven Is a Playground; Kid Who Loved Christmas, The

Warren, Nancy: Where's the Money, Noreen?

Warren, Todd: Sleeping with Strangers

Warrender, Harry: Pandora and the Flying Dutchman

Warrick, Ruth: China Sky; Citizen Kane; Corsican Brothers, The (1941); Great Dan Patch, The; Guest in the House; Iron Major, The; Journey into Fear (1942); Let's Dance; Mr. Winkle Goes to War; Ride Beyond Vengeance

Warrington, Don: Bloodbath at the House of Death; Lion of Africa, The

Warry-Smith, Dan: Legend of Gator Face, The

Warwick, James: Partners in Crime (Secret Adversary) (TV Series); Seven Dials Mystery, The; Why Didn't They Ask Evans?

Warwick, John: Face at the Window, The; Ticket of Leave Man, The

Warwick, Richard: If ... ; Lost Language of Cranes, The

Warwick, Robert: Adventures of Don Juan, The; Bold Caballero, The; Gangster's Boy; In a Lonely Place; Kismet (1944); Private Lives of Elizabeth and Essex, The; Sudan; Sullivan's Travels; Woman's Face, A

Washbourne, Mona: Billy Liar; Brides of Dracula; Brideshead Revisited; Collector, The; Driver's Seat, The; Stevie

Washburn, Beverly: Wagon Train (TV Series)

Washburn, Bryant: Falcon in Mexico, The; Night of Terror; Return of Chandu (Magician, The)

Washburne, Rick: Comrades in Arms; Hangmen; Little Patriot, The

Washington, Blue: Haunted Gold

Washington, Denzel: Bone Collector, The; Carbon Copy; Courage Under Fire; Crimson Tide; Cry Freedom; Devil in a Blue Dress; Fallen; For Queen and Country; George McKenna Story, The (1999); Glory; He Got Game; Heart Condition; Hurricane, The (1999); Malcolm X; Mighty Quinn, The; Mississippi Masala; Mo' Better Blues; Much Ado About Nothing; Pelican Brief, The; Philadelphia; Power (1986); Preacher's Wife, The; Ricochet; Siege, The; St. Elsewhere (TV Series); Virtuosity

Washington, Dinah: Ladies Sing the Blues, The

Washington, Isaiah: Always Outnumbered; Girl 6; Joe Torre: Curveballs Along the Way; Love Jones; Mr. and Mrs. Loving; Romeo Must Die; True Crime (1999)

Washington, Kenneth: Hogan's Heroes (TV Series)

Washio, Isako: Fist of the North Star (1995)

Wass, Ted: Canterville Ghost, The (1986); Curse of the Pink Panther, The; Longshot, The (1985); Oh, God, You Devil!; Pancho Barnes; Sheena; Triplecross (1985)

Wasserman, Jerry: Cooler Climate, A; Quarantine

Wasson, Craig: Body Double; Four Friends; Ghost Story; Go Tell the Spartans; Men's Club, The; Nightmare on Elm Street 3, A: The Dream Warriors; Schizoid; Sister-in-Law, The (1995); Skag; Strapped; Trapped in Space

Watanabe, Eriko: Shall We Dance? (1996)

Watanabe, Fumio: Lone Wolf and Cub: Sword of Vengeance

Watanabe, Gedde: Gung Ho (1985); Vamp; Volunteers

Watanabe, Tetsu: Fireworks; Sonatine

Watase, Tsunehiko: Antarctica

Waterman, Dennis: Cold Justice; Scars of Dracula

Waterman, Felicity: Lena's Holiday; Miracle Beach; Thunder in Paradise

Waters, Crystal: Wigstock: The Movie

Waters, Ethel: Cabin in the Sky; Cairo; Member of the Wedding, The; Pinky; Tales of Manhattan

Waters, John: Alice to Nowhere; Attack Force Z; Boulevard of Broken Dreams; Breaker Morant; Ebbtide; Grievous Bodily Harm; Heaven Tonight; Miracle Down Under; Three's Trouble; Which Way Home

Waters, Muddy: Last Waltz, The

Waterston, Sam: Assault at West Point; Capricorn One; Captive in the Land, A; Crimes and Misdemeanors;

Dempsey; Eagle's Wing; Enemy Within, The; Finnegan Begin Again; Friendly Fire; Generation; Gore Vidal's Lincoln; Great Gatsby, The; Hannah and Her Sisters; Heaven's Gate; Interiors; Journey into Fear (1975); Journey of August King, The; Just Between Friends; Killing Fields, The; Lantern Hill; Man in the Moon, The; Mindwalk; Nightmare Years, The; Proprietor, The; Rancho Deluxe; Reflections of Murder; September; Serial Mom; Shadow Conspiracy; Sweet William; Trade Secrets; Warning Sign; Welcome Home; Who Killed Mary What's 'Er Name?

Watford, Gwen: Body in the Library, The; Fall of the House of Usher, The (1949); Ghoul, The (1975); Taste the Blood of Dracula

Watkin, Pierre: Atom Man vs. Superman; Shock (1946); Story of Seabiscuit, The; Superman—The Serial; Two Lost Worlds

Watkins, Gary: Wheels of Fire

Watkins, Linda: From Hell It Came

Watkins, Tionne "T-Boz": Belly

Watkins, Tuc: I Think I Do

Watson, Alberta: Best Revenge; Destiny to Order; Hitman; The; Keep, The; Spanking the Monkey; Women of Valor

Watson, Anthony: Long Day Closes, The

Watson, Barry: Teaching Mrs. Tingle

Watson, Bill: Stingray

Watson, Bobs: Men of Boys Town; On Borrowed Time

Watson, Douglas: Parker Adderson, Philosopher; Trial of the Cantonsville Nine, The

Watson, Emily: Angela's Ashes; Boxer, The; Breaking the Waves; Cradle Will Rock; Hilary and Jackie; Metroland

Watson, Jack: King Arthur, The Young Warlord; Schizo; Sleeping Murder; Wild Geese, The

Watson, Jennia: Ragdoll

Watson, Lucile: Emperor Waltz, The; Footsteps in the Dark; Great Lie, The; Julia Misbehaves; Made for Each Other; My Forbidden Past; Thin Man Goes Home, The; Three Smart Girls; Tomorrow Is Forever; Uncertain Glory; Waterloo Bridge

Watson, Michael: Subspecies

Watson, Mills: Heated Vengeance; Kansas City Massacre, The

Watson, Minor: Adventures of Huckleberry Finn, The (1939); Beyond the Forest; Jackie Robinson Story, The; Navy Blue and Gold; Star, The (1952); Virginian, The (1946)

Watson, Moray: Body in the Library, The; Pride and Prejudice (1985)

Watson, Muse: Acts of Betrayal; From Dusk Till Dawn 2: Texas Blood Money; I Still Know What You Did Last Summer; Something to Talk About

Watson, Vernee: Death Drug

Watt, Marty: Almost You

Watt, Nathan: Unstrung Heroes

Watt, Richard C.: Deathshot

Watters, William (Hall Sr., Arch): Eegah!; Wild Guitar

Wattis, Richard: Colditz Story, The; Importance of Being Earnest, The

Watts, Naomi: Brides of Christ; Children of the Corn IV: The Gathering; Persons Unknown; Tank Girl

Wauthion, Claire: Flight of Rainbirds, A

Waxman, Al: Clown Murders, The; Collision Course (1989); Hitman, The; Iron Eagle IV; Live Wire; Malarek; Meatballs III; Mob Story; Rescuers, Stories of Courage, "Two Women"; Spasms; Summer's End; Tulips; Wild Horse Hank

Way, Eileen: Queen of Hearts

Wayans, Damon: Blankman; Bulletproof (1996); Celtic Pride; Earth Girls Are Easy; Great White Hype, The; Last Boy Scout, The; Major Payne; Mo' Money

Wayans, Keenen Ivory: Glimmer Man, The; I'm Gonna Git You Sucka!; Low Down Dirty Shame, A

Wayans, Kim: Floundering; Talking About Sex

Wayans, Marlon: Above the Rim; Don't Be a Menace to South Central while Drinking Your Juice in the 'Hood; Mo' Money; Senseless; Sixth Man, The

Wayans, Shawn: Don't Be a Menace to South Central while Drinking Your Juice in the 'Hood; New Blood

Wayborn, Kristine: Little Ghost

Wayne, David: Adam's Rib (1949); American Christmas Carol, An; Andromeda Strain, The; Apple Dumpling Gang, The; As Young as You Feel; Front Page, The (1974); How to Marry a Millionaire; Huckleberry Finn (1974); Last Angry

Man, The; Poker Alice; Portrait of Jennie; Prizefighter, The; Sad Sack, The; Stella (1950); Survivalist, The; Tender Trap, The; Three Faces of Eve, The; We're Not Married

Wayne, Ethan: Operation 'Nam

Wayne, John: Alamo, The; Allegheny Uprising; Angel and the Badman; Baby Face; Back to Bataan; Barbarian and the Geisha, The; Big Jake; Big Jim McLain; Big Stampede, The; Big Trail, The; Blood Alley; Blue Steel (1934); Brannigan; Cahill—US Marshal; Chisum; Circus World; Comancheros, The; Conqueror, The; Cowboys, The; Dakota (1945); Dark Command; Dawn Rider; Donovan's Reef; El Dorado; Fighting Kentuckian, The; Fighting Seabees, The; Flame of the Barbary Coast; Flying Leathernecks; Flying Tigers, The; Fort Apache; Frontier Horizon; Greatest Story Ever Told, The; Green Berets, The; Hatari!; Haunted Gold; Hell Town; Hellfighters; High and the Mighty, The; His Private Secretary; Hondo; Horse Soldiers, The; How the West Was Won; Hurricane Express; In Harm's Way; In Old California; Island in the Sky; King of the Pecos; Lady for a Night; Lady from Louisiana; Lady Takes a Chance, A; Lawless Frontier; Lawless Nineties, The; Legend of the Lost; Lonely Trail, The; Long Voyage Home, The; Longest Day, The; Lucky Texan; Man from Monterey, The; Man from Utah, The; Man Who Shot Liberty Valance, The; McLintock!; McQ; 'Neath Arizona Skies; New Frontier; Night Riders, The; North to Alaska; Operation Pacific; Overland Stage Raiders; Pals of the Saddle; Pittsburgh; Quiet Man, The; Rainbow Valley; Randy Rides Alone; Range Feud; Reap the Wild Wind; Red River; Red River Range; Reunion in France; Ride Him Cowboy; Riders of Destiny; Rio Bravo; Rio Grande; Rio Lobo; Rooster Cogburn; Sagebrush Trail; Sands of Iwo Jima; Santa Fe Stampede; Sea Chase, The; Searchers, The; Seven Sinners; Shadow of the Eagle; She Wore a Yellow Ribbon; Shepherd of the Hills, The; Shootist, The; Somewhere in Sonora; Sons of Katie Elder, The; Spoilers, The; Stagecoach (1939); Star Packer, The; Tall in the Saddle; Telegraph Trail, The; Texas Cyclone; Texas Terror; They Were Expendable, The; Three Faces West; Three Godfathers, The; Three Musketeers, The (1933); Three Texas Steers; Trail Beyond, The; Train Robbers, The; Trouble Along the Way; True Grit; Two-Fisted Law; Tycoon; Undefeated, The; Wake of the Red Witch; War of the Wildcats; War Wagon, The; West of the Divide; Westward Ho; Wheel of Fortune; Winds of the Wasteland; Wings of Eagles, The; Without Reservations; Wyoming Outlaw

Wayne, John Ethan: Scream (1982)

Wayne, Keith: Night of the Living Dead (1968)

Wayne, Michael: Danger Zone, The (1986); Island Fury

Wayne, Naunton: Night Train to Munich (Night Train); Passport to Pimlico; Quartet (1948)

Wayne, Norma Jean: Blondie's Blessed Event

Wayne, Patrick: Beyond Atlantis; Big Jake; Deserter, The; Green Berets, The; Her Alibi; McLintock!; People That Time Forgot, The; Rustler's Rhapsody; Searchers, The; Shenandoah; Sinbad and the Eye of the Tiger; Talion; Young Guns

Wayne, Sarah: Magic in the Water, The

Wazaki, Toshiya: X from Outer Space, The

Weatherly, Michael: Cabin by the Lake

Weatherly, Shawn: Amityville 1992: It's About Time; Mindgames; Shadowzone; Thieves of Fortune

Weathers, Carl: Action Jackson; Dangerous Passion; Death Hunt; Force Ten from Navarone; Fortune Dane; Friday Foster; Happy Gilmore; Hurricane Smith; Predator; Rocky; Rocky II; Rocky III; Rocky IV

Weaver, Blayne: Good Old Boys, The

Weaver, Dennis: Best Christmas Pageant Ever, The; Cocaine: One Man's Seduction; Disaster at Silo 7; Don't Go to Sleep; Dragnet (1954); Duel; Duel at Diablo; Gallant Hours, The; Gentle Giant; Gunsmoke (TV Series); Intimate Strangers; Ordeal of Dr. Mudd, The; Redhead from Wyoming, The; Ten Wanted Men; Two Bits & Pepper; Virginian, The (1999); What's the Matter with Helen?

Weaver, Doodles: 30 Foot Bride of Candy Rock, The

Weaver, Fritz: Black Sunday (1977); Blind Spot; Creepshow; Day of the Dolphin, The; Demon Seed; Fail-Safe; Hearst and Davies Affair, The; Holocaust; Hunter (1971); Ironclads; Jaws of Satan; Jolly Corner, The; My Name Is Bill W; Rescuers, Stories of Courage, "Two Women"; Thomas Crown Affair, The (1999); Walk in the Spring Rain, A

Weaver, Jacki: Caddie; Picnic at Hanging Rock; Squizzy Taylor; Three's Trouble

Weaver, Marjorie: Charlie Chan's Murder Cruise; Gentleman from California; Murder over New York; Young Mr. Lincoln

Weaver, Robert "Wingnut": Endless Summer II

Weaver, Sigourney: Alien; Aliens; Alien 3; Alien Resurrection; Copycat; Dave; Deal of the Century; Death and the Maiden; Eyewitness; 1492: The Conquest of Paradise; Galaxy Quest; Ghostbusters; Ghostbusters II; Gorillas in the Mist; Half-Moon Street; Ice Storm, The; Jeffrey; Map of the World, A; One Woman or Two; Snow White: A Tale of Terror; Working Girl; Year of Living Dangerously, The

Weaving, Hugo: Adventures of Priscilla, Queen of the Desert, The; Bedrooms and Hallways; Custodian, The; For Love Alone; Frauds; Matrix, The; Proof; Reckless Kelly; Right Hand Man, The

Webb, Alan: Challenge to Lassie; Chimes at Midnight (Falstaff); Entertaining Mr. Sloane; Great Train Robbery, The; King Lear (1971); Women in Love

Webb, Chloe: Belly of an Architect, The; China Beach (TV Series); Dangerous Woman, A; Heart Condition; Sid and Nancy; Twins

Webb, Clifton: Dark Corner, The; Laura; Man Who Never Was, The; Razor's Edge, The (1946); Stars and Stripes Forever; Titanic (1953); Woman's World

Webb, Daniel: Unapproachable, The

Webb, Gregg: Running Mates (1985)

Webb, Gregory: Puppet Master II

Webb, Jack: D.I., The; Dragnet (1954); Halls of Montezuma; He Walked by Night; Men, The (1950); Pete Kelly's Blues; Sunset Boulevard

Webb, Julie: Billy Jack

Webb, Lucy: Outside Ozona

Webb, Richard: Distant Drums; Out of the Past

Webb, Veronica: In Too Deep

Webber, Brian: Bent

Webber, Jake: Meet Joe Black; Skin Art; U-571; What the Deaf Man Heard

Webber, Mark: Whiteboyz

Webber, Peggy: Screaming Skull, The

Webber, Robert: Assassin; Bring Me the Head of Alfredo Garcia; Casey's Shadow; Dead Heat on a Merry-Go-Round; $ (Dollars); Don't Go to Sleep; Final Option, The; French Woman, The; Hysteria; Nuts; Outer Limits, The, (TV Series); Private Benjamin; Revenge of the Pink Panther, The; Starflight One; Streets of L.A., The; Stripper, The; 10; 12 Angry Men (1957); Wrong Is Right

Webber, Timothy: Grey Fox, The; John and the Missus; That's My Baby; Toby McTeague

Weber, Amy: Kolobos

Weber, Andrea: Everything Relative

Weber, Catherine: Body Strokes (Siren's Call); Virtual Desire

Weber, Jacques: Cyrano De Bergerac (1990); Northern Passage

Weber, Rick: Somewhere, Tomorrow

Weber, Steven: At First Sight (1999); Break Up; Cop for the Killing, A; Dracula: Dead and Loving It; Hamburger Hill; Jeffrey; Single White Female; Stephen King's The Shining

Weber, Suzanna: Cold River

Weborg, Jeff: Islander, The

Webster, Derek: Josh Kirby, Time Warrior (Series); Josh Kirby … Time Warrior: Trapped on Toy World; Josh Kirby … Time Warrior: Journey to the Magic Cavern

Webster, Hugh: King of the Grizzlies

Weck, Peter: Almost Angels

Wedgeworth, Ann: Birch Interval, The; Bogie; Catamount Killing, The; Citizen's Band; Cooperstown; Far North; Men's Club, The; Sweet Dreams; Tiger's Tale, A; Whole Wide World, The

Weeden, Bill: Sgt. Kabukiman N.Y.P.D.

Weeks, Alan: Truck Turner

Weeks, Barbara: Forbidden Trail; Sundown Rider, The; Violent Years, The

Wegener, Paul: Golem, The (How He Came into the World) (Der Golem, Wie Er in die Welt)

Weibel, Peter: Invisible Adversaries

Weidler, Virginia: All This and Heaven Too; Babes on Broadway; Best Foot Forward; Great Man Votes, The; Too Hot to Handle; Young Tom Edison

Weigel, Rafer: Free Enterprise

Weil, Liza: Stir of Echoes; Whatever

Weingraf, John E.: Disembodied, The

Weintraub, Carl: Sorry, Wrong Number (1989)

Weir, Benjamin: Double Jeopardy (1999)

Weisman, Robin: Three Men and a Little Lady; Thunder in Paradise

Weiss, George: Glen or Glenda

Weiss, Michael T.: Howling IV; Jeffrey

Weiss, Roberta: Abducted; High Stakes (1986)

Weiss, Shaun: Heavyweights

Weisser, Morgan: Long Road Home, The; Mother (1994)

Weisser, Norbert: Adrenalin: Fear the Rush; Android; Arcade; Deceit; Heatseeker; My Antonia; Nemesis 3: Time Lapse; Nemesis 4; Omega Doom; Radioactive Dreams; Riders of the Purple Sage

Weissmuller, Johnny: Fury of the Congo; Jungle Jim; Tarzan and His Mate; Tarzan and the Leopard Woman; Tarzan Escapes; Tarzan Finds a Son; Tarzan the Ape Man (1932); Tarzan Triumphs; Tarzan's New York Adventure; Tarzan's Secret Treasure

Weist, Lucinda: Haunting of Sea Cliff Inn, The

Weisz, Rachel: Chain Reaction (1996); Going All the Way; I Want You; Land Girls, The; Mummy, The (1999); Stealing Beauty; Swept from the Sea

Weitz, Bruce: Breaking the Surface: The Greg Louganis Story; Death of a Centerfold; Hill Street Blues (TV Series); Landlady, The; Liars' Club, The; Molly & Gina; No Place To Hide; O. J. Simpson Story, The; Rainbow Drive; Velocity Trap; Windrunner

Welch, Elisabeth: Big Fella; Song of Freedom

Welch, Joseph: Anatomy of a Murder

Welch, Niles: Phantom, The (1931)

Welch, Raquel: Bandolero!; Bedazzled; Bluebeard (1972); Chairman of the Board; Fantastic Voyage; Four Musketeers, The; Fuzz; Hannie Caulder; Lady in Cement; Last of Sheila, The; Legend of Walks Far Woman, The; Magic Christian, The; Mother, Jugs, and Speed; Myra Breckenridge; Oldest Profession, The; 100 Rifles; Restless; Scandal in a Small Town; Shoot Loud, Louder ... I Don't Understand; Swingin' Summer, A; Tainted Blood; Three Musketeers, The (1973); Trouble in Paradise; Wild Party, The (1975)

Welch, Tahnee: Cocoon; Cocoon: The Return; Criminal Mind, The; Johnny 2.0; Lethal Obsession; Night Train to Venice

Weld, Tuesday: Author! Author!; Cincinnati Kid, The; Falling Down; Feeling Minnesota; Five Pennies, The; Heartbreak Hotel; I'll Take Sweden; Looking for Mr. Goodbar; Lord Love a Duck; Once Upon a Time in America (Long Version); Pretty Poison; Reflections of Murder; Return to Peyton Place; Rock, Rock, Rock; Serial; Soldier in the Rain; Thief (1981); Who'll Stop the Rain; Wild in the Country

Welden, Ben: Kid Galahad (1937)

Welker, Frank: Pagemaster, The

Welland, Colin: Spymaker: The Secret Life of Ian Fleming

Weller, Frederick: Stonewall

Weller, Mary Louise: Evil, The; Forced Vengeance

Weller, Peter: Adventures of Buckaroo Banzai, The; Apology; Cat Chaser; Decoy; Diplomatic Siege; End of Summer; Firstborn; Fifty/Fifty; Just Tell Me What You Want; Killing Affair, A; Leviathan; Naked Lunch; New Age, The; Of Unknown Origin; Rainbow Drive; Road to Ruin (1991); RoboCop; RoboCop 2; Screamers (1996); Substitute Wife, The; Sunset Grill; Tunnel, The; Women & Men: Stories of Seduction

Welles, Gwen: Between the Lines; Desert Hearts; Eating; Hit! (1973); New Year's Day; Sticky Fingers

Welles, Mel: Attack of the Crab Monsters; Commando Squad; Dr. Heckyl and Mr. Hype; Little Shop of Horrors, The (1960); She Beast, The

Welles, Orson: Battle of Austerlitz, The; Black Magic (1949); Blood and Guns (Tepepa); Butterfly; Casino Royale (1967); Chimes at Midnight (Falstaff); Citizen Kane; Compulsion; F for Fake; Follow the Boys; Get to Know Your Rabbit; Immortal Story; Is Paris Burning?; It's All True; Jane Eyre (1944); Journey into Fear (1942); Lady from Shanghai; Long Hot Summer, The (1958); Macbeth (1948); Man for All Seasons, A; Mr. Arkadin (Confidential Report); Moby Dick (1956); Muppet Movie, The; Napoleon (1955); Othello (1952); Scene of the Crime (1985); Someone to Love; Stranger, The (1947); Ten Days Wonder; Third Man, The;

Three Cases of Murder; Tomorrow Is Forever; Touch of Evil; Trial, The (1963); Trouble in the Glen; V.I.P.s, The; Voyage of the Damned; Waterloo; Witching, The (Necromancy)

Welles, Steve: Puppet Master II

Welles, Virginia: Francis in the Haunted House

Welling, Miki: Alex's Apartment

Wellington, James: Too Fast Too Young

Welliver, Titus: Zero Tolerance

Wellman Jr., William: Black Caesar; Born Losers; Swingin' Summer, A

Wells, Dawn: Return to Boggy Creek; Town That Dreaded Sundown, The

Wells, Doris: Oriane

Wells, Jacqueline: Black Cat, The (1934); Kansas Terrors; Ranger and the Lady, The; Tarzan the Fearless

Wells, Mel: Wizard of the Lost Kingdom II

Wells, Tico: Five Heartbeats, The; Mississippi Masala

Wells, Tracy: Mirror, Mirror 2: Raven Dance

Wells, Vernon: Bounty Hunter 2002; Circle of Fear; Circuitry Man; Circuitry Man II: Plughead Rewired; Enemy Unseen; Last Man Standing (1988); Road Warrior, The; Stranglehold

Welsh, John: Nightmare (1964)

Welsh, Kenneth: Adrift; And Then You Die; Big Slice, The; Dead Silence (1996); Death Wish V: The Face of Death; Escape Clause; Good Fight, The; Joe Torre: Curveballs Along the Way; Last Best Year, The; Love and Hate; Loyalties; Margaret's Museum; Screwball Academy; Straight Line; War Boy, The

Welti, Lisa: Don't Sleep Alone

Wen, Jiang: Emperor's Shadow, The

Wen, Ming-Na: Hong Kong '97; Joy Luck Club, The; One Night Stand (1997); Star Quest; Street Fighter (1994)

Wences, Señor: Mother Wore Tights

Wenders, Wim: Lightning over Water

Wendt, George: Alice in Wonderland (1999); Aliens Among Us; Guilty by Suspicion; Gung Ho (1985); Hostage for a Day; House; Man of the House; Outside Providence; Plain Clothes; Spice World

Weng, Jian: Red Sorghum

Weng, Weng: For Your Height Only

Wenli, Jiang: Story of Xinghua, The

Wenner, Jann: Perfect

Went, Johanna: Living End, The

Wepper, Fritz: Bridge, The; Final Combat, The

Werle, Barbara: Gone with the West; Little Moon & Jud McGraw

Werner, Oskar: Fahrenheit 451; Jules and Jim; Lola Montes; Ship of Fools; Shoes of the Fisherman; Spy Who Came in from the Cold, The; Voyage of the Damned

Wernicke, Otto: Testament of Dr. Mabuse

Wert, Doug: Assassination Game, The; Baby Face Nelson; Dracula Rising; Wasp Woman, The (1995)

Wesley, Charles: Murdercycle

Wessel, Dick: Dick Tracy versus Cueball; Gazebo, The; Pitfall

Wesson, Dick: Destination Moon; Jim Thorpe—All American

Wesson, Eileen: Zarkorr! The Invader

Wesson, Jessica: Flipper (1996)

West, Adam: Batman (1966); Doin' Time on Planet Earth; For the Love of It; Happy Hooker Goes Hollywood, The; Joyride (1997); Mad About You; New Age, The; Night of the Kickfighters; Omega Cop; One Dark Night; Tammy and the Doctor; Young Philadelphians, The; Zombie Nightmare

West, Chandra: Puppet Master Four; Puppet Master 5: The Final Chapter; Universal Soldier II: Brothers in Arms

West, Charles: D. W. Griffith Triple Feature

West, Dean: Blood Harvest

West, Dominic: 28 Days; William Shakespeare's A Midsummer Night's Dream

West, Dottie: Aurora Encounter

West, Jeremy: Curse IV: The Ultimate Sacrifice

West, Julian: Vampyr (1931)

West, Kevin: Expose; Santa with Muscles

West, Mae: Belle of the Nineties; Every Day's a Holiday; Go West, Young Man; Goin' to Town; Heat's On, The; I'm No Angel; Klondike Annie; My Little Chickadee; Myra Breckenridge; Night after Night; Sextette; She Done Him Wrong

West, Martin: Swingin' Summer, A

West, Samuel: Carrington; Howards End

West, Shane: Whatever It Takes

West, Timothy: Hedda; Messenger: The Story of Joan of Arc, The; Oliver Twist (1982); Pocketful of Rye, A

Westaway, Simon: Sahara (1995)

Westbrook, Wendi: Under Lock and Key*

Westcott, Helen: Gunfighter, The (1950)

Wester, Travis: Paper Brigade, The

Westerman, Floyd Red Crow: Clearcut; Lakota Woman: Siege at Wounded Knee; Last Assassins; One Riot, One Ranger

Westhead, David: Mrs. Brown

Westheimer, Dr. Ruth: Forever Lulu; One Woman or Two

Westhof, Kelly: My Daughter's Keeper

Westley, Helen: Anne of Green Gables (1934); Dimples; Rebecca of Sunnybrook Farm (1938); Roberta; Stowaway

Westman, Nydia: Sweet Adeline

Westmoreland, James: Don't Answer the Phone

Weston, Celin: Lost Angels

Weston, David: Masque of the Red Death, The (1964)

Weston, Jack: All in a Night's Work; Can't Stop the Music; Cuba; Dirty Dancing; Four Seasons, The; Gator; High Road to China; Honeymoon Machine, The; Incredible Mr. Limpet, The; Ishtar; Longshot, The (1985); Mirage (1965); New Leaf, A; Palm Springs Weekend; Please Don't Eat the Daisies; Rad; Ritz, The; Short Circuit 2

Westrick, Bobby: Goblin

Wettig, Patricia: City Slickers; City Slickers II; Guilty by Suspicion; Langoliers, The; Me & Veronica; Parallel Lives; Silent Motive

Wever, Merrit: Strike! (1998)

Weyand, Ron: Deadly Hero; Music School, The

Weyers, Marius: African Rage; Bopha!; Gods Must Be Crazy, The; Power of One, The

Weyher, Ruth: Warning Shadows (1923)

Whalen, Michael: Batman and Robin (Adventures of Batman and Robin); Missile to the Moon; Poor Little Rich Girl (1936)

Whaley, Frank: Back in the U.S.S.R.; Bombshell (1997); Broken Arrow (1996); Cafe Society; Career Opportunities; Desperate Trail; Doors, The; Hoffa; Homage; I.Q.; Little Monsters; Midnight Clear, A; Swimming with Sharks; Swing Kids; Wall, The (1998) (U.S.); When Trumpets Fade

Whalin, Justin: Child's Play 3; Perfect Harmony

Whalley, Joanne: Big Man; Edge of Darkness (1986); Good Father, The; Good Man in Africa, A; Kill Me Again; Man Who Knew Too Little, The; Mother's Boys; Navy Seals; No Surrender; Scandal; Scarlett; Secret Rapture, The; Shattered (1991); To Kill a Priest; Trial by Jury; Willow

Whately, Kevin: English Patient, The; Inspector Morse (TV Series)

Wheatley, Leo: Little Kidnappers

Wheaton, Wil: Buddy System, The; Curse, The; December; Flubber; Last Prostitute, The; Liars' Club, The; Mr. Stitch; Stand by Me (1986); Star Trek: The Next Generation (TV Series); Toy Soldiers (1991)

Wheeler, Bert: Cockeyed Cavaliers; Diplomaniacs; Dixiana; Hips, Hips, Hooray; Hold 'em Jail; Hook, Line and Sinker; Kentucky Kernels

Wheeler, Jane: Marked Man

Wheeler, Kay: Rock, Baby, Rock It

Wheeler, Lois: My Foolish Heart

Wheeler-Nicholson, Dana: Circuitry Man; Denise Calls Up; Fletch; Frank & Jesse; Living in Peril; Tombstone

Whelan, Arleen: Castle in the Desert; Ramrod; Senator Was Indiscreet, The; Sun Shines Bright, The

Whelan, Wendy: George Balanchine's The Nutcracker

Whelchel, Lisa: Double McGuffin, The; Magician of Lublin, The

Whitely, Arkie: Gallowglass

Whipp, Joseph: Amazons

Whipple, Shonda: Magic Kid

Whirry, Shannon: Animal Instincts; Animal Instincts 2; Body of Influence; Dangerous Prey; Exit; Granny, The; Mirror Images II; Omega Doom; Playback; Private Obsession

Whitaker, Christina: Assault of the Killer Bimbos; Love Street

Whitaker, Duane: From Dusk Till Dawn 2: Texas Blood Money; Saturday Night Special; Within the Rock

Whitaker, Forest: Article 99; Bank Robber; Battlefield Earth; Bird; Bloodsport; Blown Away (1994); Body Count (1997); Body Snatchers, The (1993); Consenting Adults

(1992); Criminal Justice; Crying Game, The; Diary of a Hitman; Downtown; Enemy Within, The; Fast Times at Ridgemont High; Fast Times at Ridgemont High; Ghost Dog: The Way of the Samurai; Good Morning, Vietnam; Jason's Lyric; Johnny Handsome; Last Light; Light It Up; Lush Life; Phenomenon; Platoon; Rage in Harlem, A; Rebound; Smoke (1995); Species; Stakeout; Witness Protection

Whitaker, Johnny: Littlest Angel, The; Napoleon and Samantha; Snowball Express; Tom Sawyer (1973)

Whitaker, Slim: Arizona Bound; Bold Caballero, The; Ghost Patrol; Haunted Gold; Man from Monterey, The

Whitcraft, Liza: Object of Obsession

White, Alice: Sweethearts on Parade

White, Barry: Streetfight (Coonskin)

White, Bernie: Body Count (1988)

White, Betty: Hard Rain; Lake Placid; Story of Us, The; Weekend in the Country, A

White, Bill: Vampires & Other Stereotypes

White, Bo: Very Natural Thing, A

White, Carol: Daddy's Gone A-Hunting; Man Who Had Power over Women, The; Never Let Go; Some Call It Loving; Squeeze, The (1977)

White, David: Amazing Spiderman, The

White, Diz: Bullshot (Bullshot Crummond)

White, Earl: Nemesis 2

White, Henry: Raising Heroes

White, Jacqueline: Narrow Margin, The (1952)

White, Jan: Season of the Witch

White, Jesse: Bedtime for Bonzo; Bless the Beasts and Children; Dear Brigitte; Francis Goes to the Races; Matinee; Million Dollar Mermaid; Reluctant Astronaut, The; Rise and Fall of Legs Diamond, The; Tomboy and the Champ

White, John: Legend of Gator Face, The

White, Johnny: Johnny & Clyde

White, Leo: Charlie Chaplin—The Early Years Vol. 1–4; Charlie Chaplin Cavalcade

White, Marjorie: Diplomaniacs; Just Imagine

White, Michael Jai: Freedom Song; Spawn; Tyson

White, Patricia: Riders of the Whistling Pines

White, Pearl: Great Chase, The

White, Peter: Boys in the Band, The

White, Reggie: Reggie's Prayer

White, Ron: Conundrum; Kissinger and Nixon; Last Train Home; Screamers (1996); Shadow Zone: The Undead Express; Silent Witness: What a Child Saw

White, Vanna: Gypsy Angels

White, Wally: Lie Down with Dogs

Whitehead, Mike: Dinosaur Babes

Whitehead, O. Z.: Ma and Pa Kettle (The Further Adventures of Ma and Pa Kettle)

Whitehead, Paxton: Boris and Natasha; Child of Darkness, Child of Light; Chips, the War Dog; Primal Secrets

Whitelaw, Billie: Dressmaker, The; Gumshoe; Jane Eyre (1996); Krays, The; Leopard in the Snow; Lorna Doone; Make Mine Mink; Murder Elite; Night Watch; No Love for Johnnie; Omen, The; Secret Garden, The (1987); Shadey; Slayground; Strange Case of Dr. Jekyll and Mr. Hyde, The (1968); Tale of Two Cities, A (1980); Water Babies, The

Whiteman, Paul: Fabulous Dorseys, The; King of Jazz, The; Strike Up the Band

Whitfield, June: Absolutely Fabulous

Whitfield, Lynn: Color of Courage, The; Eve's Bayou; George McKenna Story, The; Josephine Baker Story, The; Junior's Groove; State of Emergency; Taking the Heat; Thin Line Between Love and Hate, A

Whitfield, Mitchell: Best Men; Dogfight; I Love You, Don't Touch Me!; My Cousin Vinny

Whitfield, Raymond: How U Like Me Now

Whitford, Bradley: Billy Madison; Masterminds; Muse, The; My Fellow Americans; Red Corner

Whiting, Barbara: Beware, My Lovely

Whiting, Jack: Give Me a Sailor

Whiting, Leonard: Romeo and Juliet (1968); Royal Hunt of the Sun

Whiting, Margaret: Sinbad and the Eye of the Tiger; Taking My Turn

Whitley, Ray: Land of the Open Range; Renegade Ranger

Whitlow, Jill: Adventures Beyond Belief; Ghost Chase; Night of the Creeps; Thunder Run; Twice Dead

Whitman, Ernest: Among the Living

Whitman, Mae: Gingerbread Man, The; Hope Floats; One Fine Day; When a Man Loves a Woman

Whitman, Stuart: Captain Apache; Comancheros, The; Crazy Mama; Crime of Passion; Day And The Hour; Delta Fox; Demonoid; Eaten Alive; Girl in Black Stockings, The; Kill Castro (Cuba Crossing, Mercenaries (1978), Sweet Violent Tony); Las Vegas Lady; Mean Johnny Barrows; Mob Boss; Monster Club, The; Omega Cop; Private Wars; Ransom (1977); Revenge (1971) (Shelley Winters); Rio Conchos; Ruby (1977); Run for the Roses (Thoroughbred); Sandman (1992); Seekers, The; Shatter; Smooth Talker; Story of Ruth, The; Strange Shadows in an Empty Room; Texas Guns; Those Magnificent Men in Their Flying Machines; Treasure of the Amazon; Trial by Jury; Vultures; Walker: Texas Ranger; White Buffalo; Wounded Heart

Whitmore, James: Above and Beyond; All My Sons (1986); All the Brothers Were Valiant; Asphalt Jungle, The; Battleground; Because You're Mine; Black Like Me; Chato's Land; Chuka; Eddy Duchin Story, The; First Deadly Sin, The; Force of One; Girl Who Had Everything, The; Give 'em Hell, Harry!; Glory! Glory!; Golden Honeymoon, The; Guns of the Magnificent Seven; Harrad Experiment, The; High Crime; I Will Fight No More Forever; It's a Big Country; Kiss Me Kate; Madigan; McConnell Story, The; Next Voice You Hear, The; Nuts; Old Explorers; Rage (1980); Relic, The; Serpent's Egg, The; Shawshank Redemption, The; Them!; Tora! Tora! Tora!; Waterhole #3; Where the Red Fern Grows; Word, The

Whitmore Jr., James: Boys in Company C, The; Gypsy Warriors, The

Whitney, Grace Lee: Star Trek (TV Series)

Whitrow, Benjamin: Belfast Assassin; Pride and Prejudice (1996)

Whitt, Garland: Blind Faith

Whittaker, Forest: Ready to Wear

Whitten, Frank: Vigil

Whitten, Margaret: Two-Gun Man from Harlem

Whitthorne, Paul: Critters 4

Whittingtonn, Shawn: Barn Burning

Whittle, Brenton: Sara Dane

Whitton, Margaret: Best of Times, The; Big Girls Don't Cry—They Get Even; Little Monsters; Major League; Man without a Face, The; 9 1/2 Weeks; Secret of My Success, The; Trial by Jury

Whitworth, James: Planet of the Dinosaurs

Whitworth, Johnny: Empire Records; Somebody is Waiting

Who, The: Kids Are Alright, The; Monterey Pop; Rock and Roll Circus, The

Wholihan, Kit: Islander, The

Whorf, Richard: Chain Lightning; Keeper of the Flame; Midnight (1934); Yankee Doodle Dandy

Whylie, James: Place of Weeping

Wickes, Mary: Blondie's Blessed Event; By the Light of the Silvery Moon; Don't Go Near the Water; How to Murder your Wife; I'll See You In My Dreams; June Bride; Ma and Pa Kettle at Home; Man Who Came to Dinner, The; On Moonlight Bay; Postcards from the Edge; Sister Act; Sister Act 2: Back in the Habit; Touched by Love

Wickham, Jeffrey: Terrorists, The

Wickham, Saskia: Leo Tolstoy's Anna Karenina (1997)

Wicki, Bernhard: Crime & Passion; Killing Cars; Love in Germany, A; Mysterious Stranger, The; Spring Symphony

Wicks, Rebecca: Jack-O

Widdoes, Kathleen: Mafia Princess; Without a Trace

Widmark, Richard: Alamo, The; All God's Children; Alvarez Kelly; Bear Island; Bedford Incident, The; Blackout (1985); Broken Lance; Cheyenne Autumn; Cold Sassy Tree; Coma; Death of a Gunfighter; Domino Principle, The; Don't Bother to Knock; Final Option, The; Halls of Montezuma; Hanky Panky; How the West Was Won; Judgment at Nuremberg; Kiss of Death (1947); Law and Jake Wade, The; Madigan; Mr. Horn; Murder on the Bayou; Night and the City (1950); Panic in the Streets; Pickup on South Street; Road House (1948); Rollercoaster; Run for the Sun; Saint Joan; Sell-Out, The; Street with No Name; Swarm, The; Texas Guns; To the Devil, a Daughter; Trap, The; True Colors; Tunnel of

Love, The; Twilight's Last Gleaming; Two Rode Together; Warlock (1959); Way West, The (1967); Whale for the Killing, A; When the Legends Die

Wieck, Dorothea: Maedchen in Uniform

Wiemann, Mathias: Fear (1955)

Wiesendanger, Alex: Little Buddha

Wiesinger, Kai: BackBeat

Wiesmeiser, Lynda: Wheels of Fire

Wiest, Dianne: Associate, The (1996); Birdcage, The; Bright Lights, Big City; Bullets over Broadway; Cookie; Cops and Robbersons; Drunks; Edward Scissorhands; Footloose; Hannah and Her Sisters; Horse Whisperer, The; Independence Day; Little Man Tate; Lost Boys, The; Parenthood; Practical Magic; Radio Days; Scout, The; September

Wiggins, Al: My Stepson, My Lover

Wiggins, Chris: American Christmas Carol, An; Fish Hawk; High-Ballin'; Kavik the Wolf Dog; King of the Grizzlies; Why Shoot the Teacher?

Wignacci, Darlene: Psycho Girls

Wilborn, Carlton: Dance

Wilby, James: Handful of Dust, A; Howards End; Maurice; Summer Story, A; Tale of Two Cities, A (1991)

Wilcox, Claire: Forty Pounds of Trouble

Wilcox, Frank: Clay Pigeon, The

Wilcox, Larry: Dirty Dozen, The: The Next Mission; Last Ride of the Dalton Gang, The; Sky Heist

Wilcox, Lisa: Nightmare on Elm Street 4, A: The Dream Master; Nightmare on Elm Street 5: The Dream Child

Wilcox, Mary: Beast of the Yellow Night

Wilcox, Robert: Dreaming Out Loud; Man They Could Not Hang, The; Mysterious Dr. Satan

Wilcox, Shannon: Hollywood Harry; Triplecross (1985)

Wilcox-Horne, Colin: Baby Maker, The

Wilcoxon, Henry: Against a Crooked Sky; Cleopatra (1934); Corsican Brothers, The (1941); Crusades, The (1935); Dragnet (1947); If I Were King; Jericho; Last of the Mohicans, The (1936); Man in the Wilderness; Miniver Story, The; Mrs. Miniver; Mysterious Mr. Moto; Pony Express Rider; Tarzan Finds a Son; Two Worlds of Jennie Logan, The; War Lord, The

Wild, Christopher: Knights and Emeralds

Wild, Jack: Melody; Oliver

Wild, Susanne: Invisible Adversaries

Wilde, Cornel: At Sword's Point; Big Combo, The; Fifth Musketeer, The; Forever Amber; Gargoyles (1972); Greatest Show on Earth, The; Leave Her to Heaven; Naked Prey, The; Norseman, The; Omar Khayyam; Passion (1954); Road House (1948); Shark's Treasure; Song to Remember, A; Sword of Lancelot; Wintertime; Woman's World

Wilde, Lois: Brothers of the West; Hopalong Rides Again; Undersea Kingdom

Wilde, Steven: Shaking the Tree

Wilder, Gene: Adventure of Sherlock Holmes' Smarter Brother, The; Alice in Wonderland (1999); Another You; Blazing Saddles; Bonnie and Clyde; Everything You Always Wanted to Know About Sex but Were Afraid to Ask; Frisco Kid, The; Funny About Love; Hanky Panky; Haunted Honeymoon; Little Prince, The; Producers, The; Quackser Fortune Has a Cousin in the Bronx; See No Evil, Hear No Evil; Silver Streak (1976); Start the Revolution Without Me; Stir Crazy; Thursday's Game; Willy Wonka and the Chocolate Factory; Woman in Red, The; World's Greatest Lover, The; Young Frankenstein

Wilder, Giselle: Unexpected Encounters

Wilder, James: Murder One; Nevada; Our Mother's Murder; Prey of the Chameleon; Scorchers; Zombie High

Wilding, Michael: Convoy (1940); Courtney Affair, The; Egyptian, The; Glass Slipper, The; In Which We Serve; Naked Edge, The; Ships with Wings; Stage Fright; Torch Song; Under Capricorn; Waterloo; World of Suzie Wong, The

Wildman, John: American Boyfriends; My American Cousin

Wildman, Steve: Super Soul Brother

Wildman, Valerie: Inner Sanctum

Wildsmith, Dawn: Surf Nazis Must Die

Wiles, Jason: Kicking and Screaming; Roadracers; Windrunner

Wiley, Jan: Dick Tracy vs. Crime Inc.

Wilferson, Guy: Enemy of the Law

Wilhoite, Kathleen: Campus Man; Everybody Wins; Fire in the Sky; Live! From Death Row; Lorenzo's Oil; Murphy's Law; Single Bars, Single Women; Tales of Erotica; Undercover (1987); Witchboard

Wilker, José: Bye Bye Brazil; Dona Flor and Her Two Husbands; Medicine Man

Wilkerson, Guy: Hanging Tree, The

Wilkes, Donna: Angel

Wilkes, Elaine: Killer Party

Wilkinson, Elizabeth: Suburban Roulette

Wilkinson, June: Bellboy and the Playgirls, The; Sno-Line

Wilkinson, Tom: Full Monty, The; Ghost and the Darkness, The; Governess, The; Letting the Birds Go Free; Paper Mask; Pocketful of Rye, A; Priest; Rush Hour; Sylvia; Wetherby; Wilde

Willard, Fred: Americathon; High Strung; How to Beat the High Co$t of Living; Lots of Luck; Moving Violations; Prehysteria! 3; Roxanne; Sodbusters; Waiting for Guffman

Wilbern, David: Midnight Confessions

Willenborg, Amber: Basket, The

Willes, Jean: King and Four Queens, The

Willets, Kathy: Creep

Willett, Chad: Annie O

Willette, Jo Ann: Welcome to 18

William, Warren: Arizona; Case of the Curious Bride, The; Case of the Howling Dog, The; Case of the Lucky Legs, The; Case of the Velvet Claws, The; Cleopatra (1934); Employees' Entrance; Firefly, The; Go West, Young Man; Lady for a Day; Madame X (1937); Man in the Iron Mask, The (1939); Private Affairs of Bel Ami, The; Satan Met a Lady; Skyscraper Souls; Stage Struck (1936); Wives Under Suspicion; Wolf Man, The

Williams, Adam: Fear Strikes Out

Williams, Amir: Silent Witness: What a Child Saw

Williams, Anson: I Married a Centerfold

Williams, Barbara: Bone Daddy; City of Hope; Digger; Family of Cops; Indecency; Jo Jo Dancer, Your Life Is Calling; Joe Torre: Curveballs Along the Way; Oh, What a Night; Spenser: Ceremony; Spenser: Pale Kings & Princes; Thief of Hearts; Tiger Warsaw; Watchers

Williams, Bill: Buckskin; Cariboo Trail; Clay Pigeon, The; Deadline at Dawn; Son of Paleface; Stratton Story, The; Those Endearing Young Charms; Torpedo Alley; Woman's Secret, A

Williams, Billy Dee: Alien Intruder; Batman (1989); Bingo Long Traveling All-Stars and Motor Kings, The; Brian's Song; Chiefs; Christmas Lilies of the Field; Dangerous Passion; Driving Me Crazy; Empire Strikes Back, The; Fear City; Final Comedown, The; Glass House, The; Hard Time; Hit! (1973); Hostage Tower, The; Imposter, The; Jacksons, The: An American Dream; Lady Sings the Blues; Mahogany; Marvin and Tige; Mask of Death; Moving Target (1996); Nighthawks; Number One with a Bullet; Oceans of Fire; Out of Towners, The (1970); Percy & Thunder; Return of the Jedi; Steel Sharks; Triplecross (1995)

Williams, Brook: Plague of the Zombies

Williams, Burt: Public Access

Williams, Cara: Doctors' Wives; Never Steal Anything Small

Williams, Carlton: Crooklyn

Williams, Caroline: Stepfather II; Texas Chainsaw Massacre 2, The

Williams, Cindy: American Graffiti; Big Man on Campus; Bingo; Conversation, The; First Nudie Musical, The; Gas-s-s-s; Meet Wally Sparks; Migrants, The; More American Graffiti; Rude Awakening (1989); Son of Blob (Beware! The Blob); Spaceship (Naked Space); Stepford Husbands, The; Travels with My Aunt; Tricks of the Trade; Uforia

Williams, Clara: Hell's Hinges

Williams III, Clarence: Against the Wall; Dangerous Relations; Deep Cover (1992); 52 Pick-Up; Frogs for Snakes; General's Daughter, The; George Wallace; Half Baked; Hoodlum; Immortals, The; Legend of 1900; Maniac Cop 2; Mod Squad, The (TV Series); My Heroes Have Always Been Cowboys; Rebound; Reindeer Games; Shepherd; Sprung; Sugar Hill

Williams, Cress: Doom Generation, The

Williams, Cynda: Black Rose of Harlem; Condition Red; Gang in Blue; Ghost Brigade; Introducing Dorothy Dandridge; Mo' Better Blues; One False Move; Relax ... It's Just Sex; Spirit Lost; Sweeper, The; Tales of Erotica

Williams, Darnell: How U Like Me Now

Williams, Dean: Distant Voices/Still Lives

Williams, Dlahn: Deadly Hero

Williams, Dick Anthony: Gardens of Stone; Gun in the House, A; Mo' Better Blues; Sophisticated Gents, The; Tap

Williams, Don: Ghastly Ones, The

Williams, Edy: Bad Girls from Mars; Hellhole; Mankillers; Secret Life of an American Wife, The; Seven Minutes, The

Williams, Emlyn: Citadel, The; Iron Duke, The; Jamaica Inn; Major Barbara; Stars Look Down, The; Wreck of the Mary Deare, The

Williams II, Ernest: Black Sister's Revenge

Williams, Esther: Andy Hardy's Double Life; Bathing Beauty; Dangerous When Wet; Duchess of Idaho; Easy to Love; Fiesta; Jupiter's Darling; Million Dollar Mermaid; Neptune's Daughter; On an Island with You; Pagan Love Song; Skirts Ahoy!; Take Me Out to the Ball Game; Texas Carnival; That's Entertainment; That's Entertainment! III; This Time For Keeps; Thrill of a Romance; Ziegfeld Follies

Williams, Gareth: Palookaville

Williams, Grant: Brain of Blood; Incredible Shrinking Man, The; Leech Woman, The; Monolith Monsters, The; PT 109

Williams, Guinn: American Empire; Bad Lands (1939); Billy the Kid; Flirtation Walk; Littlest Rebel, The; Man of the Forest; Mystery Squadron; Noah's Ark; Phantom, The (1931); Phantom Broadcast, The; Powdersmoke Range; Riders of Death Valley; Silver Queen; Station West; Vigilantes Are Coming!; Virginia City; Wolfheart's Revenge; You Only Live Once; You'll Never Get Rich

Williams, Guy: Captain Sinbad; Lost in Space (TV Series); Sign of Zorro, The

Williams, Hal: Don't Look Back: The Story of Leroy "Satchel" Paige; On the Nickel

Williams Jr., Hank: Willa

Williams, Harland: Down Periscope; Half Baked; Rocketman

Williams, Heathcote: Orlando; Tango Lesson, The

Williams, Hugh: Human Monster, The (Dark Eyes of London); One of Our Aircraft Is Missing; Ships with Wings

Williams, Ian: Heaven's a Drag

Williams, Ian Patrick: Bad Channels

Williams, James K.: Cybernator

Williams, Jamie: Second Jungle Book, The; Mowgli and Baloo

Williams, Jane: Small Time

Williams, Jason: Danger Zone, The (1986); Flesh Gordon; Vampire at Midnight

Williams, JoBeth: Adam; American Dreamer; Backlash (1998); Big Chill, The; Chantilly Lace; Child in the Night; Day After, The; Desert Bloom; Dutch; Endangered Species; Final Appeal; Jungle 2 Jungle; Just Write; Kramer vs. Kramer; Little City; Me, Myself & I; Memories of Me; My Name Is Bill W; Parallel Lives; Poltergeist; Poltergeist II: The Other Side; Ruby Jean and Joe; Sex, Love, and Cold Hard Cash; Stir Crazy; Stop! Or My Mom Will Shoot; Switch; Teachers; Victim of Love; Welcome Home; When Danger Follows You Home; Wyatt Earp

Williams, John: Alfred Hitchcock Presents (TV Series); Dial M for Murder; Paradine Case, The; Sabrina (1954); To Catch a Thief; Will Success Spoil Rock Hunter?; Witness for the Prosecution (1957); Young Philadelphians, The

Williams, Kate: Melody

Williams, Kelli: Lifepod; There Goes My Baby; Till Murder Do Us Part; Wavelength (1983); Zapped Again

Williams, Kenneth: Carry on at Your Convenience; Carry on Behind; Carry on Cleo; Carry on Cowboy; Carry on Cruising; Carry on Doctor; Carry on Emmanuelle; Carry on Nurse; Follow That Camel

Williams, Kent: Rubdown; Sister-In-Law, The (1995)

Williams, Kimberly: Cold-Blooded; Father of the Bride (1991); Father of the Bride Part II; Indian Summer; Safe House

Williams, Kurt T.: Last Dance (1991)

Williams, Lia: Shot Through the Heart

Williams, Lynn Red: Mortal Kombat: Annihilation

Williams, Malinda: High School High

Williams, Mark: Borrowers, The (1997); Trained to Fight

Williams, Megan: Anzacs

Williams, Michael: Educating Rita

Williams, Michael C.: Blair Witch Project, The

Williams, Michelle: Dick; Halloween: H20; Lassie; Timemaster

Williams, Olivia: Emma (1996); Postman, The; Rushmore; Sixth Sense, The

Williams, Paul: Battle for the Planet of the Apes; Cheap Detective, The; Headless Body in Topless Bar; Muppet Movie, The; Night They Saved Christmas, The; November Men, The; Phantom of the Paradise; Smokey and the Bandit; Smokey and the Bandit II; Smokey and the Bandit III; Stone Cold Dead; Wild Wild West Revisited, The

Williams, Peter: Jungleground; Robin Hood and the Sorcerer

Williams, Rhys: Corn Is Green, The (1945); Fastest Gun Alive, The; Hills of Home; Raintree County; Showdown, The (1950); Strange Woman, The

Williams, Robert: Platinum Blonde

Williams, Robin: Adventures of Baron Münchausen, The; Aladdin & The King of Thieves; Awakenings; Being Human; Best of Times, The; Bicentennial Man; Birdcage, The; Cadillac Man; Club Paradise; Dead Again; Dead Poets Society; Deconstructing Harry; Father's Day; Fisher King, The; Flubber; Good Morning, Vietnam; Good Will Hunting; Hamlet (1996); Hook; Jack; Jakob the Liar; Jumanji; Mrs. Doubtfire; Mork & Mindy (TV Series); Moscow on the Hudson; Nine Months; Patch Adams; Popeye; Secret Agent, The (1996); Seize the Day; Survivors, The; Toys; What Dreams May Come; World According to Garp, The

Williams, Saul: Slam

Williams, Scot: BackBeat

Williams, Simon: Blood on Satan's Claw; Odd Job, The

Williams, Spencer: Two-Gun Man from Harlem

Williams Jr., Spencer: Amos and Andy (TV Series); Bronze Buckaroo

Williams, Steven: Corrina, Corrina (1994); Deep Red (1994); Jason Goes to Hell: The Final Friday; Missing in Action 2: The Beginning; Revolver; X-Files, The (TV Series)

Williams, Treat: Dead Heat; Deadly Hero; Deep End of the Ocean, The; Deep Rising; Dempsey; Devil's Own, The; Echoes in the Darkness; Escape: Human Cargo; Final Verdict; Flashpoint; Hair; Hand Gun; Heart of Dixie, The; Johnny's Girl; Late Shift, The; Max and Helen; Men's Club, The; Night of the Sharks; 1941; Once Upon a Time in America (Long Version); Parallel Lives; Phantom, The (1996); Prince of the City; Pursuit of D. B. Cooper; Ritz, The; Smooth Talk; Streetcar Named Desire, A (1983); Sweet Lies; Things to Do in Denver When You're Dead; Third Degree Burn; Third Solution, The; 36 Hours to Die; Till Death Do Us Part; Water Engine, The

Williams, Van: Green Hornet, The (TV Series)

Williams, Vanessa: Adventures of Elmo in Grouchland, The; Don Quixote (2000)

Williams, Vanessa L.: Another You; Candyman (1992); Dance with Me; Drop Squad, The; Eraser; Full Exposure; Futuresport; Harley Davidson and the Marlboro Man; Hoodlum; Jacksons, The: An American Dream; Odyssey, The; Shaft (2000); Soul Food; Under the Gun (1988)

Williams, Wade Andrew: Route 9

Williams, Wendy O.: Pucker Up and Bark Like a Dog; Reform School Girls

Williamson, David: Resurrection Man

Williamson, Fred: Adios Amigo; Big Score, The; Black Caesar; Black Cobra 3; Blackjack; Blind Rage; Boss; Bucktown; Children of the Corn V: Fields of Terror; Deadly Impact; Deadly Intent; Delta Force, Commando Two; Express to Terror; Foxtrap; From Dusk Till Dawn; Hell Up in Harlem; Mean Johnny Barrows; One Down, Two to Go; Original Gangstas; Silent Hunter; South Beach; Steele's Law; Take a Hard Ride; Three Days to a Kill; Three the Hard Way; Vigilante; Warrior of the Lost World; Warriors of the Wasteland

Williamson, Mykelti: Buffalo Soldiers; Con Air; First Power, The; Forrest Gump; Heat (1995); Miami Vice; Soul of the Game; Species II; Three Kings; Truth or Consequences, N.M.; Waiting to Exhale; You Talkin' to Me

Williamson, Nicol: Advocate, The; Black Widow; Cheap Detective, The; Christopher Columbus (1985); Excalibur; Hamlet (1969); Human Factor, The; I'm Dancing As Fast As I Can; Passion Flower; Return to Oz; Robin and Marian; Seven-Per-Cent Solution, The; Venom; Wilby Conspiracy, The

Williamson, Phillip: Angelic Conversation

Willingham, Noble: Career Opportunities; City Slickers II; Fire in the Sky; Last Boy Scout, The; Pastime; Sweet Poison; Up Close and Personal

Willis, Bruce: Armageddon; Billy Bathgate; Blind Date (1987); Bonfire of the Vanities; Color of Night; Death Becomes Her; Die Hard; Die Hard 2: Die Harder; Die Hard with a Vengeance; Fifth Element, The; Hudson Hawk; In Country; Jackal, The; Last Boy Scout, The; Last Man Standing (1996); Mercury Rising; Moonlighting (1985) (TV Pilot); Mortal Thoughts; National Lampoon's Loaded Weapon 1; Nobody's Fool (1994); North; Pulp Fiction; Siege, The; Sixth Sense, The; Story of Us, The; Striking Distance; Sunset; That's Adequate; 12 Monkeys; Whole Nine Yards, The

Willis, Hope Alexander: Pack, The

Willis, Matt: Return of the Vampire, The; So Dear to My Heart

Willman, Noel: Kiss of the Vampire; Reptile, The

Willoughby, Lewis: Trapped by the Mormons

Wills, Chill: Alamo, The; Allegheny Uprising; Arizona Legion; Billy the Kid; Boom Town; Deadly Companions, The; Francis Joins the Wacs; Harvey Girls, The; Honky Tonk; Kentucky Rifle; Lawless Valley; Loaded Pistols; Man from the Alamo, The; Mr. Billion; Ride the Man Down; Rio Grande; Rounders, The (1965); Steagle, The; Tarzan's New York Adventure; Tulsa; Western Union; Westerner, The; Wheeler Dealers, The; Yearling, The

Wilson, Barbara: Invasion of the Animal People

Wilson, Breck: Escape from Atlantis

Wilson, Brian: Theremin: An Electronic Odyssey

Wilson, Bridgette: Billy Madison; House on Haunted Hill (1999); Love Stinks; Mortal Kombat; Nevada; Stepsister, The; Sweet Evil

Wilson, Chrystale: Players Club, The

Wilson, Daniel: Wait Until Spring, Bandini

Wilson, David Lee: Pariah

Wilson, Don: Jack Benny Program, The (TV Series)

Wilson, Don "The Dragon": Blackbelt; Bloodfist; Bloodfist 2: Forced to Fight; Bloodfist IV—Die Trying; Bloodfist V: Human Target; Bloodfist VI: Ground Zero; Capitol Conspiracy, The; Cyber Tracker; Cyber Tracker 2; Hollywood Safari; Magic Kid; Night Hunter; Operation Condor (Don "The Dragon" Wilson); Out for Blood; Power Within, The; Red Sun Rising; Ring of Fire 3: Lion Strike; Virtual Combat

Wilson, Dooley: Cairo

Wilson, Elizabeth: Addams Family, The; Believers, The; Grace Quigley; Happy Hooker, The; Incredible Shrinking Woman, The; Little Murders; Prisoner of Second Avenue, The; Quiz Show; Regarding Henry; Where Are the Children?; You Can't Take it with You (1984)

Wilson, Flip: Fish That Saved Pittsburgh, The; Uptown Saturday Night

Wilson, Frank: Emperor Jones, The

Wilson, George: Attack of the Killer Tomatoes

Wilson, Georges: Empty Canvas, The; Make Room for Tomorrow

Wilson, Jackie: Go, Johnny, Go!

Wilson, Jim: Charlie, the Lonesome Cougar

Wilson, Julie: This Could Be the Night

Wilson, Kristen: Bulletproof (1996)

Wilson, Kym: Brides of Christ

Wilson, Lambert: Belly of an Architect, The; Blood of Others, The; Five Days One Summer; Frankenstein (1992); Jefferson in Paris; Leading Man, The; Red Kiss (Rouge Baiser); Rendez-Vous; Sahara (1984); Strangers

Wilson, Lois: Covered Wagon, The; Deluge (1933); Miss Lulu Bett; Show-Off, The (1926); Vanishing American, The

Wilson, Luke: Best Men; Blue Streak; Bottle Rocket; Home Fries; My Dog Skip

Wilson, Mara: Matilda (1996); Miracle on 34th Street (1994); Mrs. Doubtfire; Simple Wish, A

Wilson, Marie: Boy Meets Girl; Girl in Every Port, A (1952); Mr. Hobbs Takes a Vacation; My Friend Irma; Never Wave at a WAC (Private Wore Skirts, The); Private Affairs of Bel Ami, The; Satan Met a Lady

Wilson, Mary Louise: Cheap Shots

Wilson, Nancy: Big Score, The; Meteor Man

Wilson, Owen C.: Anaconda; Bottle Rocket; Haunting, The (1999); Minus Man, The; Permanent Midnight; Shanghai Noon

Wilson, Paul: Brainwaves; Devonsville Terror, The

Zien, Chip: Grace Quigley

Ziering, Ian: Beverly Hills 90210; Savate

Zietek, Eva: Wedding, The (1972)

Zimbalist Jr., Efrem: Avenging, The; Band of Angels; By Love Possessed; Deep Six, The; Family Upside Down, A; Gathering, Part II, The; Hot Shots; Maverick (TV series); Tempest, The (1983); Terror Out of the Sky; Wait Until Dark; Who Is the Black Dahlia?

Zimbalist, Stephanie: Awakening, The; Babysitter, The (1980); Caroline?; Dead Ahead; Great Elephant Escape, The; Jericho Fever; Killing Mind, The; Magic of Lassie, The; Remington Steele (TV series); Story Lady, The; Tomorrow's Child

Zimmer, Laurie: Assault on Precinct 13

Zimmerman, Joey: Treehouse Hostage

Zinneman, Anna: Place Called Trinity, A

Zinni, Victoria: Shoot the Living ... Pray for the Dead

Zipp, William: Death Chase; Order of the Eagle

Zirner, August: Promise, The (1995)

Zischler, Hanns: Desire; Francesco; Kings of the Road

Zito, Chuck: Red Line

Zmed, Adrian: Bachelor Party; Final Terror, The; Grease 2; Other Woman, The

Zobel, Richard: To Sleep With a Vampire

Zobian, Mark: House on Tombstone Hill, The

Zola, Jean-Pierre: Mark of the Devil, Part 2; My Uncle (Mon Oncle)

Zollner, Anian: Promise, The (1995)

Zolotin, Adam: Leave It to Beaver

Zoofoot: Redneck Zombies

Zorek, Michael: Hot Moves; Private School

Zorich, Louis: Cheap Shots

Zorina, Vera: Follow the Boys; Goldwyn Follies, The; Louisiana Purchase

Zouzou: Chloe in the Afternoon

Zuanic, Rod: Fast Talking

Zubkov, Valentin: My Name Is Ivan

Zucco, George: Adventures of Sherlock Holmes, The; Arrest Bulldog Drummond; Black Raven, The; Bride Wore Red, The; Cat and the Canary, The (1939); Charlie Chan in Honolulu; Dead Men Walk; Firefly, The; Flying Serpent, The; Fog Island; Having a Wonderful Crime; House of Frankenstein; Mad Ghoul, The; Mad Monster; Madame X (1937); Man Who Could Work Miracles, The; Monster and the Girl, The; Mummy's Hand, The; My Favorite Blonde; New Moon; Scared to Death (1946); Seventh Cross, The; Sherlock Holmes in Washington; Sudan; Voodoo Man; Woman's Face, A

Zuckerman, Alex: Me and the Kid

Zuelke, Mark: Sinful Intrigue

Zuniga, Daphne: Charlie's Ghost; 800 Leagues Down the Amazon; Fly II, The; Gross Anatomy; Last Rites (1988); Modern Girls; Prey of the Chameleon; Spaceballs; Stand-Ins; Staying Together; Sure Thing, The

Zuniga, Jose: Gun Shy

Zurk, Steve: Biohazard: The Alien Force

Zushi, Yoshitaka: Dodes 'Ka-Den

Zutaut, Brad: Hardbodies 2

Zwerling, Darrell: Doc Savage ... , The Man of Bronze

Zwick, Abe: Sometimes Aunt Martha Does Dreadful Things

Zylberman, Noam: Last Train Home

Zylberstein, Elsa: Farinelli Il Castrato; Metroland; Mina Tannenbaum

DIRECTOR INDEX

Bolognini, Mauro: Husbands and Lovers; La Grande Bourgeoise; Oldest Profession, The

Bolotin, Craig: Light It Up; That Night

Boisson, William T.: Sleeping with Strangers

Bolt, Ben: Big Town, The; Space Rangers (TV Series)

Bolt, Robert: Lady Caroline Lamb

Bond, Jack: It Couldn't Happen Here

Bond, Timothy: Deadly Harvest; Goosebumps: The Haunted Mask; Lost World, The (1992); Return to the Lost World; Running Wild (1998)

Bond III, James: Def by Temptation

Bondarchuk, Sergei: War and Peace (1968); Waterloo

Bonerz, Peter: Nobody's Perfekt; Police Academy 6: City Under Siege; When Things Were Rotten (TV Series)

Bonifer, Mike: Lipstick Camera

Bonk, Ron: City of the Vampires; Vicious Sweet, The

Bonnard, Mario: Last Days of Pompeii (1960)

Bonniere, René: Dream Man; Halfback of Notre Dame, The

Bonns, Miguel Iglesias: Night of the Howling Beast

Bookwalter, J. R.: Dead Next Door, The; Kingdom of the Vampire; Ozone; Polymorph; Robot Ninja; Sandman, The (1996)

Boorman, John: Beyond Rangoon; Deliverance; Emerald Forest, The; Excalibur; Exorcist II: The Heretic; General, The (1998); Hell in the Pacific; Hope and Glory; Point Blank (1967); Where the Heart Is; Zardoz

Boos, H. Gordon: Red Surf

Booth, Connie: Fawlty Towers (TV Series)

Borau, José Luis: On the Line

Borchers, Donald P.: Grave Secrets

Borden, John: Native Americans, The

Borden, Lizzie: Erotique; Love Crimes; Working Girls

Boris, Robert: Buy and Cell; Frank & Jesse; Oxford Blues; Steele Justice

Borman, Arthur: ... And God Spoke

Bornedal, Ole: Nightwatch

Borris, Clay: Alligator Shoes; Gunfighters, The; Prom Night IV—Deliver Us from Evil; Quiet Cool; Someone to Die For; Suspicious Agenda

Borsos, Phillip: Dr. Bethune; Far From Home: The Adventures of Yellow Dog; Grey Fox, The; Mean Season, The; One Magic Christmas

Bortman, Michael: Crooked Hearts

Borzage, Frank: Farewell to Arms, A; Flirtation Walk; His Butler's Sister; History Is Made at Night; I've Always Loved You; Mannequin (1937); Moonrise; Mortal Storm, The; Shining Hour, The; Smilin' Through (1941); Stage Door Canteen; Strange Cargo; Three Comrades

Boskovich, John: Without You I'm Nothing

Boulting, John: Heavens Above; I'm All Right Jack; Lucky Jim

Boulting, Roy: Brothers in Law; Heavens Above; Last Word, The (1979); Moving Finger, The; Run for the Sun; There's a Girl in My Soup

Bourguignon, Serge: A Coeur Joie (Head over Heels); Sundays and Cybèle

Bourla, David: When Time Expires

Bouvier, Robert: City in Panic

Bovon, Jean: Messin' with the Blues

Bowab, John: Gabe Kaplan as Groucho; Love at the Top

Bowen, David R.: Secret Life of Jeffrey Dahmer, The

Bowen, Jenny: Street Music; Wizard of Loneliness, The

Bowen, John: Dark Secrets; Lethal Games

Bowers, George: Body and Soul (1981); Hearse, The; My Tutor; Private Resort

Bowes, Tom: Two Moon July

Bowey, John R.: Mutator

Bowman, John: Nudity Required

Bowman, Richard: Tick, The (TV Series)

Bowman, Rob: Airborne; X-Files, The (1998)

Bowser, Kenneth: In a Shallow Grave

Box, Muriel: Rattle of a Simple Man; Truth About Women, The

Boxell, Tim: Aberration

Boyd, Daniel: Chillers; Heroes of the Heart; Invasion of the Space Preachers

Boyd, Don: East of Elephant Rock; Kleptomania; Twenty-One

Boyd, Julianne: Eubie!

Boyer, Jean: Circonstances Attenuantes; Crazy For Love; Fernandel the Dressmaker

Boyle, Danny: Beach, The; Life Less Ordinary, A; Shallow Grave (1994); Trainspotting

Boyum, Steve: Meet the Deedles

Bozzetto, Bruno: Allegro Non Troppo

Bradbury, Robert N.: Between Men; Blue Steel (1934); Dawn Rider; Forbidden Trails; Kid Ranger; Lawless Frontier; Lucky Texan; Man from Utah, The; Rainbow Valley; Riders of Destiny; Riders of the Rockies; Sing, Cowboy, Sing; Star Packer, The; Texas Terror; Trail Beyond, The; Trouble in Texas; West of the Divide; Westward Ho

Braddock, Reb: Curdled

Bradford, Samuel: Teen Vamp

Bradley, Al: Captive Planet; Cross Mission; Iron Warrior; Miami Cops

Bradley, David: They Saved Hitler's Brain

Bradshaw, John: Big Slice, The; Breakout (1998); Lethal Tender; Specimen; That's My Baby; Undertaker's Wedding, The

Bradshaw, Randy: Blades of Courage; Last Train Home; Song Spinner

Brahm, John: Guest in the House; Hangover Square; Man from U.N.C.L.E., The (TV Series); Miracle of Our Lady of Fatima, The; Singapore; Thriller (TV Series); Undying Monster, The; Wintertime

Brakhage, Stan: Dog Star Man

Braiver, Bob: Midnight Ride; Rush Week

Brambilla, Marco: Demolition Man; Excess Baggage

Branagh, Kenneth: Dead Again; Hamlet (1996); Henry V (1989); Mary Shelley's Frankenstein; Midwinter's Tale, A; Much Ado About Nothing; Peter's Friends

Brand, Joshua: Pyromaniac's Love Story, A

Brand, Larry: Drifter, The; Masque of the Red Death (1989); Overexposed; Paranoia (1998); Till the End of the Night

Brander, Richard: Sizzle Beach, U.S.A.

Brando, Marlon: One-Eyed Jacks

Brandon, Clark: Skeeter

Brandstrom, Charlotte: Business Affair, A; Road to Ruin (1991); Sweet Revenge (1990)

Brannon, Fred: Dangers of the Canadian Mounted; King of the Rocketmen; Purple Monster Strikes, The; Radar Men from the Moon; Zombies of the Stratosphere (Satan's Satellites) (Serial)

Braoude, Patrick: Great, My Parents Are Divorcing

Brascia, Dominick: Evil Laugh; Hard Rock Nightmare

Brass, Tinto: Caligula

Brault, Michel: Paper Wedding

Brauman, Jack: Zombie Nightmare

Brauner, Franklin: Wild Side

Braunsteen, Joseph: Rest in Pieces

Braverman, Charles: Brotherhood of Justice; Hit and Run; Prince of Bel Air

Brayne, William: Flame to the Phoenix, A

Breakston, George: Manster, The; Scarlet Spear, The

Brealey, Gil: Test of Love, A

Breathnach, Paddy: I Went Down

Breen, Julian: Alien Arsenal; Frankenstein Reborn!; Prehysteria! 3

Breen, Richard L.: Stopover Tokyo

Breillat, Catherine: Romance (1999)

Brel, Jacques: Franz

Breils, Tia: Trading Mom

Breillat, Catherine: 36 Fillette

Breman, Valerie: Going Overboard

Bren, Milton H.: Three for Bedroom C

Brenon, Herbert: Dancing Mothers; Peter Pan (1924)

Brescia, Alfonso: White Fang and the Hunter

Bresciani, Andrea: Through the Looking Glass

Bresson, Robert: Devil, Probably, The; Diary of a Country Priest; L'Argent; Lancelot of the Lake; Man Escaped, A; Mouchette; Pickpocket

Brest, Martin: Beverly Hills Cop; Going in Style; Meet Joe Black; Midnight Run; Scent of a Woman

Bretherton, Howard: Bar-20 Rides Again; Below the Border; Call of the Prairie; Carson City Cyclone; Dawn on the Great Divide; Down Texas Way; Eagle's Brood; Ghost Town Law; Hidden Valley Outlaws; In Old Colorado; Ladies They Talk About; Outlaws of the Desert; Pirates of the Prairie; Riders of the Rio Grande; San Antonio Kid; Three on the Trail; Twilight on the Trail; West of the Law

Brewer, Otto: Phantom Empire (1935); Postal Inspector; Radio Ranch (Men with Steel Faces, Phantom Empire)

Breziner, Salome: Occasional Hell, An; Tollbooth

Briant, Michael E.: Dr. Who: Revenge of the Cybermen

Brickman, Marshall: Lovesick; Manhattan Project, The; Simon

Brickman, Paul: Men Don't Leave; Risky Business

Bridges, Alan: Brief Encounter (1974); D.P.; Out of Season; Pudd'nhead Wilson; Return of the Soldier, The; Shooting Party, The

Bridges, Beau: Seven Hours to Judgment; Wild Pair, The

Bridges, James: Baby Maker, The; Bright Lights, Big City; China Syndrome, The; Mike's Murder; Paper Chase, The; Perfect; September 30, 1955; Urban Cowboy

Bright, Matthew: Freeway 2: Confessions of a Trickbaby; Freeway (1996)

Brill, Steven: Heavyweights

Brinckerhoff, Burt: Can You Hear the Laughter? The Story of Freddie Prinze; Cracker Factory; Remington Steele (TV series)

Britten, Lawrence: Whose Child Am I?

Britton, Tracy Lynch: Maximum Breakout

Brizzi, Gaetan: Fantasia 2000

Brizzi, Paul: Fantasia 2000

Brock, Deborah: Rock 'n' Roll High School Forever; Slumber Party Massacre II

Brocka, Lino: Fight for Us

Broderick, John: Swap, The (Sam's Song); Warrior and the Sorceress, The

Broderick, Matthew: Infinity

Brodie, Kevin: Dog of Flanders, A (1999); Mugsy's Girls; Treacherous

Bromfield, Rex: Cafe Romeo; Home Is Where the Hart Is; Love at First Sight; Melanie

Bromley-Davenport, Harry: Erasable You

Bromski, Jacek: Alice (1981)

Brook, Clive: On Approval

Brook, Peter: King Lear (1971); Lord of the Flies (1963); Mahabharata, The; Marat/Sade; Meetings with Remarkable Men

Brookner, Howard: Bloodhounds of Broadway

Brooks, Adam: Almost You

Brooks, Albert: Defending Your Life; Lost in America; Modern Romance; Mother (1996); Muse, The; Real Life

Brooks, Anthony: Nudes on the Moon

Brooks, Bob: Tattoo

Brooks, James L.: As Good as It Gets; Broadcast News; I'll Do Anything; Terms of Endearment

Brooks, Joseph: If Ever I See You Again; Invitation to the Wedding; You Light Up My Life

Brooks, Mel: Blazing Saddles; Dracula: Dead and Loving It; High Anxiety; History of the World, Part One, The; Life Stinks; Producers, The; Robin Hood: Men in Tights; Silent Movie; Spaceballs; Twelve Chairs, The; Young Frankenstein

Brooks, Richard: Battle Circus; Bite the Bullet; Blackboard Jungle, The; Brothers Karamazov, The; Cat on a Hot Tin Roof (1958); Catered Affair, The; Deadline USA; $ (Dollars); Elmer Gantry; Fever Pitch; In Cold Blood; Last Hunt, The; Last Time I Saw Paris, The; Looking for Mr. Goodbar; Lord Jim; Professionals, The; Something of Value; Sweet Bird of Youth (1962); Wrong Is Right

Brooks, Robert: Who Shot Pat?

Broomfield, Nick: Aileen Wuornos: Selling of a Serial Killer; Chicken Ranch; Dark Obsession; Heidi Fleiss, Hollywood Madame; Monster in a Box

Brophy, Philip: Body Melt

Bross, Eric: Restaurant; Ten Benny

Brower, Otto: Devil Horse, The; Fighting Caravans; Hard Hombre; Law of the Sea; Scarlet River; Spirit of the West

Brown, Barry: Cloud Dancer

Brown, Barry Alexander: Lonely in America

Brown, Bruce: Endless Summer, The; Endless Summer II

Brown, Clarence: Ah, Wilderness; Angels in the Outfield (1951); Anna Christie (1930); Anna Karenina (1935); Chained; Conquest; Eagle, The; Edison, The Man; Emma; Flesh and the Devil; Free Soul, A; Goose Woman, The; Gorgeous Hussy, The; Human Comedy, The; Idiot's Delight; Inspiration; Intruder in the Dust; It's a Big Country; Last of the Mohicans, The (1920); National Velvet; Of Human Hearts; Possessed (1931); Rains Came, The; Romance; Sadie McKee; Song of Love; They Met in Bombay; To Please a Lady;

White Cliffs of Dover, The; Wife vs. Secretary; Woman of Affairs, A; Yearling, The

Brown, Edwin Scott: Prey, The

Brown, Evert: This Is America, Charlie Brown

Brown, Georg Stanford: Alone in the Neon Jungle; Dangerous Relations; Miracle of the Heart; Roots: The Next Generation; Vietnam War Story

Brown, Gregory: Dead Man Walking (1987); Stranger by Night; Street Asylum

Brown, Harry: Knickerbocker Holiday

Brown, Jim: Woody Guthrie—Hard Travelin'

Brown, Karl: White Legion

Brown, Larry: Pink Angels; Psychopath, The

Brown, Melville: Check and Double Check

Brown, Mitch: Deathshot

Brown, Richard: True Story of Frankenstein, The

Brown, Rowland: Blood Money

Brown, William H.: Casino Royale (1954)

Browning, Kirk: You Can't Take it with You (1984)

Browning, Philip: Shapeshifter

Browning, Ricou: Daring Game

Browning, Tod: Blackbird, The; Devil Doll, The (1936); Dracula (1931); Freaks; Mark of the Vampire; Outside the Law (1921); Unknown, The; West of Zanzibar; Where East Is East; White Tiger

Brownlow, Kevin: Buster Keaton: A Hard Act to Follow; Unknown Chaplin

Brownrigg, S. F.: Don't Look in the Basement; Poor White Trash II; Thinkin' Big

Bruce, James: Headless Body in Topless Bar; Love to Kill; Suicide Club, The

Bruce, John: Adventures of Sherlock Holmes, The (Series)

Brunel, Adrian: Old Spanish Custom, An

Bruno, John: Virus (1999)

Brusati, Franco: Bread and Chocolate; Sleazy Uncle, The; To Forget Venice

Brustellin, Alf: Germany In Autumn

Bryant, Charles: Salome (1923)

Buchanan, Larry: Beyond the Doors; Free, White, and 21; Goodbye, Norma Jean; Loch Ness Horror, The; Mars Needs Women

Buchowetzki, Dimitri: Othello (1922); Swan, The (1925)

Buchs, Julio: Bullet for Sandoval, A

Buck, Chris: Tarzan (1999)

Buck, Douglas: Cutting Moments

Buckalew, Bethel: My Boys Are Good Boys

Buckhantz, Allan A.: Last Contract, The

Bucksey, Colin: Blue Money; Curiosity Kills; Dealers; McGuffin, The; Midnight's Child

Bucquet, Harold S.: Adventures of Tartu; Dr. Kildare's Strange Case; Dragon Seed; On Borrowed Time; Without Love

Budd, Colin: Hurricane Smith

Buechler, John Carl: Cellar Dweller; Dungeonmaster, The; Friday the 13th, Part VII: The New Blood; Ghoulies III; Troll

Bugajski, Richard: Clearcut; Interrogation

Bui, Tony: Three Seasons

Buitenhuis, Penelope: Boulevard

Bulajic, Veljko: Day that Shook the World, The

Bunce, Alan: Babar: The Movie

Bunche, Peter Gathings: Never 2 Big

Buntzman, Mark: Exterminator 2, The

Buñuel, Joyce: Dirty Dishes

Buñuel, Luis: Age of Gold; Ascent to Heaven (Mexican Bus Ride); Belle de Jour; Criminal Life of Archibaldo de la Cruz, The; Death in the Garden; Diary of a Chambermaid (1964); Discreet Charm of the Bourgeoisie, The; El (This Strange Passion); El Bruto (The Brute); Exterminating Angel, The; Great Madcap, The; Illusion Travels by Streetcar; Land Without Bread; L'Age D'Or; Los Olvidados; Milky Way, The (1970); Nazarin; Phantom of Liberty, The; Simon of the Desert; Susanna; That Obscure Object of Desire; Tristana; Un Chien Andalou; Viridiana; Woman without Love, A; Wuthering Heights (1953)

Buravsky, Alexander: Sacred Cargo

Burchett, Mark: Vamps: Deadly Dream Girls

Burdeau, George: Native Americans, The

Burge, Robert: Keaton's Cop; Vasectomy

Burge, Stuart: Julius Caesar (1970); Othello (1965)

Burke, James: In Dark Places

Chappelle, Joe: Halloween: The Curse of Michael Myers; Phantoms

Charlson, Carl: Murder of the Century

Charlton, Robert: No Big Deal

Charr, Henri: Cellblock Sisters; Hollywood Safari; Illegal Entry; Island Fury; Under Lock and Key

Chase, Richard: Hell's Angels Forever

Chatiliez, Étienne: Tatie Danielle

Chaudhri, Amin Q.: Tiger Warsaw; Unremarkable Life, An

Chavarri, Jaime: I'm the One You're Looking For

Chechik, Jeremiah S.: Avengers, The; Benny & Joon; Diabolique (1996); National Lampoon's Christmas Vacation; Tall Tale: The Unbelievable Adventures of Pecos Bill

Cheek, Douglas: C.H.U.D.

Chekmayan, Ara: Forever James Dean

Chelsom, Peter: Funnybones; Hear My Song; Mighty, The

Chen, Joan: Xiu Xiu: The Sent Down Girl

Chenal, Pierre: Crime and Punishment (1935); Man from Nowhere, The; Native Son (1950)

Cher: If These Walls Could Talk

Chereau, Patrice: L'Homme Blessé (The Wounded Man); Queen Margot

Cherot, Christopher Scott: Hav Plenty

Cherry, John: Ernest Goes to Africa; Ernest in the Army

Cherry III, John R.: Dr. Otto and the Riddle of the Gloom Beam; Ernest Goes to Camp; Ernest Goes to Jail; Ernest Rides Again; Ernest Saves Christmas; Ernest Scared Stupid; Slam Dunk Ernest

Chetwynd, Lionel: Color of Justice; Hanoi Hilton, The

Cheveldave, Randolph: Deathgame

Chiaramonte, Andrew: Twogether

Chiodo, Stephen: Killer Klowns from Outer Space

Chionglo, Mel: Midnight Dancer (1994)

Chivers, Colin: Michael Jackson Moonwalker

Cholodenko, Lisa: High Art

Chomsky, Marvin J.: Anastasia: The Mystery of Anna; Attica; Billionaire Boys Club; Brotherhood of the Rose; Deliberate Stranger, The; Evel Knievel; Holocaust; Inside the Third Reich; Little Ladies of the Night; Murph the Surf; Nairobi Affair; Roots; Shaming, The; Tank; Victory at Entebbe

Chong, Thomas: Cheech and Chong's Next Movie; Corsican Brothers, The (1984); Far Out Man; Nice Dreams; Still Smokin'

Chopra, Joyce: Danger of Love; Lemon Sisters, The; Murder in New Hampshire; Smooth Talk

Chouraqui, Elie: Love Songs (Paroles et Musique); Man on Fire

Christensen, Benjamin: Mockery; Seven Footprints to Satan; Witchcraft Through the Ages (HAXAN)

Christian, Nathaniel: California Casanova; Club Fed

Christian, Roger: Battlefield Earth; Final Cut, The; Masterminds; Nostradamus; Sender, The; Starship; Underworld (1996)

Christian-Jaque: Legend of Frenchie King, The; Love and the Frenchwoman; Nana; Pearls of the Crown, The

Christopher, Anthony: Fatal Pulse

Christopher, Mark: 54

Chubbuck, Lyndon: Naked Souls

Chudnow, Byron: Amazing Dobermans; Daring Dobermans, The; Doberman Gang, The

Chudnow, David: Amazing Dobermans

Chukhrai, Grigori: Ballad of a Soldier

Chukhrai, Pavel: Thief, The (1997)

Chung, Sun: City War

Ciccoritti, Gerard: Graveyard Shift (1987); Paris France; Psycho Girls; Understudy, The: Graveyard Shift II; Prayer in the Dark, A

Cicero, Nando: Twice a Judas

Cimber, Matt: Butterfly; Fakeout; Single Room Furnished; Time to Die, A (1983); Yellow Hair and the Fortress of Gold

Cimino, Michael: Deer Hunter, The; Desperate Hours (1990); Heaven's Gate; Sicilian, The; Sunchaser; Thunderbolt and Lightfoot; Year of the Dragon

Cirivani, Osvaldo: Dead for a Dollar

Clair, René: A Nous la Liberte; And Then There Were None; Avant Garde Program #2; Beauties of the Night; Crazy Ray, The; Forever and a Day; Ghost Goes West, The; I Married a Witch; Italian Straw Hat, The; Le Million; Le Voyage Imaginaire; Love and the Frenchwoman; Quatorze Juliet; Under the Roofs of Paris

Clark, B. D.: Galaxy of Terror; Protector

Clark, Bob: American Clock, The; Baby Geniuses; Black Christmas; Children Shouldn't Play with Dead Things; Christmas Story, A; Deathdream; From the Hip; Loose Cannons; Murder by Decree; My Summer Story; Porky's; Porky's II: The Next Day; Rhinestone; Tribute; Turk 182

Clark, Brandon: Alligator II

Clark, Colbert: Mystery Squadron; Three Musketeers, The (1933); Warning Shadows (1933)

Clark, Duane: Bitter Harvest (1993); Shaking the Tree

Clark, Greydon: Danse Macabre; Final Justice (1984); Forbidden Dance, The; Joy Sticks; Killer Instinct; Out of Sight Out of Mind; Return, The (1980); Satan's Cheerleaders; Skinheads; Uninvited, The (1987); Wacko; Without Warning

Clark, James B.: Dog of Flanders, A; Flipper (1963); Island of the Blue Dolphins; Misty; My Side of the Mountain

Clark, Jim: Madhouse (1972)

Clark, John: Fast Lane Fever

Clark, Larry: Another Day in Paradise; Kids

Clark, Lawrence Gordon: Belfast Assassin; Midnight Man; On Dangerous Ground (1995); Romance on the Orient Express

Clark, Matt: Da

Clark, William: Goodbye Bird, The; Windrunner

Clarke, Alan: Rita, Sue and Bob Too; Scum

Clarke, James Keneim: Going Undercover

Clarke, Malcolm: Voices From a Locked Room

Clarke, Richard: Doctor Hackenstein

Clarke, Robert: Hideous Sun Demon, The

Clarke, Shirley: Connection, The (1961)

Clarke-Williams, Zoe: Men

Claxton, William F.: Bonanza (TV Series)

Clayton, Jack: Great Gatsby, The; Innocents, The (1961); Lonely Passion of Judith Hearne, The; Room at the Top; Something Wicked This Way Comes

Cleese, John: Fawlty Towers (TV Series)

Clegg, Tom: Any Man's Death; Children of the Full Moon; House That Bled to Death, The; Inside Man, The; McVicar; Sharpe (TV Series); Stroke of Midnight

Clemens, Brian: Captain Kronos: Vampire Hunter

Clemens, William: Case of the Stuttering Bishop, The; Case of the Velvet Claws, The

Clement, Dick: Bullshot (Bullshot Crummond); Catch Me a Spy; Water

Clement, René: And Hope to Die; Day and the Hour; Forbidden Games (1951); Gervaise; Is Paris Burning?; Joy House; Purple Noon; Rider on the Rain

Clements, Ron: Adventures of the Great Mouse Detective, The; Aladdin (1992); Great Mouse Detective, The; Hercules (Animated) (1997); Little Mermaid, The (1989)

Clifford, Graeme: Burke and Wills; Deception (1993); Frances; Gleaming the Cube; Last Don, The; My Husband's Secret Life; Past Tense; Turn of the Screw, The (1989)

Clift, Denison: Mystery of the Marie Celeste, The (The Phantom Ship)

Clifton, Elmer: Assassin of Youth (Marijuana); Captain America (1944); Cyclone in the Saddle; Days of Old Cheyenne; Deep in the Heart of Texas; Down to the Sea in Ships; Not Wanted; Seven Doors to Death; Skull and Crown

Clifton, Peter: Song Remains the Same, The

Cline, Eddie: Art of Buster Keaton, The; Bank Dick, The; Breaking the Ice; Buster Keaton Festival Vol. 1–3; Cowboy Millionaire; Dude Ranger; Ghost Catchers; The Hook, Line and Sinker; My Little Chickadee; Never Give a Sucker an Even Break; Peck's Bad Boy with the Circus; Private Buckaroo; Private Snuffy Smith; Three Ages, The; Villain Still Pursued Her, The

Cloche, Maurice: Monsieur Vincent

Clokey, Art: Gumby The Movie

Cloos, Hans Peter: Germany In Autumn

Clouse, Robert: Amsterdam Kill, The; Big Brawl, The; Black Belt Jones; China O'Brien; China O'Brien 2; Deadly Eyes; Enter the Dragon; Force Five; Game of Death; Gymkata; Ironheart; Pack, The; Ultimate Warrior, The

Clouzot, Henri-Georges: Diabolique (1955); Jenny Lamour; Le Corbeau (The Raven (1943)); Manon; Mystery of Picasso, The; Wages of Fear, The

Corbucci, Bruno: Aladdin (1987); Cop in Blue Jeans, The; Miami Supercops

Corbucci, Sergio: Con Artists, The; Django; Hellbenders, The; Sonny and Jed; Super Fuzz

Corcoran, Bill: Sherlock Holmes and the Incident at Victoria Falls; Survive the Night

Corea, Nicholas: Incredible Hulk Returns, The

Corea, Nick: Archer: Fugitive from the Empire

Corley, David L.: Angel's Dance

Corley, David R.: Executive Power

Corlish, Frank B.: Longest Hunt, The

Corman, Roger: Apache Woman; Atlas; Attack of the Crab Monsters; Bloody Mama; Bucket of Blood, A; Carnival Rock; Creature from the Haunted Sea, The; Day the World Ended, The; Fall of the House of Usher, The (1960); Frankenstein Unbound; Gas-s-s-s; Gunslinger; Haunted Palace, The; I, Mobster; Intruder, The (1961); It Conquered the World; Little Shop of Horrors, The (1960); Machine-Gun Kelly; Masque of the Red Death, The (1964); Pit and the Pendulum, The (1961); Premature Burial, The; Raven, The (1963); Saga of the Viking Women and Their Voyage to the Waters of the Great Sea Serpent, The (Viking Women and the Sea Serpent, The); St. Valentine's Day Massacre, The; Sorority Girl; Swamp Women; Tales of Terror; Terror, The; Tomb of Ligeia; Tower of London (1962); Trip, The; Undead, The; War of the Satellites; Wasp Woman (1960); Wild Angels, The; X (The Man with the X-Ray Eyes)

Corneau, Alain: Choice of Arms, A; Fort Saganne; Tous les Matins du Monde

Cornelius, Henry: Genevieve; I Am a Camera; Passport to Pimlico

Cornell, John: Almost an Angel; "Crocodile" Dundee II

Cornfield, Hubert: Night of the Following Day, The; Plunder Road; Pressure Point

Cornwell, Stephen: Killing Streets; Marshal Law; Philadelphia Experiment 2, The

Corona, Alfonso: Deathstalker III—The Warriors from Hell; World of the Vampires

Corr, Eugene: Desert Bloom

Correll, Charles: Cry in the Wind; Deadly Desire; Fortune Dane; In the Deep Woods; Stepsister, The

Correll, Richard: Ski Patrol

Corrente, Michael: American Buffalo; Federal Hill; Outside Providence

Corrigan, Lloyd: Daughter of the Dragon

Corson, Ian: Malicious (1995)

Cort, Bud: Ted & Venus

Corti, Axel: King's Whore, The

Coscarelli, Don: Beastmaster, The; Phantasm; Phantasm II; Phantasm III: Lord of the Dead; Phantasm IV: Oblivion; Survival Quest

Cosmatos, George Pan: Cassandra Crossing, The; Cobra (1986); Escape to Athena; Leviathan; Massacre in Rome; Of Unknown Origin; Rambo: First Blood II; Restless; Shadow Conspiracy; Tombstone

Costa, Mario: Rough Justice

Costa-Gavras, Constantin: Betrayed (1988); Hanna K.; Mad City; Missing; Music Box, The; Sleeping Car Murders, The; State of Siege; Z

Costner, Kevin: Dances with Wolves; Postman, The

Coto, Manny: Cover-Up; Dr. Giggles; Playroom; Star Kid

Cottafavi, Vittorio: Goliath and the Dragon; Hercules and the Captive Women

Cotter, John: Mountain Family Robinson

Couffer, Jack: Living Free; Nikki, Wild Dog of the North; Ring of Bright Water

Coughlan, Ian: Alison's Birthday

Coulter, Allen: Stephen King's Golden Years (TV Series)

Courtland, Jerome: Diamonds on Wheels

Couturie, Bill: Dear America: Letters Home from Vietnam; Ed

Covert, Michael: American Strays

Covington, Hil: Adventures in Spying

Cowan, Rich: Basket, The

Cowan, Will: Thing that Couldn't Die, The

Coward, Noel: In Which We Serve

Cowen, William: Oliver Twist (1933)

Cox, Alex: Repo Man; Sid and Nancy; Straight to Hell; Walker; Winner, The

Cox, Brian: Scorpion Spring

Cox, Mitchell: Rule #3

Cox, Paul: Cactus; Kostas; Lonely Hearts (1981); Man of Flowers; My First Wife; Woman's Tale, A

Crabtree, Arthur: Fiend without a Face; Horrors of the Black Museum; Quartet (1948)

Crain, William: Blacula; Dr. Black and Mr. Hyde

Cramer, Ronnie: Back Street Jane

Crane, Kenneth: Manster, The; Monster from Green Hell

Craven, Jay: Stranger in the Kingdom, A; Where the Rivers Flow North

Craven, Wes: Chiller; Deadly Blessing; Deadly Friend; Hills Have Eyes, The; Hills Have Eyes, The: Part Two; Invitation to Hell; Last House on the Left; Music of the Heart; Nightmare on Elm Street, A; People Under the Stairs, The; Scream 2; Scream 3; Scream (1996); Serpent and the Rainbow, The; Shocker; Summer of Fear; Swamp Thing; Vampire in Brooklyn; Wes Craven's New Nightmare

Crawford, Wayne: American Cop; Crime Lords

Creme, Lol: Lunatic, The

Cremin, Kevin G.: Siringo

Crenna, Richard: Better Late than Never

Cribben, Mik: Beware! Children at Play

Crichton, Charles: Battle of the Sexes, The; Dead of Night (1945); Fish Called Wanda, A; Lavender Hill Mob, The

Crichton, Michael: Coma; Great Train Robbery, The; Looker; Physical Evidence; Runaway; Westworld

Crichton, Robin: Silent Mouse

Crisp, Donald: Don Q, Son of Zorro; Navigator, The (1924)

Crispino, Armando: Autopsy; Commandos

Cristallini, Giorgio: You're Jinxed Friend, You Just Met Sacramento

Cristofer, Michael: Body Shots

Croghan, Emma-Kate: Love and Other Catastrophes

Crombie, Donald: Caddie; Irishman, The; Killing of Angel Street, The; Kitty and the Bagman

Cromwell, John: Abe Lincoln in Illinois; Ann Vickers; Anna and the King of Siam; Dead Reckoning (1947); Enchanted Cottage, The; Goddess, The; I Dream Too Much; In Name Only; Little Lord Fauntleroy (1936);-Made for Each Other; Of Human Bondage (1934); Prisoner of Zenda, The (1937); Racket, The; Since You Went Away; So Ends Our Night; Son of Fury; Spitfire (1934); Tom Sawyer (1930)

Cronenberg, David: Brood, The; Crash (1996); Dead Ringers; Dead Zone, The; eXistenZ; Fly, The (1986); M. Butterfly; Naked Lunch; Rabid; Scanners; They Came from Within; Videodrome

Crooke, Evan: Killing Jar, The

Crosland, Alan: Beloved Rogue; Case of the Howling Dog, The; Don Juan; Jazz Singer, The (1927)

Crouch, William Forest: Reet, Petite and Gone

Crounse, Avery: Cries of Silence; Eyes of Fire; Invisible Kid, The

Crowe, Cameron: Jerry Maguire; Say Anything; Singles

Crowe, Christopher: Off Limits (1988); Whispers in the Dark

Crowe, Russell: Crossing, The

Cruise, Tom: Fallen Angels

Crump, Owen: Gateway to the Mind

Cruze, James: Covered Wagon, The; Great Gabbo, The; Helldorado (1934); I Cover the Waterfront; Mr. Skitch; Old Ironsides; Roaring Road, The

Crystal, Billy: Forget Paris; Mr. Saturday Night

Cuaron, Alfonso: Fallen Angels; Great Expectations (1998); Little Princess, A (1995)

Cukor, George: Adam's Rib (1949); Bhowani Junction; Bill of Divorcement, A; Born Yesterday (1950); Camille; Corn Is Green, The (1979); David Copperfield; Dinner at Eight (1933); Double Life, A; Gaslight (1944); Heller in Pink Tights; Holiday; It Should Happen to You; Justine; Keeper of the Flame; Les Girls; Let's Make Love; Life of Her Own, A; Little Women (1933); Love Among the Ruins; My Fair Lady; Pat and Mike; Philadelphia Story, The; Rich and Famous; Romeo and Juliet (1936); Song Without End; Star Is Born, A (1954); Susan and God; Sylvia Scarlett; Travels with My Aunt; Two-Faced Woman; What Price Hollywood?; Woman's Face, A; Women, The

Cullingham, Mark: Cinderella (1985); Dead on the Money; Princess Who Had Never Laughed, The

Cummings, Bill: Bad Attitude

Cummings, Howard: Courtship

Cummings, Irving: Curly Top; Dolly Sisters, The; Double Dynamite; Down Argentine Way; Everything Happens at

Night; Flesh and Blood (1922); Hollywood Cavalcade; In Old Arizona; Just Around the Corner; Little Miss Broadway; Louisiana Purchase; Poor Little Rich Girl (1936); Springtime in the Rockies (1942)

Cummins, James: Boneyard, The

Cundey, Dean: Honey, We Shrunk Ourselves

Cundieff, Rusty: Fear of a Black Hat; Sprung; Tales from the Hood

Cunha, Richard: Frankenstein's Daughter; Giant from the Unknown; Missile to the Moon; She Demons

Cunningham, Sean S.: Deepstar Six; Friday the 13th; Manny's Orphans (Come the Tigers); New Kids, The; Stranger Is Watching, A

Curran, William: Love, Cheat & Steal

Currie, Anthony: Pink Chiquitas, The

Currier, Lavinia: Passion in the Desert

Curtis, Dan: Burnt Offerings; Curse of the Black Widow; Dead of Night (1977); Dracula (1973); Express to Terror; House of Dark Shadows; Intruders; Kansas City Massacre, The; Last Ride of the Dalton Gang, The; Love Letter, The (1998); Me and the Kid; Melvin Purvis: G-Man; Night of Dark Shadows; Night Strangler, The; Trilogy of Terror; Trilogy of Terror II; War and Remembrance; Winds of War, The

Curtis, Douglas: Sleeping Car, The

Curtis, Jack: Flesh Eaters, The

Curtis-Hall, Vondie: Gridlock'd

Curtiz, Michael: Adventures of Huckleberry Finn, The (1960); Adventures of Robin Hood, The; Angels with Dirty Faces; Black Fury; Breath of Scandal, A; Cabin in the Cotton; Captain Blood; Captains of the Clouds; Casablanca; Case of the Curious Bride, The; Charge of the Light Brigade, The (1936); Comancheros, The; Dive Bomber; Doctor X; Dodge City; Egyptian, The; Female; Flamingo Road; Force of Arms; Four Daughters; Helen Morgan Story, The; I'll See You in My Dreams; Jazz Singer, The (1953); Jim Thorpe—All American; Kennel Murder Case, The; Kid Galahad (1937); King Creole; Life with Father; Mildred Pierce; My Dream Is Yours; Mystery of the Wax Museum; Night and Day (1946); Noah's Ark; Passage to Marseilles; Private Lives of Elizabeth and Essex, The; Proud Rebel, The; Romance on the High Seas; Santa Fe Trail; Sea Hawk, The; Sea Wolf, The (1941); Strange Love of Molly Louvain, The; This Is the Army; Trouble Along the Way; Virginia City; We're No Angels (1955); White Christmas; Yankee Doodle Dandy; Young Man with a Horn

Cybulski, Mary: Hellcab

Cypher, Julie: Teresa's Tattoo

Cyran, Catherine: Hostile Intentions; In the Heat of Passion II: Unfaithful; Sawbones; True Heart; White Wolves: A Cry in the Wild II

Czinner, Paul: As You Like It; Catherine the Great

D'Esposito, Louis: Opposite Corners

Daalder, Renee: Habitat; Massacre at Central High

Daboul, Samer: Suicide Ride

Da Costa, Morton: Auntie Mame; Music Man, The

Dahl, John: Kill Me Again; Last Seduction, The; Red Rock West; Rounders; Rounders (1998); Unforgettable

Dahlin, Bob: Monster in the Closet

Dahms, Heinrich: My Daughter's Keeper

Dale, Holly: Blood & Donuts

Dalen, Zale: Expect No Mercy

Daley, Tom: Outing, The

Dali, Salvador: Un Chien Andalou

Dallamano, Massimo: Black Veil for Lisa, A; Dorian Gray

D'Almeida, Neville: Lady on the Bus

Dalrymple, Ian: Storm in a Teacup

Dalva, Robert: Black Stallion Returns, The

D'Amato (Aristide Massaccesi), Joe: Buried Alive (1979); Grim Reaper, The (1980); Trap Them and Kill Them

Damiani, Damiano: Amityville II: The Possession; Bullet for the General, A; Confessions of a Police Captain; Empty Canvas, The; Inquiry, The; Warning, The

D'Amico, Louis: Playing the Field

Damski, Mel: Badge of the Assassin; For Ladies Only; Happy Together; Legend of Walks Far Woman, The; Mischief; Wild Card; Yellowbeard

D'Andrea, Anthony: Thrillkill

Dane, Lawrence: Heavenly Bodies

Daniel, Rod: Beethoven's 2nd; K-9; Like Father, Like Son; Super, The; Teen Wolf

Daniels, Harold: Poor White Trash; Terror in the Haunted House

Daniels, Marc: I Married Joan (TV Series); Planet Earth; Star Trek (TV Series); Star Trek: The Menagerie

Danielsson, Tage: Adventures of Picasso, The

D'Anna, Claude: Salome (1985)

Danniel, Danniel: Egg

Danska, Herbert: Sweet Love, Bitter

Dante, Joe: Amazon Women on the Moon; 'Burbs, The; Explorers; Gremlins; Gremlins 2: The New Batch; Hollywood Boulevard; Howling, The; Innerspace; Matinee; Piranha (1978); Police Squad!; Second Civil War, The; Small Soldiers; Twilight Zone—The Movie

Danton, Ray: Crypt of the Living Dead; Psychic Killer; Tales of the Unexpected; Vietnam War Story

D'Antoni, Philip: Seven-Ups, The

Danus, Richard: No Place to Hide

Darabont, Frank: Buried Alive (1990); Green Mile, The; Shawshank Redemption, The

Darby, Jonathan: Enemy Within, The

Dardenne, Jean-Pierre: La Promesse

Dardenne, Luc: La Promesse

Darling, Joan: Check Is in the Mail, The; First Love (1977); Mary Hartman, Mary Hartman (TV Series); Willa

Darlow, Michael: Merlin of the Crystal Cave

Darnell, Eric: Antz

D'Arrast, Harry: Topaze (1933)

Dash, Julie: Daughters of the Dust

Dash, Sean: Breakaway

Dassin, Jules: Brute Force; Canterville Ghost, The (1944); Circle of Two; Dream of Passion, A; Naked City, The; Never on Sunday; Night and the City (1950); Reunion in France; Rififi; Topkapi

Daugherty, Herschel: Light in the Forest, The; Wagon Train (TV Series)

Davenport, Harry: Xtro; Xtro II; Xtro: Watch the Skies (Xtro 3)

Davenport, Harry Bromley: Adventures of Young Brave, The

Daves, Delmer: Badlanders, The; Broken Arrow (1950); Dark Passage; Demetrius and the Gladiators; Destination Tokyo; Drum Beat; Hanging Tree, The; Hollywood Canteen; Jubal; Kings Go Forth; Never Let Me Go; Parrish; Red House, The; Rome Adventure; Spencer's Mountain; Summer Place, A; Task Force; 3:10 to Yuma

David, Charles: Lady on a Train

David, Pierre: Scanner Cop; Serial Killer

Davidson, Boaz: American Cyborg: Steel Warrior; Going Bananas; Hospital Massacre; Outside the Law (1994); Salsa; Solar Force

Davidson, Gordon: Trial of the Cantonsville Nine, The

Davidson, John-Paul: Grave Indiscretion

Davidson, Martin: Eddie and the Cruisers; Hard Promises; Heart of Dixie, The; Hero at Large; Long Gone; Lords of Flatbush, The

Davies, Howard: Secret Rapture, The

Davies, John: Married Man, A; Sleeping Murder; Why Didn't They Ask Evans?

Davies, John Howard: Mr. Bean

Davies, Robert: Saturday Night at the Palace

Davies, Terence: Distant Voices/Still Lives; Long Day Closes, The; Neon Bible, The

Davies, Valentine: Benny Goodman Story, The

Davis, Andrew: Above the Law; Chain Reaction (1996); Code of Silence; Final Terror, The; Fugitive, The (1993); Package, The; Perfect Murder, A; Steal Big, Steal Little; Under Siege

Davis, B. J.: White Ghost

Davis, Barry: Don't Hang Up

Davis, Beau: Laser Mission

Davis, Charles: Die Watching

Davis, Desmond: Clash of the Titans; Love with a Perfect Stranger; Nice Girl Like Me, A; Ordeal by Innocence; Sign of Four, The

Davis, Eddie: Cisco Kid (TV Series); Color Me Dead

Davis, Gary: Conflict of Interest

Davis, Julie: I Love You, Don't Touch Me!; Witchcraft VI: The Devil's Mistress

Davis, Michael: Eight Days a Week

Davis, Michael Paul: Beanstalk

Davis, Ossie: Cotton Comes to Harlem; Gordon's War

Deschanel, Caleb: Crusoe; Escape Artist, The

Desfontanes, Henri: Queen Elizabeth

De Sica, Vittorio: After the Fox; Bicycle Thief, The; Boccaccio 70; Garden of the Finzi-Continis, The; Gold of Naples, The; Indiscretion of an American Wife; Marriage Italian Style; Miracle in Milan; Shoeshine; Two Women; Umberto D; Woman Times Seven; Yesterday, Today and Tomorrow

DeSimone, Tom: Concrete Jungle, The (1982); Hell Night; Reform School Girls

Desmarais, James: Road Lawyers and Other Briefs

Desmond, Brian: River of Unrest

De Sota, Bruno: Invasion of the Star Creatures

de Souza, Stephen: Street Fighter (1994)

de Toth, André: Dark Waters; House of Wax; Last of the Comanches; Man in the Saddle; Morgan the Pirate; Pitfall; Ramrod; Stranger Wore a Gun, The

Deutch, Howard: Article 99; Getting Even with Dad; Great Outdoors, The; Grumpier Old Men; Odd Couple II, The; Pretty in Pink; Some Kind of Wonderful

Deval, Jacques: Club des Femmes

Devenish, Ross: Bleak House; Overindulgence; Touch of Frost, A (TV Series)

Devereaux, Marcus: Lady of the Lake

Deville, Michel: La Lectrice (The Reader); La Petite Bande; Peril; Voyage en Douce

DeVito, Danny: Amazing Stories (TV Series); Hoffa; Matilda (1996); Ratings Game, The; Throw Momma from the Train; War of the Roses, The

Dewey, Richard Lloyd: Rockwell: A Legend of the Wild West

De Witt, Elmo: Enemy Unseen

DeWolf, Patrick: Innocent Lies

Dexter, John: I Want What I Want; Virgin Soldiers, The

Dey, Tom: Shanghai Noon

Tetsu, Dezuki: Urusei Yatsura: Inaba the Dreammaker

Dhomme, Sylvain: Seven Deadly Sins, The

Diamonde, Lucian S.: Forbidden Zone: Alien Abduction

DiBergi, Jim: Return of Spinal Tap, The

DiCillo, Tom: Box of Moonlight; Johnny Suede; Living in Oblivion; Real Blonde, The

Dick, Kirby: Sick: The Life and Death of Bob Flanagan, Supermasochist

Dick, Nigel: Dead Connection; Deadly Intent; Private Investigations

Dickerson, Ernest R.: Blind Faith; Bulletproof (1996); Futuresport; Juice; Strange Justice; Surviving the Game; Tales from the Crypt: Demon Knight

Dickinson, Thorold: Gaslight (1940); High Command, The

Dickson, Lance: Hollywood Heartbreak

Dickson, Paul: Satellite in the Sky

Didden, Marc: Istanbul

Diege, Samuel: Ride 'em Cowgirl

Diegues, Carlos: Bye Bye Brazil; Subway to the Stars

Dienstag, Alan: Moneytree, The

Dieterle, William: Boots Malone; Devil and Daniel Webster, The; Elephant Walk; Hunchback of Notre Dame, The (1939); Juarez; Kismet (1944); Life of Emile Zola, The; Omar Khayyam; Portrait of Jennie; Quick, Let's Get Married; Salome (1953); Satan Met a Lady; Scarlet Dawn; September Affair; Story of Louis Pasteur, The

Dignam, Erin: Denial

Dilello, Richard: Riot (1996) (TV Movie)

Di Leo, Fernando: Kidnap Syndicate, The; Manhunt (1973) (The Italian Connection); Violent Breed, The

Di Leo, Mario: Final Alliance

Diling, Bert: Dead Easy

Dillon, John Francis: Behind the Mask; Call Her Savage

DiMarco, Steve: Back in Action; Prisoner of Love

Dimsey, Ross: Blue Fire Lady

Dimster-Denk, Dennis: Mikey

Dindal, Mark: Cats Don't Dance

Dingo, Pece: Midnight Cabaret

Dingwall, John: Custodian, The

Dinner, Michael: Heaven Help Us; Hot to Trot; Off Beat

Dippe, Mark A. Z.: Spawn

Dirlam, John: Fatal Instinct (1992)

DiSalle, Mark: Kickboxer; Perfect Weapon

Disbrow, Warren F.: Invasion from Flesh and Blood

Disney, Walt: Fantasia; Fun and Fancy Free; Officer and a Duck, An (Limited Gold Edition 2); Peter and the Wolf; Pinocchio (1940); Three Caballeros, The

Dixon, Ivan: Percy & Thunder

Dixon, Jamie: Bram Stoker's Shadowbuilder

Dixon, Ken: Slave Girls from Beyond Infinity

Dizdar, Jasmin: Beautiful People

Dmytryk, Edward: Alvarez Kelly; Anzio; Back to Bataan; Behind the Rising Sun; Bluebeard (1972); Broken Lance; Caine Mutiny, The; Captive Wild Woman; Carpetbaggers, The; Cornered; Crossfire (1947); Devil Commands, The; Hitler's Children; Left Hand of God, The; Mirage (1965); Mountain, The; Murder My Sweet; Raintree County; Shalako; Soldier of Fortune; Tender Comrade; Till the End of Time; Walk on the Wild Side; Warlock (1959); Where Love Has Gone; Young Lions, The

Dobb, Tony: Blue Tornado

Dobbs, Frank Q.: Uphill All the Way

Dobkin, David: Clay Pigeons

Dobson, Kevin James: Gold Diggers: The Secret of Bear Mountain; Miracle in the Wilderness; Squizzy Taylor

Dodson, James: Deadly Rivals; Quest of the Delta Knights

Dohler, Don: Alien Factor, The

Doillon, Jacques: La Puritaine; Ponette

Dolman, Martin: After the Fall of New York; American Tiger; Hands of Steel

Domaradzki, Jerzy: Legend of the White Horse

Donahue, Patrick G.: Savage Instinct

Donaldson, Roger: Bounty, The; Cadillac Man; Cocktail; Dante's Peak; Getaway, The (1994); Marie; No Way Out; Sleeping Dogs; Smash Palace; Species; White Sands

Donavan, Tom: Love Spell

Done, Harris: Storm Tracker

Donehue, Vincent J.: Lonelyhearts; Peter Pan (1960); Sunrise at Campobello

Donen, Stanley: Arabesque; Bedazzled; Blame It on Rio; Charade; Damn Yankees; Deep in My Heart; Funny Face; Give a Girl a Break; Grass Is Greener, The; Indiscreet (1958); It's Always Fair Weather; Little Prince, The; Love Is Better Than Ever; Movie Movie; On the Town; Pajama Game, The; Royal Wedding; Saturn 3; Seven Brides for Seven Brothers; Singin' in the Rain; Staircase; Surprise Package; Two for the Road

Dong, Arthur: Coming Out Under Fire

Doniger, Walter: Mad Bull

Donnelly, Thomas Michael: Garden of Redemption, The; Soldier's Sweetheart, A

Donnelly, Tom: Blindsided; Quicksilver

Donner, Clive: Babes in Toyland (1986); Charlie Chan and the Curse of the Dragon Queen; Christmas Carol, A (1984); Luv; Merlin & the Sword; Not a Penny More, Not a Penny Less; Nude Bomb, The (Return of Maxwell Smart, The); Oliver Twist (1982); Scarlet Pimpernel, The (1982); Stealing Heaven; Terror Stalks the Class Reunion; Thief of Baghdad (1978); To Catch a King; What's New, Pussycat?

Donner, Richard: Conspiracy Theory; Fugitive, The (TV Series); Goonies, The; Inside Moves; Ladyhawke; Lethal Weapon; Lethal Weapon 2; Lethal Weapon 3; Lethal Weapon 4; Maverick; Omen, The; Radio Flyer; Scrooged; Superman; Tales from the Crypt (TV Series); Toy, The; Twilight Zone, The (TV Series); Wanted: Dead or Alive (TV Series)

Donoghue, Mary Agnes: Paradise (1991)

Donohue, Jack: Assault on a Queen; Babes in Toyland (1961); Lucky Me; Watch the Birdie; Yellow Cab Man, The

Donohue, John Clark: Marvelous Land of Oz, The

Donovan, Jim: Provocateur

Donovan, King: Promises, Promises

Donovan, Martin: Apartment Zero; Death Dreams; Mad at the Moon; Somebody's Waiting; Substitute, The (1993)

Donovan, Paul: Def-Con 4; George's Island; I Worship His Shadow; Norman's Awesome Experience; Northern Extremes; Tomcat: Dangerous Desires

Doran, Thomas: Spookies

Dorfmann, Jacques: Shadow of the Wolf

Dornhelm, Robert: Cold Feet (1989); Echo Park; Requiem for Dominic

Dörrie, Doris: Me and Him; Men ... (1985); Nobody Loves Me

Dotan, Shimon: Finest Hour, The; Sworn Enemies; Warriors (1994)

Douchet, Jean: Six in Paris (Paris Vue par ...)

Doueiri, Ziad: West Beirut

Douglas, Gordon: Black Arrow, The (1948); Call Me Bwana; Chuka; Detective, The (1968); Dick Tracy versus Cueball; Doolins of Oklahoma; First Yank into Tokyo; Follow That Dream; General Spanky; Girl Rush; Great Missouri Raid, The; Harlow; If You Knew Susie; In Like Flint; Kiss Tomorrow Goodbye; Lady in Cement; McConnell Story, The; Nevadan, The; Only the Valiant; Rio Conchos; Robin & the Seven Hoods; Saps at Sea; Sincerely Yours; Slaughter's Big Rip-Off; Them!; They Call Me Mister Tibbs; Tony Rome; Up Periscope; Viva Knievel; Young at Heart; Zenobia; Zombies on Broadway

Douglas, Kirk: Posse (1975)

Douglas, Peter: Tiger's Tale, A

Doumani, Lorenzo: Amore! (1993); Bug Buster; Knockout; Mad About You; Storybook

Douy, Max: Seven Deadly Sins, The

Dovzhenko, Alexander: Arsenal; Earth; Zvenigora

Dowdey, Kathleen: Blue Heaven

Dowling, Kevin: Last Rites; Mojave Moon; Sum of Us, The

Downey, Robert: America; Greaser's Palace; Hugo Pool; Putney Swope; Rented Lips; Too Much Sun; Up the Academy

Doyle, Tim: Road Lawyers and Other Briefs

Drach, Michel: Les Violons du Bal

Dragin, Bert L.: Summer Camp Nightmare; Twice Dead

Dragoti, Stan: Love at First Bite; Man with One Red Shoe, The; Mr. Mom; Necessary Roughness; She's Out of Control

Drake, Jim: Awakening of Cassie, The; Based on an Untrue Story; Legacy for Leonette; Mary Hartman, Mary Hartman (TV Series); Police Academy 4: Citizens on Patrol; Speed Zone

Drake, Oliver: Across the Rio Grande; Mummy and the Curse of the Jackals, The

Drake, T. Y.: Keeper, The

Draskovic, Boro: Vukovar

Drazan, Anthony: Hurlyburly; Imaginary Crimes; Zebrahead

Dresch, Fred: My Samurai

Dreville, Jean: Sputnik

Drew, Di: Right Hand Man, The; Trouble in Paradise

Dreyer, Carl: Day of Wrath; Gertrude; Leaves from Satan's Book; Master of the House (Du Skal Aere Din Hustru); Ordet; Passion of Joan of Arc, The; Vampyr (1931)

Dreyfuss, Richard: Anything for Love

Dridi, Karim: Bye-Bye

Driscoll, Richard: Comic, The (1985)

Driver, Charla: Deadly Target

Driver, John: Marvelous Land of Oz, The

Driver, Sara: Sleepwalker

Drove, Antonio: Tunnel, The

Drury, David: Defense of the Realm; Forever Young (1983); Hostile Waters; Intrigue; Prime Suspect 3; Rhodes; Split Decisions

Dryfoos, Susan W.: Line King, The

Dryhurst, Michael: Hard Way, The (1979)

Drysdale, Lee: Leather Jackets

Dubin, Charles S.: Cinderella (1964); Gathering, Part II, The; Meanest Men in the West, The; Moving Violation; Roots: The Next Generation; Silent Rebellion

Dubov, Adam: Dead Beat

Dubroux, Daniele: Diary of a Seducer

Du Chau, Frederik: Quest for Camelot

Duchemin, Remy: A La Mode

Dudley, Terence: All Creatures Great and Small

Duffell, Peter: Experience Preferred … But Not Essential; Far Pavilions, The; House That Dripped Blood, The; Inside Out (1975); King of the Wind; Letters to an Unknown Lover

Duffy, Martin: Bumblebee Flies Anyway, The

Dugan, Dennis: Beverly Hills Ninja; Big Daddy; Brain Donors; Happy Gilmore; Problem Child

Dugdale, George: Slaughter High

Dugowson, Martine: Mina Tannenbaum

Duguay, Christian: Adrift; Assignment, The; Live Wire; Model by Day; Scanners 2: The New Order; Scanners 3: The Takeover; Screamers (1996)

Duigan, John: Flirting; Journey of August King, The; Lawn Dogs; Leading Man, The; Molly; Romero; Sirens; Wide Sargasso Sea; Winter of Our Dreams; Year My Voice Broke, The

Duke, Bill: America's Dream; Cemetery Club, The; Deep Cover (1992); Hoodlum; Killing Floor, The; Rage in Harlem,

A; Raisin in the Sun, A (1988); Sister Act 2: Back in the Habit

Duke, Daryl: Griffin and Phoenix: A Love Story; I Heard the Owl Call My Name; Payday; President's Plane Is Missing, The; Silent Partner, The; Tai-Pan; Thornbirds, The

Dumoulin, Georges: Nous N'Irons Plus Au Bois

Duncan, Patrick: 84 Charlie Mopic; Live! From Death Row

Duncan, Peter: Children of the Revolution

Dunham, Duwayne: Homeward Bound: The Incredible Journey; Little Giants

Dunne, Griffin: Addicted to Love; Practical Magic

Dunne, Philip: Wild in the Country

Dunning, George: Yellow Submarine

Dunsky, Evan: Alarmist, The

Dupeyron, Francois: La Machine

Dupont, E. A.: Neanderthal Man, The; Variety

Duran, Ciro: Tropical Snow

Durand, Rudy: Tilt

Durgay, Attila: Matt the Gooseboy

Durlow, David: Tailspin

Durston, David E.: I Drink Your Blood; Stigma

Dutcher, Richard: God's Army

Dutton, Charles S.: First Time Felon

Duvall, Robert: Angelo, My Love; Apostle, The

Duvivier, Julien: Anna Karenina (1947); Black Jack; Burning Court, The; Diabolically Yours; Golgotha; Great Waltz, The; Little World of Don Camillo, The; Lydia; Panique; Pepe Le Moko; Tales of Manhattan

Dwan, Allan: Around the World; Brewster's Millions (1945); Cattle Queen of Montana; Enchanted Island; Escape to Burma; Gorilla, The; Heidi (1937); Hollywood Party; Iron Mask, The; Look Who's Laughing; Manhandled; Montana Belle; Northwest Outpost; Passion (1954); Pearl of the South Pacific; Rebecca of Sunnybrook Farm (1938); Restless Breed, The; Robin Hood (1923); Sands of Iwo Jima; Silver Lode; Slightly Scarlet; Tennessee's Partner; Three Musketeers, The (1939)

Dwan, Robert: You Bet Your Life (TV Series)

Dyal, H. Kaye: Project: Eliminator

Dyke, Robert: Moon Trap

Dzhordzhadze, Nan: Chef in Love, A

Dziki, Waldemar: Young Magician, The

Eady, David: Three Cases of Murder

Earnshaw, Ellen: Human Desires

Eason, B. Reeves "Breezy": Adventures of Rex and Rinty; Blue Montana Skies; Empty Holsters; Fighting Marines, The; Galloping Ghost, The; Law for Tombstone; Man of the Frontier (West River Valley); Phantom Empire (1935); Radio Ranch (Men with Steel Faces, Phantom Empire); Rimfire; Undersea Kingdom

Eason, Walter B.: Sea Hound, The

Eastman, Allan: Crazy Moon; Danger Zone (1995); Ford: The Man & the Machine; War Boy, The

Eastman, G. L.: Metamorphosis

Eastwood, Clint: Absolute Power; Bird; Bridges of Madison County, The; Bronco Billy; Eiger Sanction, The; Firefox; Gauntlet, The; Heartbreak Ridge; High Plains Drifter; Honkytonk Man; Midnight in the Garden of Good and Evil; Outlaw Josey Wales, The; Pale Rider; Perfect World, A; Play Misty for Me; Rookie, The; Sudden Impact; True Crime (1999); Unforgiven (1992); White Hunter Black Heart

Ebata, Hiroyuki: Dog Soldier: Shadows of the Past

Eberhardt, Thom: Captain Ron; Face Down; Gross Anatomy; Night Before, The; Night of the Comet; Sole Survivor; Without a Clue

Ebishima, Toyo: Serendipity, the Pink Dragon

Ecare, Desire: Faces of Women

Echevarria, Nicolas: Cabeza de Vaca

Edel, Uli: Body of Evidence; Christiane F.; Last Exit to Brooklyn; Purgatory; Rasputin (1996); Tyson

Edgren, Gustaf: Walpurgis Night

Edmunds, Don: Bare Knuckles

Edwards, Anthony: Charlie's Ghost

Edwards, Blake: Blind Date (1987); Breakfast at Tiffany's; Curse of the Pink Panther, The; Darling Lili; Days of Wine and Roses (1962); Experiment in Terror; Fine Mess, A; Great Race, The; Man Who Loved Women, The (1983); Micki & Maude; Operation Petticoat; Party, The; Perfect Furlough; Peter Gunn (TV Series); Pink Panther, The; Pink Panther Strikes Again, The; Return of the Pink Panther, The; Revenge of the Pink Panther, The; Shot in the Dark, A; Skin

Deep; S.O.B.; Son of the Pink Panther; Sunset; Switch; Tamarind Seed, The; 10; That's Life; This Happy Feeling; Trail of the Pink Panther, The; Victor/Victoria; Wild Rovers, The

Edwards, Dan: Black Cobra 3

Edwards, Dave: Secret Garden, The (1994)

Edwards, George: Attic, The

Edwards, Henry: Juggernaut (1936); Scrooge (1935)

Edwards, Vince: Mission Galactica: The Cylon Attack

Edzard, Christine: Little Dorrit

Egerton, Mark: Winds of Jarrah, The

Eggeling: Avant Garde Program #2

Eggleston, Colin: Cassandra; Long Weekend; Sky Pirates; Wicked, The

Egleson, Jan: Last Hit, The; Shock to the System, A

Egoyan, Atom: Adjuster, The; Exotica; Family Viewing; Felicia's Journey; Next of Kin (1984); Speaking Parts; Sweet Hereafter, The

Eichorn, Franz: Violent Years, The

Eisenman, Rafael: Business for Pleasure; Lake Consequence; Red Shoe Diaries 3: Another Woman's Lipstick

Eisenstein, Sergei: Alexander Nevsky; Battleship Potemkin, The; Ivan the Terrible—Part I & Part II; October (Ten Days That Shook the World); Strike (1924)

Elanjian Jr., George: Syngenor

Elfman, Richard: Forbidden Zone; Shrunken Heads

Elfont, Harry: Can't Hardly Wait

Elias, Michael: Lush Life; No Laughing Matter

Eliasberg, Jan: Past Midnight

Elikann, Larry: Blue River; Disaster at Silo 7; Fever; God Bless the Child; Great Los Angeles Earthquake, The; Great Wallendas, The; Inconvenient Woman, An; Mother's Prayer, A; One Against the Wind; Poison Ivy (1985); Story Lady, The; Stranger on My Land; Unexpected Family, An

Ellenshaw, Harrison: Dead Silence (1989)

Ellin, Doug: Kissing a Fool; Phat Beach

Elliot, Michael: Fatal Games; King Lear (1984)

Elliott, Lang: Cage; Cage II: Arena of Death, The; Private Eyes, The

Elliott, Scott: Map of the World, A

Elliott, Stephan: Adventures of Priscilla, Queen of the Desert, The; Eye of the Beholder; Frauds; Welcome to Woop Woop

Elliotts, Paul: Great Adventure, The

Ellis, Bob: Nostradamus Kid, The; Warm Nights on a Slow Moving Train

Ellis, David R.: Homeward Bound II: Lost in San Francisco

Ellison, James: Don't Go in the House

Elman, Luis: Matt the Gooseboy

Elvey, Maurice: Evil Mind, The (The Clairvoyant); School for Scandal; Sons of the Sea; Spy of Napoleon; Transatlantic Tunnel

Elwes, Cassian: Blue Flame

Emerson, John: Down to Earth; His Picture in the Papers; Reaching for the Moon (1917); Wild and Woolly

Emes, Ian: Knights and Emeralds

Emmerich, Roland: Ghost Chase; Godzilla (1998); Independence Day (1996); Making Contact; Moon 44; Patriot, The; Stargate; Universal Soldier

Enders, Robert: Stevie

Endfield, Cy: Mysterious Island; Try and Get Me; Underworld Story; Zulu

Engel, Thomas E.: Rich Little—One's a Crowd

English, John: Adventures of Captain Marvel, The; Adventures of Red Ryder; Arizona Days; Beyond the Purple Hills; Captain America (1944); Cow Town; Dead Man's Gulch; Death Valley Manhunt; Dick Tracy Returns; Dick Tracy vs. Crime Inc.; Dick Tracy's G-Men; Don't Fence Me In; Drums of Fu Manchu; Gangs of Sonora; Hawk of the Wilderness; Hills of Utah, The; Hi-Yo Silver; Last Round-Up; Loaded Pistols; Lone Ranger, The (1938); Mule Train; Mysterious Dr. Satan; Riders for Justice; Riders of the Whistling Pines; Rim of the Canyon; San Fernando Valley; Utah; Zorro Rides Again; Zorro's Fighting Legion

Englund, George: Christmas to Remember, A; Dixie Changing Habits; Ugly American, The; Zachariah

Englund, Robert: 976-EVIL

Enrico, Robert: Le Secret; Les Grandes Gueules (Jailbirds' Vacation); Occurrence at Owl Creek Bridge, An

Enright, Ray: China Sky; Coroner Creek; Dames; Earthworm Tractors; Gung Ho! (1943); Iron Major, The; Return of the Bad Men; South of St. Louis; Spoilers, The; Tomorrow at Seven; Trail Street; Wagons Roll at Night, The

Enyedi, Ildiko: Magic Hunter; My 20th Century

Ephron, Nora: Michael; Mixed Nuts; Sleepless in Seattle; This Is My Life; You've Got Mail

Epstein, Jean: La Chute de la Maison Usher

Epstein, Marcelo: Body Rock

Epstein, Robert: Celluloid Closet, The; Common Threads: Stories from the Quilt

Eram, Rene: Sweet Evil; Voodoo

Erdman, Dave: Soundstage: Blues Summit in Chicago

Ereira, Alan: Crusades, The (1995)

Erice, Victor: Spirit of the Beehive, The

Erman, John: Attic: The Hiding of Anne Frank; Boys Next Door, The (1996); Breathing Lessons; Carolina Skeletons; Child of Glass; Early Frost, An; Eleanor: First Lady of the World; Ellen Foster; Last Best Year, The; My Old Man; Only Love; Our Sons; Outer Limits, The (TV Series); Roots: The Next Generation; Scarlett; Stella (1990); Streetcar Named Desire, A (1983); When the Time Comes

Ernest, Karl: Stripteaser 2

Erschbamer, George: Bounty Hunters; Final Round; Flinch; Snake Eater; Snake Eater 2, the Drug Buster; Snake Eater III: His Law

Ersgard, Jack: Backlash (1998); Invisible: The Chronicles of Benjamin Knight; Living in Peril; Mandroid

Ersgard, Joakim: Acts of Betrayal; Visitors, The

Erskine, Chester: Androcles and the Lion; Egg and I, The; Frankie and Johnny (1934); Girl in Every Port, A (1952); Midnight (1934)

Esper, Dwain: Maniac (1934); Sex Madness

Esposito, Joe: South Beach Academy

Essex, Harry: Cremators, The; Octaman

Estevez, Emilio: Men at Work; Wisdom

Esway, Alexander: Mauvaise Graine (Bad Seed)

Eubanks, Corey Michael: Bigfoot: The Unforgettable Encounter; Two Bits & Pepper

Eustache, Jean: Mother and the Whore, The

Evans, Bruce A.: Kuffs

Evans, David Mickey: First Kid; Sandlot, The

Evans, John: Black Godfather, The

Evans, Marc: Resurrection Man; Thicker Than Water

Evans, Roger D.: Jet Benny Show, The

Everitt, Tim: Fatally Yours; Too Fast Too Young

Export, Valie: Invisible Adversaries

Eyre, Chris: Smoke Signals

Eyre, Richard: Loose Connections; Ploughman's Lunch, The; Singleton's Pluck

Eyres, John: Armed and Deadly; Conspiracy of Fear, The; Goodnight, God Bless; Judge and Jury; Monolith; Nightsiege-Project: Shadowchaser 2; Project Shadowchaser 3000

Ezra, Mark: Savage Hearts

Faber, Christian: Bail Jumper

Faenza, Roberto: Bachelor, The (1993); Corrupt

Faiman, Peter: "Crocodile" Dundee; Dutch

Fairchild, William: Horsemasters; Silent Enemy, The

Faircloth, Tommy: Crinoline Head

Fairfax, Ferdinand: Nate and Hayes; Rescue, The; Spymaker: The Secret Life of Ian Fleming

Fakasaku, Kinji: Tora! Tora! Tora!

Falk, Harry: Beulah Land; Death Squad, The; High Desert Kill; Night the City Screamed, The; Scene of the Crime (1985); Sophisticated Gents, The

Falkenstein, Jun: Tigger Movie, The

Fall, Jim: Trick

Famuyiwa, Rick: Wood, The

Fanaka, Jamaa: Black Sister's Revenge; Penitentiary; Penitentiary II; Penitentiary III; Soul Vengeance (Welcome Home Brother Charles); Street Wars

Fancher, Hampton: Minus Man, The

Fansten, Jacques: Cross My Heart (1991)

Fargo, James: Born to Race; Caravans; Enforcer, The (1976); Every Which Way But Loose; Forced Vengeance; Game for Vultures; Riding the Edge

Farino, Ernest: Josh Kirby, Time Warrior (Series); Josh Kirby … Time Warrior: Journey to the Magic Cavern; Steel and Lace

Farmer, Donald: Scream Dream; Vampire Cop

Farrelly, Bobby: Kingpin; Me, Myself & Irene; There's Something About Mary

Farrelly, Peter: Dumb and Dumber; Kingpin; Me, Myself & Irene; There's Something About Mary

Farris, John: Dear Dead Delilah

Farrow, John: Back from Eternity; Botany Bay; Commandos Strike at Dawn; Copper Canyon; Five Came Back; His Kind of Woman; Hondo; John Paul Jones; Saint Strikes Back, The; Sea Chase, The; Wake Island

Farwagi, André: Boarding School

Fasano, John: Black Roses

Fassbinder, Rainer Werner: Ali: Fear Eats the Soul; American Soldier, The; Berlin Alexanderplatz; Beware of a Holy Whore; Bitter Tears of Petra Von Kant, The; Chinese Roulette; Despair; Effi Briest; Fox and His Friends; Germany in Autumn; Gods of the Plague; I Only Want You to Love Me; In a Year of 13 Moons; Lili Marleen; Lola (1982); Marriage of Maria Braun, The; Merchant of Four Seasons, The; Mother Kusters Goes to Heaven; Querelle; Satan's Brew; Veronika Voss; Why Does Herr R. Run Amok?

Faulkner, Brenden: Spookies

Faure, William C.: Shaka Zulu

Fawcett, John: Boys Club, The

Fearnley, Neill L.: Black Ice; Escape from Mars; Johnny 2.0

Feferman, Linda: Seven Minutes in Heaven

Feijoo, Beda Docampo: Debajo del Mundo (Under Earth)

Feist, Felix: Big Trees, The; Deluge (1933); Devil Thumbs a Ride, The; Donovan's Brain; George White's Scandals; Man Who Cheated Himself, The; Threat, The

Fei, Xie: Girl from Hunan; Women from the Lake of the Scented Souls

Feldman, Jon Harmon: Lovelife

Feldman, Dennis: Real Men

Feldman, Gene: Danny

Feldman, John: Alligator Eyes; Dead Funny

Feldman, Marty: Last Remake of Beau Geste, The; When Things Were Rotten (TV Series)

Fellini, Federico: Amarcord; And the Ship Sails On; Boccaccio 70; Casanova (1976); City of Women; Clowns, The; 8; Fellini Satyricon; Fellini's Roma; Ginger and Fred; I Vitelloni; Il Bidone; Juliet of the Spirits; La Dolce Vita; La Strada; Nights of Cabiria; Orchestra Rehearsal; Variety Lights; White Sheik, The

Fenady, Georg: Arnold; Terror in the Wax Museum

Fengler, Michael: Why Does Herr R. Run Amok?

Fenton, Leslie: Saint's Vacation, The

Fenton, Thomas: Striking Point

Feraldo, Claude: Trade Secrets

Feret, René: Alexina; Mystery of Alexina, The

Ferguson, Larry: Beyond the Law (1992); Gunfighter's Moon

Ferguson, Michael: Glory Boys, The

Ferland, Guy: Babysitter, The (1995); Telling Lies in America

Fernandez, Emilio: Flor Sylvestre; Pearl, The

Ferrandini, Dean: Overkill (1996)

Ferrara, Abel: Addiction, The; Bad Lieutenant; Body Snatchers, The (1993); Cat Chaser; China Girl; Dangerous Game, A (1993); Driller Killer, The; Fear City; Funeral, The (1996); Gladiator, The (1986) (Television); King of New York; Ms. .45; New Rose Hotel; Subway Stories

Ferrell, Jeff: Revenge of the Teenage Vixens from Outer Space

Ferrer, José: Return to Peyton Place; State Fair (1962)

Ferrer, Mel: Green Mansions

Ferreri, Marco: Tales of Ordinary Madness

Ferretti, A.: Fear (1988)

Ferris, Stan: Tulips

Ferro, Pablo: Me, Myself & I

Ferroni, Giorgio: Mill of the Stone Women; Night of the Devils; Scalawag Bunch, The

Fessenden, Larry: Habit; No Telling

Feuillade, Louis: Vampires, The (1915) (Les Vampires)

Feyder, Jacques: Carnival in Flanders; Kiss, The (1929); Knight Without Armour

Fields, Michael: Bright Angel; Noon Wine

Fierberg, Steven: Voodoo Dawn

Figgis, Mike: Browning Version, The (1994); Internal Affairs; Leaving Las Vegas; Liebestraum; Loss of Sexual Innocence, The; Miss Julie (1999); Mr. Jones; One Night Stand (1997); Stormy Monday; Women & Men 2

Finch, Charles: Circle of Passion; Priceless Beauty; Where Sleeping Dogs Lie

Finch, Nigel: Lost Language of Cranes, The; Stonewall; 25 X 5: The Continuing History of the Rolling Stones; Vampyr, The (1992)

Fincher, David: Alien 3; Fight Club; Game, The (1997); Seven

Findlay, Michael: Snuff

Findlay, Roberta: Blood Sisters; Lurkers; Oracle, The; Prime Evil

Findlay, Seaton: Janis

Fink, Kenneth: Road to Freedom: The Vernon Johns Story; Stephen King's Golden Years (TV Series); Tall, Dark and Deadly; Tricks

Finkleman, Ken: Airplane II: The Sequel; Head Office

Finley, George: Gentleman Killer

Finley, Joe: Barbarian Queen II: Empress Strikes Back

Fiore, Robert: Pumping Iron

Firkin, Rex: Death of Adolf Hitler, The

Firstenberg, Sam: Agent of Death; American Ninja; American Ninja II; Avenging Force; Blood Warriors; Breakin' 2 Electric Boogaloo; Cyborg Cop; Cyborg Soldier; Delta Force 3; McCinsey's Island; Ninja III: The Domination; Operation Delta Force; Revenge of the Ninja

Firth, Michael: Heart of the Stag; Sylvia

Fischa, Michael: Crack House; Death Spa; Delta Heat; My Mom's a Werewolf

Fischer, Fred: New York The Way It Was

Fischer, Max: Entangled; Killing 'Em Softly

Fisher, David: Liar's Moon; Toy Soldiers (1983)

Fisher, Jack: Torn Apart

Fisher, Mary Ann: Lords of the Deep

Fisher, Terence: Brides of Dracula; Curse of Frankenstein, The; Curse of the Werewolf, The; Devil Rides Out, The; Dracula—Prince of Darkness; Frankenstein and the Monster from Hell; Frankenstein Created Woman; Gorgon, The; Horror of Dracula; Hound of the Baskervilles, The (1959); Island of Terror; Mummy, The (1959); Phantom of the Opera (1962); Revenge of Frankenstein; Sherlock Holmes and the Deadly Necklace; Stolen Face

Fishman, Bill: Car 54, Where Are You? (1991); Tapeheads

Fisk, Jack: Daddy's Dyin' and Who's Got the Will; Final Verdict; Raggedy Man; Violets Are Blue

Fitzgerald, Ed: Blue Movies

FitzGerald, Jon: Apart from Hugh

Fitzgerald, Thom: Hanging Garden, The

Fitzmaurice, George: As You Desire Me; Mata Hari (1931); Son of the Sheik; Suzy

Fiveson, Robert S.: Clonus Horror, The

Flaherty, Paul: Clifford; 18 Again; Who's Harry Crumb?

Flaherty, Robert: Elephant Boy; Louisiana Story, The; Nanook of the North

Flanagan, David Michael: My Sweet Suicide

Fleder, Gary: Companion, The; Kiss the Girls; Things to Do in Denver When You're Dead

Fleischer, Dave: Fabulous Fleischer Folio, The (Volume Five); Gulliver's Travels (1939); Hoppity Goes to Town; Superman Cartoons; TV's Best Adventures of Superman

Fleischer, Richard: Amin: The Rise and Fall; Amityville III: The Demon; Ashanti; Barabbas; Between Heaven and Hell; Boston Strangler, The; Clay Pigeon, The; Compulsion; Conan the Destroyer; Doctor Dolittle; Don is Dead, The; Fantastic Voyage; Follow Me Quietly; Incredible Sarah, The; Jazz Singer, The (1980); Mandingo; Million Dollar Mystery; Mr. Majestyk; Narrow Margin, The (1952); New Centurions, The; Prince and the Pauper, The (1978); Red Sonja; See No Evil; Soylent Green; 10 Rillington Place; Tora! Tora! Tora!; Tough Enough; 20,000 Leagues Under the Sea (1954); Vikings, The

Fleming, Andrew: Bad Dreams; Craft, The; Dick; Threesome

Fleming, Edward: Topsy Turvy

Fleming, Erik: Cyber Bandits

Fleming, Victor: Adventure; Bombshell (1933); Captains Courageous (1937); Dr. Jekyll and Mr. Hyde (1941); Gone with the Wind; Guy Named Joe, A; Hula; Joan of Arc; Reckless (1935); Red Dust; Test Pilot; Tortilla Flat; Treasure Island (1934); Virginian, The (1929); When the Clouds Roll By; Wizard of Oz, The

of Living; Main Street to Broadway; Mrs. Parkington; One Minute to Zero; Postman Always Rings Twice, The (1946); Seven Sinners; Slightly Honorable; Stand-In

Garrett, Roy: Eyes Behind the Stars

Garris, Mick: Critters 2: The Main Course; Psycho 4: The Beginning; Quicksilver Highway; Stand, The; Stephen King's Sleepwalkers; Stephen King's The Shining

Gasnier, Louis J.: Reefer Madness

Gast, Leon: Hell's Angels Forever; When We Were Kings

Gates, Jim: Hey Abbott!

Gates, Martin: Adventures of Mole, The

Gatlif, Tony: Gadjo Dilo; Latcho Drom; Mondo

Gaudioz, Tony: Border Heat

Gaup, Nils: North Star (1996); Pathfinder; Shipwrecked

Gavaldon, Roberto: Littlest Outlaw, The; Macario

Gawor, Eleanor: Slipping into Darkness

Gayton, Joe: Mind Ripper; Warm Summer Rain

Gazarian, Armand: Prison Planet

Gazdag, Gyula: Hungarian Fairy Tale, A

Gebhard, Glenn: Blood Screams; One Last Run

Geller, Bruce: Savage Bees, The

Gemes, Jozsef: Princess and the Goblin, The

Genina, Augusto: Cyrano de Bergerac (1925); Prix De Beaute (Beauty Prize)

Gentilomo, Giacomo: Goliath and the Vampires

George, George W.: James Dean Story, The

George, Jim: Rover Dangerfield

George, Matthew: Under the Gun (1995)

George, Peter: Surf Nazis Must Die

George, Screaming Mad: Guyver, The

George, Terry: Bright Shining Lie, A; Some Mother's Son

Gerard, Bernard: Gone with the West

Gerber, Fred: Coming Unglued; Lifeline; Rent-A-Kid

Gering, Marion: Thunder in the City

Germi, Pietro: Alfredo Alfredo; Divorce—Italian Style; Seduced and Abandoned

Gerolmo, Chris: Citizen X

Geronimi, Clyde: Alice in Wonderland (1951); Cinderella (1950); Lady and the Tramp; Legend of Sleepy Hollow, The (1949); One Hundred and One Dalmatians; Peter Pan (1953); Sleeping Beauty (1959)

Gerretsen, Peter: Night Friend

Gershuny, Theodore: Silent Night, Bloody Night

Gerstad, Harry: TV's Best Adventures of Superman

Gessner, Nicolas: Black Water; It Rained All Night the Day I Left; Little Girl Who Lives Down the Lane, The; Quicker Than the Eye; Someone Behind the Door

Gethers, Steven: Hillside Stranglers, The; Jenny's War

Giancola, David: Time Chasers

Gibbins, Duncan: Case for Murder, A; Eve of Destruction; Fire with Fire

Gibbons, Cedric: Tarzan and His Mate

Gibbons, Pamela: Midnight Dancer

Gibbons, Rodney: Little Men (1998); Neighbor, The; Stranger in the House

Gibby, Gwyneth: Dark Prince: The Intimate Diary of the Marquis de Sade; Dark Prince: The Intimate Tales of Marquis de Sade; Eruption; Marquis de Sade

Gibson, Alan: Dracula A.D. 1972; Martin's Day; Satanic Rites of Dracula, The; Twinsanity; Witness for the Prosecution (1982); Woman Called Golda, A

Gibson, Brian: Breaking Glass; Josephine Baker Story, The; Juror, The; Murderers Among Us: The Simon Wiesenthal Story; Poltergeist II: The Other Side; Still Crazy; What's Love Got to Do with It?

Gibson, Mel: Braveheart; Man without a Face, The

Giddins, Gary: Celebrating Bird: The Triumph of Charlie Parker

Gieras, Gregory: Whispering, The

Giggie, Bill: Pippi Longstocking

Giglio, Tony: Soccer Dog: The Movie

Gilbert, Brian: French Lessons; Not Without My Daughter; Tom & Viv; Vice Versa; Wilde

Gilbert, Lewis: Admirable Crichton, The; Alfie; Damn the Defiant!; Educating Rita; Haunted; Moonraker; Not Quite Paradise; Sea Shall Not Have Them, The; Shirley Valentine; Sink the Bismarck; Spy Who Loved Me, The; Stepping Out; You Only Live Twice

Giler, David: Black Bird, The

Giles, David: Murder Is Announced, A

Gilhuis, Mark G.: Bloody Wednesday

Gill, David: Buster Keaton: A Hard Act to Follow; Unknown Chaplin

Gill, Jack: Body Armor

Gillard, Stuart: Escape, The; Man Called Sarge, A; Paradise (1982); Poltergeist: The Legacy; Rocketman; Teenage Mutant Ninja Turtles III

Gillen, Jeff: Deranged

Gillespie, Jim: I Know What You Did Last Summer

Gilliam, Terry: Adventures of Baron Münchausen, The; Brazil; Fear and Loathing in Las Vegas; Fisher King, The; Jabberwocky; Monty Python and the Holy Grail; Time Bandits; 12 Monkeys

Gilliat, Sidney: Endless Night; Great St. Trinian's Train Robbery, The; Green for Danger; Only Two Can Play

Gilling, John: Gamma People, The; Mania; Mummy's Shroud, The; Night Caller from Outer Space; Plague of the Zombies; Reptile, The; Vampire over London

Gilman Jr., Mark S.: Lugosi, The Forgotten King

Gilmore, Stuart: Half-Breed, The; Hot Lead; Virginian, The (1946)

Gilroy, Bert: Lawless Valley

Gilroy, Frank D.: Gig, The; Once in Paris

Ginsberg, Milton Moses: Werewolf of Washington

Ginty, Robert: Bounty Hunter; Vietnam, Texas; Woman of Desire

Gion, Christian: Here Comes Santa Claus

Giordana, Marco Tuilio: Who Killed Pasolini?

Giovanni, Marita: Bar Girls

Giovinazzo, Buddy: No Way Home

Giraldi, Bob: Club Med; Hiding Out

Giraldi, Franco: Minute to Pray, A Second to Die, A

Girard, Bernard: Dead Heat on a Merry-Go-Round; Little Moon & Jud McGraw; Mind Snatchers, The

Girard, Francois: Red Violin, The; Thirty-Two Short Films About Glenn Gould

Girard, Michael Paul: Witchcraft 7: Judgment Hour

Girdler, William: Asylum of Satan; Day of the Animals; Grizzly; Manitou, The; Sheba Baby; Three on a Meathook

Girod, Francis: Elegant Criminal, The; Infernal Trio, The; L'Etat Sauvage (The Savage State)

Gisler, Marcel: Blue Hour, The

Glaser, Paul Michael: Air Up There, The; Band of the Hand; Cutting Edge, The; Kazaam; Miami Vice: "The Prodigal Son"; Running Man, The

Glatter, Lesli Linka: Into the Homeland; Now and Then; State of Emergency

Glatzer, Richard: Grief

Gleason, Michie: Summer Heat (1987)

Glebas, Francis: Fantasia 2000

Glen, John: Aces: Iron Eagle III; Checkered Flag; Christopher Columbus: The Discovery (1992); For Your Eyes Only; License to Kill; Living Daylights, The; Octopussy; View to a Kill, A

Glenister, John: After Julius

Glenville, Peter: Becket; Comedians, The; Hotel Paradiso; Prisoner, The (1955); Summer and Smoke

Glickenhaus, James: Exterminator, The; McBain; Protector, The; Slaughter of the Innocents; Soldier, The; Timemaster

Glicker, Paul: Running Scared (1980)

Glimcher, Arne: Just Cause; Mambo Kings, The

Glinsky, Robert: Poisonous Plants

Gluck, Wolfgang: 38 Vienna Before the Fall

Glut, Donald F.: Dinosaur Valley Girls

Godard, Jean-Luc: Alphaville; Aria; Band of Outsiders; Breathless (1959); Classic Foreign Shorts: Volume 2; Contempt; First Name: Carmen; Hail Mary; Le Gai Savoir (The Joy of Knowledge); Les Carabiniers; Married Woman, A; Masculine Feminine; My Life to Live; Oldest Profession, The; Pierrot Le Fou; Seven Deadly Sins, The; Six in Paris (Paris Vue par ...); Two or Three Things I Know About Her; Weekend; Woman Is a Woman, A

Goddard, Gary: Masters of the Universe

Goddard, Jim: Impossible Spy, The; Kennedy (TV Miniseries); Reilly: The Ace of Spies; Shanghai Surprise; Tale of Two Cities, A (1980)

Godfrey, Peter: Christmas in Connecticut (1945); Cry Wolf; Escape Me Never; Two Mrs. Carrolls, The

Godmilow, Jill: Waiting for the Moon

Godoy, Armando Robles: Green Wall, The

Goei, Glen: That's the Way I Like It

Green, Bruce Seth: Hunt for the Night Stalker; In Self Defense; Rags to Riches; Running Against Time

Green, David: Children of the Dust

Green, Guy: Diamond Head; Incredible Journey of Dr. Meg Laurel, The; Luther; Once Is Not Enough; Patch of Blue, A; Walk in the Spring Rain, A

Green, Jack: Traveller

Green, Joseph: Brain That Wouldn't Die, The

Green, Terry: Cold Justice

Green, Walon: Hellstrom Chronicle, The

Greenaway, Peter: Belly of an Architect, The; Cook, the Thief, His Wife & Her Lover, The; Draughtsman's Contract, The; Drowning by Numbers; Pillow Book, The; Prospero's Books; Zed and Two Noughts, A

Greenburg, Richard Alan: Little Monsters

Greene, Danford B.: Secret Diary of Sigmund Freud, The

Greene, David: After the Promise; Bella Mafia; Buster; Choice, The; Count of Monte Cristo, The (1975); Fatal Vision; Fire Birds; Friendly Fire; Gray Lady Down; Guardian, The (1984); Hard Country; In a Stranger's Hands; Madame Sin; Miles to Go; Penthouse, The; Prototype; Rehearsal for Murder; Shuttered Room, The; Small Sacrifices; Triplecross (1985); Vanishing Act; What Ever Happened To … ?; World War III

Greene, Herbert: Cosmic Man, The

Greene, Martin: Dark Sanity

Greengrass, Paul: Theory of Flight, The

Greenspan, Bud: Wilma

Greenstands, Arthur: Stocks and Blondes

Greenwald, Maggie: Ballad of Little Jo, The; Home Remedy; Kill-Off, The

Greenwald, Robert: Breaking Up; Burning Bed, The; Flatbed Annie and Sweetie Pie: Lady Truckers; Forgotten Prisoners; Hear no Evil; Shattered Spirits; Sweethearts' Dance; Woman of Independent Means, A; Xanadu

Greenwalt, David: Secret Admirer

Grefe, William: Impulse (1974); Jaws of Death, The; Stanley

Gregg, Colin: To the Lighthouse; We Think the World of You

Greggio, Ezio: Silence of the Hams

Greif, Leslie: Keys to Tulsa

Gremillon, Jean: Pattes Blanches (White Paws); Stormy Waters

Gremm, Wolf: Kamikaze 89

Grenville, Edmond T.: Beat Girl

Gréville, Edmond: Liars, The; Princess Tam Tam

Greyson, John: Lilies; Urinal

Gribbins, James: Shadow Creature

Gribble, Mike: Spike & Mike's Festival of Animation

Griedanus, T. Jardus: Quest for the Lost City

Gries, Tom: Breakheart Pass; Breakout (1975); Connection (1973); Fools; Glass House, The; Greatest, The; Helter Skelter; Lady Ice; Migrants, The; 100 Rifles; QB VII; Will Penny

Grieve, Andrew: Lorna Doone; Suspicion (1987)

Grieve, Ken: Adventures of Sherlock Holmes, The (Series)

Griffi, Giuseppe Patroni: Collector's Item; Divine Nymph, The; Driver's Seat, The

Griffith, Charles B.: Dr. Heckyl and Mr. Hype; Eat My Dust; Smokey Bites the Dust; Up from the Depths; Wizard of the Lost Kingdom II

Griffith, D. W.: Abraham Lincoln; Avenging Conscience, The; Birth of a Nation, The; Broken Blossoms; Dream Street; D. W. Griffith Triple Feature; Hearts of the World; Home, Sweet Home (1914); Idol Dancer, The; Intolerance; Judith of Bethulia; Mother and the Law, The; Orphans of the Storm; Sally of the Sawdust; Sorrows of Satan, The; True Heart Susie; Way Down East; White Rose, The (1923)

Griffith, Edward H.: Animal Kingdom, The; My Love for Yours (Honeymoon in Bali); Sky's the Limit, The; Young and Willing

Griffiths, Mark: Cheyenne Warrior; Cry in the Wild, A; Hardbodies; Hardbodies 2; Heroes Stand Alone; Max Is Missing; Running Hot; Tactical Assault; Ultraviolet

Grillo, Gary: American Justice

Grimaldi, Hugo: Human Duplicators, The; Mutiny in Outer Space

Grimm, Douglas K.: Laser Moon

Grindé, Nick: Before I Hang; Hitler—Dead or Alive; Man They Could Not Hang, The; Stone of Silver Creek

Grint, Alan: Adventures of Sherlock Holmes, The (Series); Secret Garden, The (1987)

Grinter, Brad F.: Blood Freak; Flesh Feast

Grissell, Wallace: Federal Operator 99

Grissmer, John: Blood Rage; Scalpel

Grlic, Rajko: That Summer of White Roses

Grofe Jr., Ferde: Proud and the Damned, The

Grosbard, Ulu: Deep End of the Ocean, The; Falling in Love; Georgia (1995); Straight Time; Subject Was Roses, The; True Confessions

Gross, Larry: 3:15—The Moment of Truth

Gross, Yoram: Dot and the Bunny; Toby and the Koala Bear

Grossman, Adam: Sometimes They Come Back Again

Grossman, David: Joe Piscopo Live!; Yo-Yo Man

Grossman, Douglas: Hell High

Grossman, Goetz: Tar

Grossman, Sam: Van, The (1976)

Grosvenor, Charles: Once Upon a Forest

Grune, Karl: Street, The

Gruza, Jerzy: Alice (1981)

Guenette, Robert: Man Who Saw Tomorrow, The

Guercio, James William: Electra Glide in Blue

Guerra, Ruy: Erendira; Opera do Malandro

Guerrieri, Romolo: Final Executioner, The

Guerrini, Mino: Mines of Kilimanjaro

Guest, Christopher: Almost Heroes; Attack of the 50-Foot Woman (1993); Big Picture, The; Waiting for Guffman

Guest, Cliff: Disturbance, The

Guest, Val: Abominable Snowman of the Himalayas, The; Carry on Admiral; Casino Royale (1967); Day the Earth Caught Fire, The; Enemy from Space; Just William's Luck; Killer Force; Men of Sherwood Forest; Persuaders, The (TV Series); Quatermass Experiment, The; Up the Creek (1958); When Dinosaurs Ruled the Earth

Guggenheim, Charles: Great St. Louis Bank Robbery, The

Guggenheim, Davis: Gossip

Guillermin, John: Blue Max, The; Bridge at Remagen, The; Death on the Nile; El Condor; King Kong (1976); King Kong Lives; Never Let Go; Sheena; Towering Inferno, The; Tracker, The; Waltz of the Toreadors

Guiol, Fred L.: Battling Orioles, The

Guitry, Sacha: Napoleon (1955); Pearls of the Crown, The

Guney, Yilmaz: Wall, The (1998) (Foreign)

Gunn, Gilbert: Cosmic Monsters, The

Gunnarsson, Sturla: Joe Torre: Curveballs Along the Way; We the Jury

Guralnick, Robert: Portfolio

Gurney Jr., Robert: Terror from the Year 5,000

Guthrie, Tyrone: Oedipus Rex (1957)

Gutierrez, Sebastian: Judas Kiss

Gutman, Nathaniel: Deadline (1987); Linda; When the Dark Man Calls

Guttfreund, Andre: Femme Fatale

Guzman, Claudio: Hostage Tower, The; Willa

Gyllenhaal, Stephen: Certain Fury; Dangerous Woman, A; Homegrown; Killing in a Small Town; Losing Isaiah; Paris Trout; Promised a Miracle; Question of Faith; Waterland

Gyongyossy, Imre: Revolt of Job, The

Gyorgy, Appel: Pebble and the Penguin, The

Haak, Diane: Secrets in the Attic

Haas, Charles: Girls Town (1959); New Adventures of Charlie Chan, The (TV Series); Outer Limits, The (TV Series); Platinum High School

Haas, Philip: Angels and Insects; Music of Chance, The

Haber, Mark: Daisies in December

Hachuel, Herve: Immortal Sins; Last of Philip Banter, The

Hackford, Taylor: Against All Odds (1984); Bound by Honor; Chuck Berry Hail! Hail! Rock 'n' Roll; Devil's Advocate; Dolores Claiborne; Everybody's All-American; Idolmaker, The; Officer and a Gentleman, An; White Nights (1985)

Haedrick, Rolf: Among the Cinders

Haft, Jeremy: Grizzly Mountain

Hafter, Petra: Demon in My View, A

Hagen, Ross: B.O.R.N.

Haggard, Mark: First Nudie Musical, The

Haggard, Piers: Back Home; Blood on Satan's Claw; Fiendish Plot of Dr. Fu Manchu, The; Fulfillment; Lifeforce Experiment, The; Quatermass Conclusion, The; Return to Treasure Island; Summer Story, A; Venom

Haggis, Paul: Red Hot

Hagman, Larry: Son of Blob (Beware! The Blob)

Hagmann, Stuart: Strawberry Statement, The; Tarantulas—The Deadly Cargo

Haid, Charles: Buffalo Soldiers; Children of Fury; Cooperstown; Iron Will; Nightman, The; Riders of the Purple Sage

Haig, Roul: Okefenokee

Haines, Fred: Steppenwolf

Haines, Randa: Children of a Lesser God; Dance with Me; Doctor, The; Wrestling Ernest Hemingway

Haines, Richard W.: Alien Space Avenger; Class of Nuke 'em High; Splatter University

Halas, John: Animal Farm

Haldane, Don : Reincarnate, The

Hale, William: Murder in Texas; Murder of Mary Phagan, The; One Shoe Makes It Murder; Red Alert; S.O.S. Titanic

Haley Jr., Jack: Love Machine, The; That's Entertainment

Halicki, H. B.: Gone in 60 Seconds; Junkman, The

Hall, Alexander: Because You're Mine; Doctor Takes a Wife, The; Forever Darling; Goin' to Town; Great Lover, The; Here Comes Mr. Jordan; I Am the Law; Little Miss Marker (1934)

Hall, Anthony Michael: Hail Caesar

Hall, Gary Skeen: Prime Time Murder

Hall, Godfrey: Honor and Glory; Undefeatable

Hall, Ivan: Kill and Kill Again; Kill or Be Killed

Hall, Kenneth J.: Evil Spawn; Ghost Writer

Hall, Mark: Wind in the Willows, The (1983)

Hall, Peter: Homecoming, The (1973); Jacob; Midsummer Night's Dream, A (1968); Never Talk to Strangers; Orpheus Descending

Hallenbeck, Bruce G.: Vampyre (1990)

Haller, Daniel: Buck Rogers in the 25th Century; Die, Monster, Die!; Dunwich Horror, The; Follow That Car; Paddy

Hallowell, Todd: Love or Money?

Hallstrom, Lasse: Children of Noisy Village, The; Cider House Rules, The; My Life as a Dog; Once Around; Something to Talk About; What's Eating Gilbert Grape?

Halperin, Victor: Revolt of the Zombies; Supernatural; White Zombie

Halvorson, Gary: Adventures of Elmo in Grouchland, The; Country Girl, The (1982)

Hamann, Craig: Boogie Boy

Hamatsu, Mamoru: Heroic Legend of Arislan

Hamburg, John: Safe Men

Hamer, Robert: Dead of Night (1945); Detective, The (1954); Kind Hearts and Coronets; School for Scoundrels; To Paris with Love

Hamilton, David: Bilitis; Tendres Cousines

Hamilton, Dean: Road Home, The; Savage Land; Strike a Pose

Hamilton, Guy: Battle of Britain; Colditz Story, The; Devil's Disciple, The; Diamonds Are Forever; Evil Under the Sun; Force Ten from Navarone; Funeral in Berlin; Goldfinger; Live and Let Die; Man with the Golden Gun, The; Mirror Crack'd, The; Remo Williams: The Adventure Begins

Hamilton, Strathford: Betrayal of the Dove; Blueberry Hill; Diving In; Escape from Atlantis; Proposition, The; Set-Up, The (1995); Temptation

Hamm, Nick: Talk of Angels

Hammer, Robert: Don't Answer the Phone

Hammond, Peter: Dark Angel, The; Inspector Morse (TV Series)

Hampton, Christopher: Carrington; Secret Agent, The (1996)

Hampton (Riccardo Freda), Robert: Caltiki, the Immortal Monster; Ghost, The (1963); Horrible Dr. Hichcock, The (Terror of Dr. Hichcock, The)

Hanbury, Victor: Hotel Reserve

Hancock, John: Bang the Drum Slowly; California Dreaming; Let's Scare Jessica to Death; Prancer; Steal the Sky; Weeds

Hand, David: Bambi; Snow White and the Seven Dwarfs (1938)

Handler, Ken: Delivery Boys

Handley, Alan: Alice Through the Looking Glass (1966)

Hanks, Tom: Fallen Angels; That Thing You Do!

Hanna, William: Hey There, It's Yogi Bear; Jetsons: The Movie; Man Called Flintstone, A

Hannam, Ken: Sunday Too Far Away

Hannant, Brian: Time Guardian, The

Hanooka, Izhak: Red Nights

Hansel, Marion: Dust

Hansen, Ed: Bikini Carwash Company, The; Party Plane; Robo C.H.I.C.

Hanson, Curtis: Arousers, The; Bad Influence; Bedroom Window, The; Children of Times Square, The; Hand That Rocks the Cradle, The; L.A. Confidential; Losin' It; River Wild, The; Wonder Boys

Hanson, David W.: Night of the Bloody Transplant

Hanson, John: Northern Lights; Wild Rose

Hardwicke, Cedric: Forever and a Day

Hardy, Joseph: Love's Savage Fury; Users, The

Hardy, Robin: Fantasist, The; Wicker Man, The

Hardy, Rod: Buffalo Girls; Rio Diablo; Sara Dane; Thirst; 20,000 Leagues Under the Sea (1996)

Hare, David: Strapless; Wetherby

Hargrove, Dean: Dear Detective

Hark, Tsui: Aces Go Places (1–3) (Mad Mission 1–3); Better Tomorrow 3, A: Love and Death in Saigon; Double Team; Knock Off; Peking Opera Blues; Twin Dragons; We're Going to Eat You!; Zu: Warriors from the Magic Mountain

Harlan, Veidt: Jud Suss

Harlin, Renny: Adventures of Ford Fairlane, The; Born American; Cliffhanger; Cutthroat Island; Deep Blue Sea; Die Hard 2: Die Harder; Long Kiss Goodnight, The; Nightmare on Elm Street 4, A: The Dream Master; Prison

Harling, Robert: Evening Star, The

Harlow, John: Candles at Nine

Harmon, Robert: Eyes of an Angel; Gotti; Hitcher, The; Nowhere to Run (1993)

Harrington, Curtis: Dead Don't Die, The; Devil Dog: The Hound of Hell; Mata Hari (1985); Night Tide; Planet of Blood (Queen of Blood); Ruby (1977); What's the Matter with Helen?; Who Slew Auntie Roo?

Harrington, Rowdy: Striking Distance

Harris, Damian: Bad Company (1995); Deceived; Discovery Program; Mercy (1999); Rachel Papers

Harris, Denny: Silent Scream

Harris, Frank: Low Blow; Patriot

Harris, Harry: Alice in Wonderland (1985); Alice Through the Looking Glass (1985)

Harris, Jack H.: Unkissed Bride

Harris, James B.: Bedford Incident, The; Boiling Point (1993); Cop; Fast-Walking; Some Call It Loving

Harris, Leslie: Just Another Girl on the I.R.T.

Harris, Monika: Legal Deceit

Harris, Richard: Hero, The (1971)

Harris, Trent: Plan from Outer Space; Rubin & Ed

Harris Jr., Wendell B.: Chameleon Street

Harrison, John: Assassination File, The; Donor Unknown; Tales from the Darkside, The Movie

Harrison, John Kent: Beautiful Dreamers; Johnny's Girl; Old Man; Sound and the Silence,The; What the Deaf Man Heard; You Know My Name

Harrison, Jules: Exterminators of the Year 3000

Harrison, Ken: 1918; On Valentine's Day

Harrison, Matthew: Kicked in the Head

Harrison, Paul: House of Seven Corpses, The

Harrison Jr., Hal: Pony Express Rider

Harron, Mary: American Psycho; I Shot Andy Warhol

Harry, Gail: Striking Poses

Harry, Lee: Silent Night, Deadly Night Part 2; Street Soldiers

Hart, Bruce: Sooner or Later

Hart, Harvey: Beverly Hills Madam; East of Eden (1982); Fortune and Men's Eyes; High Country, The; Prince of Central Park, The; Pyx, The; Shoot (1976); Standing Tall; Stone Fox, The; Utilities

Hart, Jacobsen: Steel Frontier

Hart, William S.: Hell's Hinges; Tumbleweeds

Hartford, David M.: Nomads of the North

Hartford, Kenneth: Hell Squad (1985)

Hartl, Carl: Mozart Story, The

Hartley, Hal: Amateur (1995); Flirt; Henry Fool; Simple Men; Surviving Desire; Trust; Unbelievable Truth, The

Hartman, Don: Every Girl Should Be Married; Holiday Affair (1949); It's a Big Country; Mr. Imperium

Hartwell, David: Love Is a Gun

Harvey, Anthony: Disappearance of Aimee, The; Eagle's Wing; Grace Quigley; Lion in Winter, The; Players; Richard's Things; Svengali (1983); They Might Be Giants

Harvey, Gail: Cold Sweat (1993)

Hess, David: To All a Good Night

Hess, Eugene: Don't Do It

Hess, Jon: Excessive Force; Watchers

Hessler, Gordon: Cry of the Banshee; Girl in a Swing, The; Golden Voyage of Sinbad, The; Journey of Honor; Kiss Meets the Phantom of the Park; Misfit Brigade, The; Murders in the Rue Morgue (1971); Oblong Box, The; Out on Bail; Pray for Death; Rage of Honor; Scream and Scream Again; Tales of the Unexpected

Heston, Charlton: Antony and Cleopatra (1973); Mother Lode

Heston, Fraser: Alaska; Crucifer of Blood; Needful Things; Treasure Island (1990)

Hewitt, David L.: Bloodsuckers, The; Journey to the Center of Time (Time Warp); Wizard of Mars, The

Hewitt, Jean: Blood of Dracula's Castle

Hewitt, Paul: Wild Palms

Hewitt, Peter: Bill and Ted's Bogus Journey; Borrowers, The (1997); Tom and Huck

Hewitt, Rod: Dangerous, The (1994); Verne Miller

Heyes, Douglas: Powderkeg; Thriller (TV Series); Twilight Zone, The (TV Series)

Heynemann, Laurent: Birgit Haas Must Be Killed; Old Lady Who Walked in the Sea, The

Hibbs, Jesse: To Hell and Back

Hickenlooper, George: Big Brass Ring, The; Ghost Brigade; Hearts of Darkness; Low Life, The; Persons Unknown

Hickey, Bruce: Necropolis

Hickner, Steve: Prince of Egypt

Hickox, Anthony: Full Eclipse; Hellraiser 3: Hell On Earth; Invasion of Privacy (1996); Payback (1994); Prince Valiant (1997); Sundown (1990); Warlock: The Armageddon; Waxwork; Waxwork II: Lost in Time

Hickox, Douglas: Blackout (1985); Brannigan; Entertaining Mr. Sloane; Hound of the Baskervilles, The (1983); Mistral's Daughter; Theatre of Blood; Zulu Dawn

Hickox, James: Children of the Corn III: Urban Harvest

Hicks, Scott: Shine; Snow Falling on Cedars

Higgin, Howard: Hell's House; High Voltage (1929); Painted Desert, The; Racketeer

Higgins, Colin: Best Little Whorehouse in Texas, The; Foul Play; Nine to Five

Hiken, Nat: Car 54 Where Are You? (TV Series); Love God?, The

Hill, George: Big House, The; Min and Bill; Tell It to the Marines

Hill, George Roy: Butch Cassidy and the Sundance Kid; Funny Farm; Great Waldo Pepper, The; Hawaii; Little Drummer Girl, The; Little Romance, A; Period of Adjustment; Slap Shot; Slaughterhouse Five; Sting, The; Thoroughly Modern Millie; Toys in the Attic; World According to Garp, The; World of Henry Orient, The

Hill, Jack: Big Bird Cage, The; Chamber of Fear; Coffy; Foxy Brown; Macabre Serenade; Sinister Invasion; Snake People; Spider Baby; Switchblade Sisters

Hill, James: Belstone Fox, The; Black Beauty (1971); Born Free; Christian the Lion; Corrupt Ones, The; Seaside Swingers; Study in Terror, A

Hill, Robert: Adventures of Tarzan, The; Tarzan the Fearless

Hill, Terence: Lucky Luke; Troublemakers

Hill, Tim: Muppets From Space

Hill, Walter: Another 48 Hrs.; Brewster's Millions (1985); Crossroads; Driver, The; Extreme Prejudice; 48 Hrs.; Geronimo: An American Legend (1994); Hard Times; Johnny Handsome; Last Man Standing (1996); Long Riders, The; Red Heat (1988); Southern Comfort; Streets of Fire; Tales from the Crypt (TV Series); Trespass; Warriors, The (1979); Wild Bill

Hillenbrand, David: King Cobra

Hillenbrand, Scott: King Cobra

Hiller, Arthur: Addams Family, The (TV Series); Americanization of Emily, The; Author! Author!; Babe, The (1992); Carpool; Hospital, The; In-Laws, The; Lonely Guy, The; Love Story; Making Love; Man in the Glass Booth; Man of La Mancha; Married to It; Miracle of the White Stallions; Nightwing; Out of Towners, The (1970); Outrageous Fortune; Plaza Suite; Popi; Promise Her Anything; Romantic Comedy; See No Evil, Hear No Evil; Silver Streak (1976);

Taking Care of Business; Teachers; Tobruk; Wheeler Dealers, The

Hillman, David Michael: Strangeness, The

Hillman, Wiliam Byron: Double Exposure (1982)

Hills, David: Ator: The Fighting Eagle; Blade Master, The; Caligula, the Untold Story; Quest for the Mighty Sword

Hills, Paul: Boston Kickout

Hillyer, Lambert: Dracula's Daughter; Fighting Code; Forbidden Trail; Hatbox Mystery, The; Invisible Ray, The; Narrow Trail, The; Shock, The (1923); Sundown Rider, The; Sundown Riders; Three-Word Brand, The

Hilton, Arthur: Cat Women of the Moon; Misadventures of Buster Keaton, The; Return of Jesse James, The

Hilton-Jacobs, Lawrence: Quiet Fire

Hiltzik, Robert: Sleepaway Camp

Himelstein, Howard: Power of Attorney

Hinzman, Bill: Majorettes, The

Hippolyte, Alexander Gregory: Animal Instincts; Animal Instincts 2; Animal Instincts: The Seductress; Body of Influence; Carnal Crimes; Mirror Images; Mirror Images II; Night Rhythms; Object of Obsession; Secret Games; Secret Games 3; Undercover (1995)

Hirano, Toshihiro: Dangaio; Vampire Princess Miyu

Hiroaki, Gooda: Bubblegum Crisis, Vols. 1–8

Hiroki, Hayashi: Bubblegum Crisis, Vols. 1–8

Hiroshi, Ishiodori: Bubblegum Crash, Vols. 1–3

Hiroya, Oohira: Riding Bean

Hiroyuki, Fukushima: Bubblegum Crash, Vols. 1–3; Ten Little Gall Force/Scramble Wars

Hiroyuki, Ochi: Armitage III: Electro Blood

Hirsch, Bettina: Munchies

Hirschman, Ray: Plutonium Baby

Hirtz, Dagmar: Moondance

Hiscott, Leslie S.: Triumph of Sherlock Holmes, The

Hitchcock, Alfred: Alfred Hitchcock Presents (TV Series); Alfred Hitchcock's Bon Voyage and Aventure Malgache; Birds, The; Blackmail (1929); Champagne; Dial M for Murder; Easy Virtue; Family Plot; Farmer's Wife, The; Foreign Correspondent; Frenzy; I Confess; Jamaica Inn; Juno and the Paycock; Lady Vanishes, The (1938); Lifeboat; Lodger, The; Man Who Knew Too Much, The (1934); Man Who Knew Too Much, The (1955); Manxman, The; Marnie; Mr. and Mrs. Smith; Murder; North by Northwest; Notorious; Number 17; Paradine Case, The; Psycho (1960); Rear Window; Rebecca; Rich and Strange; Ring, The; Rope; Sabotage (1936); Saboteur; Secret Agent, The; Shadow of a Doubt; Skin Game, The (1931); Spellbound; Stage Fright; Strangers on a Train; Suspicion (1941); Thirty-Nine Steps, The (1935); To Catch a Thief; Topaz; Torn Curtain; Trouble with Harry, The; Under Capricorn; Vertigo; Waltzes from Vienna; Wrong Man, The (1956); Young and Innocent

Hittleman, Carl K.: Kentucky Rifle

Hitzig, Rupert: Backstreet Dreams; Night Visitor (1989)

Hively, Jack B.: Adventures of Huckleberry Finn, The (1978); California Gold Rush; Four Jacks and a Jill; Panama Lady

Ho, Yim: Day the Sun Turned Cold, The

Hobbs, Lyndall: Back to the Beach

Hobin, Bill: Judy Garland and Friends

Hoblit, Gregory: Class of '61; Fallen; Frequency; L.A. Law; Primal Fear; Roe vs. Wade

Hochberg, Victoria: Jacob I Have Loved; Sweet 15

Hodges, Mike: Black Rainbow; Flash Gordon; Florida Straits; Get Carter; Hitchhiker, The (Series); Morons from Outer Space; Prayer for the Dying, A; Pulp; Terminal Man, The

Hodi, Jeno: Deadly Obsession; Triplecross (1995)

Hodson, Christopher: Partners in Crime (Secret Adversary) (TV Series)

Hoey, Michael: Navy vs. the Night Monsters, The

Hoffman, Herman: Invisible Boy, The; It's a Dog's Life

Hoffman, Jerzy: Deluge, The (Potop) (1973)

Hoffman, John: Strange Confession

Hoffman, Michael: One Fine Day; Promised Land; Restless Natives; Restoration; Soapdish; Some Girls; William Shakespeare's A Midsummer Night's Dream

Hoffman, Peter: Valentino Returns

Hoffs, Tamar Simon: Allnighter, The

Hofmeyr, Gary: Dirty Games; Light in the Jungle, The

Jackson, Larry: Bugs Bunny, Superstar

Jackson, Lewis: Christmas Evil

Jackson, Mick: Bodyguard, The; Chattahoochee; Clean Slate (1994); Indictment: The McMartin Trial; L.A. Story; Threads; Very British Coup, A; Volcano; Yuri Nosenko, KGB

Jackson, Pat: Encore; King Arthur, The Young Warlord; Prisoner, The (1968) (TV Series)

Jackson, Peter: Bad Taste; Dead Alive; Forgotten Silver; Frighteners, The; Heavenly Creatures; Meet the Feebles

Jackson, Philip: Project: Genesis

Jackson, Richard: Big Bust Out, The

Jackson, Wilfred: Alice in Wonderland (1951); Cinderella (1950); Lady and the Tramp; Peter Pan (1953)

Jacobs, Alan: Nina Takes a Lover

Jacobs, Jerry P.: Dangerous Place, A

Jacobs, Jon: Girl with the Hungry Eyes, The

Jacobs, Werner: Heidi (1965)

Jacobson, Rick: Bloodfist VI: Ground Zero; Full Contact; Interlocked; Night Hunter; Reasons of the Heart; Ring of Fire 3: Lion Strike; Shadow Warriors; Star Quest; Strategic Command; Suspect Device; Unborn II, The

Jacobsson, Anders: Evil Ed

Jacoby, Joseph: Great Bank Hoax, The; Hurry Up or I'll Be 30

Jacopetti, Gualtiero: Mondo Cane II

Jacquot, Benoit: School of Flesh; Single Girl

Jaeckin, Just: Emmanuelle; French Woman, The; Lady Chatterley's Lover (1981); Story of O, The

Jaffe, Stanley: Without a Trace

Jaglom, Henry: Always (1984); Babyfever; Can She Bake a Cherry Pie?; Déjà Vu (1998); Eating; Last Summer in the Hamptons; New Year's Day; Sitting Ducks; Someone to Love; Tracks; Venice/Venice

Jaimes, Sam: Snoopy: The Musical; Snoopy's Reunion; This Is America, Charlie Brown; What Next, Charlie Brown?; Why, Charlie Brown, Why?

Jaissle, Matt: Legion of the Night

Jamain, Patrick: Honeymoon

James, Alan: Come on Tarzan; Dick Tracy (1937); Phantom Thunderbolt; Red Barry; SOS Coast Guard; Trail Drive; When a Man Sees Red

James, Pedr: Martin Chuzzlewit

James, Steve: Hoop Dreams; Passing Glory; Prefontaine

Jameson, Jerry: Airport '77; Bat People; Cowboy and the Ballerina, The; High Noon, Part Two; Killing at Hell's Gate; Raise the Titanic; Starflight One; Terror on the 40th Floor

Jancso, Miklos: Red and the White, The; Round-Up, The

Janis, Conrad: November Conspiracy, The

Jankel, Annabel: D.O.A. (1988); Max Headroom; Super Mario Brothers, The

Janot, Charles: Lucy and Desi: Before the Laughter

Jaque, Christian: Fanfan the Tulip

Jarman, Derek: Angelic Conversation; Aria; Caravaggio; Edward II; Garden, The; In the Shadow of the Sun; Jubilee; Last of England, The; War Requiem

Jarmusch, Jim: Dead Man; Down by Law; Ghost Dog: The Way of the Samurai; Mystery Train; Night on Earth; Stranger Than Paradise

Jarrott, Charles: Amateur, The (1982); Anne of the Thousand Days; Boy in Blue, The; Condorman; Last Flight of Noah's Ark; Littlest Horse Thieves, The; Night of the Fox; Other Side of Midnight, The; Poor Little Rich Girl: The Barbara Hutton Story; Strange Case of Dr. Jekyll and Mr. Hyde, The (1968)

Jasny, Vojta: Great Land of Small, The

Jason, Leigh: Bride Walks Out, The; Lady for a Night; Mad Miss Manton, The; Out of the Blue

Jean, Mark: Homecoming (1996)

Jean, Vadim: Leon the Pig Farmer; Nightscare; Real Howard Spritz, The

Jeffrey, Tom: Odd Angry Shot, The

Jeffries, Lionel: Amazing Mr. Blunden, The; Baxter (1973); Railway Children, The; Water Babies, The

Jeffries, Richard: Bloodtide

Jenkins, Michael: Rebel (1985); Sweet Talker

Jenkins, Tamara: Slums of Beverly Hills

Jenz, Tom: Ladies Sing the Blues, The

Jessner, Leopold: Backstairs

Jeunet, Jean-Pierre: Alien Resurrection; City of Lost Children, The; Delicatessen

Jewison, Norman: Agnes of God; ... And Justice for A[?] Best Friends; Bogus; Cincinnati Kid, The; Fiddler on t[?] Roof; F.I.S.T.; Forty Pounds of Trouble; Hurricane, T[?] (1999); In Country; In the Heat of the Night; Jesus Chris[?] Superstar; Moonstruck; Only You (1994); Other People[?] Money; Picture Windows; Rollerball; Russians Are Co[?]ing, the Russians Are Coming, The; Send Me No Flower[?] Soldier's Story, A; Thomas Crown Affair, The (1968); Thr[?] of It All, The

Jhabvala, Ruth Prawer: Courtesans of Bombay

Jianxin, Huang: Wooden Man's Bride, The

Jimenez, Neal: Waterdance, The

Jiras, Robert: I Am the Cheese

Ji-Shun, Duan: Go-Masters, The

Jittlov, Mike: Wizard of Speed and Time, The

Joannon, Léo: Atoll K (Utopia)

Joanou, Phil: Entropy; Fallen Angels; Final Analysi[?] Heaven's Prisoners; State of Grace; Three O'Clock Hig[?] U2: Rattle and Hum; Wild Palms

Jobson, Dickie: Countryman

Jodorowsky, Alejandro: Rainbow Thief, The; Santa Sang[?]

Jodrell, Steve: Shame (1987)

Joens, Michael: My Little Pony: The Movie

Joffe, Arthur: Alberto Express; Harem

Joffe, Mark: Cosi; Efficiency Expert, The (Spotswood Grievous Bodily Harm; Matchmaker, The (1997)

Joffe, Roland: City of Joy; Fat Man and Little Boy; Goodby[?] Lover; Killing Fields, The; Mission, The; Scarlet Letter, Th[?] (1995)

Johnson, Alan: Solarbabies; To Be or Not to Be (1983)

Johnson, David C.: Drop Squad, The; Riot (1996) (T[?] Movie)

Johnson, Hugh: Chill Factor

Johnson, Irvin: Fist of Steel

Johnson, Jed: Andy Warhol's Bad

Johnson, John H.: Curse of the Blue Lights

Johnson, Kenneth: Alien Nation, Dark Horizon; Incredibl[?] Hulk, The; Short Circuit 2; Steel (1997); V

Johnson, Lamont: Broken Chain, The; Crisis at Centra[?] High; Dangerous Company; Execution of Private Slovik[?] The; Gore Vidal's Lincoln; Groundstar Conspiracy, The[?] Gunfight, A; Last American Hero, The; Lipstick; My Swee[?] Charlie; One on One; Paul's Case; Spacehunter: Adventures[?] in the Forbidden Zone; Thousand Heroes, A; Twilight Zone[?] (the TV Series); Unnatural Causes

Johnson, Mark Steven: Simon Birch

Johnson, Nunnally: Man in the Gray Flannel Suit, The[?] Three Faces of Eve, The

Johnson, Patrick Read: Angus; Baby's Day Out; Spaced In[?] vaders

Johnson, Tim: Antz

Johnston, Aaron Kim: For the Moment

Johnston, Jim: Blue de Ville

Johnston, Joe: Honey, I Shrunk the Kids; Jumanji; October[?] Sky; Pagemaster, The; Rocketeer, The

Johnstone, Tucker: Blood Salvage

Jonasson, Oskar: Remote Control (1992)

Jones, Amy: Love Letters; Maid to Order; Slumber Party[?] Massacre

Jones, Amy Holden: Rich Man's Wife, The

Jones, Brian Thomas: Escape from Safehaven; Rejuvena[?]tor, The

Jones, Buck: Law for Tombstone

Jones, Chris: Escape from Survival Zone

Jones, Chuck: Adventures of Milo in the Phantom Toll[?]booth, The; Bugs Bunny/Road Runner Movie, The; 1001 Rabbit Tales

Jones, David: Betrayal (1983); Christmas Carol, A (1999); Christmas Wife, The; 84 Charing Cross Road; Jackknife; Look Back in Anger (1989); Trial, The (1992); Unexpected Life, An

Jones, David Hugh: Confession, The

Jones, Dick: Extra Girl, The

Jones, Don: Forest, The; Housewife from Hell; Love Butcher; Sweater Girls

Jones, F. Richard: Bulldog Drummond

Jones, Gary: Mosquito

Jones, Harmon: As Young as You Feel; Bullwhip; Gorilla at Large; Pride of St. Louis, The

Jones, James Cellan: Fortunes of War (1987)

Jones, Kirk: Waking Ned Devine

Lang, Krzysztof: Paper Marriage (1992)

Lang, Michel: Gift, The; Holiday Hotel

Lang, Perry: Little Vegas; Men of War

Lang, Richard: Change of Seasons, A; Don't Go to Sleep; Fantasy Island; Kung Fu—The Movie (1986); Mountain Men, The; Texas (1994); Vega$; Word, The

Lang, Rocky: Nervous Ticks; Race for Glory

Lang, Walter: Blue Bird, The; But Not for Me; Can-Can; Desk Set; Jackpot, The; King and I, The (1956); Little Princess, The (1939); Moon over Miami; Mother Wore Tights; Red Kimono, The; Snow White and the Three Stooges; Song of the Islands; State Fair (1945); There's No Business Like Show Business; Tin Pan Alley; Weekend in Havana

Langley, Noel: Adventures of Sadie; Pickwick Papers, The; Search for Bridey Murphy, The

Langston, Murray: Wishful Thinking (1992)

Langton, Simon: Act of Passion; Anna Karenina (1985); Casanova (1987); Laguna Heat; Pride and Prejudice (1996); Upstairs, Downstairs; Whistle Blower, The

Langway, Douglas: Raising Heroes

Lanoff, Lawrence: Miami Hustle; Temptress

Lantz, Walter: World of Andy Panda, The

Lanza, Anthony M.: Glory Stompers, The; Incredible Two-Headed Transplant, The

Lapine, James: Earthly Possessions; Impromptu; Life with Mikey; Sunday in the Park with George

Lardnerward, Donald: My Life's in Turnaround

Large, Brian: Elektra

Larkin, Christopher: Very Natural Thing, A

La Rocque, Stephen: Samantha

Larraz, Joseph: House That Vanished, The; Vampyres

Larry, Sheldon: Terminal Choice

Larsen, Keith: Whitewater Sam

La Salle, Eriq: Rebound

Lasseter, John: Bug's Life, A; Toy Story; Toy Story 2

Lathan, Stan: Almos' a Man; Beat Street; Sky Is Gray, The

Latshaw, Steve: Biohazard: The Alien Force; Dark Universe, The; Jack-O

Latt, David Michael: Sorority House Party

Lattuada, Alberto: Christopher Columbus (1985); Cricket, The; Stay as You Are; Variety Lights

Laughlin, Michael: Mesmerized (Shocked); Strange Behavior; Strange Invaders

Laughlin, Tom: Billy Jack

Laughton, Charles: Night of the Hunter

Launder, Frank: Belles of St. Trinian's, The; Blue Murder at St. Trinian's; Great St. Trinian's Train Robbery, The; I See a Dark Stranger

Launer, Dale: Love Potion #9

Lautner, Georges: Icy Breasts; La Cage aux Folles III, The Wedding; My Other Husband

Lauzier, Gerard: Petit Con

Lauzon, Jean-Claude: Leolo; Night Zoo

Laven, Arnold: Monster That Challenged the World, The; Rough Night in Jericho

Lavin, Julianna: Live Nude Girls

Lavut, Martin: Palais Royale; Smokescreen

Law, Alex: Painted Faces

Law, Clara: Erotique; Reincarnation of Golden Lotus, The; Temptation of a Monk

Law, Joe: Crippled Masters, The

Lawick, Hugo van: Leopard Son, The

Lawrence, Denny: Archer's Adventure

Lawrence, Diarmuid: Emma (1996)

Lawrence, Marc: Pigs (Daddy's Deadly Darling)

Lawrence, Martin: Thin Line Between Love and Hate, A

Lawrence, Quentin: Crawling Eye, The

Lawrence, Ray: Bliss (1986)

Lawton, J. F.: Hunted, The

Layton, Joe: Littlest Angel, The

Le Moine, Yvonne: Red Dwarf, The

Leach, Wilford: Pirates of Penzance, The; Wedding Party, The

Leacock, Philip: Angel City; Curse of King Tut's Tomb, The; Thanksgiving Story, The; Three Sovereigns for Sarah; War Lover, The

Leacock, Robert: Catwalk

Leader, Tony: Children of the Damned; Lost in Space (TV Series)

Leahy, Larry: Confessions of a Hitman

Lean, David: Blithe Spirit; Bridge on the River Kwai, The; Brief Encounter (1945); Dr. Zhivago; Great Expectations (1946); Hobson's Choice (1954); In Which We Serve; Lawrence of Arabia; Oliver Twist (1948); Passage to India, A; Ryan's Daughter; Summertime; This Happy Breed

Lear, Norman: Cold Turkey

Leary, Denis: National Lampoon's Favorite Deadly Sins

Lease, Maria: Dolly Dearest

Leaver, Don: Avengers, The (TV Series); Touch of Frost, A (TV Series); Witching Time

LeBorg, Reginald: Calling Dr. Death; Dead Man's Eyes; Diary of a Madman; Jungle Woman; Mummy's Ghost, The; Psycho Sisters (1972); Voodoo Island; Weird Woman

Leboursier, Raymond: Nais

Lecallier, Adeline: Love Without Pity

Le Chanois, Jean-Paul: Le Cas du Dr. Laurent; L'Ecole Buissonniere; Les Miserables (1957); Passion for Life

Leconte, Patrice: Hairdresser's Husband, The; Monsieur Hire; Ridicule

Leddy, Bruce: My Teacher's Wife

Leder, Herbert J.: Candyman, The (1968)

Leder, Mimi: Deep Impact; Peacemaker, The (1997); Woman with a Past

Leder, Paul: Baby Doll Murders, The; Body Count (1988); Exiled in America; Frame Up; I Dismember Mama; Molly & Gina; Murder by Numbers; Sketches of a Strangler; Vultures

Lederer, Charles: Fingers at the Window; Never Steal Anything Small

Lederman, D. Ross: End of the Trail; Range Feud; Riding Tornado, The; Tarzan's Revenge; Texas Cyclone; Two-Fisted Law

Leduc, Paul: Frida

Lee, Ang: Eat Drink Man Woman; Ice Storm, The; Pushing Hands; Sense and Sensibility; Wedding Banquet, The

Lee, Bruce: Return of the Dragon

Lee, Chris Chan: Yellow

Lee, Damien: Abraxas Guardian of the Universe; Donor, The; Fatal Combat; Food of the Gods Part II; Last Man Standing (1988); Moving Target (1996); Ski School; Street Law; When the Bullet Hits the Bone

Lee, Daniel: Black Mask

Lee, Evan: Hollywood Meatcleaver Massacre

Lee, Iara: Synthetic Pleasures

Lee, Jack: Captain's Table; Wooden Horse, The

Lee, Malcolm: Best Man, The (1999)

Lee, Norman: Chamber of Horrors (1940)

Lee, Robert: Hostage Train; Virtual Assassin

Lee, Rowland V.: Bridge of San Luis Rey, The; Captain Kidd; Count of Monte Cristo, The (1934); Love from a Stranger (1937); Mysterious Dr. Fu Manchu; One Rainy Afternoon; Return of Dr. Fu Manchu; Sea Lion, The; Son of Frankenstein; Son of Monte Cristo, The; Three Musketeers, The (1935); Toast of New York, The; Tower of London (1939)

Lee, Spike: Clockers; Crooklyn; Do the Right Thing; Get on the Bus; Girl 6; He Got Game; Jungle Fever; Malcolm X; Mo' Better Blues; School Daze; She's Gotta Have It; Summer of Sam

Lee, Thomas: Supernova

Leeds, Herbert: Charlie Chan in City in Darkness; Mr. Moto in Danger Island

Leeson, Lynn Hershman: Conceiving Ada

Lefler, Doug: Hercules and the Circle of Fire

Legend, Johnny: Sleazemania Strikes Back

Legge, Michael: Alien Agenda, The (TV Series)

Legrand, François: Tower of Screaming Virgins, The

Lehman, Ernest: Portnoy's Complaint

Lehmann, Michael: Airheads; Heathers; Hudson Hawk; Meet the Applegates; My Giant; Truth About Cats and Dogs, The

Lehner, Peter: Megaville

Leiberman, Robert: Will, G. Gordon Liddy

Leibovit, Arnold: Puppetoon Movie, The

Leifer, Neil: Trading Hearts; Yesterday's Hero

Leigh, Mike: Abigail's Party; Career Girls; Four Days in July; High Hopes; Home Sweet Home (1982); Life Is Sweet; Meantime; Naked; Secrets and Lies; Topsy-Turvy; Who's Who

Leighton, Eric: Dinosaur

Leisen, Mitchell: Big Broadcast of 1938, The; Death Takes a Holiday; Girl Most Likely, The; Golden Earrings; Hands Across the Table; Lady Is Willing, The; Midnight (1939); Murder at the Vanities; Remember the Night; Swing High, Swing Low

Leitch, Christopher: Courage Mountain; I've Been Waiting for You; Teen Wolf, Too

Leitzes, Jennifer: Montana (1997)

Leker, Larry: All Dogs Go to Heaven 2

Leland, David: Big Man; Checking Out; Land Girls, The; Wish You Were Here

Lelouch, Claude: And Now, My Love; Another Man, Another Chance; Bandits (1987); Bolero (1982); Cat and Mouse; Edith and Marcel; Happy New Year (1973) (La Bonne Année); Les Misérables (1995); Man and a Woman, A; Man and a Woman, A: 20 Years Later; Robert et Robert

Lemmo, James: Dream a Little Dream 2; Heart; Relentless 3; Tripwire; We're Talking Serious Money

Lemmon, Jack: Kotch

Lemmons, Kasi: Eve's Bayou

Lemont, John: Konga

Lemorande, Rusty: Journey to the Center of the Earth (1987); Turn of the Screw (1992)

Leni, Paul: Cat and the Canary, The (1927); Last Warning, The; Man Who Laughs, The; Waxworks

Lenica, Jan: Ubu and the Great Gidouille

Lennon, Terry: Daffy Duck's Quackbusters

Lent, Dean: Border Radio

Lente, Miklos: Oddballs

Lenzi, Umberto: Almost Human; Battle of the Commandos; Bridge to Hell; Eyeball; Make Them Die Slowly; Paranoia

Leo, Malcolm: This Is Elvis

Leonard, Brett: Dead Pit, The; Hideaway; Lawnmower Man, The; Virtuosity

Leonard, Robert Z.: Broadway Serenade; Clown, The; Dancing Lady; Divorcee, The; Duchess of Idaho; Firefly, The; Girl of the Golden West, The; Great Ziegfeld, The; In the Good Old Summertime; Maytime; Nancy Goes to Rio; New Moon; Pride and Prejudice (1940); Strange Interlude (1932); Susan Lenox: Her Fall and Rise; Weekend at the Waldorf; When Ladies Meet; Ziegfeld Girl

Leonard, Sheldon: Danny Thomas Show, The (TV Series)

Leonard, Terry: Death Before Dishonor

Leondopoulos, Jordan: Swap, The (Sam's Song)

Leone, John: Great Smokey Roadblock, The

Leone, Sergio: Fistful of Dollars, A; Fistful of Dynamite, A; For a Few Dollars More; Good the Bad and the Ugly, The; Once Upon a Time in America (Long Version); Once Upon a Time in the West

Leonetti, John R.: Mortal Kombat: Annihilation

Leong, Po-Chih: Banana Cop; Cabin by the Lake; Ping Pong

Lerner, Carl: Black Like Me

Lerner, Dan: Shame (1992)

Lerner, Irving: Cry of Battle; Royal Hunt of the Sun; Studs Lonigan

Lerner, Richard: Revenge of the Cheerleaders

LeRoy, Mervyn: Anthony Adverse; Any Number Can Play; Bad Seed, The; Devil at 4 O'Clock, The; East Side, West Side; FBI Story, The; Gold Diggers of 1933; Gypsy (1962); Homecoming (1948); I Am a Fugitive from a Chain Gang; Johnny Eager; Latin Lovers; Little Caesar; Little Women (1949); Lovely to Look At; Madame Curie; Majority of One, A; Million Dollar Mermaid; Mister Roberts; No Time for Sergeants; Quo Vadis (1951); Random Harvest; Rose Marie (1954); Sweet Adeline; Three Men on a Horse; Thirty Seconds Over Tokyo; Waterloo Bridge; Without Reservations

Lessac, Michael: House of Cards

Lester, Mark L.: Armed and Dangerous; Base, The; Bobbie Jo and the Outlaw; Class of 1984; Class of 1999; Commando; Double Take; Ex, The; Extreme Justice; Firestarter; Night of the Running Man; Public Enemy #1; Showdown in Little Tokyo; Truckstop Women

Lester, Richard: Butch and Sundance: The Early Days; Cuba; Four Musketeers, The; Funny Thing Happened on the Way to the Forum, A; Hard Day's Night, A; Help!; How I Won the War; Juggernaut (1974); Knack ... and How to Get It, The; Petulia; Return of the Musketeers, The; Ritz, The; Robin

and Marian; Superman II; Superman III; Three Musketeers The (1973)

Letterier, François: Goodbye Emmanuelle

Lettich, Sheldon: Double Impact; Lionheart (1991); Onl the Strong

Letts, Barry: Gulliver in Lilliput

Leung, Tony: Bloodmoon (1997)

Leva, Gary: Plan B

Levant, Brian: Beethoven; Flintstones in Viva Rock Vegas The; Flintstones, The; Jingle All the Way; Problem Child 2

Leven, Jeremy: Don Juan DeMarco

Levering, Joseph: In Early Arizona

Levesque, Michel: Werewolves on Wheels

Levey, Jay: UHF

Levey, William A.: Blackenstein; Committed; Happ Hooker Goes to Washington, The; Hellgate; Lightning, th White Stallion; Slumber Party 57

Levi, Alan J.: Deadman's Revenge; Quantum Leap (TV Se ries); Riding with Death

Levick, David: Gospel

Levin, Henry: Ambushers, The; Desperados, The; Farme Takes a Wife, The; Jolson Sings Again; Journey to the Cen ter of the Earth (1959); Lonely Man, The; Man from Col orado, The; Murderers' Row; Run for the Roses (Thor oughbred); Two of a Kind (1951); Warriors, The (1955 Where the Boys Are (1960); Wonderful World of the Broth ers Grimm, The

Levin, Marc: Last Party, The; Slam; Whiteboyz

Levin, Peter: Comeback Kid, The; Gone to Texas; Rape anc Marriage: The Rideout Case

Levin, Thunder: Evil Lives

Levine, Michael: Checkered Flag

Levine, Paul: Operation Intercept

Levinson, Barry: Avalon; Bugsy; Diner; Disclosure; Good Morning, Vietnam; Jimmy Hollywood; Liberty Heights; Nat ural, The; Rain Man; Sleepers; Sphere; Tin Men; Toys; Wag the Dog; Young Sherlock Holmes

Levitow, Abe: Adventures of Milo in the Phantom Toll booth, The; Gay Purr-ee; Mr. Magoo's Christmas Carol

Levy, Eugene: Once Upon a Crime; Sodbusters

Levy, Jefery: Inside Monkey Zetterland; S.F.W.

Levy, Ralph: Bedtime Story; Beverly Hillbillies, The (TV Se ries); George Burns and Gracie Allen Show, The (TV Series)

Levy, Scott: Alien Within; The; Baby Face Nelson; Beneath the Bermuda Triangle; Midnight Tease; Piranha (1995); Spectre; Unknown Origin

Levy, Shawn: Address Unknown

Levy, Shuki: Blind Vision; Turbo: A Power Rangers Adven ture

Lewin, Albert: Moon and Sixpence, The; Pandora and the Flying Dutchman; Picture of Dorian Gray, The; Private Af fairs of Bel Ami, The

Lewin, Ben: Favor, the Watch and the Very Big Fish, The; Georgia (1987); Paperback Romance

Lewis, Al: Our Miss Brooks (TV Series)

Lewis, Christopher: Ripper, The (1985)

Lewis, David: Dangerous Curves

Lewis, Herschell Gordon: Blood Feast; Color Me Blood Red; Gruesome Twosome; Just for the Hell of It; Living Venus; She-Devils on Wheels; Something Weird; Suburban Roulette; Taste of Blood, A; 2,000 Maniacs; Wizard of Gore, The

Lewis, Jerry: Bellboy, The; Big Mouth, The; Cracking Up; Errand Boy, The; Family Jewels, The; Hardly Working; Ladies' Man, The; Nutty Professor, The; Patsy, The; Which Way to the Front?

Lewis, Joseph H.: Big Combo, The; Boys of the City; Gun Crazy (1950); Invisible Ghost; Lawless Street, A; Mad Doc tor of Market Street, The; Pride of the Bowery; Retreat Hell; Return of October, The; 7th Cavalry

Lewis, Mark: Gordy

Lewis, Robert: Circumstances Unknown; Crying Child, The; Dead Reckoning (1990); Don't Talk to Strangers; Lady Killers; Memories of Murder; Perfect Crime; S.H.E.; Sum mer to Remember, A

Lewis, Robert Michael: Child Bride of Short Creek; Fallen Angel; Pray for the Wildcats

Lewiston, Denis: Hot Target

Lewnes, Pericles: Redneck Zombies

Liatowitsch, Daniel: Kolobos

Libman, Leslie: Path to Paradise

Libov, Howard: Midnight Edition

Liconti, Carlo: Concrete Angels; Good Night, Michelangelo

Lieberman, Jeff: Blue Sunshine; Just Before Dawn; Remote Control (1987); Squirm

Lieberman, Robert: All I Want for Christmas; D3: The Mighty Ducks; Fire in the Sky; Table for Five; Titanic (1996)

Liebman, Max: 10 from Your Show of Shows

Lifton, Jimmy: Mirror, Mirror 2: Raven Dance

Light, Warren: Night We Never Met, The

Lima, Kevin: Goofy Movie, A; Tarzan (1999)

Liman, Doug: Getting In; Go

Lincoln, F. J.: Wild Man

Lindberg, Per: June Night

Lindenmuth, Kevin J.: Addicted to Murder; Alien Agenda, The (TV Series); Twisted Tales; Vampires & Other Stereotypes

Linder, Max: Seven Years' Bad Luck

Lindsay, Lance: Star Crystal

Lindsay-Hogg, Michael: As Is; Brideshead Revisited; Frankie Starlight; Habitation of Dragons, The; Let It Be; Master Harold and the Boys; Murder by Moonlight; Nasty Habits; Object of Beauty, The; Rock and Roll Circus, The; Running Mates (1992); Strange Case of Dr. Jekyll and Mr. Hyde, The (1989); Thumbelina (1983)

Lindtberg, Leopold: Four in a Jeep

Link, Caroline: Beyond Silence

Link, Ron: Zombie High

Linklater, Richard: Before Sunrise; Dazed and Confused; Newton Boys, The; Slacker; SubUrbia (1997)

Linman, Doug: Swingers

Linson, Art: Where the Buffalo Roam; Wild Life, The

Lion, Mickey: House of Exorcism, The

Lipman, David: Road Lawyers and Other Briefs

Lipstadt, Aaron: Android; City Limits; Pair of Aces

Lisberger, Steven: Animalympics; Hot Pursuit; Slipstream; Tron

Lishman, Eda Lever: Primo Baby

Lister, David: Rutanga Tapes, The; Trigger Fast

Lit, Law: Mr. Vampire (Vol. 1–4)

Litten, Peter Mackenzie: Heaven's a Drag

Littin, Miguel: Alsino and the Condor

Little, Dwight H.: Bloodstone; Free Willy 2: The Adventure Home; Getting Even; Halloween IV: The Return of Michael Myers; Marked for Death; Murder at 1600; Phantom of the Opera (1989); Rapid Fire

Littman, Lynne: Freak City; Testament

Litvak, Anatole: All This and Heaven Too; Amazing Dr. Clitterhouse, The; Anastasia (1956); City for Conquest; Goodbye Again; Mayerling; Night of the Generals; Sisters, The (1938); Snake Pit, The; Sorry, Wrong Number (1948); Tovaritch

Lively, Gerry: Body Moves

Livingston, Jennie: Paris Is Burning

Livingston, Robert H.: Taking My Turn

Livingston, William: Great Indian Railway, The

Livingstone, Joe: Robo Vampire

Llosa, Luis: Anaconda; Crime Zone; 800 Leagues Down the Amazon; Hour of the Assassin; Sniper; Specialist, The

Lloyd, Frank: Blood on the Sun; Cavalcade; Howards of Virginia, The; If I Were King; Last Command, The (1955); Mutiny on the Bounty (1935); Oliver Twist (1922)

Lloyd, Harold: Harold Lloyd's Comedy Classics

Lloyd, Norman: Tales of the Unexpected

Lo, Lucas: No Retreat, No Surrender 3: Blood Brothers

Loach, Kenneth: Carla's Song; Family Life; Hidden Agenda; Ladybird, Ladybird; Land and Freedom; My Name is Joe; Raining Stones; Riff-Raff (1992); Singing the Blues in Red

Loader, Jayne: Atomic Cafe, The

Lobl, Victor: Beauty and the Beast (TV Series); Eden (1993 TV Series)

Locke, Sondra: Impulse (1990); Ratboy; Trading Favors

Loftis, Norman: Messenger, The; Small Time

Logan, Bob: Meatballs 4; Repossessed; Up Your Alley

Logan, Bruce: Vendetta (1985)

Logan, Joshua: Bus Stop; Camelot; Ensign Pulver; Fanny (1961); Paint Your Wagon; Picnic; Sayonara; South Pacific; Tall Story

Logan, Stanley: Falcon's Brother, The

Logan, Tom: Shakma

Logothetis, Dimitri: Body Shot; Closer, The; Pretty Smart

Loma, J. Anthony: Counterforce; Man of Passion, A; Target Eagle

Loman (Jose Antonio De La Loma), Joseph: Boldest Job in the West, The

Lomas, Raoul: Minor Miracle, A

Lombardo, Lou: P.K. & the Kid; Russian Roulette

Lommel, Ulli: Big Sweat, The; Boogeyman, The; Brainwaves; Cocaine Cowboys; Cold Heat; Devonsville Terror, The; Overkill (1986); Warbirds

Loncraine, Richard: Bellman and True; Brimstone and Treacle; Deep Cover (1980); Haunting of Julia, The; Missionary, The; Richard III (1995); Wedding Gift, The

London, James: Place Called Trinity, A

London, Jerry: Chiefs; Ellis Island; Haunting of Sarah Hardy, The; Kiss Shot; Manhunt for Claude Dallas; Rent-a-Cop; Scarlet and the Black, The; Season of Giants, A; Shogun (Full-Length Version); Victim of Love

London, Roy: Diary of a Hitman

Long, Stanley: Adventures of a Private Eye

Longo, Robert: Johnny Mnemonic

Longon, Humphrey: Battle Force

Longstreet, Harry S.: Perfect Daughter, The; Sex, Love, and Cold Hard Cash; Vow to Kill, A

Lopez, Temistocles: Bird of Prey; Chain of Desire

Lord, Del: Trapped by Television

Lord, Jean-Claude: Eddie and the Cruisers II: Eddie Lives!; Landslide; Mind Field; Toby McTeague; Vindicator, The; Visiting Hours

Lord, Peter: Chicken Run

Lord, Stephen: Fall of the House of Usher, The (1979)

Lorentz, Pare: Plow That Broke the Plains, The

Loring, Ken: Combat Killers

Losey, Joseph: Accident; Assassination of Trotsky, The; Boy with Green Hair, The; Concrete Jungle, The (1962) (Criminal, The); Doll's House, A (1973); Go-Between, The; La Truite (The Trout); Mr. Klein; Roads to the South; Romantic Englishwoman, The; Secret Ceremony; Servant, The; Sleeping Tiger, The; Steaming; Time Without Pity

Lotterby, Sydney: Yes, Prime Minister

Lottimer, Eb: Love Matters; Twisted Love

Louis, Larry: Body Puzzle

Leunguine, Pavel: Luna Park; Taxi Blues

Lounsbery, John: Rescuers, The

Lourie, Eugene: Beast from 20,000 Fathoms, The; Colossus of New York, The; Giant Behemoth, The; Gorgo

Louzil, Eric: Class of Nuke 'em High 2: Subhumanoid Meltdown; Class of Nuke 'em High III; Fortress of Amerikkka; Lust for Freedom; Wilding, The Children of Violence

Loventhal, Charlie: First Time, The; Mr. Write; My Demon Lover

Lovy, Robert: Circuitry Man II: Plughead Rewired

Lovy, Steven: Circuitry Man; Circuitry Man II: Plughead Rewired

Low, Stephen: Titanica

Lowe, Lucas: American Shaolin: King of the Kickboxers II; King of the Kickboxers, The

Lowe, William: Slaughter in San Francisco

Lowenstein, Richard: Dogs in Space

Lowry, Dick: Cop for the Killing, A; Coward of the County; FBI Murders, The; Gambler, The (1980); Gambler, Part II—The Adventure Continues, The; Gambler, Part III—The Legend Continues, The; Gambler Returns, The: Luck of the Draw; Horse for Danny, A; In the Line of Duty: Ambush in Waco; Jayne Mansfield Story, The; Last Stand at Saber River; Living Proof: The Hank Williams, Jr., Story; Midnight Murders; Mr. Murder; Murder with Mirrors; Smokey and the Bandit III; Till Murder Do Us Part; Urban Crossfire; Wet Gold

Loy, Nanni: Cafe Express; Where's Piccone?

Lubin, Arthur: Ali Baba and the Forty Thieves; Black Friday; Buck Privates; Escapade in Japan; Francis Goes to the Races; Francis in the Navy; Francis Joins the Wacs; Francis, the Talking Mule; Hold That Ghost; Impact; Incredible Mr. Limpet, The; Lady Godiva; Maverick (TV Series); Phantom of the Opera (1943); Ride 'em Cowboy

Lubitsch, Ernst: Bluebeard's Eighth Wife; Gypsy Blood; Heaven Can Wait (1943); Lady Windermere's Fan; Marriage Circle, The; Merry Widow, The; Ninotchka; One Arabian Night; Passion (1919); Shop Around the Corner, The; Student Prince in Old Heidelberg, The; That Uncertain Feeling; To Be or Not to Be (1942)

Luby, S. Roy: Arizona Stagecoach; Black Market Rustlers; Boothill Bandits; Border Phantom; Desert Phantom; Fugitive Valley; Saddle Mountain Roundup; Trail of the Silver Spurs

Lucas, George: American Graffiti; Star Wars; Star Wars: Episode I The Phantom Menace; THX 1138

Lucas, Phil: Native Americans, The

Lucente, Francesco: Virgin Queen of St. Francis High, The

Lucidi, Maurizio: Saddle Tramps; Stateline Motel; Street People

Ludman, Larry: Deadly Impact; Operation 'Nam; Thunder Warrior; Thunder Warrior II

Ludwig, Edward: Big Jim McLain; Big Wheel, The; Bonanza (TV Series); Fabulous Texan, The; Fighting Seabees, The; Wake of the Red Witch

Luhrmann, Baz: Strictly Ballroom; William Shakespeare's Romeo and Juliet

Luke, Eric: Not Quite Human 2; Still Not Quite Human

Lumet, Sidney: Anderson Tapes, The; Critical Care; Danger; Daniel; Deathtrap; Dog Day Afternoon; Equus; Fail-Safe; Family Business; Fugitive Kind, The; Garbo Talks; Gloria (1999); Group, The; Guilty as Sin; Hill, The; Just Tell Me What You Want; Long Day's Journey into Night (1962); Morning After, The; Murder on the Orient Express; Network; Night Falls on Manhattan; Offence, The; Pawnbroker, The; Power (1986); Prince of the City; Q & A; Running on Empty; Serpico; Stage Struck (1958); Stranger Among Us, A; 12 Angry Men (1957); Verdict, The; Wiz, The

Luna, Bigas: Anguish; Chambermaid on the *Titanic*, The; Jamon, Jamon

Lunch, Lydia: Gun is Loaded, The

Lupino, Ida: Bigamist, The; Not Wanted; Trouble with Angels, The

Lusk, Don: Pirates of Dark Waters, The; The Saga Begins

Luske, Hamilton: Alice in Wonderland (1951); Cinderella (1950); Lady and the Tramp; One Hundred and One Dalmatians; Peter Pan (1953); Reluctant Dragon, The

Lussier, Patrick: Prophecy 3: The Ascent

Lustig, Dana: Wedding Bell Blues

Lustig, William: Hit List (1988); Maniac (1980); Maniac Cop; Maniac Cop 2; Maniac Cop 3: Badge of Silence; Relentless; Vigilante

Luther, Salvo: Forget Mozart

Lyman, Michel: Phantom 2040 (TV Series)

Lynch, David: Blue Velvet; Dune; Elephant Man, The (1980); Eraserhead; Hotel Room; Industrial Symphony No. 1 The Dream of the Broken Hearted; Lost Highway; Straight Story, The; Twin Peaks (Movie); Twin Peaks: Fire Walk with Me; Wild at Heart

Lynch, Jennifer Chambers: Boxing Helena

Lynch, Paul: Blindside; Bullies; Cross Country; Dream to Believe; Drop Dead Gorgeous (1991); Face the Evil; Humongous; No Contest; Prom Night; Really Weird Tales; Star Trek: The Next Generation (TV Series)

Lyne, Adrian: Fatal Attraction (1987); Flashdance; Foxes; Indecent Proposal; Jacob's Ladder; Lolita (1997); 9 1/2 Weeks

Lynn, Jonathan: Clue; Distinguished Gentleman, The; Greedy; My Cousin Vinny; Nuns on the Run; Sgt. Bilko; Trial and Error (1997); Whole Nine Yards, The

Lyon, Francis D.: Castle of Evil; Cult of the Cobra; Great Locomotive Chase, The; Oklahoman, The; Tomboy and the Champ

Maak, Karoly: Cat's Play

Maas, Dick: Amsterdamned; Lift, The

Mabe, Byron: She Freak, The

MacArthur, Charles: Scoundrel, The

Macartney, Syd: Prince Brat and the Whipping Boy

MacCorkindale, Simon: House That Mary Bought, The

MacDonald, David: Devil Girl from Mars; Never Too Late

MacDonald, Heather: Ballot Measure 9

Macdonald, Hettie: Beautiful Thing

MacDonald, Peter: Legionnaire; Mo' Money; Neverending Story III, The: Escape to Fantasia; Rambo III

MacFadden, Hamilton: Black Camel, The; Stand Up and Cheer

MacFarland, Mike: Hanging on a Star; Pink Motel

MacGregor, Sean: Gentle Savage

Machaty, Gustav: Ecstasy

Mack, Brice: Jennifer

Mackay, David: Breaking Free; Lesser Evil, The; Route 9

Mackendrick, Alexander: Ladykillers, The; Man in the White Suit, The; Sweet Smell of Success; Tight Little Island

Mackenzie, John: Act of Vengeance; Aldrich Ames: Traitor Within; Beyond the Limit; Deadly Voyage; Fourth Protocol, The; Infiltrator, The; Last of the Finest, The; Long Good Friday, The; Ruby (1991); Sense of Freedom, A; Voyage

Mackenzie, Will: Perfect Harmony; Worth Winning

MacKinnon, Gillies: Hideous Kinky; Playboys, The; Simple Twist of Fate, A; Small Faces

MacLachlan, Duncan: Second Jungle Book, The: Mowgli and Baloo

Maclean, Alison: Crush (1994)

MacLean, Stephen: Around the World in 80 Ways

Macy, W. H.: Lip Service

Madden, David: Separate Lives

Madden, John: Ethan Frome; Golden Gate; Grown-Ups; Mrs. Brown; Shakespeare in Love

Madden, Lee: Hell's Angels '69; Night Creature

Maddin, Guy: Careful; Tales from the Gimli Hospital

Madison, Alan: Trouble on the Corner

Madjidi, Majid: Children of Heaven

Madsen, Kenneth: Day in October, A

Magalhaes, Ana Maria: Erotique

Magar, Guy: Retribution; Stepfather III: Father's Day

Maggenti, Maria: Incredibly True Adventure of Two Girls in Love, The

Magnatta, Constantino: Dark Side, The; Darkside, The

Magni, Luigi: In Nome del Papa Re (In the Name of the Pope-King)

Magnoli, Albert: American Anthem; Born to Run; Dark Planet; Purple Rain; Street Knight

Magnuson, John: Lenny Bruce Performance Film, The

Magyar, Dezso: No Secrets; Rappaccini's Daughter

Mahaffey, Redge: Life 101

Maharaj, Anthony: Deathfight; Kick Fighter; Revenge of the Kickfighter

Mahon, Barry: Assault of the Rebel Girls (Cuban Rebel Girls); Rocket Attack USA

Mailer, Norman: Tough Guys Don't Dance

Main, Stewart: Desperate Remedies

Mainka, Maximiliane: Germany In Autumn

Mainka-Jellinghaus, Beate: Germany In Autumn

Maitland, George: Invasion Earth: The Aliens Are Here

Mak, Michael: Sex and Zen

Makavejev, Dusan: Coca Cola Kid, The; Innocence Unprotected; Man Is Not A Bird; Manifesto; Montenegro; Sweet Movie; WR: Mysteries of the Organism

Makhmalbaf, Mohsen: Gabbeh

Makhmalbaf, Samirah: Apple, The

Makin, Kelly: Kids in the Hall: Brain Candy; Mickey Blue Eyes; National Lampoon's Senior Trip

Makk, Karoly: Lily in Love; Love

Malenfant, Robert: Landlady, The; Nurse, The

Malick, Terence: Badlands (1973); Days of Heaven; Thin Red Line, The

Malle, Louis: Alamo Bay; Atlantic City; Au Revoir, Les Enfants; Crackers; Damage; Elevator to the Gallows; Fire Within, The; Lovers, The (1958); May Fools; Murmur of the Heart; My Dinner with Andre; Pretty Baby; Vanya on 42nd Street; Very Private Affair, A; Viva Maria!; Zazie dans le Metro

Mallet, David: Cats

Mallon, James: Mystery Science Theatre 3000: The Movie

Malmuth, Bruce: Hard to Kill; Man Who Wasn't There, The; Nighthawks; Pentathlon; Where Are the Children?

Malone, Mark: Bulletproof Heart; Hoods; Last Stop

Malone, Nancy: I Married A Monster

Malone, William: Creature; House on Haunted Hill (1999); Scared to Death (1980)

Mamet, David: Homicide; House of Games; Oleanna; Spanish Prisoner, The; Things Change; Winslow Boy, The (1999)

Mamin, Yuri: Window to Paris

Mamoru, Oshii: Ghost in the Shell

Mamoulian, Rouben: Applause; Becky Sharp; Blood and Sand (1941); Dr. Jekyll and Mr. Hyde (1932); Golden Boy; Love Me Tonight; Mark of Zorro, The (1940); Queen Christina; Silk Stockings; Summer Holiday

Manchevski, Milcho: Before the Rain

Mancuso (Joe d'Amato), Kevin: 2020 Texas Gladiators

Mandel, Jeff: Elves; Robo C.H.I.C.

Martinez, Chuck: Nice Girls Don't Explode

Martinez, Rene: Super Soul Brother

Martini, Richard: Limit Up; You Can't Hurry Love

Martino, Francesco: Dr. Butcher, M.D. (Medical Deviate)

Martino, Raymond: Davinci's War; Skyscraper; To The Limit

Martino, Sergio: Great Alligator, The; Opponent, The; Screamers (1979); Sex with a Smile; Slave of the Cannibal God; Torso

Marlins, W. Mel: Alex's Apartment

Martinson, Leslie: Atomic Kid, The; Batman (1966); Cheyenne (TV Series); Kid with the Broken Halo, The; Kid with the 200 I.Q., The; Maverick (TV Series); PT 109

Marton, Andrew: Africa—Texas Style!; Around the World Under the Sea; Clarence, the Cross-Eyed Lion; Gypsy Colt; King Solomon's Mines (1950); Longest Day, The; Men of the Fighting Lady

Marvin, Mike: Hamburger—The Motion Picture; Wraith, The

Marvin, R.: Renegade

Mas, Juan A.: Coroner, The

Masahiro, Tanaka: Riding Bean

Masaki, Shin-Ichi: Humanoid, The

Masami, Oobari: Bubblegum Crisis, Vols. 1–8

Masano, Anton Giulio: Atom Age Vampire

Mascarelli, Robert: I Don't Buy Kisses Anymore

Maseba, Yutaka: Ambassador Magma

Massaro, Francesco: Private Affairs

Massetti, Ivana: Domino

Massi, Stelvio: Fearless (1978)

Massot, Joe: Song Remains the Same, The; Wonderwall

Master P: I Got the Hook Up

Masters, Quentin: Dangerous Summer, A; Stud, The

Masterson, Peter: Arctic Blue; Blood Red; Full Moon in Blue Water; Lily Dale; Night Game; Only Thrill, The; Trip to Bountiful, The

Mastorakis, Nico: Blind Date (1984); Double Exposure (1987); Glitch!; Hired to Kill; In the Cold of the Night; Next One, The; Nightmare at Noon; Wind, The (1986)

Mastrocinque, Camillo: Full Hearts and Empty Pockets

Mastroianni, Armand: Cameron's Closet; Deep Trouble; Distortions; Double Revenge; He Knows You're Alone; Killing Hour, The; Robin Cook's Invasion; Supernaturals, The

Masuda, Toshio: Tora! Tora! Tora!

Matalon, Eddy: Blackout (1978); Cathy's Curse; Sweet Killing

Maté, Rudolph: Branded; Dark Past, The; Deep Six, The; D.O.A. (1949); For the First Time; Second Chance; Three Violent People; Union Station; Violent Men, The; When Worlds Collide

Matheson, Tim: Breach of Conduct; Buried Alive II; In the Company of Spies; Tails You Live, Heads You're Dead

Mathias, Sean: Bent

Matmor, Daniel: Homeboys II: Crack City; Urban Jungle

Matsumiya, Masuzumi: Wannabes

Matsutani, Rainer: Eating Pattern

Matsuura, Johei: Crying Freeman, Vols. 1–3

Matsuzono, Tohru: Rumik World: Laughing Target

Mattei, Bruno: Night of the Zombies (1983); Seven Magnificent Gladiators, The

Mattei, Marius: Moving Target (1990)

Matthau, Charles: Doin' Time on Planet Earth; Grass Harp, The

Matthau, Walter: Gangster Story

Matthews, Paul: Breeders (1996); Grim

Mattison, Bunny: Adventures of the Great Mouse Detective, The; Great Mouse Detective, The

Mattison, Sally: Slumber Party Massacre 3

Mattson, Arne: Doll; Girl, The

Mauri, Roberto: Animal Called Man, An; Slaughter of the Vampires

Maxwell, Garth: Jack Be Nimble

Maxwell, Peter: Highest Honor, The; Run, Rebecca, Run; Secret Agent (TV Series)

Maxwell, Ronald F.: Gettysburg; Little Darlings; Night the Lights Went Out in Georgia, The

May, Bradford: Darkman II: The Return of Durant; Darkman III: Die, Darkman, Die; Drive Like Lightning; Legacy of Lies; Lethal Lolita—Amy Fisher: My Story; Madonna: Innocence Lost; Marilyn & Bobby: Her Final Affair; Mortal Sins (1992)

May, Elaine: Heartbreak Kid, The; Ishtar; Mikey and Nicky; New Leaf, A

May, Joe: House of the Seven Gables, The; Invisible Man Returns

Mayberry, Russ: Brady Bunch, The (TV series); Challenge of a Lifetime; Fer-de-Lance; Probe; Rebels, The; Side by Side: The True Story of the Osmond Family; Unidentified Flying Oddball

Maybury, John: Love is the Devil

Mayer, Gerald: Man Inside, The (1984)

Mayers, Janet: Letter to My Killer

Mayersberg, Paul: Captive; Nightfall

Mayfield, Les: Blue Streak; Encino Man; Flubber; Miracle on 34th Street (1994)

Mayiam, Tony: Burning, The; Riddle of the Sands; Sins of Dorian Gray, The; Split Second (1992)

Maynard, Ken: Fiddlin' Buckaroo

Mayo, Archie: Adventures of Marco Polo, The; Angel on My Shoulder (1946); Black Legion; Case of the Lucky Legs, The; Go into Your Dance; House Across the Bay, The; Illicit; Night after Night; Night in Casablanca, A; Orchestra Wives; Petrified Forest, The; Svengali (1931); They Shall Have Music

Mayron, Melanie: Baby-Sitters Club, The

Maysles, Albert: Gimme Shelter

Maysles, David: Gimme Shelter

Mazo, Michael: Crackerjack; Downdraft; Last of the Warriors; Time Runner

Mazursky, Paul: Alex in Wonderland; Blume in Love; Bob & Carol & Ted & Alice; Down and Out in Beverly Hills; Enemies—A Love Story; Faithful; Harry and Tonto; Moon over Parador; Moscow on the Hudson; Next Stop, Greenwich Village; Pickle, The; Scenes from a Mall; Tempest (1982); Unmarried Woman, An; Willie and Phil; Winchell

Mazzucato, Paolo: Moonbase

McAnuff, Des: Cousin Bette

McBrearty, Don: Child's Christmas in Wales, A; Coming Out Alive; Really Weird Tales; Strange Tales: Ray Bradbury Theater

McBrearty, John: Sorority Girls and the Creature from Hell

McBride, Jim: Big Easy, The; Blood Ties (1993); Breathless (1983); David Holzman's Diary; Glen and Randa; Great Balls of Fire; Informant, The; Pronto; Wrong Man, The (1993)

McCain, Howard: No Dessert Dad Until You Mow the Lawn; Shadow of a Scream; Unspeakable, The

McCall, Cheryl: Streetwise

McCall, Rod: Cheatin' Hearts

McCalmont, James: Escape from Safehaven

McCanlies, Tim: Dancer, Texas: Pop. 81

McCann, Tim: Desolation Angels

McCarey, Leo: Affair to Remember, An; Awful Truth, The; Belle of the Nineties; Bells of St. Mary's, The; Duck Soup; Going My Way; Good Sam; Indiscreet (1931); Love Affair (1939); Milky Way, The (1936); Once Upon a Honeymoon; Ruggles of Red Gap

McCarey, Ray: So This Is Washington; You Can't Fool Your Wife

McCarthy, John P.: Forty-Niners; Trailin' North

McCarthy, Michael: Operation Amsterdam; Thieves of Fortune

McCarthy, Peter: Floundering

McCarthy, John Michael: Sore Losers

McClary, J. Michael: Annie O; Curse of the Starving Class

McClatchy, Greggor: Vampire at Midnight

McCleery, Mick: Alien Agenda; The (TV Series); Twisted Tales

McCormick, Bret: Blood on the Badge; Rumble in the Streets

McCowan, George: Frogs; Murder on Flight 502; Return to Fantasy Island

McCrae, Scooter: Shatter Dead

McCubbin, Peter: Home for Christmas

McCulloch, Bruce: Superstar: Dare to Dream

McCullough, Jim: Aurora Encounter; Mountaintop Motel Massacre

McDonald, Bruce: Dance Me Outside; Hard Core Logo; Highway 61; Scandalous Me: The Jacqueline Susann Story

McDonald, Frank: Along the Navajo Trail; Bells of Rosarita; Big Sombrero, The; Flying Blind; Gun Smugglers; Lights of Old Santa Fe; My Pal Trigger; One Body Too Many; Take It Big; Thunder Pass; Wyatt Earp: Return to Tombstone

McDonald, J. Farrell: Patchwork Girl of Oz, The

McDonald, Michael James: Crazysitter, The; Death Artist

McDonald, Rodney: Scorned 2; Steel Sharks; Surface to Air

McDougall, Don: Bonanza (TV Series); Chinese Web, The; Riding with Death

McElwee, Ross: Sherman's March

McEveety, Bernard: Brotherhood of Satan; Longest Drive, The; Napoleon and Samantha; Ride Beyond Vengeance; Roughnecks

McEveety, Vincent: Amy; Apple Dumpling Gang Rides Again, The; Castaway Cowboy, The; Charley and the Angel; Firecreek; Gunsmoke: Return to Dodge; Gus; Herbie Goes Bananas; Herbie Goes to Monte Carlo; Menace on the Mountain; Million Dollar Duck, The; Smoke (1970); Star Trek (TV Series); Superdad

McGann, William: American Empire; Case of the Black Cat, The; Dr. Christian Meets the Women; In Old California

McGaugh, W. F.: New Adventures of Tarzan

McGavin, Darren: Run Stranger Run

McGehee, Scott: Suture

McGinnis, Scott: Caroline at Midnight; Last Gasp

McGoohan, Patrick: Prisoner, The (1968) (TV Series)

McGowan, Darrell: Showdown, The (1950)

McGowan, J. P.: Drum Taps; Hurricane Express; Tarzan and the Golden Lion

McGowan, Robert: Old Swimmin' Hole, The

McGowan, Stuart E.: Billion Dollar Hobo, The; Showdown, The (1950); They Went That-A-Way and That-A-Way

McGowan, Tom: Savage Journey

McGrath, Douglas: Emma (1996)

McGrath, Joseph: Bliss of Mrs. Blossom, The; Casino Royale (1967); Magic Christian, The; 30 Is a Dangerous Age, Cynthia

McGrath, Martin: Wet and Wild Summer

McGuane, Thomas: 92 in the Shade

McGuckian, Mary: This Is the Sea

McGuire, Don: Delicate Delinquent, The

McHenry, Doug: House Party 2; Jason's Lyric

McIntyre, C. J.: Border Shootout

McIntyre, Chris: Backstreet Justice; Captured Alive

McIntyre, Thom: Rutherford County Line

McKay, Cole: Game, The (1988); Star Hunter

McKay, Jim: Girls Town (1996)

McKellar, Don: Last Night

McKellips, Paul: Reggie's Prayer

McKeown, Douglas: Return of the Alien's Deadly Spawn, The

McKimmie, Jackie: Waiting

McLachlan, Duncan: Born Wild; Double-O Kid, The; Scavengers

McLaglen, Andrew V.: Bandolero!; Blue and the Gray, The; Breakthrough; Cahill—US Marshal; Chisum; Devil's Brigade, The; Dirty Dozen, The: The Next Mission; ffolkes; Have Gun, Will Travel (TV Series); Hellfighters; McLintock!; Monkeys Go Home; On Wings of Eagles; Rare Breed, The (1966); Sahara (1984); Sea Wolves, The; Shadow Riders, The; Shenandoah; Undefeated, The; Way West, The (1967); Wild Geese, The

McLennan, Don: Slate, Wyn, and Me

McLeod, Norman Z.: Casanova's Big Night; Horse Feathers; It's a Gift; Kid from Brooklyn, The; Lady Be Good; Let's Dance; Little Men (1940); Monkey Business (1931); Never Wave at a WAC (Private Wore Skirts, The); Paleface, The; Panama Hattie; Road to Rio; Secret Life of Walter Mitty, The; Topper; Topper Takes a Trip

McLoughlin, Tom: Date with an Angel; Fire Next Time, The; Friday the 13th, Part VI: Jason Lives; Journey; One Dark Night; Sometimes They Come Back; Yarn Princess, The

McMurray, Mary: At Bertram's Hotel; Office Romances

McNamara, Sean: Adventures of Galgameth, The; Casper: A Spirited Beginning; P.U.N.K.S.; Treehouse Hostage

McNaughton, Ian: And Now for Something Completely Different; Monty Python's Flying Circus (TV Series)

McNaughton, John: Borrower, The; Girls in Prison; Henry: Portrait of a Serial Killer; Lansky; Mad Dog and Glory; Normal Life; Sex, Drugs, Rock & Roll; Wild Things

McPherson, John: Dirty Work; Fade to Black (1993); Incident at Deception Ridge; Strays

McRae, Henry: Tarzan the Tiger

McRae, Peter: Endurance (1985)

McTiernan, John: Die Hard; Die Hard with a Vengeance; Hunt for Red October, The; Last Action Hero, The; Medicine Man; Nomads; Predator; Thomas Crown Affair, The (1999); 13th Warrior, The

McWhinnie, Donald: Elizabeth R; Mapp & Lucia

Mead, Nick: Bank Robber

Meadows, Shane: Twentyfourseven (English); Twentyfourseven (boxing)

Meckler, Nancy: Alive & Kicking; Sister, My Sister

Medak, Peter: Babysitter, The (1980); Changeling, The; Day in the Death of Joe Egg, A; Ghost in the Noonday Sun; Hunchback, The (1997); Krays, The; Let Him Have It; Men's Club, The; Negatives; Odd Job, The; Pinocchio (1983); Pontiac Moon; Romeo Is Bleeding; Ruling Class, The; Snow Queen; Snow White and the Seven Dwarfs (1983); Species II; Zorro, the Gay Blade

Medem, Julio: Lovers of the Arctic Circle; Red Squirrel, The

Medford, Don: Fugitive, The: The Last Episode (TV Series); Organization, The; Sizzle

Medina, Nicholas: Friend of the Family II

Medoway, Cary: Heavenly Kid, The; Paradise Motel

Meerapfel, Jeanine: Malou

Meffre, Pomme: Grain of Sand, The

Megahey, Leslie: Advocate, The

Megahy, Francis: Carpathian Eagle; Great Riviera Bank Robbery, The; Red Sun Rising; Taffin

Mehrez, Alan: Bloodsport II; Bloodsport III

Mehta, Deepa: Camilla (1994); Earth (1998)

Mehta, Ketan: Spices

Meins, Gus: Gentleman from California; March of the Wooden Soldiers (Babes in Toyland (1934))

Meisel, Myron: It's All True

Meisel, Norbert: Adultress, The

Mekas, Adolfas: Brig, The

Mekas, Jonas: Brig, The

Melançon, André: Bach and Broccoli

Melchior, Ib: Angry Red Planet, The; Time Travelers, The

Mele, Arthur N.: Soldier's Fortune

Melendez, Bill: Bon Voyage, Charlie Brown; Boy Named Charlie Brown, A; Lion, the Witch and the Wardrobe, The; Play It Again, Charlie Brown; Race for Your Life, Charlie Brown; Snoopy, Come Home; This Is America, Charlie Brown; What Next, Charlie Brown?; You're Not Elected, Charlie Brown

Melford, George: Dracula (Spanish); East of Borneo; Moran of the Lady Letty; Sheik, The

Melkonian, James: Jerky Boys, The; Stoned Age, The

Mellencamp, John: Falling from Grace

Melton, Frank: Othello (1982)

Melville, Jean-Pierre: Bob le Flambeur; Le Doulos; Le Samourai; Les Enfants Terribles

Menaul, Chris: Fatherland; Feast of July; Passion of Ayn Rand, The; Prime Suspect 1

Mendelsohn, Eric: Judy Berlin

Menduluk, George: Doin' Time; Kidnapping of the President, The; Meatballs III; Stone Cold Dead

Mendes, Lothar: Man Who Could Work Miracles, The

Mendez, Fernando: Vampire, The

Mendez, Mike: Bimbo Movie Bash

Menendez, Ramon: Money for Nothing; Stand and Deliver

Menges, Chris: Crisscross (1992); Second Best; World Apart, A

Meng-Hua, Ho: Mighty Peking Man

Menshov, Vladimir: Moscow Does Not Believe in Tears

Menzel, Jiri: Closely Watched Trains; Larks on a String

Menzies, William Cameron: Chandu the Magician; Drums in the Deep South; Invaders from Mars (1953); Things to Come

Merchant, Ismail: Courtesans of Bombay; In Custody; Proprietor, The

Meredino, James: Hard Drive

Meredith, Burgess: Man in the Eiffel Tower, The; Yin and Yang of Mr. Go, The

Merendino, James: Real Thing, The; Terrified

Merhi, Jalal: Operation Golden Phoenix

Mitchell, Mike: Deuce Bigalow: Male Gigolo

Mitchell, Oswald: Danny Boy (1941)

Mitchell, Sollace: Call Me

Miterrand, Frederic: Madame Butterfly

Miyazaki, Hayao: Castle of Cagliostro, The; Lupin III: Tales of the Wolf (TV Series); My Neighbor Totoro; Princess Mononoke

Mizoguchi, Kenji: Chikamatsu Monogatari; Forty Seven Ronin; Geisha, A; Life of Oharu; Osaka Elegy; Princess Yang Kwei Fei; Sansho the Bailiff; Shin Heinke Monogatari; Sisters of the Gion; Story of the Late Chrysanthemums, The; Street of Shame; Ugetsu

Mizrahi, Moshe: Every Time We Say Goodbye; I Sent a Letter to My Love; La Vie Continue; Madame Rosa

Moctezuma, Juan Lopez: Dr. Tarr's Torture Dungeon; Mary, Mary, Bloody Mary

Moder, Richard: Bionic Woman, The

Möhr, Hanro: Hostage (1987)

Moeller, Phillip: Break of Hearts

Moffitt, John: Love at Stake

Mogherini, Flavio: Lunatics & Lovers

Moguy, Leonide: Action in Arabia; Whistle Stop

Moland, Hans Petter: Zero Kelvin

Molander, Gustav: Dollar; Intermezzo (1936); Only One Night

Moleon, Rafael: Baton Rouge

Molina, Jack: Craving, The

Molina, William H.: Last Assassins

Molinaro, Edouard: Beaumarchais the Scoundrel; Dracula and Son; Just the Way You Are; La Cage aux Folles; La Cage aux Folles II; Pain in the A——, A; Ravishing Idiot, The; Seven Deadly Sins, The

Moll, James: Last Days, The

Moloney, Paul: I Live With Me Dad

Monahan, Dave: Adventures of Milo in the Phantom Tollbooth, The

Mondshein, Andrew: Evidence of Blood

Mones, Paul: Fathers & Sons; Saints & Sinners

Monger, Christopher: Englishman Who Went up a Hill But Came down a Mountain, The; Just Like a Woman; Waiting for the Light

Monicelli, Mario: Big Deal on Madonna Street; Laugh for Joy (Passionate Thief (1954)); Lovers and Liars; Organizer, The; Passionate Thief, The (1961)

Monnier, Philippe: Tale of Two Cities, A (1991)

Monroe, Phil: Bugs Bunny/Road Runner Movie, The

Montagne, Edward: Reluctant Astronaut, The; They Went That-A-Way and That-A-Way

Montaldo, Giuliano: Sacco and Vanzetti; Time to Kill (1990)

Montero, Roberto: Monster of the Island, The; Slasher

Montes, Eduardo: Double Obsession

Montesi, Jorge: Bloodknot; Hush Little Baby; Omen IV: The Awakening; Soft Deceit

Montgomery, George: From Hell to Borneo

Montgomery, Monty: Loveless, The

Montgomery, Patrick: Compleat Beatles, The

Montgomery, Robert: Gallant Hours, The; Lady in the Lake

Moody, Ralph: Stage to Tucson

Moore, Charles Philip: Angel of Destruction; Blackbelt; Dance with Death; Demon Wind

Moore, Michael: Big One, The; Canadian Bacon; Roger & Me

Moore, Michael: Buckskin; Fastest Guitar Alive, The; Paradise Hawaiian Style; Talion

Moore, Richard: Circle of Iron

Moore, Robert: Chapter Two; Cheap Detective, The; Murder by Death; Thursday's Game

Moore, Ronald W.: Future-Kill

Moore, Simon: Under Suspicion

Moore, Tara: Tusks

Moore, Tom: Danielle Steel's Fine Things; 'Night, Mother; Return to Boggy Creek

Moorhouse, Jocelyn: How to Make an American Quilt; Proof; Thousand Acres, A

Mora, Philippe: Back in Business; Beast Within, The; Breed Apart, A; Communion; Death of a Soldier; Howling II ... Your Sister Is a Werewolf; Howling III; Mad Dog Morgan; Mercenary 2: Thick and Thin; Precious Find; Return of Captain Invincible, The

Morahan, Andy: Highlander: The Final Dimension; Murder in Mind

Morahan, Christopher: After Pilkington; Clockwise; Jewel in the Crown, The; Paper Mask; Unnatural Pursuits

Moranis, Rick: Strange Brew

Mordente, Tony: Love in the Present Tense

Mordillat, Gérard: Billy Ze Kick; My Life and Times with Antonin Artaud

Moreau, Jeanne: Lumiere

Moreton, David: Edge of Seventeen

Moretti, Nanni: Caro Diario; Palombella Rossa

Morgan, W. T.: Matter of Degrees, A

Morgenstern, Janusz: Legend of the White Horse

Morita, Yoshimitsu: Family Game, The

Moriyama, Yuuji: Urusei Yatsura (TV Series) Vols. 1–45; Urusei Yatsura: Only You

Morneau, Louis: Bats; Carnosaur 2; Final Judgment; Quake; To Die Standing

Moroder, Giorgio: Metropolis (1984 Musical Version)

Morris, David: Patti Rocks; Vietnam War Story—Part Two

Morris, David Burton: Hometown Boy Makes Good; Jersey Girl; Three Lives of Karen, The

Morris, Ernest: Tell-Tale Heart, The

Morris, Errol: Dark Wind; Fast, Cheap and Out of Control; Mr. Death: The Rise and Fall of Fred A. Leuchter Jr.; Thin Blue Line, The; Vernon, Florida

Morris, Howard: Don't Drink the Water; Who's Minding the Mint?; With Six You Get Eggroll

Morrison, Bruce: Shaker Run; Tearaway

Morrissey, Kevin: Witchcraft IV

Morrissey, Paul: Andy Warhol's Dracula; Andy Warhol's Frankenstein; Beethoven's Nephew; Flesh; Heat (1972); Hound of the Baskervilles, The (1977); Mixed Blood; Spike of Bensonhurst; Trash

Morse, Hollingsworth: Daughters of Satan; Justin Morgan Had a Horse

Morse, Terrel O.: Unknown World

Morse, Terry: Fog Island; Godzilla, King of the Monsters

Morton, Rocky: D.O.A. (1988); Max Headroom; Super Mario Brothers, The

Morton, Vincent: Windrider

Moses, Ben: Nickel & Dime

Moses, Gilbert: Fish That Saved Pittsburgh, The

Moses, Harry: Assault at West Point

Mosher, Gregory: Life in the Theater, A

Moshinsky, Elijah: Genghis Cohn; Green Man, The

Moskov, George: Married Too Young

Moskowitz, Steward: Adventures of an American Rabbit, The

Mosquera, Gustavo: Times to Come

Mostow, Jonathan: Beverly Hills Bodysnatchers; Breakdown; Flight of Black Angel; U-571

Mottola, Greg: Daytrippers, The

Mourneau, Louis: Soldier Boyz

Mowhray, Malcolm: Don't Tell Her It's Me; Out Cold; Private Function, A

Moxey, John Llewellyn: Bounty Man, The; Children of An Lac, The; Circus of Fear; Cradle Will Fall, The; Detective Sadie and Son; Home for the Holidays (1972) (Television); Horror Hotel; Intimate Strangers; Lady Mobster; Mating Season, The; Night Stalker, The (1971); Sanctuary of Fear; Through Naked Eyes

Moyle, Alan: Empire Records; Gun in Betty Lou's Handbag, The; Pump Up the Volume; Times Square

Müller, Ray: Wonderful Horrible Life of Leni Riefenstahl

Mulcahy, Russell: Blue Ice; Highlander; Highlander 2: The Quickening; Razorback; Real McCoy, The; Resurrection (1998); Ricochet; Russell Mulcahy's Tale of the Mummy; Shadow, The; Silent Trigger

Mullen, Mark: Cool Blue

Mulligan, Robert: Baby the Rain Must Fall; Bloodbrothers; Clara's Heart; Come September; Fear Strikes Out; Great Impostor, The; Inside Daisy Clover; Kiss Me Goodbye; Love with the Proper Stranger; Man in the Moon, The; Other, The; Pursuit of Happiness, The; Same Time Next Year; Stalking Moon, The; Summer of '42; To Kill a Mockingbird; Up the Down Staircase

Mulot, Claude: Black Venus; Blood Rose

Munch, Christopher: Hours and Times

Newman, Joseph M.: Great Dan Patch, The; Jungle Patrol; King of the Roaring Twenties; Love Nest; Pony Soldier; This Island Earth

Newman, Paul: Effect of Gamma Rays on Man-in-the-Moon Marigolds, The; Glass Menagerie, The; Harry and Son; Rachel, Rachel; Shadow Box, The; Sometimes a Great Notion

Newmeyer, Fred: Freshman, The (1925); General Spanky; Grandma's Boy; Safety Last

Niami, Ramin: Somewhere in the City

Nibbelink, Phil: American Tail, An: Fievel Goes West; We're Back! A Dinosaur's Story

Niblo, Fred: Ben-Hur (1926); Blood and Sand (1922); Mark of Zorro, The (1920); Mysterious Lady, The; Three Musketeers, The (1921)

Nic, Ted: Dungeonmaster, The

Niccol, Andrew: Gattaca

Nichetti, Maurizio: Icicle Thief, The; Volere Volare

Nicholas, Gregor: Broken English

Nicholas, Paul: Chained Heat

Nicholls Jr., J. George: Anne of Green Gables (1934); Finishing School; Return of Peter Grimm, The

Nichols, Charles A.: Charlotte's Web

Nichols, Dudley: Sister Kenny

Nichols, Mike: Biloxi Blues; Birdcage, The; Carnal Knowledge; Catch-22; Day of the Dolphin, The; Fortune, The; Gilda Live; Gin Game, The; Graduate, The; Heartburn; Postcards from the Edge; Primary Colors; Regarding Henry; Silkwood; What Planet Are You From?; Who's Afraid of Virginia Woolf?; Wolf; Working Girl

Nicholson, Arch: Dark Age; Fortress (1985)

Nicholson, Jack: Goin' South; Two Jakes, The

Nicholson, James H.: Alakazam the Great

Nicholson, Martin: This Is America, Charlie Brown; What Next, Charlie Brown?

Nicholson, Sam: This Is America, Charlie Brown; What Next, Charlie Brown?

Nicholson, William: Firelight

Nicol, Alex: Screaming Skull, The

Nicolaou, Ted: Bad Channels; Bloodlust: Subspecies III; Bloodstone: Subspecies II; Dragonworld; Leapin' Leprechauns; Magic in the Mirror; Ragdoll; Remote; Spellbreaker: Secret of the Leprechauns; Subspecies; Terror Vision; Vampire Journals

Nicolella, John: Finish Line; Kull the Conqueror; Runaway Father; Sunset Heat

Nielsen, Thomas Birch: Webmaster

Nielson, James: Tom Sawyer (1973)

Nierenberg, George T.: Say Amen, Somebody

Nigh, William: Ape, The; Black Dragons; Corregidor; Doomed to Die; Fatal Hour, The; Gangster's Boy; Hoosier Schoolboy; Mr. Wong, Detective; Mr. Wong in Chinatown; Mysterious Mr. Wong, The; Strange Case of Dr. Rx, The; That Brennan Girl

Nihonmatzu, Kazui: X from Outer Space, The

Nilsson, Rob: Heat and Sunlight; Northern Lights; On the Edge; Signal 7

Nimoy, Leonard: Funny About Love; Good Mother, The; Holy Matrimony; Star Trek III: The Search for Spock; Star Trek IV: The Voyage Home; Three Men and a Baby

Nishi, Yoshikuni: Serendipity, the Pink Dragon

Nishijima, Katsuhiko: Project A-KO

Nishio, Daisuke: 3 x 3 Eyes, Vols. 1–4

Nizet, Charles: Rescue Force

Noble, Henri: Virtual Desire

Noboru, Furuse: New Dominion Tank Police

Nobuyuki, Aramaki: Madox-01

Noëlte, Rudolf: Castle, The (1963)

Noguchi, Haruyasu: Monster from a Prehistoric Planet

Nolbandov, Sergei: Ships with Wings

Noonan, Chris: Babe (1995)

Noonan, Tommy: Three Nuts in Search of a Bolt; What Happened Was . . . ; Wife, The

Norbu, Khyentse: Cup, The

Norgard, Lindsay: Homeboys; Princess Warrior

Norman, Leslie: Saint, The (TV Series); X—The Unknown

Normand, Mabel: Charlie Chaplin ... Our Hero

Norrington, Stephen: Blade (1998); Death Machine

Norris, Aaron: Braddock: Missing in Action III; Delta Force 2; Forest Warrior; Hellbound; Hitman, The; Platoon Leader; Sidekicks; Top Dog

Norris, Guy: Rage and Honor II: Hostile Takeover

Norton, B.W.L.: Baby—Secret of the Lost Legend; More American Graffiti; Three for the Road; Tour of Duty

Norton, Bill L.: Every Mother's Worst Fear; False Arrest; Gargoyles (1972); Hercules and the Amazon Women; Hercules in the Underworld; Our Mother's Murder

Norton, Charles: Kick or Die

Norton, Edward: Keeping the Faith

Nosseck, Max: Black Beauty (1946); Brighton Strangler, The; Dillinger (1945)

Nosseck, Noel: Down, Out & Dangerous; Dreamer; French Silk; Full Exposure; Fury Within, The; King of the Mountain; Las Vegas Lady; Silent Predators; Sister-In-Law, The (1995); Tornado!

Nossiter, Jonathan: Sunday

Notz, Thierry: Fortunes of War (1993); Terror Within, The; Watchers II

Novak, Blaine: Short Fuse

Novaro, Maria: Danzon

Noyce, Phillip: Blind Fury; Bone Collector, The; Clear and Present Danger; Dead Calm; Heatwave (1983); Hitchhiker, The (Series); Newsfront; Patriot Games; Saint, The (1997); Sliver

Nuchtern, Simon: Savage Dawn; Silent Madness

Nugent, Elliott: Cat and the Canary, The (1939); Give Me a Sailor; My Favorite Brunette; My Girl Tisa; Up in Arms; Welcome, Stranger

Nunez, Victor: Flash of Green, A; Gal Young 'Un; Ruby in Paradise; Ulee's Gold

Nunn, Trevor: Hedda; Lady Jane; Twelfth Night

Nuridsnay, Claude: Microcosmos

Nuse, Deland: Chilling, The

Nussbaum, Raphael: Speak of the Devil

Nutley, Colin: House of Angels

Nutter, David: Cease Fire; Disturbing Behavior; Millennium (1996); Trancers 4: Jack of Swords; Trancers 5: Sudden Deth

Nuytten, Bruno: Camille Claudel

Nyby, Christian: Elfego Baca: Six Gun Law; Operation C.I.A.; Thing (From Another World), The (1951)

Nyby II, Christian I.: Devlin Connection III, The; Whisper Kills, A

Nygard, Roger: High Strung; Trekkies

Nykvist, Carl-Gustav: Women on the Roof, The

Nyswander, Ron: Prince of Pennsylvania

Oakley, Vern: Modern Affair, A

Oaks, Joe: Deadly Twins

O'Bannon, Dan: Resurrected, The; Return of the Living Dead, The

O'Bannon, Rockne S.: Fear (1990)

Oblowitz, Michael: This World, Then the Fireworks

Oblowsky, Stephan: Other Hell, The

Oboler, Arch: Twonky, The

O'Brien, Jack: All My Sons (1986)

O'Brien, Jim: Dressmaker, The; Foreign Affairs; Jewel in the Crown, The

O'Brien, John: Vermont Is for Lovers

Obrow, Jeffrey: Bram Stoker's The Mummy; Dorm That Dripped Blood, The (Pranks); Kindred, The; Power, The (1980); Servants of Twilight

O'Callaghan, Maurice: Broken Harvest

O'Connolly, Jim: Berserk; Crooks and Coronets (Sophie's Place); Valley of Gwangi

O'Connor, Kevin: Great Expectations (1989); House Where Evil Dwells, The

O'Connor, Pat: Cal; Circle of Friends; Dancing at Lughnasa; Fools of Fortune; Inventing the Abbotts; January Man, The; Month in the Country, A; Stars and Bars; Zelda

Ocvirk, David Todd: Kolobos

Odell, David: Martians Go Home

Odendal, Sias: Nukie

Odets, Clifford: None But the Lonely Heart

Odorisio, Luciano: Sacrilege

Oedekerk, Steve: Ace Ventura: When Nature Calls; Nothing to Lose

O'Fallon, Peter: Suicide Kings

O'Ferrall, George More: Three Cases of Murder

Ofteringer, Suzanne: Nico Icon

Ogilvie, George: Mad Max Beyond Thunderdome

Ogorodnikov, Valery: Burglar (Russian)

Ogrodnik, Mo: Ripe

O'Hara, Gerry: Bitch, The; Leopard in the Snow; Maroc 7

Parker, Albert: Black Pirate, The

Parker, Brian: Inspector Morse (TV Series)

Parker, Cary: Girl in the Picture, The

Parker, Christine: Women from Down Under

Parker, David: Bimbo Movie Bash; Dead Hate the Living, The

Parker, John: Daughter of Horror

Parker, Norton S.: Road to Ruin, The (1928)

Parker, Oliver: Othello (1995)

Parker, Percy G.: Castle of the Creeping Flesh

Parker, Trey: Cannibal! The Musical; Orgazmo; South Park: Bigger, Longer & Uncut

Parkinson, Andrew: I, Zombie

Parkinson, Eric: Future Shock

Parkinson, H. B.: Trapped by the Mormons

Parks, Hugh: Shakma; Shoot (1991)

Parks, Michael: Return of Josey Wales

Parks Jr., Gorden: Aaron Loves Angela; Learning Tree, The; Shaft; Shaft's Big Score!; Superfly; Three the Hard Way

Parolini, Gianfranco: Fury of Hercules, The; Samson

Parr, John H.: Prey for the Hunter; Pursuit

Parr, Larry: Soldier's Tale, A

Parriott, James D.: Heart Condition; Misfits of Science

Parrish, Robert: Bobo, The; Casino Royale (1967); Cry Danger; Destructors, The; Journey to the Far Side of the Sun; Mississippi Blues; Town Called Hell, A

Parrott, James: Laurel and Hardy Classics: Vol. 1–9; Pardon Us

Parry, Gordon: Tom Brown's Schooldays (1950)

Parsons, John: Watched!

Parsons, Nicholas: Dead Heart

Part, Michael: Starbirds

Pascal, Gabriel: Caesar and Cleopatra; Major Barbara

Pascal, Michel: Francois Truffaut: Stolen Moments

Paseornek, Michael: Vibrations

Paskaljevic, Goran: Cabaret Balkan; Someone Else's America

Pasolini, Pier Paolo: Accattone; Arabian Nights (1974); Canterbury Tales, The; Decameron, The; Gospel According to Saint Matthew, The; Hawks and the Sparrows, The; Love Meetings; Mamma Roma; Medea; Oedipus Rex (1967); Pigsty; Salo: 120 Days of Sodom; Teorema

Pasquin, John: Jungle 2 Jungle; Nightmare (1991); Santa Clause, The

Passer, Ivan: Born to Win; Creator; Crime & Passion; Cutter's Way; Fourth Story; Haunted Summer; Silver Bears; Stalin

Pastrone, Giovanni: Cabiria

Pataki, Michael: Cinderella (1976); Mansion of the Doomed

Patchett, Tom: Best Legs in the 8th Grade, The

Pate, Jonas: Deceiver; Grave, The

Pate, Josh: Deceiver

Pate, Michael: Tim

Patel, Raju: In the Shadow of Kilimanjaro

Paterson, Daniel M.: Girlfriend from Hell

Paton, Stuart: In Old Cheyenne; 20,000 Leagues Under the Sea (1916)

Patrick, Daniel: Haunted Sea, The

Patrick, Matthew: Hider in the House; Tainted Blood

Patrick, Michael: Drop Dead Gorgeous (1999)

Patterson, John: Grave Secrets: The Legacy of Hilltop Drive; Taken Away

Patterson, Pat: Doctor Gore

Patterson, Willi: Dreams Lost, Dreams Found

Pattinson, Michael: ... Almost; Ground Zero; Limbic Region, The; One Crazy Night

Patton-Spruill, Robert: Body Count (1997); Squeeze

Patzack, Peter: Lethal Obsession

Paul, Byron: Lt. Robin Crusoe, U.S.N.

Paul, Don: Road to El Dorado, The

Paul, Stefan: Jimmy Cliff—Bongo Man

Paul, Steven: Eternity; Falling in Love Again; Slapstick of Another Kind

Paul, Stuart: Emanon; Fate

Paulsen, David: Schizoid

Pavia, Mark: Night Flier, The

Pavlou, George: Rawhead Rex; Transmutations

Pavone, Michael: Chameleon (1995)

Payne, Alexander: Citizen Ruth

Payne, David: Addams Family Reunion; Alien Terminator; Aliens Among Us; Concealed Weapon; Criminal Hearts; Not Like Us

Payson, John: Joe's Apartment

Pearce, Michael: James Joyce's Women

Pearce, Richard: Country; Dead Man Out; Family Thing, A; Final Days, The; Heartland; Leap of Faith; Long Walk Home, The; No Mercy; Sessions; Threshold; Witness Protection

Pearl, Steven: At First Sight (1995)

Pecas, Max: Daniella by Night

Peck, Brian: Willies, The

Peck, Ron: Empire State

Peckinpah, David: When Danger Follows You Home

Peckinpah, Sam: Ballad of Cable Hogue, The; Bring Me the Head of Alfredo Garcia; Convoy (1978); Cross of Iron; Deadly Companions, The; Getaway, The (1972); Junior Bonner; Killer Elite, The; Major Dundee; Osterman Weekend, The; Pat Garrett and Billy the Kid; Ride the High Country; Straw Dogs; Wild Bunch, The

Peeples, Quinton: Joyride (1997)

Peerce, Larry: Ash Wednesday; Bell Jar, The; Court-martial of Jackie Robinson, The; Elvis and Me; Goodbye Columbus; Hard to Hold; Incident, The (1967); Love Child; Murder So Sweet; Neon Empire; Other Side of the Mountain, The; Other Side of the Mountain, Part II, The; Prison for Children; Queenie; Separate Peace, A; Sporting Club, The; That Was Rock; Two-Minute Warning; Wired; Woman Named Jackie, A

Peeters, Barbara: Summer School Teachers

Pelaez, Antonio: Crystalstone

Pelissier, Anthony: Encore; Rocking Horse Winner, The

Pellerin, Jean: Clown at Midnight, The; For Hire

Pelletier, Andre: Voodoo Dolls

Pellington, Mark: Arlington Road; Going All the Way

Pellizzari, Monica: Women from Down Under

Peltier, Melissa: Titanic (1995)

Penczner, Marius: I Was a Zombie for the FBI

Penn, Arthur: Alice's Restaurant; Bonnie and Clyde; Chase, The (1966); Dead of Winter; Four Friends; Inside; Left Handed Gun, The; Little Big Man; Miracle Worker, The (1962); Missouri Breaks, The; Night Moves; Penn & Teller Get Killed; Portrait, The; Target

Penn, Leo: Dark Secret of Harvest Home, The; Judgment in Berlin; Lost in Space (TV Series); Man Called Adam, A

Penn, Sean: Crossing Guard, The; Indian Runner, The

Pennebaker, D. A.: Don't Look Back (1967); Monterey Pop; Moon Over Broadway; War Room, The

Pennell, Eagle: Last Night at the Alamo

Peoples, David: Blood of Heroes

Pepin, Richard: Cyber Tracker; Cyber Tracker 2; Dark Breed; Firepower (1993); T-Force

Peploe, Clare: High Season; Rough Magic

Peploe, Mark: Afraid of the Dark

Perello, Hope: Howling VI: The Freaks; Pet Shop

Perennou, Marie: Microcosmos

Perez, Jack: America's Deadliest Home Video

Perier, Etienne: Investigation; Zeppelin

Perisic, Zoran: Sky Bandits

Perkins, Anthony: Lucky Stiff; Psycho III

Perry, Frank: Compromising Positions; David and Lisa; Diary of a Mad Housewife; Hello Again; Last Summer; Mommie Dearest; Monsignor; Rancho Deluxe; Skag; Swimmer, The

Persky, Bill: Serial

Pesce, P. J.: Desperate Trail

Peters, Brooke L.: Unearthly, The

Peters, Charlie: Music from Another Room; Passed Away

Petersen, Wolfgang: Air Force One; Das Boot (The Boat); Enemy Mine; For Your Love Only; In the Line of Fire; Never-Ending Story, The; Outbreak; Perfect Storm, The; Shattered (1991)

Peterson, Kristine: Critters 3; Deadly Dreams; Hard Truth; Kickboxer 5: Redemption; Lower Level; Slaves to the Underground

Petipa, Marius: Don Quixote (1988)

Petit, Christopher: Caribbean Mystery, A; Chinese Boxes

Petri, Elio: Tenth Victim, The

Petrie, Ann: Mother Teresa

Petrie, Daniel: Bay Boy, The; Betsy, The; Bramble Bush, The; Buster and Billie; Calm at Sunset; Cocoon: The Return; Dollmaker, The; Fort Apache—The Bronx; Inherit the Wind

Rankin Jr., Arthur: Around the World in 80 Days (1974); Flight of Dragons, The; Hobbit, The; Last Unicorn, The; Mad, Mad Monsters, The; Twenty Thousand Leagues Under the Sea; Willie McBean and His Magic Machine

Ransen, Mort: Margaret's Museum; Shades of Love: Sincerely, Violet

Ransick, Whitney: Hand Gun

Rao, Krishna: Crossworlds

Raphael, Frederic: Women & Men: Stories of Seduction

Rapp, Philip: Adventures of Topper, The; I Married Joan (TV Series)

Rappaport, Mark: From the Journals of Jean Seberg

Rappeneau, Jean-Paul: Cyrano De Bergerac (1990); Horseman on the Roof, The; Swashbuckler, The (1984)

Rapper, Irving: Adventures of Mark Twain, The (1944); Born Again; Brave One, The; Corn Is Green, The (1945); Deception (1946); Marjorie Morningstar; Miracle, The (1959); Now, Voyager; Rhapsody in Blue; Sextette

Rash, Steve: Buddy Holly Story, The; Can't Buy Me Love; Eddie; Held Up; Queens Logic; Son-in-Law; Under the Rainbow

Raskin, Jay: I Married a Vampire

Raskov, Daniel: Masters of Menace

Rasmussen, Lars: Littlest Viking, The

Rathborne, Tina: Zelly and Me

Ratner, Brett: Money Talks; Rush Hour

Ratoff, Gregory: Adam Had Four Sons; Black Magic (1949); Corsican Brothers, The (1941); Footlight Serenade; Heat's On, The; Intermezzo (1939); Rose of Washington Square

Rautenbach, Jans: No One Cries Forever

Ravenscroft, Alan: Titanic: A Question of Murder

Ravich, Rand: Astronaut's Wife, The

Rawi, Ousama: Housekeeper, The

Rawlins, John: Arabian Nights (1942); Arizona Ranger; Dick Tracy Meets Gruesome; Dick Tracy's Dilemma; Sherlock Holmes and the Voice of Terror; Sudan

Ray, Albert: Shriek in the Night, A; Thirteenth Guest, The

Ray, Bernard B.: Roamin' Wild; Smokey Trails

Ray, Fred Olen: Alien Dead; Alienator; Armed Response; Attack of the 60 Ft. Centerfold; Bad Girls from Mars; Beverly Hills Vamp; Biohazard; Capitol Conspiracy, The; Commando Squad; Cyberzone; Cyclone; Deep Space; Dinosaur Island; Evil Toons; Fugitive Rage; Hollywood Chainsaw Hookers; Inner Sanctum; Inner Sanctum 2; Invisible Dad; Invisible Mom; Maximum Security; Mindtwister; Mob Boss; Operation Condor (Don "The Dragon" Wilson); Phantom Empire, The (1986); Possessed by the Night; Scalps; Spirits; Star Slammer; Tomb, The; Warlords

Ray, Man: Avant Garde Program #2; Man Ray Classic Shorts

Ray, Nicholas: Born to Be Bad; 55 Days at Peking; Flying Leathernecks; In a Lonely Place; Johnny Guitar; King of Kings (1961); Knock on Any Door; Lusty Men, The; On Dangerous Ground (1951); Party Girl (1958); Rebel Without a Cause; They Live By Night; Woman's Secret, A

Ray, Satyajit: Adversary, The; Aparajito; Days and Nights in the Forest; Devi (The Goddess); Distant Thunder (1974); Home and the World; Pather Panchali; Stranger, The (1992); Two Daughters; World of Apu, The

Raye, Michael: Laserblast

Raymond, Alan: Elvis '56; Sweet Home Chicago

Raymond, Jack: Speckled Band, The

Raymond, Susan: Elvis '56; Sweet Home Chicago

Raynr, David: Trippin'; Whatever It Takes

Razatos, Spiro: Class of 1999 II: The Substitute; Fast Getaway

Reardon, John: Whoops Apocalypse

Rebane, Bill: Alpha Incident, The; Blood Harvest

Red, Eric: Bad Moon; Body Parts; Cohen and Tate; Undertow

Redford, Robert: Horse Whisperer, The; Milagro Beanfield War, The; Ordinary People; Quiz Show; River Runs Through It, A

Redmond, Lee: Final Mission (1994)

Reed, Bill: Secret of the Sword, The

Reed, Carol: Agony and the Ecstasy, The; Fallen Idol, The; Immortal Battalion, The (The Way Ahead); Key, The; Kid for Two Farthings, A; Night Train to Munich (Night Train); Odd Man Out; Oliver; Stars Look Down, The; Third Man, The; Trapeze; Unicorn, The

Reed, Jerry: What Comes Around

Reed, Joel M.: Bloodsucking Freaks (The Incredible Torture Show); Night of the Zombies (1981)

Reed, Luther: Dixiana

Reed, Ted: Nut, The

Rees, Clive: Blockhouse, The; When the Whales Came

Rees, Jerry: Brave Little Toaster, The; Marrying Man, The

Reeve, Christopher: In the Gloaming

Reeve, Geoffrey: Caravan to Vaccares; Puppet on a Chain; Souvenir

Reeves, George: TV's Best Adventures of Superman

Reeves, Matt: Pallbearer, The

Reeves, Michael: Conqueror Worm, The; She Beast, The

Regan, Patrick: Kiss Daddy Goodbye

Reggio, Godfrey: Koyaanisqatsi; Powaqqatsi

Reichert, Mark: Union City

Reichmann, Thomas: Mingus

Reid, Alastair: Inspector Morse (TV Series); Shatter (1972); Teamster Boss: The Jackie Presser Story

Reid, Max: Eye of the Snake; Wild Thing

Reid, Tim: Little Mermaid, The (1978); Once Upon a Time ... When We Were Colored

Reilly, William: Men of Respect

Reiner, Carl: All of Me; Bert Rigby, You're a Fool; Dead Men Don't Wear Plaid; Dick Van Dyke Show, The (TV Series); Enter Laughing; Fatal Instinct (1993); Jerk, The; Man with Two Brains, The; Oh, God!; One and Only, The; Sibling Rivalry; Summer Rental; Summer School; That Old Feeling; Where's Poppa?

Reiner, Jeffrey: Blood and Concrete, A Love Story; Evolution's Child; Huntress, The; Serpent's Lair; Trouble Bound

Reiner, Lucas: Spirit of '76, The

Reiner, Rob: American President, The; Few Good Men, A; Ghosts of Mississippi; Misery; North; Princess Bride, The; Stand by Me (1986); Story of Us, The; Sure Thing, The; This Is Spinal Tap; When Harry Met Sally

Reinhardt, Gottfried: Betrayed (1954)

Reinhardt, Max: Midsummer Night's Dream, A (1935)

Reinisch, Deborah: Caught in the Act

Reinl, Harald: Chariots of the Gods; Hell Hounds of Alaska; Torture Chamber of Dr. Sadism, The

Reis, Irving: All My Sons (1948); Bachelor and the Bobby Soxer, The; Big Street, The; Crack-Up; Enchantment; Falcon Takes Over, The; Hitler's Children

Reisner, Allen: All Mine to Give

Reisner, Charles F.: Art of Buster Keaton, The; Steamboat Bill Jr.

Reisz, Karel: Everybody Wins; French Lieutenant's Woman, The; Gambler, The (1974); Isadora (1969); Morgan; Sweet Dreams; Who'll Stop the Rain

Reitherman, Wolfgang: Aristocats, The; Jungle Book, The (1967); One Hundred and One Dalmatians; Rescuers, The; Robin Hood (1973); Sword in the Stone, The; Wind in the Willows, The (1949)

Reitman, Ivan: Dave; Father's Day; Ghostbusters; Ghostbusters II; Junior (1994); Kindergarten Cop; Legal Eagles; Meatballs; Six Days, Seven Nights; Stripes; Twins

Reitz, Edgar: Germany in Autumn

René, Norman: Longtime Companion; Prelude to a Kiss; Reckless (1995)

Renoir, Jean: Boudu Saved from Drowning; Crime of Monsieur Lange, The; Day in the Country, A; Diary of a Chambermaid (1946); Elena and Her Men; Elusive Corporal, The; French Can Can; Golden Coach, The; Grand Illusion; La Bête Humaine; La Chienne; La Marseillaise; Little Theatre of Jean Renoir, The; Lower Depths (1936); Madame Bovary (1934); Picnic on the Grass; River, The (1951); Rules of the Game, The; Southerner, The; Testament of Dr. Cordelier, The; This Land Is Mine; Toni

Resnais, Alain: Hiroshima, Mon Amour; Last Year at Marienbad; Melo; Mon Oncle d'Amerique; Muriel; Providence; Stavisky

Resnick, Adam: Cabin Boy

Resnikoff, Robert: First Power, The

Restaino, Elvis: Bloodsport IV: The Dark Kumite

Revier, Harry: Lost City, The

Revon, Bernard: Rascals, The

Reyes, Buddy: Night of the Kickfighters

Reynolds, Burt: End, The; Gator; Hard Time; Man from Left Field, The; Sharky's Machine; Stick

Reynolds, C.D.H.: Day of Judgment, A

Rocco, Marc: Dream a Little Dream; Murder in the First; Scenes from the Goldmine; Where the Day Takes You
Rocha, Glauber: Black God (White Devil)
Rochat, Eric: Fifth Monkey, The
Roche, Sean: Chasing Dreams
Rockwell, Alexandre: Four Rooms; In the Soup; Somebody to Love
Roddam, Franc: Aria; Bride, The; K2; Lords of Discipline, The; Moby Dick (1998); Quadrophenia; War Party
Rodnunsky, Serge: Dead Tides; Final Equinox; Lovers' Lovers
Rodriguez, Paul: Million to Juan, A
Rodriguez, Robert: Desperado; El Mariachi; Faculty, The; Four Rooms; From Dusk Till Dawn; Roadracers
Roeg, Nicolas: Aria; Castaway; Cold Heaven; Don't Look Now; Eureka; Full Body Massage; Heart of Darkness; Insignificance; Man Who Fell to Earth, The; Performance; Samson and Delilah (1996); Sweet Bird of Youth (1989); Track 29; Two Deaths; Walkabout; Witches, The (1990)
Roemer, Michael: Nothing But a Man; Plot Against Harry, The
Roessler, Rick: Slaughterhouse
Roffman, Julian: Mask, The (1961)
Rogell, Albert S.: Admiral Was a Lady, The; Li'l Abner (1940); Thundering Hoofs; War of the Wildcats
Rogers, Charles R.: Bohemian Girl, The; Devil's Brother, The; Laurel and Hardy Classics: Vol. 1–9
Rogers, Doug: Dennis the Menace: Dinosaur Hunter
Rogers, Maclean: Down Among the "Z" Men
Rogosin, Lionel: Come Back Africa; On the Bowery
Rohmer, Eric: Autumn Tale; Aviator's Wife, The; Boyfriends and Girlfriends; Chloe in the Afternoon; Claire's Knee; Four Adventures of Reinette and Mirabelle; Full Moon in Paris; Le Beau Mariage; My Night at Maud's; Pauline at the Beach; Rendezvous in Paris; Six in Paris (Paris Vue par …); Summer; Tale of Springtime, A
Roley, Sutton: Snatched
Rollin, Jean: Zombie Lake
Rollins, Bernie: Getting Over
Roman, Phil: Tom & Jerry: the Movie; What Next, Charlie Brown?
Romanek, Mark: Static
Romero, Eddie: Beast of the Yellow Night; Beyond Atlantis; Brides of the Beast; Twilight People
Romero, George A.: Crazies, The; Creepshow; Dark Half, The; Dawn of the Dead; Day of the Dead; Knightriders; Martin; Monkey Shines: An Experiment in Fear; Night of the Living Dead (1968); Season of the Witch; Two Evil Eyes
Romero, Joey: Savage Justice
Romine, Charles: Behind Locked Doors
Rondell, Ronnie: No Safe Haven
Roodt, Darrell: Cry, the Beloved Country (1995); Dangerous Ground; Father Hood; Place of Weeping; Sarafina!
Room, Abram: Bed and Sofa
Roos, Don: Opposite of Sex, The
Root, Wells: Bold Caballero, The
Ropelewski, Tom: Look Who's Talking Now; Madhouse (1990)
Roper, Mark: Alien Chaser; Live Wire: Human Timebomb; Warhead
Rose, Bernard: Candyman (1992); Chicago Joe and the Showgirl; Immortal Beloved; Leo Tolstoy's Anna Karenina (1997); Paperhouse
Rose, Lee: Color of Courage, The
Rose, Les: Gas
Rose, Mickey: Student Bodies
Rose, Reuben: Screwball Academy
Rosen, Dan: Dead Man's Curve
Rosen, Gary: Sink or Swim
Rosen, Martin: Plague Dogs, The; Stacking; Watership Down
Rosen, Phil: Charlie Chan in the Secret Service; Chinese Cat, The; Gangs, Inc. (Paper Bullets); Jade Mask, The; Little Men (1935); Meeting at Midnight; Phantom Broadcast, The; Return of the Ape Man; Scarlet Clue, The; Sphinx, The (1933); Spooks Run Wild
Rosen, Robert L.: Raw Courage
Rosenberg, Anita: Assault of the Killer Bimbos
Rosenberg, Craig: Hotel de Love
Rosenberg, Stuart: Amityville Horror, The; April Fools, The; Brubaker; Cool Hand Luke; Drowning Pool, The;

Laughing Policeman, The; Love and Bullets; My Heroes Have Always Been Cowboys; Pocket Money; Pope of Greenwich Village, The; Voyage of the Damned
Rosenberg, Tanya: Blood Games
Rosenbloom, Dale: Shiloh
Rosenblum, Ralph: Any Friend of Nicholas Nickleby Is Friend of Mine; Greatest Man in the World, The; Man That Corrupted Hadleyburg, The
Rosenfeld, Keva: Twenty Bucks
Rosenfelt, Scott: Family Prayers
Rosenthal, Rick: American Dreamer; Bad Boys (1983); Birds II, The: Land's End; Devlin; Distant Thunder (1988); Halloween II; Russkies
Rosenthal, Robert J.: Zapped!
Rosi, Francesco: Big Rip-off, The; Bizet's Carmen; Christ Stopped at Eboli; Lucky Luciano; Palermo Connection, The; Three Brothers; Truce, The
Rosman, Mark: Blue Yonder, The; Evolver; Force, The; House on Sorority Row; Invader, The
Rosner, Mark: Empire City
Ross, Benjamin: RKO 281; Young Poisoner's Handbook, The
Ross, Gary: Pleasantville
Ross, Herbert: Boys on the Side; California Suite; Dancers; Footloose; Funny Lady; Goodbye Girl, The; Goodbye, Mr. Chips (1969); I Ought to Be in Pictures; Last of Sheila, The; Max Dugan Returns; My Blue Heaven; Nijinsky; Owl and the Pussycat, The; Pennies from Heaven; Play It Again, Sam; Protocol; Secret of My Success, The; Seven-Per-Cent Solution, The; Steel Magnolias; Sunshine Boys, The; True Colors; Turning Point, The; Undercover Blues
Rossati, Nello: Sensuous Nurse, The; Tides of War
Rossellini, Roberto: Amore (1948); Fear (1955); General Della Rovere; Open City; Paisan; Rise of Louis XIV, The; Stromboli; Vanina Vanini; Voyage in Italy
Rossen, Robert: Alexander the Great; All the King's Men; Body and Soul (1947); Hustler, The; Lilith; Mambo; They Came to Cordura
Rossi, Franco: Quo Vadis? (1985)
Rosson, Arthur: Long Long Trail
Rostrup, Kaspar: Memories of a Marriage
Roth, Bobby: Baja Oklahoma; Boss' Son, The; Dead Solid Perfect; Game of Love, The; Heartbreakers; Keeper of the City; Man Inside, The (1990); Rainbow Drive
Roth, Joe: Coupe De Ville; Revenge of the Nerds II: Nerds in Paradise; Streets of Gold
Roth, Lynn: Changing Habits
Roth, Phillip: Apex; Digital Man; Prototype X29A; Velocity Trap
Roth, Tim: War Zone, The
Rothman, Stephanie: Student Nurses, The; Terminal Island; Velvet Vampire, The
Rothstein, Richard: Hitchhiker, The (Series)
Rotundo, Nick: Gladiator Cop II: The Swordsman
Rouan, Brigitte: Overseas; Post Coitum
Rouch, Jean: Six in Paris (Paris Vue par …)
Rouffio, Jaques: La Passante
Rouse, Russell: Caper of the Golden Bulls, The; Fastest Gun Alive, The; Oscar, The (1966); Thief, The (1952); Well, The
Rowe, George: Fatal Mission
Rowe, Peter: Lost!
Rowland, E. G.: Final Defeat, The
Rowland, Roy: Bugles in the Afternoon; Five Thousand Fingers of Dr. T, The; Girl Hunters, The; Hit the Deck; Hollywood Party; Meet Me in Las Vegas; Our Vines Have Tender Grapes; Seven Hills of Rome, The; Two Weeks with Love
Royle, David: Mafia: The History of the Mob in America
Rozema, Patricia: I've Heard the Mermaids Singing; Mansfield Park; When Night is Falling
Ruane, John: Death in Brunswick
Rubbo, Michael: Peanut Butter Solution, The
Ruben, Andy: Club Vampire
Ruben, J. Walter: Ace of Aces; RiffRaff (1936)
Ruben, Joseph: Dreamscape; Good Son, The; Gorp; Joyride (1977); Money Train; Return to Paradise (1998); Sister-in-Law, The (1974); Sleeping with the Enemy; Stepfather, The; True Believer
Ruben, Katt Shea: Dance of the Damned; Last Exit to Earth; Poison Ivy (1992); Streets
Rubens, Percival: Survival Zone; Sweet Murder

Rubie, Howard: Island Trader
Rubin, Bruce Joel: My Life
Rubin, C. B.: Fraternity Demon
Rubini, Sergio: Station, The
Rubino, John: Lotto Land
Rudnick, B. A.: Expose
Rudolph, Alan: Afterglow; Choose Me; Endangered Species; Equinox (1993); Love at Large; Made in Heaven (1987); Mrs. Parker and the Vicious Circle; Moderns, The; Mortal Thoughts; Nightmare Circus (Barn of the Living Dead) (Terror Circus); Songwriter; Trouble in Mind; Welcome to L.A.
Rudolph, Louis: Double Standard
Rudolph, Oscar: Brady Bunch, The (TV series); Twist Around the Clock
Ruggles, Wesley: Arizona; Cimarron (1931); I'm No Angel; No Man of Her Own; Somewhere I'll Find You
Ruiz, Raúl: Genealogies of a Crime; Shattered Image (1998)
Ruiz, Raúl: On Top of the Whale; Three Lives and Only One Death
Rumar, Craig T.: Instant Justice
Rundle, Robert: Cybernator
Rupe, Katja: Germany In Autumn
Rush, Richard: Color of Night; Freebie and the Bean; Getting Straight; Hell's Angels on Wheels; Psych-Out; Stunt Man, The
Ruskin, Coby: When Things Were Rotten (TV Series)
Rusnak, Josef: Thirteenth Floor, The (1999)
Russell, Charles: Blob, The (1988); Eraser; Mask, The (1994); Nightmare on Elm Street 3, A: The Dream Warriors
Russell, David O.: Flirting with Disaster; Spanking the Monkey; Three Kings
Russell, Jay: End of the Line; My Dog Skip
Russell, Ken: Altered States; Boy Friend, The; Crimes of Passion; Dante's Inferno; Devils, The; Gothic; Lair of the White Worm; Lisztomania; Mahler; Music Lovers, The; Prisoner of Honor; Rainbow, The; Salome's Last Dance; Savage Messiah; Tales of Erotica; Tommy; Tracked; Valentino; Whore; Women & Men: Stories of Seduction; Women in Love
Russell, William D.: Best of the Badmen; Green Promise, The; Hazel Christmas Show, The, (TV Series)
Russo, Aaron: Rude Awakening (1989)
Russo, John: Heartstopper; Midnight (1980); Midnight 2; Santa Claws
Rust, John: Smurfs and the Magic Flute, The
Rustam, Mardi: Evils of the Night
Ruzowitzky, Stefan: Inheritors, The
Ryan, Frank: Call Out the Marines; Can't Help Singing
Ryan, Terence: Brylcreem Boys, The
Ryan, William: Reach the Rock
Ryazanov, Eldar: Forgotten Tune for the Flute, A
Rydell, Mark: Cinderella Liberty; Cowboys, The; Crime of the Century; For the Boys; Harry and Walter Go to New York; Intersection; On Golden Pond; Reivers, The; River, The (1984); Rose, The
Rye, Renny: Poirot (Series)
Ryman, John: Galaxies Are Colliding
Rymer, Judy: Who Killed Baby Azaria?
Rymer, Michael: Angel Baby; In Too Deep
Sabal, Rob: Escape to White Mountain
Sabella, Paul: All Dogs Go to Heaven 2
Sachs, William: Galaxina; Hitz; Incredible Melting Man, The; Last Hour, The
Sacks, Alan: Du-Beat-E-O
Saeta, Eddie: Dr. Death: Seeker of Souls
Safran, Henri: Norman Loves Rose; Wild Duck, The
Sagal, Boris: Angela; Dial M for Murder (1981); Girl Happy; Ike: The War Years; Masada; Night Gallery; Omega Man, The; Peter Gunn (TV Series)
Sagan, Leontine: Maedchen in Uniform
Saget, Bob: Dirty Work (1998)
Saia, Louis: Boys, The (1997)
St. Clair, Malcolm: Are Parents People?; Bullfighters, The; Buster Keaton Festival Vol. 1–3; Show-Off, The (1926)
Saks, Gene: Barefoot in the Park; Brighton Beach Memoirs; Cactus Flower; Fine Romance, A; Last of the Red Hot Lovers; Mame; Odd Couple, The
Sala, H.: Nightmare Weekend
Sale, Richard: Let's Make It Legal

Sales, Leander: Don't Let Your Meat Loaf
Salkow, Sidney: City Without Men; Last Man on Earth, The; Twice-Told Tales
Salle, David: Search and Destroy (1995)
Salles Jr., Walter: Central Station; Exposure
Salomon, Mikael: Far Off Place, A; Hard Rain
Saltzman, Mark: Three Ninjas Kick Back
Salva, Victor: Clownhouse; Nature of the Beast; Powder; Rites of Passage
Salvador, Jaime: Boom in the Moon
Salvatores, Gabriele: Mediterraneo
Salwen, Hal: Denise Calls Up
Salzman, Barnard: Diamondbacks
Salzman, Glen: Rubberface
Samperi, Salvatore: Malicious (1974)
Samples, Keith: Smile Like Yours, A
Samson, Barry: Ice Runner; Yesterday's Target
Samuels, Stuart: Rockin' Ronnie
Samuelson, G. B.: She (1925)
San Fernando, Manuel: Rock 'n' Roll Wrestling Women vs. the Aztec Mummy
Sanchez, Eduardo: Blair Witch Project, The
Sanders, Denis: Elvis—That's the Way It Is; Invasion of the Bee Girls; One Man's Way
Sandgren, Ake: Slingshot, The
Sandrich, Jay: For Richer, for Poorer; Seems Like Old Times
Sandrich, Mark: Aggie Appleby, Maker of Men; Buck Benny Rides Again; Carefree; Cockeyed Cavaliers; Follow the Fleet; Gay Divorcée, The; Here Come the Waves; Hips, Hips, Hooray; Holiday Inn; Melody Cruise; Shall We Dance? (1937); So Proudly We Hail; Top Hat; Woman Rebels, A
Sands, Sompote: Crocodile
Sands, Trevor: Suicide Ride
Sanford, Arlene: I'll Be Home for Christmas; Very Brady Sequel, A
Sanforth, Clifford: Murder by Television
Sanger, Jonathan: Code Name: Emerald; Down Came a Blackbird
Sangster, Jimmy: Dynasty of Fear; Fear in the Night (Dynasty of Fear); Horror of Frankenstein; Lust for a Vampire
Santamaran, Enrick: Playgirl Killer, The
Santell, Alfred: Hairy Ape, The; Having a Wonderful Time; Interns Can't Take Money; Jack London; Winterset
Santiago, Cirio H.: Angel Fist; Beyond the Call of Duty; Caged Heat 2: Stripped of Freedom; Demon of Paradise; Devastator, The; Dune Warriors; Eye of the Eagle; Eye of the Eagle 3; Field of Fire; Final Mission (1984); Firehawk; Future Hunters; Kill Zone; Live by the Fist; Naked Vengeance; One Man Army; Raiders of the Sun; Silk 2; Sisterhood, The; Stranglehold; Stryker; TNT Jackson; Vampire Hookers (Sensuous Vampires); Wheels of Fire
Santley, Joseph: Cocoanuts; Harmony Lane; Melody Ranch
Santostefano, Damon: Severed Ties; Three to Tango
Saperstein, David: Beyond the Stars; Killing Affair, A
Sarafian, Deran: Alien Predators; Back in the U.S.S.R.; Death Warrant; Gunmen; Interzone; Road Killers, The; Terminal Velocity; To Die For (1989)
Sarafian, Richard C.: Eye of the Tiger; Gangster Wars; I Spy (TV Series); Man in the Wilderness; Man Who Loved Cat Dancing, The; Street Justice; Sunburn; Vanishing Point
Sargent, Joseph: Abraham; Caroline?; Coast to Coast; Colossus: The Forbin Project; Day One; Goldengirl; Hustling; Incident, The (1989); Ivory Hunters; Jaws: The Revenge; MacArthur; Man from U.N.C.L.E., The (TV Series); Man on a String; Mandela and De Klerk; Memorial Day; Miss Evers' Boys; Miss Rose White; My Antonia; Never Forget; Nightmares; Of Pure Blood; Passion Flower; Skylark; Streets of Laredo; Taking of Pelham One Two Three, The; Tomorrow's Child; Tribes; Wall, The (1998) (U.S.); White Lightning
Sargenti, Marina: Child of Darkness, Child of Light; Mirror Mirror
Sarin, Vic: Cold Comfort; Hearts Adrift; In His Father's Shoes; Legend of Gator Face, The; Sea People; Spenser: Pale Kings & Princes; Wounded Heart
Sarne, Michael: Myra Breckenridge
Sarno, Jonathan: Plants Are Watching, The
Sasdy, Peter: Devil Within Her, The; Devil's Undead, The; Doomwatch; Hands of the Ripper; King Arthur, The Young

Schultz, Michael: Car Wash; Carbon Copy; Cooley High; Disorderlies; For Us the Living: The Medgar Evers Story; Greased Lightning; Great American Sex Scandal, The; Killers in the House; Krush Groove; Last Dragon, The; Livin' Large; Scavenger Hunt; Sgt. Pepper's Lonely Hearts Club Band; Time Stalkers; Which Way Is Up?

Schulz, Bob: Robbers of the Sacred Mountain

Schulze, Douglas: Hellmaster

Schumacher, Joel: Batman Forever; Batman & Robin; Client, The; Cousins, The; D.C. Cab; Dying Young; 8MM; Falling Down; Flatliners; Flawless; Incredible Shrinking Woman, The; Lost Boys, The; St. Elmo's Fire; Time to Kill, A (1996)

Schunzel, Reinhold: Balalaika; Fortune's Fool; Melody Master (The Great Awakening) (New Wine)

Schuster, Harold: Breakfast in Hollywood; Dinner at the Ritz; Finger Man (1955); Marine Raiders; My Friend Flicka; So Dear to My Heart; Tender Years, The

Schuttes, Jan: Dragon Chow

Schwartz, Douglas: Baywatch: The Movie; Thunder in Paradise II; Thunder in Paradise

Schwartz, Maurice: Tevye

Schwartz, Stefan: Shooting Fish

Schwarzenegger, Arnold: Christmas in Connecticut (1992)

Schwimmer, David: Since You've Been Gone

Sciamma, Alberto: Killer Tongue

Scoffield, Jon: To See Such Fun

Scola, Ettore: Down and Dirty; Family, The (1987); La Nuit de Varennes; Le Bal; Macaroni; Passion of Love; Special Day, A; We All Loved Each Other So Much

Scorsese, Martin: After Hours; Age of Innocence, The; Alice Doesn't Live Here Anymore; Boxcar Bertha; Bringing Out the Dead; Cape Fear (1991); Casino (1995); Color of Money, The; Goodfellas; King of Comedy, The; Kundun; Last Temptation of Christ, The; Last Waltz, The; Mean Streets; New York, New York; New York Stories; Raging Bull; Taxi Driver; Two by Scorsese; Who's That Knocking at My Door?

Scott, Campbell: Big Night

Scott, Cynthia: Strangers in Good Company

Scott, Darin: Love & a .45

Scott, Gene: Windjammer

Scott, Gene: Mystery Island

Scott, George C.: Andersonville Trial, The; Rage (1972); Savage Is Loose, The

Scott, Jake: Plunkett & Macleane

Scott, James: Strike It Rich

Scott, Michael: Dangerous Heart; Heck's Way Home; Ladykiller; Sharon's Secret

Scott, Oz: Bustin' Loose

Scott, Ridley: Alien; Black Rain (1989); Blade Runner; Duellists, The; 1492: The Conquest of Paradise; G.I. Jane; Gladiator (2000); Legend; Someone to Watch Over Me; Thelma & Louise; White Squall

Scott, T.J.: TC 2000; Young Hercules

Scott, Tony: Beverly Hills Cop II; Crimson Tide; Days of Thunder; Enemy of the State; Fan, The (1996); Hunger, The (1983); Last Boy Scout, The; Revenge (1990); Top Gun; True Romance

Scribner, George: Oliver & Company

Seacat, Sandra: In the Spirit

Seagal, Steven: On Deadly Ground

Seale, James: Asylum (1996)

Seale, John: Till There Was You

Sears, Fred F.: Earth vs. the Flying Saucers; Giant Claw, The

Sears, Phil: Ripper Man

Seaton, George: Airport; Big Lift, The; Counterfeit Traitor, The; Country Girl, The (1954); Little Boy Lost; Miracle on 34th Street (1947); Showdown (1973); Teacher's Pet; 36 Hours

Sebastian, Beverly: Delta Fox; Flash and the Firecat; Gator Bait II—Cajun Justice; Rocktober Blood; Running Cool

Sebastian, Ferd: Delta Fox; Flash and the Firecat; Gator Bait II—Cajun Justice; Hitchhikers; Rocktober Blood; Running Cool

Sebastian, Jonathan: Voyage to the Prehistoric Planet

Sedan, Mike: Lap Dancing; Married People, Single Sex; Night Fire

Sedgwick, Edward: Air Raid Wardens; Beware of Spooks; Cameraman, The; Doughboys; Free and Easy; Ma and Pa Kettle Back on the Farm; Movie Struck (Pick a Star); Parlor, Bedroom and Bath; Riding on Air; Southern Yankee, A; Speak Easily; Spite Marriage; What! No Beer?

Sedwick, John: Best of Dark Shadows, The; Dark Shadows (TV Series)

Seed, Paul: Affair, The (1995); Dead Ahead: The Exxon Valdez Disaster

Seely, Bob: Rover Dangerfield

Segal, Alex: No Time for Sergeants (Television); Story of David, The

Segal, Peter: My Fellow Americans; Naked Gun 33 1/3, The—The Final Insult; Tommy Boy

Segall, Stuart: Drive-In Massacre; Illegal in Blue

Seidelman, Arthur Allan: Body Language (1992); Caller, The; Children of Rage; Dying to Remember; Friendship in Vienna, A; Glory Years; Grace and Glorie; Harvest of Fire; Hercules Goes Bananas; Kid Who Loved Christmas, The; Macbeth (1981); Poker Alice; Rescue Me; Summer of Ben Tyler, The; Trapped in Space

Seidelman, Susan: Cookie; Cooler Climate, A; Desperately Seeking Susan; Making Mr. Right; She-Devil; Smithereens; Tales of Erotica

Seiler, Lewis: Charlie Chan in Paris; Doll Face; Guadalcanal Diary; Here Comes Trouble; Pittsburgh; Smiling Ghost, The; Tanks Are Coming, The; Winning Team, The

Seiter, William A.: Allegheny Uprising; Big Business Girl; Dimples; Diplomaniacs; Four Jills in a Jeep; In Person; It's a Date; Lady Takes a Chance, A; Little Giant; Make Haste to Live; One Touch of Venus; Roberta; Room Service; Sons of the Desert; Stowaway; Susannah of the Mounties; This Is My Affair; Way Back Home; You Were Never Lovelier

Seitz, George B.: Andy Hardy Meets a Debutante; Andy Hardy's Double Life; Andy Hardy's Private Secretary; Danger Lights; Drums of Jeopardy; Fighting Ranger, The; Kit Carson; Last of the Mohicans, The (1936); Life Begins for Andy Hardy; Love Finds Andy Hardy; Vanishing American, The

Seitzman, Michael: Farmer and Chase

Sekely, Steve: Day of the Triffids, The; Revenge of the Zombies; Scar, The; Waterfront

Selander, Lesley: Arizona Bushwhackers; Border Patrol; Brothers in the Saddle; Buckskin Frontier; Doomed Caravan; Fighter Attack; Flat Top; Flight to Mars; Fort Osage; Forty Thieves; Guns of Hate; Heart of Arizona; Hellgate of the Desert; Hidden Gold; Hopalong Rides Again; Lone Ranger and the Lost City of Gold, The; Mysterious Desperado; Out California Way; Phantom of the Plains; Pirates on Horseback; Range War; Renegade Trail; Rider from Tucson; Riders of the Timberline; Road Agent; Robin Hood of Texas; Rustlers, The; Santa Fe Marshal; Sheriff of Las Vegas; Short Grass; Shotgun; Silver on the Sage; Stagecoach War; Stampede; Stick to Your Guns; Three Men from Texas; Wide-Open Town

Selick, Henry: James and the Giant Peach; Nightmare Before Christmas, The

Selignac, Arnaud: Eye of the Wolf; Northern Passage

Sell, Jack M.: Deadly Spygames

Sellier Jr., Charles E.: Annihilators, The; Silent Night, Deadly Night

Selman, David: Fighting Shadows; Texas Trail

Seltzer, David: Lucas; Punchline; Shining Through

Selwyn, Edgar: Sin of Madelon Claudet, The; Skyscraper Souls

Selznick, Aran: Care Bears Movie, The

Semler, Dean: Firestorm

Sena, Dominic: Gone in 60 Seconds; Kalifornia

Senelka, Peter: Teen Alien

Senensky, Ralph: Dream for Christmas, A

Sennett, Mack: Charlie Chaplin ... Our Hero; Dough and Dynamite/Knockout, The; These Girls Won't Talk

Sequi, Mario: Cobra, The (1967)

Sereny, Eva: Foreign Student

Seresin, Michael: Homeboy

Serious, Yahoo: Reckless Kelly; Young Einstein

Serreau, Coline: Mama, There's a Man in Your Bed; Three Men and a Cradle

Sessa, Alex: Amazons; Stormquest

Setbon, Philip: Mr. Frost

Sewell, Vernon: Blood Beast Terror, The; Curse of the Crimson Altar; Ghost Ship; Ghosts of Berkeley Square; Horrors of Burke and Hare

Seymour, Jeff: Rave Review

Sgarro, Nicholas: Fortune Dane; Happy Hooker, The

Shackleton, Michael: Survivor

Shadburne, Susan: Shadow Play

Shade, John: Swap, The (Sam's Song)

Shadyac, Tom: Ace Ventura: Pet Detective; Liar, Liar; Nutty Professor, The (1996); Patch Adams

Shafer, Dirk: Man of the Year

Shah, Krishna: Hard Rock Zombies

Shaner, Pete: Lover's Knot

Shanley, John Patrick: Joe Versus the Volcano

Shaoul, Jack: Robot in the Family

Shapiro, Alan: Crush, The (1993); Flipper (1996); Tiger Town

Shapiro, Ken: Groove Tube, The; Modern Problems

Shapiro, Paul: Dead Husbands; Heads; Invaders, The; Kurt Vonnegut's Monkey House; Lotus Eaters, The

Sharman, Jim: Rocky Horror Picture Show, The; Shock Treatment

Sharp, Alan: Little Treasure

Sharp, Don: Bear Island; Curse of the Fly; Dark Places; Four Feathers, The (1978); Guardian of the Abyss; Hennessy; Hold the Dream; Kiss of the Vampire; Psychomania; Rasputin: The Mad Monk; Thirty-Nine Steps, The (1978); What Waits Below; Woman of Substance, A

Sharp, Ian: Codename: Kyril; Final Option, The; Robin Hood and the Sorcerer; Secret Weapon

Sharpstein, Ben: Dumbo

Shatner, William: Star Trek V: The Final Frontier; Tekwar: The Original Movie

Shaughnessy, Alfred: Cat Girl

Shavelson, Melville: Cast a Giant Shadow; Five Pennies, The; Houseboat; Ike: The War Years; It Started in Naples; Legend of Valentino; New Kind of Love, A; Seven Little Foys, The; Yours, Mine and Ours

Shaver, Helen: Summer's End

Shaye, Robert: Book of Love

Shayne, Linda: Little Ghost; Purple People Eater

Shbib, Bashar: Julia Has Two Lovers

Shea, Jack: Dayton's Devils

Shea, James K.: Planet of the Dinosaurs

Shea, John: Southie

Shea, Katt: Rage, The; Carrie 2

Shear, Barry: Across 110th Street; Crash of Flight 401; Deadly Trackers, The; Night Gallery; Strike Force; Todd Killings, The; Wild in the Streets

Shebib, Donald: Ascent, The; Climb, The; Fish Hawk; Heartaches; Little Kidnappers; Pathfinder, The; Running Brave

Sheen, Martin: Cadence

Sheen, Simon S.: Three Ninjas Knuckle Up

Sheerer, Robert: Ants!

Sheets, Todd: Bimbos B.C.; Dominion (1994); Edgar Allan Poe's Madhouse; Goblin; Moonchild; Prehistoric Bimbos in Armageddon City; Shivers, The; Violent New Breed; Zombie Bloodbath; Zombie Bloodbath 2

Sheff, Stanley: Lobster Man from Mars

Shelach, Riki: Last Winter, The; Mercenary Fighters

Sheldon, David: Lovely But Deadly

Shelton, Millicent: Ride

Shelton, Ron: Blaze; Bull Durham; Cobb; Play It to the Bone; Tin Cup; White Men Can't Jump

Shelton, Toby: Return of Jafar, The

Shepard, Gerald S.: Heroes Die Young

Shepard, Richard: Cool Blue; Linguini Incident, The; Mercy; Oxygen

Shepard, Sam: Far North; Silent Tongue

Shepphird, John: Snowboard Academy; Teenage Bonnie and Klepto Clyde

Sher, Jack: Three Worlds of Gulliver, The

Sheridan, Jim: Boxer, The; Field, The; In the Name of the Father; My Left Foot

Sheridan, Michael J.: That's Entertainment! III

Sherin, Edwin: My Old Man's Place; Valdez Is Coming

Sherman, Cindy: Office Killer

Sherman, Eric: Trained to Fight

Sherman, Gary A.: After the Shock; Dead and Buried; Lisa; Murderous Vision; Poltergeist III; Raw Meat; Vice Squad; Wanted: Dead or Alive

Sherman, George: Against All Flags; Big Jake; Colorado Sunset; Comanche Territory; Covered Wagon Days; Fron-

tier Horizon; Kansas Cyclone; Kansas Terrors; Last of the Redmen; Lone Star Raiders; Mexicali Rose; Night Riders, The; Outlaws of Sonora; Overland Stage Raiders; Pals of the Saddle; Panic Button; Red River Range; Riders of the Black Hills; Rocky Mountain Rangers; Santa Fe Stampede; South of the Border; Three Texas Steers; Trail Blazers; Treasure of Pancho Villa, The; Tulsa Kid; Under Texas Skies; War Arrow; Wyoming Outlaw

Sherman, Jon: Breathing Room

Sherman, Lowell: Bachelor Apartment; Morning Glory (1933); She Done Him Wrong; Three Broadway Girls

Sherman, Vincent: Adventures of Don Juan, The; Affair in Trinidad; All Through the Night; Bogie; Hard Way, The (1942); Ice Palace; Lady of the House; Lone Star (1952); Mr. Skeffington; Return of Dr. X; Young Philadelphians, The

Shervan, Amir: Hollywood Cop

Sherwood, Bill: Parting Glances

Sherwood, John: Creature Walks Among Us, The; Monolith Monsters, The

Shibayama, Tsutomu: Ranma (TV Series)

Shields, Brent: Cupid and Cate; Durango

Shields, Frank: Project: Alien; Savage Attraction

Shields, Pat: Frasier the Lovable Lion (Frasier the Sensuous Lion)

Shigeru, Morikawa: Kimagure Orange Road, Vols. 1—4

Shils, Barry: Motorama; Wigstock: The Movie

Shilton, Gilbert: Kurt Vonnegut's Monkey House

Shima, Koji: Golden Demon

Shin, Nelson: Transformers, the Movie

Shindo, Kaneto: Island, The (1962); Onibaba

Shing, Sung Kam: Mr. Vampire (Vol. 1—4)

Shinoda, Masahiro: Double Suicide; Gonza the Spearman; MacArthur's Children

Shire, Talia: One Night Stand (1995)

Sholder, Jack: Alone in the Dark; By Dawn's Early Light; Hidden, The; Nightmare on Elm Street 2, A: Freddy's Revenge; Renegades; Sketch Artist II: Hands That See; 12:01; Vietnam War Story—Part Two; Wishmaster 2: Evil Never Dies

Sholem, Lee: Cheyenne (TV Series); Hell Ship Mutiny; Ma and Pa Kettle at Waikiki; Redhead from Wyoming, The; Superman and the Mole Men; Tobor the Great

Shonteff, Lindsay: Devil Doll (1963); Killing Edge, The; Number One of the Secret Service

Shoor, Richard: Witches' Brew

Shore, Sig: Act, The; Return of Superfly, The; Sudden Death (1986); Survivalist, The

Shore, Simon: Get Real

Shores, Lynn: Charlie Chan at the Wax Museum; Shadow Strikes, The

Shum, Mina: Double Happiness

Shumlin, Herman: Watch on the Rhine

Shustak, Allan: Midnight Confessions

Shyamalan, M. Night: Sixth Sense, The; Wide Awake

Shyer, Charles: Baby Boom; Father of the Bride (1991); Father of the Bride Part II; I Love Trouble; Irreconcilable Differences

Shyman, James: Slash Dance

Sibay, Mussef: Woman, Her Men and Her Futon, A

Sichel, Alex: All over Me

Sidaris, Andy: Day of the Warrior; Fit to Kill; Hard Ticket to Hawaii; Malibu Express; Return to Savage Beach; Savage Beach

Siddon, David: Their Only Chance

Sidney, George: Anchors Aweigh; Annie Get Your Gun; Bathing Beauty; Bye Bye Birdie; Cass Timberlane; Eddy Duchin Story, The; Half a Sixpence; Harvey Girls, The; Holiday in Mexico; Jupiter's Darling; Key to the City; Kiss Me Kate; Pal Joey; Scaramouche; Show Boat (1951); Thousands Cheer; Three Musketeers, The (1948); Viva Las Vegas; Young Bess

Sidney, Scott: Madame Behave; Tarzan of the Apes

Siegel, David: Suture

Siegel, Don: Annapolis Story, An; Beguiled, The; Big Steal, The; Black Windmill, The; Charley Varrick; Coogan's Bluff; Dirty Harry; Escape from Alcatraz; Flaming Star; Hell Is for Heroes; Invasion of the Body Snatchers (1956); Jinxed; Killers, The; Madigan; Private Hell 36; Riot in Cell Block Eleven; Rough Cut; Shootist, The; Telefon; Two Mules for Sister Sara

Sigl, Robert: Gigashadow

Signorelli, James: Easy Money; Elvira, Mistress of the Dark; Hotel Room

Sijie, Dai: China, My Sorrow

Silberg, Joel: Bad Guys; Breakin'; Catch the Heat; Lambada; Rappin'

Silberling, Brad: Casper; City of Angels

Silver, Andrew: Return (1984)

Silver, Joan Micklin: Bernice Bobs Her Hair; Between the Lines; Big Girls Don't Cry—They Get Even; Chilly Scenes of Winter; Crossing Delancey; Finnegan Begin Again; Hester Street; In the Presence of Mine Enemies; Loverboy; Prison Stories: Women on the Inside; Private Matter, A

Silver, Marisa: He Said, She Said; Indecency; Old Enough; Permanent Record; Vital Signs

Silver, Raphael D.: On the Yard

Silver, Ron: Lifepod

Silver, Scott: Johns; Mod Squad, The

Silverstein, Elliot: Car, The; Cat Ballou; Flashfire; Man Called Horse, A

Silvester, Dario: Between God, the Devil and a Winchester

Simandl, Lloyd A.: Dangerous Prey; Last of the Warriors; Ultimate Desires

Simenon, Marc: By the Blood of Others

Simeone, Lawrence L.: Blindfold: Acts of Obsession; Cop-Out; Eyes of the Beholder

Simmonds, Allen: Striker's Mountain

Simmons, Anthony: Little Sweetheart

Simmons, Kendrick: Celebrating Bird: The Triumph of Charlie Parker

Simo, Sandor: Train Killer, The

Simon, Adam: Brain Dead; Carnosaur

Simon, Francis: Chicken Chronicles, The

Simon, Juan Piquer: Cthulhu Mansion; Endless Descent; Pieces; Slugs, the Movie

Simon, Roger L.: Lies & Whispers; My Man Adam

Simon, S. Sylvan: Abbott and Costello in Hollywood; Fuller Brush Man, The; Lust for Gold; Rio Rita; Son of Lassie; Whistling in Brooklyn; Whistling in Dixie; Whistling in the Dark

Simone, Lawrence: Presumed Guilty

Simoneau, Yves: Amelia Earhart: The Final Flight; Blind Trust (Pouvoir. Intime); Dead Man's Walk; Free Money; Memphis; Mother's Boys; Perfectly Normal; 36 Hours to Die; Till Death Do Us Part

Simons, Edward: Endurance (1985)

Simpson, Jane: Little Witches; Number One Fan

Simpson, Megan: Alex

Simpson, Michael A.: Fast Food; Funland; Impure Thoughts; Sleepaway Camp II: Unhappy Campers; Sleepaway Camp III

Simpson, Peter: Prom Night III—Last Kiss

Sinatra, Frank: None But the Brave

Sinclair, Andrew: Tuxedo Warrior; Under Milk Wood

Sindell, Gerald: H.O.T.S.

Singer, Alexander: Bunco; Captain Apache; Lost in Space (TV Series); Love Has Many Faces

Singer, Bryan: Apt Pupil; Public Access; Usual Suspects, The

Singleton, John: Boyz N the Hood; Higher Learning; Poetic Justice; Rosewood; Shaft (2000)

Singleton, Ralph S.: Stephen King's Graveyard Shift (1990)

Sinise, Gary: Miles from Home; Of Mice and Men (1992); True West

Sinkel, Bernhard: Germany In Autumn

Sinofsky, Bruce: Brother's Keeper; Paradise Lost: The Child Murders at Robin Hood Hills

Sinyor, Gary: Bachelor, The (1999); Leon the Pig Farmer; Solitaire for 2

Siodmak, Curt: Bride of the Gorilla; Magnetic Monster, The

Siodmak, Robert: Cobra Woman; Crimson Pirate, The; Criss Cross (1948); Dark Mirror, The; Son of Dracula (1943); Spiral Staircase, The (1946); Strange Affair of Uncle Harry, The

Sipes, Andrew: Fair Game (1995)

Sirk, Douglas: All I Desire; All That Heaven Allows; Battle Hymn; Imitation of Life; Magnificent Obsession; Tarnished Angels, The; Time to Love and a Time to Die, A; Written on the Wind

Sissel, Sandi: Chicken Ranch

Sitch, Rob: Castle, The (1997)

Sivan, Santosh: Terrorist, The

Sivo, Yuri: Mortal Sins (1990) (Dangerous Obsession)

Sjoberg, Alf: Miss Julie

Sjoman, Vilgot: I Am Curious Blue; I Am Curious Yellow

Sjorgen, John: Money to Burn; Mosaic Project, The; Red Line

Sjöström, Victor: He Who Gets Slapped; Outlaw and His Wife, The; Phantom Chariot; Scarlet Letter, The (1926); Wind, The (1928)

Skerritt, Tom: Divided by Hate

Skjoldbjærg, Erik: Insomnia

Skogland, Kari: Children of the Corn 666: Isaac's Return

Skolimowski, Jerzy: Deep End; King, Queen and Knave; Le Départ; Lightship, The; Moonlighting (1983); Shout, The (1979); Success Is the Best Revenge; Torrents of Spring

Skoog, Susan: Whatever

Slapczynski, Richard: Adventures of Sinbad, The; Through the Looking Glass

Slater, Christian: Anything for Love

Slater, Guy: Pocketful of Rye, A

Slatzer, Robert F.: Big Foot; Hellcats, The

Sloan, Brian: I Think I Do

Sloan, Holly Goldberg: Big Green, The

Sloan, Victoria: Shrieker

Sloane, Paul: Consolation Marriage; Terror Aboard

Sloane, Rick: Visitants, The

Slocum, James: American Summer, An

Slovin, Karl: Sex and the Other Man

Sluizer, George: Crimetime; Utz; Vanishing, The (1988); Vanishing, The (1993)

Smallcombe, John: African Dream, An

Smart, Ralph: Quartet (1948)

Smawley, Robert J.: American Eagle; River of Diamonds

Smight, Jack: Airport 1975; Damnation Alley (Survival Run); Fast Break; Harper; Illustrated Man, The; Intimate Power; Loving Couples; Midway; No Way to Treat a Lady; Number One with a Bullet; Rabbit Run; Roll of Thunder, Hear My Cry; Secret War of Harry Frigg, The

Smiley, Rob: Our Friend, Martin

Smith, Bernie: You Bet Your Life (TV Series)

Smith, Brian J.: Body of Influence 2

Smith, Bruce: Bebe's Kids

Smith, Bud: Johnny Be Good

Smith, Charles Martin: Air Bud; Boris and Natasha; Fifty/Fifty; Trick or Treat (1986)

Smith, Chris: American Movie

Smith, Cliff: Ace Drummond

Smith, Clive: Pippi Longstocking; Rock and Rule

Smith, Gregg: Cover Story

Smith, Howard: Marjoe

Smith, John N.: Boys of St. Vincent; Cool, Dry Place, A; Dangerous Minds; Sugartime

Smith, Kevin: Chasing Amy; Clerks; Dogma; Mall Rats

Smith, Marshall: Satan's Bed

Smith, Mel: Bean; Radioland Murders; Tall Guy, The

Smith, Peter: No Surrender

Smith, Richard Dana: Dentist 2, The: Brace Yourself

Smith, Roy Allen: Land Before Time II, The; Land Before Time III, The

Smith, Yvonne: Ray Charles: The Genius of Soul

Smithee, Alan: Appointment with Fear; Bloodsucking Pharaohs in Pittsburgh; Call of the Wild (1992); Death of a Gunfighter; Fatal Charm; Ghost Fever; Gypsy Angels; Hellraiser: Bloodline; I Love N.Y.; Let's Get Harry; Morgan Stewart's Coming Home; O. J. Simpson Story, The; Raging Angels; Red Shoe Diaries 4: Auto Erotica; Shrimp on the Barbie; Solar Crisis; Stitches; Sub Down

Smoke, Stephen: Final Impact; Street Crimes

Smolan, Sandy: Rachel River

Snedon, Greg: Dunera Boys, The

Snider, Skott: Miracle Beach

Snyder, Robert: Henry Miller Odyssey

Soavi, Michele: Church, The; Dellamorte, Dellamore; Sect, The

Sobel, Mark: Access Code; Ordeal in the Arctic; Sweet Revenge (1987); Trial & Error (1992)

Soderbergh, Steven: Erin Brockovich; Fallen Angels; Kafka; King of the Hill; Limey, The; Out of Sight; Schizopolis; sex, lies and videotape; Underneath, The

Softley, Iain: BackBeat; East Is East; Hackers; Wings of the Dove, The

The; Gunga Din; I Remember Mama; Kentucky Kernels; More the Merrier, The; Penny Serenade; Place in the Sun, A; Quality Street; Shane; Swing Time; Talk of the Town, The; Vivacious Lady; Woman of the Year

Stevens Jr., George: Separate But Equal

Stevens, Robert: Never Love a Stranger

Stevenson, Andy: Knights and Armor

Stevenson, Rick: Magic in the Water, The

Stevenson, Robert: Absent-Minded Professor, The; Bed-knobs and Broomsticks; Blackbeard's Ghost; Darby O'Gill and the Little People; Dishonored Lady; Forever and a Day; Gnome-Mobile, The; Herbie Rides Again; In Search of the Castaways; Island at the Top of the World, The; Jane Eyre (1944); Joan of Paris; Johnny Tremain; Kidnapped (1960); King Solomon's Mines (1937); Las Vegas Story, The; Love Bug, The; Man Who Lived Again, The; Mary Poppins; Misadventures of Merlin Jones, The; Monkey's Uncle, The; My Forbidden Past; Nine Days a Queen; Old Yeller; One of Our Dinosaurs Is Missing; Shaggy D.A., The; Son of Flubber; That Darn Cat (1965); Tom Brown's School Days (1940); Walk Softly, Stranger

Stewart, Alan A.: Ghetto Blaster

Stewart, Alan L.: Ghostriders

Stewart, Douglas Day: Listen to Me; Thief of Hearts

Stewart, John: Hidden Obsession

Stewart, Peter: Dear Santa; Gun Code

Stiller, Ben: Cable Guy, The; Reality Bites

Stiller, Mauritz: Thomas Graal's Best Child; Thomas Graal's Best Film; Treasure of Arne

Stillman, Whit: Barcelona; Last Days of Disco, The; Metropolitan

Stitt, Alexander: Grendel, Grendel, Grendel

Stix, John: Great St. Louis Bank Robbery, The

Stock, Mark: Midnight Movie Massacre

Stockwell, John: Undercover (1987)

Stoeffhaas, Jerry: Cheap Shots

Stoller, Bryan Michael: Undercover Angel

Stoloff, Ben: Affairs of Annabel, The; It's a Joke, Son!; Night of Terror; Palooka; Sea Devils; Transatlantic Merry-Go-Round

Stoloff, Victor: Washington Affair, The

Stone, Andrew L.: Julie; Last Voyage, The; Sensations of 1945; Song of Norway; Stormy Weather

Stone, Norman: Mirror Crack'd from Side to Side, The; They Do It with Mirrors

Stone, Oliver: Any Given Sunday; Born on the Fourth of July; Doors, The; Hand, The; Heaven and Earth (1993); JFK; Natural Born Killers; Nixon; Platoon; Salvador; Seizure; Talk Radio; U-Turn; Wall Street

Stone, Virginia Lively: Run If You Can

Stones, Tad: Aladdin & the King of Thieves; Return of Jafar, The

Stopkewich, Lynne: Kissed

Stoppard, Tom: Rosencrantz and Guildenstern Are Dead

Storm, Esben: In Search of Anna

Storm, Howard: Mork & Mindy (TV Series); Once Bitten

Strayer, Frank: Blondie; Blondie Takes a Vacation; Blondie Has Servant Trouble; Blondie in Society; Blondie's Blessed Event; Daring Young Man, The; Fugitive Road; Ghost Walks, The; It's a Great Life; Monster Walks, The; Vampire Bat, The

Streisand, Barbra: Mirror Has Two Faces, The; Prince of Tides, The; Yentl

Streitfeld, Susan: Female Perversions

Strick, Joseph: Balcony, The; Portrait of the Artist as a Young Man, A; Tropic of Cancer

Strick, Wesley: Tie That Binds, The

Strickland, John: Prime Suspect 2

Strock, Herbert L.: Blood of Dracula; Crawling Hand, The; Devil's Messenger, The; How to Make a Monster; I Was a Teenage Frankenstein; Witches' Brew

Strock, Robert L.: Bronco (TV Series)

Stromberg, William R.: Crater Lake Monster, The

Stroud, Richard: Deadline (1988)

Stryker, Jonathan: Curtains

Stuart, Brian: Sorceress (1982)

Stuart, Jeb: Switchback

Stuart, Mel: Chisholms, The; I Love My Wife; If It's Tuesday, This Must Be Belgium; Sophia Loren: Her Own Story; Willy Wonka and the Chocolate Factory

Stuckey, Dave: Lugosi, the Forgotten King

Sturges, John: Bad Day at Black Rock; By Love Possessed; Chino; Eagle Has Landed, The; Escape from Fort Bravo; Great Escape, The; Gunfight at the O.K. Corral; Hallelujah Trail, The; Hour of the Gun, The; Ice Station Zebra; It's a Big Country; Joe Kidd; Last Train from Gun Hill; Law and Jake Wade, The; Magnificent Seven, The; Magnificent Yankee, The; Marooned; McQ; Never So Few; Old Man and the Sea, The (1958); Underwater!

Sturges, Preston: Beautiful Blonde from Bashful Bend, The; Christmas in July; Great McGinty, The; Great Moment, The; Hail the Conquering Hero; Lady Eve, The; Mad Wednesday (see also Sin of Harold Diddlebock); Miracle of Morgan's Creek, The; Palm Beach Story, The; Sin of Harold Diddlebock (Mad Wednesday); Sullivan's Travels; Unfaithfully Yours (1948)

Sturridge, Charles: Brideshead Revisited; Fairy Tale: A True Story; Foreign Field, A; Gulliver's Travels (1996) (Television); Handful of Dust, A; Where Angels Fear to Tread

Styles, Eric: Dreaming of Joseph Lees

Styles, Richard: Shallow Grave (1987)

Styron, Susanna: Shadrach

Suarez, Bobby A.: Warriors of the Apocalypse

Suarez, Gonzalo: Rowing with the Wind

Subiela, Eliseo: Man Facing Southeast

Sugai, Hisashi: Roots Search

Suissa, Daniele J.: Shades of Love: The Rose Cafe

Sullivan, Daniel: Substance of Fire, The

Sullivan, Fred G.: Cold River

Sullivan, Kevin: Anne of Avonlea; Anne of Green Gables (1985); Cosmic Slop; How Stella Got Her Groove Back; Lantern Hill; Looking for Miracles

Sullivan, Kevin Rodney: America's Dream; Soul of the Game

Sullivan, Tim: Jack and Sarah

Summers, Jeremy: Five Golden Dragons; House of 1,000 Dolls

Summers, Walter: Human Monster, The (Dark Eyes of London); River of Unrest

Sun, Shirley: Iron & Silk

Sundstrom, Cedric: American Ninja III; American Ninja IV: The Annihilation; Captive Rage

Sundstrom, Neal: Howling V—The Rebirth

Sunseri, Jack A.: Chilling, The

Suo, Masayuki: Shall We Dance? (1996)

Surjik, Stephen: Wayne's World 2; Weapons of Mass Distraction

Suso, Henry: Deathsport

Sutherland, A. Edward: Beyond Tomorrow; Every Day's a Holiday; Flying Deuces; Follow the Boys; Having a Wonderful Crime; International House; Invisible Woman, The; Mississippi; Mr. Robinson Crusoe; Murders in the Zoo; One Night in the Tropics; Saturday Night Kid, The

Sutherland, Hal: Journey Back to Oz; Pinocchio and the Emperor of the Night

Sutherland, Kiefer: Last Light; Truth or Consequences, N.M.

Svankmajer, Jan: Alice (1988)

Svatek, Peter: Bleeders; Call of the Wild: The Dog of the Yukone; Sci-Fighters

Sverak, Jan: Elementary School, The; Kolya

Swackhamer, E. W.: Amazing Spiderman, The; Are You Lonesome Tonight; Dain Curse, The; Death at Love House; Longshot (1981); Man and Boy; Night Terror; Perfect Family; Rousters, The; Secret Passion of Robert Clayton, The; Terror at London Bridge; Winds of Kitty Hawk, The

Swaim, Bob: Half-Moon Street; La Balance; Masquerade (1988); Target of Suspicion

Swanson, Donald: Magic Garden, The

Sweeney, Bob: Return to Mayberry

Sweeney, Julia: God Said, Ha!

Swenson, Charles: Mouse and His Child, The; Twice Upon a Time

Swerdlove, Larry: Skateboard Kid, The

Swickard, Charles: Hell's Hinges

Swift, David: Good Neighbor Sam; How to Succeed in Business without Really Trying; Interns, The; Parent Trap, The (1961); Pollyanna (1960)

Swift, Lela: Best of Dark Shadows, The; Dark Shadows (TV Series)

Swimmer, Saul: Mrs. Brown You've Got a Lovely Daughter

Swirnoff, Brad: Tunnelvision (1976)

Switzer, Michael: Lightning Incident, The; Nitti: The Enforcer; Past the Bleachers; Summer Dreams; Unlikely Angel

Sykes, Peter: Demons of the Mind; Jesus; To the Devil, a Daughter

Sylbert, Paul: Steagle, The

Szabo, Istvan: Colonel Redl; Father (1966); Hanussen; Meeting Venus; Mephisto; 25, Firemen's Street

Szulzinger, Boris: Mamma Dracula

Szwarc, Jeannot: Bug; Enigma; Grand Larceny; Jaws 2; Murders in the Rue Morgue (1986); Santa Claus—The Movie; Somewhere in Time; Supergirl

Taav, Michael: Paint Job, The

Tabet, Sylvio: Beastmaster 2: Through the Portal of Time

Tabio, Juan Carlos: Guantanamera!; Strawberry and Chocolate

Tacchella, Jean-Charles: Blue Country; Cousin, Cousine

Tadashi, Okuda: Riding Bean

Taft, Gene: Blame It on the Night

Tahimik, Kidlat: Perfumed Nightmare

Taicher, Robert: Inside Out (1986)

Tai-Kit, Mak: Wicked City, The (1992)

Takabayashi, Yoichi: Irezumi (Spirit of Tattoo)

Takacs, Tibor: Bad Blood (1994); Deadly Past; Gate, The; Gate II; I, Madman; Red Shoe Diaries II: Double Dare; Redline; Sabotage (1996); Sabrina, the Teenage Witch

Takahata, Isao: Grave of the Fireflies

Takakjian, Glen: Metamorphosis: The Alien Factor

Takamasa, Ikegami: A.D. Police Files, Vols. 1–3

Takamoto, Iwao: Charlotte's Web

Takayama, Hideki: Urotsukidoji: Legend of the Overfiend; Urotsukidoji II: Legend of the Demon Womb

Takeshi, Mori: Otaku No Video

Talalay, Rachel: Freddy's Dead: The Final Nightmare; Ghost in the Machine; Tank Girl

Talbot, Paul: Freakshow

Talbot, Robert: Head of the Family; Mystery Monsters

Tallas, Gregg: Prehistoric Women (1950)

Talmadge, Richard: Devil Horse, The; Project Moon Base

Tamahori, Lee: Edge, The; Mulholland Falls; Once Were Warriors

Tamayo, Augusto: Ultrawarrior

Tampa, Harry: Fairy Tales; Nocturna

Tanaka, Shigeo: Gamera Versus Barugon

Tanaka, Tokuzo: Zatoichi: The Blind Swordsman's Vengeance

Tannen, Terrell: Shadows in the Storm

Tannen, William: Flashpoint; Hero and the Terror

Tanner, Alain: In the White City; Jonah Who Will Be 25 in the Year 2000

Tansey, Robert Emmett: Caravan Trail; Colorado Serenade; Driftin' Kid; Dynamite Canyon; Where Trails End; Wild West (1946); Wildfire (1945)

Taplitz, Daniel: Black Magic (1992); Commandments; Nightlife

Tarantino, Quentin: Four Rooms; Jackie Brown; Pulp Fiction; Reservoir Dogs

Tarkovsky, Andrei: Andrei Rublev; Mirror, The; My Name Is Ivan; Nostalghia; Sacrifice, The; Solaris; Stalker

Taro, Rin: Dagger of Kamui, The; Doomed Megalopolis, Parts 1–4; Neo-Tokyo

Tash, Max: Running Kind, The

Tashlin, Frank: Alphabet Murders, The; Artists and Models; Cinderfella; Disorderly Orderly, The; Girl Can't Help It, The; Glass Bottom Boat, The; Hollywood or Bust; Private Navy of Sgt. O'Farrell, The; Son of Paleface; Susan Slept Here; Will Success Spoil Rock Hunter?

Tass, Nadia: Mr. Reliable; Pure Luck; Rikki and Pete

Tassie, Paul: Pig's Tale, A

Tati, Jacques: Jour de Fête; Mr. Hulot's Holiday; My Uncle (Mon Oncle); Parade; Playtime; Traffic

Tato, Anna Maria: Night and the Moment, The

Tatoulis, John: Silver Stallion, The

Taurog, Norman: Adventures of Tom Sawyer, The; Birds and the Bees, The; Blue Hawaii; Boys' Town; Broadway Melody of 1940; Bundle of Joy; Caddy, The; Dr. Goldfoot and the Bikini Machine; Double Trouble (1967); G.I. Blues; Girl Crazy; Girls! Girls! Girls!; Hold 'em Jail; It Happened at the World's Fair; Jumping Jacks; Little Nellie Kelly; Live a Little, Love a Little; Mad About Music; Men of Boys Town; Mrs. Wiggs of the Cabbage Patch; Onionhead; Palm Springs Weekend; Presenting Lily Mars; Rhythm on the Range; Rich, Young and Pretty; Speedway; Spinout; That Midnight Kiss; Tickle Me; Toast of New Orleans; We're Not Dressing; Words and Music; Young Tom Edison

Tausik, David: Blood Song (Haunted Symphony); Homicidal Impulse

Taverna, Michele: Managua

Tavernier, Bertrand: Beatrice; Clean Slate (Coup de Torchon) (1981); Clockmaker, The (1973); Daddy Nostalgia; Death Watch; Judge and the Assassin, The; Life and Nothing But; Mississippi Blues; Revenge of the Musketeers; Round Midnight; Sunday in the Country, A

Taviani, Paolo: Allonsonfan; Good Morning, Babylon; Kaos; Night of the Shooting Stars; Padre Padrone; Wild Flower (1993) (Fiorile)

Taviani, Vittorio: Allonsonfan; Good Morning, Babylon; Kaos; Night of the Shooting Stars; Padre Padrone; Wild Flower (1993) (Fiorile)

Taylor, Alan: Palookaville

Taylor, Baz: Near Misses; Shooting Elizabeth; Tattle Tale

Taylor, Don: Damien: Omen II; Diamond Trap, The; Escape from the Planet of the Apes; Final Countdown, The; Great Scout and Cathouse Thursday, The; Listen to Your Heart; My Wicked, Wicked Ways; Night Games; Red Flag: The Ultimate Game; Ride the Wild Surf; Secret Weapons; September Gun; Tom Sawyer (1973)

Taylor, Finn: Dream with the Fishes

Taylor, Jud: Broken Vows; Christmas Coal Mine Miracle, The; City in Fear; Clover; Danielle Steel's Kaleidoscope; Foxfire; Great Escape II, The; Old Man and the Sea, The (1990); Out of the Darkness; Packin' It In; Question of Honor, A; Revenge (1971) (Shelley Winters); Say Goodbye, Maggie Cole; Search for the Gods

Taylor, Ray: Cheyenne Takes Over; Dick Tracy (1937); Flash Gordon Conquers the Universe; Ghost Town Renegades; Ivory-Handled Gun, The; Lone Star Trail; Mystery of the Hooded Horsemen; Painted Stallion, The; Perils of Pauline, The, (1933); Rawhide (1938); Return of Chandu (Magician, The); Riders of Death Valley; Stage to Mesa City; Vigilantes Are Coming!; Winners of the West

Taylor, Renee: Love Is All There Is

Taylor, Richard: Stingray

Taylor, Robert: Heidi's Song; Nine Lives of Fritz the Cat

Taylor, Roderick: Instant Karma

Taylor, Sam: Ambassador Bill; Coquette; Freshman, The (1925); Nothing But Trouble (1944); Safety Last; Taming of the Shrew, The (1929); Tempest (1928)

Taylor, William Desmond: Tom Sawyer (1917)

Taymor, Julie: Titus

Tchernia, Pierre: Holes, The

Teague, Lewis: Alligator; Cat's Eye; Collision Course (1989); Cujo; Deadlock; Fighting Back; Jewel of the Nile, The; Lady in Red; Navy Seals; Saved by the Light; TBone N Weasel

Teche, Gary: Nevada

Téchiné, André: Les Voleurs; Ma Saison Preferée; Rendez-Vous; Scene of the Crime (1987); Thieves (Les Voleurs); Wild Reeds

Telford, Frank: Bamboo Saucer (Collision Course)

Temple, Julien: Absolute Beginners; Bullet; Earth Girls Are Easy; Great Rock and Roll Swindle, The

Templeton, George: Sundowners, The (1950)

Tennant, Andy: Amy Fisher Story, The; Anna and the King; Ever After; Fools Rush In; It Takes Two (1995); Keep the Change

Tenney, Del: Horror of Party Beach, The

Tenney, Kevin S.: Arrival II, The; Cellar, The; Night of the Demons; Peacemaker (1990); Pinocchio's Revenge; Witchboard; Witchboard 2; Witchtrap

Tennyson, Pen: Convoy (1940)

Tent, Kevin: Ultrawarrior

Terada, Kazuo: Gargoyles: The Movie

Terasawa, Buichi: Raven Tengu Kabuto

Terlesky, John: Judgment Day; Pandora Project, The; Supreme Sanction

Teshigahara, Hiroshi: Face of Another, The; Rikyu; Woman in the Dunes

Tess, Nadia: Malcolm

Tessari, Duccio: Beyond Justice; Long Live Your Death; Tex and the Lord of the Deep; Zorro

Tetzlaff, Ted: Fighting Father Dunne; RiffRaff (1947); White Tower, The; Window, The

Teuber, Monica: Magdalene

Tewkesbury, Joan: Cold Sassy Tree; Old Boyfriends; Strangers; Sudie & Simpson; Tenth Month, The

Tewksbury, Peter: Emil and the Detectives; Stay Away Joe; Trouble with Girls, The

Tezuka, Osamu: Legend of the Forest

Thau, Leon: Save the Lady

Theakston, Graham: Money Kings; Tripods

Thiele, Rolf: Tonio Kroger

Thiele, William: Tarzan Triumphs

Thies, Christopher: Winterbeast

Thomas, Albie: Palm Beach

Thomas, Antony: Code Name: Chaos

Thomas, Betty: Brady Bunch Movie, The; Dr. Dolittle (1998); Late Shift, The; Only You (1991); Private Parts (1997); 28 Days

Thomas, Dave: Experts, The; Strange Brew

Thomas, Gerald: Carry on at Your Convenience; Carry on Behind; Carry on Cleo; Carry on Cowboy; Carry on Cruising; Carry on Doctor; Carry on Emmanuelle; Carry on Nurse; Follow That Camel

Thomas, John G.: Arizona Heat; Tin Man

Thomas, Ralph: Clouded Yellow, The; Doctor at Large; Doctor at Sea; Doctor in Distress; Doctor in the House; No Love for Johnnie; Tale of Two Cities, A (1967); Thirty-Nine Steps, The (1959)

Thomas, Ralph L.: Apprentice to Murder; Terry Fox Story, The; Ticket to Heaven

Thomas, Scott: Silent Assassins

Thomas, Theodore: Frank and Ollie

Thomason, Harry: Encounter with the Unknown

Thomburg, Lee: Hollywood High, Part II

Thompson, Brett: Adventures in Dinosaur City

Thompson, Caroline: Black Beauty (1994); Buddy

Thompson, Chris: Bosom Buddies (TV Series)

Thompson, Ernest: 1969

Thompson, J. Lee: Ambassador, The; Battle for the Planet of the Apes; Blue Knight, The (1975); Cabo Blanco; Cape Fear (1962); Conquest of the Planet of the Apes; Death Wish IV: The Crackdown; Evil That Men Do, The; Firewalker; Flame over India; Greek Tycoon, The; Guns of Navarone, The; Happy Birthday to Me; Huckleberry Finn (1974); King Solomon's Mines (1985); Kinjite (Forbidden Subjects); Mackenna's Gold; Messenger of Death; Murphy's Law; Reincarnation of Peter Proud, The; St. Ives; Taras Bulba; Ten to Midnight; Tiger Bay; White Buffalo

Thompson, Robert C.: Bud and Lou; Dog Trouble

Thomsen, Christian Braad: Ladies on the Rocks

Thomson, Chris: Meteorites!; Morrison Murders, The; Swimsuit; Three's Trouble; Trucks

Thor, Cameron: Brutal Truth, The

Thornhill, Michael: Between Wars; Everlasting Secret Family, The

Thornton, Billy Bob: Sling Blade

Thorpe, Jerry: All God's Children; Kung Fu (1971); Lazarus Syndrome, The; Possessed, The (1977); Smile, Jenny, You're Dead

Thorpe, Richard: Above Suspicion (1943); Adventures of Huckleberry Finn, The (1939); All the Brothers Were Valiant; Athena; Black Hand, The; Challenge to Lassie; Date with Judy, A; Double Wedding; Fiesta; Fun in Acapulco; Girl Who Had Everything, The; Great Caruso, The; Honeymoon Machine, The; Horizontal Lieutenant, The; It's a Big Country; Ivanhoe (1952); Jailhouse Rock; Knights of the Round Table; Lone Defender, The; Night Must Fall; On an Island with You; Prisoner of Zenda, The (1952); Prodigal, The; Student Prince, The; Sun Comes Up, The; Tarzan Escapes; Tarzan Finds a Son; Tarzan's New York Adventure; Tarzan's Secret Treasure; Thin Man Goes Home, The; This Time For Keeps; Three Little Words; Thrill of a Romance; Two Girls and a Sailor; Vengeance Valley; White Cargo

Thurow, Nany: Islander, The

Tianming, Wu: King of Masks, The

Tiffe, Robert: Sword of Honor

Till, Eric: American Christmas Carol, An; Bethune; Buffalo Jump; Case of Libel, A; Challengers, The; Clarence; Final Appeal; Hot Millions; If You Could See What I Hear; Improper Channels; Mary and Joseph: A Story of Faith; Oh, What a Night; To Catch a Killer; Wild Horse Hank

Tillman Jr., George: Soul Food

Tillmans, R. L.: Witchcraft III, The Kiss of Death

Timm, Bruce W.: Batman: Mask of the Phantasm

Tinling, James: Charlie Chan in Shanghai; Mr. Moto's Gamble

Tinnell, Robert: Believe; Frankenstein and Me

Tintori, John: Hellcab

Tirola, Douglas: Reason to Believe, A

Title, Stacy: Last Supper, The (1996)

Toback, James: Black and White (2000); Exposed; Fingers; Pick-Up Artist, The

Tognazzi, Ricky: Excellent Cadavers; La Scorta

Tokar, Norman: Apple Dumpling Gang, The; Big Red; Boatniks, The; Candleshoe; Cat from Outer Space, The; Follow Me, Boys!; Happiest Millionaire, The; Horse in the Gray Flannel Suit, The; No Deposit, No Return; Sammy, the Way-Out Seal; Savage Sam; Snowball Express; Those Calloways; Tiger Walks, A; Ugly Dachshund, The; Where the Red Fern Grows

Toland, Gregg: December 7th: The Movie

Toledo, Sergio: One Man's War

Tolkin, Michael: New Age, The; Rapture, The

Tolkin, Stephen: Daybreak (1993); Stephen King's Golden Years (TV Series)

Tollin, Mike: Hank Aaron: Chasing the Dream

Tomblin, David: Invasion UFO; Prisoner, The (1968) (TV Series)

Tomomichi, Mochizuki: Kimagure Orange Road: The Movie

Tompson, Marcus: Adventures Beyond Belief

Tong, Stanley: Jackie Chan's First Strike; Mr. Magoo; Police Story III—Super Cop; Rumble in the Bronx; Supercop

Topor, Tom: Judgment

Toporoff, Ralph: American Blue Note

Topper, Burt: Soul Hustler; Strangler, The

Torn, Rip: Telephone, The

Tornatore, Giuseppe: Cinema Paradiso; Everybody's Fine; Legend of 1900, The; Pure Formality, A; Star Maker, The

Tornatore, Joe: Curse of the Crystal Eye; Demon Keeper; Grotesque

Torrance, Robert: Mutant on the Bounty

Torres, Fina: Celestial Clockwork; Oriane

Torres, Gabe: December

Torrini, Cinzia: Hotel Colonial

Tors, Ivan: Zebra in the Kitchen

Toshifumi, Kiyotsumu: Bubblegum Crash, Vols. 1–3

Totten, Robert: Huckleberry Finn (1975); Sacketts, The

Toubiana, Serge: Francois Truffaut: Stolen Moments

Tourneur, Jacques: Appointment in Honduras; Berlin Express; Cat People (1942); Circle of Danger; Comedy of Terrors; Curse of the Demon; Days of Glory; Easy Living; Flame and the Arrow, The; I Walked with a Zombie; Leopard Man, The; Out of the Past; Stars In My Crown

Tourneur, Maurice: Last of the Mohicans, The (1920); Poor Little Rich Girl, The (1917); Pride of the Clan, The; Victory (1919); Volpone

Towers, Derek: King Tut: The Face of Tutankhamun

Towne, Robert: Personal Best; Tequila Sunrise

Townsend, Bud: Coach; Nightmare in Wax (Crimes in the Wax Museum); Terror at the Red Wolf Inn (Terror House)

Townsend, Pat: Beach Girls, The

Townsend, Robert: B.A.P.S; Five Heartbeats, The; Hollywood Shuffle; Meteor Man

Toye, Wendy: Three Cases of Murder

Toynton, Ian: Annie, a Royal Adventure!; Maid, The

Toyoda, Shiro: Mistress, The (1953); Snow Country

Tramont, Jean-Claude: All Night Long; As Summers Die

Travers, Alfred: Meet the Navy

Travers, Bill: Christian the Lion

Travis, Mark W.: Going Under

Travolta, Joey: Detour (1999); Navajo Blues

Traxler, Stephen: Slithis

Trbovich, Tom: Free Ride

Treas, Terri: Play Nice

Trenchard-Smith, Brian: Atomic Dog; BMX Bandits; Day of the Assassin; Dead-End Drive-In; Escape Clause; Escape 2000; Leprechaun 3; Leprechaun 4 in Space; Night of the Demons 2; Official Denial; Quest, The (1985); Sahara (1995); Siege of Firebase Gloria, The

Trent, Barbara: Panama Deception, The

Wells, Simon: American Tail, An: Fievel Goes West; Balto; Prince of Egypt; We're Back! A Dinosaur's Story

Wenders, Wim: Alice in the City; American Friend, The; Buena Vista Social Club, The; End of Violence, The; Faraway, So Close; Goalie's Anxiety at the Penalty Kick; Hammett; Kings of the Road; Lightning over Water; Lisbon Story; Paris, Texas; Scarlet Letter (1973); State of Things, The; Tokyo-Ga; Until the End of the World; Wings of Desire; Wrong Move, The

Wendkos, Paul: Betrayal (1978); Blood Vows: The Story of a Mafia Wife; Celebrity; Cocaine: One Man's Seduction; Cry for Love, A; Execution, The; From the Dead of Night; Gidget; Gidget Goes Hawaiian; Gidget Goes to Rome; Great Escape II, The; Guns of the Magnificent Seven; Haunts of the Very Rich; Honor Thy Father; I Spy (TV Series); Johnny Tiger; Mephisto Waltz, The; Ordeal of Dr. Mudd, The; White Hot: The Mysterious Murder of Thelma Todd; Wing and a Prayer, A (1997); Woman Called Moses, A

Wenk, Richard: Just the Ticket; National Lampoon's Attack of the 5' 2" Women; Vamp

Werker, Alfred: Adventures of Sherlock Holmes, The; At Gunpoint; Devil's Canyon; He Walked by Night; Shock (1946)

Werner, Jeff: Die Laughing

Werner, Peter: Barn Burning; Battered; Don't Cry, It's Only Thunder; Hiroshima: Out of the Ashes; I Married a Centerfold; Image, The; LBJ: The Early Years; Lone Justice; No Man's Land; Substitute Wife, The

Wertmuller, Lina: All Screwed Up; Blood Feud; Camorra; Ciao Professore; Joke of Destiny; Love and Anarchy; Night Full of Rain, A; Seduction of Mimi, The; Seven Beauties; Sotto Sotto; Summer Night; Swept Away

Wesley, William: Scarecrows

West, Jake: Razor Blade Smile

West, Roland: Bat Whispers, The; Monster, The (1925)

West, Simon: Con Air; General's Daughter, The

Weston, Armand: Nesting, The

Weston, Eric: Evilspeak; Iron Triangle, The; Marvin and Tige; To Protect and Serve

Wetzl, Fulvio: Rorret

Wetzler, Gwen: Secret of the Sword, The

Wexler, Haskell: Latino; Medium Cool

Whale, James: Bride of Frankenstein; Frankenstein (1931); Invisible Man, The; Man in the Iron Mask, The (1939); Old Dark House, The (1932); Show Boat (1936); Sinners in Paradise; Wives Under Suspicion

Wharmby, Tony: Covert Assassin; Equalizer, The: "Memories of Manon"; Kissing Place, The; Lillie; Partners in Crime (Secret Adversary) (TV Series); Seven Dials Mystery, The; Sorry, Wrong Number (1989); Treacherous Crossing

Whatham, Claude: Buddy's Song; Elizabeth R; Murder Elite; Sweet William; That'll Be the Day

Wheat, Jim: After Midnight; Ewoks: The Battle for Endor; Lies

Wheat, Ken: After Midnight; Ewoks: The Battle for Endor; Lies

Wheatley, David: Hostages; Nobody's Children

Wheeler, Anne: Better Than Chocolate; Loyalties

Whelan, Tim: Badman's Territory; Clouds over Europe; Divorce of Lady X, The; Higher and Higher; Mill on the Floss, The; Rage at Dawn; Seven Day's Leave; Sidewalks of London; Step Lively; Texas Lady; Thief of Bagdad, The (1940)

Whitaker, Forest: Hope Floats; Strapped; Waiting to Exhale

White, Jules: Sidewalks of New York

White, Nathan J.: Carrier

White, Sam: People Are Funny

White, Steve: Amityville Dollhouse

White, Wally: Lie Down with Dogs

Whitelaw, Alexander: Lifespan; Vicious Circles

Whitesell, John: Calendar Girl

Whitman, Philip H.: His Private Secretary

Whitmore II, Preston A.: Walking Dead, The

Whorf, Richard: Champagne for Caesar; It Happened in Brooklyn; Love from a Stranger; Luxury Liner; Till the Clouds Roll By

Whyte, Michael: Railway Station Man, The

Wiard, William: Tom Horn

Wickes, David: Frankenstein (1992); Hitchhiker, The (Series); Jack the Ripper (1988); Jekyll & Hyde; Silver Dream Racer

Wicki, Bernhard: Bridge, The; Longest Day, The; Morituri

Widen, Gregory: Prophecy, The (1995)

Widerberg, Bo: Elvira Madigan; Man on the Roof

Wiederhorn, Ken: Eyes of a Stranger; House in the Hills, A; Meatballs Part II; Return of the Living Dead Part II; Shock Waves (Death Corps)

Wiemer, Robert: Anna to the Infinite Power; Night Train to Katmandu; Somewhere, Tomorrow

Wiene, Robert: Cabinet of Doctor Caligari, The; Hands of Orlac

Wilbur, Crane: Bat, The

Wilcox, Fred M.: Courage of Lassie; Forbidden Planet; Hills of Home; Lassie Come Home; Secret Garden, The (1949); Three Daring Daughters

Wilcox, Herbert: Courtney Affair, The; Forever and a Day; Lilacs in the Spring (Let's Make Up); London Melody; No, No Nanette; Nurse Edith Cavell; Trouble in the Glen

Wild, Andrew: Spenser: Ceremony

Wilde, Cornel: Naked Prey, The; Shark's Treasure; Sword of Lancelot

Wilde, Ted: Battling Orioles, The

Wilder, Billy: Apartment, The; Avanti!; Buddy, Buddy; Double Indemnity; Emperor Waltz, The; Fedora; Five Graves to Cairo; Fortune Cookie, The; Front Page, The (1974); Irma La Douce; Kiss Me, Stupid; Lost Weekend, The; Love in the Afternoon; Mauvaise Graine (Bad Seed); One, Two, Three; Private Life of Sherlock Holmes, The; Sabrina (1954); Seven Year Itch, The; Some Like It Hot; Spirit of St. Louis, The; Stalag 17; Sunset Boulevard; Witness for the Prosecution (1957)

Wilder, Gene: Adventure of Sherlock Holmes' Smarter Brother, The; Haunted Honeymoon; Woman in Red, The; World's Greatest Lover, The

Wilder, Glenn: Master Blaster

Wilder, John: Breaking Home Ties

Wilder, W. Lee: Big Bluff, The; Killers from Space; Manfish; Snow Creature, The

Wilding, Gavin: Listen; Raffle, The; Stag

Wiles, Gordon: Charlie Chan's Secret; Gangster, The; Ginger in the Morning

Wiley, Ethan: Children of the Corn V: Fields of Terror; House II: The Second Story

Wilkinson, Charles: Breach of Trust; Quarantine

Willeg, Edward: Mad Executioners, The

Williams, Anson: All-American Murder; Dream Date; Little White Lies; Perfect Little Murder, A

Williams, Bob: Gross Jokes

Williams, Elmo: Hell Ship Mutiny

Williams, Hype: Belly

Williams, Larry: Path to Paradise

Williams, Matt: Where the Heart Is (2000)

Williams, Oscar: Death Drug; Final Comedown, The

Williams, Paul: Mirage (1995); Miss Right; November Men, The

Williams, Richard: Arabian Knight

Williams, Scott: Man with Two Heads

Williams, Stephen: Shadow Zone: The Undead Express

Williams, Tod: Adventures of Sebastian Cole, The

Williams, Tony: Next of Kin (1987); Solo (1977)

Williamson, Fred: Adios Amigo; Big Score, The; Foxtrap; Mean Johnny Barrows; One Down, Two to Go; Silent Hunter; South Beach; Steele's Law; Three Days to a Kill

Williamson, Kevin: Teaching Mrs. Tingle

Willing, Nick: Alice in Wonderland (1999); Jason and the Argonauts (2000); Photographing Fairies

Wills, J. Elder: Big Fella; Song of Freedom

Wilson, Andy: Playing God

Wilson, Hugh: Blast from the Past; Burglar (U.S.); Dudley Do-Right; First Wives Club, The; Guarding Tess; Police Academy; Rustler's Rhapsody

Wilson, Jim: Stacy's Knights

Wilson, Richard: Al Capone; Invitation to a Gunfighter; It's All True; Pay or Die; Three in the Attic

Wilson, S. S.: Tremors 2: Aftershocks

Wilson, Sandy: American Boyfriends; Harmony Cats; My American Cousin

Wilson, Yale: Truth or Dare? A Critical Madness

Wimmer, Kurt: One Man's Justice

Winant, Scott: 'Til There Was You

Wincer, Simon: Dark Forces; D.A.R.Y.L.; Echo of Thunder, The; Escape: Human Cargo; Free Willy; Girl Who Spelled Freedom, The; Harley Davidson and the Marlboro Man;

Lighthorsemen, The; Lightning Jack; Lonesome Dove; Operation Dumbo Drop; Phantom, The (1996); Phar Lap; Quigley Down Under

Windom, Lawrence: Headin' Home

Windust, Bretaigne: Enforcer, The (1951); June Bride; Winter Meeting

Winer, Harry: House Arrest; JFK: Reckless Youth; Mirrors; Single Bars, Single Women; SpaceCamp

Winfrey, Jonathan: Assassination Game, The; Black Scorpion; Black Scorpion II: Aftershock; Carnosaur 3: Primal Species; Excessive Force II: Force on Force; Legend of the Lost Tomb; New Crime City: Los Angeles 2020

Winick, Gary: Out of the Rain; Sweet Nothing

Winkler, Charles: Disturbed; Rocky Marciano; You Talkin' to Me

Winkler, David: Finding Graceland

Winkler, Henry: Cop and a Half; Memories of Me; Smoky Mountain Christmas

Winkler, Irwin: At First Sight (1999); Guilty by Suspicion; Net, The; Night and the City (1992)

Winkless, Terence H.: Berlin Conspiracy, The; Bloodfist; Corporate Affairs; Ladykiller (1996); Nest, The (1988); Not of This Earth (1995); Rage and Honor; Westing Game, The

Winner, James: Night That Never Happened, The

Winner, Michael: Appointment with Death; Big Sleep, The (1978); Bullseye; Chato's Land; Chorus of Disapproval, A; Death Wish; Death Wish II; Death Wish III; Firepower (1979); Lawman; Mechanic, The; Nightcomers, The; Scream for Help; Sentinel, The; Stone Killer, The; Wicked Lady, The (1983)

Winning, David: Killer Image; Profile for Murder; Storm; Turbo: A Power Rangers Adventure

Winograd, Peter: One Last Run

Winston, Stan: Adventures of a Gnome Named Gnorm, The; Pumpkinhead

Winter, Alex: Freaked

Winterbottom, Michael: Butterfly Kiss; Go Now; I Want You; Jude; Welcome to Sarajevo

Winters, David: Dr. Jekyll and Mr. Hyde (1973); Last Horror Film, The; Thrashin'

Winters, Howard: Dead Boyz Can't Fly

Winters, Paul: Freeway Maniac

Winterstein, Frank: Sherlock Holmes and the Deadly Necklace

Wisbar, Frank: Devil Bat's Daughter; Strangler of the Swamp

Wise, Herbert: Castle of the Living Dead; Elizabeth R; Gathering Storm; I, Claudius; Norman Conquests, The, Episode 1: Table Manners; Norman Conquests, The, Episode 2: Living Together; Norman Conquests, The, Episode 3: Round and Round the Garden; Pope John Paul II; Skokie; Strange Interlude (1988)

Wise, Kirk: Beauty and the Beast (1991); Hunchback of Notre Dame, The (1997)

Wise, Robert: Andromeda Strain, The; Audrey Rose; Blood on the Moon; Body Snatcher, The (1945); Born to Kill; Curse of the Cat People, The; Day the Earth Stood Still, The; Desert Rats, The; Executive Suite; Haunting, The (1963); Helen of Troy; Hindenburg, The; I Want to Live!; Mademoiselle Fifi; Rooftops; Run Silent, Run Deep; Sand Pebbles, The; Set-Up, The (1949); Somebody Up There Likes Me; Sound of Music, The; Star! (1968); Star Trek—The Motion Picture; This Could Be the Night; Three Secrets; Tribute to a Bad Man; Two for the Seesaw; Until They Sail; West Side Story

Wiseman, Carol: Does This Mean We're Married?; Face the Music; Little Princess, A (1986); May Wine

Wishman, Doris: Bad Girls Go to Hell; Blaze Starr: The Original; Night to Dismember, A

Witcher, Theodore: Love Jones

Withrow, Stephen: Friends, Lovers & Lunatics

Witliff, William: Red-Headed Stranger, The

Witney, William: Adventures of Captain Marvel, The; Adventures of Red Ryder; Apache Rose; Arizona Raiders; Bells of Coronado; Bells of San Angelo; Dick Tracy Returns; Dick Tracy vs. Crime Inc.; Dick Tracy's G-Men; Down Dakota Way; Drums of Fu Manchu; Eyes of Texas; Far Frontier; G-Men vs. The Black Dragon; Golden Stallion, The; Hawk of the Wilderness; Helldorado (1946); Hi-Yo Silver; In Old Amarillo; Island of Dr. Moreau, The; Lone Ranger, The (1938); Master of the World; Mysterious Dr. Satan; Night-

time in Nevada; Outcast, The; Painted Stallion, The; Paratroop Command; Roll on Texas Moon; SOS Coast Guard; Springtime in the Sierras; Spy Smasher; Trail of Robin Hood; Trigger, Jr.; Under California Stars; Zorro Rides Again; Zorro's Fighting Legion

Wolcott, James L.: Wild Women of Wongo

Wolf, Fred: Mouse and His Child, The; Point, The

Wolfe, Donald: Savage Intruder, The

Wolk, Andy: Criminal Justice; Defenders, The: Taking the First; Defenders, The; Traces of Red

Wolk, Peter: Defenders, The: Taking the First

Wolman, Dan: Soldier of the Night; Up Your Anchor

Wolodarsky, M. Wallace: Cold-Blooded

Wolpaw, James: It's a Complex World

Wong, Che-Kirk: Big Hit, The; Crime Story

Wong, James: Final Destination

Woo, John: Better Tomorrow, A; Better Tomorrow 2, A; Blackjack; Broken Arrow (1996); Bullet in the Head; Face/Off; Hard Boiled; Hard Target; John Woo's Once a Thief; Killer, The; Mission: Impossible 2; Once a Thief

Wood, Sam: Casanova Brown; Command Decision; Day at the Races, A; Devil and Miss Jones, The; For Whom the Bell Tolls; Goodbye, Mr. Chips (1939); Guest Wife; Hold Your Man; King's Row; Kitty Foyle; Madame X (1937); Navy Blue and Gold; Night at the Opera, A; Our Town (1940); Peck's Bad Boy; Pride of the Yankees, The; Stratton Story, The

Wood Jr., Edward D.: Bride of the Monster; Glen or Glenda; Bad Boy; Hellborn; Jail Bait (1954); Night of the Ghouls; Plan 9 from Outer Space; Sinister Urge, The

Woodhead, Leslie: Endurance; Tragedy of Flight 103, The: The Inside Story

Woodman, William: King Richard II; Romeo and Juliet (1983); Tempest, The (1983)

Woodruff, Frank: Lady Scarface

Woods, Jack: Equinox (1971) (The Beast)

Woods, James: Dr. Jekyll's Dungeon of Death

Woods, Mark: Witchcraft II: The Temptress

Woodward, Joanne: Come Along with Me

Woodward, John: Neurotic Cabaret

Wool, Abbe: Roadside Prophets

Woolnough, Jeff: First Degree; Universal Soldier II: Brothers in Arms

Woo-Ping, Yuen: Twin Warriors

Workman, Chuck: Andy Warhol: Superstar; Source, The; Stoogemania

Worsley, Wallace: Ace of Hearts; Hunchback of Notre Dame, The (1923)

Worswick, Clark: Agent on Ice

Worth, Aaron: 9 Ninjas

Worth, David: Chain of Command; Kickboxer; Lady Dragon; Lady Dragon 2; Warrior of the Lost World

Wortmann, Sonke: Maybe, Maybe Not

Woster, Eric: Sandman (1992)

Wragge, Martin: Last Warrior, The

Wray, John Griffith: Anna Christie (1922)

Wrede, Caspar: One Day in the Life of Ivan Denisovich; Terrorists, The

Wright, Alexander: Fast Money (1996); First 9 Weeks, The

Wright, Allen: Slow Bullet

Wright, Geoffrey: Romper Stomper

Wright, Kay: Snow White Christmas, A

Wright, Mack V.: Haunted Gold; Hit the Saddle; Man from Monterey, The; Range Defenders; Riders of the Whistling Skull; Sea Hound, The; Somewhere in Sonora; Vigilantes Are Coming!; Winds of the Wasteland

Wright, Patrick: Hollywood High

Wright, Tenny: Big Stampede, The; Telegraph Trail, The

Wright, Thomas: Bodily Harm; Chrome Soldiers; Deadly Game; Fatal Image, The; Highlander: The Gathering; No Holds Barred; Snow Kill

Wrye, Donald: Born Innocent; Ice Castles; Not In This Town

Wuhl, Robert: Open Season

Wurlitzer, Rudy: Candy Mountain

Wyler, William: Ben-Hur (1959); Best Years of Our Lives, The; Big Country, The; Carrie (1952); Children's Hour, The; Collector, The; Come and Get It; Dead End; Desperate Hours, The (1955); Dodsworth; Friendly Persuasion; Funny Girl; Heiress, The; How to Steal a Million; Jezebel; Letter, The; Liberation of L. B. Jones, The; Little Foxes, The; Mrs.

Miniver; Roman Holiday; These Three; Westerner, The; Wuthering Heights (1939)

Wyles, David: Man with a Gun

Wynn, Bob: Resurrection of Zachary Wheeler, The

Wynn, Tracy Keenan: Hit Lady

Wynne, Paul: Bombshell (1997)

Wynorski, Jim: Big Bad Mama II; Chopping Mall; Deathstalker II: Duel of the Titans; Dinosaur Island; Ghoulies IV; Hard Bounty; Hard to Die; Haunting of Morella, The; Little Miss Millions; Lost Empire, The; Munchie; Munchie Strikes Back; 976-EVIL II: The Astral Factor; Not of This Earth; Return of the Swamp Thing; Sorceress (1994); Sorority House Massacre 2; Transylvania Twist; Vampirella; Wasp Woman, The (1995)

Wynorsky, Jim: Pandora Project, The

Xhonneux, Henri: Marquis

Xiaowen, Zhou: Emperor's Shadow, The; Ermo

Yablonsky, Yabo: Manipulator, The

Yabuki, Kimio: Twelve Months

Yaitanes, Greg: Double Tap; Hard Justice

Yakin, Boaz: Fresh; Price Above Rubies, A

Yamamoto, Michio: Evil of Dracula

Yamamoto, Yoshikio: Rei-Rei

Yamazaki, Kazuo: Urusei Yatsura (TV Series) Vols. 1–45; Urusei Yatsura: Only You; Urusei Yatsura: Remember Love

Yanagimachi, Mitsuo: Himatsuri; Shadow of China

Yansen, Louis: Misplaced

Yarbrough, Jean: Brute Man, The; Creeper, The; Devil Bat, The; Here Come the Co-Eds; Hillbillys in a Haunted House; House of Horrors; In Society; King of the Zombies; Lost in Alaska; Naughty Nineties, The

Yari, Bob: Mindgames

Yasuhiko, Yoshikazu: Venus Wars, The

Yasuyuki, Noda: Bubblegum Crash, Vols. 1–3

Yates, Hal: Flustered Comedy of Leon Errol, The

Yates, Peter: Breaking Away; Bullitt; Deep, The; Don Quixote (2000); Dresser, The; Eleni; Eyewitness; For Pete's Sake; Hot Rock, The; House on Carroll Street, The; Innocent Man, An; Koroshi; Krull; Mother, Jugs, and Speed; Murphy's War; Robbery; Roommates; Run of the Country, The; Suspect; Year of the Comet

Yates, Rebecca: Rubberface

Yau, Herman: Untold Story, The

Yeager, Steve: On the Block

Yeaton, Brook: Ice

Yeaworth Jr., Irvin S.: Blob, The (1958); Dinosaurus!; 4D Man

Yellen, Linda: Chantilly Lace; End of Summer; Parallel Lives

Yen, Chang Hsin: Shaolin Temple

Yevtushenko, Yevgenii: Kindergarten

Yolles, Edie: That's My Baby

Yonis, Jeff: Bloodfist V: Human Target; Born Bad; Humanoids from the Deep (1996)

Yorkin, Bud: Arthur 2: On the Rocks; Come Blow Your Horn; Divorce American Style; Love Hurts; Start the Revolution Without Me; Thief Who Came to Dinner, The; Twice in a Lifetime

Yoshida, Hiroaki: Iron Maze

Young, Freddie: Arthur's Hallowed Ground

Young, Harold: Dreaming Out Loud; Frozen Ghost, The; Jungle Captive; Mummy's Tomb, The; Scarlet Pimpernel, The (1934)

Young, John Scaret: Sirens (1999)

Young, Lance: Bliss (1997)

Young, Lee Doo: Silent Assassins

Young, Robert: Charlie Boy; Doomsday Gun; Fierce Creatures; Getting Gotti; Hostage (1992); Jeeves and Wooster (TV Series); Robin Hood: Herne's Son; Robin Hood: The Swords of Wayland; Romance with a Double Bass; Soldier's Home; Splitting Heirs; World Is Full of Married Men, The; Worst Witch, The

Young, Robert M.: Ballad of Gregorio Cortez, The; Caught (1996); Dominick and Eugene; Extremities; One Trick Pony; Rich Kids; Roosters; Saving Grace; Short Eyes; Slave of Dreams; Solomon and Sheba (1995); Talent for the Game; Triumph of the Spirit; We Are the Children

Young, Robert W.: Scandalous (1988)

Young, Roger: Bitter Harvest (1981); Bourne Identity, The; Doublecrossed; Geronimo (1993); Gulag; Joseph; Kiss the Sky; Lassiter; Mercy Mission (The Rescue of Flight 711); Moses (1996); Squeeze, The (1987); Two of a Kind (1982)

Young, Terence: Amorous Adventures of Moll Flanders, The; Black Tights; Bloodline; Cold Sweat (1970); Corridor of Mirrors; Dr. No; From Russia with Love; Klansman, The; Poppy Is Also a Flower, The; Red Sun; Thunderball; Wait Until Dark; When Wolves Cry

Younger, Ben: Boiler Room

Youngson, Robert: Days of Thrills and Laughter; Golden Age of Comedy, The; MGM's The Big Parade of Comedy; When Comedy Was King

Yu, Ronny: Bride of Chucky; Bride with White Hair, The; China White; Warriors of Virtue

Yuasa, Noriyaki: Gamera the Invincible; Gamera Versus Gaos; Gamera Versus Guiron; Gamera Versus Zigra

Yuen, Corey: Jet Li's the Enforcer; No Retreat, No Surrender; No Retreat, No Surrender II

Yuen, Galen: Riot (1996) (TV Movie)

Yuhas, Robert: Infamous Dorothy Parker, The

Yukich, Jim: Double Dragon

Yune, Johnny: They Still Call Me Bruce

Yust, Larry: Homebodies; Say Yes

Yuval, Peter: Firehead

Yuyama, Kunihiko: Goshogun—The Time Stranger; Pokémon the First Movie: Mewtwo Strikes Back

Yuzna, Brian: Bride of Re-Animator; Dentist, The; H. P. Lovecraft's Necronomicon: Book of the Dead; Progeny; Return of the Living Dead 3; Silent Night, Deadly Night 4—Initiation; Society

Zabalza, José Maria: Fury of the Wolf Man

Zacharias, Alfredo: Bandits (1967); Bees, The; Crossfire (1986); Demonoid

Zacharias, Steve: Revenge of the Nerds IV: Nerds in Love

Zahr, Raja: Last Season, The

Zaillian, Steven: Civil Action, A; Searching for Bobby Fischer

Zaks, Jerry: Marvin's Room

Zala, Nancy: Round Numbers

Zaloum, Alain: Canvas; Madonna; Suspicious Minds

Zamm, Alex: Chairman of the Board

Zampi, Mario: Five Golden Hours; Naked Truth (Your Past Is Showing)

Zanke, Susanne: Scorpion Woman, The

Zanuck, Lili Fini: Rush

Zanussi, Krzysztof: Camouflage; Catamount Killing, The; Contract; From a Far Country; Silent Touch, The; Unapproachable, The; Year of the Quiet Sun

Zaorski, Janusz: Baritone

Zaphiratos, Fabrice A.: Bloodbeat

Zappa, Frank: 200 Motels

Zarchi, Meir: Don't Mess with My Sister; I Spit on Your Grave

Zarindast, Tony: Werewolf

Zaslove, Alan: Return of Jafar, The

Zea, Kristi: Women & Men 2

Zeffirelli, Franco: Brother Sun, Sister Moon; Champ, The (1979); Endless Love; Hamlet (1990); Jane Eyre (1996); Jesus of Nazareth; La Traviata; Otello; Romeo and Juliet (1968); Taming of the Shrew, The (1966); Tea with Mussolini

Zeglio, Primo: Mission Stardust; Morgan the Pirate

Zeilinger, Jimmy: Little Sister

Zeisler, Alfred: Amazing Adventure

Zeltser, Yuri: Black & White; Eye of the Storm; Playmaker

Zeman, Karel: Baron Munchausen (1961)

Zemeckis, Robert: Amazing Stories (TV Series); Back to the Future; Back to the Future II; Back to the Future III; Contact; Death Becomes Her; Forrest Gump; I Wanna Hold Your Hand; Romancing the Stone; Tales from the Crypt (TV Series); Used Cars; Who Framed Roger Rabbit

Zens, Will: Fix, The

Zetlin, Barry: Dogfighters, The

Zetterling, Mai: Hitchhiker, The (Series); Scrubbers

Zhang, Yimou: Ju Dou; Not One Less; Raise the Red Lantern; Red Sorghum; Shanghai Triad; Story of Qiu Ju, The; To Live

Zhelyabuzhsky, Yuri: Cigarette Girl from Mosselprom, The

Zhuangzhuang, Tian: Blue Kite, The; Horse Thief, The

Zidi, Claude: My New Partner

Zieff, Howard: Dream Team, The; Hearts of the West; House Calls; Main Event, The; My Girl; My Girl 2; Private Benjamin; Slither; Unfaithfully Yours (1984)

Ziehl, Scott: Broken Vessels

Ziehm, Howard: Flesh Gordon; Flesh Gordon 2: Flesh Gordon meets the Cosmic Cheerleaders

Zielinski, Rafal: Babe (1982); Fun; Ginger Ale Afternoon; Jailbait (1992); National Lampoon's Last Resort; Night of the Warrior; Recruits; Screwballs; Spellcaster

Ziller, Paul: Back in Action; Bloodfist IV—Die Trying; Breaking Point (1993); Deadly Surveillance; Ms. Bear; Pledge Night; Probable Cause; Shootfighter 2: Kill or Be Killed; Virtual Seduction

Zimmerman, Jerry: Mausoleum

Zimmerman, Vernon: Fade to Black (1980)

Zinberg, Michael: Accidental Meeting

Zinnemann, Fred: Behold a Pale Horse; Day of the Jackal, The; Five Days One Summer; From Here to Eternity (1953); High Noon; Julia; Man for All Seasons, A; Member of the Wedding, The; Men, The (1950); Nun's Story, The; Oklahoma!; Search, The; Seventh Cross, The; Sundowners, The (1960)

Zinner, Peter: Salamander, The

Zito, Joseph: Abduction; Friday the 13th—The Final Chapter; Invasion U.S.A. (1985); Missing in Action; Prowler, The; Red Scorpion

Zivkovich, Milas: Concealed Weapon

Zlotoff, Lee David: Spitfire Grill, The

Zonca, Erick: Dreamlife of Angels, The

Zondag, Dick: We're Back! A Dinosaur's Story

Zondag, Ralph: Dinosaur; We're Back! A Dinosaur's Story

Zucker, David: Airplane!; Basketball; Naked Gun, The; Naked Gun 2 , The; Police Squad!; Ruthless People; Top Secret

Zucker, Jerry: Airplane!; First Knight; Ghost (1990); Police Squad!; Ruthless People; Top Secret

Zucker (Massimo Pupillo), Ralph: Terror Creatures from the Grave

Zuckerman, Steve: North Shore Fish

Zuniga, Frank: Fist Fighter; Golden Seal, The; Wilderness Family, Part 2, The

Zurinaga, Marcos: Disappearance of García Lorca, The; Tango Bar

Zurlini, Valerio: Girl with a Suitcase

Zwerin, Charlotte: Gimme Shelter

Zwick, Edward: About Last Night … ; Courage Under Fire; Glory; Having It All; Leaving Normal; Legends of the Fall; Siege, The; Special Bulletin

Zwick, Joel: Bosom Buddies (TV Series); Second Sight

Zwicky, Karl: Contagion; Vicious

Zwigoff, Terry: Crumb

ACADEMY AWARD WINNERS

1927–28
Best Picture: WINGS
Best Actor: Emil Jannings, in THE LAST COMMAND and THE WAY OF ALL FLESH
Best Actress: Janet Gaynor, in SEVENTH HEAVEN, STREET ANGEL, and SUNRISE
Best Director: Frank Borzage, for SEVENTH HEAVEN

1928–29
Best Picture: BROADWAY MELODY
Best Actor: Warner Baxter, in IN OLD ARIZONA
Best Actress: Mary Pickford, in COQUETTE
Best Director: Frank Lloyd, for THE DIVINE LADY

1929–30
Best Picture: ALL QUIET ON THE WESTERN FRONT
Best Actor: George Arliss, in DISRAELI
Best Actress: Norma Shearer, in THE DIVORCÉE
Best Director: Lewis Milestone, for ALL QUIET ON THE WESTERN FRONT

1930–31
Best Picture: CIMARRON
Best Actor: Lionel Barrymore, in A FREE SOUL
Best Actress: Marie Dressler, in MIN AND BILL
Best Director: Norman Taurog, for SKIPPY

1931–32
Best Picture: GRAND HOTEL
Best Actor: Wallace Beery, in THE CHAMP
Fredric March, in DR. JEKYLL AND MR. HYDE (tie)
Best Actress: Helen Hayes, in THE SIN OF MADELON CLAUDET
Best Director: Frank Borzage, for BAD GIRL

1932–33
Best Picture: CAVALCADE
Best Actor: Charles Laughton, in THE PRIVATE LIFE OF HENRY VIII
Best Actress: Katharine Hepburn, in MORNING GLORY
Best Director: Frank Lloyd, for CAVALCADE

1934
Best Picture: IT HAPPENED ONE NIGHT
Best Actor: Clark Gable, in IT HAPPENED ONE NIGHT
Best Actress: Claudette Colbert, in IT HAPPENED ONE NIGHT
Best Director: Frank Capra, for IT HAPPENED ONE NIGHT

1935
Best Picture: MUTINY ON THE BOUNTY
Best Actor: Victor McLaglen, in THE INFORMER
Best Actress: Bette Davis, in DANGEROUS
Best Director: John Ford, for THE INFORMER

1936

Best Picture:	THE GREAT ZIEGFELD
Best Actor:	Paul Muni, in THE STORY OF LOUIS PASTEUR
Best Actress:	Luise Rainer, in THE GREAT ZIEGFELD
Best Director:	Frank Capra, for MR. DEEDS GOES TO TOWN

1937

Best Picture:	THE LIFE OF EMILE ZOLA
Best Actor:	Spencer Tracy, in CAPTAINS COURAGEOUS
Best Actress:	Luise Rainer, in THE GOOD EARTH
Best Director:	Leo McCarey, for THE AWFUL TRUTH

1938

Best Picture:	YOU CAN'T TAKE IT WITH YOU
Best Actor:	Spencer Tracy, in BOYS TOWN
Best Actress:	Bette Davis, in JEZEBEL
Best Director:	Frank Capra, for YOU CAN'T TAKE IT WITH YOU

1939

Best Picture:	GONE WITH THE WIND
Best Actor:	Robert Donat, in GOODBYE, MR. CHIPS
Best Actress:	Vivien Leigh, in GONE WITH THE WIND
Best Director:	Victor Fleming, for GONE WITH THE WIND

1940

Best Picture:	REBECCA
Best Actor:	James Stewart, in THE PHILADELPHIA STORY
Best Actress:	Ginger Rogers, in KITTY FOYLE
Best Director:	John Ford, for THE GRAPES OF WRATH

1941

Best Picture:	HOW GREEN WAS MY VALLEY
Best Actor:	Gary Cooper, in SERGEANT YORK
Best Actress:	Joan Fontaine, in SUSPICION
Best Director:	John Ford, for HOW GREEN WAS MY VALLEY

1942

Best Picture:	MRS. MINIVER
Best Actor:	James Cagney, in YANKEE DOODLE DANDY
Best Actress:	Greer Garson, in MRS. MINIVER
Best Director:	William Wyler, for MRS. MINIVER

1943

Best Picture:	CASABLANCA
Best Actor:	Paul Lukas, in WATCH ON THE RHINE
Best Actress:	Jennifer Jones, in THE SONG OF BERNADETTE
Best Director:	Michael Curtiz, for CASABLANCA

1944

Best Picture:	GOING MY WAY
Best Actor:	Bing Crosby, in GOING MY WAY
Best Actress:	Ingrid Bergman, in GASLIGHT
Best Director:	Leo McCarey, for GOING MY WAY

1945

Best Picture:	THE LOST WEEKEND
Best Actor:	Ray Milland, in THE LOST WEEKEND
Best Actress:	Joan Crawford, in MILDRED PIERCE
Best Director:	Billy Wilder, for THE LOST WEEKEND

1946

Best Picture:	THE BEST YEARS OF OUR LIVES
Best Actor:	Fredric March, in THE BEST YEARS OF OUR LIVES
Best Actress:	Olivia de Havilland, in TO EACH HIS OWN
Best Director:	William Wyler, for THE BEST YEARS OF OUR LIVES

1947

Best Picture:	GENTLEMAN'S AGREEMENT
Best Actor:	Ronald Coleman, in A DOUBLE LIFE
Best Actress:	Loretta Young, in THE FARMER'S DAUGHTER
Best Director:	Elia Kazan, for GENTLEMAN'S AGREEMENT

1948

Best Picture:	HAMLET
Best Actor:	Laurence Olivier, in HAMLET
Best Actress:	Jane Wyman, in JOHNNY BELINDA
Best Director:	John Huston, for TREASURE OF SIERRA MADRE

1949

Best Picture:	ALL THE KING'S MEN
Best Actor:	Broderick Crawford, in ALL THE KING'S MEN
Best Actress:	Olivia de Havilland, in THE HEIRESS
Best Director:	Joseph L. Mankiewicz, for A LETTER TO THREE WIVES

1950

Best Picture:	ALL ABOUT EVE
Best Actor:	José Ferrer, in CYRANO DE BERGERAC
Best Actress:	Judy Holliday, in BORN YESTERDAY
Best Director:	Joseph L. Mankiewicz, for ALL ABOUT EVE

1951

Best Picture:	AN AMERICAN IN PARIS
Best Actor:	Humphrey Bogart, in THE AFRICAN QUEEN
Best Actress:	Vivien Leigh, in A STREETCAR NAMED DESIRE
Best Director:	George Stevens, for A PLACE IN THE SUN

1952

Best Picture:	THE GREATEST SHOW ON EARTH
Best Actor:	Gary Cooper, in HIGH NOON
Best Actress:	Shirley Booth, in COME BACK, LITTLE SHEBA
Best Director:	John Ford, for THE QUIET MAN

1953

Best Picture:	FROM HERE TO ETERNITY
Best Actor:	William Holden, in STALAG 17
Best Actress:	Audrey Hepburn, in ROMAN HOLIDAY
Best Director:	Fred Zinnemann, for FROM HERE TO ETERNITY

1954

Best Picture:	ON THE WATERFRONT
Best Actor:	Marlon Brando, in ON THE WATERFRONT
Best Actress:	Grace Kelly, in THE COUNTRY GIRL
Best Director:	Elia Kazan, for ON THE WATERFRONT

1955

Best Picture:	MARTY
Best Actor:	Ernest Borgnine, in MARTY
Best Actress:	Anna Magnani, in THE ROSE TATTOO
Best Director:	Delbert Mann, for MARTY

1956

Best Picture:	AROUND THE WORLD IN 80 DAYS
Best Actor:	Yul Brynner, in THE KING AND I
Best Actress:	Ingrid Bergman, in ANASTASIA
Best Director:	George Stevens, for GIANT

1957

Best Picture:	THE BRIDGE ON THE RIVER KWAI
Best Actor:	Alec Guinness, in THE BRIDGE ON THE RIVER KWAI
Best Actress:	Joanne Woodward, in THE THREE FACES OF EVE
Best Director:	David Lean, for THE BRIDGE ON THE RIVER KWAI

1958

Best Picture:	GIGI
Best Actor:	David Niven, in SEPARATE TABLES
Best Actress:	Susan Hayward, in I WANT TO LIVE!
Best Director:	Vincente Minnelli, for GIGI

1959

Best Picture:	BEN-HUR
Best Actor:	Charlton Heston, in BEN-HUR
Best Actress:	Simone Signoret, in ROOM AT THE TOP
Best Director:	William Wyler, for BEN-HUR

1960

Best Picture:	THE APARTMENT
Best Actor:	Burt Lancaster, in ELMER GANTRY
Best Actress:	Elizabeth Taylor, in BUTTERFIELD 8
Best Director:	Billy Wilder, for THE APARTMENT

1961

Best Picture:	WEST SIDE STORY
Best Actor:	Maximilian Schell, in JUDGMENT AT NUREMBERG
Best Actress:	Sophia Loren, in TWO WOMEN
Best Director:	Robert Wise and Jerome Robbins, for WEST SIDE STORY

1962

Best Picture:	LAWRENCE OF ARABIA
Best Actor:	Gregory Peck, in TO KILL A MOCKINGBIRD
Best Actress:	Anne Bancroft, in THE MIRACLE WORKER
Best Director:	David Lean, for LAWRENCE OF ARABIA

1963

Best Picture:	TOM JONES
Best Actor:	Sidney Poitier, in LILIES OF THE FIELD
Best Actress:	Patricia Neal, in HUD
Best Director:	Tony Richardson, for TOM JONES

1964

Best Picture:	MY FAIR LADY
Best Actor:	Rex Harrison, in MY FAIR LADY
Best Actress:	Julie Andrews, in MARY POPPINS
Best Director:	George Cukor, for MY FAIR LADY

1965

Best Picture:	THE SOUND OF MUSIC
Best Actor:	Lee Marvin, in CAT BALLOU
Best Actress:	Julie Christie, in DARLING
Best Director:	Robert Wise, for THE SOUND OF MUSIC

1966

Best Picture:	A MAN FOR ALL SEASONS
Best Actor:	Paul Scofield, in A MAN FOR ALL SEASONS
Best Actress:	Elizabeth Taylor, in WHO'S AFRAID OF VIRGINIA WOOLF?
Best Director:	Fred Zinnemann, for A MAN FOR ALL SEASONS

1967

Best Picture:	IN THE HEAT OF THE NIGHT
Best Actor:	Rod Steiger, in IN THE HEAT OF THE NIGHT
Best Actress:	Katharine Hepburn, in GUESS WHO'S COMING TO DINNER
Best Director:	Mike Nichols, for THE GRADUATE

1968

Best Picture:	OLIVER!
Best Actor:	Cliff Robertson, in CHARLY
Best Actress:	Katharine Hepburn, in THE LION IN WINTER
	Barbra Streisand, in FUNNY GIRL (tie)
Best Director:	Carol Reed, for OLIVER!

1969

Best Picture:	MIDNIGHT COWBOY
Best Actor:	John Wayne, in TRUE GRIT
Best Actress:	Maggie Smith, in THE PRIME OF MISS JEAN BRODIE
Best Director:	John Schlesinger, for MIDNIGHT COWBOY

1970

Best Picture:	PATTON
Best Actor:	George C. Scott, in PATTON
Best Actress:	Glenda Jackson, in WOMEN IN LOVE
Best Director:	Franklin J. Schaffner, for PATTON

1971

Best Picture:	THE FRENCH CONNECTION
Best Actor:	Gene Hackman, in THE FRENCH CONNECTION
Best Actress:	Jane Fonda, in KLUTE
Best Director:	William Friedkin, for THE FRENCH CONNECTION

1972

Best Picture:	THE GODFATHER
Best Actor:	Marlon Brando, in THE GODFATHER
Best Actress:	Liza Minnelli, in CABARET
Best Director:	Bob Fosse, for CABARET

1973

Best Picture:	THE STING
Best Actor:	Jack Lemmon, in SAVE THE TIGER
Best Actress:	Glenda Jackson, in A TOUCH OF CLASS
Best Director:	George Roy Hill, for THE STING

1974

Best Picture:	THE GODFATHER, PART II
Best Actor:	Art Carney, in HARRY AND TONTO
Best Actress:	Ellen Burstyn, in ALICE DOESN'T LIVE HERE ANYMORE
Best Director:	Francis Ford Coppola, for THE GODFATHER, PART II

1975

Best Picture:	ONE FLEW OVER THE CUCKOO'S NEST
Best Actor:	Jack Nicholson, in ONE FLEW OVER THE CUCKOO'S NEST
Best Actress:	Louise Fletcher, in ONE FLEW OVER THE CUCKOO'S NEST
Best Director:	Milos Forman, for ONE FLEW OVER THE CUCKOO'S NEST

1976

Best Picture:	ROCKY
Best Actor:	Peter Finch, in NETWORK
Best Actress:	Faye Dunaway, in NETWORK
Best Director:	John G. Avildsen, for ROCKY

1977

Best Picture:	ANNIE HALL
Best Actor:	Richard Dreyfuss, in THE GOODBYE GIRL
Best Actress:	Diane Keaton, in ANNIE HALL
Best Director:	Woody Allen, for ANNIE HALL

1978

Best Picture:	THE DEER HUNTER
Best Actor:	Jon Voight, in COMING HOME
Best Actress:	Jane Fonda, in COMING HOME
Best Director:	Michael Cimino, for THE DEER HUNTER

1979

Best Picture:	KRAMER VS. KRAMER
Best Actor:	Dustin Hoffman, in KRAMER VS. KRAMER
Best Actress:	Sally Field, in NORMA RAE
Best Director:	Robert Benton, for KRAMER VS. KRAMER

1980

Best Picture:	ORDINARY PEOPLE
Best Actor:	Robert De Niro, in RAGING BULL
Best Actress:	Sissy Spacek, in COAL MINER'S DAUGHTER
Best Director:	Robert Redford, for ORDINARY PEOPLE

1981

Best Picture:	CHARIOTS OF FIRE
Best Actor:	Henry Fonda, in ON GOLDEN POND
Best Actress:	Katharine Hepburn, in ON GOLDEN POND
Best Director:	Warren Beatty, for REDS

1982

Best Picture:	GANDHI
Best Actor:	Ben Kingsley, in GANDHI
Best Actress:	Meryl Streep, in SOPHIE'S CHOICE
Best Director:	Richard Attenborough, for GANDHI

1983

Best Picture:	TERMS OF ENDEARMENT
Best Actor:	Robert Duvall, in TENDER MERCIES
Best Actress:	Shirley MacLaine, in TERMS OF ENDEARMENT
Best Director:	James L. Brooks, for TERMS OF ENDEARMENT

1984

Best Picture:	AMADEUS
Best Actor:	F. Murray Abraham, in AMADEUS
Best Actress:	Sally Field, in PLACES IN THE HEART
Best Director:	Milos Forman, for AMADEUS

1985

Best Picture:	OUT OF AFRICA
Best Actor:	William Hurt, in KISS OF THE SPIDER WOMAN
Best Actress:	Geraldine Page, in THE TRIP TO BOUNTIFUL
Best Director:	Sydney Pollack, for OUT OF AFRICA

1986

Best Picture:	PLATOON
Best Actor:	Paul Newman, in THE COLOR OF MONEY
Best Actress:	Marlee Matlin, in CHILDREN OF A LESSER GOD
Best Director:	Oliver Stone, for PLATOON

1987

Best Picture:	THE LAST EMPEROR
Best Actor:	Michael Douglas, in WALL STREEET
Best Actress:	Cher, in MOONSTRUCK
Best Director:	Bernardo Bertolucci, for THE LAST EMPEROR

1988

Best Picture:	RAIN MAN
Best Actor:	Dustin Hoffman, in RAIN MAN
Best Actress:	Jodie Foster, in THE ACCUSED
Best Director:	Barry Levinson, for RAIN MAN

1989

Best Picture:	DRIVING MISS DAISY
Best Actor:	Daniel Day-Lewis, in MY LEFT FOOT
Best Actress:	Jessica Tandy, in DRIVING MISS DAISY
Best Director:	Oliver Stone, for BORN ON THE FOURTH OF JULY

1990

Best Picture:	DANCES WITH WOLVES
Best Actor:	Jeremy Irons, in REVERSAL OF FORTUNE
Best Actress:	Kathy Bates, in MISERY
Best Director:	Kevin Costner, for DANCES WITH WOLVES

1991

Best Picture:	THE SILENCE OF THE LAMBS
Best Actor:	Anthony Hopkins, in THE SILENCE OF THE LAMBS
Best Actress:	Jodie Foster, in THE SILENCE OF THE LAMBS
Best Director:	Jonathan Demme, for THE SILENCE OF THE LAMBS

1992

Best Picture:	UNFORGIVEN
Best Actor:	Al Pacino, in SCENT OF A WOMAN
Best Actress:	Emma Thompson, in HOWARD'S END
Best Director:	Clint Eastwood, for UNFORGIVEN

1993

Best Picture:	SCHINDLER'S LIST
Best Actor:	Tom Hanks, in PHILADELPHIA
Best Actress:	Holly Hunter, in THE PIANO
Best Director:	Steven Spielberg, for SCHINDLER'S LIST

1994

Best Picture:	FORREST GUMP
Best Actor:	Tom Hanks, in FORREST GUMP
Best Actress:	Jessica Lange, in BLUE SKY
Best Director:	Robert Zemeckis, for FORREST GUMP

1995

Best Picture:	BRAVEHEART
Best Actor:	Nicolas Cage, in LEAVING LAS VEGAS
Best Actress:	Susan Sarandon, in DEAD MAN WALKING
Best Director:	Mel Gibson, for BRAVEHEART

1996

Best Picture:	THE ENGLISH PATIENT
Best Actor:	Geoffrey Rush, in SHINE
Best Actress:	Frances McDormand, in FARGO
Best Director:	Anthony Minghella, for THE ENGLISH PATIENT

1997

Best Picture:	TITANIC
Best Actor:	Jack Nicholson, in AS GOOD AS IT GETS
Best Actress:	Helen Hunt, in AS GOOD AS IT GETS
Best Director:	James Cameron, for TITANIC

1998

Best Picture:	SHAKESPEARE IN LOVE
Best Actor:	Roberto Benigni, in LIFE IS BEAUTIFUL
Best Actress:	Gwyneth Paltrow, in SHAKESPEARE IN LOVE
Best Director:	Steven Spielberg, for SAVING PRIVATE RYAN

1999

Best Picture:	AMERICAN BEAUTY
Best Actor:	Kevin Spacey, in AMERICAN BEAUTY
Best Actress:	Hilary Swank, in BOYS DON'T CRY
Best Director:	Sam Mendes for AMERICAN BEAUTY

COMPLETE ALTERNATE
TITLES LIST

Party, Inc., see *Party Girls*
Passion of Beatrice, The, see *Beatrice*
Passionate Thief, see *Laugh for Joy*
Payment in Blood, see *Final Defeat, The*
Pencil, The (1983), see *Philip Marlowe, Private Eye: The Pencil*
Perils from Planet Mongo, see *Flash Gordon: Rocketship*
Perils of Nyoka, see *Nyoka and the Tiger Men*
Peuple Singe, see *Monkey People*
Phantom Tollbooth, The, see *Adventures of Milo in the Phantom Tollbooth, The*
Pick a Star, see *Movie Struck*
Piece of Pleasure, see *Une Partie de Plaisir*
Place Called Today, see *City in Fear*
Planet Outlaws, see *Buck Rogers: Destination Saturn*
Pool Sharks, see *Fatal Glass of Beer, A*
Portrait of a Woman, Nude, see *Nudo di Donna*
Potop, see *Deluge, The*
Prague Duet, see *Lies & Whispers*
Pranks, see *Dorm That Dripped Blood, The*
Private Wore Skirts, The, see *Never Wave at a WAC*
Psycho Circus, see *Circus of Fear*
Quatermass II: Enemy from Space, see *Enemy from Space*
Queen of Blood, see *Planet of Blood*
Raven, The (1943), see *Le Corbeau*
Reader, The, see *La Lectrice*
Reason to Live . . . Reason to Die, A, see *Massacre at Fort Holman*
Red River Valley, see *Man of the Frontier*
Return from the Past, see *Bloodsuckers, The*
Return of Maxwell Smart, The, see *Nude Bomb, The*
Revenge of the Zombie, see *Kiss Daddy Goodbye*
Revolutions Per Minute, see *R.P.M.*
Rhodes, see *Rhodes of Africa*
Ripper, see *Fear City*
Ripper of Notre Dame, see *Demoniac*
Rise of Catherine the Great, The, see *Catherine the Great*
Rocket to the Moon, see *Cat Women of the Moon*
Rocky Mountain Mystery, see *Fighting Westerner, The*
Rouge Baiser, see *Red Kiss*
St. Martin's Lane, see *Sidewalks of London*
Sam's Song, see *Swap, The*
Scandal Man, see *L'Odeur des Fauves*
Scarface Mob, The, see *Untouchables: Scarface Mob*
Scream and Die, see *House That Vanished, The*
Scream of the Demon Lover, see *Blood Castle*
Secret Adversary, see *Partners in Crime*
Secret Life of Ian Fleming, The, see *Spymaker: The Secret Life of Ian Fleming*
Secret of Dorian Gray, The, see *Dorian Gray*
Secret Service in Darkest Africa, see *Manhunt in the African Jungle*
Sensuous Vampires, see *Vampire Hookers*
Seven Notes in Black, see *The Psychic*
Shame (1961), see *Intruder, The*
She Was a Hippy Vampire, see *Wild World of Batwoman, The*
Shocked, see *Mesmerized*
Smuggler, The, see *Contraband*
Sophie's Place, see *Crooks and Coronets*
Space Zombies, see *Astro Zombies*
Spaceship to the Unknown, see *Flash Gordon: Rocketship*
Spider Woman, see *Sherlock Holmes and the Spider Woman*
Spirit of Tattoo, see *Irezumi*

Spotswood, see *Efficiency Expert, The*
Star Quest, see *Beyond the Rising Moon*
Stowaway to the Stars, see *Voyage en Ballon*
Street Fight, see *Coonskin*
Suicide Squadron, see *Dangerous Moonlight*
Sullivans, The, see *Fighting Sullivans, The*
Survival Run (1977), see *Damnation Alley*
Survival Run (1979), see *Soldier of Orange*
Sweet, Violent Tony, see *Kill Castro*
Sword and the Rose, The, see *Flesh and Blood*
Taste for Flesh and Blood, A, see *Invasion for Flesh and Blood*
Taxi to the Toilet, see *Taxi Zum Klo*
Teenage Monster, see *Meteor Monster*
Ten Days That Shook the World, see *October*
Tenebrae, see *Unsane*
Tepepa, see *Blood and Guns*
Terror Circus, see *Nightmare Circus*
Terror House, see *Terror at the Red Wolf Inn*
Terror of Dr. Hichcock, The, see *Horrible Dr. Hichcock, The*
They Call Me Hallelujah, see *Guns for Dollars*
They Watch, see *They*
Thief and the Cobbler, The, see *Arabian Knight*
Things in Life, The, see *Les Choses de la Vie*
This Strange Passion, see *El*
Ticks, see *Infested*
Tiger Woman, see *Perils of the Darkest Jungle*
Time Warp, see *Journey to the Center of Time*
Trip to Mars, see *Flash Gordon: Mars Attacks the World*
Trout, The, see *La Truite*
Twilight of the Dead, see *Gates of Hell*
Under Earth, see *Debajo del Mundo*
Underworld, see *Transmutations*
Unfinished Piece for a Mechanical Piano, An, see *Unfinished Piece for the Player Piano*
Utopia, see *Atoll K*
Vacation, see *National Lampoon's Vacation*
Valley Obscured by Clouds, see *Valley, The*
Vampire Men of the Lost Planet, see *Horror of the Blood Monsters*
Vampires, The, see *Goliath and the Vampires*
Vengeful Dead, The, see *Kiss Daddy Goodbye*
Vig, see *Money Kings*
Viking Women and the Sea Serpent, The, see *Saga of the Viking Women and Their Voyage to the Waters of the Great Sea Serpent, The*
Waiting Woman, see *Secrets of Women*
Walking Tall: The Final Chapter, see *Final Chapter— Walking Tall*
War Between the Planets, see *Planet on the Prowl*
Warriors Rest, see *Le Repos du Guerrier*
Way Ahead, The, see *Immortal Battalion, The*
Welcome to Oblivion, see *Ultrawarrior*
Werewolf Versus the Vampire Woman, The, see *Blood Moon*
Whiskey Galore, see *Tight Little Island*
Whispering Shadow, The, see *Warning Shadows*
White Paws, see *Pattes Blanches*
Will You Dance with Me?, see *Voulez Vous Danser avec Moi?*
Wishmaster, see *Wes Craven's Wishmaster*
Wizard of Mars, see *Horrors of the Red Planet*
Wounded Man, The, see *L'Homme Blessé*
Young Emmanuelle, A, see *Nea*
Your Past Is Showing, see *Naked Truth*
Zombie Holocaust, see *Dr. Butcher, MD*